
Manufactured in the United States of America

Published by Beckett Media LP, an Apprise Media Company

Beckett Media LP
4635 McEwen Road
Dallas, TX 75244
(972) 991-6657
www.beckett.com

Apprise Media LLC
450 Park Avenue
New York, NY 10022
(212) 751-3182
www.apprisemedia.com

First Printing
ISBN 1-930692-58-7

The Beckett Hockey Card Price Guide and Alphabetical Checklist # 18 already is being researched and prepared for release in November, 2008. In order for it to be the best resource on the market, it requires your help. If you know of any sets or singles not listed in this edition, or if you have pricing data to update the information herein, please contact us. You can send your information by email to hockeymag@beckett.com, or via the regular mail at Beckett Hockey Annual, 4635 McEwen Rd. Dallas, TX 75244. Please be sure to include your full contact information. We'll forward a complimentary copy of next year's book to 10 randomly selected hobbyists who make a contribution to that edition.

DE '07

Sportkings™ Series A
Some of the greatest signings in sports history.

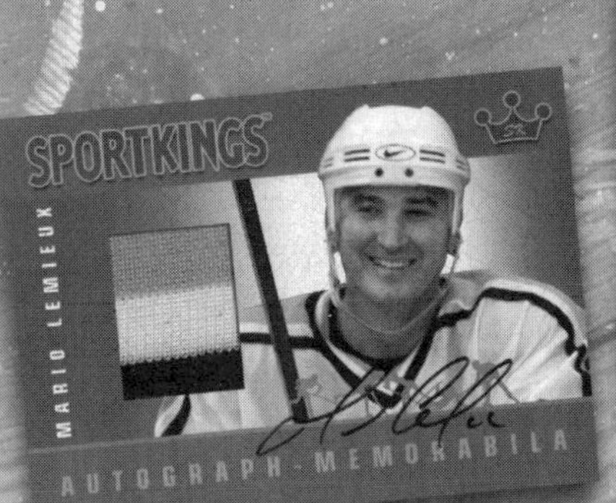

PATRICK
ROY
SPORTKINGS
SINGLE
MEMORABILIA

- 1 hard signed autograph card
- 2 additional inserts (memorabilia or autograph)
- 3 base cards
- 1 parallel base card (vintage size)

Production extremely limited - October 25, 2007

For more information visit www.sportkingsgum.com

BECKETT HOCKEY CARD PRICE GUIDE

AND ALPHABETICAL CHECKLIST

Number 17

THE HOBBY'S MOST RELIABLE AND RELIED UPON SOURCE™

Founder & Advisor: Dr. James Beckett III

Edited By
Allan Muir
with the staff of
BECKETT HOCKEY

Beckett Media LP - Dallas, Texas

NHL

1989-90 Action Packed Prototypes

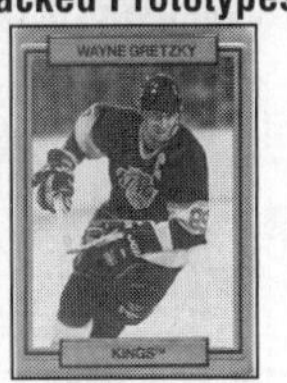

s three-card set was produced by Action ·ked to show the NHL and NHLPA a ıple in order to obtain a license for ·key cards. The cards are unnumbered l listed below in alphabetical order. ·ortedly only 1000 cards of Gretzky and ıieux were produced and only 300 of ·rman. These cards are standard size with rounded corners.

MPLETE SET (4) 125.00 300.00
Vayne Gretzky 50.00 100.00
Mario Lemieux 30.00 75.00
lario Lemieux 30.00 75.00
White border
teve Yzerman 50.00 100.00

993 Action Packed HOF Induction

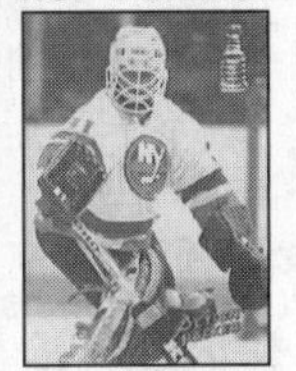

s special limited edition standard-size set s produced by Action Packed to ımemorate the 1993 Hockey Hall Of ıe induction on November 16, 1993, and ors the ten inductees. It was given to ndees at the induction and was on sale at Hockey Hall of Fame. This set was ased in a special black cardboard display uring all ten cards (in two rows of five) which could be placed in a black dboard sleeve with the Hall of Fame logo the words "1993 Hockey Hall of Fame uction, November 16, 1993" printed in er letters on the front. The back of the ·ve gives the set serial number out of a l of 5,000 sets produced.

MPLETE SET (10) 8.00 20.00
dgar Laprade .80 2.00
uy Lapointe 2.00 5.00
illy Smith 3.20 8.00
teve Shutt 2.00 5.00
ohn D'Amico .40 1.00
l Shaver .20 .50
eymour Knox III .20 .50
rank Griffiths .20 .50
red Page .20 .50
Al Strachan .20 .50

993 Action Packed Prototypes

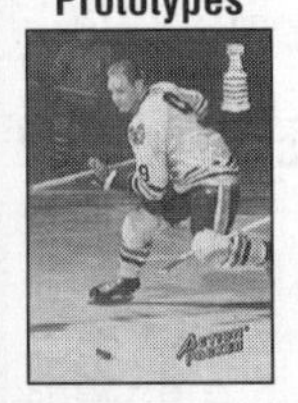

h prototype cards measure the standard and feature Bobby Hull. The first card a borderless embossed color photo, le the second card has the same design is all in gold. Both cards feature a silver nley Cup in the upper right corner. The izontal backs carry biographical (in glish and French) and statistical ·rmation, the Blackhawks logo on a puck, the word "Prototype" printed vertically the left. The cards are numbered on the k with a "BH" prefix.

MPLETE SET (2) 3.20 8.00
Bobby Hull 1.60 4.00
(Color)
obby Hull 2.00 5.00
(Gold)

1994 Action Packed Badge of Honor Promos

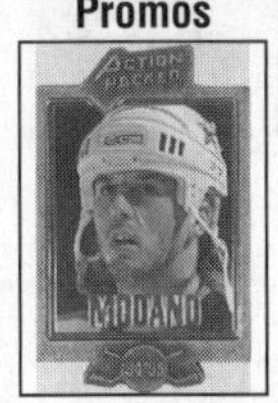

Issued to herald the release of a new product, each of these four pins measures approximately 1 1/2" by 1". They were packaged together in a cardboard sleeve which carries a checklist on its back. On a bronze background, the fronts feature color player portraits with a gold border. The player's last name appears in gold lettering at the bottom. The Action Packed logo is above the picture, while the year 1994 inside a puck and hockey sticks icon is below. The backs carry the copyrights "Action Packed 1994" and "NHL 1994", and "NHLPA 1994." The pins are unnumbered and checklisted below in alphabetical order. By all accounts, the actual set these pins were designed to promote never was released.

COMPLETE SET (4) 10.00 25.00
1 Sergei Fedorov 4.00 10.00
2 Doug Gilmour 2.00 5.00
3 Mike Modano 3.20 8.00
Dallas Star
4 Patrick Roy 4.80 12.00

1994-95 Action Packed Big Picture Promos

These four standard-size cards were issued to preview a proposed (but never released) Action Packed product, "Big Picture" cards. The fronts have borderless embossed color action photos. On a team color-coded background, the backs have a color close-up inside a gold foil circle, the player's name and team in gold foil lettering, and player profile. The front and back are hinged at the top, and the card opens up to reveal a 5 3/4" by 6 1/2" mini-poster, with a movie-frame design.

COMPLETE SET (4) 8.00 20.00
BP1 Jeremy Roenick 1.20 3.00
BP2 John Vanbiesbrouck 1.20 3.00
BP3 Jaromir Jagr 4.00 10.00
BP4 Steve Yzerman 4.00 10.00

1994-95 Action Packed Mammoth

The cards measure approximately 7 1/2" by 10 1/2". The fronts have borderless embossed color action photos with rounded corners. The player's last name is gold foil stamped on the bottom. The backs carry a color player cutout superimposed over the team logo. Player biography, profile and career totals are superimposed over the cutout. The player's name, team and position appear in a black bar alongside the left. The cards were issued in a plastic sleeve and are individually numbered out of 25,000 on the back.

COMPLETE SET (16) 4.80 12.00
MM1 Chris Chelios 1.00 2.50
MM2 Brett Hull 1.20 3.00
MM3 Pavel Bure 2.40 6.00
MM4 Adam Oates .80 2.00

1956 Adventure R749

This set features athletes from across the realm of sporting endeavours, but includes just the one hockey card listed below. The cards were slightly undersized, at 2 1/2 by 3 1/2.

63 Gordie Howe 50.00 100.00
Chuck Rayner

1990-91 Alberta International Team Canada

This 24-card set features the Canadian National Team and a bonus card of Vladislav Tretiak, the honorary captain of the Soviet Olympic team during the Pre-Olympic Hockey Tour. The cards are slightly smaller than standard size, measuring approximately 2 7/16" by 3 1/2".

COMPLETE SET (24) 4.80 12.00
1 Craig Billington .30 .75
2 Doug Dadswell .30 .75
3 Greg Andrusak .20 .50
4 Karl Dykhuis .20 .50
5 Gord Hynes .20 .50
6 Ken MacArthur .20 .50
7 Jim Paek .20 .50
8 Brad Schlegel .20 .50
9 Dave Archibald .20 .50
10 Stu Barnes .30 .75
11 Brad Bennett .20 .50
12 Todd Brost .20 .50
13 Jose Charbonneau .20 .50
14 Jason Lafreniere .20 .50
15 Chris Lindberg .20 .50
16 Ken Priestlay .20 .50
17 Stephane Roy .20 .50
18 Randy Smith .20 .50
19 Todd Strueby .20 .50
20 Vladislav Tretiak 1.20 3.00
21 Dave King CO .20 .50
23 Checklist Card .04 .10
NNO Title Card .04 .10

1991-92 Alberta International Team Canada

Sponsored by Alberta Lotteries, this 24-card standard-size set features the Canadian National Team. The fronts feature posed player photos on the ice that are full-bleed on the left and bottom. The cards are unnumbered and checklisted below in alphabetical order.

COMPLETE SET (24) 4.80 12.00
1 Dave Archibald .20 .50
2 Todd Brost .20 .50
3 Sean Burke .80 2.00
4 Terry Crisp ACO .20 .50
5 Kevin Dahl .20 .50
6 Karl Dykhuis .20 .50
7 Wayne Fleming AGM/ACO .04 .10
8 Curt Giles .20 .50
9 Gord Hynes .20 .50
10 Fabian Joseph .20 .50
11 Joe Juneau .40 1.00
12 Trevor Kidd .40 1.00
13 Dave King GM/CO .20 .50
14 Chris Kontos .20 .50
15 Chris Lindberg .20 .50
16 Kent Manderville .20 .50
17 Adrien Plavsic .20 .50
18 Dan Ratushny .20 .50
19 Stephane Roy .20 .50
20 Brad Schlegel .20 .50
21 Scott Scissons .20 .50
22 Randy Smith .20 .50
23 Jason Woolley .30 .75
24 Title Card .04 .10

1992-93 Alberta International Team Canada

This 22-card set features the Canadian National Team as well as bonus cards of Mike Myers, honorary captain of the team, and of Vladislav Tretiak, honorary captain of Russia's National Team. The cards are slightly smaller than standard size,

measuring 2 1/2" by 3 7/16". The cards are unnumbered and checklisted below in alphabetical order.

COMPLETE SET (22) 8.00 20.00
1 Dominic Amodeo .20 .50
2 Mark Astley .20 .50
3 Adrian Aucoin .40 1.00
4 Mark Bassen .20 .50
5 Eric Bellerose .20 .50
6 Mike Brewer .20 .50
7 Dany Dube CO .04 .10
8 Mike Fountain .30 .75
9 Todd Hlushko .20 .50
10 Hank Lammens .20 .50
11 Derek Laxdal .20 .50
12 Derek Mayer .20 .50
13 Keith Morris .20 .50
14 Mike Myers SNL 4.00 10.00
15 Jackson Penney .20 .50
16 Garth Premak .20 .50
17 Tom Renney CO .20 .50
18 Allain Roy .30 .75
19 Stephane Roy .20 .50
20 Trevor Sim .20 .50
21 Vladislav Tretiak 1.20 3.00
22 Title Card .04 .10

1993-94 Alberta International Team Canada

This 23-card standard-size set features players on the 1994 Canadian National Hockey Team. The cards are unnumbered and checklisted below in alphabetical order.

COMPLETE SET (23) 12.00 30.00
1 Adrian Aucoin .30 .75
2 Todd Brost .20 .50
3 Dany Dube ACO .04 .10
4 David Harlock .20 .50
5 Corey Hirsch .30 .75
6 Todd Hlushko .20 .50
7 Fabian Joseph .20 .50
8 Paul Kariya 6.00 15.00
9 Chris Kontos .20 .50
10 Manny Legace 2.00 5.00
11 Brett Lindros .20 .50
12 Ken Lovsin .20 .50
13 Jason Marshall .20 .50
14 Derek Mayer .20 .50
15 Dwayne Norris .20 .50
16 Tom Refiney CO .20 .50
17 Russ Romaniuk .20 .50
18 Brian Savage .60 1.50
19 Trevor Sim .20 .50
20 Chris Therien .30 .75
21 Todd Warriner .20 .50
22 Craig Woodcroft .20 .50
23 Title Card .04 .10

1992-93 All World Mario Lemieux Promos

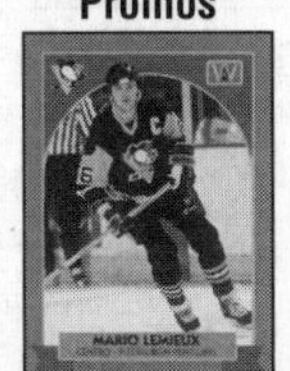

This set consists of six standard-size cards. All cards feature the same color action photo of Mario Lemieux, skating with stick in both hands. On the first three cards, the top of the photo is oval-shaped and framed by yellow stripes. The space above the oval as well as the stripe at the bottom carrying player information are purple. The outer border is green. Inside green borders, the horizontal back has a color close-up photo, biography and statistics. On the second three cards listed below, the player photo is tilted slightly to the right and framed by a thin green border. Yellow stripes above and below the picture carry information, and the outer border is black-and-white speckled. The back has a similar design and displays a close-up color head shot and biographical and statistical information on a pastel green panel. All cards are numbered as number 1. The cards were issued three different ways, in Spanish, French, and English. The design and concept of these cards is very similar to the 1992 All World Troy Aikman promos.

COMPLETE SET (6) 10.00 25.00
COMMON CARD (1A-1F) 2.00 5.00

1993 American Licorice Sour Punch Caps

Printed in Canada and sponsored by the American Licorice Co., these individually wrapped cards were inserted in specially-marked packages of 4 1/2 oz. Sour Punch Candy Straws. Each package contained one card, measuring the standard size with two punch-out caps, each measuring 1 1/2" in diameter. One cap carries the Sour Punch logo and where appropriate, a flavor, while the other cap features a color player portrait with a black border. The cards are numbered on the front, and the backs are blank. There is a special promotion cap featuring Bobby Hull with no number, but the letter "P." This promo cap was used by the American Licorice sales brokerage as a sales sample.

COMPLETE SET (8) 4.80 12.00
1 Theo Fleury .50 1.25
Sour Apple Cap
2 Guy Lafleur 1.00 2.50
Blue Raspberry Cap
3 Chris Chelios .50 1.25
Strawberry Cap
4 Stan Mikita .50 1.25
Sour Apple Cap
5 Rocket Richard 1.00 2.50
Strawberry Cap
6 Steve Thomas .20 .50
Blue Raspberry Cap
7 Checklist 1 .10 .25
Sour Punch Cap Logo
8 Checklist 2 .10 .25
Sour Punch Cap Logo
P Bobby Hull 1.00 2.50
Sour Punch Cap Logo

1924-28 Anonymous NHL

Honestly, we're not quite sure what to make of this checklist, which was provided by vintage expert Mike Jaspersen. It is thought that there are probably cards from at least two and possibly three different sets in this checklist, but because there are no distinguishing marks, it is impossible to accurately state to which single set each card belongs. It's noteworthy that at least two different sets appear to have been issued during the 1925-26 season as several players appear on two distinct cards with different numbers that only played that season. If anyone has further info and can help sort these very important cards out, please contact us at hockeymag@beckett.com. Because so little is known about these sets, they are checklisted below without pricing.

COMPLETE SET (?)
1 George Hainsworth
1 Billy Boucher
2 Billy Coutu
2 Billy Boucher
3 Georges Vezina
3 Sylvio Mantha
4 Roland Paulhus
4 Roland Paulhus
{white background
4 Sylvio Mantha
5 George Prodgers
5 Alphonse Lacroix
6 Albert Leduc
7 Wildor Larochelle VAR
{no border
7 Wildor Larochelle UER
{first name listed as Victor
8 Aurele Joliat
9 Howie Morenz
10 Hec Lepine
11 Alphonse Lacroix
11 Amby Moran
12 Art Gagne
12 Herb Rheaume
13 Pit Lepine
14 Bill Holmes
15 Leo Dandurand
16 Alex Connell
16 Frank Nighbor
17 Cy Denneny
17 King Clancy
18 King Clancy
19 Hec Kilrea
19 Billy Boucher
20 Hec Kilrea
21 Hooley Smith
22 Alex Smith VAR
{no border
22 Alex Smith
25 Ed Gorman
28 Alex Connell
31 Sprague Cleghorn
31 Carson Cooper
32 Carson Cooper
36 Hugo Harrington
38 Herb Mitchell
39 Herb Mitchell
39 Charles Stewart
40 Red Stuart
41 Lloyd Cook
41 Sprague Cleghorn
42 Billy Coutu VAR
{no border
42 Billy Coutu
46 Odie Cleghorn VAR
{no border, Pittsburgh
46 Odie Cleghorn
46 Odie Cleghorn VAR
{no border, Montreal
47 Louis Berlinquette
47 Roy Worters
48 Hib Milks
52 Hib Milks
57 Odie Cleghorn
61 Pete Bellefeuille
76 Charlie Langlois
77 Jake Forbes
79 Billy Burch
82 Joe Simpson VAR
{Montreal
82 Joe Simpson VAR
{Americans
91 Dutch Cain VAR
{Bruins
91 Dutch Cain VAR
{Maroons
91 Dunc Munro
92 Dunc Munro
95 Clint Benedict
96 Reg Noble
97 Nels Stewart
100 Sam Rothschild UER
{name misspelled Rotchild
121 Harry Holmes
127 Clem Loughlin
129 Johnny Sheppard
136 Gord Fraser
138 Dick Irvin

1993 Anti-Gambling Postcards

Each card measures 5" x 7" and is part of a multi-sport set which was created to allow voters to express their opinion to legislators on sports team-based lotteries in the U.S.

NNO Andy Moog .80 2.00
NNO Chris Chelios 2.00 5.00

2001-02 Atomic

Released in late November 2001, this 125-card base set featured die-cut cards printed on styrene stock and carried an SRP of $5.99 for a 5-card hobby pack. Rookies were short printed to just 500 copies each and were inserted at a rate of 1:21. Retail packs contained 3 cards.

COMP.SET w/o SP's (100) 30.00 60.00
SP STAT.PRINT RUN 500 SER.#'d SETS
1 Paul Kariya .60 1.50
2 Steve Shields .50 1.25
3 Milan Hnilicka .30 .75
4 Patrik Stefan .30 .75
5 Jason Allison .30 .75
6 Byron Dafoe .50 1.25
7 Bill Guerin .50 1.25
8 Sergei Samsonov .50 1.25
9 Joe Thornton 1.00 2.50
10 Martin Biron .50 1.25
11 Tim Connolly .30 .75
12 J-P Dumont .50 1.25
13 Jarome Iginla .75 2.00
14 Marc Savard .30 .75
15 Roman Turek .50 1.25
16 Ron Francis .50 1.25
17 Arturs Irbe .50 1.25
18 Jeff O'Neill .30 .75
19 Tony Amonte .50 1.25
20 Steve Sullivan .30 .75
21 Jocelyn Thibault .50 1.25
22 Rob Blake .50 1.25
23 Chris Drury .50 1.25
24 Peter Forsberg 1.50 4.00
25 Milan Hejduk .60 1.50
26 Patrick Roy 3.00 8.00
27 Joe Sakic 1.25 3.00
28 Alex Tanguay .50 1.25
29 Marc Denis .50 1.25
30 Geoff Sanderson .30 .75
31 Ed Belfour .60 1.50
32 Mike Modano 1.00 2.50
33 Joe Nieuwendyk .50 1.25
34 Pierre Turgeon .50 1.25
35 Sergei Fedorov 1.00 2.50
36 Dominik Hasek 1.25 3.00
37 Brett Hull .75 2.00
38 Luc Robitaille .50 1.25
39 Brendan Shanahan .60 1.50
40 Steve Yzerman 3.00 8.00
41 Mike Comrie .50 1.25
42 Tommy Salo .50 1.25
43 Ryan Smyth .30 .75
44 Pavel Bure .60 1.50
45 Valeri Bure .30 .75
46 Roberto Luongo .75 2.00
47 Zigmund Palffy .50 1.25
48 Felix Potvin .60 1.50
49 Manny Fernandez .50 1.25
50 Marian Gaborik 1.25 3.00
51 Saku Koivu .60 1.50
52 Yanic Perreault .30 .75
53 Jose Theodore .75 2.00
54 Mike Dunham .50 1.25
55 David Legwand .50 1.25
56 Jason Arnott .30 .75
57 Martin Brodeur 1.50 4.00
58 Patrik Elias .50 1.25
59 Mariusz Czerkawski .30 .75
60 Rick DiPietro .50 1.25
61 Michael Peca .30 .75
62 Alexei Yashin .30 .75
63 Theo Fleury .30 .75
64 Brian Leetch .50 1.25
65 Eric Lindros .60 1.50
66 Mark Messier .60 1.50
67 Daniel Alfredsson .50 1.25
68 Martin Havlat .50 1.25
69 Marian Hossa .60 1.50
70 Patrick Lalime .50 1.25
71 Roman Cechmanek .50 1.25
72 John LeClair .60 1.50
73 Mark Recchi .50 1.25
74 Jeremy Roenick .75 2.00
75 Sean Burke .50 1.25
76 Daymond Langkow .30 .75
77 Johan Hedberg .50 1.25
78 Alexei Kovalev .50 1.25
79 Mario Lemieux 4.00 10.00
80 Martin Straka .30 .75
81 Brent Johnson .50 1.25
82 Chris Pronger .50 1.25
83 Keith Tkachuk .60 1.50
84 Doug Weight .50 1.25
85 Evgeni Nabokov .50 1.25
86 Owen Nolan .50 1.25
87 Teemu Selanne .60 1.50
88 Nikolai Khabibulin .60 1.50
89 Vincent Lecavalier .60 1.50
90 Brad Richards .50 1.25
91 Curtis Joseph .60 1.50
92 Alexander Mogilny .50 1.25
93 Mats Sundin .60 1.50
94 Markus Naslund .60 1.50
95 Daniel Sedin .30 .75
96 Henrik Sedin .30 .75
97 Peter Bondra .60 1.50
98 Jaromir Jagr 1.00 2.50
99 Olaf Kolzig .50 1.25
100 Adam Oates .50 1.25
101 Ilja Bryzgalov RC 5.00 12.00
102 Timo Parssinen RC 5.00 12.00
103 Dany Heatley SP 8.00 20.00
104 Ilya Kovalchuk RC 20.00 50.00
105 Kamil Piros RC 5.00 12.00
106 Erik Cole RC 8.00 20.00
107 Vaclav Nedorost RC 5.00 12.00
108 Pavel Datsyuk RC 15.00 40.00
109 Niklas Hagman RC 5.00 12.00
110 Kristian Huselius RC 8.00 20.00
111 Jaroslav Bednar RC 5.00 12.00
112 Pascal Dupuis RC 5.00 12.00

113 Martin Erat RC 5.00 12.00
114 Scott Clemmensen RC 5.00 12.00
115 Radek Martinek RC 5.00 12.00
116 Dan Blackburn RC 6.00 15.00
117 Ivan Ciernik RC 5.00 12.00
118 Chris Neil RC 5.00 12.00
119 Pavel Brendl SP 5.00 12.00
120 Jiri Dopita RC 5.00 12.00
121 Krystofer Kolanos RC 5.00 12.00
122 Mark Rycroft RC 5.00 12.00
123 Jeff Jillson RC 5.00 12.00
124 Nikita Alexeev RC 5.00 12.00
125 Brian Sutherby RC 5.00 12.00

2001-02 Atomic Blue

STATED ODDS 1:161
PRINT RUN LIMITED TO PLAYER'S JSY #
NOT PRICED DUE TO SCARCITY

2001-02 Atomic Gold

*GOLD: 3X TO 8X BASIC CARD
STATED ODDS 2:21 HOBBY PACKS
PRINT RUN 200 SER.#'d SETS

2001-02 Atomic Premiere Date

*STARS: 5X TO 12X BASIC CARD
*SP's: .5X TO 1X BASIC CARD
STATED ODDS 1:21 HOBBY PACKS
STATED PRINT RUN 90 SER.#'d SETS

2001-02 Atomic Red

*RED: 2.5X TO 6X BASIC CARD
STATED ODDS 4:25 RETAIL
STATED PRINT RUN 290 SER.#'d SETS

2001-02 Atomic Blast

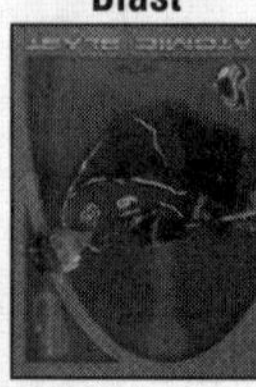

STATED ODDS 1:321 HOBBY/1:481 RETAIL
STATED PRINT RUN 55 SER.#'d SETS
1 Paul Kariya 8.00 20.00
2 Peter Forsberg 12.50 30.00
3 Joe Sakic 10.00 25.00
4 Steve Yzerman 25.00 60.00
5 Mike Comrie 8.00 20.00
6 Pavel Bure 6.00 15.00
7 Alexei Yashin 8.00 20.00
8 Eric Lindros 10.00 25.00
9 Mario Lemieux 30.00 80.00
10 Jaromir Jagr 8.00 20.00

2001-02 Atomic Core Players

COMPLETE SET (20) 40.00 80.00
STATED ODDS 1:21 HOBBY/1:25 RETAIL
1 Paul Kariya 1.25 3.00
2 Joe Thornton 2.00 5.00
3 Patrick Roy 6.00 15.00
4 Mike Modano 2.00 5.00
5 Steve Yzerman 6.00 15.00
6 Pavel Bure 1.50 4.00
7 Zigmund Palffy 1.00 2.50
8 Marian Gaborik 2.50 6.00
9 Saku Koivu 1.25 3.00
10 Martin Brodeur 3.00 8.00
11 Alexei Yashin 1.00 2.50
12 Mark Messier 1.50 4.00
13 Marian Hossa 1.25 3.00
14 John LeClair 1.50 4.00
15 Mario Lemieux 8.00 20.00
16 Chris Pronger 1.00 2.50
17 Teemu Selanne 1.25 3.00
18 Vincent Lecavalier 1.25 3.00
19 Curtis Joseph 1.25 3.00
20 Jaromir Jagr 2.00 5.00

2001-02 Atomic Jerseys

Please note that card #46 does not exist.
STATED ODDS 3:21
1 J-S Giguere 3.00 8.00
2 Steve Rucchin 3.00 8.00
3 Byron Dafoe 3.00 8.00
4 Erik Rasmussen 3.00 8.00
5 Phil Housley 3.00 8.00
6 Marc Savard 3.00 8.00

7 Jeff Shantz 3.00 8.00
8 Tony Amonte 3.00 8.00
9 Eric Daze 3.00 8.00
10 Jocelyn Thibault 3.00 8.00
11 Peter Forsberg 6.00 15.00
12 Dave Reid 3.00 8.00
13 Patrick Roy 12.00 30.00
14 Joe Sakic 8.00 20.00
15 Lyle Odelein 3.00 8.00
16 Ed Belfour 3.00 8.00
17 Benoit Hogue 3.00 8.00
18 Jyrki Lumme 3.00 8.00
19 Mike Modano 3.00 8.00
20 Sergei Zubov 3.00 8.00
21 Mathieu Dandenault 3.00 8.00
22 Dominik Hasek 6.00 15.00
23 Darren McCarty 3.00 8.00
24 Chris Osgood 3.00 8.00
25 Brendan Shanahan 3.00 8.00
26 Steve Yzerman 10.00 25.00
27 Valeri Bure 3.00 8.00
28 Wade Flaherty 3.00 8.00
29 Felix Potvin 3.00 8.00
30 Sergei Zholtok 3.00 8.00
31 Benoit Brunet 3.00 8.00
32 Jeff Hackett 3.00 8.00
33 Saku Koivu 3.00 8.00
34 Mike Dunham 3.00 8.00
35 Tom Fitzgerald 3.00 8.00
36 Scott Walker 3.00 8.00
37 Scott Niedermayer 3.00 8.00
38 Mariusz Czerkawski 3.00 8.00
39 Chris Terreri 3.00 8.00
40 Guy Hebert 3.00 8.00
41 Mike York 3.00 8.00
42 Mika Alatalo 3.00 8.00
43 Rene Corbet 3.00 8.00
44 Jan Hrdina 3.00 8.00
45 Mario Lemieux 12.00 30.00
47 Teemu Selanne 3.00 8.00
48 Mats Sundin 3.00 8.00
49 Dimitri Yushkevich 3.00 8.00
50 Jaromir Jagr 6.00 15.00

2001-02 Atomic Patches

STATED ODDS 1:21 HOBBY
PRINT RUNS VARY
1 J-S Giguere/403 6.00 15.00
2 Steve Rucchin/303 6.00 15.00
3 Byron Dafoe/128 6.00 15.00
4 Erik Rasmussen/153 6.00 15.00
5 Phil Housley/106 6.00 15.00
6 Marc Savard/403 6.00 15.00
7 Jeff Shantz/203 6.00 15.00
8 Tony Amonte/403 6.00 15.00
9 Eric Daze/328 6.00 15.00
10 Jocelyn Thibault/328 6.00 15.00
12 Dave Reid/328 6.00 15.00
13 Patrick Roy/53 40.00 100.00
14 Joe Sakic/308 12.00 30.00
15 Lyle Odelein/153 6.00 15.00
16 Ed Belfour/48 20.00 50.00
17 Benoit Hogue/123 6.00 15.00
18 Jyrki Lumme/303 6.00 15.00
19 Mike Modano/128 12.00 30.00
20 Sergei Zubov/268 6.00 15.00
21 Mathieu Dandenault/178 6.00 15.00
22 Dominik Hasek/283 10.00 25.00
23 Darren McCarty/16
24 Chris Osgood/203 6.00 15.00
26 Steve Yzerman/53 30.00 80.00
27 Valeri Bure/428 6.00 15.00
28 Wade Flaherty/302 6.00 15.00
29 Felix Potvin/103 10.00 25.00
30 Sergei Zholtok/138 6.00 15.00
33 Saku Koivu/53 15.00 40.00
34 Mike Dunham/193 6.00 15.00
35 Tom Fitzgerald/378 6.00 15.00
36 Scott Walker/428 6.00 15.00
37 Scott Niedermayer/478 6.00 15.00
38 Mariusz Czerkawski/503 6.00 15.00
39 Chris Terreri/153 6.00 15.00
40 Guy Hebert/115 6.00 15.00
41 Mike York/403 6.00 15.00
42 Mika Alatalo/228 6.00 15.00
43 Rene Corbet/53 12.00 30.00
44 Jan Hrdina/353 6.00 15.00
46 Kevin Stevens/353 6.00 15.00
47 Teemu Selanne/153 8.00 20.00
48 Mats Sundin/203 8.00 20.00
49 Dimitri Yushkevich/128 6.00 15.00
50 Jaromir Jagr/78 15.00 40.00

2001-02 Atomic Power Play

COMPLETE SET (36) 15.00 30.00
STATED ODDS 1:1
1 Paul Kariya .50 1.25
2 Patrik Stefan .25 .60
3 Sergei Samsonov .40 1.00
4 Joe Thornton .75 2.00
5 Jarome Iginla .60 1.50

6 Jeff O'Neill .25 .60
7 Tony Amonte .40 1.00
8 Peter Forsberg 1.25 3.00
9 Milan Hejduk .50 1.25
10 Joe Sakic 1.00 2.50
11 Mike Modano .75 2.00
12 Sergei Fedorov .75 2.00
13 Brendan Shanahan .50 1.25
14 Steve Yzerman 2.50 6.00
15 Mike Comrie .40 1.00
16 Pavel Bure .50 1.25
17 Zigmund Palffy .40 1.00
18 Marian Gaborik 1.00 2.50
19 Saku Koivu .50 1.25
20 Jason Arnott .25 .60
21 Alexei Yashin .25 .60
22 Theo Fleury .25 .60
23 Eric Lindros .50 1.25
24 Mark Messier .50 1.25
25 Marian Hossa .50 1.25
26 John LeClair .50 1.25
27 Mario Lemieux 3.00 8.00
28 Chris Pronger .40 1.00
29 Keith Tkachuk .50 1.25
30 Teemu Selanne .50 1.25
31 Vincent Lecavalier .50 1.25
32 Mats Sundin .50 1.25
33 Daniel Sedin .25 .60
34 Henrik Sedin .25 .60
35 Peter Bondra .50 1.25
36 Jaromir Jagr .75 2.00

2001-02 Atomic Rookie Reaction

COMPLETE SET (10) 10.00 25.00
STATED ODDS 1:41
1 Dany Heatley 2.00 5.00
2 Ilya Kovalchuk 6.00 15.00
3 Vaclav Nedorost .40 1.00
4 Rostislav Klesla .75 2.00
5 Rick DiPietro 2.00 5.00
6 Pavel Brendl .40 1.00
7 Jiri Dopita .40 1.00
8 Kris Beech .40 1.00
9 Johan Hedberg .75 2.00
10 Nikita Alexeev .40 1.00

2001-02 Atomic Statosphere

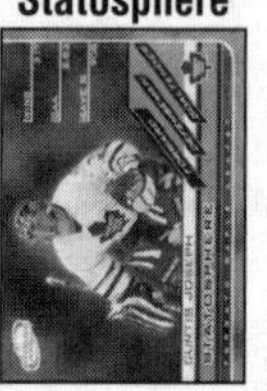

COMPLETE SET (20) 40.00 80.00
STATED ODDS 1:21 HOBBY/1:25 RETAIL
CARDS 1-10 AVAIL. HOBBY ONLY/
CARDS 11-20 AVAIL. RETAIL ONLY
1 Patrick Roy 6.00 15.00
2 Ed Belfour 1.25 3.00
3 Dominik Hasek 2.50 6.00
4 Martin Brodeur 3.00 8.00
5 Rick DiPietro 1.00 2.50
6 Mike Richter 1.25 3.00
7 Roman Cechmanek 1.00 2.50
8 Johan Hedberg 1.00 2.50
9 Evgeni Nabokov 1.00 2.50
10 Curtis Joseph 1.25 3.00
11 Peter Forsberg 3.00 8.00
12 Joe Sakic 2.50 6.00
13 Brett Hull 1.50 4.00
14 Pavel Bure 1.50 4.00
15 Zigmund Palffy 1.00 2.50
16 Alexei Yashin 1.00 2.50
17 Alexei Kovalev 1.00 2.50
18 Mario Lemieux 8.00 20.00
19 Martin Straka 1.00 2.50
20 Jaromir Jagr 2.00 5.00

2001-02 Atomic Team Nucleus

COMPLETE SET (15) 30.00 60.00
STATED ODDS 1:21 HOBBY/1:25 RETAIL
1 Bill Guerin 2.00 5.00
Sergei Samsonov
Joe Thornton
2 Jarome Iginla 2.00 5.00
Serge Savard
Roman Turek
3 Ron Francis 2.00 5.00
Arturs Irbe
Jeff O'Neill
4 Peter Forsberg 4.00 10.00
Patrick Roy
Joe Sakic
5 Ed Belfour 2.00 5.00
Mike Modano
Joe Niewendyk
6 Dominik Hasek 4.00 10.00
Brendan Shanahan
Steve Yzerman
7 Mike Comrie 2.00 5.00
Tommy Salo
Ryan Smyth
8 Jason Arnott 2.00 5.00
Martin Brodeur
Patrik Elias
9 Rick DiPietro 2.00 5.00
Mike Peca
Alexei Yashin
10 Theo Fleury 2.00 5.00
Eric Lindros
Mark Messier
11 Johan Hedberg 2.00 5.00
Alexei Kovalev
Mario Lemieux
12 Evgeni Nabokov 2.00 5.00
Owen Nolan
Teemu Selanne
13 Curtis Joseph 2.00 5.00
Alexander Mogilny
Mats Sundin
14 Markus Naslund 2.00 5.00
Daniel Sedin
Henrik Sedin
15 Peter Bondra 2.00 5.00
Jaromir Jagr
Adam Oates

2001-02 Atomic Toronto Fall Expo

Available only by wrapper redemption at the 2001 Toronto Fall Expo, this 25-card set paralleled the Atomic rookies, but carried a Fall Expo gold stamp. Each card was serial numbered out of 500.

COMPLETE SET (25) 30.00 80.00
STATED PRINT RUN 500 SETS
101 Ilja Bryzgalov 2.00 5.00
102 Timo Parssinen .75 2.00
103 Dany Heatley 4.00 10.00
104 Ilya Kovalchuk 8.00 20.00
105 Kamil Piros .75 2.00
106 Erik Cole 2.00 5.00
107 Vaclav Nedorost .75 2.00
108 Pavel Datsyuk 4.00 10.00
109 Niklas Hagman .75 2.00
110 Kristian Huselius 2.00 5.00
111 Jaroslav Bednar .75 2.00
112 Pascal Dupuis .75 2.00
113 Martin Erat .75 2.00
114 Scott Clemmensen 1.25 3.00
115 Radek Martinek .75 2.00
116 Dan Blackburn 1.25 3.00
117 Ivan Ciernik .75 2.00
118 Chris Neil 1.25 3.00
119 Pavel Brendl .75 2.00
120 Jiri Dopita .75 2.00
121 Krystofer Kolanos .75 2.00
122 Mark Rycroft .75 2.00
123 Jeff Jillson .75 2.00
124 Nikita Alexeev .75 2.00
125 Brian Sutherby .75 2.00

2002-03 Atomic

Released in mid-November, this 125-card set sported a die-cut design. Cards 101-125 were shortprinted to just 1300 copies each. Cards 126-131 were available in packs of Private Stock Reserve at a rate of 1:9 hobby packs and 1:49 retail.

COMP.SET w/o SP's (100) 25.00 60.00
SP PRINT RUN 1300 SER.#'d SETS
126-131 AVAIL. 1:9 PVT.STK HBBY PACKS
1 J-S Giguere .30 .75
2 Paul Kariya .60 1.50
3 Adam Oates .30 .75
4 Dany Heatley .75 2.00
5 Ilya Kovalchuk .75 2.00
6 Glen Murray .20 .50
7 Sergei Samsonov .30 .75
8 Joe Thornton 1.00 2.50
9 Martin Biron .30 .75
10 J-P Dumont .20 .50
11 Miroslav Satan .30 .75
12 Craig Conroy .20 .50
13 Jarome Iginla .75 2.00
14 Roman Turek .30 .75
15 Erik Cole .20 .50
16 Ron Francis .30 .75
17 Arturs Irbe .30 .75
18 Jeff O'Neill .20 .50
19 Mark Bell .20 .50
20 Eric Daze .30 .75
21 Jocelyn Thibault .30 .75
22 Rob Blake .30 .75
23 Chris Drury .30 .75
24 Peter Forsberg 1.00 2.50
25 Steven Reinprecht .20 .50
26 Patrick Roy 2.50 6.00
27 Joe Sakic 1.25 3.00
28 Marc Denis .30 .75
29 Espen Knutsen .20 .50
30 Ray Whitney .20 .50
31 Jason Arnott .20 .50
32 Bill Guerin .30 .75
33 Mike Modano 1.00 2.50
34 Marty Turco .30 .75
35 Pavel Datsyuk .60 1.50
36 Sergei Fedorov .60 1.50
37 Brett Hull .60 1.50
38 Curtis Joseph .60 1.50
39 Nicklas Lidstrom .30 .75
40 Brendan Shanahan .60 1.50
41 Steve Yzerman 2.00 5.00
42 Mike Comrie .30 .75
43 Tommy Salo .30 .75
44 Ryan Smyth .20 .50
45 Kristian Huselius .20 .50
46 Roberto Luongo .75 2.00
47 Stephen Weiss .20 .50
48 Jason Allison .20 .50
49 Zigmund Palffy .30 .75
50 Felix Potvin .60 1.50
51 Andrew Brunette .20 .50
52 Manny Fernandez .30 .75
53 Marian Gaborik 1.25 2.50
54 Doug Gilmour .30 .75
55 Saku Koivu .60 1.50
56 Yanic Perreault .20 .50
57 Jose Theodore .60 1.50
58 Denis Arkhipov .20 .50
59 Mike Dunham .30 .75
60 Martin Brodeur 1.50 4.00
61 Patrik Elias .30 .75
62 Joe Nieuwendyk .30 .75
63 Chris Osgood .30 .75
64 Michael Peca .20 .50
65 Alexei Yashin .20 .50
66 Dan Blackburn .30 .75
67 Pavel Bure .60 1.50
68 Eric Lindros .60 1.50
69 Mike Richter .30 .75
70 Daniel Alfredsson .30 .75
71 Marian Hossa .30 .75
72 Patrick Lalime .30 .75
73 Roman Cechmanek .20 .50
74 Simon Gagne .30 .75
75 Jeremy Roenick .60 1.50
76 Tony Amonte .30 .75
77 Daniel Briere .20 .50
78 Sean Burke .30 .75
79 Johan Hedberg .30 .75
80 Mario Lemieux 2.50 6.00
81 Alexei Morozov .20 .50
82 Brent Johnson .30 .75
83 Chris Pronger .30 .75
84 Keith Tkachuk .30 .75
85 Patrick Marleau .30 .75
86 Evgeni Nabokov .30 .75
87 Owen Nolan .30 .75
88 Teemu Selanne .60 1.50
89 Nikolai Khabibulin .30 .75
90 Vincent Lecavalier .60 1.50
91 Ed Belfour .30 .75
92 Alexander Mogilny .30 .75
93 Gary Roberts .20 .50
94 Mats Sundin .60 1.50
95 Todd Bertuzzi .30 .75
96 Dan Cloutier .30 .75
97 Markus Naslund .30 .75
98 Peter Bondra .30 .75
99 Jaromir Jagr 1.00 2.50
100 Olaf Kolzig .30 .75
101 Stanislav Chistov RC 2.00 5.00
102 Martin Gerber RC 2.50 6.00
103 Alexei Smirnov RC 1.50 4.00
104 Chuck Kobasew RC 2.50 6.00
105 Rick Nash RC 6.00 15.00
106 Dmitri Bykov RC 2.00 5.00
107 Henrik Zetterberg RC 6.00 15.00
108 Kari Haakana RC 2.00 5.00
109 Ales Hemsky RC 4.00 10.00
110 Alex Henry RC 2.00 5.00
111 Jay Bouwmeester RC 3.00 8.00
112 Alexander Frolov RC 4.00 10.00
113 P-M Bouchard RC 4.00 10.00
114 Sylvain Blouin RC 2.00 5.00
115 Ron Hainsey RC 2.00 5.00
116 Adam Hall RC 2.00 5.00
117 Scottie Upshall RC 2.00 5.00
118 Mike Danton SP 2.00 5.00
119 Ray Schultz RC 2.00 5.00
120 Anton Volchenkov RC 2.00 5.00
121 Dennis Seidenberg RC 2.00 5.00
122 Patrick Sharp RC 2.00 5.00
123 Dick Tarnstrom RC 2.00 5.00
124 Alexander Svitov RC 2.00 5.00
125 Steve Eminger RC 2.00 5.00
126 Jordan Leopold RC 2.00 5.00
127 Stephane Veilleux RC 1.50 4.00
128 Jason Spezza RC 8.00 20.00
129 Radovan Somik RC 1.50 4.00
130 Jeff Taffe RC 1.50 4.00
131 Tom Koivisto RC 1.50 4.00

2002-03 Atomic Blue

*STARS: 1.25X TO 3X BASIC CARDS
*ROOKIES: .5X TO 1.25X
STATED ODDS 1:6 US
PRINT RUN 175 SER.#'d SETS

2002-03 Atomic Gold

*GOLD: X TO X BASIC CARDS
*ROOKIES: .6X TO 1.5X
STATED ODDS 1:11 HOBBY
PRINT RUN 99 SER.#'d SETS

2002-03 Atomic Red

*STARS:1.5X TO 4X BASIC CARDS
*ROOKIES: .6X TO 1.5X
STATED ODDS 1:6
PRINT RUN 125 SER.#'d SETS

2002-03 Atomic Cold Fusion

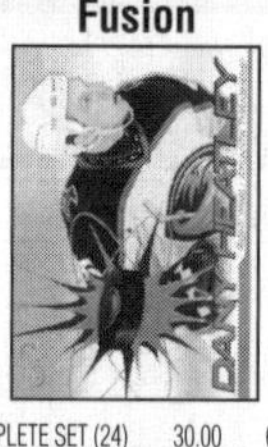

COMPLETE SET (24) 30.00 60.00
STATED ODDS 1:11
1 Paul Kariya .75 2.00
2 Dany Heatley 1.00 2.50
3 Ilya Kovalchuk 1.00 2.50
4 Joe Thornton 1.25 3.00
5 Jarome Iginla 1.00 2.50
6 Jeff O'Neill .60 1.50
7 Eric Daze .60 1.50
8 Peter Forsberg 2.00 5.00
9 Joe Sakic 1.50 4.00
10 Pavel Datsyuk .75 2.00
11 Brendan Shanahan 1.25 3.00
12 Steve Yzerman 3.00 8.00
13 Mike Comrie .60 1.50
14 Kristian Huselius .60 1.50
15 Saku Koivu .75 2.00
16 Pavel Bure 1.00 2.50
17 Eric Lindros .75 2.00
18 Daniel Alfredsson .60 1.50
19 Simon Gagne .75 2.00
20 Mario Lemieux 5.00 12.00
21 Teemu Selanne .75 2.00
22 Mats Sundin .75 2.00
23 Markus Naslund .75 2.00
24 Jaromir Jagr 1.25 3.00

2002-03 Atomic Denied

COMPLETE SET (20) 20.00 40.00
STATED ODDS 1:41
1 J-S Giguere .75 2.00
2 Roman Turek .75 2.00
3 Arturs Irbe .75 2.00
4 Jocelyn Thibault .75 2.00
5 Patrick Roy 5.00 12.00
6 Marty Turco .75 2.00
7 Curtis Joseph 1.00 2.50
8 Roberto Luongo 1.25 1.00
9 Felix Potvin 1.00 2.50
10 Jose Theodore 1.25 3.00
11 Martin Brodeur 2.50 6.00
12 Chris Osgood .75 2.00
13 Mike Richter .75 2.00
14 Patrick Lalime .75 2.00
15 Roman Cechmanek .75 2.00
16 Sean Burke .75 2.00
17 Brent Johnson .75 2.00
18 Evgeni Nabokov .75 2.00
19 Nikolai Khabibulin 1.00 2.50
20 Ed Belfour 1.00 2.50

2002-03 Atomic Hobby Parallel

*STARS: .75X TO 2X BASIC CARDS
*ROOKIES: .25X TO .75X
STATED ODDS 3:4
PRINT RUN 775 SER.#'d SETS

2002-03 Atomic Jerseys

STATED ODDS 4:21
1 Adam Oates 2.00 5.00
2 Roman Turek 2.00 5.00
3 Jason Arnott 2.00 5.00
4 Bill Guerin 2.00 5.00
5 Scott Young 2.00 5.00
6 Dominik Hasek 8.00 20.00
7 Brett Hull 4.00 10.00
8 Curtis Joseph 3.00 8.00
9 Luc Robitaille 3.00 8.00
10 Ryan Smyth 2.00 5.00
11 Jose Theodore 6.00 15.0
12 Jeff Friesen 2.00 5.0
13 Oleg Tverdovsky 2.00 5.0
14 Alexei Yashin 2.00 5.0
15 Pavel Bure 4.00 10.0
16 Mark Messier 4.00 10.0
17 John LeClair 2.00 5.0
18 Daymond Langkow 2.00 5.0
19 Mario Lemieux 12.00 30.0
20 Pavol Demitra 2.00 5.0
21 Ray Ferraro 2.00 5.0
22 Tom Barrasso 2.00 5.0
23 Darcy Tucker 2.00 5.0
24 Jaromir Jagr 8.00 20.0
25 Robert Lang 2.00 5.0

2002-03 Atomic Patches

*PATCHES: 1X TO 2.5X JERSEY

2002-03 Atomic National Pride

COMP.CANADA SET (10) 20.00 40.0
COMP.US SET (10) 8.00 15.0
STATED ODDS 1:21
C1-C10 AVAIL.CANADA PACKS ONLY
U1-U10 AVAIL.US PACKS ONLY
C1 Paul Kariya .75 2.0
C2 Jarome Iginla 1.00 2.5
C3 Rob Blake .60 1.5
C4 Joe Sakic 1.50 4.0
C5 Curtis Joseph .75 2.0
C6 Brendan Shanahan 1.00 2.5
C7 Steve Yzerman 4.00 10.0
C8 Martin Brodeur 2.00 5.0
C9 Mario Lemieux 5.00 12.0
C10 Chris Pronger .60 1.5
U1 Bill Guerin .60 1.5
U2 Mike Modano 1.25 3.0
U3 Chris Chelios .75 2.0
U4 Brett Hull 1.00 2.5
U5 Brian Leetch .60 1.5
U6 Mike Richter .60 1.5
U7 Jeremy Roenick 1.00 2.5
U8 Tony Amonte .60 1.5
U9 Keith Tkachuk .75 2.0
U10 Tom Barrasso .60 1.5

2002-03 Atomic Power Converters

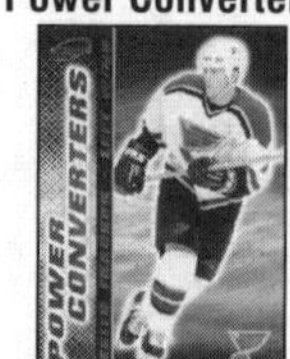

COMPLETE SET (20) 15.00 40.0
STATED ODDS 1:21
1 Dany Heatley 1.50 4.0
2 Ilya Kovalchuk 1.50 4.0
3 Miroslav Satan 1.25 3.0
4 Jarome Iginla 1.50 4.0
5 Ron Francis 1.25 3.0
6 Sami Kapanen .75 2.0
7 Nicklas Lidstrom 1.25 3.0
8 Luc Robitaille 1.25 3.0
9 Jason Allison .75 2.0
10 Zigmund Palffy .75 2.0
11 Andrew Brunette .75 2.0
12 Alexei Yashin .75 2.0
13 Pavel Bure 1.25 3.0
14 Eric Lindros 1.25 3.0
15 Daniel Briere .75 2.0
16 Pavol Demitra .75 2.0
17 Keith Tkachuk 1.25 3.0
18 Todd Bertuzzi 1.25 3.0
19 Markus Naslund 1.25 3.0
20 Peter Bondra 1.25 3.0

2002-03 Atomic Super Colliders

COMPLETE SET (16) 12.00 30.0
STATED ODDS 1:21
1 Ilya Kovalchuk 2.00 5.0
2 Joe Thornton 2.00 5.0
3 Jarome Iginla 2.00 5.0
4 Erik Cole .75 2.0
5 Jason Arnott .75 2.0
6 Brendan Shanahan 1.25 3.0
7 Ryan Smyth .75 2.0
8 Jason Allison .75 2.0
9 Michael Peca .75 2.0
10 Eric Lindros 1.25 3.0
11 Jeremy Roenick 1.25 3.0

Chris Pronger .75 2.00
Keith Tkachuk .75 2.00
Owen Nolan .75 2.00
Gary Roberts .75 2.00
Todd Bertuzzi 1.25 3.00

1998-99 Aurora

e 1998-99 Pacific Aurora set was issued one series with a total of 200 standard ze cards. The six-card packs retail for .99 each. The fronts feature color game-tion photos with a smaller head-shot of e featured player in the upper right hand rner. The super-thick card also offers a allenging trivia question on the back.

OMPLETE SET (200) 25.00 50.00
Travis Green .08 .20
Guy Hebert .20 .50
Paul Kariya .25 .60
Steve Rucchin .08 .20
Tomas Sandstrom .08 .20
Teemu Selanne .25 .60
Jason Allison .08 .20
Ray Bourque .40 1.00
Anson Carter .20 .50
Byron Dafoe .20 .50
Ted Donato .08 .20
Dave Ellett .08 .20
Dimitri Khristich .08 .20
Sergei Samsonov .20 .50
Matthew Barnaby .08 .20
Michal Grosek .08 .20
Dominik Hasek .50 1.25
Brian Holzinger .08 .20
Michael Peca .08 .20
Miroslav Satan .20 .50
Dixon Ward .08 .20
Alexei Zhitnik .08 .20
Andrew Cassels .08 .20
Theo Fleury .08 .20
Jarome Iginla .30 .75
Marty McInnis .08 .20
Derek Morris .08 .20
Michael Nylander .08 .20
Cory Stillman .08 .20
Kevin Dineen .08 .20
Nelson Emerson .08 .20
Martin Gelinas .08 .20
Sami Kapanen .08 .20
Trevor Kidd .20 .50
Robert Kron .08 .20
Jeff O'Neill .08 .20
Keith Primeau .08 .20
Tony Amonte .20 .50
Chris Chelios .25 .60
Eric Daze .20 .50
Jeff Hackett .20 .50
Jean-Yves Leroux .08 .20
Jeff Shantz .08 .20
Alexei Zhamnov .08 .20
Adam Deadmarsh .08 .20
Peter Forsberg .60 1.50
Valeri Kamensky .08 .20
Claude Lemieux .08 .20
Eric Messier .08 .20
Sandis Ozolinsh .08 .20
Patrick Roy 1.25 3.00
Joe Sakic .50 1.25
Ed Belfour .25 .60
Derian Hatcher .08 .20
Brett Hull .30 .75
Jamie Langenbrunner .08 .20
Jere Lehtinen .08 .20
Mike Modano .40 1.00
Joe Nieuwendyk .20 .50
Darryl Sydor .08 .20
Sergei Zubov .08 .20
Sergei Fedorov .40 1.00
Vyacheslav Kozlov .20 .50
Igor Larionov .20 .50
Nicklas Lidstrom .25 .60
Darren McCarty .08 .20
Chris Osgood .20 .50
Brendan Shanahan .25 .60
Steve Yzerman 1.25 3.00
Kelly Buchberger .08 .20
Mike Grier .08 .20
Bill Guerin .20 .50
Roman Hamrlik .08 .20
Boris Mironov .08 .20
Janne Niinimaa .08 .20
Ryan Smyth .20 .50
Doug Weight .20 .50
Dino Ciccarelli .20 .50
Dave Gagner .08 .20
Ed Jovanovski .08 .20
Viktor Kozlov .08 .20
Paul Laus .08 .20
Scott Mellanby .08 .20
Ray Whitney .08 .20
Rob Blake .20 .50
Stephane Fiset .08 .20
Yanic Perreault .08 .20
Luc Robitaille .20 .50
Jamie Storr .20 .50
Jozef Stumpel .20 .50
Vladimir Tsyplakov .08 .20
Shayne Corson .08 .20
Vincent Damphousse .08 .20
Saku Koivu .25 .60
Mark Recchi .20 .50
Martin Rucinsky .08 .20
Brian Savage .08 .20
Jocelyn Thibault .20 .50
Andrew Brunette .20 .50
00 Mike Dunham .20 .50
01 Tom Fitzgerald .08 .20
102 Sergei Krivokrasov .08 .20
103 Denny Lambert .08 .20
104 Mikhail Shtalenkov .08 .20
105 Darren Turcotte .08 .20
106 Dave Andreychuk .20 .50
107 Jason Arnott .08 .20
108 Martin Brodeur .60 1.50
109 Patrik Elias .20 .50
110 Bobby Holik .08 .20
111 Randy McKay .08 .20
112 Scott Niedermayer .08 .20
113 Scott Stevens .20 .50
114 Bryan Berard .20 .50
115 Jason Dawe .08 .20
116 Trevor Linden .20 .50
117 Zigmund Palffy .20 .50
118 Robert Reichel .08 .20
119 Tommy Salo .20 .50
120 Bryan Smolinski .08 .20
121 Adam Graves .08 .20
122 Wayne Gretzky 1.50 4.00
123 Alexei Kovalev .08 .20
124 Brian Leetch .25 .60
125 Mike Richter .25 .60
126 Ulf Samuelsson .08 .20
127 Kevin Stevens .20 .50
128 Daniel Alfredsson .20 .50
129 Andreas Dackell .08 .20
130 Igor Kravchuk .08 .20
131 Shawn McEachern .08 .20
132 Chris Phillips .08 .20
133 Damian Rhodes .20 .50
134 Alexei Yashin .08 .20
135 Rod Brind'Amour .20 .50
136 Alexandre Daigle .08 .20
137 Eric Desjardins .20 .50
138 Chris Gratton .20 .50
139 Ron Hextall .20 .50
140 John LeClair .25 .60
141 Eric Lindros .25 .60
142 John Vanbiesbrouck .20 .50
143 Dainius Zubrus .08 .20
144 Brad Isbister .08 .20
145 Nikolai Khabibulin .20 .50
146 Jeremy Roenick .30 .75
147 Cliff Ronning .08 .20
148 Keith Tkachuk .25 .60
149 Rick Tocchet .20 .50
150 Oleg Tverdovsky .08 .20
151 Stu Barnes .08 .20
152 Tom Barrasso .20 .50
153 Kevin Hatcher .08 .20
154 Jaromir Jagr .40 1.00
155 Darius Kasparaitis .08 .20
156 Alexei Morozov .08 .20
157 Martin Straka .08 .20
158 Jim Campbell .08 .20
159 Geoff Courtnall .08 .20
160 Grant Fuhr .20 .50
161 Al MacInnis .20 .50
162 Jamie McLennan .20 .50
163 Chris Pronger .20 .50
164 Pierre Turgeon .20 .50
165 Tony Twist .08 .20
166 Jeff Friesen .08 .20
167 Tony Granato .08 .20
168 Patrick Marleau .08 .20
169 Marty McSorley .08 .20
170 Owen Nolan .20 .50
171 Marco Sturm .08 .20
172 Mike Vernon .20 .50
173 Karl Dykhuis .08 .20
174 Mikael Renberg .20 .50
175 Stephane Richer .20 .50
176 Alexander Selivanov .08 .20
177 Paul Ysebaert .08 .20
178 Rob Zamuner .08 .20
179 Sergei Berezin .20 .50
180 Tie Domi .20 .50
181 Mike Johnson .20 .50
182 Curtis Joseph .25 .60
183 Igor Korolev .08 .20
184 Mathieu Schneider .08 .20
185 Mats Sundin .25 .60
186 Todd Bertuzzi .25 .60
187 Donald Brashear .08 .20
188 Pavel Bure .25 .60
189 Mark Messier .25 .60
190 Alexander Mogilny .20 .50
191 Mattias Ohlund .08 .20
192 Garth Snow .20 .50
193 Brian Bellows .08 .20
194 Peter Bondra .20 .50
195 Sergei Gonchar .08 .20
196 Calle Johansson .08 .20
197 Joe Juneau .20 .50
198 Olaf Kolzig .20 .50
199 Adam Oates .20 .50
200 Richard Zednik .08 .20
S108 Martin Brodeur SAMPLE .08 .20

1998-99 Aurora Atomic Laser Cuts

COMPLETE SET (20) 25.00 50.00
STATED ODDS 4:37 HOBBY
1 Paul Kariya .75 2.00
2 Teemu Selanne .75 2.00
3 Sergei Samsonov .60 1.50
4 Dominik Hasek 1.50 4.00
5 Peter Forsberg 2.00 5.00
6 Patrick Roy 4.00 10.00
7 Joe Sakic 1.50 4.00
8 Mike Modano 1.25 3.00
9 Sergei Fedorov 1.25 3.00
10 Brendan Shanahan .75 2.00
11 Steve Yzerman 4.00 10.00
12 Martin Brodeur 2.00 5.00
13 Wayne Gretzky 5.00 12.00
14 John LeClair .75 2.00
15 Eric Lindros .75 2.00
16 Jaromir Jagr 1.25 3.00
17 Mats Sundin .75 2.00
18 Pavel Bure .75 2.00
19 Mark Messier .75 2.00
20 Peter Bondra .60 1.50

1998-99 Aurora Championship Fever

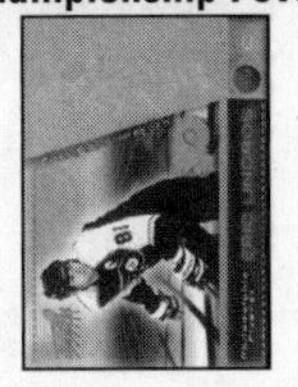

COMPLETE SET (50) 15.00 40.00
STATED ODDS 1:1
COPPER PRINT RUN 20 SETS
COPPER NOT PRICED DUE TO SCARCITY
*ICE BLUES: 6X TO 15X BASIC INSERTS
ICE BLUE PRINT RUN 100 SETS
*REDS: .75X TO 2X BASIC INSERTS
RED STATED ODDS 1:4 TREAT
*SILVERS: 2.5X TO 6X BASIC INSERTS
SILVER STATED PRINT RUN 250 SETS
1 Paul Kariya .30 .75
2 Teemu Selanne .30 .75
3 Ray Bourque .50 1.25
4 Byron Dafoe .25 .60
5 Sergei Samsonov .25 .60
6 Dominik Hasek .60 1.50
7 Michael Peca .25 .60
8 Theo Fleury .25 .60
9 Keith Primeau .25 .60
10 Chris Chelios .30 .75
11 Peter Forsberg .75 2.00
12 Patrick Roy 1.50 4.00
13 Joe Sakic .60 1.50
14 Ed Belfour .30 .75
15 Mike Modano .50 1.25
16 Sergei Fedorov .50 1.25
17 Nicklas Lidstrom .30 .75
18 Chris Osgood .25 .60
19 Brendan Shanahan .30 .75
20 Steve Yzerman 1.50 4.00
21 Doug Weight .25 .60
22 Dino Ciccarelli .25 .60
23 Rob Blake .25 .60
24 Saku Koivu .30 .75
25 Mark Recchi .25 .60
26 Martin Brodeur .75 2.00
27 Patrik Elias .25 .60
28 Trevor Linden .25 .60
29 Zigmund Palffy .25 .60
30 Wayne Gretzky 2.00 5.00
31 Mike Richter .30 .75
32 Daniel Alfredsson .25 .60
33 Damian Rhodes .25 .60
34 Alexei Yashin .25 .60
35 John LeClair .30 .75
36 Eric Lindros .30 .75
37 Dainius Zubrus .25 .60
38 Keith Tkachuk .30 .75
39 Tom Barrasso .25 .60
40 Jaromir Jagr .50 1.25
41 Grant Fuhr .25 .60
42 Pierre Turgeon .25 .60
43 Patrick Marleau .25 .60
44 Mike Vernon .25 .60
45 Rob Zamuner .25 .60
46 Mats Sundin .30 .75
47 Pavel Bure .30 .75
48 Mark Messier .30 .75
49 Peter Bondra .25 .60
50 Olaf Kolzig .25 .60
NNO M.Brodeur Gold AU/97 75.00 150.00

1998-99 Aurora Cubes

COMPLETE SET (20) 40.00 100.00
ONE PER HOBBY BOX
1 Paul Kariya 1.50 4.00
2 Teemu Selanne 1.50 4.00
3 Dominik Hasek 3.00 8.00
4 Peter Forsberg 3.00 8.00
5 Patrick Roy 6.00 15.00
6 Joe Sakic 3.00 8.00
7 Mike Modano 2.50 6.00
8 Sergei Fedorov 2.50 6.00
9 Brendan Shanahan 1.50 4.00
10 Steve Yzerman 5.00 12.00
11 Martin Brodeur 4.00 10.00
12 Wayne Gretzky 8.00 20.00
13 John LeClair 1.50 4.00
14 Eric Lindros 1.50 4.00
15 Jaromir Jagr 2.50 6.00
16 Mats Sundin 1.50 4.00
17 Pavel Bure 1.50 4.00
18 Mark Messier 1.50 4.00
19 Peter Bondra 1.25 3.00
20 Olaf Kolzig 1.25 3.00

1998-99 Aurora Front Line Copper

STATED ODDS 1:97 CANADIAN
STATED PRINT RUN 80 SETS
ICE BLUE PRINT RUN 15 SETS
ICE BLUE NOT PRICED DUE TO SCARCITY

RED STATED PRINT RUN 5 SETS
RED PARALLEL NOT PRICED DUE TO SCARCITY
1 Dominik Hasek 30.00 80.00
2 Peter Forsberg 30.00 80.00
3 Patrick Roy 50.00 125.00
4 Joe Sakic 30.00 80.00
5 Steve Yzerman 50.00 125.00
6 Daniel Alfredsson 10.00 25.00
7 Eric Lindros 20.00 50.00
8 Jaromir Jagr 25.00 60.00
9 Wayne Gretzky 75.00 200.00
10 Tie Domi 10.00 25.00

1998-99 Aurora Front Line Ice Blue

STATED ODDS 1:97 CANADIAN
STATED PRINT RUN 15 SETS
NOT PRICED DUE TO SCARCITY

1998-99 Aurora Man Advantage

COMPLETE SET (20) 50.00 100.00
STATED ODDS 1:73
1 Paul Kariya 2.00 5.00
2 Teemu Selanne 2.00 5.00
3 Ray Bourque 3.00 8.00
4 Michael Peca .60 1.50
5 Peter Forsberg 5.00 12.00
6 Joe Sakic 4.00 10.00
7 Mike Modano 3.00 8.00
8 Joe Nieuwendyk 1.50 4.00
9 Brendan Shanahan 2.00 5.00
10 Steve Yzerman 10.00 25.00
11 Shayne Corson .60 1.50
12 Zigmund Palffy 1.50 4.00
13 Wayne Gretzky 12.50 30.00
14 John LeClair 2.00 5.00
15 Eric Lindros 2.00 5.00
16 Jaromir Jagr 3.00 8.00
17 Mats Sundin 2.00 5.00
18 Pavel Bure 2.00 5.00
19 Mark Messier 2.00 5.00
20 Peter Bondra 1.50 4.00

1998-99 Aurora NHL Command

STATED ODDS 1:361
1 Teemu Selanne 3.00 8.00
2 Dominik Hasek 6.00 15.00
3 Peter Forsberg 8.00 20.00
4 Patrick Roy 15.00 40.00
5 Mike Modano 5.00 12.00
6 Steve Yzerman 15.00 40.00
7 Martin Brodeur 8.00 20.00
8 Wayne Gretzky 20.00 50.00
9 Eric Lindros 3.00 8.00
10 Jaromir Jagr 5.00 12.00

1999-00 Aurora

Cards feature one large color action photo, and one small color action photo on each cardfront. Card backs feature current statistics with another color action photo. Cardstock is thicker than most cards and were available at both hobby and retail outlets.

COMPLETE SET (150) 20.00 40.00
1 Guy Hebert .20 .50
2 Paul Kariya .25 .60
3 Marty McInnis .08 .20
4 Steve Rucchin .08 .20
5 Teemu Selanne .25 .60
6 Andrew Brunette .08 .20
7 Kelly Buchberger .08 .20
8 Damian Rhodes .08 .20
9 Jason Allison .08 .20
10 Ray Bourque .40 1.00
11 Anson Carter .20 .50
12 Byron Dafoe .20 .50
13 Sergei Samsonov .20 .50
14 Joe Thornton .40 1.00
15 Curtis Brown .08 .20
16 Dominik Hasek .50 1.25
17 Joe Juneau .20 .50
18 Michael Peca .20 .50
19 Miroslav Satan .20 .50
20 Valeri Bure .08 .20
21 J-S Giguere .20 .50
22 Phil Housley .08 .20
23 Jarome Iginla .30 .75
24 Cory Stillman .08 .20
25 Ron Francis .20 .50
26 Arturs Irbe .20 .50
27 Sami Kapanen .08 .20
28 Keith Primeau .08 .20
29 Ray Sheppard .20 .50
30 Tony Amonte .20 .50
31 J-P Dumont .20 .50
32 Doug Gilmour .20 .50
33 Jocelyn Thibault .20 .50
34 Alexei Zhamnov .08 .20
35 Adam Deadmarsh .08 .20
36 Chris Drury .20 .50
37 Theo Fleury .08 .20
38 Peter Forsberg .60 1.50
39 Milan Hejduk .30 .75
40 Claude Lemieux .08 .20
41 Patrick Roy 1.25 3.00
42 Joe Sakic .50 1.25
43 Ed Belfour .25 .60
44 Brett Hull .25 .75
45 Jamie Langenbrunner .08 .20
46 Jere Lehtinen .20 .50
47 Mike Modano .40 1.00
48 Joe Nieuwendyk .20 .50
49 Chris Chelios .25 .60
50 Sergei Fedorov .40 1.00
51 Nicklas Lidstrom .25 .60
52 Darren McCarty .08 .20
53 Chris Osgood .20 .50
54 Brendan Shanahan .25 .60
55 Steve Yzerman 1.25 3.00
56 Bill Guerin .08 .20
57 Mike Grier .20 .50
58 Tommy Salo .20 .50
59 Ryan Smyth .20 .50
60 Doug Weight .20 .50
61 Pavel Bure .25 .60
62 Sean Burke .20 .50
63 Viktor Kozlov .08 .20
64 Rob Niedermayer .08 .20
65 Mark Parrish .08 .20
66 Ray Whitney .08 .20
67 Donald Audette .08 .20
68 Rob Blake .08 .20
69 Zigmund Palffy .20 .50
70 Luc Robitaille .20 .50
71 Jamie Storr .20 .50
72 Jozef Stumpel .20 .50
73 Shayne Corson .08 .20
74 Jeff Hackett .20 .50
75 Saku Koivu .25 .60
76 Martin Rucinsky .08 .20
77 Brian Savage .08 .20
78 Mike Dunham .20 .50
79 Sergei Krivokrasov .08 .20
80 David Legwand .20 .50
81 Cliff Ronning .08 .20
82 Scott Walker .08 .20
83 Jason Arnott .08 .20
84 Martin Brodeur .60 1.50
85 Patrik Elias .20 .50
86 Bobby Holik .20 .50
87 Brendan Morrison .20 .50
88 Petr Sykora .08 .20
89 Mariusz Czerkawski .08 .20
90 Kenny Jonsson .08 .20
91 Felix Potvin .25 .60
92 Mike Watt .08 .20
93 Adam Graves .08 .20
94 Brian Leetch .25 .60
95 John MacLean .08 .20
96 Petr Nedved .20 .50
97 Mike Richter .25 .60
98 Magnus Arvedson .08 .20
99 Marian Hossa .25 .60
100 Shawn McEachern .08 .20
101 Ron Tugnutt .20 .50
102 Alexei Yashin .08 .20
103 Rod Brind'Amour .20 .50
104 Eric Desjardins .20 .50
105 John LeClair .25 .60
106 Eric Lindros .25 .60
107 Mark Recchi .20 .50
108 John Vanbiesbrouck .20 .50
109 Nikolai Khabibulin .20 .50
110 Teppo Numminen .08 .20
111 Jeremy Roenick .30 .75
112 Rick Tocchet .20 .50
113 Keith Tkachuk .25 .60
114 Matthew Barnaby .08 .20
115 Tom Barrasso .08 .20
116 Jaromir Jagr .40 1.00
117 Alexei Kovalev .08 .20
118 Martin Straka .08 .20
119 Vincent Damphousse .08 .20
120 Jeff Friesen .08 .20
121 Patrick Marleau .20 .50
122 Steve Shields .20 .50
123 Mike Vernon .20 .50
124 Pavol Demitra .20 .50
125 Grant Fuhr .20 .50
126 Al MacInnis .20 .50
127 Chris Pronger .20 .50
128 Pierre Turgeon .20 .50
129 Chris Gratton .08 .20
130 Kevin Hodson .20 .50
131 Vincent Lecavalier .08 .20
132 Paul Mara .20 .50
133 Darcy Tucker .08 .20
134 Sergei Berezin .20 .50
135 Mike Johnson .20 .50
136 Curtis Joseph .25 .60
137 Yanic Perreault .08 .20
138 Mats Sundin .25 .60
139 Steve Thomas .08 .20
140 Mark Messier .25 .60
141 Bill Muckalt .20 .50
142 Alexander Mogilny .20 .50
143 Markus Naslund .25 .60
144 Mattias Ohlund .08 .20
145 Garth Snow .20 .50
146 Peter Bondra .20 .50
147 Sergei Gonchar .08 .20
148 Benoit Gratton RC .08 .20
149 Olaf Kolzig .20 .50
150 Adam Oates .20 .50

1999-00 Aurora Premiere Date

*STARS: 15X TO 40X BASIC CARD
STATED PRINT RUN 60 SERIAL #'d SETS
*STRIPED CARDS: SAME VALUE

1999-00 Aurora Canvas Creations

COMPLETE SET (10) 60.00 150.00
STATED ODDS 1:193
1 Paul Kariya 6.00 15.00
2 Teemu Selanne 6.00 15.00
3 Dominik Hasek 12.00 30.00
4 Peter Forsberg 10.00 25.00
5 Patrick Roy 25.00 60.00
6 Steve Yzerman 20.00 50.00
7 Pavel Bure 6.00 15.00
8 John LeClair 4.00 10.00
9 Eric Lindros 6.00 15.00
10 Jaromir Jagr 8.00 20.00

1999-00 Aurora Championship Fever

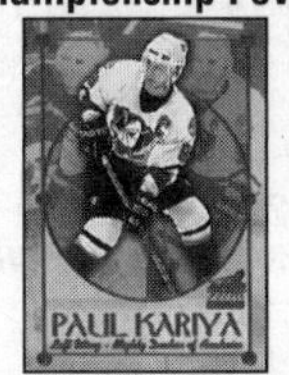

Martin Brodeur autographed 197 copies of his insert card and one each of the parallel cards; these were inserted randomly.

COMPLETE SET (20) 40.00 80.00
STATED ODDS 4:25
COPPER STATED PRINT RUN 20 SETS
COPPER NOT PRICED DUE TO SCARCITY
*ICE BLUE STARS: 15X TO 40X BASIC CARDS
ICE BLUE STATED PRINT RUN 100 SETS
*SILVER STARS: 6X TO 15X BASIC CARDS
SILVER STATED PRINT RUN 250 SETS
1 Paul Kariya .60 1.50
2 Teemu Selanne .60 1.50
3 Ray Bourque 1.00 2.50
4 Dominik Hasek 1.25 3.00
5 Michael Peca .50 1.25
6 Theo Fleury .50 1.25
7 Peter Forsberg 1.50 4.00
8 Patrick Roy 3.00 8.00
9 Joe Sakic 1.50 4.00
10 Ed Belfour .60 1.50
11 Mike Modano 1.00 2.50
12 Brendan Shanahan .60 1.50
13 Steve Yzerman 3.00 8.00
14 Pavel Bure .60 1.50
15 Martin Brodeur 1.50 4.00
16 John LeClair .60 1.50
17 Eric Lindros .60 1.50
18 Jaromir Jagr 1.00 2.50
19 Curtis Joseph .60 1.50
20 Mats Sundin .60 1.50
NNO M.Brodeur AU/197 30.00 80.00

1999-00 Aurora Complete Players

COMPLETE SET (10) 150.00 300.00
PRINT RUN 299 SERIAL #'d SETS
*PARALLEL STARS: 2.5X TO 6X BASIC CARD
PARALLEL PRINT RUN 25 SERIAL #'d SETS
1 Paul Kariya 10.00 25.00
2 Teemu Selanne 10.00 25.00
3 Dominik Hasek 12.50 30.00
4 Peter Forsberg 15.00 40.00
5 Patrick Roy 30.00 80.00
6 Mike Modano 12.50 30.00
7 Steve Yzerman 40.00 100.00
8 John LeClair 10.00 25.00
9 Eric Lindros 10.00 25.00
10 Jaromir Jagr 10.00 25.00

1999-00 Aurora Glove Unlimited

COMPLETE SET (20) 50.00 100.00
STATED ODDS 2:25
1 Guy Hebert 1.50 4.00
2 Byron Dafoe 1.50 4.00
3 Dominik Hasek 4.00 10.00
4 Arturs Irbe 1.50 4.00
5 Jocelyn Thibault 1.50 4.00
6 Patrick Roy 12.50 25.00
7 Ed Belfour 2.00 5.00
8 Chris Osgood 1.50 4.00
9 Tommy Salo 1.50 4.00
10 Jeff Hackett 1.50 4.00
11 Martin Brodeur 6.00 12.00
12 Felix Potvin 2.00 5.00
13 Mike Richter 2.00 5.00
14 Ron Tugnutt 1.50 4.00
15 John Vanbiesbrouck 1.50 4.00
16 Nikolai Khabibulin 1.50 4.00
17 Grant Fuhr 1.50 4.00
18 Steve Shields 1.50 4.00
19 Curtis Joseph 2.00 5.00
20 Olaf Kolzig 1.50 4.00

1999-00 Aurora Styrotechs

COMPLETE SET (20) 25.00 60.00
STATED ODDS 1:25
1 Paul Kariya 1.50 3.00
2 Teemu Selanne 1.50 3.00
3 Dominik Hasek 3.00 8.00
4 Theo Fleury .40 1.00
5 Peter Forsberg 3.00 8.00
6 Patrick Roy 8.00 20.00
7 Ed Belfour 1.50 3.00
8 Mike Modano 2.00 5.00
9 Brendan Shanahan 1.50 3.00
10 Steve Yzerman 6.00 15.00
11 Pavel Bure 1.50 3.00
12 Martin Brodeur 5.00 12.00
13 Alexei Yashin .40 1.00
14 John LeClair .40 1.00
15 Eric Lindros 1.50 3.00
16 Keith Tkachuk 1.50 2.00
17 Jaromir Jagr 3.00 8.00
18 Curtis Joseph 1.50 3.00
19 Mats Sundin 1.50 3.00
20 Mark Messier 1.50 4.00

2000-01 Aurora

Released as a 150-card set, Aurora base cards feature a white borderd card with two player photos on the card front. A full color action photo appears set against a background that fades from green to blue, top to bottom, and a smaller brown tone player action photo set against a blue triangle. Cards are highlighted with bronze foil. Aurora was packaged in 36-pack boxes with each pack containing six cards. A parallel with a striped background was also created and inserted randomly. The striped set was complete at 50 cards and was skip numbered.

COMPLETE SET (150) 20.00 40.00
*STRIPED: .75X TO 2X BASIC CARD
1 Guy Hebert .20 .50
2 Paul Kariya .25 .60
3 Steve Rucchin .08 .20
4 Teemu Selanne .25 .60
5 Andrew Brunette .20 .50
6 Scott Fankhouser .20 .50
7 Damian Rhodes .20 .50
8 Patrik Stefan .08 .20
9 Jason Allison .08 .20
10 Anson Carter .20 .50
11 Paul Coffey .25 .60
12 Byron Dafoe .20 .50
13 John Grahame .20 .50
14 Sergei Samsonov .20 .50

15 Joe Thornton .40 1.00
16 Maxim Afinogenov .08 .20
17 Martin Biron .20 .50
18 Doug Gilmour .20 .50
19 Dominik Hasek .50 1.25
20 Michael Peca .20 .50
21 Miroslav Satan .20 .50
22 Fred Brathwaite .20 .50
23 Valeri Bure .08 .20
24 Jarome Iginla .30 .75
25 Derek Morris .08 .20
26 Marc Savard .20 .50
27 Rod Brind'Amour .20 .50
28 Ron Francis .20 .50
29 Arturs Irbe .20 .50
30 Sami Kapanen .08 .20
31 Tony Amonte .20 .50
32 Eric Daze .20 .50
33 Steve Sullivan .08 .20
34 Jocelyn Thibault .20 .50
35 Alexei Zhamnov .20 .50
36 Ray Bourque .50 1.25
37 Chris Drury .20 .50
38 Peter Forsberg .60 1.50
39 Milan Hejduk .25 .60
40 Patrick Roy 1.25 3.00
41 Joe Sakic .50 1.25
42 Alex Tanguay .20 .50
43 Ed Belfour .25 .60
44 Brett Hull .25 .75
45 Mike Modano .40 1.00
46 Brenden Morrow .20 .50
47 Joe Nieuwendyk .20 .50
48 Chris Chelios .25 .60
49 Sergei Fedorov .40 1.00
50 Nicklas Lidstrom .25 .60
51 Chris Osgood .20 .50
52 Brendan Shanahan .25 .60
53 Pat Verbeek .08 .20
54 Steve Yzerman 1.25 3.00
55 Mike Grier .08 .20
56 Bill Guerin .20 .50
57 Tommy Salo .20 .50
58 Ryan Smyth .20 .50
59 Doug Weight .20 .50
60 Pavel Bure .25 .60
61 Trevor Kidd .20 .50
62 Viktor Kozlov .20 .50
63 Roberto Luongo .30 .75
64 Ray Whitney .20 .50
65 Rob Blake .20 .50
66 Stephane Fiset .20 .50
67 Zigmund Palffy .20 .50
68 Luc Robitaille .20 .50
69 Jamie Storr .20 .50
70 Jozef Stumpel .20 .50
71 Jeff Hackett .20 .50
72 Saku Koivu .25 .60
73 Trevor Linden .20 .50
74 Martin Rucinsky .08 .20
75 Jose Theodore .30 .75
76 Mike Dunham .20 .50
77 Patric Kjellberg .08 .20
78 David Legwand .20 .50
79 Cliff Ronning .08 .20
80 Jason Arnott .08 .20
81 Martin Brodeur .60 1.50
82 Patrik Elias .20 .50
83 Scott Gomez .08 .20
84 John Madden .20 .50
85 Scott Stevens .20 .50
86 Petr Sykora .08 .20
87 Tim Connolly .08 .20
88 Mariusz Czerkawski .08 .20
89 Brad Isbister .08 .20
90 Mark Parrish .08 .20
91 John Vanbiesbrouck .20 .50
92 Theo Fleury .08 .20
93 Adam Graves .08 .20
94 Jan Hlavac .20 .50
95 Brian Leetch .20 .50
96 Mark Messier .25 .60
97 Petr Nedved .20 .50
98 Mike Richter .25 .60
99 Daniel Alfredsson .20 .50
100 Radek Bonk .08 .20
101 Marian Hossa .25 .60
102 Shawn McEachern .20 .50
103 Vaclav Prospal .08 .20
104 Brian Boucher .25 .60
105 Eric Desjardins .20 .50
106 Simon Gagne .25 .60
107 John LeClair .25 .60
108 Eric Lindros .25 .60
109 Mark Recchi .20 .50
110 Shane Doan .20 .50
111 Joe Juneau .08 .20
112 Jeremy Roenick .30 .75
113 Keith Tkachuk .25 .60
114 Jean-Sebastien Aubin .20 .50
115 Jan Hrdina .08 .20
116 Jaromir Jagr .40 1.00
117 Alexei Kovalev .08 .20
118 Martin Straka .08 .20
119 Pavol Demitra .20 .50
120 Dallas Drake .08 .20
121 Michal Handzus .20 .50
122 Al MacInnis .20 .50
123 Chris Pronger .20 .50
124 Roman Turek .20 .50
125 Pierre Turgeon .20 .50
126 Vincent Damphousse .08 .20
127 Jeff Friesen .08 .20
128 Patrick Marleau .20 .50
129 Owen Nolan .20 .50
130 Steve Shields .20 .50
131 Dan Cloutier .20 .50
132 Matt Elich RC .20 .50
133 Mike Johnson .08 .20
134 Vincent Lecavalier .25 .60
135 Kevin Weekes .20 .50
136 Nikolai Antropov .08 .20
137 Tie Domi .20 .50
138 Jeff Farkas .08 .20
139 Curtis Joseph .25 .60
140 Mats Sundin .25 .60
141 Steve Thomas .08 .20
142 Andrew Cassels .08 .20
143 Steve Kariya .08 .20
144 Markus Naslund .25 .60
145 Felix Potvin .25 .60
146 Peter Bondra .25 .60
147 Jeff Halpern .20 .50
148 Olaf Kolzig .20 .50
149 Adam Oates .20 .50
150 Chris Simon .08 .20

2000-01 Aurora Premiere Date

*PREM.DATE STARS: 20X TO 50X BASIC CARD
STATED PRINT RUN 50 SER.#'d SETS
*PINSTRIPES: .4X TO 1X BASIC INSERTS

2000-01 Aurora Autographs

23 Valeri Bure/300 6.00 15.00
37 Chris Drury/250 8.00 20.00
42 Alex Tanguay/500 8.00 20.00
46 Brenden Morrow/500 6.00 15.00
55 Mike Grier/500 6.00 15.00
75 Jose Theodore/500 12.50 30.00
78 David Legwand/500 8.00 20.00
81 Martin Brodeur/197 40.00 80.00
115 Jean-Sebastien Aubin/500 8.00 20.00
135 Nikolai Antropov/500 6.00 15.00
148 Olaf Kolzig/250 8.00 20.00

2000-01 Aurora Canvas Creations

COMPLETE SET (10) 60.00 100.00
STATED ODDS 1:361
1 Paul Kariya 2.00 5.00
2 Peter Forsberg 6.00 15.00
3 Patrick Roy 12.50 30.00
4 Mike Modano 3.00 8.00
5 Steve Yzerman 10.00 25.00
6 Pavel Bure 2.00 5.00
7 Martin Brodeur 12.50 30.00
8 John LeClair 2.00 5.00
9 Jaromir Jagr 3.00 8.00
10 Curtis Joseph 2.00 5.00

2000-01 Aurora Championship Fever

COMPLETE SET (20) 30.00 60.00
STATED ODDS 4:37
*COPPER STARS: 10X TO 25X BASIC CARDS
COPPER PRINT RUN 90 SER.#'d SETS
*PLAT.BLUE STARS: 10X TO 25X BASIC CARDS
BLUE PRINT RUN 92 SER.#'d SETS
*SILVER STARS: 6X TO 15X BASIC CARDS
SILVER PRINT RUN 221 SER.#'d SETS
1 Paul Kariya .75 2.00
2 Teemu Selanne .75 2.00
3 Dominik Hasek 1.50 4.00
4 Ray Bourque 1.50 4.00
5 Peter Forsberg 2.00 5.00
6 Patrick Roy 4.00 10.00
7 Ed Belfour .75 2.00
8 Brett Hull 1.00 2.50
9 Mike Modano 1.25 3.00
10 Sergei Fedorov 1.25 3.00
11 Brendan Shanahan .75 2.00
12 Steve Yzerman 4.00 10.00
13 Pavel Bure .75 2.00
14 Martin Brodeur 2.00 5.00
15 Scott Gomez .75 2.00
16 Mark Messier .75 2.00
17 Brian Boucher .75 2.00
18 John LeClair .75 2.00
19 Jaromir Jagr 1.25 3.00
20 Curtis Joseph .75 2.00
NNO J.LeClair AU/197 15.00 40.00

2000-01 Aurora Dual Game-Worn Jerseys

STATED PRINT RUN 200 SER.#'d SETS
1 Petr Sykora 15.00 40.00
Saku Koivu
2 John Vanbiesbrouck 15.00 40.00
Roberto Luongo
3 S.Yzerman/B.Shanahan 20.00 50.00
4 Jaromir Jagr 15.00 40.00
Peter Bondra

2000-01 Aurora Game-Worn Jerseys

1 Paul Coffey 5.00 12.00
2 Brendan Shanahan 5.00 12.00
3 Steve Yzerman 12.50 30.00
4 Roberto Luongo 10.00 25.00
5 Saku Koivu 5.00 12.00
6 John Vanbiesbrouck 5.00 12.00
7 Mark Messier 10.00 25.00
8 Petr Sykora 5.00 12.00
9 Eric Lindros 6.00 15.00
10 Peter Bondra 5.00 12.00

2000-01 Aurora Game-Worn Jersey Patches

STATED PRINT RUN 10 SER.#'d SETS
NOT PRICED DUE TO SCARCITY

2000-01 Aurora Scouting Reports

COMPLETE SET (20) 50.00 100.00
STATED ODDS 2:37 HOBBY
1 Paul Kariya 2.00 5.00
2 Teemu Selanne 2.00 5.00
3 Patrik Stefan 1.50 4.00
4 Joe Thornton 3.00 8.00
5 Peter Forsberg 5.00 12.00
6 Milan Hejduk 2.00 5.00
7 Brett Hull 2.50 6.00
8 Ed Belfour 2.00 5.00
9 Sergei Fedorov 3.00 8.00
10 Brendan Shanahan 2.00 5.00
11 Pavel Bure 2.00 5.00
12 Roberto Luongo 2.50 6.00
13 Martin Brodeur 5.00 12.00
14 Scott Gomez 1.50 4.00
15 Marian Hossa 1.50 4.00
16 Brian Boucher 2.00 5.00
17 John LeClair 2.00 5.00
18 Vincent Lecavalier 2.00 5.00
19 Curtis Joseph 2.00 5.00
20 Mats Sundin 2.00 5.00

2000-01 Aurora Styrotechs

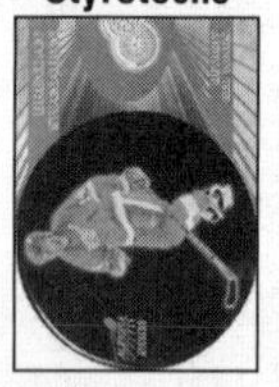

COMPLETE SET (20) 25.00 60.00
A VERSION ODDS 1:37 HOBBY
B VERSION ODDS 1:37 RETAIL
1A Paul Kariya 1.00 2.50
1B Teemu Selanne 1.00 2.50
2A Doug Gilmour 1.00 2.50
2B Dominik Hasek 2.50 6.00
3A Peter Forsberg 2.50 6.00
3B Patrick Roy 8.00 20.00
4A Joe Sakic 2.50 6.00
4B Ray Bourque 2.00 5.00
5A Brett Hull 1.00 2.50
5B Mike Modano 2.00 5.00
6A Brendan Shanahan 1.00 2.50
6B Steve Yzerman 6.00 15.00
7A Scott Gomez .40 1.00
7B Martin Brodeur 4.00 10.00
8A John LeClair .40 1.00
8B Brian Boucher .40 1.00
9A Jaromir Jagr 3.00 8.00
9B Jean-Sebastien Aubin .40 1.00
10A Curtis Joseph 1.00 2.50
10B Mats Sundin 1.00 2.50

1996 Avalanche Photo Pucks

COMPLETE SET (5) 6.00 15.00
1 Claude Lemieux 2.00 5.00
Peter Forsberg
2 Joe Sakic 1.60 4.00
Adam Deadmarsh
3 Patrick Roy 2.00 5.00
Adam Foote
4 Valeri Kamensky 1.20 3.00
Mike Ricci
5 Colorado Avalanche 1.20 3.00

1997 Avalanche Pins

This set of promotional giveaway pins was sponsored by Denver Post. One pin was given out per special event night.

1 Team Logo .40 1.00
2 Joe Sakic 1.50 4.00
3 Patrick Roy 2.50 6.00
4 Marc Crawford CO .40 1.00
5 Peter Forsberg 1.50 4.00
6 Claude Lemieux .40 1.00
7 Olympic Break .40 1.00
8 Sandiz Ozolinsh .40 1.00
9 Adam Foote .75 2.00

1999-00 Avalanche Pins

Released as a limited edition set in conjunction with the Denver Post, this 8-pin set commemorates the innagural season of the Pepsi Center. These pins were available for purchase on April 2 at the Pepsi Center vs. the Dallas Stars. Each pin was shrinkwraped with an oversized card featuring the respective player and logos of both the Pepsi Center and The Denver Post.

COMPLETE SET (8)
1 Joe Sakic 1.50 4.00
2 Adam Foote 1.25 3.00
3 Adam Deadmarsh .40 1.00
4 Patrick Roy 2.50 6.00
5 Peter Forsberg 2.00 5.00
6 Sandis Ozolinsh .40 1.00
7 Chris Drury .40 1.00
8 Milan Hejduk 1.25 3.00

1999-00 Avalanche Team Issue

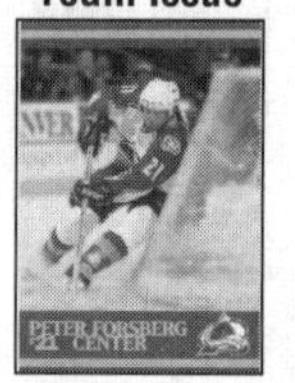

This set was issued as a promotional giveaway by the Avs. Each card in this set measures 3 1/2" x 5" and card backs are blank. The cards are unnumbered, so are listed below alphabetically.

COMPLETE SET (24) 8.00 20.00
1 Greg DeVries .10 .25
2 Adam Deadmarsh .20 .50
3 Marc Denis .30 1.00
4 Chris Dingman .10 .25
5 Chris Drury .80 1.00
6 Adam Foote .20 .50
7 Peter Forsberg 1.20 3.00
8 Alexei Gusarov .10 .25
9 Milan Hejduk .80 1.50
10 Sami Helenius .10 .25
11 Dan Hinote .40 .75
12 Jon Klemm .14 .35
13 Eric Messier .10 .25
14 Aaron Miller .10 .25
15 Jeff Odgers .10 .25
16 Sandis Ozolinsh .20 .50
17 Shjon Podein .10 .25
18 Dave Reid .10 .25
19 Brian Rolston .20 .50
20 Patrik Roy 2.00 5.00
21 Joe Sakic .80 2.00
22 Martin Skoula .20 .50
23 Alex Tanguay .80 1.50
24 Stephane Yelle .14 .35

2001-02 Avalanche Team Issue

This 23-card set measured approx. 3 1/2" X 5". Each card carried the players jersey number, name and position diagonally along the bottom of the card with the team logo at the top.

COMPLETE SET (22) 15.00 30.00
1 David Aebischer .75 2.00
2 Stephane Yelle .40 1.00
3 Rob Blake .75 2.00
4 Shjon Podein .40 1.00
5 Scott Parker .40 1.00
6 Brian Willsie .40 1.00
7 Brad Larsen .40 1.00
8 Radim Vrbata .40 1.00
9 Rick Berry .40 1.00
10 Adam Foote .40 1.00
11 Chris Drury .40 1.00
12 Alex Tanguay .75 2.00
13 Dan Hinote .40 1.00
14 Eric Messier .40 1.00
15 Joe Sakic 1.25 3.00
16 Pascal Trepanier .40 1.00
17 Martin Skoula .40 1.00
18 Steven Reinprecht .40 1.00
19 Patrick Roy 2.00 5.00
20 Milan Hejduk .75 2.00
21 Todd Gill .40 1.00
22 Greg DeVries .40 1.00
23 Peter Forsberg 1.50 4.00

2002-03 Avalanche Postcards

This postcard sized set was used as a promotional item by the team and featured player action photos on team colored card fronts. Card backs were blank.

COMPLETE SET (18) 10.00 25.00
1 Mike Keane .40 1.00
2 Riku Hahl .60 1.50
3 Scott Parker .60 1.50
4 David Aebischer .60 1.50
5 Steven Reinprecht .40 1.00
6 Greg deVries .40 1.00
7 Eric Messier .40 1.00
8 Peter Forsberg 2.00 5.00
9 Joe Sakic 2.00 5.00
10 Martin Skoula .40 1.00
11 Adam Foote .40 1.00
12 Derek Morris .40 1.00
13 Brian Willsie .40 1.00
14 Jeff Shantz .40 1.00
15 Milan Hejduk .60 1.50
16 Rob Blake .60 1.50
17 Dan Hinote .40 1.00
18 Bryan Muir .40 1.00

2003-04 Avalanche Team Issue

These team issued cards were sponsored by Conoco and each handed out at one home game each. This checklist may be incomplete. Any additional information can be forwarded to hockeymag@beckett.com.

COMPLETE SET (20) 12.00 25.00
1 David Aebischer .40 1.00
2 Rob Blake .75 2.00
3 Jim Cummins .40 1.00
4 Adam Foote .40 1.00
5 Peter Forsberg 1.25 3.00
6 Chris Gratton .40 1.00
7 Riku Hahl .40 1.00
8 Milan Hejduk .75 2.00
9 Dan Hinote .40 1.00
10 Paul Kariya .75 2.00
11 Steve Konowalchuk .40 1.00
12 John-Michael Liles .40 1.00
13 Andrei Nikolishin .40 1.00
14 Joe Sakic 1.25 3.00
15 Phil Sauve .40 1.00
16 Teemu Selanne .75 2.00
17 Karlis Skrastins .40 1.00
18 Marek Svatos .75 2.00
19 Alex Tanguay .75 2.00
20 Peter Worrell .40 1.00

2006-07 Avalanche Team Postcards

COMPLETE SET (21) 15.00 30.00
1 Tyler Arnason .40 1.00
2 Patrice Brisebois .40 1.00
3 Andrew Brunette .40 1.00
4 Peter Budaj .75 2.00
5 Brett Clark .40 1.00
6 Milan Hejduk .75 2.00
7 Ken Klee .40 1.00
8 Ian Laperriere .40 1.00
9 Jordan Leopold .40 1.00
10 Brett McLean .40 1.00
11 Brad Richardson .40 1.00
12 Mark Rycroft .40 1.00
13 Joe Sakic 2.00 5.00
14 Kurt Sauer .40 1.00
15 Karlis Skrastins .40 1.00
16 Paul Stastny 2.00 5.00
17 Marek Svatos .75 2.00
18 Jose Theodore .75 2.00
19 Pierre Turgeon .40 1.00
20 Ossi Vaananen .40 1.00
21 Wojtek Wolski .75 2.00

2003-04 Backcheck: A Hockey Retrospective

Produced by the National Library of Canada, this sepia-toned set features a look back at some early photos from hockey's history.

COMPLETE SET (20) 8.00 20.00
1 Choosing Sides .20 .50
2 Outdoor Game .20 .50
3 Early Skating .20 .50
4 Ottawa Rebels .40 1.00
5 Renfrew hockey team .40 1.00
6 Oxford Canadian Hockey Club .40 1.00
7 Gore Bay Hockey Club .40 1.00
8 Ottawa Silver Seven .75 2.00
9 Maurice Richard 2.00 5.00
10 Clarence Campbell .40 1.00
11 Bodychecking 2.00 .50
12 Asahi Athletic Club .40 1.00
13 Lester B. Pearson .20 .50
14 Prisoners' hockey team .40 1.00
15 Sydney Millionaires .40 1.00
16 Jacques Plante 2.00 5.00
17 Shinny .20 .50
18 Montreal Canadiens 1942 .75 2.00
19 Eva Ault .20 .50
20 Orillia Hockey Club .40 1.00

1995-96 Bashan Super Stickers

COMPLETE SET (135) 15.00 30.00
1 Oleg Tverdovsky TC .10 .25
2 Paul Kariya .60 1.50
3 Chad Kilger .10 .25
4 Oleg Tverdovsky .10 .25
5 Adam Oates TC .10 .25
6 Ray Bourque .60 1.50
7 Cam Neely .60 1.50
8 Adam Oates .20 .50
9 Kevin Stevens .20 .50
10 Dominik Hasek TC .10 .25
11 Pat LaFontaine .20 .50
12 Dominik Hasek .75 2.00
13 Alexei Zhitnik .10 .25
14 Theo Fleury TC .10 .25
15 Theo Fleury .40 1.00
16 Phil Housley .10 .25
17 Trevor Kidd .20 .50
18 Joe Nieuwendyk .20 .50
19 Zarley Zalapski .10 .25
20 Ed Belfour TC .10 .25
21 Jeremy Roenick .60 1.50
22 Chris Chelios .40 1.00
23 Ed Belfour .60 1.50
24 Joe Murphy .10 .25
25 Patrick Poulin .10 .25
26 Peter Forsberg TC .10 .25
27 Joe Sakic .75 2.00
28 Peter Forsberg 1.00 2.50
29 Sandis Ozolinsh .10 .25
30 Mike Ricci .10 .25
31 Valeri Kamensky .10 .25
32 Mike Modano TC .10 .25
33 Mike Modano .60 1.50
34 Kevin Hatcher .10 .25
35 Andy Moog .20 .50
36 Sergei Fedorov TC .10 .25
37 Steve Yzerman 1.25 3.00
38 Sergei Fedorov .60 1.50
39 Paul Coffey .40 1.00
40 Keith Primeau .10 .25
41 Nick Lidstrom .40 1.00
42 Bill Ranford TC .10 .25
43 Doug Weight .10 .25
44 Jason Arnott .10 .25
45 Bill Ranford .20 .50
46 John Vanbiesbrouck TC .10 .25
47 John Vanbiesbrouck .40 1.00
48 Stu Barnes .10 .25
49 Scott Mellanby .10 .25
50 Rob Niedermayer .10 .25
51 Geoff Sanderson TC .10 .25
52 Brendan Shanahan .40 1.00
53 Geoff Sanderson .10 .25
54 Sean Burke .20 .50
55 Jeff O'Neill .10 .25
56 Rob Blake TC .10 .25
57 Wayne Gretzky 2.00 5.00
58 Rob Blake .20 .50
59 Rick Tocchet .20 .50
60 Dimitri Khristich .10 .25
61 Kelly Hrudey .20 .50
62 Vincent Damphousse TC .10 .25
63 Pierre Turgeon .10 .25
64 Mark Recchi .20 .50
65 Saku Koivu .40 1.00
66 Patrick Roy 1.50 4.00
67 Vincent Damphousse .10 .25
68 Scott Stevens TC .10 .25
69 Stephane Richer .10 .25
70 Martin Brodeur 1.25 3.00
71 Scott Niedermayer .10 .25
72 Scott Stevens .10 .25
73 Matt Schneider TC .10 .25
74 Kirk Muller .10 .25
75 Mathieu Schneider .10 .25
76 Derek King .10 .25
77 Wendel Clark .20 .50
78 Mark Messier TC .10 .25
79 Brian Leetch .40 1.00
80 Mark Messier .60 1.50
81 Alexei Kovalev .10 .25
82 Luc Robitaille .40 1.00
83 Mike Richter .40 1.00
84 Radek Bonk TC .10 .25
85 Dan Quinn .10 .25
86 Alexandre Daigle .10 .25
87 Steve Duchesne .10 .25
88 Radek Bonk .10 .25
90 Eric Lindros .60 1.50
91 Mikael Renberg .10 .25
92 John LeClair .20 .50
93 Eric Desjardins .10 .25
94 Rod Brind'Amour .10 .25
95 Ron Francis TC .10 .25
96 Jaromir Jagr .75 2.00
97 Mario Lemieux 1.50 4.00
98 Ron Francis .20 .50
99 Sergei Zubov .10 .25
100 Al MacInnis TC .10 .25
101 Brett Hull .60 1.50
102 Al MacInnis .20 .50
103 Dale Hawerchuk .20 .50
104 Chris Pronger .40 1.00
105 Craig Janney TC .10 .25
106 Craig Janney .10 .25
107 Pat Falloon .10 .25
108 Arturs Irbe .40 1.00
109 Ulf Dahlen .10 .25
110 Owen Nolan .20 .50
111 Brian Bradley TC .10 .25
112 Roman Hamrlik .10 .25
113 Brian Bradley .10 .25
114 Chris Gratton .10 .25
115 Brian Bellows .10 .25
116 Doug Gilmour TC .10 .25
117 Doug Gilmour .40 1.00
118 Mats Sundin .60 1.50
119 Dave Andreychuk .10 .25
120 Felix Potvin .40 1.00
121 Larry Murphy .10 .25
122 Alex Mogilny TC .10 .25
123 Pavel Bure .40 1.00
124 Alex Mogilny .20 .50
125 Trevor Linden .20 .50
126 Jeff Brown .10 .25
127 Kirk McLean .20 .50
128 Jim Carey TC .10 .2
129 Joe Juneau .10 .2
130 Peter Bondra .20 .5
131 Jim Carey .20 .5
132 Calle Johansson .10 .2
133 Teemu Selanne TC .10 .2
134 Teemu Selanne .60 1.5
135 Alexei Zhamnov .10 .2
136 Keith Tkachuk .40 1.0

1995-96 Bashan Super Stickers Die-Cut

COMPLETE SET (25) 8.00 20.0
1 Pierre Turgeon .10 .2
2 Patrick Roy 1.50 4.0
3 Pat LaFontaine .20 .5
4 Joe Sakic 1.00 2.5
5 Paul Coffey .40 1.0
6 Ray Bourque .60 1.5
7 Brian Leetch .40 1.0
8 Joe Juneau .10 .2
9 Jeremy Roenick .60 1.5
10 Chris Chelios .40 1.0
11 Brett Hull .60 1.5
12 Paul Kariya .40 1.0
13 Jason Arnott .10 .2
14 Pavel Bure .40 1.0
15 Steve Duchesne .10 .2
16 Martin Brodeur 1.25 3.0
17 Eric Lindros .60 1.5
18 Mikael Renberg .10 .2
19 Felix Potvin .40 1.0
20 Roman Hamrlik .10 .2
21 Wayne Gretzky 2.00 5.0
22 Brendan Shanahan .60 1.5
23 Jaromir Jagr .75 2.0
24 Mario Lemieux 1.50 4.0
25 Steve Yzerman 1.25 3.0

1968 Bauer Ads

These oversized cards are approximately x 10" and feature full color fronts, with bla backs. They were issued as premiums wi Bauer skates. Since they are unnumbere they are checklisted below in alphabetic order.

COMPLETE SET (21) 300.00 600.0
1 Andy Bathgate 12.50 25.0
2 Gary Bergman 12.50 25.0
3 Charlie Burns 12.50 25.0
4 Ray Cullen 12.50 25.0
5 Gary Dornhoeffer 12.50 25.0
6 Kent Douglas 12.50 25.0
7 Tim Ecclestone 12.50 25.0
8 Bill Flett 12.50 25.0
9 Ed Giacomin 20.00 40.0
10 Ted Harris 12.50 25.0
11 Paul Henderson 20.00 40.0
12 Ken Hodge 12.50 25.0
13 Harry Howell 12.50 25.0
14 Earl Ingarfield 12.50 25.0
15 Gilles Marotte 12.50 25.0
16 Doug Mohns 12.50 25.0
17 Bobby Orr 75.00 150.0
18 Claude Provost 12.50 25.0
19 Gary Sabourin 12.50 25.0
20 Brian Smith 12.50 25.0
21 Bob Woytowich 12.50 25.0

1991-92 BayBank Bobby Orr

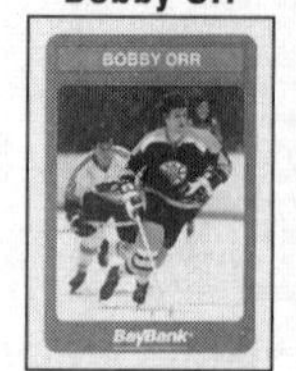

These promotional cards were sponsored BayBank and measure approximately 2 1/ by 3 1/2". A player card and a spons advertisement were packaged inside hockey puck-shaped holder (bearing th Bruins logo) and passed out to ticket holde on BayBank Night at the Bruins game. Th fronts of the first two cards have a col action player photo framed by a blue ar green inner border design. The white out border on card 1 is slightly thicker than card 2, and the positions of the player name and the sponsor name are reverse when one compares the two cards. The thi card has a green border. Against a pa green background, the back presen biography, statistics (career and playoffs and career awards. The card number appea in a green box in the upper left corner.

COMPLETE SET (4) 12.00 30.0
1 Bobby Orr 3.20 8.0
(Skating with Flyer in pursuit)
2 Bobby Orr 3.20 8.0
(Skating alone with puck)
3 Bobby Orr 3.20 8.0
(Skating behind the net)
NNO Bobby Orr 4.00 10.0
(8 1/2" by 11")
(Skating without puck)

1995 BayBank Bobby Orr

This set consists of a 10" by 8" shee featuring a color action photo of Bobby O and a standard-size card carrying the sam picture. The sheet has a blank back; the ca back salutes the Boston Bruins on the 25 Anniversary of the 1970 Stanley Cu Championship.

OMPLETE SET (2) 6.00 15.00
Bobby Orr 4.00 10.00
(Oversized card)
Bobby Orr 2.00 5.00
(Regular size card)

1971-72 Bazooka

ne 1971-72 Bazooka set contains 36 cards. ne cards, nearly identical in design to the 971-72 Topps and O-Pee-Chee hockey ards, were distributed in 12 three-card anels as the bottoms of Bazooka bubble um boxes. The cards are numbered at the ottom of each obverse. The cards are blank acked and are about 2/3 the size of andard cards. The panels of three are in umerical order, e.g., cards 1-3 are a panel, ards 4-6 form a panel, etc. The prices elow refer to cut-apart individual cards; alues for panels are 50 percent more than ne values below. This is one of the scarcest ets in the trading card hobby, and because the lack of confirmed sales, prices below e based on dealer buy prices.

OMPLETE SET (36) 4500.00 9000.00
Phil Esposito 375.00 750.00
Frank Mahovlich 200.00 400.00
Ed Van Impe 25.00 50.00
Bobby Hull 500.00 1000.00
Henri Richard 150.00 300.00
Gilbert Perreault 375.00 750.00
Alex Delvecchio 125.00 250.00
Denis DeJordy 75.00 150.00
Ted Harris 30.00 60.00
) Gilles Villemure 75.00 150.00
1 Dave Keon 150.00 300.00
2 Derek Sanderson 150.00 300.00
3 Orland Kurtenbach 30.00 60.00
4 Bob Nevin 30.00 60.00
5 Yvan Cournoyer 100.00 200.00
6 Andre Boudrias 25.00 50.00
7 Frank St.Marseille 25.00 50.00
3 Norm Ullman 100.00 200.00
9 Garry Unger 40.00 80.00
) Pierre Bouchard 25.00 50.00
Roy Edwards 75.00 150.00
2 Ralph Backstrom 30.00 60.00
3 Guy Trottier 25.00 50.00
4 Serge Bernier 25.00 50.00
5 Bert Marshall 25.00 50.00
6 Wayne Hillman 25.00 50.00
7 Tim Ecclestone 25.00 50.00
3 Walt McKechnie 25.00 50.00
) Tony Esposito 375.00 750.00
) Rod Gilbert 100.00 200.00
1 Walt Tkaczuk 30.00 60.00
2 Roger Crozier 75.00 150.00
3 Ken Schinkel 25.00 50.00
4 Ron Ellis 25.00 50.00
5 Stan Mikita 300.00 600.00
6 Bobby Orr 1250.00 2500.00

1994 Be A Player Magazine

ards were inserted into the NHLPA's Be A ayer magazine. Cards are full color and are rger than standard size.

'OMPLETE SET (4) 4.00 10.00
Paul Kariya 2.00 5.00
Felix Potvin .60 1.50
Joe Sakic 1.20 3.00
Teemu Selanne .80 2.00

1994-95 Be A Player

his set was issued by Upper Deck in onjunction with the NHL Players ssociation. The set contained 180 andard-size cards, each numbered with an R" prefix. The card backs contained text and ersonal information. The set was released hobby (blue) and retail (purple) ackaging. Production total for both was nnounced at 1,995 cases. Each box was dividually numbered on the side. Each ack included 11 cards and one autographed ard. Suggested retail was $5.95 per pack. ne NNO Wayne Gretzky promo card was cluded as a premium in an NHLPA hockey os video. The card is slightly different from s R99 regular issue card. This set was not licensed by the National Hockey League and did not use any NHL team logos.

COMPLETE SET (180) 20.00 40.00
R1 Doug Gilmour .07 .20
R2 Joel Otto .02 .10
R3 Kirk Muller .02 .10
R4 Marty McInnis .02 .10
R5 Dave Gagner .02 .10
R6 Geoff Courtnall .02 .10
R7 Dale Hawerchuk .07 .20
R8 Mike Modano .25 .60
R9 Roman Hamrlik .07 .20
R10 Marty McSorley .07 .20
R11 Teemu Selanne .15 .40
R12 Jeremy Roenick .20 .50
R13 Glenn Healy .07 .20
R14 Darren Turcotte .02 .10
R15 Derian Hatcher .02 .10
R16 Enrico Ciccone .02 .10
R17 Tony Amonte .07 .20
R18 Mark Recchi .07 .20
R19 Eric Weinrich .02 .10
R20 John Vanbiesbrouck .07 .20
R21 Nick Kypreos .02 .10
R22 Gilbert Dionne .02 .10
R23 Theo Fleury .02 .10
R24 Todd Gill .02 .10
R25 Jari Kurri .07 .20
R26 Brad May .02 .10
R27 Russ Courtnall .02 .10
R28 Bill Ranford .07 .20
R29 Steve Yzerman .75 2.00
R30 Alexandre Daigle .02 .10
R31 Mike Hudson .02 .10
R32 Ray Bourque .25 .60
R33 Dave Andreychuk .07 .20
R34 Jason Arnott .02 .10
R35 Pavel Bure .15 .40
R36 Keith Tkachuk .15 .40
R37 Scott Niedermayer .02 .10
R38 Johan Garpenlov .02 .10
R39 Dino Ciccarelli .07 .20
R40 Rob Blake .07 .20
R41 Dave Manson .02 .10
R42 Adam Foote .07 .20
R43 Chris Pronger .15 .40
R44 Scott Lachance .02 .10
R45 Adam Oates .07 .20
R46 Brian Leetch .15 .40
R47 Guy Hebert .07 .20
R48 Brett Hull .20 .50
R49 Mike Ricci .07 .20
R50 Dave Ellett .02 .10
R51 Owen Nolan .07 .20
R52 Craig Janney .02 .10
R53 Trevor Linden .07 .20
R54 Ray Sheppard .02 .10
R55 Rob Niedermayer .07 .20
R56 Kevin Haller .02 .10
R57 Jeff Norton .02 .10
R58 Martin Brodeur .40 1.00
R59 Robb Stauber .02 .10
R60 Sylvain Turgeon .02 .10
R61 Pat Verbeek .02 .10
R62 Steve Smith .02 .10
R63 Jaromir Jagr .25 .60
R64 Steve Duchesne .02 .10
R65 Tie Domi .07 .20
R66 Sylvain Lefebvre .02 .10
R67 Guy Carbonneau .02 .10
R68 Alexander Mogilny .07 .20
R69 Mario Lemieux 1.25 3.00
R70 Neil Wilkinson .02 .10
R71 Curtis Joseph .15 .40
R72 Wendel Clark .07 .20
R73 Kirk McLean .07 .20
R74 Mikael Renberg .07 .20
R75 Shawn McEachern .02 .10
R76 Mats Sundin .15 .40
R77 Craig Simpson .02 .10
R78 Phil Housley .07 .20
R79 Pat LaFontaine .15 .40
R80 Pierre Turgeon .07 .20
R81 Felix Potvin .15 .40
R82 Kevin Stevens .02 .10
R83 Steve Chiasson .02 .10
R84 Robert Petrovicky .02 .10
R85 Joe Juneau .07 .20
R86 Brendan Shanahan .15 .40
R87 Joe Sacco .02 .10
R88 David Reid .02 .10
R89 Louie DeBrusk .02 .10
R90 Darryl Sydor .02 .10
R91 Paul Coffey .15 .40
R92 Alexei Yashin .02 .10
R93 Jason Arnott .02 .10
R94 Gary Suter .02 .10
R95 Luc Robitaille .07 .20
R96 Joe Sakic .30 .75
R97 Chris Chelios .15 .40
R98 Tony Granato .02 .10
R99 Wayne Gretzky 1.50 4.00
R100 Joe Juneau .07 .20
R101 Curtis Joseph .15 .40
R102 Vincent Damphousse .02 .10
R103 Paul Kariya .15 .40
R104 Brendan Shanahan .15 .40
R105 Eric Desjardins .07 .20
R106 Eric Lindros .15 .40
R107 Kirk McLean .07 .20
R108 Mike Ricci .07 .20
R109 Chris Chelios .15 .40
R110 Chris Gratton .02 .10
R111 Doug Gilmour .07 .20
R112 Vincent Damphousse .02 .10
R113 Mark Osborne .02 .10
R114 Mike Modano .15 .40
R115 Steve Yzerman .75 2.00
R116 Garry Valk .02 .10
R117 Adam Graves .02 .10
R118 Doug Weight .07 .20
R119 Rob Niedermayer .07 .20
R120 Craig Simpson .02 .10
R121 Patrick Roy 1.25 3.00
R122 Ronnie Stern .02 .10
R123 Jiri Slegr .02 .10
R124 Darren Turcotte .02 .10
R125 Vladimir Malakhov .02 .10
R126 Paul Kariya .15 .40
R127 Mike Gartner .07 .20
R128 Scott Niedermayer .02 .10
R129 Dino Ciccarelli .07 .20
R130 Martin Brodeur TN .20 .50
R131 Kevin Hatcher .02 .10
R132 Pat LaFontaine .07 .20
R133 Joel Otto .02 .10
R134 Jason Arnott .02 .10
R135 John Vanbiesbrouck .07 .20
R136 Derian Hatcher .02 .10
R137 Brendan Shanahan .15 .40
R138 Felix Potvin .15 .40
R139 Trevor Linden .07 .20
R140 Ken Baumgartner .02 .10
R141 Denis Leary .02 .10
R142 Wendel Clark .07 .20
R143 Cam Neely .15 .40
R144 Jeremy Roenick .20 .50
R145 Sergei Fedorov .25 .60
R146 Scott Stevens .07 .20
R147 Wayne Gretzky 1.50 4.00
R148 Darius Kasparaitis .02 .10
R149 Brian Leetch .15 .40
R150 Marty McSorley .07 .20
R151 Paul Kariya .15 .40
R152 Peter Forsberg .50 1.25
R153 Brett Lindros .02 .10
R154 Kenny Jonsson .02 .10
R155 Jason Allison .02 .10
R156 Aaron Gavey .02 .10
R157 Jamie Storr .07 .20
R158 Viktor Kozlov .07 .20
R159 Valeri Bure .02 .10
R160 Oleg Tverdovsky .07 .20
R161 Brent Gretzky .02 .10
R162 Todd Harvey .02 .10
R163 Todd Warriner .02 .10
R164 Jeff Friesen .02 .10
R165 Adam Deadmarsh .02 .10
R166 Ken Baumgartner .02 .10
R167 Terry Carkner .02 .10
R168 Tie Domi .07 .20
R169 Steve Larmer .07 .20
R170 Larry Murphy .07 .20
R171 Steve Thomas .02 .10
R172 Alexei Yashin .02 .10
R173 Felix Potvin .15 .40
R174 Curtis Joseph .15 .40
R175 Rob Zamuner .02 .10
R176 Wayne Gretzky 2.00 5.00
R177 Pavel Bure .15 .40
R178 Eric Lindros .15 .40
R179 Patrick Roy 1.25 3.00
R180 Doug Gilmour .07 .20
NNO Wayne Gretzky PROMO 4.00 10.00

1994-95 Be A Player 99 All-Stars

COMPLETE SET (19) 40.00 100.00
STATED ODDS 1:14
G1 Wayne Gretzky 15.00 40.00
G2 Paul Coffey 2.00 5.00
G3 Rob Blake 2.00 5.00
G4 Pat Conacher 1.00 2.50
G5 Russ Courtnall 1.00 2.50
G6 Sergei Fedorov 4.00 10.00
G7 Grant Fuhr 3.00 8.00
G8 Todd Gill 1.00 2.50
G9 Tony Granato 1.00 2.50
G10 Brett Hull 4.00 10.00
G11 Charlie Huddy 1.00 2.50
G12 Steve Larmer 2.00 5.00
G13 Kelly Hrudey 2.00 5.00
G14 Al MacInnis 2.00 5.00
G15 Marty McSorley 2.00 5.00
G16 Jari Kurri 2.00 5.00
G17 Kirk Muller 1.00 2.50
G18 Rick Tocchet 2.00 5.00
G19 Steve Yzerman 8.00 20.00

1994-95 Be A Player Signature Cards

These authentic signature cards were issued one per foil pack. All autographs were guaranteed by the National Hockey League Players Association. The Jiri Slegr card (#119) was only available through a mail-in offer. The set is considered complete without it. Reportedly, most players signed approximately 2,400 of each card (including Slegr). Players who signed fewer are indicated below with parenthesis indicating approximately how many cards they signed.

ONE SIGNATURE CARD PER PACK
EACH PLAYER SIGNED APPROX.2400
UNLESS OTHERWISE MARKED
1 Doug Gilmour (1250) 6.00 15.00
2 Adam Foote 2.00 5.00
3 Martin Brodeur 20.00 50.00
4 Alexander Semak 2.00 5.00
5 Dale Hawerchuk 4.00 10.00
6 Derek King 2.00 5.00
7 Mark Recchi 4.00 10.00
8 Fredrik Olausson 2.00 5.00
9 Dave McLlwain 2.00 5.00
10 Marc Bergevin 2.00 5.00
11 Teemu Selanne (600) 75.00 200.00
12 Jeremy Roenick (600) 30.00 80.00
13 Eric Lacroix 2.00 5.00
14 Marty McInnis 2.00 5.00
15 Kris King 2.00 5.00
16 Bill Ranford 4.00 10.00
17 Gary Roberts 2.00 5.00
18 Mark Osborne 2.00 5.00
19 Dmitri Mironov 2.00 5.00
20 John Vanbiesbrouck (600) 40.00 100.00
21 Alexei Zhamnov 2.00 5.00
22 Brad May 2.00 5.00
23 Doug Lidster 2.00 5.00
24 Mikael Renberg 2.00 5.00
25 Kris Draper 4.00 10.00
26 Darryl Sydor 4.00 10.00
27 Claude Lemieux 2.00 5.00
28 Doug Brown 2.00 5.00
29 Louie DeBrusk 2.00 5.00
30 Andy Moog 6.00 15.00
31 Donald Audette 2.00 5.00
32 Ray Bourque (600) 60.00 150.00
33 Brian Rolston 2.00 5.00
34 Ted Drury 2.00 5.00
35 Darren Turcotte 2.00 5.00
36 Gary Shuchuk 2.00 5.00
37 Mike Ricci 2.00 5.00
38 Kirk Maltby 2.00 5.00
39 Doug Bodger 2.00 5.00
40 Kirk Muller 2.00 5.00
41 Sylvain Lefebvre 2.00 5.00
42 Brent Grieve 2.00 5.00
43 Bill Houlder 2.00 5.00
44 Neil Wilkinson 2.00 5.00
45 Donald Dufresne 2.00 5.00
46 Brian Leetch (600) 30.00 80.00
47 Bryan Smolinski 2.00 5.00
48 Kevin Hatcher 2.00 5.00
49 Steven Rice 2.00 5.00
50 Bill Guerin 4.00 10.00
51 Grant Jennings 2.00 5.00
52 Dave Andreychuk 4.00 10.00
53 Sean Burke 4.00 10.00
54 Nick Kypreos 2.00 5.00
55 Drake Berehowsky 2.00 5.00
56 Kevin Haller 2.00 5.00
57 Bill Berg 2.00 5.00
58 Chris Simon 2.00 5.00
59 Owen Nolan 4.00 10.00
(Wrong birthdate blacked out on back)
60 Don Sweeney 2.00 5.00
61 Johan Garpenlov 2.00 5.00
62 Garry Galley 2.00 5.00
63 Pat LaFontaine 4.00 10.00
64 Craig Berube 2.00 5.00
65 Dave Ellett 2.00 5.00
66 Robert Kron 2.00 5.00
67 Alexander Godynyuk 2.00 5.00
68 Markus Naslund 6.00 15.00
69 Joel Otto 2.00 5.00
70 Igor Ulanov 2.00 5.00
71 Pat Verbeek 2.00 5.00
72 Craig MacTavish 2.00 5.00
73 Gary Leeman 2.00 5.00
74 Kevin Todd 2.00 5.00
75 Mike Sullivan 2.00 5.00
76 Rob Pearson 2.00 5.00
77 Dave Gagner 2.00 5.00
78 Dirk Graham 2.00 5.00
79 Joe Sacco 2.00 5.00
80 Jassen Cullimore 2.00 5.00
81 Glen Featherstone 2.00 5.00
82 Scott Lachance 2.00 5.00
83 Kerry Huffman 2.00 5.00
84 Troy Loney 2.00 5.00
85 Rob Gaudreau 2.00 5.00
86 Brendan Shanahan (600) 75.00 150.00
87 Joe Murphy 2.00 5.00
88 Scott Niedermayer 4.00 10.00
89 Dan Quinn 2.00 5.00
90 Jeff Norton 2.00 5.00
91 Jim Dowd 2.00 5.00
92 Ray Ferraro 2.00 5.00
93 Shawn Burr 2.00 5.00
94 Denis Savard 4.00 10.00
95 Dave Manson 2.00 5.00
96 Joe Nieuwendyk 4.00 10.00
97 Tony Amonte 4.00 10.00
98 James Patrick 2.00 5.00
99 Guy Hebert 2.00 5.00
100 Peter Zezel 2.00 5.00
101 Shawn McEachern 2.00 5.00
102 Dave Lowry 2.00 5.00
103 David Reid 2.00 5.00
104 Todd Gill 2.00 5.00
105 John Cullen 2.00 5.00
106 Guy Carbonneau 2.00 5.00
107 Jeff Beukeboom 2.00 5.00
108 Wayne Gretzky (300) 250.00 500.00
109 Curtis Joseph 6.00 15.00
110 Jason Arnott 2.00 5.00
112 Gary Suter 2.00 5.00
113 Luc Robitaille 6.00 15.00
114 Tony Granato 2.00 5.00
115 Steve Yzerman (600) 100.00 200.00
116 Chris Gratton 2.00 5.00
117 Doug Weight 4.00 10.00
118 Garry Valk 2.00 5.00
119 Jiri Slegr 8.00 20.00
120 Vincent Damphousse 2.00 5.00
121 Vladimir Malakhov 2.00 5.00
122 Craig Simpson 2.00 5.00
123 Theoren Fleury 4.00 10.00
124 Dave Poulin 2.00 5.00
125 Derian Hatcher 2.00 5.00
126 Jimmy Waite 2.00 5.00
127 Norm Maciver 2.00 5.00
128 Glenn Healy 2.00 5.00
129 Jocelyn Lemieux 2.00 5.00
130 Steve Chiasson 4.00 10.00
131 Keith Jones 2.00 5.00
132 Enrico Ciccone 2.00 5.00
133 Martin Lapointe 2.00 5.00
134 John MacLean 2.00 5.00
135 Geoff Courtnall 2.00 5.00
136 David Shaw 2.00 5.00
137 Steve Duchesne 2.00 5.00
138 Dean Evason 2.00 5.00
139 Eric Weinrich 2.00 5.00
140 Kelly Hrudey 4.00 10.00
141 Ted Donato 2.00 5.00
142 Darius Kasparaitis 2.00 5.00
143 Tie Domi 4.00 10.00
144 Terry Carkner 2.00 5.00
145 Steve Thomas 2.00 5.00
146 Steve Larmer 2.00 5.00
147 Rob Zamuner 2.00 5.00
148 Larry Murphy 2.00 5.00
149 Ken Baumgartner 2.00 5.00
150 Alexei Yashin (600) 15.00 40.00
151 Paul Kariya (600) 60.00 150.00
152 Todd Harvey 2.00 5.00
153A Viktor Kozlov 4.00 10.00
(VK variation)
153B Viktor Kozlov 75.00 200.00
(Full Signature)
154 Brent Gretzky 2.00 5.00
155 Petr Klima 2.00 5.00
156 Kent Manderville 2.00 5.00
157 Mike Eagles 2.00 5.00
158 Valeri Kamensky 2.00 5.00
159 Thomas Steen 2.00 5.00
160 Michal Pivonka 2.00 5.00
161 Steve Heinze 2.00 5.00
162 Nicklas Lidstrom 6.00 15.00
163 Uwe Krupp 2.00 5.00
164 Pat Elynuik 2.00 5.00
165 Mike Peca 4.00 10.00
166 Sylvain Cote 2.00 5.00
167 Trevor Kidd 2.00 5.00
168 Patrick Poulin 2.00 5.00
169 Shane Churla 2.00 5.00
170 Scott Mellanby 2.00 5.00
171 Mike Sillinger 2.00 5.00
172 Shayne Corson 2.00 5.00
173 Micah Aivazoff 2.00 5.00
174 Robert Lang 2.00 5.00
175 Rod Brind'Amour 4.00 10.00
176 Troy Murray 2.00 5.00
177 Mike Krushelnyski 2.00 5.00
178 Sergio Momesso 2.00 5.00

1994-95 Be A Player Up Close and Personal

This 10-card set was inserted two per box (1:8 packs) in Be A Player product. The cards featured an "Up Close" photo of the player and Roy Firestone, a popular ESPN show host. The text on the back was written by Firestone. The cards are numbered with an "UC" prefix.

COMPLETE SET (10) 20.00 50.00
STATED ODDS 1:14
UC1 Wayne Gretzky 10.00 25.00
UC2 Eric Lindros 1.00 2.50
UC3 Pavel Bure 1.00 2.50
UC4 Teemu Selanne 1.00 2.50
UC5 Steve Yzerman 4.00 10.00
UC6 Jeremy Roenick 1.25 3.00
UC7 Sergei Fedorov 1.50 4.00
UC8 Patrick Roy 6.00 15.00
UC9 Paul Kariya 1.00 2.50
UC10 Doug Gilmour .50 1.25

1995-96 Be A Player

This 225-card set was released in June 1996. It was released by Upper Deck, in conjunction with the NHLPA. The set was not licensed by the NHL, hence the absence of logos and insignia from player uniforms, and the color changes on the sweaters of players from Colorado and the Islanders. Suggested retail was $7.99 per ten-card pack, although packs tended to sell for more due to the allure of the one-per-pack autographs.

COMPLETE SET (225) 15.00 40.00
1 Brett Hull .40 1.00
2 Jyrki Lumme .05 .15
3 Shean Donovan .05 .15
4 Yuri Khmylev .05 .15
5 Stephane Matteau .05 .15
6 Basil McRae .05 .15
7 Dimitri Yushkevich .05 .15
8 Ron Francis .10 .30
9 Keith Carney .05 .15
10 Brad Dalgarno .05 .15
11 Bob Carpenter .05 .15
12 Kevin Stevens .05 .15
13 Patrick Flatley .05 .15
14 Craig Muni .05 .15
15 Travis Green .10 .30
16 Derek Plante .05 .15
17 Mike Craig .05 .15
18 Chris Pronger .25 .60
19 Bret Hedican .05 .15
20 Mathieu Schneider .05 .15
21 Chris Therien .05 .15
22 Greg Adams .05 .15
23 Arturs Irbe .10 .30
24 Zigmund Palffy .10 .30
25 Peter Douris .05 .15
26 Bob Sweeney .05 .15
27 Chris Terreri .10 .30
28 Alexei Zhitnik .05 .15
29 Jay Wells .05 .15
30 Andrew Cassels .05 .15
31 Radek Bonk .05 .15
32 Brian Bellows .10 .30
33 Frantisek Kucera .05 .15
34 Valeri Bure .05 .15
35 Randy Wood .05 .15
36 Dimitri Khristich .05 .15
37 Randy Ladouceur .05 .15
38 Nelson Emerson .05 .15
39 Robert Marchment .05 .15
40 Kevin Lowe .10 .30
41 Trevor Linden .10 .30
42 Neal Broten .10 .30
43 Tom Chorske .05 .15
44 Patrice Brisebois .05 .15
45 Wayne Presley .05 .15
46 Murray Craven .05 .15
47 Craig Janney .05 .15
48 Ken Daneyko .05 .15
49 Dino Ciccarelli .10 .30
50 Jason Dawe .05 .15
51 Brad McCrimmon .05 .15
52 Randy McKay .05 .15
53 Rudy Poeschek .05 .15
54 Calle Johansson .05 .15
55 Wendel Clark .10 .30
56 Rob Ray .20 .50
57 Garth Snow .10 .30
58 Joe Juneau .05 .15
59 Craig Wolanin .05 .15
60 Ray Sheppard .05 .15
61 Oleg Tverdovsky .05 .15
62 Geoff Sanderson .05 .15
63 Mike Ridley .05 .15
64 David Oliver .05 .15
65 Russ Courtnall .05 .15
66 Joe Reekie .05 .15
67 Ken Wregget .10 .30
68 Teppo Numminen .05 .15
69 Mikhail Shtalenkov .05 .15
70 Luke Richardson .05 .15
71 Brent Gilchrist .05 .15
72 Phil Housley .10 .30
73 Greg Johnson .05 .15
74 Sean Hill .05 .15
75 Karl Dykhuis .05 .15
76 Tim Cheveldae .10 .30
77 Shjon Podein .05 .15
78 Rene Corbet .05 .15
79 Ronnie Stern .05 .15
80 Mike Donnelly .05 .15
81 Randy Cunneyworth .05 .15
82 Rick Tocchet .10 .30
83 Dallas Drake .05 .15
84 Cam Russell .05 .15
85 Daren Puppa .10 .30
86 Benoit Brunet .05 .15
87 Paul Ranheim .05 .15
88 Bob Rouse .05 .15
89 Todd Elik .05 .15
90 Darcy Wakaluk .10 .30
91 Cliff Ronning .05 .15
92 Pat Conacher .05 .15
93 Todd Krygier .05 .15
94 Dave Babych .05 .15
95 Pat Falloon .05 .15
96 Don Beaupre .10 .30
97 Wayne Gretzky 2.00 5.00
98 Chris Joseph .05 .15
99 Vyacheslav Kozlov .10 .30
100 Brent Fedyk .05 .15
101 Tim Taylor .05 .15
102 Mike Eastwood .05 .15
103 Mike Keane .05 .15
104 Grant Ledyard .05 .15
105 Rob Dimaio .05 .15
106 Martin Straka .05 .15
107 Scott Young .05 .15
108 Zarley Zalapski .05 .15
109 Steve Leach .05 .15
110 Jody Hull .05 .15
111 Lyle Odelein .05 .15
112 Bob Corkum .05 .15
113 Rob Blake .10 .30
114 Randy Burridge .05 .15
115 Keith Primeau .05 .15
116 Glen Wesley .05 .15
117 Brian Bradley .05 .15
118 Andrei Kovalenko .05 .15
119 Patrik Juhlin .05 .15
120 John Tucker .05 .15
121 Stephane Fiset .10 .30
122 Mike Hough .05 .15
123 Steve Smith .05 .15
124 Tom Barrasso .10 .30
125 Ray Whitney .10 .30
126 Benoit Hogue .05 .15
127 Stu Barnes .05 .15
128 Craig Ludwig .10 .30
129 Curtis Leschyshyn .05 .15
130 John LeClair .25 .60
131 Dennis Vial .05 .15
132 Cory Stillman .05 .15
133 Roman Hamrlik .10 .30
134 Al MacInnis .10 .30
135 Igor Korolev .05 .15
136 Rick Zombo .05 .15
137 Zdeno Ciger .05 .15
138 Brian Savage .05 .15
139 Paul Ysebaert .05 .15
140 Brent Sutter .05 .15
141 Ed Olczyk .05 .15
142 Adam Creighton .05 .15
143 Jesse Belanger .05 .15
144 Glen Murray .05 .15
145 Alexander Selivanov .05 .15
146 Trent Yawney .05 .15
147 Bruce Driver .05 .15
148 Michael Nylander .05 .15
149 Martin Gelinas .05 .15
150 Yanic Perreault .05 .15
151 Craig Billington .10 .30
152 Pierre Turgeon .10 .30
153 Mike Modano .50 1.25
154 Joe Mullen .10 .30
155 Todd Ewen .05 .15
156 Petr Nedved .10 .30
157 Dominic Roussel .10 .30
158 Murray Baron .05 .15
159 Robert Dirk .05 .15
160 Tomas Sandstrom .05 .15
161 Brian Holzinger .20 .50
162 Ken Klee RC .05 .15
163 Radek Dvorak RC .20 .50
164 Marcus Ragnarsson .10 .30
165 Aaron Gavey .05 .15
166 Jeff O'Neill .05 .15
167 Chad Kilger .10 .30
168 Todd Bertuzzi RC .75 2.00
169 Robert Svehla .05 .15
170 Eric Daze .10 .30
171 Daniel Alfredsson RC .75 2.00
172 Shane Doan RC .75 2.00
173 Kyle McLaren .10 .30
174 Saku Koivu .25 .60
175 Jere Lehtinen .10 .30
176 Nikolai Khabibulin .10 .30
177 Niklas Sundstrom .10 .30
178 Ed Jovanovski .25 .60
179 Jason Bonsignore .05 .15
180 Kenny Jonsson .05 .15
181 Vitali Yachmenev .05 .15
182 Alexei Kovalev .05 .15
183 Sandis Ozolinsh .05 .15
184 Rob Niedermayer .10 .30
185 Richard Park .05 .15
186 Adam Deadmarsh .05 .15
187 Sergei Krivokrasov .05 .15
188 Alexandre Daigle .05 .15
189 Jim Carey .10 .30
190 Todd Marchant .05 .15
191 Mike Richter .25 .60
192 Dominik Hasek .50 1.25
193 Chris Osgood .10 .30
194 Ed Belfour .25 .60
195 Felix Potvin .25 .60
196 Grant Fuhr .25 .60
197 Patrick Roy 1.25 3.00
198 Ron Hextall .10 .30
199 Jocelyn Thibault .25 .60
200 Kirk McLean .10 .30
201 Jari Kurri .25 .60
202 Bobby Holik .05 .15
203 Mats Sundin .25 .60
204 Alexander Mogilny .10 .30
205 Valeri Karpov .05 .15
206 Igor Larionov .05 .15
207 Valeri Zelepukin .05 .15
208 Jozef Stumpel .05 .15
209 Sergei Nemchinov .05 .15
210 Peter Bondra .10 .30
211 Chris Chelios .25 .60
212 Adam Graves .05 .15
213 Dale Hunter .10 .30
214 Tony Twist .10 .30
215 Keith Tkachuk .25 .60
216 Vladimir Konstantinov .10 .30
217 Sandy McCarthy .05 .15
218 Jamie Macoun .05 .15
219 Scott Stevens .10 .30
220 Mark Tinordi .05 .15
221 Bob Probert .10 .30
222 Gino Odjick .05 .15
223 Ulf Samuelsson .05 .15
224 Stu Grimson .10 .30
225 Marty McSorley .05 .15

1995-96 Be A Player Signatures

These authentic signed cards were inserted at a rate of one per pack. Every seventh pack featured a special signed card which was distinguished by unique die-cut corners. Because these cards were tougher to pull, they command a premium; multipliers for these cards are listed below. The card fronts are the same as the regular cards, but the backs of the signed cards feature a certificate of authenticity. Although production numbers were not officially revealed, documents suggest approximately 3,000 regular and 400 die-cut versions of each signed card were released. The quantities of the Wayne Gretzky cards (#S97) were intially reported at 802 signed and 99 die-cut copies. Upper Deck later announced the actual numbers as being 648 regular and 234 die-cut. The Mike Richter card (#191) was not inserted in packs, but was made available through a mail-in offer. The set is considered complete without this card.

*DIE CUTS: .75X TO 1.5X BASIC SIGS
ONE PER PACK
3000 AU'S PER PLAYER PRODUCED
400 DIE CUT AU'S PER PLAYER PRODUCED
SET PRICE EXCLUDES RICHTER MAIL-IN
S1 Brett Hull 10.00 25.00
S2 Jyrki Lumme 2.00 5.00
S3 Shean Donovan 2.00 5.00
S4 Yuri Khmylev 2.00 5.00
S5 Stephane Matteau 2.00 5.00
S6 Basil McRae 2.00 5.00
S7 Dimitri Yushkevich 2.00 5.00
S8 Ron Francis 4.00 10.00
S9 Keith Carney 2.00 5.00
S10 Brad Dalgarno 2.00 5.00
S11 Bob Carpenter 2.00 5.00
S12 Kevin Stevens 2.00 5.00
S13 Pat Flatley 2.00 5.00
S14 Craig Muni 2.00 5.00
S15 Travis Green 2.00 5.00
S16 Derek Plante 2.00 5.00
S17 Mike Craig 2.00 5.00

S18 Chris Pronger 6.00 15.00
S19 Bret Hedican 2.00 5.00
S20 Mathieu Schneider 2.00 5.00
S21 Chris Therien 2.00 5.00
S22 Greg Adams 2.00 5.00
S23 Arturs Irbe 4.00 10.00
S24 Zigmund Palffy 4.00 10.00
S25 Peter Douris 2.00 5.00
S26 Bob Sweeney 2.00 5.00
S27 Chris Terreri 2.00 5.00
S28 Alexei Zhitnik 2.00 5.00
S29 Jay Wells 2.00 5.00
S30 Andrew Cassels 2.00 5.00
S31 Radek Bonk 2.00 5.00
S32 Brian Bellows 2.00 5.00
S33 Frantisek Kucera 2.00 5.00
S34 Valeri Bure 2.00 5.00
S35 Randy Wood 2.00 5.00
S36 Dimitri Khristich 2.00 5.00
S37 Randy Ladouceur 2.00 5.00
S38 Nelson Emerson 2.00 5.00
S39 Bryan Marchment 2.00 5.00
S40 Kevin Lowe 4.00 10.00
S41 Trevor Linden 4.00 10.00
S42 Neal Broten 4.00 10.00
S43 Tom Chorske 2.00 5.00
S44 Patrice Brisebois 2.00 5.00
S45 Wayne Presley 2.00 5.00
S46 Murray Craven 2.00 5.00
S47 Craig Janney 2.00 5.00
S48 Ken Daneyko 2.00 5.00
S49 Dino Ciccarelli 4.00 10.00
S50 Jason Dawe 2.00 5.00
S51 Brad McCrimmon 2.00 5.00
S52 Randy McKay 2.00 5.00
S53 Rudy Poeschek 2.00 5.00
S54 Calle Johansson 2.00 5.00
S55 Wendel Clark 4.00 10.00
S56 Rob Ray 4.00 10.00
S57 Garth Snow 4.00 10.00
S58 Joe Juneau 4.00 10.00
S59 Craig Wolanin 2.00 5.00
S60 Ray Sheppard 2.00 5.00
S61 Oleg Tverdovsky 2.00 5.00
S62 Geoff Sanderson 2.00 5.00
S63 Mike Ridley 2.00 5.00
S64 David Oliver 2.00 5.00
S65 Russ Courtnall 2.00 5.00
S66 Joe Reekie 2.00 5.00
S67 Ken Wregget 4.00 10.00
S68 Teppo Numminen 2.00 5.00
S69 Mikhail Shtalenkov 2.00 5.00
S70 Luke Richardson 2.00 5.00
S71 Brent Gilchrist 2.00 5.00
S72 Phil Housley 2.00 5.00
S73 Greg Johnson 2.00 5.00
S74 Sean Hill 2.00 5.00
S75 Karl Dykhuis 2.00 5.00
S76 Tim Cheveldae 2.00 5.00
S77 Shjon Podein 2.00 5.00
S78 Rene Corbet 2.00 5.00
S79 Ron Stern 2.00 5.00
S80 Mike Donnelly 2.00 5.00
S81 Randy Cunneyworth 2.00 5.00
S82 Rick Tocchet 4.00 10.00
S83 Dallas Drake 2.00 5.00
S84 Cam Russell 2.00 5.00
S85 Daren Puppa 2.00 5.00
S86 Benoit Brunet 2.00 5.00
S87 Paul Ranheim 2.00 5.00
S88 Bob Rouse 2.00 5.00
S89 Todd Elik 2.00 5.00
S90 Darcy Wakaluk 2.00 5.00
S91 Cliff Ronning 2.00 5.00
S92 Pat Conacher 2.00 5.00
S93 Todd Krygier 2.00 5.00
S94 Dave Babych 2.00 5.00
S95 Pat Falloon 2.00 5.00
S96 Don Beaupre 4.00 10.00
S97 Wayne Gretzky (648) 75.00 200.00
S98 Chris Joseph 2.00 5.00
S99 Vyacheslav Kozlov 4.00 10.00
S100 Brent Fedyk 2.00 5.00
S101 Tim Taylor 2.00 5.00
S102 Mike Eastwood 2.00 5.00
S103 Mike Keane 2.00 5.00
S104 Grant Ledyard 2.00 5.00
S105 Rob Dimaio 2.00 5.00
S106 Martin Straka 2.00 5.00
S107 Scott Young 2.00 5.00
S108 Zarley Zalapski 2.00 5.00
S109 Steve Leach 2.00 5.00
S110 Jody Hull 2.00 5.00
S111 Lyle Odelein 2.00 5.00
S112 Bob Corkum 2.00 5.00
S113 Rob Blake 4.00 10.00
S114 Randy Burridge 2.00 5.00
S115 Keith Primeau 2.00 5.00
S116 Glen Wesley 2.00 5.00
S117 Brian Bradley 2.00 5.00
S118 Andrei Kovalenko 2.00 5.00
S119 Patrik Juhlin 2.00 5.00
S120 John Tucker 2.00 5.00
S121 Stephane Fiset 4.00 10.00
S122 Mike Hough 2.00 5.00
S123 Steve Smith 2.00 5.00
S124 Tom Barrasso 4.00 10.00
S125 Ray Whitney 2.00 5.00
S126 Benoit Hogue 2.00 5.00
S127 Stu Barnes 2.00 5.00
S128 Craig Ludwig 2.00 5.00
S129 Curtis Leschyshyn 2.00 5.00
S130 John LeClair 6.00 15.00
S131 Dennis Vial 2.00 5.00
S132 Cory Stillman 2.00 5.00
S133 Roman Hamrlik 2.00 5.00
S134 Al MacInnis 4.00 10.00
S135 Igor Korolev 2.00 5.00
S136 Rick Zombo 2.00 5.00
S137 Zdeno Ciger 2.00 5.00
S138 Brian Savage 2.00 5.00
S139 Paul Ysebaert 2.00 5.00
S140 Brent Sutter 2.00 5.00
S141 Ed Olczyk 2.00 5.00
S142 Adam Creighton 2.00 5.00
S143 Jesse Belanger 2.00 5.00
S144 Glen Murray 2.00 5.00
S145 Alexander Selivanov 2.00 5.00
S146 Trent Yawney 2.00 5.00
S147 Bruce Driver 2.00 5.00
S148 Michael Nylander 2.00 5.00
S149 Martin Gelinas 2.00 5.00
S150 Yanic Perreault 2.00 5.00
S151 Craig Billington 4.00 10.00
S152 Pierre Turgeon 4.00 10.00
S153 Mike Modano 10.00 25.00
S154 Joe Mullen 4.00 10.00
S155 Todd Ewen 2.00 5.00
S156 Petr Nedved 2.00 5.00
S157 Dominic Roussel 2.00 5.00
S158 Murray Baron 2.00 5.00
S159 Robert Dirk 2.00 5.00
S160 Tomas Sandstrom 2.00 5.00
S161 Brian Holzinger 2.00 5.00
S162 Ken Klee 2.00 5.00
S163 Radek Dvorak 2.00 5.00
S164 Marcus Ragnarsson 2.00 5.00
S165 Aaron Gavey 2.00 5.00
S166 Jeff O'Neill 2.00 5.00
S167 Chad Kilger 2.00 5.00
S168 Todd Bertuzzi 6.00 15.00
S169 Robert Svehla 2.00 5.00
S170 Eric Daze 2.00 5.00
S171 Daniel Alfredsson 4.00 15.00
S172 Shane Doan 4.00 10.00
S173 Kyle McLaren 2.00 5.00
S174 Saku Koivu 6.00 15.00
S175 Jere Lehtinen 4.00 10.00
S176 Nikolai Khabibulin 4.00 10.00
S177 Niklas Sundstrom 2.00 5.00
S178 Ed Jovanovski 4.00 10.00
S179 Jason Bonsignore 2.00 5.00
S180 Kenny Jonsson 2.00 5.00
S181 Vitali Yachmenev 2.00 5.00
S182 Alexei Kovalev 4.00 10.00
S183 Sandis Ozolinsh 2.00 5.00
S184 Rob Niedermayer 4.00 10.00
S185 Richard Park 2.00 5.00
S186 Adam Deadmarsh 2.00 5.00
S187 Sergei Krivokrasov 2.00 5.00
S188 Alexandre Daigle 2.00 5.00
S189 Jim Carey 4.00 10.00
S190 Todd Marchant 4.00 10.00
S191 Mike Richter 60.00 150.00
S192 Dominik Hasek 12.50 30.00
S193 Chris Osgood 4.00 10.00
S194 Ed Belfour 6.00 15.00
S195 Felix Potvin 6.00 15.00
S196 Grant Fuhr 6.00 15.00
S197 Patrick Roy 40.00 100.00
S198 Ron Hextall 4.00 10.00
S199 Jocelyn Thibault 4.00 10.00
S200 Kirk McLean 4.00 10.00
S201 Jari Kurri 4.00 10.00
S202 Bobby Holik 4.00 10.00
S203 Mats Sundin 6.00 15.00
S204 Alexander Mogilny 4.00 10.00
S205 Valeri Karpov 2.00 5.00
S206 Igor Larionov 2.00 5.00
S207 Valeri Zelepukin 2.00 5.00
S208 Jozef Stumpel 2.00 5.00
S209 Sergei Nemchinov 2.00 5.00
S210 Peter Bondra 4.00 10.00
S211 Chris Chelios 6.00 15.00
S212 Adam Graves 2.00 5.00
S213 Dale Hunter 4.00 10.00
S214 Tony Twist 6.00 15.00
S215 Keith Tkachuk 6.00 15.00
S216 Vladimir Konstantinov 25.00 50.00
S217 Sandy McCarthy 2.00 5.00
S218 Jamie Macoun 2.00 5.00
S219 Scott Stevens 4.00 10.00
S220 Mark Tinordi 2.00 5.00
S221 Bob Probert 4.00 10.00
S222 Gino Odjick 2.00 5.00
S223 Ulf Samuelsson 2.00 5.00
S224 Stu Grimson 4.00 10.00
S225 Marty McSorley 2.00 5.00
*S97 W.Gretzky DC (234) 300.00 500.00

1995-96 Be A Player Gretzky's Great Memories

COMPLETE SET (10) 40.00 80.00
COMMON GRETZKY (GM1-GM10) 4.00 10.00
GRETZKY MEMORIES STATED ODDS 1:15

1995-96 Be A Player Lethal Lines

COMPLETE SET (15) 30.00 60.00
STATED ODDS 1:7
LL1 Keith Tkachuk 1.50 4.00
LL2 Wayne Gretzky 6.00 15.00
LL3 Brett Hull 1.50 4.00
LL4 Eric Daze 1.50 4.00
LL5 Saku Koivu 1.50 4.00
LL6 Daniel Alfredsson 1.50 4.00
LL7 Pavel Bure 1.50 4.00
LL8 Sergei Fedorov 1.50 4.00
LL9 Alexander Mogilny 1.50 4.00
LL10 Paul Kariya 1.50 4.00
LL11 Mario Lemieux 5.00 12.00
LL12 Jaromir Jagr 1.50 4.00
LL13 Brendan Shanahan 1.50 4.00
LL14 Eric Lindros 1.50 4.00
LL15 Alexei Kovalev 1.25 3.00

1996-97 Be A Player

This 220-card set was issued by Pinnacle in two series and was distributed in eight-card packs with a suggested retail price of $6.99. For the first time, the series was licensed by the NHL, as well as the NHLPA, and thus the players were allowed to be seen in their own uniforms. Promotional cards were issued to dealers in six-card and two-card packs. These cards mirror those in the regular set save for the addition of the word PROMO written on the card back. The numbering, however, is the same as the base cards. The P prefix has been added for checklist purposes only.

COMPLETE SET (220) 12.00 30.00
COMPLETE SERIES 1 (110) 6.00 15.00
COMPLETE SERIES 2 (110) 6.00 15.00
1 Todd Gill .10 .25
2 Dave Andreychuk .10 .25
3 Igor Kravchuk .10 .25
4 Tom Fitzgerald .10 .25
5 Jeremy Roenick .40 1.00
6 Peter Popovic .10 .25
7 Andy Moog .20 .50
8 Steven Rice .10 .25
9 Darren Langdon .10 .25
10 Mark Fitzpatrick .20 .50
11 Alexei Zhamnov .10 .25
12 Luc Robitaille .20 .50
13 Michal Pivonka .10 .25
14 Kevin Hatcher .10 .25
15 Stephane Yelle .10 .25
16 Bill Ranford .20 .50
17 Jamie Baker .10 .25
18 Sean Burke .20 .50
19 Al Iafrate .10 .25
20 Mark Recchi .20 .50
21 Rod Brind'Amour .20 .50
22 Doug Gilmour .20 .50
23 Mike Wilson .10 .25
24 Barry Potomski RC .10 .25
25 Mike Gartner .20 .50
26 Jason Wiemer .10 .25
27 Scott Lachance .10 .25
28 Joe Murphy .10 .25
29 Bill Guerin .10 .25
30 Byron Dafoe .20 .50
31 Esa Tikkanen .10 .25
32 Ken Baumgartner .10 .25
33 Valeri Kamensky .20 .50
34 J.J. Daigneault .10 .25
35 Ulf Dahlen .10 .25
36 Jason Allison .10 .25
37 Ted Donato .10 .25
38 Pat Verbeek .10 .25
39 Miroslav Satan .10 .25
40 Eric Desjardins .20 .50
41 Dave Karpa .10 .25
42 Jeff Hackett .20 .50
43 Doug Brown .10 .25
44 Gord Murphy .10 .25
45 Kelly Hrudey .20 .50
46 Kelly Miller .10 .25
47 Tie Domi .20 .50
48 Alexei Yashin .10 .25
49 German Titov .10 .25
50 Stephane Richer .20 .50
51 Corey Hirsch .20 .50
52 Brad May .20 .50
53 Joe Nieuwendyk .20 .50
54 Sylvain Lefebvre .10 .25
55 Brian Leetch .30 .75
56 Petr Svoboda .10 .25
57 Dave Manson .10 .25
58 Jason Woolley .10 .25
59 Scott Niedermayer .10 .25
60 Kelly Chase .10 .25
61 Guy Hebert .20 .50
62 Shayne Corson .10 .25
63 Jon Casey .20 .50
64 Rob Zettler .10 .25
65 Mikael Andersson .10 .25
66 Tony Amonte .20 .50
67 Johan Garpenlov .10 .25
68 Denny Lambert .10 .25
69 Jim McKenzie .10 .25
70 Darren Turcotte .10 .25
71 Eric Weinrich .10 .25
72 Troy Mallette .10 .25
73 Donald Audette .10 .25
74 Philippe Boucher .10 .25
75 Shawn Chambers .10 .25
76 Joel Otto .10 .25
77 Tommy Salo .20 .50
78 Olaf Kolzig .30 .75
79 Adrian Aucoin .10 .25
80 Alek Stojanov .10 .25
81 Robert Reichel .10 .25
82 Marc Bureau .10 .25
83 Alexander Godynyuk .10 .25
84 Bill Berg .10 .25
85 Marc Bergevin .10 .25
86 Kevin Kaminski .10 .25
87 Uwe Krupp .10 .25
88 Boris Mironov .10 .25
89 Bob Bassen .10 .25
90 Darryl Shannon .10 .25
91 Mikael Renberg .20 .50
92 Mike Stapleton .10 .25
93 David Roberts .10 .25
94 Peter Zezel .10 .25
95 Mathieu Dandenault .10 .25
96 Bobby Dollas .10 .25
97 Don Sweeney .10 .25
98 Niklas Andersson .10 .25
99 Pat Jablonski .20 .50
100 John Slaney .10 .25
101 Kevin Todd .10 .25
102 Jamie Pushor .10 .25
103 Andreas Johansson RC .10 .25
104 Corey Schwab .20 .50
105 Todd Simpson RC .10 .25
106 Landon Wilson .10 .25
107 Daniel Goneau RC .20 .50
108 David Wilkie .10 .25
109 Andreas Dackell RC .10 .25
110 Marek Malik .10 .25
111 Mark Messier .30 .75
112 Francois Leroux .10 .25
113 Michal Sykora .10 .25
114 Rob Zamuner .10 .25
115 Craig Berube .10 .25
116 Mike Ricci .10 .25
117 Adam Burt .10 .25
118 Alexander Karpovtsev .10 .25
119 Shawn McEachern .10 .25
120 Shawn Antoski .10 .25
121 Dave Reid .10 .25
122 Todd Warriner .10 .25
123 Markus Naslund .20 .50
124 Martin Rucinsky .10 .25
125 Bob Carpenter .10 .25
126 Dean McAmmond .10 .25
127 Trevor Kidd .20 .50
128 Martin Lapointe .10 .25
129 Enrico Ciccone .10 .25
130 Dixon Ward .10 .25
131 Jason Muzzatti .20 .50
132 Bryan Smolinski .10 .25
133 Norm Maciver .10 .25
134 Fredrik Olausson .10 .25
135 Daniel Lacroix .10 .25
136 Mike Peluso .10 .25
137 Andrei Nikolishin .10 .25
138 Rhett Warrener .10 .25
139 Ray Ferraro .10 .25
140 Glenn Healy .20 .50
141 Steve Duchesne .10 .25
142 Tony Granato .10 .25
143 Cory Cross .10 .25
144 Jon Klemm .10 .25
145 Sami Kapanen .10 .25
146 Grant Marshall .10 .25
147 Matthew Barnaby .10 .25
148 Lyle Odelein .10 .25
149 Joe Dziedzic .10 .25
150 Sergei Gonchar .10 .25
151 Doug Zmolek .10 .25
152 Sean O'Donnell RC .10 .25
153 Scott Thornton .10 .25
154 Steve Heinze .10 .25
155 Garry Valk .10 .25
156 Jeff Finley .10 .25
157 Trent Klatt .10 .25
158 Jeff Beukeboom .10 .25
159 Theo Fleury .10 .25
160 Dana Murzyn .10 .25
161 Tommy Albelin .20 .50
162 Bryan McCabe .10 .25
163 Shaun Van Allen .10 .25
164 Rick Tabaracci .20 .50
165 Kevin Miller .10 .25
166 Mariusz Czerkawski .10 .25
167 Gerald Diduck .10 .25
168 Brad McCrimmon .10 .25
169 Stephane Matteau .10 .25
170 Scott Daniels .10 .25
171 Scott Mellanby .20 .50
172 Sandy Moger .10 .25
173 Steve Konowalchuk .10 .25
174 Doug Weight .20 .50
175 Darren McCarty .10 .25
176 Darryl Sydor .10 .25
177 Dave Ellett .10 .25
178 Bob Boughner RC .10 .25
179 Derek Armstrong .10 .25
180 Gary Suter .10 .25
181 Donald Brashear .10 .25
182 Chris Tamer .10 .25
183 Darrin Shannon .10 .25
184 Stanislav Neckar .10 .25
185 Brent Severyn .10 .25
186 Steve Rucchin .10 .25
187 Jeff Norton .10 .25
188 Steven Finn .10 .25
189 Kjell Samuelsson .10 .25
190 Jeff Friesen .10 .25
191 Shawn Burr .10 .25
192 Paul Laus .10 .25
193 Jeff Odgers .10 .25
194 Keith Jones .10 .25
195 Richard Matvichuk .10 .25
196 Adam Foote .10 .25
197 Bob Errey .10 .25
198 Ryan Smyth .20 .50
199 Mark Janssens .10 .25
200 Claude Lapointe .10 .25
201 Brian Noonan .10 .25
202 Damian Rhodes .20 .50
203 Dale Hawerchuk .20 .50
204 Bill Lindsay .10 .25
205 Brian Skrudland .10 .25
206 Curtis Joseph .30 .75
207 Jon Rohloff .10 .25
208 Doug Bodger .10 .25
209 Steve Sullivan RC .20 .50
210 Ricard Persson .10 .25
211 Dwayne Roloson RC 1.25 3.00
212 Mike Dunham .20 .50
213 Marcel Cousineau RC .10 .25
214 Eric Fichaud .20 .50
215 Matt Johnson .10 .25
216 Fredrik Modin RC .20 .50
217 Denis Pederson .10 .25
218 Kevin Hodson RC .20 .50
219 Drew Bannister .10 .25
220 Mike Grier RC .50 1.25
P44 Gord Murphy PROMO .10 .25
P52 Brad May PROMO .10 .25
P55 Brian Leetch PROMO .10 .25
P67 Johan Garpenlov PROMO .10 .25
P89 Bob Bassen PROMO .10 .25
P91 Mikael Renberg PROMO .10 .25
P119 Shawn MacEachern PROMO .10 .25
P176 Darryl Sydor PROMO .10 .25
P181 Donald Brashear PROMO .10 .25
P217 Denis Pederson PROMO .10 .25
P218 Kevin Hodson PROMO .10 .25
P219 Drew Bannister PROMO .10 .25

1996-97 Be A Player Autographs

These autographs were inserted one per pack. Gold foil distinguishes them from base cards. Alexei Zhamnov did not sign, and thus the set is considered complete at 219 cards. A silver parallel version of the autograph set existed as well. The cards were distinguishable by the silver foil backing on the card fronts. Although no odds were published, these cards were inserted at a rate of about 1:30 packs.

ONE AUTO.CARD PER PACK
*SILVER AUTOS: .75X TO 1.5X BASIC AUTOS
SILVER AU STATED ODDS 1:7
1 Todd Gill 1.50 4.00
2 Dave Andreychuk 3.00 8.00
3 Igor Kravchuk 1.50 4.00
4 Tom Fitzgerald 1.50 4.00
5 Jeremy Roenick 6.00 15.00
6 Peter Popovic 1.50 4.00
7 Andy Moog 2.50 6.00
8 Steven Rice 1.50 4.00
9 Darren Langdon 1.50 4.00
10 Mark Fitzpatrick 2.50 6.00
12 Luc Robitaille 6.00 15.00
13 Michal Pivonka 1.50 4.00
14 Kevin Hatcher 1.50 4.00
15 Stephane Yelle 1.50 4.00
16 Bill Ranford 3.00 8.00
17 Jamie Baker 1.50 4.00
18 Sean Burke 3.00 8.00
19 Al Iafrate 2.50 6.00
20 Mark Recchi 3.00 8.00
21 Rod Brind'Amour 3.00 8.00
22 Doug Gilmour 6.00 15.00
23 Mike Wilson 1.50 4.00
24 Barry Potomski 1.50 4.00
25 Mike Gartner 3.00 8.00
26 Jason Wiemer 1.50 4.00
27 Scott Lachance 1.50 4.00
28 Joe Murphy 1.50 4.00
29 Bill Guerin 3.00 8.00
30 Byron Dafoe 2.50 6.00
31 Esa Tikkanen 1.50 4.00
32 Ken Baumgartner 1.50 4.00
33 Valeri Kamensky 1.50 4.00
34 J.J. Daigneault 1.50 4.00
35 Ulf Dahlen 1.50 4.00
36 Jason Allison 1.50 4.00
37 Ted Donato 1.50 4.00
38 Pat Verbeek 1.50 4.00
39 Miroslav Satan 3.00 8.00
40 Eric Desjardins 2.50 6.00
41 Dave Karpa 1.50 4.00
42 Jeff Hackett 2.50 6.00
43 Doug Brown 1.50 4.00
44 Gord Murphy 1.50 4.00
45 Kelly Hrudey 2.50 6.00
46 Kelly Miller 1.50 4.00
47 Tie Domi 3.00 8.00
48 Alexei Yashin 1.50 4.00
49 German Titov 1.50 4.00
50 Stephane Richer 1.50 4.00
51 Corey Hirsch 2.50 6.00
52 Brad May 1.50 4.00
53 Joe Nieuwendyk 3.00 8.00
54 Sylvain Lefebvre 1.50 4.00
55 Brian Leetch 5.00 12.00
56 Petr Svoboda 1.50 4.00
57 Dave Manson 1.50 4.00
58 Jason Woolley 1.50 4.00
59 Scott Niedermayer 1.50 4.00
60 Kelly Chase 1.50 4.00
61 Guy Hebert 2.50 6.00
62 Shayne Corson 1.50 4.00
63 Jon Casey 2.50 6.00
64 Rob Zettler 1.50 4.00
65 Mikael Andersson 1.50 4.00
66 Tony Amonte 3.00 8.00
67 Johan Garpenlov 1.50 4.00
68 Denny Lambert 1.50 4.00
69 Jim McKenzie 1.50 4.00
70 Darren Turcotte 1.50 4.00
71 Eric Weinrich 1.50 4.00
72 Troy Mallette 1.50 4.00
73 Donald Audette 1.50 4.00
74 Philippe Boucher 1.50 4.00
75 Shawn Chambers 1.50 4.00
76 Joel Otto 1.50 4.00
77 Tommy Salo 2.50 6.00
78 Olaf Kolzig 3.00 8.00
79 Adrian Aucoin 1.50 4.00
80 Alek Stojanov 1.50 4.00
81 Robert Reichel 1.50 4.00
82 Marc Bureau 1.50 4.00
83 Alexander Godynyuk 1.50 4.00
84 Bill Berg 1.50 4.00
85 Marc Bergevin 1.50 4.00
86 Kevin Kaminski 1.50 4.00
87 Uwe Krupp 1.50 4.00
88 Boris Mironov 1.50 4.00
89 Bob Bassen 1.50 4.00
90 Darryl Shannon 1.50 4.00
91 Mikael Renberg 1.50 4.00
92 Mike Stapleton 1.50 4.00
93 David Roberts 1.50 4.00
94 Peter Zezel 1.50 4.00
95 Mathieu Dandenault 1.50 4.00
96 Bobby Dollas 1.50 4.00
97 Don Sweeney 1.50 4.00
98 Niklas Andersson 1.50 4.00
99 Pat Jablonski 1.50 4.00
100 John Slaney 1.50 4.00
101 Kevin Todd 1.50 4.00
102 Jamie Pushor 1.50 4.00
103 Andreas Johansson 1.50 4.00
104 Corey Schwab 1.50 4.00
105 Todd Simpson 1.50 4.00
106 Landon Wilson 1.50 4.00
107 Daniel Goneau 1.50 4.00
108 David Wilkie 1.50 4.00
109 Andreas Dackell 1.50 4.00
110 Marek Malik 1.50 4.00
111 Mark Messier 30.00 80.00
112 Francois Leroux 1.50 4.00
113 Michal Sykora 1.50 4.00
114 Rob Zamuner 1.50 4.00
115 Craig Berube 1.50 4.00
116 Mike Ricci 2.50 6.00
117 Adam Burt 1.50 4.00
118 Alexander Karpovtsev 1.50 4.00
119 Shawn McEachern 1.50 4.00
120 Shawn Antoski 1.50 4.00
121 Dave Reid 1.50 4.00
122 Todd Warriner 1.50 4.00
123 Markus Naslund 4.00 10.00
124 Martin Rucinsky 1.50 4.00
125 Bob Carpenter 1.50 4.00
126 Dean McAmmond 1.50 4.00
127 Trevor Kidd 2.50 6.00
128 Martin Lapointe 2.50 6.00
129 Enrico Ciccone 1.50 4.00
130 Dixon Ward 1.50 4.00
131 Jason Muzzatti 1.50 4.00
132 Bryan Smolinski 1.50 4.00
133 Norm Maciver 1.50 4.00
134 Fredrik Olausson 1.50 4.00
135 Daniel Lacroix 1.50 4.00
136 Mike Peluso 1.50 4.00
137 Andrei Nikolishin 1.50 4.00
138 Rhett Warrener 1.50 4.00
139 Ray Ferraro 1.50 4.00
140 Glenn Healy 1.50 4.00
141 Steve Duchesne 1.50 4.00
142 Tony Granato 1.50 4.00
143 Cory Cross 1.50 4.00
144 Jon Klemm 1.50 4.00
145 Sami Kapanen 1.50 4.00
146 Grant Marshall 1.50 4.00
147 Matthew Barnaby 2.50 6.00
148 Lyle Odelein 1.50 4.00
149 Joe Dziedzic 1.50 4.00
150 Sergei Gonchar 1.50 4.00
151 Doug Zmolek 1.50 4.00
152 Sean O'Donnell 1.50 4.00
153 Scott Thornton 1.50 4.00
154 Steve Heinze 1.50 4.00
155 Garry Valk 1.50 4.00
156 Jeff Finley 1.50 4.00
157 Trent Klatt 1.50 4.00
158 Jeff Beukeboom 1.50 4.00
159 Theo Fleury 1.50 4.00
160 Dana Murzyn 1.50 4.00
161 Tommy Albelin 1.50 4.00
162 Bryan McCabe 1.50 4.00
163 Shaun Van Allen 1.50 4.00
164 Rick Tabaracci 2.50 6.00
165 Kevin Miller 1.50 4.00
166 Mariusz Czerkawski 1.50 4.00
167 Gerald Diduck 1.50 4.00
168 Brad McCrimmon 1.50 4.00
169 Stephane Matteau 1.50 4.00
170 Scott Daniels 1.50 4.00
171 Scott Mellanby 1.50 4.00
172 Sandy Moger 1.50 4.00
173 Steve Konowalchuk 1.50 4.00
174 Doug Weight 2.50 6.00
175 Darren McCarty 3.00 8.00
176 Darryl Sydor 1.50 4.00
177 Dave Ellett 1.50 4.00
178 Bob Boughner 1.50 4.00
179 Derek Armstrong 1.50 4.00
180 Gary Suter 1.50 4.00
181 Donald Brashear 1.50 4.00
182 Chris Tamer 1.50 4.00
183 Darrin Shannon 1.50 4.00
184 Stanislav Neckar 1.50 4.00
185 Brent Severyn 1.50 4.00
186 Steve Rucchin 1.50 4.00
187 Jeff Norton 1.50 4.00
188 Steven Finn 1.50 4.00
189 Kjell Samuelsson 1.50 4.00
190 Jeff Friesen 1.50 4.00
191 Shawn Burr 1.50 4.00
192 Paul Laus 1.50 4.00
193 Jeff Odgers 1.50 4.00
194 Keith Jones 1.50 4.00
195 Richard Matvichuk 1.50 4.00
196 Adam Foote 1.50 4.00
197 Bob Errey 1.50 4.00
198 Ryan Smyth 3.00 8.00
199 Mark Janssens 1.50 4.00
200 Claude Lapointe 1.50 4.00
201 Brian Noonan 1.50 4.00
202 Damian Rhodes 2.50 6.00
203 Dale Hawerchuk 3.00 8.00
204 Bill Lindsay 1.50 4.00
205 Brian Skrudland 1.50 4.00
206 Curtis Joseph 10.00 20.00
207 Jon Rohloff 1.50 4.00
208 Doug Bodger 1.50 4.00
209 Steve Sullivan 2.50 6.00
210 Ricard Persson 1.50 4.00
211 Dwayne Roloson 3.00 8.00
212 Mike Dunham 3.00 8.00
213 Marcel Cousineau 1.50 4.00
214 Eric Fichaud 1.50 4.00
215 Matt Johnson 1.50 4.00
216 Fredrik Modin 1.50 4.00
217 Denis Pederson 1.50 4.00
218 Kevin Hodson 2.50 6.00
219 Drew Bannister 1.50 4.00
220 Mike Grier 1.50 4.00

1996-97 Be A Player Biscuit In The Basket

COMPLETE SET (25) 25.00 60.00
STATED ODDS 1:17
1 Wayne Gretzky 6.00 15.00
2 Mario Lemieux 4.00 10.00
3 Eric Lindros 1.25 3.00
4 Theo Fleury .75 2.00
5 Peter Forsberg 2.00 5.00
6 Keith Tkachuk .75 2.00
7 Sergei Fedorov 1.50 4.00
8 Mike Modano 1.50 4.00
9 Jaromir Jagr 2.00 5.00
10 Brendan Shanahan 1.25 3.00
11 Teemu Selanne 1.25 3.00
12 Mats Sundin 1.25 3.00
13 Steve Yzerman 3.00 8.00
14 Brett Hull 1.50 4.00
15 Zigmund Palffy .75 2.00
16 Joe Sakic 2.50 6.00
17 John LeClair .40 1.00
18 Pavel Bure 1.25 3.00
19 Mark Messier 1.25 3.00
20 Paul Kariya 1.25 3.00
21 Jason Arnott .40 1.00
22 Saku Koivu 1.25 3.00
23 Daniel Alfredsson .75 2.00
24 Alexander Mogilny .75 2.00
25 Owen Nolan .75 2.00

1996-97 Be A Player Lemieux Die Cut

This two-card set commemorated the caree of future Hall-of-Famer, Mario Lemieux, wit a special interlocking, all-foil Dufex, die-cu insert. The first card was randomly inserte in Series 1 packs with it's matching interlocking counterpart inserted in Series packs. Only 66 of each card was produce and sequentially numbered.

COMPLETE SET (2)
STATED PRINT RUN 66 SERIAL #'d SETS
1 Mario Lemieux 100.00 200.00
2 Mario Lemieux 100.00 200.00

1996-97 Be A Player Lindros Die Cut

This two-card set honored the supersta center, Eric Lindros, with a specia interlocking, all-foil Dufex, die-cut inser Each card carried an authentic autograph The first card was randomly inserted i Series 1 packs with it's matching interlocking counterpart inserted in Series packs. Only 88 of each card was produce and sequentially numbered.

COMPLETE SET (2) 100.00 200.00
RANDOM INSERTS IN PACKS
STATED PRINT RUN 88 SERIAL #'d SETS
1 Eric Lindros AU 60.00 150.00
2 Eric Lindros AU 60.00 150.00

1996-97 Be A Player Link to History

Randomly inserted at an approximate rate of 1:2 packs, cards from this 20-card se featured ten top rookie standouts matche with their 10 mega-star veteran counterparts The first five rookie "Links" appeared i Series I with the second five veteran "Links and featured silver foil with blue accents The second five rookie "Links" appeared i Series II with the first five veteran "Links and featured silver foil with red accents.

COMPLETE SET (20) 8.00 20.00
COMPLETE SERIES 1 (10) 4.00 10.00
COMPLETE SERIES 2 (10) 4.00 10.00
STATED ODDS 1:2
1A Jarome Iginla .50 1.25
1B Teemu Selanne .40 1.00
2A Harry York .20 .50
2B Peter Forsberg 1.00 2.50
3A Sergei Berezin .40 1.00
3B Brendan Shanahan .40 1.00
4A Ethan Moreau .40 1.00
4B Pavel Bure .40 1.00
5A Rem Murray .20 .50
5B Jason Arnott .20 .50
6A Jamie Langenbrunner .20 .50
6B Paul Kariya .40 1.00
7A Jim Campbell .40 1.00
7B Eric Lindros .40 1.00
8A Jonas Hoglund .20 .50
8B Pat LaFontaine .40 1.00
9A Wade Redden .20 .50
9B Steve Yzerman 2.00 5.00
10A Patrick Lalime .40 1.00
10B John Vanbiesbrouck .30 .75
2B Peter Forsberg PROMO 2.00 5.00

1996-97 Be A Player Link to History Autographs

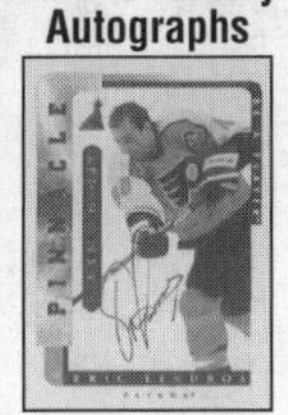

n authentic autograph and gold foil on each ard front make these parallel cards easy to entify from their more common Link to story counterparts. Exact odds per pack ere not released, but they're significantly ugher to pull than the non-autographed ards. Because of a delayed return, Ethan oreau's cards were inserted in Series II acks only; Teemu Selanne's autographed ards replaced them in Series I packs. A lver parallel version of the autograph was so created. The cards were distinguishable the silver foil backing on the card fronts. though no odds were published, these ards were inserted at a rate of about 1:30 cks.

SILVER AUs: .75X TO 2X BASIC AUTOS
A Jarome Iginla 15.00 40.00
B Teemu Selanne 6.00 15.00
A Harry York 1.50 4.00
B Peter Forsberg 15.00 40.00
A Sergei Berezin 4.00 10.00
B Brendan Shanahan 6.00 15.00
A Ethan Moreau 1.50 4.00
B Pavel Bure 6.00 15.00
A Rem Murray 1.50 4.00
B Jason Arnott 1.50 4.00
A Jamie Langenbrunner 1.50 4.00
B Paul Kariya 15.00 40.00
A Jim Campbell 4.00 10.00
B Eric Lindros 6.00 15.00
A Jonas Hoglund 1.50 4.00
B Pat LaFontaine 1.50 4.00
A Wade Redden 1.50 4.00
B Steve Yzerman 20.00 50.00
)A Patrick Lalime 4.00 10.00
)B John Vanbiesbrouck 4.00 10.00

1996-97 Be A Player Messier Die Cut

is two-card set featured superstar, Mark essier, with a special interlocking, all-foil ufex, die-cut insert. Each card was ersonally autographed. The first card was ndomly inserted in Series 1 packs with it's atching, interlocking counterpart inserted Series 2 packs. Only 11 of each card was oduced and sequentially numbered.

OMPLETE SET (2)
ANDOM INSERTS IN PACKS
TATED PRINT RUN 11 SERIAL #'d SETS
Mark Messier AU
Mark Messier AU

1996-97 Be A Player Stacking the Pads

OMPLETE SET (15) 12.00 30.00
TATED ODDS 1:35
Patrick Lalime .75 2.00
Chris Osgood .75 2.00
Ron Hextall .75 2.00
John Vanbiesbrouck .75 2.00
Martin Brodeur 2.50 6.00
Felix Potvin 1.25 3.00
Nikolai Khabibulin .75 2.00
Jim Carey .75 2.00
Grant Fuhr .75 2.00
) Mike Richter 1.25 3.00
1 Dominik Hasek 2.00 5.00
2 Andy Moog .75 2.00
3 Patrick Roy 4.00 10.00
4 Curtis Joseph 1.25 3.00
5 Jocelyn Thibault .75 2.00

1997-98 Be A Player

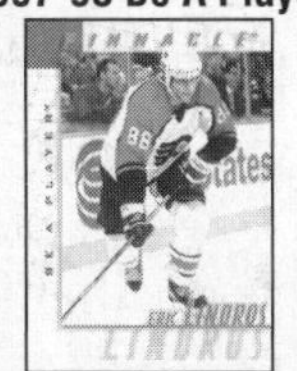

he 1997-98 Be A Player set was issued by nnacle in two series totalling 250 cards d was distributed in eight-card packs with uggested retail price of $6.99. The fronts atured color action photos of players with a eavy emphasis on rookies and Calder ophy candidates in a white and net-adow border. The backs carried a head oto with player information and career atistics.

COMPLETE SET (250) 5.00 15.00
1 Eric Lindros .25 .60
2 Martin Brodeur .60 1.50
3 Saku Koivu .25 .60
4 Felix Potvin .25 .60
5 Adam Oates .15 .35
6 Rob DiMaio .08 .25
7 Jari Kurri .15 .35
8 Andrew Cassels .08 .25
9 Trevor Linden .15 .35
10 Jocelyn Thibault .15 .35
11 Chris Chelios .25 .60
12 Paul Coffey .25 .60
13 Nikolai Khabibulin .15 .35
14 Robert Lang .08 .25
15 Brett Hull .30 .75
16 Mike Sillinger .08 .25
17 Lyle Odelein .08 .25
18 Bryan Berard .08 .25
19 Craig Muni .08 .25
20 Kris Draper .08 .25
21 Ed Jovanovski .15 .35
22 Keith Tkachuk .25 .60
23 Dean Malkoc .08 .25
24 Cory Stillman .08 .25
25 Chris Osgood .25 .60
26 Dainius Zubrus .08 .25
27 Yves Racine .08 .25
28 Eric Cairns RC .08 .25
29 Dan Bylsma .08 .25
30 Chris Terreri .08 .25
31 Bill Huard .08 .25
32 Warren Rychel .08 .25
33 Scott Walker .08 .25
34 Brian Holzinger .08 .25
35 Roman Turek .10 .25
36 Ron Tugnutt .15 .35
37 Mike Richter .25 .60
38 Mattias Norstrom .08 .25
39 Joe Sacco .08 .25
40 Derek King .08 .25
41 Brad Werenka .08 .25
42 Paul Kruse .08 .25
43 Mike Knuble RC .08 .25
44 Mike Peca .08 .25
45 Jean-Yves Leroux RC .08 .25
46 Ray Sheppard .08 .25
47 Reid Simpson .08 .25
48 Rob Brown .08 .25
49 Dave Babych .08 .25
50 Scott Pellerin .08 .25
51 Bruce Gardiner RC .08 .25
52 Adam Deadmarsh .08 .25
53 Curtis Brown .08 .25
54 Jason Marshall .08 .25
55 Gerald Diduck .08 .25
56 Mick Vukota .08 .25
57 Kevin Dean .08 .25
58 Adam Graves .08 .25
59 Craig Conroy .08 .25
60 Cale Hulse .08 .25
61 Dimitri Khristich .08 .25
62 Chris Wells .08 .25
63 Travis Green .08 .25
64 Tyler Wright .08 .25
65 Chris Simon .08 .25
66 Mikhail Shtalenkov .08 .25
67 Anson Carter .15 .35
68 Zarley Zalapski .08 .25
69 Per Gustafsson .08 .25
70 Jayson More .08 .25
71 Steve Thomas .08 .25
72 Todd Marchant .08 .25
73 Gary Roberts .08 .25
74 Richard Smehlik .08 .25
75 Aaron Miller .08 .25
76 Daren Puppa .08 .25
77 Garth Snow .15 .35
78 Greg DeVries .08 .25
79 Randy Burridge .08 .25
80 Jim Cummins .08 .25
81 Rich Pilon .08 .25
82 Chris McAlpine .08 .25
83 Joe Sakic .50 1.25
84 Ted Drury .08 .25
85 Brent Gilchrist .08 .25
86 Dallas Eakins RC .08 .25
87 Bruce Driver .08 .25
88 Jamie Huscroft .08 .25
89 Jeff Brown .08 .25
90 Janne Laukkanen .08 .25
91 Ken Klee .08 .25
92 Peter Bondra .15 .35
93 Ian Moran .08 .25
94 Stephane Quintal .08 .25
95 Jason York .08 .25
96 Todd Harvey .08 .25
97 Slava Kozlov .08 .25
98 Kevin Haller .08 .25
99 Alexei Zhamnov .08 .25
100 Craig Johnson .08 .25
101 Mike Keane .08 .25
102 Craig Rivet .08 .25
103 Roman Vopat .08 .25
104 Jim Johnson .08 .25
105 Ray Whitney .08 .25
106 Ron Sutter .08 .25
107 Jamie McLennan .15 .35
108 Kris King .08 .25
109 Lance Pitlick RC .08 .25
110 Mike Dunham .15 .35
111 Jim Dowd .08 .25
112 Geoff Sanderson .15 .35
113 Vladimir Vujtek .08 .25
114 Tim Taylor .08 .25
115 Sandis Ozolinsh .08 .25
116 Scott Daniels .08 .25
117 Bob Corkum .08 .25
118 Kirk McLean .15 .35
119 Darcy Tucker .08 .25
120 Dennis Vaske .08 .25
121 Kirk Muller .08 .25
122 Jay McKee .08 .25
123 Jere Lehtinen .08 .25
124 Ruslan Salei .08 .25
125 Al MacInnis .08 .25
126 Ulf Samuelsson .08 .25
127 Rick Tocchet .15 .35
128 Nick Kypreos .08 .25
129 Joel Bouchard .08 .25
130 Jeff O'Neill .08 .25
131 Daniel McGillis RC .08 .25
132 Sean Pronger .08 .25
133 Vladimir Malakhov .08 .25
134 Petr Sykora .08 .25
135 Zigmund Palffy .15 .35
136 Joe Reekie .08 .25
137 Chris Gratton .08 .25
138 Craig Billington .15 .35
139 Steve Washburn .08 .25
140 Robert Kron .08 .25
141 Larry Murphy .08 .25
142 Shean Donovan .08 .25
143 Scott Young .08 .25
144 Janne Niinimaa .15 .35
145 Ken Belanger RC .08 .25
146 Pavol Demitra .15 .35
147 Roman Hamrlik .08 .25
148 Lonny Bohonos .08 .25
149 Mike Eagles .08 .25
150 Kelly Buchberger .08 .25
151 Mattias Timander .08 .25
152 Benoit Hogue .08 .25
153 Joey Kocur .08 .25
154 Mats Lindgren .08 .25
155 Aki Berg .08 .25
156 Tim Sweeney .08 .25
157 Vincent Damphousse .08 .25
158 Dan Kordic .08 .25
159 Darius Kasparaitis .08 .25
160 Randy McKay .08 .25
161 Steve Staios .08 .25
162 Brendan Witt .08 .25
163 Paul Ysebaert .08 .25
164 Greg Adams .08 .25
165 Kent Manderville .08 .25
166 Steve Dubinsky .08 .25
167 David Nemirovsky .08 .25
168 Todd Bertuzzi .25 .60
169 Frederic Chabot .08 .25
170 Dmitri Mironov .08 .25
171 Pat Peake .08 .25
172 Ed Ward .08 .25
173 Jeff Shantz .08 .25
174 Dave Gagner .08 .25
175 Randy Cunneyworth .08 .25
176 Daymond Langkow .15 .35
177 Alex Hicks .08 .25
178 Darby Hendrickson .08 .25
179 Mike Sullivan .08 .25
180 Anders Eriksson .08 .25
181 Turner Stevenson .08 .25
182 Shane Churla .08 .25
183 Dave Lowry .08 .25
184 Joe Juneau .08 .25
185 Bob Essensa .08 .25
186 James Black .08 .25
187 Michal Grosek .08 .25
188 Tomas Holmstrom .08 .25
189 Ian Laperriere .08 .25
190 Terry Yake .08 .25
191 Jason Smith .08 .25
192 Sergei Zholtok .08 .25
193 Doug Houda .08 .25
194 Guy Carbonneau .08 .25
195 Terry Carkner .08 .25
196 Alexei Gusarov .08 .25
197 Vladimir Tsyplakov .08 .25
198 Jarrod Skalde .08 .25
199 Marty Murray .08 .25
200 Aaron Ward .08 .25
201 Bobby Holik .08 .25
202 Steve Chiasson .08 .25
203 Brantt Myhres .08 .25
204 Eric Messier RC .15 .35
205 Rene Corbet .08 .25
206 Mathieu Schneider .08 .25
207 Tom Chorske .08 .25
208 Doug Lidster .08 .25
209 Igor Ulanov .08 .25
210 Blair Atcheynum RC .08 .25
211 Sebastien Bordeleau .08 .25
212 Alexei Morozov .15 .35
213 Vaclav Prospal RC .40 1.00
214 Brad Bombardir RC .08 .25
215 Mattias Ohlund .15 .35
216 Chris Dingman RC .08 .25
217 Erik Rasmussen .08 .25
218 Mike Johnson RC .15 .35
219 Chris Phillips .08 .25
220 Sergei Samsonov .15 .35
221 Patrick Marleau .40 1.00
222 Alyn McCauley .15 .35
223 Ryan VandenBussche RC .08 .25
224 Daniel Cleary .08 .25
225 Magnus Arvedson RC .08 .25
226 Brad Isbister .08 .25
227 Pascal Rheaume RC .08 .25
228 Patrik Elias RC .60 1.50
229 Krzysztof Oliwa RC .08 .25
230 Tyler Moss RC .08 .25
231 Jamie Rivers .08 .25
232 Joe Thornton .40 1.00
233 Steve Shields RC .20 .50
234 Dave Scatchard RC .08 .25
235 Patrick Cote RC .08 .25
236 Rich Brennan RC .08 .25
237 Boyd Devereaux .08 .25
238 Per Johan Axelsson RC .08 .25
239 Craig Millar RC .08 .25
240 Juha Ylonen .08 .25
241 Donald MacLean .08 .25
242 Jaroslav Svejkovsky .08 .25
243 Marco Sturm RC .40 1.00
244 Steve McKenna RC .08 .25
245 Derek Morris RC .30 .75
246 Dean Chynoweth .08 .25
247 Alexander Mogilny .15 .35
248 Ray Bourque .40 1.00
249 Ed Belfour .25 .60
250 John LeClair .25 .60
P3 Saku Koivu PROMO .75 2.00

1997-98 Be A Player Autographs

Inserted one per pack, this 250-card set was an autographed gold foil enhanced parallel version of the base set. Die-cut and limited prismatic die-cut parallel autographed versions of the base set were also produced. Die-cut auto stated odds were 1:7. The prismatic parallel had a stated print run of 100 sets.

STATED ODDS 1:1
*DIE CUT STARS: 1X TO 2X BASIC AUTOS
*DIE CUT SP's: .6X TO 1.25X BASIC AUTOS
DIE CUT STATED ODDS 1:7
*PRISM.STARS: 1.5X TO 3X BASIC AUTOS
*PRISM.SP's: .75X TO 1.5X BASIC AUTOS
PRISMATIC STATED PRINT RUN 100 SETS
1 Eric Lindros SP 10.00 25.00
2 Martin Brodeur SP 40.00 100.00
3 Saku Koivu 3.00 8.00
4 Felix Potvin 3.00 8.00
5 Adam Oates 2.00 5.00
6 Rob DiMaio 1.00 2.50
7 Jari Kurri 4.00 10.00
8 Andrew Cassels 1.00 2.50
9 Trevor Linden 1.00 2.50
10 Jocelyn Thibault 2.00 5.00
11 Chris Chelios 2.00 5.00
12 Paul Coffey 4.00 10.00
13 Nikolai Khabibulin 4.00 10.00
14 Robert Lang 1.00 2.50
15 Brett Hull SP 30.00 80.00
16 Mike Sillinger 1.00 2.50
17 Lyle Odelein 1.00 2.50
18 Bryan Berard 1.00 2.50
19 Craig Muni 1.00 2.50
20 Kris Draper 1.00 2.50
21 Ed Jovanovski 1.00 2.50
22 Keith Tkachuk 2.00 5.00
23 Dean Malkoc 1.00 2.50
24 Cory Stillman 1.00 2.50
25 Chris Osgood 2.00 5.00
26 Dainius Zubrus 1.00 2.50
27 Yves Racine 1.00 2.50
28 Eric Cairns 1.00 2.50
29 Dan Bylsma 1.00 2.50
30 Chris Terreri 1.00 2.50
31 Bill Huard 1.00 2.50
32 Warren Rychel 1.00 2.50
33 Scott Walker 1.00 2.50
34 Brian Holzinger 1.00 2.50
35 Roman Turek 1.00 2.50
36 Ron Tugnutt 2.00 5.00
37 Mike Richter 2.00 5.00
38 Mattias Norstrom 1.00 2.50
39 Joe Sacco 1.00 2.50
40 Derek King 1.00 2.50
41 Brad Werenka 1.00 2.50
42 Paul Kruse 1.00 2.50
43 Mike Knuble 1.00 2.50
44 Mike Peca 2.00 5.00
45 Jean-Yves Leroux 1.00 2.50
46 Ray Sheppard 1.00 2.50
47 Reid Simpson 1.00 2.50
48 Rob Brown 1.00 2.50
49 Dave Babych 1.00 2.50
50 Scott Pellerin 1.00 2.50
51 Bruce Gardiner 1.00 2.50
52 Adam Deadmarsh 1.00 2.50
53 Curtis Brown 1.00 2.50
54 Jason Marshall 1.00 2.50
55 Gerald Diduck 1.00 2.50
56 Mick Vukota 1.00 2.50
57 Kevin Dean 1.00 2.50
58 Adam Graves 1.00 2.50
59 Craig Conroy 1.00 2.50
60 Cale Hulse 1.00 2.50
61 Dimitri Khristich 1.00 2.50
62 Chris Wells 1.00 2.50
63 Travis Green 1.00 2.50
64 Tyler Wright 1.00 2.50
65 Chris Simon 1.00 2.50
66 Mikhail Shtalenkov 1.00 2.50
67 Anson Carter 1.00 2.50
68 Zarley Zalapski 1.00 2.50
69 Per Gustafsson 1.00 2.50
70 Jayson More 1.00 2.50
71 Steve Thomas 1.00 2.50
72 Todd Marchant 1.00 2.50
73 Gary Roberts 1.00 2.50
74 Richard Smehlik 1.00 2.50
75 Aaron Miller 1.00 2.50
76 Daren Puppa 2.00 5.00
77 Garth Snow 2.00 5.00
78 Greg DeVries 1.00 2.50
79 Randy Burridge 1.00 2.50
80 Jim Cummins 1.00 2.50
81 Rich Pilon 1.00 2.50
82 Chris McAlpine 1.00 2.50
83 Joe Sakic SP 30.00 80.00
84 Ted Drury 1.00 2.50
85 Brent Gilchrist 1.00 2.50
86 Dallas Eakins 1.00 2.50
87 Bruce Driver 1.00 2.50
88 Jamie Huscroft 1.00 2.50
89 Jeff Brown 1.00 2.50
90 Janne Laukkanen 1.00 2.50
91 Ken Klee 1.00 2.50
92 Peter Bondra 2.00 5.00
93 Ian Moran 1.00 2.50
94 Stephane Quintal 1.00 2.50
95 Jason York 1.00 2.50
96 Todd Harvey 1.00 2.50
97 Slava Kozlov 2.00 5.00
98 Kevin Haller 1.00 2.50
99 Alexei Zhamnov 1.00 2.50
100 Craig Johnson 1.00 2.50
101 Mike Keane 1.00 2.50
102 Craig Rivet 1.00 2.50
103 Roman Vopat 1.00 2.50
104 Jim Johnson 1.00 2.50
105 Ray Whitney 2.00 5.00
106 Ron Sutter 1.00 2.50
107 Jamie McLennan 2.00 5.00
108 Kris King 1.00 2.50
109 Lance Pitlick 1.00 2.50
110 Mike Dunham 2.00 5.00
111 Jim Dowd 1.00 2.50
112 Geoff Sanderson 1.00 2.50
113 Vladimir Vujtek 1.00 2.50
114 Tim Taylor 1.00 2.50
115 Sandis Ozolinsh 1.00 2.50
116 Scott Daniels 1.00 2.50
117 Bob Corkum 1.00 2.50
118 Kirk McLean 2.00 5.00
119 Darcy Tucker 1.00 2.50
120 Dennis Vaske 1.00 2.50
121 Kirk Muller 1.00 2.50
122 Jay McKee 1.00 2.50
123 Jere Lehtinen 2.00 5.00
124 Ruslan Salei 1.00 2.50
125 Al MacInnis SP 12.50 30.00
126 Ulf Samuelsson 1.00 2.50
127 Rick Tocchet 2.00 5.00
128 Nick Kypreos 1.00 2.50
129 Joel Bouchard 1.00 2.50
130 Jeff O'Neill 1.00 2.50
131 Daniel McGillis 1.00 2.50
132 Sean Pronger 1.00 2.50
133 Vladimir Malakhov 1.00 2.50
134 Petr Sykora 1.00 2.50
135 Zigmund Palffy 2.00 5.00
136 Joe Reekie 1.00 2.50
137 Chris Gratton 1.00 2.50
138 Craig Billington 2.00 5.00
139 Steve Washburn 1.00 2.50
140 Robert Kron 1.00 2.50
141 Larry Murphy 1.00 2.50
142 Shean Donovan 1.00 2.50
143 Scott Young 1.00 2.50
144 Janne Niinimaa 1.00 2.50
145 Ken Belanger 1.00 2.50
146 Pavol Demitra 2.00 5.00
147 Roman Hamrlik 1.00 2.50
148 Lonny Bohonos 1.00 2.50
149 Mike Eagles 1.00 2.50
150 Kelly Buchberger 1.00 2.50
151 Mattias Timander 1.00 2.50
152 Benoit Hogue 1.00 2.50
153 Joey Kocur 1.00 2.50
154 Mats Lindgren 1.00 2.50
155 Aki Berg 1.00 2.50
156 Tim Sweeney 1.00 2.50
157 Vincent Damphousse 1.00 2.50
158 Dan Kordic 1.00 2.50
159 Darius Kasparaitis 1.00 2.50
160 Randy McKay 1.00 2.50
161 Steve Staios 1.00 2.50
162 Brendan Witt 1.00 2.50
163 Paul Ysebaert 1.00 2.50
164 Greg Adams 1.00 2.50
165 Kent Manderville 1.00 2.50
166 Steve Dubinsky 1.00 2.50
167 David Nemirovsky 1.00 2.50
168 Todd Bertuzzi 2.00 5.00
169 Frederic Chabot 1.00 2.50
170 Dmitri Mironov 1.00 2.50
171 Pat Peake 1.00 2.50
172 Ed Ward 1.00 2.50
173 Jeff Shantz 1.00 2.50
174 Dave Gagner 1.00 2.50
175 Randy Cunneyworth 1.00 2.50
176 Daymond Langkow 1.00 2.50
177 Alex Hicks 1.00 2.50
178 Darby Hendrickson 1.00 2.50
179 Mike Sullivan 1.00 2.50
180 Anders Eriksson 1.00 2.50
181 Turner Stevenson 1.00 2.50
182 Shane Churla 1.00 2.50
183 Dave Lowry 1.00 2.50
184 Joe Juneau 1.00 2.50
185 Bob Essensa 1.00 2.50
186 James Black 1.00 2.50
187 Michal Grosek 1.00 2.50
188 Tomas Holmstrom 1.00 2.50
189 Ian Laperriere 1.00 2.50
190 Terry Yake 1.00 2.50
191 Jason Smith 1.00 2.50
192 Sergei Zholtok 1.00 2.50
193 Doug Houda 1.00 2.50
194 Guy Carbonneau 1.00 2.50
195 Terry Carkner 1.00 2.50
196 Alexei Gusarov 1.00 2.50
197 Vladimir Tsyplakov 1.00 2.50
198 Jarrod Skalde 1.00 2.50
199 Marty Murray 1.00 2.50
200 Aaron Ward 1.00 2.50
201 Bobby Holik 1.00 2.50
202 Steve Chiasson 1.00 2.50
203 Brantt Myhres 1.00 2.50
204 Eric Messier 1.00 2.50
205 Rene Corbet 1.00 2.50
206 Mathieu Schneider 1.00 2.50
207 Tom Chorske 1.00 2.50
208 Doug Lidster 1.00 2.50
209 Igor Ulanov 1.00 2.50
210 Blair Atcheynum 1.00 2.50
211 Sebastien Bordeleau 1.00 2.50
212 Alexei Morozov 1.00 2.50
213 Vaclav Prospal 1.00 2.50
214 Brad Bombardir 1.00 2.50
215 Mattias Ohlund 1.00 2.50
216 Chris Dingman 1.00 2.50
217 Erik Rasmussen 1.00 2.50
218 Mike Johnson 1.00 2.50
219 Chris Phillips 1.00 2.50
220 Sergei Samsonov 3.00 8.00
221 Patrick Marleau 4.00 10.00
222 Alyn McCauley 1.00 2.50
223 Ryan Vandenbussche 1.00 2.50
224 Daniel Cleary 1.00 2.50
225 Magnus Arvedson 1.00 2.50
226 Brad Isbister 1.00 2.50
227 Pascal Rheaume 1.00 2.50
228 Patrik Elias 3.00 8.00
229 Krzysztof Oliwa 1.00 2.50
230 Tyler Moss 1.00 2.50
231 Jamie Rivers 1.00 2.50
232 Joe Thornton 10.00 25.00
233 Steve Shields 2.00 5.00
234 Dave Scatchard 1.00 2.50
235 Patrick Cote 1.00 2.50
236 Rich Brennan 1.00 2.50
237 Boyd Devereaux 1.00 2.50
238 Per Johan Axelsson 1.00 2.50
239 Craig Millar 1.00 2.50
240 Juha Ylonen 1.00 2.50
241 Donald MacLean 1.00 2.50
242 Jaroslav Svejkovsky 1.00 2.50
243 Marco Sturm 2.00 5.00
244 Steve McKenna 1.00 2.50
245 Derek Morris 1.00 2.50
246 Dean Chynoweth 1.00 2.50
247 Alexander Mogilny SP 12.50 30.00
248 Ray Bourque SP 25.00 60.00
249 Ed Belfour SP 20.00 50.00
250 John LeClair SP 12.50 30.00

1997-98 Be A Player One Timers

COMPLETE SET (20) 12.50 30.00
STATED ODDS 1:7
1 Wayne Gretzky 2.50 6.00
2 Keith Tkachuk .40 1.00
3 Eric Lindros .75 2.00
4 Brendan Shanahan .75 2.00
5 Paul Kariya .75 2.00
6 Brett Hull .75 2.00
7 Jaromir Jagr 1.25 3.00
8 Teemu Selanne .75 2.00
9 John LeClair .40 1.00
10 Mike Modano .75 2.00
11 Peter Forsberg 1.25 3.00
12 Pavel Bure .75 2.00
13 Peter Bondra .40 1.00
14 Saku Koivu .75 2.00
15 Pat LaFontaine .40 1.00
16 Patrik Elias .40 1.00
17 Richard Zednik .40 1.00
18 Mike Johnson .40 1.00
19 Marco Sturm .40 1.00
20 Joe Thornton 1.25 3.00

1997-98 Be A Player Stacking the Pads

COMPLETE SET (15) 15.00 40.00
STATED ODDS 1:15
1 Guy Hebert .75 2.00
2 Dominik Hasek 2.00 5.00
3 Felix Potvin 1.00 2.50
4 Patrick Roy 4.00 10.00
5 Ed Belfour 1.00 2.50
6 Chris Osgood .75 2.00
7 Curtis Joseph 1.00 2.50
8 John Vanbiesbrouck .75 2.00
9 Jocelyn Thibault .75 2.00
10 Mike Richter 1.00 2.50
11 Martin Brodeur 3.00 8.00
12 Garth Snow .75 2.00
13 Nikolai Khabibulin .75 2.00
14 Tommy Salo .75 2.00
15 Byron Dafoe .75 2.00

1997-98 Be A Player Take A Number

COMPLETE SET (20) 30.00 60.00
STATED ODDS 1:15
1 Ray Bourque 2.00 5.00
2 Eric Daze 2.00 2.00
3 Ed Belfour 1.00 2.50
4 Patrick Roy 5.00 12.00
5 Sergei Fedorov 1.25 3.00
6 John Vanbiesbrouck 2.00 2.00
7 Doug Gilmour 2.00 2.00
8 Wayne Gretzky 6.00 15.00
9 Bryan Berard .75 2.00
10 Eric Lindros 1.00 2.50
11 Paul Coffey 1.00 2.50
12 Jeremy Roenick 1.25 3.00
13 Brett Hull 1.25 3.00
14 Pierre Turgeon 2.00 2.00
15 Keith Primeau .75 2.00
16 Daren Puppa 2.00 2.00
17 Mark Messier 1.00 2.50
18 Alexander Mogilny 2.00 2.00
19 Joe Sakic 2.00 5.00
20 Jaromir Jagr 1.50 4.00

1998-99 Be A Player

The 1998-99 Be A Player set was issued in two series totalling 300 cards and was distributed in eight-card packs with an SRP of $6.99. The fronts featured color action photos of players with a heavy emphasis on rookies and Calder Trophy candidates printed on 30 pt. card stock with a full foil treatment. The backs carried a head photo with player information and career statistics. A gold-foiled parallel version was also created and inserted into random packs.

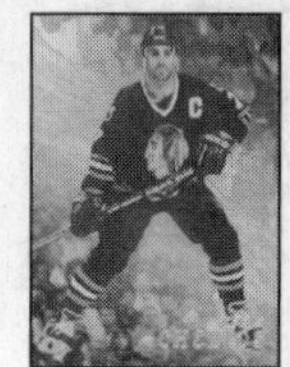

COMPLETE SET (300) 75.00 150.00
COMP.SERIES 1 (150) 50.00 100.00
COMP.SERIES 2 (150) 50.00 100.00
COMP.GOLD SET (300) 350.00 700.00
COMP.SER.1 GOLD (150) 200.00 400.00
COMP.SER.2 GOLD (150) 150.00 300.00
*GOLD STARS: 2X TO 5X BASIC CARDS
*GOLD RC's: 1.5X TO 3X BASIC CARDS
GOLD RANDOM INSERTS IN PACKS
1 Jason Marshall .15 .40
2 Paul Kariya .60 1.50
3 Teemu Selanne .60 1.50
4 Guy Hebert .50 1.25
5 Ted Drury .15 .40
6 Byron Dafoe .50 1.25
7 Rob Dimaio .15 .40
8 Ray Bourque 1.00 2.50
9 Joe Thornton 1.00 2.50
10 Sergei Samsonov .50 1.25
11 Dimitri Khristich .15 .40
12 Michael Peca .15 .40
13 Jason Woolley .15 .40
14 Matthew Barnaby .15 .40
15 Brian Holzinger .15 .40
16 Dixon Ward .15 .40
17 Tyler Moss .15 .40
18 Jarome Iginla .75 2.00
19 Marty McInnis .15 .40
20 Andrew Cassels .15 .40
21 Jason Wiemer .15 .40
22 Trevor Kidd .15 .40
23 Keith Primeau .15 .40
24 Sami Kapanen .15 .40
25 Robert Kron .15 .40
26 Glen Wesley .15 .40
27 Jeff Hackett .50 1.25
28 Tony Amonte .50 1.25
29 Alexei Zhamnov .15 .40
30 Eric Weinrich .15 .40
31 Jeff Shantz .15 .40
32 Christian Laflamme .15 .40
33 Adam Foote .15 .40
34 Patrick Roy 3.00 8.00
35 Peter Forsberg 1.50 4.00
36 Adam Deadmarsh .15 .40
37 Joe Sakic 1.25 3.00
38 Eric Lacroix .15 .40
39 Guy Carbonneau .15 .40
40 Mike Modano 1.00 2.50
41 Roman Turek .15 .40
42 Mike Keane .15 .40
43 Sergei Zubov .15 .40
44 Jere Lehtinen .15 .40
45 Sergei Fedorov 1.00 2.50
46 Steve Yzerman 3.00 8.00
47 Chris Osgood .50 1.25
48 Larry Murphy .15 .40
49 Vyacheslav Kozlov .15 .40
50 Darren McCarty .15 .40
51 Boris Mironov .15 .40
52 Roman Hamrlik .15 .40
53 Bill Guerin .50 1.25
54 Mike Grier .15 .40
55 Todd Marchant .15 .40
56 Ray Whitney .15 .40
57 Dave Gagner .15 .40
58 Scott Mellanby .15 .40
59 Robert Svehla .15 .40
60 Viktor Kozlov .15 .40
61 Luc Robitaille .50 1.25
62 Yanic Perreault .15 .40
63 Jozef Stumpel .50 1.25
64 Sandy Moger .15 .40
65 Ian Laperriere .15 .40
66 Jocelyn Thibault .50 1.25
67 Dave Manson .15 .40
68 Mark Recchi .50 1.25
69 Patrick Poulin .15 .40
70 Benoit Brunet .15 .40
71 Turner Stevenson .15 .40
72 Mike Dunham .50 1.25
73 Tom Fitzgerald .15 .40
74 Darren Turcotte .15 .40
75 Brad Smyth .15 .40
76 J.J. Daigneault .15 .40
77 Dave Andreychuk .50 1.25
78 Jason Arnott .15 .40
79 Martin Brodeur 1.50 4.00
80 Randy McKay .15 .40
81 Patrik Elias .50 1.25
82 Kevin Dean .15 .40
83 Tommy Salo .15 .40
84 Scott Lachance .15 .40
85 Bryan Berard .50 1.25
86 Robert Reichel .15 .40
87 Kenny Jonsson .15 .40
88 Kevin Stevens .15 .40
89 Mike Richter .60 1.50
90 Wayne Gretzky 4.00 10.00
91 Adam Graves .15 .40
92 Alexei Kovalev .15 .40
93 Ulf Samuelsson .15 .40
94 Radek Bonk .15 .40
95 Wade Redden .15 .40
96 Damian Rhodes .50 1.25
97 Bruce Gardiner .15 .40
98 Daniel Alfredsson .50 1.25
99 Ron Hextall .15 .40
100 Eric Lindros .60 1.50
101 Chris Gratton .50 1.25
102 Dainius Zubrus .15 .40
103 Luke Richardson .15 .40
104 Petr Svoboda .15 .40

105 Rick Tocchet .15 .40
106 Teppo Numminen .15 .40
107 Jeremy Roenick .75 2.00
108 Nikolai Khabibulin .50 1.25
109 Brad Isbister .15 .40
110 Peter Skudra .15 .40
111 Alexei Morozov .15 .40
112 Kevin Hatcher .15 .40
113 Darius Kasparaitis .15 .40
114 Stu Barnes .15 .40
115 Martin Straka .15 .40
116 Andrei Zyuzin .15 .40
117 Marcus Ragnarsson .15 .40
118 Murray Craven .15 .40
119 Marco Sturm .15 .40
120 Patrick Marleau .15 .40
121 Shawn Burr .15 .40
122 Grant Fuhr .50 1.25
123 Chris Pronger .50 1.25
124 Geoff Courtnall .15 .40
125 Jim Campbell .15 .40
126 Pavol Demitra .50 1.25
127 Todd Gill .15 .40
128 Cory Cross .15 .40
129 Daymond Langkow .50 1.25
130 Alexander Selivanov .15 .40
131 Mikael Renberg .50 1.25
132 Rob Zamuner .15 .40
133 Stephane Richer .15 .40
134 Fredrik Modin .15 .40
135 Derek King .15 .40
136 Mats Sundin .60 1.50
137 Mike Johnson .15 .40
138 Alyn McCauley .15 .40
139 Jason Smith .15 .40
140 Markus Naslund .60 1.50
141 Alexander Mogilny .50 1.25
142 Mattias Ohlund .15 .40
143 Donald Brashear .15 .40
144 Garth Snow .50 1.25
145 Brian Bellows .15 .40
146 Peter Bondra .15 .40
147 Joe Juneau .50 1.25
148 Steve Konowalchuk .15 .40
149 Ken Klee .15 .40
150 Michal Pivonka .15 .40
151 Steve Rucchin .15 .40
152 Stu Grimson .15 .40
153 Tomas Sandstrom .15 .40
154 Fredrik Olausson .15 .40
155 Travis Green .15 .40
156 Jason Allison .15 .40
157 Steve Heinze .15 .40
158 Rob Tallas .15 .40
159 Darren Van Impe .15 .40
160 Ken Baumgartner .15 .40
161 Peter Ferraro .15 .40
162 Dominik Hasek 1.25 3.00
163 Geoff Sanderson .15 .40
164 Miroslav Satan .15 .40
165 Rob Ray .15 .40
166 Alexei Zhitnik .15 .40
167 Phil Housley .15 .40
168 Theo Fleury .15 .40
169 Ken Wregget .15 .40
170 Valeri Bure .15 .40
171 Rico Fata .15 .40
172 Arturs Irbe .15 .40
173 Sean Hill .15 .40
174 Ron Francis .15 .40
175 Jeff O'Neill .15 .40
176 Paul Ranheim .15 .40
177 Paul Coffey .60 1.50
178 Doug Gilmour .50 1.25
179 Eric Daze .50 1.25
180 Chris Chelios .15 .40
181 Bob Probert .15 .40
182 Mark Fitzpatrick .15 .40
183 Alexei Gusarov .15 .40
184 Sylvain Lefebvre .15 .40
185 Craig Billington .15 .40
186 Valeri Kamensky .15 .40
187 Milan Hejduk RC 1.50 4.00
188 Sandis Ozolinsh .15 .40
189 Brett Hull .75 2.00
190 Ed Belfour .15 .40
191 Darryl Sydor .15 .40
192 Sergei Gusev RC .15 .40
193 Joe Nieuwendyk .15 .40
194 Derian Hatcher .15 .40
195 Brendan Shanahan .60 1.50
196 Tomas Holmstrom .15 .40
197 Nicklas Lidstrom .60 1.50
198 Martin Lapointe .15 .40
199 Igor Larionov .15 .40
200 Kris Draper .15 .40
201 Kelly Buchberger .15 .40
202 Andrei Kovalenko .15 .40
203 Josef Beranek .15 .40
204 Mikhail Shtalenkov .15 .40
205 Pat Falloon .15 .40
206 Mark Parrish RC .60 1.50
207 Terry Carkner .15 .40
208 Rob Niedermayer .15 .40
209 Sean Burke .15 .40
210 Oleg Kvasha RC .60 1.50
211 Pavel Bure .60 1.50
212 Rob Blake .15 .40
213 Vladimir Tsyplakov .15 .40
214 Stephane Fiset .15 .40
215 Steve Duchesne .15 .40
216 Patrice Brisebois .15 .40
217 Vincent Damphousse .15 .40
218 Saku Koivu .60 1.50
219 Jose Theodore .75 2.00
220 Brett Clark RC .15 .40
221 Martin Rucinsky .15 .40
222 Vladimir Malakhov .15 .40
223 Sergei Krivokrasov .15 .40
224 Scott Walker .15 .40
225 Greg Johnson .15 .40
226 Cliff Ronning .15 .40
227 Eric Fichaud .15 .40
228 Bob Carpenter .15 .40
229 Scott Daniels .15 .40
230 Brian Rolston .15 .40
231 Sergei Brylin .15 .40
232 Scott Niedermayer .15 .40
233 Bryan Smolinski .15 .40
234 Trevor Linden .15 .40
235 Eric Brewer .15 .40
236 Zigmund Palffy .15 .40
237 Sergei Nemchinov .15 .40
238 Brian Leetch .15 .40
239 Mathieu Schneider .15 .40
240 Niklas Sundstrom .15 .40
241 Manny Malhotra .50 1.25
242 Jeff Beukeboom .15 .40
243 Petr Nedved .15 .40
244 Ron Tugnutt .15 .40
245 Shawn Van Allen .15 .40
246 Alexei Yashin .15 .40
247 Jason York .15 .40
248 Shawn McEachern .15 .40
249 Marian Hossa .60 1.50
250 John LeClair .60 1.50
251 Rod Brind'Amour .15 .40
252 John Vanbiesbrouck .50 1.25
253 Eric Desjardins .50 1.25
254 Valeri Zelepukin .15 .40
255 Karl Dykhuis .15 .40
256 Keith Tkachuk .60 1.50
257 Dallas Drake .15 .40
258 Oleg Tverdovsky .15 .40
259 Jyrki Lumme .15 .40
260 Jimmy Waite .15 .40
261 Jaromir Jagr 1.00 2.50
262 German Titov .15 .40
263 Robert Lang .15 .40
264 Brad Werenka .15 .40
265 Rob Brown .15 .40
266 Bobby Dollas .15 .40
267 Jeff Friesen .15 .40
268 Andy Sutton RC .15 .40
269 Steve Shields .15 .40
270 Mike Ricci .15 .40
271 Joe Murphy .15 .40
272 Tony Granato .15 .40
273 Jamie McLennan .50 1.25
274 Al MacInnis .15 .40
275 Pierre Turgeon .15 .40
276 Kelly Chase .15 .40
277 Craig Conroy .15 .40
278 Scott Young .15 .40
279 Vincent Lecavalier 1.25 3.00
280 Wendel Clark .15 .40
281 Daren Puppa .15 .40
282 Sandy McCarthy .15 .40
283 Daniil Markov .15 .40
284 Curtis Joseph .60 1.50
285 Sergei Berezin .50 1.25
286 Steve Sullivan .15 .40
287 Tomas Kaberle RC .75 2.00
288 Kris King .15 .40
289 Igor Korolev .15 .40
290 Mark Messier .60 1.50
291 Bill Muckalt RC .15 .40
292 Todd Bertuzzi .60 1.50
293 Brad May .15 .40
294 Peter Zezel .15 .40
295 Dmitri Mironov .15 .40
296 Adam Oates .15 .40
297 Calle Johansson .15 .40
298 Craig Berube .15 .40
299 Sergei Gonchar .15 .40
300 Andrei Nikolishin .15 .40

1998-99 Be A Player Press Release

This 300-card set paralleled the basic series, but carried a gold foil "Press Release" stamp on the card fronts. The cards were rumored to be available only to members of the media. Due to the scarcity and method of distribution, the set is not priced, but the few singles we have seen have sold for anywhere from 10 X to 50X the base price.
NOT PRICED DUE TO SCARCITY

2006-07 Be A Player

COMPLETE SET (215) 30.00 60.00
RC STATED PRINT RUN 999 #'d SETS
1 Dainius Zubrus .15 .40
2 Nikolai Zherdev .15 .40
3 Alexei Yashin .15 .40
4 Curtis Joseph .30 .75
5 Justin Williams .15 .40
6 Todd White .15 .40
7 Kyle Wellwood .15 .40
8 Doug Weight .15 .40
9 Cam Ward .30 .75
10 Aaron Ward .15 .40
11 Scott Walker .15 .40
12 David Vyborny .15 .40
13 Radim Vrbata .15 .40
14 Antoine Vermette .15 .40
15 Stephane Veilleux .15 .40
16 Thomas Vanek .25 .60
17 Mike Van Ryn .15 .40
18 R.J. Umberger .15 .40
19 Marty Turco .25 .60
20 Darcy Tucker .15 .40
21 Vesa Toskala .25 .60
22 Kimmo Timonen .15 .40
23 Joe Thornton .50 1.25
24 Jose Theodore .30 .75
25 Tim Taylor .15 .40
26 Alex Tanguay .25 .60
27 Steve Sullivan .15 .40
28 Brad Stuart .15 .40
29 Martin Straka .15 .40
30 Jarret Stoll .15 .40
31 Lee Stempniak .15 .40
32 Matt Stajan .15 .40
33 Eric Staal .30 .75
34 Martin St. Louis .25 .60
35 Jason Spezza .30 .75
36 Sheldon Souray .15 .40
37 Ryan Smyth .25 .60
38 Jason Smith .15 .40
39 Chris Simon .15 .40
40 Mike Sillinger .15 .40
41 Jody Shelley .15 .40
42 Teemu Selanne .30 .75
43 Henrik Sedin .15 .40
44 Brent Seabrook .15 .40
45 Nick Schultz .15 .40
46 Marc Savard .15 .40
47 Sergei Samsonov .25 .60
48 Sami Salo .15 .40
49 Joe Sakic .60 1.50
50 Michael Ryder .25 .60
51 Tuomo Ruutu .15 .40
52 Derek Roy .15 .40
53 Dwayne Roloson .30 .75
54 Mike Richards .25 .60
55 Brad Richards .25 .60
56 Robyn Regehr .15 .40
57 Wade Redden .15 .40
58 Andrew Raycroft .25 .60
59 Brian Rafalski .15 .40
60 Petr Prucha .15 .40
61 Wayne Primeau .15 .40
62 Tom Poti .15 .40
63 Joni Pitkanen .15 .40
64 Dion Phaneuf .40 1.00
65 Andrew Peters .15 .40
66 Yanic Perreault .15 .40
67 Dustin Penner .15 .40
68 Michael Peca .15 .40
69 Mark Parrish .15 .40
70 Alexander Ovechkin 1.00 2.50
71 Steve Ott .15 .40
72 Michael Nylander .15 .40
73 Mattias Norstrom .15 .40
74 Antero Niittymaki .25 .60
75 Scott Niedermayer .15 .40
76 Markus Naslund .30 .75
77 Glen Murray .15 .40
78 Bryan Muir .15 .40
79 Brendan Morrison .15 .40
80 Steve Montador .15 .40
81 Ryan Miller .30 .75
82 Milan Michalek .15 .40
83 Andrej Meszaros .15 .40
84 Andy McDonald .15 .40
85 Jamal Mayers .15 .40
86 Patrick Marleau .25 .60
87 Andrei Markov .15 .40
88 Ryan Malone .15 .40
89 Manny Malhotra .15 .40
90 Roberto Luongo .40 1.00
91 Henrik Lundqvist .40 1.00
92 John-Michael Liles .15 .40
93 Nicklas Lidstrom .30 .75
94 Jordan Leopold .15 .40
95 Jere Lehtinen .15 .40
96 David Legwand .15 .40
97 Vincent Lecavalier .30 .75
98 Georges Laraque .15 .40
99 Andrew Ladd .15 .40
100 Chris Kunitz .15 .40
101 Slava Kozlov .15 .40
102 Alexei Kovalev .15 .40
103 Olaf Kolzig .30 .75
104 Saku Koivu .30 .75
105 Chuck Kobasew .15 .40
106 Mike Knuble .15 .40
107 Nikolai Khabibulin .30 .75
108 Duncan Keith .15 .40
109 Olli Jokinen .15 .40
110 Jarome Iginla .40 1.00
111 Trent Hunter .15 .40
112 Cristobal Huet .40 1.00
113 Marian Hossa .25 .60
114 Shawn Horcoff .15 .40
115 Bobby Holik .15 .40
116 Chris Higgins .15 .40
117 Dany Heatley .40 1.00
118 Martin Havlat .25 .60
119 Dan Hamhuis .15 .40
120 Bill Guerin .15 .40
121 Mike Green .15 .40
122 Hal Gill .15 .40
123 Martin Gerber .30 .75
124 Simon Gagne .30 .75
125 Alexander Frolov .15 .40
126 Kurtis Foster .15 .40
127 Peter Forsberg .50 1.25
128 Marc-Andre Fleury .30 .75
129 Ruslan Fedotenko .15 .40
130 Sergei Federov .30 .75
131 Garnet Exelby .15 .40
132 Robert Esche .25 .60
133 Steve Eminger .15 .40
134 Patrik Elias .15 .40
135 Patrick Eaves .15 .40
136 J.P. Dumont .15 .40
137 Chris Drury .15 .40
138 Shane Doan .15 .40
139 Marc Denis .25 .60
140 Craig Conroy .15 .40
141 Erik Cole .15 .40
142 Chris Clark .15 .40
143 Jonathan Cheechoo .30 .75
144 Zdeno Chara .15 .40
145 Jeff Carter .30 .75
146 Brian Campbell .15 .40
147 Mike Cammalleri .15 .40
148 Kyle Calder .15 .40
149 Brent Burns .15 .40
150 Gilbert Brule .30 .75
151 Dustin Brown .15 .40
152 Curtis Brown .15 .40
153 Rod Brind`Amour .25 .60
154 Daniel Briere .25 .60
155 Eric Brewer .15 .40
156 Dan Boyle .15 .40
157 Brad Boyes .15 .40
158 Jay Bouwmeester .15 .40
159 Pierre-Marc Bouchard .15 .40
160 Rob Blake .25 .60
161 Steve Bernier .15 .40
162 Patrice Bergeron .30 .75
163 Mark Bell .15 .40
164 Keith Ballard .15 .40
165 Sean Avery .15 .40
166 Adrian Aucoin .15 .40
167 Daniel Alfredsson .25 .60
168 Maxim Afinogenov .15 .40
169 Kevyn Adams .15 .40
170 Shawn Bates .15 .40
201 Evgeni Malkin RC 12.00 30.00
202 Phil Kessel RC 5.00 12.00
203 Luc Bourdon RC 2.50 6.00
204 Dustin Boyd RC 2.50 6.00
205 Patrick O'Sullivan RC 2.50 6.00
206 Blake Comeau RC 1.50 4.00
207 Shea Weber RC 2.50 6.00
208 Matt Carle RC 2.50 6.00
209 Loui Eriksson RC 1.50 4.00
210 Mark Stuart RC 1.50 4.00
211 Eric Fehr RC 2.50 6.00
212 Travis Zajac RC 3.00 8.00
213 Anze Kopitar RC 6.00 15.00
214 Ladislav Smid RC 1.50 4.00
215 Noah Welch RC 1.50 4.00
216 Jordan Staal RC 12.00 30.00
217 Alexander Radulov RC 5.00 12.00
218 Drew Stafford RC 5.00 12.00
219 Paul Stastny RC 8.00 20.00
220 Dave Bolland RC 1.50 4.00
221 Marek Schwarz RC 2.50 6.00
222 Ryan Potulny RC 2.50 6.00
223 Marc-Antoine Pouliot RC 2.50 6.00
224 Jarkko Immonen RC 1.50 4.00
225 Josh Hennessy RC 1.50 4.00
226 Benoit Pouliot RC 2.50 6.00
227 Nigel Dawes RC 1.50 4.00
228 Matt Lashoff RC 1.50 4.00
229 Keith Yandle RC 1.50 4.00
230 Karri Ramo RC 1.50 4.00
231 Guillaume Latendresse RC 6.00 15.00
232 Marc-Edouard Vlasic RC 1.50 4.00
233 Patrick Thoresen RC 2.50 6.00
234 Niklas Grossman RC 1.50 4.00
235 Ian White RC 1.50 4.00
236 Clarke MacArthur RC 1.50 4.00
237 Jesse Schultz RC 1.50 4.00
238 David Booth RC 1.50 4.00
239 Joe Pavelski RC 2.50 6.00
240 Martin Houle RC 1.50 4.00
241 Mikhail Grabovski RC 1.50 4.00
242 David McKee RC 2.50 6.00
243 Brandon Prust RC 1.50 4.00
244 Kristopher Letang RC 2.50 6.00
245 Shawn Belle RC 1.50 4.00

2006-07 Be A Player Profiles

STATED PRINT RUN 499 #'d SETS
PP1 Vincent Lecavalier 1.00 2.50
PP2 Thomas Vanek .75 2.00
PP3 Teemu Selanne 1.00 2.50
PP4 Simon Gagne 1.00 2.50
PP5 Sergei Federov 1.00 2.50
PP6 Scott Niedermayer .50 1.25
PP7 Saku Koivu 1.00 2.50
PP8 Ryan Smyth .75 2.00
PP9 Pierre-Marc Bouchard .50 1.25
PP10 Phil Kessel 1.50 4.00
PP11 Peter Forsberg 1.50 4.00
PP12 Paul Stastny 2.50 6.00
PP13 Patrice Bergeron 1.00 2.50
PP14 Nicklas Lidstrom 1.00 2.50
PP15 Markus Naslund 1.00 2.50
PP16 Marian Hossa .75 2.00
PP17 Marc-Andre Fleury 1.00 2.50
PP18 Jordan Staal 4.00 10.00
PP19 Jonathan Cheechoo 1.00 2.50
PP20 Joe Thornton 1.50 4.00
PP21 Joe Sakic 2.00 5.00
PP22 Jay Bouwmeester .50 1.25
PP23 Jarome Iginla 1.25 3.00
PP24 Guillaume Latendresse 2.00 5.00
PP25 Eric Staal 1.00 2.50
PP26 Dion Phaneuf 1.25 3.00
PP27 Dany Heatley 1.25 3.00
PP28 Daniel Alfredsson .75 2.00
PP29 Alexander Ovechkin 3.00 8.00
PP30 Alexander Frolov .50 1.25

2006-07 Be A Player Profiles Autographs

STATED PRINT RUN 5 #'d SETS
NOT PRICED DUE TO SCARCITY
PP1 Vincent Lecavalier
PP2 Thomas Vanek
PP3 Teemu Selanne
PP4 Simon Gagne
PP5 Sergei Federov
PP6 Scott Niedermayer
PP7 Saku Koivu
PP8 Ryan Smyth
PP9 Pierre-Marc Bouchard
PP10 Phil Kessel
PP11 Peter Forsberg
PP12 Paul Stastny
PP13 Patrice Bergeron
PP14 Nicklas Lidstrom
PP15 Markus Naslund
PP16 Marian Hossa
PP17 Marc-Andre Fleury
PP18 Jordan Staal
PP19 Jonathan Cheechoo
PP21 Joe Sakic
PP22 Jay Bouwmeester
PP23 Jarome Iginla
PP24 Guillaume Latendresse
PP25 Eric Staal
PP26 Dion Phaneuf
PP27 Dany Heatley
PP28 Daniel Alfredsson
PP29 Alexander Ovechkin
PP30 Alexander Frolov

2006-07 Be A Player Signatures

AA Adrian Aucoin 2.50 6.00
AD Daniel Alfredsson 4.00 10.00
AF Alexander Frolov 2.50 6.00
AK Alexei Kovalev 2.50 6.00
AL Andrew Ladd 2.50 6.00
AM Andrei Markov 2.50 6.00
AN Antero Niittymaki 4.00 10.00
AO Alexander Ovechkin 30.00 80.00
AP Andrew Peters 2.50 6.00
AR Andrew Raycroft 4.00 10.00
AS Sean Avery 2.50 6.00
AT Alex Tanguay 4.00 10.00
AV Antoine Vermette 2.50 6.00
AW Aaron Ward 2.50 6.00
AY Alexei Yashin 2.50 6.00
BA Shawn Bates 2.50 6.00
BB Brad Boyes 2.50 6.00
BC Brian Campbell 2.50 6.00
BD Daniel Briere 4.00 10.00
BE Patrice Bergeron 5.00 12.00
BG Bill Guerin 2.50 6.00
BH Bobby Holik 2.50 6.00
BL Rob Blake 4.00 10.00
BM Bryan Muir 2.50 6.00
BO Dan Boyle 2.50 6.00
BR Brad Richards 4.00 10.00
BS Brad Stuart 2.50 6.00
BU Brent Burns 2.50 6.00
CA Jeff Carter 5.00 12.00
CB Curtis Brown 2.50 6.00
CC Craig Conroy 2.50 6.00
CD Chris Drury 2.50 6.00
CH Chuck Kobasew 2.50 6.00
CJ Curtis Joseph 5.00 12.00
CK Chris Kunitz 2.50 6.00
CL Chris Clark 2.50 6.00
CM Mike Cammalleri 2.50 6.00
CR Cristobal Huet 6.00 15.00
CS Chris Simon 2.50 6.00
CW Cam Ward 5.00 12.00
DA Dan Hamhuis 2.50 6.00
DB Dustin Brown 2.50 6.00
DH Dany Heatley 6.00 15.00
DK Duncan Keith 2.50 6.00
DL David Legwand 2.50 6.00
DP Dion Phaneuf 6.00 15.00
DR Derek Roy 2.50 6.00
DT Darcy Tucker 2.50 6.00
DV David Vyborny 2.50 6.00
DW Doug Weight 2.50 6.00
DZ Dainius Zubrus 2.50 6.00
EA Patrick Eaves 2.50 6.00
EB Eric Brewer 2.50 6.00
EC Erik Cole 2.50 6.00
EL Patrik Elias 2.50 6.00
EM Steve Eminger 2.50 6.00
ES Eric Staal 5.00 12.00
EX Garnet Exelby 2.50 6.00
GA Simon Gagne 5.00 12.00
GB Gilbert Brule 5.00 12.00
GE Martin Gerber 5.00 12.00
GL Georges Laraque 4.00 10.00
GM Glen Murray 2.50 6.00
HA Martin Havlat 4.00 10.00
HG Hal Gill 2.50 6.00
HI Chris Higgins 4.00 10.00
HL Henrik Lundqvist 6.00 15.00
HO Shawn Horcoff 2.50 6.00
HS Henrik Sedin 2.50 6.00
HU Trent Hunter 2.50 6.00
JA Jason Smith 2.50 6.00
JB Jay Bouwmeester 2.50 6.00
JC Jonathan Cheechoo 5.00 12.00
JD J.P. Dumont 2.50 6.00
JE Jere Lehtinen 2.50 6.00
JI Jarome Iginla 6.00 15.00
JL John-Michael Liles 2.50 6.00
JM Jamal Mayers 2.50 6.00
JO Joe Sakic 30.00 60.00
JP Joni Pitkanen 2.50 6.00
JS Jarret Stoll 2.50 6.00
JT Joe Thornton SP
JW Justin Williams 2.50 6.00
KA Kevyn Adams 2.50 6.00
KB Keith Ballard 2.50 6.00
KC Kyle Calder 2.50 6.00
KF Kurtis Foster 2.50 6.00
KN Mike Knuble 2.50 6.00
KO Saku Koivu 5.00 12.00
KT Kimmo Timonen 2.50 6.00
KW Kyle Wellwood 10.00 25.00
KZ Slava Kozlov 2.50 6.00
LE Jordan Leopold 2.50 6.00
LS Lee Stempniak 2.50 6.00
MA Manny Malhotra 2.50 6.00
MB Mark Bell 2.50 6.00
MC Andy McDonald 2.50 6.00
MD Marc Denis 4.00 10.00
MF Marc-Andre Fleury 5.00 12.00
MG Mike Green 2.50 6.00
MH Marian Hossa 4.00 10.00
MI Milan Michalek 2.50 6.00
MN Michael Nylander 2.50 6.00
MO Brendan Morrison 2.50 6.00
MP Michael Peca 2.50 6.00
MS Marc Savard 2.50 6.00
MT Marty Turco 4.00 10.00
MV Mike Van Ryn 2.50 6.00
MX Maxim Afinogenov 2.50 6.00
MZ Andrej Meszaros 2.50 6.00
NA Markus Naslund 5.00 12.00
NK Nikolai Khabibulin 5.00 12.00
NL Nicklas Lidstrom 5.00 12.00
NO Mattias Norstrom 2.50 6.00
NS Nick Schultz 2.50 6.00
NZ Nikolai Zherdev 2.50 6.00
OJ Olli Jokinen 2.50 6.00
OK Olaf Kolzig 5.00 12.00
OT Steve Ott 2.50 6.00
PA Mark Parrish 2.50 6.00
PB Pierre-Marc Bouchard 2.50 6.00
PE Dustin Penner 4.00 10.00
PF Peter Forsberg 25.00 60.00
PM Patrick Marleau 4.00 10.00
PP Petr Prucha 2.50 6.00
RA Brian Rafalski 2.50 6.00
RB Rod Brind`Amour 4.00 10.00
RD Michael Ryder 4.00 10.00
RE Robert Esche 4.00 10.00
RF Ruslan Fedotenko 2.50 6.00
RI Mike Richards 4.00 10.00
RL Roberto Luongo 25.00 60.00
RM Ryan Malone 2.50 6.00
RO Dwayne Roloson 5.00 12.00
RR Robyn Regehr 2.50 6.00
RS Ryan Smyth 4.00 10.00
RU R.J. Umberger 2.50 6.00
RV Radim Vrbata 2.50 6.00
RY Ryan Miller 5.00 12.00
SB Steve Bernier 2.50 6.00
SD Shane Doan 2.50 6.00
SE Sergei Samsonov 4.00 10.00
SF Sergei Federov 5.00 12.00
SH Jody Shelley 2.50 6.00
SI Mike Sillinger 2.50 6.00
SJ Matt Stajan 2.50 6.00
SK Brent Seabrook 2.50 6.00
SL Martin St. Louis 4.00 10.00
SM Steve Montador 2.50 6.00
SN Scott Niedermayer 2.50 6.00
SO Sheldon Souray 2.50 6.00
SP Jason Spezza 5.00 12.00
SS Sami Salo 2.50 6.00
ST Martin Straka 2.50 6.00
SU Steve Sullivan 2.50 6.00
TH Jose Theodore 5.00 12.00
TP Tom Poti 2.50 6.00
TR Tuomo Ruutu 2.50 6.00
TS Teemu Selanne 12.00 30.00
TT Tim Taylor 2.50 6.00
TV Thomas Vanek 6.00 15.00
TW Todd White 2.50 6.00
VE Stephane Veilleux 2.50 6.00
VL Vincent Lecavalier 5.00 12.00
VT Vesa Toskala 4.00 10.00
WA Scott Walker 2.50 6.00
WP Wayne Primeau 2.50 6.00
WR Wade Redden 2.50 6.00
YP Yanic Perreault 2.50 6.00
ZC Zdeno Chara 2.50 6.00

2006-07 Be A Player Signatures 10

STATED PRINT RUN 10 #'d SETS
NOT PRICED DUE TO SCARCITY
1 Dainius Zubrus
2 Nikolai Zherdev
3 Alexei Yashin
5 Justin Williams
10 Doug Weight
11 Cam Ward
18 Thomas Vanek
21 Marty Turco
22 Darcy Tucker
23 Vesa Toskala
26 Jose Theodore
28 Alex Tanguay
32 Martin Straka
34 Lee Stempniak
35 Matt Stajan
36 Eric Staal
37 Martin St. Louis
38 Jason Spezza
39 Sheldon Souray
40 Ryan Smyth
45 Teemu Selanne
46 Henrik Sedin
49 Marc Savard
53 Joe Sakic
54 Michael Ryder
55 Tuomo Ruutu
57 Dwayne Roloson
58 Mike Richards
59 Brad Richards
62 Wade Redden
63 Andrew Raycroft
64 Brian Rafalski
65 Petr Prucha
68 Joni Pitkanen
69 Dion Phaneuf
71 Yanic Perreault
74 Mark Parrish
76 Alexander Ovechkin
81 Scott Niedermayer
82 Markus Naslund
83 Glen Murray
86 Brendan Morrison
88 Ryan Miller
89 Milan Michalek
93 Patrick Marleau
95 Ryan Malone
97 Roberto Luongo
98 Henrik Lundqvist
100 Nicklas Lidstrom
103 Jere Lehtinen
104 David Legwand
105 Vincent Lecavalier
110 Alexei Kovalev
112 Olaf Kolzig
113 Saku Koivu
117 Nikolai Khabibulin
119 Olli Jokinen
121 Jarome Iginla
123 Cristobal Huet
124 Marian Hossa
129 Dany Heatley
132 Bill Guerin
137 Martin Gerber
138 Simon Gagne
139 Alexander Frolov
141 Peter Forsberg
142 Marc-Andre Fleury
144 Sergei Federov
149 Patrik Elias
152 Chris Drury
154 Marc Denis
156 Erik Cole
158 Jonathan Cheechoo
159 Zdeno Chara
160 Jeff Carter
162 Mike Cammalleri
168 Rod Brind`Amour
169 Daniel Briere
172 Brad Boyes
173 Jay Bouwmeester
174 Pierre-Marc Bouchard
176 Rob Blake
178 Steve Bernier
179 Patrice Bergeron
185 Daniel Alfredsson
186 Maxim Afinogenov
202 Phil Kessel
203 Luc Bourdon
205 Patrick O'Sullivan
208 Matt Carle
216 Jordan Staal
219 Paul Stastny
231 Guillaume Latendresse

2006-07 Be A Player Signatures 25

STATED PRINT RUN 25 #'d SETS
3 Alexei Yashin 8.00 20.00
5 Justin Williams 8.00 20.00
8 Kyle Wellwood 8.00 20.00
10 Doug Weight 8.00 20.00
13 Scott Walker 8.00 20.00
14 David Vyborny 8.00 20.00
19 Mike Van Ryn 8.00 20.00
20 R.J. Umberger 8.00 20.00
21 Marty Turco 15.00 40.00
22 Darcy Tucker 8.00 20.00
24 Kimmo Timonen 8.00 20.00
28 Alex Tanguay 15.00 40.00
30 Steve Sullivan 8.00 20.00
31 Brad Stuart 8.00 20.00
33 Jarret Stoll 8.00 20.00
36 Eric Staal 15.00 40.00
37 Martin St. Louis 15.00 40.00
38 Jason Spezza 15.00 40.00
40 Ryan Smyth 15.00 40.00
41 Jason Smith 8.00 20.00
44 Jody Shelley 8.00 20.00
45 Teemu Selanne 15.00 100.00
47 Brent Seabrook 8.00 20.00
51 Sergei Samsonov 15.00 40.00
52 Sami Salo 8.00 20.00
53 Joe Sakic 30.00 80.00
54 Michael Ryder 15.00 40.00
56 Derek Roy 8.00 20.00
57 Dwayne Roloson 15.00 40.00
59 Brad Richards 15.00 40.00
63 Andrew Raycroft 15.00 40.00
67 Tom Poti 8.00 20.00
69 Dion Phaneuf 20.00 50.00
70 Andrew Peters 8.00 20.00
72 Dustin Penner 15.00 40.00
73 Michael Peca 8.00 20.00
76 Alexander Ovechkin 75.00 150.00
78 Michael Nylander 8.00 20.00
81 Scott Niedermayer 8.00 20.00
82 Markus Naslund 15.00 40.00
83 Glen Murray 8.00 20.00
88 Ryan Miller 15.00 40.00
91 Andy McDonald 8.00 20.00
93 Patrick Marleau 15.00 40.00
97 Roberto Luongo 30.00 80.00
98 Henrik Lundqvist 20.00 50.00
99 John-Michael Liles 8.00 20.00
100 Nicklas Lidstrom 15.00 40.00
101 Jordan Leopold 8.00 20.00
105 Vincent Lecavalier 15.00 40.00
107 Andrew Ladd 8.00 20.00
108 Chris Kunitz 8.00 20.00
109 Slava Kozlov 8.00 20.00
113 Saku Koivu 15.00 40.00
115 Chuck Kobasew 8.00 20.00
116 Mike Knuble 8.00 20.00
118 Duncan Keith 8.00 20.00
119 Olli Jokinen 8.00 20.00
121 Jarome Iginla 25.00 60.00
122 Trent Hunter 8.00 20.00
123 Cristobal Huet 20.00 50.00
124 Marian Hossa 15.00 40.00
126 Shawn Horcoff 8.00 20.00
127 Bobby Holik 8.00 20.00
128 Chris Higgins 15.00 40.00
129 Dany Heatley 20.00 50.00
132 Bill Guerin 8.00 20.00
138 Simon Gagne 15.00 40.00
141 Peter Forsberg 30.00 80.00
142 Marc-Andre Fleury 15.00 40.00
143 Ruslan Fedotenko 8.00 20.00
144 Sergei Federov 15.00 40.00
149 Patrik Elias 8.00 20.00
152 Chris Drury 8.00 20.00
155 Craig Conroy 8.00 20.00
157 Chris Clark 8.00 20.00
158 Jonathan Cheechoo 15.00 40.00
161 Brian Campbell 8.00 20.00
163 Kyle Calder 8.00 20.00
166 Dustin Brown 8.00 20.00
170 Eric Brewer 8.00 20.00
176 Rob Blake 15.00 40.00
179 Patrice Bergeron 15.00 40.00
185 Daniel Alfredsson 15.00 40.00
186 Maxim Afinogenov 8.00 20.00
202 Phil Kessel 15.00 40.00
207 Shea Weber 8.00 20.00
216 Jordan Staal 30.00 80.00
219 Paul Stastny 25.00 60.00
227 Nigel Dawes 8.00 20.00
231 Guillaume Latendresse 20.00 50.00
233 Patrick Thoresen 8.00 20.00

2006-07 Be A Player Signatures Duals

DAS Chris Simon / Sean Avery 6.00 15.00
DBC Rob Blake / Mike Cammalleri 6.00 15.00
DBK Patrice Bergeron / Phil Kessel 10.00 25.00
DBO Marc Savard / Glen Murray 6.00 15.00
DBP Mark Parrish / Pierre-Marc Bouchard 6.00 15.00
DBU Daniel Briere / Thomas Vanek 10.00 25.00
DBV David Vyborny / Gilbert Brule 6.00 15.00
DCA Craig Conroy / Alex Tanguay 6.00 15.00
DCB Steve Bernier / Matt Carle 8.00 20.00
DCH Brent Seabrook / Duncan Keith 6.00 15.00
DCW Aaron Ward / Zdeno Chara 6.00 15.00
DDR Chris Drury / Derek Roy 6.00 15.00
DED Jason Smith / Dwayne Roloson 6.00 15.00
DER Brian Rafalski / Patrik Elias 6.00 15.00
DEV Antoine Vermette / Patrick Eaves 6.00 15.00
DFL Nicklas Lidstrom / Peter Forsberg 25.00 50.00
DFS Marc-Andre Fleury / Jordan Staal 30.00 60.00
DFZ Nikolai Zherdev / Sergei Federov 15.00 30.00
DGC Simon Gagne / Jeff Carter 15.00 30.00
DGE Steve Eminger / Mike Green 4.00 10.00
DHK Saku Koivu 20.00 40.00

Cristobal Huet
)HM Martin Straka 8.00 20.00
Henrik Lundqvist
)HS Jason Spezza 15.00 30.00
Dany Heatley
)IH Jarome Iginla 25.00 50.00
Dany Heatley
)IP Jarome Iginla 25.00 50.00
Dion Phaneuf
)JS Jarret Stoll 4.00 10.00
Shawn Horcoff
)KH Marian Hossa 6.00 15.00
Slava Kozlov
)KR Tuomo Ruutu 6.00 15.00
Nikolai Khabibulin
)KS Sergei Samsonov 6.00 15.00
Alexei Kovalev
)LN Markus Naslund 20.00 40.00
Roberto Luongo
)LS Vincent Lecavalier 10.00 25.00
Martin St. Louis
)MB Brendan Morrison 8.00 20.00
Luc Bourdon
)MC Brian Campbell 10.00 25.00
Ryan Miller
)MG Patrick Marleau 5.00 12.00
Bill Guerin
)MK Andy McDonald 5.00 12.00
Chris Kunitz
)MS Manny Malhotra 4.00 10.00
Jody Shelley
)NA David Legwand 4.00 10.00
Steve Sullivan
)NE Robert Esche 8.00 20.00
Antero Niittymaki
)OC Alexander Ovechkin 40.00 60.00
Chris Clark
)PL Georges Laraque 4.00 10.00
Andrew Peters
)RF Brad Richards 4.00 10.00
Ruslan Fedotenko
)RH Michael Ryder 15.00 30.00
Chris Higgins
)RM Wade Redden 6.00 15.00
Andrej Meszaros
)RS Robyn Regehr 4.00 10.00
Brad Stuart
)RT Darcy Tucker 8.00 20.00
Andrew Raycroft
)RU Mike Richards 6.00 15.00
R.J. Umberger
)SA Daniel Alfredsson 20.00 40.00
Jason Spezza
)SB Rod Brind'Amour 8.00 20.00
Eric Staal
)SH Mike Sillinger 4.00 10.00
Trent Hunter
)SK Teemu Selanne 30.00 80.00
Saku Koivu
)SM Andrei Markov 6.00 15.00
Sheldon Souray
)SN Teemu Selanne 20.00 40.00
Scott Niedermayer
)SO Jody Shelley 5.00 12.00
Steve Ott
)SS Joe Sakic 30.00 80.00
Paul Stastny
)SY Alexei Yashin 6.00 15.00
Ryan Smyth
)TL Jere Lehtinen 6.00 15.00
Marty Turco
)VB Mike Van Ryn 5.00 12.00
Jay Bouwmeester
)WB Doug Weight 5.00 12.00
Brad Boyes
)WS Kyle Wellwood 10.00 25.00
Matt Stajan

2006-07 Be A Player Signatures Trios

STATED PRINT RUN 25 #'d SETS
'BKS Marc Savard 75.00 125.00
Patrice Bergeron
Phil Kessel
'CWB Shea Weber 50.00 100.00
Matt Carle
Luc Bourdon
'DBV Chris Drury 50.00 100.00
Daniel Briere
Thomas Vanek
'FCO Alexander Frolov 30.00 80.00
Mike Cammalleri
Patrick O'Sullivan
'FLS Steve Sullivan
David Legwand
Peter Forsberg
'FSM Ryan Malone 75.00 125.00
Marc-Andre Fleury
Jordan Staal
'FVB David Vyborny
Sergei Federov
Gilbert Brule
'GCR Simon Gagne 75.00 125.00
Mike Richards
Jeff Carter
'HHK Cristobal Huet 50.00 100.00
Chris Higgins
Alexei Kovalev
'HKH Marian Hossa
Bobby Holik
Slava Kozlov
'IPT Jarome Iginla 75.00 150.00
Alex Tanguay
Dion Phaneuf
'JBM Olli Jokinen
Jay Bouwmeester
Steve Montador
'KRL Saku Koivu 75.00 125.00
Michael Ryder
Guillaume Latendresse
'LNM Markus Naslund 60.00 100.00
Roberto Luongo
Brendan Morrison
'LRS Vincent Lecavalier 75.00 150.00
Brad Richards
Martin St. Louis
'MAR Maxim Afinogenov 50.00 100.00
Derek Roy
Ryan Miller

TOKC Olaf Kolzig
Alexander Ovechkin
Chris Clark
TRKS Tuomo Ruutu 60.00 100.00
Brent Seabrook
Nikolai Khabibulin
TRPP Michael Peca
Yanic Perreault
Andrew Raycroft
TRSH Jarret Stoll 40.00 80.00
Shawn Horcoff
Dwayne Roloson
TSAH Daniel Alfredsson
Jason Spezza
Dany Heatley
TSBC Erik Cole 50.00 100.00
Rod Brind'Amour
Eric Staal
TSNP Martin Straka 50.00 100.00
Michael Nylander
Petr Prucha
TSTS Joe Sakic 75.00 125.00
Jose Theodore
Paul Stastny
TTBM Vesa Toskala 30.00 80.00
Milan Michalek
Steve Bernier
TTCM Patrick Marleau 30.00 80.00
Joe Thornton
Jonathan Cheechoo
TTLO Jere Lehtinen
Marty Turco
Steve Ott
TTWS Darcy Tucker 30.00 60.00
Kyle Wellwood
Matt Stajan
TWBS Doug Weight 30.00 60.00
Brad Boyes
Lee Stempniak
TYSS Alexei Yashin 80.00
Ryan Smyth
Mike Sillinger

2006-07 Be A Player Signatures Foursomes

STATED PRINT RUN 10 #'d SETS
NOT PRICED DUE TO SCARCITY
FFLNA Markus Naslund
Nicklas Lidstrom
Peter Forsberg
Daniel Alfredsson
FIBRC Jarome Iginla
Jonathan Cheechoo
Michael Ryder
Patrice Bergeron
FLTFR Roberto Luongo
Marty Turco
Andrew Raycroft
Marc-Andre Fleury
FLTKG Olaf Kolzig
Vesa Toskala
Henrik Lundqvist
Martin Gerber
FMSRS Patrick Marleau
Brad Richards
Marc Savard
Jason Spezza
FNBRB Wade Redden
Jay Bouwmeester
Rob Blake
Scott Niedermayer
FOFKF Alexander Frolov
Alexei Kovalev
Sergei Federov
Alexander Ovechkin
FSKJL Teemu Selanne
Jere Lehtinen
Saku Koivu
Olli Jokinen
FSLST Joe Sakic
Vincent Lecavalier
Joe Thornton
Eric Staal
FSSLK Phil Kessel
Paul Stastny
Jordan Staal
Guillaume Latendresse

2006-07 Be A Player Unmasked Warriors

STATED PRINT RUN 99 #'d SETS 6.00 15.00
AUTO'D 1/1 VERSION ALSO EXISTS
AUTO NOT PRICED DUE TO SCARCITY
UM1 Ryan Miller 8.00 20.00
UM2 Jose Theodore 8.00 20.00
UM3 Marty Turco 6.00 15.00
UM4 Dwayne Roloson 6.00 15.00
UM5 Cristobal Huet 8.00 20.00
UM6 Henrik Lundqvist 8.00 20.00
UM7 Cam Ward 6.00 15.00
UM8 Marc-Andre Fleury 8.00 20.00
UM9 Andrew Raycroft 6.00 15.00
UM10 Roberto Luongo 8.00 20.00

2006-07 Be A Player Up Close and Personal

STATED PRINT RUN 999 #'d SETS
AUTO'D VERSION /10 EXISTS
AUTOS NOT PRICED DUE TO SCARCITY
UC1 Alex Tanguay .50 1.25
UC2 Justin Williams .30 .75
UC3 Alexander Ovechkin 2.00 5.00
UC4 Alexei Yashin .30 .75
UC5 Andrew Raycroft .50 1.25
UC6 Andy McDonald .30 .75
UC7 Bill Guerin .30 .75
UC8 Brad Richards .50 1.25
UC9 Brian Campbell .30 .75
UC10 Chris Drury .30 .75
UC11 Cristobal Huet .75 2.00
UC12 Dany Heatley .75 2.00
UC13 Darcy Tucker .30 .75
UC14 Ryan Miller .60 1.50
UC15 Dion Phaneuf .75 2.00
UC16 Doug Weight .30 .75
UC17 Dwayne Roloson .60 1.50
UC18 Eric Staal .60 1.50
UC19 Henrik Lundqvist .75 2.00
UC20 Henrik Sedin .30 .75
UC21 Jarome Iginla .75 2.00
UC22 Jason Spezza .60 1.50
UC23 Jonathan Cheechoo .60 1.50
UC24 Daniel Briere .50 1.25
UC25 Joe Sakic 1.25 3.00
UC26 Joe Thornton 1.00 2.50
UC27 Lee Stempniak .30 .75
UC28 Marc Savard .30 .75
UC29 Marc-Andre Fleury .60 1.50
UC30 Marian Hossa .50 1.25
UC31 Mark Parrish .30 .75
UC32 Markus Naslund .60 1.50
UC33 Martin St. Louis .50 1.25
UC34 Martin Straka .30 .75
UC35 Marty Turco .50 1.25
UC36 Michael Peca .30 .75
UC37 Michael Ryder .50 1.25
UC38 Nicklas Lidstrom .60 1.50
UC39 Nikolai Khabibulin .60 1.50
UC40 Olaf Kolzig .60 1.50
UC41 Martin Havlat .50 1.25
UC42 Patrice Bergeron .60 1.50
UC43 Patrick Marleau .50 1.25
UC44 Patrik Elias .30 .75
UC45 Paul Stastny 1.50 4.00
UC46 Peter Forsberg 1.00 2.50
UC47 Rob Blake .50 1.25
UC48 Roberto Luongo .75 2.00
UC49 Rod Brind'Amour .50 1.25
UC50 Ryan Smyth .50 1.25
UC51 Saku Koivu .60 1.50
UC52 Scott Niedermayer .30 .75
UC53 Sergei Federov .60 1.50
UC54 Simon Gagne .60 1.50
UC55 Kimmo Timonen .30 .75
UC56 Teemu Selanne .60 1.50
UC57 Jordan Staal 2.50 6.00
UC58 Vincent Lecavalier .60 1.50
UC59 Wade Redden .30 .75
UC60 Zdeno Chara .30 .75

1998-99 BAP Autographs

Inserted one per pack, this 300-card set was an autographed version of the base set. SP's had a stated print run of 450 except for the Gretzky card which was reported to be limited to 90 copies. A gold-foil parallel to the set was also created and inserted in random packs. Gold SP's had a stated print run of 50 except for the Gretzky gold parallel which was numbered out of 9.

STATED ODDS ONE PER PACK
SP's STATED PRINT RUN 450 SETS
*GOLD STARS: 1X TO 2X BASIC AUTOS
*GOLD SP's: 1X TO 1.5X BASIC AUTOS
GOLD SP's STATED PRINT RUN 50 SETS
1 Jason Marshall 1.50 4.00
2 Paul Kariya SP 15.00 40.00
3 Teemu Selanne SP 20.00 50.00
4 Guy Hebert 4.00 10.00
5 Ted Drury 1.50 4.00
6 Byron Dafoe 1.50 4.00
7 Rob Dimaio 1.50 4.00
8 Ray Bourque SP 20.00 50.00
9 Joe Thornton 8.00 20.00
10 Sergei Samsonov 4.00 10.00
11 Dimitri Khristich 1.50 4.00
12 Michael Peca 1.50 4.00
13 Jason Woolley 1.50 4.00
14 Matthew Barnaby 1.50 4.00
15 Brian Holzinger 1.50 4.00
16 Dixon Ward 1.50 4.00
17 Tyler Moss 1.50 4.00
18 Jarome Iginla 8.00 20.00
19 Marty McInnis 1.50 4.00
20 Andrew Cassels 1.50 4.00
21 Jason Wiemer 1.50 4.00
22 Trevor Kidd 4.00 10.00
23 Keith Primeau 1.50 4.00
24 Sami Kapanen 1.50 4.00
25 Robert Kron 1.50 4.00
26 Glen Wesley 1.50 4.00
27 Jeff Hackett 4.00 10.00
28 Tony Amonte SP 6.00 15.00
29 Alexei Zhamnov 1.50 4.00
30 Eric Weinrich 1.50 4.00
31 Jeff Shantz 1.50 4.00
32 Christian Laflamme 1.50 4.00
33 Adam Foote 1.50 4.00
34 Patrick Roy SP 40.00 100.00
35 Peter Forsberg SP 20.00 50.00
36 Adam Deadmarsh 1.50 4.00
37 Joe Sakic SP 30.00 80.00
38 Eric Lacroix 1.50 4.00
39 Guy Carbonneau 1.50 4.00
40 Mike Modano SP 15.00 40.00
41 Roman Turek 1.50 4.00
42 Mike Keane 1.50 4.00
43 Sergei Zubov 1.50 4.00
44 Jere Lehtinen 4.00 10.00
45 Sergei Fedorov SP 10.00 25.00
46 Steve Yzerman SP 40.00 100.00
47 Chris Osgood 4.00 10.00
48 Larry Murphy 1.50 4.00
49 Vyacheslav Kozlov 4.00 10.00
50 Darren McCarty 4.00 10.00
51 Boris Mironov 1.50 4.00
52 Roman Hamrlik 1.50 4.00
53 Bill Guerin 1.50 4.00
54 Mike Grier 1.50 4.00
55 Todd Marchant 1.50 4.00
56 Ray Whitney 1.50 4.00
57 Dave Gagner 1.50 4.00
58 Scott Mellanby 1.50 4.00
59 Robert Svehla 1.50 4.00
60 Viktor Kozlov 1.50 4.00
61 Luc Robitaille 6.00 15.00
62 Yanic Perreault 1.50 4.00
63 Jozef Stumpel 1.50 4.00
64 Sandy Moger 1.50 4.00
65 Ian Laperriere 1.50 4.00
66 Jocelyn Thibault 4.00 10.00
67 Dave Manson 1.50 4.00
68 Mark Recchi SP 6.00 15.00
69 Patrick Poulin 1.50 4.00
70 Benoit Brunet 1.50 4.00
71 Turner Stevenson 1.50 4.00
72 Mike Dunham 4.00 10.00
73 Tom Fitzgerald 1.50 4.00
74 Darren Turcotte 1.50 4.00
75 Brad Smyth 1.50 4.00
76 J.J. Daigneault 1.50 4.00
77 Dave Andreychuk 4.00 10.00
78 Jason Arnott 1.50 4.00
79 Martin Brodeur SP 30.00 80.00
80 Randy McKay 1.50 4.00
81 Patrik Elias 4.00 10.00
82 Kevin Dean 1.50 4.00
83 Tommy Salo 4.00 10.00
84 Scott Lachance 1.50 4.00
85 Bryan Berard 1.50 4.00
86 Robert Reichel 1.50 4.00
87 Kenny Jonsson 1.50 4.00
88 Kevin Stevens 1.50 4.00
89 Mike Richter SP 10.00 25.00
90 Wayne Gretzky/90 200.00 400.00
91 Adam Graves 1.50 4.00
92 Alexei Kovalev 4.00 10.00
93 Ulf Samuelsson 1.50 4.00
94 Radek Bonk 1.50 4.00
95 Wade Redden 1.50 4.00
96 Damian Rhodes 1.50 4.00
97 Bruce Gardiner 1.50 4.00
98 Daniel Alfredsson 4.00 10.00
99 Ron Hextall 4.00 10.00
100 Eric Lindros SP 6.00 15.00
101 Chris Gratton 1.50 4.00
102 Dainius Zubrus 1.50 4.00
103 Luke Richardson 1.50 4.00
104 Petr Svoboda 1.50 4.00
105 Rick Tocchet 4.00 10.00
106 Teppo Numminen 1.50 4.00
107 Jeremy Roenick SP 12.00 30.00
108 Nikolai Khabibulin 4.00 10.00
109 Brad Isbister 1.50 4.00
110 Peter Skudra 1.50 4.00
111 Alexei Morozov 1.50 4.00
112 Kevin Hatcher 1.50 4.00
113 Darius Kasparaitis 1.50 4.00
114 Stu Barnes 1.50 4.00
115 Martin Straka 1.50 4.00
116 Andrei Zyuzin 1.50 4.00
117 Marcus Ragnarsson 1.50 4.00
118 Murray Craven 1.50 4.00
119 Marco Sturm 1.50 4.00
120 Patrick Marleau 4.00 10.00
121 Shawn Burr 1.50 4.00
122 Grant Fuhr 4.00 10.00
123 Chris Pronger 4.00 10.00
124 Geoff Courtnall 1.50 4.00
125 Jim Campbell 1.50 4.00
126 Pavol Demitra 4.00 10.00
127 Todd Gill 1.50 4.00
128 Cory Cross 1.50 4.00
129 Daymond Langkow 1.50 4.00
130 Alexander Selivanov 1.50 4.00
131 Mikael Renberg 1.50 4.00
132 Rob Zamuner 1.50 4.00
133 Stephane Richer 1.50 4.00
134 Fredrik Modin 1.50 4.00
135 Derek King 1.50 4.00
136 Mats Sundin SP 10.00 25.00
137 Mike Johnson 1.50 4.00
138 Alyn McCauley 1.50 4.00
139 Jason Smith 1.50 4.00
140 Markus Naslund 6.00 15.00
141 Alexander Mogilny SP 6.00 15.00
142 Mattias Ohlund 1.50 4.00
143 Donald Brashear 1.50 4.00
144 Garth Snow 1.50 4.00
145 Brian Bellows 1.50 4.00
146 Peter Bondra SP 6.00 15.00
147 Joe Juneau 1.50 4.00
148 Steve Konowalchuk 1.50 4.00
149 Ken Klee 1.50 4.00
150 Michal Pivonka 1.50 4.00
151 Steve Rucchin 1.50 4.00
152 Stu Grimson 1.50 4.00
153 Tomas Sandstrom 1.50 4.00
154 Fredrik Olausson 1.50 4.00
155 Travis Green 1.50 4.00
156 Jason Allison 1.50 4.00
157 Steve Heinze 1.50 4.00
158 Rob Tallas 1.50 4.00
159 Darren Van Impe 1.50 4.00
160 Ken Baumgartner 1.50 4.00
161 Peter Ferraro 1.50 4.00
162 Dominik Hasek SP 25.00 60.00
163 Geoff Sanderson 1.50 4.00
164 Miroslav Satan 4.00 10.00
165 Rob Ray 4.00 10.00
166 Alexei Zhitnik 1.50 4.00
167 Phil Housley 1.50 4.00
168 Theo Fleury SP 10.00 25.00
169 Ken Wregget 1.50 4.00
170 Valeri Bure 1.50 4.00
171 Rico Fata 1.50 4.00
172 Arturs Irbe 4.00 10.00
173 Sean Hill 1.50 4.00
174 Ron Francis SP 6.00 15.00
175 Jeff O'Neill 1.50 4.00
176 Paul Ranheim 1.50 4.00
177 Paul Coffey SP 10.00 25.00
178 Doug Gilmour SP 8.00 20.00
179 Eric Daze 1.50 4.00
180 Chris Chelios SP 10.00 25.00
181 Bob Probert 4.00 10.00
182 Mark Fitzpatrick 1.50 4.00
183 Alexei Gusarov 1.50 4.00
184 Sylvain Lefebvre 1.50 4.00
185 Craig Billington 1.50 4.00
186 Valeri Kamensky 1.50 4.00
187 Milan Hejduk 6.00 15.00
188 Sandis Ozolinsh 1.50 4.00
189 Brett Hull SP 15.00 40.00
190 Ed Belfour SP 10.00 25.00
191 Darryl Sydor 1.50 4.00
192 Sergei Gusev 1.50 4.00
193 Joe Nieuwendyk SP 6.00 15.00
194 Derian Hatcher 1.50 4.00
195 Brendan Shanahan SP 8.00 20.00
196 Tomas Holmstrom 4.00 10.00
197 Nicklas Lidstrom 6.00 15.00
198 Martin Lapointe 4.00 10.00
199 Igor Larionov 1.50 4.00
200 Kris Draper 1.50 4.00
201 Kelly Buchberger 1.50 4.00
202 Andrei Kovalenko 1.50 4.00
203 Josef Beranek 1.50 4.00
204 Mikhail Shtalenkov 1.50 4.00
205 Pat Falloon 1.50 4.00
206 Mark Parrish 1.50 4.00
207 Terry Carkner 1.50 4.00
208 Rob Niedermayer 1.50 4.00
209 Sean Burke 4.00 10.00
210 Oleg Kvasha 1.50 4.00
211 Pavel Bure SP 15.00 40.00
212 Rob Blake 4.00 10.00
213 Vladimir Tsyplakov 1.50 4.00
214 Stephane Fiset 1.50 4.00
215 Steve Duchesne 1.50 4.00
216 Patrice Brisebois 1.50 4.00
217 Vincent Damphousse 1.50 4.00
218 Saku Koivu 6.00 15.00
219 Jose Theodore 8.00 20.00
220 Brett Clark 1.50 4.00
221 Martin Rucinsky 1.50 4.00
222 Vladimir Malakhov 1.50 4.00
223 Sergei Krivokrasov 1.50 4.00
224 Scott Walker 1.50 4.00
225 Greg Johnson 1.50 4.00
226 Cliff Ronning 1.50 4.00
227 Eric Fichaud 1.50 4.00
228 Bob Carpenter 1.50 4.00
229 Scott Daniels 1.50 4.00
230 Brian Rolston 1.50 4.00
231 Sergei Brylin 1.50 4.00
232 Scott Niedermayer 1.50 4.00
233 Bryan Smolinski 1.50 4.00
234 Trevor Linden 4.00 10.00
235 Eric Brewer 1.50 4.00
236 Zigmund Palffy SP 6.00 15.00
237 Sergei Nemchinov 1.50 4.00
238 Brian Leetch SP 6.00 15.00
239 Mathieu Schneider 1.50 4.00
240 Niklas Sundstrom 1.50 4.00
241 Manny Malhotra 1.50 4.00
242 Jeff Beukeboom 1.50 4.00
243 Petr Nedved 1.50 4.00
244 Ron Tugnutt 1.50 4.00
245 Shawn Van Allen 1.50 4.00
246 Alexei Yashin 1.50 4.00
247 Jason York 1.50 4.00
248 Shawn McEachern 1.50 4.00
249 Marian Hossa 6.00 15.00
250 John LeClair SP 8.00 20.00
251 Rod Brind'Amour 4.00 10.00
252 John Vanbiesbrouck 4.00 10.00
253 Eric Desjardins 1.50 4.00
254 Valeri Zelepukin 1.50 4.00
255 Karl Dykhuis 1.50 4.00
256 Keith Tkachuk 4.00 10.00
257 Dallas Drake 1.50 4.00
258 Oleg Tverdovsky 1.50 4.00
259 Jyrki Lumme 1.50 4.00
260 Jimmy Waite 1.50 4.00
261 Jaromir Jagr SP 20.00 50.00
262 German Titov 1.50 4.00
263 Robert Lang 1.50 4.00
264 Brad Werenka 1.50 4.00
265 Rob Brown 1.50 4.00
266 Bobby Dollas 1.50 4.00
267 Jeff Friesen 1.50 4.00
268 Andy Sutton 1.50 4.00
269 Steve Shields 4.00 10.00
270 Mike Ricci 1.50 4.00
271 Joe Murphy 1.50 4.00
272 Tony Granato 1.50 4.00
273 Jamie McLennan 1.50 4.00
274 Al MacInnis SP 10.00 25.00
275 Pierre Turgeon 1.50 4.00
276 Kelly Chase 1.50 4.00
277 Craig Conroy 1.50 4.00
278 Scott Young 1.50 4.00
279 Vincent Lecavalier 8.00 20.00
280 Wendel Clark 4.00 10.00
281 Daren Puppa 1.50 4.00
282 Sandy McCarthy 1.50 4.00
283 Daniil Markov 1.50 4.00
284 Curtis Joseph SP 10.00 25.00
285 Sergei Berezin 1.50 4.00
286 Steve Sullivan 1.50 4.00
287 Tomas Kaberle 1.50 4.00
288 Kris King 1.50 4.00
289 Igor Korolev 1.50 4.00
290 Mark Messier SP 50.00 100.00
291 Bill Muckalt 1.50 4.00
292 Todd Bertuzzi 6.00 15.00
293 Brad May 1.50 4.00
294 Peter Zezel 1.50 4.00
295 Dmitri Mironov 1.50 4.00
296 Adam Oates SP 6.00 15.00
297 Calle Johansson 1.50 4.00
298 Craig Berube 1.50 4.00
299 Sergei Gonchar 1.50 4.00
300 Andrei Nikolishin 1.50 4.00

1998-99 BAP AS Game Used Stick Cards

STATED PRINT RUN 100 SETS
S1 Eric Lindros 15.00 40.00
S2 Peter Forsberg 25.00 60.00
S3 Teemu Selanne 15.00 40.00
S4 Mike Modano 15.00 40.00
S5 Mats Sundin 15.00 40.00
S6 Patrick Roy 40.00 100.00
S7 Paul Kariya 15.00 40.00
S8 Martin Brodeur 30.00 80.00
S9 Steve Yzerman 40.00 100.00

S10 Mark Messier 15.00 40.00
S11 Brett Hull 15.00 40.00
S12 Joe Sakic 25.00 60.00
S13 Alexander Mogilny 15.00 40.00
S14 Sergei Fedorov 20.00 50.00
S15 Ray Bourque 25.00 60.00
S16 Jeremy Roenick 15.00 40.00
S17 Jaromir Jagr 30.00 80.00
S18 Dominik Hasek 15.00 40.00
S19 Chris Chelios 15.00 40.00
S20 John LeClair 15.00 40.00
S21 Brendan Shanahan 15.00 40.00
S22 Ed Belfour 15.00 40.00
S23 Wayne Gretzky 125.00 300.00

1998-99 BAP AS Game Used Jersey Cards

STATED PRINT RUN 100 SETS
AS1 Eric Lindros 12.50 30.00
AS2 Peter Forsberg 20.00 50.00
AS3 Teemu Selanne 12.50 30.00
AS4 Mike Modano 12.50 30.00
AS5 Mats Sundin 12.50 30.00
AS6 Patrick Roy 30.00 80.00
AS7 Paul Kariya 12.50 30.00
AS8 Martin Brodeur 25.00 60.00
AS9 Steve Yzerman 30.00 80.00
AS10 Mark Messier 12.50 30.00
AS11 Paul Coffey 12.50 30.00
AS12 Brett Hull 12.50 30.00
AS13 Joe Sakic 15.00 40.00
AS14 Alexander Mogilny 8.00 20.00
AS15 Sergei Fedorov 15.00 40.00
AS16 Ray Bourque 20.00 50.00
AS17 Jeremy Roenick 12.50 30.00
AS18 Jaromir Jagr 15.00 40.00
AS19 Pavel Bure 12.50 30.00
AS20 Dominik Hasek 20.00 50.00
AS21 Chris Chelios 12.50 30.00
AS22 John LeClair 12.50 30.00
AS23 Brendan Shanahan 12.50 30.00
AS24 Ed Belfour 12.50 30.00
AS25 Wayne Gretzky 100.00 200.00

1998-99 BAP AS Legend Gordie Howe

Randomly inserted in packs, this two-card set honored Hall-of-Famer Gordie Howe. One card in the set carried a piece of Howe's Detroit Red Wings jerseys embedded in the cards. Each card was autographed by Gordie Howe and eachc ard was limited to just 90 copies.

STAT.PRINT RUN 90 SETS
GH1 Gordie Howe GJ AU 125.00 250.00
GH2 Gordie Howe AU 100.00 200.00

1998-99 BAP AS Milestones

COMPLETE SET (22) 50.00 100.00
RANDOM INSERTS IN PACKS
M1 Wayne Gretzky 4.00 10.00
M2 Mark Messier 2.00 5.00
M3 Dino Ciccarelli 1.50 4.00
M4 Steve Yzerman 3.00 8.00
M5 Dave Andreychuk 1.50 4.00
M6 Brett Hull 2.50 6.00
M7 Wayne Gretzky 4.00 10.00
M8 Mark Messier 2.00 5.00
M9 Dino Ciccarelli 1.50 4.00
M10 Steve Yzerman 3.00 8.00
M11 Bernie Nicholls 1.50 4.00
M12 Ron Francis 1.50 4.00
M13 Ray Bourque 2.50 6.00
M14 Paul Coffey 2.00 5.00
M15 Adam Oates 1.50 4.00
M16 Phil Housley 1.50 4.00
M17 Dale Hunter 1.50 4.00
M18 Luc Robitaille 1.50 4.00
M19 Doug Gilmour 1.50 4.00
M20 Larry Murphy 1.50 4.00
M21 Dave Andreychuk 1.50 4.00
M22 Al MacInnis 1.50 4.00

1998-99 BAP Playoff Game Used Jerseys

STATED PRINT RUN 100 SETS
G1 Wayne Gretzky 75.00 200.00
G2 Mats Sundin 12.50 30.00
G3 Jeremy Roenick 12.50 30.00
G4 Eric Lindros 12.50 30.00
G5 John LeClair 12.50 30.00
G6 Joe Sakic 15.00 40.00
G7 Peter Forsberg 20.00 50.00
G8 Patrick Roy 40.00 100.00
G9 Martin Brodeur 25.00 60.00
G10 Pavel Bure 12.50 30.00
G11 Teemu Selanne 12.50 30.00
G12 Paul Kariya 12.50 30.00
G13 Ray Bourque 20.00 50.00
G14 Brendan Shanahan 12.50 30.00
G15 Steve Yzerman 30.00 80.00
G16 Sergei Fedorov 15.00 40.00
G17 Mike Modano 12.50 30.00
G18 Brett Hull 12.50 30.00
G19 Ed Belfour 12.50 30.00
G20 Mark Messier 12.50 30.00
G21 Alexander Mogilny 8.00 20.00
G22 Tony Amonte 8.00 20.00
G23 Jaromir Jagr 15.00 40.00
G24 Alexei Yashin 8.00 20.00

1998-99 BAP Playoff Game Used Jersey Autographs

STATED PRINT RUN 10 SETS
G1 Wayne Gretzky
G2 Mats Sundin
G4 Eric Lindros
G5 John LeClair
G6 Joe Sakic
G8 Patrick Roy
G9 Martin Brodeur
G10 Pavel Bure
G11 Teemu Selanne
G12 Paul Kariya
G14 Brendan Shanahan
G15 Steve Yzerman
G16 Sergei Fedorov
G22 Alexei Yashin

1998-99 BAP Playoff Highlights

COMPLETE SET (18) 60.00 125.00
H1 Mark Messier 2.00 5.00
H2 Peter Forsberg 5.00 12.00
H3 Wayne Gretzky 12.50 30.00
H4 Martin Brodeur 5.00 12.00
H5 Jaromir Jagr 3.00 8.00
H6 Mike Richter 2.00 5.00
H7 Steve Yzerman 10.00 25.00
H8 Patrick Roy 10.00 25.00
H9 Paul Coffey 2.00 5.00
H10 Joe Sakic 4.00 10.00
H11 John Vanbiesbrouck 2.00 5.00
H12 Pavel Bure 2.00 5.00
H13 Chris Osgood 2.00 5.00
H14 Chris Chelios 2.00 5.00
H15 Curtis Joseph 2.00 5.00
H16 Brian Leetch 2.00 5.00
H17 Sergei Fedorov 3.00 8.00
H18 Doug Gilmour 2.00 5.00

1998-99 BAP Playoff Legend Mario Lemieux

Randomly inserted in packs, this 4-card set was limited to a print run of just 66 sets.

Each card featured one or two pieces of game-used memorabilia and an autograph from Mario Lemieux.
STATED PRINT RUN 66 CARDS
L1 All-Star Jersey/AU Card 150.00 300.00
L2 Penguins Jersey/AU Card 150.00 300.00
L3 All-Star Jsy/Stick/AU Card 200.00 400.00
L4 Peng.Jsy/Stick/AU Card 200.00 400.00

1998-99 BAP Playoff Practice Used Jerseys

STATED PRINT RUN 100 SETS
P1 Brett Hull 10.00 25.00
P2 Alexander Mogilny 6.00 15.00
P3 Ray Bourque 15.00 40.00
P4 Pavel Bure 10.00 25.00
P5 Steve Yzerman 30.00 80.00
P6 Ed Belfour 10.00 25.00
P7 Jaromir Jagr 12.50 30.00
P8 Sergei Fedorov 12.50 30.00
P9 Teemu Selanne 10.00 25.00
P10 Eric Lindros 10.00 25.00
P11 Tony Amonte 8.00 20.00
P12 Jeremy Roenick 10.00 25.00
P13 John LeClair 10.00 25.00
P14 Mike Modano 10.00 25.00
P15 Joe Sakic 12.50 30.00
P16 Patrick Roy 30.00 80.00
P17 Mark Messier 10.00 25.00
P18 Paul Kariya 10.00 25.00
P19 Martin Brodeur 20.00 50.00
P20 Mats Sundin 25.00 60.00
P21 Brendan Shanahan 10.00 25.00
P22 Peter Forsberg 20.00 50.00
P23 Alexei Yashin 6.00 15.00
P24 Wayne Gretzky 100.00 150.00

2005-06 Be A Player

Released in August 2005, Be A Player was produced by Upper Deck for the first time. Each pack contained 5 cards including one autograph card and carried a $20 SRP, each box carried 10 packs.
COMPLETE SET (90) 15.00 40.00
1 J-S Giguere .40 1.00
2 Joffrey Lupul .25 .60
3 Ilya Kovalchuk .60 1.50
4 Dany Heatley .60 1.50
5 Kari Lehtonen .50 1.25
6 Glen Murray .25 .60
7 Joe Thornton .75 2.00
8 Andrew Raycroft .40 1.00
9 Miroslav Satan .25 .60
10 Chris Drury .40 1.00
11 Daniel Briere .25 .60
12 Jarome Iginla .60 1.50
13 Miikka Kiprusoff .50 1.25
14 Martin Gelinas .25 .60
15 Erik Cole .25 .60
16 Eric Staal .40 1.00
17 Tuomo Ruutu .25 .60
18 Eric Daze .40 1.00
19 Joe Sakic 1.00 2.50
20 Peter Forsberg .75 2.00
21 Milan Hejduk .50 1.25
22 Rob Blake .40 1.00
23 Alex Tanguay .40 1.00
24 Rick Nash .60 1.50
25 Nikolai Zherdev .40 1.00
26 Todd Marchant .25 .60
27 Marty Turco .40 1.00
28 Brenden Morrow .40 1.00
29 Mike Modano .50 1.25
30 Brendan Shanahan .50 1.25
31 Nicklas Lidstrom .50 1.25
32 Pavel Datsyuk .50 1.25
33 Steve Yzerman 2.00 5.00
34 Curtis Joseph .50 1.25
35 Ryan Smyth .40 1.00
36 Jason Smith .25 .60
37 Ty Conklin .40 1.00
38 Olli Jokinen .40 1.00
39 Roberto Luongo .60 1.50
40 Jay Bouwmeester .25 .60
41 Zigmund Palffy .40 1.00
42 Luc Robitaille .40 1.00
43 Alexander Frolov .40 1.00
44 Marian Gaborik .75 2.00
45 Dwayne Roloson .40 1.00
46 Saku Koivu .50 1.25
47 Jose Theodore .50 1.25
48 Michael Ryder .40 1.00
49 Tomas Vokoun .40 1.00
50 Steve Sullivan .25 .60
51 Jordin Tootoo .25 .60
52 Martin Brodeur 1.50 4.00
53 Patrik Elias .40 1.00
54 Scott Gomez .40 1.00
55 Rick DiPietro .40 1.00
56 Mike Peca .25 .60
57 Trent Hunter .25 .60
58 Jaromir Jagr .75 2.00
59 Bobby Holik .25 .60
60 Dan Blackburn
61 Marian Hossa .40 1.00
62 Jason Spezza .50 1.25
63 Daniel Alfredsson .40 1.00
64 Keith Primeau .25 .60
65 Simon Gagne .50 1.25
66 Robert Esche .40 1.00
67 Brett Hull .50 1.25
68 Shane Doan .25 .60
69 Mike Comrie .40 1.00
70 Marc-Andre Fleury .40 1.00
71 Mark Recchi .40 1.00
72 Mario Lemieux 2.50 6.00
73 Patrick Marleau .40 1.00
74 Jonathan Cheechoo .50 1.25
75 Evgeni Nabokov .40 1.00
76 Chris Pronger .40 1.00
77 Doug Weight .40 1.00
78 Keith Tkachuk .50 1.25
79 Martin St. Louis .40 1.00
80 Vincent Lecavalier .50 1.25
81 Nikolai Khabibulin .50 1.25
82 Brad Richards .40 1.00
83 Dave Andreychuk .25 .60
84 Gary Roberts .25 .60
85 Mats Sundin .50 1.25
86 Joe Nieuwendyk .40 1.00
87 Markus Naslund .50 1.25
88 Brendan Morrison .25 .60
89 Ed Jovanovski .40 1.00
90 Olaf Kolzig .40 1.00

2005-06 Be A Player First Period

*STARS: 2X TO 5X BASIC CARDS
PRINT RUN 100 SER.#'d SETS

2005-06 Be A Player Second Period

*STARS: 5X TO 12X BASIC CARDS
PRINT RUN 50 SER.#'d SETS

2005-06 Be A Player Third Period

PRINT RUN 10 SER.#'d SETS
NOT PRICED DUE TO SCARCITY

2005-06 Be A Player Overtime

PRINT RUN 1 SER.#'d SET
NOT PRICED DUE TO SCARCITY

2005-06 Be A Player Class Action

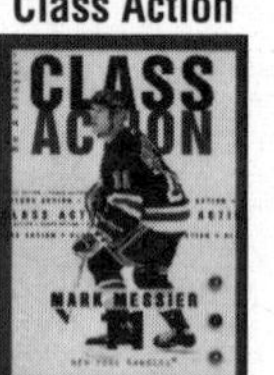

COMPLETE SET
PRINT RUN 299 SER.#'d SETS
CA1 Keith Tkachuk 1.50 4.00
CA2 Dany Heatley 2.00 5.00
CA3 Ilya Kovalchuk 2.00 5.00
CA4 Joe Thornton 2.50 6.00
CA5 Jarome Iginla 2.00 5.00
CA6 Peter Forsberg 2.50 6.00
CA7 Joe Sakic 3.00 8.00
CA8 Rick Nash 2.00 5.00
CA9 Mike Modano 1.50 4.00
CA10 Steve Yzerman 5.00 12.00
CA11 Mats Sundin 1.50 4.00
CA12 Martin St. Louis 1.25 3.00
CA13 Jose Theodore 2.00 5.00
CA14 Miikka Kiprusoff 1.50 4.00
CA15 Martin Brodeur 5.00 12.00
CA16 Mark Messier 1.50 4.00
CA17 Markus Naslund 1.50 4.00
CA18 Jeremy Roenick 2.00 5.00
CA19 Brett Hull 2.00 5.00
CA20 Mario Lemieux 6.00 15.00

2005-06 Be A Player Dual Signatures

STATED ODDS 1:10
AR D.Andreychuk/L.Robitaille 8.00 20.00
BD Daniel Briere 8.00 20.00
Chris Drury
BF Martin Brodeur 40.00 100.00
Marc-Andre Fleury
BS Brian Rafalski 5.00 12.00
Scott Niedermayer
DK Dany Heatley 15.00 40.00
Kari Lehtonen
DL Kris Draper 20.00 50.00
Nicklas Lidstrom
DR M.Denis/D.Roloson 8.00 20.00
DT E.Daze/J.Thibault 5.00 12.00
FL Marc Andre Fleury 20.00 50.00
Roberto Luongo
GB Bill Guerin 5.00 12.00
Brenden Morrow
GD Bill Guerin/C.Drury 5.00 12.00
HH Marian Hossa 15.00 40.00
Dominik Hasek
HR Marian Hossa 8.00 20.00
Wade Redden
HT Gordie Howe 125.00 250.00
Joe Thornton
IM Jarome Iginla 10.00 25.00
Patrick Marleau
JE J.Spezza/E.Staal 15.00 40.00
KC K.Tkachuk/C.Pronger 10.00 25.00
LI Martin St. Louis 15.00 40.00
Jarome Iginla
LL Martin St.Louis 12.50 30.00
Vincent Lecavalier
LP Nicklas Lidstrom 20.00 50.00
Chris Pronger
LW Roberto Luongo 8.00 20.00
Stephen Weiss
MA Michael Peca 5.00 12.00
Adrian Aucoin
MC P.Marleau/J.Cheechoo 10.00 25.00
ND R.Nash/M.Denis 12.00 30.00
NL Markus Naslund 12.00 30.00
Trevor Linden
NT R.Nash/J.Thornton 15.00 40.00
PA Paul Kariya 12.00 30.00
Alex Tanguay
PE Keith Primeau 5.00 12.00
Robert Esche
PP Michael Peca 5.00 12.00
Mark Parrish
RB Luc Robitaille 5.00 12.00
Dustin Brown
RJ Rob Blake 5.00 12.00
Jay Bouwmeester
RL Roberto Luongo 20.00 50.00
Kari Lehtonen
RR Michael Ryder 5.00 12.00
Mike Ribeiro
RT Michael Ryder 10.00 25.00
Jose Theodore
SB Joe Sakic 25.00 60.00
Rob Blake
SR J.Spezza/M.Ryder 12.00 30.00
SS R.Smyth/J.Smith 8.00 20.00
ST Mike Sillinger 5.00 12.00
Keith Tkachuk
TL Marty Turco 12.00 30.00
Roberto Luongo
TM Joe Thornton 10.00 25.00
Glen Murray
TP Joe Thornton 10.00 25.00
Keith Primeau
TR Jose Theodore 8.00 20.00
Mike Ribeiro
VR Vincent Lecavalier 10.00 25.00
Ruslan Fedotenko

2005-06 Be A Player Ice Icons

PRINT RUN 99 SER.#'d SETS
ICE1 Martin Brodeur 15.00 40.00
ICE2 Mario Lemieux 20.00 50.00
ICE3 Joe Sakic 6.00 15.00
ICE4 Peter Forsberg 5.00 12.00
ICE5 Steve Yzerman 12.00 30.00

2005-06 Be A Player Outtakes

PRINT RUN 499 SER.#'d SETS
OT1 J-S Giguere 1.00 2.50
OT2 Sergei Fedorov 1.25 3.00
OT3 Dany Heatley 1.50 4.00
OT4 Ilya Kovalchuk 1.50 4.00
OT5 Andrew Raycroft 1.00 2.50
OT6 Joe Thornton 2.00 5.00
OT7 Chris Drury 1.00 2.50
OT8 Jarome Iginla 1.50 4.00
OT9 Miikka Kiprusoff 1.25 3.00
OT10 Eric Staal 1.00 2.50
OT11 Tuomo Ruutu .60 1.50
OT12 Peter Forsberg 2.00 5.00
OT13 Rob Blake 1.00 2.50
OT14 Alex Tanguay 1.00 2.50
OT15 Joe Sakic 2.50 6.00
OT16 Nikolai Zherdev 1.00 2.50
OT17 Rick Nash 1.50 4.00
OT18 Mike Modano 1.25 3.00
OT19 Marty Turco 1.00 2.50
OT20 Pavel Datsyuk 1.25 3.00
OT21 Brendan Shanahan 1.25 3.00
OT22 Steve Yzerman 5.00 12.00
OT23 Ryan Smyth 1.00 2.50
OT24 Roberto Luongo 1.50 4.00
OT25 Luc Robitaille 1.00 2.50
OT26 Marian Gaborik 2.50 6.00
OT27 Saku Koivu 1.25 3.00
OT28 Jose Theodore 1.50 4.00
OT29 Tomas Vokoun 1.00 2.50
OT30 Steve Sullivan .60 1.50
OT31 Martin Brodeur 6.00 15.00
OT32 Jaromir Jagr 2.00 5.00
OT33 Mark Messier 1.25 3.00
OT34 Michael Peca .60 1.50
OT35 Daniel Alfredsson 1.00 2.50
OT36 Jason Spezza 1.25 3.00
OT37 Jeremy Roenick 1.50 4.00
OT38 Simon Gagne 1.25 3.00
OT39 Shane Doan .60 1.50
OT40 Mario Lemieux 6.00 15.00
OT41 Patrick Marleau 1.00 2.50
OT42 Keith Tkachuk 1.25 3.00
OT43 Chris Pronger 1.00 2.50
OT44 Vincent Lecavalier 1.25 3.00
OT45 Martin St. Louis 1.00 2.50
OT46 Mats Sundin 1.25 3.00
OT47 Ed Belfour 1.25 3.00
OT48 Markus Naslund 1.25 3.00
OT49 Ed Jovanovski 1.00 2.50
OT50 Olaf Kolzig 1.00 2.50

2005-06 Be A Player Quad Signatures

STATED ODDS 1:180
BLTG Martin Brodeur 250.00 500.00
Roberto Luongo
Jose Theodore
Jean Sebastien Giguere
BLUE Chris Pronger 30.00 80.00
Keith Tkachuk
Eric Weinrich
Mike Sillinger
BOST Joe Thornton 100.00 200.00
Andrew Raycroft
Glen Murray
Patrice Bergeron
COLO Alex Tanguay 75.00 150.00
Joe Sakic
David Aebischer
Vincent Damphousse
GDEF Chris Pronger 100.00 200.00
Nicklas Lidstrom
Rob Blake
Jay Bouwmeester
GOAL Martin Brodeur 200.00 400.00
Jose Theodore
Jean-Sebastien Giguere
Marc-Andre Fleury
HAWK Tuomo Ruutu 30.00 80.00
Eric Daze
Jocelyn Thibault
Bryan Berard
HSNT Heatly/Sakic/Nash/Thorntn
IMPL Jarome Iginla 50.00 100.00
Patrick Marleau
Keith Primeau
Martin St. Louis
ITLB Iginla/Tangy/St.Lou/Bergrn 50.00 125.00
MAPL Sundn/Stajn/McCbe/Robrts 75.00 150.00
MONT Theo/Ryder/Ribeiro/Souray 125.00 250.00
OTWA Marian Hossa 100.00 200.00
Wade Redden
Peter Bondra
Dominik Hasek
RBSS Ruutu/Bergrn/Staal/Stajan 60.00 125.00
SCCH Andrychk/St.Lou/Richrds/Stllmn
60.00 100.00
SDPH Ryan Smyth 30.00 80.00
Eric Daze
Keith Primeau
Bobby Holik
SHSL Sakic/Heatly/Sundn/St.Lou 60.00 125.00
SSIR Ryan Smyth 100.00 200.00
Jason Smith
Jarome Iginla
Robyn Regehr
TLAL Marty Turco 100.00 200.00
Roberto Luongo
David Aebischer
Kari Lehtonen

2005-06 Be A Player Signatures

ONE PER PACK
GOLD PRINT RUN 10 SER.#'d SETS
GOLD NOT PRICED DUE TO SCARCITY
AA Adrian Aucoin 2.00 5.00
AB Andrew Brunette 2.00 5.00
AC Andrew Cassels 2.00 5.00
AE David Aebischer 4.00 10.00
AH Adam Hall 2.00 5.00
AL Andreas Lilja 2.00 5.00
AM Alyn McCauley 2.00 5.00
AN Dave Andreychuk 4.00 10.00
AR Andrew Raycroft 5.00 12.00
AT Alex Tanguay 4.00 10.00
AV Sean Avery 2.00 5.00
BA Matthew Barnaby 2.00 5.00
BB Bryan Berard 2.00 5.00
BD Boyd Devereaux 2.00 5.00
BE Brenden Morrow 4.00 10.00
BG Bill Guerin SP 8.00 20.00
BH Bobby Holik 2.00 5.00
BI Martin Biron 4.00 10.00
BJ Barret Jackman 4.00 10.00
BM Brendan Morrison 4.00 10.00
BN Brian Boucher 4.00 10.00
BO Bob Boughner 2.00 5.00
BR Brian Rolston 2.00 5.00
BS Brendan Shanahan 15.00 40.00
BT Brent Sopel 2.00 5.00
BW Brendan Witt 2.00 5.00
BY Bryan McCabe 2.00 5.00
CC Carlo Colaiacovo 2.00 5.00
CD Chris Drury SP 40.00 100.00
CO Craig Conroy 2.00 5.00
CP Chris Pronger 4.00 10.00
CR Craig Rivet 2.00 5.00
CS Cory Stillman 2.00 5.00
DB Daniel Briere 2.00 5.00
DC Daniel Cleary 2.00 5.00
DD Dallas Drake 2.00 5.00
DE Derian Hatcher 2.00 5.00
DI Daniel Alfredsson 6.00 15.00
DL David Legwand 4.00 10.00
DN Dan Cloutier 4.00 10.00
DO Sean Donovan 2.00 5.00
DR Dwayne Roloson 4.00 10.00
DT Mathieu Schneider 4.00 10.00
DU Dustin Brown 5.00 12.00
DY Darryl Sydor 2.00 5.00
EB Eric Brewer 2.00 5.00
EC Erik Cole 5.00 12.00
EI Eric Staal 8.00 20.00
EL Eric Lindros 8.00 20.00
ER Eric Belanger 2.00 5.00
ES Robert Esche 4.00 10.00
EW Eric Weinrich 2.00 5.00
FA Brian Rafalski 2.00 5.00
FE Ruslan Fedotenko 2.00 5.00
GI Brian Gionta 2.00 5.00
GL Martin Gelinas 2.00 5.00
GM Glen Murray 2.00 5.00
GS Garth Snow 2.00 5.00
HA Dominik Hasek 25.00 60.00
HE Bret Hedican 2.00 5.00
HF Shawn Horcoff 2.00 5.00
HO Gordie Howe SP 250.00 400.00
HT Dany Heatley 8.00 20.00
HZ Henrik Zetterberg 10.00 25.00
IG Jarome Iginla 12.00 30.00
IL Ian Laperriere 2.00 5.00
JA Jason Arnott 2.00 5.00
JB Jay Bouwmeester 6.00 15.00
JC Jonathan Cheechoo 10.00 25.00
JD Jody Shelley 2.00 5.00
JG J-S Giguere 4.00 10.00
JI Jim Dowd 2.00 5.00
JL Joffrey Lupul 2.00 5.00
JM John-Michael Liles 2.00 5.00
JO Jeff O'Neill 2.00 5.00
JP J-P Dumont 2.00 5.00
JS Jason Smith 2.00 5.00
JT Jocelyn Thibault 4.00 10.00
JW Justin Williams 2.00 5.00
KA Trent Klatt 2.00 5.00
KD Kris Draper 4.00 10.00
KE Kevyn Adams 2.00 5.00
KL Kari Lehtonen 12.00 30.00
KP Keith Primeau SP 10.00 25.00
KT Keith Tkachuk SP 25.00 60.00
KW Kevin Weekes 4.00 10.00
LA Robert Lang 5.00 12.00
LE Jordan Leopold 2.00 5.00
LU Luc Robitaille SP 20.00 50.00
LW Daymond Langkow 2.00 5.00
MA Brad May 2.00 5.00
MD Mathieu Dandenault 2.00 5.00
ME Mike Knuble 2.00 5.00
MF Marc-Andre Fleury 12.50 30.00
MH Marian Hossa 12.00 30.00
MI Mike Comrie 4.00 10.00
ML Martin Lapointe 2.00 5.00
MO Mattias Ohlund 2.00 5.00
MP Mark Parrish 2.00 5.00
MR Marc Denis 4.00 10.00
MS Matt Stajan 2.00 5.00
MT Martin Brodeur SP 150.00 250.00
MU Bryan Muir 2.00 5.00
MW Mattias Weinhandl 2.00 5.00
NA Markus Naslund SP 15.00 40.00
NB Nick Boynton 2.00 5.00
ND Niko Dimitrakos 2.00 5.00
NH Nathan Horton 5.00 12.00
NI Rob Niedermayer 2.00 5.00
NL Nicklas Lidstrom SP 25.00 60.00
OK Olaf Kolzig 6.00 15.00
OR Brooks Orpik 2.00 5.00
OT Steve Ott 2.00 5.00
PA Paul Martin 2.00 5.00
PB Peter Bondra 4.00 10.00
PC Patrice Bergeron 8.00 20.00
PD Pascal Dupuis 2.00 5.00
PE Mike Peca 5.00 12.00
PK Paul Kariya 15.00 40.00
PM Patrick Marleau SP 40.00 100.00
PT Pierre Turgeon 2.00 5.00
RA Rod Brind'Amour 4.00 10.00
RB Rob Blake 4.00 10.00
RC Brad Richards 5.00 12.00
RD Rick DiPietro 6.00 15.00
RF Rico Fata 2.00 5.00
RI Mike Ribeiro 5.00 12.00
RK Ryan Kesler 2.00 5.00
RL Roberto Luongo SP 25.00 60.00
RN Rick Nash 10.00 25.00
RO Gary Roberts 2.00 5.00
RR Robyn Regehr 2.00 5.00
RS Ryan Smyth 2.00 5.00
RU Tuomo Ruutu 4.00 10.00
RW Ray Whitney 2.00 5.00
RY Michael Ryder SP 15.00 40.00
SA Joe Sakic 25.00 60.00
SB Sean Burke 4.00 10.00
SC Scott Niedermayer 2.00 5.00
SD Shane Doan 2.00 5.00
SE Steve Sullivan 2.00 5.00
SG Mike Sillinger 2.00 5.00
SH Shawn McEachern 2.00 5.00
SI Steve Shields 4.00 10.00
SJ Joe Thornton 20.00 50.00
SL Martin St. Louis 4.00 10.00
SM Scott Mellanby 2.00 5.00
SN Geoff Sanderson 2.00 5.00
SO Steve Staios 2.00 5.00
SP Jason Spezza 10.00 25.00
SQ Stephane Quintal 2.00 5.00
SR Steve Rucchin 2.00 5.00
SS Sheldon Souray 2.00 5.00
SU Mats Sundin 12.00 30.00
TE Mikael Tellqvist 4.00 10.00
TH Jose Theodore 10.00 25.00
TI Mattias Timander 2.00 5.00
TL Trevor Linden 2.00 5.00
TM Todd Marchant 2.00 5.00
TN Tyson Nash 2.00 5.00
TO Steve Thomas 2.00 5.00
TP Tom Poti 2.00 5.00
TR Trent Hunter 2.00 5.00
TT Tim Taylor 2.00 5.00
TU Marty Turco 4.00 10.00
TW Todd White 2.00 5.00
VD Vincent Damphousse 2.00 5.00
VL Vincent Lecavalier 25.00 60.00
WA Scott Walker 2.00 5.00
WE Stephen Weiss 2.00 5.00
WR Wade Redden 2.00 5.00
YO Scott Young 2.00 5.00
ZE Eric Daze 4.00 10.00

2005-06 Be A Player Triple Signatures

STATED ODDS 1:90
AVS Sakic/Tanguay/Kariya SP 30.00 80.00
BSH Bondra/Spezza/Hossa SP 40.00 100.00
BUF Drury/Briere/Biron 20.00 50.00
DAL Turco/Morrow/Guerin SP 20.00 50.00
DEV Brodeur/Niedrmyr/Rafalski SP 125.00 250.00
DRL Dipietro/Raycroft/Luongo SP 30.00 80.00
FGR Fleury/Giguere/Raycroft SP 30.00 80.00
HGT Howe/Guerin/Tkachuk SP 100.00 200.00
HSN Hossa/Sundin/Naslund SP 30.00 80.00
IBM Iginla/Bergeron/Marleau SP 30.00 75.00
LBP Lidstrom/Blake/Pronger SP 30.00 80.00
LLA Luongo/Lehtnen/Aebischr SP 30.00 80.00
MTL Theodore/Ryder/Ribeiro SP 30.00 80.00
NKI Naslund/Kariya/Iginla SP 50.00 100.00
NMS Naslund/Morrison/Sopel 20.00 50.00
PAN Weiss/Horton/Bouwmeester 20.00 50.00
PDL Keith Primeau 20.00 50.00
Eric Daze
Eric Lindros
PTS Keith Primeau 30.00 80.00
Joe Thornton
Mats Sundin
SIS Joe Sakic 75.00 150.00
Jarome Iginla
Mats Sundin
SNL Mats Sundin 20.00 50.00
Markus Naslund
Nicklas Lidstrom
STL Keith Tkachuk 20.00 50.00
Chris Pronger
Dallas Drake
STS Joe Sakic 100.00 200.00
Joe Thornton
Jason Spezza
TBL Martin St. Louis 75.00 150.00
Brad Richards
Vincent Lecavalier
TGR Marty Turco 25.00 60.00
Jean-Sebastien Giguere
Andrew Raycroft
TLP Joe Thornton 75.00 150.00
Vincent Lecavalier
Keith Primeau

2005-06 Be A Player World Cup Salute

PRINT RUN 199 SER.#'d SETS
WCS1 Fredrik Modin 1.50 4.00
WCS2 Vincent Lecavalier 2.50 6.00
WCS3 Keith Tkachuk 1.50 4.00
WCS4 Joe Sakic 4.00 10.00
WCS5 Martin Havlat 1.50 4.00
WCS6 Kimmo Timonen 1.50 4.00
WCS7 Joe Thornton 3.00 8.00
WCS8 Mike Modano 3.00 8.00
WCS9 Daniel Alfredsson 1.50 4.00
WCS10 Patrik Elias 1.50 4.00
WCS11 Martin Brodeur 8.00 20.00
WCS12 Tomas Vokoun 2.50 6.00
WCS13 Miikka Kiprusoff 2.50 6.00
WCS14 Robert Esche 1.50 4.00
WCS15 Bill Guerin 1.50 4.00

2006-07 Be A Player Portraits

1 Jean-Sebastien Giguere .30 .75
2 Chris Pronger .30 .75
3 Teemu Selanne .40 1.00
4 Scott Niedermayer .20 .50
5 Ilya Kovalchuk .50 1.25
6 Kari Lehtonen .40 1.00
7 Marian Hossa .30 .75
8 Marc Savard .20 .50
9 Brad Boyes .20 .50
10 Patrice Bergeron .40 1.00
11 Hannu Toivonen .40 1.00
12 Zdeno Chara .20 .50
13 Daniel Briere .30 .75
14 Chris Drury .20 .50
15 Ryan Miller .40 1.00
16 Jarome Iginla .50 1.25
17 Miikka Kiprusoff .40 1.00
18 Dion Phaneuf .50 1.25
19 Alex Tanguay .30 .75
20 Rod Brind'Amour .30 .75
21 Erik Cole .20 .50
22 Eric Staal .40 1.00
23 Cam Ward .40 1.00
24 Nikolai Khabibulin .40 1.00
25 Martin Havlat .30 .75
26 Tuomo Ruutu .20 .50
27 Marek Svatos .20 .50
28 Joe Sakic .75 2.00
29 Jose Theodore .40 1.00
30 Milan Hejduk .20 .50
31 Rick Nash .40 1.00
32 Pascal LeClaire .30 .75
33 Sergei Fedorov .40 1.00
34 Gilbert Brule .40 1.00
35 Mike Modano .40 1.00
36 Marty Turco .30 .75
37 Brenden Morrow .30 .75
38 Eric Lindros .40 1.00
39 Dominik Hasek .60 1.50
40 Pavel Datsyuk .30 .75
41 Nicklas Lidstrom .40 1.00
42 Henrik Zetterberg .40 1.00
43 Ales Hemsky .20 .50
44 Ryan Smyth .30 .75
45 Joffrey Lupul .20 .50
46 Shawn Horcoff .20 .50
47 Ed Belfour .40 1.00
48 Olli Jokinen .20 .50
49 Nathan Horton .20 .50
50 Todd Bertuzzi .30 .75
51 Rob Blake .30 .75
52 Alexander Frolov .20 .50
53 Pavol Demitra .20 .50
54 Manny Fernandez .30 .75
55 Marian Gaborik .50 1.25
56 Cristobal Huet .50 1.25
57 Sergei Samsonov .20 .50
58 Saku Koivu .40 1.00
59 Michael Ryder .30 .75
60 Paul Kariya .40 1.00
61 Tomas Vokoun .30 .75
62 Martin Brodeur 1.00 2.50
63 Patrik Elias .20 .50
64 Brian Gionta .20 .50
65 Alexei Yashin .20 .50
66 Miroslav Satan .20 .50
67 Rick DiPietro .30 .75
68 Jaromir Jagr .60 1.50
69 Henrik Lundqvist .50 1.25
70 Brendan Shanahan .40 1.00
71 Dany Heatley .50 1.25
72 Jason Spezza .40 1.00
73 Wade Redden .20 .50
74 Daniel Alfredsson .30 .75
75 Peter Forsberg .60 1.50
76 Antero Niittymaki .30 .75
77 Jeff Carter .40 1.00
78 Simon Gagne .40 1.00
79 Curtis Joseph .40 1.00
80 Jeremy Roenick .50 1.25
81 Shane Doan .20 .50
82 Marc-Andre Fleury .40 1.00
83 Sidney Crosby 2.00 5.00
84 Joe Thornton .60 1.50
85 Patrick Marleau .30 .75
86 Jonathan Cheechoo .40 1.00
87 Keith Tkachuk .30 .75
88 Doug Weight .20 .50
89 Brad Richards .30 .75
90 Vincent Lecavalier .40 1.00
91 Martin St. Louis .30 .75
92 Mats Sundin .40 1.00
93 Alexander Steen .30 .75
94 Michael Peca .20 .50
95 Andrew Raycroft .30 .75
96 Markus Naslund .40 1.00
97 Brendan Morrison .20 .50
98 Roberto Luongo .50 1.25
99 Alexander Ovechkin 1.00 2.50
100 Olaf Kolzig .40 1.00
101 Yan Stastny RC 1.00 2.50
102 Mark Stuart RC 1.00 2.50
103 Evgeni Malkin RC 6.00 15.00
104 Patrick Thoresen RC 1.25 3.00
105 Patrick O'Sullivan RC 1.25 3.00
106 Tomas Kopecky RC 1.25 3.00
107 Marc-Antoine Pouliot RC 1.25 3.00
108 Konstantin Pushkaryov RC 1.00 2.50
109 Phil Kessel RC 2.50 6.00
110 Luc Bourdon RC 1.25 3.00
111 Shea Weber RC 1.25 3.00
112 Guillaume Latendresse RC 3.00 8.00
113 Jordan Staal RC 6.00 15.00
114 Paul Stastny RC 4.00 10.00
115 Anze Kopitar RC 3.00 8.00
116 Jarkko Immonen RC .75 2.00
117 Travis Zajac RC 1.50 4.00
118 Nigel Dawes RC 1.00 2.50
119 Kristopher Letang RC 1.25 3.00
120 Ryan Potulny RC 1.25 3.00
121 Ryan Shannon RC 1.00 2.50
122 Marc-Edouard Vlasic RC 1.00 2.50
123 Noah Welch RC 1.00 2.50
124 Ladislav Smid RC 1.00 2.50
125 Matt Carle RC 1.25 3.00
126 Loui Eriksson RC 1.00 2.50
127 Brendan Bell RC 1.00 2.50
128 Ian White RC 1.00 2.50
129 Jeremy Williams RC 1.00 2.50
130 Eric Fehr RC 1.25 3.00

2006-07 Be A Player Portraits Dual Signature Portraits

ODDS 1:6
DSBB Brad Boyes 8.00 20.00
Patrice Bergeron
DSCJ Zdeno Chara 8.00 20.00
Milan Jurcina
DSCT Joe Thornton 30.00 80.00
Jonathan Cheechoo SP
DSDB Chris Drury 15.00 40.00
Daniel Briere
DSDJ Jason Spezza 20.00 50.00
Dany Heatley
DSFN Rick Nash 15.00 40.00
Sergei Federov
DSFW Marc-Andre Fleury 15.00 40.00
Ryan Whitney
DSGC Simon Gagne 12.00 30.00
Jeff Carter
DSGN Scott Niedermayer 20.00 50.00
Jean-Sebastien Giguere
DSHL Dominik Hasek 40.00 80.00
Nicklas Lidstrom
DSHS Milan Hejduk 6.00 15.00
Marek Svatos
DSIT Jarome Iginla 15.00 40.00
Alex Tanguay
DSJB Olli Jokinen 6.00 15.00
Jay Bouwmeester
DSKK Saku Koivu 15.00 30.00
Mikko Koivu
DSKV Paul Kariya 20.00 40.00
Tomas Vokoun
DSLN Markus Naslund 25.00 50.00
Roberto Luongo
DSLP Henrik Lundqvist 15.00 40.00
Petr Prucha
DSMT Mike Modano 20.00 40.00
Marty Turco
DSNT Tuomo Ruutu 8.00 20.00
Nikolai Khabibulin
DSOK Olaf Kolzig 40.00 80.00
Alexander Ovechkin
DSRU Mike Richards 6.00 15.00
R.J. Umberger
DSSM Joe Sakic 50.00 80.00
Mike Modano SP
DSWG Doug Weight 6.00 15.00
Bill Guerin
DSWS Eric Staal 12.00 30.00
Cam Ward

2006-07 Be A Player Portraits First Exposures

ODS 1 PER PACK
EAK Andrei Kostitsyn 2.50 6.00
EAL Andrew Ladd 2.50 6.00
EAM Andrej Meszaros 2.50 6.00
EAO Alexander Ovechkin 6.00 15.00
EAP Alexander Perezhogin 2.50 6.00
EAS Alexander Steen 3.00 8.00
EBB Brandon Bochenski 2.50 6.00
EBW Brad Winchester 2.50 6.00
ECB Cam Barker 2.50 6.00
ECP Corey Perry 4.00 10.00
ECW Cam Ward 4.00 10.00
EDB Derek Boogaard 2.50 6.00
EDP Daniel Paille 2.50 6.00
EDP Dion Phaneuf 4.00 10.00
EEN Eric Nystrom 2.50 6.00
EGB Gilbert Brule 3.00 8.00
EHL Henrik Lundqvist 5.00 12.00
EHT Hannu Toivonen 3.00 8.00
EJC Jeff Carter 3.00 8.00
EJF Johan Franzen 2.50 6.00
EJG Josh Gorges 2.50 6.00
EJH Jim Howard 3.00 8.00
EJJ Jussi Jokinen 2.00 5.00
EJK Jakub Klepis 2.50 6.00
EJT Jeff Tambellini 2.50 6.00
EMJ Milan Jurcina 2.50 6.00
EMK Mikko Koivu 2.00 5.00
EMR Mike Richards 3.00 8.00
EPB Peter Budaj 3.00 8.00
EPN Petteri Nokelainen 2.50 6.00
EPP Petr Prucha 2.50 6.00
ERG Ryan Getzlaf 4.00 10.00
ERO Rostislav Olesz 2.00 5.00
ERS Ryan Suter 2.50 6.00
ERU R.J. Umberger 2.50 6.00
ERW Ryan Whitney 2.50 6.00
ESC Sidney Crosby 25.00 60.00
ETV Thomas Vanek 3.00 8.00
EVF Valtteri Filppula 2.50 6.00
EWW Wojtek Wolski 2.50 6.00
EYD Yann Danis 3.00 8.00
EZP Zach Parise 3.00 8.00

2006-07 Be A Player Portraits Quadruple Signature Portraits

RINT RUN 10 #'d SETS
OT PRICED DUE TO SCARCITY
HVHH Tomas Vokoun
Marian Hossa
Dominik Hasek
Milan Hejduk
KIHN Paul Kariya
Jarome Iginla
Dany Heatley
Rick Nash
KJP Saku Koivu
Olli Jokinen
Miikka Kiprusoff
Joni Pitkanen
SSTS Joe Sakic
Joe Thornton
Jason Spezza
Eric Staal

2006-07 Be A Player Portraits Sensational Six

RINT RUN 5 #'d SETS
OT PRICED DUE TO SCARCITY
S1ST Mike Modano
Mats Sundin
Joe Thornton
Rick Nash
Marc-Andre Fleury
Alexander Ovechkin
SCDN Jarome Iginla
Simon Gagne
Jason Spezza
Dany Heatley
Rick Nash
Eric Staal
SGOL Dominik Hasek
Roberto Luongo
Jean-Sebastien Giguere
Marty Turco
Marc-Andre Fleury
Cam Ward
SSJM Joe Sakic
Mats Sundin
Patrick Marleau
Saku Koivu
Markus Naslund
Joe Thornton
SSTR Nicklas Lidstrom
Sergei Fedorov
Joe Sakic
Mike Modano
Mats Sundin
Dominik Hasek

2006-07 Be A Player Portraits Signature Portraits

NE PER PACK
PAL Andrew Ladd 6.00 15.00
PAO Alexander Ovechkin 50.00 100.00
PAT Alex Tanguay 6.00 15.00
PBB Brad Boyes 6.00 15.00
PBG Bill Guerin 6.00 15.00
PBH Bobby Holik 6.00 15.00
PBL Brian Leetch 12.00 30.00
PBM Brenden Morrow 8.00 20.00
PBR Brian Rolston 6.00 15.00
PBS Brent Seabrook 6.00 15.00
PBW Brad Winchester 6.00 15.00
PCA Colby Armstrong 8.00 20.00
PCB Cam Barker 6.00 15.00
PCD Chris Drury SP 20.00 50.00
SPCH Jonathan Cheechoo 8.00 20.00
SPCW Cam Ward 10.00 25.00
SPDB Daniel Briere SP 25.00 50.00
SPDH Dany Heatley 12.00 30.00
SPDP Daniel Paille 8.00 20.00
SPDR Dwayne Roloson 10.00 25.00
SPDW Doug Weight SP 15.00 40.00
SPEJ Ed Jovanovski 6.00 15.00
SPEM Evgeni Malkin 40.00 80.00
SPEN Evgeni Nabokov 6.00 15.00
SPES Robert Esche 8.00 20.00
SPGM Glen Murray 6.00 15.00
SPHA Jeff Halpern 6.00 15.00
SPHE Milan Hejduk 6.00 15.00
SPHK Dominik Hasek 20.00 50.00
SPHL Henrik Lundqvist 20.00 40.00
SPHT Hannu Toivonen 6.00 15.00
SPJB Jay Bouwmeester SP 20.00 40.00
SPJC Jeff Carter 8.00 20.00
SPJG Jean-Sebastien Giguere SP 25.00 60.00
SPJI Jarome Iginla 12.00 30.00
SPJJ Jussi Jokinen 6.00 15.00
SPJO Joe Thornton 40.00 80.00
SPJP Joni Pitkanen 6.00 15.00
SPJS Joe Sakic 30.00 60.00
SPKB Keith Ballard 6.00 15.00
SPKL Kari Lehtonen 12.00 30.00
SPKO Mikko Koivu 6.00 15.00
SPKP Keith Primeau 6.00 15.00
SPLE John LeClair 10.00 25.00
SPLS Lee Stempniak 8.00 20.00
SPMA Marc-Andre Fleury 20.00 40.00
SPMB Mark Bell 6.00 15.00
SPMG Martin Gerber 10.00 25.00
SPMH Marian Hossa 12.00 30.00
SPMJ Milan Jurcina 6.00 15.00
SPMK Miikka Kiprusoff 15.00 40.00
SPMM Mike Modano SP 60.00 100.00
SPMN Markus Naslund 12.00 30.00
SPMO Brendan Morrison 6.00 15.00
SPMS Marek Svatos 6.00 15.00
SPMT Marty Turco 8.00 20.00
SPNH Nathan Horton 6.00 15.00
SPNK Nikolai Khabibulin SP 25.00 50.00
SPNL Nicklas Lidstrom 20.00 50.00
SPNZ Nikolai Zherdev 6.00 15.00
SPOJ Olli Jokinen SP 25.00 50.00
SPOK Olaf Kolzig 12.00 30.00
SPPB Patrice Bergeron 12.00 30.00
SPPK Paul Kariya 25.00 50.00
SPPM Patrick Marleau 8.00 20.00
SPPP Petr Prucha 6.00 15.00
SPRB Rob Blake 8.00 20.00
SPRD Mike Richards 8.00 20.00
SPRJ R.J. Umberger 6.00 15.00
SPRL Roberto Luongo 30.00 60.00
SPRM Ryan Miller 20.00 40.00
SPRN Rick Nash 10.00 25.00
SPRO Rostislav Olesz 6.00 15.00
SPRW Ryan Whitney 8.00 20.00
SPSB Steve Bernier 6.00 15.00
SPSC Sidney Crosby SP 300.00 450.00
SPSD Shane Doan 6.00 15.00
SPSF Sergei Fedorov SP 20.00 50.00
SPSG Simon Gagne SP 20.00 50.00
SPSJ Matt Stajan 6.00 15.00
SPSK Saku Koivu 10.00 25.00
SPSM Mats Sundin 25.00 50.00
SPSN Scott Niedermayer 10.00 25.00
SPSP Jason Spezza 10.00 25.00
SPSR Ryan Suter 6.00 15.00
SPSS Steve Sullivan 6.00 15.00
SPST Eric Staal 10.00 25.00
SPTP Tom Poti 6.00 15.00
SPTR Tuomo Ruutu 6.00 15.00
SPTV Thomas Vanek 10.00 25.00
SPVO Tomas Vokoun 10.00 25.00
SPWR Wade Redden 6.00 15.00
SPWW Wojtek Wolski 6.00 15.00
SPZC Zdeno Chara 8.00 20.00

2006-07 Be A Player Portraits Timeless Tens

PRINT RUN 3 #'d SETS
NOT PRICED DUE TO SCARCITY
TTCAN Joe Thornton
Jarome Iginla
Simon Gagne
Jason Spezza
Alex Tanguay
Jonathan Cheechoo
Dany Heatley
Rick Nash
Patrice Bergeron
Eric Staal
TTNET Tomas Vokoun
Dominik Hasek
Roberto Luongo
Jean-Sebastien Giguere
Evgeni Nabokov
Henrik Lundqvist
Martin Gerber
Miikka Kiprusoff
Cam Ward
Nikolai Khabibulin

2006-07 Be A Player Portraits Triple Signature Portraits

PRINT RUN 25 #'d SETS
TBOS Glen Murray 40.00 80.00
Brad Boyes
Patrice Bergeron
TBUF Chris Drury 60.00 125.00
Daniel Briere
Ryan Miller
TCGY Alex Tanguay
Miikka Kiprusoff
Jarome Iginla
TCLB Rick Nash 75.00 150.00
Nikolai Zherdev
Sergei Fedorov
TCOL Joe Sakic 75.00 150.00
Milan Hejduk
Marek Svatos
TLWF Roberto Luongo 75.00 150.00
Marc-Andre Fleury
Cam Ward
TNSS Jason Spezza 75.00 150.00
Rick Nash
Eric Staal
TOTT Dany Heatley 75.00 150.00
Wade Redden
Jason Spezza
TSJS Joe Thornton 50.00 125.00
Mark Bell
Jonathan Cheechoo
TSSM Joe Sakic 75.00 175.00
Mike Modano
Mats Sundin

2002-03 BAP All-Star Edition

Released to coincide with the 2003 NHL All-Star game, this 150-card set featured players who made appearances in past all-star games. Cards 101-150 were short-printed to just 100 copies each and featured rookies.

COMP.SET w/o SP's (100) 40.00 80.00
101-150 SP/RC PRINT RUN 100 SER.#'d SETS
1 Daniel Alfredsson .25 .60
2 Tony Amonte .25 .60
2001 Denver
3 Ed Belfour .30 .75
1996 Boston
4 Rob Blake .25 .60
2002 Los Angeles
5 Peter Bondra .25 .60
1999 Tampa Bay
6 Radek Bonk .10 .25
2000 Toronto
7 Martin Brodeur .75 2.00
8 Martin Brodeur .75 2.00
9 Martin Brodeur .75 2.00
10 Valeri Bure .10 .25
2000 Toronto
11 Pavel Bure .30 .75
1997 San Jose
12 Pavel Bure .50 1.25
1997 San Jose
13 Sean Burke .25 .60
2002 Los Angeles
14 Roman Cechmanek .25 .60
2001 Denver
15 Chris Chelios .30 .75
2002 Los Angeles
16 Vincent Damphousse .10 .25
2002 Los Angeles
17 Eric Daze .25 .60
2002 Los Angeles
18 Pavol Demitra .25 .60
2000 Toronto
19 Patrik Elias .25 .60
2002 Los Angeles
20 Sergei Fedorov .50 1.25
21 Sergei Fedorov .60 1.50
1996 Boston
22 Theo Fleury .10 .25
1997 San Jose
23 Peter Forsberg .75 2.00
24 Peter Forsberg .75 2.00
1996 Boston
25 Peter Forsberg .75 2.00
1998 Vancouver
26 Simon Gagne .30 .75
2001 Denver
27 Scott Gomez .10 .25
2000 Toronto
28 Bill Guerin .25 .60
2001 Denver
29 Milan Hejduk .30 .75
2001 Denver
30 Phil Housley .10 .25
2000 Toronto
31 Brett Hull .40 1.00
32 Jarome Iginla .40 1.00
33 Arturs Irbe .25 .60
1999 Tampa Bay
34 Jaromir Jagr .50 1.25
35 Jaromir Jagr .50 1.25
1998 Vancouver
36 Jaromir Jagr .50 1.25
1996 Boston
37 Curtis Joseph .30 .75
2000 Toronto
38 Ed Jovanovski .25 .60
2002 Los Angeles
39 Tomas Kaberle .10 .25
2002 Los Angeles
40 Sami Kapanen .10 .25
2002 Los Angeles
41 Paul Kariya .30 .75
1997 San Jose
42 Paul Kariya .30 .75
2001 Denver
43 Paul Kariya .30 .75
1996 Boston
44 Nikolai Khabibulin .30 .75
2002 Los Angeles
45 Saku Koivu .30 .75
1998 Vancouver
46 Olaf Kolzig .25 .60
2000 Toronto
47 Alex Kovalev .25 .60
2001 Denver
48 John LeClair .30 .75
1997 San Jose
49 Brian Leetch .25 .60
2001 Denver
50 Brian Leetch .25 .60
1994 New York
51 Mario Lemieux 2.00 5.00
52 Mario Lemieux 2.00 5.00
53 Mario Lemieux 2.00 5.00
54 Nicklas Lidstrom .30 .75
1999 Tampa Bay
55 Nicklas Lidstrom .30 .75
2001 Denver
56 Eric Lindros .30 .75
2000 Toronto
57 Al MacInnis .25 .60
2000 Toronto
58 Mark Messier .30 .75
1994 New York
59 Mark Messier .30 .75
1996 Boston
60 Mike Modano .50 1.25
61 Mike Modano .50 1.25
62 Alexander Mogilny .25 .60
1996 Boston
63 Evgeni Nabokov .25 .60
2001 Denver
64 Markus Naslund .30 .75
2001 Denver
65 Scott Niedermayer .10 .25
1998 Vancouver
66 Owen Nolan .25 .60
2002 Los Angeles
67 Teppo Numminen .10 .25
2001 Denver
68 Chris Osgood .25 .60
1996 Boston
69 Sandis Ozolinsh .10 .25
2002 Los Angeles
70 Zigmund Palffy .25 .60
2001 Denver
71 Felix Potvin .30 .75
1996 Boston
72 Chris Pronger .25 .60
2000 Toronto
73 Mark Recchi .25 .60
2000 Toronto
74 Mike Richter .25 .60
2000 Toronto
75 Luc Robitaille .25 .60
1999 Tampa Bay
76 Jeremy Roenick .40 1.00
77 Patrick Roy 1.50 4.00
78 Patrick Roy 1.50 4.00
2001 Denver
79 Patrick Roy 1.50 4.00
1994 New York
80 Joe Sakic .60 1.50
81 Joe Sakic .60 1.50
2001 Denver
82 Tommy Salo .25 .60
2000 Toronto
83 Teemu Selanne .30 .75
2002 Los Angeles
84 Brendan Shanahan .30 .75
2002 Los Angeles
85 Brendan Shanahan .50 1.25
2000 Toronto
86 Brendan Shanahan .50 1.25
1996 Boston
87 Scott Stevens .25 .60
2000 Toronto
88 Mats Sundin .30 .75
2000 Toronto
89 Mats Sundin .30 .75
1997 San Jose
90 Darryl Sydor .10 .25
1999 Tampa Bay
91 Jose Theodore .40 1.00
92 Joe Thornton .30 .75
2002 Los Angeles
93 Keith Tkachuk .30 .75
1999 Tampa Bay
94 Ron Tugnutt .25 .60
1999 Tampa Bay
95 Roman Turek .25 .60
2000 Toronto
96 Doug Weight .25 .60
2001 Denver
97 Alexei Yashin .10 .25
1994 New York
98 Steve Yzerman 1.50 4.00
99 Steve Yzerman 1.50 4.00
100 Alexei Zhamnov .25 .60
2002 Los Angeles
101 Dany Heatley SP 6.00 15.00
102 Ilya Kovalchuk SP 6.00 15.00
103 Marian Gaborik SP 10.00 25.00
104 Marty Turco SP 5.00 12.00
105 Mike Comrie SP 5.00 12.00
106 Cody Rudkowsky RC 4.00 10.00
107 Levente Szuper RC 4.00 10.00
108 Alex Henry RC 4.00 10.00
109 Lynn Loyns RC 4.00 10.00
110 Tomi Pettinen RC 4.00 10.00
111 Micki Dupont RC 4.00 10.00
112 Shaone Morrisonn RC 6.00 15.00
113 Ryan Miller RC 40.00 100.00
114 Mikael Tellqvist RC 10.00 25.00
115 Dany Sabourin RC 6.00 15.00
116 Tim Thomas RC 10.00 25.00
117 Kurt Sauer RC 4.00 10.00
118 Kari Haakana RC 4.00 10.00
119 Lasse Pirjeta RC 4.00 10.00
120 Shawn Thornton RC 6.00 15.00
121 Curtis Sanford RC 6.00 15.00
122 Dick Tarnstrom RC 4.00 10.00
123 Radovan Somik RC 4.00 10.00
124 Martin Gerber RC 10.00 25.00
125 Dennis Seidenberg RC 4.00 10.00
126 P-M Bouchard RC 10.00 25.00
127 Alexei Smirnov RC 4.00 10.00
128 Ales Hemsky RC 30.00 80.00
129 Stephane Veilleux RC 4.00 10.00
130 Tom Koivisto RC 4.00 10.00
131 Jeff Taffe RC 4.00 10.00
132 Jordan Leopold RC 6.00 15.00
133 Stanislav Chistov RC 6.00 15.00
134 Rick Nash RC 75.00 150.00
135 Chuck Kobasew RC 10.00 25.00
136 Alexander Svitov RC 4.00 10.00
137 Carlo Colaiacovo RC 10.00 25.00
138 Jason Spezza RC 75.00 200.00
139 Henrik Zetterberg RC 40.00 100.00
140 Anton Volchenkov RC 6.00 15.00
141 Ron Hainsey RC 4.00 10.00
142 Jay Bouwmeester RC 15.00 40.00
143 Adam Hall RC 4.00 10.00
144 Steve Eminger RC 4.00 10.00
145 Mike Cammalleri RC 12.00 30.00
146 Dmitri Bykov RC 4.00 10.00
147 Ivan Majesky RC 4.00 10.00
148 Alexander Frolov RC 25.00 60.00
149 Scottie Upshall RC 10.00 25.00
150 Patrick Sharp RC 6.00 15.00

2002-03 BAP All-Star Edition Gold

PRINT RUN 1 SER.#'d SET
NOT PRICED DUE TO SCARCITY

2002-03 BAP All-Star Edition Silver

SILVER PRINT RUN 20 SER.#'d SETS
NOT PRICED DUE TO SCARCITY

2002-03 BAP All-Star Edition Bobble Heads

ONE PER BOX
STATED PRINT RUNS LISTED BELOW
1 Mario Lemieux/1066 20.00 50.00
2 Jose Theodore/1560 10.00 25.00
3 Pavel Bure/2010 10.00 25.00
4 Curtis Joseph/1031 10.00 25.00
5 Martin Brodeur/1530 12.50 30.00
6 Peter Forsberg/2031 12.50 30.00
7 Steve Yzerman/2019 12.50 30.00
8 Jaromir Jagr/2068 10.00 25.00
9 Joe Sakic/1519 10.00 25.00
10 Patrick Roy/1033 20.00 50.00

2002-03 BAP All-Star Edition He Shoots-He Scores Points

ONE PER PACK
RED.PROGRAM HAS EXPIRED
1 Brian Leetch 1 pt. .10 .25
2 Eric Lindros 1 pt. .10 .25
3 Mark Messier 1 pt. .10 .25
4 Owen Nolan 1 pt. .10 .25
5 Teemu Selanne 1 pt. .10 .25
6 Brendan Shanahan 1 pt. .10 .25
7 Mats Sundin 1 pt. .10 .25
8 Alexei Yashin 1 pt. .10 .25
9 Martin Brodeur 2 pt. .10 .25
10 Pavel Bure 2 pt. .10 .25
11 Sergei Fedorov 2 pt. .10 .25
12 Jaromir Jagr 2 pt. .10 .25
13 Curtis Joseph 2 pt. .10 .25
14 Nicklas Lidstrom 2 pt. .10 .25
15 Mike Modano 2 pt. .10 .25
16 Patrick Roy 2 pt. .10 .25
17 Joe Sakic 2 pt. .10 .25
18 Peter Forsberg 3 pt. .10 .25
19 Mario Lemieux 3 pt. .10 .25
20 Steve Yzerman 3 pt. .10 .25

2002-03 BAP All-Star Edition He Shoots-He Score Prizes

STATED PRINT RUN 20 SETS
NOT PRICED DUE TO SCARCITY
1 Tony Amonte
2 Ed Belfour
3 Martin Brodeur
4 Pavel Bure
5 Chris Chelios
6 Sergei Fedorov
7 Peter Forsberg
8 Jaromir Jagr
9 Curtis Joseph
10 Paul Kariya
11 Nikolai Khabibulin
12 John LeClair
13 Brian Leetch
14 Mario Lemieux
15 Nicklas Lidstrom
16 Eric Lindros
17 Al MacInnis
18 Mark Messier
19 Mike Modano
20 Markus Naslund
21 Owen Nolan
22 Chris Pronger
23 Mark Recchi
24 Patrick Roy
25 Joe Sakic
26 Teemu Selanne
27 Brendan Shanahan
28 Mats Sundin
29 Alexei Yashin
30 Steve Yzerman

2002-03 BAP All-Star Edition Jerseys

*MULT.COLOR SWATCH: .75X TO 1.5X HI
STAT.PRINT RUN 100 SETS
1 Daniel Alfredsson 6.00 15.00
1997 San Jose
2 Tony Amonte 6.00 15.00
2001 Denver
3 Ed Belfour 8.00 20.00
1996 Boston
4 Rob Blake 6.00 15.00
2002 Los Angeles
5 Peter Bondra 6.00 15.00
1999 Tampa Bay
6 Radek Bonk 4.00 10.00
2000 Toronto
7 Martin Brodeur 15.00 40.00
8 Martin Brodeur 15.00 40.00
9 Martin Brodeur 15.00 40.00
10 Valeri Bure 4.00 10.00
2000 Toronto
11 Pavel Bure 8.00 20.00
1997 San Jose
12 Pavel Bure 8.00 20.00
1997 San Jose
13 Sean Burke 4.00 10.00
2002 Los Angeles
14 Roman Cechmanek 4.00 10.00
2001 Denver
15 Chris Chelios 8.00 20.00
2002 Los Angeles
16 Vincent Damphousse 4.00 10.00
2002 Los Angeles
17 Eric Daze 4.00 10.00
2002 Los Angeles
18 Pavol Demitra 4.00 10.00
2000 Toronto
19 Patrik Elias 4.00 10.00
2002 Los Angeles
20 Sergei Fedorov 8.00 20.00
2002 Los Angeles
21 Sergei Fedorov 8.00 20.00
1996 Boston
22 Theo Fleury 6.00 15.00
1997 San Jose
23 Peter Forsberg 12.50 25.00
2001 Denver
24 Peter Forsberg 10.00 25.00
1996 Boston
25 Peter Forsberg 10.00 25.00
1998 Vancouver
26 Simon Gagne 8.00 20.00
2001 Denver
27 Scott Gomez 6.00 15.00
2000 Toronto
28 Bill Guerin 6.00 15.00
2001 Denver
29 Milan Hejduk 8.00 20.00
2001 Denver
30 Phil Housley 4.00 10.00
2000 Toronto
31 Brett Hull 10.00 25.00
1994 New York
32 Jarome Iginla 10.00 25.00
2002 Los Angeles
33 Arturs Irbe 6.00 15.00
1999 Tampa Bay
34 Jaromir Jagr 10.00 25.00
2000 Toronto
35 Jaromir Jagr 10.00 25.00
1998 Vancouver
36 Jaromir Jagr 10.00 25.00
1996 Boston
37 Curtis Joseph 8.00 20.00
2000 Toronto
38 Ed Jovanovski 4.00 10.00
2002 Los Angeles
39 Tomas Kaberle 4.00 10.00
2002 Los Angeles
40 Sami Kapanen 4.00 10.00
2002 Los Angeles
41 Paul Kariya 8.00 20.00
1997 San Jose
42 Paul Kariya 8.00 20.00
2001 Denver
43 Paul Kariya 8.00 20.00
1996 Boston
44 Nikolai Khabibulin 8.00 20.00
2002 Los Angeles
45 Saku Koivu 8.00 20.00
1998 Vancouver
46 Olaf Kolzig 6.00 15.00
2000 Toronto
47 Alex Kovalev 4.00 10.00
2001 Denver
48 John LeClair 6.00 15.00
1997 San Jose
49 Brian Leetch 6.00 15.00
2001 Denver
50 Brian Leetch 6.00 15.00
1994 New York
51 Mario Lemieux 20.00 50.00
52 Mario Lemieux 20.00 50.00
53 Mario Lemieux 20.00 50.00
54 Nicklas Lidstrom 8.00 20.00
1999 Tampa Bay
55 Nicklas Lidstrom 8.00 20.00
2001 Denver
56 Eric Lindros 8.00 20.00
2000 Toronto
57 Al MacInnis 6.00 15.00
2000 Toronto
58 Mark Messier 15.00 40.00
1994 New York
59 Mark Messier 15.00 40.00
1996 Boston
60 Mike Modano 8.00 20.00
61 Mike Modano 8.00 20.00
62 Alexander Mogilny 6.00 15.00
1996 Boston
63 Evgeni Nabokov 6.00 15.00
2001 Denver
64 Markus Naslund 8.00 20.00
2001 Denver
65 Scott Niedermayer 6.00 15.00
1998 Vancouver
66 Owen Nolan 6.00 15.00
2002 Los Angeles
67 Teppo Numminen 4.00 10.00
2001 Denver
68 Chris Osgood 6.00 15.00
1996 Boston
69 Sandis Ozolinsh 4.00 10.00
2002 Los Angeles
70 Zigmund Palffy 6.00 15.00
2001 Denver
71 Felix Potvin 8.00 20.00
1996 Boston
72 Chris Pronger 6.00 15.00
2000 Toronto
73 Mark Recchi 6.00 15.00
2000 Toronto
74 Mike Richter 6.00 15.00
2000 Toronto
75 Luc Robitaille 6.00 15.00
1999 Tampa Bay
76 Jeremy Roenick 10.00 25.00
2000 Toronto
77 Patrick Roy 20.00 50.00
2002 Los Angeles
78 Patrick Roy 20.00 50.00
2001 Denver
79 Patrick Roy 20.00 50.00
1994 New York
80 Joe Sakic 15.00 40.00
1998 Vancouver
81 Joe Sakic 15.00 40.00
2001 Denver
82 Tommy Salo 4.00 10.00
2000 Toronto
83 Teemu Selanne 8.00 20.00
2002 Los Angeles
84 Brendan Shanahan 8.00 20.00
2002 Los Angeles
85 Brendan Shanahan 8.00 20.00
2000 Toronto
86 Brendan Shanahan 8.00 20.00
1996 Boston
87 Scott Stevens 4.00 10.00
2000 Toronto
88 Mats Sundin 8.00 20.00
2000 Toronto
89 Mats Sundin 8.00 20.00
1997 San Jose
90 Darryl Sydor 4.00 10.00
1999 Tampa Bay
91 Jose Theodore 8.00 20.00
2002 Los Angeles
92 Joe Thornton 12.00 30.00
2002 Los Angeles
93 Keith Tkachuk 8.00 20.00
1999 Tampa Bay
94 Ron Tugnutt 4.00 10.00
1999 Tampa Bay
95 Roman Turek 4.00 10.00
2000 Toronto
96 Doug Weight 4.00 10.00
2001 Denver
97 Alexei Yashin 4.00 10.00
1994 New York
98 Steve Yzerman 15.00 40.00
99 Steve Yzerman 15.00 40.00
100 Alexei Zhamnov 4.00 10.00
2002 Los Angeles

2002-03 BAP All-Star Edition Jerseys Gold

STATED PRINT RUN 10 SETS
NOT PRICED DUE TO SCARCITY

2002-03 BAP All-Star Edition Jerseys Silver

*SILVER: .5X TO 1.25X BASIC JERSEY
STATED PRINT RUN 30 SETS

2002-03 BAP First Edition

This 440-card set contained two different subsets; "Statistical Leaders" and "Draft Picks". The draft picks cards featured different players in retail and hobby packs and are noted below with "H" or "R" suffixes. Cards 426-440 (both retail and hobby) were available by a mail-in redemption found in packs only.

COMPLETE SET (425)
CARDS 401H-425H AVAIL.HOBBY PACKS
CARDS 401R-425R AVAIL.RETAIL PACKS
CARDS 426H-440H AVAIL.BY MAIL-IN
CARDS 426R-440R AVAIL.BY MAIL-IN
1 Mario Lemieux 2.00 5.00
2 Sergei Gonchar .10 .25
3 Brian Leetch .25 .60
4 Felix Potvin .30 .75
5 Sandis Ozolinsh .10 .25
6 Steven Reinprecht .10 .25
7 Byron Dafoe .25 .60

8 Mark Bell .10 .25
9 Jeff O'Neill .10 .25
10 Sean Burke .25 .60
11 Darcy Tucker .10 .25
12 Scott Stevens .25 .60
13 David Aebischer .25 .60
14 Jocelyn Thibault .25 .60
15 Radek Bonk .10 .25
16 Milan Hejduk .30 .75
17 Zigmund Palffy .25 .60
18 Luc Robitaille .25 .60
19 Tomas Kaberle .10 .25
20 Rostislav Klesla .10 .25
21 Alexei Zhamnov .10 .25
22 Ron Francis .25 .60
23 Mike Fisher .10 .25
24 Dany Heatley .40 1.00
25 Kyle McLaren .10 .25
26 Doug Weight .25 .60
27 Henrik Sedin .10 .25
28 Roman Turek .25 .60
29 Adam Deadmarsh .10 .25
30 Sami Kapanen .10 .25
31 Sergei Samsonov .25 .60
32 Kristian Huselius .10 .25
33 Dimitri Yushkevich .10 .25
34 Patrik Elias .25 .60
35 Nick Boynton .10 .25
36 Martin Biron .25 .60
37 Brad Richards .25 .60
38 Alyn McCauley .10 .25
39 Daniel Sedin .10 .25
40 Teppo Numminen .10 .25
41 Luke Richardson .10 .25
42 Manny Fernandez .25 .60
43 Vincent Lecavalier .30 .75
44 Mattias Ohlund .10 .25
45 Milan Kraft .10 .25
46 Mike Dunham .25 .60
47 Derian Hatcher .10 .25
48 Oleg Tverdovsky .10 .25
49 Shane Doan .10 .25
50 Martin Skoula .10 .25
51 John LeClair .30 .75
52 Tommy Salo .25 .60
53 Miroslav Satan .25 .60
54 Bryan Berard .10 .25
55 Roman Cechmanek .25 .60
56 Alexei Morozov .10 .25
57 J-S Giguere .25 .60
58 Pierre Turgeon .25 .60
59 Martin Straka .10 .25
60 Stephane Yelle .10 .25
61 Marc Savard .10 .25
62 Sergei Zubov .10 .25
63 Jeff Friesen .10 .25
64 Daniel Briere .10 .25
65 Patrik Stefan .10 .25
66 Pavol Demitra .25 .60
67 Radek Dvorak .10 .25
68 Marty Turco .25 .60
69 Keith Tkachuk .30 .75
70 Maxim Afinogenov .10 .25
71 Mika Noronen .25 .60
72 Evgeni Nabokov .25 .60
73 Todd Bertuzzi .30 .75
74 Valeri Bure .10 .25
75 Marian Hossa .30 .75
76 J-P Dumont .10 .25
77 Niklas Sundstrom .10 .25
78 Eric Daze .25 .60
79 Brian Boucher .25 .60
80 Nikolai Khabibulin .30 .75
81 Darren McCarty .10 .25
82 Pavel Brendl .10 .25
83 Mark Recchi .25 .60
84 Dan Cloutier .25 .60
85 Manny Legace .25 .60
86 Keith Primeau .10 .25
87 Alex Tanguay .25 .60
88 Ed Jovanovski .25 .60
89 Roberto Luongo .40 1.00
90 Andreas Johansson .10 .25
91 Steve Shields .25 .60
92 Saku Koivu .30 .75
93 Chris Drury .25 .60
94 Olaf Kolzig .25 .60
95 Jan Hrdina .10 .25
96 Ivan Novoseltsev .10 .25
97 Kenny Jonsson .10 .25
98 Martin Havlat .25 .60
99 Scott Niedermayer .10 .25
100 Chris Phillips .10 .25
101 Tony Amonte .25 .60
102 Alexander Mogilny .25 .60
103 Chris Pronger .25 .60
104 Chris Gratton .10 .25
105 Sergei Fedorov .50 1.25
106 David Legwand .25 .60
107 Ron Tugnutt .25 .60
108 Steven McCarthy .10 .25
109 Brian Rolston .10 .25
110 Bobby Holik .10 .25
111 Darryl Sydor .10 .25
112 Steve Sullivan .10 .25
113 Toby Petersen .10 .25
114 Scott Gomez .10 .25
115 Adam Foote .10 .25
116 Rob Niedermayer .10 .25
117 Arturs Irbe .25 .60
118 Al MacInnis .25 .60
119 Jeff Hackett .25 .60
120 Pavel Bure .30 .75
121 Patrick Lalime .25 .60
122 Vincent Damphousse .10 .25
123 Steve Passmore .25 .60
124 Simon Gagne .30 .75
125 Shawn McEachern .10 .25
126 Bryan McCabe .10 .25
127 Jamie Storr .25 .60
128 Mike Richter .30 .75
129 Petr Sykora .10 .25
130 Trevor Kidd .25 .60
131 Jaromir Jagr .50 1.25
132 Bill Guerin .25 .60
133 Mark Messier .30 .75
134 Ilya Kovalchuk .40 1.00
135 Teemu Selanne .30 .75
136 Dominik Hasek .60 1.50
137 Mats Sundin .30 .75
138 Jose Theodore .40 1.00
139 Brendan Shanahan .30 .75
140 Daniel Alfredsson .25 .60
141 Martin Brodeur .75 2.00
142 Jarome Iginla .40 1.00
143 Peter Bondra .30 .75
144 Peter Forsberg .75 2.00
145 Curtis Joseph .30 .75
146 Alexei Yashin .10 .25
147 Patrick Roy 1.50 4.00
148 Markus Naslund .30 .75
149 Jeremy Roenick .40 1.00
150 Eric Lindros .30 .75
151 Steve Yzerman 1.50 4.00
152 Marian Gaborik .60 1.50
153 Mike Modano .50 1.25
154 Joe Sakic .60 1.50
155 Paul Kariya .30 .75
156 Owen Nolan .25 .60
157 Rob Blake .25 .60
158 Nicklas Lidstrom .30 .75
159 Joe Thornton .50 1.25
160 Mario Lemieux 2.00 5.00
161 Magnus Arvedson .10 .25
162 Chris Clark .10 .25
163 Don Sweeney .10 .25
164 Fredrik Modin .10 .25
165 Matt Cooke .10 .25
166 Rhett Warrener .10 .25
167 Tim Taylor .10 .25
168 Viktor Kozlov .10 .25
169 Michal Rozsival .10 .25
170 Mathieu Schneider .10 .25
171 Matt Cullen .10 .25
172 Vladimir Malakhov .10 .25
173 Mattias Norstrom .10 .25
174 Greg Johnson .10 .25
175 Eric Desjardins .10 .25
176 Damian Rhodes .10 .25
177 Stephane Quintal .10 .25
178 Sami Salo .10 .25
179 Craig Rivet .10 .25
180 Oleg Saprykin .10 .25
181 Chris Therien .10 .25
182 Robyn Regehr .10 .25
183 Erik Cole .10 .25
184 Ed Belfour .30 .75
185 Chris Chelios .30 .75
186 Pavel Datsyuk .30 .75
187 Mike Comrie .25 .60
188 Doug Gilmour .25 .60
189 Johan Hedberg .25 .60
190 Brett Hull .40 1.00
191 Theo Fleury .10 .25
192 Rick DiPietro .25 .60
193 Marcus Ragnarsson .10 .25
194 Mike Peca .10 .25
195 Ryan Smyth .10 .25
196 Ruslan Salei .10 .25
197 Anson Carter .25 .60
198 Eric Brewer .10 .25
199 Alexei Kovalev .25 .60
200 Gary Roberts .10 .25
201 Micki Dupont RC .10 .25
202 Pat Verbeek .10 .25
203 Dmitri Kalinin .10 .25
204 Brad Stuart .25 .60
205 Brent Johnson .25 .60
206 Todd White .10 .25
207 Andy McDonald .10 .25
208 Glen Murray .10 .25
209 Chris Osgood .25 .60
210 Tim Connolly .10 .25
211 Scott Hartnell .10 .25
212 Radim Vrbata .10 .25
213 Dimitri Khristich .10 .25
214 Brendan Morrison .25 .60
215 Matt Henderson RC .10 .25
216 Jason Allison .10 .25
217 Ray Whitney .10 .25
218 Niklas Hagman .10 .25
219 Andrew Brunette .10 .25
220 Brian Rafalski .10 .25
221 Mark Parrish .10 .25
222 Dave Andreychuk .10 .25
223 Dainius Zubrus .10 .25
224 P.J. Stock .10 .25
225 Espen Knutsen .10 .25
226 Jiri Dopita .10 .25
227 Jeff Jillson .10 .25
228 Tie Domi .25 .60
229 Milan Hnilicka .25 .60
230 Martin Lapointe .10 .25
231 Taylor Pyatt .10 .25
232 Kyle Calder .10 .25
233 Marc Denis .25 .60
234 Brenden Morrow .25 .60
235 Cliff Ronning .10 .25
236 Wade Redden .10 .25
237 Kris Beech .10 .25
238 Patrick Marleau .25 .60
239 Corey Schwab .25 .60
240 Nikita Alexeev .10 .25
241 Miikka Kiprusoff .25 .60
242 Jason Arnott .10 .25
243 Joe Nieuwendyk .25 .60
244 Adam Oates .25 .60
245 Darius Kasparaitis .10 .25
246 Mike York .10 .25
247 Donald Brashear .10 .25
248 Kevin Weekes .25 .60
249 Jaroslav Spacek .10 .25
250 Alex Auld .10 .25
251 Denis Arkhipov .10 .25
252 Cory Stillman .10 .25
253 Craig Conroy .10 .25
254 Dan Blackburn .25 .60
255 Vaclav Nedorost .25 .60
256 Ladislav Nagy .10 .25
257 Lukas Krajicek .10 .25
258 Raffi Torres .10 .25
259 Richard Zednik .10 .25
260 Brad Bombardir .10 .25
261 Ilja Bryzgalov .25 .60
262 Frederic Cassivi .10 .25
263 Geoff Sanderson .10 .25
264 Dwayne Roloson .10 .25
265 Jani Hurme .25 .60
266 Sebastien Centomo .25 .60
267 Jeff Halpern .10 .25
268 Mikael Renberg .10 .25
269 Vaclav Prospal .10 .25
270 Sylvain Blouin RC .10 .25
271 Olivier Michaud .25 .60
272 Pascal Dupuis .10 .25
273 Michael Nylander .10 .25
274 Daymond Langkow .25 .60
275 Mike Sillinger .10 .25
276 Yanic Perreault .10 .25
277 Oleg Petrov .10 .25
278 Rod Brind'Amour .25 .60
279 Scott Clemmensen .25 .60
280 Jason Smith .10 .25
281 Vladimir Orszagh .10 .25
282 Stephen Weiss .10 .25
283 Tony Hrkac .10 .25
284 Ty Conklin .25 .60
285 Ulf Dahlen .10 .25
286 Karel Pilar .10 .25
287 Krys Kolanos .10 .25
288 Marcel Hossa .10 .25
289 Martin Prusek .25 .60
290 Robert Svehla .10 .25
291 Radoslav Suchy .10 .25
292 Alexander Khavanov .10 .25
293 Andy Delmore .10 .25
294 Adrian Aucoin .10 .25
295 Bates Battaglia .10 .25
296 Jussi Markkanen .10 .25
297 Martin Erat .10 .25
298 Jim Dowd .10 .25
299 Mark Hartigan .10 .25
300 Neil Little .10 .25
301 Markus Naslund UC .40 1.00
302 Bill Guerin UC .30 .75
303 Nicklas Lidstrom UC .40 1.00
304 Sergei Fedorov UC .75 2.00
305 Mats Sundin UC .40 1.00
306 Teemu Selanne UC .40 1.00
307 Sergei Gonchar UC .12 .30
308 Brian Leetch UC .40 1.00
309 Jeremy Roenick UC .50 1.25
310 Jaromir Jagr UC .60 1.50
311 Mark Recchi UC .30 .75
312 Sandis Ozolinsh UC .12 .30
313 Jarome Iginla UC .50 1.25
314 Jose Theodore UC .50 1.25
315 Steve Yzerman UC 2.00 5.00
316 Paul Kariya UC .40 1.00
317 Eric Daze UC .30 .75
318 Ilya Kovalchuk UC .50 1.25
319 Brendan Shanahan UC .40 1.00
320 Marian Gaborik UC .75 2.00
321 Joe Sakic UC .75 2.00
322 Peter Forsberg UC 1.00 2.50
323 Mario Lemieux UC 2.50 6.00
324 Luc Robitaille UC .40 1.00
325 Eric Lindros UC .40 1.00
326 Mike Modano UC .60 1.50
327 Patrick Roy UC 2.00 5.00
328 Dominik Hasek UC .75 2.00
329 Scott Stevens UC .30 .75
330 Martin Brodeur UC 1.00 2.50
331 Keith Tkachuk UC .40 1.00
332 Rostislav Klesla UC .30 .75
333 Joe Thornton UC .60 1.50
334 Alexei Yashin UC .12 .30
335 Brett Hull UC .50 1.25
336 Olaf Kolzig UC .30 .75
337 Roberto Luongo UC .40 1.00
338 Pavel Bure UC .40 1.00
339 Chris Chelios UC .40 1.00
340 Owen Nolan UC .30 .75
341 Paul Kariya FP .40 1.00
342 Ilya Kovalchuk FP .50 1.25
343 Joe Thornton FP .60 1.50
344 Miroslav Satan FP .30 .75
345 Jarome Iginla FP .50 1.25
346 Jeff O'Neill FP .12 .30
347 Eric Daze FP .30 .75
348 Patrick Roy FP 2.00 5.00
349 Rostislav Klesla FP .30 .75
350 Mike Modano FP .60 1.50
351 Steve Yzerman FP 2.00 5.00
352 Mike Comrie FP .30 .75
353 Roberto Luongo FP .40 1.00
354 Zigmund Palffy FP .30 .75
355 Marian Gaborik FP .75 2.00
356 Jose Theodore FP .50 1.25
357 Scott Hartnell FP .12 .30
358 Martin Brodeur FP 1.00 2.50
359 Alexei Yashin FP .12 .30
360 Pavel Bure FP .40 1.00
361 Marian Hossa FP .40 1.00
362 Simon Gagne FP .40 1.00
363 Daniel Briere FP .12 .30
364 Mario Lemieux FP 2.50 6.00
365 Chris Pronger FP .30 .75
366 Owen Nolan FP .30 .75
367 Nikolai Khabibulin FP .40 1.00
368 Mats Sundin FP .40 1.00
369 Markus Naslund FP .40 1.00
370 Jaromir Jagr FP .60 1.50
371 Jarome Iginla .30 .75
Markus Naslund
Todd Bertuzzi
372 Jarome Iginla .30 .75
Mats Sundin
Glen Murray
Bill Guerin
373 Oates/Allison/Sakic .40 1.00
374 Chris Chelios .30 .75
Jeremy Roenick
Glen Murray
Simon Gagne
375 Peter Worrell .30 .75
Brad Ference
Chris Neil
376 Roy/Cechmanek/Turco .40 1.00
377 Theodore/Roy/Cech./Turco .50 1.25
378 Pavol Demitra .30 .75
Glen Murray
Mats Sundin
379 Brian Rolston .30 .75
Michael Peca
Miroslav Satan
380 Hasek/Brodeur/Nabokov .40 1.00
381 Robert Svehla .30 .75
Darius Kasparaitis
Derian Hatcher
382 Nicklas Lidstrom .30 .75
Sergei Gonchar
383 Heatley/Kovalchuk/Huselius .50 1.25
384 Kovalchuk/Heatley/Huselius .50 1.25
385 Adrian Aucoin .30 .75
Chris Pronger
Nicklas Lidstrom
386 Yanic Perreault .30 .75
Rod Brind'Amour
Ron Francis
387 Peter Bondra .30 .75
Jarome Iginla
388 Daniel Briere .30 .75
Adam Deadmarsh
Jan Hrdina
389 Patrick Roy AS 2.00 5.00
390 Chris Pronger AS .30 .75
391 Rob Blake AS .30 .75
392 Vincent Damphousse AS .30 .75
393 Owen Nolan AS .30 .75
394 Brendan Shanahan AS .60 1.50
395 Dominik Hasek AS .75 2.00
396 Nicklas Lidstrom AS .40 1.00
397 Sandis Ozolinsh AS .30 .75
398 Sergei Fedorov AS .75 2.00
399 Jaromir Jagr AS .60 1.50
400 Teemu Selanne AS .40 1.00
401H Mike Modano DP .60 1.50
401R Trevor Linden DP .12 .30
402H Jeremy Roenick DP .50 1.25
402R Mats Sundin DP .40 1.00
403H Bill Guerin DP .30 .75
403R Olaf Kolzig DP .30 .75
404H Owen Nolan DP .30 .75
404R Jaromir Jagr DP .60 1.50
405H Martin Brodeur DP 1.00 2.50
405R Eric Lindros DP .60 1.50
406H Scott Niedermayer DP .30 .75
406R Peter Forsberg DP 1.00 2.50
407H Markus Naslund DP .30 .75
407R Alexei Yashin DP .12 .30
408H Chris Pronger DP .30 .75
408R Paul Kariya DP .40 1.00
409H Jason Arnott DP .10 .25
409R Jocelyn Thibault DP .30 .75
410H Adam Deadmarsh DP .12 .30
410R Jason Allison DP .12 .30
411H Todd Bertuzzi DP .30 .75
411R Ed Jovanovski DP .30 .75
412H Jeff O'Neill DP .30 .75
412R Ryan Smyth DP .12 .30
413H Dan Cloutier DP .30 .75
413R Jarome Iginla DP .50 1.25
414H J-S Giguere DP .30 .75
414R Martin Biron DP .30 .75
415H Petr Sykora DP .30 .75
415R Brian Boucher DP .30 .75
416H Marc Denis DP .30 .75
416R Joe Thornton DP .60 1.50
417H Roberto Luongo DP .40 1.00
417R Eric Brewer DP .12 .30
418H Sergei Samsonov DP .30 .75
418R Marian Hossa DP .40 1.00
419H Vincent Lecavalier DP .30 .75
419R Mark Bell DP .12 .30
420H Alex Tanguay DP .40 1.00
420R Simon Gagne DP .40 1.00
421H Martin Havlat DP .30 .75
421R Rick DiPietro DP .30 .75
422H Dany Heatley DP .40 1.00
422R Marian Gaborik DP .30 .75
423H Rostislav Klesla DP .30 .75
423R Scott Hartnell DP .12 .30
424H Ilya Kovalchuk DP .50 1.25
424R Stephen Weiss DP .40 1.00
425H Dan Blackburn DP .30 .75
425R Lukas Krajicek DP .12 .30
426H Steve Yzerman DP 6.00 15.00
426R Mario Lemieux DP 8.00 20.00
427H Gary Roberts DP .40 1.00
427R Brian Leetch DP 1.00 2.50
428H Brendan Shanahan DP 2.00 5.00
428R Pierre Turgeon DP 1.00 2.50
429H Joe Sakic DP 2.50 6.00
429R Teemu Selanne DP 2.00 5.00
430H Keith Tkachuk DP 1.25 3.00
430R H.Sedin/D.Sedin DP 1.00 2.50
431H Steve Ott DP RC 3.00 8.00
431R Brooks Orpik DP RC 2.00 5.00
432H Pascal Leclaire DP RC 3.00 8.00
432R Shaone Morrisonn DP RC 2.00 5.00
433H Alexei Smirnov DP RC 2.00 5.00
433R Ron Hainsey DP RC 2.00 5.00
434H Alexander Frolov DP RC 4.00 10.00
434R Anton Volchenkov DP RC 2.00 5.00
435H Jeff Taffe DP RC 2.00 5.00
435R Jason Spezza DP RC 6.00 15.00
436H Alexander Svitov DP RC 2.50 6.00
436R Stanislav Chistov DP RC 2.50 6.00
437H Chuck Kobasew DP RC 2.50 6.00
437R Ales Hemsky DP RC 6.00 15.00
438H Carlo Colaiacovo DP RC 2.50 6.00
438R Jay Bouwmeester DP RC 3.00 8.00
439H Rick Nash DP RC 8.00 20.00
439R Scottie Upshall DP RC 3.00 8.00
440H P-M Bouchard DP RC 4.00 10.00
440R Steve Eminger DP RC 2.00 5.00

2002-03 BAP First Edition Debut Jerseys

This 160-card set was inserted at a overall rate for memorabilia of 1:36 hobby and 1:48 retail. Each card was limited to a production run of 50 copies.

*MULT.COLOR SWATCH: .75X TO 1.5X
OVERALL MEM.ODDS 1:36 HBBY/1:48 RET.
STATED PRINT RUN 50 SETS

1 Pavel Bure 15.00 40.00
2 Patrick Roy 40.00 100.00
3 Curtis Joseph 15.00 40.00
4 Mats Sundin 15.00 40.00
5 Ed Belfour 15.00 40.00
6 Teemu Selanne 15.00 40.00
7 Martin Brodeur 25.00 60.00
8 Owen Nolan 10.00 25.00
9 Jarome Iginla 20.00 50.00
10 Steve Yzerman 30.00 80.00
11 Marian Gaborik 20.00 50.00
12 Jaromir Jagr 15.00 40.00
13 Eric Lindros 15.00 40.00
14 Ilya Kovalchuk 20.00 50.00
15 Nicklas Lidstrom 10.00 25.00
16 Paul Kariya 15.00 40.00
17 Joe Thornton 25.00 60.00
18 Mark Messier 20.00 50.00
19 Keith Tkachuk 10.00 25.00
20 Joe Sakic 20.00 50.00

2002-03 BAP First Edition He Shoots-He Score Points

ONE PER PACK
RED.PROGRAM HAS EXPIRED

1 Ron Francis 1 pt. .10 .25
2 Sergei Fedorov 1 pt. .10 .25
3 Milan Hejduk 1 pt. .10 .25
3 Saku Koivu 1 pt. .10 .25
4 Dany Heatley 1 pt. .10 .25
5 Ilya Kovalchuk 1 pt. .10 .25
7 Teemu Selanne 1 pt. .10 .25
8 Eric Lindros 1 pt. .10 .25
9 Mark Messier 1 pt. .10 .25
10 Owen Nolan 1 pt. .10 .25
11 Joe Thornton 1 pt. .10 .25
12 Pavel Bure 2 pts. .10 .25
13 Jarome Iginla 2 pts. .10 .25
14 Paul Kariya 2 pts. .10 .25
15 Joe Sakic 2 pts. .10 .25
16 Steve Yzerman 2 pts. .10 .25
17 Mike Modano 2 pts. .10 .25
18 Peter Forsberg 3 pts. .10 .25
19 Mats Sundin 3 pts. .10 .25
20 Mario Lemieux 3 pts. .10 .25

2002-03 BAP First Edition He Shoots-He Scores Prizes

PRINT RUN 20 SER. #'d SETS
NOT PRICED DUE TO SCARCITY

1 Peter Forsberg
2 Mario Lemieux
3 Mats Sundin
4 Jarome Iginla
5 Pavel Bure
6 Joe Sakic
7 Steve Yzerman
8 Paul Kariya
9 Mike Modano
10 Mark Messier
11 Milan Hejduk
12 Ron Francis
13 Saku Koivu
14 Owen Nolan
15 Joe Thornton
16 Ilya Kovalchuk
17 Dany Heatley
18 Eric Lindros
19 Teemu Selanne
20 Sergei Fedorov
21 Brendan Shanahan
22 Marian Gaborik
23 Patrick Roy
24 Martin Brodeur
25 Jose Theodore
26 Dominik Hasek
27 Jeremy Roenick
28 Jaromir Jagr
29 Keith Tkachuk
30 Markus Naslund

2002-03 BAP First Edition Jerseys

*MULT.COLOR SWATCH: .75X TO 1.5X
CARDS 1-130 AVAIL. RETAIL/HOBBY
CARDS 131-160 AVAIL.HOBBY ONLY
STATED PRINT RUN 100 SETS

1 Mario Lemieux 15.00 40.00
2 Sergei Gonchar 5.00 12.00
3 Brian Leetch 5.00 12.00
4 Felix Potvin 6.00 15.00
5 Sandis Ozolinsh 5.00 12.00
6 Steven Reinprecht 5.00 12.00
7 Byron Dafoe 5.00 12.00
8 Mark Bell 5.00 12.00
9 Jeff O'Neill 5.00 12.00
10 Sean Burke 5.00 12.00
11 Darcy Tucker 5.00 12.00
12 Scott Stevens 5.00 12.00
13 David Aebischer 5.00 12.00
14 Jocelyn Thibault 5.00 12.00
15 Radek Bonk 5.00 12.00
16 Milan Hejduk 6.00 15.00
17 Zigmund Palffy 5.00 12.00
18 Luc Robitaille 5.00 12.00
19 Tomas Kaberle 5.00 12.00
20 Rostislav Klesla 5.00 12.00
21 Alexei Zhamnov 5.00 12.00
22 Ron Francis 5.00 12.00
23 Mike Fisher 5.00 12.00
24 Dany Heatley 8.00 20.00
25 Kyle McLaren 5.00 12.00
26 Doug Weight 5.00 12.00
27 Henrik Sedin 5.00 12.00
28 Roman Turek 5.00 12.00
29 Adam Deadmarsh 5.00 12.00
30 Sami Kapanen 5.00 12.00
31 Sergei Samsonov 5.00 12.00
32 Kristian Huselius 5.00 12.00
33 Dimitri Yushkevich 5.00 12.00
34 Patrik Elias 5.00 12.00
35 Nick Boynton 5.00 12.00
36 Martin Biron 5.00 12.00
37 Brad Richards 5.00 12.00
38 Alyn McCauley 5.00 12.00
39 Daniel Sedin 5.00 12.00
40 Teppo Numminen 5.00 12.00
41 Luke Richardson 5.00 12.00
42 Manny Fernandez 5.00 12.00
43 Vincent Lecavalier 6.00 15.00
44 Mattias Ohlund 5.00 12.00
45 Milan Kraft 5.00 12.00
46 Mike Dunham 5.00 12.00
47 Derian Hatcher 5.00 12.00
48 Oleg Tverdovsky 5.00 12.00
49 Shane Doan 5.00 12.00
50 Martin Skoula 5.00 12.00
51 John LeClair 6.00 15.00
52 Tommy Salo 5.00 12.00
53 Miroslav Satan 5.00 12.00
54 Bryan Berard 5.00 12.00
55 Roman Cechmanek 5.00 12.00
56 Alexei Morozov 5.00 12.00
57 J-S Giguere 5.00 12.00
58 Pierre Turgeon 5.00 12.00
59 Martin Straka 5.00 12.00
60 Stephane Yelle 5.00 12.00
61 Marc Savard 5.00 12.00
62 Sergei Zubov 5.00 12.00
63 Jeff Friesen 5.00 12.00
64 Daniel Briere 5.00 12.00
65 Patrik Stefan 5.00 12.00
66 Pavol Demitra 5.00 12.00
67 Radek Dvorak 5.00 12.00
68 Marty Turco 5.00 12.00
69 Keith Tkachuk 6.00 15.00
70 Maxim Afinogenov 5.00 12.00
71 Mika Noronen 5.00 12.00
72 Evgeni Nabokov 5.00 12.00
73 Todd Bertuzzi 6.00 15.00
74 Valeri Bure 5.00 12.00
75 Marian Hossa 6.00 15.00
76 J-P Dumont 5.00 12.00
77 Niklas Sundstrom 5.00 12.00
78 Eric Daze 5.00 12.00
79 Brian Boucher 5.00 12.00
80 Nikolai Khabibulin 6.00 15.00
81 Darren McCarty 5.00 12.00
82 Pavel Brendl 5.00 12.00
83 Mark Recchi 5.00 12.00
84 Dan Cloutier 5.00 12.00
85 Manny Legace 5.00 12.00
86 Keith Primeau 5.00 12.00
87 Alex Tanguay 5.00 12.00
88 Ed Jovanovski 5.00 12.00
89 Roberto Luongo 10.00 25.00
90 Andreas Johansson 5.00 12.00
91 Steve Shields 5.00 12.00
92 Saku Koivu 6.00 15.00
93 Chris Drury 5.00 12.00
94 Olaf Kolzig 5.00 12.00
95 Jan Hrdina 5.00 12.00
96 Ivan Novoseltsev 5.00 12.00
97 Kenny Jonsson 5.00 12.00
98 Martin Havlat 5.00 12.00
99 Scott Niedermayer 5.00 12.00
100 Chris Phillips 5.00 12.00
101 Tony Amonte 5.00 12.00
102 Alexander Mogilny 5.00 12.00
103 Chris Pronger 5.00 12.00
104 Chris Gratton 5.00 12.00
105 Sergei Fedorov 8.00 20.00
106 David Legwand 5.00 12.00
107 Ron Tugnutt 5.00 12.00
108 Steven McCarthy 5.00 12.00
109 Brian Rolston 5.00 12.00
110 Bobby Holik 5.00 12.00
111 Darryl Sydor 5.00 12.00
112 Steve Sullivan 5.00 12.00
113 Toby Petersen 5.00 12.00
114 Scott Gomez 5.00 12.00
115 Adam Foote 5.00 12.00
116 Rob Niedermayer 5.00 12.00
117 Arturs Irbe 5.00 12.00
118 Al MacInnis 5.00 12.00
119 Jeff Hackett 5.00 12.00
120 Pavel Bure 6.00 15.00
121 Patrick Lalime 5.00 12.00
122 Vincent Damphousse 5.00 12.00
123 Steve Passmore 5.00 12.00
124 Simon Gagne 6.00 15.00
125 Shawn McEachern 5.00 12.00
126 Bryan McCabe 5.00 12.00
127 Jamie Storr 5.00 12.00
128 Mike Richter 6.00 15.00
129 Petr Sykora 5.00 12.00
130 Trevor Kidd 5.00 12.00
131 Jaromir Jagr 10.00 25.00
132 Bill Guerin 5.00 12.0
133 Mark Messier 6.00 15.0
134 Ilya Kovalchuk 10.00 25.0
135 Teemu Selanne 6.00 15.0
136 Dominik Hasek 15.00 40.0
137 Mats Sundin 6.00 15.0
138 Jose Theodore 10.00 25.0
139 Brendan Shanahan 6.00 15.0
140 Daniel Alfredsson 5.00 12.0
141 Martin Brodeur 15.00 40.0
142 Jarome Iginla 10.00 25.0
143 Peter Bondra 6.00 15.0
144 Peter Forsberg 15.00 40.0
145 Curtis Joseph 6.00 15.0
146 Alexei Yashin 5.00 12.0
147 Patrick Roy 20.00 50.0
148 Markus Naslund 6.00 15.0
149 Jeremy Roenick 10.00 25.0
150 Eric Lindros 6.00 15.0
151 Steve Yzerman 15.00 40.0
152 Marian Gaborik 12.50 30.0
153 Mike Modano 8.00 20.0
154 Joe Sakic 12.50 30.0
155 Paul Kariya 6.00 15.0
156 Owen Nolan 5.00 12.0
157 Rob Blake 5.00 12.0
158 Nicklas Lidstrom 6.00 15.0
159 Joe Thornton 10.00 25.0
160 Mario Lemieux 15.00 40.0

2002-03 BAP First Edition Magnificent Inserts

This 10-card set featured game-use equipment from the career of Mari Lemieux. Cards MI1-MI5 had a print run 40 copies each and cards MI6-MI10 we limited to just 10 copies each. Cards MI MI10 are not priced due to scarcity.

CARDS MI1-MI5 PRINT RUN 40 SETS
CARDS MI6-MI10 PRINT RUN 10 SETS
MI6-MI10 NOT PRICED DUE TO SCARCIT

MI1 2000-01 Jersey 30.00 80.0
MI2 1985-86 Jersey 30.00 80.0
MI3 2002 All-Star Jersey 30.00 80.0
MI4 1987 Canada Cup Jersey 30.00 80.0
MI5 Dual Jersey 50.00 125.0
MI6 Number
MI7 Emblem
MI8 Triple Jersey
MI9 Quad Jersey
MI10 Complete Package

2002-03 BAP First Edition Scoring Leaders

*MULT.COLOR SWATCH: .75X TO 1.5X
STATED PRINT RUN 50 SETS

1 Paul Kariya 12.50 30.0
2 Dany Heatley 20.00 50.0
3 Sergei Samsonov 12.50 30.0
4 Jarome Iginla 15.00 40.0
5 Ron Francis 12.50 30.0
6 Eric Daze 12.50 30.0
7 Joe Sakic 20.00 50.0
8 Mike Modano 15.00 40.0
9 Brendan Shanahan 12.50 30.0
10 Patrik Elias 12.50 30.0
11 Alexei Yashin 12.50 30.0
12 Eric Lindros 12.50 30.0
13 Daniel Alfredsson 12.50 30.0
14 Jeremy Roenick 15.00 40.0
15 Alexei Kovalev 12.50 30.0
16 Owen Nolan 12.50 30.0
17 Brad Richards 12.50 30.0
18 Mats Sundin 12.50 30.0
19 Markus Naslund 12.50 30.0
20 Jaromir Jagr 15.00 40.0

1999-00 BAP Memorabilia

Released as two series, the base 300-car set was released under Be A Playe Memorabilia, and the last 100-cards wer released as Be A Player Memorabilia A Update. Base cards feature color actio photos and are enhanced with blue fo highlights. Gold and silver parallels of th t were also created and inserted into ndom packs. Gold parallels had a stated int run of 100 sets and silver parallels had stated print run of 1000 sets. Be A Player emorabilia was packaged in 24-pack xes with packs containing eight cards and rried a suggested retail price of $3.29 US d $4.99 CAN.

OMPLETE SET (400) 40.00 100.00
OMP.SER.1 (300) 30.00 80.00
OMP.UPDATE SET (100) 8.00 20.00
OMP.FACT.UPD.SET (100) 15.00 40.00
Patrik Stefan RC .25 .60
Glen Murray .08 .25
Nicklas Lidstrom .30 .75
Arturs Irbe .25 .60
Viktor Kozlov .08 .25
Dimitri Yushkevich .08 .25
Byron Ritchie RC .08 .25
Robert Svehla .08 .25
Jeremy Roenick .40 1.00
0 Ron Francis .25 .60
1 Oleg Kvasha .08 .25
2 Marian Hossa .30 .75
3 Mark Recchi .25 .60
4 Scott Mellanby .08 .25
5 Adam Graves .08 .25
6 Boris Mironov .08 .25
7 Derian Hatcher .08 .25
8 Brian Leetch .30 .75
9 Mattias Ohlund .08 .25
0 Ray Whitney .08 .25
1 Mike Richter .30 .75
2 Paul Mara .08 .25
3 Todd Bertuzzi .30 .75
4 Sergei Zubov .08 .25
5 Cliff Ronning .08 .25
6 Anson Carter .25 .60
7 Dmitri Mironov .08 .25
8 Shane Willis .08 .25
9 Shayne Corson .08 .25
0 Chris Chelios .30 .75
1 Pavel Kubina .08 .25
2 Michal Grosek .08 .25
3 Gary Suter .08 .25
4 Greg Adams .08 .25
5 Joe Thornton .50 1.25
6 Matt Higgins .08 .25
7 Chris Gratton .08 .25
8 Ray Bourque .50 1.25
9 Tommy Salo .25 .60
0 Igor Kravchuk .08 .25
1 Byron Dafoe .25 .60
2 Larry Murphy .08 .25
3 Bryan McCabe .08 .25
4 John Vanbiesbrouck .25 .60
5 Brett Hull .40 1.00
6 Christian Dube .08 .25
7 Kyle McLaren .08 .25
8 Jere Lehtinen .25 .60
9 Petr Nedved .25 .60
0 Jason Allison .08 .25
1 Brad Lukowich RC .08 .25
2 Scott Stevens .25 .60
3 Sergei Krivokrasov .08 .25
4 Olaf Kolzig .25 .60
5 Sami Kapanen .08 .25
6 Sami Salo .08 .25
7 Cory Stillman .08 .25
8 Darcy Tucker .08 .25
9 Rod Brind'Amour .25 .60
0 John Jakopin RC .08 .25
1 Martin Brodeur .75 2.00
2 Jiri Slegr .08 .25
3 Rem Murray .08 .25
4 Jason Arnott .08 .25
5 Jon Sim RC .25 .60
6 Cory Sarich .08 .25
7 Brian Rafalski RC .25 .60
8 Kevin Hatcher .08 .25
9 Ted Donato .08 .25
0 Dan LaCouture .08 .25
1 Alexei Kovalev .08 .25
2 Peter Bondra .25 .60
3 John LeClair .30 .75
4 Matthew Barnaby .08 .25
5 Adam Oates .25 .60
6 Janne Niinimaa .08 .25
7 Tom Barrasso .25 .60
8 Sergei Gonchar .08 .25
9 Alex Tanguay .25 .60
0 Jean-Luc Grand-Pierre RC .08 .25
1 Alexei Tezikov RC .25 .60
2 Doug Gilmour .08 .25
3 Sergei Brylin .08 .25
4 Ron Tugnutt .25 .60
5 Stephane Richer .08 .25
6 Marc Denis .25 .60
7 Sergei Fedorov .50 1.25
8 Brian Rolston .08 .25
9 Chris Pronger .25 .60
0 Dan Cloutier .25 .60
1 Anders Eriksson .08 .25
2 Donald Audette .08 .25
3 Ed Jovanovski .08 .25
4 Tony Amonte .25 .60
5 Jamie Storr .25 .60
6 German Titov .08 .25
7 Eric Daze .25 .60
8 Zigmund Palffy .25 .60
9 Dan McGillis .08 .25
00 Nikolai Khabibulin .25 .60
01 Mathieu Schneider .08 .25
02 Magnus Arvedson .25 .60
03 Joe Sakic .60 1.50
04 Brian Campbell RC .08 .25
05 Wade Redden .08 .25
06 Andrei Nikolishin .08 .25
07 Steve Rucchin .08 .25
08 Shawn McEachern .08 .25
09 Alexander Karpovtsev .08 .25
10 Miroslav Satan .25 .60
11 Andreas Dackell .08 .25
12 Niklas Sundstrom .08 .25
13 Scott Niedermayer .08 .25
14 Ken Wregget .25 .60
15 Olli Jokinen .25 .60
16 Vincent Lecavalier .30 .75
17 Paul Kariya .30 .75
18 Alexei Zhamnov .08 .25
19 Martin Rucinsky .08 .25
120 Daniel Cleary .08 .25
121 Yanic Perreault .08 .25
122 Alexei Zhitnik .08 .25
123 Vadim Sharifijanov .08 .25
124 Derek King .08 .25
125 Jason Woolley .08 .25
126 Pavel Bure .30 .75
127 Darius Kasparaitis .08 .25
128 Stu Barnes .08 .25
129 Josef Beranek .08 .25
130 Milan Hejduk .30 .75
131 Michael Peca .25 .60
132 Tomas Holmstrom .08 .25
133 Patrick Marleau .30 .75
134 Dominik Hasek .60 1.50
135 Chris Osgood .25 .60
136 Radek Bonk .08 .25
137 Martin Biron .25 .60
138 Igor Larionov .08 .25
139 Felix Potvin .30 .75
140 Oleg Tverdovsky .08 .25
141 Steve Yzerman 1.50 4.00
142 Bobby Holik .08 .25
143 Landon Wilson .08 .25
144 Marty McInnis .08 .25
145 Remi Royer .08 .25
146 Brendan Morrison .25 .60
147 Jaromir Jagr .50 1.25
148 Steve Thomas .08 .25
149 Rico Fata .08 .25
150 John Madden RC .40 1.00
151 Miroslav Guren .08 .25
152 Jochen Hecht RC .75 2.00
153 Gary Roberts .08 .25
154 Patrik Elias .25 .60
155 Al MacInnis .25 .60
156 Jonathan Girard .08 .25
157 Jan Hlavac .08 .25
158 Pierre Turgeon .25 .60
159 Matt Cullen .08 .25
160 Trevor Letowski .08 .25
161 Roman Turek .25 .60
162 Luc Robitaille .25 .60
163 Marcus Nilsson .08 .25
164 Pavol Demitra .25 .60
165 Fredrik Olausson .08 .25
166 Blake Sloan .30 .75
167 Eric Lindros .30 .75
168 Guy Hebert .25 .60
169 Adam Deadmarsh .08 .25
170 Mike Leclerc .08 .25
171 Teemu Selanne .30 .75
172 Ty Jones .08 .25
173 Calle Johansson .08 .25
174 Ed Belfour .30 .75
175 Craig MacDonald RC .08 .25
176 Todd Harvey .08 .25
177 Martin Straka .08 .25
178 Mariusz Czerkawski .08 .25
179 Grant Fuhr .25 .60
180 Mark Parrish .08 .25
181 Sandis Ozolinsh .08 .25
182 Patrice Brisebois .08 .25
183 Geoff Courtnall .08 .25
184 Chris Drury .25 .60
185 Saku Koivu .30 .75
186 Teppo Numminen .08 .25
187 Alexei Morozov .08 .25
188 Stephane Quintal .08 .25
189 Eric Desjardins .25 .60
190 Pavel Patera RC .08 .25
191 Vladimir Malakhov .08 .25
192 J-S Giguere .25 .60
193 Niclas Havelid RC .25 .60
194 Trevor Linden .08 .25
195 Simon Gagne .30 .75
196 Kevin Weekes .25 .60
197 Joe Nieuwendyk .25 .60
198 Cameron Mann .08 .25
199 Adam Mair RC .25 .60
200 Kim Johnsson RC .25 .60
201 Mikael Renberg .25 .60
202 Curtis Joseph .30 .75
203 Juha Lind .08 .25
204 Doug Weight .25 .60
205 Mats Lindgren .08 .25
206 Marcus Ragnarsson .08 .25
207 Igor Korolev .08 .25
208 Claude Lemieux .08 .25
209 Jeff Hackett .25 .60
210 Brendan Witt .08 .25
211 Steve Kariya RC .25 .60
212 Jarome Iginla .40 1.00
213 Pavel Rosa .08 .25
214 Andrei Zyuzin .08 .25
215 Oleg Saprykin RC .20 .50
216 Sean Burke .25 .60
217 Mike Modano .50 1.25
218 Phil Housley .08 .25
219 Ryan Smyth .08 .25
220 Daren Puppa .25 .60
221 Aki Berg .08 .25
222 Mike Grier .08 .25
223 Keith Jones .08 .25
224 Marc Savard .08 .25
225 Bill Guerin .25 .60
226 Theo Fleury .08 .25
227 Shawn Heins RC .08 .25
228 Tom Poti .08 .25
229 Tim Connolly .08 .25
230 Glen Wesley .08 .25
231 Brendan Shanahan .30 .75
232 Kenny Jonsson .08 .25
233 Mats Sundin .30 .75
234 Damian Rhodes .25 .60
235 Martin Lapointe .08 .25
236 David Legwand .25 .60
237 Rob Niedermayer .08 .25
238 Bill Muckalt .08 .25
239 Valeri Bure .08 .25
240 Manny Malhotra .25 .60
241 Jozef Stumpel .25 .60
242 Brad Stuart .25 .60
243 Curtis Brown .08 .25
244 Alexei Yashin .08 .25
245 Owen Nolan .25 .60
246 Shawn Bates .08 .25
247 Jan Hrdina .08 .25
248 Marco Sturm .08 .25
249 Nelson Emerson .08 .25
250 Stephane Fiset .25 .60
251 Mike Vernon .25 .60
252 Jason Botterill .08 .25
253 Marty Reasoner .25 .60
254 Roman Hamrlik .08 .25
255 Ray Ferraro .08 .25
256 Jamie Langenbrunner .08 .25
257 Brian Holzinger .08 .25
258 Andrew Brunette .25 .60
259 Peter Forsberg .75 2.00
260 Jyrki Lumme .08 .25
261 Keith Primeau .08 .25
262 Patrick Roy 1.50 4.00
263 Dmitri Nabokov .08 .25
264 Darryl Laplante .08 .25
265 Mark Messier .30 .75
266 Benoit Gratton RC .08 .25
267 Bryan Berard .25 .60
268 Wendel Clark .08 .25
269 Vincent Damphousse .08 .25
270 J-P Dumont .25 .60
271 Darryl Sydor .08 .25
272 Darren Turcotte .08 .25
273 Sergei Berezin .08 .25
274 Jeff Friesen .08 .25
275 Ville Peltonen .08 .25
276 Rick Tocchet .25 .60
277 Darren McCarty .08 .25
278 Greg Johnson .08 .25
279 Dan Smith RC .08 .25
280 Sergei Samsonov .25 .60
281 Petr Sykora .08 .25
282 Dallas Drake .08 .25
283 Steve Konowalchuk .08 .25
284 Yan Golubovsky .08 .25
285 Dan Boyle RC .25 .60
286 Alexander Mogilny .25 .60
287 Daniel Alfredsson .25 .60
288 Steve Shields .25 .60
289 Markus Naslund .30 .75
290 Vyacheslav Kozlov .08 .25
291 Keith Tkachuk .30 .75
292 Adrian Aucoin .08 .25
293 JocelynThibault .25 .60
294 Kevin Stevens .08 .25
295 John MacLean .08 .25
296 Mike Ricci .08 .25
297 Rob Blake .08 .25
298 Radek Dvorak .08 .25
299 Mike Dunham .25 .60
300 Richard Matvichuk .08 .25
301 Scott Gomez .08 .25
302 Nikolai Antropov RC .40 1.00
303 Glen Metropolit RC .30 .75
304 Robyn Regehr .08 .25
305 Mathieu Biron .08 .25
306 Nathan Dempsey RC .08 .25
307 Roberto Luongo .40 1.00
308 Andreas Karlsson RC .08 .25
309 Ray Bourque .60 1.50
310 Artem Chubarov .08 .25
311 Mike Fisher RC .25 .60
312 Andrew Ference .08 .25
313 Todd Reirden RC .08 .25
314 Martin Skoula RC .25 .60
315 Radislav Suchy RC .08 .25
316 Joel Prpic RC .25 .60
317 Yuri Butsayev RC .08 .25
318 Andy Delmore RC .25 .60
319 Steve McCarthy .08 .25
320 Brian Rolston .08 .25
321 Dimitri Kalinin RC .08 .25
322 Brenden Morrow .30 .75
323 Mike Vernon .25 .60
324 Nils Ekman RC .08 .25
325 Felix Potvin .30 .75
326 Jan Nemecek RC .08 .25
327 Michael York .08 .25
328 Evgeni Nabokov RC 2.50 6.00
329 Rick Tocchet .25 .60
330 Vitali Vishnevsky .08 .25
331 Francis Bouillon RC .08 .25
332 Robert Esche RC .75 2.00
333 Ray Giroux RC .08 .25
334 Per Svartvadet RC .08 .25
335 Kyle Calder RC .40 1.00
336 Brian Boucher .40 1.00
337 Dan Hinote RC .25 .60
338 Darrel Scoville RC .08 .25
339 Ivan Novoseltsev RC .25 .60
340 Petr Schastlivy RC .25 .60
341 Andre Savage RC .30 .75
342 Michal Grosek .08 .25
343 Richard Lintner RC .08 .25
344 Tyson Nash RC .25 .60
345 Tommy Westlund RC .08 .25
346 Jason Krog RC .08 .25
347 Jarkko Ruutu RC .08 .25
348 Mike Ribeiro .08 .25
349 Alexander Mogilny .25 .60
350 Maxim Afinogenov .08 .25
351 Ron Tugnutt .25 .60
352 Jaroslav Spacek .25 .60
353 Petr Buzek .25 .60
354 Sami Helenius RC .25 .60
355 Peter Schaefer .25 .60
356 Alan Letang RC .25 .60
357 Keith Primeau .08 .25
358 Jay Henderson RC .08 .25
359 Dave Tanabe .25 .60
360 Fred Brathwaite .25 .60
361 Chris Gratton .25 .60
362 Maxim Balmochnyk .25 .60
363 John Emmons .08 .25
364 Mark Eaton RC .25 .60
365 Kevyn Adams .08 .25
366 Alfie Michaud RC .25 .60
367 Chris Herperger RC .25 .60
368 Scott Langkow .25 .60
369 Marquis Mathieu RC .08 .25
370 Milan Hnilicka RC .25 .60
371 Michal Rozsival RC .25 .60
372 Sergei Krivokrasov .08 .25
373 Brad Chartrand RC .08 .25
374 Ryan Bonni RC .08 .25
375 Roman Lyashenko .08 .25
376 Denis Hamel RC .08 .25
377 Stephane Robidas RC .08 .25
378 Jeff Halpern RC .25 .60
379 Karlis Skrastins RC .08 .25
380 Jeff Zehr RC .08 .25
381 Brian Holzinger .08 .25
382 Josef Beranek .25 .60
383 Harold Druken .25 .60
384 Doug Gilmour .25 .60
385 Ladislav Nagy RC .75 2.00
386 Bert Robertsson RC .08 .25
387 Scott Fankhouser RC .25 .60
388 Brian Willsie .25 .60
389 Eric Boguniecki RC .40 1.00
390 Dmitri Yakushin RC .25 .60
391 Chris Clark RC .25 .60
392 Paul Comrie RC .30 .75
393 John Grahame RC .25 .60
394 Rod Brind'Amour .25 .60
395 Vladimir Malakhov .08 .25
396 Jiri Fischer .25 .60
397 Kimmo Timonen .08 .25
398 Brad Ference .08 .25
399 Marc Lamothe RC .08 .25
400 Radek Dvorak .08 .25
DT5 Dimitri Tertyshny TRIB .30 .75
SC3 Steve Chiasson TRIB .40 1.00

1999-00 BAP Memorabilia Gold

*STARS: 15X TO 30X HI COLUMN
*ROOKIES: 8X TO 20X
STATED PRINT RUN 100 SER.#'d SETS

1999-00 BAP Memorabilia Silver

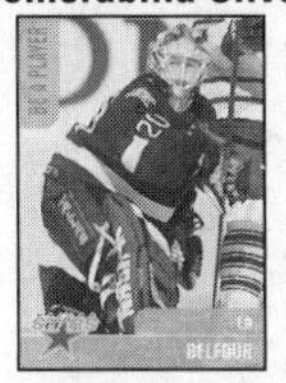

*STARS: 1.5X TO 4X HI COLUMN
*ROOKIES: 1X TO 2.5X
STATED PRINT RUN 1000 SER.#'d SETS

1999-00 BAP Memorabilia Jersey Cards

*MULT.COLOR SWATCH: 1X TO 1.5X HI
STATED ODDS 1:250
J1 Eric Lindros 10.00 25.00
J2 Peter Forsberg 15.00 40.00
J3 Teemu Selanne 10.00 25.00
J4 Mike Modano 12.00 30.00
J5 Mats Sundin 10.00 30.00
J6 Patrick Roy 40.00 100.00
J7 Paul Kariya 10.00 30.00
J8 Martin Brodeur 25.00 60.00
J9 Ray Bourque 15.00 40.00
J10 Mark Messier 10.00 25.00
J11 Curtis Joseph 10.00 25.00
J12 Brett Hull 10.00 30.00
J13 Al MacInnis 8.00 20.00
J14 Theo Fleury 8.00 20.00
J15 Sergei Fedorov 12.00 30.00
J16 Brian Leetch 8.00 20.00
J17 Alexei Yashin 8.00 20.00
J18 Jaromir Jagr 15.00 40.00
J19 Pavel Bure 12.00 30.00
J20 Dominik Hasek 20.00 50.00
J21 Chris Chelios 8.00 20.00
J22 John LeClair 8.00 20.00
J23 Brendan Shanahan 10.00 30.00
J24 Ed Belfour 10.00 30.00
J25 Wayne Gretzky 60.00 150.00
J26 Saku Koivu 8.00 20.00
J27 Tony Amonte 8.00 20.00
J28 Peter Bondra 8.00 20.00

1999-00 BAP Memorabilia Jersey Emblems

*EMBLEMS: 1X TO 2X JERSEY CARDS
STATED ODDS 1:999

1999-00 BAP Memorabilia Jersey Numbers

*NUMBERS: 1X TO 1.75X JERSEY CARDS
STATED ODDS 1:999

1999-00 BAP Memorabilia Jersey and Stick Cards

*JERSEY/STICK: .5X TO 1.25X JERSEY CARD
STATED ODDS 1:999

1999-00 BAP Memorabilia Selects Silver

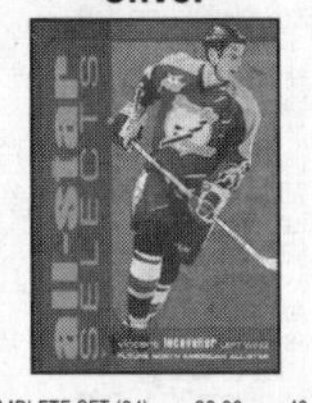

COMPLETE SET (24) 20.00 40.00
STATED ODDS 1:25
*GOLD STARS: 2X TO 5X BASIC CARDS
GOLD STATED ODDS 1:250
SL1 Peter Forsberg 2.50 6.00
SL2 Pavol Demitra .75 2.00
SL3 Jaromir Jagr 1.50 4.00
SL4 Sandis Ozolinsh .50 1.25
SL5 Nicklas Lidstrom 1.00 2.50
SL6 Dominik Hasek 2.00 5.00
SL7 Eric Lindros 1.00 2.50
SL8 Paul Kariya 1.00 2.50
SL9 Tony Amonte .75 2.00
SL10 Brian Leetch 1.00 2.50
SL11 Al MacInnis 1.00 2.50
SL12 Martin Brodeur 2.50 6.00
SL13 Petr Sykora .50 1.25
SL14 Sergei Samsonov .75 2.00
SL15 Marian Hossa 1.00 2.50
SL16 Andrei Zyuzin .50 1.25
SL17 Sami Salo .50 1.25
SL18 Roman Turek 1.00 2.50
SL19 Chris Drury .75 2.00
SL20 Vincent Lecavalier 1.00 2.50
SL21 J-P Dumont .75 2.00
SL22 Kyle McLaren .50 1.25
SL23 Adrian Aucoin .50 1.25
SL24 Marc Denis 1.00 2.50

1999-00 BAP Memorabilia AS American Hobby

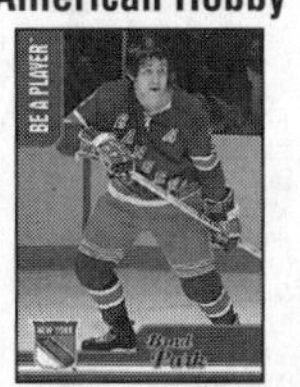

Randomly inserted in American hobby packs at the rate of 1:32, this 12-card set featured former NHL greats from the New York Rangers and the Boston Bruins.

COMPLETE SET (12) 15.00 30.00
STATED ODDS 1:32
AH1 Ken Hodge 1.25 3.00
AH2 Cam Neely 2.50 6.00
AH3 Derek Sanderson 2.00 5.00
AH4 Gerry Cheevers 2.00 5.00
AH5 Johnny Bucyk 1.25 3.00
AH6 Wayne Cashman 1.25 3.00
AH7 Vic Hadfield 1.25 3.00
AH8 Andy Bathgate 1.25 3.00
AH9 Brad Park 1.25 3.00
AH10 Ed Giacomin 1.50 4.00
AH11 John Davidson 1.50 4.00
AH12 Rod Gilbert 1.25 3.00

1999-00 BAP Memorabilia AS American Hobby Autographs

Randomly inserted in American hobby packs at the rate of 1:320, this 12-card set paralleled the base Channel Specific American insert set in an autographed version.

STATED ODDS 1:320
AH1 Ken Hodge 15.00 40.00
AH2 Cam Neely 25.00 60.00
AH3 Derek Sanderson 25.00 60.00
AH4 Gerry Cheevers 25.00 60.00
AH5 Johnny Bucyk 15.00 40.00
AH6 Wayne Cashman 15.00 40.00
AH7 Vic Hadfield 15.00 40.00
AH8 Andy Bathgate 15.00 40.00
AH9 Brad Park 15.00 40.00
AH10 Ed Giacomin 20.00 50.00
AH11 John Davidson 20.00 50.00
AH12 Rod Gilbert 15.00 40.00

1999-00 BAP Memorabilia AS Canadian Hobby

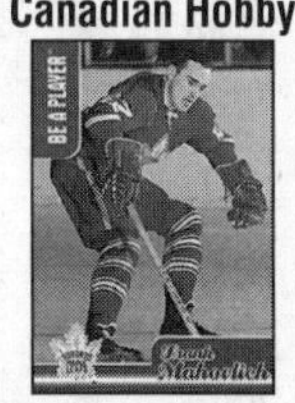

Randomly inserted in Canadian hobby packs at the rate of 1:32, this 12-card set featured former NHL greats from the Toronto Maple Leafs and the Montreal Canadians.

COMPLETE SET (12) 15.00 30.00
STATED ODDS 1:32
CH1 Borje Salming 1.50 4.00
CH2 Dave Keon 2.00 5.00
CH3 Darryl Sittler 2.00 5.00
CH4 Frank Mahovlich 2.00 5.00
CH5 Johnny Bower 2.00 5.00
CH6 Lanny McDonald 1.25 3.00
CH7 Peter Mahovlich 1.25 3.00
CH8 Dickie Moore 1.25 3.00
CH9 John Ferguson 1.25 3.00
CH10 Larry Robinson 1.25 3.00
CH11 Yvan Cournoyer 1.25 3.00
CH12 Serge Savard 1.25 3.00

1999-00 BAP Memorabilia AS Canadian Hobby Autographs

Randomly inserted in Canadian Hobby packs at the rate of 1:320, this 12-card set paralleled the base Channel Specific Canadian insert set in an autographed version.

STATED ODDS 1:320
CH1 Borje Salming 20.00 50.00
CH2 Dave Keon 20.00 60.00
CH3 Darryl Sittler 20.00 60.00
CH4 Frank Mahovlich 25.00 60.00
CH5 Johnny Bower 25.00 60.00
CH6 Lanny McDonald 15.00 40.00
CH7 Peter Mahovlich 15.00 40.00
CH8 Dickie Moore 15.00 40.00
CH9 John Ferguson 15.00 40.00
CH10 Larry Robinson 15.00 40.00
CH11 Yvan Cournoyer 15.00 40.00

1999-00 BAP Memorabilia AS Retail

Randomly inserted in retail packs at the rate of 1:32, this 12-card set featured former NHL greats from the Chicago Blackhawks and the Detroit Red Wings.

COMPLETE SET (12) 20.00 40.00
STATED ODDS 1:32
R1 Bobby Hull 4.00 10.00
R2 Dennis Hull 1.25 3.00
R3 Denis Savard 1.25 3.00
R4 Pierre Pilote 1.25 3.00
R5 Stan Mikita 2.50 6.00
R6 Tony Esposito 2.00 5.00
R7 Alex Delvecchio 1.50 4.00
R8 Bill Gadsby 1.25 3.00
R9 Mickey Redmond 2.00 5.00
R10 Norm Ullman 1.25 3.00
R11 Red Kelly 1.50 4.00
R12 Ted Lindsay 1.50 4.00

1999-00 BAP Memorabilia AS Retail Autographs

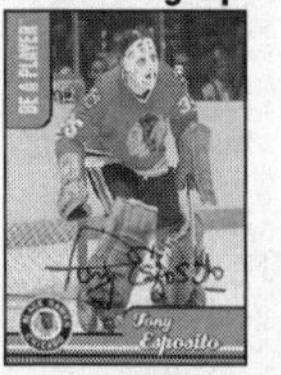

Randomly inserted in retail packs at the rate of 1:320, this 12-card set paralleled the base Channel Specific Retail insert set in an autographed version.

STATED ODDS 1:320
R1 Bobby Hull 30.00 80.00
R2 Dennis Hull 20.00 40.00
R3 Denis Savard 20.00 40.00
R4 Pierre Pilote 20.00 40.00
R5 Stan Mikita 30.00 80.00
R6 Tony Esposito 30.00 80.00
R7 Alex Delvecchio 20.00 40.00
R8 Bill Gadsby 20.00 40.00
R9 Mickey Redmond 25.00 60.00
R10 Norm Ullman 20.00 40.00
R11 Red Kelly 20.00 40.00
R12 Ted Lindsay 25.00 50.00

1999-00 BAP Memorabilia AS Heritage Ruby

Randomly inserted in packs, this 24-card set featured NHL stars in their first team uniform and their current team uniform. The base set was red and sequentially numbered to 1000. Sapphire and emerald parallels were also created. Sapphire parallels were blue in color and had a stated print run of 100 sets. Emerald parallels were green in color and had a stated print run of 10 sets. Emerald parallels were not priced due to scarcity.

COMPLETE SET (24) 60.00 125.00
STATED PRINT RUN 1000 SERIAL #'d SETS*SAPPHIRE: 4X TO 10X BASIC CARDS
SAPPHIRE STATED PRINT RUN 100 SETS
EMERALD STATED PRINT RUN 10 SETS
EMERALD: NOT PRICED DUE TO SCARCITY
H1 Brendan Shanahan 2.00 5.00
H2 John LeClair 2.00 5.00
H3 Jeremy Roenick 2.50 6.00
H4 John Vanbiesbrouck 1.50 4.00
H5 Dominik Hasek 4.00 10.00
H6 Adam Oates 1.50 4.00
H7 Teemu Selanne 2.00 5.00
H8 Ron Francis 1.50 4.00
H9 Al MacInnis 1.50 4.00
H10 Patrick Roy 10.00 25.00
H11 Doug Gilmour 1.50 4.00
H12 Brett Hull 2.50 6.00
H13 Curtis Joseph 2.00 5.00
H14 Mark Messier 2.00 5.00
H15 Paul Coffey 2.00 5.00
H16 Byron Dafoe 2.00 5.00
H17 Ed Belfour 2.00 5.00
H18 Wayne Gretzky 12.50 30.00
H19 Pavel Bure 2.00 5.00
H20 Chris Chelios 2.00 5.00
H21 Mats Sundin 2.00 5.00
H22 Joe Nieuwendyk 1.50 4.00
H23 Pavol Demitra 1.50 4.00
H24 Grant Fuhr 2.00 5.00

1999-00 BAP Update Double AS Jersey Cards

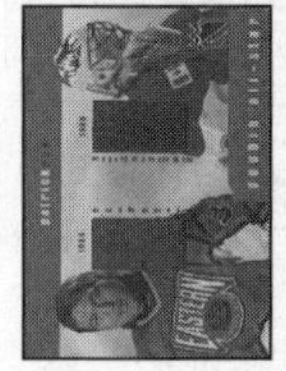

Randomly inserted in Update Factory Sets at the rate of 1:5, this 20-card set featured player photos coupled with two swatches of game-worn jerseys.

STATED ODDS 1:5 UPD.FACTORY SETS
D1 Jaromir Jagr 15.00 40.00
D2 Eric Lindros 12.50 40.00
D3 Peter Forsberg 20.00 50.00
D4 Patrick Roy 30.00 80.00
D5 Paul Kariya 12.50 40.00
D6 Mats Sundin 12.50 40.00
D7 Ray Bourque 20.00 50.00
D8 Ed Belfour 12.50 40.00
D9 Wayne Gretzky 75.00 200.00
D10 Teemu Selanne 12.50 40.00
D11 Brendan Shanahan 12.50 40.00
D12 Dominik Hasek 25.00 60.00
D13 Pavel Bure 12.50 40.00
D14 John LeClair 12.50 40.00
D15 Al MacInnis 10.00 25.00
D16 Brett Hull 15.00 40.00
D17 Brian Leetch 12.50 40.00
D18 Mark Messier 12.50 40.00
D19 Martin Brodeur 30.00 80.00
D20 Sergei Fedorov 20.00 50.00

1999-00 BAP Update Teammates Jersey Cards

STATED ODDS 1:5 UPD.FACTORY SETS
TM1 Curtis Joseph / Jeremy Roenick 12.50 30.00
TM2 Wayne Gretzky / Rob Blake 40.00 100.00
TM3 Patrick Roy / Mark Messier 30.00 80.00
TM4 Teemu Selanne / Brett Hull 12.50 30.00

TM5 Brendan Shanahan 20.00 50.00
Sergei Fedorov
TM6 Ray Bourque 25.00 60.00
Brian Leetch
TM7 Eric Lindros 12.50 30.00
John LeClair
TM8 Jaromir Jagr 20.00 50.00
Mark Messier
TM9 Martin Brodeur 15.00 40.00
Brendan Shanahan
TM10 Peter Forsberg 25.00 60.00
Paul Kariya
TM11 Ed Belfour 12.50 30.00
Chris Chelios
TM12 Teemu Selanne 12.50 30.00
Paul Kariya
TM13 Dominik Hasek 12.50 30.00
Peter Bondra
TM14 Steve Yzerman 30.00 80.00
Pavel Bure
TM15 John LeClair 25.00 60.00
Ray Bourque
TM16 Theo Fleury 12.50 30.00
Owen Nolan
TM17 Martin Brodeur 25.00 60.00
Paul Coffey
TM18 John LeClair 12.50 30.00
Eric Lindros
TM19 Jaromir Jagr 25.00 60.00
Pavel Bure
TM20 Dominik Hasek 25.00 60.00
Nikolai Khabibulin
TM21 Patrick Roy 25.00 60.00
Brian Leetch
TM22 Wayne Gretzky 40.00 100.00
Mike Modano
TM23 Peter Forsberg 15.00 40.00
Sandis Ozolinsh
TM24 Chris Chelios 25.00 60.00
Ray Bourque
TM25 Mats Sundin 12.50 30.00
Nicklas Lidstrom
TM26 Paul Kariya 12.50 30.00
Mike Modano
TM27 Theo Fleury 12.50 30.00
Tony Amonte
TM28 Peter Forsberg 25.00 60.00
Teemu Selanne
TM29 Eric Lindros 12.50 30.00
Darryl Sydor
TM30 Pavel Bure 12.50 30.00
Mats Sundin
TM31 Jeremy Roenick 12.50 30.00
Scott Stevens
TM32 Jaromir Jagr 15.00 40.00
Olaf Kolzig
TM33 Mike Richter 12.50 30.00
Tony Amonte
TM34 Chris Pronger 12.50 30.00
Al MacInnis
TM35 Brendan Shanahan 20.00 50.00
Martin Brodeur
TM36 Alexander Mogilny 12.50 30.00
Mark Messier
TM37 Steve Yzerman 40.00 100.00
Sergei Fedorov
TM38 Brendan Shanahan 25.00 60.00
Sergei Fedorov
TM39 Steve Yzerman 20.00 50.00
Chris Chelios
TM40 Steve Yzerman 25.00 60.00
Brendan Shanahan
TM41 Mats Sundin 12.50 30.00
Curtis Joseph
TM42 Peter Forsberg 40.00 100.00
Patrick Roy
TM43 Peter Forsberg 30.00 80.00
Joe Sakic
TM44 Joe Sakic 30.00 80.00
Patrik Roy
TM45 Teemu Selanne 12.50 30.00
Paul Kariya
TM46 B.Hull/M.Modano 20.00 50.00
TM47 Brett Hull 12.50 30.00
Ed Belfour
TM48 E.Belfour/M.Modano 15.00 40.00
TM49 Eric Lindros 12.50 30.00
John LeClair
TM50 Brian Leetch 15.00 40.00
Theo Fleury

2000-01 BAP Memorabilia

Released as a 521-card base set, including two update sets, Be A Player Memorabilia cards featured full color player action shots with white borders on three sides and black lettering. Be A Player was packaged in 24-pack boxes with packs containing eight cards and carried an American SRP of $3.29 and a Canadian SRP of $4.99. A Trevor Linden Autograph redemption card was randomly inserted in series one packs. For a $20.00 donation to the Trevor Linden foundation, an autographed card was returned. Be A Player Memorabilia Update, card numbers 397-497 and inserts were issued in factory set form only. Be A Player Final Update was issued by mail redemption as a 24-card set numbered 498-521.

COMPLETE SET (521) 75.00 150.00
COMP.SER 1 (396) 60.00 120.00
COMP.UPDATE SET (101) 15.00 30.00
COMP. FINAL UPDATE SET (24) 15.00 30.00
1 Jaromir Jagr .50 1.25
2 Scott Mellanby .08 .25
3 Mike Fisher .08 .25
4 Slava Kozlov .08 .25
5 Steve Valiquette RC .40 1.00
6 Simon Gagne .30 .75
7 Alexei Morozov .08 .25
8 Alexei Zhitnik .08 .25
9 Jochen Hecht .08 .25
10 Jamie Allison .08 .25
11 Olli Jokinen .25 .60
12 Bobby Holik .08 .25
13 Keith Primeau .08 .25
14 Bryan McCabe .08 .25
15 Tim Connolly .08 .25
16 Marco Sturm .08 .25
17 Craig Darby .08 .25
18 Jeff Cowan RC .40 1.00
19 Brad Stuart .08 .25
20 Sean O'Donnell .08 .25
21 Mike Minard RC .40 1.00
22 Rob Blake .08 .25
23 Marek Malik .08 .25
24 Marek Posmyk .08 .25
25 Alex Tanguay .25 .60
26 Steven McCarthy .08 .25
27 Bill Guerin .25 .60
28 Ed Jovanovski .08 .25
29 Martin Skoula .08 .25
30 Jeff Hackett .25 .60
31 Vladimir Tsyplakov .08 .25
32 Sergei Zubov .08 .25
33 Damian Rhodes .25 .60
34 Brent Sopel RC .40 1.00
35 Frantisek Kaberle .08 .25
36 Michael Peca .08 .25
37 Steve Kelly .08 .25
38 Geoff Sanderson .08 .25
39 Petr Svoboda .08 .25
40 Martin Brodeur .75 2.00
41 Markus Naslund .30 .75
42 Steve Thomas .08 .25
43 Anson Carter .25 .60
44 Theo Fleury .30 .75
45 Felix Potvin .30 .75
46 Adam Deadmarsh .08 .25
47 Dave Tanabe .08 .25
48 Trevor Kidd .25 .60
49 Jeff Friesen .08 .25
50 Marc Moro RC .40 1.00
51 Luc Robitaille .25 .60
52 Mike Richter .30 .75
53 Eric Desjardins .08 .25
54 Jean-Sebastien Aubin .25 .60
55 Paul Laus .08 .25
56 Kimmo Timonen .08 .25
57 Steve Sullivan .08 .25
58 Eric Cairns .08 .25
59 Scott Stevens .25 .60
60 Andy Delmore .08 .25
61 Jeff Nielsen .08 .25
62 Mathieu Biron .08 .25
63 Juha Lind .08 .25
64 Maxim Afinogenov .08 .25
65 Guy Hebert .25 .60
66 Sergei Brylin .08 .25
67 Mike Modano .50 1.25
68 Tommy Salo .25 .60
69 Bryan Smolinski .08 .25
70 Sergei Varlamov .08 .25
71 Paul Mara .08 .25
72 Peter Forsberg .75 2.00
73 Doug Weight .25 .60
74 Peter Bondra .30 .75
75 Marc Denis .25 .60
76 Jamie Storr .25 .60
77 Alexei Kovalev .25 .60
78 Dainius Zubrus .08 .25
79 Mike Grier .08 .25
80 Olaf Kolzig .25 .60
81 Bryan Adams RC .40 1.00
82 Scott Niedermayer .08 .25
83 David Gosselin RC .40 1.00
84 Boris Mironov .08 .25
85 Kyle McLaren .08 .25
86 Steve Kariya .08 .25
87 Dimitri Yushkevich .08 .25
88 Paul Kariya .30 .75
89 Brian Leetch .30 .75
90 Jeff Daniels .08 .25
91 Brendan Morrison .25 .60
92 Brian Campbell .08 .25
93 Ray Whitney .08 .25
94 Marian Hossa .30 .75
95 Sergei Samsonov .30 .75
96 Mike York .08 .25
97 Mark Eaton .08 .25
98 Ryan VandenBussche .08 .25
99 Vladimir Malakhov .08 .25
100 Jeff Finley .08 .25
101 John Vanbiesbrouck .25 .60
102 Brad Isbister .08 .25
103 John Madden .08 .25
104 Patrick Roy 1.50 4.00
105 Radek Bonk .08 .25
106 Brett Hull .40 1.00
107 Andreas Dackell .08 .25
108 Pierre Turgeon .08 .25
109 Jason Woolley .08 .25
110 Jeff O'Neill .08 .25
111 John LeClair .30 .75
112 Darryl Sydor .08 .25
113 Ryan Smyth .08 .25
114 Curtis Joseph .30 .75
115 Gary Roberts .08 .25
116 Pavel Kubina .08 .25
117 Roman Hamrlik .08 .25
118 Sandis Ozolinsh .08 .25
119 Manny Fernandez .25 .60
120 Adam Oates .25 .60
121 Darby Hendrickson .08 .25
122 Glen Murray .08 .25
123 Jiri Slegr .08 .25
124 Steve Yzerman 1.50 4.00
125 Mats Lindgren .08 .25
126 Sergei Gonchar .08 .25
127 Joe Thornton .50 1.25
128 Petr Sykora .08 .25
129 Pavol Demitra .25 .60
130 Tyler Wright .08 .25
131 Johan Davidsson .08 .25
132 Brian Rolston .08 .25
133 Mark Messier .30 .75
134 Darcy Tucker .08 .25
135 Oleg Tverdovsky .08 .25
136 Petr Nedved .08 .25
137 Harold Druken .08 .25
138 Valeri Bure .08 .25
139 Mikael Andersson .08 .25
140 Evgeni Nabokov .25 .60
141 Janne Laukkanen .08 .25
142 Radek Dvorak .08 .25
143 Brian Boucher .30 .75
144 Eric Daze .25 .60
145 Dan Cloutier .08 .25
146 Scott Gomez .08 .25
147 Dallas Drake .08 .25
148 Shawn McEachern .08 .25
149 Joe Nieuwendyk .25 .60
150 Kenny Jonsson .08 .25
151 Saku Koivu .30 .75
152 Roman Turek .25 .60
153 Chris Gratton .08 .25
154 Steve Rucchin .08 .25
155 Teppo Numminen .08 .25
156 Jamie Langenbrunner .08 .25
157 Johnathan Aitken RC .40 1.00
158 Nikolai Antropov .08 .25
159 Stephane Fiset .08 .25
160 Manny Malhotra .08 .25
161 Pavel Bure .30 .75
162 Chris Drury .25 .60
163 Roberto Luongo .40 1.00
164 Norm Maracle .25 .60
165 Brendan Shanahan .30 .75
166 Calle Johansson .08 .25
167 Cory Stillman .08 .25
168 Jozef Stumpel .08 .25
169 Ron Tugnutt .25 .60
170 Brian Savage .08 .25
171 Viktor Kozlov .08 .25
172 Chris Simon .08 .25
173 Chris Joseph .08 .25
174 Willie Mitchell RC .40 1.00
175 Randy Robitaille .08 .25
176 Sami Kapanen .08 .25
177 Jonathan Girard .08 .25
178 Andrew Cassels .08 .25
179 Jani Hurme RC .40 1.00
180 Maxim Balmochnyk .08 .25
181 Adam Graves .08 .25
182 Steve Shields .08 .25
183 Marc Savard .08 .25
184 Zigmund Palffy .30 .75
185 Magnus Arvedson .08 .25
186 Byron Dafoe .25 .60
187 Jan Hlavac .08 .25
188 Len Barrie .08 .25
189 Jocelyn Thibault .25 .60
190 Fred Brathwaite .25 .60
191 Fredrik Modin .08 .25
192 Shane Doan .08 .25
193 Petr Mika RC .40 1.00
194 Larry Murphy .08 .25
195 Daniel Alfredsson .25 .60
196 Brenden Morrow .25 .60
197 Martin Rucinsky .08 .25
198 Michal Handzus .08 .25
199 Dominik Hasek .60 1.50
200 Rod Brind'Amour .25 .60
201 Trevor Letowski .08 .25
202 Derian Hatcher .08 .25
203 Phil Housley .08 .25
204 Martin Biron .25 .60
205 Sergei Berezin .08 .25
206 Ron Francis .25 .60
207 Cliff Ronning .08 .25
208 Robert Svehla .08 .25
209 Vincent Lecavalier .30 .75
210 Kent Manderville .08 .25
211 Andrew Brunette .08 .25
212 Chris Chelios .30 .75
213 Alexander Karpovtsev .08 .25
214 Robyn Regehr .08 .25
215 Mika Alatalo .08 .25
216 Jan Hrdina .08 .25
217 Nicklas Lidstrom .30 .75
218 Ivan Novoseltsev .08 .25
219 Alexander Mogilny .25 .60
220 Chris Pronger .25 .60
221 Paul Coffey .30 .75
222 John Grahame .25 .60
223 Jeff Farkas .08 .25
224 Eric Lindros .30 .75
225 Jorgen Jonsson .08 .25
226 Jean-Francois Labbe RC .40 1.00
227 Owen Nolan .25 .60
228 Oleg Saprykin .08 .25
229 Patrick Marleau .25 .60
230 Aaron Downey RC .40 1.00
231 Chris Osgood .25 .60
232 Mike Wilson .08 .25
233 Joe Sakic .60 1.50
234 Dieter Kochan RC .40 1.00
235 Jeremy Roenick .40 1.00
236 Alexei Zhamnov .08 .25
237 Sergei Fedorov .50 1.25
238 Petr Schastlivy .08 .25
239 Milan Hejduk .30 .75
240 Patrice Brisebois .08 .25
241 Marty Reasoner .08 .25
242 Ed Belfour .30 .75
243 Vitali Vishnevsky .08 .25
244 Keith Tkachuk .30 .75
245 Petr Buzek .08 .25
246 Miroslav Satan .25 .60
247 Adam Mair .08 .25
248 Jere Karalahti .08 .25
249 Mike Dunham .25 .60
250 Mike Sillinger .08 .25
251 Andrei Skopintsev RC .40 1.00
252 Sergei Vyshedkevich .40 1.00
253 Steve Duchesne .08 .25
254 Tomas Kaberle .08 .25
255 Arturs Irbe .25 .60
256 Niklas Sundstrom .08 .25
257 Al MacInnis .25 .60
258 Mike Ribeiro .08 .25
259 Rob Niedermayer .08 .25
260 Jean-Guy Trudel RC .40 1.00
261 Martin Straka .08 .25
262 Jason Arnott .08 .25
263 David Legwand .25 .60
264 Tony Amonte .25 .60
265 Jason Allison .08 .25
266 Patrik Elias .25 .60
267 Mark Recchi .25 .60
268 Patrik Stefan .08 .25
269 Mariusz Czerkawski .08 .25
270 Vincent Damphousse .08 .25
271 Sergei Krivokrasov .08 .25
272 Teemu Selanne .30 .75
273 Patrick Lalime .25 .60
274 Nick Boynton .08 .25
275 Darren McCarty .08 .25
276 Jaroslav Spacek .08 .25
277 Chris Dingman .08 .25
278 Jarome Iginla .40 1.00
279 Andrei Zyuzin .08 .25
280 Jyrki Lumme .08 .25
281 Michal Grosek .08 .25
282 Janne Niinimaa .08 .25
283 Wade Redden .08 .25
284 Ray Bourque .60 1.50
285 Trevor Linden .08 .25
286 Ladislav Nagy .08 .25
287 Jose Theodore .40 1.00
288 Bates Battaglia .08 .25
289 Mikael Renberg .08 .25
290 Donald Audette .08 .25
291 Doug Gilmour .30 .75
292 Yanic Perreault .08 .25
293 Anders Eriksson .08 .25
294 Gary Suter .08 .25
295 Brad Ference .08 .25
296 Mats Sundin .30 .75
297 Ray Ferraro .08 .25
298 Jiri Fischer .08 .25
299 Todd Bertuzzi .30 .75
300 Derek Morris .08 .25
301 Patric Kjellberg .08 .25
302 Pat Verbeek .08 .25
303 Kip Miller .08 .25
304 Alexei Vasilyev .08 .25
305 Marcus Ragnarsson .08 .25
306 Arron Asham .08 .25
307 Sylvain Cote .08 .25
308 Vaclav Prospal .08 .25
309 Aki Berg .08 .25
310 Alexander Selivanov .08 .25
311 Wayne Primeau .08 .25
312 Brian Rafalski .08 .25
313 Jonas Hoglund .08 .25
314 Adam Foote .08 .25
315 Steve Konowalchuk .08 .25
316 Robert Dome .08 .25
317 Antti Laaksonen .08 .25
318 Mike Ricci .08 .25
319 Gino Odjick .08 .25
320 Eric Weinrich .08 .25
321 Jason Strudwick .08 .25
322 Kim Johnsson .08 .25
323 Dimitri Kalinin .08 .25
324 Daymond Langkow .08 .25
325 Todd Marchant .08 .25
326 Richard Matvichuk .08 .25
327 Travis Green .08 .25
328 Igor Larionov .08 .25
329 Mattias Ohlund .08 .25
330 Igor Kravchuk .08 .25
331 Richard Zednik .08 .25
332 Curtis Brown .08 .25
333 Krzysztof Oliwa .08 .25
334 Darius Kasparaitis .08 .25
335 Michael Nylander .08 .25
336 Stan Drulia .08 .25
337 Nelson Emerson .08 .25
338 Greg Johnson .08 .25
339 Sean Hill .08 .25
340 Keith Jones .08 .25
341 Bill Muckalt .08 .25
342 Randy McKay .08 .25
343 Stu Grimson .08 .25
344 Tyson Nash .08 .25
345 Dan Hinote .08 .25
346 Mike Rathje .08 .25
347 Brian Holzinger .08 .25
348 Eric Nickulas RC .40 1.00
349 Alexandre Daigle .08 .25
350 Jan Bulis .08 .25
351 Tom Poti .08 .25
352 Kevyn Adams .08 .25
353 Scott Thornton .08 .25
354 Sean Burke .08 .25
355 Peter Worrell .08 .25
356 Josef Beranek .08 .25
357 Matt Cullen .08 .25
358 Sandy McCarthy .08 .25
359 Sergei Zholtok .08 .25
360 Darren Langdon .08 .25
361 Martin Lapointe .08 .25
362 Adrian Aucoin .08 .25
363 Dmitri Nabokov .08 .25
364 Jason Blake .08 .25
365 Jeff Halpern .08 .25
366 Rico Fata .08 .25
367 Dave Reid .08 .25
368 Vitali Yachmenev .08 .25
369 Hnat Domenichelli .08 .25
370 Rick Tocchet .08 .25
371 Tommy Westlund .08 .25
372 Chris Phillips .08 .25
373 Claude Lemieux .08 .25
374 Greg Adams .08 .25
375 Todd Simpson .08 .25
376 Ken Klee .08 .25
377 Andre Savage .08 .25
378 Bryan Marchment .08 .25
379 Dean McAmmond .08 .25
380 Mike Johnson .08 .25
381 Tomas Holmstrom .08 .25
382 Robert Lang .08 .25
383 Dan McGillis .08 .25
384 Jamie Rivers .08 .25
385 Dave Andreychuk .25 .60
386 Marty McInnis .08 .25
387 Sami Salo .08 .25
388 Daniel Cleary .08 .25
389 Robert Esche .08 .25
390 Aaron Gavey .08 .25
391 Andrei Nikolishin .08 .25
392 Jason Krog .08 .25
393 Stu Barnes .08 .25
394 Tomas Vokoun .08 .25
395 Peter Schaefer .08 .25
396 Daniil Markov .08 .25
397 Daniel Sedin .08 .25
398 Kris Beech .08 .25
399 Samuel Pahlsson .08 .25
400 Gary Roberts .08 .25
401 Marian Gaborik RC 2.50 6.00
402 Oleg Kvasha .08 .25
403 Martin Havlat RC 1.50 4.00
404 Roman Simicek RC .40 1.00
405 Dallas Drake .08 .25
406 Jakub Cutta RC .40 1.00
407 German Titov .08 .25
408 Jarno Kultanen RC .40 1.00
409 Sandis Ozolinsh .08 .25
410 David Vyborny .08 .25
411 Olli Jokinen .25 .60
412 Maxim Sushinski .08 .25
413 John Vanbiesbrouck .25 .60
414 Shane Hnidy RC .40 1.00
415 Milan Kraft .08 .25
416 Alexander Kharitonov RC .40 1.00
417 Andrei Nazarov .08 .25
418 Dave Andreychuk .25 .60
419 Niclas Wallin RC .40 1.00
420 Rostislav Klesla RC .60 1.50
421 Denis Shvidki .08 .25
422 Mathieu Garon .08 .25
423 Taylor Pyatt .08 .25
424 Roman Cechmanek RC .40 1.00
425 Mark Smith RC .40 1.00
426 Shayne Corson .08 .25
427 Jonas Ronnqvist RC .40 1.00
428 J-P Dumont .08 .25
429 Josef Vasicek RC .40 1.00
430 Tyler Bouck RC .40 1.00
431 Matt Schneider .08 .25
432 Andrei Markov .08 .25
433 Vladimir Malakhov .08 .25
434 Maxime Ouellet .08 .25
435 Matt Bradley .08 .25
436 Dave Manson .08 .25
437 Brad Tapper RC .40 1.00
438 Eric Boulton RC .40 1.00
439 Brent Johnson .08 .25
440 Marty Turco RC 1.50 4.00
441 Tomas Vlasak .08 .25
442 Greg Classen RC .40 1.00
443 Mark Messier .30 .75
444 Justin Williams RC 1.00 2.50
445 Sean Hill .08 .25
446 Bryan McCabe .08 .25
447 Andreas Karlsson .08 .25
448 Mika Noronen .08 .25
449 Alexander Karpovtsev .08 .25
450 Boyd Devereaux .08 .25
451 Lubomir Visnovsky RC .40 1.00
452 Scott Hartnell RC .60 1.50
453 Jason Labarbera RC .60 1.50
454 Petr Hubacek RC .40 1.00
455 Alexander Khavanov RC .40 1.00
456 Petr Svoboda RC .40 1.00
457 Tomi Kallio .08 .25
458 Mike Vernon .08 .25
459 Reto Von Arx RC .40 1.00
460 Maxim Kuznetsov .08 .25
461 Steven Reinprecht RC .40 1.00
462 Turner Stevenson .08 .25
463 Roberto Luongo .40 1.00
464 Brad Richards .08 .25
465 Bryce Salvador RC .40 1.00
466 Kevin Hatcher .08 .25
467 Paul Coffey .30 .75
468 Marty Murray .08 .25
469 Todd Fedoruk RC .40 1.00
470 Brian Swanson RC .40 1.00
471 Christian Matte .08 .25
472 Sascha Goc RC .40 1.00
473 Dale Purinton RC .40 1.00
474 Brad May .08 .25
475 Brad Brown .08 .25
476 Petteri Nummelin RC .40 1.00
477 Ruslan Fedotenko RC .40 1.00
478 Ronald Petrovicky RC .40 1.00
479 David Aebischer RC 1.00 2.50
480 Michel Riesen RC .40 1.00
481 Ladislav Benysek RC .40 1.00
482 Mark Parrish .08 .25
483 Mike Mottau .08 .25
484 Ossi Vaananen RC .40 1.00
485 Andrew Raycroft RC 1.25 3.00
486 Sylvain Cote .08 .25
487 Richard Jackman .08 .25
488 Toni Lydman .08 .25
489 Ron Tugnutt .08 .25
490 Igor Larionov .08 .25
491 Lubomir Sekeras RC .40 1.00
492 Roman Hamrlik .08 .25
493 Johan Holmqvist RC .40 1.00
494 Josef Melichar RC .08 .25
495 Sheldon Keefe .08 .25
496 Henrik Sedin .08 .25
497 Rick DiPietro RC 1.50 4.00
498 Teemu Selanne .30 .75
499 Keith Tkachuk .30 .75
500 Rob Blake .25 .60
501 Mario Lemieux 2.00 5.00
502 Johan Hedberg RC .60 1.50
503 Felix Potvin .30 .75
504 Branislav Mezei .08 .25
505 Mike Comrie RC 1.00 2.50
506 Miikka Kiprusoff .40 1.00
507 Petr Tenkrat RC .40 1.00
508 Mark Bell .08 .25
509 Steve Gainey RC .40 1.00
510 Jason Williams RC .40 1.00
511 Shawn Horcoff RC .75 2.00
512 Eric Chouinard .08 .25
513 Derek Gustafson RC .40 1.00
514 Bryan Allen .08 .25
515 Kristian Kudroc .08 .25
516 Gregg Naumenko RC .40 1.00
517 Pierre Dagenais .08 .25
518 Juraj Kolnik RC .40 1.00
519 Tomas Kloucek RC .40 1.00
520 Andreas Lilja RC .40 1.00
521 Alexei Ponikarovsky RC .40 1.00
*NNO Trevor Linden AU 15.00 25.00

2000-01 BAP Memorabilia Emerald

EMERALD STAT.PRINT RUN 10 SERIAL #'d SETS
NOT PRICED DUE TO SCARCITY

2000-01 BAP Memorabilia Ruby

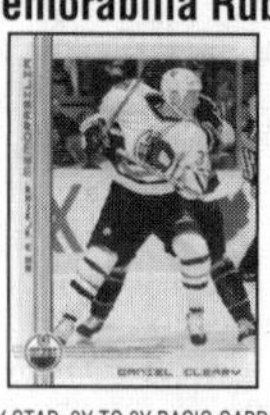

*RUBY STAR: 3X TO 8X BASIC CARDS
*RUBY RC's: 1.5X TO 3X BASIC CARDS
PRINT RUN 200 SERIAL #'d SETS

2000-01 BAP Memorabilia Sapphire

*SAPPHIRE STARS: 6X TO 15X BASIC CARDS
*SAPPHIRE RC's: 5X TO 10X BASIC CARDS
PRINT RUN 100 SERIAL #'d SETS

2000-01 BAP Memorabilia Promos

This 396-card set paralleled the base series but carried the word promo on the card backs. The cards were issued as promotional materila to announce the products release. Due to the distribution method and scarcity, they were not priced.
NOT PRICED DUE TO SCARCITY

2000-01 BAP Memorabilia All-Star Tickets

Randomly seeded in packs at the rate of 1:864, this 10-card set featured swatches of All-Star Game tickets with the respective year's All-Star Game logo faded into the background.

COMPLETE SET (10) 150.00 300.00
STATED ODDS 1:864
AST1 1990 All-Star Game 12.50 30.00
AST2 1991 All-Star Game 12.50 30.00
AST3 1992 All-Star Game 12.50 30.00
AST4 1993 All-Star Game 12.50 30.00
AST5 1994 All-Star Game 12.50 30.00
AST6 1996 All-Star Game 12.50 30.00
AST7 1997 All-Star Game 12.50 30.00
AST8 1998 All-Star Game 12.50 30.00
AST9 1999 All-Star Game 12.50 30.00
AST10 2000 All-Star Game 12.50 30.00

2000-01 BAP Memorabilia Georges Vezina

Randomly inserted in packs at the rate of 1:2400, this 16-card set features today's top goalies coupled with a swatch of a Georges Vezina goalie pad. The Vezina pad used was believed to be the only one in existance.

V1 Olaf Kolzig 150.00 400.00
V2 Dominik Hasek 150.00 400.00
V3 Dominik Hasek 150.00 400.00
V4 Dominik Hasek 150.00 400.00
V5 Jim Carey 150.00 400.00
V6 Dominik Hasek 150.00 400.00
V7 Dominik Hasek 150.00 400.00
V8 Ed Belfour 150.00 400.00
V9 Patrick Roy 200.00 500.00
V10 Ed Belfour 150.00 300.00
V11 Patrick Roy 200.00 500.00
V12 Patrick Roy 200.00 500.00
V13 Grant Fuhr 150.00 300.00
V14 John Vanbiesbrouck 150.00 300.00
V15 Tom Barrasso 150.00 300.00
V16 Georges Vezina 600.00 1000.00

2000-01 BAP Memorabilia Goalie Memorabilia

Randomly inserted in packs at the rate of 1:999, this 30-card set featured swatches of goalie worn jerseys, sticks, pads and gloves. Cards G1-G11 were single player cards with two swatches of memorabilia, card numbers G12-G28 were dual player cards with two swatches of memorabilia, and card numbers G29 and G30 were triple player cards with three swatches of memorabilia.

STATED ODDS 1:999
G1 Mike Richter J/S 30.00 80.00
G2 Patrick Roy G/S 100.00 250.00
G3 Dominik Hasek G/S 60.00 150.00
G4 Ed Belfour J/S 30.00 80.00
G5 Curtis Joseph G/S 30.00 80.00
G6 Terry Sawchuk G/S 125.00 300.00
G7 Vladislav Tretiak J/G 100.00 250.00
G8 Gerry Cheevers S/P 30.00 80.00
G9 Felix Potvin G/J 30.00 80.00
G10 Frank Brimsek G/J 40.00 100.00
G11 Bernie Parent P/J 30.00 80.00
G12 Bernie Parent Jersey 40.00 100.00
Tony Esposito Jersey
G13 Johnny Bower Stick 60.00 150.00
Curtis Joseph Stick
G14 Frank Brimsek Glove 40.00 100.00
Gerry Cheevers Stick
G15 Patrick Roy Stick 125.00 300.00
Jacques Plante Glove
G16 Vlatislav Tretiak Jersey 100.00 250.00
Tony Esposito Jersey
G17 Terry Sawchuk Stick 125.00 300.00
Curtis Joseph Jersey
G18 Turk Broda Glove 40.00 100.00
Curtis Joseph Jersey
G19 Johnny Bower Glove 40.00 100.00
Turk Broda Glove
G20 Felix Potvin Glove 75.00 200.00
Curtis Joseph Stick
G21 Ed Belfour Jersey 100.00 250.00
Patrick Roy Jersey
G22 Ed Belfour Jersey 100.00 250.00
Vladislav Tretiak Jersey
G23 Terry Sawchuk Stick 150.00 400.00
Jacques Plante Glove
G24 Johnny Bower Stick 125.00 300.00
Terry Sawchuk Stick
G25 Tony Esposito Glove 40.00 100.00
Gerry Cheevers Pad
G26 Frank Brimsek Glove 40.00 100.00
Gerry Cheevers Pad
G27 Curtis Joseph Glove 40.00 100.00
Turk Broda Glove
G28 Patrick Roy Glove 200.00 500.00
Terry Sawchuk Glove
G29 Curtis Joseph Stick 125.00 300.00
Johnny Bower Stick
Terry Sawchuk Stick
G30 Gerry Cheevers Stick 75.00 200.00
Bernie Parent Stick
Tony Esposito Stick

2000-01 BAP Memorabilia Jersey Cards

*MULT.COLOR SWATCH: 1X TO 1.5X JERSEY CARD
STATED ODDS 1:360
J1 Jeremy Roenick 10.00 25.00
J2 Mats Sundin 8.00 20.00
J3 Pavel Bure 8.00 20.00
J4 Martin Brodeur 15.00 40.00
J5 Mike Richter 8.00 20.00
J6 Brendan Shanahan 8.00 20.00
J7 Chris Pronger 8.00 20.00
J8 Al MacInnis 8.00 20.00
J9 Jaromir Jagr 12.00 30.00
J10 Olaf Kolzig 8.00 20.00
J11 Tony Amonte 8.00 20.00
J12 Scott Stevens 8.00 20.00
J13 Dominik Hasek 12.00 30.00
J14 Peter Forsberg 12.00 30.00
J15 Teemu Selanne 8.00 20.00
J16 Eric Lindros 8.00 20.00
J17 Nicklas Lidstrom 8.00 20.00

J18 Theo Fleury 8.00 20.00
J19 Darryl Sydor 8.00 20.00
J20 Mike Modano 12.00 30.00
J21 Nikolai Khabibulin 8.00 20.00
J22 Sandis Ozolinsh 8.00 20.00
J23 Mark Messier 8.00 20.00
J24 Joe Sakic 12.00 30.00
J25 Wayne Gretzky 40.00 100.00
J26 Owen Nolan 8.00 20.00
J27 Daniel Alfredsson 8.00 20.00
J28 Paul Coffey 8.00 20.00
J29 Steve Yzerman 15.00 40.00
J30 Brett Hull 12.00 30.00
J31 Paul Kariya 8.00 20.00
J32 John LeClair 8.00 20.00
J33 Ed Belfour 10.00 25.00
J34 Patrick Roy 20.00 50.00
J35 Sergei Fedorov 12.00 30.00
J36 Mark Recchi 8.00 20.00
J37 Ray Bourque 12.00 30.00
J38 Brian Leetch 8.00 20.00
J39 Rob Blake 8.00 20.00
J40 Curtis Joseph 8.00 20.00

2000-01 BAP Memorabilia Jersey Emblems

*EMBLEMS: 1X TO 2.5X JERSEY CARDS
STATED ODDS 1:999

2000-01 BAP Memorabilia Jersey Numbers

*NUMBERS: 1X TO 2.5X JERSEY CARDS
STATED ODDS 1:999

2000-01 BAP Memorabilia Jersey and Stick Cards

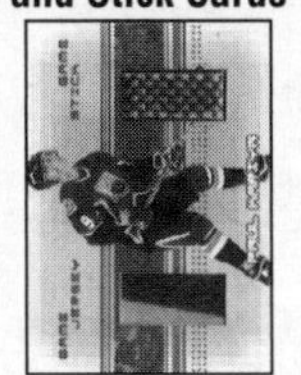

*JSY/STICKS: .75X TO 1.25X JERSEY CARDS
STATED ODDS 1:999

2000-01 BAP Memorabilia Mario Lemieux Legends

Randomly inserted in packs at the rate of 1:4800, this 10-card set featured game-used memorabilia swatches from Mario Lemieux. Memorabilia combinations are listed below. The stated print run on each card was an estimated 30 sets.
STATED PRINT RUN 30 SETS
L1 1987-88 Jsy 50.00 125.00
L2 1991-92 Jsy 50.00 125.00
L3 1987 Jsy/1991 Glove 60.00 150.00
L4 1991-92 Jsy/Glove 60.00 150.00
L5 1991-92 Jsy Emblem 150.00 400.00
L6 1991-92 Jsy Number 150.00 400.00
L7 1991-92 Glove 50.00 125.00
L8 1996 AS Jsy 50.00 125.00
L9 1987 Jsy/1996 AS Jsy 60.00 150.00
L10 1991 Jsy/1996 Jsy 60.00 150.00

2000-01 BAP Memorabilia Mario Lemieux Legends Autographs

Randomly seeded in packs, this 10-card set paralleled the base Legends set enhanced with an autograph. The stated print run on each card was an estimated 6 sets.
STATED PRINT RUN 6 SETS
NOT PRICED DUE TO SCARCITY

2000-01 BAP Memorabilia Patent Power Jerseys

STATED ODDS 1:4800
PP1 M.Lemieux/W.Gretzky 250.00 600.00
PP2 P.Kariya/S.Yzerman 150.00 400.00
PP3 Pavel Bure 100.00 250.00

Jaromir Jagr
PP4 Mats Sundin 40.00 100.00
Peter Forsberg
PP5 Teemu Selanne 40.00 100.00
Brett Hull
PP6 Brendan Shanahan 40.00 100.00
John LeClair

2000-01 BAP Memorabilia Update Heritage Jersey Cards

Inserts were placed in the Be A Player Memorabilia Update set on top of the sealed 100 cards along with the DiPietro Rookie card. Sets contained either four random insert cards, or one memorabilia card. Memorabilia cards were inserted at approximately one in five sets. The Heritage Jersey Cards featured a gold background, full color player action photography and a swatch of a game-used jersey in the upper right hand corner of the card front. Gold parallels numbered 1/1 were also created and inserted randomly, but are not priced due to scarcity.
*MULT.COLOR SWATCH: 1X TO 2X
MEMORABILIA STATED ODDS 1:5
FACT.SETS
GOLD 1 OF 1's EXIST
H1 Mark Messier 20.00 60.00
H2 Pavel Bure 20.00 50.00
H3 Paul Coffey 15.00 40.00
H4 Mats Sundin 20.00 50.00
H5 Curtis Joseph 15.00 40.00
H6 Ed Belfour 15.00 40.00
H7 Mike Modano 25.00 60.00
H8 Brett Hull 25.00 60.00
H9 Teemu Selanne 20.00 50.00
H10 Keith Tkachuk 10.00 25.00
H11 Patrick Roy 100.00 250.00
H12 Chris Chelios 10.00 25.00
H13 Al MacInnis 10.00 25.00
H14 Theo Fleury 10.00 25.00
H15 Keith Primeau 10.00 25.00
H16 Ray Bourque 40.00 100.00
H17 Brendan Shanahan 20.00 50.00
H18 Owen Nolan 10.00 25.00
H19 Felix Potvin 20.00 50.00
H20 Trevor Linden 10.00 25.00
H21 Scott Stevens 10.00 25.00
H22 Adam Oates 10.00 25.00

2000-01 BAP Memorabilia Update Record Breakers

Inserts were placed in the Be A Player Memorabilia Update set on top of the sealed 100 cards along with the DiPietro Rookie card. Sets contained either four random insert cards, or one memorabilia card. Memorabilia cards were inserted at approximately one in five sets. This 2-card set featured full color player action photography on a white card stock with two swatches of game used memorabilia. Gold parallels numbered 1/1 were also created and inserted randomly, but are not priced due to scarcity.
MEMORABILIA STATED ODDS 1:5
FACT.SETS
GOLD 1 OF 1's EXIST
BB1 Pavel Bure 50.00 125.00
Valeri Bure
RB1 Patrick Roy 275.00 600.00
Terry Sawchuk

2000-01 BAP Memorabilia Update Teammates

*MULT.COLOR SWATCH:1X TO 2X
MEMORABILIA STATED ODDS 1:5
FACT.SETS
GOLD 1 OF 1's EXIST
TM1 Petr Sykora 25.00 60.00
Martin Brodeur
TM2 Sergei Gonchar 10.00 25.00

Adam Oates
TM3 Jaromir Jagr 40.00 100.00
Mario Lemieux
TM4 Tony Amonte 10.00 25.00
Bob Probert
TM5 Jeremy Roenick 10.00 25.00
Keith Tkachuk
TM6 Michael Peca 10.00 25.00
Dominik Hasek
TM7 Mark Messier 25.00 60.00
Brian Leetch
TM8 Pavel Bure 10.00 25.00
Paul Laus
TM9 Tie Domi 10.00 25.00
Mats Sundin
TM10 M.Brodeur/S.Niedermayer 25.00 60.00
TM11 Kyle McLaren 10.00 25.00
Byron Dafoe
TM12 Nicklas Lidstrom 20.00 50.00
Chris Chelios
TM13 Darren McCarty 20.00 50.00
Steve Yzerman
TM14 Darryl Sydor 10.00 25.00
Ed Belfour
TM15 B.Hull/M.Modano 15.00 40.00
TM16 Brendan Shanahan 20.00 50.00
Sergei Fedorov
TM17 Nicklas Lidstrom 10.00 25.00
Slava Kozlov
TM18 Patrick Roy 40.00 100.00
Peter Forsberg
TM19 Mike Richter 10.00 25.00
Theo Fleury
TM20 Martin Straka 10.00 25.00
Jaromir Jagr
TM21 Jason Arnott 10.00 25.00
Scott Stevens
TM22 Brendan Shanahan 10.00 25.00
Chris Osgood
TM23 Paul Kariya 10.00 25.00
Guy Hebert
TM24 Curtis Joseph 10.00 25.00
Mats Sundin
TM25 Tony Amonte 10.00 25.00
Eric Daze
TM26 Teemu Selanne 10.00 25.00
Paul Kariya
TM27 Petr Sykora 10.00 25.00
Jason Arnott
TM28 Patrick Roy 40.00 100.00
Joe Sakic
TM29 Steve Yzerman 20.00 50.00
Sergei Fedorov
TM30 Keith Tkachuk 10.00 25.00
Teppo Numminen
TM31 Scott Niedermayer 10.00 25.00
Scott Stevens
TM32 Mark Messier 10.00 25.00
Mike Richter
TM33 Teppo Numminen 10.00 25.00
Nikolai Khabibulin
TM34 Peter Forsberg 30.00 80.00
Joe Sakic
TM35 Chris Osgood 10.00 25.00
Slava Kozlov
TM36 E.Belfour/M.Modano 12.50 30.00
TM37 Tie Domi 10.00 25.00
Curtis Joseph
TM38 Jeremy Roenick 10.00 25.00
Nikolai Khabibulin
TM39 Guy Hebert 10.00 25.00
Teemu Selanne
TM40 Theo Fleury 10.00 25.00
Brian Leetch

2000-01 BAP Memorabilia Update Tough Materials

*MULT.COLOR SWATCH: 1X TO 2X
MEMORABILIA STATED ODDS 1:5
FACT.SETS
GOLD 1 OF 1's EXIST
T1 Bob Probert 20.00 50.00
T2 Tie Domi 30.00 80.00
T3 Stu Grimson 25.00 60.00
T4 Eric Cairns 10.00 25.00
T5 Paul Laus 10.00 25.00
T6 Donald Brashear 15.00 40.00
T7 Rob Ray 15.00 40.00
T8 Wade Belak 10.00 25.00
T9 Kelly Chase 10.00 25.00
T10 Peter Worrell 10.00 25.00
T11 Darren McCarty 20.00 50.00
T12 Todd Simpson 10.00 25.00
T13 Krzysztof Oliwa 15.00 40.00
T14 Sandy McCarthy 10.00 25.00
T15 Brad Brown 10.00 25.00
T16 Luke Richardson 10.00 25.00
T17 Jeff Odgers 10.00 25.00
T18 Chris Dingman 10.00 25.00
T19 Enrico Ciccone 10.00 25.00
T20 Ryan VandenBussche 15.00 40.00
T21 Bob Boughner 10.00 25.00
T22 Gino Odjick 10.00 25.00
T23 Matt Johnson 10.00 25.00
T24 Jean-Luc Grand-Pierre 10.00 25.00
T25 Craig Berube 20.00 50.00
T26 Ian Laperriere 10.00 25.00

2001-02 BAP Memorabilia

Released in August 2001, this 300-card set featured color action photos on gray and black bordered card fronts.
COMP.SER.1 SET (300) 30.00 80.00
CARDS 301-500 AVAIL.IN BAP UPD.PACKS
1 Rick DiPietro .25 .60
2 Radek Dvorak .10 .25
3 Radek Bonk .10 .25
4 Evgeni Nabokov .25 .60
5 Roman Turek .25 .60
6 Daniel Sedin .10 .25
7 Jeff Halpern .10 .25
8 Joe Thornton .50 1.25
9 Maxim Afinogenov .10 .25
10 Oleg Saprykin .10 .25
11 Shane Willis .10 .25
12 Jocelyn Thibault .25 .60
13 Alex Tanguay .25 .60
14 Brenden Morrow .25 .60
15 Steve Yzerman 1.50 4.00
16 Anson Carter .25 .60
17 Brad Richards .25 .60
18 Mike York .10 .25
19 Brian Rafalski .10 .25
20 Maxime Ouellet .25 .60
21 Ruslan Fedotenko .10 .25
22 Brad Stuart .25 .60
23 Daniel Corso .10 .25
24 Mika Noronen .25 .60
25 Jason Williams .10 .25
26 Scott Stevens .25 .60
27 Patrick Lalime .25 .60
28 Johan Hedberg .25 .60
29 Vincent Damphousse .10 .25
30 Jochen Hecht .10 .25
31 Ed Jovanovski .25 .60
32 J-S Giguere .25 .60
33 Fred Brathwaite .25 .60
34 Arturs Irbe .25 .60
35 Ron Tugnutt .25 .60
36 Ed Belfour .30 .75
37 Chris Osgood .25 .60
38 Mike Comrie .25 .60
39 Aaron Miller .10 .25
40 Martin Brodeur .75 2.00
41 Martin Havlat .25 .60
42 Roman Cechmanek .25 .60
43 Teppo Numminen .10 .25
44 Milan Kraft .10 .25
45 Pavol Demitra .25 .60
46 Henrik Sedin .10 .25
47 Byron Dafoe .25 .60
48 Dave Tanabe .10 .25
49 Chris Drury .25 .60
50 Tommy Salo .25 .60
51 Lubomir Visnovsky .10 .25
52 Andrei Markov .10 .25
53 Jason Arnott .10 .25
54 Adam Foote .10 .25
55 Vitali Vishnevski .10 .25
56 Ville Nieminen .10 .25
57 Mike Mottau .10 .25
58 Brendan Morrison .25 .60
59 Lee Goren .10 .25
60 Scott Gomez .10 .25
61 Tim Connolly .10 .25
62 Daniel Alfredsson .25 .60
63 Owen Nolan .25 .60
64 Chris Pronger .25 .60
65 Fredrik Modin .10 .25
66 Mario Lemieux 2.00 5.00
67 Olaf Kolzig .25 .60
68 Jeff Friesen .10 .25
69 Patrik Stefan .10 .25
70 Sergei Samsonov .25 .60
71 J-P Dumont .10 .25
72 Sandis Ozolinsh .10 .25
73 Milan Hejduk .30 .75
74 Sergei Zubov .10 .25
75 Sergei Fedorov .50 1.25
76 Janne Niinimaa .10 .25
77 Roberto Luongo .40 1.00
78 Felix Potvin .30 .75
79 Petr Sykora .10 .25
80 Petr Nedved .10 .25
81 Shawn McEachern .10 .25
82 Simon Gagne .30 .75
83 Sean Burke .25 .60
84 Al MacInnis .25 .60
85 Vincent Lecavalier .30 .75
86 Sergei Gonchar .10 .25
87 Oleg Tverdovsky .10 .25
88 Bill Guerin .25 .60
89 Miroslav Satan .25 .60
90 Marc Savard .10 .25
91 Peter Forsberg .60 1.50
92 Brett Hull .40 1.00
93 Nicklas Lidstrom .30 .75
94 Ryan Smyth .10 .25
95 Luc Robitaille .25 .60
96 Alexander Mogilny .25 .60
97 Mark Messier .30 .75
98 Marian Hossa .30 .75
99 Keith Primeau .10 .25
100 Todd Bertuzzi .30 .75
101 Justin Williams .10 .25
102 Ossi Vaananen .10 .25
103 Robert Lang .10 .25
104 Pavel Bure .30 .75
105 Tomas Kaberle .10 .25
106 Nikolai Antropov .10 .25
107 Tomi Kallio .10 .25
108 David Vyborny .10 .25
109 Denis Shvidki .10 .25
110 Jozef Stumpel .10 .25
111 Dimitri Kalinin .10 .25
112 Stephane Robidas .10 .25
113 Scott Walker .10 .25
114 Jamie Langenbrunner .10 .25
115 Maxim Kuznetsov .10 .25
116 Mike Grier .10 .25
117 Michael Nylander .10 .25
118 Derian Hatcher .10 .25
119 Scott Niedermayer .10 .25
120 Petr Schastlivy .10 .25
121 Tomas Divisek RC .15 .40
122 Toby Petersen .10 .25
123 Jarkko Ruutu .10 .25
124 Chris Chelios .30 .75
125 Andrew Raycroft .25 .60
126 Jason Woolley .10 .25
127 Derek Morris .10 .25
128 David Legwand .25 .60
129 Jaromir Jagr .50 1.25
130 Serge Aubin .10 .25
131 Jere Lehtinen .25 .60
132 Manny Legace .25 .60
133 Patrick Roy 1.50 4.00
134 Glen Murray .10 .25
135 Jan Bulis .10 .25
136 Mike Dunham .25 .60
137 Jan Hlavac .10 .25
138 Wade Redden .10 .25
139 Jan Hrdina .10 .25
140 Keith Tkachuk .30 .75
141 Yanic Perreault .10 .25
142 Jonas Ronnqvist .10 .25
143 John Madden .10 .25
144 Jani Hurme .25 .60
145 Chris Gratton .10 .25
146 Toni Lydman .10 .25
147 Mike Modano .50 1.25
148 Boris Mironov .10 .25
149 Joe Sakic .60 1.50
150 Chris Nielsen .10 .25
151 Marty Turco .25 .60
152 Bryan Smolinski .10 .25
153 Daniel Cleary .10 .25
154 Anders Eriksson .10 .25
155 Pierre Dagenais .10 .25
156 Wes Walz .10 .25
157 Brian Savage .10 .25
158 Stu Barnes .10 .25
159 Eric Desjardins .10 .25
160 Juraj Kolnik .10 .25
161 Brendan Shanahan .30 .75
162 Karel Rachunek .10 .25
163 Marc Denis .25 .60
164 Martin Straka .10 .25
165 Alexander Kharitonov .10 .25
166 Sergei Brylin .10 .25
167 Eric Daze .25 .60
168 Alexei Kovalev .25 .60
169 Jiri Slegr .10 .25
170 Brian Rolston .10 .25
171 Phil Housley .10 .25
172 Josef Vasicek .10 .25
173 Patrick Marleau .25 .60
174 Steven Reinprecht .10 .25
175 Gary Roberts .10 .25
176 Darryl Sydor .10 .25
177 Michel Riesen .10 .25
178 Kevyn Adams .10 .25
179 Andreas Lilja .10 .25
180 Roman Hamrlik .10 .25
181 Mathieu Garon .25 .60
182 Scott Hartnell .10 .25
183 Kenny Jonsson .10 .25
184 Jeff Ulmer .10 .25
185 Petr Hubacek .10 .25
186 Jeremy Roenick .40 1.00
187 Scott Young .10 .25
188 Sergei Berezin .10 .25
189 Steve Konowalchuk .10 .25
190 Curtis Joseph .30 .75
191 Jonathan Girard .10 .25
192 Brian Campbell .10 .25
193 Markus Naslund .30 .75
194 David Aebischer .25 .60
195 Peter Bondra .30 .75
196 Paul Kariya .30 .75
197 Jason Allison .10 .25
198 Dominik Hasek .60 1.50
199 Branislav Mezei .10 .25
200 Peter Smrek RC .15 .40
201 Miikka Kiprusoff .25 .60
202 Kristian Kudroc .10 .25
203 Kyle McLaren .10 .25
204 Calle Johansson .10 .25
205 Gregg Naumenko .10 .25
206 Damian Rhodes .25 .60
207 Willie Mitchell .10 .25
208 Daniel Tkaczuk .10 .25
209 Mike Ribeiro .10 .25
210 Rostislav Klesla .10 .25
211 Denis Arkhipov .10 .25
212 Andy McDonald .10 .25
213 Ivan Novoseltsev .10 .25
214 Manny Fernandez .25 .60
215 Reto Von Arx .10 .25
216 Ray Bourque .60 1.50
217 Mike Jefferson RC .15 .40
218 Jason Chimera RC .15 .40
219 Mattias Ohlund .10 .25
220 Rico Fata .10 .25
221 Brad Tapper .10 .25
222 Mike Richter .30 .75
223 Nick Boynton .10 .25
224 Harold Druken .10 .25
225 Chris Clark .10 .25
226 Colin White .10 .25
227 Tyler Bouck .10 .25
228 Jesse Wallin .10 .25
229 Jeff Hackett .10 .25
230 Greg Classen .10 .25
231 Adam Mair .10 .25
232 Ivan Ciernik RC .15 .40
233 Marc Chouinard .10 .25
234 Chris Mason .10 .25
235 Ronald Petrovicky .10 .25
236 Kyle Calder .10 .25
237 Rick Berry .10 .25
238 Mathieu Darche RC .15 .40
239 Theo Fleury .10 .25
240 Mike Commodore .10 .25
241 Michal Handzus .10 .25
242 Bill Tibbetts RC .15 .40
243 Cory Stillman .10 .25
244 Valeri Bure .10 .25
245 Matt Pettinger .10 .25
246 Rod Brind'Amour .25 .60
247 Pascal Dupuis RC .15 .40
248 Martin Rucinsky .10 .25
249 Cliff Ronning .10 .25
250 Brad Isbister .10 .25
251 Antti-Jussi Niemi .10 .25
252 Mark Bell .10 .25
253 Martin Spanhel RC .15 .40
254 Andrew Cassels .10 .25
255 Andrew Brunette .10 .25
256 Ron Francis .25 .60
257 Tony Amonte .25 .60
258 Espen Knutsen .10 .25
259 Viktor Kozlov .10 .25
260 Sergei Krivokrasov .10 .25
261 Richard Zednik .10 .25
262 Bubba Berenzweig .10 .25
263 Pavel Patera .10 .25
264 Mike Johnson .10 .25
265 Teemu Selanne .30 .75
266 John LeClair .30 .75
267 Adam Deadmarsh .10 .25
268 Herbert Vasilijevs .10 .25
269 Steven McCarthy .10 .25
270 Mathieu Schneider .10 .25
271 Peter Bartos .10 .25
272 Ray Ferraro .10 .25
273 Eric Chouinard .10 .25
274 Marian Cisar .10 .25
275 Jarome Iginla .40 1.00
276 Jeff O'Neill .10 .25
277 Steve Sullivan .10 .25
278 Rob Blake .25 .60
279 Geoff Sanderson .10 .25
280 Niclas Wallin .10 .25
281 Vitali Yeremeyev .10 .25
282 Doug Weight .25 .60
283 Martin Skoula .10 .25
284 Zigmund Palffy .25 .60
285 Marian Gaborik .60 1.50
286 Saku Koivu .30 .75
287 Joe Nieuwendyk .25 .60
288 Patrik Elias .25 .60
289 Mariusz Czerkawski .10 .25
290 Brian Leetch .25 .60
291 Alexei Yashin .10 .25
292 Mark Recchi .25 .60
293 Shane Doan .10 .25
294 Brian Holzinger .10 .25
295 Mikael Samuelsson RC .15 .40
296 Pierre Turgeon .25 .60
297 Sheldon Keefe .10 .25
298 Mats Sundin .30 .75
299 Bryan Allen .10 .25
300 Adam Oates .25 .60
301 Ilja Bryzgalov RC 1.25 3.00
302 Erik Cole RC .15 .40
303 Pavel Datsyuk RC 1.50 4.00
304 Nikolai Khabibulin .30 .75
305 Dan Blackburn RC .40 1.00
306 Jeff Jillson RC .15 .40
307 Brian Sutherby RC .15 .40
308 Vaclav Nedorost RC .15 .40
309 Byron Ritchie .10 .25
310 Martin Erat RC .15 .40
311 Vaclav Pletka RC .15 .40
312 Karel Pilar RC .15 .40
313 Jaroslav Obsut RC .15 .40
314 Jason Allison .10 .25
315 Eric Lindros .30 .75
316 Mike Farrell RC .15 .40
317 Doug Gilmour .25 .60
318 Bruno St. Jacques RC .15 .40
319 Martin Lapointe .10 .25
320 Dan Focht RC .15 .40
321 Ben Simon RC .15 .40
322 Mile Peluso RC .15 .40
323 Martin Cibak RC .15 .40
324 Marcel Hossa RC .15 .40
325 Chris Neil .10 .25
326 Mark Rycroft RC .15 .40
327 Timo Parssinen RC .15 .40
328 Sebastien Charpentier RC .15 .40
329 Kip Brennan RC .15 .40
330 Christian Berglund RC .15 .40
331 Tom Kostopoulos RC .15 .40
332 Pat Kavanagh RC .15 .40
333 Sebastien Centomo RC .15 .40
334 Andrew Brunette .10 .25
335 Toni Dahlman RC .15 .40
336 Kamil Piros RC .15 .40
337 Robert Schnabel RC .15 .40
338 Radim Vrbata .10 .25
339 Chris Osgood .25 .60
340 Steve Montador RC .15 .40
341 Reinhard Divis RC .15 .40
342 Steve Moore RC .40 1.00
343 Branko Radivojevic RC .15 .40
344 Zdenek Kutlak RC .15 .40
345 Jiri Dopita RC .15 .40
346 Josef Boumedienne RC .15 .40
347 Phil Housley .10 .25
348 Niko Kapanen RC .40 1.00
349 Travis Roche RC .15 .40
350 Raffi Torres RC .20 .50
351 Randy Robitaille .10 .25
352 Chris Corrinet RC .15 .40
353 Pierre Turgeon .25 .60
354 Pavel Skrbek RC .15 .40
355 Jeremy Roenick .40 1.00
356 Riku Hahl RC .15 .40
357 Stanislav Gron RC .15 .40
358 Pasi Nurminen RC .20 .50
359 Nick Smith RC .15 .40
360 Shane Endicott RC .15 .40
361 Ales Kotalik RC 1.25 3.00
362 Blake Bellefeuille RC .15 .40
363 Jaroslav Bednar RC .15 .40
364 Andreas Salomonsson RC .15 .40
365 Krystofer Kolanos RC .15 .40
366 Tim Connolly .10 .25
367 Ivan Huml RC .15 .40
368 Sean Avery RC .15 .40
369 Trent Hunter RC .75 2.00
370 Richard Scott RC .15 .40
371 Doug Weight .25 .60
372 Ilya Kovalchuk RC 2.50 6.00
373 Dominik Hasek .60 1.50
374 Scott Clemmensen RC .15 .40
375 Nikita Alexeev RC .15 .40
376 Luc Robitaille .25 .60
377 Mike Peca .10 .25
378 Brett Hull .40 1.00
379 Valeri Bure .10 .25
380 Pavel Brendl .10 .25
381 Jukka Hentunen RC .15 .40
382 John Erskine RC .15 .40
383 Nick Schultz RC .15 .40
384 Radek Martinek RC .15 .40
385 Dany Heatley .40 1.00
386 Alex Auld .10 .25
387 Tyler Arnason RC .40 1.00
388 Ty Conklin RC .15 .40
389 Olivier Michaud RC .15 .40
390 Sandis Ozolinsh .10 .25
391 Evgeny Konstantinov RC .15 .40
392 Roman Turek .25 .60
393 Kristian Huselius RC .50 1.25
394 Alexei Yashin .10 .25
395 Alexander Mogilny .25 .60
396 Eric Meloche RC .15 .40
397 Andy McDonald .10 .25
398 Niklas Hagman RC .15 .40
399 Ryan Flinn RC .15 .40
400 Mike Weaver RC .15 .40
401 Nolan Yonkman .10 .25
402 Ryan Jardine .10 .25
403 Andrej Nedorost RC .15 .40
404 Andrej Podkonicky RC .15 .40
405 Hnat Domenichelli .10 .25
406 Bob Wren RC .15 .40
407 Brad Norton RC .15 .40
408 Brian Pothier RC .15 .40
409 Trevor Letowski .10 .25
410 Chris Bala RC .15 .40
411 Tom Fitzgerald .25 .60
412 Petr Tenkrat .10 .25
413 Dan Snyder RC .40 1.00
414 David Cullen RC .15 .40
415 David Ling RC .15 .40
416 Dean Melanson RC .15 .40
417 Duvie Westcott RC .15 .40
418 Eric Beaudoin RC .15 .40
419 Marty McInnis .10 .25
420 Francis Lessard RC .15 .40
421 Frederic Cassivi RC .15 .40
422 Bill Lindsay .10 .25
423 Kim Johnsson .10 .25
424 Daniil Markov .10 .25
425 Guillaume Lefebvre RC .15 .40
426 Hannes Hyvonen RC .15 .40
427 Jeff Daw RC .15 .40
428 Jody Shelley RC .60 1.50
429 Joel Kwiatkowski RC .15 .40
430 Josh Langfeld RC .15 .40
431 Kelly Fairchild RC .15 .40
432 Kevin Sawyer RC .15 .40
433 Kriby Law RC .15 .40
434 Kyle Rossiter RC .15 .40
435 Lukas Krajicek RC .15 .40
436 Mark Hartigan RC .15 .40
437 Martin Prusek RC .15 .40
438 Matt Davidson RC .15 .40
439 Andre Roy .10 .25
440 Chris Kelleher RC .15 .40
441 Mike Matteucci RC .15 .40
442 Nathan Perrott RC .15 .40
443 Neil Little RC .15 .40
444 Rocky Thompson RC .15 .40
445 Ryan Tobler RC .15 .40
446 Scott Nichol RC .15 .40
447 Jiri Slegr .10 .25
448 Stephen Weiss RC .75 2.00
449 Jeff Cowan .10 .25
450 Thomas Ziegler RC .15 .40
451 Todd Rohloff RC .15 .40
452 Blake Sloan .10 .25
453 Tony Tuzzolino RC .15 .40
454 Tony Virta RC .15 .40
455 Adam Oates .25 .60
456 Benoit Brunet .10 .25
457 Benoit Hogue .10 .25
458 Brian Savage .10 .25
459 Cliff Ronning .10 .25
460 Darius Kasparaitis .10 .25
461 Dean McAmmond .10 .25
462 Donald Brashear .10 .25
463 Glen Murray .10 .25
464 Jamie Allison .10 .25
465 Jamie Langenbrunner .10 .25
466 Jan Hlavac .10 .25
467 Jason Arnott .10 .25
468 Joe Nieuwendyk .25 .60
469 Jozef Stumpel .10 .25
470 Juha Ylonen .10 .25
471 Kevin Weekes .25 .60
472 Kirill Safronov .10 .25
473 Manny Malhotra .10 .25
474 Martin Rucinsky .10 .25
475 Matthew Barnaby .10 .25
476 Mike Keane .10 .25
477 Mike York .10 .25
478 Mikko Eloranta .10 .25
479 Pascal Rheaume .10 .25
480 Pavel Bure .30 .75
481 Pierre Dagenais .10 .25
482 Randy McKay .10 .25
483 Ray Ferraro .10 .25
484 Rem Murray .10 .25
485 Rick Berry .10 .25
486 Sean Brown .10 .25
487 Sean Hill .10 .25
488 Sergei Berezin .10 .25
489 Shane Willis .10 .25
490 Stephane Fiset .10 .25
491 Stephane Richer .10 .25
492 Steve Thomas .10 .25
493 Tom Barrasso .25 .60
494 Tom Poti .10 .25
495 Trevor Linden .10 .25
496 Valeri Kamensky .10 .25

497 Ville Nieminen .10 .25
498 Zdeno Chara .10 .25
499 Shjon Podein .10 .25
500 Shaun Van Allen .10 .25

2001-02 BAP Memorabilia Emerald

STATED PRINT RUN 10 SER.#'d SETS
NOT PRICED DUE TO SCARCITY

2001-02 BAP Memorabilia Ruby

*STARS: 5X TO 12X BASIC CARDS
*RUBY RC'S: 1.5X TO 4X BASIC CARDS
STATED PRINT RUN 200 SER.#'d SETS

2001-02 BAP Memorabilia Sapphire

*STARS:8X TO 20X BASIC CARDS
*ROOKIES: 3X TO 8X BASIC CARDS
STATED PRINT RUN 100 SER.#'d SETS

2001-02 BAP Memorabilia All-Star Jerseys

*MULT.COLORS: 1X TO 1.5X BASIC CARDS
STATED PRINT RUN 98 SETS
ASJ1 Evgeni Nabokov 6.00 15.00
ASJ2 Paul Kariya 6.00 15.00
ASJ3 Zigmund Palffy 6.00 15.00
ASJ4 Milan Hejduk 6.00 15.00
ASJ5 Patrick Roy 15.00 40.00
ASJ6 Rob Blake 6.00 15.00
ASJ7 Nicklas Lidstrom 6.00 15.00
ASJ8 Martin Brodeur 12.00 30.00
ASJ9 Doug Weight 4.00 10.00
ASJ10 Bill Guerin 4.00 10.00
ASJ11 Dominik Hasek 12.50 30.00
ASJ12 Joe Sakic 12.50 30.00
ASJ13 Alexei Kovalev 4.00 10.00
ASJ14 Roman Cechmanek 4.00 10.00
ASJ15 Pavel Bure 6.00 15.00
ASJ16 Mario Lemieux 20.00 50.00
ASJ17 Ray Bourque 10.00 25.00
ASJ18 Teppo Numminen 4.00 10.00
ASJ19 Sandis Ozolinsh 4.00 10.00
ASJ20 Tony Amonte 6.00 15.00
ASJ21 Peter Forsberg 10.00 25.00
ASJ22 Brian Leetch 6.00 15.00
ASJ23 Radek Bonk 4.00 10.00
ASJ24 Theo Fleury 6.00 15.00
ASJ25 Simon Gagne 6.00 15.00
ASJ26 Valeri Bure 4.00 10.00
ASJ27 Pavol Demitra 4.00 10.00
ASJ28 Scott Gomez 6.00 15.00
ASJ29 Curtis Joseph 6.00 15.00
ASJ30 Viktor Kozlov 4.00 10.00
ASJ31 Mark Messier 8.00 20.00
ASJ32 Mike Modano 8.00 20.00
ASJ33 Owen Nolan 6.00 15.00
ASJ34 Tommy Salo 4.00 10.00
ASJ35 Roman Turek 4.00 10.00
ASJ36 Steve Yzerman 15.00 40.00
ASJ37 Jaromir Jagr 10.00 25.00
ASJ38 Mats Sundin 6.00 15.00
ASJ39 Nikolai Khabibulin 6.00 15.00
ASJ40 Markus Naslund 6.00 15.00
ASJ41 Keith Tkachuk 6.00 15.00
ASJ42 Alexei Yashin 4.00 10.00
ASJ43 Chris Pronger 6.00 15.00
ASJ44 Al MacInnis 6.00 15.00
ASJ45 Peter Bondra 4.00 10.00
ASJ46 Arturs Irbe 4.00 10.00
ASJ47 Eric Lindros 6.00 15.00
ASJ48 Teemu Selanne 6.00 15.00
ASJ49 Daniel Alfredsson 6.00 15.00
ASJ50 Brett Hull 10.00 25.00

2001-02 BAP Memorabilia All-Star Emblems

STATED PRINT RUN 10 SETS
NOT PRICED DUE TO SCARCITY

2001-02 BAP Memorabilia All-Star Numbers

STATED PRINT RUN 10 SETS
NOT PRICED DUE TO SCARCITY

2001-02 BAP Memorabilia All-Star Jersey Doubles

*MULT.COLOR: 1X TO 1.5X BASIC CARDS
STATED PRINT RUN 60 SETS
DASJ1 Paul Kariya 10.00 25.00
DASJ2 Patrick Roy 25.00 60.00
DASJ3 Rob Blake 10.00 25.00
DASJ4 Nicklas Lidstrom 10.00 25.00
DASJ5 Martin Brodeur 25.00 60.00
DASJ6 Dominik Hasek 25.00 60.00
DASJ7 Joe Sakic 20.00 50.00
DASJ8 Ray Bourque 20.00 50.00
DASJ9 Tony Amonte 10.00 25.00
DASJ10 Peter Forsberg 20.00 50.00
DASJ11 Brian Leetch 10.00 25.00
DASJ12 Theo Fleury 10.00 25.00
DASJ13 Mats Sundin 10.00 25.00
DASJ14 Pavel Bure 10.00 25.00
DASJ15 Steve Yzerman 25.00 60.00
DASJ16 Mike Modano 12.50 30.00
DASJ17 Mark Messier 10.00 25.00
DASJ18 Curtis Joseph 10.00 25.00
DASJ19 Brendan Shanahan 10.00 25.00
DASJ20 Jaromir Jagr 15.00 40.00
DASJ21 Eric Lindros 10.00 25.00
DASJ22 Mario Lemieux 30.00 80.00
DASJ23 Al MacInnis 10.00 25.00
DASJ24 John LeClair 10.00 25.00
DASJ25 Chris Pronger 10.00 25.00
DASJ26 Wayne Gretzky 75.00 200.00
DASJ27 Teemu Selanne 10.00 25.00
DASJ28 Owen Nolan 10.00 25.00
DASJ29 Alexei Yashin 10.00 25.00
DASJ30 Jeremy Roenick 12.50 30.00

2001-02 BAP Memorabilia All-Star Starting Lineup

With a print run of just 70 sets, this 12-card set featured game-worn jersey swatches from starters of the 2001 NHL All-Star Game.

*MULT.COLORS: 1X TO 1.5X BASIC CARDS
STATED PRINT RUN 70 SETS
S1 Dominik Hasek 12.50 30.00
S2 Nicklas Lidstrom 10.00 25.00
S3 Sandis Ozolinsh 10.00 25.00
S4 Milan Hejduk 10.00 25.00
S5 Peter Forsberg 20.00 50.00
S6 Pavel Bure 10.00 25.00
S7 Patrick Roy 30.00 80.00
S8 Ray Bourque 25.00 60.00
S9 Rob Blake 10.00 25.00
S10 Paul Kariya 10.00 25.00
S11 Theo Fleury 10.00 25.00
S12 Joe Sakic 20.00 50.00

2001-02 BAP Memorabilia All-Star Teammates

This 50-card set highlighted players who were teammates at either the 1994, 1996, 1997, 1998, 1999, 2000, or 2001 NHL All-Star Game. Each card carried a swatch of All-Star Game jersey from each player depicted. Each card was limited to just 80 copies.

*MULT.COLORS: 1X TO 1.5X BASIC CARDS
STATED PRINT RUN 80 SETS
AST1 Evgeni Nabokov 12.50 30.00
Milan Hejduk
Zigmund Palffy
AST2 Kariya/Lemieux/Gagne 30.00 80.00
AST3 Rob Blake 40.00 100.00
Patrick Roy
Joe Sakic
AST4 Martin Brodeur 20.00 50.00
Doug Weight
Brian Leetch
AST5 Roman Cechmanek 20.00 50.00
Pavel Bure
Peter Forsberg
AST6 Dominik Hasek 12.50 30.00
Alexei Kovalev
Nicklas Lidstrom
AST7 Raymond Bourque 20.00 50.00
Brian Leetch
Theo Fleury
AST8 Tony Amonte 12.50 30.00
Bill Guerin
Doug Weight
AST9 Evgeni Nabokov 15.00 40.00
Roman Cechmanek
Dominik Hasek
AST10 Paul Kariya 20.00 50.00
Joe Sakic
Theo Fleury
AST11 Peter Forsberg 20.00 50.00
Milan Hejduk
AST12 P.Roy/M.Lemieux 50.00 125.00
AST13 Raymond Bourque 20.00 50.00
Rob Blake
AST14 Pavel Bure 12.50 30.00
Valeri Bure
Viktor Kozlov
AST15 Martin Brodeur 40.00 100.00
Scott Gomez
Scott Stevens
AST16 Chris Pronger 12.50 30.00
Al MacInnis
AST17 Tony Amonte 20.00 50.00
Mike Modano
Jeremy Roenick
AST18 Olaf Kolzig 12.50 30.00
Tommy Salo
Roman Turek
AST19 Brendan Shanahan 20.00 50.00
Steve Yzerman
AST20 Mats Sundin 15.00 40.00
Tommy Salo
AST21 Jaromir Jagr 12.50 30.00
Pavel Bure
AST22 Modno/Joseph/Yzrmn 25.00 60.00
AST23 Pavel Bure 12.50 30.00
Valeri Bure
AST24 Steve Yzerman 25.00 60.00
Mark Messier
Scott Gomez
AST25 Mike Modano 12.50 30.00
Eric Lindros
AST26 Peter Forsberg 20.00 50.00
Teemu Selanne
AST27 Markus Naslund 12.50 30.00
Alexei Yashin
Peter Bondra
AST28 Dominik Hasek 15.00 40.00
Arturs Irbe
Nikolai Khabibulin
AST29 Mats Sundin 12.50 30.00
Nicklas Lidstrom
Markus Naslund
AST30 Chris Pronger 12.50 30.00
Al MacInnis
AST31 Paul Kariya 12.50 30.00
Tony Amonte
AST32 Peter Forsberg 20.00 50.00
Jaromir Jagr
AST33 Mike Modano 12.50 30.00
John LeClair
AST34 Wayne Gretzky 75.00 200.00
Mike Modano
Eric Lindros
AST35 Patrick Roy 30.00 80.00
Joe Sakic
AST36 Jaromir Jagr 25.00 60.00
Peter Forsberg
Pavel Bure
AST37 Wayne Gretzky 125.00 300.00
Patrick Roy
AST38 Bourque/Chelios/Leetch 20.00 50.00
AST39 Eric Lindros 12.50 30.00
Mark Messier
AST40 Dominik Hasek 12.50 30.00
Nikolai Khabibulin
AST41 J.Sakic/M.Modano 20.00 50.00
AST42 Dominik Hasek 15.00 40.00
Raymond Bourque
AST43 Steve Yzerman 20.00 50.00
Mats Sundin
AST44 Paul Kariya 12.50 30.00
Pavel Bure
AST45 Mats Sundin 12.50 30.00
Teemu Selanne
AST46 Brett Hull 12.50 30.00
Ed Belfour
AST47 Jaromir Jagr 12.50 30.00
Eric Lindros
AST48 Peter Forsberg 15.00 40.00
Paul Kariya
AST49 Wayne Gretzky 30.00 80.00
Curtis Joseph
AST50 Patrick Roy 25.00 60.00
Raymond Bourque

2001-02 BAP Memorabilia Country of Origin

This 60-card set featured swatches of the national flag emblem from the highlighted player's All-Star Game jersey. Cards CO41-60 were available in random packs of BAP Update and were limited to 10 copies each. Cards CO1-40 were limited to 12 copies each. The cards are not priced due to scarcity.

CO1-CO40 PRINT RUN 12 SETS
CO41-CO60 PRINT RUN 10 SETS
NOT PRICED DUE TO SCARCITY
CO1 Mario Lemieux
CO2 Eric Lindros
CO3 Theo Fleury
CO4 Paul Kariya
CO5 Joe Sakic
CO6 Ray Bourque
CO7 Al MacInnis
CO8 Rob Blake
CO9 Steve Yzerman
CO10 Patrick Roy
CO11 Martin Brodeur
CO12 Curtis Joseph
CO13 Scott Niedermayer
CO14 Bill Guerin
CO15 Mike Modano
CO16 Brian Leetch
CO17 Doug Weight
CO18 Jeremy Roenick
CO19 Tony Amonte
CO20 Keith Tkachuk
CO21 Teppo Numminen
CO22 Teemu Selanne
CO23 Dominik Hasek
CO24 Jaromir Jagr
CO25 Milan Hejduk
CO26 Radek Bonk
CO27 Roman Cechmanek
CO28 Peter Forsberg
CO29 Tommy Salo
CO30 Daniel Alfredsson
CO31 Nicklas Lidstrom
CO32 Markus Naslund
CO33 Alexei Kovalev
CO34 Pavel Bure
CO35 Alexei Yashin
CO36 Valeri Bure
CO37 Peter Bondra
CO38 Pavol Demitra
CO39 Zigmund Palffy
CO40 Sandis Ozolinsh
CO41 Patrik Elias
CO42 Sami Kapanen
CO43 Tomas Kaberle
CO44 Nikolai Khabibulin
CO45 Vincent Damphousse
CO46 Eric Daze
CO47 Jarome Iginla
CO48 Mario Lemieux
CO49 Owen Nolan
CO50 Joe Thornton
CO51 Sean Burke
CO52 Jose Theodore
CO53 Brendan Shanahan
CO54 Mats Sundin
CO55 Mark Recchi
CO56 Luc Robitaille
CO57 Ed Jovanovski
CO58 John LeClair
CO59 Sergei Fedorov
CO60 Chris Pronger

2001-02 BAP Memorabilia Draft Redemptions

Inserted randomly in packs, this 30-card set featured cards representing the top thirty draft picks in 2001. Each card was redeemable for the player it represented once that player made his NHL debut. Collectors had six months to redeem the cards once the player was available. The redemption cards themselves were hand-numbered out of 100. If by 11/1/2005, the player has still not played in the NHL, the collector has the choice of redeeming the card for others in the set or continuing to wait. Expiration dates of the redeemable cards are listed below.

STATED PRINT RUN 100 SETS
EXPIRED CARD PRINT RUNS BELOW
1 Ilya Kovalchuk/74 75.00 200.00
Expired 4/2/2002
2 Jason Spezza/55 125.00 250.00
Expired 4/24/2003
3 Alexander Svitov/52 20.00 50.00
Expired 4/10/2003
4 Stephen Weiss/55 40.00 80.00
5 Stanislav Chistov/53 15.00 40.00
6 Mikko Koivu EXCH 10.00 25.00
7 Mike Komisarek/47 25.00 60.00
Expired 8/19/2003
8 Pascal Leclaire/49 25.00 60.00
Expired 6/12/2003
9 Tuomo Ruutu/64 50.00 100.00
Expired 12/17/2003
10 Dan Blackburn/67 15.00 40.00
Expired 4/10/2002
11 Fredrik Sjostrom 10.00 25.00
Expired 4/30/2004
12 Dan Hamhuis/63 25.00 60.00
Expired 4/9/2004
13 Ales Hemsky/52 60.00 150.00
Expired 4/10/2003
14 Chuck Kobasew/50 25.00 60.00
Expired 4/10/2003
15 Carolina Hurricanes 8.00 20.00
16 R.J. Umberger EXCH 10.00 25.00
17 Carlo Colaiacovo/50 25.00 60.00
Expired 4/23/2003
18 Los Angeles Kings 8.00 20.00
19 Shaone Morrisonn/48 20.00 50.00
Expired 4/19/2003
20 Marcel Goc 10.00 25.00
21 Colby Armstrong EXCH 10.00 25.00
22 Buffalo Sabres 8.00 20.00
23 Tim Gleason/61 15.00 40.00
Expired 4/9/2004
24 Lukas Krajicek/31 25.00 60.00
Expired 10/6/2002
25 Alexander Perezhogin EXCH 10.00 25.00
26 Jason Bacashihua/46 25.00 60.00
Expired 9/5/2003
27 Jeff Woywitka EXCH 8.00 20.00
28 New Jersey Devils 8.00 20.00
29 Adam Munro 8.00 20.00
30 Dave Steckel EXCH 8.00 20.00

2001-02 BAP Memorabilia 500 Goal Scorers

This 28-card set featured players who hit the milestone of 500 goals in their career. Each card featured an action photo of the given player alongside a game-worn swatch of his jersey on the card front. Each card was printed in quantities of 99,50,40 or 20 only. The Shanahan and Francis cards were available in random BAP Update packs only. Cards with print runs of 20 or less are not priced due to scarcity.

*MULT.COLOR: 1X TO 1.5X BASIC CARDS
STATED ODDS 1:269
NNO CARDS AVAIL.IN BAP UPD.PACKS
GS1 Wayne Gretzky/20
GS2 Gordie Howe/20
GS3 Marcel Dionne/50 20.00 50.00
GS4 Phil Esposito/40 40.00 100.00
GS5 Mike Gartner/99 10.00 25.00
GS6 Mark Messier/99 25.00 60.00
GS7 Steve Yzerman/99 30.00 80.00
GS8 Brett Hull/99 25.00 60.00
GS9 Mario Lemieux/20
GS10 Dino Ciccarelli/99 10.00 25.00
GS11 Jari Kurri/99 12.50 30.00
GS12 Luc Robitaille/99 10.00 25.00
GS13 Mike Bossy/50 10.00 25.00
GS14 Dave Andreychuk/99 10.00 25.00
GS15 Guy Lafleur/50 25.00 60.00
GS16 John Bucyk/99 10.00 25.00
GS17 Maurice Richard/20
GS18 Stan Mikita/40 25.00 60.00
GS19 Frank Mahovlich/40 30.00 80.00
GS20 Bryan Trottier/99 10.00 25.00
GS21 Dale Hawerchuk/99 10.00 25.00
GS22 Gilbert Perreault/99 15.00 40.00
GS23 Jean Beliveau/20
GS24 Pat Verbeek/99 10.00 25.00
GS25 Michel Goulet/99 10.00 25.00
GS26 Joe Mullen/99 10.00 25.00
GS27 Lanny McDonald/99 10.00 25.00
GS28 Bobby Hull/40 30.00 80.00
NNO Brendan Shanahan/25 25.00 60.00
NNO Ron Francis/25 20.00 50.00

2001-02 BAP Memorabilia Goalies Jerseys

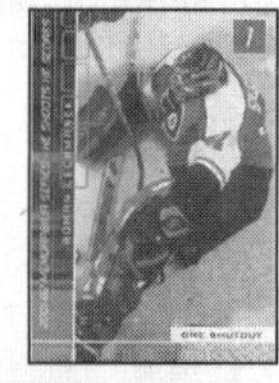

*MULT.COLORS: 1X TO 1.5X BASIC CARDS
STATED PRINT RUN 80 SETS
GJ1 Byron Dafoe 10.00 25.00
GJ2 Dominik Hasek 15.00 40.00
GJ3 Mike Vernon 10.00 25.00
GJ4 Arturs Irbe 10.00 25.00
GJ5 Jocelyn Thibault 10.00 25.00
GJ6 Patrick Roy 20.00 50.00
GJ7 Ed Belfour 10.00 25.00
GJ8 Chris Osgood 10.00 25.00
GJ9 Johan Hedberg 10.00 25.00
GJ10 Roberto Luongo 10.00 25.00
Trevor Kid
GJ11 Jose Theodore 12.00 30.00
Jeff Hackett
GJ12 Mike Dunham 10.00 25.00
GJ13 Martin Brodeur 20.00 50.00
GJ14 Mike Richter 10.00 25.00
GJ15 Roman Cechmanek 10.00 25.00
Brian Boucher
GJ16 Jean-Sebastien Aubin 10.00 25.00
GJ17 Roman Turek 10.00 25.00
GJ18 Curtis Joseph 10.00 25.00
GJ19 Olaf Kolzig 10.00 25.00
GJ20 Felix Potvin 10.00 25.00

2001-02 BAP Memorabilia Goalie Traditions

This 42-card set featured game-worn goalie gear swatches of one, two or three goalies from the past and present. Single player cards were limited to 60 sets, two player cards were limited to 50 sets, and three player cards were limited to 20 sets. Triple player cards were not priced due to scarcity.

SNGL.STATED PRINT RUN 60 SETS
DBL.STATED PRINT RUN 50 SETS
TRPL.STATED PRINT RUN 20 SETS
TRIPLES NOT PRICED DUE TO SCARCITY
GT1 Curtis Joseph 12.50 30.00
GT2 Johnny Bower 20.00 50.00
GT3 Turk Broda 30.00 80.00
GT4 Patrick Roy 30.00 80.00
GT5 Jacques Plante 25.00 60.00
GT6 Jose Theodore 15.00 40.00
GT7 Glenn Hall 12.50 30.00
GT8 Tony Esposito 12.50 30.00
GT9 Jocelyn Thibault 12.50 30.00
GT10 Chuck Rayner 12.50 30.00
GT11 Ed Giacomin 25.00 60.00
GT12 Mike Richter 12.50 30.00
GT13 Frank Brimsek 12.50 30.00
GT14 Gerry Cheevers 12.50 30.00
GT15 Byron Dafoe 12.50 30.00
GT16 Terry Sawchuk 30.00 80.00
GT17 Glenn Hall 12.50 30.00
GT18 Chris Osgood 12.50 30.00
GT19 Curtis Joseph 40.00 100.00
Turk Broda
GT20 Curtis Joseph 40.00 100.00
Johnny Bower
GT21 Johnny Bower 20.00 50.00
Turk Broda
GT22 Terry Sawchuk 50.00 125.00
Glenn Hall
GT23 Glenn Hall 20.00 50.00
Chris Osgood
GT24 Terry Sawchuck 40.00 100.00
Chris Osgood
GT25 Glenn Hall 20.00 50.00
Jocelyn Thibault
GT26 Glenn Hall 20.00 50.00
Tony Esposito
GT27 Tony Esposito 20.00 50.00
Jocelyn Thibault
GT28 Jacques Plante 50.00 125.00
Patrick Roy
GT29 Jacques Plante 40.00 100.00
Jose Theodore
GT30 Patrick Roy 50.00 125.00
Jose Theodore
GT31 Frank Brimsek 20.00 50.00
Byron Dafoe
GT32 Frank Brimsek 20.00 50.00
Gerry Cheevers
GT33 Gerry Cheevers 20.00 50.00
Byron Dafoe
GT34 Chuck Rayner 20.00 50.00
Ed Giacomin
GT35 Chuck Rayner 20.00 50.00
Mike Richter
GT36 Ed Giacomin 20.00 50.00
Mike Richter
GT37 Curtis Joseph
Johnny Bower
Turk Broda
GT38 Terry Sawchuk
Glenn Hall
Chris Osgood
GT39 Tony Esposito
Glenn Hall
Jocelyn Thibault
GT40 Jacques Plante
Patrick Roy
Jose Theodore
GT41 Frank Brimsek
Gerry Cheevers
Byron Dafoe
GT42 Mike Richter
Chuck Rayner
Ed Giacomin

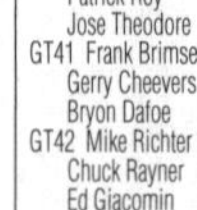

2001-02 BAP Memorabilia He Shoots-He Scores Points

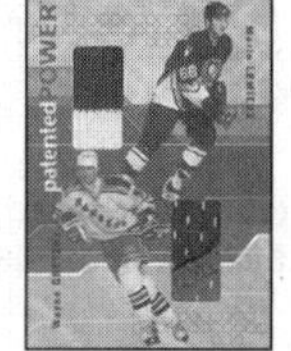

ONE PER PACK
RED.PROGRAM EXPIRED
1 Roman Cechmanek 1 pt. .20 .50
2 Martin Havlat 1 pt. .20 .50
3 Milan Hejduk 1 pt. .20 .50
4 Curtis Joseph 1 pt. .20 .50
5 Saku Koivu 1 pt. .20 .50
6 Mark Messier 1 pt. .20 .50
7 Mike Modano 1 pt. .20 .50
8 Evgeni Nabokov 1 pt. .20 .50
9 Chris Pronger 1 pt. .20 .50
10 Mats Sundin 1 pt. .20 .50
11 Martin Brodeur 2 pts. .20 .50
12 Peter Forsberg 2 pts. .20 .50
13 Paul Kariya 2 pts. .20 .50
14 Vincent Lecavalier 2 pts. .20 .50
15 Patrick Roy 2 pts. .20 .50
16 Joe Sakic 2 pts. .20 .50
17 Steve Yzerman 2 pts. .20 .50
18 Pavel Bure 3 pts. .20 .50
19 Mario Lemieux 3 pts. .20 .50
20 Teemu Selanne 3 pts. .20 .50

2001-02 BAP Memorabilia He Shoots-He Scores Prizes

STAT.PRINT RUN 20 SER.#'d SETS
NOT PRICED DUE TO SCARCITY
1 Daniel Sedin
2 Jaromir Jagr
3 Alex Tanguay
4 Steve Yzerman
5 Scott Stevens
6 Ed Belfour
7 Martin Brodeur
8 Roman Cechmanek
9 Teemu Selanne
10 Jason Arnott
11 Scott Gomez
12 Owen Nolan
13 Chris Pronger
14 Mario Lemieux
15 Olaf Kolzig
16 Patrik Stefan
17 Milan Hejduk
18 Sergei Fedorov
19 Roberto Luongo
20 Al MacInnis
21 Vincent Lecavalier
22 Peter Forsberg
23 Marian Hossa
24 Keith Primeau
25 Pavel Bure
26 Patrick Roy
27 Mike Modano
28 Joe Sakic
29 Brendan Shanahan
30 Martin Straka
31 Keith Tkachuk
32 Curtis Joseph
33 Peter Bondra
34 Ron Francis
35 Tony Amonte
36 Saku Koivu
37 Brian Leetch
38 Mark Recchi
39 Mats Sundin
40 Wayne Gretzky

2001-02 BAP Memorabilia Patented Power

This six card set featured game-worn jersey swatches from both player's featured. Each card was limited to just 20 copies.

*MULT.COLORS: 1X TO 1.5X BASIC CARDS
STATED PRINT RUN 20 SETS
PP1 Jaromir Jagr 40.00 100.00
Mats Sundin
PP2 M.Lemieux/W.Gretzky 200.00 500.00
PP3 Pavel Bure 40.00 100.00
Milan Hejduk
PP4 Mike Modano 40.00 100.00
Chris Pronger
PP5 Paul Kariya 60.00 150.00
Jose Sakic
PP6 Peter Forsberg 75.00 200.00
Steve Yzerman

2001-02 BAP Memorabilia Rocket's Mates

This 10-card set featured game-used jersey swatches from players who played with Hall-of-Famer Maurice "Rocket" Richard. The card fronts carried a small action photo of the featured player on the right side and a black-and-white head shot of Richard on the left. Each card was limited to 50 copies.

*MULT.COLORS: 1X TO 1.5X BASIC CARDS
STATED PRINT RUN 50 SETS
RM1 Jacques Plante 50.00 125.00
Rocket Richard
RM2 Doug Harvey 25.00 60.00
Rocket Richard
RM3 Jean Beliveau 30.00 80.00
Rocket Richard
RM4 Henri Richard 25.00 60.00
Rocket Richard
RM5 Bernie Geoffrion 30.00 80.00
RM6 Dollard St. Laurent 25.00 60.00
Rocket Richard
RM7 Elmer Lach 25.00 60.00
Rocket Richard
RM8 Dickie Moore 25.00 60.00
Rocket Richard
RM9 Butch Bouchard 25.00 60.00
Rocket Richard

RM10 Jean-Guy Talbot 25.00 60.00
Rocket Richard

2001-02 BAP Memorabilia Stanley Cup Champions

This 14-card set honored the winners of the 2001 Stanley Cup, the Colorado Avalanche. Each card carried a full-color photo of the featured player and a swatch of game-used jersey on the card front. Each card was limited to just 40 copies.

*MULT.COLORS: 1X TO 1.5X HI
STATED PRINT RUN 40 SETS
CA1 Patrick Roy 100.00 250.00
CA2 Adam Foote 15.00 40.00
CA3 Ray Bourque 75.00 200.00
CA4 Martin Skoula 15.00 40.00
CA5 Shjon Podein 15.00 40.00
CA6 Alex Tanguay 15.00 40.00
CA7 Chris Dingman 15.00 40.00
CA8 Milan Hejduk 15.00 40.00
CA9 Peter Forsberg 60.00 150.00
CA10 Joe Sakic 40.00 100.00
CA11 Eric Messier 15.00 40.00
CA12 Jon Klemm 15.00 40.00
CA13 Dave Reid 15.00 40.00
CA14 Chris Drury 15.00 40.00

2001-02 BAP Memorabilia Stanley Cup Playoffs

This 32-card set featured players who participated in the 2001 Stanley Cup Playoffs. Each card carried a full-color photo and a swatch of game-used jersey on the card front. Cards SC1-16 were limited to 95 copies each, cards SC17-24 were limited to 80, cards SC25-60 were limited to 40, and cards SC31 and 32 were limited to just 10 copies each. Cards SC31-32 are not priced due to scarcity.

*MULT.COLORS: 1X TO 1.5X BASIC CARDS
PRINT RUNS LISTED BELOW
SC31-SC32 NOT PRICED DUE TO SCARCITY
SC1 Mats Sundin/95 10.00 25.00
SC2 Daniel Alfredsson/95 10.00 25.00
SC3 Scott Stevens/95 10.00 25.00
SC4 Arturs Irbe/95 10.00 25.00
SC5 Martin Straka/95 10.00 25.00
SC6 Olaf Kolzig/95 10.00 25.00
SC7 Doug Gilmour/95 10.00 25.00
SC8 Roman Cechmanek/95 10.00 25.00
SC9 Joe Sakic/95 15.00 40.00
SC10 Daniel Sedin/95 10.00 25.00
SC11 Zigmund Palffy/95 10.00 25.00
SC12 Sergei Fedorov/95 12.50 30.00
SC13 Ed Belfour/95 10.00 25.00
SC14 Tommy Salo/95 10.00 25.00
SC15 Roman Turek/95 10.00 25.00
SC16 Owen Nolan/95 10.00 25.00
SC17 Patrick Roy/80 20.00 50.00
SC18 Luc Robitaille/80 10.00 25.00
SC19 Chris Pronger/80 10.00 25.00
SC20 Mike Modano/80 12.50 30.00
SC21 Martin Brodeur/80 20.00 50.00
SC22 Curtis Joseph/80 10.00 25.00
SC23 Dominik Hasek/80 12.50 30.00
SC24 Mario Lemieux/80 30.00 80.00
SC25 Jason Arnott/60 10.00 25.00
SC26 Johan Hedberg/60 10.00 25.00
SC27 Ray Bourque/60 15.00 40.00
SC28 Al MacInnis/60 10.00 25.00
SC29 Scott Gomez/40 10.00 25.00
SC30 Chris Drury/40 10.00 25.00
SC31 R.Bourque/10 Cup Winners
SC32 Patrick Roy/10 Conn Smythe

2002-03 BAP Memorabilia

Released in mid-November 2002, this 300-card base set featured 200 veteran cards, 30 shortprinted rookie cards and the following shortprinted subsets: Franchise Players (201-230) and the Big Deal (231-270). Shortprinted cards were inserted at a rate of one per pack. Cards 301-400 were only available via mail-in offer found in packs.

COMP.SET w/o UPDATE (300) 200.00 400.00
COMP.SET w/o SP's (200) 25.00 50.00
CARDS 271-400 ODDS 1:1
CARDS 301-400 AVAIL.VIA MAIL-IN
1 Steve Yzerman 1.50 4.00
2 Steve Reinprecht .10 .25
3 J-S Giguere .25 .60
4 Chris Simon .10 .25
5 Dany Heatley .40 1.00
6 Brendan Morrison .25 .60
7 Bill Guerin .25 .60
8 Alexander Mogilny .25 .60
9 Martin Biron .25 .60
10 Brad Richards .25 .60
11 Craig Conroy .10 .25
12 Al MacInnis .25 .60
13 Arturs Irbe .25 .60
14 Evgeni Nabokov .25 .60
15 Alexei Zhamnov .10 .25
16 Daniel Briere .10 .25
17 Alex Tanguay .25 .60
18 Milan Kraft .10 .25
19 Marc Denis .25 .60
20 Adam Oates .25 .60
21 Darryl Sydor .10 .25
22 Daniel Alfredsson .25 .60
23 Brendan Shanahan .30 .75
24 Brian Leetch .25 .60
25 Anson Carter .25 .60
26 Adrian Aucoin .10 .25
27 Kristian Huselius .10 .25
28 Jamie Langenbrunner .10 .25
29 Adam Deadmarsh .10 .25
30 Denis Arkhipov .10 .25
31 Andrew Brunette .10 .25
32 Donald Audette .10 .25
33 Rob Blake .25 .60
34 Jaromir Jagr .50 1.25
35 Felix Potvin .30 .75
36 Dan Cloutier .25 .60
37 Niklas Hagman .10 .25
38 Alyn McCauley .10 .25
39 Eric Brewer .10 .25
40 Nikolai Khabibulin .30 .75
41 Brett Hull .40 1.00
42 Brent Johnson .25 .60
43 Brenden Morrow .25 .60
44 Mike Ricci .10 .25
45 Ray Whitney .10 .25
46 Alexei Kovalev .25 .60
47 Chris Drury .25 .60
48 Daymond Langkow .10 .25
49 Eric Daze .25 .60
50 Pavel Brendl .10 .25
51 Bates Battaglia .10 .25
52 Jani Hurme .25 .60
53 Dean McAmmond .10 .25
54 Dan Blackburn .25 .60
55 Maxim Afinogenov .10 .25
56 Alexei Yashin .10 .25
57 Steve Shields .25 .60
58 Joe Nieuwendyk .25 .60
59 Frantisek Kaberle .10 .25
60 Jan Lasak .10 .25
61 Ron Francis .25 .60
62 Jeff Friesen .10 .25
63 Doug Gilmour .25 .60
64 Jeff Halpern .10 .25
65 Ilya Kovalchuk .40 1.00
66 Daniel Sedin .10 .25
67 Glen Murray .10 .25
68 Bryan McCabe .10 .25
69 Miroslav Satan .25 .60
70 Pavel Kubina .10 .25
71 Derek Morris .10 .25
72 Chris Pronger .25 .60
73 Erik Cole .10 .25
74 Owen Nolan .25 .60
75 Jocelyn Thibault .25 .60
76 Jan Hrdina .10 .25
77 Greg DeVries .10 .25
78 Krystofer Kolanos .10 .25
79 David Vyborny .10 .25
80 Jeremy Roenick .40 1.00
81 Jason Arnott .10 .25
82 Mike Leclerc .10 .25
83 Marian Hossa .30 .75
84 Chris Chelios .30 .75
85 Eric Lindros .30 .75
86 Jochen Hecht .10 .25
87 Chris Osgood .25 .60
88 Roberto Luongo .40 1.00
89 Martin Brodeur .75 2.00
90 Jaroslav Modry .10 .25
91 Martin Erat .10 .25
92 Manny Fernandez .25 .60
93 Jose Theodore .40 1.00
94 Olaf Kolzig .25 .60
95 Ed Jovanovski .25 .60
96 Sandis Ozolinsh .10 .25
97 Corey Schwab .25 .60
98 Sami Kapanen .10 .25
99 Mike Comrie .25 .60
100 Shane Willis .10 .25
101 Dominik Hasek .60 1.50
102 Jason Allison .10 .25
103 Doug Weight .25 .60
104 Marty Turco .25 .60
105 Patrick Marleau .25 .60
106 Rostislav Klesla .10 .25
107 Johan Hedberg .25 .60
108 Joe Sakic .60 1.50
109 Marian Gaborik .60 1.50
110 Sean Burke .25 .60
111 Mark Bell .10 .25
112 John LeClair .30 .75
113 Jaroslav Svoboda .10 .25
114 Todd Bertuzzi .30 .75
115 Martin Havlat .25 .60
116 Pavel Datsyuk .30 .75
117 Jarome Iginla .40 1.00
118 Mark Messier .30 .75
119 Stu Barnes .10 .25
120 Shayne Corson .10 .25
121 Mark Parrish .10 .25
122 Joe Thornton .50 1.25
123 Patrik Elias .25 .60
124 Milan Hnilicka .25 .60
125 Mike Dunham .25 .60
126 Oleg Tverdovsky .10 .25
127 Richard Zednik .10 .25
128 Peter Forsberg .75 2.00
129 Mikko Eloranta .10 .25
130 Zdeno Chara .10 .25
131 Curtis Joseph .30 .75
132 Steve Rucchin .10 .25
133 Sergei Fedorov .50 1.25
134 Josef Vasicek .10 .25
135 Ryan Smyth .10 .25
136 Scott Niedermayer .10 .25
137 Shane Doan .10 .25
138 Steve Sullivan .10 .25
139 Stephen Weiss .10 .25
140 Alexander Daigle .10 .25
141 Fred Brathwaite .25 .60
142 Peter Bondra .30 .75
143 Patrik Stefan .10 .25
144 Tony Amonte .25 .60
145 Valeri Bure .10 .25
146 Rick DiPietro .25 .60
147 Martin Straka .10 .25
148 Jeff O'Neill .10 .25
149 Milan Hejduk .30 .75
150 Kirk Maltby .10 .25
151 Mike York .10 .25
152 Scott Gomez .10 .25
153 Mike Peca .10 .25
154 Mike Richter .30 .75
155 Patrick Lalime .25 .60
156 Justin Williams .10 .25
157 Mario Lemieux 2.00 5.00
158 Kevin Weekes .25 .60
159 Scott Young .10 .25
160 Tommy Salo .25 .60
161 Steve Webb .10 .25
162 Teemu Selanne .30 .75
163 Jozef Stumpel .10 .25
164 Patrick Roy 1.50 4.00
165 Zigmund Palffy .25 .60
166 Pavel Bure .30 .75
167 Vincent Damphousse .10 .25
168 Sergei Gonchar .10 .25
169 Sergei Samsonov .25 .60
170 Luc Robitaille .25 .60
171 Scott Stevens .25 .60
172 Robert Lang .10 .25
173 Henrik Sedin .10 .25
174 Tim Connolly .10 .25
175 Pierre Turgeon .25 .60
176 Yanic Perreault .10 .25
177 Radek Bonk .10 .25
178 Keith Tkachuk .30 .75
179 Paul Kariya .30 .75
180 Mike Modano .50 1.25
181 Saku Koivu .30 .75
182 Mark Recchi .25 .60
183 Roman Turek .25 .60
184 Kris Draper .10 .25
185 Scott Hartnell .10 .25
186 Keith Primeau .10 .25
187 Vincent Lecavalier .30 .75
188 Darcy Tucker .10 .25
189 Markus Naslund .30 .75
190 Pavol Demitra .25 .60
191 Gary Roberts .10 .25
192 Rod Brind'Amour .25 .60
193 Radim Vrbata .10 .25
194 Nicklas Lidstrom .30 .75
195 Tom Poti .10 .25
196 Roman Cechmanek .25 .60
197 Scott Mellanby .10 .25
198 Mats Sundin .30 .75
199 Filip Kuba .10 .25
200 Simon Gagne .30 .75
201 Paul Kariya FP .50 1.25
202 Ilya Kovalchuk FP .60 1.50
203 Joe Thornton FP .75 2.00
204 Miroslav Satan FP .40 1.00
205 Jarome Iginla FP .60 1.50
206 Ron Francis FP .40 1.00
207 Eric Daze FP .40 1.00
208 Patrick Roy FP 2.50 6.00
209 Rostislav Klesla FP .40 1.00
210 Mike Modano FP .75 2.00
211 Steve Yzerman FP 2.50 6.00
212 Mike Comrie FP .40 1.00
213 Roberto Luongo FP .50 1.25
214 Zigmund Palffy FP .50 1.25
215 Marian Gaborik FP .40 1.00
216 Jose Theodore FP .50 1.25
217 Scott Hartnell FP .15 .40
218 Martin Brodeur FP 1.25 3.00
219 Alexei Yashin FP .30 .75
220 Pavel Bure FP .60 1.50
221 Marian Hossa FP .50 1.25
222 Simon Gagne FP .50 1.25
223 Daniel Briere FP .15 .40
224 Mario Lemieux FP 3.00 8.00
225 Chris Pronger FP .40 1.00
226 Owen Nolan FP .40 1.00
227 Nikolai Khabibulin FP .40 1.00
228 Mats Sundin FP .50 1.25
229 Markus Naslund FP .40 1.00
230 Jaromir Jagr FP .75 2.00
231 P.Forsberg/E.Lindros 1.50 4.00
232 P.Roy/J.Thibault 2.00 5.00
233 T.Sawchuk/J.Bucyk 2.00 5.00
234 J.Plante/G.Worsley 1.50 4.00
235 Chris Pronger .75 2.00
Brendan Shanahan
236 Eric Lindros .75 2.00
Pavel Brendl
237 Kris Beech .75 2.00
Jaromir Jagr
238 Ed Jovanovski .75 2.00
Pavel Bure
239 Jarome Iginla .75 2.00
Joe Nieuwendyk
240 Dominik Hasek .75 2.00
Eric Daze
241 Denis Savard .75 2.00
Chris Chelios
242 Adam Oates .75 2.00
Jason Allison
243 Dominik Hasek .75 2.00
Slava Kozlov
244 Robert Svehla .75 2.00
Dimitri Yushkevich
245 Trevor Linden .75 2.00
Todd Bertuzzi
246 Guy Lafleur .75 2.00
Sergei Zubov
247 Jason Arnott .75 2.00
Bill Guerin
248 Alexander Mogilny .75 2.00
Mike Peca
249 Brendan Shanahan .75 2.00
Keith Primeau
250 John LeClair .75 2.00
Mark Recchi
251 Rob Blake .75 2.00
Adam Deadmarsh
252 Jeremy Roenick .75 2.00
Alexei Zhamnov
253 Mike Peca .75 2.00
Tim Connolly
254 Sandis Ozolinsh .75 2.00
Owen Nolan
255 Chris Drury .75 2.00
Manny Fernandez
256 Roman Turek .75 2.00
Fred Braithwaite
257 Jason Arnott .75 2.00
Joe Nieuwendyk
258 Dave Andreychuk .75 2.00
Brian Rolston
259 Bryan Berard .75 2.00
Felix Potvin
260 Valeri Bure .75 2.00
Rob Niedermayer
261 Brian Boucher .75 2.00
Michal Handzus
262 Adam Oates .75 2.00
263 Bobby Holik .75 2.00
264 Robert Lang .75 2.00
265 Curtis Joseph .75 2.00
266 Ed Belfour .75 2.00
267 Darius Kasparaitis .75 2.00
268 Bill Guerin .75 2.00
269 Petr Sykora .75 2.00
Oleg Tverdovsky
270 Tony Amonte .75 2.00
271 P-M Bouchard RC 2.00 5.00
272 Rick Nash RC 4.00 10.00
273 Dennis Seidenberg RC 1.50 4.00
274 Jay Bouwmeester RC 2.00 5.00
275 Stanislav Chistov RC 1.50 4.00
276 Kurt Sauer RC 1.25 3.00
277 Ivan Majesky RC 1.25 3.00
278 Chuck Kobasew RC 1.25 3.00
279 Jeff Taffe RC 1.25 3.00
280 Mikael Tellqvist RC 1.25 3.00
281 Ales Hemsky RC 3.00 8.00
282 Patrick Sharp RC 1.25 3.00
283 Jordan Leopold RC 1.25 3.00
284 Dmitri Bykov RC 1.25 3.00
285 Alex Henry RC 1.25 3.00
286 Henrik Zetterberg RC 5.00 12.00
287 Alexander Frolov RC 2.00 5.00
288 Steve Eminger RC 1.25 3.00
289 Carlo Colaiacovo RC 1.50 4.00
290 Tom Koivisto RC 1.25 3.00
291 Shawn Thornton RC 1.25 3.00
292 Ron Hainsey RC 1.25 3.00
293 Martin Gerber RC 1.25 3.00
294 Adam Hall RC 1.25 3.00
295 Jason Spezza RC 4.00 10.00
296 Anton Volchenkov RC 1.25 3.00
297 Jeff Paul RC 1.25 3.00
298 Scottie Upshall RC 1.50 4.00
299 Alexander Svitov RC 1.50 4.00
300 Alexei Smirnov RC 1.25 3.00
301 Ed Belfour .30 .75
302 Ryan Bayda RC 1.25 3.00
303 Jerred Smithson RC 1.25 3.00
304 Mike Komisarek RC 3.00 8.00
305 Jarret Stoll RC 3.00 8.00
306 Radovan Somik RC 1.25 3.00
307 Rob Davison RC 1.25 3.00
308 Jason King RC 3.00 8.00
309 Tony Amonte .25 .60
310 Cam Severson RC 1.25 3.00
311 Matt Walker RC 1.25 3.00
312 Jesse Fibiger RC 1.25 3.00
313 Ray Emery RC 3.00 8.00
314 Vernon Fiddler RC 1.25 3.00
315 Alex Kovalev .25 .60
316 Marc-Andre Bergeron RC 1.25 3.00
317 Jason Elliott RC 1.25 3.00
318 Craig Andersson RC 1.25 3.00
319 Sandis Ozolinsh .10 .25
320 Ryan Miller RC 2.00 5.00
321 Chris Osgood .25 .60
322 Michael Garnett RC 1.25 3.00
323 Bobby Allen RC 1.25 3.00
324 Cristobal Huet RC 4.00 10.00
325 Curtis Murphy RC 1.25 3.00
326 Darren Haydar RC 1.25 3.00
327 Mathieu Schneider .10 .25
328 Ray Schultz RC 1.25 3.00
329 Jim Vandermeer RC 1.25 3.00
330 Miroslav Zalesak RC 1.25 3.00
331 Christian Backman RC 1.25 3.00
332 John Craighead RC 1.25 3.00
333 Doug Gilmour .25 .60
334 Dick Tarnstrom RC 1.25 3.00
335 Chad Wiseman RC 1.25 3.00
336 John Tripp RC 1.25 3.00
337 Ari Ahonen RC 1.25 3.00
338 Rickard Wallin RC 1.25 3.00
339 Jonathan Hedstrom RC 1.25 3.00
340 Daniel Briere .10 .25
341 Paul Manning RC 1.25 3.00
342 Igor Radulov RC 1.25 3.00
343 Tomas Malec RC 1.25 3.00
344 Sean McMorrow RC 1.25 3.00
345 Dany Sabourin RC 1.25 3.00
346 Steve Thomas .10 .25
347 Shaone Morrisonn RC 1.25 3.00
348 Brad Defauw RC 1.25 3.00
349 Michael Leighton RC 1.25 3.00
350 Pascal Leclaire RC 1.50 4.00
351 Chris Schmidt RC 1.25 3.00
352 Stephane Veilleux RC 1.25 3.00
353 Jim Fahey RC 1.25 3.00
354 Konstantin Koltsov RC 1.50 4.00
355 Cody Rudkowsky RC 1.25 3.00
356 Anson Carter .25 .60
357 Francois Beauchemin RC 1.25 3.00
358 Patrick Boileau RC 1.25 3.00
359 Sylvain Blouin RC 1.25 3.00
360 Eric Bertrand RC 1.25 3.00
361 Jamie Hodson RC 1.25 3.00
362 Curtis Sanford RC 1.50 4.00
363 Ryan Kraft RC 1.25 3.00
364 Owen Nolan .25 .60
365 Niko Dimitrakos RC 1.25 3.00
366 Simon Gamache RC 1.25 3.00
367 Doug Janik RC 1.25 3.00
368 Tomas Kurka RC 1.25 3.00
369 Josh Harding RC 10.00 25.00
370 Radoslav Hecl RC 1.25 3.00
371 Kris Vernarsky RC 1.25 3.00
372 Steve Ott RC 2.50 6.00
373 Frederic Cloutier RC 1.25 3.00
374 Eric Godard RC 1.25 3.00
375 Kari Haakana RC 1.25 3.00
376 Tomi Pettinen RC 1.25 3.00
377 Brooks Orpik RC 1.25 3.00
378 Lynn Loyns RC 1.25 3.00
379 Radim Vrbata .10 .25
380 Fernando Pisani RC 1.25 3.00
381 Alexei Semenov RC 1.25 3.00
382 Burke Henry RC 1.25 3.00
383 Tim Thomas RC 1.25 3.00
384 Mike Siklenka RC 3.00 8.00
385 Lasse Pirjeta RC 1.25 3.00
386 Tomas Zizka RC 1.25 3.00
387 Tomas Surovy RC 1.25 3.00
388 Paul Gaustad RC 1.25 3.00
389 Martin Samuelsson RC 1.25 3.00
390 Matt Henderson RC 1.25 3.00
391 Mike Dunham .25 .60
392 Levente Szuper RC 1.25 3.00
393 Jared Aulin RC 1.25 3.00
394 Brandon Reid RC 1.25 3.00
395 Mike Cammalleri RC 2.00 5.00
396 Ian MacNeil RC 1.25 3.00
397 Brad Isbister .10 .25
398 Garnet Exelby RC 1.25 3.00
399 Jason Bacashihua RC 3.00 8.00
400 Sami Kapanen .10 .25

2002-03 BAP Memorabilia Emerald

EMERALD PRINT RUN 10 SER.#'d SETS
EMERALD NOT PRICED DUE TO SCARCITY

2002-03 BAP Memorabilia Ruby

*STARS: 2.5X TO 6X BASIC CARD
*SP's: .75X TO 2X
*ROOKIES: .5X TO 1.25 X
RUBY PRINT RUN 200 SER.#'d SETS

2002-03 BAP Memorabilia Sapphire

*STARS: 4X TO 10X BASIC CARDS
*SP's: 1.25X TO 3X
*ROOKIES: .75X TO 2X
SAPPHIRE PRINT RUN 100 SER.#'d SETS

2002-03 BAP Memorabilia All-Star Jerseys

This 60-card set featured swatches of all-star game-used jerseys. Each card was limited to just 90 copies each.

*MULT.COLOR: 1X TO 1.5X HI
STATED PRINT RUN 90 SETS
ASJ-1 Daniel Alfredsson 6.00 15.00
ASJ-2 Tony Amonte 6.00 15.00
ASJ-3 Ed Belfour 6.00 15.00
ASJ-4 Rob Blake 6.00 15.00
ASJ-5 Peter Bondra 6.00 15.00
ASJ-6 Martin Brodeur 12.50 30.00
ASJ-7 Pavel Bure 6.00 15.00
ASJ-8 Chris Chelios 6.00 15.00
ASJ-9 Eric Daze 6.00 15.00
ASJ-10 Pavol Demitra 6.00 15.00
ASJ-11 Patrik Elias 6.00 15.00
ASJ-12 Sergei Fedorov 10.00 25.00
ASJ-13 Theo Fleury 6.00 15.00
ASJ-14 Peter Forsberg 12.50 30.00
ASJ-15 Simon Gagne 6.00 15.00
ASJ-16 Bill Guerin 6.00 15.00
ASJ-17 Dominik Hasek 12.50 30.00
ASJ-18 Milan Hejduk 6.00 15.00
ASJ-19 Brett Hull 12.50 30.00
ASJ-20 Jarome Iginla 8.00 20.00
ASJ-21 Arturs Irbe 6.00 15.00
ASJ-22 Jaromir Jagr 12.50 30.00
ASJ-23 Curtis Joseph 6.00 15.00
ASJ-24 Ed Jovanovski 6.00 15.00
ASJ-25 Paul Kariya 6.00 15.00
ASJ-26 Nikolai Khabibulin 6.00 15.00
ASJ-27 Saku Koivu 6.00 15.00
ASJ-28 Alexei Kovalev 6.00 15.00
ASJ-29 John LeClair 6.00 15.00
ASJ-30 Brian Leetch 6.00 15.00
ASJ-31 Mario Lemieux 15.00 40.00
ASJ-32 Nicklas Lidstrom 6.00 15.00
ASJ-33 Eric Lindros 6.00 15.00
ASJ-34 Al MacInnis 6.00 15.00
ASJ-35 Mark Messier 6.00 15.00
ASJ-36 Mike Modano 8.00 20.00
ASJ-37 Alexander Mogilny 6.00 15.00
ASJ-38 Evgeni Nabokov 6.00 15.00
ASJ-39 Markus Naslund 6.00 15.00
ASJ-40 Scott Niedermayer 6.00 15.00
ASJ-41 Owen Nolan 6.00 15.00
ASJ-42 Felix Potvin 6.00 15.00
ASJ-43 Sandis Ozolinsh 6.00 15.00
ASJ-44 Zigmund Palffy 6.00 15.00
ASJ-45 Chris Pronger 6.00 15.00
ASJ-46 Mark Recchi 6.00 15.00
ASJ-47 Mike Richter 6.00 15.00
ASJ-48 Luc Robitaille 6.00 15.00
ASJ-49 Jeremy Roenick 8.00 20.00
ASJ-50 Patrick Roy 20.00 50.00
ASJ-51 Joe Sakic 12.50 30.00
ASJ-52 Teemu Selanne 6.00 15.00
ASJ-53 Brendan Shanahan 6.00 15.00
ASJ-54 Mats Sundin 6.00 15.00
ASJ-55 Jose Theodore 8.00 20.00
ASJ-56 Joe Thornton 8.00 20.00
ASJ-57 Keith Tkachuk 6.00 15.00
ASJ-58 Doug Weight 6.00 15.00
ASJ-59 Alexei Yashin 6.00 15.00
ASJ-60 Steve Yzerman 15.00 40.00

2002-03 BAP Memorabilia All-Star Emblems

PRINT RUN 10 SETS
EMBLEMS NOT PRICED DUE TO SCARCITY
ASE-1 Martin Brodeur
ASE-2 Pavel Bure
ASE-3 Sergei Fedorov
ASE-4 Peter Forsberg
ASE-5 Dominik Hasek
ASE-6 Brett Hull
ASE-7 Jarome Iginla
ASE-8 Jaromir Jagr
ASE-9 Curtis Joseph
ASE-10 Paul Kariya
ASE-11 Brian Leetch
ASE-12 Mario Lemieux
ASE-13 Nicklas Lidstrom
ASE-14 Eric Lindros
ASE-15 Mark Messier
ASE-16 Mike Modano
ASE-17 Owen Nolan
ASE-18 Luc Robitaille
ASE-19 Patrick Roy
ASE-20 Joe Sakic
ASE-21 Teemu Selanne
ASE-22 Brendan Shanahan
ASE-23 Mats Sundin
ASE-24 Jose Theodore
ASE-25 Steve Yzerman

2002-03 BAP Memorabilia All-Star Numbers

PRINT RUN 10 SETS
NUMBERS NOT PRICED DUE TO SCARCITY
ASN-1 Martin Brodeur
ASN-2 Pavel Bure
ASN-3 Sergei Fedorov
ASN-4 Peter Forsberg
ASN-5 Dominik Hasek
ASN-6 Brett Hull
ASN-7 Jarome Iginla
ASN-8 Jaromir Jagr
ASN-9 Curtis Joseph
ASN-10 Paul Kariya
ASN-11 Brian Leetch
ASN-12 Mario Lemieux
ASN-13 Nicklas Lidstrom
ASN-14 Eric Lindros
ASN-15 Mark Messier
ASN-16 Mike Modano
ASN-17 Owen Nolan
ASN-18 Luc Robitaille
ASN-19 Patrick Roy
ASN-20 Joe Sakic
ASN-21 Teemu Selanne
ASN-22 Brendan Shanahan
ASN-23 Mats Sundin
ASN-24 Jose Theodore
ASN-25 Steve Yzerman

2002-03 BAP Memorabilia All-Star Starting Lineup

This 12-card set featured swatches of all-star game jerseys and was limited to just 40 copies each.

*MULT.COLOR: 1X TO 1.5X HI
STATED PRINT RUN 40 SETS
AS-1 Patrick Roy 60.00 150.00
AS-2 Chris Pronger 20.00 50.00
AS-3 Rob Blake 20.00 50.00
AS-4 Vincent Damphousse 20.00 50.00
AS-5 Owen Nolan 20.00 50.00
AS-6 Brendan Shanahan 20.00 50.00
AS-7 Dominik Hasek 30.00 80.00
AS-8 Nicklas Lidstrom 20.00 50.00
AS-9 Sandis Ozolinsh 20.00 50.00
AS-10 Sergei Fedorov 25.00 60.00
AS-11 Jaromir Jagr 30.00 80.00
AS-12 Teemu Selanne 20.00 50.00

2002-03 BAP Memorabilia All-Star Teammmates

STATED PRINT RUN 75 SETS
AST-1 Sergei Fedorov 12.50 30.00
Teemu Selanne
AST-2 Curtis Joseph 12.50 30.00
Jeremy Roenick
AST-3 Patrick Roy 25.00 60.00
Mark Messier
AST-4 M.Lemieux/M.Messier 30.00 80.00
AST-5 Brendan Shanahan 12.50 30.00
Jaromir Jagr
AST-6 Alexander Mogilny 12.50 30.00
Paul Kariya
AST-7 S.Yzerman/O.Nolan 25.00 60.00
AST-8 Theo Fleury 12.50 30.00
Mats Sundin
AST-9 Martin Brodeur 25.00 60.00
Dominik Hasek
AST-10 Pavel Bure 12.50 30.00
Peter Forsberg
AST-11 Jaromir Jagr 12.50 30.00
Dominik Hasek
AST-12 E.Lindros/M.Modano 12.50 30.00
AST-13 Eric Lindros 12.50 30.00
Keith Tkachuk
AST-14 Peter Forsberg 15.00 40.00
Dominik Hasek
AST-15 Alexei Yashin 12.50 30.00
Teemu Selanne
AST-16 Jaromir Jagr 12.50 30.00
Mats Sundin
AST-17 S.Yzerman/J.Roenick 20.00 50.00
AST-18 Martin Brodeur 25.00 60.00
Curtis Joseph
AST-19 Chris Pronger 12.50 30.00
Tony Amonte
AST-20 Eric Lindros 20.00 50.00
Mark Messier
AST-21 Joe Sakic 12.50 30.00
Bill Guerin
AST-22 M.Lemieux/P.Roy 30.00 80.00
AST-23 Evgeni Nabokov 12.50 30.00
Dominik Hasek
AST-24 Peter Forsberg 20.00 50.00
Pavel Bure
AST-25 P.Kariya/M.Brodeur 20.00 50.00
AST-26 Jose Theodore 30.00 80.00
Patrick Roy
AST-27 Brendan Shanahan 12.50 30.00
Owen Nolan
AST-28 J.Iginla/M.Lemieux 25.00 60.00
AST-29 Jaromir Jagr 12.50 30.00
Nicklas Lidstrom
AST-30 Teemu Selanne 12.50 30.00
Sergei Fedorov

2002-03 BAP Memorabilia All-Star Triple Jerseys

Limited to just 50 copies, this 20-card set featured triple swatches of jerseys from three different all-star games.

STATED PRINT RUN 50 SETS
ASTJ-1 Rob Blake 12.50 30.00
ASTJ-2 Martin Brodeur 30.00 80.00
ASTJ-3 Pavel Bure 12.50 30.00
ASTJ-4 Peter Forsberg 30.00 80.00
ASTJ-5 Dominik Hasek 15.00 40.00
ASTJ-6 Jaromir Jagr 15.00 40.00
ASTJ-7 Paul Kariya 12.50 30.00
ASTJ-8 John LeClair 12.50 30.00
ASTJ-9 Brian Leetch 12.50 30.00
ASTJ-10 Mario Lemieux 60.00 150.00
ASTJ-11 Nicklas Lidstrom 12.50 30.00
ASTJ-12 Eric Lindros 12.50 30.00
ASTJ-13 Al MacInnis 12.50 30.00
ASTJ-14 Mark Messier 25.00 60.00
ASTJ-15 Mike Modano 15.00 40.00
ASTJ-16 Owen Nolan 12.50 30.00
ASTJ-17 Patrick Roy 50.00 125.00
ASTJ-18 Teemu Selanne 12.50 30.00
ASTJ-19 Brendan Shanahan 12.50 30.00
ASTJ-20 Mats Sundin 12.50 30.00

2002-03 BAP Memorabilia Draft Redemptions

Inserted randomly in packs, this 30-card set featured cards representing the top thirty draft picks in 2002. Each card was redeemable for the player it represented once that player made his NHL debut. Collectors had six months to redeem the cards once the player was available. The redemption cards themselves were hand-numbered out of 100.

PRINT RUN 100 SER.#'d SETS
EXPIRED CARD PRINT RUNS BELOW
1 Rick Nash/67 75.00 200.00
2 Kari Lehtonen/64 60.00 125.00
3 Jay Bouwmeester/63 50.00 100.00
Expired 4/20/2003
4 Joni Pitkanen/68 25.00 60.00
Expired 4/9/2004
5 Ryan Whitney EXCH 15.00 40.00
6 Scottie Upshall/52 25.00 60.00
Expired 4/20/2003
7 Joffrey Lupul/56 30.00 80.00
Expired 4/8/2004
8 P-M Bouchard/50 25.00 60.00
Expired 4/20/2003
9 Petr Taticek 8.00 20.00
10 Eric Nystrom EXCH 6.00 15.00
11 Keith Ballard EXCH 5.00 15.00
12 Steve Eminger/51 15.00 40.00
Expired 4/20/2003
13 Alexander Semin/45 30.00 80.00
Expired 4/14/2004
14 Chris Higgins/61 25.00 60.00
Expired 4/11/2004
15 Edmonton Oilers 12.50 30.00
16 Jakub Klepis EXCH 8.00 20.00
17 Boyd Gordon/54 12.00 30.00
Expired 4/9/2004
18 Denis Grebeshkov 10.00 25.00
Expired 8/28/2004
19 Phoenix Coyotes 8.00 20.00
20 Daniel Paille 20.00 50.00
21 Anton Babchuk 10.00 25.00
Expired 7/8/2004
22 Sean Bergenheim/45 10.00 25.00
Expired 4/9/2004
23 Ben Eager 10.00 25.00
24 Alexander Steen 15.00 40.00
25 Cam Ward EXCH 15.00 40.00
26 Dallas Stars 8.00 20.00
27 San Jose Sharks 8.00 20.00
28 Colorado Avalanche 8.00 20.00
29 Hannu Toivonen EXCH 15.00 40.00
30 Jim Slater EXCH 6.00 15.00

2002-03 BAP Memorabilia Franchise Players

*MULT.COLOR: 1X TO 1.5X HI
STATED PRINT RUN 40 SETS
FP-1 Paul Kariya 10.00 25.00
FP-2 Ilya Kovalchuk 12.50 30.00
FP-3 Joe Thornton 15.00 40.00
FP-4 Miroslav Satan 10.00 25.00
FP-5 Jarome Iginla 12.50 30.00
FP-6 Ron Francis 10.00 25.00
FP-7 Eric Daze 10.00 25.00
FP-8 Patrick Roy 20.00 50.00
FP-9 Rostislav Klesla 10.00 25.00
FP-10 Mike Modano 12.50 30.00
FP-11 Steve Yzerman 20.00 50.00
FP-12 Mike Comrie 10.00 25.00
FP-13 Roberto Luongo 12.50 30.00
FP-14 Zigmund Palffy 10.00 25.00
FP-15 Marian Gaborik 15.00 40.00
FP-16 Jose Theodore 12.50 30.00
FP-17 Scott Hartnell 10.00 25.00
FP-18 Martin Brodeur 20.00 50.00
FP-19 Alexei Yashin 10.00 25.00
FP-20 Pavel Bure 10.00 25.00
FP-21 Marian Hossa 10.00 25.00
FP-22 Simon Gagne 10.00 25.00
FP-23 Daniel Briere 10.00 25.00
FP-24 Mario Lemieux 25.00 60.00
FP-25 Chris Pronger 10.00 25.00
FP-26 Owen Nolan 10.00 25.00
FP-27 Nikolai Khabibulin 10.00 25.00
FP-28 Mats Sundin 10.00 25.00
FP-29 Markus Naslund 10.00 25.00
FP-30 Jaromir Jagr 12.50 30.00

2002-03 BAP Memorabilia Future of the Game

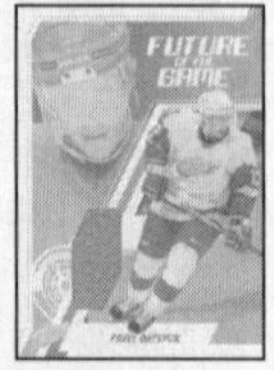

*MULT.COLOR: 1X TO 1.5X HI
STATED PRINT RUN 30 SETS
FG-1 Pavel Datsyuk 15.00 40.00
FG-2 Dan Blackburn 15.00 40.00
FG-3 Ilya Kovalchuk 20.00 50.00
FG-4 Roberto Luongo 20.00 50.00
FG-5 Dany Heatley 20.00 50.00
FG-6 Jose Theodore 20.00 50.00
FG-7 Mike Comrie 15.00 40.00
FG-8 Marian Gaborik 25.00 60.00
FG-9 Simon Gagne 15.00 40.00
FG-10 Joe Thornton 25.00 60.00
FG-11 Trent Hunter 15.00 40.00
FG-12 Martin Havlat 15.00 40.00
FG-13 Scott Hartnell 15.00 40.00
FG-14 Kristian Huselius 15.00 40.00
FG-15 Rick DiPietro 15.00 40.00
FG-16 Kyle Calder 15.00 40.00
FG-17 Alex Tanguay 15.00 40.00
FG-18 Brad Richards 15.00 40.00
FG-19 Rostislav Klesla 15.00 40.00
FG-20 Justin Williams 15.00 40.00
FG-21 Jason Spezza 30.00 80.00
FG-22 Jay Bouwmeester 15.00 40.00

2002-03 BAP Memorabilia He Shoots-He Scores Points

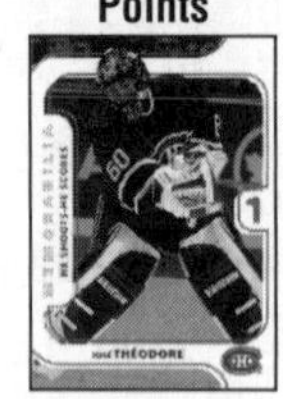

COMMON CARD .10 .25
ONE PER PACK
RED.PROGRAM EXPIRED
1 Mike Modano 1 pt. .10 .25
2 Jeremy Roenick 1 pt. .10 .25
3 Owen Nolan 1 pt. .10 .25
4 Chris Pronger 1 pt. .10 .25
5 Ron Francis 1 pt. .10 .25
6 Jose Theodore 1 pt. .10 .25
7 Brendan Shanahan 1 pt. .10 .25
8 Dany Heatley 1 pt. .10 .25
9 Paul Kariya 2 pts. .10 .25
10 Pavel Bure 2 pts. .10 .25
11 Peter Forsberg 2 pts. .10 .25
12 Joe Sakic 2 pts. .10 .25
13 Dominik Hasek 2 pts. .10 .25
14 Martin Brodeur 2 pts. .10 .25
15 Eric Lindros 2 pts. .10 .25
16 Ilya Kovalchuk 2 pts. .10 .25
17 Jaromir Jagr 2 pts. .10 .25
18 Patrick Roy 3 pts. .10 .25
19 Mario Lemieux 3 pts. .10 .25
20 Steve Yzerman 3 pts. .10 .25

2002-03 BAP Memorabilia He Shoots-He Scores Prizes

PRINT RUN 20 SER.#'d SETS
NOT PRICED DUE TO SCARCITY
1 Steve Yzerman
2 Mario Lemieux
3 Patrick Roy
4 Jaromir Jagr
5 Ilya Kovalchuk
6 Eric Lindros
7 Martin Brodeur
8 Dominik Hasek
9 Joe Sakic
10 Peter Forsberg
11 Pavel Bure
12 Paul Kariya
13 Dany Heatley
14 Brendan Shanahan
15 Jose Theodore
16 Ron Francis
17 Chris Pronger
18 Owen Nolan
19 Jeremy Roenick
20 Mike Modano
21 Roberto Luongo
22 Marian Gaborik
23 Todd Bertuzzi
24 Pavel Datsyuk
25 Jarome Iginla
26 Mats Sundin
27 Mark Messier
28 Sergei Fedorov
29 Nicklas Lidstrom
30 Teemu Selanne

2002-03 BAP Memorabilia Magnificent Inserts

This 10-card set featured game-used equipment from the career of Mario Lemieux. Cards MI1-MI5 had a print run of 40 copies each and cards MI6-MI10 were limited to just 10 copies each. Cards MI6-MI10 are not priced due to scarcity.
MI1-MI5 PRINT RUN 40 SETS
MI6-MI10 PRINT RUN 10 SETS
MI6-MI10 NOT PRICED DUE TO SCARCITY
MI1 2000-01 Jersey 30.00 80.00
MI2 1985-86 Jersey 30.00 80.00

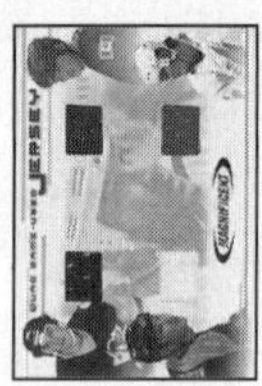

MI3 2002 All-Star Jersey 30.00 80.00
MI4 1987 Canada Cup Jersey 30.00 80.00
MI5 Dual Jersey 50.00 125.00
MI6 Number
MI7 Emblem
MI8 Triple Jersey
MI9 Quad Jersey
MI10 Complete Package

2002-03 BAP Memorabilia Magnificent Inserts Autographs

This 10-card set paralleled the base Magnificent Inserts but carried certified autographs and each card was hand numbered. Cards MI1-MI5 were serial-numbered to 15 each and cards MI6-MI10 were serial numbered out of 5.
MI1-MI5 PRINT RUN 15 SER.#'d SETS
MI6-MI10 PRINT RUN 5 SER.#'d SETS
NOT PRICED DUE TO SCARCITY

2002-03 BAP Memorabilia Mini Stanley Cups

Inserted one per hobby box, these miniature Stanley Cup replicas featured a player picture from a cup winning team on the front.
ONE PER HOBBY BOX
1 Johnny Bower 8.00 20.00
2 Tim Horton 12.00 30.00
3 Jean Beliveau 15.00 40.00
4 Lorne Worsley 8.00 20.00
5 Terry Sawchuk 12.00 30.00
6 Serge Savard 8.00 20.00
7 Henri Richard 8.00 20.00
8 Phil Esposito 8.00 20.00
9 Frank Mahovlich 8.00 20.00
10 Gerry Cheevers 8.00 20.00
11 Yvan Cournoyer 8.00 20.00
12 Bobby Clarke 8.00 20.00
13 Bernie Parent 8.00 20.00
14 Steve Shutt 8.00 20.00
15 Larry Robinson 8.00 20.00
16 Guy Lafleur 15.00 40.00
17 Guy Lapointe 8.00 20.00
18 Bryan Trottier 8.00 20.00
19 Mike Bossy 8.00 20.00
20 Denis Potvin 8.00 20.00
21 Bob Nystrom 8.00 20.00
22 Mark Messier 8.00 20.00
23 Andy Moog 8.00 20.00
24 Patrick Roy 20.00 50.00
25 Jari Kurri 15.00 40.00
26 Grant Fuhr 8.00 20.00
27 Doug Gilmour 8.00 20.00
28 Adam Graves 8.00 20.00
29 Mario Lemieux 20.00 50.00
30 Jaromir Jagr 15.00 40.00
31 John LeClair 8.00 20.00
32 Brian Leetch 8.00 20.00
33 Martin Brodeur 15.00 40.00
34 Peter Forsberg 12.00 30.00
35 Steve Yzerman 15.00 40.00
36 Nicklas Lidstrom 12.00 30.00
37 Mike Modano 12.00 30.00
38 Scott Stevens 8.00 20.00
39 Joe Sakic 12.00 30.00
40 Dominik Hasek 12.00 30.00

2002-03 BAP Memorabilia Stanley Cup Champions

This 15-card set featured swatches of game-worn jersey from the 2002 Stanley Cup Champion Detroit Red Wings. Cards were limited to just 40 copies each.
STATED PRINT RUN 40 SETS
SCC-1 Jiri Fischer 15.00 40.00
SCC-2 Mathieu Dandenault 15.00 40.00
SCC-3 Chris Chelios 15.00 40.00
SCC-4 Dominik Hasek 15.00 40.00
SCC-5 Steve Yzerman 40.00 100.00
SCC-6 Brendan Shanahan 15.00 40.00
SCC-7 Luc Robitaille 15.00 40.00
SCC-8 Nicklas Lidstrom 15.00 40.00
SCC-9 Manny Legace 30.00 80.00
SCC-10 Sergei Fedorov 30.00 80.00
SCC-11 Darren McCarty 15.00 40.00
SCC-12 Jason Williams 15.00 40.00
SCC-13 Pavel Datsyuk 15.00 40.00
SCC-14 Tomas Holmstrom 15.00 40.00
SCC-15 Brett Hull 25.00 60.00

2002-03 BAP Memorabilia Stanley Cup Playoffs

This 32-card set featured swatches of game-worn jersey. Print runs are listed below.
*MULT.COLOR: 1X TO 1.5X HI
PRINT RUNS LISTED BELOW
LOWER PRINT RUNS NOT PRICED
DUE TO SCARCITY
SC-1 Roman Cechmanek/90 8.00 20.00
SC-2 Patrick Lalime/90 8.00 20.00
SC-3 Gary Roberts/90 8.00 20.00
SC-4 Alexei Yashin/90 8.00 20.00
SC-5 Joe Thornton/90 12.50 30.00
SC-6 Jose Theodore/90 30.00 80.00
SC-7 Ron Francis/90 12.50 30.00
SC-8 Martin Brodeur/90 20.00 50.00
SC-9 Owen Nolan/90 8.00 20.00
SC-10 Sean Burke/90 8.00 20.00
SC-11 Felix Potvin/90 8.00 20.00
SC-12 Peter Forsberg/90 15.00 40.00
SC-13 Todd Bertuzzi/90 8.00 20.00
SC-14 Steve Yzerman/90 20.00 50.00
SC-15 Eric Daze/90 8.00 20.00
SC-16 Brent Johnson/90 8.00 20.00
SC-17 Teemu Selanne/60 8.00 20.00
SC-18 Chris Drury/60 8.00 20.00
SC-19 Alexander Mogilny/60 8.00 20.00
SC-20 Daniel Alfredsson/60 8.00 20.00
SC-21 Sergei Fedorov/60 15.00 40.00
SC-22 Keith Tkachuk/60 15.00 40.00
SC-23 Saku Koivu/60 8.00 20.00
SC-24 Jeff O'Neill/60 8.00 20.00
SC-25 Curtis Joseph/40 15.00 40.00
SC-26 Arturs Irbe/40 12.50 30.00
SC-27 Dominik Hasek/40 40.00 100.00
SC-28 Patrick Roy/40 40.00 100.00
SC-29 Ron Francis/30 25.00 60.00
SC-30 Dominik Hasek/30 30.00 80.00
SC-31 Steve Yzerman/10
SC-32 Nicklas Lidstrom
Conn Smythe Winner/10

2002-03 BAP Memorabilia Teammates

STATED PRINT RUN 70 SETS
TM-1 Dominik Hasek 25.00 60.00
Steve Yzerman
TM-2 Sergei Fedorov 15.00 40.00
Brendan Shanahan
TM-3 Luc Robitaille 12.50 30.00
Brett Hull
TM-4 Joe Sakic 30.00 80.00
Peter Forsberg
TM-5 Rob Blake 30.00 80.00
Patrick Roy
TM-6 Pavel Bure 12.50 30.00
Eric Lindros
TM-7 Brian Leetch 12.50 30.00
Mark Messier
TM-8 Mats Sundin 12.50 30.00
Curtis Joseph
TM-9 Jeremy Roenick 12.50 30.00
Roman Cechmanek
TM-10 Mark Recchi 12.50 30.00
Simon Gagne
TM-11 Jaromir Jagr 12.50 30.00
Peter Bondra
TM-12 Jose Theodore 12.50 30.00
Saku Koivu
TM-13 Zigmund Palffy 12.50 30.00
Felix Potvin
TM-14 Martin Brodeur 12.50 30.00
Patrik Elias
TM-15 Mario Lemieux 25.00 60.00
Alexei Kovalev
TM-16 Chris Pronger 12.50 30.00
Al MacInnis
TM-17 Doug Weight 12.50 30.00
Keith Tkachuk
TM-18 Teemu Selanne 12.50 30.00
Owen Nolan
TM-19 Ed Jovanovski 12.50 30.00
Markus Naslund
TM-20 Jarome Iginla 12.50 30.00
Roman Turek

2003-04 BAP Memorabilia

This 250-card set came in packs as a 200-card base set including 100 veteran skaters,

a 70-card Between the Pipes subset, and 30 rookies that were short-printed. Cards 201-250 were available via an online offer only for $29 US.
COMP. SET w/o UPDATE (200) 75.00 150.00
COMP.SET w/o SP's (170) 25.00 50.00
201-250 AVAIL.VIA ONLINE OFFER ONLY
1 Al MacInnis .20 .50
2 Alexei Morozov .05 .20
3 Ales Hemsky .20 .50
4 Ales Kotalik .05 .20
5 Alex Kovalev .20 .50
6 Alexander Frolov .05 .20
7 Alexander Mogilny .20 .50
8 Alexei Yashin .05 .20
9 Alexei Zhamnov .05 .20
10 Anson Carter .20 .50
11 Barret Jackman .20 .50
12 Bill Guerin .20 .50
13 Brad Richards .20 .50
14 Brad Stuart .05 .20
15 Brendan Shanahan .25 .60
16 Chris Drury .20 .50
17 Brett Hull .30 .75
18 Daniel Alfredsson .20 .50
19 Daniel Briere .05 .20
20 Dany Heatley .30 .75
21 David Legwand .20 .50
22 Daymond Langkow .20 .50
23 Derian Hatcher .05 .20
24 Doug Weight .20 .50
25 Ed Jovanovski .20 .50
26 Eric Daze .20 .50
27 Eric Lindros .25 .60
28 Geoff Sanderson .05 .20
29 Glen Murray .05 .20
30 Henrik Zetterberg .25 .60
31 Ilya Kovalchuk .30 .75
32 Jamie Langenbrunner .05 .20
33 Jarome Iginla .30 .75
34 Jaromir Jagr .40 1.00
35 Jason Allison .05 .20
36 Jason Spezza .25 .60
37 Jay Bouwmeester .05 .20
38 Jeff O'Neill .05 .20
39 Jere Lehtinen .20 .50
40 Jeremy Roenick .30 .75
41 Joe Sakic .50 1.25
42 Joe Thornton .40 1.00
43 John LeClair .25 .60
44 Keith Tkachuk .25 .60
45 Kristian Huselius .05 .20
46 Marian Gaborik .50 1.25
47 Marian Hossa .25 .60
48 Mario Lemieux 1.50 4.00
49 Mark Messier .25 .60
50 Markus Naslund .25 .60
51 Martin Havlat .20 .50
52 Martin St. Louis .20 .50
53 Mats Sundin .25 .60
54 Michael Peca .05 .20
55 Mike Comrie .20 .50
56 Mike Johnson .05 .20
57 Mike Komisarek .05 .20
58 Mike Modano .40 1.00
59 Milan Hejduk .25 .60
60 Miroslav Satan .20 .50
61 Nicklas Lidstrom .25 .60
62 Olli Jokinen .20 .50
63 Owen Nolan .20 .50
64 Pascal Dupuis .05 .20
65 Patrick Marleau .20 .50
66 Patrik Elias .20 .50
67 Patrik Stefan .05 .20
68 Paul Kariya .25 .60
69 Pavel Bure .25 .60
70 Pavol Demitra .05 .20
71 Peter Bondra .20 .50
72 Peter Forsberg .60 1.50
73 Petr Sykora .05 .20
74 Ray Whitney .05 .20
75 Richard Zednik .05 .20
76 Rick Nash .30 .75
77 Rob Blake .20 .50
78 Ron Francis .20 .50
79 Ryan Smyth .05 .20
80 Saku Koivu .25 .60
81 Sandis Ozolinsh .05 .20
82 Scott Hartnell .05 .20
83 Scott Niedermayer .05 .20
84 Scottie Upshall .05 .20
85 Sergei Fedorov .40 1.00
86 Sergei Gonchar .05 .20
87 Sergei Samsonov .20 .50
88 Sergei Zubov .05 .20
89 Simon Gagne .25 .60
90 Zdeno Chara .05 .20
91 Chuck Kobasew .05 .20
92 Steve Yzerman 1.25 3.00
93 Teemu Selanne .25 .60
94 Todd Bertuzzi .25 .60
95 Tony Amonte .20 .50
96 Vaclav Prospal .05 .20
97 Vincent Lecavalier .25 .60
98 Slava Kozlov .05 .20
99 Sylvester Flis .50 1.25
100 Zigmund Palffy .20 .50
101 Alex Auld .20 .50
102 Andrew Raycroft .20 .50
103 Ari Ahonen .20 .50
104 Brent Johnson .20 .50
105 Brian Boucher .20 .50
106 Brian Finley .20 .50
107 Byron Dafoe .20 .50
108 Chris Osgood .20 .50
109 Cristobal Huet .20 .50
110 Corey Schwab .20 .50
111 Curtis Joseph .25 .60
112 Curtis Sanford .20 .50
113 Dan Blackburn .20 .50
114 Dan Cloutier .20 .50
115 David Aebischer .20 .50
116 Dwayne Roloson .20 .50
117 Ed Belfour .25 .60
118 Evgeni Nabokov .20 .50
119 Felix Potvin .25 .60
120 Fred Brathwaite .20 .50
121 Garth Snow .20 .50
122 Jani Hurme .20 .50
123 Jason Bacashihua .20 .50
124 J-S Giguere .20 .50
125 Jeff Hackett .20 .50
126 Jocelyn Thibault .20 .50
127 Johan Hedberg .20 .50
128 John Grahame .20 .50
129 Jose Theodore .30 .75
130 Josh Harding .20 .50
131 Jussi Markkanen .20 .50
132 Kevin Weekes .20 .50
133 Manny Fernandez .20 .50
134 Manny Legace .20 .50
135 Marc Denis .20 .50
136 Martin Biron .20 .50
137 Martin Brodeur .60 1.50
138 Martin Gerber .20 .50
139 Martin Prusek .20 .50
140 Marty Turco .20 .50
141 Mathieu Garon .20 .50
142 Maxime Ouellet .20 .50
143 Michael Leighton .20 .50
144 Miikka Kiprusoff .20 .50
145 Mika Noronen .20 .50
146 Mikael Tellqvist .20 .50
147 Mike Dunham .20 .50
148 Nikolai Khabibulin .25 .60
149 Olaf Kolzig .20 .50
150 Pascal Leclaire .20 .50
151 Pasi Nurminen .20 .50
152 Patrick Lalime .20 .50
153 Patrick Roy 1.25 3.00
154 Ray Emery .20 .50
155 Rick DiPietro .20 .50
156 Robert Esche .20 .50
157 Roberto Luongo .30 .75
158 Roman Cechmanek .20 .50
159 Roman Turek .20 .50
160 Ron Tugnutt .20 .50
161 Ryan Miller .20 .50
162 Sean Burke .20 .50
163 Sebastien Caron .20 .50
164 Sebastien Charpentier .20 .50
165 Steve Shields .20 .50
166 Tomas Vokoun .20 .50
167 Tommy Salo .20 .50
168 Trevor Kidd .20 .50
169 Vesa Toskala .20 .50
170 Zac Bierk .20 .50
171 Tuomo Ruutu RC 1.25 3.00
172 Jordin Tootoo RC 1.25 3.00
173 Joni Pitkanen RC 1.00 2.50
174 Peter Sejna RC .50 1.25
175 Dan Hamhuis RC .75 2.00
176 Eric Staal RC 2.00 5.00
177 Dan Fritsche RC .50 1.25
178 Dustin Brown RC .50 1.25
179 Christopher Higgins RC 1.00 2.50
180 Nathan Horton RC 1.25 3.00
181 Milan Michalek RC .75 2.00
182 Boyd Gordon RC .50 1.25
183 Marc-Andre Fleury RC 2.50 6.00
184 Joffrey Lupul RC 1.00 2.50
185 David Hale RC .50 1.25
186 Sean Bergenheim RC .50 1.25
187 Tim Gleason RC .50 1.25
188 Pavel Vorobiev RC .50 1.25
189 Paul Martin RC .50 1.25
190 Marek Svatos RC .50 1.25
191 Antoine Vermette RC .50 1.25
192 Matt Stajan RC 1.25 3.00
193 Alexander Semin RC 1.00 2.50
194 Brent Burns RC .50 1.25
195 Jiri Hudler RC .75 2.00
196 Matthew Lombardi RC .50 1.25
197 Maxim Kondratiev RC .50 1.25
198 Brent Krahn RC .50 1.25
199 Antti Miettinen RC .50 1.25
200 Patrice Bergeron RC 2.00 5.00
201 Cover Card/Checklist .05 .20
202 Marek Zidlicky XRC .60 1.50
203 John-Michael Liles XRC .60 1.50
204 Ryan Malone XRC .60 1.50
205 Tom Preissing XRC .60 1.50
206 Rastislav Stana XRC .60 1.50
207 Mike Commodore .05 .20
208 Jaromir Jagr .40 1.00
209 Fredrik Sjostrom XRC .60 1.50
210 Nikolai Zherdev XRC 1.50 4.00
211 Derek Roy XRC .60 1.50
212 Marcus Nilsson .05 .20
213 Milan Michalek XRC .60 1.50
214 Tomas Plekanec XRC .60 1.50
215 Mark Popovic XRC .60 1.50
216 Frederic Henry XRC .60 1.50
217 Nolan Schaefer XRC .60 1.50
218 Colton Orr XRC .60 1.50
219 Mike Smith XRC 2.00 5.00
220 Cory Stillman .05 .20
221 Carl Corazzini XRC .60 1.50
222 Eric Heffler XRC .60 1.50
223 Dimitri Afanasenkov .05 .20
224 Garth Murray .05 .20
225 Matt Ellison XRC .60 1.50
226 Ville Nieminen .05 .20
227 Brooks Laich XRC .60 1.50
228 Sergei Gonchar .05 .20
229 Fedor Tyutin XRC .60 1.50
230 Ron Francis .20 .50
231 Phil Osaer XRC .60 1.50
232 Miikka Kiprusoff .20 .50
233 Michal Barinka XRC .60 1.50
234 Brad Boyes XRC .60 1.50
235 Erik Westrum XRC .60 1.50
236 Kari Lehtonen XRC 3.00 8.00
237 Chad Alban XRC .60 1.50
238 Thomas Pock XRC .60 1.50
239 Darryl Sydor .05 .20
240 Greg Mauldin XRC .60 1.50
241 Eric Perrin XRC .60 1.50
242 Michael Ryder .05 .20
243 Esa Pirnes XRC .60 1.50
244 Matt Murley XRC .60 1.50
245 Trevor Daley XRC .60 1.50
246 Libor Pivko XRC .60 1.50
247 John Pohl XRC .60 1.50
248 Seamus Kotyk XRC .60 1.50
249 Sergei Zinovjev XRC .60 1.50
250 Joe Nieuwendyk .20 .50

2003-04 BAP Memorabilia Emerald

PRINT RUN 10 SER.#'d SETS
NOT PRICED DUE TO SCARCITY

2003-04 BAP Memorabilia Gold

AVAIL.IN BAP UPD.BOXES ONLY
PRINT RUN 1 SET
NOT PRICED DUE TO SCARCITY

2003-04 BAP Memorabilia Ruby

*STARS: 2.5X TO 6X BASIC CARDS
*ROOKIES: .5X TO 1.25X
PRINT RUN 200 SER.#'d SETS

2003-04 BAP Memorabilia Sapphire

*STARS: 4X TO 10X BASE HI
*ROOKIES : .75X TO 2X
PRINT RUN 100 SER.#'d SETS

2003-04 BAP Memorabilia All-Star Complete Jerseys

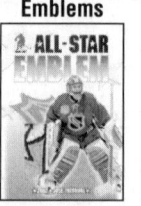

STATED PRINT RUN 10 SETS
NOT PRICED DUE TO SCARCITY
ASCJ1 Peter Forsberg
ASCJ2 Paul Kariya
ASCJ3 Patrick Roy
ASCJ4 Dany Heatley
ASCJ5 Mike Modano
ASCJ6 Joe Thornton
ASCJ7 Jose Theodore
ASCJ8 Joe Sakic
ASCJ9 Martin Brodeur
ASCJ10 Steve Yzerman

2003-04 BAP Memorabilia All-Star Emblems

STATED PRINT RUN 10 SETS
NOT PRICED DUE TO SCARCITY
ASE-1 Mike Modano
ASE-2 Paul Kariya
ASE-3 Nicklas Lidstrom
ASE-4 Patrick Roy
ASE-5 Dany Heatley
ASE-6 Peter Forsberg
ASE-7 Alex Kovalev
ASE-8 Jaromir Jagr
ASE-9 Brian Leetch
ASE-10 Joe Thornton
ASE-11 Brendan Shanahan
ASE-12 Chris Pronger
ASE-13 Jose Theodore
ASE-14 Martin Brodeur
ASE-15 Pavel Bure
ASE-16 Joe Sakic
ASE-17 Markus Naslund
ASE-18 John LeClair
ASE-19 Al MacInnis
ASE-20 Steve Yzerman

2003-04 BAP Memorabilia All-Star Jerseys

*MULT.COLOR SWATCH: .75X TO 1.5X
STATED PRINT RUN 90 SETS
MVP CARDS PRINT RUN 10 SETS

MVP CARDS NOT PRICED DUE TO SCARCITY
ASJ-1 Peter Forsberg 10.00 25.00
ASJ-2 Jaromir Jagr 10.00 25.00
ASJ-3 Mike Modano 8.00 20.00
ASJ-4 Bill Guerin 6.00 15.00
ASJ-5 Paul Kariya 6.00 15.00
ASJ-6 Nicklas Lidstrom 6.00 15.00
ASJ-7 Teemu Selanne 6.00 15.00
ASJ-8 Patrick Roy 12.50 30.00
ASJ-9 Alex Kovalev 6.00 15.00
ASJ-10 Dany Heatley MVP
ASJ-11 Sergei Fedorov 10.00 25.00
ASJ-12 Jaromir Jagr 10.00 25.00
ASJ-13 Brian Leetch 6.00 15.00
ASJ-14 Joe Thornton 8.00 20.00
ASJ-15 Jose Theodore 8.00 20.00
ASJ-16 Brendan Shanahan 6.00 15.00
ASJ-17 Patrick Roy 15.00 40.00
ASJ-18 Chris Pronger 6.00 15.00
ASJ-19 Nicklas Lidstrom 6.00 15.00
ASJ-20 Eric Daze MVP
ASJ-21 Martin Brodeur 12.50 30.00
ASJ-22 Pavel Bure 6.00 15.00
ASJ-23 Peter Forsberg 12.50 30.00
ASJ-24 Paul Kariya 6.00 15.00
ASJ-25 Brian Leetch 6.00 15.00
ASJ-26 Nicklas Lidstrom 6.00 15.00
ASJ-27 Markus Naslund 6.00 15.00
ASJ-28 Patrick Roy 15.00 40.00
ASJ-29 Joe Sakic 10.00 25.00
ASJ-30 Bill Guerin MVP
ASJ-31 Al MacInnis 6.00 15.00
ASJ-32 Jaromir Jagr 10.00 25.00
ASJ-33 John LeClair 6.00 15.00
ASJ-34 Martin Brodeur 12.50 30.00
ASJ-35 Mike Modano 8.00 20.00
ASJ-36 Jeremy Roenick 8.00 20.00
ASJ-37 Brendan Shanahan 6.00 15.00
ASJ-38 Mats Sundin 6.00 15.00
ASJ-39 Steve Yzerman 12.50 30.00
ASJ-40 Pavel Bure MVP

2003-04 BAP Memorabilia All-Star Numbers

STATED PRINT RUN 20 SETS
NOT PRICED DUE TO SCARCITY
ASN-1 Mike Modano
ASN-2 Paul Kariya
ASN-3 Nicklas Lidstrom
ASN-4 Patrick Roy
ASN-5 Dany Heatley
ASN-6 Peter Forsberg
ASN-7 Alex Kovalev
ASN-8 Jaromir Jagr
ASN-9 Brian Leetch
ASN-10 Joe Thornton
ASN-11 Brendan Shanahan
ASN-12 Chris Pronger
ASN-13 Jose Theodore
ASN-14 Martin Brodeur
ASN-15 Pavel Bure
ASN-16 Joe Sakic
ASN-17 Markus Naslund
ASN-18 John LeClair
ASN-19 Al MacInnis
ASN-20 Steve Yzerman

2003-04 BAP Memorabilia All-Star Staring Lineup

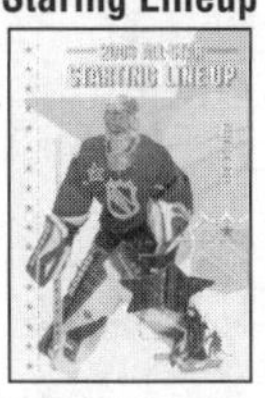

1 Nikolai Khabibulin 8.00 20.00
2 Brian Leetch 8.00 20.00
3 Sandis Ozolinsh 8.00 20.00
4 Mario Lemieux 15.00 40.00
5 Jaromir Jagr 10.00 25.00
6 Alex Kovalev 8.00 20.00
7 Patrick Roy 15.00 40.00
8 Nicklas Lidstrom 8.00 20.00
9 Rob Blake 8.00 20.00
10 Mike Modano 10.00 25.00
11 Bill Guerin 8.00 20.00
12 Teemu Selanne 8.00 20.00

2003-04 BAP Memorabilia All-Star Teammates

STATED PRINT RUN 30 SETS
AST1 P.Forsberg/P.Roy 30.00 80.00
AST2 D.Heatley/J.Jagr 20.00 50.00
AST3 M.Modano/B.Guerin 20.00 50.00
AST4 N.Lidstrom/P.Kariya 20.00 50.00
AST5 B.Leetch/J.Thornton 25.00 60.00
AST6 J.Theodore/P.Roy 40.00 100.00
AST7 B.Shanahan/B.Leetch 20.00 50.00
AST8 M.Brodeur/P.Roy 40.00 100.00
AST9 P.Forsberg/N.Lidstrom 25.00 60.00
AST10 J.Sakic/B.Leetch 30.00 80.00

2003-04 BAP Memorabilia Brush with Greatness

This 25-card set featured artist renderings on the card fronts along with foil highlights. Foil cards were inserted at one per box. A contest entry parallel without the foil effect was also created and more plentiful. On the back of the contest cards were rules and instructions for entering a drawing for a jersey of the given player with the artist's rendering painted on the jersey. Some of the jerseys also included the player's autograph. Entry deadlines were staggered, but the last deadline was August 2004.
FOIL ODDS 1 PER BOX
COMMON CONTEST CARD .60 1.50
1 Mario Lemieux 6.00 15.00
2 Martin Brodeur 5.00 12.00
3 Marian Gaborik 4.00 10.00
4 Paul Kariya 2.00 5.00
5 Peter Forsberg 5.00 12.00
6 Jason Spezza 2.00 5.00
7 Maurice Richard 4.00 10.00
8 Jacques Plante 3.00 8.00
9 Henrik Zetterberg 2.00 5.00
10 Ed Belfour 2.00 5.00
11 Nicklas Lidstrom 2.00 5.00
12 Rick Nash 2.50 6.00
13 Bill Barilko 2.00 5.00
14 J-S Giguere 2.00 5.00
15 Jose Theodore 2.00 5.00
16 Pavel Bure 2.00 5.00
17 Ilya Kovalchuk 2.50 6.00
18 Mats Sundin 2.00 5.00
19 Terry Sawchuk 3.00 8.00
20 Joe Thornton 3.00 8.00
21 Dominik Hasek 4.00 10.00
22 Joe Sakic 4.00 10.00
23 Dany Heatley 2.50 6.00
24 Steve Yzerman 5.00 12.00
25 Patrick Roy 6.00 15.00

2003-04 BAP Memorabilia Deep in the Crease

COMPLETE SET (15) 12.00 30.00
D1 Pasi Nurminen .75 2.00
Byron Dafoe
Jani Hurme
Frederic Cassivi
D2 Jocelyn Thibault .75 2.00
Michael Leighton
Craig Andersson
Steve Passmore
D3 Jose Theodore .75 2.00
Mathieu Garon
Eric Fichaud
J-F Damphousse
Oliver Michaud
D4 New Jersey Devils .75 2.00
D5 Mike Dunham .75 2.00
Dan Blackburn
Jussi Markkanen
Jason Labarbera
D6 Tomas Vokoun .75 2.00
Jan Lasek
Brian Finley
Chris Mason
D7 J-S Giguere .75 2.00
Martin Gerber
Ilya Bryzgalov
Gregg Naumenko
D8 Dominik Hasek 3.00 8.00
Curtis Joseph
Manny Legace
Marc Lamothe
D9 Ed Belfour 1.50 4.00
Trevor Kidd
Mikael Tellqvist
Sebastien Centomo
Jamie Hodson
D10 Dan Cloutier .75 2.00
Johan Hedberg
Alex Auld
Tyler Moss
D11 Manny Fernandez .75 2.00
Dwayne Roloson
Johan Holmqvist
Josh Harding
Frederic Cloutier
D12 Chris Osgood .75 2.00
Brent Johnson
Curtis Sanford
Reinhard Divis
Cody Rudkowsky
D13 Martin Biron .75 2.00
Mika Noronen
Ryan Miller
Tom Askey
D14 Roberto Luongo .75 2.00
Steve Shields
Simon Lajeunesse
Travis Scott
D15 Marc-Andre Fleury 2.00 5.00
Sebastien Caron
J-S Aubin
Martin Brochu

2003-04 BAP Memorabilia Draft Redemptions

Inserted randomly in packs, this 30-card set featured cards representing the top thirty draft picks in 2003. Each card was redeemable for the player it represented once that player made his NHL debut. Collectors had six months to redeem the cards once the player was available. The redemption cards themselves were hand-numbered out of 100.
STATED PRINT RUN 100 SETS
EXPIRED CARD PRINT RUNS BELOW
1 Marc-Andre Fleury/56 75.00 200.00
Expired 6/11/2004
2 Eric Staal/51 40.00 100.00
Expired 6/11/2004
3 Nathan Horton/48 40.00 100.00
Expired 6/11/2004
4 Nikolai Zherdev/52 25.00 60.00
Expired 6/11/2004
5 Thomas Vanek EXCH 25.00 60.00
6 Milan Michalek/41 25.00 60.00
Expired 6/11/2004
7 Ryan Suter EXCH 15.00 40.00
8 Braydon Coburn EXCH 8.00 20.00
9 Dion Phaneuf EXCH 30.00 80.00
10 Andrei Kostitsyn EXCH 12.00 30.00
11 Jeff Carter EXCH 20.00 50.00
12 New York Rangers 12.50 30.00
13 Dustin Brown/43 12.50 30.00
Expired 6/11/2004
14 Brent Seabrook EXCH 10.00 25.00
15 Robert Nilsson EXCH 12.50 30.00
16 Steve Bernier EXCH 15.00 40.00
17 Zach Parise EXCH 25.00 60.00
18 Eric Fehr EXCH 15.00 40.00
19 Ryan Getzlaf EXCH 25.00 60.00
20 Brent Burns/46 25.00 60.00
Expired 6/11/2004
21 Mark Stuart EXCH 8.00 20.00
22 Edmonton Oilers 15.00 40.00
23 Ryan Kesler/40 25.00 60.00
24 Mike Richards EXCH 15.00 40.00
25 Anthony Stewart EXCH 12.50 30.00
26 Los Angeles Kings 12.50 30.00
27 Jeff Tambellini EXCH 8.00 20.00
28 Corey Perry EXCH 15.00 40.00
29 Patrick Eaves EXCH 15.00 40.00
30 St. Louis Blues 8.00 20.00

2003-04 BAP Memorabilia Future of the Game

STATED PRINT RUN 30 SETS
FG-1 Scottie Upshall 10.00 25.00
FG-2 Ray Emery 10.00 25.00
FG-3 Rick Nash 25.00 60.00
FG-4 Stanislav Chistov 10.00 25.00
FG-5 Ryan Miller 10.00 25.00
FG-6 Henrik Zetterberg 20.00 50.00
FG-7 Alexander Frolov 10.00 25.00
FG-8 Barret Jackman 10.00 25.00
FG-9 Brandon Reid 10.00 25.00
FG-10 Mike Komisarek 10.00 25.00
FG-11 Alexei Smirnov 10.00 25.00
FG-12 Steve Ott 10.00 25.00
FG-13 Mike Cammalleri 10.00 25.00
FG-14 Jason Spezza 25.00 60.00
FG-15 Carlo Colaiacovo 10.00 25.00
FG-16 Jared Aulin 10.00 25.00
FG-17 Ales Hemsky 10.00 25.00
FG-18 Marc-Andre Fleury 30.00 80.00
FG-19 Eric Staal 25.00 60.00
FG-20 Dustin Brown 10.00 25.00

2003-04 BAP Memorabilia Future Wave

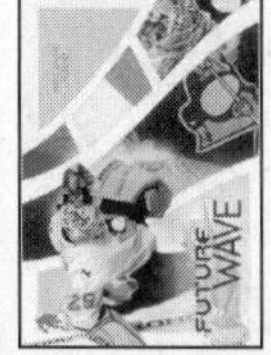

STATED PRINT RUN 60 SETS
FW-1 Marc-Andre Fleury 30.00 80.00
FW-2 Ray Emery 12.00 30.00
FW-3 David Aebischer 12.00 30.00
FW-4 Rick DiPietro 12.00 30.00
FW-5 Dan Blackburn 8.00 20.00
FW-6 Mathieu Garon 8.00 20.00
FW-7 Ryan Miller 15.00 40.00
FW-8 Brian Finley 8.00 20.00
FW-9 Alex Auld 8.00 20.00
FW-10 Mika Noronen 8.00 20.00
FW-11 Mikael Tellqvist 12.00 30.00
FW-12 Andrew Raycroft 12.00 30.00

2003-04 BAP Memorabilia Gloves

STATED PRINT RUN 30 SETS
GUG1 J-S Giguere 15.00 40.00
GUG2 Patrick Roy 30.00 80.00
GUG3 Marty Turco 15.00 40.00
GUG4 Olaf Kolzig 15.00 40.00
GUG5 Patrick Lalime 15.00 40.00
GUG6 Jacques Plante 30.00 80.00
GUG7 Bill Durnan 15.00 40.00
GUG8 Bernie Parent 15.00 40.00
GUG9 Vladislav Tretiak 50.00 100.00
GUG10 Charlie Hodge 15.00 40.00
GUG11 Keith Tkachuk 15.00 40.00
GUG12 Mario Lemieux 30.00 80.00
GUG13 Eric Lindros 15.00 40.00
GUG14 Sergei Samsonov 15.00 40.00
GUG15 Jarome Iginla 20.00 50.00
GUG16 Wendel Clark 15.00 40.00
GUG17 Dickie Moore 15.00 40.00
GUG18 Bill Gadsby 30.00 80.00
GUG19 Bernie Geoffrion 15.00 40.00
GUG20 Eddie Shore 30.00 80.00

2003-04 BAP Memorabilia He Shoots-He Scores Points

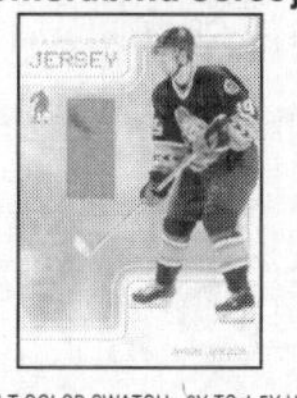

ONE PER PACK
RED.PROGRAM EXPIRED
1 Jose Theodore 1 Pt. .40 1.00
2 Jeremy Roenick 1 Pt. .40 1.00
3 Chris Pronger 1 Pt. .40 1.00
4 Markus Naslund 1 Pt. .40 1.00
5 Nicklas Lidstrom 1 Pt. .40 1.00
6 Dany Heatley 1 Pt. .40 1.00
7 Bill Guerin 1 Pt. .40 1.00
8 Pavel Bure 1 Pt. .40 1.00
9 Steve Yzerman 2 Pts. .40 1.00
10 Joe Thornton 2 Pts. .40 1.00
11 Mats Sundin 2 Pts. .40 1.00
12 Brendan Shanahan 2 Pts. .40 1.00
13 Teemu Selanne 2 Pts. .40 1.00
14 Joe Sakic 2 Pts. .40 1.00
15 Mike Modano 2 Pts. .40 1.00
16 Paul Kariya 2 Pts. .40 1.00
17 Sergei Fedorov 2 Pts. .40 1.00
18 Patrick Roy 3 Pts. .40 1.00
19 Peter Forsberg 3 Pts. .40 1.00
20 Martin Brodeur 3 Pts. .40 1.00

2003-04 BAP Memorabilia He Shoots-He Scores Prizes

PRINT RUN 20 SER.#'d SETS
NOT PRICED DUE TO SCARCITY
1 Peter Forsberg
2 Mike Modano
3 Bill Guerin
4 Paul Kariya
5 Nicklas Lidstrom
6 Teemu Selanne
7 Patrick Roy
8 Dany Heatley
9 Sergei Fedorov
10 Joe Thornton
11 Jose Theodore
12 Brendan Shanahan
13 Chris Pronger
14 Martin Brodeur
15 Pavel Bure
16 Markus Naslund
17 Joe Sakic
18 Jeremy Roenick
19 Mats Sundin
20 Steve Yzerman
21 Ed Belfour
22 Mario Lemieux
23 Jaromir Jagr
24 Curtis Joseph
25 Keith Tkachuk
26 Tony Amonte
27 Jarome Iginla
28 Eric Lindros
29 Brian Leetch
30 Milan Hejduk

2003-04 BAP Memorabilia Jersey and Stick

STATED PRINT RUN 90 SETS
SJ-1 Joe Thornton 15.00 40.00
SJ-2 Sergei Samsonov 8.00 20.00
SJ-3 Jarome Iginla 10.00 25.00
SJ-4 Ron Francis 8.00 20.00
SJ-5 Jocelyn Thibault 8.00 20.00
SJ-6 Mats Sundin 8.00 20.00
SJ-7 Rob Blake 8.00 20.00
SJ-8 Al MacInnis 8.00 20.00
SJ-9 Rick Nash 15.00 40.00
SJ-10 Marty Turco 8.00 20.00
SJ-11 Bill Guerin 8.00 20.00
SJ-12 Chris Chelios 8.00 20.00
SJ-13 Luc Robitaille 8.00 20.00
SJ-14 Mike Comrie 8.00 20.00
SJ-15 Markus Naslund 8.00 20.00
SJ-16 Roberto Luongo 10.00 25.00
SJ-17 Peter Bondra 8.00 20.00
SJ-18 John LeClair 8.00 20.00
SJ-19 Rick DiPietro 8.00 20.00
SJ-20 Tony Amonte 8.00 20.00
SJ-21 Eric Lindros 8.00 20.00
SJ-22 Jeremy Roenick 12.50 30.00
SJ-23 Ilya Kovalchuk 12.50 30.00
SJ-24 Dany Heatley 12.50 30.00
SJ-25 Patrick Roy 20.00 50.00
SJ-26 Joe Sakic 15.00 40.00
SJ-27 Peter Forsberg 15.00 40.00
SJ-28 Mike Modano 10.00 25.00
SJ-29 Steve Yzerman 20.00 50.00
SJ-30 Nicklas Lidstrom 8.00 20.00
SJ-31 Brett Hull 12.50 30.00
SJ-32 Jose Theodore 10.00 25.00
SJ-33 Martin Brodeur 15.00 40.00
SJ-34 Pavel Bure 8.00 20.00
SJ-35 Mario Lemieux 20.00 50.00
SJ-36 Jaromir Jagr 12.50 30.00
SJ-37 Marian Gaborik 20.00 50.00
SJ-38 Brendan Shanahan 8.00 20.00
SJ-39 Dominik Hasek 12.50 30.00
SJ-40 Todd Bertuzzi 8.00 20.00

2003-04 BAP Memorabilia Jerseys

*MULT.COLOR SWATCH: .6X TO 1.5X HI
STATED PRINT RUN 90 SETS
GJ-1 Joe Thornton 10.00 25.00
GJ-2 Dominik Hasek 10.00 25.00
GJ-3 Jarome Iginla 10.00 25.00
GJ-4 Ron Francis 6.00 15.00
GJ-5 Henrik Zetterberg 6.00 15.00
GJ-6 Mats Sundin 6.00 15.00
GJ-7 Rob Blake 6.00 15.00
GJ-8 Al MacInnis 6.00 15.00
GJ-9 Milan Hejduk 6.00 15.00
GJ-10 Rick Nash 10.00 25.00
GJ-11 Marty Turco 6.00 15.00
GJ-12 J-S Giguere 6.00 15.00
GJ-13 Jason Spezza 8.00 20.00
GJ-14 Luc Robitaille 6.00 15.00
GJ-15 Alexander Mogilny 6.00 15.00
GJ-16 Mike Comrie 6.00 15.00
GJ-17 Markus Naslund 6.00 15.00
GJ-18 Roberto Luongo 10.00 25.00
GJ-19 Jay Bouwmeester 6.00 15.00
GJ-20 Marian Hossa 6.00 15.00
GJ-21 Todd Bertuzzi 6.00 15.00
GJ-22 Saku Koivu 6.00 15.00
GJ-23 Curtis Joseph 6.00 15.00
GJ-24 Rick DiPietro 6.00 15.00
GJ-25 Ed Belfour 6.00 15.00
GJ-26 Eric Lindros 6.00 15.00
GJ-27 Jeremy Roenick 10.00 25.00
GJ-28 Brian Leetch 6.00 15.00
GJ-29 Owen Nolan 6.00 15.00
GJ-30 Simon Gagne 6.00 15.00
GJ-31 Brendan Shanahan 6.00 15.00
GJ-32 Ilya Kovalchuk 10.00 25.00
GJ-33 Dany Heatley 10.00 25.00
GJ-34 Patrick Roy 15.00 40.00
GJ-35 Joe Sakic 12.00 30.00
GJ-36 Peter Forsberg 10.00 25.00
GJ-37 Mike Modano 10.00 25.00
GJ-38 Steve Yzerman 15.00 40.00
GJ-39 Nicklas Lidstrom 6.00 15.00
GJ-40 Brett Hull 10.00 25.00
GJ-41 Jose Theodore 8.00 20.00
GJ-42 Martin Brodeur 12.00 30.00
GJ-43 Pavel Bure 6.00 15.00
GJ-44 Mark Messier 6.00 15.00
GJ-45 Mario Lemieux 15.00 40.00
GJ-46 Jaromir Jagr 10.00 25.00
GJ-47 Marian Gaborik 12.00 30.00
GJ-48 Teemu Selanne 6.00 15.00
GJ-49 Paul Kariya 6.00 15.00
GJ-50 Sergei Fedorov 8.00 20.00

2003-04 BAP Memorabilia Jersey Autographs

STATED PRINT RUN 10 SETS
NOT PRICED DUE TO SCARCITY

2003-04 BAP Memorabilia Masks III

COMPLETE SET (20) 40.00 80.00
1 J-S Giguere 4.00 10.00
2 Roman Cechmanek 4.00 10.00
3 Dominik Hasek 6.00 15.00
4 Roberto Luongo 5.00 12.00
5 Ryan Miller 4.00 10.00
6 Sean Burke 4.00 10.00
7 Kevin Weekes 4.00 10.00
8 Mike Dunham 4.00 10.00
9 Jeff Hackett 4.00 10.00
10 Martin Prusek 4.00 10.00
11 Olaf Kolzig 4.00 10.00
12 Nikolai Khabibulin 4.00 10.00
13 Pasi Nurminen 4.00 10.00
14 Johan Hedberg 4.00 10.00
15 Marty Turco 4.00 10.00
16 Felix Potvin 4.00 10.00
17 Marc Denis 4.00 10.00
18 Marc-Andre Fleury 8.00 20.00
19 David Aebischer 4.00 10.00
20 Jocelyn Thibault 4.00 10.00

2003-04 BAP Memorabilia Masks III Gold

*GOLD: 2.5X TO 6X BASIC MASKS
STATED PRINT RUN 30 SETS

2003-04 BAP Memorabilia Masks III Silver

*SILVER: 1X TO 2.5X BASIC MASKS
PRINT RUN SERIAL 300 SETS

2003-04 BAP Memorabilia Masks III Autographs

This 16-card set paralleled the regular insert set but carried certified player autographs. Cards were limited to 10 copies each and were not priced due to scarcity.
STATED PRINT RUN 10 SETS
NOT PRICED DUE TO SCARCITY
M-DA David Aebischer
M-DH Mike Dunham
M-FP Felix Potvin
M-JH Jeff Hackett
M-JT Jocelyn Thibault
M-KW Kevin Weekes
M-MDE Marc Denis
M-MDU Mike Dunham
M-MF Marc-Andre Fleury
M-MT Marty Turco
M-NK Nikolai Khabibulin
M-OK Olaf Kolzig
M-PN Pasi Nurminen
M-RC Roman Cechmanek
M-RL Roberto Luongo
M-RM Ryan Miller

2003-04 BAP Memorabilia Masks III Memorabilia

This 20-card set paralleled the regular insert set but carried swatches of game-used memorabilia. Cards were limited to 10 copies each and were not priced due to scarcity.
STATED PRINT RUN 10 SETS
NOT PRICED DUE TO SCARCITY

2003-04 BAP Memorabilia Practice Jerseys

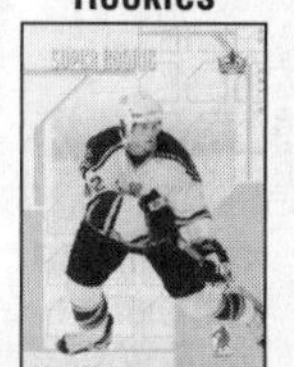

STATED PRINT RUN 40 SETS
PMP1 Curtis Joseph 10.00 25.00
PMP2 Martin Brodeur 15.00 40.00
PMP3 Ed Jovanovski 10.00 25.00
PMP4 Scott Neidermayer 10.00 25.00
PMP5 Al MacInnis 10.00 25.00
PMP6 Rob Blake 10.00 25.00
PMP7 Chris Pronger 10.00 25.00
PMP8 Owen Nolan 10.00 25.00
PMP9 Eric Lindros 10.00 25.00
PMP10 Paul Kariya 10.00 25.00
PMP11 Steve Yzerman 15.00 40.00
PMP12 Brendan Shanahan 10.00 25.00
PMP13 Theo Fleury 10.00 25.00
PMP14 Ryan Smyth 10.00 25.00
PMP15 Joe Nieuwendyk 10.00 25.00
PMP16 Jarome Iginla 12.50 30.00

2003-04 BAP Memorabilia Stanley Cup Champions

STATED PRINT RUN 40 SETS
SCC-1 Martin Brodeur 40.00 100.00
SCC-2 Jamie Langenbrunner 20.00 40.00
SCC-3 Scott Gomez 20.00 40.00
SCC-4 Joe Nieuwendyk 20.00 40.00
SCC-5 John Madden 20.00 40.00
SCC-6 Scott Niedermayer 20.00 40.00
SCC-7 Jeff Friesen 20.00 40.00
SCC-8 Scott Stevens 25.00 60.00
SCC-9 Patrik Elias 20.00 40.00
SCC-10 Corey Schwab 20.00 40.00

2003-04 BAP Memorabilia Stanley Cup Playoffs

CARDS 1-16 PRINT RUN 90 SETS
CARDS 17-24 PRINT RUN 80 SETS
CARDS 25-28 PRINT RUN 60 SETS
CARDS 29-30 PRINT RUN 20 SETS
CARDS 31-32 PRINT RUN 10 SETS
29-32 NOT PRICED DUE TO SCARCITY
SCP-1 Steve Yzerman 15.00 40.00
SCP-2 J-S Giguere 6.00 15.00
SCP-3 Doug Weight 6.00 15.00
SCP-4 Ed Jovanovski 6.00 15.00
SCP-5 Joe Sakic 15.00 40.00
SCP-6 Marian Gaborik 12.50 30.00
SCP-7 Mike Modano 10.00 25.00
SCP-8 Georges Laraque 6.00 15.00
SCP-9 Marian Hossa 8.00 20.00
SCP-10 Alexei Yashin 6.00 15.00
SCP-11 Scott Niedermayer 6.00 15.00
SCP-12 Jeff Hackett 6.00 15.00
SCP-13 Martin St.Louis 6.00 15.00
SCP-14 Jaromir Jagr 10.00 25.00
SCP-15 Mark Recchi 6.00 15.00
SCP-16 Alex Mogilny 6.00 15.00
SCP-17 Paul Kariya 8.00 20.00
SCP-18 Marty Turco 6.00 15.00
SCP-19 Dwayne Roloson 6.00 15.00
SCP-20 Markus Naslund 8.00 20.00
SCP-21 Daniel Alfredsson 6.00 15.00
SCP-22 Jeremy Roenick 10.00 25.00
SCP-23 Vincent Lecavalier 8.00 20.00
SCP-24 Jamie Langenbrunner 6.00 15.00
SCP-25 J-S Giguere 6.00 15.00
SCP-26 Manny Fernandez 6.00 15.00
SCP-27 Jason Spezza 12.50 30.00
SCP-28 John Madden 6.00 15.00
SCP-29 Paul Kariya
SCP-30 Martin Brodeur
SCP-31 Scott Stevens Cup Winners
SCP-32 J-S Giguere Conn Smythe

2003-04 BAP Memorabilia Super Rookies

This 12-card set was randomly inserted and featured rookies from the 2003-04 season. A silver parallel serial-numbered out of 100 and gold parallel 1/1's were also created. Prices for the silver parallel can be found by using the multiplier below.
COMPLETE SET (12) 20.00 50.00
*SILVER: .75X TO 2X BASE HI
SILVER PRINT RUN 100 SER.#'d SETS
UNPRICED GOLD 1/1's EXIST
SR1 Tuomo Ruutu 4.00 10.00
SR2 Joffrey Lupul 3.00 8.00
SR3 Brent Burns 2.00 5.00
SR4 David Hale 2.00 5.00

SR5 Patrice Bergeron 5.00 12.00
SR6 Joni Pitkanen 3.00 8.00
SR7 Sean Bergenheim 2.00 5.00
SR8 Boyd Gordon 2.00 5.00
SR9 Eric Staal 5.00 12.00
SR10 Nathan Horton 4.00 10.00
SR11 Dustin Brown 2.00 5.00
SR12 Tim Gleason 2.00 5.00
SR13 Dan Hamhuis 2.00 5.00
SR14 Jordin Tootoo 5.00 12.00
SR15 Jiri Hudler 4.00 10.00
SR16 Marc-Andre Fleury 8.00 20.00
SR17 Christopher Higgins 3.00 8.00
SR18 Pavel Vorobiev 2.00 5.00
SR19 Alexander Semin 2.00 5.00
SR20 Brent Krahn 2.00 5.00

2003-04 BAP Memorabilia Tandems

STATED PRINT RUN 60 SETS
T-1 D.Roloson/M.Fernandez 12.50 30.00
T-2 P.Lalime/M.Prusek 20.00 50.00
T-3 D.Hasek/M.Legace 25.00 60.00
T-4 M.Biron/R.Miller 12.50 30.00
T-5 M.Brodeur/C.Schwab 15.00 40.00
T-6 M.Turco/R.Tugnutt 12.50 30.00
T-7 J.Giguere/M.Gerber 12.50 30.00
T-8 J.Theodore/M.Garon 20.00 50.00
T-9 R.Luongo/J.Hurme 12.50 30.00
T-10 E.Belfour/T.Kidd 15.00 40.00

2003-04 BAP Memorabilia Vintage Memorabilia

STATED PRINT RUN 15 SETS
NOT PRICED DUE TO SCARCITY
VM-1 Tiny Thompson
VM-2 Chuck Gardiner
VM-3 Tim Horton
VM-4 Gerry Cheevers
VM-5 Bernie Parent
VM-6 Maurice Richard
VM-7 Terry Sawchuk
VM-8 Newsy Lalonde
VM-9 Doug Harvey
VM-10 Ted Lindsay
VM-11 Henri Richard
VM-12 Bill Mosienko
VM-13 Aurel Joliat
VM-14 Alex Delvecchio
VM-15 Bobby Clarke
VM-16 Eddie Shore
VM-17 Marcel Dionne
VM-18 Jean Beliveau
VM-19 Bill Durnan
VM-20 George Hainsworth

2003-04 BAP Memorabilia Cleveland National

STATED PRINT RUN 10 SER.#'d SETS
NOT PRICED DUE TO SCARCITY

1999-00 BAP Millennium Prototypes

This 8-card set was issued to dealers as a promo to introduce the Be A Player Millennium brand.
COMPLETE SET (8) 4.80 12.00
1 Teemu Selanne 1.20 3.00
2 Sergei Samsonov .60 1.50
3 Mike Modano .80 2.00
4 Sergei Fedorov 1.20 3.00
5 Saku Koivu .60 1.50
6 John Vanbiesbrouck .60 1.50
7 Sergei Berezin .20 .50
8 Olaf Kolzig .60 1.50

1999-00 BAP Millennium

Released as a 250-card set, Be A Player Millennium featured all silver foil base cards with full color action photography. Ruby, sapphire and emerald parallels were also created and inserted randomly. Ruby parallels are red in color and have a stated print run of 1000 sets. Sapphire parallels are blue in color and have a stated print run of 100 sets. Emerald parallels are green in color and have a stated print run of 10 sets. Emerald parallels are not priced due to scarcity. Millennium was packaged in 12-pack boxes with packs containing five cards. Each pack contained one authentic autograph card. Due to a difficulty in obtaining the Jaromir Jagr Signature cards, BAP offered a special Game Jersey card to those that sent in the redemption for the autographed card. The jersey card has been added to the bottom of the checklist.
COMPLETE SET (250) 125.00 250.00
JAGR GJ SPECIAL MADE AVAILABLE WITH EXCH. SIGNATURE CARD
1 Paul Kariya .60 1.50
2 Teemu Selanne .60 1.50
3 Oleg Tverdovsky .25 .60
4 Niclas Havelid RC .40 1.50
5 Guy Hebert .50 1.25
6 Stu Grimson .25 .60
7 Pavel Trnka .25 .60
8 Ladislav Kohn .25 .60
9 Matt Cullen .25 .60
10 Steve Rucchin .25 .60
11 Dominic Roussel .50 1.25
12 Patrik Stefan RC .40 1.25
13 Damian Rhodes .50 1.25
14 Ray Ferraro .25 .60
15 Andrew Brunette .50 1.25
16 Johan Garpenlov .25 .60
17 Nelson Emerson .25 .60
18 Jason Botterill .25 .60
19 Kelly Buchberger .25 .60
20 Ray Bourque 1.00 2.50
21 Ken Belanger .25 .60
22 Sergei Samsonov .50 1.25
23 Byron Dafoe .50 1.25
24 Joe Thornton 1.00 2.50
25 Kyle McLaren .25 .60
26 Cameron Mann .25 .60
27 Mikko Eloranta RC .50 1.25
28 Jonathan Girard .25 .60
29 Dominik Hasek 1.25 3.00
30 Michael Peca .50 1.25
31 Erik Rasmussen .25 .60
32 Brian Campbell RC .25 .60
33 Miroslav Satan .50 1.25
34 Vaclav Varada .25 .60
35 Martin Biron .50 1.25
36 Dixon Ward .25 .60
37 Cory Sarich .25 .60
38 Grant Fuhr .50 1.25
39 Jarome Iginla .75 2.00
40 Valeri Bure .25 .60
41 Oleg Saprykin RC .50 1.25
42 Rene Corbet .25 .60
43 Cory Stillman .25 .60
44 Denis Gauthier .25 .60
45 Steve Dubinsky .25 .60
46 Rico Fata .25 .60
47 Steve Halko RC .25 .60
48 Keith Primeau .25 .60
49 Sami Kapanen .25 .60
50 Arturs Irbe .50 1.25
51 Jeff O'Neill .25 .60
52 Kent Manderville .25 .60
53 Gary Roberts .25 .60
54 Nolan Pratt .50 1.25
55 Brad Brown .25 .60
56 Tony Amonte .50 1.25
57 J-P Dumont .50 1.25
58 Anders Eriksson .25 .60
59 Bryan Muir .25 .60
60 Dean McAmmond .25 .60
61 Jocelyn Thibault .50 1.25
62 Eric Daze .50 1.25
63 Shean Donovan .25 .60
64 Scott Parker .25 .60
65 Peter Forsberg 1.00 2.50
66 Patrick Roy 2.00 5.00
67 Joe Sakic 1.25 3.00
68 Sandis Ozolinsh .25 .60
69 Chris Drury .50 1.25
70 Milan Hejduk .60 1.50
71 Shjon Podein .25 .60
72 Marc Denis .50 1.25
73 Alex Tanguay .50 1.25
74 Blake Sloan .60 1.50
75 Jamie Langenbrunner .25 .60
76 Mike Modano 1.00 2.50
77 Derian Hatcher .25 .60
78 Joe Nieuwendyk .50 1.25
79 Ed Belfour .60 1.50
80 Brad Lukowich RC .25 .60
81 Jere Lehtinen .50 1.25
82 Brett Hull .75 2.00
83 Shawn Chambers .25 .60
84 Pavel Patera RC .25 .60
85 Darryl Sydor .25 .60
86 Jiri Fischer .25 .60
87 Nicklas Lidstrom .60 1.50
88 Steve Yzerman 2.00 5.00
89 Sergei Fedorov 1.00 2.50
90 Brendan Shanahan .60 1.50
91 Chris Chelios .60 1.50
92 Aaron Ward .25 .60
93 Kirk Maltby .25 .60
94 Yuri Butsayev RC .25 .60
95 Mathieu Dandenault .25 .60
96 Doug Weight .50 1.25
97 Bill Guerin .50 1.25
98 Tom Poti .25 .60
99 Wayne Gretzky 3.00 8.00
100 Georges Laraque RC .50 1.25
101 Sean Brown .25 .60
102 Mike Grier .25 .60
103 Tommy Salo .50 1.25
104 Rem Murray .25 .60
105 Paul Comrie RC .50 1.25
106 Pavel Bure .60 1.50
107 Rob Niedermayer .25 .60
108 Oleg Kvasha .25 .60
109 Filip Kuba RC .50 1.25
110 Viktor Kozlov .25 .60
111 Radek Dvorak .25 .60
112 Ray Whitney .25 .60
113 Mark Parrish .25 .60
114 Dan Boyle RC .50 1.25
115 Marcus Nilsson .25 .60
116 Lance Pitlick .25 .60
117 Paul Laus .25 .60
118 Rob Blake .25 .60
119 Stephane Fiset .50 1.25
120 Zigmund Palffy .50 1.25
121 Donald Audette .25 .60
122 Luc Robitaille .50 1.25
123 Jamie Storr .50 1.25
124 Dan Bylsma .25 .60
125 Pavel Rosa .25 .60
126 Jason Blake RC .50 1.25
127 Mattias Norstrom .25 .60
128 Saku Koivu .60 1.50
129 Trevor Linden .25 .60
130 Arron Asham .25 .60
131 Matt Higgins .25 .60
132 Martin Rucinsky .25 .60
133 Brian Savage .25 .60
134 Jeff Hackett .50 1.25
135 Scott Thornton .25 .60
136 David Legwand .50 1.25
137 Cliff Ronning .25 .60
138 Ville Peltonen .25 .60
139 Tomas Vokoun .50 1.25
140 Sergei Krivokrasov .25 .60
141 Greg Johnson .25 .60
142 Mike Dunham .50 1.25
143 Martin Brodeur 1.50 4.00
144 Scott Niedermayer .25 .60
145 Petr Sykora .25 .60
146 Vadim Sharifijanov .25 .60
147 Denis Pederson .25 .60
148 Jason Arnott .25 .60
149 Brendan Morrison .50 1.25
150 Bobby Holik .25 .60
151 Brian Rafalski RC .60 1.50
152 Olli Jokinen .50 1.25
153 Tim Connolly .25 .60
154 Gino Odjick .25 .60
155 Zdeno Chara .25 .60
156 Kenny Jonsson .25 .60
157 Mariusz Czerkawski .25 .60
158 Kim Johnsson RC .50 1.00
159 Brian Leetch .60 1.50
160 Theo Fleury .25 .60
161 Petr Nedved .50 1.25
162 John MacLean .25 .60
163 Manny Malhotra .50 1.25
164 Jan Hlavac .25 .60
165 Valeri Kamensky .50 1.25
166 Adam Graves .25 .60
167 Michael York .25 .60
168 Mike Richter .60 1.50
169 Chris Phillips .25 .60
170 Marian Hossa .60 1.50
171 Magnus Arvedson .25 .60
172 Ron Tugnutt .50 1.25
173 Vaclav Prospal .25 .60
174 Sami Salo .25 .60
175 Jason York .25 .60
176 Shawn McEachern .25 .60
177 Rob Zamuner .25 .60
178 Eric Lindros .60 1.50
179 John LeClair .60 1.50
180 Eric Desjardins .50 1.25
181 Rod Brind'Amour .50 1.25
182 Mark Recchi .50 1.25
183 Simon Gagne .60 1.50
184 Sandy McCarthy .25 .60
185 John Vanbiesbrouck .50 1.25
186 Dan McGillis .25 .60
187 Keith Jones .25 .60
188 Keith Tkachuk .60 1.50
189 Teppo Numminen .25 .60
190 Jeremy Roenick .75 2.00
191 Nikolai Khabibulin .50 1.25
192 Deron Quint .25 .60
193 Trevor Letowski .25 .60
194 Jaromir Jagr 1.00 2.50
195 Jan Hrdina .25 .60
196 Andrew Ference .25 .60
197 Alexei Kovalev .25 .60
198 Martin Straka .25 .60
199 Kip Miller .25 .60
200 Martin Sonnenberg RC .25 .60
201 Alexei Morozov .25 .60
202 Chris Pronger .50 1.25
203 Al MacInnis .50 1.25
204 Pavol Demitra .50 1.25
205 Pierre Turgeon .50 1.25
206 Jamal Mayers .25 .60
207 Chris McAlpine .25 .60
208 Ron Sutter .25 .60
209 Mike Rathje .25 .60
210 Patrick Marleau .60 1.50
211 Jeff Friesen .25 .60
212 Niklas Sundstrom .25 .60
213 Steve Shields .50 1.25
214 Brad Stuart .50 1.25
215 Alexander Korolyuk .25 .60
216 Mike Ricci .25 .60
217 Paul Mara .25 .60
218 Fredrik Modin .25 .60
219 Dan Cloutier .50 1.25
220 Vincent Lecavalier .60 1.50
221 Pavel Kubina .25 .60
222 Chris Gratton .25 .60
223 Mike Sillinger .25 .60
224 Nikolai Antropov RC .60 1.50
225 Todd Warriner .25 .60
226 Mats Sundin .60 1.50
227 Curtis Joseph .60 1.50
228 Chris McAllister RC .25 .60
229 Bryan Berard .50 1.25
230 Tomas Kaberle .25 .60
231 Igor Korolev .25 .60
232 Sergei Berezin .25 .60
233 Artem Chubarov .25 .60
234 Ed Jovanovski .25 .60
235 Mark Messier .60 1.50
236 Bill Muckalt .25 .60
237 Brad May .25 .60
238 Adrian Aucoin .25 .60
239 Mattias Ohlund .25 .60
240 Greg Hawgood .25 .60
241 Steve Kariya RC .75 1.00
242 Markus Naslund .60 1.50
243 Alexander Mogilny .50 1.25
244 Jamie Huscroft .25 .60
245 Peter Bondra .50 1.25
246 Olaf Kolzig .50 1.25
247 Brendan Witt .25 .60
248 Adam Oates .50 1.25
249 Sergei Gonchar .25 .60
250 Jan Bulis .25 .60
NNO J.Jagr GJ Special 40.00 100.00

1999-00 BAP Millennium Emerald

STATED PRINT RUN 10 SER.#'d SETS
NOT PRICED DUE TO SCARCITY

1999-00 BAP Millennium Ruby

*STARS: 1.5X TO 4X HI COL.
*ROOKIES: .75X TO 2X
STATED PRINT RUN 1000 SER.#'d SETS

1999-00 BAP Millennium Sapphire

*STARS: 12.5X TO 30X HI COL.
*ROOKIES: 4X TO 10X HI
STATED PRINT RUN 100 SER.#'d SETS

1999-00 BAP Millennium Signatures

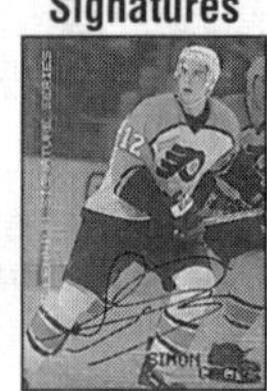

Inserted one per pack, this 250-card set paralleled the base set with player autographs and a congratulatory note on the back. Gold parallels were also created and inserted randomly into packs. Gold SP's had a print run of 50 sets.
*GOLD STARS: 1.25X TO 3X BASIC CARDS
*GOLD SP's: .75X TO 2X BASIC CARDS
GOLD SP PRINT RUN 50 SETS
1 Paul Kariya SP 20.00 50.00
2 Teemu Selanne SP 12.50 30.00
3 Oleg Tverdovsky 2.00 5.00
4 Niclas Havelid 2.00 5.00
5 Guy Hebert 4.00 10.00
6 Stu Grimson 2.00 5.00
7 Pavel Trnka 2.00 5.00
8 Ladislav Kohn 2.00 5.00
9 Matt Cullen 2.00 5.00
10 Steve Rucchin 2.00 5.00
11 Dominic Roussel 2.00 5.00
12 Patrik Stefan 2.00 5.00
13 Damian Rhodes 4.00 10.00
14 Ray Ferraro 2.00 5.00
15 Andrew Brunette 2.00 5.00
16 Johan Garpenlov 2.00 5.00
17 Nelson Emerson 2.00 5.00
18 Jason Botterill 2.00 5.00
19 Kelly Buchberger 2.00 5.00
20 Ray Bourque SP 25.00 60.00
21 Ken Belanger 2.00 5.00
22 Sergei Samsonov SP 6.00 15.00
23 Byron Dafoe SP 6.00 15.00
24 Joe Thornton 8.00 20.00
25 Kyle McLaren 2.00 5.00
26 Cameron Mann 2.00 5.00
27 Mikko Eloranta 2.00 5.00
28 Jonathan Girard 2.00 5.00
29 Dominik Hasek SP 150.00 300.00
30 Michael Peca SP 6.00 15.00
31 Erik Rasmussen 2.00 5.00
32 Brian Campbell 2.00 5.00
33 Miroslav Satan 4.00 10.00
34 Vaclav Varada 2.00 5.00
35 Martin Biron 4.00 10.00
36 Dixon Ward 2.00 5.00
37 Cory Sarich 2.00 5.00
38 Grant Fuhr SP 6.00 15.00
39 Jarome Iginla 6.00 15.00
40 Valeri Bure 2.00 5.00
41 Oleg Saprykin 2.00 5.00
42 Rene Corbet 2.00 5.00
43 Cory Stillman 2.00 5.00
44 Denis Gauthier 2.00 5.00
45 Steve Dubinsky 2.00 5.00
46 Rico Fata 2.00 5.00
47 Steve Halko 2.00 5.00
48 Keith Primeau SP 6.00 15.00
49 Sami Kapanen 2.00 5.00
50 Arturs Irbe 4.00 10.00
51 Jeff O'Neill 2.00 5.00
52 Kent Manderville 2.00 5.00
53 Gary Roberts 2.00 5.00
54 Nolan Pratt 2.00 5.00
55 Brad Brown 2.00 5.00
56 Tony Amonte SP 6.00 15.00
57 J-P Dumont 2.00 5.00
58 Anders Eriksson 2.00 5.00
59 Bryan Muir 2.00 5.00
60 Dean McAmmond 2.00 5.00
61 Jocelyn Thibault 4.00 10.00
62 Eric Daze 4.00 10.00
63 Shean Donovan 2.00 5.00
64 Scott Parker 2.00 5.00
65 Peter Forsberg SP 25.00 60.00
66 Patrick Roy SP 50.00 125.00
67 Joe Sakic SP 30.00 80.00
68 Sandis Ozolinsh 2.00 5.00
69 Chris Drury 4.00 10.00
70 Milan Hejduk 5.00 12.00
71 Shjon Podein 2.00 5.00
72 Marc Denis 4.00 10.00
73 Alex Tanguay 2.00 5.00
74 Blake Sloan 2.00 5.00
75 Jamie Langenbrunner 2.00 5.00
76 Mike Modano SP 20.00 50.00
77 Derian Hatcher 2.00 5.00
78 Joe Nieuwendyk SP 6.00 15.00
79 Ed Belfour SP 20.00 50.00
80 Brad Lukowich 2.00 5.00
81 Jere Lehtinen 4.00 10.00
82 Brett Hull SP 15.00 40.00
83 Shawn Chambers 2.00 5.00
84 Pavel Patera 2.00 5.00
85 Darryl Sydor 2.00 5.00
86 Jiri Fischer 2.00 5.00
87 Nicklas Lidstrom 5.00 12.00
88 Steve Yzerman SP 40.00 100.00
89 Sergei Fedorov SP 15.00 40.00
90 Brendan Shanahan SP 10.00 25.00
91 Chris Chelios SP 10.00 25.00
92 Aaron Ward 2.00 5.00
93 Kirk Maltby 2.00 5.00
94 Yuri Butsayev 2.00 5.00
95 Mathieu Dandenault 2.00 5.00
96 Doug Weight SP 6.00 15.00
97 Bill Guerin 4.00 10.00
98 Tom Poti 2.00 5.00
99 Wayne Gretzky SP 300.00 500.00
100 Georges Laraque 5.00 12.00
101 Sean Brown 2.00 5.00
102 Mike Grier 2.00 5.00
103 Tommy Salo 4.00 10.00
104 Rem Murray 2.00 5.00
105 Paul Comrie 2.00 5.00
106 Pavel Bure SP 12.50 30.00
107 Rob Niedermayer 2.00 5.00
108 Oleg Kvasha 2.00 5.00
109 Filip Kuba 2.00 5.00
110 Viktor Kozlov 2.00 5.00
111 Radek Dvorak 2.00 5.00
112 Ray Whitney 2.00 5.00
113 Mark Parrish 2.00 5.00
114 Dan Boyle 2.00 5.00
115 Marcus Nilsson 2.00 5.00
116 Lance Pitlick 2.00 5.00
117 Paul Laus 2.00 5.00
118 Rob Blake 4.00 10.00
119 Stephane Fiset 2.00 5.00
120 Zigmund Palffy SP 6.00 15.00
121 Donald Audette 2.00 5.00
122 Luc Robitaille 4.00 10.00
123 Jamie Storr 4.00 10.00
124 Dan Bylsma 2.00 5.00
125 Pavel Rosa 2.00 5.00
126 Jason Blake 2.00 5.00
127 Mattias Norstrom 2.00 5.00
128 Saku Koivu SP 12.00 30.00
129 Trevor Linden 2.00 5.00
130 Arron Asham 2.00 5.00
131 Matt Higgins 2.00 5.00
132 Martin Rucinsky 2.00 5.00
133 Brian Savage 2.00 5.00
134 Jeff Hackett 4.00 10.00
135 Scott Thornton 2.00 5.00
136 David Legwand 4.00 10.00
137 Cliff Ronning 2.00 5.00
138 Ville Peltonen 2.00 5.00
139 Tomas Vokoun 4.00 10.00
140 Sergei Krivokrasov 2.00 5.00
141 Greg Johnson 2.00 5.00
142 Mike Dunham 4.00 10.00
143 Martin Brodeur SP 40.00 100.00
144 Scott Niedermayer SP 8.00 20.00
145 Petr Sykora 2.00 5.00
146 Vadim Sharifijanov 2.00 5.00
147 Denis Pederson 2.00 5.00
148 Jason Arnott SP 6.00 15.00
149 Brendan Morrison 4.00 10.00
150 Bobby Holik 2.00 5.00
151 Brian Rafalski 2.00 5.00
152 Olli Jokinen 4.00 10.00
153 Tim Connolly 2.00 5.00
154 Gino Odjick 2.00 5.00
155 Zdeno Chara 2.00 5.00
156 Kenny Jonsson 2.00 5.00
157 Mariusz Czerkawski 2.00 5.00
158 Kim Johnsson 2.00 5.00
159 Brian Leetch SP 12.00 30.00
160 Theo Fleury SP 8.00 20.00
161 Petr Nedved 2.00 5.00
162 John MacLean 2.00 5.00
163 Manny Malhotra 2.00 5.00
164 Jan Hlavac 2.00 5.00
165 Valeri Kamensky 2.00 5.00
166 Adam Graves 2.00 5.00
167 Michael York 2.00 5.00
168 Mike Richter SP 10.00 25.00
169 Chris Phillips 2.00 5.00
170 Marian Hossa 5.00 12.00
171 Magnus Arvedson 2.00 5.00
172 Ron Tugnutt 4.00 10.00
173 Vaclav Prospal 2.00 5.00
174 Sami Salo 2.00 5.00
175 Jason York 2.00 5.00
176 Shawn McEachern 2.00 5.00
177 Rob Zamuner 2.00 5.00
178 Eric Lindros SP 10.00 25.00
179 John LeClair SP 6.00 15.00
180 Eric Desjardins 2.00 5.00
181 Rod Brind'Amour 4.00 10.00
182 Mark Recchi 4.00 10.00
183 Simon Gagne 5.00 12.00
184 Sandy McCarthy 2.00 5.00
185 John Vanbiesbrouck SP 6.00 15.00
186 Dan McGillis 2.00 5.00
187 Keith Jones 2.00 5.00
188 Keith Tkachuk SP 6.00 15.00
189 Teppo Numminen 2.00 5.00
190 Jeremy Roenick SP 12.50 30.00
191 Nikolai Khabibulin 4.00 10.00
192 Deron Quint 2.00 5.00
193 Trevor Letowski 2.00 5.00
194 Jaromir Jagr SP 25.00 60.00
195 Jan Hrdina 2.00 5.00
196 Andrew Ference 2.00 5.00
197 Alexei Kovalev 4.00 10.00
198 Martin Straka 2.00 5.00
199 Kip Miller 2.00 5.00
200 Martin Sonnenberg 2.00 5.00
201 Alexei Morozov 2.00 5.00
202 Chris Pronger SP 6.00 15.00
203 Al MacInnis SP 6.00 15.00
204 Pavol Demitra 4.00 10.00
205 Pierre Turgeon 4.00 10.00
206 Jamal Mayers 2.00 5.00
207 Chris McAlpine 2.00 5.00
208 Ron Sutter 2.00 5.00
209 Mike Rathje 2.00 5.00
210 Patrick Marleau 4.00 10.00
211 Jeff Friesen SP 6.00 15.00
212 Niklas Sundstrom 4.00 10.00
213 Steve Shields 4.00 10.00
214 Brad Stuart 4.00 10.00
215 Alexander Korolyuk 2.00 5.00
216 Mike Ricci 2.00 5.00
217 Paul Mara 2.00 5.00
218 Fredrik Modin 2.00 5.00
219 Dan Cloutier 4.00 10.00
220 Vincent Lecavalier 5.00 12.00
221 Pavel Kubina 2.00 5.00
222 Chris Gratton SP 6.00 15.00
223 Mike Sillinger 2.00 5.00
224 Nikolai Antropov 2.00 5.00
225 Todd Warriner 2.00 5.00
226 Mats Sundin SP 10.00 25.00
227 Curtis Joseph SP 15.00 40.00
228 Chris McAllister 2.00 5.00
229 Bryan Berard SP 6.00 15.00
230 Tomas Kaberle 2.00 5.00
231 Igor Korolev 2.00 5.00
232 Sergei Berezin 2.00 5.00
233 Artem Chubarov 2.00 5.00
234 Ed Jovanovski 2.00 5.00
235 Mark Messier SP 30.00 80.00
236 Bill Muckalt 2.00 5.00
237 Brad May 2.00 5.00
238 Adrian Aucoin 2.00 5.00
239 Mattias Ohlund 2.00 5.00
240 Greg Hawgood 2.00 5.00
241 Steve Kariya 2.00 5.00
242 Markus Naslund 5.00 12.00
243 Alexander Mogilny SP 6.00 15.00
244 Jamie Huscroft 2.00 5.00
245 Peter Bondra SP 6.00 15.00
246 Olaf Kolzig SP 8.00 20.00
247 Brendan Witt 2.00 5.00
248 Adam Oates SP 8.00 20.00
249 Sergei Gonchar 2.00 5.00
250 Jan Bulis 2.00 5.00

1999-00 BAP Millennium Calder Candidates Ruby

Randomly inserted in packs, this 50-card set featured top Calder trophy prospects. Cards contained full-color action photography and were set off by a red border. Ruby versions were serial numbered 0101/1000 to 1000/1000. Sapphire and emerald parallels were also created and randomly inserted. Sapphire parallels were blue in color and had a stated print run of 100 sets. Emerald parallels were green in color and had a stated print run of 10 sets. Emerald parallels are not priced due to scarcity.
COMPLETE SET (50) 100.00 200.00
STATED PRINT RUN 1000 SETS
*SAPPHIRE: 1.5X TO 4X BASIC CARDS
SAPPHIRE PRINT RUN 100 SETS
EMERALD PRINT RUN 10 SETS
NOT PRICED DUE TO SCARCITY
C1 Alex Tanguay 2.50 6.00
C2 Simon Gagne 3.00 8.00
C3 Kyle Calder 2.00 5.00
C4 Ryan Johnson 2.00 5.00
C5 Dave Tanabe 2.00 5.00
C6 Scott Gomez 2.00 5.00
C7 Patrik Stefan 2.00 5.00
C8 Jiri Fischer 2.00 5.00
C9 Blake Sloan 2.00 5.00
C10 Trevor Letowski 2.00 5.00
C11 Michael York 2.00 5.00
C12 Mike Ribeiro 2.00 5.00
C13 Ladislav Kohn 2.00 5.00
C14 Martin Skoula 2.00 5.00
C15 Steve Kariya 2.00 5.00
C16 Nikolai Antropov 2.00 5.00
C17 David Legwand 2.50 6.00
C18 J-P Dumont 2.00 5.00
C19 Filip Kuba 2.00 5.00
C20 Mike Fisher 2.00 5.00
C21 Tim Connolly 2.00 5.00
C22 Martin Biron 2.50 6.00
C23 Oleg Saprykin 2.00 5.00
C24 Maxim Afinogenov 2.00 5.00
C25 Petr Buzek 2.00 5.00
C26 Paul Comrie 2.00 5.00
C27 Brian Boucher 2.50 6.00
C28 Peter Schaefer 2.00 5.00
C29 Alex Tezikov 2.00 5.00
C30 Milan Hnilicka 2.50 6.00
C31 Brian Rafalski 2.00 5.00
C32 Sami Helenius 2.00 5.00
C33 Frantisek Kaberle 2.00 5.00
C34 Jochen Hecht 2.00 5.00
C35 Mathieu Biron 2.00 5.00
C36 Randy Robitaille 2.00 5.00
C37 Roberto Luongo 4.00 10.00
C38 Steve McCarthy 2.00 5.00
C39 Brad Lukowich 2.00 5.00
C40 Kim Johnsson 2.00 5.00
C41 Brad Stuart 2.00 5.00
C42 Glen Metropolit 2.00 5.00
C43 Marc Denis 2.50 6.00
C44 Robyn Regehr 2.00 5.00
C45 Per Svartvadet 2.00 5.00
C46 Jonathan Girard 2.00 5.00
C47 Mark Eaton 2.00 5.00
C48 Ivan Novoseltsev 2.00 5.00
C49 Jan Hlavac 2.00 5.00
C50 Richard Jackman 2.00 5.00

1999-00 BAP Millennium Goalie Memorabilia

STATED PRINT RUN 30 SETS
G1 Curtis Joseph 125.00 300.00
G2 Patrick Roy 200.00 400.00
G3 Grant Fuhr 60.00 150.00
G4 Garth Snow 50.00 125.00
G5 Jeff Hackett 30.00 80.00
G6 Chris Osgood 30.00 80.00
G7 Dominik Hasek 150.00 300.00
G8 Arturs Irbe 30.00 80.00

1999-00 BAP Millennium Jerseys

STATED PRINT RUN 100 SETS
J1 Theo Fleury 8.00 20.00
J2 Brendan Shanahan 10.00 30.00
J3 Curtis Joseph 10.00 30.00
J4 Saku Koivu 10.00 30.00
J5 Dominik Hasek 25.00 60.00
J6 Al MacInnis 8.00 20.00
J7 John LeClair 10.00 30.00
J8 Teemu Selanne 10.00 30.00
J9 Wayne Gretzky 60.00 150.00
J10 Pavel Bure 10.00 30.00
J11 Mark Messier 10.00 30.00
J12 Jaromir Jagr 20.00 50.00
J13 Ray Bourque 20.00 50.00
J14 Chris Chelios 10.00 30.00
J15 Mats Sundin 10.00 30.00
J16 Paul Kariya 10.00 30.00
J17 Peter Bondra 8.00 20.00
J18 Eric Lindros 10.00 30.00
J19 Sergei Fedorov 15.00 40.00
J20 Peter Forsberg 20.00 50.00
J21 Brett Hull 12.50 30.00
J22 Tony Amonte 8.00 20.00
J23 Patrick Roy 30.00 80.00
J24 Ed Belfour 10.00 30.00
J25 Martin Brodeur 30.00 80.00
J26 Brian Leetch 8.00 20.00
J27 Mike Modano 12.50 30.00
J28 Joe Sakic 15.00 40.00
J29 Jeremy Roenick 12.50 30.00
J30 Steve Yzerman 30.00 80.00
J31 Alexander Mogilny 8.00 20.00
J32 Paul Coffey 10.00 30.00

1999-00 BAP Millennium Jersey Autographs

STATED PRINT RUN 10 SETS
NOT PRICED DUE TO SCARCITY

1999-00 BAP Millennium Jersey and Stick Cards

*JERSEY/STICKS: .5X TO 1.25X JERSEY CARDS
STATED PRINT RUN 40 SETS

1999-00 BAP Millennium Jersey Emblems

*EMBLEMS: 1.25X TO 1.75X JERSEY CARDS
STATED PRINT RUN 20 SETS

1999-00 BAP Millennium Jersey Numbers

*NUMBERS: 1X TO 1.5X JERSEY CARDS
STATED PRINT RUN 30 SETS

1999-00 BAP Millennium Pearson

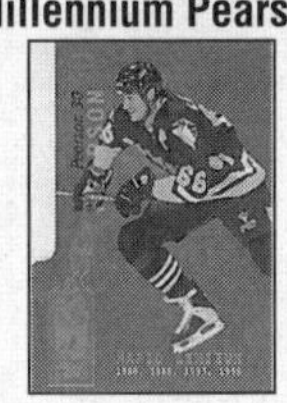

Randomly inserted in packs, this 16-card set features recipients of the Lester B. Pearson Trophy for outstanding play. Cards are foil and picture the Pearson trophy in the lower right hand corner. Stated print run for this set is 300 cards.

COMPLETE SET (16) 125.00 250.00
STATED PRINT RUN 300 SETS
P1 Jaromir Jagr 10.00 25.00
P2 Dominik Hasek 10.00 25.00
P3 Mario Lemieux 20.00 50.00
P4 Eric Lindros 2.50 6.00
P5 Sergei Fedorov 8.00 20.00
P6 Mark Messier 2.50 6.00
P7 Brett Hull 6.00 15.00
P8 Steve Yzerman 15.00 40.00
P9 Wayne Gretzky 25.00 60.00
P10 Mike Liut 2.50 6.00
P11 Marcel Dionne 4.00 10.00
P12 Guy Lafleur 5.00 12.00
P13 Bobby Orr 25.00 60.00
P14 Phil Esposito 6.00 15.00
P15 Bobby Clarke 6.00 15.00
P16 Jean Ratelle 2.50 6.00

1999-00 BAP Millennium Pearson Autographs

Randomly seeded in packs, this 16-card set parallels the base Be A Player Millennium Pearson set and is enhanced with player autographs. Players signed 30 cards each.

STATED PRINT RUN 30 SETS
PLAYERS SIGNED FIRST 30 OF 300 CARDS
P1 Jaromir Jagr 75.00 200.00
P2 Dominik Hasek 75.00 200.00
P3 Mario Lemieux 150.00 300.00
P4 Eric Lindros 40.00 80.00
P5 Sergei Fedorov 40.00 100.00
P6 Mark Messier 75.00 200.00
P7 Brett Hull 40.00 100.00
P8 Steve Yzerman 75.00 200.00
P9 Wayne Gretzky 300.00 600.00
P10 Mike Liut 30.00 60.00
P11 Marcel Dionne 30.00 80.00
P12 Guy Lafleur 60.00 150.00
P13 Bobby Orr 400.00 600.00
P14 Phil Esposito 30.00 80.00
P15 Bobby Clarke 40.00 100.00
P16 Jean Ratelle 30.00 60.00

1999-00 BAP Millennium Players of the Decade

Randomly inserted in packs, this 10-card set features top players from the last two decades. Base cards contain full color action photography set against a blue foil background. Stated print run for this set is 1000 cards.

COMPLETE SET (10) 60.00 125.00
STATED PRINT RUN 1000 SETS
D1 Wayne Gretzky 15.00 40.00
D2 Mark Messier 3.00 8.00
D3 Patrick Roy 12.50 30.00
D4 Dominik Hasek 5.00 12.00
D5 Jaromir Jagr 4.00 10.00
D6 Eric Lindros 5.00 10.00
D7 Sergei Fedorov 5.00 12.00
D8 Brett Hull 3.00 8.00
D9 Ray Bourque 4.00 10.00
D10 Steve Yzerman 12.50 30.00

1999-00 BAP Millennium Players of the Decade Autographs

Randomly inserted in packs, this 10-card set parallels the base Players of the Decade insert set and is enhanced with player autographs. The first 90 cards in the 1000 set print run were autographed. Jagr, Hull, and Yzerman were exchange cards.

STATED PRINT RUN 90 SETS
PLYRS.SIGNED FIRST 90 OF 1000
D1 Wayne Gretzky 125.00 300.00
D2 Mark Messier 75.00 200.00
D3 Patrick Roy 75.00 200.00
D4 Dominik Hasek 60.00 150.00
D5 Jaromir Jagr 60.00 150.00
D6 Eric Lindros 25.00 60.00
D7 Sergei Fedorov 40.00 100.00
D8 Brett Hull 30.00 80.00
D9 Ray Bourque 40.00 100.00
D10 Steve Yzerman 75.00 200.00

2002 BAP NHL All-Star History

Available at the In the Game, Inc. booth during the All-Star Fantasy show, this 52-card set featured past and present players from every year of the All-Star Game. Collectors had to open a box of 2001-02 BAP product to receive one card serial-numbered out of 10. Gold 1 of 1's also were randomly available. Due to the scarcity and limited distribution of these cards, they are not priced.

PRINT RUN 10 SETS
UNPRICED GOLD 1/1'S EXIST
1 Turk Broda
2 Frank Brimsek
3 Ted Kennedy
4 Maurice Richard
5 Chuck Rayner
6 Bill Mosienko
7 Jean Beliveau
8 Doug Harvey
9 Ted Lindsay
10 Henri Richard
11 Jacques Plante
12 Glenn Hall
13 Terry Sawchuk
14 Bobby Hull
15 Johnny Bower
16 Tim Horton
17 Johnny Bucyk
18 Stan Mikita
19 Bill Gadsby
20 Gordie Howe
21 Ed Giacomin
22 Bernie Parent
23 Bobby Clarke
24 Gilbert Perreault
25 Frank Mahovlich
26 Tony Esposito
27 Denis Potvin
28 Guy Lafleur
29 Bryan Trottier
30 Lanny McDonald
31 Marcel Dionne
32 Wayne Gretzky
33 Mike Bossy
34 Mark Messier
35 Paul Coffey
36 Steve Yzerman
37 Mario Lemieux
38 Grant Fuhr
39 Patrick Roy
40 Brett Hull
41 Brian Leetch
42 Jeremy Roenick
43 Jaromir Jagr
44 Luc Robitaille
45 Joe Sakic
46 Eric Lindros
47 Paul Kariya
48 Mike Modano
49 Peter Forsberg
50 Pavel Bure
51 Milan Hejduk
52 Mats Sundin

2000-01 BAP Parkhurst 2000

Randomly inserted in packs of Be A Player Memorabilia, Be A Player Memorabilia Update, and Be A Player Signature Series at the rate of 1:5, this 250-card set features the Parkhurst name and logo. Player action shots are framed by a green and gray border along the left and bottom of the card. Each card is enhanced with a Parkhurst 50th anniversary gold foil stamp.

COMPLETE SET (250) 50.00 125.00
COMP.SERIES 1 (100) 20.00 50.00
COMP.UPDATE SET (50) 10.00 25.00
COMP.SIG.SERIES SET (100) 20.00 50.00
STATED ODDS 1:5 SER.1/SIG.SERIES
P1 Pavel Bure .40 1.00
P2 Tony Amonte .30 .75
P3 Chris Pronger .30 .75
P4 John Madden .20 .50
P5 Kimmo Timonen .20 .50
P6 Marc Savard .20 .50
P7 Peter Forsberg .75 2.00
P8 Arturs Irbe .30 .75
P9 Mike York .20 .50
P10 Brendan Shanahan .40 1.00
P11 Simon Gagne .40 1.00
P12 Maxim Afinogenov .20 .50
P13 Joe Sakic 1.25 3.00
P14 Curtis Joseph .40 1.00
P15 Jozef Stumpel .20 .50
P16 Vitali Vishnevsky .20 .50
P17 Owen Nolan .30 .75
P18 Jan Hrdina .20 .50
P19 Brenden Morrow .30 .75
P20 Todd Bertuzzi .40 1.00
P21 Vincent Lecavalier .40 1.00
P22 Andrew Brunette .20 .50
P23 Brendan Morrison .30 .75
P24 Rod Brind'Amour .30 .75
P25 Patrik Elias .20 .50
P26 Joe Thornton 1.00 2.50
P27 Roman Turek .20 .50
P28 Fred Brathwaite .20 .50
P29 Brian Leetch .30 .75
P30 Trevor Linden .20 .50
P31 Janne Niinimaa .20 .50
P32 Nikolai Antropov .20 .50
P33 Teemu Selanne .40 1.00
P34 Calle Johansson .20 .50
P35 Boris Mironov .20 .50
P36 Eric Desjardins .20 .50
P37 Mark Parrish .20 .50
P38 Alex Tanguay .30 .75
P39 Jason Arnott .20 .50
P40 Vincent Damphousse .20 .50
P41 Dominik Hasek 1.25 3.00
P42 Teppo Numminen .20 .50
P43 Patrick Lalime .20 .50
P44 Valeri Bure .20 .50
P45 Adam Oates .30 .75
P46 Sergei Zubov .20 .50
P47 Tim Connolly .20 .50
P48 Pavel Kubina .20 .50
P49 Nicklas Lidstrom .40 1.00
P50 Mark Recchi .30 .75
P51 Chris Drury .20 .50
P52 Kyle McLaren .20 .50
P53 Steve Kariya .20 .50
P54 Scott Gomez .20 .50
P55 Rob Blake .30 .75
P56 Miroslav Satan .20 .50
P57 Cliff Ronning .20 .50
P58 Radek Dvorak .20 .50
P59 Jeff O'Neill .20 .50
P60 Dainius Zubrus .20 .50
P61 Brad Ference .20 .50
P62 Jarome Iginla .60 1.50
P63 Chris Simon .30 .75
P64 Darryl Sydor .20 .50
P65 Daniel Alfredsson .30 .75
P66 Sandis Ozolinsh .20 .50
P67 Brian Rafalski .20 .50
P68 Ryan Smyth .30 .75
P69 John LeClair .40 1.00
P70 Patrik Stefan .20 .50
P71 Patrick Marleau .30 .75
P72 Roberto Luongo .60 1.50
P73 Chris Osgood .30 .75
P74 Pierre Turgeon .30 .75
P75 Zigmund Palffy .30 .75
P76 Jeff Farkas .20 .50
P77 Milan Hejduk .40 1.00
P78 Ray Whitney .30 .75
P79 Felix Potvin .40 1.00
P80 Chris Gratton .20 .50
P81 Brad Stuart .20 .50
P82 Ron Francis .30 .75
P83 Oleg Tverdovsky .20 .50
P84 Alexei Kovalev .30 .75
P85 Sergei Fedorov .60 1.50
P86 Nick Boynton .20 .50
P87 David Legwand .20 .50
P88 Robyn Regehr .20 .50
P89 Brian Boucher .20 .50
P90 Roman Hamrlik .20 .50
P91 Jochen Hecht .20 .50
P92 Alexei Zhamnov .20 .50
P93 Olaf Kolzig .30 .75
P94 Jose Theodore .60 1.50
P95 Jeremy Roenick .60 1.50
P96 Theo Fleury .20 .50
P97 Patrick Roy 3.00 8.00
P98 Marian Hossa .40 1.00
P99 Martin Brodeur 1.50 4.00
P100 Brett Hull .60 1.50
P101 Daniel Sedin .20 .50
P102 Paul Coffey .40 1.00
P103 Ray Bourque .75 2.00
P104 Glen Murray .20 .50
P105 Mariusz Czerkawski .20 .50
P106 Jeff Friesen .20 .50
P107 Sergei Samsonov .30 .75
P108 Tyler Wright .20 .50
P109 Manny Fernandez .30 .75
P110 Mike Richter .40 1.00
P111 Pavol Demitra .20 .50
P112 Brian Rolston .20 .50
P113 Ron Tugnutt .30 .75
P114 Alexander Mogilny .30 .75
P115 Radek Bonk .20 .50
P116 Al MacInnis .30 .75
P117 J-P Dumont .20 .50
P118 Ed Belfour .60 1.50
P119 Jeff Hackett .20 .50
P120 Shawn McEachern .20 .50
P121 Dan Cloutier .20 .50
P122 Mika Noronen .20 .50
P123 Derian Hatcher .20 .50
P124 Saku Koivu .40 1.00
P125 Keith Primeau .20 .50
P126 Mats Sundin .40 1.00
P127 Damian Rhodes .20 .50
P128 Chris Chelios .40 1.00
P129 Mike Dunham .20 .50
P130 Keith Tkachuk .20 .50
P131 Steve Thomas .20 .50
P132 Phil Housley .20 .50
P133 Doug Weight .30 .75
P134 Kris Beech .20 .50
P135 Jyrki Lumme .20 .50
P136 Guy Hebert .20 .50
P137 Sami Kapanen .20 .50
P138 Trevor Kidd .20 .50
P139 Marian Gaborik 1.00 2.50
P140 Martin Straka .20 .50
P141 Ed Jovanovski .20 .50
P142 Jean-Sebastien Aubin .20 .50
P143 Viktor Kozlov .20 .50
P144 Scott Stevens .30 .75
P145 Jiri Slegr .20 .50
P146 Steve Yzerman 2.50 6.00
P147 Jocelyn Thibault .30 .75
P148 Stephane Fiset .20 .50
P149 Kenny Jonsson .20 .50
P150 Steve Shields .20 .50
P151 Paul Kariya .40 1.00
P152 Shane Willis .20 .50
P153 Martin Lapointe .20 .50
P154 Brian Savage .20 .50
P155 Alexei Yashin .20 .50
P156 Marcus Ragnarsson .20 .50
P157 Petr Tenkrat .20 .50
P158 Sandis Ozolinsh .20 .50
P159 Anson Carter .20 .50
P160 Scott Hartnell .20 .50
P161 Rick Tocchet .20 .50
P162 Brad Richards .30 .75
P163 Byron Dafoe .20 .50
P164 Marc Denis .30 .75
P165 Steve Reinprecht .20 .50
P166 Mario Lemieux 3.00 8.00
P167 Taylor Pyatt .20 .50
P168 Mike Vernon .30 .75
P169 Scott Niedermayer .20 .50
P170 Milan Kraft .20 .50
P171 Donald Audette .20 .50
P172 Steve Sullivan .20 .50
P173 Todd Marchant .20 .50
P174 Scott Walker .20 .50
P175 Daymond Langkow .20 .50
P176 Fredrik Modin .20 .50
P177 Ray Ferraro .20 .50
P178 Michael Nylander .20 .50
P179 Robert Svehla .20 .50
P180 Petr Sykora .20 .50
P181 Claude Lemieux .20 .50
P182 Sergei Berezin .20 .50
P183 Doug Gilmour .30 .75
P184 Jere Lehtinen .20 .50
P185 Maxim Sushinski .20 .50
P186 Jan Hlavac .20 .50
P187 Michal Handzus .20 .50
P188 Jamie Langenbrunner .20 .50
P189 John Vanbiesbrouck .30 .75
P190 Brent Johnson .20 .50
P191 Jason Allison .20 .50
P192 Adam Deadmarsh .20 .50
P193 Scott Mellanby .20 .50
P194 Sergei Brylin .20 .50
P195 Shane Doan .20 .50
P196 Jonas Hoglund .20 .50
P197 Bill Guerin .20 .50
P198 Espen Knutsen .20 .50
P199 Bryan Smolinski .20 .50
P200 Brad Isbister .20 .50
P201 Robert Lang .20 .50
P202 Andrew Cassels .20 .50
P203 Daniel Tkaczuk .20 .50
P204 Igor Larionov .20 .50
P205 Andrei Markov .20 .50
P206 Magnus Arvedson .20 .50
P207 Henrik Sedin .20 .50
P208 Manny Legace .20 .50
P209 Adam Graves .20 .50
P210 Marty Turco .30 .75
P211 Stu Barnes .20 .50
P212 Geoff Sanderson .20 .50
P213 Luc Robitaille .30 .75
P214 Roman Hamrlik .20 .50
P215 Jaromir Jagr 1.00 2.50
P216 Markus Naslund .40 1.00
P217 Alexei Zhitnik .20 .50
P218 Joe Nieuwendyk .30 .75
P219 Lubomir Sekeras .20 .50
P220 Petr Nedved .20 .50
P221 Dallas Drake .20 .50
P222 Sergei Gonchar .20 .50
P223 Dave Tanabe .20 .50
P224 Tommy Salo .20 .50
P225 Rick DiPietro .40 1.00
P226 Justin Williams .20 .50
P227 Dimitri Khristich .20 .50
P228 Lubomir Visnovsky .20 .50
P229 Jani Hurme .20 .50
P230 Roman Cechmanek .30 .75
P231 Cory Stillman .20 .50
P232 Mike Modano .60 1.50
P233 Scott Pellerin .20 .50
P234 Mark Messier .40 1.00
P235 Scott Young .20 .50
P236 Petr Bondra .20 .50
P237 Oleg Saprykin .20 .50
P238 Pat Verbeek .20 .50
P239 Martin Rucinsky .20 .50
P240 Martin Havlat .40 1.00
P241 Evgeni Nabokov .30 .75
P242 Tomi Kallio .20 .50
P243 Eric Daze .20 .50
P244 Roberto Luongo .60 1.50
P245 Bobby Holik .20 .50
P246 Sean Burke .20 .50
P247 Martin Biron .20 .50
P248 Mathieu Garon .30 .75
P249 Jamie Storr .20 .50
P250 Maxime Ouellet .20 .50

2000-01 BAP Signature Series

Released in February 2001 as a 300-card set with 5 cards per pack, Be A Player Signature Series featured full color action photos on silver metallic stock with the set name on the left border and the players name in the lower right corner. Cards 251-275 were short-printed to just 1000 serial-numbered sets, and cards 276-300 were short-printed to just 500 serial-numbered sets.

COMP.SET w/o SP's (250) 50.00 100.00
SP's 251-275 PRINT RUN 1000 SER.#'ed SETS
SP's 276-300 PRINT RUN 500 SER.#'ed SETS
1 Doug Gilmour .50 1.25
2 Todd Reirden .30 .75
3 Mike Johnson .30 .75
4 Scott Walker .30 .75
5 Mike York .30 .75
6 Roman Turek .50 1.25
7 Sergei Zubov .30 .75
8 Brad Stuart .50 1.25
9 Michael Peca .50 1.25
10 Jyrki Lumme .30 .75
11 Steve Yzerman 3.00 8.00
12 Olaf Kolzig .50 1.25
13 Ray Bourque 1.25 3.00
14 Clarke Wilm .30 .75
15 Eric Desjardins .50 1.25
16 Rod Brind'Amour .50 1.25
17 Marc Savard .30 .75
18 Jarome Iginla .75 2.00
19 Daniel Alfredsson .50 1.25
20 Alexei Yashin .30 .75
21 Keith Tkachuk .60 1.50
22 Jaromir Jagr 1.00 2.50
23 Trevor Kidd .50 1.25
24 Alexei Kovalev .50 1.25
25 Jan Hrdina .30 .75
26 Tom Poti .30 .75
27 Jere Karalahti .30 .75
28 Janne Niinimaa .30 .75
29 Ray Whitney .30 .75
30 Nicklas Lidstrom .60 1.50
31 Martin Lapointe .30 .75
32 Matt Cullen .30 .75
33 Theo Fleury .30 .75
34 Mats Sundin .60 1.50
35 Kimmo Timonen .30 .75
36 Joe Thornton 1.00 2.50
37 Adam Graves .30 .75
38 Andrei Zyuzin .30 .75
39 Michal Handzus .30 .75
40 Jamie Storr .50 1.25
41 Teemu Selanne .60 1.50
42 Brian Rafalski .30 .75
43 Aaron Gavey .30 .75
44 Jose Theodore .75 2.00
45 Tyler Wright .30 .75
46 Alexander Mogilny .50 1.25
47 Brad Isbister .30 .75
48 Guy Hebert .50 1.25
49 Chris Simon .30 .75
50 Dominik Hasek 1.25 3.00
51 Dan Cloutier .30 .75
52 Brian Holzinger .30 .75
53 Dimitri Khristich .30 .75
54 Tyson Nash .30 .75
55 Patrick Marleau .50 1.25
56 Marty Reasoner .30 .75
57 Manny Fernandez .50 1.25
58 Brenden Morrow .50 1.25
59 Darren McCarty .30 .75
60 Milan Hejduk .60 1.50
61 Darius Kasparaitis .30 .75
62 Jere Lehtinen .50 1.25
63 Andrew Brunette .30 .75
64 Wayne Gretzky 4.00 10.00
65 Robyn Regehr .30 .75
66 Travis Green .30 .75
67 John Grahame .50 1.25
68 Mike Fisher .30 .75
69 Josef Marha .30 .75
70 Randy McKay .30 .75
71 Brett Hull .75 2.00
72 Anson Carter .50 1.25
73 Owen Nolan .50 1.25
74 Sean Burke .50 1.25
75 Mario Lemieux 4.00 10.00
76 Brian Savage .30 .75
77 Jason Ward .30 .75
78 Patrick Lalime .50 1.25
79 Glen Murray .30 .75
80 Mathieu Biron .30 .75
81 Todd Bertuzzi .60 1.50
82 Chris Drury .50 1.25
83 Maxim Afinogenov .30 .75
84 Michal Rozsival .30 .75
85 Glen Metropolit .30 .75
86 Mariusz Czerkawski .30 .75
87 Byron Dafoe .50 1.25
88 Mark Recchi .50 1.25
89 Mike Modano 1.00 2.50
90 Felix Potvin .60 1.50
91 Saku Koivu .60 1.50
92 Jay Pandolfo .30 .75
93 Todd Simpson .30 .75
94 Calle Johansson .30 .75
95 Bill Guerin .50 1.25
96 Oleg Tverdovsky .30 .75
97 Kyle McLaren .30 .75
98 Mark Messier .60 1.50
99 Chris Gratton .30 .75
100 Sergei Brylin .30 .75
101 David Legwand .50 1.25
102 Jason Allison .30 .75
103 Daniel Cleary .30 .75
104 Curtis Joseph .60 1.50
105 Sergei Fedorov 1.00 2.50
106 Jeremy Roenick .75 2.00
107 Frantisek Kaberle .30 .75
108 Chris Pronger .50 1.25
109 Martin Skoula .50 1.25
110 Jiri Slegr .30 .75
111 Trevor Letowski .30 .75
112 Colin Forbes .30 .75
113 Sergei Zholtok .30 .75
114 David Harlock .30 .75
115 Scott Stevens .50 1.25
116 Dave Tanabe .30 .75
117 Mattias Timander .30 .75
118 Stu Barnes .30 .75
119 Simon Gagne .60 1.50
120 Paul Coffey .60 1.50
121 Peter Bondra .60 1.50
122 Ed Jovanovski .50 1.25
123 J-P Dumont .30 .75
124 Pavol Demitra .50 1.25
125 Mike Vernon .50 1.25
126 Brendan Morrison .50 1.25
127 Dainius Zubrus .30 .75
128 Al MacInnis .50 1.25
129 Kevyn Adams .30 .75
130 Petr Buzek .30 .75
131 Steve Kariya .30 .75
132 Keith Primeau .30 .75
133 Kenny Jonsson .30 .75
134 Lance Pitlick .30 .75
135 Randy Robitaille .30 .75
136 Brian Rolston .30 .75
137 Alex Tanguay .50 1.25
138 Alexei Zhamnov .30 .75
139 Peter Forsberg 1.50 4.00
140 Cam Stewart .30 .75
141 Vitali Vishnevsky .30 .75
142 Tim Connolly .30 .75
143 Tie Domi .50 1.25
144 Jaroslav Modry .30 .75
145 Jarno Kultanen RC .30 .75
146 Igor Larionov .30 .75
147 Derian Hatcher .30 .75
148 Scott Niedermayer .30 .75
149 Shawn McEachern .30 .75
150 Sergei Berezin .30 .75
151 Rob Blake .50 1.25
152 Steve Thomas .30 .75
153 Ryan Smyth .30 .75
154 Petr Nedved .30 .75
155 Jochen Hecht .30 .75
156 Richard Zednik .30 .75
157 Tommy Salo .50 1.25
158 Ed Belfour .60 1.50
159 Lyle Odelein .30 .75
160 Steve Sullivan .30 .75
161 Vincent Damphousse .30 .75
162 Andy Delmore .30 .75
163 Harold Druken .30 .75
164 Martin Brodeur 1.50 4.00
165 Mike Richter .60 1.50
166 Radek Bonk .30 .75
167 Joe Sakic 1.25 3.00
168 John Vanbiesbrouck .50 1.25
169 Jeff Shantz .30 .75
170 Jean-Sebastien Aubin .50 1.25
171 Shayne Corson .30 .75
172 Jeff Friesen .30 .75
173 Jeff Hackett .50 1.25
174 Jozef Stumpel .30 .75
175 Daymond Langkow .50 1.25
176 Nikolai Antropov .30 .75
177 Ron Tugnutt .50 1.25
178 Viktor Kozlov .50 1.25
179 Adam Oates .50 1.25
180 Steve Webb .30 .75
181 Pierre Turgeon .50 1.25
182 Fred Brathwaite .50 1.25
183 Martin Biron .50 1.25
184 John LeClair .60 1.50
185 Steve Rucchin .30 .75
186 Patrik Elias .50 1.25
187 Boris Mironov .30 .75
188 Mika Alatalo .30 .75
189 Jocelyn Thibault .50 1.25
190 Jason York .30 .75
191 Zigmund Palffy .50 1.25
192 Paul Kariya .60 1.50
193 Stu Grimson .30 .75
194 Jeff Halpern .30 .75
195 Scott Gomez .30 .75
196 Tomas Vlasak .30 .75
197 Roman Hamrlik .30 .75
198 Radek Dvorak .30 .75
199 Martin Straka .30 .75
200 Martin Rucinsky .30 .75
201 Valeri Bure .30 .75
202 Scott Mellanby .30 .75
203 Steve McKenna .30 .75
204 Luc Robitaille .50 1.25
205 Joe Nieuwendyk .50 1.25
206 Brendan Shanahan .60 1.50
207 Robert Lang .30 .75
208 Todd Marchant .30 .75
209 Doug Weight .50 1.25
210 Andre Roy .30 .75
211 Patrick Roy 3.00 8.00
212 Vincent Lecavalier .60 1.50
213 Trevor Linden .50 1.25
214 Patrik Stefan .30 .75
215 Jan Hlavac .30 .75
216 Ron Francis .50 1.25
217 Brian Boucher .60 1.50
218 Tony Hrkac .30 .75
219 Brian Leetch .50 1.25
220 Tony Amonte .50 1.25
221 Nikolai Khabibulin .50 1.25
222 Sandis Ozolinsh .30 .75
223 Darryl Sydor .30 .75
224 Bobby Holik .30 .75
225 Sami Kapanen .30 .75
226 Pavel Bure .60 1.50
227 Steve Konowalchuk .30 .75
228 Brent Gilchrist .30 .75
229 Jeff O'Neill .30 .75
230 Andre Savage .30 .75
231 Pavel Kubina .30 .75
232 Jason Arnott .30 .75
233 Petr Sykora .30 .75
234 Miroslav Satan .50 1.25
235 Chris Osgood .50 1.25
236 Sergei Samsonov .50 1.25
237 Marian Hossa .60 1.50
238 Arturs Irbe .50 1.25
239 Josh Holden .30 .75
240 Phil Housley .30 .75
241 Dimitri Yushkevich .30 .75
242 Cliff Ronning .30 .75
243 John Madden .30 .75
244 Jaroslav Spacek .30 .75
245 Craig Darby .30 .75
246 Eric Lindros .60 1.50
247 Markus Naslund .60 1.50
248 Sergei Gonchar .30 .75
249 Gary Roberts .30 .75
250 Steve Shields .50 1.25
251 Petteri Nummelin SP RC 1.00 2.50
252 Mika Noronen SP 1.00 2.50
253 Andrew Raycroft SP RC 3.00 8.00
254 Taylor Pyatt SP 1.00 2.50
255 Toni Lydman SP 1.00 2.50
256 Matt Bradley SP 1.00 2.50
257 Petr Hubacek SP RC 1.00 2.50
258 Ossi Vaananen SP RC 1.00 2.50
259 Dimitri Kalinin SP 1.00 2.50
260 Justin Williams SP RC 3.00 8.00
261 Jeff Farkas SP 1.00 2.50
262 Brent Sopel SP RC 1.00 2.50
263 Samuel Pahlsson SP 1.00 2.50
264 Josef Vasicek SP RC 1.00 2.50
265 Shane Willis SP 1.00 2.50
266 Petr Svoboda SP RC 1.00 2.50
267 Petr Schastlivy SP 1.00 2.50
268 Roman Simicek SP RC 1.00 2.50
269 Reto Von Arx SP RC 1.00 2.50
270 Colin White SP RC 1.00 2.50
271 Lubomir Sekeras SP RC 1.00 2.50
272 Alexander Kharitonov SP RC 1.00 2.50
273 Maxim Sushinski SP 1.00 2.50
274 Sergei Vyshedkevich SP RC 1.00 2.50
275 Brad Ference SP 1.00 2.50
276 Martin Havlat SP RC 6.00 15.00
277 Maxime Ouellet SP 3.00 8.00
278 Roberto Luongo SP 4.00 10.00
279 Marian Gaborik RC 10.00 25.00
280 Daniel Sedin SP 3.00 8.00
281 Henrik Sedin SP 3.00 8.00
282 Milan Kraft SP 3.00 8.00
283 Denis Shvidki SP 3.00 8.00
284 Kris Beech SP 3.00 8.00
285 Rostislav Klesla SP RC 3.00 8.00
286 Jani Hurme SP RC 3.00 8.00
287 Oleg Saprykin SP 3.00 8.00
288 Marty Turco RC 5.00 12.00
289 Brad Richards SP 3.00 8.00
290 Steve McCarthy SP 3.00 8.00
291 Tomi Kallio SP 3.00 8.00
292 Evgeni Nabokov SP 3.00 8.00
293 Steven Reinprecht SP RC 3.00 8.00
294 Andrei Markov SP 3.00 8.00
295 Brent Johnson SP 3.00 8.00
296 Rick DiPietro SP RC 6.00 15.00
297 Roman Cechmanek SP RC 3.00 8.00
298 Daniel Tkaczuk SP 3.00 8.00
299 Mathieu Garon SP 3.00 8.00
300 Scott Hartnell SP RC 4.00 10.00

2000-01 BAP Signature Series Emerald

STAT.PRINT RUN 10 SER.#'ed SETS
NOT PRICED DUE TO SCARCITY

2000-01 BAP Signature Series Ruby

*STARS: 2X TO 4X BASIC CARDS
*SP's 251-275: .3X TO .75X BASIC CARDS
*SP's 276-300: .25X TO .5X BASIC CARDS
STAT.PRINT RUN 200 SER.#'ed SETS

2000-01 BAP Signature Series Sapphire

*STARS: 4X TO 8X BASIC CARDS
*SP's 251-275: .5X TO 1X BASIC CARDS
*SP'S 276-300: .3X TO .75X
STAT.PRINT RUN 100 SER.#'d SETS

2000-01 BAP Signature Series Autographs

Randomly inserted in packs at the rate of one in one, this 250-card set paralleld the base set with player autographs.

ONE PER PACK
*GOLD AUTOS: .5X TO 1.25X HI
1 Pavel Bure SP 12.50 30.00
2 Valeri Bure SP 10.00 25.00
3 Mike Johnson 2.00 5.00
4 Rob Blake 4.00 10.00
5 Brendan Morrison 2.00 5.00
6 David Legwand 2.00 5.00
7 Dimitri Kalinin 2.00 5.00

8 Jeff Farkas 2.00 5.00
9 Brian Savage 2.00 5.00
10 Dan Cloutier 2.00 5.00
11 Tom Poti 2.00 5.00
12 Doug Gilmour SP 10.00 25.00
13 Steve Konowalchuk 2.00 5.00
14 Scott Mellanby 2.00 5.00
15 Brent Sopel 2.00 5.00
16 Ron Tugnutt SP 10.00 25.00
17 Steve Thomas 2.00 5.00
18 Dainius Zubrus 2.00 5.00
19 Jason Allison SP 10.00 25.00
20 Jason Ward 2.00 5.00
21 Brian Holzinger 2.00 5.00
22 Jere Karalahti 2.00 5.00
23 Todd Reirden 2.00 5.00
24 Brent Gilchrist 2.00 5.00
25 Steve McKenna 2.00 5.00
26 Viktor Kozlov 2.00 5.00
27 Ryan Smyth 2.00 5.00
28 Al MacInnis SP 10.00 25.00
29 Daniel Cleary 2.00 5.00
30 Patrick Lalime 2.00 5.00
31 Dimitri Khristich 2.00 5.00
32 Janne Niinimaa 2.00 5.00
33 Mike Johnson 2.00 5.00
34 Jeff O'Neill SP 10.00 25.00
35 Luc Robitaille SP 10.00 25.00
36 Adam Oates SP 10.00 25.00
37 Petr Nedved 2.00 5.00
38 Kevyn Adams 2.00 5.00
39 Curtis Joseph SP 12.50 30.00
40 Glen Murray 2.00 5.00
41 Tyson Nash 2.00 5.00
42 Ray Whitney 2.00 5.00
43 Scott Walker 2.00 5.00
44 Andre Savage 2.00 5.00
45 Joe Nieuwendyk SP 10.00 25.00
46 Steve Webb 2.00 5.00
47 Jochen Hecht 2.00 5.00
48 Petr Buzek 2.00 5.00
49 Sergei Fedorov SP 20.00 50.00
50 Mathieu Biron 2.00 5.00
51 Patrick Marleau 4.00 10.00
52 Nicklas Lidstrom SP 12.50 30.00
53 Mike York 2.00 5.00
54 Pavel Kubina 2.00 5.00
55 Brendan Shanahan SP 12.50 30.00
56 Pierre Turgeon SP 10.00 25.00
57 Richard Zednik 2.00 5.00
58 Steve Kariya 2.00 5.00
59 Jeremy Roenick SP 15.00 40.00
60 Todd Bertuzzi 4.00 10.00
61 Marty Reasoner 2.00 5.00
62 Martin Lapointe 2.00 5.00
63 Roman Turek 2.00 5.00
64 Jason Arnott SP 10.00 25.00
65 Robert Lang 2.00 5.00
66 Fred Brathwaite 2.00 5.00
67 Tommy Salo 2.00 5.00
68 Keith Primeau SP 10.00 25.00
69 Frantisek Kaberle 2.00 5.00
70 Chris Drury 4.00 10.00
71 Manny Fernandez 4.00 10.00
72 Shane Willis 2.00 5.00
73 Matt Cullen 2.00 5.00
74 Sergei Zubov 2.00 5.00
75 Petr Sykora 2.00 5.00
76 Todd Marchant 2.00 5.00
77 Martin Biron 4.00 10.00
78 Ed Belfour SP 15.00 40.00
79 Kenny Jonsson SP 10.00 25.00
80 Chris Pronger SP 10.00 25.00
81 Maxim Afinogenov 2.00 5.00
82 Brenden Morrow 4.00 10.00
83 Theo Fleury SP 10.00 25.00
84 Brad Stuart 2.00 5.00
85 Miroslav Satan 4.00 10.00
86 Doug Weight SP 10.00 25.00
87 John LeClair SP 12.50 30.00
88 Lyle Odelein 2.00 5.00
89 Lance Pitlick 2.00 5.00
90 Martin Skoula 2.00 5.00
91 Michal Rozsival 2.00 5.00
92 Darren McCarty 4.00 10.00
93 Mats Sundin SP 20.00 50.00
94 Michael Peca 2.00 5.00
95 Chris Osgood SP 10.00 25.00
96 Andre Roy 2.00 5.00
97 Steve Rucchin 2.00 5.00
98 Steve Sullivan 2.00 5.00
99 Randy Robitaille 2.00 5.00
100 Jiri Slegr 2.00 5.00
101 Glen Metropolit 2.00 5.00
102 Milan Hejduk 4.00 10.00
103 Kimmo Timonen 2.00 5.00
104 Jyrki Lumme 2.00 5.00
105 Sergei Samsonov SP 10.00 25.00
106 Patrick Roy SP 60.00 125.00
107 Patrik Elias 4.00 10.00
108 Vincent Damphousse 2.00 5.00
109 Brian Rolston 2.00 5.00
110 Peter Forsberg SP 20.00 50.00
111 Mariusz Czerkawski 2.00 5.00
112 Darius Kasparaitis 2.00 5.00
113 Joe Thornton 10.00 25.00
114 Steve Yzerman SP 40.00 100.00
115 Marian Hossa 6.00 15.00
116 Vincent Lecavalier 6.00 15.00
117 Colin White 2.00 5.00
118 Boris Mironov 2.00 5.00
119 Andy Delmore 2.00 5.00
120 Alex Tanguay 4.00 10.00
121 Colin Forbes 2.00 5.00
122 Byron Dafoe 2.00 5.00
123 Jere Lehtinen 4.00 10.00
124 Adam Graves 2.00 5.00
125 Olaf Kolzig SP 10.00 25.00
126 Arturs Irbe 4.00 10.00
127 Trevor Linden 4.00 10.00
128 Mika Alatalo 2.00 5.00
129 Harold Druken 2.00 5.00
130 Alexei Zhamnov 2.00 5.00
131 Sergei Zholtok 2.00 5.00
132 Mark Recchi SP 10.00 25.00
133 Andrew Brunette 2.00 5.00
134 Andrei Zyuzin 2.00 5.00
135 Ray Bourque SP 20.00 50.00
136 Josh Holden 2.00 5.00
137 Patrik Stefan 2.00 5.00
138 Jocelyn Thibault 4.00 10.00
139 Martin Brodeur SP 30.00 80.00
140 Trevor Letowski 2.00 5.00
141 David Harlock 2.00 5.00
142 Mike Modano SP 12.50 30.00
143 Wayne Gretzky SP 400.00 800.00
144 Michal Handzus 2.00 5.00
145 Clarke Wilm 2.00 5.00
146 Phil Housley 2.00 5.00
147 Jan Hlavac 2.00 5.00
148 Jason York 2.00 5.00
149 Mike Richter SP 12.50 30.00
150 Sergei Vyshedkevich 2.00 5.00
151 Cam Stewart 2.00 5.00
152 Scott Stevens SP 10.00 25.00
153 Felix Potvin 6.00 15.00
154 Robyn Regehr 2.00 5.00
155 Jamie Storr 2.00 5.00
156 Eric Desjardins 2.00 5.00
157 Dimitri Yushkevich 2.00 5.00
158 Ron Francis SP 10.00 25.00
159 Zigmund Palffy SP 10.00 25.00
160 Radek Bonk 2.00 5.00
161 Vitali Vishnevsky 2.00 5.00
162 Dave Tanabe 2.00 5.00
163 Saku Koivu 6.00 15.00
164 Travis Green 2.00 5.00
165 Teemu Selanne SP 12.50 30.00
166 Rod Brind'Amour 2.00 5.00
167 Cliff Ronning 2.00 5.00
168 Brian Boucher 4.00 10.00
169 Paul Kariya SP 20.00 50.00
170 Joe Sakic SP 40.00 100.00
171 Tim Connolly 2.00 5.00
172 Mattias Timander 2.00 5.00
173 Jay Pandolfo 2.00 5.00
174 John Grahame 2.00 5.00
175 Brian Rafalski 2.00 5.00
176 Marc Savard 2.00 5.00
177 John Madden 2.00 5.00
178 Tony Hrkac 2.00 5.00
179 Stu Grimson 2.00 5.00
180 John Vanbiesbrouck SP 10.00 25.00
181 Tie Domi 4.00 10.00
182 Stu Barnes 2.00 5.00
183 Todd Simpson 2.00 5.00
184 Mike Fisher 2.00 5.00
185 Aaron Gavey 2.00 5.00
186 Jarome Iginla 8.00 20.00
187 Jaroslav Spacek 2.00 5.00
188 Brian Leetch SP 12.50 30.00
189 Jeff Halpern 2.00 5.00
190 Jeff Shantz 2.00 5.00
191 Jaroslav Modry 2.00 5.00
192 Simon Gagne 6.00 15.00
193 Calle Johansson 2.00 5.00
194 Josef Marha 2.00 5.00
195 Jose Theodore 8.00 20.00
196 Daniel Alfredsson 4.00 10.00
197 Craig Darby 2.00 5.00
198 Tony Amonte SP 10.00 25.00
199 Scott Gomez 2.00 5.00
200 Jean-Sebastien Aubin 4.00 10.00
201 Jarno Kultanen 2.00 5.00
202 Paul Coffey SP 12.50 30.00
203 Bill Guerin SP 10.00 25.00
204 Roberto Luongo 8.00 20.00
205 Randy McKay 2.00 5.00
206 Tyler Wright 2.00 5.00
207 Alexei Yashin 2.00 5.00
208 Eric Lindros SP 15.00 40.00
209 Nikolai Khabibulin 6.00 15.00
210 Tomas Vlasak 2.00 5.00
211 Shayne Corson 2.00 5.00
212 Igor Larionov SP 10.00 25.00
213 Peter Bondra SP 12.50 30.00
214 Mika Noronen 2.00 5.00
215 Andrew Raycroft 8.00 20.00
216 Taylor Pyatt 2.00 5.00
217 Toni Lydman 2.00 5.00
218 Matt Bradley 2.00 5.00
219 Brad Richards 4.00 10.00
220 Steve McCarthy 2.00 5.00
221 Tomi Kallio 2.00 5.00
222 Justin Williams 2.00 5.00
223 Brad Ference 2.00 5.00
224 Steven Reinprecht 2.00 5.00
225 Samuel Pahlsson 2.00 5.00
226 Josef Vasicek 2.00 5.00
227 Jani Hurme 2.00 5.00
228 Petr Svoboda 2.00 5.00
229 Petr Schastlivy 2.00 5.00
230 Roman Simicek 2.00 5.00
231 Reto Von Arx 2.00 5.00
232 Oleg Saprykin 2.00 5.00
233 Lubomir Sekeras 2.00 5.00
234 Alexander Kharitonov 2.00 5.00
235 Maxim Sushinski 2.00 5.00
236 Andrei Markov 2.00 5.00
237 Scott Hartnell 2.00 5.00
238 Martin Havlat 4.00 10.00
239 Maxime Ouellet 2.00 5.00
240 Petteri Nummelin 2.00 5.00
241 Marian Gaborik 12.00 30.00
242 Daniel Sedin 2.00 5.00
243 Henrik Sedin 2.00 5.00
244 Milan Kraft 2.00 5.00
245 Denis Shvidki 2.00 5.00
246 Kris Beech 2.00 5.00
247 Rostislav Klesla 2.00 5.00
248 Petr Hubacek 2.00 5.00
249 Ossi Vaananen 2.00 5.00
250 Marty Turco 4.00 10.00

2000-01 BAP Signature Series Department of Defense

Randomly inserted in packs, this 20-card set featured a game-used swatch of jersey and a action player photo on a background of computer generated steel girders and rivets. Each card had a stated print run of 100 each.

*MULT.COLOR SWATCH: 1X TO 2X
STAT.PRINT RUN 100 SETS
DD1 Brian Leetch 10.00 25.00
DD2 Ray Bourque 25.00 60.00
DD3 Chris Chelios 15.00 40.00
DD4 Nicklas Lidstrom 20.00 50.00

DD5 Sandis Ozolinsh 8.00 20.00
DD6 Scott Stevens 10.00 25.00
DD7 Al MacInnis 10.00 25.00
DD8 Kyle McLaren 8.00 20.00
DD9 Kenny Jonsson 8.00 20.00
DD10 Teppo Numminen 8.00 20.00
DD11 Sergei Zubov 8.00 20.00
DD12 Scott Niedermayer 8.00 20.00
DD13 Paul Coffey 25.00 60.00
DD14 Adam Foote 8.00 20.00
DD15 Sergei Gonchar 8.00 20.00
DD16 Phil Housley 8.00 20.00
DD17 Eric Desjardins 8.00 20.00
DD18 Dimitri Yushkevich 8.00 20.00
DD19 Chris Pronger 10.00 25.00
DD20 Rob Blake 10.00 25.00

2000-01 BAP Signature Series Franchise Players

STAT.PRINT RUN 30 SETS
F1 Paul Kariya 15.00 40.00
F2 Patrik Stefan 8.00 20.00
F3 Joe Thornton 25.00 60.00
F4 Dominik Hasek 25.00 60.00
F5 Jarome Iginla 20.00 50.00
F6 Jeff O'Neill 15.00 40.00
F7 Tony Amonte 15.00 40.00
F8 Peter Forsberg 25.00 60.00
F9 Ron Tugnutt 15.00 40.00
F10 Mike Modano 20.00 40.00
F11 Steve Yzerman 50.00 125.00
F12 Doug Weight 15.00 40.00
F13 Pavel Bure 15.00 40.00
F14 Rob Blake 15.00 40.00
F15 Marian Gaborik 25.00 60.00
F16 Saku Koivu 15.00 40.00
F17 David Legwand 15.00 40.00
F18 Martin Brodeur 50.00 125.00
F19 Mariusz Czerkawski 15.00 40.00
F20 Brian Leetch 15.00 40.00
F21 Marian Hossa 15.00 40.00
F22 John LeClair 15.00 40.00
F23 Keith Tkachuk 15.00 40.00
F24 Jaromir Jagr 30.00 80.00
F25 Chris Pronger 15.00 40.00
F26 Owen Nolan 15.00 40.00
F27 Vincent Lecavalier 15.00 40.00
F28 Curtis Joseph 15.00 40.00
F29 Daniel Sedin 15.00 40.00
F30 Olaf Kolzig 15.00 40.00

2000-01 BAP Signature Series Goalie Memorabilia Autographs

Randomly inserted in packs, this 5-card set featured a game-used swatch of equipment and an autograph beside a color action photo of the player. The player's name was printed along the left border and the words "Goalie Legend" appeared on the top of each card. Each card had a stated print run of 150 sets.

STAT.PRINT RUN 150 SETS
GLS1 Gerry Cheevers 50.00 125.00
GLS2 Vladislav Tretiak 100.00 250.00
GLS3 Tony Esposito 50.00 125.00
GLS4 Johnny Bower 50.00 125.00
GLS5 Bernie Parent 50.00 125.00

2000-01 BAP Signature Series He Shoots-He Scores Points

ONE PER PACK
RED.PROGRAM HAS EXPIRED
1 P.Bure 3pts. .20 .50
2 M.Brodeur 1pts. .20 .50
3 T.Fleury 3pts. .20 .50
4 P.Forsberg 1pts. .20 .50
5 P.Forsberg 3pts. .20 .50
6 D.Hasek 2pts. .20 .50
7 B.Hull 2pts. .20 .50
8 J.Jagr 3pts. .20 .50
9 C.Joseph 1pts. .20 .50
10 P.Kariya 2pts. .20 .50
11 M.Lemieux 3pts. .20 .50
12 M.Messier 2pts. .20 .50
13 M.Modano 2pts. .20 .50
14 Z.Palffy 1pts. .20 .50
15 L.Robitaille 2pts. .20 .50
16 P.Roy 2pts. .20 .50
17 J.Sakic 2pts. .20 .50
18 B.Shanahan 1pts. .20 .50
19 M.Sundin 1pts. .20 .50
20 S.Yzerman 3pts. .20 .50

2000-01 BAP Signature Series He Shoots-He Scores Prizes

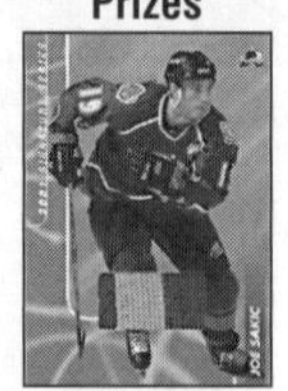

STAT.PRINT RUN 20 SER.#'d SETS
NOT PRICED DUE TO SCARCITY
1 Pavel Bure
2 Milan Hejduk
3 Patrick Roy
4 Roberto Luongo
5 Alexei Yashin
6 Peter Bondra
7 Martin Brodeur
8 Steve Yzerman
9 Vincent Lecavalier
10 Mike Modano
11 Wayne Gretzky
12 Peter Forsberg
13 Mark Recchi
14 Olaf Kolzig
15 Arturs Irbe
16 Patrik Stefan
17 Al MacInnis
18 Luc Robitaille
19 Dominik Hasek
20 Curtis Joseph
21 Paul Kariya
22 Joe Sakic
23 Sergei Fedorov
24 Ed Belfour
25 Keith Tkachuk
26 Chris Pronger
27 Nicklas Lidstrom
28 Brendan Shanahan
29 Brett Hull
30 Brian Leetch
31 Mark Messier
32 Jeremy Roenick
33 Keith Primeau
34 Tony Amonte
35 Scott Gomez
36 Jason Arnott
37 Mats Sundin
38 Chris Osgood
39 Mario Lemieux
40 Jaromir Jagr

2000-01 BAP Signature Series Jersey Cards

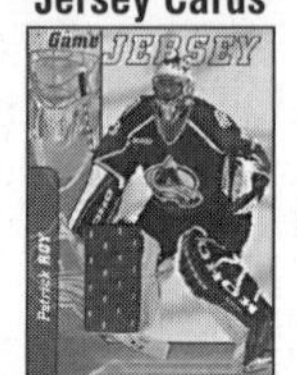

*MULT.COLOR SWATCH: 1X TO 2X
STAT.PRINT RUN 100 SETS
J1 Theo Fleury 10.00 25.00
J2 Brendan Shanahan 10.00 25.00
J3 Curtis Joseph 10.00 25.00
J4 Saku Koivu 10.00 25.00
J5 Dominik Hasek 20.00 50.00
J6 Al MacInnis 10.00 25.00
J7 John LeClair 10.00 25.00
J8 Teemu Selanne 10.00 25.00
J9 Scott Niedermayer 10.00 25.00
J10 Pavel Bure 10.00 25.00
J11 Mark Messier 10.00 25.00
J12 Jaromir Jagr 15.00 40.00
J13 Chris Pronger 10.00 25.00
J14 Chris Osgood 10.00 25.00
J15 Mats Sundin 10.00 25.00
J16 Paul Kariya 10.00 25.00
J17 Scott Stevens 10.00 25.00
J18 Kenny Jonsson 10.00 25.00
J19 Sergei Fedorov 12.50 30.00
J20 Peter Forsberg 15.00 40.00
J21 Brett Hull 12.50 30.00
J22 Tony Amonte 10.00 25.00
J23 Patrick Roy 30.00 80.00
J24 Ed Belfour 10.00 25.00
J25 Martin Brodeur 25.00 60.00
J26 Brian Leetch 10.00 25.00
J27 Mike Modano 12.50 30.00
J28 Jeff Friesen 10.00 25.00
J29 Jeremy Roenick 12.50 30.00
J30 Steve Yzerman 30.00 80.00
J31 Joe Sakic 20.00 50.00
J32 Mike Peca 10.00 25.00
J33 Luc Robitaille 10.00 25.00
J34 Adam Oates 10.00 25.00
J35 Valeri Bure 10.00 25.00
J36 Kyle McLaren 10.00 25.00
J37 Nicklas Lidstrom 10.00 25.00
J38 Jason Arnott 10.00 25.00
J39 Mike Richter 10.00 25.00
J40 Keith Tkachuk 10.00 25.00

2000-01 BAP Signature Series Jersey and Stick Cards

*JSY/STICK: .5X TO 1.25X JERSEY CARDS
STAT.PRINT RUN 100 SETS

2000-01 BAP Signature Series Jersey Cards Autographs

*STAT.PRINT RUN 10 SER.#'d SETS
CARD J28 NOT RELEASED
NOT PRICED DUE TO SCARCITY

2000-01 BAP Signature Series Jersey Emblems

STAT.PRINT RUN 10 SETS
NOT PRICED DUE TO SCARCITY

2000-01 BAP Signature Series Jersey Numbers

STAT.PRINT RUN 10 SETS
NOT PRICED DUE TO SCARCITY

2000-01 BAP Signature Series Mario Lemieux Legend

Randomly inserted in packs, this 5-card set features two swatches of game-used equipment per card, accompanied by a photo of Mario Lemieux. Each card has a stated print run of 30, but the cards are not serial numbered.

STAT.PRINT RUN 30 SETS
LM1 M.Lemieux #/EMB 250.00 500.00
LM2 M.Lemieux Jsy/GLOVE 100.00250.00
LM3 M.Lemieux Jsy/GLOVE 100.00250.00
LM4 M.Lemieux Jsy/Jsy 100.00 250.00
LM5 M.Lemieux Jsy/Jsy/Jsy 250.00500.00

2000-01 BAP Signature Series Mario Lemieux Legend Autographs

Randomly inserted in packs, this 5-card set parallels the Be A Player Signature Series Mario Lemieux Legends cards, but with an autograph on each card. Each card has a stated print run of 6, but the cards are not serial numbered.

STAT.PRINT RUN 6 SETS
NOT PRICED DUE TO SCARCITY

2000-01 BAP Signature Series Mario Lemieux Retrospective

Randomly inserted in packs, this 20-card set highlights the career of Mario Lemieux. Each card portrays a specific milestone in his career.

COMPLETE SET (20) 50.00 100.00
COMMON CARD (MLR1-MLR20) 2.00 5.00

2001-02 BAP Signature Series

This 250-card set featured full-color action photos on silver-mirrored card fronts. Cards 226-250 were available in BAP Update packs only.

COMP.SER. 1 SET (225) 100.00 200.00
CARDS 225-250 AVAIL.IN BAP UPD.PACKS
1 Rick DiPietro .50 1.25
2 Patrik Stefan .30 .75
3 Hal Gill .30 .75
4 J-P Dumont .30 .75
5 Jarome Iginla .75 2.00
6 Shane Willis .30 .75
7 Chris Phillips .30 .75
8 Rostislav Klesla .30 .75
9 Brenden Morrow .50 1.25
10 Manny Legace .50 1.25
11 Anson Carter .50 1.25
12 Roberto Luongo .75 2.00
13 Aaron Miller .30 .75
14 Wayne Primeau .30 .75
15 Brian Savage .30 .75
16 John Jakopin .30 .75
17 Greg Johnson .30 .75
18 Marc Chouinard .30 .75
19 Steve Martins .30 .75
20 Marian Hossa .60 1.50
21 Brent Johnson .50 1.25
22 Sean Burke .50 1.25
23 Jan Hrdina .30 .75
24 Evgeni Nabokov .50 1.25
25 Adam Deadmarsh .30 .75
26 Brad Richards .50 1.25
27 Wade Redden .30 .75
28 David Legwand .50 1.25
29 J-S Giguere .50 1.25
30 Ray Ferraro .30 .75
31 Denis Hamel .30 .75
32 Marc Savard .30 .75
33 Craig Adams .30 .75
34 Landon Wilson .30 .75
35 Marc Denis .50 1.25
36 Roman Lyashenko .30 .75
37 Tomas Holmstrom .30 .75
38 Mike Comrie .50 1.25
39 Scott Hartnell .30 .75
40 Sergei Krivokrasov .30 .75
41 Mathieu Garon .50 1.25
42 Denis Arkhipov .30 .75
43 Roman Hamrlik .30 .75
44 Mike Mottau .30 .75
45 Shawn McEachern .30 .75
46 Peter White .30 .75
47 Shane Doan .30 .75
48 Janne Laukkanen .30 .75
49 Martin St. Louis .50 1.25
50 Tomas Kaberle .30 .75
51 Daniel Sedin .30 .75
52 Jonas Ronnqvist .30 .75
53 Damian Rhodes .50 1.25
54 Vaclav Varada .30 .75
55 Ronald Petrovicky .30 .75
56 Tommy Westlund .30 .75
57 Michael Nylander .30 .75
58 Serge Aubin .30 .75
59 Jiri Fischer .30 .75
60 Shawn Horcoff .30 .75
61 Peter Worrell .30 .75
62 Willie Mitchell .30 .75
63 Oleg Petrov .30 .75
64 Scott Walker .30 .75
65 Tomi Kallio .30 .75
66 Jason Strudwick .30 .75
67 Magnus Arvedson .30 .75
68 Eric Daze .50 1.25
69 Johan Hedberg .50 1.25
70 Fredrik Modin .30 .75
71 Nathan Dempsey .30 .75
72 Henrik Sedin .30 .75
73 Mike LeClerc .30 .75
74 Hnat Domenichelli .30 .75
75 Jeff Cowan .30 .75
76 Brad Stuart .30 .75
77 Bryan Allen .30 .75
78 Wes Walz .30 .75
79 Patrick Traverse .30 .75
80 Markus Naslund .60 1.50
81 Brad Isbister .30 .75
82 Jan Hlavac .30 .75
83 Steve Sullivan .30 .75
84 Marian Gaborik 1.00 2.50
85 Kristian Kudroc .30 .75
86 Peter Schaefer .30 .75
87 Pascal Trepanier .30 .75
88 Milan Hnilicka .50 1.25
89 Dave Lowry .30 .75
90 Jamie Allison .30 .75
91 Jeff Nielsen .30 .75
92 Sheldon Souray .30 .75
93 Mike Dunham .50 1.25
94 Branislav Mezei .30 .75
95 Dale Purinton .30 .75
96 Cory Sarich .30 .75
97 Jarkko Ruutu .30 .75
98 Kyle Calder .30 .75
99 Frantisek Musil .30 .75
100 Tomas Kloucek .30 .75
101 Karel Rachunek .30 .75
102 Darcy Tucker .30 .75
103 Alex Tanguay .50 1.25
104 Patrick Lalime .50 1.25
105 Ossi Vaananen .30 .75
106 Martin Skoula .30 .75
107 Lubomir Visnovsky .30 .75
108 Richard Zednik .30 .75
109 Jani Hurme .50 1.25
110 Teppo Numminen .30 .75
111 Scott Young .30 .75
112 Robert Reichel .30 .75
113 Dave Tanabe .30 .75
114 Steven Reinprecht .30 .75
115 Ryan Smyth .30 .75
116 Jozef Stumpel .30 .75
117 Martin Rucinsky .30 .75
118 Radek Dvorak .30 .75
119 Chris Herperger .30 .75
120 Eric Weinrich .30 .75
121 Claude Lemieux .30 .75
122 Mike Ricci .30 .75
123 Cory Stillman .30 .75
124 Alyn McCauley .30 .75
125 Trevor Linden .30 .75
126 Vitali Vishnevsky .30 .75
127 Tim Connolly .30 .75
128 Oleg Saprykin .30 .75
129 Arturs Irbe .50 1.25
130 Ville Nieminen .30 .75
131 David Vyborny .30 .75
132 Janne Niinimaa .30 .75
133 Joey Tetarenko .30 .75
134 Bryan Smolinski .30 .75
135 Stacy Roest .30 .75
136 Mikael Renberg .30 .75
137 Gino Odjick .30 .75
138 Petr Sykora .30 .75
139 Alexei Yashin .30 .75
140 Martin Havlat .50 1.25
141 Rick Tocchet .30 .75
142 Daymond Langkow .30 .75
143 Kevin Stevens .30 .75
144 Patrick Marleau .50 1.25
145 Reed Low .30 .75
146 Bryan McCabe .30 .75
147 Dimitri Khristich .30 .75
148 Oleg Tverdovsky .30 .75
149 Yannick Tremblay .30 .75
150 Martin Biron .50 1.25
151 Rob Niedermayer .30 .75
152 Rod Brind'Amour .50 1.25
153 Adam Foote .30 .75
154 Geoff Sanderson .30 .75
155 Pat Verbeek .30 .75
156 Nicklas Lidstrom .60 1.50
157 Jochen Hecht .30 .75
158 Robert Svehla .30 .75
159 Mathieu Schneider .30 .75
160 Antti Laaksonen .30 .75
161 Jeff Hackett .50 1.25
162 Scott Niedermayer .30 .75
163 Sandis Ozolinsh .30 .75
164 Radek Bonk .30 .75
165 Roman Cechmanek .50 1.25
166 Mike Johnson .30 .75
167 Milan Kraft .30 .75
168 Adam Graves .30 .75
169 Pavol Demitra .50 1.25
170 Kevin Weekes .50 1.25
171 Travis Green .30 .75
172 Jeff Halpern .30 .75
173 Steve Shields .50 1.25
174 Lubos Bartecko .30 .75
175 P.J. Stock .30 .75
176 Maxim Afinogenov .30 .75
177 Derek Morris .30 .75
178 Bates Battaglia .30 .75
179 Boris Mironov .30 .75
180 David Aebischer .50 1.25
181 Espen Knutsen .30 .75
182 Darryl Sydor .30 .75
183 Igor Larionov .30 .75
184 Eric Brewer .30 .75
185 Trevor Kidd .50 1.25
186 Eric Belanger .30 .75
187 Manny Fernandez .50 1.25
188 Francois Bouillon .30 .75
189 Patrik Elias .50 1.25
190 Mariusz Czerkawski .30 .75
191 Daniel Alfredsson .50 1.25
192 Brian Boucher .50 1.25
193 Sergei Berezin .30 .75
194 Kris Beech .30 .75
195 Vincent Damphousse .30 .75
196 Fred Brathwaite .50 1.25
197 Ben Clymer .30 .75
198 Wade Belak .30 .75
199 Ed Jovanovski .50 1.25
200 Sergei Gonchar .30 .75
201 Dan Blackburn RC .75 2.00
202 Daniel Tjarnqvist .30 .75
203 Andreas Salomonsson RC 1.00 2.50
204 Vaclav Nedorost RC 1.00 2.50
205 Justin Kurtz RC 1.00 2.50
206 Jiri Dopita RC 1.00 2.50
207 Ilya Kovalchuk RC 4.00 10.00
208 Richard Jackman .30 .75
209 Scott Nichol RC 1.00 2.50
210 Brad Larsen .30 .75
211 Jason Williams .30 .75
212 Kristian Huselius RC 1.50 4.00
213 Andreas Lilja .30 .75
214 Nick Schultz RC 1.00 2.50
215 Marc Moro .30 .75
216 Scott Clemmensen RC 1.00 2.50
217 Brad Tapper .30 .75
218 Barrett Heisten .30 .75
219 Chris Neil RC 1.00 2.50
220 Pavel Brendl .30 .75
221 Miikka Kiprusoff .50 1.25
222 Jimmie Olvestad .30 .75
223 Brian Sutherby RC 1.00 2.50
224 Timo Parssinen RC 1.00 2.50
225 Sascha Goc .30 .75
226 Dany Heatley .75 2.00
227 Nick Boynton .30 .75
228 Steve Begin .30 .75
229 Erik Cole RC 1.00 2.50
230 Mark Bell .30 .75
231 Rick Berry .30 .75
232 Niko Kapanen RC 1.00 2.50
233 Pavel Datsyuk RC 2.00 5.00
234 Niklas Hagman RC 1.00 2.50
235 Jaroslav Bednar RC 1.00 2.50
236 Pascal Dupuis RC 1.00 2.50
237 Mike Ribeiro .30 .75
238 Martin Erat RC 1.00 2.50
239 Jiri Bicek .30 .75
240 Radek Martinek RC 1.00 2.50
241 Ivan Ciernik RC 1.00 2.50
242 Jesse Boulerice .30 .75
243 Krys Kolanos RC 1.00 2.50
244 Toby Petersen .30 .75
245 Jeff Jillson RC 1.00 2.50
246 Mark Hycroft RC 1.00 2.50
247 Kamil Piros RC 1.00 2.50
248 Nikita Alexeev RC 1.00 2.50
249 Stephen Peat .30 .75
250 Pierre Dagenais .30 .75

2001-02 BAP Signature Series Certified 100

his 60-card set resembled the base set, but arried a light purple background and the ords "Signature Series Certified" on the ard front and was numbered on the back "1 f 100". Players featured in this set were not cluded in the base set.

TATED PRINT RUN 100 SETS
1 Al MacInnis 4.00 10.00
2 Adam Oates 4.00 10.00
3 Byron Dafoe 4.00 10.00
4 Bill Guerin 4.00 10.00
5 Brian Leetch 4.00 10.00
6 Brendan Shanahan 3.00 8.00
7 Chris Drury 4.00 10.00
8 Chris Gratton 2.50 6.00
9 Curtis Joseph 3.00 8.00
10 Chris Pronger 2.50 6.00
11 Donald Audette 2.50 6.00
12 Doug Weight 2.50 6.00
13 Ed Belfour 3.00 8.00
14 Eric Lindros 3.00 8.00
15 Jason Allison 2.50 6.00
16 Jason Arnott 2.50 6.00
17 John LeClair 3.00 8.00
18 Jeff O'Neill 2.50 6.00
19 Jeremy Roenick 3.00 8.00
20 Joe Sakic 5.00 12.00
21 Joe Thornton 4.00 10.00
22 Kyle McLaren 2.50 6.00
23 Luc Robitaille 4.00 10.00
24 Martin Brodeur 8.00 20.00
25 Milan Hejduk 3.00 8.00
26 Martin Lapointe 2.50 6.00
27 Mike Modano 4.00 10.00
28 Mark Recchi 2.50 6.00
29 Mats Sundin 3.00 8.00
30 Olaf Kolzig 2.50 6.00
31 Peter Bondra 3.00 8.00
32 Pavel Bure 3.00 8.00
33 Paul Kariya 3.00 8.00
34 Pierre Turgeon 2.50 6.00
35 Rob Blake 2.50 6.00
36 Ron Francis 2.50 6.00
37 Roman Turek 2.50 6.00
38 Sergei Fedorov 4.00 10.00
39 Scott Gomez 2.50 6.00
40 Saku Koivu 3.00 8.00
41 Sami Kapanen 2.50 6.00
42 Sergei Samsonov 2.50 6.00
43 Scott Stevens 2.50 6.00
44 Steve Yzerman 8.00 20.00
45 Tony Amonte 4.00 10.00
46 Theo Fleury 2.50 6.00
47 Teemu Selanne 3.00 8.00
48 Tommy Salo 2.50 6.00
49 Vincent Lecavalier 3.00 8.00
50 Zigmund Palffy 4.00 10.00
51 Brett Hull 3.00 8.00
52 Dominik Hasek 5.00 12.00
53 Jaromir Jagr 4.00 10.00
54 Mario Lemieux 12.50 30.00
55 Mark Messier 3.00 8.00
56 Mike Vernon 2.50 6.00
57 Owen Nolan 2.50 6.00
58 Peter Forsberg 8.00 20.00
59 Patrick Roy 8.00 20.00
60 Wayne Gretzky 12.50 30.00

2001-02 BAP Signature Series Certified 50

his 60-card set resembled the base set, but arried a dark purple background and the ords "Signature Series Certified" on the ard front and is numbered on the back "1 of)". Players featured in this set were not cluded in the base set.

CERTIFIED 50 : .75X TO 2X CERTIFIED 00 BASE
TATED PRINT RUN 50 SETS

2001-02 BAP Signature Series Certified 1 of 1's

his 60-card set paralleled the base set, but arried a dark green background and the ords "Signature Series Certified" on the ard front and each card was numbered on e back "1 of 1".

TATED PRINT RUN 1 SET
OT PRICED DUE TO SCARCITY

2001-02 BAP Signature Series Autographs

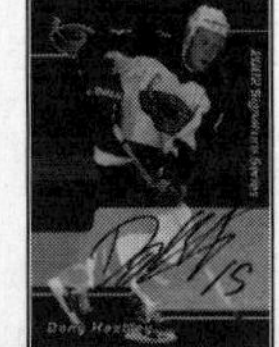

This 297-card set partially paralleled the base set but carried player autographs in a muted area on the card front. Card numbers that carried a "L" or "XL" prefix were short printed, but no numbers are known at this time. Cards 226-250 and numbers LTS, LPF, LSY, LSF, LTA, LJR and XLMM were available in BAP Update packs only.

ONE PER PACK
1 Rick DiPietro 6.00 15.00
2 Patrik Stefan 2.00 5.00
3 Hal Gill 2.00 5.00
4 J-P Dumont 2.00 5.00
5 Jarome Iginla 10.00 25.00
6 Shane Willis 2.00 5.00
7 Chris Phillips 2.00 5.00
8 Rostislav Klesla 2.00 5.00
9 Brenden Morrow 4.00 10.00
10 Manny Legace 4.00 10.00
11 Anson Carter SP 20.00 50.00
12 Roberto Luongo 8.00 20.00
13 Aaron Miller 2.00 5.00
14 Wayne Primeau 2.00 5.00
15 Brian Savage 2.00 5.00
16 John Jakopin 2.00 5.00
17 Greg Johnson 2.00 5.00
18 Marc Chouinard 2.00 5.00
19 Steve Martins 2.00 5.00
20 Marian Hossa 6.00 15.00
21 Brent Johnson SP 60.00 125.00
22 Sean Burke 4.00 10.00
23 Jan Hrdina 2.00 5.00
24 Evgeni Nabokov 4.00 10.00
25 Adam Deadmarsh 2.00 5.00
26 Brad Richards 4.00 10.00
27 Wade Redden 2.00 5.00
28 David Legwand 5.00 5.00
29 J-S Giguere 4.00 10.00
30 Ray Ferraro 2.00 5.00
31 Denis Hamel 2.00 5.00
32 Marc Savard 2.00 5.00
33 Craig Adams 2.00 5.00
34 Landon Wilson 2.00 5.00
35 Marc Denis 4.00 10.00
36 Roman Lyashenko 2.00 5.00
37 Tomas Holmstrom 2.00 5.00
38 Mike Comrie 5.00 5.00
39 Scott Hartnell 2.00 5.00
40 Sergei Krivokrasov 2.00 5.00
41 Mathieu Garon 3.00 8.00
42 Denis Arkhipov 2.00 5.00
43 Roman Hamrlik 2.00 5.00
44 Mike Mottau 2.00 5.00
45 Shawn McEachern 2.00 5.00
46 Peter White SP 60.00 150.00
47 Shane Doan 2.00 5.00
48 Janne Laukkanen 2.00 5.00
49 Martin St. Louis 10.00 25.00
50 Tomas Kaberle 2.00 5.00
51 Daniel Sedin 2.00 5.00
52 Jonas Ronnqvist 2.00 5.00
53 Damian Rhodes 3.00 8.00
54 Vaclav Varada 2.00 5.00
55 Ronald Petrovicky 2.00 5.00
56 Tommy Westlund 2.00 5.00
57 Michael Nylander 2.00 5.00
58 Serge Aubin 2.00 5.00
59 Jiri Fischer SP 50.00 125.00
60 Shawn Horcoff 2.00 5.00
61 Peter Worrell 2.00 5.00
62 Willie Mitchell 2.00 5.00
63 Oleg Petrov 2.00 5.00
64 Scott Walker 2.00 5.00
65 Tomi Kallio 2.00 5.00
66 Jason Strudwick 2.00 5.00
67 Magnus Arvedson 2.00 5.00
68 Eric Daze 5.00 12.00
69 Johan Hedberg 3.00 8.00
70 Fredrik Modin 2.00 5.00
71 Nathan Dempsey 2.00 5.00
72 Henrik Sedin 2.00 5.00
73 Mike LeClerc 2.00 5.00
74 Hnat Domenichelli 2.00 5.00
75 Jeff Cowan 2.00 5.00
76 Brad Stuart 2.00 5.00
77 Bryan Allen 2.00 5.00
78 Wes Walz 2.00 5.00
79 Patrick Traverse 2.00 5.00
80 Markus Naslund 4.00 10.00
81 Brad Isbister 2.00 5.00
82 Jan Hlavac SP 50.00 125.00
83 Steve Sullivan 2.00 5.00
84 Marian Gaborik 12.50 30.00
85 Kristian Kudroc 2.00 5.00
86 Peter Schaefer 2.00 5.00
87 Pascal Trepanier 2.00 5.00
88 Milan Hnilicka 3.00 8.00
89 Dave Lowry 2.00 5.00
90 Jamie Allison 2.00 5.00
91 Jeff Nielsen 2.00 5.00
92 Sheldon Souray 2.00 5.00
93 Mike Dunham 3.00 8.00
94 Branislav Mezei 2.00 5.00
95 Dale Purinton 2.00 5.00
96 Cory Sarich 2.00 5.00
97 Jarkko Ruutu 2.00 5.00
98 Kyle Calder 2.00 5.00
99 Frantisek Musil 2.00 5.00
100 Tomas Kloucek 2.00 5.00
101 Karel Rachunek 2.00 5.00
102 Darcy Tucker 2.00 5.00
103 Alex Tanguay 4.00 10.00
104 Patrick Lalime 3.00 8.00
105 Ossi Vaananen 2.00 5.00
106 Martin Skoula 2.00 5.00
107 Lubomir Visnovsky 2.00 5.00
108 Richard Zednik 2.00 5.00
109 Jani Hurme 3.00 8.00
110 Teppo Numminen 2.00 5.00
111 Scott Young 2.00 5.00
112 Robert Reichel 2.00 5.00
113 Dave Tanabe 2.00 5.00
114 Steven Reinprecht 2.00 5.00
115 Ryan Smyth 2.00 5.00
116 Jozef Stumpel 2.00 5.00
117 Martin Rucinsky 2.00 5.00
118 Radek Dvorak 2.00 5.00
119 Chris Herperger 2.00 5.00
120 Eric Weinrich 2.00 5.00
121 Claude Lemieux 2.00 5.00
122 Mike Ricci 2.00 5.00
123 Cory Stillman 2.00 5.00
124 Alyn McCauley 2.00 5.00
125 Trevor Linden 2.00 5.00
126 Vitaly Vishnevsky 2.00 5.00
127 Tim Connolly 2.00 5.00
128 Oleg Saprykin 2.00 5.00
129 Arturs Irbe 3.00 8.00
130 Ville Nieminen 2.00 5.00
131 David Vyborny 2.00 5.00
132 Janne Niinimaa 2.00 5.00
133 Joey Tetarenko 2.00 5.00
134 Bryan Smolinski 2.00 5.00
135 Stacy Roest 2.00 5.00
136 Mikael Renberg 2.00 5.00
137 Gino Odjick 2.00 5.00
138 Petr Sykora 2.00 5.00
139 Alexei Yashin 2.00 5.00
140 Martin Havlat 4.00 10.00
141 Rick Tocchet 2.00 5.00
142 Daymond Langkow 2.00 5.00
143 Kevin Stevens 2.00 5.00
144 Patrick Marleau 4.00 10.00
145 Reed Low 2.00 5.00
146 Bryan McCabe 2.00 5.00
147 Dimitri Khristich 2.00 5.00
148 Oleg Tverdovsky 2.00 5.00
149 Yannick Tremblay 2.00 5.00
150 Martin Biron 4.00 10.00
151 Rob Niedermayer 2.00 5.00
152 Rod Brind'Amour 4.00 10.00
153 Adam Foote 2.00 5.00
154 Geoff Sanderson 2.00 5.00
155 Pat Verbeek 2.00 5.00
156 Nicklas Lidstrom 8.00 20.00
157 Jochen Hecht 2.00 5.00
158 Robert Svehla 2.00 5.00
159 Mathieu Schneider 2.00 5.00
160 Antti Laaksonen 2.00 5.00
161 Jeff Hackett 4.00 10.00
162 Scott Niedermayer 2.00 5.00
163 Sandis Ozolinsh 2.00 5.00
164 Radek Bonk 2.00 5.00
165 Roman Cechmanek 3.00 8.00
166 Mike Johnson 2.00 5.00
167 Milan Kraft 2.00 5.00
168 Adam Graves 2.00 5.00
169 Pavol Demitra 3.00 8.00
170 Kevin Weekes 3.00 8.00
171 Travis Green 2.00 5.00
172 Jeff Halpern 2.00 5.00
173 Steve Shields 3.00 8.00
174 Lubos Bartecko 2.00 5.00
175 P.J. Stock 3.00 8.00
176 Maxim Afinogenov 2.00 5.00
177 Derek Morris 2.00 5.00
178 Bates Battaglia 2.00 5.00
179 Boris Mironov 2.00 5.00
180 David Aebischer 8.00 20.00
181 Espen Knutsen 2.00 5.00
182 Darryl Sydor 2.00 5.00
183 Igor Larionov 2.00 5.00
184 Eric Brewer 2.00 5.00
185 Trevor Kidd 3.00 8.00
186 Eric Belanger 2.00 5.00
187 Manny Fernandez 20.00 50.00
188 Francois Bouillon 2.00 5.00
189 Patrik Elias 4.00 10.00
190 Mariusz Czerkawski 2.00 5.00
191 Daniel Alfredsson 4.00 10.00
192 Brian Boucher 3.00 8.00
193 Sergei Berezin 2.00 5.00
194 Kris Beech 2.00 5.00
195 Vincent Damphousse 2.00 5.00
196 Fred Brathwaite 3.00 8.00
197 Ben Clymer 2.00 5.00
198 Wade Belak 2.00 5.00
199 Ed Jovanovski 3.00 8.00
200 Sergei Gonchar 2.00 5.00
201 Dan Blackburn 3.00 8.00
202 Daniel Tjarnqvist 2.00 5.00
203 Andreas Salomonsson 5.00 12.00
204 Vaclav Nedorost 2.00 5.00
205 Justin Kurtz 2.00 5.00
206 Jiri Dopita 2.00 5.00
207 Ilya Kovalchuk 10.00 25.00
208 Richard Jackman 2.00 5.00
209 Scott Nichol 2.00 5.00
210 Brad Larsen 2.00 5.00
211 Jason Williams 2.00 5.00
212 Kristian Huselius 2.00 5.00
213 Andreas Lilja 2.00 5.00
214 Nick Schultz 2.00 5.00
215 Marc Moro 2.00 5.00
216 Scott Clemmensen 3.00 8.00
217 Brad Tapper 2.00 5.00
218 Barrett Heisten 2.00 5.00
219 Chris Neil 2.00 5.00
220 Pavel Brendl 2.00 5.00
221 Miikka Kiprusoff 8.00 20.00
222 Jimmie Olvestad 2.00 5.00
223 Brian Sutherby 2.00 5.00
224 Timo Parssinen 2.00 5.00
225 Sascha Goc 2.00 5.00
226 Dany Heatley 10.00 25.00
227 Nick Boynton 2.00 5.00
228 Steve Begin 2.00 5.00
229 Erik Cole 2.00 5.00
230 Mark Bell 2.00 5.00
231 Rick Berry 2.00 5.00
232 Niko Kapanen 2.00 5.00
233 Pavel Datsyuk 8.00 20.00
234 Niklas Hagman 2.00 5.00
235 Jaroslav Bednar 2.00 5.00
236 Pascal Dupuis 2.00 5.00
237 Mike Ribeiro 2.00 5.00
238 Martin Erat 2.00 5.00
239 Jiri Bicek 2.00 5.00
240 Radek Martinek 2.00 5.00
241 Ivan Ciernik 2.00 5.00
242 Jesse Boulerice 2.00 5.00
243 Krystofer Kolanos 2.00 5.00
244 Toby Petersen 2.00 5.00
245 Jeff Jillson 2.00 5.00
246 Mark Rycroft 2.00 5.00
247 Kamil Piros 2.00 5.00
248 Nikita Alexeev 2.00 5.00
249 Stephen Peat 2.00 5.00
250 Pierre Dagenais 2.00 5.00
LAM Al MacInnis SP 8.00 20.00
LBD Byron Dafoe SP 10.00 25.00
LBG Bill Guerin SP 8.00 20.00
LBL Brian Leetch SP 12.50 30.00
LBS Brendan Shanahan SP 15.00 40.00
LCD Chris Drury SP 8.00 20.00
LCG Chris Gratton SP 8.00 20.00
LCP Chris Pronger SP 8.00 20.00
LDA Donald Audette SP 8.00 20.00
LDW Doug Weight SP 8.00 20.00
LEB Ed Belfour SP 20.00 50.00
LJL John LeClair SP 12.50 30.00
LJO Jeff O'Neill SP 8.00 20.00
LJR Jeremy Roenick SP 20.00 50.00
LJS Joe Sakic SP 25.00 60.00
LJT Joe Thornton SP 12.50 30.00
LKM Kyle McLaren SP 8.00 20.00
LLR Luc Robitaille SP 8.00 20.00
LMH Milan Hejduk SP 12.50 30.00
LML Martin Lapointe SP 8.00 20.00
LMR Mark Recchi SP 8.00 20.00
LOK Olaf Kolzig SP 8.00 20.00
LPK Paul Kariya SP 25.00 50.00
LPT Pierre Turgeon SP 8.00 20.00
LRB Rob Blake SP 8.00 20.00
LRF Ron Francis SP 8.00 20.00
LRT Roman Turek SP 8.00 20.00
LSF Sergei Fedorov SP 15.00 40.00
LSK Sami Kapanen SP 8.00 20.00
LSY Steve Yzerman SP 50.00 125.00
LTA Tony Amonte SP 8.00 20.00
LTS Teemu Selanne SP 12.50 30.00
LVL Vincent Lecavalier SP 12.50 30.00
LZP Zigmund Palffy SP 12.50 30.00
LJAL Jason Allison SP 8.00 20.00
LPBO Peter Bondra SP 8.00 20.00
LPBU Pavel Bure SP 12.50 30.00
LSSA Sergei Samsonov SP 8.00 20.00
LSST Scott Stevens SP 8.00 20.00
LTSA Tommy Salo SP 8.00 20.00
XLDH Dominik Hasek SP 100.00 250.00
XLML Mario Lemieux SP 250.00 500.00
XLMM Mark Messier SP 200.00 400.00
XLMV Mike Vernon SP 30.00 80.00
XLON Owen Nolan SP 40.00 100.00
XLPF Peter Forsberg SP 60.00 150.00
XLWG Wayne Gretzky SP 250.00 500.00

2001-02 BAP Signature Series Autographs Gold

This 297-card set paralleled the base autograph set but carried a gold tone card front. Gold cards were advertised as being more scarce, but no information on production numbers is known at this time.

GOLD: 1X TO 1.5X BASIC AUTO
11 Anson Carter 25.00 60.00
21 Brent Johnson 40.00 100.00
46 Peter White 25.00 60.00
59 Jiri Fischer 40.00 100.00
82 Jan Hlavac 25.00 60.00

2001-02 BAP Signature Series Department of Defense

STATED PRINT RUN 40 SETS
DD-1 Rob Blake 12.50 30.00
DD-2 Brian Leetch 12.50 30.00
DD-3 Nicklas Lidstrom 12.50 30.00
DD-4 Oleg Tverdovsky 12.50 30.00
DD-5 Chris Pronger 12.50 30.00
DD-6 Al MacInnis 12.50 30.00
DD-7 Kyle McLaren 12.50 30.00
DD-8 Sergei Gonchar 12.50 30.00
DD-9 Tomas Kaberle 12.50 30.00
DD-10 Sandis Ozolinsh 12.50 30.00
DD-11 Darius Kasparaitis 12.50 30.00
DD-12 Rostislav Klesla 12.50 30.00

2001-02 BAP Signature Series 500 Goal Scorers

This 28-card set featured game-worn jersey swatches of members of the exclusive 500-goal club. Print runs were varied and are listed below. Cards ML, MM and SY were available in random packs of BAP Update. All cards carried a S500 prefix. Cards with less than 20 copies are not priced due to scarcity.

*MULT.COLOR SWATCH: .5X TO 1.5X HI
STATED PRINT RUNS LISTED BELOW
PRINT RUNS OF 20 OR LESS NOT PRICED DUE TO SCARCITY
UNPRICED AUTOS/10 EXIST
1 Gordie Howe/10
2 Steve Yzerman/30 60.00 150.00
3 Jean Beliveau/20
4 Frank Mahovlich/30 30.00 80.00
5 Stan Mikita/30 30.00 80.00
6 Guy Lafleur/30 25.00 60.00
7 Marcel Dionne/30 10.00 25.00
8 Bobby Hull/20
9 Phil Esposito/30 30.00 80.00
10 Mike Bossy/50 20.00 50.00
11 Luc Robitaille/30 25.00 60.00
12 Jari Kurri/90 10.00 25.00
13 Dave Andreychuk/90 10.00 25.00
14 Mike Gartner/90 10.00 25.00
15 John Bucyk/30 25.00 60.00
16 Michel Goulet/90 10.00 25.00
17 Dino Ciccarelli/90 10.00 25.00
18 Pat Verbeek/90 10.00 25.00
19 Bryan Trottier/50 10.00 25.00
20 Dale Hawerchuk/90 10.00 25.00
21 Gilbert Perreault/90 10.00 25.00
22 Joe Mullen/90 10.00 25.00
23 Lanny McDonald/90 10.00 25.00
24 Brett Hull/30 40.00 80.00
25 Mark Messier/30 50.00 125.00
26 Mario Lemieux/20
27 Maurice Richard/10
28 Ron Francis/10
29 Brendan Shanahan/10
ML Mario Lemieux/10 AU
MM Mark Messier/10 AU
SY Steve Yzerman/10 AU

2001-02 BAP Signature Series Franchise Jerseys

STATED PRINT RUN 28 SETS
FP-1 Paul Kariya 12.50 30.00
FP-2 Ilya Kovalchuk 20.00 50.00
FP-3 Joe Thornton 15.00 40.00
FP-4 Miroslav Satan 12.50 30.00
FP-5 Jarome Iginla 15.00 40.00
FP-6 Sami Kapanen 12.50 30.00
FP-7 Tony Amonte 12.50 30.00
FP-8 Joe Sakic 20.00 50.00
FP-9 Rostislav Klesla 12.50 30.00
FP-10 Mike Modano 15.00 40.00
FP-11 Steve Yzerman 30.00 80.00
FP-12 Tommy Salo 12.50 30.00
FP-13 Pavel Bure 12.50 30.00
FP-14 Zigmund Palffy 12.50 30.00
FP-15 Marian Gaborik 25.00 60.00
FP-16 Jose Theodore 15.00 40.00
FP-17 David Legwand 12.50 30.00
FP-18 Martin Brodeur 30.00 80.00
FP-19 Eric Lindros 12.50 30.00
FP-20 Alexei Yashin 12.50 30.00
FP-21 Daniel Alfredsson 12.50 30.00
FP-22 John LeClair 12.50 30.00
FP-23 Sean Burke 12.50 30.00
FP-24 Mario Lemieux 40.00 100.00
FP-25 Owen Nolan 12.50 30.00
FP-26 Doug Weight 12.50 30.00
FP-27 Vincent Lecavalier 12.50 30.00
FP-28 Mats Sundin 12.50 30.00
FP-29 Markus Naslund 12.50 30.00
FP-30 Jaromir Jagr 20.00 50.00

2001-02 BAP Signature Series He Shoots-He Scores Points

ONE PER PACK
RED.PROGRAM HAS EXPIRED
1 Tony Amonte 1pt. .20 .50
2 Sergei Fedorov 1pt. .20 .50
3 Bill Guerin 1pt. .20 .50
4 John Leclair 1pt. .20 .50
5 Eric Lindros 1pt. .20 .50
6 Mark Messier 1 pt. .20 .50
7 Mike Modano 1pt. .20 .50
8 Luc Robitaille 1pt. .20 .50
9 Jeremy Roenick 1pt. .20 .50
10 Teemu Selanne 1pt. .20 .50
11 Mats Sundin 1pt. .20 .50
12 Pavel Bure 2 pts. .20 .50
13 Jarome Iginla 2 pts. .20 .50
14 Jaromir Jagr 2 pts. .20 .50
15 Paul Kariya 2 pts. .20 .50
16 Ilya Kovalchuk 2 pts. .20 .50
17 Brendan Shanahan 2 pts. .20 .50
18 Mario Lemieux 3 pts. .20 .50
19 Joe Sakic 3 pts. .20 .50
20 Steve Yzerman 3 pts. .20 .50

2001-02 BAP Signature Series He Shoots-He Scores Prizes

STATED PRINT RUN 20 SER.#'d SETS
NOT PRICED DUE TO SCARCITY
1 Steve Yzerman

2 Joe Sakic
3 Mario Lemieux
4 Ron Francis
5 Ilya Kovalchuk
6 Brendan Shanahan
7 Paul Kariya
8 Jaromir Jagr
9 Jarome Iginla
10 Eric Lindros
11 Mats Sundin
12 Teemu Selanne
13 Mike Modano
14 John LeClair
15 Tony Amonte
16 Luc Robitaille
17 Sergei Fedorov
18 Bill Guerin
19 Jeremy Roenick
20 Mark Messier
21 Joe Thornton
22 Sami Kapanen
23 Mark Recchi
23 Alexander Mogilny
24 Sergei Samsonov
25 Saku Koivu
26 Kristian Huselius
27 Milan Hejduk
28 Peter Forsberg
29 Chris Drury
30 Doug Weight
31 Zigmund Palffy
33 Owen Nolan
34 Daniel Alfredsson
35 Markus Naslund
36 Eric Daze
37 Keith Tkachuk
38 Alexei Yashin
39 Peter Bondra
40 Rob Blake

2001-02 BAP Signature Series International Medals

Limited to just 30 copies each, this 42-card set features game-worn jersey swatches from NHL players who participated in the 2002 Winter Olympics. The card fronts carried a color head shot photo of the featured player along with the jersey swatch under the player to appear as if it was a medal around his neck.

STATED PRINT RUN 30 SER.#'d SETS
IB-1 Nikolai Khabibulin 12.50 30.00
IB-2 Sergei Samsonov 12.50 30.00
IB-3 Darius Kasparaitis 12.50 30.00
IB-4 Alexei Yashin 12.50 30.00
IB-5 Oleg Tverdovsky 12.50 30.00
IB-6 Pavel Bure 12.50 30.00
IB-7 Ilya Kovalchuk 15.00 40.00
IB-8 Alexei Kovalev 12.50 30.00
IS-1 Mike Richter 12.50 30.00
IS-2 Tony Amonte 12.50 30.00
IS-3 Chris Chelios 12.50 30.00
IS-4 Doug Weight 12.50 30.00
IS-5 John LeClair 12.50 30.00
IS-6 Mike Modano 15.00 40.00
IS-7 Bill Guerin 12.50 30.00
IS-8 Brian Rolston 12.50 30.00
IG-1 Martin Brodeur 30.00 80.00
IG-2 Rob Blake 12.50 30.00
IG-3 Al MacInnis 12.50 30.00
IG-4 Theo Fleury 12.50 30.00
IG-5 Paul Kariya 12.50 30.00
IG-6 Mario Lemieux 30.00 80.00
IG-7 Eric Lindros 12.50 30.00
IG-8 Steve Yzerman 30.00 80.00

2001-02 BAP Signature Series Jerseys

*MULT.COLOR SWATCH: .5X TO 1.5X HI
GJ1-GJ70 PRINT RUN 60 SETS
GJ71-GJ98 PRINT RUN 90 SETS
GJ71-GJ98 AVAIL.IN BAP UPD.PACKS
GJ-1 Paul Kariya 10.00 25.00
GJ-2 Rostislav Klesla 4.00 10.00
GJ-3 Joe Thornton 12.50 30.00
GJ-4 Martin Havlat 10.00 25.00
GJ-5 Byron Dafoe 10.00 25.00
GJ-6 Dominik Hasek 15.00 40.00
GJ-7 Miroslav Satan 10.00 25.00
GJ-8 Teemu Selanne 10.00 25.00
GJ-9 Jarome Iginla 12.50 30.00
GJ-10 Ron Francis 10.00 25.00
GJ-11 Pierre Turgeon 10.00 25.00
GJ-12 Tony Amonte 10.00 25.00
GJ-13 Henrik Sedin 8.00 20.00
GJ-14 Alex Tanguay 10.00 25.00
GJ-15 Marian Gaborik 12.00 30.00
GJ-16 Joe Sakic 15.00 40.00
GJ-17 Patrick Roy 25.00 60.00
GJ-18 Chris Drury 10.00 25.00
GJ-19 Rob Blake 10.00 25.00
GJ-20 Mike Modano 12.50 30.00
GJ-21 Sergei Fedorov 12.50 30.00
GJ-22 Nicklas Lidstrom 10.00 25.00
GJ-23 Steve Yzerman 20.00 50.00
GJ-24 Milan Hejduk 8.00 20.00
GJ-25 Jeff O'Neill 4.00 10.00
GJ-26 Luc Robitaille 10.00 25.00
GJ-27 Brendan Shanahan 10.00 25.00
GJ-28 Pavel Bure 10.00 25.00
GJ-29 Roberto Luongo 12.50 30.00
GJ-30 Zigmund Palffy 10.00 25.00
GJ-31 Brian Savage 4.00 10.00
GJ-32 Saku Koivu 10.00 25.00
GJ-33 Scott Stevens 10.00 25.00
GJ-34 Scott Gomez 8.00 20.00
GJ-35 Martin Brodeur 20.00 50.00
GJ-36 Jason Arnott 4.00 10.00
GJ-37 Scott Niedermayer 8.00 20.00
GJ-38 Eric Lindros 10.00 25.00
GJ-39 Brian Leetch 10.00 25.00
GJ-40 Mark Messier 10.00 25.00
GJ-41 Mike Richter 10.00 25.00
GJ-42 Kenny Jonsson 8.00 20.00
GJ-43 Alexei Yashin 8.00 20.00
GJ-44 Radek Bonk 8.00 20.00
GJ-45 Ilya Kovalchuk 12.00 30.00
GJ-46 Marian Hossa 10.00 25.00
GJ-47 Roman Cechmanek 4.00 10.00
GJ-48 Mark Recchi 10.00 25.00
GJ-49 John LeClair 10.00 25.00
GJ-50 Brian Boucher 10.00 25.00
GJ-51 Keith Primeau 8.00 20.00
GJ-52 Jeremy Roenick 12.00 30.00
GJ-53 Jaromir Jagr 15.00 40.00
GJ-54 Mario Lemieux 25.00 60.00
GJ-55 Owen Nolan 10.00 25.00
GJ-56 Doug Weight 10.00 25.00
GJ-57 Chris Pronger 10.00 25.00
GJ-58 Al MacInnis 10.00 25.00
GJ-59 Vincent Lecavalier 10.00 25.00
GJ-60 Brad Richards 10.00 25.00
GJ-61 Curtis Joseph 10.00 25.00
GJ-62 Mats Sundin 10.00 25.00
GJ-63 Daniel Sedin 8.00 20.00
GJ-64 Peter Bondra 10.00 25.00
GJ-65 Adam Oates 10.00 25.00
GJ-66 Olaf Kolzig 10.00 25.00
GJ-67 Sergei Gonchar 8.00 20.00
GJ-68 Todd Bertuzzi 10.00 25.00
GJ-69 Theo Fleury 8.00 20.00
GJ-70 Markus Naslund 10.00 25.00
GJ-71 Alexander Mogilny 8.00 20.00
GJ-72 Nikolai Khabibulin 10.00 25.00
GJ-73 Ed Belfour 10.00 25.00
GJ-74 Petr Sykora 4.00 10.00
GJ-75 Peter Forsberg 12.00 30.00
GJ-76 Patrick Lalime 8.00 20.00
GJ-77 Keith Tkachuk 10.00 25.00
GJ-78 Daniel Alfredsson 8.00 20.00
GJ-79 Chris Chelios 10.00 25.00
GJ-80 Sean Burke 4.00 10.00
GJ-81 Eric Daze 4.00 10.00
GJ-82 Patrik Elias 4.00 10.00
GJ-83 Adam Foote 4.00 10.00
GJ-84 Bill Guerin 8.00 20.00
GJ-85 Jose Theodore 12.00 30.00
GJ-86 Sandis Ozolinsh 4.00 10.00
GJ-87 Felix Potvin 10.00 25.00
GJ-88 Tommy Salo 8.00 20.00
GJ-89 Martin Straka 4.00 10.00
GJ-90 Jocelyn Thibault 8.00 20.00
GJ-91 Pavel Bure 10.00 25.00
GJ-92 Roman Turek 4.00 10.00
GJ-93 Sergei Samsonov 8.00 20.00
GJ-94 Dan Cloutier 8.00 20.00
GJ-95 Kristian Huselius 4.00 10.00
GJ-96 Arturs Irbe 8.00 20.00
GJ-97 Sami Kapanen 4.00 10.00
GJ-98 Evgeni Nabokov 8.00 20.00

2001-02 BAP Signature Series Jersey Autographs

This 50-card set featured autographs and game-worn jersey swatches on each card. Each card was serial-numbered out of 10. The Yzerman, Lemieux, Messier, Richter, Bonk, Roenick, Amonte, and Fedorov cards were only available in random BAP Update packs. This set is not priced due to scarcity.

STATED PRINT RUN 10 SER.#'d SETS
NOT PRICED DUE TO SCARCITY
GUAM Al MacInnis
GUAT Alex Tanguay
GUAY Alexei Yashin
GUBB Brian Boucher
GUBD Byron Dafoe
GUBL Brian Leetch
GUBR Brad Richards
GUBS Brendan Shanahan
GUBSA Brian Savage
GUCD Chris Drury
GUCP Chris Pronger
GUDH Dominik Hasek
GUDS Daniel Sedin
GUDW Doug Weight
GUHS Henrik Sedin
GUIK Ilya Kovalchuk
GUJI Jarome Iginla
GUJL John LeClair
GUJO Jeff O'Neill
GUJS Joe Sakic
GUJT Joe Thornton
GUKJ Kenny Jonsson
GUKP Keith Primeau

GULR Luc Robitaille
GUMG Marian Gaborik
GUMH Milan Hejduk
GUMHA Martin Havlat
GUMHO Marian Hossa
GUML Mario Lemieux
GUMME Mark Messier
GUMN Markus Naslund
GUMR Mike Richter
GUMS Miroslav Satan
GUNL Nicklas Lidstrom
GUOK Olaf Kolzig
GUON Owen Nolan
GUPB Pavel Bure
GUPBO Peter Bondra
GUPK Paul Kariya
GUPT Pierre Turgeon
GURB Rob Blake
GURBO Radek Bonk
GURC Roman Cechmanek
GURF Ron Francis
GURK Rostislav Klesla
GURL Roberto Luongo
GUSF Sergei Fedorov
GUSG Sergei Gonchar
GUSN Scott Niedermayer
GUSS Scott Stevens
GUSY Steve Yzerman
GUTB Todd Bertuzzi
GUTS Teemu Selanne
GUVL Vincent Lecavalier
GUZP Zigmund Palffy

2001-02 BAP Signature Series Jersey and Stick Cards

*JERSEY/STICK: .5X TO 1.25X JERSEY CARD
JERSEY/STICK PRINT RUN 60 SETS

2001-02 BAP Signature Series Emblems

STATED PRINT RUN 10 SETS
NOT PRICED DUE TO SCARCITY
GUE-1 Paul Kariya
GUE-2 Ilya Kovalchuk
GUE-3 Joe Thornton
GUE-4 Bill Guerin
GUE-5 Byron Dafoe
GUE-6 Dominik Hasek
GUE-7 Miroslav Satan
GUE-8 Teemu Selanne
GUE-9 Mike Vernon
GUE-10 Ron Francis
GUE-11 Jarome Iginla
GUE-12 Tony Amonte
GUE-13 Mario Lemieux
GUE-14 Peter Forsberg
GUE-15 Joe Sakic
GUE-16 Patrick Roy
GUE-17 Chris Drury
GUE-18 Brendan Shanahan
GUE-19 Mike Modano
GUE-20 Sergei Fedorov
GUE-21 Nicklas Lidstrom
GUE-22 Steve Yzerman
GUE-23 Chris Pronger
GUE-24 Curtis Joseph
GUE-25 Doug Weight
GUE-26 Pavel Bure
GUE-27 Roberto Luongo
GUE-28 Al MacInnis
GUE-29 Jeremy Roenick
GUE-30 Luc Robitaille
GUE-31 Olaf Kolzig
GUE-32 Peter Bondra
GUE-33 Adam Oates
GUE-34 Martin Brodeur
GUE-35 Jason Arnott
GUE-36 Eric Lindros
GUE-37 Brian Leetch
GUE-38 Mark Messier
GUE-39 Mike Richter
GUE-40 Mats Sundin
GUE-41 Owen Nolan
GUE-42 Alexei Yashin
GUE-43 Jaromir Jagr
GUE-44 Daniel Alfredsson
GUE-45 Marian Hossa
GUE-46 Roman Cechmanek
GUE-47 Mark Recchi
GUE-48 John LeClair
GUE-49 Brian Boucher
GUE-50 Vincent Lecavalier

2001-02 BAP Signature Series Numbers

STATED PRINT RUN 10 SETS
NOT PRICED DUE TO SCARCITY

2001-02 BAP Signature Series Teammates

STATED PRINT RUN 40 SETS
TM-1 Paul Kariya 12.50 30.00
Jeff Friesen
TM-2 Patrik Stefan 12.50 30.00
Ilya Kovalchuk
TM-3 Bill Guerin 8.00 20.00
Byron Dafoe
TM-4 Martin Biron 8.00 20.00
Miroslav Satan
TM-5 Jarome Iginla 12.50 30.00
Roman Turek
TM-6 Ron Francis 8.00 20.00
Sami Kapanen
TM-7 Tony Amonte 8.00 20.00
Eric Daze
TM-8 Joe Sakic 40.00 100.00
Patrick Roy
TM-9 Chris Drury 12.50 30.00
Milan Hejduk
TM-10 Mike Modano 15.00 40.00
Ed Belfour
TM-11 Steve Yzerman 20.00 50.00
Brendan Shanahan
TM-12 Luc Robitaille 25.00 60.00
Dominik Hasek
TM-13 Pavel Bure 12.50 30.00
Roberto Luongo
TM-14 Zigmund Palffy 12.50 30.00
Felix Potvin
TM-15 Marian Gaborik 12.50 30.00
Manny Fernandez
TM-16 Brian Savage 15.00 40.00
Jose Theodore
TM-17 Jason Arnott 20.00 50.00
Martin Brodeur
TM-18 Scott Niedermayer 8.00 20.00
Scott Stevens
TM-19 Mark Messier 15.00 40.00
Eric Lindros
TM-20 Kenny Jonsson 8.00 20.00
Alexei Yashin
TM-21 Daniel Alfredsson 12.50 30.00
Patrick Lalime
TM-22 Mark Recchi 12.50 30.00
Jeremy Roenick
TM-23 John LeClair 8.00 20.00
Brian Boucher
TM-24 Mario Lemieux 30.00 80.00
Milan Kraft
TM-25 Owen Nolan 12.50 30.00
Teemu Selanne
TM-26 Doug Weight 8.00 20.00
Keith Tkachuk
TM-27 Vincent Lecavalier 12.50 30.00
Nikolai Khabibulin
TM-28 Mats Sundin 12.50 30.00
Curtis Joseph
TM-29 Daniel Sedin 12.50 30.00
Markus Naslund
TM-30 Peter Bondra 25.00 60.00
Jaromir Jagr

2001-02 BAP Signature Series Vintage Autographs

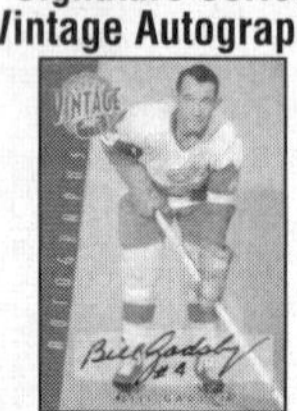

This 40-card set featured autographs of retired NHL stars. Autographs were positioned beneath a full-color player photo on the card fronts. Print runs for each card are listed below. Card #VA16 was supposed to be Woody Dumart, but he passed away before he could sign, therefore that card does not exist.

STATED PRINT RUNS LISTED BELOW
CARD NUMBER VA16 NOT PRODUCED
PRINT RUNS OF 20 OR LESS NOT PRICED DUE TO SCARCITY
VA-1 Tony Esposito/60 25.00 60.00
VA-2 Phil Esposito/40 30.00 80.00
VA-3 Gordie Howe/20 75.00 200.00
VA-4 Gordie Howe/20 75.00 200.00
VA-5 Jean Beliveau/40 25.00 60.00
VA-6 Jean Beliveau/40 25.00 60.00
VA-7 Bobby Hull/40 20.00 50.00
Winnipeg
VA-8 Bobby Hull/40 20.00 50.00
Chicago
VA-9 Ted Lindsay/40 12.50 30.00
VA-10 Johnny Bower/60 12.50 30.00
VA-11 Milt Schmidt/80 20.00 50.00
VA-12 Red Kelly/80 12.50 30.00
VA-13 Glenn Hall/40 15.00 40.00
VA-14 Chuck Rayner/40 20.00 50.00
VA-15 Elmer Lach/80 15.00 40.00
VA-17 Gerry Cheevers/40 20.00 50.00
VA-18 Gump Worsley/40 30.00 80.00
VA-19 Butch Bouchard/80 12.50 30.00
VA-20 Henri Richard/80 12.50 30.00
VA-21 Henri Richard/80 15.00 40.00
VA-22 Bernie Geoffrion/80 20.00 50.00
VA-23 Dollard St. Laurent/80 12.50 30.00
VA-24 Dickie Moore/70 12.50 30.00
VA-25 Jean-Guy Talbot/80 12.50 30.00
VA-26 Bill Gadsby/80 12.50 30.00
VA-27 Frank Mahovlich/40 25.00 60.00
VA-28 Dino Ciccarelli/70 12.50 30.00
VA-29 Jari Kurri/70 15.00 40.00
VA-30 Mike Bossy/70 12.50 30.00
VA-31 Johnny Bucyk/90 12.50 30.00
VA-32 Michel Goulet/90 12.50 30.00
VA-33 Stan Mikita/40 20.00 50.00
VA-34 Bryan Trottier/70 12.50 30.00
VA-35 Dale Hawerchuk/70 15.00 40.00
VA-36 Gilbert Perreault/40 12.50 30.00
VA-37 Marcel Dionne/40 20.00 50.00
VA-38 Mike Gartner/70 12.50 30.00
VA-39 Lanny McDonald/70 12.50 30.00
VA-40 Guy Lafleur/40 40.00 100.00

2002-03 BAP Signature Series

Released in mid-May, this 200-card base set consisted of 177 veterans and 23 rookies.
COMPLETE SET (200) 75.00 150.00
1 Dany Heatley .50 1.25
2 Alexei Zhamnov .20 .50
3 Mike Comrie .30 .75
4 Dwayne Roloson .30 .75
5 Mike Dunham .30 .75
6 Simon Gagne .40 1.00
7 Evgeni Nabokov .30 .75
8 Bryan McCabe .20 .50
9 Todd Bertuzzi .40 1.00
10 Alex Kovalev .30 .75
11 Dave Andreychuk .20 .50
12 Daniel Alfredsson .30 .75
13 Marian Gaborik .75 2.00
14 J-S Aubin .30 .75
15 Andy McDonald .20 .50
16 Brad Richards .30 .75
17 Henrik Sedin .20 .50
18 Mark Bell .20 .50
19 Adam Deadmarsh .20 .50
20 Marc Denis .30 .75
21 Mike York .20 .50
22 Johan Hedberg .30 .75
23 Vincent Damphousse .20 .50
24 Marian Hossa .40 1.00
25 Richard Zednik .20 .50
26 Alexei Yashin .20 .50
27 Sergei Gonchar .20 .50
28 Martin Straka .20 .50
29 Ed Jovanovski .30 .75
30 Robert Lang .20 .50
31 Markus Naslund .40 1.00
32 Mike Sillinger .20 .50
33 Jamie Storr .30 .75
34 Kimmo Timonen .20 .50
35 Patrick Lalime .30 .75
36 Alyn McCauley .20 .50
37 Scott Walker .20 .50
38 Trevor Linden .20 .50
39 Ilya Kovalchuk .50 1.25
40 Jarome Iginla .50 1.25
41 Alex Tanguay .30 .75
42 Yanic Perreault .20 .50
43 Jocelyn Thibault .30 .75
44 Eric Brewer .20 .50
45 Ray Whitney .20 .50
46 Ryan Smyth .20 .50
47 Steven Reinprecht .20 .50
48 Phil Housley .20 .50
49 Milan Hnilicka .30 .75
50 Maxim Afinogenov .20 .50
51 Andrew Brunette .20 .50
52 Miroslav Satan .30 .75
53 Glen Murray .20 .50
54 Mark Parrish .20 .50
55 Daniel Sedin .20 .50
56 Brendan Morrison .30 .75
57 Brian Rafalski .20 .50
58 Dan Cloutier .30 .75
59 Espen Knutsen .20 .50
60 Radim Vrbata .20 .50
61 Patrik Stefan .20 .50
62 Eric Daze .30 .75
63 Felix Potvin .40 1.00
64 Darcy Tucker .20 .50
65 Jose Theodore .50 1.25
66 Scott Hartnell .20 .50
67 Martin Havlat .30 .75
68 Radek Bonk .20 .50
69 Patrick Marleau .30 .75
70 Andy Delmore .20 .50
71 Rostislav Klesla .20 .50
72 David Aebischer .30 .75
73 Steve Shields .30 .75
74 Stu Barnes .20 .50
75 Tim Connolly .20 .50
76 J-S Giguere .30 .75
77 Shane Doan .20 .50
78 Brian Rolston .20 .50
79 Shawn McEachern .20 .50
80 Martin Biron .30 .75
81 Craig Conroy .20 .50
82 Mika Noronen .20 .50
83 Brian Boucher .30 .75
84 Kyle Calder .20 .50
85 Cliff Ronning .20 .50
86 Brian Gionta .20 .50
87 Shawn Bates .20 .50
88 Michal Handzus .20 .50
89 Daniel Briere .20 .50
90 Adam Graves .20 .50
91 Martin St. Louis .30 .75
92 Ladislav Nagy .20 .50
93 Oleg Tverdovsky .20 .50
94 Pavel Brendl .20 .50
95 Alexei Morozov .20 .50
96 Daymond Langkow .20 .50
97 Krys Kolanos .20 .50
98 Sean Burke .30 .75
99 Chris Drury .30 .75
100 Steve Sullivan .20 .50
101 Paul Kariya .40 1.00
102 Peter Forsberg 1.00 2.50
103 Ron Tugnutt .30 .75
104 Manny Legace .30 .75
105 Tommy Salo .30 .75
106 Kristian Huselius .20 .50
107 Jason Allison .20 .50
108 Mariusz Czerkawski .20 .50
109 Jeff Friesen .20 .50
110 Chris Osgood .30 .75
111 Martin Prusek .30 .75
112 Steve Yzerman 1.50 4.00
113 John LeClair .40 1.00
114 Jan Hrdina .20 .50
115 Tony Amonte .30 .75
116 Teemu Selanne .40 1.00
117 Cory Stillman .20 .50
118 Nikolai Khabibulin .40 1.00
119 Mats Sundin .40 1.00
120 Olaf Kolzig .30 .75
121 Petr Sykora .20 .50
122 Joe Thornton .60 1.50
123 Roman Turek .30 .75
124 Derek Morris .20 .50
125 Bill Guerin .30 .75
126 Brendan Shanahan .40 1.00
127 Roberto Luongo .50 1.25
128 Zigmund Palffy .30 .75
129 Pavol Demitra .30 .75
130 Saku Koivu .40 1.00
131 Joe Nieuwendyk .30 .75
132 Mike Peca .20 .50
133 Petr Schastlivy .20 .50
134 Jeremy Roenick .50 1.25
135 Mario Lemieux 2.00 5.00
136 Petr Cajanek .20 .50
137 Vincent Lecavalier .40 1.00
138 Peter Bondra .30 .75
139 Brent Johnson .30 .75
140 Sergei Samsonov .30 .75
141 Joe Sakic .75 2.00
142 Brenden Morrow .30 .75
143 Arturs Irbe .30 .75
144 Chris Chelios .40 1.00
145 Sandis Ozolinsh .20 .50
146 Doug Gilmour .30 .75
147 Scott Stevens .30 .75
148 Sergei Fedorov .60 1.50
149 Keith Primeau .20 .50
150 Eric Boguniecki .20 .50
151 Shane Willis .20 .50
152 Rob Blake .30 .75
153 Luc Robitaille .30 .75
154 Pierre Turgeon .30 .75
155 Curtis Joseph .40 1.00
156 Stephen Weiss .20 .50
157 Patrik Elias .30 .75
158 Mark Recchi .30 .75
159 Al MacInnis .30 .75
160 Patrick Roy 1.50 4.00
161 Darryl Sydor .20 .50
162 Nicklas Lidstrom .40 1.00
163 Doug Weight .30 .75
164 Roman Cechmanek .30 .75
165 Marty Turco .30 .75
166 Pavel Datsyuk .40 1.00
167 Chris Pronger .30 .75
168 Scott Young .20 .50
169 Igor Larionov .20 .50
170 Keith Tkachuk .40 1.00
171 Ron Francis .30 .75
172 Dan Blackburn .30 .75
173 Jeff O'Neill .20 .50
174 Bobby Holik .20 .50
175 Erik Cole .20 .50
176 Pavel Bure .40 1.00
177 Brian Leetch .30 .75
178 Curtis Sanford RC 1.50 4.00
179 Carlo Colaiacovo RC 1.50 4.00
180 Dennis Seidenberg RC 1.50 4.00
181 Adam Hall RC 1.25 3.00
182 Ivan Majesky RC 1.25 3.00
183 Rick Nash RC 4.00 10.00
184 Alexei Smirnov RC 1.25 3.00
185 Chuck Kobasew RC 1.50 4.00
186 Ron Hainsey RC 1.25 3.00
187 Stephane Veilleux RC 1.25 3.00
188 Scottie Upshall RC 1.50 4.00
189 Lasse Pirjeta RC 1.25 3.00
190 Henrik Zetterberg RC 4.00 10.00
191 Jay Bouwmeester RC 2.00 5.00
192 Alexander Frolov RC 2.50 6.00
193 Dmitri Bykov RC 1.25 3.00
194 Stanislav Chistov RC 1.50 4.00
195 Jordan Leopold RC 1.25 3.00
196 P-M Bouchard RC 2.50 6.00
197 Mike Cammalleri RC 1.50 4.00
198 Anton Volchenkov RC 1.25 3.00
199 Lynn Loyns RC 1.25 3.00
200 Steve Eminger RC 1.25 3.00

2002-03 BAP Signature Series All-Rookie

This 12-card set featured game-worn equipment from some of the leagues most promising young players. Each card was limited to just 50 copies.
*MULT.COLOR SWATCH: .75X TO 1.5X
STATED PRINT RUN 50 SETS
AR1 Ryan Miller 15.00 40.00
AR2 Jay Bouwmeester 15.00 40.00
AR3 Dennis Seidenberg 10.00 25.00
AR4 Stephen Weiss 12.00 30.00
AR5 Marcel Hossa 12.00 30.00
AR6 Radovan Somik 10.00 25.00
AR7 Jan Lasak 10.00 25.00
AR8 Jordan Leopold 10.00 25.00
AR9 Barret Jackman 12.00 30.00
AR10 Mike Cammalleri 15.00 40.00
AR11 Henrik Zetterberg Skate 20.00 50.00
AR12 Rick Nash 20.00 50.00

2002-03 BAP Signature Series Autographs

This 200-card set paralleled the base set but carried certified autographs on the card fronts. They were inserted one per pack and short prints are designated below.
ONE PER PACK
*GOLD: .75X TO 1.25X
1 Dany Heatley 8.00 20.00
2 Alexei Zhamnov 2.00 5.00
3 Mike Comrie 4.00 10.00
4 Dwayne Roloson 4.00 10.00
5 Mike Dunham 4.00 10.00
6 Simon Gagne 6.00 15.00
7 Evgeni Nabokov 4.00 10.00
8 Bryan McCabe 2.00 5.00
9 Todd Bertuzzi 4.00 10.00
10 Alexei Kovalev 4.00 10.00
11 Dave Andreychuk 4.00 10.00
12 Daniel Alfredsson 4.00 10.00
13 Marian Gaborik 12.50 30.00
14 J-S Aubin 2.00 5.00
15 Andy McDonald 2.00 5.00
16 Brad Richards 4.00 10.00
17 Henrik Sedin 2.00 5.00
18 Mark Bell 2.00 5.00
19 Adam Deadmarsh 2.00 5.00
20 Marc Denis 4.00 10.00
21 Mike York 2.00 5.00
22 Johan Hedberg 2.00 5.00
23 Vincent Damphousse 2.00 5.00
24 Marian Hossa 6.00 15.00
25 Richard Zednik 2.00 5.00
26 Alexei Yashin 2.00 5.00
27 Sergei Gonchar 2.00 5.00
28 Martin Straka 2.00 5.00
29 Ed Jovanovski 4.00 10.00
30 Robert Lang 2.00 5.00
31 Markus Naslund 6.00 15.00
32 Mike Sillinger 2.00 5.00
33 Jamie Storr 2.00 5.00
34 Kimmo Timonen 2.00 5.00
35 Patrick Lalime 2.00 5.00
36 Alyn McCauley 2.00 5.00
37 Scott Walker 2.00 5.00
38 Trevor Linden 4.00 10.00
39 Ilya Kovalchuk 12.50 30.00
40' Jarome Iginla 8.00 20.00
41 Alex Tanguay 4.00 10.00
42 Yanic Perreault 2.00 5.00
43 Jocelyn Thibault 2.00 5.00
44 Eric Brewer 2.00 5.00
45 Ray Whitney 2.00 5.00
46 Ryan Smyth 2.00 5.00
47 Steven Reinprecht 2.00 5.00
48 Phil Housley 2.00 5.00
49 Milan Hnilicka 2.00 5.00
50 Maxim Afinogenov 2.00 5.00
51 Andrew Brunette 2.00 5.00
52 Miroslav Satan 4.00 10.00
53 Glen Murray 2.00 5.00
54 Mark Parrish 2.00 5.00
55 Daniel Sedin 2.00 5.00
56 Brendan Morrison 2.00 5.00
57 Brian Rafalski 2.00 5.00
58 Dan Cloutier 4.00 10.00
59 Espen Knutsen 2.00 5.00
60 Radim Vrbata 2.00 5.00
61 Patrik Stefan 2.00 5.00
62 Eric Daze 2.00 5.00
63 Felix Potvin 4.00 10.00
64 Darcy Tucker 2.00 5.00
65 Jose Theodore 6.00 15.00
66 Scott Hartnell 2.00 5.00
67 Martin Havlat 4.00 10.00
68 Radek Bonk 2.00 5.00
69 Patrick Marleau 4.00 10.00
70 Andy Delmore 2.00 5.00
71 Rostislav Klesla 2.00 5.00
72 David Aebischer 4.00 10.00
73 Steve Shields 2.00 5.00
74 Stu Barnes 2.00 5.00
75 Tim Connolly 2.00 5.00
76 J-S Giguere 6.00 15.00
77 Shane Doan 2.00 5.00
78 Brian Rolston 2.00 5.00
79 Shawn McEachern 2.00 5.00
80 Martin Biron 2.00 5.00
81 Craig Conroy 2.00 5.00
82 Mika Noronen 2.00 5.00
83 Brian Boucher 2.00 5.00
84 Kyle Calder 2.00 5.00
85 Cliff Ronning 2.00 5.00
86 Brian Gionta 2.00 5.00
87 Shawn Bates 2.00 5.00
88 Michal Handzus 2.00 5.00
89 Daniel Briere 4.00 10.00
90 Adam Graves 2.00 5.00
91 Martin St. Louis 4.00 10.00
92 Ladislav Nagy 2.00 5.00
93 Oleg Tverdovsky 2.00 5.00
94 Pavel Brendl 2.00 5.00
95 Alexei Morozov 2.00 5.00
96 Daymond Langkow 2.00 5.00
97 Krys Kolanos 2.00 5.00
98 Sean Burke 4.00 10.00
99 Chris Drury 4.00 10.00
100 Steve Sullivan 2.00 5.00
101 Paul Kariya SP 15.00 40.00
102 Peter Forsberg SP 25.00 60.00
103 Ron Tugnutt SP 8.00 20.00
104 Manny Legace 4.00 10.00
105 Tommy Salo SP 8.00 20.00
106 Kristian Huselius 2.00 5.00
107 Jason Allison SP 8.00 20.00
108 Mariusz Czerkawski 2.00 5.00
109 Jeff Friesen SP 8.00 20.00
110 Chris Osgood SP 8.00 20.00
111 Martin Prusek 2.00 5.00
112 Steve Yzerman SP 30.00 80.00
113 John LeClair SP 8.00 20.00
114 Jan Hrdina 2.00 5.00
115 Tony Amonte SP 8.00 20.00
116 Teemu Selanne SP 8.00 20.00
117 Cory Stillman 2.00 5.00
118 Nikolai Khabibulin SP 10.00 25.00
119 Mats Sundin SP 20.00 50.00
120 Olaf Kolzig SP 12.00 30.00
121 Petr Sykora 8.00 20.00
122 Joe Thornton SP 15.00 40.00
123 Roman Turek SP 8.00 20.00
124 Derek Morris SP 8.00 20.00
125 Bill Guerin SP 8.00 20.00
126 Brendan Shanahan SP 15.00 40.00
127 Roberto Luongo 8.00 20.00
128 Zigmund Palffy SP 8.00 20.00
129 Pavol Demitra SP 8.00 20.00
130 Saku Koivu SP 8.00 20.00
131 Joe Nieuwendyk SP 8.00 20.00
132 Mike Peca SP 8.00 20.00
133 Petr Schastlivy 2.00 5.00
134 Jeremy Roenick SP 15.00 40.00
135 Mario Lemieux SP 125.00 300.00
136 Petr Cajanek 2.00 5.00
137 Vincent Lecavalier SP 12.00 30.00
138 Peter Bondra SP 8.00 20.00
139 Brent Johnson SP 8.00 20.00
140 Sergei Samsonov SP 8.00 20.00
141 Joe Sakic SP 20.00 50.00
142 Brenden Morrow 4.00 10.00
143 Arturs Irbe 2.00 5.00
144 Chris Chelios SP 12.50 30.00
145 Sandis Ozolinsh 2.00 5.00
146 Doug Gilmour SP 8.00 20.00
147 Scott Stevens SP 10.00 25.00
148 Sergei Fedorov SP 12.50 30.00
149 Keith Primeau SP 8.00 20.00
150 Eric Boguniecki 2.00 5.00
151 Shane Willis 2.00 5.00
152 Rob Blake SP 8.00 20.00
153 Luc Robitaille SP 12.50 30.00
154 Pierre Turgeon SP 8.00 20.00
155 Curtis Joseph SP 12.50 30.00
156 Stephen Weiss 2.00 5.00
157 Patrik Elias SP 8.00 20.00
158 Mark Recchi SP 8.00 20.00
159 Al MacInnis SP 8.00 20.00
160 Patrick Roy SP 60.00 150.00
161 Darryl Sydor SP 8.00 20.00
162 Nicklas Lidstrom SP 15.00 40.00
163 Doug Weight SP 8.00 20.00
164 Roman Cechmanek 2.00 5.00
165 Marty Turco 4.00 10.00
166 Pavel Datsyuk 12.50 30.00
167 Chris Pronger SP 8.00 20.00
168 Scott Young 2.00 5.00
169 Igor Larionov SP 10.00 25.00
170 Keith Tkachuk SP 8.00 20.00
171 Ron Francis SP 8.00 20.00
172 Dan Blackburn 2.00 5.00
173 Jeff O'Neill SP 8.00 20.00
174 Bobby Holik SP 8.00 20.00
175 Erik Cole 2.00 5.00
176 Pavel Bure SP 8.00 20.00
177 Brian Leetch SP 8.00 20.00
178 Curtis Sanford 4.00 10.00
179 Carlo Colaiacovo 2.00 5.00
180 Dennis Seidenberg 2.00 5.00
181 Adam Hall 2.00 5.00
182 Ivan Majesky 2.00 5.00
183 Rick Nash 15.00 40.00
184 Alexei Smirnov 2.00 5.00
185 Chuck Kobasew 2.00 5.00
186 Ron Hainsey 2.00 5.00
187 Stephane Veilleux 2.00 5.00
188 Scottie Upshall 4.00 10.00
189 Lasse Pirjeta 2.00 5.00
190 Henrik Zetterberg 20.00 50.00
191 Jay Bouwmeester 6.00 15.00
192 Alexander Frolov 6.00 15.00
193 Dmitri Bykov 2.00 5.00
194 Stanislav Chistov 2.00 5.00
195 Jordan Leopold 2.00 5.00
196 P-M Bouchard 4.00 10.00
197 Mike Cammalleri 4.00 10.00
198 Anton Volchenkov 2.00 5.00
199 Lynn Loyns 2.00 5.00
200 Steve Eminger 2.00 5.00

2002-03 BAP Signature Series Autograph Buybacks 1998

Available randomly in packs of 2002-03 BAP Signature Series, these cards were older BAP autograph cards that were "bought back" by ITG and inserted into the product on a average of two per box. These cards are distinguishable by the silver foil "10th Anniversary" stamp they carry on the card fronts. Several different years are represented in this buyback series.
*BUYBACKS: .6X TO 1.5X ORIGINAL VALUES

2002-03 BAP Signature Series Autograph Buybacks 1999

*BUYBACKS: .6X TO 1.5X ORIGINAL VALUES

2002-03 BAP Signature Series Autograph Buybacks 2000

*BUYBACKS: .6X TO 1.5X ORIGINAL VALUES

2002-03 BAP Signature Series Autograph Buybacks 2001

*BUYBACKS: .6X TO 1.5X ORIGINAL VALUES

2002-03 BAP Signature Series Complete Jersey

This 10-card set featured four swatches c game-used jersey, including pieces c emblems and numbers. Cards were limite to 10 copies each and are not priced due t scarcity.
STATED PRINT RUN 10 SETS
NOT PRICED DUE TO SCARCITY
CJ1 Mario Lemieux
CJ2 Patrick Roy
CJ3 Steve Yzerman
CJ4 Paul Kariya
CJ5 Jaromir Jagr
CJ6 Marian Gaborik
CJ7 Peter Forsberg
CJ8 Pavel Bure
CJ9 Joe Sakic
CJ10 Teemu Selanne

2002-03 BAP Signature Series Defensive Wall

This 10-card set featured pieces of game used jersey from starting defensive trios Each card was limited to 50 copies each.
STATED PRINT RUN 50 SETS
DW1 Rob Blake 40.00 100.00
Patrick Roy
Adam Foote
DW2 Tomas Kaberle 25.00 60.00
Ed Belfour
Bryan McCabe
DW3 Eric Desjardins 15.00 40.00
Roman Cechmanek
Dennis Seidenberg
DW4 Brian Leetch 15.00 40.00
Dan Blackburn
Darius Kasparitis
DW5 Sergei Zubov 25.00 60.00
Marty Turco
Derian Hatcher
DW6 Scott Stevens 30.00 80.00
Martin Brodeur
Scott Niedermayer
DW7 Chris Pronger 15.00 40.00
Brent Johnson
Al MacInnis
DW8 Wade Redden 15.00 40.00
Patrick Lalime
Chris Phillips
DW9 Brendan Witt 15.00 40.00
Olaf Kolzig
Sergei Gonchar
DW10 Ed Jovanovski 15.00 40.00
Dan Cloutier
Mattias Ohlund

2002-03 BAP Signature Series Famous Scraps

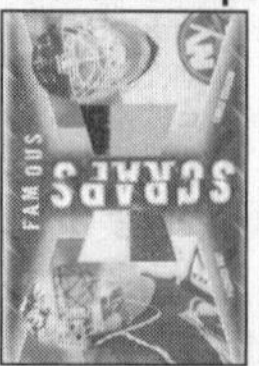

This 12-card set highlighted two player who have "mixed it up" at various time during their careers. Each card was limted t just 50 copies and carried pieces of jerse from each player.
STATED PRINT RUN 50 SETS
FS1 Dave Schultz 20.00 50.00
Dave Williams
FS2 Bob Probert 20.00 50.00

Wendel Clark
S3 Ian Laperriere 20.00 50.00
Bill Guerin
S4 Peter Worrell 20.00 50.00
Chris Gratton
S5 Bill Guerin 20.00 50.00
Jarome Iginla
S6 Tie Domi 30.00 80.00
Rob Ray
S7 Mike Comrie 20.00 50.00
Ilya Kovalchuk
S8 Felix Potvin 20.00 50.00
Ron Hextall
S9 Owen Nolan 20.00 50.00
Bob Probert
S10 Patrick Roy 30.00 80.00
Chris Osgood
S11 Donald Brashear 20.00 50.00
Georges Laraque
S12 Matt Johnson 20.00 50.00
Sandy McCarthy

2002-03 BAP Signature Series Franchise Players

MULT.COLOR SWATCH: .75X TO 1.5X
STATED PRINT RUN 50 SETS
J1 Paul Kariya 8.00 20.00
J2 Dany Heatley 12.50 30.00
J3 Joe Thornton 15.00 40.00
J4 Miroslav Satan 8.00 20.00
J5 Jarome Iginla 10.00 25.00
J6 Ron Francis 8.00 20.00
J7 Jocelyn Thibault 8.00 20.00
J8 Rick Nash 15.00 40.00
J9 Joe Sakic 15.00 40.00
J10 Mike Modano 12.50 30.00
J11 Steve Yzerman 20.00 50.00
J12 Mike Comrie 8.00 20.00
J13 Roberto Luongo 12.50 30.00
J14 Jason Allison 8.00 20.00
J15 Marian Gaborik 15.00 40.00
J16 Jose Theodore 8.00 20.00
J17 David Legwand 8.00 20.00
J18 Martin Brodeur 20.00 50.00
J19 Mike Peca 8.00 20.00
J20 Pavel Bure 8.00 20.00
J21 Marian Hossa 8.00 20.00
J22 Jeremy Roenick 10.00 25.00
J23 Daniel Briere 8.00 20.00
J24 Mario Lemieux 20.00 50.00
J25 Teemu Selanne 8.00 20.00
J26 Chris Pronger 8.00 20.00
J27 Vincent Lecavalier 8.00 20.00
J28 Mats Sundin 8.00 20.00
J29 Markus Naslund 8.00 20.00
J30 Jaromir Jagr 12.50 30.00

2002-03 BAP Signature Series Golf

his 100-card set was inserted one per pack nd pictured players enjoying the game of olf.
OMPLETE SET (100) 50.00 100.00
NE PER PACK
S1 Adam Foote .50 1.25
S2 Adam Oates .50 1.25
S3 Adrian Aucoin .30 .75
S4 Alex Tanguay .50 1.25
S5 Alexander Mogilny .50 1.25
S6 Alexei Yashin .30 .75
S7 Alyn McCauley .30 .75
S8 Andy McDonald .30 .75
S9 Brian Leetch .50 1.25
S10 Bates Battaglia .30 .75
S11 Bobby Holik .30 .75
S12 Brad Isbister .30 .75
S13 Brendan Morrison .50 1.25
S14 Arturs Irbe .50 1.25
S15 Brian Savage .30 .75
S16 Bryan Marchment .30 .75
S17 Bryan McCabe .30 .75
S18 Carlo Colaiacovo .30 .75
S19 Chris Drury .50 1.25
S20 Chris Gratton .30 .75
S21 Chris Neil .30 .75
S22 Chris Osgood .50 1.25
S23 Chris Simon .30 .75
S24 Curtis Joseph .60 1.50
S25 Daniel Sedin .30 .75
S26 Darius Kasparaitis .30 .75
S27 Darren McCarty .30 .75
S28 Darryl Sittler .60 1.50
S29 David Aebischer .50 1.25
S30 David Legwand .50 1.25
S31 Denis Arkhipov .30 .75
S32 Derek Morris .30 .75
S33 Donald Brashear .30 .75
S34 Doug Gilmour .50 1.25
S35 Ed Belfour .60 1.50
S36 Ed Jovanovski .50 1.25
GS37 Erik Cole .30 .75
GS38 Eric Lindros .60 1.50
GS39 Grant Fuhr .50 1.25
GS40 Jaroslav Svoboda .30 .75
GS41 Jeff O'Neill .30 .75
GS42 Jarome Iginla .75 2.00
GS43 Joe Sakic 1.25 3.00
GS44 Johan Hedberg .50 1.25
GS45 Josef Vasicek .30 .75
GS46 J-S Giguere .50 1.25
GS47 Kenny Jonsson .30 .75
GS48 Luc Robitaille .50 1.25
GS49 Mario Lemieux 4.00 10.00
GS50 Mark Parrish .30 .75
GS51 Martin Brodeur 1.50 4.00
GS52 Martin Erat .30 .75
GS53 Martin Skoula .30 .75
GS54 Mats Sundin .60 1.50
GS55 Matt Cooke .30 .75
GS56 Mattias Ohlund .30 .75
GS57 Mike Dunham .50 1.25
GS58 Mike Fisher .30 .75
GS59 Mike Keane .30 .75
GS60 Mike Peca .30 .75
GS61 Mike Ricci .30 .75
GS62 Milan Hejduk .60 1.50
GS63 Miroslav Satan .50 1.25
GS64 Nik Antropov .30 .75
GS65 Olaf Kolzig .50 1.25
GS66 Owen Nolan .50 1.25
GS67 Pat Verbeek .30 .75
GS68 Patrick Marleau .50 1.25
GS69 Patrick Roy 3.00 8.00
GS70 Paul Kariya .60 1.50
GS71 Peter Bondra .50 1.25
GS72 Peter Forsberg 1.50 4.00
GS73 Petr Sykora .30 .75
GS74 Radek Dvorak .30 .75
GS75 Rick DiPietro .50 1.25
GS76 Rob Blake .50 1.25
GS77 Robert Lang .30 .75
GS78 Roman Hamrlik .30 .75
GS79 Dany Heatley .50 1.25
GS80 Ron Francis .50 1.25
GS81 Ryan Smyth .30 .75
GS82 Sami Kapanen .30 .75
GS83 Scott Hartnell .30 .75
GS84 Scott Stevens .50 1.25
GS85 Scott Walker .30 .75
GS86 Stan Mikita .75 2.00
GS87 Stanislav Chistov .30 .75
GS88 Steve Konowalchuk .30 .75
GS89 Steve Rucchin .30 .75
GS90 Steve Yzerman 3.00 8.00
GS91 Stephen Peat .30 .75
GS92 Steven Reinprecht .30 .75
GS93 Teemu Selanne .60 1.50
GS94 Tie Domi .50 1.25
GS95 Todd Bertuzzi .60 1.50
GS96 Todd White .30 .75
GS97 Tom Poti .30 .75
GS98 Trent Klatt .30 .75
GS99 Trevor Kidd .50 1.25
GS100 Wade Redden .30 .75

2002-03 BAP Signature Series Jerseys

*MULT.COLOR SWATCH: .75X TO 1.5X
STATED PRINT RUN 90 SETS
SGJ1 Mario Lemieux 20.00 50.00
SGJ2 Steve Yzerman 20.00 50.00
SGJ3 Peter Forsberg 12.50 30.00
SGJ4 Patrick Roy 20.00 50.00
SGJ5 Jarome Iginla 10.00 25.00
SGJ6 Pavel Bure 8.00 20.00
SGJ7 Jaromir Jagr 10.00 25.00
SGJ8 Eric Lindros 8.00 20.00
SGJ9 Paul Kariya 8.00 20.00
SGJ10 Ilya Kovalchuk 10.00 25.00
SGJ11 Mike Modano 10.00 25.00
SGJ12 Joe Thornton 12.50 30.00
SGJ13 Jose Theodore 10.00 25.00
SGJ14 Jeremy Roenick 10.00 25.00
SGJ15 Martin Brodeur 20.00 50.00
SGJ16 Mats Sundin 8.00 20.00
SGJ17 Mark Messier 8.00 20.00
SGJ18 Alexei Yashin 6.00 15.00
SGJ19 Marian Gaborik 12.50 30.00
SGJ20 Brendan Shanahan 8.00 20.00
SGJ21 Owen Nolan 6.00 15.00
SGJ22 Joe Sakic 12.50 30.00
SGJ23 Daniel Alfredsson 6.00 15.00
SGJ24 Teemu Selanne 8.00 20.00
SGJ25 Nicklas Lidstrom 8.00 20.00
SGJ26 John LeClair 8.00 20.00
SGJ27 Keith Tkachuk 8.00 20.00
SGJ28 Brian Leetch 6.00 15.00
SGJ29 Milan Hejduk 8.00 20.00
SGJ30 Dany Heatley 10.00 25.00
SGJ31 Sergei Samsonov 6.00 15.00
SGJ32 Todd Bertuzzi 8.00 20.00
SGJ33 Markus Naslund 8.00 20.00
SGJ34 Chris Chelios 8.00 20.00
SGJ35 Rob Blake 6.00 15.00
SGJ36 Sergei Fedorov 10.00 25.00
SGJ37 Al MacInnis 6.00 15.00
SGJ38 Luc Robitaille 6.00 15.00
SGJ39 Martin Havlat 6.00 15.00
SGJ40 Ron Francis 6.00 15.00
SGJ41 Alexander Mogilny 6.00 15.00
SGJ42 Chris Pronger 6.00 15.00
SGJ43 Doug Weight 6.00 15.00
SGJ44 Zigmund Palffy 8.00 20.00
SGJ45 Peter Bondra 6.00 15.00
SGJ46 Mike Comrie 6.00 15.00
SGJ47 Pavel Datsyuk 10.00 25.00
SGJ48 Marian Hossa 8.00 20.00
SGJ49 Saku Koivu 8.00 20.00
SGJ50 Dan Blackburn 6.00 15.00
SGJ51 Steve Shields 6.00 15.00
SGJ52 Bill Guerin 6.00 15.00
SGJ53 Doug Gilmour 6.00 15.00
SGJ54 Jason Spezza 12.50 30.00
SGJ55 Jay Bouwmeester 6.00 15.00
SGJ56 Alexei Smirnov 6.00 15.00
SGJ57 Stanislav Chistov 6.00 15.00
SGJ58 Chuck Kobasew 6.00 15.00
SGJ59 Jordan Leopold 6.00 15.00
SGJ60 Niko Kapanen 6.00 15.00
SGJ61 Scottie Upshall 6.00 15.00
SGJ62 Ron Hainsey 6.00 15.00
SGJ63 Alexander Frolov 6.00 15.00
SGJ64 Mike Cammalleri 6.00 15.00
SGJ65 Dennis Seidenberg 6.00 15.00
SGJ66 Rick Nash 10.00 25.00
SGJ67 Carlo Colaiacovo 6.00 15.00
SGJ68 Marty Turco 6.00 15.00
SGJ69 Alex Kovalev 6.00 15.00
SGJ70 Vincent Lecavalier 6.00 15.00

2002-03 BAP Signature Series Jersey Autographs

PRINT RUN 10 SER.#'d SETS
NOT PRICED DUE TO SCARCITY

2002-03 BAP Signature Series Magnificent Inserts

This 10-card set featured game-used equipment from the career of Mario Lemieux. Cards MI1-MI5 had a print run of 40 copies each and cards MI6-MI10 were limited to just 10 copies each. Cards MI6-MI10 are not priced due to scarcity.
MI1-MI5 PRINT RUN 40 SETS
MI6-MI10 PRINT RUN 10 SETS
MI6-MI10 NOT PRICED DUE TO SCARCITY
MI1 2000-01 Season 30.00 80.00
MI2 1985-86 Season 30.00 80.00
MI3 2002 NHL All-Star 30.00 80.00
MI4 1987 Canada Cup 30.00 80.00
MI5 Dual Jersey 50.00 125.00
MI6 Number
MI7 Emblem
MI8 Triple Jersey
MI9 Quad Jersey
MI10 Complete Package

2002-03 BAP Signature Series Magnificent Inserts Autographs

This 10-card set paralleled the base Magnificent Inserts but carried certified autographs and each card was hand numbered. Cards MI1-MI5 were serial-numbered to 15 each and cards MI6-MI10 were serial numbered out of 5.
MI1-MI4 PRINT RUN 15 SETS
MI5-MI10 PRINT RUN 5 SETS
NOT PRICED DUE TO SCARCITY

2002-03 BAP Signature Series Phenoms

This 12-card set featured players in their 4th year in the league and included swatches of game jerseys. Cards were limited to just 40 copies each.
*MULT.COLOR SWATCH: .75X TO 1.5X
STATED PRINT RUN 40 SETS
YP1 Mike Fisher 10.00 25.00
YP2 Simon Gagne 10.00 25.00
YP3 Scott Gomez 10.00 25.00
YP4 David Legwand 10.00 25.00
YP5 Patrik Stefan 10.00 25.00
YP6 Brad Stuart 10.00 25.00
YP7 Alex Tanguay 10.00 25.00
YP8 Brent Johnson 10.00 25.00
YP9 Roberto Luongo 20.00 50.00
YP10 Evgeni Nabokov 10.00 25.00
YP11 Nik Antropov 20.00 50.00
YP12 Espen Knutsen 10.00 25.00

2002-03 BAP Signature Series Team Quads

Limited to just 10 copies each, this 20-card set featured jersey swatches from four teammates. This set is not priced due to scarcity.
STATED PRINT RUN 10 SETS
NOT PRICED DUE TO SCARCITY
TQ1 Joe Sakic
Peter Forsberg
Rob Blake
Patrick Roy
TQ2 Ed Belfour
Mats Sundin
Alexander Mogilny
Tie Domi
TQ3 Jeremy Roenick
John LeClair
Mark Recchi
Roman Cechmanek
TQ4 Eric Lindros
Brian Leetch
Pavel Bure
Dan Blackburn
TQ5 Roberto Luongo
Kristian Huselius
Jay Bouwmeester
Stephen Weiss
TQ6 Saku Koivu
Marcel Hossa
Doug Gilmour
Jose Theodore
TQ7 Scott Stevens
Scott Niedermayer
Martin Brodeur
Patrik Elias
TQ8 Mario Lemieux
Alex Kovalev
Johan Hedberg
Martin Straka
TQ9 Jaromir Jagr
Peter Bondra
Olaf Kolzig
Sergei Gonchar
TQ10 Felix Potvin
Alexander Frolov
Jason Allison
Adam Deadmarsh
TQ11 Steve Shields
Sergei Samsonov
Joe Thornton
Glen Murray
TQ12 Dany Heatley
Ilya Kovalchuk
Pasi Nurminen
Patrik Stefan
TQ13 Steve Yzerman
Sergei Fedorov
Brett Hull
Nicklas Lidstrom
TQ14 Todd Bertuzzi
Markus Naslund
Henrik Sedin
Daniel Sedin
TQ15 Keith Tkachuk
Chris Pronger
Doug Weight
Al MacInnis
TQ16 Marty Turco
Jason Arnott
Mike Modano
Bill Guerin
TQ17 Eric Brewer
Georges Laraque
Mike Comrie
Tommy Salo
TQ18 Vincent Damphousse
Teemu Selanne
Evgeni Nabokov
Owen Nolan
TQ19 Adam Oates
Paul Kariya
J-S Giguere
Stanislav Chistov
TQ20 Patrick Lalime
Marian Hossa
Martin Havlat
Jason Spezza

2002-03 BAP Signature Series Triple Memorabilia

STATED PRINT RUN 30 SETS
TM1 Mario Lemieux 100.00 250.00
TM2 Mats Sundin 20.00 50.00
TM3 Steve Yzerman 60.00 150.00
TM4 Joe Thornton 30.00 80.00
TM5 Eric Lindros 20.00 50.00
TM6 Patrick Roy 60.00 150.00
TM7 Brett Hull 30.00 80.00
TM8 Sergei Fedorov 30.00 80.00
TM9 Martin Brodeur 50.00 125.00
TM10 Joe Sakic 30.00 80.00

2000-01 BAP Ultimate Memorabilia Autographs

Be A Player Ultimate Memorabilia was released in May 2001 and boasted one memorabilia card per pack and a SRP of approximately $100 per pack. There were 5 packs in a box and 1 card per pack. This 50-card set featured certified player autographs under color action photos on silver and purple die-cut card stock. Each card in Ultimate Memorabilia was sealed in a clear plastic slab with a descriptive label at the top.
STATED PRINT RUN 90 SER.#'d SETS
GOLD AUTO STAT.PRINT RUN 10 SER.#'d SETS
GOILD NOT PRICED DUE TO SCARCITY
1 Theo Fleury 10.00 25.00
2 Brendan Shanahan 15.00 40.00
3 Curtis Joseph 15.00 40.00
4 Saku Koivu 15.00 40.00
5 Olaf Kolzig 10.00 25.00
6 Al MacInnis 10.00 25.00
7 John LeClair 15.00 40.00
8 Teemu Selanne 15.00 40.00
9 Wayne Gretzky 150.00 350.00
10 Pavel Bure 15.00 40.00
11 Mario Lemieux 100.00 250.00
12 Milan Hejduk 15.00 40.00
13 Ray Bourque 25.00 60.00
14 Daniel Alfredsson 10.00 25.00
15 Mats Sundin 15.00 40.00
16 Paul Kariya 15.00 40.00
17 Scott Gomez 10.00 25.00
18 Eric Lindros 15.00 40.00
19 Sergei Fedorov 20.00 50.00
20 Peter Forsberg 25.00 60.00
21 Vincent Lecavalier 10.00 25.00
22 Tony Amonte
23 Patrick Roy 60.00 150.00
24 Ed Belfour 15.00 40.00
25 Martin Brodeur 40.00 100.00
26 Brian Leetch 10.00 25.00
27 Mike Modano 20.00 50.00
28 Joe Sakic 40.00 100.00
29 Jeremy Roenick 15.00 40.00
30 Steve Yzerman 60.00 150.00
31 Nikolai Khabibulin 10.00 25.00
32 Roman Turek 10.00 25.00
33 Keith Primeau 10.00 25.00
34 Mike Richter 15.00 40.00
35 Patrik Stefan 10.00 25.00
36 Scott Stevens 10.00 25.00
37 Valeri Bure 10.00 25.00
38 Doug Weight 10.00 25.00
39 Nicklas Lidstrom 15.00 40.00
40 Chris Drury 10.00 25.00
41 Mike Peca 10.00 25.00
42 Chris Pronger 10.00 25.00
43 Rob Blake 10.00 25.00
44 Luc Robitaille 10.00 25.00
45 Joe Thornton 25.00 60.00
46 Jason Arnott 10.00 25.00
47 Daniel Sedin 10.00 25.00
48 Pierre Turgeon 10.00 25.00
49 Brad Stuart 10.00 25.00
50 Adam Oates 10.00 25.00

2000-01 BAP Ultimate Memorabilia Active Eight

This 8-card set featured three players on each card along with a game-used jersey swatch of each. Each card recognized the three statistical leaders in a featured category. Each card was sealed in a clear plastic slab with a descriptive label at the top. Stated print run on these cards was 30 sets.
*MULT.COLOR SWATCH: 1X TO 1.5X HI
STATED PRINT RUN 30 SERIAL #'d SETS
AE1 Messier/Yzerman/Lemieux 200.00 400.00
AE2 Messier/Yzerman/Francis 60.00 150.00
AE3 Lemieux/Hull/Bure 75.00 200.00
AE4 Mario Lemieux 150.00 300.00
Eric Lindros
Jaromir Jagr
AE5 Patrick Roy 60.00 150.00
Mike Vernon
John Vanbiesbrouck
AE6 Ed Belfour 60.00 150.00
Patrick Roy
Dominik Hasek
AE7 Martin Brodeur 60.00 150.00
Dominik Hasek
Chris Osgood
AE8 Dominik Hasek 60.00 150.00
Martin Brodeur
Guy Hebert

2000-01 BAP Ultimate Memorabilia Captain's C

This 10-card set featured a swatch of the captain's "C" patch from a game-used jersey of the featured player. The swatch was affixed in the middle of the card in the shape of the letter C. Each card was sealed in a clear plastic slab with a descriptive label at the top. Stated print run on these cards was 5 sets. This set is not priced due to scarcity.
STATED PRINT RUN 5 SERIAL #'d SETS
NOT PRICED DUE TO SCARCITY
C1 Steve Yzerman
C2 Keith Tkachuk
C3 Mats Sundin
C4 Saku Koivu
C5 Jaromir Jagr
C6 Paul Kariya
C7 Mark Messier
C8 Joe Sakic
C9 Wayne Gretzky
C10 Mario Lemieux

2000-01 BAP Ultimate Memorabilia Dynasty Jerseys

This 20-card set featured a swatch of game-used jersey of the depicted player and commemorates that player's time with a championship team. The jersey swatch was affixed on the card in the shape of the Stanley Cup. Each card was sealed in a clear plastic slab with a descriptive label at the top. Stated print run on these cards was 50 sets.
*MULT.COLOR SWATCH:1X TO 2X BASIC CARDS
PRINT RUN 50 SERIAL #'d SETS
EMBLEM PRINT RUN 10 SER.#'d SETS
EMBLEMS NOT PRICED DUE TO SCARCITY
D1 Wayne Gretzky 150.00 300.00
D2 Mark Messier 40.00 100.00
D3 Grant Fuhr 30.00 80.00
D4 Paul Coffey 25.00 60.00
D5 Bill Ranford 30.00 80.00
D6 Mario Lemieux 100.00 200.00
D7 Paul Coffey 25.00 60.00
D8 Jaromir Jagr 40.00 100.00
D9 Tom Barrasso 25.00 60.00
D10 Ron Francis 30.00 80.00
D11 Larry Murphy 25.00 60.00
D12 Ulf Samuelsson 25.00 60.00
D13 Steve Yzerman 60.00 150.00
D14 Chris Osgood 25.00 60.00
D15 Nicklas Lidstrom 25.00 60.00
D16 Sergei Fedorov 30.00 80.00
D17 Brendan Shanahan 25.00 60.00
D18 Darren McCarty 25.00 60.00
D19 Slava Kozlov 25.00 60.00
D20 Mike Vernon 25.00 60.00

2000-01 BAP Ultimate Memorabilia Game-Used Jerseys

*MULT.COLOR SWATCH: 1X TO 2X BASIC CARDS
STATED PRINT RUN 60 SER.#'d SETS
GJ1 Theo Fleury 8.00 20.00
GJ2 Brendan Shanahan 10.00 25.00
GJ3 Curtis Joseph 10.00 25.00
GJ4 Roman Turek 10.00 25.00
GJ5 Dominik Hasek 20.00 50.00

GJ6 Al MacInnis 10.00 25.00
GJ7 John LeClair 10.00 25.00
GJ8 Teemu Selanne 10.00 25.00
GJ9 Wayne Gretzky 75.00 200.00
GJ10 Pavel Bure 10.00 25.00
GJ11 Mark Messier 10.00 25.00
GJ12 Jaromir Jagr 15.00 40.00
GJ13 Arturs Irbe 8.00 20.00
GJ14 Vincent Lecavalier 10.00 25.00
GJ15 Mats Sundin 12.50 30.00
GJ16 Paul Kariya 10.00 25.00
GJ17 Marian Hossa 10.00 25.00
GJ18 Owen Nolan 8.00 20.00
GJ19 Sergei Fedorov 15.00 40.00
GJ20 Peter Forsberg 20.00 50.00
GJ21 Brett Hull 12.50 30.00
GJ22 Tony Amonte 8.00 20.00
GJ23 Patrick Roy 40.00 100.00
GJ24 Ed Belfour 10.00 25.00
GJ25 Martin Brodeur 30.00 80.00
GJ26 Brian Leetch 8.00 20.00
GJ27 Mike Modano 15.00 40.00
GJ28 Joe Sakic 20.00 50.00
GJ29 Jeremy Roenick 12.50 30.00
GJ30 Steve Yzerman 30.00 80.00
GJ31 Jason Allison 8.00 20.00
GJ32 Milan Hejduk 10.00 25.00
GJ33 Mike Richter 10.00 25.00
GJ34 Patrik Stefan 8.00 20.00
GJ35 Kyle McLaren 8.00 20.00
GJ36 Valeri Bure 8.00 20.00
GJ37 Felix Potvin 10.00 25.00
GJ38 Chris Pronger 8.00 20.00
GJ39 Scott Stevens 8.00 20.00
GJ40 Luc Robitaille 8.00 20.00
GJ41 Roberto Luongo 12.50 30.00
GJ42 Chris Osgood 8.00 20.00
GJ43 Olaf Kolzig 8.00 20.00
GJ44 Scott Gomez 8.00 20.00
GJ45 Jason Arnott 8.00 20.00
GJ46 Rob Blake 8.00 20.00
GJ47 Keith Tkachuk 10.00 25.00
GJ48 Saku Koivu 8.00 20.00
GJ49 Alexei Yashin 8.00 20.00
GJ50 Nicklas Lidstrom 10.00 25.00

2000-01 BAP Ultimate Memorabilia Game-Used Emblems

STATED PRINT RUN 10 SERIAL #'d SETS
NOT PRICED DUE TO SCARCITY
E1 Brendan Shanahan
E2 Curtis Joseph
E3 Roman Turek
E4 Dominik Hasek
E5 John LeClair
E6 Teemu Selanne
E7 Wayne Gretzky
E8 Pavel Bure
E9 Mark Messier
E10 Jaromir Jagr
E11 Arturs Irbe
E12 Vincent Lecavalier
E13 Mats Sundin
E14 Paul Kariya
E15 Marian Hossa
E16 Owen Nolan
E17 Sergei Fedorov
E18 Peter Forsberg
E19 Brett Hull
E20 Tony Amonte
E21 Patrick Roy
E22 Ed Belfour
E23 Martin Brodeur
E24 Mike Modano
E25 Joe Sakic
E26 Steve Yzerman
E27 Jason Allison
E28 Milan Hejduk
E29 Mike Richter
E30 Patrik Stefan
E31 Chris Pronger
E32 Luc Robitaille
E33 Roberto Luongo
E34 Chris Osgood
E35 Olaf Kolzig
E36 Scott Gomez
E37 Jason Arnott
E38 Rob Blake
E39 Keith Tkachuk
E40 Alexei Yashin

2000-01 BAP Ultimate Memorabilia Game-Used In The Numbers

STATED PRINT RUN 10 SERIAL #'d SETS
NOT PRICED DUE TO SCARCITY

2000-01 BAP Ultimate Memorabilia Game-Used Sticks

*SINGLE COLOR SWATCH: .25X TO .75X
STATED PRINT RUN 90 SER.#'d SETS
GS1 Theo Fleury 8.00 20.00
GS2 Brendan Shanahan 10.00 25.00
GS3 Curtis Joseph 10.00 25.00

GS4 Roman Turek 8.00 20.00
GS5 Dominik Hasek 20.00 50.00
GS6 Al MacInnis 8.00 20.00
GS7 John LeClair 10.00 25.00
GS8 Teemu Selanne 10.00 25.00
GS9 Wayne Gretzky 50.00 125.00
GS10 Pavel Bure 10.00 25.00
GS11 Mark Messier 10.00 25.00
GS12 Jaromir Jagr 20.00 50.00
GS13 Arturs Irbe 8.00 20.00
GS14 Vincent Lecavalier 10.00 25.00
GS15 Mats Sundin 10.00 25.00
GS16 Paul Kariya 10.00 25.00
GS17 Marian Hossa 10.00 25.00
GS18 Owen Nolan 8.00 20.00
GS19 Sergei Fedorov 15.00 40.00
GS20 Peter Forsberg 20.00 50.00
GS21 Brett Hull 15.00 40.00
GS22 Tony Amonte 8.00 20.00
GS23 Patrick Roy 40.00 100.00
GS24 Ed Belfour 10.00 25.00
GS25 Martin Brodeur 30.00 80.00
GS26 Brian Leetch 10.00 25.00
GS27 Mike Modano 20.00 50.00
GS28 Joe Sakic 25.00 60.00
GS29 Jeremy Roenick 15.00 40.00
GS30 Steve Yzerman 30.00 80.00
GS31 Jason Allison 8.00 20.00
GS32 Milan Hejduk 10.00 25.00
GS33 Mike Richter 10.00 25.00
GS34 Patrik Stefan 8.00 20.00
GS35 Kyle McLaren 8.00 20.00
GS36 Valeri Bure 8.00 20.00
GS37 Felix Potvin 15.00 40.00
GS38 Chris Pronger 10.00 25.00
GS39 Scott Stevens 10.00 25.00
GS40 Luc Robitaille 10.00 25.00
GS41 Roberto Luongo 15.00 40.00
GS42 Chris Osgood 10.00 25.00
GS43 Olaf Kolzig 10.00 25.00
GS44 Scott Gomez 10.00 25.00
GS45 Jason Arnott 8.00 20.00
GS46 Rob Blake 8.00 20.00
GS47 Keith Tkachuk 10.00 25.00
GS48 Saku Koivu 10.00 25.00
GS49 Alexei Yashin 8.00 20.00
GS50 Nicklas Lidstrom 10.00 25.00

2000-01 BAP Ultimate Memorabilia Goalie Memorabilia

This 20-card set featured swatches of game-used equipment from each of the depicted goalies on the card. Each card was sealed in a clear plastic slab with a descriptive label at the top. Stated print run on these cards was 30 sets.

*MULT COLOR SWATCH:1X TO 1.5X BASIC CARDS
STATED PRINT RUN 30 SERIAL #'d SETS
GM1 Jacques Plante 75.00 200.00
Patrick Roy
GM2 Terry Sawchuk 75.00 . 200.00
Patrick Roy
GM3 Mike Vernon 25.00 60.00
Chris Osgood
GM4 Curtis Joseph 25.00 60.00
Felix Potvin
GM5 Tony Esposito 30.00 80.00
Ed Belfour
GM6 Turk Broda 30.00 80.00
Johnny Bower
GM7 Bernie Parent 25.00 60.00
Brian Boucher
GM8 Tony Esposito 40.00 100.00
Gerry Cheevers
GM9 Bernie Parent 50.00 125.00
Gerry Cheevers
GM10 Jacques Plante G/J 60.00 150.00
GM11 Patrick Roy 60.00 150.00
Eddie Belfour
GM12 Curtis Joseph 30.00 80.00
Dominik Hasek
GM13 Roman Turek 25.00 60.00
Ed Belfour
GM14 Martin Brodeur 60.00 150.00
Jacques Plante
GM15 Mike Richter 25.00 60.00
John Vanbiesbrouck
GM16 Jacques Plante G/S/J 60.00 150.00
GM17 Tony Esposito 75.00 200.00
Bernie Parent
Vladislav Tretiak
GM18 Frank Brimsek 50.00 125.00
Byron Dafoe
Gerry Cheevers
GM19 Johnny Bower 75.00 200.00
Turk Broda
Terry Sawchuk
GM20 Patrick Roy 125.00 300.00
Georges Vezina
Terry Sawchuk

2000-01 BAP Ultimate Memorabilia Goalie Memorabilia Autographed

This 5-card set featured a swatch of game-used equipment and an autograph from the depicted goalie. Each card was sealed in a

clear plastic slab with a descriptive label at the top. Stated print run on these cards was 50 sets.

*MULT.COLOR SWATCH:1X TO 1.5X BASIC CARDS
STATED PRINT RUN 50 SERIAL #'d SETS
UG1 Gerry Cheevers 40.00 100.00
UG2 Vladislav Tretiak 75.00 200.00
UG3 Tony Esposito 40.00 100.00
UG4 Johnny Bower 40.00 100.00
UG5 Bernie Parent 50.00 125.00

2000-01 BAP Ultimate Memorabilia Goalie Sticks

*SINGLE COLOR STICKS: .5X TO 1X HI
STATED PRINT RUN 50 SERIAL #'d SETS
G1 Guy Hebert 12.50 30.00
G2 Damian Rhodes 12.50 30.00
G3 Byron Dafoe 12.50 30.00
G4 Dominik Hasek 15.00 40.00
G5 Mike Vernon 12.50 30.00
G6 Arturs Irbe 12.50 30.00
G7 Jocelyn Thibault 12.50 30.00
G8 Patrick Roy 50.00 125.00
G9 Marc Denis 12.50 30.00
G10 Ed Belfour 12.50 30.00
G11 Chris Osgood 12.50 30.00
G12 Tommy Salo 12.50 30.00
G13 Roberto Luongo 25.00 60.00
G14 Jamie Storr 12.50 30.00
G15 Manny Fernandez 12.50 30.00
G16 Jeff Hackett 12.50 30.00
G17 Mike Dunham 12.50 30.00
G18 Martin Brodeur 30.00 80.00
G19 John Vanbiesbrouck 12.50 30.00
G20 Mike Richter 12.50 30.00
G21 Patrick Lalime 12.50 30.00
G22 Brian Boucher 12.50 30.00
G23 Nikolai Khabibulin 12.50 30.00
G24 J-S Aubin 12.50 30.00
G25 Roman Turek 12.50 30.00
G26 Steve Shields 12.50 30.00
G27 Dan Cloutier 12.50 30.00
G28 Curtis Joseph 12.50 30.00
G29 Felix Potvin 12.50 30.00
G30 Olaf Kolzig 12.50 30.00

2000-01 BAP Ultimate Memorabilia Gordie Howe No. 9

This 3-card set featured swatches of game-used jerseys of Gordie Howe from one of the three professional teams he played for during his career. The cards carried a color action photo of Howe in the team's jersey in the forefront and the shape of the number 9 in the background with another action shot and a head shot on it. The jersey swatch was affixed in the shape of the hollow of the number 9. Each card was sealed in a clear plastic slab with a descriptive label at the top. Stated print run on these cards was 50 sets.

*MULT.COLOR SWATCH: 1X TO 1.5X BASIC CARDS
JERSEY PRINT RUN 50 SERIAL #'d SETS
COMMON JSY/AUTO 125.00 250.00
JSY/AUTO PRINT RUN 20 SER.#'d SETS
9-1 Gordie Howe 50.00 125.00
Detroit
9-2 Gordie Howe 50.00 125.00
New England
9-3 Gordie Howe 50.00 125.00
Houston

2000-01 BAP Ultimate Memorabilia Gordie Howe Retrospective Jerseys

This 7-card set featured game-used swatches of Gordie Howe's jerseys from the three teams he played for during his professional career. The cards carried a color action photo of Howe in the team's jersey in the forefront and the words "Howe Legend" in the background. Cards with one or two jersey swatches also carried larger headshots and the depicted team logo in the background. Each card was sealed in a clear plastic slab with a descriptive label at the top. Stated print run on these cards was 50 sets.

*MULT.COLOR SWATCH:1X TO 1.5X BASIC CARDS

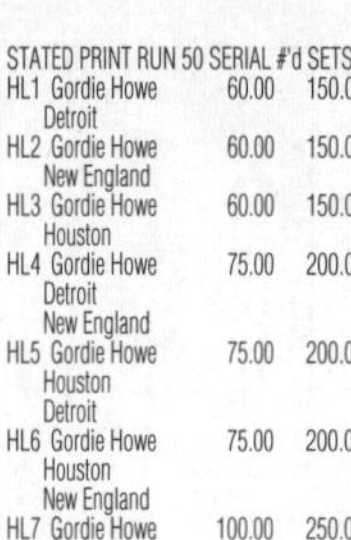

STATED PRINT RUN 50 SERIAL #'d SETS
HL1 Gordie Howe 60.00 150.00
Detroit
HL2 Gordie Howe 60.00 150.00
New England
HL3 Gordie Howe 60.00 150.00
Houston
HL4 Gordie Howe 75.00 200.00
Detroit
New England
HL5 Gordie Howe 75.00 200.00
Houston
Detroit
HL6 Gordie Howe 75.00 200.00
Houston
New England
HL7 Gordie Howe 100.00 250.00
Detroit
New England
Houston

2000-01 BAP Ultimate Memorabilia Gordie Howe Retrospective Jerseys Autograph

This set paralleled the Be A Player Ultimate Memorabilia Gordie Howe Retrospective Jerseys set except that each card carries an autograph of Gordie Howe along with the words "Mr. Hockey" in his handwriting. Each card was sealed in a clear plastic slab with a descriptive label at the top. Stated print run on these cards was 20 sets.

*MULT.COLOR SWATCH:1X TO 1.5X BASIC CARDS
STATED PRINT RUN 20 SERIAL #'d SETS
GH1 Gordie Howe 125.00 250.00
Detroit
GH2 Gordie Howe 125.00 250.00
New England
GH3 Gordie Howe 125.00 250.00
Houston
GH4 Gordie Howe 125.00 250.00
Detroit
New England
GH5 Gordie Howe 125.00 250.00
Houston
Detroit
GH6 Gordie Howe 125.00 250.00
Houston
New England
GH7 Gordie Howe 400.00 800.00
Detroit
New England
Houston

2000-01 BAP Ultimate Memorabilia Hart Trophy

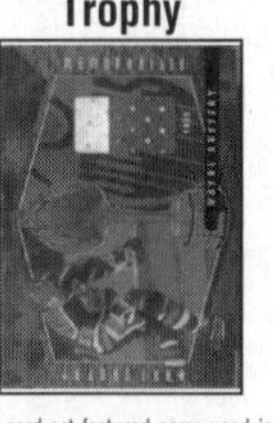

This 20-card set featured game-used jersey swatches of past winners of the Hart trophy. Each card carried a color action photo of the given player and a picture of the trophy alongside the jersey swatch. Some players in the set have multiple cards to mirror the amount times they have won the trophy. Each card was sealed in a clear plastic slab with a descriptive label at the top. Stated print run on these cards was 30 sets.

*MULT.COLOR SWATCH:1X TO 1.5X BASIC CARDS
STATED PRINT RUN 30 SERIAL #'d SETS
H1 Chris Pronger 30.00 80.00
H2 Jaromir Jagr 40.00 100.00
H3 Dominik Hasek 40.00 100.00
H4 Dominik Hasek 40.00 100.00
H5 Mario Lemieux 60.00 150.00
H6 Eric Lindros 30.00 80.00
H7 Sergei Fedorov 30.00 80.00
H8 Mario Lemieux 60.00 150.00
H9 Mark Messier 50.00 125.00
H10 Brett Hull 40.00 100.00
H11 Mark Messier 50.00 125.00
H12 Wayne Gretzky 75.00 200.00
H13 Mario Lemieux 60.00 150.00
H14 Wayne Gretzky 75.00 200.00
H15 Wayne Gretzky 75.00 200.00
H16 Wayne Gretzky 75.00 200.00
H17 Wayne Gretzky 75.00 200.00
H18 Wayne Gretzky 75.00 200.00
H19 Wayne Gretzky 75.00 200.00
H20 Wayne Gretzky 75.00 200.00

2000-01 BAP Ultimate Memorabilia Jacques Plante Jersey Cards

This 15-card set featured a game-used jersey swatch of goalie great Jacques Plante. Each card also carried a photo of a current day goalie and the cards are listed below based on those players. Each card was sealed in a clear plastic slab with a descriptive label at the top. Stated print run on these cards was 30 sets.

*MULT.COLOR SWATCH:1X TO 1.5X BASIC CARDS

STATED PRINT RUN 30 SERIAL #'d SETS
*SKATE CARDS: .6X TO 1.5X JSY HI
SKATE PRINT RUN 20 SER.#'d SETS
PJ1 Patrick Roy 75.00 200.00
PJ2 Ed Belfour 30.00 80.00
PJ3 Martin Brodeur 60.00 150.00
PJ4 Dominik Hasek 40.00 100.00
PJ5 Chris Osgood 30.00 80.00
PJ6 Curtis Joseph 30.00 80.00
PJ7 Tommy Salo 30.00 80.00
PJ8 Mike Richter 30.00 80.00
PJ9 Byron Dafoe 30.00 80.00
PJ10 Roberto Luongo 30.00 80.00
PJ11 Roman Turek 30.00 80.00
PJ12 Olaf Kolzig 30.00 80.00
PJ13 Felix Potvin 30.00 80.00
PJ14 Jocelyn Thibault 30.00 80.00
PJ15 Brian Boucher 30.00 80.00

2000-01 BAP Ultimate Memorabilia Journey Jerseys

This 20-card set features game-used jersey swatches of players who played for at least two different franchises during their career. Each card carries a swatch of the player's jersey for both teams depicted as well as photos of the player in each team's jersey. Each card was sealed in a clear plastic slab with a descriptive label at the top. Stated print run on these cards was 50 sets.

*MULT.COLOR SWATCH:1X TO 1.5X BASIC CARDS
PRINT RUN 50 SERIAL #'d SETS
EMBLM/NMBR PRINT RUN 10 SER.#'d SETS
JJ1 Wayne Gretzky 150.00 350.00
JJ2 Mark Messier 25.00 60.00
JJ3 Pavel Bure 20.00 50.00
JJ4 Jeff Hackett 20.00 50.00
JJ5 Mats Sundin 20.00 50.00
JJ6 Curtis Joseph 20.00 50.00
JJ7 Ed Belfour 20.00 50.00
JJ8 Mike Modano 20.00 50.00
JJ9 Brett Hull 30.00 80.00
JJ10 Teemu Selanne 20.00 50.00
JJ11 Keith Tkachuk 20.00 50.00
JJ12 Patrick Roy 125.00 300.00
JJ13 Chris Chelios 20.00 50.00
JJ14 Al MacInnis 20.00 50.00
JJ15 Theo Fleury 20.00 50.00
JJ16 Jason Allison 20.00 50.00
JJ17 Jeremy Roenick 25.00 60.00
JJ18 Brendan Shanahan 20.00 50.00
JJ19 Owen Nolan 20.00 50.00
JJ20 Felix Potvin 20.00 50.00

2000-01 BAP Ultimate Memorabilia Magnificent Ones

This 10-card set featured game-used jersey swatches from Mario Lemieux and another star player on each card. The cards carry a small headshot of Lemieux beside his jersey swatch on the right side of the card and an action shot of the other player on the left beside his jersey swatch. The words "Magnificent Ones" is printed across the top border. Each card was sealed in a clear plastic slab with a descriptive label at the top. Stated print run on these cards was 40 sets.

*MULT.COLOR SWATCH:1X TO 1.5X BASIC CARDS
STATED PRINT RUN 40 SERIAL #'d SETS
M.ONES AU STAT.PRINT RUN 6 SER.#'d SETS
M.ONES AU SIGN.BY LEMIEUX ONLY
ML1 S.Yzerman/M.Lemieux 75.00 200.00
ML2 J.Jagr/M.Lemieux 60.00 150.00
ML3 M.Brodeur/M.Lemieux 60.00 150.00
ML4 M.Messier/M.Lemieux 40.00 100.00
ML5 P.Roy/M.Lemieux 75.00 200.00
ML6 R.Bourque/M.Lemieux 60.00 150.00
ML7 R.Francis/M.Lemieux 30.00 80.00
ML8 D.Hasek/M.Lemieux 60.00 150.00
ML9 W.Gretzky/M.Lemieux 125.00 300.00
ML10 P.Coffey/M.Lemieux 30.00 80.00

2000-01 BAP Ultimate Memorabilia Maurice Richard Autographs

This 5-card set remembers one of the greats of the game, Rocket Richard. Each card

features a photo of Richard and a cut autograph. The autographs were originally on 8x10 reprints of Richard's 1953-54 Parkhurst card. In the Game, Inc. obtained the autographs through a private signing with Richard. The autographs were then cut and affixed to the cards in this set as swatches. Each card was sealed in a clear plastic slab with a descriptive label at the top. Stated print run on these cards was 10 sets.

COMMON CARD (R1-R5) 300.00 500.00
STATED PRINT RUN 10 SERIAL #'d SETS

2000-01 BAP Ultimate Memorabilia NHL Records

This 10-card set recognized 10 different players who hold various NHL records. Each card featured a photo and a swatch of game-used jersey of that player. A brief explanation of the record was on the back of each card. Each card was sealed in a clear plastic slab with a descriptive label at the top. Stated print run on these cards was 30 sets.

*MULT.COLOR SWATCH:1X TO 1.5X BASIC CARDS
STATED PRINT RUN 30 SERIAL #'d SETS
R1 Terry Sawchuk 50.00 125.00
R2 Patrick Roy 60.00 150.00
R3 Tony Esposito 25.00 60.00
R4 Jacques Plante 40.00 100.00
R5 Bill Mosienko 25.00 60.00
R6 Teemu Selanne 25.00 60.00
R7 Mario Lemieux 60.00 150.00
R8 Ray Bourque 30.00 80.00
R9 Gordie Howe 40.00 100.00
R10 Wayne Gretzky 75.00 200.00

2000-01 BAP Ultimate Memorabilia Norris Trophy

This 10-card set featured game-used jersey swatches of winners of the Norris trophy. The cards carried an action photo of the given player, a picture of the Norris trophy, and a square piece of jersey. Each card was sealed in a clear plastic slab with a descriptive label at the top. Stated print run on these cards was 50 sets.

*MULT.COLOR SWATCH:1X TO 1.5X BASIC CARDS
STATED PRINT RUN 50 SER.#'d SETS
N1 Chris Pronger 20.00 50.00
N2 Al MacInnis 20.00 50.00
N3 Rob Blake 20.00 50.00
N4 Brian Leetch 20.00 50.00
N5 Chris Chelios 20.00 50.00
N6 Paul Coffey 20.00 50.00
N7 Ray Bourque 30.00 80.00
N8 Chris Chelios 20.00 50.00
N9 Brian Leetch 20.00 50.00
N10 Ray Bourque 30.00 80.00

2000-01 BAP Ultimate Memorabilia Retro-Active

This 10-card set featured a player from the past and from the present who have both won the same award. Each card carries a photo of each player along side a game-used jersey swatch of each. A photo of the shared award is in the middle of the two swatches. Each card was sealed in a clear plastic slab with a descriptive label at the top. Stated print run on these cards was 30 sets.

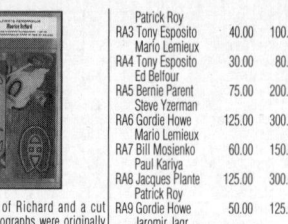

*MULT.COLOR SWATCH:1X TO 1.5X BASIC CARDS
STATED PRINT RUN 30 SER.#'d SETS
RA1 Gordie Howe 50.00 125.00
Chris Pronger
RA2 Terry Sawchuk 150.00 300.00
Patrick Roy
RA3 Tony Esposito 40.00 100.00
Mario Lemieux
RA4 Tony Esposito 30.00 80.00
Ed Belfour
RA5 Bernie Parent 75.00 200.00
Steve Yzerman
RA6 Gordie Howe 125.00 300.00
Mario Lemieux
RA7 Bill Mosienko 60.00 150.00
Paul Kariya
RA8 Jacques Plante 125.00 300.00
Patrick Roy
RA9 Gordie Howe 50.00 125.00
Jaromir Jagr
RA10 Wayne Gretzky 150.00 400.00
Mark Messier

2000-01 BAP Ultimate Memorabilia Teammates

*MULT.COLOR SWATCH: 1X TO 2X BASIC CARDS
STATED PRINT RUN 70 SER.#'d SETS
TM1 Steve Yzerman 20.00 50.00
Sergei Fedorov
TM2 Brendan Shanahan 12.00 30.00
Slava Kozlov
TM3 S.Yzerman/C.Chelios 20.00 50.00
TM4 S.Yzerman/B.Shanahan 30.00 80.00
TM5 Jeremy Roenick 12.00 30.00
Keith Tkachuk
TM6 Nicklas Lidstom 15.00 40.00
Sergei Fedorov
TM7 Nicklas Lidstrom 12.00 30.00
Chris Osgood
TM8 Nicklas Lidstrom 15.00 40.00
Brendan Shanahan
TM9 Chris Osgood 12.00 30.00
Sergei Fedorov
TM10 Nikolai Khabibulin 8.00 20.00
Jeremy Roenick
TM11 Sergei Gonchar 8.00 20.00
Adam Oates
TM12 Curtis Joseph 12.00 30.00
Mats Sundin
TM13 Curtis Joseph 8.00 20.00
Tie Domi
TM14 Mats Sundin 8.00 20.00
Tie Domi
TM15 Peter Forsberg 50.00 125.00
Patrick Roy
TM16 Peter Forsberg 25.00 60.00
Joe Sakic
TM17 Joe Sakic 60.00 150.00
Patrick Roy
TM18 Boris Mironov 8.00 20.00
Tony Amonte
TM19 Pavel Bure 8.00 20.00
Paul Laus
TM20 Mike Peca 15.00 40.00
Dominik Hasek
TM21 Paul Kariya 15.00 40.00
Teemu Selanne
TM22 Teemu Selanne 8.00 20.00
Guy Hebert
TM23 Paul Kariya 8.00 20.00
Guy Hebert
TM24 B.Hull/M.Modano 15.00 40.00
TM25 Brett Hull 12.00 30.00
Ed Belfour
TM26 E.Belfour/M.Modano 15.00 40.00
TM27 Sergei Zubov 8.00 20.00
Ed Belfour
TM28 Brett Hull 8.00 20.00
Darryl Sydor
TM29 Eric Desjardins 8.00 20.00
John LeClair
TM30 Jason Arnott 20.00 50.00
Martin Brodeur
TM31 S.Yzerman/M.Vernon 20.00 50.00
TM32 Brett Hull 20.00 50.00
Curtis Joseph
TM33 Keith Tkachuk 12.00 30.00
Teemu Selanne
TM34 Mats Sundin 12.00 30.00
Owen Nolan
TM35 Ed Belfour 12.00 30.00
Chris Chelios
TM36 Mark Messier 100.00 250.00
Wayne Gretzky
TM37 Theo Fleury 8.00 20.00
Al MacInnis
TM38 Felix Potvin 12.00 30.00
Mats Sundin
TM39 Mario Lemieux 60.00 150.00
Jaromir Jagr
TM40 Ray Bourque 20.00 50.00
Adam Oates

2001-02 BAP Ultimate Memorabilia Active Eight

All cards in this product were graded by Beckett Grading Services and available only in graded form. Due to the various amount of grading ranges, only a median price for Mint/NmMt+ copies was assigned below.

STATED PRINT RUN 30 SER.#'d SETS
1 Kariya/Lemieux/Sakic 60.00 150.00
2 Patrick Roy 50.00 125.00

Mike Vernon
Tom Barrasso
3 Ron Francis 40.00 100.00
Mark Messier
Steve Yzerman
4 Mario Lemieux 50.00 125.00
Luc Robitaille
Jaromir Jagr
5 Messier/Hull/Lemieux 60.00 150.00
6 Teemu Selanne 40.00 100.00
Joe Nieuwendyk
Luc Robitaille
7 Mark Messier 40.00 100.00
Ron Francis
Scott Stevens
8 Mario Lemieux 40.00 100.00
Mats Sundin
Steve Yzerman

2001-02 BAP Ultimate Memorabilia All-Star History

STATED PRINT RUN 40 SER.#'d SETS
1 Turk Broda 20.00 50.00
2 Frank Brimsek 15.00 40.00
3 Ted Kennedy 15.00 40.00
4 Maurice Richard 60.00 150.00
5 Chuck Rayner 15.00 40.00
6 Bill Mosienko 15.00 40.00
7 Jean Beliveau 30.00 80.00
8 Doug Harvey 15.00 40.00
9 Ted Lindsay 15.00 40.00
10 Henri Richard 20.00 50.00
11 Jacques Plante 30.00 80.00
12 Glenn Hall 15.00 40.00
13 Terry Sawchuk 40.00 100.00
14 Bobby Hull 15.00 40.00
15 Johnny Bower 15.00 40.00
16 Tim Horton 40.00 100.00
17 Johnny Bucyk 15.00 40.00
18 Stan Mikita 15.00 40.00
19 Bill Gadsby 15.00 40.00
20 Gordie Howe 40.00 100.00
21 Ed Giacomin 15.00 40.00
22 Bernie Parent 20.00 50.00
23 Bobby Clarke 15.00 40.00
24 Gilbert Perreault 15.00 40.00
25 Frank Mahovlich 15.00 40.00
26 Tony Esposito 25.00 60.00
27 Denis Potvin 15.00 40.00
28 Guy Lafleur 25.00 60.00
29 Bryan Trottier 15.00 40.00
30 Lanny McDonald 15.00 40.00
31 Marcel Dionne 15.00 40.00
32 Wayne Gretzky 75.00 200.00
33 Mike Bossy 15.00 40.00
34 Mark Messier 15.00 40.00
35 Paul Coffey 25.00 60.00
36 Steve Yzerman 40.00 100.00
37 Mario Lemieux 40.00 100.00
38 Grant Fuhr 15.00 40.00
39 Patrick Roy 40.00 100.00
40 Brett Hull 25.00 60.00
41 Brian Leetch 15.00 40.00
42 Jeremy Roenick 20.00 50.00
43 Jaromir Jagr 25.00 60.00
44 Luc Robitaille 15.00 40.00
45 Joe Sakic 30.00 80.00
46 Eric Lindros 15.00 40.00
47 Paul Kariya 15.00 40.00
48 Mike Modano 15.00 40.00
49 Peter Forsberg 25.00 60.00
50 Pavel Bure 15.00 40.00
51 Milan Hejduk 15.00 40.00
52 Mats Sundin 15.00 40.00

2001-02 BAP Ultimate Memorabilia Autographs

PRINT RUNS LISTED BELOW
UNDER 25 NOT PRICED DUE TO SCARCITY
1 Alexei Yashin/40 15.00 40.00
2 Brian Leetch/40 25.00 60.00
3 Daniel Alfredsson/40 15.00 40.00
4 Keith Tkachuk/40 25.00 60.00
5 Milan Hejduk/40 25.00 60.00

Mark Recchi/40 15.00 40.00
Paul Kariya/40 25.00 60.00
Scott Stevens/40 15.00 40.00
Joe Sakic/40 40.00 100.00
0 Al MacInnis/30 15.00 40.00
1 Peter Bondra/40 15.00 40.00
2 John LeClair/40 25.00 60.00
3 Brendan Shanahan/40 25.00 60.00
4 Rob Blake/40 15.00 40.00
5 Luc Robitaille/40 15.00 40.00
6 Jarome Iginla/40 30.00 80.00
7 Pavel Bure/40 25.00 60.00
8 Marcel Dionne/40 15.00 40.00
9 Gordie Howe/40 50.00 125.00
0 Phil Esposito/40 15.00 40.00
1 Guy Lafleur/40 30.00 80.00
2 Gilbert Perreault/40 15.00 40.00
3 Bobby Hull/40 30.00 80.00
4 Jean Beliveau/40 25.00 60.00
5 Stan Mikita/40 30.00 80.00
6 Ted Lindsay/20
7 Frank Mahovlich/30 25.00 60.00
8 Mario Lemieux/30 100.00 250.00
9 Tony Amonte/30 15.00 40.00
0 Jeremy Roenick/30 30.00 80.00
1 Owen Nolan/40 15.00 40.00
2 Mark Messier/40 40.00 100.00
3 Steve Yzerman/40 60.00 150.00
4 Sergei Fedorov/40 30.00 80.00
5 Wayne Gretzky/30 200.00 400.00

2001-02 BAP Ultimate Memorabilia Bloodlines

TATED PRINT RUN 20 SERIAL #'d SETS
OT PRICED DUE TO SCARCITY
Pavel Bure
Valeri Bure
Scott Niedermayer
Rob Niedermayer
Henri Richard
Rocket Richard
Peter Mahovlich
Frank Mahovlich
Tony Esposito
Phil Esposito
Brett Hull
Dennis Hull
Bobby Hull
Sid Abel
Brent Johnson
Paul Kariya
Steve Kariya

2001-02 BAP Ultimate Memorabilia Calder Trophy

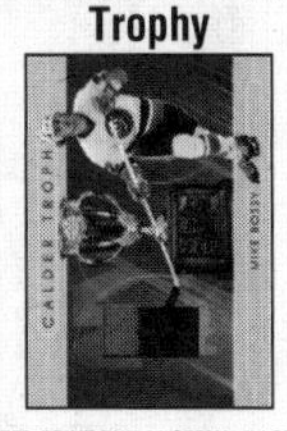

TATED PRINT RUN 30 SERIAL #'d SETS
Evgeni Nabokov 15.00 40.00
Scott Gomez 10.00 40.00
Chris Drury 15.00 25.00
Sergei Samsonov 15.00 40.00
Bryan Berard 10.00 25.00
Daniel Alfredsson 10.00 40.00
Peter Forsberg 25.00 60.00
Martin Brodeur 40.00 100.00
Teemu Selanne 20.00 50.00
0 Pavel Bure 20.00 50.00
1 Ed Belfour 20.00 50.00
2 Tom Barrasso 15.00 40.00
3 Brian Leetch 15.00 40.00
4 Joe Nieuwendyk 15.00 40.00
5 Luc Robitaille 15.00 40.00
6 Mario Lemieux 40.00 100.00
7 Dale Hawerchuk 15.00 40.00
8 Mike Bossy 20.00 50.00
9 Bryan Trottier 15.00 40.00
0 Denis Potvin 20.00 50.00
1 Gilbert Perreault 15.00 40.00
2 Tony Esposito 20.00 50.00
3 Glenn Hall 20.00 50.00
4 Terry Sawchuk 40.00 100.00
5 Frank Brimsek 20.00 50.00

2001-02 BAP Ultimate Memorabilia Captain's C

TATED PRINT RUN 5 SETS
OT PRICED DUE TO SCARCITY
Daniel Alfredsson
Jean Beliveau
Johnny Bucyk
Ron Francis
Wayne Gretzky
Jaromir Jagr
Paul Kariya

8 Brian Leetch
9 Mario Lemieux
10 Gilbert Perreault
11 Denis Potvin
12 Chris Pronger
13 Henri Richard
14 Mats Sundin
15 Steve Yzerman

2001-02 BAP Ultimate Memorabilia Complete Package

STATED PRINT RUN 10 SETS
NOT PRICED DUE TO SCARCITY
1 Wayne Gretzky
2 Tim Horton
3 Jarome Iginla
4 Curtis Joseph
5 Guy Lafleur
6 Eric Lindros
7 Jacques Plante
8 Patrick Roy
9 Terry Sawchuk
10 Mats Sundin

2001-02 BAP Ultimate Memorabilia Cornerstones

STATED PRINT RUN 20 SERIAL #'d SETS
NOT PRICED DUE TO SCARCITY
1 Ace Bailey
Johnny Bower
Lanny McDonald
Mats Sundin
2 Patrick Roy
Maurice Richard
Jean Beliveau
Guy Lafleur
3 Bobby Hull
Glenn Hall
Stan Mikita
Tony Amonte
4 Ted Lindsay
Gordie Howe
Terry Sawchuk
Steve Yzerman
5 Chuck Rayner
Ed Giacomin
Phil Esposito
Brian Leetch
6 Frank Brimsek
Johnny Bucyk
Cam Neely
Joe Thornton

2001-02 BAP Ultimate Memorabilia Decades

STATED PRINT RUN 50 SER.#'d SETS
1 Chuck Rayner 20.00 50.00
2 Frank Brimsek 20.00 50.00
3 Terry Sawchuk 40.00 100.00
4 Jacques Plante 50.00 125.00
5 Doug Harvey 20.00 50.00
6 Bill Gadsby 20.00 50.00
7 Gordie Howe 40.00 100.00
8 Ted Lindsay 20.00 50.00
9 Johnny Bower 20.00 50.00
10 Glenn Hall 20.00 50.00
11 Bobby Hull 25.00 60.00

12 Stan Mikita 20.00 50.00
13 Tony Esposito 25.00 60.00
14 Gerry Cheevers 20.00 50.00
15 Guy Lafleur 25.00 60.00
16 Bobby Clarke 20.00 50.00
17 Denis Potvin 20.00 50.00
18 Serge Savard 20.00 50.00
19 Patrick Roy 40.00 100.00
20 Grant Fuhr 20.00 50.00
21 Larry Robinson 20.00 50.00
22 Al MacInnis 20.00 50.00
23 Cam Neely 30.00 80.00
24 Mike Bossy 20.00 50.00

2001-02 BAP Ultimate Memorabilia Dynamic Duos

STATED PRINT RUN 30 SERIAL #'D SETS
1 M.Modano/W.Gretzky 50.00 125.00
2 Jaromir Jagr 20.00 50.00
John LeClair
3 Luc Robitaille 25.00 60.00
Joe Sakic
4 Milan Hejduk 25.00 60.00
Brett Hull
5 Pavel Bure 20.00 50.00
Alexei Yashin
6 Steve Yzerman 30.00 80.00
Mats Sundin
7 Paul Kariya 25.00 60.00
Peter Forsberg
8 Teemu Selanne 20.00 50.00
Brendan Shanahan
9 Mark Messier 25.00 60.00
Jarome Iginla
10 Alexander Mogilny 20.00 50.00
Mark Recchi
11 Peter Bondra 20.00 50.00
Theo Fleury
12 Jeremy Roenick 60.00 150.00
Mario Lemieux
13 Eric Lindros 25.00 60.00
Ilya Kovalchuk
14 Keith Tkachuk 20.00 50.00
Tony Amonte
15 Doug Weight 20.00 50.00
Daniel Alfredsson
16 Vincent Damphousse 20.00 50.00
Sergei Fedorov

2001-02 BAP Ultimate Memorabilia Dynasty Jerseys

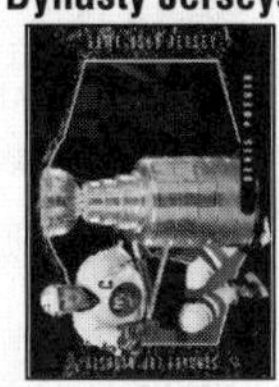

STATED PRINT RUN 50 SER.#'d SETS
1 Bill Barber 20.00 50.00
2 Mike Bossy 20.00 50.00
3 Bobby Clarke 20.00 50.00
4 Yvan Cournoyer 20.00 50.00
5 Bob Gainey 20.00 50.00
6 Guy Lafleur 25.00 60.00
7 Guy Lapointe 20.00 50.00
8 Reggie Leach 20.00 50.00
9 Bob Nystrom 20.00 50.00
10 Bernie Parent 20.00 50.00
11 Denis Potvin 20.00 50.00
12 Larry Robinson 20.00 50.00
13 Serge Savard 20.00 50.00
14 Dave Schultz 20.00 50.00
15 Steve Shutt 20.00 50.00
16 Billy Smith 20.00 50.00
17 Bryan Trottier 20.00 50.00
18 Joe Watson 20.00 50.00

2001-02 BAP Ultimate Memorabilia Dynasty Emblems

STATED PRINT RUN 10 SETS
NOT PRICED DUE TO SCARCITY

2001-02 BAP Ultimate Memorabilia Dynasty Numbers

STATED PRINT RUN 10 SETS
NOT PRICED DUE TO SCARCITY

2001-02 BAP Ultimate Memorabilia Emblems

STATED PRINT RUN 10 SERIAL #'d SETS
NOT PRICED DUE TO SCARCITY
1 Paul Kariya
2 Martin Brodeur
3 John LeClair
4 Ilya Kovalchuk
5 Bill Guerin
6 Dominik Hasek
7 Keith Tkachuk
8 Pavel Bure
9 Brian Leetch
10 Mario Lemieux
11 Mats Sundin
12 Owen Nolan
13 Mark Messier
14 Jaromir Jagr
15 Joe Sakic
16 Rob Blake
17 Brendan Shanahan
18 Eric Lindros
19 Mike Modano
20 Sergei Fedorov
21 Nicklas Lidstrom
22 Steve Yzerman
23 Teemu Selanne
24 Alexei Yashin
25 Doug Weight
26 Chris Pronger
27 Patrick Roy
28 Curtis Joseph
29 Jeremy Roenick
30 Luc Robitaille

2001-02 BAP Ultimate Memorabilia Emblem Attic

STATED PRINT RUN 5 SETS
NOT PRICED DUE TO SCARCITY
1 Jean Beliveau
2 Bobby Clarke
3 Phil Esposito
4 Wayne Gretzky
5 Glenn Hall
6 Doug Harvey
7 Gordie Howe
8 Bobby Hull
9 Guy Lafleur
10 Ted Lindsay
11 Frank Mahovlich
12 Mark Messier
13 Stan Mikita
14 Jacques Plante
15 Denis Potvin
16 Henri Richard
17 Rocket Richard
18 Larry Robinson
19 Terry Sawchuk
20 Bryan Trottier

2001-02 BAP Ultimate Memorabilia 500 Goal Scorers

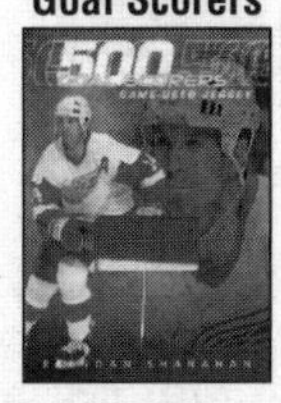

PRINT RUNS LISTED BELOW
UNDER 30 NOT PRICED DUE TO SCARCITY
1 Wayne Gretzky/10
2 Gordie Howe/10
3 Mario Lemieux/10
4 Bobby Hull/10
5 Mike Bossy/30 20.00 50.00

6 Guy Lafleur/30 30.00 80.00
7 Jean Beliveau/10
8 Stan Mikita/30 20.00 50.00
9 Marcel Dionne/30 20.00 50.00
10 Phil Esposito/30 30.00 80.00
11 Frank Mahovlich/10
12 Mark Messier/30 20.00 50.00
13 Steve Yzerman/30 75.00 200.00
14 Brett Hull/30 40.00 100.00
15 Mike Gartner/30 20.00 50.00
16 Bryan Trottier/30 20.00 50.00
17 Gilbert Perreault/30 25.00 60.00
18 Lanny McDonald/30 20.00 50.00
19 Jari Kurri/30 30.00 80.00
20 Dale Hawerchuk/30 20.00 50.00
21 Luc Robitaille/30 20.00 50.00
22 Dave Andreychuk/30 20.00 50.00
23 John Bucyk/30 25.00 60.00
24 Michel Goulet/30 20.00 50.00
25 Joe Mullen/30 20.00 50.00
26 Dino Ciccarelli/30 20.00 50.00
27 Pat Verbeek/30 20.00 50.00
28 Maurice Richard/10
29 Ron Francis/30 20.00 50.00
30 Brendan Shanahan/30 30.00 80.00

2001-02 BAP Ultimate Memorabilia 500 Goal Scorers Autographs

PRINT RUNS LISTED BELOW
PRINT RUNS UNDER 25 NOT PRICED
DUE TO SCARCITY
1 Bobby Hull/25 60.00 150.00
2 Bryan Trottier/15
3 Dale Hawerchuk/25 30.00 80.00
4 Dave Andreychuk/30 30.00 80.00
5 Dino Ciccarelli/10
6 Frank Mahovlich/25 40.00 100.00
7 Gilbert Perreault/15
8 Guy Lafleur/20
9 Jari Kurri/20
10 Jean Beliveau/15
11 John Bucyk/25 40.00 100.00
12 Lanny McDonald/20
13 Luc Robitaille/15
14 Marcel Dionne/25 30.00 80.00
15 Mario Lemieux/10
16 Michel Goulet/30 30.00 80.00
17 Mike Bossy/25 50.00 125.00
18 Mike Gartner/30 30.00 80.00
19 Gordie Howe/20
20 Pat Verbeek/10
21 Phil Esposito/15
22 Rocket Richard/10
23 Stan Mikita/25 30.00 80.00
24 Steve Yzerman/15
25 Joe Mullen/20

2001-02 BAP Ultimate Memorabilia 500 Goal Scorers Jerseys and Sticks

*JSY AND STICK: .5X TO 1.25X 500 GOAL JSY
STAT.PRINT RUN 40 SER.#'d SETS UNLESS
OTHERWISE NOTED
7 Jean Beliveau/40 25.00 60.00
11 Frank Mahovlich/40 25.00 60.00

2001-02 BAP Ultimate Memorabilia 500 Goal Scorers Emblems

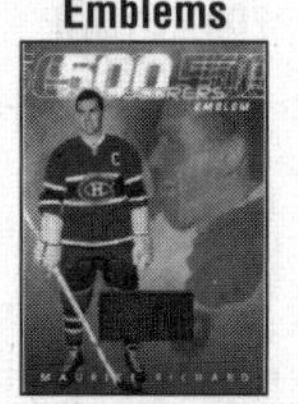

STATED PRINT RUN 10 SETS
NOT PRICED DUE TO SCARCITY

2001-02 BAP Ultimate Memorabilia Gloves Are Off

STATED PRINT RUN 30 SER.#'d SETS
1 Rocket Richard 50.00 125.00
2 Gordie Howe 40.00 100.00
3 Mario Lemieux 40.00 100.00
4 Wayne Gretzky 75.00 200.00
5 Bill Gadsby 20.00 50.00
6 Doug Harvey 15.00 40.00
7 Ted Kennedy 20.00 50.00
8 King Clancy 40.00 100.00
9 Joe Sakic 30.00 80.00
10 Guy Lafleur 25.00 60.00
11 Eric Lindros 15.00 40.00

13 Mats Sundin 15.00 40.00
14 Al MacInnis 15.00 40.00
15 Doug Weight 15.00 40.00
16 Simon Gagne 15.00 40.00
17 Scott Niedermayer 15.00 40.00
18 Sergei Samsonov 15.00 40.00
19 Alexei Yashin 15.00 40.00
20 John LeClair 15.00 40.00
21 Sergei Fedorov 25.00 60.00
22 Chris Chelios 15.00 40.00
23 Jarome Iginla 25.00 60.00
24 Ace Bailey 30.00 80.00
25 Dickie Moore 15.00 40.00

2001-02 BAP Ultimate Memorabilia Jerseys

STATED PRINT RUN 50 SERIAL #'d SETS
1 Paul Kariya 12.50 30.00
2 Martin Brodeur 25.00 60.00
3 John LeClair 12.50 30.00
4 Ilya Kovalchuk 15.00 40.00
5 Bill Guerin 10.00 25.00
6 Dominik Hasek 15.00 40.00
7 Keith Tkachuk 12.50 30.00
8 Pavel Bure 12.50 30.00
9 Brian Leetch 10.00 25.00
10 Mario Lemieux 25.00 60.00
11 Mats Sundin 12.50 30.00
12 Owen Nolan 10.00 25.00
13 Mark Messier 12.50 30.00
14 Jaromir Jagr 15.00 40.00
15 Joe Sakic 20.00 50.00
16 Rob Blake 10.00 25.00
17 Brendan Shanahan 12.50 30.00
18 Eric Lindros 12.50 30.00
19 Mike Modano 15.00 40.00
20 Sergei Fedorov 15.00 40.00
21 Nicklas Lidstrom 12.50 30.00
22 Steve Yzerman 25.00 60.00
23 Teemu Selanne 12.50 30.00
24 Alexei Yashin 10.00 25.00
25 Doug Weight 10.00 25.00
26 Chris Pronger 10.00 25.00
27 Patrick Roy 25.00 60.00
28 Curtis Joseph 12.50 30.00
29 Jeremy Roenick 15.00 40.00
30 Luc Robitaille 10.00 25.00

2001-02 BAP Ultimate Memorabilia Jerseys and Sticks

*JSY/STK: .5X TO 1.25X JSY HI
STATED PRINT RUN 50 SERIAL #'d SETS

2001-02 BAP Ultimate Memorabilia Journey Jerseys

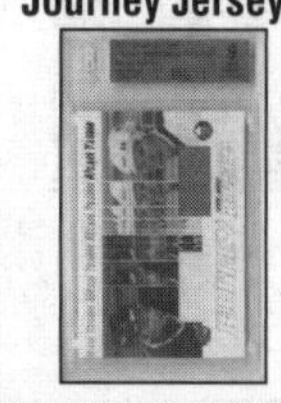

STATED PRINT RUN 50 SER.#'d SETS
1 Mark Messier 15.00 40.00
2 Curtis Joseph 15.00 40.00
3 Alexei Yashin 12.50 30.00
4 Gordie Howe 60.00 150.00
5 Felix Potvin 15.00 40.00
6 Rob Blake 12.50 30.00
7 Pavel Bure 20.00 50.00
8 Mats Sundin 15.00 40.00
9 Ed Belfour 15.00 40.00
10 Mike Modano 20.00 50.00
11 Brett Hull 20.00 50.00
12 Brendan Shanahan 15.00 40.00
13 Teemu Selanne 15.00 40.00

14 Keith Tkachuk 12.50 30.00
15 Patrick Roy 50.00 125.00
16 Luc Robitaille 12.50 30.00
17 Jeremy Roenick 20.00 50.00
18 Alexander Mogilny 12.50 30.00
19 Dominik Hasek 20.00 50.00
20 Jaromir Jagr 25.00 60.00
21 Roman Turek 12.50 30.00
22 Wayne Gretzky 125.00 300.00

2001-02 BAP Ultimate Memorabilia Journey Emblems

STATED PRINT RUN 10 SETS
NOT PRICED DUE TO SCARCITY

2001-02 BAP Ultimate Memorabilia Legend Terry Sawchuk

All cards in this product were graded by Beckett Grading Services and are available only in graded form. Cards in this 16-card set honored legendary goalie Terry Sawchuk by combining a swatch of his game-worn jersey with a swatch of game jersey from a current NHL goalie. Cards from this set were serial-numbered out of 20 on the back of the grading label. Cards were unnumbered and are listed below in checklist order.

STATED PRINT RUN 20 SER.#'d SETS
NOT PRICED DUE TO SCARCITY
1 Patrick Roy
2 Martin Brodeur
3 Dominik Hasek
4 Curtis Joseph
5 Nikolai Khabibulin
6 Johan Hedberg
7 Ed Belfour
8 Mike Richter
9 Felix Potvin
10 Tommy Salo
11 Roberto Luongo
12 Byron Dafoe
13 Jose Theodore
14 Jocelyn Thibault
15 Evgeni Nabokov
16 Olaf Kolzig

2001-02 BAP Ultimate Memorabilia Les Canadiens

STATED PRINT RUN 40 SER.#'d SETS
1 Mark Recchi 20.00 50.00
2 Yvan Cournoyer 20.00 50.00
3 Steve Shutt 20.00 50.00
4 Maurice Richard 75.00 200.00
5 Bob Gainey 25.00 60.00
6 Larry Robinson 20.00 50.00
7 Henri Richard 20.00 50.00
8 Jose Theodore 25.00 60.00
9 Saku Koivu 20.00 50.00
10 Patrick Roy 50.00 125.00
11 Jean Beliveau 30.00 80.00
12 Doug Harvey 20.00 50.00
13 Frank Mahovlich 20.00 50.00
14 Peter Mahovlich 20.00 50.00
15 Guy Lafleur 25.00 60.00
16 Serge Savard 20.00 50.00
17 Guy Lapointe 20.00 50.00
18 Jacques Plante 50.00 125.00

2001-02 BAP Ultimate Memorabilia Made to Order

Ten Made to Order redemption cards were randomly inserted into packs. Each redemption card entitled the holder to a 1 of 1 jersey card of the player they chose from a list provided by BAP.
1 Wayne Gretzky NYR

2 Wayne Gretzky Edmonton
3 Mario Lemieux Away
4 Mario Lemieux Home Left Profile
5 Mario Lemieux Home Right Profile
6 Pavel Bure
7 Marian Gaborik
NNO Redemption Card

2001-02 BAP Ultimate Memorabilia MVP

Ten MVP Winner Redemption cards were randomly inserted into packs. The redemption cards entitled the holder to a jersey card of the Hart Trophy winner for 2001-02. The cards were then graded by Beckett Grading Services and numbered out of 10.

PRINT RUN 10 CARDS
NOT PRICED DUE TO SCARCITY
1 Jose Theodore

2001-02 BAP Ultimate Memorabilia Numbers

STATED PRINT RUN 20 SERIAL #'d SETS
NOT PRICED DUE TO SCARCITY
1 Paul Kariya
2 John LeClair
3 Ilya Kovalchuk
4 Bill Guerin
5 Dominik Hasek
6 Keith Tkachuk
7 Pavel Bure
8 Brian Leetch
9 Mario Lemieux
10 Mats Sundin
11 Mark Messier
12 Joe Sakic
13 Rob Blake
14 Mike Modano
15 Sergei Fedorov
16 Martin Brodeur
17 Jaromir Jagr
18 Brendan Shanahan
19 Owen Nolan
20 Eric Lindros
21 Nicklas Lidstrom
22 Steve Yzerman
23 Teemu Selanne
24 Alexei Yashin
25 Doug Weight
26 Chris Pronger
27 Patrick Roy
28 Curtis Joseph
29 Jeremy Roenick
30 Luc Robitaille

2001-02 BAP Ultimate Memorabilia Name Plates

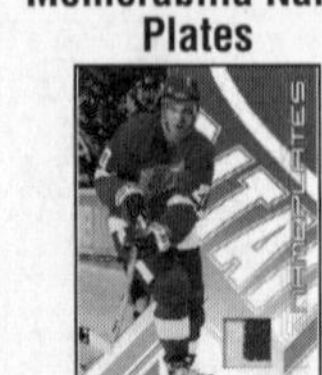

PRINT RUNS LISTED BELOW
1 Wayne Gretzky LA/40 75.00 200.00
2 Mario Lemieux/50 40.00 100.00
3 Paul Kariya/40 15.00 40.00
4 Pavel Bure/40 15.00 40.00
5 Mats Sundin/40 15.00 40.00
6 Mark Recchi/40 10.00 25.00
7 Dominik Hasek/40 20.00 50.00
8 Luc Robitaille/50 10.00 25.00
9 Bill Guerin/50 10.00 25.00
10 Eric Lindros/50 15.00 40.00
11 Patrick Roy/40 30.00 80.00
12 Nikolai Khabibulin/50 15.00 40.00
13 Teemu Selanne/50 15.00 40.00
14 Mark Messier/50 15.00 40.00
15 Steve Yzerman/50 30.00 80.00
16 Brian Leetch/50 10.00 25.00
17 Owen Nolan/50 10.00 25.00
18 Jarome Iginla/50 20.00 50.00
19 Gordie Howe Aeros/50 30.00 80.00
20 Roman Cechmanek/50 10.00 25.00
21 Joe Thornton/50 20.00 50.00
22 Ilya Kovalchuk/50 20.00 50.00
23 Curtis Joseph/50 15.00 40.00
24 Jeremy Roenick/50 20.00 50.00
25 Keith Tkachuk/50 15.00 40.00
26 Joe Sakic/50 20.00 50.00
27 Jaromir Jagr/50 20.00 50.00
28 Rob Blake/40 10.00 25.00
29 Mike Modano/50 20.00 50.00
30 Martin Brodeur/50 30.00 80.00
31 Nicklas Lidstrom/50 15.00 40.00
32 John LeClair/50 15.00 40.00
33 Gordie Howe NE/50 30.00 80.00
34 Chris Pronger/50 10.00 25.00
35 Sergei Fedorov/50 20.00 50.00
36 Jason Arnott/50 10.00 25.00
37 Marcel Dionne/40 10.00 25.00
38 Phil Esposito/50 20.00 50.00
39 Wayne Gretzky NYR/50 75.00 200.00
40 Doug Weight/40 10.00 25.00

2001-02 BAP Ultimate Memorabilia Playoff Records

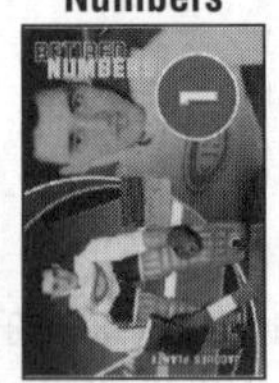

STATED PRINT RUNS LISTED BELOW
1 Patrick Roy/50 30.00 80.00
219 Games
2 Patrick Roy/50 30.00 80.00
137 Wins
3 Larry Robinson/50 20.00 50.00
20 Years
4 Mark Messier/50 20.00 50.00
14 Goals
5 Wayne Gretzky/50 50.00 125.00
382 Points
6 Reggie Leach/50 20.00 50.00
19 Goals
7 Jari Kurri/50 25.00 60.00
12 Goals
8 Jari Kurri/50 25.00 60.00
19 Goals
9 Wayne Gretzky/50 50.00 125.00
260 Assists
10 Wayne Gretzky/10
14 Assists in a Six-Game Series
11 Wayne Gretzky/10
6 Assists in one Playoff Game
12 Wayne Gretzky/10
31 Assists
13 Wayne Gretzky/50 50.00 125.00
133 Goals
14 Wayne Gretzky/10
47 Points in 1985 Playoffs
15 Mario Lemieux/50 40.00 100.00
16 Mike Bossy/50 20.00 50.00
35 Goals
17 Mark Messier/50 20.00 50.00
236 Games
18 Wayne Gretzky/10
24 Career Playoff Game-Winning Goals
19 Joe Sakic/50 30.00 80.00
6 Goals
20 Maurice Richard/10
6 Playoff Overtime Goals

2001-02 BAP Ultimate Memorabilia Production Line

All cards in this product were graded by Beckett Grading Services and are available only in graded form. Cards from this set feature game-used jersey swatches from the legendary Production Line of the Detroit Red Wings. Each card was serial-numbered out of 20 on the back of the grading label. Cards are unnumbered and are listed below in checklist order.

STATED PRINT RUN 20 SERIAL #'d SETS
NOT PRICED DUE TO SCARCITY
1 Gordie Howe
2 Sid Abel
3 Ted Lindsay
4 Gordie Howe
Sid Abel
Ted Lindsay
5 Gordie Howe
Sid Abel
Ted Lindsay

2001-02 BAP Ultimate Memorabilia Prototypical Players

STATED PRINT RUN 40 SERIAL #'d SETS
1 Jacques Plante 60.00 150.00
Patrick Roy
2 Jacques Plante 60.00 150.00
Martin Brodeur
3 Jacques Plante 40.00 100.00
Dominik Hasek
4 Doug Harvey 25.00 60.00
Chris Pronger
5 Doug Harvey 25.00 60.00
Rob Blake
6 Doug Harvey 25.00 60.00
Nicklas Lidstrom
7 Jean Beliveau 50.00 125.00
Steve Yzerman
8 J.Beliveau/M.Lemieux 50.00 125.00
9 Jean Beliveau 40.00 100.00
Joe Sakic
10 Bobby Hull 25.00 60.00
Luc Robitaille
11 Bobby Hull 25.00 60.00
Paul Kariya
12 Bobby Hull 25.00 60.00
Brendan Shanahan
13 Gordie Howe 40.00 100.00
Jaromir Jagr
14 Gordie Howe 25.00 60.00
Pavel Bure
15 Gordie Howe 25.00 60.00
Brett Hull

2001-02 BAP Ultimate Memorabilia Retired Numbers

STATED PRINT RUN 5 SETS
NOT PRICED DUE TO SCARCITY
1 Sid Abel
2 Bill Barber
3 Jean Beliveau
4 Mike Bossy
5 Johnny Bucyk
6 Bobby Clarke
7 Marcel Dionne
8 Tony Esposito
9 Wayne Gretzky
10 Glenn Hall
11 Doug Harvey
12 Gordie Howe
13 Bobby Hull
14 Guy Lafleur
15 Ted Lindsay
16 Stan Mikita
17 Bernie Parent
18 Gilbert Perreault
19 Jacques Plante
20 Denis Potvin
21 Henri Richard
22 Rocket Richard
23 Terry Sawchuk
24 Billy Smith

2001-02 BAP Ultimate Memorabilia Retro Trophies

STATED PRINT RUN 25 SER.#'d SETS
1 Wayne Gretzky 60.00 150.00
Joe Sakic
Hart Trophy
2 Gordie Howe 40.00 100.00
Jaromir Jagr
Hart Trophy
3 Wayne Gretzky 60.00 150.00
Jaromir Jagr
Art Ross Trophy
4 W.Gretzky/M.Lemieux 75.00 200.00
5 Bobby Clarke 50.00 125.00
Mario Lemieux
Masterton Trophy
6 Mike Bossy 30.00 80.00
Joe Sakic
Lady Byng Trophy
7 Jari Kurri 25.00 60.00
Paul Kariya
Lady Byng Trophy
8 Lanny McDonald 25.00 60.00
Curtis Joseph
King Clancy Trophy
9 Terry Sawchuk 30.00 80.00
Dominik Hasek
Vezina Trophy
10 Glenn Hall 50.00 125.00
Patrick Roy
Calder Trophy
11 Terry Sawchuk 40.00 100.00
Evgeni Nabokov
Calder Trophy
12 Tony Esposito 40.00 100.00
Martin Brodeur
Calder Trophy
13 Bobby Clarke 30.00 80.00
Steve Yzerman
Selke Trophy
14 Glenn Hall 50.00 125.00
Patrick Roy
Conn Smythe Trophy
15 Bernie Parent 50.00 125.00
Patrick Roy
Conn Smythe Trophy
16 W.Gretzky/M.Lemieux 75.00 200.00
17 G.Lafleur/M.Lemieux 50.00 125.00
18 Doug Harvey 25.00 60.00
Nicklas Lidstrom
Norris Trophy
19 W.Gretzky/M.Lemieux 75.00 200.00
20 Guy Lafleur 40.00 100.00
Joe Sakic
Lester B. Pearson Award

2001-02 BAP Ultimate Memorabilia Retro Teammates

STATED PRINT RUNS LISTED BELOW
1 Beliveau/H.Richard/M.Richard/10
2 M.Richard/Plante/Harvey/10
3 Howe/Lindsay/Sawchuk/30 100.00 250.00
4 Gretzky/Messier/Coffey/10
5 Bossy/Trottier/Potvin/30 40.00 100.00
6 Clarke/Barber/Schultz/30 40.00 100.00
7 Hull/Hall/Mikita/30 75.00 200.00
8 Horton/Bower/Sawchuk/30 75.00 200.00
9 Lapointe/Savard/Mahovlich/30 40.00 100.00
10 Lafleur/Cournoyer/Beliveau/30 60.00 150.00
11 Lemieux/Coffey/Jagr/30 50.00 125.00
12 Gretzky/Leetch/Messier/30 100.00 250.00
13 Gretzky/Kurri/Robitaille/30 100.00 250.00
14 H.Richard/Harvey/M.Richard/10

2001-02 BAP Ultimate Memorabilia ROY

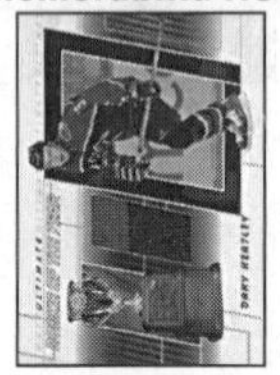

Ten Calder Winner Redemption cards were randomly inserted into packs.

PRINT RUN 10 SETS
NOT PRICED DUE TO SCARCITY
1 Dany Heatley

2001-02 BAP Ultimate Memorabilia Scoring Leaders

STATED PRINT RUN 40 SER.#'d SETS
1 Wayne Gretzky 1982 60.00 150.00
2 Wayne Gretzky 1983 60.00 150.00
3 Wayne Gretzky 1984 60.00 150.00
4 Wayne Gretzky 1985 60.00 150.00
5 Jari Kurri 1986 25.00 60.00
6 Wayne Gretzky 1987 60.00 150.00
7 Mario Lemieux 1988 30.00 80.00
8 Mario Lemieux 1989 30.00 80.00
9 Brett Hull 1990 15.00 40.00
10 Brett Hull 1991 15.00 40.00
11 Brett Hull 1992 15.00 40.00
12 Teemu Selanne 15.00 40.00
Alexander Mogilny
1993
13 Pavel Bure 1994 15.00 40.00
14 Peter Bondra 1995 15.00 40.00
15 Mario Lemieux 1996 30.00 80.00
16 Keith Tkachuk 1997 15.00 40.00
17 Teemu Selanne 15.00 40.00
Peter Bondra
1998
18 Teemu Selanne 1999 15.00 40.00
19 Pavel Bure 2000 15.00 40.00
20 Pavel Bure 2001 15.00 40.00
21 Jarome Iginla 2002 20.00 50.00

2001-02 BAP Ultimate Memorabilia Stanley Cup Winners

STATED PRINT RUN 50 SER.#'d SETS
1 Henri Richard 20.00 50.00
2 Jean Beliveau 30.00 80.00
3 Yvan Cournoyer 20.00 50.00
4 Red Kelly 20.00 50.00
5 Maurice Richard 75.00 200.00
6 Serge Savard 20.00 50.00
7 Jacques Plante/10
8 Johnny Bower 20.00 50.00
9 Bryan Trottier 20.00 50.00
10 Larry Robinson 20.00 50.00
11 Mark Messier 30.00 80.00
12 Jacques Laperriere 20.00 50.00
13 Doug Harvey 20.00 50.00
14 Frank Mahovlich 20.00 50.00
15 Guy Lapointe 20.00 50.00
16 Jari Kurri 25.00 60.00
17 Guy Lafleur 25.00 60.00
18 Bob Gainey 30.00 80.00
19 Grant Fuhr 20.00 50.00
20 Turk Broda/10
21 Ted Kennedy 20.00 50.00
22 Steve Shutt 20.00 50.00
23 Wayne Gretzky 75.00 200.00
24 Terry Sawchuk 40.00 100.00
25 Denis Potvin 20.00 50.00
26 Ted Lindsay 20.00 50.00
27 Billy Smith 20.00 50.00
28 Gordie Howe/10

2001-02 BAP Ultimate Memorabilia Vezina Winner

Ten Vezina Winner Redemption cards were randomly inserted into packs.

PRINT RUN 10 SETS
NOT PRICED DUE TO SCARCITY
1 Jose Theodore

2001-02 BAP Ultimate Memorabilia Waving the Flag

STATED PRINT RUN 30 SER.#'d SETS
1 Mario Lemieux 30.00 80.00
2 Joe Sakic 20.00 50.00
3 Steve Yzerman 25.00 60.00
4 Paul Kariya 15.00 40.00
5 Curtis Joseph 12.50 30.00
6 Martin Brodeur 25.00 60.00
7 Eric Lindros 12.50 30.00
8 Chris Pronger 10.00 25.00
9 Jaromir Jagr 15.00 40.00
10 Milan Hejduk 12.50 30.00
11 Dominik Hasek 20.00 50.00
12 Martin Havlat 10.00 25.00
13 Teemu Selanne 15.00 40.00
14 Jani Hurme 10.00 25.00
15 Miikka Kiprusoff 15.00 40.00
16 Sami Kapanen 10.00 25.00
17 Mats Sundin 12.50 30.00
18 Nicklas Lidstrom 12.50 30.00
19 Tommy Salo 10.00 25.00
20 Markus Naslund 12.50 30.00
21 Jeremy Roenick 15.00 40.00
22 Doug Weight 10.00 25.00
23 Tony Amonte 10.00 25.00
24 Brian Leetch 12.00 30.00
25 Mike Modano 15.00 40.00
26 Brett Hull 15.00 40.00
27 John Leclair 12.50 30.00
28 Keith Tkachuk 12.50 30.00
29 Alexei Yashin 10.00 25.00
30 Pavel Bure 12.50 30.00
31 Nikolai Khabibulin 12.50 30.00
32 Darius Kasparaitis 10.00 25.00

2002-03 BAP Ultimate Memorabilia

Released in May 2003, BAP Ultimate Memorabilia contained a graded rookie card numbered out of 250 and an encapsulated memorabilia card per pack. Rookie cards were not numbered and are listed below in checklist order. Since they were only available in graded form, raw cards were not priced.

COMPLETE SET (100)
1 P-M Bouchard
2 Rick Nash
3 Dennis Seidenberg
4 Jay Bouwmeester
5 Stanislav Chistov
6 Kurt Sauer
7 Ivan Majesky
8 Chuck Kobasew
9 Jordan Leopold
10 Steve Ott
11 Ales Hemsky
12 Patrick Sharp
13 Kari Haakana
14 Dmitri Bykov
15 Alex Henry
16 Henrik Zetterberg
17 Alexander Frolov
18 Steve Eminger
19 Scottie Upshall
20 Tom Koivisto
21 Ari Ahonen
22 Ron Hainsey
23 Martin Gerber
24 Adam Hall
25 Lasse Pirjeta
26 Anton Volchenkov
27 Jeff Paul
28 Carlo Colaiacovo
29 Alexander Svitov
30 Alexei Smirnov
31 Jeff Taffe
32 Mikael Tellqvist
33 Radovan Somik
34 Mike Komisarek
35 Chris Schmidt
36 Dick Tarnstrom
37 Ryan Bayda
38 Sylvain Blouin
39 Ray Emery
40 Stephane Veilleux
41 Curtis Sanford
42 Eric Godard
43 Pascal Leclaire
44 Patrick Boileau
45 Tim Thomas
46 Mike Cammalleri
47 Jason Spezza
48 Cody Rudkowsky
49 Darren Haydar
50 Ryan Miller
51 Brandon Reid
52 Christian Backman
53 Niko Dimitrakos
54 Garnet Exelby
55 Jason King
56 Martin Samuelsson
57 Miroslav Zalesak
58 Tomas Malec
59 Michael Garnett
60 Matt Walker
61 Shaone Morrisonn
62 Chad Wiseman
63 Michael Leighton
64 Tomas Surovy
65 Jason Bacashihua
66 Jim Vandermeer
67 Konstantin Koltsov
68 Fernando Pisani
69 Rickard Wallin
70 Brooks Orpik
71 Tomas Zizka
72 Jarret Stoll
73 Cristobal Huet
74 Levente Szuper
75 Jared Aulin
76 Simon Gamache
77 Kris Vernarsky
78 Radoslav Hecl
79 Jamie Hodson
80 Marc-Andre Bergeron
81 Mike Siklenka
82 Igor Radulov
83 Paul Manning
84 John Tripp
85 Ian MacNeil
86 Jim Fahey
87 Dany Sabourin
88 Alexei Semenov
89 Curtis Murphy
90 Jerred Smithson
91 Francois Beauchemin
92 Vernon Fiddler
93 Cam Severson
94 Burke Henry
95 Brad Defauw
96 Craig Andersson
97 Frederic Cloutier
98 Tomas Kurka
99 Jonathan Hedstrom
100 Valeri Kharlamov

2002-03 BAP Ultimate Memorabilia Active Eight

PRINT RUN 30 SER.#'d SETS
1 Messier/Francis/Yzerman 40.00 100.00
2 Lemieux/Forsberg/Oates 40.00 100.00
3 Roy/Belfour/Brodeur 100.00 250.00
4 Hull/Messier/Yzerman 40.00 100.00
5 Messier/Francis/Yzerman 40.00 100.00
6 Patrick Roy 60.00 150.00
Ed Belfour
Curtis Joseph
7 Lemieux/Sakic/Leetch 50.00 125.00
8 Lemieux/Yzerman/Oates 60.00 150.00

2002-03 BAP Ultimate Memorabilia All-Star MVP

*MULT.COLOR SWATCH: .75X TO 1.5X
PRINT RUN 40 SER.#'d SETS
1 Bill Guerin 12.50 30.00
2 Bobby Hull/1970 15.00 40.00
3 Bobby Hull/1971 15.00 40.00
4 Brett Hull 20.00 50.00
5 Dany Heatley 15.00 40.00
6 Eric Daze 12.50 30.00
7 Frank Mahovlich 15.00 40.00
8 Grant Fuhr 25.00 60.00
9 Henri Richard 12.50 30.00
10 Jean Beliveau 25.00 60.00
11 Mario Lemieux 25.00 60.00
12 Mario Lemieux 25.00 60.00
13 Mario Lemieux 25.00 60.00
14 Mark Recchi 12.50 30.00
15 Mike Bossy 12.50 30.00
16 Mike Gartner 12.50 30.00
17 Mike Richter 12.50 30.00
18 Pavel Bure 12.50 30.00
19 Peter Mahovlich 15.00 40.00
20 Reggie Leach 12.50 30.00
21 Vincent Damphousse 12.50 30.00
22 Teemu Selanne 12.50 30.00

2002-03 BAP Ultimate Memorabilia Autographs

PRINT RUN 30 SER.#'d SETS
GOLD 1 OF 1's EXIST
1 Alexander Frolov 25.00 60.00
2 Alexei Smirnov 12.50 30.00
3 Anton Volchenkov 12.50 30.00
4 Carlo Colaiacovo 12.50 30.00
5 Chuck Kobasew 12.50 30.00
6 Jay Bouwmeester 25.00 60.00
7 Jordan Leopold 12.50 30.00
8 Mike Cammalleri 12.50 30.00
9 P-M Bouchard 20.00 50.00
10 Rick Nash 40.00 80.00
11 Ron Hainsey 12.50 30.00
12 Scottie Upshall 12.50 30.00
13 Stanislav Chistov 12.00 30.00
14 Sergei Fedorov 25.00 60.00
15 Patrick Roy 100.00 250.00
16 Mario Lemieux 100.00 250.00
17 Brian Leetch 20.00 50.00
18 Dany Heatley 30.00 80.00
19 Jarome Iginla 25.00 60.00
20 Joe Sakic 50.00 125.00
21 Joe Thornton 30.00 80.00
22 Jose Theodore 25.00 60.00
23 Pavel Bure 20.00 50.00
24 Peter Forsberg 40.00 100.00
25 Saku Koivu 20.00 50.00
26 Alexander Svitov 12.50 30.00
27 Stephane Veilleux 12.50 30.00
28 Adam Hall 12.50 30.00
29 Henrik Zetterberg 40.00 100.00
30 Steve Eminger 12.50 30.00

2002-03 BAP Ultimate Memorabilia Blades of Steel

PRINT RUN 10 SER.#'d SETS
NOT PRICED DUE TO SCARCITY
1 Nels Stewart
2 Georges Vezina
3 Jean Beliveau
4 Tim Horton
5 Maurice Richard

Jacques Plante
Bill Barilko
Mario Lemieux
Aurel Joliat
0 Jarome Iginla

2002-03 BAP Ultimate Memorabilia Calder Candidates

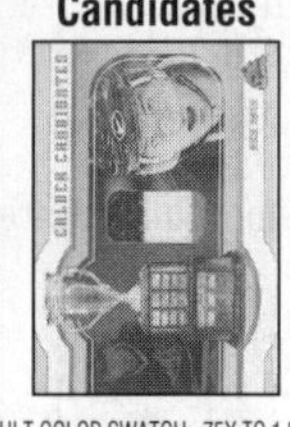

MULT.COLOR SWATCH: .75X TO 1.5X
RINT RUN 40 SER.#'d SETS

Henrik Zetterberg 30.00 80.00
Niko Kapanen 12.50 30.00
Ron Hainsey 12.50 30.00
Jason Spezza 30.00 80.00
Anton Volchenkov 12.50 30.00
Ivan Huml 12.50 30.00
Tyler Arnason 12.50 30.00
Dennis Seidenberg 12.50 30.00
Alexander Frolov 12.50 30.00
0 Alexei Smirnov 12.50 30.00
1 Jay Bouwmeester 12.50 30.00
2 Ales Hemsky 20.00 50.00
3 Rick Nash 30.00 80.00
4 Jordan Leopold 12.50 30.00
5 Stephen Weiss 12.50 30.00
6 Ryan Miller 12.50 30.00
7 Chuck Kobasew 12.50 30.00
8 Alexander Svitov 12.50 30.00
9 Adam Hall 12.50 30.00
0 Stanislav Chistov 12.50 30.00

2002-03 BAP Ultimate Memorabilia Captains

his 8-card set featured swatches from the aptain's C on the featured player's jersey. ards were serial-numbered to just 5 and ach card was encapsulated in a clear plastic ab with a descriptive label encased at the p. This set is not priced due to scarcity. he set is unnumbered and listed below in hecklist order.
RINT RUN 5 SER.#'d SETS
OT PRICED DUE TO SCARCITY

Paul Kariya
Mario Lemieux
Joe Thornton
Saku Koivu
Markus Naslund
Mats Sundin
Steve Yzerman
Joe Sakic

2002-03 BAP Ultimate Memorabilia Complete Package

his 10-card set featured 4 swatches of ame-used memorabilia per card. Cards ere serial-numbered to just 10 and each ard was encapsulated in a clear plastic slab ith a descriptive label encased at the top. he set is unnumbered and listed below in hecklist order. This set is not priced due to carcity.
RINT RUN 10 SER.#'d SETS
OT PRICED DUE TO SCARCITY

Curtis Joseph
Eric Lindros
Guy Lafleur
Jacques Plante
Mario Lemieux
Mats Sundin
Maurice Richard
Patrick Roy
Terry Sawchuk
0 Tim Horton

2002-03 BAP Ultimate Memorabilia Conn Smythe

*MULT.COLOR SWATCH: .75X TO 1.5X
PRINT RUN 30 SER.#'d SETS

1 Jean Beliveau/1965 30.00 80.00
2 Roger Crozier/1966 15.00 40.00
3 Glenn Hall/1968 20.00 50.00
4 Serge Savard/1969 15.00 40.00
5 Yvan Cournoyer/1973 20.00 50.00
6 Bernie Parent/1974 20.00 50.00
7 Bernie Parent/1975 20.00 50.00
8 Reggie Leach/1976 15.00 40.00
9 Guy Lafleur/1977 25.00 60.00
10 Larry Robinson/1978 15.00 40.00
11 Bryan Trottier/1980 15.00 40.00
12 Mike Bossy/1982 15.00 40.00
13 Billy Smith/1983 15.00 40.00
14 Mark Messier/1984 25.00 60.00
15 Patrick Roy/1986 40.00 100.00
16 Ron Hextall/1987 20.00 50.00
17 Al MacInnis/1989 15.00 40.00
18 Bill Ranford/1990 15.00 40.00
19 Mario Lemieux 40.00 100.00
20 Mario Lemieux 40.00 100.00
21 Patrick Roy/1993 40.00 100.00
22 Brian Leetch/1994 20.00 50.00
23 Claude Lemieux/1995 15.00 40.00
24 Joe Sakic/1996 30.00 80.00
25 Mike Vernon/1997 25.00 60.00
26 Steve Yzerman 30.00 80.00
27 Joe Nieuwendyk/1999 15.00 40.00
28 Scott Stevens/2000 15.00 40.00
29 Patrick Roy/2001 40.00 100.00
30 Nicklas Lidstrom/2002 15.00 40.00

2002-03 BAP Ultimate Memorabilia Cornerstones

This 8-card set featured swatches of game-used jerseys from 4 different players considered the greatest to play in that given city. Cards were serial-numbered to just 20 and each card was encapsulated in a clear plastic slab with a descriptive label encased at the top. The set is unnumbered and listed below in checklist order. This set is not priced due to scarcity.
PRINT RUN 20 SER.#'d SETS
NOT PRICED DUE TO SCARCITY

1 Tiny Thompson
Gerry Cheevers
Cam Neely
Joe Thornton
2 Bill Mosienko
Bobby Hull
Michel Goulet
Eric Daze
3 Ted Lindsay
Terry Sawchuk
Alex Delvecchio
Steve Yzerman
4 Aurel Joliat
Jean Beliveau
Guy Lafleur
Saku Koivu
5 Chuck Rayner
Ed Giacomin
Phil Esposito
Mark Messier
6 King Clancy
Teeder Kennedy
Lanny McDonald
Mats Sundin
7 Bernie Parent
Bobby Clarke
Eric Lindros
Simon Gagne
8 Denis Potvin
Bryan Trottier
Mike Bossy
Alexei Yashin

2002-03 BAP Ultimate Memorabilia Cup Duels

*MULT.COLOR SWATCH: .75X TO 1.5X
PRINT RUN 40 SER.#'d SETS
GOLD 1 OF 1's EXIST

1 George Hainsworth 40.00 100.00
Tiny Thompson
2 Terry Sawchuk 75.00 200.00
Jacques Plante
3 Jacques Plante 30.00 80.00
Johnny Bower

4 Glenn Hall 40.00 100.00
Terry Sawchuk
5 Johnny Bower 30.00 80.00
Terry Sawchuk
6 Roger Crozier 20.00 50.00
Gump Worsley
7 Gerry Cheevers 20.00 50.00
Ed Giacomin
8 Gilles Gilbert 20.00 50.00
Bernie Parent
9 Billy Smith 20.00 50.00
Grant Fuhr
10 Patrick Roy 30.00 80.00
Mike Vernon
11 Ron Hextall 20.00 50.00
Grant Fuhr
12 Andy Moog 20.00 50.00
Grant Fuhr
13 Patrick Roy 30.00 80.00
Mike Vernon
14 Andy Moog 20.00 50.00
Bill Ranford
15 Tom Barrasso 20.00 50.00
Ed Belfour
16 Martin Brodeur 40.00 100.00
Mike Vernon
17 John Vanbiesbrouck 40.00 100.00
Patrick Roy
18 Olaf Kolzig 20.00 50.00
Chris Osgood
19 Martin Brodeur 30.00 80.00
Ed Belfour
20 P.Roy/M.Broduer 75.00 150.00

2002-03 BAP Ultimate Memorabilia Customer Appreciation Card

This special memorabilia card was only available to collectors who held a Henrik Zetterberg autograph redemption card. The card was sent back along with the autograph card as a token of appreciation. The card was serial-numbered to just 31 copies and was sealed in a plastic card slab.

1 Henrik Zetterberg 40.00 100.00

2002-03 BAP Ultimate Memorabilia Dynamic Duos

PRINT RUN 30 SER.#'d SETS

1 M.Lemieux/J.Thornton 30.00 80.00
2 Peter Forsberg 20.00 50.00
Mats Sundin
3 I.Kovalchuk/S.Fedorov 25.00 60.00
4 S.Yzerman/D.Heatley 30.00 80.00
5 M.Modano/B.Hull 25.00 60.00
6 Brendan Shanahan 20.00 50.00
Paul Kariya
7 Joe Sakic 20.00 50.00
Eric Lindros
8 Saku Koivu 20.00 50.00
Teemu Selanne
9 J.Jagr/M.Gaborik 25.00 60.00
10 Pavel Bure 20.00 50.00
Sergei Samsonov

2002-03 BAP Ultimate Memorabilia Dynasty Jerseys

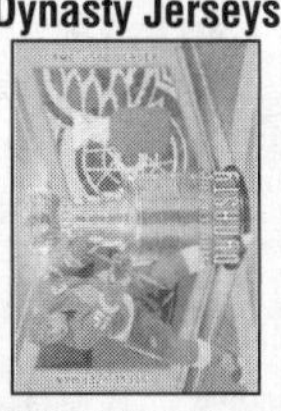

*MULT.COLOR SWATCH: .75X TO 1.5X
PRINT RUN 50 SER.#'d SETS

1 Brendan Shanahan 25.00 60.00
2 Brett Hull 30.00 80.00
3 Chris Chelios 25.00 60.00
4 Chris Osgood 20.00 50.00
5 Darren McCarty 20.00 50.00
6 Igor Larionov 20.00 50.00
7 Jiri Fischer 20.00 50.00
8 Kirk Maltby 20.00 50.00
9 Kris Draper 20.00 50.00
10 Luc Robitaille 20.00 50.00
11 Manny Legace 25.00 60.00
12 Martin Lapointe 20.00 50.00
13 Mathieu Dandenault 20.00 50.00
14 Mike Vernon 20.00 50.00
15 Nicklas Lidstrom 25.00 60.00
16 Pavel Datsyuk 25.00 60.00
17 Sergei Fedorov 30.00 80.00
18 Steve Yzerman 40.00 100.00
19 Tomas Holmstrom 20.00 50.00
20 Slava Kozlov 20.00 50.00

2002-03 BAP Ultimate Memorabilia Dynasty Emblems

PRINT RUN 10 SER.#'d SETS
NOT PRICED DUE TO SCARCITY

2002-03 BAP Ultimate Memorabilia Dynasty Numbers

PRINT RUN 10 SER.#'d SETS
NOT PRICED DUE TO SCARCITY

2002-03 BAP Ultimate Memorabilia Emblem Attic

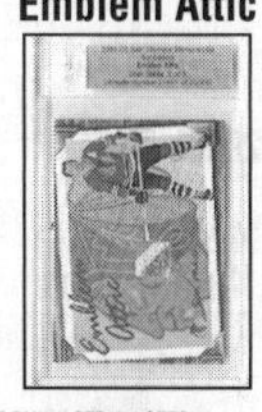

PRINT RUN 5 SER.#'d SETS
NOT PRICED DUE TO SCARCITY.

1 George Hainsworth
2 Bernie Parent
3 Marcel Dionne
4 Gerry Cheevers
5 Frank Mahovlich
6 Roy Worters
7 Jean Beliveau
8 Doug Harvey
9 John Bucyk
10 Tony Esposito
11 Jacques Plante
12 Guy Lafleur
13 Ted Lindsay
14 Terry Sawchuk
15 Bobby Hull
16 Harry Lumley
17 Glenn Hall
18 Stan Mikita
19 Roger Crozier
20 Ed Giacomin
21 Rocket Richard
22 Frank Brimsek
23 Phil Esposito
24 Mike Bossy
25 Aurel Joliat
26 Red Kelly
27 Henri Richard
28 Bobby Clarke

2002-03 BAP Ultimate Memorabilia Emblems

PRINT RUN 10 SER.#'d SETS
NOT PRICED DUE TO SCARCITY
GOLD 1 OF 1's EXIST

1 Mats Sundin
2 Joe Thornton
3 Steve Yzerman
4 Pavel Bure
5 Dany Heatley
6 Chris Chelios
7 Markus Naslund
8 Jaromir Jagr
9 Mario Lemieux
10 Brendan Shanahan
11 Peter Forsberg
12 Paul Kariya
13 Joe Sakic
14 Brett Hull
15 Martin Brodeur
16 Mike Comrie
17 Brian Leetch
18 Nicklas Lidstrom
19 Jeremy Roenick
20 Mike Modano
21 Patrick Roy
22 Sergei Fedorov
23 Luc Robitaille
24 John LeClair
25 Eric Lindros
26 Mark Messier
27 Saku Koivu
28 Ilya Kovalchuk
29 Marian Gaborik
30 Valeri Kharlamov

2002-03 BAP Ultimate Memorabilia Finals Showdown

This 40-card set featured jersey swatches from players who have faced off in the finals in years past. Cards were serial-numbered to just 40 and each card was encapsulated in a clear plastic slab with a descriptive label encased at the top. The set is unnumbered and listed below in checklist order.
*MULT.COLOR SWATCH: .75X TO 1.5X
PRINT RUN 40 SER.#'d SETS

1 Alex Delvecchio 20.00 50.00
Doug Harvey
2 Bernie Geoffrion 20.00 50.00
Ted Lindsay
3 Henri Richard 30.00 80.00
Tim Horton
4 Maurice Richard 40.00 100.00
Frank Mahovlich
5 Stan Mikita 30.00 80.00
Terry Sawchuk
6 Frank Mahovlich 20.00 50.00
Bobby Hull
7 Red Kelly 25.00 60.00
Terry Sawchuk
8 Tim Horton 40.00 100.00
Alex Delvecchio
9 Jean Beliveau 20.00 50.00
Glenn Hall
10 Jean Beliveau 20.00 50.00
Roger Crozier
11 Johnny Bower 20.00 50.00
John Ferguson
12 Peter Mahovlich 20.00 50.00
Bobby Hull
13 Gerry Cheevers 20.00 50.00
Rod Gilbert
14 Yvan Cournoyer 20.00 50.00
Bobby Hull
15 Bernie Parent 20.00 50.00
John Bucyk
16 Bobby Clarke 20.00 50.00
Gilbert Perreault
17 Steve Shutt 20.00 50.00
Dave Schultz
18 Guy Lapointe 20.00 50.00
Gerry Cheevers
19 Larry Robinson 20.00 50.00
Gerry Cheevers
20 Guy Lafleur 40.00 100.00
Phil Esposito
21 Billy Smith 25.00 60.00
Bobby Clarke
22 Bryan Trottier 30.00 80.00
Grant Fuhr
23 Mark Messier 20.00 50.00
Felix Potvin
24 Patrick Roy 40.00 100.00
Lanny McDonald
25 Jari Kurri 40.00 100.00
Ron Hextall
26 Kevin Lowe 20.00 50.00
Cam Neely
27 Al MacInnis 30.00 80.00
Patrick Roy
28 Mark Messier 20.00 50.00
Cam Neely
29 Mario Lemieux 50.00 125.00
Mike Modano
30 Jaromir Jagr 25.00 60.00
Jeremy Roenick
31 Patrick Roy 30.00 80.00
Luc Robitaille
32 Mark Messier 30.00 80.00
Pavel Bure
33 Martin Brodeur 40.00 100.00
Steve Yzerman
34 Patrick Roy 40.00 100.00
Rob Niedermayer
35 Steve Yzerman 50.00 125.00
Eric Lindros
36 Sergei Fedorov 20.00 50.00
Olaf Kolzig
37 Brett Hull 20.00 50.00
Mike Peca
38 Jason Arnott 20.00 50.00
Ed Belfour
39 Joe Sakic 30.00 80.00
Martin Brodeur
40 Nicklas Lidstrom 20.00 50.00
Ron Francis

2002-03 BAP Ultimate Memorabilia First Overall

This 15-card set featured players chosen first in the NHL entry draft and featured a swatch of game-worn jersey. Cards were serial-numbered to just 20 and each card was encapsulated in a clear plastic slab with a descriptive label encased at the top. The set is unnumbered and listed below in checklist order. This set is not priced due to scarcity.
PRINT RUN 20 SER.#'d SETS
NOT PRICED DUE TO SCARCITY

1 Alexandre Daigle
2 Bryan Berard
3 Chris Phillips
4 Ed Jovanovski
5 Eric Lindros
6 Ilya Kovalchuk
7 Joe Thornton
8 Mats Sundin
9 Mike Modano
10 Owen Nolan
11 Patrik Stefan
12 Rick DiPietro
13 Rick Nash
14 Roman Hamrlik
15 Vincent Lecavalier

2002-03 BAP Ultimate Memorabilia 500 Goal Scorers

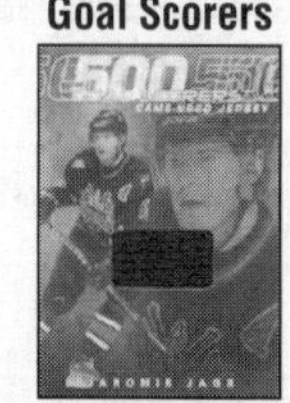

This 3-card set honored the 3 latest players to hit the 500 goal mark. Cards were serial-numbered to just 30 and each card was encapsulated in a clear plastic slab with a descriptive label encased at the top. The set is unnumbered and listed below in checklist order.
*MULT.COLOR SWATCH: .75X TO 1.5X
PRINT RUN 30 SER.#'d SETS

1 Joe Nieuwendyk 15.00 40.00
2 Joe Sakic 30.00 80.00
3 Jaromir Jagr 25.00 60.00

2002-03 BAP Ultimate Memorabilia 500 Goal Scorers Jersey and Stick

This 3-card set paralleled the regular insert set but included piece of stick with the swatch of jersey. Cards were serial-numbered to just 30 and were encapsulated in a clear plastic holder with a descriptive label encased at the top. Cards were unnumbered and are listed in checklist order.
*JSY/STK: .5X TO 1.25X JERSEY
PRINT RUN 30 SER.#'d SETS

2002-03 BAP Ultimate Memorabilia 500 Goal Scorers Emblems

PRINT RUN 10 SER.#'d SETS
NOT PRICED DUE TO SCARCITY

2002-03 BAP Ultimate Memorabilia Global Dominators

This 10-card set featured game-worn jersey swatches of players who regularly represent their nation in competition. Cards were serial-numbered to just 30 and each card was encapsulated in a clear plastic slab with a descriptive label encased at the top. The set is unnumbered and listed below in checklist order. Unpriced gold one of ones were also created.
*MULT.COLOR SWATCH: .75X TO 1.5X
PRINT RUN 30 SER.#'d SETS
GOLD 1 OF 1's EXIST

1 Mario Lemieux 40.00 100.00
2 Al MacInnis 15.00 40.00
3 Rob Blake 15.00 40.00
4 Peter Forsberg 25.00 60.00
5 Igor Larionov 15.00 40.00
6 Joe Sakic 30.00 80.00
7 Steve Yzerman 40.00 100.00
8 Alexander Mogilny 15.00 40.00
9 Theo Fleury 15.00 40.00
10 Brendan Shanahan 15.00 40.00

2002-03 BAP Ultimate Memorabilia Gloves Are Off

PRINT RUN 30 SER.#'d SETS

1 Ace Bailey 40.00 100.00
2 Mario Lemieux 30.00 80.00
3 Joe Sakic 20.00 50.00
4 Aurel Joliat 40.00 100.00
5 Guy Lafleur 30.00 80.00
6 Al MacInnis 15.00 40.00
7 Dickie Moore 15.00 40.00
8 Chris Chelios 15.00 40.00
9 Sergei Fedorov 20.00 50.00
10 Eddie Shore 20.00 50.00
11 Ted Kennedy 25.00 60.00
12 Eric Lindros 15.00 40.00
13 Mats Sundin 15.00 40.00
14 Doug Harvey 20.00 50.00
15 Bill Gadsby 30.00 80.00
16 Jarome Iginla 20.00 50.00
17 Joe Thornton 20.00 50.00
18 Maurice Richard 30.00 80.00
19 Brett Hull 20.00 50.00
20 King Clancy 30.00 80.00

2002-03 BAP Ultimate Memorabilia Great Moments

This 17-card set reflected on some of the best moments in NHL history and included pieces of game-used memorabilia from the featured play. Cards were serial-numbered to just 30 unless otherwise noted below and each card was encapsulated in a clear plastic slab with a descriptive label encased at the top. The set is unnumbered and listed below in checklist order.
*MULT.COLOR SWATCH: .75X TO 1.5X
PRINT RUN 30 SER.#'d SETS/
UNLESS OTHERWISE NOTED
LOWER PRINT RUNS NOT
PRICED DUE TO SCARCITY

1 Teeder Kennedy
And Royalty
2 Eddie Shore
Ace Bailey
Shake Hands
3 Maurice Richard
Jim Henry
Shake Hands
4 Mario Lemieux 50.00 125.00
5 Darryl Sittler 50.00 125.00
10 Points In A Game
6 Bill Barilko
The Goal/10
7 Frank Brimsek 25.00 60.00
First All-Star Game
8 Teemu Selanne 25.00 60.00
Rookie Record
9 Mark Messier 25.00 60.00
Rangers First Cup
In 54 Years
10 Patrick Roy 50.00 125.00
Breaks Sawchuk's Record
11 Jacques Plante 30.00 80.00
Donning the Mask
12 Jean Beliveau 30.00 80.00
First Conn Smythe
13 Glenn Hall 25.00 60.00
500 Straight Games
14 Maurice Richard 40.00 100.00
Five Goals In Playoff Game
15 Georges Hainsworth
22 Shutouts In One Year
16 Maurice Richard 40.00 100.00
Canadiens Win 5th
Consecutive Cup
17 Bill Mosienko 25.00 60.00
Fastest Hat Trick
18 M.Richard/Fifty in Fifty 40.00 100.00
19 Terry Sawchuk 40.00 100.00
100 Shutouts
20 Stan Mikita 25.00 60.00
Second Triple Crown

2002-03 BAP Ultimate Memorabilia Hat Tricks

This 20-card set featured 3 different swatches of game-used memorabilia from the featured player. Cards were serial-numbered to just 30 and each card was encapsulated in a clear plastic slab with a descriptive label encased at the top. The set is unnumbered and listed below in checklist order.

PRINT RUN 30 SER.#'d SETS
1 Simon Gagne 20.00 50.00
2 John LeClair 20.00 50.00
3 Adam Deadmarsh 10.00 25.00
4 Jeff O'Neill 10.00 25.00
5 Keith Tkachuk 20.00 50.00
6 Joe Thornton 30.00 80.00
7 Rob Blake 10.00 25.00
8 Alexei Yashin 10.00 25.00
9 Sergei Fedorov 30.00 80.00
10 Mario Lemieux 75.00 200.00
11 Jarome Iginla 25.00 60.00
12 Doug Weight 15.00 40.00
13 Brett Hull 30.00 80.00
14 Joe Sakic 50.00 125.00
15 Sergei Samsonov 10.00 25.00
16 Al MacInnis 15.00 40.00
17 Eric Lindros 20.00 50.00
18 Steve Yzerman 60.00 150.00
19 Mats Sundin 20.00 50.00
20 Chris Chelios 20.00 50.00

2002-03 BAP Ultimate Memorabilia Jerseys

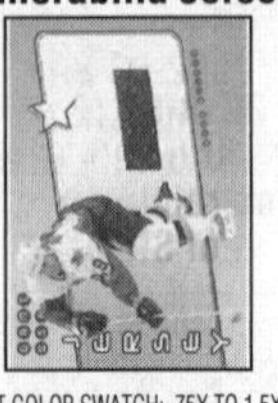

*MULT.COLOR SWATCH: .75X TO 1.5X
PRINT RUN 50 SER.#'d SETS
GOLD 1/1's EXIST
1 Bill Guerin 10.00 25.00
2 Jarome Iginla 15.00 40.00
3 Jose Theodore 15.00 40.00
4 Mario Lemieux 30.00 80.00
5 Martin Brodeur 25.00 60.00
6 Brendan Shanahan 10.00 25.00
7 Brett Hull 20.00 50.00
8 Dany Heatley 15.00 40.00
9 Ed Belfour 10.00 25.00
10 Eric Lindros 10.00 25.00
11 Ilya Kovalchuk 15.00 40.00
12 Jaromir Jagr 15.00 40.00
13 Jason Spezza 15.00 40.00
14 Jay Bouwmeester 20.00 50.00
15 Jeremy Roenick 12.50 30.00
16 Joe Sakic 15.00 40.00
17 Joe Thornton 12.50 30.00
18 John LeClair 10.00 25.00
19 Marian Gaborik 20.00 50.00
20 Marian Hossa 10.00 25.00
21 Mark Messier 10.00 25.00
22 Markus Naslund 10.00 25.00
23 Marty Turco 10.00 25.00
24 Mats Sundin 10.00 25.00
25 Mike Modano 12.50 30.00
26 Milan Hejduk 10.00 25.00
27 Nicklas Lidstrom 10.00 25.00
28 Patrick Roy 25.00 60.00
29 Paul Kariya 10.00 25.00
30 Pavel Bure 10.00 25.00
31 Peter Forsberg 25.00 60.00
32 Rick Nash 25.00 60.00
33 Saku Koivu 10.00 25.00
34 Sergei Fedorov 15.00 40.00
35 Sergei Samsonov 10.00 25.00
36 Steve Yzerman 25.00 60.00
37 Teemu Selanne 10.00 25.00
38 Todd Bertuzzi 10.00 25.00
39 Valeri Kharlamov 25.00 60.00
40 Vincent Lecavalier 10.00 25.00

2002-03 BAP Ultimate Memorabilia Jersey and Stick

*JSY/STK: .5X TO 1.25X BASIC JERSEY
PRINT RUN 50 SER.#'d SETS
GOLD 1 OF 1's EXIST
19 Roberto Luongo 15.00 40.00

2002-03 BAP Ultimate Memorabilia Journey Jerseys

This 10-card set featured swatches of game-worn jerseys from every team the given player played for. Cards were serial-numbered to just 50 and each card was

encapsulated in a clear plastic slab with a descriptive label encased at the top. The set is unnumbered and listed below in checklist order. Unpriced gold one of ones were also created.
PRINT RUN 50 SER.#'d SETS
GOLD 1 OF 1's EXIST
1 Patrick Roy 50.00 125.00
2 Ed Belfour 25.00 60.00
3 Jaromir Jagr 25.00 60.00
4 Brett Hull 40.00 100.00
5 Adam Oates 20.00 50.00
6 Eric Lindros 20.00 50.00
7 Bill Guerin 20.00 50.00
8 Jeremy Roenick 25.00 60.00
9 Pavel Bure 20.00 50.00
10 Alexander Mogilny 20.00 50.00

2002-03 BAP Ultimate Memorabilia Journey Emblems

PRINT RUN 10 SER.#'d SETS
NOT PRICED DUE TO SCARCITY
GOLD 1 OF 1's EXIST

2002-03 BAP Ultimate Memorabilia Legend

This 10-card set highlighted the career of Rocket Richard. Each card carried a piece of memorabilia and dual player cards carried two pieces. Cards in this set were serial-numbered to 15 unless otherwise noted below.. This set is not priced due to scarcity.
PRINT RUN 15 SER.#'d SETS
NOT PRICED DUE TO SCARCITY
1 Maurice Richard JSY/AUTO
2 Maurice Richard GLOVE
3 Maurice Richard SKATE
4 Maurice Richard STICK
5 Maurice Richard
Complete Package
6 Maurice Richard
Doug Harvey
7 Maurice Richard
Jacques Plante
8 Maurice Richard
Jean Beliveau
9 Maurice Richard
Henri Richard
10 Maurice Richard
Complete Package Auto/5

2002-03 BAP Ultimate Memorabilia Lifetime Achievers

This 20-card set featured swatches of game-worn jerseys. Cards were serial-numbered to just 40 and each card was encapsulated in a clear plastic slab with a descriptive label encased at the top. The set is unnumbered and listed below in checklist order.
*MULT.COLOR SWATCH: .75X TO 1.5X
PRINT RUN 40 SER.#'d SETS
1 Sergei Fedorov 15.00 40.00
2 Nicklas Lidstrom 12.50 30.00
3 Brendan Shanahan 12.50 30.00
4 Ed Belfour 12.50 30.00
5 Doug Gilmour 12.50 30.00
6 Jaromir Jagr 20.00 50.00
7 Patrick Roy 30.00 80.00
8 Eric Lindros 12.50 30.00
9 Brian Leetch 12.50 30.00
10 Pavel Bure 12.50 30.00
11 Brett Hull 20.00 50.00
12 Martin Brodeur 30.00 80.00
13 Curtis Joseph 12.50 30.00
14 Mario Lemieux 30.00 80.00
15 Steve Yzerman 30.00 80.00
16 Luc Robitaille 12.50 30.00
17 Mark Messier 12.50 30.00
18 Chris Chelios 12.50 30.00
19 Ron Francis 12.50 30.00
20 Joe Sakic 25.00 60.00

2002-03 BAP Ultimate Memorabilia Made to Order

Limited to just 10 copies each, these redemption cards entitiled the holder to a special one of one memorabilia card of a player they could choose from a specific list. Exchange cards were available for single, double or triple memorabilia cards. The redemption cards and the one of ones are not priced due to scarcity.
PRINT RUN 10 SER.#'d SETS
NOT PRICED DUE TO SCARCITY

2002-03 BAP Ultimate Memorabilia Magnificent Inserts

This 10-card set featured game-used equipment from the career of Mario Lemieux. Cards 1-5 had a print run of 30 copies each and cards 6-10 were limited to just 10 copies each. Cards 6-10 are not priced due to scarcity. Each card was encapsulated in a clear plastic slab with a descriptive label encased at the top.
1-5 PRINT RUN 30 SER.#'d SETS
6-10 PRINT RUN 10 SER.#'d SETS
6-10 NOT PRICED DUE TO SCARCITY
1 1985-86 Season 50.00 125.00
2 2000-01 Season 50.00 125.00
3 2002 NHL All-Star 50.00 125.00
4 1987 Canada Cup 50.00 125.00
5 Dual Jersey 60.00 150.00
6 Number
7 Emblem
8 Triple Jersey
9 Quad Jersey
10 Complete Package

2002-03 BAP Ultimate Memorabilia Magnificent Insert Autographs

This 10-card set paralleled the basic insert set but each card also carried a certified Mario Lemieux autograph. Cards 1-5 were serial-numbered to just 15 copies each and cards 6-10 were serial-numbered to just 5 copies each. This set is not priced due to scarcity.
1-5 PRINT RUN 15 SER.#'d SETS
6-10 PRINT RUN 5 SER.#'d SETS
NOT PRICED DUE TO SCARCITY

2002-03 BAP Ultimate Memorabilia Magnificent Ones

This 10-card set featured dual swatches of jerseys from Mario Lemieux and a player he recognized as one of the best in the game. Cards were serial-numbered to just 30 and each card was encapsulated in a clear plastic slab with a descriptive label encased at the top. The set is unnumbered and listed below in checklist order.
*MULT.COLOR SWATCH: .75X TO 1.5X
PRINT RUN 30 SER.#'d SETS
1 M.Lemieux/P.Roy 75.00 200.00
2 M.Lemieux/S.Yzerman 50.00 125.00
3 M.Lemieux/J.Jagr 25.00 60.00
4 M.Lemieux/M.Modano 25.00 60.00
5 M.Lemieux/M.Brodeur 60.00 150.00
6 M.Lemieux/P.Kariya 25.00 60.00
7 M.Lemieux/J.Sakic 25.00 60.00
8 M.Lemieux/P.Forsberg 25.00 60.00
9 M.Lemieux/P.Bure 25.00 60.00
10 M.Lemieux/B.Shanahan 25.00 60.00

2002-03 BAP Ultimate Memorabilia Magnificent Ones Autographs

PRINT RUN 10 SER.#'d SETS
NOT PRICED DUE TO SCARCITY
SIGNED BY LEMIEUX ONLY

2002-03 BAP Ultimate Memorabilia MVP Winner

Limited to only 10 copies, collectors could redeem this card for a memorabilia card of Peter Forsberg, the winner of the Hart trophy.
STATED PRINT RUN 10 SER.#'d SETS
NOT PRICED DUE TO SCARCITY
1 Peter Forsberg

2002-03 BAP Ultimate Memorabilia Nameplates

PRINT RUN 40 SER.#'d SETS
GOLD 1 OF 1's EXIST
1 Jaromir Jagr 30.00 80.00
2 Mike Modano 15.00 40.00
3 Joe Thornton 20.00 50.00
4 Nicklas Lidstrom 12.50 30.00
5 Jay Bouwmeester 10.00 25.00
6 Jason Spezza 25.00 60.00
7 Patrick Roy 40.00 100.00
8 Peter Forsberg 25.00 60.00
9 Steve Yzerman 40.00 100.00
10 Marian Hossa 12.50 30.00
11 Ilya Kovalchuk 25.00 60.00
12 Ed Belfour 12.50 30.00
13 Mario Lemieux 40.00 100.00
14 Joe Sakic 25.00 60.00
15 Marian Gaborik 30.00 80.00
16 Pavel Bure 12.50 30.00
17 Martin Brodeur 30.00 80.00
18 Markus Naslund 12.50 30.00
19 Curtis Joseph 12.50 30.00
20 Paul Kariya 12.50 30.00

2002-03 BAP Ultimate Memorabilia Number Ones

This 10-card set highlighted players who wore the jersey number one and featured a swatch of the jersey number. Cards were serial-numbered to just 10 and each card was encapsulated in a clear plastic slab with a descriptive label encased at the top. The set is unnumbered and listed below in checklist order. This set is not priced due to scarcity.
PRINT RUN 10 SER.#'d SETS
NOT PRICED DUE TO SCARCITY
1 Arturs Irbe
2 Ed Giacomin
3 Glenn Hall
4 Jacques Plante
5 Johan Hedberg
6 Roberto Luongo
7 Roger Crozier
8 Roman Turek
9 Sean Burke
10 Terry Sawchuk

2002-03 BAP Ultimate Memorabilia Numbers

PRINT RUN 10 SER.#'d SETS
NOT PRICED DUE TO SCARCITY
1 Mike Modano

2 Mario Lemieux
3 Sergei Fedorov
4 Ilya Kovalchuk
5 Patrick Roy
6 Jaromir Jagr
7 Eric Lindros
8 Peter Forsberg
9 Brendan Shanahan
10 Marian Gaborik
11 Markus Naslund
12 John LeClair
13 Saku Koivu
14 Chris Chelios
15 Dany Heatley
16 Brian Leetch
17 Mark Messier
18 Steve Yzerman
19 Pavel Bure
20 Valeri Kharlamov
21 Luc Robitaille
22 Paul Kariya
23 Brett Hull
24 Jeremy Roenick
25 Joe Sakic
26 Martin Brodeur
27 Mike Comrie
28 Joe Thornton
29 Mats Sundin
30 Nicklas Lidstrom

2002-03 BAP Ultimate Memorabilia Numerology

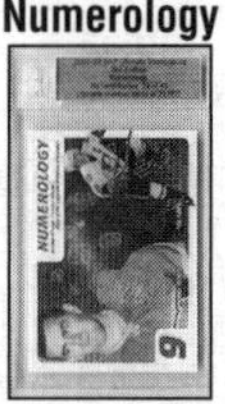

This 30-card set featured dual swatches of game-used jersey from the 2 featured players; who both wore the same jersey number. Cards were serial-numbered to just 40 and each card was encapsulated in a clear plastic slab with a descriptive label encased at the top. The set is unnumbered and listed below in checklist order.
*MULT.COLOR SWATCH: .75X TO 1.5X
PRINT RUN 40 SER.#'d SETS
1 Glenn Hall 15.00 40.00
Johan Hedberg
2 Terry Sawchuk 30.00 80.00
Roman Turek
3 Jacques Plante 20.00 50.00
Sean Burke
4 Bernie Parent 15.00 40.00
Roberto Luongo
5 Doug Harvey 15.00 40.00
Brian Leetch
6 Jean Beliveau 30.00 80.00
Vincent Lecavalier
7 Red Kelly 15.00 40.00
Rob Blake
8 Denis Potvin 15.00 40.00
Nicklas Lidstrom
9 Phil Esposito 30.00 80.00
Keith Tkachuk
10 Rod Gilbert 15.00 40.00
Gary Roberts
11 Maurice Richard 40.00 100.00
Paul Kariya
12 B.Hull/M.Modano 15.00 40.00
13 Johnny Bucyk 15.00 40.00
Pavel Bure
14 G.Lafleur/M.Gaborik 40.00 100.00
15 Alex Delvecchio 15.00 40.00
Ron Francis
16 Gilbert Perreault 15.00 40.00
Mark Messier
17 Yvan Cournoyer 15.00 40.00
Jarome Iginla
18 Marcel Dionne 15.00 40.00
Trevor Linden
19 Valeri Kharlamov 40.00 100.00
Ilya Kovalchuk
20 Serge Savard 15.00 40.00
Marian Hossa
21 L.Robinson/S.Yzerman 30.00 80.00
22 Bryan Trottier 15.00 40.00
Joe Sakic
23 Vladislav Tretiak 30.00 80.00
Ed Belfour
24 Stan Mikita 15.00 40.00
Peter Forsberg
25 Mike Bossy 15.00 40.00
Kristian Huselius
26 Bobby Nystrom 15.00 40.00
Milan Hejduk
27 Frank Mahovlich 15.00 40.00
Mike Peca
28 Billy Smith 15.00 40.00
Curtis Joseph
29 Grant Fuhr 40.00 100.00
Dan Blackburn
30 Tony Esposito 15.00 40.00
Marty Turco

2002-03 BAP Ultimate Memorabilia Paper Cuts Autographs

This 36-card set featured cut-signatures from some of the greatest legends in NHL history. Each card was a one-of-one and was encapsulated in a clear plastic slab with a descriptive label encased at the top. The set is unnumbered and listed below in checklist order. This set is not priced due to scarcity.
PRINT RUN 1 SET
NOT PRICED DUE TO SCARCITY
1 Harold Cotton
2 Toe Blake
3 Bun Cook
4 Bill Cook
5 Tiny Thompson
6 Ace Bailey
7 Bryan Hextall
8 Doug Harvey
9 Max Bentley
10 Harry Lumley
11 Sweeney Schriner
12 Bill Cowley
13 Flash Hollett
14 Jack Stewart
15 Bill Mosienko
16 Ebbie Goodfellow
17 Joe Primeau
18 Turk Broda
19 Busher Jackson
20 Ching Johnson
21 King Clancy
22 Terry Sawchuk
23 Neil Colville
24 Jacques Plante
25 Babe Pratt
26 Bill Barilko
27 Tim Horton
28 Hap Day
29 Sid Abel
30 Gordie Drillon
31 Harry Oliver
32 Syl Apps
33 Aurel Joliat
34 Charlie Conacher
35 Frank Boucher
36 Red Dutton

2002-03 BAP Ultimate Memorabilia Playoff Scorers

*MULT.COLOR SWATCH: .75X TO 1.5X
PRINT RUN 30 SER.#'d SETS
GOLD 1 OF 1's EXIST
1 Peter Forsberg 20.00 50.00
2 Joe Sakic 30.00 80.00
3 Brett Hull 20.00 50.00
4 Peter Forsberg 20.00 50.00
5 Steve Yzerman 30.00 80.00
6 Eric Lindros 15.00 40.00
7 Joe Sakic 30.00 80.00
8 Sergei Fedorov 20.00 50.00
9 Brian Leetch 15.00 40.00
10 Mario Lemieux 40.00 100.00
11 Mark Messier 15.00 40.00
12 Mike Bossy 25.00 60.00
13 Maurice Richard 40.00 100.00
14 Jean Beliveau 20.00 50.00
15 Brett Hull 25.00 60.00
16 Bryan Trottier 15.00 40.00
17 Mario Lemieux 40.00 100.00
18 Bobby Hull 25.00 60.00
19 Phil Esposito 30.00 80.00
20 Steve Yzerman 30.00 80.00

2002-03 BAP Ultimate Memorabilia Retro Teammates

PRINT RUN 30 SER.#'d SETS
1 Darryl Sittler 30.00 80.00
Lanny McDonald
Tiger Williams
2 Gilles Gilbert 30.00 80.00
Gerry Cheevers
John Bucyk
3 Bobby Hull 30.00 80.00
Stan Mikita
Glenn Hall
4 Guy Lafleur 75.00 200.00
Yvan Cournoyer
Serge Savard
5 Rod Gilbert 30.00 80.00
Ed Giacomin
Phil Esposito
6 Mario Lemieux 75.00 200.00
Jaromir Jagr
Ron Francis
7 Maurice Richard 75.00 200.00
JacquesPlante
Jean Beliveau
8 Tim Horton 75.00 200.00
Johnny Bower
Red Kelly
9 Dave Schultz 30.00 80.00
Bobby Clarke
Bernie Parent
10 Alex Delvecchio 30.00 80.00
Terry Sawchuk
Sid Abel

2002-03 BAP Ultimate Memorabilia Retro Trophies

*MULT.COLOR SWATCH: .75X TO 1.5X
PRINT RUN 40 SER.#'d SETS
UNLESS OTHERWISE NOTED
1 D.Heatley/M.Lemieux 40.00 100.00
2 Patrick Roy 75.00 200.00
Terry Sawchuk
3 Mike Peca 20.00 50.00
Bobby Clarke
4 Saku Koivu 20.00 50.00
Henri Richard
5 Paul Kariya 30.00 80.00
Marcel Dionne
6 Jaromir Jagr 20.00 50.00
Stan Mikita
7 S.Yzerman/J.Beliveau 25.00 60.00
8 Ed Belfour 20.00 50.00
Glenn Hall
9 M.Lemieux/H.Morenz/10
10 Jose Theodore 30.00 80.00
Jacques Plante
11 Nicklas Lidstrom 20.00 50.00
Larry Robinson
12 M.Lemieux/P.Esposito 40.00 100.00
13 Jarome Iginla 20.00 50.00
Bobby Hull
14 Mark Messier 20.00 50.00
Ron Hextall
15 Martin Brodeur 30.00 80.00
Frank Brimsek
16 Nicklas Lidstrom 20.00 50.00
Rogier Crozier
17 M.Lemieux/L.McDonald 40.00 100.00
18 Peter Forsberg 20.00 50.00
Bryan Trottier
19 Brett Hull 30.00 80.00
Bobby Hull
20 Joe Sakic 40.00 100.00
Maurice Richard

2002-03 BAP Ultimate Memorabilia Scoring Leaders

*MULT.COLOR SWATCH: .75X TO 1.5X
PRINT RUN 40 SER.#'d SETS
1 Peter Forsberg 25.00 60.00
2002-03
2 Jarome Iginla 15.00 40.00
2001-02
3 Mario Lemieux 2000-01 25.00 60.00
4 Jaromir Jagr 15.00 40.00
1999-00
5 Jaromir Jagr 15.00 40.00
1998-99
6 Jaromir Jagr 15.00 40.00
1997-98
7 Mario Lemieux 1996-97 25.00 60.00
8 Mario Lemieux 1995-96 25.00 60.00
9 Jaromir Jagr 15.00 40.00
1994-95
10 Mario Lemieux 1992-93 25.00 60.00
11 Mario Lemieux 1991-92 25.00 60.00
12 Mario Lemieux 1988-89 25.00 60.00
13 Mario Lemieux 1987-88 25.00 60.00
14 Marcel Dionne 12.50 30.00
1979-80
15 Bryan Trottier 12.50 30.00
1978-79
16 Guy Lafleur 12.50 30.00

1977-78		
Guy Lafleur	12.50	30.00
1976-77		
Guy Lafleur	12.50	30.00
1975-76		
Phil Esposito	20.00	50.00
Phil Esposito	20.00	50.00
1972-73		
Phil Esposito	20.00	50.00
1971-72		
Phil Esposito	20.00	50.00
1970-71		
Phil Esposito	20.00	50.00
1968-69		
Stan Mikita	12.50	30.00
1967-68		
Stan Mikita	12.50	30.00
1966-67		
Bobby Hull	20.00	50.00
1965-66		
Stan Mikita	12.50	30.00
1964-65		
Stan Mikita	12.50	30.00
1963-64		
Bobby Hull	20.00	50.00
1961-62		
Bernie Geoffrion	12.50	30.00
1960-61		
Bobby Hull	20.00	50.00
1959-60		
Dickie Moore	12.50	30.00
1958-59		
Dickie Moore	12.50	30.00
1957-58		
Jean Beliveau	20.00	50.00
1956-57		
Bernie Geoffrion	12.50	30.00
1955-56		

2002-03 BAP Ultimate lemorabilia Seams Unbelievable

s 8-card set featured swatches of game-d jersey with the seam exposed. Cards e serial-numbered to just 10 and each d was encapsulated in a clear plastic slab n a descriptive label encased at the top. set is unnumbered and listed below in cklist order. This set is not priced due to rcity.

INT RUN 10 SER.#'d SETS
T PRICED DUE TO SCARCITY
Mario Lemieux
Ted Lindsay
Glenn Hall
George Hainsworth
Guy Lafleur
Gerry Cheevers
Bill Durnan
Bill Mosienko

2002-03 BAP Ultimate lemorabilia Storied Franchise

s 25-card set honored the Montreal nadiens and featured a swatch of game-d memorabilia on the card fronts. Cards e serial-numbered to just 20 (unless erwise noted below) and each card was apsulated in a clear plastic slab with a criptive label encased at the top. The set nnumbered and listed below in checklist er. This set is not priced due to scarcity.

INT RUN 20 SER.#'d SETS
T PRICED DUE TO SCARCITY
Bernie Geoffrion
Charlie Hodge
Howie Morenz
Larry Robinson
Jacques Plante
John LeClair
Patrick Roy
Maurice Richard
Serge Savard
Bill Durnan
Guy Lafleur
Guy Lapointe
Lorne Worsley
George Hainsworth
Jacques Laperriere
Yvan Cournoyer
Henri Richard
Frank Mahovlich
Doug Harvey
Rogie Vachon
Steve Shutt
Jean Beliveau
Henri Richard

24 Georges Vezina/10
25 Aurel Joliat

2002-03 BAP Ultimate Memorabilia Vezina Winner

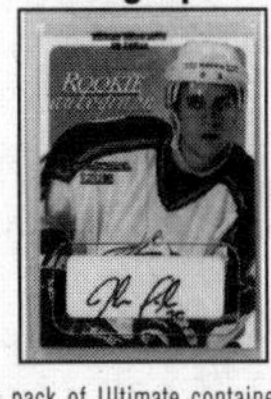

Limited to only 10 copies, collectors could redeem this card for a memorabilia card of the winner of the Vezina trophy.

PRINT RUN 10 SER.#'d SETS
NOT PRICED DUE TO SCARCITY
1 Martin Brodeur

2002-03 BAP Ultimate Memorabilia Vintage Hat Tricks

This 6-card set featured 3 pieces of game-used memorabilia from the featured player. Cards were serial-numbered to just 10 and each card was encapsulated in a clear plastic slab with a descriptive label encased at the top. The set is unnumbered and listed below in checklist order. This set is not priced due to scarcity.

PRINT RUN 10 SER.#'d SETS
NOT PRICED DUE TO SCARCITY
1 Eddie Shore
2 Aurel Joliat
3 Rocket Richard
4 Tim Horton
5 Guy Lafleur
6 Jean Beliveau

2002-03 BAP Ultimate Memorabilia Vintage Jerseys

This 40-card set featured jersey swatches from past hockey greats. Cards were serial-numbered to just 40 and each card was encapsulated in a clear plastic slab with a descriptive label encased at the top. The set is unnumbered and listed below in checklist order. Unpriced gold one of one's exist.

*MULT.COLOR SWATCH: .75X TO 1.5X
PRINT RUN 40 SER.#'d SETS
UNPRICED GOLD 1 OF 1's EXIST

1 Stan Mikita	12.50	30.00
2 Alex Delvecchio	12.50	30.00
3 Aurel Joliat	30.00	80.00
4 Bernie Parent	12.50	30.00
5 Bill Barber	12.50	30.00
6 Bobby Clarke	12.50	30.00
7 Bobby Hull	12.50	30.00
8 Bryan Trottier	12.50	30.00
9 Dennis Hull	12.50	30.00
10 Doug Harvey	12.50	30.00
11 Ed Giacomin	12.50	30.00
12 Frank Brimsek	12.50	30.00
13 Frank Mahovlich	12.50	30.00
14 George Hainsworth	20.00	50.00
15 Gerry Cheevers	12.50	30.00
16 Gilbert Perreault	12.50	30.00
17 Glenn Hall	12.50	30.00
18 Guy Lafleur	12.50	30.00
19 Harry Lumley	20.00	50.00
20 Henri Richard	12.50	30.00
21 Jacques Plante	30.00	80.00
22 Jean Beliveau	25.00	60.00
23 John Bucyk	12.50	30.00
24 Lanny McDonald	12.50	30.00
25 Larry Robinson	12.50	30.00
26 Marcel Dionne	12.50	30.00
27 Maurice Richard	30.00	80.00
28 Mike Bossy	12.50	30.00
29 Peter Mahovlich	12.50	30.00
30 Phil Esposito	12.50	30.00
31 Red Kelly	20.00	50.00
32 Roger Crozier	12.50	30.00
33 Roy Worters	20.00	50.00
34 Sid Abel	12.50	30.00
35 Ted Lindsay	12.50	30.00
36 Terry Sawchuk	50.00	125.00
37 Tim Horton	30.00	80.00
38 Tony Esposito	12.50	30.00
39 Valeri Kharlamov	25.00	60.00
40 Vladislav Tretiak	40.00	100.00

2002-03 BAP Ultimate Memorabilia Vintage Jersey Autographs

PRINT RUN 10 SER.#'d SETS
NOT PRICED DUE TO SCARCITY
1 Jean Beliveau
2 John Bucyk
3 Marcel Dionne
4 Ed Giacomin
5 Glenn Hall
6 Red Kelly
7 Guy Lafleur
8 Ted Lindsay
9 Frank Mahovlich
10 Stan Mikita
11 Henri Richard
12 Bobby Hull
13 Phil Esposito

2003-04 BAP Ultimate Memorabilia Autographs

Each pack of Ultimate contained one memorabilia card that was slabbed by BGS and one unslabbed card of either an auto, gold auto, auto/jersey, auto/stick, auto/emblem or auto/number. The auto/memorabilia cards were found in sealed toploaders.

1-89 PRINT RUN 135 SER.#'d SETS
ROOKIE AU PRINT RUN 100 SER.#'d SETS
131-165 PRINT RUN 19 SER.#'d SETS

1 Alexei Kovalev	6.00	15.00
2 Shane Doan	6.00	15.00
3 Ales Hemsky	6.00	15.00
4 Ray Whitney	6.00	15.00
5 Alexander Frolov	6.00	15.00
6 Mike Peca	6.00	15.00
7 Chris Drury	6.00	15.00
8 Chris Osgood	6.00	15.00
9 Andrew Raycroft	10.00	25.00
10 Rick DiPietro	6.00	15.00
11 Chuck Kobasew	6.00	15.00
12 Vincent Lecavalier	8.00	20.00
13 Olaf Kolzig	8.00	20.00
14 Erik Cole	6.00	15.00
15 Ryan Smyth	6.00	15.00
16 Anson Carter	6.00	15.00
17 Jocelyn Thibault	6.00	15.00
18 Alexei Yashin	6.00	15.00
19 David Aebischer	6.00	15.00
20 Chris Pronger	6.00	15.00
21 Ron Francis	6.00	15.00
22 Markus Naslund	8.00	20.00
23 Tommy Salo	6.00	15.00
24 Patrick Lalime	6.00	15.00
25 Joe Nieuwendyk	6.00	15.00
26 Vincent Damphousse	6.00	15.00
27 Bill Guerin	6.00	15.00
28 Jeremy Roenick	15.00	40.00
29 Barret Jackman	6.00	15.00
30 Curtis Joseph	8.00	20.00
31 Jason Spezza	12.50	30.00
32 Sergei Fedorov	15.00	40.00
33 Gary Roberts	6.00	15.00
34 Glen Murray	6.00	15.00
35 Adam Oates	6.00	15.00
36 Felix Potvin	8.00	20.00
37 Eric Brewer	6.00	15.00
38 Jeff O'Neill	6.00	15.00
39 Tomas Vokoun	8.00	20.00
40 Olli Jokinen	6.00	15.00
41 Martin Prusek	6.00	15.00
42 Sergei Gonchar	6.00	15.00
43 Kevin Weekes	6.00	15.00
44 Roman Cechmanek	6.00	15.00
45 Scott Stevens	6.00	15.00
46 Dwayne Roloson	6.00	15.00
47 Martin Biron	6.00	15.00
48 Keith Tkachuk	6.00	15.00
49 Pasi Nurminen	6.00	15.00
50 Saku Koivu	8.00	20.00
51 David Legwand	6.00	15.00
52 Jay Bouwmeester	6.00	15.00
53 Patrik Elias	6.00	15.00
54 Zigmund Palffy	6.00	15.00
55 Tyler Arnason	6.00	15.00
56 Sergei Samsonov	6.00	15.00
57 Ryan Miller	15.00	40.00
58 Mike Dunham	6.00	15.00
59 Nikolai Khabibulin	8.00	20.00
60 Roman Turek	6.00	15.00
61 Marian Hossa	8.00	20.00
62 Marc Denis	6.00	15.00
63 Peter Bondra	10.00	25.00
64 Marty Turco	8.00	20.00
65 John LeClair	8.00	20.00
66 Johan Hedberg	6.00	15.00
67 Sean Burke	6.00	15.00
68 Ed Jovanovski	6.00	15.00
69 Tony Amonte	6.00	15.00
70 Daymond Langkow	6.00	15.00
71 Miroslav Satan	6.00	15.00
72 J-S Giguere	6.00	15.00
73 Evgeni Nabokov	6.00	15.00
74 Rostislav Klesla	6.00	15.00
75 Al MacInnis	6.00	15.00
76 Niko Kapanen	6.00	15.00
77 Manny Fernandez	6.00	15.00
78 Milan Hejduk	8.00	20.00
79 Doug Weight	6.00	15.00
80 Jarome Iginla	12.50	30.00
81 Martin St. Louis	8.00	20.00
82 Daniel Alfredsson	6.00	15.00
83 Marian Gaborik	12.50	30.00
84 Rob Blake	6.00	15.00
85 Dan Cloutier	6.00	15.00
86 Simon Gagne	8.00	20.00
87 Mark Recchi	6.00	15.00
88 Teemu Selanne	8.00	20.00
89 Todd Bertuzzi	8.00	20.00
90 Chris Kunitz	10.00	25.00
91 Eric Staal	60.00	125.00
92 Nathan Horton	15.00	40.00
93 Andrew Peters	10.00	25.00
94 Alexander Semin	20.00	50.00
95 Matthew Lombardi	10.00	25.00
96 Joffrey Lupul	15.00	40.00
97 John-Michael Liles	10.00	25.00
98 Jiri Hudler	12.50	30.00
99 Tuomo Ruutu	20.00	50.00
100 Anton Babchuk	10.00	25.00
101 Dan Fritsche	10.00	25.00
102 Derek Roy	12.50	30.00
103 Paul Martin	10.00	25.00
104 Pavel Vorobiev	10.00	25.00
105 Matthew Spiller	10.00	25.00
106 Patrice Bergeron	25.00	60.00
107 Chris Higgins	25.00	60.00
108 Noah Clarke	10.00	25.00
109 Nikolai Zherdev	15.00	30.00
110 Brent Burns	10.00	25.00
111 Dustin Brown	10.00	25.00
112 Michael Ryder	20.00	50.00
113 Joni Pitkanen	12.00	30.00
114 Jordin Tootoo	25.00	60.00
115 Ryan Malone	10.00	25.00
116 David Hale	10.00	25.00
117 Antti Miettinen	10.00	25.00
118 Doug Lynch	10.00	25.00
119 Tim Gleason	10.00	25.00
120 Dan Hamhuis	10.00	25.00
121 Fredrik Sjostrom	10.00	25.00
122 Kari Lehtonen	50.00	125.00
123 Marc-Andre Fleury	40.00	100.00
124 Marek Zidlicky	10.00	25.00
125 Milan Michalek	15.00	40.00
126 Matt Stajan	20.00	50.00
127 Peter Sarno	10.00	25.00
128 Antoine Vermette	10.00	25.00
129 Boyd Gordon	10.00	25.00
130 Kyle Wellwood	25.00	60.00
131 Steve Yzerman		
132 Rick Nash		
133 Roberto Luongo		
134 Joe Thornton		
135 Joe Sakic		
136 Pavel Datsyuk		
137 Martin Brodeur		
138 Mike Modano		
139 Brian Leetch		
140 Peter Forsberg		
141 Owen Nolan		
142 Brett Hull		
143 Jaromir Jagr		
144 Dominik Hasek		
145 Ilya Kovalchuk		
146 Jose Theodore		
147 Mario Lemieux		
148 Mats Sundin		
149 Eric Lindros		
150 Henrik Zetterberg		
151 Dany Heatley		
152 Nicklas Lidstrom		
153 Bobby Orr		
154 Ted Kennedy		
155 Ray Bourque		
156 Jean Beliveau		
157 Tony Esposito		
158 Patrick Roy		
159 Ted Lindsay		
160 Frank Mahovlich		
161 Guy Lafleur		
162 Henri Richard		
163 Maurice Richard		
164 Phil Esposito		
165 Johnny Bower		

2003-04 BAP Ultimate Memorabilia Autographs Gold

*GOLD 1-89: 1X TO 2.5X BASE HI
1-89 PRINT RUN 35 SER.#'d SETS
*GOLD 90-130: .6X TO 1.5X
90-130 PRINT RUN 20 SER.#'d SETS
131-165 PRINT RUN 1 SET

2003-04 BAP Ultimate Memorabilia Autographed Jerseys

10-89/PRINT RUN 30 SER.#'d SETS
91-129 PRINT RUN 20 SER.#'d SETS
91-129 NOT PRICED DUE TO SCARCITY

10 Rick DiPietro	20.00	50.00
12 Vincent Lecavalier	30.00	80.00
13 Olaf Kolzig	25.00	60.00
17 Jocelyn Thibault	20.00	50.00
19 David Aebischer	20.00	50.00
20 Chris Pronger	20.00	50.00
21 Ron Francis	20.00	50.00
22 Markus Naslund	25.00	60.00
24 Patrick Lalime	20.00	50.00
27 Bill Guerin	20.00	50.00
28 Jeremy Roenick	30.00	80.00
29 Barret Jackman	20.00	50.00
30 Curtis Joseph	25.00	60.00
31 Jason Spezza	25.00	60.00
33 Gary Roberts	20.00	50.00
39 Tomas Vokoun	20.00	50.00
48 Keith Tkachuk	25.00	60.00
50 Saku Koivu	25.00	60.00
52 Jay Bouwmeester	20.00	50.00
56 Sergei Samsonov	20.00	50.00
57 Ryan Miller	25.00	60.00
58 Mike Dunham	20.00	50.00
59 Nikolai Khabibulin	25.00	60.00
60 Roman Turek	20.00	50.00
61 Marian Hossa	25.00	60.00
62 Marc Denis	20.00	50.00
65 John LeClair	25.00	60.00
66 Johan Hedberg	20.00	50.00
68 Ed Jovanovski	20.00	50.00
69 Tony Amonte	20.00	50.00
72 J-S Giguere	20.00	50.00
75 Al MacInnis	20.00	50.00
77 Manny Fernandez	20.00	50.00
78 Milan Hejduk	25.00	60.00
79 Doug Weight	20.00	50.00
81 Martin St.Louis	25.00	60.00
82 Daniel Alfredsson	20.00	50.00
83 Marian Gaborik	40.00	100.00
85 Dan Cloutier	20.00	50.00
86 Simon Gagne	20.00	50.00
87 Mark Recchi	20.00	50.00
88 Teemu Selanne	30.00	80.00
89 Todd Bertuzzi	25.00	60.00
91 Eric Staal		
92 Nathan Horton		
94 Alexander Semin		
95 Matthew Lombardi		
96 Joffrey Lupul		
99 Tuomo Ruutu		
101 Dan Fritsche		
102 Derek Roy		
106 Patrice Bergeron		
107 Christopher Higgins		
109 Nikolai Zherdev		
110 Brent Burns		
111 Dustin Brown		
112 Michael Ryder		
113 Joni Pitkanen		
114 Jordin Tootoo		
115 Ryan Malone		
119 Tim Gleason		
120 Dan Hamhuis		
126 Matt Stajan		
128 Antoine Vermette		
129 Boyd Gordon		
131 Steve Yzerman	50.00	125.00
132 Rick Nash	30.00	80.00
133 Roberto Luongo	30.00	80.00
134 Joe Thornton	30.00	80.00
135 Joe Sakic	40.00	100.00
136 Pavel Datsyuk	25.00	60.00
137 Martin Brodeur	100.00	200.00
138 Mike Modano	30.00	80.00
139 Brian Leetch	25.00	60.00
140 Peter Forsberg	40.00	100.00
141 Owen Nolan	20.00	50.00
142 Brett Hull	30.00	80.00
144 Dominik Hasek	40.00	100.00
145 Ilya Kovalchuk	30.00	80.00
146 Jose Theodore	25.00	60.00
147 Mario Lemieux	75.00	200.00
148 Mats Sundin	25.00	60.00
149 Eric Lindros	25.00	60.00
150 Henrik Zetterberg	30.00	80.00
151 Dany Heatley	30.00	80.00
152 Nicklas Lidstrom	30.00	80.00
153 Bobby Orr	175.00	400.00
155 Ray Bourque	40.00	100.00
157 Tony Esposito	30.00	80.00
158 Patrick Roy	125.00	250.00
165 Johnny Bower	30.00	80.00

2003-04 BAP Ultimate Memorabilia Autographed Emblems

PRINT RUN 10 SER.#'d SETS
NOT PRICED DUE TO SCARCITY
12 Vincent Lecavalier
20 Chris Pronger
22 Markus Naslund
27 Bill Guerin
28 Jeremy Roenick
31 Jason Spezza
48 Keith Tkachuk
64 Marty Turco
65 John LeClair
78 Milan Hejduk
79 Doug Weight
81 Martin St. Louis
82 Daniel Alfredsson
83 Marian Gaborik
89 Todd Bertuzzi
91 Eric Staal
92 Nathan Horton
94 Alexander Semin
95 Matthew Lombardi
96 Joffrey Lupul
99 Tuomo Ruutu
101 Dan Fritsche
102 Derek Roy
106 Patrice Bergeron
107 Christopher Higgins
109 Nikolai Zherdev
110 Brent Burns
111 Dustin Brown
112 Michael Ryder
113 Joni Pitkanen
114 Jordin Tootoo
115 Ryan Malone
119 Tim Gleason
120 Dan Hamhuis
126 Matt Stajan
128 Antoine Vermette
129 Boyd Gordon
131 Steve Yzerman
132 Rick Nash
133 Roberto Luongo
134 Joe Thornton
135 Joe Sakic
136 Pavel Datsyuk
137 Martin Brodeur
138 Mike Modano
139 Brian Leetch
140 Peter Forsberg
141 Owen Nolan
142 Brett Hull
144 Dominik Hasek
145 Ilya Kovalchuk
146 Jose Theodore
147 Mario Lemieux
148 Mats Sundin
149 Eric Lindros
150 Henrik Zetterberg
151 Dany Heatley
152 Nicklas Lidstrom
153 Bobby Orr
155 Ray Bourque
158 Patrick Roy

2003-04 BAP Ultimate Memorabilia Autographed Numbers

PRINT RUN 20 SER.#'d SETS
NOT PRICED DUE TO SCARCITY
91 Eric Staal
92 Nathan Horton
94 Alexander Semin
95 Matthew Lombardi
96 Joffrey Lupul
99 Tuomo Ruutu
101 Dan Fritsche
102 Derek Roy
106 Patrice Bergeron
107 Christopher Higgins
109 Nikolai Zherdev
110 Brent Burns
111 Dustin Brown
112 Michael Ryder
113 Joni Pitkanen
114 Jordin Tootoo
115 Ryan Malone
119 Tim Gleason
120 Dan Hamhuis
126 Matt Stajan
128 Antoine Vermette
129 Boyd Gordon

2003-04 BAP Ultimate Memorabilia Autographed Sticks

PRINT RUN 30 SER.#'d SETS

32 Sergei Fedorov	25.00	60.00
45 Scott Stevens	15.00	40.00
56 Sergei Samsonov	15.00	40.00
86 Simon Gagne	15.00	40.00
123 Marc-Andre Fleury	40.00	100.00
131 Steve Yzerman	40.00	100.00
132 Rick Nash	30.00	80.00
134 Joe Thornton	25.00	60.00
135 Joe Sakic	30.00	80.00
136 Pavel Datsyuk	25.00	60.00
138 Mike Modano	20.00	50.00
140 Peter Forsberg	30.00	80.00
142 Brett Hull	30.00	80.00
143 Jaromir Jagr	50.00	125.00
145 Ilya Kovalchuk	30.00	80.00
147 Mario Lemieux	75.00	200.00
151 Dany Heatley	30.00	80.00
153 Bobby Orr	150.00	350.00
158 Patrick Roy	125.00	250.00
165 Johnny Bower	25.00	60.00

2003-04 BAP Ultimate Memorabilia Active Eight

PRINT RUN 30 SER.#'d SETS

1 Belfour/Brodeur/Hasek	50.00	125.00
2 Belfour/Joseph/Brodeur	50.00	125.00
3 Lemieux/Hull/Mogilny	40.00	100.00
4 Sundin/Lidstrom/Forsberg	30.00	80.00
5 Lemieux/Messier/Forsberg	50.00	125.00
6 Yzerman/Sakic/Stevens	40.00	100.00
7 Roenick/Modano/Leetch	30.00	80.00
8 Lemieux/Hull/Yzerman	50.00	125.00

2003-04 BAP Ultimate Memorabilia Always An All-Star

PRINT RUN 50 SER.#'d SETS
UNPRICED GOLD 1/1's EXIST

1 Martin Brodeur	25.00	60.00
2 Mike Modano	15.00	40.00
3 Brian Leetch	12.50	30.00
4 Brett Hull	20.00	50.00
5 Al MacInnis	12.50	30.00
6 Paul Kariya	12.50	30.00
7 Eric Lindros	12.50	30.00
8 Teemu Selanne	12.50	30.00
9 Nicklas Lidstrom	12.50	30.00
10 Sergei Fedorov	20.00	50.00
11 Patrick Roy	30.00	80.00
12 Peter Forsberg	20.00	50.00
13 Mark Messier	20.00	50.00
14 Jaromir Jagr	15.00	40.00
15 Ray Bourque	25.00	60.00
16 Mario Lemieux	40.00	100.00
17 Brendan Shanahan	12.50	30.00
18 Chris Pronger	12.50	30.00
19 Dominik Hasek	15.00	40.00
20 Mats Sundin	12.50	30.00

2003-04 BAP Ultimate Memorabilia Blades of Steel

This 7-card set featured swatches of game-used skates. Each card was limited to just 20 copies.

PRINT RUN 20 SER.#'d SETS
NOT PRICED DUE TO SCARCITY
1 Mario Lemieux
2 Henrik Zetterberg
3 Al MacInnis
4 Pavel Bure
5 Jarome Iginla
6 Raymond Bourque
7 Pavel Datsyuk

2003-04 BAP Ultimate Memorabilia Bleu,Blanc et Rouge

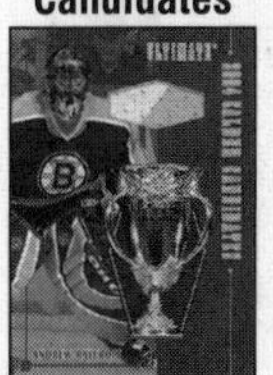

This 18-card set featured "cut" autographs of legendary Canadiens players. Each card was a 1/1.

PRINT RUN 1 SET
NOT PRICED DUE TO SCARCITY
1 Aurel Joliat
2 Jacques Plante
3 Sylvio Mantha
4 Newsy Lalonde
5 Johnny Gagnon
6 Toe Blake
7 Doug Harvey
8 Ken Reardon
9 Maurice Richard
10 George Hainsworth
11 Jean Beliveau
12 Guy Lafleur
13 Bill Durnan
14 Phil Watson
15 Murph Chamberlain
16 Elmer Lach
17 Dick Irvin
18 Patrick Roy

2003-04 BAP Ultimate Memorabilia Calder Candidates

PRINT RUN 50 SER.#'d SETS
UNPRICED GOLD 1/1's EXIST

1 Andrew Raycroft	10.00	25.00
2 Eric Staal	15.00	40.00
3 Michael Ryder	15.00	40.00
4 Marc-Andre Fleury	20.00	50.00
5 Ryan Malone	10.00	25.00

6 Trent Hunter 10.00 25.00
7 Patrice Bergeron 15.00 40.00
8 Joni Pitkanen 10.00 25.00
9 Matthew Lombardi 10.00 25.00
10 Nikolai Zherdev 12.00 30.00
11 Tuomo Ruutu 12.00 30.00
12 Joffrey Lupul 10.00 25.00

2003-04 BAP Ultimate Memorabilia Career Year

PRINT RUN 40 SER.#'d SETS
1 Martin Brodeur 30.00 80.00
2 Cam Neely 15.00 40.00
3 Ray Bourque 15.00 40.00
4 Patrick Roy 30.00 80.00
5 Rick Nash 20.00 50.00
6 Steve Yzerman 30.00 80.00
7 Bobby Orr 60.00 150.00
8 Mario Lemieux 40.00 100.00

2003-04 BAP Ultimate Memorabilia Complete Jersey

PRINT RUN 30 SER.#'d SETS
UNPRICED GOLD 1/1's EXIST
1 Joe Thornton 40.00 100.00
2 Mario Lemieux 100.00 250.00
3 Marian Gaborik 50.00 125.00
4 Brett Hull 40.00 100.00
5 Dany Heatley 40.00 100.00
6 Joe Sakic 60.00 150.00
7 Paul Kariya 30.00 80.00
8 Steve Yzerman 60.00 150.00
9 Rick Nash 50.00 125.00
10 Nicklas Lidstrom 30.00 80.00
11 Sergei Fedorov 40.00 100.00
12 Patrick Roy 75.00 200.00
13 Peter Forsberg 50.00 125.00
14 Henrik Zetterberg 30.00 80.00
15 Dominik Hasek 40.00 100.00
16 Martin Brodeur 75.00 150.00
17 Mike Modano 40.00 100.00
18 Brendan Shanahan 30.00 80.00
19 Ilya Kovalchuk 50.00 125.00
20 Saku Koivu 30.00 80.00

2003-04 BAP Ultimate Memorabilia Complete Package

This 11-card set featured 4 different swatches per card from the featured player's equipment. Included in the memorabilia were items such as skates, jerseys, sticks, pants, socks, and pads. Cards were limited to 10 copies each.
PRINT RUN 10 SER.#'d SETS
NOT PRICED DUE TO SCARCITY
UNPRICED GOLD 1/1's EXIST
1 Mario Lemieux
2 Steve Yzerman
3 Nikolai Khabibulin
4 Al MacInnis
5 Jarome Iginla
6 Mats Sundin
7 Marty Turco
8 Eric Lindros
9 Curtis Joseph
10 JosÃ© ThÃ©odore
11 David Aebischer

2003-04 BAP Ultimate Memorabilia Cornerstones

PRINT RUN 20 SER.#'d SETS
NOT PRICED DUE TO SCARCITY
1 Vezina/Plante/Roy/Theodore
2 Plante/Richard/Harve/Beliveau
3 H.Richard/Lafleur/Robinson/Savard
4 Bower/F.Mahovlich/Kelly/Horton

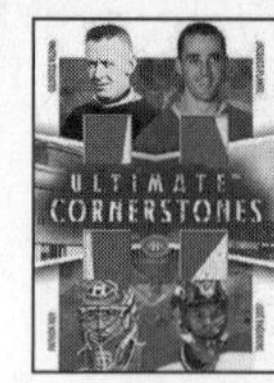

5 Shore/Orr/Bourque/Thornton
6 Brimsek/Lumley/Hall/Esposito
7 Lindsay/Sawchuk/Delvecchio/Yzerman
8 Bossy/Trottier/Potvin/Smith

2003-04 BAP Ultimate Memorabilia Dynamic Duos

PRINT RUN 30 SER.#'d SETS
1 T.Selanne/S.Koivu 20.00 50.00
2 M.Sundin/P.Forsberg 20.00 50.00
3 M.Lemieux/S.Yzerman 50.00 125.00
4 J.Sakic/B.Shanahan 20.00 50.00
5 E.Lindros/P.Kariya 20.00 50.00
6 J.Roenick/K.Tkachuk 20.00 50.00
7 I.Kovalchuk/S.Fedorov 20.00 50.00
8 R.Nash/J.Thornton 20.00 50.00
9 B.Hull/M.Modano 20.00 50.00
10 M.Messier/J.Spezza 20.00 50.00

2003-04 BAP Ultimate Memorabilia Emblem Attic

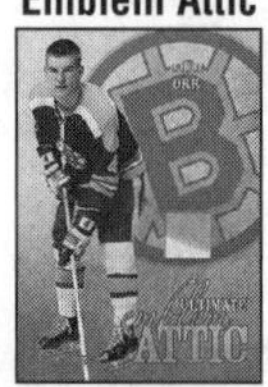

PRINT RUN 5 SER.#'d SETS
NOT PRICED DUE TO SCARCITY
UNPRICED GOLD 1/1's EXIST
1 Bobby Orr
2 Johnny Bower
3 Roy Worters
4 Raymond Bourque
5 Roger Crozier
6 Frank Brimsek
7 Harry Lumley
8 Sid Abel
9 Jean Beliveau
10 Gump Worsley
11 Henri Richard
12 George Hainsworth
13 Aurel Joliat
14 Terry Sawchuk
15 Jacques Plante
16 Tony Esposito
17 Bobby Hull
18 Marcel Dionne
19 Frank Mahovlich
20 Glenn Hall

2003-04 BAP Ultimate Memorabilia Emblems

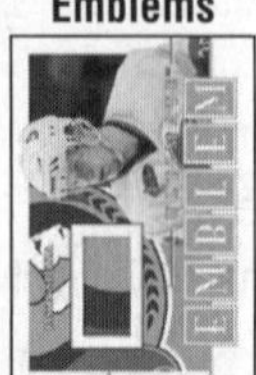

PRINT RUN 10 SER.#'d SETS
NOT PRICED DUE TO SCARCITY
UNPRICED GOLD 1/1's EXIST
1 Dany Heatley
2 Dominik Hasek
3 Ed Belfour
4 Eric Lindros
5 Henrik Zetterberg
6 Ilya Kovalchuk
7 Jarome Iginla
8 Jason Spezza
9 Joe Sakic
10 Joe Thornton
11 Jose Theodore
12 Brian Leetch
13 Marian Gaborik
14 Mario Lemieux
15 Markus Naslund
16 Martin Brodeur
17 Mats Sundin
18 Mike Modano
19 Nicklas Lidstrom
20 Paul Kariya
21 Pavel Datsyuk
22 Peter Forsberg
23 Rick Nash
24 Roberto Luongo
25 Roberto Luongo
26 Saku Koivu
27 Sergei Fedorov
28 Steve Yzerman
29 Todd Bertuzzi
30 Vincent Lecavalier

2003-04 BAP Ultimate Memorabilia First Trophy Winners

This 9-card set featured "cut" signatures of players who were the first to win league trophies. Cards were 1/1's.
PRINT RUN 1 SET
NOT PRICED DUE TO SCARCITY
1 Elmer Lach
2 Syl Apps
3 Frank Nighbor
4 Red Kelly
5 George Hainsworth
6 Jean Beliveau
7 Phil Esposito
8 Fred Shero
9 Jack Adams

2003-04 BAP Ultimate Memorabilia Franchise Present and Future

PRINT RUN 40 SER.#'d SETS
1 S.Fedorov/J.Lupul 15.00 40.00
2 I.Kovalchuk/D.Heatley 25.00 60.00
3 J.Thornton/P.Bergeron 20.00 50.00
4 M.Satan/D.Roy 15.00 40.00
5 J.Iginla/M.Lombardi 15.00 40.00
6 J.O'Neill/E.Staal 15.00 40.00
7 J.Thibault/T.Ruutu 12.00 30.00
8 P.Forsberg/D.Aebischer 15.00 40.00
9 R.Nash/N.Zherdev 20.00 50.00
10 M.Modano/S.Ott 15.00 40.00
11 S.Yzerman/P.Datsyuk 30.00 80.00
12 R.Smyth/A.Hemsky 15.00 40.00
13 R.Luongo/J.Bouwmeester 20.00 50.00
14 Z.Palffy/A.Frolov 15.00 40.00
15 M.Gaborik/P.Bouchard 30.00 80.00
16 J.Theodore/M.Ryder 25.00 60.00
17 D.Legwand/J.Tootoo 15.00 40.00
18 M.Brodeur/P.Martin 30.00 80.00
19 A.Yashin/R.DiPietro 15.00 40.00
20 M.Messier/F.Tyutin 20.00 50.00
21 M.Hossa/J.Spezza 15.00 40.00
22 J.LeClair/J.Pitkanen 15.00 40.00
23 S.Doan/B.Boucher 15.00 40.00
24 M.Lemieux/M.Fleury 50.00 125.00
25 C.Pronger/B.Jackman 15.00 40.00
26 E.Nabokov/J.Cheechoo 30.00 80.00
27 N.Khabibulin/V.Lecavalier 15.00 40.00
28 M.Sundin/M.Stajan 15.00 40.00
29 M.Naslund/A.Auld 15.00 40.00
30 O.Kolzig/A.Semin 15.00 40.00

2003-04 BAP Ultimate Memorabilia Gloves Are Off

PRINT RUN 25 SER.#'d SETS
1 Joe Thornton 20.00 50.00
2 Brett Hull 20.00 50.00
3 Mario Lemieux 30.00 80.00
4 Joe Sakic 20.00 50.00
5 Jarome Iginla 20.00 50.00
6 Sergei Samsonov 15.00 40.00
7 Mats Sundin 15.00 40.00
8 Eric Lindros 15.00 40.00
9 Rob Blake 15.00 40.00
10 John LeClair 15.00 40.00
11 Stan Mikita 15.00 40.00
12 Bill Gadsby 15.00 40.00
13 Aurel Joliat 25.00 60.00
14 Bernie Geoffrion 15.00 40.00
15 Dickie Moore 15.00 40.00
16 Howie Morenz 50.00 125.00
17 Doug Harvey 20.00 50.00
18 King Clancy 30.00 80.00
19 Ray Bourque 15.00 40.00
20 Eddie Shore 30.00 80.00

2003-04 BAP Ultimate Memorabilia Great Moments

COMMON CARD(1-12) 12.50 30.00
PRINT RUN 40 SER.#'d SETS
1 Bobby Orr 50.00 125.00
2 S.Mikita/B.Hull 25.00 60.00
3 Patrick Roy 30.00 80.00
4 Steve Yzerman 25.00 60.00
5 M.Messier/J.Theodore 25.00 60.00
6 Ray Bourque 15.00 40.00
7 B.Clarke/B.Barber 15.00 40.00
8 Henri Richard 12.50 30.00
9 Mike Bossy 15.00 40.00
10 Maurice Richard 30.00 80.00
11 Mark Messier 25.00 60.00
12 Cam Neely 20.00 50.00

2003-04 BAP Ultimate Memorabilia Hat Tricks

This 20-card set featured three different pieces of memorabilia. Cards were limited to 30 cards each.
PRINT RUN 30 SER.#'d SETS
1 Keith Tkachuk 15.00 40.00
2 Henrik Zetterberg 25.00 60.00
3 Alexei Yashin 12.50 30.00
4 Mats Sundin 15.00 40.00
5 Joe Thornton 25.00 60.00
6 Pavel Datsyuk 25.00 60.00
7 Joe Sakic 30.00 80.00
8 Mario Lemieux 50.00 125.00
9 Milan Hejduk 15.00 40.00
10 Eric Lindros 15.00 40.00
11 Jarome Iginla 25.00 60.00
12 Steve Yzerman 40.00 100.00
13 Sergei Samsonov 12.50 30.00
14 Brett Hull 25.00 60.00
15 Chris Chelios 15.00 40.00
16 Al MacInnis 12.50 30.00
17 Doug Weight 12.50 30.00
18 John LeClair 15.00 40.00
19 Rob Blake 12.50 30.00
20 Scott Niedermayer 15.00 40.00

2003-04 BAP Ultimate Memorabilia Heroes

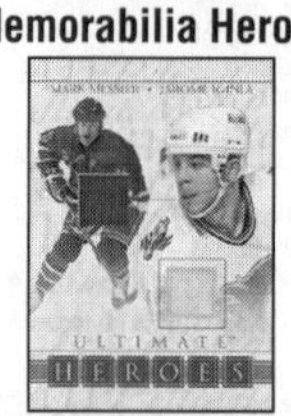

PRINT RUN 30 SER.#'d SETS
UNPRICED AUTO 1/1's EXIST
1 Ilya Kovalchuk 30.00 80.00
Valeri Kharlamov
2 J.Thornton/S.Yzerman 25.00 60.00
3 Jarome Iginla 20.00 50.00
Mark Messier
4 S.Yzerman/B.Trottier 25.00 60.00
5 M.Lemieux/G.Lafleur 40.00 100.00
6 R.Nash/M.Sundin 20.00 50.00
7 Dany Heatley 20.00 50.00
Brett Hull
8 Patrick Roy 50.00 125.00
Jacques Plante
9 Terry Sawchuk 40.00 100.00
George Hainsworth
10 Jose Theodore 40.00 100.00
Patrick Roy
11 Roberto Luongo 40.00 100.00
Patrick Roy
12 Ed Belfour 30.00 80.00
Vladislav Tretiak
13 M.Brodeur/P.Roy 40.00 100.00
14 Mike Richter 20.00 50.00
Gerry Cheevers
15 Teemu Selanne 30.00 80.00
Jarri Kurri
16 Alex Tanguay 25.00 60.00
Joe Sakic
17 P.Marleau/M.Lemieux 30.00 80.00
18 V.Lecavalier/S.Yzerman 25.00 60.00
19 M.St.Louis/M.Lemieux 30.00 80.00
20 Tuomo Ruutu 20.00 50.00
Peter Forsberg

2003-04 BAP Ultimate Memorabilia Hometown Heroes

PRINT RUN 50 SER.#'d SETS
UNPRICED GOLD 1/1's EXIST
1 Maurice Richard 40.00 100.00
Henri Richard
2 M.Brodeur/R.Luongo 20.00 50.00
3 Ray Bourque 20.00 50.00
Doug Harvey
4 Peter Forsberg 25.00 60.00
Markus Naslund
5 M.Gaborik/Z.Chara 15.00 40.00
6 George Hainsworth 15.00 40.00
Brad Park
7 Marcel Dionne 15.00 40.00
Yvan Cournoyer
8 Eric Staal 20.00 50.00
Alex Delvecchio
9 Frank Mahovlich 15.00 40.00
Pete Mahovlich
10 Rob Blake 15.00 40.00
Red Kelly
11 Brett Hull 15.00 40.00
Andrew Raycroft
12 Jose Theodore 25.00 60.00
Martin St.Louis
13 Joe Thornton 15.00 40.00
Eric Lindros
14 Mark Messier 15.00 40.00
Jarome Iginla
15 Bill Durnan 20.00 50.00
Conacher
16 Phil Esposito 20.00 50.00
Tony Esposito
17 Jarri Kurri 40.00 100.00
Kari Lehtonen
18 Terry Sawchuk 25.00 60.00
Bill Mosienko
19 Aurel Joliat 20.00 50.00
Denis Potvin
20 M.Bossy/M.Lemieux 40.00 100.00

2003-04 BAP Ultimate Memorabilia Jerseys

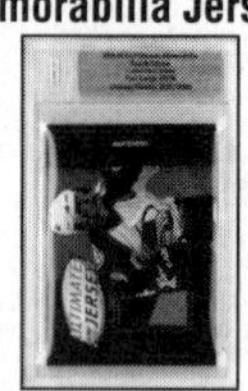

PRINT RUN 50 SER.#'d SETS
UNPRICED GOLD 1/1's EXIST
1 Paul Kariya 10.00 25.00
2 Teemu Selanne 10.00 25.00
3 Sergei Fedorov 12.50 30.00
4 Mario Lemieux 25.00 60.00
5 Dany Heatley 15.00 40.00
6 Joe Thornton 15.00 40.00
7 Steve Yzerman 25.00 60.00
8 Bill Guerin 8.00 20.00
9 Ilya Kovalchuk 15.00 40.00
10 Chris Pronger 8.00 20.00
11 Mats Sundin 10.00 25.00
12 Peter Forsberg 15.00 40.00
13 Rick Nash 12.50 30.00
14 Mike Modano 12.50 30.00
15 Martin Brodeur 25.00 60.00
16 Jason Spezza 10.00 25.00
17 Brett Hull 15.00 40.00
18 Jeremy Roenick 15.00 40.00
19 Joe Sakic 15.00 40.00
20 Ed Belfour 10.00 25.00
21 Jose Theodore 12.50 30.00
22 Roberto Luongo 12.50 30.00
23 Henrik Zetterberg 10.00 25.00
24 Dominik Hasek 12.50 30.00
25 Jarome Iginla 12.50 30.00
26 Eric Lindros 10.00 25.00
27 Keith Tkachuk 10.00 25.00
28 Marian Gaborik 15.00 40.00
29 Nicklas Lidstrom 10.00 25.00
30 John LeClair 10.00 25.00
31 Pavel Datsyuk 10.00 25.00
32 Vincent Lecavalier 10.00 25.00
33 Markus Naslund 10.00 25.00
34 Milan Hejduk 10.00 25.00
35 Todd Bertuzzi 10.00 25.00
36 Marty Turco 8.00 20.00
37 Rob Blake 8.00 20.00
38 Andrew Raycroft 12.50 30.00
39 Martin St. Louis 8.00 20.00
40 Saku Koivu 10.00 25.00

2003-04 BAP Ultimate Memorabilia Jersey and Emblems

PRINT RUN 10 SER.#'d SETS
NOT PRICED DUE TO SCARCITY
UNPRICED GOLD 1/1's EXIST
1 Alexander Mogilny
2 Bill Guerin
3 Bobby Orr
4 Brendan Shanahan
5 Brett Hull
6 Brian Leetch
7 Chris Pronger
8 Curtis Joseph
9 Dany Heatley
10 Dominik Hasek
11 Ed Belfour
12 Eric Lindros
13 Ilya Kovalchuk
14 Jarome Iginla
15 Jason Spezza
16 Jeremy Roenick
17 Joe Sakic
18 Joe Thornton
19 Jose Theodore
20 Keith Tkachuk
21 Marian Gaborik
22 Mario Lemieux
23 Markus Naslund
24 Martin Brodeur
25 Martin St. Louis
26 Marty Turco
27 Mats Sundin
28 Mike Modano
29 Nicklas Lidstrom
30 Owen Nolan
31 Patrick Roy
32 Pavel Datsyuk
33 Peter Forsberg
34 Ray Bourque
35 Rick Nash
36 Roberto Luongo
37 Sergei Fedorov
38 Sergei Samsonov
39 Steve Yzerman
40 Teemu Selanne

2003-04 BAP Ultimate Memorabilia Jersey and Numbers

PRINT RUN 10 SER.#'d SETS
NOT PRICED DUE TO SCARCITY
UNPRICED GOLD 1/1's EXIST

2003-04 BAP Ultimate Memorabilia Jersey and Stick

PRINT RUN 50 SER.#'d SETS
UNPRICED GOLD 1/1's EXIST
1 Jason Spezza 15.00 40.00
2 Brian Leetch 15.00 40.00
3 Dany Heatley 25.00 60.00
4 Mario Lemieux 40.00 100.00
5 Mats Sundin 15.00 40.00
6 Jarome Iginla 20.00 50.00
7 Mike Modano 20.00 50.00
8 Rick Nash 20.00 50.00
9 Steve Yzerman 40.00 100.00
10 Keith Tkachuk 15.00 40.00
11 Joe Thornton 25.00 60.00
12 Martin Brodeur 40.00 100.00
13 Dominik Hasek 20.00 50.00
14 Nikolai Khabibulin 15.00 40.00
15 Joe Sakic 25.00 60.00
16 Vincent Lecavalier 15.00 40.00
17 Peter Forsberg 25.00 60.00
18 Brendan Shanahan 15.00 40.00
19 Marc-Andre Fleury 30.00 80.00
20 Chris Pronger 12.50 30.00
21 Patrick Roy 40.00 100.00
22 Johnny Bower 25.00 60.00
23 Ray Bourque 20.00 50.00
24 Jacques Plante 30.00 80.00
25 Jean Beliveau 25.00 60.00
26 Gump Worsley 25.00 60.00
27 Gilbert Perreault
28 Bryan Trottier
29 Mike Bossy
30 Marcel Dionne

2003-04 BAP Ultimate Memorabilia Journey Jerseys

PRINT RUN 50 SER.#'d SETS
UNPRICED GOLD 1/1's EXIST
1 Sergei Fedorov 15.00 40.00
2 Paul Kariya 12.50 30.00
3 Teemu Selanne 12.50 30.00
4 Ed Belfour 15.00 40.00
5 Brian Leetch 12.50 30.00
6 Patrick Roy 40.00 100.00
7 Brett Hull 25.00 60.00
8 Mark Messier 20.00 50.00

9 Jeremy Roenick 15.00 40.0
10 Ray Bourque 25.00 60.0

2003-04 BAP Ultimate Memorabilia Journey Emblems

PRINT RUN 10 SER.#'d SETS
NOT PRICED DUE TO SCARCITY
UNPRICED GOLD 1/1's EXIST

2003-04 BAP Ultimate Memorabilia Lifetime Achievers

PRINT RUN 30 SER.#'d SETS
1 Mario Lemieux 30.00 80.0
2 Patrick Roy 30.00 80.0
3 Bobby Orr 50.00 125.0
4 Ray Bourque 20.00 50.0
5 Mark Messier 25.00 60.0
6 Brett Hull 15.00 40.0
7 Brian Leetch 15.00 40.0
8 Steve Yzerman 30.00 80.0

2003-04 BAP Ultimate Memorabilia Linemates

PRINT RUN 10 SER.#'d SETS
NOT PRICED DUE TO SCARCITY
1 Doug Mohns
Stan Mikita
Ken Wharram
2 John LeClair
Eric Lindros
Mikael Renberg
3 Charlie Hodge
Phil Esposito
Wayne Cashman
4 Moore/Geoffrion/Beliveau
5 Stan Mikita
Jim Pappin
Bobby Hull
6 Marcel Dionne
Charlie Simmer
Dave Taylor
7 Bryan Trottier
Clark Gillies
Mike Bossy
8 Guy Lafleur
Pete Mahovlich
Steve Shutt
9 Brett Hull
Henrik Zetterberg
Pavel Datsyuk
10 Maurice Richard
Elmer Lach
Toe Blake
11 Joe Primeau
Charlie Conacher
Busher Jackson
12 Vladimir Krutov
Igor Larionov
Sergei Makarov

2003-04 BAP Ultimate Memorabilia Lumbergraphs

s 50-card set featured "cut" signatures
oved from actual autographed sticks.
h card was a 1/1.
NT RUN 1 SET
T PRICED DUE TO SCARCITY
ooney Weiland
Voody Dumart
Dit Clapper
Bobby Bauer
rank Brimsek
Ace Bailey
ionel Conacher
Roy Worters
Charlie Conacher
Lorne Chabot
Howie Morenz
Black Jack Stewart
Sid Abel
Tommy Ivan
Boom Boom Geoffrion
Sweeney Schriner
Gordie Drillon
Bill Barilko
Syl Apps
Turk Broda
Jack Adams
Tim Horton
Toe Blake
Doug Harvey
Jacques Plante
Frank Selke
Red Horner
Harold Baldy Cotton
Hooley Smith
Leo Reise
Cy Wentworth
Mud Bruneteau
Ebbie Goodfellow
Elmer Lach
Joe Primeau
King Clancy
Cecil Hart
Ted Lindsay
Red Kelly
Harry Watson
Max Bentley
Bob Davidson
Roger Crozier
Frank Mahovlich
Babe Seibert
Aurel Joliat
George Hainsworth
Hap Day
Henri Richard
Maurice Richard

2003-04 BAP Ultimate Memorabilia Made to Order

D.CARDS 10 COPIES EACH
Bobby Orr Jersey
H.Zetterberg Triple Mem
H.Zetterberg Emblem
H.Zetterberg Jsy/Emblem
H.Zetterberg Comp.Jsy

2003-04 BAP Ultimate Memorabilia Aagnificent Career

NT RUN 40 SER.#'d SETS
TO PRINT RUN 10 SETS
TOS NOT PRICED DUE TO SCARCITY
Mario Lemieux 30.00 80.00
A Grand Entrance
Mario Lemieux 30.00 80.00
Twice Is Nice
Mario Lemieux 30.00 80.00
A Scoring Machine
Mario Lemieux 30.00 80.00
A Canadian Hero
Mario Lemieux 30.00 80.00
A Hoard Of Hardware
Mario Lemieux 30.00 80.00
Farewell For Now
Mario Lemieux 30.00 80.00
600-Goal Man
Mario Lemieux 30.00 80.00
International Star
Mario Lemieux 30.00 80.00
1,700th Point
Quad Jersey 75.00 150.00

2003-04 BAP Ultimate Memorabilia Magnificent Prospects

NT RUN 30 SER.#'d SETS
TO PRINT RUN 10 SETS
TOS NOT PRICED DUE TO SCARCITY
TOS SIGNED BY LEMIEUX ONLY
Mario Lemieux AU 60.00 150.00
Marc Andre Fleury
Mario Lemieux AU 40.00 100.00
Eric Staal
Mario Lemieux AU 40.00 100.00
Patrice Bergeron
Mario Lemieux AU 30.00 80.00
Michael Ryder

5 Mario Lemieux AU 40.00 100.00
Ryan Malone
6 Mario Lemieux AU 30.00 80.00
Tuomo Ruutu
7 Mario Lemieux AU 30.00 80.00
Joffrey Lupul
8 Mario Lemieux AU 30.00 80.00
Jordin Tootoo
9 Mario Lemieux AU 30.00 80.00
Andrew Raycroft
10 Mario Lemieux AU 30.00 80.00
Nikolai Zherdev

2003-04 BAP Ultimate Memorabilia Maple Leafs Forever

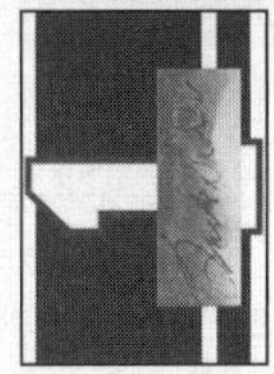

This 19-card set featured "cut" signatures from former Toronto greats on 1/1 cards.
PRINT RUN 1 SET
NOT PRICED DUE TO SCARCITY
1 Frank McCool
2 Syl Apps
3 Turk Broda
4 Babe Pratt
5 King Clancy
6 Frank Finnigan
7 Bob Davidson
8 Tim Horton
9 Harry Lumley
10 Gordie Drillon
11 Ace Bailey
12 Joe Primeau
13 Harry Watson
14 Ted Kennedy
15 Hap Day
16 Lorne Carr
17 Bill Barilko
18 Sweeney Schriner
19 Foster Hewitt

2003-04 BAP Ultimate Memorabilia Memorialized

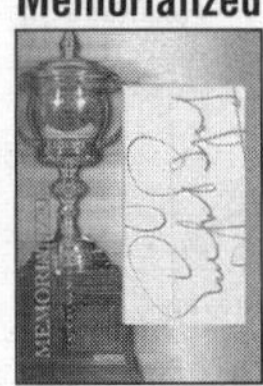

This 14-card set featured "cut" signatures of some of hockey's pioneers on 1/1 cards.
PRINT RUN 1 SET
NOT PRICED DUE TO SCARCITY
1 Lady Byng
2 Jack Adams
3 Rocket Richard
4 Conn Smythe
5 James Norris
6 Lester Patrick
7 Frank Calder
8 Art Ross
9 Edward VIII
Prince of Wales
10 King Clancy
11 Frank J. Selke Sr.
12 Clarence Campbell
13 Lester B. Pearson
14 Cecil Hart

2003-04 BAP Ultimate Memorabilia Nameplates

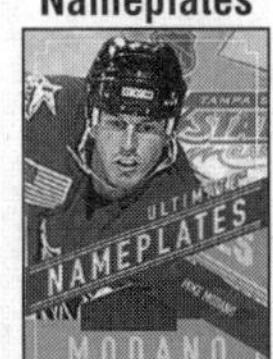

PRINT RUN 40 SER.#'d SETS
UNLESS OTHERWISE NOTED
UNPRICED GOLD 1/1's EXIST
1 Sergei Fedorov 20.00 50.00
2 Dominik Hasek 20.00 50.00
3 Dany Heatley 20.00 50.00
4 Markus Naslund 12.50 30.00
5 Curtis Joseph 12.50 30.00
6 Mike Modano 15.00 40.00
7 Paul Kariya 12.50 30.00
8 Mark Messier 25.00 60.00
9 Teemu Selanne 12.50 30.00
10 Martin Brodeur 30.00 80.00
11 Brian Leetch 15.00 40.00
12 Joe Thornton 15.00 40.00
13 Mario Lemieux 40.00 100.00
14 Steve Yzerman 25.00 60.00
15 Eric Lindros 12.50 30.00
16 Peter Forsberg 25.00 60.00
17 Zigmund Palffy 12.50 30.00
18 Jeremy Roenick 15.00 40.00
19 Chris Pronger 12.50 30.00
20 Nicklas Lidstrom 12.50 30.00
21 Mats Sundin 12.50 30.00
22 Brendan Shanahan 12.50 30.00
23 Henrik Zetterberg 15.00 40.00
24 Jose Theodore 15.00 40.00
25 Marc-Andre Fleury 25.00 60.00
26 Kari Lehtonen 25.00 60.00
27 Andrew Raycroft 20.00 50.00
28 Ray Bourque 25.00 60.00
29 Cam Neely 20.00 50.00
30 Patrick Roy/20 75.00 200.00

2003-04 BAP Ultimate Memorabilia Numbers

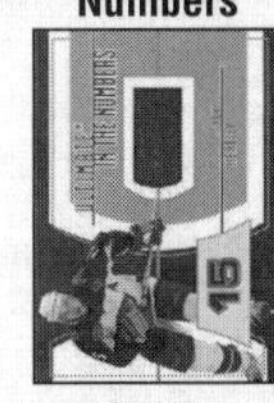

PRINT RUN 10 SER.#'d SETS
NOT PRICED DUE TO SCARCITY
UNPRICED GOLD 1/1's EXIST
1 Paul Kariya
2 Sergei Fedorov
3 Mario Lemieux
4 Dany Heatley
5 Joe Thornton
6 Steve Yzerman
7 Ilya Kovalchuk
8 Mats Sundin
9 Peter Forsberg
10 Rick Nash
11 Mike Modano
12 Martin Brodeur
13 Jason Spezza
14 Joe Sakic
15 Ed Belfour
16 JosÃ© ThÃ©odore
17 Roberto Luongo
18 Henrik Zetterberg
19 Dominik Hasek
20 Jarome Iginla
21 Eric Lindros
22 Marian Gaborik
23 Nicklas Lidstrom
24 Pavel Datsyuk
25 Vincent Lecavalier
26 Markus Naslund
27 Todd Bertuzzi
28 Rob Blake
29 Saku Koivu
30 Patrick Roy

2003-04 BAP Ultimate Memorabilia Paper Cuts

This 19-card set featured "cut" signatures from former NHL greats on 1/1 cards.
PRINT RUN 1 SET
NOT PRICED DUE TO SCARCITY
1 Jacques Plante
2 Ace Bailey
3 Joe Primeau
4 Frank Brimsek
5 Bill Mosienko
6 Aurel Joliat
7 King Clancy
8 Toe Blake
9 Frank Patrick
10 Bill Durnan
11 Mel Hill
12 Flash Hollett
13 Foster Hewitt
14 Frank Selke
15 Gordie Drillon
16 Bill Cowley
17 Dit Clapper
18 Turk Broda
19 Terry Sawchuk
20 Red Dutton
21 Doug Harvey
22 Harry Oliver
23 Syl Apps
24 Ebbie Goodfellow
25 Mud Bruneteau
26 Muzz Patrick
27 James D. Norris
28 Bryan Hextall
29 Max Bentley
30 Charlie Conacher
31 Busher Jackson
32 Hooley Smith
33 Sweeney Schriner
34 Babe Siebert
35 Sid Abel
36 Maurice Richard
37 Art Coulter
38 Babe Pratt
39 Eddie Shore
40 Roy Worters
41 Dave Kerr
42 Bill Cook
43 Howie Morenz
44 Bill Barilko
45 Dick Irvin
46 Frank Calder
47 Lester Patrick
48 Frank Boucher
49 Lynn Patrick
50 Newsy Lalonde

2003-04 BAP Ultimate Memorabilia Perennial Powerhouse Jersey

PRINT RUN 30 SER.#'d SETS
1 Patrick Roy 30.00 80.00
2 Joe Sakic 20.00 50.00
3 Peter Forsberg 20.00 50.00
4 Ray Bourque 20.00 50.00
5 Rob Blake 12.50 30.00
6 Alex Tanguay 12.50 30.00
7 Milan Hejduk 12.50 30.00
8 David Aebischer 12.50 30.00
9 Paul Kariya 12.50 30.00
10 Teemu Selanne 12.50 30.00

2003-04 BAP Ultimate Memorabilia Perennial Powerhouse Jersey and Stick

*JSY/STK: .6X TO 1.5X JSY HI
PRINT RUN 30 SER.#'d SETS

2003-04 BAP Ultimate Memorabilia Perennial Powerhouse Emblem

PRINT RUN 10 SER.#'d SETS
NOT PRICED DUE TO SCARCITY

2003-04 BAP Ultimate Memorabilia Raised to the Rafters

This 20-card set commemorated past stars who's respective teams have retired their jersey numbers. Cards were limited to just 30 copies each.
PRINT RUN 30 SER.#'d SETS
1 Cam Neely 30.00 60.00
2 Doug Harvey 30.00 60.00
3 Mike Richter 40.00 80.00
4 Bobby Orr 150.00 250.00
5 Johnny Bower 20.00 50.00
6 Ray Bourque 30.00 60.00
7 Sid Abel 20.00 50.00
8 Ted Lindsay 20.00 40.00
9 Rod Gilbert 20.00 50.00
10 Maurice Richard 40.00 80.00
11 Jean Beliveau 40.00 80.00
12 Bobby Hull 20.00 40.00
13 Stan Mikita 20.00 40.00
14 Bobby Clarke 25.00 60.00
15 Bernie Parent 25.00 60.00
16 Jacques Plante 40.00 80.00
17 Mike Bossy 20.00 40.00
18 Marcel Dionne 20.00 40.00
19 Bryan Trottier 20.00 40.00
20 Eddie Shore 40.00 80.00

2003-04 BAP Ultimate Memorabilia Redemption Cards

This 4-card set was inserted as redemption cards redeemable for a card of the winner(s) of the Vezina, Richard, Norris and Perason awards.
PRINT RUN 10 SER.#'d SETS
NOT PRICED DUE TO SCARCITY
1 M.Brodeur/G.Vezina/Vezina
2 Scott Niedermayer
Bobby Orr
Norris Trophy
3 Martin St. Louis
Phil Epsosito
Pearson Award
4 Richard/Kovy/Nash/Iginla/Richard

2003-04 BAP Ultimate Memorabilia Retro Teammates

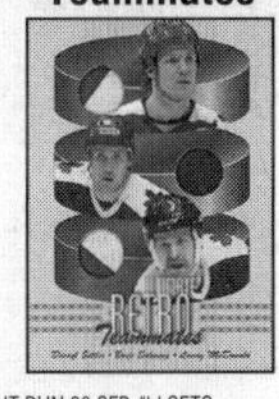

PRINT RUN 30 SER.#'d SETS
1 Bourque/Neely/Oates 40.00 100.00
2 M.Richard/Harvey/Plante 75.00 200.00
3 Sawchuk/Lindsay/Abel 40.00 100.00
4 Messier/Richter/Leetch 75.00 200.00
5 Orr/Cheevers/Bucyk 125.00 300.00
6 Trottier/Bossy/Potvin 40.00 100.00
7 Beliveau/H.Richard/Worsley 40.00100.00
8 Clarke/Barber/Parent 40.00 100.00
9 Sittler/McDonald/Salming 40.00 100.00
10 Shore/Thompson/Stewart 40.00 100.00

2003-04 BAP Ultimate Memorabilia Retro-Active Trophies

PRINT RUN 50 SER.#'d SETS
1 T.Lindsay/J.Iginla 15.00 40.00
2 B.Orr/P.Forsberg 40.00 100.00
3 J.Beliveau/M.Lemieux 30.00 80.00
4 R.Bourque/P.Forsberg 25.00 60.00
5 B.Orr/M.Lemieux 75.00 200.00
6 T.Sawchuk/M.Brodeur 30.00 80.00
7 R.Worters/D.Hasek 15.00 40.00
8 E.Shore/M.Messier 20.00 50.00
9 M.Richard/M.Lemieux 40.00 100.00
10 D.Harvey/N.Lidstrom 15.00 40.00
11 B.Orr/B.Leetch 40.00 100.00
12 R.Bourque/C.Pronger 15.00 40.00
13 B.Mosienko/J.Sakic 20.00 50.00
14 M.Dionne/Br.Hull 15.00 40.00
15 J.Plante/M.Brodeur 25.00 60.00
16 J.Bower/E.Belfour 15.00 40.00
17 P.Roy/J.Theodore 30.00 80.00
18 J.Beliveau/S.Yzerman 25.00 60.00
19 P.Roy/J.Sakic 30.00 80.00
20 G.Lafleur/M.Lemieux 30.00 80.00

2003-04 BAP Ultimate Memorabilia Rookie Jersey and Emblems

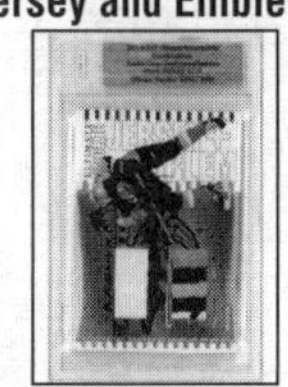

PRINT RUN 10 SER.#'d SETS
NOT PRICED DUE TO SCARCITY
UNPRICED GOLD 1/1'S EXIST
1 Kari Lehtonen
2 Joni Pitkanen
3 Tim Gleason
4 Chris Higgins
5 Nathan Horton
6 Marek Zidlicky
7 Antti Miettinen
8 Patrice Bergeron
9 Ryan Malone
10 Matthew Lombardi
11 David Hale
12 Tuomo Ruutu
13 Derek Roy
14 Paul Martin
15 Jordin Tootoo
16 Dustin Brown
17 Antoine Vermette
18 Matt Stajan
19 Nikolai Zherdev
20 Marc-Andre Fleury
21 Fedor Tyutin
22 Niklas Kronwall
23 Eric Staal
24 Andrew Raycroft
25 Trent Hunter
26 Christian Ehrhoff
27 Alexander Semin
28 Brent Burns
29 Boyd Kane
30 Sean Bergenheim
31 Ryan Kesler
32 Peter Sejna
33 Michael Ryder
34 John-Michael Liles
35 Joffrey Lupul
36 Esa Pirnes
37 Antero Niittymaki
38 Mark Popovic
39 Patrick Leahy
40 Rastislav Stana

2003-04 BAP Ultimate Memorabilia Rookie Jersey and Numbers

PRINT RUN 10 SER.#'d SETS
NOT PRICED DUE TO SCARCITY
UNPRICED GOLD 1/1's EXIST
1 Kari Lehtonen
2 Joni Pitkanen
3 Tim Gleason
4 Christopher Higgins
5 Nathan Horton
6 Marek Zidlicky
7 Antti Miettinen
8 Patrice Bergeron
9 Ryan Malone
10 Matthew Lombardi
11 David Hale
12 Tuomo Ruutu
13 Derek Roy
14 Paul Martin
15 Jordin Tootoo
16 Dustin Brown
17 Antoine Vermette
18 Matt Stajan
19 Nikolai Zherdev
20 Marc-Andre Fleury
21 Fedor Tyutin
22 Niklas Kronwall
23 Eric Staal
24 Andrew Raycroft
25 Trent Hunter
26 Christian Ehrhoff
27 Alexander Semin
28 Brent Burns
29 Boyd Kane
30 Sean Bergenheim
31 Ryan Kesler
32 Peter Sejna
33 Michael Ryder
34 John-Michael Liles
35 Joffrey Lupul
36 Esa Pirnes
37 Antero Niittymaki
38 Mark Popovic
39 Patrick Leahy
40 Rastislav Stana

2003-04 BAP Ultimate Memorabilia Seams Unbelievable

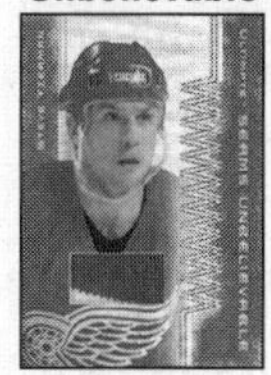

PRINT RUN 20 SER.#'d SETS
NOT PRICED DUE TO SCARCITY
1 Mario Lemieux
2 Patrick Roy
3 Steve Yzerman
4 Bobby Orr
5 Raymond Bourque
6 Martin Brodeur
7 Ilya Kovalchuk
8 Rick Nash

2003-04 BAP Ultimate Memorabilia The Goal

This 14-card set commemorated probably the most famous goal in hockey history. Known now as "The Goal", this image of Bobby Orr flying through the air after being tripped by Noel Picard and scoring on Glenn Hall to lead the Bruins to a defeat over the Blues to win the Stanley Cup is probably one of the most recognizable in hockey. Single jersey and stick cards were limited to 35 copies. Jersey autographs were limited to 10 copies each. All other print runs are listed below.
SINGLE JSY PRINT RUN 35 SER.#'d SETS
SINGLE STK PRINT RUN 35 SER.#'d SETS
JSY AU PRINT RUN 10 SER.#'d SETS
PRINT RUNS OF 10 NOT
PRICED DUE TO SCARCITY
1 Bobby Orr JSY 75.00 200.00
2 B.Orr JSY AU
3 Noel Picard JSY 20.00 50.00
4 Glenn Hall JSY 25.00 60.00
5 B.Orr/N.Picard JSY/30 100.00 250.00
6 B.Orr/G.Hall JSY/30 125.00 250.00
7 B.Orr/G.Hall JSY AU
8 B.Orr STK 75.00 200.00
9 G.Hall STK 25.00 60.00
10 N.Picard STK 20.00 50.00
11 Orr/Hall/Picard STK/10
12 Orr/Hall/Picard JSY/10
13 Orr/Hall/Picard JSY AU/10
14 N.Picard/G.Hall JSY/29 25.00 60.00

2003-04 BAP Ultimate Memorabilia Triple Threads

PRINT RUN 40 SER.#'d SETS
1 Brodeur/Potvin/DiPietro 40.00 100.00
2 Hasek/Cloutier/Aebischer 25.00 60.00
3 Joseph/Khabibulin/Giguere 20.00 50.00
4 Belfour/Turco/Cechmanek 20.00 50.00
5 Theodore/Osgood/Luongo 25.00 60.00
6 Kolzig/Biron/Nabokov 15.00 40.00
7 Roy/Crozier/Bower 30.00 80.00
8 Sawchuk/Lumley/Plante 40.00 100.00
9 Hainsworth/Brimsek/Worters 30.00 80.00
10 Blake/Bouwmeester/Pronger 12.50 30.00
11 Lidstrom/Brewer/MacInnis 12.50 30.00
12 Leetch/Chara/Foote 15.00 40.00
13 Orr/T.Horton/Robinson 75.00 200.00
14 Harvey/Bourque/Salming 20.00 50.00
15 Sundin/Modano/Alfredsson 15.00 40.00
16 Lemieux/Hossa/Hull 40.00 100.00
17 St.Louis/Mogilny/Kovalchuk 20.00 50.00
18 Heatley/Thornton/Koivu 30.00 80.00
19 Weight/Palffy/Kariya 12.50 30.00
20 Selanne/Lindros/Tkachuk 15.00 40.00
21 Sakic/Bertuzzi/Yzerman 30.00 80.00
22 Forsberg/Amonte/Naslund 20.00 50.00
23 Nolan/Roenick/Zetterberg 15.00 40.00
24 Nash/Shanahan/Arnott 15.00 40.00
25 Gaborik/Elias/LeClair 15.00 40.00
26 Beliveau/F.Mahovlich/Bossy 25.00 60.00
27 Lindsay/H.Richard/Clarke 20.00 50.00
28 Neely/P.Esposito/McDonald 30.00 80.00
29 Bergeron/Horton/Bergenheim 25.00 60.00
30 Hunter/Gordon/Hale 12.50 30.00
31 Ruutu/Semin/Martin 15.00 40.00
32 Tootoo/Lombardi/Pitkanen 12.00 30.00
33 Staal/Ryder/Brown 30.00 80.00
34 Fleury/Zherdev/Raycroft 25.00 60.00

2003-04 BAP Ultimate Memorabilia Ultimate Captains

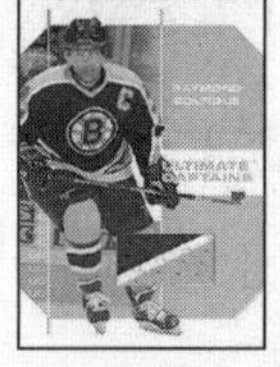

This 8-card set featured swatches cut from the captain's C of the featured player. Cards were limited to 5 copies each.
PRINT RUN 5 SER.#'d SETS
NOT PRICED DUE TO SCARCITY
1 Ray Bourque
2 Mike Peca
3 Chris Pronger
4 Scott Stevens
5 Vincent Lecavalier
6 Jean Beliveau
7 Mario Lemieux
8 Mario Lemieux

2003-04 BAP Ultimate Memorabilia Ultimate Defenseman

PRINT RUN 20 SER.#'d SETS
AUTO PRINT RUN 4 SER.#'d SETS
NOT PRICED DUE TO SCARCITY
1 Bobby Orr/Jersey
2 Bobby Orr/Number
3 Bobby Orr/Jersey/Stick
4 Bobby Orr/Stick
5 Bobby Orr/Skate
6 Bobby Orr/Triple Memorabilia

2003-04 BAP Ultimate Memorabilia Ultimate Forward

PRINT RUN 20 SER.#'d SETS
AUTO PRINT RUN 6 SER.#'d SETS
NOT PRICED DUE TO SCARCITY
1 Mario Lemieux/Jersey
2 Mario Lemieux/Number
3 Mario Lemieux/Jersey/Stick
4 Mario Lemieux/Glove
5 Mario Lemieux/Pants
6 Mario Lemieux/Triple Memorabilia

2003-04 BAP Ultimate Memorabilia Ultimate Goaltender

PRINT RUN 20 SER.#'d SETS
AUTO PRINT RUN 3 SER.#'d SETS
NOT PRICED DUE TO SCARCITY
1 Patrick Roy/Jersey
2 Patrick Roy/Jersey
3 Patrick Roy/Jersey/Stick
4 Patrick Roy/Number
5 Patrick Roy/Pad
6 Patrick Roy/Triple Memorabilia

2003-04 BAP Ultimate Memorabilia Vintage Blades of Steel

PRINT RUN 20 SER.#'d SETS
NOT PRICED DUE TO SCARCITY
1 Bill Barilko
2 Georges Vezina
3 Rocket Richard
4 Cyclone Taylor
5 Frank Patrick
6 Frank Nighbor
7 Hap Day
8 Clint Benedict
9 Elmer Lach
10 Busher Jackson
11 Eddie Shore
12 Jacques Plante
13 Toe Blake
14 Jack Adams
15 Bobby Orr
16 Tim Horton
17 Aurel Joliat
18 Nels Stewart
19 Paddy Moran
20 Jean Beliveau

2003-04 BAP Ultimate Memorabilia Vintage Complete Jersey

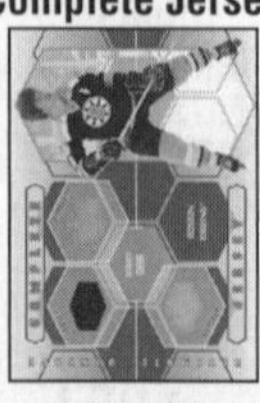

This 10-card set featured swatches of game-used jersey, numbers, emblems and fight straps. Cards were limited to just 10 copies each.

PRINT RUN 10 SER.#'d SETS
NOT PRICED DUE TO SCARCITY
UNPRICED GOLD 1/1's EXIST
1 Bobby Orr
2 Ray Bourque
3 Johnny Bower
4 Aurel Joliat
5 George Hainsworth
6 Roy Worters
7 Jean Beliveau
8 Bill Mosienko
9 Ted Lindsay
10 Jacques Plante

2003-04 BAP Ultimate Memorabilia Vintage Complete Package

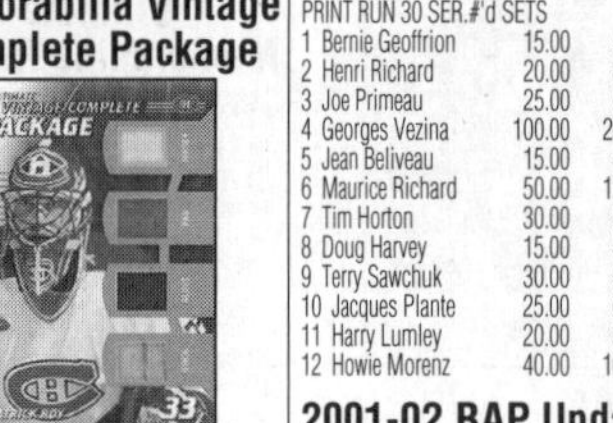

This 8-card set featured 4 different swatches per card of the featured players. Included in the memorabilia were items such as skates, jerseys, sticks, pants, socks, and pads. Cards were limited to 10 copies each.

PRINT RUN 10 SER.#'d SETS
NOT PRICED DUE TO SCARCITY
UNPRICED GOLD 1/1's EXIST
1 Terry Sawchuk
2 Jacques Plante
3 Maurice Richard
4 Ray Bourque
5 Stan Mikita
6 Patrick Roy
7 Guy Lafleur
8 Bernie Parent

2003-04 BAP Ultimate Memorabilia Vintage Hat Tricks

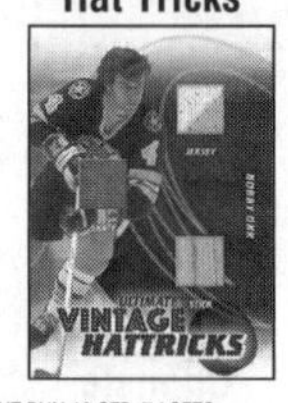

PRINT RUN 10 SER.#'d SETS
NOT PRICED DUE TO SCARCITY
1 Bobby Orr
2 Cam Neely
3 Ray Bourque
4 Eddie Shore
5 Stan Mikita
6 Aurel Joliat

2003-04 BAP Ultimate Memorabilia Vintage Jerseys

PRINT RUN 40 SER.#'d SETS
NOT PRICED DUE TO SCARCITY
UNPRICED GOLD 1/1's EXIST

1 Aurel Joliat	30.00	80.00
2 Bobby Orr	75.00	150.00
3 Doug Harvey	12.50	30.00
4 Roy Worters	20.00	50.00
5 Jacques Plante	25.00	60.00
6 Jean Beliveau	25.00	60.00
7 Johnny Bower	20.00	50.00
8 George Hainsworth	15.00	40.00
9 Frank Brimsek	15.00	40.00
10 Roger Crozier	12.50	30.00
11 Harry Lumley	20.00	50.00
12 Sid Abel	12.50	30.00
13 Bill Mosienko	12.50	30.00
14 John Bucyk	12.50	30.00
15 Ted Lindsay	12.50	30.00
16 Alex Delvecchio	12.50	30.00
17 Phil Esposito	15.00	40.00
18 Frank Mahovlich	12.50	30.00
19 Maurice Richard	30.00	80.00
20 Dennis Hull	12.50	30.00
21 Marcel Dionne	12.50	30.00
22 Terry O'Reilly	15.00	40.00
23 Vladislav Tretiak	40.00	100.00
24 Henri Richard	12.50	30.00
25 Larry Robinson	12.50	30.00
26 Mike Bossy	12.50	30.00
27 Bryan Trottier	12.50	30.00
28 Gump Worsley	12.50	30.00
29 Bobby Clarke	12.50	30.00
30 Red Kelly	15.00	40.00
31 Gilbert Perreault	12.50	30.00
32 Lanny McDonald	12.50	30.00
33 Ray Bourque	15.00	40.00
34 Ed Giacomin	15.00	40.00
35 Valeri Kharlamov	20.00	50.00
36 Stan Mikita	12.50	30.00
37 Denis Potvin	12.50	30.00
38 Bobby Hull	20.00	50.00
39 Patrick Roy	25.00	60.00
40 Cam Neely	15.00	40.00

2003-04 BAP Ultimate Memorabilia Vintage Lumber

PRINT RUN 30 SER.#'d SETS

1 Bernie Geoffrion	15.00	40.00
2 Henri Richard	20.00	50.00
3 Joe Primeau	25.00	60.00
4 Georges Vezina	100.00	250.00
5 Jean Beliveau	15.00	40.00
6 Maurice Richard	50.00	125.00
7 Tim Horton	30.00	80.00
8 Doug Harvey	15.00	40.00
9 Terry Sawchuk	30.00	80.00
10 Jacques Plante	25.00	60.00
11 Harry Lumley	20.00	50.00
12 Howie Morenz	40.00	100.00

2001-02 BAP Update

ALL BASE CARDS LISTED UNDER
ORIGINAL BASE SETS

2001-02 BAP Update He Shoots-He Scores Points

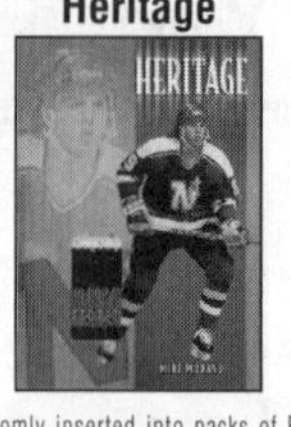

Inserted one per pack, these cards carried a value of 1, 2 or 3 points. The points could be redeemed for special memorabilia cards. The cards are unnumbered and are listed below in alphabetical order by point value. Redemption cards expired May 2003.

ONE PER PACK
RED.PROGRAM HAS EXPIRED

1 Todd Bertuzzi 1 pt.	.20	.50
2 Theo Fleury 1 pt.	.20	.50
3 Marian Gaborik 1 pt.	.20	.50
4 Bill Guerin 1 pt.	.20	.50
5 Martin Havlat 1 pt.	.20	.50
6 Marian Hossa 1 pt.	.20	.50
7 Nicklas Lidstrom 1 pt.	.20	.50
8 Alexei Yashin 1 pt.	.20	.50
9 Ed Belfour 2 pts.	.20	.50
10 Martin Brodeur 2 pts.	.20	.50
11 Pavel Bure 2 pts.	.20	.50
12 Ron Francis 2 pts.	.20	.50
13 Luc Robitaille 2 pts.	.20	.50
14 Jose Theodore 2 pts.	.20	.50
15 Peter Forsberg 3 pts.	.20	.50
16 Dominik Hasek 3 pts.	.20	.50
17 Curtis Joseph 3 pts.	.20	.50
18 Patrick Roy 3 pts.	.20	.50

2001-02 BAP Update He Shoots-He Scores Prizes

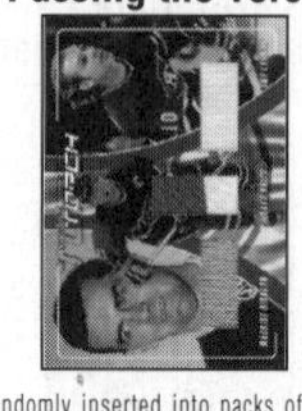

Available only by redeeming 400 BAP Update He Shoots-He Scores points, this 40-card set featured game-used swatches of jersey and a color photo of the player. There were 14 card that resembled the Memorabilia series, 13 cards that resembled the Signature Series set and 13 cards that resembled the Parkhurst set. Each card had a stated print run of 20 serial-numbered sets and each was encased in a clear plastic slab with a descriptive label at the top. This set is unpriced due to scarcity and volatility.

STATED PRINT RUN 20 SER.#'d SETS
NOT PRICED DUE TO SCARCITY
1 Ilya Kovalchuk M
2 Patrik Elias M
3 Jose Theodore M
4 Luc Robitaille M
5 Jarome Iginla M
6 Paul Kariya M
7 Patrick Lalime M
8 Pavel Bure M
9 Markus Naslund M
10 Evgeni Nabokov M
11 Eric Lindros M
12 Jeremy Roenick M
13 Alexander Mogilny M
14 Dominik Hasek M
15 Bill Guerin S
16 Marty Turco S
17 Vincent Lecavalier S
18 Zigmund Palffy S
19 Nicklas Lidstrom S
20 Sami Kapanen S
21 Peter Forsberg S
22 Marian Hossa S
23 Alexei Yashin S
24 Ron Francis S
25 Luc Robitaille S
26 Joe Thornton S
27 Peter Bondra S
28 Roberto Luongo P
29 Theo Fleury P
30 Todd Bertuzzi P
31 Jose Theodore P
32 Marian Gaborik P
33 Pavel Bure P
34 Ed Belfour P
35 Martin Havlat P
36 Martin Brodeur P
37 Alex Tanguay P
38 Curtis Joseph P
39 Dominik Hasek P
40 Patrick Roy P

2001-02 BAP Update Heritage

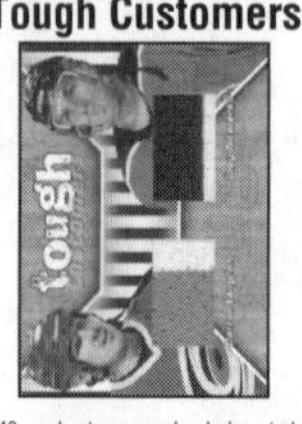

Randomly inserted into packs of BAP Update, this 30-card set featured game-worn jersey swatches of the featured players affixed beside a color action photo of the player on a blue card front. Cards in this set were limited to 90 copies each.

STATED PRINT RUN 90 SETS

Card		
H1 Wayne Gretzky	30.00	80.00
H2 Curtis Joseph	10.00	25.00
H3 Felix Potvin	10.00	25.00
H4 Mark Messier	12.50	30.00
H5 Doug Gilmour	10.00	25.00
H6 Keith Tkachuk	10.00	25.00
H7 Teemu Selanne	10.00	25.00
H8 Adam Oates	10.00	25.00
H9 Pavel Bure	6.00	15.00
H10 Mats Sundin	10.00	25.00
H11 Ed Belfour	10.00	25.00
H12 Mike Modano	8.00	20.00
H13 Brett Hull	12.50	30.00
H14 Brendan Shanahan	10.00	25.00
H15 Al MacInnis	10.00	25.00
H16 Theo Fleury	6.00	15.00
H17 Ed Jovanovski	6.00	15.00
H18 Keith Primeau	6.00	15.00
H19 Patrick Roy	20.00	50.00
H20 Jeff Hackett	10.00	25.00
H21 Owen Nolan	10.00	25.00
H22 Jeremy Roenick	12.50	30.00
H23 Mark Recchi	10.00	25.00
H24 Roman Turek	10.00	25.00
H25 Alexander Mogilny	10.00	25.00
H26 Jason Allison	6.00	15.00
H27 Luc Robitaille	10.00	25.00
H28 Bill Guerin	10.00	25.00
H29 Rob Blake	10.00	25.00
H30 Gary Roberts	6.00	15.00

2001-02 BAP Update Passing the Torch

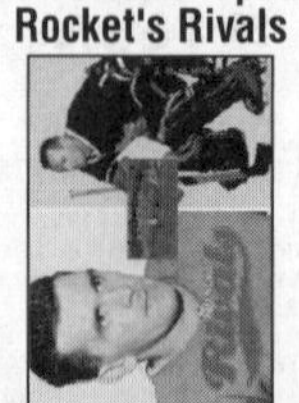

Randomly inserted into packs of BAP Update, this 6-card set featured game-worn swatches from the three players featured on each card. Two black-and-white photos flanked a smaller color photo on the card front with the jersey swatches under each photo. Cards from this set were limited to 25 copies each.

STATED PRINT RUN 25 SETS

Card		
PTT1 Johnny Bucyk	20.00	50.00
Cam Neely		
Joe Thornton		
PTT2 Bobby Hull	20.00	50.00
Michel Goulet		
Tony Amonte		
PTT3 Sid Abel	60.00	150.00
Gordie Howe		
Steve Yzerman		
PTT4 Rocket Richard	60.00	150.00
Guy Lafleur		
Saku Koivu		
PTT5 Ed Giacomin	20.00	50.00
Rod Gilbert		
Brian Leetch		
PTT6 King Clancy	60.00	150.00
Tim Horton		
Mats Sundin		

2001-02 BAP Update Rocket's Rivals

Randomly inserted into packs of BAP Update, this 10-card set featured game-worn jersey swatches of the featured player. Each card carried a black-and-white photo of Rocket Richard on the left side and a color photo of the featured player on the right. The jersey swatch was affixed in the middle. Exact print runs for each card are printed below.

STATED PRINT RUNS LISTED BELOW
LOWER PRINT RUNS NOT PRICED
DUE TO SCARCITY

RR-1 Gordie Howe		
Rocket Richard/10		
RR-2 Ted Lindsay	40.00	100.00
Rocket Richard/30		
RR-3 Johnny Bower	40.00	100.00
Rocket Richard/30		
RR-4 Terry Sawchuk	40.00	100.00
Rocket Richard/30		
RR-5 Frank Brimsek	20.00	50.00
Rocket Richard/40		
RR-6 Turk Broda		
Rocket Richard/10		
RR-7 Bill Gadsby	20.00	50.00
Rocket Richard/30		
RR-8 Chuck Rayner		
Rocket Richard/10		
RR-9 Glenn Hall	20.00	50.00
Rocket Richard/30		
RR-10 Bill Mosienko	40.00	100.00
Rocket Richard/40		

2001-02 BAP Update Tough Customers

This 40-card set was randomly inserted into packs of BAP Update. Each card carried two jersey swatches from some of the league's most notorious enforcers. Jersey swatches were affixed under color photos of each player. Cards from this set were limited to 90 copies each.

*MULT.COLOR SWATCH: .75X TO 1.5X
STATED PRINT RUN 90 SETS

TC1 Dave Schultz	30.00	80.00
Tiger Williams		
TC2 Bob Probert	15.00	40.00
Tie Domi		
TC3 Ian Laperriere	15.00	40.00
Stu Grimson		
TC4 Peter Worrell	8.00	20.00
Craig Berube		
TC5 Jamal Mayers	8.00	20.00
Ken Belanger		
TC6 Stu Grimson	30.00	80.00
Bob Probert		
TC7 Paul Laus	8.00	20.00
Matt Johnson		
TC8 Rob Ray	12.00	30.00
Chris Neil		
TC9 Andrei Nazarov	8.00	20.00
Brad Brown		
TC10 Joey Tetarenko	8.00	20.00
Darren Langdon		
TC11 Tie Domi	12.00	30.00
Rob Ray		
TC12 Krzysztof Oliwa	8.00	20.00
Peter Worrell		
TC13 Luke Richardson	8.00	20.00
Jeff Odgers		
TC14 P.J.Stock	8.00	20.00
Matthew Barnaby		
TC15 Wade Belak	8.00	20.00
Sandy McCarthy		
TC16 Donald Brashear	15.00	40.00
Georges Laraque		
TC17 Andre Roy	8.00	20.00
Jeff Odgers		
TC18 Andre Roy	8.00	20.00
Tie Domi		
TC19 Donald Brashear	20.00	50.00
Bob Probert		
TC20 Darren Langdon	8.00	20.00
Rocky Thompson		
TC21 Ryan Vandenbussche	10.00	25.00
Chris Simon		
TC22 Matt Johnson	8.00	20.00
Craig Berube		
TC23 Scott Parker	8.00	20.00
Denny Lambert		
TC24 Georges Laraque	8.00	20.00
Jeff Odgers		
TC25 Luke Richardson	8.00	20.00
Wade Belak		
TC26 Chris Dingman	8.00	20.00
Paul Laus		
TC27 Gino Odjick	8.00	20.00
Chris Simon		
TC28 Ian Laperriere	8.00	20.00
Andrei Nazarov		
TC29 Georges Laraque	8.00	20.00
Paul Laus		
TC30 Krzysztof Oliwa	8.00	20.00
Eric Cairns		
TC31 Maurice Richard	60.00	150.00
Ted Lindsay		
TC32 Gordie Howe	100.00	200.00
Stan Mikita		
TC33 Denny Lambert	8.00	20.00
Andre Roy		
TC34 Wendel Clark	25.00	60.00
Bob Probert		
TC35 Ryan Vandenbussche	8.00	20.00
Jamal Mayers		
TC36 Rocky Thompson	8.00	20.00
P.J. Stock		
TC37 Scott Parker	8.00	20.00
Ken Belanger		
TC38 Chris Neil	8.00	20.00
Matthew Barnaby		
TC39 Chris Dingman	15.00	40.00
Sandy McCarthy		
TC40 Gino Odjick	8.00	20.00
Eric Cairns		

2001-02 BAP Update Travel Plans

Randomly inserted into packs of BAP Update, this 16-card set featured game-worn jersey swatches of the featured player from two different teams. Each card carried small color photos of the player in the two different uniforms alongside the two jersey swatches. Cards in this set were limited to 50 copies each.

*MULT.COLOR SWATCH: .75X TO 1.5X
STATED PRINT RUN 50 SETS

TP1 Jaromir Jagr	20.00	50.00
TP2 Dominik Hasek	20.00	50.00
TP3 Roman Turek	8.00	20.00
TP4 Teemu Selanne	12.50	30.00
TP5 Keith Tkachuk	12.50	30.00
TP6 Rob Blake	12.50	30.00
TP7 Alexander Mogilny	8.00	20.00
TP8 Luc Robitaille	12.50	30.00
TP9 Alexei Yashin	8.00	20.00
TP10 Eric Lindros	12.50	30.00
TP11 Jeremy Roenick	15.00	40.00
TP12 Doug Weight	8.00	20.00
TP13 Felix Potvin	12.50	30.00
TP14 Nikolai Khabibulin	15.00	40.00
TP15 Dave Andreychuk	8.00	20.00
TP16 Dan Cloutier	8.00	20.00

1934-44 Beehive Group I Photos

The 1934-44 Beehive photos are the first of three groups. Production was suspended in 1944 due to wartime priorities. The photos include a facsimile autograph, small script or occasionally block letters. Complete set price is not given due to an ongoing debate over what constitutes a complete set. A number of unconfirmed photos are scattered throughout the Beehive master checklist. If anyone has information to corroborate the existence of any of these cards, please forward it to Beckett Publications.

Card		
COMMON PHOTO	7.50	15.00
1 Bobby Bauer	7.50	15.00
2 Red Beattie	12.50	25.00
3 Buzz Boll (Unconfirmed)		
4 Yank Boyd	75.00	150.00
5A Frankie Brimsek (With Net)	12.50	25.00
5B Frankie Brimsek (Without Net)	15.00	30.00
8 Dit Clapper	10.00	20.00
9 Roy Conacher	10.00	20.00
10 Bun Cook	10.00	20.00
11 Bill Cowley	10.00	20.00
12 John Crawford	7.50	15.00
13 Woody Dumart	12.50	25.00
14 Don Gallinger	87.50	175.00
15 Ray Getiffe	15.00	30.00
17 Bep Guidolin	50.00	100.00
18 Red Hamill	15.00	30.00
19 Mel Hill	10.00	20.00
24 Pat McReavy	7.50	15.00
25 Alex Motter	15.00	30.00
26 Peggy O'Neil	10.00	20.00
29 Charlie Sands	10.00	20.00
30 Jackie Schmidt	87.50	175.00
31 Milt Schmidt	10.00	20.00
32 Jack Shewchuk	10.00	20.00
33 Eddie Shore	50.00	100.00
35 Tiny Thompson	25.00	50.00
36 Cooney Weiland	10.00	20.00
38 George Allen	12.50	25.00
39 Doug Bentley	15.00	30.00
40 Max Bentley	20.00	40.00
42 Glenn Brydson	62.50	125.00
43 Marty Burke	7.50	15.00
44 Bill Carse	7.50	15.00
45 Bob Carse	7.50	15.00
46 Lorne Chabot	25.00	50.00
47 John Chad	15.00	30.00
49 Les Cunningham	15.00	30.00
50 Cully Dahlstrom	10.00	20.00
53 Leroy Goldsworthy	12.50	25.00
54 Paul Goodman	20.00	40.00
55 Johnny Gottselig	12.50	25.00
56 Philip Hergesheimer	7.50	15.00
58 George(Wingy) Johnston	87.50	175.00
59 Alex Kaleta	15.00	30.00
60 Mike Karakas	15.00	30.00
63 Alex Levinsky	12.50	25.00
64 Sam LoPresti	25.00	50.00
65 Dave Mackay	125.00	250.00
66 Bill MacKenzie (Unconfirmed)		
67 Mush March	7.50	15.00
68 John Mariucci	25.00	50.0
69 Joe Matte	62.50	125.0
70 Red Mitchell UER (Name misspelled Mitchel)	87.50	175.0
72 Peter Palangio	40.00	80.0
73 Joe Papike	50.00	100.0
75 Cliff Purpur	87.50	175.0
77 Doc Romnes	25.00	50.0
78 Earl Seibert	10.00	20.0
81 Paul Thompson	15.00	30.0
83 Louis Trudel UER (Name misspelled Trudell)	20.00	40.0
84 Audley Tuten	87.50	175.0
85 Art Wiebe	12.50	25.0
86 Sid Abel	15.00	30.0
87 Larry Aurie	7.50	15.0
88 Marty Barry	12.50	25.0
89 Ralph Bowman	12.50	25.0
90 Adam Brown	40.00	80.0
91 Connie Brown	50.00	100.0
92 Jerry Brown	150.00	300.0
93 Mud Bruneteau	10.00	20.0
94 Eddie Bush	125.00	250.0
95 Joe Carveth	7.50	15.0
99 Les Douglas	50.00	100.0
100 Gus Biesebrecht UER (Name misspelled Geisebrech)	7.50	15.0
101 Ebbie Goodfellow	10.00	20.0
102 Don Grosso	7.50	15.0
104 Syd Howe	10.00	20.0
105 Bill Jennings	40.00	80.0
106 Jack Keating	15.00	30.0
107 Pete Kelly	10.00	20.0
108 Hec Kilrea	10.00	20.0
109 Ken Kilrea	10.00	20.0
110 Wally Kilrea	10.00	20.0
111 Herb Lewis	10.00	20.0
112 Carl Liscombe	7.50	15.0
114 Douglas McCaig	40.00	80.0
115A Bucko McDonald (Ice photo)	50.00	100.0
115B Bucko McDonald (Dressing room photo)	50.00	100.0
116 Pat McReavy	40.00	80.0
118 Johnny Mowers	12.50	25.0
119 Jimmy Orlando	7.50	15.0
120 Gord Pettinger	20.00	40.0
121 John Sherf	20.00	40.0
123 Norm Smith	15.00	30.0
124 John Sorrell	12.50	25.0
125 Jack Stewart	20.00	40.0
128 Carl Voss	50.00	100.0
129 Eddie Wares	150.00	300.0
131 Arch Wilder	12.50	25.0
132 Douglas Young	12.50	25.0
133 Jack Adams	12.50	25.0
134 Marty Barry	200.00	400.0
135 Joe Benoit	10.00	20.
136 Paul Bibeault	25.00	50.
137 Toe Blake	15.00	30.0
138 Butch Bouchard	7.50	15.
139 Claude Bourque	20.00	40.
140 George Allan Brown	62.50	125.0
141 Walt Buswell	20.00	40.0
143 Murph Chamberlain	25.00	50.0
144 Wilf Cude	15.00	30.0
145 Bunny Dame	25.00	50.0
146 Tony DeMeres UER (Name misspelled Dremers)	7.50	15.0
147 Joffre Desilets	10.00	20.0
148 Gordie Drillon	350.00	700.0
149 Polly Drouin	7.50	15.0
151 Johnny Gagnon	7.50	15.0
152 Bert Gardiner	15.00	30.0
153 Ray Getiffe	40.00	80.0
154 Red Goupille	10.00	20.0
155 Tony Graboski	10.00	20.0
157 Paul Haynes	7.50	15.0
158 Gerry Heffernan	75.00	150.0
160 Roger Jenkins	30.00	60.0
161 Aurel Joliat	20.00	40.0
162 Elmer Lach	20.00	40.0
163 Leo Lamoreux UER (Name misspelled Camoreaux)	62.50	125.0
164 Pit Lepine	7.50	15.
165 Rod Lorraine	15.00	30.
166 Georges Mantha	10.00	20.
167 Sylvio Mantha	10.00	20.0
169 Armand Mondou	7.50	15.0
170 Howie Morenz	375.00	750.0
171 Pete Morin	75.00	150.0
172 Buddy O'Connor	75.00	150.0
175 Jack Portland	7.50	15.0
176 John Quilty	12.50	25.0
177 Ken Reardon	20.00	40.0
178 Terry Reardon	50.00	100.0
179 Maurice Richard	20.00	40.0
180 Earl Robinson	200.00	400.0
181 Charlie Sands	30.00	60.0
182 Babe Siebert	20.00	40.0
183 Alex Singbush	50.00	100.0
184 Bill Summerhill	87.50	175.0
185 Louis Trudel	40.00	80.0
187 Cy Wentworth	1500.00	3000.0
188 Douglas Young	50.00	100.0
189 Bill Beveridge	30.00	60.0
190 Russ Blinco	20.00	40.0
191 Herb Cain	30.00	60.0
192 Gerry Carson UER (Name misspelled Jerry)	87.50	175.0
194 Alex Connell	30.00	60.0
195 Tom Cook	20.00	40.0
196 Stewart Evans	15.00	30.0
197 Bob Gracie	50.00	100.0
198 Max Kaminsky	87.50	175.0
199 Bill MacKenzie	62.50	125.0
200 Gus Marker	100.00	200.0
201 Baldy Northcott	30.00	60.0
202 Earl Robinson	25.00	50.0
203 Paul Runge	87.50	175.0
204 Gerry Shannon UER (Name misspelled Jerry)	87.50	175.0
206 Des Smith	20.00	40.0
207 Hooley Smith	20.00	40.0

Dave Trottier 50.00 100.00
Jimmy Ward 20.00 40.00
Cy Wentworth 25.00 50.00
Viv Allen 30.00 60.00
Tom Anderson 20.00 40.00
Bill Benson 25.00 50.00
Lorne Carr 25.00 50.00
Art Chapman 20.00 40.00
Red Dutton 25.00 50.00
Pat Egan 20.00 40.00
Hap Emms 40.00 80.00
Wilf Field 20.00 40.00
John Gallagher 20.00 40.00
Joe Jerwa 25.00 50.00
Jim Klein 50.00 100.00
Joe Krol 625.00 1250.00
Joe Lamb 40.00 80.00
Red Heron 20.00 40.00
Hazen McAndrew 750.00 1500.00
Ken Mosdell 200.00 400.00
Al Murray 15.00 30.00
John O'Flaherty 30.00 60.00
Chuck Rayner 100.00 200.00
Earl Robertson 25.00 50.00
Sweeny Schriner 20.00 40.00
Al Shields 50.00 100.00
Pete Slobodzian UER 30.00 60.00
(Name misspelled Slobodian)
Nels Stewart 25.00 50.00
Fred Thurier 62.50 125.00
Harry Watson 112.50 225.00
Eddie Wiseman 15.00 30.00
Roy Worters 30.00 60.00
Ralph Wycherly 30.00 60.00
Frank Boucher 20.00 40.00
Norm Burns 50.00 100.00
Mac Colville 7.50 15.00
Neil Colville 10.00 20.00
Bill Cook 12.50 25.00
Joe Cooper 7.50 15.00
Art Coulter 7.50 15.00
Gord Davidson 30.00 60.00
Cecil Dillon 10.00 20.00
Jim Franks 100.00 200.00
Red Garrett 75.00 150.00
Ott Heller 7.50 15.00
A Jim Henry 50.00 100.00
(Vertical photo)
B Jim Henry 30.00 60.00
(Horizontal photo)
Bryan Hextall Sr. 15.00 30.00
Dutch Hiller 10.00 20.00
Ching Johnson 12.50 25.00
Bill Juzda 10.00 20.00
Butch Keeling 10.00 20.00
Davey Kerr 15.00 30.00
Bobby Kirk 50.00 100.00
Bob Kirkpatrick 50.00 100.00
Kilby MacDonald 10.00 20.00
Larry Molyneaux 15.00 30.00
John Murray Murdoch 20.00 40.00
Vic Myles 87.50 175.00
Lynn Patrick 10.00 20.00
Murray Patrick 7.50 15.00
Alf Pike 7.50 15.00
Babe Pratt 12.50 25.00
Alex Shibicky 7.50 15.00
Clint Smith 7.50 15.00
Norman Tustin 50.00 100.00
Grant Warwick 50.00 100.00
Phil Watson 7.50 15.00
Syl Apps Sr. 12.50 25.00
Murray Armstrong 7.50 15.00
Andy Blair 10.00 20.00
Buzz Boll 10.00 20.00
George Boothman 125.00 250.00
Turk Broda 12.50 25.00
Lorne Carr 30.00 60.00
Murph Chamberlain 7.50 15.00
Lex Chisholm 10.00 20.00
Jack Church 10.00 20.00
Francis Clancy 15.00 30.00
Charlie Conacher 12.50 25.00
Bob Copp 30.00 60.00
Baldy Cotton 10.00 20.00
Bob Davidson 7.50 15.00
Hap Day 7.50 15.00
Ernie Dickens 100.00 200.00
Gordie Drillon 7.50 15.00
Frank Finnigan 12.50 25.00
Jack Forsey 100.00 200.00
Jimmy Fowler UER 7.50 15.00
(Name misspelled Jimmie)
Bob Goldham 100.00 200.00
Hank Goldup 7.50 15.00
George Hainsworth 20.00 40.00
Reg Hamilton 7.50 15.00
Red Heron 10.00 20.00
Mel Hill 150.00 300.00
Frank Hollett 7.50 15.00
Red Horner 10.00 20.00
Art Jackson 7.50 15.00
Harvey Jackson 7.50 15.00
Bingo Kampman 20.00 40.00
Reg Kelly 10.00 20.00
William Kendall 40.00 80.00
Hec Kilrea 25.00 50.00
Pete Langelle 10.00 20.00
Bucko McDonald 10.00 20.00
A Norm Mann 12.50 25.00
B Norm Mann 87.50 175.00
(Name overlaps stick)
Gus Marker 7.50 15.00
Johnny McCreedy 20.00 40.00
Jack McLean 50.00 100.00
Don Metz 7.50 15.00
Nick Metz 7.50 15.00
George Parsons 12.50 25.00
Bud Poile 87.50 175.00
Babe Pratt 125.00 250.00
Joe Primeau 12.50 25.00
Doc Romnes 25.00 50.00
Sweeny Schriner 15.00 30.00
Jack Shill 12.50 25.00
Wally Stanowski UER 7.50 15.00
(Name misspelled Stanowsky)
Phil Stein 25.00 50.00
A Gaye Stewart 175.00 350.00
(Home Sweater)
350B Gaye Stewart 100.00 200.00
(Away Sweater)
351 Billy Taylor 7.50 15.00
352 Rhys Thompson 200.00 400.00
353 Bill Thoms 7.50 15.00
354 1944-45 Maple Leafs 150.00 300.00
355 1937 Winnipeg Monarchs 75.00150.00
356 Foster Hewitt 40.00 80.00
357 Wes McKnight 62.50 125.00
358A Allan Cup 30.00 60.00
(Dated on back)
358B Allan Cup 62.50 125.00
(Blank Back)
359A Lady Byng Trophy 30.00 60.00
(Dated on back)
359B Lady Byng Trophy 62.50 125.00
(Blank back)
360A Calder Trophy 30.00 60.00
(Dated on back)
360B Calder Trophy 62.50 125.00
(Blank back)
361A Hart Trophy 30.00 60.00
(Dated on back)
361B Hart Trophy 62.50 125.00
(Blank back)
362A Memorial Cup 40.00 80.00
(Dated on back)
362B Memorial Cup 75.00 150.00
(Blank back)
363A Prince of Wales Trophy 87.50175.00
(Dated on back)
363B Prince of Wales Trophy 100.00200.00
(Blank back)
364A Stanley Cup 30.00 60.00
(Dated on back)
364B Stanley Cup 50.00 100.00
(Blank back)
364C Stanley Cup 50.00 100.00
(Name horizontal)
365A Georges Vezina Trophy 30.00 60.00
(Dated on back)
365B Georges Vezina Trophy 62.50 125.00
(Blank back)

1944-63 Beehive Group II Photos

The 1944-63 Beehive photos are the second of three groups. Issued after World War II, this group generally had new photos and a larger script than was typical of Group I. Facsimile autographs were again featured. There are a number of unconfirmed photos that appeared on the Beehive checklist, among these are the Allan and Memorial Cup trophies in either of their varieties. Because of the lack of confirmation, those cards are not listed below. Information regarding the existence of any of these unconfirmed photos can be forwarded it to Beckett Publications.

1 Bob Armstrong 5.00 10.00
2 Pete Babando 25.00 50.00
3 Ray Barry 25.00 50.00
4 Gus Bodnar 40.00 80.00
5 Leo Boivin 6.00 12.00
6 Frankie Brimsek 12.50 25.00
8 John Bucyk 7.50 15.00
9 Charlie Burns 5.00 10.00
10 Jack Caffery 30.00 60.00
11 Real Chevrefils 5.00 10.00
12A Wayne Connelly 10.00 20.00
12B Wayne Connelly 30.00 60.00
(Name overlaps skate)
14 John Crawford 10.00 20.00
15A Dave Creighton 6.00 12.00
(White sweater)
15B Dave Creighton 30.00 60.00
(Photo on ice)
16 Woody Dumart 12.50 25.00
17 Pat Egan 15.00 30.00
19 Lorne Ferguson 6.00 12.00
20 Fern Flaman 5.00 10.00
21 Bruce Gamble 6.00 12.00
22 Cal Gardner 6.00 12.00
23 Ray Gariepy 10.00 20.00
24 Jack Gelineau 12.50 25.00
25 Jean-Guy Gendron 5.00 10.00
26A Warren Godfrey 6.00 12.00
(A on sweater)
26B Warren Godfrey 30.00 60.00
(With puck)
26C Warren Godfrey 50.00 100.00
(Without puck)
27 Ed Harrison 5.00 10.00
28 Don Head 5.00 10.00
29 Andy Hebenton 7.50 15.00
30 Murray Henderson 7.50 15.00
31 Jim Henry 15.00 30.00
32 Larry Hillman 20.00 40.00
33 Pete Horeck 10.00 20.00
34 Bronco Horvath 5.00 10.00
35 Tom Johnson 5.00 10.00
36 Eddie Johnston 7.50 15.00
38 Joe Klukay 90.00 175.00
39 Edward Kryznowski 6.00 12.00
40 Orland Kurtenbach 20.00 40.00
41 Leo Labine 5.00 10.00
42 Hal Laycoe 5.00 10.00
43 Harry Lumley 7.50 15.00
44 Pentti Lund 500.00 1000.00
45 Fleming Mackell 5.00 10.00
46 Phil Maloney 10.00 20.00
47 Frank Martin 10.00 20.00
48 Jack McIntyre 10.00 20.00
49 Don McKenney 5.00 10.00
50 Dick Meissner 5.00 10.00
51 Doug Mohns 5.00 10.00
52 Murray Oliver 5.00 10.00
53 Willie O'Ree 7.50 15.00
54A John Peirson 6.00 12.00
54B Johnny Peirson 50.00 100.00
55A Cliff Pennington 10.00 20.00
(Name away from skate)
55B Cliff Pennington 50.00 100.00
(Name near skate)
56A Bob Perreault 12.50 25.00
(Name away from skate)
56B Bob Perreault 50.00 100.00
(Name overlaps skate)
57 Jim Peters 10.00 20.00
58 Dean Prentice 6.00 12.00
59 Andre Pronovost 5.00 10.00
60 Bill Quackenbush 10.00 20.00
61 Larry Regan 25.00 50.00
62 Earl Reibel 20.00 40.00
63 Paul Ronty 6.00 12.00
64 Ed Sandford 5.00 10.00
65 Terry Sawchuk 60.00 125.00
66A Don Simmons ERR 75.00 150.00
(Photo of Norm Defelice)
66B Don Simmons COR 5.00 10.00
67 Kenny Smith 6.00 12.00
68A Pat Stapleton 10.00 20.00
(Name away from skate)
68B Pat Stapleton 50.00 100.00
(Name near skate)
69 Vic Stasiuk 7.50 15.00
70 Red Sullivan 12.50 25.00
71 Jerry Toppazzini 5.00 10.00
72 Zellio Toppazzini 6.00 12.00
73 Grant Warwick 20.00 40.00
74 Tom Williams 5.00 10.00
75 Al Arbour 6.00 12.00
76 Pete Babando 10.00 20.00
77 Earl Balfour 5.00 10.00
78 Murray Balfour 5.00 10.00
79 Jim Bedard 10.00 20.00
80 Doug Bentley 12.50 25.00
81 Gus Bodnar 6.00 12.00
82 Frankie Brimsek 20.00 40.00
83 Adam Brown 10.00 20.00
84 Hank Ciesla 20.00 40.00
85 Jim Conacher 7.50 15.00
86 Pete Conacher 5.00 10.00
87 Roy Conacher 5.00 10.00
88 Joe Conn 40.00 80.00
89 Murray Costello 40.00 80.00
90 Gerry Couture 12.50 25.00
91 Al Dewsbury 6.00 12.00
92 Ernie Dickens 5.00 10.00
93 Jack Evans 5.00 10.00
94 Reggie Fleming 5.00 10.00
95 Lee Fogolin 7.50 15.00
96 Bill Gadsby 5.00 10.00
97 George Gee 6.00 12.00
98 Bob Goldham 12.50 25.00
99 Bep Guidolin 6.00 12.00
100 Glenn Hall 6.00 12.00
101 Murray Hall 15.00 30.00
102 Red Hamill 15.00 30.00
103 Billy Hay 5.00 10.00
104 Jim Henry 15.00 30.00
105 Wayne Hillman 12.50 25.00
107 Bronco Horvath 6.00 12.00
108 Fred Hucul 12.50 25.00
109A Bobby Hull 100.00 200.00
(Jersey 9)
109B Bobby Hull 15.00 30.00
(Jersey 16)
110 Lou Jankowski 12.50 25.00
111 Forbes Kennedy 25.00 50.00
112 Ted Lindsay 7.50 15.00
113 Ed Litzenberger 5.00 10.00
114 Harry Lumley 20.00 40.00
Goalie
115A Len Lunde 30.00 60.00
(Name away from stick)
115B Len Lunde 10.00 20.00
(Name overlaps stick)
116 Pat Lundy 7.50 15.00
117 Vic Lynn
(Unconfirmed)
118A Al MacNeil 20.00 40.00
(Name overlaps stick and skate)
118B Al MacNeil 6.00 12.00
(Name overlaps stick)
119A Chico Maki 7.50 15.00
(Name away from stick)
119B Chico Maki 60.00 125.00
(Name overlaps stick)
120 Doug McCaig 12.50 25.00
121 Ab McDonald 5.00 10.00
122 Jim McFadden 20.00 40.00
124 Gerry Melnyk UER 5.00 10.00
(Name misspelled Jerry)
125 Stan Mikita 6.00 12.00
127 Gus Mortson 5.00 10.00
128 Bill Mosienko 7.50 15.00
129 Ron Murphy 5.00 10.00
130 Ralph Nattrass 12.50 25.00
131 Eric Nesterenko 5.00 10.00
132 Bert Olmstead 12.50 25.00
133 Jim Peters 20.00 40.00
134 Pierre Pilote 5.00 10.00
135 Metro Prystai 6.00 12.00
137 Clare Raglan 15.00 30.00
138A Al Rollins 50.00 100.00
(Vertical photo)
138B Al Rollins 15.00 30.00
(Horizontal photo)
139 Tod Sloan 5.00 10.00
140 Dollard St. Laurent 5.00 10.00
141 Gaye Stewart 10.00 20.00
142 Jack Stewart 20.00 40.00
143A Bob Turner 25.00 50.00
(Name away from stick)
143B Bob Turner 15.00 30.00
(Name overlaps stick)
144 Elmer Vasko 5.00 10.00
145 Kenny Wharram 5.00 10.00
146 Larry Wilson 10.00 20.00
147 Howie Young 12.50 25.00
149 Sid Abel 10.00 20.00
150 Al Arbour 20.00 40.00
151 Pete Babando 12.50 25.00
152A Doug Barkley 30.00 60.00
(Stick blade showing)
152B Doug Barkley 10.00 20.00
(No blade showing)
153 Hank Bassen 6.00 12.00
154 Stephen Black 15.00 30.00
155 Marcel Bonin 7.50 15.00
156 John Bucyk 25.00 50.00
157 John Conacher 100.00 200.00
158 Gerry Couture UER 6.00 12.00
(Name misspelled Jerry)
159 Billy Dea 12.50 25.00
160 Alex Delvecchio 5.00 10.00
162 Bill Dineen 5.00 10.00
163 Jim Enio 30.00 60.00
164 Alex Faulkner 25.00 50.00
165 Lee Fogolin 6.00 12.00
166 Val Fonteyne 5.00 10.00
167 Bill Gadsby 7.50 15.00
168 Fern Gauthier 20.00 40.00
169 George Gee 7.50 15.00
170 Fred Glover 5.00 10.00
171 Howie Glover 5.00 10.00
172 Warren Godfrey 5.00 10.00
173 Peter Goegan 5.00 10.00
174 Bob Goldham 6.00 12.00
175 Glenn Hall 40.00 80.00
176 Larry Hillman 25.00 50.00
177 Pete Horeck 20.00 40.00
178A Gordie Howe 25.00 50.00
178B Gordie Howe 40.00 80.00
(C on sweater)
179 Ron Ingram 20.00 40.00
180 Larry Jeffrey 15.00 30.00
181 Al Johnson 5.00 10.00
182 Red Kelly 5.00 10.00
183 Forbes Kennedy 5.00 10.00
184 Leo Labine 5.00 10.00
185 Tony Leswick 5.00 10.00
186 Ted Lindsay 6.00 12.00
187 Ed Litzenberger 15.00 30.00
188 Harry Lumley 12.50 25.00
189 Len Lunde 5.00 10.00
190 Parker MacDonald 5.00 10.00
191 Bruce MacGregor 5.00 10.00
192 Clare Martin 12.50 25.00
193 Jim McFadden 7.50 15.00
194 Max McNab 12.50 25.00
195 Gerry Melnyk UER 5.00 10.00
(Name misspelled Jerry)
196 Don Morrison 12.50 25.00
197 Rod Morrison 25.00 50.00
198 Gerry Odrowski 5.00 10.00
199 Murray Oliver 5.00 10.00
200 Marty Pavelich 5.00 10.00
201 Jim Peters 25.00 50.00
202 Bud Poile 75.00 150.00
203 Andre Pronovost 6.00 12.00
204 Marcel Pronovost 5.00 10.00
205 Metro Prystai 5.00 10.00
206 Bill Quackenbush 25.00 50.00
207 Earl Reibel 5.00 10.00
208 Leo Reise Jr. 6.00 12.00
209 Terry Sawchuk 20.00 40.00
210 Glen Skov 5.00 10.00
211 Floyd Smith 6.00 12.00
212A Vic Stasiuk 12.50 25.00
(Home sweater; full stick showing)
212B Vic Stasiuk 20.00 40.00
(Home sweater; partial stick showing)
212C Vic Stasiuk 7.50 15.00
(Away sweater)
213 Gaye Stewart 15.00 30.00
214 Jack Stewart 15.00 30.00
215 Norm Ullman 5.00 10.00
216 Johnny Wilson 5.00 10.00
217 Benny Woit 5.00 10.00
218 Howie Young 6.00 12.00
219 Larry Zeidel 12.50 25.00
220 Ralph Backstrom 5.00 10.00
221 Dave Balon 5.00 10.00
222 Jean Beliveau 10.00 20.00
223A Red Berenson 12.50 25.00
(White script)
223B Red Berenson 100.00 200.00
(Black script)
224 Marcel Bonin 5.00 10.00
225 Butch Bouchard 5.00 10.00
226 Tod Campeau 50.00 100.00
227 Joe Carveth 6.00 12.00
228 Murph Chamberlain 25.00 50.00
229 Doc Couture 20.00 40.00
230 Floyd Curry UER 5.00 10.00
(Name misspelled Currie)
231 Ian Cushenan 7.50 15.00
232 Lorne Davis 6.00 12.00
233 Eddie Dorohoy 12.50 25.00
234 Gilles Dube 30.00 60.00
235 Bill Durnan 20.00 40.00
236 Norm Dussault 12.50 25.00
237 John Ferguson 6.00 12.00
238 Bob Fillion 7.50 15.00
239 Louie Fontinato 5.00 10.00
240 Dick Gamble 10.00 20.00
241 Bernard Geoffrion 7.50 15.00
242 Phil Goyette 5.00 10.00
243 Leo Gravelle 12.50 25.00
244 John Hanna 30.00 60.00
245 Glen Harmon 10.00 20.00
246 Terry Harper 5.00 10.00
247 Doug Harvey 7.50 15.00
248 Bill Hicke 5.00 10.00
250 Bert Hirschfeld
(Unconfirmed)
251A Charlie Hodge 40.00 80.00
(White script)
251B Charlie Hodge 6.00 12.00
(Black script)
252 Tom Johnson 6.00 12.00
253 Vern Kaiser 20.00 40.00
254 Frank King 20.00 40.00
255 Elmer Lach 6.00 12.00
256 Al Langlois 5.00 10.00
257 Jacques Laperriere 5.00 10.00
258 Hal Laycoe 6.00 12.00
259 Jackie Leclair 5.00 10.00
260 Roger Leger 10.00 20.00
261 Ed Litzenberger 12.50 25.00
262 Ross Lowe 20.00 40.00
263 Al MacNeil 5.00 10.00
264 Bud MacPherson 5.00 10.00
265 Cesare Maniago 6.00 12.00
266 Don Marshall 5.00 10.00
267 Paul Masnick 5.00 10.00
268 Eddie Mazur 10.00 20.00
269 John McCormack 6.00 12.00
270 Alvin McDonald 5.00 10.00
271 Calum MacKay 6.00 12.00
272 Gerry McNeil 7.50 15.00
273 Paul Meger 10.00 20.00
274 Dickie Moore 6.00 12.00
275 Kenny Mosdell 10.00 20.00
276 Bert Olmstead 5.00 10.00
277 Gerry Plamondon 10.00 20.00
278 Jacques Plante 20.00 40.00
279 Andre Pronovost 5.00 10.00
280 Claude Provost 5.00 10.00
281 Ken Reardon 12.50 25.00
282 Billy Reay 6.00 12.00
283 Henri Richard 10.00 20.00
284 Maurice Richard 20.00 40.00
285 Rip Riopelle 15.00 30.00
286 George Robertson 50.00 100.00
287 Bobby Rousseau 5.00 10.00
288 Dollard St. Laurent 5.00 10.00
289 Jean-Guy Talbot 5.00 10.00
290A Gilles Tremblay 5.00 10.00
(Dark background)
290B Gilles Tremblay 100.00 200.00
(Light background)
291A J.C. Tremblay 5.00 10.00
(Dark background)
291B J.C. Tremblay 100.00 200.00
(Light background)
292 Bob Turner 5.00 10.00
293 Grant Warwick 20.00 40.00
294 Gump Worsley 12.50 25.00
295 Clint Albright 6.00 12.00
296A Dave Balon 12.50 25.00
(Name high on photo)
296B Dave Balon 5.00 10.00
(Name low on photo)
297A Andy Bathgate 6.00 12.00
(Home sweater)
297B Andy Bathgate 10.00 20.00
(Away sweater)
298 Max Bentley 25.00 50.00
299 Johnny Bower 25.00 50.00
300 Hy Buller 10.00 20.00
301A Larry Cahan 6.00 12.00
(Home sweater)
301B Larry Cahan 12.50 25.00
(Away sweater)
302 Bob Crystal 15.00 30.00
304 Brian Cullen 5.00 10.00
305 Ian Cushenan 5.00 10.00
306 Billy Dea 15.00 30.00
307 Frank Eddolls 5.00 10.00
308 Pat Egan 20.00 40.00
309A Jack Evans 5.00 10.00
(Name parallel to bottom)
309B Jack Evans 20.00 40.00
(Name printed diagonally)
310 Dunc Fisher 7.50 15.00
311 Louie Fontinato 5.00 10.00
312 Bill Gadsby 5.00 10.00
313 Jean-Guy Gendron 5.00 10.00
314 Rod Gilbert 6.00 12.00
315 Howie Glover 20.00 40.00
317 Phil Goyette 5.00 10.00
318 Aldo Guidolin 25.00 50.00
319 Vic Hadfield 6.00 12.00
320 Ted Hampson 5.00 10.00
321 Doug Harvey 6.00 12.00
322 Andy Hebenton 5.00 10.00
323 Camille Henry 5.00 10.00
324 Wally Hergesheimer 5.00 10.00
325 Ike Hildebrand 15.00 30.00
326 Bronco Horvath 6.00 12.00
327 Harry Howell 5.00 10.00
328A Earl Ingarfield Sr. 5.00 10.00
(Name away from stick)
328B Earl Ingarfield Sr. 12.50 25.00
(Name near stick)
329 Bing Juckes 15.00 30.00
330 Alex Kaleta 7.50 15.00
331 Stephen Kraftcheck 20.00 40.00
332 Eddie Kullman 7.50 15.00
333 Gus Kyle 6.00 12.00
334 Gord Labossiere 25.00 50.00
335 Al Langlois 5.00 10.00
336 Edgar Laprade 7.50 15.00
337 Tony Leswick 6.00 12.00
338 Danny Lewicki 5.00 10.00
339 Pentti Lund 10.00 20.00
340 Don Marshall 12.50 25.00
341 Jack McCartan 6.00 12.00
342 Bill McDonagh 12.50 25.00
343 Don McKenney 10.00 20.00
344 Jackie McLeod 10.00 20.00
345 Nick Mickoski 6.00 12.00
346 Billy Moe 7.50 15.00
348 Ron Murphy 5.00 10.00
349 Buddy O'Connor 7.50 15.00
350 Marcel Paille 50.00 100.00
351 Jacques Plante 50.00 100.00
352 Bud Poile 20.00 40.00
353 Larry Popein 5.00 10.00
354A Dean Prentice 5.00 10.00
(Home sweater)
354B Dean Prentice 7.50 15.00
(Away sweater)
355 Don Raleigh 7.50 15.00
356A Jean Ratelle ERR 25.00 50.00
(Name misspelled John)
356B Jean Ratelle COR 20.00 40.00
357 Chuck Rayner 12.50 25.00
358 Leo Reise Jr. 6.00 12.00
359 Paul Ronty 6.00 12.00
360 Ken Schinkel 5.00 10.00
361 Eddie Shack 15.00 30.00
362 Fred Shero 15.00 30.00
363 Reg Sinclair 20.00 40.00
364 Eddie Slowinski 7.50 15.00
365 Allan Stanley 5.00 10.00
366 Wally Stanowski 6.00 12.00
367 Red Sullivan 5.00 10.00
369 Gump Worsley 5.00 10.00
370 Gary Aldcorn 10.00 20.00
371 Syl Apps Sr. 90.00 175.00
372 Al Arbour 5.00 10.00
373A George Armstrong 6.00 12.00
373B George Armstrong 12.50 25.00
(Dark background)
373C George Armstrong 100.00 200.00
(Light background)
374 Bob Bailey 20.00 40.00
375 Earl Balfour 10.00 20.00
376 Bill Barilko 25.00 50.00
377 Andy Bathgate 25.00 50.00
378 Bob Baun 5.00 10.00
379 Max Bentley 12.50 25.00
380 Jack Bionda 75.00 150.00
381 Garth Boesch 6.00 12.00
382 Leo Boivin 7.50 15.00
383 Hugh Bolton 5.00 10.00
384 Johnny Bower 10.00 20.00
385 Carl Brewer 5.00 10.00
386 Turk Broda 12.50 25.00
387 Larry Cahan 7.50 15.00
388 Ray Ceresino 50.00 100.00
389 Ed Chadwick 6.00 12.00
390 Pete Conacher 50.00 100.00
391 Les Costello 20.00 40.00
392 Dave Creighton 10.00 20.00
393 Barry Cullen 12.50 25.00
394 Brian Cullen 5.00 10.00
395 Robert Dawes 12.50 25.00
396 Kent Douglas 5.00 10.00
397 Dick Duff 5.00 10.00
398 Gary Edmundson 5.00 10.00
399 Gerry Ehman 5.00 10.00
400 Bill Ezinicki 10.00 20.00
401 Fern Flaman 25.00 50.00
402 Cal Gardner 10.00 20.00
403 Ted Hampson 5.00 10.00
404 Gord Hannigan 10.00 20.00
405 Billy Harris 5.00 10.00
406 Bob Hassard 40.00 80.00
407 Larry Hillman 5.00 10.00
408 Tim Horton 12.50 25.00
409 Bronco Horvath 10.00 20.00
410 Ron Hurst 75.00 150.00
411 Gerry James UER 15.00 30.00
(Name misspelled Jerry)
412 Bill Juzda 7.50 15.00
413A Red Kelly 6.00 12.00
(Bare-headed)
413B Red Kelly 15.00 30.00
(Wearing helmet)
414 Ted Kennedy 10.00 20.00
415 Dave Keon 7.50 15.00
416 Joe Klukay 6.00 12.00
417 Stephen Kraftcheck 20.00 40.00
418 Danny Lewicki 12.50 25.00
419 Ed Litzenberger 6.00 12.00
420 Harry Lumley 12.50 25.00
421 Vic Lynn 6.00 12.00
422 Fleming MacKell 7.50 15.00
423 John MacMillan 5.00 10.00
424 Al MacNeil 10.00 20.00
425 Frank Mahovlich 12.50 25.00
426 Phil Maloney 75.00 150.00
427 Cesare Maniago 6.00 12.00
428 Frank Mathers 20.00 40.00
429 John McCormack 30.00 60.00
430 Parker MacDonald 12.50 25.00
431 Don McKenney 20.00 40.00
432 Howie Meeker 7.50 15.00
433 Don Metz 150.00 300.00
434 Nick Metz 100.00 200.00
435 Rudy Migay 5.00 10.00
436 Jim Mikol 5.00 10.00
437 Jim Morrison 5.00 10.00
438 Gus Mortson 6.00 12.00
439 Eric Nesterenko 7.50 15.00
440 Bob Nevin 5.00 10.00
441 Mike Nykoluk 25.00 50.00
442 Bert Olmstead 6.00 12.00
443 Bob Pulford 6.00 12.00
444 Marc Reaume 7.50 15.00
445 Larry Regan 5.00 10.00
446 Dave Reid 75.00 150.00
447 Al Rollins 15.00 30.00
448A Eddie Shack 150.00 300.00
(Dark background)
449 Don Simmons 6.00 12.00
450 Tod Sloan 5.00 10.00
451 Sid Smith 5.00 10.00
452 Bob Solinger 30.00 60.00
453A Allan Stanley ERR 6.00 12.00
(Name misspelled Alan; dark background)
453B Allan Stanley COR 12.50 25.00
(Light background)
454 Wally Stanowski 200.00 400.00
455 Ron Stewart 5.00 10.00
456 Harry Taylor 20.00 40.00
457 Jim Thomson 6.00 12.00
458 Ray Timgren 7.50 15.00
459 Harry Watson 6.00 12.00
460 Johnny Wilson 5.00 10.00
461 1962-63 Maple Leafs 200.00 400.00
(Team picture)
462A Lady Byng Trophy 150.00 300.00
(Four white borders)
462B Lady Byng Trophy 60.00 125.00
(White bottom border only)
463A Calder Memorial Trophy 150.00 300.00
(Four white borders)
463B Calder Memorial Trophy 60.00125.00
(White bottom border only)
464A Hart Trophy 150.00 300.00
(Four white borders)
464B Hart Trophy 60.00 125.00
(White bottom border only)
465A James Norris 150.00 300.00
Memorial Trophy
(Four white borders)
465B James Norris 60.00 125.00
Memorial Trophy
(White bottom border only)
466A Prince of Wales Trophy 150.00300.00
(Four white borders)
466B Prince of Wales Trophy 60.00 125.00
(White bottom border only)
467A Art Ross Trophy 150.00 300.00
(Four white borders)
467B Art Ross Trophy 60.00 125.00
(White bottom border only)
468A Stanley Cup 150.00 300.00
(Four white borders)
468B Stanley Cup 60.00 125.00
(White bottom border only)
469A Georges Vezina Trophy 150.00300.00
(Four white borders)
469B Georges Vezina Trophy 60.00 125.00
(White bottom border only)

1964-67 Beehive Group III Photos

The 1964-67 Beehive photo set is the third of three groups. These photos were issued by St. Lawrence Starch and measure 5 3/8" by 8". The fronts display black-and-white action poses inside a white inner border and a simulated wood-grain outer border. The player's name is displayed on an plaque in the lower wooden border. The backs are blank. A number of unconfirmed photos are part of the Beehive checklist, but have yet to be confirmed.and therefore are not listed below.

1 Murray Balfour 12.50 25.00
2 Leo Boivin 6.00 12.00
3 John Bucyk 7.50 15.00
4 Wayne Connelly 90.00 175.00
5 Bob Dillabough 6.00 12.00
6 Gary Dornhoefer 7.50 15.00
7 Reggie Fleming 6.00 12.00
8 Guy Gendron 60.00 125.00
9 Warren Godfrey 150.00 300.00
10 Ted Green 6.00 12.00
11 Andy Hebenton 90.00 175.00
12 Eddie Johnston 7.50 15.00
13 Tom Johnson 7.50 15.00
14 Forbes Kennedy 10.00 20.00
15 Orland Kurtenbach 20.00 40.00
16 Bobby Leiter 6.00 12.00
17 Parker MacDonald 6.00 12.00
18 Bob McCord 10.00 20.00
19 Ab McDonald 6.00 12.00
20 Murray Oliver 6.00 12.00
21 Bernie Parent 40.00 80.00
22 Cliff Pennington 100.00 225.00
23 Bob Perreault 175.00 350.00
24 Dean Prentice 6.00 12.00
25 Ron Schock UER 6.00 12.00
(Name misspelled Shock)
26 Pat Stapleton 25.00 50.00
27 Ron Stewart 7.50 15.00
28 Ed Westfall 6.00 12.00
29 Tom Williams 6.00 12.00
30 Lou Angotti 6.00 12.00
31 Wally Boyer 6.00 12.00
32 Denis DeJordy 7.50 15.00
33 Dave Dryden 15.00 30.00
34A Phil Esposito 40.00 80.00
(Full Blade showing)
34B Phil Esposito 10.00 20.00
(Partial blade showing)
35 Glenn Hall ERR 10.00 20.00
(Name misspelled Glen)
36 Murray Hall 100.00 225.00
37 Billy Hay 6.00 12.00
38 Camille Henry 10.00 20.00
39 Wayne Hillman 75.00 150.00
40 Ken Hodge Sr. 7.50 15.00
41A Bobby Hull 100.00 225.00
(Home sweater)
41B Bobby Hull 200.00 400.00
(Home sweater; negative reversed)
41C Bobby Hull 15.00 30.00
(Away sweater; blade showing)
41D Bobby Hull 15.00 30.00
(Away sweater; no blade showing)
41E Bobby Hull 200.00 400.00
(Home portrait)
41F Bobby Hull 15.00 30.00
(Promotional portrait)
42 Dennis Hull 6.00 12.00
43 Doug Jarrett 6.00 12.00
44 Len Lunde 6.00 12.00
45 Al MacNeil 6.00 12.00
46A Chico Maki 50.00 100.00
(In action)
46B Chico Maki 6.00 12.00
(Portrait)
47 John McKenzie 15.00 30.00
49 Stan Mikita 10.00 20.00
50 Doug Mohns 6.00 12.00
51A Eric Nesterenko 100.00 225.00
(Light background)
51B Eric Nesterenko 6.00 12.00
(Dark background)
52A Pierre Pilote 125.00 250.00
(Home sweater)
52B Pierre Pilote 7.50 15.00
(Away sweater)
53 Matt Ravlich 6.00 12.00
55A Fred Stanfield 75.00 150.00
55B Fred Stanfield 50.00 100.00
(Reversed negative)
56 Pat Stapleton 6.00 12.00
57 Bob Turner 125.00 250.00
58 Ed Van Impe 6.00 12.00
59 Elmer Vasko 7.50 15.00
60 Kenny Wharram 6.00 12.00

61 Doug Barkley 6.00 12.00
62 Hank Bassen 7.50 15.00
63A Andy Bathgate 6.00 12.00
(Number visible on sleeve)
63B Andy Bathgate 6.00 12.00
(Partial number visible)
64 Gary Bergman 6.00 12.00
65 Leo Boivin 7.50 15.00
66 Roger Crozier 7.50 15.00
67A Alex Delvecchio 10.00 20.00
(Home sweater)
67B Alex Delvecchio 150.00 300.00
(Away sweater)
68 Alex Faulkner 175.00 350.00
69 Val Fonteyne 6.00 12.00
70 Bill Gadsby 6.00 12.00
71 Warren Godfrey 12.50 25.00
72 Pete Goegan 12.50 25.00
73 Murray Hall 6.00 12.00
74 Ted Hampson 6.00 12.00
75 Billy Harris 15.00 30.00
76 Paul Henderson 10.00 20.00
77A Gordie Howe 20.00 40.00
77B Gordie Howe 100.00 225.00
(C on sweater)
78 Ron Ingram 150.00 300.00
79A Larry Jeffrey 50.00 100.00
(Home sweater)
79B Larry Jeffrey 30.00 60.00
(Away sweater)
80A Eddie Joyal 12.50 25.00
80B Eddie Joyal 100.00 225.00
(Reversed negative)
81 Al Langlois 6.00 12.00
82 Ted Lindsay 10.00 20.00
83 Parker MacDonald 6.00 12.00
84A Bruce MacGregor 7.50 15.00
(Home sweater)
84B Bruce MacGregor 50.00 100.00
(Away sweater)
85 Pete Mahovlich 6.00 12.00
86 Bert Marshall 6.00 12.00
87 Pit Martin 6.00 12.00
89 Ab McDonald 6.00 12.00
90 Ron Murphy 6.00 12.00
91 Dean Prentice 6.00 12.00
92 Andre Pronovost 10.00 20.00
93 Marcel Pronovost 5.00 10.00
(Unconfirmed)
94A Floyd Smith 7.50 15.00
(Home sweater)
94B Floyd Smith 100.00 225.00
(Home sweater; reversed negative)
94C Floyd Smith 90.00 175.00
(Away sweater)
95 Norm Ullman 10.00 20.00
96 Bob Wall 6.00 12.00
97 Ralph Backstrom 6.00 12.00
98 Dave Balon 6.00 12.00
99 Jean Beliveau 12.50 25.00
100 Red Berenson 6.00 12.00
101 Yvan Cournoyer 10.00 20.00
102 Dick Duff 7.50 15.00
103 John Ferguson 6.00 12.00
104 John Hanna 100.00 200.00
105A Terry Harper 6.00 12.00
(Posed)
105B Terry Harper 100.00 225.00
(In action)
106 Ted Harris 6.00 12.00
107 Bill Hicke 7.50 15.00
108 Charlie Hodge 10.00 20.00
109 Jacques Laperriere 6.00 12.00
110A Claude Larose 6.00 12.00
110B Claude Larose 250.00 450.00
(Reversed negative)
111 Claude Provost 6.00 12.00
112 Henri Richard 12.50 25.00
113 Maurice Richard 30.00 60.00
114 Jim Roberts 6.00 12.00
115 Bobby Rousseau 6.00 12.00
116 Jean-Guy Talbot 6.00 12.00
117A Gilles Tremblay 6.00 12.00
(Sweater 21)
117B Gilles Tremblay 50.00 100.00
(Sweater 24)
118 J.C. Tremblay 6.00 12.00
119 Gump Worsley 10.00 20.00
120 Lou Angotti 6.00 12.00
121 Arnie Brown 6.00 12.00
122 Larry Cahan 150.00 300.00
124 Reggie Fleming 6.00 12.00
125 Bernie Geoffrion 10.00 20.00
126 Ed Giacomin 12.50 25.00
127 Rod Gilbert 10.00 20.00
128 Phil Goyette 6.00 12.00
129 Vic Hadfield 7.50 15.00
131 Camille Henry 75.00 150.00
132 Bill Hicke 6.00 12.00
133 Wayne Hillman 6.00 12.00
134 Harry Howell 7.50 15.00
135 Earl Ingarfield Sr. 6.00 12.00
137 Orland Kurtenbach 10.00 20.00
138 Gord Labossiere 75.00 150.00
139 Al MacNeil 6.00 12.00
140 Cesare Maniago 10.00 20.00
141 Don Marshall 6.00 12.00
143 Jim Neilson 6.00 12.00
144 Bob Nevin 6.00 12.00
145 Marcel Paille 20.00 40.00
146 Jacques Plante 40.00 80.00
147 Jean Ratelle 12.50 25.00
148 Rod Seiling 6.00 12.00
151 George Armstrong 10.00 20.00
152 Andy Bathgate 10.00 20.00
153A Bob Baun 60.00 125.00
(Number visible)
153B Bob Baun 10.00 20.00
(No number visible)
154A Johnny Bower 90.00 175.00
(Number visible)
154B Johnny Bower 12.50 25.00
(No number visible)
155 Wally Boyer 15.00 30.00
156 John Brenneman 6.00 12.00
157 Carl Brewer 12.50 25.00
158 Turk Broda 15.00 30.00
159 Brian Conacher 6.00 12.00
160 Kent Douglas 6.00 12.00
161 Ron Ellis 6.00 12.00
162 Bruce Gamble 10.00 20.00
163A Billy Harris 50.00 100.00
(Number visible)
163B Billy Harris 100.00 225.00
(No number visible)
164 Larry Hillman 12.50 25.00
165A Tim Horton 90.00 175.00
(Number visible)
165B Tim Horton 15.00 30.00
(No number visible)
166 Bronco Horvath 90.00 175.00
167 Larry Jeffrey 15.00 30.00
168 Eddie Joyal 20.00 40.00
169 Red Kelly 10.00 20.00
170 Ted Kennedy 10.00 20.00
171A Dave Keon 75.00 150.00
(Number visible)
171B Dave Keon 12.50 25.00
(No number visible)
172 Orland Kurtenbach 7.50 20.00
173 Ed Litzenberger 10.00 20.00
174A Frank Mahovlich 90.00 175.00
(Number visible)
174B Frank Mahovlich 15.00 30.00
(No number visible)
175A Don McKenney 50.00 100.00
(Small photo)
175B Don McKenney 10.00 20.00
(Large photo)
176 Dickie Moore 10.00 20.00
177 Jim Pappin 6.00 12.00
178A Marcel Pronovost 7.50 15.00
(Blade showing)
178B Marcel Pronovost 15.00 30.00
(No Blade showing)
180A Bob Pulford 50.00 100.00
(Number visible)
180B Bob Pulford 10.00 20.00
(No number visible)
181 Terry Sawchuk 15.00 30.00
182 Brit Selby 6.00 12.00
183 Eddie Shack 12.50 25.00
184 Don Simmons 12.50 25.00
185 Allan Stanley 10.00 20.00
186 Pete Stemkowski 6.00 12.00
187A Ron Stewart 90.00 175.00
(Number visible)
187B Ron Stewart 30.00 60.00
(No number visible)
188 Mike Walton 15.00 30.00
189 Bernie Geoffrion 25.00 50.00
190 Lady Byng Trophy 60.00 125.00
191 Calder Memorial Trophy 60.00 125.00
192 Hart Trophy 60.00 125.00
193 Prince of Wales Trophy 60.00 125.00
194 James Norris Memorial Trophy 60.00 125.00
195 Art Ross Trophy 60.00 125.00
196 Stanley Cup 60.00 125.00
197 Vezina Trophy 60.00 125.00

1997-98 Beehive

The Beehives set was issued in one series totaling 75 cards and was distributed in four-card packs with a suggested retail price of $4.99. This set is a revival of the 1934-67 Beehive Photos sets produced by the St. Lawrence Starch Co. of Port Credit, Ontario. This new version features color player portraits printed on 5" by 7" cards. The backs carry a black-and-white action player photos with player information and career statistics. The player information as well as a trivia question is printed in both French and English. The set contains the topical subsets: Golden Originals (57-62), and Junior League Stars (63-74).

COMPLETE SET (75) 12.00 30.00
1 Eric Lindros .25 .60
2 Teemu Selanne .25 .60
3 Brendan Shanahan .25 .60
4 Joe Sakic .60 1.50
5 John LeClair .25 .60
6 Brett Hull .30 .75
7 Jaromir Jagr .50 1.25
8 Bryan Berard .15 .40
9 Peter Forsberg .60 1.50
10 Ed Belfour .25 .60
11 Steve Yzerman 1.25 3.00
12 Curtis Joseph .25 .60
13 Saku Koivu .25 .60
14 Keith Tkachuk .25 .60
15 Pavel Bure .25 .60
16 Felix Potvin .25 .60
17 Ray Bourque .50 1.00
18 Theo Fleury .10 .25
19 Patrick Roy 1.50 4.00
20 Joe Nieuwendyk .15 .40
21 Alexei Yashin .10 .25
22 Owen Nolan .15 .40
23 Mark Recchi .15 .40
24 Dominik Hasek .60 1.50
25 Chris Chelios .25 .60
26 Mike Modano .40 1.00
27 John Vanbiesbrouck .15 .40
28 Brian Leetch .25 .60
29 Dino Ciccarelli .10 .25
30 Mark Messier .25 .60
31 Paul Kariya .25 .60
32 Jocelyn Thibault .15 .40
33 Wayne Gretzky 2.00 5.00
34 Doug Weight .15 .40
35 Yanic Perreault .10 .25
36 Luc Robitaille .15 .40
37 Chris Osgood .15 .40
38 Adam Oates .15 .40
39 Mats Sundin .25 .60
40 Trevor Linden .15 .40
41 Mike Richter .25 .60
42 Zigmund Palffy .15 .40
43 Pat LaFontaine .25 .60
44 Grant Fuhr .15 .40
45 Martin Brodeur .75 2.00
46 Sergei Fedorov .40 1.00
47 Doug Gilmour .15 .40
48 Daniel Alfredsson .15 .40
49 Ron Francis .15 .40
50 Geoff Sanderson .15 .40
51 Joe Thornton .60 1.50
52 Vaclav Prospal RC .25 .60
53 Patrik Elias RC 1.00 2.50
54 Mike Johnson RC .25 .60
55 Alyn McCauley .15 .40
56 Brendan Morrison RC .40 1.00
57 Johnny Bower GO .30 .75
58 John Bucyk GO .30 .75
59 Stan Mikita GO .30 .75
60 Ted Lindsay GO .30 .75
61 Maurice Richard GO 1.25 3.00
62 Andy Bathgate GO .30 .75
63 Stefan Cherneski JLS RC .15 .40
64 Craig Hillier JLS RC .25 .60
65 Daniel Tkaczuk JLS .25 .60
66 Josh Holden JLS .15 .40
67 Marian Cisar JLS RC .15 .40
68 J-P Dumont JLS RC .60 1.50
69 Roberto Luongo JLS RC 3.00 8.00
70 Aren Miller JLS RC .15 .40
71 Mathieu Garon JLS .25 .60
72 Charlie Stephens JLS RC .25 .60
73 Sergei Varlamov JLS RC .30 .75
74 Pierre Dagenais JLS RC .40 1.00
75 Willie O'Ree CC RC .75 2.00
P1 Eric Lindros PROMO .10 .25
R1 Redemption .10 .25

1997-98 Beehive Authentic Autographs

Randomly inserted in packs at the rate of 1:12, this 19-card set features autographed cards of CHL stars that seem to have an outstanding chance of becoming NHL stars as well as some of the NHL's top rookies.

STATED ODDS 1:12
51 Joe Thornton 10.00 25.00
52 Vaclav Prospal 2.00 5.00
53 Patrik Elias 6.00 15.00
54 Mike Johnson 2.00 5.00
55 Alyn McCauley 4.00 10.00
56 Brendan Morrison 4.00 10.00
63 Stefan Cherneski 2.00 5.00
64 Craig Hillier 2.00 5.00
65 Daniel Tkaczuk 2.00 5.00
66 Josh Holden 2.00 5.00
67 Marian Cisar 2.00 5.00
68 J-P Dumont 3.00 8.00
69 Roberto Luongo 15.00 40.00
70 Aren Miller 2.00 5.00
71 Mathieu Garon 4.00 10.00
72 Charlie Stephens 2.00 5.00
73 Sergei Varlamov 2.00 5.00
74 Pierre Dagenais 2.00 5.00
75 Willie O'Ree 10.00 25.00

1997-98 Beehive Golden Portraits

Randomly inserted in packs at the rate of 1:3, this 75-card set is a gold-foil parallel version of the base set.

*STARS: 2X TO 5X BASIC CARD
*ROOKIES: 1X TO 2.5X BASIC CARD
STATED ODDS 1:3

1997-98 Beehive Golden Originals Autographs

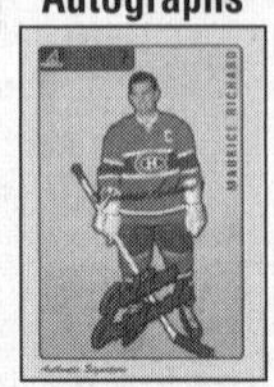

Randomly inserted in packs at the rate of 1:36, this six-card set features autographed color photos of six top retired players.

STATED ODDS 1:36
57 Johnny Bower 8.00 20.00
58 John Bucyk 8.00 20.00
59 Stan Mikita 8.00 20.00
60 Ted Lindsay 8.00 20.00
61 Maurice Richard 40.00 80.00
62 Andy Bathgate 8.00 20.00

1997-98 Beehive Team

Randomly inserted in packs at the rate of 1:11, this 25-card set features color photos of some of Hockey's best players. The backs carry player information. A Beehive Gold Team set was also produced which is a parallel version to this insert set and has an insertion rate of 1:49.

COMPLETE SET (25) 60.00 150.00
STATED ODDS 1:11
*GOLD TEAM: .75X TO 2X BASIC INSERTS
GOLD TEAM STATED ODDS 1:49
1 Paul Kariya 2.50 6.00
2 Mark Messier 2.50 6.00
3 Mike Modano 3.00 8.00
4 Brendan Shanahan 2.50 6.00
5 John Vanbiesbrouck 1.50 4.00
6 Martin Brodeur 6.00 15.00
7 Wayne Gretzky 12.00 30.00
8 Eric Lindros 2.50 6.00
9 Peter Forsberg 4.00 10.00
10 Jaromir Jagr 4.00 10.00
11 Teemu Selanne 2.50 6.00
12 John LeClair 1.50 4.00
13 Saku Koivu 2.50 6.00
14 Brett Hull 3.00 8.00
15 Patrick Roy 10.00 25.00
16 Steve Yzerman 8.00 20.00
17 Keith Tkachuk 1.50 4.00
18 Pat LaFontaine 1.50 4.00
19 Joe Sakic 5.00 12.00
20 Patrik Elias 1.50 4.00
21 Vaclav Prospal 1.00 2.50
22 Joe Thornton 4.00 10.00
23 Sergei Samsonov 2.00 5.00
24 Alexei Morozov 1.00 2.50
25 Marco Sturm 1.00 2.50

2003-04 Beehive

This 250-card set was designed to reflect the design of the original Beehive photos with "woodgrain" borders and color player photos. The set consisted of 200 veterans and 50 short-printed rookies inserted at 1:5 packs.

COMPLETE SET (250) 100.00 200.00
COMP.SET w/o SP's (200) 15.00 40.00
RC STATED ODDS 1:5
1 Petr Sykora .08 .20
2 Martin Gerber .20 .50
3 Vaclav Prospal .08 .20
4 J-S Giguere .20 .50
5 Sergei Fedorov .30 .75
6 Stanislav Chistov .08 .20
7 Sandis Ozolinsh .08 .20
8 Pasi Nurminen .20 .50
9 Marc Savard .08 .20
10 Vyacheslav Kozlov .08 .20
11 Dany Heatley .30 .75
12 Ilya Kovalchuk .30 .75
13 Andrew Raycroft .20 .50
14 Glen Murray .08 .20
15 Brian Rolston .08 .20
16 Jeff Jillson .08 .20
17 Don Cherry .50 1.25
18 Nick Boynton .08 .20
19 Felix Potvin .20 .50
20 Joe Thornton .40 1.00
21 Sergei Samsonov .20 .50
22 Ales Kotalik .08 .20
23 Alexei Zhitnik .08 .20
24 Maxim Afinogenov .08 .20
25 Chris Drury .20 .50
26 Daniel Briere .08 .20
27 Martin Biron .20 .50
28 Steve Reinprecht .08 .20
29 Jamie McLennan .08 .20
30 Martin Gelinas .08 .20
31 Jarome Iginla .30 .75
32 Roman Turek .20 .50
33 Jeff O'Neill .08 .20
34 Danny Markov .08 .20
35 Erik Cole .08 .20
36 Rod Brind'Amour .08 .20
37 Jamie Storr .20 .50
38 Ron Francis .20 .50
39 Bryan Berard .08 .20
40 Eric Daze .20 .50
41 Kyle Calder .08 .20
42 Michael Leighton .20 .50
44 Jocelyn Thibault .20 .50
45 Tyler Arnason .20 .50
46 Philippe Sauve .20 .50
47 Teemu Selanne .25 .60
48 Alex Tanguay .20 .50
49 Derek Morris .08 .20
50 Milan Hejduk .25 .60
51 Patrick Roy 1.25 3.00
52 David Aebischer .20 .50
53 Joe Sakic .50 1.25
54 Paul Kariya .25 .60
55 Peter Forsberg .60 1.50
56 Darryl Sydor .08 .20
57 Trevor Letowski .08 .20
58 Marc Denis .20 .50
59 Rick Nash .30 .75
60 Todd Marchant .08 .20
61 Brenden Morrow .20 .50
62 Jere Lehtinen .20 .50
63 Sergei Zubov .08 .20
64 Stu Barnes .08 .20
65 Teppo Numminen .08 .20
66 Bill Guerin .20 .50
67 Marty Turco .20 .50
68 Mike Modano .40 1.00
69 Gordie Howe 1.25 3.00
70 Brendan Shanahan .25 .60
71 Brett Hull .30 .75
72 Nicklas Lidstrom .25 .60
73 Dominik Hasek .50 1.00
74 Henrik Zetterberg .25 .60
75 Steve Yzerman 1.25 3.00
76 Eric Brewer .08 .20
77 Adam Oates .20 .50
78 Ryan Smyth .08 .20
79 Ales Hemsky .08 .20
80 Raffi Torres .08 .20
81 Wayne Gretzky 1.50 4.00
82 Tommy Salo .20 .50
83 Steve Shields .08 .20
84 Jay Bouwmeester .08 .20
85 Olli Jokinen .20 .50
86 Roberto Luongo .30 .75
87 Marcel Dionne .30 .75
88 Alexander Frolov .08 .20
89 Adam Deadmarsh .08 .20
90 Jason Allison .08 .20
91 Luc Robitaille .20 .50
92 Roman Cechmanek .20 .50
93 Zigmund Palffy .20 .50
94 Andrew Brunette .08 .20
95 Dwayne Roloson .20 .50
96 Pascal Dupuis .08 .20
97 Wes Walz .08 .20
98 Manny Fernandez .20 .50
99 Marian Gaborik .50 1.00
100 Pierre-Marc Bouchard .08 .20
101 Andrei Markov .08 .20
102 Guy Lafleur .60 2.50
103 Mike Ribeiro .08 .20
104 Jose Theodore .30 .75
105 Marcel Hossa .25 .60
106 Michael Ryder .08 .20
107 Saku Koivu .25 .60
108 Greg Johnson .08 .20
109 David Legwand .20 .50
110 Tomas Vokoun .20 .50
111 Jamie Langenbrunner .08 .20
112 Jeff Friesen .08 .20
113 John Madden .08 .20
114 Scott Niedermayer .08 .20
115 Martin Brodeur .60 1.50
116 Patrik Elias .20 .50
117 Scott Gomez .20 .50
118 Scott Stevens .20 .50
119 Brian Gionta .08 .20
119B Alexei Zhamnov .08 .20
120 Mariusz Czerkawski .08 .20
121 Eric Godard .08 .20
122 Jason Blake .08 .20
123 Mark Parrish .08 .20
124 Alexei Yashin .08 .20
125 Michael Peca .08 .20
126 Rick DiPietro .20 .50
127 Alex Kovalev .20 .50
128 Anson Carter .20 .50
129 Brian Leetch .20 .50
130 Petr Nedved .08 .20
131 Eric Lindros .25 .60
132 Mark Messier .25 .60
133 Mike Dunham .20 .50
134 Daniel Alfredsson .20 .50
135 Zdeno Chara .08 .20
136 Jason Spezza .25 .60
137 Marian Hossa .25 .60
138 Patrick Lalime .20 .50
139 Bobby Clarke .40 1.00
140 John LeClair .25 .60
141 Justin Williams .08 .20
142 Mark Recchi .20 .50
143 Robert Esche .20 .50
144 Tony Amonte .20 .50
145 Jeff Hackett .20 .50
146 Jeremy Roenick .30 .75
147 Simon Gagne .25 .60
148 Brian Boucher .20 .50
149 Chris Gratton .08 .20
150 David Tanabe .08 .20
151 Jan Hrdina .08 .20
152 Mike Johnson .20 .50
153 Sean Burke .20 .50
154 Brooks Orpik .08 .20
155 Konstantin Koltsov .08 .20
156 Rico Fata .08 .20
157 Sebastien Caron .20 .50
158 Mario Lemieux 1.50 4.00
159 Martin Straka .08 .20
160 Jonathan Cheechoo .10 .25
161 Kyle McLaren .08 .20
162 Niko Dimitrakos .08 .20
163 Evgeni Nabokov .20 .50
164 Patrick Marleau .20 .50
165 Vincent Damphousse .20 .50
166 Chris Pronger .20 .50
167 Reed Low .08 .20
168 Chris Osgood .20 .50
169 Doug Weight .20 .50
170 Keith Tkachuk .25 .60
171 Pavol Demitra .20 .50
172 Dave Andreychuk .20 .50
173 Martin St. Louis .20 .50
174 Nikolai Khabibulin .25 .60
175 Vincent Lecavalier .25 .60
176 Brad Richards .20 .50
177 Fredrik Modin .08 .20
178 Gary Roberts .08 .20
179 Joe Nieuwendyk .20 .50
180 Tie Domi .20 .50
181 Alexander Mogilny .20 .50
182 Ed Belfour .25 .60
183 Mats Sundin .25 .60
184 Owen Nolan .20 .50
185 Daniel Sedin .08 .20
186 Magnus Arvedson .08 .20
187 Dan Cloutier .20 .50
188 Henrik Sedin .08 .20
189 Brendan Morrison .20 .50
190 Jason King .08 .20
191 Trevor Linden .08 .20
192 Ed Jovanovski .20 .50
193 Johan Hedberg .20 .50
194 Markus Naslund .25 .60
195 Todd Bertuzzi .25 .60
196 Robert Lang .08 .20
197 Sergei Gonchar .08 .20
198 Jaromir Jagr .40 1.00
199 Olaf Kolzig .20 .50
200 Peter Bondra .20 .50
201 Joffrey Lupul RC 1.50 4.00
202 Patrice Bergeron RC 2.50 6.00
203 Niklas Kronwall RC 1.50 4.00
204 Eric Staal RC 4.00 10.00
205 Pavel Vorobiev RC 1.25 3.00
206 Tuomo Ruutu RC 2.00 5.00
207 Tomas Plekanec RC 1.25 3.00
208 Timofei Shishkanov RC 1.25 3.00
209 Tuomas Pihlman RC 1.25 3.00
210 Dan Fritsche RC 1.25 3.00
211 Antti Miettinen RC 1.25 3.00
212 Jiri Hudler RC 2.00 5.00
213 Nathan Horton RC 3.00 5.00
214 Dustin Brown RC 1.50 4.00
215 Kyle Wellwood RC 2.00 5.00
216 Mike Smith RC 2.00 5.00
217 Ryan Kesler RC 1.25 3.00
218 Fredrik Sjostrom RC 1.25 3.00
219 Chris Higgins RC 3.00 8.00
220 Dan Hamhuis RC 1.25 3.00
221 Jordin Tootoo RC 2.50 6.00
222 Carl Corazzini RC 1.25 3.00
223 Tony Martensson RC 1.25 3.00
224 Aaron Johnson RC 1.25 3.00
225 Anton Babchuk RC 1.25 3.00
226 Jozef Balej RC 1.25 3.00
227 Joni Pitkanen RC 1.50 4.00
228 Aleksander Suglobov RC 1.25 3.00
229 Marc-Andre Fleury RC 6.00 15.00
230 Nikolai Zherdev RC 1.50 4.00
231 Gavin Morgan RC 1.25 3.00
232 Milan Michalek RC 1.50 4.00
233 Peter Sejna RC 1.25 3.00
234 Matt Stajan RC 2.50 6.00
235 Maxim Kondratiev RC 1.25 3.00
236 Alexander Semin RC 4.00 10.00
237 Zbynek Michalek RC 1.25 3.00
238 Jeff Hamilton RC 1.25 3.00
239 Andrew Hutchinson RC 1.25 3.00
240 Mikhail Yakubov RC 1.25 3.00
241 Sergei Zinovjev RC 1.25 3.00
242 Noah Clarke RC 1.25 3.00
243 Tim Jackman RC 1.25 3.00
244 Jason Pominville RC 2.00 5.00
245 Tony Salmelainen RC 1.25 3.00
246 Rastislav Stana RC 1.25 3.00
247 Darryl Bootland RC 1.25 3.00
248 Trevor Daley RC 1.25 3.00
249 Peter Sarno RC 1.25 3.00
250 Nathan Smith RC 1.25 3.00

2003-04 Beehive Variations

This partial parallel set featured varying photos from the base set and could be distinguished by the lighter borders.

STATED ODDS 1:3
5 Sergei Fedorov .60 1.50
12 Ilya Kovalchuk .60 1.50
17 Don Cherry 1.00 2.50
20 Joe Thornton .75 2.00
21 Sergei Samsonov .40 1.00
25 Chris Drury .40 1.00
31 Jarome Iginla .60 1.50
35 Erik Cole .15 .40
44 Jocelyn Thibault .40 1.00
51 Patrick Roy 2.50 6.00
53 Joe Sakic 1.00 2.50
55 Peter Forsberg 1.25 3.00
59 Rick Nash .60 1.50
67 Marty Turco .40 1.00
68 Mike Modano .75 2.00
69 Gordie Howe 2.50 6.00
74 Henrik Zetterberg .50 1.25
75 Steve Yzerman 2.50 6.00
79 Ales Hemsky .15 .40
80 Raffi Torres .15 .40
81 Wayne Gretzky 3.00 8.00
86 Roberto Luongo .60 1.50
87 Marcel Dionne .60 1.50
91 Luc Robitaille .40 1.00
93 Zigmund Palffy .40 1.00
99 Marian Gaborik .75 2.00
102 Guy Lafleur 2.00 5.00
104 Jose Theodore .60 1.50
107 Saku Koivu .50 1.25
110 Tomas Vokoun .40 1.00
115 Martin Brodeur 1.25 3.00
120 Mariusz Czerkawski .15 .40
126 Rick DiPietro .40 1.00
132 Mark Messier .50 1.25
136 Jason Spezza .50 1.25
137 Marian Hossa .50 1.25
139 Bobby Clarke .75 2.00
144 Tony Amonte .40 1.00
146 Jeremy Roenick .60 1.50
153 Sean Burke .40 1.00
158 Mario Lemieux 3.00 8.00
164 Patrick Marleau .40 1.00
170 Keith Tkachuk .50 1.25
174 Nikolai Khabibulin .50 1.25
175 Vincent Lecavalier .50 1.25
182 Ed Belfour .50 1.25
183 Mats Sundin .50 1.25
190 Jason King .40 1.00
195 Todd Bertuzzi .50 1.25
198 Jaromir Jagr .75 2.00

2003-04 Beehive Gold

PRINT RUN 15 SER.#'d SETS
NOT PRICED DUE TO SCARCITY

2003-04 Beehive Silver

*STARS: 3X TO 8X BASIC CARDS
*ROOKIES: 1.25X TO 3X
PRINT RUN 67 SER.#'d SETS

2003-04 Beehive Jumbos

These large box toppers were found one box in an indivdual "jumbo" pack carried a jumbo jersey and a jumbo bas variation card.

ONE PER BOX
1 J-S Giguere 1.00 2
2 Sergei Fedorov 1.50 4
3 Ilya Kovalchuk 1.50 4
4 Joe Thornton 2.00 5
5 Don Cherry 3.00 8
6 Ron Francis 1.00 2
7 Jocelyn Thibault 1.00 2
8 Peter Forsberg 3.00 8
9 Rick Nash 1.50 4
10 Marty Turco 1.00 2
11 Gordie Howe 4.00 10
12 Steve Yzerman 4.00 10
13 Roberto Luongo 1.50 4
14 Don Cherry 2.00 5
15 Marian Gaborik 2.50 6
16 Guy Lafleur 1.50 4
17 Scotty Bowman 1.50 4
18 Martin Brodeur 4.00 10
19 Jason Spezza 1.25 3
20 Marian Hossa 1.25 3
21 Jeremy Roenick 1.50 4
22 Mario Lemieux 5.00 12
23 Ed Belfour 1.25 3
24 Markus Naslund 1.25 3
25 Todd Bertuzzi 1.25 3

2003-04 Beehive Jumbo Variations

STATED ODDS 1:3
1 Joffrey Lupul 3.00 8
2 Sergei Fedorov 4.00 10
3 Ilya Kovalchuk 4.00 10
4 Joe Thornton 5.00 12
5 Don Cherry 8.00 20
6 Eric Staal 4.00 10
7 Tuomo Ruutu 3.00 8
8 Peter Forsberg 8.00 20
9 Rick Nash 4.00 10
10 Marty Turco 2.50 6
11 Gordie Howe 10.00 25
12 Jiri Hudler 4.00 10
13 Nathan Horton 4.00 10
14 Don Cherry 8.00 20
15 Marian Gaborik 6.00 15
16 Guy Lafleur 4.00 10
17 Scotty Bowman 4.00 10
18 Martin Brodeur 10.00 25
19 Jason Spezza 3.00 8
20 Marian Hossa 3.00 8
21 Joni Pitkanen 3.00 8
22 Marc-Andre Fleury 8.00 20
23 Ed Belfour 3.00 8
24 Markus Naslund 3.00 8
25 Todd Bertuzzi 3.00 8

2003-04 Beehive Jumbo Jerseys

These large box toppers were found one box in an indivdual "jumbo" pack carried a jumbo jersey and a jumbo bas variation card. Each card carried two je swatches.

*MULT.COLOR SWATCH: .75X TO 2X
ONE PER JUMBO PACK
BH1 Jeremy Roenick 6.00 15
BH2 Marty Turco 5.00 12
BH3 Mario Lemieux 40.00 100
BH4 Todd Bertuzzi 6.00 15
BH5 Jarome Iginla 6.00 15
BH6 Dominik Hasek 10.00 25
BH7 Chris Drury 5.00 12
BH8 Jose Theodore 8.00 20
BH9 Joe Sakic 8.00 20
BH10 Mike Modano 6.00 15
BH11 Mats Sundin 6.00 15
BH12 Sergei Fedorov 6.00 15
BH13 Keith Tkachuk 6.00 15
BH14 Ed Belfour 6.00 15
BH15 Sean Burke 5.00 12
BH16 Tony Amonte 5.00 12
BH17 Joe Thornton 8.00 20

8 Vincent Lecavalier 5.00 12.00
9 Roberto Luongo 8.00 20.00
0 Steve Yzerman 15.00 40.00
1 Jason Spezza 8.00 20.00
2 Rick Nash 8.00 20.00

2003-04 Beehive Jerseys

LT.COLOR SWATCH: .6X TO 1.5X
TED ODDS 1:15
Mike Modano 5.00 12.00
Zigmund Palffy 3.00 8.00
Jason Spezza 4.00 10.00
Tony Amonte 3.00 8.00
Jeremy Roenick 5.00 12.00
Vincent Lecavalier 3.00 8.00
Marian Gaborik 8.00 20.00
Alexei Yashin 3.00 8.00
Ilya Kovalchuk 5.00 12.00
0 Keith Tkachuk 4.00 10.00
1 Markus Naslund 4.00 10.00
2 Bill Guerin 3.00 8.00
3 Brendan Shanahan 4.00 10.00
4 Dominik Hasek 6.00 15.00
5 Jose Theodore 5.00 12.00
6 Eric Lindros 4.00 10.00
7 Martin Brodeur 10.00 25.00
8 Patrick Lalime 3.00 8.00
9 Rick Nash 5.00 12.00
0 Ryan Smyth 3.00 8.00
1 Marty Turco 3.00 8.00
2 Roberto Luongo 5.00 12.00
3 J-S Giguere 3.00 8.00
4 Ed Belfour 6.00 15.00
5 Joe Thornton 5.00 12.00
6 Todd Bertuzzi 4.00 10.00
7 Steve Yzerman 10.00 25.00
8 Saku Koivu 4.00 10.00
9 Jarome Iginla 5.00 12.00
0 Chris Drury 3.00 8.00
1 Joe Sakic 8.00 20.00
2 Paul Kariya 4.00 10.00
3 Marian Hossa 4.00 10.00
4 Doug Weight 3.00 8.00
5 Sergei Fedorov 5.00 12.00
6 Mats Sundin 4.00 10.00
7 Mario Lemieux 12.50 30.00
8 Teemu Selanne 4.00 10.00
9 Jocelyn Thibault 4.00 10.00
0 Ron Francis 3.00 8.00

2003-04 Beehive Jersey Autographs

TED ODDS 1:240
Martin Brodeur/20
Saku Koivu/25 40.00 100.00
Ilya Kovalchuk/25 60.00 150.00
Eric Lindros/25 40.00 100.00
Patrick Roy/25 200.00 400.00
Jason Spezza/25 50.00 100.00
Marty Turco/25 30.00 80.00
Jarome Iginla/30 25.00 60.00
Wayne Gretzky/10
0 Marian Hossa/50 20.00 50.00
1 Gordie Howe
2 Roberto Luongo/50 30.00 80.00
3 Zigmund Palffy/25 15.00 40.00
4 Jeremy Roenick/50 30.00 80.00
5 Jose Theodore/25 40.00 100.00
6 Joe Thornton/50 40.00 100.00
7 David Aebischer/50 25.00 60.00
8 Todd Bertuzzi/75 20.00 50.00
9 Mike Comrie/75 12.50 30.00
0 Marcel Hossa/75 12.50 30.00
1 Markus Naslund/75 20.00 50.00
2 Rick DiPietro/50 25.00 60.00
3 Scott Hartnell/50 12.50 30.00
4 Ales Hemsky/90 15.00 40.00
5 Henrik Zetterberg/90 20.00 50.00

2003-04 Beehive Signatures

f press time, not all cards have been ied.
TED ODDS 1:240
WN PRINT RUNS BELOW
Martin Brodeur
Patrick Roy
Jason Spezza/25 75.00 150.00
Wayne Gretzky/10
Gordie Howe/10
Jose Theodore/25 40.00 100.00
David Aebischer/25 25.00 60.00
Marian Gaborik
Jarome Iginla/25 50.00 125.00
0 Marian Hossa/50 30.00 80.00
1 Joe Thornton/100 15.00 40.00
2 Anson Carter/25 15.00 40.00
3 Chuck Kobasew/50 15.00 40.00
4 Roberto Luongo/25 50.00 125.00
5 Jeremy Roenick/25 60.00 150.00
6 Mike Comrie/100 8.00 20.00
7 Markus Naslund/100 12.50 30.00
8 Rick DiPietro/50 25.00 60.00
9 Henrik Zetterberg/100 15.00 40.00
0 Jared Aulin/50 12.50 30.00
1 Rick Nash/25 40.00 100.00
2 Owen Nolan/25 25.00 60.00
3 Marcel Hossa/50 6.00 15.00
4 Scott Hartnell/90 6.00 15.00
5 Ales Hemsky/75 6.00 15.00

2003-04 Beehive Sticks Beige Border

STATED ODDS 1:30
BE1 Jarome Iginla 5.00 12.00
BE2 J-S Giguere 2.50 6.00
BE3 Keith Tkachuk 4.00 10.00
BE4 Jocelyn Thibault 2.50 6.00
BE5 Martin Brodeur 10.00 25.00
BE6 Joe Sakic 8.00 20.00
BE7 Mike Modano 6.00 15.00
BE8 Johan Hedberg 2.50 6.00
BE9 Mats Sundin 4.00 10.00
BE10 Brendan Shanahan 4.00 10.00
BE11 Owen Nolan 2.50 6.00
BE12 Marc Denis 2.50 6.00
BE13 Teemu Selanne 4.00 10.00
BE14 Curtis Joseph 4.00 10.00
BE15 Patrik Stefan 2.50 6.00
BE16 Mike Comrie 2.50 6.00
BE17 Milan Hejduk 4.00 10.00
BE18 Ed Jovanovski 2.50 6.00
BE19 Luc Robitaille 2.50 6.00
BE20 Olaf Kolzig 2.50 6.00
BE21 Mika Noronen 2.50 6.00
BE22 Jeremy Roenick 6.00 15.00
BE23 Mike Dunham 2.50 6.00
BE24 Rick DiPietro 2.50 6.00
BE25 Peter Bondra 2.50 6.00
BE26 Ed Belfour 4.00 10.00
BE27 Felix Potvin 4.00 10.00
BE28 Peter Forsberg 10.00 25.00
BE29 Gordie Howe 10.00 25.00
BE30 Brian Boucher 2.50 6.00
BE31 Brett Hull 6.00 15.00
BE32 Sean Burke 2.50 6.00
BE33 Ilya Kovalchuk 6.00 15.00
BE34 Roman Cechmanek 2.50 6.00
BE35 Jaromir Jagr 6.00 15.00
BE36 David Aebischer 2.50 6.00
BE37 Dominik Hasek 8.00 20.00
BE38 Tommy Salo 2.50 6.00
BE39 Guy Lafleur 2.50 6.00
BE40 Jose Theodore 5.00 12.00
BE41 Marcel Dionne 2.50 6.00
BE42 Vincent Lecavalier 4.00 10.00

2003-04 Beehive Sticks Blue Border

STATED ODDS 1:60
BL1 Sean Burke 3.00 8.00
BL2 Zigmund Palffy 3.00 8.00
BL3 Simon Gagne 5.00 12.00
BL4 Justin Williams 3.00 8.00
BL5 Jean-Sebastien Giguere 3.00 8.00
BL6 Chris Chelios 5.00 12.00
BL7 John LeClair 5.00 12.00
BL8 Rick DiPietro 3.00 8.00
BL9 Peter Bondra 3.00 8.00
BL10 Pavel Bure 5.00 12.00
BL11 Mark Messier 5.00 12.00
BL12 Olaf Kolzig 3.00 8.00
BL13 Martin Brodeur 12.50 30.00
BL14 Felix Potvin 3.00 8.00
BL15 Owen Nolan 3.00 8.00
BL16 Patrik Stefan 3.00 8.00
BL17 Jaromir Jagr 8.00 20.00
BL18 Tommy Salo 3.00 8.00
BL19 Mark Recchi 3.00 8.00
BL20 Ed Belfour 5.00 12.00
BL21 Roman Cechmanek 3.00 8.00

2003-04 Beehive Sticks Red Border

STATED ODDS 1:60
RE1 Dominik Hasek 10.00 25.00
RE2 Brett Hull 8.00 20.00
RE3 Peter Forsberg 12.50 30.00
RE4 Jose Theodore 6.00 15.00
RE5 Marc Denis 3.00 8.00
RE6 Mike Modano 8.00 20.00
RE7 Mark Messier 6.00 15.00
RE8 Mats Sundin 5.00 12.00
RE9 Brendan Shanahan 5.00 12.00
RE10 Eric Lindros 5.00 12.00
RE11 Ron Francis 6.00 15.00
RE12 Jeremy Roenick 8.00 20.00
RE13 Ilya Kovalchuk 8.00 20.00
RE14 Martin Brodeur 12.50 30.00
RE15 Joe Sakic 10.00 25.00
RE16 Keith Tkachuk 5.00 12.00
RE17 David Aebischer 3.00 8.00
RE18 Marcel Dionne 3.00 8.00
RE19 Owen Nolan 3.00 8.00
RE20 Sergei Fedorov 8.00 20.00
RE21 Gordie Howe 12.50 30.00

2005-06 Beehive

COMP.SET w/o SP's (90) 10.00 25.00
RC ODDS 1:4
JUMBOS 1 PER PACK
1 Teemu Selanne .25 .60
2 Joffrey Lupul .12 .30
3 J-S Giguere .20 .50
4 Ilya Kovalchuk .30 .75
5 Kari Lehtonen .25 .60
6 Marian Hossa .25 .60
7 Patrice Bergeron .20 .50
8 Sergei Samsonov .20 .50
9 Andrew Raycroft .20 .50
10 Brian Leetch .25 .60
11 Glen Murray .15 .30
12 Chris Drury .20 .50
13 Daniel Briere .15 .30
14 Jarome Iginla .30 .75
15 Miikka Kiprusoff .25 .60
16 Tony Amonte .20 .50
17 Erik Cole .15 .30
18 Eric Staal .20 .50
19 Nikolai Khabibulin .25 .60
20 Tuomo Ruutu .15 .30
21 Eric Daze .20 .50
22 Joe Sakic .50 1.25
23 Milan Hejduk .25 .60
24 Alex Tanguay .20 .50
25 Rob Blake .20 .50
26 Rick Nash .30 .75
27 Sergei Fedorov .30 .75
28 Mike Modano .25 .60
29 Bill Guerin .20 .50
30 Marty Turco .20 .50
31 Steve Yzerman 1.00 2.50
32 Brendan Shanahan .25 .60
33 Pavel Datsyuk .25 .60
34 Nicklas Lidstrom .25 .60
35 Ty Conklin .20 .50
36 Chris Pronger .20 .50
37 Ryan Smyth .20 .50
38 Roberto Luongo .30 .75
39 Jay Bouwmeester .15 .30
40 Olli Jokinen .20 .50
41 Luc Robitaille .20 .50
42 Jeremy Roenick .30 .75
43 Pavol Demitra .20 .50
44 Marian Gaborik .50 1.25
45 Dwayne Roloson .20 .50
46 Saku Koivu .25 .60
47 Jose Theodore .30 .75
48 Michael Ryder .20 .50
49 Mike Ribeiro .15 .30
50 Paul Kariya .25 .60
51 Tomas Vokoun .20 .50
52 Martin Brodeur 1.25 3.00
53 Patrik Elias .20 .50
54 Scott Gomez .20 .50
55 Alexander Mogilny .20 .50
56 Miroslav Satan .20 .50
57 Alexei Yashin .15 .30
58 Rick DiPietro .20 .50
59 Jaromir Jagr .40 1.00
60 Dominik Hasek .50 1.25
61 Dany Heatley .30 .75
62 Martin Havlat .20 .50
63 Jason Spezza .25 .60
64 Daniel Alfredsson .20 .50
65 Peter Forsberg .40 1.00
66 Robert Esche .12 .30
67 Keith Primeau .12 .30
68 Simon Gagne .25 .60
69 Curtis Joseph .25 .60
70 Shane Doan .15 .30
71 Mario Lemieux 1.50 4.00
72 Mark Recchi .20 .50
73 Zigmund Palffy .20 .50
74 Joe Thornton .40 1.00
75 Patrick Marleau .25 .60
76 Jonathan Cheechoo .25 .60
77 Evgeni Nabokov .20 .50
78 Doug Weight .20 .50
79 Keith Tkachuk .25 .60
80 Martin St. Louis .20 .50
81 Vincent Lecavalier .25 .60
82 Brad Richards .20 .50
83 Mats Sundin .25 .60
84 Ed Belfour .25 .60
85 Eric Lindros .25 .60
86 Jason Allison .15 .30
87 Markus Naslund .25 .60
88 Brendan Morrison .10 .30
89 Todd Bertuzzi .25 .60
90 Olaf Kolzig .20 .50
91 Brandon Bochenski RC 1.50 4.00
92 Patrick Eaves RC 2.50 6.00
93 Derek Boogaard RC 2.00 5.00
94 Brad Richardson RC 1.50 4.00
95 Ole-Kristian Tollefsen RC 1.50 4.00
96 Dennis Wideman RC 1.50 4.00
97 Lee Stempniak RC 1.50 4.00
98 Maxim Lapierre RC 1.50 4.00
99 Andrei Kostitsyn RC 2.50 6.00
100 Rob McVicar RC 1.50 4.00
101 Sidney Crosby RC 40.00 80.00
102 Alexander Ovechkin RC 12.00 30.00
103 Jeff Carter RC 3.00 8.00
104 Corey Perry RC 3.00 8.00
105 Rostislav Olesz RC 2.00 5.00
106 Gilbert Brule RC 2.50 6.00
107 Zach Parise RC 4.00 10.00
108 Alexander Perezhogin RC 2.00 5.00
109 Hannu Toivonen RC 2.50 6.00
110 Wojtek Wolski RC 3.00 8.00
111 Jeff Woywitka RC 1.50 4.00
112 Alexander Steen RC 3.00 8.00
113 Ryan Getzlaf RC 3.00 8.00
114 Dion Phaneuf RC 6.00 15.00
115 Ryan Suter RC 2.00 5.00
116 Mike Richards RC 2.50 6.00
117 Cam Ward RC 3.00 8.00
118 Robert Nilsson RC 1.50 4.00
119 Jim Howard RC 2.50 6.00
120 Thomas Vanek RC 5.00 12.00
121 Braydon Coburn RC 1.50 4.00
122 Brent Seabrook RC 1.50 4.00
123 Peter Budaj RC 2.50 6.00
124 Yann Danis RC 2.00 4.00
125 David Leneveu RC 1.50 4.00
126 Henrik Lundqvist RC 6.00 15.00
127 Johan Franzen RC 1.50 4.00
128 Andrej Meszaros RC 1.50 4.00
129 Jussi Jokinen RC 2.50 6.00
130 Rene Bourque RC 1.50 4.00
131 Jay McClement RC 1.50 4.00
132 Keith Ballard RC 1.50 4.00
133 Evgeny Artyukhin RC 1.50 4.00
134 R.J. Umberger RC 2.00 5.00
135 Petteri Nokelainen RC 1.50 4.00
136 Petr Prucha RC 2.50 6.00
137 Ryan Whitney RC 2.00 5.00
138 Matt Foy RC 1.50 4.00
139 Ryane Clowe RC 2.00 5.00
140 Andrew Wozniewski RC 1.50 4.00
141 Maxime Talbot RC 1.50 4.00
142 Anthony Stewart RC 2.00 5.00
143 Andrew Alberts RC 1.50 4.00
144 Jakub Klepis RC 1.50 4.00
145 Mikko Koivu RC 2.50 6.00
146 Ryan Hollweg RC 1.50 4.00
147 Jim Slater RC 1.50 4.00
148 Chris Campoli RC 1.50 4.00
149 Jordan Sigalet RC 2.00 5.00
150 Steve Bernier RC 2.50 6.00
151 Tomas Fleischmann RC 1.50 4.00
152 Matt Jones RC 1.50 4.00
153 Barry Tallackson RC 2.00 5.00
154 Ben Eager RC 1.50 4.00
155 Danny Richmond RC 1.50 4.00
156 Andrew Ladd RC 2.00 5.00
157 Jeremy Colliton RC 1.50 4.00
158 Bruno Gervais RC 1.50 4.00
159 Jeff Tambellini RC 1.50 4.00
160 Gerald Coleman RC 1.50 4.00
161 Paul Ranger RC 1.50 4.00
162 Staffan Kronwall RC 1.50 4.00
163 Dustin Penner RC 2.50 6.00
164 Kyle Brodziak RC 1.50 4.00
165 Greg Jacina RC 1.50 4.00
166 Erik Christensen RC 1.50 4.00
167 Kyle Quincey RC 1.50 4.00
168 Chris Thorburn RC 1.50 4.00
169 Christoph Schubert RC 1.50 4.00
170 Dimitri Patzold RC 1.50 4.00
171 Junior Lessard RC 1.50 4.00
172 Vojtech Polak RC 1.50 4.00
173 Adam Berkhoel RC 1.50 4.00
174 Cam Barker RC 1.50 4.00
175 Kevin Dallman RC 1.50 4.00
176 Milan Jurcina RC 1.50 4.00
177 Brad Winchester RC 1.50 4.00
178 George Parros RC 1.50 4.00
179 Al Montoya RC 2.50 6.00
180 Brett Lebda RC 1.50 4.00
181 Joe Sakic 2.50 6.00
182 Alex Tanguay 1.00 2.50
183 Milan Hejduk 1.25 3.00
184 Rick Nash 1.50 4.00
185 Mike Modano 2.00 5.00
186 Bill Guerin .60 1.50
187 Steve Yzerman 3.00 8.00
188 Brendan Shanahan 1.25 3.00
189 Chris Pronger 1.00 2.50
190 Roberto Luongo 1.50 4.00
191 Jeremy Roenick 1.50 4.00
192 Luc Robitaille 1.00 2.50
193 Marian Gaborik 2.00 5.00
194 Saku Koivu 1.25 3.00
195 Jose Theodore 1.50 4.00
196 Paul Kariya 1.25 3.00
197 Martin Brodeur 3.00 8.00
198 Patrik Elias 1.00 2.50
199 Miroslav Satan .60 1.50
200 Alexei Yashin .60 1.50
201 Jaromir Jagr 2.00 5.00
202 Dominik Hasek 2.00 5.00
203 Dany Heatley 1.50 4.00
204 Jason Spezza 1.25 3.00
205 Peter Forsberg 2.00 5.00
206 Keith Primeau 1.00 2.50
207 Curtis Joseph 1.25 3.00
208 Brett Hull 1.50 4.00
209 Mario Lemieux 4.00 10.00
210 Evgeni Nabokov 1.00 2.50
211 Jonathan Cheechoo 1.25 3.00
212 Keith Tkachuk 1.25 3.00
213 Doug Weight 1.00 2.50
214 Martin St. Louis 1.00 2.50
215 Vincent Lecavalier 1.25 3.00
216 Mats Sundin 1.25 3.00
217 Ed Belfour 1.25 3.00
218 Eric Lindros 1.25 3.00
219 Markus Naslund 1.25 3.00
220 Olaf Kolzig 1.00 2.50
221 Mike Bossy 1.25 3.00
222 Wayne Cashman .60 1.50
223 Gerry Cheevers 1.00 2.50
224 Bobby Clarke 1.25 3.00
225 Phil Esposito 2.00 5.00
226 Tony Esposito 1.25 3.00
227 Grant Fuhr 1.50 4.00
228 Glenn Hall 1.25 3.00
229 Jari Kurri 1.25 3.00
230 Guy Lafleur 1.50 4.00
231 Lanny McDonald 1.00 2.50
232 Gilbert Perreault 1.25 3.00
233 Jean Beliveau 1.25 3.00
234 Johnny Bucyk 1.25 3.00
235 Gordie Howe 2.00 5.00
236 Wayne Gretzky 6.00 15.00
237 Bernie Geoffrion 1.25 3.00
238 Red Kelly .75 2.00
239 Stan Mikita 1.25 3.00
240 Bryan Trottier 1.00 2.50
241 J-S Giguere 1.00 2.50
242 Sergei Fedorov 1.25 3.00
243 Teemu Selanne 1.25 3.00
244 Ilya Kovalchuk 1.50 4.00
245 Marian Hossa 1.00 2.50
246 Patrice Bergeron 1.25 3.00
247 Joe Thornton 2.00 5.00
248 Jarome Iginla 1.50 4.00
249 Miikka Kiprusoff 1.25 3.00
250 Nikolai Khabibulin 1.25 3.00

2005-06 Beehive Beige

*STARS: 5X TO 12X BASE HI
*ROOKIES: .2X TO .5X
BEIGE ODDS 1:15
SKIP-NUMBERED SET
101 Sidney Crosby 30.00 80.00
102 Alexander Ovechkin 20.00 50.00

2005-06 Beehive Blue

*STARS: 4X TO 10X BASE HI
*ROOKIES: .15X TO .4X
BLUE ODDS 1:5
SKIP-NUMBERED SET

2005-06 Beehive Gold

*STARS: 10X TO 25X BASE HI
*ROOKIES: 2X TO 5X
ODDS 1:240
SKIP-NUMBERED SET
101 Sidney Crosby 125.00 250.00
102 Alexander Ovechkin 75.00 150.00

2005-06 Beehive Red

*STARS: 2X TO 5X BASE HI
*ROOKIES: .10X TO .25X
ODDS 1:2
SKIP-NUMBERED SET
101 Sidney Crosby 15.00 40.00

2005-06 Beehive Rookie Jumbos

COMPLETE SET (5) 20.00 40.00
R1 Sidney Crosby 8.00 20.00
R2 Alexander Ovechkin 3.00 8.00
R3 Jeff Carter 2.00 5.00
R4 Alexander Perezhogin 1.50 4.00
R5 Corey Perry 2.00 5.00

2005-06 Beehive Matte

*STARS: 6X TO 15X BASE HI
1-100 PRINT RUN 100 SER.#'d SETS
*ROOKIES: 1.5X TO 4X
101-180 PRINT RUN 25 SER.#'d SETS
101 Sidney Crosby 200.00 400.00

2005-06 Beehive Matted Materials

ODDS 1:7.5
MMAF Adam Foote 2.50 6.00
MMAH Ales Hemsky 2.50 6.00
MMAK Alex Kovalev 4.00 10.00
MMAR Andrew Raycroft 4.00 10.00
MMAY Alexei Yashin 2.50 6.00
MMBG Bill Guerin 2.50 6.00
MMBM Brendan Morrison 2.00 5.00
MMBR Brad Richards 4.00 10.00
MMBW Brendan Witt 2.50 6.00
MMCD Chris Drury 4.00 10.00
MMCJ Curtis Joseph 4.00 10.00
MMCO Chris Osgood 4.00 10.00
MMDA Daniel Alfredsson 4.00 10.00
MMDB Dustin Brown 2.50 6.00
MMDC Dan Cloutier 4.00 10.00
MMDE Pavol Demitra 4.00 10.00
MMDH Dany Heatley 5.00 12.00
MMDR Dwayne Roloson 4.00 10.00
MMDW Doug Weight 4.00 10.00
MMEL Eric Lindros 4.00 10.00
MMGA Mathieu Garon 4.00 10.00
MMGI Brian Gionta 2.50 6.00
MMGL Guy Lafleur 6.00 15.00
MMGM Glen Murray 2.50 6.00
MMGO Scott Gomez 4.00 10.00
MMHJ Milan Hejduk 4.00 10.00
MMHO Marian Hossa 4.00 10.00
MMHS Henrik Sedin 2.50 6.00
MMHZ Henrik Zetterberg 4.00 10.00
MMIK Ilya Kovalchuk 5.00 12.00
MMJB Jay Bouwmeester 2.50 6.00
MMJG J-S Giguere 4.00 10.00
MMJO Jose Theodore 4.00 10.00
MMJR Jeremy Roenick 5.00 12.00
MMJS Jason Spezza 4.00 10.00
MMJT Joe Thornton 6.00 15.00
MMJW Jason Williams 2.50 6.00
MMKP Keith Primeau 2.50 6.00
MMKT Keith Tkachuk 4.00 10.00
MMLN Ladislav Nagy 2.50 6.00
MMLR Luc Robitaille 4.00 10.00
MMLU Joffrey Lupul 2.50 6.00
MMMB Martin Brodeur 8.00 20.00
MMMC Bryan McCabe 2.50 6.00
MMMD Marc Denis 4.00 10.00
MMMF Manny Fernandez 4.00 10.00
MMMG Martin Gerber 4.00 10.00
MMMH Marcel Hossa 2.50 6.00
MMMI Milan Michalek 2.50 6.00
MMMK Miikka Kiprusoff 4.00 10.00
MMML Mario Lemieux 12.00 30.00
MMMM Mike Modano 5.00 12.00
MMMN Markus Naslund 4.00 10.00
MMMP Mark Parrish 2.50 6.00
MMMR Michael Ryder 4.00 10.00
MMMS Mats Sundin 4.00 10.00
MMMT Marty Turco 4.00 10.00
MMMW Brenden Morrow 4.00 10.00
MMNA Nik Antropov 2.50 6.00
MMNH Nathan Horton 2.50 6.00
MMNK Nikolai Khabibulin 4.00 10.00
MMOJ Olli Jokinen 4.00 10.00
MMPA Patrik Elias 4.00 10.00
MMPB Pierre-Marc Bouchard 2.50 6.00
MMPD Pavel Datsyuk 4.00 10.00
MMPE Michael Peca 2.50 6.00
MMPF Peter Forsberg 5.00 12.00
MMRB Rob Blake 4.00 10.00
MMRE Robert Esche 4.00 10.00
MMRM Ryan Miller 4.00 10.00
MMRN Rick Nash 5.00 12.00
MMSA Joe Sakic 6.00 15.00
MMSC Sidney Crosby 40.00 80.00
MMSF Sergei Fedorov 4.00 10.00
MMSG Simon Gagne 4.00 10.00
MMSK Saku Koivu 4.00 10.00
MMSL Martin St. Louis 4.00 10.00
MMSS Sergei Samsonov 4.00 10.00
MMST Matt Stajan 2.50 6.00
MMSY Steve Yzerman 8.00 20.00
MMTB Todd Bertuzzi 4.00 10.00
MMTC Ty Conklin 4.00 10.00
MMWG Wayne Gretzky 15.00 40.00

2005-06 Beehive Matted Materials Remarkable

AU 2.5X to 4X MATTED MATERIALS
PRINT RUN 50 SER.#'d SETS
RMSC Sidney Crosby 300.00 500.00

2005-06 Beehive PhotoGraphs

ODDS 1:60
PGAO Alexander Ovechkin 25.00 60.00
PGBH Bobby Hull 40.00 100.00
PGCO Corey Perry 10.00 25.00
PGCP Chris Pronger 12.00 30.00
PGDW Doug Weight 8.00 20.00
PGES Eric Staal 12.00 30.00
PGGH Gordie Howe 50.00 125.00
PGGL Guy LaFleur 30.00 80.00
PGJC Jeff Carter 10.00 25.00
PGJI Jarome Iginla 15.00 40.00
PGJS Jason Spezza 10.00 25.00
PGJT Joe Thornton 12.00 30.00
PGLA Guy Lapointe 8.00 20.00
PGMB Mike Bossy 10.00 25.00
PGMD Marcel Dionne 10.00 25.00
PGMM Mike Modano 12.00 30.00
PGMN Markus Naslund 8.00 20.00
PGMT Marty Turco 8.00 20.00
PGPE Phil Esposito SP 40.00 80.00
PGRB Ray Bourque 30.00 80.00
PGRN Rick Nash 12.00 30.00
PGSC Sidney Crosby 150.00 250.00
PGSL Martin St. Louis 8.00 20.00
PGTE Tony Esposito 20.00 50.00
PGWG Wayne Gretzky SP 200.00 300.00

2005-06 Beehive Signature Scrapbook

ODDS 1:30
SSAA Andrew Alberts 3.00 8.00
SSAM Andrej Meszaros 3.00 8.00
SSAO Alexander Ovechkin 30.00 80.00
SSAP Alexander Perezhogin 8.00 20.00
SSAR Andrew Raycroft 6.00 15.00
SSAS Anthony Stewart 5.00 12.00
SSBA Matthew Barnaby 3.00 8.00
SSBB Brandon Bochenski 3.00 8.00
SSBC Bobby Clarke 12.00 30.00
SSBE Steve Bernier 8.00 20.00
SSBM Brenden Morrow 5.00 12.00
SSBO Mike Bossy SP 20.00 50.00
SSBP Brad Park 6.00 15.00
SSBR Brad Richards 6.00 15.00
SSBS Borje Salming 8.00 20.00
SSBU Peter Budaj 6.00 15.00
SSCB Cam Barker 3.00 8.00
SSCC Chris Campoli 3.00 8.00
SSCH Jonathan Cheechoo 8.00 20.00
SSCK Chris Kunitz 5.00 12.00
SSCL Ryane Clowe 3.00 8.00
SSCN Craig Conroy 3.00 8.00
SSCO Braydon Coburn 5.00 12.00
SSCP Corey Perry 8.00 20.00
SSCS Cory Stillman 3.00 8.00
SSCW Cam Ward 8.00 20.00
SSDA Daniel Alfredsson 8.00 20.00
SSDC Don Cherry 15.00 40.00
SSDF Dan Fritsche 3.00 8.00
SSDH Dany Heatley SP 20.00 50.00
SSDI Dickie Moore 6.00 15.00
SSDK Duncan Keith 3.00 8.00
SSDL David Leneveu 5.00 12.00
SSDM Darren McCarty 6.00 15.00
SSDP Dion Phaneuf 15.00 40.00
SSDS Derek Sanderson 8.00 20.00
SSDT Dave Taylor 5.00 12.00
SSEA Patrick Eaves 6.00 15.00
SSED Eric Daze 3.00 8.00
SSFC Fred Cusick 3.00 8.00
SSFT Fedor Tjutin 3.00 8.00
SSGB Gilbert Brule 5.00 12.00
SSGH Gordie Howe SP 60.00 150.00
SSGL Guy Lafleur SP 50.00 100.00
SSGP Gilbert Perreault 10.00 25.00
SSHO Marian Hossa 6.00 15.00
SSHV Martin Havlat 5.00 12.00
SSHZ Henrik Zetterberg 10.00 25.00
SSJB Jay Bouwmeester SP 15.00 40.00
SSJC Jeff Carter 8.00 20.00
SSJF Johan Franzen 6.00 15.00
SSJH Jim Howard 6.00 15.00
SSJI Jarome Iginla SP 12.00 30.00
SSJM Jay McClement 3.00 8.00
SSJO Jeff O'Neill 3.00 8.00
SSJR Jeremy Roenick 15.00 40.00
SSJS Jason Spezza SP
SSJT Joe Thornton SP 20.00 40.00
SSJV Josef Vasicek 3.00 8.00
SSKM Ken Morrow 3.00 8.00
SSKN Kevin Nastiuk 5.00 12.00
SSKP Keith Primeau SP 8.00 20.00
SSLM Lanny McDonald 5.00 12.00
SSLR Luc Robitaille SP 30.00 80.00
SSLS Lee Stempniak 3.00 8.00
SSLU Roberto Luongo SP 12.00 30.00
SSMB Martin Brodeur SP 75.00 150.00
SSMC Mike Cammalleri 8.00 20.00
SSMD Marcel Dionne SP 15.00 40.00
SSMG Marian Gaborik SP 40.00 80.00
SSMH Marcel Hossa 3.00 8.00
SSMI Miroslav Satan 3.00 8.00
SSMJ Milan Jurcina 3.00 8.00
SSMK Mikko Koivu 8.00 20.00
SSMM Mike Modano SP 20.00 50.00
SSMN Markus Naslund SP 12.00 30.00
SSMP Michael Peca 3.00 8.00
SSMR Mike Ribeiro SP 8.00 20.00
SSMS Marco Sturm 3.00 8.00
SSMT Marty Turco 6.00 15.00
SSMU Larry Murphy 3.00 8.00
SSNH Nathan Horton 3.00 8.00
SSNK Nikolai Khabibulin 8.00 20.00
SSNY Michael Nylander 3.00 8.00
SSNZ Nikolai Zherdev 5.00 12.00
SSON Owen Nolan 5.00 12.00
SSPB Patrice Bergeron SP 12.00 30.00
SSPE Phil Esposito SP 20.00 50.00
SSPN Petteri Nokelainen 3.00 8.00
SSPP Petr Prucha 6.00 15.00
SSRB Rob Blake 5.00 12.00
SSRE Robert Esche 3.00 8.00
SSRI Michael Richards 6.00 15.00
SSRL Reggie Leach 5.00 12.00
SSRM Ryan Miller 6.00 15.00
SSRN Rick Nash SP 15.00 40.00
SSRS Ryan Smyth 12.00 30.00
SSRV Rogie Vachon 8.00 20.00
SSRW Ryan Whitney 6.00 15.00
SSRY Michael Ryder 6.00 15.00
SSSB Scotty Bowman SP 20.00 40.00
SSSC Sidney Crosby SP 175.00 300.00
SSSD Shane Doan 3.00 8.00
SSSE Brent Seabrook 3.00 8.00
SSSG Simon Gagne 6.00 15.00
SSSL Martin St. Louis SP 12.00 30.00
SSST Alexander Steen 8.00 20.00
SSSZ Sergei Zubov 3.00 8.00
SSTA Tyler Arnason 3.00 8.00
SSTB Todd Bertuzzi SP 6.00 15.00
SSTE Tony Esposito SP 20.00 40.00
SSTO Terry O'Reilly 6.00 15.00
SSTV Thomas Vanek 10.00 25.00
SSVP Vaclav Prospal 3.00 8.00
SSWC Wayne Cashman 6.00 15.00
SSYD Yann Danis 6.00 15.00
SSZC Zdeno Chara 5.00 12.00
SSZP Zach Parise 8.00 20.00

2006-07 Beehive

COMPLETE SET w/o SPs (100) 12.00 30.00
5 X 7 ONE PER PACK
1 Alexander Ovechkin 1.00 2.50
2 Olaf Kolzig .25 .60
3 Markus Naslund .25 .60
4 Roberto Luongo .30 .75
5 Mats Sundin .25 .60
6 Michael Peca .12 .30
7 Alexander Steen .20 .50
8 Andrew Raycroft .20 .50
9 Vincent Lecavalier .25 .60
10 Brad Richards .20 .50
11 Martin St. Louis .20 .50
12 Manny Legace .20 .50
13 Keith Tkachuk .20 .50
14 Doug Weight .12 .30
15 Joe Thornton .40 1.00
16 Patrick Marleau .20 .50
17 Jonathan Cheechoo .25 .60
18 Vesa Toskala .20 .50
19 Sidney Crosby 2.00 5.00
20 Mark Recchi .12 .30
21 Marc-Andre Fleury .25 .60
22 Colby Armstrong .12 .30
23 Shane Doan .12 .30
24 Ed Jovanovski .12 .30
25 Jeremy Roenick .30 .75
26 Owen Nolan .20 .50
27 Peter Forsberg .40 1.00
28 Simon Gagne .25 .60
29 Jeff Carter .25 .60
30 Joni Pitkanen .12 .30
31 Jason Spezza .25 .60
32 Dany Heatley .30 .75
33 Martin Gerber .25 .60
34 Daniel Alfredsson .20 .50
35 Jaromir Jagr .40 1.00
36 Brendan Shanahan .25 .60
37 Henrik Lundqvist .30 .75
38 Alexei Yashin .12 .30
39 Rick DiPietro .20 .50
40 Miroslav Satan .12 .30
41 Martin Brodeur .75 2.00
42 Patrik Elias .12 .30
43 Brian Gionta .12 .30
44 Paul Kariya .25 .60
45 Tomas Vokoun .20 .50
46 Jason Arnott .12 .30
47 Saku Koivu .25 .60
48 Cristobal Huet .30 .75
49 Michael Ryder .20 .50
50 Alexei Kovalev .12 .30
51 Marian Gaborik .30 .75
52 Manny Fernandez .20 .50
53 Pavol Demitra .12 .30
54 Mark Parrish .12 .30
55 Alexander Frolov .12 .30
56 Rob Blake .20 .50
57 Ed Belfour .25 .60
58 Todd Bertuzzi .20 .50
59 Olli Jokinen .12 .30
60 Ales Hemsky .12 .30
61 Jarret Stoll .12 .30
62 Ryan Smyth .20 .50
63 Joffrey Lupul .12 .30
64 Henrik Zetterberg .25 .60
65 Dominik Hasek .40 1.00
66 Pavel Datsyuk .20 .50

67 Nicklas Lidstrom .25 .60
68 Mike Modano .25 .60
69 Marty Turco .20 .50
70 Eric Lindros .25 .60
71 Rick Nash .25 .60
72 Pascal LeClaire .20 .50
73 Gilbert Brule .25 .60
74 Sergei Fedorov .25 .60
75 Joe Sakic .50 1.25
76 Milan Hejduk .12 .30
77 Jose Theodore .25 .60
78 Marek Svatos .12 .30
79 Nikolai Khabibulin .25 .60
80 Tuomo Ruutu .12 .30
81 Martin Havlat .20 .50
82 Eric Staal .25 .60
83 Cam Ward .25 .60
84 Rod Brind`Amour .20 .50
85 Jarome Iginla .30 .75
86 Miikka Kiprusoff .25 .60
87 Alex Tanguay .20 .50
88 Dion Phaneuf .30 .75
89 Chris Drury .12 .30
90 Ryan Miller .25 .60
91 Patrice Bergeron .25 .60
92 Hannu Toivonen .20 .50
93 Brad Boyes .12 .30
94 Zdeno Chara .12 .30
95 Ilya Kovalchuk .30 .75
96 Kari Lehtonen .25 .60
97 Marian Hossa .20 .50
98 Teemu Selanne .25 .60
99 Chris Pronger .20 .50
100 Jean-Sebastien Giguere .20 .50
101 David McKee RC 1.50 4.00
102 Ryan Shannon RC 1.25 3.00
103 Shane O'Brien RC 1.25 3.00
104 Matt Lashoff RC 1.25 3.00
105 Phil Kessel RC 2.50 6.00
106 Mark Stuart RC 1.25 3.00
107 Yan Stastny RC 1.25 3.00
108 Clarke MacArthur RC 1.25 3.00
109 Drew Stafford RC 2.50 6.00
110 Brandon Prust RC 1.25 3.00
111 Dustin Boyd RC 2.00 5.00
112 Michael Blunden RC 1.25 3.00
113 Dave Bolland RC 1.25 3.00
114 Paul Stastny RC 3.00 8.00
115 Fredrik Norrena RC 1.50 4.00
116 Loui Eriksson RC 1.25 3.00
117 Tomas Kopecky RC 2.00 5.00
118 Stefan Liv RC 1.50 4.00
119 Jeff Drouin-Deslauriers RC 1.25 3.00
120 Alexei Mikhnov RC 1.25 3.00
121 Ladislav Smid RC 1.25 3.00
122 Patrick Thoresen RC 2.00 5.00
123 Marc-Antoine Pouliot RC 1.50 4.00
124 David Booth RC 1.25 3.00
125 Anze Kopitar RC 3.00 8.00
126 Patrick O'Sullivan RC 1.50 4.00
127 Konstantin Pushkaryov RC 1.25 3.00
128 Benoit Pouliot RC 2.00 5.00
129 Mikhail Grabovski RC 1.25 3.00
130 Guillaume Latendresse RC 3.00 8.00
131 Alexander Radulov RC 3.00 8.00
132 Shea Weber RC 1.50 4.00
133 Travis Zajac RC 2.00 5.00
134 Johnny Oduya RC 1.25 3.00
135 Blake Comeau RC 1.25 3.00
136 Nigel Dawes RC 1.25 3.00
137 Jarkko Immonen RC 1.25 3.00
138 Josh Hennessy RC 1.25 3.00
139 Kelly Guard RC 1.25 3.00
140 Martin Houle RC 1.25 3.00
141 Ryan Potulny RC 2.00 5.00
142 Enver Lisin RC 1.25 3.00
143 Keith Yandle RC 1.25 3.00
144 Evgeni Malkin RC 6.00 15.00
145 Kristopher Letang RC 1.50 4.00
146 Jordan Staal RC 6.00 15.00
147 Michel Ouellet RC 2.00 5.00
148 Noah Welch RC 1.25 3.00
149 Joe Pavelski RC 2.00 5.00
150 Marc-Edouard Vlasic RC 1.25 3.00
151 Matt Carle RC 1.50 4.00
152 Marek Schwarz RC 2.00 5.00
153 Blair Jones RC 1.25 3.00
154 Ian White RC 1.25 3.00
155 Brendan Bell RC 1.25 3.00
156 Kris Newbury RC 1.25 3.00
157 Jesse Schultz RC 1.25 3.00
158 Alexander Edler RC 1.25 3.00
159 Luc Bourdon RC 1.50 4.00
160 Eric Fehr RC 1.50 4.00
161 Alexander Ovechkin 2.50 6.00
162 Roberto Luongo 1.50 4.00
163 Markus Naslund 1.25 3.00
164 Michael Peca .60 1.50
165 Mats Sundin 1.25 3.00
166 Vincent Lecavalier 1.25 3.00
167 Joe Thornton 2.00 5.00
168 Jonathan Cheechoo 1.25 3.00
169 Sidney Crosby 6.00 15.00
170 Mario Lemieux 4.00 10.00
171 Marc-Andre Fleury 1.25 3.00
172 Jeremy Roenick 1.50 4.00
173 Shane Doan .60 1.50
174 Bobby Clarke 1.25 3.00
175 Peter Forsberg 2.00 5.00
176 Simon Gagne 1.25 3.00
177 Jason Spezza 1.25 3.00
178 Dany Heatley 1.50 4.00
179 Jaromir Jagr 2.00 5.00
180 Brendan Shanahan 1.25 3.00
181 Henrik Lundqvist 1.50 4.00
182 Mike Bossy 1.00 2.50
183 Billy Smith 1.25 3.00
184 Miroslav Satan .60 1.50
185 Martin Brodeur 2.50 6.00
186 Patrik Elias .60 1.50
187 Paul Kariya 1.25 3.00
188 Tomas Vokoun 1.00 2.50
189 Patrick Roy 4.00 10.00
190 Michael Ryder 1.00 2.50
191 Saku Koivu 1.25 3.00
192 Guy Lafleur 2.00 5.00
193 Marian Gaborik 1.50 4.00
194 Manny Fernandez 1.00 2.50
195 Rob Blake 1.00 2.50
196 Alexander Frolov .60 1.50
197 Luc Robitaille 1.00 2.50
198 Marcel Dionne 1.25 3.00
199 Ed Belfour 1.25 3.00
200 Todd Bertuzzi 1.00 2.50
201 Ryan Smyth 1.00 2.50
202 Ales Hemsky .60 1.50
203 Grant Fuhr 1.50 4.00
204 Gordie Howe 2.50 6.00
205 Henrik Zetterberg 1.25 3.00
206 Nicklas Lidstrom 1.25 3.00
207 Dominik Hasek 2.00 5.00
208 Mike Modano 1.50 4.00
209 Marty Turco 1.00 2.50
210 Eric Lindros 1.25 3.00
211 Rick Nash 1.50 4.00
212 Pascal LeClaire 1.00 2.50
213 Joe Sakic 2.50 6.00
214 Milan Hejduk .60 1.50
215 Jose Theodore 1.25 3.00
216 Ray Bourque 2.00 5.00
217 Bobby Hull 1.50 4.00
218 Tony Esposito 1.25 3.00
219 Martin Havlat 1.00 2.50
220 Cam Ward 1.25 3.00
221 Eric Staal 1.25 3.00
222 Jarome Iginla 1.50 4.00
223 Dion Phaneuf 1.50 4.00
224 Miikka Kiprusoff 1.25 3.00
225 Alex Tanguay 1.00 2.50
226 Chris Drury .60 1.50
227 Ryan Miller 1.25 3.00
228 Patrice Bergeron 1.25 3.00
229 Cam Neely 1.50 4.00
230 Brad Boyes .60 1.50
231 Bobby Orr 3.00 8.00
232 Ilya Kovalchuk 1.50 4.00
233 Kari Lehtonen 1.25 3.00
234 Teemu Selanne 1.25 3.00
235 Chris Pronger 1.00 2.50

2006-07 Beehive Blue

*STARS: 3X TO 8X BASE HI
*RCs: .3X TO .8X BASE HI
STATED ODDS 1:15
SKIP-NUMBERED SET
19 Sidney Crosby 12.00 30.00
144 Evgeni Malkin 12.00 30.00

2006-07 Beehive Gold

*STARS: 10X TO 25X BASE HI
*RCs: NOT PRICED DUE TO SCARCITY
STATED ODDS 1:240
SKIP-NUMBERED SET
1 Alexander Ovechkin 20.00 50.00
3 Markus Naslund 6.00 15.00
4 Roberto Luongo 8.00 20.00
5 Mats Sundin 6.00 15.00
8 Andrew Raycroft 5.00 12.00
9 Vincent Lecavalier 6.00 15.00
11 Martin St. Louis 5.00 12.00
13 Keith Tkachuk 5.00 12.00
14 Doug Weight 3.00 8.00
15 Joe Thornton 10.00 25.00
16 Patrick Marleau 5.00 12.00
17 Jonathan Cheechoo 6.00 15.00
19 Sidney Crosby 50.00 125.00
21 Marc-Andre Fleury 6.00 15.00
23 Shane Doan 3.00 8.00
25 Jeremy Roenick 8.00 20.00
27 Peter Forsberg 10.00 25.00
28 Simon Gagne 6.00 15.00
31 Jason Spezza 6.00 15.00
32 Dany Heatley 8.00 20.00
35 Jaromir Jagr 10.00 25.00
36 Brendan Shanahan 6.00 15.00
37 Henrik Lundqvist 8.00 20.00
38 Alexei Yashin 3.00 8.00
40 Miroslav Satan 3.00 8.00
41 Martin Brodeur 20.00 50.00
42 Patrik Elias 3.00 8.00
43 Brian Gionta 3.00 8.00
44 Paul Kariya 6.00 15.00
45 Tomas Vokoun 5.00 12.00
47 Saku Koivu 6.00 15.00
49 Michael Ryder 5.00 12.00
51 Marian Gaborik 8.00 20.00
52 Manny Fernandez 5.00 12.00
55 Alexander Frolov 3.00 8.00
56 Rob Blake 5.00 12.00
57 Ed Belfour 6.00 15.00
60 Ales Hemsky 3.00 8.00
62 Ryan Smyth 5.00 12.00
64 Henrik Zetterberg 6.00 15.00
65 Dominik Hasek 10.00 25.00
66 Pavel Datsyuk 5.00 12.00
67 Nicklas Lidstrom 6.00 15.00
68 Mike Modano 6.00 15.00
69 Marty Turco 5.00 12.00
70 Eric Lindros 6.00 15.00
71 Rick Nash 6.00 15.00
74 Sergei Fedorov 6.00 15.00
75 Joe Sakic 12.00 30.00
76 Milan Hejduk 3.00 8.00
77 Jose Theodore 6.00 15.00
79 Nikolai Khabibulin 6.00 15.00
81 Martin Havlat 5.00 12.00
82 Eric Staal 6.00 15.00
83 Cam Ward 6.00 15.00
85 Jarome Iginla 8.00 20.00
86 Miikka Kiprusoff 6.00 15.00
88 Dion Phaneuf 8.00 20.00
89 Chris Drury 3.00 8.00
90 Ryan Miller 6.00 15.00
91 Patrice Bergeron 6.00 15.00
94 Zdeno Chara 3.00 8.00
95 Ilya Kovalchuk 8.00 20.00
96 Kari Lehtonen 6.00 15.00
97 Marian Hossa 5.00 12.00
98 Teemu Selanne 6.00 15.00
99 Chris Pronger 5.00 12.00
PT President's Trophy
SC Stanley Cup 20.00 50.00
100 Jean-Sebastien Giguere 5.00 12.00
105 Phil Kessel
109 Drew Stafford
111 Dustin Boyd
114 Paul Stastny
116 Loui Eriksson
125 Anze Kopitar
126 Patrick O'Sullivan
128 Benoit Pouliot
130 Guillaume Latendresse
131 Alexander Radulov
133 Travis Zajac
144 Evgeni Malkin
146 Jordan Staal
151 Matt Carle
157 Jesse Schultz
ART Art Ross Trophy 15.00 40.00
BMT Bill Masterton Memorial 15.00 40.00
CCT Clarence Campbell Trophy 15.0040.00
CMT Calder Memorial Trophy 15.00 40.00
CST Conn Smythe Trophy 15.00 40.00
FST Frank Selke Memorial 15.00 40.00
HMT Hart Memorial Trophy 15.00 40.00
JAA Jack Adams Award 15.00 40.00
KCT King Clancy Trophy 15.00 40.00
LBT Lady Byng Trophy 15.00 40.00
LBT Lady Byng Trophy 15.00 40.00
MRT Rocket Richard Trophy 15.00 40.00
PWT Prince of Wales Trophy 15.00 40.00
VT Vezina Trophy 20.00 50.00
WJT William B. Jennings Trophy 15.00 40.00
LBP Lester B. Pearson Award 15.00 40.00

2006-07 Beehive Matte

*STARS: 5X TO 12X BASE HI
*RCs: .75X TO 2X BASE HI
PRINT RUN 100 #'d SETS
1 Alexander Ovechkin 10.00 25.00
2 Olaf Kolzig 3.00 8.00
3 Markus Naslund 3.00 8.00
4 Roberto Luongo 4.00 10.00
5 Mats Sundin 3.00 8.00
6 Michael Peca 1.50 4.00
7 Alexander Steen 2.50 6.00
8 Andrew Raycroft 2.50 6.00
9 Vincent Lecavalier 3.00 8.00
10 Brad Richards 2.50 6.00
11 Martin St. Louis 2.50 6.00
12 Manny Legace 2.50 6.00
13 Keith Tkachuk 2.50 6.00
14 Doug Weight 1.50 4.00
15 Joe Thornton 5.00 12.00
16 Patrick Marleau 2.50 6.00
17 Jonathan Cheechoo 3.00 8.00
18 Vesa Toskala 2.50 6.00
19 Sidney Crosby 30.00 80.00
20 Mark Recchi 1.50 4.00
21 Marc-Andre Fleury 3.00 8.00
22 Colby Armstrong 1.50 4.00
23 Shane Doan 1.50 4.00
24 Ed Jovanovski 1.50 4.00
25 Jeremy Roenick 4.00 10.00
26 Owen Nolan 2.50 6.00
27 Peter Forsberg 5.00 12.00
28 Simon Gagne 3.00 8.00
29 Jeff Carter 3.00 8.00
30 Joni Pitkanen 1.50 4.00
31 Jason Spezza 3.00 8.00
32 Dany Heatley 4.00 10.00
33 Martin Gerber 3.00 8.00
34 Daniel Alfredsson 2.50 6.00
35 Jaromir Jagr 5.00 12.00
36 Brendan Shanahan 3.00 8.00
37 Henrik Lundqvist 4.00 10.00
38 Alexei Yashin 1.50 4.00
39 Rick DiPietro 2.50 6.00
40 Miroslav Satan 1.50 4.00
41 Martin Brodeur 10.00 25.00
42 Patrik Elias 1.50 4.00
43 Brian Gionta 1.50 4.00
44 Paul Kariya 3.00 8.00
45 Tomas Vokoun 2.50 6.00
46 Jason Arnott 1.50 4.00
47 Saku Koivu 3.00 8.00
48 Cristobal Huet 4.00 10.00
49 Michael Ryder 2.50 6.00
50 Alexei Kovalev 1.50 4.00
51 Marian Gaborik 4.00 10.00
52 Manny Fernandez 2.50 6.00
53 Pavol Demitra 1.50 4.00
54 Mark Parrish 1.50 4.00
55 Alexander Frolov 1.50 4.00
56 Rob Blake 2.50 6.00
57 Ed Belfour 3.00 8.00
58 Todd Bertuzzi 2.50 6.00
59 Olli Jokinen 1.50 4.00
60 Ales Hemsky 1.50 4.00
61 Jarret Stoll 1.50 4.00
62 Ryan Smyth 2.50 6.00
63 Joffrey Lupul 1.50 4.00
64 Henrik Zetterberg 3.00 8.00
65 Dominik Hasek 5.00 12.00
66 Pavel Datsyuk 2.50 6.00
67 Nicklas Lidstrom 3.00 8.00
68 Mike Modano 3.00 8.00
69 Marty Turco 2.50 6.00
70 Eric Lindros 3.00 8.00
71 Rick Nash 3.00 8.00
72 Pascal LeClaire 2.50 6.00
73 Gilbert Brule 3.00 8.00
74 Sergei Fedorov 3.00 8.00
75 Joe Sakic 6.00 15.00
76 Milan Hejduk 1.50 4.00
77 Jose Theodore 3.00 8.00
78 Marek Svatos 1.50 4.00
79 Nikolai Khabibulin 3.00 8.00
80 Tuomo Ruutu 1.50 4.00
81 Martin Havlat 2.50 6.00
82 Eric Staal 3.00 8.00
83 Cam Ward 3.00 8.00
84 Rod Brind`Amour 2.50 6.00
85 Jarome Iginla 4.00 10.00
86 Miikka Kiprusoff 3.00 8.00
87 Alex Tanguay 2.50 6.00
88 Dion Phaneuf 4.00 10.00
89 Chris Drury 1.50 4.00
90 Ryan Miller 3.00 8.00
91 Patrice Bergeron 3.00 8.00
92 Hannu Toivonen 2.50 6.00
93 Brad Boyes 1.50 4.00
94 Zdeno Chara 1.50 4.00
95 Ilya Kovalchuk 4.00 10.00
96 Kari Lehtonen 3.00 8.00
97 Marian Hossa 2.50 6.00
98 Teemu Selanne 3.00 8.00
99 Chris Pronger 2.50 6.00
100 Jean-Sebastien Giguere 2.50 6.00
101 David McKee 5.00 12.00
102 Ryan Shannon 3.00 8.00
103 Shane O'Brien 3.00 8.00
104 Matt Lashoff 3.00 8.00
105 Phil Kessel 10.00 25.00
106 Mark Stuart 3.00 8.00
107 Yan Stastny 3.00 8.00
108 Clarke MacArthur 3.00 8.00
109 Drew Stafford 8.00 20.00
110 Brandon Prust 3.00 8.00
111 Dustin Boyd 5.00 12.00
112 Michael Blunden 3.00 8.00
113 Dave Bolland 3.00 8.00
114 Paul Stastny 15.00 40.00
115 Fredrik Norrena 5.00 12.00
116 Loui Eriksson 3.00 8.00
117 Tomas Kopecky 5.00 12.00
118 Stefan Liv 5.00 12.00
119 Jeff Drouin-Deslauriers 3.00 8.00
120 Alexei Mikhnov 3.00 8.00
121 Ladislav Smid 3.00 8.00
122 Patrick Thoresen 5.00 12.00
123 Marc-Antoine Pouliot 5.00 12.00
124 David Booth 3.00 8.00
125 Anze Kopitar 12.00 30.00
126 Patrick O'Sullivan 5.00 12.00
127 Konstantin Pushkaryov 3.00 8.00
128 Benoit Pouliot 5.00 12.00
129 Mikhail Grabovski 3.00 8.00
130 Guillaume Latendresse 12.00 30.00
131 Alexander Radulov 10.00 25.00
132 Shea Weber 5.00 12.00
133 Travis Zajac 6.00 15.00
134 Johnny Oduya 3.00 8.00
135 Blake Comeau 3.00 8.00
136 Nigel Dawes 3.00 8.00
137 Jarkko Immonen 3.00 8.00
138 Josh Hennessy 3.00 8.00
139 Kelly Guard 3.00 8.00
140 Martin Houle 3.00 8.00
141 Ryan Potulny 5.00 12.00
142 Enver Lisin 3.00 8.00
143 Keith Yandle 3.00 8.00
144 Evgeni Malkin 20.00 50.00
145 Kristopher Letang 5.00 12.00
146 Jordan Staal 20.00 50.00
147 Michel Ouellet 6.00 15.00
148 Noah Welch 3.00 8.00
149 Joe Pavelski 5.00 12.00
150 Marc-Edouard Vlasic 3.00 8.00
151 Matt Carle 5.00 12.00
152 Marek Schwarz 5.00 12.00
153 Blair Jones 3.00 8.00
154 Ian White 3.00 8.00
155 Brendan Bell 3.00 8.00
156 Kris Newbury 3.00 8.00
157 Jesse Schultz 3.00 8.00
158 Alexander Edler 3.00 8.00
159 Luc Bourdon 5.00 12.00
160 Eric Fehr 5.00 12.00

2006-07 Beehive Red Facsimile Signatures

*STARS: 2X TO 5X HI
*RCs:.2X TO .5X HI
SKIP-NUMBERED SET
STATED ODDS 1:8
1 Alexander Ovechkin 4.00 10.00
3 Markus Naslund 1.25 3.00
4 Roberto Luongo 1.50 4.00
5 Mats Sundin 1.25 3.00
8 Andrew Raycroft 1.00 2.50
9 Vincent Lecavalier 1.25 3.00
10 Brad Richards 1.00 2.50
11 Martin St. Louis 1.00 2.50
13 Keith Tkachuk 1.00 2.50
15 Joe Thornton 2.00 5.00
16 Patrick Marleau 1.00 2.50
17 Jonathan Cheechoo 1.25 3.00
19 Sidney Crosby 10.00 25.00
21 Marc-Andre Fleury 1.25 3.00
23 Shane Doan .60 1.50
24 Ed Jovanovski .60 1.50
25 Jeremy Roenick 1.50 4.00
26 Owen Nolan 1.00 2.50
27 Peter Forsberg 2.00 5.00
28 Simon Gagne 1.25 3.00
31 Jason Spezza 1.25 3.00
32 Dany Heatley 1.50 4.00
34 Daniel Alfredsson 1.00 2.50
35 Jaromir Jagr 2.00 5.00
36 Brendan Shanahan 1.25 3.00
37 Henrik Lundqvist 1.50 4.00
38 Alexei Yashin .60 1.50
40 Miroslav Satan .60 1.50
41 Martin Brodeur 4.00 10.00
42 Patrik Elias .60 1.50
43 Brian Gionta .60 1.50
44 Paul Kariya 1.25 3.00
45 Tomas Vokoun 1.50 4.00
47 Saku Koivu 2.00 5.00
48 Cristobal Huet 2.50 6.00
49 Michael Ryder 1.00 2.50
51 Marian Gaborik 1.50 4.00
52 Manny Fernandez 1.00 2.50
55 Alexander Frolov .60 1.50
56 Rob Blake 1.00 2.50
57 Ed Belfour 1.25 3.00
58 Todd Bertuzzi 1.00 2.50
59 Olli Jokinen .60 1.50
60 Ales Hemsky .60 1.50
62 Ryan Smyth 1.00 2.50
64 Henrik Zetterberg 1.25 3.00
65 Dominik Hasek 3.00 8.00
66 Pavel Datsyuk 1.00 2.50
67 Nicklas Lidstrom 1.25 3.00
68 Mike Modano 2.00 5.00
69 Marty Turco 1.00 2.50
70 Eric Lindros 1.25 3.00
71 Rick Nash 1.25 3.00
72 Pascal LeClaire 1.00 2.50
74 Sergei Fedorov 1.25 3.00
75 Joe Sakic 2.50 6.00
76 Milan Hejduk .60 1.50
77 Jose Theodore 1.25 3.00
79 Nikolai Khabibulin 1.25 3.00
81 Martin Havlat 1.00 2.50
82 Eric Staal 1.25 3.00
83 Cam Ward 1.25 3.00
85 Jarome Iginla 1.50 4.00
86 Miikka Kiprusoff 1.25 3.00
87 Alex Tanguay 1.00 2.50
88 Dion Phaneuf 1.50 4.00
89 Chris Drury .60 1.50
90 Ryan Miller 1.25 3.00
91 Patrice Bergeron 1.25 3.00
95 Ilya Kovalchuk 1.50 4.00
96 Kari Lehtonen 1.25 3.00
97 Marian Hossa 1.00 2.50
98 Teemu Selanne 1.25 3.00
99 Chris Pronger 1.00 2.50
100 Jean-Sebastien Giguere 1.00 2.50
105 Phil Kessel 2.50 6.00
109 Drew Stafford 2.50 6.00
111 Dustin Boyd 1.25 3.00
114 Paul Stastny 4.00 10.00
116 Loui Eriksson .75 2.00
117 Tomas Kopecky 1.50 4.00
121 Ladislav Smid .75 2.00
123 Marc-Antoine Pouliot 1.25 3.00
125 Anze Kopitar 4.00 10.00
126 Patrick O'Sullivan 1.50 4.00
128 Benoit Pouliot 1.25 3.00
130 Guillaume Latendresse 3.00 8.00
131 Alexander Radulov 2.50 6.00
132 Shea Weber 1.50 4.00
133 Travis Zajac 1.50 4.00
137 Nigel Dawes .75 2.00
138 Josh Hennessy .75 2.00
141 Ryan Potulny 1.25 3.00
142 Enver Lisin .75 2.00
144 Evgeni Malkin 8.00 20.00
146 Jordan Staal 5.00 12.00
151 Matt Carle 1.50 4.00
157 Jesse Schultz .75 2.00
159 Luc Bourdon 1.25 3.00
160 Eric Fehr 1.25 3.00

2006-07 Beehive Wood

*STARS: 1.5X TO 4X BASE HI
*RCs: .15X TO .4X BASE HI
STATED ODDS 1:2
SKIP-NUMBERED SET
1 Alexander Ovechkin 3.00 8.00
3 Markus Naslund 1.00 2.50
4 Roberto Luongo 1.25 3.00
5 Mats Sundin 1.00 2.50
8 Andrew Raycroft .75 2.00
9 Vincent Lecavalier 1.00 2.50
10 Brad Richards .75 2.00
11 Martin St. Louis .75 2.00
13 Keith Tkachuk .75 2.00
15 Joe Thornton 1.50 4.00
16 Patrick Marleau .75 2.00
17 Jonathan Cheechoo 1.00 2.50
19 Sidney Crosby 8.00 20.00
21 Marc-Andre Fleury 1.00 2.50
23 Shane Doan .50 1.25
24 Ed Jovanovski .50 1.25
25 Jeremy Roenick 1.25 3.00
26 Owen Nolan .75 2.00
27 Peter Forsberg 1.50 4.00
28 Simon Gagne 1.00 2.50
31 Jason Spezza 1.00 2.50
32 Dany Heatley 1.25 3.00
34 Daniel Alfredsson .75 2.00
35 Jaromir Jagr 1.50 4.00
36 Brendan Shanahan 1.00 2.50
37 Henrik Lundqvist 1.25 3.00
38 Alexei Yashin .50 1.25
40 Miroslav Satan .50 1.25
41 Martin Brodeur 3.00 8.00
42 Patrik Elias .50 1.25
43 Brian Gionta .50 1.25
44 Paul Kariya 1.00 2.50
45 Tomas Vokoun .75 2.00
47 Saku Koivu 1.00 2.50
48 Cristobal Huet 1.25 3.00
49 Michael Ryder .75 2.00
51 Marian Gaborik 1.25 3.00
52 Manny Fernandez .75 2.00
55 Alexander Frolov .50 1.25
56 Rob Blake .75 2.00
57 Ed Belfour 1.00 2.50
58 Todd Bertuzzi .75 2.00
59 Olli Jokinen .50 1.25
60 Ales Hemsky .50 1.25
62 Ryan Smyth .75 2.00
64 Henrik Zetterberg 1.00 2.50
65 Dominik Hasek 1.50 4.00
66 Pavel Datsyuk .75 2.00
67 Nicklas Lidstrom 1.00 2.50
68 Mike Modano 1.00 2.50
69 Marty Turco .75 2.00
70 Eric Lindros 1.00 2.50
71 Rick Nash 1.00 2.50
72 Pascal LeClaire .75 2.00
74 Sergei Fedorov 1.00 2.50
75 Joe Sakic 2.00 5.00
76 Milan Hejduk .50 1.25
77 Jose Theodore 1.00 2.50
79 Nikolai Khabibulin 1.00 2.50
81 Martin Havlat .75 2.00
82 Eric Staal 1.00 2.50
83 Cam Ward 1.00 2.50
85 Jarome Iginla 1.25 3.00
86 Miikka Kiprusoff 1.00 2.50
87 Alex Tanguay .75 2.00
88 Dion Phaneuf 1.25 3.00
89 Chris Drury .50 1.25
90 Ryan Miller 1.00 2.50
91 Patrice Bergeron 1.00 2.50
95 Ilya Kovalchuk 1.25 3.00
96 Kari Lehtonen 1.00 2.50
97 Marian Hossa .75 2.00
98 Teemu Selanne 1.00 2.50
99 Chris Pronger .75 2.00
100 Jean-Sebastien Giguere .75 2.00
105 Phil Kessel 1.50 4.00
109 Drew Stafford 1.25 3.00
111 Dustin Boyd .75 2.00
114 Paul Stastny 3.00 8.00
116 Loui Eriksson .50 1.25
117 Tomas Kopecky 1.00 2.50
121 Ladislav Smid .50 1.25
123 Marc-Antoine Pouliot .75 2.00
125 Anze Kopitar 2.50 6.00
126 Patrick O'Sullivan 1.00 2.50
128 Benoit Pouliot .75 2.00
130 Guillaume Latendresse 2.00 5.00
131 Alexander Radulov 1.50 4.00
132 Shea Weber 1.00 2.50
133 Travis Zajac 1.00 2.50
137 Nigel Dawes .50 1.25
138 Josh Hennessy .50 1.25
141 Ryan Potulny .75 2.00
142 Enver Lisin .50 1.25
144 Evgeni Malkin 6.00 15.00
146 Jordan Staal
151 Matt Carle
157 Jesse Schultz
159 Luc Bourdon
160 Eric Fehr

2006-07 Beehive 5 X 7 Black and White

*STARS: .6X TO 1.5X JUMBO HI
*RCs: .2X TO .5X BASE HI
STATED ODDS 1:15
SKIP-NUMBERED SET
5 Mats Sundin 2.00 5.00
17 Jonathan Cheechoo 2.00 5.00
28 Simon Gagne 2.00 5.00
45 Tomas Vokoun 1.50 4.00
47 Saku Koivu 2.00 5.00
49 Michael Ryder 1.50 4.00
51 Marian Gaborik 2.50 6.00
57 Ed Belfour 2.00 5.00
67 Nicklas Lidstrom 2.00 5.00
74 Sergei Fedorov 2.00 5.00
83 Cam Ward 2.00 5.00
85 Jarome Iginla 2.50 6.00
91 Patrice Bergeron 2.00 5.00
96 Kari Lehtonen 2.00 5.00
98 Teemu Selanne 2.00 5.00
100 Jean-Sebastien Giguere 1.50 4.00
174 Bobby Clarke 2.00 5.00
182 Mike Bossy 1.50 4.00
183 Billy Smith 2.00 5.00
192 Guy Lafleur 3.00 8.00
203 Grant Fuhr 2.50 6.00
216 Ray Bourque 2.50 6.00
217 Bobby Hull 3.00 8.00
218 Tony Esposito 2.00 5.00
229 Cam Neely 2.50 6.00

2006-07 Beehive 5 X 7 Cherry Wood

STATED ODDS 1:240
SKIP-NUMBERED SET
1 Alexander Ovechkin 10.00 25.00
15 Joe Thornton 10.00 25.00
27 Peter Forsberg 10.00 25.00
35 Jaromir Jagr
41 Martin Brodeur
65 Dominik Hasek 10.00 25.00
75 Joe Sakic 15.00 40.00
PT President's Trophy 15.00 40.00
SC Stanley Cup 40.00 80.00
VT Vezina Trophy 25.00 50.00
ART Art Ross Trophy 25.00 50.00
BMT Bill Masterton Trophy 15.00 40.00
CCT Campbell Trophy 15.00 40.00
CMT Calder Memorial Trophy 15.00 40.00
CST Conn Smythe Trophy 15.00 40.00
FST Selke Trophy 15.00 40.00
HMT Hart Memorial Trophy
JAA Jack Adams Award 15.00 40.00
JNT James Norris Trophy 15.00 40.00
KCT King Clancy Trophy 15.00 40.00
LBP Pearson Award 15.00 40.00
LBT Lady Byng Trophy 15.00 40.00
MRT Rocket Richard Trophy 15.00 40.00
PWT Prince of Wales Trophy 15.00 40.00
WJT William M. Jennings Trophy 15.00 40.00

2006-07 Beehive 5 X 7 Dark Wood

STATED ODDS 1:150
SKIP-NUMBERED SET
3 Markus Naslund 6.00 15.00
4 Roberto Luongo 8.00 20.00
9 Vincent Lecavalier 8.00 20.00
19 Sidney Crosby 15.00 40.00
21 Marc-Andre Fleury
31 Jason Spezza
32 Dany Heatley 6.00 15.00
36 Brendan Shanahan 5.00 12.00
37 Henrik Lundqvist 6.00 15.00
44 Paul Kariya 5.00 12.00
64 Henrik Zetterberg 6.00 15.00
68 Mike Modano 6.00 15.00
71 Rick Nash 5.00 12.00
82 Eric Staal 6.00 15.00
86 Miikka Kiprusoff 6.00 15.00
90 Ryan Miller 5.00 12.00
95 Ilya Kovalchuk 6.00 15.00
105 Phil Kessel 4.00 10.00
144 Evgeni Malkin 12.00 30.00
146 Jordan Staal 8.00 20.00
170 Mario Lemieux 10.00 25.00
189 Patrick Roy 10.00 25.00
198 Marcel Dionne 4.00 10.00
204 Gordie Howe 10.00 25.00
231 Bobby Orr 20.00 50.00

2006-07 Beehive Matted Materials

STATED ODDS 1:8
MMAE David Aebischer 4.00 10.00
MMAF Alexander Frolov 2.50 6.00
MMAH Ales Hemsky 2.50 6.00
MMAO Alexander Ovechkin 12.00 30.00
MMAS Alexander Steen 4.00 10.00
MMAT Alex Tanguay 4.00 10.00
MMBB Brad Boyes 2.50 6.00
MMBO Pierre-Marc Bouchard 2.50 6.00
MMCD Chris Drury 2.50 6.00
MMCN Cam Neely 5.00 12.
MMCP Corey Perry 4.00 10.
MMCS Cory Stillman 2.50 6.
MMCW Cam Ward 5.00 12.
MMDA Daniel Alfredsson 4.00 10.
MMDH Dany Heatley 6.00 15.
MMDR Dwayne Roloson 5.00 12.
MMEB Ed Belfour 4.00 10.
MMES Eric Staal 5.00 12.
MMHA Martin Havlat 4.00 10.
MMHT Hannu Toivonen 4.00 10.
MMHZ Henrik Zetterberg 5.00 12.
MMIK Ilya Kovalchuk 6.00 15.
MMJB Jay Bouwmeester 2.50 6.
MMJC Jeff Carter 5.00 12.
MMJI Jarome Iginla 6.00 15.
MMJJ Jaromir Jagr 6.00 15.
MMJL Joffrey Lupul 2.50 6.
MMJS Joe Sakic 8.00 20.
MMJT Joe Thornton 6.00 15.
MMLE Jere Lehtinen 2.50 6.
MMLN Ladislav Nagy 2.50 6.
MMMB Martin Brodeur 10.00 25.
MMMG Marian Gaborik 6.00 15.
MMMH Milan Hejduk 2.50 6.
MMML Mario Lemieux SP 20.00 50.
MMMM Mike Modano 5.00 12.
MMMP Michael Peca 2.50 6.
MMMS Mats Sundin 5.00 12.
MMMT Marty Turco 4.00 10.
MMNL Nicklas Lidstrom 4.00 10.
MMPB Patrice Bergeron 5.00 12.
MMPF Peter Forsberg 6.00 15.
MMPK Paul Kariya 4.00 10.
MMPM Patrick Marleau 4.00 10.
MMRB Ray Bourque 6.00 15.
MMRL Roberto Luongo 6.00 15.
MMRM Ryan Miller 5.00 12.
MMRN Rick Nash 4.00 10.
MMRS Ryan Smyth 4.00 10.
MMSA Marc Savard 2.50 6.
MMSC Sidney Crosby SP 25.00 50.
MMSG Scott Gomez 2.50 6.
MMSK Saku Koivu 4.00 10.
MMSS Sergei Samsonov 4.00 10.
MMST Jarret Stoll 2.00 5.
MMSV Marek Svatos 2.50 6.
MMSZ Sergei Zubov 2.50 6.
MMTH Tomas Holmstrom 2.50 6.
MMTV Tomas Vokoun 4.00 10.
MMZC Zdeno Chara 2.50 6.

2006-07 Beehive PhotoGraphs

STATED ODDS 1:240
PGAR Andrew Raycroft 12.00 30.
PGBO Bobby Orr SP 150.00 300.
PGDH Dominik Hasek SP 75.00 150.
PGES Eric Staal 20.00 50.
PGGH Gordie Howe 75.00 125.
PGGL Guy Lafleur 25.00 50.
PGHE Dany Heatley 15.00 40.
PGJI Jarome Iginla 15.00 40.
PGJT Joe Thornton 20.00 50.
PGKL Kari Lehtonen 15.00 40.
PGMB Martin Brodeur 60.00 125.
PGMG Marian Gaborik 25.00 60.
PGML Mario Lemieux SP
PGMM Mike Modano 20.00 50.
PGMR Michael Ryder 20.00 50.
PGNL Nicklas Lidstrom 20.00 50.
PGPB Patrice Bergeron 20.00 50.
PGPR Patrick Roy 100.00 175.
PGRB Ray Bourque 40.00 80.
PGRL Roberto Luongo 40.00 100.
PGRN Rick Nash 20.00 50.
PGSC Sidney Crosby 150.00 200.
PGTE Tony Esposito 15.00 40.
PGVL Vincent Lecavalier 30.00 60.
PGWG Wayne Gretzky 150.00 250.

2006-07 Beehive Remarkable Matte Materials

STATED PRINT RUN 15 #'d SETS
NOT PRICED DUE TO SCARCITY
MMAE David Aebischer
MMAF Alexander Frolov
MMBB Brad Boyes
MMBO Pierre-Marc Bouchard
MMCD Chris Drury
MMCP Corey Perry
MMCS Cory Stillman
MMDH Dany Heatley
MMDR Dwayne Roloson
MMES Eric Staal
MMHA Martin Havlat
MMHT Hannu Toivonen
MMIK Ilya Kovalchuk
MMJC Jeff Carter
MMJI Jarome Iginla
MMJT Joe Thornton
MMLN Ladislav Nagy
MMMB Martin Brodeur
MMMG Marian Gaborik
MMMH Milan Hejduk
MMMM Mike Modano
MMMP Michael Peca
MMMT Marty Turco
MMNL Nicklas Lidstrom
MMPB Patrice Bergeron
MMPM Patrick Marleau
MMRB Ray Bourque
MMRL Roberto Luongo
MMRM Ryan Miller
MMRN Rick Nash
MMRS Ryan Smyth
MMSC Sidney Crosby
MMSG Scott Gomez
MMSK Saku Koivu
MMSS Sergei Samsonov
MMST Jarret Stoll
MMSV Marek Svatos
MMTH Tomas Holmstrom
MMZC Zdeno Chara

2006-07 Beehive gnature Scrapbook

TED ODDS 1:15
F Alexander Frolov 5.00 12.00
H Ales Hemsky 3.00 8.00
B Brad Boyes 3.00 8.00
G Brian Gionta 3.00 8.00
O Bobby Orr SP
A Colby Armstrong 3.00 8.00
C Chris Campoli 3.00 8.00
H Chris Higgins 5.00 12.00
P Chris Phillips 3.00 8.00
C Don Cherry 15.00 40.00
L David Leneveu 3.00 8.00
R Dwayne Roloson 5.00 12.00
S Darryl Sittler 10.00 25.00
T Darcy Tucker 5.00 12.00
S Eric Staal SP 12.00 30.00
E Martin Gerber 5.00 12.00
H Gordie Howe SP 40.00 80.00
E Milan Hejduk 3.00 8.00
U Cristobal Huet 10.00 25.00
A Jason Arnott 3.00 8.00
B Johnny Bucyk 5.00 12.00
C Jonathan Cheechoo 6.00 15.00
I Jarome Iginla 10.00 25.00
P Joni Pitkanen 3.00 8.00
S Jarret Stoll 3.00 8.00
T Jose Theodore SP 8.00 20.00
D Kris Draper 3.00 8.00
N Ladislav Nagy 3.00 8.00
B Mike Bossy SP 12.00 30.00
C Mike Cammalleri 3.00 8.00
F Marc-Andre Fleury 10.00 25.00
G Marian Gaborik 10.00 25.00
H Martin Havlat 5.00 12.00
P Michael Peca 3.00 8.00
R Mike Richards 3.00 8.00
S Marek Svatos 3.00 8.00
A J.P. Parise 3.00 8.00
B Pierre-Marc Bouchard 3.00 8.00
E Patrik Elias 3.00 8.00
M Patrick Marleau SP 12.00 30.00
P Petr Prucha 3.00 8.00
R Patrick Roy SP 100.00 200.00
S Peter Stastny 8.00 20.00
B Rene Bourque 3.00 8.00
M Ryan Miller 8.00 20.00
W Ryan Whitney 3.00 8.00
A Marc Savard 3.00 8.00
B Steve Bernier 3.00 8.00
S Sergei Samsonov SP 10.00 25.00
H Tomas Holmstrom 5.00 12.00
L Ted Lindsay SP 12.00 30.00
O Terry O'Reilly SP 15.00 40.00
T Vesa Toskala SP 10.00 25.00
G Wayne Gretzky SP 150.00 300.00

2001-02 Between the Pipes

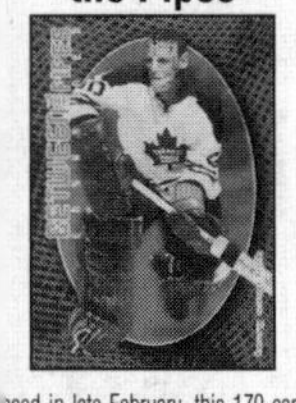

ased in late February, this 170-card set the first to focus exclusively on the inders of the past and present NHL. sets included trophy winners and netcam ography. The last twenty cards in the set available in BAP Update packs only. production for this product was limited 0 cases.

MPLETE SET (150) 50.00 100.00
MP.SET w/UPDATE (170) 75.00 150.00
DS 151-170 AVAIL. IN BAP
.PACKS
atrick Roy 1.50 4.00
S Giguere .50 1.00
on Tugnutt .50 1.00
ick DiPietro .50 1.00
ilan Hnilicka .50 1.00
ean-Sebastien Aubin .50 1.00
raig Billington .50 1.00
yron Dafoe .50 1.00
axime Ouellet .50 1.00
Ed Belfour .75 2.00
John Grahame .50 1.00
Mathieu Garon .50 1.00
Martin Biron .50 1.00
Dan Cloutier .50 1.00
Tomas Vokoun .50 1.00
Arturs Irbe .50 1.00
Curtis Joseph .75 2.00
Jocelyn Thibault .50 1.00
Roman Cechmanek .50 1.00
Miikka Kiprusoff .50 1.00
Olaf Kolzig .50 1.00
Jani Hurme .50 1.00
David Aebischer .50 1.00
Damian Rhodes .50 1.00
Marc Denis .50 1.00
Marty Turco .50 1.00
Evgeni Nabokov .50 1.00
Manny Legace .50 1.00
Mike Dunham .50 1.00
Tommy Salo .50 1.00
Sean Burke .50 1.00
Andrew Raycroft .50 1.00
Roberto Luongo 1.00 2.50
Johan Holmqvist .50 1.00
Felix Potvin .75 2.00
Martin Brodeur 1.25 3.00
Gregg Naumenko .50 1.00
Travis Scott .50 1.00
Manny Fernandez .50 1.00
Kevin Weekes .50 1.00
Steve Passmore .50 1.00
Johan Hedberg .50 1.00
Patrick Lalime .50 1.00
44 Jose Theodore 1.00 2.50
45 Mika Noronen .50 1.00
46 Brent Johnson .50 1.00
47 Chris Mason .50 1.00
48 Mike Fountain .50 1.00
49 Jamie McLennan .50 1.00
50 Mike Richter .75 2.00
51 Eric Fichaud .50 1.00
52 Steve Shields .50 1.00
53 Rich Parent .50 1.00
54 Mike Vernon .50 1.00
55 Jason LaBarbera .50 1.00
56 Dominik Hasek 1.25 3.00
57 Dan Blackburn RC 2.00 5.00
58 Robert Esche .50 1.00
59 Joaquin Gage .50 1.00
60 Jamie Storr .50 1.00
61 Brian Boucher .50 1.00
62 Trevor Kidd .50 1.00
63 Nikolai Khabibulin .75 2.00
64 Norm Maracle .50 1.00
65 Roman Turek .50 1.00
66 Tyler Moss .50 1.00
67 Fred Brathwaite .50 1.00
68 Garth Snow .50 1.00
69 Dieter Kochan .50 1.00
70 Bob Essensa .50 1.00
71 Kirk McLean .50 1.00
72 Chris Osgood .50 1.00
73 Jeff Hackett .50 1.00
74 Stephane Fiset .50 1.00
75 Dominic Roussel .50 1.00
76 Corey Hirsch .50 1.00
77 Vitali Yeremeyev .50 1.00
78 Tom Barrasso .50 1.00
79 Scott Clemmensen RC 1.50 4.00
80 Martin Brochu .50 1.00
81 Corey Schwab .50 1.00
82 Ty Conklin RC 1.50 4.00
83 Dwayne Roloson .50 1.00
84 Ilja Bryzgalov RC 1.50 4.00
85 Olivier Michaud RC 5.00 12.00
86 Vesa Toskala .50 1.00
87 Jussi Markkanen .50 1.00
88 Patrick Desrochers .50 1.00
89 Peter Skudra .50 1.00
90 J-F Damphousse .50 1.00
91 Mike Dunham .50 1.00
92 Mike Richter .75 2.00
93 Brian Boucher .50 1.00
94 Patrick Roy 1.50 4.00
95 Martin Biron .50 1.00
96 Jean-Sebastien Aubin .50 1.00
97 Curtis Joseph .75 2.00
98 Martin Brodeur 1.25 3.00
99 Arturs Irbe .50 1.00
100 Jeff Hackett .50 1.00
101 Ed Belfour .75 2.00
102 Jocelyn Thibault .50 1.00
103 Roman Cechmanek .50 1.00
104 Patrick Lalime .50 1.00
105 Olaf Kolzig .50 1.00
106 Byron Dafoe .50 1.00
107 Johan Hedberg .50 1.00
108 Dan Cloutier .50 1.00
109 Dominik Hasek 1.25 3.00
110 Olaf Kolzig .50 1.00
111 Patrick Roy 1.50 4.00
112 Ed Belfour .75 2.00
113 Grant Fuhr .75 2.00
114 Ron Hextall .75 2.00
115 Pelle Lindbergh 1.25 3.00
116 Tom Barrasso .75 2.00
117 Billy Smith 1.00 2.50
118 Bernie Parent .75 2.00
119 Tony Esposito 1.00 2.50
120 Gump Worsley .75 2.00
121 Glenn Hall 1.00 2.50
122 Jacques Plante 1.25 3.00
123 Johnny Bower .75 2.00
124 Terry Sawchuk 1.25 3.00
125 Harry Lumley .75 2.00
126 Bill Durnan .75 2.00
127 Turk Broda .75 2.00
128 Frank Brimsek .75 2.00
129 Tiny Thompson .75 2.00
130 George Hainsworth .75 2.00
131 Gump Worsley .75 2.00
132 Georges Vezina 1.50 4.00
133 Vladislav Tretiak 1.25 3.00
134 Tiny Thompson .75 2.00
135 Terry Sawchuk 1.25 3.00
136 Jacques Plante 1.25 3.00
137 Chuck Rayner .75 2.00
138 Bernie Parent .75 2.00
139 Harry Lumley .75 2.00
140 Glenn Hall 1.00 2.50
141 George Hainsworth .75 2.00
142 Ed Giacomin .75 2.00
143 Charlie Gardiner .75 2.00
144 Tony Esposito 1.00 2.50
145 Bill Durnan .75 2.00
146 Gerry Cheevers 1.00 2.50
147 Turk Broda .75 2.00
148 Frank Brimsek .75 2.00
149 Johnny Bower .75 2.00
150 Roy Worters .75 2.00
151 Pasi Nurminen RC 2.50 6.00
152 Alex Auld .50 1.00
153 John Vanbiesbrouck .50 1.00
154 Wade Flaherty .50 1.00
155 Kevin Weekes .50 1.00
156 Tom Barrasso .50 1.00
157 Stephane Fiset .50 1.00
158 Sebastien Centomo RC 3.00 8.00
159 Jean-Francois Labbe .50 1.00
160 Simon Lajeunesse .50 1.00
161 Frederic Cassivi RC 1.50 4.00
162 Martin Prusek RC 1.50 4.00
163 Dominik Hasek 1.25 3.00
164 David Aebischer .50 1.00
165 Dan Cloutier .50 1.00
166 Byron Dafoe .50 1.00
167 Curtis Joseph .75 2.00
168 Ed Belfour .75 2.00
169 Tommy Salo .50 1.00
170 Jose Theodore 1.00 2.50

2001-02 Between the Pipes All-Star Jerseys

Limited to just 60 copies each, this 16-card set featured goalies who played in the last several All-Star Games alongside a swatch of their jersey from the game.

STATED PRINT RUN 60 SETS
ASJ1 Ed Belfour 10.00 25.00
1996 All-Star
ASJ2 Arturs Irbe 10.00 25.00
1999 All-Star
ASJ3 Martin Brodeur 25.00 60.00
ASJ4 Roman Cechmanek 10.00 25.00
2001 All-Star
ASJ5 Dominik Hasek 15.00 40.00
1998 All-Star
ASJ6 Olaf Kolzig 10.00 25.00
2000 All-Star
ASJ7 Curtis Joseph 10.00 25.00
2000 All-Star
ASJ8 Mike Richter 10.00 25.00
2000 All-Star
ASJ9 Patrick Roy 30.00 80.00
1994 All-Star
ASJ10 Evgeni Nabokov 10.00 25.00
2001 All-Star
ASJ11 Tommy Salo 10.00 25.00
2000 All-Star
ASJ12 Curtis Joseph 10.00 25.00
1994 All-Star
ASJ13 Dominik Hasek 15.00 40.00
1997 All-Star
ASJ14 Roman Turek 10.00 25.00
2000 All-Star
ASJ15 Nikolai Khabibulin 10.00 25.00
1998 All-Star
ASJ16 Patrick Roy 30.00 80.00
2001 All-Star

2001-02 Between the Pipes Double Memorabilia

This 30-card set featured both a game-worn jersey swatch and a stick or pad swatch from the featured goalie. Each card was limited to 50 copies.

STATED PRINT RUN 50 SETS
DM1 Felix Potvin 15.00 40.00
DM2 Mike Vernon 15.00 40.00
DM3 Johan Hedberg 15.00 40.00
DM4 Olaf Kolzig 15.00 40.00
DM5 Jeff Hackett 15.00 40.00
DM6 Martin Brodeur 40.00 100.00
DM7 Mike Dunham 15.00 40.00
DM8 Trevor Kidd 15.00 40.00
DM9 Damian Rhodes 15.00 40.00
DM10 John Grahame 15.00 40.00
DM11 Roberto Luongo 20.00 50.00
DM12 Manny Legace 15.00 40.00
DM13 Evgeni Nabokov 15.00 40.00
DM14 Jose Theodore 20.00 50.00
DM15 Robert Esche 15.00 40.00
DM16 Chris Osgood 15.00 40.00
DM17 Sean Burke 15.00 40.00
DM18 Martin Biron 15.00 40.00
DM19 Jocelyn Thibault 15.00 40.00
DM20 Brian Boucher 15.00 40.00
DM21 Curtis Joseph 15.00 40.00
DM22 Roman Turek 15.00 40.00
DM23 Gerry Cheevers 15.00 40.00
DM24 Terry Sawchuk 50.00 125.00
DM25 Grant Fuhr 15.00 40.00
DM26 Bernie Parent 40.00 100.00
DM27 Ron Hextall 15.00 40.00
DM28 Gump Worsley 30.00 80.00
DM29 Tony Esposito 15.00 40.00
DM30 Ed Giacomin 15.00 40.00

2001-02 Between the Pipes Future Wave

This 10-card set featured younger goalies from around the league alongside a game-worn jersey swatch. The word "Future Wave" were printed vertically on the right border and the player's name is printed in the right bottom corner. Each card was limited to just 22 copies. The set is not priced due to scarcity.

STATED PRINT RUN 22 SETS
NOT PRICED DUE TO SCARCITY
FW1 Johan Hedberg
FW2 Martin Biron
FW3 Patrick Lalime
FW4 Roberto Luongo
FW5 Johan Holmqvist
Dan Blackburn
FW6 Dan Cloutier
FW7 Miikka Kiprusoff
Evgeni Nabokov
FW8 Brian Boucher
FW9 Mathieu Garon
FW10 Rick DiPietro

2001-02 Between the Pipes Goalie Gear

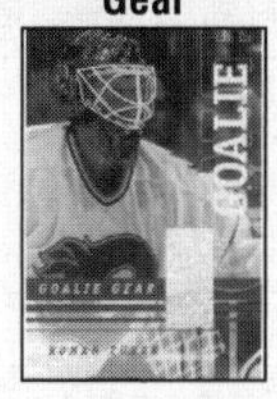

This 30-card set featured an up close color photo beside a game-used swatch of goalie pad or glove. The word "goalie" was printed vertically along the right border and the goalie's name was printed under the photo. Cards from this set were limited to just 70 copies each (unless noted differently below). Cards with fewer than 25 copies are not priced due to scarcity.

STATED PRINT RUN 70 SETS/
UNLESS OTHERWISE NOTED
PRINT RUNS OF LESS THAN 25/
NOT PRICED DUE TO SCARCITY
GG1 Felix Potvin 15.00 40.00
GG2 Jeff Hackett 10.00 25.00
GG3 Mike Vernon 10.00 25.00
GG4 Sean Burke 10.00 25.00
GG5 Johan Hedberg 10.00 25.00
GG6 Jose Theodore 15.00 40.00
GG7 Robert Esche 10.00 25.00
GG8 Dan Cloutier 10.00 25.00
GG9 Olaf Kolzig 12.50 30.00
GG10 Roberto Luongo 20.00 50.00
GG11 Manny Legace 10.00 25.00
GG12 Martin Brodeur 40.00 100.00
GG13 Marty Turco 12.50 30.00
GG14 Arturs Irbe 12.50 30.00
GG15 Damian Rhodes 10.00 25.00
GG16 Trevor Kidd 10.00 25.00
GG17 Mike Dunham 10.00 25.00
GG18 Evgeni Nabokov 12.50 30.00
GG19 Roman Turek 10.00 25.00
GG20 Brian Boucher 10.00 25.00
GG21 Jocelyn Thibault 10.00 25.00
GG22 Dominik Hasek/20
GG23 Patrick Roy/20
GG24 Curtis Joseph/20
GG25 Brent Johnson 10.00 25.00
GG26 Patrick Lalime 10.00 25.00
GG27 J-S Aubin 10.00 25.00
GG28 Martin Biron 10.00 25.00
GG29 Chris Osgood 12.50 30.00
GG30 Rick DiPietro 12.50 30.00

2001-02 Between the Pipes He Shoots-He Saves Points

Inserted one per pack, these cards carry a value of 1, 2 or 3 points. The points could be redeemed for special memorabilia cards. The cards are unnumbered and are listed below in alphabetical order by point value. The redemption program ended November 2002.

ONE PER PACK
RED.PROGRAM HAS EXPIRED
1 Brian Boucher 1pt. .20 .50
2 Sean Burke 1pt. .20 .50
3 Byron Dafoe 1pt. .20 .50
4 Nikolai Khabibulin 1pt. .20 .50
5 Olaf Kolzig 1pt. .20 .50
6 Roberto Luongo 1pt. .20 .50
7 Evgeni Nabokov 1pt. .20 .50
8 Jose Theodore 1pt. .20 .50
9 Jocelyn Thibault 1 pt. .20 .50
10 Roman Turek 1pt. .20 .50
11 Ed Belfour 2 pts. .20 .50
12 Martin Brodeur 2 pts. .20 .50
13 Grant Fuhr 2 pts. .20 .50
14 Glenn Hall 2 pts. .20 .50
15 Jacques Plante 2 pts. .20 .50
16 Tommy Salo 2 pts. .20 .50
17 Dominik Hasek 3 pts. .20 .50
18 Curtis Joseph 3 pts. .20 .50
19 Patrick Roy 3 pts. .20 .50
20 Terry Sawchuk 3 pts. .20 .50

2001-02 Between the Pipes He Shoots-He Saves Prizes

Available only by redeeming 400 Between the Pipes He Shoots-He Saves points, this 40-card set featured game-used swatches of jersey and a color photo of the player. Each card had a stated print run of 20 serial-numbered sets and each was encased in a clear plastic slab with a descriptive label at the top. This set is unpriced due to scarcity and volatility.

STATED PRINT RUN 20 SER.#'d SETS
NOT PRICED DUE TO SCARCITY
1 Dominik Hasek
2 Ron Tugnutt
3 Mike Dunham
4 Marty Turco
5 Glenn Hall
6 Grant Fuhr
7 J-S Aubin
8 Mike Richter
9 Dan Cloutier
10 Tommy Salo
11 Roman Turek
12 Evgeni Nabokov
13 Nikolai Khabibulin
14 Patrick Lalime
15 Brian Boucher
16 Byron Dafoe
17 Olaf Kolzig
18 Jose Theodore
19 Jocelyn Thibault
20 Sean Burke
21 Felix Potvin
22 Arturs Irbe
23 Curtis Joseph
24 Jeff Hackett
25 Roman Cechmanek
26 Martin Brodeur
27 Patrick Roy
28 Manny Legace
29 Steve Shields
30 Ed Belfour
31 Martin Biron
32 Miikka Kiprusoff
33 Johan Hedberg
34 Ron Hextall
35 Manny Fernandez
36 Damian Rhodes
37 Bernie Parent
38 Billy Smith
39 Jani Hurme
40 Roberto Luongo

2001-02 Between the Pipes Jerseys

This 42-card set featured game-worn jersey swatches affixed to the right of full-color action photos on a two color background. The words "game used jersey" are printed at the card top and the player's name is printed on the right hand border. Each card was limited to 90 copies.

STATED PRINT RUN 90 SETS
*MULT.COLOR SWATCH: .5X TO 1.25X HI
GJ1 Byron Dafoe 6.00 15.00
GJ2 Dominik Hasek 15.00 40.00
GJ3 Mike Vernon 10.00 25.00
GJ4 Arturs Irbe 10.00 25.00
GJ5 Jocelyn Thibault 6.00 15.00
GJ6 Patrick Roy 25.00 60.00
GJ7 Ed Belfour 10.00 25.00
GJ8 Chris Osgood 10.00 25.00
GJ9 Johan Hedberg 6.00 15.00
GJ10 Roberto Luongo 12.50 30.00
GJ11 Jose Theodore 12.50 30.00
GJ12 Mike Dunham 6.00 15.00
GJ13 Martin Brodeur 20.00 50.00
GJ14 Mike Richter 10.00 25.00
GJ15 Roman Cechmanek 6.00 15.00
GJ16 J-S Aubin 6.00 15.00
GJ17 Roman Turek 6.00 15.00
GJ18 Curtis Joseph 10.00 25.00
GJ19 Olaf Kolzig 10.00 25.00
GJ20 Felix Potvin 10.00 25.00
GJ21 Trevor Kidd 6.00 15.00
GJ22 Tommy Salo 6.00 15.00
GJ23 Jeff Hackett 6.00 15.00
GJ24 Brian Boucher 6.00 15.00
GJ25 Dan Cloutier 6.00 15.00
GJ26 Damian Rhodes 6.00 15.00
GJ27 Ron Tugnutt 6.00 15.00
GJ28 Marty Turco 10.00 25.00
GJ29 Manny Fernandez 6.00 15.00
GJ30 Marc Denis 6.00 15.00
GJ31 Evgeni Nabokov 10.00 25.00
GJ32 Nikolai Khabibulin 10.00 25.00
GJ33 Sean Burke 6.00 15.00
GJ34 Gregg Naumenko 6.00 15.00
GJ35 Steve Shields 6.00 15.00
GJ36 Mathieu Garon 6.00 15.00
GJ37 Manny Legace 6.00 15.00
GJ38 Johan Holmqvist 6.00 15.00
GJ39 Martin Biron 6.00 15.00
GJ40 David Aebischer 10.00 25.00
GJ41 Miikka Kiprusoff 10.00 25.00
GJ42 John Grahame 6.00 15.00

2001-02 Between the Pipes Emblems

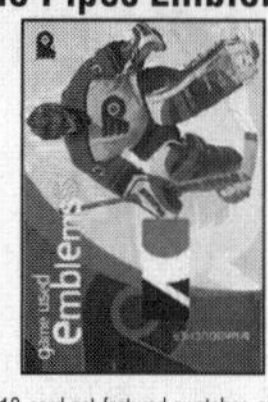

This 10-card set featured swatches of jersey emblem of the featured player. The words "game-used emblem is printed along the card top and the player's name is printed vertically along the left hand border. Each card was limited to just 20 copies. The set is not priced due to scarcity.

STATED PRINT RUN 20 SETS
NOT PRICED DUE TO SCARCITY
GUE1 Dominik Hasek
GUE2 Jocelyn Thibault
GUE3 Patrick Roy
GUE4 Johan Hedberg
GUE5 Roman Turek
GUE6 Curtis Joseph
GUE7 Olaf Kolzig
GUE8 Tommy Salo
GUE9 Brian Boucher
GUE10 Evgeni Nabokov

2001-02 Between the Pipes Jersey and Stick Cards

This 42-card set featured swatches of both game-worn jerseys and game-used sticks from the featured player. Each card was limited to 90 copies.

STATED PRINT RUN 90 SETS
GSJ1 Byron Dafoe 10.00 25.00
GSJ2 Dominik Hasek 20.00 50.00
GSJ3 Mike Vernon 10.00 25.00
GSJ4 Arturs Irbe 12.00 30.00
GSJ5 Jocelyn Thibault 10.00 25.00
GSJ6 Patrick Roy 40.00 100.00
GSJ7 Ed Belfour 12.00 30.00
GSJ8 Johan Hedberg 10.00 25.00
GSJ9 Roberto Luongo 20.00 50.00
GSJ10 Jose Theodore 12.00 30.00
GSJ11 Mike Dunham 10.00 25.00
GSJ12 Martin Brodeur 30.00 80.00
GSJ13 Mike Richter 12.00 30.00
GSJ14 Roman Cechmanek 10.00 25.00
GSJ15 J-S Aubin 10.00 25.00
GSJ16 Roman Turek 10.00 25.00
GSJ17 Curtis Joseph 12.00 30.00
GSJ18 Olaf Kolzig 12.00 30.00
GSJ19 Felix Potvin UER 12.00 30.00
GSJ20 Trevor Kidd 10.00 25.00
GSJ21 Tommy Salo 10.00 25.00
GSJ22 Jeff Hackett 10.00 25.00
GSJ23 Brian Boucher 10.00 25.00
GSJ24 Dan Cloutier 10.00 25.00
GSJ25 Manny Legace 10.00 25.00
GSJ26 Damian Rhodes 10.00 25.00
GSJ27 Martin Biron 10.00 25.00
GSJ28 Ron Tugnutt 10.00 25.00
GSJ29 Evgeni Nabokov 12.00 30.00
GSJ30 Nikolai Khabibulin 12.00 30.00
GSJ31 Sean Burke 10.00 25.00
GSJ32 Patrick Lalime 10.00 25.00
GSJ33 Steve Shields 10.00 25.00
GSJ34 Tomas Vokoun 12.00 30.00
GSJ35 Manny Fernandez 10.00 25.00
GSJ36 David Aebischer 10.00 25.00
GSJ37 Tony Esposito 30.00 80.00
GSJ38 Bernie Parent 40.00 100.00
GSJ39 Glenn Hall 40.00 100.00
GSJ40 Jacques Plante 50.00 125.00
GSJ41 Grant Fuhr 30.00 80.00
GSJ42 Terry Sawchuk 60.00 150.00

2001-02 Between the Pipes Numbers

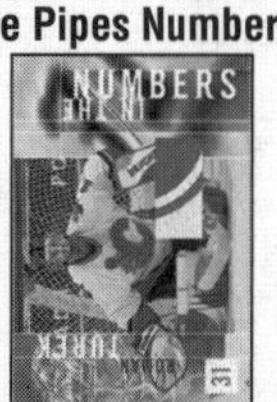

Limited to just 20 copies each, this 10 card set featured game-worn swatches from the featured player's jersey number. The words "in the numbers" appear vertically along the right hand border and the player's name appears along the left hand border. This set is not priced due to scarcity.

STATED PRINT RUN 20 SETS
NOT PRICED DUE TO SCARCITY
ITN1 Dominik Hasek
ITN2 Jocelyn Thibault
ITN3 Patrick Roy
ITN4 Johan Hedberg
ITN5 Roman Turek
ITN6 Curtis Joseph
ITN7 Olaf Kolzig
ITN8 Tommy Salo
ITN9 Brian Boucher
ITN10 Evgeni Nabokov

2001-02 Between the Pipes Masks

This 40-card set featured some of the more memorable goalie masks from the past and present NHL. Dufex technology was used to give the cards an overall foil effect. Cards were unnumbered and are listed below in checklist order. Cards 31-40 were available in BAP Update packs only.

COMPLETE SET (40) 100.00 200.00
CARDS 31-40 AVAIL.IN BAP UPD.PACKS
*SILVER: 1.25X TO 3X BASE HI
SILVER PRINT RUN 300 SETS
*GOLD: 3X TO 8X BASE HI
GOLD PRINT RUN 30 SETS
1 Jacques Plante 6.00 15.00
2 Curtis Joseph 4.00 10.00
3 Ed Giacomin 4.00 10.00
4 Gilles Gratton 2.50 6.00
5 Murray Bannerman 2.50 6.00
6 John Vanbiesbrouck 2.50 6.00
7 Gerry Cheevers 5.00 12.00
8 Steve Shields 2.50 6.00
9 Damian Rhodes 2.50 6.00
10 Byron Dafoe 2.50 6.00
11 Martin Biron 2.50 6.00
12 Roman Turek 2.50 6.00
13 Patrick Roy 8.00 20.00
14 Ed Belfour 4.00 10.00
15 Manny Legace 2.50 6.00
16 Tommy Salo 2.50 6.00
17 Roberto Luongo 5.00 12.00
18 Felix Potvin 4.00 10.00
19 Manny Fernandez 2.50 6.00
20 Jose Theodore 5.00 12.00
21 Mike Dunham 2.50 6.00
22 Mike Richter 4.00 10.00
23 Patrick Lalime 2.50 6.00
24 Roman Cechmanek 5.00 12.00
25 Sean Burke 2.50 6.00
26 Johan Hedberg 2.50 6.00
27 Evgeni Nabokov 5.00 12.00
28 Brent Johnson 2.50 6.00
29 Curtis Joseph 4.00 10.00
30 Olaf Kolzig 2.50 6.00
31 Ed Belfour 4.00 10.00
32 Grant Fuhr 2.50 6.00
33 Brian Hayward 2.50 6.00
34 Milan Hnilicka 2.50 6.00
35 Jocelyn Thibault 2.50 6.00
36 Ron Tugnutt 2.50 6.00
37 Jeff Hackett 2.50 6.00
38 Rick DiPietro 2.50 6.00
39 Miikka Kiprusoff 2.50 6.00
40 Nikolai Khabibulin 4.00 10.00

2001-02 Between the Pipes Record Breakers

This 20-card set featured record setting goalies along side swatches of game-used jerseys. The words "Record Breakers" appeared along the top left border and the goalie's feat was printed in the bottom right border. Each card was limited to just 50 copies each.

STATED PRINT RUN 50 SETS
RB1 Patrick Roy 30.00 80.00
Most Playoff Wins
RB2 Terry Sawchuk 150.00 400.00
Martin Brodeur
Jacques Plante
Most 40 Win Seasons
RB3 Jacques Plante 30.00 80.00
Most Vezina Trophies
RB4 Martin Brodeur 40.00 100.00
RB5 Terry Sawchuk 40.00 100.00
Most Career Games
RB6 Bernie Parent 15.00 40.00
Most Wins in a Season
RB7 Tony Esposito 15.00 40.00
Most Consecutive 30 Win Seasons
RB8 Ed Belfour 15.00 40.00
Most Shutouts (Active Goalie)
RB9 Grant Fuhr 15.00 40.00
Longest Undefeated Streak by a Rookie
RB10 Patrick Roy 30.00 80.00
Most Playoff Shutouts
RB11 Patrick Roy 30.00 80.00
Most Conn Smythe Trophies
RB12 Ed Belfour 15.00 40.00
Most Consecutive Playoff Wins
RB13 Jacques Plante 30.00 80.00
Most Stanley Cup Wins
RB14 Gerry Cheevers 15.00 40.00
Longest Undefeated Streak
RB15 Terry Sawchuk 40.00 100.00
Most Career Shutouts
RB16 Patrick Roy 30.00 80.00
Most 30 Win Seasons
RB17 Patrick Roy 30.00 80.00
Most Career Wins

RB18 Chris Osgood 15.00 40.00
Best Winning Percentage
RB19 Tony Esposito 15.00 40.00
Most Shutouts by a Rookie
RB20 Glenn Hall 15.00 40.00
Most Consecutive Games Played

2001-02 Between the Pipes Tandems

This 13-card set featured goalie duos from specific teams around the league. Each card included a full-color photo of each goalie and a game-worn jersey swatch on the card front. The words "Goalie Tandems" were printed on the bottom border of each card. This set was limited to just 50 copies of each card.

STATED PRINT RUN 50 SETS
GT1 Evgeni Nabokov 30.00 80.00
Miika Kiprusoff
GT2 Roman Cechmanek 15.00 40.00
Brian Boucher
GT3 Jose Theodore 25.00 60.00
Jeff Hackett
GT4 Roberto Luongo 15.00 40.00
Trevor Kidd
GT5 Patrick Roy 50.00 125.00
David Aebischer
GT6 Steve Shields 15.00 40.00
J-S Giguere
GT7 Ed Belfour 15.00 40.00
Marty Turco
GT8 Roman Turek 15.00 40.00
Mike Vernon
GT9 Dominik Hasek 15.00 40.00
Manny Legace
GT10 Byron Dafoe 15.00 40.00
John Grahame
GT11 Sean Burke 15.00 40.00
Robert Esche
GT12 Jocelyn Thibault 20.00 50.00
Steve Passmore
GT13 J-S Aubin 15.00 40.00
Johan Hedberg

2001-02 Between the Pipes Trophy Winners

This 24-card set honored goalies who have won various league awards through the years. Each card featured a color photo in the card center accompanied by a swatch of game-used jersey. On the right side of the card front the player's name and the trophy he won was printed vertically. On the left side of the card was a picture of the award itself. Each card was limited to 50 copies.

STATED PRINT RUN 40 SETS
TW1 Patrick Roy 40.00 100.00
Conn Smythe Winner
TW2 Dominik Hasek 20.00 50.00
Vezina Winner
TW3 Evgeni Nabokov 15.00 40.00
Calder Winner
TW4 Jacques Plante 40.00 100.00
Vezina Winner
TW5 Olaf Kolzig 15.00 40.00
Vezina Winner
TW6 Terry Sawchuk 60.00 150.00
Vezina Winner
TW7 Glenn Hall 15.00 40.00
Conn Smythe Winner
TW8 Billy Smith 15.00 40.00
Conn Smythe Winner
TW9 Turk Broda 15.00 40.00
Vezina Winner
TW10 Ron Hextall 15.00 40.00
Vezina Winner
TW11 Tiny Thompson 30.00 80.00
Vezina Winner
TW12 Bill Durnan 15.00 40.00
Vezina Winner
TW13 Glenn Hall 15.00 40.00
Vezina Winner
TW14 Terry Sawchuk 60.00 150.00
Calder Winner
TW15 Tony Esposito 20.00 50.00
Calder Winner
TW16 Glenn Hall 15.00 40.00
Calder Winner
TW17 Martin Brodeur 30.00 80.00
TW18 Jacques Plante 40.00 100.00
Hart Winner
TW19 Dominik Hasek 20.00 50.00
Hart Winner
TW20 Billy Smith 15.00 40.00
Vezina Winner
TW21 Bernie Parent 15.00 40.00
Conn Smythe Winner
TW22 Ed Belfour 20.00 50.00
Calder Winner
TW23 Frank Brimsek 15.00 40.00
Calder Winner
TW24 Dominik Hasek 20.00 50.00
Lester B. Pearson Award Winner

2001-02 Between the Pipes Vintage Memorabilia

This 20-card set featured game-used equipment from retired goalies. Each card carried a full color photo of the featured goalie on the right side of the card front and a larger black-and-white up close photo on the left side of the card front. The game-used swatch was affixed in the center of the two photos. Each card was limited to just 40 sets.

STATED PRINT RUN 40 SETS
VM1 Grant Fuhr 15.00 40.00
VM2 Turk Broda 25.00 60.00
VM3 Gerry Cheevers 15.00 40.00
VM4 Bernie Parent 15.00 40.00
VM5 Jacques Plante 30.00 80.00
VM6 Terry Sawchuk 50.00 125.00
VM7 Frank Brimsek 15.00 40.00
VM8 Glenn Hall 15.00 40.00
VM9 Tony Esposito 15.00 40.00
VM10 Vladislav Tretiak 60.00 150.00
VM11 Billy Smith 15.00 40.00
VM12 Johnny Bower 15.00 40.00
VM13 Georges Vezina 300.00 600.00
VM14 Ron Hextall 15.00 40.00
VM15 Ed Giacomin 15.00 40.00
VM16 Gump Worsley 25.00 60.00
VM17 Bill Durnan 15.00 40.00
VM18 Rogie Vachon 25.00 60.00
VM19 Tiny Thompson 15.00 40.00
VM20 Charlie Gardner 15.00 40.00

2002-03 Between the Pipes

This 150-card set highlighted the goal keepers, past and present, of the NHL. The set included two subsets; "enshrined", which featured retired goalies, and "home and away", which featured goalies in their home and road uniforms.

COMPLETE SET (150) 20.00 50.00
1 Patrick Roy 1.50 4.00
2 Jose Theodore 1.00 2.50
3 Olaf Kolzig .40 1.00
4 Roberto Luongo 1.00 2.50
5 Tommy Salo .20 .50
6 Dan Blackburn .20 .50
7 Patrick Lalime .20 .50
8 Martin Brodeur 1.25 3.00
9 Evgeni Nabokov .20 .50
10 Jani Hurme .20 .50
11 Dan Cloutier .20 .50
12 Mike Dunham .20 .50
13 Miika Kiprusoff .40 1.00
14 Rick DiPietro .40 1.00
15 Martin Biron .20 .50
16 Steve Passmore .20 .50
17 Curtis Joseph .60 1.50
18 Manny Fernandez .20 .50
19 Kevin Weekes .20 .50
20 Stephane Fiset .20 .50
21 Jocelyn Thibault .20 .50
22 David Aebischer .20 .50
23 Marty Turco .40 1.00
24 Jamie Storr .20 .50
25 Marc Denis .20 .50
26 Arturs Irbe .20 .50
27 Felix Potvin .60 1.50
28 Manny Legace .20 .50
29 Mike Richter .60 1.50
30 J-S Aubin .20 .50
31 Sean Burke .20 .50
32 Milan Hnilicka .20 .50
33 Ed Belfour .60 1.50
34 Roman Turek .20 .50
35 Frederic Cassivi .20 .50
36 Tomas Vokoun .40 1.00
37 Travis Scott .20 .50
38 Dwayne Roloson .20 .50
39 Roman Cechmanek .20 .50
40 Johan Hedberg .20 .50
41 Neil Little .20 .50
42 Jeff Hackett .20 .50
43 John Grahame .20 .50
44 Norm Maracle .20 .50
45 Ty Conklin .20 .50
46 Trevor Kidd .20 .50
47 Nikolai Khabibulin .60 1.50
48 Dieter Kochan .20 .50
49 Robert Esche .20 .50
50 Chris Osgood .20 .50
51 J-S Giguere .20 .50
52 Steve Shields .20 .50
53 Wade Flaherty .20 .50
54 Peter Skudra .20 .50
55 Brent Johnson .20 .50
56 Brian Boucher .20 .50
57 Garth Snow .20 .50
58 Fred Brathwaite .20 .50
59 Ron Tugnutt .20 .50
60 Craig Billington .20 .50
61 Martin Brochu .20 .50
62 Corey Schwab .20 .50
63 Tim Thomas RC 1.50 4.00
64 J-F Labbe .20 .50
65 Damian Rhodes .20 .50
66 Kevin Hodson .20 .50
67 Jamie McLennan .20 .50
68 Tyler Moss .20 .50
69 Tom Barrasso .20 .50
70 Corey Hirsch .20 .50
71 Eric Fichaud .20 .50
72 Byron Dafoe .20 .50
73 Mika Noronen .20 .50
74 Alex Auld .20 .50
75 Curtis Sanford RC 1.00 2.50
76 Martin Gerber RC 1.00 2.50
77 Mikael Tellqvist RC 1.25 3.00
78 J-M Pelletier .20 .50
79 J-F Damphousse .20 .50
80 Johan Holmqvist .20 .50
81 Mathieu Garon .20 .50
82 Martin Prusek .20 .50
83 Ilja Bryzgalov .20 .50
84 Andrew Raycroft .20 .50
85 Derek Gustafson .20 .50
86 Jason LaBarbera .20 .50
87 Marc Lamothe .20 .50
88 Scott Clemmensen .20 .50
89 Cody Rudkowsky RC .60 1.50
90 Craig Andersson RC .60 1.50
91 Maxime Ouellet .20 .50
92 Jan Lasak .20 .50
93 Patrick DesRochers .20 .50
94 Pasi Nurminen .20 .50
95 Sebastien Centomo .20 .50
96 Jussi Markkanen .20 .50
97 Sebastien Charpentier .20 .50
98 Reinhard Divis .20 .50
99 Simon Lajeunesse .20 .50
100 Vesa Toskala .20 .50
101 Olivier Michaud .20 .50
102 Levente Szuper RC .60 1.50
103 Philippe Sauve .20 .50
104 Dany Sabourin RC .60 1.50
105 Ryan Miller RC 3.00 8.00
106 Chris Mason .40 1.00
107 Steve Valiquette .20 .50
108 Pascal Leclaire RC 1.00 2.50
109 Jason Elliott RC .60 1.50
110 Michael Garnett RC .60 1.50
111 Tiny Thompson .60 1.50
112 Frank Brimsek .60 1.50
113 Jacques Plante 1.25 3.00
114 Terry Sawchuk 1.25 3.00
115 Georges Vezina 1.50 4.00
116 Chuck Rayner .60 1.50
117 Glenn Hall .60 1.50
118 Turk Broda .60 1.50
119 George Hainsworth .60 1.50
120 Roy Worters .60 1.50
121 J-S Giguere HA .20 .50
122 Milan Hnilicka HA .20 .50
123 Steve Shields HA .20 .50
124 Martin Biron HA .20 .50
125 Roman Turek HA .20 .50
126 Arturs Irbe HA .20 .50
127 Jocelyn Thibault HA .20 .50
128 Patrick Roy HA 1.50 4.00
129 Marc Denis HA .20 .50
130 Marty Turco HA .40 1.00
131 Curtis Joseph HA .60 1.50
132 Tommy Salo HA .20 .50
133 Roberto Luongo HA 1.00 2.50
134 Felix Potvin HA .60 1.50
135 Manny Fernandez HA .20 .50
136 Jose Theodore HA 1.00 2.50
137 Tomas Vokoun HA .40 1.00
138 Martin Brodeur HA 1.25 3.00
139 Chris Osgood HA .20 .50
140 Mike Richter HA .60 1.50
141 Patrick Lalime HA .20 .50
142 Roman Cechmanek HA .20 .50
143 Sean Burke HA .20 .50
144 Johan Hedberg HA .20 .50
145 Brent Johnson HA .20 .50
146 Evgeni Nabokov HA .20 .50
147 Nikolai Khabibulin HA .60 1.50
148 Ed Belfour HA .60 1.50
149 Dan Cloutier HA .20 .50
150 Olaf Kolzig HA .40 1.00

2002-03 Between the Pipes Gold

This 110-card set paralleled the first 110 cards of the base set but carried gold foil backgrounds on the card fronts. Each card was individually numbered out of 10.

GOLD PRINT RUN 10 SER.#'d SETS
NOT PRICED DUE TO SCARCITY

2002-03 Between the Pipes Silver

This 110-card set paralleled the first 110 cards of the base set but carried silver foil backgrounds on the card fronts. Each card was individually numbered out of 100.

*STARS: 3X TO 8X BASE HI
*ROOKIES: .75X TO 2X
SILVER PRINT RUN 100 SER.#'d SETS

2002-03 Between the Pipes All-Star Stick and Jersey

Limited to just 40-copies each, this 16-card set featured pieces of all-star game jerseys and sticks.

STATED PRINT RUN 40 SETS
1 Eddie Belfour 20.00 50.00
1996 Boston
2 Curtis Joseph 20.00 50.00
2000 Toronto

3 Martin Brodeur 40.00 100.00
4 Patrick Roy 50.00 125.00
1994 New York
5 Mike Richter 20.00 50.00
2000 Toronto
6 Evgeni Nabokov 20.00 50.00
2001 Denver
7 Olaf Kolzig 20.00 50.00
2000 Toronto
8 Felix Potvin 20.00 50.00
1996 Boston
9 Tommy Salo 20.00 50.00
2000 Toronto
10 Jose Theodore 25.00 60.00
2002 Los Angeles
11 Nikolai Khabibulin 20.00 50.00
2002 Los Angeles
12 Roman Turek 20.00 50.00
2000 Toronto
13 Sean Burke 20.00 50.00
2002 Los Angeles
14 Roman Cechmanek 20.00 50.00
2001 Denver
15 Arturs Irbe 20.00 50.00
1999 Tampa Bay
16 Chris Osgood 20.00 50.00
1996 Boston

2002-03 Between the Pipes Behind the Mask

This 20-card set featured swatches of game jerseys. Cards were limited to 30 copies each.

STATED PRINT RUN 30 SETS
1 Marty Turco 15.00 40.00
2 Martin Brodeur 25.00 60.00
3 Patrick Roy 30.00 80.00
4 Roberto Luongo 20.00 50.00
5 Tommy Salo 15.00 40.00
6 Nikolai Khabibulin 15.00 40.00
7 Sean Burke 15.00 40.00
8 Patrick Lalime 15.00 40.00
9 Arturs Irbe 15.00 40.00
10 Jocelyn Thibault 15.00 40.00
11 Jose Theodore 15.00 40.00
12 Rick DiPietro 15.00 40.00
13 Marc Denis 15.00 40.00
14 Mike Dunham 15.00 40.00
15 Johan Hedberg 15.00 40.00
16 Olaf Kolzig 15.00 40.00
17 Dan Cloutier 15.00 40.00
18 Felix Potvin 15.00 40.00
19 Ed Belfour 15.00 40.00
20 Steve Shields 15.00 40.00

2002-03 Between the Pipes Blockers

Limited to just 50 copies each, this 18-card set featured pieces of game-used goalie blockers.

*MULT.COLOR SWATCH: .75X TO 1.5X
STATED PRINT RUN 50 SETS
1 Curtis Joseph 15.00 40.00
2 Jani Hurme 10.00 25.00
3 Evgeni Nabokov 10.00 25.00
4 Felix Potvin 15.00 40.00
5 J-S Giguere 10.00 25.00
6 Jocelyn Thibault 10.00 25.00
7 Marty Turco 20.00 50.00
8 Mike Dunham 10.00 25.00
9 Johan Hedberg 10.00 25.00
10 Roman Cechmanek 10.00 25.00
11 Olaf Kolzig 10.00 25.00
12 Patrick Lalime 10.00 25.00
13 Roberto Luongo 12.50 30.00
14 Roman Turek 10.00 25.00
15 Nikolai Khabibulin 10.00 25.00
16 Tommy Salo 10.00 25.00
17 Trevor Kidd 10.00 25.00
18 Sean Burke 10.00 25.00

2002-03 Between the Pipes Complete Package

Limited to just 10 copies each, this 12-card set featured four pieces of game-used

memorabilia. This set is not priced due to scarcity.

STATED PRINT RUN 10 SETS
NOT PRICED DUE TO SCARCITY
CP1 Patrick Roy
CP2 Curtis Joseph
CP3 Terry Sawchuk
CP4 Jacques Plante
CP5 Marty Turco
CP6 Johan Hedberg
CP7 Sean Burke
CP8 Jocelyn Thibault
CP9 Bernie Parent
CP10 Nikolai Khabibulin
CP11 Grant Fuhr
CP12 Roman Cechmanek

2002-03 Between the Pipes Double Memorabilia

This 20-card set carried dual swatches of game-used memorabilia. Each card was limited to just 40 copies each.

STATED PRINT RUN 40 SETS
1 Martin Brodeur 30.00 80.00
2 Sean Burke 12.50 30.00
3 Dan Cloutier 12.50 30.00
4 Chris Osgood 12.50 30.00
5 Jose Theodore 25.00 60.00
6 Olaf Kolzig 12.50 30.00
7 Patrick Roy 30.00 80.00
8 Tommy Salo 12.50 30.00
9 Marty Turco 12.50 30.00
10 Roman Turek 12.50 30.00
11 Mike Dunham 12.50 30.00
12 Manny Legace 12.00 30.00
13 Jocelyn Thibault 12.50 30.00
14 Nikolai Khabibulin 12.50 30.00
15 Johan Hedberg 12.50 30.00
16 Trevor Kidd 12.50 30.00
17 J-S Aubin 12.50 30.00
18 Jacques Plante 40.00 100.00
19 Terry Sawchuk 40.00 100.00
20 Roger Crozier 12.00 30.00

2002-03 Between the Pipes Emblems

Limited to 10 copies each, this 30-card set carried pieces of jersey emblems on the card fronts. This set is not priced due to scarcity.

STATED PRINT RUN 10 SETS
NOT PRICED DUE TO SCARCITY
1 Arturs Irbe
2 Miikka Kiprusoff
3 Rick DiPietro
4 Dan Blackburn
5 Dan Cloutier
6 David Aebischer
7 Evgeni Nabokov
8 Felix Potvin
9 Manny Fernandez
10 J-S Aubin
11 J-S Giguere
12 Jani Hurme
13 Jocelyn Thibault
14 Jose Theodore
15 Mike Dunham
16 Martin Biron
17 Johan Hedberg
18 Martin Brodeur
19 Marty Turco
20 Mika Noronen
21 Mike Richter
22 Nikolai Khabibulin
23 Olaf Kolzig
24 Patrick Lalime
25 Patrick Roy
26 Roberto Luongo
27 Roman Cechmanek
28 Roman Turek
29 Sean Burke
30 Tommy Salo

2002-03 Between the Pipes Future Wave

STATED PRINT RUN 60 SETS
1 Miikka Kiprusoff 20.00 50.00

2 Jose Theodore 20.00 50.00
3 Roberto Luongo 20.00 50.00
4 Rick DiPietro 12.00 30.00
5 Dan Blackburn 8.00 20.00
6 Mathieu Garon 8.00 20.00
7 Johan Hedberg 8.00 20.00
8 Dan Cloutier 8.00 20.00
9 Martin Biron 8.00 20.00
10 Marty Turco 12.00 30.00
11 Alex Auld 8.00 20.00
12 Brent Johnson 8.00 20.00

2002-03 Between the Pipes Goalie Autographs

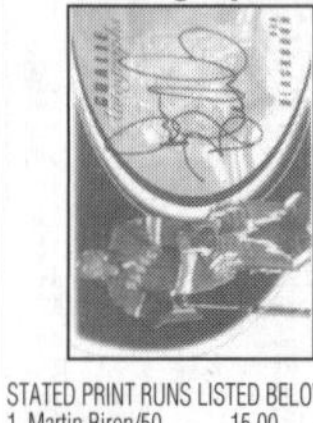

STATED PRINT RUNS LISTED BELOW
1 Martin Biron/50 15.00 40.00
2 Dan Blackburn/50 15.00 40.00
3 Sean Burke/50 15.00 40.00
4 Dan Cloutier/50 15.00 40.00
5 Marc Denis/50 15.00 40.00
6 J-S Giguere/50 15.00 40.00
7 Johan Hedberg/50 15.00 40.00
8 Milan Hnilicka/50 15.00 40.00
9 Arturs Irbe/50 15.00 40.00
10 Brent Johnson/50 15.00 40.00
11 Curtis Joseph/50 20.00 50.00
12 Nikolai Khabibulin/50 20.00 50.00
13 Olaf Kolzig/50 15.00 40.00
14 Patrick Lalime/50 15.00 40.00
15 Roberto Luongo/50 20.00 50.00
16 Evgeni Nabokov/50 15.00 40.00
17 Chris Osgood/50 15.00 40.00
18 Felix Potvin/50 25.00 60.00
19 Dwayne Roloson/50 15.00 40.00
20 Tommy Salo/50 15.00 40.00
21 Steve Shields/50 15.00 40.00
22 Jose Theodore/50 20.00 50.00
23 Jocelyn Thibault/50 15.00 40.00
24 Marty Turco/50 20.00 50.00
25 Roman Turek/50 15.00 40.00
26 Johnny Bower/90 15.00 40.00
27 Bernie Parent/90 15.00 40.00
28 Ed Giacomin/90 15.00 40.00
29 Gerry Cheevers/90 15.00 40.00
30 Vladislav Tretiak/90 60.00 125.00
31 Gump Worsley/40 30.00 80.00
32 Tony Esposito/90 25.00 60.00
33 John Davidson/90 15.00 40.00
34 Glenn Hall/90 15.00 40.00
35 Charlie Hodge/90 15.00 40.00
36 Rogie Vachon/90 15.00 40.00

2002-03 Between the Pipes He Shoots-He Saves Points

Inserted one per pack, these cards carried a value of 1, 2 or 3 points. The points could be redeemed for special memorabilia cards. The cards are unnumbered and are listed below in alphabetical order by point value. The redemption program ended December 31, 2003.

ONE PER PACK
RED.PROGRAM HAS EXPIRED
1 Sean Burke 1 pt. .40 1.00
2 Roman Cechmanek 1 pt. .40 1.00
3 Dan Cloutier 1 pt. .40 1.00
4 Johan Hedberg 1 pt. .40 1.00
5 Arturs Irbe 1 pt. .40 1.00
6 Patrick Lalime 1 pt. .40 1.00
7 Evgeni Nabokov 1 pt. .40 1.00
8 Felix Potvin 1 pt. .40 1.00
9 Mike Richter 1 pt. .40 1.00
10 Marty Turco 1 pt. .40 1.00
11 Roman Turek 1 pt. .40 1.00
12 Dan Blackburn 2 pt. .40 1.00
13 Nikolai Khabibulin 2 pt. .40 1.00
14 Olaf Kolzig 2 pt. .40 1.00
15 Roberto Luongo 2 pt. .40 1.00
16 Tommy Salo 2 pt. .40 1.00
17 Jocelyn Thibault 2 pt. .40 1.00
18 Martin Brodeur 3 pt. .40 1.00
19 Patrick Roy 3 pt. .40 1.00
20 Jose Theodore 3 pt. .40 1.00

2002-03 Between the Pipes He Shoots He Saves Prizes

Available only by redeeming 400 Betw the Pipes He Shoots-He Scores points, 30-card set featured game-used swatches jersey and a color photo of the player. E card had a stated print run of 20 ser numbered sets and each was encased i clear plastic slab with a descriptive labe the top. This set is unpriced due to scar and volatility.

STATED PRINT RUN 20 SETS
NOT PRICED DUE TO SCARCITY
1 Patrick Roy
2 Roberto Luongo
3 Olaf Kolzig
4 Marty Turco
5 Mike Richter
6 Dan Blackburn
7 Tommy Salo
8 Sean Burke
9 Roman Cechmanek
10 Patrick Lalime
11 Roman Turek
12 Evgeni Nabokov
13 Nikolai Khabibulin
14 Johan Hedberg
15 Felix Potvin
16 Martin Brodeur
17 Arturs Irbe
18 Jocelyn Thibault
19 Dan Cloutier
20 Jose Theodore
21 Harry Lumley
22 Roy Worters
23 Roger Crozier
24 George Hainsworth
25 Tony Esposito
26 Gerry Cheevers
27 Ed Giacomin
28 Terry Sawchuk
29 Bernie Parent
30 Glenn Hall

2002-03 Between the Pipes Inspirations

These dual jersey cards were limited to 40 copies each.

STATED PRINT RUN 40 SETS
I1 Patrick Roy 50.00 125.
Jacques Plante
I2 Terry Sawchuk 50.00 125.
George Hainsworth
I3 Jose Theodore 60.00 150.
Patrick Roy
I4 Roberto Luongo 30.00 80.
Patrick Roy
I5 Sean Burke 25.00 60.
Bernie Parent
I6 Eddie Belfour 40.00 100.
Vladislav Tretiak
I7 Dan Blackburn 25.00 60.
Curtis Joseph
I8 M.Brodeur/P.Roy 50.00 125.
I9 Mike Richter 25.00 60.
Gerry Cheevers
I10 Rick DiPietro 25.00 60.
Ron Hextall

2002-03 Between the Pipes Jerseys

*MULT.COLOR SWATCH: .5X TO 1.25X
STATED PRINT RUN 90 SETS
1 Arturs Irbe 8.00 20.
2 Miikka Kiprusoff 8.00 20.
3 Rick DiPietro 8.00 20.
4 Dan Blackburn 8.00 20.
5 Dan Cloutier 8.00 20.
6 David Aebischer 8.00 20.
7 Evgeni Nabokov 8.00 20.
8 Felix Potvin 8.00 20.
9 Manny Fernandez 8.00 20.
10 J-S Aubin 8.00 20.
11 J-S Giguere 8.00 20.
12 Jani Hurme 8.00 20.
13 Jocelyn Thibault 8.00 20.

Jose Theodore	12.50	30.00
Mike Dunham	8.00	20.00
Martin Biron	8.00	20.00
Johan Hedberg	8.00	20.00
Martin Brodeur	15.00	40.00
Marty Turco	8.00	20.00
Mika Noronen	8.00	20.00
Mike Richter	8.00	20.00
Nikolai Khabibulin	8.00	20.00
Olaf Kolzig	8.00	20.00
Patrick Lalime	8.00	20.00
Patrick Roy	20.00	50.00
Roberto Luongo	12.50	30.00
Roman Cechmanek	8.00	20.00
Roman Turek	8.00	20.00
Sean Burke	8.00	20.00
Tommy Salo	8.00	20.00
Maxime Ouellet	8.00	20.00
Ed Belfour	8.00	20.00
Sebastien Charpentier	8.00	20.00
Robert Esche	8.00	20.00
Curtis Sanford	8.00	20.00
Milan Hnilicka	8.00	20.00
Steve Shields	8.00	20.00
Tim Thomas	12.50	30.00
Trevor Kidd	8.00	20.00
Fred Brathwaite	8.00	20.00
Martin Prusek	8.00	20.00
John Grahame	8.00	20.00
Jamie Storr	8.00	20.00
Sebastien Centomo	8.00	20.00
Ron Tugnutt	8.00	20.00
Martin Gerber	8.00	20.00
Jussi Markkanen	8.00	20.00
Simon Lajeunesse	8.00	20.00
Reinhard Divis	8.00	20.00
Jeff Hackett	8.00	20.00

2002-03 Between he Pipes Masks II

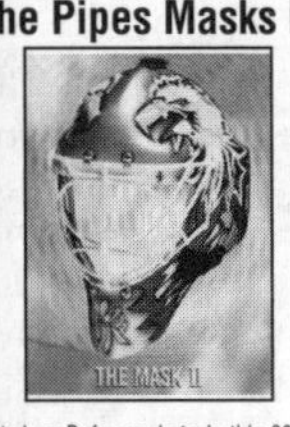

ted on Dufex card stock, this 30-card eatured artist renderings of the masks e famous by the goalies who wore them.

MPLETE SET (30)	30.00	60.00

VER: 1.25X TO 3X BASE HI
VER PRINT RUN 300 SETS
LD: 3X TO 8X BASE HI
D PRINT RUN 30 SETS

-S Giguere	2.00	5.00
ilan Hnilicka	2.00	5.00
teve Shields	2.00	5.00
artin Biron	2.00	5.00
oman Turek	2.00	5.00
evin Weekes	2.00	5.00
ocelyn Thibault	2.00	5.00
atrick Roy	6.00	15.00
arc Denis	2.00	5.00
Marty Turco	2.00	5.00
Curtis Joseph	2.50	6.00
Tommy Salo	2.00	5.00
Roberto Luongo	4.00	10.00
Felix Potvin	2.50	6.00
Manny Fernandez	2.00	5.00
Jose Theodore	4.00	10.00
Mike Dunham	2.00	5.00
Mike Richter	2.50	6.00
Rick DiPietro	2.00	5.00
Patrick Lalime	2.00	5.00
Roman Cechmanek	2.00	5.00
Sean Burke	2.00	5.00
Johan Hedberg	2.00	5.00
Evgeni Nabokov	2.00	5.00
Miikka Kiprusoff	4.00	10.00
Brent Johnson	2.00	5.00
Nikolai Khabibulin	2.50	6.00
Ed Belfour	2.50	6.00
Jeff Hackett	2.00	5.00
Olaf Kolzig	2.00	5.00

2002-03 Between the Pipes Nightmares

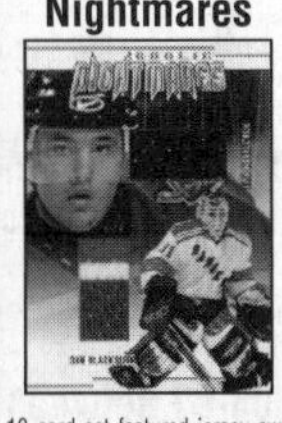

10-card set featured jersey swatches NHL goalies and shooters who had a ry of scoring against them. Production limited to 60 copies each.
TED PRINT RUN 60 SETS

DanBlackburn	15.00	40.00
Ilya Kovalchuk		
M.Richter/M.Lemieux	25.00	60.00
Tommy Salo	15.00	40.00
Jaromir Jagr		
F.Potvin/S.Yzerman	30.00	80.00
Stephane Fiset	12.50	30.00
Pavel Bure		
Mike Richter	15.00	40.00
Jarome Iginla		
Tommy Salo	12.50	30.00
Peter Forsberg		
Curtis Joseph	25.00	60.00
Joe Sakic		
Olaf Kolzig	12.50	30.00

Eric Lindros		
GN10 Tom Barrasso	12.50	30.00
Mats Sundin		

2002-03 Between the Pipes Numbers

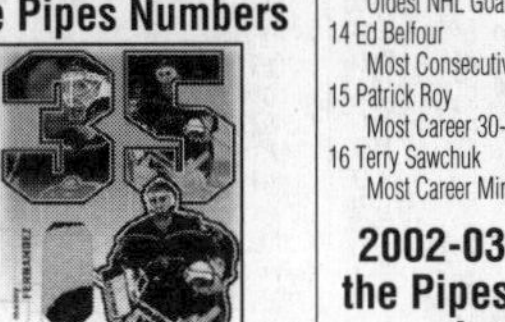

This 30-card set partially paralleled the base jersey set but carried a piece jersey number. Each card was limited to just 10 copies each. This set is not priced due to scarcity.
STATED PRINT RUN 10 SETS
NOT PRICED DUE TO SCARCITY

1 Arturs Irbe
2 Miikka Kiprusoff
3 Rick DiPietro
4 Dan Blackburn
5 Dan Cloutier
6 David Aebischer
7 Evgeni Nabokov
8 Felix Potvin
9 Manny Fernandez
10 J-S Aubin
11 J-S Giguere
12 Jani Hurme
13 Jocelyn Thibault
14 Jose Theodore
15 Mike Dunham
16 Martin Biron
17 Johan Hedberg
18 Martin Brodeur
19 Marty Turco
20 Mika Noronen
21 Mike Richter
22 Nikolai Khabibulin
23 Olaf Kolzig
24 Patrick Lalime
25 Patrick Roy
26 Roberto Luongo
27 Roman Cechmanek
28 Roman Turek
29 Sean Burke
30 Tommy Salo

2002-03 Between the Pipes Pads

Limited to just 50 copies each, this 14-card set featured pieces of game-used goalie pads.
*MULT.COLOR SWATCH: .75X TO 1.5X
STAT.PRINT RUN 50 SETS

1 Martin Brodeur	30.00	80.00
2 Patrick Roy	30.00	80.00
3 Marty Turco	10.00	25.00
4 Curtis Joseph	15.00	40.00
5 Ed Belfour	15.00	40.00
6 Jose Theodore	20.00	50.00
7 Sean Burke	10.00	25.00
8 Dan Cloutier	10.00	25.00
9 Chris Osgood	10.00	25.00
10 Nikolai Khabibulin	15.00	40.00
11 J-S Aubin	10.00	25.00
12 Steve Shields	10.00	25.00
13 Mike Dunham	10.00	25.00
14 Jocelyn Thibault	10.00	25.00

2002-03 Between the Pipes Record Breakers

This 16-card memorabilia set was limited to just 40 copies each.
STATED PRINT RUN 40 SETS

1 Terry Sawchuk	30.00	80.00
Most Career Games Played		
2 Patrick Roy	20.00	50.00
Most Career Playoff Games		
3 George Hainsworth	20.00	50.00
4 Jacques Plante	25.00	60.00
Most Vezina Trophies		
5 Patrick Roy	20.00	50.00
Most Career Wins		
6 Glenn Hall	12.50	30.00
Most Consecutive Complete Games		
7 Tony Esposito	12.50	30.00
Most Shutouts by a Rookie		
8 Gerry Cheevers	12.50	30.00
Longest Undefeated Streak-Season		
9 Martin Brodeur	30.00	80.00
10 Bernie Parent	12.50	30.00
Most Wins-Season		
11 Terry Sawchuk	30.00	80.00
Most Career Shutouts		
12 Patrick Roy	20.00	50.00
Most Career Playoff Wins		
13 Johnny Bower	12.50	30.00
Oldest NHL Goalie		
14 Ed Belfour	12.50	30.00
Most Consecutive Playoff Wins		
15 Patrick Roy	20.00	50.00
Most Career 30-Win Seasons		
16 Terry Sawchuk	30.00	80.00
Most Career Minutes		

2002-03 Between the Pipes Stick and Jerseys

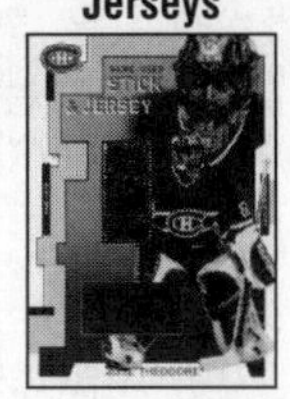

This 30-card set partially paralleled the base jersey set but also carried a piece of game-used stick. Print run was 90 copies each.
STATED PRINT RUN 90 SETS

1 Arturs Irbe	10.00	25.00
2 Miikka Kiprusoff	10.00	25.00
3 Rick DiPietro	10.00	25.00
4 Dan Blackburn	10.00	25.00
5 Dan Cloutier	10.00	25.00
6 David Aebischer	10.00	25.00
7 Evgeni Nabokov	10.00	25.00
8 Felix Potvin	10.00	25.00
9 Manny Fernandez	10.00	25.00
10 J-S Aubin	10.00	25.00
11 J-S Giguere	10.00	25.00
12 Jani Hurme	10.00	25.00
13 Jocelyn Thibault	10.00	25.00
14 Jose Theodore	15.00	40.00
15 Mike Dunham	10.00	25.00
16 Martin Biron	10.00	25.00
17 Johan Hedberg	10.00	25.00
18 Martin Brodeur	20.00	50.00
19 Marty Turco	10.00	25.00
20 Mika Noronen	10.00	25.00
21 Mike Richter	10.00	25.00
22 Nikolai Khabibulin	10.00	25.00
23 Olaf Kolzig	10.00	25.00
24 Patrick Lalime	10.00	25.00
25 Patrick Roy	25.00	60.00
26 Roberto Luongo	15.00	40.00
27 Roman Cechmanek	10.00	25.00
28 Roman Turek	10.00	25.00
29 Sean Burke	10.00	25.00
30 Tommy Salo	10.00	25.00

2002-03 Between the Pipes Tandems

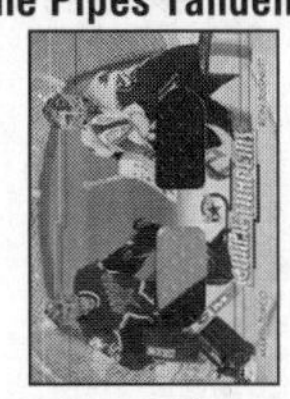

This 20-card memorabilia set featured starting goalies and their backups. Each card was limited to 30 copies.
STATED PRINT RUN 30 SETS

1 Mike Richter	15.00	40.00
Dan Blackburn		
2 Patrick Roy	50.00	125.00
David Aebischer		
3 Jocelyn Thibault	15.00	40.00
Steve Passmore		
4 Evgeni Nabokov	25.00	60.00
Miikka Kiprusoff		
5 Patrick Lalime	15.00	40.00
Martin Prusek		
6 Martin Biron	15.00	40.00
Mika Noronen		
7 Johan Hedberg	15.00	40.00
J-S Aubin		
8 Roman Cechmanek	15.00	40.00
Robert Esche		
9 Jose Theodore	15.00	40.00
Jeff Hackett		
10 Felix Potvin	15.00	40.00
Jamie Storr		
11 Mike Dunham	15.00	40.00
Tomas Voukon		
12 Dan Cloutier	15.00	40.00
Alex Auld		
13 J-S Giguere	15.00	40.00
Martin Gerber		
14 Ed Belfour	30.00	80.00
Trevor Kidd		
15 Brent Johnson	15.00	40.00
Fred Brathwaite		
16 Chris Osgood	15.00	40.00
Rick Dipietro		
17 Steve Shields	15.00	40.00
John Grahame		
18 Tommy Salo	15.00	40.00
Jussi Markkanen		
19 Marty Turco	15.00	40.00
Ron Tugnutt		
20 Olaf Kolzig	15.00	40.00
Maxime Ouellet		

2002-03 Between the Pipes Trappers

Limited to just 60 copies each, this 18-card set featured pieces of game-used goalie trappers.
*MULT.COLOR SWATCH: .75X TO 1.5X
STATED PRINT RUN 60 SETS

GT1 Vladislav Tretiak	50.00	100.00
GT2 Bill Durnan	20.00	50.00
GT3 Dan Cloutier	10.00	25.00
GT4 Byron Dafoe	10.00	25.00
GT5 Johan Hedberg	10.00	25.00
GT6 Charlie Hodge	30.00	80.00
GT7 Nikolai Khabibulin	10.00	25.00
GT8 Jacques Plante	30.00	80.00
GT9 Olaf Kolzig	12.00	30.00
GT10 Harry Lumley	10.00	25.00
GT11 Bernie Parent	25.00	60.00
GT12 Patrick Roy	40.00	100.00
GT13 Terry Sawchuk	30.00	80.00
GT14 Jocelyn Thibault	10.00	25.00
GT15 Marty Turco	12.00	30.00
GT16 Roger Crozier	15.00	40.00
GT17 Sean Burke	10.00	25.00
GT18 Grant Fuhr	20.00	50.00

2002-03 Between the Pipes Vintage Memorabilia

This 20-card memorabilia set was limited to just 20 copies per card. This set is not priced due to scarcity.
STATED PRINT RUN 20 SETS
NOT PRICED DUE TO SCARCITY

1 Johnny Bower
2 Harry Lumley
3 Roger Crozier
4 Ed Giacomin
5 Bill Durnan
6 George Hainsworth
7 Gerry Cheevers
8 Bernie Parent
9 Tony Esposito
10 Jacques Plante
11 Charlie Hodge
12 Glenn Hall
13 Roy Worters
14 Tiny Thompson
15 Charlie Gardiner
16 Terry Sawchuk
17 Frank Brimsek
18 Vladislav Tretiak
19 Bernie Parent
20 Ed Giacomin

2005 Between the Pipes

COMPLETE SET (25)	6.00	15.00
1 Johnny Bower	.40	1.00
2 Turk Broda	.40	1.00
3 Martin Brodeur	1.25	3.00
4 Richard Brodeur	.20	.50
5 Gerry Cheevers	.40	1.00
6 Tony Esposito	.40	1.00
7 Grant Fuhr	.40	1.00
8 Ed Giacomin	.30	.75
9 Glenn Hall	.30	.75
10 Ron Hextall	.40	1.00
11 Charlie Hodge	.20	.50
12 Mike Palmateer	.30	.75
13 Bernie Parent	.40	1.00
14 Jacques Plante	.75	2.00
15 Bill Ranford	.20	.50
16 Chico Resch	.20	.50
17 Patrick Roy	1.25	3.00
18 Terry Sawchuk	.75	2.00
19 Billy Smith	.40	1.00
20 Jose Theodore	.40	1.00
21 Tiny Thompson	.40	1.00
22 Vladislav Tretiak	.40	1.00
23 Rogie Vachon	.30	.75
24 Georges Vezina	.40	1.00
25 Gump Worsley	.40	1.00

2005 Between the Pipes Autographs

COMPLETE SET (20)
RANDOM INSERTS IN BTP BOX SETS

A-BP Bernie Parent	12.00	30.00
A-BR Bill Ranford	6.00	15.00
A-BS Billy Smith	10.00	25.00
A-CH Charlie Hodge	8.00	20.00
A-CR Chico Resch	6.00	15.00
A-EG Ed Giacomin	10.00	25.00
A-GC Gerry Cheevers	10.00	25.00
A-GH Glenn Hall	10.00	25.00
A-GR Grant Fuhr	10.00	25.00
A-GW Gump Worsley	10.00	25.00
A-JB Johnny Bower	12.00	30.00
A-JT Jose Theodore	10.00	25.00
A-MB Martin Brodeur	60.00	100.00
A-MP Mike Palmateer	10.00	25.00
A-PR Patrick Roy	60.00	100.00
A-RB Richard Brodeur	6.00	15.00
A-RH Ron Hextall	10.00	25.00
A-RV Rogie Vachon	8.00	20.00
A-TO Tony Esposito	12.00	30.00
A-VT Vladislav Tretiak	15.00	40.00

2005 Between the Pipes Complete Package

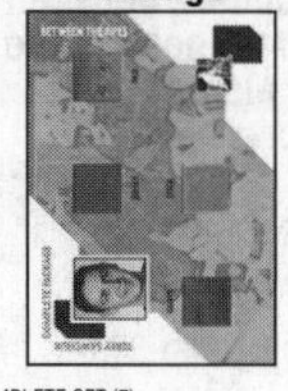

COMPLETE SET (7)
RANDOM INSERTS IN BTP BOX SETS
NOT PRICED DUE TO SCARCITY

CP-1 Grant Fuhr
CP-2 Patrick Roy
CP-3 Jacques Plante
CP-4 Gerry Cheevers
CP-5 Terry Sawchuk
CP-6 Bernie Parent
CP-7 Jose Theodore

2005 Between the Pipes Double Memorabilia

COMPLETE SET (8)
PRINT RUN 40 SER. #'d SETS

DM-1 Patrick Roy	20.00	50.00
DM-2 Patrick Roy	20.00	50.00
DM-3 Martin Brodeur	15.00	40.00
DM-4 Ron Hextall	10.00	25.00
DM-5 Tony Esposito	10.00	25.00
DM-6 Gerry Cheevers	10.00	25.00
DM-7 Vladislav Tretiak	12.00	30.00
DM-8 Jose Theodore	12.00	30.00

2005 Between the Pipes Gloves

COMPLETE SET (8)
RANDOM INSERTS IN BTP BOX SETS

GUG-1 Tony Esposito	10.00	25.00
GUG-2 Patrick Roy	25.00	60.00
GUG-3 Gilles Gilbert	10.00	25.00
GUG-4 Vladislav Tretiak	15.00	40.00
GUG-5 Jose Theodore	10.00	25.00
GUG-6 Rogie Vachon	8.00	20.00
GUG-7 Charlie Hodge	8.00	20.00
GUG-8 Grant Fuhr	10.00	25.00

2005 Between the Pipes Jerseys

COMPLETE SET (12)
RANDOM INSERTS IN BTP BOX SETS

GUJ-1 Patrick Roy	12.00	30.00
GUJ-2 Patrick Roy	12.00	30.00
GUJ-3 Martin Brodeur	12.00	30.00
GUJ-4 Tony Esposito	8.00	20.00
GUJ-5 Vladislav Tretiak	8.00	20.00
GUJ-6 Glenn Hall	8.00	20.00
GUJ-7 Mike Richter	8.00	20.00
GUJ-8 Jose Theodore	8.00	20.00
GUJ-9 Billy Smith	8.00	20.00
GUJ-10 Grant Fuhr	8.00	20.00
GUJ-11 Bill Ranford	5.00	12.00
GUJ-12 Richard Brodeur	5.00	12.00

2005 Between the Pipes Jersey and Sticks

COMPLETE SET (10)
RANDOM INSERTS IN BTP BOX SETS

SJ-1 Patrick Roy		
SJ-2 Patrick Roy	20.00	50.00
SJ-3 Martin Brodeur	15.00	40.00
SJ-4 Ed Giacomin	10.00	25.00
SJ-5 Johnny Bower	10.00	25.00
SJ-6 Tony Esposito	10.00	25.00
SJ-7 Mike Richter	10.00	25.00
SJ-8 Ron Hextall	10.00	25.00
SJ-9 Jose Theodore	10.00	25.00
SJ-10 Grant Fuhr	10.00	25.00

2005 Between the Pipes Pads

COMPLETE SET (8)
PRINT RUN 20 SER. #'d SETS

GUP-1 Bernie Parent	12.00	30.00
GUP-2 Grant Fuhr	12.00	30.00
GUP-3 Gerry Cheevers	12.00	30.00
GUP-4 Ron Hextall	12.00	30.00
GUP-5 Martin Brodeur	15.00	40.00
GUP-6 Patrick Roy	20.00	50.00
GUP-7 Jacques Plante	25.00	60.00
GUP-8 Jose Theodore	12.00	30.00

2005 Between the Pipes Signed Memorabilia

COMPLETE SET (10)
RANDOM INSERTS IN BTP BOX SETS
NOT PRICED DUE TO LACK OF MARKET INFO

SM-1 Patrick Roy
SM-2 Patrick Roy
SM-3 Martin Brodeur
SM-4 Glenn Hall
SM-5 Johnny Bower
SM-6 Gerry Cheevers
SM-7 Ed Giacomin
SM-8 Jose Theodore
SM-9 Grant Fuhr
SM-10 Bernie Parent

2006-07 Between The Pipes

COMPLETE SET (150)	25.00	60.00
1 Al Montoya	.30	.75
2 Andrew Penner	.15	.40
3 Barry Brust	.15	.40
4 Brent Krahn	.15	.40
5 Bryan Pitton	.15	.40
6 Brian Finley		.40
7 Carey Price	1.25	3.00
8 Chris Beckford-Tseu	.30	.75
9 Corey Crawford	.15	.40
10 Craig Anderson	.15	.40
11 Curtis McElhinney	.15	.40
12 David LeNeveu	.25	.60
13 Frank Doyle	.25	.60
14 Frederic Cassivi	.15	.40
15 Gerald Coleman	.15	.40
16 Hannu Toivonen	.30	.75
17 Jaroslav Halak	1.25	3.00
18 Jason Bacashihua	.15	.40
19 Jason LaBarbera	.15	.40
20 Jeff Glass	.25	.60
21 J-F Racine	.15	.40
22 Jimmy Howard	.25	.60
23 John Murray	.15	.40
24 Jonathan Bernier	.25	.60
25 Jordan Parise	.15	.40
26 Josh Harding	.30	.75
27 J-P Levasseur	.15	.40
28 Julien Ellis	.15	.40
29 Justin Leclerc	.15	.40
30 Justin Pogge	.60	1.50
31 Kelly Guard	.15	.40
32 Kevin Lalande	.15	.40
33 Kurt Mucha	.15	.40
34 Kyle Moir	.15	.40
35 Leland Irving	.30	.75
36 Marek Schwarz	.30	.75
37 Martin Houle	.15	.40
38 Michael Leighton	.15	.40
39 Mikael Tellqvist	.30	.75
40 Mike Smith	.30	.75
41 Nicola Riopel	.15	.40
42 Pekka Rinne	.15	.40
43 Philippe Sauve	.15	.40
44 Rejean Beauchemin	.15	.40
45 Ryan Daniels	.15	.40
46 Stefan Liv	.25	.60
47 Tobias Stephan	.15	.40
48 Steve Mason	.15	.40
49 Trevor Cann	.25	.60
50 Tuukka Rask	.40	1.00
51 Tyler Plante	.15	.40
52 Tyson Sexsmith	.15	.40
53 Wade Dubielewicz	.15	.40
54 Yann Danis	.25	.60
55 Yutaka Fukufuji	1.00	2.50
56 Alex Auld	.25	.60
57 Antero Niittymaki	.30	.75
58 Cam Ward	.30	.75
59 Cristobal Huet	.40	1.00
60 Peter Budaj	.25	.60
61 Dominik Hasek	.50	1.25
62 Dwayne Roloson	.25	.60
63 Henrik Lundqvist	.50	1.25
64 Ilya Bryzgalov	.25	.60
65 Ed Belfour	.40	1.00
66 Johan Holmqvist	.25	.60
67 Kari Lehtonen	.30	.75
68 Manny Fernandez	.30	.75
69 Marc-Andre Fleury	.30	.75
70 Martin Brodeur	1.00	2.50
71 Martin Gerber	.30	.75
72 Pascal Leclaire	.30	.75
73 Ray Emery	.30	.75
74 Rick DiPietro	.25	.60
75 Roberto Luongo	.50	1.25
76 Ryan Miller	.40	1.00
77 Tim Thomas	.30	.75
78 Andy Moog	.25	.60
79 Bernie Parent	.25	.60
80 Billy Smith	.30	.75
81 Brian Hayward	.15	.40
82 Charlie Hodge	.15	.40
83 Chico Resch	.15	.40
84 Dan Bouchard	.25	.60
85 Doug Favell	.30	.75
86 Ed Giacomin	.30	.75
87 Emile Francis	.30	.75
88 Felix Potvin	.40	1.00
89 Gerry Cheevers	.40	1.00
90 Gilles Gilbert	.30	.75
91 Glenn Hall	.30	.75
92 Grant Fuhr	.40	1.00
93 Gump Worsley	.30	.75
94 John Davidson	.30	.75
95 Johnny Bower	.30	.75
96 Ken Wregget	.30	.75
97 Mike Palmateer	.40	1.00
98 Patrick Roy	1.50	4.00
99 Richard Brodeur	.25	.60
100 Rogie Vachon	.40	1.00
101 Ron Hextall	.40	1.00
102 Tom Barrasso	.15	.40
103 Tony Esposito	.25	.60
104 Vladislav Tretiak	.75	2.00
105 Al Montoya	.30	.75
106 Cam Ward	.30	.75
107 Carey Price	1.25	3.00
108 Grant Fuhr	.40	1.00
109 Hannu Toivonen	.30	.75
110 Kari Lehtonen	.40	1.00
111 Leland Irving	.25	.60
112 Marc-Andre Fleury	.30	.75
113 Marek Schwarz	.25	.60
114 Martin Brodeur	1.00	2.50
115 Rick DiPietro	.30	.75
116 Tuukka Rask	.50	1.25
117 Martin Brodeur	1.00	2.50
118 Patrick Roy	1.50	4.00
119 Roberto Luongo	.50	1.25
120 Marc-Andre Fleury	.40	1.00
121 Carey Price	1.25	3.00
122 Justin Pogge	.50	1.25
123 Jeff Glass	.30	.75
124 Bill Ranford	.30	.75
125 Ed Belfour	.30	.75
126 George Hainsworth	.30	.75
127 Georges Vezina	.40	1.00
128 Jacques Plante	.40	1.00
129 Pelle Lindbergh	.40	1.00
130 Roger Crozier	.30	.75
131 Roy Worters	.30	.75
132 Terry Sawchuk	.40	1.00
133 Tiny Thompson	.30	.75
134 Turk Broda	.30	.75
135 Bower/Sawchuk	.25	.60
136 Parent/Favell	.60	1.50
137 Smith/Resch	.40	1.00
138 Worsley/Vachon	.30	.75
139 Belfour/Hasek	.50	1.25
140 Giacomin/Davidson	.40	1.00
141 Plante/Hall	.75	2.00
142 Hasek/Fuhr	.50	1.25
143 Patrick Roy	1.50	4.00
144 Terry Sawchuk	.40	1.00
145 Bernie Parent	.30	.75
146 George Hainsworth	.30	.75
147 Glenn Hall	.30	.75
148 Grant Fuhr	.30	.75
149 Martin Brodeur	1.00	2.50
150 Gerry Cheevers	.30	.75

2006-07 Between The Pipes Aspiring

STATED PRINT RUN 50 SETS

AS01 Martin Brodeur	15.00	40.00
Cam Ward		
AS02 Patrick Roy	25.00	60.00
Cristobal Huet		
AS03 Dominik Hasek	15.00	40.00
Ryan Miller		
AS04 Roberto Luongo	15.00	40.00
Leland Irving		
AS05 Patrick Roy	40.00	80.00
Carey Price		
AS06 Dominik Hasek	12.00	30.00
Marek Schwarz		
AS07 Grant Fuhr	12.00	30.00
Ray Emery		
AS08 Pelle Lindbergh	25.00	60.00
Henrik Lundqvist		
AS09 Martin Brodeur	12.00	30.00
Jeff Glass		
AS10 Patrick Roy	25.00	60.00
Jonathan Bernier		

2006-07 Between The Pipes Aspiring Gold

STATED PRINT RUN 10 SETS
NOT PRICED DUE TO SCARCITY

2006-07 Between The Pipes Autographs

ODDS 1:24
AMF2 Marc-Andre Fleury SP 40.00 100.00
AAM2 Al Montoya SP 8.00 20.00
ACW2 Cam Ward SP 12.00 30.00
ACP2 Carey Price SP 50.00 125.00
AGF2 Grant Fuhr SP 8.00 20.00
AHT2 Hannu Toivonen SP 8.00 20.00
ALI2 Leland Irving SP 12.00 30.00
AMS2 Marek Schwarz SP 20.00 50.00
AMB2 Martin Brodeur SP 40.00 100.00
ARDI Rick DiPietro SP 10.00 25.00
ATR2 Tuukka Rask SP 15.00 40.00
AKL2 Kari Lehtonen SP 20.00 50.00
AAP Andrew Penner 6.00 15.00
ABF Brian Finley 5.00 12.00
AFD Frank Doyle 6.00 15.00
AJHA Jaroslav Halak 15.00 40.00
AJDL Jeff Deslauriers 5.00 12.00
AJFR J-F Racine 6.00 15.00
AJPA Jordan Parise 10.00 25.00
AJL Justin Leclerc 5.00 12.00
AKG Kelly Guard 6.00 15.00
AKMU Kurt Mucha 5.00 12.00
ANR Nicola Riopel 5.00 12.00
ATST Tobias Stephan 4.00 10.00
ATC Trevor Cann 4.00 10.00
AAM Al Montoya 6.00 15.00
ABB Barry Brust 4.00 10.00
ABK Brent Krahn 6.00 15.00
ABPI Bryan Pitton 4.00 10.00
ACP Carey Price 30.00 80.00
ACC Corey Crawford 4.00 10.00
ACA Craig Anderson 4.00 10.00
ACM Curtis McElhinney 4.00 10.00
ADD Devan Dubnyk 6.00 15.00
AFC Frederic Cassivi 4.00 10.00
AHT Hannu Toivonen 10.00 25.00
AJBA Jason Bacashihua 6.00 15.00
AJG Jeff Glass 12.00 30.00
AJH Jimmy Howard 6.00 15.00
AJM John Murray 4.00 10.00
AJBE Jonathan Bernier 8.00 20.00
AJHR Josh Harding 6.00 15.00
AJPL J-P Levasseur 4.00 10.00
AJE Julien Ellis 4.00 10.00
AJP Justin Pogge 15.00 40.00
AKLA Kevin Lalande 4.00 10.00
AKM Kyle Moir 4.00 10.00
ALI Leland Irving 12.00 30.00
AMS Marek Schwarz 15.00 40.00
AMH Martin Houle 6.00 15.00
AMSM Mike Smith 10.00 25.00
APRI Pekka Rinne 4.00 10.00
APS Philippe Sauve 4.00 10.00
ARB Rejean Beauchemin 6.00 15.00
ARD Ryan Daniels 6.00 15.00
ASL Stefan Liv 6.00 15.00
ASM Steve Mason 4.00 10.00
ATR Tuukka Rask 15.00 40.00
ATP Tyler Plante 4.00 10.00
ATS Tyson Sexsmith 4.00 10.00
AWD Wade Dubielewicz 6.00 15.00
AYD Yann Danis 6.00 15.00
ATM Thomas McCollum 4.00 10.00
AYFA Yutaka Fukufuji 50.00 125.00
AML Michael Leighton 6.00 15.00
AJLB Jason LaBarbera 6.00 15.00
ACBT Chris Beckford-Tseu 8.00 20.00
ADL David LeNeveu 5.00 12.00
AAMO Andy Moog 6.00 15.00
ABP Bernie Parent 10.00 25.00
ABS Billy Smith 8.00 20.00
ABH Brian Hayward 6.00 15.00
ACHO Charlie Hodge 12.00 30.00
ACR Chico Resch 10.00 25.00
ADB Dan Bouchard 6.00 15.00
ADF Doug Favell 6.00 15.00
AEG Ed Giacomin 10.00 30.00
AEF Emile Francis 10.00 25.00
AFP Felix Potvin 12.00 30.00
AGC Gerry Cheevers 8.00 20.00
AGG Gilles Gilbert 8.00 20.00
AGH Glenn Hall 12.00 30.00
AGF Grant Fuhr 8.00 20.00
AGW Gump Worsley 20.00 40.00
AJD John Davidson 10.00 25.00
AJB Johnny Bower 10.00 25.00
AKW Ken Wregget 6.00 15.00
AMP Mike Palmateer 10.00 25.00
APR Patrick Roy SP 40.00 100.00
ARBR Richard Brodeur 6.00 15.00
ARV Rogie Vachon 8.00 20.00
ARH Ron Hextall 10.00 25.00
ATB Tom Barrasso 10.00 25.00
ATE Tony Esposito 8.00 20.00
AVT Vladislav Tretiak 20.00 50.00
ABR Bill Ranford 10.00 25.00
AJV John Vanbiesbrouck 10.00 25.00
AAA Alex Auld 8.00 20.00
AAN Antero Niittymaki 10.00 25.00
ACW Cam Ward 15.00 30.00
ACH Cristobal Huet 12.00 30.00
ADH Dominik Hasek SP 25.00 50.00
ADR Dwayne Roloson 6.00 15.00
AEB Ed Belfour 20.00 50.00
AHL Henrik Lundqvist 12.00 30.00
AIB Ilya Bryzgalov 6.00 15.00
AJHO Johan Holmqvist 6.00 15.00
AMFR Manny Fernandez 8.00 20.00
AMF Marc-Andre Fleury SP 12.00 30.00
AMB Martin Brodeur SP 50.00 100.00
AMG Martin Gerber 10.00 25.00
APL Pascal Leclaire 6.00 15.00
ARE Ray Emery 8.00 20.00
ARL Roberto Luongo 15.00 40.00
ARM Ryan Miller 10.00 25.00
ATT Tim Thomas 6.00 15.00
AKL Kari Lehtonen 10.00 25.00
ACP3 Carey Price SP 25.00 60.00
AEB2 Ed Belfour SP 20.00 50.00
AJG2 Jeff Glass SP 4.00 10.00
AJP2 Justin Pogge SP 25.00 60.00
AMF3 Marc-Andre Fleury SP 15.00 40.00
AMB3 Martin Brodeur SP 50.00 125.00
APR2 Patrick Roy SP 75.00 150.00
ARL2 Roberto Luongo SP 40.00 100.00
AYFB Yutaka Fukufuji KANJI 175.00325.00

2006-07 Between The Pipes Complete Jersey

STATED PRINT RUN 10 SETS
NOT PRICED DUE TO SCARCITY
CJ01 Cam Ward
CJ02 Glenn Hall
CJ03 Martin Brodeur
CJ04 Ray Emery
CJ05 Tony Esposito
CJ06 Manny Fernandez
CJ07 Marc-Andre Fleury
CJ08 Dominik Hasek
CJ09 Mike Palmateer
CJ10 Cristobal Huet
CJ11 Vladislav Tretiak
CJ12 Kari Lehtonen
CJ13 Tom Barrasso
CJ14 Roberto Luongo
CJ15 Ryan Miller
CJ16 Rogie Vachon
CJ17 Patrick Roy (MTL)
CJ18 Curtis Joseph
CJ19 Patrick Roy (COL)
CJ20 Felix Potvin

2006-07 Between The Pipes Complete Jersey Gold

STATED PRINT RUN 1 SET
NOT PRICED DUE TO SCARCITY

2006-07 Between The Pipes Complete Package

STATED PRINT RUN 10 SETS
NOT PRICED DUE TO SCARCITY
CP01 Gerry Cheevers
CP02 Grant Fuhr
CP03 Bernie Parent
CP04 Jacques Plante
CP05 Patrick Roy (MTL)
CP06 Patrick Roy (COL)
CP07 Terry Sawchuk
CP08 Marc-Andre Fleury
CP09 Martin Brodeur
CP10 Dominik Hasek

2006-07 Between The Pipes Complete Package Gold

STATED PRINT RUN 1 SET
NOT PRICED DUE TO SCARCITY

2006-07 Between The Pipes Double Jerseys

STATED PRINT RUN 40 SETS
DJ01 Al Montoya 10.00 25.00
John Davidson
DJ02 Dwayne Roloson 8.00 20.00
Manny Fernandez
DJ03 Ron Hextall 25.00 60.00
Bernie Parent
DJ04 Cam Ward 15.00 40.00
Martin Brodeur
DJ05 Cristobal Huet 25.00 60.00
Patrick Roy
DJ06 Dominik Hasek 15.00 40.00
Ryan Miller
DJ07 Dominik Hasek 15.00 40.00
Terry Sawchuk
DJ08 Ed Giacomin 30.00 80.00
Henrik Lundqvist
DJ09 Vladislav Tretiak 15.00 40.00
Vladimir Myshkin
DJ10 Gerry Cheevers 12.00 30.00
Tim Thomas
DJ11 Glenn Hall 12.00 30.00
Tony Esposito
DJ12 Grant Fuhr 15.00 40.00
Bill Ranford
DJ13 Jacques Plante 30.00 60.00
Gump Worsley
DJ14 John Davidson 12.00 30.00
Mike Richter
DJ15 Felix Potvin 15.00 40.00
Justin Pogge
DJ16 Antero Niittymaki 8.00 20.00
Kari Lehtonen
DJ17 Dan Bouchard 20.00 50.00
Patrick Roy
DJ18 Marc-Andre Fleury 15.00 40.00
Tom Barrasso
DJ19 Martin Brodeur 30.00 80.00
Terry Sawchuk
DJ20 Ilya Bryzgalov 15.00 40.00
Vladislav Tretiak
DJ21 Patrick Roy 30.00 80.00
Carey Price
DJ22 Patrick Roy 40.00 100.00
Martin Brodeur
DJ23 Ray Emery 12.00 30.00
Dominik Hasek
DJ24 Rick DiPietro 15.00 40.00
Billy Smith
DJ25 Roberto Luongo 20.00 50.00
Martin Brodeur
DJ26 Roy Worters 8.00 20.00
Frank Brimsek
DJ27 John Vanbiesbrouck 30.00 60.00
Mike Richter
DJ28 Felix Potvin 15.00 40.00
Andrew Raycroft
DJ29 Roberto Luongo 20.00 50.00
Patrick Roy

2006-07 Between The Pipes Double Jerseys Gold

STATED PRINT RUN 10 SETS
NOT PRICED DUE TO SCARCITY

2006-07 Between The Pipes Double Memorabilia

STATED PRINT RUN 40 SETS
DM01 Rogie Vachon 12.00 30.00
DM02 Martin Brodeur 20.00 50.00
DM03 Gerry Cheevers 12.00 30.00
DM04 Tony Esposito 10.00 25.00
DM05 Marc-Andre Fleury 10.00 25.00
DM06 Ed Giacomin 15.00 40.00
DM07 Dominik Hasek 12.00 30.00
DM08 Ron Hextall 20.00 50.00
DM09 Leland Irving 15.00 40.00
DM10 Roberto Luongo 15.00 40.00
DM11 Al Montoya 10.00 25.00
DM12 Bernie Parent 15.00 40.00
DM13 Jacques Plante 15.00 40.00
DM14 Patrick Roy (COL) 20.00 50.00
DM15 Patrick Roy (MTL) 20.00 50.00
DM16 Terry Sawchuk 20.00 50.00
DM17 Tiny Thompson 10.00 25.00
DM18 Hannu Toivonen 10.00 25.00
DM19 Vladislav Tretiak 15.00 40.00
DM20 Felix Potvin 15.00 40.00

2006-07 Between The Pipes Double Memorabilia Gold

STATED PRINT RUN 10 SETS
NOT PRICED DUE TO SCARCITY

2006-07 Between The Pipes Emblems

STATED PRINT RUN 10 SETS
NOT PRICED DUE TO SCARCITY
GUE01 Rogie Vachon
GUE02 Marc-Andre Fleury
GUE03 Henrik Lundqvist
GUE04 Tony Esposito
GUE05 Manny Fernandez
GUE06 Jeff Glass
GUE07 Kelly Guard
GUE08 Ron Hextall
GUE09 Kari Lehtonen
GUE10 Roberto Luongo
GUE11 Antero Niittymaki
GUE12 Billy Smith
GUE13 Mike Smith
GUE14 Hannu Toivonen
GUE15 Gump Worsley
GUE16 Tom Barrasso
GUE17 Richard Brodeur
GUE18 Barry Brust
GUE19 Dwayne Roloson
GUE20 Martin Gerber
GUE21 Jason Bacashihua
GUE22 Jonathan Bernier
GUE23 Rejean Beauchemin
GUE24 Ryan Daniels
GUE25 Yann Danis
GUE26 Curtis McElhinney
GUE27 Brian Finley
GUE28 Mathieu Garon
GUE29 Johan Holmqvist
GUE30 Mikael Tellqvist
GUE31 Pekka Rinne
GUE32 Bill Ranford
GUE33 Andrew Penner
GUE34 Corey Crawford
GUE35 Andy Moog
GUE36 Jimmy Howard
GUE37 Josh Harding
GUE38 Martin Houle
GUE39 Pascal Leclaire
GUE40 Vladislav Tretiak
GUE41 Leland Irving
GUE42 Philippe Sauve
GUE43 Brent Krahn
GUE44 Maxime Ouellet
GUE45 Grant Fuhr
GUE46 Cristobal Huet
GUE47 Ryan Miller
GUE48 Carey Price
GUE49 Terry Sawchuk
GUE50 Tim Thomas
GUE51 Justin Pogge
GUE52 Ed Giacomin
GUE53 Andrew Raycroft
GUE54 Frank Brimsek
GUE55 Glenn Hall
GUE56 Ray Emery
GUE57 J-S Aubin
GUE58 Ilya Bryzgalov
GUE59 Marek Schwarz
GUE60 Peter Budaj
GUE61 Dominik Hasek
GUE62 Curtis Joseph
GUE63 Felix Potvin
GUE64 Cam Ward
GUE65 Mike Richter
GUE66 Patrick Roy
GUE67 David LeNeveu
GUE68 Alex Auld
GUE69 Rick DiPietro
GUE70 Martin Brodeur
GUE71 Ed Belfour

2006-07 Between The Pipes Emblems Gold

STATED PRINT RUN 1 SET
NOT PRICED DUE TO SCARCITY

2006-07 Between The Pipes Emblems Autographs

STATED PRINT RUN 10 SETS
NOT PRICED DUE TO SCARCITY
GUE01 Rogie Vachon
GUE02 Marc-Andre Fleury
GUE03 Henrik Lundqvist
GUE04 Tony Esposito
GUE05 Manny Fernandez
GUE06 Jeff Glass
GUE07 Kelly Guard
GUE08 Ron Hextall
GUE10 Roberto Luongo
GUE11 Antero Niittymaki
GUE12 Billy Smith
GUE13 Mike Smith
GUE14 Hannu Toivonen
GUE15 Gump Worsley
GUE16 Tom Barrasso
GUE17 Richard Brodeur
GUE18 Barry Brust
GUE19 Dwayne Roloson
GUE20 Martin Gerber
GUE21 Jason Bacashihua
GUE22 Jonathan Bernier
GUE23 Rejean Beauchemin
GUE24 Ryan Daniels
GUE25 Yann Danis
GUE26 Curtis McElhinney
GUE27 Brian Finley
GUE29 Johan Holmqvist
GUE31 Pekka Rinne
GUE32 Bill Ranford
GUE33 Andrew Penner
GUE34 Corey Crawford
GUE35 Andy Moog
GUE36 Jimmy Howard
GUE37 Josh Harding
GUE38 Martin Houle
GUE39 Pascal Leclaire
GUE40 Vladislav Tretiak
GUE41 Leland Irving
GUE42 Philippe Sauve
GUE43 Brent Krahn
GUE45 Grant Fuhr
GUE46 Cristobal Huet
GUE47 Ryan Miller
GUE48 Carey Price
GUE50 Tim Thomas
GUE51 Justin Pogge
GUE55 Glenn Hall
GUE56 Ray Emery
GUE58 Ilya Bryzgalov
GUE59 Marek Schwarz
GUE61 Dominik Hasek
GUE63 Felix Potvin
GUE64 Cam Ward
GUE66 Patrick Roy
GUE68 Alex Auld
GUE70 Martin Brodeur
GUE71 Ed Belfour

2006-07 Between The Pipes Forgotten Franchises

COMPLETE SET (10) 12.00 30.00
ODDS 1:12 PACKS
FF01 Chuck Rayner 1.50 4.00
FF02 Hap Holmes 1.50 4.00
FF03 Alex Connell 1.50 4.00
FF04 Jake Forbes 1.50 4.00
FF05 Lorne Chabot 1.50 4.00
FF06 Earl Robertson 1.50 4.00
FF07 Clint Benedict 1.50 4.00
FF08 Wilf Cude 1.50 4.00
FF09 Roy Worters 1.50 4.00
FF10 Paddy Moran 1.50 4.00

2006-07 Between The Pipes Gloves

STATED PRINT RUN 50 SETS
GG01 Martin Brodeur 20.00 50.00
GG02 Rick DiPietro 12.00 30.00
GG03 Tony Esposito 12.00 30.00
GG04 Marc-Andre Fleury 12.00 30.00
GG05 Grant Fuhr 12.00 30.00
GG06 Ed Giacomin 20.00 50.00
GG07 Gilles Gilbert 15.00 40.00
GG08 David LeNeveu 8.00 20.00
GG09 Dominik Hasek 15.00 40.00
GG10 Charlie Hodge 12.00 30.00
GG11 Leland Irving 10.00 25.00
GG12 Curtis Joseph 15.00 40.00
GG13 Felix Potvin 15.00 40.00
GG14 Al Montoya 8.00 20.00
GG15 Jacques Plante
GG16 Patrick Roy 20.00 50.00
GG17 Hannu Toivonen 10.00 25.00
GG18 Gump Worsley 12.00 30.00
GG19 Glenn Hall

2006-07 Between The Pipes Gloves Gold

STATED PRINT RUN 10 SETS
NOT PRICED DUE TO SCARCITY

2006-07 Between The Pipes Jerseys

STATED PRINT RUN 90 SETS
GUJ01 Rogie Vachon 6.00 20.00
GUJ02 Marc-Andre Fleury 8.00 20.00
GUJ03 Henrik Lundqvist 10.00 25.00
GUJ04 Tony Esposito 8.00 20.00
GUJ05 Manny Fernandez 6.00 15.00
GUJ06 Jeff Glass 6.00 15.00
GUJ07 Kelly Guard 6.00 15.00
GUJ08 Ron Hextall 8.00 20.00
GUJ09 Kari Lehtonen 8.00 20.00
GUJ10 Roberto Luongo 10.00 25.00
GUJ11 Antero Niittymaki 6.00 15.00
GUJ12 Billy Smith 8.00 20.00
GUJ13 Mike Smith 6.00 15.00
GUJ14 Hannu Toivonen 6.00 15.00
GUJ15 Gump Worsley 8.00 20.00
GUJ16 Tom Barrasso 6.00 15.00
GUJ17 Richard Brodeur 6.00 15.00
GUJ18 Barry Brust 6.00 15.00
GUJ19 Dwayne Roloson 8.00 20.00
GUJ20 Martin Gerber 8.00 20.00
GUJ21 Jason Bacashihua 6.00 15.00
GUJ22 Jonathan Bernier 6.00 15.00
GUJ23 Rejean Beauchemin 6.00 15.00
GUJ24 Ryan Daniels 6.00 15.00
GUJ25 Yann Danis 6.00 15.00
GUJ26 Curtis McElhinney 6.00 15.00
GUJ27 Brian Finley 6.00 15.00
GUJ28 Mathieu Garon 6.00 15.00
GUJ29 Johan Holmqvist 6.00 15.00
GUJ30 Mikael Tellqvist 6.00 15.00
GUJ31 Pekka Rinne 6.00 15.00
GUJ32 Bill Ranford 8.00 20.00
GUJ33 Andrew Penner 6.00 15.00
GUJ34 Corey Crawford 6.00 15.00
GUJ35 Andy Moog 6.00 15.00
GUJ36 Jimmy Howard 6.00 15.00
GUJ37 Josh Harding 6.00 15.00
GUJ38 Martin Houle 6.00 15.00
GUJ39 Pascal Leclaire 6.00 15.00
GUJ40 Vladislav Tretiak 10.00 25.00
GUJ41 Leland Irving 6.00 15.00
GUJ42 Philippe Sauve 6.00 15.00
GUJ43 Brent Krahn 6.00 15.00
GUJ44 Maxime Ouellet 6.00 15.00
GUJ45 Grant Fuhr 10.00 25.00
GUJ46 Cristobal Huet 10.00 25.00
GUJ47 Ryan Miller 8.00 20.00
GUJ48 Carey Price 8.00 20.00
GUJ49 Terry Sawchuk 10.00 25.00
GUJ50 Tim Thomas 6.00 15.00
GUJ51 Justin Pogge 8.00 20.00
GUJ52 Ed Giacomin 10.00 25.00
GUJ53 Andrew Raycroft 6.00 15.00
GUJ54 Frank Brimsek 8.00 20.00
GUJ55 Glenn Hall 8.00 20.00
GUJ56 Ray Emery 6.00 15.00
GUJ57 J-S Aubin 6.00 15.00
GUJ58 Ilya Bryzgalov 6.00 15.00
GUJ59 Marek Schwarz 6.00 15.00
GUJ60 Peter Budaj 6.00 15.00
GUJ61 Dominik Hasek 10.00 25.00
GUJ62 Curtis Joseph 8.00 20.00
GUJ63 Felix Potvin 8.00 20.00
GUJ64 Cam Ward 8.00 20.00
GUJ65 Mike Richter 6.00 15.00
GUJ66 Patrick Roy 15.00 40.00
GUJ67 David LeNeveu 6.00 15.00
GUJ68 Alex Auld 6.00 15.00
GUJ69 Rick DiPietro 6.00 15.00
GUJ70 Martin Brodeur 12.00 30.00
GUJ71 Ed Belfour 8.00 20.00

2006-07 Between The Pipes Jerseys Gold

STATED PRINT RUN 10 SETS
NOT PRICED DUE TO SCARCITY

2006-07 Between The Pipes Jerseys Autographs

STATED PRINT RUN 10 SETS
NOT PRICED DUE TO SCARCITY
GUJ01 Rogie Vachon
GUJ02 Marc-Andre Fleury
GUJ03 Henrik Lundqvist
GUJ04 Tony Esposito
GUJ05 Manny Fernandez
GUJ06 Jeff Glass
GUJ07 Kelly Guard
GUJ08 Ron Hextall
GUJ10 Roberto Luongo
GUJ11 Antero Niittymaki
GUJ12 Billy Smith
GUJ13 Mike Smith
GUJ14 Hannu Toivonen
GUJ15 Gump Worsley
GUJ16 Tom Barrasso
GUJ17 Richard Brodeur
GUJ18 Barry Brust
GUJ19 Dwayne Roloson
GUJ20 Martin Gerber
GUJ21 Jason Bacashihua
GUJ22 Jonathan Bernier
GUJ23 Rejean Beauchemin
GUJ24 Ryan Daniels
GUJ25 Yann Danis
GUJ26 Curtis McElhinney
GUJ27 Brian Finley
GUJ29 Johan Holmqvist
GUJ31 Pekka Rinne
GUJ32 Bill Ranford
GUJ33 Andrew Penner
GUJ34 Corey Crawford
GUJ35 Andy Moog
GUJ36 Jimmy Howard
GUJ37 Josh Harding
GUJ38 Martin Houle
GUJ39 Pascal Leclaire
GUJ40 Vladislav Tretiak
GUJ41 Leland Irving
GUJ42 Philippe Sauve
GUJ43 Brent Krahn
GUJ45 Grant Fuhr
GUJ46 Cristobal Huet
GUJ47 Ryan Miller
GUJ48 Carey Price
GUJ50 Tim Thomas
GUJ51 Justin Pogge
GUJ55 Glenn Hall
GUJ56 Ray Emery
GUJ58 Ilya Bryzgalov
GUJ59 Marek Schwarz
GUJ61 Dominik Hasek
GUJ63 Felix Potvin
GUJ64 Cam Ward
GUJ66 Patrick Roy
GUJ68 Alex Auld
GUJ70 Martin Brodeur
GUJ71 Ed Belfour

2006-07 Between The Pipes Numbers

STATED PRINT RUN 10 SETS
NOT PRICED DUE TO SCARCITY
GUN01 Rogie Vachon
GUN02 Marc-Andre Fleury
GUN03 Henrik Lundqvist
GUN04 Tony Esposito
GUN05 Manny Fernandez
GUN06 Jeff Glass
GUN07 Kelly Guard
GUN08 Ron Hextall
GUN09 Kari Lehtonen
GUN10 Roberto Luongo
GUN11 Antero Niittymaki
GUN12 Billy Smith
GUN13 Mike Smith
GUN14 Hannu Toivonen
GUN15 Gump Worsley
GUN16 Tom Barrasso
GUN17 Richard Brodeur
GUN18 Barry Brust
GUN19 Dwayne Roloson
GUN20 Martin Gerber
GUN21 Jason Bacashihua
GUN22 Jonathan Bernier
GUN23 Rejean Beauchemin
GUN24 Ryan Daniels
GUN25 Yann Danis
GUN26 Curtis McElhinney
GUN27 Brian Finley
GUN28 Mathieu Garon
GUN29 Johan Holmqvist
GUN30 Mikael Tellqvist
GUN31 Pekka Rinne
GUN32 Bill Ranford
GUN33 Andrew Penner
GUN34 Corey Crawford
GUN35 Andy Moog
GUN36 Jimmy Howard
GUN37 Josh Harding
GUN38 Martin Houle
GUN39 Pascal Leclaire
GUN40 Vladislav Tretiak
GUN41 Leland Irving
GUN42 Philippe Sauve
GUN43 Brent Krahn
GUN44 Maxime Ouellet
GUN45 Grant Fuhr
GUN46 Cristobal Huet
GUN47 Ryan Miller
GUN48 Carey Price
GUN49 Terry Sawchuk
GUN50 Tim Thomas
GUN51 Justin Pogge
GUN52 Ed Giacomin
GUN53 Andrew Raycroft
GUN54 Frank Brimsek
GUN55 Glenn Hall
GUN56 Ray Emery
GUN57 J-S Aubin
GUN58 Ilya Bryzgalov
GUN59 Marek Schwarz
GUN60 Peter Budaj
GUN61 Dominik Hasek
GUN62 Curtis Joseph
GUN63 Felix Potvin
GUN64 Cam Ward
GUN65 Mike Richter
GUN66 Patrick Roy
GUN67 David LeNeveu
GUN68 Alex Auld
GUN69 Rick DiPietro
GUN70 Martin Brodeur
GUN71 Ed Belfour

2006-07 Between The Pipes Numbers Gold

STATED PRINT RUN 1 SET
NOT PRICED DUE TO SCARCITY

2006-07 Between The Pipes Numbers Autographs

STATED PRINT RUN 10 SETS
NOT PRICED DUE TO SCARCITY

2006-07 Between The Pipes Pads

STATED PRINT RUN 70 SETS
GP01 Martin Brodeur 20.00 50.00
GP02 Gerry Cheevers 8.00 20.00
GP03 Grant Fuhr 8.00 20.00
GP04 Bernie Parent 8.00 20.00
GP05 Jacques Plante 12.00 30.00
GP06 Patrick Roy 25.00 60.00
GP07 Tiny Thompson 8.00 20.00
GP08 Vladislav Tretiak 25.00 60.00
GP09 Curtis Joseph 10.00 25.00
GP10 Ron Hextall 10.00 25.00
GP11 Ed Belfour 10.00 25.00

2006-07 Between The Pipes Pads Gold

STATED PRINT RUN 10 SETS
NOT PRICED DUE TO SCARCITY

2006-07 Between The Pipes Playing For Your Country

STATED PRINT RUN 40 SETS
PC01 Jonathan Bernier 10.00 25.00
PC02 Martin Brodeur 15.00 40.00
PC03 Ilya Bryzgalov 10.00 25.00
PC04 Roberto Luongo 12.00 30.00
PC05 Tom Barrasso 12.00 30.00
PC06 Vladimir Dzurilla 10.00 25.00
PC07 Grant Fuhr 12.00 30.00
PC08 Dominik Hasek 12.00 30.0
PC09 Cristobal Huet 12.00 30.0
PC10 Marc-Andre Fleury 12.00 30.0
PC11 Carey Price 20.00 50.0
PC12 John Vanbiesbrouck 10.00 25.0
PC13 Henrik Lundqvist 12.00 30.0
PC14 Rogie Vachon 10.00 25.0
PC15 Al Montoya 10.00 25.0
PC16 Vladimir Myshkin 12.00 30.0
PC17 Antero Niittymaki 10.00 25.0
PC18 Justin Pogge 12.00 30.0
PC19 Tony Esposito 10.00 25.0
PC20 Mike Richter 10.00 25.0
PC21 Patrick Roy 25.00 60.
PC22 Marek Schwarz 10.00 25.
PC23 Hannu Toivonen 10.00 25.
PC24 Vladislav Tretiak 15.00 40.
PC25 Curtis Joseph 10.00 25.
PC26 Kari Lehtonen 10.00 25.0

2006-07 Between The Pipes Playing For Your Country Gold

STATED PRINT RUN 10 SETS
NOT PRICED DUE TO SCARCITY

2006-07 Between The Pipes Prospect Trios

STATED PRINT RUN 40 SETS
PT01 Tim Thomas 15.00 40.0
Brian Finley
Hannu Toivonen
PT02 Pascal Leclaire
Peter Budaj
Josh Harding
PT03 Ray Emery 15.00 40.0
Jeff Glass
Kelly Guard
PT04 Antero Niittymaki 15.00 40.
Martin Houle
Rejean Beauchemin
PT05 Curtis McElhinney 10.00 25.
Kevin Lalande
Leland Irving
PT06 Leland Irving 20.00 50.
Jonathan Bernier
Trevor Cann
PT07 Carey Price 15.00 40.0
Jean-Philippe Levasseur
Steve Mason
PT08 Julien Ellis 10.00 25.0
Dan LaCosta
Justin Peters
PT09 Carey Price 20.00 50.0
Kristofer Westblom
Leland Irving
PT10 Kevin Lalande 10.00 25.0
Tyler Plante
Kyle Moir
PT11 Ryan Daniels 10.00 25.0
Alexandre Vincent
Julien Ellis
PT12 Carey Price 20.00 50.
Jonathan Boutin
Jonathan Bernier
PT13 Marc-Andre Fleury 20.00 50.
Alex Auld
Kari Lehtonen
PT14 Jonathan Bernier 15.00 40.
Barry Brust
Jason Labarbera
PT15 Cristobal Huet 20.00 50.
Carey Price
Yann Danis
PT16 Chris Beckford-Tseu
Marek Schwarz
Jason Bacashihua
PT17 J-S Aubin 10.00 25.0
Gerald Coleman
Corey Crawford
PT18 Justin Pogge
Ilya Bryzgalov
Al Montoya
PT19 Billy Thompson 10.00 25.0
Jonathan Boutin
Adam Munro
PT20 David LeNeveu 10.00 25.0
Frederic Cassivi
Maxime Ouellet

2006-07 Between The Pipes Prospect Trios Gold

STATED PRINT RUN 10 SETS
NOT PRICED DUE TO SCARCITY

2006-07 Between The Pipes Roy vs. Brodeur

JSY PRINT RUN 25 SETS
PATCH PRINT RUN 10 SETS
NOT PRICED DUE TO SCARCITY
AU PRINT RUN 10 SETS
NOT PRICED DUE TO SCARCITY
RB01 Roy (MTL)/Brodeur JSY 40.00 80.0
RB02 Roy (COL)/Brodeur JSY 40.00 80.0
RB03 Roy (MTL)/Brodeur JSY 40.00 80.0
RB04 Roy (COL)/Brodeur JSY 40.00 80.0
RB05 Roy/Brodeur JSY 40.00 80.0
RB06 Roy/Brodeur JSY 40.00 80.0
RB07 Roy/Brodeur Patch/10
RB08 Roy/Brodeur Patch/10
RB09 Roy (MTL)/Brodeur AU/10
RB10 Roy (COL)/Brodeur AU/10

006-07 Between he Pipes Roy vs. Brodeur Gold

ED PRINT RUN 1 SET
PRICED DUE TO SCARCITY

006-07 Between e Pipes Shooting Gallery

ED PRINT RUN 30 SETS
Vezina 250.00 400.00
lante
achon
oy
uet
rice
Bower 125.00 250.00
awchuk
almateer
otvin
aycroft
ogge
Thompson 100.00 175.00
heevers
ilbert
loog
homas
oivonen
Gardiner 125.00 250.00
rancis
rimsek
umley
all
sposito
Giacomin 150.00 300.00
avidson
anbiesbrouck
ichter
undqvist
ontoya
Sawchuk 150.00 300.00
rozier
iacomin
ernon
asek
loward
Parent 125.00 250.00
indbergh
extall
iittymaki
oule
eauchemin
Tretiak 150.00 300.00
asek
ichter
rodeur
ehtonen
undqvist
Sawchuk 125.00 250.00
ante
ower
all
heevers
iacomin
Durnan 250.00 400.00
ante
all
oy
asek
rodeur

006-07 Between e Pipes Shooting Gallery Gold

ED PRINT RUN 10 SETS
RICED DUE TO SCARCITY

006-07 Between e Pipes Stick and Jersey

ED PRINT RUN 40 SETS
Manny Fernandez 10.00 25.00
Johnny Bower 10.00 25.00
Martin Brodeur 20.00 50.00
Gerry Cheevers 12.00 30.00
John Davidson 10.00 25.00
Rick DiPietro 15.00 40.00
Ray Emery 10.00 25.00
Tony Esposito 12.00 30.00
Marc-Andre Fleury 15.00 40.00
Grant Fuhr 12.00 30.00
Ed Giacomin 12.00 30.00
Glenn Hall 12.00 30.00
Dominik Hasek 12.00 30.00
Ron Hextall 15.00 40.00
Cristobal Huet 12.00 30.00
Leland Irving 12.00 30.00
Jason LaBarbera 10.00 25.00
Roberto Luongo 15.00 40.00
Henrik Lundqvist 12.00 30.00
Ryan Miller 15.00 40.00
Al Montoya 10.00 25.00
Antero Niittymaki 10.00 25.00
Felix Potvin 15.00 40.00
Bernie Parent 15.00 40.00
Jacques Plante 20.00 50.00
Andrew Raycroft 10.00 25.00
Mike Richter 10.00 25.00
Pekka Rinne 10.00 25.00
Patrick Roy (COL) 20.00 50.00
Patrick Roy (MTL) 25.00 60.00
Terry Sawchuk 20.00 50.00
Billy Smith 12.00 30.00
Roger Crozier 10.00 25.00
Tim Thomas 10.00 25.00
Hannu Toivonen 10.00 25.00
Rogie Vachon 12.00 30.00
John Vanbiesbrouck 12.00 30.00
Gump Worsley 12.00 30.00
Richard Brodeur 15.00 40.00
Tom Barrasso 12.00 30.00

2006-07 Between The Pipes Stick and Jersey Gold

STATED PRINT RUN 10 SETS
NOT PRICED DUE TO SCARCITY

2006-07 Between The Pipes Stick and Jersey Autographs

STATED PRINT RUN 10 SETS
NOT PRICED DUE TO SCARCITY
SJ01 Manny Fernandez
SJ02 Johnny Bower
SJ03 Martin Brodeur
SJ04 Gerry Cheevers
SJ05 John Davidson
SJ07 Ray Emery
SJ08 Tony Esposito
SJ09 Marc-Andre Fleury
SJ10 Grant Fuhr
SJ12 Glenn Hall
SJ13 Dominik Hasek
SJ14 Ron Hextall
SJ15 Cristobal Huet
SJ16 Leland Irving
SJ18 Roberto Luongo
SJ19 Henrik Lundqvist
SJ20 Ryan Miller
SJ21 Al Montoya
SJ22 Antero Niittymaki
SJ23 Felix Potvin
SJ24 Bernie Parent
SJ28 Pekka Rinne
SJ29 Patrick Roy (COL)
SJ30 Patrick Roy (MTL)
SJ32 Billy Smith
SJ34 Tim Thomas
SJ35 Hannu Toivonen
SJ36 Rogie Vachon
SJ38 Gump Worsley
SJ39 Richard Brodeur
SJ40 Tom Barrasso

2006-07 Between The Pipes Stick Work

STATED PRINT RUN 50 SETS
SW01 Patrick Roy 50.00 125.00
Martin Brodeur
Roberto Luongo
SW02 Roger Crozier 40.00 80.00
Dominik Hasek
Ryan Miller
SW03 Bernie Parent 40.00 80.00
Pelle Lindbergh
Ron Hextall
SW04 Gump Worsley 50.00 100.00
Patrick Roy
Cristobal Huet
SW05 Tony Esposito 30.00 60.00
Gerry Cheevers
Ed Giacomin
SW06 Johnny Bower 30.00 60.00
Mike Palmateer
Felix Potvin

2006-07 Between The Pipes Stick Work Gold

STATED PRINT RUN 10 SETS
NOT PRICED DUE TO SCARCITY

2006-07 Between The Pipes The Mask

COMPLETE SET (40) 125.00 250.00
ODDS 1:24
M01 Al Montoya 4.00 10.00
M02 Kari Lehtonen 5.00 12.00
M03 Miikka Kiprusoff 5.00 12.00
M04 Antero Niittymaki 3.00 8.00
M05 Ray Emery 3.00 8.00
M06 Andrew Raycroft 3.00 8.00
M07 Ryan Miller 5.00 12.00
M08 Martin Gerber 3.00 8.00
M09 Ken Dryden 8.00 20.00
M10 Marc-Andre Fleury 5.00 12.00
M11 Joey MacDonald 3.00 8.00
M12 Henrik Lundqvist 5.00 12.00
M13 Cam Ward 4.00 10.00
M14 Cristobal Huet 5.00 12.00
M15 Rick DiPietro 4.00 10.00
M16 Ilya Bryzgalov 3.00 8.00
M17 Jose Theodore 4.00 10.00
M18 Dominik Hasek 8.00 20.00
M19 Nikolai Khabibulin 4.00 10.00
M20 Marty Turco 4.00 10.00
M21 Marek Schwarz 4.00 10.00
M22 Patrick Roy 10.00 25.00
M23 Dominik Hasek 8.00 20.00
M24 Ed Belfour 4.00 10.00
M25 Manny Legace 3.00 8.00
M26 Curtis Joseph 4.00 10.00
M27 Hannu Toivonen 3.00 8.00
M28 Martin Biron 3.00 8.00
M29 Dan Cloutier 3.00 8.00
M30 Kevin Weekes 3.00 8.00
M31 Jimmy Howard 3.00 8.00
M32 Devan Dubnyk 3.00 8.00
M33 Mikael Tellqvist 3.00 8.00
M34 Jacques Plante 6.00 15.00
M35 Jeff Glass 3.00 8.00
M36 Henrik Lundqvist 5.00 12.00
M37 Vesa Toskala 3.00 8.00
M38 Johan Hedberg 3.00 8.00
M39 Tomas Vokoun 4.00 10.00
M40 Carey Price 8.00 20.00

2006-07 Between The Pipes The Mask Gold

STATED PRINT RUN 10 SETS
NOT PRICED DUE TO SCARCITY

2006-07 Between The Pipes The Mask Silver

*SILVER: .5X to 1.5X MASK HI
STATED PRINT RUN 100 SETS

2006-07 Between The Pipes The Mask Game-Used

STATED PRINT RUN 25 SETS
MGU01 Martin Biron 15.00 40.00
MGU02 Ilya Bryzgalov 15.00 40.00
MGU03 Rick DiPietro 25.00 50.00
MGU04 Ken Dryden 150.00 250.00
MGU05 Ray Emery 25.00 50.00
MGU06 Marc-Andre Fleury 30.00 60.00
MGU07 Dominik Hasek 40.00 80.00
MGU08 Cristobal Huet 30.00 60.00
MGU09 Miikka Kiprusoff 40.00 80.00
MGU10 Kari Lehtonen 30.00 60.00
MGU11 Henrik Lundqvist 30.00 60.00
MGU12 Ryan Miller 30.00 60.00
MGU13 Al Montoya 25.00 50.00
MGU14 Antero Niittymaki 15.00 40.00
MGU15 Jacques Plante 40.00 80.00
MGU16 Andrew Raycroft 25.00 50.00
MGU17 Patrick Roy 60.00 125.00
MGU18 Marty Turco 30.00 60.00
MGU19 Cam Ward 25.00 50.00
MGU20 Hannu Toivonen 15.00 40.00

2006-07 Between The Pipes The Mask Game-Used Gold

STATED PRINT RUN 1 SET
NOT PRICED DUE TO SCARCITY

1951 Berk Ross

These four cards are part of a larger 72-card mult-sport set. The cards are undersized, and were issued in 18-card boxes.
COMPLETE SET (4) 125.00 250.00
1 Sid Abel 37.50 75.00
2 Bill Durnan 50.00 100.00
3 Bill Quackenbush 37.50 75.00
4 Jack Stewart 20.00 40.00

1996-97 Black Diamond

This hobby-only set was issued in one series totaling 180 cards, with three varying levels of difficulty: Single Black Diamond (1-90), Double Black Diamond (91-150), and Triple Black Diamond (151-180). Doubles were inserted 1:4 packs and Triples 1:30 packs. Packs of six cards retailed for $3.49. This set is most noteworthy because of the inlcusion of one of the most sought after RCs to date, #160 Joe Thornton. The Gretzky promo mirrors the regular issue, aside from the word SAMPLE which runs across his portrait on the card back. This set was extremely condition sensitive.
COMPLETE SET (180) 350.00 600.00
COMP.SINGLE SET (90) 10.00 25.00
DBL.DIAMOND (91-150) STAT.ODDS 1:4
TRIP.DIAMOND (150-180) STAT.ODDS 1:30
CONDITION SENSITIVE SET
1 Roman Turek RC .40 1.00
2 Slava Fetisov .08 .25
3 Mike Dunham .20 .50
4 Jean-Francois Fortin RC .20 .50
5 Keith Primeau .08 .25
6 Zigmund Palffy .20 .50
7 Curtis Leschyshyn .08 .25
8 Vladimir Tsyplakov .20 .50
9 Adam Graves .08 .25
10 Ian Laperriere .08 .25
11 Bill Lindsay .08 .25
12 Brian Leetch .40 1.00
13 Martin Lapointe .08 .25
14 Scott Barney RC .40 1.00
15 Mike Grier RC .75 2.00
16 Vladimir Konstantinov .20 .50
17 Rem Murray RC .20 .50
18 Ed Jovanovski .20 .50
19 Chris O'Sullivan .08 .25
20 Steve Rucchin .08 .25
21 Jay Pandolfo .08 .25
22 Nick Boynton RC .60 1.50
23 Greg Adams .08 .25
24 Adam Colagiacomo RC .40 1.00
25 Vincent Damphousse .08 .25
26 Shane Willis RC .60 1.50
27 Alexei Kovalev .08 .25
28 Doug Gilmour .20 .50
29 Joel Otto .08 .25
30 Donald Audette .08 .25
31 Tommy Salo .20 .50
32 Rob Ray .08 .25
33 Kris Draper .08 .25
34 Ed Belfour .40 1.00
35 Mike Richter .40 1.00
36 Nikolai Khabibulin .20 .50
37 Eric Desjardins .20 .50
38 Daniel Tkaczuk RC .40 1.00
39 Keith Jones .20 .50
40 Per Gustafsson RC .20 .50
41 Jocelyn Thibault .40 1.00
42 Mike Gartner .20 .50
43 Vitali Yachmenev .08 .25
44 Jonas Hoglund .08 .25
45 Craig Janney .08 .25
46 Daymond Langkow .20 .50
47 Mattias Timander RC .20 .50
48 Scott Young .08 .25
49 Mikael Renberg .08 .25
50 Nicklas Lidstrom .40 1.00
51 Andrei Kovalenko .08 .25
52 Adam Foote .08 .25
53 Guy Hebert .20 .50
54 Kevin Hatcher .08 .25
55 Rick Tocchet .08 .25
56 Sergei Zubov .08 .25
57 Chris Phillips .08 .25
58 Denis Savard .20 .50
59 Bernie Nicholls .08 .25
60 Jozef Stumpel .08 .25
61 Darius Kasparaitis .08 .25
62 Kelly Hrudey .20 .50
63 Marcel Cousineau RC .40 1.00
64 Brian Skrudland .08 .25
65 Byron Dafoe .20 .50
66 Ray Sheppard .08 .25
67 Chris Simon .08 .25
68 Dainius Zubrus RC .75 2.00
69 Ethan Moreau RC .40 1.00
70 Theo Fleury .08 .25
71 Damian Rhodes .20 .50
72 Kevin Dineen .08 .25
73 Kenny Jonsson .08 .25
74 Ray Ferraro .08 .25
75 Jaromir Jagr .60 1.50
76 Wayne Primeau .08 .25
77 Chris Gratton .08 .25
78 Alyn McCauley .40 1.00
79 Christian Dube .20 .50
80 Bill Ranford .20 .50
81 Adam Deadmarsh .08 .25
82 Dale Hunter .20 .50
83 Derek Plante .08 .25
84 Todd Bertuzzi .40 1.00
85 Stephane Fiset .20 .50
86 Boyd Devereaux RC .40 1.00
87 Jere Lehtinen .08 .25
88 Peter Schaefer RC 1.00 2.50
89 Alexander Mogilny .20 .50
90 Joe Juneau .20 .50
91 Alexandre Daigle .60 1.50
92 Jeff O'Neill .60 1.50
93 Todd Warriner .60 1.50
94 Sergei Berezin RC .75 2.00
95 Petr Nedved .60 1.50
96 Phil Housley .60 1.50
97 Jason Arnott 1.25 3.00
98 Sandis Ozolinsh .60 1.50
99 Mike Modano 2.00 5.00
100 Mark Messier 2.00 5.00
101 Ron Francis 1.25 3.00
102 Oleg Tverdovsky .60 1.50
103 Patrick Marleau RC 25.00 60.00
104 Brian Bellows .60 1.50
105 Eric Fichaud .60 1.50
106 Alexei Zhamnov .60 1.50
107 Wendel Clark .60 1.50
108 Dimitri Khristich .60 1.50
109 Mike Ricci .60 1.50
110 John LeClair 2.00 5.00
111 Owen Nolan 1.25 3.00
112 Bill Guerin 1.25 3.00
113 Vyacheslav Kozlov .60 1.50
114 Brendan Shanahan 2.00 5.00
115 Trevor Linden .60 1.50
116 Jose Theodore 2.00 5.00
117 Rod Brind'Amour 1.25 3.00
118 Brian Holzinger .60 1.50
119 Shayne Corson .60 1.50
120 Bryan Smolinski .60 1.50
121 Tony Granato .60 1.50
122 Mariusz Czerkawski .60 1.50
123 Andrew Cassels .60 1.50
124 Scott Stevens 1.25 3.00
125 Mike Ridley .60 1.50
126 Jamie Langenbrunner .60 1.50
127 Scott Mellanby .60 1.50
128 Grant Fuhr 1.25 3.00
129 Felix Potvin 1.25 3.00
130 Marc Denis .75 2.00
131 Corey Hirsch .60 1.50
132 Chris Osgood 1.25 3.00
133 Peter Bondra 1.25 3.00
134 Martin Brodeur 4.00 10.00
135 Pierre Turgeon 1.25 3.00
136 Pat Verbeek .60 1.50
137 Scott Niedermayer .60 1.50
138 Geoff Sanderson .60 1.50
139 Jason Dawe .60 1.50
140 Rob Niedermayer .60 1.50
141 Daniel Alfredsson 1.25 3.00
142 Jim Campbell .60 1.50
143 Roman Hamrlik .60 1.50
144 Rob Blake 1.25 3.00
145 Chris Chelios 2.00 5.00
146 Teemu Selanne .40 1.00
147 Jim Carey 1.25 3.00
148 Dino Ciccarelli .60 1.50
149 Mark Recchi 1.25 3.00
150 Chris Pronger 1.25 3.00
151 Paul Coffey 4.00 8.00
152 Adam Oates 3.00 6.00
153 Keith Tkachuk 4.00 8.00
154 Janne Niinimaa 2.00 5.00
155 Sergei Fedorov 6.00 15.00
156 Dominik Hasek 10.00 25.00
157 Eric Lindros 4.00 10.00
158 Curtis Joseph 4.00 10.00
159 Alexei Yashin 2.00 5.00
160 Joe Thornton RC 250.00 400.00
161 Bryan Berard 2.00 5.00
162 Steve Yzerman 15.00 40.00
163 Mats Sundin 5.00 12.00
164 Jarome Iginla 6.00 15.00
165 John Vanbiesbrouck 3.00 6.00
166 Mario Lemieux 20.00 50.00
167 Jeremy Roenick 8.00 20.00
168 Patrick Lalime RC 25.00 60.00
169 Joe Sakic 10.00 25.00
170 Brett Hull 5.00 12.00
171 Peter Forsberg 8.00 20.00
172 Doug Weight 3.00 6.00
173 Tony Amonte 3.00 6.00
174 Patrick Roy 20.00 50.00
175 Paul Kariya 5.00 12.00
176 Pavel Bure 5.00 12.00
177 Ray Bourque 8.00 20.00
178 Saku Koivu 5.00 12.00
179 Wade Redden 2.00 5.00
180 Wayne Gretzky 30.00 80.00
P180 Wayne Gretzky Promo 1.00 2.50

1996-97 Black Diamond Gold

This was a gold-foil parallel to the three-tiered Upper Deck Black Diamond set. Single golds were inserted 1:15 packs, Doubles 1:46, and Triples, for which an insertion ratio was not announced, were limited to just 50 sets.
*SINGLE DIAM.STARS: 3X TO 8X BASIC CARDS
*SINGLE DIAM.RC's: 1.25X TO 3X BASIC CARDS
SINGLE DIAMOND STATED ODDS 1:15
*DOUBLE DIAM.STARS: 1.5X TO 3X BASIC CARDS
*DOUBLE DIAM.RCs: .75X TO 2X BASIC CARDS
DOUBLE DIAMOND STATED ODDS 1:46
*TRIPLE DIAM.STARS: 3X TO 6X BASIC CARDS
*TRIPLE DIAM.YOUNG STARS: 1.25X TO 3X BASIC CARDS
TRIPLE STATED PRINT RUN 50 SETS

1996-97 Black Diamond Run for the Cup

Ultra-rare and individually crash-numbered to just 100 sets, these 20 cel-chrome inserts featured high profile players with their eyes set on the Stanley Cup.
RANDOM INSERTS IN PACKS
STATED PRINT RUN 100 SERIAL #'d SETS
RC1 Wayne Gretzky 125.00 300.00
RC2 Saku Koivu 15.00 40.00
RC3 Mario Lemieux 75.00 200.00
RC4 Patrick Roy 75.00 200.00
RC5 Jaromir Jagr 25.00 60.00
RC6 John Vanbiesbrouck 8.00 20.00
RC7 Peter Forsberg 30.00 80.00
RC8 Paul Kariya 15.00 40.00
RC9 Steve Yzerman 60.00 150.00
RC10 Joe Sakic 30.00 80.00
RC11 Mark Messier 20.00 50.00
RC12 Sergei Fedorov 15.00 40.00
RC13 Mats Sundin 15.00 40.00
RC14 Pavel Bure 20.00 50.00
RC15 Ed Jovanovski 8.00 20.00
RC16 Mike Modano 25.00 60.00
RC17 Curtis Joseph 15.00 40.00
RC18 Teemu Selanne 20.00 50.00
RC19 Jarome Iginla 25.00 60.00
RC20 Eric Lindros 15.00 40.00

1997-98 Black Diamond

The 1997-98 Upper Deck Black Diamond set was issued in one series totaling 150 cards and distributed in six-card packs with a suggested retail price of $3.49. The fronts feature color action player photos reproduced on Light F/X card stock with foil treatment and one, two, three, or four Black Diamonds on the front designating its rarity. The backs carry player information and statistics.
COMPLETE SET (150) 60.00 120.00
1 Alexei Zhitnik .08 .20
2 Adam Graves .08 .20
3 Keith Primeau .08 .20
4 Mike Richter .25 .60
5 Felix Potvin .25 .60
6 Valeri Bure .08 .20
7 Mark Messier .25 .60
8 Dainius Zubrus .25 .60
9 Owen Nolan .20 .50
10 Kenny Jonsson .08 .20
11 Ron Francis .20 .50
12 Bryan Berard .08 .20
13 Eric Messier RC .20 .50
14 Paul Kariya .25 .60
15 Teemu Elomo RC .20 .50
16 Joe Nieuwendyk .08 .20
17 Scott Stevens .20 .50
18 Zigmund Palffy .20 .50
19 Brett Hull .30 .75
20 Dominik Hasek .50 1.25
21 Dino Ciccarelli .08 .20
22 Rob Niedermayer .08 .20
23 Mark Recchi .20 .50
24 Brad Isbister .08 .20
25 Timo Vertala RC .20 .50
26 Mika Noronen RC .75 2.00
27 Sandis Ozolinsh .08 .20
28 Chris Phillips .08 .20
29 Chris Chelios .25 .60
30 Jason Dawe .08 .20
31 Kirk McLean .20 .50
32 Jason Allison .08 .20
33 Brian Leetch .25 .60
34 Guy Hebert .08 .20
35 David Legwand RC 1.00 2.50
36 Pierre Hedin RC .20 .50
37 Sergei Samsonov .20 .50
38 Bill Guerin .20 .50
39 Chris Osgood .20 .50
40 Jere Lehtinen .08 .20
41 Patrick Roy 1.25 3.00
42 John Vanbiesbrouck .20 .50
43 Maxim Afinogenov RC 2.00 5.00
44 Patrik Elias RC 2.00 5.00
45 Josh Holden .08 .20
46 Saku Koivu .25 .60
47 Maxim Balmochnykh RC .40 1.00
48 Pasi Petrilainen .08 .20
49 Robert Reichel .08 .20
50 Wade Redden .08 .20
51 Richard Zednik .08 .20
52 Ty Jones RC .30 .75
53 Nikolai Khabibulin .20 .50
54 Kyle McLaren .08 .20
55 Daniel Tkaczuk .25 .60
56 Alexei Zhamnov .08 .20
57 Donald MacLean .08 .20
58 Dave Gagner .08 .20
59 Jeremy Roenick .30 .75
60 Ray Bourque .40 1.00
61 Rod Brind'Amour .20 .50
62 Miroslav Satan .08 .20
63 Eric Daze .20 .50
64 Mike Ricci .08 .20
65 John LeClair .25 .60
66 Bryan Marchment .08 .20
67 Henrik Petre RC .20 .50
68 John MacLean .08 .20
69 Artem Chubarov RC .20 .50
70 Doug Gilmour .20 .50
71 Marco Sturm RC 1.00 2.50
72 Jaromir Jagr .40 1.00
73 Daniel Alfredsson .20 .50
74 Daren Puppa .20 .50
75 Adam Deadmarsh .08 .20
76 Luc Robitaille .20 .50
77 Mats Sundin .25 .60
78 Dan Cloutier .08 .20
79 Manny Malhotra RC .75 2.00
80 Mike Modano .40 1.00
81 Espen Knutsen RC .75 2.00
82 Sergei Fedorov .40 1.00
83 Chris Pronger .20 .50
84 Doug Weight .20 .50
85 Dmitri Nabokov .08 .20
86 Gary Roberts .08 .20
87 Peter Bondra .20 .50
88 Robert Dome RC .08 .20
89 Jan Bulis RC .08 .20
90 Eric Brewer RC 1.25 3.00
91 Nikos Tselios RC .08 .20
92 Scott Mellanby .08 .20
93 Vitali Vishnevsky RC .40 1.00
94 Derian Hatcher .08 .20
95 Teemu Selanne .25 .60
96 Joe Sakic .50 1.25
97 Alexander Mogilny .20 .50
98 Jesse Boulerice RC .40 1.00
99 Johan Forsander RC .08 .20
100 Pierre Turgeon .20 .50
101 Tony Amonte .20 .50
102 Timo Ahmaoja RC .08 .20
103 Rob Blake .08 .20
104 Derek Morris RC .40 1.00
105 Alex Tanguay RC 4.00 10.00
106 Peter Forsberg .60 1.50
107 Shayne Corson .08 .20
108 Tyler Moss RC .20 .50
109 Adam Oates .20 .50
110 Keith Tkachuk .25 .60
111 Alexei Yashin .08 .20
112 Joe Thornton .60 1.50
113 Andy Moog .20 .50
114 Daniel Sedin RC 2.00 5.00
115 Pavel Bure .25 .60
116 Denis Shvidki RC .40 1.00
117 Jason Arnott .08 .20
118 Mike Johnson RC .40 1.00
119 Nicklas Lidstrom .25 .60
120 Mattias Ohlund .20 .50
121 Alexander Selivanov .08 .20
122 Martin Brodeur .60 1.50
123 Steve Yzerman 1.25 3.00
124 Dimitri Vlassenkov RC .20 .50
125 Jeff Farkas RC .40 1.00
126 Curtis Joseph .25 .60
127 Yanic Perreault .08 .20
128 Alyn McCauley .20 .50
129 Vyacheslav Kozlov .08 .20
130 Alexei Morozov .20 .50
131 Roberto Luongo RC 10.00 25.00
132 Jarome Iginla .30 .75
133 Pat LaFontaine .25 .60
134 Ed Belfour .25 .60
135 Toby Petersen RC .75 2.00
136 Henrik Sedin RC 2.00 5.00
137 Marcus Nilson .08 .20
138 Cameron Mann .25 .60
139 Eero Somervuori RC .20 .50
140 Patrick Marleau .40 1.00
141 Ed Jovanovski .20 .50
142 Roman Hamrlik .08 .20
143 Theo Fleury .08 .20
144 Wayne Gretzky 1.50 4.00
145 Eric Lindros .25 .60
146 Boyd Deveraux .08 .20
147 Sami Kapanen .08 .20
148 Grant Fuhr .08 .20
149 Brendan Shanahan .25 .60
150 Vincent Lecavalier RC 6.00 15.00

1997-98 Black Diamond Double Diamond

Inserted one in every pack, this 150-card set is a two black diamond parallel version of the Upper Deck Black Diamond base set.
*STARS: .75X TO 2X BASIC CARD
*ROOKIES: .6X TO 1.5X BASIC CARDS
STATED ODDS 1:1

1997-98 Black Diamond Triple Diamond

Randomly inserted in packs at the rate of 1:3, this 150-card set is an all-gold Light F/X parallel version of the base set with three black diamonds printed on the card fronts.
*STARS: 3X TO 8X BASIC CARD
*ROOKIES: 1.25X TO 3X BASIC CARDS
STATED ODDS 1:3

1997-98 Black Diamond Quadruple Diamond

Randomly inserted in packs, this 150-card set is an all-black Light F/X parallel version of the base set with four black diamonds printed on the card fronts. Only 50 sets were produced.
*STARS: 40X TO 100X BASIC CARDS
*ROOKIES: 4X TO 10X HI
STATED PRINT RUN 50 SETS
150 Vincent Lecavalier 75.00 150.00

1997-98 Black Diamond Premium Cut

Randomly inserted in packs at the rate of 1:7, this 30-card set features color action photos of top stars printed in a Light F/X card design with a single black diamond.
COMPLETE SET (30) 100.00 200.00
SINGLE DIAMOND STATED ODDS 1:7
*DOUBLES: .75X TO 1.5X BASIC INSERTS
DOUBLE DIAMOND STATED ODDS 1:15
*TRIPLES: 1.25X TO 2.5X BASIC INSERTS
TRIPLE DIAMOND STATED ODDS 1:30
PC1 Wayne Gretzky 12.50 30.00
PC2 Patrick Roy 10.00 25.00
PC3 Brendan Shanahan 2.00 5.00
PC4 Ray Bourque 2.00 5.00
PC5 Alexei Morozov 1.50 4.00
PC6 John LeClair 2.00 5.00
PC7 Steve Yzerman 10.00 25.00
PC8 Patrik Elias 1.50 4.00
PC9 Pavel Bure 2.00 5.00
PC10 Brian Leetch 2.00 5.00
PC11 Peter Forsberg 5.00 12.00
PC12 Marco Sturm 2.00 5.00
PC13 Eric Lindros 2.00 5.00
PC14 Keith Tkachuk 2.00 5.00
PC15 Teemu Selanne 2.00 5.00
PC16 Bryan Berard 1.50 4.00
PC17 Joe Thornton 3.00 8.00
PC18 Brett Hull 2.50 6.00
PC19 Nicklas Lidstrom 2.00 5.00
PC20 Jaromir Jagr 3.00 8.00
PC21 Vaclav Prospal 2.00 5.00
PC22 Pat LaFontaine 2.00 5.00
PC23 Mark Messier 2.00 5.00
PC24 Martin Brodeur 5.00 12.00
PC25 Mike Modano 3.00 8.00
PC26 Paul Kariya 2.00 5.00
PC27 Mike Johnson 2.00 5.00
PC28 Sergei Samsonov 1.50 4.00
PC29 Joe Sakic 4.00 10.00
PC30 Mats Sundin 2.00 5.00

1997-98 Black Diamond Premium Cut Quadruple Diamond Horizontal

This 30-card hobby only set is a special black Light F/X, embossed, horizontal, die-cut version of the regular insert set with various insertion rates. Cards #8, 10, 16, 17, 18, 19, 23, 27, 29 and 30 have an insertion rate of 1:30; #4, 5, 7, 12, 14, 15, 21, 22, 25 and 26 have a 1:90 insertion rate; #6, 9, 11, 20, 24 and 28 have a 1:2000 insertion rate; #3 and 13 have a 1:15,000 insertion rate; and #1 and 2 have a 1:30,000 insertion rate.

8/10/16/17/18/19/23/27/29/30 ODDS 1:30
4/5/7/12/14/15/21/22/25/26 ODDS 1:90
6/9/11/20/24/28 ODDS 1:2000,
3/13 ODDS 1:15,000

PC1 Wayne Gretzky 300.00 800.00
PC2 Patrick Roy 200.00 500.00
PC3 Brendan Shanahan 60.00 150.00
PC4 Ray Bourque 6.00 15.00
PC5 Alexei Morozov 4.00 10.00
PC6 John LeClair 1.50 4.00
PC7 Steve Yzerman 20.00 50.00
PC8 Patrik Elias 3.00 8.00
PC9 Pavel Bure 60.00 150.00
PC10 Brian Leetch 1.50 4.00
PC11 Peter Forsberg 60.00 150.00
PC12 Marco Sturm 8.00 20.00
PC13 Eric Lindros 60.00 150.00
PC14 Keith Tkachuk 1.50 4.00
PC15 Teemu Selanne 5.00 12.00
PC16 Bryan Berard 1.50 4.00
PC17 Joe Thornton 5.00 12.00
PC18 Brett Hull 2.50 6.00
PC19 Nicklas Lidstrom 2.00 5.00
PC20 Jaromir Jagr 50.00 125.00
PC21 Vaclav Prospal 1.50 4.00
PC22 Pat LaFontaine 4.00 10.00
PC23 Mark Messier 1.50 4.00
PC24 Martin Brodeur 50.00 125.00
PC25 Mike Modano 8.00 20.00
PC26 Paul Kariya 12.50 30.00
PC27 Mike Johnson 1.50 4.00
PC28 Sergei Samsonov 30.00 80.00
PC29 Joe Sakic 4.00 10.00
PC30 Mats Sundin 2.00 5.00

1997-98 Black Diamond Premium Cut Quadruple Diamond Verticals

Randomly inserted in packs at the rate of 1:180, this 30-card set is a parallel version of the regular insert set with four black diamonds on the card fronts.

STATED ODDS 1:180
PC1 Wayne Gretzky 50.00 125.00
PC2 Patrick Roy 40.00 100.00
PC3 Brendan Shanahan 20.00 50.00
PC4 Ray Bourque 20.00 50.00
PC5 Alexei Morozov 20.00 50.00
PC6 John LeClair 20.00 50.00
PC7 Steve Yzerman 40.00 100.00
PC8 Patrik Elias 20.00 50.00
PC9 Pavel Bure 20.00 50.00
PC10 Brian Leetch 20.00 50.00
PC11 Peter Forsberg 30.00 80.00
PC12 Marco Sturm 20.00 50.00
PC13 Eric Lindros 20.00 50.00
PC14 Keith Tkachuk 20.00 50.00
PC15 Teemu Selanne 20.00 50.00
PC16 Bryan Berard 20.00 50.00
PC17 Joe Thornton 20.00 50.00
PC18 Brett Hull 20.00 50.00
PC19 Nicklas Lidstrom 20.00 50.00
PC20 Jaromir Jagr 20.00 50.00
PC21 Vaclav Prospal 20.00 50.00
PC22 Pat LaFontaine 20.00 50.00
PC23 Mark Messier 20.00 50.00
PC24 Martin Brodeur 40.00 100.00
PC25 Mike Modano 10.00 30.00
PC26 Paul Kariya 20.00 50.00
PC27 Mike Johnson 20.00 50.00
PC28 Sergei Samsonov 20.00 50.00
PC29 Joe Sakic 20.00 50.00
PC30 Mats Sundin 20.00 50.00

1998-99 Black Diamond

The 1998-99 Upper Deck Black Diamond set was issued in one series for a total of 120 cards and was distributed in six-card packs with a suggested retail price of $3.99. The fronts feature color action player photos reproduced on Light F/X card stock with foil treatment and one, two, three, or four Black Diamonds designating its rarity. Cards 1-90

are regular player cards with cards 91-120 displaying top prospect players and an insertion rate of 1:4 for the single diamond cards. The backs carry player information and statistics. Only 2,000 Double Diamond sets were produced, 1,000 Triple Diamond sets, and 100 Quadruple Diamond sets.

COMPLETE SET (120) 60.00 125.00
COMP.SET w/o SP's (90) 10.00 20.00
SP 91-120 STATED ODDS 1:4
1 Paul Kariya .25 .60
2 Teemu Selanne .25 .60
3 Johan Davidsson .10 .25
4 Ray Bourque .40 1.00
5 Sergei Samsonov .20 .50
6 Jason Allison .10 .25
7 Joe Thornton .40 1.00
8 Miroslav Satan .20 .50
9 Brian Holzinger .10 .25
10 Dominik Hasek .50 1.25
11 Rico Fata .10 .25
12 Jarome Iginla .30 .75
13 Theo Fleury .10 .25
14 Ron Francis .20 .50
15 Gary Roberts .10 .25
16 Keith Primeau .10 .25
17 Sami Kapanen .10 .25
18 Doug Gilmour .20 .50
19 Chris Chelios .25 .60
20 Tony Amonte .20 .50
21 Peter Forsberg .60 1.50
22 Patrick Roy 1.25 3.00
23 Joe Sakic .50 1.25
24 Chris Drury .20 .50
25 Brett Hull .30 .75
26 Ed Belfour .25 .60
27 Mike Modano .40 1.00
28 Darryl Sydor .10 .25
29 Sergei Fedorov .40 1.00
30 Steve Yzerman 1.25 3.00
31 Nicklas Lidstrom .25 .60
32 Chris Osgood .20 .50
33 Brendan Shanahan .25 .60
34 Doug Weight .20 .50
35 Bill Guerin .10 .25
36 Tom Poti .10 .25
37 Pavel Bure .25 .60
38 Mark Parrish RC 1.25 3.00
39 Rob Niedermayer .10 .25
40 Pavel Rosa RC .10 .25
41 Rob Blake .10 .25
42 Olli Jokinen .20 .50
43 Vincent Damphousse .10 .25
44 Mark Recchi .20 .50
45 Terry Ryan .10 .25
46 Saku Koivu .25 .60
47 Mike Dunham .20 .50
48 Sergei Krivokrasov .10 .25
49 Scott Stevens .20 .50
50 Martin Brodeur .60 1.50
51 Brendan Morrison .20 .50
52 Eric Brewer .10 .25
53 Zigmund Palffy .20 .50
54 Felix Potvin .25 .60
55 Wayne Gretzky 1.50 4.00
56 Brian Leetch .25 .60
57 Manny Malhotra .10 .25
58 Mike Richter .25 .60
59 Alexei Yashin .10 .25
60 Wade Redden .10 .25
61 Daniel Alfredsson .20 .50
62 Eric Lindros .25 .60
63 John LeClair .25 .60
64 John Vanbiesbrouck .20 .50
65 Rod Brind'Amour .20 .50
66 Keith Tkachuk .25 .60
67 Daniel Briere .20 .50
68 Jeremy Roenick .30 .75
69 Jaromir Jagr .40 1.00
70 German Titov .20 .50
71 Alexei Morozov .20 .50
72 Patrick Marleau .10 .25
73 Andrei Zyuzin .10 .25
74 Mike Vernon .20 .50
75 Owen Nolan .20 .50
76 Marty Reasoner .20 .50
77 Al MacInnis .20 .50
78 Chris Pronger .20 .50
79 Wendel Clark .20 .50
80 Vincent Lecavalier .60 1.50
81 Craig Janney .10 .25
82 Tomas Kaberle RC .60 1.50
83 Curtis Joseph .25 .60
84 Mats Sundin .25 .60
85 Mark Messier .25 .60
86 Bill Muckalt RC .20 .50
87 Mattias Ohlund .20 .50
88 Peter Bondra .20 .50
89 Olaf Kolzig .20 .50
90 Richard Zednik .10 .25
91 Harold Druken SP 1.25 3.00
92 Roberto Luongo SP 1.25 3.00
93 Daniel Tkaczuk SP 1.00 2.50
94 Brenden Morrow SP RC 2.00 5.00
95 Mike Van Ryn SP 1.00 2.50
96 Brian Finley SP RC 1.00 2.50
97 Jani Rita SP RC 1.25 3.00
98 Iikka Mikkola SP RC 1.25 3.00
99 Mikko Jokela SP RC 1.25 3.00
100 Tommi Santala SP RC 1.25 3.00
101 Teemu Virkkunen SP RC 1.25 3.00
102 Arto Laatikainen SP RC 1.25 3.00
103 Kirill Safronov SP RC 1.25 3.00
104 Alexei Volkov SP RC 1.25 3.00
105 Denis Arkhipov SP RC 1.25 3.00
106 Alexander Zevakhin SP RC 1.25 3.00
107 Denis Shvidki SP 1.25 3.00
108 Maxim Afinogenov SP 1.25 3.00
109 Daniel Sedin SP 1.25 3.00
110 Henrik Sedin SP 1.25 3.00
111 Jimmie Olvestad SP RC 1.25 3.00
112 Mathias Weinhandl SP RC 1.25 3.00
113 Mathias Tjarnqvist SP RC 1.25 3.00
114 Jakob Johnansson SP RC 1.25 3.00
115 David Legwand SP 1.25 3.00
116 Barrett Heisten SP RC 1.25 3.00
117 Tim Connolly SP RC 1.50 4.00
118 Andy Hilbert SP RC 1.25 3.00
119 Joe Blackburn SP RC 1.25 3.00
120 Dave Tanabe SP RC 1.25 3.00

1998-99 Black Diamond Double Diamond

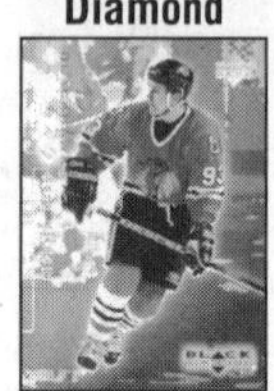

Randomly inserted into packs, this 120-card set is a parallel version of the base set displaying two black diamonds on the card fronts. Only 2,000 sets were made.

*STARS: 2X TO 5X BASIC CARDS
*SP's: .6X TO 1.5X BASIC CARDS
STATED PRINT RUN 2000 SETS

1998-99 Black Diamond Triple Diamond

Randomly inserted into packs, this 120-card set is a parallel version of the base set displaying three black diamonds on the card fronts. Only 1,000 sets were made.

*STARS: 3X TO 8X BASIC CARDS
*SP's: 1X TO 2.5X BASIC CARDS
STATED PRINT RUN 1000 SETS

1998-99 Black Diamond Quadruple Diamond

Randomly inserted into packs, this 120-card set is a parallel version of the base set displaying four black diamonds on the card fronts. Only 100 sets were made.

*STARS: 30X TO 80X BASIC CARDS
*SP's: 5X TO 10X BASIC CARDS
STATED PRINT RUN 100 SETS

1998-99 Black Diamond Myriad

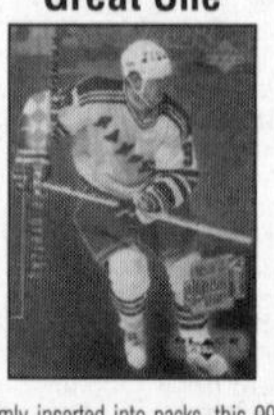

Randomly inserted into packs, this 30-card set features color action photos of the current top NHL's superstars. Only 1,500 serially numbered sets were produced. A limited edition parallel version of this set, Myriad 2, was produced and numbered 1 of 1.

STATED PRINT RUN 1500 SERIAL #'d SETS
MYRIAD 2 ONE OF ONE PARALLEL EXISTS
M1 Vincent Lecavalier 6.00 15.00
M2 John Vanbiesbrouck 2.00 5.00
M3 Paul Kariya 2.50 6.00
M4 Keith Tkachuk 2.50 6.00
M5 Mike Modano 4.00 10.00
M6 Dominik Hasek 5.00 12.00
M7 Teemu Selanne 2.50 6.00
M8 Manny Malhotra 1.00 2.50
M9 Brendan Shanahan 2.50 6.00
M10 Pavel Bure 2.50 6.00
M11 Chris Drury 2.00 5.00
M12 Curtis Joseph 2.50 6.00
M13 Joe Sakic 5.00 12.00
M14 Eric Lindros 2.50 6.00
M15 Peter Bondra 2.00 5.00
M16 Brett Hull 3.00 8.00
M17 Ray Bourque 4.00 10.00
M18 Jaromir Jagr 4.00 10.00
M19 Steve Yzerman 12.50 30.00
M20 Mark Parrish 4.00 10.00
M21 Martin Brodeur 6.00 15.00
M22 Saku Koivu 2.50 6.00
M23 Patrick Roy 12.50 30.00
M24 John LeClair 2.50 6.00
M25 Doug Gilmour 2.00 5.00
M26 Sergei Fedorov 4.00 10.00
M27 Wayne Gretzky 15.00 40.00
M28 Peter Forsberg 6.00 15.00
M29 Eric Brewer 1.00 2.50
M30 Sergei Samsonov 2.00 5.00

1998-99 Black Diamond Winning Formula Gold

Randomly inserted into hobby packs only, this 30-card set features color photos of top players and goalies. Each card is sequentially numbered to the pictured player's goals or goalie's wins multiplied times 50.

PRINT RUN EQUALS GOALS/WINS X 50
WF1 Paul Kariya/850 3.00 8.00
WF2 Teemu Selanne/2600 3.00 8.00
WF3 Sergei Samsonov/1100 2.50 6.00
WF4 Dominik Hasek/1650 6.00 15.00
WF5 Vincent Lecavalier/2200 5.00 12.00
WF6 Patrick Roy/1550 15.00 40.00
WF7 Peter Forsberg/1250 8.00 20.00
WF8 Joe Sakic/1350 5.00 12.00
WF9 Ed Belfour/1850 3.00 8.00
WF10 Brendan Shanahan/1400 3.00 8.00
WF11 Steve Yzerman/1200 20.00 50.00
WF12 Chris Osgood/1650 2.50 6.00
WF13 Curtis Joseph/1450 3.00 8.00
WF14 Manny Malhotra/800 2.50 6.00
WF15 Martin Brodeur/2150 6.00 15.00
WF16 Chris Drury/1400 2.50 6.00
WF17 Zigmund Palffy/2250 2.50 6.00
WF18 Wayne Gretzky/1150 25.00 50.00
WF19 Theo Fleury/1350 2.50 6.00
WF20 Alexei Yashin/1650 2.50 6.00
WF21 Eric Lindros/1500 3.00 8.00
WF22 John LeClair/2550 2.50 6.00
WF23 Keith Tkachuk/2000 3.00 8.00
WF24 Mark Messier/1100 3.00 8.00
WF25 Jaromir Jagr/1750 5.00 12.00
WF26 Brett Hull/1350 5.00 12.00
WF27 Mats Sundin/1650 3.00 8.00
WF28 Pavel Bure/2550 3.00 8.00
WF29 Peter Bondra/2600 2.50 6.00
WF30 Mike Modano/1050 8.00 20.00

1998-99 Black Diamond Winning Formula Platinum

Randomly inserted into packs, this 30-card set is a platinum foil parallel version of the regular Winning Formula set. Each card is numbered to the player's actual accomplishments. Scarcer cards are not priced.

LOW PRINT RUNS NOT PRICED DUE TO SCARCITY
WF1 Paul Kariya/17
WF2 Teemu Selanne/52 50.00 100.00
WF3 Sergei Samsonov/22
WF4 Dominik Hasek/33 100.00 200.00
WF5 Vincent Lecavalier/44 100.00 200.00
WF6 Patrick Roy/31 250.00 500.00
WF7 Peter Forsberg/25
WF8 Joe Sakic/27
WF9 Ed Belfour/37 60.00 120.00
WF10 Brendan Shanahan/28
WF11 Steve Yzerman/24
WF12 Chris Osgood/33 75.00 150.00
WF13 Curtis Joseph/29
WF14 Manny Malhotra/16 25.00 60.00
WF15 Martin Brodeur/43 100.00 200.00
WF16 Chris Drury/28
WF17 Zigmund Palffy/45 60.00 120.00
WF18 Wayne Gretzky/23
WF19 Theo Fleury/27
WF20 Alexei Yashin/33 25.00 60.00
WF21 Eric Lindros/30 50.00 100.00
WF22 John LeClair/51 50.00 100.00
WF23 Keith Tkachuk/40 75.00 150.00
WF24 Mark Messier/22
WF25 Jaromir Jagr/35 60.00 150.00
WF26 Brett Hull/27
WF27 Mats Sundin/33 50.00 100.00
WF28 Pavel Bure/51 50.00 100.00
WF29 Peter Bondra/52 50.00 100.00
WF30 Mike Modano/21

1998-99 Black Diamond Year of the Great One

Randomly inserted into packs, this 99-card set features color photos of the great Wayne Gretzky. Cards 1-45 are marked with a single diamond; 46-75 display double diamonds; 76-90 show triple diamonds; and 91-99 carry quadruple diamonds. Each card is sequentially numbered to 99.

COMMON YOTG (1-99) 125.00 300.00
EACH CARD SERIAL NUMBERED TO 99

1999-00 Black Diamond

The 1999-00 Black Diamond set was released as 120-card set comprised of 90 veteran cards and 30 Diamonds in the Rough cards, short printed and inserted at one in three packs, which feature future NHL stars. Player action shots are set against a card background where the middle 2/3 is silver foil and the top and bottom are colored to match the player's team colors. Black Diamond was packaged in 24-pack boxes with 6-card packs, carried an SRP of $3.99, and was released as both hobby and retail.

COMPLETE SET (120) 60.00 150.00
COMP.SET w/o SP's (90) 20.00 50.00
COMMON CARD (1-90) .10 .25
SP 91-120 ODDS 1:3
1 Paul Kariya .25 .60
2 Teemu Selanne .25 .60
3 Guy Hebert .20 .50
4 Damian Rhodes .20 .50
5 Patrik Stefan RC .60 1.50
6 Dean Sylvester RC .20 .50
7 Sergei Samsonov .20 .50
8 Byron Dafoe .20 .50
9 Ray Bourque .40 1.00
10 Joe Thornton .40 1.00
11 Dominik Hasek .50 1.25
12 Michael Peca .20 .50
13 Miroslav Satan .20 .50
14 Martin Biron .20 .50
15 Oleg Saprykin RC .60 1.50
16 Valeri Bure .10 .25
17 Robyn Regehr .10 .25
18 Dave Tanabe .10 .25
19 Arturs Irbe .20 .50
20 Sami Kapanen .10 .25
21 Kyle Calder RC .20 .50
22 Tony Amonte .20 .50
23 Doug Gilmour .20 .50
24 Patrick Roy 1.25 3.00
25 Joe Sakic .50 1.25
26 Peter Forsberg .60 1.50
27 Chris Drury .20 .50
28 Milan Hejduk .25 .60
29 Mike Modano .40 1.00
30 Brett Hull .30 .75
31 Ed Belfour .25 .60
32 Jon Sim RC .20 .50
33 Nicklas Lidstrom .25 .60
34 Sergei Fedorov .40 1.00
35 Brendan Shanahan .25 .60
36 Steve Yzerman 1.25 3.00
37 Chris Osgood .20 .50
38 Paul Comrie RC .10 .25
39 Bill Guerin .10 .25
40 Doug Weight .20 .50
41 Pavel Bure .25 .60
42 Ivan Novoseltsev RC .20 .50
43 Trevor Kidd .20 .50
44 Zigmund Palffy .20 .50
45 Luc Robitaille .20 .50
46 Stephane Fiset .20 .50
47 Mike Ribeiro .10 .25
48 Saku Koivu .25 .60
49 David Legwand .20 .50
50 Robert Valicevic RC .10 .25
51 Martin Brodeur .60 1.50
52 Scott Gomez .20 .50
53 Brian Rafalski RC .20 .50
54 Tim Connolly .10 .25
55 Jorgen Jonsson RC .10 .25
56 Theo Fleury .10 .25
57 Brian Leetch .25 .60
58 Mike Richter .25 .60
59 Marian Hossa .25 .60
60 Radek Bonk .10 .25
61 Mike Fisher RC .60 1.50
62 Eric Lindros .25 .60
63 Keith Primeau .10 .25
64 John LeClair .25 .60
65 Jeremy Roenick .30 .75
66 Keith Tkachuk .25 .60
67 Mika Alatalo RC .20 .50
68 Jaromir Jagr .40 1.00
69 Martin Straka .10 .25
70 Alexei Kovalev .10 .25
71 Jochen Hecht RC .20 .50
72 Pavol Demitra .20 .50
73 Chris Pronger .20 .50
74 Patrick Marleau .20 .50
75 Owen Nolan .20 .50
76 Jeff Friesen .10 .25
77 Steve Shields .20 .50
78 Vincent Lecavalier .25 .60
79 Dan Cloutier .10 .25
80 Adam Mair RC .20 .50
81 Mike Johnson .20 .50
82 Mats Sundin .25 .60
83 Nikolai Antropov RC .75 2.00
84 Curtis Joseph .25 .60
85 Steve Kariya RC .20 .50
86 Mark Messier .25 .60
87 Alexander Mogilny .20 .50
88 Olaf Kolzig .20 .50
89 Peter Bondra .20 .50
90 Alexandre Volchkov RC .20 .50
91 Pavel Brendl SP RC 2.50 6.00
92 Jamie Lundmark SP .50 1.25
93 Kris Beech SP .50 1.25
94 Michael Zigomanis SP .50 1.25
95 Branislav Mezei SP RC .50 1.25
96 Sheldon Keefe SP RC .50 1.25
97 Brian Finley SP .50 1.25
98 Taylor Pyatt SP .50 1.25
99 Denis Shvidki SP .50 1.25
100 Barret Jackman SP .50 1.25
101 Maxime Ouellet SP .50 1.25
102 Milan Kraft SP RC 3.00 8.00
103 Brad Ralph SP RC .50 1.25
104 Alexei Volkov SP .50 1.25
105 Mathieu Chouinard SP .50 1.25
106 Mark Bell SP .50 1.25
107 Ryan Jardine SP RC .50 1.25
108 Kristian Kudroc SP RC .50 1.25
109 Norm Milley SP .50 1.25
110 Alexander Buturlin .50 1.25
111 Jaroslav Kristek SP RC .50 1.25
112 Luke Sellars SP RC .50 1.25
113 Bryan Kazarian SP RC .50 1.25
114 Brett Lysak SP RC .50 1.25
115 Andrei Shefer SP RC .50 1.25
116 Michal Sivek SP RC .50 1.25
117 Justin Papineau SP .50 1.25
118 Mattias Weinhandl SP .50 1.25
119 Daniel Sedin SP .50 1.25
120 Henrik Sedin SP .50 1.25

1999-00 Black Diamond Diamond Cut

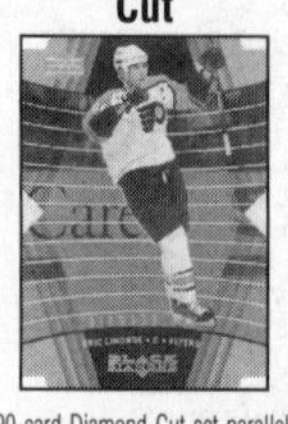

The 90-card Diamond Cut set parallels the Black Diamond base 90-card set in a die cut version and is seeded at 1:6 packs; and the 30-card Diamond Cut Diamonds in the Rough set parallels the 30 prospect cards in a die cut version and is seeded at 1:11 packs. On the front of these parallels, the words "Diamond Cut" appear just above the player's name.

*STARS: 2X TO 5X BASIC CARDS
*RC's (non SP's): 1.25X TO 3X BASIC CARDS
*SP's: .75X TO 2X BASIC CARDS
1-90 STATED ODDS 1:6
91-120 STATED ODDS 1:3

1999-00 Black Diamond Final Cut

The 90-card Final Cut set parallels the Black Diamond base 90-card set in a die cut holographic foil version and is numbered on the back out of 100; and the 30-card Final Cut Diamonds in the Rough set parallels the 30 prospect cards at the end of the set in a die cut holographic foil version and is numbered on the back out of 50. On the front of these parallels, the words "Final Cut" appear just above the player's name.

*STARS: 30X TO 80X BASIC CARDS
*RC's (non SP's): 5X TO 10X BASIC CARDS
*SP's: 4X TO 10X BASIC CARDS
STATED PRINT RUN 100 SERIAL #'d SETS
SP STATED PRINT RUN 50 SERIAL #'d SETS

1999-00 Black Diamond A Piece of History

Randomly inserted in hobby packs at 1:179 and retail packs at 1:336, this 20-card set features NHL players with a single diamond-cut swatch of a game-used stick. Hobby cards feature a red foil shift, and retail cards feature a blue foil shift. Double and triple diamond parallels of this set were also created. These parallels carry two or three swatches of memorabilia respectively. Double diamonds were seeded at 1:1008, and triple diamonds were numbered one of one. Triple diamonds not priced due to scarcity.

STATED ODDS 1:336
*DBL.DIAM.STARS: 1X TO 2X BASIC CARDS
DBL DIAM STATED ODDS 1:1008
TRIPLE DIAMOND 1/1's EXIST
BH Brett Hull 10.00 25.00
DH Dominik Hasek 10.00 25.00
EB Ed Belfour 10.00 25.00
EL Eric Lindros 10.00 25.00
GH Gordie Howe 20.00 50.00
JJ Jaromir Jagr 12.50 30.00
JL John LeClair 10.00 25.00
JS Joe Sakic 12.50 30.00
KT Keith Tkachuk 10.00 25.00
MB Martin Brodeur 20.00 5[...]
MM Mike Modano 10.00 2[...]
PB Pavel Bure 10.00 2[...]
PF Peter Forsberg 15.00 4[...]
PK Paul Kariya 10.00 2[...]
PR Patrick Roy 20.00 5[...]
RB Ray Bourque 10.00 2[...]
SY Steve Yzerman 20.00 5[...]
TC Tim Connolly 8.00 2[...]
TS Teemu Selanne 10.00 2[...]
WG Wayne Gretzky 30.00 8[...]

1999-00 Black Diamond Diamonation

Randomly inserted in packs at 1:4, this card set showcases NHL's most colle[...] players on a foil card with laser-et[...] diamonds in the background.

COMPLETE SET (20) 15.00 3[...]
STATED ODDS 1:4
D1 Paul Kariya .50
D2 Patrik Stefan .75
D3 Sergei Samsonov .50
D4 Teemu Selanne .50
D5 Patrick Roy 2.50
D6 Mike Modano .75
D7 Sergei Fedorov 1.00
D8 Pavel Bure .60
D9 David Legwand .50
D10 Martin Brodeur 1.25
D11 Theo Fleury .50
D12 Eric Lindros .75
D13 Keith Tkachuk .50
D14 Jaromir Jagr .75
D15 Mats Sundin .50
D16 Steve Kariya .60
D17 Peter Bondra .50
D18 Peter Forsberg 1.25
D19 Steve Yzerman 2.50
D20 Zigmund Palffy .50

1999-00 Black Diamond Diamon[...] Might

Randomly inserted in packs at 1:9, this card set pictures NHL's toughest playe[...] against a colored foil background.

COMPLETE SET (10) 8.00 1[...]
STATED ODDS 1:9
DM1 Peter Forsberg 1.50
DM2 Brendan Shanahan 1.00
DM3 Eric Lindros 1.00
DM4 John LeClair .75
DM5 Jaromir Jagr 1.00
DM6 Keith Tkachuk .60
DM7 Teemu Selanne .60
DM8 Mats Sundin .60
DM9 Mark Messier .75
DM10 Theo Fleury .60

1999-00 Black Diamond Diamon[...] Skills

Randomly inserted in packs at 1:24, this card set features top players who mak[...] highlight reel night after night. Action p[...] photos on a foil-front card are set agai[...] centered diamond background that is fr[...] by horizontal laser-etched lines.

COMPLETE SET (10) 25.00 5[...]
STATED ODDS 1:24
DS1 Teemu Selanne 1.25
DS2 Paul Kariya 3.00
DS3 Patrick Roy 6.00 1[...]
DS4 Pavel Bure 1.50
DS5 Sergei Fedorov 2.50
DS6 Eric Lindros 2.00
DS7 Jaromir Jagr 2.00
DS8 Martin Brodeur 3.00
DS9 Theo Fleury 1.25
DS10 Curtis Joseph 1.25

1999-00 Black Diamond Gordie Howe Gallery

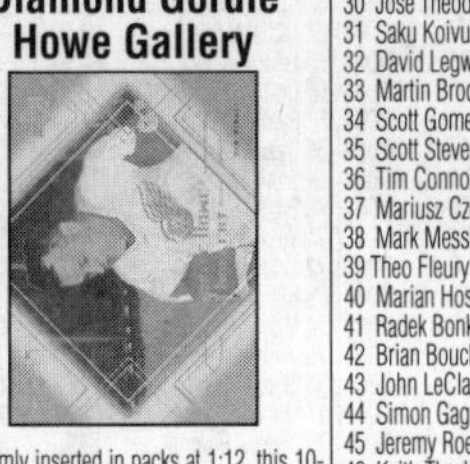

ndomly inserted in packs at 1:12, this 10-rd set pays tribute to one of hockey's eatest legends. A centered picture framed a diamond is centered on a holographic 1 background. Card backs carry a "GH" efix.

OMPLETE SET (10) 40.00 80.00
OMMON CARD (GH1-GH10) 5.00 10.00
ATED ODDS 1:12

1999-00 Black Diamond Myriad

ndomly inserted in packs at 1:24, this 10-rd set showcases 10 of the NHL's most lectible stars in action.

OMPLETE SET (10) 20.00 40.00
ATED ODDS 1:24
1 Patrik Stefan 2.00 5.00
2 Teemu Selanne 1.25 3.00
3 Sergei Samsonov 1.25 3.00
4 Joe Sakic 2.50 6.00
5 Brett Hull 1.50 4.00
6 Pavel Bure 1.50 4.00
7 Steve Yzerman 6.00 15.00
8 Jaromir Jagr 2.00 5.00
9 Eric Lindros 2.00 5.00
10 Paul Kariya 3.00 8.00

2000-01 Black Diamond

eased in early December 2000, Black amond featured a 132-card base set nsisting of 82 regular issue cards and 50 ort printed Precious Gems cards divided into three tiers. Tier 1, numbers 61-75 d 112-132, were sequentially numbered to 99, tier 2, card numbers 76-84, were quentially numbered to 1250, and tier 3, d numbers 85-90, were sequentially mbered to 500. Cards 91-132 were only ailable in packs of Upper Deck Rookie date. Base cards were all foil and have ored borders along the top and bottom of card to match each respective player's m colors. Black Diamond was packaged 24-pack boxes with packs containing six ds and carried a suggested retail price of 99.

OMPLETE SET (90) 300.00 600.00
OMP.SET w/o SP's (82) 15.00 30.00
OMP.SET w/UPD (132)
-75, 112-132 PRINT RUN 1999 SER.#'d TS
-84 STAT.PRINT RUN 1250 SER.#'d TS
-90 STAT.PRINT RUN 500 SER.#'d SETS
ARDS 91-132 AVAIL.IN UD ROOK.UPD. CKS
Paul Kariya .25 .60
Teemu Selanne .25 .60
Patrik Stefan .10 .25
Joe Thornton .40 1.00
Sergei Samsonov .20 .50
Dominik Hasek .50 1.25
Maxim Afinogenov .10 .25
Valeri Bure .10 .25
Marc Savard .10 .25
Ron Francis .20 .50
Jeff O'Neill .10 .25
Tony Amonte .20 .50
Michal Grosek .10 .25
Patrick Roy 1.25 3.00
Ray Bourque .50 1.25
Milan Hejduk .25 .60
Peter Forsberg .50 1.25
Brett Hull .30 .75
Ed Belfour .25 .60
Mike Modano .40 1.00
Brendan Shanahan .25 .60
Chris Osgood .20 .50
Steve Yzerman 1.25 3.00
Doug Weight .20 .50
Tommy Salo .20 .50
Pavel Bure .25 .60
Trevor Kidd .20 .50
28 Rob Blake .20 .50
29 Luc Robitaille .20 .50
30 Jose Theodore .30 .75
31 Saku Koivu .25 .60
32 David Legwand .20 .50
33 Martin Brodeur .60 1.50
34 Scott Gomez .10 .25
35 Scott Stevens .20 .50
36 Tim Connolly .10 .25
37 Mariusz Czerkawski .10 .25
38 Mark Messier .25 .60
39 Theo Fleury .10 .25
40 Marian Hossa .25 .60
41 Radek Bonk .10 .25
42 Brian Boucher .25 .60
43 John LeClair .25 .60
44 Simon Gagne .25 .60
45 Jeremy Roenick .30 .75
46 Keith Tkachuk .25 .60
47 Jaromir Jagr .40 1.00
48 Martin Straka UER .10 .25
(Name missing on card front)
49 Steve Shields .20 .50
50 Jeff Friesen .10 .25
51 Chris Pronger .20 .50
52 Roman Turek .20 .50
53 Vincent Lecavalier .25 .60
54 Dan Cloutier .10 .25
55 Curtis Joseph .25 .60
56 Mats Sundin .25 .60
57 Markus Naslund .25 .60
58 Felix Potvin .25 .60
59 Olaf Kolzig .20 .50
60 Jeff Halpern .10 .25
61 Matt Pettinger RC 2.00 5.00
62 Chris Nielsen RC 2.00 5.00
63 Dany Heatley RC 60.00 125.00
64 Matt Zultek RC 2.00 5.00
65 Dmitri Afanasenkov RC 2.00 5.00
66 Tyler Bouck RC 2.00 5.00
67 Jonas Andersson RC 2.00 5.00
68 Marc-Andre Thinel RC 2.00 5.00
69 Jaroslav Svoboda RC 2.00 5.00
70 Josef Vasicek RC 2.00 5.00
71 Andrew Raycroft RC 6.00 15.00
72 Juraj Kolnik RC 2.00 5.00
73 Zdenek Blatny RC 2.00 5.00
74 Sebastien Caron RC 2.00 5.00
75 Michael Ryder RC 15.00 40.00
76 Eric Nickulas RC 2.00 5.00
77 Jeff Cowan RC 2.00 5.00
78 Steven Reinprecht RC 2.00 5.00
79 David Gosselin RC 2.00 5.00
80 Colin White RC 2.00 5.00
81 Steve Valiquette RC 2.00 5.00
82 Jani Hurme RC 2.00 5.00
83 Jean-Guy Trudel RC 2.00 5.00
84 Dieter Kochan RC 2.00 5.00
85 Paul Kariya PG 10.00 25.00
86 Patrick Roy PG 15.00 40.00
87 Steve Yzerman PG 12.00 30.00
88 Pavel Bure PG 6.00 15.00
89 Martin Brodeur PG 10.00 25.00
90 Jaromir Jagr PG 10.00 25.00
91 Samuel Pahlsson .10 .25
92 Eric Boulton RC .30 .75
93 Daniel Tkaczuk .10 .25
94 Rob Shearer RC .30 .75
95 David Vyborny .10 .25
96 Tyler Bouck UD .40 1.00
97 Mike Comrie RC 4.00 10.00
98 Anson Carter .20 .50
99 Roman Simicek RC .30 .75
100 Andrei Markov .10 .25
101 Jason Arnott .10 .25
102 Mike Mottau .10 .25
103 Taylor Pyatt .10 .25
104 Alexei Yashin .10 .25
105 Todd Fedoruk RC .30 .75
106 Milan Kraft .20 .50
107 Mario Lemieux 1.50 4.00
108 Evgeni Nabokov .20 .50
109 Brad Richards .20 .50
110 Daniel Sedin .10 .25
111 Henrik Sedin .10 .25
112 Petr Tenkrat RC 2.00 5.00
113 Lee Goren RC 2.00 5.00
114 David Aebischer RC 3.00 8.00
115 Yuri Babenko RC 2.00 5.00
116 Rostislav Klesla RC 3.00 8.00
117 Marty Turco RC 8.00 20.00
118 Jason Williams RC 4.00 10.00
119 Michel Riesen RC 2.00 5.00
120 Lubomir Visnovsky RC 2.00 5.00
121 Travis Scott RC 2.00 5.00
122 Peter Bartos RC 2.00 5.00
123 Marian Gaborik RC 10.00 25.00
124 Scott Hartnell RC 2.00 5.00
125 Rick DiPietro RC 6.00 15.00
126 Vitali Yeremeyev RC 2.00 5.00
127 Martin Havlat RC 6.00 15.00
128 Roman Cechmanek RC 2.00 5.00
129 Justin Williams RC 3.00 8.00
130 Ruslan Fedotenko RC 2.00 5.00
131 Alexander Kharitonov RC 2.00 5.00
132 Alexei Ponikarovsky RC 2.00 5.00

2000-01 Black Diamond Gold

Randomly inserted in hobby packs, this 90-card set paralleled the base set enhanced with a gold stamp across the middle of the card reading "Diamond Gold." Each card was sequentially numbered to 100.

*GOLD STARS: 10X TO 25X BASIC CARD
*61-75 GOLD PG RC's: 1X TO 2X BASIC CARDS
*76-84 GOLD PG RC's: 1X TO 2X BASIC CARDS
*85-90 GOLD PG's: 1X TO 2X BASIC CARDS
GOLD STAT.PRINT RUN 100 SER.#'d SETS
63 Dany Heatley 150.00 300.00

2000-01 Black Diamond Diamonation

Randomly inserted in packs at the rate of 1:12, this nine card set features full color player action photography set against a red and silver foil background with gold foil highlights.

COMPLETE SET (9) 15.00 30.00
STATED ODDS 1:12
IG1 Paul Kariya 1.00 2.50
IG2 Patrick Roy 5.00 12.00
IG3 Sergei Fedorov 2.00 5.00
IG4 Pavel Bure 1.25 3.00
IG5 Scott Gomez 1.00 2.50
IG6 John LeClair 1.25 3.00
IG7 Jaromir Jagr 1.50 4.00
IG8 Vincent Lecavalier 1.00 2.50
IG9 Curtis Joseph 1.00 2.50

2000-01 Black Diamond Diamond Might

Randomly seeded in packs at the rate of 1:12, this nine card set features full color action photography set on an all foil card with red highlights along the card bottom in the shape of a "V." Cards have gold foil stamping highlights.

COMPLETE SET (9) 15.00 30.00
STATED ODDS 1:12
FP1 Teemu Selanne 1.25 3.00
FP2 Peter Forsberg 2.50 6.00
FP3 Ray Bourque 2.00 5.00
FP4 Mike Modano 1.50 4.00
FP5 Brendan Shanahan 1.50 4.00
FP6 Pavel Bure 1.25 3.00
FP7 Martin Brodeur 2.50 6.00
FP8 John LeClair 1.25 3.00
FP9 Jaromir Jagr 1.50 4.00

2000-01 Black Diamond Diamond Skills

Randomly inserted in packs at the rate of 1:17, this six card set features full color action photography set against a foil backdrop with cardboard borders along the top and bottom left hand corners. Cards contain gold foil stamping highlights.

COMPLETE SET (6) 20.00 40.00
STATED ODDS 1:17
IC1 Patrick Roy 6.00 15.00
IC2 Mike Modano 2.00 5.00
IC3 Steve Yzerman 6.00 15.00
IC4 Martin Brodeur 3.00 8.00
IC5 John LeClair 1.50 4.00
IC6 Jaromir Jagr 2.00 5.00

2000-01 Black Diamond Game Gear

Randomly inserted in Black Diamond packs at the rate of 1:23 and 1:30 in UD Update packs, this 32-card set features player action shots coupled with a swatch of game used memorabilia. Update cards are marked below.

STATED ODDS 1:23/1:30 UPDATE
BJV J.Vanbiesbrouck Blocker 6.00 15.00
BSB Sean Burke Blocker 6.00 15.00
BTB Tom Barrasso Blocker 6.00 15.00
BTS Tommy Salo Blocker 6.00 15.00
CJV John Vanbiesbrouck Glove 6.00 15.00
CKM Kirk McLean Glove 6.00 15.00
CSB Sean Burke Glove 6.00 15.00
CTB Tom Barrasso Glove 6.00 15.00
CTS Tommy Salo Glove 6.00 15.00
GEL Eric Lindros Glove SP 6.00 15.00
GTS Teemu Selanne Glove SP 8.00 20.00
GWG Wayne Gretzky Glove SP 40.00 100.00
LBD Byron Dafoe Pad 6.00 15.00
LCJ Curtis Joseph Pad 6.00 15.00
LDH Dominik Hasek Pad 15.00 40.00
LGF Grant Fuhr Pad 20.00 50.00
LJV John Vanbiesbrouck Pad 6.00 15.00
LMB Martin Biron Pad 6.00 15.00
LOK Olaf Kolzig Pad 6.00 15.00
LRL Roberto Luongo Pad 8.00 20.00
LSS Steve Shields Pad 6.00 15.00
SMM Mark Messier Skate SP 30.00 80.00
GDR Chris Drury Glove Upd 6.00 15.00
GFE Sergei Fedorov Glove Upd 12.50 30.00
GSA Joe Sakic Glove Upd 12.50 30.00
GTH Joe Thornton Glove Upd 12.50 30.00
GYA Alexei Yashin Glove Upd 6.00 15.00
LAU J.S. Aubin Pad 6.00 15.00
LDE Marc Denis Pad Upd 6.00 15.00
LOS Chris Osgood Pad Upd 6.00 15.00
LTU Roman Turek Pad Upd 6.00 15.00
SJA Jaromir Jagr Skate Upd 20.00 50.00

2000-01 Black Diamond Myriad

Randomly inserted in packs at the rate of 1:17, this six card set features player action photography set against a blue and silver foil background with a black and silver border along the left side of the card. Cards contain gold foil highlights.

COMPLETE SET (6) 12.00 25.00
STATED ODDS 1:17
CC1 Paul Kariya 1.50 4.00
CC2 Peter Forsberg 3.00 8.00
CC3 Pavel Bure 1.50 4.00
CC4 Scott Gomez 1.50 4.00
CC5 Jaromir Jagr 2.00 5.00
CC6 Curtis Joseph 1.50 4.00

2003-04 Black Diamond

This 198-card set consisted of four distinct tiers. Single diamond cards (1-84); double diamond cards (85-126) inserted at 1:2; triple diamond cards (127-168) inserted at 1:8 and quadruple diamond cards inserted at 1:24.

COMPLETE SET (198) 200.00 400.00
COMP.SET w/o SP's (126) 40.00 80.00
DOUBLE 85-126 ODDS 1:2
TRIPLE 127-168 ODDS 1:8
QUAD 169-198 ODDS 1:24
1 Mike York .08 .25
2 Pavel Bure .40 1.00
3 Steve Reinprecht .08 .25
4 Vincent Lecavalier .40 1.00
5 Alex Auld .08 .25
6 Eric Daze .30 .75
7 Jeff Hackett .30 .75
8 Manny Fernandez .08 .25
9 Alexei Zhamnov .08 .25
10 Bryan Marchment .08 .25
11 Jason Allison .08 .25
12 Tony Amonte .30 .75
13 David Legwand .30 .75
14 Geoff Sanderson .08 .25
15 Olaf Kolzig .30 .75
16 Vaclav Prospal .08 .25
17 Sebastien Caron .30 .75
18 Daniel Alfredsson .30 .75
19 Martin Biron .30 .75
20 Jay Bouwmeester .08 .25
21 Nikolai Khabibulin .40 1.00
22 Keith Tkachuk .40 1.00
23 Miroslav Satan .30 .75
24 Rick DiPietro .30 .75
25 Ryan Smyth .08 .25
26 Alexander Mogilny .30 .75
27 Daniil Markov .08 .25
28 Jason Spezza .40 1.00
29 Roman Cechmanek .30 .75
30 Brendan Morrison .30 .75
31 Chris Gratton .08 .25
32 Joe Sakic .75 2.00
33 Jose Theodore .50 1.25
34 Dwayne Roloson .30 .75
35 Ed Jovanovski .30 .75
36 Peter Forsberg .75 2.00
37 Robert Esche .30 .75
38 Daniel Briere .08 .25
39 Doug Weight .30 .75
40 Mike Comrie .30 .75
41 Michael Peca .08 .25
42 Ales Kotalik .08 .25
43 Alexei Kovalev .30 .75
44 Tommy Salo .30 .75
45 Pavol Demitra .30 .75
46 Alex Tanguay .30 .75
47 Johan Hedberg .30 .75
48 Jan Hrdina .08 .25
49 Mike Komisarek .08 .25
50 Petr Sykora .08 .25
51 Ilya Kovalchuk .50 1.25
52 Mike Modano .60 1.50
53 Scottie Upshall .08 .25
54 Rico Fata .08 .25
55 Sergei Gonchar .08 .25
56 Mike Dunham .30 .75
57 Olli Jokinen .30 .75
58 Roman Turek .30 .75
59 Alexander Svitov .08 .25
60 Bill Guerin .30 .75
61 Byron Dafoe .30 .75
62 Patrick Marleau .30 .75
63 Patrik Elias .30 .75
64 Brett Hull .50 1.25
65 Marco Sturm .08 .25
66 Andrew Raycroft .08 .25
67 Peter Sejna RC .08 .25
68 John LeClair .40 1.00
69 Kyle Calder .08 .25
70 Pierre-Marc Bouchard .08 .25
71 Nikolai Antropov .08 .25
72 J-S Giguere .30 .75
73 Marc Denis .30 .75
74 Martin Straka .08 .25
75 Peter Bondra .30 .75
76 Ron Hainsey .08 .25
77 Brendan Shanahan .40 1.00
78 Evgeni Nabokov .30 .75
79 Glen Murray .08 .25
80 Martin Brodeur 1.00 2.50
81 Adam Deadmarsh .08 .25
82 Kevin Weekes .30 .75
83 Owen Nolan .30 .75
84 Zdeno Chara .08 .25
85 Andrew Cassels .40 .75
86 Simon Gagne .75 2.00
87 Derian Hatcher .40 .75
88 Mats Sundin 1.00 2.50
89 Chris Osgood .75 2.00
90 Henrik Zetterberg 1.00 2.50
91 Saku Koivu 1.00 2.50
92 Sergei Samsonov .75 2.00
93 Arron Asham .40 .75
94 Teppo Numminen .40 .75
95 Philippe Sauve .75 2.00
96 Jeff O'Neill .40 .75
97 Luc Robitaille .75 2.00
98 Marty Turco .75 2.00
99 Niko Dimitrakos .40 .75
100 Markus Naslund 1.00 2.50
101 Stephen Weiss .40 .75
102 Ed Belfour 1.00 2.50
103 Roberto Luongo 1.25 3.00
104 Eric Lindros 1.00 2.50
105 Jocelyn Thibault .75 2.00
106 Marian Hossa 1.00 2.50
107 Teemu Selanne 1.00 2.50
108 Jaromir Jagr 2.50 6.00
109 Stanislav Chistov .40 .75
110 Zigmund Palffy .75 2.00
111 P.J. Axelsson .40 .75
112 Denis Arkhipov .40 .75
113 Sean Burke .75 2.00
114 Todd Marchant .40 .75
115 Maxim Afinogenov .40 .75
116 Tomas Vokoun .75 2.00
117 Jason Blake .40 .75
118 Jordan Leopold .40 .75
119 Martin St. Louis .75 2.00
120 Pavel Datsyuk 1.00 2.50
121 Marc Savard .40 .75
122 Marian Gaborik 3.00 8.00
123 Jamie Langenbrunner .40 .75
124 Jarome Iginla 1.25 3.00
125 Al MacInnis .75 2.00
126 Nicklas Lidstrom 1.00 2.50
127 Georges Laraque 3.00 8.00
128 Justin Williams 3.00 8.00
129 Anson Carter 3.00 8.00
130 Chris Drury 3.00 8.00
131 Willie Mitchell 3.00 8.00
132 Rick Nash 4.00 10.00
133 Scott Stevens 3.00 8.00
134 Chris Pronger 3.00 8.00
135 Mario Lemieux 10.00 25.00
136 Steve Ott 3.00 8.00
137 Steve Yzerman 8.00 20.00
138 Dany Heatley 4.00 10.00
139 Ron Francis 3.00 8.00
140 Alexander Frolov 3.00 8.00
141 Tyler Arnason 3.00 8.00
142 Rob Blake 3.00 8.00
143 Patrick Lalime 3.00 8.00
144 Joe Thornton 5.00 12.00
145 David Aebischer 3.00 8.00
146 Alexei Yashin 3.00 8.00
147 Felix Potvin 3.00 8.00
148 Boyd Gordon RC 4.00 10.00
149 Tom Preissing RC 4.00 10.00
150 Brent Burns RC 4.00 10.00
151 Antoine Vermette RC 4.00 10.00
152 Antti Miettinen RC 4.00 10.00
153 Maxim Kondratiev RC 4.00 10.00
154 Christian Ehrhoff RC 4.00 10.00
155 Jiri Hudler RC 5.00 12.00
156 David Hale RC 4.00 10.00
157 Marek Svatos RC 8.00 20.00
158 Matthew Lombardi RC 4.00 10.00
159 Alexander Semin RC 10.00 25.00
160 John-Michael Liles RC 4.00 10.00
161 Dan Fritsche RC 4.00 10.00
162 Esa Pirnes RC 4.00 10.00
163 Cody McCormick RC 4.00 10.00
164 Lasse Kukkonen RC 4.00 10.00
165 Tim Gleason RC 4.00 10.00
166 Marek Zidlicky RC 4.00 10.00
167 Christoph Brandner RC 4.00 10.00
168 Sean Bergenheim RC 4.00 10.00
169 Mike Johnson 6.00 15.00
170 Erik Cole 6.00 15.00
171 Barret Jackman 6.00 15.00
172 Marcel Hossa 6.00 15.00
173 Tie Domi 6.00 15.00
174 Michael Rupp 6.00 15.00
175 Jeremy Roenick 10.00 25.00
176 Sergei Fedorov 10.00 25.00
177 Paul Kariya 8.00 20.00
178 Mike Ricci 8.00 20.00
179 Brenden Morrow 6.00 15.00
180 Dominik Hasek 10.00 25.00
181 P.J. Stock 6.00 15.00
182 Ales Hemsky 8.00 20.00
183 Todd Bertuzzi 8.00 20.00
184 Patrice Bergeron RC 12.00 30.00
185 Pavel Vorobiev RC 4.00 10.00
186 Milan Michalek RC 8.00 20.00
187 Matt Stajan RC 8.00 20.00
188 Dan Hamhuis RC 5.00 12.00
189 Joffrey Lupul RC 8.00 20.00
190 Eric Staal RC 15.00 40.00
191 Tuomo Ruutu RC 6.00 15.00
192 Nathan Horton RC 8.00 20.00
193 Dustin Brown RC 6.00 15.00
194 Jordin Tootoo RC 8.00 20.00
195 Joni Pitkanen RC 5.00 12.00
196 Peter Sejna RC 4.00 10.00
197 Chris Higgins RC 10.00 25.00
198 Marc-Andre Fleury RC 25.00 60.00

2003-04 Black Diamond Black

This set is also referred to as the "Clarity" parallel.

NOT PRICED DUE TO SCARCITY
STATED PRINT RUN 10 SER.#'d SETS

2003-04 Black Diamond Green

This set is also referred to as the "Color" parallel.

*SINGLE STARS: 3X TO 8X BASIC CARDS
*DOUBLE STARS: 2X TO 5X
*TRIPLE STARS: 1X TO 2.5X
*TRIPLE ROOKIES: .5X TO 1.25X
*QUAD STARS: .5X TO 1.25X
*QUAD ROOKIES: .4X TO 1X
STATED PRINT RUN 100 SER.#'d SETS

2003-04 Black Diamond Red

This set is also referred to as the "Cut" parallel.

*SINGLE STARS: 5X TO 12X BASIC CARDS
*DOUBLE STARS: 3X TO 8X
*TRIPLE STARS: 1.5X TO 4X
*TRIPLE ROOKIES: .75X TO 2X
*QUAD STARS: .75X TO 2X
*QUAD ROOKIES: .5X TO 1.25X
STATED PRINT RUN 50 SER.#'d SETS

2003-04 Black Diamond Signature Gems

This 36-card autograph set featured certified autographs on diamond-mirrored stickers affixed to the cards.

STATED ODDS 1:48
SG-1 Maxim Afinogenov 6.00 15.00
SG-2 Ray Bourque 15.00 40.00
SG-4 Pavel Bure 10.00 25.00
SG-5 Erik Cole 6.00 15.00
SG-6 Mike Comrie 6.00 15.00
SG-7 Simon Gagne 6.00 15.00
SG-8 Rick Nash 12.50 30.00
SG-9 Wayne Gretzky 100.00 250.00
SG-10 Scott Hartnell 6.00 15.00
SG-11 Martin Havlat 6.00 15.00
SG-12 Ilya Kovalchuk 15.00 40.00
SG-13 Gordie Howe 60.00 150.00
SG-14 Curtis Joseph 8.00 20.00
SG-15 Alexander Svitov 6.00 15.00
SG-16 John LeClair 10.00 25.00
SG-17 Steve Ott 6.00 15.00
SG-18 Bobby Orr 75.00 200.00
SG-19 Joe Thornton 15.00 40.00
SG-20 Henrik Zetterberg 10.00 25.00
SG-21 Marty Turco 8.00 20.00
SG-22 Marian Hossa 12.00 30.00
SG-23 Patrick Roy/24 300.00 500.00
SG-24 J-S Giguere 6.00 15.00
SG-25 Marian Gaborik 15.00 40.00
SG-26 Todd Bertuzzi 8.00 20.00
SG-27 Jason Spezza 12.50 30.00
SG-28 Jarome Iginla 15.00 40.00
SG-29 Sergei Samsonov 6.00 15.00
SG-30 Jose Theodore 12.50 30.00
SG-31 Justin Williams 6.00 15.00
SG-32 Alexander Frolov 6.00 15.00
SG-33 Brooks Orpik 6.00 15.00
SG-34 Kurt Sauer 6.00 15.00
SG-35 Steve Yzerman 25.00 60.00
SG-36 Ed Belfour 25.00 60.00
SG-37 Jeff Taffe 6.00 15.00

2003-04 Black Diamond Threads

*MULT.COLOR SWATCH: .5X TO 1.25X
STATED ODDS 1:12
DT-RN Rick Nash 8.00 20.00
DT-BS Brendan Shanahan 6.00 15.00
DT-JB Jay Bouwmeester 5.00 12.00
DT-MA Maxim Afinogenov 5.00 12.00
DT-AS Alexander Svitov 5.00 12.00
DT-TE Jose Theodore 8.00 20.00
DT-KC Kyle Calder 5.00 12.00
DT-KP Keith Primeau 5.00 12.00
DT-TH Jocelyn Thibault 5.00 12.00
DT-MH Marian Hossa 6.00 15.00
DT-ED Eric Daze 5.00 12.00
DT-JG J-S Giguere 5.00 12.00
DT-JR Jeremy Roenick 6.00 15.00
DT-MT Marty Turco 6.00 15.00
DT-DA David Aebischer 5.00 12.00
DT-IK Ilya Kovalchuk 8.00 20.00
DT-MD Marc Denis 5.00 12.00
DT-DU Mike Dunham 5.00 12.00
DT-CP Chris Pronger 5.00 12.00
DT-DW Doug Weight 5.00 12.00
DT-AF Alexander Frolov 5.00 12.00
DT-MO Mike Modano 8.00 20.00
DT-AZ Alexei Zhamnov 5.00 12.00
DT-BM Brenden Morrow 5.00 12.00
DT-DH Dany Heatley 8.00 20.00
DT-MS Mats Sundin 6.00 15.00
DT-PK Paul Kariya 6.00 15.00
DT-RL Roberto Luongo 8.00 20.00
DT-SN Scott Niedermayer 5.00 12.00
DT-DB Daniel Briere 5.00 12.00
DT-MM Mark Messier 12.50 30.00
DT-ML Mario Lemieux 12.50 30.00
DT-EB Ed Belfour 6.00 15.00
DT-PB Peter Bondra 5.00 12.00
DT-PF Peter Forsberg 8.00 20.00
DT-MB Martin Brodeur 12.50 30.00
DT-EJ Ed Jovanovski 5.00 12.00
DT-JS Jason Spezza 6.00 15.00
DT-MN Markus Naslund 6.00 15.00
DT-JT Joe Thornton 8.00 20.00
DT-AT Alex Tanguay 5.00 12.00
DT-EL Eric Lindros 6.00 15.00

2003-04 Black Diamond Threads Green

This set is also referred to as the "Color" parallel.

*STARS: .6X TO 1.5X BASIC INSERTS
STATED PRINT RUN 99 SER.#'d SETS

2003-04 Black Diamond Threads Red

This set is also referred to as the "Cut" parallel.

*STARS: 1X TO 2.5X BASIC INSERTS
STATED PRINT RUN 50 SER.#'d SETS

2003-04 Black Diamond Threads Black

This set is also referred to as the "Clarity" parallel.

STATED PRINT RUN 10 SER.#'d SETS
NOT PRICED DUE TO SCARCITY

2005-06 Black Diamond

COMPLETE SET
COMP.SET w/o SP's (84) 10.00 20.00
DOUBLE ODDS 1:4
TRIPLE ODDS 1:8
QUAD ODDS 1:24
1 Joffrey Lupul .15 .40
2 Steve Rucchin .15 .40
3 Riku Hahl .15 .40
4 Shawn McEachern .15 .40
5 Marc Savard .15 .40
6 Philippe Sauve .20 .50
7 Nick Boynton .15 .40
8 Martin Lapointe .15 .40
9 Maxim Afinogenov .15 .40
10 Chris Drury .20 .50
11 Mike Grier .15 .40
12 Jordan Leopold .15 .40
13 Darren McCarty .15 .40
14 Martin Gelinas .15 .40
15 Eric Staal .20 .50
16 Jeff O'Neill .15 .40
17 Erik Cole .15 .40
18 Rod Brind'Amour .15 .40
19 Jocelyn Thibault .20 .50
20 Tyler Arnason .15 .40
21 Bryan Berard .15 .40
22 Eric Daze .20 .50
23 Rob Blake .20 .50
24 Nikolai Zherdev .15 .40
25 Marc Denis .20 .50
26 Justin Williams .15 .40
27 Brenden Morrow .20 .50
28 Sergei Zubov .15 .40
29 Jere Lehtinen .20 .50

30 Henrik Zetterberg .25 .60
31 Ty Conklin .20 .50
32 Ryan Smyth .15 .40
33 Jason Smith .15 .40
34 Chris Chelios .20 .50
35 Stephen Weiss .15 .40
36 Olli Jokinen .20 .50
37 Gary Roberts .15 .40
38 Alexander Frolov .15 .40
39 Mathieu Garon .20 .50
40 Lubomir Visnovsky .15 .40
41 Dwayne Roloson .20 .50
42 Pascal Dupuis .15 .40
43 Brian Rolston .20 .50
44 Filip Kuba .15 .40
45 Richard Zednik .15 .40
46 Sheldon Souray .15 .40
47 Steve Sullivan .15 .40
48 Jordin Tootoo .15 .40
49 Tomas Vokoun .20 .50
50 Scott Walker .15 .40
51 Martin Brodeur 1.50 4.00
52 Scott Niedermayer .15 .40
53 Brian Rafalski .15 .40
54 Alexander Mogilny .20 .50
55 Bobby Holik .15 .40
56 Kevin Weekes .20 .50
57 Jamie Lundmark .15 .40
58 Michael Peca .15 .40
59 Mark Parrish .15 .40
60 Adrian Aucoin .15 .40
61 Wade Redden .15 .40
62 Zdeno Chara .15 .40
63 Simon Gagne .25 .60
64 Robert Esche .20 .50
65 Mike Comrie .20 .50
66 Shane Doan .15 .40
67 Derian Hatcher .15 .40
68 Ladislav Nagy .15 .40
69 Milan Kraft .15 .40
70 Ryan Malone .15 .40
71 Marco Sturm .15 .40
72 Brad Stuart .15 .40
73 Alyn McCauley .15 .40
74 Patrick Lalime .20 .50
75 Dustin Brown .15 .40
76 Fredrik Modin .15 .40
77 Dave Andreychuk .20 .50
78 Brian Leetch .25 .60
79 Tie Domi .20 .50
80 Ed Jovanovski .20 .50
81 Brendan Morrison .20 .50
82 Dan Cloutier .20 .50
83 Brendan Witt .15 .40
84 Martin Biron .20 .50
85 Manny Legace 1.00 2.50
86 J-S Giguere 1.00 2.50
87 Sergei Fedorov 1.50 4.00
88 Andrew Raycroft 1.00 2.50
89 Sergei Samsonov 1.00 2.50
90 Miroslav Satan 1.00 2.50
91 Miikka Kiprusoff 1.00 2.50
92 David Aebischer 1.00 2.50
93 Milan Hejduk 1.25 3.00
94 Marty Turco 1.00 2.50
95 Curtis Joseph 1.25 3.00
96 Nicklas Lidstrom 1.25 3.00
97 Roberto Luongo 1.00 2.50
98 Zigmund Palffy 1.00 2.50
99 Luc Robitaille 1.00 2.50
100 Mike Ribeiro 1.00 2.50
101 Michael Ryder 1.00 2.50
102 Scott Gomez 1.00 2.50
103 Patrik Elias 1.00 2.50
104 Alexei Yashin 1.00 2.50
105 Daniel Alfredsson 1.00 2.50
106 Martin Havlat 1.00 2.50
107 Tony Amonte 1.00 2.50
108 John LeClair 1.25 3.00
109 Brett Hull 1.50 4.00
110 Marc-Andre Fleury 1.00 2.50
111 Mark Recchi 1.00 2.50
112 Patrick Marleau 1.00 2.50
113 Jonathan Cheechoo 1.50 4.00
114 Chris Pronger 1.00 2.50
115 Doug Weight 1.00 2.50
116 Brad Richards 1.00 2.50
117 Glen Murray 1.00 2.50
118 Tuomo Ruutu 1.00 2.50
119 Pavol Demitra 1.00 2.50
120 David Legwand 1.00 2.50
121 Eric Lindros 1.25 3.00
122 Rick DiPietro 1.00 2.50
123 Al MacInnis 1.00 2.50
124 Joe Nieuwendyk 1.00 2.50
125 Trevor Linden 1.00 2.50
126 Olaf Kolzig 1.00 2.50
127 Dany Heatley 4.00 10.00
128 Kari Lehtonen 3.00 8.00
129 Patrice Bergeron 3.00 8.00
130 Alex Tanguay 3.00 8.00
131 Paul Kariya 3.00 8.00
132 Mike Modano 4.00 10.00
133 Bill Guerin 3.00 8.00
134 Pavel Datsyuk 3.00 8.00
135 Brendan Shanahan 3.00 8.00
136 Saku Koivu 3.00 8.00
137 Marian Hossa 3.00 8.00
138 Jason Spezza 3.00 8.00
139 Jeremy Roenick 4.00 10.00
140 Keith Primeau 3.00 8.00
141 Evgeni Nabokov 3.00 8.00
142 Vincent Lecavalier 3.00 8.00
143 Ed Belfour 3.00 8.00
144 Jason Allison 3.00 8.00
145 Markus Naslund 3.00 8.00
146 Keith Tkachuk 3.00 8.00
147 Nikolai Khabibulin 3.00 8.00
148 Andrew Alberts RC 2.50 6.00
149 Andy Wozniewski RC 2.50 6.00
150 Brandon Bochenski RC 3.00 8.00
151 Brent Seabrook RC 4.00 10.00
152 Cam Ward RC 6.00 15.00
153 Chris Campoli RC 2.50 6.00
154 David Leneveu RC 3.00 8.00
155 Duncan Keith RC 2.50 6.00
156 Henrik Lundqvist RC 10.00 25.00
157 Jay McClement RC 2.50 6.00
158 Johan Franzen RC 3.00 8.00
159 Jussi Jokinen RC 3.00 8.00
160 Keith Ballard RC 2.50 6.00
161 Kevin Dallman RC 2.50 6.00
162 Maxime Talbot RC 2.50 6.00
163 Niklas Nordgren RC 2.50 6.00
164 Peter Budaj RC 3.00 8.00
165 Petteri Nokelainen RC 2.50 6.00
166 Rene Bourque RC 2.50 6.00
167 Jeff Woywitka RC 2.50 6.00
168 Ryan Hollweg RC 2.50 6.00
169 Ilya Kovalchuk 5.00 12.00
170 Joe Thornton 6.00 15.00
171 Jarome Iginla 5.00 12.00
172 Joe Sakic 8.00 20.00
173 Peter Forsberg 8.00 20.00
174 Rick Nash 4.00 10.00
175 Steve Yzerman 10.00 25.00
176 Marian Gaborik 5.00 12.00
177 Jose Theodore 4.00 10.00
178 Jaromir Jagr 6.00 15.00
179 Mark Messier 8.00 20.00
180 Dominik Hasek 6.00 15.00
181 Mario Lemieux 12.50 30.00
182 Martin St. Louis 4.00 10.00
183 Mats Sundin 3.00 10.00
184 Wayne Gretzky 15.00 40.00
185 Gordie Howe 8.00 20.00
186 Ray Bourque 5.00 12.00
187 Patrick Roy 12.50 30.00
188 Bryan Trottier 4.00 10.00
189 Cam Neely 4.00 10.00
190 Gilbert Brule RC 15.00 40.00
191 Alexander Ovechkin RC 50.00 125.00
192 Zach Parise RC 10.00 25.00
193 Sidney Crosby RC 225.00 400.00
194 Dion Phaneuf RC 30.00 60.00
195 Jeff Carter RC 8.00 20.00
196 Corey Perry RC 10.00 25.00
197 Thomas Vanek RC 15.00 40.00
198 Ryan Getzlaf RC 15.00 40.00
199 Mike Richards RC 6.00 15.00
200 Robert Nilsson RC 5.00 12.00
201 Alexander Steen RC 6.00 15.00
202 Rostislav Olesz RC 5.00 12.00
203 Wojtek Wolski RC 10.00 25.00
204 Ryan Suter RC 5.00 12.00
205 Hannu Toivonen RC 6.00 15.00
206 Yann Danis RC 5.00 12.00
207 Jim Howard RC 6.00 15.00
208 Andrej Meszaros RC 6.00 15.00
209 Braydon Coburn RC 4.00 10.00
210 Alexander Perezhogin RC 5.00 12.00
211 Dustin Penner RC 5.00 12.00
212 Zenon Konopka RC 2.50 6.00
213 Jim Slater RC 3.00 8.00
214 Adam Berkhoel RC 3.00 8.00
215 Jordan Sigalet RC 3.00 8.00
216 Milan Jurcina RC 2.50 6.00
217 Ben Walter RC 2.50 6.00
218 Chris Thorburn RC 2.50 6.00
219 Daniel Paille RC 2.50 6.00
220 Nathan Paetsch RC 2.50 6.00
221 Andrew Ladd RC 4.00 10.00
222 Kevin Nastiuk RC 3.00 8.00
223 Danny Richmond RC 2.50 6.00
224 Cam Barker RC 3.00 8.00
225 Corey Crawford RC 3.00 8.00
226 James Wisniewski RC 2.50 6.00
227 Brad Richardson RC 2.50 6.00
228 Vitaly Kolesnik RC 3.00 8.00
229 Ole-Kristian Tollefsen RC 2.50 6.00
230 Jaroslav Balastik RC 2.50 6.00
231 Geoff Platt RC 2.50 6.00
232 Alexandre Picard RC 2.50 6.00
233 Joakim Lindstrom RC 2.50 6.00
234 Junior Lessard RC 2.50 6.00
235 Vojtech Polak RC 2.50 6.00
236 Kyle Quincey RC 3.00 8.00
237 Valtteri Filppula RC 3.00 8.00
238 Brett Lebda RC 2.50 6.00
239 Kyle Brodziak RC 2.50 6.00
240 Brad Winchester RC 2.50 6.00
241 Danny Syvret RC 2.50 6.00
242 Matt Greene RC 2.50 6.00
243 J-F Jacques RC 2.50 6.00
244 Anthony Stewart RC 2.50 6.00
245 Rob Globke RC 2.50 6.00
246 Petr Taticek RC 2.50 6.00
247 Jeff Tambellini RC 3.00 8.00
248 Petr Kanko RC 2.50 6.00
249 George Parros RC 2.50 6.00
250 Yanick Lehoux RC 2.50 6.00
251 Richard Petiot RC 2.50 6.00
252 Mikko Koivu RC 4.00 10.00
253 Derek Boogaard RC 3.00 8.00
254 Matt Foy RC 2.50 6.00
255 Andrei Kostitsyn RC 4.00 10.00
256 Maxim Lapierre RC 2.50 6.00
257 Kevin Klein RC 2.50 6.00
258 Pekka Rinne RC 3.00 8.00
259 Barry Tallackson RC 3.00 8.00
260 Jason Ryznar RC 2.50 6.00
261 Jeremy Colliton RC 3.00 8.00
262 Bruno Gervais RC 2.50 6.00
263 Petr Prucha RC 4.00 10.00
264 Al Montoya RC 4.00 10.00
265 Christoph Schubert RC 2.50 6.00
266 Patrick Eaves RC 4.00 10.00
267 R.J. Umberger RC 4.00 10.00
268 Ben Eager RC 2.50 6.00
269 Alexandre Picard RC 2.50 6.00
270 Stefan Ruzicka RC 2.50 6.00
271 Ryan Whitney RC 3.00 8.00
272 Erik Christensen RC 2.50 6.00
273 Colby Armstrong RC 4.00 10.00
274 Steve Bernier RC 4.00 10.00
275 Dimitri Patzold RC 3.00 8.00
276 Ryane Clowe RC 2.50 6.00
277 Josh Gorges RC 2.50 6.00
278 Grant Stevenson RC 2.50 6.00
279 Lee Stempniak RC 2.50 6.00
280 Colin Hemingway RC 2.50 6.00
281 Dennis Wideman RC 2.50 6.00
282 Evgeny Artyukhin RC 2.50 6.00
283 Ryan Craig RC 2.50 6.00
284 Paul Ranger RC 2.50 6.00
285 Darren Reid RC 2.50 6.00
286 Gerald Coleman RC 3.00 8.00
287 Staffan Kronwall RC 2.50 6.00
288 Jay Harrison RC 2.50 6.00
289 Kevin Bieksa RC 2.50 6.00
290 Rob McVicar RC 3.00 8.00
291 Tomas Mojzis RC 2.50 6.00
292 Jakub Klepis RC 2.50 6.00
293 Tomas Fleischmann RC 2.50 6.00
294 Mike Green RC 2.50 6.00

2005-06 Black Diamond Emerald

COMMON SINGLE DIAMOND 8.00 20.00
*DOUBLE STARS.: 4X TO 10X
*TRIPLE STARS.: 1.5X TO 4X
*TRIPLE ROOKIE: 1.25X TO 3X
*QUAD STARS.: .75X TO 2X
*QUAD ROOKIE: 1X TO 2.5X
PRINT RUN 25 SER.#'d SETS

2005-06 Black Diamond Gold

PRINT RUN 10 SER.#'d SETS
NOT PRICED DUE TO SCARCITY

2005-06 Black Diamond Onyx

STATED PRINT RUN 1 SET
NOT PRICED DUE TO SCARCITY

2005-06 Black Diamond Ruby

COMMON SINGLE DIAMOND (1-84) 4.00 10.00
COMMON DOUBLE DIAM. (85-126) 5.00 12.00
*TRIPLE STARS.: .75X TO 2X
*TRIPLE ROOKIE: 1X TO 2.5X
*QUAD STARS.: .5X TO 1.25X
*QUAD ROOKIE: .5X TO 1.25X
PRINT RUN 100 SER.#'d SETS
191 Alexander Ovechkin 200.00 300.00
193 Sidney Crosby 300.00 500.00

2005-06 Black Diamond Gemography

Overall auto odds 1:48.
STATED ODDS 1:62
G-AC Anson Carter 5.00 12.00
G-AV Antoine Vermette 6.00 12.00
G-BA Milan Bartovic 4.00 10.00
G-BB Brad Boyes 6.00 12.00
G-BI Martin Biron 6.00 12.00
G-CD Chris Drury 6.00 12.00
G-DB Dustin Brown 5.00 12.00
G-DH Dany Heatley 15.00 40.00
G-EC Erik Cole 5.00 12.00
G-FS Fredrik Sjostrom 4.00 10.00
G-GH Gordie Howe 40.00 100.00
G-HA Dominik Hasek 20.00 50.00
G-HO Marcel Hossa 4.00 10.00
G-IK Ilya Kovalchuk 15.00 40.00
G-JC Jonathan Cheechoo 10.00 25.00
G-JI Jarome Iginla 20.00 50.00
G-JR Jeremy Roenick 15.00 40.00
G-JT Joe Thornton 20.00 50.00
G-KD Kris Draper 6.00 12.00
G-LR Luc Robitaille 8.00 20.00
G-MB Martin Brodeur 50.00 125.00
G-MC Mike Comrie 4.00 10.00
G-MF Marc-Andre Fleury 15.00 40.00
G-MG Marian Gaborik 20.00 50.00
G-MH Martin Havlat 6.00 12.00
G-MN Markus Naslund 8.00 15.00
G-MP Mark Popovic 4.00 10.00
G-MR Michael Ryder 8.00 15.00
G-NK Nikolai Khabibulin 8.00 15.00
G-NZ Nikolai Zherdev 4.00 10.00
G-PB Patrice Bergeron 10.00 25.00
G-RB Ray Bourque 30.00 80.00
G-RE Robert Esche 5.00 12.00
G-RK Ryan Kesler 5.00 12.00
G-SB Sean Bergenheim 4.00 10.00
G-SL Martin St. Louis 6.00 15.00
G-SP Jason Spezza 12.00 30.00
G-SS Sheldon Souray 4.00 10.00
G-TM Travis Moen 4.00 10.00
G-TR Tuomo Ruutu 6.00 12.00
G-TS Timofei Shishkanov 4.00 10.00
G-WG Wayne Gretzky 200.00 300.00

2005-06 Black Diamond Gemography Emerald

*EMERALD: .6X TO 1.5X BASIC INSERTS
PRINT RUN 25 SER.#'d SETS

2005-06 Black Diamond Gemography Gold

PRINT RUN 10 SER.#'d SETS
NOT PRICED DUE TO SCARCITY

2005-06 Black Diamond Gemography Onyx

PRINT RUN 1 SER.#'d SET
NOT PRICED DUE TO SCARCITY

2005-06 Black Diamond Gemography Ruby

*RUBY: .5X TO 1.25X BASIC INSERT
PRINT RUN 50 SER.#'d SET

2005-06 Black Diamond Jerseys

STATED ODDS 1:12
J-AM Al MacInnis 4.00 10.00
J-BH Brett Hull 5.00 12.00
J-BO Mike Bossy 5.00 12.00
J-BS Brendan Shanahan 5.00 12.00
J-CC Chris Chelios 5.00 12.00
J-CJ Curtis Joseph 5.00 12.00
J-EB Ed Belfour 5.00 12.00
J-EJ Ed Jovanovski 3.00 8.00
J-GL Guy Lafleur 6.00 15.00
J-HA Dominik Hasek 6.00 15.00
J-JF Jeff Friesen 3.00 8.00
J-JI Jarome Iginla 6.00 15.00
J-JJ Jaromir Jagr 6.00 15.00
J-JN Joe Nieuwendyk 3.00 8.00
J-JO Jose Theodore 5.00 12.00
J-JR Jeremy Roenick 5.00 12.00
J-JS Joe Sakic 8.00 20.00
J-JT Joe Thornton 6.00 15.00
J-KP Keith Primeau 3.00 8.00
J-MB Martin Brodeur 10.00 25.00
J-MG Marian Gaborik 6.00 15.00
J-MH Milan Hejduk 3.00 8.00
J-ML Mario Lemieux 15.00 40.00
J-MM Mike Modano 5.00 12.00
J-MS Mark Messier 8.00 20.00
J-OJ Olli Jokinen 3.00 8.00
J-ON Owen Nolan 4.00 8.00
J-PB Pavel Bure 5.00 12.00
J-PE Peter Bondra 4.00 10.00
J-PF Peter Forsberg 6.00 15.00
J-PK Paul Kariya 5.00 12.00
J-PL Patrick Lalime 3.00 8.00
J-RL Roberto Luongo 6.00 15.00
J-RN Rick Nash 5.00 12.00
J-SF Sergei Fedorov 5.00 12.00
J-SK Saku Koivu 5.00 12.00
J-SL Martin St. Louis 4.00 10.00
J-SU Mats Sundin 5.00 12.00
J-SY Steve Yzerman 12.00 30.00
J-TS Teemu Selanne 5.00 12.00
J-WG Wayne Gretzky 20.00 50.00

2005-06 Black Diamond Jerseys Ruby

*RUBY: .5X TO 1.25X
PRINT RUN 100 SER.#'d SETS
J-DH Dany Heatley 8.00 20.00

2005-06 Black Diamond Jersey Duals

*DUAL: 1.25X TO 3X SINGLE
PRINT RUN 25 SER.#'d SETS
DJ-DH Dany Heatley 12.50 30.00

2005-06 Black Diamond Jersey Triples

PRINT RUN 10 SER.#'d SETS
NOT PRICED DUE TO SCARCITY

2005-06 Black Diamond Jersey Quads

PRINT RUN 1 SET
NOT PRICED DUE TO SCARCITY

2006-07 Black Diamond

DOUBLE ODDS 1:4
TRIPLE ODDS 1:8
QUAD ODDS 1:24
CARDS 169-189 DO NOT EXIST
1 Corey Perry .25 .60
2 Ilya Bryzgalov .25 .60
3 Scott Niedermayer .15 .40
4 Slava Kozlov .15 .40
5 Jim Slater .15 .40
6 Hannu Toivonen .30 .75
7 Marc Savard .15 .40
8 Zdeno Chara .15 .40
9 Glen Murray .15 .40
10 Daniel Briere .15 .40
11 Maxim Afinogenov .15 .40
12 Thomas Vanek .15 .40
13 Daymond Langkow .15 .40
14 Chuck Kobasew .15 .40
15 Rod Brind'Amour .25 .60
16 Justin Williams .15 .40
17 Mike Commodore .15 .40
18 Michal Handzus .15 .40
19 Brent Seabrook .15 .40
20 Nikolai Khabibulin .30 .75
21 Peter Budaj .25 .60
22 Wojtek Wolski .15 .40
23 Fredrik Modin .15 .40
24 Pascal Leclaire .25 .60
25 Bryan Berard .15 .40
26 Brenden Morrow .25 .60
27 Sergei Zubov .15 .40
28 Jere Lehtinen .15 .40
29 Kris Draper .15 .40
30 Tomas Holmstrom .15 .40
31 Dwayne Roloson .25 .60
32 Jarret Stoll .15 .40
33 Shawn Horcoff .15 .40
34 Fernando Pisani .15 .40
35 Olli Jokinen .15 .40
36 Nathan Horton .15 .40
37 Todd Bertuzzi .25 .60
38 Mike Cammalleri .15 .40
39 Craig Conroy .15 .40
40 Pavol Demitra .15 .40
41 Mark Parrish .15 .40
42 Manny Fernandez .25 .60
43 Pierre-Marc Bouchard .15 .40
44 Sergei Samsonov .25 .60
45 Alex Kovalev .15 .40
46 Jason Arnott .15 .40
47 Steve Sullivan .15 .40
48 Scott Hartnell .15 .40
49 Scott Gomez .15 .40
50 Brian Gionta .15 .40
51 Zach Parise .25 .60
52 Rick DiPietro .25 .60
53 Robert Nilsson .15 .40
54 Jason Blake .15 .40
55 Petr Prucha .15 .40
56 Martin Straka .15 .40
57 Martin Gerber .25 .60
58 Wade Redden .15 .40
59 Patrick Eaves .15 .40
60 Joni Pitkanen .15 .40
61 Mike Richards .25 .60
62 Antero Niittymaki .25 .60
63 Curtis Joseph .30 .75
64 Ladislav Nagy .15 .40
65 Ed Jovanovski .15 .40
66 Colby Armstrong .15 .40
67 Ryan Whitney .15 .40
68 Ryan Malone .15 .40
69 Steve Bernier .15 .40
70 Evgeni Nabokov .25 .60
71 Vesa Toskala .25 .60
72 Keith Tkachuk .25 .60
73 Bill Guerin .15 .40
74 Manny Legace .25 .60
75 Vaclav Prospal .15 .40
76 Marc Denis .25 .60
77 Martin St. Louis .25 .60
78 Andrew Raycroft .25 .60
79 Darcy Tucker .15 .40
80 Daniel Sedin .15 .40
81 Henrik Sedin .15 .40
82 Brendan Morrison .15 .40
83 Dainius Zubrus .15 .40
84 Olaf Kolzig .30 .75
85 Teemu Selanne 2.00 5.00
86 Jean-Sebastien Giguere 1.50 4.00
87 Chris Pronger 1.50 4.00
88 Marian Hossa 1.50 4.00
89 Brad Boyes 1.00 2.50
90 Chris Drury 1.00 2.50
91 Ryan Miller 2.00 5.00
92 Alex Tanguay 1.50 4.00
93 Erik Cole 1.00 2.50
94 Tuomo Ruutu 1.00 2.50
95 Martin Havlat 1.50 4.00
96 Jose Theodore 2.00 5.00
97 Marek Svatos 1.00 2.50
98 Sergei Fedorov 2.00 5.00
99 Gilbert Brule 2.00 5.00
100 Eric Lindros 2.00 5.00
101 Marty Turco 1.50 4.00
102 Pavel Datsyuk 1.50 4.00
103 Ales Hemsky 1.00 2.50
104 Ryan Smyth 1.50 4.00
105 Jay Bouwmeester 1.00 2.50
106 Rob Blake 1.50 4.00
107 Alexander Frolov 1.00 2.50
108 Mikko Koivu 1.00 2.50
109 Cristobal Huet 2.50 6.00
110 Mike Ribeiro 1.00 2.50
111 Tomas Vokoun 1.50 4.00
112 Patrik Elias 1.00 2.50
113 Alexei Yashin 1.00 2.50
114 Miroslav Satan 1.00 2.50
115 Henrik Lundqvist 2.50 6.00
116 Daniel Alfredsson 1.50 4.00
117 Simon Gagne 2.00 5.00
118 Jeff Carter 1.50 4.00
119 Shane Doan 1.00 2.50
120 Jeremy Roenick 2.00 5.00
121 Mark Recchi 1.00 2.50
122 Patrick Marleau 1.50 4.00
123 Doug Weight 1.00 2.50
124 Brad Richards 1.50 4.00
125 Alexander Steen 1.50 4.00
126 Michael Peca 1.00 2.50
127 Kari Lehtonen 3.00 8.00
128 Patrice Bergeron 3.00 8.00
129 Miikka Kiprusoff 3.00 8.00
130 Dion Phaneuf 4.00 10.00
131 Eric Staal 3.00 8.00
132 Cam Ward 3.00 8.00
133 Milan Hejduk 2.00 5.00
134 Mike Modano 2.50 6.00
135 Henrik Zetterberg 3.00 8.00
136 Nicklas Lidstrom 3.00 8.00
137 Ed Belfour 3.00 8.00
138 Saku Koivu 3.00 8.00
139 Michael Ryder 3.00 8.00
140 Paul Kariya 3.00 8.00
141 Brendan Shanahan 3.00 8.00
142 Dany Heatley 4.00 10.00
143 Marc-Andre Fleury 3.00 8.00
144 Jonathan Cheechoo 3.00 8.00
145 Vincent Lecavalier 3.00 8.00
146 Markus Naslund 3.00 8.00
147 Roberto Luongo 4.00 10.00
148A Roman Polak RC 2.00 5.00
148B Ilya Kovalchuk 4.00 10.00
149A Joel Perrault RC 2.00 5.00
149B Ray Bourque 4.00 10.00
150A Yan Stastny RC 2.50 6.00
150B Cam Neely 3.00 8.00
151A Konstantin Pushkarev RC 2.00 5.00
151B Jarome Iginla 4.00 10.00
152A Jarkko Immonen RC 2.50 6.00
152B Joe Sakic 4.00 10.00
153A Marc-Antoine Pouliot RC 3.00 8.00
153B Patrick Roy 6.00 15.00
154A Jeremy Williams RC 2.00 5.00
154B Rick Nash 3.00 8.00
155A Michel Ouellet RC 3.00 8.00
155B Dominik Hasek 4.00 10.00
156A Tomas Kopecky RC 2.50 6.00
156B Gordie Howe 5.00 12.00
157A Keith Yandle RC 2.00 5.00
157B Wayne Gretzky 8.00 20.00
158A Marc-Edouard Vlasic RC 2.50 6.00
158B Marian Gaborik 4.00 10.00
159A Shane O'Brien RC 2.50 6.00
159B Jean Beliveau 3.00 8.00
160A Ryan Shannon RC 2.00 5.00
160B Martin Brodeur 5.00 12.00
161A John Oduya RC 2.00 5.00
161B Jaromir Jagr 4.00 10.00
162A Fredrik Norrena RC 2.50 6.00
162B Jason Spezza 3.00 8.00
163A Kristopher Letang RC 2.50 6.00
163B Peter Forsberg 4.00 10.00
164A Niklas Backstrom RC 3.00 8.00
164B Sidney Crosby 20.00 40.00
165A D.J. King RC 2.00 5.00
165B Mario Lemieux 6.00 15.00
166A Patrick Thoresen RC 2.50 6.00
166B Joe Thornton 4.00 10.00
167A Patrick Fischer RC 2.00 5.00
167B Mats Sundin 3.00 8.00
168A Mikko Lehtonen RC 2.00 5.00
168B Alexander Ovechkin 5.00 12.00
190 Mark Stuart RC 2.50 6.00
191 Eric Fehr RC 3.00 8.00
192 Ryan Potulny RC 3.00 8.00
193 Ian White RC 2.50 6.00
194 Alexei Kaigorodov RC 2.50 6.00
195 Noah Welch RC 2.50 6.00
196 Shea Weber RC 5.00 10.00
197 Enver Lisin RC 2.50 6.00
198 Matt Carle RC 4.00 10.00
199 Patrick O'Sullivan RC 6.00 15.00
200 Anze Kopitar RC 15.00 40.00
201 Travis Zajac RC 5.00 12.00
202 Phil Kessel RC 12.00 30.00
203 Guillaume Latendresse RC 12.00 30.00
204 Nigel Dawes RC 2.50 6.00
205 Jordan Staal RC 40.00 80.00
206 Paul Stastny RC 12.00 30.00
207 Luc Bourdon RC 5.00 12.00
208 Ladislav Smid RC 2.50 6.00
209 Loui Eriksson RC 4.00 10.00
210 Evgeni Malkin RC 75.00 125.00

2006-07 Black Diamond Black

STATED PRINT RUN 1/1
NOT PRICED DUE TO SCARCITY

2006-07 Black Diamond Gold

COMPLETE SET (210)
STATED PRINT RUN 10 #'d SETS
NOT PRICED DUE TO SCARCITY

2006-07 Black Diamond Ruby

COMPLETE SET (210)
STATED PRINT RUN 100 #'d SETS
1 Corey Perry 4.00 10.00
2 Ilya Bryzgalov 4.00 10.00
3 Scott Niedermayer 2.50 6.00
4 Slava Kozlov 2.50 6.00
5 Jim Slater 2.50 6.00
6 Hannu Toivonen 4.00 10.00
7 Marc Savard 2.50 6.00
8 Zdeno Chara 2.50 6.00
9 Glen Murray 2.50 6.00
10 Daniel Briere 4.00 10.00
11 Maxim Afinogenov 2.50 6.00
12 Thomas Vanek 4.00 10.00
13 Daymond Langkow 2.50 6.00
14 Chuck Kobasew 2.50 6.00
15 Rod Brind'Amour 4.00 10.00
16 Justin Williams 2.50 6.00
17 Mike Commodore 2.50 6.00
18 Michal Handzus 2.50 6.00
19 Brent Seabrook 2.50 6.00
20 Nikolai Khabibulin 5.00 12.00
21 Peter Budaj 4.00 10.00
22 Wojtek Wolski 2.50 6.00
23 Fredrik Modin 2.50 6.00
24 Pascal Leclaire 4.00 10.00
25 Bryan Berard 2.50 6.00
26 Brenden Morrow 4.00 10.00
27 Sergei Zubov 2.50 6.00
28 Jere Lehtinen 2.50 6.00
29 Kris Draper 2.50 6.00
30 Tomas Holmstrom 2.50 6.00
31 Dwayne Roloson 5.00 12.00
32 Jarret Stoll 2.50 6.00
33 Shawn Horcoff 2.50 6.00
34 Fernando Pisani 2.50 6.00
35 Olli Jokinen 2.50 6.00
36 Nathan Horton 2.50 6.00
37 Todd Bertuzzi 4.00 10.00
38 Mike Cammalleri 2.50 6.00
39 Craig Conroy 2.50 6.00
40 Pavol Demitra 2.50 6.00
41 Mark Parrish 2.50 6.00
42 Manny Fernandez 4.00 10.00
43 Pierre-Marc Bouchard 2.50 6.00
44 Sergei Samsonov 4.00 10.00
45 Alex Kovalev 2.50 6.00
46 Jason Arnott 2.50 6.00
47 Steve Sullivan 2.50 6.00
48 Scott Hartnell 2.50 6.00
49 Scott Gomez 2.50 6.00
50 Brian Gionta 2.50 6.00
51 Zach Parise 4.00 10.00
52 Rick DiPietro 4.00 10.00
53 Robert Nilsson 2.50 6.00
54 Jason Blake 2.50 6.00
55 Petr Prucha 2.50 6.00
56 Martin Straka 2.50 6.00
57 Martin Gerber 5.00 12.00
58 Wade Redden 2.50 6.00
59 Patrick Eaves 2.50 6.00
60 Joni Pitkanen 2.50 6.00
61 Mike Richards 4.00 10.0
62 Antero Niittymaki 4.00 10.0
63 Curtis Joseph 5.00 12.0
64 Ladislav Nagy 2.50 6.0
65 Ed Jovanovski 2.50 6.0
66 Colby Armstrong 2.50 6.0
67 Ryan Whitney 2.50 6.0
68 Ryan Malone 2.50 6.0
69 Steve Bernier 2.50 6.0
70 Evgeni Nabokov 4.00 10.0
71 Vesa Toskala 4.00 10.0
72 Keith Tkachuk 4.00 10.0
73 Bill Guerin 2.50 6.0
74 Manny Legace 4.00 10.0
75 Vaclav Prospal 2.50 6.0
76 Marc Denis 4.00 10.0
77 Martin St. Louis 4.00 10.0
78 Andrew Raycroft 4.00 10.0
79 Darcy Tucker 2.50 6.0
80 Daniel Sedin 2.50 6.0
81 Henrik Sedin 2.50 6.0
82 Brendan Morrison 2.50 6.0
83 Dainius Zubrus 2.50 6.0
84 Olaf Kolzig 5.00 12.0
85 Teemu Selanne 5.00 12.0
86 Jean-Sebastien Giguere 4.00 10.0
87 Chris Pronger 4.00 10.0
88 Marian Hossa 4.00 10.0
89 Brad Boyes 2.50 6.0
90 Chris Drury 2.50 6.0
91 Ryan Miller 5.00 12.0
92 Alex Tanguay 4.00 10.0
93 Erik Cole 2.50 6.0
94 Tuomo Ruutu 2.50 6.0
95 Martin Havlat 4.00 10.0
96 Jose Theodore 5.00 12.0
97 Marek Svatos 2.50 6.0
98 Sergei Fedorov 5.00 12.0
99 Gilbert Brule 5.00 12.0
100 Eric Lindros 5.00 12.0
101 Marty Turco 4.00 10.0
102 Pavel Datsyuk 4.00 10.0
103 Ales Hemsky 2.50 6.0
104 Ryan Smyth 4.00 10.0
105 Jay Bouwmeester 2.50 6.0
106 Rob Blake 4.00 10.0
107 Alexander Frolov 2.50 6.0
108 Mikko Koivu 2.50 6.0
109 Cristobal Huet 6.00 15.0
110 Mike Ribeiro 2.50 6.0
111 Tomas Vokoun 4.00 10.0
112 Patrik Elias 2.50 6.0
113 Alexei Yashin 2.50 6.0
114 Miroslav Satan 2.50 6.0
115 Henrik Lundqvist 6.00 15.0
116 Daniel Alfredsson 4.00 10.0
117 Simon Gagne 5.00 12.0
118 Jeff Carter 5.00 12.0
119 Shane Doan 2.50 6.0
120 Jeremy Roenick 6.00 15.0
121 Mark Recchi 2.50 6.0
122 Patrick Marleau 4.00 10.0
123 Doug Weight 2.50 6.0
124 Brad Richards 4.00 10.0
125 Alexander Steen 4.00 10.0
126 Michael Peca 2.50 6.0
127 Kari Lehtonen 5.00 12.0
128 Patrice Bergeron 5.00 12.0
129 Miikka Kiprusoff 5.00 12.0
130 Dion Phaneuf 6.00 15.0
131 Eric Staal 5.00 12.0
132 Cam Ward 5.00 12.0
133 Milan Hejduk 2.50 6.0
134 Mike Modano 5.00 12.0
135 Henrik Zetterberg 5.00 12.0
136 Nicklas Lidstrom 5.00 12.0
137 Ed Belfour 5.00 12.0
138 Saku Koivu 5.00 12.0
139 Michael Ryder 4.00 10.0
140 Paul Kariya 5.00 12.0
141 Brendan Shanahan 5.00 12.0
142 Dany Heatley 6.00 15.0
143 Marc-Andre Fleury 5.00 12.0
144 Jonathan Cheechoo 5.00 12.0
145 Vincent Lecavalier 5.00 12.0
146 Markus Naslund 5.00 12.0
147 Roberto Luongo 6.00 15.0
148A Roman Polak 2.50 6.0
148B Ilya Kovalchuk 6.00 15.0
149A Joel Perrault 2.50 6.0
149B Ray Bourque 8.00 20.0
150A Yan Stastny 2.50 6.0
150B Cam Neely 6.00 15.0
151A Konstantin Pushkarev 2.50 6.0
151B Jarome Iginla 6.00 15.0
152A Jarkko Immonen 2.50 6.0
152B Joe Sakic 10.00 25.0
153A Marc-Antoine Pouliot 4.00 10.0
153B Patrick Roy 15.00 40.0
154A Jeremy Williams 2.50 6.0
154B Rick Nash 5.00 12.0
155A Michel Ouellet 5.00 12.0
155B Dominik Hasek 6.00 15.0
156A Tomas Kopecky 4.00 10.0
156B Gordie Howe 10.00 25.0
157A Keith Yandle 2.50 6.0
157B Wayne Gretzky 25.00 60.0
158A Marc-Edouard Vlasic 2.50 6.0
158B Marian Gaborik 6.00 15.0
159A Shane O'Brien 2.50 6.0
159B Jean Beliveau 6.00 15.0
160A Ryan Shannon 2.50 6.0
160B Martin Brodeur 8.00 20.0
161A John Oduya 2.50 6.0
161B Jaromir Jagr 8.00 20.0
162A Fredrik Norrena 4.00 10.0
162B Jason Spezza 5.00 12.0
163A Kristopher Letang 4.00 10.0
163B Peter Forsberg 6.00 15.0
164A Niklas Backstrom 5.00 12.0
164B Sidney Crosby 40.00 100.0
165A D.J. King 2.50 6.0
165B Mario Lemieux 15.00 40.0
166A Patrick Thoresen 4.00 10.0
166B Joe Thornton 8.00 20.0
167A Patrick Fischer 2.50 6.0
167B Mats Sundin 5.00 12.0
168A Mikko Lehtonen 2.50 6.0
168B Alexander Ovechkin 15.00 40.0
190 Mark Stuart 3.00 8.0
191 Eric Fehr 5.00 12.0

Ryan Potulny 5.00 12.00
Ian White 3.00 8.00
Alexei Kaigorodov 3.00 8.00
Noah Welch 3.00 8.00
Shea Weber 5.00 12.00
Enver Lisin 3.00 8.00
Matt Carle 5.00 12.00
Patrick O'Sullivan 5.00 12.00
Anze Kopitar 25.00 60.00
Travis Zajac 10.00 25.00
Phil Kessel 20.00 50.00
Guillaume Latendresse 25.00 60.00
Nigel Dawes 8.00 20.00
Jordan Staal 60.00 150.00
Paul Stastny 25.00 60.00
Luc Bourdon 10.00 25.00
Ladislav Smid 8.00 20.00
Loui Eriksson 6.00 15.00
Evgeni Malkin 150.00 250.00

2006-07 Black Diamond Gemography

TED ODDS 1:48
Adam Berkhoel 6.00 15.00
Andrew Ladd 4.00 10.00
Alexander Ovechkin SP 125.00250.00
Brandon Bochenski 4.00 10.00
Brian Leetch SP 30.00 80.00
Bryan McCabe 4.00 10.00
Brad Winchester 4.00 10.00
Jeff Carter 8.00 20.00
Cam Barker 4.00 10.00
Chuck Kobasew 4.00 10.00
Chris Phillips 4.00 10.00
Cory Stillman 4.00 10.00
David Aebischer 6.00 15.00
Dion Phaneuf 10.00 25.00
Danny Richmond 4.00 10.00
Doug Weight 4.00 10.00
Erik Christensen 6.00 15.00
Gordie Howe SP 50.00 125.00
Georges Laraque 4.00 10.00
Glen Murray 4.00 10.00
Scott Hartnell 4.00 10.00
Henrik Zetterberg SP 20.00 40.00
Jonathan Cheechoo 8.00 20.00
Josh Gorges 4.00 10.00
Jim Howard 6.00 15.00
Jarome Iginla SP 15.00 40.00
Jussi Jokinen 4.00 10.00
Jeff O'Neill 4.00 10.00
Joni Pitkanen SP 10.00 25.00
Jim Slater 4.00 10.00
Jose Theodore 10.00 25.00
Kris Draper SP 20.00 40.00
Kari Lehtonen SP 15.00 40.00
Kimmo Timonen 4.00 10.00
Marian Gaborik SP 15.00 40.00
Marian Hossa SP 12.00 30.00
Miikka Kiprusoff SP 15.00 40.00
Mario Lemieux SP 75.00 150.00
Mark Parrish 4.00 10.00
Mike Ribeiro 4.00 10.00
Miroslav Satan 6.00 15.00
Marty Turco SP 15.00 30.00
Mike Van Ryn 4.00 10.00
Marek Zidlicky 4.00 10.00
Nathan Horton 4.00 10.00
Patrice Bergeron SP 25.00 60.00
Patrick Marleau 6.00 15.00
Petr Prucha 4.00 10.00
Paul Ranger 4.00 10.00
Rene Bourque 4.00 10.00
Ryan Miller SP 20.00 40.00
Rick Nash SP 20.00 50.00
Sidney Crosby 150.00 250.00
Shawn Horcoff 4.00 10.00
Ty Conklin 6.00 15.00
Vesa Toskala 6.00 15.00
Wayne Gretzky SP 150.00 250.00

2006-07 Black Diamond Jerseys

TED ODDS 1:13
Arron Asham 3.00 8.00
Alexander Frolov 3.00 8.00
Ales Hemsky 3.00 8.00
Alex Kovalev 3.00 8.00
Jason Allison 3.00 8.00
Andrej Meszaros 3.00 8.00
Alexander Ovechkin SP 12.00 30.00
Alexander Steen 4.00 10.00
Alex Tanguay 4.00 10.00
Brad Boyes 3.00 8.00
Patrice Bergeron 6.00 15.00
Bill Guerin 3.00 8.00
Barret Jackman 3.00 8.00
Brian Leetch 6.00 15.00
Brendan Morrison 3.00 8.00
Brandon Bochenski 3.00 8.00
Martin Brodeur 12.00 30.00
Brad Stuart 3.00 8.00
Peter Budaj 4.00 10.00
Chris Drury 3.00 8.00
Curtis Joseph 5.00 12.00
Chuck Kobasew 3.00 8.00
Mike Comrie 3.00 8.00
Corey Perry 4.00 10.00
Cam Ward 5.00 12.00
Donald Brashear 3.00 8.00
Dan Cloutier 4.00 10.00
Pavol Demitra 3.00 8.00
Dan Hamhuis 3.00 8.00
Duncan Keith 3.00 8.00
Dion Phaneuf 6.00 15.00
Doug Weight 3.00 8.00
Evgeni Artyukhin 3.00 8.00
Ed Belfour 5.00 12.00
Eric Lindros 5.00 12.00
Simon Gagne 5.00 12.00
Milan Hejduk 3.00 8.00
Henrik Zetterberg 5.00 12.00
Ilya Kovalchuk 8.00 20.00
Jason Arnott 3.00 8.00
Jay Bouwmeester 3.00 8.00
Jeff Friesen 3.00 8.00
Jean-Sebastien Giguere 4.00 10.00
JJH Jeff Hoggan 3.00 8.00
JJJ Jaromir Jagr 10.00 25.00
JJK Jakub Klepis 3.00 8.00
JJL Joffrey Lupul 3.00 8.00
JJN Joe Nieuwendyk 4.00 10.00
JJS Joe Sakic 10.00 25.00
JJT Joe Thornton 8.00 20.00
JKD Kris Draper 3.00 8.00
JKO Andrei Kostitsyn 3.00 8.00
JKT Keith Tkachuk 4.00 10.00
JLA Andrew Ladd 3.00 8.00
JLE Jere Lehtinen 3.00 8.00
JMA Mark Bell 3.00 8.00
JMB Martin Biron 4.00 10.00
JMC Mike Cammalleri 3.00 8.00
JMH Marian Hossa 4.00 10.00
JMI Mike Komisarek 3.00 8.00
JMJ Milan Jurcina 3.00 8.00
JMK Miikka Kiprusoff 6.00 15.00
JMM Mike Modano 8.00 20.00
JMN Markus Naslund 5.00 12.00
JMO Shaone Morrisonn 3.00 8.00
JMP Michael Peca 3.00 8.00
JMR Mark Recchi 3.00 8.00
JMS Marek Svatos 3.00 8.00
JNH Nathan Horton 3.00 8.00
JNK Nikolai Khabibulin 5.00 12.00
JPA Daniel Paille 3.00 8.00
JPB Peter Bondra 4.00 10.00
JPD Pavel Datsyuk 4.00 10.00
JPF Peter Forsberg 10.00 25.00
JPK Paul Kariya 5.00 12.00
JRB Rod Brind'Amour 4.00 10.00
JRC Ryan Craig 3.00 8.00
JRD Rick DiPietro 4.00 10.00
JRH Ryan Hollweg 3.00 8.00
JRK Rostislav Klesla 3.00 8.00
JRM Ryan Miller 6.00 15.00
JRO Rob Blake 4.00 10.00
JRU R.J. Umberger 3.00 8.00
JRY Michael Ryder 4.00 10.00
JSA Miroslav Satan 3.00 8.00
JSC Sidney Crosby SP 30.00 80.00
JSF Sergei Fedorov 6.00 15.00
JSG Scott Gomez 3.00 8.00
JSH Jody Shelley 3.00 8.00
JSM Mats Sundin 5.00 12.00
JSN Brendan Shanahan 5.00 12.00
JSS Sergei Samsonov 4.00 10.00
JST Matt Stajan 3.00 8.00
JSU Scottie Upshall 3.00 8.00
JSW Stephen Weiss 3.00 8.00
JTC Ty Conklin 4.00 10.00
JTH Tomas Holmstrom 3.00 8.00
JTP Tom Poti 3.00 8.00
JVN Ville Nieminen 3.00 8.00
JWG Wayne Gretzky 30.00 80.00

2006-07 Black Diamond Jerseys Black

COMPLETE SET (100)
STATED PRINT RUN 1/1
NOT PRICED DUE TO SCARCITY

2006-07 Black Diamond Jerseys Gold

COMPLETE SET (100)
STATED PRINT RUN 10 #'d SETS
NOT PRICED DUE TO SCARCITY

2006-07 Black Diamond Jerseys Ruby

COMPLETE SET (100)
*RUBY: .5X TO 1.5X BASE HI
STATED PRINT RUN 100 #'d SETS
JSC Sidney Crosby/25 75.00 175.00
JWG Wayne Gretzky/25 125.00 200.00

2006-07 Black Diamond Jerseys Black Autographs

STATED PRINT RUN 1/1
NOT PRICED DUE TO SCARCITY
JAF Alexander Frolov
JAH Ales Hemsky
JAO Alexander Ovechkin
JAT Alex Tanguay
JBB Brad Boyes
JBI Martin Biron
JBL Brian Leetch
JBO Brandon Bochenski
JCA Mike Cammalleri
JCD Chris Drury
JCK Chuck Kobasew
JDC Dan Cloutier
JDP Dion Phaneuf
JDW Doug Weight
JGO Scott Gomez
JHO Marian Hossa
JHZ Henrik Zetterberg
JIK Ilya Kovalchuk
JJB Jay Bouwmeester
JJH Jeff Hoggan
JJL Joffrey Lupul
JJT Joe Thornton
JKD Kris Draper
JKI Miikka Kiprusoff
JMB Martin Brodeur
JMH Milan Hejduk
JMN Markus Naslund
JMP Michael Peca
JMS Marek Svatos
JNH Nathan Horton
JNK Nikolai Khabibulin
JPB Patrice Bergeron
JRK Rostislav Klesla
JRM Ryan Miller
JRO Rob Blake
JRY Michael Ryder
JSA Miroslav Satan
JSC Sidney Crosby
JSS Sergei Samsonov
JSW Stephen Weiss
JWG Wayne Gretzky

1968-69 Blackhawks Team Issue

This 8-card set measures approximately 4" by 6".
COMPLETE SET (8) 25.00 50.00
1 Dennis Hull 4.00 8.00
2 Doug Jarrett 2.50 5.00
3 Chico Maki 3.00 6.00
4 Gilles Marotte 2.50 5.00
5 Stan Mikita 10.00 20.00
6 Jim Pappin 2.50 5.00
7 Pat Stapleton 2.50 5.00
8 Ken Wharram 3.00 6.00

1970-71 Blackhawks Postcards

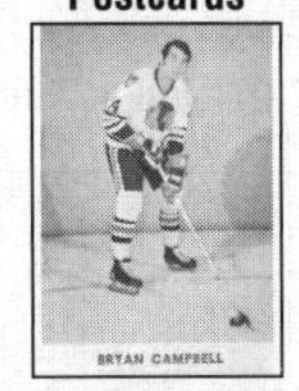

This 14-card set measures approximately 4" by 6". T
COMPLETE SET (14) 25.00 50.00
1 Lou Angotti 1.50 3.00
2 Bryan Campbell 1.50 3.00
3 Bobby Hull 10.00 20.00
Bill Wirtz OWN
Stan Mikita
4 Dennis Hull 3.00 6.00
5 Tommy Ivan GM 1.50 3.00
Billy Reay CO
6 Doug Jarrett 1.50 3.00
7 Keith Magnuson 2.50 5.00
8 Pit Martin 1.50 3.00
9 Stan Mikita 5.00 10.00
10 Eric Nesterenko 2.50 5.00
11 Jim Pappin 2.00 4.00
12 Allan Pinder 1.50 3.00
13 Paul Shmyr 1.50 3.00
14 Bill White 2.00 4.00

1979-80 Blackhawks Postcards

COMPLETE SET (21) 12.50 25.00
1 Keith Brown .50 1.00
2 J.P. Bordeleau .50 1.00
3 Ted Bully .50 1.00
4 Alain Daigle .50 1.00
5 Tony Esposito 3.00 6.00
6 Greg Fox .50 1.00
7 Tim Higgins .50 1.00
8 Reggie Kerr .50 1.00
9 Cliff Koroll .50 1.00
10 Tom Lysiak .50 1.00
11 Keith Magnuson 1.00 2.00
12 John Marks .50 1.00
13 Stan Mikita 4.00 8.00
14 Grant Mulvey 1.00 2.00
15 Bob Murray 1.00 2.00
16 Mike O'Connell .50 1.00
17 Rich Preston .50 1.00
18 Bob Pulford 1.00 2.00
19 Terry Ruskowski .50 1.00
20 Mike Veisor .50 1.00
21 Doug Wilson 2.00 4.00

1980-81 Blackhawks Postcards

These postcard-size cards measure approximately 4" by 6".
COMPLETE SET (16) 12.50 25.00
1 Keith Brown 1.00 2.00
2 Greg Fox .50 1.00
3 Dave Hutchison .50 1.00
4 Cliff Koroll ACO .50 1.00
5 Keith Magnuson CO .75 1.50
6 Peter Marsh .75 1.50
7 Grant Mulvey .75 1.50
8 Rich Preston .50 1.00
9 Florent Robidoux .50 1.00
10 Terry Ruskowski .75 1.50
11 Denis Savard 2.50 5.00
12 Al Secord 1.00 2.00
13 Ron Sedlbauer .50 1.00
14 Glen Sharpley .50 1.00
15 Darryl Sutter 1.00 2.00
16 Miles Zaharko .50 1.00

1980-81 Blackhawks White Border

These 14 blank-backed photos measure approximately 5 1/2" by 8 1/2".
COMPLETE SET (14) 10.00 20.00
1 Murray Bannerman .75 1.50
2 J.P. Bordeleau .50 1.00
3 Keith Brown 1.00 2.00
4 Tony Esposito 2.50 5.00
5 Greg Fox .50 1.00
6 Tim Higgins .50 1.00
7 Doug Lecuyer .50 1.00
8 John Marks .50 1.00
9 Grant Mulvey .75 1.50
10 Rich Preston .50 1.00
11 Terry Ruskowski .75 1.50
12 Denis Savard 2.50 5.00
13 Darryl Sutter 1.00 2.00
14 Tim Trimper .50 1.00

1981-82 Blackhawks Borderless Postcards

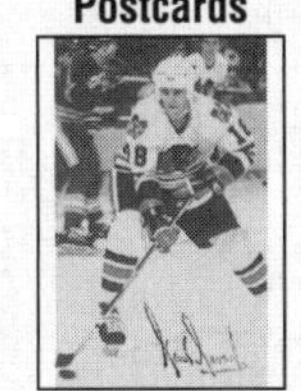

These 28 postcards measure approximately 3 1/2" by 5 1/2"..
COMPLETE SET (28) 12.00 30.00
1 Murray Bannerman .60 1.50
2 Keith Brown .60 1.50
3 Ted Bulley .30 .75
4 Doug Crossman .60 1.50
5 Jerome Dupont .30 .75
6 Tony Esposito 2.00 5.00
7 Greg Fox .30 .75
8 Bill Gardner .30 .75
9 Tim Higgins .30 .75
10 Dave Hutchison .30 .75
11 Reg Kerr .30 .75
12 Cliff Koroll ACO .30 .75
13 Tom Lysiak .60 1.50
14 Keith Magnuson CO .60 1.50
15 John Marks .30 .75
16 Peter Marsh .30 .75
17 Grant Mulvey .30 .75
18 Bob Murray .30 .75
19 Rick Paterson .30 .75
20 Rich Preston .30 .75
21 Bob Pulford GM .60 1.50
22 Terry Ruskowski .30 .75
23 Denis Savard 2.00 5.00
24 Al Secord .80 2.00
25 Glen Sharpley .30 .75
26 Darryl Sutter .80 2.00
27 Toni Tanti .80 2.00
28 Doug Wilson 1.20 3.00

1981-82 Blackhawks Brown Background

These 17 postcards measure approximately 4" by 6"..
COMPLETE SET (17) 10.00 25.00
1 Keith Brown .80 2.00
2 Greg Fox .40 1.00
3 Dave Hutchison .40 1.00
4 Cliff Koroll ACO .40 1.00
5 Keith Magnuson CO .80 2.00
6 Peter Marsh .80 2.00
7 Grant Mulvey .80 2.00
8 Bob Pulford GM/CO 1.20 3.00
9 Rich Preston .40 1.00
10 Florent Robidoux .40 1.00
11 Terry Ruskowski .80 2.00
12 Denis Savard 3.00 7.50
13 Al Secord .80 2.00
14 Ron Sedlbauer .40 1.00
15 Glen Sharpley .40 1.00
16 Darryl Sutter 1.20 3.00
17 Miles Zaharko .40 1.00

1982-83 Blackhawks Postcards

COMPLETE SET (23) 12.00 30.00
1 Murray Bannerman .50 1.25
2 Keith Brown .50 1.25
3 Doug Crossman .40 1.00
4 Dennis Cyr .30 .75
5 Tony Esposito 1.60 4.00
6 Dave Feamster .30 .75
7 Bill Gardner .30 .75
8 Greg Fox .30 .75
9 Tim Higgins .30 .75
10 Steve Larmer 2.00 5.00
11 Steve Ludzik .60 1.50
12 Tom Lysiak .50 1.25
13 Peter Marsh .30 .75
14 Grant Mulvey .30 .75
15 Bob Murray .30 .75
16 Troy Murray .40 1.00
17 Rick Paterson .30 .75
18 Rich Preston .30 .75
19 Denis Savard 1.60 4.00
20 Al Secord .80 2.00
21 Darryl Sutter .60 1.50
22 Orval Tessier CO .40 1.00
23 Doug Wilson 1.00 2.50

1983-84 Blackhawks Postcards

These 27 postcards measure approximately 3 1/2" by 5 1/2".
COMPLETE SET (27) 14.00 35.00
1 Murray Bannerman .60 1.50
2 Keith Brown .40 1.00
3 Denis Cyr .30 .75
4 Jerome Dupont .30 .75
5 Tony Esposito 1.60 4.00
6 Dave Feamster .30 .75
7 Curt Fraser .40 1.00
8 Bill Gardner .30 .75
9 Bob Janecyk .60 1.50
10 Cliff Koroll ACO .20 .50
11 Steve Larmer 2.80 7.00
12 Steve Ludzik .60 1.50
13 Tom Lysiak .60 1.50
14 Peter Marsh .30 .75
15 Bob Murray .30 .75
16 Troy Murray .60 1.50
17 Jack O'Callahan .30 .75
18 Rick Paterson .30 .75
19 Rich Preston .30 .75
20 Denis Savard 1.60 4.00
21 Al Secord .80 2.00
22 Darryl Sutter .80 2.00
23 Orval Tessier CO .20 .50
24 Behn Wilson .30 .75
25 Doug Wilson 1.00 2.50
26 Ken Yaremchuk .30 .75
27 Title Card .20 .50

1985-86 Blackhawks Team Issue

COMPLETE SET (26) 20.00 40.00
1 Steve Larmer 1.25 3.00
2 Keith Brown .75 2.00
3 Cliff Koroll .40 1.00
4 Roger Neilson .40 1.00
5 Bob Pulford .40 1.00
6 Behn Wilson .75 2.00
7 Jerome Dupont .75 2.00
8 Rick Paterson .40 1.00
9 Al Secord 1.25 3.00
10 Marc Bergevin .40 1.00
11 Darryl Sutter 1.25 3.00
12 Murray Bannerman .75 2.00
13 Bruce Cassidy .40 1.00
14 Bill Watson .40 1.00
15 Curt Fraser .40 1.00
16 Warren Skorodenski .75 2.00
17 Troy Murray .40 1.00
18 Bill Gardner .40 1.00
19 Ken Yaremchuk .40 1.00
20 Steve Ludzik .40 1.00
21 Jack O'Callahan .75 2.00
22 Tom Lysiak .40 1.00
23 Bob Murray .40 1.00
24 Ed Olczyk .75 2.00
25 Denis Savard 1.25 3.00
26 Doug Wilson 1.25 3.00

1986-87 Blackhawks Coke

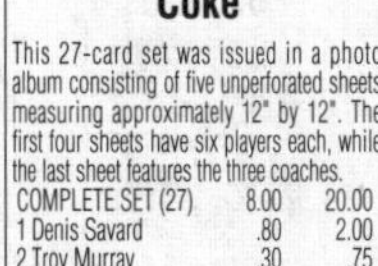

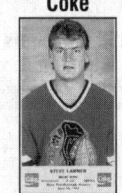

The cards measure approximately 3 1/2" by 6 1/2".
COMPLETE SET (24) 8.00 20.00
1 Murray Bannerman .40 1.00
2 Marc Bergevin .30 .75
3 Keith Brown .30 .75
4 Dave Donnelly .30 .75
5 Curt Fraser .30 .75
6 Steve Larmer 1.20 3.00
7 Steve Ludzik .30 .75
8 Dave Manson .60 1.50
9 Bob Murray .30 .75
10 Troy Murray .30 .75
11 Gary Nylund .30 .75
12 Jack O'Callahan .30 .75
13 Ed Olczyk .40 1.00
14 Rick Paterson .30 .75
15 Wayne Presley .30 .75
16 Rich Preston .30 .75
17 Bob Sauve .40 1.00
18 Denis Savard 1.20 3.00
19 Al Secord .40 1.00
20 Mike Stapleton .30 .75
21 Darryl Sutter .40 1.00
22 Bill Watson .30 .75
23 Behn Wilson .30 .75
24 Doug Wilson .60 1.50

1987-88 Blackhawks Coke

The cards measure approximately 3 1/2" by 6 1/2".
COMPLETE SET (30) 8.00 20.00
1 Murray Bannerman .40 1.00
2 Marc Bergevin .30 .75
3 Keith Brown .30 .75
4 Glen Cochrane .30 .75
5 Curt Fraser .30 .75
6 Steve Larmer 1.00 2.50
7 Mark LaVarre .30 .75
8 Steve Ludzik .30 .75
9 Dave Manson .60 1.50
10 Bob Mason .40 1.00
11 Bob McGill .30 .75
12 Bob Murdoch CO .30 .75
13 Bob Murray .30 .75
14 Troy Murray .40 1.00
15 Brian Noonan .30 .75
16 Gary Nylund .30 .75
17 Darren Pang .60 1.50
18 Wayne Presley .30 .75
19 Everett Sanipass .30 .75
20 Denis Savard 1.00 2.50
21 Mike Stapleton .30 .75
22 Darryl Sutter CO .30 .75
23 Duane Sutter .40 1.00
24 Steve Thomas .50 1.25
25 Wayne Thomas CO .30 .75
26 Rick Vaive .40 1.00
27 Dan Vincelette .30 .75
28 Bill Watson .30 .75
29 Behn Wilson .30 .75
30 Doug Wilson .60 1.50

1988-89 Blackhawks Coke

The cards measure approximately 3 1/2" by 6 1/2".
COMPLETE SET (25) 8.00 20.00
1 Ed Belfour 4.00 10.00
2 Keith Brown .20 .50
3 Bruce Cassidy .20 .50
4 Mike Eagles .20 .50
5 Dirk Graham .40 1.00
6 Mike Hudson .20 .50
7 Mike Keenan CO .60 1.50
8 Steve Larmer .60 1.50
9 Dave Manson .40 1.00
10 Jacques Martin CO .10 .25
11 Bob McGill .20 .50
12 E.J. McGuire CO .10 .25
13 Troy Murray .40 1.00
14 Brian Noonan .20 .50
15 Darren Pang .30 .75
16 Wayne Presley .20 .50
17 Everett Sanipass .20 .50
18 Denis Savard .80 2.00
19 Duane Sutter .30 .75
20 Steve Thomas .40 1.00
21 Rick Vaive .30 .75
22 Dan Vincelette .20 .50
23 Jimmy Waite .30 .75
24 Doug Wilson .40 1.00
25 Trent Yawney .20 .50

1989-90 Blackhawks Coke

This 27-card set was issued in a photo album consisting of five unperforated sheets measuring approximately 12" by 12". The first four sheets have six players each, while the last sheet features the three coaches.
COMPLETE SET (27) 8.00 20.00
1 Denis Savard .80 2.00
2 Troy Murray .30 .75
3 Steve Larmer .60 1.50
4 Doug Wilson .60 1.50
5 Bob Murray .20 .50
6 Jeremy Roenick 3.20 8.00

7 Duane Sutter .30 .75
8 Greg Gilbert .20 .50
9 Trent Yawney .20 .50
10 Bob McGill .20 .50
11 Jacques Cloutier .30 .75
12 Bob Bassen .20 .50
13 Steve Thomas .40 1.00
14 Adam Creighton .30 .75
15 Wayne Van Dorp .20 .50
16 Dirk Graham .40 1.00
17 Mike Hudson .20 .50
18 Al Secord .30 .75
19 Alain Chevrier .30 .75
20 Wayne Presley .20 .50
21 Steve Konroyd .20 .50
22 Everett Sanipass .20 .50
23 Keith Brown .20 .50
24 Dave Manson .40 1.00
25 Mike Keenan CO .40 1.00
26 E.J. McGuire CO .10 .25
27 Jacques Martin CO .10 .25

1990-91 Blackhawks Coke

This 28-card set was issued in a photo album consisting of five unperforated sheets measuring approximately 11 3/4" by 12 1/4".
COMPLETE SET (28) 8.00 20.00
1 Dirk Graham .30 .75
2 Troy Murray .30 .75
3 Steve Larmer .40 1.00
4 Doug Wilson .40 1.00
5 Chris Chelios 1.00 2.50
6 Jeremy Roenick 2.00 5.00
7 Steve Thomas .30 .75
8 Greg Gilbert .20 .50
9 Trent Yawney .20 .50
10 Bob McGill .20 .50
11 Jacques Cloutier .24 .60
12 Jocelyn Lemieux .20 .50
13 Michel Goulet .40 1.00
14 Adam Creighton .24 .60
15 Mike McNeill .20 .50
16 Ed Belfour 2.40 6.00
17 Mike Hudson .20 .50
18 Greg Millen .30 .75
19 Stu Grimson .30 .75
20 Wayne Presley .20 .50
21 Steve Konroyd .20 .50
22 Mike Peluso .30 .75
23 Keith Brown .20 .50
24 Dave Manson .30 .75
25 Mike Keenan CO .30 .75
26 Darryl Sutter CO .30 .75
27 E.J. McGuire CO .10 .25
28 Vladislav Tretiak CO 1.00 2.50

1991-92 Blackhawks Coke

This photo album measured approximately 11 5/8" by 12 1/4".
COMPLETE SET (28) 8.00 20.00
1 Ed Belfour 1.25 3.00
2 Keith Brown .20 .50
3 Rod Buskas .20 .50
4 Chris Chelios .75 2.00
5 Karl Dykhuis .20 .50
6 Greg Gilbert .20 .50
7 Michel Goulet .30 .75
8 Dirk Graham .30 .75
9 Stu Grimson .40 1.00
10 Mike Hudson .20 .50
11 Mike Keenan GM/CO .40 1.00
12 Steve Konroyd .20 .50
13 Frantisek Kucera .20 .50
14 Steve Larmer .40 1.00
15 Brad Lauer .20 .50
16 Jocelyn Lemieux .20 .50
17 Bryan Marchment .20 .50
18 Dave McDowall CO .10 .25
19 Brian Noonan .20 .50
20 Mike Peluso .20 .50
21 Rich Preston CO .10 .25
22 Jeremy Roenick 1.25 3.00
23 Steve Smith .30 .75
24 Mike Stapleton .20 .50
25 Brent Sutter .30 .75
26 Darryl Sutter CO .30 .75
27 John Tonelli .30 .75
28 Jimmy Waite .30 .75

1992-93 Blackhawks Coke

COMPLETE SET (20) 10.00 25.00
1 Adam Bennett .30 .75
2 Cam Russell .30 .75
3 Christian Ruuttu .30 .75
4 Stu Grimson .75 2.00
5 Brent Sutter .75 2.00
6 Dave Christian .40 1.00

7 Mike Hudson	.30	.75
8 Rob Brown	.30	.75
9 Steve Larmer	.75	2.00
10 Bryan Marchment	.30	.75
11 Igor Kravchuk	.30	.75
12 Paul Baxter	.30	.75
13 Vladislav Tretiak	.75	2.00
14 Rich Preston	.30	.75
15 Darryl Sutter	.75	2.00
16 Keith Brown	.30	.75
17 Bob Pulford	.30	.75
18 Jimmy Waite	.40	1.00
19 Ed Belfour	1.25	3.00
20 Jeremy Roenick	1.25	3.00

1993-94 Blackhawks Coke

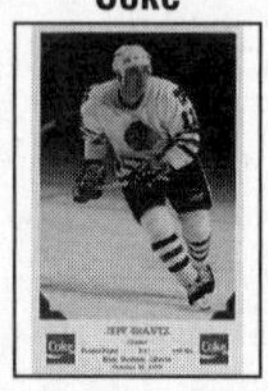

This team photo album measured approximately 11 1/2" by 12 1/4". Each of the four glossy pages features two rows with three player cards per row; the final six player cards are printed on the inside of the back cover.

COMPLETE SET (30)	6.00	15.00
1 Joe Murphy	.30	.75
2 Chris Chelios	.80	2.00
3 Rich Sutter	.20	.50
4 Frantisek Kucera	.20	.50
5 Jeff Shantz	.20	.50
6 Brian Noonan	.20	.50
7 Michel Goulet	.30	.75
8 Jeremy Roenick	.80	2.00
9 Dave Christian	.20	.50
10 Patrick Poulin	.20	.50
11 Brent Sutter	.20	.50
12 Cam Russell	.20	.50
13 Stephane Matteau	.20	.50
14 Ed Belfour	1.00	2.50
15 Neil Wilkinson	.20	.50
16 Eric Weinrich	.20	.50
17 Christian Ruuttu	.20	.50
18 Kevin Todd	.20	.50
19 Jeff Hackett	.40	1.00
20 Steve Smith	.24	.60
21 Jocelyn Lemieux	.20	.50
22 Keith Carney	.20	.50
23 Troy Murray	.20	.50
24 Darin Kimble	.20	.50
25 Dirk Graham	.30	.75
26 Bob Pulford GM	.20	.50
27 Darryl Sutter CO	.20	.50
28 Paul Baxter ACO	.10	.25
29 Rich Preston ACO	.10	.25
30 Phil Myre ACO	.10	.25

1994-95 Blackhawks Coke

These cards are more like oversized photos, and came complete with an album.

COMPLETE SET(21)	6.00	15.00
1 Tony Amonte	.80	2.00
2 Ed Belfour	1.00	2.50
3 Keith Carney	.20	.50
4 Chris Chelios	.80	2.00
5 Dirk Graham	.30	.75
6 Brent Grieve	.20	.50
7 Jeff Hackett	.40	1.00
8 Roger Johansson	.20	.50
9 Darin Kimble	.20	.50
10 Sergei Krivokrasov	.20	.50
11 Joe Murphy	.20	.50
12 Bernie Nicholls	.40	1.00
13 Patrick Poulin	.20	.50
14 Bob Probert	.40	1.00
15 Cam Russell	.20	.50
16 Jeff Shantz	.20	.50
17 Steve Smith	.20	.50
18 Greg Smyth	.20	.50
19 Gary Suter	.30	.75
20 Brent Sutter	.20	.50
21 Eric Weinrich	.20	.50

1995-96 Blackhawks Coke

COMPLETE SET (19)	6.00	15.00
1 Tony Amonte	.80	2.00
2 Ed Belfour	1.00	2.50
3 Keith Carney	.20	.50
4 Chris Chelios	.80	2.00
5 Murray Craven	.20	.50
6 Jim Cummins	.20	.50
7 Eric Daze	.40	1.00
8 Jeff Hackett	.40	1.00
9 Sergei Krivokrasov	.20	.50
10 Joe Murphy	.20	.50
11 Bernie Nicholls	.40	1.00
12 Bob Probert	.40	1.00
13 Cam Russell	.20	.50
14 Denis Savard	.40	1.00
15 Jeff Shantz	.20	.50
16 Steve Smith	.20	.50
17 Gary Suter	.20	.50
18 Brent Sutter	.20	.50
19 Eric Weinrich	.20	.50

1998 Blackhawks Legends

Made and distributed by Pizza Hut in 1998, these cards feature rounded corners, and full color photos on the front.

COMPLETE SET (5)	4.80	12.00
1 Tony Esposito	1.25	3.00
2 Glenn Hall	1.25	3.00

3 Bobby Hull	1.25	5.00
4 Steve Larmer	1.25	1.50
5 Denis Savard	1.25	1.50

1998-99 Blackhawks Chicago Sun-Times

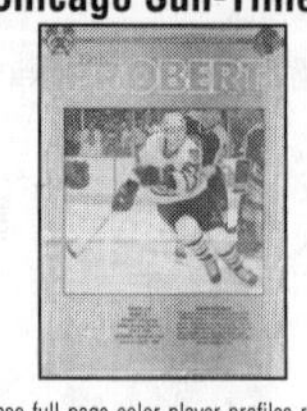

These full-page color player profiles ran in the Chicago Sun-Times during the 1998-99 season. Each page contains a action photo along with player stats and career highlights. The pages are unnumbered and are listed below in alphabetical order.

COMPLETE SET	3.00	8.00
1 Chris Chelios	1.25	3.00
2 Mark Fitzpatrick	.40	1.00
3 Doug Gilmour	.75	2.00
4 Christian Laflamme	.40	1.00
5 Bob Probert	1.25	3.00
6 Jocelyn Thibault	.40	1.00

1999-00 Blackhawks Chicago Sun-Times

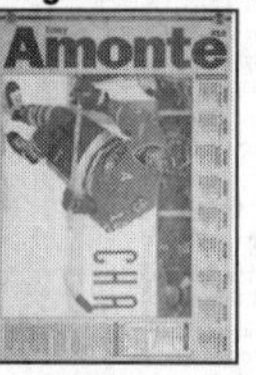

These full-page color player profiles ran in the Chicago Sun-Times during the 1999-2000 season. Each page contains a action photo along with player stats and career highlights. The pages are unnumbered and are listed below in alphabetical order.

COMPLETE SET (12)	4.00	10.00
1 Tony Amonte	.80	2.00
2 Brad Brown	.40	1.00
3 Mark Janssens	.40	1.00
4 Jean-Yves Leroux	.40	1.00
5 Dave Manson	.40	1.00
6 Bryan McCabe	.40	1.00
7 Boris Mironov	.40	1.00
8 Michael Nylander	.40	1.00
9 Doug Zmolek	.40	1.00
10 Denis Savard	.40	1.00
Trent Yawney		
Lorne Molliken		
Bob Pulford		
11 Team photo	.40	1.00

1999-00 Blackhawks Lineup Cards

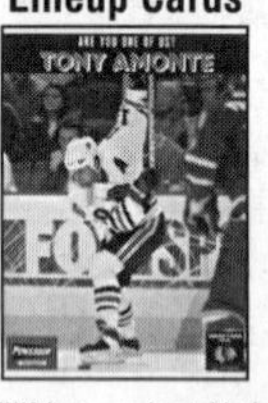

These 8X10 items were inserted in the first 4,000 copies of each Blackhawks game program.

COMPLETE SET (10)	8.00	20.00
1 Tony Amonte	1.60	4.00
2 Brad Brown	.40	1.00
3 Eric Daze	1.20	3.00
4 Doug Gilmour	1.60	4.00
5 Dean McAmmond	.40	1.00
6 Bryan McCabe	.40	1.00
7 Boris Mironov	.40	1.00
8 Steve Sullivan	.80	2.00
9 Jocelyn Thibault	1.20	3.00
10 Alexei Zhamnov	.40	1.00

2002-03 Blackhawks Postcards

These are standard postcard size and feature blank backs. Please forward additional information to hockeymag@beckett.com

COMPLETE SET (?)		
1 Eric Daze	.40	1.00
2 Steve Poapst	.40	1.00
3 Jason Strudwick	.40	1.00
4 Brian Sutter CO	.40	1.00
5 Jocelyn Thibault	.75	2.00
6 Ryan Vandenbussche	.40	1.00
7 Alexei Zhamnov	.40	1.00

2003-04 Blackhawks Postcards

COMPLETE SET (31)	10.00	25.00
1 Craig Andersson	.40	1.00
2 Tyler Arnason	.30	.75
3 Anton Babchuk	.20	.50
4 Mark Bell	.40	1.00
5 Kyle Calder	.40	1.00
6 Eric Daze	.40	1.00
7 Nathan Dempsey	.20	.50
8 Alexander Karpovtsev	.20	.50
9 Igor Korolev	.20	.50
10 Lasse Kukkonen	.20	.50
11 Michael Leighton	.40	1.00
12 Al MacAdam ACO	.02	.10
13 Steve McCarthy	.20	.50
14 Brett McLean	.20	.50
15 Travis Moen	.20	.50
16 Scott Nichol	.20	.50
17 Ville Nieminen	.20	.50
18 Steve Passmore	.40	1.00
19 Steve Poapst	.20	.50
20 Deron Quint	.20	.50
21 Igor Radulov	.40	1.00
22 Tuomo Ruutu	2.00	5.00
23 Denis Savard ACO	.30	.75
24 Jason Strudwick	.20	.50
25 Steve Sullivan	.40	1.00
26 Brent Sutter CO	.10	.25
27 Jocelyn Thibault	.75	2.00
28 Vladislav Tretiak ACO	.40	1.00
29 Ryan VandenBussche	.20	.50
30 Pavel Vorobiev	.20	.50
31 Alexei Zhamnov	.20	.50

2006-07 Blackhawks Postcards

COMPLETE SET (23)	10.00	20.00
1 Adrian Aucoin	.40	1.00
2 Denis Arkhipov	.40	1.00
3 Jeff Hamilton	.40	1.00
4 Martin Lapointe	.40	1.00
5 Tony Salmelainen	.40	1.00
6 Jassen Cullimore	.40	1.00
7 Martin Havlat	.60	1.50
8 Patrick Sharp	.40	1.00
9 Michael Holmqvist	.40	1.00
10 Brent Seabrook	.40	1.00
11 Rene Bourque	.40	1.00
12 Jim Vandermeer	.40	1.00
13 Duncan Keith	.40	1.00
14 Nikolai Khabibulin	.75	2.00
15 Michal Handzus	.40	1.00
16 Tuomo Ruutu	.75	2.00
17 Radim Vrbata	.40	1.00
18 Brian Boucher	.60	1.50
19 Bryan Smolinski	.40	1.00
20 Lasse Kukkonen	.40	1.00
21 Denis Savard CO	.75	2.00
22 Mark Hardy CO	.20	.50
23 Stephane Waite ACO	.20	.50

2006-07 Blackhawks Postcards Glossy

We have no pricing information on this set. It is believed that there are other singles not yet catalogued. Please forward any additional information to hockeymag@beckett.com.

1 Troy Brouwer
2 Peter Bondra
3 James Wisniewski
4 Karl Stewart
5 Ryan Stewart CO

1993 Bleachers 23K Manon Rheaume

This four-card standard-size set featured 23 Karat gold borders. The production run was reportedly 10,000 numbered sets and 1,500 uncut numbered strips.

COMPLETE SET (4)	2.00	5.00

1996 Bleachers Lemieux

This one-card set featured an embossed image of Mario Lemieux on a 23 Karat all-gold sculptured card. The card was packaged in a clear acrylic holder along with a Certificate of Authenticity inside a collectible foil-stamped box. Only 10,000 of the card were produced and are serially numbered.

1 Mario Lemieux	7.50	5.00

2001-02 Blizzak Kim St-Pierre

This single card was issued as a promotional premium with the purchase of a set of Bridgestone Blizzak tires in the province of Quebec during the winter of 2001-02. The card features a photo of Canadian National Women's team goalie St-Pierre wearing a Bridgestone jersey on the front, and features personal and statistical data on the back in French. It is believed that 2,000 of these cards were produced, but less than 500 were actually given out in the promotion.

NNO Kim St-Pierre	2.00	5.00

2001-02 Blue Jackets Donatos Pizza

Sponsored by Donatos Pizza, this 24-card set was issued in sheets containing 6 cards, a pizza coupon and a merchandise coupon.

COMPLETE SET (24)	5.00	12.00
1 Geoff Sanderson	.20	.50
2 Grant Marshall	.20	.50
3 Serge Aubin	.20	.50
4 Robert Kron	.20	.50
5 Blake Sloan	.20	.50
6 Mattias Timander	.20	.50
7 Tyler Wright	.20	.50
8 Espen Knutsen	.40	1.00
9 Rostislav Klesla	.40	1.00
10 Kevin Dineen	.20	.50
11 Deron Quint	.20	.50
12 Ron Tugnutt	.40	1.00
13 Marc Denis	.40	1.00
14 David Vyborny	.20	.50
15 Lyle Odelein	.20	.50
16 Jean-Luc Grand-Pierre	.20	.50
17 Radim Bicanek	.20	.50
18 Geoff Sanderson	.20	.50
19 Ron Tugnutt	.40	1.00
20 Ray Whitney	.20	.50
21 Mike Sillinger	.20	.50
22 Chris Nielsen	.20	.50
23 Jamie Pushor	.20	.50
24 Jamie Heward	.20	.50

1971-72 Blues Postcards

This 30-card set measures approximately 3 1/2" by 5 1/2".

COMPLETE SET (30)	35.00	70.00
1 Al Arbour CO	2.50	5.00
2 John Arbour	1.00	2.00
3 Curt Bennett	1.00	2.00
4 Chris Bordeleau	1.00	2.00
5 Carl Brewer	1.50	3.00
6 Jacques Caron	1.00	2.00
7 Terry Crisp	2.00	4.00
8 Andre Dupont	1.50	3.00
9 Jack Egers	1.00	2.00
10 Larry Hornung	1.00	2.00
11 Brian Lavender	1.00	2.00
11 Mike Murphy	1.00	2.00
12 Gordon Marchant ATR	.50	1.00
Alex McPherson ATR		
12 Gerry Odrowski	1.00	2.00
13 Bill McCreary AGM	.50	1.00
14 Danny O'Shea	1.00	2.00
15 Mike Parizeau	1.00	2.00
16 Noel Picard	1.00	2.00
17 Barclay Plager	2.00	4.00
18 Bill Plager	1.50	3.00
19 Bob Plager	2.00	4.00
20 Phil Roberto	1.50	3.00
21 Gary Sabourin	1.00	2.00
22 Jim Shires	1.00	2.00
23 Frank St. Marseille	1.50	3.00
24 Floyd Thomson	1.00	2.00
25 Garry Unger	2.50	5.00
26 Garry Unger action	2.50	5.00
27 Ernie Wakely	1.50	3.00
28 Tom Woodcock TR	.50	1.00

1972-73 Blues White Border

Printed on thin white stock, this set of 22 photos measures approximately 6 7/8" by 8 3/4".

COMPLETE SET (22)	30.00	60.00
1 Jacques Caron	1.50	3.00

2 Steve Durbano	2.00	4.00
3 Jack Egers	1.50	3.00
4 Chris Evans	1.50	3.00
5 Jean Hamel	1.50	3.00
6 Fran Huck	1.50	3.00
7 Brent Hughes	1.50	3.00
8 Bob Johnson	2.00	4.00
9 Mike Lampman	1.50	3.00
10 Bob McCord	1.50	3.00
11 Wayne Merrick	2.00	4.00
12 Mike Murphy	1.50	3.00
13 Danny O'Shea	1.50	3.00
14 Barclay Plager	2.50	5.00
15 Bob Plager	2.50	5.00
16 Pierre Plante	1.50	3.00
17 Phil Roberto	2.00	4.00
18 Gary Sabourin	1.50	3.00
19 Wayne Stephenson	2.50	5.00
20 Jean-Guy Talbot CO	1.50	3.00
21 Floyd Thomson	1.50	3.00
22 Garry Unger	2.50	5.00
AC1 Garry Unger	2.50	5.00
AC2 Phil Roberto	2.00	4.00

1973-74 Blues White Border

Printed on thin white stock, this set of 24 photos measures approximately 6 7/8" by 8 3/4". The set is dated by the Glen Sather photo; 1973-74 was his only season with the team.

COMPLETE SET (24)	25.00	50.00
1 Lou Angotti	.75	1.50
2 Don Awrey	.75	1.50
3 John Davidson	2.50	5.00
4 Ab Demarco	.75	1.50
5 Steve Durbano	.75	1.50
6 Chris Evans	.75	1.50
7 Larry Giroux	.75	1.50
8 Jean Hamel	.75	1.50
9 Nick Harbaruk	.75	1.50
10 J.Bob Kelly	1.00	2.00
11 Mike Lampman	.75	1.50
12 Wayne Merrick	.75	1.50
13 Barclay Plager	2.00	4.00
14 Bob Plager	2.00	4.00
15 Pierre Plante	1.50	3.00
16 Phil Roberto	2.50	5.00
17 Gary Sabourin	.75	1.50
18 Glen Sather	2.00	4.00
19 Wayne Stephenson	2.00	4.00
20 Jean-Guy Talbot CO	.75	1.50
21 Floyd Thomson	.75	1.50
22 Garry Unger	1.25	2.50
23 Garry Unger action	1.25	2.50
24 Team Photo	1.50	3.00
(1972-73 team)		

1978-79 Blues Postcards

This 21-postcard set of the St. Louis Blues measures approximately 3 1/2" by 5 1/2".

COMPLETE SET (24)	15.00	30.00
1 Wayne Babych	1.00	2.00
2 Curt Bennett	1.00	2.00
3 Harvey Bennett	.50	1.00
4 Red Berenson	1.50	3.00
5 Blue Angels	1.00	2.00
6 Jack Brownschidle	1.00	2.00
7 Mike Crombeen	.50	1.00
8 Tony Currie	.50	1.00
9 Fanvan	.10	.25
10 Bernie Federko	2.00	4.00
11 Barry Gibbs	.50	1.00
12 Larry Giroux	.50	1.00
13 Inge Hammarstrom	1.00	2.00
14 Neil Labatte	.50	1.00
15 Bob Murdoch	.50	1.00
16 Phil Myre	1.00	2.00
17 Larry Patey	.50	1.00
18 Barclay Plager CO	1.00	2.00
19 Rick Shinske	.50	1.00
20 John Smrke	.50	1.00
21 Ed Staniowski	.50	1.00
22 Bob Stewart	.50	1.00
23 Brian Sutter	2.00	4.00
24 Garry Unger	1.50	3.00

1987-88 Blues Team Photos

The 20 team photos in this set each measure approximately 8 1/2" by 11".

COMPLETE SET (20)	6.00	15.00
1 1967-68 Team Photo	.60	1.50
2 1968-69 Team Photo	.40	1.00
3 1969-70 Team Photo	.40	1.00
4 1970-71 Team Photo	.40	1.00
5 1971-72 Team Photo	.40	1.00
6 1972-73 Team Photo	.40	1.00
7 1973-74 Team Photo	.40	1.00
8 1974-75 Team Photo	.40	1.00
9 1975-76 Team Photo	.40	1.00
10 1976-77 Team Photo	.40	1.00
11 1977-78 Team Photo	.40	1.00
12 1978-79 Team Photo	.40	1.00
13 1979-80 Team Photo	.40	1.00
14 1980-81 Team Photo	.40	1.00
15 1981-82 Team Photo	.40	1.00
16 1982-83 Team Photo	.40	1.00
17 1983-84 Team Photo	.40	1.00
18 1984-85 Team Photo	.40	1.00
19 1985-86 Team Photo	.40	1.00
20 1986-87 Team Photo	.40	1.00

1987-88 Blues Kodak

The 1987-88 St. Louis Blues Team Photo Album was sponsored by Kodak in conjunction with KMOX Radio. The set consists of three large sheets, each measuring approximately 11" by 8 1/4" and joined together to form one continuous sheet.

COMPLETE SET (26)	12.00	30.00
1 Brian Benning	.40	1.00
2 Tim Bothwell	.30	.75
3 Charlie Bourgeois	.30	.75
4 Paul Cavallini	.40	1.00
5 Gino Cavallini	.40	1.00
6 Michael Dark	.30	.75
7 Doug Evans	.30	.75
8 Todd Ewen	.60	1.50
9 Bernie Federko	1.20	3.00
10 Ron Flockhart	.30	.75
11 Doug Gilmour	2.40	6.00
12 Gaston Gingras	.30	.75
13 Tony Hrkac	.40	1.00
14 Mark Hunter	.40	1.00
15 Jocelyn Lemieux	.30	.75
16 Tony McKegney	.40	1.00
17 Rick Meagher	.40	1.00
18 Greg Millen	.60	1.50
19 Robert Nordmark	.30	.75
20 Greg Paslawski	.30	.75
21 Herb Raglan	.30	.75
22 Rob Ramage	.40	1.00
23 Cliff Ronning	1.00	2.50
24 Brian Sutter	.60	1.50
25 Perry Turnbull	.30	.75
26 Rick Wamsley	.60	1.50

1987-88 Blues Team Issue

This 24-card set measures 3 1/2" by 5 1/2".

COMPLETE SET (24)	14.00	35.00
1 Brian Benning	.40	1.00
2 Mike Bullard	.80	2.00
3 Gino Cavallini	.40	1.00
4 Paul Cavallini	.40	1.00
5 Craig Coxe	.30	.75
6 Robert Dirk	.30	.75
7 Doug Evans	.30	.75
8 Todd Ewen	.60	1.50
9 Bernie Federko	1.20	3.00
10 Gaston Gingras	.30	.75
11 Tony Hrkac	.40	1.00
12 Brett Hull	6.00	15.00
13 Tony McKegney	.40	1.00
14 Rick Meagher	.40	1.00
15 Greg Millen	.60	1.50
16 Sergio Momesso	.30	.75
17 Greg Paslawski	.30	.75
18 Herb Raglan	.30	.75
19 Dave Richter	.30	.75
20 Vincent Riendeau	.40	1.00
21 Gordie Roberts	.40	1.00
22 Brian Sutter	.60	1.50
23 Tom Tilley	.30	.75
24 Steve Tuttle	.30	.75

1988-89 Blues Kodak

The 1988-89 St. Louis Blues Team Photo Album was sponsored by Kodak. It consists of three large sheets, each measuring approximately 11" by 8 1/4" and joined together to form one continuous sheet.

COMPLETE SET (25)	10.00	25.00
1 Brian Benning	.30	
2 Tim Bothwell	.30	
3 Gino Cavallini	.30	
4 Paul Cavallini	.30	
5 Craig Coxe	.30	
6 Doug Evans	.30	
7 Todd Ewen	.40	1.
8 Bernie Federko	.80	2.
9 Gaston Gingras	.30	
10 Tony Hrkac	.40	1.
11 Brett Hull	4.80	12.
12 Mike Lalor	.30	
13 Tony McKegney	.40	1.
14 Rick Meagher	.30	
15 Greg Millen	.40	1.
16 Sergio Momesso	.30	
17 Greg Paslawski	.30	
18 Herb Raglan	.30	
19 Vincent Riendeau	.40	1.
20 Dave Richter	.30	
21 Gordie Roberts	.30	
22 Cliff Ronning	.80	2.
23 Tom Tilley	.30	
24 Steve Tuttle	.30	
25 Peter Zezel	.40	1.(

1988-89 Blues Team Issue

This 24-card set measures approximatel 1/2" by 5 1/4".

COMPLETE SET (24)	10.00	25.
1 Brian Benning	.30	
2 Mike Bullard	.60	1.
3 Gino Cavallini	.30	
4 Paul Cavallini	.30	
5 Craig Coxe	.30	
6 Robert Dirk	.30	
7 Doug Evans	.30	
8 Todd Ewen	.40	1.
9 Bernie Federko	.80	2.
10 Gaston Gingras	.30	
11 Tony Hrkac	.40	1.
12 Brett Hull	4.80	12.
13 Tony McKegney	.40	1.
14 Rick Meagher	.30	
15 Greg Millen	.40	1.
16 Sergio Momesso	.30	
17 Greg Paslawski	.30	
18 Herb Raglan	.30	
19 Dave Richter	.30	
20 Vincent Riendeau	.40	1.
21 Gordie Roberts	.30	
22 Brian Sutter CO	.40	1.
23 Tom Tilley	.30	
24 Steve Tuttle	.30	

1989-90 Blues Kodak

This 25-card set of St. Louis Blues measu approximately 2 3/8" by 3 1/2" and ha portrait shot of the player surrounded yellow borders. The set was suppose passed out to the first 15,000 ticket-holc at the Blues vs. Buffalo Sabres game February 27th.

COMPLETE SET (25)	10.00	25.
1 Pat Jablonski	.40	1.
4 Gordie Roberts	.20	
6 Tony Twist	.60	1.
9 Peter Zezel	.30	
10 Dave Lowry	.20	
12 Adam Oates	1.20	3.
14 Paul Cavallini	.20	
15 Paul MacLean	.30	
16 Brett Hull	2.00	5.
17 Gino Cavallini	.20	
19 Rod Brind'Amour	1.20	3.
20 Tom Tilley	.20	
21 Jeff Brown	.40	1.
22 Rick Meagher	.20	
23 Adrien Plavsic	.20	
25 Herb Raglan	.20	
26 Mike Lalor	.20	
27 Sergio Momesso	.20	
30 Vincent Riendeau	.40	1.(
31 Curtis Joseph	4.00	10.
35 Steve Tuttle	.20	
38 Dominic Lavoie	.20	
39 Kelly Chase	.20	
40 Dave Thomlinson	.20	
NNO Brian Sutter CO	.30	

1990-91 Blues Kodak

This 25-card standard-size set w sponsored by Kodak in conjunction w KMOX Radio.

COMPLETE SET (25)	10.00	25.(
1 Bob Bassen	.20	
2 Rod Brind'Amour	1.20	3.(
3 Jeff Brown	.30	
4 David Bruce	.20	

ino Cavallini .20 .50
aul Cavallini .20 .50
eoff Courtnall .40 1.00
obert Dirk .20 .50
len Featherstone .20 .50
Brett Hull 2.00 5.00
Curtis Joseph 1.20 3.00
Dave Lowry .20 .50
Paul MacLean .20 .50
Mario Marois .20 .50
Rick Meagher .20 .50
Sergio Momesso .20 .50
Adam Oates 1.20 3.00
Vincent Riendeau .30 .75
Cliff Ronning .50 1.25
Harold Snepsts .40 1.00
Scott Stevens .60 1.50
Brian Sutter CO .20 .50
Rich Sutter .20 .50
Steve Tuttle .20 .50
Ron Wilson .20 .50

1991-92 Blues Postcards

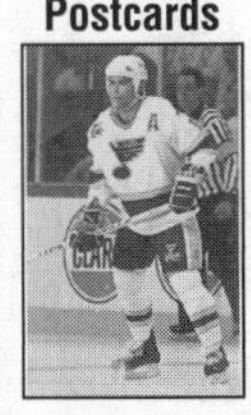

s 22-card set measures approximately 3 " by 5 1/2".

MPLETE SET (22) 8.00 20.00
Murray Baron .20 .50
ob Bassen .20 .50
eff Brown .40 1.00
arth Butcher .30 .75
ino Cavallini .20 .50
aul Cavallini .20 .50
elly Chase .24 .60
ave Christian .30 .75
elson Emerson .30 .75
Brett Hull 1.60 4.00
Pat Jablonski .30 .75
Curtis Joseph 1.20 3.00
Darin Kimble .20 .50
Dave Lowry .20 .50
Michel Mongeau .20 .50
Adam Oates .80 2.00
Rob Robinson .20 .50
Brendan Shanahan 1.60 4.00
Rich Sutter .30 .75
Ron Sutter .30 .75
Ron Wilson .20 .50
Rick Zombo .20 .50

1992-93 Blues UD Best of the Blues

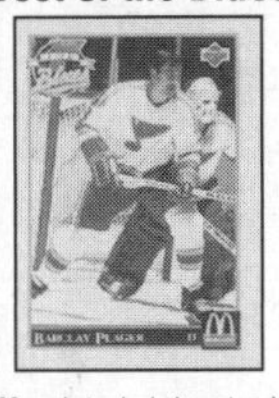

s 28-card standard-size set, subtitled est of the Blues" was distributed at Donald's restaurants of St. Louis and ro East and showcases St. Louis Blues' yers from the past 25 years.

MPLETE SET (28) 12.00 30.00
lenn Hall 1.20 3.00
oug Gilmour 1.20 3.00
l Arbour .40 1.00
Mike Liut .40 1.00
lake Dunlop .20 .50
oel Picard .20 .50
ob Plager .40 1.00
b McDonald .20 .50
urtis Joseph 2.00 5.00
Wayne Babych .20 .50
Red Berenson .40 1.00
Brett Hull 1.60 4.00
Bob Gassoff .40 1.00
Bernie Federko .40 1.00
Gary Sabourin .20 .50
Joe Mullen .40 1.00
Adam Oates .80 2.00
Jorgen Pettersson .20 .50
Frank St. Marseille .30 .75
Scott Stevens .60 1.50
Rob Ramage .40 1.00
Jacques Plante 1.20 3.00
Rick Meagher .20 .50
Barclay Plager .40 1.00
Brian Sutter .40 1.00
Perry Turnbull .20 .50
Garry Unger .40 1.00
Checklist SP 2.00 5.00
0 Brett Hull AU 60.00 150.00

1996-97 Blues Dispatch 30th Anniversary

This set was created by the St. Louis Post-Dispatch to commemorate the 30th anniversary of the Blues joining the NHL. Additional information can be forwarded to hockeymag@beckett.com.

COMPLETE SET (5) 4.00 10.00
1 Grant Fuhr .80 2.00
2 Brett Hull 1.60 4.00
3 Al MacInnis .80 2.00
4 Chris Pronger .80 2.00
5 Tony Twist .80 2.00

1999-00 Blues Taco Bell

Released by In the Game in conjunction with Taco Bell, this 24-card set features the 1999-2000 St. Louis Blues on four different six card sheets with a Taco Bell coupon.

COMPLETE SET (24) 6.00 15.00
1 Marc Bergevin .10 .25
2 Jochen Hecht .20 .50
3 Jamie McLennan .20 .50
4 Pierre Turgeon .40 .75
5 Scott Young .20 .50
6 Dave Ellett .10 .25
7 Lubos Bartecko .10 .25
8 Pavol Demitra .40 1.00
9 Michal Handzus .20 .50
10 Jeff Finley .10 .25
11 Ricard Persson .10 .25
12 Bob Bassen .10 .25
13 Craig Conroy .10 .25
14 Mike Eastwood .10 .25
15 Scott Pellerin .10 .25
16 Chris Pronger 1.20 3.00
17 Todd Reirden .10 .25
18 Roman Turek .40 .75
19 Kelly Chase .20 .50
20 Al MacInnis .80 2.00
21 Jamal Mayers .20 .50
22 Pascal Rheaume .10 .25
23 Tyson Nash .80 2.00
24 Stephane Richer .10 .25

2002-03 Blues Magnets

These magnets were handed out at home games throughout the 2002-03 season. Please forward any further information to us at hockeymag@beckett.com.

COMPLETE SET (?)
1 Pavol Demitra 2.00 5.00
2 Martin Rucinsky 1.25 3.00
3 Doug Weight 2.00 5.00

2002-03 Blues Team Issue

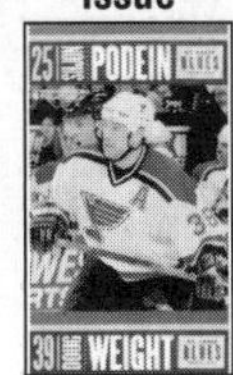

This set was handed out at a home game during the 2002-03 season. The cards came attached in a large foldout format.

COMPLETE SET (24) 8.00 20.00
1 Fred Brathwaite .30 .75
2 Petr Cajanek .20 .50
3 Daniel Corso .20 .50
4 Pavol Demitra .40 1.00
5 Dallas Drake .20 .50
6 Mike Eastwood .20 .50
7 Jeff Finley .20 .50
8 Barret Jackman .80 2.00
9 Brent Johnson .40 1.00
10 Alexander Khavanov .20 .50
11 Tom Koivisto .20 .50
12 Christian Laflamme .20 .50
13 Reed Low .20 .50
14 Al MacInnis .60 1.50
15 Jamal Mayers .30 .75
16 Scott Mellanby .20 .50
17 Tyson Nash .40 1.00
18 Shjon Podein .20 .50
19 Chris Pronger .60 1.50
20 Bryce Salvador .20 .50
21 Cory Stillman .20 .50
22 Keith Tkachuk .80 2.00
23 Mike Van Ryn .20 .50
24 Doug Weight .60 1.50

1938 Bocnal Tobacco Luminous

Cards measure 1 3/8 x 2 1/2 and feature white design on a black background. They are meant to glow in the dark. Produced for Newgent Cigarettes in London.

19 Field Hockey 15.00 30.00
20 Ice Hockey 25.00 50.00

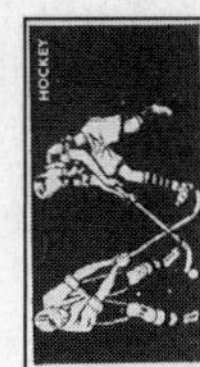

1990-91 Bowman

The 1990-91 Bowman set contains 264 standard-size cards.

COMPLETE SET (264) 8.00 20.00
COMP.FACT.SET (264) 8.00 20.00
1 Jeremy Roenick RC .50 1.25
2 Doug Wilson .01 .05
3 Greg Millen .01 .05
4 Steve Thomas .02 .10
5 Steve Larmer .02 .10
6 Denis Savard .02 .10
7 Ed Belfour RC .75 2.00
8 Dirk Graham .01 .05
9 Adam Creighton .01 .05
10 Keith Brown .01 .05
11 Jacques Cloutier .01 .05
12 Al Secord .01 .05
13 Troy Murray .01 .05
14 Kelly Chase .01 .05
15 Dave Lowry .01 .05
16 Adam Oates .02 .10
17 Sergio Momesso RC .02 .10
18 Paul MacLean .01 .05
19 Peter Zezel .01 .05
20 Vincent Riendeau RC .02 .10
21 Dave Thomlinson .01 .05
22 Paul Cavallini .01 .05
23 Rod Brind'Amour RC .40 1.00
24 Brett Hull .25 .60
25 Jeff Brown .01 .05
26 Dominic Lavoie .01 .05
27 Andy Brickley .01 .05
28 Bob Sweeney .01 .05
29 Cam Neely .08 .25
30 Bob Carpenter .01 .05
31 Ray Bourque .15 .40
32 Rejean Lemelin .02 .10
33 Craig Janney .02 .10
34 Bob Beers RC .02 .10
35 Andy Moog .08 .25
36 Dave Poulin .01 .05
37 Brian Propp .01 .05
38 John Byce .01 .05
39 John Carter .01 .05
40 Dave Christian .01 .05
41 Shayne Corson .02 .10
42 Chris Chelios .08 .25
43 Mike McPhee .01 .05
44 Guy Carbonneau .02 .10
45 Stephane Richer .02 .10
46 Petr Svoboda .01 .05
Chris Chelios actually pictured
47 Russ Courtnall .01 .05
48 Sylvain Lefebvre .01 .05
49 Brian Skrudland .01 .05
50 Patrick Roy .50 1.25
51 Bobby Smith .02 .10
52 Mathieu Schneider RC .08 .25
53 Stephan Lebeau RC .02 .10
54 Petri Skriko .01 .05
55 Jim Sandlak .01 .05
56 Doug Lidster .01 .05
57 Kirk McLean .02 .10
58 Brian Bradley .01 .05
59 Greg Adams .01 .05
60 Paul Reinhart .01 .05
61 Trevor Linden .02 .10
62 Adrien Plavsic .01 .05
63 Igor Larionov RC .20 .50
64 Steve Bozek .01 .05
65 Dan Quinn .01 .05
66 Mike Liut .02 .10
67 Nick Kypreos .01 .05
68 Michal Pivonka RC .02 .10
69 Dino Ciccarelli .02 .10
70 Kevin Hatcher .01 .05
71 Dale Hunter .01 .05
72 Don Beaupre .02 .10
73 Geoff Courtnall .01 .05
74 Rob Murray .01 .05
75 Calle Johansson .01 .05
76 Kelly Miller .01 .05
77 Mike Ridley .01 .05
78 Alan May .01 .05
79 Bob Brooke .01 .05
80 Slava Fetisov RC .08 .25
81 Sylvain Turgeon .01 .05
82 Kirk Muller .01 .05
83 John MacLean .02 .10
84 Jon Morris .01 .05
85 Brendan Shanahan .08 .25
86 Peter Stastny .02 .10
87 Bruce Driver .01 .05
88 Neil Brady .01 .05
89 Patrik Sundstrom .01 .05
90 Eric Weinrich RC .08 .25
91 Joe Nieuwendyk .02 .10
92 Sergei Makarov RC .08 .25
93 Al MacInnis .02 .10
94 Mike Vernon .02 .10
95 Gary Roberts .02 .10
96 Doug Gilmour .02 .10
97 Joe Mullen .02 .10
98 Rick Wamsley .02 .10
99 Joel Otto .01 .05
100 Paul Ranheim RC .02 .10
101 Gary Suter .01 .05
102 Theo Fleury .01 .05
103 Sergei Priakin .01 .05
104 Tony Horacek .01 .05
105 Ron Hextall .02 .10
106 Gord Murphy RC .02 .10
107 Pelle Eklund .01 .05
108 Rick Tocchet .02 .10
109 Murray Craven .01 .05
110 Doug Sulliman .01 .05
111 Kjell Samuelsson .01 .05
112 Ilkka Sinisalo .01 .05
113 Keith Acton .01 .05
114 Mike Bullard .01 .05
115 Doug Crossman .01 .05
116 Tom Fitzgerald .01 .05
117 Don Maloney .01 .05
118 Alan Kerr .01 .05
119 Mark Fitzpatrick RC .08 .25
120 Hubie McDonough .01 .05
121 Randy Wood .01 .05
122 Jeff Norton .01 .05
123 Pat LaFontaine .08 .25
124 Pat Flatley .01 .05
125 Joe Reekie .01 .05
126 Brent Sutter .01 .05
127 David Volek .01 .05
128 Shawn Cronin RC .01 .05
129 Dale Hawerchuk .02 .10
130 Brent Ashton .01 .05
131 Bob Essensa RC .20 .50
132 Dave Ellett .01 .05
133 Thomas Steen .01 .05
134 Doug Smail .01 .05
135 Fredrik Olausson .01 .05
136 Dave McLlwain .01 .05
137 Pat Elynuik .01 .05
138 Teppo Numminen RC .02 .10
139 Paul Fenton .01 .05
140 Tony Granato .01 .05
141 Tomas Sandstrom .01 .05
142 Rob Blake RC .25 .60
143 Wayne Gretzky .60 1.50
144 Kelly Hrudey .02 .10
145 Mike Krushelnyski .01 .05
146 Steve Duchesne .01 .05
147 Steve Kasper .01 .05
148 John Tonelli .01 .05
149 Dave Taylor .02 .10
150 Larry Robinson .02 .10
151 Todd Elik RC .01 .05
152 Luc Robitaille .02 .10
153 Al Iafrate .02 .10
154 Allan Bester .02 .10
155 Gary Leeman .01 .05
156 Mark Osborne .01 .05
157 Tom Fergus .01 .05
158 Brad Marsh .01 .05
159 Wendel Clark .02 .10
160 Daniel Marois .01 .05
161 Ed Olczyk .01 .05
162 Rob Ramage .01 .05
163 Vincent Damphousse .01 .05
164 Lou Franceschetti .01 .05
165 Paul Gillis .01 .05
166 Craig Wolanin .01 .05
167 Marc Fortier .01 .05
168 Tony McKegney .01 .05
169 Joe Sakic .30 .75
170 Michel Petit .01 .05
171 Scott Gordon .01 .05
172 Tony Hrkac .01 .05
173 Bryan Fogarty .01 .05
174 Mike Hough .01 .05
175 Claude Loiselle .01 .05
176 Ulf Dahlen .01 .05
177 Larry Murphy .02 .10
178 Neal Broten .02 .10
179 Don Barber .01 .05
180 Shawn Chambers .01 .05
181 Clark Donatelli .01 .05
182 Brian Bellows .01 .05
183 Jon Casey .02 .10
184 Neil Wilkinson RC .01 .05
185 Aaron Broten .01 .05
186 Dave Gagner .02 .10
187 Basil McRae .01 .05
188 Mike Modano RC .60 1.50
189 Grant Fuhr .08 .25
190 Martin Gelinas RC .10 .30
191 Jari Kurri .08 .25
192 Geoff Smith .01 .05
193 Craig MacTavish .01 .05
194 Esa Tikkanen .01 .05
195 Glenn Anderson .02 .10
196 Joe Murphy RC .02 .10
197 Petr Klima .01 .05
198 Kevin Lowe .01 .05
199 Mark Messier .08 .25
200 Steve Smith .01 .05
201 Craig Simpson .01 .05
202 Rob Brown .01 .05
203 Wendell Young .02 .10
204 Mario Lemieux .60 1.50
205 Phil Bourque .01 .05
206 Mark Recchi RC .40 1.00
207 Zarley Zalapski .01 .05
208 Kevin Stevens RC .08 .25
209 Tom Barrasso .02 .10
210 John Cullen .01 .05
211 Paul Coffey .08 .25
212 Bob Errey .01 .05
213 Tony Tanti .01 .05
214 Carey Wilson .01 .05
215A Brian Leetch ERR .25 .60
(Name spelled eetch)
215B Brian Leetch COR .12 .30
216 Darren Turcotte RC .02 .10
217 Brian Mullen .01 .05
218 Mike Richter RC .40 1.00
219 Troy Mallette .01 .05
220 Mike Gartner .02 .10
221 Bernie Nicholls .02 .10
222 John Vanbiesbrouck .02 .10
223 John Ogrodnick .01 .05
224 Paul Broten .01 .05
225 James Patrick .01 .05
226 Mark Janssens .01 .05
227 Randy McKay .01 .05
228 Marc Habscheid .01 .05
229 Jimmy Carson .01 .05
230 Yves Racine RC .02 .10
231 Dave Barr .01 .05
232 Shawn Burr .01 .05
233 Steve Yzerman .40 1.00
234 Steve Chiasson .01 .05
235 Daniel Shank .01 .05
236 John Chabot .01 .05
237 Gerard Gallant .01 .05
238 Bernie Federko .01 .05
239 Phil Housley .02 .10
240 Alexander Mogilny RC .50 1.25
241 Pierre Turgeon .08 .25
242 Daren Puppa .02 .10
243 Scott Arniel .01 .05
244 Christian Ruuttu .01 .05
245 Doug Bodger .01 .05
246 Dave Andreychuk .02 .10
247 Mike Foligno .01 .05
248 Dean Kennedy .01 .05
249 Dave Snuggerud .01 .05
250 Rick Vaive .01 .05
251 Todd Krygier .01 .05
252 Adam Burt RC .01 .05
253 Scott Young .01 .05
254 Ron Francis .02 .10
255 Peter Sidorkiewicz .02 .10
256 Dave Babych .01 .05
257 Pat Verbeek .01 .05
258 Ray Ferraro .01 .05
259 Chris Govedaris .01 .05
260 Brad Shaw .01 .05
261 Kevin Dineen .01 .05
262 Dean Evason .01 .05
263 Checklist 1-132 .01 .05
264 Checklist 133-264 .01 .05

1990-91 Bowman Tiffany

Parallel to base set, Topps only produced 3000 sets. Cards can be distinguished by a glossy coating not found on regular issued cards.

COMPLETE SET (264) 60.00 125.00
*STARS: 12.5X TO 25X BASIC CARDS
*RC's: 4X TO 10X BASIC CARDS

1990-91 Bowman Hat Tricks

This 22-card standard size set was issued as an insert in the 1990-91 Bowman hockey wax packs. This set honored the 14 players (1-14) who scored three or more goals (a hat trick) in a game at least twice during the 1989-90 regular season and the eight players (15-22) who performed the feat during the 1990 NHL playoffs. The fronts of the cards have a glossy sheen to them while the backs talk about the hat tricks of the players. There are two Mike Gartner cards as he had hat tricks for two different teams.

COMPLETE SET (22) 2.40 6.00
1 Brett Hull .24 .60
2 Mario Lemieux 1.00 2.50
3 Rob Brown .06 .15
4 Mark Messier .24 .60
5 Steve Yzerman .60 1.50
6 Vincent Damphousse .16 .40
7 Kevin Dineen .06 .15
8 Mike Gartner .16 .40
9 Pat LaFontaine .20 .50
10 Gary Leeman .06 .15
11 Stephane Richer .16 .40
12 Luc Robitaille .16 .40
13 Steve Thomas .16 .40
14 Rick Tocchet .16 .40
15 Dino Ciccarelli .16 .40
16 John Druce .06 .15
17 Mike Gartner .16 .40
18 Tony Granato .06 .15
19 Jari Kurri .16 .40
20 Bernie Nicholls .16 .40
21 Tomas Sandstrom .16 .40
22 Dave Taylor .06 .15

1991-92 Bowman

The 1991-92 Bowman hockey set contains 429 standard-size cards. On a white card face, the fronts display color action player photos enclosed by blue and tan border stripes. The player's name appears in a purple stripe below the picture. The backs are colorful (displaying blue, green, and red fading to yellow sections) and present biography and statistics (career and for the 1990-91 season). The season statistics are broken down to show the player's performance against each NHL team. The cards are numbered on the back and checklisted below according to teams. The only Rookie Card worthy of note is John LeClair.

COMPLETE SET (429) 5.00 12.00
COMP.FACT.SET (429) 6.00 15.00
1 John Cullen .01 .05
2 Todd Krygier .01 .05
3 Kay Whitmore .02 .10
4 Terry Yake .01 .05
5 Randy Ladouceur .01 .05
6 Kevin Dineen .01 .05
7 Jim McKenzie .01 .05
8 Brad Shaw .01 .05
9 Mark Hunter .01 .05
10 Dean Evason .01 .05
11 Mikael Andersson .01 .05
12 Pat Verbeek .01 .05
13 Peter Sidorkiewicz .02 .10
14 Mike Tomlak .01 .05
15 Zarley Zalapski .01 .05
16 Rob Brown .01 .05
17 Sylvain Cote .01 .05
18 Bobby Holik .02 .10
19 Daryl Reaugh .02 .10
20 Paul Cyr .01 .05
21 Doug Bodger .01 .05
22 Dave Andreychuk .02 .10
23 Clint Malarchuk .02 .10
24 Darrin Shannon .01 .05
25 Christian Ruuttu .01 .05
26 Uwe Krupp .01 .05
27 Pierre Turgeon .02 .10
28 Kevin Haller RC .01 .05
29 Dave Snuggerud .01 .05
30 Alexander Mogilny .07 .20
31 Dale Hawerchuk .02 .10
32 Mike Ramsey .01 .05
33 Darcy Wakaluk RC .02 .10
34 Tony Tanti .01 .05
35 Jay Wells .01 .05
36 Mikko Makela .01 .05
37 Daren Puppa .02 .10
38 Benoit Hogue .01 .05
39 Rick Vaive .01 .05
40 Grant Ledyard .01 .05
41 Steve Yzerman HT .20 .40
42 Steve Yzerman .40 1.00
43 Shawn Burr .01 .05
44 Yves Racine .01 .05
45 Johan Garpenlov .01 .05
46 Keith Primeau .01 .05
47 Tim Cheveldae .02 .10
48 Brad McCrimmon .01 .05
49 Dave Barr .01 .05
50 Sergei Fedorov .12 .30
51 Brent Fedyk .01 .05
52 Jimmy Carson .01 .05
53 Paul Ysebaert .01 .05
54 Rick Zombo .01 .05
55 Bob Probert .02 .10
56 Gerard Gallant .01 .05
57 Kevin Miller .01 .05
58 Randy Moller .01 .05
59 Kris King .01 .05
60 Corey Millen RC .01 .05
61 Brian Mullen .01 .05
62 Darren Turcotte .01 .05
63 Ray Sheppard .01 .05
64 David Shaw .01 .05
65 Troy Mallette .01 .05
66 James Patrick .01 .05
67 Mark Janssens .01 .05
68 John Vanbiesbrouck .02 .10
69 Joey Kocur .02 .10
70 Mike Richter .07 .20
71 John Ogrodnick .01 .05
72 Kelly Kisio .01 .05
73 Normand Rochefort .01 .05
74 Mike Gartner .02 .10
75 Brian Leetch .07 .20
76 Bernie Nicholls .02 .10
77 Jan Erixon .01 .05
78 Larry Murphy .02 .10
79 Joe Mullen .02 .10
80 Tom Barrasso .02 .10
81 Paul Coffey .07 .20
82 Jiri Hrdina .01 .05
83 Mark Recchi .07 .20
84 Randy Gilhen .01 .05
85 Bob Errey .01 .05
86 Scott Young .01 .05
87 Mario Lemieux .50 1.25
88 Ulf Samuelsson .01 .05
89 Frank Pietrangelo .01 .05
90 Ron Francis .02 .10
91 Paul Stanton .01 .05
92 Kevin Stevens .01 .05
93 Bryan Trottier .07 .20
94 Phil Bourque .01 .05
95 Jaromir Jagr .12 .30
96 Petr Klima HT .01 .05
97 Adam Graves .02 .10
98 Esa Tikkanen .01 .05
99 Norm Maciver RC .01 .05
100 Craig MacTavish .01 .05
101 Bill Ranford .02 .10
102 Martin Gelinas .01 .05
103 Charlie Huddy .01 .05
104 Petr Klima .01 .05
105 Ken Linseman .01 .05
106 Steve Smith .01 .05
107 Craig Simpson .01 .05
108 Chris Joseph .01 .05
109 Joe Murphy .01 .05
110 Jeff Beukeboom .01 .05
111 Grant Fuhr .07 .20
112 Geoff Smith .01 .05
113 Anatoli Semenov .01 .05
114 Mark Messier .07 .20
115 Kevin Lowe .02 .10
116 Glenn Anderson .02 .10
117 Bobby Smith .02 .10
118 Doug Smail .01 .05
119 Jon Casey .02 .10
120 Gaetan Duchesne .01 .05
121 Neal Broten .02 .10
122 Brian Hayward .02 .10
123 Brian Propp .01 .05
124 Mark Tinordi .01 .05
125 Mike Modano .15 .40
126 Marc Bureau .01 .05
127 Ulf Dahlen .01 .05
128 Chris Dahlquist .01 .05
129 Brian Bellows .01 .05
130 Mike Craig .01 .05
131 Dave Gagner .01 .05
132 Brian Glynn .01 .05
133 Joe Sakic .15 .40
134 Owen Nolan .07 .20
135 Everett Sanipass .01 .05
136 Jamie Baker RC .01 .05
137 Mats Sundin .07 .20
138 Craig Wolanin .01 .05
139 Kip Miller .01 .05
140 Steven Finn .01 .05
141 Tony Hrkac .01 .05
142 Curtis Leschyshyn .01 .05
143 Mike McNeil .01 .05
144 Mike Hough .01 .05
145 Alexei Gusarov RC .02 .10
146 Jacques Cloutier .02 .10
147 Shawn Anderson .01 .05
148 Stephane Morin .01 .05
149 Bryan Fogarty .01 .05
150 Scott Pearson .01 .05
151 Ron Tugnutt .02 .10
152 Randy Velischek .01 .05
153 David Reid .01 .05
154 Rob Ramage .01 .05
155 Dave Hannan .01 .05
156 Wendel Clark .02 .10
157 Peter Ing .02 .10
158 Michel Petit .01 .05
159 Brian Bradley .01 .05
160 Rob Cimetta .01 .05
161 Gary Leeman .01 .05
162 Aaron Broten .01 .05
163 Dave Ellett .01 .05
164 Peter Zezel .01 .05
165 Daniel Marois .01 .05
166 Mike Krushelnyski .01 .05
167 Luke Richardson .01 .05
168 Scott Thornton .01 .05
169 Mike Foligno .01 .05
170 Vincent Damphousse .01 .05
171 Todd Gill .01 .05
172 Kevin Maguire .01 .05
173 Wayne Gretzky HT .30 .75
174 Tomas Sandstrom HT .01 .05
175 John Tonelli .01 .05
176 Wayne Gretzky .50 1.25
177 Larry Robinson .02 .10
178 Jay Miller .01 .05
179 Tomas Sandstrom .01 .05
180 John McIntyre .01 .05
181 Brad Jones .01 .05
182 Rob Blake .02 .10
183 Kelly Hrudey .02 .10
184 Marty McSorley .01 .05
185 Todd Elik .01 .05
186 Dave Taylor .02 .10
187 Steve Kasper .01 .05
188 Luc Robitaille .02 .10
189 Bob Kudelski .01 .05
190 Daniel Berthiaume .02 .10
191 Steve Duchesne .01 .05
192 Tony Granato .01 .05
193 Bob Essensa .02 .10
194 Phil Sykes .01 .05
195 Paul MacDermid .01 .05
196 Dave McLlwain .01 .05
197 Phil Housley .02 .10
198 Pat Elynuik .01 .05
199 Randy Carlyle .01 .05
200 Thomas Steen .01 .05
201 Teppo Numminen .01 .05
202 Danton Cole .01 .05
203 Doug Evans .01 .05
204 Ed Olczyk .01 .05
205 Moe Mantha .01 .05
206 Scott Arniel .01 .05
207 Rick Tabaracci .02 .10
208 Bryan Marchment RC .02 .10
209 Mark Osborne .01 .05
210 Fredrik Olausson .01 .05
211 Brent Ashton .01 .05
212 Ray Ferraro .01 .05
213 Mark Fitzpatrick .02 .10
214 Hubie McDonough .01 .05
215 Joe Reekie .01 .05
216 Bill Berg .01 .05
217 Wayne McBean .01 .05
218 Pat Flatley .01 .05
219 Jeff Hackett .02 .10
220 Derek King .01 .05
221 Craig Ludwig .01 .05
222 Pat LaFontaine .07 .20
223 David Volek .01 .05
224 Glenn Healy .02 .10
225 Jeff Norton .01 .05
226 Brent Sutter .01 .05
227 Randy Wood .01 .05
228 Gary Nylund .01 .05
229 Dave Chyzowski .01 .05
230 Rick Tocchet .02 .10
231 Ken Wregget .02 .10
232 Terry Carkner .01 .05
233 Martin Hostak .01 .05
234 Ron Hextall .02 .10
235 Gord Murphy .01 .05
236 Scott Mellanby .01 .05
237 Pete Peeters .02 .10
238 Ron Sutter .01 .05
239 Murray Craven .01 .05
240 Kjell Samuelsson .01 .05
241 Pelle Eklund .01 .05
242 Mark Pederson .01 .05
243 Murray Baron .01 .05
244 Keith Acton .01 .05
245 Derrick Smith .01 .05
246 Mike Ricci .07 .20
247 Dale Kushner .01 .05
248 Normand Lacombe .01 .05
249 Theo Fleury HT .01 .05
250 Sergei Makarov HT .01 .05
251 Paul Ranheim .01 .05
252 Joe Nieuwendyk .02 .10
253 Mike Vernon .02 .10
254 Gary Suter .01 .05
255 Doug Gilmour .02 .10
256 Paul Fenton .01 .05
257 Roger Johansson .01 .05
258 Stephane Matteau .01 .05

259 Frank Musil .01 .05
260 Joel Otto .01 .05
261 Tim Sweeney .01 .05
262 Al MacInnis .02 .10
263 Gary Roberts .02 .10
264 Sergei Makarov .01 .05
265 Carey Wilson .01 .05
266 Ric Nattress .01 .05
267 Robert Reichel .01 .05
268 Rick Wamsley .02 .10
269 Brian MacLellan .01 .05
270 Theo Fleury .01 .05
271 Claude Lemieux .01 .05
272 John MacLean .02 .10
273 Slava Fetisov .01 .05
274 Kirk Muller .01 .05
275 Sean Burke .02 .10
276 Alexei Kasatonov .01 .05
277 Claude Lemieux .01 .05
278 Eric Weinrich .01 .05
279 Patrik Sundstrom .01 .05
280 Zdeno Ciger .01 .05
281 Bruce Driver .01 .05
282 Laurie Boschman .01 .05
283 Chris Terreri .02 .10
284 Ken Daneyko .01 .05
285 Doug Brown .01 .05
286 Jon Morris .01 .05
287 Peter Stastny .02 .10
288 Brendan Shanahan .07 .20
289 John MacLean .02 .10
290 Mike Liut .02 .10
291 Michal Pivonka .01 .05
292 Kelly Miller .01 .05
293 John Druce .01 .05
294 Calle Johansson .01 .05
295 Alan May .01 .05
296 Kevin Hatcher .02 .10
297 Tim Bergland .01 .05
298 Mikhail Tatarinov .01 .05
299 Peter Bondra .02 .10
300 Al Iafrate .02 .10
301 Nick Kypreos .01 .05
302 Dino Ciccarelli .02 .10
303 Dale Hunter .01 .05
304 Don Beaupre .02 .10
305 Jim Hrivnak .02 .10
306 Stephen Leach .01 .05
307 Dimitri Khristich .01 .05
308 Mike Ridley .01 .05
309 Sergio Momesso .01 .05
310 Kirk McLean .02 .10
311 Greg Adams .01 .05
312 Adrien Plavsic .01 .05
313 Cliff Ronning .01 .05
314 Garry Valk .01 .05
315 Troy Gamble .01 .05
316 Gino Odjick .01 .05
317 Doug Lidster .01 .05
318 Geoff Courtnall .02 .10
319 Tom Kurvers .01 .05
320 Robert Kron .01 .05
321 Jyrki Lumme .01 .05
322 Jay Mazur .01 .05
323 Dave Capuano .01 .05
324 Petr Nedved .02 .10
325 Steve Bozek .01 .05
326 Igor Larionov .01 .05
327 Trevor Linden .02 .10
328 Shayne Corson .01 .05
329 Eric Desjardins .02 .10
330 Stephane Richer .02 .10
331 Brian Skrudland .01 .05
332 Sylvain Lefebvre .01 .05
333 Stephan Lebeau .01 .05
334 Mike Keane .01 .05
335 Patrick Roy .40 1.00
336 Brent Gilchrist .01 .05
337 Andre Racicot RC .01 .05
338 Guy Carbonneau .02 .10
339 Mike McPhee .01 .05
340 Andrew Cassels .01 .05
341 Petr Svoboda .01 .05
342 Denis Savard .02 .10
343 Mathieu Schneider .01 .05
344 John LeClair RC .50 1.25
345 Tom Chorske .01 .05
346 Russ Courtnall .01 .05
347 Ken Hodge Jr. HT .01 .05
348 Cam Neely HT .02 .10
349 Randy Burridge .01 .05
350 Glen Wesley .01 .05
351 Chris Nilan .01 .05
352 Jeff Lazaro .01 .05
353 Wes Walz .01 .05
354 Rejean Lemelin .02 .10
355 Craig Janney .02 .10
356 Ray Bourque .10 .30
357 Bob Sweeney .01 .05
358 Dave Christian .01 .05
359 Dave Poulin .01 .05
360 Garry Galley .01 .05
361 Andy Moog .07 .20
362 Ken Hodge Jr. .01 .05
363 Jim Wiemer .01 .05
364 Petri Skriko .01 .05
365 Don Sweeney .01 .05
366 Cam Neely .07 .20
367 Brett Hull HT .07 .20
368 Gino Cavallini .01 .05
369 Scott Stevens .02 .10
370 Rich Sutter .01 .05
371 Glen Featherstone .01 .05
372 Vincent Riendeau .02 .10
373 Dave Lowry .01 .05
374 Rod Brind'Amour .07 .20
375 Brett Hull .08 .25
376 Dan Quinn .01 .05
377 Tom Tilley .01 .05
378 Paul Cavallini .01 .05
379 Bob Bassen .01 .05
380 Mario Marois .01 .05
381 Darin Kimble .01 .05
382 Ron Wilson .01 .05
383 Garth Butcher .01 .05
384 Adam Oates .02 .10
385 Jeff Brown .01 .05
386 Jeremy Roenick HT .07 .20
387 Tony McKegney .01 .05
388 Troy Murray .01 .05
389 Dave Manson .01 .05
390 Ed Belfour .07 .20
391 Steve Thomas .01 .05
392 Michel Goulet .02 .10
393 Trent Yawney .01 .05
394 Adam Creighton .01 .05
395 Steve Larmer .02 .10
396 Jimmy Waite .02 .10
397 Dirk Graham .01 .05
398 Chris Chelios .07 .20
399 Mike Hudson .01 .05
400 Doug Wilson .02 .10
401 Greg Gilbert .01 .05
402 Wayne Presley .01 .05
403 Jeremy Roenick .07 .20
404 Frantisek Kucera .01 .05
405 Blackhawks/North Stars .01 .05
406 Blues/Red Wings .01 .05
407 Flames/Oilers .01 .05
408 Penguins/Devils .01 .05
409 Rangers/Capitals .01 .05
410 Bruins/Whalers .01 .05
411 Canadiens/Sabres .01 .05
412 Kings/Canucks .01 .05
413 Penguins/Capitals .01 .05
414 Bruins/Canadiens .01 .05
415 North Stars/Blues .01 .05
416 Kings/Oilers .01 .05
417 North Stars/Oilers .01 .05
418 Bruins/Penguins .01 .05
419 Game 1 Cup Finals .02 .10
420 Game 2 Cup Finals .02 .10
421 Game 3 Cup Finals .02 .10
422 Game 4 Cup Finals .02 .10
423 Game 5 Cup Finals .02 .10
424 Game 6 Cup Finals .02 .10
425 Mario Lemieux Smythe .10 .30
426 Checklist 1-108 .01 .05
427 Checklist 109-216 .01 .05
428 Checklist 217-324 .01 .05
429 Checklist 325-429 .01 .05

1992-93 Bowman

The 1992-93 Bowman hockey set contains 442 standard-size cards. Reportedly only 2,000 16-box wax cases were produced. One of 45 gold-foil engraved cards was inserted in each 15-card pack. These gold-foil cards feature 44 All-Stars (Campbell Conference on cards 199-220 and Wales Conference on cards 222-243) and a special card commemorating Mario Lemieux as the winner of the Conn Smythe trophy (440). The 18 gold-foil All-Stars that were single printed are listed in the checklist below as SP. The basic card fronts feature color action player photos with white borders. A magenta bar at the top left corner carries the Bowman "B". A gradated turquoise bar at the bottom right displays the player's name. The backs have a burlap-textured background and carry a close-up photo, a yellow and white statistics box presenting the player's performance vs. other teams, and biography. The only noteworthy Rookie Card in the set is Guy Hebert. There are a number of non glossy Eric Lindros (No. 442) cards on the market. These are unauthorized releases and should be avoided by collectors.

COMPLETE SET (442) 100.00 200.00
FOIL ODDS 1:15
1 Wayne Gretzky 2.50 6.00
2 Mike Krushelnyski .08 .25
3 Ray Bourque .75 2.00
4 Keith Brown .08 .25
5 Bob Sweeney .08 .25
6 Dave Christian .08 .25
7 Frantisek Kucera .08 .25
8 John LeClair .40 1.00
9 Jamie Macoun .08 .25
10 Bob Carpenter .08 .25
11 Garry Galley .08 .25
12 Bob Kudelski .08 .25
13 Doug Bodger .08 .25
14 Craig Janney .20 .50
15 Glen Wesley .08 .25
16 Daren Puppa .20 .50
17 Andy Brickley .08 .25
18 Steve Konroyd .08 .25
19 Dave Poulin .08 .25
20 Phil Housley .20 .50
21 Kevin Todd .08 .25
22 Tomas Sandstrom .08 .25
23 Pierre Turgeon .20 .50
24 Steve Smith .08 .25
25 Ray Sheppard .08 .25
26 Stu Barnes .08 .25
27 Grant Ledyard .08 .25
28 Benoit Hogue .08 .25
29 Randy Burridge .08 .25
30 Clint Malarchuk .20 .50
31 Steve Duchesne .08 .25
32 Guy Hebert RC 1.50 4.00
33 Steve Kasper .08 .25
34 Alexander Mogilny .20 .50
35 Marty McSorley .08 .25
36 Doug Weight .60 1.50
37 Dave Taylor .20 .50
38 Guy Carbonneau .20 .50
39 Brian Benning .08 .25
40 Nelson Emerson .08 .25
41 Craig Wolanin .08 .25
42 Kelly Hrudey .20 .50
43 Chris Chelios .50 1.25
44 Dave Andreychuk .20 .50
45 Russ Courtnall .08 .25
46 Stephane Richer .08 .25
47 Petr Svoboda .08 .25
48 Barry Pederson .08 .25
49 Claude Lemieux .08 .25
50 Tony Granato .08 .25
51 Al MacInnis .20 .50
52 Luciano Borsato .08 .25
53 Sergei Makarov .08 .25
54 Bobby Smith .20 .50
55 Gary Suter .08 .25
56 Tom Draper .08 .25
57 Corey Millen .08 .25
58 Joe Mullen .20 .50
59 Joe Nieuwendyk .20 .50
60 Brian Hayward .20 .50
61 Steve Larmer .20 .50
62 Cam Neely .50 1.25
63 Ric Nattress .08 .25
64 Denis Savard .20 .50
65 Gerald Diduck .08 .25
66 Pat Jablonski .20 .50
67 Brad McCrimmon .08 .25
68 Dirk Graham .08 .25
69 Joel Otto .08 .25
70 Luc Robitaille .20 .50
71 Dana Murzyn .08 .25
72 Jocelyn Lemieux .08 .25
73 Mike Hudson .08 .25
74 Patrick Roy 2.00 5.00
75 Doug Wilson .20 .50
76 Wayne Presley .08 .25
77 Felix Potvin .50 1.25
78 Jeremy Roenick .50 1.25
79 Andy Moog .50 1.25
80 Joey Kocur .20 .50
81 Neal Broten .20 .50
82 Shayne Corson .08 .25
83 Doug Gilmour .20 .50
84 Rob Zettler .08 .25
85 Bob Probert .20 .50
86 Mike Vernon .20 .50
87 Rick Zombo .08 .25
88 Adam Creighton .08 .25
89 Mike McPhee .08 .25
90 Ed Belfour .50 1.25
91 Steve Chiasson .08 .25
92 Dominic Roussel .20 .50
93 Troy Murray .08 .25
94 Jari Kurri .50 1.25
95 Geoff Smith .08 .25
96 Paul Ranheim .08 .25
97 Rick Wamsley .20 .50
98 Brian Noonan .08 .25
99 Kevin Lowe .20 .50
100 Josef Beranek .08 .25
101 Michel Petit .08 .25
102 Craig Billington .20 .50
103 Steve Yzerman 1.50 4.00
104 Glenn Anderson .20 .50
105 Perry Berezan .08 .25
106 Bill Ranford .20 .50
107 Randy Ladouceur .08 .25
108 Jimmy Carson .20 .50
109 Gary Roberts .08 .25
110 Checklist 1-110 .08 .25
111 Brad Shaw .08 .25
112 Pat Verbeek .08 .25
113 Mark Messier .50 1.25
114 Grant Fuhr .50 1.25
115 Sylvain Cote .08 .25
116 Mike Sullivan .08 .25
117 Steve Thomas .20 .50
118 Craig MacTavish .08 .25
119 Dave Babych .08 .25
120 Jim Waite .20 .50
121 Kevin Dineen .20 .50
122 Shawn Burr .08 .25
123 Ron Francis .20 .50
124 Garth Butcher .08 .25
125 Jarmo Myllys .08 .25
126 Doug Brown .08 .25
127 James Patrick .08 .25
128 Ray Ferraro .08 .25
129 Terry Carkner .08 .25
130 John MacLean .20 .50
131 Randy Velischek .08 .25
132 John Vanbiesbrouck .20 .50
133 Dean Evason .08 .25
134 Patrick Flatley .08 .25
135 Petr Klima .08 .25
136 Geoff Sanderson .20 .50
137 Joe Reekie .08 .25
138 Kirk Muller .08 .25
139 Brian Mullen .08 .25
140 Daniel Berthiaume .20 .50
141 David Shaw .08 .25
142 Pat LaFontaine .50 1.25
143 Ulf Dahlen .08 .25
144 Esa Tikkanen .08 .25
145 Slava Fetisov .08 .25
146 Mike Gartner .20 .50
147 Brent Sutter .08 .25
148 Darcy Wakaluk .20 .50
149 Brian Leetch .50 1.25
150 Craig Simpson .08 .25
151 Mike Modano .60 1.50
152 Bryan Trottier .20 .50
153 Larry Murphy .20 .50
154 Pavel Bure .50 1.25
155 Kay Whitmore .20 .50
156 Darren Turcotte .08 .25
157 Frank Musil .08 .25
158 Mikael Andersson .08 .25
159 Rick Tocchet .20 .50
160 Scott Stevens .20 .50
161 Bernie Nicholls .20 .50
162 Peter Sidorkiewicz .20 .50
163 Scott Mellanby .08 .25
164 Alexander Semak .08 .25
165 Kjell Samuelsson .08 .25
166 Kelly Kisio .08 .25
167 Sylvain Turgeon .08 .25
168 Rob Brown .08 .25
169 Gerard Gallant .08 .25
170 Jyrki Lumme .08 .25
171 Dave Gagner .20 .50
172 Tony Tanti .08 .25
173 Zarley Zalapski .08 .25
174 Joe Murphy .08 .25
175 Ron Sutter .08 .25
176 Dino Ciccarelli .20 .50
177 Jim Johnson .08 .25
178 Mike Hough .08 .25
179 Pelle Eklund .08 .25
180 John Druce .08 .25
181 Paul Coffey .50 1.25
182 Ken Wregget .20 .50
183 Brendan Shanahan .50 1.25
184 Keith Acton .08 .25
185 Steven Finn .08 .25
186 Brett Hull .75 2.00
187 Rollie Melanson .20 .50
188 Derek King .08 .25
189 Mario Lemieux 2.00 5.00
190 Mathieu Schneider .08 .25
191 Claude Vilgrain .08 .25
192 Gary Leeman .08 .25
193 Paul Cavallini .08 .25
194 John Cullen .08 .25
195 Ron Hextall .20 .50
196 David Volek .08 .25
197 Gordie Roberts .08 .25
198 Dale Craigwell .08 .25
199 Ed Belfour FOIL 2.00 5.00
200 Brian Bellows FOIL SP 2.00 5.00
201 Chris Chelios FOIL .60 1.50
202 Tim Cheveldae FOIL SP 2.00 5.00
203A Vincent Damphousse AFOIL ERR (Team name missing on card back) .60 1.50
203B Vincent Damphousse FOIL COR .60 1.50
204 Dave Ellett FOIL .60 1.50
205 Sergei Fedorov FOIL SP 6.00 15.00
206 Theo Fleury FOIL 1.50 4.00
207 Wayne Gretzky FOIL SP 6.00 15.00
208 Phil Housley FOIL .60 1.50
209 Brett Hull FOIL 2.00 5.00
210 Trevor Linden FOIL SP 2.00 5.00
211 Al MacInnis FOIL .20 .50
212 Kirk McLean FOIL SP 2.00 5.00
213 Adam Oates FOIL .60 1.50
214 Gary Roberts FOIL SP 2.00 5.00
215 Larry Robinson FOIL .20 .50
216 Luc Robitaille FOIL .60 1.50
217 Jeremy Roenick FOIL SP 6.00 15.00
218 Mark Tinordi FOIL .20 .50
219 Doug Wilson FOIL .60 1.50
220 Steve Yzerman FOIL 4.00 10.00
221 Checklist 111-220 .08 .25
222 Don Beaupre FOIL SP 2.00 5.00
223 Ray Bourque FOIL SP 2.00 5.00
224 Rod Brind'Amour UER FOIL SP (Apostrophe in last name is missing) 2.00 5.00
225 Randy Burridge FOIL SP 2.00 5.00
226 Paul Coffey FOIL SP 2.50 6.00
227 John Cullen FOIL SP .08 .25
228 Eric Desjardins FOIL SP 2.00 5.00
229 Ray Ferraro FOIL SP .08 .25
230 Kevin Hatcher FOIL .60 1.50
231 Jaromir Jagr FOIL 1.50 4.00
232 Brian Leetch FOIL SP 2.50 6.00
233 Mario Lemieux FOIL SP 4.00 10.00
234 Mark Messier FOIL .50 1.25
235 Alexander Mogilny FOIL .60 1.50
236 Kirk Muller FOIL .60 1.50
237 Owen Nolan FOIL .60 1.50
238 Mike Richter FOIL .60 1.50
239 Patrick Roy FOIL SP 4.00 10.00
240 Joe Sakic FOIL SP 8.00 20.00
241 Kevin Stevens FOIL .60 1.50
242 Scott Stevens FOIL .20 .50
243 Bryan Trottier FOIL SP 2.50 6.00
244 Joe Sakic 1.25 3.00
245 Daniel Marois .08 .25
246 Randy Wood .08 .25
247 Jeff Brown .08 .25
248 Peter Bondra .20 .50
249 Peter Stastny .20 .50
250 Tom Barrasso .20 .50
251 Al Iafrate .20 .50
252 James Black .08 .25
253 Jan Erixon .08 .25
254 Brian Lawton .08 .25
255 Luke Richardson .08 .25
256 Rob Zamuner .08 .25
257 Jeff Chychrun .08 .25
258 Adam Oates .20 .50
259 Tom Kurvers .08 .25
260 Brian Bellows .08 .25
261 Trevor Linden .20 .50
262 Vincent Riendeau .20 .50
263 Peter Zezel .08 .25
264 Rich Pilon .08 .25
265 Paul Broten .08 .25
266 Gaetan Duchesne .08 .25
267 Doug Lidster .08 .25
268 Rod Brind'Amour .20 .50
269 Jon Casey .20 .50
270 Pat Elynuik .08 .25
271 Kevin Hatcher .08 .25
272 Brian Propp .08 .25
273 Tom Fergus .08 .25
274 Steve Weeks .20 .50
275 Calle Johansson .08 .25
276 Russ Romaniuk .08 .25
277 Greg Paslawski .08 .25
278 Ed Olczyk .08 .25
279 Rod Langway .08 .25
280 Murray Craven .08 .25
281 Guy Larose .08 .25
282 Paul MacDermid .08 .25
283 Brian Bradley .08 .25
284 Paul Stanton .08 .25
285 Kirk McLean .20 .50
286 Andrei Lomakin .08 .25
287 Randy Carlyle .08 .25
288 Donald Audette .08 .25
289 Dan Quinn .08 .25
290 Mike Keane .08 .25
291 Dave Ellett .08 .25
292 Joe Juneau UER (Card back says shoots right& should be left) .20 .50
293 Phil Bourque .08 .25
294 Michal Pivonka .08 .25
295 Fredrik Olausson .08 .25
296 Randy McKay .08 .25
297 Don Beaupre .20 .50
298 Steve Leach .08 .25
299 Teppo Numminen .08 .25
300 Slava Kozlov .20 .50
301 Kevin Haller .08 .25
302 Jaromir Jagr .75 2.00
303 Dale Hunter .20 .50
304 Bob Errey .08 .25
305 Nicklas Lidstrom .75 2.00
306 Bob Essensa .20 .50
307 Sylvain Lefebvre .08 .25
308 Dale Hawerchuk .20 .50
309 Dave Snuggerud .08 .25
310 Michel Goulet .20 .50
311 Eric Desjardins .20 .50
312 Thomas Steen .08 .25
313 Scott Niedermayer .08 .25
314 Mark Recchi .20 .50
315 Gord Murphy .08 .25
316 Sergio Momesso .08 .25
317 Todd Elik .08 .25
318 Louie DeBrusk .08 .25
319 Mike Lalor .08 .25
320 Jamie Leach .08 .25
321 Darryl Sydor .08 .25
322 Brent Gilchrist .08 .25
323 Alexei Kasatonov .08 .25
324 Rick Tabaracci .20 .50
325 Wendel Clark .20 .50
326 Vladimir Konstantinov .50 1.25
327 Randy Gilhen .08 .25
328 Owen Nolan .20 .50
329 Vincent Damphousse .08 .25
330 Checklist 221-331 .08 .25
331 Yves Racine .08 .25
332 Jacques Cloutier .20 .50
333 Greg Adams .08 .25
334 Mike Craig .08 .25
335 Curtis Leschyshyn .08 .25
336 John McIntyre .08 .25
337 Stephane Quintal .08 .25
338 Kelly Miller .08 .25
339 Dave Manson .08 .25
340 Stephane Matteau .08 .25
341 Christian Ruuttu .08 .25
342 Mike Donnelly .08 .25
343 Eric Weinrich .08 .25
344 Mats Sundin .50 1.25
345 Geoff Courtnall .08 .25
346 Stephan Lebeau .08 .25
347 Jeff Beukeboom .08 .25
348 Jeff Hackett .20 .50
349 Uwe Krupp .08 .25
350 Igor Larionov .08 .25
351 Ulf Samuelsson .08 .25
352 Marty McInnis .08 .25
353 Peter Ahola .08 .25
354 Mike Richter .50 1.25
355 Theo Fleury .08 .25
356 Dan Lambert .08 .25
357 Brent Ashton .08 .25
358 David Bruce .08 .25
359 Chris Dahlquist .08 .25
360 Mike Ridley .08 .25
361 Pat Falloon .08 .25
362 Doug Smail .08 .25
363 Adrien Plavsic .08 .25
364 Ron Wilson .08 .25
365 Derian Hatcher .08 .25
366 Kevin Stevens .08 .25
367 Rob Blake .50 1.25
368 Curtis Joseph .50 1.25
369 Tom Fitzgerald .08 .25
370 Dave Lowry .08 .25
371 J.J. Daigneault .08 .25
372 Jim Hrivnak .20 .50
373 Adam Graves .08 .25
374 Brad May .08 .25
375 Todd Gill .08 .25
376 Paul Ysebaert .08 .25
377 David Williams RC .08 .25
378 Bob Bassen .08 .25
379 Brian Glynn .08 .25
380 Kris King .08 .25
381 Rob Pearson .08 .25
382 Marc Bureau .08 .25
383 Jim Paek .08 .25
384 Tomas Forslund .08 .25
385 Darrin Shannon .08 .25
386 Chris Terreri .20 .50
387 Andrew Cassels .08 .25
388 Jay More .08 .25
389 Tony Amonte .20 .50
390 Mark Pederson .08 .25
391 Kevin Miller .08 .25
392 Igor Ulanov .08 .25
393 Kelly Buchberger .08 .25
394 Mark Fitzpatrick .20 .50
395 Mikhail Tatarinov .08 .25
396 Petr Nedved .20 .50
397 Jeff Odgers .08 .25
398 Stephane Fiset .20 .50
399 Mark Tinordi .08 .25
400 Johan Garpenlov .08 .25
401 Robert Reichel .08 .25
402 Don Sweeney UER (Back photo actually Bob Sweeney) .08 .25
403 Rob DiMaio .08 .25
404 Bill Lindsay RC .08 .25
405 Steph Beauregard .20 .50
406 Mike Ricci .20 .50
407 Bobby Holik .20 .50
408 Igor Kravchuk .08 .25
409 Murray Baron .08 .25
410 Troy Gamble .20 .50
411 Cliff Ronning .08 .25
412 Jeff Reese .08 .25
413 Robert Kron .08 .25
414 Benoit Brunet .08 .25
415 Shawn McEachern .08 .25
416 Sergei Fedorov .75 2.00
417 Joe Sacco .08 .25
418 Bryan Marchment .08 .25
419 John LeBlanc RC .08 .25
420 Tim Cheveldae .20 .50
421 Claude LaPointe .08 .25
422 Ken Sutton .08 .25
423 Anatoli Semenov .08 .25
424 Mike McNeil .08 .25
425 Norm Maciver .08 .25
426 Sergei Nemchinov .08 .25
427 Dimitri Khristich .08 .25
428 Dominik Hasek 1.25 3.00
429 Bob McGill .08 .25
430 Valeri Zelepukin .08 .25
431 Vladimir Ruzicka .08 .25
432 Valeri Kamensky .08 .25
433 Pat MacLeod .08 .25
434 Glenn Healy .20 .50
435 Patrice Brisebois .08 .25
436 James Baker .08 .25
437 Michel Picard .08 .25
438 Scott Lachance UER (Back photo actually Brad Turner) .08 .25
439 Gilbert Dionne .08 .25
440 Mario Lemieux Smythe FOIL 4.00 10.00
441 Checklist 332-441 .08 .25
442 Eric Lindros UER (Acquired 6-30-92& not 6-20-92 as in bio) .50 1.25

1995-96 Bowman

The 1995-96 Bowman set - the first hockey release under that name by the Topps company since 1992-93 - was issued in one series totaling 165 cards. The 9-card packs had a suggested retail price of $2.00. The highlight of the set is an extended Rookies subset (91-165). Rookie Cards in the set include Daniel Alfredsson and Petr Sykora. The Cool Trade redemption offer expired on October 15, 1996.

COMPLETE SET (165) 12.50 25.00
1 Wayne Gretzky .75 2.00
2 Ray Bourque .20 .50
3 Craig Janney .02 .10
4 Andrew Cassels .02 .10
5 Alexander Mogilny .05 .15
6 Pierre Turgeon .05 .15
7 Dave Andreychuk .05 .15
8 Mark Messier .10 .30
9 Igor Korolev .02 .10
10 Tomas Sandstrom .02 .10
11 Shayne Corson .02 .10
12 Chris Chelios .10 .30
13 Claude Lemieux .02 .10
14 Stephane Richer .05 .15
15 Patrick Roy .60 1.50
16 Al MacInnis .05 .15
17 Cam Neely .10 .30
18 Doug Gilmour .05 .15
19 Steve Thomas .05 .15
20 Jeremy Roenick .15 .40
21 Steve Yzerman .60 1.50
22 Petr Klima .02 .10
23 Luc Robitaille .05 .15
24 Bill Ranford .05 .15
25 Grant Fuhr .10 .30
26 Sean Burke .05 .15
27 John MacLean .05 .15
28 Brendan Shanahan .10 .30
29 Pat LaFontaine .10 .30
30 John Vanbiesbrouck .05 .15
31 Ron Francis .05 .15
32 Brian Leetch .05 .15
33 Dave Gagner .05 .15
34 Larry Murphy .05 .15
35 Mike Modano .20 .50
36 Rick Tocchet .05 .15
37 Scott Mellanby .02 .10
38 Ron Hextall .05 .15
39 Joe Juneau .02 .10
40 Mario Lemieux .60 1.50
41 Paul Coffey .10 .30
42 Joe Sakic .25 .60
43 Brett Hull .15 .40
44 Adam Oates .05 .1
45 Wendel Clark .05 .1
46 Trevor Linden .05 .1
47 Tom Barrasso .05 .1
48 Kevin Hatcher .02 .1
49 Mats Sundin .10 .3
50 Scott Stevens .05 .1
51 Mark Recchi .05 .1
52 Theo Fleury .02 .1
53 Ed Belfour .10 .3
54 Adam Graves .02 .1
55 Peter Bondra .05 .1
56 Dominik Hasek .25 .6
57 Jaromir Jagr .20 .5
58 Owen Nolan .05 .1
59 Kevin Stevens .02 .1
60 Alexei Zhamnov .05 .1
61 Dimitri Khristich .02 .1
62 Chris Pronger .10 .3
63 John LeClair .10 .3
64 Scott Niedermayer .02 .1
65 Pavel Bure .10 .3
66 Chris Osgood .05 .1
67 Geoff Sanderson .02 .1
68 Doug Weight .05 .1
69 Keith Tkachuk .10 .3
70 Martin Brodeur .30 .7
71 Eric Lindros .10 .3
72 Martin Straka .02 .1
73 Alexander Selivanov .02 .1
74 Jim Carey .05 .1
75 Teemu Selanne .10 .3
76 Rob Niedermayer .05 .1
77 Vyacheslav Kozlov .05 .1
78 Todd Harvey .05 .1
79 Felix Potvin .10 .3
80 Sergei Fedorov .15 .4
81 Mathieu Schneider .02 .1
82 Roman Hamrlik .05 .1
83 Mikael Renberg .05 .1
84 Jeff Friesen .02 .1
85 Peter Forsberg .30 .7
86 Kenny Jonsson .02 .1
87 Brian Savage .02 .1
88 Oleg Tverdovsky .02 .1
89 Nikolai Khabibulin .05 .1
90 Paul Kariya .10 .3
91 Zdenek Nedved .02 .1
92 Darren Langdon .02 .1
93 Lonny Bohonos RC .02 .1
94 Mike Wilson .02 .1
95 Landon Wilson RC .02 .1
96 Bryan McCabe .02 .1
97 Byron Dafoe .05 .1
98 Denny Lambert .02 .1
99 Craig Mills .02 .1
100 Ed Jovanovski .10 .3
101 Jason Bonsignore .02 .1
102 Clayton Beddoes UER back reads Bleddoes .02 .1
103 Jamie Pushor .02 .1
104 Drew Bannister .02 .1
105 Ed Ward .02 .1
106 Todd Warriner .02 .1
107 Deron Quint .02 .1
108 Rhett Warrener .02 .1
109 Marko Kiprusoff .02 .1
110 Daniel Alfredsson RC .75 2.0
111 Marcus Ragnarsson UER RC .05 .1
Spelled Ragnarasson
112 Miroslav Satan RC .75 2.0
113 Niklas Sundstrom .05 .1
114 Mathieu Dandenault .02 .1
115 Vitali Yachmenev .02 .1
116 Petr Sykora RC .75 2.0
117 Antti Tormanen .02 .1
118 Jeff O'Neill .02 .1
119 David Nemirovsky RC .02 .1
120 Jason Doig .02 .1
121 Aaron Gavey .02 .1
122 Ladislav Kohn .02 .1
123 Richard Park .02 .1
124 Stephane Yelle .02 .1
125 Eric Daze .05 .1
126 Niclas Andersson .02 .1
127 Brendan Witt .02 .1
128 Jamie Storr .05 .1
129 Darby Hendrickson .02 .1
130 Radek Dvorak RC .20 .5
131 Cory Stillman .02 .1
132 Jamie Rivers .02 .1
133 Ville Peltonen .02 .1
134 Peter Ferraro .02 .1
135 Trent McCleary RC .02 .1
136 Chris Wells .02 .1
137 Chad Kilger RC .02 .1
138 Denis Pederson .02 .1
139 Roman Vopat .02 .1
140 Shean Donovan .02 .1
141 Alex Stojanov .02 .1
142 Mark Kolesar .02 .1
143 Scott Walker RC .02 .1
144 Dave Roche RC .02 .1
145 Corey Hirsch .05 .1
146 Aki Berg .02 .1
147 Stefan Ustorf .02 .1
148 Saku Koivu .10 .3
149 Shane Doan RC .30 .7
150 Jere Lehtinen .05 .1
151 Kyle McLaren RC .02 .1
152 Marty Murray .02 .1
153 Sean Pronger RC .02 .1
154 Joaquin Gage RC .02 .1
155 Eric Fichaud .05 .1
156 Todd Bertuzzi RC 1.25 3.0
157 Wayne Primeau .02 .1
158 Scott Bailey .02 .1
159 Viktor Kozlov .05 .1
160 Valeri Bure .02 .1
161 Dody Wood .02 .1
162 Grant Marshall .02 .1
163 Ken Klee RC .02 .1
164 Corey Schwab RC .20 .5
165 Brian Holzinger RC .10 .3
NNO Cool Trade Exchange EXP. .40 1.0

1995-96 Bowman All-Foil

The 1995-96 Bowman All-Foil set is a 16
card parallel of the regular version. The

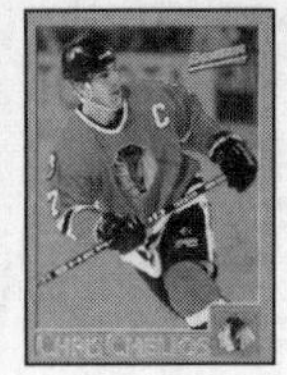

rds, which were inserted one per pack, ature a stylish metallicized front, while the acks remain the same as the basic cards.
STARS: 4X TO 8X BASIC CARDS
RCs: 1.5X TO 3X BASIC CARDS
NE PER PACK

1995-96 Bowman Draft Prospects

serted one in every pack, this 40-card set atures the players who participated in the st annual 1996 CHL Draft Prospects game Toronto. Fourteen of the players pictured ent on to become first-round selections in e 1996 NHL entry draft.

OMPLETE SET (40) 4.00 10.00
NE PER PACK
1 Johnathan Aitken .10 .25
2 Chris Allen .10 .25
3 Matt Bradley .10 .25
4 Daniel Briere 1.00 2.50
5 Jeff Brown .10 .25
6 Jan Bulis .10 .25
7 Daniel Corso .40 1.00
8 Luke Curtin .10 .25
9 Matthieu Descoteaux .10 .25
10 Boyd Devereaux .10 .25
11 Jason Doyle .10 .25
12 Etienne Drapeau .10 .25
13 J-P Dumont .75 2.00
14 Mathieu Garon .60 1.50
15 Josh Green .10 .25
16 Chris Hajt .10 .25
17 Matt Higgins .10 .25
18 Craig Hillier .10 .25
19 Josh Holden .10 .25
20 Dan Focht .10 .25
21 Henry Kuster .10 .25
22 Francis Larivee .10 .25
23 Mario Larocque .10 .25
24 Wes Mason .10 .25
25 Francois Methot .10 .25
26 Geoff Peters .10 .25
27 Randy Petruk .10 .25
28 Chris Phillips .40 1.00
29 Boris Protsenko .10 .25
30 Remi Royer .10 .25
31 Cory Sarich .10 .25
32 Jaroslav Svejkovsky .10 .25
33 Curtis Tipler .10 .25
34 Darren Van Oene .10 .25
35 Jesse Wallin .10 .25
36 Kurt Walsh .10 .25
37 Lance Ward .10 .25
38 Steve Wasylko .10 .25
39 Trevor Wasyluk .10 .25
40 Jon Zukiwsky .10 .25

1995-96 Bowman's Best

ndomly inserted in packs at a rate of 1:12, s 30-card set is dedicated to the finest ars and up'n'comers in the NHL. A fractor parallel to this set was also created d inserted at a rate of 1:36.

OMPLETE SET (30) 40.00 100.00
TATED ODDS 1:12
B1 Peter Forsberg 3.00 8.00
B2 Teemu Selanne 1.50 4.00
B3 Eric Lindros 1.50 4.00
B4 Scott Stevens .75 2.00
B5 Wayne Gretzky 8.00 20.00
B6 Mark Messier 1.50 4.00
B7 Jaromir Jagr 2.50 6.00
B8 Martin Brodeur 4.00 10.00
B9 Alexander Mogilny .75 2.00
B10 Mario Lemieux 6.00 15.00
B11 Joe Sakic 3.00 8.00
B12 Sergei Fedorov 2.00 5.00
B13 Pavel Bure 1.50 4.00
B14 Brian Leetch .75 2.00
B15 Paul Kariya 1.50 4.00
B16 Daniel Alfredsson 2.00 5.00
B17 Saku Koivu 1.50 4.00
B18 Eric Daze .40 1.00
B19 Ed Jovanovski 1.50 4.00
B20 Vitali Yachmenev .40 1.00
B21 Niklas Sundstrom .40 1.00
B22 Radek Dvorak .40 1.00
B23 Byron Dafoe .75 2.00
BB24 Shane Doan 1.50 4.00
BB25 Chad Kilger .20 .50
BB26 Jeff O'Neill .50 1.25
BB27 Cory Stillman .50 1.25
BB28 Valeri Bure .50 1.25
BB29 Marcus Ragnarsson .30 .75
BB30 Todd Bertuzzi 2.00 5.00

1995-96 Bowman's Best Refractors

COMPLETE REFRACTOR SET 600.00 900.00
*STARS: 1.25X TO 3X BASIC INSERTS
*ROOKIES: 6X TO 15X
RANDOM INSERTS IN PACKS

1998-99 Bowman's Best

This 150-card set was distributed in six-card packs with a suggested retail price of $5. The set features color action photos of 100 key veterans printed on cards with a gold design and 35 top NHL rookies and 14 CHL stars showcased on silver-designed cards. The cards are all printed on thick 26-pt. stock. The backs carry player information and career statistics.

COMPLETE SET (150) 90.00 150.00
COMP.SET w/o SP's (100) 15.00 25.00
1 Steve Yzerman 1.50 4.00
2 Paul Kariya .30 .75
3 Wayne Gretzky 2.00 5.00
4 Jaromir Jagr .50 1.25
5 Mark Messier .30 .75
6 Keith Tkachuk .30 .75
7 John LeClair .30 .75
8 Martin Brodeur .75 2.00
9 Rob Blake .25 .60
10 Brett Hull .40 1.00
11 Dominik Hasek .60 1.50
12 Peter Forsberg .75 2.00
13 Doug Gilmour .25 .60
14 Vincent Damphousse .08 .25
15 Zigmund Palffy .25 .60
16 Daniel Alfredsson .25 .60
17 Mike Vernon .25 .60
18 Chris Pronger .25 .60
19 Wendel Clark .25 .60
20 Curtis Joseph .30 .75
21 Peter Bondra .25 .60
22 Grant Fuhr .25 .60
23 Nikolai Khabibulin .25 .60
24 Kevin Hatcher .08 .25
25 Brian Leetch .30 .75
26 Patrik Elias .25 .60
27 Chris Osgood .25 .60
28 Patrick Roy 1.50 4.00
29 Chris Chelios .30 .75
30 Trevor Kidd .08 .25
31 Theo Fleury .08 .25
32 Michael Peca .08 .25
33 Ray Bourque .50 1.25
34 Ed Belfour .30 .75
35 Sergei Fedorov .50 1.25
36 Adrian Aucoin .08 .25
37 Alexei Yashin .08 .25
38 Rick Tocchet .25 .60
39 Mats Sundin .30 .75
40 Alexander Mogilny .25 .60
41 Jeff Friesen .08 .25
42 Eric Lindros .30 .75
43 Mike Richter .30 .75
44 Saku Koivu .30 .75
45 Teemu Selanne .30 .75
46 Doug Weight .25 .60
47 Nicklas Lidstrom .30 .75
48 Mike Modano .50 1.25
49 Joe Sakic .60 1.50
50 Ron Francis .25 .60
51 Jason Allison .08 .25
52 Brendan Shanahan .30 .75
53 Bobby Holik .08 .25
54 Damian Rhodes .25 .60
55 Jeremy Roenick .40 1.00
56 Tom Barrasso .08 .25
57 Al MacInnis .25 .60
58 Pavel Bure .30 .75
59 Olaf Kolzig .25 .60
60 Patrick Marleau .08 .25
61 Cliff Ronning .08 .25
62 Joe Nieuwendyk .25 .60
63 Jeff Hackett .25 .60
64 Keith Primeau .08 .25
65 Jarome Iginla .40 1.00
66 Sergei Samsonov .25 .60
67 Rod Brind'Amour .25 .60
68 Dino Ciccarelli .25 .60
69 Ryan Smyth .25 .60
70 Owen Nolan .25 .60
71 Mike Johnson .25 .60
72 Adam Oates .08 .25
73 Mattias Ohlund .25 .60
74 Jamie Heward RC .08 .25
75 Mike Dunham .25 .60
76 Jere Lehtinen .25 .60
77 Tony Amonte .25 .60
78 Derek Morris .08 .25
79 Darren McCarty .08 .25
80 Bryan Berard .25 .60
81 Adam Graves .08 .25
82 John Vanbiesbrouck .25 .60
83 Marco Sturm .08 .25
84 Joe Thornton .50 1.25
85 Wade Redden .08 .25
86 Pierre Turgeon .25 .60
87 Bill Ranford .25 .60
88 Alexei Zhitnik .08 .25
89 Valeri Kamensky .08 .25
90 Dean McAmmond .08 .25
91 Jozef Stumpel .25 .60
92 Jocelyn Thibault .25 .60
93 Joe Juneau .25 .60
94 Craig Janney .25 .60
95 Robert Reichel .25 .60
96 Mark Recchi .25 .60
97 Sami Kapanen .08 .25
98 Shayne Corson .08 .25
99 Scott Niedermayer .08 .25
100 Trevor Linden .25 .60
101 Olli Jokinen SP 1.50 3.00
102 Chris Drury SP 2.00 5.00
103 Daniel Cleary SP 1.00 2.50
104 Yan Golubovsky SP RC 1.25 3.00
105 Brendan Morrison SP 1.50 3.00
106 Manny Malhotra SP 1.50 3.00
107 Marian Hossa SP 1.25 3.00
108 Daniel Briere SP 1.00 2.50
109 Vincent Lecavalier SP 1.50 4.00
110 Milan Hejduk SP RC 3.00 8.00
111 Tom Poti SP 1.00 2.50
112 Mike Maneluk SP RC 1.50 3.00
113 Marty Reasoner SP 1.00 2.50
114 Rico Fata SP 1.00 2.50
115 Eric Brewer SP 1.00 2.50
116 Dan Cloutier SP 1.00 2.50
117 Mike Leclerc SP 1.00 2.50
118 Dimitri Tertyshny SP RC 1.00 2.50
119 Josh Green SP RC 1.50 4.00
120 Mark Parrish SP RC 1.50 4.00
121 Jamie Wright SP 1.00 2.50
122 Fred Lindquist SP RC 1.00 2.50
123 Daniil Markov SP RC 1.00 2.50
124 Bill Muckalt SP RC 1.50 3.00
125 Johan Davidsson SP 1.00 2.50
126 Oleg Kvasha SP RC 1.25 3.00
127 Cameron Mann SP 1.00 2.50
128 Pascal Trepanier SP RC 1.00 2.50
129 Clarke Wilm SP RC 1.00 2.50
130 Alain Nasreddine SP RC 1.00 2.50
131 Bryan Helmer SP RC 1.00 2.50
132 Michal Handzus SP RC 1.50 4.00
133 Pavel Kubina SP RC 1.25 3.00
134 Zdeno Chara SP 1.00 2.50
135 Matt Higgins SP RC 1.00 2.50
136 David Legwand SP 1.50 4.00
137 Brad Stuart SP RC 2.50 6.00
138 Mark Bell SP RC 3.00 8.00
139 Eric Chouinard SP 1.00 2.50
140 Simon Gagne SP 1.50 4.00
141 Ramzi Abid SP RC 2.50 6.00
142 Sergei Varlamov SP 1.50 3.00
143 Mike Ribeiro SP 1.00 2.50
144 Derrick Walser SP RC 1.00 2.50
145 Mathieu Garon SP 1.00 2.50
146 Daniel Tkaczuk SP 1.00 2.50
147 Jeff Heerema SP RC 1.50 4.00
148 Sebastien Roger SP RC 1.00 2.50
149 Bret DeCecco SP 1.00 2.50
150 Checklist SP 1.50 3.00

1998-99 Bowman's Best Refractors

Randomly inserted in packs at the rate of 1:52, this 150-card set is a refractive parallel version of the base set. Only 400 of each card were produced and sequentially numbered.

*STARS: 8X TO 20X BASIC CARDS
*SP's: 2X TO 5X BASIC CARDS
STATED ODDS 1:387

1998-99 Bowman's Best Atomic Refractors

Randomly inserted into packs at the rate of 1:1549, this 150-card set is a parallel version of the base set and is similar in design. The difference is seen in the special sparkling refractive sheen of the cards. Only 100 of each card was produced and sequentially numbered.

*STARS: 20X TO 50X BASIC CARDS
*SP's: 7.5X TO 15X BASIC CARDS
STATED ODDS 1:1549
STATED PRINT RUN 100 SERIAL #'d SETS
1 Steve Yzerman 40.00 100.00
3 Wayne Gretzky 60.00 150.00
28 Patrick Roy 40.00 100.00

1998-99 Bowman's Best Autographs

Randomly inserted in packs at the rate of 1:97, this 20-card set displays autographed color photos of five rookie and five veteran players each featured in two different photos. Both versions of the rookies carry silver backgrounds, with gold backgrounds for the veterans. Each card is stamped with the

Topps "Certified Autograph Issue" logo.

STATED ODDS 1:97
*REFRACTORS: .75X TO 2X BASIC INSERTS
REF.STATED ODDS 1:516
*ATOMIC REF: 1.5X TO 4X BASIC INSERTS
ATOM REF.STATED ODDS 1:1549
A1A Dominik Hasek 15.00 40.00
A1B Dominik Hasek 25.00 50.00
A2A Jaromir Jagr 15.00 40.00
A2B Jaromir Jagr 25.00 60.00
A3A Peter Bondra 6.00 15.00
A3B Peter Bondra 6.00 15.00
A4A Sergei Fedorov 15.00 40.00
A4B Sergei Fedorov 25.00 50.00
A5A Ray Bourque 20.00 50.00
A5B Ray Bourque 25.00 60.00
A6A Bill Muckalt 3.00 8.00
A6B Bill Muckalt 3.00 8.00
A7A Brendan Morrison 6.00 15.00
A7B Brendan Morrison 6.00 15.00
A8A Chris Drury 6.00 15.00
A8B Chris Drury 6.00 15.00
A9A Mark Parrish 3.00 8.00
A9B Mark Parrish 3.00 8.00
A10A Manny Malhotra 3.00 8.00
A10B Manny Malhotra 3.00 8.00

1998-99 Bowman's Best Mirror Image Fusion

Randomly inserted in packs at the rate of 1:12, this 20-card set features color action photos of Western and Eastern Conference players printed on die-cut, double-sided cards. Each card features a veteran on one side and a rising star on the other and can be married to its die-cut counterpart from the opposite conference.

COMPLETE SET (20) 60.00 125.00
STATED ODDS 1:12
*REFRACTORS: 4X TO 10X BASIC INSERTS
REF.STATED ODDS 1:387
REF.PRINT RUN 100 SERIAL #'d SETS
*ATOMIC REF: 12.5X TO 30X BASIC INSERTS
ATOM REF.STATED ODDS 1:1549
ATOM REF.PRINT RUN 25 SERIAL #'d SETS
F1 John LeClair 2.00 5.00
Bates Battaglia
F2 Paul Kariya 2.00 5.00
Mike LeClerc
F3 Jaromir Jagr 4.00 10.00
Mark Parrish
F4 Teemu Selanne 2.00 5.00
Frederik Lindquist
F5 Eric Lindros 2.00 5.00
Vincent Lecavalier
F6 Peter Forsberg 5.00 12.00
Olli Jokinen
F7 Brian Leetch 1.25 3.00
Daniil Markov
F8 Nicklas Lidstrom 2.00 5.00
Yan Golubovsky
F9 Dominik Hasek 4.00 10.00
Dan Cloutier
F10 Patrick Roy 10.00 25.00
Tyler Moss
F11 Sergei Samsonov 1.25 3.00
Mike Watt
F12 Keith Tkachuk 2.50 6.00
Jamie Wright
F13 Peter Bondra 2.50 6.00
Marian Hossa
F14 Pavel Bure 2.00 5.00
Bill Muckalt
F15 Wayne Gretzky 12.00 30.00
Brendan Morrison
F16 Sergei Fedorov 3.00 8.00
Marty Reasoner
F17 Ray Bourque 3.00 8.00
Eric Brewer
F18 Chris Pronger 1.25 3.00
Tom Poti
F19 Martin Brodeur 5.00 12.00
Jose Theodore
F20 Chris Osgood 1.25 3.00
Jamie Storr

1998-99 Bowman's Best Performers

Randomly inserted in packs at the rate of 1:12, this 10-card set features action color photos of top young stars and rookies.

COMPLETE SET (10) 10.00 25.00
STATED ODDS 1:12
*REFRACTORS: 4X TO 10X BASIC INSERTS
REF.STATED ODDS 1:387
REF.PRINT RUN 200 SERIAL #'d SETS
*ATOMIC REF: 10X TO 25X BASIC INSERTS
ATOM REF.STATED ODDS 1:1549
ATOM REF. PRINT RUN 50 SERIAL #'d SETS
BP1 Mike Johnson .75 2.00
BP2 Sergei Samsonov 1.25 3.00
BP3 Patrik Elias .75 2.00
BP4 Patrick Marleau 1.25 3.00
BP5 Mattias Ohlund .75 2.00
BP6 Manny Malhotra .75 2.00
BP7 Chris Drury .75 2.00
BP8 Daniel Briere 1.25 3.00
BP9 Brendan Morrison .75 2.00
BP10 Vincent Lecavalier 4.00 10.00

1998-99 Bowman's Best Scotty Bowman's Best

Randomly inserted into packs at the rate of 1:6, this 11-card set features color photos of ten of the best present day players in the NHL according to Scotty Bowman who is one of the greatest coaches of all time. Card #11 is a card of the coach himself and 100 of these cards were autographed with an insertion rate of 1:7,745.

COMPLETE SET (11) 25.00 50.00
STATED ODDS 1:6
*REFRACTORS: 3X TO 8X BASIC INSERTS
REF.STATED ODDS 1:704
REF.PRINT RUN 200 SERIAL #'d SETS
*ATOMIC REF: 10X TO 20X BASIC INSERTS
ATOM REF.STATED ODDS 1:2816
ATOM REF.PRINT RUN 50 SERIAL #'d SETS
SB1 Dominik Hasek 2.50 6.00
SB2 Martin Brodeur 3.00 8.00
SB3 Chris Osgood 1.00 3.00
SB4 Nicklas Lidstrom 1.25 3.00
SB5 Eric Lindros 1.25 3.00
SB6 Jaromir Jagr 2.00 5.00
SB7 Steve Yzerman 6.00 15.00
SB8 Peter Forsberg 3.00 8.00
SB9 Paul Kariya 1.25 3.00
SB10 Ray Bourque 2.00 5.00
SB11 Scotty Bowman 1.25 3.00
SB11S Scotty Bowman AU 40.00 100.00

2001-02 Bowman YoungStars

Released in late May, this 165-card set carried an SRP of $3.00. Card fronts carried gold foil accents and black borders on full-color action photos. The Topps/NHL Young Stars logo appeared in the bottom left hand corner.

COMPLETE SET (165) 75.00 150.00
1 Patrick Roy 2.50 6.00
2 Brett Hull .60 1.50
3 Mario Lemieux 3.00 8.00
4 Jaromir Jagr .75 2.00
5 Mats Sundin .50 1.25
6 Mike Modano .75 2.00
7 Jarome Iginla .60 1.50
8 Jason Allison .20 .50
9 Mike Richter .50 1.25
10 Chris Pronger .40 1.00
11 Patrik Elias .40 1.00
12 Tommy Salo .40 1.00
13 Tony Amonte .40 1.00
14 Joe Thornton .75 2.00
15 Joe Sakic 1.00 2.50
16 Pavel Bure .50 1.25
17 Teemu Selanne .50 1.25
18 Markus Naslund .50 1.25
19 Nikolai Khabibulin .50 1.25
20 Paul Kariya .50 1.25
21 Dominik Hasek 1.00 2.50
22 Ron Francis .40 1.00
23 Ray Ferraro .20 .50
24 Miroslav Satan .40 1.00
25 Milan Hejduk .50 1.25
26 Jose Theodore .50 1.25
27 Daniel Alfredsson .40 1.00
28 Michael Peca .20 .50
29 Keith Primeau .20 .50
30 Doug Weight .40 1.00
31 Sean Burke .40 1.00
32 Adam Oates .40 1.00
33 Brian Rolston .20 .50
34 Rob Blake .40 1.00
35 Steve Yzerman 2.50 6.00
36 Eric Lindros .50 1.25
37 Keith Tkachuk .50 1.25
38 Dan Cloutier .40 1.00
39 Chris Osgood .40 1.00
40 Zigmund Palffy .40 1.00
41 Jocelyn Thibault .40 1.00
42 Roman Turek .40 1.00
43 Ed Belfour .50 1.25
44 Adam Deadmarsh .20 .50
45 Marian Hossa .50 1.25
46 Owen Nolan .40 1.00
47 Curtis Joseph .50 1.25
48 Peter Bondra .40 1.00
49 Jeremy Roenick .60 1.50
50 Brendan Shanahan .50 1.25
51 Eric Daze .40 1.00
52 J-P Dumont .20 .50
53 Bill Guerin .40 1.00
54 Jukka Hentunen RC .75 2.00
55 Brian Leetch .40 1.00
56 Alexei Kovalev .40 1.00
57 Olaf Kolzig .40 1.00
58 Mike York .20 .50
59 Felix Potvin .50 1.25
60 Pierre Turgeon .40 1.00
61 Luc Robitaille .40 1.00
62 Sami Kapanen .20 .50
63 Byron Dafoe .40 1.00
64 Ryan Smyth .20 .50
65 John LeClair .50 1.25
66 Pavol Demitra .40 1.00
67 Alexei Yashin .20 .50
68 Vincent Lecavalier .50 1.25
69 Chris Drury .40 1.00
70 Mike Dunham .40 1.00
71 Patrick Lalime .40 1.00
72 Derek Morris .20 .50
73 Peter Forsberg 1.25 3.00
74 Sergei Fedorov .75 2.00
75 Mark Parrish .20 .50
76 Simon Gagne .50 1.25
77 Jeff O'Neill .20 .50
78 Alexander Mogilny .40 1.00
79 Johan Hedberg .40 1.00
80 Martin Brodeur 1.25 3.00
81 Claude Lemieux .20 .50
82 Mark Messier .50 1.25
83 Nicklas Lidstrom .50 1.25
84 Stu Barnes .20 .50
85 Steve Sullivan .20 .50
86 Jeff Friesen .20 .50
87 Brent Johnson .40 1.00
88 Marc Denis .40 1.00
89 Jason Arnott .20 .50
90 Brendan Morrison .40 1.00
91 Jere Lehtinen .40 1.00
92 Craig Conroy .20 .50
93 Petr Sykora .20 .50
94 Gary Roberts .40 1.00
95 Saku Koivu .50 1.25
96 Scott Stevens .40 1.00
97 Radek Bonk .20 .50
98 Roman Cechmanek .40 1.00
99 Robert Lang .20 .50
100 Tom Barrasso .40 1.00
101 Yanic Perreault .20 .50
102 Joe Nieuwendyk .40 1.00
103 Al MacInnis .40 1.00
104 Vincent Damphousse .20 .50
105 Anson Carter .40 1.00
106 Sergei Samsonov .40 1.00
107 Theo Fleury .20 .50
108 Mark Recchi .40 1.00
109 Marco Sturm .20 .50
110 Jiri Dopita RC .75 2.00
111 Tim Connolly .20 .50
112 Mike Fisher .20 .50
113 Alex Tanguay .40 1.00
114 Christian Berglund RC .75 2.00
115 Olivier Michaud RC 1.25 3.00
116 John Erskine RC .75 2.00
117 Mikael Samuelsson RC .75 2.00
118 Radek Martinek RC .75 2.00
119 Mark Rycroft RC .75 2.00
120 Mike Ribeiro .20 .50
121 Vaclav Pletka RC .75 2.00
122 Toni Dahlman RC .75 2.00
123 Brian Sutherby RC .75 2.00
124 Karel Rachunek .75 2.00
125 Robyn Regehr .75 2.00
126 Martin Erat RC .75 2.00
127 Nick Boynton .75 2.00
128 Nick Schultz RC .75 2.00
129 Timo Parssinen RC .75 2.00
130 Jaroslav Bednar RC .75 2.00
131 Roberto Luongo .60 1.50
132 Pascal Dupuis RC .75 2.00
133 Dave Tanabe .20 .50
134 Dany Heatley .60 1.50
135 Jeff Jillson RC .75 2.00
136 Marian Gaborik 1.00 2.50
137 Radim Vrbata .20 .50
138 Andrew Ference .20 .50
139 Rostislav Klesla .20 .50
140 Dan Blackburn RC .60 1.50
141 Andy Hilbert .20 .50
142 Martin Havlat .40 1.00
143 Niko Kapanen RC .75 2.00
144 Brenden Morrow .40 1.00
145 Scott Hartnell .20 .50
146 Raffi Torres RC 1.00 2.50
147 Vaclav Nedorost RC .75 2.00
148 Krys Kolanos RC .75 2.00
149 Kyle Calder .20 .50
150 Niklas Hagman RC .75 2.00
151 Brian Gionta .20 .50
152 Kristian Huselius RC .75 2.00
153 Mike Comrie .40 1.00
154 Ty Conklin RC .75 2.00
155 Justin Williams .20 .50
156 Erik Cole RC .75 2.00
157 Nikita Alexeev RC .75 2.00
158 Paul Mara .20 .50
159 Ilya Kovalchuk RC 4.00 10.00
160 David Legwand .40 1.00
161 Ilja Bryzgalov RC .75 2.00
162 Brad Richards .40 1.00
163 Evgeni Nabokov .40 1.00
164 Kris Beech .20 .50
165 Pavel Datsyuk RC 3.00 8.00

2001-02 Bowman YoungStars Gold

This 165-card set paralleled the base set, but card fronts had a gold glitter effect added. Each card was serial-numbered out of 250.

*GOLD: 1.5X TO 4X BASIC CARD
STATED PRINT RUN 250 SER.#'d SETS

2001-02 Bowman YoungStars Ice Cubed

This 165-card set paralleled the base set, but the card stock was approximately 3 times thicker and the card fronts were high gloss. These cards were inserted into every pack that did not contain a memorabilia card to prevent pack searching.

*ICE CUBED: .5X TO 1.25X BASIC CARD
ONE PER NON-MEMORABILIA PACK

2001-02 Bowman YoungStars Autographs

This 23-card set featured certified autographs of players who participated in the 2002 Topps/NHL Young Stars Game. All cards carried a YSA prefix.

STATED ODDS 1:478
ALL CARDS CARRY YSA PREFIX
AF Andrew Ference 10.00 25.00
BM Brenden Morrow 15.00 40.00
BR Brad Richards 25.00 60.00
DB Dan Blackburn 10.00 25.00
DH Dany Heatley 25.00 60.00
DL David Legwand 10.00 25.00
DT Dave Tanabe 10.00 25.00
IK Ilya Kovalchuk 30.00 80.00
JW Justin Williams 10.00 25.00
KC Kyle Calder 10.00 25.00
KH Kristian Huselius 10.00 25.00
KR Karel Rachunek 10.00 25.00
MC Mike Comrie 10.00 25.00
MF Mike Fisher 10.00 25.00
MG Marian Gaborik 25.00 60.00
MR Mike Ribeiro 10.00 25.00
NB Nick Boynton 10.00 25.00
PD Pavel Datsyuk 25.00 60.00
PM Paul Mara 10.00 25.00
RL Roberto Luongo 20.00 50.00
RR Robyn Regehr 10.00 25.00
SH Scott Hartnell 10.00 25.00
TC Tim Connolly 10.00 25.00

2001-02 Bowman YoungStars Autographed Puck Redemptions

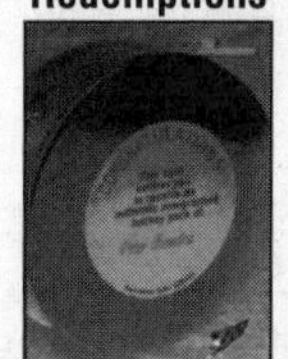

Inserted at overall odds of 1:186, this set of redemption cards entitled the holder to an autographed team logo puck. Redemption cards expired 5/30/03. The Ilya Kovalchuk redemption card was inserted at odds of 1:1978.

COMMON EXPIRED CARD .20 .50
OVERALL ODDS 1:186
ALL CARDS HAVE EXPIRED

2001-02 Bowman YoungStars Relics

This 69-card set featured swatches of jerseys and sticks used in the 2002 Topps/NHL Young Stars Game. Jersey swatches were

inserted at a rate of 1:6. Stick swatches were inserted at a rate of 1:193. Combo cards with both jersey and stick swatches were serial-numbered out of 25. All cards carried a FF prefix.

JERSEY STATED ODDS 1:6
STICK STATED ODDS 1:193
JSY/STK PRINT RUN 25 SER.#'d SETS
ALL CARDS CARRY FF PREFIX
JAF Andrew Ference 2.00 5.00
JBM Brenden Morrow 3.00 8.00
JBR Brad Richards 3.00 8.00
JDB Dan Blackburn 2.00 5.00
JDH Dany Heatley 4.00 10.00
JDL David Legwand 2.00 5.00
JDT Dave Tanabe 2.00 5.00
JIK Ilya Kovalchuk 6.00 15.00
JJW Justin Williams 2.00 5.00
JKC Kyle Calder 2.00 5.00
JKH Kristian Huselius 2.00 5.00
JKR Karel Rachunek 2.00 5.00
JMC Mike Comrie 2.00 5.00
JMF Mike Fisher 2.00 5.00
JMG Marian Gaborik 12.00 30.00
JMR Mike Ribeiro 2.00 5.00
JNB Nick Boynton 2.00 5.00
JPD Pavel Datsyuk 4.00 10.00
JPM Paul Mara 2.00 5.00
JRL Roberto Luongo 4.00 10.00
JRR Robyn Regehr 2.00 5.00
JSH Scott Hartnell 2.00 5.00
JTC Tim Connolly 2.00 5.00
SAF Andrew Ference 8.00 20.00
SBM Brenden Morrow 10.00 25.00
SBR Brad Richards 8.00 20.00
SDB Dan Blackburn 8.00 20.00
SDH Dany Heatley 10.00 25.00
SDL David Legwand 8.00 20.00
SDT Dave Tanabe 8.00 20.00
SIK Ilya Kovalchuk 20.00 50.00
SJW Justin Williams 10.00 25.00
SKC Kyle Calder 8.00 20.00
SKH Kristian Huselius 8.00 20.00
SKR Karel Rachunek 8.00 20.00
SMC Mike Comrie 8.00 20.00
SMF Mike Fisher 8.00 20.00
SMG Marian Gaborik 15.00 40.00
SMR Mike Ribeiro 8.00 20.00
SNB Nick Boynton 8.00 20.00
SPD Pavel Datsyuk 10.00 25.00
SPM Paul Mara 8.00 20.00
SRL Roberto Luongo 10.00 25.00
SRR Robyn Regehr 8.00 20.00
SSH Scott Hartnell 8.00 20.00
STC Tim Connolly 8.00 20.00
DSAF Andrew Ference 15.00 40.00
DSBM Brenden Morrow 15.00 40.00
DSBR Brad Richards 25.00 60.00
DSDB Dan Blackburn 25.00 60.00
DSDH Dany Heatley 50.00 125.00
DSDL David Legwand 12.00 30.00
DSDT Dave Tanabe 15.00 40.00
DSIK Ilya Kovalchuk 75.00 200.00
DSJW Justin Williams 15.00 40.00
DSKC Kyle Calder 15.00 40.00
DSKH Kristian Huselius 15.00 40.00
DSKR Karel Rachunek 15.00 40.00
DSMC Mike Comrie 25.00 60.00
DSMF Mike Fisher 15.00 40.00
DSMG Marian Gaborik 50.00 125.00
DSMR Mike Ribeiro 25.00 60.00
DSNB Nick Boynton 15.00 40.00
DSPD Pavel Datsyuk 50.00 125.00
DSPM Paul Mara 15.00 40.00
DSRL Roberto Luongo 40.00 100.00
DSRR Robyn Regehr 15.00 40.00
DSSH Scott Hartnell 15.00 40.00
DSTC Tim Connolly 15.00 40.00

2001-02 Bowman YoungStars Rivals

This 11-card set featured dual game-worn swatches from players who participated in the 2002 Topps Young Stars game. Each card was serial-numbered out of 250. All cards carried a FF prefix.

STATED PRINT RUN 250 SER.#'d SETS
ALL CARDS CARRY FF PREFIX
R1 Roberto Luongo 15.00 40.00
Dan Blackburn
R2 Karel Rachunek 12.00 30.00
Brad Richards
R3 Andrew Ference 10.00 25.00
Dave Tanabe
R4 Nick Boynton 12.00 30.00
Robyn Regehr
R5 M.Gaborik/I.Kovalchuk 20.00 50.00
R6 M.Comrie/D.Heatley 15.00 40.00
R7 Mike Ribeiro 10.00 25.00
Justin Williams
R8 Tim Connolly 10.00 25.00
David Legwand
R9 Mike Fisher 15.00 40.00
Pavel Datsyuk
R10 Scott Hartnell 12.00 30.00
Brenden Morrow
R11 Kristian Huselius 10.00 25.00
Kyle Calder

2002 Bowman Toronto Spring Expo

This 10-card set was part of a wrapper redemption program at the Topps booth during the 2002 Toronto Spring Expo. A total of 500 sets were made available, with the first 300 including a card autographed by top prospect Ilya Kovalchuk. The remaining 200 sets included a non-signed Kovalchuk card.

COMPLETE SET (10) 10.00 25.00
1 Ilya Kovalchuk 6.00 15.00
1B Ilya Kovalchuk AU 20.00 50.00
2 Curtis Joseph .80 2.00
3 Pavel Datsyuk 2.00 5.00
4 Jose Theodore .80 2.00
5 Jarome Iginla .40 1.00
6 Martin Brodeur .80 2.00
7 Patrick Roy 1.20 3.00
8 Dany Heatley 1.20 3.00
9 Dan Blackburn 1.20 3.00
10 Mats Sundin .40 1.00

2002-03 Bowman YoungStars

Released in April 2003, this 165-card set featured color action photos on black-bordered card fronts. The set highlighted the annual Topps YoungStars game held on All-Star weekend.

COMPLETE SET (165) 25.00 60.00
1 Nicklas Lidstrom .50 1.25
2 Martin Brodeur 1.25 3.00
3 Tony Amonte .40 1.00
4 Todd Bertuzzi .50 1.25
5 Joe Thornton .75 2.00
6 Ron Francis .40 1.00
7 Paul Kariya .50 1.25
8 Eric Lindros .50 1.25
9 John LeClair .50 1.25
10 Doug Weight .40 1.00
11 Jaromir Jagr .75 2.00
12 Mats Sundin .50 1.25
13 Saku Koivu .50 1.25
14 Peter Forsberg 1.25 3.00
15 Alexei Yashin .20 .50
16 Mike Modano .75 2.00
17 Chris Drury .40 1.00
18 Ryan Smyth .20 .50
19 Tomas Vokoun .40 1.00
20 Marian Hossa .50 1.25
21 Owen Nolan .40 1.00
22 Vincent Lecavalier .50 1.25
23 Jocelyn Thibault .40 1.00
24 Marc Denis .40 1.00
25 Roberto Luongo .60 1.50
26 Mario Lemieux 3.00 8.00
27 Keith Tkachuk .50 1.25
28 Radek Bonk .20 .50
29 Bill Guerin .40 1.00
30 Jason Allison .20 .50
31 Jeff O'Neill .20 .50
32 Alexei Zhamnov .20 .50
33 Scott Stevens .40 1.00
34 Mark Recchi .40 1.00
35 Alexander Mogilny .40 1.00
36 Olaf Kolzig .40 1.00
37 Sean Burke .40 1.00
38 Brett Hull .60 1.50
39 Andrew Cassels .20 .50
40 Jarome Iginla .60 1.50
41 Joe Sakic 1.00 2.50
42 Brian Leetch .40 1.00
43 Simon Gagne .50 1.25
44 Dan Cloutier .40 1.00
45 Brian Rolston .20 .50
46 Milan Hejduk .50 1.25
47 Steve Yzerman 2.50 6.00
48 Martin Havlat .40 1.00
49 Alexei Kovalev .40 1.00
50 Pavol Demitra .40 1.00
51 Mark Parrish .20 .50
52 Felix Potvin .50 1.25
53 Brenden Morrow .40 1.00
54 Steve Sullivan .20 .50
55 Patrick Roy 2.50 6.00
56 Manny Fernandez .40 1.00
57 Vincent Damphousse .20 .50
58 Michael Peca .20 .50
59 Anson Carter .40 1.00
60 Kevin Weekes .20 .50
61 Peter Bondra .40 1.00
62 Brad Richards .40 1.00
63 Johan Hedberg .40 1.00
64 Olli Jokinen .40 1.00
65 Miroslav Satan .40 1.00
66 Petr Sykora .20 .50
67 Al MacInnis .40 1.00
68 Markus Naslund .50 1.25
69 Mark Messier .50 1.25
70 Rob Blake .40 1.00
71 Sergei Samsonov .40 1.00
72 Jose Theodore .60 1.50
73 Eric Boguniecki .20 .50
74 Nikolai Khabibulin .50 1.25
75 Marco Sturm .20 .50
76 Patrick Lalime .40 1.00
77 Jeremy Roenick .60 1.50
78 John Madden .20 .50
79 Steve Rucchin .20 .50
80 Jere Lehtinen .40 1.00
81 Stu Barnes .20 .50
82 Roman Turek .40 1.00
83 Curtis Joseph .50 1.25
84 Evgeni Nabokov .40 1.00
85 Daniel Alfredsson .40 1.00
86 Brendan Morrison .40 1.00
87 Roman Cechmanek .40 1.00
88 Chris Osgood .40 1.00
89 Tommy Salo .40 1.00
90 Craig Conroy .20 .50
91 Zigmund Palffy .40 1.00
92 Pavel Bure .50 1.25
93 Brent Johnson .40 1.00
94 Ed Belfour .50 1.25
95 Shane Doan .20 .50
96 David Legwand .40 1.00
97 Sergei Fedorov .75 2.00
98 Jason Arnott .20 .50
99 Keith Primeau .20 .50
100 Martin St. Louis .40 1.00
101 Teemu Selanne .50 1.25
102 Patrik Elias .40 1.00
103 Ray Whitney .20 .50
104 Brendan Shanahan .50 1.25
105 Taylor Pyatt .20 .50
106 Niklas Hagman .20 .50
107 Henrik Tallinder .20 .50
108 Rostislav Klesla .20 .50
109 David Aebischer .40 1.00
110 Marcel Hossa .50 1.25
111 Pavel Brendl .20 .50
112 Ossi Vaananen .20 .50
113 Erik Cole .20 .50
114 Marian Gaborik 1.25 3.00
115 Alexander Svitov RC .75 2.00
116 Stanislav Chistov RC 1.00 2.50
117 Jordan Leopold RC .75 2.00
118 Ryan Miller RC 2.00 5.00
119 Kurt Sauer RC .75 2.00
120 Jonathan Cheechoo .20 .50
121 Radovan Somik RC .75 2.00
122 Anton Volchenkov RC .75 2.00
123 Pavel Datsyuk .50 1.25
124 Alexander Frolov RC 1.00 2.50
125 Steve Ott RC 1.00 2.50
126 Jason Spezza RC 4.00 10.00
127 Barret Jackman .40 1.00
128 Steve Eminger RC .75 2.00
129 Pascal Dupuis .20 .50
130 Brian Sutherby .20 .50
131 Dan Blackburn .40 1.00
132 Ron Hainsey RC .75 2.00
133 Jay Bouwmeester RC 1.00 2.50
134 Adam Hall RC .75 2.00
135 Mike Comrie .40 1.00
136 Nick Schultz .20 .50
137 Henrik Zetterberg RC 2.50 6.00
138 Radim Vrbata .20 .50
139 Jaroslav Svoboda .20 .50
140 Tyler Arnason .40 1.00
141 Dany Heatley .60 1.50
142 Ivan Huml .20 .50
143 Kristian Huselius .20 .50
144 Martin Gerber RC .75 2.00
145 Tom Koivisto RC .75 2.00
146 Mikael Tellqvist RC .75 2.00
147 Dennis Seidenberg RC 1.00 2.50
148 Mike Cammalleri RC .75 2.00
149 Niko Kapanen .20 .50
150 Shawn Thornton RC .75 2.00
151 Alexei Smirnov RC .75 2.00
152 Jamie Lundmark .20 .50
153 Shawn Horcoff .20 .50
154 Branko Radivojevic .20 .50
155 Rick Nash RC 3.00 8.00
156 Mattias Weinhandl .20 .50
157 Stephen Weiss .20 .50
158 Dmitri Bykov RC .75 2.00
159 Ales Hemsky RC 2.00 5.00
160 Chuck Kobasew RC .75 2.00
161 P-M Bouchard RC 1.00 2.50
162 Scottie Upshall RC 1.00 2.50
163 Patrick Sharp RC .75 2.00
164 Derrick Walser .20 .50
165 Ilya Kovalchuk .60 1.50
NNO Jerry Walsh .01 .01
Honorary Eqmt. Mgr.

2002-03 Bowman YoungStars Gold

Inserted at 1:11, this 165-card set paralleled the base ste but carried a gold "glitter" effect on the card fronts. Each card was serial-numbered out of 250 on the card back.

*STARS: 1.5X TO 4X BASE HI
*ROOKIES: .75X TO 2X
STATED ODDS 1:11
STATED PRINT RUN 250 SER.#'d SETS

2002-03 Bowman YoungStars Silver

Inserted one per non-memorabilia pack, this 165-card set paralleled the base set but carried a silver "glitter" effect on the card fronts.

*STARS: .5X TO1.25X BASIC CARD
*ROOKIES: .3X TO .75X
ONE PER PACK

2002-03 Bowman YoungStars Autographs

Inserted at 1:333, this 27-card set featured certified autographs of players who competed in the annual Topps YoungStars game.

STATED ODDS 1:333
STATED PRINT RUN 50 SER.#'d SETS
AF Alexander Frolov 25.00 60.00
AH Adam Hall 15.00 40.00
AS Alexander Svitov 15.00 40.00
AV Anton Volchenkov 15.00 40.00
BJ Barret Jackman 15.00 20.00
BR Branko Radivojevic 15.00 40.00
BS Brian Sutherby 15.00 40.00
DA David Aebischer 25.00 60.00
DS Dennis Seidenberg 15.00 40.00
HT Henrik Tallinder 15.00 40.00
JB Jay Bouwmeester 30.00 80.00
JL Jordan Leopold 15.00 40.00
MH Marcel Hossa 15.00 40.00
MW Mattias Weinhandl 15.00 40.00
NH Niklas Hagman 15.00 40.00
NK Niko Kapanen 15.00 40.00
NS Nick Schultz 15.00 40.00
OV Ossi Vaananen 15.00 40.00
PB Pavel Brendl 15.00 40.00
RK Rostislav Klesla 15.00 40.00
RM Ryan Miller 40.00 100.00
RN Rick Nash 40.00 100.00
SC Stanislav Chistov 15.00 40.00
SH Shawn Horcoff 15.00 40.00
SW Stephen Weiss 15.00 40.00
TA Tyler Arnason 20.00 50.00
TP Taylor Pyatt 15.00 40.00

2002-03 Bowman YoungStars Autograph Puck Redemptions

Inserted at 1:3262, this 28-card set entitled the bearer to an autographed puck of the featured player. Though the cards were not serial-numbered, it was announced that each player signed 10 pucks each.

STATED ODDS 1:3263
STATED PRINT RUN 10 SETS
NOT PRICED DUE TO SCARCITY
1 Rick Nash
2 Niko Kapanen
3 Shawn Horcoff
4 Marcel Hossa
5 Henrik Tallinder
6 Nick Schultz
7 Adam Hall
8 Brian Sutherby
9 Alexander Frolov
10 Alexander Svitov
11 Anton Volchenkov
12 Barrett Jackman
13 Branko Radivojevec
14 Brian Sutherby
15 David Aebischer
16 Dennis Seidenberg
17 Jay Bouwmeester
18 Jordan Leopold
19 Mattias Weinhandl
20 Ossi Vaananen
21 Niklas Hagman
22 Pavel Brendl
23 Rostislav Klesla
24 Ryan Miller
25 Stanislav Chistov
26 Stephen Weiss
27 Taylor Pyatt
28 Tyler Arnason

2002-03 Bowman YoungStars Jerseys

Inserted at 1:7, this 27-card set featured a swatch of player jersey worn during the annual Topps YoungStars game. All cards carried a "FFJ" prefix on the card back.

*MULT.COLOR SWATCH: .75X TO 1.5X HI
STATED ODDS 1:7
AF Alexander Frolov 4.00 10.00
AH Adam Hall 3.00 8.00
AS Alexander Svitov 3.00 8.00
AV Anton Volchenkov 3.00 8.00
BJ Barret Jackman 3.00 8.00
BR Branko Radivojevic 3.00 8.00
BS Brian Sutherby 3.00 8.00
DA David Aebischer 4.00 10.00
DS Dennis Seidenberg 3.00 8.00
HT Henrik Tallinder 3.00 8.00
JB Jay Bouwmeester 5.00 12.00
JL Jordan Leopold 3.00 8.00
MH Marcel Hossa 3.00 8.00
MW Mattias Weinhandl 3.00 8.00
NH Niklas Hagman 3.00 8.00
NK Niko Kapanen 3.00 8.00
NS Nick Schultz 3.00 8.00
OV Ossi Vaananen 3.00 8.00
PB Pavel Brendl 3.00 8.00
RK Rostislav Klesla 3.00 8.00
RM Ryan Miller 5.00 12.00
RN Rick Nash 8.00 20.00
SC Stanislav Chistov 3.00 8.00
SH Shawn Horcoff 3.00 8.00
SW Stephen Weiss 3.00 8.00
TA Tyler Arnason 3.00 8.00
TP Taylor Pyatt 3.00 8.00

2002-03 Bowman YoungStars Patches

Inserted at 1:333, this 27-card set paralleled the basic jersey set but the jersey swatch was replaced with a patch variation. All cards carried "FFP" prefix on the card back.

STATED ODDS 1:333
STATED PRINT RUN 50 SER.#'d SETS

2002-03 Bowman YoungStars Double Stuff

Inserted at 1:667, this 27-card set paralleled the basic jersey set but also included a piece of game-used stick. All cards carried a "FFDS" prefix on the card back.

STATED ODDS 1:667
STATED PRINT RUN 25 SER.#'d SETS

2002-03 Bowman YoungStars Triple Stuff

Inserted at 1:1203, this 27-card set paralleled the basic jersey set but also included a piece of game-used stick and a swatch of jersey patch. All cards carried a "FFTS" prefix on the card back and were serial-numbered out of 10. The cards are not priced due to scarcity.

STATED ODDS 1:1203
STATED PRINT RUN 10 SER.#'d SETS
NOT PRICED DUE TO SCARCITY

2002-03 Bowman YoungStars MVP Puck Relic

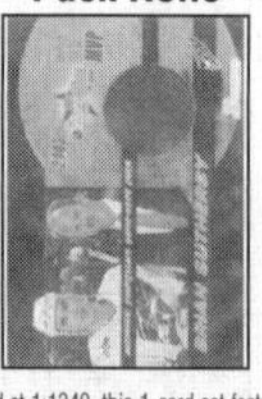

Inserted at 1:1340, this 1-card set featured a piece of puck used during the Topps YoungStars game during the 2003 NHL All-Star weekend. The card front pictured the game MVP, Brian Sutherby and Topps representative J.Peter Sawkins. Each card was serial-numbered out of 100.

STATED ODDS 1:1340
STATED PRINT RUN 100 SER.#'d SETS
1 Brian Sutherby 20.00 50.00

2002-03 Bowman YoungStars Rivals

Inserted at 1:139, this 13-card set featured game-worn jersey swatches of the two players pictured. All cards carry a "FFR" prefix on the card backs and were serial-numbered out of 250.

*MULT.COLOR SWATCH: .5X TO 1.25X HI
STATED ODDS 1:139
STATED PRINT RUN 250 SER.#'d SETS
AFAS Alexander Frolov 8.00 20.00
Alexander Svitov
AHMW Adam Hall 8.00 20.00
Mattias Weinhandl
BJDS Barret Jackman 8.00 20.00
Dennis Seidenberg
BRPB Branko Radivojevic 8.00 20.00
Pavel Brendl
DARM David Aebischer 10.00 25.00
Ryan Miller
JLTP Jordan Leopold 8.00 20.00
Taylor Pyatt
NKMH Niko Kapanen 8.00 20.00
Marcel Hossa
NSNH Nick Schultz 8.00 20.00
Niklas Hagman
OVHT Ossi Vaananen 8.00 20.00
Henrik Tallinder
RKAV Rostislav Klesla 8.00 20.00
Anton Volchenkov
RNJB R.Nash/J.Bouwmeester 10.00 25.00
SCSW Stanislav Chistov 8.00 20.00
Stephen Weiss
TABS Tyler Arnason 8.00 20.00
Brian Sutherby

2002-03 Bowman YoungStars Rivals Patches

Inserted at 1:3446, this 13-card set paralleled the basic Rivals set but each card carried two swatches of jersey patch on the card front. Each card was serial-numbered out of 10, and the cards are not priced due to scarcity.

STATED ODDS 1:3446
STATED PRINT RUN 10 SER.#'d SETS
NOT PRICED DUE TO SCARCITY

2002-03 Bowman YoungStars Sticks

Inserted at 1:167, this 27-card set featured pieces of game-used sticks from the annual Topps YoungStars game. Each card carried a "FFS" prefix on the card back.

STATED ODDS 1:167
AF Alexander Frolov 12.50 30.00
AH Adam Hall 8.00 20.00
AS Alexander Svitov 8.00 20.00
AV Anton Volchenkov 8.00 20.00
BJ Barret Jackman 8.00 20.00
BR Branko Radivojevic 8.00 20.00
BS Brian Sutherby 8.00 20.00
DA David Aebischer 15.00 40.00
DS Dennis Seidenberg 8.00 20.00
HT Henrik Tallinder 8.00 20.00
JB Jay Bouwmeester 12.50 30.00
JL Jordan Leopold 10.00 25.00
MH Marcel Hossa 8.00 20.00
MW Mattias Weinhandl 8.00 20.00
NH Niklas Hagman 8.00 20.00
NK Niko Kapanen 8.00 20.00
NS Nick Schultz 8.00 20.00
OV Ossi Vaananen 8.00 20.00
PB Pavel Brendl 8.00 20.00
RK Rostislav Klesla 8.00 20.00
RM Ryan Miller 15.00 40.00
RN Rick Nash 25.00 60.00
SC Stanislav Chistov 10.00 25.00
SH Shawn Horcoff 8.00 20.00
SW Stephen Weiss 8.00 20.00
TA Tyler Arnason 8.00 20.00
TP Taylor Pyatt 8.00 20.00

2003-04 Bowman

2003-04 Bowman/Bowman Chrome was packaged as one product consisting of two distinct brands.

COMP.SET w/o SP's (110) 20.00 40.00
1 Rick Nash .30 .75
2 Brian Leetch .20 .50
3 Pasi Nurminen .20 .50
4 Vincent Lecavalier .25 .60
5 Nicklas Lidstrom .25 .60
6 Barret Jackman .20 .50
7 Stanislav Chistov .12 .30
8 Patrick Marleau .20 .50
9 Paul Kariya .25 .60
10 Joe Thornton .40 1.00
11 Daniel Alfredsson .20 .50
12 Bill Guerin .20 .50
13 Tyler Arnason .20 .50
14 Dwayne Roloson .20 .50
15 Dany Heatley .30 .75
16 Brett Hull .30 .75
17 Ilya Kovalchuk .30 .75
18 Marian Hossa .25 .60
19 Joe Sakic .50 1.25
20 Henrik Zetterberg .25 .6
21 Peter Forsberg .60 1.5
22 Ales Kotalik .12 .3
23 Jamie Lundmark .12 .3
24 Brian Sutherby .12 .3
25 Patrik Elias .20 .5
26 Tomas Vokoun .20 .5
27 Jeremy Roenick .25 .6
28 Alexander Svitov .12 .3
29 Josef Vasicek .12 .3
30 Martin Brodeur .60 1.5
31 Chuck Kobasew .12 .3
32 Kyle Calder .12 .3
33 Daymond Langkow .20 .5
34 Marc Denis .20 .5
35 Sergei Samsonov .20 .5
36 Chris Pronger .20 .5
37 Sebastien Caron .20 .5
38 Markus Naslund .25 .6
39 Dominik Hasek .50 1.2
40 Alex Kovalev .20 .5
41 Roman Turek .20 .5
42 Petr Sykora .20 .5
43 Niko Kapanen .12 .3
44 Todd Bertuzzi .25 .6
45 Aleksey Morozov .12 .3
46 Ed Belfour .25 .6
47 David Aebischer .20 .5
48 Mike Johnson .12 .3
49 Jose Theodore .30 .7
50 Marian Gaborik .50 1.2
51 Evgeni Nabokov .20 .5
52 Eric Brewer .12 .3
53 Chris Osgood .20 .5
54 Sergei Gonchar .12 .3
55 Michael Rupp .12 .3
56 Olaf Kolzig .20 .5
57 Jan Bulis .12 .3
58 Dan Cloutier .20 .5
59 Nik Antropov .12 .3
60 Roberto Luongo .30 .7
61 Ales Hemsky .20 .5
62 Robert Esche .20 .5
63 Adam Hall .12 .3
64 Chris Drury .20 .5
65 Alyn McCauley .12 .3
66 Mario Lemieux .75 2.0
67 Pierre-Marc Bouchard .12 .3
68 Jaromir Jagr .40 1.0
69 Alexei Yashin .12 .3
70 Patrick Lalime .20 .5
71 Miroslav Satan .20 .5
72 Michael Peca .12 .3
73 Ziggy Palffy .20 .5
74 Jason Spezza .25 .6
75 Jay Bouwmeester .12 .3
76 Tommy Salo .20 .5
77 Simon Gagne .25 .6
78 Nick Schultz .12 .3
79 Scott Stevens .20 .5
80 Jarome Iginla .30 .7
81 Roman Cechmanek .20 .5
82 Alexander Mogilny .20 .5
83 Ron Francis .20 .5
84 Mike Dunham .20 .5
85 Glen Murray .12 .3
86 Rick DiPietro .20 .5
87 David Legwand .20 .5
88 Nikolai Khabibulin .25 .6
89 Mike Comrie .20 .5
90 Marty Turco .20 .5
91 Sergei Fedorov .30 .7
92 Brian Boucher .20 .5
93 Kristian Huselius .12 .3
94 Saku Koivu .25 .6
95 Justin Papineau .12 .3
96 Martin Biron .20 .5
97 Derian Hatcher .12 .3
98 Martin St. Louis .20 .5
99 Mike Modano .40 1.0
100 J-S Giguere .20 .5
101 Pavol Demitra .12 .3
102 Olli Jokinen .20 .5
103 Kevin Weekes .20 .5
104 Steve Shields .20 .5
105 Mats Sundin .25 .6
106 Artem Chubarov .12 .3
107 Alexander Frolov .12 .3
108 Jocelyn Thibault .20 .5
109 Martin Havlat .20 .5
110 Milan Hejduk .25 .6
111 Nathan Horton RC 2.50 6.0
112 Joffrey Lupul RC 1.50 4.0
113 Tuomo Ruutu RC 2.00 5.0
114 Jiri Hudler RC 1.50 4.0
115 Marek Svatos RC 4.00 10.0
116 Milan Michalek RC 1.25 3.0
117 Maxim Kondratiev RC 1.25 3.0
118 Dan Hamhuis RC 1.25 3.0
119 Boyd Gordon RC 1.25 3.0
120 Eric Staal RC 8.00 20.0
121 Dan Fritsche RC 1.25 3.0
122 Matthew Spiller RC 1.25 3.0
123 Ryan Malone RC 1.50 4.0
124 Cody McCormick RC 1.25 3.0
125 Tom Preissing RC 1.25 3.0
126 Dominic Moore RC 1.25 3.0
127 Matthew Lombardi RC 1.25 3.0
128 Chris Higgins RC 2.00 5.0
129 Pavel Vorobiev RC 1.25 3.0
130 Wade Brookbank RC 1.25 3.0
131 Tim Gleason RC 1.25 3.0
132 Matt Murley RC 1.25 3.0
133 Andrew Peters RC 1.25 3.0
134 Gregory Campbell RC 1.25 3.0
135 John-Michael Liles RC 1.25 3.0
136 Sergei Zinovjev RC 1.25 3.0
137 Alexander Semin RC 2.00 5.0
138 Lasse Kukkonen RC 1.25 3.0
139 Marek Zidlicky RC 1.25 3.0
140 Tony Salmelainen RC 1.25 3.0
141 Travis Moen RC 1.25 3.0
142 Nikolai Zherdev RC 2.00 5.0
143 Paul Martin RC 1.25 3.0
144 Peter Sarno RC 1.25 3.0
145 David Hale RC 1.25 3.0
146 Dustin Brown RC 1.25 3.0
147 Matt Stajan AU RC 10.00 25.0
148 Peter Sejna AU RC 6.00 15.0
149 S.Bergenheim AU RC 6.00 15.0
150 Antti Miettinen AU RC 6.00 15.0

51 Patrice Bergeron AU RC 20.00 50.00
52 Marc-Andre Fleury AU RC 40.00 80.00
53 Antoine Vermette AU RC 6.00 15.00
54 Jordin Tootoo AU RC 10.00 25.00
55 Rick Mrozik AU RC 6.00 15.00
56 Joni Pitkanen AU RC 10.00 25.00

2003-04 Bowman Gold

STARS: 2.5X TO 6X BASE HI
ROOKIES 111-146: .2X TO .5X
ROOKIES 147-156: .08X TO .2X
NE PER PACK

2003-04 Bowman Future Fabrics

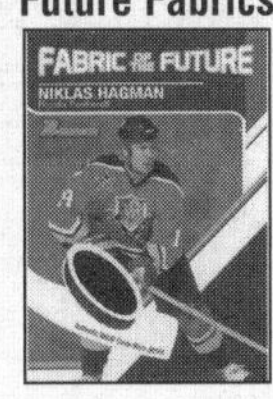

MULT.COLOR SWATCH: .75X TO 1.5X
TATED ODDS 1:178
F-MW Mattias Weinhandl 3.00 8.00
F-SHO Shawn Horcoff 3.00 8.00
F-AF Alexander Frolov 5.00 12.00
F-DA David Aebischer 5.00 12.00
F-KH Kristian Huselius 3.00 8.00
F-AS Alexander Svitov 3.00 8.00
F-RM Ryan Miller 8.00 20.00
F-TA Tyler Arnason 3.00 8.00
F-AH Adam Hall 3.00 8.00
F-NH Niklas Hagman 3.00 8.00
F-JL Jordan Leopold 3.00 8.00
F-SH Scott Hartnell 3.00 8.00
F-SC Stanislav Chistov 3.00 8.00
F-BS Brian Sutherby 3.00 8.00
F-JB Jay Bouwmeester 3.00 8.00
F-NK Niko Kapanen 3.00 8.00
F-DB Dan Blackburn 4.00 10.00
F-BJ Barret Jackman 3.00 8.00
F-JLU Jamie Lundmark 3.00 8.00
F-JS Jason Spezza 8.00 20.00

2003-04 Bowman Future Fabric Patches

TATED ODDS 1:437
RINT RUN 20 SER.#'d SETS
OT PRICED DUE TO SCRACITY

2003-04 Bowman Future Rivals

MULT.COLOR SWATCH .75X TO 1.5X
TATED ODDS 1:187
K T.Arnason/N.Kapanen 4.00 10.00
T D.Aebischer/M.Turco 8.00 20.00
H S.Chistov/M.Hejduk 4.00 10.00
I M.Comrie/J.Iginla 8.00 20.00
H M.Gaborik/D.Heatley 12.00 30.00
D M.Hejduk/P.Datsyuk 8.00 20.00
G K.Huselius/S.Gagne 4.00 10.00
H S.Horcoff/A.Hall 4.00 10.00
F B.Jackman/A.Frolov 4.00 10.00
D N.Kapanen/P.Datsyuk 6.00 15.00
K V. Lecavalier/I.Kovalchuk 10.00 25.00
T P.Lalime/J.Theodore 6.00 15.00
L R.Miller/R.Luongo 10.00 25.00
M P.Marleau/B.Morrison 6.00 15.00
C R.Nash/S.Chistov 10.00 25.00
G R.Nash/M.Gaborik 12.00 30.00
S B.Richards/B.Sutherby 6.00 15.00
H J.Spezza/N.Hagman 8.00 20.00
L M. Weinhandl/J.Lundmark 4.00 10.00

2003-04 Bowman Future Rivals Patches

TATED ODDS 1:450
RINT RUN 20 SER.#'d SETS
OT PRICED DUE TO SCARCITY

2003-04 Bowman Goal to Goal

is 9-card set featured swatches of game-orn jerseys of both players featured along th a piece of all-star goal net.
TATED ODDS 1:299
Y D.Alfredsson/A.Yashin 12.00 30.00
C M.Gaborik/S.Chistov 20.00 50.00
HG D.Heatley/B.Guerin 12.00 30.00
JH J.Jagr/M.Hejduk 20.00 50.00
KN N.Kapanen/R.Nash 25.00 60.00
MN M.Modano/M.Naslund 15.00 40.00
SG J.Spezza/S.Gagne 15.00 40.00
SI M.Satan/J.Iginla 12.00 30.00
TK J.Thornton/I.Kovalchuk 25.00 60.00

2003-04 Bowman Premier Performance

*MULT.COLOR SWATCH: .75X TO 1.5X
STATED ODDS 1:28
PP-JL Joffrey Lupul 3.00 8.00
PP-AV Antoine Vermette 2.50 6.00
PP-AM Antti Miettinen 2.50 6.00
PP-DH Dan Hamhuis 2.50 6.00
PP-MS Marek Svatos 10.00 25.00
PP-PS Peter Sejna 2.50 6.00
PP-MST0 Matt Stajan 4.00 10.00
PP-NH Nathan Horton 4.00 10.00
PP-JP Joni Pitkanen 2.50 6.00
PP-SB Sean Bergenheim 2.50 6.00

2003-04 Bowman Premier Performance Patches

*PATCHES: .75X TO 2X JSY HI
PRINT RUN 50 SER.#'d SETS

2003-04 Bowman Signs of the Future

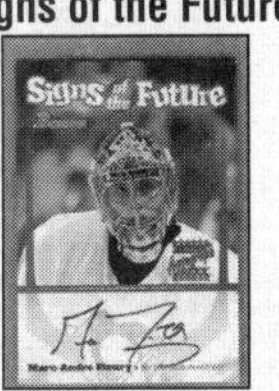

STATED ODDS 1:81
SOF-ES Eric Staal 8.00 20.00
SOF-AM Antti Miettinen 5.00 12.00
SOF-PS Peter Sejna 5.00 12.00
SOF-MAF Marc-Andre Fleury 15.00 40.00
SOF-MZ Miroslav Zalesak 5.00 12.00
SOF-MS Matt Stajan 8.00 20.00
SOF-AV Antoine Vermette 5.00 12.00
SOF-RN Rick Nash 10.00 25.00
SOF-PMB Pierre-Marc Bouchard 5.00 12.00

2003-04 Bowman Chrome

2003-04 Bowman/Bowman Chrome was packaged as one product consisting of two distinct brands.
COMP.SET w/o SP's (110) 30.00 60.00
RC AUTO PRINT RUN 250 SER.#'d SETS
1 Rick Nash .50 1.25
2 Brian Leetch .30 .75
3 Pasi Nurminen .30 .75
4 Vincent Lecavalier .40 1.00
5 Nicklas Lidstrom .40 1.00
6 Barret Jackman .30 .75
7 Stanislav Chistov .20 .50
8 Patrick Marleau .30 .75
9 Paul Kariya .40 1.00
10 Joe Thornton .60 1.50
11 Daniel Alfredsson .30 .75
12 Bill Guerin .30 .75
13 Tyler Arnason .30 .75
14 Dwayne Roloson .30 .75
15 Dany Heatley .50 1.25
16 Brett Hull .50 1.25
17 Ilya Kovalchuk .50 1.25
18 Marian Hossa .40 1.00
19 Joe Sakic .75 2.00
20 Henrik Zetterberg .40 1.00
21 Peter Forsberg 1.00 2.50
22 Ales Kotalik .20 .50
23 Jamie Lundmark .20 .50
24 Brian Sutherby .20 .50
25 Patrik Elias .30 .75
26 Tomas Vokoun .30 .75
27 Jeremy Roenick .50 1.25
28 Alexander Svitov .20 .50
29 Josef Vasicek .20 .50
30 Martin Brodeur 1.00 2.50
31 Chuck Kobasew .20 .50
32 Kyle Calder .20 .50
33 Daymond Langkow .30 .75
34 Marc Denis .30 .75
35 Sergei Samsonov .30 .75
36 Chris Pronger .30 .75
37 Sebastien Caron .30 .75
38 Markus Naslund .40 1.00
39 Dominik Hasek .75 2.00
40 Alex Kovalev .30 .75
41 Roman Turek .30 .75
42 Petr Sykora .30 .75
43 Niko Kapanen .20 .50
44 Todd Bertuzzi .40 1.00
45 Aleksey Morozov .20 .50
46 Ed Belfour .40 1.00
47 David Aebischer .30 .75
48 Mike Johnson .20 .50
49 Jose Theodore .50 1.25
50 Marian Gaborik .75 2.00
51 Evgeni Nabokov .30 .75
52 Eric Brewer .20 .50
53 Chris Osgood .30 .75
54 Sergei Gonchar .20 .50
55 Michael Rupp .20 .50
56 Olaf Kolzig .30 .75
57 Jan Bulis .20 .50
58 Dan Cloutier .30 .75
59 Nik Antropov .20 .50
60 Roberto Luongo .50 1.25
61 Ales Hemsky .30 .75
62 Robert Esche .30 .75
63 Adam Hall .20 .50
64 Chris Drury .30 .75
65 Alyn McCauley .20 .50
66 Mario Lemieux 1.25 3.00
67 Pierre-Marc Bouchard .20 .50
68 Jaromir Jagr .60 1.50
69 Alexei Yashin .20 .50
70 Patrick Lalime .30 .75
71 Miroslav Satan .30 .75
72 Michael Peca .20 .50
73 Ziggy Palffy .30 .75
74 Jason Spezza .40 1.00
75 Jay Bouwmeester .20 .50
76 Tommy Salo .30 .75
77 Simon Gagne .40 1.00
78 Nick Schultz .20 .50
79 Scott Stevens .30 .75
80 Jarome Iginla .50 1.25
81 Roman Cechmanek .30 .75
82 Alexander Mogilny .30 .75
83 Ron Francis .30 .75
84 Mike Dunham .30 .75
85 Glen Murray .20 .50
86 Rick DiPietro .30 .75
87 David Legwand .30 .75
88 Nikolai Khabibulin .40 1.00
89 Mike Comrie .30 .75
90 Marty Turco .30 .75
91 Sergei Fedorov .50 1.25
92 Brian Boucher .30 .75
93 Kristian Huselius .20 .50
94 Saku Koivu .40 1.00
95 Justin Papineau .20 .50
96 Martin Biron .30 .75
97 Derian Hatcher .20 .50
98 Martin St. Louis .30 .75
99 Mike Modano .60 1.50
100 Jean-Sebastien Giguere .30 .75
101 Pavol Demitra .20 .50
102 Olli Jokinen .30 .75
103 Kevin Weekes .30 .75
104 Steve Shields .30 .75
105 Mats Sundin .40 1.00
106 Artem Chubarov .20 .50
107 Alexander Frolov .20 .50
108 Jocelyn Thibault .30 .75
109 Martin Havlat .30 .75
110 Milan Hejduk .40 1.00
111 Nathan Horton RC 3.00 8.00
112 Joffrey Lupul RC 2.00 5.00
113 Tuomo Ruutu RC 2.50 6.00
114 Jiri Hudler RC 2.00 5.00
115 Marek Svatos RC 3.00 8.00
116 Milan Michalek RC 1.50 4.00
117 Maxim Kondratiev RC 1.50 4.00
118 Dan Hamhuis RC 1.50 4.00
119 Boyd Gordon RC 1.50 4.00
120 Eric Staal RC 10.00 25.00
121 Dan Fritsche RC 1.50 4.00
122 Matthew Spiller RC 1.50 4.00
123 Ryan Malone RC 1.50 4.00
124 Cody McCormick RC 1.50 4.00
125 Tom Preissing RC 1.50 4.00
126 Dominic Moore RC 1.50 4.00
127 Matthew Lombardi RC 2.00 5.00
128 Chris Higgins RC 3.00 8.00
129 Pavel Vorobiev RC 1.50 4.00
130 Wade Brookbank RC 1.50 4.00
131 Tim Gleason RC 1.50 4.00
132 Matt Murley RC 1.50 4.00
133 Andrew Peters RC 1.50 4.00
134 Gregory Campbell RC 1.50 4.00
135 John-Michael Liles RC 1.50 4.00
136 Sergei Zinovjev RC 1.50 4.00
137 Alexander Semin RC 2.50 6.00
138 Lasse Kukkonen RC 1.50 4.00
139 Marek Zidlicky RC 1.50 4.00
140 Tony Salmelainen RC 1.50 4.00
141 Travis Moen RC 1.50 4.00
142 Nikolai Zherdev RC 2.00 5.00
143 Paul Martin RC 1.50 4.00
144 Peter Sarno RC 1.50 4.00
145 David Hale RC 1.50 4.00
146 Dustin Brown RC 1.50 4.00
147 Matt Stajan AU RC 15.00 40.00
148 Peter Sejna AU RC 8.00 20.00
149 Sean Bergenheim AU RC 8.00 20.00
150 Antti Miettinen AU RC 8.00 20.00
151 Patrice Bergeron AU RC 30.00 80.00
152 Marc-Andre Fleury AU RC 50.00 125.00
153 Antoine Vermette AU RC 8.00 20.00
154 Jordin Tootoo AU RC 15.00 40.00
155 Rick Mrozik AU RC 8.00 20.00
156 Joni Pitkanen AU RC 10.00 25.00

2003-04 Bowman Chrome Refractors

*STARS: 3X TO 8X BASE HI
*ROOKIES 111-146: .6X TO 1.5X
1-146 PRINT RUN 300 SER.#'d SETS
*ROOKIE AU: .5X TO 1.25X
ROOKIE AU PRINT RUN 50 SER.#'d SETS
152 Marc-Andre Fleury 60.00 150.00

2003-04 Bowman Chrome Gold Refractors

*STARS: 6X TO 15X
*ROOKIES 111-146: 1.25X TO 3X

2003-04 Bowman Chrome Xfractors

*STARS: 4X TO 10X BASE HI
*ROOKIES 111-146: .75X TO 2X
CARDS 1-146 PRINT RUN 150 SER.#'d SETS
*ROOKIES AU: .6X TO 1.5X
ROOKIE AU PRINT RUN 25 SER.#'d SETS
152 Marc-Andre Fleury AU 100.00 250.00

1938-39 Bruins Garden Magazine Supplement

These large (8 X 10") photos were printed on very thin, sepia-toned stock and inserted in game programs issued at the Boston Gardens. Any additional information would be appreciated.

COMPLETE SET (9) 350.00 700.00
1 Red Beattie 20.00 40.00
2 Walter Galbraith 20.00 40.00
3 Lionel Hitchman 40.00 80.00
4 Joseph Lamb 20.00 40.00
5 Harry Oliver 20.00 40.00
6 Art Ross 75.00 150.00
7 Eddie Shore 125.00 250.00
8 Nels Stewart 40.00 80.00
9 Tiny Thompson 50.00 100.00

1955-56 Bruins Photos

These black and white photos measure approximately 6" x 8" and were distributed in an envelope bearing the Bruins logo.

COMPLETE SET (17) 100.00 200.00
1 Bob Armstrong 5.00 10.00
2 Marcel Bonin 5.00 10.00
3 Leo Boivin 7.50 15.00
4 Real Chevrefils 5.00 10.00
5 Fern Flaman 7.50 15.00
6 Cal Gardner 2.50 5.00
7 Lionel Heinrich 2.50 5.00
8 Leo Labine 7.50 15.00
9 Hal Laycoe 5.00 10.00
10 Fleming Mackell 5.00 10.00
11 Don McKenney 5.00 10.00
12 Doug Mohns 7.50 15.00
13 Bill Quackenbush 7.50 15.00
14 Johnny Peirson 5.00 10.00
15 Terry Sawchuk 25.00 50.00
16 Vic Stasiuk 5.00 10.00
17 Jerry Toppazzini 5.00 10.00
NNO Envelope 10.00 20.00

1957-58 Bruins Photos

This 14-card set measures approximately 6 5/8" by 8 1/8".

COMPLETE SET (20) 100.00 200.00
1 Bob Armstrong 5.00 10.00
2 Jack Bionda 2.50 5.00
3 Leo Boivin 5.00 10.00
4 Johnny Bucyk 25.00 50.00
5 Real Chevrefils 4.00 8.00
6 Fern Flaman 6.00 12.00
7 Jean-Guy Gendron 5.00 10.00
8 Larry Hillman 5.00 10.00
9 Bronco Horvath 6.00 12.00
10 Norm Johnson 6.00 12.00
11 Leo Labine 5.00 10.00
12 Fleming Mackell 4.00 8.00
13 Don McKenney 4.00 8.00
14 Doug Mohns 6.00 12.00
15 Jim Morrison 2.50 5.00
16 Johnny Peirson 2.50 5.00
17 Larry Regan 2.50 5.00
18 Milt Schmidt CO 10.00 20.00
19 Vic Stasiuk 6.00 12.00
20 Jerry Toppazzini 2.50 5.00

1958-59 Bruins Photos

These 6X8 photos were issued by the team.

COMPLETE SET (15) 75.00 150.00
1 Bob Armstrong 5.00 10.00
2 Johnny Bucyk 15.00 30.00
3 Real Chevrefils 5.00 10.00
4 Fern Flaman 6.00 12.00
5 Jean-Guy Gendron 5.00 10.00
6 Larry Hillman 5.00 10.00
7 Leo Labine 5.00 10.00
8 Fleming MacKell 5.00 10.00
9 Don McKenney 5.00 10.00
10 Jim Morrison 5.00 10.00
11 Larry Regan 5.00 10.00
12 Dutch Reibel 5.00 10.00
13 Don Simmons 10.00 20.00
14 Vic Stasiuk 5.00 10.00
15 Jerry Toppazzini 5.00 10.00

1970-71 Bruins Postcards

Cards are standard postcard size and were issued in a binder with perforations.

COMPLETE SET (21) 75.00 150.00
1 Team Photo 2.50 5.00
2 Ed Johnston 2.50 5.00
3 Gerry Cheevers 7.50 15.00
4 Wayne Cashman 2.50 5.00
5 Garnet Bailey 5.00 10.00
6 Don Marcotte 1.50 3.00
7 John Bucyk 5.00 10.00
8 Wayne Carleton 1.50 3.00
9 Reggie Leach 4.00 8.00
10 Ken Hodge 2.50 5.00
11 Ed Westfall 2.00 4.00
12 John McKenzie 2.00 4.00
13 Phil Esposito 10.00 20.00
14 Fred Stanfield 1.50 3.00
15 Derek Sanderson 5.00 10.00
16 Bobby Orr 25.00 50.00
17 Dallas Smith 2.00 4.00
18 Rick Smith 1.50 3.00
19 Ted Green 2.00 4.00
20 Don Awrey 1.50 3.00
21 Tom Johnson CO 2.00 4.00

1970-71 Bruins Team Issue

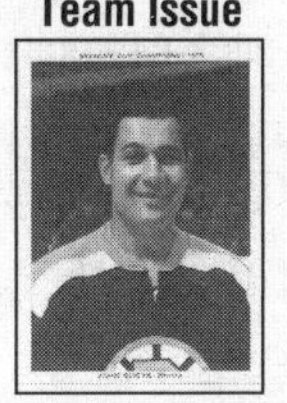

This set of 18 team-issue photos commemorates the Boston Bruins as 1970 Stanley Cup Champions. The set was issued in two different photo packs of nine photos each. The photos measure approximately 6" by 8".

COMPLETE SET (18) 50.00 100.00
1 Garnet Bailey 5.00 10.00
2 Johnny Bucyk 5.00 10.00
3 Gary Doak 2.00 4.00
4 Phil Esposito 10.00 20.00
5 Ed Johnston 2.50 5.00
6 Don Marcotte 1.50 3.00
7 Derek Sanderson 5.00 10.00
8 Dallas Smith 2.00 4.00
9 Ed Westfall 2.00 4.00
10 Don Awrey 1.50 3.00
11 Wayne Carleton 1.50 3.00
12 Wayne Cashman 2.50 5.00
13 Gerry Cheevers 7.50 15.00
14 Ken Hodge 2.50 5.00
15 John McKenzie 2.00 4.00
16 Bobby Orr 25.00 50.00
17 Rick Smith 1.50 3.00
18 Fred Stanfield 1.50 3.00

1971-72 Bruins Postcards

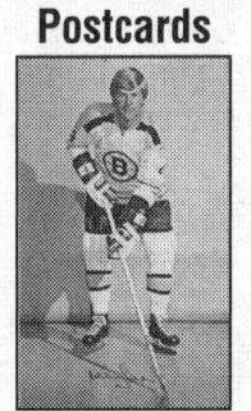

Originally issued in booklet form, these 20 photo cards measure 3 1/2" by 5 1/2". The cards have perforated tops that allow them to be detached from the yellow booklet, which bears the Bruins logo and crossed hockey sticks on its front.

COMPLETE SET (20) 50.00 100.00
1 Ed Johnston 2.00 4.00
2 Bobby Orr 20.00 40.00
3 Teddy Green 1.50 3.00
4 Phil Esposito 10.00 20.00
5 Ken Hodge 2.00 4.00
6 John Bucyk 4.00 8.00
7 Rick Smith 1.00 2.00
8 Mike Walton 1.50 3.00
9 Wayne Cashman 2.00 4.00
10 Ace Bailey 5.00 10.00
11 Derek Sanderson 4.00 8.00
12 Fred Stanfield 1.00 2.00
13 Ed Westfall 1.50 3.00
14 John McKenzie 1.50 3.00
15 Dallas Smith 1.00 2.00
16 Don Marcotte 1.00 2.00
17 Garry Peters 1.00 2.00
18 Don Awrey 1.00 2.00
19 Reggie Leach 2.00 4.00
20 Gerry Cheevers 5.00 10.00

1983-84 Bruins Team Issue

This 17-card set measures approximately 3 1/8" by 4 1/8".

COMPLETE SET (17) 10.00 25.00
1 Ray Bourque 4.00 10.00
2 Bruce Crowder .40 1.00
3 Keith Crowder .60 1.50
4 Luc Dufour .40 1.00
5 Tom Fergus .40 1.00
6 Randy Hillier .40 1.00
7 Steve Kasper .60 1.50
8 Gord Kluzak .60 1.50
9 Mike Krushelnyski .40 1.00
10 Peter McNab .60 1.50
11 Rick Middleton 1.20 3.00
12 Mike Milbury .60 1.50
13 Mike O'Connell .60 1.50
14 Terry O'Reilly .80 2.00
15 Brad Palmer .40 1.00
16 Barry Pederson .60 1.50
17 Pete Peeters .80 2.00

1984-85 Bruins Postcards

This set features 20 postcard-size issues of the Bruins. It is believed they were issued as giveaways at player signing appearances.

COMPLETE SET (20) 12.00 30.00
1 Ray Bourque 3.20 8.00
2 Lyndon Byers 1.20 3.00
3 Geoff Courtnall .80 2.00
4 Keith Crowder .60 1.50
5 Tom Fergus .40 1.00
6 Mike Gillis .40 1.00
7 Steve Kasper .60 1.50
8 Doug Keans .60 1.50
9 Gord Kluzak .60 1.50
10 Ken Linseman .60 1.50
11 Nevin Markwart .60 1.50
12 Rick Middleton 1.20 3.00
13 Mike Milbury .60 1.50
14 Mike O'Connell .40 1.00
15 Terry O'Reilly 1.20 3.00
16 Barry Pederson .60 1.50
17 Pete Peeters .80 2.00
18 Charlie Simmer .60 1.50
19 Lou Sleigher .60 1.50
20 Mats Thelin .40 1.00

1988-89 Bruins Sports Action

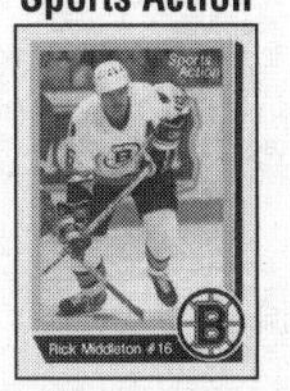

This 24-card set measures the standard size and was issued by Sports Action.

COMPLETE SET (24) 6.00 15.00
1 Ray Bourque 1.20 3.00
2 Randy Burridge .16 .40
3 Lyndon Byers .40 1.00
4 Keith Crowder .20 .50
5 Craig Janney .20 .50
6 Bob Joyce .10 .25
7 Steve Kasper .20 .50
8 Gord Kluzak .20 .50
9 Reed Larson .10 .25
10 Rejean Lemelin .30 .75
11 Ken Linseman .20 .50
12 Tom McCarthy .10 .25
13 Rick Middleton .60 1.50
14 Jay Miller .40 1.00
15 Andy Moog .60 1.50
16 Cam Neely 1.00 2.50
17 Terry O'Reilly CO .20 .50
18 Allen Pederson .10 .25
19 Willi Plett .10 .25
20 Bob Sweeney .10 .25
21 Michael Thelven .10 .25
22 Glen Wesley .20 .50
23 Bob Joyce .20 .50
Craig Janney
24 Dynamic Duo .80 2.00
Ray Bourque
Cam Neely

1988-89 Bruins Postcards

This 20-postcard set of the Boston Bruins was produced by Sports Action Marketing.

COMPLETE SET (20) 8.00 20.00
1 Ray Bourque 1.60 4.00
2 Andy Brickley .20 .50
3 John Carter .20 .50
4 Garry Galley .30 .75
5 Craig Janney .60 1.50
6 Greg Johnston .20 .50
7 Bob Joyce .20 .50
8 Steve Kasper .30 .75
9 Gord Kluzak .30 .75
10 Rejean Lemelin .40 1.00
11 Ken Linseman .30 .75
12 Rick Middleton .60 1.50
13 Andy Moog 1.00 2.50
14 Cam Neely 1.60 4.00
15 Bill O'Dwyer .20 .50
16 Allen Pedersen .20 .50
17 Stephane Quintal .20 .50
18 Bob Sweeney .20 .50
19 Michael Thelven .20 .50
20 Glen Wesley .40 1.00

1989-90 Bruins Sports Action

This standard sized 24-card set was issued by Sports Action.

COMPLETE SET (24) 4.80 12.00
1 Ray Bourque .80 2.00
2 Andy Brickley .20 .50
3 Randy Burridge .20 .50
4 Lyndon Byers .20 .50

5 Bob Carpenter .20 .50
6 John Carter .20 .50
7 Rob Cimetta .20 .50
8 Garry Galley .30 .75
9 Bob Gould .20 .50
10 Greg Hawgood .20 .50
11 Craig Janney .30 .75
12 Bob Joyce .20 .50
13 Rejean Lemelin .30 .75
14 Ken Linseman .20 .50
15 Andy Moog .40 1.00
16 Nevin Markwart .20 .50
17 Cam Neely .60 1.50
18 Allen Pedersen .20 .50
19 Stephane Quintal .20 .50
20 Bob Sweeney .20 .50
21 Michael Thelven .20 .50
22 Glen Wesley .30 .75
23 Bruins Top 10 Scorers .40 1.00
24 Stanley Cup Champions .40 1.00

1989-90 Bruins Sports Action Update

This 12-card standard-size set was issued by Sports Action.

COMPLETE SET (12) 3.20 8.00
1 Ray Bourque .80 2.00
2 Dave Christian .30 .75
3 Peter Douris .20 .50
4 Gord Kluzak .30 .75
5 Brian Lawton .20 .50
6 Mike Millar .20 .50
7 Dave Poulin .30 .75
8 Brian Propp .30 .75
9 Don Sweeney .30 .75
10 Graeme Townshend .20 .50
11 Jim Wiemer .20 .50
12 Bruins Leaders .80 2.00
Ray Bourque
Rejean Lemelin
Cam Neely

1990-91 Bruins Sports Action

The Markwart and Quintal cards were reportedly only issued in the first print run of 400 24-card sets. In the second and larger print run, these cards were replaced by Byers and Hodge. Consequently, the Markwart and Quintal cards are more difficult to find than the Byers and Hodge cards.

COMPLETE SET (26) 8.00 20.00
1 Bob Beers .20 .50
2 Ray Bourque 1.20 3.00
3 Andy Brickley .20 .50
4 Randy Burridge .24 .60
5 John Byce .20 .50
6 Lyndon Byers .30 .75
7 Bob Carpenter .20 .50
8 John Carter .20 .50
9 Dave Christian .24 .60
10 Peter Douris .20 .50
11 Garry Galley .20 .50
12 Ken Hodge Jr. .20 .50
13 Craig Janney .30 .75
14 Rejean Lemelin .30 .75
15 Nevin Markwart SP 1.20 3.00
16 Andy Moog .60 1.50
17 Cam Neely .80 2.00
18 Chris Nilan .24 .60
19 Allen Pedersen .20 .50
20 Dave Poulin .24 .60
21 Stephane Quintal SP 1.20 3.00
22 Bob Sweeney .20 .50
23 Don Sweeney .24 .60
24 Wes Walz .20 .50
25 Glen Wesley .30 .75
26 Rejean Lemelin .40 1.00
Andy Moog

1991-92 Bruins Sports Action

This 24-card standard-size set was issued by Sports Action.

COMPLETE SET (24) 4.80 12.00
1 Brent Ashton .16 .40
2 Bob Beers .16 .40
3 Daniel Berthiaume .20 .50
4 Ray Bourque 1.00 2.50

5 Bob Carpenter	.16	.40
6 Peter Douris	.10	.25
7 Glen Featherstone	.10	.25
8 Ken Hodge Jr.	.10	.25
9 Jeff Lazaro	.10	.25
10 Stephen Leach	.16	.40
11 Andy Moog	.40	1.00
12 Gord Murphy	.10	.25
13 Cam Neely	.80	2.00
14 Adam Oates	.40	1.00
15 Dave Poulin	.20	.50
16 David Reid	.16	.40
17 Vladimir Ruzicka	.16	.40
18 Bob Sweeney	.16	.40
19 Don Sweeney	.16	.40
20 Jim Vesey	.10	.25
21 Glen Wesley	.16	.40
22 Jim Wiemer	.10	.25
23 Chris Winnes	.10	.25
24 The Big Three	.60	1.50
Andy Moog		
Ray Bourque		
Cam Neely		

1991-92 Bruins Sports Action Legends

COMPLETE SET (36)	6.00	15.00
1 Bob Armstrong	.10	.25
2 Leo Boivin	.16	.40
3 Ray Bourque	.80	2.00
4 Frank Brimsek	.30	.75
5 Johnny Bucyk	.40	1.00
6 Wayne Cashman	.10	.25
7 Gerry Cheevers	.40	1.00
8 Dit Clapper	.30	.75
9 Bill Cowley	.10	.25
10 Phil Esposito	.50	1.25
11 Fernie Flaman	.16	.40
12 Mel Hill	.16	.40
Bill Cowley		
Roy Conacher		
13 Lionel Hitchman	.16	.40
14 Fleming Mackell	.10	.25
15 Don Marcotte	.10	.25
16 Don McKenney	.10	.25
17 Rick Middleton	.20	.50
18 Doug Mohns	.10	.25
19 Terry O'Reilly	.16	.40
20 Bobby Orr	1.20	3.00
21 Brad Park	.30	.75
22 John Peirson	.10	.25
23 Bill Quackenbush	.20	.50
24 Jean Ratelle	.30	.75
25 Art Ross CO/GM	.20	.50
26 Ed Sandford	.10	.25
27 Terry Sawchuk	.60	1.50
28 Milt Schmidt	.40	1.00
29 Milt Schmidt	.20	.50
Cooney Weiland		
Bill Cowley		
30 Eddie Shore	.40	1.00
31 Harry Sinden CO/GM	.20	.50
and President		
32 Tiny Thompson	.16	.40
33 Cooney Weiland	.16	.40
34 Ed Westfall	.10	.25
35 Bruins Defense	.20	.50
1955-56		
Bill Quackenbush		
Fern Flaman		
Terry Sawchuk		
Bob Armstrong		
Leo Boivin		
36 The Kraut Line	.30	.75
Milt Schmidt		
Woody Dumart		
Bobby Bauer		

1992-93 Bruins Postcards

This set measures approximately 3 1/2" by 5 1/2".

COMPLETE SET (12)	4.00	10.00
1 Ray Bourque	1.20	3.00
2 Ted Donato	.20	.50
3 Joe Juneau	.30	.75
4 Dimitri Kvartalnov	.20	.50
5 Stephen Leach	.20	.50
6 Andy Moog	.80	2.00
7 Adam Oates	.80	2.00
8 Dave Poulin	.30	.75
9 Gordie Roberts	.20	.50
10 Vladimir Ruzicka	.20	.50
11 Don Sweeney	.30	.75
12 Glen Wesley	.30	.75

1998 Bruins Alumni

Released for sale at the Fleet Center, this 35-card set features Boston Bruins from the past. The sets were sold for $18, and each set contained one autographed card.

COMPLETE SET (35)	8.00	20.00
1 Reggie Lemelin	.20	.50
2 Harry Sinden	.10	.25
3 Jim Craig	.20	.50
4 Bobby Orr	2.00	5.00
5 Ferny Flaman	.20	.50
6 Bob Beers	.10	.25
7 Ken Hodge	.20	.50
8 Cam Neely	1.00	3.00
9 John Bucyk	.40	1.00
10 Jean Ratelle	.20	.50
11 Bob Miller	.04	.10
12 Ed Sandford	.04	.10
13 Ken Linseman	.20	.50
14 Woody Dumart	.20	.50
15 Milt Schmidt	.30	.75
16 Derek Sanderson	.40	1.00
17 Fred Stanfield	.10	.25
18 Garnet Bailey	.80	2.00
19 John McKenzie	.20	.50
20 Dallas Smith	.10	.25
21 Don Marcotte	.10	.25
22 Brad Park	.30	.75
23 Matt Glennon	.04	.10
24 Terry O'Reilly	.30	1.00
25 Gary Doak	.10	.25
26 Don Awrey	.10	.25
27 Billy O'Dwyer	.04	.10
28 Dave Hynes	.04	.10
29 Tom Songin	.04	.10
30 Gerry Cheevers	.40	1.00
31 Don McKenney	.10	.25
32 Frank Simonetti	.04	.10
33 Bronco Horvath	.10	.25
34 Doug Mohns	.10	.25
35 Header Card	.04	.01

1998 Bruins Alumni Autographs

One autographed card was inserted in each set of 1998 Boston Bruins Alumni. Since so many sets would need to be purchase to complete a set, it's quite possible that no complete sets exist. The autographs of Bobby Orr and Cam Neely have not yet been confirmed, and so prices are not listed (nor are they included in the complete set value). If you can confirm either of these cards, please write to hockeymag@beckett.com. The Ace Bailey card is believed to be his only certified autographed single. Bailey was killed in the 9/11 plane hijackings.

COMPLETE SET (35)	120.00	300.00
1 Reggie Lemelin	4.00	10.00
2 Harry Sinden	4.00	10.00
3 Jim Craig	6.00	15.00
4 Bobby Orr		
5 Ferny Flaman	2.00	5.00
6 Bob Beers	.80	2.00
7 Ken Hodge	3.20	8.00
8 Cam Neely		
9 John Bucyk	8.00	25.00
10 Jean Ratelle	6.00	20.00
11 Bob Miller	.40	1.00
12 Ed Sandford	.40	1.00
13 Ken Linseman	2.00	5.00
14 Woody Dumart	12.00	40.00
15 Milt Schmidt	10.00	25.00
16 Derek Sanderson	14.00	40.00
17 Fred Stanfield	1.20	3.00
18 Garnet Bailey	16.00	40.00
19 John McKenzie	3.20	8.00
20 Dallas Smith	4.00	10.00
21 Don Marcotte	1.20	3.00
22 Brad Park	6.00	15.00
23 Matt Glennon	.40	1.00
24 Terry O'Reilly	14.00	40.00
25 Gary Doak	1.20	3.00
26 Don Awrey	1.20	3.00
27 Billy O'Dwyer	.40	1.00
28 Dave Hynes	.40	1.00
29 Tom Songin	.40	1.00
30 Gerry Cheevers	10.00	25.00
31 Don McKenney	1.20	3.00
32 Frank Simonetti	.40	1.00
33 Bronco Horvath	4.00	10.00
34 Doug Mohns	2.00	5.00
35 Header Card	.40	1.00

1999-00 Bruins Season Ticket Offer

This two card set was mailed to Bruins season ticket holders in an effort to bolster the renewal rate. The cards were perforated at the end of the offer. They are regular card stock and, because of the nature of distribution, are extremely rare in the hobby.

COMPLETE SET (2)	25.00	60.00
1 Joe Thornton	20.00	50.00
2 Sergei Samsonov	6.00	15.00

2002-03 Bruins Team Issue

These oversized (4X6) player photos feature action photos on the front and blank backs. They were distributed through the Bruins marketing department and were used mainly for autograph signings.

COMPLETE SET (8)	6.00	15.00
1 Blades MASCOT	.20	.50
2 Nick Boynton	.40	1.00
3 Hal Gill	.40	1.00
4 Glen Murray	.75	2.00
5 Brian Rolston	.75	2.00

6 Sergei Samsonov	1.25	3.00
7 P.J. Stock	1.25	3.00
8 Joe Thornton	2.00	5.00

2003-04 Bruins Team Issue

These oversized,very thin cards were available only in singles form at team events or through by-mail requests. It's possible that the checklist not complete. Send additional info to hockeymag@beckett.com

COMPLETE SET (14)	8.00	20.00
1 Nick Boynton	.40	1.00
2 Hal Gill	.40	1.00
3 Mike Knuble	.40	1.00
4 Martin Lapointe	.60	1.50
5 Dan McGillis	.40	1.00
6 Glen Murray	.60	1.50
7 Sean O'Donnell	.40	1.00
8 Felix Potvin	.40	1.00
9 Andrew Raycroft	1.25	3.00
10 Sergei Samsonov	1.25	3.00
11 Mike Sullivan CO	.10	.25
12 Joe Thornton	2.00	5.00
13 Blades MASCOT	.10	.25
14 Team photo	.40	1.00

2005-06 Bruins Boston Globe

Produced by Upper Deck, this set was distributed in two unperforated sheets with the purchase of a Sunday Boston Globe newspaper on consecutive weekends in late 2005.

COMPLETE SET (24)	8.00	20.00
1 Glen Murray	.20	.50
2 Hannu Toivonen	1.00	2.50
3 Andrew Alberts	.20	.50
4 Hal Gill	.20	.50
5 Tom Fitzgerald	.20	.50
6 Milan Jurcina	.20	.50
7 Brad Boyes	.30	.75
8 David Tanabe	.20	.50
9 Wayne Primeau	.20	.50
10 Brad Stuart	.20	.50
11 Alexei Zhamnov	.20	.50
12 Brian Leetch	.75	2.00
13 Patrice Bergeron	.75	2.00
14 Marco Sturm	.20	.50
15 Nick Boynton	.20	.50
16 Brad Isbister	.20	.50
17 Sergei Samsonov	.40	1.00
18 Pat Leahy	.20	.50
19 Andrew Raycroft	.40	1.00
20 Tim Thomas	.75	2.00
21 Travis Green	.20	.50
22 Josh Langfeld	.20	.50
23 Dan LaCouture	.20	.50
24 P.J. Axelsson	.20	.50

1911-12 C55

The C55 Hockey set, probably issued during the 1911-12 season, contains 45 numbered cards. Being one of the early Canadian cigarette cards, the issuer of this set is unknown, although there is speculation that it may have been Imperial Tobacco. These small cards measure approximately 1 1/2" by 2 1/2". The line drawing, color portrait on the front of the card is framed by two hockey sticks. The number of the card appears on both the front and back as does the player's name. The players in the set were members of the NHA: Quebec Bulldogs, Ottawa Senators, Montreal Canadiens, Montreal Wanderers, and Renfrew Millionaires. This set is prized highly by collectors but is the easiest of the three early sets (C55, C56, or C57) to find. The complete set price includes either variety of the Small variation.

COMPLETE SET (45)	7500.00	15000.00
1 Paddy Moran	250.00	500.00
2 Joe Hall RC	200.00	400.00
3 Barney Holden	100.00	200.00
4 Joe Malone RC	500.00	1000.00
5 Ed Oatman RC	100.00	200.00
6 Tom Dunderdale	150.00	300.00
7 Ken Mallen RC	100.00	200.00
8 Jack MacDonald RC	100.00	200.00
9 Fred Lake	100.00	200.00
10 Albert Kerr RC	100.00	250.00
11 Marty Walsh	150.00	300.00
12 Hamby Shore RC	100.00	200.00
13 Alex Currie RC	100.00	200.00
14 Bruce Ridpath	100.00	200.00
15 Bruce Stuart	150.00	300.00
16 Percy Lesueur	150.00	300.00
17 Jack Darragh RC	150.00	300.00
18 Steve Vair RC	100.00	200.00
19 Don Smith RC	100.00	200.00
20 Cyclone Taylor	750.00	1500.00
21 Bert Lindsay RC	125.00	250.00
22 H.L.(Larry) Gilmour RC	150.00	300.00
23 Bobby Rowe RC	100.00	200.00
24 Sprague Cleghorn RC	250.00	500.00
25 Odie Cleghorn RC	150.00	300.00
26 Skene Ronan RC	100.00	200.00
27A W.Smaill RC Hand on stk	350.00	700.00
27B W.Smaill RC Hand on hip	400.00	800.00
28 Ernest(Moose) Johnson	200.00	400.00
29 Jack Marshall	150.00	300.00
30 Harry Hyland	125.00	250.00
31 Art Ross	750.00	1500.00
32 Riley Hern	150.00	300.00
33 Gordon Roberts	150.00	300.00
34 Frank Glass	100.00	200.00
35 Ernest Russell	150.00	300.00
36 James Gardner RC	150.00	300.00
37 Art Bernier	100.00	200.00
38 Georges Vezina RC	3000.00	6000.00
39 G.(Henri) Dallaire RC	100.00	200.00
40 R.(Rocket) Power RC	100.00	200.00
41 Didier(Pit) Pitre	150.00	300.00
42 Newsy Lalonde	750.00	1500.00
43 Eugene Payan RC	100.00	200.00
44 George Poulin RC	100.00	200.00
45 Jack Laviolette	150.00	300.00

1910-11 C56

One of the first hockey sets to appear (circa 1910-11), this full-color set of unknown origin (although there is speculation that the issuer was Imperial Tobacco) features 36 cards. The card numbering appears in the upper left part of the front of the card. These small cards measure approximately 1 1/2" by 2 5/8". The player's name and affiliation appear at the bottom within the border. The backs feature the player's name and career affiliations below crossed hockey sticks, a puck and the words "Hockey Series."

COMPLETE SET (36)	5000.00	10000.00
1 Frank Patrick RC	300.00	600.00
2 Percy Lesueur RC	150.00	300.00
3 Gordon Roberts RC	150.00	300.00
4 Barney Holden RC	75.00	150.00
5 Frank(Pud) Glass RC	75.00	150.00
6 Edgar Dey RC	75.00	150.00
7 Marty Walsh RC	125.00	250.00
8 Art Ross RC	500.00	1000.00
9 Angus Campbell RC	125.00	250.00
10 Harry Hyland RC	175.00	350.00
11 Herb Clark RC	75.00	150.00
12 Art Ross RC	500.00	1000.00
13 Ed Decary RC	75.00	150.00
14 Tom Dunderdale RC	200.00	400.00
15 Cyclone Taylor RC	500.00	1000.00
16 Joseph Cattarinich RC	100.00	200.00
17 Bruce Stuart RC	175.00	350.00
18 Nick Bawlf RC	75.00	150.00
19 Jim Jones RC	100.00	200.00
20 Ernest Russell RC	175.00	350.00
21 Jack Laviolette RC	125.00	250.00
22 Riley Hern RC	150.00	300.00
23 Didier(Pit) Pitre RC	150.00	300.00
24 Skinner Poulin RC	75.00	150.00
25 Art Bernier RC	75.00	150.00
26 Lester Patrick RC	400.00	700.00
27 Fred Lake RC	75.00	150.00
28 Paddy Moran RC	300.00	600.00
29 C.Toms RC	75.00	150.00
30 Ernest(Moose) Johnson RC UER	275.00	550.00
Misspelled Johnston		
31 Horace Gaul RC	75.00	150.00
32 Harold McNamara RC	75.00	150.00
33 Jack Marshall RC	125.00	250.00
34 Bruce Ridpath RC	75.00	150.00
35 Jack Marshall RC	125.00	250.00
36 Newsy Lalonde RC	500.00	1000.00

1912-13 C57

This set of 50 black and white cards was produced circa 1912-13. These small cards measure approximately 1 1/2" by 2 5/8". The player's name and affiliation are printed on both the front and back. The card number appears on the back only with the words "Series of 50." Although the origin of the set is unknown, it is safe to assume that the producer who issued the C56 series issued this as well, as the backs of the cards are quite similar. A brief career outline in English is contained on the back. This set is considered to be the toughest to find of the three early hockey sets.

COMPLETE SET (50)	12000.00	20000.00
1 Georges Vezina	1500.00	2500.00
2 Punch Broadbent RC	350.00	600.00
3 Clint Benedict RC	350.00	600.00
4 A. Atchinson RC	150.00	300.00
5 Tom Dunderdale	200.00	400.00
6 Art Bernier	150.00	300.00
7 G.(Henri) Dallaire	150.00	300.00
8 George Poulin	150.00	300.00
9 Eugene Payan	150.00	300.00
10 Steve Vair	150.00	300.00
11 Bobby Rowe	150.00	300.00
12 Don Smith	150.00	300.00
13 Bert Lindsay	150.00	300.00
14 Skene Ronan	150.00	300.00
15 Sprague Cleghorn	350.00	600.00
16 Joe Hall	200.00	400.00
17 Jack MacDonald	150.00	300.00
18 Paddy Moran	200.00	400.00
19 Harry Hyland	150.00	300.00
20 Art Ross	600.00	1000.00
21 Frank Glass	150.00	300.00
22 Walter Smaill	150.00	300.00
23 Gordon Roberts	150.00	300.00
24 James Gardner	200.00	400.00
25 Ernest(Moose) Johnson	200.00	400.00
26 Ernie Russell	200.00	400.00
27 Percy Lesueur	200.00	400.00
28 Bruce Ridpath	150.00	300.00
29 Jack Darragh	200.00	400.00
30 Hamby Shore	150.00	300.00
31 Fred Lake	150.00	300.00
32 Alex Currie	150.00	300.00
33 Albert Kerr	150.00	300.00
34 Eddie Gerard RC	200.00	400.00
35 Carl Kendall RC	150.00	300.00
36 Jack Fournier RC	150.00	300.00
37 Goldie Prodgers RC	150.00	300.00
38 Jack Marks RC	150.00	300.00
39 George Broughton RC	150.00	300.00
40 Arthur Boyce RC	150.00	300.00
41 Lester Patrick	400.00	800.00
42 Joe Dennison RC	150.00	300.00
43 Cyclone Taylor	600.00	1000.00
44 Newsy Lalonde	600.00	1000.00
45 Didier(Pit) Pitre	150.00	300.00
46 Jack Laviolette	150.00	300.00
47 Ed Oatman	150.00	300.00
48 Joe Malone	400.00	800.00
49 Marty Walsh	200.00	400.00
50 Odie Cleghorn	150.00	300.00

1912 C61 Lacrosse

This set, produced by Imperial Tobacco, features prominent lacrosse stars of the day, but is included in this book because it features several prominent hockey players of the day, including Newsy Lalonde, Jack Laviolette and Clint Benedict.

1 Charlie Querrie	150.00	400.00
2 Dolly Durkin	60.00	150.00
3 Fred Rowntree	60.00	150.00
4 Fred Graydon	60.00	150.00
5 Kid Kinsman	60.00	150.00
6 Al Dade	60.00	150.00
7 Jimmy Hogan	60.00	150.00
8 A. Kenna	60.00	150.00
9 W. Oâ ™Kane	60.00	150.00
10 F. Scott	60.00	150.00
11 Newsy Lalonde	500.00	800.00
12 Mickey Ion	100.00	200.00
13 Mag MacGregor	60.00	150.00
14 Dot Phelan	60.00	150.00
15 Spike Griffiths	60.00	150.00
16 Whitey Eastwood	60.00	150.00
17 Red McCarthy	60.00	150.00
18 Jack Shea	60.00	150.00
19 Clint Benedict	250.00	500.00
20 Bobby Pringle	60.00	150.00
21 A. Ranson	60.00	150.00
22 Lawrence Degray	60.00	150.00
23 Francis Cummings	60.00	150.00
24 Fred Degan	60.00	150.00
25 Don Cameron	60.00	150.00
26 James Gifford	60.00	150.00
27 Archie Hall	60.00	150.00
28 W. Turnbull	60.00	150.00
29 Punk Wintermute	60.00	150.00
30 Tom Gifford	60.00	150.00
31 O. Secours	60.00	150.00
32 Dr. Lachapelle	60.00	150.00
33 Joe Cattarinich	100.00	200.00
34 Dare Devil Gauthier	60.00	150.00
35 Jack Laviolette	100.00	200.00
36 George Roberts	60.00	150.00
37 Steve Rochford	60.00	150.00
38 Henry Scott	60.00	150.00
39 J. McIlwane	60.00	150.00
40 Nick Neville	60.00	150.00
41 P.J. Brennan	60.00	150.00
42 Howie McIntyre	60.00	150.00
43 Gus Dillon	60.00	150.00
44 J. Barry	60.00	150.00
45 Johnny Howard	60.00	150.00
46 Eddie Powers	60.00	150.00
47 Art Warwick	60.00	150.00
48 Ernie Menary	60.00	150.00
49 Georgie Kalls	60.00	150.00
50 Fred Stagg	60.00	150.00

1924-25 C144 Champ's Cigarettes

This unnumbered 60-card set was issued during the 1924-25 season by Champ's Cigarettes. There is a brief biography on the card back written in English. The cards are sepia tone and measure approximately 1 1/2" by 2 1/2". Since the cards are unnumbered, they are checklisted in alphabetical order by subject.

COMPLETE SET (60)	10000.00	20000.00
1 Jack Adams	150.00	250.00
2 Lloyd Andrews	125.00	200.00
3 Clint Benedict	250.00	400.00
4 Louis Berlinquette RC	125.00	200.00
5 Eddie Bouchard	125.00	200.00
6 Billy Boucher	150.00	250.00
7 Bob Boucher RC	125.00	200.00
8 Punch Broadbent	200.00	350.00
9 Billy Burch	200.00	350.00
10 Dutch Cain RC	125.00	200.00
11 Earl Campbell RC	125.00	200.00
12 George Carroll RC	125.00	200.00
13 King Clancy	1000.00	1750.00
14 Odie Cleghorn	150.00	250.00
15 Sprague Cleghorn	250.00	400.00
16 Alex Connell RC	250.00	400.00
17 Carson Cooper RC	125.00	200.00
18 Bert Corbeau	150.00	250.00
19 Billy Coutu	125.00	200.00
20 Clarence (Hap) Day RC	250.00	400.00
21 Cy Denneny	200.00	350.00
22 Charles A. Dinsmore RC	125.00	200.00
23 Babe Dye	200.00	350.00
24 Frank Finnigan RC	200.00	350.00
25 Vernon Forbes	125.00	200.00
26 Norman (Heck) Fowler RC	150.00	250.00
27 Red Green	125.00	200.00
28 Shorty Green	200.00	350.00
29 Curly Headley RC	125.00	200.00
30 Jim Herberts RC	125.00	200.00
31 Fred Hitchman RC	125.00	200.00
32 Albert Holway RC	125.00	200.00
33 Stan Jackson	125.00	200.00
34 Aurel Joliat	800.00	1400.00
35 Louis C. Langlois RC	125.00	200.00
36 Fred (Frock) Lowrey RC	125.00	200.00
37 Sylvio Mantha	200.00	350.00
38 Albert McCaffrey RC	125.00	200.00
39 Robert McKinnon RC	125.00	200.00
40 Herbie Mitchell RC	125.00	200.00
41 Howie Morenz	2000.00	3500.00
42 Dunc Munro RC	150.00	250.00
43 Gerald J.M. Munro RC	125.00	200.00
44 Frank Nighbor	250.00	400.00
45 Reg Noble	200.00	350.00
46 Mickey O'Leary RC	125.00	200.00
47 Goldie Prodgers	125.00	200.00
48 Ken Randall	125.00	200.00
49 George Redding RC	125.00	200.00
50 John Ross Roach	150.00	250.00
51 Mickey Roach	125.00	200.00
52 Sam Rothschild RC	125.00	200.00
53 Werner Schnarr RC	125.00	200.00
54 Ganton Scott RC	125.00	200.00
55 Alf Skinner RC	125.00	200.00
56 Hooley Smith RC	200.00	350.00
57 Chris Speyers RC	125.00	200.00
58 Jesse Spring	125.00	200.00
59 The Stanley Cup	350.00	600.00
60 Georges Vezina	1200.00	2000.00

1930 Campbell's Soup

Measures approximately 2" x 7" and is black and white. Lower portion of card features a Campbell's slogan. The player pictured is unidentified.

COMPLETE SET (1)	50.00	100.00
NNO Hockey Player	50.00	100.00

1994-95 Canada Games NHL POGS

Produced by Canada Games Company Limited, this set includes 376 POGS and 8 checklist cards. Each POG measures 1 5/8" in diameter; the checklist cards measure 2 3/8" by 3 1/2". Each cello pack featured 5 POGS and one checklist card; also one in every five packs contained a bonus kini. The fronts display color action head shots framed by foil and color geometric designs. The team name, player's name, and his position are printed on the fronts. In black on white, the backs carry biography, 1993-94 season statistics, NHL totals, and various logos. The POGS are numbered on the back.

COMPLETE SET (376)	40.00	100.00
1 Kini-Kings	.20	.50
2 Kini-Rangers	.20	.50
3 Kini-Penguins	.20	.50
4 Kini-Stars	.20	.50
5 Kini-Senators	.20	.50
6 Kini-Jets	.20	.50
7 Kini-Canucks	.20	.50
8 Kini-Capitals	.20	.50
9 Kini-Ducks	.20	.50
10 Kini-Bruins	.20	.50
11 Kini-Sabres	.20	.50
12 Kini-Flames	.20	.50
13 Kini-Blackhawks	.20	.50
14 Kini-Red Wings	.20	.50
15 Kini-Oilers	.20	.50
16 Kini-Panthers	.20	.50
17 Kini-Whalers	.20	.50
18 Kini-Canadiens	.20	.50
19 Kini-Devils	.20	.50
20 Kini-Islanders	.20	.50
21 Kini-Flyers	.20	.50
22 Kini-Nordiques	.20	.50
23 Kini-Sharks	.20	.50
24 Kini-Blues	.20	.50
25 Kini-Lightning	.20	.50
26 Kini-Leafs	.20	.50
27 Cliff Ronning	.04	.10
28 Bob Corkum	.04	.10
29 Joe Sacco	.04	.10
30 Peter Douris	.04	.10
31 Shaun Van Allen	.04	.10
32 Stephan Lebeau	.04	.10
33 Stu Grimson	.04	.10
34 Tim Sweeney	.04	.10
35 Adam Oates	.20	.50
36 Al Iafrate	.06	.15
37 Alexei Kastanov	.04	.10
38 Bryan Smolinski	.10	.25
39 Cam Neely	.30	.7
40 Don Sweeney	.04	.1
41 Glen Murray	.04	.1
42 Ray Bourque	.40	1.0
43 Ted Donato	.04	.1
44 Alexander Mogilny	.40	1.0
45 Doug Gilmour	.40	1.0
46 Dale Hawerchuk	.20	.5
47 Derek Plante	.10	.2
48 Donald Audette	.10	.2
49 Doug Bodger	.04	.1
50 Pat LaFontaine	.20	.5
51 Randy Wood	.04	.1
52 Richard Smehlik	.04	.1
53 Yuri Khmylev	.04	.1
54 Theo Fleury	.30	.7
55 Kelly Kisio	.04	.1
56 Joe Nieuwendyk	.10	.2
57 Michael Nylander	.04	.1
58 Joel Otto	.04	.1
59 James Patrick	.04	.1
60 Robert Reichel	.10	.2
61 Gary Roberts	.10	.2
62 Wes Walz	.04	.1
63 Ulf Dahlen	.04	.1
64 Zarley Zalapski	.04	.1
65 Tony Amonte	.30	.7
66 Dirk Graham	.04	.1
67 Joe Murphy	.06	.1
68 Bernie Nicholls	.10	.2
69 Patrick Poulin	.04	.1
70 Jeremy Roenick	.40	1.0
71 Christian Ruutu	.04	.1
72 Brent Sutter	.04	.1
73 Chris Chelios	.60	1.5
74 Steve Smith	.04	.1
75 Gary Suter	.04	.1
76 Neal Broten	.06	.1
77 Russ Courtnall	.04	.1
78 Dean Evason	.04	.1
79 Dave Gagner	.06	.1
80 Mike McPhee	.04	.1
81 Mike Modano	.30	.7
82 Paul Cavallini	.04	.1
83 Derian Hatcher	.04	.1
84 Grant Ledyard	.04	.1
85 Mark Tinordi	.04	.1
86 Dino Ciccarelli	.16	.4
87 Sergei Fedorov	1.20	3.0
88 Slava Kozlov	.10	.2
89 Darren McCarty	.10	.2
90 Keith Primeau	.10	.2
91 Ray Sheppard	.10	.2
92 Steve Yzerman	2.00	5.0
93 Paul Coffey	.40	1.0
94 Vladimir Konstantinov	.04	.1
95 Nicklas Lidstrom	.16	.4
96 Greg Adams	.04	.1
97 Jason Arnott	.30	.7
98 Kelly Buchberger	.04	.1
99 Shayne Corson	.04	.1
100 Scott Pearson	.04	.1
101 Doug Weight	.20	.5
102 Boris Mironov	.10	.2
103 Fredrik Olausson	.04	.1
104 Stu Barnes	.04	.1
105 Bob Kudelski	.04	.1
106 Andrei Lomakin	.04	.1
107 Dave Lowry	.04	.1
108 Scott Mellanby	.10	.2
109 Rob Niedermayer	.20	.5
110 Brian Skrudland	.04	.1
111 Brian Benning	.04	.1
112 Gord Murphy	.04	.1
113 Andrew Cassels	.04	.1
114 Robert Kron	.04	.1
115 Jocelyn Lemieux	.04	.1
116 Paul Ranheim	.04	.1
117 Geoff Sanderson	.20	.5
118 Jim Sandlak	.04	.1
119 Darren Turcotte	.04	.1
120 Pat Verbeek	.10	.2
121 Chris Pronger	.16	.4
122 Pat Conacher	.04	.1
123 Mike Donnelly	.04	.1
124 John Druce	.04	.1
125 Tony Granato	.06	.1
126 Wayne Gretzky	4.00	10.0
127 Jari Kurri	.10	.2
128 Warren Rychel	.04	.1
129 Rob Blake	.08	.2
130 Marty McSorley	.10	.2
131 Alexei Zhitnik	.04	.1
132 Brian Bellows	.04	.1
133 Vince Damphousse	.20	.5
134 Gilbert Dionne	.04	.1
135 Mike Keane	.04	.1
136 John LeClair	1.00	2.5
137 Kirk Muller	.10	.2
138 Oleg Petrov	.04	.1
139 Eric Desjardins	.04	.1
140 Lyle Odelein	.04	.1
141 Peter Popovic	.04	.1
142 Mathieu Schneider	.04	.1
143 Trent Klatt	.04	.1
144 Bobby Holik	.04	.1
145 Claude Lemieux	.16	.4
146 John MacLean	.08	.2
147 Corey Millen	.04	.1
148 Stephane Richer	.06	.1
149 Valeri Zelepukin	.04	.1
150 Bruce Driver	.04	.1
151 Gino Odjick	.04	.1
152 Scott Stevens	.10	.2
153 Brad Dalgarno	.04	.1
154 Ray Ferraro	.04	.1
155 Pat Flatley	.04	.1
156 Travis Green	.06	.1
157 Derek King	.04	.1
158 Marty McInnis	.04	.1
159 Steve Thomas	.10	.2
160 Pierre Turgeon	.20	.5
161 Darius Kasparaitis	.04	.1
162 Vladimir Malakhov	.04	.1
163 Alexei Kovalev	.10	.2
164 Steve Larmer	.10	.2
165 Stephane Matteau	.04	.1
166 Mark Messier	.80	2.0
167 Sergei Nemchinov	.04	.1
168 Brian Noonan	.04	.1
169 Petr Nedved	.10	.2

170 Brian Leetch .60 1.50
171 Kevin Lowe .04 .10
172 Sergei Zubov .04 .10
173 Sylvain Turgeon .04 .10
174 Alexei Yashin .20 .50
175 Norm Maciver .04 .10
176 Brad Shaw .04 .10
177 Brent Fedyk .04 .10
178 Mark Lamb .04 .10
179 Don McSween .04 .10
180 Mark Recchi .20 .50
181 Mikael Renberg .30 .75
182 Gary Galley .04 .10
183 Ron Francis .20 .50
184 Jaromir Jagr 2.00 5.00
185 Mario Lemieux 3.20 8.00
186 Shawn McEachern .04 .10
187 Joe Mullen .08 .20
188 Tomas Sandstrom .06 .15
189 Kevin Stevens .08 .20
190 Martin Straka .04 .10
191 Larry Murphy .10 .25
192 Kjell Samuelsson .04 .10
193 Ulf Samuelsson .04 .10
194 Wendel Clark .16 .40
195 Valeri Kamensky .16 .40
196 Andrei Kovalenko .04 .10
197 Owen Nolan .20 .50
198 Mike Ricci .04 .10
199 Joe Sakic 1.20 3.00
200 Scott Young .04 .10
201 Uwe Krupp .04 .10
202 Curtis Leschyshyn .04 .10
203 Brett Hull .80 2.00
204 Craig Janney .10 .25
205 Kevin Miller .04 .10
206 Vitali Prokhorov .04 .10
207 Brendan Shanahan 1.20 3.00
208 Peter Stastny .10 .25
209 Esa Tikkanen .08 .20
210 Steve Duchesne .04 .10
211 Gaeten Duchesne .04 .10
212 Todd Elik .04 .10
213 Pogman .20 .50
214 Pat Falloon .04 .10
215 Johan Garpenlov .04 .10
216 Igor Larionov .10 .25
217 Sergei Makarov .06 .15
218 Jeff Norton .04 .10
219 Sandis Ozolinsh .20 .50
220 Mikael Andersson .04 .10
221 Brian Bradley .10 .25
222 Danton Cole .04 .10
223 Chris Gratton .20 .50
224 Petr Klima .04 .10
225 Denis Savard .10 .25
226 John Tucker .04 .10
227 Shawn Chambers .04 .10
228 Chris Joseph .04 .10
229 Dave Andreychuk .10 .25
230 Nikolai Borschevsky .04 .10
231 Mike Craig .04 .10
232 Mike Eastwood .04 .10
233 Mike Gartner .20 .50
234 Doug Gilmour .40 1.00
235 Kent Manderville .04 .10
236 Mike Ridley .04 .10
237 Mats Sundin .30 .75
238 Dave Ellett .04 .10
239 Todd Gill .04 .10
240 Jamie Macoun .04 .10
241 Dmitri Mironov .04 .10
242 Peter Bondra .40 1.00
243 Randy Burridge .04 .10
244 Dale Hunter .04 .10
245 Joe Juneau .16 .40
246 Dmitri Khristich .10 .25
247 Kelly Miller .04 .10
248 Michal Pivonka .04 .10
249 Sylvain Cote .04 .10
250 Tie Domi .20 .50
251 Dallas Drake .04 .10
252 Nelson Emerson .04 .10
253 Teemu Selanne 1.20 3.00
254 Darrin Shannon .04 .10
255 Thomas Steen .04 .10
256 Keith Tkachuk .60 1.50
257 Dave Manson .04 .10
258 Stephane Quintal .04 .10
259 Adam Graves AS .10 .25
260 Brian Leetch AS .40 1.00
261 John Vanbiesbrouck AS .60 1.50
262 Scott Stevens AS .10 .25
263 Ray Bourque AS .40 1.00
264 Al MacInnis AS .10 .25
265 Brendan Shanahan AS 1.20 3.00
266 Pavel Bure AS 1.60 4.00
267 Sergei Fedorov AS 1.20 3.00
268 Wayne Gretzky AS 4.00 10.00
269 Guy Hebert .20 .50
270 Kirk McLean .20 .50
271 John Blue .10 .25
272 Vincent Riendeau .10 .25
273 Grant Fuhr .20 .50
274 Dominik Hasek 1.20 3.00
275 Trevor Kidd .16 .40
276 Ed Belfour .60 1.50
277 Andy Moog .20 .50
278 Mike Vernon .20 .50
279 Bill Ranford .20 .50
280 John Vanbiesbrouck 1.00 2.50
281 Sean Burke .20 .50
282 Kelly Hrudey .20 .50
283 Patrick Roy 3.20 8.00
284 Martin Brodeur 1.60 4.00
285 Chris Terreri .06 .15
286 Jamie McLennan .08 .20
287 Glenn Healy .10 .25
288 Mike Richter .60 1.50
289 Craig Billington .10 .25
290 Dominic Roussel .08 .20
291 Tom Barrasso .10 .25
292 Stephane Fiset .10 .25
293 Curtis Joseph .80 2.00
294 Arturs Irbe .40 1.00
295 Daren Puppa .20 .50
296 Felix Potvin .60 1.50
297 Tim Cheveldae .10 .25
298 Don Beaupre .10 .25
299 Rick Tabaracci .08 .20
300 Anaheim Mighty Ducks .16 .40
301 Boston Bruins .16 .40
302 Buffalo Sabres .04 .10
303 Calgary Flames .04 .10
304 Chicago Blackhawks .10 .25
305 Dallas Stars .04 .10
306 Detroit Red Wings .16 .40
307 Edmonton Oilers .04 .10
308 Florida Panthers .04 .10
309 Hartford Whalers .04 .10
310 Los Angeles Kings .16 .40
311 Montreal Canadiens .16 .40
312 New Jersey Devils .04 .10
313 Jeff Brown .04 .10
314 New York Rangers .16 .40
315 Ottawa Senators .04 .10
316 Philadelphia Flyers .04 .10
317 Pittsburgh Penguins .04 .10
318 Quebec Nordiques .04 .10
319 St. Louis Blues .04 .10
320 San Jose Sharks .10 .25
321 Tampa Bay Lightning .04 .10
322 Toronto Maple Leafs .10 .25
323 Vancouver Canucks .04 .10
324 Washington Capitals .04 .10
325 Winnipeg Jets .04 .10
326 Martin Brodeur AW 1.60 4.00
327 Brian Leetch AW .40 1.00
328 Cam Neely AW .30 .75
329 Geoff Courtnall .04 .10
330 Pogman .20 .50
331 Sergei Fedorov AW 1.20 3.00
332 Dominik Hasek AW 1.20 3.00
333 Dominik Hasek 1.20 3.00
Grant Fuhr AW
334 Brian Leetch .40 1.00
335 Martin Gelinas .08 .20
336 Cam Neely .20 .50
337 Mike Richter .60 1.50
338 Luke Richardson .04 .10
339 Jyrki Lumme .04 .10
340 Nathan Lafayette .04 .10
341 Pavel Bure 1.00 2.50
342 Sergio Momesso .04 .10
343 Trevor Linden .20 .50
344 Tie Domi .16 .40
345 Scott Stevens .10 .25
346 Teppo Numminen .04 .10
347 Anatoli Semenov .04 .10
348 Steve Heinze .04 .10
349 Tom Chorske .04 .10
350 Bill Guerin .08 .20
351 Scott Niedermayer .10 .25
352 Adam Graves .10 .25
353 Alexandre Daigle .20 .50
354 Troy Mallette .04 .10
355 Dave McLlwain .04 .10
356 Jesse Beranek .04 .10
357 Kevin Dineen .04 .10
358 Eric Lindros 1.60 4.00
359 Bob Rouse .04 .10
360 Sergei Fedorov AW 1.20 3.00
361 Bob Errey .04 .10
362 Brad May .04 .10
363 Kevin Hatcher .04 .10
364 New York Islanders .04 .10
365 Randy Ladouceur .04 .10
366 Bobby Dollas .04 .10
367 Igor Kravchuk .04 .10
368 Jesse Belanger .04 .10
369 Pogman .20 .50
370 Gary Valk .04 .10
371 Pogman .20 .50
372 Ron Hextall .20 .50
373 Rod Brind'Amour .20 .50
374 Benoit Hogue .04 .10
375 Alexei Zhamnov .10 .25
376 Pavel Bure AW 1.60 4.00
NNO Checklist 1-47 .04 .10
NNO Checklist 48-94 .04 .10
NNO Checklist 95-141 .04 .10
NNO Checklist 142-188 .04 .10
NNO Checklist 189-235 .04 .10
NNO Checklist 236-282 .04 .10
NNO Checklist 283-329 .04 .10
NNO Checklist 330-376 .04 .10

1995-96 Canada Games NHL POGS

This set of 296 POGS was produced by Canada Games. The POGS were distributed in packs of five, with every fifth pack containing a bonus Kini. These Kinis are listed at the end of the checklist with a K-prefix. They do not picture the trophy mentioned. The POGS themselves feature a colorful action shot of the player, while the backs feature abbreviated stats.

COMPLETE SET (296) 32.00 80.00
1 Wayne Gretzky 2.40 6.00
2 Mario Lemieux 2.00 5.00
3 Cam Neely .40 1.00
4 Ray Bourque .80 2.00
5 Patrick Roy 1.60 4.00
6 Mark Messier .50 1.25
7 Brett Hull .50 1.25
8 Grant Fuhr .30 .75
9 Eric Lindros 1.00 2.50
10 John LeClair .60 1.50
11 Jaromir Jagr 1.20 3.00
12 Chris Chelios .40 1.00
13 Paul Coffey .40 1.00
14 Dominik Hasek .80 2.00
15 Alexei Zhamnov .30 .75
16 Keith Tkachuk .40 1.00
17 Theo Fleury .40 1.00
18 Ray Bourque .80 2.00
19 Larry Murphy .30 .75
20 Ed Belfour .40 1.00
21 Pavel Bure 1.00 2.50
22 Doug Gilmour .40 1.00
23 Brett Hull .50 1.25
24 Mark Messier .50 1.25
25 Cam Neely .40 1.00
26 Jeremy Roenick .40 1.00
27 Patrick Roy 1.60 4.00
28 Jim Carey .30 .75
29 Peter Forsberg 1.00 2.50
30 Jeff Friesen .04 .10
31 Kenny Jonsson .30 .75
32 Paul Kariya 1.20 3.00
33 Ian Laperriere .04 .10
34 David Oliver .04 .10
35 Kyle McLaren .30 .75
36 Ray Bourque .50 1.25
37 Alexei Kasatonov .04 .10
38 Blaine Lacher .30 .75
39 Brian Holzinger .30 .75
40 Derek Plante .04 .10
41 Mike Peca .04 .10
42 Pat LaFontaine .40 1.00
43 Jason Dawe .04 .10
44 Brad May .04 .10
45 Yuri Khmylev .04 .10
46 Garry Galley .04 .10
47 Alexei Zhitnik .04 .10
48 Dominik Hasek .80 2.00
49 Joe Nieuwendyk .30 .75
50 German Titov .04 .10
51 Cory Stillman .04 .10
52 Theo Fleury .40 1.00
53 Paul Kruse .04 .10
54 Michael Nylander .04 .10
55 Gary Roberts .04 .10
56 Phil Housley .04 .10
57 Steve Chiasson .04 .10
58 Zarley Zalapski .04 .10
59 Ron Stern .04 .10
60 Trevor Kidd .30 .75
61 Jeremy Roenick .40 1.00
62 Denis Savard .40 1.00
63 Tony Amonte .40 1.00
64 Bernie Nicholls .04 .10
65 Sergei Krivokrasov .04 .10
66 Joe Murphy .04 .10
67 Patrick Poulin .04 .10
68 Bob Probert .30 .75
69 Gary Suter .04 .10
70 Chris Chelios .40 1.00
71 Ed Belfour .40 1.00
72 Joe Sakic .80 2.00
73 Mike Ricci .04 .10
74 Valeri Kamensky .30 .75
75 Andrei Kovalenko .04 .10
76 Owen Nolan .30 .75
77 Peter Forsberg 1.00 2.50
78 Scott Young .04 .10
79 Uwe Krupp .04 .10
80 Curtis Leschyshyn .04 .10
81 Adam Deadmarsh .30 .75
82 Stephane Fiset .30 .75
83 Bob Bassen .04 .10
84 Corey Millen .04 .10
85 Mike Modano .50 1.25
86 Dave Gagner .30 .75
87 Mike Donnelly .04 .10
88 Trent Klatt .04 .10
89 Kevin Hatcher .04 .10
90 Grant Ledyard .04 .10
91 Greg Adams .04 .10
92 Andy Moog .30 .75
93 Keith Primeau .30 .75
94 Kris Draper .04 .10
95 Sergei Fedorov .80 2.00
96 Steve Yzerman 1.20 3.00
97 Vyacheslav Kozlov .04 .10
98 Ray Sheppard .30 .75
99 Dino Ciccarelli .30 .75
100 Slava Fetisov .04 .10
101 Nicklas Lidstrom .40 1.00
102 Paul Coffey .40 1.00
103 Darren McCarty .30 .75
104 Mike Vernon .30 .75
105 Doug Weight .30 .75
106 Jason Arnott .30 .75
107 Todd Marchant .04 .10
108 David Oliver .04 .10
109 Igor Kravchuk .04 .10
110 Jiri Slegr .04 .10
111 Kelly Buchberger .04 .10
112 Scott Thornton .04 .10
113 Bill Ranford .30 .75
114 Jesse Belanger .04 .10
115 Stu Barnes .04 .10
116 Scott Mellanby .30 .75
117 Bill Lindsay .04 .10
118 Dave Lowry .04 .10
119 Gaetan Duchesne .04 .10
120 Johan Garpenlov .04 .10
121 Paul Laus .04 .10
122 Gord Murphy .04 .10
123 John Vanbiesbrouck .40 1.00
124 Andrew Cassels .04 .10
125 Geoff Sanderson .30 .75
126 Brendan Shanahan .80 2.00
127 Paul Ranheim .04 .10
128 Steven Rice .04 .10
129 Frantisek Kucera .04 .10
130 Glen Wesley .04 .10
131 Sean Burke .30 .75
132 Wayne Gretzky 2.40 6.00
133 Dimitri Khristich .04 .10
134 Jari Kurri .30 .75
135 John Druce .04 .10
136 Pat Conacher .04 .10
137 Rick Tocchet .30 .75
138 Rob Blake .30 .75
139 Tony Granato .04 .10
140 Marty McSorley .30 .75
141 Darryl Sydor .30 .75
142 Eric Lacroix .04 .10
143 Kelly Hrudey .30 .75
144 Brian Savage .04 .10
145 Pierre Turgeon .30 .75
146 Benoit Brunet .04 .10
147 Valeri Bure .04 .10
148 Vincent Damphousse .30 .75
149 Mike Keane .04 .10
150 Mark Recchi .30 .75
151 Vladimir Malakhov .04 .10
152 Patrice Brisebois .04 .10
153 J.J. Daigneault .04 .10
154 Yves Racine .04 .10
155 Patrick Roy 1.60 4.00
156 Bob Carpenter .04 .10
157 Neal Broten .04 .10
158 Steve Thomas .30 .75
159 Bobby Holik .30 .75
160 John MacLean .30 .75
161 Mike Peluso .04 .10
162 Randy McKay .04 .10
163 Stephane Richer .30 .75
164 Scott Niedermayer .30 .75
165 Scott Stevens .30 .75
166 Bill Guerin .30 .75
167 Martin Brodeur 1.00 2.50
168 Kirk Muller .30 .75
169 Zigmund Palffy .40 1.00
170 Travis Green .04 .10
171 Brett Lindros .04 .10
172 Derek King .04 .10
173 Pat Flatley .04 .10
174 Wendel Clark .30 .75
175 Bryan McCabe .04 .10
176 Mathieu Schneider .04 .10
177 Eric Fichaud .04 .10
178 Ray Ferraro .04 .10
179 Adam Graves .30 .75
180 Mark Messier .50 1.25
181 Sergei Nemchinov .04 .10
182 Pat Verbeek .30 .75
183 Luc Robitaille .30 .75
184 Alexei Kovalev .30 .75
185 Jeff Beukeboom .04 .10
186 Brian Leetch .40 1.00
187 Ulf Samuelsson .04 .10
188 Alexander Karpovtsev .04 .10
189 Mike Richter .40 1.00
190 Alexandre Daigle .30 .75
191 Alexei Yashin .30 .75
192 Dan Quinn .04 .10
193 Martin Straka .04 .10
194 Radek Bonk .04 .10
195 Pavol Demitra .30 .75
196 Steve Duchesne .30 .75
197 Chris Dahlquist .04 .10
198 Sean Hill .04 .10
199 Stanislav Neckar .04 .10
200 Don Beaupre .30 .75
201 Eric Lindros 1.00 2.50
202 Rod Brind'Amour .30 .75
203 Shjon Podein .04 .10
204 Brent Fedyk .04 .10
205 Joel Otto .04 .10
206 John LeClair .60 1.50
207 Kevin Dineen .04 .10
208 Petr Svoboda .04 .10
209 Eric Desjardins .04 .10
210 Ron Hextall .30 .75
211 Mario Lemieux 2.00 5.00
212 Petr Nedved .30 .75
213 Bryan Smolinski .30 .75
214 Tomas Sandstrom .30 .75
215 Ron Francis .30 .75
216 Jaromir Jagr 1.20 3.00
217 Sergei Zubov .04 .10
218 Drake Berehowsky .04 .10
219 Dmitri Mironov .04 .10
220 Ken Wregget .30 .75
221 Tom Barrasso .30 .75
222 Igor Larionov .30 .75
223 Jeff Friesen .30 .75
224 Kevin Miller .04 .10
225 Ray Whitney .04 .10
226 Craig Janney .30 .75
227 Pat Falloon .04 .10
228 Ulf Dahlen .04 .10
229 Viktor Kozlov .30 .75
230 Michal Sykora .04 .10
231 Sandis Ozolinsh .30 .75
232 Jamie Baker .04 .10
233 Arturs Irbe .30 .75
234 Adam Creighton .04 .10
235 Ian Laperriere .04 .10
236 Brett Hull .50 1.25
237 Brian Noonan .04 .10
238 Dale Hawerchuk .30 .75
239 Esa Tikkanen .30 .75
240 Geoff Courtnall .04 .10
241 Shayne Corson .04 .10
242 Al MacInnis .30 .75
243 Chris Pronger .30 .75
244 Jeff Norton .04 .10
245 Grant Fuhr .30 .75
246 Brian Bradley .04 .10
247 Chris Gratton .30 .75
248 John Cullen .04 .10
249 John Tucker .04 .10
250 Paul Ysebaert .04 .10
251 Petr Klima .04 .10
252 Alexander Selivanov .04 .10
253 Brian Bellows .04 .10
254 Enrico Ciccone .04 .10
255 Roman Hamrlik .30 .75
256 Daren Puppa .30 .75
257 Doug Gilmour .40 1.00
258 Benoit Hogue .04 .10
259 Mats Sundin .40 1.00
260 Dave Andreychuk .30 .75
261 Mike Gartner .30 .75
262 Randy Wood .04 .10
263 Tie Domi .04 .10
264 Dave Ellett .04 .10
265 Todd Gill .04 .10
266 Larry Murphy .30 .75
267 Kenny Jonsson .30 .75
268 Felix Potvin .40 1.00
269 Cliff Ronning .04 .10
270 Mike Ridley .04 .10
271 Trevor Linden .30 .75
272 Alexander Mogilny .30 .75
273 Martin Gelinas .30 .75
274 Pavel Bure .80 2.00
275 Russ Courtnall .04 .10
276 Jeff Brown .04 .10
277 Jyrki Lumme .04 .10
278 Kirk McLean .30 .75
279 Steve Konowalchuk .04 .10
280 Kelly Miller .04 .10
281 Peter Bondra .40 1.00
282 Keith Jones .04 .10
283 Joe Juneau .30 .75
284 Mark Tinordi .04 .10
285 Calle Johansson .04 .10
286 Sergei Gonchar .04 .10
287 Jim Carey .30 .75
288 Dallas Drake .04 .10
289 Alexei Zhamnov .30 .75
290 Mike Eastwood .04 .10
291 Igor Korolev .04 .10
292 Teemu Selanne .80 2.00
293 Keith Tkachuk .40 1.00
294 Teppo Numminen .04 .10
295 Dave Manson .04 .10
296 Tim Cheveldae .30 .75
K1 Lester B. Pearson .30 .75
K2 Art Ross .30 .75
K3 Bill Masterton .30 .75
K4 Calder .30 .75
K5 Clarence S. Campbell .30 .75
K6 Conn Smythe .30 .75
K7 Frank J. Selke .30 .75
K8 Hart .30 .75
K9 Jack Adams .30 .75
K10 James Norris .30 .75
K11 King Clancy .30 .75
K12 Lady Byng .30 .75
K13 Prince of Wales .30 .75
K14 Stanley Cup .30 .75
K15 Vezina .30 .75
K16 William M. Jennings .30 .75

1983 Canadian National Juniors

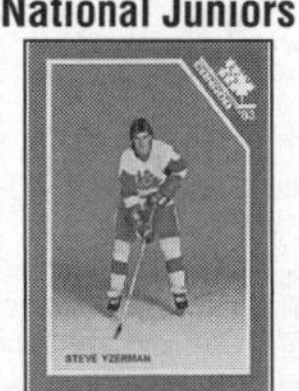

This 21-card set features Canada's 1983 National Junior Team. The cards measure approximately 3 1/2" by 5" and feature on the fronts either color posed action shots or close-up photos, shot against a blue background. On a red card face, the photos are enclosed by white borders, and the upper right corner of the picture is cut off to allow space for the team logo. The backs are blank and the unnumbered cards are checklisted below in alphabetical order. The set includes early cards of Mario Lemieux, Steve Yzerman, Mike Vernon, Dave Andreychuk, and Pat Verbeek. Three other players on the team who were not at the photo session and therefore not represented in the set are Paul Boutillier, Marc Habscheid, and Brad Shaw. A large team card (approximately 5" by 10 1/4") featuring all the players (except Marc Habscheid) and coaches was also produced. A two-thirds size (measuring approximately 5" by 7 1/4") team card entitled Celebration '82 with Troy Murray holding the Championship Plate as well as a (7 1/4" by 10 1/4") '82 team card were also produced. These special oversized cards are not typically included as part of the complete set as listed and valued below.

COMPLETE SET (21) 60.00 150.00
1 Dave Andreychuk 3.20 8.00
2 Joe Cirella .80 2.00
3 Paul Cyr .40 1.00
4 Dale Derkatch .40 1.00
5 Mike Eagles .40 1.00
6 Pat Flatley UER .80 2.00
(Misspelled Flately)
7 Mario Gosselin .80 2.00
8 Gary Leeman .80 2.00
9 Mario Lemieux 32.00 80.00
10 Mark Morrison .40 1.00
11 James Patrick .80 2.00
12 Mike Sands .60 1.50
13 Gord Sherven .40 1.00
14 Tony Tanti .80 2.00
15 Larry Trader .40 1.00
16 Sylvain Turgeon .60 1.50
17 Pat Verbeek 3.20 8.00
18 Mike Vernon 3.20 8.00
19 Steve Yzerman 24.00 60.00
20 Checklist Card .20 .50
21 Title Card .20 .50
NNO Team Card 3.20 8.00
(Regular size)
NNO Large Team Card 4.00 10.00
NNO Team Card '82 2.00 5.00
NNO Celebration '82 2.00 5.00
(Troy Murray)

2003 Canada Post

Released in early 2003, this 24-card set, produced by Pacific Trading Cards, featured actual Canada Post stamps on the cards. Packs were sold exclusively at Canada Post offices and contained six cards.

COMPLETE SET (24) 30.00 75.00
1 Wayne Gretzky 4.00 10.00
2 Gordie Howe 3.20 8.00
3 Maurice Richard 1.60 5.00
4 Doug Harvey 1.20 3.00
5 Bobby Orr 4.00 10.00
6 Jacques Plante 2.40 5.00
7 Jean Beliveau 2.40 5.00
8 Terry Sawchuk 2.40 5.00
9 Eddie Shore 2.00 5.00
10 Denis Potvin 1.20 3.00
11 Bobby Hull 2.00 5.00
12 Syl Apps 1.20 3.00
13 Tim Horton 1.60 4.00
14 Guy Lafleur 1.60 4.00
15 Howie Morenz 1.20 4.00
16 Glenn Hall 1.20 5.00
17 Red Kelly 1.20 3.00
18 Phil Esposito 1.60 4.00
19 Frank Mahovlich 1.20 3.00
20 Ray Bourque 1.60 4.00
21 Serge Savard 1.20 3.00
22 Stan Mikita 1.20 3.00
23 Mike Bossy 1.20 3.00
24 Bill Durnan 1.20 4.00

2003 Canada Post Autographs

These autographed versions of the Canada Post cards were randomly inserted into packs. Each player signed just 100 cards. We were unable to confirm enough sales of any of these singles to provide accurate pricing, so we are simply checklisting them below.

COMPLETE SET (4) 200.00 350.00
7 Jean Beliveau 40.00 100.00
11 Bobby Hull 40.00 100.00
14 Guy Lafleur 40.00 100.00
16 Glenn Hall 30.00 80.00

2004 Canada Post

This 6-card set, produced by Pacific Trading Cards, updated the 2003 set and featured actual Canada Post stamps on the cards. Packs were sold exclusively at Canada Post offices.

COMPLETE SET (6) 6.00 15.00
25 Johnny Bower 1.50 4.00
26 Marcel Dionne 1.25 3.00
27 Larry Robinson 1.25 3.00
28 Milt Schmidt 1.25 3.00
29 Ted Lindsay 1.25 3.00
30 Brad Park 1.25 3.00

2004 Canada Post Autographs

Randomly inserted in Canada Post packs, found only at Canada Post outlets, at a rate of about 1:9 packs. Limited to 300 serial numbered sets.

COMPLETE SET (6) 150.00 250.00
PRINT RUN 300 SER.#'d SETS
1 Johnny Bower 25.00 50.00
2 Marcel Dionne 20.00 40.00
3 Larry Robinson 20.00 50.00
4 Milt Schmidt 20.00 50.00
5 Ted Lindsay 25.00 60.00
6 Brad Park 20.00 50.00

2005 Canada Post

This 6-card set, produced by Pacific Trading Cards, updated further the set that featured actual Canada Post stamps on the cards. Packs were sold exclusively at Canada Post offices.

COMPLETE SET (6) 6.00 15.00
31 Henri Richard 1.25 3.00
32 Grant Fuhr 1.25 3.00
33 Allan Stanley 1.25 3.00
34 Pierre Pilote 1.25 3.00
35 Bryan Trottier 1.25 3.00
36 John Bucyk 1.25 3.00

2005 Canada Post Autographs

This 6-card set was randomly inserted in Canada Post packs, found only at Canada Post outlets, at a rate of about 1:10 packs.

COMPLETE SET (6) 125.00 200.00
31 Henri Richard 15.00 40.00
32 Grant Fuhr 15.00 40.00
33 Allan Stanley 15.00 40.00
34 Pierre Pilote 15.00 40.00
35 Bryan Trottier 15.00 40.00
36 John Bucyk 15.00 40.00

2004 Canadian Women's World Championship Team

This oversized (3 3/4 by 5 1/4) series features players who competed for Team Canada at the 2004 World Women's Championships in Halifax. It's believed they were sold in set form at the event. The cards are unnumbered and so are listed in alphabetical order.

COMPLETE SET (22) 25.00
1 Dana Antal .40 1.00
2 Gillian Apps .60 1.50
3 Kelly Bechard .40 1.00
4 Jennifer Botterill .40 1.00
5 Therese Brisson .40 1.00
6 Cassie Campbell 1.25 3.00
7 Delaney Collins .40 1.00
8 Gillian Ferrari .40 1.00
9 Danielle Goyette .40 1.00
10 Jayna Hefford .75 2.00
11 Becky Kellar .40 1.00
12 Gina Kingsbury .40 1.00
13 Charline Labonte 1.25 3.00
14 Caroline Ouellette .40 1.00
15 Cherie Piper .40 1.00
16 Cheryl Pounder .40 1.00
17 Sami Jo Small .75 2.00
18 Colleen Sostorics .40 1.00
19 Kim St-Pierre .75 2.00
20 Vicky Sunohara .75 2.00
21 Sarah Vaillancourt .40 1.00
22 Hayley Wickenheiser 1.25 3.00

1964-65 Canadiens Postcards

This 24-postcard set features the Montreal Canadiens. The standard-size postcards feature action, black and white photography on the front, with the player's autograph stamped on in blue ink. The backs are blank. The set is noteworthy for including collectibles of HOFers Yvan Cournoyer and Rogatien Vachon before their RCs were issued.

COMPLETE SET (24) 100.00 200.00
1 Ralph Backstrom 2.50 5.00
2 Jean Beliveau 12.50 25.00
3 Toe Blake 5.00 10.00
4 Yvan Cournoyer 15.00 30.00
5 Dick Duff 2.50 5.00
6 John Ferguson 5.00 10.00
7 Danny Grant 2.50 5.00
8 Terry Harper 2.50 5.00
9 Ted Harris 2.50 5.00
10 Jacques Laperriere 4.00 8.00
11 Claude Larose 2.50 5.00
12 Jacques Lemaire 10.00 20.00
13 Garry Monahan 2.50 5.00
14 Claude Provost 2.50 5.00
15 Mickey Redmond 10.00 20.00
16 Henri Richard 7.50 15.00
17 Bobby Rousseau 2.50 5.00
18 Serge Savard 5.00 10.00
19 Gilles Tremblay 2.50 5.00
20 J.C. Tremblay 2.50 5.00
21 Carol Vadnais 1.50 3.00
22 Rogatien Vachon 15.00 30.00
23 Bryan Watson 1.50 3.00
24 Gump Worsley 5.00 10.00

1965-66 Canadiens Steinberg Glasses

This set of plastic glasses honoring members of the Montreal Canadiens were issued in the mid 1960's. As they are unnumbered, we are sequencing them in alphabetical order.

COMPLETE SET (12) 75.00 150.00
1 Ralph Backstrom 5.00 10.00
2 Jean Beliveau 15.00 30.00
3 John Ferguson 7.50 15.00
4 Charlie Hodge 7.50 15.00
5 Jacques Laperierre 5.00 10.00
6 Claude Provost 5.00 10.00
7 Henri Richard 10.00 20.00
8 Bob Rousseau 5.00 10.00
9 Jean Guy Talbot 5.00 10.00
10 Gilles Trembley 5.00 10.00
11 J.C. Tremblay 6.00 12.00
12 Gump Worsley 10.00 20.00

1966-67 Canadiens IGA

The 1966-67 Canadiens IGA set apparently is comprised of 10 small, postage stamp sized (3/4" by 3/4") cards which likely were part of a larger coupon book. With no attention to date on the card, it has been set by the Gilles Tremblay issue. The cards feature a head shot on a pinkish-red background. If anyone knows of other cards in this set, please forward the information to Beckett Publications.

COMPLETE SET (10) 150.00 300.00
1 J.C. Tremblay 15.00 30.00
2 Ralph Backstrom 15.00 30.00
3 Dick Duff 15.00 30.00
4 Ted Harris 12.50 25.00
5 Claude Larose 12.50 25.00
6 Bobby Rousseau 15.00 30.00
7 Terry Harper 15.00 30.00
8 Gilles Tremblay 12.50 25.00
9 John Ferguson 15.00 30.00
10 Gump Worsley 40.00 80.00

1967-68 Canadiens IGA

The 1967-68 IGA Montreal Canadiens set includes 23 color cards measuring approximately 1 5/8" by 1 7/8". The cards are unnumbered other than by jersey number which is how they are listed below. The cards were part of a game involving numerous prizes. The card backs contain no personal information about the player (only information about the IGA game) and are written in French and English. The set features early cards of Jacques Lemaire and Rogatien Vachon in their Rookie Card year as well as Serge Savard two years prior to his Rookie Card year.

COMPLETE SET (30) 325.00 650.00
1 Gump Worsley 25.00 50.00
2 Jacques Laperriere 15.00 30.00
3 J.C. Tremblay 12.50 25.00

4 Jean Beliveau 40.00 80.00
5 Gilles Tremblay 10.00 20.00
6 Ralph Backstrom 10.00 20.00
8 Dick Duff 12.50 25.00
10 Ted Harris 10.00 20.00
11 Claude Larose 10.00 20.00
12 Yvan Cournoyer 20.00 40.00
14 Claude Provost 10.00 20.00
15 Bobby Rousseau 10.00 20.00
16 Henri Richard 25.00 50.00
17 Carol Vadnais 10.00 20.00
18 Serge Savard 25.00 50.00
19 Terry Harper 12.50 25.00
20 Garry Monahan 10.00 20.00
22 John Ferguson 12.50 25.00
23 Danny Grant 12.50 25.00
24 Mickey Redmond 20.00 40.00
25 Jacques Lemaire 30.00 60.00
30 Rogatien Vachon 40.00 80.00
NNO Hector(Toe) Blake CO 15.00 30.00

1968-69 Canadiens IGA

The 1968-69 IGA Montreal Canadiens set includes 19 color cards measuring approximately 1 1/4" by 2 1/4". The cards are unnumbered other than by jersey number which is how they are listed below. The cards were part of a game involving numerous prizes. The card backs contain no personal information about the player (only information about the IGA game) and are written in French and English.

COMPLETE SET (30) 300.00 600.00
1 Gump Worsley 30.00 60.00
2 Jacques Laperriere 15.00 30.00
3 J.C. Tremblay 12.50 25.00
4 Jean Beliveau 40.00 80.00
5 Gilles Tremblay 10.00 20.00
6 Ralph Backstrom 12.50 25.00
8 Dick Duff 12.50 25.00
10 Ted Harris 10.00 20.00
12 Yvan Cournoyer 25.00 50.00
14 Claude Provost 10.00 20.00
15 Bobby Rousseau 12.50 25.00
16 Henri Richard 25.00 50.00
18 Serge Savard 20.00 40.00
19 Terry Harper 12.50 25.00
20 Garry Monahan 10.00 20.00
22 John Ferguson 15.00 30.00
24 Mickey Redmond 20.00 40.00
25 Jacques Lemaire 30.00 60.00
30 Rogatien Vachon 30.00 60.00

1968-69 Canadiens Postcards BW

This 20-card set of black and white postcards features full-bleed posed player photos with facsimile autographs in white. This set marks the last year the Canadiens' organization issued black and white postcards. The cards are unnumbered and checklisted below in alphabetical order. Serge Savard appears in this set prior to his Rookie Card year.

COMPLETE SET (20) 40.00 80.00
1 Ralph Backstrom 1.50 3.00
2 Jean Beliveau 7.50 15.00
3 Yvan Cournoyer 4.00 8.00
4 Dick Duff 1.50 3.00
5 John Ferguson 2.50 5.00
6 Terry Harper 1.50 3.00
7 Ted Harris 1.25 2.50
8 Jacques Laperriere 2.00 4.00
9 Jacques Lemaire 5.00 10.00
10 Garry Monahan 1.25 2.50
11 Claude Provost 1.25 2.50
12 Mickey Redmond 4.00 8.00
13 Henri Richard 4.00 8.00
14 Bobby Rousseau 1.50 3.00
15 Claude Ruel CO 1.25 2.50
16 Serge Savard 4.00 8.00
17 Gilles Tremblay 1.25 2.50
18 J.C. Tremblay 1.50 3.00
19 Rogatien Vachon 5.00 10.00
20 Gump Worsley 5.00 10.00

1969-71 Canadiens Postcards Color

This 31-card set of postcards features full-bleed posed color player photos with facsimile autographs in black across the bottom of the pictures. These postcards were also issued without facsimile autographs. For the 1969-70, 1970-71, and 1971-72 seasons, many of the same postcards were issued. The cards are unnumbered and checklisted below in alphabetical order.

COMPLETE SET (31) 50.00 100.00
1 Ralph Backstrom 1.50 3.00
2 Jean Beliveau 6.00 12.00
3 Chris Bordeleau 1.25 2.50
4 Pierre Bouchard 1.25 2.50
5 Guy Charron 1.25 2.50
6 Bill Collins 1.25 2.50
7 Yvan Cournoyer 4.00 8.00
8 John Ferguson 2.00 4.00
9 Terry Harper 1.50 3.00
10 Ted Harris 1.25 2.50
11 Rejean Houle 2.00 4.00
12 Jacques Laperriere 2.00 4.00
13 Guy Lapointe 3.00 6.00
14 Claude Larose 1.25 2.50
15 Jacques Lemaire 4.00 8.00
16 Al MacNeil CO 1.25 2.50
17 Frank Mahovlich 4.00 8.00
18 Peter Mahovlich 3.00 6.00
19 Phil Myre 2.00 4.00
20 Larry Pleau 1.50 3.00
21 Claude Provost 1.50 3.00
22 Mickey Redmond 4.00 8.00
23 Henri Richard 4.00 8.00
24 Phil Roberto 1.25 2.50
25 Jim Roberts 1.25 2.50
26 Bobby Rousseau 1.50 3.00
27 Claude Ruel CO 1.25 2.50
28 Serge Savard 4.00 8.00
29 Marc Tardif 1.50 3.00
30 J.C. Tremblay 1.50 3.00
31 Rogatien Vachon 5.00 10.00

1970-72 Canadiens Pins

This 22-pin set features members of the Montreal Canadiens. Each pin measures approximately 1 3/4" in diameter and has a black and white picture of the player. With the exception of Guy Lafleur, Frank Mahovlich, and Claude Ruel, who are pictured from the waist up, the other pictures are full body shots. The player's name appears below the picture. The pins are made of metal and have a metal clasp on the back. The pins are undated; since Bobby Rousseau's last season with the Canadiens was 1969-70 and 1971-72 was Ken Dryden, Guy Lafleur, and Frank Mahovlich's first season with Montreal, we have assigned 1970-72 to the set, meaning the set was likely issued over a period of years and may, in fact, comprise two distinct sets entirely.

COMPLETE SET (22) 75.00 150.00
1 Jean Beliveau 10.00 20.00
2 Yvan Cournoyer 4.00 8.00
3 Ken Dryden 20.00 40.00
4 John Ferguson 2.50 5.00
5 Terry Harper 2.00 4.00
6 Guy Lafleur 12.50 25.00
7 Jacques Laperriere 2.50 5.00
8 Guy Lapointe 2.50 5.00
9 Jacques Lemaire 4.00 8.00
10 Frank Mahovlich 5.00 10.00
11 Peter Mahovlich 2.50 5.00
12 Henri Richard 5.00 10.00
13 Bobby Rousseau 2.50 5.00
14 Claude Ruel CO 1.50 3.00
15 Serge Savard 2.50 5.00
16 J.C. Tremblay 2.00 4.00
17 Rogatien Vachon 4.00 8.00
18 Ted Harris 2.50 5.00
19 Claude Provost 2.50 5.00
20 Mickey Redmond 3.00 6.00
21 Ralph Backstrom 2.50 5.00
22 Gump Worsley 5.00 10.00

1971-72 Canadiens Postcards

This 25-card set of postcards features full-bleed posed color player photos with facsimile autographs in black across the pictures. For the 1969-70, 1970-71, and 1971-72 seasons, many of the same poses were issued. The cards are unnumbered and checklisted below in alphabetical order. The key cards in the set are Ken Dryden and Guy Lafleur appearing in their Rookie Card year. Also noteworthy is Coach Scotty Bowman's first card.

COMPLETE SET (25) 75.00 150.00
1 Pierre Bouchard .75 1.50
2 Scotty Bowman CO 4.00 8.00
3 Yvan Cournoyer 4.00 8.00
4 Denis DeJordy 1.50 3.00
5 Ken Dryden 20.00 40.00
6 Terry Harper 1.00 2.00
7 Dale Hoganson .75 1.50
8 Rejean Houle 1.00 2.00
9 Guy Lafleur 15.00 30.00
10 Jacques Laperriere 2.00 4.00
11 Guy Lapointe 2.00 4.00
12 Claude Larose .75 1.50
13 Jacques Lemaire 4.00 8.00
14 Frank Mahovlich 4.00 8.00
15 Peter Mahovlich 1.50 3.00
16 Phil Myre 1.50 3.00
17 Larry Pleau 1.00 2.00
18 Henri Richard 4.00 8.00
19 Phil Roberto .75 1.50
20 Jim Roberts .75 1.50
21 Leon Rochefort .75 1.50
22 Serge Savard 2.00 4.00
23 Marc Tardif 1.25 2.50
24 J.C. Tremblay 1.25 2.50
25 Rogatien Vachon 4.00 8.00

1972-73 Canadiens Postcards

This 22-card set features white bordered posed color player photos with pale green

backgrounds. A facsimile autograph appears across the picture. The words "Pro Star Promotions, Inc." are printed in the border at the bottom. The Scotty Bowman card is the same as in the 1971-72 set. The cards are unnumbered and checklisted below in alphabetical order. The card of Steve Shutt predates his Rookie Card by two years.

COMPLETE SET (22) 62.50 125.00
1 Chuck Arnason 1.00 2.00
2 Pierre Bouchard 1.50 3.00
3 Scotty Bowman CO 5.00 10.00
4 Yvan Cournoyer 2.50 5.00
5 Ken Dryden 17.50 35.00
6 Rejean Houle 1.50 3.00
7 Guy Lafleur 10.00 20.00
8 Jacques Laperriere 2.00 4.00
9 Guy Lapointe 2.00 4.00
10 Claude Larose 1.00 2.00
11 Chuck Lefley 1.00 2.00
12 Jacques Lemaire 2.50 5.00
13 Frank Mahovlich 2.50 5.00
14 Peter Mahovlich 2.00 4.00
15 Bob Murdoch 1.00 2.00
16 Michel Plasse 2.00 4.00
17 Henri Richard 2.50 5.00
18 Jim Roberts 1.00 2.00
19 Serge Savard 2.00 4.00
20 Steve Shutt 4.00 8.00
21 Marc Tardif 1.50 3.00
22 Murray Wilson 1.00 2.00

1972 Canadiens Great West Life Prints

Cards measure 11" x 14" and were produced by Great West Life Insurance Company. Backs are blank. Cards are unnumbered and checklisted below in alphabetical order.

COMPLETE SET (6) 50.00 100.00
1 Pierre Bouchard 5.00 10.00
2 Yvan Cournoyer 5.00 10.00
3 Ken Dryden 20.00 40.00
4 Pete Mahovlich 5.00 10.00
5 Guy Lafleur 12.50 25.00
6 Steve Shutt 5.00 10.00

1973-74 Canadiens Postcards

This 24-card set features full-bleed color action player photos. The player's name, number and a facsimile autograph are printed on the back. Reportedly distribution problems limited sales to the public. The cards are unnumbered and checklisted below in alphabetical order. The card of Bob Gainey predates his Rookie Card by one year.

COMPLETE SET (24) 40.00 80.00
1 Jean Beliveau 6.00 12.00
(Portrait)
2 Pierre Bouchard .75 1.50
3 Scotty Bowman CO 3.00 6.00
(At bench)
4 Yvan Cournoyer 2.50 5.00
5 Bob Gainey 4.00 8.00
6 Dave Gardner .75 1.50
7 Guy Lafleur 5.00 10.00
8 Yvon Lambert .75 1.50
9 Jacques Laperriere 1.25 2.50
10 Guy Lapointe 1.25 2.50
11 Michel Larocque 1.50 3.00
12 Claude Larose SP 2.50 5.00
13 Chuck Lefley .75 1.50
14 Jacques Lemaire 1.50 3.00
15 Frank Mahovlich 2.50 5.00
16 Peter Mahovlich 1.25 2.50
17 Michel Plasse SP 2.50 5.00
18 Henri Richard 2.50 5.00
19 Jim Roberts SP 2.50 5.00
20 Larry Robinson 5.00 10.00
21 Serge Savard 1.25 2.50
22 Steve Shutt 2.50 5.00
23 Wayne Thomas 1.25 2.50
24 Murray Wilson SP 2.50 5.00

1974-75 Canadiens Postcards

This 27-card set features full-bleed color photos of players seated on a bench in the forum. The cards were issued with and without facsimile autographs. Claude Larose (13) and Chuck Lefley (14) went to St. Louis mid-season resulting in limited distribution of their cards. The Mario Tremblay card (25) was issued only without a facsimile autograph. The cards are unnumbered and checklisted below in alphabetical order.

COMPLETE SET (27) 37.50 75.00
1 Pierre Bouchard .75 1.50
2 Scotty Bowman CO 2.00 4.00
3 Rick Chartraw .75 1.50
4 Yvan Cournoyer 2.00 4.00
5 Ken Dryden 6.00 12.00
6 Bob Gainey 4.00 8.00
7 Glenn Goldup .75 1.50
8 Guy Lafleur 4.00 8.00
9 Yvon Lambert .75 1.50
10 Jacques Laperriere 1.00 2.00
11 Guy Lapointe 1.50 3.00
12 Michel Larocque 1.00 2.00
13 Claude Larose SP 1.50 3.00
14 Chuck Lefley SP 1.50 3.00
15 Jacques Lemaire 2.00 4.00
16 Peter Mahovlich 1.00 2.00
17 Henri Richard 2.00 4.00
18 Doug Risebrough 1.00 2.00
19 Jim Roberts SP 1.50 3.00
20 Larry Robinson 4.00 8.00
21 Glen Sather 1.50 3.00
22 Serge Savard 1.00 2.00
23 Steve Shutt 2.00 4.00
24 Wayne Thomas 1.00 2.00
25 Mario Tremblay 1.00 2.00
26 John Van Boxmeer .75 1.50
27 Murray Wilson SP 1.50 3.00

1975-76 Canadiens Postcards

This 20-card set features posed color photos of players on ice. A facsimile autograph appears in a white bottom border. The cards are unnumbered and checklisted below in alphabetical order. The Doug Jarvis card predates his Rookie Card by one year.

COMPLETE SET (20) 25.00 50.00
1 Don Awrey .75 1.50
2 Pierre Bouchard .75 1.50
3 Scotty Bowman CO 2.00 4.00
(Portrait)
4 Yvan Cournoyer 2.00 4.00
5 Ken Dryden 6.00 12.00
6 Bob Gainey 2.00 4.00
7 Doug Jarvis 2.00 4.00
(White uniform)
8 Guy Lafleur 4.00 8.00
9 Yvon Lambert .75 1.50
10 Guy Lapointe 1.25 2.50
11 Michel Larocque 1.00 2.00
12 Jacques Lemaire 2.00 4.00
13 Peter Mahovlich 1.00 2.00
14 Doug Risebrough .75 1.50
15 Jim Roberts .75 1.50
16 Larry Robinson 3.00 6.00
17 Serge Savard 1.25 2.50
18 Steve Shutt 2.00 4.00
19 Mario Tremblay 1.00 2.00
20 Murray Wilson .75 1.50

1976-77 Canadiens Postcards

This 23-card set features posed color photos of players seated in front of a light blue studio background. A facsimile autograph appears in a white bottom border. The cards are unnumbered and checklisted below in alphabetical order.

COMPLETE SET (23) 25.00 50.00
1 Pierre Bouchard .75 1.50
2 Scotty Bowman CO 2.00 4.00
3 Rick Chartraw .75 1.50
4 Yvan Cournoyer 1.50 3.00
5 Ken Dryden 5.00 10.00
6 Bob Gainey 2.00 4.00
7 Rejean Houle .75 1.50
8 Doug Jarvis 1.00 2.00
9 Guy Lafleur 4.00 8.00
10 Yvon Lambert .75 1.50
11 Guy Lapointe 1.00 2.00
12 Michel Larocque 1.25 2.50
13 Jacques Lemaire 1.50 3.00
14 Peter Mahovlich 1.00 2.00
15 Bill Nyrop .75 1.50
16 Doug Risebrough .75 1.50
17 Jim Roberts .75 1.50
18 Larry Robinson 2.50 5.00
19 Claude Ruel CO .50 1.00
20 Serge Savard 1.00 2.00
21 Steve Shutt 1.50 3.00
22 Mario Tremblay 1.00 2.00
23 Murray Wilson .75 1.50

1977-78 Canadiens Postcards

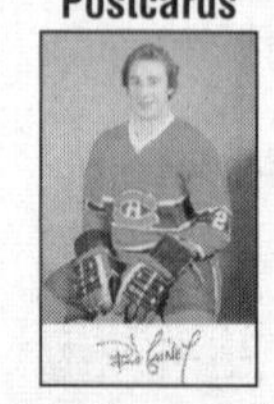

This 25-card set features posed action color photos of players on the ice. A facsimile autograph appears in a white bottom bottom. New players were photographed from the shoulders up. Many of the cards are the same as in the 1975-76 set. The cards are unnumbered and checklisted below in alphabetical order.

COMPLETE SET (25) 25.00 50.00
1 Pierre Bouchard .50 1.00
2 Scotty Bowman CO 1.50 3.00
3 Rick Chartraw .50 1.00
4 Yvan Cournoyer 1.50 3.00
5 Ken Dryden 4.50 9.00
6 Brian Engblom .75 1.50
7 Bob Gainey 1.50 3.00
8 Rejean Houle .50 1.00
9 Doug Jarvis .75 1.50
10 Guy Lafleur 3.00 6.00
11 Yvon Lambert .50 1.00
12 Guy Lapointe 1.00 2.00
13 Michel Larocque .75 1.50
14 Pierre Larouche 1.00 2.00
15 Jacques Lemaire 1.25 2.50
16 Gilles Lupien .50 1.00
17 Pierre Mondou .50 1.00
18 Bill Nyrop .50 1.00
19 Doug Risebrough .50 1.00
20 Larry Robinson 2.00 4.00
21 Claude Ruel CO .50 1.00
22 Serge Savard 1.00 2.00
23 Steve Shutt 1.50 3.00
24 Mario Tremblay .75 1.50
25 Murray Wilson .50 1.00

1978-79 Canadiens Postcards

This 26-card set features posed color player photos taken from the shoulders up. All the pictures have a red background except for Ruel and Cournoyer who are shown against blue. A facsimile autograph appears in a white bottom border. The cards are unnumbered and checklisted below in alphabetical order. The key card in the set is Rod Langway, appearing two years before his Rookie Card.

COMPLETE SET (26) 25.00 50.00
1 Scotty Bowman CO 1.50 3.00
2 Rick Chartraw .50 1.00
3 Cam Connor .50 1.00
4 Yvan Cournoyer 1.50 3.00
5 Ken Dryden 4.00 8.00
6 Brian Engblom .50 1.00
7 Bob Gainey 1.50 3.00
8 Rejean Houle .50 1.00
9 Pat Hughes .50 1.00
10 Doug Jarvis .75 1.50
11 Guy Lafleur 3.00 6.00
12 Yvon Lambert .50 1.00
13 Rod Langway 2.00 4.00
14 Guy Lapointe 1.00 2.00
15 Michel Larocque .75 1.50
16 Pierre Larouche 1.00 2.00
17 Jacques Lemaire 1.25 2.50
18 Gilles Lupien .50 1.00
19 Pierre Mondou .50 1.00
20 Mark Napier .50 1.00
21 Doug Risebrough .50 1.00
22 Larry Robinson 2.00 4.00
23 Claude Ruel CO .50 1.00
24 Serge Savard 1.00 2.00
25 Steve Shutt 1.50 3.00
26 Mario Tremblay .50 1.00

1979-80 Canadiens Postcards

This 25-card set features posed color player photos taken from the waist up. All the pictures have a red background except for Ruel who is shown against blue. A facsimile autograph appears in a white bottom border. Several cards are the same as the 1978-79 issue. Bernie Geoffrion's card was not distributed after he resigned as coach on December 12, 1980. Richard Sevigny's card received limited distribution because of late issue. The cards are unnumbered and checklisted below in alphabetical order. The cards measure approximately 3 1/2" by 5 1/2" and the backs are blank.

COMPLETE SET (25) 20.00 40.00
1 Rick Chartraw .50 1.00
2 Normand Dupont .50 1.00
3 Brian Engblom .50 1.00
4 Bob Gainey 1.50 3.00
5 Bernie Geoffrion CO SP 2.50 5.00
6 Danny Geoffrion .50 1.00
7 Denis Herron .75 1.50
8 Rejean Houle .50 1.00
9 Doug Jarvis .50 1.00
10 Guy Lafleur 2.50 5.00
11 Yvon Lambert .50 1.00
12 Rod Langway 1.00 2.00
13 Guy Lapointe 1.00 2.00
14 Michel Larocque .75 1.50
15 Pierre Larouche 1.00 2.00
16 Gilles Lupien .50 1.00
17 Pierre Mondou .50 1.00
18 Mark Napier .75 1.50
19 Doug Risebrough .75 1.50
20 Larry Robinson 1.50 3.00
21 Claude Ruel CO .50 1.00
22 Serge Savard .75 1.50
23 Richard Sevigny SP 2.50 5.00
24 Steve Shutt 1.00 2.00
25 Mario Tremblay .75 1.50

1980-81 Canadiens Postcards

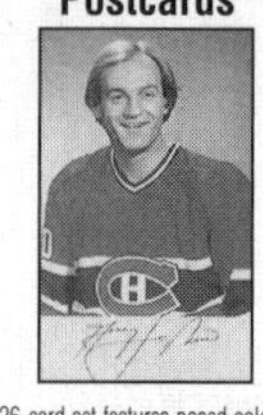

This 26-card set features posed color player photos taken from the waist up against a blue background. A facsimile autograph appears in a white bottom border. The cards are unnumbered and checklisted below in alphabetical order. The cards measure approximately 3 1/2" by 5 1/2" and the backs are blank.

COMPLETE SET (26) 17.50 35.00
1 Keith Acton .75 1.50
2 Bill Baker .50 1.00
3 Rick Chartraw .50 1.00
4 Brian Engblom .50 1.00
5 Bob Gainey 1.00 2.00
6 Gaston Gingras .50 1.00
7 Denis Herron 1.00 2.00
8 Rejean Houle .75 1.50
9 Doug Jarvis .50 1.00
10 Guy Lafleur 2.50 5.00
11 Yvon Lambert .50 1.00
12 Rod Langway .75 1.50
13 Guy Lapointe 1.00 2.00
14 Michel Larocque 1.00 2.00
15 Pierre Larouche .75 1.50
16 Pierre Mondou .50 1.00
17 Mark Napier .50 1.00
18 Chris Nilan 1.00 2.00
19 Doug Risebrough .50 1.00
20 Larry Robinson 1.50 3.00
21 Claude Ruel CO .50 1.00
22 Serge Savard .75 1.50
23 Richard Sevigny .50 1.00
24 Steve Shutt 1.00 2.00
25 Mario Tremblay .75 1.50
26 Doug Wickenheiser .50 1.00

1981-82 Canadiens Postcards

This 28-card set features posed color player photos taken from the waist up against a blue or blue-white background. A facsimile autograph appears in a white bottom border. Many cards are the same as in the 1980-81 set. The Gilbert Delorme card was short-printed. The cards are unnumbered and checklisted below in alphabetical order.

COMPLETE SET (28) 14.00 35.00
1 Team Photo 1.20 3.00
2 Keith Acton .40 1.00
3 Bob Berry CO .30 .75
4 Jeff Brubaker .30 .75
5 Gilbert Delorme SP 1.60 4.00
6 Brian Engblom .30 .75
7 Bob Gainey .80 2.00
8 Gaston Gingras .30 .75
9 Denis Herron .50 1.25
10 Rejean Houle .40 1.00
11 Mark Hunter .30 .75
12 Doug Jarvis .30 .75
13 Guy Lafleur 2.00 5.00
14 Rod Langway .60 1.50
15 Jacques Laperriere .60 1.50
16 Guy Lapointe .60 1.50
17 Craig Laughlin .30 .75
18 Pierre Mondou .30 .75
19 Mark Napier .40 1.00
20 Chris Nilan .40 1.00
21 Robert Picard .30 .75
22 Doug Risebrough .30 .75
23 Larry Robinson 1.20 3.00
24 Richard Sevigny .50 1.25
25 Steve Shutt .80 2.00
26 Mario Tremblay .40 1.00
27 Rick Wamsley .50 1.25
28 Doug Wickenheiser .30 .75

1982-83 Canadiens Postcards

This 28-card set features posed color player photos taken from the waist up against a blue background. A facsimile autograp appears in a white bottom panel. Man photos are the same as in the 1980-81 an 1981-82 sets. Player information, jerse number, and the team logo are on the back The Richard card has the same style but it i not originally part of the set; it was issued i 1983. The Root card was issued late in th year and thus was limited in its distributior Some color variations appear in the Gaine and Picard cards. The cards are unnumbere and checklisted below in alphabetical orde Notable cards in the set include Gu Carbonneau and Mats Naslund appearin the year before their Rookie Card.

COMPLETE SET (28) 12.00 30.00
1 Keith Acton .30 .75
2 Bob Berry CO .30 .75
3 Guy Carbonneau 1.60 4.00
4 Dan Daoust .30 .75
5 Gilbert Delorme .30 .75
6 Bob Gainey .80 2.00
7 Gaston Gingras .30 .75
8 Rick Green .30 .75
9 Rejean Houle .30 .75
10 Mark Hunter .30 .75
11 Guy Lafleur 2.00 5.00
12 Jacques Laperriere .40 1.00
13 Craig Ludwig .60 1.50
14 Pierre Mondou .30 .75
15 Mark Napier .40 1.00
16 Mats Naslund 1.20 3.00
17 Ric Nattress .30 .75
18 Chris Nilan .40 1.00
19 Robert Picard .30 .75
20 Henri Richard 1.20 3.00
21 Larry Robinson 1.20 3.00
22 Bill Root SP .80 2.00
23 Richard Sevigny .50 1.25
24 Steve Shutt .80 2.00
25 Mario Tremblay .40 1.00
26 Ryan Walter .40 1.00
27 Rick Wamsley .50 1.25
28 Doug Wickenheiser .30 .75

1982-83 Canadiens Steinberg

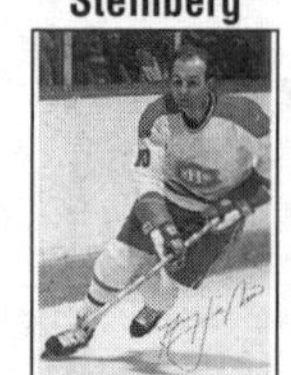

This 24-card set was sponsored b Steinberg and the Montreal Canadien Hockey Club as the "Follow the Play promotion. The cards were issued in a sma vinyl photo album with one card per binde and measure approximately 3 1/2" by 15/16". For a few of the players, th biography on the card back is written i French; those players are so noted in th checklist below. We have checklisted th cards below in alphabetical order.

COMPLETE SET (24) 10.00 25.00
1 Keith Acton .20 .50
2 Guy Carbonneau 1.20 3.00
3 Gilbert Delorme .20 .50
{(French bio)
4 Bob Gainey .60 1.50
5 Rick Green .20 .50
6 Mark Hunter .20 .50
7 Rejean Houle .20 .50
8 Guy Lafleur 1.60 4.00
9 Craig Ludwig .40 1.00
10 Pierre Mondou .20 .50
11 Mark Napier .30 .75
12 Mats Naslund .80 2.00
13 Ric Nattress .20 .50
{(French bio)
14 Chris Nilan .30 .75
15 Robert Picard .20 .50
16 Larry Robinson .80 2.00
17 Bill Root .20 .50
18 Richard Sevigny .40 1.00
19 Steve Shutt .60 1.50
20 Mario Tremblay .30 .75
21 Ryan Walter .30 .75
22 Rick Wamsley .40 1.00
{(French bio)
23 Doug Wickenheiser .20 .50
24 Title Card .50 1.25
Team photo (Canadiens celebrating on ice)
xx Vinyl Card Album 2.00 5.00

1983-84 Canadiens Postcards

This 33-card set features color photos c players posed on the ice. A facsimil autograph appears at the bottom. Playe information, jersey number, and the tean logo are on the back. The team continued t issue cards throughout the season, s several card were distributed on a limite basis. The Laperriere card (number 14) i the same card as in the 1982-83 set. Th Delorme and Wickenheiser cards were no issued as part of the set because of trade issued in 1984, the Beliveau card was not part of the team set but has the same style. The cards are unnumbered and checklisted below in alphabetical order. The key card in the set is Chris Chelios appearing the year before his Rookie Card.

COMPLETE SET (33) 16.00 40.00
1 Jean Beliveau 1.20 3.00
2 Bob Berry CO .30 .75
3 Guy Carbonneau .80 2.00
4 Kent Carlson .30 .75
5 John Chabot .30 .75
6 Chris Chelios 4.00 10.00
7 Gilbert Delorme SP 1.20 3.00
8 Bob Gainey .60 1.50
9 Rick Green .30 .75
10 Jean Hamel .30 .75
11 Mark Hunter .30 .75
12 Guy Lafleur 1.60 4.00
13 Jacques Lemaire .60 1.50
14 Jacques Laperriere .40 1.00
(Action shot)
15 Jacques Laperriere .40 1.00
(Head shot)
16 Craig Ludwig .40 1.00
17 Pierre Mondou .30 .75
18 Mats Naslund .80 2.00
19 Ric Nattress .30 .75
20 Chris Nilan .40 1.00
21 Steve Penney .40 1.00
22 Jacques Plante 1.20 3.00
23 Larry Robinson 1.00 2.50
24 Bill Root .30 .75
25 Richard Sevigny .40 1.00
26 Steve Shutt .60 1.50
27 Bobby Smith .60 1.50
28 Mario Tremblay .40 1.00
29 Alfie Turcotte .30 .75
30 Perry Turnbull .30 .75
31 Ryan Walter .30 .75
32 Rick Wamsley .50 1.25
33 Doug Wickenheiser SP 1.20 3.00

1984-85 Canadiens Postcards

This 31-card set features color photos of players posed on the ice. A facsimile autograph appears at the bottom. Player information, jersey number, and the team logo are on the back. Many cards are the same as in the 1983-84 set. The cards are unnumbered and checklisted below in alphabetical order.

COMPLETE SET (31) 12.00 30.00
1 Guy Carbonneau .60 1.50
(Action on ice& foot raised& with puck)
2 Guy Carbonneau .60 1.50
(Still& both feet on ice& no puck)
3 Kent Carlson .30 .75
4 Chris Chelios 2.40 6.00
Same card as 1983-84, but with autograph on front
5 Lucien Deblois .30 .75
6 Ron Flockhart .30 .75
7 Bob Gainey .60 1.50
8 Rick Green .30 .75
9 Jean Hamel .30 .75
10 Mark Hunter .30 .75
11 Tom Kurvers .30 .75
12 Guy Lafleur 1.60 4.00
13 Jacques Laperriere .40 1.00
14 Jacques Lemaire .60 1.50
15 Craig Ludwig .40 1.00
16 Mike McPhee .60 1.50
17 Pierre Mondou .30 .75
18 Mats Naslund .80 2.00
19 Ric Nattress .30 .75
20 Chris Nilan .40 1.00
21 Steve Penney .40 1.00
(Same card as 1983-84)
22 Steve Penney .40 1.00
23 Jean Perron .30 .75
24 Larry Robinson 1.00 2.50
25 Bobby Smith .60 1.50
26 Doug Soetaert .40 1.00
27 Petr Svoboda .60 1.50
28 Mario Tremblay .30 .75
29 Alfie Turcotte .30 .75
(Same card as 1983-84)
30 Alfie Turcotte .30 .75
(Autograph on front)
31 Ryan Walter .40 1.00

1985-86 Canadiens Placemats

Sponsored by Pepsi-Cola and 7-Up, this set of seven placemats was issued to commemorate the Montreal Canadiens as the 1984-85 Division Champions. Each placemat measures approximately 11" by 17". On an yellow-orange background with a white border, the front carries a painted portrait, action shot and a facsimile autograph of two different players. Player name, position, and number, date and place of birth, and career statistics in French and English are also found on the front. The sponsors' logos appear in the upper right corner. The backs feature a red-and-white plaid design. The placemats are unnumbered. One placemat shows portraits of all twelve players with their facsimile autographs.

COMPLETE SET (7) 8.00 20.00
1 Bob Gainey 1.60 4.00
Guy Carbonneau
2 Mats Naslund .80 2.00
Tom Kurvers
3 Chris Nilan .80 2.00
Petr Svoboda
4 Steve Penney 2.00 5.00
Chris Chelios
5 Larry Robinson 1.60 4.00
Serge Boisvert
6 Mario Tremblay .80 2.00
Bobby Smith
7 Hockey Stars 2.00 5.00
Steve Penney
Chris Chelios
Larry Robinson
Serge Boisvert
Mario Tremblay
Bobby Smith
Mats Naslund
Tom Kurvers
Bob Gainey
Guy Carbonneau
Chris Nilan
Petr Svoboda

1985-86 Canadiens Postcards

This 40-card set features color photos of players posed in red uniforms against a white background. A facsimile autograph appears on a red diagonal line in the lower right corner on most cards. However, there is some variation in the autograph location. Player information and the team logo are on the back. Several cards (1, 2, 3, 11, 14, 17, 19) were issued late in the season. The cards are unnumbered and checklisted below in alphabetical order. The key card in this set is Patrick Roy, which pre-dates his Rookie Card by one year. Other notable early cards include Claude Lemieux, Stephane Richer, and Brian Skrudland.

COMPLETE SET (40) 24.00 60.00
1 Serge Boisvert SP .60 1.50
(No red line or autograph)
2 Serge Boisvert SP .60 1.50
(Portrait)
3 Randy Bucyk SP .60 1.50
(No red line or autograph)
4 Guy Carbonneau .40 1.00
5 Chris Chelios 1.60 4.00
6 Kjell Dahlin .20 .50
(J in autograph on stick)
7 Kjell Dahlin .20 .50
(E in autograph on stick)
8 Lucien Deblois .20 .50
9 Bob Gainey .60 1.50
(B in autograph on stick)
10 Bob Gainey .60 1.50
(G in autograph on stick)
11 Gaston Gingras SP .60 1.50
12 Rick Green .20 .50
(No letters on stick)
13 Rick Green .20 .50
(C in autograph on stick)
14 John Kordic SP 2.00 5.00
(No red line or autograph)
15 Tom Kurvers .20 .50
16 Mike Lalor .20 .50
17 Claude Lemieux SP 3.20 8.00
(No red line or autograph)
18 Craig Ludwig .30 .75
19 David Maley SP .60 1.50
(No red line or autograph)
20 Mike McPhee .40 1.00
21 Sergio Momesso .30 .75
22 Mats Naslund .60 1.50
23 Chris Nilan .30 .75
(Dot from i in Nilan touching toe)
24 Chris Nilan .30 .75
(Dot from i in Nilan away from toe)
25 Steve Penney .30 .75
26 Jean Perron .20 .50
(Portrait)
27 Stephane Richer .80 2.00
28 Larry Robinson 1.00 2.50
29 Steve Rooney .20 .50
(Loop in R through skate toe)
30 Steve Rooney .20 .50
(Loop in R through skate laces)
31 Patrick Roy 10.00 25.00
32 Brian Skrudland .80 2.00
33 Bobby Smith .40 1.00
(B in autograph touching stick)
34 Bobby Smith .40 1.00
(O in autograph on stick)
35 Doug Soetaert .30 .75
(T at end of name by pad)
36 Doug Soetaert .30 .75
(T at end of name away from pad)
37 Petr Svoboda .30 .75
38 Mario Tremblay .30 .75
(T in autograph touching blade)
39 Mario Tremblay .30 .75
(T in autograph away from blade)
40 Ryan Walter .30 .75

1985-86 Canadiens Provigo

This 25-sticker set of the Montreal Canadiens was produced by Provigo. The puffy (Styrofoam-backed) stickers measure approximately 1 1/8" by 2 1/4" and feature a color head and shoulders photo of the player, with the player's number and name bordered by star-studded banners across the bottom of the picture. The Canadiens' logo is superimposed over the banner at its right end. The backs are blank. We have checklisted them below in alphabetical order, with the uniform number to the right of the player's name. The 25 stickers were to be attached to a cardboard poster. The poster measures approximately 20" by 11" and has 25 white spaces designated for the stickers on a red background. At the center is a picture of a goalie mask, with the Canadiens' logo above and slightly to the right. The back of the poster has a checklist, stripes in the team's colors, and two team logos. The set features early cards of Stephane Richer and Patrick Roy pre-dating their actual Rookie Cards.

COMPLETE SET (25) 16.00 40.00
1 Guy Carbonneau 21 .50 1.25
2 Chris Chelios 24 1.60 4.00
3 Kjell Dahlin 20 .20 .50
4 Lucien Deblois 27 .20 .50
5 Bob Gainey 23 .60 1.50
6 Rick Green 5 .20 .50
7 Tom Kurvers 18 .20 .50
8 Mike Lalor 38 .20 .50
9 Craig Ludwig 17 .30 .75
10 Mike McPhee 35 .40 1.00
11 Sergio Momesso 36 .30 .75
12 Mats Naslund 26 .60 1.50
13 Chris Nilan 30 .30 .75
14 Steve Penney 37 .30 .75
15 Jean Perron CO .20 .50
16 Stephane Richer 44 .80 2.00
17 Larry Robinson 19 1.00 2.50
18 Steve Rooney 28 .20 .50
19 Patrick Roy 33 10.00 25.00
20 Brian Skrudland 39 .80 2.00
21 Bobby Smith 15 .40 1.00
22 Doug Soetaert 1 .20 .50
23 Petr Svoboda 25 .30 .75
24 Mario Tremblay 14 .30 .75
25 Ryan Walter 11 .30 .75
NNO Provigo Poster 2.00 5.00

1986-87 Canadiens Postcards

Each of the 25 cards in this set measures approximately 3 3/8" by 5 1/2". The front features a color posed photo (without borders) of the player. The information on the back has a diagonal orientation and is printed in the Canadiens' team colors read and blue. At the top on the back appears the Canadiens' logo, followed by the player's name, his signature, and brief biographical information (in French and English). Notably, the Shayne Corson card in this set pre-dates his RC by three years.

COMPLETE SET (25) 14.00 35.00
1 Guy Carbonneau 21 .40 1.00
2 Chris Chelios 24 1.20 3.00
3 Shayne Corson 34 .80 2.00
4 Kjell Dahlin 20 .20 .50
5 Bob Gainey 23 .40 1.00
6 Rick Green 5 .20 .50
7 Brian Hayward 1 .40 1.00
8 John Kordic 31 .60 1.50
9 Mike Lalor 38 .20 .50
10 Jacques Laperriere ACO .30 .75
11 Claude Lemieux 1.60 4.00
12 Craig Ludwig 17 .20 .50
13 Mike McPhee 35 .30 .75
14 Sergio Momesso 36 .20 .50
15 Mats Naslund 26 .40 1.00
16 Chris Nilan 30 .30 .75
17 Jean Perron CO .20 .50
18 Stephane Richer 44 .80 2.00
19 Larry Robinson 19 .80 2.00
20 Patrick Roy 33 6.00 15.00
21 Scott Sandelin 3 .20 .50
22 Brian Skrudland 39 .60 1.50
23 Bobby Smith 15 .30 .75
24 Petr Svoboda 25 .20 .50
25 Ryan Walter 11 .30 .75
26 Serge Savard
27 Larry Trader
28 Francois Allaire

1987 Canadiens Kodak

Little is known about this set. It is believed that the cards below represent a partial checklist for what likely was a promotional giveaway. Any additional information may be forwarded to hockeymag@beckett.com.

COMPLETE SET (7) 2.40 6.00
1 Guy Carbonneau .40 1.00
2 Bob Gainey .50 1.25
3 Mike McPhee .30 .75
4 Mats Naslund .40 1.00
5 Chris Nilan .30 .75
6 Larry Robinson .80 2.00
7 Bobby Smith .30 .75

1987-88 Canadiens Postcards

This 35-card set is in the postcard size format, with each card measuring approximately 3 1/2" by 5 1/2". The fronts feature full-bleed posed color action shots. In a diagonal format at the top of the back appears the team logo, followed by the player's name, his signature, and brief biographical information (in French and English). The cards are unnumbered and checklisted below in alphabetical order. There are two versions of the Stephane Richer postcard (#23); both are included in the complete set price.

COMPLETE SET (35) 12.00 30.00
1 Francois Allaire ACO .10 .25
2 Guy Carbonneau .40 1.00
3 Jose Charbonneau .20 .50
4 Chris Chelios 1.00 2.50
5 Shayne Corson .40 1.00
6 Kjell Dahlin .20 .50
7 Bob Gainey .50 1.25
8 Rick Green .20 .50
9 Gaston Gingras .20 .50
10 Brian Hayward .30 .75
11 John Kordic .60 1.50
12 Mike Lalor .20 .50
13 Jacques Laperriere ACO .20 .50
14 Claude Lemieux 1.20 3.00
15 Craig Ludwig .20 .50
16 David Maley .20 .50
17 Mike McPhee .30 .75
18 Sergio Momesso .20 .50
19 Claude Mouton ANN .10 .25
20 Mats Naslund .40 1.00
21 Chris Nilan .30 .75
22 Jean Perron CO .10 .25
23A Stephane Richer .60 1.50
(With moustache)
23B Stephane Richer .60 1.50
(No moustache)
24 Larry Robinson .80 2.00
25 Steve Rooney .20 .50
26 Patrick Roy 6.00 15.00
27 Scott Sandelin .20 .50
28 Serge Savard DIR .30 .75
29 Brian Skrudland .50 1.25
30 Bobby Smith .30 .75
31 Petr Svoboda .20 .50
32 Gilles Thibaudeau .20 .50
33 Larry Trader .20 .50
34 Ryan Walter .30 .75

1987-88 Canadiens Vachon Stickers

Featuring the Montreal Canadiens, this set consists of 28 panels, each measuring approximately 2 7/8" by 5 9/16". Each panel is made up of five stickers, two that measure approximately 1 1/2" by 2 5/8", and three that measure approximately 1" by 1 11/16". The larger stickers carry color action player photos or team pictures. The smaller ones are close-ups of players or action shots. The stickers appear in a variety of combinations on the panels, with one panel showing small player shots and another panel carrying the same player shots but with different action photos. All told, 88 different stickers were printed. The back of the panel explains in French and English that albums are available for 49 cents at participating supermarkets and at "Les Canadiens" souvenir boutiques, and that collectors can send in 2.00 to Super Series Vachon and receive the album through the mail. The first six stickers can be pieced together to form a composite team photo. The stickers are numbered on the front.

COMPLETE SET (88) 16.00 40.00
1 Canadiens Team Photo .10 .25
(Top left)
2 Canadiens Team Photo .10 .25
(Top middle)
3 Canadiens Team Photo .10 .25
(Top right)
4 Canadiens Team Photo .10 .25
(Bottom left)
5 Canadiens Team Photo .10 .25
(Bottom middle)
6 Canadiens Team Photo .10 .25
(Bottom right)
7 Jean Perron CO .10 .25
8 Jacques Laperriere ACO .10 .25
9 Francois Allaire ACO .10 .25
10 Jean Perron CO .10 .25
11 Jacques Laperriere .10 .25
12 Bob Gainey .30 .75
13 Bob Gainey .30 .75
14 Guy Carbonneau .16 .40
15 Guy Carbonneau .16 .40
16 Guy Carbonneau .16 .40
17 Michael McPhee .16 .40
18 Bob Gainey .30 .75
19 Chris Nilan .16 .40
20 Chris Nilan .16 .40
21 Guy Carbonneau .16 .40
22 Mike Lalor .10 .25
23 Patrick Roy and 1.60 4.00
Guy Carbonneau
24 Ryan Walter .10 .25
25 Ryan Walter .10 .25
26 Bobby Smith .16 .40
27 Mats Naslund .16 .40
28 Bobby Smith .16 .40
29 Mike McPhee .16 .40
30 Bobby Smith .16 .40
31 Claude Lemieux .80 2.00
32 Brian Skrudland .10 .25
33 Craig Ludwig .16 .40
34 Brian Skrudland .16 .40
35 Craig Ludwig .10 .25
36 Brian Skrudland .16 .40
37 Mike McPhee .16 .40
38 Mike McPhee .16 .40
39 Kjell Dahlin .10 .25
40 Kjell Dahlin .10 .25
41 Bobby Smith .16 .40
42 Patrick Roy 2.00 5.00
43 Patrick Roy 2.00 5.00
44 Larry Trader .10 .25
45 Mats Naslund .20 .50
46 Mats Naslund .20 .50
47 Mats Naslund .20 .50
48 Mats Naslund .20 .50
49 Shayne Corson .20 .50
50 Shayne Corson .20 .50
51 Stephane Richer .20 .50
52 Stephane Richer .20 .50
53 Bob Gainey .30 .75
54 Stephane Richer .20 .50
55 Sergio Momesso .10 .25
56 Sergio Momesso .10 .25
57 John Kordic .40 1.00
58 John Kordic .40 1.00
59 Mike Lalor .10 .25
60 Mike Lalor .10 .25
61 Brian Hayward .16 .40
62 Guy Carbonneau .16 .40
63 Guy Carbonneau .16 .40
64 Brian Hayward .16 .40
65 Rick Green .10 .25
66 Rick Green .10 .25
67 Brian Hayward .16 .40
68 Rick Green .10 .25
69 Patrick Roy 2.00 5.00
70 Rick Green .10 .25
71 Patrick Roy 2.00 5.00
72 Larry Robinson .40 1.00
73 Larry Robinson .40 1.00
74 Patrick Roy 2.00 5.00
75 Petr Svoboda .10 .25
76 Patrick Roy 2.00 5.00
77 Petr Svoboda .10 .25
78 Chris Chelios .60 1.50
79 Chris Chelios .60 1.50
80 Craig Ludwig .16 .40
81 Craig Ludwig .16 .40
82 Chris Chelios .60 1.50
83 Chris Chelios .60 1.50
84 Brian Hayward .16 .40
85 Craig Ludwig .16 .40
86 Bobby Smith .16 .40
87 Mats Naslund .16 .40
88 Bob Gainey .30 .75
xx Sticker Album 2.00 5.00

1988-89 Canadiens Postcards

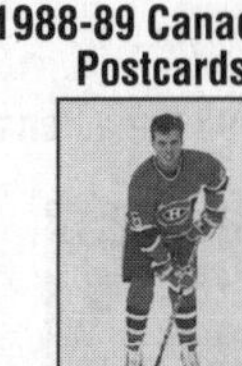

This 30-card, team-issued set measures approximately 3 1/2" by 5 1/2" and features full-bleed color player photos. The players are posed on the ice against a white background. The coaches' cards feature color portraits against a black background. The backs are white and show the team name and logo in large red letters at the top. The player's name, number, and biography are printed in blue. A facsimile autograph at the bottom rounds out the back. The cards are unnumbered and checklisted below in alphabetical order.

COMPLETE SET (30) 10.00 25.00
1 Francois Allaire ACO .10 .25
2 Pat Burns CO .40 1.00
3 Guy Carbonneau .40 1.00
4 Jose Charbonneau .20 .50
5 Chris Chelios .80 2.00
6 Ronald Corey PRES .10 .25
7 Shayne Corson .40 1.00
8 Russ Courtnall .40 1.00
9 Eric Desjardins .60 1.50
10 Bob Gainey .40 1.00
11 Brent Gilchrist .30 .75
12 Rick Green .20 .50
13 Brian Hayward .30 .75
14 Mike Keane .40 1.00
15 Mike Lalor .20 .50
16 Jacques Laperriere ACO .20 .50
17 Claude Lemieux .60 1.50
18 Craig Ludwig .30 .75
19 Steven Martinson .20 .50
20 Mike McPhee .30 .75
21 Mats Naslund .40 1.00
22 Stephane Richer .40 1.00
23 Larry Robinson .80 2.00
24 Patrick Roy 4.00 10.00
25 Serge Savard DIR .40 1.00
26 Brian Skrudland .40 1.00
27 Bobby Smith .30 .75
28 Petr Svoboda .20 .50
30 Ryan Walter .20 .50
39 Gilles Thibaudeau .20 .50

1989-90 Canadiens Kraft

This 24-card set of Montreal Canadiens was sponsored by Le Journal de Montreal and Kraft Foods. The cards were issued as two four-card insert sheets in Les Canadiens magazine. The cards measure approximately 3 3/4" by 5 7/16". The front features a posed color photo of the player on white card stock. The cards are unnumbered and hence are listed below in alphabetical order.

COMPLETE SET (24) 10.00 25.00
1 Pat Burns CO .40 1.00
2 Guy Carbonneau .40 1.00
3 Chris Chelios 1.00 2.50
4 Shayne Corson .60 1.50
5 Russ Courtnall .30 .75
6 J.J. Daigneault .30 .75
7 Eric Desjardins .40 1.00
8 Todd Ewen .30 .75
9 Brent Gilchrist .30 .75
10 Brian Hayward .30 .75
11 Mike Keane .40 1.00
12 Stephan Lebeau .50 1.25
13 Sylvain Lefebvre .30 .75
14 Claude Lemieux .80 2.00
15 Craig Ludwig .40 1.00
16 Mike McPhee .30 .75
17 Mats Naslund .60 1.50
18 Stephane Richer .60 1.50
19 Patrick Roy 3.20 8.00
20 Mathieu Schneider .60 1.50
21 Brian Skrudland .30 .75
22 Bobby Smith .30 .75
23 Petr Svoboda .30 .75
24 Ryan Walter .30 .75

1989-90 Canadiens Postcards

This 32-card set measures approximately 3 7/16" by 5 7/16" and features borderless color player photos. The players are posed on the ice against a white background. The coaches' cards feature color portraits against a black background. The backs are white and carry the team name and logo in large red letters at the top. The player's name, jersey number, and biography are printed in blue. A facsimile autograph at the bottom rounds out the back. The cards are unnumbered and checklisted below in alphabetical order.

COMPLETE SET (32) 10.00 25.00
1 Francois Allaire ACO .10 .25
2 Pat Burns CO .40 1.00
3 Guy Carbonneau .30 .75
4 Chris Chelios .60 1.50
5 Tom Chorske .20 .50
6 Ronald Corey PR .10 .25
7 Shayne Corson .40 1.00
8 Russ Courtnall .40 1.00
9 Jean-Jacques Daigneault .20 .50
10 Eric Desjardins .40 1.00
11 Martin Desjardins .20 .50
12 Donald Dufresne .20 .50
13 Brent Gilchrist .20 .50
14 Brian Hayward .30 .75
15 Mike Keane .30 .75
16 Jacques Laperriere ACO .20 .50
17 Stephan Lebeau .30 .75
18 Sylvain Lefebvre .40 1.00
19 Claude Lemieux .40 1.00
20 Jocelyn Lemieux .20 .50
21 Craig Ludwig .20 .50
22 Jyrki Lumme .40 1.00
23 Steven Martinson .20 .50
24 Mike McPhee .30 .75
25 Mats Naslund .40 1.00
26 Stephane Richer .40 1.00
27 Patrick Roy 2.40 6.00
28 Serge Savard DIR .20 .50
29 Brian Skrudland .40 1.00
30 Bobby Smith .30 .75
31 Petr Svoboda .30 .75
32 Ryan Walter .20 .50

1989-90 Canadiens Provigo Figurines

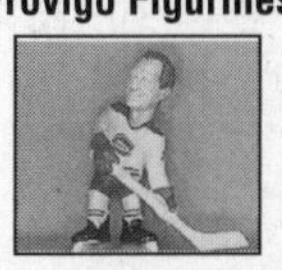

These 13 plastic figurines of the 1989-90 Canadiens are approximately 3" tall and show the players in their white home jerseys, wearing skates and holding white hockey sticks. The players' names and uniform numbers appear on their jersey backs. The figurines are numbered on the backs of the hockey sticks. The original issue price for these figurines was 1.99 Canadian. The figurines were distributed in a package with a coupon booklet.

COMPLETE SET (13) 28.00 70.00
6 Russ Courtnall 1.60 4.00
15 Bobby Smith 1.60 4.00
17 Craig Ludwig 1.20 3.00
21 Guy Carbonneau 1.60 4.00
23 Bob Gainey 2.00 5.00
24 Chris Chelios 3.20 8.00
25 Petr Svoboda 1.20 3.00
26 Mats Naslund 2.00 5.00
27 Shayne Corson 2.00 5.00
33 Patrick Roy 10.00 25.00
35 Mike McPhee 1.20 3.00
39 Brian Skrudland 1.60 4.00
44 Stephane Richer 2.00 5.00

1990-91 Canadiens Postcards

This 33-card set measures approximately 3 1/2" by 5 1/2" and features borderless color player photos. The players are posed on the ice against a white background. The coaches' cards feature color portraits against a black background. The backs are white and carry the team name and logo in large red letters at the top. The player's name, jersey number, and biography are printed in blue. A facsimile autograph at the bottom rounds out the back. The cards are unnumbered and checklisted below in alphabetical order.

COMPLETE SET (33) 10.00 25.00
1 Francois Allaire ACO .10 .25
2 Jean-Claude Bergeron .30 .75
3 Benoit Brunet .20 .50
4 Pat Burns CO .30 .75
5 Guy Carbonneau .30 .75
6 Andrew Cassels .30 .75
7 Tom Chorske .20 .50
8 Ronald Corey PR .10 .25
9 Shayne Corson .40 1.00
10 Russ Courtnall .30 .75
11 Jean-Jacques Daigneault .20 .50
12 Eric Desjardins .40 1.00
13 Gerald Diduck .20 .50
14 Donald Dufresne .20 .50
15 Todd Ewen .24 .60
16 Brent Gilchrist .20 .50
17 Mike Keane .30 .75
18 Jacques Laperriere ACO .20 .50
19 Stephan Lebeau .20 .50
20 Sylvain Lefebvre .30 .75
21 Mike McPhee .30 .75
22 Lyle Odelein .40 1.00
23 Mark Pederson .20 .50
24 Stephane Richer .30 .75
25 Patrick Roy 2.40 6.00
26 Denis Savard .60 1.50
27 Serge Savard DIR .30 .75
28 Mathieu Schneider .40 1.00
29 Brian Skrudland .40 1.00
30 Petr Svoboda .30 .75
31 Charles Thiffault ACO .10 .25
32 Sylvain Turgeon .20 .50
33 Ryan Walter .20 .50

1991 Canadiens Panini Team Stickers

This 32-sticker set was issued in a plastic bag that contained two 16-sticker sheets (approximately 9" by 12") and a foldout poster, "Super Poster - Hockey 91", on which the stickers could be affixed. The players' names appear only on the poster, not on the stickers. Each sticker measures about 2 1/8" by 2 7/8" and features a color player action shot on its white-bordered front. The back of the white sticker sheet is lined off into 16 panels, each carrying the logos for Panini, the NHL, and the NHLPA, as well as the same number that appears on the front of the sticker. Every Canadian NHL team was featured in this promotion. Each team set was available by mail-order from Panini Canada Ltd. for 2.99 plus 50 cents for shipping and handling.

COMPLETE SET (32)	2.00	5.00
1 Jean-Claude Bergeron	.04	.10
2 Guy Carbonneau	.04	.10
3 Andrew Cassels	.06	.15
4 Tom Chorske	.02	.05
5 Shayne Corson	.06	.15
6 Russ Courtnall	.06	.15
7 Jean-Jacques Daigneault	.04	.10
8 Eric Desjardins	.04	.10
9 Gerald Diduck	.02	.05
10 Donald Dufresne	.02	.05
11 Todd Ewen	.02	.05
12 Brent Gilchrist	.04	.10
13 Mike Keane	.04	.10
14 Stephan Lebeau	.04	.10
15 Sylvain Lefebvre	.04	.10
16 Mike McPhee	.04	.10
17 Mark Pederson	.02	.05
18 Stephane Richer	.10	.25
19 Patrick Roy	1.00	2.50
20 Denis Savard	.16	.40
21 Mathieu Schneider	.04	.10
22 Brian Skrudland	.04	.10
23 Petr Svoboda	.04	.10
24 Ryan Walter	.04	.10
A Team Logo Left Side	.06	.15
B Team Logo Right Side	.06	.15
C Canadiens in Action Upper Left Corner	.06	.15
D Canadiens in Action Lower Left Corner	.06	.15
E Game Action Upper Right Corner	.06	.15
F Game Action Lower Right Corner	.06	.15
G Patrick Roy	.80	2.00
H Game Action	.10	.25

1991-92 Canadiens Postcards

This 31-card team-issued set measures approximately 3 1/2" by 5 1/2". The fronts feature full-bleed color photos, with the players posed in front of a white background. The backs are white and show the team name in large red letters at the top. The player's name, number, and biography (in French and English) are printed in blue. A facsimile autograph at the bottom rounds out the back. The cards are unnumbered and checklisted below in alphabetical order.

COMPLETE SET (31)	10.00	25.00
1 Francois Allaire ACO	.10	.25
2 Patrice Brisebois	.30	.75
3 Pat Burns CO	.30	.75
4 Guy Carbonneau	.30	.75
5 Ronald Corey PRES	.10	.25
6 Shayne Corson	.40	1.00
7 Alain Cote	.20	.50
8 Russ Courtnall	.40	1.00
9 Jean-Jacques Daigneault	.20	.50
10 Eric Desjardins	.30	.75
11 Donald Dufresne	.20	.50
12 Todd Ewen	.20	.50
13 Brent Gilchrist	.30	.75
14 Mike Keane	.30	.75
15 Jacques Laperriere ACO	.20	.50
16 Stephan Lebeau	.20	.50
17 John LeClair	2.40	6.00
18 Sylvain Lefebvre	.30	.75
19 Mike McPhee	.30	.75
20 Kirk Muller	.40	1.00
21 Lyle Odelein	.30	.75
22 Andre Racicot	.30	.75
23 Mario Roberge	.20	.50
24 Patrick Roy	2.00	5.00
25 Denis Savard	.40	1.00
26 Serge Savard DIR	.30	.75
27 Mathieu Schneider	.30	.75
28 Brian Skrudland	.30	.75
29 Petr Svoboda	.20	.50
30 Charles Thiffault ACO	.10	.25
31 Sylvain Turgeon	.20	.50
32 Roland Melanson		

1992-93 Canadiens Postcards

This 27-card team-issued set measures 3 1/2" by 5 1/2" and features full-bleed glossy color player photos. The players are posed on the ice against a white background. The backs are white and show the team name in large red letters at the top. The player's name, number, and biography are printed in blue. A facsimile autograph at the bottom rounds out the back. The cards are unnumbered and checklisted below in alphabetical order.

COMPLETE SET (27)	7.20	18.00
1 Brian Bellows	.30	.75
2 Patrice Brisebois	.20	.50
3 Benoit Brunet	.20	.50
4 Guy Carbonneau	.30	.75
5 Jean-Jacques Daigneault	.20	.50
6 Vincent Damphousse	.40	1.00
7 Eric Desjardins	.30	.75
8 Jacques Demers CO	.30	.75
9 Gilbert Dionne	.20	.50
10 Donald Dufresne	.20	.50
11 Todd Ewen	.20	.50
12 Kevin Haller	.20	.50
13 Sean Hill	.20	.50
14 Mike Keane	.30	.75
15 Patric Kjellberg	.20	.50
16 Stephan Lebeau	.20	.50
17 John LeClair	1.20	3.00
18 Kirk Muller	.40	1.00
19 Lyle Odelein	.30	.75
20 Oleg Petrov	.20	.50
21 Andre Racicot	.24	.60
22 Mario Roberge	.20	.50
23 Ed Ronan	.20	.50
24 Patrick Roy	1.60	4.00
25 Denis Savard	.40	1.00
26 Mathieu Schneider	.30	.75
27 Brian Skrudland	.30	.75

1993-94 Canadiens Molson

Measuring approximately 8" by 10 1/2", this ten-card set was sponsored by Molson and was apparently distributed in conjunction with certain games throughout the season. The fronts feature full-bleed posed color photos. The photos are accented by a red line on the top and each side; at the bottom, a blue stripe carries the player's name and his uniform number. Inside a white outer border and a fading team color-coded inner border, the backs present team line-ups in English and French for the Canadiens and the respective visiting team. The cards are unnumbered and checklisted below in alphabetical order.

COMPLETE SET (10)	20.00	50.00
1 Brian Bellows	2.40	6.00
2 Benoit Brunet	2.00	5.00
3 Guy Carbonneau	2.40	6.00
4 Vincent Damphousse	4.00	10.00
5 Jean-Jacques Daigneault	3.20	8.00
6 Kevin Haller	2.00	5.00
7 Mike Keane	2.40	6.00
8 Kirk Muller	2.40	6.00
9 Peter Popovic	2.00	5.00
10 Mathieu Schneider	2.40	6.00

1993-94 Canadiens Postcards

This 26-card, team-issued set measures approximately 3 1/2" by 5 1/2" and features full-bleed glossy color player photos. The players are posed on the ice against a white background. The bilingual (French and English) backs are white and show the team name in large red letters at the top. The player's name, number, and biography are printed in blue. A facsimile autograph at the bottom rounds out the back. The cards are unnumbered and checklisted below in alphabetical order.

COMPLETE SET (26)	8.00	20.00
1 Brian Bellows	.30	.75
2 Patrice Brisebois	.24	.60
3 Benoit Brunet	.20	.50
4 Guy Carbonneau	.30	.75
5 Jean-Jacques Daigneault	.20	.50
6 Vincent Damphousse	.40	1.00
7 Jacques Demers CO	.20	.50
8 Eric Desjardins	.30	.75
9 Gilbert Dionne	.20	.50
10 Paul DiPietro	.20	.50
11 Kevin Haller	.20	.50
12 Mike Keane	.24	.60
13 Stephan Lebeau	.20	.50
14 John LeClair	1.00	2.50
15 Gary Leeman	.20	.50
16 Kirk Muller	.30	.75
17 Lyle Odelein	.30	.75
18 Peter Popovic	.20	.50
19 Andre Racicot	.24	.60
20 Rob Ramage	.20	.50
21 Mario Roberge	.20	.50
22 Ed Ronan	.20	.50
23 Patrick Roy	2.00	5.00
24 Mathieu Schneider	.30	.75
25 Pierre Sevigny	.20	.50
26 Ron Wilson	.20	.50

1994-95 Canadiens Postcards

This 27-card set measures approximately 3 1/2" by 5 1/2" and features borderless color player photos. The players are posed on the ice against a white background. The backs are white and carry the team name and logo in large red letters at the top. The player's name, jersey number, and biography are printed in blue. A facsimile autograph at the bottom rounds out the back. The cards are unnumbered and checklisted below in alphabetical order.

COMPLETE SET (27)	6.00	15.00
1 Brian Bellows	.30	.75
2 Donald Brashear	.20	.50
3 Patrice Brisebois	.20	.50
4 Benoit Brunet	.20	.50
5 J.J Daigneault	.20	.50
6 Vincent Damphousse	.30	.75
7 Jacques Demers CO	.20	.50
8 Eric Desjardins	.30	.75
9 Gilbert Dionne	.20	.50
10 Paul DiPietro	.20	.50
11 Gerry Fleming	.20	.50
12 Bryan Fogarty	.20	.50
13 Mike Keane	.20	.50
14 John LeClair	.80	2.00
15 Jim Montgomery	.20	.50
16 Kirk Muller	.30	.75
17 Lyle Odelein	.30	.75
18 Oleg Petrov	.20	.50
19 Peter Popovic	.20	.50
20 Yves Racine	.20	.50
21 Ed Ronan	.20	.50
22 Patrick Roy	1.60	4.00
23 Brian Savage	.30	.75
24 Mathieu Schneider	.30	.75
25 Pierre Sevigny	.20	.50
26 Turner Stevenson	.20	.50
27 Ron Tugnutt	.40	1.00

1995-96 Canadiens Postcards

This 20-card set measures approximately 3 1/2" by 5 1/2" and features borderless color player photos. The players are posed on the ice against a white background. The backs are white and carry the team name and logo in large red letters at the top. The player's name, jersey number, and biography are printed in blue. A facsimile autograph at the bottom rounds out the back. The cards are unnumbered and checklisted below in alphabetical order.

COMPLETE SET (20)	6.00	15.00
1 Donald Brashear	.20	.50
2 Patrice Brisebois	.20	.50
3 Benoit Brunet	.20	.50
4 Valeri Bure	.20	.50
5 Marc Bureau	.20	.50
6 Vincent Damphousse	.40	1.00
7 Mike Keane	.24	.60
8 Saku Koivu	1.60	4.00
9 Vladimir Malakhov	.20	.50
10 Lyle Odelein	.20	.50
11 Oleg Petrov	.20	.50
12 Peter Popovic	.20	.50
13 Stephane Quintal	.20	.50
14 Yves Racine	.20	.50
15 Mark Recchi	.40	1.00
16 Patrick Roy	1.60	4.00
17 Brian Savage	.24	.60
18 Turner Stevenson	.20	.50
19 Mario Tremblay CO	.20	.50
20 Pierre Turgeon	.40	1.00

1995-96 Canadiens Sheets

These 12 sheets were inserted in Montreal Canadiens game programs during the 1995-96 season. The fronts of the 8 1/2" by 11" sheets feature black and white photos of Montreal players in construction gear, while the backs feature lineups for that evening's match. There are reports that the Bure sheet is the toughest to find; hence a premium has been attached. The cards are dated, but unnumbered, and thus have been checklisted alphabetically below.

COMPLETE SET (12)	48.00	120.00
1 Valeri Bure	8.00	20.00
2 Benoit Brunet	4.00	10.00
3 Peter Popovic	4.00	10.00
4 Saku Koivu	6.00	15.00
5 Turner Stevenson	4.00	10.00
6 Mark Recchi	4.80	12.00
7 Vladimir Malakhov	4.00	10.00
8 Stephane Quintal	4.00	10.00
9 Brian Savage	4.00	10.00
10 Patrice Brisebois	4.00	10.00
11 Vincent Damphousse	4.80	12.00
12 Pierre Turgeon	4.80	12.00

1996-97 Canadiens Postcards

This 33-card postcard set was produced by the team for distribution in set form through the club store, or as autographable handouts by the players. They are standard postcard size and feature full-bleed color photos on the front. The backs include biographical information. The unnumbered cards are listed below alphabetically.

COMPLETE SET (33)	8.00	20.00
1 Murray Baron	.20	.50
2 Sebastien Bordeleau	.20	.50
3 Patrice Brisebois	.20	.50
4 Benoit Brunet	.20	.50
5 Valeri Bure	.20	.50
6 Marc Bureau	.20	.50
7 Ronald Corey PRES	.20	.50
8 Shayne Corson	.40	1.00
9 Yvan Cournoyer	.60	1.50
10 Jassen Cullimore	.20	.50
11 Vincent Damphousse	.40	1.00
12 Rejean Houle	.20	.50
13 Pat Jablonski	.30	.75
14 Saku Koivu	1.20	3.00
15 Jacques Laperierre	.30	.75
16 Vladimir Malakhov	.20	.50
17 Dave Manson	.20	.50
18 Chris Murray	.20	.50
19 Peter Popovic	.20	.50
20 Stephane Qunital	.20	.50
21 Mark Recchi	.40	1.00
22 Stephane Richer	.40	1.00
23 Craig Rivet	.20	.50
24 Martin Rucinsky	.30	.75
25 Brian Savage	.30	.75
26 Steve Shutt	.30	.75
27 Turner Stevenson	.20	.50
28 Jose Theodore	4.00	10.00
29 Jocelyn Thibault	.80	2.00
30 Scott Thornton	.20	.50
31 Mario Trembley	.20	.50
32 Darcy Tucker	.40	1.00
33 David Wilkie	.20	.50

1996-97 Canadiens Sheets

These large (8.5" X 11") sheets were distributed one per issue of the Montreal Canadiens game program during the exhibition and regular season. The fronts are dominated by a posed head shot, with a smaller action photo superimposed. The player's name and sweater number also appear. The back features the lineups for both teams from that evening's contest, as well as the logo of sponsor Molson Export. Unnumbered, the set is listed below in alphabetical order.

COMPLETE SET (28)	40.00	100.00
1 Patrice Brisebois	1.20	3.00
2 Benoit Brunet	1.20	3.00
3 Valeri Bure	1.60	4.00
4 Marc Bureau	1.20	3.00
5 Shayne Corson	1.60	4.00
6 Jassen Cullimore	1.20	3.00
7 Vincent Damphousse	2.00	5.00
8 Rory Fitzpatrick	1.20	3.00
9 Saku Koivu	4.00	10.00
10 Vladimir Malakhov	1.20	3.00
11 Dave Manson	1.60	4.00
12 Chris Murray	1.20	3.00
13 Peter Popovic	1.20	3.00
14 Stephane Quintal	1.20	3.00
15 Mark Recchi	2.00	5.00
16 Stephane Richer	1.60	4.00
17 Craig Rivet	1.20	3.00
18 Martin Rucinsky	1.60	4.00
19 Brian Savage	1.60	4.00
20 Turner Stevenson	1.20	3.00
21 Jose Theodore	8.00	20.00
22 Jocelyn Thibault	3.20	8.00
23 Scott Thornton	1.20	3.00
24 Darcy Tucker	1.60	4.00
25 Pierre Turgeon	2.00	5.00
26 David Wilkie	1.20	3.00
27 Centre Molson First Anniversary	.40	1.00
28 Canadiens Line-up	1.20	3.00

1997-98 Canadiens Postcards

This 26-card set was produced by the team and measures the standard postcard size. The fronts feature color player photos. The backs carry player information. The cards are unnumbered and checklisted below in alphabetical order.

COMPLETE SET (26)	6.00	15.00
1 Sebastien Bordeleau	.20	.50
2 Patrice Brisebois	.20	.50
3 Benoit Brunet	.20	.50
4 Valeri Bure	.20	.50
5 Marc Bureau	.20	.50
6 Brett Clark	.20	.50
7 Shayne Corson	.40	1.00
8 Jassen Cullimore	.20	.50
9 Vincent Damphousse	.40	1.00
10 Saku Koivu	1.20	3.00
11 Vladimir Malakhov	.20	.50
12 Dave Manson	.20	.50
13 Andy Moog	.40	1.00
14 Peter Popovic	.20	.50
15 Stephane Quintal	.20	.50
16 Mark Recchi	.30	.75
17 Stephane Richer	.40	1.00
18 Craig Rivet	.20	.50
19 Martin Rucinsky	.30	.75
20 Brian Savage	.30	.75
21 Turner Stevenson	.20	.50
22 Jocelyn Thibault	.40	1.00
23 Scott Thornton	.20	.50
24 Darcy Tucker	.20	.50
25 Alain Vigneault	.20	.50
26 David Wilkie	.20	.50

1998-99 Canadiens Team Issue

This 26-card set pictures the 1998-99 Montreal Canadiens team on 3.5X5.5" cards. Each card back contains a facsimile signature of the respective player. Cards are numbered alphabetically.

COMPLETE SET (26)	4.00	15.00
1 Benoit Brunet	.20	.50
2 Brett Clark	.20	.50
3 Shayne Corson	.20	.50
4 Vincent Damphousse	.40	1.00
5 Jeff Hackett	.40	1.00
6 Matt Higgins	.20	.50
7 Jonas Hoglund	.20	.50
8 Eric Houde	.20	.50
9 Saku Koivu	.80	2.00
10 Vladimir Malakhov	.20	.50
11 Trent McCleary	.20	.50
12 Dave Morissette	.20	.50
13 Alain Nasreddine	.20	.50
14 Patrick Poulin	.20	.50
15 Stephane Quintal	.20	.50
16 Marc Recchi	.30	.75
17 Craig Rivet	.20	.50
18 Martin Rucinsky	.20	.50
19 Brian Savage	.30	.75
20 Turner Stevenson	.20	.50
21 Jose Theodore	1.20	3.00
22 Scott Thornton	.20	.50
23 Igor Ulanov	.20	.50
24 Alain Vigneault	.20	.50
25 Eric Weinrich	.20	.50
26 Sergei Zholtok	.20	.50

2000-01 Canadiens Postcards

This set features the Canadiens of the NHL. These postcard-like collectibles were issued by the team to each player to be used for autograph signing sessions. Sets were also available directly through the team.

COMPLETE SET (34)	8.00	20.00
1 Francois Bouillon	.20	.50
2 Andrei Bashkirov	.20	.50
3 Mathieu Garon	.60	1.50
4 Karl Dykhuis	.20	.50
5 Xavier Delisle	.20	.50
6 Patrice Brisebois	.20	.50
7 Benoit Brunet	.20	.50
8 Jose Theodore	1.20	3.00
9 Craig Darby	.20	.50
10 Eric Chouinard	.30	.75
11 Jeff Hackett	.40	1.00
12 Chad Kilger	.20	.50
13 Jim Campbell	.20	.50
14 Christian Laflamme	.20	.50
15 Eric Landry	.20	.50
16 Juha Lind	.20	.50
17 Trevor Linden	.40	1.00
18 Andrei Markov	.20	.50
19 Gino Odjick	.30	.75
20 Patrick Poulin	.20	.50
21 Oleg Petrov	.20	.50
22 Craig Rivet	.20	.50
23 Stephane Robidas	.20	.50
24 Martin Rucinsky	.20	.50
25 Brian Savage	.40	1.00
26 Sheldon Souray	.20	.50
27 Saku Koivu	.60	1.50
28 Johan Witehall	.20	.50
29 Eric Weinrich	.20	.50
30 Dainius Zubrus	.20	.50
31 Michel Therrien CO	.10	.25
32 Guy Carbonneau CO	.40	1.00
33 Rick Green CO	.10	.25
34 Andre Savard GM	.20	.50

2001-02 Canadiens Postcards

This set is a postcard-sized issue capturing the members of the 2001-02 Canadiens. The cards were available at team appearances in singles form. They were not believed to be issued in set form. The cards are unnumbered and are listed in alphabetical order.

COMPLETE SET (32)	9.78	24.44
1 Donald Audette	.30	.75
2 Shaun Van Allen	.30	.75
3 Patrice Brisebois	.30	.75
4 Benoit Brunet	.30	.75
5 Jan Bulis	.30	.75
6 Andreas Dackell	.30	.75
7 Karl Dykhuis	.30	.75
8 Mathieu Garon	.60	1.50
9 Doug Gilmour	.80	2.00
10 Jeff Hackett	.60	1.50
11 Joe Juneau	.30	.75
12 Chad Kilger	.30	.75
13 Saku Koivu	.80	2.00
14 Gino Odjick	.30	.75
15 Yanic Perreault	.30	.75
16 Oleg Petrov	.30	.75
17 Patrick Poulin	.30	.75
18 Stephane Quintal	.30	.75
19 Mike Ribeiro	.40	1.00
20 Craig Rivet	.30	.75
21 Stephane Robidas	.30	.75
22 Martin Rucinsky	.30	.75
23 Jose Theodore	1.20	3.00
24 Brian Savage	.30	.75
25 Reid Simpson	.30	.75
26 Sheldon Souray	.30	.75
27 Patrick Traverse	.30	.75
28 Richard Zednik	.30	.75
29 Michel Therrien HCO	.10	.25
30 Guy Carbonneau CO	.30	.75
31 Rick Green CO	.10	.25
32 Roland Melanson CO	.20	.50

2002 Canadiens AGF

These four cards were distributed as a complete set inside a single package that was distributed as a promotional giveaway by Quebec-based mutual fund firm AGF. The cards mimic OPC designs from the 1970s, and feature each player involved in a typical post-retirement activity such as golfing and fishing. Although it is believed they were issued in 2002, that has not been confirmed.

COMPLETE SET (4)	2.00	5.00
NNO Yvan Cournoyer	.80	2.00
NNO Rejean Houle	.40	1.00
NNO Steve Shutt	.80	2.00
NNO Henri Richard	.80	2.00

2002-03 Canadiens Postcards

This postcard sized set resembled many of the Canadiens issues of the past with color action photos on the fronts and the player/coach's name, position, birthday, and birth place on the back in both French and English. A facsimile autograph adorned the card backs as well. Cards measured approximately 3 1/2 X 5 1/2.

COMPLETE SET (31)	7.20	18.00
1 Stephane Quintal	.20	.50
2 Saku Koivu	.80	2.00
3 Oleg Petrov	.20	.50
4 Richard Zednik	.20	.50
5 Randy McKay	.20	.50
6 Bill Lindsay	.20	.50
7 Andreas Dackell	.20	.50
8 Chad Kilger	.20	.50
9 Sylvain Blouin	.20	.50
10 Mariusz Czerkawski	.20	.50
11 Karl Dykhuis	.20	.50
12 Mathieu Garon	.40	1.00
13 Jeff Hackett	.40	1.00
14 Jan Bulis	.20	.50
15 Patrice Brisebois	.20	.50
16 Sheldon Souray	.20	.50
17 Craig Rivet	.20	.50
18 Patrick Traverse	.20	.50
19 Jose Theodore	.80	2.00
20 Ron Hainsey	.80	1.50
21 Mike Ribeiro	.20	.50
22 Andrei Markov	.20	.50
23 Donald Audette	.20	.50
24 Joe Juneau	.20	.50
25 Doug Gilmour	.40	1.00
26 Yanic Perreault	.20	.50
27 Michel Therrien HCO	.04	.10
28 Guy Charron ACO	.04	.10
29 Rick Green ACO	.04	.10
30 Clement Jodoin ACO	.04	.10
31 Roland Melanson ACO	.10	.25

2003-04 Canadiens Postcards

Team-issued cards feature a blurred player image on the front, with player name, number, facsimile autograph and bio info in French and English on the back.

COMPLETE SET (30)	10.00	25.00
1 Donald Audette	.20	.50
2 Steve Begin	.20	.50
3 Francois Bouillon	.20	.50
4 Patrice Brisebois	.20	.50
5 Jan Bulis	.20	.50
6 Andreas Dackell	.20	.50
7 Karl Dykhuis	.20	.50
8 Bob Gainey GM	.20	.50
9 Mathieu Garon	.40	1.00
10 Ron Hainsey	.20	.50
11 Chris Higgins	1.00	2.50
12 Marcel Hossa	.40	1.00
13 Claude Julien CO	.10	.25
14 Joe Juneau	.20	.50
15 Chad Kilger	.20	.50
16 Saku Koivu	.75	2.00
17 Mike Komisarek	.40	1.00
18 Darren Langdon	.40	1.00
19 Andrei Markov	.20	.50
20 Yanic Perreault	.20	.50
21 Stephane Quintal	.20	.50
22 Mike Ribeiro	.40	1.00
23 Craig Rivet	.20	.50
24 Michael Ryder	1.25	3.00
25 Sheldon Souray	.40	1.00
26 Niklas Sundstrom	.20	.50
27 Jose Theodore	1.25	3.00
28 Jason Ward	.20	.50
29 Richard Zednik	.20	.50
30 Team Photo	.20	.50

2005-06 Canadiens Team Issue

COMPLETE SET (25)	15.00	30.00
1 Steve Begin	.40	1.00
2 Radek Bonk	.40	1.00
3 Francis Bouillon	.40	1.00
4 Jan Bulis	.40	1.00
5 Pierre Dagenais	.40	1.00
6 Mathieu Dandenault	.40	1.00
7 Yann Danis	.60	1.50
8 Chris Higgins	.40	1.00
9 Cristobal Huet	1.00	2.50
10 Raitis Ivanans	.75	2.00
11 Saku Koivu	.75	2.00
12 Mike Komisarek	.40	1.00
13 Alexei Kovalev	.40	1.00
14 Andrei Markov	.40	1.00
15 Alexander Perezhogin	.40	1.00
16 Tomas Plekanec	.40	1.00
17 Mike Ribeiro	.40	1.00
18 Craig Rivet	.40	1.00
19 Michael Ryder	.75	2.00
20 Sheldon Souray	.40	1.00
21 Mark Streit	.40	1.00
22 Niklas Sundstrom	.40	1.00
23 Jose Theodore	1.00	2.50
24 Richard Zednik	.40	1.00
25 Youppi MASCOT	.10	.25

2006-07 Canadiens Postcards

1 David Aebischer	.60	1.50
2 Cristobal Huet	.75	2.00
3 Steve Begin	.40	1.00
4 Radek Bonk	.40	1.00
5 Francis Bouillon	.40	1.00
6 Mathieu Dandenault	.40	1.00
7 Aaron Downey	.60	1.50
8 Christopher Higgins	.60	1.50
9 Mike Johnson	.40	1.00
10 Mike Komisarek	.40	1.00
11 Alex Kovalev	.40	1.00
12 Guillaume Latendresse	1.25	3.00
13 Andrei Markov	.40	1.00
14 Garth Murray	.40	1.00
15 Janne Niinimaa	.40	1.00
16 Alexander Perezhogin	.40	1.00
17 Tomas Plekanec	.40	1.00
18 Craig Rivet	.40	1.00
19 Michael Ryder	.60	1.50
20 Mark Streit	.75	2.00
21 Sheldon Souray	.40	1.00
22 Sergei Samsonov	.40	1.00
23 Team Photo	.40	1.00
24 Youppi MASCOT	.10	.25

1970-71 Canucks Royal Bank

This 20-card set of Vancouver Canucks was sponsored by Royal Bank, whose company logo appears at the lower left corner on the front. The set is subtitled Royal Bank Leo's Leaders Canucks Player of the Week. The black and white posed player photos measure approximately 5" by 7" and have white borders. The player's signature is inscribed across the bottom of the picture, and the backs are blank. The cards are unnumbered and checklisted below in alphabetical order.

COMPLETE SET (20)	30.00	60.00
1 Andre Boudrias	2.00	4.00
2 Mike Corrigan	1.50	3.00
3 Ray Cullen	2.50	5.00
4 Gary Doak	1.50	3.00

George Gardner 1.50 3.00
Murray Hall 1.50 3.00
Charlie Hodge 4.00 8.00
Danny Johnson 1.50 3.00
Orland Kurtenbach 2.50 5.00
Wayne Maki 1.50 3.00
Rosaire Paiement 2.00 4.00
Paul Popiel 2.00 4.00
Pat Quinn 4.00 8.00
Marc Reaume 1.50 3.00
Darryl Sly 1.50 3.00
Dale Tallon 2.50 5.00
Ted Taylor 1.50 3.00
Barry Wilkins 1.50 3.00
Dunc Wilson 2.50 5.00
Jim Wiste 1.50 3.00

1971-72 Canucks Royal Bank

is 20-card set of Vancouver Canucks was onsored by Royal Bank, whose company go appears at the lower left corner on the nt. The set is subtitled Royal Bank Leo's aders Canucks Player of the Week. The ack and white posed player photos easure approximately 5" by 7" and have iite borders. The player's signature is scribed across the bottom of the picture, d the backs are blank. The cards are mbered by week of issue. Card number 10 unknown and may have never been sued.

OMPLETE SET (20) 25.00 50.00
Bobby Lalonde 1.00 2.00
Mike Corrigan 1.00 2.00
Murray Hall 1.00 2.00
Jocelyn Guevremont 2.00 4.00
Pat Quinn 3.00 6.00
Orland Kurtenbach 2.00 4.00
Paul Popiel 2.00 4.00
Ron Ward 1.00 2.00
Rosaire Paiement 1.50 3.00
1 Dale Tallon 2.00 4.00
2 Bobby Schmautz 2.00 4.00
3 Dennis Kearns 1.00 2.00
4 Barry Wilkins 1.00 2.00
5 Dunc Wilson 2.50 5.00
6 Andre Boudrias 2.00 4.00
7 Ted Taylor 1.50 3.00
8 George Gardner 1.00 2.00
9 John Schella 1.00 2.00
0 Wayne Maki 1.50 3.00
1 Gary Doak 1.00 2.00

1972-73 Canucks Nalley's

is six-card set was available on the backs specially marked Nalley's Triple Pak tato Chips boxes. The back yellow panel s a 6 3/4" by 5 3/8" (approximately) action ot of a Canuck player beside the goalie d net. One player card is superimposed er the lower left corner of this large action oto. The card is framed by a thin rforated line; if the card were cut out, it ould measure about 3" by 3 3/4". The front atures a close-up posed color player photo om the waste up) with white borders. The ayer's name and position appear in white ttom border. The backs are blank. At the ttom of each back panel are miniature ue-tinted versions of all six player cards. e cards are unnumbered and checklisted low in alphabetical order.

OMPLETE SET (6) 62.50 125.00
Andre Boudrias 10.00 20.00
George Gardner 10.00 20.00
Wayne Maki 12.50 25.00
Rosaire Paiement 12.50 25.00
Pat Quinn 20.00 40.00
Barry Wilkins 10.00 20.00

1972-73 Canucks Royal Bank

is 21-card set of Vancouver Canucks was onsored by Royal Bank, whose company go appears at the lower left corner on the ont. The set is subtitled Leo's Leaders anucks Player of the Week. These colorful ll body player photos measure pproximately 5" by 7" and have white orders. The background of the photos nges from light blue to royal blue. The ayer's facsimile signature is inscribed ross the bottom of the picture, and the cks are blank. The cards are unnumbered the front and checklisted below in phabetical order.

OMPLETE SET (21) 20.00 40.00
Dave Balon 1.50 3.00
Gregg Boddy 1.00 2.00
Larry Bolonchuk 1.00 2.00
4 Andre Boudrias 1.00 2.00
5 Ed Dyck 1.00 2.00
6 Jocelyn Guevremont 1.50 3.00
7 James Hargreaves 1.00 2.00
8 Dennis Kearns 1.00 2.00
9 Orland Kurtenbach 1.50 3.00
10 Bobby Lalonde 1.00 2.00
11 Richard Lemieux 1.00 2.00
12 Don Lever 1.50 3.00
13 Wayne Maki 1.50 3.00
14 Bryan McSheffrey 1.00 2.00
15 Gerry O'Flaherty 1.00 2.00
16 Bobby Schmautz 1.50 3.00
17 Dale Tallon 1.50 3.00
18 Don Tannahill 1.00 2.00
19 Barry Wilkins 1.00 2.00
20 Dunc Wilson 1.50 3.00
21 John Wright 1.00 2.00

1973-74 Canucks Royal Bank

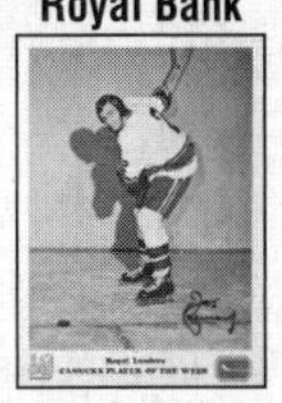

This 21-card set of Vancouver Canucks was sponsored by Royal Bank, whose company logo appears at the lower left corner on the front. The set is subtitled Royal Leaders Canucks Player of the Week. These colorful full body player photos measure approximately 5" by 7" and have white borders. The background of the photos ranges from yellowish green to green. The player's facsimile signature is inscribed across the bottom of the picture, and the backs are blank. The cards are unnumbered on the front and checklisted below in alphabetical order.

COMPLETE SET (21) 20.00 40.00
1 Paulin Bordeleau 1.00 2.00
2 Andre Boudrias 1.00 2.00
3 Jacques Caron 1.00 2.00
4 Bob Dailey 1.00 2.00
5 Dave Dunn 1.00 2.00
6 Jocelyn Guevremont 1.50 3.00
7 Dennis Kearns 1.00 2.00
8 Jerry Korab 1.00 2.00
9 Orland Kurtenbach 2.00 4.00
10 Bobby Lalonde 1.00 2.00
11 Richard Lemieux 1.00 2.00
12 Don Lever 1.50 3.00
13 Bill McCreary 1.00 2.00
14 Bryan McSheffrey 1.00 2.00
15 Gerry O'Flaherty 1.00 2.00
16 Bobby Schmautz 2.00 4.00
17 Gary Smith 2.00 4.00
18 Don Tannahill 1.00 2.00
19 Dennis Ververgaert 1.50 3.00
20 Barry Wilkins 1.00 2.00
21 John Wright 1.00 2.00

1974-75 Canucks Royal Bank

This 20-card set of Vancouver Canucks was sponsored by Royal Bank, whose company logo appears at the lower left corner on the front. The set is subtitled Royal Leaders Player of the Week. These colorful head and shoulders player photos are presented on a white background with a thin black border. The cards measure approximately 5" by 7", have white borders, and are printed on glossy paper. The player's facsimile signature is inscribed across the bottom of the picture, and the backs are blank. The cards are unnumbered on the front and checklisted below in alphabetical order.

COMPLETE SET (20) 20.00 40.00
1 Gregg Boddy 1.00 2.00
2 Paulin Bordeleau 1.50 3.00
3 Andre Boudrias 1.50 3.00
4 Bob Dailey 1.00 2.00
5 Ab DeMarco 1.00 2.00
6 John Gould 1.00 2.00
7 John Grisdale 1.00 2.00
8 Dennis Kearns 1.00 2.00
9 Bobby Lalonde 1.00 2.00
10 Don Lever 1.50 3.00
11 Ken Lockett 1.00 2.00
12 Gerry Meehan 1.50 3.00
13 Garry Monahan 1.00 2.00
14 Chris Oddleifson 1.00 2.00
15 Gerry O'Flaherty 1.00 2.00
16 Tracy Pratt 1.00 2.00
17 Mike Robitaille 1.00 2.00
18 Leon Rochefort 1.00 2.00
19 Gary Smith 1.50 3.00
20 Dennis Ververgaert 1.50 3.00

1975-76 Canucks Royal Bank

This 22-card set of Vancouver Canucks was sponsored by Royal Bank, whose company logo appears at the lower left corner on the front. The set is subtitled Royal Leaders

Player of the Week. The cards measure approximately 4 3/4" by 7 1/4" and are printed on glossy paper. The fronts feature a color head and shoulders shot of the player on white background with a thin black border. The player's facsimile autograph appears below the picture. The backs are blank. The cards are unnumbered and we have checklisted them below in alphabetical order.

COMPLETE SET (22) 20.00 40.00
1 Rick Blight 1.00 2.00
2 Gregg Boddy 1.00 2.00
3 Paulin Bordeleau 1.00 2.00
4 Andre Boudrias 1.00 2.00
5 Bob Dailey 1.00 2.00
6 Ab DeMarco 1.00 2.00
7 John Gould 1.00 2.00
8 John Grisdale 1.00 2.00
9 Dennis Kearns 1.00 2.00
10 Bobby Lalonde 1.00 2.00
11 Don Lever 1.50 3.00
12 Ken Lockett 1.00 2.00
13 Garry Monahan 1.00 2.00
14 Bob Murray 1.00 2.00
15 Chris Oddleifson 1.00 2.00
16 Gerry O'Flaherty 1.00 2.00
17 Tracy Pratt 1.00 2.00
18 Mike Robitaille 1.00 2.00
19 Ron Sedlbauer 1.00 2.00
20 Gary Smith 1.50 3.00
21 Harold Snepsts 3.00 6.00
22 Dennis Ververgaert 1.50 3.00

1976-77 Canucks Royal Bank

This 23-card set of Vancouver Canucks was sponsored by Royal Bank, whose company logo appears at the lower left corner on the front. The set is subtitled Royal Leaders Player of the Week. The cards measure approximately 4 3/4" by 7 1/4" and are printed on glossy paper. The fronts feature a color head and shoulders shot of the player on white background with a thin black border. The player's facsimile autograph appears below the picture. The backs are blank. The cards are unnumbered and we have checklisted them below in alphabetical order.

COMPLETE SET (23) 20.00 40.00
1 Rick Blight 1.00 2.00
2 Bob Dailey 1.00 2.00
3 Dave Fortier 1.00 2.00
4 Brad Gassoff 1.00 2.00
5 John Gould 1.00 2.00
6 John Grisdale 1.00 2.00
7 Dennis Kearns 1.00 2.00
8 Bobby Lalonde 1.00 2.00
9 Don Lever 1.50 3.00
10 Cesare Maniago 2.00 4.00
11 Garry Monahan 1.00 2.00
12 Bob Murray 1.00 2.00
13 Chris Oddleifson 1.00 2.00
14 Gerry O'Flaherty 1.00 2.00
15 Curt Ridley 1.00 2.00
16 Mike Robitaille 1.00 2.00
17 Ron Sedlbauer 1.00 2.00
18 Harold Snepsts 2.50 5.00
19 Andy Spruce 1.00 2.00
20 Ralph Stewart 1.00 2.00
21 Dennis Ververgaert 1.50 3.00
22 Mike Walton 1.50 3.00
23 Jim Wiley 1.50 3.00

1977-78 Canucks Canada Dry Cans

This extremely scarce set features the Canucks of the NHL. Each specially-marked regular sized ginger ale can sold in the Vancouver area for a limited time featured a headshot of a player on the back side. Unopened cans sell for a premium of 100 percent.

COMPLETE SET (16) 20.00 40.00
1 Rick Blight 1.00 2.00
2 Brad Gassoff 1.00 2.00
3 Jere Gillis 1.00 2.00
4 Larry Goodenough 1.00 2.00
5 Hilliard Graves 1.00 2.00
6 Dennis Kearns 1.00 2.00
7 Don Lever 1.00 2.00
8 Cesare Maniago 2.50 5.00
9 Jack McIlhargey 1.00 2.00
10 Garry Monahan 1.00 2.00
11 Chris Oddleifson 1.00 2.00
12 Curt Ridley 1.00 2.00
13 Derek Sanderson 2.50 5.00
14 Harold Snepsts 2.00 4.00
15 Mike Walton 1.00 2.00
16 Dennis Ververgaert 1.00 2.00

1977-78 Canucks Royal Bank

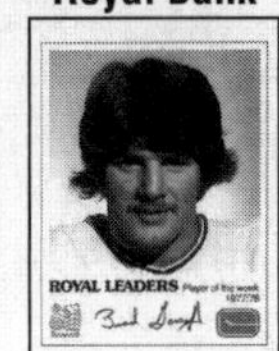

This 21-card set of Vancouver Canucks was sponsored by Royal Bank, whose company logo appears at the lower left corner on the front. The set is subtitled Royal Leaders Player of the Week. The cards measure approximately 4 1/4" by 5 1/2" and are printed on thin cardboard stock. The fronts feature a color head and shoulders shot of the player on white background with a thin black border. The player's facsimile autograph appears below the picture. The backs are blank. The cards are unnumbered; they are checklisted below in alphabetical order.

COMPLETE SET (21) 20.00 40.00
1 Rick Blight 1.00 2.00
2 Larry Carriere 1.00 2.00
3 Rob Flockhart 1.00 2.00
4 Brad Gassoff 1.00 2.00
5 Jere Gillis 1.00 2.00
6 Larry Goodenough 1.00 2.00
7 Hilliard Graves 1.00 2.00
8 John Grisdale 1.00 2.00
9 Dennis Kearns 1.00 2.00
10 Don Lever 1.50 3.00
11 Cesare Maniago 2.00 4.00
12 Bob Manno 1.00 2.00
13 Jack McIlhargey 1.00 2.00
14 Garry Monahan 1.00 2.00
15 Chris Oddleifson 1.00 2.00
16 Gerry O'Flaherty 1.00 2.00
17 Curt Ridley 1.50 3.00
18 Ron Sedlbauer 1.00 2.00
19 Harold Snepsts 2.00 4.00
20 Dennis Ververgaert 1.50 3.00
21 Mike Walton 1.00 2.00

1978-79 Canucks Royal Bank

This 23-card set of Vancouver Canucks was sponsored by Royal Bank, whose company logo appears at the upper left corner on the front. The cards measure approximately 4 1/4" by 5 1/2" and are printed on thin cardboard stock. The fronts feature a color head and shoulders shot of the player on white background with a thin blue border. The player's facsimile autograph and the team logo appear above the picture. The backs present biographical and statistical information. The cards are unnumbered; they are checklisted below in alphabetical order.

COMPLETE SET (23) 20.00 40.00
1 Rick Blight .75 1.50
2 Gary Bromley 1.00 2.00
3 Bill Derlago .75 1.50
4 Roland Eriksson .75 1.50
5 Curt Fraser 1.00 2.00
6 Jere Gillis .75 1.50
7 Thomas Gradin 2.00 4.00
8 Hilliard Graves .75 1.50
9 John Grisdale .75 1.50
10 Glen Hanlon 1.25 2.50
11 Randy Holt .75 1.50
12 Dennis Kearns .75 1.50
13 Don Lever 1.00 2.00
14 Lars Lindgren .75 1.50
15 Bob Manno .75 1.50
16 Pit Martin 1.00 2.00
17 Jack McIlhargey .75 1.50
18 Chris Oddleifson .75 1.50
19 Ron Sedlbauer .75 1.50
20 Stan Smyl 2.00 4.00
21 Harold Snepsts 2.00 4.00
22 Dennis Ververgaert 1.00 2.00
23 Lars Zetterstrom .75 1.50

1979-80 Canucks Royal Bank

This 22-card set features posed color player photos from the shoulders up of the Vancouver Canucks. There are actually two different sets with the same value, a team-issued (no reference to Royal Bank) blank back set and a Royal Bank set; the card pictures (and values) are the same in both versions of the set. The sponsor name appears in black print at the card top, with the words "Player of the Week 1979/80" immediately below. The cards measure approximately 4 1/4" by 5 1/2". The front features a color head shot with a blue background and black and white borders. The player's jersey number, facsimile autograph, and team logo appear in the bottom white border. Since this is an unnumbered set, the cards are listed alphabetically. The Royal Bank backs carry biography, career summary, and complete statistical information (season by season, regular schedule, and playoffs).

COMPLETE SET (22) 15.00 30.00
1 Brent Ashton 1.00 2.00
2 Rick Blight .75 1.50
3 Gary Bromley 1.00 2.00
4 Drew Callander .75 1.50
5 Bill Derlago 1.00 2.00
6 Curt Fraser 1.00 2.00
7 Jere Gillis .75 1.50
8 Thomas Gradin 1.50 3.00
9 Glen Hanlon 1.25 2.50
10 John Hughes .75 1.50
11 Dennis Kearns .75 1.50
12 Don Lever 1.00 2.00
13 Lars Lindgren .75 1.50
14 Bob Manno .75 1.50
15 Kevin McCarthy .75 1.50
16 Jack McIlhargey .75 1.50
17 Chris Oddleifson .75 1.50
18 Curt Ridley .75 1.50
19 Ron Sedlbauer .75 1.50
20 Stan Smyl 1.50 3.00
21 Harold Snepsts 1.50 3.00
22 Rick Vaive 1.25 2.50

1980-81 Canucks Silverwood Dairies

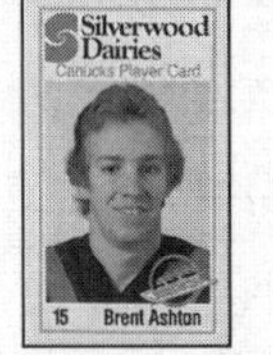

This 24-card set of Vancouver Canucks was sponsored by Silverwood Dairies. The cards measure approximately 2 1/2" by 3 1/2" individually but were issued as perforated panels of three. The cards are checklisted below in alphabetical order.

COMPLETE SET (24) 20.00 40.00
1 Brent Ashton 1.00 2.00
2 Ivan Boldirev 1.00 2.00
3 Per-Olov Brasar .75 1.50
4 Richard Brodeur 2.00 4.00
5 Gary Bromley 1.00 2.00
6 Jerry Butler .75 1.50
7 Colin Campbell 1.25 2.50
8 Curt Fraser 1.00 2.00
9 Thomas Gradin 1.25 2.50
10 Glen Hanlon 1.25 2.50
11 Dennis Kearns .75 1.50
12 Rick Lanz .75 1.50
13 Lars Lindgren .75 1.50
14 Dave Logan .75 1.50
15 Gary Lupul .75 1.50
16 Bob Manno .75 1.50
17 Kevin McCarthy .75 1.50
18 Gerry Minor .75 1.50
19 Kevin Primeau .75 1.50
20 Darcy Rota .75 1.50
21 Stan Smyl 1.50 3.00
22 Harold Snepsts 1.50 3.00
23 Bobby Schmautz .75 1.50
24 Dave(Tiger) Williams 2.00 4.00

1980-81 Canucks Team Issue

This 22-card set measures approximately 3 3/4" by 4 7/8" and features posed color head and shoulder player photos against a light blue-gray background. The pictures have rounded corners and are enclosed by thick black and thin red border stripes. The player's name, uniform number, position, and the team logo appear in the thicker bottom border. A facsimile autograph runs vertically to the left of the player's head. The backs are blank.

COMPLETE SET (22) 15.00 30.00
1 Brent Ashton 1.00 2.00
2 Ivan Boldirev 1.00 2.00
3 Per-Olov Brasar .75 1.50
4 Richard Brodeur 2.00 4.00
5 Gary Bromley 1.00 2.00
6 Jerry Butler .75 1.50
7 Colin Campbell 1.25 2.50
8 Curt Fraser 1.00 2.00
9 Thomas Gradin 1.25 2.50
10 Glen Hanlon 1.25 2.50
11 Dennis Kearns .75 1.50
12 Rick Lanz .75 1.50
13 Lars Lindgren .75 1.50
14 Dave Logan .75 1.50
15 Gary Lupul .75 1.50
16 Kevin McCarthy .75 1.50
17 Gerry Minor .75 1.50
18 Darcy Rota .75 1.50
19 Bobby Schmautz .75 1.50
20 Stan Smyl 1.50 3.00
21 Harold Snepsts 1.50 3.00
22 Tiger Williams 2.00 4.00

1981-82 Canucks Silverwood Dairies

This 24-card set of Vancouver Canucks was sponsored by Silverwood Dairies, and the sponsor's name and logo appear at the top

of the card face. The cards measure approximately 2 7/16" by 4 1/16" and feature a color action player photo, with the team logo superimposed at the lower right corner of the picture. The cards are unnumbered and so are checklisted in alphabetical order.

COMPLETE SET (24) 10.00 25.00
1 Per-Olov Brasar .40 1.00
2 Richard Brodeur 1.00 2.50
3 Ivan Boldirev .50 1.25
4 Jiri Bubla .40 1.00
5 Jerry Butler .40 1.00
6 Colin Campbell .60 1.50
7 Marc Crawford .80 2.00
8 Anders Eldebrink .40 1.00
9 Curt Fraser .40 1.00
10 Thomas Gradin .80 2.00
11 Doug Halward .40 1.00
12 Darcy Rota .40 1.00
12 Glen Hanlon .60 1.50
13 Stan Smyl 1.00 2.50
13 Ivan Hlinka .40 1.00
14 Rick Lanz .40 1.00
15 Lars Lindgren .40 1.00
16 Blair MacDonald .40 1.00
17 Gerry Minor .40 1.00
18 Gary Lupul .40 1.00
22 Kevin McCarthy .40 1.00
24 Lars Molin .40 1.00
24 Dave(Tiger) Williams 1.00 2.50
25 Harold Snepsts 1.00 2.50

1981-82 Canucks Team Issue

This 20-card set measures approximately 3 3/4" by 4 7/8" and features posed color head and shoulder player photos against a blue background. The pictures have rounded corners and are enclosed by thick black and thin red border stripes. The player's name, uniform number, position, and the team logo appear in the thicker bottom border. A facsimile autograph runs vertically to the left of the player's head. The backs are blank. The card of Richard Brodeur is the same one used in the 1980-81 team-issued set.

COMPLETE SET (20) 8.00 20.00
1 Ivan Boldirev .60 1.50
2 Per-Olov Brasar .40 1.00
3 Richard Brodeur 1.00 2.50
4 Jiri Bubla .40 1.00
5 Jerry Butler .40 1.00
6 Colin Campbell 1.00 2.50
7 Anders Eldebrink .40 1.00
8 Curt Fraser .60 1.50
9 Thomas Gradin .80 2.00
10 Doug Halward .40 1.00
11 Glen Hanlon .60 1.50
12 Rick Lanz .40 1.00
13 Gary Lupul .40 1.00
14 Blair MacDonald .40 1.00
15 Kevin McCarthy .40 1.00
16 Gerry Minor .40 1.00
17 Lars Molin .40 1.00
18 Darcy Rota .40 1.00
19 Stan Smyl .80 2.00
20 Tiger Williams 1.00 2.50

1982-83 Canucks Team Issue

This 23-card set of the Vancouver Canucks was issued in three panels of six cards each with a fourth panel having five cards because the team photo fills the space of two player cards. The cards measure approximately 3 3/4" by 4 7/8". The fronts feature a color posed photo of the player with rounded corners and surrounded by a thick black and a thin red border. The player's name, position, jersey number and team logo appear below the photo in a wide black border. The horizontal backs carry the player's name, position, jersey number, biographical and statistical information. The cards are unnumbered and checklisted below in alphabetical order.

COMPLETE SET (23) 8.00 20.00
1 Ivan Boldirev .40 1.00
2 Richard Brodeur 1.00 2.50
3 Jiri Bubla .30 .75
4 Garth Butcher .40 1.00
5 Ron Delorme .30 .75
6 Ken Ellacott .30 .75
7 Curt Fraser .30 .75
8 Thomas Gradin .60 1.50
9 Doug Halward .30 .75
10 Ivan Hlinka .30 .75
11 Rick Lanz .30 .75
12 Moe Lemay .30 .75
13 Lars Lindgren .30 .75
14 Kevin McCarthy .30 .75
15 Gerry Minor .30 .75
16 Lars Molin .30 .75
17 Jim Nill .30 .75
18 Darcy Rota .30 .75
19 Stan Smyl .60 1.50
20 Harold Snepsts 1.00 2.50
21 Patrik Sundstrom .80 2.00
22 Dave Williams .80 2.00
23 Team Photo .30 .75

1983-84 Canucks Team Issue

This 23-card set of Vancouver Canucks was issued in three panels of six cards each, with the fourth panel having 5 cards (the team photo card fills the space of two player cards). The cards measure approximately 3 11/16" by 4 5/8". The front features a color posed photo (with rounded corners) of the player, surrounded by a thick black and a thin red border. The Canucks' logo and player information appear below the picture. The back has biographical and statistical information in a horizontal format. We have checklisted the names below in alphabetical order, with the uniform number to the right of the name.

COMPLETE SET (23) 10.00 25.00
1 Richard Brodeur 35 .80 2.00
2 Jiri Bubla 29 .20 .50
3 Garth Butcher 5 .40 1.00
4 Marc Crawford 28 .40 1.00
5 Ron Delorme 19 .20 .50
6 John Garrett 31 .40 1.00
7 Jere Gillis 4 .20 .50
8 Thomas Gradin 23 .60 1.50
9 Doug Halward 2 .20 .50
10 Mark Kirton 16 .20 .50
11 Rick Lanz 4 .20 .50
12 Gary Lupul 7 .20 .50
13 Kevin McCarthy 25 .20 .50
14 Lars Molin 26 .20 .50
15 Jim Nill 8 .20 .50
16 Michel Petit 3 .40 1.00
17 Darcy Rota 18 .20 .50
18 Stan Smyl 12 .60 1.50
19 Harold Snepsts 27 .80 2.00
20 Patrik Sundstrom 17 .60 1.50
21 Tony Tanti 9 .60 1.50
22 Dave(Tiger) Williams 22 .80 2.00
23 Team Photo .40 1.00

1984-85 Canucks Team Issue

This 26-card set of Vancouver Canucks was issued in four six-card panels plus a larger team photo card and an Air Canucks advertisement card (the latter two measure approximately 4 5/8" by 7"). The player cards measure 3 5/16" by 4 1/4". The key card in the set is Cam Neely appearing in his Rookie Card year. The cards are unnumbered and checklisted below in alphabetical order.

COMPLETE SET (26) 10.00 25.00
1 Neil Belland .20 .50
2 Richard Brodeur .60 1.50
3 Jiri Bubla .20 .50
4 Garth Butcher .30 .75
5 Frank Caprice .30 .75
6 J.J. Daigneault .30 .75
7 Ron Delorme .20 .50
8 John Garrett .40 1.00
9 Thomas Gradin .60 1.50
10 Taylor Hall .20 .50
11 Doug Halward .20 .50
12 Rick Lanz .20 .50
13 Moe Lemay .20 .50
14 Doug Lidster .30 .75
15 Gary Lupul .20 .50
16 Al MacAdam .20 .50
17 Peter McNab .30 .75
18 Cam Neely 4.00 10.00
19 Michel Petit .30 .75
20 Darcy Rota .20 .50
21 Petri Skriko .40 1.00
22 Stan Smyl .40 1.00
23 Patrik Sundstrom .40 1.00
24 Tony Tanti .40 1.00
25 Team Photo (Large size) .60 1.50
26 Air Canucks (Advertisement) .10 .25

1985-86 Canucks Team Issue

This 25-card set of Vancouver Canucks was issued in four panels of six cards each, with a separate team photo card. The player cards measure approximately 3 3/8" by 4 1/4". The team photo measures approximately 7" by 4 5/8". The fronts feature color posed player photos (with rounded corners) surrounded by thick black and thin red borders. The

Canucks' logo and player information appear below the picture. The backs are blank. The cards are unnumbered and checklisted below in alphabetical order.

COMPLETE SET (25)	7.20	18.00
1 Richard Brodeur	.60	1.50
2 Jiri Bubla	.20	.50
3 Garth Butcher	.30	.75
4 Frank Caprice	.30	.75
5 Glen Cochrane	.20	.50
6 Craig Coxe	.20	.50
7 J.J. Daigneault	.30	.75
8 Thomas Gradin	.40	1.00
9 Taylor Hall	.20	.50
10 Doug Halward	.20	.50
11 Jean-Marc Lanthier	.20	.50
12 Rick Lanz	.20	.50
13 Moe Lemay	.20	.50
14 Doug Lidster	.30	.75
15 Dave Lowry	.20	.50
16 Gary Lupul	.20	.50
17 Cam Neely	3.00	7.50
18 Brent Peterson	.20	.50
19 Jim Sandlak	.30	.75
20 Petri Skriko	.40	1.00
21 Stan Smyl	.40	1.00
22 Patrik Sundstrom	.40	1.00
23 Steve Tambellini	.20	.50
24 Tony Tanti	.40	1.00
25 Team Photo (Large size)	1.20	3.00

1986-87 Canucks Team Issue

This 24-card set of Vancouver Canucks was issued in four panels of six cards each; after perforation, the cards measure the standard size (2 1/2" by 3 1/2"). The front design has color head and shoulder shots with white borders. Below the picture the player's name and number appear between two team logos. The horizontally oriented backs have biography and career statistics. The cards are unnumbered and checklisted below in alphabetical order, with the uniform number after the name.

COMPLETE SET (24)	4.80	12.00
1 Richard Brodeur 35	.60	1.50
2 Garth Butcher 5	.30	.75
3 Frank Caprice 30	.30	.75
4 Glen Cochrane 29	.20	.50
5 Craig Coxe 32	.20	.50
6 Taylor Hall 8	.20	.50
7 Stu Kulak 16	.20	.50
8 Moe Lemay 14	.20	.50
9 Dave Lowry 22	.20	.50
10 Brad Maxwell 27	.20	.50
11 Petri Skriko 26	.30	.75
12 Barry Pederson 7	.40	1.00
13 Rick Lanz 4	.20	.50
14 Doug Lidster 3	.30	.75
15 Brent Peterson 10	.20	.50
16 Michel Petit 24	.30	.75
17 Dave Richter 6	.20	.50
18 Stan Smyl 12	.40	1.00
19 Jim Sandlak 33	.20	.50
20 Patrik Sundstrom 17	.40	1.00
21 Rich Sutter 15	.20	.50
22 Steve Tambellini 20	.20	.50
23 Tony Tanti 9	.40	1.00
24 Wendell Young 1	.40	1.00

1987-88 Canucks Shell Oil

This 24-card set of Vancouver Canucks was sponsored by Shell Oil and released only in British Columbia. It was issued as eight different three-card panels, with the cards measuring the standard size, 2 1/2" by 3 1/2", after perforation. The cards were distributed as a promotion for Shell Oil, with one panel set per week given out at participating Shell stations. Included with the cards was a coupon offering a 5.00 discount on tickets to the Canucks games. The front features a color head and shoulders shot of the player, with the Canucks' logo superimposed at the upper left hand corner of the picture. The player's name, position, and the "Formula Shell" logo appear below the picture. The back has biographical and career information on the player. The cards are unnumbered and checklisted below in alphabetical order. Kirk McLean's card predates his Rookie Card by two years.

COMPLETE SET (24)	3.20	8.00
1 Greg Adams	.30	.75
2 Jim Benning	.10	.25
3 Randy Boyd	.10	.25
4 Richard Brodeur	.40	1.00
5 David Bruce	.10	.25
6 Garth Butcher	.10	.25
7 Frank Caprice	.16	.40
8 Craig Coxe	.10	.25
9 Willie Huber	.10	.25
10 Doug Lidster	.20	.50
11 Dave Lowry	.10	.25
12 Kirk McLean	1.00	2.50
13 Larry Melnyk	.10	.25
14 Barry Pederson	.20	.50
15 Dave Richter	.10	.25
16 Jim Sandlak	.10	.25
17 Dave Saunders	.10	.25
18 Petri Skriko	.20	.50
19 Stan Smyl	.30	.75
20 Daryl Stanley	.10	.25
21 Rich Sutter	.10	.25
22 Steve Tambellini	.10	.25
23 Tony Tanti	.30	.75
24 Doug Wickenheiser	.10	.25

1988-89 Canucks Mohawk

This 24-card standard-size set of Vancouver Canucks was sponsored by Mohawk and issued in six panels of four cards each. The cards feature on the front a color head and shoulders shot of the player on white card stock. The Canucks' and Mohawk logos appear at the bottom of the card. The player's name, position, and number are given in black lettering running the bottom to top on the left side of the picture. The backs are blank. We have checklisted the cards below in alphabetical order, with the player's number to the right of his name. The cards of Trevor Linden and Kirk McLean's predate their Rookie Cards by one year.

COMPLETE SET (24)	6.00	15.00
1 Greg Adams 8	.40	1.00
2 Jim Benning 4	.20	.50
3 Ken Berry 18	.20	.50
4 Randy Boyd 29	.20	.50
5 Steve Bozek 14	.20	.50
6 Brian Bradley 10	.60	1.50
7 David Bruce 25	.20	.50
8 Garth Butcher 5	.20	.50
9 Kevan Guy 2	.20	.50
10 Doug Lidster 3	.20	.50
11 Trevor Linden 16	2.00	5.00
12 Kirk McLean 1	1.20	3.00
13 Larry Melnyk 24	.20	.50
14 Robert Nordmark 6	.20	.50
15 Barry Pederson 7	.30	.75
16 Paul Reinhart 23	.30	.75
17 Jim Sandlak 19	.20	.50
18 Petri Skriko 26	.30	.75
19 Stan Smyl 12	.30	.75
20 Harold Snepsts 27	.60	1.50
21 Ronnie Stern 20	.20	.50
22 Rich Sutter 15	.20	.50
23 Tony Tanti 9	.30	.75
24 Steve Weeks 31	.30	.75

1989-90 Canucks Mohawk

This 24-card standard-size set was sponsored by Mohawk to commemorate the Vancouver Canucks' 20th year in the NHL and was issued in six panels of four cards each. The cards feature a color head and shoulders shot of the player on white card stock. The Canucks' and Mohawk logos appear at the bottom of the card, and the Canucks' logo has the number "2" before it joining with the circular shape of the logo to suggest "20." The player's name, position, and number are given in black lettering running the bottom to top on the left side of the picture. The backs are blank. We have checklisted the cards below in alphabetical order, with the player's number to the right of his name.

COMPLETE SET (24)	6.00	15.00
1 Greg Adams 8	.30	.75
2 Jim Benning 4	.20	.50
3 Steve Bozek 14	.20	.50
4 Brian Bradley 10	.40	1.00
5 Garth Butcher 5	.20	.50
6 Craig Coxe 22	.20	.50
7 Vladimir Krutov 17	.40	1.00
8 Igor Larionov 18	.80	2.00
9 Doug Lidster 3	.20	.50
10 Trevor Linden 16	1.60	4.00
11 Kirk McLean 1	.80	2.00
12 Larry Melnyk 24	.20	.50
13 Robert Nordmark 6	.20	.50
14 Barry Pederson 7	.30	.75
15 Paul Reinhart 23	.30	.75
16 Jim Sandlak 19	.20	.50
17 Petri Skriko 26	.30	.75
18 Doug Smith	.20	.50
19 Stan Smyl 12	.40	1.00
20 Harold Snepsts 27	.40	1.00
21 Daryl Stanley 29	.20	.50
22 Rich Sutter 15	.20	.50
23 Tony Tanti 9	.30	.75
24 Steve Weeks 31	.30	.75

1990-91 Canucks Mohawk

This 29-card set of Vancouver Canucks was sponsored by Mohawk and issued in panels. After perforation, the cards measure the standard size. The front features color mug shots of the players, with thin red borders on a white card face. The player's name and position appear in black lettering above the picture, while the team logo in the lower right corner rounds out the card face. The horizontally oriented backs have biographical information and statistics (regular season and playoff). The cards are unnumbered and checklisted below in alphabetical order.

COMPLETE SET (29)	6.00	15.00
1 Greg Adams	.30	.75
2 Jim Agnew	.20	.50
3 Steve Bozek	.20	.50
4 Garth Butcher	.20	.50
5 Dave Capuano	.20	.50
6 Craig Coxe	.20	.50
7 Gerald Diduck	.20	.50
8 Troy Gamble	.30	.75
9 Don Gibson	.20	.50
10 Kevan Guy	.20	.50
11 Robert Kron	.20	.50
12 Tom Kurvers	.20	.50
13 Igor Larionov	.60	1.50
14 Doug Lidster	.20	.50
15 Trevor Linden	.80	2.00
16 Jyrki Lumme	.30	.75
17 Jay Mazur	.20	.50
18 Andrew McBain	.20	.50
19 Kirk McLean	.60	1.50
20 Rob Murphy	.20	.50
21 Petr Nedved	.60	1.50
22 Robert Nordmark	.20	.50
23 Gino Odjick	.30	.75
24 Adrien Plavsic	.20	.50
25 Dan Quinn	.20	.50
26 Jim Sandlak	.20	.50
27 Stan Smyl	.30	.75
28 Ronnie Stern	.20	.50
29 Garry Valk	.20	.50

1990-91 Canucks Molson

This set features large (approximately 8" by 10") glossy color close-up photos of Canucks, who were honored as the Molson Canadian Player of the Month. The photos are enclosed by a gold border. The player's name appears in the bottom gold border. At the bottom center is a picture of the Molson Cup. The team logo and a Molson logo in the lower corners round out the front. The backs are blank, and the unnumbered photos are checklisted below in alphabetical order.

COMPLETE SET (6)	16.00	40.00
1 Brian Bradley	2.00	5.00
2 Troy Gamble	2.00	5.00
3 Doug Lidster	2.00	5.00
4 Trevor Linden	4.00	10.00
5 Kirk McLean (Facing right)	3.20	8.00
6 Kirk McLean (Facing front)	3.20	8.00

1991 Canucks Panini Team Stickers

This 32-sticker set was issued in a plastic bag that contained two 16-sticker sheets (approximately 9" by 12") and a foldout poster, "Super Poster - Hockey 91", on which the stickers could be affixed. The players' names appear only on the poster, not on the stickers. Each sticker measures about 2 1/8" by 2 7/8" and features a color player action shot on its white-bordered front. The back of the white sticker sheet is lined off into 16 panels, each carrying the logos for Panini, the NHL, and the NHLPA, as well as the same number that appears on the front of the sticker. Every Canadian NHL team was featured in this promotion. Each team set was available by mail-order from Panini Canada Ltd. for 2.99 plus 50 cents for shipping and handling.

COMPLETE SET (32)	1.60	4.00
1 Greg Adams	.04	.10
2 Jim Agnew	.02	.05
3 Steve Bozek	.02	.05
4 Brian Bradley	.08	.20
5 Garth Butcher	.02	.05
6 Dave Capuano	.02	.05
7 Craig Coxe	.02	.05
8 Troy Gamble	.04	.10
9 Kevan Guy	.02	.05
10 Robert Kron	.02	.05
11 Igor Larionov	.10	.25
12 Doug Lidster	.04	.10
13 Trevor Linden	.20	.50
14 Jyrki Lumme	.04	.10
15 Andrew McBain	.02	.05
16 Rob Murphy	.02	.05
17 Petr Nedved	.20	.50
18 Robert Nordmark	.02	.05
19 Adrien Plavsic	.02	.05
20 Dan Quinn	.04	.10
21 Jim Sandlak	.02	.05
22 Petri Skriko	.04	.10
23 Stan Smyl	.08	.20
24 Ronnie Stern	.02	.05
A Team Logo Left Side	.06	.15
B Team Logo Right Side	.06	.15
C Canucks in Action Upper Left Corner	.06	.15
D Canucks in Action Lower Left Corner	.06	.15
E Game Action Upper Right Corner	.06	.15
F Game Action Lower Right Corner	.06	.15
G Kirk McLean	.20	.50
H Trevor Linden	.20	.50

1991-92 Canucks Autograph Cards

These autograph cards, each measuring approximately 3 3/4" by 8 1/2", were issued by the team with a large white area at the bottom for the players to sign. The front features a glossy color close-up photo, with the year and the team logo in the white border above the picture. In cursive lettering, the player's name and number appear below the picture, with his position printed in block lettering. The unnumbered cards are blank on the back and checklisted below in alphabetical order.

COMPLETE SET (23)	10.00	25.00
1 Greg Adams	.40	1.00
2 Pavel Bure	3.00	8.00
3 Dave Babych	.40	1.00
4 Geoff Courtnall	.40	1.00
5 Gerald Diduck	.20	.50
6 Robert Dirk	.20	.50
7 Troy Gamble	.30	.75
8 Randy Gregg	.20	.50
9 Robert Kron	.20	.50
10 Igor Larionov	.60	1.50
11 Doug Lidster	.20	.50
12 Trevor Linden	1.00	2.50
13 Jyrki Lumme	.30	.75
14 Kirk McLean	1.20	3.00
15 Sergio Momesso	.20	.50
16 Rob Murphy	.20	.50
17 Dana Murzyn	.20	.50
18 Petr Nedved	1.20	3.00
19 Gino Odjick	.30	.75
20 Adrien Plavsic	.20	.50
21 Cliff Ronning	.60	1.50
22 Jim Sandlak	.20	.50
23 Ryan Walter	.20	.50

1991-92 Canucks Molson

This set features large (approximately 8" by 10") glossy color close-up photos of Canucks who were honored as the Molson Canadian Player of the Month or Player of the Year. The photos are enclosed by white, red, and blue border stripes. A gold leaf appear above the picture, while a gold plaque identifying the player appears below the picture. The team logo and a Molson logo appear in the lower corners. The backs are blank, and the unnumbered photos are checklisted below in alphabetical order.

COMPLETE SET (7)	20.00	50.00
1 Greg Adams	1.60	4.00
2 Pavel Bure (White uniform)	6.00	15.00
3 Pavel Bure POY (Black uniform)	6.00	15.00
4 Igor Larionov	2.40	6.00
5 Trevor Linden	2.80	7.00
6 Kirk McLean	2.80	7.00
7 Cliff Ronning	2.00	5.00

1991-92 Canucks Team Issue 8x10

This set features 8" by 10" glossy color close-up photos of the Vancouver Canucks. The photos are enclosed by a thin black border. In cursive lettering, the player's name and number appear below the picture, with his position printed in block lettering. The team logo in the lower left corner completes the front. The backs carry a black and white head shot, biography, 1990-91 season summary, career highlights, personal information, and complete statistics. The cards are unnumbered and checklisted below in alphabetical order.

COMPLETE SET (23)	30.00	75.00
1 Greg Adams	1.60	4.00
2 Pavel Bure	6.00	15.00
3 Dave Babych	1.20	3.00
4 Geoff Courtnall	1.60	4.00
5 Gerald Diduck	1.20	3.00
6 Robert Dirk	1.20	3.00
7 Troy Gamble	1.60	4.00
8 Randy Gregg	1.20	3.00
9 Robert Kron	1.20	3.00
10 Igor Larionov	1.60	4.00
11 Doug Lidster	1.20	3.00
12 Trevor Linden	2.00	5.00
13 Jyrki Lumme	1.20	3.00
14 Kirk McLean	2.00	5.00
15 Sergio Momesso	1.20	3.00
16 Rob Murphy	1.20	3.00
17 Dana Murzyn	1.20	3.00
18 Petr Nedved	2.00	5.00
19 Gino Odjick	1.60	4.00
20 Adrien Plavsic	1.20	3.00
21 Cliff Ronning	2.00	5.00
22 Jim Sandlak	1.20	3.00
23 Ryan Walter	1.20	3.00

1992-93 Canucks Road Trip Art

Dubbed "Road Trip Art Cards," this set of 25 approximately 4 3/4" by 7" player portraits was available only at Subway and Payless stores. Each week for six weeks, a set of four player portraits was released at a suggested price of 2.29 per pack. Also there was a tab inside each package and one could win a pair of 1993-94 season tickets, autographed Road Trip prints, limited edition Road Trip prints, Road Trip puzzles, and Road Trip coloring books. The photos are black-and-white and picture the Canuck players dressed in western garb. A gold foil facsimile autograph is printed near the bottom. The backs carry the player's name in a wide red stripe at the top. Humorous text in the form of player quotes rests against a white background along with the team logo and the words "Road Trip." A bright yellow stripe accents the bottom of the card and contains manufacturer information. The portraits are listed below in alphabetical order with the week issued denoted.

COMPLETE SET (25)	6.00	15.00
1 Greg Adams W1	.30	.75
2 Shawn Antoski W5	.20	.50
3 Dave Babych W5	.30	.75
4 Pavel Bure W3	2.00	5.00
5 Geoff Courtnall W5	.30	.75
6 Gerald Diduck W4	.20	.50
7 Robert Dirk W5	.20	.50
8 Tom Fergus W3	.20	.50
9 Robert Kron W2	.20	.50
10 Doug Lidster W2	.20	.50
11 Trevor Linden W1	.60	1.50
12 Jyrki Lumme W1	.30	.75
13 Kirk McLean W2	.60	1.50
14 Sergio Momesso W2	.20	.50
15 Dana Murzyn W3	.20	.50
16 Petr Nedved W4	.60	1.50
17 Gino Odjick W4	.40	1.00
18 Adrien Plavsic W6	.20	.50
19 Cliff Ronning W6	.30	.75
20 Jim Sandlak W6	.20	.50
21 Jiri Slegr W1	.20	.50
22 Garry Valk W4	.20	.50
23 Ryan Walter W5	.20	.50
24 Dixon Ward W3	.20	.50
25 Kay Whitmore W6	.30	.75

1994-95 Canucks Program Inserts

Measuring approximately 8" by 10 1/2", these program inserts feature the 1994-95 Vancouver Canucks. The fronts have color action player shots with white borders. The player's name, number and position appear on the fronts, along with the words "Canucks Collector Series" in a bar at the top. The backs are blank. The inserts are unnumbered and checklisted below in alphabetical order.

COMPLETE SET (22)	32.00	80.00
1 Greg Adams	1.60	4.00
2 Shawn Antoski	1.60	4.00
3 Dave Babych	1.60	4.00
4 Jeff Brown	1.60	4.00
5 Pavel Bure	4.00	10.00
6 Geoff Courtnall	1.60	4.00
7 Gerald Diduck	1.60	4.00
8 Robert Dirk	1.60	4.00
9 Martin Gelinas	1.60	4.00
10 Brian Glynn	1.60	4.00
11 Tim Hunter	1.60	4.00
12 Nathan LaFayette	1.60	4.00
13 Trevor Linden	2.00	5.00
14 Jyrki Lumme	1.60	4.00
15 Kirk McLean	2.00	5.00
16 Dana Murzyn	1.60	4.00
17 Gino Odjick	1.60	4.00
18 Adrien Plavsic	1.60	4.00
19 Cliff Ronning	1.60	4.00
20 Jiri Slegr	1.60	4.00
21 Dixon Ward	1.60	4.00
22 Kay Whitmore	2.00	5.00

1995-96 Canucks Building the Dream Art

This 18-card set of the Vancouver Canucks features 5" by 7" borderless black-and-white player photos in construction worker poses with gold facsimile autographs at the bottom. The backs carry player information. This set continues the tradition begun in 1992-93 with the Canucks Road Trip Art set.

COMPLETE SET (18)	6.00	15.00
1 Kirk McLean	.40	1.00
2 Kay Whitmore	.24	.60
3 Bret Hedican	.20	.50
4 Tim Hunter	.20	.50
5 Dana Murzyn	.20	.50
6 Jyrki Lumme	.24	.60
7 Cliff Ronning	.30	.75
8 Jeff Brown	.30	.75
9 Martin Gelinas	.40	1.00
10 Pavel Bure	2.00	5.00
11 Jiri Slegr	.20	.50
12 Sergio Momesso	.20	.50
13 Gino Odjick	.40	1.00
14 Geoff Courtnall	.20	.50
15 John McIntyre	.20	.50
16 Trevor Linden	.80	2.00
17 Mike Peca	.40	1.00
18 Dave Babych	.20	.50

1996-97 Canucks Postcards

This extremely attractive, 27-postcard set was produced by the Canucks and sponsored by IGA grocery stores as a promotional giveaway. The highly stylized fronts have an action color photo with the team name above, and a row of team logos to the right. Immediately below the photo is a strip for autographing. The backs are blank. As the postcards are unnumbered, they are listed according to their sweater number, which is displayed on the lower right hand front corner.

COMPLETE SET (27)	6.00	15.00
1 Kirk McLean	.30	.75
3 Bret Hedican	.10	.25
4 Mark Wotton	.10	.25
5 Dana Murzyn	.10	.25
6 Adrian Aucoin	.10	.25
7 David Roberts	.10	.25
8 Donald Brashear	.10	.25
9 Russ Courtnall	.20	.50
10 Esa Tikkanen	.20	.50
16 Trevor Linden	.30	.75
17 Mike Ridley	.20	.50
18 Troy Crowder	.10	.25
19 Markus Naslund	.20	.50
20 Alexander Semak	.10	.25
21 Jyrki Lumme	.20	.50
23 Martin Gelinas	.30	.75
24 Scott Walker	.20	.50
26 Mike Sillinger	.10	.25
27 Leif Rohlin	.10	.25
29 Gino Odjick	.30	.75
30 Mike Fountain	.20	.50
31 Corey Hirsch	.30	.75
32 Chris Joseph	.10	.25
44 Dave Babych	.20	.50
89 Alexander Mogilny	.60	1.50
96 Pavel Bure	1.60	4.00
NNO Team Photo	.20	.50

2002-03 Canucks Team Issue

These singles were offered at tear appearances. The checklist is believed to b incomplete. If you have additiona information, contact us a hockeymag@beckett.com.

COMPLETE SET (?)	
1 Murray Baron	1.00
2 Todd Bertuzzi	5.00
3 Dan Cloutier	3.00
4 Matt Cooke	3.00
5 Artem Chubarov	1.00
6 Ed Jovanovski	3.00
7 Trent Klatt	1.00
8 Trevor Linden	3.00
9 Marek Malik	1.00
10 Brendan Morrison	3.00
11 Markus Naslund	5.00
12 Mattias Ohlund	1.00
13 Sami Salo	1.00
14 Daniel Sedin	3.00
15 Henrik Sedin	3.00

2003-04 Canucks Postcards

COMPLETE SET (28)	18.00
1 Bryan Allen	.50
2 Magnus Arvedson	.50
3 Todd Bertuzzi	1.00
4 Brian Burke GM	.10
5 Artem Chubarov	.50
6 Dan Cloutier	1.00
7 Matt Cooke	1.00
8 Marc Crawford CO	.25
9 Johan Hedberg	.50
10 Mike Johnston ACO	.10
11 Ed Jovanovski	1.00
12 Mike Keane	.50
13 Jason King	.50
14 Trevor Linden	1.00
15 Mats Lindgren	.50
16 Marek Malik	.50
17 Brad May	.50
18 Jack McIlhargey ACO	.10
19 Brendan Morrison	1.00
20 Markus Naslund	2.00
21 Mattias Ohlund	.50
22 Jarkko Ruutu	.50
23 Sami Salo	.50
24 Daniel Sedin	1.00
25 Henrik Sedin	1.00
26 Jiri Slegr	.50
27 Brent Sopel	.50
28 Finn MASCOT	.10

2003-04 Canucks Sav-on-Foods

Created by Pacific Trading Cards, this 24 card set featured players from the Vancouve Canucks and were sold exclusively at Sav on-Foods stores. Cards were sold in 4-car packs for an SRP of $2.99. Autographs Markus Naslund, Todd Bertuzzi and Brenda Morrison were also randomly insertec Because of lack of market information, the are unpriced.

COMPLETE SET (30)	6.00	15.00
1 Trevor Linden	.60	1.50
2 Johan Hedberg	.20	.50
3 Mike Keane	.20	.50
4 Todd Bertuzzi / Brendan Morrison / Markus Naslund	.40	1.00
5 Markus Naslund	.60	1.50
6 Daniel Sedin	.40	1.00
7 Marek Malik	.20	.50
8 Brad May	.20	.50
9 Brendan Morrison	.20	.50
10 Mattias Ohlund	.20	.50
11 Magnus Arvedson	.20	.50
12 Bryan Allen	.20	.50
13 Jason King	.20	.50
14 Henrik Sedin	.40	1.00
15 Brent Sopel	.20	.50
16 Ed Jovanovski / Dan Cloutier / Mattias Ohlund	.40	1.00
17 Dan Cloutier	.40	1.00
18 Artem Chubarov	.20	.50
19 Jarkko Ruutu	.20	.50
20 Daniel Sedin / Henrik Sedin / Jason King	.40	1.00
21 Ed Jovanovski	.40	1.00
22 Todd Bertuzzi	.40	1.00
23 Matt Cooke	.40	1.00
24 Sami Salo	.20	.50

NO Markus Naslund AU		
NO Brendan Morrison AU		
NO Todd Bertuzzi AU		

2006-07 Canucks Postcards

COMPLETE SET (25)	15.00	25.00
Kevin Bieksa	.60	1.50
Luc Bourdon	.40	1.00
Jan Bulis	.40	1.00
Alexandre Burrows	.40	1.00
Marc Chouinard	.40	1.00
Matt Cooke	.60	1.50
Rory Fitzpatrick	.40	1.00
Josh Green	.40	1.00
Ryan Kesler	.40	1.00
0 Lukas Krajicek	.40	1.00
1 Trevor Linden	.75	2.00
2 Roberto Luongo	1.25	3.00
3 Willie Mitchell	.40	1.00
4 Brendan Morrison	.40	1.00
5 Markus Naslund	.75	2.00
6 Mattias Ohlund	.40	1.00
7 Taylor Pyatt	.40	1.00
8 Dany Sabourin	.40	1.00
9 Sami Salo	.40	1.00
0 Tommi Santala	.40	1.00
1 Daniel Sedin	.75	2.00
2 Henrik Sedin	.75	2.00
3 Alain Vigneault CO	.10	.25
4 Fin MASCOT	.10	.25
5 Logo Card	.10	.25

1974-75 Capitals White Borders

his 25-card set measures approximately 5" / 7" is printed on very thin paper stock. The onts have black-and-white player portraits ith white borders. The player's name and ie team logo appear under the photo. The acks are blank. The cards are unnumbered id checklisted below in alphabetical order.

OMPLETE SET (25)	30.00	60.00
John Adams	1.00	2.00
Jim Anderson CO	1.00	2.00
Ron Anderson	1.00	2.00
Steve Atkinson	1.00	2.00
Michel Belhumeur	2.00	4.00
Mike Bloom	1.00	2.00
Gord Brooks	1.00	2.00
Bruce Cowick	1.00	2.00
Denis Dupere	1.00	2.00
0 Jack Egers	1.00	2.00
1 Jim Hrycuik	1.00	2.00
2 Greg Joly	1.50	3.00
3 Dave Kryskow	1.00	2.00
4 Yvon Labre	1.50	3.00
5 Pete Laframboise	1.00	2.00
6 Bill Lesuk	1.00	2.00
7 Ron Low	2.00	4.00
8 Joe Lundrigan	1.00	2.00
9 Mike Marson	1.50	3.00
0 Bill Mikkelson	1.00	2.00
1 Doug Mohns	2.00	4.00
2 Andre Peloffy	1.00	2.00
3 Milt Schmidt GM	2.50	5.00
4 Gord Smith	1.00	2.00
5 Tom Williams	1.50	3.00

1978-79 Capitals Team Issue

his set features the Capitals of the NHL. ie oversized cards feature black and white ead shots on thin paper stock. It is believed iey were issued as a set to fans who quested them by mail.

OMPLETE SET (18)	7.50	15.00
Michel Bergeron	.75	1.50
Greg Carroll	.50	1.00
Guy Charron	.50	1.00
Rolf Edberg	.50	1.00
Rick Green	.50	1.00
Gordie Lane	.50	1.00
Mark Lofthouse	.50	1.00
Jack Lynch	.50	1.00
Dennis Maruk	.75	1.50
0 Paul Mulvey	.50	1.00
1 Robert Picard	.50	1.00
2 Bill Riley	.50	1.00
3 Tom Rowe	.50	1.00
4 Bob Sirois	.50	1.00
5 Gord Smith	.50	1.00
6 Leif Svensson	.75	1.50
7 Ryan Walter	.50	1.00
8 Bernie Wolf	.50	1.00

1979-80 Capitals Team Issue

his set features the Capitals of the NHL. ie oversized cards feature black and white ead shots on thin paper stock. It is believed iey were issued as a set to fans who equested them by mail.

OMPLETE SET (23)	20.00	40.00
Pierre Bouchard	.50	1.00
Guy Charron	.50	1.00
Rolf Edberg	.50	1.00
Mike Gartner	12.50	25.00
Rick Green	.50	1.00
Bengt Gustafsson	.75	1.50
Dennis Hextall	.75	1.50
Gary Inness	.50	1.00
Yvon Labre	.50	1.00
10 Antero Lehtonen	.50	1.00
11 Mark Lofthouse	.50	1.00
12 Paul McKinnon	.50	1.00
13 Dennis Maruk	.75	1.50
14 Paul Mulvey	.50	1.00
15 Robert Picard	.75	1.50
16 Greg Polis	.50	1.00
17 Errol Rausse	.50	1.00
18 Tom Rowe	.50	1.00
19 Peter Scamurra	.50	1.00
20 Bob Sirois	.50	1.00
21 Wayne Stephenson	.50	1.00
22 Leif Svensson	.75	1.50
23 Ryan Walter	.50	1.00

1981-82 Capitals Team Issue

This 21-card set measures approximately 5" by 7". The fronts have black-and-white player portraits with white borders. The player's name, position, jersey number, and the team logo appear under the photo. The backs are blank. The cards are unnumbered and checklisted below in alphabetical order.

COMPLETE SET (21)	12.00	30.00
1 Timo Blomqvist	.40	1.00
2 Bobby Carpenter	1.20	3.00
3 Glen Currie	.40	1.00
4 Gaetan Duchesne	.60	1.50
5 Mike Gartner	4.00	10.00
6 Rick Green	.60	1.50
7 Randy Holt	.40	1.00
8 Wes Jarvis	.40	1.00
9 Al Jensen	.60	1.50
10 Dennis Maruk	1.20	3.00
11 Terry Murray	.40	1.00
12 Lee Norwood	.40	1.00
13 Mike Palmateer	1.20	3.00
14 Dave Parro	.60	1.50
15 Torrie Robertson	.60	1.50
16 Greg Theberge	.60	1.50
17 Chris Valentine	.40	1.00
18 Darren Veitch	.40	1.00
19 Howard Walker	.40	1.00
21 Ryan Walter	.80	2.00

1982-83 Capitals Team Issue

This 25-card set measures approximately 5" by 7". The fronts have black-and-white player portraits with white borders. The player's name, position, jersey number, and the team logo appear under the photo. The backs are blank. The cards are unnumbered and checklisted below in alphabetical order. The card of Scott Stevens appears one year before his Rookie Card.

COMPLETE SET (25)	16.00	40.00
1 Timo Blomqvist	.40	1.00
2 Ted Bulley	.40	1.00
3 Bobby Carpenter	.80	2.00
4 Glen Currie	.40	1.00
5 Brian Engblom	.60	1.50
6 Mike Gartner	3.20	8.00
7 Bob Gould	.40	1.00
8 Bengt Gustafsson	.80	2.00
9 Alan Haworth	.40	1.00
10 Randy Holt	.40	1.00
11 Ken Houston	.40	1.00
12 Doug Jarvis	.80	2.00
13 Rod Langway	1.60	4.00
14 Craig Laughlin	.40	1.00
15 Dennis Maruk	.80	2.00
16 Bryan Murray CO	.40	1.00
17 Terry Murray ACO	.40	1.00
18 Lee Norwood	.40	1.00
19 Milan Novy	.40	1.00
20 Dave Parro	.60	1.50
21 David Poile GM	.40	1.00
22 Pat Riggin	1.00	2.50
23 Scott Stevens	4.00	10.00
24 Chris Valentine	.40	1.00
25 Darren Veitch	.40	1.00

1984-85 Capitals Pizza Hut

These cards of Washington Capitals were given out to members of the Junior Capitals Club and measure approximately 4 1/2" by 6". The front features a color action photo of the player, with three blue stripes on the picture. The back has a small head shot of the player and his career statistics. The cards are unnumbered and hence are listed below alphabetically by player name.

COMPLETE SET (15)	14.00	35.00
1 Bob Carpenter	.80	2.00
2 Dave Christian	1.00	2.50
3 Glen Currie	.60	1.50
4 Gaetan Duchesne	.60	1.50
5 Mike Gartner	3.00	7.50
6 Bob Gould	.60	1.50
7 Bengt Gustafsson	.80	2.00
8 Alan Haworth	.60	1.50
9 Doug Jarvis	.80	2.00
10 Al Jensen	.80	2.00
11 Rod Langway	1.20	3.00
12 Craig Laughlin	.60	1.50
13 Larry Murphy	2.00	5.00
14 Pat Riggin	.80	2.00
15 Scott Stevens	3.00	7.50

1985-86 Capitals Pizza Hut

These cards of members of the Washington Capitals were mailed three at a time to members of the Junior Capitals Club and measure approximately 4 1/2" by 6". The front features a color action photo of the player, with three red stripes on the picture. The back has a small head shot of the player and his career statistics. When Doug Jarvis, Pat Riggin, and Darren Veitch were traded, supposedly their cards were pulled and never mailed to club members. It is alleged that these cards were destroyed and only a few were kept. Consequently, these player cards are scarce.

COMPLETE SET (15)	14.00	35.00
1 Bob Carpenter	.80	2.00
2 Dave Christian	1.00	2.50
3 Gaetan Duchesne	.60	1.50
4 Mike Gartner	2.40	6.00
5 Bob Gould	.60	1.50
6 Bengt Gustafsson	.80	2.00
7 Alan Haworth	.60	1.50
8 Doug Jarvis SP	1.60	4.00
9 Al Jensen	.80	2.00
10 Rod Langway	1.20	3.00
11 Craig Laughlin	.60	1.50
12 Larry Murphy	2.00	5.00
13 Pat Riggin SP	2.00	5.00
14 Scott Stevens	2.40	6.00
15 Darren Veitch SP	1.60	4.00

1986-87 Capitals Kodak

The 1986-87 Washington Capitals Team Photo Album was sponsored by Kodak. It consists of three large sheets joined together to form one continuous sheet. The first panel has a team photo measuring approximately 10" by 8". The second and third panels consist of player cards; after perforation, they measure approximately 2" by 2 5/8". The cards feature color posed photos, with player information below. The cards are unnumbered and we have checklisted them below in alphabetical order. Kevin Hatcher's card predates his Rookie Card by one year.

COMPLETE SET (26)	12.00	30.00
1 Greg Adams	.60	1.50
2 John Barrett	.30	.75
3 John Blum	.30	.75
4 Dave Christian	.40	1.00
5 Bob Crawford	.30	.75
6 Gaetan Duchesne	.30	.75
7 Lou Franceschetti	.30	.75
8 Mike Gartner	1.60	4.00
9 Bob Gould	.30	.75
10 Jeff Greenlaw	.30	.75
11 Kevin Hatcher	.80	2.00
12 Alan Haworth	.30	.75
13 David A. Jensen	.30	.75
14 Rod Langway	.80	2.00
15 Craig Laughlin	.30	.75
16 Bob Mason	.40	1.00
17 Kelly Miller	.40	1.00
18 Larry Murphy	1.00	2.50
19 Bryan Murray CO	.30	.75
20 Pete Peeters	.80	2.00
21 Michal Pivonka	1.20	3.00
22 Mike Ridley	.80	2.00
23 Gary Sampson	.30	.75
24 Greg Smith	.30	.75
25 Scott Stevens	1.60	4.00
26 Large Team Photo	.80	2.00

1986-87 Capitals Police

This 24-card police set features players of the Washington Capitals. The cards measure approximately 2 5/8" by 3 3/4" and were issued in two-card panels. The front has a color action photo on white card stock, with player information and the Capitals' logo below the picture. Inside a thin black border the back features a hockey tip ("Caps Tips"), an anti-crime tip, and logos of sponsoring police agencies. The cards are unnumbered and we have checklisted them below in alphabetical order, with the jersey number to the right of the player's name. Kevin Hatcher's card predates his Rookie Card by one year.

COMPLETE SET (24)	6.00	15.00
1 Greg Adams 22	.40	1.00
2 John Barrett 6	.20	.50
3 Bob Carpenter 10	.20	.50
4 Dave Christian 27	.30	.75
5 Yvon Corriveau 26	.20	.50
6 Gaetan Duchesne 14	.20	.50
7 Lou Franceschetti 32	.20	.50
8 Mike Gartner 11	1.20	3.00
9 Bob Gould 23	.20	.50
10 Kevin Hatcher 4	.60	1.50
11 Alan Haworth 15	.20	.50
12 Al Jensen 35	.24	.60
13 David A. Jensen 9	.20	.50
14 Rod Langway 5	.60	1.50
15 Craig Laughlin 18	.20	.50
16 Stephen Leach 21	.30	.75
17 Larry Murphy 8	.80	2.00
18 Bryan Murray CO	.20	.50
19 Pete Peeters 1	.60	1.50
20 Jorgen Pettersson 12	.20	.50
21 Michal Pivonka 17	.80	2.00
22 David Poile VP/GM	.20	.50
23 Greg Smith 19	.20	.50
24 Scott Stevens 3	1.20	3.00

1987-88 Capitals Kodak

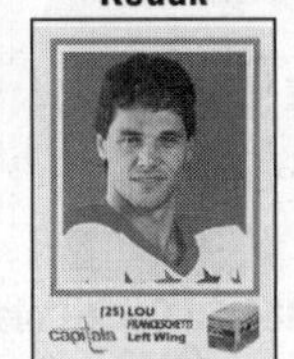

The 1987-88 Washington Capitals Team Photo Album was sponsored by Kodak. It consists of three large sheets, each measuring approximately 11" by 8 1/4" and joined together to form one continuous sheet. The first panel has a team photo, with the players' names listed according to rows below the picture. While the second panel presents three rows of five cards each, the third panel presents two rows of five cards, with five Kodak coupons completing the left over portion of the panel. After perforation, the cards measure approximately 2 3/16" by 2 15/16". They feature color-posed photos bordered in red, with player information below the picture. The Capitals' logo and a picture of a Kodak film box complete the card face. The back has biographical and statistical information in a horizontal format. The cards are checklisted below by sweater number.

COMPLETE SET (26)	8.00	20.00
1 Pete Peeters	.40	1.00
2 Garry Galley	.40	1.00
3 Scott Stevens	.80	2.00
4 Kevin Hatcher	.80	2.00
5 Rod Langway	.40	1.00
6 John Barrett	.20	.50
8 Larry Murphy	.60	1.50
10 Kelly Miller	.30	.75
11 Mike Gartner	1.00	2.50
12 Peter Sundstrom	.30	.75
16 Bengt Gustafsson	.30	.75
17 Mike Ridley	.60	1.50
18 Craig Laughlin	.20	.50
19 Greg Smith	.20	.50
20 Michal Pivonka	.60	1.50
22 Greg Adams	.40	1.00
23 Bob Gould	.20	.50
25 Lou Franceschetti	.20	.50
27 Dave Christian	.40	1.00
29 Ed Kastelic	.20	.50
30 Clint Malarchuk	.40	1.00
32 Dale Hunter	.60	1.50
34 Bill Houlder	.30	.75
xx Bryan Murray CO	.20	.50
XX Team Photo	.20	.50
xx David Poile VP/GM	.20	.50

1987-88 Capitals Team Issue

This 23-card set measures 5 1/4" by 8". The fronts feature autographed color action photos. The backs carry a head shot, biography, 1986-87 recap, career highlights, personal information and complete statistics with the player's name, position and jersey number at the top. The cards are unnumbered and checklisted below in alphabetical order.

COMPLETE SET (23)	10.00	25.00
1 Greg Adams	.50	1.25
2 John Barrett	.30	.75
3 Dave Christian	.50	1.25
4 Lou Franceschetti	.30	.75
5 Garry Galley	.60	1.50
6 Mike Gartner	1.20	3.00
7 Bob Gould	.30	.75
8 Bengt Gustafsson	.40	1.00
9 Kevin Hatcher	1.20	3.00
10 Dale Hunter	.80	2.00
11 David Jensen	.30	.75
12 Ed Kastelic	.30	.75
13 Rod Langway	.50	1.25
14 Craig Laughlin	.30	.75
15 Clint Malarchuk	.50	1.25
16 Kelly Miller	.40	1.00
17 Larry Murphy	.80	2.00
18 Pete Peeters	.60	1.50
19 Michal Pivonka	.80	2.00
20 Mike Ridley	.80	2.00
21 Greg Smith	.30	.75
22 Scott Stevens	1.00	2.50
23 Peter Sundstrom	.40	1.00

1988-89 Capitals Borderless

Measuring approximately 5" by 7", this 21-card set features the 1988-89 Washington Capitals. The fronts have borderless color action player photos. The backs carry player biography and statistics, season and career highlights, and short personal information. The cards are unnumbered and checklisted below in alphabetical order.

COMPLETE SET (21)	6.00	15.00
1 Dave Christian	.40	1.00
2 Yvon Corriveau	.30	.75
3 Geoff Courtnall	.80	2.00
4 Lou Franceschetti	.30	.75
5 Mike Gartner	.80	2.00
6 Bob Gould	.30	.75
7 Bengt Gustafsson	.40	1.00
8 Kevin Hatcher	.60	1.50
9 Dale Hunter	.60	1.50
10 Rod Langway	.60	1.50
11 Stephen Leach	.30	.75
12 Grant Ledyard	.30	.75
13 Clint Malarchuk	.40	1.00
14 Kelly Miller	.30	.75
15 Larry Murphy	.60	1.50
16 Pete Peeters	.40	1.00
17 Michal Pivonka	.80	2.00
18 Mike Ridley	.60	1.50
19 Neil Sheehy	.30	.75
20 Scott Stevens	.80	2.00
21 Peter Sundstrom	.40	1.00

1988-89 Capitals Smokey

This 24-card safety set features players of the Washington Capitals. The cards measure approximately 2 5/8" by 3 3/4" and were issued in two-card panels. The front has a color action photo on white card stock, with player information and logos below the picture. Inside a thin black border the back features a hockey tip ("Caps Tips") and a fire prevention cartoon starring Smokey. The cards are unnumbered and we have checklisted them below in alphabetical order, with the sweater number to the right of the player's name. Geoff Courtnall's card predates his Rookie Card by a year.

COMPLETE SET (24)	6.00	15.00
1 Dave Christian 27	.30	.75
2 Yvon Corriveau 26	.20	.50
3 Geoff Courtnall 14	.60	1.50
4 Lou Franceschetti 25	.20	.50
5 Mike Gartner 11	.60	1.50
6 Bob Gould 23	.20	.50
7 Bengt Gustafsson 16	.30	.75
8 Kevin Hatcher 4	.40	1.00
9 Dale Hunter 32	.40	1.00
10 Rod Langway 5	.40	1.00
11 Stephen Leach 21	.20	.50
12 Grant Ledyard 6	.20	.50
13 Clint Malarchuk 30	.30	.75
14 Kelly Miller 10	.20	.50
15 Larry Murphy 8	.40	1.00
16 Bryan Murray CO	.30	.75
17 Pete Peeters 1	.30	.75
18 Michal Pivonka 20	.60	1.50
19 David Poile VP/GM	.20	.50
20 Mike Ridley 17	.40	1.00
21 Neil Sheehy 15	.20	.50
22 Scott Stevens 3	.60	1.50
23 Peter Sundstrom 12	.30	.75
24 Title Card Smokey the Bear	.20	.50

1989-90 Capitals Kodak

The 1989-90 Washington Capitals Team Photo Album was co-sponsored by Kodak and W. Bell and Co. It consists of three large sheets, each measuring approximately 11" by 8 1/4" and joined together to form one continuous sheet. The first panel has a large blue square designated for autographs. While the second panel presents three rows of five cards each, the third panel presents two rows of five cards, with Kodak advertisements completing the left over portion of the panel. After perforation, the cards measure approximately 2 3/16" by 2 1/2". They feature color action photos bordered in red, with player information below the picture. The Capitals' logo and a picture of a Kodak film box complete the card face. The back has biographical and statistical information in a horizontal format. The cards are checklisted below by sweater number.

COMPLETE SET (25)	8.00	20.00
1 Mike Liut	.40	1.00
3 Scott Stevens	.80	2.00
4 Kevin Hatcher	.60	1.50
5 Rod Langway	.60	1.50
6 Calle Johansson	.40	1.00
8 Bob Rouse	.30	.75
10 Kelly Miller	.40	1.00
11 Tim Bergland	.30	.75
12 John Tucker	.30	.75
14 Geoff Courtnall	.60	1.50
15 Neil Sheehy	.30	.75
16 Alan May	.30	.75
17 Mike Ridley	.40	1.00
19 John Druce	.30	.75
20 Michal Pivonka	.40	1.00
21 Stephen Leach	.30	.75
22 Dino Ciccarelli	.80	2.00
26 Steve Maltais	.30	.75
27 Bob Joyce	.30	.75
29 Scot Kleinendorst	.30	.75
32 Dale Hunter	.60	1.50
33 Don Beaupre	.40	1.00
xx Rob Laird ACO	.20	.50
xx Terry Murray CO	.20	.50
xx David Poile VP/GM	.20	.50

1989-90 Capitals Team Issue

This 23-card set measures approximately 5" by 7". The fronts feature full-bleed, posed color photos with the player's jersey as a background. The backs are blank. The cards are unnumbered and checklisted below in alphabetical order.

COMPLETE SET (23)	7.20	18.00
1 Don Beaupre	.30	.75
2 Dave Christian	.30	.75
3 Dino Ciccarelli	.60	1.50
4 Yvon Corriveau	.20	.50
5 Geoff Courtnall	.40	1.00
6 Kevin Hatcher	.40	1.00
7 Bill Houlder	.30	.75
8 Dale Hunter	.40	1.00
9 Calle Johansson	.30	.75
10 Dimitri Khristich	.60	1.50
11 Scot Kleinendorst	.20	.50
12 Nick Kypreos	.20	.50
13 Rod Langway	.40	1.00
14 Stephen Leach	.20	.50
15 Bob Mason	.30	.75
16 Alan May	.20	.50
17 Kelly Miller	.30	.75
18 Michal Pivonka	.30	.75
19 Mike Ridley	.30	.75
20 Bob Rouse	.20	.50
21 Neil Sheehy	.20	.50
22 Scott Stevens	.60	1.50
23 Doug Wickenheiser	.20	.50

1990-91 Capitals Kodak

The 1990-91 Washington Capitals Team Photo Album was sponsored by Kodak. It consists of three large sheets joined together to form one continuous sheet. The first panel has a team photo measuring approximately 10" by 8". The second and third panels consist of player cards; after perforation, they measure approximately 2" by 2 5/8". The cards feature color posed photos, with player information below. The cards are unnumbered and we have checklisted them below in alphabetical order.

COMPLETE SET (25)	6.00	15.00
1 Don Beaupre	.40	1.00
2 Tim Bergland	.20	.50
3 Peter Bondra	2.00	5.00
4 Dino Ciccarelli	.40	1.00
5 John Druce	.20	.50
6 Kevin Hatcher	.40	1.00
7 Dale Hunter	.40	1.00
8 Al Iafrate	.60	1.50
9 Calle Johansson	.30	.75
10 Dimitri Khristich	.40	1.00
11 Nick Kypreos	.20	.50
12 Mike Lalor	.20	.50
13 Rod Langway	.40	1.00
14 Stephen Leach	.20	.50
15 Mike Liut	.40	1.00
16 Alan May	.20	.50
17 Kelly Miller	.20	.50
18 Terry Murray CO	.10	.25
19 John Perpich	.10	.25
20 Michal Pivonka	.40	1.00
21 David Poile VP/GM	.10	.25
22 Mike Ridley	.40	1.00
23 Ken Sabourin	.20	.50
24 Mikhail Tatarinov	.20	.50
25 Dave Tippett	.20	.50

1990-91 Capitals Postcards

This 5 x 7 set features full color photos on the front and a blank back. Cards are unnumbered and checklisted below in alphabetical order.

COMPLETE SET (22)	8.00	20.00
1 Don Beaupre	.40	1.00
2 Tim Bergland	.20	.50
3 Peter Bondra	2.00	5.00
4 Dino Ciccarelli	.40	1.00
5 John Druce	.20	.50
6 Kevin Hatcher	.40	1.00
7 Jim Hrivnak	.24	.60
8 Dale Hunter	.40	1.00
9 Al Iafrate	.60	1.50
10 Calle Johansson	.30	.75
11 Nick Kypreos	.20	.50
12 Mike Lalor	.20	.50
13 Rod Langway	.40	1.00
14 Steve Leach	.20	.50
15 Mike Liut	.40	1.00
16 Alan May	.20	.50
17 Kelly Miller	.20	.50
18 Rob Murray	.20	.50
19 Michal Pivonka	.40	1.00
20 Mike Ridley	.40	1.00
21 Neil Sheehy	.20	.50
22 Dave Tippett	.20	.50

1990-91 Capitals Smokey

This fire safety set contains 22 cards and features members of the Washington Capitals. The cards measure approximately 2 1/2" by 3 3/4" and were issued in two-card panels. The front has a color action photo of the player, with player information below the picture between the Smokey the Bear and team logos. The back includes %%Caps Tips– and a fire prevention message from Smokey.

COMPLETE SET (22)	4.80	12.00
1 Don Beaupre	.30	.75
2 Tim Bergland	.16	.40
3 Peter Bondra	1.60	4.00
4 Dino Ciccarelli	.40	1.00
5 John Druce	.16	.40
6 Kevin Hatcher	.30	.75
7 Jim Hrivnak	.20	.50
8 Dale Hunter	.30	.75
9 Calle Johansson	.20	.50
10 Nick Kypreos	.16	.40
11 Mike Lalor	.16	.40
12 Rod Langway	.30	.75
13 Stephen Leach	.20	.50
14 Mike Liut	.40	1.00
15 Alan May	.16	.40
16 Kelly Miller	.16	.40
17 Rob Murray	.16	.40
18 Michal Pivonka	.40	1.00
19 Mike Ridley	.30	.75
20 Neil Sheehy	.16	.40
21 Mikhail Tatarinov	.16	.40
22 Dave Tippett	.16	.40

1991-92 Capitals Junior 5x7

This 25-card set measures approximately 5" by 7" and features full-bleed glossy action photos; in small black type across the bottom, the uniform number, name, and position are burned in. The backs are blank.

COMPLETE SET (25)	7.20	18.00
1 Don Beaupre	.40	1.00
2 Tim Bergland	.20	.50
3 Peter Bondra	1.60	4.00
4 Randy Burridge	.30	.75
5 Shawn Chambers	.20	.50
6 Dino Ciccarelli	.60	1.50
7 Sylvain Cote	.20	.50
8 John Druce	.20	.50
9 Jeff Greenlaw	.20	.50
10 Kevin Hatcher	.60	1.50
11 Dale Hunter	.60	1.50
12 Al Iafrate	.60	1.50
13 Calle Johansson	.30	.75
14 Dimitri Khristich	.60	1.50
15 Todd Krygier	.20	.50
16 Nick Kypreos	.20	.50
17 Mike Lalor	.20	.50
18 Rod Langway	.40	1.00
19 Mike Liut	.40	1.00
20 Alan May	.20	.50
21 Kelly Miller	.20	.50
22 Michal Pivonka	.60	1.50
23 Mike Ridley	.40	1.00
24 Ken Sabourin	.20	.50
25 Dave Tippett	.20	.50

1991-92 Capitals Kodak

The 1991-92 Washington Capitals Team Photo Album was sponsored by Kodak. It consists of three large sheets joined together to form one continuous sheet. The first panel measures approximately 11" by 8," and it has blank space allotted for autographs. The second panel carries three rows with five player cards each; after perforation, they measure approximately 2 3/16" by 2 3/4." The third panel has two rows with five player cards each, and a final row consisting of two Kodak coupons. The cards feature color head shots, with player information, team logo, and a picture of a Kodak film box below. In a horizontal format, the backs have biographical and statistical information. Though the cards are unnumbered, they are arranged in alphabetical order by players' last names and checklisted below accordingly.

COMPLETE SET (25)	4.80	12.00
1 Don Beaupre	.30	.75
2 Tim Bergland	.16	.40
3 Peter Bondra	1.00	2.50
4 Randy Burridge	.20	.50
5 Shawn Chambers	.16	.40
6 Dino Ciccarelli	.40	1.00
7 Sylvain Cote	.20	.50
8 John Druce	.16	.40
9 Kevin Hatcher	.30	.75
10 Jim Hrivnak	.20	.50
11 Dale Hunter	.30	.75
12 Al Iafrate	.40	1.00
13 Calle Johansson	.20	.50
14 Dimitri Khristich	.40	1.00
15 Todd Krygier	.16	.40
16 Nick Kypreos	.16	.40
17 Rod Langway	.30	.75
18 Mike Liut	.30	.75
19 Paul MacDermid	.16	.40
20 Alan May	.16	.40
21 Kelly Miller	.16	.40
22 Michal Pivonka	.40	1.00
23 Mike Ridley	.30	.75
24 Brad Schlegel	.16	.40
25 Dave Tippett	.16	.40

1992-93 Capitals Kodak

The 1992-93 Washington Capitals Team Photo Album was sponsored by Kodak. It consists of three 8 1/4" by 11" sheets joined together to form one continuous sheet. The

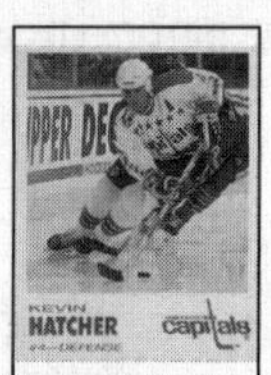

first panel has a slot for collecting autographs. The second and third panels consist of player cards; after perforation, they measure approximately 2 3/16" by 2 3/4". The fronts feature color action player photos with white borders. Player information and the team logo are printed in the bottom white border. The horizontal backs carry biography and complete statistical information. Though the cards are unnumbered, they are arranged alphabetically on the sheet and checklisted below accordingly.

COMPLETE SET (25)	6.00	15.00
1 Shawn Anderson	.20	.50
2 Don Beaupre	.40	1.00
3 Peter Bondra	1.00	2.50
4 Randy Burridge	.24	.60
5 Bobby Carpenter	.24	.60
6 Paul Cavallini	.20	.50
7 Sylvain Cote	.20	.50
8 Pat Elynuik	.20	.50
9 Kevin Hatcher	.30	.75
10 Jim Hrivnak	.24	.60
11 Dale Hunter	.40	1.00
12 Al Iafrate	.40	1.00
13 Calle Johansson	.24	.60
14 Keith Jones	.24	.60
15 Dimitri Khristich	.40	1.00
16 Steve Konowalchuk	.30	.75
17 Todd Krygier	.20	.50
18 Rod Langway	.30	.75
19 Paul MacDermid	.20	.50
20 Alan May	.20	.50
21 Kelly Miller	.20	.50
22 Michal Pivonka	.40	1.00
23 Mike Ridley	.30	.75
24 Reggie Savage	.20	.50
25 Jason Woolley	.24	.60

1995-96 Capitals Team Issue

This 28-card set was given away as a premium in complete sheet form at a game late in the '95-96 season. The cards -- which feature the Caps in their new sweaters -- are perforated to be removed. As the cards are unnumbered, they are listed below in alphabetical order.

COMPLETE SET (28)	4.80	12.00
1 Jason Allison	.60	1.50
2 Craig Berube	.14	.35
3 Peter Bondra	1.20	3.00
4 Jim Carey	.20	.50
5 Sylvain Cote	.14	.35
6 Mike Eagles	.14	.35
7 Martin Gendron	.14	.35
8 Sergei Gonchar	.14	.35
9 Dale Hunter	.30	.75
10 Calle Johansson	.20	.50
11 Jim Johnson	.14	.35
12 Keith Jones	.20	.50
13 Joe Juneau	.30	.75
14 Kevin Kaminski	.14	.35
15 Ken Klee	.14	.35
16 Olaf Kolzig	.60	1.50
17 Steve Konowalchuk	.30	.75
18 Kelly Miller	.14	.35
19 Jeff Nelson	.14	.35
20 Pat Peake	.14	.35
21 Michal Pivonka	.20	.50
22 Joe Reekie	.14	.35
23 Jim Schoenfeld CO	.10	.25
24 Slapshot Mascot	.04	.10
25 Slapshot Mascot	.04	.10
26 Mark Tinordi	.14	.35
27 Stefan Ustorf	.14	.35
28 Brendan Witt	.20	.50

1998-99 Capitals Kids and Cops

This set features the Capitals of the NHL. These slightly oversized singles were given out to kids by local police officers. A completed set could be turned in at local police stations for a "special gift." If anyone knows what that gift was, we'd love to hear about it.

COMPLETE SET (7)	4.00	10.00
1 Olaf Kolzig	1.20	3.00
2 Peter Bondra	1.20	3.00
3 Adam Oates	.80	2.00
4 Dale Hunter	.80	2.00
5 Calle Johansson	.40	1.00
6 Steve Konowalchuk	.40	1.00
7 Slapshot MAS	.40	1.00

2002-03 Capitals Team Issue

Checklist is incomplete. We are looking for additional information on this set.

COMPLETE SET (?)		
1 Peter Bondra	.60	1.50
2 Jason Doig	.40	1.00
3 Sergei Gonchar	.40	1.00
4 Jaromir Jagr	1.25	3.00
5 Olaf Kolzig	1.25	3.00
6 Steve Konowalchuk	.40	1.00
7 Robert Lang	.40	1.00
8 Brendan Witt	.40	1.00
9 Dainius Zubrus	.40	1.00

1949 Carrera Ltd Sports Series

Cards feature blank backs, and come from a multi-sport series of 50 cards. Each card was cutout of a tobacco pack. The Anning single recently was discovered by collector Barry Chreptyk. Based on the numbering, it's possible there may be other hockey players in the set.

44 Les Anning		35.00
46 Duke Campbell	17.50	35.00

1934-35 CCM Brown Border Photos

These lovely oversized (11 X 9) photos were issued as premiums inside boxes of CCM skates. One such premium was included per box. The photos showed teams of the day and thus are highly prized by today's collectors. They are rarely seen in high grade and when offered, typically bring prices well above those listed below. Since the photos are unnumbered, they are listed below in alphabetical order.

COMPLETE SET (12)	500.00	1000.00
1 Boston Bruins	50.00	100.00
2 Chicago Blackhawks	50.00	100.00
3 Detroit Red Wings	50.00	100.00
4 Montreal Canadiens	62.50	125.00
5 Montreal Maroons	62.50	125.00
6 New York Americans	62.50	125.00
7 New York Rangers	50.00	100.00
8 Toronto Maple Leafs	50.00	100.00
9 All-Star Game	75.00	150.00
10 Allan Cup Champs, Moncton	25.00	50.00
11 Can-Am Champs, Providence	30.00	60.00
12 Memorial Cup Champs, St. Mike's	25.00	50.00

1935-36 CCM Green Border Photos

Like the previous year's offering, singles from this set were offered as a premium with the purchase of a new pair of CCM skates. This season, however, individual players were offered, along with teams. As they are unnumbered, they are listed below in alphabetical order.

COMPLETE SET (10)	375.00	750.00
1 Boston Cubs (Can-Am champs)		25.00 50.00
2 Boston Bruins	62.50	125.00
3 Halifax (Allan Cup)	25.00	50.00
4 Montreal Maroons	75.00	150.00
5 Toronto Maple Leafs	62.50	125.00
6 Winnipeg (Memorial Cup)	25.00	50.00
7 Frank Boucher	37.50	75.00
8 Lorne Chabot	50.00	100.00
9 Charlie Conacher	50.00	100.00
10 Foster Hewitt	37.50	75.00

1936 Champion Postcards

The set is in the same format as the 1936 Triumph set and was issued in the same manner as the Triumph set, except as an insert in "Boys" magazine published weekly in Great Britain. Three cards were issued in the first week of the promotion in "The Champion" and then one per week in "Boys" magazine. The cards are sepia toned and are postcard size, measuring approximately 3 1/2" by 5 1/2". The set is subtitled "Stars of the Ice Rinks". The cards are unnumbered and hence presented in alphabetical order. The date mentioned below is the issue date as noted on the card back in Canadian style, day/month/year.

COMPLETE SET (10)	875.00	1750.00
1 Marty Barry 18/1/36	40.00	80.00
2 Harold(Mush) March 8/2/36	40.00	80.00
3 Reg(Hooley) Smith 18/1/36	87.50	175.00
4 Sweeney Schriner 22/2/36	87.50	175.00
5 King Clancy 18/1/36	250.00	500.00
6 Bill Cook 1/2/36	100.00	200.00
7 Pep Kelly 25/1/36	40.00	80.00
8 Aurel Joliat 15/2/36	225.00	450.00
9 Charles Conacher 29/2/36	200.00	400.00
10 Fred(Bun) Cook 7/3/36	100.00	200.00

1963-65 Chex Photos

The 1963-65 Chex Photos measure approximately 5" by 7". This unnumbered set depicts players from four NHL teams, Chicago Blackhawks, Detroit Red Wings, Toronto Maple Leafs, and Montreal Canadiens. These blank-backed, stiff-cardboard photos are thought to have been issued during the 1963-64 (Canadiens and Maple Leafs) and 1964-65 (Blackhawks, Red Wings, and Canadiens again) seasons. Since these photo cards are unnumbered, they are ordered and numbered below alphabetically according to the player's name. There is rumored to be a Denis DeJordy in this set. The complete set price below includes both varieties of Beliveau and Rousseau.

COMPLETE SET (60)	1000.00	2000.00
1 George Armstrong	20.00	40.00
2 Ralph Backstrom	10.00	20.00
3 Dave Balon	20.00	40.00
4 Bob Baun	20.00	40.00
5A Jean Beliveau (Looking ahead)	20.00	40.00
5B Jean Beliveau (Looking left)	25.00	50.00
6 Red Berenson	10.00	20.00
7 Hector(Toe) Blake CO	25.00	50.00
8 Johnny Bower	20.00	40.00
9 Alex Delvecchio	20.00	40.00
10 Kent Douglas	25.00	50.00
11 Dick Duff	15.00	30.00
12 Phil Esposito	75.00	150.00
13 John Ferguson	12.50	25.00
14 Bill Gadsby	30.00	60.00
15 Jean Gauthier	30.00	60.00
16 BoomBoom Geoffrion	10.00	20.00
17 Glenn Hall	25.00	50.00
18 Terry Harper	15.00	30.00
19 Billy Harris	7.50	15.00
20 Bill(Red) Hay	30.00	60.00
21 Paul Henderson	50.00	100.00
22 Bill Hicke	20.00	40.00
23 Wayne Hillman	20.00	40.00
24 Charlie Hodge	20.00	40.00
25 Tim Horton	50.00	100.00
26 Gordie Howe	50.00	100.00
27 Bobby Hull	50.00	100.00
28 Punch Imlach CO	20.00	40.00
29 Red Kelly	20.00	40.00
30 Dave Keon	20.00	40.00
31 Jacques Laperriere	12.50	25.00
32 Ed Litzenberger	20.00	40.00
33 Parker MacDonald	30.00	60.00
34 Bruce MacGregor	40.00	80.00
35 Frank Mahovlich	20.00	40.00
36 Chico Maki	30.00	60.00
37 Pit Martin	30.00	60.00
38 John MacMillan	30.00	60.00
39 Stan Mikita	30.00	60.00
40 Bob Nevin	10.00	20.00
41 Pierre Pilote	20.00	40.00
42 Marcel Pronovost	30.00	60.00
43 Claude Provost	10.00	20.00
44 Bob Pulford	10.00	20.00
45 Marc Reaume	40.00	80.00
46 Henri Richard	15.00	30.00
47A Bobby Rousseau	40.00	80.00
47B Bob Rousseau	30.00	60.00
48 Eddie Shack	20.00	40.00
49 Don Simmons	30.00	60.00
50 Allan Stanley	30.00	60.00
51 Ron Stewart	7.50	15.00
52 Jean-Guy Talbot	10.00	20.00
53 Gilles Tremblay	15.00	30.00
54 J.C. Tremblay	25.00	50.00
55 Norm Ullman	20.00	40.00
56 Elmer(Moose) Vasko	40.00	80.00
57 Ken Wharram	50.00	100.00
58 Gump Worsley	15.00	30.00

1992-93 Clark Candy Mario Lemieux

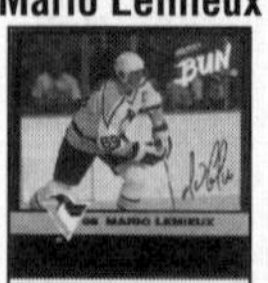

Issued by Clark Candy, this three-card set features three different color player photos of the Pittsburgh Penguins' Mario Lemieux. One card was inserted in each Bun candy bar pack. Each card measures approximately 3" by 3" and has a facsimile autograph in black inscribed across the picture. The pictures have black borders, and a gold stripe carrying the team logo cuts across the bottom of the card. The backs present biographical information, career summary, honors and awards, or career playing record. Only card number 3 listed below has a black-and-white close-up photo on its back. The cards are unnumbered and checklisted below in alphabetical order. There are reports that Lemieux may have signed some cards for insertion; to date, these rumors remain unsubstantiated.

COMPLETE SET (3)	2.40	6.00
COMMON CARD (1-3)	1.00	2.50

1972-73 Cleveland Crusaders WHA

This 15-card set measures 8 1/2" x 11" and features a black and white head shot on the front along with a facsimile autograph, and a Cleveland Crusaders color logo in the lower left corner. Featured portraits were done by Charles Linnett. The cards are unnumbered and checklisted below in alphabetical order.

COMPLETE SET (15)	25.00	50.00
1 Ron Buchanan	2.00	4.00
2 Ray Clearwater	2.00	4.00
3 Bob Dillabough	2.00	4.00
4 Grant Erickson	2.00	4.00
5 Ted Hodgson	2.00	4.00
6 Ralph Hopiavouri	2.00	4.00
7 Bill Horton	2.00	4.00
8 Gary Jarrett	2.00	4.00
9 Skip Krake	2.00	4.00
10 Wayne Muloin	2.00	4.00
11 Bill Needham CO	2.00	4.00
12 Rick Pumple	2.50	5.00
13 Paul Shmyr	2.00	4.00
14 Robert Whidden	2.00	4.00
15 Jim Wiste	2.50	5.00

1964-65 Coca-Cola Caps

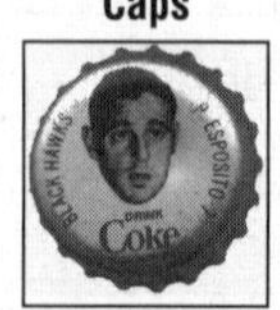

The 1964-65 Coca-Cola Caps set contains 108 bottle caps measuring approximately 1 1/8" in diameter. The caps feature a black and white picture on the tops, and are unnumbered except for uniform numbers (which is listed to the right of the player's name in the checklist below). These caps were issued with both Coke and Sprite. Because Sprite was sold in lesser quantities than Coke, those caps tend to be harder to find. As such, some dealers charge a slight premium for those caps. There are also rumored to be French variations for both the Coke and the Sprite caps, making a total of four possible ways to put the set together. While no transactions have been reported for these French versions, it's fair to assume that their scarcity alone might earn them a slight premium over the prices listed below. The set numbering below is by teams and numerically within teams as follows: Boston Bruins (1-18), Chicago Blackhawks (19-36), Detroit Red Wings (37-54), Montreal Canadiens (55-72, New York Rangers (73-90), and Toronto Maple Leafs (91-108). A plastic holder (in the shape of a rink) was also available for holding and displaying the caps; the holder is not included in the complete set price below.

COMPLETE SET (108)	375.00	750.00
1 Ed Johnston 1	2.50	5.00
2 Bob McCord 4	1.50	3.00
3 Ted Green 6	2.00	4.00
4 Orland Kurtenbach 7	2.00	4.00
5 Gary Dornhoefer 8	2.00	4.00
6 Johnny Bucyk 9	5.00	10.00
7 Tom Johnson 10	2.00	4.00
8 Tom Williams 11	1.50	3.00
9 Murray Balfour 12	1.50	3.00
10 Forbes Kennedy 14	1.50	3.00
11 Murray Oliver 16	1.50	3.00
12 Dean Prentice 17	2.00	4.00
13 Ed Westfall 18	2.00	4.00
14 Reg Fleming 19	1.50	3.00
15 Leo Boivin 20	2.00	4.00
16 Ab McDonald 21	1.50	3.00
17 Ron Schock 23	1.50	3.00
18 Bob Leiter 24	1.50	3.00
19 Glenn Hall 1	6.00	12.00
20 Doug Mohns 2	2.00	4.00
21 Pierre Pilote 3	2.50	5.00
22 Elmer Vasko 4	1.50	3.00
23 Fred Stanfield 6	1.50	3.00
24 Phil Esposito 7	20.00	40.00
25 Bobby Hull 9	25.00	50.00
26 Bill(Red) Hay 11	1.25	2.50
27 John Brenneman 12	1.25	2.50
28 Doug Robinson 14	1.50	3.00
29 Eric Nesterenko 15	2.00	4.00
30 Chico Maki 16	2.00	4.00
31 Ken Wharram 17	1.50	3.00
32 John McKenzie 18	1.50	3.00
33 Al MacNeil 19	1.50	3.00
34 Wayne Hillman 20	1.50	3.00
35 Stan Mikita 21	7.50	15.00
36 Denis DeJordy 30	2.00	4.00
37 Roger Crozier 1	2.50	5.00
38 Albert Langlois 2	1.50	3.00
39 Marcel Pronovost 3	2.00	4.00
40 Bill Gadsby 4	2.00	4.00
41 Doug Barkley 5	1.50	3.00
42 Norm Ullman 7	4.00	8.00
43 Pit Martin 8	2.00	4.00
44 Gordie Howe 9	30.00	60.00
45A Gordie Howe 10	40.00	80.00
45B Alex Delvecchio 10	15.00	30.00
46 Ron Murphy 12	1.50	3.00
47 Larry Jeffrey 14	1.50	3.00
48 Ted Lindsay 15	5.00	10.00
49 Bruce MacGregor 16	1.50	3.00
50 Floyd Smith 17	1.50	3.00
51 Gary Bergman 18	1.50	3.00
52 Paul Henderson 19	3.00	6.00
53 Parker MacDonald 20	1.50	3.00
54 Eddie Joyal 21	1.50	3.00
55 Charlie Hodge 1	2.00	4.00
56 Jacques Laperriere 2	2.00	4.00
57 J.C. Tremblay 3	2.00	4.00
58 Jean Beliveau 4	10.00	20.00
59 Ralph Backstrom 6	2.00	4.00
60 Bill Hicke 8	1.50	3.00
61 Ted Harris 10	1.50	3.00
62 Claude Larose 11	1.50	3.00
63 Yvan Cournoyer 12	7.50	15.00
64 Claude Provost 14	1.50	3.00
65 Bobby Rousseau 15	2.00	4.00
66 Henri Richard 16	6.00	12.00
67 Jean-Guy Talbot 17	2.00	4.00
68 Terry Harper 19	2.00	4.00
69 Dave Balon 20	1.50	3.00
70 Gilles Tremblay 21	1.50	3.00
71 John Ferguson 22	2.50	5.00
72 Jim Roberts 26	1.50	3.00
73 Jacques Plante 1	10.00	20.00
74 Harry Howell 3	2.00	4.00
75 Arnie Brown 4	1.50	3.00
76 Don Johns 6	1.50	3.00
77 Rod Gilbert 7	4.00	8.00
78 Bob Nevin 8	1.50	3.00
79 Dick Duff 9	2.00	4.00
80 Earl Ingarfield 10	1.50	3.00
81 Vic Hadfield 11	2.00	4.00
82 Jim Mikol 12	1.50	3.00
83 Val Fonteyne 14	1.50	3.00
84 Jim Neilson 15	1.50	3.00
85 Rod Seiling 16	1.50	3.00
86 Lou Angotti 17	1.50	3.00
87 Phil Goyette 20	1.50	3.00
88 Camille Henry 21	2.00	4.00
89 Don Marshall 22	2.00	4.00
90 Marcel Paille 23	2.00	4.00
91 Johnny Bower 1	5.00	10.00
92 Carl Brewer 2	2.00	4.00
93 Red Kelly 4	5.00	10.00
94 Tim Horton 7	7.50	15.00
95 George Armstrong 9	4.00	8.00
96 Andy Bathgate 10	4.00	8.00
97 Ron Ellis 11	2.00	4.00
98 Ralph Stewart 12	1.50	3.00
99 Dave Keon 14	4.00	8.00
100 Dickie Moore 16	2.50	5.00
101 Don McKenney 17	1.50	3.00
102 Kent Douglas 19	1.50	3.00
103 Bob Pulford 20	2.50	5.00
104 Bob Baun 21	2.50	5.00
105 Eddie Shack 23	4.00	8.00
106 Terry Sawchuk 24	10.00	20.00
107 Allan Stanley 26	2.50	5.00
108 Frank Mahovlich 27	6.00	12.00
xx Cap Holder (Plastic Rink)	50.00	100.00

1965-66 Coca-Cola

This set contains 108 unnumbered black and white cards featuring 18 players from each of the six NHL teams. The cards were issued in perforated team panels of 18 cards. The cards are priced below as perforated cards; the value of unperforated strips is approximately 20-30 percent more than the sum of the individual prices. The cards are approximately 2 3/4" by 3 1/2" and have bi-lingual (French and English) write-ups on the card backs. An album to hold the cards was available from the company on a mail-order basis. It retails in the $50-$75 range in Near Mint. The set numbering below is by teams and numerically within teams as follows: Boston Bruins (1-18), Chicago Blackhawks (19-36), Detroit Red Wings (37-54), Montreal Canadiens (55-72, New York Rangers (73-90), and Toronto Maple Leafs (91-108).

COMPLETE SET (108)	250.00	500.00
1 Gerry Cheevers	15.00	30.00
2 Albert Langlois	.75	1.50
3 Ted Green	1.00	2.00
4 Ron Stewart	.75	1.50
5 Bob Woytowich	.75	1.50
6 Johnny Bucyk	3.00	6.00
7 Tom Williams	.75	1.50
8 Forbes Kennedy	.75	1.50
9 Murray Oliver	.75	1.50
10 Dean Prentice	1.00	2.00
11 Ed Westfall	1.00	2.00
12 Reg Fleming	.75	1.50
13 Leo Boivin	1.50	3.00
14 Parker MacDonald	.75	1.50
15 Bob Dillabough	.75	1.50
16 Barry Ashbee	2.50	5.00
17 Don Awrey	.75	1.50
18 Bernie Parent	15.00	30.00
19 Glenn Hall	5.00	10.00
20 Doug Mohns	1.00	2.00
21 Pierre Pilote	1.50	3.00
22 Elmer Vasko	.75	1.50
23 Matt Ravlich	.75	1.50
24 Fred Stanfield	.75	1.50
25 Phil Esposito	20.00	40.00
26 Bobby Hull	20.00	40.00
27 Dennis Hull	2.50	5.00
28 Bill(Red) Hay	1.00	2.00
29 Ken Hodge	1.50	3.00
30 Eric Nesterenko	1.00	2.00
31 Chico Maki	1.00	2.00
32 Ken Wharram	1.00	2.00
33 Al MacNeil	.75	1.50
34 Doug Jarrett	.75	1.50
35 Stan Mikita	6.00	12.00
36 Dave Dryden	1.25	2.50
37 Roger Crozier	1.50	3.00
38 Warren Godfrey	.75	1.50
39 Bert Marshall	.75	1.50
40 Bill Gadsby	1.50	3.00
41 Doug Barkley	.75	1.50
42 Norm Ullman	2.00	4.00
43 Gordie Howe	30.00	60.00
44 Alex Delvecchio	2.50	5.00
45 Val Fonteyne	.75	1.50
46 Ron Murphy	.75	1.50
47 Billy Harris	.75	1.50
48 Bruce MacGregor	.75	1.50
49 Floyd Smith	.75	1.50
50 Paul Henderson	4.00	8.00
51 Andy Bathgate	1.75	3.50
52 Ab McDonald	.75	1.50
53 Gary Bergman	.75	1.50
54 Hank Bassen	1.25	2.50
55 Charlie Hodge	1.50	3.00
56 Jacques Laperriere	1.50	3.00
57 Jean-Claude Tremblay	1.00	2.00
58 Jean Beliveau	7.50	15.00
59 Ralph Backstrom	1.00	2.00
60 Dick Duff	1.25	2.50
61 Ted Harris	1.00	2.00
62 Claude Larose	.75	1.50
63 Yvan Cournoyer	10.00	20.00
64 Claude Provost	1.00	2.00
65 Bobby Rousseau	1.00	2.00
66 Henri Richard	5.00	10.00
67 Jean-Guy Talbot	1.25	2.50
68 Terry Harper	1.00	2.00
69 Gilles Tremblay	.75	1.50
70 John Ferguson	1.25	2.50
71 Jim Roberts	1.00	2.00
72 Gump Worsley	5.00	10.00
73 Ed Giacomin	12.50	25.00
74 Wayne Hillman	.75	1.50
75 Harry Howell	2.00	4.00
76 Arnie Brown	.75	1.50
77 Doug Robinson	.75	1.50
78 Mike McMahon	.75	1.50
79 Rod Gilbert	2.50	5.00
80 Bob Nevin	.75	1.50
81 Earl Ingarfield	.75	1.50
82 Vic Hadfield	1.25	2.50
83 Bill Hicke	.75	1.50
84 John McKenzie	1.00	2.00
85 Jim Neilson	.75	1.50
86 Jean Ratelle	2.50	5.00
87 Phil Goyette	.75	1.50
88 Garry Peters	.75	1.50
89 Don Marshall	.75	1.50
90 Don Simmons	1.25	2.50
91 Johnny Bower	5.00	10.00
92 Marcel Pronovost	2.00	4.00
93 Red Kelly	2.50	5.00
94 Tim Horton	7.50	15.00
95 Ron Ellis	1.00	2.00
96 George Armstrong	2.00	4.00
97 Brit Selby	.75	1.50
98 Pete Stemkowski	.75	1.50
99 Dave Keon	5.00	10.00
100 Mike Walton	1.00	2.00
101 Kent Douglas	.75	1.50
102 Bob Pulford	2.00	4.00
103 Bob Baun	2.00	4.00
104 Eddie Shack	2.50	5.00
105 Orland Kurtenbach	1.00	2.00
106 Allan Stanley	1.50	3.00
107 Frank Mahovlich	5.00	10.00
108 Terry Sawchuk	10.00	20.00
NNO Album	40.00	80.00

1965-66 Coca-Cola Booklets

These four "How To Play" booklets are illustrated with cartoon-like drawings, each measure approximately 4 7/8" by 3 1/2", and are printed on newsprint. Booklets A and B have yellow covers, while booklets C and D have blue covers. The 31-page booklets could be obtained through a mail-in offer. Under bottle caps of Coke or Sprite (marked with a hockey stick) were cork liners bearing the name of the player who wrote a booklet. To receive a booklet, the collector had to send in ten cork liners (with name of the player whose booklet was desired), ten cents, and the correct answer to a trivia question. Issued by Coca-Cola to promote hockey among the school-aged, they are designed in comic book fashion showing correct positions and moves for goalie, forward (both defensive and offensive), and defenseman. They are authored by the hockey players listed below. They are lettered rather than numbered and we have checklisted them below accordingly. The booklets were available in both English and French.

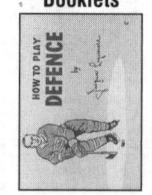

COMPLETE SET (4)	75.00	150.00
A Johnny Bower How To Play Goal	25.00	50.00
B Dave Keon How To Play Forward (Defensive)	25.00	50.00
C Jacques Laperriere How To Play Defence	12.50	25.00
D Henri Richard How To Play Forward (Offensive)	25.00	50.00

1977-78 Coca-Cola

Each of these mini-cards measures approximately 1 3/8" by 1 3/8". The fronts feature a color "mug shot" of the player, with his name given above the picture. Red and blue lines form the borders on the sides of the picture. The year 1978, the city from which the team hails, and the Coke logo appear below the picture. Inside a black border (with rounded corners) the back has basic biographical information. These unnumbered cards are listed alphabetically below.

COMPLETE SET (30)	62.50	300.00
1 Syl Apps	.75	3.00
2 Dave Burrows	.75	3.00
3 Bobby Clarke	6.00	25.00
4 Yvan Cournoyer	2.50	10.00
5 John Davidson	1.50	10.00
6 Marcel Dionne	4.00	15.00
7 Doug Favell	1.25	5.00
8 Rod Gilbert	1.50	10.00
9 Brian Glennie	.75	3.00
10 Butch Goring	.75	3.00
11 Lorne Henning	.75	3.00
12 Cliff Koroll	.75	3.00
13 Guy Lapointe	1.50	5.00
14 Dave Maloney	.75	3.00
15 Pit Martin	.75	3.00
16 Lou Nanne	.75	3.00
17 Bobby Orr	30.00	125.00
18 Brad Park	2.50	10.00
19 Craig Ramsay	.75	3.00
20 Larry Robinson	5.00	20.00
21 Jim Rutherford	1.25	5.00
22 Don Saleski	.75	3.00
23 Steve Shutt	2.50	8.00
24 Darryl Sittler	4.00	20.00
25 Billy Smith	3.00	10.00
26 Bob Stewart	.75	3.00
27 Rogatien Vachon	2.50	10.00
28 Jimmy Watson	.75	3.00
29 Joe Watson	.75	3.00
30 Ed Westfall	.75	3.00

1994 Coca-Cola Wayne Gretzky Cups

Standing approximately 6" high, these full color cups featuring an image of Wayne along with a biographical fact from the appropriate year. Set may be incomplete and we welcome any additional information you may have.

COMPLETE SET (5)	8.00	20.00
COMMON CUP	1.60	4.00

1994 Coke/Mac's Milk Gretzky POGs

This 18-disc set features POGs measuring approximately 1 5/8" in diameter. These cards were offered through Mac's Milk stores in Canada (primarily Ontario); they were available at the store counter with the purchase of any Coke bottled product from May through middle of June of 1994. Inside a gold-foil holographic border, the front feature action color player photos with the words "The Great One" printed in black letters above the photo and a Coca-Cola Future Stars emblem at the bottom. The backs feature Gretzky's most prolific records and accomplishments.

COMPLETE SET (18)	6.00	15.00
COMMON POG (1-18)	.40	1.00

1970-71 Colgate Stamps

The 1970-71 Colgate Stamps set includes 93 small color stamps measuring approximately 1" by 1 1/4". The set was distributed in three sheets of 31. Sheet one featured centers (numbered 1-31) and was available with the giant size of toothpaste, sheet two featured wings (numbered 32-62) and was available with the family size of toothpaste, and sheet three featured goalies and defensemen (numbered 63-93) and was available with king and super size toothpaste. The cards are priced below as individual stamps; the value of a complete sheet would be approximately 20 percent more than the sum of the individual stamp prices. Colgate also issued three calendars so that brushers could stick a stamp on each day for brushing regularly. These calendars retail in the $5-$10 range. The cards were numbered in a star in the upper left corner of the card face.

COMPLETE SET (93)	100.00	200.00
1 Walt McKechnie	.50	1.00
2 Bob Pulford	1.50	3.00
3 Mike Walton	.50	1.00
4 Alex Delvecchio	2.50	5.00
5 Tom Williams	.50	1.00
6 Derek Sanderson	5.00	10.00
7 Garry Unger	1.00	2.00

8 Lou Angotti .50 1.00
9 Ted Hampson .50 1.00
10 Phil Goyette .50 1.00
11 Juha Widing .50 1.00
12 Norm Ullman 2.00 4.00
13 Garry Monahan .50 1.00
14 Henri Richard 2.50 5.00
15 Ray Cullen .50 1.00
16 Danny O'Shea .50 1.00
17 Marc Tardif .75 1.50
18 Jude Drouin .50 1.00
19 Charlie Burns .50 1.00
20 Gerry Meehan .75 1.50
21 Ralph Backstrom .75 1.50
22 Frank St.Marseille .50 1.00
23 Orland Kurtenbach .50 1.00
24 Red Berenson 1.00 2.00
25 Jean Ratelle 2.00 4.00
26 Syl Apps .75 1.50
27 Don Marshall .50 1.00
28 Gilbert Perreault 5.00 10.00
29 Andre Lacroix .75 1.50
30 Jacques Lemaire 1.50 3.00
31 Pit Martin .75 1.50
32 Dennis Hull .75 1.50
33 Dave Balon .50 1.00
34 Keith McCreary .50 1.00
35 Bobby Rousseau .75 1.50
36 Danny Grant .75 1.50
37 Brit Selby .50 1.00
38 Bob Nevin .50 1.00
39 Rosaire Paiement .50 1.00
40 Gary Dornhoefer 1.00 2.00
41 Eddie Shack 2.00 4.00
42 Ron Schock .50 1.00
43 Jim Pappin .50 1.00
44 Mickey Redmond 1.50 3.00
45 Vic Hadfield .75 1.50
46 Johnny Bucyk 2.00 4.00
47 Gordie Howe 12.00 30.00
48 Ron Anderson .50 1.00
49 Gary Jarrett .50 1.00
50 Jean Pronovost .75 1.50
51 Simon Nolet .50 1.00
52 Bill Goldsworthy .75 1.50
53 Rod Gilbert 2.00 4.00
54 Ron Ellis .75 1.50
55 Mike Byers .50 1.00
56 Norm Ferguson .50 1.00
57 Gary Sabourin .50 1.00
58 Tim Ecclestone .50 1.00
59 John McKenzie .50 1.00
60 Yvan Cournoyer 2.00 4.00
61 Ken Schinkel .50 1.00
62 Ken Hodge 1.00 2.00
63 Cesare Maniago 1.50 3.00
64 J.C. Tremblay .75 1.50
65 Gilles Marotte .50 1.00
66 Bob Baun 1.00 2.00
67 Gerry Desjardins 1.00 2.00
68 Charlie Hodge 1.50 3.00
69 Matt Ravlich .50 1.00
70 Ed Giacomin 3.00 6.00
71 Gerry Cheevers 4.00 8.00
72 Pat Quinn .75 1.50
73 Gary Bergman .50 1.00
74 Serge Savard 1.00 2.00
75 Les Binkley 1.00 2.00
76 Arnie Brown .50 1.00
77 Pat Stapleton .50 1.00
78 Ed Van Impe .50 1.00
79 Jim Dorey .50 1.00
80 Dave Dryden 1.50 3.00
81 Dale Tallon .75 1.50
82 Bruce Gamble 1.50 3.00
83 Roger Crozier 1.50 3.00
84 Denis DeJordy 1.50 3.00
85 Rogatien Vachon 2.00 4.00
86 Carol Vadnais .50 1.00
87 Bobby Orr 20.00 50.00
88 Noel Picard .50 1.00
89 Gilles Villemure 1.50 3.00
90 Gary Smith 1.50 3.00
91 Doug Favell 1.50 3.00
92 Ernie Wakely 1.50 3.00
93 Bernie Parent 5.00 10.00
NNO Stamp Calendar Sheet 5.00 10.00

1971-72 Colgate Heads

The 16 hockey collectibles in this set measure approximately 1 1/4" in height with a base of 7/8" and are made out of cream-colored or beige plastic. The promotion lasted approximately five months during the winter of 1972. The busts were issued in series of four in the various sizes of Colgate Toothpaste. The player's last name is found only on the back of the base of the head. The Ullmann error is not included in the complete set price below. The heads are unnumbered and checklisted below in alphabetical order.

COMPLETE SET (16) 100.00 200.00
1 Yvon Cournoyer 3.00 8.00
2 Marcel Dionne UER 6.00 15.00
(Head actually Stan Mikita)
3 Ken Dryden 8.00 20.00
4 Paul Henderson 2.50 6.00
5 Guy Lafleur 8.00 20.00
6 Frank Mahovlich 4.00 10.00
7 Richard Martin SP 15.00 30.00
8 Bobby Orr 20.00 40.00
9 Brad Park SP 20.00 40.00
10 Jacques Plante 6.00 15.00
11 Jean Ratelle 3.00 8.00
12 Derek Sanderson 6.00 15.00
13 Dale Tallon 2.00 5.00
14 Walt Tkaczuk 2.00 4.00
15A Norm Ullman ERR 4.00 10.00
(Misspelled Ullmann)
15B Norm Ullman COR 10.00 25.00
16 Garry Unger 2.00 5.00

1995-96 Collector's Choice

This 396 card standard-size set was issued in 12-card packs with a suggested retail price of 99 cents per pack. The design is similar to the 1995 Collector Choice issues in baseball, basketball and football. Each card features a photo framed by white borders. The player's name and team is identified in the lower right-hand corner. The backs contain another photograph, biographical information and statistics. The last 70 cards of the set are dedicated to the following subsets: 1995 European Junior Championship (325-354), What's Your Game? (355-369), and Hardware Heroes (370-394). Rookie Cards in this set include Teemu Riihijarvi and Marcus Nilsson. In addition, 15-card set was available only to collectors who redeemed through the mail a Young Guns Trade card, which was inserted at a rate of 1:34 packs. The cards were intended to "complete" the Collector's Choice set by including several of the top rookies of 1995-96, and thus bear the same design and continue the numbering from that set.

COMPLETE SET (396) 10.00 20.00
1 Wayne Gretzky .60 1.50
2 Darius Kasparaitis .01 .05
3 Scott Niedermayer .01 .05
4 Brendan Shanahan .08 .25
5 Doug Gilmour .02 .10
6 Lyle Odelein .01 .05
7 Dave Gagner .01 .05
8 Gary Suter .01 .05
9 Sandis Ozolinsh .01 .05
10 Sergei Zubov .01 .05
11 Don Beaupre .02 .10
12 Bill Lindsay .01 .05
13 David Oliver .01 .05
14 Bob Corkum .01 .05
15 German Titov .01 .05
16 Jari Kurri .08 .25
17 Cliff Ronning .01 .05
18 Paul Coffey .08 .25
19 Ian Laperriere .01 .05
20 Dave Andreychuk .02 .10
21 Andrei Nikolishin .01 .05
22 Blaine Lacher .02 .10
23 Yuri Khmylev .01 .05
24 Darren Turcotte .01 .05
25 Joe Mullen .02 .10
26 Peter Forsberg .25 .60
27 Paul Ysebaert .01 .05
28 Tommy Soderstrom .02 .10
29 Rod Brind'Amour .02 .10
30 Jim Carey .02 .10
31 Geoff Courtnall .01 .05
32 Slava Kozlov .02 .10
33 Ray Ferraro .01 .05
34 John MacLean .02 .10
35 Benoit Brunet .01 .05
36 Trent Klatt .01 .05
37 Chris Chelios .08 .25
38 Tom Pederson .01 .05
39 Pat Elynuik .01 .05
40 Rob Niedermayer .02 .10
41 Jason Arnott .01 .05
42 Patrik Carnback .01 .05
43 Steve Chiasson .01 .05
44 Marty McSorley .01 .05
45 Pavel Bure .08 .25
46 Glenn Anderson .08 .25
47 Doug Brown .01 .05
48 Mike Ridley .01 .05
49 Alexei Zhamnov .02 .10
50 Mariusz Czerkawski .01 .05
51 Derek Plante .01 .05
52 Andrew Cassels .01 .05
53 Tom Barrasso .02 .10
54 Andrei Kovalenko .01 .05
55 Pat Verbeek .01 .05
56 Alexander Semak .01 .05
57 Eric Lindros .08 .25
58 Peter Bondra .02 .10
59 Marty McInnis .01 .05
60 Bill Guerin .02 .10
61 Patrice Brisebois .01 .05
62 Andy Moog .08 .25
63 Eric Weinrich .01 .05
64 Arturs Irbe .02 .10
65 Sean Hill .01 .05
66 Jesse Belanger .01 .05
67 Bryan Marchment .01 .05
68 Joe Sacco .01 .05
69 Trevor Kidd .02 .10
70 Dan Quinn .01 .05
71 Kirk McLean .02 .10
72 Benoit Hogue .01 .05
73 Garry Galley .01 .05
74 Randy Wood .01 .05
75 Nikolai Khabibulin .02 .10
76 Ted Donato .01 .05
77 Doug Bodger .01 .05
78 Paul Ranheim .01 .05
79 Ulf Samuelsson .01 .05
80 Uwe Krupp .01 .05
81 Oleg Tverdovsky .01 .05
82 Kelly Miller .01 .05
83 Darryl Sydor .02 .10
84 Brian Bellows .01 .05
85 Jeremy Roenick .12 .30
86 Phil Bourque .01 .05
87 Louie DeBrusk .01 .05
88 Joel Otto .01 .05
89 Dino Ciccarelli .02 .10
90 Mats Sundin .08 .25
91 Don Sweeney .01 .05
92 Roman Hamrlik .02 .10
93 Petr Svoboda .01 .05
94 Zigmund Palffy .02 .10
95 Patrick Roy .40 1.00
96 Sergei Krivokrasov .01 .05
97 Wade Flaherty RC .02 .10
98 Fredrik Olausson .01 .05
99 Sergio Momesso .01 .05
100 Mike Vernon .02 .10
101 Todd Gill .01 .05
102 Cam Neely .08 .25
103 Wendel Clark .02 .10
104 John Tucker .01 .05
105 Eric Desjardins .02 .10
106 Ed Olczyk .01 .05
107 Bob Beers .01 .05
108 Mark Recchi .02 .10
109 Ed Belfour .08 .25
110 Radek Bonk .01 .05
111 Cory Stillman .01 .05
112 Jeff Norton .01 .05
113 Terry Carkner .01 .05
114 Felix Potvin .08 .25
115 Alexei Kasatonov .01 .05
116 Brian Noonan .01 .05
117 Daren Puppa .02 .10
118 Joe Juneau .01 .05
119 Valeri Bure .01 .05
120 Murray Craven .01 .05
121 Marko Tuomainen .01 .05
122 Trevor Linden .02 .10
123 Zarley Zalapski .01 .05
124 Jeff Shantz .01 .05
125 Dmitri Mironov .01 .05
126 Jamie Huscroft .01 .05
127 Jaromir Jagr .15 .40
128 Brian Bradley .01 .05
129 Brett Lindros .01 .05
130 Calle Johansson .01 .05
131 Pierre Turgeon .02 .10
132 Denis Savard .02 .10
133 Joe Nieuwendyk .02 .10
134 Petr Klima .01 .05
135 John Druce .01 .05
136 Chris Osgood .02 .10
137 Kenny Jonsson .01 .05
138 Jocelyn Lemieux .01 .05
139 Tomas Sandstrom .01 .05
140 Chris Gratton .01 .05
141 Mark Tinordi .01 .05
142 Kirk Muller .01 .05
143 Vladimir Malakhov .01 .05
144 Jiri Slegr .01 .05
145 Shawn McEachern .01 .05
146 Shayne Corson .01 .05
147 Kelly Hrudey .02 .10
148 Sergei Fedorov .12 .30
149 Mike Gartner .02 .10
150 Stephane Fiset .02 .10
151 Larry Murphy .02 .10
152 Enrico Ciccone .01 .05
153 Mike Keane .01 .05
154 Steve Larmer .02 .10
155 Dale Hunter .02 .10
156 Joe Murphy .01 .05
157 Pat LaFontaine .08 .25
158 Rob Gaudreau .01 .05
159 Paul Kariya .08 .25
160 Rob Blake .02 .10
161 Keith Primeau .01 .05
162 Dave Ellett .01 .05
163 Alexander Mogilny .02 .10
164 Luc Robitaille .02 .10
165 Alexander Selivanov .01 .05
166 Keith Jones .02 .10
167 Turner Stevenson .01 .05
168 Keith Tkachuk .08 .25
169 Bernie Nicholls .01 .05
170 Stanislav Neckar .01 .05
171 Scott Mellanby .01 .05
172 Doug Weight .02 .10
173 Shaun Van Allen .01 .05
174 Gary Roberts .01 .05
175 Robert Lang .01 .05
176 Martin Gelinas .01 .05
177 Ray Sheppard .01 .05
178 Bryan Smolinski .01 .05
179 Wayne Presley .01 .05
180 Jimmy Carson .01 .05
181 John Cullen .01 .05
182 Mikael Andersson .01 .05
183 Dimitri Khristich .01 .05
184 Chris Therien .01 .05
185 Bobby Holik .01 .05
186 Kevin Hatcher .01 .05
187 Patrick Poulin .01 .05
188 Pat Falloon .01 .05
189 Alexei Yashin .01 .05
190 Gord Murphy .01 .05
191 Kirk Maltby .02 .10
192 Dave Karpa .01 .05
193 Kelly Kisio .01 .05
194 Tony Granato .01 .05
195 Al Iafrate .02 .10
196 Nelson Emerson .01 .05
197 Adam Oates .02 .10
198 Rob Ray .08 .25
199 Sean Burke .02 .10
200 Ron Francis .02 .10
201 Theo Fleury .02 .10
202 Patrick Flatley .01 .05
203 Ron Hextall .02 .10
204 Martin Brodeur .25 .60
205 Mike Kennedy RC .01 .05
206 Tony Amonte .02 .10
207 Sergei Makarov .01 .05
208 Alexandre Daigle .01 .05
209 Stu Barnes .01 .05
210 Todd Marchant .01 .05
211 Valeri Karpov .01 .05
212 Phil Housley .02 .10
213 Jamie Storr .02 .10
214 Brett Hull .10 .30
215 Kris King .01 .05
216 Ray Bourque .15 .40
217 Donald Audette .01 .05
218 Steven Rice .01 .05
219 Kevin Stevens .01 .05
220 Mark Messier .08 .25
221 Valeri Kamensky .02 .10
222 Mikael Renberg .02 .10
223 Scott Stevens .02 .10
224 Derian Hatcher .01 .05
225 Ray Whitney .02 .10
226 Bob Kudelski .01 .05
227 Mikhail Shtalenkov .01 .05
228 Nicklas Lidstrom .08 .25
229 Adam Creighton .01 .05
230 Dave Manson .01 .05
231 Craig Simpson .01 .05
232 Chris Pronger .08 .25
233 Adrien Plavsic .01 .05
234 Alexei Kovalev .01 .05
235 Tommy Salo RC .40 1.00
236 Patrik Juhlin .01 .05
237 Tom Chorske .01 .05
238 Mike Modano .15 .40
239 Igor Larionov .01 .05
240 Johan Garpenlov .01 .05
241 Todd Krygier .01 .05
242 Tie Domi .02 .10
243 Bill Houlder .01 .05
244 Teemu Selanne .08 .25
245 Dale Hawerchuk .08 .25
246 Bill Ranford .02 .10
247 Brian Leetch .02 .10
248 Steve Thomas .02 .10
249 Dimitri Yushkevich .01 .05
250 Stephane Richer .02 .10
251 Todd Harvey .02 .10
252 Viktor Kozlov .02 .10
253 John Vanbiesbrouck .02 .10
254 Rick Tocchet .02 .10
255 Bret Hedican .01 .05
256 Mario Lemieux .50 1.25
257 Igor Korolev .01 .05
258 Dominik Hasek .20 .50
259 Owen Nolan .02 .10
260 Michal Pivonka .01 .05
261 John LeClair .08 .25
262 Claude Lemieux .01 .05
263 Mike Donnelly .01 .05
264 Craig Janney .01 .05
265 Milos Holan .01 .05
266 Steve Yzerman .50 1.25
267 Russ Courtnall .01 .05
268 Esa Tikkanen .01 .05
269 Dallas Drake .01 .05
270 Norm Maciver .01 .05
271 Scott Young .01 .05
272 Glenn Healy .02 .10
273 Brian Rolston .01 .05
274 Corey Millen .01 .05
275 Kevin Miller .01 .05
276 Eric LaCroix .01 .05
277 Adam Graves .01 .05
278 Christian Ruuttu .01 .05
279 Steve Duchesne .01 .05
280 Stephane Quintal .01 .05
281 Brent Gretzky .01 .05
282 Mike Ricci .02 .10
283 Sergei Nemchinov .01 .05
284 Sylvain Cote .01 .05
285 Neal Broten .02 .10
286 Greg Adams .01 .05
287 Guy Hebert .02 .10
288 Joe Sakic .20 .50
289 Bobby Dollas .01 .05
290 Gino Odjick .01 .05
291 Curtis Joseph .08 .25
292 Teppo Numminen .01 .05
293 Geoff Sanderson .01 .05
294 Adam Deadmarsh .01 .05
295 Kevin Haller .01 .05
296 Sergei Brylin .01 .05
297 Ulf Dahlen .01 .05
298 Robert Kron .01 .05
299 Dave Lowry .01 .05
300 Nikolai Borschevsky .01 .05
301 Jeff Brown .01 .05
302 Guy Carbonneau .08 .25
303 Alexei Zhitnik .01 .05
304 Frantisek Kucera .01 .05
305 Curtis Leschyshyn .01 .05
306 Mike Richter .08 .25
307 Dean Evason .01 .05
308 Jozef Stumpel .01 .05
309 Jeff Friesen .01 .05
310 Kelly Buchberger .01 .05
311 Michael Nylander .01 .05
312 Josef Beranek .01 .05
313 Al MacInnis .02 .10
314 Ken Wregget .02 .10
315 Glen Wesley .01 .05
316 Jocelyn Thibault .08 .25
317 Jeff Beukeboom .01 .05
318 Steve Konowalchuk .01 .05
319 Tim Cheveldae .02 .10
320 Vincent Damphousse .01 .05
321 Mats Naslund .01 .05
322 Mathieu Schneider .01 .05
323 Petr Nedved .02 .10
324 Brent Fedyk .01 .05
325 Jussi Tie RC .01 .05
326 Mikko Markkanen RC .02 .10
327 Timo Hakanen RC .02 .10
328 Sami Salonen RC .02 .10
329 Juha Viinikainen RC .02 .10
330 Jani Riihinen RC .02 .10
331 Teemu Riihijarvi RC .02 .10
332 Jaakko Niskavaara RC .02 .10
333 Miika Elomo .02 .10
334 Tomi Kallio RC .40 1.00
335 Vesa Toskala RC .02 .10
336 Tuomas Reijonen RC .02 .10
337 Aki-Petteri Berg RC .01 .05
338 Tomi Hirvonen RC .02 .10
339 Jussi Salminen RC .02 .10
340 Andreas Sjolund RC .02 .10
341 Johan Ramstedt RC .01 .05
342 Bjorn Danielsson RC .02 .10
343 Per Gustavsson RC .02 .10
344 Niklas Anger RC .02 .10
345 Marcus Nilsson RC .10 .25
346 Per Anton Lundstrom RC .02 .10
347 Henrik Rehnberg RC .02 .10
348 Robert Borgqvist RC .02 .10
349 Ted Christensen RC .02 .10
350 Samuel Phalsson RC .01 .05
351 Fredrik Loven RC .01 .05
352 Patrik Wallenberg RC .02 .10
353 Jan Labraaten RC .02 .10
354 Peter Wallin RC .01 .05
355 Cam Neely .08 .25
356 Keith Tkachuk .08 .25
357 Chris Gratton .01 .05
358 Adam Graves .01 .05
359 Doug Gilmour .02 .10
360 Adam Deadmarsh .01 .05
361 Wayne Gretzky .08 .25
362 Joe Sakic .08 .25
363 Paul Kariya .08 .25
364 Brett Hull .08 .25
365 Sergei Fedorov .08 .25
366 Brian Rolston .01 .05
367 Dominik Hasek .08 .25
368 John Vanbiesbrouck .02 .10
369 Jim Carey .01 .05
370 Paul Kariya .08 .25
371 Peter Forsberg .08 .25
372 Jeff Friesen .01 .05
373 Kenny Jonsson .01 .05
374 Chris Therien .01 .05
375 Jim Carey .01 .05
376 John LeClair .08 .25
377 Eric Lindros .08 .25
378 Jaromir Jagr .08 .25
379 Paul Coffey .08 .25
380 Chris Chelios .08 .25
381 Dominik Hasek .08 .25
382 Keith Tkachuk .08 .25
383 Alexei Zhamnov .02 .10
384 Theo Fleury .01 .05
385 Ray Bourque .08 .25
386 Larry Murphy .02 .10
387 Ed Belfour .08 .25
388 Eric Lindros .08 .25
389 Jaromir Jagr .08 .25
390 Paul Coffey .08 .25
391 Peter Forsberg .08 .25
392 Claude Lemieux .01 .05
393 Ron Francis .02 .10
394 Dominik Hasek .08 .25
395 Wayne Gretzky CL .08 .25
396 Wayne Gretzky CL .08 .25
397 Saku Koivu TRADE 1.25 3.00
398 Radek Dvorak TRADE .08 .25
399 Ed Jovanovski TRADE
400 Brendan Witt TRADE .08 .25
401 Jeff O'Neill TRADE .08 .25
402 Daymond Langkow TRADE .08 .25
403 Shane Doan TRADE RC 1.25 3.00
404 Bryan McCabe TRADE .08 .25
405 Marty Murray TRADE .08 .25
406 Daniel Alfredsson TRADE 1.00 2.50
407 Jason Doig TRADE .08 .25
408 Niklas Sundstrom TRADE .08 .25
409 Vitali Yachmenev TRADE .08 .25
410 Aki Berg TRADE .08 .25
411 Eric Daze TRADE .40 1.00
NNO Young Guns Trade Card .08 .25

1995-96 Collector's Choice Player's Club

Issued one per pack, this 396 card standard-size set is a parallel to the regular Collector's Choice issue. These cards have silver borders and the words "Players Club" are printed vertically on the left side of the card in silver-foil.

COMPLETE SET (396) 60.00 100.00
*STARS: 5X TO 10X BASIC CARDS
*RCs: 2X TO 4X BASIC CARDS
395 Checklist 1-200 .10 .25
396 Checklist 201-396 .10 .25

1995-96 Collector's Choice Player's Club Platinum

This 396-card standard size set is a parallel to the regular Collector's Choice set. Issued a rate of 1:34 packs, these cards are printed on silver-foil paper stock. Although difficult to pull from packs, many of the cards came over from Europe, where they were readily available from collectors clubs. This added supply dampened demand somewhat for these cards in North America.

*STARS: 30X TO 75X BASIC CARDS
*RCs: 15X TO 40X BASIC CARDS
395 Checklist 1-200 .75 2.00
396 Checklist 201-396 .75 2.00

1995-96 Collector's Choice Crash The Game

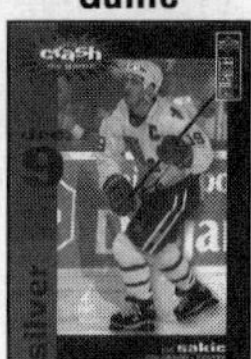

Consisting of 90 cards, this interactive set featured 30 players. Each player had three cards with different dates on the front. If the player scored a goal on either of the dates, the card with the corresponding date could be redeemed for a special 30-card set. Randomly inserted in packs, these cards came in silver (1:5 packs) and gold (1:34 packs) foil versions. The words "silver" or "gold" were in their respective color foil at bottom left and the date was also done in foil. There are also several parallels of this set, including gold and silver redeemed winner sets, and gold and silver bonus cards awarded of the redeemed player along with the gold or silver set. Multipliers can be found in the header below to determine values for these versions. Because not every player had a winning card, however, the gold and silver bonus sets are considered complete at 23 cards each. It should be noted however that a few copies of the bonus cards have been confirmed to exist of the seven players that did not have winning cards. Also, several erroneous variation cards have been reported featuring game dates on which that player's team did not play. These cards appear to be in short supply, but do not demand exorbitant premiums. To differentiate between each of the player's three insert cards, they are numbered here with A, B and C suffixes. The expiration date for redeeming cards was July 1st, 1996.

*GOLD STARS: 1.5X TO 4X BASIC CARDS
*EXCHANGE CARDS: .1X TO .25X BASIC CARDS
*GOLD EXCH.CARDS: .4X TO .8X BASIC CARDS
*BONUS CARDS: 1X TO 2X BASIC CARDS
*GOLD BONUS CARDS: 2.5X TO 5X BASIC CARDS
C1A Pavel Bure 10/12/95 .30 .75
C1B Pavel Bure 12/17/95 .50 1.25
C1C Pavel Bure 3/23/96 .50 1.25
C2A Sergei Fedorov 10/19/95 .50 1.25
C2B Sergei Fedorov 12/31/95 .60 1.50
C2C Sergei Fedorov 3/12/96 .60 1.50
C3A Wayne Gretzky 10/7/95 2.00 5.00
C3B Wayne Gretzky 12/31/95 2.00 5.00
C3C Wayne Gretzky 2/10/96 2.00 5.00
C4A Eric Lindros 11/12/95 .30 .75
C4B Eric Lindros 1/3/96 .50 1.25
C4C Eric Lindros 3/3/96 .50 1.25
C5A Brett Hull 10/10/95 .50 1.25
C5B Brett Hull 12/19/95 .50 1.25
C5C Brett Hull 3/24/96 .50 1.25
C6A Mark Messier 11/8/95 .30 .75
C6B Mark Messier 1/22/96 .50 1.25
C6C Mark Messier 3/31/96 .50 1.25
C7A Jaromir Jagr 10/14/95 .50 1.25
C7B Jaromir Jagr 12/17/95 .50 1.25
C7C Jaromir Jagr 3/5/96 .50 1.25
C8A Alexei Zhamnov 10/9/95 .25 .60
C8B Alexei Zhamnov 12/28/95 .25 .60
C8C Alexei Zhamnov 2/21/96 .25 .60
C9A Joe Sakic 10/6/95 .60 1.50
C9B Joe Sakic 12/9/95 .60 1.50
C9C Joe Sakic 2/3/96 .60 1.50
C10A Paul Kariya 10/18/95 .30 .75
C10B Paul Kariya 12/19/95 .30 .75
C10C Paul Kariya 3/17/96 .30 .75
C11A Theo Fleury 10/27/95 .20 .50
C11B Theo Fleury 12/11/95 .20 .50
C11C Theo Fleury 2/6/96 .20 .50
C12A Owen Nolan 11/1/95 .25 .60
C12B Owen Nolan 1/4/96 .25 .60
C12C Owen Nolan 3/17/96 .25 .60
C13A Peter Bondra 10/13/95 .25 .60
C13B Peter Bondra 12/2/95 .25 .60
C13C Peter Bondra 3/12/96 .25 .60
C14A Cam Neely 11/7/95 .30 .75
C14B Cam Neely 1/11/96 .30 .75
C14C Cam Neely 3/23/96 .30 .75
C15A Pierre Turgeon 10/25/95 .25 .60
C15B Pierre Turgeon 12/23/95 .25 .60
C15C Pierre Turgeon 2/21/96 .25 .60
C16A Mike Modano 11/1/95 .60 1.50
C16B Mike Modano 1/5/96 .60 1.50
C16C Mike Modano 2/22/96 .60 1.50
C17A Bernie Nicholls 10/10/95 .20 .50
C17B Bernie Nicholls 12/15/95 .20 .50
C17C Bernie Nicholls 3/24/96 .20 .50
C18A Alexei Yashin 11/4/95 .20 .50
C18B Alexei Yashin 12/23/95 .20 .50
C18C Alexei Yashin 3/21/96 .20 .50
C19A Jason Arnott 10/27/95 .20 .50
C19B Jason Arnott 12/18/95 .20 .50
C19C Jason Arnott 2/28/96 .20 .50
C20A Peter Forsberg 11/22/95 .75 2.00
C20B Peter Forsberg 2/15/96 .75 2.00
C20C Peter Forsberg 3/27/96 .75 2.00
C21A Doug Gilmour 10/17/95 .25 .60
C21B Doug Gilmour 12/16/95 .25 .60
C21C Doug Gilmour 2/18/96 .25 .60
C22A G. Sanderson 10/11/95 .20 .50
C22B G. Sanderson 12/18/95 .20 .50
C22C G. Sanderson 3/6/96 .20 .50
C23A John LeClair 10/15/95 .50 1.25
C23B John LeClair 12/16/95 .50 1.25
C23C John LeClair 2/19/96 .50 1.25
C24A Ray Bourque 10/11/95 .60 1.50
C24B Ray Bourque 12/16/95 .20 .50
C24C Ray Bourque 2/6/96 .20 .50
C25A Mario Lemieux 1.50 4.00
C25B Mario Lemieux 1.50 4.00
C25C Mario Lemieux 1.50 4.00
C26A Steve Yzerman 11/7/95 1.50 4.00
C26B Steve Yzerman 1/24/96 1.50 4.00
C26C Steve Yzerman 2/27/96 1.50 4.00
C27A Pat LaFontaine 10/20/95 .30 .75
C27B Pat LaFontaine 12/27/95 .30 .75
C27C Pat LaFontaine 2/17/96 .30 .75
C28A Claude Lemieux 10/7/95 .20 .50
C28B Claude Lemieux 12/15/95 .20 .50
C28C Claude Lemieux 2/10/96 .20 .50
C29A Paul Coffey 10/15/95 .30 .75
C29B Paul Coffey 12/5/95 .30 .75
C29C Paul Coffey 2/13/96 .30 .75
C30A Mats Sundin 11/7/95 .30 .75
C30B Mats Sundin 1/3/96 .30 .75
C30C Mats Sundin 3/15/96 .30 .75

1996-97 Collector's Choice

The '96-97 Collector's Choice set was issued in one series totaling 348 cards. The 12-card packs retailed for $.99 each. The set contains three subsets: Scotty Bowman's Winning Formula (289-308), Three-Star Selection (309-336) and Captain Tomorrow (337-346). Fifteen additional Young Guns cards (numbered 349-363) were available via mail in exchange for the randomly inserted Young Guns Trade card (1:35 packs). They are not considered part of the complete set, but are listed below as they are numbered consecutively to the regular set. The Gretzky 4 X 6 cards were received when redeeming winning trivia cards from the Meet the Stars contest.

COMPLETE SET (348) 8.00 20.00
1 Paul Kariya .08 .25
2 Teemu Selanne .08 .25
3 Steve Rucchin .01 .05
4 Mikhail Shtalenkov .01 .05
5 Guy Hebert .02 .10
6 Shaun Van Allen .01 .05
7 Anatoli Semenov .01 .05
8 J.F. Jomphe RC .01 .05
9 Alex Hicks .01 .05
10 Roman Oksiuta .01 .05
11 Todd Ewen .01 .05
12 Adam Oates .02 .10
13 Ray Bourque .15 .40
14 Don Sweeney .01 .05
15 Kyle McLaren .01 .05
16 Cam Neely .08 .25
17 Bill Ranford .02 .10
18 Rick Tocchet .02 .10
19 Ted Donato .01 .05
20 Shawn McEachern .01 .05
21 Jon Rohloff .01 .05
22 Joe Mullen .02 .10
23 Pat LaFontaine .08 .25
24 Brian Holzinger .02 .10
25 Wayne Primeau .01 .05
26 Alexei Zhitnik .01 .05
27 Derek Plante .01 .05
28 Randy Burridge .01 .05
29 Brad May .02 .10
30 Dominik Hasek .20 .50
31 Jason Dawe .01 .05
32 Mike Peca .01 .05
33 Matthew Barnaby .02 .10
34 Trevor Kidd .02 .10
35 Theo Fleury .01 .05
36 Cale Hulse .01 .05
37 Bob Sweeney .01 .05
38 Michael Nylander .01 .05
39 German Titov .01 .05
40 Cory Stillman .01 .05
41 Zarley Zalapski .01 .05
42 Jocelyn Lemieux .01 .05
43 Sandy McCarthy .01 .05
44 Gary Roberts .01 .05
45 Eric Daze .02 .10
46 Jeremy Roenick .12 .30
47 Chris Chelios .08 .25
48 Joe Murphy .01 .05
49 Tony Amonte .02 .10
50 Bernie Nicholls .01 .05
51 Eric Weinrich .01 .05
52 Gary Suter .01 .05
53 Jeff Shantz .01 .05
54 Jeff Hackett .02 .10
55 Ed Belfour .08 .25
56 Uwe Krupp .01 .05
57 Claude Lemieux .01 .05
58 Adam Deadmarsh .01 .05
59 Stephane Fiset .02 .10
60 Sandis Ozolinsh .01 .05
61 Stephane Yelle .01 .05
62 Valeri Kamensky .02 .10
63 Peter Forsberg .25 .60
64 Joe Sakic .20 .50
65 Patrick Roy .50 1.25
66 Chris Simon .01 .05
67 Todd Harvey .01 .05
68 Joe Nieuwendyk .02 .10
69 Mike Modano .15 .40
70 Derian Hatcher .01 .05
71 Kevin Hatcher .01 .05
72 Benoit Hogue .01 .05
73 Guy Carbonneau .01 .05
74 Jamie Langenbrunner .01 .05
75 Jere Lehtinen .01 .05
76 Craig Ludwig .01 .05
77 Grant Marshall .01 .05
78 Greg Johnson .01 .05

79 Steve Yzerman .40 1.00
80 Sergei Fedorov .12 .30
81 Vyacheslav Kozlov .01 .05
82 Vladimir Konstantinov .02 .10
83 Igor Larionov .01 .05
84 Chris Osgood .02 .10
85 Paul Coffey .08 .25
86 Nicklas Lidstrom .08 .25
87 Keith Primeau .01 .05
88 Dino Ciccarelli .02 .10
89 Darren McCarty .01 .05
90 Curtis Joseph .08 .25
91 Doug Weight .02 .10
92 Jason Arnott .01 .05
93 Mariusz Czerkawski .01 .05
94 Kelly Buchberger .01 .05
95 Zdeno Ciger .01 .05
96 David Oliver .01 .05
97 Todd Marchant .01 .05
98 Miroslav Satan .01 .05
99 Bryan Marchment .01 .05
100 Louie DeBrusk .01 .05
101 John Vanbiesbrouck .02 .10
102 Scott Mellanby .02 .10
103 Rob Niedermayer .02 .10
104 Robert Svehla .01 .05
105 Ed Jovanovski .02 .10
106 Johan Garpenlov .01 .05
107 Jody Hull .01 .05
108 Bill Lindsay .01 .05
109 Terry Carkner .01 .05
110 Stu Barnes .01 .05
111 Ray Sheppard .02 .10
112 Brendan Shanahan .08 .25
113 Geoff Sanderson .02 .10
114 Andrei Nikolishin .01 .05
115 Andrew Cassels .01 .05
116 Nelson Emerson .01 .05
117 Jason Muzzatti .02 .10
118 Marek Malik .01 .05
119 Sean Burke .02 .10
120 Jeff Brown .01 .05
121 Jeff O'Neill .01 .05
122 Kelly Chase .01 .05
123 Dimitri Khristich .01 .05
124 Kevin Stevens .01 .05
125 Vitali Yachmenev .01 .05
126 Yanic Perreault .01 .05
127 Kevin Todd .01 .05
128 Aki Berg .01 .05
129 Craig Johnson .01 .05
130 Mattias Norstrom .01 .05
131 Ray Ferraro .01 .05
132 Steven Finn .01 .05
133 Pierre Turgeon .02 .10
134 Saku Koivu .08 .25
135 Mark Recchi .02 .10
136 Jocelyn Thibault .08 .25
137 Andrei Kovalenko .01 .05
138 Vincent Damphousse .01 .05
139 Vladimir Malakhov .01 .05
140 Brian Savage .01 .05
141 Valeri Bure .01 .05
142 Patrice Brisebois .01 .05
143 Martin Rucinsky .01 .05
144 Martin Brodeur .25 .60
145 Steve Thomas .01 .05
146 Bill Guerin .01 .05
147 Petr Sykora .01 .05
148 Scott Stevens .02 .10
149 Scott Niedermayer .01 .05
150 Phil Housley .02 .10
151 Brian Rolston .01 .05
152 Neal Broten .02 .10
153 Dave Andreychuk .02 .10
154 Randy McKay .01 .05
155 Eric Fichaud .02 .10
156 Zigmund Palffy .02 .10
157 Travis Green .02 .10
158 Darby Hendrickson .01 .05
159 Kenny Jonsson .01 .05
160 Marty McInnis .01 .05
161 Bryan McCabe .01 .05
162 Darius Kasparaitis .01 .05
163 Alexander Semak .01 .05
164 Todd Bertuzzi .08 .25
165 Niclas Andersson .01 .05
166 Mark Messier .08 .25
167 Mike Richter .08 .25
168 Niklas Sundstrom .01 .05
169 Brian Leetch .08 .25
170 Wayne Gretzky .75 2.00
171 Luc Robitaille .02 .10
172 Marty McSorley .01 .05
173 Jari Kurri .02 .10
174 Adam Graves .01 .05
175 Sergei Nemchinov .01 .05
176 Alexei Kovalev .01 .05
177 Daniel Alfredsson .02 .10
178 Randy Cunneyworth .01 .05
179 Alexei Yashin .01 .05
180 Alexandre Daigle .01 .05
181 Radek Bonk .01 .05
182 Steve Duchesne .01 .05
183 Ted Drury .01 .05
184 Antti Tormanen .01 .05
185 Stan Neckar .01 .05
186 Damian Rhodes .02 .10
187 Janne Laukkanen .01 .05
188 Eric Lindros .08 .25
189 Mikael Renberg .02 .10
190 John LeClair .08 .25
191 Ron Hextall .02 .10
192 Rod Brind'Amour .02 .10
193 Joel Otto .01 .05
194 Pat Falloon .01 .05
195 Eric Desjardins .02 .10
196 Dale Hawerchuk .02 .10
197 Chris Therien .01 .05
198 Dan Quinn .01 .05
199 Oleg Tverdovsky .02 .10
200 Chad Kilger .01 .05
201 Keith Tkachuk .08 .25
202 Igor Korolev .01 .05
203 Alexei Zhamnov .02 .10
204 Nikolai Khabibulin .02 .10
205 Shane Doan .01 .05
206 Deron Quint .01 .05
207 Craig Janney .02 .10
208 Norm Maciver .01 .05
209 Teppo Numminen .01 .05
210 Mario Lemieux .50 1.25
211 Jaromir Jagr .15 .40
212 Ron Francis .02 .10
213 Tom Barrasso .02 .10
214 Sergei Zubov .01 .05
215 Tomas Sandstrom .01 .05
216 Joe Dziedzic .01 .05
217 Richard Park .01 .05
218 Bryan Smolinski .01 .05
219 Petr Nedved .02 .10
220 Ken Wregget .02 .10
221 Dmitri Mironov .01 .05
222 Peter Zezel .01 .05
223 Brett Hull .10 .30
224 Grant Fuhr .02 .10
225 Shayne Corson .01 .05
226 Chris Pronger .02 .10
227 Craig MacTavish .01 .05
228 Al MacInnis .02 .10
229 Geoff Courtnall .01 .05
230 Stephane Matteau .01 .05
231 Tony Twist .01 .05
232 Brian Noonan .01 .05
233 Owen Nolan .02 .10
234 Shean Donovan .01 .05
235 Darren Turcotte .01 .05
236 Marcus Ragnarsson .01 .05
237 Viktor Kozlov UER .01 .05
(has Slava Kozlov's stats)
238 Jeff Friesen .01 .05
239 Chris Terreri .02 .10
240 Ray Whitney .01 .05
241 Ville Peltonen .01 .05
242 Andrei Nazarov .01 .05
243 Ulf Dahlen .01 .05
244 Roman Hamrlik .02 .10
245 Chris Gratton .02 .10
246 Petr Klima .01 .05
247 Daren Puppa .02 .10
248 Rob Zamuner .01 .05
249 Aaron Gavey .01 .05
250 Brian Bradley .01 .05
251 Paul Ysebaert .01 .05
252 Igor Ulanov .01 .05
253 Alexander Selivanov .01 .05
254 Shawn Burr .01 .05
255 Mats Sundin .08 .25
256 Doug Gilmour .02 .10
257 Felix Potvin .08 .25
258 Wendel Clark .02 .10
259 Kirk Muller .01 .05
260 Dave Gagner .02 .10
261 Tie Domi .02 .10
262 Mathieu Schneider .01 .05
263 Dimitri Yushkevich .01 .05
264 Don Beaupre .02 .10
265 Larry Murphy .02 .10
266 Pavel Bure .08 .25
267 Alexander Mogilny .02 .10
268 Trevor Linden .02 .10
269 Jyrki Lumme .01 .05
270 Cliff Ronning .01 .05
271 Kirk McLean .02 .10
272 Corey Hirsch .02 .10
273 Esa Tikkanen .01 .05
274 Gino Odjick .01 .05
275 Markus Naslund .08 .25
276 Russ Courtnall .01 .05
277 Joe Juneau .01 .05
278 Jim Carey .08 .25
279 Peter Bondra .02 .10
280 Michal Pivonka .01 .05
281 Steve Konowalchuk .01 .05
282 Pat Peake .01 .05
283 Brendan Witt .01 .05
284 Stefan Ustorf .01 .05
285 Keith Jones .01 .05
286 Sergei Gonchar .01 .05
287 Sylvain Cote .01 .05
288 Dale Hunter .01 .05
289 Paul Kariya SB .08 .25
290 Wayne Gretzky SB .08 .25
291 Eric Lindros SB .08 .25
292 Steve Yzerman SB .08 .25
293 Mario Lemieux SB .08 .25
294 Jaromir Jagr SB .08 .25
295 Keith Tkachuk SB .08 .25
296 Mark Messier SB .08 .25
297 Jeremy Roenick SB .12 .30
298 Peter Forsberg SB .08 .25
299 Joe Sakic SB .08 .25
300 Theo Fleury SB .01 .05
301 Chris Chelios SB .08 .25
302 Vlad Konstantinov SB .01 .05
303 Brian Leetch SB .08 .25
304 Ray Bourque SB .08 .25
305 Scott Stevens SB .02 .10
306 Martin Brodeur SB .08 .25
307 Patrick Roy SB .08 .25
308 Scotty Bowman .02 .10
309 Paul Kariya .01 .05
Teemu Selanne
Guy Hebert
310 Adam Oates .02 .10
Ray Bourque
Cam Neely
311 Pat LaFontaine .02 .10
Alexei Zhitnik
Dominik Hasek
312 Theo Fleury .02 .10
Michael Nylander
Trevor Kidd
313 Jeremy Roenick .02 .10
Chris Chelios
Eric Daze
314 Joe Sakic .30 .75
Patrick Roy
Peter Forsberg
315 Mike Modano .02 .10
Joe Nieuwendyk
Todd Harvey
316 Sergei Fedorov .08 .25
Vladimir Konstantinov
Paul Coffey
317 Doug Weight .10 .30
Jason Arnott
Curtis Joseph
318 Ed Jovanovski .02 .10
John Vanbiesbrouck
Rob Niedermayer
319 Brendan Shanahan .02 .10
Geoff Sanderson
Sean Burke
320 Vitali Yachmenev .01 .05
Dimitri Khristich
Ray Ferraro
321 Jocelyn Thibault .08 .25
Pierre Turgeon
Saku Koivu
322 Martin Brodeur .02 .10
Steve Thomas
Scott Stevens
323 Todd Bertuzzi .02 .10
Eric Fichaud
Zigmund Palffy
324 Brian Leetch .08 .25
Adam Graves
Mike Richter
325 Alexander Daigle .01 .05
Alexei Yashin
Damian Rhodes
326 Ron Hextall .02 .10
John LeClair
Mikael Renberg
327 Alexei Zhamnov .02 .10
Keith Tkachuk
Oleg Tverdovsky
328 Jaromir Jagr .08 .25
Petr Nedved
Ron Francis
329 Wayne Gretzky .40 1.00
Brett Hull
Al MacInnis
330 Owen Nolan .02 .10
Darren Turcotte
Chris Terreri
331 Roman Hamrlik .02 .10
Chris Gratton
Darren Puppa
332 Doug Gilmour .02 .10
Felix Potvin
Mats Sundin
333 Alexander Mogilny .02 .10
Pavel Bure
Trevor Linden
334 Jim Carey .02 .10
Joe Juneau
Peter Bondra
335 Mario Lemieux .08 .25
Mark Messier
Eric Lindros
336 Wayne Gretzky .40 1.00
Teemu Selanne
Joe Sakic
337 Chad Kilger .01 .05
338 Todd Bertuzzi .08 .25
339 Petr Sykora .01 .05
340 Ed Jovanovski .02 .10
341 Kyle McLaren .01 .05
342 Brian Holzinger .02 .10
343 Jeff O'Neill .01 .05
344 Daniel Alfredsson .02 .10
345 Brendan Witt .01 .05
346 Daymond Langkow .02 .10
347 Checklist .01 .05
348 Checklist .01 .05
349 Jarome Iginla YG .75 2.00
350 Sergei Berezin YG .20 .50
351 Jose Theodore YG .75 2.00
352 Rem Murray YG .08 .25
353 Daniel Goneau YG .08 .25
354 Ethan Moreau YG .08 .25
355 Jonas Hoglund YG .08 .25
356 Anders Eriksson YG .08 .25
357 Christian Dube YG .08 .25
358 Roman Turek YG .20 .50
359 Bryan Berard YG .08 .25
360 Jim Campbell YG .08 .25
361 Janne Niinimaa YG .08 .25
362 Wade Redden YG .20 .50
363 Marc Denis YG .20 .50
P222 Wayne Gretzky PROMO 2.00 5.00
NNO Young Guns Trade .40 1.00
NNO1 Wayne Gretzky '79-80 2.50 6.00
Meet the Stars 4X6
NNO2 Wayne Gretzky 802 2.50 6.00
Meet the Stars 4X6

1996-97 Collector's Choice Jumbos

These 5 X 7 cards were inserted as box toppers.

COMPLETE SET (5) 8.00
1 Theo Fleury 2.00
2 Curtis Joseph 3.00
3 Jose Theodore 2.50
4 Wade Redden 1.00
5 Mats Sundin 2.50

1996-97 Collector's Choice MVP

This set consists of 45 of the NHL's top stars and rookies. Silver versions are found one per pack, while the tougher gold parallel version is found 1:35 packs. These cards can be differentiated by the color of the foil on the left-hand border. The card fronts feature a color action photo with abbreviation "MVP" appearing in either silver or gold (depending on the version) at the bottom of the card. Values for the gold cards can be determined by utilizing the multiplier below.

COMPLETE SET (45) 10.00 25.00
*GOLD STARS: 2.5X TO 6X BASIC INSERTS
UD1 Wayne Gretzky 2.00 5.00
UD2 Ron Francis .10 .25
UD3 Peter Forsberg .60 1.50
UD4 Alexander Mogilny .10 .25
UD5 Joe Sakic .50 1.25
UD6 Claude Lemieux .05 .15
UD7 Teemu Selanne .25 .60
UD8 John LeClair .25 .60
UD9 Doug Weight .10 .25
UD10 Paul Kariya .25 .60
UD11 Theo Fleury .05 .15
UD12 John Vanbiesbrouck .10 .25
UD13 Sergei Fedorov .30 .75
UD14 Steve Yzerman 1.25 3.00
UD15 Adam Oates .10 .25
UD16 Keith Tkachuk .25 .60
UD17 Mike Modano .40 1.00
UD18 Jeremy Roenick .30 .75
UD19 Patrick Roy 1.25 3.00
UD20 Felix Potvin .25 .60
UD21 Martin Brodeur .60 1.50
UD22 Pavel Bure .25 .60
UD23 Peter Bondra .10 .25
UD24 Zigmund Palffy .10 .25
UD25 Roman Hamrlik .10 .25
UD26 Brendan Shanahan .25 .60
UD27 Ray Bourque .40 1.00
UD28 Paul Coffey .25 .60
UD29 Brett Hull .30 .75
UD30 Brian Leetch .25 .60
UD31 Chris Chelios .25 .60
UD32 Vitali Yachmenev .05 .15
UD33 Nicklas Lidstrom .25 .60
UD34 Ed Jovanovski .10 .25
UD35 Sandis Ozolinsh .05 .15
UD36 Scott Stevens .10 .25
UD37 Eric Daze .10 .25
UD38 Saku Koivu .25 .60
UD39 Daniel Alfredsson .10 .25
UD40 Pat LaFontaine .25 .60
UD41 Cam Neely .25 .60
UD42 Owen Nolan .10 .25
UD43 Jaromir Jagr .40 1.00
UD44 Mats Sundin .25 .60
UD45 Doug Gilmour .10 .25

1996-97 Collector's Choice Stick'Ums

This unusual set consists of 30 stickers, the first 25 of which feature the NHL's top players. The remaining stickers feature a variety of hockey-oriented doo-daddery. These stickers were randomly inserted at 1:3 packs.

COMPLETE SET (30) 10.00 20.00
S1 Wayne Gretzky 2.50 6.00
S2 Brett Hull .40 1.00
S3 Peter Forsberg .75 2.00
S4 Patrick Roy 1.50 4.00
S5 Cam Neely .30 .75
S6 Jeremy Roenick .40 1.00
S7 Mario Lemieux 1.50 4.00
S8 Jaromir Jagr .50 1.25
S9 Eric Lindros .30 .75
S10 Mark Messier .30 .75
S11 Felix Potvin .30 .75
S12 Brendan Shanahan .30 .75
S13 Teemu Selanne .30 .75
S14 Paul Kariya .30 .75
S15 Mike Modano .50 1.25
S16 Pavel Bure .30 .75
S17 Jim Carey .30 .75
S18 Roman Hamrlik .15 .30
S19 Pierre Turgeon .15 .30
S20 Theo Fleury .05 .15
S21 Pat LaFontaine .30 .75
S22 Steve Yzerman 1.50 4.00
S23 Sergei Fedorov .40 1.00
S24 Martin Brodeur .75 2.00
S25 Owen Nolan .15 .30
S26 Ice Machine .05 .15
S27 Champions .05 .15
S28 Slap Shot .05 .15
S29 Stripes .05 .15
S30 Goal .05 .15

1996-97 Collector's Choice Crash the Game

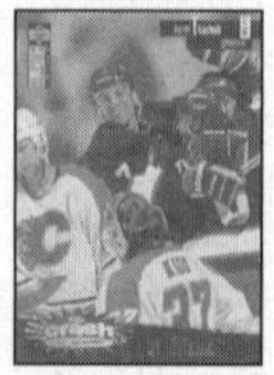

This interactive set features 30 NHL stars on a total of 88 cards. 28 players appear on 3 variations each, while two (Joe Sakic and Adam Oates) are featured on but two by virtue of an error by Upper Deck. Randomly inserted in packs, these cards come in silver (1:5 packs) and gold (1:44 packs) foil versions. If the player scored a goal against the team featured on his card, the winning card could be redeemed for a special exchange card. There are two versions of this set as well. Both versions feature the same design and photos, but they are different from the Crash cards for which they were redeemed. Furthermore, the gold versions of the exchange cards were die-cut. To differentiate between each of the player's three insert cards, they are numbered here with A, B and C suffixes. These suffixes do not appear on the cards themselves. The expiration date for these cards was July 1, 1997.

COMPLETE SET (88) 40.00 80.00
*GOLD: 1.25X TO 3X BASIC INSERTS
*EXCH.STARS: 1.25X TO 3X BASIC INSERTS
*GOLD EXCH: 4X TO 10X BASIC INSERTS
ONE EXCH.CARD VIA MAIL PER WINNER
EXCH.CARDS 20 AND 25 NOT ISSUED
C1A Wayne Gretzky 2.00 5.00
C1B Wayne Gretzky 2.00 5.00
C1C Wayne Gretzky 2.00 5.00
C2A Doug Gilmour .25 .60
C2B Doug Gilmour .25 .60
C2C Doug Gilmour .25 .60
C3A Alexander Mogilny .25 .60
C3B Alexander Mogilny .25 .60
C3C Alexander Mogilny .25 .60
C4A Peter Bondra .25 .60
C4B Peter Bondra .25 .60
C4C Peter Bondra .25 .60
C5A Mario Lemieux 1.50 4.00
C5B Mario Lemieux 1.50 4.00
C5C Mario Lemieux 1.50 4.00
C6A Jaromir Jagr .50 1.25
C6B Jaromir Jagr .50 1.25
C6C Jaromir Jagr .50 1.25
C7A Joe Sakic .60 1.50
C7B Joe Sakic .60 1.50
C8A Vitali Yachmenev .20 .50
C8B Vitali Yachmenev .20 .50
C8C Vitali Yachmenev .20 .50
C9A Doug Weight .25 .60
C9B Doug Weight .25 .60
C9C Doug Weight .25 .60
C10A Steve Yzerman 1.50 4.00
C10B Steve Yzerman 1.50 4.00
C10C Steve Yzerman 1.50 4.00
C11A Alexei Zhamnov .20 .50
C11B Alexei Zhamnov .20 .50
C11C Alexei Zhamnov .20 .50
C12A John LeClair .30 .75
C12B John LeClair .30 .75
C12C John LeClair .30 .75
C13A Daniel Alfredsson .25 .60
C13B Daniel Alfredsson .25 .60
C13C Daniel Alfredsson .25 .60
C14A Brendan Shanahan .30 .75
C14B Brendan Shanahan .50 1.25
C14C Brendan Shanahan .50 1.25
C15A Saku Koivu .30 .75
C15B Saku Koivu .30 .75
C15C Saku Koivu .30 .75
C16A Steve Thomas .20 .50
C16B Steve Thomas .20 .50
C16C Steve Thomas .20 .50
C17A Pavel Bure .30 .75
C17B Pavel Bure .50 1.25
C17C Pavel Bure .50 1.25
C18A Slava Kozlov .20 .50
C18B Slava Kozlov .20 .50
C18C Slava Kozlov .20 .50
C19A Teemu Selanne .30 .75
C19B Teemu Selanne .30 .75
C19C Teemu Selanne .30 .75
C20A Eric Daze .20 .50
C20B Eric Daze .20 .50
C20C Eric Daze .20 .50
C21A Adam Oates .25 .60
C21B Adam Oates .25 .60
C22A Ray Bourque .50 1.25
C22B Ray Bourque .50 1.25
C22C Ray Bourque .50 1.25
C23A Jason Arnott .20 .50
C23B Jason Arnott .20 .50
C23C Jason Arnott .20 .50
C24A Paul Kariya .30 .75
C24B Paul Kariya .30 .75
C24C Paul Kariya .30 .75
C25A Mikael Renberg .20 .50
C25B Mikael Renberg .20 .50
C25C Mikael Renberg .20 .50
C26A Keith Tkachuk .30 .75
C26B Keith Tkachuk .30 .75
C26C Keith Tkachuk .30 .75
C27A Brian Leetch .25 .60
C27B Brian Leetch .25 .60
C27C Brian Leetch .25 .60
C28A Eric Lindros .30 .75
C28B Eric Lindros .50 1.25
C28C Eric Lindros .50 1.25
C29A Mats Sundin .30 .75
C29B Mats Sundin .30 .75
C29C Mats Sundin .30 .75
C30A Mark Messier .40 1.00
C30B Mark Messier .40 1.00
C30C Mark Messier .40 1.00

1996-97 Collector's Choice Blow-Ups

The ten cards in this set were issued one per special retail box of Collector's Choice. The cards are identical in every way to their corresponding regular version, except for the size; these cards measure 4 X 6 inches.

COMPLETE SET (10) 10.00 25.00
13 Ray Bourque .80 2.00
23 Pat LaFontaine .50 1.25
35 Theo Fleury .60 1.50
62 Valeri Kamensky .50 1.25
69 Mike Modano .80 2.00
84 Chris Osgood .60 1.50
133 Pierre Turgeon .50 1.25
170 Wayne Gretzky 4.00 10.00
244 Roman Hamrlik .40 1.00
257 Felix Potvin .50 1.25

1996-97 Collector's Choice Blow-Ups Bi-Way

These eight oversized (4 by 6 inches) cards mirrored the regular edition Collector's Choice cards, save for the numbering on the back. The cards were inserted one per box sold through the Bi-Way discount chain in Canada.

COMPLETE SET (8) 12.00 30.00
1 Wayne Gretzky 4.00 10.00
2 Theo Fleury .60 1.50
3 Jason Arnott .50 1.25
4 Saku Koivu .60 1.50
5 Pierre Turgeon .50 1.25
6 Daniel Alfredsson .50 1.25
7 Felix Potvin .50 1.25
8 Alexander Mogilny .50 1.25

1997-98 Collector's Choice

This 320-card set features color photos of approximately ten players from each of the NHL's 26 teams and was distributed in 14-card packs with a suggested retail price of $1.29. The set contains 275 regular player cards and two subsets: National Heroes (36 cards) which includes some of the most talented junior players, and Chippy's Checklist (9 cards) which highlights nine of the mascot's favorite players on the set's checklist cards. The cards are dual numbered and are checklisted in team order alphabetized by city.

COMPLETE SET (320) 8.00 20.00
1 Guy Hebert .08 .25
2 Sean Pronger .03 .10
3 Dmitri Mironov .03 .10
4 Darren Van Impe .03 .10
5 Joe Sacco .03 .10
6 Ted Drury .03 .10
7 Steve Rucchin .03 .10
8 Teemu Selanne .10 .30
9 Paul Kariya .10 .30
10 Jari Kurri .08 .25
11 Kevin Todd .03 .10
12 Ray Bourque .20 .50
13 Anson Carter .08 .25
14 Ted Donato .03 .10
15 Kyle McLaren .03 .10
16 Jason Allison .03 .10
17 Jim Carey .08 .25
18 Jozef Stumpel .08 .25
19 Jean-Yves Roy .03 .10
20 Steve Heinze .03 .10
21 Sheldon Kennedy .03 .10
22 Dominik Hasek .25 .60
23 Rob Ray .03 .10
24 Derek Plante .03 .10
25 Brian Holzinger .03 .10
26 Mike Peca .03 .10
27 Matthew Barnaby .03 .10
28 Donald Audette .03 .10
29 Alexei Zhitnik .03 .10
30 Garry Galley .03 .10
31 Pat LaFontaine .10 .30
32 Jason Dawe .03 .10
33 Hnat Domenichelli .03 .10
34 Jarome Iginla .12 .40
35 Chris O'Sullivan .03 .10
36 Todd Simpson .03 .10
37 Trevor Kidd .08 .25
38 Dave Gagner .03 .10
39 German Titov .08 .25
40 Theo Fleury .03 .10
41 Dwayne Roloson .03 .10
42 Marty McInnis .03 .10
43 Jonas Hoglund .03 .10
44 Tony Amonte .08 .25
45 Gary Suter .03 .10
46 Chris Chelios .10 .30
47 Jeff Hackett .08 .25
48 Ulf Dahlen .03 .10
49 Bob Probert .03 .10
50 Kevin Miller .03 .10
51 Ethan Moreau .03 .10
52 Eric Weinrich .03 .10
53 Eric Daze .08 .25
54 Peter Forsberg .30 .75
55 Joe Sakic .25 .60
56 Patrick Roy .60 1.50
57 Adam Deadmarsh .03 .10
58 Valeri Kamensky .08 .25
59 Keith Jones .03 .10
60 Sandis Ozolinsh .03 .10
61 Mike Ricci .03 .10
62 Claude Lemieux .03 .10
63 Mike Keane .03 .10
64 Adam Foote .03 .10
65 Mike Modano .20 .50
66 Pat Verbeek .03 .10
67 Andy Moog .08 .25
68 Joe Nieuwendyk .08 .25
69 Jamie Langenbrunner .03 .10
70 Derian Hatcher .03 .10
71 Greg Adams .03 .10
72 Daryll Sydor .03 .10
73 Dave Reid .03 .10
74 Jere Lehtinen .03 .10
75 Todd Harvey .03 .10
76 Brendan Shanahan .10 .30
77 Mike Vernon .08 .25
78 Steve Yzerman .60 1.50
79 Sergei Fedorov .20 .50
80 Chris Osgood .08 .25
81 Nicklas Lidstrom .10 .30
82 Vladimir Konstantinov .08 .25
83 Darren McCarty .03 .10
84 Kirk Maltby .03 .10
85 Vyacheslav Kozlov .03 .10
86 Martin Lapointe .03 .10
87 Doug Weight .08 .25
88 Mike Grier .03 .10
89 Curtis Joseph .10 .30
90 Andrei Kovalenko .03 .10
91 Rem Murray .03 .10
92 Ryan Smyth .08 .25
93 Mariusz Czerkawski .03 .10
94 Drew Bannister .03 .10
95 Jason Arnott .03 .10
96 Luke Richardson .03 .10
97 Dean McAmmond .03 .10
98 Kirk Muller .03 .10
99 Ray Sheppard .03 .10
100 Scott Mellanby .03 .10
101 Ed Jovanovski .08 .25
102 John Vanbiesbrouck .08 .25
103 Radek Dvorak .03 .10
104 Robert Svehla .03 .10
105 Rob Niedermayer .03 .10
106 Dave Nemirovsky .03 .10
107 Steve Washburn .03 .10
108 Bill Lindsay .03 .10
109 Kevin Dineen .03 .10
110 Keith Primeau .03 .10
111 Sean Burke .08 .25
112 Derek King .03 .10
113 Andrew Cassels .03 .10
114 Glen Wesley .03 .10
115 Nelson Emerson .03 .10
116 Geoff Sanderson .08 .25
117 Jeff O'Neill .03 .10
118 Kent Manderville .03 .10
119 Dimitri Khristich .03 .10
120 Ian Laperriere .03 .10
121 Aki Berg .03 .10
122 Vladimir Tsyplakov .03 .10
123 Vitali Yachmenev .03 .10
124 Roman Vopat .03 .10
125 Rob Blake .08 .25
126 Jan Vopat .03 .10
127 Jeff Shevalier RC .03 .10
128 Byron Dafoe .08 .25
129 Saku Koivu .10 .30
130 Vincent Damphousse .03 .10
131 Brian Savage .03 .10
132 Valeri Bure .03 .10
133 Mark Recchi .08 .25
134 Jocelyn Thibault .08 .25
135 Jose Theodore .12 .40
136 Dave Manson .03 .10
137 Shayne Corson .03 .10
138 Stephane Richer .03 .10
139 Doug Gilmour .08 .25
140 Scott Stevens .08 .25
141 Martin Brodeur .30 .75
142 Dave Andreychuk .03 .10
143 Bobby Holik .03 .10
144 Brian Rolston .03 .10
145 Jay Pandolfo .03 .10
146 John MacLean .03 .10
147 Bill Guerin .08 .25
148 Scott Niedermayer .03 .10
149 Denis Pederson .03 .10
150 Zigmund Palffy .08 .25
151 Robert Reichel .03 .10
152 Bryan Smolinski .03 .10
153 Eric Fichaud .08 .25
154 Todd Bertuzzi .10 .30
155 Bryan Berard .08 .25
156 Niklas Anderson .03 .10
157 Bryan McCabe .03 .10
158 Tommy Salo .08 .25
159 Kenny Jonsson .03 .10
160 Travis Green .03 .10
161 Mike Richter .10 .30
162 Brian Leetch .10 .30
163 Adam Graves .03 .10
164 Vladimir Vorobiev RC .03 .10
165 Niklas Sundstrom .03 .10
166 Russ Courtnall .03 .10
167 Wayne Gretzky .75 2.00
168 Mark Messier .10 .30
169 Alexander Karpovtsev .03 .10
170 Luc Robitaille .08 .25
171 Ulf Samuelsson .03 .10
172 Daniel Alfredsson .08 .25
173 Alexei Yashin .03 .10
174 Alexandre Daigle .03 .10
175 Andreas Dackell .03 .10
176 Wade Redden .03 .10
177 Sergei Zholtok .03 .10
178 Damian Rhodes .08 .25
179 Steve Duchesne .03 .10
180 Shawn McEachern .03 .10
181 Ron Tugnutt .08 .25
182 John Leclair .10 .30
183 Janne Niinimaa .08 .25
184 Mikael Renberg .08 .25
185 Vaclav Prospal RC .10 .30
186 Eric Lindros .10 .30
187 Dainius Zubrus .10 .30
188 Ron Hextall .08 .25
189 Paul Coffey .10 .30
190 Dale Hawerchuk .08 .25
191 Trent Klatt .03 .10
192 Rod Brind'Amour .08 .25
193 Nikolai Khabibulin .08 .25
194 Keith Tkachuk .08 .25
195 Jeremy Roenick .15 .40
196 Mike Gartner .08 .25
197 Dallas Drake .03 .10
198 Oleg Tverdovsky .03 .10
199 Cliff Ronning .03 .10
200 Teppo Numminen .03 .10
201 Craig Janney .03 .10
202 Deron Quint .03 .10
203 Jason Wooley .03 .10
204 Ron Francis .08 .25
205 Jaromir Jagr .20 .50
206 Greg Johnson .03 .10
207 Kevin Hatcher .03 .10
208 Patrick Lalime .08 .25
209 Petr Nedved .08 .25
210 Ken Wregget .08 .25
211 Darius Kasparaitis .03 .10
212 Stu Barnes .03 .10
213 Joe Dziedzic .03 .10
214 Owen Nolan .08 .25
215 Jeff Friesen .03 .10
216 Ed Belfour .10 .30
217 Viktor Kozlov .03 .10
218 Tony Granato .03 .10
219 Darren Turcotte .03 .10

220 Stephen Guolla RC .03 .10
221 Marty McSorley .03 .10
222 Marcus Ragnarsson .03 .10
223 Al Iafrate .03 .10
224 Brett Hull .15 .40
225 Grant Fuhr .08 .25
226 Pierre Turgeon .08 .25
227 Geoff Courtnall .03 .10
228 Jim Campbell .03 .10
229 Harry York .03 .10
230 Tony Twist .08 .25
231 Joe Murphy .03 .10
232 Pavol Demitra .08 .25
233 Chris Pronger .08 .25
234 Al MacInnis .08 .25
235 Daren Puppa .08 .25
236 Chris Gratton .08 .25
237 Dino Ciccarelli .03 .10
238 Rob Zamuner .03 .10
239 Igor Ulanov .03 .10
240 Roman Hamrlik .03 .10
241 Alexander Selivanov .03 .10
242 Patrick Poulin .03 .10
243 Daymond Langkow .08 .25
244 Corey Schwab .08 .25
245 Mats Sundin .10 .30
246 Wendel Clark .08 .25
247 Sergei Berezin .03 .10
248 Steve Sullivan .03 .10
249 Fredrik Modin .03 .10
250 Darby Hendrickson .03 .10
251 Jason Podollan .03 .10
252 Felix Potvin .10 .30
253 Tie Domi .08 .25
254 Todd Warriner .03 .10
255 Pavel Bure .10 .30
256 Alexander Mogilny .08 .25
257 Martin Gelinas .03 .10
258 Corey Hirsch .08 .25
259 Trevor Linden .08 .25
260 Mike Sillinger .03 .10
261 Markus Naslund .10 .30
262 Jyrki Lumme .03 .10
263 Gino Odjick .03 .10
264 Mike Ridley .03 .10
265 Dave Roberts .03 .10
266 Adam Oates .08 .25
267 Bill Ranford .08 .25
268 Joe Juneau .08 .25
269 Chris Simon .03 .10
270 Peter Bondra .08 .25
271 Dale Hunter .03 .10
272 Jaroslav Svejkovski .08 .25
273 Sergei Gonchar .03 .10
274 Steve Konowalchuk .03 .10
275 Phil Housley .03 .10
276 Angela James RC .40 1.00
277 Nancy Drolet RC .03 .10
278 Lesley Reddon RC .40 1.00
279 Hayley Wickenheiser RC 1.00 2.50
280 Vicky Sunohara RC .60 1.50
281 Cassie Campbell RC .75 2.00
282 Geraldine Heaney RC .03 .10
283 Judy Diduck RC .03 .10
284 France St. Louis RC .03 .10
285 Danielle Goyette RC .03 .10
286 Therese Brisson RC .03 .10
287 Stacey Wilson RC .03 .10
288 Danielle Dube RC .03 .10
289 Jayna Hefford RC .60 1.50
290 Luce Letendre RC .03 .10
291 Lori Dupuis RC .03 .10
292 Rebecca Fahey RC .03 .10
293 Fiona Smith RC .03 .10
294 Laura Schuler RC .03 .10
295 Karen Nystrom RC .03 .10
296 Joe Thornton .30 .75
297 Peter Schaefer .20 .50
298 Daniel Tkaczuk .15 .40
299 Alyn McCauley .08 .25
300 Shane Willis .03 .10
301 Chris Phillips .03 .10
302 Marc Denis .08 .25
303 Jason Ward .03 .10
304 Patrick Marleau .20 .50
305 Brad Isbister .03 .10
306 Cameron Mann .15 .40
307 Daniel Cleary .08 .25
308 Brad Larsen .03 .10
309 Nick Boynton .08 .25
310 Scott Barney .08 .25
311 Boyd Devereaux .03 .10
312 Wayne Gretzky CL .10 .30
313 Steve Yzerman CL .10 .30
314 Jaromir Jagr CL .10 .30
315 Jarome Iginla CL .10 .30
316 Patrick Roy CL .10 .30
317 John Vanbiesbrouck CL .08 .25
318 Paul Kariya CL .10 .30
319 Doug Weight CL .03 .10
320 Mats Sundin CL .08 .25

1997-98 Collector's Choice Blow-Ups

Very little is known about this oversized set that consisted of 5 cards other than the two mentioned below. Cards were numbered "X of 5" on the card backs. Any further inofrmation can be sent to hockeymag@beckett.com

1 Wayne Gretzky
2 Tony Amonte

1997-98 Collector's Choice Crash the Game

Randomly inserted in packs at the rate of 1:5, this 90-card set features color player photos. If the pictured player scores against the designated team, the card could be redeemed for a special high quality redemption card of that player (expired 7/1/1998).

COMPLETE SET (90) 15.00 30.00
COMP.EXCH.SET (30) 25.00 50.00
*EXCH.CARDS: 2X TO 4X BASIC INSERTS
C1A Wayne Gretzky 1.50 4.00
C1B Wayne Gretzky 1.50 4.00
C1C Wayne Gretzky 1.50 4.00
C2A Mike Modano .40 1.00
C2B Mike Modano .40 1.00
C2C Mike Modano .40 1.00
C3A Doug Weight .25 .60
C3B Doug Weight .25 .60
C3C Doug Weight .25 .60
C4A Brendan Shanahan .25 .60
C4B Brendan Shanahan .75 2.00
C4C Brendan Shanahan .75 2.00
C5A Ray Sheppard .15 .40
C5B Ray Sheppard .15 .40
C5C Ray Sheppard PHO .15 4.00
C6A Keith Primeau .15 .40
C6B Keith Primeau .15 .40
C6C Keith Primeau .15 .40
C7A Ray Bourque CHI L .40 1.00
C7B Ray Bourque .40 1.00
C7C Ray Bourque .40 1.00
C8A Teemu Selanne .25 .60
C8B Teemu Selanne .25 .60
C8C Teemu Selanne .25 .60
C9A Paul Kariya .25 .60
C9B Paul Kariya .25 .60
C9C Paul Kariya TB .25 .60
C10A Tony Amonte .20 .50
C10B Tony Amonte .20 .50
C10C Tony Amonte .20 .50
C11A Saku Koivu .40 1.00
C11B Saku Koivu .40 1.00
C11C Saku Koivu .40 1.00
C12A Donald Audette .15 .40
C12B Donald Audette .15 .40
C12C Donald Audette .15 .40
C13A Doug Gilmour .40 1.00
C13B Doug Gilmour STL .40 1.00
C13C Doug Gilmour .40 1.00
C14A Theo Fleury .25 .60
C14B Theo Fleury FLO .25 .60
C14C Theo Fleury .25 .60
C15A Alexei Yashin COL .08 .20
C15B Alexei Yashin .08 .20
C15C Alexei Yashin .08 .20
C16A Zigmund Palffy .50 1.25
C16B Zigmund Palffy .50 1.25
C16C Zigmund Palffy .50 1.25
C17A Dimitri Khristich .25 .60
C17B Dimitri Khristich .25 .60
C17C Dimitri Khristich .25 .60
C18A Joe Sakic 1.00 2.50
C18B Joe Sakic 1.00 2.50
C18C Joe Sakic 1.00 2.50
C19A Steve Yzerman 2.00 5.00
C19B Steve Yzerman 2.00 5.00
C19C Steve Yzerman 2.00 5.00
C20A Eric Lindros .25 .60
C20B Eric Lindros .40 1.00
C20C Eric Lindros .40 1.00
C21A Peter Forsberg FLO .60 1.50
C21B Peter Forsberg .60 1.50
C21C Peter Forsberg .60 1.50
C22A Dino Ciccarelli .15 .40
C22B Dino Ciccarelli .15 .40
C22C Dino Ciccarelli .15 .40
C23A Mats Sundin .25 .60
C23B Mats Sundin .25 .60
C23C Mats Sundin .25 .60
C24A Pavel Bure .25 .60
C24B Pavel Bure .40 1.00
C24C Pavel Bure .40 1.00
C25A Peter Bondra CHI .25 .60
C25B Peter Bondra .25 .60
C25C Peter Bondra .25 .60
C26A Brett Hull .30 .75
C26B Brett Hull .30 .75
C26C Brett Hull .30 .75
C27A Keith Tkachuk BOS .30 .75
C27B Keith Tkachuk .30 .75
C27C Keith Tkachuk .30 .75
C28A Jaromir Jagr .40 1.00
C28B Jaromir Jagr .40 1.00
C28C Jaromir Jagr .40 1.00
C29A Jarome Iginla .30 .75
C29B Jarome Iginla .30 .75
C29C Jarome Iginla .30 .75
C30A Owen Nolan .15 .40
C30B Owen Nolan .15 .40
C30C Owen Nolan NYI L .15 .40

1997-98 Collector's Choice Magic Men

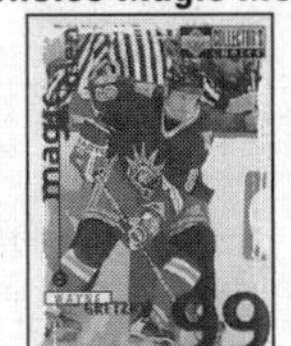

Randomly inserted in Canadian packs at the rate of 1:32, this 10-card set features five color photos each of Wayne Gretzky and Patrick Roy.

COMMON GRETZKY (MM1-MM5) 5.00 10.00
COMMON ROY (MM6-MM10) 4.00 8.00

1997-98 Collector's Choice Star Quest

This 90-card, four-tier insert set features color photos of some of the top NHL Superstars printed using the hobby's top

technology. The 45 cards in Tier One (SQ1-SQ45) were randomly inserted one in every pack; the 20 cards in Tier Two (SQ45-SQ65) were randomly inserted 1:21 packs; the 15 cards of Tier Three (SQ66-SQ80) were randomly inserted 1:71 packs; the 10 cards of Tier Four were randomly inserted 1:145 packs.

COMPLETE SET (90) 125.00 250.00
SQ1 Bryan Berard .15 .40
SQ2 Robert Svehla .08 .20
SQ3 Petr Nedved .15 .40
SQ4 Steve Sullivan .08 .20
SQ5 Nicklas Lidstrom .20 .50
SQ6 Wade Redden .08 .20
SQ7 Jason Arnott .08 .20
SQ8 Martin Gelinas .08 .20
SQ9 Mikael Renberg .08 .20
SQ10 Jeff Friesen .08 .20
SQ11 Chris Chelios .20 .50
SQ12 Jarome Iginla .25 .60
SQ13 Vyacheslav Kozlov .08 .20
SQ14 Brian Holzinger .08 .20
SQ15 Eric Daze .15 .40
SQ16 Pat Verbeek .08 .20
SQ17 Jozef Stumpel .15 .40
SQ18 Rob Niedermayer .15 .40
SQ19 Sergei Fedorov .30 .75
SQ20 Brian Leetch .20 .50
SQ21 Bill Guerin .08 .20
SQ22 Dino Ciccarelli .08 .20
SQ23 Adam Oates .15 .40
SQ24 Mike Grier .08 .20
SQ25 Alexandre Daigle .08 .20
SQ26 Janne Niinimaa .15 .40
SQ27 Dimitri Khristich .08 .20
SQ28 Oleg Tverdovsky .08 .20
SQ29 Felix Potvin .20 .50
SQ30 Mike Richter .20 .50
SQ31 Curtis Joseph .20 .50
SQ32 Vincent Damphousse .08 .20
SQ33 Vladimir Konstantinov .15 .40
SQ34 Andy Moog .15 .40
SQ35 Nikolai Khabibulin .15 .40
SQ36 Ed Belfour .20 .50
SQ37 Scott Mellanby .08 .20
SQ38 Sandis Ozolinsh .08 .20
SQ39 Travis Green .08 .20
SQ40 Patrick Lalime .15 .40
SQ41 Niklas Sundstrom .08 .20
SQ42 Guy Hebert .15 .40
SQ43 Vitali Yachmenev .08 .20
SQ44 Roman Hamrlik .08 .20
SQ45 Adam Deadmarsh .08 .20
SQ46 Alexei Zhamnov .75 1.50
SQ47 Saku Koivu 1.25 3.00
SQ48 Sergei Berezin 1.00 2.50
SQ49 Mark Messier 1.25 3.00
SQ50 Martin Brodeur 3.00 8.00
SQ51 Daniel Alfredsson 1.00 2.50
SQ52 John LeClair 1.25 3.00
SQ53 Mike Vernon 1.00 2.50
SQ54 Ron Francis 1.00 2.50
SQ55 Keith Primeau .75 1.50
SQ56 Pierre Turgeon 1.00 2.50
SQ57 Jim Carey 1.00 2.50
SQ58 Peter Bondra 1.00 2.50
SQ59 Pavel Bure 1.25 3.00
SQ60 Ray Sheppard .75 1.50
SQ61 Chris Gratton 1.00 2.50
SQ62 Derek Plante .75 1.50
SQ63 Joe Sakic 2.50 6.00
SQ64 Theo Fleury .75 1.50
SQ65 Tony Amonte 1.00 2.50
SQ66 Zigmund Palffy 2.00 5.00
SQ67 Steve Yzerman 10.00 25.00
SQ68 Doug Weight 2.00 5.00
SQ69 Alexander Mogilny 2.00 5.00
SQ70 Doug Gilmour 2.50 5.00
SQ71 Peter Forsberg 6.00 15.00
SQ72 Alexei Yashin 2.00 5.00
SQ73 Geoff Sanderson 2.00 5.00
SQ74 Brendan Shanahan 2.50 6.00
SQ75 Mark Recchi 2.00 5.00
SQ76 Brett Hull 3.00 8.00
SQ77 Ray Bourque 4.00 10.00
SQ78 Owen Nolan 2.00 5.00
SQ79 Jeremy Roenick 3.00 8.00
SQ80 Teemu Selanne 2.50 6.00
SQ81 Dominik Hasek 6.00 15.00
SQ82 Mike Modano 4.00 10.00
SQ83 Mats Sundin 4.00 10.00
SQ84 John Vanbiesbrouck 4.00 10.00
SQ85 Paul Kariya 2.50 6.00
SQ86 Patrick Roy 10.00 25.00
SQ87 Keith Tkachuk 4.00 10.00
SQ88 Eric Lindros 4.00 10.00
SQ89 Jaromir Jagr 6.00 15.00
SQ90 Wayne Gretzky 15.00 40.00

1997-98 Collector's Choice Stick'Ums

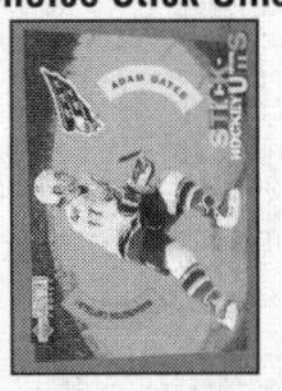

Randomly inserted in packs at the rate of 1:3, this 30-card set features color action player photos printed on re-stickable stickers that stick anywhere.

COMPLETE SET (30) 15.00 30.00
S1 Wayne Gretzky 2.50 5.00
S2 John Vanbiesbrouck .30 .60
S3 Martin Brodeur 1.00 2.00
S4 Rob Blake .30 .60
S5 Saku Koivu .40 .75
S6 Curtis Joseph .40 .75
S7 Chris Chelios .40 .75
S8 Mike Modano .60 1.25
S9 Paul Kariya .40 .75
S10 Eric Lindros .40 .75
S11 Daniel Alfredsson .30 .60
S12 Jarome Iginla .50 1.00
S13 Jeremy Roenick .50 1.00
S14 Brendan Shanahan .40 .75
S15 Jaromir Jagr .60 1.25
S16 Zigmund Palffy .30 .60
S17 Mats Sundin .40 .75
S18 Teemu Selanne .40 .75
S19 Joe Sakic .75 1.50
S20 Ed Belfour .40 .75
S21 Peter Forsberg 1.00 2.00
S22 Dino Ciccarelli .15 .25
S23 Patrick Roy 2.00 4.00
S24 Doug Gilmour .30 .60
S25 Pavel Bure .40 .75
S26 Brett Hull .50 1.00
S27 Ray Bourque .60 1.25
S28 Adam Oates .30 .60
S29 Steve Yzerman 2.00 4.00
S30 Dominik Hasek .75 1.50

1997-98 Collector's Choice World Domination

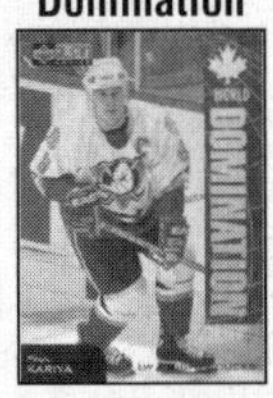

Randomly inserted in Canadian packs at the rate of 1:4, this 20-card set features color photos of top players. The backs carry player information.

COMPLETE SET (20) 25.00 50.00
W1 Wayne Gretzky 5.00 12.00
W2 Mark Messier .75 2.00
W3 Steve Yzerman 4.00 10.00
W4 Brendan Shanahan .75 2.00
W5 Paul Kariya .75 2.00
W6 Joe Sakic 1.50 4.00
W7 Eric Lindros .75 2.00
W8 Rod Brind'Amour .60 1.50
W9 Keith Primeau .60 1.50
W10 Trevor Linden .60 1.50
W11 Theo Fleury .60 1.50
W12 Scott Niedermeyer .60 1.50
W13 Rob Blake .60 1.50
W14 Chris Pronger .60 1.50
W15 Eric Desjardins .60 1.50
W16 Adam Foote .60 1.50
W17 Scott Stevens .60 1.50
W18 Patrick Roy 4.00 10.00
W19 Curtis Joseph .75 2.00
W20 Martin Brodeur 2.00 5.00

1996-97 Coyotes Coca-Cola

This set features the Coyotes of the NHL. The postcard-sized set was issued for autograph sessions and other personal appearances by team players. There are multiple versions of the cards of some players. These cards features different front photos, but identical backs.

COMPLETE SET (37) 10.00 25.00
1 Bob Corkum .20 .50
2 Shane Doan .60 1.50
3 Dallas Drake .20 .50
4 Dallas Eakins .20 .50
5 Mike Eastwood .20 .50
6 Jeff Finley .20 .50
7 Mike Gartner .30 .75
8 Mike Gartner .30 .75
9 Mike Hudson .20 .50
10 Craig Janney .20 .50
11 Jim Johnson .20 .50
12 Nikolai Khabibulin .60 1.50
13 Nikolai Khabibulin .60 1.50
14 Chad Kilger .20 .50
15 Kris King .20 .50
16 Kris King .20 .50
17 Igor Korolev .20 .50
18 Norm Maciver .20 .50
19 Dave Manson .20 .50
20 Brad McCrimmon .20 .50
21 Jim McKenzie .20 .50
22 Teppo Numminen .30 .75
23 Deron Quint .20 .50
24 Jeremy Roenick .80 2.00
25 Jeremy Roenick .80 2.00
26 Jeremy Roenick .80 2.00
27 Cliff Ronning .20 .50
28 Darrin Shannon .20 .50
29 Mike Stapleton .20 .50
30 Keith Tkachuk .80 2.00
31 Keith Tkachuk .80 2.00
32 Oleg Tverdovsky .20 .50
33 Darcy Wakaluk .24 .60
34 Zinetula Bilyaletinov CO .10 .25
34 Don Hay CO .10 .25
34 Paul MacLean CO .10 .25
36 Team Photo .20 .50

2001-02 Coyotes Team Issue

This set features the Phoenix Coyotes. This set was given away a few cards at a time at various home games, as well as at player autograph appearances. The oversized cards measure approximately 3 X 6. It is believed the checklist is complete, but due to the nature of the distribution, there may be other singles out there. If you discover one, please contact us at hockeymag@beckett.com.

COMPLETE SET (22) 10.00 25.00
1 Drake Berehowsky .40 1.00
2 Sergei Berezin .40 1.00
3 Daniel Briere .80 2.00
4 Sean Burke .80 2.00
5 Shane Doan .80 2.00
6 Robert Esche .80 2.00
7 Michal Handzus .40 1.00
8 Mike Johnson .40 1.00
9 Krys Kolanos 1.20 3.00
10 Daymond Langkow .80 2.00
11 Claude Lemieux .40 1.00
12 Paul Mara .40 1.00
13 Daniil Markov .40 1.00
14 Brad May .40 1.00
15 Ladislav Nagy .40 1.00
16 Teppo Numminen .40 1.00
17 Denis Pederson .40 1.00
18 Todd Simpson .40 1.00
19 Radoslav Suchy .40 1.00
20 Mike Sullivan .40 1.00
21 Ossi Vaananen .60 1.00
22 Landon Wilson .40 1.00

2002-03 Coyotes Team Issue

Cards were issued by the team in an unknown fashion. Cards are oversized (3X6), unnumbered and are blank backed.

COMPLETE SET (25) 15.00 30.00
1 Header .10 .25
2 Todd Simpson .40 1.00
3 Ossi Vaananen .40 1.00
4 Drake Berehowsky .40 1.00
5 Deron Quint .40 1.00
6 Daymond Langkow .60 1.50
7 Mike Johnson .40 1.00
8 Radoslav Suchy .40 1.00
9 Kelly Buchberger .40 1.00
10 Ladislav Nagy .75 2.00
11 Shane Doan .75 2.00
12 Paul Mara .40 1.00
13 Teppo Numminen .40 1.00
14 Landon Wilson .40 1.00
15 Branko Radivojevic .60 1.50
16 Brian Boucher .60 1.50
17 Krys Kolanos .40 1.00
18 Andrei Nazarov .40 1.00
19 Brian Savage .40 1.00
20 Danny Markov .40 1.00
21 Sean Burke .75 2.00
22 Benoit Allaire ACO .10 .25
23 Pat Conacher ACO .10 .25
24 Rick Bowness ACO .10 .25
25 Bob Francis CO .10 .25
26 Scott Pellerin .40 1.00
27 Paul Ranheim .40 1.00
28 Zac Bierk .60 1.50
29 Tony Amonte .75 2.00
30 Charlie Simmer ANN .20 .50
31 Curt Keilback ANN .10 .25
32 Ramzi Abid .40 1.00
33 Dan Focht .40 1.00
34 Daniel Briere .75 2.00
35 Brad May .40 1.00

2003-04 Coyotes Postcards

This checklist may be incomplete. Send additional info to hockeymag@beckett.com.

COMPLETE SET (27) 10.00 20.00
1 Zac Bierk .40 1.00
2 Brian Boucher .30 .75
3 Sean Burke .40 1.00
4 Daniel Cleary .20 .50
5 Shane Doan 1.00 2.50
6 Brad Ference .20 .50
7 Dave Tanabe .20 .50
8 Jan Hrdina .20 .50
9 Cale Hulse .20 .50
10 Mike Johnson .20 .50
11 Krystofer Kolanos .20 .50
12 Daymond Langkow .30 .75
13 Paul Mara .20 .50
14 Ladislav Nagy .60 1.50
15 Tyson Nash .40 1.00
16 Andrei Nazarov .20 .50
17 Ivan Novoseltsev .20 .50
18 Branko Radivojevic .40 1.00
19 Brian Savage .20 .50
20 Mike Sillinger .20 .50
21 Fredrik Sjostrom .30 .75
22 Matthew Spiller .20 .50
23 Radoslav Suchy .20 .50
24 Jeff Taffe .20 .50
25 Dave Tanabe .20 .50
26 Ossi Vaananen .20 .50
27 Landon Wilson .20 .50

1924-25 Crescent Falcon-Tigers

The 1924-25 Crescent Ice Cream Falcon-Tigers set contains 13 black and white cards measuring approximately 1 9/16" by 2 3/8". The back has the card number (at the top) and two offers: 1) a brick of ice cream to any person bringing to the Crescent Ice Cream plant any 14 Crescent Hockey Pictures bearing consecutive numbers; and 2) a hockey stick to anyone bringing to the ice cream plant three sets of Crescent Hockey Pictures bearing consecutive numbers from 1-14. The complete set price below does not include the unknown card 6, which is believed to have been short printed.

COMPLETE SET (13) 1200.00 2400.00
1 Bill Cockburn 112.50 225.00
2 Wally Byron 100.00 200.00
3 Wally Fridfinson 100.00 200.00
4 Murray Murdoch 125.00 250.00
5 Oliver Redpath 100.00 200.00
7 Ward McVey 100.00 200.00
8 Tote Mitchell 100.00 200.00
9 Lorne Carrol 100.00 200.00
10 Tony Wise 100.00 200.00
11 Johnny Myres 100.00 200.00
12 Gordon McKenzie 100.00 200.00
13 Harry Neal 112.50 225.00
14 Blake Watson 112.50 225.00

1923-24 Crescent Selkirks

The 1923-24 Crescent Ice Cream set contains 14 cards measuring approximately 1 9/16" by 2 3/8". The set features the Selkirks hockey club and was produced by Crescent Ice Cream of Winnipeg, Manitoba. The front shows a black and white head and shoulders shot of the player, with the team name written in a crescent over the player's head. At the bottom of the picture, the player's name and position appear in white lettering in a black stripe. The back has the card number (at the top) and two offers: 1) a brick of ice cream to any person bringing to the Crescent Ice Cream plant any 14 Crescent Hockey Pictures bearing consecutive numbers; and 2) a hockey stick to anyone bringing to the ice cream plant three sets of Crescent Hockey Pictures bearing consecutive numbers from 1-14. The complete set price below does not include the unknown card number 6.

COMPLETE SET (13) 600.00 1200.00
1 Cliff O'Meara 62.50 125.00
2 Leo Benard 50.00 100.00
3 Pete Speirs 50.00 100.00
4 Howard Brandon 50.00 100.00
5 George A. Clark 50.00 100.00
7 Cecil Browne 50.00 100.00
8 Jack Connelly 50.00 100.00
9 Charlie Gardner 100.00 200.00
10 Ward Turvey 50.00 100.00
11 Connie Johanneson 50.00 100.00
12 Frank Woodall 50.00 100.00
13 Harold McMunn 50.00 100.00
14 Connie Neil 62.50 125.00

1924-25 Crescent Selkirks

The 1924-25 Crescent Ice Cream Selkirks set contains 14 black and white cards measuring approximately 1 9/16" by 2 3/8". The back has the card number (at the top) and two offers: 1) a brick of ice cream to any person bringing to the Crescent Ice Cream plant any 14 Crescent Hockey Pictures bearing consecutive numbers; and 2) a hockey stick to anyone bringing to the ice cream plant three sets of Crescent Hockey Pictures bearing consecutive numbers from 1-14.

COMPLETE SET (14) 850.00 1700.00
1 Howard Brandon 50.00 100.00
2 Jack Hughes 50.00 100.00
3 Tony Baril 50.00 100.00
4 Bill Bowman 50.00 100.00
5 W. Roberts 50.00 100.00
6 Cecil Browne SP 375.00 750.00
7 Errol Gillis 50.00 100.00
8 Selkirks Team 100.00 200.00
On The Ice
9 Fred Comfort 50.00 100.00
10 Cliff O'Meara 50.00 100.00
11 Leo Benard 50.00 100.00
12 Pete Speirs 50.00 100.00
13 Peter Meurer 50.00 100.00
14 Bill Borland 50.00 100.00

1997-98 Crown Royale

The 1997-98 Pacific Crown Royale set was issued in one series totaling 144 cards and was distributed in four-card packs. The fronts features color player images printed on an all-die-cut crown format. The backs carry player information.

COMPLETE SET (144) 40.00 100.00
1 Guy Hebert .40 1.00
2 Paul Kariya .60 1.50
3 Steve Rucchin .20 .50
4 Tomas Sandstrom .20 .50
5 Teemu Selanne .60 1.50
6 Jason Allison .20 .50
7 Ray Bourque 1.00 2.50
8 Anson Carter .40 1.00
9 Byron Dafoe .40 1.00
10 Ted Donato .20 .50
11 Joe Thornton 1.50 4.00
12 Jason Dawe .20 .50
13 Michal Grosek .20 .50
14 Dominik Hasek 1.25 3.00
15 Michael Peca .20 .50
16 Miroslav Satan .20 .50
17 Chris Dingman RC .20 .50
18 Theo Fleury .20 .50
19 Jarome Iginla .75 2.00
20 Tyler Moss RC .20 .50
21 Cory Stillman .20 .50
22 Kevin Dineen .20 .50
23 Nelson Emerson .20 .50
24 Trevor Kidd .40 1.00
25 Keith Primeau .40 1.00
26 Geoff Sanderson .20 .50
27 Tony Amonte .40 1.00
28 Chris Chelios .60 1.50
29 Eric Daze .20 .50
30 Jeff Hackett .40 1.00
31 Chris Terreri .40 1.00
32 Adam Deadmarsh .20 .50
33 Peter Forsberg 1.00 2.50
34 Valeri Kamensky .20 .50
35 Jari Kurri .40 1.00
36 Claude Lemieux .20 .50
37 Patrick Roy 2.00 5.00
38 Joe Sakic 1.25 3.00
39 Ed Belfour .60 1.50
40 Derian Hatcher .20 .50
41 Mike Modano 1.00 2.50
42 Joe Nieuwendyk .40 1.00
43 Pat Verbeek .20 .50
44 Sergei Zubov .20 .50
45 Sergei Fedorov 1.00 2.50
46 Vyacheslav Kozlov .20 .50
47 Nicklas Lidstrom .60 1.50
48 Darren McCarty .20 .50
49 Chris Osgood .40 1.00
50 Brendan Shanahan .60 1.50
51 Steve Yzerman 2.00 5.00
52 Jason Arnott .20 .50
53 Curtis Joseph .60 1.50
54 Ryan Smyth .40 1.00
55 Doug Weight .40 1.00
56 Dave Gagner .20 .50
57 Ed Jovanovski .40 1.00
58 Viktor Kozlov .20 .50
59 Scott Mellanby .20 .50
60 John Vanbiesbrouck .40 1.00
61 Kevin Weekes RC .60 1.50
62 Rob Blake .40 1.00
63 Donald MacLean .20 .50
64 Yanic Perreault .20 .50
65 Luc Robitaille .40 1.00
66 Jozef Stumpel .20 .50
67 Shayne Corson .20 .50
68 Vincent Damphousse .20 .50
69 Saku Koivu .60 1.50
70 Andy Moog .40 1.00
71 Mark Recchi .40 1.00
72 Stephane Richer .20 .50
73 Martin Brodeur 1.50 4.00
74 Patrik Elias RC 1.25 3.00
75 Doug Gilmour .40 1.00
76 Bobby Holik .20 .50
77 Scott Stevens .40 1.00
78 Bryan Berard .20 .50
79 Zigmund Palffy .40 1.00
80 Robert Reichel .20 .50
81 Tommy Salo .40 1.00
82 Bryan Smolinski .20 .50
83 Adam Graves .20 .50
84 Wayne Gretzky 3.00 8.00
85 Pat LaFontaine .60 1.50
86 Brian Leetch .60 1.50
87 Mike Richter .60 1.50
88 Niklas Sundstrom .20 .50
89 Daniel Alfredsson .40 1.00
90 Alexandre Daigle .20 .50
91 Shawn McEachern .20 .50
92 Chris Phillips .20 .50
93 Ron Tugnutt .40 1.00
94 Alexei Yashin .20 .50
95 Rod Brind'Amour .40 1.00
96 Chris Gratton .20 .50
97 Ron Hextall .40 1.00
98 John LeClair .60 1.50
99 Eric Lindros .60 1.50
100 Vaclav Prospal RC .60 1.50
101 Dainius Zubrus .60 1.50
102 Mike Gartner .40 1.00
103 Brad Isbister .20 .50
104 Nikolai Khabibulin .40 1.00
105 Jeremy Roenick .75 2.00
106 Cliff Ronning .20 .50
107 Keith Tkachuk .60 1.50

108 Tom Barrasso .40 1.00
109 Ron Francis .40 1.00
110 Jaromir Jagr 1.00 2.50
111 Alexei Morozov .20 .50
112 Ed Olczyk .20 .50
113 Jim Campbell .20 .50
114 Pavol Demitra .40 1.00
115 Steve Duchesne .20 .50
116 Grant Fuhr .40 1.00
117 Brett Hull .75 2.00
118 Pierre Turgeon .40 1.00
119 Jeff Friesen .20 .50
120 Patrick Marleau .60 1.50
121 Owen Nolan .40 1.00
122 Marco Sturm RC 1.00 2.50
123 Mike Vernon .40 1.00
124 Dino Ciccarelli .20 .50
125 Roman Hamrlik .20 .50
126 Daren Puppa .40 1.00
127 Paul Ysebaert .20 .50
128 Sergei Berezin .20 .50
129 Wendel Clark .40 1.00
130 Alyn McCauley .20 .50
131 Felix Potvin .60 1.50
132 Mats Sundin .60 1.50
133 Pavel Bure .60 1.50
134 Martin Gelinas .20 .50
135 Trevor Linden .40 1.00
136 Mark Messier .60 1.50
137 Alexander Mogilny .40 1.00
138 Peter Bondra .40 1.00
139 Dale Hunter .20 .50
140 Joe Juneau .20 .50
141 Olaf Kolzig .40 1.00
142 Adam Oates .40 1.00
143 Jaroslav Svejkovsky .20 .50
144 Richard Zednik .20 .50

1997-98 Crown Royale Emerald Green

Randomly inserted in Canadian packs only at the rate of 4:25, this 144-card set is a parallel version of the base set with green foil highlights.
*STARS: 2.5X TO 5X BASIC CARDS
*RC's: 1.5X TO 3X BASIC CARDS

1997-98 Crown Royale Ice Blue

Randomly inserted in packs at the rate of 1:25, this 144-card set is a parallel version of the base set with blue foil highlights.
*STARS: 10X TO 20X BASIC CARDS
RC's: 4X TO 10X BASIC CARDS

1997-98 Crown Royale Silver

Randomly inserted in U.S. packs only at the rate of 4:25, this 144-card set is a parallel version of the base set with silver foil highlights.
*STARS: 2.5X TO 5X BASIC CARDS
*RC's: 1.5X TO 3X BASIC CARDS

1997-98 Crown Royale Blades of Steel Die-Cuts

Randomly inserted in packs at the rate of 1:49, this 20-card set features color images of top NHL players on a laser-cut and die-cut skate background.
COMPLETE SET (20) 50.00 125.00
1 Paul Kariya 2.00 5.00
2 Teemu Selanne 2.00 5.00
3 Joe Thornton 4.00 10.00
4 Chris Chelios 1.50 4.00
5 Peter Forsberg 4.00 10.00
6 Patrick Roy 10.00 25.00
7 Mike Modano 2.50 6.00
8 Sergei Fedorov 2.50 6.00
9 Brendan Shanahan 2.00 5.00
10 Steve Yzerman 8.00 20.00
11 Ryan Smyth 1.50 4.00
12 Saku Koivu 2.00 5.00
13 Bryan Berard .75 2.00
14 Wayne Gretzky 12.00 30.00
15 Brian Leetch 1.50 4.00
16 Eric Lindros 2.00 5.00
17 Jaromir Jagr 4.00 10.00
18 Brett Hull 2.50 6.00
19 Pavel Bure 2.00 5.00
20 Mark Messier 2.50 6.00

1997-98 Crown Royale Cramer's Choice Jumbos

Inserted one per box, this ten-card set features top NHL Hockey players as chosen by Pacific President and CEO, Michael Cramer. The fronts display a color action player cut-out on a pyramid die-cut shaped background printed on a premium-sized card.
COMPLETE SET (10) 15.00 40.00
UNPRICED SIGNED PARALLELS #'d OF 10 EXIST
1 Paul Kariya 1.50 4.00
2 Teemu Selanne 1.25 3.00
3 Joe Thornton 2.50 6.00
4 Peter Forsberg 1.50 4.00
5 Patrick Roy 3.00 8.00
6 Steve Yzerman 2.50 6.00
7 Wayne Gretzky 4.00 10.00
8 Eric Lindros 1.25 3.00
9 Jaromir Jagr 1.50 4.00
10 Pavel Bure 1.25 3.00

1997-98 Crown Royale Freeze Out Die-Cuts

Randomly inserted in packs at the rate of 1:25, this 20-card set features color action photos of top goalies on a background of shattering ice and printed on a die-cut card.
COMPLETE SET (20) 30.00 80.00
1 Guy Hebert 1.00 2.50
2 Byron Dafoe 1.00 2.50
3 Dominik Hasek 4.00 10.00
4 Tyler Moss 1.00 2.50
5 Patrick Roy 10.00 25.00
6 Ed Belfour 2.00 5.00
7 Chris Osgood 1.00 2.50
8 Curtis Joseph 2.00 5.00
9 John Vanbiesbrouck 2.00 5.00
10 Andy Moog 2.00 5.00
11 Martin Brodeur 6.00 15.00
12 Mike Richter 2.00 5.00
13 Ron Hextall 2.00 5.00
14 Garth Snow 1.00 2.50
15 Nikolai Khabibulin 2.00 5.00
16 Tom Barrasso 1.00 2.50
17 Grant Fuhr 2.00 5.00
18 Mike Vernon 2.00 5.00
19 Felix Potvin 2.00 5.00
20 Olaf Kolzig 2.00 5.00

1997-98 Crown Royale Hat Tricks Die-Cuts

Randomly inserted in packs at the rate of 1:25, this 20-card set features color photos of top NHL scorers printed on a hat-shaped die-cut card.
COMPLETE SET (20) 40.00 100.00
1 Paul Kariya 2.50 6.00
2 Teemu Selanne 2.50 6.00
3 Joe Thornton 4.00 10.00
4 Peter Forsberg 4.00 10.00
5 Joe Sakic 5.00 12.00
6 Mike Modano 4.00 10.00
7 Brendan Shanahan 2.50 6.00
8 Steve Yzerman 6.00 15.00
9 Ryan Smyth 1.50 4.00
10 Zigmund Palffy 1.50 4.00
11 Wayne Gretzky 10.00 25.00
12 John LeClair 1.50 4.00
13 Eric Lindros 2.00 5.00
14 Keith Tkachuk 1.50 4.00
15 Jaromir Jagr 4.00 10.00
16 Brett Hull 3.00 8.00
17 Mats Sundin 2.00 5.00
18 Pavel Bure 2.00 5.00
19 Mark Messier 2.00 5.00
20 Peter Bondra 1.50 4.00

1997-98 Crown Royale Lamplighters Cel-Fusion Die-Cuts

Randomly inserted in packs at the rate of 1:73, this 20-card set features color photos of the NHL's top goal scorers with a net and goal light as background and printed on a die-cut cel-fusion card.
COMPLETE SET (20) 60.00 150.00
1 Paul Kariya 2.00 5.00
2 Teemu Selanne 2.00 5.00
3 Joe Thornton 6.00 15.00
4 Michael Peca 1.00 2.50
5 Peter Forsberg 6.00 15.00
6 Joe Sakic 8.00 20.00
7 Mike Modano 4.00 10.00
8 Brendan Shanahan 2.00 5.00
9 Steve Yzerman 12.00 30.00
10 Saku Koivu 2.00 5.00
11 Wayne Gretzky 20.00 50.00
12 Pat LaFontaine 1.00 2.50
13 John LeClair 1.00 2.50
14 Eric Lindros 2.00 5.00
15 Dainius Zubrus 1.00 2.50
16 Keith Tkachuk 2.00 5.00
17 Jaromir Jagr 6.00 15.00
18 Brett Hull 2.00 5.00
19 Pavel Bure 2.00 5.00
20 Mark Messier 4.00 10.00

1998-99 Crown Royale

The 1998-99 Pacific Crown Royale set was issued in one series totaling 144 cards and was distributed in six-card packs with a suggested retail price of $5.99. The set features color action player photos printed on cards with silver and gold foil highlights, dual etching and a die-cut crown as background.
COMPLETE SET (144) 30.00 80.00
1 Travis Green .20 .50
2 Guy Hebert .30 .75
3 Paul Kariya .40 1.00
4 Tomas Sandstrom .20 .50
5 Teemu Selanne .40 1.00
6 Jason Allison .20 .50
7 Ray Bourque 1.00 2.50
8 Byron Dafoe .30 .75
9 Dimitri Khristich .20 .50
10 Sergei Samsonov .30 .75
11 Matthew Barnaby .20 .50
12 Michal Grosek .20 .50
13 Dominik Hasek 1.25 3.00
14 Michael Peca .20 .50
15 Miroslav Satan .20 .50
16 Andrew Cassels .20 .50
17 Rico Fata .20 .50
18 Theo Fleury .20 .50
19 Jarome Iginla .75 2.00
20 Martin St. Louis RC 4.00 10.00
21 Ken Wregget .30 .75
22 Ron Francis .30 .75
23 Arturs Irbe .30 .75
24 Sami Kapanen .20 .50
25 Trevor Kidd .30 .75
26 Keith Primeau .20 .50
27 Tony Amonte .30 .75
28 Chris Chelios .40 1.00
29 Eric Daze .20 .50
30 Doug Gilmour .30 .75
31 Jocelyn Thibault .30 .75
32 Chris Drury .30 .75
33 Peter Forsberg 1.25 3.00
34 Milan Hejduk RC 2.00 5.00
35 Patrick Roy 2.50 6.00
36 Joe Sakic 1.25 3.00
37 Ed Belfour .40 1.00
38 Brett Hull .40 1.00
39 Jamie Langenbrunner .20 .50
40 Jere Lehtinen .20 .50
41 Mike Modano 1.00 2.50
42 Joe Nieuwendyk .30 .75
43 Darryl Sydor .20 .50
44 Sergei Fedorov 1.00 2.50
45 Nicklas Lidstrom .40 1.00
46 Darren McCarty .20 .50
47 Chris Osgood .30 .75
48 Brendan Shanahan .40 1.00
49 Steve Yzerman 2.50 6.00
50 Bob Essensa .30 .75
51 Bill Guerin .20 .50
52 Janne Niinimaa .20 .50
53 Tom Poti .20 .50
54 Ryan Smyth .20 .50
55 Doug Weight .30 .75
56 Sean Burke .30 .75
57 Dino Ciccarelli .20 .50
58 Ed Jovanovski .20 .50
59 Viktor Kozlov .20 .50
60 Oleg Kvasha RC .40 1.00
61 Mark Parrish RC .75 2.00
62 Rob Blake .30 .75
63 Manny Legace .40 1.00
64 Yanic Perreault .20 .50
65 Luc Robitaille .30 .75
66 Jozef Stumpel .50 1.25
67 Shayne Corson .20 .50
68 Vincent Damphousse .20 .50
69 Jeff Hackett .30 .75
70 Saku Koivu .40 1.00
71 Mark Recchi .30 .75
72 Andrew Brunette .50 1.25
73 Mike Dunham .30 .75
74 Tom Fitzgerald .20 .50
75 Greg Johnson .20 .50
76 Sergei Krivokrasov .20 .50
77 Jason Arnott .20 .50
78 Martin Brodeur 1.50 4.00
79 Patrik Elias .30 .75
80 Bobby Holik .20 .50
81 Brendan Morrison .30 .75
82 Bryan Berard .20 .50
83 Trevor Linden .30 .75
84 Zigmund Palffy .30 .75
85 Robert Reichel .20 .50
86 Tommy Salo .30 .75
87 Adam Graves .20 .50
88 Wayne Gretzky 3.00 8.00
89 Brian Leetch .40 1.00
90 Manny Malhotra .20 .50
91 Mike Richter .40 1.00
92 Daniel Alfredsson .30 .75
93 Igor Kravchuk .20 .50
94 Shawn McEachern .20 .50
95 Damian Rhodes .30 .75
96 Alexei Yashin .20 .50
97 Rod Brind'Amour .30 .75
98 Ron Hextall .30 .75
99 John LeClair .40 1.00
100 Eric Lindros .40 1.00
101 John Vanbiesbrouck .30 .75
102 Dainius Zubrus .20 .50
103 Nikolai Khabibulin .30 .75
104 Jeremy Roenick .75 2.00
105 Keith Tkachuk .40 1.00
106 Rick Tocchet .30 .75
107 Oleg Tverdovsky .20 .50
108 Tom Barrasso .30 .75
109 Jan Hrdina RC .40 1.00
110 Jaromir Jagr 1.00 2.50
111 Alexei Morozov .20 .50
112 German Titov .20 .50
113 Jim Campbell .20 .50
114 Grant Fuhr .30 .75
115 Al MacInnis .30 .75
116 Chris Pronger .30 .75
117 Pierre Turgeon .30 .75
118 Jeff Friesen .20 .50
119 Patrick Marleau .30 .75
120 Owen Nolan .20 .50
121 Marco Sturm .20 .50
122 Mike Vernon .30 .75
123 Wendel Clark .30 .75
124 Vincent Lecavalier 1.25 3.00
125 Bill Ranford .30 .75
126 Stephane Richer .30 .75
127 Rob Zamuner .20 .50
128 Sergei Berezin .20 .50
129 Tie Domi .30 .75
130 Mike Johnson .20 .50
131 Curtis Joseph .40 1.00
132 Mats Sundin .40 1.00
133 Donald Brashear .20 .50
134 Pavel Bure .40 1.00
135 Mark Messier .40 1.00
136 Alexander Mogilny .30 .75
137 Bill Muckalt RC .20 .50
138 Mattias Ohlund .20 .50
139 Garth Snow .30 .75
140 Peter Bondra .30 .75
141 Matthew Herr RC .20 .50
142 Joe Juneau .30 .75
143 Olaf Kolzig .30 .75
144 Adam Oates .30 .75

1998-99 Crown Royale Limited Series

Randomly inserted into packs, this 144-card set is a limited parallel edition of the base set printed on 24-point card stock. Only 99 serial-numbered sets were produced.
*STARS: 4X TO 8X BASIC CARDS
*ROOKIES: 2.5X TO 6X BASIC CARDS

1998-99 Crown Royale Cramer's Choice Jumbos

Inserted one per box, this 10-card set features color action cut-outs of top NHL players as chosen by Pacific President and CEO, Michael Cramer, printed on premium-sized, dual-foiled, die-cut pyramid-shaped cards. Six different serial-numbered parallel sets were also produced: 35 serial-numbered dark blue foil sets, 30 serial-numbered green foil sets, 25 serial-numbered red foil sets, 20 serial-numbered light blue foil sets, 10 serial-numbered gold foil sets, and 1 serial-numbered purple foil set.
COMPLETE SET (10) 20.00 40.00
*DARK BLUES: 10X TO 25X BASIC INSERTS
*GOLD: 20X TO 50X BASIC INSERTS
*GREEN: 10X TO 25X BASIC INSERTS
*LT.BLUE: 15X TO 40X BASIC INSERTS
*RED: 10X TO 25X BASIC INSERTS
PURPLE 1/1's NOT PRICE DUE TO SCARCITY
1 Paul Kariya 1.25 3.00
2 Teemu Selanne 1.25 3.00
3 Dominik Hasek 2.00 5.00
4 Peter Forsberg 2.50 6.00
5 Patrick Roy 3.00 8.00
6 Steve Yzerman 3.00 8.00
7 Martin Brodeur 3.00 8.00
8 Wayne Gretzky 4.00 10.00
9 Eric Lindros 1.25 3.00
10 Jaromir Jagr 1.50 4.00

1998-99 Crown Royale Living Legends

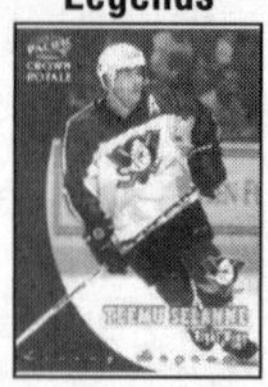

Randomly inserted in hobby packs at the rate of 1:73, this 10-card set features color action photos of some of the NHL's all-time great players. Only 375 serial-numbered sets were produced.
COMPLETE SET (10) 100.00 200.00
1 Paul Kariya 12.50 30.00
2 Teemu Selanne 8.00 20.00
3 Dominik Hasek 8.00 20.00
4 Peter Forsberg 10.00 25.00
5 Patrick Roy 20.00 50.00
6 Steve Yzerman 12.50 30.00
7 Martin Brodeur 10.00 25.00
8 Wayne Gretzky 20.00 60.00
9 Eric Lindros 8.00 20.00
10 Jaromir Jagr 25.00 60.00

1998-99 Crown Royale Master Performers

Randomly inserted in hobby packs at the rate of 2:25, this 20-card set features color action photos of some of the most popular players printed on fully foiled, etched cards.
COMPLETE SET (20) 40.00 100.00
1 Paul Kariya 2.00 5.00
2 Teemu Selanne 2.00 5.00
3 Dominik Hasek 4.00 10.00
4 Peter Forsberg 3.00 8.00
5 Patrick Roy 8.00 20.00
6 Joe Sakic 4.00 10.00
7 Brett Hull 2.50 6.00
8 Mike Modano 3.00 8.00
9 Sergei Fedorov 2.50 6.00
10 Brendan Shanahan 2.00 5.00
11 Steve Yzerman 6.00 15.00
12 Saku Koivu 2.00 5.00
13 Martin Brodeur 5.00 12.00
14 Wayne Gretzky 10.00 25.00
15 John LeClair 1.50 4.00
16 Eric Lindros 2.00 5.00
17 Jaromir Jagr 3.00 8.00
18 Mats Sundin 2.00 5.00
19 Mark Messier 2.00 5.00
20 Peter Bondra 1.50 4.00

1998-99 Crown Royale Pillars of the Game

Inserted one at the bottom of every pack, this 25-card set features color action photos of popular players with a hockey puck in the background and printed on holographic gold foil cards.
COMPLETE SET (25) 10.00 20.00
1 Teemu Selanne .30 .75
2 Ray Bourque .50 1.25
3 Michael Peca .10 .25
4 Theo Fleury .10 .25
5 Chris Chelios .30 .75
6 Doug Gilmour .25 .60
7 Patrick Roy 1.50 4.00
8 Joe Sakic .60 1.50
9 Ed Belfour .30 .75
10 Brett Hull .40 1.00
11 Mike Modano .50 1.25
12 Sergei Fedorov .50 1.25
13 Brendan Shanahan .50 1.25
14 Steve Yzerman 1.50 4.00
15 Saku Koivu .30 .75
16 Martin Brodeur .75 2.00
17 John LeClair .30 .75
18 Eric Lindros .30 .75
19 John Vanbiesbrouck .25 .60
20 Keith Tkachuk .30 .75
21 Jaromir Jagr .50 1.25
22 Curtis Joseph .30 .75
23 Mats Sundin .30 .75
24 Mark Messier .30 .75
25 Peter Bondra .25 .60

1998-99 Crown Royale Pivotal Players

Inserted one at the top of every pack, this 25-card set features color action photos of top stars and rookies printed on holographic silver foil cards.
COMPLETE SET (25) 10.00 20.00
1 Paul Kariya .30 .75
2 Dominik Hasek .60 1.50
3 Michael Peca .10 .25
4 Peter Forsberg .75 2.00
5 Joe Sakic .60 1.50
6 Brett Hull .40 1.00
7 Mike Modano .50 1.25
8 Sergei Fedorov .50 1.25
9 Chris Osgood .25 .60
10 Brendan Shanahan .30 .75
11 Ryan Smyth .10 .25
12 Mark Parrish .40 1.00
13 Saku Koivu .30 .75
14 Martin Brodeur .75 2.00
15 Trevor Linden .10 .25
16 Wayne Gretzky 2.00 5.00
17 Alexei Yashin .10 .25
18 John LeClair .30 .75
19 John Vanbiesbrouck .25 .60
20 Keith Tkachuk .30 .75
21 Vincent Lecavalier .75 2.00
22 Mats Sundin .30 .75
23 Mark Messier .30 .75
24 Peter Bondra .25 .60
25 Olaf Kolzig .25 .60

1998-99 Crown Royale Rookie Class

Randomly inserted in packs at the rate of 1:25, this 10-card set features color action photos of top rookies printed on full-foil designed cards.
COMPLETE SET (10) 15.00 40.00
1 Chris Drury 2.00 5.00
2 Milan Hejduk 2.00 5.00
3 Mark Parrish 1.25 3.00
4 Manny Legace 2.00 5.00
5 Brendan Morrison 1.25 3.00
6 Manny Malhotra 1.25 3.00
7 Daniel Briere 2.00 5.00
8 Vincent Lecavalier 4.00 10.00
9 Tomas Kaberle 1.25 3.00
10 Bill Muckalt 1.25 3.00

1999-00 Crown Royale

The 1999-00 Pacific Crown Royale set was issued in one series totaling 144 cards and was distributed in six-card packs with a suggested retail price of $5.99. The set features color action player photos printed on cards with silver and gold foil highlights, dual etching and a die-cut crown as background.
COMPLETE SET (144) 40.00 100.00
1 Guy Hebert .30 .75
2 Paul Kariya 1.25 3.00
3 Steve Rucchin .20 .50
4 Teemu Selanne .60 1.50
5 Andrew Brunette .20 .50
6 Scott Fankhouser RC 1.25 3.00
7 Andreas Karlsson RC .75 2.00
8 Damian Rhodes .20 .50
9 Patrik Stefan SP RC 1.00 2.50
10 Jason Allison .20 .50
11 Ray Bourque 1.00 2.50
12 Byron Dafoe .30 .75
13 Mikko Eloranta RC .20 .50
14 Sergei Samsonov .30 .75
15 Joe Thornton 1.00 2.50
16 Maxim Afinogenov SP .75 2.00
17 Martin Biron SP .75 2.00
18 Dominik Hasek 1.25 3.00
19 Michael Peca .20 .50
20 Miroslav Satan .30 .75
21 Valeri Bure .20 .50
22 Grant Fuhr .30 .75
23 Jarome Iginla .75 2.00
24 Robyn Regehr SP .75 2.00
25 Oleg Saprykin SP RC 1.00 2.50
26 Ron Francis .30 .75
27 Arturs Irbe .30 .75
28 Sami Kapanen .20 .50
29 Jeff O'Neill .20 .50
30 Tony Amonte .30 .75
31 Kyle Calder SP RC 1.00 2.50
32 Eric Daze .20 .50
33 Doug Gilmour .30 .75
34 Jocelyn Thibault .30 .75
35 Marc Denis SP .75 2.00
36 Chris Drury .30 .75
37 Peter Forsberg 1.25 3.00
38 Milan Hejduk .60 1.50
39 Patrick Roy 2.50 6.00
40 Joe Sakic 1.25 3.00
41 Alex Tanguay SP 1.50 4.00
42 Ed Belfour .60 1.50
43 Ryan Christie RC .75 2.00
44 Brett Hull .75 2.00
45 Jere Lehtinen .30 .75
46 Mike Modano 1.00 2.50
47 Joe Nieuwendyk .30 .75
48 Chris Chelios .60 1.50
49 Sergei Fedorov 1.00 2.50
50 Nicklas Lidstrom .60 1.50
51 Chris Osgood .30 .75
52 Brendan Shanahan .60 1.50
53 Steve Yzerman 2.50 6.00
54 Bill Guerin .30 .75
55 Tommy Salo .30 .75
56 Alexander Selivanov .20 .50
57 Ryan Smyth .30 .75
58 Doug Weight .30 .75
59 Pavel Bure .60 1.50
60 Trevor Kidd .30 .75
61 Ivan Novoseltsev SP RC 1.25 2.50
62 Ray Whitney .20 .50
63 Mike Vernon .30 .75
64 Rob Blake .30 .75
65 Stephane Fiset .30 .75
66 Zigmund Palffy .30 .75
67 Luc Robitaille .30 .75
68 Brian Smolinski .20 .50
69 Jeff Hackett .30 .75
70 Saku Koivu .60 1.50
71 Trevor Linden .20 .50
72 Brian Savage .20 .50
73 Jose Theodore .75 2.00
74 Mike Dunham .30 .75
75 Sergei Krivokrasov .20 .50
76 David Legwand SP .75 2.00
77 Cliff Ronning .20 .50
78 Martin Brodeur 1.50 4.00
79 Patrik Elias .30 .75
80 Scott Gomez SP .75 2.00
81 Bobby Holik .20 .50
82 Claude Lemieux .20 .50
83 Petr Sykora .20 .50
84 Tim Connolly SP .75 2.00
85 Mariusz Czerkawski .20 .50
86 Brad Isbister .20 .50
87 Kenny Jonsson .20 .50
88 Roberto Luongo SP .75 2.00
89 Theo Fleury .20 .50
90 Milan Hnilicka RC 1.25 3.00
91 Brian Leetch .60 1.50
92 Mike Richter .60 1.50
93 Michael York SP .75 2.00
94 Daniel Alfredsson .30 .75
95 Radek Bonk .20 .50
96 Mike Fisher RC .75 2.00
97 Marian Hossa .60 1.50
98 Joe Juneau .20 .50
99 Ron Tugnutt .30 .75
100 Alexei Yashin .20 .50
101 Simon Gagne SP 1.50 4.00
102 John LeClair .30 .75
103 Eric Lindros .60 1.50
104 Keith Primeau .20 .50
105 Mark Recchi .30 .75
106 John Vanbiesbrouck .30 .75
107 Travis Green .20 .50
108 Nikolai Khabibulin .30 .75
109 Jermy Roenick .75 2.00
110 Keith Tkachuk .60 1.50
111 Tom Barrasso .30 .75
112 Jaromir Jagr 1.00 2.50
113 Alexei Kovalev .20 .50
114 Robert Lang .20 .50
115 Pavol Demitra .20 .50
116 Jochen Hecht SP RC 1.50 4.00
117 Al MacInnis .30 .75
118 Ladislav Nagy RC 1.50 4.00
119 Chris Pronger .30 .75
120 Roman Turek .20 .50
121 Pierre Turgeon .20 .50
122 Vincent Damphousse .20 .50
123 Jeff Friesen .20 .50
124 Patrick Marleau .30 .75
125 Owen Nolan .30 .75
126 Steve Shields .30 .75
127 Dan Cloutier .20 .50
128 Chris Gratton .20 .50
129 Vincent Lecavalier .60 1.50
130 Mike Sillinger .20 .50
131 Nikolai Antropov SP RC 1.25 3.00
132 Sergei Berezin .20 .50
133 Tie Domi .20 .50
134 Curtis Joseph .60 1.50
135 Mats Sundin .60 1.50
136 Steve Kariya SP RC 1.25 3.00
137 Mark Messier .60 1.50
138 Markus Naslund .60 1.50
139 Peter Schaefer SP .75 2.00
140 Garth Snow .30 .75
141 Peter Bondra .30 .75
142 Jan Bulis .20 .50
143 Olaf Kolzig .30 .75
144 Adam Oates .30 .75

1999-00 Crown Royale Limited Series

Randomly inserted in packs, This 144-card parallel set features the base card with a red foil Limited Series logo and box with the serial number in the lower front right corner. This set is serial numbered out of 99.
*STARS: 5X TO 12X BASIC CARDS
*SP's: 3X TO 8X BASIC CARDS

1999-00 Crown Royale Premiere Date

Randomly inserted in packs, This 144-card parallel set features the base card with a gold foil Premier Date logo and box with the serial number in the lower front right corner. This set is serial numbered out of 73.
*STARS: 6X TO 15X BASIC CARDS
*SP's: 4X TO 10X BASIC CARDS

1999-00 Crown Royale Prospects Parallel

Randomly inserted at 1:24 packs, this 23-card parallel set showcases the prospect cards with a gold foil box on the bottom right-front corner of the card. This set is skip-numbered. The cards are serial numbered out of 450.
*PROSPECT PAR: 1.25X TO 3X BASIC CARDS

1999-00 Crown Royale Card-Supials

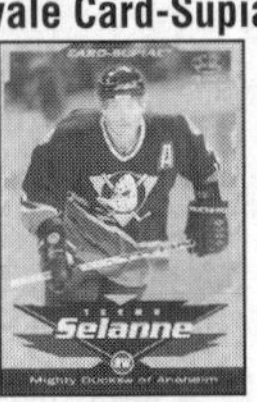

Randomly inserted in packs at 2:25, this 25-card set was issued in two versions. The large version features player action-shots with a rainbow holo-foil border and a cut on the back where a Card-Supials Mini card is inserted. The Mini's may or may not match the large card.
COMP.LARGE SET (20) 20.00 50.00
1 Paul Kariya 1.00 2.50
2 Teemu Selanne 1.00 2.50
3 Patrik Stefan 1.50 4.00
4 Joe Thornton 1.25 3.00
5 Dominik Hasek 2.00 5.00
6 Peter Forsberg 1.50 4.00
7 Patrick Roy 4.00 10.00
8 Alex Tanguay 1.00 2.50
9 Mike Modano 1.50 4.00
10 Brendan Shanahan 1.00 2.50
11 Steve Yzerman 3.00 8.00
12 Pave Bure 1.00 2.50
13 Martin Brodeur 2.50 6.00
14 Scott Gomez 1.00 2.50
15 Roberto Luongo 1.50 4.00
16 Eric Lindros 1.00 2.50
17 John Vanbiesbrouck 1.00 2.50
18 Jaromir Jagr 1.50 4.00
19 Mats Sundin 1.00 2.50
20 Steve Kariya 1.50 4.00

1999-00 Crown Royale Century 21

Randomly inserted in packs, this 10-card set is out of this world. Player photos are set against an outer-space background and a rainbow foil "21." Each card is serial numbered out of 375.

COMPLETE SET (10) 30.00 60.00
1 Paul Kariya 4.00 10.00
2 Patrik Stefan 1.25 3.00
3 Chris Drury 4.00 10.00
4 Peter Forsberg 8.00 20.00
5 Pave Bure 3.00 8.00
6 Scott Gomez 1.25 3.00
7 Roberto Luongo 4.00 10.00
8 Marian Hossa 2.00 5.00
9 Jaromir Jagr 5.00 12.00
10 Vincent Lecavalier 3.00 8.00

1999-00 Crown Royale Cramer's Choice Jumbos

Inserted one per box, this 10-card set features color action cut-outs of top NHL players as chosen by Pacific President and CEO, Michael Cramer, printed on premium-sized, dual-foiled, die-cut pyramid-shaped cards. Six different serial-numbered parallel sets were also produced: 35 serial-numbered dark blue foil sets, 30 serial-numbered green foil sets, 25 serial-numbered red foil sets, 20 serial-numbered light blue foil sets, 10 serial-numbered gold foil sets, and 1 serial-numbered purple foil set. Purple and gold parallels are not priced due to scarcity.
COMPLETE SET (10) 15.00 30.00
*DARK BLUE: 12.5X TO 25X BASIC CARDS
*GREEN: 12.5X TO 25X BASIC CARDS
*LT.BLUE: 20X TO 40X BASIC CARDS
*RED: 15X TO 30X BASIC CARDS
1 Paul Kariya 1.00 2.50
2 Teemu Selanne 1.00 2.50
3 Peter Forsberg 2.00 5.00
4 Patrick Roy 3.00 8.00
5 Mike Modano 1.25 3.00
6 Steve Yzerman 3.00 8.00
7 Pave Bure 1.00 2.50
8 Martin Brodeur 3.00 8.00
9 Eric Lindros 1.00 2.50
10 Jaromir Jagr 1.25 3.00

1999-00 Crown Royale Gold Crown Die-Cuts Jumbos

Inserted at six in 10 boxes, this 6-card jumbo set is an enhanced version of the base cards. The jumbos are vertical instead of horizontal, and feature rainbow foil on the die-cut crown background. Each card is serial numbered out of 960.
COMPLETE SET (6) 25.00 50.00
1 Teemu Selanne 3.00 8.00
2 Dominik Hasek 3.00 8.00
3 Patrick Roy 8.00 20.00
4 Steve Yzerman 8.00 20.00
5 Martin Brodeur 4.00 10.00
6 John LeClair 2.00 5.00

1999-00 Crown Royale Ice Elite

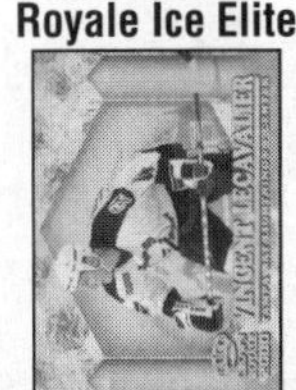

Inserted in packs at a rate of 1:1, this 25-card set silhouettes 25 of the NHL's most exciting players against a blue-ice background. A parallel of this set was also created and randomly inserted. The parallel was numbered to just 10.
COMPLETE SET (25) 10.00 20.00
1 Paul Kariya .30 .75
2 Teemu Selanne .30 .75
3 Joe Thornton .50 1.25
4 Dominik Hasek .60 1.50
5 Tony Amonte .25 .60
6 Milan Hejduk .30 .75
7 Patrick Roy 1.50 4.00
8 Joe Sakic .60 1.50
9 Ed Belfour .30 .75
10 Brett Hull .40 1.00
11 Brendan Shanahan .30 .75
12 Steve Yzerman 1.50 4.00
13 Luc Robitaille .25 .60
14 Trevor Linden .25 .60
15 David Legwand .25 .60
16 Martin Brodeur .75 2.00
17 Theo Fleury .25 .60
18 Marian Hossa .30 .75
19 John LeClair .30 .75
20 Mark Recchi .25 .60
21 Jeremy Roenick .40 1.00
22 Owen Nolan .25 .60
23 Vincent Lecavalier .30 .75
24 Curtis Joseph .30 .75
25 Steve Kariya .25 .60

1999-00 Crown Royale Ice Elite Parallel

STATED PRINT RUN 10 SERIAL #'d SETS
RANDOM INSERTS IN PACKS
NOT PRICED DUE TO SCARCITY

1999-00 Crown Royale International Glory

Inserted in packs at a rate of one in one, this 25-card set places 25 of the NHL's top players in action to the background of their home country's flag. A parallel of this set was also created and randomly inserted in packs. The parallel was numbered to just 20.
COMPLETE SET (25) 10.00 20.00
*PARALLEL's: 60X TO 150X BASIC CARDS
1 Teemu Selanne .30 .75
2 Patrik Stefan .25 .60
3 Dominik Hasek .60 1.50
4 Arturs Irbe .25 .60
5 Chris Drury .25 .60
6 Peter Forsberg .75 2.00
7 Patrick Roy 1.50 4.00
8 Mike Modano .50 1.25
9 Sergei Fedorov .50 1.25
10 Brendan Shanahan .30 .75
11 Pave Bure .30 .75
12 Zigmund Palffy .25 .60
13 Saku Koivu .30 .75
14 Martin Brodeur .75 2.00
15 Scott Gomez .25 .60
16 Theo Fleury .25 .60
17 Simon Gagne .30 .75
18 Eric Lindros .30 .75
19 John Vanbiesbrouck .30 .75
20 Keith Tkachuk .30 .75
21 Jaromir Jagr .50 1.25
22 Pavol Demitra .25 .60
23 Jochen Hecht .25 .60
24 Jeff Friesen .25 .60
25 Mats Sundin .30 .75

1999-00 Crown Royale Team Captain Die-Cuts

Randomly inserted in packs at 1:25, this 10-card set showcases hockey's most respected team captains. Player action shots are set against a die-cut "C" background.
COMPLETE SET (10) 25.00 50.00
1 Paul Kariya 4.00 10.00
2 Ray Bourque 2.50 6.00
3 Joe Sakic 3.00 8.00
4 Steve Yzerman 8.00 20.00
5 Eric Lindros 2.50 6.00
6 Keith Tkachuk 1.50 4.00
7 Jaromir Jagr 2.50 6.00
8 Owen Nolan 1.25 3.00
9 Mats Sundin 1.50 4.00
10 Mark Messier 2.00 5.00

2000-01 Crown Royale

The 2000-01 Crown Royale set was issued in March 2001. The 6-card packs carried an SRP of $6.99. The set was issued as one series totaling 144 cards of which the last 35 were sequentially numbered to 400. The set features color action player photos printed on cards with silver and gold foil highlights, dual etching and a die-cut crown as background.
COMP. SET w/o SP's (108) 20.00 50.00
1 Guy Hebert .30 .75
2 Paul Kariya .60 1.50
3 Teemu Selanne .60 1.50
4 Donald Audette .20 .50
5 Andrew Brunette .20 .50
6 Damian Rhodes .20 .50
7 Patrik Stefan .20 .50
8 Jason Allison .20 .50
9 Byron Dafoe .30 .75
10 Bill Guerin .30 .75
11 Sergei Samsonov .30 .75
12 Joe Thornton 1.00 2.50
13 Doug Gilmour .30 .75
14 Chris Gratton .20 .50
15 Dominik Hasek 1.25 3.00
16 Michael Peca .20 .50
17 Valeri Bure .20 .50
18 Jarome Iginla .75 2.00
19 Marc Savard .20 .50
20 Ron Francis .30 .75
21 Arturs Irbe .30 .75
22 Sami Kapanen .20 .50
23 Tony Amonte .30 .75
24 Jocelyn Thibault .30 .75
25 Alexei Zhamnov .20 .50
26 Ray Bourque 1.25 3.00
27 Chris Drury .30 .75
28 Peter Forsberg 1.50 4.00
29 Milan Hejduk .30 .75
30 Patrick Roy 2.50 6.00
31 Joe Sakic 1.25 3.00
32 Geoff Sanderson .20 .50
33 Ron Tugnutt .30 .75
34 Ed Belfour .40 1.00
35 Brett Hull .75 2.00
36 Mike Modano 1.00 2.50
37 Joe Nieuwendyk .30 .75
38 Sergei Fedorov 1.00 2.50
39 Chris Osgood .30 .75
40 Brendan Shanahan .60 1.50
41 Steve Yzerman 2.00 5.00
42 Tommy Salo .30 .75
43 Ryan Smyth .20 .50
44 Doug Weight .30 .75
45 Pavel Bure .60 1.50
46 Rob Niedermayer .30 .75
47 Ray Whitney .20 .50
48 Stephane Fiset .20 .50
49 Zigmund Palffy .30 .75
50 Luc Robitaille .30 .75
51 Jamie Storr .30 .75
52 Jim Dowd .20 .50
53 Jamie McLennan .20 .50
54 Scott Pellerin .20 .50
55 Saku Koivu .60 1.50
56 Martin Rucinsky .20 .50
57 Brian Savage .20 .50
58 Jose Theodore .75 2.00
59 Mike Dunham .20 .50
60 David Legwand .20 .50
61 Vitali Yachmenev .20 .50
62 Martin Brodeur 1.50 4.00
63 Patrik Elias .30 .75
64 Scott Gomez .20 .50
65 Alexander Mogilny .30 .75
66 Tim Connolly .20 .50
67 Brad Isbister .20 .50
68 John Vanbiesbrouck .30 .75
69 Theo Fleury .20 .50
70 Brian Leetch .30 .75
71 Mark Messier .60 1.50
72 Mike Richter .40 1.00
73 Daniel Alfredsson .30 .75
74 Radek Bonk .20 .50
75 Marian Hossa .40 1.00
76 Patrick Lalime .30 .75
77 Alexei Yashin .20 .50
78 Brian Boucher .30 .75
79 Simon Gagne .40 1.00
80 John LeClair .40 1.00
81 Eric Lindros .60 1.50
82 Sean Burke .30 .75
83 Shane Doan .20 .50
84 Jeremy Roenick .75 2.00
85 Keith Tkachuk .40 1.00
86 Jaromir Jagr 1.00 2.50
87 Mario Lemieux 2.50 6.00
88 Martin Straka .20 .50
89 Chris Pronger .30 .75
90 Roman Turek .30 .75
91 Pierre Turgeon .30 .75
92 Scott Young .20 .50
93 Patrick Marleau .30 .75
94 Owen Nolan .30 .75
95 Steve Shields .30 .75
96 Vincent Lecavalier .40 1.00
97 Fredrik Modin .20 .50
98 Kevin Weekes .20 .50
99 Sergei Berezin .20 .50
100 Curtis Joseph .40 1.00
101 Gary Roberts .20 .50
102 Mats Sundin .60 1.50
103 Andrew Cassels .20 .50
104 Markus Naslund .40 1.00
105 Felix Potvin .40 1.00
106 Peter Bondra .40 1.00
107 Olaf Kolzig .30 .75
108 Adam Oates .30 .75
109 Samuel Pahlsson SP 1.50 4.00
110 Tomi Kallio SP 1.50 4.00
111 Andrew Raycroft RC 6.00 15.00
112 Eric Boulton RC 1.50 4.00
113 Dimitri Kalinin SP 1.50 4.00
114 Oleg Saprykin SP 1.50 4.00
115 Josef Vasicek RC 1.50 4.00
116 Shane Willis SP 1.50 4.00
117 Steven McCarthy SP 1.50 4.00
118 David Aebischer RC 8.00 20.00
119 Serge Aubin RC 1.50 4.00
120 Marc Denis SP 1.50 4.00
121 David Vyborny SP 1.50 4.00
122 Marty Turco RC 10.00 25.00
123 Roberto Luongo SP 8.00 20.00
124 Ivan Novoseltsev SP 1.50 4.00
125 Denis Shvidki SP 1.50 4.00
126 Steven Reinprecht RC 1.50 4.00
127 Marian Gaborik RC 12.00 30.00
128 Filip Kuba SP 1.50 4.00
129 Andrei Markov SP 1.50 4.00
130 Scott Hartnell RC 5.00 12.00
131 Colin White RC 1.50 4.00
132 Rick DiPietro RC 8.00 20.00
133 Taylor Pyatt SP 1.50 4.00
134 Martin Havlat RC 10.00 25.00
135 Jani Hurme RC 1.50 4.00
136 Justin Williams RC 4.00 10.00
137 Robert Esche SP 1.50 4.00
138 Milan Kraft SP 1.50 4.00
139 Brent Johnson SP 1.50 4.00
140 Evgeni Nabokov SP 6.00 15.00
141 Sheldon Keefe SP 1.50 4.00
142 Brad Richards SP 6.00 15.00
143 Daniel Sedin SP 1.50 4.00
144 Henrik Sedin SP 1.50 4.00

2000-01 Crown Royale Ice Blue

This set paralleled the first 108 cards of the base set.
*STARS: 10X TO 20X BASIC CARDS
PRINT RUN 75 SER.#'d SETS

2000-01 Crown Royale Limited Series

This set paralleled the first 108 cards of the base set.The cards look the same as the base set except for silver foil in place of the gold and a serial number to 25 on the card front.
*STARS: 15X TO 30X BASIC CARDS

2000-01 Crown Royale Premiere Date

This set paralleled the first 108 cards of the base set.
*STARS: 10X TO 20X BASIC CARDS

2000-01 Crown Royale Red

Randomly inserted in retail packs, this 108-card set parallels the base set with red foil highlights.
*RED: 1X TO 2X BASIC CARD
RANDOM INSERTS IN RETAIL PACKS

2000-01 Crown Royale 21st Century Rookies

This 25-card set was inserted at the stated rate of 1:1. The set features color action photos of each player on a mostly green background accompanied by the players name, position, and team.
COMPLETE SET (25) 15.00 30.00
1 Tomi Kallio .20 .50
2 Andrew Raycroft 2.00 5.00
3 Eric Boulton .20 .50
4 Oleg Saprykin .20 .50
5 Shane Willis .20 .50
6 Steven McCarthy .20 .50
7 David Aebischer 1.25 3.00
8 Marc Denis .75 2.00
9 Marty Turco 1.25 3.00
10 Roberto Luongo .75 2.00
11 Steven Reinprecht .20 .50
12 Marian Gaborik 2.00 5.00
13 Andrei Markov .20 .50
14 Colin White .20 .50
15 Rick DiPietro 1.25 3.00
16 Taylor Pyatt .20 .50
17 Martin Havlat 1.50 4.00
18 Jani Hurme .40 1.00
19 Justin Williams 1.00 2.50
20 Milan Kraft .20 .50
21 Brent Johnson .40 1.00
22 Evgeni Nabokov 1.25 3.00
23 Brad Richards 1.25 3.00
24 Daniel Sedin .20 .50
25 Henrik Sedin .20 .50

2000-01 Crown Royale Game-Worn Jerseys

Randomly inserted in packs, this 25-card set featured game-used jersey swatches and full-color player photographs on a mostly

gray background. Please note that the cards have different print runs which are player specific. They are listed below, following the player's name.
*MULT.COLOR SWATCH:1X TO 2X HI COL.
1 Byron Dafoe/602 3.00 8.00
2 Valeri Bure/599 3.00 8.00
3 Rico Fata/596 3.00 8.00
4 Phil Housley/599 3.00 8.00
5 Marc Savard/597 3.00 8.00
6 Peter Forsberg/624 6.00 15.00
7 Ed Belfour/608 4.00 10.00
8 Brett Hull/591 5.00 12.00
9 Jamie Langenbrunner/599 3.00 8.00
10 Grant Marshall/593 3.00 8.00
11 Mike Modano/587 5.00 12.00
12 Joe Nieuwendyk/597 3.00 8.00
13 Chris Chelios/1157 4.00 10.00
14 Chris Osgood/592 3.00 8.00
15 Brendan Shanahan/781 4.00 10.00
16 Patric Kjellberg/594 3.00 8.00
17 Mike Richter/596 4.00 10.00
18 Alexei Yashin/946 3.00 8.00
19 Eric Desjardins/594 3.00 8.00
20 John LeClair/594 4.00 10.00
21 Jyrki Lumme/592 3.00 8.00
22 Michal Rozsival/591 3.00 8.00
23 Martin Straka/581 3.00 8.00
24 Mats Sundin/343 4.00 10.00
25 Felix Potvin/585 4.00 10.00

2000-01 Crown Royale Game-Worn Jersey Patches

This randomly inserted set paralleled the Crown Royale Game-Worn Jerseys set, but each card carries a swatch of jersey patch. Please note that the cards have different print runs which are player specific. They are listed below, following the player's name.
1 Byron Dafoe/141 15.00 40.00
2 Valeri Bure/145 15.00 40.00
3 Rico Fata/144 15.00 40.00
4 Phil Housley/144 15.00 40.00
5 Marc Savard/144 15.00 40.00
6 Peter Forsberg/141 15.00 40.00
7 Ed Belfour/145 20.00 50.00
8 Brett Hull/144 15.00 40.00
9 Jamie Langenbrunner/143 15.00 40.00
10 Grant Marshall/144 15.00 40.00
11 Mike Modano/143 20.00 50.00
12 Joe Nieuwendyk/142 15.00 40.00
13 Chris Chelios/192 20.00 50.00
14 Chris Osgood/143 15.00 40.00
15 Brendan Shanahan/163 20.00 50.00
16 Patric Kjellberg/136 15.00 40.00
17 Mike Richter/135 20.00 50.00
18 Alexei Yashin/283 15.00 40.00
19 Eric Desjardins/145 15.00 40.00
20 John LeClair/144 20.00 50.00
21 Jyrki Lumme/144 15.00 40.00
22 Michal Rozsival/144 15.00 40.00
23 Martin Straka/144 15.00 40.00
24 Mats Sundin/104 20.00 50.00
25 Felix Potvin/144 20.00 50.00

2000-01 Crown Royale Premium-Sized Game-Worn Jerseys

This 25-card set was inserted one per hobby box. Individual cards measured 3 1/2" x 5" and carry a premium-sized jersey swatch that measured 1 1/2" x 2". Each card also carried a color action photo of each player, and the back describes when the jersey was worn. Please note that the cards have different print runs which are player specific. They are listed below, following the player's name.
*MULT.COLOR SWATCH: 1X TO 2X HI COL.
1 Byron Dafoe/343 10.00 25.00
2 Valeri Bure/349 10.00 25.00
3 Rico Fata/343 10.00 25.00
4 Phil Housley/344 10.00 25.00
5 Marc Savard/343 10.00 25.00
6 Peter Forsberg/95 25.00 60.00
7 Ed Belfour/352 10.00 25.00
8 Brett Hull/317 15.00 40.00
9 Jamie Langenbrunner/338 10.00 25.00
10 Grant Marshall/342 10.00 25.00
11 Mike Modano/320 15.00 40.00
12 Joe Nieuwendyk/333 8.00 20.00
13 Chris Chelios/94 10.00 25.00
14 Chris Osgood/351 8.00 20.00
15 Brendan Shanahan/96 10.00 25.00
16 Patric Kjellberg/327 10.00 25.00
17 Mike Richter/346 10.00 25.00
18 Alexei Yashin/345 10.00 25.00
19 Eric Desjardins/349 10.00 25.00
20 John LeClair/330 10.00 25.00
21 Jyrki Lumme/336 10.00 25.00
22 Michal Rozsival/357 10.00 25.00
23 Martin Straka/334 10.00 25.00
25 Felix Potvin/345 10.00 25.00

2000-01 Crown Royale Game-Worn Jersey Redemptions

This 11-card set was inserted into random packs as redemption cards only. It was substituted into the product at the last minute in place of the Crown Royale Road To The Gold insert set. The cards are serial numbered to 475 unless noted differently below.
1 Stu Barnes 10.00 25.00
2 Jarome Iginla 12.50 30.00
3 Joe Sakic 20.00 50.00
4 David Legwand 10.00 25.00
5 Scott Niedermayer 10.00 25.00
6 Theo Fleury 10.00 25.00
7 Daniel Alfredsson 10.00 25.00
8 Jeremy Roenick 12.50 30.00
9 Jaromir Jagr 15.00 40.00
10 Curtis Joseph 10.00 25.00
11 Mario Lemieux/100 40.00 100.00

2000-01 Crown Royale Jewels of the Crown

Inserted at a rate of 1:1, this 25-card set features full-color action photos of top stars on front with computer-generated purple jewels in each corner.
COMPLETE SET (25) 20.00 40.00
1 Paul Kariya .60 1.50
2 Teemu Selanne .60 1.50
3 Patrik Stefan .40 1.00
4 Jason Allison .40 1.00
5 Joe Thornton 1.00 2.50
6 Dominik Hasek 1.25 3.00
7 Ray Bourque 1.25 3.00
8 Peter Forsberg 1.50 4.00
9 Patrick Roy 3.00 8.00
10 Joe Sakic 1.25 3.00
11 Brett Hull .75 2.00
12 Mike Modano 1.00 2.50
13 Brendan Shanahan 1.00 2.50
14 Steve Yzerman 3.00 8.00
15 Doug Weight .40 1.00
16 Pavel Bure .75 2.00
17 Martin Brodeur 1.50 4.00
18 Mark Messier .75 2.00
19 John LeClair .75 2.00
20 Eric Lindros 1.00 2.50
21 Jaromir Jagr 1.00 2.50
22 Mario Lemieux 4.00 10.00
23 Vincent Lecavalier .60 1.50
24 Curtis Joseph .60 1.50
25 Mats Sundin .60 1.50

2000-01 Crown Royale Landmarks

Randomly inserted in packs, this 10-card set features color action photos in the forefront and the skyline of the depicted player's team city in the background. Each card was serial numbered out of 102.
COMPLETE SET (10) 75.00 150.00
1 Paul Kariya 6.00 15.00
2 Dominik Hasek 10.00 25.00
3 Peter Forsberg 12.50 30.00
4 Patrick Roy 25.00 60.00
5 Steve Yzerman 25.00 60.00
6 Pavel Bure 6.00 15.00

7 Martin Brodeur 12.50 30.00
8 Jaromir Jagr 8.00 20.00
9 Mario Lemieux 30.00 80.00
10 Curtis Joseph 6.00 15.00

2000-01 Crown Royale Now Playing

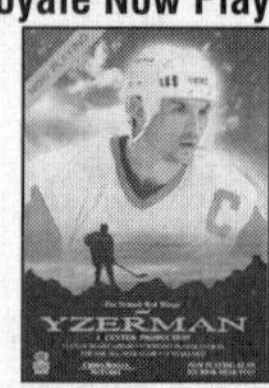

Randomly inserted at a rate of 1:25, this 20-card set features a movie poster look, that carries a large color player photo over a small silhouette. The words "Now Playing" run diagonally in the left hand corner, and the player's name in bold is at the bottom above mock movie credits.

COMPLETE SET (20) 50.00 100.00
1 Paul Kariya 1.50 4.00
2 Teemu Selanne 1.50 4.00
3 Jason Allison 1.25 3.00
4 Ray Bourque 3.00 8.00
5 Peter Forsberg 4.00 10.00
6 Patrick Roy 8.00 20.00
7 Brett Hull 2.00 5.00
8 Steve Yzerman 6.00 15.00
9 Pavel Bure 2.00 5.00
10 Marian Gaborik 4.00 10.00
11 Martin Brodeur 4.00 10.00
12 Theo Fleury 1.25 3.00
13 John LeClair 1.50 4.00
14 Jaromir Jagr 2.50 6.00
15 Mario Lemieux 10.00 25.00
16 Vincent Lecavalier 1.50 4.00
17 Curtis Joseph 1.50 4.00
18 Mats Sundin 1.50 4.00
19 Daniel Sedin 1.25 3.00
20 Henrik Sedin 1.25 3.00

2001 Crown Royale Calder Collection Gold Edition

Available only through a mail-in offer, this 8-card set used the Crown Royale die-cut design to highlight several young players considered to be contenders for the Calder trophy. Each card was highlighted with gold foil. The set cost $39.95 US and each card was serial-numbered out of 1000. The offers were found in packs of 2000-01 Pacific products.

COMPLETE SET (8) 24.00 60.00
1 Evgeni Nabokov 6.00 15.00
2 Daniel Sedin 2.40 6.00
3 Henrik Sedin 1.60 4.00
4 Marian Gaborik 6.00 15.00
5 Rick DiPietro 4.80 12.00
6 Martin Havlat 6.00 15.00
7 Brad Richards 2.40 6.00
8 David Aebischer 4.00 10.00

2001 Crown Royale Calder Collection All-Star Edition

This 8-card set was produced by Pacific as a wrapper redemption for the 2001 All-Star Fan Fest. Base cards feature full color player portrait photos on a silver and maroon crown die-cut card. Each card is sequentially numbered to 2,001.

COMPLETE SET (8) 20.00 50.00
C1 David Aebischer 3.20 8.00
C2 Marian Gaborik 4.00 10.00
C3 Rick DiPietro 3.20 8.00
C4 Martin Havlat 4.00 10.00
C5 Evgeni Nabokov 3.20 8.00
C6 Brad Richards 1.60 4.00
C7 Daniel Sedin 1.60 4.00
C8 Henrik Sedin 1.20 3.00

2001-02 Crown Royale

Released in both hobby and retail channels, this 180-card set featured die-cut base cards and 35 short printed rookies with a crown style die-cut. Rookies were serial-numbered out of 267. Hobby versions were enhanced with gold foil, retail versions with green foil. Hobby packs carried a SRP $5.99 for a 3-card pack. Retail packs included 5 cards.

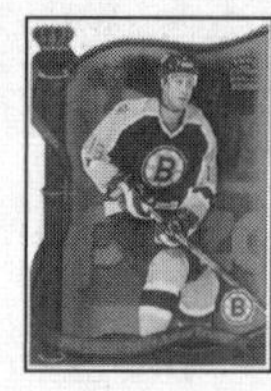

COMP.SET w/o SP's (144) 30.00 80.00
1 Matt Cullen .20 .50
2 Jeff Friesen .20 .50
3 J-S Giguere .30 .75
4 Paul Kariya .60 1.00
5 Ray Ferraro .20 .50
6 Dany Heatley .75 2.00
7 Milan Hnilicka .30 .75
8 Patrik Stefan .20 .50
9 Byron Dafoe .30 .75
10 Glen Murray .20 .50
11 Brian Rolston .20 .50
12 Sergei Samsonov .30 .75
13 Joe Thornton 1.00 2.50
14 Stu Barnes .20 .50
15 Martin Biron .30 .75
16 Tim Connolly .20 .50
17 J-P Dumont .20 .50
18 Miroslav Satan .30 .75
19 Craig Conroy .20 .50
20 Jarome Iginla .75 2.00
21 Dean McAmmond .20 .50
22 Derek Morris .20 .50
23 Marc Savard .20 .50
24 Roman Turek .20 .50
25 Ron Francis .30 .75
26 Arturs Irbe .30 .75
27 Sami Kapanen .20 .50
28 Jeff O'Neill .20 .50
29 Tony Amonte .30 .75
30 Mark Bell .20 .50
31 Kyle Calder .20 .50
32 Eric Daze .20 .50
33 Steve Sullivan .20 .50
34 Jocelyn Thibault .30 .75
35 Rob Blake .30 .75
36 Chris Drury .30 .75
37 Peter Forsberg 1.50 2.50
38 Milan Hejduk .30 .75
39 Patrick Roy 4.00 5.00
40 Joe Sakic 1.25 2.50
41 Alexei Tanguay .30 .75
42 Marc Denis .30 .75
43 Rostislav Klesla .20 .50
44 Geoff Sanderson .20 .50
45 Ron Tugnutt .30 .75
46 Ed Belfour .60 1.00
47 Jere Lehtinen .30 .75
48 Mike Modano 1.00 2.50
49 Joe Nieuwendyk .30 .75
50 Pierre Turgeon .30 .75
51 Sergei Fedorov 1.00 2.50
52 Dominik Hasek 1.25 2.50
53 Brett Hull .75 1.00
54 Nicklas Lidstrom .60 1.00
55 Luc Robitaille .60 1.00
56 Brendan Shanahan .60 1.00
57 Steve Yzerman 3.00 4.00
58 Anson Carter .20 .50
59 Daniel Cleary .20 .50
60 Mike Comrie .20 .50
61 Tommy Salo .30 .75
62 Ryan Smyth .30 .75
63 Pavel Bure .60 1.00
64 Viktor Kozlov .20 .50
65 Roberto Luongo .75 2.00
66 Jason Allison .20 .50
67 Adam Deadmarsh .20 .50
68 Steve Heinze .20 .50
69 Zigmund Palffy .30 .75
70 Felix Potvin .60 1.00
71 Andrew Brunette .20 .50
72 Jim Dowd .20 .50
73 Manny Fernandez .30 .75
74 Marian Gaborik 1.25 2.50
75 Doug Gilmour .30 .75
76 Jeff Hackett .30 .75
77 Yanic Perreault .20 .50
78 Brian Savage .20 .50
79 Jose Theodore .75 2.00
80 Mike Dunham .30 .75
81 David Legwand .20 .50
82 Cliff Ronning .20 .50
83 Scott Walker .20 .50
84 Jason Arnott .20 .50
85 Martin Brodeur 1.50 3.00
86 Patrik Elias .30 .75
87 Scott Stevens .30 .75
88 Petr Sykora .20 .50
89 Rick DiPietro .30 .75
90 Chris Osgood .30 .75
91 Mark Parrish .20 .50
92 Mike Peca .20 .50
93 Alexei Yashin .20 .50
94 Theo Fleury .20 .50
95 Brian Leetch .30 .75
96 Eric Lindros .60 1.00
97 Mark Messier .60 1.00
98 Mike Richter .60 1.00
99 Daniel Alfredsson .30 .75
100 Martin Havlat .30 .75
101 Marian Hossa .60 1.00
102 Patrick Lalime .30 .75
103 Todd White .20 .50
104 Brian Boucher .20 .50
105 Roman Cechmanek .20 .50
106 Simon Gagne .60 1.00
107 John LeClair .30 .75
108 Mark Recchi .30 .75
109 Jeremy Roenick .75 2.00
110 Daniel Briere .20 .50
111 Sean Burke .30 .75
112 Shane Doan .20 .50
113 Claude Lemieux .20 .50
114 Johan Hedberg .30 .75
115 Alexei Kovalev .30 .75
116 Roberto Lang .20 .50
117 Mario Lemieux 2.50 6.00
118 Pavol Demitra .30 .75
119 Brent Johnson .30 .75
120 Chris Pronger .30 .75
121 Keith Tkachuk .60 1.00
122 Doug Weight .30 .75
123 Vincent Damphousse .20 .50
124 Evgeni Nabokov .30 .75
125 Owen Nolan .30 .75
126 Teemu Selanne .60 1.00
127 Nikolai Khabibulin .60 1.00
128 Vincent Lecavalier .60 1.00
129 Brad Richards .30 .75
130 Martin St. Louis .30 .75
131 Curtis Joseph .60 1.00
132 Alexander Mogilny .30 .75
133 Gary Roberts .20 .50
134 Mats Sundin .60 1.00
135 Darcy Tucker .20 .50
136 Dan Cloutier .30 .75
137 Brendan Morrison .30 .75
138 Markus Naslund .30 .75
139 Daniel Sedin .20 .50
140 Henrik Sedin .20 .50
141 Peter Bondra .60 1.00
142 Jaromir Jagr 1.00 2.50
143 Olaf Kolzig .30 .75
144 Adam Oates .30 .75
145 Ilja Bryzgalov RC 6.00 15.00
146 Timo Parssinen RC 4.00 10.00
147 Ilya Kovalchuk RC 40.00 100.00
148 Brian Pothier RC 4.00 10.00
149 Jukka Hentunen RC 4.00 10.00
150 Erik Cole RC 6.00 15.00
151 Vaclav Nedorost RC 4.00 10.00
152 Brian Gionta SP 4.00 10.00
153 Mathieu Darche RC 4.00 10.00
154 Jody Shelley RC 8.00 20.00
155 Martin Spanhel RC 4.00 10.00
156 Niko Kapanen RC 4.00 10.00
157 Pavel Datsyuk RC 20.00 50.00
158 Jason Chimera RC 4.00 10.00
159 Ty Conklin RC 4.00 10.00
160 Jussi Markkanen SP 4.00 10.00
161 Niklas Hagman RC 4.00 10.00
162 Kristian Huselius RC 8.00 20.00
163 Jaroslav Bednar RC 4.00 10.00
164 David Cullen RC 4.00 10.00
165 Pascal Dupuis RC 4.00 10.00
166 Nick Schultz RC 4.00 10.00
167 Martin Erat RC 6.00 15.00
168 Andreas Salomonsson RC 4.00 10.00
169 Radek Martinek RC 4.00 10.00
170 Raffi Torres RC 8.00 20.00
171 Dan Blackburn RC 4.00 10.00
172 Chris Neil RC 6.00 15.00
173 Jiri Dopita RC 4.00 10.00
174 Krystofer Kolanos RC 4.00 10.00
175 Billy Tibbetts RC 4.00 10.00
176 Mark Rycroft RC 4.00 10.00
177 Jeff Jillson RC 4.00 10.00
178 Nikita Alexeev RC 4.00 10.00
179 Chris Corrinet RC 4.00 10.00
180 Brian Sutherby RC 4.00 10.00

2001-02 Crown Royale Blue

This 144-card set paralleled the base set not including the SP's, but carried blue foil in place of the green and were serial-numbered out of 89. These cards were found in retail packs only at a stated rate of 2:25.
BLUE: 5X TO 12X BASIC CARD

2001-02 Crown Royale Premiere Date

This 144-card set paralleled the base set not including the SP's, but carried a premiere date stamp and were serial-numbered out of 60. These cards were found in hobby packs only at a stated rate of 1:25.
PREM.DATE: 4X TO 10X BASIC CARD

2001-02 Crown Royale Red

This 144-card set paralleled the base set not including the SP's, but carried red foil in place of the gold and were serial-numbered out of 35. These cards were found in hobby packs only at a stated rate of 1:49.
RED: 5X TO 12X BASIC CARD

2001-02 Crown Royale All-Star Honors

COMPLETE SET (1-20) 60.00 125.00
STATED ODDS 1:49 HOBBY/1:97 RETAIL
1 Paul Kariya 2.00 5.00
2 Roman Turek 1.50 4.00
3 Rob Blake 1.50 4.00

4 Patrick Roy 10.00 25.00
5 Joe Sakic 4.00 10.00
6 Mike Modano 3.00 8.00
7 Dominik Hasek 4.00 10.00
8 Brett Hull 2.50 6.00
9 Brendan Shanahan 3.00 8.00
10 Steve Yzerman 10.00 25.00
11 Pavel Bure 3.00 8.00
12 Martin Brodeur 5.00 12.00
13 Patrik Elias 1.50 4.00
14 Alexei Yashin 1.50 4.00
15 Eric Lindros 3.00 8.00
16 Mark Messier 2.50 6.00
17 Mario Lemieux 12.50 30.00
18 Doug Weight 1.50 4.00
19 Curtis Joseph 2.00 5.00
20 Mats Sundin 2.00 5.00

2001-02 Crown Royale Crowning Achievement

COMPLETE SET (20) 50.00 100.00
CARDS 1-10 INSERTED IN RETAIL PACKS
CARDS 11-20 INSERTED IN HOBBY PACKS
STATED ODDS 1:25
1 Dany Heatley 3.00 8.00
2 Ilya Kovalchuk 8.00 20.00
3 Mark Bell .75 2.00
4 Rostislav Klesla 2.00 5.00
5 Kristian Huselius .75 2.00
6 Martin Erat .75 2.00
7 Rick Dipietro 1.50 4.00
8 Dan Blackburn 1.50 4.00
9 Krystofer Kolanos .75 2.00
10 Johan Hedberg 1.50 4.00
11 Jarome Iginla 2.50 6.00
12 Patrick Roy 6.00 15.00
13 Joe Sakic 2.50 6.00
14 Dominik Hasek 2.50 6.00
15 Steve Yzerman 6.00 15.00
16 Pavel Bure 2.00 5.00
17 Martin Brodeur 3.00 8.00
18 Eric Lindros 2.00 5.00
19 Mario Lemieux 8.00 20.00
20 Jaromir Jagr 2.00 5.00

2001-02 Crown Royale Jewels of the Crown

COMPLETE SET (1-30) 60.00 125.00
STATED ODDS 1:25 HOBBY/RETAIL
1 Paul Kariya 1.00 2.50
2 Joe Thornton 2.00 5.00
3 Jarome Iginla 1.25 3.00
4 Roman Turek .75 2.00
5 Jeff O'Neill .75 2.00
6 Peter Forsberg 3.00 8.00
7 Patrick Roy 6.00 15.00
8 Joe Sakic 2.50 6.00
9 Mike Modano 2.00 5.00
10 Dominik Hasek 2.50 6.00
11 Brendan Shanahan 2.00 5.00
12 Steve Yzerman 6.00 15.00
13 Ryan Smyth .75 2.00
14 Pavel Bure 1.50 4.00
15 Jason Allison .75 2.00
16 Marian Gaborik 2.00 5.00
17 Saku Koivu 1.00 2.50
18 Martin Brodeur 3.00 8.00
19 Patrik Elias .75 2.00
20 Alexei Yashin .75 2.00
21 Eric Lindros 2.00 5.00
22 Mark Messier 1.50 4.00
23 Marian Hossa 1.00 2.50
24 Jeremy Roenick 1.25 3.00
25 Mario Lemieux 8.00 20.00
26 Keith Tkachuk 1.00 2.50
27 Teemu Selanne 1.00 2.50
28 Curtis Joseph 1.00 2.50
29 Mats Sundin 1.00 2.50
30 Jaromir Jagr 2.00 5.00

2001-02 Crown Royale Legendary Heroes

Inserted at a stated rate of 1:48 hobby boxes and 1:60 retail boxes, this 10-card set featured both a small full body photo on the left side of the card front and a larger head shot in the center under the players number. Each card was serial-numbered out of 31.

1 Paul Kariya 20.00 50.00
2 Patrick Roy 40.00 100.00
3 Dominik Hasek 12.50 30.00
4 Steve Yzerman 40.00 100.00
5 Martin Brodeur 20.00 50.00
6 Eric Lindros 12.50 30.00
7 Mark Messier 10.00 25.00
8 Mario Lemieux 50.00 125.00
9 Curtis Joseph 10.00 25.00
10 Jaromir Jagr 15.00 40.00

2001-02 Crown Royale Rookie Royalty

COMPLETE SET (1-20) 25.00 60.00
STATED ODDS 1:49 HOBBY/1:97 RETAIL
1 Dany Heatley 4.00 10.00
2 Ilya Kovalchuk 8.00 20.00
3 Erik Cole 1.25 3.00
4 Mark Bell 1.25 3.00
5 Vaclav Nedorost .75 2.00
6 Brian Willsie .75 2.00
7 Rostislav Klesla .75 2.00
8 Pavel Datsyuk 6.00 15.00
9 Ty Conklin .75 2.00
10 Kristian Huselius .75 2.00
11 Jaroslav Bednar .75 2.00
12 Martin Erat .75 2.00
13 Rick Dipietro 2.00 5.00
14 Dan Blackburn .75 2.00
15 Krystofer Kolanos .75 2.00
16 Kris Beech .75 2.00
17 Johan Hedberg .75 2.00
18 Toby Petersen .75 2.00
19 Jeff Jillson .75 2.00
20 Nikita Alexeev .75 2.00

2001-02 Crown Royale Triple Threads

Inserted at a rate of 2:25 hobby and 1:97 retail, this 20-card set featured three swatches of game-used sweaters from the players featured. The swatches were affixed beside a small color photo of each player and arranged vertically.

1 Paul Kariya 10.00 25.00
Steve Rucchin
Oleg Tverdovsky
2 Craig Conroy 5.00 12.00
Marc Savard
Roman Turek
3 Sergei Samsonov 5.00 12.00
Valeri Bure
Sergei Zubov
4 Jean-Sebastien Giguere 12.00 30.00
Jose Theodore
Patrick Roy
5 J-P Dumont 5.00 12.00
Richard Smehlik
Alexei Zhitnik
6 Kyle Calder 5.00 12.00
Matthieu Dandenault
Eric Daze
7 Joe Sakic 10.00 25.00
Patrick Roy
Greg DeVries
8 Dallas Stars 10.00 25.00
9 Jarome Iginla 8.00 20.00
Jochen Hecht
Andrew Cassels
10 Tom Fitzgerald 5.00 12.00
Cliff Ronning
Vitali Yachmenev
11 Steve Yzerman 15.00 40.00
Joe Sakic
Eric Lindros
12 Saku Koivu 8.00 20.00
Mats Sundin
Roman Turek
13 Scott Niedermayer 5.00 12.00
Chris Terreri
Manny Malhotra
14 Mariusz Czerkawski 5.00 12.00
Mats Lindgren
Mika Alatalo
15 Petr Nedved 8.00 20.00
Mike Richter
Theo Fleury
16 Mike Dunham 5.00 12.00
Scott Walker
Tom Fitzgerald
17 Mario Lemieux 15.00 40.00
Martin Straka
Alexei Kovalev
18 Scott Young 5.00 12.00
Jamie McLennan
Mike Eastwood
19 Cory Stillman 5.00 12.00
Jochen Hecht
Pierre Turgeon
20 Peter Bondra 8.00 20.00
Jaromir Jagr
Martin Straka

2001 Crown Royale Toronto Expo Rookie Collection

This set was issued by Pacific in a wrapper redemption program at the Toronto Spring Expo, May 4-6, 2001. The set features top rookies on the Crown Royale base card design with a blue background. Each card is serial numbered out of 499.

COMPLETE SET (8) 32.00 80.00
G1 Marty Turco 4.80 12.00
G2 Mike Comrie 10.00 25.00
G3 Rick DiPietro 6.00 15.00
G4 Martin Havlat 10.00 25.00
G5 Roman Cechmanek 4.00 10.00
G6 Brent Johnson 3.20 8.00
G7 Evgeni Nabokov 4.00 10.00
G8 Brad Richards 4.00 10.00

2002-03 Crown Royale

This 140-card set contained 100 veteran base cards and 40 shortprinted rookie cards that were inserted at 1:2 and serial-numbered to 2299 copies each.

COMPLETE SET (140) 75.00 150.00
COMP.SET w/o SP's (100) 40.00 80.00
1 J-S Giguere .50 1.25
2 Paul Kariya .60 1.50
3 Adam Oates .50 1.25
4 Dany Heatley .75 2.00
5 Ilya Kovalchuk .75 2.00
6 Glen Murray .30 .75
7 Sergei Samsonov .50 1.25
8 Steve Shields .50 1.25
9 Joe Thornton 1.00 2.50
10 Martin Biron .50 1.25
11 Chris Gratton .30 .75
12 Miroslav Satan .50 1.25
13 Chris Drury .50 1.25
14 Jarome Iginla .75 2.00
15 Roman Turek .50 1.25
16 Rod Brind'Amour .50 1.25
17 Ron Francis .50 1.25
18 Arturs Irbe .50 1.25
19 Jeff O'Neill .30 .75
20 Eric Daze .50 1.25
21 Jocelyn Thibault .50 1.25
22 Alexei Zhamnov .30 .75
23 Peter Forsberg 1.50 4.00
24 Milan Hejduk .60 1.50
25 Patrick Roy 3.00 8.00
26 Joe Sakic 1.25 3.00
27 Andrew Cassels .30 .75
28 Marc Denis .50 1.25
29 Bill Guerin .50 1.25
30 Mike Modano 1.00 2.50
31 Marty Turco .50 1.25
32 Sergei Fedorov 1.00 2.50
33 Brett Hull .75 2.00
34 Curtis Joseph .60 1.50
35 Nicklas Lidstrom .60 1.50
36 Brendan Shanahan .60 1.50
37 Steve Yzerman 3.00 8.00
38 Anson Carter .50 1.25
39 Mike Comrie .50 1.25
40 Tommy Salo .50 1.25
41 Ryan Smyth .30 .75
42 Kristian Huselius .30 .75
43 Roberto Luongo .75 2.00
44 Jason Allison .30 .75
45 Zigmund Palffy .50 1.25
46 Felix Potvin .50 1.25
47 Manny Fernandez .50 1.25
48 Marian Gaborik 1.25 3.00
49 Bill Muckalt .30 .75
50 Jeff Hackett .50 1.25
51 Saku Koivu .60 1.50
52 Jose Theodore .75 2.00
53 Richard Zednik .30 .75
54 David Legwand .50 1.25
55 Tomas Vokoun .50 1.25
56 Martin Brodeur 1.50 4.00
57 Patrik Elias .50 1.25
58 Scott Gomez .30 .75
59 Joe Nieuwendyk .50 1.25
60 Chris Osgood .50 1.25
61 Michael Peca .30 .75
62 Alexei Yashin .30 .75
63 Pavel Bure .60 1.50
64 Eric Lindros .60 1.50
65 Mike Richter .60 1.50
66 Daniel Alfredsson .50 1.25
67 Marian Hossa .60 1.50
68 Patrick Lalime .50 1.25
69 Roman Cechmanek .50 1.25
70 Simon Gagne .60 1.50
71 John LeClair .60 1.50
72 Jeremy Roenick .75 2.00
73 Tony Amonte .50 1.25
74 Daniel Briere .30 .75
75 Sean Burke .50 1.25
76 Johan Hedberg .50 1.25
77 Alexei Kovalev .50 1.25
78 Mario Lemieux 4.00 10.00
79 Alexei Morozov .30 .75
80 Pavol Demitra .50 1.25
81 Brent Johnson .50 1.25
82 Keith Tkachuk .60 1.50
83 Doug Weight .50 1.25
84 Vincent Damphousse .30 .75
85 Evgeni Nabokov .50 1.25
86 Teemu Selanne .60 1.50
87 Nikolai Khabibulin .60 1.50
88 Vincent Lecavalier .60 1.50
89 Martin St. Louis .50 1.25
90 Ed Belfour .60 1.50
91 Trevor Kidd .50 1.25
92 Alexander Mogilny .50 1.25
93 Mats Sundin .60 1.50
94 Todd Bertuzzi .60 1.50
95 Dan Cloutier .50 1.25
96 Brendan Morrison .50 1.25
97 Markus Naslund .60 1.50
98 Peter Bondra .50 1.25
99 Jaromir Jagr 1.00 2.50
100 Olaf Kolzig .50 1.25
101 Stanislav Chistov RC 2.00 5.00
102 Martin Gerber RC 1.50 4.00
103 Alexei Smirnov RC 1.50 4.00
104 Tim Thomas RC 2.00 5.00
105 Ryan Miller RC 2.50 6.00
106 Chuck Kobasew RC 1.50 4.00
107 Jordan Leopold RC 1.50 4.00
108 Pascal Leclaire RC 2.00 5.00
109 Rick Nash RC 8.00 20.00
110 Lasse Pirjeta RC 1.50 4.00
111 Steve Ott RC 2.50 6.00
112 Dmitri Bykov RC 1.50 4.00
113 Henrik Zetterberg RC 4.00 10.00
114 Ales Hemsky RC 4.00 10.00
115 Jay Bouwmeester RC 2.50 6.00
116 Ivan Majesky RC 1.50 4.00
117 Mike Cammalleri RC 2.00 5.00
118 Alexander Frolov RC 2.50 6.00
119 P-M Bouchard RC 2.50 6.00
120 Stephane Veilleux RC 1.50 4.00
121 Kyle Wanvig SP 1.50 4.00
122 Sylvain Blouin RC 1.50 4.00
123 Ron Hainsey RC 1.50 4.00
124 Adam Hall RC 1.50 4.00
125 Scottie Upshall RC 2.50 6.00
126 Ray Schultz RC 1.50 4.00
127 Jason Spezza RC 6.00 15.00
128 Anton Volchenkov RC 1.50 4.00
129 Dennis Seidenberg RC 1.50 4.00
130 Patrick Sharp RC 1.50 4.00
131 Radovan Somik RC 1.50 4.00
132 Jeff Taffe RC 1.50 4.00
133 Dick Tarnstrom RC 1.50 4.00
134 Tom Koivisto RC 1.50 4.00
135 Curtis Sanford RC 2.00 5.00
136 Lynn Loyns RC 1.50 4.00
137 Alexander Svitov RC 1.50 4.00
138 Carlo Colaiacovo RC 1.50 4.00
139 Steve Eminger RC 1.50 4.00
140 Alex Henry RC 1.50 4.00

2002-03 Crown Royale Blue

*STARS: X TO X BASIC CARDS
BLUE VETERAN ODDS 1:2 RETAIL PACKS
*ROOKIES (101-140): .75X TO 2X
ROOKIE PRINT RUN 350 SER.#'d SETS

2002-03 Crown Royale Purple

This 40-card hobby only set paralleled the last 40 cards of the base set but carried purple foil highlights. These cards were inserted at 1:5 and were serial-numbered out of 799.
*PURPLE: .3X TO .75X BASIC CARDS

2002-03 Crown Royale Red

*STARS: .75X TO 2X BASIC CARDS
RED VETERANS ODDS 1:4
*ROOKIES (101-140): .5X TO 1.25X
RED ROOKIE ODDS 1:12
RED ROOKIE PRINT RUN 350 SER.#'d SETS

2002-03 Crown Royale Retail

This 140-card set resembled the Hobby version but each card was highlighted with silver foil accents. Cards 101-140 were inserted at 1:7 packs.
*STARS: SAME VALUE AS HOBBY
*SP's: .3X TO .75X HOBBY HI

2002-03 Crown Royale Jerseys

*MULT.COLOR SWATCH: .75X TO 1.5X
STATED ODDS 2:23 HBBY/1:25 RETAIL
1 Dany Heatley/755 6.00 15.00

Ilya Kovalchuk/762 8.00 20.00
Joe Sakic/513 10.00 25.00
Geoff Sanderson/758 5.00 12.00
Marty Turco/763 5.00 12.00
Mike Comrie/762 5.00 12.00
Valeri Bure/760 5.00 12.00
Zigmund Palffy/512 5.00 12.00
Jose Theodore/513 6.00 15.00
Martin Brodeur 12.50 30.00
Patrik Elias/503 5.00 12.00
Mike Peca/762 5.00 12.00
Brian Leetch/762 5.00 12.00
Martin Havlat/757 5.00 12.00
Jeremy Roenick/746 6.00 15.00
Mario Lemieux 12.50 30.00
Alexei Morozov/753 5.00 12.00
Chris Pronger/763 5.00 12.00
Sergei Varlamov 5.00 12.00
Owen Nolan/513 5.00 12.00
Fredrik Modin/759 5.00 12.00
Alexander Mogilny/762 5.00 12.00
Markus Naslund/754 5.00 12.00
Peter Bondra/761 5.00 12.00
Jaromir Jagr/763 10.00 25.00

2002-03 Crown Royale Jerseys Gold

GOLD: .75X TO 2X BASIC JERSEYS
STATED PRINT RUN 25 SER.#'d SETS

2002-03 Crown Royale Dual Patches

Inserted as box toppers in hobby boxes, this -card set featured dual pieces of jersey patches. Print runs are listed below.

Dany Heatley 30.00 80.00
Ilya Kovalchuk/63
Martin Biron 12.50 30.00
J-P Dumont/273
Rod Brind'Amour 12.50 30.00
Erik Cole
Alexei Zhamnov 12.50 30.00
Steve Sullivan/209
Patrick Roy 60.00 125.00
Peter Forsberg SP
Joe Sakic 15.00 40.00
Alex Tanguay/228
Geoff Sanderson 12.50 30.00
Rostislav Klesla/403
M.Modano/P.Turgeon SP 15.00 40.00
Sergei Fedorov 12.50 30.00
Luc Robitaille/117
Tommy Salo 12.50 30.00
Ryan Smyth/188
1 Valeri Bure 12.50 30.00
Kristian Huselius/403
2 Adam Deadmarsh 12.50 30.00
Bryan Smolinski/403
3 M.Gaborik/M.Fernandez 25.00 60.00
4 Martin Brodeur 20.00 50.00
Patrik Elias/153
5 Michael Peca 12.50 30.00
Alexei Yashin/253
6 Brian Leetch 15.00 40.00
Mike Richter/213
7 M.Lemieux/A.Morozov 25.00 60.00
8 Alexei Kovalev 15.00 40.00
Martin Straka/403
9 Evgeni Nabokov 15.00 40.00
Patrick Marleau/163
0 Nikolai Khabibulin 20.00 40.00
Brad Richards/303
1 Alexander Mogilny 12.50 30.00
Darcy Tucker/203
2 Daniel Sedin 12.50 30.00
Henrik Sedin/243
3 Peter Bondra 12.50 30.00
Olaf Kolzig/347

2002-03 Crown Royale Coats of Armor

COMPLETE SET (10) 20.00 40.00
STATED ODDS 1:8 HBBY/1:25 RETAIL
Patrick Roy 4.00 10.00
Marty Turco .60 1.50
Curtis Joseph .75 2.00
Roberto Luongo 1.00 2.50
Jose Theodore 1.00 2.50
Martin Brodeur 2.00 5.00
Mike Richter .75 2.00
Patrick Lalime .60 1.50
Nikolai Khabibulin .75 2.00
0 Ed Belfour .75 2.00

2002-03 Crown Royale Lords of the Rink

COMPLETE SET (20) 30.00 60.00
STATED ODDS 1:5

1 Paul Kariya .75 2.00
2 Dany Heatley 1.00 2.50
3 Ilya Kovalchuk 1.00 2.50
4 Joe Thornton 1.25 3.00
5 Jarome Iginla 1.00 2.50
6 Peter Forsberg 2.00 5.00
7 Joe Sakic 1.50 4.00
8 Mike Modano 1.25 3.00
9 Brendan Shanahan 1.25 3.00
10 Steve Yzerman 4.00 10.00
11 Zigmund Palffy .60 1.50
12 Marian Gaborik 1.50 4.00
13 Saku Koivu .75 2.00
14 Pavel Bure 1.00 2.50
15 Eric Lindros .75 2.00
16 Mario Lemieux 5.00 12.00
17 Teemu Selanne .75 2.00
18 Vincent Lecavalier .75 2.00
19 Mats Sundin .75 2.00
20 Jaromir Jagr 1.25 3.00

2002-03 Crown Royale Rookie Royalty

COMPLETE SET (20) 12.00 25.00
STATED ODDS 1:5 HBBY/1:13 RETAIL
1 Stanislav Chistov .75 2.00
2 Martin Gerber .75 2.00
3 Alexei Smirnov .75 2.00
4 Ivan Huml .75 2.00
5 Chuck Kobasew .75 2.00
6 Tyler Arnason .75 2.00
7 Rick Nash 1.50 4.00
8 Dmitri Bykov .75 2.00
9 Henrik Zetterberg 1.50 4.00
10 Ales Hemsky .75 2.00
11 Jay Bouwmeester .75 2.00
12 Stephen Weiss .75 2.00
13 Alexander Frolov .75 2.00
14 Scottie Upshall .75 2.00
15 Justin Mapletoft .75 2.00
16 Jamie Lundmark .75 2.00
17 Jason Spezza 1.50 4.00
18 Petr Cajanek .75 2.00
19 Jonathan Cheechoo .75 2.00
20 Alexander Svitov .75 2.00

2002-03 Crown Royale Royal Portraits

STATED ODDS 1:45 HBBY/1:97 RETAIL
1 Paul Kariya 2.50 6.00
2 Ilya Kovalchuk 3.00 8.00
3 Patrick Roy 12.50 30.00
4 Joe Sakic 5.00 12.00
5 Rick Nash 15.00 40.00
6 Steve Yzerman 12.50 30.00
7 Martin Brodeur 6.00 15.00
8 Jason Spezza 12.50 30.00
9 Mario Lemieux 15.00 40.00
10 Jaromir Jagr 4.00 10.00

2003-04 Crown Royale

This 136-card die-cut set consisted of 100 veteran cards and 36 rookie cards short-printed to 575 serial-numbered copies each.

COMPLETE SET (136)
COMP.SET w/o SP's (100) 20.00 50.00
1 Sergei Fedorov .60 1.50
2 Martin Gerber .30 .75
3 J-S Giguere .30 .75
4 Ilya Kovalchuk .60 1.50
5 Pasi Nurminen .30 .75
6 Marc Savard .20 .50
7 Glen Murray .20 .50
8 Felix Potvin .50 1.25
9 Joe Thornton .75 2.00
10 Martin Biron .30 .75
11 J-P Dumont .20 .50
12 Taylor Pyatt .20 .50
13 Jarome Iginla .60 1.50
14 Chuck Kobasew .20 .50
15 Roman Turek .30 .75
16 Erik Cole .20 .50
17 Jeff O'Neill .30 .75
18 Kevin Weekes .30 .75
19 Tyler Arnason .30 .75
20 Brett McLean .20 .50
21 Jocelyn Thibault .30 .75
22 David Aebischer .30 .75
23 Peter Forsberg 1.00 2.50
24 Milan Hejduk .30 .75
25 Paul Kariya .50 1.25
26 Joe Sakic 1.00 2.50
27 Philippe Sauve .30 .75
28 Marc Denis .30 .75
29 Todd Marchant .20 .50
30 Rick Nash .60 1.50
31 Jason Arnott .20 .50
32 Bill Guerin .30 .75
33 Mike Modano .75 2.00
34 Marty Turco .30 .75
35 Dominik Hasek 1.00 2.50
36 Nicklas Lidstrom .50 1.25
37 Brendan Shanahan .50 1.25
38 Ray Whitney .20 .50
39 Steve Yzerman 1.50 4.00
40 Georges Laraque .20 .50
41 Tommy Salo .30 .75
42 Ryan Smyth .20 .50
43 Jay Bouwmeester .20 .50
44 Olli Jokinen .30 .75
45 Roberto Luongo .60 1.50
46 Jason Allison .20 .50
47 Roman Cechmanek .30 .75
48 Ziggy Palffy .30 .75
49 Luc Robitaille .30 .75
50 Pierre-Marc Bouchard .20 .50
51 Marian Gaborik .75 2.00
52 Dwayne Roloson .30 .75
53 Mathieu Garon .20 .50
54 Saku Koivu .50 1.25
55 Mike Ribeiro .20 .50
56 Jose Theodore .50 1.25
57 Scottie Upshall .20 .50
58 Tomas Vokoun .30 .75
59 Martin Brodeur 1.25 3.00
60 Patrik Elias .30 .75
61 Jeff Friesen .30 .75
62 Scott Gomez .20 .50
63 Mariusz Czerkawski .20 .50
64 Jason Blake .20 .50
65 Rick DiPietro .30 .75
66 Mike Dunham .30 .75
67 Alex Kovalev .30 .75
68 Mark Messier .50 1.25
69 Daniel Alfredsson .30 .75
70 Marian Hossa .50 1.25
71 Patrick Lalime .30 .75
72 Jason Spezza .50 1.25
73 Jeff Hackett .30 .75
74 Mark Recchi .30 .75
75 Jeremy Roenick .50 1.25
76 Justin Williams .20 .50
77 Sean Burke .30 .75
78 Ladislav Nagy .20 .50
79 Rico Fata .20 .50
80 Mario Lemieux 2.00 5.00
81 Chris Osgood .30 .75
82 Chris Pronger .30 .75
83 Keith Tkachuk .30 .75
84 Doug Weight .30 .75
85 Jonathan Cheechoo .30 .75
86 Alyn McCauley .20 .50
87 Evgeni Nabokov .30 .75
88 Nikolai Khabibulin .50 1.25
89 Vincent Lecavalier .50 1.25
90 Brad Richards .30 .75
91 Martin St. Louis .30 .75
92 Ed Belfour .50 1.25
93 Alexander Mogilny .30 .75
94 Owen Nolan .30 .75
95 Mats Sundin .50 1.25
96 Todd Bertuzzi .30 .75
97 Jason King .20 .50
98 Markus Naslund .30 .75
99 Jaromir Jagr .60 1.50
100 Olaf Kolzig .30 .75
101 Garrett Burnett RC 1.50 4.00
102 Joffrey Lupul RC 2.00 5.00
103 Patrice Bergeron RC 6.00 15.00
104 Sergei Zinovjev RC 1.50 4.00
105 Brent Krahn RC 1.50 4.00
106 Matthew Lombardi RC 1.50 4.00
107 Eric Staal RC 6.00 15.00
108 Tuomo Ruutu RC 3.00 8.00
109 Pavel Vorobiev RC 1.50 4.00
110 John-Michael Liles RC 1.50 4.00
111 Cody McCormick RC 1.50 4.00
112 Dan Fritsche RC 1.50 4.00
113 Nikolai Zherdev RC 2.50 6.00
114 Trevor Daley RC 1.50 4.00
115 Antti Miettinen RC 1.50 4.00
116 Jiri Hudler RC 2.00 5.00
117 Gregory Campbell RC 1.50 4.00
118 Nathan Horton RC 3.00 8.00
119 Dustin Brown RC 1.50 4.00
120 Tim Gleason RC 1.50 4.00
121 Brent Burns RC 1.50 4.00
122 Christopher Higgins RC 4.00 10.00
123 Dan Hamhuis RC 1.50 4.00
124 Jordin Tootoo RC 2.50 6.00
125 Marek Zidlicky RC 1.50 4.00
126 Paul Martin RC 1.50 4.00
127 Sean Bergenheim RC 1.50 4.00
128 Antoine Vermette RC 1.50 4.00
129 Joni Pitkanen RC 1.50 4.00
130 Matthew Spiller RC 1.50 4.00
131 Marc-Andre Fleury RC 10.00 25.00
132 Peter Sejna RC 1.50 4.00
133 Milan Michalek RC 2.00 5.00
134 Tom Preissing RC 1.50 4.00
135 Matt Stajan RC 2.50 6.00
136 Boyd Gordon RC 1.50 4.00

2003-04 Crown Royale Blue

*STARS: 1.25X TO 3X BASE HI
STATED PRINT RUN 850 SER.#'d SETS

2003-04 Crown Royale Red

STATED PRINT RUN 5 SER.#'d SETS
NOT PRICED DUE TO SCARCITY

2003-04 Crown Royale Retail

The retail version of this product carried silver foil highlights. Rookies in the retail set were serial-numbered out of 899.

*STARS: SAME VALUE HOBBY
*RCs: .3X TO .75X
RC PRINT RUN 899 SER.#'d SETS

2003-04 Crown Royale Gauntlet of Glory

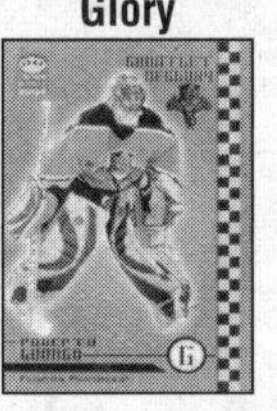

COMPLETE SET (20) 10.00 20.00
STATED ODDS 1:6
1 J-S Giguere .50 1.25
2 Pasi Nurminen .50 1.25
3 Felix Potvin .60 1.50
4 Martin Biron .50 1.25
5 Jocelyn Thibault .50 1.25
6 David Aebischer .50 1.25
7 Marc Denis .50 1.25
8 Marty Turco .50 1.25
9 Dominik Hasek 1.25 3.00
10 Roberto Luongo .75 2.00
11 Jose Theodore .75 2.00
12 Martin Brodeur 1.50 4.00
13 Rick DiPietro .50 1.25
14 Patrick Lalime .50 1.25
15 Sean Burke .50 1.25
16 Marc-Andre Fleury 1.50 4.00
17 Evgeni Nabokov .50 1.25
18 Nikolai Khabibulin .60 1.50
19 Ed Belfour .60 1.50
20 Dan Cloutier .50 1.25

2003-04 Crown Royale Global Conquest

STATED ODDS 1:11
1 M.Brodeur/M.Lemieux 2.00 5.00
2 Dominik Hasek .75 2.00
Jaromir Jagr
3 Teemu Selanne .60 1.50
Saku Koivu
4 Olaf Kolzig .60 1.50
Marco Sturm
5 Evgeni Nabokov .60 1.50
Nik Antropov
6 Sergei Fedorov 1.25 3.00
Ilya Kovalchuk
7 M.Gaborik/M.Hossa 1.00 2.50
8 Markus Naslund 1.25 3.00
Peter Forsberg
9 David Aebischer .60 1.50
Martin Gerber
10 Mike Modano .60 1.50
Jeremy Roenick

2003-04 Crown Royale Jerseys

STATED ODDS 3:20
1 Sergei Fedorov 4.00 10.00
2 Ilya Kovalchuk 5.00 12.00
3 Joe Thornton 5.00 12.00
4 Ryan Miller 3.00 8.00
5 Matthew Lombardi 2.00 5.00
6 Peter Forsberg 6.00 15.00
7 Teemu Selanne 3.00 8.00
8 Mike Modano 4.00 10.00
9 Steve Yzerman 8.00 20.00
10 Ales Hemsky 2.50 6.00
11 Jay Bouwmeester 2.00 5.00
12 Nathan Horton 4.00 10.00
13 Saku Koivu 3.00 8.00
14 Martin Brodeur 8.00 20.00
15 Rick DiPietro 2.50 6.00
16 Eric Lindros 3.00 8.00
17 Jason Spezza 6.00 15.00
18 Antoine Vermette 2.00 5.00
19 Jeremy Roenick 4.00 10.00
20 Mario Lemieux 10.00 25.00
21 Barret Jackman 2.00 5.00
22 Vincent Lecavalier 3.00 8.00
23 Ed Belfour 3.00 8.00
24 Owen Nolan 2.50 6.00
25 Markus Naslund 3.00 8.00

2003-04 Crown Royale Patches

*PATCHES: .75X TO 2X JERSEY CARDS
STATED ODDS 1:20
20 Mario Lemieux/25 50.00 125.00

2003-04 Crown Royale Lords of the Rink

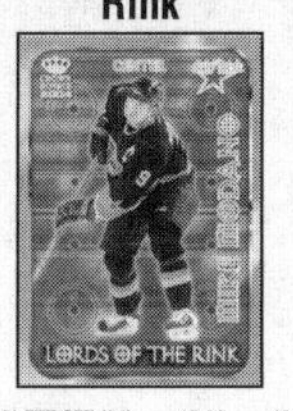

COMPLETE SET (24) 15.00 40.00
STATED ODDS 1:6
1 Sergei Fedorov .75 2.00
2 Ilya Kovalchuk .75 2.00
3 Joe Thornton 1.00 2.50
4 Eric Staal .50 1.25
5 Peter Forsberg 1.50 4.00
6 Milan Hejduk .60 1.50
7 Paul Kariya .60 1.50
8 Joe Sakic 1.25 3.00
9 Rick Nash .75 2.00
10 Mike Modano 1.00 2.50
11 Steve Yzerman 2.00 5.00
12 Henrik Zetterberg .60 1.50
13 Jay Bouwmeester .50 1.25
14 Ziggy Palffy .50 1.25
15 Marian Hossa .60 1.50
16 Jason Spezza .60 1.50
17 Jeremy Roenick .60 1.50
18 Mario Lemieux 2.50 6.00
19 Keith Tkachuk .60 1.50
20 Vincent Lecavalier .50 1.25
21 Mats Sundin .60 1.50
22 Todd Bertuzzi .60 1.50
23 Markus Naslund .60 1.50
24 Jaromir Jagr .75 2.00

2003-04 Crown Royale Royal Portraits

COMPLETE SET (10) 12.50 25.00
STATED ODDS 1:11
1 Joffrey Lupul 1.00 2.50
2 Patrice Bergeron 2.00 5.00
3 Eric Staal 2.00 5.00
4 Jiri Hudler 1.00 2.50
5 Nathan Horton 1.50 4.00
6 Jordin Tootoo 1.50 4.00
7 Joni Pitkanen 1.00 2.50
8 Marc-Andre Fleury 3.00 8.00
9 Milan Michalek 1.00 2.50
10 Matt Stajan 1.50 4.00

1970-71 Dad's Cookies

The 1970-71 Dad's Cookies set contains 144 unnumbered color cards. Each card measures approximately 1 7/8" by 5 3/8". Each player is pictured on the front dressed in an "NHL Players" emblazoned jersey. The fronts contain player statistics for the 1969-70 season and for his career. The backs, in both English and French, are the same for all cards. The backs contain an ad for these cards and Dad's Cookies, a special offer for an NHL Players Association decal and a 1969 NHL Players Association copyright line.

COMPLETE SET (144) 100.00 200.00
1 Lou Angotti .75 1.50
2 Don Awrey .50 1.00
3 Bob Baun .75 1.50
4 Jean Beliveau 4.00 8.00
5 Red Berenson .75 1.50
6 Gary Bergman .50 1.00
7 Les Binkley 1.00 2.00
8 Andre Boudrias .50 1.00
9 Wally Boyer .50 1.00
10 Arnie Brown .50 1.00
11 Johnny Bucyk 1.50 3.00
12 Charlie Burns .50 1.00
13 Larry Cahan .50 1.00
14 Gerry Cheevers 2.50 5.00
15 Bobby Clarke 6.00 12.00
16 Wayne Connelly .50 1.00
17 Yvan Cournoyer 1.50 3.00
18 Roger Crozier 1.00 2.00
19 Ray Cullen .50 1.00
20 Denis DeJordy 1.00 2.00
21 Alex Delvecchio 1.50 3.00
22 Gary Dillabough .50 1.00
23 Gary Doak .50 1.00
24 Gary Dornhoefer 1.00 2.00
25 Dick Duff .75 1.50
26 Tim Ecclestone .50 1.00
27 Roy Edwards 1.00 2.00
28 Gerry Ehman .50 1.00
29 Ron Ellis .75 1.50
30 Phil Esposito 5.00 10.00
31 Tony Esposito 5.00 10.00
32 Doug Favell 1.00 2.00
33 John Ferguson .75 1.50
34 Norm Ferguson .50 1.00
35 Reg Fleming .50 1.00
36 Bill Flett .50 1.00
37 Bruce Gamble 1.00 2.00
38 Jean-Guy Gendron .50 1.00
39 Ed Giacomin 2.00 4.00
40 Rod Gilbert 1.00 2.00
41 Bill Goldsworthy .75 1.50
42 Phil Goyette .50 1.00
43 Danny Grant .75 1.50
44 Ted Green .75 1.50
45 Vic Hadfield .75 1.50
46 Al Hamilton .50 1.00
47 Ted Hampson .50 1.00
48 Terry Harper .75 1.50
49 Ted Harris .50 1.00
50 Paul Henderson 1.50 3.00
51 Bryan Hextall .50 1.00
52 Bill Hicke .50 1.00
53 Larry Hillman .50 1.00
54 Wayne Hillman .50 1.00
55 Charlie Hodge 1.25 2.50
56 Ken Hodge .75 1.50
57 Gordie Howe 10.00 20.00
58 Harry Howell 1.00 2.00
59 Bobby Hull 7.50 15.00
60 Dennis Hull .75 1.50
61 Earl Ingarfield .50 1.00
62 Doug Jarrett .50 1.00
63 Gary Jarrett .50 1.00
64 Ed Johnston 1.00 2.00
65 Dave Keon 1.50 3.00
66 Skip Krake .50 1.00
67 Orland Kurtenbach .75 1.50
68 Andre Lacroix .75 1.50
69 Jacques Laperriere .75 1.50
70 Jacques Lemaire 1.50 3.00
71 Rick Ley .50 1.00
72 Bruce MacGregor .50 1.00
73 Keith Magnuson .75 1.50
74 Frank Mahovlich 2.00 4.00
75 Chico Maki .50 1.00
76 Gilles Marotte .50 1.00
77 Bert Marshall .50 1.00
78 Don Marshall .50 1.00
79 Pit Martin .75 1.50
80 Keith McCreary .50 1.00
81 Ab McDonald .50 1.00
82 Jim McKenny .75 1.50
83 John McKenzie .75 1.50
84 Mike McMahon .50 1.00
85 Larry Mickey .50 1.00
86 Stan Mikita 2.50 5.00
87 Doug Mohns .50 1.00
88 Wayne Muloin .50 1.00
89 Jim Neilson .50 1.00
90 Bob Nevin .50 1.00
91 Murray Oliver .50 1.00
92 Bobby Orr 20.00 40.00
93 Danny O'Shea .50 1.00
94 Rosaire Paiement .50 1.00
95 Bernie Parent 2.50 5.00
96 Jean-Paul Parise .50 1.00
97 Brad Park 1.50 3.00
98 Mike Pelyk .50 1.00
99 Gilbert Perreault 2.00 4.00
100 Noel Picard .50 1.00
101 Barclay Plager .75 1.50
102 Jacques Plante 5.00 10.00
103 Tracy Pratt .50 1.00
104 Dean Prentice .50 1.00
105 Jean Pronovost .75 1.50
106 Bob Pulford .75 1.50
107 Pat Quinn 1.00 2.00
108 Jean Ratelle 1.00 2.00
109 Matt Ravlich .50 1.00
110 Mickey Redmond 1.00 2.00
111 Henri Richard 2.00 4.00
112 Jim Roberts .50 1.00
113 Dale Rolfe .50 1.00
114 Bobby Rousseau .50 1.00
115 Gary Sabourin .50 1.00
116 Derek Sanderson 2.50 5.00
117 Glen Sather 1.50 3.00
118 Serge Savard 1.00 2.00
119 Ken Schinkel .50 1.00
120 Rod Seiling .50 1.00
121 Brit Selby .50 1.00
122 Eddie Shack 1.50 3.00
123 Floyd Smith .50 1.00
124 Fred Stanfield .50 1.00
125 Pat Stapleton .50 1.00
126 Frank St.Marseille .50 1.00
127 Dale Tallon .50 1.00
128 Walt Tkaczuk .50 1.00
129 J.C. Tremblay .50 1.00
130 Norm Ullman .75 1.50
131 Garry Unger .75 1.50
132 Rogatien Vachon 1.50 3.00
133 Carol Vadnais .50 1.00
134 Ed Van Impe .50 1.00
135 Bob Wall .50 1.00
136 Mike Walton .50 1.00
137 Bryan Watson .50 1.00
138 Joe Watson .50 1.00
139 Tom Webster .50 1.00
140 Juha Widing 1.00 2.00
141 Tom Williams .50 1.00
142 Jim Wiste .50 1.00
143 Gump Worsley 2.50 5.00
144 Bob Woytowich .75 1.50

1983-84 Devils Postcards

This set is the first confirmed to feature the franchise transferred from Colorado to New Jersey. The color postcards feature action photos and were issued by the team as promotional items at player appearances.

COMPLETE SET (25) 10.00 25.00
1 Mike Antonovich .20 .50
2 Mel Bridgman .30 .75
3 Aaron Broten .20 .50
4 Murray Brumwell .30 .75
5 Dave Cameron .30 .75
6 Rich Chernomaz .20 .50
7 Joe Cirella .30 .75
8 Ken Daneyko .60 1.50
9 Larry Floyd .20 .50
10 Paul Gagne .20 .50
11 Mike Kitchen .30 .75
12 Jeff Larmer .30 .75
13 Don Lever .20 .50
14 Dave Lewis .20 .50
15 Bob Lorimer .20 .50
16 Ron Low .30 .75
17 Jan Ludvig .20 .50
18 John Maclean 2.40 6.00
19 Bob MacMillan .30 .75
20 Hector Marini .20 .50
21 Rick Meagher .20 .50
22 Grant Mulvey .30 .75
23 Glenn Resch .60 1.50
24 Phil Russell .20 .50
25 Pat Verbeek 2.40 6.00

1984-85 Devils Postcards

This 25-card set of New Jersey Devils features on the front borderless color photos of the players, with two team logos (in green and red) in the white stripe below the picture. The cards measure approximately 3 1/4" by 6 1/8" and are in the postcard type format. On the left half of the back appear a black and white head shot of the player, basic player information, and the Devils' team logo. The cards are checklisted below according to uniform number. The side panel of the package of Colgate Dental Cream listed the checklist of the complete set. The cards of John MacLean and Kirk Muller predate their Rookie Cards.

COMPLETE SET (25) 8.00 20.00
1 Chico Resch .80 2.00
2 Joe Cirella .30 .75
4 Bob Lorimer .20 .50
5 Phil Russell .20 .50
8 Dave Pichette .20 .50
9 Don Lever .30 .75
10 Aaron Broten .20 .50
12 Pat Verbeek 2.00 5.00
14 Rich Chernomaz .20 .50
15 John MacLean 1.60 4.00
16 Rick Meagher .20 .50
17 Paul Gagne .20 .50
18 Mel Bridgman .30 .75
19 Rich Preston .20 .50
20 Tim Higgins .20 .50
21 Bob Hoffmeyer .20 .50
22 Doug Sulliman .20 .50
23 Bruce Driver .40 1.00
25 Dave Lewis .20 .50
27 Kirk Muller 2.00 5.00
28 Uli Hiemer .20 .50
29 Jan Ludvig .20 .50
30 Ron Low .30 .75
33 Hannu Kamppurri .30 .75
NNO Doug Carpenter CO .20 .50

1985-86 Devils Postcards

This ten-card set of New Jersey Devils features on the front borderless color player photos. The cards measure approximately 3 5/8" by 5 1/2" and are in the postcard format. The horizontal backs are divided in half by a thin black line and have the year, biographical information, home town, and a career highlight at the upper left corner. The cards are unnumbered and checklisted below in alphabetical order. Key cards in the set are Kirk Muller in his Rookie Card year and Craig Billington prior to his Rookie Card year.

COMPLETE SET (10) 5.60 14.00

1 Greg Adams .60 1.50
2 Perry Anderson .40 1.00
3 Craig Billington .80 2.00
4 Alain Chevrier .60 1.50
5 Paul Gagne .40 1.00
6 Mark Johnson .40 1.00
7 Kirk Muller 1.60 4.00
8 Chico Resch 1.00 2.50
9 Randy Velischek .40 1.00
10 Craig Wolanin .40 1.00

1986-87 Devils Police

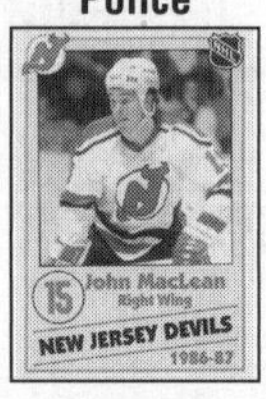

This 20-card set was jointly sponsored by the New Jersey Devils, S.O.B.E.R., Howard Bank, and Independent Insurance Agents of Bergen Country. Logos for these sponsors appear on the bottom of the card back. The front features a color action photo of the player, with the Devils' and NHL logos superimposed over the top corners of the picture. A thin black line and a green line serves as the inner and outer borders respectively; the area in between is yellow, with printing in the team's colors red and black. In addition to sponsors' logos, the back has biographical information, an anti-drug message, and career statistics. We have checklisted the cards below in alphabetical order, with uniform number to the right of the player's name.

COMPLETE SET (20) 12.00 30.00
1 Greg Adams 24 .60 1.50
2 Perry Anderson 25 .40 1.00
3 Timo Blomqvist 5 .40 1.00
4 Andy Brickley 26 .40 1.00
5 Mel Bridgman 18 .60 1.50
6 Aaron Broten 10 .40 1.00
7 Alain Chevrier 30 .60 1.50
8 Joe Cirella 2 .60 1.50
9 Ken Daneyko 3 .60 1.50
10 Bruce Driver 23 .80 2.00
11 Uli Hiemer 28 .40 1.00
12 Mark Johnson 12 .60 1.50
13 Jan Ludvig 29 .40 1.00
14 John MacLean 15 1.60 4.00
15 Peter McNab 7 .60 1.50
16 Kirk Muller 9 2.00 5.00
17 Doug Sulliman 22 .40 1.00
18 Randy Velischek 27 .40 1.00
19 Pat Verbeek 2.00 5.00
20 Craig Wolanin 6 .40 1.00

1988-89 Devils Caretta

This 30-card set has color action photos of the New Jersey Devils on the front, with a thin black border on white card stock. The cards measure approximately 2 7/8" by 4 1/4". The team name and logo on the top are printed in green and red; the text below the picture, giving player name, uniform number, and position, is printed in black. The horizontally oriented back has career statistics, a team logo, and a Carretta Trucking logo. We have checklisted the cards below in alphabetical order. Brendan Shanahan appears in his Rookie Card year.

COMPLETE SET (30) 10.00 25.00
1 Perry Anderson 25 .20 .50
2 Bob Bellemore CO .20 .50
3 Aaron Broten 10 .20 .50
4 Doug Brown 24 .20 .50
5 Sean Burke 1 1.20 3.00
6 Anders Carlsson 20 .20 .50
7 Joe Cirella 2 .20 .50
8 Pat Conacher 32 .20 .50
9 Ken Daneyko 3 .30 .75
10 Bruce Driver 23 .30 .75
11 Bob Hoffmeyer CO .20 .50
12 Jamie Huscroft 4 .20 .50
13 Mark Johnson 12 .30 .75
14 Jim Korn 14 .20 .50
15 Tom Kurvers 5 .20 .50
16 Lou Lamoriello P/GM .10 .25
17 Claude Loiselle 19 .20 .50
18 John MacLean 15 .80 2.00
19 David Maley 8 .20 .50
20 Doug McKay CO .10 .25
21 Kirk Muller 9 .80 2.00
22 Jack O'Callahan 7 .20 .50
23 Steve Rooney 18 .20 .50
24 Bob Sauve 28 .30 .75
25 Jim Schoenfeld CO .40 1.00
26 Brendan Shanahan 11 6.00 15.00
27 Patrik Sundstrom 17 .30 .75
28 Randy Velischek 27 .20 .50
29 Pat Verbeek 16 .80 2.00
30 Craig Wolanin 6 .20 .50

1989-90 Devils Caretta

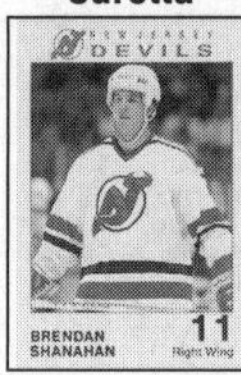

This 29-card set has color action photos of the New Jersey Devils on the front, with a thin red border on white card stock. The team name and logo on the top are printed in green and red; the text below the picture, giving player name, uniform number, and position, is printed in black. The horizontal back provides brief biographical information and career statistics, a black-and-white picture and a Caretta Trucking logo. (The set also was issued without the trucking logo.) The cards measure approximately 2 7/8" by 4 1/4". These unnumbered cards are checklisted below alphabetically with sweater number noted to the right.

COMPLETE SET (29) 8.00 20.00
1 Tommy Albelin 26 .20 .50
2 Bob Bellemore CO .10 .25
3 Neil Brady 19 .20 .50
4 Aaron Broten 10 .20 .50
5 Doug Brown 24 .20 .50
6 Sean Burke 1 .80 2.00
7 Pat Conacher 32 .20 .50
8 John Cunniff CO .10 .25
9 Ken Daneyko 3 .20 .50
10 Bruce Driver 23 .40 1.00
11 Slava Fetisov 2 .80 2.00
12 Mark Johnson 12 .20 .50
13 Jim Korn 14 .20 .50
14 Lou Lamoriello P/GM .10 .25
15 John MacLean 15 .60 1.50
16 David Maley 8 .20 .50
17 Kirk Muller 9 .80 2.00
18 Janne Ojanen 22 .20 .50
19 Walt Poddubny 21 .20 .50
20 Reijo Ruotsalainen 29 .20 .50
21 Brendan Shanahan 11 2.00 5.00
22 Sergei Starikov 4 .20 .50
23 Patrik Sundstrom 17 .20 .50
24 Peter Sundstrom 20 .20 .50
25 Chris Terreri 31 .40 1.00
26 Sylvain Turgeon 16 .20 .50
27 Randy Velischek 27 .20 .50
28 Eric Weinrich 7 .20 .50
29 Craig Wolanin 6 .20 .50

1990-91 Devils Team Issue

This set contains 30 standard-size cards and features members of the New Jersey Devils. The front has a color photo of the player, with the team logo in the upper left corner. The back has statistical information. These cards are unnumbered and are checklisted below in alphabetical order.

COMPLETE SET (30) 6.00 15.00
1 Tommy Albelin .16 .40
2 Laurie Boschman .16 .40
3 Doug Brown .20 .50
4 Sean Burke .60 1.50
5 Tim Burke .16 .40
6 Zdeno Ciger .20 .50
7 Pat Conacher .16 .40
8 Troy Crowder .20 .50
9 John Cunniff CO .10 .25
10 Ken Daneyko .30 .75
11 Bruce Driver .20 .50
12 Slava Fetisov .30 .75
13 Alexei Kasatonov .20 .50
14 Lou Lamoriello P/GM .10 .25
15 Claude Lemieux .40 1.00
16 David Maley .16 .40
17 John MacLean .40 1.00
18 Jon Morris .16 .40
19 Kirk Muller .60 1.50
20 Lee Norwood .16 .40
21 Myles O'Connor .16 .40
22 Walt Poddubny .20 .50
23 Brendan Shanahan 2.00 5.00
24 Peter Stastny .60 1.50
25 Alan Stewart .16 .40
26 Warren Strelow .16 .40
27 Doug Sulliman .16 .40
28 Patrik Sundstrom .20 .50
29 Chris Terreri .20 .50
30 Eric Weinrich .20 .50

1991-92 Devils Teams Carvel

This ten-card set features team photos of the ten Devils teams from 1982-83 through 1991-92. The cards have a coupon for Carvel Ice Cream with an entry form for the "Shoot to Win" contest. The backs list all the players who are pictured and the statistical leaders from that particular year. The cards are unnumbered and measure approximately 2 1/2" by 6" with coupon. One card was issued per spectator at certain home games during the 1991-92 season.

COMPLETE SET (10) 8.00 20.00
1 1982-83 Devils Team 1.20 3.00
2 1983-84 Devils Team 1.00 2.50
3 1984-85 Devils Team 1.00 2.50
4 1985-86 Devils Team 1.00 2.50
5 1986-87 Devils Team 1.00 2.50
6 1987-88 Devils Team 1.00 2.50
7 1988-89 Devils Team 1.00 2.50
8 1989-90 Devils Team 1.00 2.50
9 1990-91 Devils Team 1.00 2.50
10 1991-92 Devils Team 1.00 2.50

1996-97 Devils Team Issue

This attractive team-issued set is complete at 30-cards. It was apparently issued as a premium at a game sometime during the '96-97 season and was sponsored by Sharp Electronics. The fronts feature action color photos surrounded by a red border. The player's name and number appear at the top, while his position and team logo grace the bottom. The backs include a black and white head shot as well as comprehensive statistics.

COMPLETE SET (30) 12.00 30.00
1 Mike Dunham .80 2.00
3 Ken Daneyko .20 .50
4 Scott Stevens .30 .75
10 Denis Pederson .30 .75
11 Steve Sullivan .40 1.00
12 Bill Guerin .80 2.00
14 Brian Rolston .30 .75
15 John MacLean .30 .75
16 Bobby Holik .30 .75
17 Petr Sykora .80 2.00
18 Sergei Brylin .20 .50
19 Bob Carpenter .10 .25
20 Jay Pandolfo .20 .50
21 Randy McKay .30 .75
22 Patrik Elias 4.00 10.00
23 Dave Andreychuk .20 .50
24 Lyle Odelein .20 .50
25 Valeri Zelepukin .10 .25
26 Jason Smith .20 .50
27 Scott Niedermayer .40 1.00
28 Kevin Dean .10 .25
29 Shawn Chambers .10 .25
30 Martin Brodeur 2.00 5.00
32 Steve Thomas .20 .50
33 Reid Simpson .10 .25
NNO Jacques Lemaire CO .20 .50
NNO John J. McMullen CH .04 .10
NNO Lou Lamoriello GM .04 .10
NNO Robbie Ftorek ACO .10 .25
NNO Jacques Caron ACO .04 .10

1997-98 Devils Team Issue

This set features the Devils of the NHL. The cards were sponsored by Zebra Pens and were given away as a promotion at a single home game.

COMPLETE SET (32) 8.00 20.00
1 Mike Dunham .40 1.00
2 Sheldon Souray .16 .40
3 Ken Daneyko .16 .40
4 Scott Stevens .30 .75
5 Ken Sutton .16 .40
6 Brad Bombardir .16 .40
7 Vlastimil Kroupa .16 .40
8 Denis Pederson .16 .40
9 Bill Guerin .40 1.00
10 John MacLean .16 .40
11 Bobby Holik .20 .50
12 Petr Sykora .40 1.00
13 Sergei Brylin .16 .40
14 Bobby Carpenter .16 .40
15 Jay Pandolfo .16 .40
16 Randy McKay .20 .50
17 Scott Daniels .16 .40
18 Dave Andreychuk .20 .50
19 Lyle Odelein .16 .40
20 Valeri Zelepukin .16 .40
21 Patrik Elias 1.20 3.00
22 Kevin Dean .16 .40
23 Krzysztof Oliwa .30 .75
24 Martin Brodeur 1.20 3.00
25 Steve Thomas .20 .50
26 Reid Simpson .16 .40
27 Doug Gilmour .40 1.00
28 Jacques Lemaire CO .10 .25
29 Robbie Ftorek CO .04 .10
30 Jacques Caron CO .04 .10
31 Lou Lamoriello PRES .04 .10
32 John McMullen CHAIR .04 .10

1998-99 Devils Team Issue

COMPLETE SET (30) 20.00
1 Dave Andreychuk .75
2 Jason Arnott .75
3 Brad Bombardir .50
4 Martin Brodeur 5.00
5 Sergei Brylin .50
6 Jacques Caron ACO .10
7 Bob Carpenter ACO .10
8 Ken Daneyko .50
9 Kevin Dean .50
10 Patrik Elias 1.00
11 Slava Fetisov CO .25
12 Robbie Ftorek HCO .10
13 Bobby Holik .50
14 Sasha Lakovic .50
15 Lou Lamoriello GM .10
16 John Madden 1.00
17 Randy McKay .50
18 John McMullen OWN .10
19 Brendan Morrison 1.00
20 Scott Niedermayer .75
21 Lyle Odelein .50
22 Krzysztof Oliwa 1.00
23 Jay Pandolfo .75
24 Denis Pederson .50
25 Brian Rolston .75
26 Vadim Sharifijanov .50
27 Sheldon Souray .50
28 Scott Stevens 1.00
29 Petr Sykora 1.00
30 Chris Terreri .75

1999-00 Devils Team Issue

This set features the Devils of the NHL. The set is believed to have been issued as a promotional giveaway and was sponsored by PSEG Energy.

COMPLETE SET (31) 8.00 20.00
1 Scott Stevens .30 .75
2 Sheldon Souray .16 .40
3 Ken Daneyko .16 .40
4 Brad Bombardir .16 .40
5 Vadim Sharifijanov .16 .40
6 Brendan Morrison .20 1.00
7 John Madden .20 1.00
8 Sergei Nemchinov .16 .40
9 Bobby Holik .20 .50
10 Petr Sykora .60 1.00
11 Sergei Brylin .16 .40
12 Denis Pederson .16 .40
13 Jay Pandolfo .16 .40
14 Randy McKay .20 .50
15 Claude Lemieux .30 .75
16 Scott Gomez .40 1.00
17 Lyle Odelein .16 .40
18 Jason Arnott .40 .75
19 Patrik Elias .80 1.50
20 Scott Niedermayer .30 .75
21 Brian Rafalski .20 .50
22 Krzysztof Oliwa .40 1.00
23 Martin Brodeur 1.20 4.00
24 Chris Terreri .16 .50
25 Robbie Ftorek CO .16 .40
26 Slava Fetisov CO .20 .50
27 Larry Robinson CO .20 .50
28 Jacques Caron CO .04 .10
29 Lou Lamoriello GM .04 .10
30 Dr. John J. McMullen .04 .10
31 PSEG Energy .04 .10

2000-01 Devils Team Issue

This set was issued as a promotional giveaway at a single home game early in the season.

COMPLETE SET (30) 10.00 25.00
1 Jason Arnott .40 1.00
2 Martin Brodeur 2.00 5.00
3 Sergei Brylin .20 .50
4 Mike Commodore .30 .75
5 Ken Daneyko .20 .50
6 Patrik Elias .80 2.00
7 Sascha Goc .20 .50
8 Scott Gomez .40 1.00
9 Bobby Holik .30 .75
10 Steve Kelly .20 .50
11 John Madden .80 2.00
12 Randy McKay .30 .75
13 Jim McKenzie .20 .50
14 Alexander Mogilny .30 .75
15 Sergei Nemchinov .20 .50
16 Scott Niedermayer .40 1.00
17 Jay Pandolfo .20 .50
18 Brian Rafalski .20 .50
19 Scott Stevens .40 1.00
20 Turner Stevenson .20 .50
21 Ken Sutton .20 .50
22 Petr Sykora .80 2.00
23 Chris Terreri .30 .75
24 Colin White .30 .75
25 Larry Robinson CO .20 .50
26 Slava Fetisov ACO .20 .50
27 Kurt Kleinendorst ACO .04 .10
28 Jacques Caron ACO .04 .10
29 Lou Lamoriello GM .04 .10
30 2000 Stanley Cup Champions .20 .50

2001-02 Devils Team Issue

This set features the Devils of the NHL. The set was sponsored by Model's and was issued as a promotional giveaway at a home game early in the 2001-02 season.

COMPLETE SET (25) 8.00 20.00
1 Jason Arnott .40 1.00
2 Martin Brodeur 2.00 5.00
3 Sergei Brylin .20 .50
4 Jacques Caron ACO .04 .11
5 Pierre Dagenais .20 .50
6 Patrik Elias .80 2.00
7 Slava Fetisov ACO .20 .50
8 Scott Gomez .40 1.00
9 Bobby Holik .31 .78
10 Lou Lamoriello GM .04 .11
11 Jay Leach ACO .04 .11
12 John Madden .40 1.00
13 Randy McKay .31 .78
14 Jim McKenzie .20 .50
15 Sergei Nemchinov .20 .50
16 Scott Niedermayer .40 1.00
17 Devil Mascot .04 .11
18 Jay Pandolfo .20 .50
19 Brian Rafalski .20 .50
20 Larry Robinson CO .20 .50
21 Andreas Salomonsson .80 2.00
22 Scott Stevens 1.00
23 Turner Stevenson .20 .50
24 Petr Sykora .80 2.00
NNO Title Card .04 .11

2002-03 Devils Team Issue

Issued by the team at a game late in 2002, this 30-card set featured color photos on the card fronts and blank backs. The cards were unnumbered and are listed below by jersey number.

COMPLETE SET (30)
1 Ken Daneyko .10 .40
2 Scott Stevens .30 1.00
3 Colin White .10 .40
4 Tommy Albelin .10 .40
5 Steve Guolla .10 .40
6 Jiri Bicek .10 .50
7 Craig Darby .10 .40
8 Oleg Tverdovsky .10 .40
9 John Madden .30 1.00
10 Jeff Friesen .20 .75
11 Brian Gionta .30 1.00
12 Jamie Langenbrunner .20 .75
13 Christian Berglund .10 .40
14 Sergei Brylin .10 .40
15 Jim McKenzie .10 .40
16 Jay Pandolfo .10 .40
17 Scott Gomez .20 .75
18 Turner Stevenson .10 .40
19 Joe Nieuwendyk .30 1.00
20 Patrik Elias .30 .75
21 Scott Niedermayer .30 1.00
22 Brian Rafalski .10 .50
23 Martin Brodeur 2.00 5.00
24 Corey Schwab .20 .75
25 Lou Lamoriello GM .04 .10
26 Pat Burns HCO .04 .10
27 Bobby Carpenter ACO .04 .10
28 John MacLean ACO .04 .10
29 Jacques Caron CO .04 .10
30 Mascot .04 .10

2003-04 Devils Team Issue

This team set was sponsored by Verizon and handed out at a home game during the 2003-04 season. They are listed below by player number.

2 Sean Brown .20 .50
4 Scott Stevens .30 .75
5 Colin White .20 .50
6 Tommy Albelin .20 .50
7 Paul Martin .40 1.00
8 Igor Larionov .30 .75
10 Erik Rasmussen .20 .50
11 John Madden .40 1.00
12 Jeff Friesen .30 .75
14 Brian Gionta .75 2.00
15 Jamie Langenbrunner .30 .75
16 Mike Rupp .20 .50
17 Christian Berglund .20 .50
18 Sergei Brylin .20 .50
20 Jay Pandolfo .20 .50
23 Scott Gomez .40 1.00
24 Turner Stevenson .20 .50
25 David Hale .20 .50
26 Patrik Elias .40 1.00
27 Scott Niedermayer .40 1.00
28 Brian Rafalski .20 .50
29 Grant Marshall .20 .50
30 Martin Brodeur 5.00
35 Corey Schwab .30 .75
40 Scott Clemmensen .30 .75
41 Lou Lamoriello GM .02 .10
42 Pat Burns HCO .02 .10
43 Bob Carpenter ACO .02 .10
44 John MacLean ACO .02 .10
45 Jacques Laperiere ACO .02 .10
46 Jacques Caron ACO .02 .10
47 Mascot .02 .10

2005-06 Devils Team Issue

COMPLETE SET (30) 10.00 20.00
1 N.J. Devil MASCOT .02 .10
2 Jacques Caron ACO .02 .10
3 John MacLean ACO .02 .10
4 Jacques Laperriere ACO .02 .10
5 Larry Robinson CO .02 .10
6 Lou Lamoriello GM .02 .10
7 Alexander Mogilny .30 .75
8 Scott Clemmensen .30 .75
9 Ari Ahonen .30 .75
10 Martin Brodeur 2.00 5.00
11 Grant Marshall .20 .50
12 Brian Rafalski .20 .50
13 Patrik Elias .30 .75
14 David Hale .20 .50
15 Richard Matvichuk .20 .50
16 Scott Gomez .30 .75
17 Viktor Kozlov .20 .50
18 Jay Pandolfo .20 .50
19 Sergei Brylin .20 .50
20 Darren Langdon .30 .75
21 Jamie Langenbrunner .20 .50
22 Brain Gionta .40 1.00
23 John Madden .20 .50
24 Erik Rasmussen .20 .50
25 Zach Parise 2.00 5.00
26 Sean Brown .20 .50
27 Paul Martin .20 .50
28 Dan McGillis .20 .50
29 Colin White .20 .50
30 Vladimir Malakhov .20 .50

2006-07 Devils Team Set

COMPLETE SET (41) 10.00 25.00
1 Martin Brodeur 2.00 5.00
2 Alex Brooks .20 .50
3 Sergei Brylin .20 .50
4 Scott Clemmensen .20 .50
5 Jim Dowd .20 .50
6 Patrik Elias .30 .75
7 Brian Gionta .40 1.00
8 Scott Gomez .40 1.00
9 David Hale .20 .50
10 Cam Janssen .40 1.00
11 Dan LaCouture .20 .50
12 Jamie Langenbrunner .20 .50
13 Brad Lukowich .20 .50
14 John Madden .20 .50
15 Paul Martin .20 .50
16 Richard Matvichuk .20 .50
17 Alexander Mogilny .30 .75
18 Johnny Oduya .20 .50
19 Jay Pandolfo .20 .50
20 Zach Parise .75 2.00
21 Brian Rafalski .20 .50
22 Erik Rasmussen .20 .50
23 Mike Rupp .20 .50
24 Barry Tallackson .20 .50
25 Colin White .20 .50
26 Jason Wiemer .20 .50
27 Travis Zajac .40 1.00
28 Lou Lamoriello GM .10 .25
29 Claude Julien CO .10 .25
30 Jacques Laperriere ACO .10 .25
31 John MacLean ACO .10 .25
32 Jacques Caron ACO .10 .25
33 Mel Bridgman .20 .50
34 Bruce Driver .20 .50
35 Patrik Elias .30 .75
36 Don Lever .20 .50
37 Kirk Muller .20 .50
38 Scott Niedermayer .30 .75
39 Scott Stevens .30 .75
40 Ken Daneyko .20 .50
41 Scott Stevens .30 .75

1934-35 Diamond Matchbooks Silver

Covers from this first hockey matchbook issue generally feature color action shots with a silver background and green and black vertical bars on the cover's left side. "The Diamond Match Co., NYC" imprint appears on a double line below the striker. These matchbooks usually were issued in twin-packs through cigar and drug stores of the day. Complete matchbooks carry a 50 percent premium over the prices listed below.

COMPLETE SET (60) 1500.00 2400.00
1 Taffy Abel 15.00 25.00
2 Marty Barry 15.00 25.00
3 Red Beattie 15.00 25.00
4 Frank Boucher 25.00 40.00
5 Doug Brennan 15.00 25.00
6 Bill Brydge 15.00 25.00
7 Eddie Burke 35.00 50.00
8 Marty Burke 15.00 25.00
9 Gerald Carson 15.00 25.00
10 Lorne Chabot 35.00 50.00
11 Art Chapman 15.00 25.00
12 Dit Clapper 50.00 80.00
13 Lionel Conacher 50.00 80.00
14 Red Conn 15.00 25.00
15 Bill Cook 35.00 50.00
16 Bun Cook 35.00 50.00
17 Thomas Cook 18.00 30.00
18 Rosario "Lolo" Couture 15.00 25.00
19 Bob Davie 15.00 25.00
20 Cecil Dillon 15.00 25.00
21 Duke Dutkowski 15.00 25.00
22 Red Dutton 25.00 40.00
23 Johnny Gagnon 15.00 25.00
24 Chuck Gardiner 35.00 50.00
25 Johnny Gottselig 15.00 25.00
26 Robert Gracie 15.00 25.00
27 Lloyd Gross 15.00 25.00
28 Ott Heller 15.00 25.00
29 Normie Himes 15.00 25.00
30 Lionel Hitchman 35.00 50.00
31 Red Jackson 15.00 25.00
32 Roger Jenkins 15.00 25.00
33 Aurel Joliat 50.00 80.00
34 Butch Keeling 15.00 25.00
35 William Kendall 15.00 25.00
36 Jim Klein 15.00 25.00
37 Joe Lamb 15.00 25.00
38 Wildor Larochelle 18.00 30.00
39 Pit Lepine 15.00 25.00
40 Jack Leswick 15.00 25.00
41 Georges Mantha 35.00 50.00
42 Sylvio Mantha 35.00 50.00
43 Mush March 18.00 30.00
44 Ronnie Martin 15.00 25.00
45 Rabbitt McVeigh 15.00 25.00
46 Howie Morenz 200.00 350.00
47 Murray Murdoch 15.00 25.00
48 Harold Oliver 25.00 40.0
49 George Patterson 15.00 25.0
50 Hal Picketts 15.00 25.0
51 Victor Ripley 15.00 25.0
52 Doc Romnes 15.00 25.0
53 Johnny Sheppard 15.00 25.0
54 Eddie Shore 75.00 125.0
55 Art Somers 15.00 25.0
56 Chris Speyers 15.00 25.0
57 Nelson Stewart 35.00 50.0
58 Tiny Thompson 50.00 80.0
59 Louis Trudel 15.00 25.0
60 Roy Worters 35.00 50.0

1935-36 Diamond Matchbooks Tan 1

The reverse of these tan-colored cove feature a brief player history with the player name and team affiliation or positio appearing at the top. "The Diamond Matc Co., NYC" imprint appears below the strik on a single line. Complete matchbooks car a 50 percent premium over the prices belov A matchbook of Joe Starke is reported exist, but we cannot officially confirm that this point in time.

COMPLETE SET (69) 1100.00 1800.0
1 Andy Aitkenhead 15.00 25.0
2 Vern Ayres 15.00 25.0
3 Bill Beveridge 18.00 30.0
4 Ralph Bowman 15.00 25.0
5 Bill Brydge 15.00 25.0
6 Glenn Brydson 15.00 25.0
7 Eddie Burke 18.00 30.0
8 Marty Burke 15.00 25.0
9 Lorne Carr 15.00 25.0
10 Gerald Carson 15.00 25.0
11 Lorne Chabot 25.00 40.0
12 Art Chapman 15.00 25.0
13 Red Conn 15.00 25.0
14 Bert Connoly 15.00 25.0
15 Bun Cook 25.00 40.0
16 Tommy Cook 15.00 25.0
17 Art Coulter 15.00 25.0
18 Lolo Couture 15.00 25.0
19 Bill Cowley 18.00 30.0
20 Wilf Cude 18.00 30.0
21 Mervin Dutton 18.00 30.0
22 Frank Finnigan 15.00 25.0
23 Irv Frew 15.00 25.00
24 LeRoy Goldsworthy 15.00 25.00
25 Johnny Gottselig 15.00 25.00
26 Bob Gracie 15.00 25.00
27 Ott Heller 15.00 25.00
28 Normie Himes 15.00 25.00
29 Syd Howe 25.00 40.00
30 Roger Jenkins 15.00 25.00
31 Ching Johnson 30.00 50.00
32 Aurel Joliat 35.00 60.00
33 Max Kaminsky 15.00 25.00
34 Butch Keeling 15.00 25.00
35 Bill Kendall 15.00 25.00
36 Lloyd Klein 15.00 25.00
37 Joe Lamb 15.00 25.00
38 Wildor Larochelle 15.00 25.00
39 Pit Lepine 15.00 25.00
40 Norman Locking 15.00 25.00
41 Georges Mantha 25.00 40.00
42 Sylvio Mantha 25.00 40.00
43 Harold March 15.00 25.00
44 Charlie Mason 15.00 25.00
45 Donnie McFadyen 15.00 25.00
46 Jack McGill 15.00 25.00
47 Rabbit McVeigh 15.00 25.00
48 Armand Mondou 15.00 25.00
49 Howie Morenz 180.00 300.00
50 Murray Murdoch 15.00 25.00
51 Al Murray 15.00 25.00
52 Harry Oliver 25.00 40.00
53 Jean Pusie 15.00 25.00
54 Paul Marcel Raymond 15.00 25.00
55 Jack Riley 15.00 25.00
56 Vic Ripley 15.00 25.00
57 Desse Roche 15.00 25.00
58 Earl Roche 15.00 25.00
59 Doc Romnes 15.00 25.00
60 Sweeney Schriner 30.00 50.00
61 Earl Seibert 25.00 40.00
62 Gerald Shannon 15.00 25.00
63 Alex Smith 15.00 25.00
64 Joe Starke 15.00 25.00
recently confirmed
65 Nels Stewart 30.00 50.00
66 Paul Thompson 15.00 25.00
67 Louis Trudel 15.00 25.00
68 Carl Voss 15.00 25.00
69 Art Wiebe 15.00 25.00
70 Roy Worters 25.00 40.00

1935-36 Diamond Matchbooks Tan 2

The Type 2 covers are similar to the Type tan-bordered set except that the player'

position or team affiliation information has been omitted from the reverse side. "The Diamond Match Co., NYC" imprint appears in a single line. As complete matchbooks are fairly scarce, they carry a premium of 50 percent over the prices below.

COMPLETE SET (63) 1100.00 1800.00
1 Tommy Anderson 15.00 25.00
2 Vern Ayres 15.00 25.00
3 Frank Boucher 25.00 40.00
4 Frank Boucher 25.00 40.00
5 Bill Brydge 15.00 25.00
6 Marty Burke 15.00 25.00
7 Lorne Carr 15.00 25.00
8 Lorne Chabot 25.00 40.00
9 Art Chapman 15.00 25.00
10 Bert Connolly 15.00 25.00
11 Bill Cook 25.00 40.00
12 Bill Cook 25.00 40.00
13 Bun Cook 25.00 40.00
14 Tommy Cook 15.00 25.00
15 Art Coulter 15.00 25.00
16 Lolo Couture 15.00 25.00
17 Wilf Cude 25.00 40.00
18 Cecil Dillon 15.00 25.00
19 Cecil Dillon 15.00 25.00
20 Red Dutton 25.00 40.00
21 Hap Emms 25.00 40.00
22 Irv Frew 15.00 25.00
23 Johnny Gagnon 15.00 25.00
24 Leroy Goldsworthy 15.00 25.00
25 Johnny Gottselig 15.00 25.00
26 Paul Haynes 15.00 25.00
27 Ott Heller 15.00 25.00
28 Irving Jaffee 15.00 25.00
recently confirmed
29 Joe Jerwa 15.00 25.00
30 Ching Johnson 25.00 40.00
31 Aurel Joliat 30.00 50.00
32 Butch Keeling 15.00 25.00
33 William Kendall 15.00 25.00
34 Davey Kerr 25.00 40.00
35 Lloyd Klein 15.00 25.00
36 Wildor Larochelle 15.00 25.00
37 Pit Lepine 15.00 25.00
38 Arthur Lesieur 15.00 25.00
39 Alex Levinsky 15.00 25.00
40 Alex Levinsky 15.00 25.00
41 Norm Locking 15.00 25.00
42 Georges Mantha 25.00 40.00
43 Sylvio Mantha 25.00 40.00
44 Mush Marsh 15.00 25.00
45 Charlie Mason 15.00 25.00
46 Donnie McFadyen 15.00 25.00
47 Jack McGill 15.00 25.00
48 Armand Mondou 15.00 25.00
49 Howie Morenz 180.00 300.00
50 Murray Murdoch 15.00 25.00
51 Al Murray 15.00 25.00
52 Harry Oliver 25.00 40.00
53 Eddie Ouellette 15.00 25.00
54 Lynn Patrick 25.00 40.00
55 Lynn Patrick 25.00 40.00
56 Paul Runge 15.00 25.00
57 Sweeney Schriner 25.00 40.00
58 Art Somers 15.00 25.00
59 Harold Starr 15.00 25.00
recently confirmed
60 Nels Stewart 30.00 50.00
61 Paul Thompson 15.00 25.00
62 Louis Trudel 15.00 25.00
63 Carl Voss 15.00 25.00
64 Art Wiebe 25.00 40.00
65 Roy Worters 25.00 40.00

1935-36 Diamond Matchbooks Tan 3

The Type 3 matchbook covers are almost identical to the Type 2 covers except that the manufacturer's imprint "Made In The USA/The Diamond Match Co. NYC" is a double line designation. Complete matchbooks are rarely scarce and carry a 50 percent premium over the prices below.

COMPLETE SET (60) 950.00 1600.00
1 Tommy Anderson 15.00 25.00
2 Vern Ayres 15.00 25.00
3 Frank Boucher 18.00 30.00
4 Bill Brydge 15.00 25.00
5 Marty Burke 15.00 25.00
6 Walter Buswell 15.00 25.00
7 Lorne Carr 15.00 25.00
8 Lorne Chabot 25.00 40.00
9 Art Chapman 15.00 25.00
10 Bert Connolly 15.00 25.00
11 Bill Cook 25.00 40.00
12 Bun Cook 25.00 40.00
13 Tommy Cook 18.00 30.00
14 Art Coulter 15.00 25.00
15 Lolo Couture 15.00 25.00
16 Wilf Cude 18.00 30.00
17 Cecil Dillon 15.00 25.00
18 Red Dutton 18.00 30.00
19 Hap Emms 18.00 30.00
20 Irvin Frew 15.00 25.00
21 Johnny Gagnon 15.00 25.00
22 Leroy Goldsworthy 15.00 25.00
23 Johnny Gottselig 15.00 25.00
24 Paul Haynes 15.00 25.00
25 Ott Heller 15.00 25.00
26 Joe Jerwa 15.00 25.00
27 Ching Johnson 25.00 40.00
28 Aurel Joliat 30.00 50.00
29 Mike Karakas 18.00 30.00
30 Butch Keeling 15.00 25.00
31 Dave Kerr 18.00 30.00
32 Lloyd Klein 15.00 25.00
33 Wildor Larochelle 18.00 30.00
34 Pit Lepine 15.00 25.00
35 Arthur Lesieur 15.00 25.00
36 Alex Levinsky 18.00 30.00
37 Norman Locking 15.00 25.00
38 George Mantha 25.00 40.00
39 Sylvio Mantha 25.00 40.00
40 Harold "Mush" March 18.00 30.00
41 Charlie Mason 15.00 25.00
42 Charlie Mason 15.00 25.00
43 Donnie McFadyen 15.00 25.00
44 Jack McGill 15.00 25.00
45 Armand Mondou 15.00 25.00
46 Howie Morenz 180.00 300.00
47 Murray Murdoch 15.00 25.00
48 Al Murray 15.00 25.00
49 Harry Oliver 25.00 40.00
50 Eddie Ouellette 15.00 25.00
51 Lynn Patrick 25.00 40.00
52 Paul Runge 15.00 25.00
53 Sweeney Schriner 25.00 40.00
54 Harold Starr 15.00 25.00
recently confirmed
55 Nels Stewart 30.00 50.00
56 Paul Thompson 15.00 25.00
57 Louis Trudel 15.00 25.00
58 Carl Voss 18.00 30.00
59 Art Wiebe 18.00 30.00
60 Roy Worters 18.00 30.00

1935-36 Diamond Matchbooks Tan 4

This tan-bordered issue is comprised only of Chicago Blackhawks players. The set is similar to Type 1 in that the player's team name appears between the player's name and bio on the reverse. The "Made in USA/The Diamond Match Co., NYC" imprint appears on two lines. Complete matchbooks carry a 50 percent premium.

COMPLETE SET (15) 180.00 300.00
1 Andy Blair 15.00 25.00
2 Glenn Brydson 15.00 25.00
3 Marty Burke 15.00 25.00
4 Tommy Cook 18.00 30.00
5 Johnny Gottselig 15.00 25.00
6 Harold Jackson 15.00 25.00
7 Mike Karakas 18.00 30.00
8 Wildor Larochelle 18.00 30.00
9 Alex Levinsky 18.00 30.00
10 Clem Loughlin 15.00 25.00
11 Harold March 18.00 30.00
12 Earl Seibert 25.00 40.00
13 Paul Thompson 15.00 25.00
14 Louis Trudel 15.00 25.00
15 Art Wiebe 18.00 30.00

1935-36 Diamond Matchbooks Tan 5

This tan-bordered set features only players from the Chicago Blackhawks. This is the hardest match cover issue to distinguish. The difference is that the team name is not featured between the player's name and his bio on the reverse. Complete matchbooks carry a 50 percent premium over the prices below.

COMPLETE SET (14) 125.00 200.00
1 Glenn Brydson 15.00 25.00
2 Marty Burke 15.00 25.00
3 Tommy Cook 15.00 25.00
4 Cully Dahlstrom 15.00 25.00
5 Johnny Gottselig 15.00 25.00
6 Vic Heyliger 15.00 25.00
7 Mike Karakas 15.00 25.00
8 Alex Levinsky 15.00 25.00
9 Harold March 15.00 25.00
10 Earl Seibert 15.00 25.00
11 William J. Stewart 15.00 25.00
12 Paul Thompson 15.00 25.00
13 Louis Trudel 15.00 25.00
14 Art Wiebe 15.00 25.00

1937 Diamond Matchbooks Tan 6

This 14-matchbook set is actually a reissue of the Type 5 Blackhawks set, and was released one year later. The only difference between the two series is that the reissued matchbooks have black match tips while the Type 5 issue has tan match tips. Complete matchbooks carry a 50 percent premium over the prices listed below.

COMPLETE SET (14) 150.00 250.00
1 Glenn Brydson 15.00 25.00
2 Martin A. Burke 15.00 25.00
3 Tom Cook 15.00 25.00
4 Cully Dahlstrom 15.00 25.00
5 Johnny Gottselig 15.00 25.00
6 Vic Heyliger 15.00 25.00
7 Mike Karakas 15.00 25.00
8 Alex Levinsky 15.00 25.00
9 Harold March 15.00 25.00
10 Earl Seibert 18.00 30.00
11 William J. Stewart 15.00 25.00
12 Paul Thompson 15.00 25.00
13 Louis Trudel 15.00 25.00
14 Art Wiebe 15.00 25.00

1972-83 Dimanche/Derniere Heure *

The blank-backed photo sheets in this multi-sport set measure approximately 8 1/2" by 11" and feature white-bordered color sports star photos from Dimanche Derniere Heure, a Montreal newspaper. The player's name, position and biographical information appear within the lower white margin. All text is in French. A white vinyl album was available for storing the photo sheets. Printed on the album's spine are the words, "Mes Vedettes du Sport" (My Stars of Sport). The photos are unnumbered and are checklisted below in alphabetical order according to sport or team as follows: Montreal Expos baseball players (1-117; National League baseball players (118-130); Montreal Canadiens hockey players (131-177); wrestlers (178-202); prize fighters (203-204); auto racing drivers (250-208); women's golf (209); Patof the circus clown (210); and CFL (211-278).

131 Chuck Arnason .78 1.56
132 Jean Beliveau VP 2.50 5.00
133 Pierre Bouchard .78 1.56
(Action)
134 Pierre Bouchard .78 1.56
(Posed)
135 Scotty Bowman CO 2.50 5.00
136 Yvan Cournoyer 2.50 5.00
(Action)
137 Yvan Cournoyer 2.50 5.00
(Posed)
138 Ken Dryden 5.00 10.00
139 Bob Gainey 2.50 5.00
140 Dale Hoganson .78 1.56
141 Rejean Houle 1.00 2.00
142 Guy Lafleur 5.00 10.00
(Action)
143 Guy Lafleur 5.00 10.00
(Posed)
144 Yvon Lambert 1.00 2.00
145 Jacques Laperriere 2.50 5.00
(Action)
146 Jacques Laperriere 2.50 5.00
(Posed)
147 Guy Lapointe 2.50 5.00
(Action)
148 Guy Lapointe 2.50 5.00
(Posed)
149 Michel Larocque 1.22 2.44
150 Claude Larose 1.00 2.00
(Action)
151 Claude Larose 1.00 2.00
(Posed)
152 Chuck Lefley .78 1.56
(Action)
153 Chuck Lefley .78 1.56
(Posed)
154 Jacques Lemaire 2.50 5.00
(Action)
155 Jacques Lemaire 2.50 5.00
(Posed)
156 Frank Mahovlich 3.00 6.00
(Action)
157 Frank Mahovlich 3.00 6.00
(Posed)
158 Pete Mahovlich 1.50 3.00
(Action)
159 Pete Mahovlich 1.50 3.00
(Posed)
160 Bob J. Murdoch .78 1.56
161 Michel Plasse 1.22 2.44
(Action)
162 Michel Plasse 1.22 2.44
(Posed)
163 Henri Richard 3.00 6.00
(Action)
164 Henri Richard 3.00 6.00
(Posed)
165 Jim Roberts 1.00 2.00
(Action)
166 Jim Roberts 1.00 2.00
(Posed)
167 Larry Robinson 3.00 6.00
(Action)
168 Larry Robinson 3.00 6.00
(Posed)
169 Serge Savard 2.50 5.00
(Action)
170 Serge Savard 2.50 5.00
(Posed)
171 Steve Shutt 2.50 5.00
(Action)
172 Steve Shutt 2.50 5.00
(Posed)
173 Marc Tardif 1.00 2.00
174 Wayne Thomas .78 1.56
(Action)
175 Wayne Thomas 1.00 2.00
(Posed)
176 Murray Wilson .78 1.56
(Action)
177 Murray Wilson .78 1.56
(Posed)

1992 Disney Mighty Ducks Movie

Issued to promote the Walt Disney movie "The Mighty Ducks", this eight-card set measures approximately 3 1/2" by 6" and is designed in the postcard format. Each card is perforated; the left portion, measuring the standard size, displays a full-bleed color photo, while the right portion is a solid neon color with a box for the stamp at the upper right. The back of the trading card portion has a brief player profile, while the other portion has an advertisement for the movie.

The cards are unnumbered and checklisted below in alphabetical order. The character's name in the movie is given on the continuation line.

COMPLETE SET (8) 16.00 40.00
1 Brandon Adams 2.00 5.00
Jesse
2 Emilio Estevez 2.40 6.00
Coach Bombay
3 Joshua Jackson 3.20 8.00
Charlie
4 Marguerite Moreau 2.00 5.00
Connie
5 Elden Ratliff 2.00 5.00
Fulton
6 Shaun Weiss 2.00 5.00
Goldberg
7 Rollerblading in 2.00 5.00
Shopping Mall
8 Team Photo 2.00 5.00

1925 Dominion Chocolates

This set consisted of 120 multi-sport cards, 32 of which were hockey. The cards were black and white and measured approx. 3" x 1 1/4".

COMMON CARD 200.00
13 Granite Club 200.00
Olympic Champs
28 North Ontario Team 200.00
35 Peterborough Team 200.00
49 Owen Sound Jrs. 200.00
55 E.J. Collett 200.00
56 Hughie J. Fox 200.00
57 Dunc Munro 200.00
58 M.Rutherford 200.00
59 Beattie Ramsay 200.00
60 Bert McCaffrey 200.00
61 Soo Greyhounds 200.00
68 J.P. Aggatts 200.00
69 Hooley Smith 350.00
70 J.Cameron 200.00
81 William Fraser 200.00
82 Vernon Forbes 200.00
83 Shorty Green 300.00
84 Red Green 200.00
86 Jack Langtry 200.00
89 Billy Coutu 200.00
92 Jack Hughes 200.00
95 Edouard Lalonde 500.00
101 Bill Brydge 200.00
103 Cecil Browne 200.00
106 Red Porter 200.00
112 North Bay Team 200.00
113 Ross Somerville 200.00
114 Harry Watson 250.00
117 Odie Cleghorn UER 200.00
First Name Spelled Ogie
118 Lionel Conacher 500.00
119 Aurel Joliat 800.00
120 Georges Vezina 1500.00

1993-94 Donruss

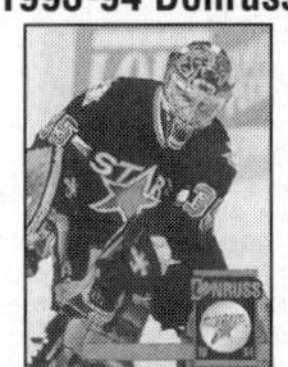

These 510 standard-size cards feature borderless color player action shots on their fronts. The player's name appears in gold foil within a team-color-coded stripe near the bottom. His team logo rests in a lower corner. The backs, some of which are horizontal, carry another borderless color player action shot. The player's name, team, position, and biography are shown within a black rectangle on the left. His statistics appear in ghosted strips below or alongside. Production of the Update set (401-510) was limited to 4,000 cases. Rookie Cards include Jason Arnott, Chris Osgood, Jocelyn Thibault and German Titov.

COMPLETE SET (510) 15.00 30.00
COMPLETE SERIES 1 (400) 12.50 25.00
COMPLETE UPDATE SET (110) 2.50 5.00
1 Steven King .02 .10
2 Joe Sacco .02 .10
3 Anatoli Semenov .02 .10
4 Terry Yake .02 .10
5 Alexei Kasatonov .02 .10
6 Patrik Carnback RC .02 .10
7 Sean Hill .02 .10
8 Bill Houlder .02 .10
9 Todd Ewen .02 .10
10 Bob Corkum .02 .10
11 Tim Sweeney .02 .10
12 Ron Tugnutt .05 .15
13 Guy Hebert .05 .15
14 Shaun Van Allen .02 .10
15 Stu Grimson .02 .10
16 Jon Casey .05 .15
17 Dan Marois .02 .10
18 Adam Oates .05 .15
19 Glen Wesley .02 .10
20 Cam Stewart RC .02 .10
21 Don Sweeney .02 .10
22 Glen Murray .02 .10
23 Jozef Stumpel .02 .10
24 Ray Bourque .20 .50
25 Ted Donato .02 .10
26 Joe Juneau .05 .15
27 Dmitri Kvartalnov .02 .10
28 Steve Leach .02 .10
29 Cam Neely .10 .30
30 Bryan Smolinski .02 .10
31 Craig Simpson .02 .10
32 Donald Audette .02 .10
33 Doug Bodger .02 .10
34 Grant Fuhr .05 .15
35 Dale Hawerchuk .05 .15
36 Yuri Khmylev .02 .10
37 Pat LaFontaine .10 .30
38 Brad May .05 .15
39 Alexander Mogilny .05 .15
40 Richard Smehlik .02 .10
41 Petr Svoboda .02 .10
42 Matthew Barnaby .05 .15
43 Sergei Petrenko .02 .10
44 Mark Astley RC .02 .10
45 Derek Plante RC .02 .10
46 Theo Fleury .02 .10
47 Al MacInnis .05 .15
48 Joe Nieuwendyk .05 .15
49 Joel Otto .02 .10
50 Paul Ranheim .02 .10
51 Robert Reichel .02 .10
52 Gary Roberts .02 .10
53 Gary Suter .02 .10
54 Mike Vernon .05 .15
55 Kelly Kisio .02 .10
56 German Titov RC .02 .10
57 Wes Walz .02 .10
58 Ted Drury .02 .10
59 Sandy McCarthy .02 .10
60 Vesa Viitakoski RC .02 .10
61 Jeff Hackett .05 .15
62 Neil Wilkinson .02 .10
63 Dirk Graham .02 .10
64 Ed Belfour .10 .30
65 Chris Chelios .10 .30
66 Joe Murphy .02 .10
67 Jeremy Roenick .15 .40
68 Steve Smith .02 .10
69 Brent Sutter .02 .10
70 Steve Dubinsky RC .02 .10
71 Michel Goulet .05 .15
72 Christian Ruuttu .02 .10
73 Bryan Marchment .02 .10
74 Sergei Krivokrasov .02 .10
75 Jeff Shantz RC .02 .10
76 Mike Modano .20 .50
77 Derian Hatcher .02 .10
78 Ulf Dahlen .02 .10
79 Mark Tinordi .02 .10
80 Russ Courtnall .02 .10
81 Mike Craig .02 .10
82 Trent Klatt .02 .10
83 Dave Gagner .05 .15
84 Chris Tancill .02 .10
85 James Black .02 .10
86 Dean Evason .02 .10
87 Andy Moog .05 .15
88 Paul Cavallini .02 .10
89 Grant Ledyard .02 .10
90 Jarkko Varvio .02 .10
91 Slava Kozlov .05 .15
92 Mike Sillinger .02 .10
93 Aaron Ward RC .02 .10
94 Greg Johnson .02 .10
95 Steve Yzerman .60 1.50
96 Tim Cheveldae .05 .15
97 Steve Chiasson .02 .10
98 Dino Ciccarelli .05 .15
99 Paul Coffey .10 .30
100 Dallas Drake RC .02 .10
101 Sergei Fedorov .20 .50
102 Nicklas Lidstrom .10 .30
103 Darren McCarty RC .25 .60
104 Bob Probert .05 .15
105 Ray Sheppard .05 .15
106 Scott Pearson .02 .10
107 Steven Rice .02 .10
108 Louie DeBrusk .02 .10
109 Dave Manson .02 .10
110 Dean McAmmond .02 .10
111 Roman Oksiuta RC .02 .10
112 Geoff Smith .02 .10
113 Zdeno Ciger .02 .10
114 Shayne Corson .02 .10
115 Luke Richardson .02 .10
116 Igor Kravchuk .02 .10
117 Bill Ranford .05 .15
118 Doug Weight .05 .15
119 Fred Brathwaite RC .25 .60
120 Jason Arnott RC .60 1.50
121 Tom Fitzgerald .02 .10
122 Mike Hough .02 .10
123 Jesse Belanger .02 .10
124 Brian Skrudland .02 .10
125 Dave Lowry .02 .10
126 Scott Mellanby .05 .15
127 Evgeny Davydov .02 .10
128 Andrei Lomakin .02 .10
129 Brian Benning .02 .10
130 Scott Levins RC .02 .10
131 Gord Murphy .02 .10
132 John Vanbiesbrouck .05 .15
133 Mark Fitzpatrick .05 .15
134 Rob Niedermayer .05 .15
135 Alexander Godynyuk .02 .10
136 Eric Weinrich .02 .10
137 Mark Greig .02 .10
138 Jim Sandlak .02 .10
139 Adam Burt .02 .10
140 Nick Kypreos .02 .10
141 Sean Burke .05 .15
142 Andrew Cassels .02 .10
143 Robert Kron .02 .10
144 Michael Nylander .02 .10
145 Robert Petrovicky .02 .10
146 Patrick Poulin .02 .10
147 Geoff Sanderson .05 .15
148 Pat Verbeek .02 .10
149 Zarley Zalapski .02 .10
150 Chris Pronger .15 .40
151 Jari Kurri .10 .30
152 Wayne Gretzky .75 2.00
153 Pat Conacher .02 .10
154 Shawn McEachern .02 .10
155 Mike Donnelly .02 .10
156 Warren Rychel .02 .10
157 Gary Shuchuk .02 .10
158 Rob Blake .05 .15
159 Jimmy Carson .02 .10
160 Tony Granato .02 .10
161 Kelly Hrudey .05 .15
162 Luc Robitaille .05 .15
163 Tomas Sandstrom .02 .10
164 Darryl Sydor .02 .10
165 Alexei Zhitnik .02 .10
166 Benoit Brunet .02 .10
167 Lyle Odelein .02 .10
168 Kevin Haller .02 .10
169 Pierre Sevigny .02 .10
170 Brian Bellows .02 .10
171 Patrice Brisebois .02 .10
172 Vincent Damphousse .02 .10
173 Eric Desjardins .05 .15
174 Gilbert Dionne .02 .10
175 Stephan Lebeau .02 .10
176 John LeClair .10 .30
177 Kirk Muller .02 .10
178 Patrick Roy .60 1.50
179 Mathieu Schneider .02 .10
180 Peter Popovic RC .02 .10
181 Corey Millen .02 .10
182 Jason Smith RC .02 .10
183 Bobby Holik .02 .10
184 John MacLean .05 .15
185 Bruce Driver .02 .10
186 Bill Guerin .02 .10
187 Claude Lemieux .02 .10
188 Bernie Nicholls .02 .10
189 Scott Niedermayer .02 .10
190 Stephane Richer .05 .15
191 Alexander Semak .02 .10
192 Scott Stevens .05 .15
193 Valeri Zelepukin .02 .10
194 Chris Terreri .05 .15
195 Martin Brodeur .40 1.00
196 Ron Hextall .05 .15
197 Brad Dalgarno .02 .10
198 Ray Ferraro .02 .10
199 Patrick Flatley .02 .10
200 Travis Green .05 .15
201 Benoit Hogue .02 .10
202 Steve Junker RC .02 .10
203 Darius Kasparaitis .02 .10
204 Derek King .02 .10
205 Uwe Krupp .02 .10
206 Scott Lachance .02 .10
207 Vladimir Malakhov .02 .10
208 Steve Thomas .02 .10
209 Pierre Turgeon .05 .15
210 Scott Scissons .02 .10
211 Glenn Healy .05 .15
212 Alexander Karpovtsev .02 .10
213 James Patrick .02 .10
214 Sergei Nemchinov .02 .10
215 Esa Tikkanen .02 .10
216 Corey Hirsch .05 .15
217 Tony Amonte .05 .15
218 Mike Gartner .05 .15
219 Adam Graves .02 .10
220 Alexei Kovalev .05 .15
221 Brian Leetch .10 .30
222 Mark Messier .10 .30
223 Mike Richter .10 .30
224 Darren Turcotte .02 .10
225 Sergei Zubov .02 .10
226 Craig Billington .05 .15
227 Troy Mallette .02 .10
228 Vladimir Ruzicka .02 .10
229 Darrin Madeley RC .02 .10
230 Mark Lamb .02 .10
231 Dave Archibald .02 .10
232 Bob Kudelski .02 .10
233 Norm Maciver .02 .10
234 Brad Shaw .02 .10
235 Sylvain Turgeon .02 .10
236 Brian Glynn .02 .10
237 Alexandre Daigle .02 .10
238 Alexei Yashin .02 .10
239 Dimitri Filimonov .02 .10
240 Pavol Demitra .05 .15
241 Jason Bowen .02 .10
242 Eric Lindros .10 .30
243 Dominic Roussel .05 .15
244 Milos Holan RC .02 .10
245 Greg Hawgood .02 .10
246 Yves Racine .02 .10
247 Josef Beranek .02 .10
248 Rod Brind'Amour .05 .15
249 Kevin Dineen .02 .10
250 Pelle Eklund .02 .10
251 Garry Galley .02 .10
252 Mark Recchi .05 .15
253 Tommy Soderstrom .05 .15
254 Dimitri Yushkevich .02 .10
255 Mikael Renberg .10 .30
256 Marty McSorley .02 .10
257 Joe Mullen .05 .15
258 Doug Brown .02 .10
259 Kjell Samuelsson .02 .10
260 Tom Barrasso .05 .15
261 Ron Francis .05 .15
262 Mario Lemieux .60 1.50
263 Larry Murphy .05 .15
264 Ulf Samuelsson .02 .10
265 Kevin Stevens .02 .10
266 Martin Straka .02 .10
267 Rick Tocchet .05 .15
268 Bryan Trottier .05 .15
269 Markus Naslund .10 .30
270 Jaromir Jagr .20 .50
271 Martin Gelinas .02 .10
272 Adam Foote .02 .10
273 Curtis Leschyshyn .02 .10
274 Stephane Fiset .05 .15
275 Jocelyn Thibault RC .40 1.00
276 Steve Duchesne .02 .10
277 Valeri Kamensky .05 .15
278 Andrei Kovalenko .02 .10
279 Owen Nolan .05 .15
280 Mike Ricci .02 .10
281 Martin Rucinsky .02 .10
282 Joe Sakic .25 .60
283 Mats Sundin .10 .30
284 Scott Young .02 .10
285 Claude Lapointe .02 .10
286 Brett Hull .15 .40
287 Vitali Karamnov .02 .10
288 Ron Sutter .02 .10
289 Garth Butcher .02 .10
290 Vitali Prokhorov .02 .10
291 Bret Hedican .02 .10
292 Tony Hrkac .02 .10
293 Jeff Brown .02 .10
294 Phil Housley .05 .15
295 Craig Janney .05 .15
296 Curtis Joseph .10 .30
297 Igor Korolev .02 .10
298 Kevin Miller .02 .10
299 Brendan Shanahan .10 .30
300 Jim Montgomery RC .02 .10
301 Gaetan Duchesne .02 .10
302 Jimmy Waite .05 .15
303 Jeff Norton .02 .10
304 Sergei Makarov .02 .10
305 Igor Larionov .02 .10
306 Mike Lalor .02 .10
307 Michal Sykora RC .02 .10
308 Pat Falloon .02 .10
309 Johan Garpenlov .02 .10
310 Rob Gaudreau RC .02 .10
311 Arturs Irbe .05 .15
312 Sandis Ozolinsh .02 .10
313 Doug Zmolek .02 .10
314 Mike Rathje .02 .10
315 Vlastimil Kroupa RC .02 .10
316 Daren Puppa .05 .15
317 Petr Klima .02 .10
318 Brent Gretzky RC .02 .10
319 Denis Savard .05 .15
320 Garard Gallant .02 .10
321 Joe Reekie .02 .10
322 Mikael Andersson .02 .10
323 Bill McDougall RC .02 .10
324 Brian Bradley .02 .10
325 Shawn Chambers .02 .10
326 Adam Creighton .02 .10
327 Roman Hamrlik .05 .15
328 John Tucker .02 .10
329 Rob Zamuner .02 .10
330 Chris Gratton .05 .15
331 Sylvain Lefebvre .02 .10
332 Nikolai Borschevsky .02 .10
333 Bob Rouse .02 .10
334 John Cullen .02 .10
335 Todd Gill .02 .10
336 Drake Berehowsky .02 .10
337 Wendel Clark .05 .15
338 Peter Zezel .02 .10
339 Rob Pearson .02 .10
340 Glenn Anderson .05 .15
341 Doug Gilmour .05 .15
342 Dave Andreychuk .05 .15
343 Felix Potvin .10 .30
344 David Ellett .02 .10
345 Alexei Kudashov RC .02 .10
346 Gino Odjick .02 .10
347 Jyrki Lumme .02 .10
348 Dana Murzyn .02 .10
349 Sergio Momesso .02 .10
350 Greg Adams .02 .10
351 Pavel Bure .10 .30
352 Geoff Courtnall .02 .10
353 Murray Craven .02 .10
354 Trevor Linden .05 .15
355 Kirk McLean .05 .15
356 Petr Nedved .05 .15
357 Cliff Ronning .02 .10
358 Jiri Slegr .02 .10
359 Kay Whitmore .05 .15
360 Gerald Diduck .02 .10
361 Pat Peake .02 .10
362 Dave Poulin .02 .10
363 Rick Tabaracci .05 .15
364 Jason Woolley .02 .10
365 Kelly Miller .02 .10
366 Peter Bondra .05 .15
367 Sylvain Cote .02 .10
368 Pat Elynuik .02 .10
369 Kevin Hatcher .02 .10
370 Dale Hunter .02 .10
371 Al Iafrate .02 .10
372 Calle Johansson .02 .10
373 Dimitri Khristich .02 .10
374 Michal Pivonka .02 .10
375 Mike Ridley .02 .10
376 Paul Ysebaert .02 .10
377 Stu Barnes .02 .10
378 Sergei Bautin .02 .10
379 Kris King .02 .10
380 Alexei Zhamnov .05 .15
381 Tie Domi .05 .15
382 Bob Essensa .05 .15
383 Nelson Emerson .02 .10
384 Boris Mironov .02 .10
385 Teppo Numminen .02 .10
386 Fredrik Olausson .02 .10
387 Teemu Selanne .10 .30
388 Darrin Shannon .02 .10
389 Thomas Steen .02 .10
390 Keith Tkachuk .10 .30
391 Opening Night .30 .75
Panthers
392 Opening Night-Ducks .30 .75
393 Alexandre Daigle .05 .15
Chris Pronger
Chris Gratton
394 Teemu Selanne .15 .40
Joe Juneau RB
395 Wayne Gretzky .30 .75
Luc Robitaille
396 Inserts Checklist .02 .10
397 Atlantic Div. Checklist .02 .10

398 Northeast Div. Checklist .02 .10
399 Central Div. Checklist .02 .10
400 Pacific Div. Checklist .02 .10
401 Garry Valk .02 .10
402 Al Iarante .02 .10
403 David Reid .02 .10
404 Jason Dawe .02 .10
405 Craig Muni .02 .10
406 Dan Keczmer RC .02 .10
407 Michael Nylander .02 .10
408 James Patrick .02 .10
409 Andrei Trefilov .02 .10
410 Zarley Zalapski .02 .10
411 Tony Amonte .05 .15
412 Keith Carney .02 .10
413 Randy Cunneyworth .02 .10
414 Ivan Droppa RC .02 .10
415 Gary Suter .02 .10
416 Eric Weinrich .02 .10
417 Paul Ysebaert .02 .10
418 Richard Matvichuk .02 .10
419 Alan May .02 .10
420 Darcy Wakaluk .05 .15
421 Micah Aivazoff RC .02 .10
422 Terry Carkner .02 .10
423 Kris Draper .02 .10
424 Chris Osgood RC .60 1.50
425 Keith Primeau .02 .10
426 Bob Beers .02 .10
427 Ilya Byakin RC .02 .10
428 Kirk Maltby RC .02 .10
429 Boris Mironov .02 .10
430 Fredrik Olausson .02 .10
431 Peter White RC .02 .10
432 Stu Barnes .02 .10
433 Mike Foligno .02 .10
434 Bob Kudelski .02 .10
435 Geoff Smith .02 .10
436 Igor Chibirev RC .02 .10
437 Ted Drury .02 .10
438 Alexander Godynyuk .02 .10
439 Frank Kucera .02 .10
440 Jocelyn Lemieux .02 .10
441 Brian Propp .02 .10
442 Paul Ranheim .02 .10
443 Jeff Reese .02 .10
444 Kevin Smyth RC .02 .10
445 Jim Storm RC .02 .10
446 Phil Crowe RC .02 .10
447 Marty McSorley .02 .10
448 Keith Redmond RC .02 .10
449 Dixon Ward .02 .10
450 Guy Carbonneau .02 .10
451 Mike Keane .02 .10
452 Oleg Petrov .02 .10
453 Ron Tugnutt .05 .15
454 Randy McKay .02 .10
455 Jaroslav Modry RC .02 .10
456 Yan Kaminsky .02 .10
457 Marty McInnis .02 .10
458 Jamie McLennan RC .05 .15
459 Zigmund Palffy .05 .15
460 Glenn Anderson .05 .15
461 Steve Larmer .05 .15
462 Craig MacTavish .02 .10
463 Stephane Matteau .02 .10
464 Brian Noonan .02 .10
465 Mattias Norstrom RC .02 .10
466 Scott Levins .02 .10
467 Derek Mayer RC .02 .10
468 Andy Schneider RC .02 .10
469 Todd Hlushko RC .02 .10
470 Stewart Malgunas RC .02 .10
471 Justin Duberman RC .02 .10
472 Ladislav Karabin RC .02 .10
473 Shawn McEachern .02 .10
474 Ed Patterson RC .02 .10
475 Tomas Sandstrom .02 .10
476 Bob Bassen .02 .10
477 Garth Butcher .02 .10
478 Iain Fraser RC .02 .10
479 Mike McKee RC .02 .10
480 Dwayne Norris RC .02 .10
481 Garth Snow RC .15 .40
482 Ron Sutter .02 .10
483 Kelly Chase .02 .10
484 Steve Duchesne .02 .10
485 Daniel Laperrire .02 .10
486 Petr Nedved .05 .15
487 Peter Stastny .05 .15
488 Ulf Dahlen .02 .10
489 Todd Elik .02 .10
490 Andrei Nazarov RC .02 .10
491 Danton Cole .02 .10
492 Chris Joseph .02 .10
493 Chris LiPuma RC .02 .10
494 Mike Gartner .05 .15
495 Mark Greig .02 .10
496 David Harlock .02 .10
497 Matt Martin RC .02 .10
498 Shawn Antoski .02 .10
499 Jeff Brown .02 .10
500 Jimmy Carson .02 .10
501 Martin Gelinas .02 .10
502 Yevgeny Namestnikov RC .02 .10
503 Randy Burridge .02 .10
504 Joe Juneau .05 .15
505 Kevin Kaminski RC .02 .10
506 Arto Blomsten .02 .10
507 Tim Cheveldae .05 .15
508 Dallas Drake .02 .10
509 Dave Manson .02 .10
510 Update Checklist .02 .10

1993-94 Donruss Elite Inserts

These 15 cards feature on their fronts color player photos framed by diamond-shaped starburst designs set within dark marbleized inner borders and prismatic foil outer borders. The player's name appears within the lower prismatic foil margin. The back carries the player's name, career highlights, and a color head shot, all set on a dark marbleized background framed by a silver border. The 10 first-series Elite cards (1-10) were random inserts in '93-94 Donruss Series 1 packs. The five Elite Update cards (U1-U5) were randomly inserted in Donruss Update packs. All Elite cards are individually numbered on the back and have a production limited to 10,000 of each.

COMPLETE SET (10) 30.00 60.00
1 Mario Lemieux 6.00 15.00
2 Alexandre Daigle 1.25 3.00
3 Teemu Selanne 1.25 3.00
4 Eric Lindros 1.25 3.00
5 Brett Hull 2.00 5.00
6 Jeremy Roenick 1.50 4.00
7 Doug Gilmour 1.25 3.00
8 Alexander Mogilny 1.25 3.00
9 Patrick Roy 6.00 15.00
10 Wayne Gretzky 8.00 20.00
U1 Mikael Renberg 1.25 3.00
U2 Sergei Fedorov 1.50 4.00
U3 Felix Potvin 1.25 3.00
U4 Cam Neely 1.25 3.00
U5 Alexei Yashin 1.25 3.00

1993-94 Donruss Ice Kings

Randomly inserted in Series 1 packs, these 10 cards feature on their fronts borderless color player drawings by noted sports artist Dick Perez. The player's name, his team's logo, and the year, 1994, appear within a blue banner near the bottom. The blue-bordered back carries the player's career highlights on a ghosted representation of a hockey rink. The cards are numbered on the back as "X of 10."

COMPLETE SET (10) 12.50 25.00
1 Patrick Roy 2.00 5.00
2 Pat LaFontaine .40 1.00
3 Jaromir Jagr .60 1.50
4 Wayne Gretzky 2.50 6.00
5 Chris Chelios .40 1.00
6 Felix Potvin .40 1.00
7 Mario Lemieux 2.00 5.00
8 Pavel Bure .40 1.00
9 Eric Lindros .40 1.00
10 Teemu Selanne .40 1.00

1993-94 Donruss Rated Rookies

Randomly inserted in Series 1 packs, these 15 cards have borderless fronts that feature color player action shots on motion streaked backgrounds. The player's name appears at the top. On its right side, the black horizontal back carries a color player action cutout superposed upon his team's logo. Biography and career highlights are shown alongside on the left. The cards are numbered on the back as "X of 15."

COMPLETE SET (15) 6.00 15.00
1 Alexandre Daigle .20 .50
2 Chris Gratton .30 .75
3 Chris Pronger .75 2.00
4 Rob Niedermayer .30 .75
5 Mikael Renberg .40 1.00
6 Jarkko Varvio .20 .50
7 Alexei Yashin .20 .50
8 Markus Naslund .60 1.50
9 Boris Mironov .20 .50
10 Martin Brodeur 2.00 5.00
11 Jocelyn Thibault .60 1.50
12 Jason Arnott .75 2.00
13 Jim Montgomery .20 .50
14 Ted Drury .20 .50
15 Roman Oksiuta .20 .50

1993-94 Donruss Special Print

Randomly inserted in Series 1 packs, these 26 cards feature on their fronts color player action shots that are borderless, except at the bottom, where the black edge carries the player's name in white cursive lettering. The prismatic foil set logo rests in a lower corner. The words "Special Print 1 of 20,000" appear in prismatic foil across the top.The cards are numbered, or rather lettered (A-Z), on the back. Two additional unnumbered special print cards (Robitaille WC and Lemieux EC) could be found at the rate of 1:360 packs.

COMPLETE SET (26) 40.00 100.00
A Ron Tugnutt .60 1.50
B Adam Oates .60 1.50
C Alexander Mogilny .60 1.50
D Theo Fleury .40 1.00
E Jeremy Roenick 1.50 4.00
F Mike Modano 1.50 4.00
G Steve Yzerman 4.00 10.00
H Jason Arnott 1.25 3.00
I Rob Niedermayer .60 1.50
J Chris Pronger 1.50 4.00
K Wayne Gretzky 8.00 20.00
L Patrick Roy 6.00 15.00
M Scott Niedermayer .40 1.00
N Pierre Turgeon .60 1.50
O Mark Messier 1.25 3.00
P Alexandre Daigle .40 1.00
Q Eric Lindros 1.25 3.00
R Mario Lemieux 6.00 15.00
S Mats Sundin 1.25 3.00
T Pat Falloon .40 1.00
U Brett Hull 1.50 4.00
V Chris Gratton .60 1.50
W Felix Potvin 1.25 3.00
X Pavel Bure 1.25 3.00
Y Al Iafrate .40 1.00
Z Teemu Selanne 1.25 3.00
NNO Luc Robitaille WC 2.00 5.00
NNO Mario Lemieux EC 6.00 15.00

1993-94 Donruss Team Canada

One of these 22 (or one of the 22 Team USA) cards were inserted in every 1993-94 Donruss Update pack. The front of each card features a player action cutout set on a red metallic background highlighted by a world map. The player's name appears at the upper left. The horizontal back carries a color player action shot on the right side. Below the photo are the player's statistics from his 1994 World Junior Championships play. On the left side are the player's name, position, biography, and NHL status. The cards are numbered on the back as "X of 22." The unnumbered checklist carries the 22 Team Canada cards, as well as the 22 Team USA cards.

COMPLETE SET (22) 5.00 10.00
1 Jason Allison .40 1.00
2 Chris Armstrong .20 .50
3 Drew Bannister .20 .50
4 Jason Botterill .20 .50
5 Joel Bouchard .20 .50
6 Curtis Bowen .20 .50
7 Anson Carter .60 1.50
8 Brandon Convery .20 .50
9 Yannick Dube .20 .50
10 Manny Fernandez .75 2.00
11 Jeff Friesen .20 .50
12 Aaron Gavey .20 .50
13 Martin Gendron .20 .50
14 Rick Girard .20 .50
15 Todd Harvey .40 1.00
16 Bryan McCabe .40 1.00
17 Marty Murray .20 .50
18 Mike Peca .60 1.50
19 Nick Stajduhar .20 .50
20 Jamie Storr .40 1.00
21 Brent Tully .20 .50
22 Brendan Witt .40 1.00
NNO WJC Checklist .20 .50

1993-94 Donruss Team USA

One of these 22 (or one of the 22 Team Canada) cards were inserted in every 1993-94 Donruss Update pack. The front of each card features a player action cutout set on a blue metallic background highlighted by a world map. The player's name appears at the upper left. The horizontal back carries a color player action shot on the right side. Below the photo are the player's statistics from his 1994 World Junior Championships play. On the left side are the player's name, position, biography, and NHL status. The cards are numbered on the back as "X of 22." The unnumbered checklist carries the 22 Team Canada cards, as well as the 22 Team USA cards.

COMPLETE SET (22) 4.00 8.00
1 Kevyn Adams .20 .50
2 Jason Bonsignore .20 .50
3 Andy Brink .20 .50
4 Jon Coleman .20 .50
5 Adam Deadmarsh .30 .75
6 Aaron Ellis .20 .50
7 John Emmons .20 .50
8 Ashlin Halfnight .20 .50
9 Kevin Hilton .20 .50
10 Jason Karmanos .20 .50
11 Toby Kvalevog .20 .50
12 Bob Lachance .20 .50
13 Jamie Langenbrunner .40 1.00
14 Jason McBain .20 .50
15 Chris O'Sullivan .20 .50
16 Jay Pandolfo .30 .75
17 Richard Park .30 .75
18 Deron Quint .20 .50
19 Ryan Sittler .20 .50
20 Blake Sloan .20 .50
21 John Varga .20 .50
22 David Wilkie .20 .50
NNO WJC Checklist .20 .50

1994-95 Donruss

This 330-card standard-size set was issued in one series. Cards were issued in 12-card hobby packs and 18-card jumbo packs. Fronts feature a near full-bleed design, other than the bottom right corner which displays player name, set name, and position stamped in a silver foil sunburst design. This silver foil area is very difficult to read. Backs feature two additional photos, team logo, and single season stats. Rookie Cards in the set include Mariusz Czerkawski, Mikhail Shtalenkov and John Gruden.

COMPLETE SET (330) 6.00 15.00
1 Steve Yzerman .60 1.50
2 Paul Ysebaert .02 .10
3 Doug Weight .05 .15
4 Trevor Kidd .05 .15
5 Mario Lemieux .60 1.50
6 Andrei Kovalenko .02 .10
7 Arturs Irbe .05 .15
8 Doug Gilmour .05 .15
9 Mark Messier .10 .30
10 Milos Holan .02 .10
11 Kevin Miller .02 .10
12 Felix Potvin .10 .30
13 Josef Beranek .02 .10
14 Mikael Andersson .02 .10
15 Stephane Matteau .02 .10
16 Todd Simon RC .02 .10
17 Darcy Wakaluk .05 .15
18 Kelly Buchberger .02 .10
19 Pavel Bure .10 .30
20 Dave Lowry .02 .10
21 Bryan Smolinski .02 .10
22 Kirk McLean .05 .15
23 Pierre Turgeon .05 .15
24 Martin Brodeur .30 .75
25 Jason Arnott .02 .10
26 Steve Dubinsky .02 .10
27 Larry Murphy .05 .15
28 Craig Janney .05 .15
29 Patrik Carnback .02 .10
30 Derek King .02 .10
31 Peter Bondra .05 .15
32 Jason Bowen .02 .10
33 Maxim Bets .02 .10
34 Matt Martin .02 .10
35 Jeff Hackett .05 .15
36 Kevin Dineen .02 .10
37 Trent Klatt .02 .10
38 Joe Murphy .02 .10
39 Sandy McCarthy .02 .10
40 Brian Bradley .02 .10
41 Scott Lachance .02 .10
42 Scott Mellanby .05 .15
43 Adam Graves .02 .10
44 Dale Hawerchuk .05 .15
45 Owen Nolan .05 .15
46 Keith Primeau .02 .10
47 Jim Dowd .02 .10
48 Dan Plante RC .02 .10
49 Rick Tabaracci .05 .15
50 Geoff Courtnall .02 .10
51 Markus Naslund .10 .30
52 Kelly Miller .02 .10
53 Kirk Maltby .02 .10
54 Paul Coffey .10 .30
55 Gord Murphy .02 .10
56 Joe Nieuwendyk .05 .15
57 Ulf Dahlen .02 .10
58 Dmitri Mironov .02 .10
59 Kevin Smyth .02 .10
60 Tie Domi .05 .15
61 Oleg Petrov .02 .10
62 Bill Guerin .05 .15
63 Alexei Yashin .02 .10
64 Joe Sacco .02 .10
65 Aris Brimanis RC .02 .10
66 Randy Burridge .02 .10
67 Neal Broten .05 .15
68 Ray Bourque .20 .50
69 Ron Tugnutt .05 .15
70 Darryl Sydor .02 .10
71 Jocelyn Thibault .10 .30
72 Shawn Chambers .02 .10
73 Alexei Zhamnov .05 .15
74 Michael Nylander .02 .10
75 Travis Green .05 .15
76 Brad May .02 .10
77 Geoff Sanderson .05 .15
78 Derek Plante .02 .10
79 Stephane Richer .05 .15
80 Rod Brind'Amour .05 .15
81 Guy Hebert .05 .15
82 Claude Lemieux .02 .10
83 Pat Falloon .02 .10
84 Alexei Kudashov .02 .10
85 Andrei Lomakin .02 .10
86 Dino Ciccarelli .05 .15
87 John Tucker .02 .10
88 Jamie McLennan .05 .15
89 Peter Taglianetti .02 .10
90 Bobby Holik .02 .10
91 Sergei Krivokrasov .02 .10
92 Alexander Mogilny .05 .15
93 Jari Kurri .05 .15
94 Dominik Hasek .30 .75
95 Shawn McEachern .02 .10
96 Bob Corkum .02 .10
97 Dimitri Filimonov .02 .10
98 John LeClair .10 .30
99 Theo Fleury .02 .10
100 Daren Puppa .05 .15
101 Greg Adams .02 .10
102 Joel Otto .02 .10
103 Sergei Makarov .02 .10
104 Mike Ricci .02 .10
105 Sylvain Turgeon .02 .10
106 Igor Larionov .02 .10
107 Tony Amonte .05 .15
108 Andy Moog .10 .30
109 Jeff Brown .02 .10
110 Checklist 1-83 .02 .10
111 Mike Gartner .05 .15
112 Craig Simpson .02 .10
113 Rob Niedermayer .05 .15
114 Robert Kron .02 .10
115 Jason York RC .02 .10
116 Valeri Kamensky .05 .15
117 Ray Whitney .02 .10
118 Chris Chelios .10 .30
119 Scott Levins .02 .10
120 Sandis Ozolinsh .02 .10
121 Mark Recchi .05 .15
122 Ron Francis .05 .15
123 Dean McAmmond .02 .10
124 Terry Yake .02 .10
125 Sergei Nemchinov .02 .10
126 Vitali Prokhorov .02 .10
127 Wayne Gretzky .75 2.00
128 Roman Hamrlik .05 .15
129 Jarkko Varvio .02 .10
130 Brian Skrudland .02 .10
131 Murray Craven .02 .10
132 Jeff Norton .02 .10
133 Pavol Demitra .05 .15
134 Mike Keane .02 .10
135 Paul Cavallini .02 .10
136 Richard Smehlik .02 .10
137 Eric Lindros .10 .30
138 Mariusz Czerkawski RC .15 .40
139 Darrin Shannon .02 .10
140 Brian Noonan .02 .10
141 Joe Sakic .25 .60
142 Steve Thomas .02 .10
143 Gary Roberts .02 .10
144 Patrick Poulin .02 .10
145 Tony Granato .02 .10
146 Donald Brashear RC .02 .10
147 Ron Hextall .05 .15
148 Corey Millen .02 .10
149 Dale Hunter .02 .10
150 Greg Johnson .02 .10
151 John MacLean .05 .15
152 Brian Leetch .10 .30
153 Sylvain Cote .02 .10
154 Thomas Steen .02 .10
155 Ted Donato .02 .10
156 Nathan Lafayette .02 .10
157 Kelly Chase .02 .10
158 Sean Burke .05 .15
159 Jaromir Jagr .20 .50
160 Checklist 84-166 .02 .10
161 Scott Niedermayer .02 .10
162 Ray Ferraro .02 .10
163 Todd Elik .02 .10
164 Dave Gagner .05 .15
165 Mike Richter .10 .30
166 Garry Galley .02 .10
167 Russ Courtnall .02 .10
168 Marty McSorley .02 .10
169 Robert Reichel .02 .10
170 Mike Rathje .02 .10
171 Bill Ranford .05 .15
172 Danton Cole .02 .10
173 Sergei Fedorov .20 .50
174 Brendan Shanahan .10 .30
175 Byron Dafoe RC .40 1.00
176 John Vanbiesbrouck .05 .15
177 Eric Desjardins .05 .15
178 Andrew Cassels .02 .10
179 John Gruden RC .02 .10
180 Slava Kozlov .05 .15
181 Trevor Linden .05 .15
182 Kris Draper .02 .10
183 Steve Smith .02 .10
184 Andre Faust .02 .10
185 James Patrick .02 .10
186 Ted Drury .02 .10
187 Dan Laperriere .02 .10
188 Benoit Hogue .02 .10
189 Chris Gratton .02 .10
190 Jyrki Lumme .02 .10
191 Peter Stastny .05 .15
192 Keith Tkachuk .10 .30
193 Mike Modano .20 .50
194 Nicklas Lidstrom .10 .30
195 Pierre Sevigny .02 .10
196 Scott Pearson .02 .10
197 Jaroslav Modry .02 .10
198 Garry Valk .02 .10
199 Kevin Hatcher .02 .10
200 Denis Tsygurov RC .02 .10
201 Paul Laus .02 .10
202 Alexander Godynyuk .02 .10
203 Brian Bellows .02 .10
204 Michal Sykora .02 .10
205 Al Iafrate .02 .10
206 Mark Tinordi .02 .10
207 Kelly Hrudey .05 .15
208 Tom Barrasso .05 .15
209 Craig Billington .05 .15
210 Teemu Selanne .10 .30
211 Alexandre Daigle .02 .10
212 Grant Fuhr .05 .15
213 Doug Brown .02 .10
214 Tim Sweeney .02 .10
215 Chris Pronger .10 .30
216 Alexei Gusarov .02 .10
217 Gary Suter .02 .10
218 Boris Mironov .02 .10
219 Sergei Zubov .02 .10
220 Checklist 167-249 .02 .10
221 Shayne Corson .02 .10
222 Jeremy Roenick .15 .40
223 John Druce .02 .10
224 Martin Straka .02 .10
225 Stephane Fiset .05 .15
226 Vincent Damphousse .02 .10
227 Bob Kudelski .02 .10
228 German Titov .02 .10
229 Kevin Stevens .02 .10
230 Dave Ellett .02 .10
231 Steve Larmer .05 .15
232 Glen Wesley .02 .10
233 Mathieu Schneider .02 .10
234 Stephan Lebeau .02 .10
235 Mark Fitzpatrick .05 .15
236 Mikael Renberg .05 .15
237 Darren McCarty .02 .10
238 Todd Nelson .02 .10
239 Igor Korolev .02 .10
240 Warren Rychel .02 .10
241 Gino Odjick .02 .10
242 Dave Manson .02 .10
243 Calle Johansson .02 .10
244 Andrei Trefilov .02 .10
245 Jason Dawe .02 .10
246 Glen Murray .02 .10
247 Jeff Shantz .02 .10
248 Zarley Zalapski .02 .10
249 Petr Klima .02 .10
250 Patrice Brisebois .02 .10
251 Chris Osgood .20 .50
252 Darius Kasparaitis .02 .10
253 Chris Joseph .02 .10
254 Glenn Anderson .05 .15
255 Kirk Muller .02 .10
256 Jason Smith .02 .10
257 Bob Bassen .02 .10
258 Joe Juneau .05 .15
259 Igor Kravchuk .02 .10
260 John Lilley .02 .10
261 Philippe Bozon .02 .10
262 Scott Stevens .05 .15
263 Dominic Roussel .05 .15
264 Dimitri Khristich .02 .10
265 Ed Patterson .02 .10
266 Mike Peca .02 .10
267 Teppo Numminen .02 .10
268 Alexei Kovalev .05 .15
269 Cam Neely .10 .30
270 Iain Fraser .02 .10
271 Tomas Sandstrom .02 .10
272 Lyle Odelein .02 .10
273 Norm Maciver .02 .10
274 Zdeno Ciger .02 .10
275 Ed Belfour .10 .30
276 Brian Savage .02 .10
277 Vlastimil Kroupa .02 .10
278 Cliff Ronning .02 .10
279 Alexei Zhitnik .02 .10
280 Jim Storm .02 .10
281 Don Sweeney .02 .10
282 Mike Donnelly .02 .10
283 Glenn Healy .05 .15
284 Denis Savard .05 .15
285 Chris Terreri .05 .15
286 Darren Turcotte .02 .10
287 Curtis Joseph .10 .30
288 Ken Baumgartner .02 .10
289 Matthew Barnaby .05 .15
290 Brent Sutter .02 .10
291 Valeri Zelepukin .02 .10
292 Michal Pivonka .02 .10
293 Ray Sheppard .05 .15
294 Jiri Slegr .02 .10
295 Vesa Viitakoski .02 .10
296 Ulf Samuelsson .02 .10
297 Nelson Emerson .02 .10
298 John Slaney .02 .10
299 Pat Verbeek .02 .10
300 Pat LaFontaine .10 .30
301 Johan Garpenlov .02 .10
302 Eric Weinrich .02 .10
303 Richard Matvichuk .02 .10
304 Steve Duchesne .02 .10
305 Donald Audette .02 .10
306 Stu Barnes .02 .10
307 Vladimir Malakhov .02 .10
308 Dimitri Yushkevich .02 .10
309 David Sacco .02 .10
310 Scott Young .02 .10
311 Marty McInnis .02 .10
312 Grant Ledyard .02 .10
313 Peter Popovic .02 .10
314 Mikhail Shtalenkov RC .02 .10
315 Dave McLlwain .02 .10
316 Cam Stewart .02 .10
317 Derian Hatcher .02 .10
318 Pat Peake .02 .10
319 Wes Walz .02 .10
320 Fred Brathwaite .05 .15
321 Jesse Belanger .02 .10
322 Jozef Stumpel .02 .10
323 Dave Andreychuk .05 .15
324 Yuri Khmylev .02 .10
325 Tim Cheveldae .05 .15
326 Anatoli Semenov .02 .10
327 Alexander Karpovtsev .02 .10
328 Patrick Roy .60 1.50
329 Troy Mallette .02 .10
330 Checklist 250-330 .02 .10

1994-95 Donruss Dominators

The eight cards in this set were randomly inserted in Donruss product at the rate of 1:36 packs. Each card features head shots of three players, grouped by position and conference, over a silver foil set logo. Individual photos appear on the back wit statistical information. Cards are numbere "X of 8."

COMPLETE SET (8) 30.00 60.00
1 Eric Lindros 3.00 8.00
Mario Lemieux
Mark Messier
2 Brian Leetch 4.00 10.00
Ray Bourque
Scott Stevens
3 Patrick Roy 6.00 15.00
Dominik Hasek
John Vanbiesbrouck
4 Cam Neely 2.00 5.00
Jaromir Jagr
Mikael Renberg
5 Sergei Fedorov 8.00 20.00
Jeremy Roenick
Wayne Gretzky
6 Chris Chelios 2.00 5.00
Paul Coffey
Al MacInnis
7 Arturs Irbe 2.00 5.00
Ed Belfour
Felix Potvin
8 Brett Hull 3.00 8.00
Pavel Bure
Teemu Selanne

1994-95 Donruss Elite Inserts

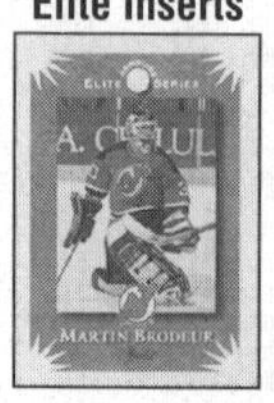

This ten-card standard-size set was issue in Donruss product at the rate of 1:72 packs The design features a silver border with deckle edge cut and rounded corner surrounding an action player photo. The se title tops the photo, with team logo, playe name and team name below it. Card back feature a small photo and persona information. Each card is individuall numbered out of 10,000 on the back.

COMPLETE SET (10) 30.00 60.00
1 Jason Arnott .40 1.00
2 Martin Brodeur 3.00 8.00
3 Pavel Bure 1.25 3.00
4 Sergei Fedorov 2.00 5.00
5 Wayne Gretzky 8.00 20.00
6 Mario Lemieux 6.00 15.00
7 Eric Lindros 1.25 3.00
8 Felix Potvin 1.25 3.00
9 Jeremy Roenick 1.50 4.00
10 Patrick Roy 6.00 15.00

1994-95 Donruss Ice Masters

This ten-card set was produced in the styl of previous Diamond King sets in basebal featuring the renderings of artist Dick Perez The cards were randomly inserted at the rat of 1:18 packs A foil logo and player name are stamped in silver foil on the front. Backs are black and have a brief paragraph o information. Cards are numbered "X of 10."

COMPLETE SET (10) 8.00 15.00
1 Ed Belfour .50 1.25
2 Sergei Fedorov .75 2.00
3 Doug Gilmour .25 .60
4 Wayne Gretzky 3.00 8.00
5 Mario Lemieux 2.50 6.00
6 Eric Lindros .50 1.25
7 Mark Messier .50 1.25
8 Mike Modano .75 2.00
9 Luc Robitaille .25 .60
10 John Vanbiesbrouck .25 .60

1994-95 Donruss Masked Marvels

The ten cards in this set of NHL goalies wer randomly inserted at a rate of 1:18 packs The card fronts display a small action photo to the left and a holographic facial image printed in a silver foil disc at right. Cards are numbered X of 10 on the back. These cards feature a removable clear plastic coating on the front which is designed to protect the hologram from scratches. A white sticker reading "Remove Protective Coating" covers a small segment of each card front. Prices

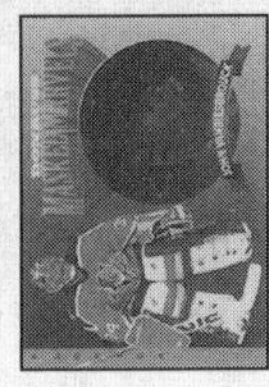

elow reflect values for cards with the oating intact; collectors are free to preserve heir cards with or without this coating.
COMPLETE SET (10) 15.00 30.00
1 Ed Belfour 1.00 2.50
2 Martin Brodeur 2.50 6.00
3 Dominik Hasek 2.00 5.00
4 Arturs Irbe .75 2.00
5 Curtis Joseph 1.25 3.00
6 Kirk McLean .75 2.00
7 Felix Potvin 1.00 2.50
8 Mike Richter 1.00 2.50
9 Patrick Roy 5.00 12.00
10 John Vanbiesbrouck 1.00 2.50

1995-96 Donruss

hese 390 standard-size cards represent the rst and second series of the 1995-96 Donruss issue. The fronts feature borderless olor action player photos. The player's ame and team is identified on the bottom of he card. The borderless backs carry a color ction photo with seasonal and career stats s an inset on the right side. Rookie Cards nclude Daniel Alfredsson and Daymond angkow.
COMPLETE SET (390) 15.00 30.00
COMPLETE SERIES 1 (205) 9.00 18.00
COMPLETE SERIES 2 (185) 6.00 12.00
1 Eric Lindros .10 .30
2 Steve Larmer .05 .15
3 Oleg Tverdovsky .02 .10
4 Vladimir Malakhov .02 .10
5 Ian Laperriere .02 .10
6 Chris Marinucci RC .02 .10
7 Nelson Emerson .02 .10
8 David Oliver .02 .10
9 Felix Potvin .10 .30
10 Manny Fernandez .10 .30
11 Jason Wiemer .02 .10
12 Dale Hunter .05 .15
13 Wayne Gretzky .75 2.00
14 Todd Gill .02 .10
15 Radim Bicanek .02 .10
16 Kirk McLean .05 .15
17 Esa Tikkanen .02 .10
18 Yuri Khmylev .02 .10
19 Peter Bondra .05 .15
20 Brian Savage .02 .10
21 Mariusz Czerkawski .02 .10
22 Rob Blake .05 .15
23 Chris Osgood .05 .15
24 Bernie Nicholls .02 .10
25 Doug Weight .05 .15
26 Shaun Van Allen .02 .10
27 Jeremy Roenick .15 .40
28 Sean Burke .05 .15
29 Pat Verbeek .02 .10
30 Dino Ciccarelli .05 .15
31 Trevor Kidd .05 .15
32 Steve Thomas .05 .15
33 Dominik Hasek .25 .60
34 Sandis Ozolinsh .05 .15
35 Bill Guerin .05 .15
36 Scott Young .02 .10
37 Scott Mellanby .05 .15
38 Joe Mullen .05 .15
39 Steve Larouche RC .02 .10
40 Joe Nieuwendyk .05 .15
41 Rick Tocchet .05 .15
42 Keith Primeau .02 .10
43 Darren Turcotte .02 .10
44 Jason Arnott .02 .10
45 Brantt Myhres RC .02 .10
46 Murray Craven .02 .10
47 Martin Gendron .02 .10
48 Mark Recchi .05 .15
49 Uwe Krupp .02 .10
50 Alexei Zhitnik .02 .10
51 Rob Niedermayer .05 .15
52 Sergei Brylin .02 .10
53 Mats Naslund .02 .10
54 Glenn Healy .05 .15
55 Mathieu Schneider .02 .10
56 Marko Tuomainen .02 .10
57 Paul Kariya .10 .30
58 Dave Gagner .02 .10
59 Mike Richter .10 .30
60 Patrik Juhlin .02 .10
61 Pierre Turgeon .05 .15
62 Mike Modano .20 .50
63 Chris Pronger .10 .30
64 Chris Joseph .02 .10
65 Peter Forsberg .30 .75
66 Roman Oksiuta .02 .10
67 Jamie Storr .05 .15
68 Brett Hull .15 .40
69 Steve Chiasson .02 .10
70 Benoit Hogue .02 .10
71 Guy Hebert .05 .15
72 Chris Therien .02 .10
73 Darryl Sydor .05 .15
74 Phil Housley .05 .15
75 Jason Allison .02 .10
76 Richard Smehlik .02 .10
77 Shean Donovan .02 .10
78 Keith Tkachuk .10 .30
79 Cliff Ronning .02 .10
80 Mikael Renberg .05 .15
81 Steven Rice .02 .10
82 Adam Graves .02 .10
83 Nicklas Lidstrom .10 .30
84 Daren Puppa .05 .15
85 Todd Warriner .02 .10
86 Jon Rohloff .02 .10
87 Patrice Tardif .02 .10
88 John MacLean .05 .15
89 Ulf Samuelsson .02 .10
90 Alexander Selivanov .02 .10
91 Chris Chelios .10 .30
92 Ulf Dahlen .02 .10
93 Brad May .02 .10
94 Ron Francis .05 .15
95 Kevin Hatcher .02 .10
96 Steve Yzerman .60 1.50
97 Jocelyn Thibault .10 .30
98 Dave Andreychuk .05 .15
99 Gary Suter .02 .10
100 Teemu Selanne .10 .30
101 Don Sweeney .02 .10
102 Valeri Bure .02 .10
103 Todd Harvey .05 .15
104 Luc Robitaille .05 .15
105 Scott Niedermayer .02 .10
106 John Vanbiesbrouck .05 .15
107 Alexei Yashin .02 .10
108 Ed Belfour .10 .30
109 Jyrki Lumme .02 .10
110 Petr Klima .02 .10
111 Tony Granato .02 .10
112 Bob Corkum .02 .10
113 Chris McAlpine RC .02 .10
114 John LeClair .10 .30
115 Kenny Jonsson .02 .10
116 Garry Galley .02 .10
117 Jeff Norton .02 .10
118 Tomas Sandstrom .02 .10
119 Paul Coffey .10 .30
120 Mike Ricci .05 .15
121 Tony Amonte .05 .15
122 Chris Gratton .02 .10
123 Blaine Lacher .05 .15
124 Andrei Nikolishin .02 .10
125 Michal Grosek .02 .10
126 Shawn Chambers .02 .10
127 Ray Bourque .20 .50
128 Jeff Nelson .02 .10
129 Kirk Muller .02 .10
130 Sergei Zubov .02 .10
131 Stanislav Neckar .02 .10
132 Stu Barnes .02 .10
133 Jari Kurri .10 .30
134 Slava Kozlov .05 .15
135 Curtis Joseph .10 .30
136 Joe Juneau .02 .10
137 Craig Janney .02 .10
138 Bryan Smolinski .02 .10
139 Brian Bradley .02 .10
140 Steve Rucchin .05 .15
141 Donald Audette .02 .10
142 Jaromir Jagr .20 .50
143 Mike Torchia RC .05 .15
144 Ray Ferraro .02 .10
145 Adam Deadmarsh .02 .10
146 Joe Murphy .02 .10
147 Ron Hextall .05 .15
148 Andrew Cassels .02 .10
149 Martin Brodeur .30 .75
150 Marek Malik .02 .10
151 Eric Desjardins .05 .15
152 Cory Stillman .02 .10
153 Owen Nolan .05 .15
154 Randy Wood .02 .10
155 Alexei Zhamnov .05 .15
156 John Cullen .02 .10
157 Zdenek Nedved .02 .10
158 Greg Adams .02 .10
159 Kelly Miller .02 .10
160 Alexander Daigle .02 .10
161 Gord Murphy .02 .10
162 Jeff Friesen .02 .10
163 Scott Stevens .05 .15
164 Denis Chasse .02 .10
165 Cam Neely .10 .30
166 Magnus Svensson RC .02 .10
167 Joe Sakic .25 .60
168 Kevin Brown .02 .10
169 Craig Conroy RC .02 .10
170 Pavel Bure .10 .30
171 Viktor Kozlov .05 .15
172 Pat LaFontaine .10 .30
173 Sergei Gonchar .02 .10
174 Brett Lindros .02 .10
175 Jassen Cullimore .02 .10
176 Mats Sundin .10 .30
177 Zarley Zalapski .02 .10
178 Stephane Richer .05 .15
179 Steve Smith .02 .10
180 Brendan Shanahan .10 .30
181 Brian Leetch .05 .15
182 Ken Wregget .05 .15
183 Jeff Brown .02 .10
184 Darby Hendrickson .02 .10
185 Nikolai Khabibulin .05 .15
186 Glen Wesley .02 .10
187 Andrei Nazarov .02 .10
188 Rod Brind'Amour .05 .15
189 Jim Carey .05 .15
190 Derek Plante .02 .10
191 Valeri Karpov .02 .10
192 Mike Kennedy RC .02 .10
193 Wendel Clark .05 .15
194 Radek Bonk .02 .10
195 Jozef Stumpel .02 .10
196 Tommy Salo RC .40 1.00
197 Michal Pivonka .02 .10
198 Ray Sheppard .02 .10
199 Russ Courtnall .02 .10
200 Todd Marchant .02 .10
201 Geoff Sanderson .02 .10
202 Vincent Damphousse .02 .10
203 Sergei Krivokrasov .02 .10
204 Jesse Belanger .02 .10
205 Al MacInnis .05 .15
206 Philippe DeRouville .02 .10
207 Mike Eastwood .02 .10
208 Travis Green .05 .15
209 Jeff Shantz .02 .10
210 Shane Doan RC .30 .75
211 Mike Sullivan .02 .10
212 Kevin Dineen .02 .10
213 Pat Falloon .02 .10
214 Rick Tabaracci .05 .15
215 Kelly Hrudey .05 .15
216 Alexei Kovalev .02 .10
217 Matt Johnson .02 .10
218 Turner Stevenson .02 .10
219 Mike Sillinger .02 .10
220 Bobby Holik .02 .10
221 Kevin Stevens .02 .10
222 Dave Lowry .02 .10
223 Martin Gelinas .02 .10
224 Darren Langdon RC .02 .10
225 Tie Domi .05 .15
226 Doug Bodger .02 .10
227 Patrick Flatley .02 .10
228 Anders Myrvold RC .02 .10
229 German Titov .02 .10
230 Pat Peake .02 .10
231 Robert Kron .02 .10
232 Mike Donnelly .02 .10
233 Denis Savard .05 .15
234 Mathieu Dandenault RC .02 .10
235 Joe Dziedzic .02 .10
236 Valeri Kamensky .05 .15
237 Joaquin Gage RC .02 .10
238 Geoff Courtnall .02 .10
239 Arturs Irbe .05 .15
240 Dan Quinn .02 .10
241 J.C. Bergeron .02 .10
242 Brian Noonan .02 .10
243 Ulf Samuelsson .02 .10
244 Jeff O'Neill .02 .10
245 Sandy Moger RC .02 .10
246 Don Beaupre .05 .15
247 Bob Probert .02 .10
248 Mattias Norstrom .02 .10
249 Jason Bonsignore .02 .10
250 Mike Ridley .02 .10
251 Joe Mullen .05 .15
252 Petr Nedved .05 .15
253 Jason Doig .02 .10
254 Olaf Kolzig .05 .15
255 Mark Tinordi .02 .10
256 Roman Hamrlik .05 .15
257 Denis Pederson .02 .10
258 Paul Ysebaert .02 .10
259 Neal Broten .05 .15
260 Jason Woolley .02 .10
261 Teppo Numminen .02 .10
262 Scott Thornton .02 .10
263 Ted Donato .02 .10
264 Marcus Ragnarsson RC .05 .15
265 Dimitri Khristich .02 .10
266 Mike Peca .05 .15
267 Dominic Roussel .05 .15
268 Owen Nolan .05 .15
269 Patrick Poulin .02 .10
270 Mario Lemieux .60 1.50
271 Mark Messier .10 .30
272 Slava Fetisov .02 .10
273 Andrei Trefilov .02 .10
274 Damian Rhodes .05 .15
275 Alexander Mogilny .05 .15
276 Ray Sheppard .02 .10
277 Radek Dvorak RC .20 .50
278 Steve Duchesne .02 .10
279 Jason Smith RC .02 .10
280 Wade Flaherty RC .05 .15
281 Lyle Odelein .02 .10
282 Keith Jones .05 .15
283 Saku Koivu .10 .30
284 Marty Murray .02 .10
285 Sergei Fedorov .15 .40
286 Brian Rolston .02 .10
287 Dave Roche RC .02 .10
288 Sylvain Lefebvre .02 .10
289 Theo Fleury .02 .10
290 Andy Moog .10 .30
291 Tom Barrasso .05 .15
292 Craig Mills RC .02 .10
293 Mike Gartner .05 .15
294 Stefan Ustorf .02 .10
295 Darren Turcotte .02 .10
296 Steve Konowalchuk .02 .10
297 Ray Ferraro .02 .10
298 Brian Holzinger RC .10 .30
299 Daniel Alfredsson RC .30 .75
300 Derek King .02 .10
301 Mark Fitzpatrick .05 .15
302 Joe Sacco .02 .10
303 Scott Walker RC .02 .10
304 Ricard Persson RC .02 .10
305 Mike Rathje .02 .10
306 Petr Svoboda .02 .10
307 Roman Vopat RC .02 .10
308 Ray Whitney .05 .15
309 Calle Johansson .02 .10
310 Grant Fuhr .10 .30
311 John Tucker .02 .10
312 Anatoli Semenov .02 .10
313 Darren McCarty .02 .10
314 Stephane Quintal .02 .10
315 Jason Dawe .02 .10
316 Zigmund Palffy .05 .15
317 Dave Manson .02 .10
318 Vitali Yachmenev .02 .10
319 Chris Pronger .10 .30
320 Valeri Zelepukin .02 .10
321 Ryan Smyth .05 .15
322 Johan Garpenlov .02 .10
323 Bill Ranford .05 .15
324 Daymond Langkow RC .20 .50
325 Aki-Petteri Berg RC .05 .15
326 Derian Hatcher .02 .10
327 Bryan Smolinski .02 .10
328 Michel Picard .02 .10
329 Alek Stojanov .02 .10
330 Trent Klatt .02 .10
331 Richard Park .02 .10
332 Jere Lehtinen .05 .15
333 Bryan McCabe .02 .10
334 Kyle McLaren RC .02 .10
335 Todd Krygier .02 .10
336 Adam Creighton .02 .10
337 Jamie Pushor .02 .10
338 Patrick Roy .60 1.50
339 Milos Holan .02 .10
340 Dave Ellett .02 .10
341 Brian Bellows .02 .10
342 Jamie Rivers .02 .10
343 Claude Lemieux .02 .10
344 Leif Rohlin RC .02 .10
345 Eric Daze .05 .15
346 Todd Bertuzzi RC .50 1.25
347 Antti Tormanen RC .02 .10
348 Luc Robitaille .05 .15
349 Tim Taylor RC .02 .10
350 Stephane Yelle RC .02 .10
351 Marko Kiprusoff .02 .10
352 Igor Korolev .02 .10
353 Scott Lachance .02 .10
354 Marty McSorley .02 .10
355 Joel Otto .02 .10
356 Josef Beranek .02 .10
357 Sergei Zubov .02 .10
358 Rhett Warrener RC .02 .10
359 Jimmy Carson .02 .10
360 Zdeno Ciger .02 .10
361 Brendan Witt .02 .10
362 Byron Dafoe .05 .15
363 Steve Thomas .05 .15
364 Deron Quint .02 .10
365 Nelson Emerson .02 .10
366 Larry Murphy .05 .15
367 Benoit Brunet .02 .10
368 Kjell Samuelsson .02 .10
369 Aaron Gavey .02 .10
370 Robert Svehla RC .02 .10
371 Rene Corbet .02 .10
372 Gary Roberts .02 .10
373 Shawn McEachern .02 .10
374 Andrei Kovalenko .02 .10
375 Yanic Perreault .02 .10
376 Shayne Corson .02 .10
377 Brendan Shanahan .10 .30
378 Sergei Nemchinov .02 .10
379 Chad Kilger RC .02 .10
380 Sergio Momesso .02 .10
381 Craig Billington .05 .15
382 Niklas Sundstrom .05 .15
383 Matthew Barnaby .10 .30
384 Dale Hawerchuk .10 .30
385 Trevor Linden .05 .15
386 Adam Oates .05 .15
387 Dimitri Yushkevich .02 .10
388 Todd Elik .02 .10
389 Wendel Clark .05 .15
390 Stephane Fiset .05 .15
NNO Checklist Card 1 .05 .15
NNO Checklist Card 2 .05 .15
NNO Checklist Card 3 .05 .15
NNO Checklist Card 4 .05 .15
NNO Checklist Card 5 .05 .15
NNO Checklist Card 6 .05 .15
NNO Checklist Card 7 .05 .15
NNO Checklist Card 8 .05 .15

1995-96 Donruss Between The Pipes

Shaped like a goal and outlined in red foil, these ten cards were randomly inserted in series 1 (1-5) and 2 (6-10) packs at a rate of 1:36. The goaltender is pictured within the goal with a solid blue background. The backs feature a brief write-up and career statistics.
COMPLETE SET (10) 40.00 80.00
COMPLETE SERIES 1 (5) 20.00 35.00
COMPLETE SERIES 2 (5) 30.00 55.00
1 Blaine Lacher 2.00 5.00
2 Dominik Hasek 6.00 15.00
3 Mike Vernon 2.00 5.00
4 Trevor Kidd 2.00 5.00
5 Martin Brodeur 8.00 20.00
6 Jim Carey 2.00 5.00
7 Patrick Roy 10.00 25.00
8 Sean Burke 2.00 5.00
9 Felix Potvin 3.00 8.00
10 Ed Belfour 3.00 8.00

1995-96 Donruss Canadian World Junior Team

These 22 standard-size cards were randomly inserted into series 1 (1-11) and series 2 (12-22) packs at a rate of 1:2. These cards honor players who represented Canada in the 1995 World Junior Championships. Large player photographs are superimposed on a maple leaf design. The backs feature two player photos. One is an inset photo in a maple leaf and the other on the left side is a black-and-white image. Information about the player is located in the upper left corner while his National Junior Team career stats are printed on the right side of the card. The cards are numbered "X of 22" in the upper right-hand corner.
COMPLETE SET (22) 6.00 12.00
COMPLETE SERIES 1 (11) 3.00 6.00
COMPLETE SERIES 2 (11) 5.00 10.00
1 Jamie Storr .75 2.00
2 Dan Cloutier .20 .50
3 Nolan Baumgartner .20 .50
4 Chad Allen .20 .50
5 Wade Redden .20 .50
6 Ed Jovanovski .75 2.00
7 Jamie Rivers .20 .50
8 Bryan McCabe .75 2.00
9 Lee Sorochan .20 .50
10 Marty Murray .20 .50
11 Larry Courville .20 .50
12 Jason Allison .20 .50
13 Darcy Tucker .20 .50
14 Jeff O'Neill .20 .50
15 Eric Daze .75 2.00
16 Alexandre Daigle .20 .50
17 Todd Harvey .75 2.00
18 Jason Botterill .20 .50
19 Shean Donovan .20 .50
20 Denis Pederson .20 .50
21 Jeff Friesen .20 .50
22 Ryan Smyth .60 1.50

1995-96 Donruss Dominators

The eight cards in this set were randomly inserted in series two hobby packs only at a rate of 1:35. Each features three of the top players at each position from each conference. The cards are individually numbered on the backs out of 5,000.
COMPLETE SET (8) 20.00 40.00
1 Peter Forsberg 4.00 10.00
Eric Lindros
Mario Lemieux
2 John LeClair 4.00 10.00
Mikael Renberg
Jaromir Jagr
3 Sergei Zubov 1.50 4.00
Ray Bourque
Brian Leetch
4 Jim Carey 3.00 8.00
Martin Brodeur
Dominik Hasek
5 Doug Gilmour 4.00 10.00
Wayne Gretzky
Sergei Fedorov
6 Brett Hull 2.00 5.00
Paul Kariya
Pavel Bure
7 Paul Coffey 1.50 4.00
Chris Chelios
Al MacInnis
8 Felix Potvin 4.00 10.00
Ed Belfour
Trevor Kidd

1995-96 Donruss Elite Inserts

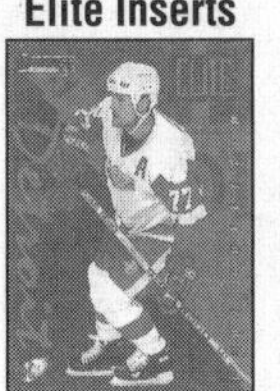

These ten standard-size cards were randomly inserted into first (1-5) and second series (6-10) Donruss at a rate of 1:116 and 1:47 packs respectively. Each card is sequentially numbered out of 10,000. The fronts feature blue holographic foil, layered with copper foil which emphasize the player's name and team logo. The word "Elite" is noted in the upper right-hand corner. The card backs are printed in metallic copper and metallic blue ink silhouetting the player's image. There is a brief blurb about the player on the left side of the card. The cards are numbered "X" of 10 in the upper right corner.
COMPLETE SET (10) 25.00 50.00
1 Alexei Zhamnov .60 1.50
2 Joe Sakic 2.50 6.00
3 Mikael Renberg .60 1.50
4 Sergei Fedorov 1.50 4.00
5 Paul Coffey 1.25 3.00
6 Paul Kariya 1.25 3.00
7 Wayne Gretzky 8.00 20.00
8 Eric Lindros 1.25 3.00
9 Mario Lemieux 6.00 15.00
10 Jaromir Jagr 2.00 5.00

1995-96 Donruss Igniters

These 10 standard-size cards were randomly inserted in Series 1 hobby packs. The horizontally-oriented cards feature the player's photo superimposed against the word "Igniters". His name and team are identified on the bottom of the card. The backs are individually numbered out of 5,000.
COMPLETE SET (10) 15.00 30.00
1 Adam Oates 1.25 3.00

2 Paul Coffey 1.50 4.00
3 Doug Gilmour 1.25 3.00
4 Pierre Turgeon 1.25 3.00
5 Mark Messier 1.50 4.00
6 Alexei Zhamnov 1.25 3.00
7 Jeremy Roenick 2.00 5.00
8 Steve Yzerman 6.00 15.00
9 Joe Nieuwendyk 1.25 3.00
10 Ron Francis 1.25 3.00

1995-96 Donruss Marksmen

The eight cards in this set were randomly inserted into series one Donruss retail packs only at a rate of 1:24. The cards showcase the top eight goal scorers of the 1994-95 season.
COMPLETE SET (8) 6.00 12.00
1 Peter Bondra .75 2.00
2 Owen Nolan .75 2.00
3 Eric Lindros .75 2.00
4 Ray Sheppard .75 2.00
5 Jaromir Jagr 1.50 3.00
6 Theo Fleury .75 2.00
7 Brett Hull 1.00 2.50
8 Brendan Shanahan .75 2.00

1995-96 Donruss Pro Pointers

Inserted one per series two pack, these twenty cards feature hockey tips from top players born in the United States (1-10) and Canada (11-20).
COMPLETE SET (20) 3.00 6.00
1 Jeremy Roenick USA .20 .50
2 Pat LaFontaine USA .15 .40
3 Jason Bonsignore USA .05 .10
4 Chris Chelios USA .15 .40
5 Brian Leetch USA .15 .40
6 Brett Hull USA .20 .50
7 Keith Tkachuk USA .15 .40
8 Mike Modano USA .25 .60
9 Brian Rolston USA .05 .10
10 Darren Turcotte USA .05 .10
11 Jeff Friesen CAN .05 .10
12 Theo Fleury CAN .05 .10
13 Eric Lindros CAN .15 .40
14 Mario Lemieux .75 2.00
15 Jamie Storr CAN .10 .20
16 Trevor Kidd CAN .10 .20
17 Chris Pronger CAN .15 .40
18 Brendan Witt CAN .05 .10
19 Paul Kariya CAN .15 .40
20 Todd Harvey CAN .10 .20

1995-96 Donruss Rated Rookies

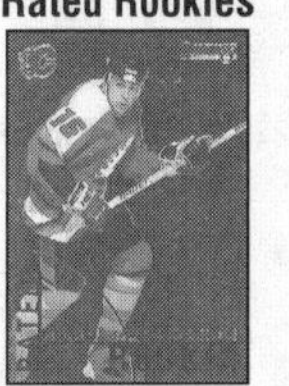

Randomly inserted at a rate of 1:24 series two retail packs, this 16-card set features a plethora of players who made their NHL debuts in the 1995-96 season.
COMPLETE SET (16) 25.00 50.00
1 Saku Koivu 5.00 12.00
2 Todd Bertuzzi 5.00 12.00
3 Niklas Sundstrom 1.00 2.50
4 Jeff O'Neill .75 2.00
5 Zdenek Nedved .75 2.00
6 Eric Daze 1.00 2.50
7 Chad Kilger 1.00 2.50
8 Shane Doan .75 2.00
9 Vitali Yachmenev 1.00 2.50
10 Radek Dvorak 5.00 12.00
11 Marty Murray .75 2.00
12 Cory Stillman .75 2.00
13 Marcus Ragnarsson 1.00 2.50
14 Daniel Alfredsson 1.00 2.50
15 Antti Tormanen .75 2.00
16 Petr Sykora 3.00 8.00

1995-96 Donruss Rookie Team

These nine standard-size cards featuring leading rookies from the 1994-95 season were issued in first series packs (1:12). The borderless fronts feature the player's photo blending into various colors which represent his team's color pattern. The player's name and team identification are located on the bottom. The horizontal back features a close-up player photo, along with a brief note. The cards are numbered on the upper right as "X" of 9.
1 Jim Carey .20 .50
2 Peter Forsberg 1.00 2.50
3 Paul Kariya .40 1.00
4 David Oliver .15 .30
5 Blaine Lacher .20 .50
6 Oleg Tverdovsky .15 .30
7 Jeff Friesen .15 .30
8 Todd Marchant .15 .30
9 Todd Harvey .20 .50

1996-97 Donruss

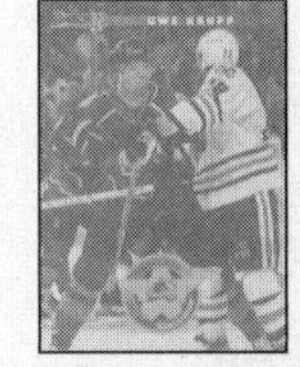

The 1996-97 Donruss set was issued in one series totaling 240 cards. The 10-card packs retailed for $1.89 each. Card fronts feature a borderless color action photo along with player name at the top and team name and logo at the bottom. Card backs feature another color action photo, along with stats and biographical information. Key Rookie Cards include Ethan Moreau and Kevin Hodson.
COMPLETE SET (240) 6.00 15.00
1 Joe Sakic .20 .50
2 Jeremy Roenick .12 .30
3 Kirk McLean .02 .10
4 Zarley Zalapski .01 .05
5 Jyrki Lumme .01 .05
6 Owen Nolan .02 .10
7 Luc Robitaille .02 .10
8 Bob Probert .02 .10
9 Ken Baumgartner .01 .05
10 Rick Tabaracci .02 .10
11 Alexei Zhitnik .01 .05
12 Al MacInnis .02 .10
13 Brian Leetch .08 .25
14 Valeri Kamensky .02 .10
15 Todd Gill .01 .05
16 Mark Messier .08 .25
17 Pierre Turgeon .02 .10
18 Mathieu Schneider .01 .05
19 Vyacheslav Kozlov .01 .05
20 Milos Holan .01 .05
21 Yanic Perreault .01 .05
22 Mike Modano .15 .40
23 Claude Lemieux .01 .05
24 Rob Niedermayer .02 .10
25 Eric Desjardins .02 .10
26 Alexander Semak .01 .05
27 Mark Recchi .02 .10
28 Slava Fetisov .01 .05
29 Kevin Hatcher .01 .05
30 Mats Sundin .08 .25
31 Jeff Reese .02 .10
32 Alexander Selivanov .01 .05
33 Jim Carey .08 .25
34 Daren Puppa .02 .10
35 Vincent Damphousse .01 .05
36 John LeClair .08 .25
37 Jon Casey .02 .10
38 Chris Terreri .02 .10
39 Larry Murphy .02 .10
40 Geoff Sanderson .02 .10
41 Adam Oates .02 .10
42 Sandy McCarthy .01 .05
43 Jaromir Jagr .15 .40
44 Roman Oksiuta .01 .05
45 Zigmund Palffy .02 .10
46 Doug Gilmour .02 .10
47 Cliff Ronning .01 .05
48 Curtis Leschyshyn .01 .05
49 Scott Mellanby .02 .10
50 Sergei Fedorov .12 .30
51 Denis Savard .02 .10
52 Mike Vernon .02 .10
53 Todd Marchant .01 .05
54 Geoff Courtnall .01 .05
55 Shayne Corson .01 .05
56 Dimitri Khristich .01 .05
57 Scott Stevens .02 .10
58 German Titov .01 .05
59 Darren Turcotte .01 .05
60 Michal Pivonka .01 .05
61 Ron Hextall .02 .10
62 Ed Belfour .08 .25
63 Chris Pronger .02 .10
64 Brian Bellows .01 .05
65 Pavel Bure .08 .25
66 Adam Graves .01 .05

1996-97 Donruss

67 Tom Barrasso .02 .10
68 Stu Barnes .01 .05
69 Norm Maciver .01 .05
70 Jesse Belanger .01 .05
71 Chris Chelios .08 .25
72 Tommy Soderstrom .02 .10
73 Nelson Emerson .01 .05
74 Kenny Jonsson .01 .05
75 Bill Lindsay .01 .05
76 Petr Nedved .02 .10
77 Robert Svehla .01 .05
78 Tomas Sandstrom .01 .05
79 Jeff Friesen .01 .05
80 Tony Amonte .02 .10
81 Sylvain Lefebvre .01 .05
82 Greg Adams .01 .05
83 Vladimir Konstantinov .02 .10
84 Roman Hamrlik .02 .10
85 Doug Weight .02 .10
86 Shaun Van Allen .01 .05
87 Bill Ranford .02 .10
88 Jeff Hackett .02 .10
89 Alexei Zhamnov .02 .10
90 Dale Hawerchuk .02 .10
91 Sergei Zubov .01 .05
92 Dan Quinn .01 .05
93 Wayne Gretzky .75 2.00
94 Todd Harvey .01 .05
95 Chris Osgood .02 .10
96 Felix Potvin .08 .25
97 Richard Matvichuk .01 .05
98 Wendel Clark .02 .10
99 Bryan Smolinski .01 .05
100 Rob Blake .02 .10
101 Jocelyn Thibault .08 .25
102 Trevor Linden .02 .10
103 Craig MacTavish .01 .05
104 Sandis Ozolinsh .01 .05
105 Oleg Tverdovsky .02 .10
106 Garry Galley .01 .05
107 Derek Plante .01 .05
108 Stephane Richer .02 .10
109 Dave Andreychuk .02 .10
110 Curtis Joseph .08 .25
111 Greg Johnson .01 .05
112 Patrick Roy .50 1.25
113 Pat LaFontaine .08 .25
114 Uwe Krupp .01 .05
115 Ulf Dahlen .01 .05
116 Brian Bradley .01 .05
117 Grant Fuhr .02 .10
118 Brian Skrudland .01 .05
119 Nicklas Lidstrom .08 .25
120 Steve Chiasson .01 .05
121 Sean Burke .02 .10
122 Rick Tocchet .02 .10
123 Martin Rucinsky .01 .05
124 Alexei Yashin .01 .05
125 Mikael Renberg .02 .10
126 Teppo Numminen .01 .05
127 Randy Burridge .01 .05
128 Radek Bonk .01 .05
129 Scott Young .01 .05
130 Gary Suter .01 .05
131 Mario Lemieux .50 1.25
132 Ray Bourque .15 .40
133 Martin Gelinas .01 .05
134 Keith Tkachuk .08 .25
135 Benoit Hogue .01 .05
136 Ken Wregget .02 .10
137 Eric Lindros .08 .25
138 Keith Primeau .01 .05
139 Peter Forsberg .25 .60
140 Paul Coffey .08 .25
141 Mike Ridley .01 .05
142 Paul Kariya .08 .25
143 Jason Arnott .01 .05
144 Joe Murphy .01 .05
145 Adam Deadmarsh .01 .05
146 John MacLean .02 .10
147 Peter Bondra .02 .10
148 Martin Brodeur .25 .60
149 Ron Francis .02 .10
150 Dino Ciccarelli .02 .10
151 Joe Juneau .02 .10
152 Matthew Barnaby .02 .10
153 Mark Tinordi .01 .05
154 Craig Janney .02 .10
155 Rod Brind'Amour .02 .10
156 Damian Rhodes .02 .10
157 Teemu Selanne .08 .25
158 James Patrick .01 .05
159 Theo Fleury .01 .05
160 Trevor Kidd .02 .10
161 Kirk Muller .01 .05
162 Andrew Cassels .01 .05
163 Brent Fedyk .01 .05
164 Guy Hebert .02 .10
165 Jason Dawe .01 .05
166 Andy Moog .02 .10
167 Igor Larionov .01 .05
168 Brian Savage .01 .05
169 Kris Draper .01 .05
170 Dave Gagner .01 .05
171 Steve Yzerman .50 1.25
172 Nikolai Khabibulin .02 .10
173 Chris Gratton .01 .05
174 Dave Lowry .01 .05
175 Travis Green .02 .10
176 Alexei Kovalev .01 .05
177 Mike Ricci .01 .05
178 Brendan Shanahan .08 .25
179 Corey Hirsch .02 .10
180 Bill Guerin .01 .05
181 Alexander Mogilny .02 .10
182 Steve Duchesne .01 .05
183 Ray Ferraro .01 .05
184 Mike Richter .08 .25
185 Yuri Khmylev .01 .05
186 Stephane Fiset .02 .10
187 John Vanbiesbrouck .02 .10
*188 Scott Niedermayer .01 .05
189 Brad May .02 .10
190 Shawn McEachern .01 .05
191 Joe Mullen .02 .10
192 Dominik Hasek .20 .50
193 Steve Thomas .01 .05
194 Russ Courtnall .01 .05
195 Joe Nieuwendyk .02 .10
196 Petr Klima .01 .05
197 Brett Hull .10 .30
198 Bernie Nicholls .01 .05
199 Dale Hunter .01 .05
200 Pat Verbeek .01 .05
201 Phil Housley .02 .10
202 Todd Krygier .01 .05
203 Zdeno Ciger .01 .05
204 Alexandre Daigle .01 .05
205 Cam Neely .08 .25
206 Mike Gartner .02 .10
207 Garth Snow .02 .10
208 Pat Falloon .01 .05
209 Kelly Hrudey .02 .10
210 Ray Sheppard .02 .10
211 Ted Donato .01 .05
212 Glenn Healy .02 .10
213 Radek Dvorak .01 .05
214 Niclas Andersson .01 .05
215 Miroslav Satan .01 .05
216 Roman Vopat .01 .05
217 Bryan McCabe .01 .05
218 Jamie Langenbrunner .01 .05
219 Kyle McLaren .01 .05
220 Stephane Yelle .01 .05
221 Byron Dafoe .02 .10
222 Grant Marshall .01 .05
223 Ryan Smyth .08 .25
224 Ville Peltonen .01 .05
225 Deron Quint .01 .05
226 Brian Holzinger .02 .10
227 Jose Theodore .10 .30
228 Ethan Moreau RC .08 .25
229 Steve Sullivan RC .20 .50
230 Kevin Hodson RC .08 .25
231 Cory Stillman .01 .05
232 Ralph Intranuovo .01 .05
233 Vitali Yachmenev .01 .05
234 Marcus Ragnarsson .01 .05
235 Nolan Baumgartner .01 .05
236 Chad Kilger .01 .05
237 Niklas Sundstrom .01 .05
238 Paul Coffey CL (1-120) .08 .25
239 Doug Gilmour CL (121-240) .08 .25
240 Steve Yzerman CL (inserts) .12 .30

1996-97 Donruss Press Proofs

This 240-card standard size set is a parallel issue to the regular Donruss set. A cut-out star in the upper right-hand corner, along with the words "First 2,000 Printed, Press Proof" printed above the set logo, along the bottom distinguish these cards from their regular counterparts.
*STARS: 4X TO 10X HI COLUMN

1996-97 Donruss Between the Pipes

This standard-size set features 10 of the NHL's top netminders. These cards are found only in retail packs and are serially numbered to 4,000.
COMPLETE SET (10) 15.00 40.00
1 Patrick Roy 6.00 15.00
2 Martin Brodeur 3.00 8.00
3 Jim Carey 1.25 3.00
4 John Vanbiesbrouck 2.00 5.00
5 Chris Osgood 2.00 5.00
6 Ed Belfour 2.00 5.00
7 Jocelyn Thibault 1.25 3.00
8 Curtis Joseph 2.00 5.00
9 Nikolai Khabibulin 2.00 5.00
10 Felix Potvin 2.00 5.00

1996-97 Donruss Dominators

The ten cards in this set were randomly inserted in hobby packs at indeterminate odds and feature three of the top players at each position. These cards are serially numbered to 5,000 and printed on laminated holographic foil stock.
COMPLETE SET (10) 20.00 40.00
1 Jim Carey 1.50 4.00
Martin Brodeur
John Vanbiesbrouck
2 Nikolai Khabibulin 1.50 4.00
Chris Osgood
Jocelyn Thibault
3 Chris Chelios 2.00 5.00
Paul Coffey
Ray Bourque
4 Mario Lemieux 4.00 10.00
Jaromir Jagr
Ron Francis
5 Eric Lindros 4.00 10.00
Wayne Gretzky
Jason Arnott
6 Doug Gilmour 1.50 4.00
Wendel Clark
Pierre Turgeon
7 Alexander Mogilny 1.50 4.00
Pavel Bure
Trevor Linden
8 Paul Kariya 1.50 4.00
Teemu Selanne
Keith Tkachuk
9 Mike Modano 1.50 4.00
Jeremy Roenick
Sergei Fedorov
10 Eric Daze 1.50 4.00
Saku Koivu
Ed Jovanovski

1996-97 Donruss Elite Inserts

These ten standard-size cards were randomly inserted into all varieties of packs. The basic version of the set has silver borders with cards serially numbered to 10,000. The tougher-to-find gold parallel version features, naturally enough, gold borders with serial numbering to 2,000.
COMPLETE SET (10) 20.00 40.00
*GOLDS: 1.5X TO 3X BASIC INSERTS
1 Pavel Bure 1.25 3.00
2 Wayne Gretzky 8.00 20.00
3 Doug Weight 1.25 3.00
4 Brett Hull 2.00 5.00
5 Mark Messier 1.25 3.00
6 Brendan Shanahan 1.25 3.00
7 Joe Sakic 2.50 6.00
8 Sergei Fedorov 1.50 4.00
9 Eric Lindros 1.25 3.00
10 Patrick Roy 6.00 15.00

1996-97 Donruss Go Top Shelf

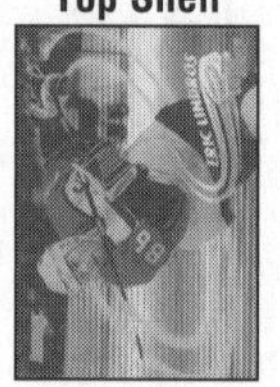

This 10-card set was distributed only through magazine packs, with each card numbered out of 2,000.
COMPLETE SET (10) 20.00 50.00
1 Mario Lemieux 8.00 20.00
2 Teemu Selanne 2.00 5.00
3 Joe Sakic 4.00 10.00
4 Alexander Mogilny 1.25 3.00
5 Jaromir Jagr 3.00 8.00
6 Brett Hull 2.50 6.00
7 Mike Modano 2.50 6.00
8 Paul Kariya 2.00 5.00
9 Eric Lindros 2.00 5.00
10 Peter Forsberg 3.00 8.00

1996-97 Donruss Hit List

This set features 20 of the NHL's top bangers and crashers. Individually numbered to 10,000, these cards feature an internal die-cut with a color photo, and the player's name and position in silver foil on the front.
COMPLETE SET (20) 10.00 25.00
1 Eric Lindros .75 2.00
2 Wendel Clark .40 1.00
3 Ed Jovanovski .20 .50
4 Jeremy Roenick 1.50 4.00
5 Doug Weight .40 1.00
6 Chris Chelios .75 2.00
7 Brendan Shanahan .75 2.00
8 Mark Messier 1.25 3.00
9 Scott Stevens .20 .50
10 Keith Tkachuk .60 1.50
11 Trevor Linden .60 1.50
12 Eric Daze .20 .50
13 John LeClair .60 1.50
14 Peter Forsberg 2.00 5.00
15 Doug Gilmour .60 1.50
16 Roman Hamrlik .20 .50
17 Owen Nolan .20 .50
18 Claude Lemieux .20 .50
19 Saku Koivu .75 2.00
20 Theo Fleury .20 .50
P1 Eric Lindros PROMO .40 1.00

1996-97 Donruss Rated Rookies

This set features ten top young superstars. A rare press proof version of these cards exists, though little about them, including quantity of production, is unknown. They are not mentioned on any product literature, nor are they widely available. They are fairly easy to distinguish by virtue of their gold foil finish. The press proof versions, when seen, have been trading with a multiplier of 5X to 10X the value of the basic cards.
COMPLETE SET (10) 8.00 20.00
1 Eric Daze .75 2.00
2 Petr Sykora .75 2.00
3 Valeri Bure .75 2.00
4 Jere Lehtinen .75 2.00
5 Jeff O'Neill .75 2.00
6 Saku Koivu 1.50 4.00
7 Ed Jovanovski .75 2.00
8 Eric Fichaud .75 2.00
9 Todd Bertuzzi 1.50 4.00
10 Daniel Alfredsson 1.50 4.00

1997-98 Donruss

The 1997-98 Donruss set was issued in one series totaling 230 cards and distributed in 10-card packs. The fronts featured color action player photos. The backs carried player information.
COMPLETE SET (230) 10.00 25.00
1 Peter Forsberg .30 .75
2 Steve Yzerman .60 1.50
3 Eric Lindros .10 .30
4 Mark Messier .10 .30
5 Patrick Roy .60 1.50
6 Jeremy Roenick .15 .40
7 Paul Kariya .10 .30
8 Valeri Bure .02 .10
9 Dominik Hasek .25 .60
10 Doug Gilmour .06 .20
11 Garth Snow .06 .20
12 Todd Bertuzzi .10 .30
13 Chris Osgood .06 .20
14 Jarome Iginla .15 .40
15 Lonny Bohonos .02 .10
16 Jeff O'Neill .02 .10
17 Daniel Alfredsson .06 .20
18 Daymond Langkow .06 .20
19 Alexei Yashin .02 .10
20 Byron Dafoe .06 .20
21 Mike Peca .02 .10
22 Jim Carey .06 .20
23 Pat Verbeek .02 .10
24 Terry Ryan .02 .10
25 Adam Oates .06 .20
26 Kevin Hatcher .02 .10
27 Ken Wregget .06 .20
28 Pierre Turgeon .06 .20
29 John LeClair .10 .30
30 Jere Lehtinen .02 .10
31 Jamie Storr .06 .20
32 Doug Weight .06 .20
33 Tommy Salo .06 .20
34 Bernie Nicholls .02 .10
35 Jocelyn Thibault .06 .20
36 Dale Hawerchuk .06 .20
UER front Dave
37 Chris Chelios .10 .30
38 Kirk Muller .02 .10
39 Steve Sullivan .02 .10
40 Andy Moog .06 .20
41 Martin Gelinas .02 .10
42 Shayne Corson .02 .10
43 Curtis Joseph .10 .30
44 Donald Audette .02 .10
45 Rick Tocchet .06 .20
46 Craig Janney .02 .10
47 Geoff Courtnall .02 .10
48 Wade Redden .02 .10
49 Steve Rucchin .02 .10
50 Ethan Moreau .02 .10
51 Steve Shields RC .20 .50
52 Jamie Pushor .02 .10
53 Saku Koivu .10 .30
54 Oleg Tverdovsky .02 .10
55 Jeff Friesen .02 .10
56 Chris Gratton .02 .10
57 Wendel Clark .06 .20
58 John Vanbiesbrouck .06 .20
59 Trevor Kidd .06 .20
60 Sandis Ozolinsh .02 .10
61 Dave Andreychuk .02 .10
62 Travis Green .02 .10
63 Paul Coffey .10 .30
64 Roman Turek .06 .20
65 Vladimir Konstantinov .06 .20
66 Ray Bourque .20 .50
67 Wayne Primeau .02 .10
68 Todd Harvey .02 .10
69 Derek King .02 .10
70 Adam Graves .02 .10
71 Brett Hull .15 .40
72 Scott Niedermayer .02 .10
73 Mike Vernon .06 .20
74 Brian Holzinger .02 .10
75 Dainius Zubrus .10 .30
76 Patrick Lalime .06 .20
77 Corey Schwab .06 .20
78 Alexandre Daigle .02 .10
79 Geoff Sanderson .06 .20
80 Dave Gagner .02 .10
81 Jose Theodore .15 .40
82 Sergei Fedorov .20 .50
83 Keith Tkachuk .10 .30
84 Owen Nolan .06 .20
85 Brandon Convery .02 .10
86 Trevor Linden .06 .20
87 Landon Wilson .02 .10
88 Claude Lemieux .02 .10
89 Dimitri Khristich .02 .10
90 Luc Robitaille .06 .20
91 Todd Warriner .02 .10
92 Kelly Hrudey .06 .20
93 Mike Dunham .06 .20
94 Mike Grier .02 .10
95 Joe Juneau .06 .20
96 Alexei Zhamnov .02 .10
97 Jamie Langenbrunner .02 .10
98 Sean Pronger .02 .10
99 Janne Niinimaa .06 .20
100 Chris Pronger .06 .20
101 Ray Sheppard .02 .10
102 Tony Amonte .06 .20
103 Ron Tugnutt .06 .20
104 Mike Modano .20 .50
105 Dan Trebil .02 .10
106 Alexander Mogilny .06 .20
107 Darren McCarty .02 .10
108 Ted Donato .02 .10
109 Brian Savage .02 .10
110 Mike Gartner .06 .20
111 Jim Campbell .02 .10
112 Roman Hamrlik .02 .10
113 Andreas Dackell .02 .10
114 Ron Hextall .06 .20
115 Steve Washburn .02 .10
116 Jeff Hackett .06 .20
117 Joe Sakic .25 .60
118 Anson Carter .06 .20
119 Vyacheslav Kozlov .02 .10
120 Nikolai Khabibulin .06 .20
121 Tony Granato .02 .10
122 Al MacInnis .06 .20
123 Daren Puppa .06 .20
124 Mike Richter .10 .30
125 Zigmund Palffy .06 .20
126 Martin Brodeur .30 .75
127 Rem Murray .02 .10
128 Sean Burke .06 .20
129 Aki Berg .02 .10
130 Dmitri Mironov .02 .10
131 Jamie Allison .02 .10
132 Valeri Kamensky .06 .20
133 Pat LaFontaine .10 .30
134 Jozef Stumpel .06 .20
135 Peter Bondra .06 .20
136 Mark Recchi .06 .20
137 Ron Francis .06 .20
138 Harry York .02 .10
139 Mats Sundin .10 .30
140 Bobby Holik .02 .10
141 Eric Desjardins .06 .20
142 Scott Lachance .02 .10
143 Wayne Gretzky .75 2.00
144 Ed Jovanovski .06 .20
145 Jason Arnott .02 .10
146 Andrew Cassels .02 .10
147 Roman Vopat .02 .10
148 Dwayne Roloson .02 .10
149 Derek Plante .02 .10
150 Phil Housley .02 .10
151 Mikael Renberg .06 .20
152 Petr Nedved .06 .20
153 Grant Fuhr .06 .20
154 Felix Potvin .10 .30
155 John MacLean .02 .10
156 Brian Leetch .10 .30
157 Rod Brind'Amour .06 .20
158 Ryan Smyth .06 .20
159 Teemu Selanne .10 .30
160 Theo Fleury .02 .10
161 Adam Deadmarsh .02 .10
162 Corey Hirsch .06 .20
163 Bryan Berard .06 .20
164 Ed Belfour .10 .30
165 Sergei Berezin .02 .10
166 Damian Rhodes .06 .20
167 Guy Hebert .06 .20
168 Derian Hatcher .02 .10
169 Jonas Hoglund .02 .10
170 Matthew Barnaby .02 .10
171 Scott Mellanby .02 .10
172 Bill Ranford .06 .20
173 Vincent Damphousse .02 .10
174 Anders Eriksson .02 .10
175 Chad Kilger .02 .10
176 Darren Turcotte .02 .10
177 Dino Ciccarelli .02 .10
178 Niklas Sundstrom .02 .10
179 Stephane Fiset .06 .20
180 Mike Ricci .02 .10
181 Brendan Shanahan .10 .30
182 Darcy Tucker .02 .10
183 Eric Fichaud .06 .20
184 Todd Marchant .02 .10
185 Keith Primeau .02 .10
186 Joe Nieuwendyk .06 .20
187 Pavel Bure .10 .30
188 Jaromir Jagr .20 .50
189 Kirk McLean .06 .20
190 Daniel Goneau .02 .10
191 Rob Niedermayer .02 .10
192 Eric Daze .06 .20
193 Richard Matvichuk .02 .10
194 Scott Stevens .06 .20
195 Dale Hunter .02 .10
196 Hnat Domenichelli .02 .10
197 Philippe DeRouville .02 .10
198 Marcel Cousineau .06 .20
199 Kevin Hodson .06 .20
200 J-S Giguere .06 .20
201 Paxton Schafer RC .06 .20
202 Marc Denis .06 .20
203 Frank Banham RC .02 .10
204 Vadim Sharifijanov .02 .10
205 Paul Healey RC .02 .10
206 D.J. Smith RC .02 .10
207 Christian Matte RC .02 .10
208 Sean Brown RC .02 .10
209 Tomas Vokoun RC .60 1.50
210 Vladimir Vorobiev RC .02 .10
211 Jean-Yves Leroux RC .02 .10
212 Domenic Pittis RC .02 .10
213 Derek Wilkinson RC .02 .10
214 Jason Holland .02 .10
215 Pascal Rheaume RC .02 .10
216 Steve Kelly RC .02 .10
217 Vaclav Varada .02 .10
218 Mike Fountain .02 .10
219 Vaclav Prospal RC .10 .30
220 Jaroslav Svejkovsky .06 .20
221 Marty Murray .02 .10
222 Wade Belak RC .06 .20
223 Jamal Mayers RC .02 .10
224 Shayne Toporowski RC .02 .10
225 Mike Knuble RC .06 .20
226 Jarome Iginla CL (1-60) .10 .30
227 Keith Tkachuk CL (61-120) .06 .20
228 Adam Oates CL (121-180) .02 .10
229 John LeClair CL (181-230) .10 .30
230 Brian Leetch CL (inserts) .06 .20

1997-98 Donruss Press Proofs Silver

Randomly inserted in packs, this 230-card set was a parallel to the Donruss base set and featured a full foil card stock with silver foil accents. Only 2000 of this set were produced.
*STARS: 20X TO 40X BASIC CARDS
*RC's: 4X TO 10X BASIC CARDS

1997-98 Donruss Press Proofs Gold

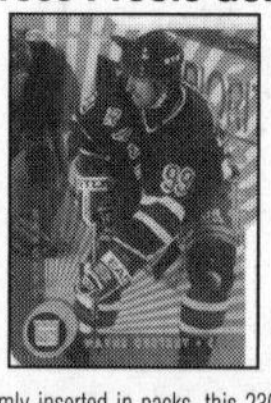

Randomly inserted in packs, this 230-card set was a parallel to the Donruss base set and featured a unique die cut design with gold foil stamping. Only 500 of this set were produced and were sequentially numbered.
*STARS: 40X TO 100X BASIC CARDS
*ROOKIES: 8X TO 20X BASIC CARDS

1997-98 Donruss Between The Pipes

Randomly inserted in hobby packs only, this 10-card set featured color photos of the league's top defensive players printed on an etched, full foil card stock with foil stamped accents. Only 3000 of this set were produced and were sequentially numbered.
COMPLETE SET (10) 50.00 125.00
1 Patrick Roy 15.00 40.00
2 Martin Brodeur 12.00 30.00
3 John Vanbiesbrouck 4.00 10.00
4 Dominik Hasek 12.00 20.00
5 Chris Osgood 4.00 10.00
6 Jose Theodore 4.00 10.00
7 Garth Snow 4.00 10.00
8 Curtis Joseph 5.00 12.00
9 Felix Potvin 5.00 12.00
10 Jocelyn Thibault 4.00 10.00

1997-98 Donruss Elite Inserts

Randomly inserted in packs, this 12-card set featured color photos of the league's most dominant superstars printed on card stock utilizing a double treatment of gold and holographic gold foils. Only 2500 of each card were produced and were sequentially numbered.
COMPLETE SET (12) 30.00 60.00
1 Wayne Gretzky 8.00 20.00
2 Jaromir Jagr 2.00 5.00
3 Eric Lindros 1.25 3.00
4 Paul Kariya 1.25 3.00
5 Patrick Roy 6.00 15.00
6 Steve Yzerman 6.00 15.00
7 Peter Forsberg 3.00 8.00
8 John Vanbiesbrouck .75 2.00
9 Brendan Shanahan 1.25 3.00
10 Martin Brodeur 3.00 8.00
11 Dominik Hasek 2.50 6.00
12 Teemu Selanne 1.25 3.00
13P Martin Brodeur PROMO 2.00 5.00

1997-98 Donruss Line 2 Line

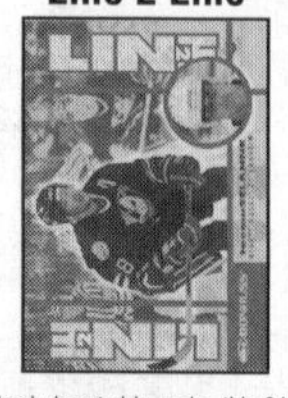

Randomly inserted in packs, this 24-card fractured insert set contained three levels of scarcity with each level printed on foil card stocks. Level one was "Red Line" which featured color photos of 12 players with red foil enhancements and each card sequentially numbered to 4000; Level two was "Blue Line" which featured color photos of eight players with blue foil enhancement and each sequentially numbered to 2000. Level three was "Gold Line" which featured color photos of four players with each sequentially numbered to 1000. The first 25 of each Line two card featured a unique die cut design.
COMPLETE SET (24) 100.00 200.00
*RED DIE CUTS: 2X TO 5X BASIC RED
*BLUE DIE CUTS: 1.25X TO 3X BASIC BLU
*GOLD DIE CUTS: 1.25X TO 3X BASIC GOLD
1 Wayne Gretzky G 20.00 50.00
2 Teemu Selanne R 4.00 10.00
3 Brian Leetch B 5.00 10.00
4 Peter Forsberg R 8.00 20.00
5 Steve Yzerman R 12.00 30.00
6 Oleg Tverdovsky B 2.50 2.00
7 Doug Gilmour R 2.50 4.00
8 Eric Lindros G 3.00 8.00
9 Bryan Berard B 2.50 6.00
10 Brendan Shanahan R 2.50 4.00
11 Pavel Bure R 3.00 8.00
12 Joe Sakic R 6.00 15.00
13 Chris Chelios B 5.00 12.00
14 Mike Modano R 5.00 12.00
15 Paul Coffey B 5.00 12.00
16 Jaromir Jagr G 10.00 25.00
17 Jarome Iginla R 4.00 10.00
18 Brett Hull R 4.00 10.00
19 Wade Redden B 2.50 6.00
20 Paul Kariya G 10.00 25.00
21 Ray Bourque B 8.00 15.00
22 Ryan Smyth R 2.50 4.00
23 Mark Messier R 3.00 8.00
24 Sandis Ozolinsh B 4.00 2.00
P4 Peter Forsberg PROMO 8.00 20.00
P5 Steve Yzerman PROMO 10.00 25.00

1997-98 Donruss Rated Rookies

Randomly inserted in packs, this 10-card set featured color action photos of the hottest young rookie prospects printed on background with the letters "RR." A "Medalist" parallel was also created and printed on foil card stock accented with both gold foil and silver holographic foil treatments.
COMPLETE SET (10) 6.00 15.00
*MEDALISTS: 1.5X TO 4X BASIC INSERTS
1 Tomas Vokoun 2.00 5.00
2 Paxton Schafer .40 1.00
3 Vaclav Prospal .75 2.00
4 Marc Denis .75 2.00
5 Domenic Pittis .40 1.00
6 Christian Matte .40 1.00
7 Marcel Cousineau .40 1.00
8 Steve Kelly .40 1.00
9 Jaroslav Svejkovsky .40 1.00
10 J-S Giguere 2.00 5.00

1997-98 Donruss Red Alert

Randomly inserted in retail packs only, this 10-card set featured color photos of the league's top goal scorers printed on thick plastic card stock, die cut in the shape of a goal light and highlighted with red holographic foil treatments. Only 5,000 of the set were produced and were sequentially

nbered.
)MPLETE SET (10) 40.00 80.00
Adam Deadmarsh 2.00 5.00
Ryan Smyth 4.00 10.00
Sergei Fedorov 6.00 15.00
Keith Tkachuk 4.00 10.00
Brett Hull 6.00 15.00
Pavel Bure 6.00 15.00
John LeClair 2.00 5.00
Zigmund Palffy 4.00 10.00
Mats Sundin 4.00 10.00
Peter Bondra 4.00 10.00

1996-97 Donruss Canadian Ice

is 150-card set was issued eight cards per ck with a suggested retail price of $2.99. ile these sets were initially made for stribution to Canada, a large amount of the oduct was shipped to the United States. rd fronts featured a full color action photo th the player's name and team appearing ar the bottom of the card. Key rookies in s set included Mike Grier, Kevin Hodson, an Moreau, and Dainius Zubrus.

)MPLETE SET (150) 10.00 25.00
Jaromir Jagr .30 .75
Jocelyn Thibault .20 .50
Paul Kariya .20 .50
Derian Hatcher .02 .10
Wayne Gretzky 1.00 2.50
Peter Forsberg .30 .75
Eric Lindros .20 .50
Adam Oates .10 .25
Paul Coffey .20 .50
) Chris Osgood .10 .25
Pat LaFontaine .20 .50
2 Mats Sundin .20 .50
3 Rob Niedermayer .10 .25
4 Doug Weight .10 .25
5 Al MacInnis .10 .25
6 Damian Rhodes .10 .25
7 Stephane Fiset .10 .25
3 Mike Gartner .10 .25
9 Patrick Roy 1.00 1.50
) Eric Daze .10 .25
1 Ray Bourque .30 .75
2 Keith Tkachuk .20 .50
3 Mark Recchi .10 .25
4 Peter Bondra .10 .25
5 Mike Modano .25 .60
6 Mike Richter .20 .50
7 Keith Primeau .02 .10
8 Todd Bertuzzi .20 .50
9 Wendel Clark .10 .25
0 Scott Young .02 .10
1 Mario Lemieux .60 1.50
2 Valeri Kamensky .10 .25
3 Kirk McLean .10 .25
4 Daniel Alfredsson .10 .25
5 Ed Jovanovski .10 .25
6 Kelly Hrudey .10 .25
7 Trevor Kidd .10 .25
8 Joe Juneau .02 .10
9 Steve Yzerman 1.00 1.25
0 Saku Koivu .20 .50
1 Alexei Kovalev .02 .10
2 Rob Blake .10 .25
3 Shayne Corson .02 .10
4 Roman Hamrlik .10 .25
5 Stephane Yelle .02 .10
6 Martin Brodeur .40 1.00
7 Kirk Muller .02 .10
8 Pat Verbeek .02 .10
9 Jari Kurri .10 .25
0 Michal Pivonka .02 .10
1 Ron Hextall .10 .25
2 Trevor Linden .10 .25
3 Vincent Damphousse .02 .10
4 Owen Nolan .10 .25
5 Sergei Fedorov .25 .60
6 Chris Chelios .20 .50
7 Jeremy Roenick .25 .60
8 Zigmund Palffy .10 .25
9 Pavel Bure .20 .50
0 Dominik Hasek .40 1.00
1 Alexei Yashin .02 .10
2 Chris Gratton .10 .25
3 Joe Nieuwendyk .10 .25
4 Luc Robitaille .10 .25
5 Brett Hull .25 .60
6 Sean Burke .10 .25
7 Felix Potvin .20 .50
8 Jason Arnott .02 .10
9 Valeri Bure .02 .10
0 Tom Barrasso .10 .25
1 Vyacheslav Kozlov .02 .10
2 Petr Sykora .02 .10
3 Corey Hirsch .10 .25
4 Joe Sakic .40 1.00
5 Bill Ranford .10 .25
6 Yanic Perreault .02 .10
7 Mikael Renberg .10 .25
8 Theo Fleury .02 .10
79 Jim Carey .10 .25
80 Vitali Yachmenev .02 .10
81 Martin Rucinsky .02 .10
82 Jeff O'Neill .02 .10
83 Marcus Ragnarsson .02 .10
84 John Vanbiesbrouck .10 .25
85 Teemu Selanne .20 .50
86 Larry Murphy .10 .25
87 Mark Messier .20 .50
88 Alexei Zhamnov .10 .25
89 Ryan Smyth .20 .50
90 Andy Moog .10 .25
91 Alexander Mogilny .10 .25
92 Kris Draper .02 .10
93 Ron Francis .10 .25
94 Mike Vernon .10 .25
95 Nikolai Khabibulin .10 .25
96 Mariusz Czerkawski .02 .10
97 Mathieu Schneider .02 .10
98 Stephane Richer .10 .25
99 Mike Ricci .02 .10
100 John LeClair .10 .25
101 Brendan Shanahan .20 .50
102 Daren Puppa .10 .25
103 Scott Stevens .10 .25
104 Alexandre Daigle .02 .10
105 Dimitri Khristich .02 .10
106 Bernie Nicholls .02 .10
107 Scott Mellanby .10 .25
108 Brian Leetch .20 .50
109 Grant Fuhr .10 .25
110 Pierre Turgeon .10 .25
111 Jere Lehtinen .02 .10
112 Doug Gilmour .20 .50
113 Ed Belfour .20 .50
114 Geoff Sanderson .10 .25
115 Claude Lemieux .02 .10
116 Curtis Joseph .20 .50
117 Igor Larionov .02 .10
118 Jamie Pushor .02 .10
119 Sergei Berezin RC .20 .50
120 Eric Fichaud .10 .25
121 Wade Redden .02 .10
122 Hnat Domenichelli .02 .10
123 Rem Murray RC .02 .10
124 Jarome Iginla .25 .60
125 Richard Zednik RC .25 .60
126 Daniel Goneau RC .02 .10
127 Ethan Moreau RC .20 .50
128 Janne Niinimaa .20 .50
129 Tomas Holmstrom RC .60 1.50
130 Fredrik Modin RC .30 .75
131 Bryan Berard .20 .50
132 Jim Campbell .02 .10
133 Chris O'Sullivan .02 .10
134 Andreas Dackell RC .02 .10
135 Daymond Langkow .10 .25
136 Kevin Hodson RC .20 .50
137 Jamie Langenbrunner .02 .10
138 Mattias Timander RC .02 .10
139 Tuomas Gronman .02 .10
140 Jonas Hoglund .02 .10
141 Mike Grier RC .40 1.00
142 Terry Ryan RC .02 .10
143 Darcy Tucker .02 .10
144 Brandon Convery .02 .10
145 Anders Eriksson .02 .10
146 Christian Dube .02 .10
147 Dainius Zubrus RC .50 1.25
148 Grant Fuhr CL .02 .10
149 Paul Coffey CL .10 .25
150 Ray Bourque CL .10 .25

1996-97 Donruss Canadian Ice Gold Press Proofs

This 150-card set was the tougher of two parallels to the base set. Production of these cards were limited to 150 sets, a fact which is noted on the card. The words Canadian Gold appeared on the top of the card, and a gold foil treatment was used to enhance the appearance.

*STARS: 12X TO 30X BASIC CARDS
*RCs: 6X TO 15X BASIC CARDS

1996-97 Donruss Canadian Ice Red Press Proofs

This 150-card set was the easier of two parallels to the base set. Production of these cards was limited to 750 sets, a fact noted on the card. The fronts featured silver and red foil enhancements, along with the words Canadian Red.

*STARS: 6X TO 15X BASIC CARDS
*RCs: 3X TO 8X BASIC CARDS

1996-97 Donruss Canadian Ice Les Gardiens

This bronze foil set featured 10 of the NHL's top netminders, each of whom were born in Quebec. A full-color portrait of each player adorned the card fronts, along with the skyline of Montreal in the background. The player's name and team were printed in gold foil along the bottom of these cards. Each card was serially numbered out of 1,500.

COMPLETE SET (10) 25.00 60.00
1 Patrick Roy 10.00 25.00
2 Jocelyn Thibault 2.00 5.00
3 Felix Potvin 3.00 8.00
4 Martin Brodeur 6.00 15.00
5 Stephane Fiset 2.00 5.00
6 Eric Fichaud 2.00 5.00
7 Dominic Roussel 2.00 5.00
8 Emmanuel Fernandez 2.00 5.00
9 Martin Biron 2.00 5.00
10 Jose Theodore 4.00 10.00

1996-97 Donruss Canadian Ice Mario Lemieux Scrapbook

This 25-card set was made as a tribute to Mario Lemieux. Each card depicted a different highlight from the storied career of the Penguins' great. Only 1,966 individually numbered copies of each card were produced. Mario also hand signed a number of these cards, and there were two distinct versions of this card. The first, numbered out of 1200, was randomly inserted into packs. The second, numbered out of 500, was available in a framed version of the set available directly through an in-pack offer from Donruss.

COMPLETE SET (25) 100.00 200.00
COMMON CARD (1-25) 5.00 10.00
NNO1 M.Lemieux AU/500 100.00 250.00
NNO2 M.Lemieux AU/1200 30.00 80.00

1996-97 Donruss Canadian Ice O Canada

This 16-card set featured some of the top players born in Canada. Card fronts contained a color action photo, with the Canadian flag in the background. Each card had die-cut corners and featured gold and red foil printing. Just 2,000 individually numbered copies of each of these cards were produced.

COMPLETE SET (16) 40.00 100.00
1 Joe Sakic 6.00 15.00
2 Paul Kariya 2.50 6.00
3 Mark Messier 2.50 6.00
4 Jarome Iginla 3.00 8.00
5 Theo Fleury .75 2.00
6 Ed Belfour 2.50 6.00
7 Wayne Gretzky 25.00 40.00
8 Chris Gratton .75 2.00
9 Doug Gilmour 2.00 5.00
10 Kirk Muller .75 2.00
11 Eric Lindros 2.50 6.00
12 Brendan Shanahan 2.50 6.00
13 Mario Lemieux 12.00 30.00
14 Eric Daze .75 2.00
15 Geoff Sanderson .75 2.00
16 Terry Ryan .75 2.00

1997-98 Donruss Canadian Ice

The 1997-98 Donruss Canadian Ice set was issued in one series totaling 150 cards and distributed in eight-card packs. The fronts featured color action player photos. The backs carryed player information.

COMPLETE SET (150) 15.00 30.00
1 Patrick Roy 1.00 2.50
2 Paul Kariya .20 .50
3 Eric Lindros .20 .50
4 Steve Yzerman 1.00 2.50
5 Wayne Gretzky 1.25 3.00
6 Peter Forsberg .50 1.25
7 John Vanbiesbrouck .08 .25
8 Jaromir Jagr .30 .75
9 Jim Campbell .02 .10
10 Dominik Hasek .40 1.00
11 Ray Bourque .30 .75
12 Jarome Iginla .25 .60
13 Mike Modano .30 .75
14 Ed Jovanovski .08 .25
15 Jocelyn Thibault .08 .25
16 Keith Tkachuk .20 .50
17 Brett Hull .25 .60
18 Pavel Bure .20 .50
19 Saku Koivu .20 .50
20 Curtis Joseph .20 .50
21 Eric Daze .08 .25
22 Keith Primeau .02 .10
23 Theo Fleury .02 .10
24 Pierre Turgeon .08 .25
25 Peter Bondra .08 .25
26 Ed Belfour .20 .50
27 Pat Verbeek .02 .10
28 Chris Osgood .08 .25
29 Ray Sheppard .02 .10
30 Stephane Fiset .08 .25
31 Wade Redden .02 .10
32 Trevor Linden .08 .25
33 Zigmund Palffy .08 .25
34 Tony Amonte .08 .25
35 Derek Plante .02 .10
36 Jonas Hoglund .02 .10
37 Guy Hebert .08 .25
38 Garth Snow .08 .25
39 Chris Gratton .08 .25
40 Mats Sundin .20 .50
41 Geoff Sanderson .08 .25
42 Martin Brodeur .50 1.25
43 Jozef Stumpel .08 .25
44 Ron Francis .08 .25
45 Alexander Mogilny .08 .25
46 Bill Ranford .08 .25
47 Kirk Muller .02 .10
48 Ron Hextall .08 .25
49 Doug Gilmour .08 .25
50 Mark Messier .20 .50
51 Joe Nieuwendyk .08 .25
52 Ryan Smyth .08 .25
53 Mark Recchi .08 .25
54 Mike Gartner .08 .25
55 Al MacInnis .08 .25
56 Felix Potvin .20 .50
57 Rob Blake .08 .25
58 Dimitri Khristich .02 .10
59 Jim Carey .08 .25
60 Trevor Kidd .08 .25
61 Martin Gelinas .02 .10
62 Oleg Tverdovsky .02 .10
63 Ron Tugnutt .08 .25
64 Paul Coffey .20 .50
65 Travis Green .02 .10
66 Andrew Cassels .02 .10
67 Brendan Shanahan .20 .50
68 Luc Robitaille .08 .25
69 Pat LaFontaine .20 .50
70 Daymond Langkow .08 .25
71 Petr Nedved .08 .25
72 Sergei Fedorov .30 .75
73 Anson Carter .08 .25
74 Teemu Selanne .20 .50
75 Nikolai Khabibulin .08 .25
76 Ken Wregget .08 .25
77 Dino Ciccarelli .02 .10
78 Adam Oates .02 .10
79 Kirk McLean .08 .25
80 Wendel Clark .08 .25
81 Jeff Friesen .02 .10
82 Valeri Kamensky .08 .25
83 Ethan Moreau .02 .10
84 Matthew Barnaby .02 .10
85 Andy Moog .08 .25
86 Doug Weight .08 .25
87 Mike Dunham .08 .25
88 Brian Leetch .20 .50
89 Mike Peca .02 .10
90 Chris Pronger .08 .25
91 Alexei Zhamnov .02 .10
92 Bryan Berard .08 .25
93 John LeClair .20 .50
94 Steve Sullivan .02 .10
95 Grant Fuhr .02 .10
96 Mikael Renberg .08 .25
97 Adam Graves .02 .10
98 Ray Ferraro .02 .10
99 Sean Burke .08 .25
100 Jeremy Roenick .25 .60
101 Jeff Hackett .08 .25
102 Joe Sakic .40 1.00
103 Jamie Langenbrunner .02 .10
104 Stephane Richer .02 .10
105 Dave Andreychuk .02 .10
106 Tommy Salo .08 .25
107 Mike Richter .20 .50
108 Owen Nolan .08 .25
109 Corey Hirsch .08 .25
110 Daren Puppa .08 .25
111 Darcy Tucker .02 .10
112 Daniel Alfredsson .08 .25
113 Rod Brind'Amour .08 .25
114 Scott Stevens .08 .25
115 Vincent Damphousse .02 .10
116 Mathieu Schneider .02 .10
117 Jason Arnott .02 .10
118 Mike Vernon .08 .25
119 Sandis Ozolinsh .02 .10
120 Chris Chelios .20 .50
121 Mike Grier .02 .10
122 Alexandre Daigle .02 .10
123 Roman Hamrlik .02 .10
124 Derian Hatcher .02 .10
125 Damian Rhodes .08 .25
126 Adam Deadmarsh .02 .10
127 Alexei Yashin .02 .10
128 Terry Ryan .02 .10
129 Jeff Ware .02 .10
130 Steve Kelly .02 .10
131 Hnat Domenichelli .02 .10
132 Steve Shields RC .30 .75
133 Paxton Schafer RC .08 .25
134 Vadim Sharifijanov .02 .10
135 Vaclav Prospal RC .20 .50
136 Mike Fountain .02 .10
137 Christian Matte RC .02 .10
138 Tomas Vokoun RC .60 1.50
139 Vladimir Vorobiev RC .02 .10
140 Domenic Pittis RC .02 .10
141 Vaclav Varada .02 .10
142 D.J. Smith RC .02 .10
143 Jaroslav Svejkovsky .08 .25
144 Jason Holland .02 .10
145 Marc Denis .08 .25
146 J-S Giguere .08 .25
147 Marcel Cousineau .08 .25
148 Dave Andreychuk CL (1-75) .02 .10
149 Mike Gartner CL (76-150) .02 .10
150 Stanley Cup .02 .10
Team Picture CL (inserts)

1997-98 Donruss Canadian Ice Dominion Series

This 150-card set was a parallel to the base set and was similar in design. Only 150 of each card were produced. Serial numbered and non-serial numbered cards carryed the same value.

*DOMINION STARS: 50X TO 125X BASIC CARDS
*DOMINION RC's: 25X TO 60X BASIC CARDS

1997-98 Donruss Canadian Ice Provincial Series

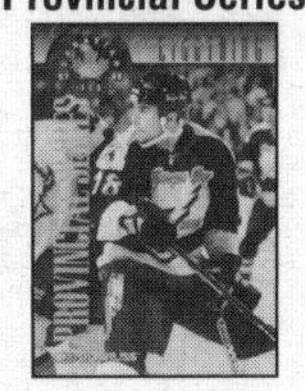

This 150-card set was a parallel to the base set and was similar in design. Only 750 of each card were produced, and were sequentially numbered.

*PROV.STARS: 12.5X TO 30X BASIC CARDS
*PROVINCIAL RC's: 6X TO 15X BASIC CARDS

1997-98 Donruss Canadian Ice Les Gardiens

Randomly inserted in packs, this 12-card set featured color photos honoring great goaltenders from Quebec printed on micro-etched foil board. Only 1500 of each card were produced and were sequentially numbered.

COMPLETE SET (12) 40.00 100.00
1 Patrick Roy 15.00 40.00
2 Felix Potvin 4.00 10.00
3 Martin Brodeur 10.00 25.00
4 J-S Giguere 4.00 10.00
5 Stephane Fiset 2.00 5.00
6 Jose Theodore 4.00 10.00
7 Jocelyn Thibault 2.00 5.00
8 Eric Fichaud 2.00 5.00
9 Patrick Lalime 2.00 5.00
10 Marcel Cousineau 2.00 5.00
11 Philippe DeRouville 2.00 5.00
12 Marc Denis 2.00 5.00

1997-98 Donruss Canadian Ice Les Gardiens Promos

This 12-card set was issued as a promotional item. The cards were a parallel to the base set except that each was numbered Promo/1500. Reportedly 1500 of each promo card were produced.

COMPLETE SET (12) 32.00 80.00
1 Patrick Roy 6.00 15.00
2 Felix Potvin 3.20 8.00
3 Martin Brodeur 8.00 20.00
4 J-S Giguere 2.40 6.00
5 Stephane Fiset 2.40 6.00
6 Jose Theodore 2.40 6.00
7 Jocelyn Thibault 3.20 8.00
8 Eric Fichaud 2.40 6.00
9 Patrick Lalime 3.20 8.00
10 Marcel Cousineau 2.40 6.00
11 Philippe DeRouville 2.40 6.00
12 Marc Denis 2.40 6.00

1997-98 Donruss Canadian Ice National Pride

Randomly inserted in packs, this 30-card set featured color photos of the most prominent native Canadian players printed on a die cut plastic card in the shape of a maple leaf and with gold foil highlights.

COMPLETE SET (30) 75.00 150.00
1 Wayne Gretzky 20.00 50.00
2 Mark Messier 3.00 8.00
3 Paul Kariya 3.00 8.00
4 Steve Yzerman 15.00 40.00
5 Brendan Shanahan 3.00 8.00
6 Chris Osgood 1.50 4.00
7 Adam Oates 1.50 4.00
8 Eric Lindros 3.00 8.00
9 Doug Gilmour 1.50 4.00
10 Ryan Smyth 1.50 4.00
11 Ray Bourque 5.00 12.00
12 Jason Arnott .60 1.50
13 Jarome Iginla 4.00 10.00
14 Geoff Sanderson 1.50 4.00
15 Alexandre Daigle .60 1.50
16 Trevor Linden 1.50 4.00
17 Joe Sakic 6.00 15.00
18 Mark Recchi 1.50 4.00
19 Theo Fleury .60 1.50
20 Ron Francis 1.50 4.00
21 Daymond Langkow 1.50 4.00
22 Ed Belfour 3.00 8.00
23 Paul Coffey 3.00 8.00
24 Pierre Turgeon 1.50 4.00
25 Claude Lemieux .60 1.50
26 Ron Hextall 1.50 4.00
27 Curtis Joseph 3.00 8.00
28 Mike Vernon 1.50 4.00
29 Vincent Damphousse .60 1.50
30 Owen Nolan 1.50 4.00

1997-98 Donruss Canadian Ice Stanley Cup Scrapbook

Randomly inserted in packs, this 33-card set was a fractured chase set which features color photos of players from each round of the 1997 Stanley Cup Playoffs. Only 2000 of the 16 Quarterfinals cards were produced and were sequentially numbered; 1500 of the eight sequentially numbered Conference Semifinals cards were produced; 1000 of the six sequentially numbered Conference Finals cards were produced; 750 of the two sequentially numbered Stanley Cup Finals cards were produced; only 250 of the one Stanley Cup Champions cards were produced and were sequentially numbered. Mike Vernon and Eric Lindros each autographed 750 of the Stanley Cup Finals cards, and Brendan Shanahan autographed 250 of the Stanley Cup Champions cards. A framed version of this set serial numbered to 500 was also available through a mail-in offer in packs. The cards were a parallel to the base set except that the words "Canadian Collectors Set" appeared at the top of the card. Sets were available for $500 through this offer, and due to the scarcity of them, they are not priced.

1 Mike Modano Q 6.00 15.00
2 Curtis Joseph Q 4.00 10.00
3 Joe Sakic Q 8.00 20.00
4 Chris Chelios Q 2.50 6.00
5 Chris Osgood Q 2.50 6.00
6 Brett Hull Q 5.00 12.00
7 Jeremy Roenick Q 4.00 10.00
8 Teemu Selanne Q 4.00 10.00
9 Jaromir Jagr Q 6.00 15.00
10 Garth Snow Q 2.50 6.00
11 Alexei Yashin Q 2.50 6.00
12 Steve Shields Q 2.50 6.00
13 Doug Gilmour Q 3.00 8.00
14 Jose Theodore Q 5.00 12.00
15 Mike Richter Q 2.50 6.00
16 John Vanbiesbrouck Q 2.50 6.00
17 Ryan Smyth CS 2.50 6.00
18 Peter Forsberg CS 12.50 30.00
19 Steve Yzerman CS 25.00 60.00
20 Paul Kariya CS 4.00 10.00
21 Janne Niinimaa CS 2.50 6.00
22 Dominik Hasek CS 10.00 25.00
23 Mark Messier CS 4.00 10.00
24 Martin Brodeur CS 12.50 30.00
25 Slava Kozlov CF 2.50 6.00
26 Sergei Fedorov CF 12.50 30.00
27 Patrick Roy CF 25.00 60.00
28 Wayne Gretzky CF 30.00 80.00
29 John LeClair CF 4.00 10.00
30 Paul Coffey CF 8.00 20.00
31 M.Vernon SCF/AU 750 12.50 25.00
32 E.Lindros SCF/AU 750 20.00 40.00
33 B.Shanahan SCC/AU 250 50.00 125.00

1995-96 Donruss Elite

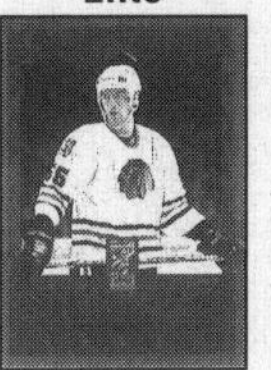

This 110-card super premium set was the last mainstream release of the 1995-96 card season. The product was distributed by Pinnacle Brands, which purchased Donruss and all of its sports licenses just prior to the set's debut. The eight-card packs had a suggested retail of $2.99. The Cool Trade Exchange card was randomly inserted 1:48 packs, although there were numerous reports of collectors finding up to eight copies per box. When found, it could be redeemed for parallel versions of the four Donruss Elite cards found in the NHL Cool Trade wrapper redemption set. This offer expired on September 30, 1996. Rookie Cards include Daniel Alfredsson, Todd Bertuzzi, Radek Dvorak, Chad Kilger and Shane Doan.

COMPLETE SET (110) 10.00 25.00
1 Jocelyn Thibault .20 .50
2 Nicklas Lidstrom .20 .50
3 Brendan Shanahan .20 .50
4 Kenny Jonsson .05 .15
5 Doug Weight .08 .25
6 Oleg Tverdovsky .05 .15
7 Brett Hull .25 .60
8 Larry Murphy .08 .25
9 Ray Bourque .30 .75
10 Adam Graves .05 .15
11 Gary Suter .05 .15
12 Bill Ranford .08 .25
13 Zigmund Palffy .08 .25
14 Cam Neely .20 .50
15 Al MacInnis .08 .25
16 Joe Sakic .40 1.00
17 Kevin Hatcher .05 .15
18 Alexander Mogilny .08 .25
19 Radek Dvorak RC .30 .75
20 Ed Belfour .20 .50
21 Jeff O'Neill .05 .15
22 Valeri Kamensky .08 .25
23 John MacLean .08 .25
24 Zdeno Ciger .05 .15
25 Daniel Alfredsson RC .50 1.25
26 Owen Nolan .08 .25
27 Wendel Clark .08 .25
28 Brian Savage .05 .15
29 Alexei Zhamnov .08 .25
30 Dominik Hasek .40 1.00
31 Paul Kariya .20 .50
32 Mike Modano .30 .75
33 Craig Janney .05 .15
34 Todd Harvey .08 .25
35 Jaromir Jagr .30 .75
36 Roman Hamrlik .08 .25
37 Sergei Zubov .05 .15
38 Marcus Ragnarsson RC .08 .25
39 Peter Forsberg .50 1.25
40 Ron Francis .08 .25
41 German Titov .05 .15
42 Grant Fuhr .20 .50
43 Martin Brodeur .50 1.25
44 Claude Lemieux .05 .15
45 Trevor Linden .08 .25
46 Mark Messier .20 .50
47 Jeremy Roenick .25 .60
48 Peter Bondra .08 .25
49 Donald Audette .05 .15
50 Joe Nieuwendyk .08 .25
51 Mario Lemieux CL .30 .75
52 Vitali Yachmenev .05 .15
53 Sergei Fedorov .30 .75
54 Kirk Muller .05 .15
55 Chad Kilger RC .05 .15
56 John LeClair .20 .50
57 Todd Bertuzzi RC .75 2.00
58 Wayne Gretzky 1.25 3.00
59 Curtis Joseph .20 .50
60 Niklas Sundstrom .08 .25
61 Chris Chelios .20 .50
62 Radek Bonk .05 .15
63 Eric Daze .08 .25
64 Patrick Roy 1.00 2.50
65 Rob Niedermayer .08 .25
66 Mario Lemieux 1.00 2.50
67 Saku Koivu .20 .50
68 Ed Jovanovski .20 .50
69 Jim Carey .08 .25
70 Scott Stevens .08 .25
71 Steve Thomas .08 .25
72 Mats Sundin .20 .50
73 Teemu Selanne .20 .50
74 Tomas Sandstrom .05 .15
75 Pat LaFontaine .20 .50
76 Pat Verbeek .05 .15
77 Pavel Bure .20 .50
78 Jeff Brown .05 .15
79 Alexei Yashin .05 .15
80 Adam Oates .08 .25

Card	Low	High
81 Keith Tkachuk	.20	.50
82 Brian Bradley	.05	.15
83 John Vanbiesbrouck	.08	.25
84 Alexander Selivanov	.05	.15
85 Paul Coffey	.20	.50
86 Scott Mellanby	.05	.15
87 Slava Kozlov	.08	.25
88 Eric Lindros	.20	.50
89 Deron Quint	.05	.15
90 Pierre Turgeon	.08	.25
91 Rod Brind'Amour	.08	.25
92 Doug Gilmour	.08	.25
93 Sandis Ozolinsh	.05	.15
94 Mikael Renberg	.08	.25
95 Kevin Stevens	.05	.15
96 Vincent Damphousse	.05	.15
97 Felix Potvin	.20	.50
98 Brian Leetch	.08	.25
99 Steve Yzerman	1.00	2.50
100 Dale Hawerchuk	.20	.50
101 Jason Arnott	.05	.15
102 Ray Sheppard	.05	.15
103 Mark Recchi	.08	.25
104 Joe Juneau	.05	.15
105 Luc Robitaille	.08	.25
106 Theo Fleury	.05	.15
107 Sean Burke	.08	.25
108 Ron Hextall	.08	.25
109 Shane Doan RC	.50	1.25
110 Eric Lindros CL	.08	.25
NNO Cool Trade Exchange	.05	.15

1995-96 Donruss Elite Die Cut Stars

This die-cut set paralleled the main Donruss Elite set. The first 500 cards off the press had the die-cut pattern. Interestingly, boxes from early in the production run contained cards intended to be die-cut which weren't. These cards were unintentionally released, and thus are considered variations, rather than a separate set. These cards were discernible from regular issue cards by a curvilinear pattern which ran across the top of the card just above the photo. Although some collectors speculated that these cards were in shorter supply than the regular die-cuts, that was not verified by the company, and unsubstantiated by market evidence. Multipliers can be found in the header below to determine values for these.

*DIE-CUT STARS: 12.5X TO 30X BASIC CARDS
*ROOKIES: 4X TO 10X BASIC CARDS
*UN-CUT STARS: 10X TO 25X BASIC CARDS
UN-CUT RC's: 5X TO 12X BASIC CARDS

1995-96 Donruss Elite Cutting Edge

This 15-card insert set celebrated the top performers of the 1995-96 season. The cards were printed and embossed on laminated polycarbonate material that simulated brushed steel. Each card was serially numbered out of 2,500. The cards were randomly inserted at a rate of 1:32 packs.

Card	Low	High
COMPLETE SET (15)	50.00	100.00
1 Eric Lindros	2.00	5.00
2 Mario Lemieux	10.00	25.00
3 Wayne Gretzky	12.50	30.00
4 Peter Forsberg	5.00	12.00
5 Paul Kariya	2.00	5.00
6 Jaromir Jagr	3.00	8.00
7 Alexander Mogilny	1.00	2.50
8 Mark Messier	2.00	5.00
9 Sergei Fedorov	3.00	8.00
10 Pierre Turgeon	1.00	2.50
11 Mats Sundin	2.00	5.00
12 Brett Hull	2.50	6.00
13 Paul Coffey	2.00	5.00
14 Jeremy Roenick	2.50	6.00
15 Teemu Selanne	2.00	5.00

1995-96 Donruss Elite Lemieux/Lindros Series

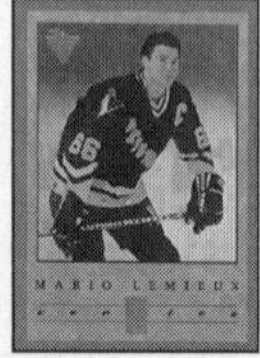

These two seven-card sets recognized two of the most dominating players in the game, Eric Lindros and Mario Lemieux, who also happened to be Donruss spokesmen. The cards were printed on gold holographic foil, with the Lindros cards serially numbered up to 1,088 and the Lemieux cards to 1,066. The seventh card in each series was autographed, giving it a considerably higher value. The seven cards were inserted at a rate of 1:160. There also was a card signed by both Lindros and Lemieux, which was not considered part of either complete set. Both this card and the Lemieux autograph were available only through redemption cards; Lemieux was unable to sign them in time for random insertion. The dual signed card was limited to 500 copies and was inserted in 1:2400 packs. Expired, unredeemed redemption cards are valued at $5-$10. The Lindros cards were assigned an E suffix for cataloguing purposes only.

Card	Low	High
COMP.LEMIEUX SET (7)	125.00	300.00
COMMON LEMIEUX (1-6)	15.00	40.00
COMP.LINDROS SET (7)	75.00	200.00
COMMON LINDROS (1-6)	10.00	25.00
7 Mario Lemieux AU	50.00	125.00
7E Eric Lindros AU	30.00	80.00
NNO Mario Lemieux Eric Lindros AU	125.00	300.00

1995-96 Donruss Elite Painted Warriors

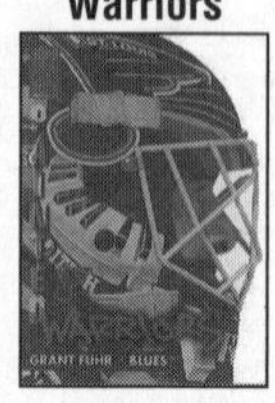

This ten card insert set focused on top goalies and their brightly painted headgear. Each card was printed on clear plastic and then die-cut around the face mask. The cards were individually numbered out of 2,500. The cards were inserted at a rate of 1:48 packs.

Card	Low	High
COMPLETE SET (10)	15.00	30.00
1 Patrick Roy	3.00	8.00
2 Felix Potvin	.75	2.00
3 Martin Brodeur	2.50	6.00
4 Ed Belfour	.75	2.00
5 Guy Hebert	.75	2.00
6 John Vanbiesbrouck	.75	2.00
7 Jocelyn Thibault	.75	2.00
8 Ron Hextall	.75	2.00
9 Grant Fuhr	.75	2.00
10 Jim Carey	.75	2.00
P3 Martin Brodeur PROMO	2.50	6.00
P4 Ed Belfour PROMO	2.50	6.00
P9 Grant Fuhr PROMO	2.50	6.00

1995-96 Donruss Elite Rookies

The fifteen cards in this set -- inserted 1:16 packs -- highlighted the top rookies of the 1995-96 season. The cards were printed on an icy silver foil background and detailed with gold trim. The cards were individually numbered out of 5,000.

Card	Low	High
COMPLETE SET (15)	15.00	40.00
1 Eric Daze	1.00	2.50
2 Vitali Yachmenev	1.00	2.50
3 Daniel Alfredsson	2.00	5.00
4 Todd Bertuzzi	2.00	5.00
5 Byron Dafoe	1.00	2.50
6 Eric Fichaud	1.00	2.50
7 Marcus Ragnarsson	1.00	2.50
8 Saku Koivu	3.00	8.00
9 Chad Kilger	1.00	2.50
10 Radek Dvorak	1.00	2.50
11 Ed Jovanovski	2.00	5.00
12 Jeff O'Neill	2.00	5.00
13 Shane Doan	2.00	5.00
14 Niklas Sundstrom	2.00	5.00
15 Kyle McLaren	1.00	2.50

1995-96 Donruss Elite World Juniors

This 44-card insert set featured the top Canadian and US players from the 1996 World Junior Championships. The cards were printed on canvas stock that simulated the flag of the player's home country. Each card was individually numbered out of 1,000. The cards were inserted 1:30 packs.

Card	Low	High
COMPLETE SET (44)	125.00	250.00
1 Marc Denis	4.00	10.00
2 Jose Theodore	10.00	15.00
3 Chad Allan	2.00	5.00
4 Nolan Baumgartner	2.00	5.00
5 Denis Gauthier	2.00	5.00
6 Jason Holland	2.00	5.00
7 Chris Phillips	2.00	5.00
8 Wade Redden	4.00	10.00
9 Rhett Warrener	2.00	5.00
10 Jason Botterill	2.00	5.00
11 Curtis Brown	2.00	5.00
12 Hnat Domenichelli	2.00	5.00
13 Christian Dube	2.00	5.00
14 Robb Gordon	2.00	5.00
15 Jarome Iginla	10.00	25.00
16 Daymond Langkow	4.00	10.00
17 Brad Larsen	2.00	5.00
18 Alyn McCauley	2.00	5.00
19 Craig Mills	2.00	5.00
20 Jason Podollan	2.00	5.00
21 Mike Watt	2.00	5.00
22 Jamie Wright	2.00	5.00
23 Brian Boucher	6.00	15.00
24 Marc Magliarditi	2.00	5.00
25 Bryan Berard	2.00	5.00
26 Chris Bogas	2.00	5.00
27 Ben Clymer	2.00	5.00
28 Jeff Kealty	2.00	5.00
29 Mike McBain	2.00	5.00
30 Jeremiah McCarthy	2.00	5.00
31 Tom Poti	2.00	5.00
32 Reg Berg	2.00	5.00
33 Matt Cullen	3.00	8.00
34 Chris Drury	8.00	20.00
35 Jeff Farkas	2.00	5.00
36 Casey Hankinson	2.00	5.00
37 Matt Herr	2.00	5.00
38 Mark Parrish	3.00	8.00
39 Erik Rasmussen	2.00	5.00
40 Marty Reasoner	2.00	5.00
41 Wyatt Smith	2.00	5.00
42 Brian Swanson	2.00	5.00
43 Mike Sylvia	2.00	5.00
44 Mike York	3.00	8.00

1996-97 Donruss Elite

The 1996-97 Donruss Elite set was issued in one series totaling 150 cards. Packs contained eight cards for a suggested retail price of $3.99, and were distributed as a hobby-only product. Card fronts featured a color action photo with a foil background. A 20-card rookie subset was found at the end of the set (#128-147). Key rookies included Sergei Berezin, Patrick Lalime, Ethan Moreau, and Dainius Zubrus.

Card	Low	High
COMPLETE SET (150)	12.50	25.00
1 Paul Kariya	.25	.60
2 Ron Hextall	.10	.30
3 Andy Moog	.10	.30
4 Brett Hull	.30	.75
5 Felix Potvin	.25	.60
6 Jocelyn Thibault	.25	.60
7 Eric Lindros	.25	.60
8 Jaromir Jagr	.40	1.00
9 Sergei Fedorov	.30	.75
10 Wayne Gretzky	1.50	4.00
11 Peter Bondra	.10	.30
12 Peter Forsberg	.60	1.50
13 Stephane Fiset	.10	.30
14 Owen Nolan	.10	.30
15 Rob Niedermayer	.10	.30
16 Martin Brodeur	.60	1.50
17 Ray Bourque	.40	1.00
18 Todd Bertuzzi	.25	.60
19 Jim Carey	.25	.60
20 Chris Chelios	.25	.60
21 Chris Osgood	.10	.30
22 Mark Messier	.25	.60
23 Roman Hamrlik	.10	.30
24 Kevin Hatcher	.05	.15
25 Doug Weight	.10	.30
26 Mark Recchi	.10	.30
27 Jeremy Roenick	.30	.75
28 Derian Hatcher	.05	.15
29 Grant Fuhr	.10	.30
30 Scott Stevens	.10	.30
31 Adam Oates	.10	.30
32 Scott Mellanby	.10	.30
33 Mikael Renberg	.10	.30
34 Corey Hirsch	.10	.30
35 Michal Pivonka	.05	.15
36 Stephane Richer	.10	.30
37 Dominik Hasek	.50	1.25
38 Steve Yzerman	1.25	3.00
39 Jeff O'Neill	.05	.15
40 Ron Francis	.10	.30
41 Alexei Yashin	.05	.15
42 Pat Verbeek	.05	.15
43 Geoff Courtnall	.05	.15
44 Doug Gilmour	.10	.30
45 Trevor Kidd	.10	.30
46 Jason Arnott	.05	.15
47 Niklas Sundstrom	.05	.15
48 Rob Blake	.10	.30
49 Nikolai Khabibulin	.10	.30
50 Igor Larionov	.05	.15
51 Sean Burke	.10	.30
52 Zigmund Palffy	.10	.30
53 Jeff Friesen	.05	.15
54 Theo Fleury	.05	.15
55 Mats Sundin	.25	.60
56 Alexander Mogilny	.10	.30
57 John LeClair	.25	.60
58 Shayne Corson	.05	.15
59 Teemu Selanne	.25	.60
60 Kelly Hrudey	.10	.30
61 Keith Tkachuk	.25	.60
62 Joe Nieuwendyk	.10	.30
63 Tom Barrasso	.10	.30
64 Aaron Gavey	.05	.15
65 Alexei Zhamnov	.10	.30
66 Patrick Roy	1.25	3.00
67 Al MacInnis	.10	.30
68 Trevor Linden	.10	.30
69 Bill Guerin	.05	.15
70 Dimitri Khristich	.05	.15
71 Eric Daze	.10	.30
72 Paul Coffey	.25	.60
73 Keith Primeau	.05	.15
74 John Vanbiesbrouck	.10	.30
75 Bernie Nicholls	.05	.15
76 Yanic Perreault	.05	.15
77 Jere Lehtinen	.05	.15
78 Luc Robitaille	.10	.30
79 Todd Gill	.05	.15
80 Saku Koivu	.25	.60
81 Vyacheslav Kozlov	.05	.15
82 Ed Jovanovski	.10	.30
83 Brendan Witt	.05	.15
84 Alexandre Daigle	.05	.15
85 Jari Kurri	.10	.30
86 Mike Vernon	.10	.30
87 Jeff Beukeboom	.05	.15
88 Mathieu Schneider	.05	.15
89 Niklas Andersson	.05	.15
90 Joe Juneau	.05	.15
91 Ed Belfour	.25	.60
92 Curtis Joseph	.25	.60
93 Rod Brind'Amour	.10	.30
94 Vitali Yachmenev	.05	.15
95 Alexander Selivanov	.05	.15
96 Mike Richter	.25	.60
97 Bill Ranford	.10	.30
98 Wendel Clark	.10	.30
99 Slava Fetisov	.05	.15
100 Daniel Alfredsson	.10	.30
101 Pat LaFontaine	.25	.60
102 Joe Murphy	.05	.15
103 Pavel Bure	.25	.60
104 Craig Janney	.10	.30
105 Radek Dvorak	.05	.15
106 Cory Stillman	.05	.15
107 Adam Graves	.05	.15
108 Aki Berg	.05	.15
109 Mario Lemieux	1.25	3.00
110 Claude Lemieux	.05	.15
111 Sergei Zubov	.05	.15
112 Pierre Turgeon	.10	.30
113 Damian Rhodes	.10	.30
114 Daren Puppa	.10	.30
115 Alexei Zhitnik	.05	.15
116 Mike Modano	.40	1.00
117 Kenny Jonsson	.05	.15
118 Valeri Kamensky	.10	.30
119 Valeri Bure	.05	.15
120 Joe Sakic	.50	1.25
121 Kirk McLean	.10	.30
122 Petr Sykora	.05	.15
123 Mike Gartner	.10	.30
124 Ryan Smyth	.25	.60
125 Brian Leetch	.25	.60
126 Brendan Shanahan	.25	.60
127 Geoff Sanderson	.10	.30
128 Corey Schwab	.10	.30
129 Anders Eriksson	.05	.15
130 Harry York RC	.25	.60
131 Jarome Iginla	.30	.75
132 Eric Fichaud	.10	.30
133 Patrick Lalime RC	1.25	3.00
134 Daymond Langkow	.10	.30
135 Mattias Timander RC	.05	.15
136 Ethan Moreau RC	.25	.60
137 Christian Dube	.05	.15
138 Sergei Berezin RC	.50	1.25
139 Jose Theodore	.30	.75
140 Wade Redden	.05	.15
141 Dainius Zubrus RC	.40	1.00
142 Jim Campbell	.05	.15
143 Daniel Goneau RC	.10	.30
144 Jamie Langenbrunner	.05	.15
145 Rem Murray RC	.05	.15
146 Jonas Hoglund	.05	.15
147 Bryan Berard	.25	.60
148 Chris Osgood CL (1-75)	.10	.30
149 Eric Lindros CL (76-150)	.25	.60
150 Jason Arnott CL (inserts)	.05	.15

1996-97 Donruss Elite Die Cut Stars

This die-cut set paralleled the main Donruss Elite set. Card fronts featured a die-cut, silver-poly laminate foil to distinguish them from their base counterparts.

*STARS: 4X TO 10X HI COLUMN
*ROOKIES: 3X TO 5X HI

1996-97 Donruss Elite Aspirations

This set featured twenty-five of the NHL's top rookies and young superstars. Each card was serially numbered out of 3,000. Card fronts featured a color action photo with blue and silver foil surrounding the photo.

Card	Low	High
COMPLETE SET (25)	12.00	30.00
1 Eric Daze	.40	1.00
2 Daniel Alfredsson	2.00	5.00
3 Petr Sykora	.40	1.00
4 Todd Bertuzzi	2.00	5.00

Card	Low	High
5 Saku Koivu	2.00	5.00
6 Ed Jovanovski	.75	2.00
7 Jim Campbell	.40	1.00
8 Valeri Bure	.40	1.00
9 Jeff O'Neill	.40	1.00
10 Jere Lehtinen	.75	2.00
11 Terry Ryan	.40	1.00
12 Jonas Hoglund	.40	1.00
13 Daymond Langkow	.75	2.00
14 Eric Fichaud	.40	1.00
15 Dainius Zubrus	.75	2.00
16 Janne Niinimaa	.40	1.00
17 Sergei Berezin	.40	1.00
18 Daniel Goneau	.40	1.00
19 Jarome Iginla	4.00	10.00
20 Ethan Moreau	.40	1.00
21 Jamie Langenbrunner	.40	1.00
22 Rem Murray	.40	1.00
23 Bryan Berard	.40	1.00
24 Wade Redden	.40	1.00
25 Christian Dube	.40	1.00

1996-97 Donruss Elite Hart to Hart

This special insert set was issued in two parts, one featuring Eric Lindros and the other featuring Mario Lemieux. Each set contained six cards. The Lindros set was serial numbered to 1,996 sets, with the first 188 signed by Lindros. The Lemieux set was serial numbered to 1,995 sets, with the first 166 signed by Lemieux. In addition, Donruss also included a dual autograph of Lemieux and Lindros, serial numbered to just 500. The prefixes listed below for the autographs are for checklisting purposes only.

Card	Low	High
COMPLETE LEMIEUX SET (6)	75.00	125.00
COMMON LEMIEUX (1-6)	12.50	25.00
COMPLETE LINDROS SET (6)	40.00	80.00
COMMON LINDROS (1-6)	6.00	15.00
1AU Eric Lindros AU/188	25.00	60.00
AU1 Mario Lemieux AU/166	30.00	80.00
NNO Eric Lindros Mario Lemieux AU	50.00	125.00

1996-97 Donruss Elite Painted Warriors

This 10-card insert set focusesd on top goalies and their brightly painted headgear. Each card was printed on clear plastic and then die-cut around the mask. The cards were individually numbered out of 2,500.

Card	Low	High
COMPLETE SET (10)	40.00	100.00
1 Patrick Roy	15.00	40.00
2 Mike Richter	4.00	10.00
3 Jim Carey	2.00	5.00
4 John Vanbiesbrouck	4.00	10.00
5 Jocelyn Thibault	2.00	5.00
6 Felix Potvin	4.00	10.00
7 Ed Belfour	4.00	10.00
8 Martin Brodeur	8.00	20.00
9 Nikolai Khabibulin	4.00	10.00
10 Stephane Fiset	2.00	5.00

1996-97 Donruss Elite Painted Warriors Promos

These cards mirrored the regular versions except in the serial number box on the back, where the number read PROMO/2500. The Brodeur was the most readily available of these cards.

Card	Low	High
COMPLETE SET (10)	30.00	75.00
P1 Patrick Roy	6.00	12.00
P2 Mike Richter	6.00	12.00
P3 Jim Carey	6.00	12.00
P4 John Vanbiesbrouck	6.00	12.00
P5 Jocelyn Thibault	6.00	12.00
P6 Felix Potvin	6.00	12.00
P7 Ed Belfour	6.00	12.00
P8 Martin Brodeur	6.00	12.00
P9 Nikolai Khabibulin	6.00	12.00
P10 Stephane Fiset	6.00	12.00

1996-97 Donruss Elite Perspective

This 12-card set focused on the NHL's veteran stars. Card fronts featured a die-cut, micro-etched, foil design. Each card was individually numbered out of 500.

Card	Low	High
COMPLETE SET (12)	40.00	100.00
1 Wayne Gretzky	15.00	40.00
2 Mark Messier	3.00	8.00
3 Steve Yzerman	10.00	25.00
4 Mario Lemieux	12.00	30.00
5 Paul Coffey	2.00	5.00
6 Doug Gilmour	2.00	5.00

Card	Low	High
7 Brendan Shanahan	3.00	8.00
8 Jaromir Jagr	5.00	12.00
9 Brett Hull	4.00	10.00
10 Pat LaFontaine	2.00	5.00
11 Chris Chelios	2.00	5.00
12 Grant Fuhr	2.00	5.00

1996-97 Donruss Elite Status

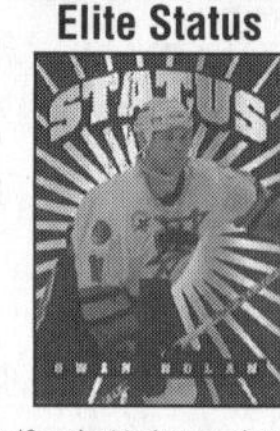

This 12-card set took an up-close look at some of the NHL's top players who were in the prime of their careers. Card fronts were foil laminate and featured a full-color photo. Each card was serially numbered out of 750.

Card	Low	High
COMPLETE SET (12)	30.00	60.00
1 Pavel Bure	2.50	6.00
2 Keith Tkachuk	2.50	6.00
3 Sergei Fedorov	3.00	8.00
4 Doug Weight	1.25	3.00
5 Paul Kariya	2.50	6.00
6 Owen Nolan	1.25	3.00
7 Peter Forsberg	6.00	15.00
8 Eric Lindros	2.50	6.00
9 Alexander Mogilny	1.25	3.00
10 Teemu Selanne	2.50	6.00
11 Joe Sakic	5.00	12.00
12 Jeremy Roenick	3.00	8.00

1997-98 Donruss Elite

The 1997-98 Donruss Elite hobby exclusive set was issued in one series totaling 150 cards and was distributed in five-card packs with a suggested retail price of $3.99. The fronts featured color player photos printed on thick foil card stock. The backs carried player information. The set contained the topical subset: Elite Generations (115-144).

Card	Low	High
COMPLETE SET (150)	15.00	40.00
1 Peter Forsberg	.60	1.50
2 Mike Modano	.40	1.00
3 John Vanbiesbrouck	.20	.50
4 Pavel Bure	.25	.60
5 Mark Messier	.25	.60
6 Joe Thornton	.60	1.50
7 Paul Kariya	.25	.60
8 Martin Brodeur	.60	1.50
9 Wayne Gretzky	1.50	4.00
10 Eric Lindros	.25	.60
11 Jaromir Jagr	.40	1.00
12 Brett Hull	.30	.75
13 Jarome Iginla	.30	.75
14 Patrick Roy	1.25	3.00
15 Steve Yzerman	1.25	3.00
16 Sergei Samsonov	.20	.50
17 Teemu Selanne	.25	.60
18 Brendan Shanahan	.25	.60
19 Curtis Joseph	.25	.60
20 Saku Koivu	.25	.60
21 Ray Bourque	.40	1.00
22 Jaroslav Svejkovsky	.20	.50
23 Keith Primeau	.08	.20
24 Alexandre Daigle	.08	.20
25 Vyacheslav Kozlov	.08	.20
26 Jozef Stumpel	.20	.50
27 Alexei Yashin	.08	.20
28 Marian Hossa RC	3.00	6.00
29 Bryan Berard	.20	.50
30 Dominik Hasek	.50	1.25
31 Chris Chelios	.25	.60
32 Derian Hatcher	.08	.20
33 Ed Jovanovski	.20	.50
34 Zigmund Palffy	.20	.50
35 Ron Hextall	.20	.50
36 Daymond Langkow	.20	.50
37 Daniel Cleary	.20	.50
38 Alyn McCauley	.20	.50
39 Sean Burke	.20	.50
40 Brian Leetch	.25	.60
41 Joe Juneau	.20	.50
42 Damian Rhodes	.20	.50
43 Dino Ciccarelli	.08	.20
44 Valeri Kamensky	.20	.50
45 Guy Hebert	.20	.50
46 Brad Isbister	.08	.20
47 Adam Graves	.08	.20
48 Andrew Cassels	.08	.20
49 Joe Sakic	.50	1.25
50 Dainius Zubrus	.25	.60
51 Roberto Luongo RC	2.00	5.00
52 Ethan Moreau	.08	.20
53 Chris Osgood	.20	.50
54 Stephane Fiset	.20	.50
55 Sergei Berezin	.08	.20
56 Mike Richter	.25	.60
57 Valeri Bure	.08	.20
58 Mats Sundin	.25	.60
59 Mike Dunham	.20	.50
60 Byron Dafoe	.20	.50
61 Joe Nieuwendyk	.20	.50
62 Mike Grier	.08	.20
63 Paul Coffey	.25	.60
64 Chris Phillips	.08	.20
65 Patrik Elias RC	1.00	2.50
66 Andy Moog	.20	.50
67 Geoff Sanderson	.20	.50
68 Jere Lehtinen	.08	.20
69 Alexander Mogilny	.20	.50
70 Ryan Smyth	.20	.50
71 John LeClair	.25	.60
72 Olli Jokinen RC	.75	2.00
73 Doug Gilmour	.20	.50
74 Theo Fleury	.08	.20
75 Adam Deadmarsh	.08	.20
76 Scott Mellanby	.08	.20
77 Jeremy Roenick	.30	.75
78 Jim Campbell	.08	.20
79 Daren Puppa	.20	.50
80 Vaclav Prospal RC	.25	.60
81 Vincent Damphousse	.08	.20
82 Derek Plante	.08	.20
83 Sandis Ozolinsh	.08	.20
84 Darren McCarty	.08	.20
85 Luc Robitaille	.20	.50
86 Wade Redden	.08	.20
87 Eric Fichaud	.20	.50
88 Jocelyn Thibault	.20	.50
89 Trevor Linden	.20	.50
90 Boyd Devereaux	.08	.20
91 Chris Gratton	.20	.50
92 Janne Niinimaa	.20	.50
93 Jeff Friesen	.08	.20
94 Roman Hamrlik	.08	.20
95 Jason Arnott	.08	.20
96 Sergei Fedorov	.40	1.00
97 Tony Amonte	.20	.50
98 Mattias Ohlund	.20	.50
99 Patrick Marleau	.40	1.00
100 Felix Potvin	.25	.60
101 Tommy Salo	.20	.50
102 Ed Belfour	.25	.60
103 Doug Weight	.20	.50
104 Daniel Alfredsson	.20	.50
105 Pierre Turgeon	.20	.50
106 Espen Knutsen RC	.30	.75
107 Trevor Kidd	.20	.50
108 Alexei Morozov	.20	.50
109 Oleg Tverdovsky	.08	.20
110 Grant Fuhr	.20	.50
111 Pat LaFontaine	.25	.60
112 Keith Tkachuk	.25	.60
113 Ron Francis	.20	.50
114 Derek Morris RC	.30	.75
115 Joe Sakic G	.25	.60
116 Brian Leetch G	.25	.60
117 Alyn McCauley G	.08	.20
118 Pavel Bure G	.15	.40
119 Eric Lindros G	.20	.50
120 Teemu Selanne G	.25	.60
121 Jarome Iginla G	.30	.75
122 Steve Yzerman G	.60	1.50
123 Daniel Cleary G	.08	.20
124 Bryan Berard G	.08	.20
125 Jaromir Jagr G	.20	.50
126 John Vanbiesbrouck G	.20	.50
127 Mark Messier G	.15	.40
128 Patrick Marleau G	.20	.50
129 Mike Modano G	.25	.60
130 Zigmund Palffy G	.20	.50
131 Felix Potvin G	.25	.60
132 Derek Morris G	.08	.20
133 Brendan Shanahan G	.20	.50
134 Sergei Samsonov G	.20	.50
135 Dainius Zubrus G	.25	.60
136 Paul Kariya G	.25	.60
137 Martin Brodeur G	.30	.75
138 Joe Thornton G	.30	.75
139 Mattias Ohlund G	.08	.20
140 Ryan Smyth G	.08	.20
141 Jaroslav Svejkovsky G	.08	.20
142 Patrick Roy G	.60	1.50
143 Wayne Gretzky G	.75	2.00
144 Espen Knutsen G	.08	.20
145 Patrick Marleau CL	.25	.60
146 Pat Lafontaine CL	.08	.20
147 Mike Gartner CL	.08	.20
148 Joe Thornton CL	.30	.75
149 Teemu Selanne CL	.25	.60
150 Mark Messier CL	.20	.50

1997-98 Donruss Elite Aspirations

Randomly inserted in packs, this 150-card set was a die-cut parallel version of the base set printed on foil board. Each card was numbered 1 of 750.

*STARS: 6X TO 15X BASIC CARDS
*RC's: 2X TO 5X BASIC CARDS

1997-98 Donruss Elite Status

Randomly inserted in packs, this 150-card set was a die-cut parallel version of the base set printed on holofoil board. Each card was sequentially numbered to 100.

STARS: 20X TO 50X HI COLUMN
ROOKIES: 8X TO 20X HI
8 Marian Hossa 30.00 75.00

1997-98 Donruss Elite Back to the Future

andomly inserted in packs, this eight-card et featured color player photos printed on ouble-sided cards. One side displayed a eteran star or Hockey HOF member while e other side highlighted a younger talent. he first 100 of each card was autographed y both of the featured players.

COMPLETE SET (8) 30.00 60.00
Eric Lindros 3.00 8.00
Joe Thornton
Jocelyn Thibault 3.00 8.00
Marc Denis
Teemu Selanne 3.00 8.00
Patrick Marleau
Jaromir Jagr 4.00 10.00
Daniel Cleary
Sergei Fedorov 5.00 12.00
Peter Forsberg
Brett Hull 4.00 10.00
Bobby Hull
Martin Brodeur 5.00 12.00
Roberto Luongo
Gordie Howe 6.00 15.00
Steve Yzerman

1997-98 Donruss Elite Back to the Future Autographs

andomly inserted in packs, this eight-card et was a parallel to the regular Back to the uture insert set and consisted of the first 00 cards of the regular set autographed by oth players.

Eric Lindros 40.00 100.00
Joe Thornton
Jocelyn Thibault 40.00 100.00
Marc Denis
Teemu Selanne 40.00 100.00
Patrick Marleau
Jaromir Jagr 40.00 100.00
Daniel Cleary
Sergei Fedorov 75.00 200.00
Peter Forsberg
Brett Hull 75.00 200.00
Bobby Hull
Martin Brodeur 150.00 300.00
Roberto Luongo
Gordie Howe 150.00 400.00
Steve Yzerman

1997-98 Donruss Elite Craftsmen

andomly inserted in packs, this 30-card set eatured color photos of top players printed n full foil board and micro-etched. The ards were sequentially numbered to 2,500.

*MAST.CRFT: 2X TO 5X BASIC INSERTS
John Vanbiesbrouck 1.00 2.50
2 Eric Lindros 1.50 4.00
3 Joe Sakic 3.00 8.00
4 Mark Messier 2.00 5.00
5 Jaroslav Svejkovsky 1.00 2.50
6 Dominik Hasek 3.00 8.00
7 Chris Osgood 1.00 2.50
8 Martin Brodeur 4.00 10.00
9 Sergei Fedorov 2.00 5.00
10 Daniel Cleary 1.00 2.50
11 Patrick Marleau 1.25 3.00
12 Sergei Samsonov 1.25 3.00
13 Felix Potvin 1.50 4.00
14 Patrick Roy 8.00 20.00
15 Teemu Selanne 1.50 4.00
16 Steve Yzerman 8.00 20.00
17 Jarome Iginla 2.00 5.00
18 Mike Modano 2.50 6.00
19 Wayne Gretzky 10.00 25.00
20 Pavel Bure 1.50 4.00
21 Ryan Smyth 1.25 3.00
22 Paul Kariya 1.50 4.00
23 Peter Forsberg 4.00 10.00
24 Joe Thornton 2.50 6.00
25 Jaromir Jagr 2.50 6.00
26 Bryan Berard 1.00 2.50
27 Brendan Shanahan 1.50 4.00
28 Keith Tkachuk 1.50 4.00
29 Curtis Joseph 1.50 4.00
30 Brian Leetch 1.00 2.50

1997-98 Donruss Elite Prime Numbers

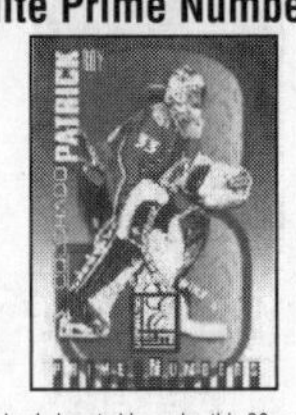

Randomly inserted in packs, this 36-card set featured color photos of 12 top stars with a number in the background. Each star appeared on three cards which, when linked together in the right order, displayed a significant career statistic. Each card in the set was sequentially numbered to the career statistic and that number followed the player's name below.

PRINT RUNS IN PARENTHESIS BELOW
LOWER PRINT RUNS NOT PRICED
DUE TO SCARCITY
1A Peter Forsberg 2 (54) 30.00 80.00
1B Peter Forsberg 5 (204) 8.00 20.00
1C Peter Forsberg 4 (250) 8.00 20.00
2A Patrick Roy 3 (49) 50.00 125.00
2B Patrick Roy 4 (309) 12.50 30.00
2C Patrick Roy 9 (340) 12.50 30.00
3A Mark Messier 2 (95) 8.00 20.00
3B Mark Messier 9 (205) 4.00 10.00
3C Mark Messier 5 (290) 4.00 10.00
4A Eric Lindros 4 (36) 15.00 40.00
4B Eric Lindros 3 (406) 4.00 10.00
4C Eric Lindros 6 (430) 4.00 10.00
5A Paul Kariya 2 (46) 30.00 80.00
5B Paul Kariya 4 (206) 8.00 20.00
5C Paul Kariya 6 (240) 4.00 10.00
6A Jaromir Jagr 2 (66) 20.00 50.00
6B Jaromir Jagr 6 (206) 10.00 25.00
6C Jaromir Jagr 6 (260) 10.00 25.00
7A Teemu Selanne 2 (37) 15.00 40.00
7B Teemu Selanne 3 (207) 4.00 10.00
7C Teemu Selanne 7 (230) 4.00 10.00
8A John Vanbiesbrouck 2 (88) 6.00 15.00
8B John Vanbiesbrouck 8 (208) 4.00 10.00
8C John Vanbiesbrouck 8 (280) 4.00 10.00
9A Brendan Shanahan 3 (35) 12.50 30.00
9B Brendan Shanahan 3 (305) 4.00 10.00
9C Brendan Shanahan 5 (330) 4.00 10.00
10A Steve Yzerman 5 (39) 60.00 150.00
10B Steve Yzerman 3 (509) 12.50 30.00
10C Steve Yzerman 9 (530) 12.50 30.00
11A Joe Sakic 3 (7)
11B Joe Sakic 0 (307) 6.00 15.00
11C Joe Sakic 7 (300) 6.00 15.00
12A Pavel Bure 3 (88) 8.00 20.00
12B Pavel Bure 8 (308) 4.00 10.00
12C Pavel Bure 8 (380) 4.00 10.00

1997-98 Donruss Elite Prime Numbers Die-Cuts

Randomly inserted in packs, this 36-card set was a die-cut parallel version of the regular Prime Numbers set. How many of each card was produced depended on the specified statistical number the card represented. Print runs of less than 10 not priced due to scarcity.

1A Peter Forsberg 2 (200) 12.50 30.00
1B Peter Forsberg 5 (50) 50.00 125.00
1C Peter Forsberg 4 (4)
2A Patrick Roy 3 (300) 15.00 40.00
2B Patrick Roy 4 (40) 60.00 150.00
2C Patrick Roy 9 (9)
3A Mark Messier 2 (200) 8.00 20.00
3B Mark Messier 9 (90) 12.50 30.00
3C Mark Messier 5 (5)
4A Eric Lindros 4 (400) 8.00 20.00
4B Eric Lindros 3 (30) 20.00 50.00
4C Eric Lindros 6 (6)
5A Paul Kariya 2 (200) 12.50 30.00
5B Paul Kariya 4 (40) 50.00 125.00
5C Paul Kariya 6 (6)
6A Jaromir Jagr 2 (200) 10.00 25.00
6B Jaromir Jagr 6 (60) 30.00 80.00
6C Jaromir Jagr 6 (6)
7A Teemu Selanne 2 (200) 8.00 20.00
7B Teemu Selanne 3 (30) 15.00 40.00
7C Teemu Selanne 7 (7)
8A John Vanbiesbrouck 2 (200) 8.00 20.00
8B John Vanbiesbrouck 8 (80) 12.50 30.00
8C John Vanbiesbrouck 8 (8)
9A Brendan Shanahan 3 (300) 8.00 20.00
9B Brendan Shanahan 3 (30) 20.00 50.00
9C Brendan Shanahan 5 (5)
10A Steve Yzerman 5 (500) 15.00 40.00
10B Steve Yzerman 3 (30) 60.00 150.00
10C Steve Yzerman 9 (9)
11A Joe Sakic 3 (300) 10.00 25.00
11B Joe Sakic 0 (0)
11C Joe Sakic 7 (7)
12A Pavel Bure 3 (300) 8.00 20.00
12B Pavel Bure 8 (80) 12.50 30.00
12C Pavel Bure 8 (8)

1998-99 Donruss Elite Promos

These cards were issued in the summer of 1998 in anticipation of an upcoming Donruss Elite hockey product. Prior to the release of the full set, Donruss went out of business. No regular cards from this set exist. Each card is marked PROMO/2500 on the back, although it is believed that far fewer than 2,500 copies were produced of each, with some probably limited to 100 or less. Some were believed to be easier to acquire than others, including the Sergei Samsonov and Dominik Hasek issue.

1 John LeClair 10.00 25.00
2 Brett Hull 6.00 15.00
3 Saku Koivu 4.00 10.00
4 Mark Messier 10.00 25.00
5 Keith Tkachuk 6.00 15.00
6 Teemu Selanne 16.00 40.00
7 Sergei Samsonov 2.00 5.00
8 Pavel Bure 16.00 40.00
9 Brendan Shanahan 10.00 25.00
10 Dominik Hasek 2.00 5.00
11 Joe Thornton 20.00 50.00
12 Joe Sakic 20.00 50.00
13 Martin Brodeur 10.00 25.00
14 Peter Forsberg 20.00 50.00
15 Steve Yzerman 40.00 100.00
16 Patrick Roy 40.00 100.00
17 Jaromir Jagr 10.00 25.00
18 Paul Kariya 20.00 50.00
19 Eric Lindros 16.00 40.00
20 Wayne Gretzky 40.00 125.00

1997-98 Donruss Limited

This 200-card set was distributed in five-card packs with a suggested retail price of $4.99 and featured full-bleed player photographs printed on double-sided cards. The set contained the following subsets: Counterparts, which displayed photos of two superstar players connected by their positions utilizing a Poly-Chromium print technology; Double Team, which featured two formidable teammates back-to-back; Star Factor, which highlighted the top stars using a different photo of the same star on each side; and Unlimited Potential/Talent, which combineed a photo of a young rookie on one side and a veteran star's photo on the other.

COMPLETE SET (200) 150.00 400.00
COMP.COUNTERPART.SET (100) 10.00 25.00
1 Brendan Shanahan .25 .60
Harry York C
2 Peter Forsberg RC .60 1.50
Michael Knuble C
3 Chris Osgood .25 .60
Kirk McLean C
4 Wayne Gretzky S 20.00 50.00
5 John Vanbiesbrouck 1.00 2.50
Ed Jovanovski D
6 Paul Coffey .25 .60
Darryl Sydor C
7 Pavel Bure .25 .60
Valeri Bure C
8 Sergei Berezin 2.00 5.00
Jaromir Jagr U
9 Saku Koivu .25 .60
Mats Sundin C
10 Trevor Kidd .10 .25
Corey Hirsch C
11 Teemu Selanne S 2.50 6.00
12 Zigmund Palffy .10 .25
Radek Bonk C
13 Mats Sundin 1.00 2.50
Sergei Berezin D
14 Jim Carey .10 .25
Bill Ranford C
15 John LeClair .10 .25
Claude Lemieux C
16 Janne Niinimaa 1.50 4.00
Chris Chelios U
17 Kevin Hodson 1.00 2.50
Michael Knuble D
18 Adam Graves .10 .25
Keith Jones C
19 M.Modano/T.Linden C .40 1.00
20 Brett Hull S 4.00 10.00
21 Derian Hatcher .10 .25
Kevin Hatcher C
22 Daniel Alfredsson .10 .25
Dave Andreychuk C
23 Steve Shields 1.00 2.50
Vaclav Varada D
24 Theo Fleury .10 .25
Geoff Courtnall C
25 Mark Messier .25 .60
Dino Ciccarelli C
26 Ryan Smyth S 2.00 5.00
27 Mike Grier 1.00 2.50
Jason Arnott D
28 Ed Belfour .25 .60
Andy Moog C
29 Jean Giguere 2.00 5.00
Felix Potvin U
30 Eric Lindros .25 .60
Todd Bertuzzi C
31 Daymond Langkow .10 .25
David Roberts C
32 Mike Richter .25 .60
Grant Fuhr C
33 Adam Oates 1.00 2.50
Jaroslav Svejkovsky D
34 Saku Koivu 1.00 2.50
Darcy Tucker D
35 Paul Kariya S 2.50 6.00
36 Joe Sakic .50 1.25
Bernie Nicholls C
37 Ed Jovanovski RC .10 .25
D.J.Smith C
38 Vaclav Prospal 1.50 4.00
Brendan Shanahan U
39 Mike Peca .10 .25
Marty Murray C
40 Mike Gartner .10 .25
Wendel Clark C
41 Steve Yzerman S 12.00 30.00
42 M.Modano/R.Turek D 1.50 4.00
43 Joe Nieuwendyk .10 .25
Jarome Iginla C
44 Patrick Roy 1.25 3.00
Jocelyn Thibault C
45 Hnat Domenichelli .10 .25
Andrew Cassels C
46 Christian Dube .10 .25
Steve Sullivan C
47 Marc Denis 1.00 2.50
Valeri Kamensky D
48 Peter Forsberg S 6.00 15.00
49 Derek Plante .10 .25
Todd Harvey C
50 Mike Grier .25 .60
Eric Lindros U
51 Brett Hull 1.25 3.00
Jim Campbell D
52 Mark Recchi .10 .25
Landon Wilson C
53 Darcy Tucker RC .10 .25
Pascal Rheaume C
54 Chris O'Sullivan .10 .25
Anders Eriksson C
55 Jaromir Jagr S 6.00 15.00
56 Paul Kariya 1.00 2.50
Teemu Selanne D
57 Felix Potvin .25 .60
Damian Rhodes C
58 Brian Holzinger .10 .25
Mike Ricci C
59 Eric Fichaud 1.00 2.50
Travis Green D
60 Ethan Moreau .10 .25
John MacLean C
61 Joe Juneau .10 .25
Jeff O'Neill C
62 John Vanbiesbrouck S 2.00 5.00
63 Byron Dafoe RC .10 .25
Steve Shields C
64 Mikael Renberg .10 .25
Niklas Sundstrom C
65 Ryan Smyth .10 .25
Eric Daze C
66 Doug Gilmour 1.00 2.50
Pascal Rheaume D
67 Jim Campbell .10 .25
Craig Janney C
68 Alexander Mogilny .10 .25
Mathew Barnaby C
69 Alexei Yashin S 2.00 5.00
70 Bryan Berard 1.50 4.00
Brian Leetch U
71 Alexei Yashin .10 .25
Brian Savage C
72 Jeff Friesen .10 .25
Darren McCarty C
73 Dimitri Khristich .10 .25
Chad Kilger C
74 Martin Brodeur 2.50 6.00
Dave Andreychuk D
75 Luc Robitaille .10 .25
Pat Verbeek C
76 Dominik Hasek .50 1.25
Jamie Storr C
77 Felix Potvin S 2.50 6.00
78 Mike Dunham 1.00 2.50
Vadim Sharifijanov D
79 Jason Arnott .10 .25
Rob Niedermayer C
80 Eric Desjardins .10 .25
Chris Phillips C
81 Curtis Joseph .25 .60
Jose Theodore C
82 Doug Gilmour .10 .25
Rod Brind'Amour C
83 Keith Tkachuk .25 .60
Rick Tocchet C
84 Mark Messier S .25 .60
85 Chris Pronger .10 .25
Aki Berg C
86 Marcel Cousineau 2.50 6.00
Dominik Hasek U
87 Ethan Moreau 1.00 2.50
Chris Chelios D
88 Jonas Hoglund .10 .25
Rob Zamuner C
89 Ron Hextall .10 .25
Kevin Hodson C
90 John LeClair S .25 .60
91 Vaclav Prospal RC .25 .60
Viktor Kozlov C
92 Ray Bourque 2.50 6.00
Joe Thornton D
93 Oleg Tverdovsky .10 .25
Sergei Zubov C
94 Ethan Moreau 1.50 4.00
John LeClair U
95 Adam Deadmarsh S 2.00 5.00
96 Jaroslav Svejkovsky .10 .25
Jozef Stumpel C
97 Wayne Gretzky 6.00 15.00
Vladimir Vorobiev D
98 Sergei Fedorov S 3.00 8.00
99 Jim Campbell 1.50 4.00
Ryan Smyth U
100 Vaclav Prospal 1.00 2.50
Paul Coffey D
101 Wayne Primeau .10 .25
Sean Pronger C
102 Jean Giguere .10 .25
Guy Hebert C
103 Curtis Joseph S 2.50 6.00
104 Pavel Bure .25 .60
Alexander Mogilny D
105 Jeremy Roenick .25 .60
Tony Amonte C
106 Sandis Ozolinsh .10 .25
Kirk McLaren C
107 Anson Carter .10 .25
Steve Kelly C
108 Paul Coffey S 2.00 5.00
109 Dainius Zubrus 3.00 8.00
Peter Forsberg U
110 Travis Green .10 .25
Scott Mellanby C
111 Pat LaFontaine .10 .25
Valeri Kamensky C
112 Adam Oates S 2.00 5.00
113 John Vanbiesbrouck .10 .25
Roman Turek C
114 Jarome Iginla 4.00 10.00
Paul Kariya U
115 Steve Yzerman 4.00 10.00
Chris Osgood D
116 Marcel Cousineau 1.00 2.50
Steve Sullivan D
117 Owen Nolan .10 .25
Steve Rucchin C
118 Donald Audette .10 .25
Ted Donato C
119 Geoff Sanderson 1.00 2.50
Sean Burke D
120 Jeremy Roenick S 4.00 10.00
121 Vladimir Vorobiev RC .10 .25
Andreas Johansson
122 Alexander Mogilny S 2.00 5.00
123 Jocelyn Thibault 1.00 2.50
Terry Ryan D
124 Eric Fichaud .10 .25
Nikolai Khabibulin C
125 Ray Bourque RC .50 1.25
Eric Messier C
126 Sergei Fedorov .30 .75
Keith Primeau C
127 Marc Denis 4.00 10.00
Martin Brodeur U
128 Mats Sundin S 2.50 6.00
129 Peter Bondra .10 .25
Roman Vopat C
130 Tommy Salo .10 .25
Corey Schwab C
131 Sergei Samsonov 1.00 2.50
Jim Carey D
132 Adam Deadmarsh 2.00 5.00
Joe Sakic D
133 Daymond Langkow 1.50 4.00
Keith Tkachuk U
134 Mike Richter S 2.50 6.00
135 Geoff Sanderson .10 .25
Jere Lehtinen C
136 Janne Niinimaa .10 .25
Jamie Pushor C
137 Andreas Dackell .10 .25
Vincent Damphousse C
138 Keith Tkachuk S 2.00 5.00
139 Ray Bourque S 4.00 10.00
140 Keith Tkachuk 1.25 3.00
Jeremy Roenick D
141 Rem Murray .10 .25
Ray Sheppard C
142 Peter Schaefer .10 .25
Patrick Lalime C
143 Jaroslav Svejkovsky .25 .60
Teemu Selanne U
144 Todd Marchant .10 .25
Tony Granato C
145 Sandis Ozolinsh S 2.00 5.00
146 Roman Hamrlik .25 .60
Nicklas Lidstrom C
147 Dominik Hasek S 6.00 15.00
148 Chris Gratton .10 .25
Daniel Goneau C
149 Martin Brodeur S 8.00 20.00
150 Martin Brodeur .60 1.50
Stephane Fiset C
151 Jose Theodore 8.00 20.00
Patrick Roy U
152 Jose Theodore 1.00 2.50
Mark Recchi D
153 Pavel Bure S 2.50 6.00
154 Sergei Berezin .10 .25
Denis Pederson C
155 Doug Gilmour S 2.00 5.00
156 Peter Nedved .10 .25
Kirk Muller C
157 Theo Fleury S 2.00 5.00
158 Harry York 1.00 2.50
Pierre Turgeon D
159 Andreas Johansson 1.00 2.50
Patrick Lalime D
160 Marcel Cousineau .10 .25
Jeff Hackett C
161 Adam Deadmarsh .10 .25
Alexandre Daigle C
162 Adam Oates .10 .25
Todd Warriner C
163 Zigmund Palffy S 2.00 5.00
164 Ed Belfour S 2.50 6.00
165 Saku Koivu 6.00 15.00
Steve Yzerman U
166 Chris Chelios .25 .60
Scott Lachance C
167 Jamie Langenbrunner .10 .25
Brandon Convery C
168 Janne Niinimaa 1.00 2.50
John LeClair D
169 Brendan Shanahan S 2.50 6.00
170 Darren Puppa .10 .25
Garth Snow C
171 Chris Osgood S 2.00 5.00
172 Pierre Turgeon .10 .25
Shane Corson C
173 Doug Weight 1.00 2.50
Rem Murray D
174 Eric Fichaud 1.50 4.00
Curtis Joseph U
175 Chris Chelios S 2.00 5.00
176 Wade Redden .10 .25
Scott Stevens C
177 Jarome Iginla 1.00 2.50
Theo Fleury D
178 Vaclav Varada .10 .25
Igor Larionov C
179 Brian Leetch S 2.00 5.00
180 Stephane Fiset 1.00 2.50
Roman Vopat D
181 Zigmund Palffy 1.00 2.50
Bryan Berard D
182 Bryan Berard 1.00 2.50
Brian Leetch
183 Eric Lindros S 2.50 6.00
184 Derek Plante 1.00 2.50
Brian Holzinger D
185 Brett Hull .30 .75
Martin Gelinas C
186 Daniel Alfredsson 1.00 2.50
Damian Rhodes D
187 Joe Thornton 4.00 10.00
Mark Messier U
188 Mike Vernon .10 .25
Ken Wregget C
189 Alexei Yashin .60 1.50
Wade Redden D
190 Joe Sakic S 8.00 20.00
191 Doug Weight .10 .25
Darren Turcotte C
192 Daymond Langkow .10 .25
Darren Puppa C
193 Mike Modano S 4.00 10.00
194 Sean Burke .10 .25
Mike Dunham C
195 Dainius Zubrus .10 .25
Sebastien Bordeleau C
196 Owen Nolan 1.00 2.50
Jeff Friesen D
197 Vladimir Vorobiev 2.00 5.00
Sergei Fedorov U
198 Patrick Roy S 15.00 40.00
199 Mike Grier .10 .25
Ron Francis C
200 Patrick Marleau 10.00 25.00
Wayne Gretzky U
P183 Eric Lindros PROMO .40 1.00

1997-98 Donruss Limited Exposure

Randomly inserted in packs, this 200-card set was a parallel to the base set and featured holographic poly-chromium technology on both sides. The set was designated by an exclusive "Limited Exposure" stamp. Less than 25 sets of the Star Factor cards and less than 40 of the Unlimited cards were produced.

*COUNTER.STARS: 5X TO 10X BASIC CARDS
*DBL.TEAM STARS: 5X TO 10X BASIC CARDS
*ST.FACT.STARS: 4X TO 8X BASIC CARDS
*UNLIMITED STARS: 2X TO 5X BASIC CARDS

1997-98 Donruss Limited Fabric of the Game

Randomly inserted in packs, this 72-card partial multi-fractured set featured color player photos distinguished by using three different technologies, each of which represented a different statistical category: Embossed Canvas (Wins), Leather (Goals), and Wood (Assists). Five more levels crossed the sections and were sequentially numbered: Legendary Material (numbered to 100), Hall of Fame Material (numbered to 250), Superstar Material (numbered to 500), Star Material (numbered to 750), and Major Material (numbered to 1000)

1 Wayne Gretzky HF 40.00 100.00
2 Martin Brodeur S 6.00 15.00
3 Dainius Zubrus M 1.00 2.50
4 Joe Sakic SS 8.00 20.00
5 Joe Sakic HF 12.00 30.00
6 Sergei Fedorov S 3.00 8.00
7 John Vanbiesbrouck HF 6.00 15.00
8 Saku Koivu M 2.50 6.00
9 J-S Giguere M 2.50 6.00
10 Paul Kariya S 3.00 8.00
11 Mike Richter SS 4.00 10.00
12 Paul Coffey L 6.00 15.00
13 Brendan Shanahan L 20.00 50.00
14 Jaromir Jagr SS 6.00 15.00
15 Felix Potvin SS 4.00 10.00
16 Mats Sundin SS 4.00 10.00
17 Mike Vernon HF 6.00 15.00
18 Keith Tkachuk S 2.00 5.00
19 Doug Gilmour HF 6.00 15.00
20 Patrick Roy L 60.00 150.00
21 Sergei Samsonov M 2.50 6.00
22 Mike Grier M 1.00 2.50
23 Curtis Joseph SS 3.00 8.00
24 Zigmund Palffy S 2.00 5.00
25 Chris Osgood S 2.00 5.00
26 Mats Sundin S 3.00 8.00
27 Kelly Hrudey HF 6.00 15.00
28 Brett Hull L 25.00 60.00
29 Ray Bourque HF 10.00 25.00
30 Nikolai Khabibulin S 2.00 5.00
31 Bryan Berard M 1.00 2.50
32 Jaroslav Svejkovsky M 1.00 2.50
33 Ed Belfour SS 4.00 10.00
34 Wayne Gretzky L 75.00 200.00
35 Jeremy Roenick SS 5.00 12.00
36 Andy Moog L 10.00 25.00
37 Eric Lindros S 3.00 8.00
38 Brett Hull SS 5.00 12.00
39 Marcel Cousineau M 1.00 2.50
40 Paul Kariya M 2.50 6.00
41 Mike Dunham M 1.00 2.50
42 Chris Phillips M 1.00 2.50
43 Teemu Selanne SS 4.00 10.00
44 Mark Messier L 25.00 60.00
45 Grant Fuhr L 15.00 40.00
46 Daniel Alfredsson M 1.50 4.00
47 Marc Denis M 1.00 2.50
48 Daymond Langkow M 1.00 2.50
49 Steve Yzerman HF 25.00 60.00
50 Ryan Smyth S 2.00 5.00
51 Alexander Mogilny HF 6.00 15.00
52 Ron Hextall HF 6.00 15.00
53 Brendan Shanahan S 3.00 8.00
54 Jim Carey S 2.00 5.00
55 Eric Lindros S 3.00 8.00
56 Eric Fichaud M 1.00 2.50
57 Sergei Berezin M 1.00 2.50
58 Chris Chelios HF 6.00 15.00
59 Mark Messier HF 10.00 25.00
60 Damian Rhodes M 2.50 6.00
61 Jarome Iginla M 3.00 8.00
62 Jocelyn Thibault S 2.00 5.00
63 John LeClair S 2.00 5.00
64 Brian Leetch SS 4.00 10.00
65 Dominik Hasek S 6.00 15.00
66 Pavel Bure SS 4.00 10.00
67 Mike Modano S 4.00 10.00
68 Daniel Cleary M 1.00 2.50
69 Janne Niinimaa M 1.00 2.50
70 Steve Yzerman L 40.00 100.00
71 Jose Theodore M 3.00 6.00
72 Peter Forsberg S 5.00 12.00

1997-98 Donruss Preferred

The 1997-98 Donruss Preferred set was issued in one series totaling 200 cards and distributed in five-card packs inside collectible tins. The set featured color player photos on an all micro-etched foil board card with bronze, silver, gold, and platinum finishes.

COMPLETE SET (200) 400.00 800.00
COMP.BRONZE SET (100) 12.50 30.00
1 Dominik Hasek G 8.00 20.00
2 Peter Forsberg G 10.00 25.00
3 Brendan Shanahan P 8.00 20.00
4 Wayne Gretzky P 25.00 60.00
5 Eric Lindros P 8.00 20.00
6 Keith Tkachuk G 4.00 10.00
7 Mark Messier P .25 .60
8 Mike Modano G 6.00 15.00
9 John Vanbiesbrouck P 8.00 20.00
10 Paul Kariya P 8.00 20.00
11 Saku Koivu G 4.00 10.00
12 Paul Coffey B .25 .60
13 Joe Juneau B .20 .50
14 Jeff Friesen S .60 1.50
15 Brett Hull G 5.00 12.00
16 Martin Brodeur G 10.00 25.00
17 Jarome Iginla G 5.00 12.00
18 Keith Primeau S .60 1.50
19 Ed Jovanovski B .20 .50
20 Jamie Langenbrunner B .10 .25
21 Derian Hatcher S .60 1.50
22 Brian Leetch G 4.00 10.00
23 Daymond Langkow S 1.50 4.00
24 Ray Bourque S 3.00 8.00
25 Pavel Bure G .25 .60
26 Janne Niinimaa S 1.50 4.00
27 Jamie Storr S 1.50 4.00
28 Darcy Tucker B .10 .25
29 Anson Carter B .20 .50
30 Jeff O'Neill B .10 .25
31 Jason Arnott G 1.25 3.00
32 Tommy Salo B .20 .50
33 Petr Nedved B .20 .50
34 Mike Peca B .20 .50
35 Ethan Moreau S .60 1.50
36 Ray Sheppard B .20 .50
37 Damian Rhodes B .20 .50
38 Mats Sundin S 2.00 5.00
39 Alexander Mogilny G 3.00 8.00
40 Mike Dunham S 1.50 4.00
41 Steve Yzerman P 20.00 50.00
42 Alexei Yashin S .60 1.50
43 Jim Carey S 1.50 4.00
44 Mike Grier S .60 1.50
45 Steve Rucchin B .10 .25
46 Mark Recchi S .60 1.50
47 Mike Gartner B .20 .50
48 Alexandre Daigle S 1.50 4.00
49 Eric Fichaud G 3.00 8.00
50 Harry York B .10 .25
51 Dino Ciccarelli B .20 .50
52 Bill Ranford B .20 .50
53 Adam Deadmarsh G 1.25 3.00
54 Ed Belfour B .25 .60
55 Jozef Stumpel S 1.50 4.00
56 Rem Murray B .10 .25
57 Pat Verbeek B .10 .25
58 Pat LaFontaine S 1.50 4.00
59 Dainius Zubrus S 1.50 4.00
60 Grant Fuhr B .20 .50
61 Rob Niedermayer B .20 .50
62 Brian Savage B .10 .25
63 Gary Roberts B .10 .25

64 Tony Amonte B .20 .50
65 Jere Lehtinen B .20 .50
66 Dave Andreychuk B .20 .50
67 Rod Brind'Amour B .20 .50
68 Mikael Renberg B .20 .50
69 Doug Gilmour S 1.50 4.00
70 Kevin Hatcher B .10 .25
71 Byron Dafoe B .20 .50
72 Derek Plante S .60 1.50
73 Trevor Kidd B .20 .50
74 Doug Weight S 1.50 4.00
75 Valeri Bure B .10 .25
76 John LeClair G 4.00 10.00
77 Sergei Berezin B .20 .50
78 Peter Bondra S 1.50 4.00
79 Bryan Berard G 3.00 8.00
80 Steve Shields B RC .40 1.00
81 Chris Osgood G 3.00 8.00
82 Mike Vernon B .20 .50
83 Martin Gelinas B .20 .50
84 Curtis Joseph S 2.00 5.00
85 Geoff Sanderson S 1.50 4.00
86 Patrick Roy P 20.00 50.00
87 Jocelyn Thibault G 3.00 8.00
88 Jeremy Roenick S 2.50 6.00
89 Trevor Linden B .20 .50
90 Daniel Alfredsson S 1.50 4.00
91 Sergei Zubov B .10 .25
92 Dimitri Khristich S .60 1.50
93 Brian Holzinger B .10 .25
94 Andrew Cassels B .10 .25
95 Teemu Selanne G 4.00 10.00
96 Ron Hextall B .20 .50
97 Wade Redden B .10 .25
98 Jim Campbell B .10 .25
99 Felix Potvin G 4.00 10.00
100 Adam Oates S 1.50 4.00
101 Nikolai Khabibulin B .20 .50
102 Jose Theodore S 2.50 6.00
103 Sandis Ozolinsh S .60 1.50
104 Sean Burke B .20 .50
105 Vaclav Prospal G RC 8.00 20.00
106 Zigmund Palffy G 3.00 8.00
107 Kyle McLaren B .10 .25
108 Owen Nolan S 1.50 4.00
109 Chris Pronger S 1.50 4.00
110 Daren Puppa B .20 .50
111 Garth Snow B .20 .50
112 Aki Berg B .10 .25
113 Andy Moog B .20 .50
114 Darren McCarty B .10 .25
115 Joe Nieuwendyk B .20 .50
116 Eric Daze S 1.50 4.00
117 Pierre Turgeon S 1.50 4.00
118 Ken Wregget B .20 .50
119 Ryan Smyth G 3.00 8.00
120 Kirk Muller B .10 .25
121 Luc Robitaille B .20 .50
122 Sergei Fedorov G 6.00 15.00
123 Sean Pronger B .10 .25
124 Mike Richter S 2.00 5.00
125 Jaromir Jagr P 10.00 25.00
126 Claude Lemieux B .10 .25
127 Chris Chelios S 2.00 5.00
128 Joe Sakic P 12.50 30.00
129 Guy Hebert S 1.50 4.00
130 Chris Gratton S 1.50 4.00
131 Steve Sullivan B .10 .25
132 Al MacInnis B .20 .50
133 Adam Graves S .60 1.50
134 Vyacheslav Kozlov B .10 .25
135 Scott Mellanby S .60 1.50
136 Stephane Fiset B .20 .50
137 Oleg Tverdovsky S .60 1.50
138 Theo Fleury S .60 1.50
139 Jeff Hackett B .20 .50
140 Vincent Damphousse B .10 .25
141 Roman Hamrlik S .60 1.50
142 Ron Francis S 1.50 4.00
143 Scott Lachance B .10 .25
144 Todd Harvey B .10 .25
145 Marc Denis S 1.50 4.00
146 Jaroslav Svejkovsky G 3.00 8.00
147 Olli Jokinen S RC 8.00 20.00
148 Sergei Samsonov G 3.00 8.00
149 Chris Phillips G 1.25 3.00
150 Patrick Marleau G 8.00 20.00
151 Joe Thornton G 10.00 25.00
152 Daniel Cleary S 1.50 4.00
153 Alyn McCauley G 3.00 8.00
154 Brad Isbister S .60 1.50
155 Alexei Morozov S 2.00 5.00
156 Shawn Bates B RC .10 .25
157 Jean-Yves Leroux B RC .10 .25
158 Marcel Cousineau B .20 .50
159 Vaclav Varada B .10 .25
160 J-S Giguere S 1.50 4.00
161 Espen Knutsen B RC .75 2.00
162 Marian Hossa S RC 20.00 50.00
163 Robert Dome B RC .10 .25
164 Juha Lind B RC .10 .25
165 Sergei Fedorov NT B .40 1.00
166 Jarome Iginla NT B .30 .75
167 Jaroslav Svejkovsky NT B .20 .50
168 Patrick Roy NT S 10.00 25.00
169 Dominik Hasek NT B .50 1.25
170 Alexander Mogilny NT B .20 .50
171 Chris Chelios NT B .25 .60
172 Wayne Gretzky NT S 12.50 30.00
173 Peter Forsberg NT B .60 1.50
174 Ray Bourque NT B .40 1.00
175 Joe Sakic NT S 4.00 10.00
176 Mike Modano NT B .25 .60
177 Mark Messier NT B .25 .60
178 Teemu Selanne NT B .25 .60
179 Steve Yzerman NT S 10.00 25.00
180 Eric Lindros NT S 2.00 5.00
181 Doug Weight NT B .20 .50
182 John Vanbiesbrouck NT B .20 .50
183 Paul Kariya NT S 2.00 5.00
184 Brendan Shanahan NT S 2.00 5.00
185 Martin Brodeur NT B .60 1.50
186 Bryan Berard NT B .20 .50
187 Marc Denis NT B .20 .50
188 Brian Leetch NT B .25 .60
189 Ryan Smyth NT S 2.00 5.00
190 Dainius Zubrus NT B .20 .50
191 Keith Tkachuk NT B .25 .60
192 Jaromir Jagr NT S 3.00 8.00
193 Brett Hull NT B .30 .75
194 Pavel Bure NT B .25 .60
195 Sergei Samsonov B .20 .50
196 Olli Jokinen B .40 1.00
197 Chris Phillips B .20 .50
198 Patrick Marleau B .50 1.25
199 Daniel Cleary B .20 .50
200 Joe Thornton B .75 2.00

1997-98 Donruss Preferred Cut to the Chase

Randomly inserted in packs, this 200-card set was a die-cut parallel version of the base set. Each card featured a background of bronze, silver gold, or platinum.
*BRONZE STARS: 4X TO 10X BASIC CARDS
*BRONZE RC's: 2X TO 5X BASIC CARDS
*SILVER STARS: 1.5X TO 4X BASIC CARDS
*SILVER RC's: 1X TO 2.5X BASIC CARDS
*GOLD STARS: 1.25X TO 3X BASIC CARDS
*PLATINUM STARS: 1X TO 2.5 X BASIC CARDS

1997-98 Donruss Preferred Color Guard

Randomly inserted in packs, this 18-card set featured color images of top puckstoppers printed on die-cut plastic cards with the player's team colors in the background. The set was sequentially numbered to 1,500.
COMPLETE SET (18) 75.00 150.00
1 Patrick Roy 15.00 40.00
2 Martin Brodeur 10.00 25.00
3 Curtis Joseph 3.00 8.00
4 John Vanbiesbrouck 3.00 8.00
5 Felix Potvin 3.00 8.00
6 Dominik Hasek 6.00 15.00
7 Chris Osgood 3.00 8.00
8 Eric Fichaud 2.00 5.00
9 Jocelyn Thibault 2.00 5.00
10 Marc Denis 2.00 5.00
11 Jose Theodore 5.00 12.00
12 Mike Vernon 3.00 8.00
13 Jim Carey 2.00 5.00
14 Ron Hextall 3.00 8.00
15 Mike Richter 3.00 8.00
16 Ed Belfour 3.00 8.00
17 Mike Dunham 2.00 5.00
18 Damian Rhodes 2.00 5.00

1997-98 Donruss Preferred Color Guard Promos

Very few copies of this 18-card set was released as a promotional item. It paralleled the base set except that all cards were numbered Promo/1500. It is believed that fewer than 50 copies exist of each of these cards.
COMPLETE SET (18) 150.00 250.00
1 Patrick Roy 20.00 50.00
2 Martin Brodeur 15.00 40.00
3 Curtis Joseph 6.00 15.00
4 John Vanbiesbrouck 6.00 15.00
5 Felix Potvin 6.00 15.00
6 Dominik Hasek 8.00 20.00
7 Chris Osgood 4.00 10.00
8 Eric Fichaud 4.00 10.00
9 Jocelyn Thibault 4.00 10.00
10 Marc Denis 4.00 10.00
11 Jose Theodore 8.00 20.00
12 Mike Vernon 4.00 10.00
13 Jim Carey 4.00 10.00
14 Ron Hextall 6.00 15.00
15 Mike Richter 8.00 20.00
16 Ed Belfour 10.00 25.00
17 Mike Dunham 4.00 10.00
18 Damian Rhodes 4.00 10.00

1997-98 Donruss Preferred Line of the Times

Randomly inserted in packs, this 24-card set featured color photos of star players printed on die-cut cards and utilizing micro-etching technology. Three cards were made to be placed side by side to form one interactive card which spelled out a particular word in the background. The set was sequentially numbered to 2,500.
COMPLETE SET (24) 125.00 250.00
1A Ryan Smyth 3.00 8.00
1B Sergei Fedorov 6.00 15.00
1C Jaromir Jagr 6.00 15.00
2A Eric Lindros 4.00 10.00
2B Joe Thornton 6.00 15.00
2C Brendan Shanahan 4.00 10.00
3A John LeClair 4.00 10.00
3B Keith Tkachuk 4.00 10.00
3C Brett Hull 5.00 12.00
4A Pavel Bure 4.00 10.00
4B Sergei Samsonov 3.00 8.00
4C Paul Kariya 4.00 10.00
5A Mike Modano 6.00 15.00
5B Teemu Selanne 4.00 10.00
5C Patrick Marleau 4.00 10.00
6A Wayne Gretzky 25.00 60.00
6B Steve Yzerman 20.00 50.00
6C Daniel Cleary 2.50 6.00
7A Jarome Iginla 5.00 12.00
7B Peter Forsberg 10.00 25.00
7C Mark Messier 4.00 10.00
8A Joe Sakic 8.00 20.00
8B Jaroslav Svejkovsky 3.00 8.00
8C Dainius Zubrus 3.00 8.00

1997-98 Donruss Preferred Line of the Times Promos

This 24-card set was released in singles form as promotional items on a very limited basis. The cards paralleled the base set except that they were numbered Promo/2500. It is believed, however, that fewer than 100 copies existed for each of these cards.
COMPLETE SET (24) 100.00 250.00
1A Ryan Smyth 2.00 5.00
1B Sergei Fedorov 6.00 15.00
1C Jaromir Jagr 10.00 25.00
2A Eric Lindros 4.00 10.00
2B Joe Thornton 4.00 10.00
2C Brendan Shanahan 4.00 10.00
3A John LeClair 4.00 10.00
3B Keith Tkachuk 4.00 10.00
3C Brett Hull 4.00 10.00
4A Pavel Bure 8.00 20.00
4B Sergei Samsonov 4.00 10.00
4C Paul Kariya 10.00 25.00
5A Mike Modano 4.00 10.00
5B Teemu Selanne 6.00 15.00
5C Patrick Marleau 4.00 10.00
6A Wayne Gretzky 20.00 50.00
6B Steve Yzerman 10.00 25.00
6C Daniel Cleary 2.00 5.00
7A Jarome Iginla 2.00 5.00
7B Peter Forsberg 8.00 20.00
7C Mark Messier 4.00 10.00
8A Joe Sakic 6.00 15.00
8B Jaroslav Svejkovsky .80 2.00
8C Dainius Zubrus .80 2.00

1997-98 Donruss Preferred Precious Metals

Randomly inserted in packs, this 15-card set was a partial parallel version of the base set. The cards were printed on card stock consisting of 1 gram of real gold or platinum. Only 100 of each card was produced.
COMPLETE SET (15) 800.00 1500.00
1 Brendan Shanahan P 60.00 150.00
2 Joe Thornton G 75.00 200.00
3 Wayne Gretzky P 200.00 500.00
4 Mark Messier P 60.00 150.00
5 Patrick Roy P 150.00 400.00
6 Martin Brodeur G 100.00 250.00
7 Eric Lindros P 50.00 100.00
8 Paul Kariya P 40.00 100.00
9 Teemu Selanne G 40.00 100.00
10 Jaromir Jagr P 60.00 150.00
11 Joe Sakic P 75.00 200.00
12 Peter Forsberg G 100.00 200.00
13 John Vanbiesbrouck P 40.00 100.00
14 Steve Yzerman P 100.00 250.00
15 Sergei Samsonov G 40.00 100.00

1997-98 Donruss Priority

The 1997-98 Donruss Priority hobby only set was issued in one series totaling 220 cards and was distributed in two-types of five-card packs--postcard and stamp packs--with a suggested retail price of $4.99. Postcard packs had a 5" by 7" horizontal format and contained only even numbered cards from the set. The odd numbered cards were twice as scarce and could be found only in the stamp packs. The fronts featured color action player photos printed with foil treatments, while the backs carried player information. The set contained the topical subset: 1st Class Package (185-214). The set was released towards the end of the 97-98 NHL season.
COMPLETE SET (220) 25.00 50.00
1 Patrick Roy SP 1.25 3.00
2 Eric Lindros .20 .50
3 Keith Tkachuk SP .15 .40
4 Steve Yzerman .75 2.00
5 John Vanbiesbrouck SP .25 .60
6 Teemu Selanne .20 .50
7 Martin Brodeur SP .60 1.50
8 Peter Forsberg .40 1.00
9 Brett Hull SP .30 .75
10 Wayne Gretzky 1.00 2.50
11 Mike Modano SP .40 1.00
12 Sergei Fedorov .25 .60
13 Paul Kariya SP .60 1.50
14 Saku Koivu .20 .50
15 Pavel Bure SP .20 .50
16 Mark Messier .20 .50
17 Joe Sakic SP .50 1.25
18 Jaromir Jagr .25 .60
19 Brendan Shanahan SP .20 .50
20 Ray Bourque .25 .60
21 Daymond Langkow SP .10 .30
22 Alexandre Daigle .07 .20
23 Dainius Zubrus SP .10 .30
24 Ryan Smyth .10 .30
25 Derek Plante SP .10 .30
26 Eric Daze .10 .30
27 Ed Jovanovski SP .10 .30
28 Sergei Berezin .07 .20
29 Roman Turek SP .15 .40
30 Derian Hatcher .07 .20
31 Jarome Iginla SP .20 .50
32 Luc Robitaille .10 .30
33 Rod Brind'Amour SP .15 .40
34 Mathieu Schneider .07 .20
35 Olaf Kolzig SP .15 .40
36 Nikolai Khabibulin .10 .30
37 Scott Niedermayer SP .10 .30
38 Keith Primeau .07 .20
39 Dimitri Khristich SP .10 .30
40 Eric Fichaud .10 .30
41 Pierre Turgeon SP .15 .40
42 Kevin Stevens .07 .20
43 Nicklas Lidstrom SP .10 .30
44 Sean Burke .10 .30
45 Sandis Ozolinsh SP .10 .30
46 Owen Nolan .10 .30
47 Peter Bondra SP .25 .60
48 Ron Hextall .10 .30
49 Rob Blake SP .10 .30
50 Geoff Sanderson .10 .30
51 Sergei Zubov SP .10 .30
52 Doug Gilmour .10 .30
53 Oleg Tverdovsky SP .10 .30
54 Bryan Berard .07 .20
55 Bill Ranford SP .15 .40
56 Mats Sundin .20 .50
57 Damian Rhodes SP .15 .40
58 Zigmund Palffy .10 .30
59 Mike Grier SP .10 .30
60 Jozef Stumpel .10 .30
61 Mark Recchi SP .10 .30
62 Alexei Zhamnov .07 .20
63 Jere Lehtinen SP .10 .30
64 Andrew Cassels .07 .20
65 Kevin Hodson SP .15 .40
66 Dino Ciccarelli .10 .30
67 Niklas Sundstrom SP .10 .30
68 Jeff Hackett .10 .30
69 Brian Holzinger SP .15 .40
70 Jeff Friesen .07 .20
71 Ed Belfour SP .25 .60
72 Wayne Primeau .07 .20
73 Sami Kapanen SP .10 .30
74 Brian Leetch .10 .30
75 Mikael Renberg SP .15 .40
76 Ron Tugnutt .10 .30
77 Ron Francis SP .15 .40
78 Jocelyn Thibault .10 .30
79 Jamie Langenbrunner SP .10 .30
80 Dominik Hasek .30 .75
81 Chris Osgood SP .15 .40
82 Grant Fuhr .10 .30
83 Adam Graves SP .10 .30
84 Janne Niinimaa .10 .30
85 Kelly Hrudey SP .15 .40
86 Mike Dunham .10 .30
87 Valeri Kamensky SP .15 .40
88 Cory Stillman .07 .20
89 Anson Carter SP .10 .30
90 Igor Larionov .07 .20
91 Chris Pronger SP .15 .40
92 Steve Sullivan .07 .20
93 Mike Gartner SP .15 .40
94 Jim Campbell .10 .30
95 Valeri Bure SP .10 .30
96 Stephane Fiset .10 .30
97 Jason Arnott SP .10 .30
98 Trevor Kidd .10 .30
99 Chris Chelios SP .25 .60
100 Kevin Hatcher .07 .20
101 Felix Potvin SP .25 .60
102 Travis Green .07 .20
103 Dave Gagner SP .10 .30
104 Byron Dafoe .10 .30
105 Rick Tabaracci SP .15 .40
106 Gary Roberts .07 .20
107 Mike Ricci SP .10 .30
108 Andy Moog .10 .30
109 Sean Pronger SP .10 .30
110 Paul Coffey .10 .30
111 Trevor Linden SP .15 .40
112 Rob Zamuner .07 .20
113 Daniel Alfredsson SP .15 .40
114 Ray Sheppard .10 .30
115 Steve Shields RC SP .40 1.00
116 Ethan Moreau .07 .20
117 Tomas Sandstrom SP .10 .30
118 Chris Gratton .10 .30
119 Alexander Mogilny SP .15 .40
120 Roman Hamrlik .07 .20
121 Tommy Salo SP .15 .40
122 Jason Allison .07 .20
123 Curtis Joseph SP .20 .50
124 Guy Hebert .10 .30
125 Jeff O'Neill SP .10 .30
126 Donald Audette .07 .20
127 Claude Lemieux SP .10 .30
128 Brian Savage .07 .20
129 Scott Mellanby SP .10 .30
130 Vyacheslav Kozlov .10 .30
131 Wade Redden SP .10 .30
132 John LeClair .20 .50
133 Jeremy Roenick SP .25 .60
134 Andreas Johansson .07 .20
135 Nelson Emerson SP .10 .30
136 Daren Puppa .10 .30
137 Joe Juneau SP .15 .40
138 Garth Snow .10 .30
139 Tom Barrasso SP .15 .40
140 Joe Nieuwendyk .10 .30
141 Theo Fleury SP .10 .30
142 Yanic Perreault .07 .20
143 Mike Richter SP .25 .60
144 Al MacInnis .10 .30
145 Mike Peca SP .15 .40
146 Darren McCarty .07 .20
147 Alexei Yashin SP .10 .30
148 Rick Tocchet .10 .30
149 Adam Oates SP .15 .40
150 Wendel Clark .07 .20
151 Tony Amonte SP .15 .40
152 Dave Andreychuk .07 .20
153 Jamie Storr SP .15 .40
154 Craig Janney .10 .30
155 Todd Bertuzzi SP
156 Harry York .07 .20
157 Todd Harvey SP .10 .30
158 Bobby Holik .07 .20
159 Mike Vernon SP .15 .40
160 Pat LaFontaine .10 .30
161 Doug Weight SP .15 .40
162 Kirk McLean .10 .30
163 Adam Deadmarsh SP .10 .30
164 Vincent Damphousse .07 .20
165 Vaclav Prospal RC SP .15 .40
166 Daniel Cleary .10 .30
167 Jaroslav Svejkovsky SP .15 .40
168 Marco Sturm RC .25 .60
169 Robert Dome RC SP .10 .30
170 Patrik Elias RC .50 1.25
171 Mattias Ohlund SP .15 .40
172 Espen Knutsen RC .20 .50
173 Joe Thornton SP .60 1.50
174 Jan Bulis RC .07 .20
175 Patrick Marleau SP .40 1.00
176 Brad Isbister .07 .20
177 Kevin Weekes RC SP 2.50 6.00
178 Sergei Samsonov .10 .30
179 Tyler Moss RC SP .10 .30
180 Chris Phillips .07 .20
181 Alyn McCauley SP .10 .30
182 Derek Morris RC .10 .30
183 Alexei Morozov SP .15 .40
184 Boyd Devereaux .07 .20
185 Peter Forsberg SP .15 .40
186 Brendan Shanahan .10 .30
187 Teemu Selanne SP .15 .40
188 Eric Lindros .10 .30
189 Mark Messier SP .15 .40
190 Vaclav Prospal .10 .30
191 Jarome Iginla SP .20 .50
192 Mike Modano .10 .30
193 John Vanbiesbrouck SP .15 .40
194 Bryan Berard .07 .20
195 Patrick Marleau SP .15 .40
196 Martin Brodeur .10 .30
197 Patrick Roy SP .15 .40
198 Felix Potvin .20 .50
199 Wayne Gretzky SP 1.50 4.00
200 Sergei Samsonov .10 .30
201 Ryan Smyth SP .15 .40
202 Keith Tkachuk .20 .50
203 Chris Osgood SP .15 .40
204 Paul Kariya .07 .20
205 John LeClair SP .20 .50
206 Alyn McCauley .10 .30
207 Joe Thornton SP .40 1.00
208 Joe Sakic .10 .30
209 Steve Yzerman SP 1.25 3.00
210 Saku Koivu .20 .50
211 Pavel Bure SP .15 .40
212 Zigmund Palffy .10 .30
213 Alexei Yashin SP .10 .30
214 Sergei Fedorov .10 .30
215 Joe Thornton CL SP .40 1.00
216 Patrick Marleau CL .10 .30
217 Daniel Cleary CL SP .10 .30
218 Sergei Samsonov CL .10 .30
219 Jaroslav Svejkovsky CL SP .10 .30
220 Alyn McCauley CL .07 .20

1997-98 Donruss Priority Stamp of Approval

This 220-card set was a parallel to the base set. Each card was randomly inserted into packs and was serial numbered out of 100. Card design featured a deckle edge similar to a postage stamp, and design front was different from that of the base set.
*EVEN NMBRS.: 20X TO 50 X BASIC CARDS
*ODD NMBRS.: 15X TO 40X

1997-98 Donruss Priority Direct Deposit

Randomly inserted in packs, this 30-card set featured color action photos of top goal scorers printed on swirled-look foil board with micro etching. The cards were sequentially numbered to just 3,000.
COMPLETE SET (30) 100.00 200.00
1 Brendan Shanahan 2.50 6.00
2 Steve Yzerman 8.00 20.00
3 Pavel Bure 2.50 6.00
4 Jaromir Jagr 4.00 10.00
5 Ryan Smyth 1.50 4.00
6 Sergei Samsonov 1.50 4.00
7 Mark Messier 2.50 6.00
8 Wayne Gretzky 10.00 25.00
9 Jarome Iginla 3.00 8.00
10 Peter Forsberg 6.00 15.00
11 Joe Sakic 5.00 12.00
12 Sergei Fedorov 4.00 10.00
13 Mike Modano 4.00 10.00
14 Paul Kariya 2.50 6.00
15 Teemu Selanne 2.50 6.00
16 Eric Lindros 2.50 6.00
17 Keith Tkachuk 2.50 6.00
18 Patrick Marleau 4.00 10.00
19 Jaroslav Svejkovsky 1.50 4.00
20 Alyn McCauley 1.50 4.00
21 Saku Koivu 2.50 6.00
22 Zigmund Palffy 1.50 4.00
23 Brett Hull 3.00 8.00
24 Patrik Elias 2.50 6.00
25 Joe Thornton 6.00 15.00
26 Espen Knutsen 1.50 4.00
27 Daniel Alfredsson 2.00 5.00
28 John LeClair 2.50 6.00
29 Dainius Zubrus 1.50 4.00
30 Jason Arnott 1.50 4.00

1997-98 Donruss Priority Direct Deposit Promos

P7 Mark Messier 2.50 6.00
P8 Wayne Gretzky 10.00 25.00
P10 Peter Forsberg
P18 Patrick Marleau 1.50 4.00
P22 Zigmund Palffy 1.50 4.00
P25 Joe Thornton 3.00 8.00

1997-98 Donruss Priority Postcards

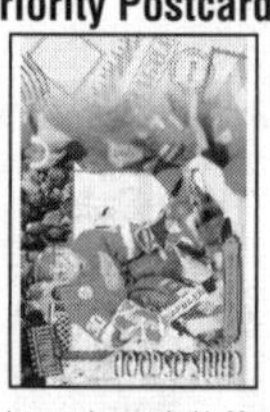

Inserted one per large pack, this 36-card set featured standard postcard sized cards.
COMPLETE SET (36) 25.00 50.00
1 Patrick Roy 2.50 6.00
2 Brendan Shanahan .50 1.25
3 Steve Yzerman 2.50 6.00
4 Jaromir Jagr .75 2.00
5 Pavel Bure .50 1.25
6 Mark Messier .50 1.25
7 Wayne Gretzky 3.00 8.00
8 Eric Lindros .50 1.25
9 Joe Sakic 1.00 2.50
10 Peter Forsberg 1.25 3.00
11 John Vanbiesbrouck .40 1.00
12 Mike Modano .75 2.00
13 Paul Kariya .50 1.25
14 Teemu Selanne .50 1.25
15 Sergei Fedorov .75 2.00
16 Joe Thornton 1.25 3.00
17 Sergei Samsonov .40 1.00
18 Patrick Marleau .75 2.00
19 Ryan Smyth .40 1.00
20 Jarome Iginla .60 1.50
21 John LeClair .50 1.25
22 Brian Leetch .50 1.25
23 Chris Chelios .50 1.25
24 Martin Brodeur 1.25 3.00
25 Bryan Berard .40 1.00
26 Keith Tkachuk .50 1.25
27 Saku Koivu .50 1.25
28 Brett Hull .60 1.50
29 Felix Potvin .50 1.25
30 Chris Osgood .40 1.00
31 Dominik Hasek 1.00 2.50
32 Zigmund Palffy .40 1.00
33 Jeremy Roenick .60 1.50
34 Dainius Zubrus .40 1.00
35 Ray Bourque .75 2.00
36 Jocelyn Thibault .40 1.00

1997-98 Donruss Priority Postcards Opening Day Issues

Randomly inserted in packs, this 30-card set featured color player photos on an all-foil postcard with gold-foil stamping and slits for the corresponding Donruss Priority Stamp card or Donruss Priority trading car with a stamp and a commemorative cance Each card was numbered just out of 1,000.
*SINGLES: 5X TO 10X REGULAR POSTCARDS
1 Patrick Roy 12.00 30.00
2 Eric Lindros 5.00 12.00
3 Keith Tkachuk 5.00 12.00
4 Steve Yzerman 12.00 30.00
5 John Vanbiesbrouck 4.00 10.00
6 Teemu Selanne 6.00 15.00
7 Martin Brodeur 10.00 25.00
8 Peter Forsberg 8.00 20.00
9 Brett Hull 6.00 15.00
10 Wayne Gretzky 15.00 40.00
11 Mike Modano 8.00 20.00
12 Paul Kariya 5.00 12.00
13 Pavel Bure 5.00 12.00
14 Mark Messier 6.00 15.00
15 Joe Sakic 8.00 20.00
16 Jaromir Jagr 8.00 20.00
17 Brendan Shanahan 5.00 12.00
18 Ryan Smyth 4.00 10.00
19 Jarome Iginla 6.00 15.00
20 Bryan Berard 4.00 10.00
21 Jocelyn Thibault 4.00 10.00
22 Dominik Hasek 8.00 20.00
23 Chris Osgood 5.00 12.00
24 Chris Chelios 5.00 12.00
25 Felix Potvin 5.00 12.00
26 John LeClair 5.00 12.00
27 Saku Koivu 5.00 12.00
28 Joe Thornton 8.00 20.00
29 Patrick Marleau 6.00 15.00
30 Sergei Samsonov 4.00 10.00

1997-98 Donruss Priority Postmaster General

Randomly inserted in packs, this 20-card se featured color photos of top goalies printe on all-foil board with foil stamping. Onl 1,500 of each card were produced an sequentially numbered.
COMPLETE SET (20) 40.00 80.00
1 Patrick Roy 12.00 30.00
2 John Vanbiesbrouck 2.00 5.00
3 Felix Potvin 3.00 8.00
4 Curtis Joseph 3.00 8.00
5 Mike Richter 2.00 5.00
6 Jocelyn Thibault 1.00 2.50
7 Ed Belfour 2.00 5.00
8 Chris Osgood 2.00 5.00
9 Ron Hextall 2.00 5.00
10 Martin Brodeur 8.00 20.00
11 Mike Vernon 2.00 5.00
12 Eric Fichaud 1.00 2.50
13 Dominik Hasek 6.00 15.00
14 Byron Dafoe 1.00 2.50
15 Tommy Salo 1.00 2.50
16 Garth Snow 1.00 2.50
17 Tom Barrasso 1.00 2.50
18 Marc Denis 1.00 2.50
19 Grant Fuhr 2.00 5.00
20 Guy Hebert 1.00 2.50

1997-98 Donruss Priority Postmaster Generals Promos

Released as a 20-card promotional set, these cards paralleled the base set except that they are numbered Promo/1500.
COMPLETE SET (20) 40.00 100.00
1 Patrick Roy 6.00 15.00
2 John Vanbiesbrouck 3.20 8.00
3 Felix Potvin 3.20 8.00
4 Curtis Joseph 4.00 10.00
5 Mike Richter 3.20 8.00
6 Jocelyn Thibault 3.20 8.00
7 Ed Belfour 3.20 8.00
8 Chris Osgood 3.20 8.00
9 Ron Hextall 2.40 6.00
10 Martin Brodeur 4.80 12.00
11 Mike Vernon 2.40 6.00
12 Eric Fichaud 2.40 6.00
13 Dominik Hasek 4.00 10.00
14 Byron Dafoe 2.40 6.00
15 Tommy Salo 2.40 6.00
16 Garth Snow 2.40 6.00
17 Tom Barrasso 2.40 6.00
18 Marc Denis 2.40 6.00
19 Grant Fuhr 2.40 6.00
20 Guy Hebert 2.40 6.00

1997-98 Donruss Priority Stamps

Randomly inserted one per small pack, this 36-card set featured color photos of top NHL players printed on real currency stamps. Printed in the country of Grenada, each stamp came protected in a stamp holder

d. Bronze, silver, and gold parallel sions of this set were also produced with insertion rate of 1:6.

MPLETE SET (36) 20.00 40.00
RONZE: 1X TO 2X BASIC INSERTS
LVER: 2X TO 4X BASIC INSERTS
OLDS: 4X TO 8X BASIC INSERTSS
Patrick Roy 2.50 6.00
Brendan Shanahan .50 1.25
Steve Yzerman 2.50 6.00
Jaromir Jagr .75 2.00
Pavel Bure .50 1.25
Mark Messier .50 1.25
Wayne Gretzky 3.00 8.00
Eric Lindros .50 1.25
Joe Sakic 1.00 2.50
Peter Forsberg 1.25 3.00
John Vanbiesbrouck .40 1.00
Mike Modano .75 2.00
Paul Kariya .50 1.25
Teemu Selanne .50 1.25
Sergei Fedorov .75 2.00
Joe Thornton 1.25 3.00
Sergei Samsonov .40 1.00
Patrick Marleau .75 2.00
Ryan Smyth .40 1.00
Jarome Iginla .60 1.50
John LeClair .50 1.25
Brian Leetch .40 1.00
Chris Chelios .40 1.00
Martin Brodeur 1.25 3.00
Bryan Berard .40 1.00
Keith Tkachuk .50 1.25
Saku Koivu .50 1.25
Brett Hull .60 1.50
Felix Potvin .50 1.25
Chris Osgood .40 1.00
Dominik Hasek 1.00 2.50
Zigmund Palffy .40 1.00
Jeremy Roenick .60 1.50
Dainius Zubrus .40 1.00
Ray Bourque .75 2.00
Jocelyn Thibault .40 1.00

993-94 Ducks Milk Caps

is set of six milk caps measured proximately 1 1/2" in diameter and uresdthe Mighty Ducks of Anaheim. The its showed a color player headshot set inst a teal green background with a neon ow stripe. The player's name appeared at bottom, along with the production ures "One of 15,000". The backs were id white. The milk caps were numbered he front.

MPLETE SET (6) 2.00 5.00
im Sweeney .40 1.00
Bobby Dollas .40 1.00
Stu Grimson .60 1.50
erry Yake .40 1.00
Bob Corkum .40 1.00
O Inaugural Season .40 1.00
First Win

1994-95 Ducks Carl's Jr.

e 28-card standard-size set was nsored by Carl's Jr. The fronts featured a or action player photo on a back ground h a purple border. The player's name and m logo was at the left. The backs carried a ad shot of the player, biographical ormation, statistics, and jersey number. e sponsor name and logo was at the tom with a saying against drug use.

MPLETE SET (28) 6.00 15.00
atrick Carnback .10 .25
Bob Corkum .10 .25
Robert Dirk .10 .25
Bobby Dollas .10 .25
Peter Douris .10 .25
Todd Ewen .20 .50
Shaun Van Allen .10 .25
Garry Valk .10 .25
Guy Hebert .60 1.50
Paul Kariya 4.00 10.00
Valeri Karpov .10 .25
Steven King .10 .25
Todd Krygier .10 .25
Tom Kurvers .10 .25
Randy Ladouceur .10 .25
Stephan Lebeau .20 .50
John Lilley .10 .25
Don McSween .10 .25
Steve Rucchin .30 .75
David Sacco .10 .25
Joe Sacco .10 .25
Mikhail Shtalenkov .30 .75
Jim Thomson .10 .25
Oleg Tverdovsky .30 .75
David Williams .10 .25
Wild Wing (Mascot) .10 .25
Carl Karcher .01
(Sponsor Owner)
28 Happy Star .01
(Sponsor Logo)

1995-96 Ducks Team Issue

These five oversized (5" X 7") black and white photos pictured members of the '95-96 Mighty Ducks of Anaheim. The cards featured a posed head shot, with the player's name and a pair of team logos along the bottom. The backs were blank. The photos were unnumbered, and were listed below alphabetically. It's highly unlikely that the checklist was complete as listed below. Additional information would be appreciated and can be forwarded to Beckett Publications.

COMPLETE SET (5) 1.20 3.00
1 Bobby Dollas .20 .50
2 David Karpa .20 .50
3 Steve Rucchin .30 .75
4 Mikhail Shtalenkov .30 .75
5 Garry Valk .20 .50

1996-97 Ducks Team Issue

This unique 26-card set was produced by Up Front Sports and sponsored by Southland Micro Systems. The first twenty cards in the set followed the standard design of action photo on the front and stats on the back. Cards 21-24, however, were die-cut pop-up cards. Reports indicated that the Garry Valk destroyed or pulled since he was traded before the set's release. It's not known how many copies may still exist, but the card has been confirmed.

COMPLETE SET (26) 8.00 20.00
1 Mikhail Shtalenkov .20 .50
2 Bobby Dollas .16 .40
3 Roman Oksiuta .16 .40
4 Kevin Todd .16 .40
5 Ted Drury .16 .40
6 Joe Sacco .16 .40
7 Dmitri Mironov .20 .50
8 Warren Rychel .20 .50
10 Shawn Antoski .16 .40
11 Steve Rucchin .20 .50
12 Ken Baumgartner .16 .40
13 Brian Bellows .16 .40
14 Nikolai Tsulygin .16 .40
15 Jason Marshall .16 .40
16 Darren Van Impe .16 .40
17 David Karpa .16 .40
18 Wild Wing .04 .10
19 J.F. Jomphe .16 .40
20 Sean Pronger .16 .40
21 Guy Hebert .60 1.50
22 Paul Kariya 2.40 6.00
23 Jari Kurri .80 2.00
24 Teemu Selanne 1.60 4.00
25 Southland .01
26 Southland .01
27 Ron Wilson CO .10 .25

2002-03 Ducks Team Issue

The singles in this odd size set were distributed at promotional events. The set listing below is not complete. If you can confirm others, please contact us at hockeymag@beckett.com.

COMPLETE SET (?)
1 Adam Oates .40 1.00
1 Dan Bylsma .20 .50
2 J-S Giguere 1.25 3.00
3 Paul Kariya 1.25 3.00
4 Ruslan Salei .20 .50
5 Petr Sykora .20 .50
6 Vitaly Vishnevski .20 .50

2005-06 Ducks Team Issue

COMPLETE SET (22) 6.00 15.00
1 Kip Brennan .20 .50
2 Ilya Bryzgalov .30 .75
3 Keith Carney .20 .50
4 Joe DiPenta .30 .75
5 Todd Fedoruk .20 .50
6 Ryan Getzlaf .75 2.00
7 Jean-Sebastien Giguere .40 1.00
8 Jonathan Hedstrom .20 .50
9 Joffrey Lupul .40 1.00
10 Jason Marshall .20 .50
11 Andy McDonald .20 .50
12 Travis Moen .20 .50
13 Rob Niedermayer .20 .50
14 Scott Niedermayer .20 .50
15 Sandis Ozolinsh .20 .50
16 Samuel Pahlsson .20 .50
17 Corey Perry .75 2.00
18 Ruslan Salei .20 .50
19 Teemu Selanne .75 2.00
20 Petr Sykora .20 .50
21 Vitali Vishnevsky .20 .50
22 Randy Carlyle HC .02 .10

1992-93 Durivage Panini

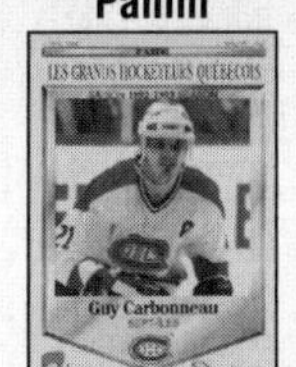
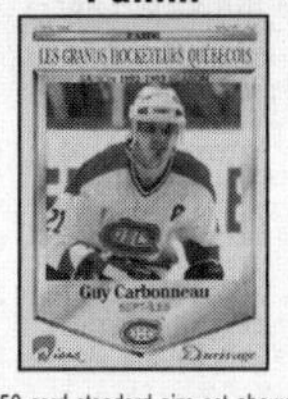

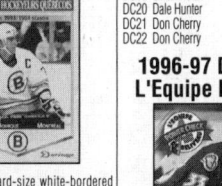

This 50-card standard-size set showcased hockey stars who were born in Quebec. The cards, which were inserted in loaves of bread, featured color, action player photos set on a gold plaque design. The player's name appeared below the photo on the plaque. The words "Les Grands Hockeyeurs Quebecois" were printed in red at the top of the card. The backs had a ghosted black-and-white player photo with biography and career summary printed in French over the picture. The Patrick Roy signed card was randomly inserted. It is believed he signed 500 copies, although that has not been confirmed.

COMPLETE SET (50) 8.00 20.00
1 Guy Carbonneau .10 .25
2 Lucien Deblois .08 .20
3 Benoit Hogue .08 .20
4 Steve Kasper .08 .20
5 Mike Krushelnyski .08 .20
6 Claude Lapointe .08 .20
7 Stephan Lebeau .08 .20
8 Mario Lemieux 1.60 4.00
9 Stephane Morin .08 .20
10 Denis Savard .10 .25
11 Pierre Turgeon .10 .25
12 Kevin Dineen .08 .20
13 Gord Donnelly .08 .20
14 Claude Lemieux .10 .25
15 Jocelyn Lemieux .08 .20
16 Daniel Marois .08 .20
17 Scott Mellanby .08 .20
18 Stephane Richer .10 .25
19 Benoit Brunet .10 .25
20 Vincent Damphousse .10 .25
21 Gilbert Dionne .10 .25
22 Gaetan Duchesne .08 .20
23 Bob Errey .08 .20
24 Michel Goulet .10 .25
25 Mike Hough .08 .20
26 Sergio Momesso .08 .20
27 Mario Roberge .08 .20
28 Luc Robitaille .12 .30
29 Sylvain Turgeon .08 .20
30 Marc Bergevin .08 .20
31 Ray Bourque .50 1.25
32 Patrice Brisebois .08 .20
33 Jeff Chychrun .08 .20
34 Sylvain Cote .08 .20
35 J.J. Daigneault .08 .20
36 Eric Desjardins .10 .25
37 Gord Dineen .08 .20
38 Steve Duchesne .08 .20
39 Donald Dufresne .08 .20
40 Steven Finn .08 .20
41 Garry Galley .08 .20
42 Kevin Lowe .10 .25
43 Michel Petit .08 .20
44 Normand Rochefort .08 .20
45 Randy Velischek .08 .20
46 Jacques Cloutier .10 .25
47 Stephane Fiset .12 .30
48 Rejean Lemelin .10 .25
49 Andre Racicot .10 .25
50 Patrick Roy 3.20 8.00
NNO Patrick Roy AU 50.00 125.00

1993-94 Durivage Score

These 50 standard-size white-bordered cards featured color player action shots "mounted" on golden plaque designs. The player's name and hometown appeared within a black stripe below the photo. All the players in the set were from the province of Quebec. His team's logo appeared further below. The white-bordered back carried a color player action photo on the right and, on the left, bilingual biography and statistics. Cards 1-6 belonged to a "Special Edition" subset and had gold-foil highlights on their fronts. The cards were numbered on the back as "X of 50."

COMPLETE SET (50) 12.00 30.00
1 Alexandre Daigle .30 .75
2 Pierre Sevigny .12 .30
3 Jocelyn Thibault .50 1.25
4 Philippe Boucher .12 .30
5 Martin Brodeur 1.60 4.00
New Jers
6 Martin Lapointe .40 1.00
7 Patrice Brisebois .40 1.00
8 Benoit Brunet .12 .30
9 Guy Carbonneau .40 1.00
10 Jean-Jacques Daigneault .12 .30
11 Vincent Damphousse .40 1.00
12 Eric Desjardins .40 1.00
13 Gilbert Dionne .12 .30
14 Stephan Lebeau .40 1.00
15 Andre Racicot .40 1.00
16 Mario Roberge .12 .30
17 Patrick Roy 3.20 8.00
18 Jacques Cloutier .40 1.00
19 Alain Cote .12 .30
20 Steven Finn .12 .30
21 Stephane Fiset .30 .75
22 Martin Gelinas .12 .30
23 Reggie Savage .12 .30
24 Claude Lapointe .12 .30
25 Denis Savard .50 1.25
26 Ray Bourque .80 2.00
27 Joe Juneau .30 .75
28 Ron Stern .12 .30
29 Benoit Hogue .40 1.00
30 Pierre Turgeon .50 1.25
31 Mike Krushelnyski .12 .30
32 Felix Potvin .50 1.25
33 Sergio Momesso .12 .30
34 Yves Racine .12 .30
35 Sylvain Cote .12 .30
36 Sylvain Turgeon .12 .30
37 Kevin Dineen .40 1.00
38 Garry Galley .40 1.00
39 Dominic Roussel .40 1.00
40 Gaetan Duchesne .12 .30
41 Luc Robitaille .50 1.25
42 Michel Goulet .50 1.25
43 Jocelyn Lemieux .12 .30
44 Stephane Matteau .12 .30
45 Mike Hough .12 .30
46 Scott Mellanby .50 1.25
47 Claude Lemieux .30 .75
48 Stephane Richer .50 1.25
49 Jimmy Waite .12 .30
50 Patrick Poulin .40 1.00
NNO Patrick Roy AU 80.00 200.00
NNO Jocelyn Thibault AU 40.00 100.00

1996-97 Duracell All-Cherry Team

This 22-card set was available in three-card packs with the purchase of specially-marked packages of Duracell batteries in English-speaking Canada and was produced by Pinnacle Brands. The players featured in the set were chosen by CBC commentator and fashion doyenne Don Cherry. The card fronts featured a color action photo, along with manufacturer logos. The backs included a brief resume. Interestingly, the player's stats could only be revealed by pressing a trio of heat-sensitive strips. There were rumored to be short printed cards in the set, but no confirmation of this has become available.

COMPLETE SET (22) 8.00 20.00
DC1 Paul Coffey .30 .75
DC2 Lyle Odelein .10 .25
DC3 Joe Sakic .50 1.25
DC4 Curtis Joseph .40 1.00
DC5 Brett Hull .40 1.00
DC6 Eric Lindros .60 1.50
DC7 Doug Gilmour .30 .75
DC8 Chris Chelios .30 .75
DC9 Marty McSorley .10 .25
DC10 Kirk Muller .10 .25
DC11 Trevor Linden .10 .25
DC12 Brendan Shanahan .60 1.50
DC13 Tie Domi .20 .50
DC14 Rick Tocchet .10 .25
DC15 Steve Yzerman 1.20 3.00
DC16 Scott Stevens .10 .25
DC17 Patrick Roy 1.60 4.00
DC18 Keith Tkachuk .30 .75
DC19 Owen Nolan .20 .50
DC20 Dale Hunter .10 .25
DC21 Don Cherry .40 1.00
DC22 Don Cherry .40 1.00

1996-97 Duracell L'Equipe Beliveau

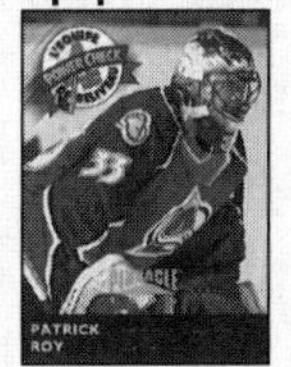

This 22-card set was available in 3-card packs with specially marked packages of Duracell batteries in French-speaking Canada. The set was produced by Pinnacle. The design was the same as that of the All-Cherry team cards, save for the different logo in the upper left corner of the front; also the text on the back of these cards is French. As the team was selected by former Habs great Jean Beliveau, the player composition was slightly different, with a notable increase in the francophone content. As this series was produced in more limited quantities than the Cherry set, the French version of the singles which appear in both sets carry a slight premium.

COMPLETE SET (22) 14.00 35.00
JB1 Paul Coffey .40 1.00
JB2 Lyle Odelein .10 .25
JB3 Joe Sakic 1.00 2.50
JB4 Eric Daze .30 .75
JB5 Brett Hull .80 2.00
JB6 Martin Brodeur 1.20 3.00
JB7 Doug Gilmour .60 1.50
JB8 Peter Forsberg 1.20 3.00
JB9 Mike Gartner .20 .50
JB10 Saku Koivu .60 1.50
JB11 Trevor Linden .10 .25
JB12 Felix Potvin .40 1.00
JB13 Mats Sundin .40 1.00
JB14 Pierre Turgeon .20 .50
JB15 Vincent Damphousse .10 .25
JB16 Scott Stevens .10 .25
JB17 Patrick Roy 2.00 5.00
JB18 Keith Tkachuk .60 1.50
JB19 Ray Bourque .80 2.00
JB20 Paul Kariya 1.20 3.00
JB21 Jean Beliveau .40 1.00
JB22 Jean Beliveau .40 1.00

2003-04 Duracell

These cards were issued as a mail-in premium with the purchase of Duracell batteries in Canada.

COMPLETE SET (15) 20.00
1 Jean-Sebastien Giguere .40 1.00
2 Patrick Lalime .20 .50
3 Curtis Joseph .75 2.00
4 Marty Turco .40 1.00
5 Ed Belfour .75 2.00
6 Sean Burke .20 .50
7 Roberto Luongo .75 2.00
8 Jose Theodore .75 2.00
9 Olaf Kolzig .20 .50
10 Martin Brodeur 1.25 3.00
11 Mike Richter .20 .50
12 Dan Blackburn .20 .50
13 Patrick Roy 1.50 4.00
14 Dwayne Roloson .20 .50
15 Dan Cloutier .20 .50

1994 EA Sports

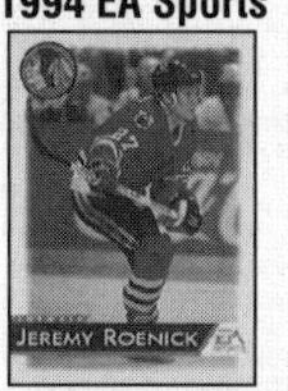

This 225-card boxed set was issued by Electronic Arts Sports as a premium with packages of its NHLPA '94 video game. Two cards were included with each game. In addition, an order form for a complete set was found inside the game box; the original price was 24.95 direct. The fronts were white with action player photos that had airbrushed edges. The team logo appeared in the upper left corner with the player's name printed on a black bar across the bottom edge. The player's position was on a team color-coded stripe above the player's name. The borderless backs displayed a head shot in the upper left corner with player performance rating below. A brief biography and career summary appeared to the right.

COMPLETE SET (225) 30.00 75.00
1 Alexei Kasatonov .02 .05
2 Randy Ladouceur .02 .05
3 Terry Yake .02 .05
4 Troy Loney .02 .05
5 Anatoli Semenov .02 .05
6 Guy Hebert .06 .15
7 Ray Bourque 1.20 3.00
8 Don Sweeney .02 .05
9 Adam Oates .20 .50
10 Joe Juneau .16 .40
11 Cam Neely .40 1.00
12 Andy Moog .10 .25
13 Doug Bodger .02 .05
14 Petr Svoboda .02 .05
15 Pat LaFontaine .20 .50
16 Dale Hawerchuk .10 .25
17 Alexander Mogilny .20 .50
18 Grant Fuhr .10 .25
19 Gary Suter .02 .05
20 Al MacInnis .06 .15
21 Joe Nieuwendyk .06 .15
22 Gary Roberts .06 .15
23 Theo Fleury .10 .25
24 Mike Vernon .06 .15
25 Chris Chelios .40 1.00
26 Steve Smith .02 .05
27 Jeremy Roenick .60 1.50
28 Michel Goulet .06 .15
29 Steve Larmer .06 .15
30 Ed Belfour .60 1.50
31 Mark Tinordi .02 .05
32 Tommy Sjodin .02 .05
33 Mike Modano .80 2.00
34 Dave Gagner .06 .15
35 Russ Courtnall .06 .15
36 Jon Casey .02 .05
37 Paul Coffey .40 1.00
38 Steve Chiasson .02 .05
39 Steve Yzerman 2.40 6.00
40 Sergei Fedorov 1.20 3.00
41 Dino Ciccarelli .06 .15
42 Tim Cheveldae .06 .15
43 Dave Manson .02 .05
44 Igor Kravchuk .02 .05
45 Doug Weight .10 .25
46 Shayne Corson .06 .15
47 Petr Klima .02 .05
48 Bill Ranford .06 .15
49 Joe Cirella .02 .05
50 Gord Murphy .02 .05
51 Brian Skrudland .02 .05
52 Andrei Lomakin .02 .05
53 Scott Mellanby .02 .05
54 John Vanbiesbrouck .40 1.00
55 Zarley Zalapski .02 .05
56 Eric Weinrich .02 .05
57 Andrew Cassels .02 .05
58 Geoff Sanderson .06 .15
59 Pat Verbeek .06 .15
60 Sean Burke .06 .15
61 Rob Blake .06 .15
62 Marty McSorley .06 .15
63 Wayne Gretzky 4.00 10.00
64 Luc Robitaille .20 .50
65 Tomas Sandstrom .06 .15
66 Kelly Hrudey .06 .15
67 Eric Desjardins .06 .15
68 Mathieu Schneider .06 .15
69 Kirk Muller .06 .15
70 Vincent Damphousse .10 .25
71 Brian Bellows .02 .05
72 Patrick Roy 3.20 8.00
73 Scott Stevens .06 .15
74 Slava Fetisov .06 .15
75 Alexander Semak .02 .05
76 Stephane Richer .06 .15
77 Claude Lemieux .10 .25
78 Chris Terreri .06 .15
79 Vladimir Malakhov .02 .05
80 Darius Kasparaitis .02 .05
81 Pierre Turgeon .20 .50
82 Steve Thomas .06 .15
83 Benoit Hogue .02 .05
84 Glenn Healy .06 .15
85 Brian Leetch .40 1.00
86 James Patrick .02 .05
87 Mark Messier .80 2.00
88 Designer Tip .02 .05
89 Mike Gartner .06 .15
90 Mike Richter .40 1.00
91 Norm Maciver .02 .05
92 Brad Shaw .02 .05
93 Jamie Baker .02 .05
94 Sylvain Turgeon .02 .05
95 Bob Kudelski .02 .05
96 Peter Sidorkiewicz .02 .05
97 Garry Galley .02 .05
98 Dimitri Yushkevich .02 .05
99 Eric Lindros 1.60 4.00
100 Rod Brind'Amour .06 .15
101 Mark Recchi .20 .50
102 Tommy Soderstrom .02 .05
103 Larry Murphy .10 .25
104 Ulf Samuelsson .06 .15
105 Mario Lemieux 3.20 8.00
106 Kevin Stevens .06 .15
107 Jaromir Jagr 2.00 5.00
108 Tom Barrasso .10 .25
109 Steve Duchesne .06 .15
110 Curtis Leschyshyn .02 .05
111 Mats Sundin .40 1.00
112 Joe Sakic 1.20 3.00
113 Owen Nolan .20 .50
114 Ron Hextall .10 .25
115 Doug Wilson .06 .15
116 Neil Wilkinson .02 .05
117 Kelly Kisio .02 .05
118 Johan Garpenlov .02 .05
119 Pat Falloon .06 .15
120 Arturs Irbe .16 .40
121 Jeff Brown .06 .15
122 Garth Butcher .06 .15
123 Craig Janney .06 .15
124 Brendan Shanahan .80 2.00
125 Brett Hull .80 2.00
126 Curtis Joseph .80 2.00
127 Bob Beers .02 .05
128 Roman Hamrlik .10 .25
129 Brian Bradley .06 .15
130 Mikael Andersson .02 .05
131 Chris Kontos .02 .05
132 Wendell Young .02 .05
133 Todd Gill .02 .05
134 Dave Ellett .02 .05
135 Doug Gilmour .40 1.00
136 Dave Andreychuk .06 .15
137 Nikolai Borschevsky .02 .05
138 Felix Potvin .40 1.00
139 Jyrki Lumme .02 .05
140 Doug Lidster .02 .05
141 Cliff Ronning .06 .15
142 Geoff Courtnall .02 .05
143 Pavel Bure 1.60 4.00
144 Kirk McLean .06 .15
145 Phil Housley .06 .15
146 Teppo Numminen .02 .05
147 Alexei Zhamnov .06 .15
148 Thomas Steen .02 .05
149 Teemu Selanne 1.20 3.00
150 Bob Essensa .06 .15
151 Kevin Hatcher .02 .05
152 Al Iafrate .06 .15
153 Mike Ridley .02 .05
154 Dimitri Khristich .02 .05
155 Peter Bondra .10 .25
156 Don Beaupre .02 .05
157 All Stars East CL .06 .15
158 All Stars West CL .06 .15
159 Mighty Ducks Team CL .10 .25
160 Bruins Team CL .10 .25
161 Sabres Team CL .06 .15
162 Flames Team CL .06 .15
163 Blackhawks Team CL .10 .25
164 Red Wings Team CL .10 .25
165 Oilers Team CL .06 .15
166 Panthers Team CL .06 .15
167 Whalers Team CL .06 .15
168 Kings Team CL .10 .25
169 Stars Team CL .06 .15
170 Canadiens Team CL .10 .25
171 Devils Team CL .06 .15
172 Islanders Team CL .06 .15
173 Rangers Team CL .10 .25
174 Senators Team CL .06 .15
175 Flyers Team CL .06 .15
176 Penguins Team CL .06 .15
177 Nordiques Team CL .06 .15
178 Sharks Team CL .10 .25
179 Blues Team CL .06 .15
180 Lightning Team CL .06 .15
181 Leafs Team CL .10 .25
182 Canucks Team CL .06 .15
183 Capitals Team CL .06 .15
184 Jets Team CL .06 .15
185 Ray Bourque SL .10 .25
186 Chris Chelios SL .10 .25
187 Ed Belfour SL .40 1.00
188 Adam Oates SL .10 .25
189 Skill Leaders 1.60 4.00
Shot Accu
190 Al Iafrate SL .06 .15
191 Alexander Mogilny SL .20 .50
192 Wayne Gretzky SL 2.00 5.00
193 New Feature .02 .05
194 Derian Hatcher .02 .05
195 Dmitri Kvartalnov .02 .05
196 Randy Wood .02 .05
197 Gord Murphy .02 .05
198 New Feature .02 .05
199 Ducks/Panthers Team Logo .10 .25
200 Luc Robitaille .10 .25
201 Terry Yake .02 .05
202 Mark Fitzpatrick .02 .05
203 Brad Shaw .02 .05
204 NHL Logos .02 .05
205 Jyrki Lumme .02 .05
206 Peter Sidorkiewicz .02 .05
207 Gord Murphy .02 .05
208 Slava Fetisov .02 .05
209 Stephan LeBeau .02 .05
210 Gord Murphy .02 .05
211 Dominik Hasek 1.20 3.00
212 Cam Neely .40 1.00
213 Designer Tips .02 .05
214 Designer Tips .02 .05
215 Designer Tips .02 .05
216 Designer Tips .02 .05
217 Designer Tips .02 .05
218 Designer Tips .02 .05
219 Designer Tips .02 .05
220 Designer Tips .02 .05
221 Designer Tips .02 .05
222 Designer Tips .02 .05
223 Designer Tips .02 .05
224 Designer Tips .02 .05
225 Designer Tips .02 .05

2001 EA Sports

This 9-card set was inserted one-card-per-game in EA Sports' NHL 2002 video game and was produced by Upper Deck. A Gold parallel was also produced and inserted randomly. An autographed Mario Lemieux card has also been rumored to exist, but no verification of that has been made.

COMPLETE SET (9)
*GOLD: 2X TO 5 X BASIC CARD
1 Mario Lemieux 4.00 15.00
2 Mario Lemieux 4.00 15.00
3 Owen Nolan .40 1.00
4 Jere Lehtinen .08 1.00
5 Martin Rucinsky .20 .50
6 Chris Pronger .40 1.00
7 Markus Naslund .40 2.00
8 Peter Forsberg 1.60 6.00
9 Steve Yzerman 3.20 12.00

1962-63 El Producto Discs

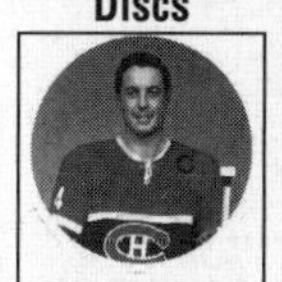

The six discs in this set measured approximately 3" in diameter. They were issued as a strip of six connected in a fragile manner and were in full color. The discs were unnumbered and checklisted below in alphabetical order. The set in unperforated form is valued 25 percent greater than the value below.

COMPLETE SET (6) 150.00 300.00
1 Jean Beliveau 30.00 60.00
2 Glenn Hall 25.00 50.00
3 Gordie Howe 75.00 150.00
4 Dave Keon 30.00 60.00
5 Frank Mahovlich 25.00 50.00
6 Henri Richard 25.00 50.00

1995-96 Emotion Promo Strip

This 6" by 3" strip was distributed by Skybox to introduce its Emotion line of cards. The front featured two cards of Jeremy Roenick of the Chicago Blackhawks: his basic Emotion issue and his X-Cited insert. They were identical to the regularly issued cards, save for the word sample found in the back upper right corner. They were separated by a white bar with the sponsor logo horizontally printed in gold and date cards premier in black.

1 Jeremy Roenick .40 1.00

1995-96 Emotion

This 200-card high end set was released in 8-card packs with an SRP of $4.99. The set was distinguished by its use of an "emotional" term to describe the action on the card face. The Jeremy Roenick SkyMotion card was obtainable in exchange for three wrappers and $25. The unique card featured three seconds of actual game footage. The offer for this card expired on June 30, 1996.

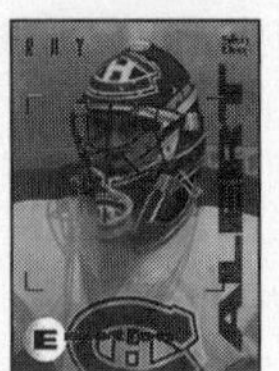

COMPLETE SET (200) 20.00 40.00
1 Bobby Dollas .05 .15
2 Guy Hebert .10 .30
3 Paul Kariya .20 .50
4 Oleg Tverdovsky .05 .15
5 Shaun Van Allen .05 .15
6 Ray Bourque .30 .75
7 Al Iafrate .10 .30
8 Blaine Lacher .10 .30
9 Joe Mullen .10 .30
10 Cam Neely .20 .50
11 Adam Oates .10 .30
12 Kevin Stevens .05 .15
13 Don Sweeney .05 .15
14 Donald Audette .05 .15
15 Garry Galley .05 .15
16 Dominik Hasek .40 1.00
17 Brian Holzinger RC .20 .50
18 Pat LaFontaine .20 .50
19 Alexei Zhitnik .05 .15
20 Steve Chiasson .05 .15
21 Theo Fleury .05 .15
22 Phil Housley .10 .30
23 Trevor Kidd .10 .30
24 Joe Nieuwendyk .10 .30
25 Gary Roberts .05 .15
26 Zarley Zalapski .05 .15
27 Ed Belfour .20 .50
28 Chris Chelios .20 .50
29 Sergei Krivokrasov .05 .15
30 Joe Murphy .05 .15
31 Bernie Nicholls .05 .15
32 Patrick Poulin .05 .15
33 Jeremy Roenick .25 .60
34 Gary Suter .05 .15
35 Corbet .05 .15
36 Peter Forsberg .50 1.25
37 Valeri Kamensky .10 .30
38 Uwe Krupp .05 .15
39 Curtis Leschyshyn .05 .15
40 Owen Nolan .10 .30
41 Mike Ricci .10 .30
42 Joe Sakic .40 1.00
43 Jocelyn Thibault .20 .50
44 Bob Bassen .05 .15
45 Dave Gagner .05 .15
46 Todd Harvey .10 .30
47 Derian Hatcher .05 .15
48 Kevin Hatcher .05 .15
49 Mike Modano .30 .75
50 Andy Moog .20 .50
51 Dino Ciccarelli .10 .30
52 Paul Coffey .20 .50
53 Sergei Fedorov .30 .75
54 Vladimir Konstantinov .10 .30
55 Slava Kozlov .10 .30
56 Nicklas Lidstrom .20 .50
57 Keith Primeau .05 .15
58 Ray Sheppard .05 .15
59 Mike Vernon .10 .30
60 Steve Yzerman 1.00 2.50
61 Jason Arnott .05 .15
62 Curtis Joseph .20 .50
63 Igor Kravchuk .05 .15
64 Todd Marchant .05 .15
65 David Oliver .05 .15
66 Bill Ranford .10 .30
67 Doug Weight .10 .30
68 Stu Barnes .05 .15
69 Jesse Belanger .05 .15
70 Gord Murphy .05 .15
71 Magnus Svensson RC .05 .15
72 John Vanbiesbrouck .10 .30
73 Sean Burke .10 .30
74 Andrew Cassels .05 .15
75 Frantisek Kucera .05 .15
76 Andrei Nikolishin .05 .15
77 Geoff Sanderson .05 .15
78 Brendan Shanahan .20 .50
79 Darren Turcotte .05 .15
80 Rob Blake .10 .30
81 Wayne Gretzky 1.50 4.00
82 Dimitri Khristich .05 .15
83 Jari Kurri .20 .50
84 Jamie Storr .10 .30
85 Darryl Sydor .10 .30
86 Rick Tocchet .10 .30
87 Vincent Damphousse .05 .15
88 Vladimir Malakhov .05 .15
89 Stephane Quintal .05 .15
90 Mark Recchi .10 .30
91 Patrick Roy 1.00 2.50
92 Brian Savage .05 .15
93 Pierre Turgeon .10 .30
94 Martin Brodeur .50 1.25
95 Neal Broten .10 .30
96 Shawn Chambers .05 .15
97 Claude Lemieux .05 .15
98 John MacLean .10 .30
99 Randy McKay .05 .15
100 Scott Niedermayer .05 .15
101 Stephane Richer .10 .30
102 Scott Stevens .10 .30
103 Todd Bertuzzi RC 1.00 2.50
104 Patrick Flatley .05 .15
105 Brett Lindros .05 .15
106 Kirk Muller .05 .15
107 Tommy Salo RC .75 2.00
108 Mathieu Schneider .05 .15
109 Alexander Semak .05 .15
110 Dennis Vaske .05 .15
111 Ray Ferraro .05 .15
112 Adam Graves .05 .15
113 Alexei Kovalev .05 .15
114 Steve Larmer .10 .30
115 Brian Leetch .10 .30
116 Mark Messier .20 .50
117 Mike Richter .20 .50
118 Luc Robitaille .10 .30
119 Ulf Samuelsson .05 .15
120 Pat Verbeek .05 .15
121 Don Beaupre .10 .30
122 Radek Bonk .05 .15
123 Alexandre Daigle .05 .15
124 Steve Duchesne .05 .15
125 Steve Larouche .05 .15
126 Dan Quinn .05 .15
127 Martin Straka .05 .15
128 Alexei Yashin .05 .15
129 Rod Brind'Amour .10 .30
130 Eric Desjardins .10 .30
131 Ron Hextall .10 .30
132 John LeClair .20 .50
133 Eric Lindros .20 .50
134 Mikael Renberg .10 .30
135 Chris Therien .05 .15
136 Ron Francis .10 .30
137 Jaromir Jagr .30 .75
138 Mario Lemieux 1.00 2.50
139 Dmitri Mironov .05 .15
140 Petr Nedved .10 .30
141 Tomas Sandstrom .05 .15
142 Bryan Smolinski .05 .15
143 Ken Wregget .10 .30
144 Sergei Zubov .05 .15
145 Shayne Corson .05 .15
146 Geoff Courtnall .05 .15
147 Dale Hawerchuk .20 .50
148 Brett Hull .25 .60
149 Ian Laperriere .05 .15
150 Al MacInnis .10 .30
151 Chris Pronger .20 .50
152 David Roberts .05 .15
153 Esa Tikkanen .05 .15
154 Ulf Dahlen .05 .15
155 Jeff Friesen .05 .15
156 Arturs Irbe .10 .30
157 Craig Janney .05 .15
158 Sergei Makarov .05 .15
159 Sandis Ozolinsh .05 .15
160 Mike Rathje .05 .15
161 Ray Whitney .10 .30
162 Brian Bradley .05 .15
163 Chris Gratton .05 .15
164 Roman Hamrlik .10 .30
165 Petr Klima .05 .15
166 Daren Puppa .10 .30
167 Paul Ysebaert .05 .15
168 Dave Andreychuk .10 .30
169 Mike Gartner .10 .30
170 Todd Gill .05 .15
171 Doug Gilmour .10 .30
172 Kenny Jonsson .05 .15
173 Larry Murphy .10 .30
174 Felix Potvin .20 .50
175 Mats Sundin .20 .50
176 Josef Beranek .05 .15
177 Jeff Brown .05 .15
178 Pavel Bure .20 .50
179 Russ Courtnall .05 .15
180 Trevor Linden .10 .30
181 Kirk McLean .10 .30
182 Alexander Mogilny .10 .30
183 Roman Oksiuta .05 .15
184 Mike Ridley .05 .15
185 Jason Allison .05 .15
186 Jim Carey .10 .30
187 Sergei Gonchar .05 .15
188 Dale Hunter .10 .30
189 Calle Johansson .05 .15
190 Joe Juneau .05 .15
191 Joe Reekie .05 .15
192 Nelson Emerson .05 .15
193 Nikolai Khabibulin .10 .30
194 Dave Manson .05 .15
195 Teppo Numminen .05 .15
196 Teemu Selanne .20 .50
197 Keith Tkachuk .20 .50
198 Alexei Zhamnov .10 .30
199 Checklist #1 .05 .15
200 Checklist #2 .05 .15
NNO J.Roenick SkyMotion 15.00 30.00
NNO Roenick SkyMotion Exch. 2.50 5.00

1995-96 Emotion generatioNext

This ten-card set took a look at those players thought to be the stars of tomorrow. The cards, which featured a player bust over a fiery metallic foil background were inserted at a rate of 1:10 packs. The cards were numbered "X of 10" on the back.

COMPLETE SET (10) 8.00 15.00
1 Brian Holzinger 1.00 2.50
2 Eric Daze .60 1.50
3 Jason Bonsignore .30 .75
4 Jamie Storr .60 1.50
5 Tommy Salo 2.00 5.00
6 Brendan Witt .30 .75
7 Saku Koivu 1.00 2.50
8 Todd Bertuzzi 3.00 8.00
9 Ed Jovanovski .30 .75
10 Chad Kilger .30 .75

1995-96 Emotion Ntense Power

This ten-card set highlighted the game's top power forwards. Utilizing a design element similar to the previous set using this name, the cards featured a cut-out player photo over a swirling foil background. The cards were randomly inserted 1:30 packs, and were numbered "X of 10" on the back.

COMPLETE SET (10) 10.00 20.00

1 Cam Neely 1.50 4.00
2 Keith Primeau .50 1.25
3 Mark Messier 1.50 4.00
4 Eric Lindros 1.50 4.00
5 Mikael Renberg 1.00 2.50
6 Owen Nolan 1.00 2.50
7 Brendan Shanahan 1.50 4.00
8 Kevin Stevens .50 1.25
9 Keith Tkachuk 1.50 4.00
10 Rick Tocchet 1.00 2.50

1995-96 Emotion Xcel

This ten-card set featured the top ten players in the league as chosen by the Fleer staff. The cards were issued randomly in packs at the rate of 1:72 packs. It was apparent, however, that a significant quantity of these cards entered the market through non-pack distribution, making them significantly easier to acquire than the long pack odds would suggest. This additional supply dampened the demand -- and hence, the prices -- for these cards.

COMPLETE SET (10) 30.00 60.00
1 Adam Oates .75 2.00
2 Jeremy Roenick 2.00 5.00
3 Sergei Fedorov 2.00 5.00
4 Wayne Gretzky 10.00 25.00
5 Alexei Yashin .60 1.50
6 Eric Lindros 1.25 3.00
7 Ron Francis .75 2.00
8 Mario Lemieux 8.00 20.00
9 Joe Sakic 3.00 8.00
10 Alexei Zhamnov .60 1.50

1995-96 Emotion Xcited

This twenty-card set was the easiest pull from this issue, randomly inserted 1:3 packs. The set included many of the top offensive players in the game.

COMPLETE SET (20) 15.00 30.00
1 Theo Fleury .20 .50
2 Jeremy Roenick .75 2.00
3 Mike Modano 1.00 2.50
4 Sergei Fedorov 1.00 2.50
5 Wayne Gretzky 5.00 12.00
6 Brian Leetch .40 1.00
7 Alexei Yashin .20 .50
8 Brett Hull .75 2.00
9 Jaromir Jagr 1.00 2.50
10 Mario Lemieux 3.00 8.00
11 Ron Francis .40 1.00
12 Keith Primeau .20 .50
13 Joe Sakic 1.25 3.00
14 Peter Forsberg 1.50 4.00
15 Paul Kariya .60 1.50
16 Pavel Bure .60 1.50
17 Alexei Zhamnov .40 1.00
18 Martin Brodeur 1.50 4.00
19 Jim Carey .40 1.00
20 Chris Chelios .60 1.50

1992-93 Enor Mark Messier

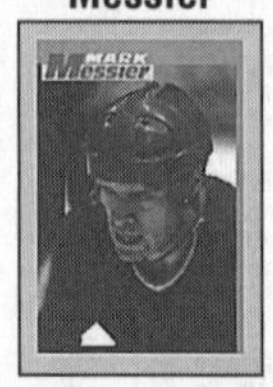

One card from this ten-card standard-size set was included in each specially marked package of Enor Progard Plus sports card pages. The cards featured color player photos with silver borders. A red stripe that ran along the right edge and top of the photo accented the card face and provided a backdrop for the player's name, which was printed in white and blue. The horizontal back showed a close-up player photo that overlaped a red border stripe similar to the one on the front and a pale blue panel. The red stripe contained the player's name. The blue panel containsedplayer information. A black vertical bar ran along the left edge of the panel and contained biographical information.

COMPLETE SET (10) 2.00 5.00
COMMON MESSIER (1-10) .20 .50

1969-73 Equitable Sports Hall of Fame

Little is known about these miniature prints beyond the confirmed checklist. Additional information can be forwarded to hockeymag@beckett.com.

COMPLETE SET (6) 62.50 125.00
1 Phil Esposito 10.00 20.00
2 Bernie Geoffrion 10.00 20.00
3 Gordie Howe 25.00 50.00
4 Ching Johnson 7.50 15.00
5 Stan Mikita 10.00 20.00
6 Maurice Richard 12.50 25.00

1970-71 Esso Power Players

The 1970-71 Esso Power Players set included 252 color stamps measuring approximately 1 1/2" by 2". The stamps were issued in six-stamp sheets and given away free with a minimum purchase of $3 of Esso gasoline. There were 18 stamps for each of the 14 teams then in the NHL. The stamps were unnumbered except for jersey (uniform) number. The set was issued with an album, which could be found in either a soft or hard bound version. The hard cover album supposedly had extra pages with additional players. The stamps and albums were available in both French and English language versions. The set was numbered below numerically within each team as follows: Montreal Canadiens (1-18), Toronto Maple Leafs (19-36), Vancouver Canucks (37-54), Boston Bruins (55-72), Buffalo Sabres (73-90), California Golden Seals (91-108), Chicago Blackhawks (109-126), Detroit Red Wings (127-144), Los Angeles Kings (145-162), Minnesota North Stars (163-180), New York Rangers (181-198), Philadelphia Flyers (199-216), Pittsburgh Penguins (217-234), and St. Louis Blues (235-252). Supposedly there were 59 stamps which are tougher to find than the others. The short-printed stamps were apparently those players who were pre-printed into the soft-cover album and hence not included in the first stamp printing.

COMPLETE SET (252) 125.00 250.00
1 Rogatien Vachon 1 1.50 3.00
2 Jacques Laperriere 2 .38 .75
3 J.C. Tremblay 3 .25 .50
4 Jean Beliveau 4 4.00 8.00
5 Guy Lapointe 5 .50 1.00
6 Fran Huck 6 .20 .40
7 Bill Collins 10 .20 .40
8 Marc Tardif 11 .25 .50
9 Yvan Cournoyer 12 .75 1.50
10 Claude Larose 15 .20 .40
11 Henri Richard 16 2.00 4.00
12 Serge Savard 18 .38 .75
13 Terry Harper 19 .25 .50
14 Pete Mahovlich 20 .38 .75
15 John Ferguson 22 .50 1.00
16 Mickey Redmond 24 .63 1.25
17 Jacques Lemaire 25 .63 1.25
18 Phil Myre 30 .38 .75
19 Jacques Plante 1 4.00 8.00
20 Rick Ley 2 .25 .50
21 Mike Pelyk 4 .20 .40
22 Ron Ellis 6 .25 .50
23 Jim Dorey 8 .20 .40
24 Norm Ullman 9 1.00 2.00
25 Guy Trottier 11 .20 .40
26 Jim Harrison 12 .20 .40
27 Dave Keon 14 1.00 2.00
28 Mike Walton 16 .25 .50
29 Jim McKenny 18 .20 .40
30 Paul Henderson 19 .50 1.00
31 Garry Monahan 20 SP .50 1.00
32 Bob Baun 21 .38 .75
33 Bill MacMillan 23 .20 .40
34 Brian Glennie 24 .20 .40
35 Darryl Sittler 27 5.00 10.00
36 Bruce Gamble 30 .50 1.00
37 Charlie Hodge 1 .63 1.25
38 Gary Doak 2 .20 .40
39 Pat Quinn 3 .38 .75
40 Barry Wilkins 4 .20 .40
41 Darryl Sly 5 SP .50 1.00
42 Marc Reaume 6 .20 .40
43 Andre Boudrias 7 .20 .40
44 Danny Johnson 8 .20 .40
45 Ray Cullen 10 SP .50 1.00
46 Wayne Maki 11 .20 .40
47 Mike Corrigan 12 .20 .40
48 Rosaire Paiement 15 .20 .40
49 Paul Popiel 18 SP .50 1.00
50 Dale Tallon 19 .25 .50
51 Murray Hall 23 SP .50 1.00
52 Len Lunde 24 .20 .40
53 Orland Kurtenbach 25 .25 .50
54 Dunc Wilson 30 SP .50 1.00
55 Ed Johnston 1 .50 1.00
56 Bobby Orr 4 12.50 25.00
57 Ted Green 6 .25 .50
58 Phil Esposito 7 2.50 5.00
59 Ken Hodge 8 .38 .75
60 Johnny Bucyk 9 1.00 2.00
61 Rick Smith 10 SP .50 1.00
62 Wayne Carleton 11 SP .50 1.00
63 Wayne Cashman 12 SP .75 1.50
64 Garnet Bailey 14 .20 .40
65 Derek Sanderson 16 2.00 4.00
66 Fred Stanfield 17 SP .50 1.00
67 Ed Westfall 18 .25 .50
68 John McKenzie 19 .20 .40
69 Dallas Smith 20 .20 .40
70 Don Marcotte 21 .20 .40
71 Don Awrey 26 SP .50 1.00
72 Gerry Cheevers 30 1.50 3.00
73 Roger Crozier 1 .75 1.50
74 Jim Watson 2 .25 .50
75 Tracy Pratt 3 .20 .40
76 Doug Barrie 5 SP .50 1.00
77 Al Hamilton 6 .25 .50
78 Cliff Schmautz 7 SP .50 1.00
79 Reg Fleming 9 .20 .40
80 Phil Goyette 10 .20 .40
81 Gilbert Perreault 11 2.50 5.00
82 Skip Krake 12 .20 .40
83 Gerry Meehan 15 .25 .50
84 Ron Anderson 16 .20 .40
85 Floyd Smith 17 SP .50 1.00
86 Steve Atkinson 19 .20 .40
87 Paul Andrea 21 SP .50 1.00
88 Don Marshall 22 .20 .40
89 Eddie Shack 23 SP 1.50 3.00
90 Larry Keenan 26 .20 .40
91 Gary Smith 1 .50 1.00
92 Doug Roberts 2 .20 .40
93 Harry Howell 3 .63 1.25
94 Wayne Muloin 4 .20 .40
95 Carol Vadnais 5 .20 .40
96 Dick Mattiussi 6 .20 .40
97 Earl Ingarfield 7 .20 .40
98 Gerry Ehman 8 .20 .40
99 Bill Hicke 9 .20 .40
100 Ted Hampson 10 .20 .40
101 Gary Jarrett 12 .20 .40
102 Joe Hardy 14 SP .50 1.00
103 Tony Featherstone 16 SP .50 1.00
104 Gary Croteau 18 .20 .40
105 Ernie Hicke 20 SP .50 1.00
106 Ron Stackhouse 21 .20 .40
107 Dennis Hextall 22 SP .75 1.50
108 Bob Sneddon 30 SP .50 1.00
109 Gerry Desjardins 1 SP .75 1.50
110 Bill White 2 .25 .50
111 Keith Magnuson 3 .25 .50
112 Doug Jarrett 4 SP .50 1.00
113 Lou Angotti 6 .20 .40
114 Pit Martin 7 .25 .50
115 Jim Pappin 8 .20 .40
116 Bobby Hull 9 5.00 10.00
117 Dennis Hull 10 SP 1.00 2.00
118 Doug Mohns 11 .25 .50
119 Pat Stapleton 12 .25 .50
120 Bryan Campbell 14 SP .50 1.00
121 Eric Nesterenko 15 .25 .50
122 Chico Maki 16 .25 .50
123 Gerry Pinder 18 .25 .50
124 Cliff Koroll 20 .20 .40
125 Stan Mikita 21 3.00 6.00
126 Tony Esposito 35 3.00 6.00
127 Jim Rutherford 1 SP 1.00 2.00
128 Gary Bergman 2 .25 .50
129 Dale Rolfe 3 .20 .40
130 Larry Brown 4 SP .50 1.00
131 Serge Lajeunesse 5 .20 .40
132 Garry Unger 7 .38 .75
133 Tom Webster 8 .25 .50
134 Gordie Howe 9 7.50 15.00
135 Alex Delvecchio 10 1.00 2.00
136 Don Luce 11 SP .50 1.00
137 Bruce MacGregor 12 .25 .50
138 Nick Libett 14 .25 .50
139 Al Karlander 15 .20 .40
140 Ron Harris 16 .20 .40
141 Wayne Connelly 17 SP .50 1.00
142 Billy Dea 21 SP .50 1.00
143 Frank Mahovlich 27 2.00 4.00
144 Roy Edwards 30 .38 .75
145 Jack Norris 1 .20 .40
146 Dale Hoganson 2 .20 .40
147 Larry Cahan 3 .20 .40
148 Gilles Marotte 4 SP .50 1.00
149 Noel Price 5 SP .50 1.00
150 Paul Curtis 6 SP .50 1.00
151 Ross Lonsberry 8 .20 .40
152 Gord Labossiere 9 .20 .40
153 Doug Robinson 11 SP .50 1.00
154 Larry Mickey 12 .20 .40
155 Juha Widing 15 .20 .40
156 Eddie Joyal 16 .20 .40
157 Bill Flett 17 .20 .40
158 Bob Berry 18 .25 .50
159 Bob Pulford 20 .38 .75
160 Matt Ravlich 21 .20 .40
161 Mike Byers 24 SP .50 1.00
162 Denis DeJordy 30 .25 .50
163 Gump Worsley 1 2.00 4.00
164 Barry Gibbs 2 SP .50 1.00
165 Fred Barrett 3 .20 .40
166 Ted Harris 4 .20 .40
167 Danny O'Shea 7 .20 .40
168 Bill Goldsworthy 8 .25 .50
169 Charlie Burns 9 .20 .40
170 Murray Oliver 10 .20 .40
171 Jean-Paul Parise 11 .25 .50
172 Tom Williams 12 SP .50 1.00
173 Bobby Rousseau 15 .25 .50
174 Buster Harvey 18 SP .50 1.00
175 Tom Reid 20 SP .50 1.00
176 Danny Grant 21 .25 .50
177 Walt McKechnie 22 .20 .40
178 Lou Nanne 23 .25 .50
179 Danny Lawson 24 SP .50 1.00
180 Cesare Maniago 30 .25 .50
181 Ed Giacomin 1 1.50 3.00
182 Brad Park 2 2.50 5.00
183 Tim Horton 3 2.50 5.00
184 Arnie Brown 4 .20 .40
185 Rod Gilbert 7 .75 1.50
186 Bob Nevin 8 .20 .40
187 Bill Fairbairn 10 SP .50 1.00
188 Vic Hadfield 11 .25 .50
189 Ron Stewart 12 .20 .40
190 Jim Neilson 15 .25 .50
191 Rod Seiling 16 SP .50 1.00
192 Dave Balon 17 SP .50 1.00
193 Walt Tkaczuk 18 .25 .50
194 Jean Ratelle 19 .75 1.50
195 Jack Egers 20 .20 .40
196 Pete Stemkowski 21 SP .50 1.00
197 Ted Irvine 27 .20 .40
198 Gilles Villemure 30 .50 1.00
199 Doug Favell 1 .75 1.50
200 Ed Van Impe 2 .20 .40
201 Larry Hillman 3 .20 .40
202 Barry Ashbee 4 .38 .75
203 Wayne Hillman 6 SP .50 1.00
204 Andre Lacroix 7 .25 .50
205 Lew Morrison 8 .20 .40
206 Bob Kelly 9 SP .50 1.00
207 Jean-Guy Gendron 11 .20 .40
208 Gary Dornhoefer 12 .38 .75
209 Joe Watson 14 .20 .40
210 Garry Peters 15 SP .50 1.00
211 Bobby Clarke 16 5.00 10.00
212 Earl Heiskala 19 SP .50 1.00
213 Jim Johnson 20 .20 .40
214 Serge Bernier 21 .20 .40
215 Larry Hale 23 SP .50 1.00
216 Bernie Parent 30 2.50 5.00
217 Al Smith 1 .38 .75
218 Duane Rupp 2 .20 .40
219 Bob Woytowich 3 .20 .40
220 Bob Blackburn 4 .20 .40
221 Bryan Watson 5 SP .50 1.00
222 Dunc McCallum 6 .25 .50
223 Bryan Hextall 7 .25 .50
224 Andy Bathgate 9 SP 1.25 2.50
225 Keith McCreary 10 SP .50 1.00
226 Nick Harbaruk 11 .20 .40
227 Ken Schinkel 12 .20 .40
228 Glen Sather 16 SP 1.25 2.50
229 Ron Schock 17 .20 .40
230 Wally Boyer 18 .20 .40
231 Jean Pronovost 19 .25 .50
232 Dean Prentice 20 .25 .50
233 Jim Morrison 27 .20 .40
234 Les Binkley 30 SP .75 1.50
235 Glenn Hall 1 2.00 4.00
236 Bob Wall 2 .20 .40
237 Noel Picard 4 .20 .40
238 Bob Plager 5 .25 .50
239 Jim Roberts 6 .25 .50
240 Red Berenson 7 .25 .50
241 Barclay Plager 8 .25 .50
242 Frank St.Marseille 9 .20 .40
243 George Morrison 10 SP .50 1.00
244 Gary Sabourin 11 .20 .40
245 Terry Crisp 12 SP 1.00 2.00
246 Tim Ecclestone 14 .20 .40
247 Bill McCreary 15 .20 .40
248 Brit Selby 18 SP .50 1.00
249 Jim Lorentz 19 SP .50 1.00
250 Ab McDonald 20 .20 .40
251 Chris Bordeleau 21 SP .50 1.00
252 Ernie Wakely 31 .50 1.00
xx Soft Cover Album 7.50 15.00
xx Hard Cover Album 25.00 50.00

1983-84 Esso

The 1983-84 Esso set contained 21 color cards measuring approximately 4 1/2" by 3" although the player photo portion of the card was only 2" by 3". There were actually two different sets, one in French and one in English. The cards were actually part of a lottery-type game where 5000.00 cash could be won instantly via a scratch-off. The card backs contained information about the contest on the back of the contest portion and player statistics on the back of the player photo portion of the card. The cards were numbered and hence they are checklisted below alphabetically. There was very little difference in availability of the English set as opposed to the French set; however there seemed to be a slight premium on the French set over the English set of about 20 percent over the prices listed below.

COMPLETE SET (21) 6.00 15.00
1 Glenn Anderson .40 1.00
2 John Anderson .20 .50
3 Dave Babych .20 .50
4 Richard Brodeur .40 1.00
5 Paul Coffey 1.60 4.00
6 Bill Derlago .20 .50
7 Bob Gainey .60 1.50
8 Michel Goulet .40 1.00
9 Dale Hawerchuk .80 2.00
10 Dale Hunter .30 .75
11 Morris Lukowich .20 .50
12 Lanny McDonald .60 1.50
13 Mark Messier 2.00 5.00
14 Jim Peplinski .20 .50
15 Paul Reinhart .20 .50
16 Larry Robinson .50 1.25
17 Stan Smyl .30 .75
18 Harold Snepsts .30 .75
19 Marc Tardif .20 .50
20 Mario Tremblay .20 .50
21 Rick Vaive .30 .75

1988-89 Esso All-Stars

The 1988-89 Esso All-Stars set contained 48 color cards (actually adhesive-backed "stickers") measuring approximately 2 1/8" by 3 1/4". The fronts featured borderless

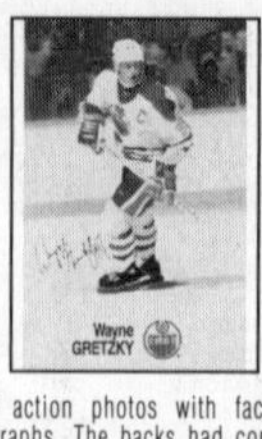

color action photos with facsim autographs. The backs had comple checklists for the whole set. The playe depicted included hockey greats from t past and present. The cards (stickers) we unnumbered and hence are checklist below in alphabetical order. There was a 3 page album (8 1/2" by 11") available either English or French, which was intend to hold the stickers. In fact each albu already contained five pasted-in cards, Giacomin, Al MacInnis, Rick Middletc Bernie Parent, and Pierre Pilote. The car were distributed in Canada in packs of with a purchase of gasoline at participati Esso service stations. The complete set pri below includes the album.

COMPLETE SET (48) 6.00 15.0
1 Jean Beliveau .30 .7
2 Mike Bossy .30 .7
3 Ray Bourque .30 .7
4 Johnny Bower .16 .4
5 Bobby Clarke .20 .5
6 Paul Coffey .30 .7
7 Yvan Cournoyer .10 .2
8 Marcel Dionne .16 .4
9 Ken Dryden .40 1.0
10 Phil Esposito .30 .7
11 Tony Esposito .20 .5
12 Grant Fuhr .16 .4
13 Clark Gillies .08 .2
14 Michel Goulet .10 .2
15 Wayne Gretzky 1.60 4.0
16 Dale Hawerchuk .10 .2
17 Ron Hextall .16 .4
18 Gordie Howe .60 1.5
19 Mark Howe .08 .2
20 Bobby Hull .30 .7
21 Tim Kerr .08 .2
22 Jari Kurri .10 .2
23 Guy Lafleur .30 .7
24 Rod Langway .08 .2
25 Jacques Laperriere .08 .2
26 Guy Lapointe .10 .2
27 Mario Lemieux 1.00 2.5
28 Frank Mahovlich .20 .5
29 Lanny McDonald .10 .2
30 Mark Messier .40 1.0
31 Stan Mikita .20 .5
32 Mats Naslund .08 .2
33 Bobby Orr .80 2.0
34 Brad Park .10 .2
35 Gilbert Perreault .10 .2
36 Denis Potvin .10 .2
37 Larry Robinson .10 .2
38 Luc Robitaille .20 .5
39 Borje Salming .08 .2
40 Denis Savard .10 .2
41 Serge Savard .10 .2
42 Steve Shutt .10 .2
43 Darryl Sittler .10 .2
44 Billy Smith .10 .2
45 John Tonelli .08 .2
46 Bryan Trottier .10 .2
47 Norm Ullman .10 .2
48 Gump Worsley .20 .5
xx Album 1.20 3.0

1997-98 Esso Olympic Hockey Heroes

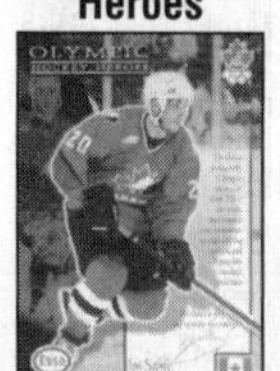

These oversized cards featured color acti photos on the front, along with biographic information on the back. Each player w pictured in his or her respective Olymp uniform. The set was available in six seri from Esso gas stations and comes comple with a black binder.

COMPLETE SET (60) 12.00 30.0
*FRENCH VERSION: 1X TO 1.5X BASIC CARDS
1 Header Card .04 .1
2 Olympic Hockey History .04 .1
3 CBC Broadcast Guide .04 .1
4 Olympic Hockey Bracket .04 .1
5 Team Canada .04 .1
6 Eric Lindros .80 2.0
7 Joe Sakic .60 1.5
8 Trevor Linden .16 .4
9 Paul Kariya .80 2.0
10 Brendan Shanahan .40 1.0
11 Rod Brind'Amour .16 .4
12 Theo Fleury .16 .4
13 Eric Desjardins .10 .2
14 Scott Niedermayer .10 .2
15 Chris Pronger .16 .4
16 Rob Blake .10 .2
17 Patrick Roy 1.00 2.5
18 Curtis Joseph .20 .5
19 Keith Primeau .16 .4
20 Mark Messier .30 .7
21 Adam Foote .10 .2
22 Team USA .04 .1

Keith Tkachuk .24 .60
Mike Modano .20 .50
John LeClair .30 .75
Doug Weight .16 .40
Brett Hull .24 .60
Jeremy Roenick .20 .50
Brian Leetch .20 .50
Chris Chelios .20 .50
Kevin Hatcher .10 .25
Derian Hatcher .10 .25
Mike Richter .20 .50
John Vanbiesbrouck .40 1.00
Team Russia .04 .10
Sergei Fedorov .40 1.00
Alexei Yashin .16 .40
Pavel Bure .40 1.00
Alexander Mogilny .16 .40
Nikolai Khabibulin .16 .40
Team Sweden .04 .10
Mats Sundin .20 .50
Peter Forsberg .60 1.50
Daniel Alfredsson .16 .40
Nicklas Lidstrom .16 .40
Kenny Jonsson .10 .25
Team Finland .04 .10
Saku Koivu .40 1.00
Esa Tikkanen .16 .40
Teemu Selanne .40 1.00
Team Czech Republic .04 .10
Jaromir Jagr .60 1.50
Roman Hamrlik .16 .40
Dominik Hasek .40 1.00
Women's Team Canada .04 .10
Nancy Drolet .20 .50
Geraldine Heaney .20 .50
Hayley Wickenheiser .20 .50
Cassie Campbell .20 .50
Stacy Wilson .20 .50
NO E.Lindros AU 150.00 100.00

2001-02 eTopps

e 2001-02 eTopps cards were issued via ps' website and initially sold exclusively eBay's eTopps Trade Floor. Owner's of cards could hold the cards on account h Topps and freely trade those cards nilar to shares of stock. They also could y a fee to take actual delivery of their ds, but most are still held on account with ps. The production quantity of each card isted beside the player's name. Prices ow are derived from sales on the eTopps ding floor on ebay.

Joe Sakic/782
Paul Kariya/1032
Curtis Joseph/714
Brendan Shanahan/2000
Patrik Elias/859
Evgeni Nabokov/549
Johan Hedberg/574
Patrick Roy/938
John LeClair/494
Martin Brodeur/663
Teemu Selanne/784
Mike Modano/559
Martin Havlat/510
Roberto Luongo/747
Peter Forsberg/598
Steve Yzerman/796
Pavel Bure/896
Mark Messier/618
Mike Comrie/809
Mats Sundin/717
Owen Nolan/457
Ed Belfour/730
Mario Lemieux/1116
Keith Tkachuk/751
Milan Hejduk/532
Rick Dipietro/579
Roman Cechmanek/511
Sergei Fedorov/710
Vincent Lecavalier/550
Eric Lindros/634
Ilya Kovalchuk/2513
Zigmund Palffy/550
Dominik Hasek/753
Jaromir Jagr/569
Doug Weight/521

2002-03 eTopps

e 2002-03 eTopps cards were issued via ops' website and initially sold exclusively eBay's eTopps Trade Floor. Owner's of cards could hold the cards on account h Topps and freely trade those cards nilar to shares of stock. They also could y a fee to take actual delivery of their rds, but most are still held on account with pps. Prices below are derived from sales the eTopps trading floor on ebay. oduction numbers are listed below.

Jarome Iginla/1668
Pavel Bure/1475
Patrick Roy/1500
4 Mats Sundin/1320
5 Jaromir Jagr/1500
6 Martin Brodeur/1459
7 Jose Theodore/1181
8 Nicklas Lidstrom/1551
9 Joe Sakic/1162
10 Ilya Kovalchuk/1500
11 Mike Modano/922
12 Sergei Fedorov/1583
13 Pavel Datsyuk/1500
14 Saku Koivu/1276
15 Peter Forsberg/1240
16 Dany Heatley/2580
17 Erik Cole/1952
18 Mario Lemieux/2000
19 Eric Lindros/1243
20 Patrik Elias/1500
21 Steve Yzerman/1500
22 Michael Peca/837
23 Todd Bertuzzi/2000
24 Evgeni Nabokov/925
25 Paul Kariya/971
26 Peter Bondra/1102
27 Chris Pronger/1147
28 Alexei Yashin/1133
29 Daniel Alfredsson/840
30 Teemu Selanne/949
31 Brendan Shanahan/1078
32 Brett Hull/1739
33 Ron Francis/1063
34 Simon Gagne/1500
35 Marty Turco/1500
36 Roberto Luongo/918
37 Joe Thornton/1500
38 Mike Comrie/1196
39 Rick Nash/3000
40 Stanislav Chistov/2000
41 Henrik Zetterberg/3000
42 Ales Hemsky/2000
43 Jay Bouwmeester/3000
44 Alexei Smirnov/2000
45 Chuck Kobasew/2000
46 P-M Bouchard/2000
47 Jason Spezza/2000
48 Alexander Svitov/2000
49 Marian Gaborik/2000
50 Jeremy Roenick/1145
51 Olli Jokinen/1260
52 Marian Hossa/1500
53 Markus Naslund/2000
54 Ryan Miller/2000
55 Martin St. Louis/1489
56 Jocelyn Thibault/930

2003-04 eTopps

The 2003-04 eTopps cards were issued via Topps' website and initially sold exclusively on eBay's eTopps Trade Floor. Owner's of the cards could hold the cards on account with Topps and freely trade those cards similar to shares of stock. They also could pay a fee to take actual delivery of their cards, but most are still held on account with Topps. Since most do not trade hands as physical cards, we've simply listed the checkliProduction numbers are listed below.

1 Pasi Nurminen/757
2 Al MacInnis/871
3 Daniel Briere/743
4 Jordan Leopold/861
5 Tyler Arnason/920
6 Niko Kapanen/780
7 Kristian Huselius/797
8 Jamie Langenbrunner/756
10 J-S Giguere/693
11 Mario Lemieux/1000
12 Patrick Lalime/832
13 Milan Hejduk/817
14 Rick DiPietro/749
15 Owen Nolan/839
16 Dany Heatley/698
17 Mattias Weinhandl/774
18 Brendan Morrison/687
19 Paul Kariya/767
20 Zigmund Palffy/636
21 Marian Gaborik/872
22 Sergei Fedorov/706
23 Tony Amonte/558
24 Roberto Luongo/674
26 Saku Koivu/651
27 Todd Bertuzzi/868
28 Patrik Elias/804
29 Jeremy Roenick/1000
30 Marian Hossa/839
31 Brad Richards/1000
32 Joe Thornton/1123
33 Peter Forsberg/1000
34 Daymond Langkow/644
35 Ed Jovanovski/873
36 Martin Brodeur/1000
37 Jarome Iginla/913
38 Jaromir Jagr/792
39 Rick Nash/1035
40 Teemu Selanne/769
41 Patrice Bergeron/1500
42 Peter Sejna/838
43 Matthew Stajan/1000
44 Eric Staal/1500
45 Nathan Horton/1000
46 Joffrey Lupul/886
47 Tuomo Ruutu/1462
48 Jordin Tootoo/990
49 Dustin Brown/918
50 Marc-Andre Fleury/2000
51 Patrick Marleau/932
52 Joni Pitkanen/1000
53 Pavel Datsyuk/1000
54 Brian Leetch/1000
55 Chris Chelios/896
56 Andrew Raycroft/1500

1948-52 Exhibits Canadian

These cards measured approximately 3 1/4" by 5 1/4" and were issued on heavy cardboard stock. The cards showed full-bleed photos with the player's name burned in toward the bottom. The hockey exhibit cards were generally considered more scarce than their baseball exhibit counterparts. Since the cards were unnumbered, the set is arranged below alphabetically within teams as follows: Montreal (1-27), Toronto (28-42), Detroit (43-46), Boston (47-48), Chicago (49-50), and New York (51). The set closes with an Action subset (52-65).

COMPLETE SET (65) 750.00 1500.00
1 Reggie Abbott 6.00 12.00
2 Jean Beliveau 37.50 75.00
3 Jean Beliveau 50.00 100.00
(Aces' captain)
4 Toe Blake 20.00 40.00
5 Butch Bouchard 10.00 20.00
6 Bob Fillion 6.00 12.00
7 Dick Gamble 7.50 15.00
8 Bernie Geoffrion 25.00 50.00
9 Doug Harvey 20.00 40.00
10 Tom Johnson 10.00 20.00
11 Elmer Lach 20.00 40.00
12 Hal Laycoe 6.00 12.00
13 Jacques Locas 6.00 12.00
14 Bud McPherson 6.00 12.00
15 Paul Maznick 6.00 12.00
16 Gerry McNeil 20.00 40.00
17 Paul Meger 6.00 12.00
18 Dickie Moore 20.00 40.00
19 Ken Mosdell 6.00 12.00
20 Bert Olmstead 10.00 20.00
21 Ken Reardon 12.50 25.00
22 Billy Reay 7.50 15.00
23 Maurice Richard 50.00 100.00
(Stick on ice)
24 Maurice Richard 50.00 100.00
(Stairs in back ground)
25 Dollard St.Laurent 7.50 15.00
26 Grant Warwick 6.00 12.00
27 Floyd Curry 7.50 15.00
28 Bill Barilko 20.00 40.00
29 Turk Broda 20.00 40.00
30 Cal Gardner 10.00 20.00
31 Bill Juzda 6.00 12.00
32 Ted Kennedy 20.00 40.00
33 Joe Klukay 6.00 12.00
34 Fleming Mackell 6.00 12.00
35 Howie Meeker 15.00 30.00
36 Gus Mortson 6.00 12.00
37 Al Rollins 12.50 25.00
38 Sid Smith 7.50 15.00
39 Tod Sloan 6.00 12.00
40 Ray Timgren 6.00 12.00
41 Jim Thomson 6.00 12.00
42 Max Bentley 12.50 25.00
43 Sid Abel 10.00 20.00
44 Gordie Howe 62.50 125.00
45 Ted Lindsay 25.00 50.00
46 Harry Lumley 20.00 40.00
47 Jack Gelineau 6.00 12.00
48 Paul Ronty 6.00 12.00
49 Doug Bentley 12.50 25.00
50 Roy Conacher 7.50 15.00
51 Chuck Rayner 12.50 25.00
52 Boston vs. Montreal 10.00 20.00
(In front of net; 23 of Boston visible)
53 Detroit vs. New York 30.00 60.00
(Howe and Ranger on goal line on ice)
54 Montreal vs. Toronto 30.00 60.00
(Richard shooting puck past Toronto goalie)
55 New York vs. Montreal 30.00 60.00
(Richard is on goalie)
56 New York vs. Montreal 10.00 20.00
(Open net; 9 of Rangers on ice)
57 Montreal vs. Boston 10.00 20.00
(Ref and several players in front of Boston goal)
58 Detroit vs. Montreal 10.00 20.00
(Two Canadiens in front of Detroit goalie)
59 Chicago vs. Montreal 10.00 20.00
(5 Blackhawks and 2 Canadiens on ice in front of goalie)
60 New York vs. Montreal 25.00 50.00
(Richard and Elmer Lach in front of Ranger and Rayner)
61 Chicago vs. Montreal 15.00 30.00
(5 Geoffrion shooting at Chicago goalie)
62 Detroit vs. Montreal 20.00 40.00
(Sawchuk saves against 8)
63 Detroit vs. Montreal 10.00 20.00
(Canadiens score)
64 Toronto vs. Montreal 10.00 20.00
(Canadiens score)
65 Chicago vs. Montreal 10.00 20.00
(Canadiens score)

1995-96 Fanfest Phil Esposito

This five-card set was sponsored by the five licensed card companies (Donruss, Fleer/Skybox, Pinnacle, Topps, and Upper Deck) who each produced one card for distribution at the 1996 All-Star Game Fanfest, which was held in Boston. The fronts featured color action photos of Phil Esposito in designs unique to each manufacturer. The backs carried information about the legendary Bruin great.

COMPLETE SET (5) 8.00 20.00
COMMON ESPO (1-5) 2.40 6.00

1994-95 Finest

This 165-card super-premium set was issued in seven-card packs, in 24-pack boxes. The cards featured a blue marbleized foil border with a centered player photo. The player's last name only, along with the Finest logo, dominated the top of the front. The card fronts also featured a clear protective peel-off coating which was designed to prevent scratches and other damage to the card. Values below reflect unpeeled cards, although hobby opinions on whether to leave the coating intact or remove it vary. Collectors are advised to make a decision based on their own preference. Card backs had player photos, brief stats, and a recap of that player's finest moment. Card numbers 5, 56, 68, and 99 had wrong photos and player names on the back. These were corrected only in the '94-95 Finest Super Team Stanley Cup Winner Redemption set. A World Junior players subset was included (112-165). Rookie cards in the set included Bryan Berard, Radek Bonk, Eric Daze, Miikka Elomo, Eric Fichaud, Sean Haggerty, Ed Jovanovski, Ryan Smyth, Jeff O'Neill and Wade Redden.

COMPLETE SET (165) 30.00 80.00
1 Peter Forsberg .75 2.00
2 Oleg Tverdovsky .50 1.25
3 Radek Bonk RC .30 .75
4 Brian Rolston .10 .30
5 Kenny Jonsson UER .10 .30
6 Patrik Juhlin RC .30 .75
7 Paul Kariya .50 1.25
8 Janne Laukkanen .10 .30
9 Brett Lindros .10 .30
10 Andrei Nikolishin .10 .30
11 Jeff Friesen .10 .30
12 Jamie Storr .20 .50
13 Chris Therien .10 .30
14 Alexander Cherbayev .10 .30
15 Kevin Brown RC .30 .75
16 Mark Messier .50 1.25
17 Kevin Hatcher .10 .30
18 Scott Stevens .20 .50
19 Keith Tkachuk .50 1.25
20 Guy Hebert .20 .50
21 Jason Arnott .10 .30
22 Cam Neely .50 1.25
23 Adam Graves .10 .30
24 Pavel Bure .50 1.25
25 Mark Tinordi .10 .30
26 Felix Potvin .50 1.25
27 Nikolai Khabibulin .20 .50
28 Theo Fleury .10 .30
29 Curtis Joseph .50 1.25
30 Patrick Roy 1.25 3.00
31 Adam Deadmarsh .10 .30
32 Pat Falloon .10 .30
33 Jaromir Jagr .75 2.00
34 Chris Chelios .50 1.25
35 Ray Bourque .75 2.00
36 Mike Vernon .20 .50
37 Steve Thomas .10 .30
38 Eric Lindros .50 1.25
39 Dave Andreychuk .20 .50
40 John Vanbiesbrouck .20 .50
41 Wayne Gretzky 2.00 5.00
42 Brett Hull .75 2.00
43 Dominik Hasek .75 2.00
44 Kirk Muller .10 .30
45 Rob Blake .20 .50
46 Viktor Kozlov .10 .30
47 Todd Harvey .10 .30
48 Valeri Bure .10 .30
49 Brian Leetch .50 1.25
50 Ray Sheppard .20 .50
51 Ed Belfour .50 1.25
52 Rick Tocchet .20 .50
53 Daren Puppa .20 .50
54 Russ Courtnall .10 .30
55 Jason Allison .10 .30
56 Alexei Yashin UER .10 .30
57 Sandis Ozolinsh .10 .30
58 Chris Gratton .10 .30
59 Mike Peca .10 .30
60 Glen Wesley .10 .30
61 Kirk McLean .20 .50
62 Chris Pronger .50 1.25
63 Steve Larmer .20 .50
64 Michal Grosek .10 .30
65 Sergei Fedorov .60 1.50
66 Stu Barnes .10 .30
67 Adam Oates .20 .50
68 Paul Coffey UER .50 1.25
69 Joe Sakic 1.00 2.50
70 Pat LaFontaine .50 1.25
71 Martin Brodeur 1.00 2.50
72 Bob Corkum .10 .30
73 Jeremy Roenick .50 1.25
74 Shayne Corson .10 .30
75 German Titov .10 .30
76 Teemu Selanne .50 1.25
77 Eric Fichaud RC .30 .75
78 Pierre Turgeon .20 .50
79 Alexander Selivanov RC .30 .75
80 Kevin Stevens .10 .30
81 Jari Kurri .20 .50
82 Gary Roberts .10 .30
83 Geoff Courtnall .10 .30
84 Steve Yzerman 1.25 3.00
85 Rod Brind'Amour .20 .50
86 Mike Richter .50 1.25
87 Bernie Nicholls .20 .50
88 Alexandre Daigle .10 .30
89 Luc Robitaille .20 .50
90 John MacLean .20 .50
91 Phil Housley .20 .50
92 Brendan Shanahan .50 1.25
93 Joe Juneau .20 .50
94 Stephane Richer .20 .50
95 Blaine Lacher RC .30 .75
96 Mike Gartner .20 .50
97 Rene Corbet .10 .30
98 Vincent Damphousse .10 .30
99 Alexander Mogilny UER .20 .50
100 Doug Gilmour .20 .50
101 Petr Nedved .20 .50
102 Alexei Zhamnov .20 .50
103 Wendel Clark .20 .50
104 Arturs Irbe .20 .50
105 Brian Bellows .10 .30
106 Mike Modano .75 2.00
107 Ravil Gusmanov .10 .30
108 Geoff Sanderson .20 .50
109 Mark Recchi .20 .50
110 Mats Sundin .50 1.25
111 Pavol Demitra .20 .50
112 Richard Park .10 .30
113 Doug Bonner RC .30 .75
114 Bryan Berard RC .30 .75
115 Rory Fitzpatrick .60 1.50
116 Deron Quint .10 .30
117 Jason Bonsignore .10 .30
118 Adam Deadmarsh .10 .30
119 Sean Haggerty RC .30 .75
120 Jamie Langenbrunner .10 .30
121 Jeff Mitchell RC .30 .75
122 Antti Aalto RC .30 .75
123 Tommi Rajamaki RC .30 .75
124 J. Markkanen RC UER 1.00 2.50
125 Miikka Kiprusoff RC 12.00 30.00
126 Jere Karalahti RC .30 .75
127 Petri Kokko RC .30 .75
128 Janne Niinimaa .50 1.25
129 Kimmo Timonen .20 .50
130 Martti Jarventie RC .30 .75
131 Mikko Helisten RC .30 .75
132 Niko Halttunen RC .30 .75
133 Tommi Miettinen .20 .50
134 Miska Kangasniemi RC .30 .75
135 Veli-Pekka Nutikka RC .30 .75
136 Jani Hassinen RC .30 .75
137 Timo Salonen RC .30 .75
138 Tommi Sova RC .30 .75
139 Toni Makiaho RC .30 .75
140 Tommi Hamalainen RC .30 .75
141 Juha Vuorivirta RC .30 .75
142 Jussi Tarvainen RC .30 .75
143 Miikka Elomo RC .30 .75
144 Jason Botterill .10 .30
145 Dan Cloutier RC .60 1.50
146 Jamie Storr .20 .50
147 Chad Allan RC .30 .75
148 Nolan Baumgartner RC .10 .30
149 Ed Jovanovski RC .30 .75
150 Bryan McCabe .10 .30
151 Wade Redden RC .30 .75
152 Jamie Rivers RC .30 .75
153 Lee Sorochan RC .30 .75
154 Jason Allison .10 .30
155 Alexandre Daigle .10 .30
156 Larry Courville RC .30 .75
157 Eric Daze RC .30 .75
158 Shean Donovan RC .30 .75
159 Jeff Friesen .10 .30
160 Todd Harvey .10 .30
161 Marty Murray .10 .30
162 Jeff O'Neill RC .30 .75
163 Denis Pederson RC .30 .75
164 Darcy Tucker RC .40 1.00
165 Ryan Smyth RC 1.00 2.50

1994-95 Finest Super Team Winners

This 165-card set was awarded to collectors who redeemed the winning New Jersey Devils team card. The cards were the same as the regular Finest cards save for the Super Team Winner embossed logo. Values for the cards can be determined by applying the multipliers below to the values listed for the regular cards.

COMPLETE SET (165) 50.00 100.00
*SUP.TM.SINGLES: 1.5X TO 3X BASE CARD

1994-95 Finest Refractors

The cards in this set were parallel to the Finest set. They were randomly inserted at the rate of 1:12 packs. These cards appeared identical to the regular issue; careful examination in the proper light revealed a reflective, rainbow-like sheen to the foil on the front. If in doubt, we recommend comparing to other cards from the set; in this setting, a refractor truly stands out. These cards also came with the clear protective peel-off coating. Multipliers can be found in the header below to determine value for these.

*STARS: 4X TO 10X BASIC CARDS
*ROOKIES: 2.5X TO 6X

1994-95 Finest Bowman's Best

This 45-card set was randomly inserted in Finest packs at the rate of 1:4. Card fronts featured a cut-out player photo over a blue or red hi-tech half moon background utilizing the Finest printing technology. The first twenty cards in the set feature NHL veterans. The second twenty consists of NHL rookies. The last five cards pair a star veteran and a top rookie in a horizontal format. The card fronts have the clear protective peel-off coating. The backs of the first forty cards have brief text information outlining the player's strong points, and a small portrait photo. The final five cards simply feature text comparing the two players. Cards are numbered with a B (1-20) prefix for veterans, R (1-20) for rookies, and X (21-25) for dual player cards.

COMPLETE SET (45) 40.00 100.00
*B1-B20 REF.STARS: 3X TO 8X BASIC CARDS
*R1-R20 REF.STARS: 2X TO 5X BASIC CARDS
*X21-X25 REF.STARS: 1.5X TO 4X BASIC CARDS
B1 Ray Bourque 2.00 5.00
B2 Mark Messier 1.25 3.00
B3 Cam Neely 2.00 5.00
B4 Theo Fleury 1.25 3.00
B5 Jeremy Roenick 2.00 5.00
B6 Mike Modano 2.00 5.00
B7 Sergei Fedorov 2.00 5.00
B8 John Vanbiesbrouck 1.25 3.00
B9 Pierre Turgeon .60 1.50
B10 Kirk Muller .60 1.50
B11 Pavel Bure 2.00 5.00
B12 Brian Leetch 1.50 4.00
B13 Mike Richter 1.50 4.00
B14 Teemu Selanne 1.25 3.00
B15 Brett Hull 1.50 4.00
B16 Eric Lindros 1.25 3.00
B17 Keith Tkachuk 1.25 3.00
B18 Joe Sakic 3.00 8.00
B19 Doug Gilmour 1.25 3.00
B20 Jaromir Jagr 2.00 5.00
R1 Paul Kariya 1.25 3.00
R2 Oleg Tverdovsky .60 1.50
R3 Blaine Lacher .60 1.50
R4 Todd Harvey .60 1.50
R5 Roman Oksiuta .60 1.50
R6 David Oliver .60 1.50
R7 Jamie Storr .60 1.50
R8 Brian Savage .60 1.50
R9 Brian Rolston .60 1.50
R10 Brett Lindros .60 1.50
R11 Radek Bonk .60 1.50
R12 Peter Forsberg 3.00 8.00
R13 Adam Deadmarsh .60 1.50
R14 Jeff Friesen .60 1.50
R15 Denis Chasse .60 1.50
R16 Jason Wiemer .60 1.50
R17 Alexander Selivanov .60 1.50
R18 Kenny Jonsson .60 1.50
R19 Todd Marchant .60 1.50
R20 Mariusz Czerkawski .60 1.50
X21 Theo Fleury 1.25 3.00
Paul Kariya
X22 Doug Gilmour 2.00 5.00
Peter Forsberg
X23 Joe Sakic 1.25 3.00
Radek Bonk
X24 Brian Leetch 1.25 3.00
Oleg Tverdovsky
X25 Cam Neely 1.25 3.00
Jason Wiemer

1994-95 Division's Finest Clear Cut

The 20 cards in this set were randomly inserted in Finest packs at the rate of 1:12.

COMPLETE SET (20) 25.00 60.00
1 Patrick Roy 5.00 12.00
2 Ray Bourque 2.00 5.00
3 Adam Oates .60 1.50
4 Luc Robitaille .60 1.50
5 Mark Recchi .60 1.50
6 Mike Richter 1.50 4.00
7 Scott Stevens .60 1.50
8 Eric Lindros 1.50 4.00
9 Adam Graves .40 1.00
10 Stephane Richer .60 1.50
11 Ed Belfour 1.50 4.00
12 Al MacInnis .60 1.50
13 Sergei Fedorov 2.00 5.00
14 Brendan Shanahan 1.50 4.00
15 Brett Hull 2.00 5.00
16 Arturs Irbe .60 1.50
17 Sandis Ozolinsh .40 1.00
18 Wayne Gretzky 8.00 20.00
19 Gary Roberts .40 1.00
20 Pavel Bure 1.50 4.00

1994-95 Finest Ring Leaders

This 20-card set was comprised of players who have earned at least two Stanley Cup rings. Unlike other Finest cards, these did not come with a peel-off coating.

COMPLETE SET (20) 50.00 100.00
STATED ODDS 1:24
1 Mark Messier 3.00 8.00
2 Kevin Lowe 1.00 2.50
3 Jari Kurri 3.00 8.00
4 Grant Fuhr 3.00 8.00
5 Wayne Gretzky 20.00 50.00
6 Paul Coffey 2.00 5.00
7 Craig Simpson 1.00 2.50
8 Craig MacTavish 1.00 2.50
9 Jeff Beukeboom 1.00 2.50
10 Joe Mullen 1.00 2.50
11 Marty McSorley 1.00 2.50
12 Steve Smith 1.00 2.50
13 Kevin Stevens 1.00 2.50
14 Patrick Roy 12.00 30.00
15 Jaromir Jagr 4.00 10.00
16 Ron Francis 2.00 5.00
17 Bill Ranford 2.00 5.00
18 Larry Murphy 2.00 5.00
19 Tom Barrasso 2.00 5.00
20 Adam Graves 1.00 2.50

1995-96 Finest

The 1995-96 Finest set was issued in one series totaling 191 cards. The 6-card hobby packs had an SRP of $5.00 each. The players were featured across three themes: Finest Rookies, Finest Performers and Finest Defenders. Within those themes, cards were produced in different quantities: some players were common, some uncommon and some rare. The breakdown for the player selection of common (bronze), uncommon (silver) and rare (gold) cards was supposedly random with no consideration given to the status of each player in the set, although many of the gold cards did feature upper-echelon stars. Odds of finding an uncommon silver card were 1:4 packs, while golds were found 1:24 packs.

COMPLETE SET (191) 150.00 400.00
1 Eric Lindros B .40 1.00
2 Ray Bourque G 8.00 20.00
3 Eric Daze B .20 .50
4 Craig Janney S 1.00 2.50
5 Wayne Gretzky B 2.00 5.00
6 Dave Andreychuk B .20 .50
7 Phil Housley B .08 .25
8 Mike Gartner B .20 .50
9 Cam Neely B .40 1.00
10 Brett Hull B .60 1.50
11 Daren Puppa S 1.50 4.00
12 Tomas Sandstrom S 1.00 2.50
13 Patrick Roy G 15.00 40.00
14 Steve Thomas B .08 .25
15 Joe Sakic B .75 2.00
16 Ray Sheppard S 1.00 2.50
17 Steve Duchesne B .08 .25
18 Shayne Corson S 1.00 2.50
19 Chris Chelios G 4.00 10.00
20 John Vanbiesbrouck B .20 .50
21 Randy Burridge B .08 .25
22 Shane Doan B RC 1.00 2.50
23 Brian Savage B .08 .25
24 Luc Robitaille B .20 .50
25 Jeremy Roenick G 8.00 20.00
26 Peter Forsberg B 1.00 2.50
27 Jeff Friesen S 1.00 2.50
28 Aaron Gavey S 1.00 2.50
29 Kenny Jonsson S 1.00 2.50
30 Theo Fleury G 4.00 10.00
31 Dave Gagner S 1.00 2.50
32 Alexander Selivanov S 1.00 2.50
33 Scott Stevens B .20 .50
34 Valeri Bure B .08 .25
35 Teemu Selanne G 6.00 15.00
36 Ray Ferraro S 1.00 2.50
37 Sylvain Cote S 1.00 2.50
38 John MacLean B .08 .25
39 Brendan Shanahan B .40 1.00

40 Pat LaFontaine B .08 .25
41 Brian Leetch G 4.00 10.00
42 Larry Murphy B .20 .50
43 Adam Oates B .20 .50
44 Rod Brind'Amour B .20 .50
45 Martin Brodeur G 10.00 25.00
46 Pierre Turgeon B .08 .25
47 Claude Lemieux B .08 .25
48 Al MacInnis S 1.50 4.00
49 Geoff Courtnall S 1.00 2.50
50 Mark Messier B .40 1.00
51 Bill Ranford B .20 .50
52 Vincent Damphousse S 1.00 2.50
53 Jere Lehtinen B .08 .25
54 Bryan McCabe S 1.00 2.50
55 Doug Gilmour G 4.00 10.00
56 Mathieu Schneider S 1.00 2.50
57 Igor Larionov S 1.00 2.50
58 Joe Murphy S 1.00 2.50
59 Niklas Sundstrom B .08 .25
60 John LeClair B .40 1.00
61 Cory Stillman B .08 .25
62 David Oliver B .08 .25
63 Nikolai Khabibulin B .40 1.00
64 Steve Rucchin B .08 .25
65 Brendan Shanahan S 2.00 5.00
66 Jim Carey B .20 .50
67 Brian Holzinger S RC 1.00 2.50
68 Stu Barnes S 1.00 2.50
69 Nicklas Lidstrom B .40 1.00
70 Jaromir Jagr B .60 1.50
71 Donald Audette S 1.00 2.50
72 Dominik Hasek B .75 2.00
73 Peter Bondra S 1.50 4.00
74 Andrew Cassels B .08 .25
75 Pavel Bure B .40 1.00
76 Marcus Ragnarsson B RC .20 .50
77 Ray Bourque S 3.00 8.00
78 Alexei Zhamnov B .08 .25
79 Travis Green S 1.00 2.50
80 Joe Sakic B .75 2.00
81 Chad Kilger B RC .08 .25
82 Bill Guerin S 1.00 2.50
83 Vyacheslav Kozlov B .08 .25
84 Igor Korolev S 1.00 2.50
85 Saku Koivu G 4.00 10.00
86 Ron Hextall B .08 .25
87 Wendel Clark S 1.00 2.50
88 Eric Lindros G 6.00 15.00
89 Richard Park B .08 .25
90 Dominik Hasek S 4.00 10.00
91 Shawn McEachern B .08 .25
92 Martin Straka S 1.00 2.50
93 Roman Hamrlik B .08 .25
94 Roman Oksiuta S 1.00 2.50
95 Sergei Fedorov B .60 1.50
96 Jeff O'Neill S 1.00 2.50
97 Todd Harvey S 1.00 2.50
98 Rob Niedermayer B .08 .25
99 Mark Messier G 6.00 15.00
100 Peter Forsberg G 8.00 20.00
101 Deron Quint B .08 .25
102 Nelson Emerson S 1.00 2.50
103 Scott Niedermayer B .08 .25
104 Doug Weight S 1.50 4.00
105 Felix Potvin B .40 1.00
106 Brendan Witt B .08 .25
107 Zdeno Ciger B .08 .25
108 Ed Belfour S 2.00 5.00
109 Jody Hull B .08 .25
110 Cam Neely S 2.00 5.00
111 Kyle McLaren B RC .08 .25
112 Petr Klima S 1.00 2.50
113 Grant Fuhr B .20 .50
114 Todd Krygier B .08 .25
115 Brian Leetch B .20 .50
116 Daniel Alfredsson S RC 6.00 15.00
117 Zigmund Palffy B .08 .25
118 Antti Tormanen B .08 .25
119 Mark Recchi B .20 .50
120 Mikael Renberg B .08 .25
121 Chris Chelios B .40 1.00
122 Guy Hebert B .20 .50
123 Keith Tkachuk G 4.00 10.00
124 Joe Juneau S 1.00 2.50
125 Radek Dvorak S RC 1.50 4.00
126 Gary Suter B .08 .25
127 Ron Francis B .20 .50
128 Mike Modano G 8.00 20.00
129 Tom Barrasso B .20 .50
130 Pat LaFontaine B .08 .25
131 Pat Verbeek B .08 .25
132 Sean Burke S 1.50 4.00
133 Rick Tocchet B .08 .25
134 Petr Sykora B RC .75 2.00
135 Felix Potvin B .40 1.00
136 Scott Mellanby B .08 .25
137 Paul Coffey B .40 1.00
138 Aki Berg G RC 4.00 10.00
139 Jason Arnott B .08 .25
140 Alexander Mogilny G 4.00 10.00
141 Sandis Ozolinsh B .08 .25
142 Owen Nolan S 1.50 4.00
143 Brian Bradley B .08 .25
144 Trevor Linden B .08 .25
145 Patrick Roy B 1.50 4.00
146 Todd Bertuzzi B RC 1.50 4.00
147 Michal Pivonka B .08 .25
148 Kevin Hatcher S 1.00 2.50
149 Chris Terreri B .20 .50
150 Mario Lemieux B 1.50 4.00
151 Alexei Yashin S 1.00 2.50
152 Scott Stevens S 1.00 2.50
153 Dale Hawerchuk B .08 .25
154 Markus Naslund B .40 1.00
155 Teemu Selanne B .40 1.00
156 Darcy Wakaluk S 1.00 2.50
157 Vitali Yachmenev B .08 .25
158 Jason Dawe B .08 .25
159 Chris Osgood B .20 .50
160 Alexander Mogilny B .20 .50
161 Kirk McLean S 1.00 2.50
162 Steve Yzerman G 12.00 30.00
163 Shean Donovan B .08 .25
164 Valeri Kamensky S 1.00 2.50
165 Paul Kariya B .40 1.00
166 Dimitri Khristich S 1.00 2.50
167 Teppo Numminen B .08 .25
168 Joe Nieuwendyk S 1.50 4.00
169 Mike Richter S 2.00 5.00
170 Doug Gilmour B .20 .50
171 Sergei Zubov B .08 .25
172 Michael Nylander B .08 .25
173 Geoff Sanderson B .08 .25
174 Eric Desjardins S 1.00 2.50
175 Jeremy Roenick B .50 1.25
176 Ed Jovanovski G 4.00 10.00
177 Mats Sundin B .40 1.00
178 Martin Brodeur B 1.00 2.50
179 John LeClair G 4.00 10.00
180 Wayne Gretzky G 20.00 50.00
181 Theo Fleury B .08 .25
182 Pierre Turgeon S 1.00 2.50
183 Robert Svehla B RC .08 .25
184 Brett Hull G 6.00 15.00
185 Jaromir Jagr G 8.00 20.00
186 Sergei Fedorov B .60 1.50
187 Pavel Bure G 6.00 15.00
188 John Vanbiesbrouck B .20 .50
189 Paul Kariya B .40 1.00
190 Mario Lemieux G 15.00 40.00
191 Checklist UER G 4.00 10.00

1995-96 Finest Refractors

The 1995-96 Finest Refractors set was issued as a parallel to the Finest set. Mirroring it's three levels of difficulty, the cards were inserted at varying rates. Common refractors could be found 1:12 packs. Uncommon refractors were 1:48, while the rare refractors were hidden 1:288 packs. It is believed there were less than 150 rare refractors, less than 450 uncommon and less than 1,000 common refractors available.
*BRONZE STARS: 4X TO 8X BASIC CARDS
*BRONZE YOUNG STARS: 6X TO 12X BASIC CARDS
*SILVER STARS: 2.5X TO 5X BASIC CARDS
*SILVER RC's: 1.25X TO 3X BASIC CARDS HI
*GOLD STARS: 1X TO 2X BASIC CARDS

1998-99 Finest

The 1998-99 Finest set was issued in one series totaling 150 cards and was distributed in six-card packs with a suggested retail price of $5. The fronts featured color action player photos printed on 29-pt. stock and identified by a different graphic according to the player's position. The backs carried player information and career statistics.

COMPLETE SET (150) 30.00 60.00
1 Teemu Selanne .30 .75
2 Theo Fleury .10 .30
3 Ed Belfour .30 .75
4 Dominik Hasek .60 1.50
5 Dino Ciccarelli .25 .60
6 Peter Forsberg .75 2.00
7 Rob Blake .25 .60
8 Martin Gelinas .10 .30
9 Vincent Damphousse .10 .30
10 Doug Brown .10 .30
11 Dave Andreychuk .25 .60
12 Bill Guerin .25 .60
13 Daniel Alfredsson .25 .60
14 Dainius Zubrus .10 .30
15 Nikolai Khabibulin .25 .60
16 Sergei Nemchinov .10 .30
17 Rod Brind'Amour .25 .60
18 Patrick Marleau .10 .30
19 Brett Hull .40 1.00
20 Rob Zamuner .10 .30
21 Anson Carter .25 .60
22 Chris Pronger .25 .60
23 Owen Nolan .25 .60
24 Alexandre Daigle .10 .30
25 Darius Kasparaitis .10 .30
26 Steve Rucchin .10 .30
27 Grant Fuhr .25 .60
28 Mike Sillinger .10 .30
29 Tony Amonte .25 .60
30 Jeremy Roenick .40 1.00
31 Garry Galley .10 .30
32 Jeff Friesen .10 .30
33 Alexei Zhitnik .10 .30
34 Sergei Fedorov .50 1.25
35 Martin Brodeur .75 2.00
36 Curtis Joseph .30 .75
37 Mike Johnson .10 .30
38 Mattias Ohlund .25 .60
39 Derian Hatcher .10 .30
40 Zigmund Palffy .25 .60
41 Rob Niedermayer .10 .30
42 Keith Primeau .10 .30
43 Valeri Kamensky .10 .30
44 Cliff Ronning .10 .30
45 Saku Koivu .30 .75
46 Jiri Slegr .10 .30
47 Igor Korolev .10 .30
48 Sergei Samsonov .25 .60
49 Vaclav Prospal .10 .30
50 Ron Francis .25 .60
51 John LeClair .30 .75
52 Peter Bondra .25 .60
53 Matt Cullen .10 .30
54 Doug Gilmour .25 .60
55 John Vanbiesbrouck .25 .60
56 Kevin Stevens .25 .60
57 Vladimir Malakhov .10 .30
58 Guy Hebert .25 .60
59 Patrik Elias .25 .60
60 Boris Mironov .10 .30
61 Rob DiMaio .10 .30
62 Pavol Demitra .25 .60
63 Michael Nylander .10 .30
64 Wayne Gretzky 2.00 5.00
65 Miroslav Satan .10 .30
66 Eric Daze .25 .60
67 Jozef Stumpel .25 .60
68 Mark Messier .30 .75
69 Pat Verbeek .10 .30
70 Felix Potvin .30 .75
71 Ethan Moreau .10 .30
72 Steve Yzerman 1.50 4.00
73 Paul Ysebaert .10 .30
74 Jaromir Jagr .50 1.25
75 Mike Modano .50 1.25
76 Chris Osgood .25 .60
77 Robert Svehla .10 .30
78 Joe Juneau .25 .60
79 Adam Deadmarsh .10 .30
80 Keith Tkachuk .30 .75
81 Mark Recchi .25 .60
82 Andrew Cassels .10 .30
83 Mike Hough .10 .30
84 Rem Murray .10 .30
85 Trevor Kidd .25 .60
86 Jeff Hackett .25 .60
87 Mikael Renberg .25 .60
88 Al MacInnis .25 .60
89 Mike Richter .30 .75
90 Markus Naslund .30 .75
91 Joe Sakic .60 1.50
92 Michael Peca .10 .30
93 Scott Thornton .10 .30
94 Vyacheslav Kozlov .25 .60
95 Bobby Holik .10 .30
96 Alexei Yashin .10 .30
97 Robert Kron .10 .30
98 Adam Oates .25 .60
99 Chris Simon .10 .30
100 Paul Kariya .30 .75
101 Ray Bourque .50 1.25
102 Eric Desjardins .25 .60
103 Glen Murray .10 .30
104 Oleg Tverdovsky .10 .30
105 Pavel Bure .30 .75
106 Mats Sundin .30 .75
107 Bryan Berard .25 .60
108 Janne Niinimaa .10 .30
109 Wade Redden .10 .30
110 Trevor Linden .25 .60
111 Jarome Iginla .40 1.00
112 Joe Nieuwendyk .25 .60
113 Alexei Kovalev .10 .30
114 Dave Gagner .10 .30
115 Dimitri Yushkevich .10 .30
116 Sandis Ozolinsh .10 .30
117 Dimitri Khristich .10 .30
118 Jim Campbell .10 .30
119 Nicklas Lidstrom .30 .75
120 Scott Niedermayer .10 .30
121 Niklas Sundstrom .10 .30
122 Karl Dykhuis .10 .30
123 Brendan Shanahan .30 .75
124 Sandy McCarthy .10 .30
125 Pierre Turgeon .25 .60
126 Olaf Kolzig .25 .60
127 Chris Chelios .30 .75
128 Luc Robitaille .25 .60
129 Alexander Mogilny .25 .60
130 Sami Kapanen .10 .30
131 Stu Barnes .10 .30
132 Scott Stevens .25 .60
133 Doug Weight .25 .60
134 Alexei Zhamnov .10 .30
135 Mike Vernon .25 .60
136 Derek Morris .10 .30
137 Brian Leetch .30 .75
138 Ray Whitney .10 .30
139 Chris Gratton .25 .60
140 Patrick Roy 1.50 4.00
141 Jason Allison .10 .30
142 Tom Barrasso .25 .60
143 Derek Plante .10 .30
144 Denis Pederson .10 .30
145 Mike Ricci .10 .30
146 Damian Rhodes .25 .60
147 Marco Sturm .10 .30
148 Darryl Sydor .10 .30
149 Eric Lindros .30 .75
150 Checklist .10 .30

1998-99 Finest No Protectors

Randomly inserted into packs at the rate of 1:4, this 150-card set was a parallel to the base set without the Finest Protector.
COMPLETE SET (150) 80.00 200.00
*STARS: 1.5X TO 3X BASIC CARDS

1998-99 Finest No Protectors Refractors

Randomly inserted into packs at the rate of 1:24, this 150-card set was a parallel to the regular refractor set without the Finest protector.
*STARS: 5X TO 10X BASIC CARDS

1998-99 Finest Refractors

Randomly inserted into packs at the rate of 1:12, this 150-card set was a parallel to the base set and was distinguished by the refractive quality of the card.
*STARS: 2X TO 5X BASIC CARDS

1998-99 Finest Centurion

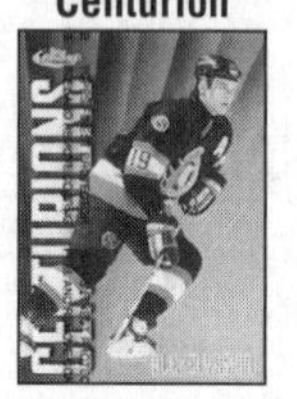

Randomly inserted into packs at the rate of 1:72, this 20-card set featured color action photos of rising NHL stars. Only 500 serial-numbered sets were produced. A refractor parallel was also produced and inserted at a rate of 1:477. Each refractor was serial numbered out of 75.
COMPLETE SET (20) 75.00 150.00
*REFRACTORS: 1.5X TO 4X HI COLUMN
C1 Patrik Elias 5.00 12.00
C2 Bryan Berard 5.00 12.00
C3 Chris Osgood 3.00 8.00
C4 Saku Koivu 6.00 15.00
C5 Alexei Yashin 3.00 8.00
C6 Zigmund Palffy 3.00 8.00
C7 Peter Forsberg 15.00 40.00
C8 Jason Allison 3.00 8.00
C9 Wade Redden 3.00 8.00
C10 Paul Kariya 6.00 15.00
C11 Martin Brodeur 15.00 40.00
C12 Patrick Marleau 3.00 8.00
C13 Jaromir Jagr 10.00 25.00
C14 Mattias Ohlund 5.00 12.00
C15 Teemu Selanne 6.00 15.00
C16 Mike Johnson 5.00 12.00
C17 Joe Thornton 8.00 20.00
C18 Jocelyn Thibault 5.00 12.00
C19 Daniel Alfredsson 5.00 12.00
C20 Sergei Samsonov 5.00 12.00

1998-99 Finest Double Sided Mystery Finest

Randomly inserted into packs at the rate of 1:36, this 50-card set featured color action photos of 20 players printed on double-sided cards with one of three other players on the back or the same player on both sides. The opaque Finest Protector had to be peeled off in order to view the card. A refractor parallel was also produced and randomly inserted at a rate of 1:144.
COMPLETE SET (50) 250.00 500.00
*REFRACTORS.STARS: 1X TO 2X HI COLUMN
M1 Jaromir Jagr / Wayne Gretzky 10.00 25.00
M2 Jaromir Jagr / Dominik Hasek 5.00 12.00
M3 Jaromir Jagr / Eric Lindros 5.00 12.00
M4 Jaromir Jagr / Jaromir Jagr 5.00 12.00
M5 Dominik Hasek / Wayne Gretzky 12.50 30.00
M6 Dominik Hasek / Eric Lindros 5.00 12.00
M7 Dominik Hasek / Dominik Hasek 5.00 12.00
M8 Wayne Gretzky / Eric Lindros 12.50 30.00
M9 Wayne Gretzky / Wayne Gretzky 20.00 50.00
M10 Eric Lindros / Eric Lindros 5.00 12.00
M11 Paul Kariya / Teemu Selanne 5.00 12.00
M12 Paul Kariya / Ray Bourque 5.00 12.00
M13 Paul Kariya / Sergei Samsonov 5.00 12.00
M14 Paul Kariya / Paul Kariya 5.00 12.00
M15 Teemu Selanne / Ray Bourque 5.00 12.00
M16 Teemu Selanne / Sergei Samsonov 5.00 12.00
M17 Teemu Selanne / Teemu Selanne 5.00 12.00
M18 Ray Bourque / Sergei Samsonov 5.00 12.00
M19 Ray Bourque / Ray Bourque 5.00 12.00
M20 Sergei Samsonov / Sergei Samsonov 5.00 12.00
M21 Martin Brodeur / Peter Forsberg 10.00 25.00
M22 M.Brodeur/P.Roy 10.00 25.00
M23 Martin Brodeur / Joe Sakic 8.00 20.00
M24 Martin Brodeur / Martin Brodeur 8.00 20.00
M25 Peter Forsberg / Patrick Roy 12.50 30.00
M26 Peter Forsberg / Joe Sakic 10.00 25.00
M27 Peter Forsberg / Peter Forsberg 10.00 25.00
M28 Patrick Roy / Joe Sakic 12.50 30.00
M29 Patrick Roy / Patrick Roy 15.00 40.00
M30 Joe Sakic / Joe Sakic 5.00 12.00
M31 M.Modano/S.Yzerman 12.50 30.00
M32 Mike Modano / Sergei Fedorov 8.00 20.00
M33 Mike Modano / Brendan Shanahan 8.00 20.00
M34 Mike Modano / Mike Modano 5.00 12.00
M35 Steve Yzerman / Sergei Fedorov 8.00 20.00
M36 Steve Yzerman / Brendan Shanahan 8.00 20.00
M37 S.Yzerman/S.Yzerman 15.00 40.00
M38 Sergei Fedorov / Brendan Shanahan 5.00 12.00
M39 Sergei Fedorov / Sergei Fedorov 5.00 12.00
M40 Brendan Shanahan / Brendan Shanahan 5.00 12.00
M41 Mark Messier / John Leclair 5.00 12.00
M42 Mark Messier / Keith Tkachuk 5.00 12.00
M43 Mark Messier / Pavel Bure 5.00 12.00
M44 Mark Messier / Mark Messier 5.00 12.00
M45 John Leclair / Keith Tkachuk 5.00 12.00
M46 John Leclair / Pavel Bure 5.00 12.00
M47 John Leclair / John Leclair 5.00 12.00
M48 Pavel Bure / Keith Tkachuk 5.00 12.00
M49 Pavel Bure / Pavel Bure 4.00 10.00
M50 Keith Tkachuk / Keith Tkachuk 5.00 12.00

1998-99 Finest Futures Finest

Randomly inserted into packs at the rate of 1:72, this 20-card set featured color action photos of hard-charging NHL prospects and CHL players. Only 500 serial-numbered sets were produced. A refractor parallel was also produced and randomly inserted at a rate of 1:238. Refractors were serial numbered to 150.
COMPLETE SET (20) 40.00 80.00
*REFRACTORS: 1X TO 1.5X BASIC INSERTS
F1 David Legwand 4.00 10.00
F2 Manny Malhotra 2.00 5.00
F3 Vincent Lecavalier 6.00 15.00
F4 Brad Stuart 2.00 5.00
F5 Bryan Allen 2.00 5.00
F6 Rico Fata 2.00 5.00
F7 Mark Bell 2.00 5.00
F8 Michael Rupp 2.00 5.00
F9 Jeff Heerema 2.00 5.00
F10 Alex Tanguay 5.00 10.00
F11 Patrick Desrochers 2.00 5.00
F12 Mathieu Chouinard 2.00 5.00
F13 Eric Chouinard 2.00 5.00
F14 Martin Skoula 4.00 10.00
F15 Robyn Regehr 2.00 5.00
F16 Marian Hossa 6.00 15.00
F17 Daniel Cleary 2.00 5.00
F18 Olli Jokinen 2.00 5.00
F19 Brendan Morrison 2.00 5.00
F20 Erik Rasmussen 2.00 5.00

1998-99 Finest Oversize

Inserted one per hobby box, this seven-card set featured color action photos of top NHL

players printed on oversized cards measuring approximately 3 1/4" by 4 9/16". A refractor parallel was also produced and inserted at a rate of 1 in 6 boxes.
COMPLETE SET (7) 15.00 30.00
*REFRACTORS: 1.5X TO 3X BASIC INSERTS
1 Teemu Selanne 1.50 4.00
2 Dominik Hasek 1.50 4.00
3 Martin Brodeur 2.00 5.00
4 Wayne Gretzky 5.00 12.00
5 Steve Yzerman 4.00 10.00
6 Jaromir Jagr 1.25 3.00
7 Eric Lindros 1.50 4.00

1998-99 Finest Promos

This six-card set featured color action player photos printed on an embossed card with faint skating marks in the background. The fronts were covered with the Finest Protector film. The backs carried another player photos, biographical information, and season and career statistics. The cards were numbered with a "PP" prefix on the backs.
COMPLETE SET (6) 2.00 5.00
PP1 Scott Stevens .20 .50
PP2 Michael Nylander .20 .50
PP3 Brendan Shanahan .60 1.50
PP4 Trevor Kidd .30 .75
PP5 Bill Guerin .40 1.00
PP6 Brian Leetch .40 1.00

1998-99 Finest Red Lighters

Randomly inserted in packs at the rate of 1:24, this 20-card set featured color action photos of top NHL scorers printed on die-cut chromium cards. A refractor parallel was also created and inserted at 1:72.
COMPLETE SET (20) 40.00 80.00
*REFRACTORS: 1X TO 2X BASIC INSERTS
R1 Jaromir Jagr 2.50 6.00
R2 Mike Modano 2.50 6.00
R3 Paul Kariya 1.25 3.00
R4 Pavel Bure 1.25 3.00
R5 Peter Bondra 1.50 4.00
R6 Sergei Fedorov 2.00 5.00
R7 Steve Yzerman 6.00 15.00
R8 Teemu Selanne 1.25 3.00
R9 Wayne Gretzky 8.00 20.00
R10 Brendan Shanahan 1.25 3.00
R11 Eric Lindros 1.25 3.00
R12 Alexei Yashin 1.25 3.00
R13 Jason Allison 1.25 3.00
R14 Joe Nieuwendyk 1.50 4.00
R15 Joe Sakic 3.00 8.00
R16 John Leclair 1.25 3.00
R17 Keith Tkachuk 1.25 3.00
R18 Mark Messier 1.25 3.00
R19 Mats Sundin 1.25 3.00
R20 Zigmund Palffy 1.50 4.00

1994-95 Flair

This 225-card super premium set was issued in 10-card packs with a suggested retail price of $3.99. The cards featured a full-bleed design with dual action photos on the front and gold foil printing. The card stock was thicker than any basic issue. Yearly stats appeared on back in silver, printed over one more photo. The cards were arranged alphabetically within teams. Rookie cards in this set included Mariusz Czerkawski, David Oliver, Eric Fichaud and Jason Wiemer. To prevent tampering or searching, Fleer employed an innovative packaging design: the packs are actually a cello-wrapped, two-piece silver foil box, with the cards inside wrapped again in a sealed cello pouch.
COMPLETE SET (225) 25.00 50.00
1 Bob Corkum .07 .20
2 Bobby Dollas .07 .20
3 Guy Hebert .15 .40
4 Paul Kariya .30 .75
5 Anatoli Semenov .07 .20
6 Tim Sweeney .07 .20
7 Garry Valk .07 .20
8 Ray Bourque .50
9 Mariusz Czerkawski RC .40
10 Al Iafrate .07
11 Cam Neely .30
12 Adam Oates .15
13 Vincent Riendeau .15
14 Don Sweeney .07
15 Donald Audette .07
16 Doug Bodger .07
17 Dominik Hasek .75
18 Dale Hawerchuk .15
19 Pat LaFontaine .30
20 Alexander Mogilny .15
21 Craig Muni .07
22 Richard Smehlik .07
23 Denis Tsygurov RC .07
24 Theo Fleury .07
25 Trevor Kidd .15
26 James Patrick .07
27 Robert Reichel .07
28 Gary Roberts .07
29 German Titov .07
30 Zarley Zalapski .07
31 Ed Belfour .30
32 Chris Chelios .30
33 Dirk Graham .07
34 Joe Murphy .07
35 Bernie Nicholls .15
36 Jeremy Roenick .40
37 Steve Smith .07
38 Gary Suter .07
39 Neal Broten .15
40 Russ Courtnall .07
41 Todd Harvey .07
42 Grant Ledyard .07
43 Mike Modano .50
44 Andy Moog .30
45 Mark Tinordi .07
46 Dino Ciccarelli .15
47 Paul Coffey .30
48 Sergei Fedorov .50
49 Vladimir Konstantinov .15
50 Slava Kozlov .15
51 Keith Primeau .07
52 Ray Sheppard .15
53 Mike Vernon .15
54 Jason York RC .07
55 Steve Yzerman 1.50
56 Jason Arnott .07
57 Shayne Corson .07
58 Igor Kravchuk .07
59 Dean McAmmond .07
60 David Oliver RC .07
61 Bill Ranford .15
62 Doug Weight .15
63 Jesse Belanger .07
64 Bob Kudelski .07
65 Scott Mellanby .15
66 Gord Murphy .07
67 Rob Niedermayer .15
68 Brian Skrudland .07
69 John Vanbiesbrouck .15
70 Sean Burke .15
71 Andrew Cassels .07
72 Alexander Godynyuk .07
73 Chris Pronger .30
74 Geoff Sanderson .15
75 Darren Turcotte .07
76 Pat Verbeek .07
77 Rob Blake .15
78 Mike Donnelly .07
79 Wayne Gretzky 2.00
80 Kelly Hrudey .15
81 Jari Kurri .15
82 Marty McSorley .07
83 Rick Tocchet .15
84 Brian Bellows .07
85 Patrice Brisebois .07
86 Valeri Bure .07
87 Vincent Damphousse .07
88 Eric Desjardins .15
89 Kirk Muller .07
90 Oleg Petrov .07
91 Patrick Roy 1.50
92 Martin Brodeur .75
93 David Emma .07
94 Bill Guerin .15
95 John MacLean .15
96 Scott Niedermayer .07
97 Stephane Richer .15
98 Brian Rolston .07
99 Alexander Semak .07
100 Scott Stevens .15
101 Valeri Zelepukin .07
102 Patrick Flatley .07
103 Derek King .07
104 Brett Lindros .07
105 Vladimir Malakhov .07
106 Marty McInnis .07
107 Jamie McLennan .15
108 Steve Thomas .07
109 Pierre Turgeon .15
110 Jeff Beukeboom .07
111 Adam Graves .07
112 Alexei Kovalev .15
113 Steve Larmer .15
114 Brian Leetch .30
115 Mark Messier .30
116 Sergei Nemchinov .07
117 Mike Richter .30
118 Sergei Zubov .07
119 Craig Billington .15
120 Alexandre Daigle .07
121 Sean Hill .07
122 Norm Maciver .07
123 Dave McLlwain .07
124 Alexei Yashin .07
125 Vladislav Boulin RC .07
126 Rod Brind'Amour .15
127 Ron Hextall .15
128 Patrik Juhlin RC .07
129 Eric Lindros .30
130 Mark Recchi .15
131 Mikael Renberg .15
132 Chris Therien .07
133 Tom Barrasso .15
134 Ron Francis .15
135 Mario Lemieux 1.50
136 Shawn McEachern .07
137 Larry Murphy .15
138 Luc Robitaille .15

9 Ulf Samuelsson .07 .20
0 Kevin Stevens .07 .20
1 Martin Straka .07 .20
2 Wendel Clark .15 .40
3 Rene Corbet .07 .20
4 Adam Deadmarsh .07 .20
5 Stephane Fiset .15 .40
6 Peter Forsberg 1.00 2.50
7 Valeri Kamensky .15 .40
8 Janne Laukkanen .07 .20
9 Sylvain Lefebvre .07 .20
0 Mike Ricci .07 .20
1 Joe Sakic .60 1.50
2 Steve Duchesne .07 .20
3 Brett Hull .40 1.00
4 Craig Janney .15 .40
5 Craig Johnson .07 .20
6 Curtis Joseph .30 .75
7 Al MacInnis .15 .40
8 Brendan Shanahan .30 .75
9 Peter Stastny .15 .40
0 Esa Tikkanen .07 .20
1 Ulf Dahlen .07 .20
2 Todd Elik .07 .20
3 Pat Falloon .07 .20
4 Jeff Friesen .07 .20
5 Johan Garpenlov .07 .20
6 Arturs Irbe .15 .40
7 Sergei Makarov .07 .20
8 Jeff Norton .07 .20
9 Sandis Ozolinsh .07 .20
0 Brian Bradley .07 .20
1 Shawn Chambers .07 .20
2 Aaron Gavey .07 .20
3 Chris Gratton .07 .20
4 Petr Klima .07 .20
5 Daren Puppa .15 .40
6 Jason Wiemer RC .07 .20
7 Dave Andreychuk .15 .40
8 Dave Ellett .07 .20
9 Eric Fichaud RC .15 .40
0 Mike Gartner .15 .40
1 Doug Gilmour .15 .40
2 Kenny Jonsson .07 .20
3 Dmitri Mironov .07 .20
4 Felix Potvin .30 .75
5 Mike Ridley .07 .20
6 Mats Sundin .30 .75
7 Greg Adams .07 .20
8 Jeff Brown .07 .20
9 Pavel Bure .30 .75
0 Nathan Lafayette .07 .20
1 Trevor Linden .15 .40
2 Jyrki Lumme .07 .20
3 Kirk McLean .15 .40
4 Cliff Ronning .07 .20
5 Jason Allison .07 .20
6 Peter Bondra .15 .40
7 Randy Burridge .07 .20
8 Sylvain Cote .07 .20
9 Dale Hunter .07 .20
0 Joe Juneau .15 .40
1 Dimitri Khristich .07 .20
2 Todd Nelson .07 .20
3 Pat Peake .07 .20
4 Rick Tabaracci .15 .40
5 Tim Cheveldae .15 .40
6 Dallas Drake .07 .20
7 Dave Manson .07 .20
8 Teppo Numminen .07 .20
9 Teemu Selanne .30 .75
0 Darrin Shannon .07 .20
1 Keith Tkachuk .30 .75
2 Alexei Zhamnov .15 .40
3 Sergei Fedorov .30 .75
4 Sergei Fedorov .30 .75
5 Sergei Fedorov .30 .75
6 Sergei Fedorov .30 .75
7 Sergei Fedorov .30 .75
8 Sergei Fedorov .30 .75
9 Sergei Fedorov .30 .75
0 Sergei Fedorov .30 .75
1 Sergei Fedorov .30 .75
2 Sergei Fedorov .30 .75
3 Checklist .07 .20
4 Checklist .07 .20
5 Checklist .07 .20

994-95 Flair Center Spotlight

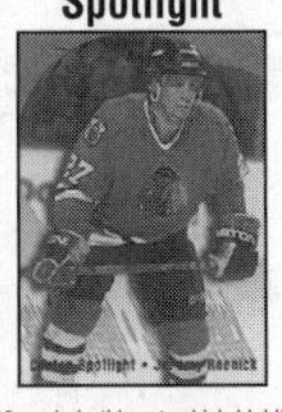

e 10 cards in this set, which highlighted me of the league's top centers, were domly inserted in Flair product at the rate 1:4 packs. The cards featured an action ot with two spotlights defining the ckground. Backs featured another action oto, along with a player profile. The cards re numbered on the back as "X of 10".

MPLETE SET (10) 10.00 20.00
Jason Arnott .15 .40
Sergei Fedorov 1.00 2.50
Doug Gilmour .30 .75
Wayne Gretzky 4.00 10.00
Pat LaFontaine .60 1.50
Mario Lemieux 3.00 8.00
Eric Lindros .60 1.50
Mark Messier .60 1.50
Mike Modano 1.00 2.50
Jeremy Roenick .75 2.00

1994-95 Flair Hot Numbers

e ten cards in this set, which highlight me of the game's deadliest snipers, were domly inserted in Flair product at the rate 1:16 packs. The cards featured an action

shot over a black background featuring a scribble of neon colors. The player, team, and set name appeared vertically along the left border of the card. Card backs had a similar style as the front and are numbered as "X of 10".

COMPLETE SET (10) 20.00 40.00
1 Pavel Bure .75 2.00
2 Wayne Gretzky 5.00 12.00
3 Dominik Hasek 2.00 5.00
4 Brett Hull 1.00 2.50
5 Mario Lemieux 4.00 10.00
6 Adam Oates .40 1.00
7 Luc Robitaille .40 1.00
8 Patrick Roy 4.00 10.00
9 Brendan Shanahan .75 2.00
10 Steve Yzerman 4.00 10.00

1994-95 Flair Scoring Power

This 10-card standard-size set was inserted in packs at a rate of 1:8. The fronts had a color action photo on the right side and the player's name and the word "Power" going down the left side in silver-foil. The background consisted of many multi-color lines scrawled about. The backs has a color photo with player information and the player's name and "Scoring Power" in silver-foil at the top. The background was similar to the front and they are numbered "X of 10" at the bottom.

COMPLETE SET (10) 6.00 12.00
1 Pavel Bure .75 2.00
2 Alexandre Daigle .20 .50
3 Sergei Fedorov 1.25 3.00
4 Alexei Kovalev .40 1.00
5 Brian Leetch .75 2.00
6 Eric Lindros .75 2.00
7 Mike Modano 1.25 3.00
8 Alexander Mogilny .40 1.00
9 Jeremy Roenick 1.00 2.50
10 Alexei Yashin .20 .50

1996-97 Flair

The 1996-97 Flair set was issued in one series totaling 125 cards. The set contained the Wave of the Future subset (101-125). Although numbered as part of the set, these cards were short printed and inserted at a rate of 1:4 packs. Card fronts featured a color action photo, and a background portrait of the player. Card backs contained a color action photo and statistics. Cards were distributed in four-card packs and carried a suggested retail price of $3.99. Key rookies include Sergei Berezin, Mike Grier, Patrick Lalime, Ethan Moreau and Dainius Zubrus.

COMPLETE SET (125) 40.00 80.00
COMP.BASE SET (100) 20.00 40.00
1 Guy Hebert .20 .50
2 Paul Kariya .30 .75
3 Teemu Selanne .30 .75
4 Ray Bourque .50 1.25
5 Adam Oates .20 .50
6 Bill Ranford .20 .50
7 Jozef Stumpel .08 .25
8 Dominik Hasek .60 1.50
9 Pat LaFontaine .30 .75
10 Alexei Zhitnik .08 .25
11 Theo Fleury .08 .25
12 Dave Gagner .20 .50
13 Trevor Kidd .20 .50
14 Tony Amonte .20 .50
15 Chris Chelios .30 .75
16 Eric Daze .20 .50
17 Alexei Zhamnov .20 .50
18 Peter Forsberg .75 2.00
19 Sandis Ozolinsh .08 .25
20 Patrick Roy 1.50 4.00
21 Joe Sakic .60 1.50
22 Derian Hatcher .08 .25
23 Mike Modano .50 1.25
24 Andy Moog .20 .50
25 Pat Verbeek .08 .25
26 Sergei Fedorov .50 1.25
27 Slava Fetisov .08 .25
28 Nicklas Lidstrom .30 .75
29 Chris Osgood .20 .50
30 Brendan Shanahan .30 .75
31 Steve Yzerman 1.50 4.00
32 Jason Arnott .08 .25
33 Curtis Joseph .30 .75
34 Boris Mironov .08 .25
35 Ryan Smyth .30 .75
36 Doug Weight .20 .50
37 Ed Jovanovski .20 .50
38 Ray Sheppard .20 .50
39 Robert Svehla .08 .25
40 John Vanbiesbrouck .20 .50
41 Andrew Cassels .08 .25
42 Jason Muzzatti .20 .50
43 Keith Primeau .08 .25
44 Geoff Sanderson .20 .50
45 Rob Blake .20 .50
46 Dimitri Khristich .08 .25
47 Vincent Damphousse .08 .25
48 Saku Koivu .30 .75
49 Mark Recchi .20 .50
50 Martin Rucinsky .08 .25
51 Jocelyn Thibault .30 .75
52 Martin Brodeur .75 2.00
53 Bill Guerin .08 .25
54 Scott Stevens .20 .50
55 Scott Lachance .08 .25
56 Zigmund Palffy .20 .50
57 Tommy Salo .20 .50
58 Bryan Smolinski .08 .25
59 Wayne Gretzky 2.50 5.00
60 Brian Leetch .30 .75
61 Mark Messier .30 .75
62 Mike Richter .30 .75
63 Daniel Alfredsson .20 .50
64 Damian Rhodes .20 .50
65 Alexei Yashin .08 .25
66 Paul Coffey .30 .75
67 Dale Hawerchuk .20 .50
68 Ron Hextall .20 .50
69 John LeClair .30 .75
70 Eric Lindros .30 .75
71 Nikolai Khabibulin .20 .50
72 Jeremy Roenick .40 1.00
73 Keith Tkachuk .30 .75
74 Oleg Tverdovsky .20 .50
75 Ron Francis .20 .50
76 Kevin Hatcher .08 .25
77 Jaromir Jagr .50 1.25
78 Mario Lemieux 1.50 4.00
79 Petr Nedved .20 .50
80 Grant Fuhr .20 .50
81 Brett Hull .40 1.00
82 Al MacInnis .20 .50
83 Ed Belfour .30 .75
84 Tony Granato .08 .25
85 Owen Nolan .20 .50
86 Dino Ciccarelli .20 .50
87 John Cullen .08 .25
88 Roman Hamrlik .20 .50
89 Wendel Clark .20 .50
90 Doug Gilmour .20 .50
91 Felix Potvin .30 .75
92 Mats Sundin .30 .75
93 Pavel Bure .30 .75
94 Corey Hirsch .20 .50
95 Trevor Linden .20 .50
96 Alexander Mogilny .20 .50
97 Peter Bondra .20 .50
98 Jim Carey .30 .75
99 Dale Hunter .08 .25
100 Chris Simon .08 .25
101 Mattias Timander RC .30 .75
102 Vaclav Varada RC .30 .75
103 Jarome Iginla SP .40 1.00
104 Ethan Moreau RC .75 2.00
105 Jamie Langenbrunner SP .30 .75
106 Roman Turek RC .75 2.00
107 Tomas Holmstrom RC .75 2.00
108 Kevin Hodson RC .75 2.00
109 Mats Lindgren SP .30 .75
110 Mike Grier RC SP 1.00 2.50
111 Rem Murray RC .75 2.00
112 Jose Theodore SP 2.00 5.00
113 David Wilkie SP .30 .75
114 Bryan Berard SP .30 .75
115 Eric Fichaud SP .30 .75
116 Daniel Goneau RC .75 2.00
117 Andreas Dackell RC .75 2.00
118 Wade Redden SP .30 .75
119 Dainius Zubrus RC .75 2.00
120 Janne Niinimaa SP .30 .75
121 Patrick Lalime RC 2.00 5.00
122 Harry York RC SP .75 2.00
123 Jim Campbell SP .30 .75
124 Sergei Berezin RC .75 2.00
125 Jaro. Svejkovsky RC .75 2.00

1996-97 Flair Blue Ice

This 125-card set paralleled the basic Flair set. The cards were randomly inserted in packs at a rate of 1:20, though many dealers suggested they were harder to obtain than the odds suggest. Each card was serial numbered tp 250, and card fronts carried a blue foil background along with the words BLUE ICE. No complete set price is listed below due to the extremely short print run of the set, and the lack of market activity in complete set form. Values can be determined by applying the multipliers below to the prices for the corresponding regular card.

*STARS: 15X TO 40X BASIC CARDS
*WAVE/FUTURE: 1.5X TO 3X BASIC CARDS

1996-97 Flair Center Ice Spotlight

This set featured ten of the NHL's top players. Card fronts featured a color action photo, with purple, red and yellow spotlights highlighting the background. The cards were randomly inserted in packs at a rate of 1:30.

COMPLETE SET (10) 15.00 40.00
1 Pavel Bure 1.50 4.00
2 Sergei Fedorov 2.00 5.00
3 Peter Forsberg 2.00 5.00
4 Brett Hull 2.00 5.00
5 Jaromir Jagr 2.50 6.00
6 Paul Kariya 1.50 4.00
7 Joe Sakic 3.00 8.00
8 Teemu Selanne 1.50 4.00
9 Mats Sundin 1.50 4.00
10 Steve Yzerman 6.00 15.00

1996-97 Flair Hot Gloves

This insert set focused on twelve of the NHL's best netminders. Card fronts featured a color action photo with the mesh of a goalie glove in the background. Card backs contained a player photo and biographical information. Each card was die-cut and randomly inserted in packs at a rate of 1:40.

COMPLETE SET (12) 40.00 100.00
1 Ed Belfour 4.00 10.00
2 Martin Brodeur 10.00 25.00
3 Jim Carey 2.00 5.00
4 Dominik Hasek 6.00 15.00
5 Curtis Joseph 4.00 10.00
6 Patrick Lalime 2.00 5.00
7 Chris Osgood 4.00 10.00
8 Felix Potvin 4.00 10.00
9 Mike Richter 4.00 10.00
10 Patrick Roy 15.00 40.00
11 Jocelyn Thibault 2.00 5.00
12 John Vanbiesbrouck 4.00 10.00

1996-97 Flair Hot Numbers

This 10-card insert set featured NHL superstars who wear double numbers on their jerseys. Card fronts featured a color photo with an orange/red background and their jersey number along the top of the card. The cards were randomly inserted in packs at a rate of 1:72.

COMPLETE SET (10) 25.00 50.00
1 Ray Bourque 2.50 6.00
2 Paul Coffey 1.50 4.00
3 Eric Daze 1.00 2.50
4 Wayne Gretzky 10.00 25.00
5 Ed Jovanovski 1.00 2.50
6 Saku Koivu 1.50 4.00
7 Mario Lemieux 8.00 20.00
8 Eric Lindros 1.50 4.00
9 Mark Messier 1.50 4.00
10 Owen Nolan 1.00 2.50

1996-97 Flair Now And Then

Each card in this set featured three players who share a common bond. They are pictured in their rookie seasons on the front, while the back gave an up-to-date look. The cards were randomly inserted in packs at a rate of 1:400.

COMPLETE SET (3) 40.00 100.00
1 Wayne Gretzky 25.00 60.00
Mark Messier
Mike Gartner
2 Mario Lemieux 15.00 40.00
Patrick Roy
Kirk Muller
3 Eric Lindros 10.00 25.00
Peter Forsberg
Scott Niedermayer

2006-07 Flair Showcase

MALKIN AVAIL. AS EXPO REDEMPTION
COMMON UPDATE RC 1.50 4.00
SEMISTAR UPDATE RC 2.50 6.00
UPD. RCs AVAIL IN UPDATE DEALER PACKS
1 Jean-Sebastien Giguere .50 1.25
2 Teemu Selanne .60 1.50
3 Corey Perry .50 1.25
4 Scott Niedermayer .30 .75
5 Joffrey Lupul .30 .75
6 Ilya Kovalchuk .75 2.00
7 Marian Hossa .50 1.25
8 Kari Lehtonen .60 1.50
9 Patrice Bergeron .60 1.50
10 Marc Savard .30 .75
11 Brad Boyes .30 .75
12 Mark Stuart RC .75 2.00
13 Chris Drury .30 .75
14 Ryan Miller .60 1.50
15 Thomas Vanek .30 .75
16 Jarome Iginla .75 2.00
17 Miikka Kiprusoff .75 2.00
18 Dion Phaneuf .75 2.00
19 Eric Staal .50 1.25
20 Cam Ward .60 1.50
21 Justin Williams .30 .75
22 Erik Cole .30 .75
23 Doug Weight .30 .75
24 Nikolai Khabibulin .60 1.50
25 Tuomo Ruutu .30 .75
26 Dustin Byfuglien RC .75 2.00
27 Milan Hejduk .50 1.25
28 Alex Tanguay .50 1.25
29 Jose Theodore .75 2.00
30 Marek Svatos .30 .75
31 Rob Blake .50 1.25
32 Rick Nash .75 2.00
33 Sergei Fedorov .60 1.50
34 Mike Modano .75 2.00
35 Marty Turco .50 1.25
36 Brenden Morrow .30 .75
37 Jere Lehtinen .30 .75
38 Steve Yzerman 2.00 5.00
39 Tomas Kopecky RC 1.25 3.00
40 Henrik Zetterberg .50 1.25
41 Pavel Datsyuk .50 1.25
42 Tomas Holmstrom .30 .75
43 Kris Draper .30 .75
44 M-A Pouliot RC 1.25 3.00
45 Ales Hemsky .30 .75
46 Roberto Luongo .75 2.00
47 Olli Jokinen .30 .75
48 Konstantin Pushkarev RC .75 2.00
49 Jeremy Roenick .75 2.00
50 Alexander Frolov .30 .75
51 Marian Gaborik 1.25 3.00
52 Manny Fernandez .50 1.25
53 Saku Koivu .60 1.50
54 Michael Ryder .50 1.25
55 Mike Ribeiro .30 .75
56 Cristobal Huet .50 1.25
57 Paul Kariya .60 1.50
58 Tomas Vokoun .50 1.25
59 Shea Weber RC .75 2.00
60 Patrik Elias .30 .75
61 Masi Marjamaki RC .40 1.00
62 Alexei Yashin .30 .75
63 Rick DiPietro .50 1.25
64 Miroslav Satan .30 .75
65 Henrik Lundqvist .75 2.00
66 Jarkko Immonen RC .75 2.00
67 Daniel Alfredsson .50 1.25
68 Martin Gerber .50 1.25
69 Jason Spezza .60 1.50
70 Dany Heatley .75 2.00
71 Martin Havlat .50 1.25
72 Zdeno Chara .30 .75
73 Simon Gagne .60 1.50
74 Ryan Potulny RC 2.00 2.50
75 Jeff Carter .50 1.25
76 Peter Forsberg 1.50 4.00
77 Shane Doan .30 .75
78 Ladislav Nagy .30 .75
79 Curtis Joseph .60 1.50
80 Marc-Andre Fleury .60 1.50
81 Noah Welch RC 1.00 .75
82 Matt Carle RC 1.50 4.00
83 Evgeni Nabokov .50 1.25
84 Jonathan Cheechoo .50 1.25
85 Patrick Marleau .50 1.25
86 Keith Tkachuk .60 1.50
87 Vincent Lecavalier .60 1.50
88 Martin St. Louis .50 1.25
89 Brad Richards .50 1.25
90 Ian White RC .75 2.00
91 Ben Ondrus RC .60 1.50
92 Eric Lindros .60 1.50
93 Alexander Steen .50 1.25
94 Jeremy Williams RC .75 2.00
95 Todd Bertuzzi .50 1.25
96 Markus Naslund .60 1.50
97 Ed Jovanovski .30 .75
98 Eric Fehr RC .75 2.00
99 Alexander Ovechkin 2.50 6.00
100 Olaf Kolzig .60 1.50
101 Teemu Selanne .60 1.50
102 Scott Niedermayer .30 .75
103 Corey Perry .50 1.25
104 Marian Hossa .50 1.25
105 Kari Lehtonen .60 1.50
106 Yan Stastny RC .75 2.00
107 Glen Murray .30 .75
108 Brian Leetch .60 1.50
109 Brad Boyes .30 .75
110 Chris Drury .30 .75
111 Ryan Miller .60 1.50
112 Thomas Vanek .30 .75
113 Dion Phaneuf .75 2.00
114 Erik Cole .30 .75
115 Cam Ward .60 1.50
116 Mark Recchi .30 .75
117 Nikolai Khabibulin .60 1.50
118 Tuomo Ruutu .30 .75
119 Rob Blake .50 1.25
120 Milan Hejduk .50 1.25
121 Marek Svatos .30 .75
122 Sergei Fedorov .60 1.50
123 Brenden Morrow .30 .75
124 Marty Turco .50 1.25
125 Tomas Kopecky RC 1.25 3.00
126 Pavel Datsyuk .50 1.25
127 Henrik Zetterberg .50 1.25
128 M-A Pouliot RC 1.25 3.00
129 Ales Hemsky .30 .75
130 Olli Jokinen .30 .75
131 Konstantin Pushkarev RC .75 2.00
132 Luc Robitaille .50 1.25
133 Jeremy Roenick .75 2.00
134 Alexander Frolov .30 .75
135 Marian Gaborik 1.25 3.00
136 Michael Ryder .50 1.25
137 Shea Weber RC .75 2.00
138 Paul Kariya .60 1.50
139 Tomas Vokoun .50 1.25
140 Patrik Elias .30 .75
141 Alexei Yashin .30 .75
142 Rick DiPietro .50 1.25
143 Miroslav Satan .30 .75
144 Henrik Lundqvist .75 2.00
145 Billy Thompson RC .75 2.00
146 Filip Novak RC .40 1.00
147 Daniel Alfredsson .50 1.25
148 Zdeno Chara .30 .75
149 Martin Havlat .50 1.25
150 Simon Gagne .60 1.50
151 Keith Primeau .30 .75
152 Jeff Carter .50 1.25
153 Shane Doan .30 .75
154 Ladislav Nagy .30 .75
155 Curtis Joseph .60 1.50
156 Noah Welch RC .30 2.50
157 Marc-Andre Fleury .60 1.50
158 Evgeni Nabokov .50 1.25
159 Jonathan Cheechoo .50 1.25
160 Patrick Marleau .50 1.25
161 Keith Tkachuk .60 1.50
162 Brad Richards .50 1.25
163 Ben Ondrus RC .75 2.00
164 Brendan Bell RC .75 2.00
165 Ian White RC .75 2.00
166 Eric Lindros .60 1.50
167 Todd Bertuzzi .50 1.25
168 Ed Jovanovski .30 .75
169 Eric Fehr RC .75 2.00
170 Olaf Kolzig .60 1.50
171 Jean-Sebastien Giguere .50 1.25
172 Ilya Kovalchuk .75 2.00
173 Patrice Bergeron .60 1.50
174 Jarome Iginla .75 2.00
175 Miikka Kiprusoff .75 2.00
176 Eric Staal .60 1.50
177 Joe Sakic 1.25 3.00
178 Jose Theodore .75 2.00
179 Alex Tanguay .50 1.25
180 Rick Nash .75 2.00
181 Mike Modano .75 2.00
182 Steve Yzerman 2.00 5.00
183 Brendan Shanahan .60 1.50
184 Chris Pronger .50 1.25
185 Roberto Luongo .75 2.00
186 Saku Koivu .60 1.50
187 Martin Brodeur 2.00 5.00
188 Jaromir Jagr 1.00 2.50
189 Jason Spezza .60 1.50
190 Dany Heatley .75 2.00
191 Martin Gerber .50 1.25
192 Peter Forsberg 1.50 4.00
193 Sidney Crosby 5.00 12.00
194 Joe Thornton 1.00 2.50
195 Vincent Lecavalier .60 1.50
196 Martin St. Louis .50 1.25
197 Mats Sundin .60 1.50
198 Andrew Raycroft .50 1.25
199 Markus Naslund .60 1.50
200 Alexander Ovechkin 3.00 8.00
201 Jean-Sebastien Giguere 1.25 3.00
202 Teemu Selanne 1.50 4.00
203 Kari Lehtonen 1.50 4.00
204 Marian Hossa 1.25 3.00
205 Ilya Kovalchuk 2.00 5.00
206 Ray Bourque 2.00 5.00
207 Patrice Bergeron 1.50 4.00
208 Brian Leetch 1.50 4.00
209 Chris Drury .75 2.00
210 Ryan Miller 1.50 4.00
211 Jarome Iginla 2.00 5.00
212 Miikka Kiprusoff 2.00 5.00
213 Dion Phaneuf 1.50 4.00
214 Eric Staal 1.50 4.00
215 Cam Ward 1.50 4.00
216 Rod Brind`Amour .75 2.00
217 Nikolai Khabibulin 1.25 3.00
218 Joe Sakic 3.00 8.00
219 Alex Tanguay .75 2.00
220 Milan Hejduk .75 2.00
221 Jose Theodore 1.50 4.00
222 Marek Svatos .75 2.00
223 Rick Nash 2.00 5.00
224 Sergei Fedorov 1.25 3.00
225 Mike Modano 2.00 5.00
226 Marty Turco 1.25 3.00
227 Brenden Morrow .75 2.00
228 Steve Yzerman 4.00 10.00
229 Gordie Howe 2.50 6.00
230 Brendan Shanahan 2.00 5.00
231 Henrik Zetterberg 1.25 3.00
232 Pavel Datsyuk 1.25 3.00
233 Chris Pronger 1.25 3.00
234 Roberto Luongo 3.00 8.00
235 Olli Jokinen 1.50 4.00
236 Luc Robitaille 2.00 5.00
237 Jeremy Roenick 2.00 5.00
238 Marian Gaborik 4.00 10.00
239 Saku Koivu 2.00 5.00
240 Patrick Roy 15.00 40.00
241 Michael Ryder 2.00 5.00
242 Paul Kariya 3.00 8.00
243 Martin Brodeur 10.00 25.00
244 Patrik Elias 2.00 5.00
245 Alexei Yashin 2.00 5.00
246 Rick DiPietro 2.00 5.00
247 Jaromir Jagr 6.00 15.00
248 Henrik Lundqvist 4.00 10.00
249 Martin Gerber 2.00 5.00
250 Dany Heatley 4.00 10.00
251 Jason Spezza 2.50 6.00
252 Daniel Alfredsson 2.00 5.00
253 Peter Forsberg 6.00 15.00
254 Simon Gagne 2.00 5.00
255 Shane Doan 2.00 5.00
256 Mario Lemieux 15.00 40.00
257 Sidney Crosby 15.00 40.00
258 Marc-Andre Fleury 3.00 8.00
259 Evgeni Nabokov 2.50 6.00
260 Joe Thornton 4.00 10.00
261 Jonathan Cheechoo 2.50 6.00
262 Vincent Lecavalier 3.00 8.00
263 Martin St. Louis 2.50 6.00
264 Brad Richards 2.50 6.00
265 Andrew Raycroft 2.50 6.00
266 Mats Sundin 2.50 6.00
267 Markus Naslund 2.50 6.00
268 Todd Bertuzzi 2.50 6.00
269 Alexander Ovechkin 8.00 20.00
270 Olaf Kolzig 2.50 6.00
271 Jean-Sebastien Giguere 2.50 6.00
272 Ilya Kovalchuk 6.00 15.00
273 Ray Bourque 6.00 15.00
274 Jarome Iginla 8.00 20.00
275 Miikka Kiprusoff 6.00 15.00
276 Eric Staal 6.00 15.00
277 Joe Sakic 10.00 25.00
278 Rick Nash 6.00 15.00
279 Mike Modano 8.00 20.00
280 Steve Yzerman 12.00 30.00
281 Gordie Howe 8.00 20.00
282 Henrik Zetterberg 6.00 15.00
283 Roberto Luongo 8.00 20.00
284 Saku Koivu 6.00 15.00
285 Patrick Roy 15.00 40.00
286 Paul Kariya 6.00 15.00
287 Martin Brodeur 15.00 40.00
288 Jaromir Jagr 8.00 20.00
289 Daniel Alfredsson 5.00 12.00
290 Dany Heatley 8.00 20.00
291 Jason Spezza 6.00 15.00
292 Peter Forsberg 10.00 25.00
293 Mario Lemieux 20.00 50.00
294 Sidney Crosby 25.00 60.00
295 Joe Thornton 10.00 25.00
296 Vincent Lecavalier 8.00 20.00
297 Andrew Raycroft 5.00 12.00
298 Mats Sundin 6.00 15.00
299 Markus Naslund 8.00 20.00
300 Alexander Ovechkin 15.00 40.00
301 Ryan Shannon RC 1.50 4.00
302 David McKee RC 2.50 6.00
303 Phil Kessel RC 5.00 12.00
304 Matt Lashoff RC 1.50 4.00
305 Drew Stafford RC 4.00 10.00
306 Clarke MacArthur RC 1.50 4.00
307 Dustin Boyd RC 2.50 6.00
308 Brandon Prust RC 1.50 4.00
309 Dave Bolland RC 1.50 4.00
310 Paul Stastny RC 6.00 15.00
311 Loui Eriksson RC 1.50 4.00
312 Ladislav Smid RC 1.50 4.00
313 Patrick O'Sullivan RC 2.00 5.00
314 Anze Kopitar RC 5.00 12.00
315 Benoit Pouliot RC 2.50 6.00
316 Guillaume Latendresse RC 6.00 15.00
317 Alexander Radulov RC 5.00 12.00
318 Travis Zajac RC 3.00 8.00
319 Nigel Dawes RC 1.50 4.00
320 Josh Hennessy RC 1.50 4.00
321 Enver Lisin RC 1.50 4.00
322 Evgeni Malkin RC 10.00 25.00
323 Jordan Staal RC 10.00 25.00
324 Kristopher Letang RC 2.50 6.00
325 Marc-Edouard Vlasic RC 1.50 4.00
326 Joe Pavelski RC 2.50 6.00
327 Marek Schwarz RC 2.50 6.00
328 Karri Ramo RC 1.50 4.00
329 Luc Bourdon RC 2.50 6.00
330 Jesse Schultz RC 1.50 4.00
FE-301 Evgeni Malkin 15.00 40.00

2006-07 Flair Showcase Parallel

1-100: 1.5X TO 3X HI COLUMN

2006-07 Flair Showcase Hot Gloves

STATED ODDS 1:72
HG1 Jean-Sebastien Giguere 6.00 15.00
HG2 Kari Lehtonen 8.00 20.00
HG3 Hannu Toivonen 6.00 15.00
HG4 Ryan Miller 8.00 20.00
HG5 Miikka Kiprusoff 8.00 20.00
HG6 Martin Gerber 8.00 20.00
HG7 Nikolai Khabibulin 8.00 20.00
HG8 Jose Theodore 8.00 20.00
HG9 Marc Denis 6.00 15.00
HG10 Marty Turco 8.00 20.00
HG11 Cam Ward 8.00 20.00
HG12 Dwayne Roloson 6.00 15.00
HG13 Roberto Luongo 8.00 20.00
HG14 Mathieu Garon 6.00 15.00
HG15 Manny Fernandez 6.00 15.00
HG16 Cristobal Huet 8.00 20.00
HG17 Tomas Vokoun 8.00 20.00
HG18 Martin Brodeur 12.00 30.00
HG19 Rick DiPietro 8.00 20.00
HG20 Henrik Lundqvist 8.00 20.00
HG21 Pascal Leclaire 8.00 20.00
HG22 Antero Niittymaki 6.00 15.00
HG23 Curtis Joseph 8.00 20.00
HG24 Marc-Andre Fleury 8.00 20.00
HG25 Evgeni Nabokov 8.00 20.00
HG26 Curtis Sanford 6.00 15.00
HG27 Vesa Toskala 6.00 15.00
HG28 Andrew Raycroft 8.00 20.00
HG29 Alex Auld 6.00 15.00
HG30 Olaf Kolzig 8.00 20.00

2006-07 Flair Showcase Hot Numbers

STATED ODDS 1:180
HN1 Teemu Selanne 8.00 20.00
HN2 Kari Lehtonen 8.00 20.00
HN3 Ray Bourque 8.00 20.00
HN4 Miikka Kiprusoff 10.00 25.00
HN5 Jarome Iginla 10.00 25.00
HN6 Martin Gerber 8.00 20.00
HN7 Eric Staal 8.00 20.00
HN8 Nikolai Khabibulin 10.00 25.00
HN9 Alex Tanguay 15.00 40.00
HN10 Jose Theodore 8.00 20.00
HN11 Joe Sakic 15.00 40.00
HN12 Milan Hejduk 6.00 15.00
HN13 Rick Nash 8.00 20.00
HN14 Sergei Fedorov 8.00 20.00
HN15 Mike Modano 8.00 20.00
HN16 Henrik Zetterberg 6.00 15.00
HN17 Gordie Howe 12.00 30.00
HN18 Brendan Shanahan 6.00 15.00
HN19 Steve Yzerman 15.00 40.00
HN20 Ales Hemsky 6.00 15.00
HN21 Jeremy Roenick 6.00 15.00
HN22 Luc Robitaille 8.00 20.00
HN23 Marian Gaborik 10.00 25.00
HN24 Patrick Roy 20.00 50.00
HN25 Michael Ryder 6.00 15.00
HN26 Saku Koivu 6.00 15.00
HN27 Martin Brodeur 15.00 40.00
HN28 Alexei Yashin 6.00 15.00
HN29 Jaromir Jagr 12.00 30.00
HN30 Dominik Hasek 10.00 25.00
HN31 Dany Heatley 10.00 25.00
HN32 Peter Forsberg 10.00 25.00
HN33 Sidney Crosby 30.00 60.00
HN34 Mario Lemieux 25.00 50.00
HN35 Joe Thornton 10.00 25.00
HN36 Vincent Lecavalier 8.00 20.00
HN37 Martin St. Louis 6.00 15.00
HN38 Mats Sundin 8.00 20.00
HN39 Eric Lindros 8.00 20.00
HN40 Todd Bertuzzi 6.00 15.00
HN41 Markus Naslund 6.00 15.00
HN42 Alexander Ovechkin 20.00 40.00

2006-07 Flair Showcase Hot Numbers Parallel

#'d to JERSEY NUMBER
PRINT RUNS UNDER 24 NOT LISTED
HN1 Teemu Selanne
HN2 Kari Lehtonen 25.00 60.00
HN3 Ray Bourque 15.00 40.00
HN4 Miikka Kiprusoff 25.00 60.00
HN5 Jarome Iginla
HN6 Martin Gerber 40.00 80.00
HN7 Eric Staal
HN8 Nikolai Khabibulin 12.00 30.00
HN9 Alex Tanguay
HN10 Jose Theodore 15.00 30.00
HN11 Joe Sakic
HN12 Milan Hejduk
HN13 Rick Nash 12.00 30.00
HN14 Sergei Fedorov 12.00 30.00
HN15 Mike Modano
HN16 Henrik Zetterberg 15.00 40.00
HN17 Gordie Howe
HN18 Brendan Shanahan
HN19 Steve Yzerman
HN20 Ales Hemsky 8.00 20.00
HN21 Jeremy Roenick 12.00 30.00
HN22 Luc Robitaille
HN23 Marian Gaborik
HN24 Patrick Roy
HN25 Michael Ryder 8.00 20.00
HN26 Saku Koivu
HN27 Martin Brodeur 25.00 80.00
HN28 Alexei Yashin 8.00 20.00
HN29 Jaromir Jagr 15.00 40.00
HN30 Dominik Hasek 20.00 50.00
HN31 Dany Heatley
HN32 Peter Forsberg
HN33 Sidney Crosby 40.00 100.00
HN34 Mario Lemieux 30.00 80.00
HN35 Joe Thornton
HN36 Vincent Lecavalier
HN37 Martin St. Louis 20.00 50.00
HN38 Mats Sundin
HN39 Eric Lindros 12.00 30.00
HN40 Todd Bertuzzi 8.00 20.00
HN41 Markus Naslund
HN42 Alexander Ovechkin

2006-07 Flair Showcase Inks

STATED ODDS 1:18
IAF Alexander Frolov 4.00 10.00
IAH Ales Hemsky 6.00 15.00
IAL Andrew Ladd 4.00 10.00
IAM Andy McDonald 4.00 10.00
IAN Antero Niittymaki 12.00 30.00
IAO Alexander Ovechkin SP 60.00 100.00
IBB Brad Boyes 6.00 15.00
IBE Ben Eager 4.00 10.00
IBG Brian Gionta 6.00 15.00
IBI Martin Biron 6.00 15.00
IBL Brian Leetch 8.00 20.00
IBR Brenden Morrow 6.00 15.00
ICD Chris Drury 4.00 10.00
ICH Cristobal Huet 10.00 25.00
ICK Chris Kunitz 4.00 10.00
IDA David Aebischer 6.00 15.00
IDB Daniel Briere 10.00 25.00
IDC Dan Cloutier 4.00 10.00
IDK Duncan Keith 4.00 10.00
IDL David Leneveu 4.00 10.00
IDP Dion Phaneuf 10.00 25.00
IDR Dwayne Roloson 6.00 15.00
IDU Dustin Brown 4.00 10.00
IED Eric Daze 4.00 10.00
IEN Evgeni Nabokov 6.00 15.00
IFP Fernando Pisani 4.00 10.00
IHA Michal Handzus 4.00 10.00
IHE Dany Heatley
IHJ Milan Hejduk 6.00 15.00
IHO Marcel Hossa 5.00 12.00
IHZ Henrik Zetterberg 15.00 40.00
IIK Ilya Kovalchuk SP 20.00 50.00
IJC Jonathan Cheechoo 6.00 15.00
IJI Jarome Iginla 12.00 30.00
IJL Joffrey Lupul 6.00 15.00
IJO Jeff O'Neill 4.00 10.00
IJP Joni Pitkanen 4.00 10.00
IJR Jeremy Roenick SP 15.00 40.00
IJT Jose Theodore 8.00 20.00
IKD Kris Draper 4.00 10.00
IKE Ryan Kesler 4.00 10.00
IKI Miikka Kiprusoff 15.00 40.00
IKL Kari Lehtonen 8.00 20.00
IKO Chuck Kobasew 4.00 10.00
ILR Luc Robitaille 10.00 25.00
ILX Mario Lemieux SP 125.00 200.00
IMA Maxim Afinogenov 5.00 12.00
IMB Martin Brodeur SP 60.00 125.00
IMC Mike Cammalleri 4.00 10.00
IMF Marc-Andre Fleury 12.00 30.00
IMG Marian Gaborik 15.00 40.00
IMH Martin Havlat 6.00 15.00
IMI Ryan Miller 10.00 25.00
IML Manny Legace 6.00 15.00
IMM Milan Michalek 6.00 15.00
IMN Markus Naslund 6.00 15.00
IMO Brendan Morrison 4.00 10.00
IMP Mark Parrish 4.00 10.00
IMR Mike Richards 6.00 15.00
IMS Marc Savard 4.00 10.00
IMT Marty Turco SP
INA Nikolai Antropov 4.00 10.00
IOJ Olli Jokinen 4.00 10.00
IOK Olaf Kolzig 8.00 20.00
IPA Jay McClement 4.00 10.00
IPB Pierre-Marc Bouchard 4.00 10.00
IPM Patrick Marleau SP 8.00 20.00
IRB Rob Blake 4.00 10.00
IRF Ruslan Fedotenko 4.00 10.00
IRI Mike Ribeiro 4.00 10.00
IRM Ryan Malone 4.00 10.00
IRS Ryan Smyth 6.00 15.00
IRY Michael Ryder 8.00 20.00
ISA Miroslav Satan 4.00 10.00
ISC Sidney Crosby SP 150.00 250.00
ISG Scott Gomez 4.00 10.00
ISH Shawn Horcoff 6.00 15.00
ISS Sergei Samsonov SP 12.00 30.00
ISV Marek Svatos SP 15.00 40.00
ITB Todd Bertuzzi SP 20.00 50.00
ITC Ty Conklin 4.00 10.00
ITE Mikael Tellqvist 6.00 15.00
ITH Joe Thornton SP 20.00 50.00
ITV Tomas Vokoun 10.00 25.00
IVL Vincent Lecavalier 15.00 40.00
IWR Wade Redden 4.00 10.00

2006-07 Flair Showcase Stitches

STATED ODDS 1:9
SSAH Ales Hemsky 3.00 8.00
SSAK Alex Kovalev 3.00 8.00
SSAO Alexander Ovechkin 12.00 30.00
SSAT Alex Tanguay 3.00 8.00
SSBG Bill Guerin 3.00 8.00
SSBL Rob Blake 4.00 10.00
SSBM Brenden Morrow 4.00 10.00
SSBO Radek Bonk 3.00 8.00
SSBR Martin Brodeur 8.00 20.00
SSBS Brad Stuart 3.00 8.00
SSCA Carlo Colaiacovo 3.00 8.00
SSCC Chris Chelios 4.00 10.00
SSCD Chris Drury 3.00 8.00
SSCO Chris Osgood 4.00 10.00
SSCP Chris Pronger 4.00 10.00
SSDA Daniel Alfredsson 4.00 10.00
SSDB Donald Brashear 3.00 8.00
SSDC Dan Cloutier 3.00 8.00
SSDE Pavol Demitra 3.00 8.00
SSDH Dan Hamhuis 3.00 8.00
SSDL David Legwand 3.00 8.00
SSDM Darren McCarty 3.00 8.00
SSDR Dwayne Roloson 4.00 10.00
SSEB Ed Belfour 4.00 10.00
SSED Eric Daze 3.00 8.00
SSEL Eric Lindros 4.00 10.00
SSEN Evgeni Nabokov 4.00 10.00
SSES Eric Staal 4.00 10.00
SSFP Fernando Pisani 3.00 8.00
SSGA Mathieu Garon 4.00 10.00
SSGM Glen Murray 3.00 8.00
SSGR Gary Roberts 3.00 8.00
SSHO Marcel Hossa 3.00 8.00
SSJA Jason Arnott 3.00 8.00
SSJB Jay Bouwmeester 3.00 8.00
SSJC Jonathan Cheechoo 3.00 8.00
SSJG Jean-Sebastien Giguere 4.00 10.00
SSJI Jarome Iginla 6.00 15.00
SSJJ Jaromir Jagr 6.00 15.00
SSJL Joffrey Lupul 3.00 8.00
SSJO Joe Thornton 6.00 15.00
SSJR Jeremy Roenick 4.00 10.00
SSJS Jason Spezza 4.00 10.00
SSJT Jose Theodore 4.00 10.00
SSJW Justin Williams 3.00 8.00
SSKP Keith Primeau 3.00 8.00
SSKT Keith Tkachuk 3.00 8.00
SSLE Jere Lehtinen 3.00 8.00
SSLM Mario Lemieux 10.00 25.00
SSLN Ladislav Nagy 3.00 8.00
SSLU Jamie Lundmark 3.00 8.00
SSMA Marian Gaborik 6.00 15.00
SSMB Martin Biron 3.00 8.00
SSMC Bryan McCabe 3.00 8.00
SSMG Martin Gerber 4.00 10.00
SSMH Marian Hossa 4.00 10.00
SSMK Miikka Kiprusoff 4.00 10.00
SSML Manny Legace 4.00 10.00
SSMM Mike Modano 5.00 12.00
SSMN Markus Naslund 4.00 10.00
SSMO Brendan Morrison 3.00 8.00
SSMP Michael Peca 3.00 8.00
SSMR Mike Ribeiro 3.00 8.00
SSMS Marek Svatos 4.00 10.00
SSNA Nikolai Antropov 3.00 8.00
SSOH Mattias Ohlund 3.00 8.00
SSOJ Olli Jokinen 3.00 8.00
SSPA Mark Parrish 3.00 8.00
SSPB Pierre-Marc Bouchard 3.00 8.00
SSPD Pavel Datsyuk 4.00 10.00
SSPE Patrik Elias 3.00 8.00
SSPF Peter Forsberg 6.00 15.00
SSRA Brian Rafalski 3.00 8.00
SSRB Rod Brind'Amour 3.00 8.00
SSRE Robert Esche 4.00 10.00
SSRL Robert Lang 3.00 8.00
SSRM Ryan Miller 4.00 10.00
SSRR Robyn Regehr 3.00 8.00
SSRT Raffi Torres 3.00 8.00
SSRY Michael Ryder 3.00 8.00
SSRZ Richard Zednik 3.00 8.00
SSSA Miroslav Satan 3.00 8.00
SSSC Sidney Crosby 20.00 50.00
SSSG Simon Gagne 4.00 10.00
SSSK Sami Kapanen 3.00 8.00
SSSM Matt Stajan 4.00 10.00
SSSN Scott Niedermayer 3.00 8.00
SSST Martin Straka 3.00 8.00
SSSU Mats Sundin 4.00 10.00
SSSW Stephen Weiss 3.00 8.00
SSSY Steve Yzerman 8.00 20.00
SSTA Tony Amonte 3.00 8.00
SSTC Ty Conklin 4.00 10.00
SSTH Tomas Holmstrom 3.00 8.00
SSTL Trevor Linden 4.00 10.00
SSTR Tuomo Ruutu 4.00 10.00
SSTS Teemu Selanne 4.00 10.00
SSWI Jason Williams 3.00 8.00
SSWR Wade Redden 3.00 8.00
SSZC Zdeno Chara 3.00 8.00

2006-07 Flair Showcase Wave of the Future

STATED ODDS 1:6
WF1 Joffrey Lupul 1.00 2.50
WF2 Kari Lehtonen 1.50 4.00
WF3 Ilya Kovalchuk 2.00 5.00
WF4 Patrice Bergeron 1.50 4.00
WF5 Brad Boyes 1.00 2.50
WF6 Ryan Miller 1.50 4.00
WF7 Dion Phaneuf 2.00 5.00
WF8 Eric Staal 1.50 4.00
WF9 Tuomo Ruutu 1.00 2.50
WF10 Marek Svatos 1.00 2.50
WF11 Rick Nash 1.50 4.00
WF12 Jussi Jokinen 1.00 2.50
WF13 Henrik Zetterberg 1.50 4.00
WF14 Ales Hemsky 1.00 2.50
WF15 Jarret Stoll 1.00 2.50
WF16 Nathan Horton 1.00 2.50
WF17 Dustin Brown 1.00 2.50
WF18 Alexander Frolov 1.00 2.50
WF19 Marian Gaborik 2.00 5.00
WF20 Mikko Koivu 1.00 2.50
WF21 Corey Perry 1.50 4.00
WF22 Thomas Vanek 1.50 4.00
WF23 Michael Ryder 1.50 4.00
WF24 Chris Higgins 1.00 2.50
WF25 Zach Parise 1.00 2.50
WF26 Rick DiPietro 1.50 4.00
WF27 Henrik Lundqvist 1.50 4.00
WF28 Petr Prucha 1.00 2.50
WF29 Jason Spezza 1.50 4.00
WF30 Dany Heatley 2.00 5.00
WF31 Martin Havlat 1.50 4.00
WF32 Jeff Carter 1.50 4.00
WF33 Joni Pitkanen 1.00 2.50
WF34 Mike Richards 1.50 4.00
WF35 Sidney Crosby 8.00 20.00
WF36 Marc-Andre Fleury 2.00 5.00
WF37 Steve Bernier 1.00 2.50
WF38 Alexander Steen 1.50 4.00
WF39 Kyle Wellwood 1.00 2.50
WF40 Andrew Raycroft 1.50 4.00
WF41 Ryan Kesler 1.00 2.50
WF42 Alexander Ovechkin 3.00 8.00

1972-73 Flames Postcards

This 20-card set of the Atlanta Flames measured 3 1/2" by 5 1/2". The fronts featured color action player photos with a white border. The player's autograph was across the bottom of the photo. The backs were blank. The cards were unnumbered and checklisted below in alphabetical order.

COMPLETE SET (20) 30.00 60.00
1 Curt Bennett 1.00 2.00
2 Dan Bouchard 2.50 5.00
3 Rey Comeau 1.00 2.00
4 BoomBoom Geoffrion CO 5.00 10.00
5 Bob Leiter 1.00 2.00
6 Kerry Ketter 1.00 2.00
7 Billy MacMillan 1.00 2.00
8 Randy Manery 1.00 2.00
9 Keith McCreary 1.00 2.00
10 Lew Morrison 1.00 2.00
11 Phil Myre 3.00 6.00
12 Bob Paradise 1.00 2.00
13 Noel Picard 1.00 2.00
14 Bill Plager 1.50 3.00
15 Noel Price 1.50 3.00
16 Pat Quinn 2.50 5.00
17 Jacques Richard 1.50 3.00
18 Leon Rochefort 1.00 2.00
19 Larry Romanchych 1.00 2.00
20 John Stewart 1.00 2.00

1978-79 Flames Majik Market

This 20 card set was issued during the 1978-79 season and features members of the Atlanta Flames. The front had an action shot as well as a facsimile autograph. The back had the player's name, uniform number and some personal statistics. At the bottom, sponsors "Coca-Cola Bottling" and radio station WTLA are credited. Pat Ribble, who was traded during the season, was the most difficult card to obtain and is listed as an SP. We have checklisted this set by the uniform number.

COMPLETE SET (19) 15.00 30.00
1 Rejean Lemelin 1.50 3.00
2 Greg Fox .50 1.00
3 Pat Ribble SP 5.00 10.00
5 Brad Marsh 2.00 4.00
6 Ken Houston .50 1.00
7 Bobby LaLonde .50 1.00
8 David Shand .50 1.00
9 Jean Pronovost .75 1.50
10 Bill Clement 1.50 3.00
11 Bob MacMillan .50 1.00
12 Tom Lysiak 1.00 2.00
15 Rod Seiling .50 1.00
16 Guy Chouinard 1.00 2.00
19 Ed Kea .50 1.00
20 Bob Murdoch .75 1.50
24 Harold Phillipoff .50 1.00
25 Willi Plett 1.00 2.00
27 Eric Vail 1.00 2.00
30 Daniel Bouchard 1.50 3.00

1979-80 Flames Postcards

This 20-card set was sponsored by the Atlanta Coca-Cola Bottling Company, Winn Dixie, and radio station WLTA-100. The set was in the postcard format, with each card measuring approximately 3 1/2" by 5 1/2". The fronts featured full-bleed color action shots; a facsimile autograph was inscribed across the lower portion of the pictures. The backs carried the player's name, uniform number, biography, and sponsor logos. The cards were unnumbered and checklisted below in alphabetical order.

COMPLETE SET (20) 15.00 30.00
1 Curt Bennett .50 1.00
2 Dan Bouchard 1.50 3.00
3 Guy Chouinard 1.00 2.00
4 Bill Clement 2.00 4.00
5 Jim Craig 2.50 5.00
6 Ken Houston .50 1.00
7 Don Lever .50 1.00
8 Bob MacMillan .50 1.00
9 Brad Marsh 2.50 5.00
10 Bob Murdoch .75 1.50
11 Kent Nilsson 2.50 5.00
12 Willi Plett 1.25 2.50
13 Jean Pronovost .75 1.50
14 Pekka Rautakallio .50 1.00
15 Paul Reinhart .75 1.50
16 Pat Riggin 1.25 2.50
17 Phil Russell .50 1.00
18 David Shand .50 1.00
19 Garry Unger 1.50 3.00
20 Eric Vail .75 1.50

1979-80 Flames Team Issue

Cards measured 3 3/4 x 5 1/4 and featured black and white action photos on the front along with a facsimile signature. Backs were blank. Cards were unnumbered and checklisted below in alphabetical order.

COMPLETE SET (22) 20.00 40.00
1 Curt Bennett .50 1.00
2 Ivan Boldirev .50 1.00
3 Dan Bouchard 1.50 3.00
4 Guy Chouinard 1.00 2.00
5 Bill Clement 1.50 3.00
6 Jim Craig 2.00 4.00
7 Ken Houston .50 1.00
8 Brad Marsh 1.50 3.00
9 Bob MacMillan .50 1.00
10 Al McNeil .50 1.00
11 Bob Murdoch .75 1.50
12 Kent Nilsson 2.00 4.00
13 Willi Plett 1.00 2.00
14 Jean Pronovost .75 1.50
15 Pekka Rautakallio .50 1.00
16 Paul Reinhart .75 1.50
17 Pat Riggin 1.00 2.00
18 Darcy Rota .50 1.00
19 Phil Russell .50 1.00
20 David Shand .50 1.00
21 Garry Unger 1.25 2.50
22 Eric Vail 1.00 2.00

1980-81 Flames Postcards

This 24-postcard set measured approximately 3 3/4" by 5". The fronts featured borderless posed color player photos. The backs were blank. The cards were unnumbered and checklisted below in alphabetical order.

COMPLETE SET (24) 20.00 40.00
1 Daniel Bouchard 1.50 3.00
2 Guy Chouinard 1.00 2.00

3 Bill Clement 1.00 2.00
4 Denis Cyr .50 1.00
5 Randy Holt .50 1.00
6 Ken Houston .50 1.00
7 Rejean Lemelin 2.50 5.00
8 Kevin Lavallee .50 1.00
9 Don Lever .50 1.00
10 Bob MacMillan .50 1.00
11 Bob Murdoch .50 1.00
12 Brad Marsh 1.25 2.50
13 Kent Nilsson 2.00 4.00
14 Willi Plett .75 1.50
15 Jim Peplinski 1.25 2.50
16 Pekka Rautakallio 1.00 2.00
17 Paul Reinhart 1.25 2.50
18 Pat Riggin 1.00 2.00
19 Phil Russell .50 1.00
20 Brad Smith .50 1.00
21 Jay Soleway .50 1.00
22 Eric Vail .75 1.50
23 Bert Wilson .50 1.00
24 Team Photo .75 1.50

1981-82 Flames Postcards

This 20-postcard set measured approximately 3 3/4" by 5". The fronts featured borderless posed color player photos. The backs were blank. The cards are unnumbered and checklisted below in alphabetical order.

COMPLETE SET (20) 10.00 25.00
1 Charlie Bourgeois .30 .75
2 Mel Bridgman .40 1.00
3 Guy Chouinard .60 1.50
4 Bill Clement .60 1.50
5 Denis Cyr .30 .75
6 Jamie Hislop .30 .75
7 Ken Houston .30 .75
8 Steve Konroyd .30 .75
9 Dan Labraaten .30 .75
10 Kevin Lavallee .30 .75
11 Rejean Lemelin 1.20 3.00
12 Lanny McDonald 1.20 3.00
13 Gary McAdam .30 .75
14 Bob Murdoch .40 1.00
15 Jim Peplinski .80 2.00
16 Willi Plett .60 1.50
17 Pekka Rautakallio .40 1.00
18 Paul Reinhart .60 1.50
19 Pat Riggin .60 1.50
20 Phil Russell .30 .75

1982-83 Flames Dollars

These six cards, measuring approximately 3" by 5" and perforated on each end, were issued with "Hockey Dollars" or what may be better described as silver-colored coins. Each coin (measuring approximately 1 1/4" in diameter) displayed an engraving of the player's face on the obverse and the team logo on the reverse. The card fronts were gray with tan lettering. They had the player's name, number, year, team logo, and a picture of the coin. In a horizontal format, the backs carried biography, career highlights, and career statistics. The cards were numbered on the back in the upper right corner. The prices below refer to the coin-card combination intact.

COMPLETE SET (6) 10.00 25.00
1 Mel Bridgman 1.60 4.00
2 Don Edwards 1.60 4.00
3 Lanny McDonald DP 3.20 8.00
4 Kent Nilsson 2.40 6.00
5 Jim Peplinski 1.60 4.00
6 Paul Reinhart 2.00 5.00

1985-86 Flames Red Rooster

This 30-card set of Calgary Flames was sponsored by Red Rooster Food Stores, Old Dutch Potato Chips, and Post Cereals. The player cards could be collected from any Red Rooster Food Stores. The cards measured approximately 2 3/4" by 3 5/8" and featured on the front a color posed head shot (with rounded corners) of the player, with a facsimile autograph in white ink in the lower right-hand corner of the picture. The player's name, uniform number, the Calgary Flames' logo, and a hockey tip appeared below the picture. The back had biographical and statistical information on the top portion, while the bottom has sponsor advertisements and the anti-crime slogan "Support Crime Stoppers." The set included two different cards of Lanny McDonald and Doug Risebrough. Al MacInnis appeared in his Rookie Card year whereas Mike Vernon's appearance predated his Rookie Card by two years.

COMPLETE SET (30) 10.00 25.00
1 Paul Baxter .14 .35
2 Ed Beers .14 .35
3 Perry Berezan .14 .35
4 Charlie Bourgeois .14 .35
5 Steve Bozek .14 .35
6 Gino Cavallini .14 .35
7 Marc D'Amour .20 .50
8 Tim Hunter .40 1.00
9 Bob Johnson CO 1.00 2.50
10 Steve Konroyd .14 .35
11 Richard Kromm .14 .35
12 Rejean Lemelin .40 1.00
13 Hakan Loob .40 1.00
14 Lanny McDonald .80 2.00
15 Lanny McDonald .80 2.00
16 Al MacInnis 2.40 6.00
17 Jamie Macoun .20 .50
18 Bob Murdoch CO .14 .35
19 Joel Otto .60 1.50
20 Pierre Page CO .20 .50
21 Colin Patterson .14 .35
22 Jim Peplinski .30 .75
23 Dan Quinn .20 .50
24 Paul Reinhart .30 .75
25 Doug Risebrough .14 .35
26 Doug Risebrough .14 .35
27 Neil Sheehy .14 .35
28 Gary Suter .40 1.00
29 Mike Vernon 2.40 6.00
(No facsimile autograph on card front)
30 Carey Wilson .14 .35

1986-87 Flames Red Rooster

This 30-card set of Calgary Flames was sponsored by Red Rooster Food Stores in conjunction with Old Dutch Potato Chips. The player cards could be collected from any Red Rooster Food Stores. The cards measured approximately 2 3/4" by 3 5/8" and featured a color posed photo (with rounded corners) of the player, with a facsimile autograph in blue ink across the bottom of the picture. The player's name, uniform number, the Calgary Flames' logo, and a hockey tip appeared below the picture. The back had biographical and statistical information on the top portion, while the bottom has sponsor advertisements and the anti-crime slogan "Support Crime Stoppers." The set included two different cards of Lanny McDonald, Joe Mullen, and Paul Reinhart. Gary Roberts' card predated his Rookie Card year by three years.

COMPLETE SET (30) 8.00 20.00
1 Paul Baxter .20 .50
2 Perry Berezan .20 .50
3 Steve Bozek .20 .50
4 Brian Bradley .40 1.00
5 Brian Engblom .20 .50
6 Nick Fotiu .20 .50
7 Tim Hunter .30 .75
8 Bob Johnson CO .80 2.00
9 Rejean Lemelin .40 1.00
10 Hakan Loob .40 1.00
11 Al MacInnis 1.20 3.00
12 Jamie Macoun .20 .50
13 Lanny McDonald .60 1.50
14 Lanny McDonald .60 1.50
15 Joe Mullen .60 1.50
16 Joe Mullen .60 1.50
17 Bob Murdoch CO .20 .50
18 Joel Otto .40 1.00
19 Pierre Page CO .20 .50
20 Colin Patterson .20 .50
21 Jim Peplinski .20 .50
22 Paul Reinhart .20 .50
23 Paul Reinhart .20 .50
24 Doug Risebrough .20 .50
25 Gary Roberts 1.60 4.00
26 Neil Sheehy .20 .50
27 Gary Suter .20 .50
28 John Tonelli .30 .75
29 Mike Vernon 1.20 3.00
30 Carey Wilson .20 .50

1987-88 Flames Red Rooster

This 30-card set of Calgary Flames was sponsored by Red Rooster Food Stores, and the player cards could be collected from a[ny] of these stores. The cards measure[d] 11/16" by 3 9/16" and featured on the fro[nt a] color posed head-and-shoulders shot (w[ith] rounded corners) of the player, wit[h a] facsimile autograph in blue ink across [the] bottom of the picture. The player's nar[me,] uniform number, the Calgary Flames' lo[go,] and a hockey tip appeared below the pict[ure.] The back had biographical and statisti[cal] information on the top portion, while [the] bottom had a sponsor advertisement and [the] anti-crime slogan "Support Crime Stoppe[rs."] The set included two different cards of Ha[kan] Loob, Lanny McDonald, and J[oe] Nieuwendyk. The Brett Hull and J[oe] Nieuwendyk cards were the key cards in [the] set since they pre-dated their O-Pee-C[hee] and Topps Rookie Cards by one year.

COMPLETE SET (30) 20.00 50.[00]
1 Perry Berezan .16 .[40]
2 Steve Bozek .16 .[40]
3 Mike Bullard .20 .5[0]
4 Shane Churla .30 .[75]
5 Terry Crisp CO .16 .[40]
6 Doug Dadswell .20 .[50]
7 Brian Glynn .16 .[40]
8 Brett Hull 12.00 30.[00]
9 Tim Hunter .20 .5[0]
10 Hakan Loob .30 .[75]
11 Hakan Loob .30 .7[5]
12 Al MacInnis .80 2.[00]
13 Brad McCrimmon .20 .5[0]
14 Lanny McDonald .40 1.[00]
15 Lanny McDonald .40 1.[00]
16 Joe Mullen .40 1.[00]
17 Dana Murzyn .16 .[40]
18 Ric Nattress .16 .[40]
19 Joe Nieuwendyk 2.40 6.[00]
20 Joe Nieuwendyk 2.40 6.[00]
21 Joel Otto .30 .7[5]
22 Pierre Page CO .16 .[40]
23 Colin Patterson .16 .[40]
24 Jim Peplinski .20 .5[0]
25 Paul Reinhart .20 .5[0]
26 Doug Risebrough CO .16 .[40]
27 Gary Roberts .80 2.[00]
28 Gary Suter .30 .7[5]
29 John Tonelli .20 .5[0]
30 Mike Vernon .80 2.[00]

1990-91 Flames IGA/McGavin's

This 30-card standard-size set w[as] sponsored by IGA food stores in conjunct[ion] with McGavin's, a distributor of bread a[nd] other products in Alberta. Protected b[y a] cello pack, one card was inserted in bre[ad] loaves distributed by McGavin's to I[GA] stores in Calgary and Edmonton. Calg[ary] consumers received a Flames' card, wh[ile] Edmonton consumers received an Oile[rs] card. Checklist and coaches cards were [not] inserted in the loaves but were included [in] five hundred individually numbered a[nd] uncut sheets not offered to the gene[ral] public. The cards were printed on thin ca[rd] stock. The fronts had posed color pla[yer] photos, with a border that shaded from [red] to orange and back to red. The player's na[me] was printed in the bottom border, and [the] uniform number was printed in a circle in [the] upper left corner of each picture. T[he] horizontally oriented backs featur[ed] biographical information, with year-by-y[ear] statistics presented in a pink rectang[le.] Sponsor logos at the bottom round ed[ ] the back. The cards were unnumbered a[nd] checklisted below in alphabetical order.

COMPLETE SET (30) 14.00 35.[00]
1 Paul Baxter CO SP 1.20 3.[00]
2 Guy Charron CO SP 1.60 4.[00]
3 Theo Fleury 2.00 5.[00]
4 Doug Gilmour 2.00 5.[00]
5 Jiri Hrdina .20 .5[0]
6 Mark Hunter .20 .5[0]
7 Tim Hunter .40 1.[00]
8 Roger Johansson .20 .5[0]
9 Al MacInnis .80 2.[00]
10 Brian MacLellan .20 .5[0]
11 Jamie Macoun .30 .7[5]
12 Sergei Makarov .60 1.5[0]
13 Sergei Makarov .60 1.5[0]
(Calder Trophy Winner)
and Al MacInnis
(NHL First AS Team& Defence 1989-90)
14 Stephane Matteau .30 .7[5]
15 Dana Murzyn .20 .5[0]
16 Frantisek Musil .20 .5[0]
17 Ric Nattress .20 .5[0]
18 Joe Nieuwendyk 1.20 3.0[0]
19 Joel Otto .40 1.0[0]
20 Colin Patterson .20 .5[0]
21 Sergei Priakin .20 .5[0]
22 Paul Ranheim .30 .7[5]
23 Robert Reichel .60 1.5[0]
24 Doug Risebrough SP 1.20 3.0[0]
CO/GM
25 Gary Roberts .80 2.0[0]
26 Gary Suter .40 1.0[0]
27 Tim Sweeney .20 .5[0]
28 Mike Vernon .80 2.0[0]
29 Rick Wamsley .40 1.0[0]
30 Checklist Card SP 1.20 3.0[0]

991 Flames Panini Team Stickers

s 32-sticker set was issued in a plastic that contained two 16-sticker sheets proximately 9" by 12") and a foldout ster, "Super Poster - Hockey 91", on ich the stickers could be affixed. The yers' names appeared only on the poster, on the stickers. Each sticker measured ut 2 1/8" by 2 7/8" and featured a color yer action shot on its white-bordered it. The back of the white sticker sheet was ed off into 16 panels, each carried the os for Panini, the NHL, and the NHLPA, well as the same number that appears on front of the sticker. Every Canadian NHL m was featured in this promotion. Each n set was available by mail-order from ini Canada Ltd. for 2.99 plus 50 cents for pping and handling.

MPLETE SET (32) 1.60 4.00
heo Fleury .30 .75
oug Gilmour .30 .75
iri Hrdina .02 .05
lark Hunter .02 .05
im Hunter .04 .10
oger Johansson .02 .05
l MacInnis .16 .40
rian MacLellan .02 .05
amie Macoun .02 .05
Sergei Makarov .10 .25
Stephane Matteau .02 .05
Dana Murzyn .02 .05
Ric Nattress .02 .05
Joe Nieuwendyk .16 .40
Joel Otto .06 .15
Colin Patterson .02 .05
Sergei Priakin .02 .05
Paul Ranheim .04 .10
Gary Roberts .16 .40
Ken Sabourin .02 .05
Gary Suter .04 .10
Tim Sweeney .02 .05
Mike Vernon .16 .40
Rick Wamsley .04 .10
eam Logo Left Side .02 .05
eam Logo Right Side .02 .05
lames' Time Out Upper Left Corner .02 .05
lames' Time Out Lower Left Corner .02 .05
lames' Time Out Upper Right Corner .02 .05
lames' Time Out Lower Right Corner .02 .05
oel Otto Roger Johansson .04 .10
ary Suter .04 .10

991-92 Flames IGA

s 30-card standard-size set of Calgary mes was sponsored by IGA food stores d included manufacturers' discount pons. One pack of cards was distributed Calgary and Edmonton IGA stores with grocery purchase of 10.00 or more. The ds were printed on thin card stock. The nts had posed color action photos dered in red. The player's name was ted vertically in the wider left border, and uniform number and the team name peared at the bottom of the picture. In ck print on a white background, the backs sented biography and statistics (regular son and playoff). Packs were kept under cash drawer, and therefore many of the ds were creased. Each pack contained ee Oilers and two Flames cards. The cklist and coaches cards for both teams re not included in the packs but were ilable on a very limited basis through an ut team sheet offer. Also the Osiecki card med to be in short supply, either because short printing or short distribution. The ds were unnumbered and checklisted ow in alphabetical order, with the coaches ds listed after the players.

MPLETE SET (30) 10.00 25.00
heo Fleury 1.00 2.50
omas Forslund .16 .40
oug Gilmour 1.00 2.50
larc Habscheid .16 .40
im Hunter .24 .60
im Kyte .16 .40
l MacInnis .40 1.00
amie Macoun .16 .40
ergei Makarov .40 1.00
Stephane Matteau .16 .40
Frantisek Musil .16 .40
Ric Nattress .16 .40
Joe Nieuwendyk .50 1.25
Mark Osiecki .80 2.00
Joel Otto .24 .60
Paul Ranheim .16 .40
Robert Reichel .30 .75
Gary Roberts .40 1.00
Neil Sheehy .16 .40
Martin Simard .16 .40
Ronnie Stern .16 .40
Gary Suter .30 .75
Tim Sweeney .16 .40
Mike Vernon .40 1.00
Rick Wamsley .30 .75
Carey Wilson .16 .40
27 Paul Baxter CO SP 1.00 2.50
28 Guy Charron CO SP 1.00 2.50
29 Doug Risebrough CO SP 1.00 2.50
30 Checklist Card SP 1.00 2.50

1992-93 Flames IGA

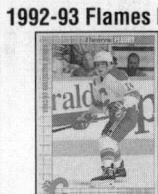

Sponsored by IGA food stores, the 30 standard-size cards comprising this Special Edition Collector Series set featured color player action shots on their fronts. Each photo was trimmed with a black line and offset flush with the thin white border on the right, which surrounds the card. On the remaining three sides, the picture was edged with a gray and white netlike pattern. The player's name appeard in the upper right and the Flames logo rested in the lower left. The back carried the player's name at the top, with his position, uniform number, biography, and stat table set within a reddish-gray screened background. The Flames logo in the upper right rounded out the card.

COMPLETE SET (30) 8.00 20.00
1 Checklist .04 .10
2 Craig Berube .20 .50
3 Gary Leeman .16 .40
4 Joel Otto .30 .75
5 Robert Reichel .40 1.00
6 Gary Roberts .40 1.00
7 Greg Smyth .16 .40
8 Gary Suter .30 .75
9 Jeff Reese .24 .60
10 Mike Vernon .40 1.00
11 Carey Wilson .16 .40
12 Trent Yawney .16 .40
13 Michel Petit .16 .40
14 Paul Ranheim .16 .40
15 Sergei Makarov .40 1.00
16 Frantisek Musil .16 .40
17 Joe Nieuwendyk .80 2.00
18 Alexander Godynyuk .16 .40
19 Roger Johansson .16 .40
20 Theo Fleury 1.00 2.50
21 Chris Lindberg .16 .40
22 Al MacInnis .60 1.50
23 Kevin Dahl .16 .40
24 Chris Dahlquist .16 .40
25 Ronnie Stern .20 .50
26 Dave King CO .16 .40
27 Guy Charron CO .04 .10
28 Slavomir Lener CO .04 .10
29 Jamie Hislop CO .04 .10
30 Franchise History .04 .10

1997-98 Flames Collector's Photos

COMPLETE SET (20) 15.00 30.00
1 Mike Vernon .75 2.00
2 Theoren Fleury 1.25 3.00
3 Trevor Kidd .75 2.00
4 Aaron Gavey .40 1.00
5 Mike Peluso .40 1.00
6 Derek Morris .40 1.00
7 Brian Sutter .40 1.00
8 Ron Stern .40 1.00
9 Joe Nieuwendyk 1.25 3.00
10 Andrew Cassels .40 1.00
11 Joel Otto .40 1.00
12 Todd Simpson .40 1.00
13 Lanny McDonald 1.25 3.00
14 Marty McInnis .40 1.00
15 Dave Gagner .40 1.00
16 Brett Hull 2.00 5.00
17 Cale Hulse .40 1.00
18 Doug Gilmour 1.50 4.00
19 Sandy McCarthy .75 2.00
20 Tim Hunter .75 2.00

1994-95 Fleer

This set was issued in a single 250-card series. Cards were issued in 12-card hobby and 18-card jumbo packs. There were four different card front designs, one unique to each of the NHL's divisions. Each card front had personal information in varying positions on the card. The card backs were all similar as they featured two photos, the player's name and expanded statistics. Rookie Cards included Mariusz Czerkawski, Blaine Lacher, David Oliver, Radek Bonk and Jim Carey.

COMPLETE SET (250) 12.50 25.00
1 Patrik Carnback .02 .10
2 Bob Corkum .02 .10
3 Paul Kariya .10 .30
4 Valeri Karpov RC .02 .10
5 Tom Kurvers .02 .10
6 John Lilley .02 .10
7 Mikhail Shtalenkov RC .02 .10
8 Oleg Tverdovsky .05 .15
9 Ray Bourque .20 .50
10 Mariusz Czerkawski RC .10 .30
11 John Gruden RC .02 .10
12 Al Iafrate .02 .10
13 Blaine Lacher RC .05 .15
14 Mats Naslund .02 .10
15 Cam Neely .10 .30
16 Adam Oates .05 .15
17 Bryan Smolinski .02 .10
18 Don Sweeney .02 .10
19 Donald Audette .02 .10
20 Dominik Hasek .25 .60
21 Dale Hawerchuk .05 .15
22 Yuri Khmylev .02 .10
23 Pat LaFontaine .10 .30
24 Brad May .02 .10
25 Alexander Mogilny .05 .15
26 Derek Plante .02 .10
27 Richard Smehlik .02 .10
28 Steve Chiasson .02 .10
29 Theo Fleury .02 .10
30 Phil Housley .05 .15
31 Trevor Kidd .05 .15
32 Joe Nieuwendyk .05 .15
33 James Patrick .02 .10
34 Robert Reichel .02 .10
35 Gary Roberts .02 .10
36 German Titov .02 .10
37 Tony Amonte .05 .15
38 Ed Belfour .10 .30
39 Chris Chelios .10 .30
40 Dirk Graham .02 .10
41 Sergei Krivokrasov .02 .10
42 Joe Murphy .02 .10
43 Bernie Nicholls .05 .15
44 Patrick Poulin .02 .10
45 Jeremy Roenick .15 .40
46 Steve Smith .02 .10
47 Gary Suter .02 .10
48 Russ Courtnall .02 .10
49 Dave Gagner .05 .15
50 Brent Gilchrist .02 .10
51 Todd Harvey .02 .10
52 Derian Hatcher .02 .10
53 Kevin Hatcher .02 .10
54 Mike Kennedy RC .02 .10
55 Mike Modano .05 .15
56 Andy Moog .10 .30
57 Dino Ciccarelli .05 .15
58 Paul Coffey .10 .30
59 Sergei Fedorov .15 .40
60 Vladimir Konstantinov .05 .15
61 Slava Kozlov .05 .15
62 Nicklas Lidstrom .10 .30
63 Chris Osgood .20 .50
64 Keith Primeau .02 .10
65 Ray Sheppard .05 .15
66 Mike Vernon .05 .15
67 Steve Yzerman .60 1.50
68 Jason Arnott .02 .10
69 Shayne Corson .02 .10
70 Igor Kravchuk .02 .10
71 Todd Marchant .02 .10
72 Roman Oksiuta .02 .10
73 Fredrik Olausson .02 .10
74 David Oliver RC .02 .10
75 Bill Ranford .05 .15
76 Stu Barnes .02 .10
77 Jesse Belanger .02 .10
78 Keith Brown .02 .10
79 Bob Kudelski .02 .10
80 Scott Mellanby .05 .15
81 Gord Murphy .02 .10
82 Rob Niedermayer .05 .15
83 John Vanbiesbrouck .05 .15
84 Sean Burke .05 .15
85 Jimmy Carson .02 .10
86 Andrew Cassels .02 .10
87 Andrei Nikolishin .02 .10
88 Chris Pronger .10 .30
89 Geoff Sanderson .05 .15
90 Darren Turcotte .02 .10
91 Pat Verbeek .02 .10
92 Glen Wesley .02 .10
93 Rob Blake .05 .15
94 Wayne Gretzky .75 2.00
95 Kelly Hrudey .05 .15
96 Jari Kurri .05 .15
97 Eric Lacroix .02 .10
98 Marty McSorley .02 .10
99 Jamie Storr .05 .15
100 Rick Tocchet .05 .15
101 Brian Bellows .02 .10
102 Patrice Brisebois .02 .10
103 Vincent Damphousse .02 .10
104 Kirk Muller .02 .10
105 Lyle Odelein .02 .10
106 Mark Recchi .05 .15
107 Patrick Roy .60 1.50
108 Brian Savage .02 .10
109 Mathieu Schneider .02 .10
110 Turner Stevenson .02 .10
111 Martin Brodeur .30 .75
112 Bill Guerin .05 .15
113 Claude Lemieux .02 .10
114 John MacLean .05 .15
115 Scott Niedermayer .02 .10
116 Stephane Richer .05 .15
117 Brian Rolston .02 .10
118 Alexander Semak .02 .10
119 Scott Stevens .05 .15
120 Ray Ferraro .02 .10
121 Patrick Flatley .02 .10
122 Darius Kasparaitis .02 .10
123 Derek King .02 .10
124 Scott Lachance .02 .10
125 Brett Lindros .02 .10
126 Vladimir Malakhov .02 .10
127 Jamie McLennan .05 .15
128 Zigmund Palffy .05 .15
129 Steve Thomas .02 .10
130 Pierre Turgeon .05 .15
131 Jeff Beukeboom .02 .10
132 Adam Graves .02 .10
133 Alexei Kovalev .05 .15
134 Steve Larmer .05 .15
135 Brian Leetch .10 .30
136 Mark Messier .10 .30
137 Petr Nedved .05 .15
138 Sergei Nemchinov .02 .10
139 Mike Richter .10 .30
140 Sergei Zubov .02 .10
141 Don Beaupre .05 .15
142 Radek Bonk RC .10 .30
143 Alexandre Daigle .02 .10
144 Pavol Demitra .05 .15
145 Pat Elynuik .02 .10
146 Rob Gaudreau .02 .10
147 Sean Hill .02 .10
148 Sylvain Turgeon .02 .10
149 Alexei Yashin .02 .10
150 Rod Brind'Amour .05 .15
151 Eric Desjardins .05 .15
152 Gilbert Dionne .02 .10
153 Garry Galley .02 .10
154 Ron Hextall .05 .15
155 Patrik Juhlin RC .02 .10
156 John LeClair .10 .30
157 Eric Lindros .10 .30
158 Mikael Renberg .05 .15
159 Chris Therien .02 .10
160 Dimitri Yushkevich .02 .10
161 Len Barrie .02 .10
162 Ron Francis .05 .15
163 Jaromir Jagr .20 .50
164 Shawn McEachern .02 .10
165 Joe Mullen .05 .15
166 Larry Murphy .05 .15
167 Luc Robitaille .05 .15
168 Ulf Samuelsson .02 .10
169 Tomas Sandstrom .02 .10
170 Kevin Stevens .02 .10
171 Martin Straka .02 .10
172 Ken Wregget .05 .15
173 Wendel Clark .05 .15
174 Adam Deadmarsh .02 .10
175 Stephane Fiset .05 .15
176 Peter Forsberg .40 1.00
177 Valeri Kamensky .05 .15
178 Andrei Kovalenko .02 .10
179 Uwe Krupp .02 .10
180 Sylvain Lefebvre .02 .10
181 Owen Nolan .05 .15
182 Mike Ricci .02 .10
183 Joe Sakic .25 .60
184 Denis Chasse RC .02 .10
185 Adam Creighton .02 .10
186 Steve Duchesne .02 .10
187 Brett Hull .15 .40
188 Curtis Joseph .10 .30
189 Ian Laperriere RC .02 .10
190 Al MacInnis .05 .15
191 Brendan Shanahan .10 .30
192 Patrice Tardif RC .02 .10
193 Esa Tikkanen .02 .10
194 Ulf Dahlen .02 .10
195 Pat Falloon .02 .10
196 Jeff Friesen .02 .10
197 Arturs Irbe .05 .15
198 Sergei Makarov .02 .10
199 Andrei Nazarov .02 .10
200 Sandis Ozolinsh .02 .10
201 Michal Sykora .02 .10
202 Ray Whitney .02 .10
203 Brian Bradley .02 .10
204 Shawn Chambers .02 .10
205 Eric Charron .02 .10
206 Chris Gratton .02 .10
207 Roman Hamrlik .05 .15
208 Petr Klima .02 .10
209 Daren Puppa .05 .15
210 Alexander Selivanov RC .05 .15
211 Jason Wiemer RC .02 .10
212 Dave Andreychuk .05 .15
213 Dave Ellett .02 .10
214 Mike Gartner .05 .15
215 Doug Gilmour .05 .15
216 Kenny Jonsson .02 .10
217 Dmitri Mironov .02 .10
218 Felix Potvin .10 .30
219 Mike Ridley .02 .10
220 Mats Sundin .10 .30
221 Josef Beranek .02 .10
222 Jeff Brown .02 .10
223 Pavel Bure .10 .30
224 Geoff Courtnall .02 .10
225 Trevor Linden .05 .15
226 Jyrki Lumme .02 .10
227 Kirk McLean .05 .15
228 Gino Odjick .02 .10
229 Mike Peca .02 .10
230 Cliff Ronning .02 .10
231 Jason Allison .02 .10
232 Peter Bondra .05 .15
233 Jim Carey RC .10 .30
234 Sylvain Cote .02 .10
235 Dale Hunter .02 .10
236 Joe Juneau .05 .15
237 Dimitri Khristich .02 .10
238 Pat Peake .02 .10
239 Mark Tinordi .02 .10
240 Nelson Emerson .02 .10
241 Michal Grosek .02 .10
242 Nikolai Khabibulin .05 .15
243 Dave Manson .02 .10
244 Stephane Quintal .02 .10
245 Teemu Selanne .10 .30
246 Keith Tkachuk .10 .30
247 Alexei Zhamnov .05 .15
248 Checklist .02 .10
249 Checklist .02 .10
250 Checklist .02 .10

1994-95 Fleer Franchise Futures

The 10-card set was randomly inserted at a rate of 1:7 12-card hobby packs. The set featured young stars of the NHL in action

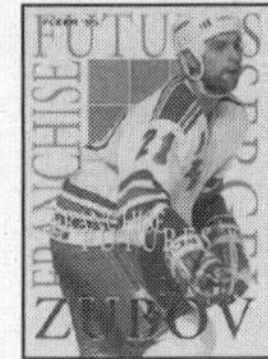

photos positioned over the card title. The background was in the color of the team. The back had a photo and player information.

COMPLETE SET (10) 5.00 10.00
1 Jason Arnott .40 1.00
2 Rob Blake .60 1.50
3 Adam Graves .40 1.00
4 Arturs Irbe .60 1.50
5 Joe Juneau .60 1.50
6 Sandis Ozolinsh .40 1.00
7 Mikael Renberg .60 1.50
8 Keith Tkachuk 1.25 3.00
9 Alexei Yashin .40 1.00
10 Sergei Zubov .40 1.00

1994-95 Fleer Headliners

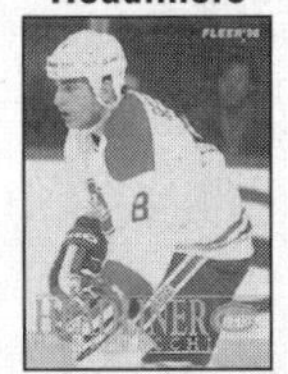

This 10-card set was randomly inserted in packs at the rate of 1:4. The set featured the superstars of the league in a borderless design. The word "Headliner", the player's name and team were printed in silver foil on the lower portion of the card front. A photo and informative text were on the back.

COMPLETE SET (10) 8.00 15.00
1 Pavel Bure .60 1.50
2 Sergei Fedorov .75 2.00
3 Doug Gilmour .30 .75
4 Wayne Gretzky 4.00 10.00
5 Brian Leetch .60 1.50
6 Eric Lindros .60 1.50
7 Mark Messier .60 1.50
8 Cam Neely .60 1.50
9 Mark Recchi .30 .75
10 Brendan Shanahan .60 1.50

1994-95 Fleer Netminders

The easiest of the Fleer insert sets, this 10-card set was found at the rate of 1:2 packs. The set featured the top goalies in the league in a silhouetted design. The word "Netminder" and the player's name were printed in gold foil on the front side portion of the card front. A portrait photo and player information were on the back.

COMPLETE SET (10) 4.00 8.00
1 Ed Belfour .30 .75
2 Martin Brodeur .75 2.00
3 Dominik Hasek .60 1.50
4 Arturs Irbe .15 .40
5 Curtis Joseph .30 .75
6 Kirk McLean .15 .40
7 Felix Potvin .30 .75
8 Mike Richter .30 .75
9 Patrick Roy 1.50 4.00
10 John Vanbiesbrouck .15 .40

1994-95 Fleer Rookie Sensations

This 10-card set was randomly inserted at a rate of 1:7 jumbo retail packs. The set featured the top first-year stars of the league over a water-splashed design. The phrase "Rookie Sensation" along with the player's name were printed in silver foil in the center portion of the card front. A photo and text information were on the back.

COMPLETE SET (10) 20.00 40.00
1 Radek Bonk .75 2.00
2 Peter Forsberg 8.00 20.00
3 Jeff Friesen .75 2.00
4 Todd Harvey .75 2.00
5 Paul Kariya 2.50 6.00
6 Blaine Lacher .75 2.00
7 Brett Lindros .75 2.00
8 Mike Peca .75 2.00
9 Jamie Storr 2.00 5.00
10 Oleg Tverdovsky 2.00 5.00

1994-95 Fleer Slapshot Artists

The most difficult of the Fleer inserts, the ten cards in this set were inserted at the rate of 1:12 packs. The cards featured a silhouetted player photo surrounded by three smaller cut-out versions of the same photo. The background was in the team's color. The back had the player's photo and career information.

COMPLETE SET (10) 10.00 20.00
1 Wendel Clark .75 2.00
2 Brett Hull 2.00 5.00
3 Al Iafrate .50 1.25
4 Jaromir Jagr 2.50 6.00
5 Al MacInnis .75 2.00
6 Mike Modano .75 2.00
7 Stephane Richer .75 2.00
8 Jeremy Roenick 2.00 5.00
9 Geoff Sanderson .75 2.00
10 Steve Thomas .50 1.25

1996-97 Fleer Promo Sheet

This sheet, which featured samples of John LeClair and Peter Ferraro regular cards, as well as a John LeClair Art Ross insert card, contained product and release date information for '96-97 Fleer. The cards were unnumbered, and would bear perforation marks if removed, distinguishing them from their regular counterparts. They are listed below as they appear on the sheet.

COMPLETE SET (3) .40 1.00
1 John LeClair .10 .25
2 John LeClair Art Ross insert .30 .75
3 Peter Ferraro .04 .10

1996-97 Fleer

This 150-card set was released in one series in 10-card packs for both the hobby and retail markets with an SRP of $1.49. Although rarely delving past first-line players, the set boasted a strong player selection. All major stars were represented, among them Wayne Gretzky's first card in a New York Rangers sweater. The only Rookie Card of note was Martin Biron.

COMPLETE SET (150) 7.50 15.00
1 Guy Hebert .05 .15
2 Paul Kariya .10 .30
3 Teemu Selanne .10 .30
4 Ray Bourque .20 .50
5 Kyle McLaren .02 .10
6 Adam Oates .05 .15
7 Bill Ranford .05 .15
8 Rick Tocchet .05 .15
9 Jason Dawe .02 .10
10 Dominik Hasek .25 .60
11 Pat LaFontaine .10 .30
12 Theo Fleury .02 .10
13 Trevor Kidd .05 .15
14 German Titov .02 .10
15 Ed Belfour .10 .30
16 Chris Chelios .10 .30
17 Eric Daze .05 .15
18 Jeremy Roenick .15 .40
19 Gary Suter .02 .10
20 Peter Forsberg .30 .75
21 Valeri Kamensky .05 .15
22 Claude Lemieux .02 .10
23 Sandis Ozolinsh .02 .10
24 Patrick Roy .60 1.50
25 Joe Sakic .25 .60
26 Derian Hatcher .02 .10
27 Mike Modano .20 .50
28 Sergei Zuboxv .02 .10
29 Paul Coffey .10 .30
30 Sergei Fedorov .15 .40
31 Vladimir Konstantinov .05 .15
32 Slava Kozlov .05 .15
33 Chris Osgood .05 .15
34 Keith Primeau .02 .10
35 Steve Yzerman .60 1.50
36 Jason Arnott .02 .10
37 Curtis Joseph .10 .30
38 Doug Weight .05 .15
39 Ed Jovanovski .05 .15
40 Scott Mellanby .05 .15
41 Rob Niedermayer .05 .15
42 Ray Sheppard .05 .15
43 Robert Svehla .02 .10
44 John Vanbiesbrouck .05 .15
45 Sean Burke .05 .15
46 Andrew Cassels .02 .10
47 Geoff Sanderson .05 .15
48 Brendan Shanahan .10 .30
49 Ray Ferraro .02 .10
50 Dimitri Khristich .02 .10
51 Vitali Yachmenev .02 .10
52 Valeri Bure .02 .10
53 Vincent Damphousse .02 .10
54 Saku Koivu .10 .30
55 Mark Recchi .05 .15
56 Jocelyn Thibault .10 .30
57 Pierre Turgeon .05 .15
58 Martin Brodeur .30 .75
59 Phil Housley .05 .15
60 Scott Niedermayer .02 .10
61 Scott Stevens .05 .15
62 Steve Thomas .02 .10
63 Todd Bertuzzi .10 .30
64 Travis Green .05 .15
65 Kenny Jonsson .02 .10
66 Zigmund Palffy .05 .15
67 Adam Graves .02 .10
68 Wayne Gretzky .75 2.00
69 Alexei Kovalev .02 .10
70 Brian Leetch .10 .30
71 Mark Messier .10 .30
72 Niklas Sundstrom .02 .10
73 Daniel Alfredsson .05 .15
74 Radek Bonk .02 .10
75 Steve Duchesne .02 .10
76 Damian Rhodes .05 .15
77 Alexei Yashin .02 .10
78 Rod Brind'Amour .05 .15
79 Eric Desjardins .05 .15
80 Ron Hextall .05 .15
81 John LeClair .10 .30
82 Eric Lindros .10 .30
83 Mikael Renberg .05 .15
84 Tom Barrasso .05 .15
85 Ron Francis .05 .15
86 Jaromir Jagr .20 .50
87 Mario Lemieux .60 1.50
88 Petr Nedved .05 .15
89 Bryan Smolinski .02 .10
90 Nikolai Khabibulin .05 .15
91 Teppo Numminen .02 .10
92 Keith Tkachuk .10 .30
93 Oleg Tverdovsky .05 .15
94 Alexei Zhamnov .05 .15
95 Shayne Corson .02 .10
96 Grant Fuhr .05 .15
97 Brett Hull .15 .40
98 Al MacInnis .05 .15
99 Chris Pronger .05 .15
100 Owen Nolan .05 .15
101 Marcus Ragnarsson .02 .10
102 Chris Terreri .05 .15
103 Brian Bradley .02 .10
104 Roman Hamrlik .05 .15
105 Daren Puppa .05 .15
106 Alexander Selivanov .02 .10
107 Doug Gilmour .05 .15
108 Larry Murphy .05 .15
109 Felix Potvin .10 .30
110 Mats Sundin .10 .30
111 Pavel Bure .10 .30
112 Trevor Linden .05 .15
113 Kirk McLean .05 .15
114 Alexander Mogilny .05 .15
115 Peter Bondra .05 .15
116 Jim Carey .10 .30
117 Sergei Gonchar .02 .10
118 Joe Juneau .02 .10
119 Michal Pivonka .02 .10
120 Brendan Witt .02 .10
121 Nolan Baumgartner .02 .10
122 Martin Biron RC 1.00 2.50
123 Jason Bonsignore .02 .10
124 Andrew Brunette RC .20 .50
125 Jason Doig .02 .10
126 Peter Ferraro .02 .10
127 Eric Fichaud .05 .15
128 Ladislav Kohn RC .02 .10
129 Jamie Langenbrunner .02 .10
130 Daymond Langkow .05 .15
131 Jay McKee RC .02 .10
132 Wayne Primeau RC .02 .10
133 Jamie Storr RC .05 .15
134 Jose Theodore .12 .40
135 Roman Vopat RC .02 .10
136 Rookie Scoring Leaders .05 .15
Daniel Alfredsson
Valeri Bure
Eric Daze
Saku Koivu
137 Points Leaders .10 .30
Ron Francis
Jaromir Jagr
Mario Lemieux
Joe Sakic
138 Goals Leaders .05 .15
Peter Bondra
Jaromir Jagr
Mario Lemieux
Alexander Mogilny
139 Assists Leaders .10 .30
Peter Forsberg
Ron Francis
Jaromir Jagr
Mario Lemieux
140 Defensive Points Leaders .10 .30
Ray Bourque
Chris Chelios
Paul Coffey
Brian Leetch
141 Mario Lemieux .10 .30
Jaromir Jagr
Paul Kariya
Keith Tkachuk
142 Jaromir Jagr .02 .10
Sergei Fedorov
John LeClair

Claude Lemieux		
143 Plus/Minus Leaders	.02	.10
Sergei Federov		
Slava Fetisov		
Vladimir Konstantinov		
Petr Nedved		
144 Goals Against Avg. Ldrs.	.05	.15
Jim Carey		
Ron Hextall		
Chris Osgood		
Mike Vernon		
145 Games Won Leaders	.05	.15
Martin Brodeur		
Jim Carey		
Ron Hextall		
Chris Osgood		
146 Shutouts Leaders	.05	.15
Martin Brodeur		
Jim Carey		
Chris Osgood		
Daren Puppa		
147 Dominik Hasek	.05	.15
Daren Puppa		
Jeff Hackett		
Guy Hebert		
148 Checklist (1-72)	.02	.10
149 Checklist (73-150)	.02	.10
150 Checklist (Inserts)	.02	.10

1996-97 Fleer Art Ross

Randomly inserted in packs at a rate of 1:6, this 25-card set featured players in contention for the Art Ross trophy as the league's leading scorer.

COMPLETE SET (25)	20.00	50.00
1 Pavel Bure	.75	1.50
2 Sergei Fedorov	1.00	2.00
3 Theo Fleury	.25	.50
4 Peter Forsberg	2.00	4.00
5 Ron Francis	.40	.75
6 Wayne Gretzky	5.00	10.00
7 Brett Hull	1.00	2.00
8 Jaromir Jagr	1.25	2.50
9 Valeri Kamensky	.40	.75
10 Paul Kariya	.75	1.50
11 Pat LaFontaine	.75	1.50
12 John LeClair	.75	1.50
13 Mario Lemieux	4.00	8.00
14 Eric Lindros	.75	1.50
15 Mark Messier	.75	1.50
16 Alexander Mogilny	.40	.75
17 Petr Nedved	.40	.75
18 Adam Oates	.40	.75
19 Jeremy Roenick	1.00	2.00
20 Joe Sakic	1.50	3.00
21 Teemu Selanne	.75	1.50
22 Keith Tkachuk	.75	1.50
23 Pierre Turgeon	.40	.75
24 Doug Weight	.40	.75
25 Steve Yzerman	4.00	8.00

1996-97 Fleer Calder Candidates

Randomly inserted in packs at a rate of 1:96, this 10-card set featured up-and-comers poised to make a run at the Calder trophy, which is awarded to the NHL's rookie of the year.

COMPLETE SET (10)	8.00	20.00
1 Andrew Brunette	.75	2.00
2 Jason Doig	.75	2.00
3 Peter Ferraro	.75	2.00
4 Eric Fichaud	.75	2.00
5 Ladislav Kohn	.75	2.00
6 Jamie Langenbrunner	1.25	3.00
7 Daymond Langkow	1.25	3.00
8 Jamie Storr	.75	2.00
9 Jose Theodore	3.00	8.00
10 Roman Vopat	.75	2.00

1996-97 Fleer Norris

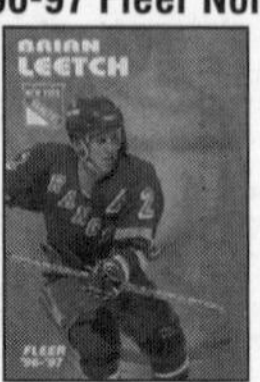

Randomly inserted in retail packs only at a rate of 1:36, this 10-card set featured veteran rearguards in contention for recognition as the game's top blueliner.

COMPLETE SET (10)	15.00	40.00
1 Ray Bourque	6.00	15.00
2 Chris Chelios	4.00	10.00
3 Paul Coffey	4.00	10.00
4 Eric Desjardins	1.25	3.00
5 Phil Housley	1.25	3.00
6 Vladimir Konstantinov	2.50	6.00
7 Brian Leetch	4.00	10.00
8 Teppo Numminen	1.25	3.00
9 Larry Murphy	1.25	3.00
10 Sandis Ozolinsh	1.25	3.00

1996-97 Fleer Pearson

Randomly inserted in packs at a rate of 1:144, this 10-card set was the most difficult to come by of this year's Fleer offering, and also the most star-studded. Gracing this set were ten top stars worthy of consideration for the NHLPA MVP award.

COMPLETE SET (10)	50.00	125.00
1 Pavel Bure	3.00	8.00
2 Sergei Fedorov	3.00	8.00
3 Peter Forsberg	5.00	12.00
4 Wayne Gretzky	15.00	40.00
5 Jaromir Jagr	5.00	12.00
6 Paul Kariya	3.00	8.00
7 Mario Lemieux	10.00	25.00
8 Eric Lindros	3.00	8.00
9 Patrick Roy	10.00	25.00
10 Joe Sakic	6.00	15.00

1996-97 Fleer Rookie Sensations

Randomly inserted in hobby packs only at a rate of 1:20, this 10-card set featured some of the top rookie attractions of the '95-96 campaign.

COMPLETE SET (10)	6.00	15.00
1 Daniel Alfredsson	1.50	4.00
2 Todd Bertuzzi	1.50	4.00
3 Valeri Bure	.40	1.00
4 Eric Daze	.40	1.00
5 Sergei Gonchar	.40	1.00
6 Ed Jovanovski	.40	1.00
7 Saku Koivu	1.50	4.00
8 Marcus Ragnarsson	.40	1.00
9 Petr Sykora	.40	1.00
10 Vitali Yachmenev	.40	1.00

1996-97 Fleer Vezina

Randomly inserted in packs at a rate of 1:60, this set featured ten netminders who are perennial favorites to win the Vezina award.

COMPLETE SET (10)	50.00	100.00
1 Ed Belfour	4.00	10.00
2 Sean Burke	3.00	8.00
3 Jim Carey	4.00	10.00
4 Dominik Hasek	8.00	20.00
5 Ron Hextall	3.00	8.00
6 Chris Osgood	4.00	10.00
7 Felix Potvin	4.00	10.00
8 Daren Puppa	3.00	8.00
9 Patrick Roy	15.00	40.00
10 John Vanbiesbrouck	4.00	10.00

1996-97 Fleer Picks

This 90-card set was a joint venture with Topps and was skip-numbered. All cards in this set had even numbers, while the Topps Picks set had the odds. The cards were issued in seven-card packs with a suggested retail price of $.99. The two card companies held a fantasy-style draft with each picking 56 forwards, 28 defensemen and six goaltenders to be included in their half of the set. The fronts featured color action player photos in a bordered design with the backs displaying projected stats for the 1996-97 season.

COMPLETE SET (92)	4.00	10.00
2 Joe Sakic	.20	.50
4 Eric Lindros	.08	.25
6 Paul Kariya	.08	.25
8 Wayne Gretzky	1.50	3.50
10 Chris Osgood	.02	.10
12 Brian Leetch	.08	.25
14 Ray Bourque	.15	.40
16 Ron Francis	.02	.10
18 Keith Tkachuk	.08	.25
20 Paul Coffey	.08	.25
22 Phil Housley	.02	.10
24 Theo Fleury	.01	.05
26 Sergei Zubov	.01	.05
28 Adam Oates	.02	.10
30 John LeClair	.08	.25
32 Pierre Turgeon	.02	.10
34 Nicklas Lidstrom	.08	.25
36 Vincent Damphousse	.01	.05
38 Pat LaFontaine	.08	.25
40 Brendan Shanahan	.08	.25
42 Robert Svehla	.01	.05
44 Peter Bondra	.02	.10
46 Mikael Renberg	.02	.10
48 Alexei Yashin	.01	.05
50 Zigmund Palffy	.02	.10
52 Larry Murphy	.02	.10
54 Rod Brind'Amour	.02	.10
56 Alexei Zhamnov	.02	.10
58 Jason Arnott	.01	.05
60 Craig Janney	.02	.10
62 Jason Woolley	.01	.05
64 Jeff Brown	.01	.05
66 Tomas Sandstrom	.01	.05
68 Doug Gilmour	.02	.10
70 Travis Green	.02	.10
72 Teppo Numminen	.01	.05
74 Petr Sykora	.01	.05
76 Saku Koivu	.08	.25
78 Daniel Alfredsson	.02	.10
80 Ron Hextall	.02	.10
82 Jocelyn Thibault	.08	.25
84 Mike Richter	.08	.25
86 Nikolai Khabibulin	.02	.10
88 John Vanbiesbrouck	.02	.10
90 Adam Graves	.01	.05
92 Kenny Jonsson	.01	.05
94 Jyrki Lumme	.01	.05
96 Zdeno Ciger	.01	.05
98 Ed Jovanovski	.02	.10
100 Greg Johnson	.01	.05
102 Pat Falloon	.01	.05
104 Andrew Cassels	.01	.05
106 German Titov	.01	.05
108 Joe Juneau	.01	.05
110 Igor Larionov	.01	.05
112 Norm Maciver	.01	.05
114 Chris Pronger	.02	.10
116 Scott Niedermayer	.01	.05
118 Vladimir Malakhov	.01	.05
120 Dale Hawerchuk	.02	.10
122 Jason Dawe	.01	.05
124 Valeri Bure	.01	.05
126 Marcus Ragnarsson	.01	.05
128 Stephane Richer	.02	.10
130 Wendel Clark	.02	.10
132 Bryan Smolinski	.01	.05
134 Dimitri Khristich	.01	.05
136 Benoit Hogue	.01	.05
138 Kirk Muller	.01	.05
140 Peter Ferraro	.01	.05
142 Vitali Yachmenev	.01	.05
144 Jere Lehtinen	.01	.05
146 Brandon Convery	.01	.05
148 Darcy Tucker	.01	.05
150 Curtis Brown	.01	.05
152 Alexei Zhitnik	.01	.05
154 John Slaney	.01	.05
156 Bruce Driver	.01	.05
158 Jeff O'Neill	.01	.05
160 Patrice Brisebois	.01	.05
162 Gord Murphy	.01	.05
164 Doug Bodger	.01	.05
166 Marty McSorley	.01	.05
168 Nolan Baumgartner	.01	.05
170 Mike Gartner	.02	.10
172 Andrei Nikolishin	.01	.05
174 Alexei Yegorov RC	.01	.05
176 Dave Reid	.01	.05
178 Marty Murray	.01	.05
180 Anders Eriksson	.01	.05
182 Checklist (2-180)	.01	.05
184 Checklist (inserts)	.01	.05

1996-97 Fleer Picks Captain's Choice

Randomly inserted in packs at a rate of 1:360, this set featured ten top team captains. The fronts carried borderless color action player photos while the backs displayed player information.

COMPLETE SET (10)	50.00	100.00
1 Eric Lindros	3.00	8.00
2 Steve Yzerman	15.00	40.00
3 Mario Lemieux	20.00	50.00
4 Wayne Gretzky	25.00	60.00
5 Mark Messier	3.00	8.00
6 Joe Sakic	6.00	15.00
7 Keith Tkachuk	3.00	8.00
8 Doug Gilmour	2.50	6.00
9 Trevor Linden	2.00	5.00
10 Brendan Shanahan	3.00	8.00

1996-97 Fleer Picks Dream Lines

Randomly inserted in packs at a rate of 1:70, this 10-card set featured three star players sharing some connection on each card.

COMPLETE SET (10)	40.00	80.00
1 Wayne Gretzky	15.00	40.00
Mario Lemieux		
Eric Lindros		
2 Jeremy Roenick	2.00	5.00
Chris Chelios		
Mike Richter		
3 Daniel Alfredsson	4.00	10.00
Peter Forsberg		
Martin Brodeur		
4 Sergei Fedorov	3.00	8.00
Alexander Mogilny		
Pavel Bure		
5 Teemu Selanne	2.00	5.00
Paul Kariya		
Keith Tkachuk		
6 Jaromir Jagr	3.00	8.00
Dominik Hasek		
Roman Hamrlik		
7 John LeClair	3.00	8.00
Brendan Shanahan		
Mike Modano		
8 Patrick Roy	12.00	30.00
Ed Belfour		
John Vanbiesbrouck		
9 Joe Sakic	3.00	8.00
Valeri Kamensky		
Sandis Ozolinsh		
10 Brett Hull	2.00	5.00
Pat Verbeek		
Pat LaFontaine		

1996-97 Fleer Picks Fabulous 50

Inserted one in every pack, this 50-card set featured color action photos of the best players in the NHL. The nature of this set allowed Fleer to include players they were unable to select in the draft, thus giving a more complete feel to the entire product.

COMPLETE SET (50)	12.50	30.00
1 Daniel Alfredsson	.20	.50
2 Peter Bondra	.20	.50
3 Ray Bourque	.50	1.25
4 Martin Brodeur	.75	2.00
5 Pavel Bure	.30	.75
6 Jim Carey	.30	.75
7 Chris Chelios	.30	.75
8 Paul Coffey	.30	.75
9 Eric Daze	.20	.50
10 Sergei Fedorov	.40	1.00
11 Theo Fleury	.07	.20
12 Peter Forsberg	.75	2.00
13 Ron Francis	.20	.50
14 Sergei Gonchar	.07	.20
15 Wayne Gretzky	2.00	5.00
16 Roman Hamrlik	.20	.50
17 Kevin Hatcher	.07	.20
18 Ron Hextall	.07	.20
19 Brett Hull	.40	1.00
20 Jaromir Jagr	.50	1.25
21 Ed Jovanovski	.20	.50
22 Valeri Kamensky	.07	.20
23 Paul Kariya	.30	.75
24 John LeClair	.30	.75
25 Brian Leetch	.30	.75
26 Mario Lemieux	1.50	4.00
27 Trevor Linden	.07	.20
28 Eric Lindros	.30	.75
29 Mark Messier	.30	.75
30 Mike Modano	.50	1.25
31 Alexander Mogilny	.20	.50
32 Petr Nedved	.07	.20
33 Joe Nieuwendyk	.07	.20
34 Owen Nolan	.20	.50
35 Adam Oates	.07	.20
36 Chris Osgood	.20	.50
37 Sandis Ozolinsh	.07	.20
38 Zigmund Palffy	.20	.50
39 Jeremy Roenick	.40	1.00
40 Patrick Roy	1.50	4.00
41 Joe Sakic	.60	1.50
42 Teemu Selanne	.30	.75
43 Brendan Shanahan	.30	.75
44 Keith Tkachuk	.30	.75
45 Pierre Turgeon	.07	.20
46 John Vanbiesbrouck	.20	.50
47 Doug Weight	.07	.20
48 Alexei Yashin	.07	.20
49 Steve Yzerman	1.50	4.00
50 Alexei Zhamnov	.20	.50

1996-97 Fleer Picks Fantasy Force

Randomly inserted in packs at a rate of 1:50, this 10-card set featured color action photos of ten of the league's most valuable assets to fantasy league owners.

COMPLETE SET (10)	25.00	60.00
1 John LeClair	1.25	3.00
2 Chris Osgood	1.25	3.00
3 Ron Hextall	1.25	3.00
4 Eric Daze	.75	2.00
5 Jaromir Jagr	4.00	10.00
6 Brett Hull	2.00	5.00
7 Ron Francis	1.25	3.00
8 Martin Brodeur	6.00	15.00
9 Sergei Fedorov	3.00	8.00
10 Petr Nedved	.75	2.00

1996-97 Fleer Picks Jagged Edge

Randomly inserted in packs at a rate of 1:18, this 20-card set featured color action photos of players with a propensity for the dramatic.

COMPLETE SET (20)	12.00	30.00
1 Daniel Alfredsson	1.25	3.00
2 Theo Fleury	.75	2.00
3 Alexander Mogilny	1.25	3.00
4 Doug Weight	.75	2.00
5 Alexei Yashin	.75	2.00
6 Paul Kariya	1.50	4.00
7 Saku Koivu	1.50	4.00
8 Sandis Ozolinsh	.40	1.00
9 Petr Nedved	.40	1.00
10 Jeremy Roenick	2.00	5.00
11 Mike Modano	2.00	5.00
12 Jim Carey	.40	1.00
13 Ed Jovanovski	.40	1.00
14 Alexei Zhamnov	.40	1.00
15 Adam Oates	.75	2.00
16 Ron Francis	.75	2.00
17 Brian Leetch	1.50	4.00
18 Paul Coffey	1.50	4.00
19 Eric Daze	.40	1.00
20 Zigmund Palffy	.75	2.00

2006-07 Fleer

COMPLETE SET (230)	50.00	100.00
1 Jean-Sebastien Giguere	.12	.30
2 Andy McDonald	.07	.20
3 Teemu Selanne	.15	.40
4 Scott Niedermayer	.07	.20
5 Chris Pronger	.12	.30
6 Ilya Bryzgalov	.12	.30
7 Ryan Getzlaf	.12	.30
8 Corey Perry	.12	.30
9 Jim Slater	.07	.20
10 Ilya Kovalchuk	.20	.50
11 Kari Lehtonen	.15	.40
12 Marian Hossa	.12	.30
13 Bobby Holik	.07	.20
14 Slava Kozlov	.07	.20
15 Patrice Bergeron	.15	.40
16 Hannu Toivonen	.15	.40
17 Brad Boyes	.07	.20
18 Zdeno Chara	.07	.20
19 Marco Sturm	.07	.20
20 Glen Murray	.07	.20
21 Marc Savard	.07	.20
22 Maxim Afinogenov	.07	.20
23 Chris Drury	.07	.20
24 Ryan Miller	.12	.30
25 Ales Kotalik	.07	.20
26 Thomas Vanek	.07	.20
27 Daniel Briere	.07	.20
28 Jaroslav Spacek	.07	.20
29 Jarome Iginla	.20	.50
30 Miikka Kiprusoff	.15	.40
31 Daymond Langkow	.07	.20
32 Dion Phaneuf	.20	.50
33 Chuck Kobasew	.07	.20
34 Alex Tanguay	.12	.30
35 Eric Staal	.20	.50
36 Justin Williams	.07	.20
37 Cam Ward	.15	.40
38 Cory Stillman	.07	.20
39 Rod Brind`Amour	.12	.30
40 Mike Commodore	.07	.20
41 Erik Cole	.07	.20
42 Andrew Ladd	.07	.20
43 Michal Handzus	.07	.20
44 Tuomo Ruutu	.07	.20
45 Nikolai Khabibulin	.15	.40
46 Martin Havlat	.12	.30
47 Rene Bourque	.07	.20
48 Brent Seabrook	.07	.20
49 Joe Sakic	.30	.75
50 Wojtek Wolski	.07	.20
51 Milan Hejduk	.12	.30
52 Marek Svatos	.07	.20
53 Jose Theodore	.20	.50
54 Pierre Turgeon	.07	.20
55 Peter Budaj	.12	.30
56 Sergei Fedorov	.15	.40
57 Fredrik Modin	.07	.20
58 Rick Nash	.15	.40
59 Pascal Leclaire	.12	.30
60 Bryan Berard	.07	.20
61 David Vyborny	.07	.20
62 Mike Modano	.15	.40
63 Marty Turco	.12	.30
64 Brenden Morrow	.15	.40
65 Eric Lindros	.15	.40
66 Jussi Jokinen	.07	.20
67 Jere Lehtinen	.07	.20
68 Sergei Zubov	.07	.20
69 Pavel Datsyuk	.12	.30
70 Tomas Holmstrom	.07	.20
71 Henrik Zetterberg	.15	.40
72 Nicklas Lidstrom	.15	.40
73 Dominik Hasek	.25	.60
74 Robert Lang	.07	.20
75 Kris Draper	.07	.20
76 Ales Hemsky	.07	.20
77 Joffrey Lupul	.07	.20
78 Dwayne Roloson	.12	.30
79 Ryan Smyth	.12	.30
80 Jarret Stoll	.07	.20
81 Shawn Horcoff	.07	.20
82 Fernando Pisani	.07	.20
83 Todd Bertuzzi	.12	.30
84 Nathan Horton	.07	.20
85 Jay Bouwmeester	.07	.20
86 Olli Jokinen	.07	.20
87 Joe Nieuwendyk	.12	.30
88 Ed Belfour	.15	.40
89 Alexander Frolov	.07	.20
90 Mike Cammalleri	.07	.20
91 Mathieu Garon	.12	.30
92 Lubomir Visnovsky	.07	.20
93 Craig Conroy	.07	.20
94 Rob Blake	.12	.30
95 Pavol Demitra	.07	.20
96 Brian Rolston	.07	.20
97 Manny Fernandez	.12	.30
98 Marian Gaborik	.25	.60
99 Pierre-Marc Bouchard	.07	.20
100 Mikko Koivu	.07	.20
101 Mark Parrish	.07	.20
102 Cristobal Huet	.20	.50
103 Saku Koivu	.15	.40
104 Alex Kovalev	.07	.20
105 Michael Ryder	.12	.30
106 Mike Ribeiro	.07	.20
107 Chris Higgins	.07	.20
108 David Aebischer	.12	.30
109 Paul Kariya	.15	.40
110 Steve Sullivan	.07	.20
111 Tomas Vokoun	.12	.30
112 David Legwand	.07	.20
113 Jason Arnott	.07	.20
114 Scott Hartnell	.07	.20
115 Martin Brodeur	.75	2.00
116 Patrik Elias	.07	.20
117 Brian Gionta	.07	.20
118 Brian Rafalski	.07	.20
119 Scott Gomez	.07	.20
120 Zach Parise	.12	.30
121 Alexei Yashin	.07	.20
122 Jason Blake	.07	.20
123 Rick DiPietro	.12	.30
124 Miroslav Satan	.07	.20
125 Trent Hunter	.07	.20
126 Mike Sillinger	.07	.20
127 Jaromir Jagr	.25	.60
128 Henrik Lundqvist	.20	.50
129 Martin Straka	.07	.20
130 Brendan Shanahan	.15	.40
131 Petr Prucha	.07	.20
132 Matt Cullen	.07	.20
133 Martin Gerber	.12	.30
134 Antoine Vermette	.07	.20
135 Daniel Alfredsson	.12	.30
136 Jason Spezza	.15	.40
137 Dany Heatley	.20	.50
138 Wade Redden	.07	.20
139 Patrick Eaves	.07	.20
140 Ray Emery	.12	.30
141 Simon Gagne	.15	.40
142 Antero Niittymaki	.12	.30
143 Peter Forsberg	.40	1.00
144 Keith Primeau	.07	.20
145 Jeff Carter	.12	.30
146 Joni Pitkanen	.07	.20
147 R.J. Umberger	.07	.20
148 Shane Doan	.07	.20
149 Curtis Joseph	.15	.40
150 Ladislav Nagy	.07	.20
151 Mike Comrie	.07	.20
152 Jeremy Roenick	.20	.50
153 Ed Jovanovski	.07	.20
154 Sidney Crosby	1.25	3.00
155 Ryan Malone	.07	.20
156 Colby Armstrong	.07	.20
157 Marc-Andre Fleury	.12	.30
158 Sergei Gonchar	.07	.20
159 John LeClair	.12	.30
160 Patrick Marleau	.12	.30
161 Jonathan Cheechoo	.15	.40
162 Vesa Toskala	.12	.30
163 Joe Thornton	.25	.60
164 Evgeni Nabokov	.12	.30
165 Steve Bernier	.07	.20
166 Keith Tkachuk	.15	.40
167 Manny Legace	.12	.30
168 Doug Weight	.07	.20
169 Petr Cajanek	.07	.20
170 Lee Stempniak	.07	.20
171 Bill Guerin	.07	.20
172 Vincent Lecavalier	.15	.40
173 Martin St. Louis	.12	.30
174 Marc Denis	.12	.30
175 Brad Richards	.12	.30
176 Vaclav Prospal	.07	.20
177 Ryan Craig	.07	.20
178 Ruslan Fedotenko	.07	.20
179 Mats Sundin	.15	.40
180 Michael Peca	.07	.20
181 Kyle Wellwood	.07	.20
182 Bryan McCabe	.07	.20
183 Alexander Steen	.12	.30
184 Andrew Raycroft	.12	.30
185 Darcy Tucker	.07	.20
186 Tomas Kaberle	.07	.20
187 Roberto Luongo	.20	.50
188 Markus Naslund	.15	.40
189 Daniel Sedin	.07	.20
190 Henrik Sedin	.07	.20
191 Mattias Ohlund	.07	.20
192 Brendan Morrison	.07	.20
193 Willie Mitchell	.07	
194 Ryan Kesler	.07	
195 Alexander Ovechkin	.75	2.
196 Olaf Kolzig	.15	
197 Dainius Zubrus	.07	
198 Brent Johnson	.12	
199 Chris Clark	.07	
200 Richard Zednik	.07	
201 Shea Weber RC	1.00	2.
202 Noah Welch RC	.75	2.
203 Eric Fehr RC	1.00	2.
204 Mark Stuart RC	1.00	2.
205 Matt Carle RC	1.25	3.
206 Jarkko Immonen RC	.75	2.
207 Michel Ouellet RC	1.00	2.
208 Konstantin Pushkarev RC	.75	2.
209 Marc-Antoine Pouliot RC	1.00	2.
210 Ian White RC	.75	2.
211 Filip Novak RC	.75	2.
212 Tomas Kopecky RC	1.00	2.
213 Billy Thompson RC	.75	2.
214 Dustin Byfuglien RC	.75	2.
215 Yan Stastny RC	1.00	2.
216 Ben Ondrus RC	.75	2.
217 Brendan Bell RC	.75	2.
218 Steve Regier RC	.75	2.
219 Erik Reitz RC	.75	2.
220 Joel Perrault RC	.75	2.
221 Bill Thomas RC	.75	2.
222 Carsen Germyn RC	.75	2.
223 Rob Collins RC	.75	2.
224 Frank Doyle RC	.75	2.
225 Dan Jancevski RC	.75	2.
226 David Liffiton RC	.75	2.
227 Matt Koalska RC	.75	2.
228 Ryan Potulny RC	1.00	2.
229 Ryan Caldwell RC	.75	2.
230 David Printz RC	.75	2.

2006-07 Fleer Oversized

COMPLETE SET (14)	12.00	30.
15 Patrice Bergeron	.75	2.
30 Miikka Kiprusoff	.75	2.
35 Eric Staal	.75	2.
49 Joe Sakic	1.50	4.
71 Henrik Zetterberg	.75	2.
103 Saku Koivu	.75	2.
115 Martin Brodeur	2.50	6.
127 Jaromir Jagr	1.25	3.
137 Dany Heatley	1.00	2.
143 Peter Forsberg	1.50	4.
154 Sidney Crosby	4.00	10.
163 Joe Thornton	1.25	3.
179 Mats Sundin	.75	2.
195 Alexander Ovechkin	3.00	8.

2006-07 Fleer Tiffany

COMMONS	1.50	4.
STARS 6X TO 15X		
STATED ODDS (1-200) 1:36		
201-230 NOT YET PRICED/ SCARCITY		
STATED ODDS (201-230) 1:360		
154 Sidney Crosby	12.00	30.
195 Alexander Ovechkin	8.00	20.

2006-07 Fleer Fabricology

STATED ODDS 1:40		
FAA Ari Ahonen	2.50	6.
FAF Alexander Frolov	2.50	6.
FAH Adam Hall	2.50	6.
FAK Alex Kovalev	2.50	6.
FAM Andrej Meszaros	2.50	6.
FAO Alexander Ovechkin SP	15.00	40.
FAR Andrew Raycroft	3.00	8.
FAU Alex Auld	3.00	8.
FBG Bill Guerin	2.50	6.
FBJ Barret Jackman	2.50	6.
FBM Brendan Morrison	2.50	6.
FBO Jay Bouwmeester	2.50	6.
FBR Brian Rolston	2.50	6.
FBS Brad Stuart	2.50	6.
FBT Barry Tallackson	2.50	6.
FCC Chris Chelios	3.00	8.
FCD Chris Drury	3.00	8.
FCO Chris Osgood	4.00	10.
FCP Chris Pronger	3.00	8.
FDB Donald Brashear	2.50	6.
FDE Pavol Demitra	2.50	6.
FDH Dan Hamhuis	2.50	6.
FDL David Legwand	2.50	6.
FDM Dominic Moore	2.50	6.
FDS Daniel Sedin	2.50	6.
FDW Doug Weight	2.50	6.
FEB Ed Belfour SP	8.00	20.
FED Eric Daze	2.50	6.
FEL Eric Lindros	4.00	10.
FEP Patrik Elias	2.50	6.
FGA Mathieu Garon	3.00	8.
FGR Gary Roberts	2.50	6.
FHO Marian Hossa	3.00	8.
FIK Ilya Kovalchuk	6.00	15.
FJA Jason Arnott	2.50	6.
FJB Jason Bacashihua	3.00	8.
FJG Jean-Sebastien Giguere	3.00	8.
FJJ Jaromir Jagr	6.00	15.
FJL Jamie Lundmark	2.50	6.
FJR Jeremy Roenick	4.00	10.
FJS Jason Spezza	4.00	10.
FJT Joe Thornton	6.00	15.
FJW Justin Williams	2.50	6.
FKL Kari Lehtonen	4.00	10.
FKO Mike Komisarek	2.50	6.
FKP Keith Primeau	2.50	6.
FKT Keith Tkachuk	3.00	8.
FLE Jere Lehtinen	3.00	8.
FMA Martin Brodeur	8.00	20.
FMB Martin Biron	3.00	8.
FMC Bryan McCabe	2.50	6.
FMG Marian Gaborik	5.00	12.
FMH Marcel Hossa	2.50	6.
FMK Miikka Kiprusoff	4.00	10.
FMM Mike Modano	6.00	15.
FMN Markus Naslund	3.00	8.
FMO Mattias Ohlund	2.50	6.

Card	Low	High
P Mark Parrish	2.50	6.00
S Martin Straka	2.50	6.00
T Marty Turco	4.00	10.00
A Nikolai Antropov	2.50	6.00
O Mika Noronen	3.00	8.00
J Olli Jokinen	2.50	6.00
K Olaf Kolzig	4.00	10.00
A Patrik Stefan	2.50	6.00
B Peter Bondra	3.00	8.00
D Pavel Datsyuk	4.00	10.00
E Michael Peca	2.50	6.00
F Peter Forsberg	6.00	15.00
L Patrick Lalime	3.00	8.00
M Patrick Marleau	3.00	8.00
S Patrick Sharp	4.00	10.00
T Pierre Turgeon	2.50	6.00
B Rob Blake	2.50	6.00
E Robert Esche	3.00	8.00
F Ruslan Fedotenko	2.50	6.00
H Ryan Hollweg	2.50	6.00
K Rostislav Klesla	2.50	6.00
L Robert Lang	2.50	6.00
M Ryan Miller	4.00	10.00
N Rob Niedermayer	2.50	6.00
O Rod Brind`Amour	2.50	6.00
T Raffi Torres	3.00	8.00
A Philippe Sauve	3.00	8.00
C Sidney Crosby SP	30.00	80.00
F Sergei Fedorov	6.00	15.00
G Simon Gagne	3.00	8.00
K Sami Kapanen	2.50	6.00
N Scott Niedermayer	2.50	6.00
S Sergei Samsonov	3.00	8.00
T Matt Stajan	2.50	6.00
W Stephen Weiss	2.50	6.00
C Tim Connolly	2.50	6.00
H Tomas Holmstrom	3.00	8.00
O Jordin Tootoo	4.00	10.00
P Tom Poti	2.50	6.00
R Tuomo Ruutu	3.00	8.00
S Teemu Selanne	4.00	10.00
Y Ty Conklin	3.00	8.00
C Zdeno Chara	2.50	6.00

2006-07 Fleer Hockey Headliners

Card	Low	High
MPLETE SET (25)	10.00	25.00
ATED ODDS 1:4		
1 Sidney Crosby	2.00	5.00
2 Alexander Ovechkin	1.50	4.00
3 Teemu Selanne	.30	.75
4 Cam Ward	.30	.75
5 Luc Robitaille	.25	.60
6 Mario Lemieux	1.50	4.00
7 Joe Thornton	.50	1.25
8 Ilya Kovalchuk	.40	1.00
9 Daniel Alfredsson	.25	.60
10 Henrik Lundqvist	.40	1.00
11 Brian Leetch	.30	.75
12 Pierre Turgeon	.15	.40
13 Fernando Pisani	.15	.40
14 Alexander Ovechkin	1.50	4.00
15 Sidney Crosby	2.00	5.00
16 Alexander Ovechkin	1.50	4.00
17 Dany Heatley	.40	1.00
18 Martin Havlat	.25	.60
19 Dion Phaneuf	.40	1.00
20 Miikka Kiprusoff	.30	.75
21 Jaromir Jagr	.50	1.25
22 Jonathan Cheechoo	.30	.75
23 Martin Brodeur	1.00	2.50
24 Ilya Bryzgalov	.25	.60
25 Marek Svatos	.15	.40

2006-07 Fleer Netminders

Card	Low	High
MPLETE SET (25)	8.00	20.00
ATED ODDS 1:4		
Ilya Bryzgalov	.40	1.00
Kari Lehtonen	.50	1.25
Ryan Miller	.50	1.25
Dominik Hasek	.75	2.00
Miikka Kiprusoff	.50	1.25
Cam Ward	.50	1.25
Nikolai Khabibulin	.50	1.25
Jose Theodore	.50	1.25
Marty Turco	.50	1.25
0 Dwayne Roloson	.40	1.00
1 Roberto Luongo	.60	1.50
2 Manny Fernandez	.40	1.00
3 Cristobal Huet	.75	2.00
4 Tomas Vokoun	.50	1.25
5 Martin Brodeur	1.50	4.00
6 Rick DiPietro	.40	1.00
7 Henrik Lundqvist	.60	1.50
8 Martin Gerber	.40	1.00
9 Antero Niittymaki	.40	1.00
0 Curtis Joseph	.50	1.25
1 Marc-Andre Fleury	.50	1.25
2 Andrew Raycroft	.40	1.00
3 Vesa Toskala	.40	1.00
4 Olaf Kolzig	.50	1.25
5 Marc Denis	.40	1.00

2006-07 Fleer Signing Day

Card	Low	High
ATED ODDS 1:432		
AA Adrian Aucoin	6.00	15.00
AF Alexander Frolov	6.00	15.00
AH Ales Hemsky	8.00	20.00
AO Alexander Ovechkin SP	250.00	350.00
BA Matthew Barnaby	6.00	15.00
BB Brad Boyes	6.00	15.00
BI Martin Biron	10.00	25.00
BL Brian Leetch	20.00	50.00
BR Dustin Brown	6.00	15.00
BS Brent Seabrook	8.00	20.00
CD Chris Drury	6.00	15.00
CK Chuck Kobasew	6.00	15.00
CP Chris Phillips	6.00	15.00
CW Cam Ward	12.00	30.00
DA David Aebischer	10.00	25.00
DB Daniel Briere	12.00	30.00
DP Dion Phaneuf	15.00	40.00
DR Dwayne Roloson	10.00	25.00
EA Evgeni Artyukhin	6.00	15.00
GL Georges Laraque	10.00	25.00
SDHO Marcel Hossa	6.00	15.00
SDJC Jonathan Cheechoo	12.00	30.00
SDJF Johan Franzen	6.00	15.00
SDJH Jeff Halpern	8.00	20.00
SDJI Jarome Iginla SP		
SDJT Jose Theodore	15.00	40.00
SDKC Kyle Calder	6.00	15.00
SDKD Kris Draper	6.00	15.00
SDKI Miikka Kiprusoff SP		
SDMB Martin Brodeur SP		
SDMG Marian Gaborik SP		
SDMH Milan Hejduk	10.00	25.00
SDMJ Milan Jurcina	6.00	15.00
SDMK Mikko Koivu	10.00	25.00
SDMR Mike Ribeiro	6.00	15.00
SDMS Marc Savard	6.00	15.00
SDMT Mikael Tellqvist	10.00	25.00
SDPB Peter Budaj	10.00	25.00
SDPN Petteri Nokelainen	6.00	15.00
SDRB Rob Blake	8.00	20.00
SDRF Ruslan Fedotenko	6.00	15.00
SDRG Ryan Getzlaf	12.00	30.00
SDRI Raitis Ivanans	6.00	15.00
SDRO Rostislav Olesz	6.00	15.00
SDRS Ryan Suter	6.00	15.00
SDRY Michael Ryder	10.00	25.00
SDSC Sidney Crosby	125.00	250.00
SDSG Scott Gomez	6.00	15.00
SDSH Scott Hartnell	6.00	15.00
SDTA Jeff Tambellini	6.00	15.00
SDTC Ty Conklin	8.00	20.00
SDTH Joe Thornton SP		
SDTV Thomas Vanek	12.00	30.00
SDVL Vincent Lecavalier SP		

2006-07 Fleer Speed Machines

Card	Low	High
COMPLETE SET (25)	6.00	15.00
STATED ODDS 1:4		
SM1 Scott Niedermayer	.15	.40
SM2 Teemu Selanne	.30	.75
SM3 Ilya Kovalchuk	.40	1.00
SM4 Marian Hossa	.25	.60
SM5 Erik Cole	.15	.40
SM6 Chris Drury	.15	.40
SM7 Alex Tanguay	.25	.60
SM8 Joe Sakic	.60	1.50
SM9 Sergei Fedorov	.30	.75
SM10 Bill Guerin	.15	.40
SM11 Mike Modano	.30	.75
SM12 Pavel Datsyuk	.25	.60
SM13 Jay Bouwmeester	.15	.40
SM14 Marian Gaborik	.40	1.00
SM15 Alex Kovalev	.15	.40
SM16 Paul Kariya	.30	.75
SM17 Miroslav Satan	.15	.40
SM18 Dany Heatley	.40	1.00
SM19 Sami Kapanen	.15	.40
SM20 Simon Gagne	.30	.75
SM21 Patrick Marleau	.25	.60
SM22 Martin St. Louis	.25	.60
SM23 Mats Sundin	.30	.75
SM24 Markus Naslund	.30	.75
SM25 Alexander Ovechkin	1.50	4.00

2006-07 Fleer Total O

Card	Low	High
COMPLETE SET (25)	8.00	20.00
STATED ODDS 1:4		
O1 Ilya Kovalchuk	.40	1.00
O2 Patrice Bergeron	.30	.75
O3 Jarome Iginla	.40	1.00
O4 Eric Staal	.30	.75
O5 Joe Sakic	.60	1.50
O6 Rick Nash	.30	.75
O7 Mike Modano	.30	.75
O8 Pavel Datsyuk	.25	.60
O9 Henrik Zetterberg	.30	.75
O10 Ales Hemsky	.15	.40
O11 Olli Jokinen	.15	.40
O12 Saku Koivu	.30	.75
O13 Paul Kariya	.30	.75
O14 Patrik Elias	.15	.40
O15 Jaromir Jagr	.50	1.25
O16 Dany Heatley	.40	1.00
O17 Daniel Alfredsson	.25	.60
O18 Jason Spezza	.30	.75
O19 Peter Forsberg	.60	1.50
O20 Sidney Crosby	2.00	5.00
O21 Joe Thornton	.50	1.25
O22 Jonathan Cheechoo	.30	.75
O23 Mats Sundin	.30	.75
O24 Markus Naslund	.30	.75
O25 Alexander Ovechkin	1.50	4.00

2001-02 Fleer Legacy

Released in mid-March 2002, this 64-card set was carried an SRP of $4.99 for a 4 card pack. Cards 1-8 resembled the design of Ultra and were short printed to 2002 copies each. Cards 9-64 were a horizontal design featuring color photos on a white card front.

Card	Low	High
COMPLETE SET (64)	40.00	80.00
1 Mario Lemieux SP	5.00	12.00
2 Bobby Hull SP	2.50	6.00
3 Guy Lafleur SP	2.00	5.00
4 Phil Esposito SP	2.50	6.00
5 Cam Neely SP	2.00	5.00
6 Jean Beliveau SP	1.50	4.00
7 Bryan Trottier SP	1.50	4.00
8 Jari Kurri SP	2.00	5.00
9 Jean Beliveau	.30	.75
10 Bob Nystrom	.12	.30
11 Phil Esposito	.50	1.25
12 Bobby Hull	.50	1.25
13 Guy Lafleur	.40	1.00
14 Gilbert Perreault	.12	.30
15 Henri Richard	.30	.75
16 Marcel Dionne	.30	.75
17 Tony Esposito	.40	1.00
18 Clark Gillies	.12	.30
19 Grant Fuhr	.25	.60
20 Brad Park	.25	.60
21 Frank Mahovlich	.30	.75
22 John Bucyk	.12	.30
23 Billy Smith	.25	.60
24 Ulf Samuelsson	.12	.30
25 Mario Lemieux	1.25	3.00
26 Rod Gilbert	.30	.75
27 Basil McRae	.12	.30
28 Dave Semenko	.12	.30
29 Neal Broten	.12	.30
30 Terry Sawchuk	.50	1.25
31 Dino Ciccarelli	.12	.30
32 Mike Bossy	.30	.75
33 Borje Salming	.25	.60
34 Stan Mikita	.40	1.00
35 Ted Lindsay	.30	.75
36 Gerry Cheevers	.40	1.00
37 Michel Goulet	.12	.30
38 Red Kelly	.30	.75
39 Bobby Clarke	.30	.75
40 Todd Ewen	.12	.30
41 Denis Potvin	.25	.60
42 Paul Henderson	.12	.30
43 Butch Goring	.25	.60
44 Nick Fotiu	.12	.30
45 Denis Savard	.25	.60
46 Larry Robinson	.25	.60
47 Joe Kocur	.40	1.00
48 Bernie Parent	.30	.75
49 Mike Liut	.25	.60
50 Bernie Geoffrion	.30	.75
51 Tony Twist	.12	.30
52 Bryan Trottier	.25	.60
53 Cam Neely	.30	.75
54 Brent Sutter	.12	.30
55 Dave Schultz	.25	.60
56 Terry O'Reilly	.12	.30
57 Jari Kurri	.25	.60
58 Lanny McDonald	.12	.30
59 Mike Gartner	.12	.30
60 Alex Delvecchio	.30	.75
61 Ron Hextall	.40	1.00
62 Darryl Sittler	.30	.75
63 Dale Hunter	.12	.30
64 John Vanbiesbrouck	.25	.60

2001-02 Fleer Legacy Ultimate

This set paralleled the entire base set and carried a serial-numbering to 202. Gold replaced the white on the card front backgrounds.

*STARS: 4X TO 10X BASIC CARD
*SP's: 1.25X TO 3X BASIC SP's

2001-02 Fleer Legacy In the Corners

Inserted at stated rates of 1:24 hobby and 1:36 retail, this 12-card set features pieces of dasher boards from Joe Louis Arena. Card fronts carry a color photo of the featured player on the left, the player's name vertically on the right and a postage stamp-sized board piece in the center. Card backs carry a congratulatory message. Cards are unnumbered and are listed below in checklist order.

Card	Low	High
1 Dino Ciccarelli	5.00	12.00
2 Jari Kurri	6.00	15.00
3 Guy Lafleur	6.00	15.00
4 Mario Lemieux	10.00	25.00
5 Lanny McDonald	5.00	12.00
6 Cam Neely	5.00	12.00
7 Denis Potvin	5.00	12.00
8 Larry Robinson	5.00	12.00
9 Borje Salming	5.00	12.00
10 Darryl Sittler	5.00	12.00
11 Billy Smith	5.00	12.00
12 Tony Twist	5.00	12.00

2001-02 Fleer Legacy Memorabilia

Inserted at stated odds of 1:24 hobby and 1:36 retail, this 25-card set featured game-used swatches of jersey or sticks. Card fronts carry a color photo on the left side and the memorabilia piece on the left. Jersey cards had the words "Tailor Made" printed under the jersey swatch and the swatch was postage stamp-sized. Stick cards had the words "Hockey Kings" above the dime-sized

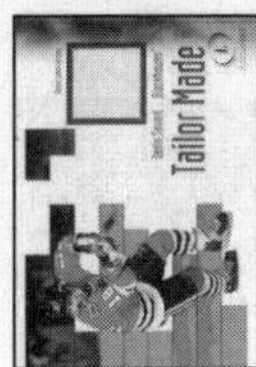

stick piece. Card backs carried a congratulatory message. Cards are unnumbered and listed below in checklist order.

*MULT.COLOR SWATCH: .5X TO 1.25X HI

Card	Low	High
1 Dino Ciccarelli	6.00	15.00
2 Tony Esposito JSY	8.00	20.00
3 Michel Goulet	6.00	15.00
4 Guy Lafleur	8.00	20.00
5 Mario Lemieux JSY	10.00	25.00
6 Larry Robinson	6.00	15.00
7 Borje Salming	6.00	15.00
8 Denis Savard	6.00	15.00
9 Jean Beliveau	8.00	20.00
10 Marcel Dionne	5.00	12.00
11 Tony Esposito	6.00	15.00
12 Phil Esposito	10.00	25.00
13 Mike Gartner	6.00	15.00
14 Bobby Hull	12.50	30.00
15 Guy Lafleur	6.00	15.00
16 Mario Lemieux STK	12.50	30.00
17 Stan Mikita	10.00	25.00
18 Cam Neely	10.00	25.00
19 Brad Park	6.00	15.00
20 Gilbert Perreault	6.00	15.00
21 Henri Richard	6.00	15.00
22 Terry Sawchuk	20.00	50.00
23 Darryl Sittler	8.00	20.00
24 Bryan Trottier	6.00	15.00
25 John Vanbiesbrouck	6.00	15.00

2001-02 Fleer Legacy Memorabilia Autographs

This 9-card set paralleled the stick cards in the memorabilia set but also carried the player's autograph under the stick piece. All cards in the checklist were only available as redemption cards out of packs. Cards were serial-numbered out of 100 each. Redemption cards expired March 2003.

Card	Low	High
1 Jean Beliveau	20.00	50.00
2 Phil Esposito	25.00	60.00
3 Bobby Hull	30.00	80.00
4 Guy Lafleur	20.00	50.00
5 Mario Lemieux	50.00	125.00
6 Stan Mikita	20.00	50.00
7 Darryl Sittler	20.00	50.00
8 Bryan Trottier	15.00	40.00

2002 Fleer Lemieux All-Star Fantasy

Available as a wrapper redemption from the Fleer booth at the NHL All-Star Game in LA, this special Mario Lemieux card was limited to 10,000 copies.

Card	Low	High
1 Mario Lemieux	2.00	5.00

2002-03 Fleer Throwbacks

This 91-card set featured players from the past and featured a few former players first main stream card. Card #92 was not available in packs, and was only available via redemption at the 2003 NHL All-Star Block Party.

Card	Low	High
COMPLETE SET (91)	20.00	40.00
1 Terry O'Reilly	.40	1.00
2 Barry Beck	.20	.50
3 Bobby Clarke	.30	.75
4 Mike Foligno	.20	.50
5 Danny Gare	.20	.50
6 Clark Gillies	.20	.50
7 Bernie Federko	.20	.50
8 Dale Hunter	.20	.50
9 Kris King	.20	.50
10 Ted Lindsay	.40	1.00
11 Tie Domi	.20	.50
12 Rob Ramage	.20	.50
13 Jim Schoenfeld	.20	.50
14 Steve Smith	.20	.50
15 Harold Snepsts	.20	.50
16 Rod Langway	.20	.50
17 Denis Potvin	.30	.75
18 John Bucyk	.25	.60
19 Dirk Graham	.20	.50
20 Lanny McDonald	.20	.50
21 Stan Smyl	.20	.50
22 Andre Dupont	.20	.50
23 Todd Ewen	.20	.50
24 George McPhee	.20	.50
25 Paul Baxter	.20	.50
26 Keith Magnuson	.20	.50
27 Kevin Kaminski	.20	.50
28 Mike Peluso	.20	.50
29 Dave Semenko	.20	.50
30 David Maley	.20	.50
31 Jeff Beukeboom	.20	.50
32 Dave Brown	.20	.50
33 Troy Crowder	.20	.50
34 Bobby Hull	.50	1.25
35 Dan Maloney	.20	.50
36 Jimmy Mann	.20	.50
37 Rudy Poeschek	.20	.50
38 John Wensink	.20	.50
39 Kim Clackson	.20	.50
40 Jay Wells	.20	.50
41 Glen Cochrane RC	.30	.75
42 Alan May	.20	.50
43 Willi Plett	.20	.50
44 Kevin McClelland	.20	.50
45 Jim Cummins	.20	.50
46 Basil McRae	.20	.50
47 Ron Delorme	.20	.50
48 John Ferguson	.20	.50
49 Gord Donnelly	.20	.50
50 Nick Kypreos	.20	.50
51 Larry Playfair	.20	.50
52 Marty McSorley	.20	.50
53 Tim Hunter	.20	.50
54 Billy Smith	.25	.60
55 Laurie Boschman	.20	.50
56 Wayne Cashman	.20	.50
57 Link Gaetz	.20	.50
58 Darin Kimble	.20	.50
59 Bob Nystrom	.25	.60
60 Ronnie Stern	.20	.50
61 Ken Baumgartner	.20	.50
62 Ken Linseman	.20	.50
63 Kelly Chase	.20	.50
64 Bob Gassoff	.20	.50
65 Joey Kocur	.20	.50
66 Chris Nilan	.20	.50
67 Dave Schultz	.20	.50
68 Tony Twist	.20	.50
69 Enrico Ciccone	.20	.50
70 Jay Miller	.20	.50
71 Phil Russell	.20	.50
72 Bryan Watson	.20	.50
73 Paul Holmgren	.20	.50
74 Garth Butcher	.20	.50
75 Al Iafrate	.20	.50
76 Barclay Plager	.20	.50
77 Brent Severyn	.20	.50
78 Ron Hextall	.25	.60
79 Shane Churla	.20	.50
80 Dino Ciccarelli	.20	.50
81 Cam Neely	.40	1.00
82 Ulf Samuelsson	.20	.50
83 Mick Vukota	.20	.50
84 Garry Howatt	.20	.50
85 Gary Rissling RC	.30	.75
86 Behn Wilson	.20	.50
87 Jack Carlson RC	.30	.75
88 Bob Bassen	.20	.50
89 Curt Brackenbury	.20	.50
90 Mario Roberge	.20	.50
91 Serge Roberge RC	.30	.75
92 Bob Probert	5.00	12.00

2002-03 Fleer Throwbacks Gold

*GOLD: 2X TO 5X BASIC CARDS
STATED ODDS 1:1

2002-03 Fleer Throwbacks Platinum

*PLATINUM: 6X TO 15X BASIC CARDS
STAT.PRINT RUN 50 SER.#' d SETS

2002-03 Fleer Throwbacks Autographs

This 23-card set featured certified player autographs and was inserted at a rate of 1:144.

Card	Low	High
1 Terry O'Reilly	12.50	30.00
2 Bobby Clarke	15.00	40.00
3 Clark Gillies	8.00	20.00
4 Dale Hunter	8.00	20.00
5 Ted Lindsay	25.00	60.00
6 Tie Domi	15.00	40.00
7 Jim Schoenfeld	15.00	40.00
8 Denis Potvin	8.00	20.00
9 Todd Ewen	8.00	20.00
10 Kevin Kaminski	8.00	20.00
11 Bob Probert	100.00	250.00
12 Dave Brown	12.50	30.00
13 Bobby Hull	40.00	100.00
14 Basil McRae	15.00	40.00
15 Larry Playfair	8.00	20.00
16 Marty McSorley	20.00	50.00
17 Billy Smith	40.00	100.00
18 Bob Nystrom	8.00	20.00
19 Ken Baumgartner	8.00	20.00
20 Kelly Chase	8.00	20.00
21 Joey Kocur	15.00	40.00
22 Dave Schultz	10.00	25.00
23 Tony Twist	25.00	60.00

2002-03 Fleer Throwbacks Drop the Gloves

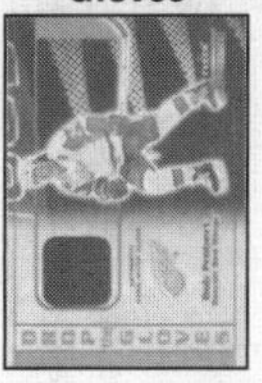

Serial-numbered to 200 copies each, this 5-card set featured pieces of game-used gloves. Cards were not numbered and are listed below in checklist order.

Card	Low	High
1 Bob Probert	40.00	100.00
2 Ron Hextall	20.00	50.00
3 Tony Twist	12.50	30.00
4 Marty McSorley	8.00	20.00
5 Jim Cummins	8.00	20.00

2002-03 Fleer Throwbacks Scraps

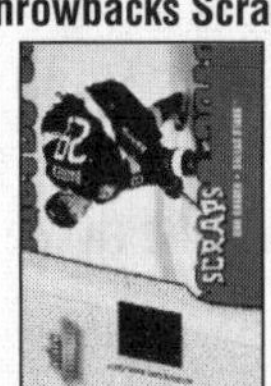

Inserted at 1:25, this 8-card set featured pieces of game jerseys. Cards were not numbered and are listed below in checklist order.

Card	Low	High
1 Basil McRae	5.00	12.00
2 Enrico Ciccone	5.00	12.00
3 Bob Bassen	6.00	15.00
4 Joey Kocur	6.00	15.00
5 Clark Gillies	5.00	12.00
6 Marty McSorley	5.00	12.00
7 Tony Twist	5.00	12.00
8 Dale Hunter	5.00	12.00

2002-03 Fleer Throwbacks Tie Downs

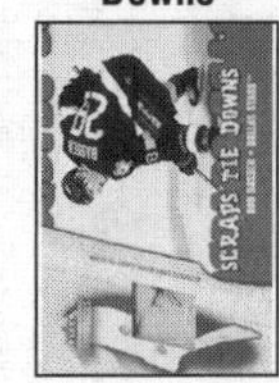

This 8-card set paralleled the basic jersey set but featured swatches of jersey tie-downs. Each card was serial-numbered out of 50.

Card	Low	High
1 Basil McRae	20.00	50.00
2 Enrico Ciccone	20.00	50.00
3 Bob Bassen	25.00	60.00
4 Joey Kocur	25.00	60.00
5 Clark Gillies	20.00	50.00
6 Marty McSorley	20.00	50.00
7 Tony Twist	20.00	50.00
8 Dale Hunter	20.00	50.00

2002-03 Fleer Throwbacks Squaring Off

Card	Low	High
COMPLETE SET (9)	15.00	30.00
STATED ODDS 1:24		
1 Bob Probert / Joey Kocur	2.50	6.00
2 Dave Schultz / Clark Gillies	1.50	4.00
3 Cam Neely / Ulf Samuelsson	2.00	5.00
4 Terry O'Reilly / Jim Schoenfeld	1.50	4.00
5 Barry Beck / Denis Potvin	1.50	4.00
6 Bobby Clarke / Dale Hunter	1.50	4.00
7 Tony Twist / Marty McSorley	2.50	6.00
8 Dave Brown / Dave Schultz	2.50	6.00
9 Ron Hextall / Billy Smith	1.50	4.00

2002-03 Fleer Throwbacks Squaring Off Memorabilia

This 8-card set was inserted at 1:48 and paralleled the basic insert set but carried dual memorabilia swatches.

Card	Low	High
1 Bob Probert JSY / Joey Kocur STK	10.00	25.00
2 Dave Schultz JSY / Clark Gillies JSY	6.00	15.00
3 Cam Neely JSY / Ulf Samuelsson JSY	8.00	20.00
4 Terry O'Reilly JSY / Jim Schoenfeld JSY	6.00	15.00
5 Barry Beck JSY / Denis Potvin JSY	6.00	15.00
6 Bobby Clarke STK / Dale Hunter JSY	6.00	15.00
7 Tony Twist JSY / Marty McSorley JSY	10.00	25.00
8 Dave Brown JSY / Dave Schultz JSY	10.00	25.00

2002-03 Fleer Throwbacks Stickwork

Cards are not numbered and are listed below in checklist order.

Card	Low	High
1 Kelly Chase	5.00	12.00
2 Dale Hunter	5.00	12.00
3 Curt Brackenbury	5.00	12.00
4 Todd Ewen	5.00	12.00
5 Jim Cummins	6.00	15.00
6 Rudy Poeschek	5.00	12.00
7 Jay Wells	5.00	12.00
8 Enrico Ciccone	5.00	12.00
9 Marty McSorley	15.00	40.00
10 Bobby Hull	8.00	20.00
11 Cam Neely	6.00	15.00
12 Bobby Clarke	8.00	20.00
13 Bob Probert	8.00	20.00

1994 Fleury Hockey Tips

Titled "Theoren Fleury Hockey School Tip of the Week," this 14-card set measuresd the standard size. The lavender-bordered fronts had color action photos illustrating each hockey tip. The backs carried the "Tip of the Week" in black lettering followed by discussion. The cards were numbered on both sides.

Card	Low	High
COMPLETE SET (14)	2.00	5.00
COMMON CARD (1-14)	.20	.50

1970-71 Flyers Postcards

This 12-card, team-issued set measured 3 1/2" by 5 1/2" and was in the postcard format. The fronts featured full-bleed color photos, with the players posed on ice at the skating rink. A facsimile autograph was inscribed across the bottom. The white backs carried player information and team logo across the top. The cards were unnumbered and checklisted below in alphabetical order.

Card	Low	High
COMPLETE SET (12)	20.00	40.00
1 Barry Ashbee	3.00	6.00
2 Gary Dornhoefer	3.00	6.00
3 Warren Elliott / Frank Leurs	1.00	2.00
4 Doug Favell	3.00	6.00

Card	Low	High
5 Earl Heiskala	1.50	3.00
6 Larry Hillman	2.50	5.00
7 Andre Lacroix	2.50	5.00
8 Lew Morrison	1.50	3.00
9 Simon Nolet	2.00	4.00
10 Garry Peters	1.50	3.00
11 Vic Stasiuk CO	1.50	3.00
12 George Swarbrick	1.50	3.00

1972 Flyers Mighty Milk

These seven panels, which were issued on the sides of half gallon cartons of Mighty Milk, featured members of the Philadelphia Flyers. After cutting, the panels measured approximately 3 5/8" by 7 1/2". All lettering and the portrait itself were in blue. Inside a frame with rounded corners, each panel displayed a portrait of the player and a player profile. The words "Philadelphia Hockey Star" and the player's name appeared above the frame, while an advertisement for Mighty Milk and another for TV Channel 29 appeared immediately below. The backs were blank. The panels were unnumbered and checklisted below in alphabetical order.

Card	Low	High
COMPLETE SET (8)	87.50	175.00
1 Serge Bernier	7.50	15.00
2 Bobby Clarke	40.00	80.00
3 Gary Dornhoefer	10.00	20.00
4 Doug Favell	15.00	30.00
5 Jean-Guy Gendron	7.50	15.00
6 Bob Kelly		
7 Bill Lesuk	7.50	15.00
8 Ed Van Impe	10.00	20.00

1973-74 Flyers Linnett

These oversize cards were produce by Charles Linnett Studios. Cards were done in black and white and featured a facsimile signature. Original price per piece was only 50 cents. Cards measure 8 1/2 x 11. They were unnumbered and checklisted below in alphabetical order.

Card	Low	High
COMPLETE SET (1-18)	40.00	80.00
1 Barry Ashbee	1.50	3.00
2 Bill Barber	5.00	10.00
3 Tom Bladon	1.50	3.00
4 Bob Clarke	5.00	10.00
5 Bill Clement	3.00	6.00
6 Terry Crisp	2.50	5.00
7 Bill Flett	2.00	4.00
8 Bob Kelly	1.50	3.00
9 Orest Kindrachuk	1.50	3.00
10 Ross Lonsberry	1.50	3.00
11 Rick Macleish	2.00	4.00
12 Simon Nolet	2.00	4.00
13 Bernard Parent	5.00	10.00
14 Don Saleski	1.50	3.00
15 Dave Schultz	3.00	6.00
16 Ed Van Impe	1.50	3.00
17 Jimmy Watson	2.00	4.00
18 Joe Watson	2.00	4.00

1983-84 Flyers J.C. Penney

Sponsored by J.C. Penney, this 22-card set measured approximately 4" by 6". The fronts featured color posed action shots of the players on ice. Beneath the picture were the team name, logo, player's name, and the phrase "Compliments of J.C. Penney Stores in the Delaware Valley." The backs were blank. The cards were unnumbered and checklisted below in alphabetical order.

Card	Low	High
COMPLETE SET (22)	14.00	35.00
1 Ray Allison	.40	1.00
2 Bill Barber	.80	2.00
3 Frank Bathe	.40	1.00
4 Lindsay Carson	.40	1.00
5 Bobby Clarke	2.00	5.00
6 Glen Cochrane	.40	1.00
7 Doug Crossman	.60	1.50
8 Miroslav Dvorak	.40	1.00
9 Thomas Eriksson	.40	1.00
10 Bob Froese	.60	1.50
11 Randy Holt	.40	1.00
12 Mark Howe	.80	2.00
13 Tim Kerr	.80	2.00
14 Pelle Lindbergh	4.80	12.00
15 Brad Marsh	.60	1.50
16 Brad McCrimmon	.60	1.50
17 Dave Poulin	.60	1.50
18 Brian Propp	.80	2.00
19 Ilkka Sinisalo	.60	1.50
20 Darryl Sittler	1.60	4.00
21 Rich Sutter	.40	1.00
22 Ron Sutter	.40	1.00

1985-86 Flyers Postcards

This 31 card set featured action photos on the front, and came complete with player name, number and statistics.

Card	Low	High
COMPLETE SET (31)	10.00	25.00
1 Bill Barber	.40	1.00
2 Dave Brown	.30	.75
3 Lindsay Carson	.20	.50
4 Bob Clarke	.80	2.00
5 Murray Craven	.20	.50
6 Pat Croce	.10	.25
7 Doug Crossman	.20	.50

Card	Low	High
8 Per-Erik Eklund	.20	.50
9 Thomas Eriksson	.20	.50
10 Bob Froese	.30	.75
11 Len Hachborn	.10	.25
12 Paul Holmgren	.20	.50
13 Ed Hospodar	.20	.50
14 Mark Howe	.30	.75
15 Mike Keenan	.40	1.00
16 Tim Kerr	.30	.75
17 Pelle Lindbergh	3.20	8.00
18 Brad Marsh	.20	.50
19 Brad McCrimmon	.30	.75
20 E.J. McGuire CO	.10	.25
21 Bernie Parent CO	.40	1.00
22 Joe Paterson	.10	.25
23 Dave Poulin	.20	.50
24 Brian Propp	.40	1.00
25 Ilkka Sinisalo	.20	.50
26 Derrick Smith	.20	.50
27 Rich Sutter	.20	.50
28 Ron Sutter	.20	.50
29 Rick Tocchet	2.40	6.00
30 Peter Zezel	.80	2.00
31 Team Photo	.80	2.00

1986-87 Flyers Postcards

This 29-card set of Philadelphia Flyers featured full-bleed, color action and posed photos. The cards measured approximately 4 1/8" by 6" and were in a postcard format. A player's autograph facsimile was printed on the front. A diagonal black stripe cut across the lower portion of the picture. Within the black stripe appeared narrow orange stripes, the Flyers logo, and player information. The horizontal white backs carryed career statistics and biography on the left, and the postcard format mailing address space on the right. The cards were unnumbered and checklisted below in alphabetical order.

Card	Low	High
COMPLETE SET (29)	10.00	25.00
1 Bill Barber CO	.40	1.00
2 Dave Brown	.30	.75
3 Lindsay Carson	.20	.50
4 Murray Craven	.20	.50
5 Pat Croce TR	.10	.25
6 Doug Crossman	.20	.50
7 Jean-Jacques Daigneault	.20	.50
8 Pelle Eklund	.30	.75
9 Ron Hextall	1.60	4.00
10 Paul Holmgren CO	.20	.50
11 Ed Hospodar	.20	.50
12 Mark Howe	.60	1.50
13 Mike Keenan CO	.40	1.00
14 Tim Kerr	.60	1.50
15 Brad Marsh	.20	.50
16 Brad McCrimmon	.30	.75
17 E.J. McGuire CO	.10	.25
18 Scott Mellanby	.60	1.50
19 Bernie Parent CO	.40	1.00
20 Dave Poulin	.30	.75
21 Brian Propp	.40	1.00
22 Glenn Resch	.40	1.00
23 Ilkka Sinisalo	.20	.50
24 Derrick Smith	.20	.50
25 Daryl Stanley	.20	.50
26 Ron Sutter	.20	.50
27 Rick Tocchet	2.00	5.00
28 Peter Zezel	.40	1.00
29 Team Photo	.80	2.00

1989-90 Flyers Postcards

This 29-card set measured 4 1/8" by 6" and was in the postcard format. The fronts featured full-bleed color action player photos. A team color-coded (black with thin orange stripes) diagonal stripe cut across the bottom portion and carried the team logo, biographical information, and jersey number. The white horizontal backs carried the team logo, biography, and career summary. The cards were unnumbered and checklisted below in alphabetical order.

Card	Low	High
COMPLETE SET (29)	8.00	20.00
1 Keith Acton	.20	.50
2 Craig Berube	.20	.50
3 Mike Bullard	.20	.50
4 Terry Carkner	.20	.50
5 Jeff Chychrun	.20	.50
6 Bob Clarke VP/GM	.80	2.00
7 Murray Craven	.20	.50
8 Mike Eaves ACO	.10	.25
9 Pelle Eklund	.30	.75
10 Ron Hextall	.80	2.00
11 Paul Holmgren CO	.20	.50
12 Mark Howe	.40	1.00
13 Kerry Huffman	.20	.50
14 Tim Kerr	.40	1.00
15 Scott Mellanby	.40	1.00
16 Gord Murphy	.20	.50
17 Andy Murray ACO	.10	.25
18 Pete Peeters	.40	1.00
19 Dave Poulin	.40	1.00
20 Brian Propp	.40	1.00
21 Kjell Samuelsson	.40	1.00
22 Ilkka Sinisalo	.20	.50
23 Derrick Smith	.20	.50
24 Doug Sulliman	.20	.50
25 Ron Sutter	.20	.50
26 Rick Tocchet	.80	2.00
27 Jay Wells	.20	.50
28 Ken Wregget	.80	2.00
29 Team Photo	.80	2.00

1990-91 Flyers Postcards

This 26-card set was issued by the Philadelphia Flyers. Each card measured approximately 4 1/8" by 6". The fronts displayed full-bleed color action photos. A team color-coded (black with thin orange stripes) diagonal stripe cut across the bottom portion and carried the team logo, biographical information, and jersey number. The horizontal backs were postcard design and, on the left, presented biography, statistics, and notes. The cards were unnumbered and checklisted below in alphabetical order.

Card	Low	High
COMPLETE SET (26)	6.00	15.00
1 Keith Acton	.30	.75
2 Murray Baron	.20	.50
3 Craig Berube	.20	.50
4 Terry Carkner	.20	.50
5 Jeff Chychrun	.20	.50
6 Murray Craven	.30	.75
7 Pelle Eklund	.30	.75
8 Ron Hextall	.60	1.50
9 Tony Horacek	.20	.50
10 Martin Hostak	.20	.50
11 Mark Howe	.40	1.00
12 Kerry Huffman	.20	.50
13 Tim Kerr	.40	1.00
14 Dale Kushner	.20	.50
15 Norman Lacombe	.20	.50
16 Jiri Latal	.20	.50
17 Scott Mellanby	.40	1.00
18 Gord Murphy	.20	.50
19 Pete Peeters	.30	.75
20 Mike Ricci	.60	1.50
21 Kjell Samuelsson	.30	.75
22 Derrick Smith	.20	.50
23 Ron Sutter	.20	.50
24 Rick Tocchet	.80	2.00
25 Ken Wregget	.40	1.00
26 Team Photo	.80	2.00

1991-92 Flyers J.C. Penney

This 26-card set was issued by the Flyers in conjunction with J.C. Penney Stores and Lee. Each card measured approximately 4 1/8" by 6". The fronts displayed full-bleed color action photos. A team color-coded (black with thin orange stripes) diagonal stripe cut across the bottom portion and carried the team logo, biographical information, and jersey number. The horizontal backs were postcard design and, on the left, presented biography, statistics, and notes. The cards were unnumbered and checklisted below in alphabetical order.

Card	Low	High
COMPLETE SET (26)	6.00	15.00
1 Keith Acton	.30	.75
2 Rod Brind'Amour	.60	1.50
3 Dave Brown	.30	.75
4 Terry Carkner	.20	.50
5 Kimbi Daniels	.20	.50
6 Kevin Dineen	.40	1.00
7 Steve Duchesne	.30	.75
8 Pelle Eklund	.20	.50
9 Corey Foster	.20	.50
10 Ron Hextall	.60	1.50
11 Tony Horacek	.20	.50
12 Mark Howe	.40	1.00
13 Kerry Huffman	.20	.50
14 Brad Jones	.20	.50
15 Steve Kasper UER (Misspelled Kaspar on front)	.20	.50
16 Dan Kordic	.20	.50
17 Jiri Latal	.20	.50
18 Andrei Lomakin	.20	.50
19 Gord Murphy	.20	.50
20 Mark Pederson	.20	.50
21 Dan Quinn	.20	.50
22 Mike Ricci	.40	1.00
23 Kjell Samuelsson	.24	.60
24 Rick Tocchet	.60	1.50
25 Ken Wregget	.40	1.00
26 Team Photo	.60	1.50

1992-93 Flyers J.C. Penney

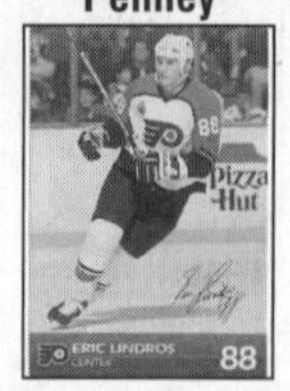

This 23-card set was sponsored by J.C. Penney Stores and Lee in the Delaware Valley. The cards measured approximately 4 1/8" by 6" and featured color, action player photos with facsimile autographs near the bottom of each picture. A gray border stripe across the bottom carried the team logo, player's name, position, and jersey number. The horizontal backs displayed biographical information, statistics, and career notes within a postcard-type format. The cards were unnumbered and checklisted below in alphabetical order.

Card	Low	High
COMPLETE SET (23)	8.00	20.00
1 Keith Acton	.24	.60
2 Stephane Beauregard	.24	.60
3 Brian Benning	.20	.50
4 Rod Brind'Amour	.60	1.50
5 Claude Boivin	.20	.50
6 Dave Brown	.30	.75
7 Terry Carkner	.20	.50
8 Shawn Cronin	.20	.50
9 Kevin Dineen	.30	.75
10 Pelle Eklund	.20	.50
11 Doug Evans	.20	.50
12 Brent Fedyk	.20	.50
13 Garry Galley	.30	.75
14 Gord Hynes	.20	.50
15 Eric Lindros	4.00	10.00
16 Andrei Lomakin	.20	.50
17 Ryan McGill	.20	.50
18 Ric Nattress	.20	.50
19 Greg Paslawski	.20	.50
20 Mark Recchi	.80	2.00
21 Dominic Roussel	.30	.75
22 Dimitri Yushkevich	.20	.50
23 Team Photo	.60	1.50

1992-93 Flyers Upper Deck Sheets

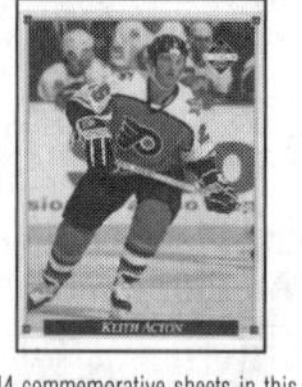

The 44 commemorative sheets in this set were distributed individually in game programs at Philadelphia Flyers home games during the 1992-93 season in Flyer magazine. The sheets measured approximately 8 1/2" by 11" and featured color, posed and action, player photos with orange and white borders. A black bar with an orange accent stripe above it carried either the player's name or a picture title. On sheets with a title, the player's name was printed on the photo in either orange or white lettering. A black diamond design was printed with the individual sheet number and the production run. The backs displayed the game date and teams playing. All sheets were the Flyers versus another NHL team. The roster and management of each team was also given. The sheets are unnumbered and checklisted below in chronological order. There was a second team photo issued March 13th. Due to a violent winter storm, only a few thousand spectators made it to the Spectrum. Play was halted when a severe wind blew out a few windows in the concourse area causing debris to scatter out into the seats. The sheets were distributed again during the make-up game on April 1.

Card	Low	High
COMPLETE SET (44)	100.00	250.00
1 Quebec Nordiques	2.00	5.00
Sept. 19& 1992 (4&500)		
Kevin Dineen		
2 New Jersey Devils	1.20	3.00
Sept. 24& 1992 (4&500)		
Brian Benning		
3 Washington Capitals	3.20	8.00
Oct. 3& 1992 (4&500)		
Mark Recchi		
4 New Jersey Devils	1.60	4.00
Oct. 9& 1992 (7&500)		
Keith Acton		
5 New York Islanders	3.20	8.00
Oct. 15& 1992 (4&500)		
Rod Brind'Amour		
6 Winnipeg Jets	1.60	4.00
Oct. 18& 1992 (4&500)		
Dave Brown		
7 Vancouver Canucks	2.00	5.00
Oct. 22& 1992 (4&500)		
Dominic Roussel		
8 Montreal Canadiens	1.20	3.00
Oct. 24& 1992 (4&500)		
Gord Hynes		
9 St. Louis Blues	1.20	3.00
Nov. 7& 1992 (4&500)		
Claude Boivin		
10 New York Islanders	1.20	3.00
Nov. 12& 1992 (4&500)		
Dimitri Yushkevich		
11 Ottawa Senators	16.00	40.00
Nov. 15& 1992 (5&500)		
Eric Lindros		
12 New York Rangers	1.60	4.00
Nov. 19& 1992 (4&500)		
Steve Kasper		
13A Buffalo Sabres	4.80	12.00
Nov. 22& 1992 (4&500)		
1992-93 Team Picture		
13B Buffalo Sabres	4.00	10.00
Nov. 22& 1992		
1992-93 Team Picture		
(Pizza Hut logo on front and Citation Graphics Ad on back)		
14 New York Islanders	1.20	3.00
Nov. 27& 1992 (5&500)		
Greg Paslawski		
15 Quebec Nordiques	1.60	4.00
Dec. 3& 1992 (4&500)		
Terry Carkner		
16 Boston Bruins	1.20	3.00
Dec. 6& 1992 (4&500)		
Shawn Cronin		
17 Washington Capitals	1.20	3.00
Dec. 12& 1992 (4&500)		
Brent Fedyk		
18 Pittsburgh Penguins	1.60	4.00
Dec. 17& 1992 (4&500)		
Garry Galley		
19 Chicago Blackhawks	1.20	3.00
Dec. 19& 1992 (5&000)		
Andrei Lomakin		
20 Pittsburgh Penguins	2.00	5.00
Dec. 23& 1992 (5&500)		
Bill and Kevin Dineen		
21 Washington Capitals	1.60	4.00
Jan. 7& 1993 (4&500)		
Stephane Beauregard		
22 New York Rangers	3.20	8.00
Jan. 9& 1993 (6&000)		
Mark Recchi		
23 Edmonton Oilers	1.20	3.00
Jan. 10& 1993 (5&000)		
Ryan McGill		
24 Calgary Flames	1.20	3.00
Jan. 14& 1993 (6&500)		
Doug Evans		
25 Detroit Red Wings	2.00	5.00
Jan. 17& 1993 (5&000)		
The Captains		
Kevin Dineen		
Keith Acton		
Terry Carkner		
26 Boston Bruins	1.20	3.00
Jan. 21& 1993 (5&000)		
Ric Nattress		
27 Hartford Whalers	3.20	8.00
Jan. 24& 1993 (5&000)		
Rod Brind'Amour		
28 Buffalo Sabres	2.00	5.00
Jan. 26& 1993 (5&000)		
Tommy Soderstrom		
29 Quebec Nordiques	1.60	4.00
Jan. 28& 1993 (5&000)		
Pelle Eklund		
30 Ottawa Senators	1.60	4.00
Feb. 9& 1993 (5&000)		
Dave Brown		
31 Montreal Canadiens	10.00	25.00
Feb. 11& 1993 (5&500)		
The Rookies		
Tommy Soderstrom		
Dimitri Yushkevich		
Dominic Roussel		
Ryan McGill		
Eric Lindros		
32 New Jersey Devils	1.20	3.00
Feb. 14& 1993 (5&000)		
Josef Beranek		
33 New Jersey Devils	1.20	3.00
Feb. 25& 1993 (6&000)		
Greg Paslawski		
34 New York Islanders	1.60	4.00
Feb. 27& 1993 (5&000)		
The Coaches		
Craig Hartsburg		
Bill Dineen		
Ken Hitchcock		
35 Pittsburgh Penguins	1.60	4.00
Mar. 2& 1993 (5&000)		
Keith Acton		
36 Washington Capitals	3.20	8.00
Mar. 11& 1993 (5&500)		
NHL All-Star		
Mark Recchi		
37A Los Angeles Kings	1.60	4.00
Mar. 13& 1993 (5&500)		
Garry Galley		
37B Los Angeles Kings	3.00	7.50
Make-up Game		
1992-93 Team Picture		
38 Minnesota North Stars	1.60	4.00
Mar. 16& 1993 (5&000)		
Terry Carkner		
39 New Jersey Devils	2.00	5.00
Mar. 21& 1993 (5&000)		
Dominic Roussel		
40 San Jose Sharks	1.20	3.00
Mar. 25& 1993 (5&000)		
Greg Hawgood		
41 Tampa Bay Lightning	1.20	3.00
Apr. 3& 1993 (5&500)		
Viacheslav Butsayev		
42 Toronto Maple Leafs	10.00	25.00
Apr. 4& 1993 (6&000)		
Crazy 8's		
Mark Recchi		
Eric Lindros		
Brent Fedyk		
43 Washington Capitals	2.00	5.00
Apr. 8& 1993 (5&500)		
European Style		
Andrei Lomakin		
Dimitri Yushkevich		
Viachesiav Butsayev		
44 New York Rangers	4.00	10.00
Apr. 12& 1993 (5&500)		
Hockey Hall of Famers		
Bob Clarke		
Ed Snider		
Bill Barber		
Bernie Parent		
Keith Allen		

1993-94 Flyers J.C. Penney

This 24-card set was issued by the Flyers as a promotional item at a home game, and was sponsored by JC Penney. These collectibles were postcard sized, featured full color action photos on the front, and player data on the back. The cards were unnumbered, and were checklisted below in alphabetical order.

Card	Low	High
COMPLETE SET (24)	8.00	20.00
1 Josef Beranek	.30	.75
2 Claude Boivin	.20	.50
3 Jason Bowen	.20	.50
4 Rod Brind'Amour	.60	1.50
5 Slava Butsayev	.20	.50
6 Dave Brown	.30	.75
7 Al Conroy	.20	.50
8 Kevin Dineen	.30	.75
9 Pelle Eklund	.20	.50
10 Brent Fedyk	.20	.50
11 Jeff Finley	.20	.50
12 Garry Galley	.30	.75
13 Eric Lindros	3.20	8.00
14 Stewart Malgunas	.20	.50
15 Ryan McGill	.20	.50
16 Rob Ramage	.20	.50
17 Mark Recchi	.80	2.00
18 Mikael Renberg	.60	1.50
19 Dominic Roussel	.30	.75
20 Yves Racine	.20	.50
21 Tommy Soderstrom	.30	.75
22 Dave Tippett	.20	.50
23 Dimitri Yuskevich	.20	.50
NNO Team Photo	.40	1.00

1993-94 Flyers Lineup Sheets

The 44 commemorative sheets in this set were distributed individually in game programs at Philadelphia Flyers home games during the 1993-94 season in Flyer magazine. The sheets measured approximately 8 1/2" by 11" and featured color, posed and action, player photos with orange and white borders. The sheets are listed below by player in alphabetical order.

Card	Low	High
COMPLETE SET (43)	50.00	125.00
1 Josef Beranek	1.00	2.50
2 Claude Boivin	1.00	2.50
3 Jason Bowen	1.00	2.50
4 Rod Brind'Amour	2.00	5.00
5 Rod Brind'Amour	2.00	5.00
6 Dave Brown	2.00	5.00
7 Slava Butsayev	1.00	2.50
8 Terry Carkner	1.00	2.50
9 Al Conroy	1.00	2.50
10 Kevin Dineen	1.00	2.50
11 Kevin Dineen	1.00	2.50
12 Pelle Eklund	1.00	2.50
13 Andre Faust	1.00	2.50
14 Brent Fedyk	1.00	2.50
15 Brent Fedyk	1.00	2.50
16 Jeff Finley	1.00	2.50
17 Garry Galley	1.00	2.50
18 Greg Hawgood	1.00	2.50
19 Tim Kerr	2.00	5.00
20 Mark Lamb	1.00	2.50
21 Eric Lindros	4.00	10.00
22 Eric Lindros	4.00	10.00
23 Eric Lindros	4.00	10.00
24 Stewart Malgunas	1.00	2.50
25 Ryan McGill	1.00	2.50
26 Yves Racine	1.00	2.50
27 Rob Ramage	1.00	2.50
28 Mark Recchi	2.00	5.00
29 Mark Recchi	2.00	5.00
30 Mikael Renberg	1.00	2.50
31 Dominic Roussel	1.50	4.00
32 Dominic Roussel	1.50	4.00
33 Dave Tippett	1.00	2.50
34 Dmitri Yushkevich	1.00	2.50
35 Dmitri Yushkevich	1.00	2.50
36 Rob Zettler	1.00	2.50
37 The Coaches	1.00	2.50
38 Team Photo	1.00	2.50
39 Team Photo	1.00	2.50
40 Renberg, Bowen, Malgunas	1.00	2.50
41 The Captains	2.00	5.00
42 Recchi, Lindros, Galley	2.00	5.00
43 Flyers and their Fans	1.00	2.50

1996-97 Flyers Postcards

This attractive 24-card set was produced late in the '96-97 season by the club. The standard-sized postcards featured an action photo on the front, along with the player's name, position and jersey number. The back contained a remarkably thorough stats package, including career numbers, awards and transaction info. Unnumbered, the cards are listed below in alphabetical order.

Card	Low	High
COMPLETE SET (24)	6.00	15.00
1 Team Photo	.20	.50
2 Rod Brind'Amour	.30	.75
3 Paul Coffey	.40	1.00
4 Scott Daniels	.10	.25
5 Eric Desjardins	.16	.40
6 John Druce	.10	.25
7 Karl Dykhuis	.10	.2
8 Pat Falloon	.10	.2
9 Dale Hawerchuk	.30	.7
10 Ron Hextall	.30	.7
11 Trent Klatt	.10	.2
12 Dan Kordic	.10	.2
13 Daniel Lacroix	.10	.2
14 John LeClair	.80	2.0
15 Eric Lindros	2.00	5.0
16 Janne Niinimaa	.60	1.5
17 Joel Otto	.10	.2
18 Shjon Podein	.10	.2
19 Mikael Renberg	.30	.7
20 Kjell Samuelsson	.10	.2
21 Garth Snow	.20	.5
22 Petr Svoboda	.10	.2
23 Chris Therien	.10	.2
24 Dainius Zubrus	.80	2.0

1997 Flyers Phone Cards

These phone cards produced by Comca were available only in the Philadelphia ar Each card was worth 15-minutes of lo distance.

Card	Low	High
COMPLETE SET (4)	3.20	8.0
1 Alexandre Daigle	.40	1.0
2 Chris Gratton	.40	1.0
3 John LeClair	1.20	3.0
4 Eric Lindros	2.00	5.0

2001-02 Flyers Postcards

This 30-card set featured full-color acti photos bordered by team colors and logo Each card measured approximately 4" X The set was unnumbered and is listed belo in alphabetical order.

Card	Low	High
COMPLETE SET (30)	9.78	24.4
1 Brian Boucher	1.00	2.5
2 Donald Brashear	.30	.7
3 Roman Cechmanek	.40	1.0
4 Eric Desjardins	.20	.5
5 Jiri Dopita	.40	1.0
6 Todd Fedoruk	.30	.7
7 Ruslan Fedotenko	.30	.7
8 Simon Gagne	1.20	3.0
9 Kim Johnsson	.20	.5
10 Kent Manderville	.20	.5
11 John LeClair	.80	2.0
12 Chris McAllister	.20	.5
13 Dam McGillis	.20	.5
14 Marty Murray	.20	.5
15 Keith Primeau	.40	1.0
16 Paul Ranheim	.20	.5
17 Mark Recchi	.40	1.0
18 Luke Richardson	.20	.5
19 Jeremy Roenick	.80	2.0
20 Chris Therien	.20	.5
21 Rick Tocchet	.30	.7
22 Eric Weinrich	.20	.5
23 Justin Williams	.40	1.0
24 Flyers Team Photo	.40	1.0
25 Bill Barber	.10	.2
Mike Stothers		
E.J. McGuire		
26 Broadcasters	.04	.1
27 Bob Clarke GM	.30	.7
28 Ron Hextall ACO	.30	.7
29 Phantoms Team Photo	.20	.5
30 Phlex MASCOT	.10	.2

2002-03 Flyers Postcards

Card	Low	High
COMPLETE SET (24)	8.00	20.0
1 Eric Weinrich	.30	.7
2 Kim Johnsson	.30	.7
3 Mark Recchi	.40	1.0
4 John LeClair	.40	1.0
5 Simon Gagne	.60	1.5
6 Justin Williams	.30	.7
7 Paul Ranheim	.30	.7
8 Radovan Somik	.30	.7
9 Chris McAllister	.30	.7
10 Keith Primeau	.40	1.0
11 Chris Therien	.30	.7
12 Michal Handzus	.30	.7
13 Todd Fedoruk	.40	1.0
14 Roman Cechmanek	.40	1.0
15 Dennis Seidenberg	.30	.7
16 Eric Desjardins	.30	.7
17 Marty Murray	.30	.7
18 Robert Esche	.40	1.0
19 Pavel Brendl	.30	.7
20 Donald Brashear	.30	.7
21 Jeremy Roenick	.75	2.0
22 The Coaches	.10	.2
23 Team Card	.20	.5
24 Philadelphia Phantoms	.20	.5

2003-04 Flyers Program Inserts

...erted into individual game programs, ...e sheets measure approximately 8 1/2" x ... and each sheet was individually serial-...bered at the top. The checklist below is ...mplete. If you have any further info on ... set, please forward it to ...keymag@beckett.com.

Jeremy Roenick 2.00 5.00
...oni Pitkanen 1.25 3.00
...ony Amonte 1.50 4.00
...obert Esche 1.50 4.00
...anny Markov 1.25 3.00
...eith Primeau 1.50 4.00

2003-04 Flyers Postcards

...s 24-card set was produced by the team ... available through the team website and ...earances.

...MPLETE SET (24) 8.00 20.00
...ony Amonte .40 1.00
...onald Brashear .40 1.00
...ike Comrie .40 1.00
...ric Desjardins .20 .50
...obert Esche .40 1.00
...odd Fedoruk .40 1.00
...imon Gagne .40 1.00
...eff Hackett .30 .75
...ichal Handzus .20 .50
Kim Johnsson .20 .50
Sami Kapanen .20 .50
Claude Lapointe .20 .50
John LeClair .40 1.00
Danny Markov .20 .50
Joni Pitkanen .40 1.00
Keith Primeau .40 1.00
Marcus Ragnarsson .20 .50
Mark Recchi .40 1.00
Jeremy Roenick .75 2.00
Radovan Somik .20 .50
Chris Therien .20 .50
Jim Vandermeer .20 .50
Eric Weinrich .20 .50
Coaches .10 .25

2005-06 Flyers Team Issue

...MPLETE SET (25) 8.00 15.00
...hiladelphia Flyers CL .01 .01
...onald Brashear .30 .75
...eff Carter .60 1.50
...ric Desjardins .20 .50
...obert Esche .30 .75
...eter Forsberg .75 2.00
...imon Gagne .40 1.00
...ichal Handzus .20 .50
...erian Hatcher .20 .50
Kim Johnsson .20 .50
Sami Kapanen .20 .50
Mike Knuble .20 .50
Antero Niittymaki .75 2.00
Joni Pitkanen .40 1.00
Keith Primeau .20 .50
Branko Radivojevic .20 .50
Mike Rathje .20 .50
Mike Richards .40 1.00
Brian Savage .20 .50
Dennis Seidenberg .20 .50
Patrick Sharp .20 .50
Jonathan Sim .20 .50
Turner Stevenson .20 .50
Chris Therien .20 .50
R.J. Umberger .40 1.00

2006-07 Flyers Postcards

...MPLETE SET (23) 10.00 25.00
...erian Hatcher .40 1.00
...ike Rathje .40 1.00
...andy Jones .40 1.00
...eoff Sanderson .40 1.00
...cottie Upshall .40 1.00
...imon Gagne .75 2.00
...eff Carter .75 2.00
...ike Richards .75 2.00
...yle Calder .40 1.00
R.J. Umberger .40 1.00
Mike Knuble .40 1.00
Denis Gauthier .40 1.00
Sami Kapanen .40 1.00
Dmitry Afanasenkov .40 1.00
Todd Fedoruk .40 1.00
Antero Niittymaki .60 1.50
Robert Esche .60 1.50
Joni Pitkanen .40 1.00
Alexandre Picard .40 1.00
Michael Leighton .60 1.50
Ben Eager .40 1.00

22 Mike York .40 1.00
23 Alexei Zhitnik .40 1.00

1971-72 Frito-Lay

This ten-card set featured members of the Toronto Maple Leafs and Montreal Canadiens. Since the cards were unnumbered, they had been listed below in alphabetical order within team, Montreal (1-5) and Toronto (6-10). The cards were paper thin, each measuring approximately 1 1/2" by 2".

COMPLETE SET (10) 50.00 100.00
1 Yvan Cournoyer 4.00 8.00
2 Ken Dryden 25.00 50.00
3 Frank Mahovlich 5.00 10.00
4 Henri Richard 5.00 10.00
5 J.C. Tremblay 2.00 4.00
6 Bobby Baun 2.00 4.00
7 Ron Ellis 2.00 4.00
8 Paul Henderson 3.00 6.00
9 Jacques Plante 10.00 20.00
10 Norm Ullman 3.00 6.00

1988-89 Frito-Lay Stickers

The 1988-89 Frito-Lay Hockey Stickers set included 42 small (1 3/8" by 1 3/4") stickers. The fronts were dominated by color photos, but also had each player's name and uniform number. The stickers were distributed in sealed plastic, and packaged one per special Frito-Lay snack bag. Reportedly distribution was via 35 million bags of Ruffles, O'Gradys, Dulac, Lays, Doritos, Fritos, Tostitos, Cheetos, and Chester Popcorn -- each containing one of the 42 players in the set. Since they were actually stickers, there was very little information on the backing. The checklist below also gave the player's uniform number as listed on each card. A poster was also available from the company by sending in 2.00 and one UPC symbol from any Frito-Lay product.

COMPLETE SET (42) 12.00 30.00
1 Mario Lemieux 66 2.40 6.00
2 Bryan Trottier 19 .20 .50
3 Steve Yzerman 19 1.60 4.00
4 Bernie Federko 24 .16 .40
5 Brian Bellows 23 .16 .40
6 Denis Savard 18 .20 .50
7 Neal Broten 7 .16 .40
8 Doug Gilmour 9 .60 1.50
9 Dale Hawerchuk 10 .20 .50
10 Luc Robitaille 20 .60 1.50
11 Ed Olczyk 16 .10 .25
12 Andrew McBain 20 .10 .25
13 Mike Gartner 11 .20 .50
14 Pat LaFontaine 16 .40 1.00
15 Scott Stevens 3 .20 .50
16 Ray Bourque 77 .80 2.00
17 Cam Neely 8 .60 1.50
18 Mike Foligno 17 .10 .25
19 Tom Barrasso 30 .20 .50
20 Ron Francis 10 .30 .75
21 Peter Stastny 26 .20 .50
22 Michel Goulet 16 .20 .50
23 Bernie Nicholls 9 .20 .50
24 Paul Coffey 77 .60 1.50
25 Mats Naslund 26 .16 .40
26 Glenn Anderson 9 .20 .50
27 Dave Poulin 20 .10 .25
28 Kevin Dineen 11 .10 .25
29 Wendel Clark 17 .30 .75
30 James Patrick 3 .10 .25
31 Al MacInnis 2 .30 .75
32 Troy Murray 19 .10 .25
33 Kirk Muller 9 .20 .50
34 Marcel Dionne 16 .20 .50
35 Mark Messier 11 .80 2.00
36 Joe Nieuwendyk 25 .60 1.50
37 Ron Hextall 27 .30 .75
38 Sean Burke 1 .20 .50
39 Barry Pederson 7 .10 .25
40 Stephane Richer 44 .20 .50
41 Bob Probert 24 .60 1.50
42 Tony Tanti 9 .10 .25
NNO Set Poster 1.20 3.00

1996-97 Frosted Flakes Masks

One of these 7 cards was inserted into specially marked boxes of Frosted Flakes in Canada early in the season. These unique die-cut cards featured a net design and a goalie mask, which could be popped up on display in front of the net. Just two of the cards featured the actual faces and mask designs of individual goalies (#1-2). Cards 3-6 featured generic masks with the design of the team logo, while the seventh featured

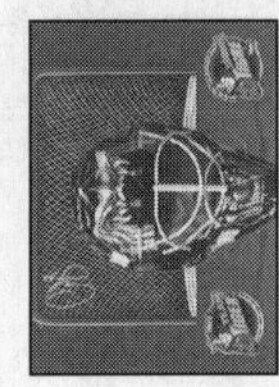

a Tony the Tiger mask. The complete set was available by mail for $2.50 plus three proofs of purchase.

COMPLETE SET (7) 8.00 20.00
1 Felix Potvin 1.20 3.00
2 Curtis Joseph 2.00 5.00
3 Montreal Canadiens 1.20 3.00
4 Ottawa Senators 1.20 3.00
5 Calgary Flames 1.20 3.00
6 Vancouver Canucks 1.20 3.00
7 Tony the Tiger 1.20 3.00

1991-92 Future Trends Canada '72 Promos

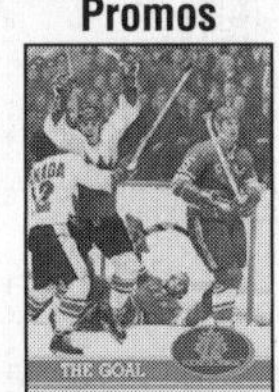

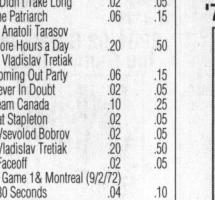

This standard-size three-card set was issued to promote the release of Future Trends' Team Canada '72 set. To commemorate Team Canada of 1972, 7200 of each promotional card were offered for sale at Canada's Hudson Bay Stores. The fronts featured full-bleed black-and-white action shots from a game between Team Canada and the Soviet team. The card title appeared in white lettering within a red stripe across the bottom of the picture. The '72 Hockey Canada logo appeared in the lower right. Except for their horizontal orientation, the backs were similar to the fronts, with full-bleed black-and-white photos, white lettering within a red stripe at the bottom, and logo in the lower right. The cards were unnumbered and checklisted below in alphabetical order by title. These promos were issued in English and French versions.

COMPLETE SET (3) 7.20 18.00
1 The Goal 3.20 8.00
The Scoreboard
2 The Leader 4.00 10.00
Phil Esposito
3 The Legend 2.40 6.00
The Kid

1991-92 Future Trends Canada '72

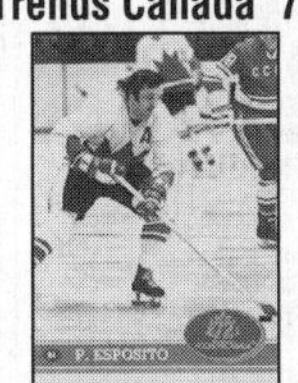

Future Trends Experience Ltd. produced this 101-card standard-size set to celebrate the 20th anniversary of the 1972 Summit Series between the Soviets and the Canadians. The cards were available initially only at the Bay and were sold in ten-card foil packs with no factory sets. The 70 players of the Canadian and Russian teams were represented, and 30 additional special cards captured unforgettable moments from the series. Between one and two special cards, signed in gold paint pen by living Canadian players, were randomly inserted into each foil case. Only one non-Canadian, Vladislav Tretiak, signed cards. Supposedly each of the signers signed only 750 cards for insertion and distribution within the packs. These cards were specially coated with a swirl pattern over the autograph. Reportedly, The Bay also issued 2500 autographed sets without the special coating, but we have no confirmation of this at this time. The cards featured on the fronts borderless black-and-white, action or posed pictures. A white, red, and gold stripe cut across the bottom of the card face and intersected the '72 Hockey Canada logo at the lower right corner. The backs carried additional photos, biographical information, series statistics, sportswriters' editorial comments, and/or player quotes. Card number 40 featured Phil Esposito's September 8, 1972, address to the nation. The card number appeared in a blue oblong design within the bottom red stripe on both sides. The '72 Hockey Canada logo also appeared in the lower right corner of the back. The set was issued in both an English and a French version. The production quantities were reportedly 9,000 English and 1,000 French 12-box cases. Also released were 1972 uncut sheet sets. Signed cards generally commanded 100 to 250 times the values below.

COMPLETE SET (101) 2.40 6.00
1 In The Beginning .06 .15
2 The Backyard Rink .02 .05
3 It Didn't Take Long .02 .05
4 The Patriarch .06 .15
Anatoli Tarasov
5 More Hours a Day .20 .50
Vladislav Tretiak
6 Coming Out Party .06 .15
7 Never In Doubt .02 .05
8 Team Canada .10 .25
9 Pat Stapleton .02 .05
10 Vsevolod Bobrov .02 .05
11 Vladislav Tretiak .20 .50
12 Faceoff .02 .05
Game 1& Montreal (9/2/72)
13 30 Seconds .04 .10
Game 1& Montreal (9/2/72)
14 Yevgeny Zimin .02 .05
15 Bill White .02 .05
16 7-3 .02 .05
Game 1 Statistics
17 Don Awrey .02 .05
18 Mickey Redmond .08 .20
19 Alexander Gusev .06 .15
20 Alexander Maltsev .10 .25
21 Rod Seiling .02 .05
22 Dale Tallon .02 .05
23 Coming Back .02 .05
Game 2& Toronto (9/4/72)
24 Unforgettable .02 .05
Game 2 Statistics
25 Wayne Cashman .06 .15
26 Frank Mahovlich .10 .25
27 Peter Mahovlich .02 .05
28 Vyacheslav Solodukhin .06 .15
Alexander Sidelnikov
29 Yuri Shatalov .06 .15
30 Brothers .06 .15
Frank Mahovlich
Peter Mahovlich
31 The Goalies .20 .50
32 Alexander Bodunov .02 .05
33 All Even .02 .05
Game 3 Statistics
34 Yuri Blinov .02 .05
35 Jocelyn Guevremont .02 .05
36 Vic Hadfield .02 .05
37 Yuri Lebedev .02 .05
38 Yevgeny Poladiev .06 .15
Vyacheslav Starshinov
39 Disaster .02 .05
Game 4 Statistics
40 Address to The Nation .10 .25
Phil Esposito
41 Victor Kuzkin .02 .05
42 Vladimir Lutchenko .10 .25
43 Boris Mikhailov .16 .40
44 Grace Under Pressure .02 .05
Game 5& Moscow (9/22/72)
45 Afraid to Lose .02 .05
46 Ready To Win .02 .05
Game 5 Statistics
47 Vladimir Vikulov .02 .05
48 Red Berenson .02 .05
49 Richard Martin .02 .05
50 Alexander Martynyuk .02 .05
51 Gilbert Perreault .10 .25
52 Vladimir Petrov .16 .40
53 Serge Savard .06 .15
54 Vladimir Shadrin .02 .05
55 DA DA KA-NA-DA .02 .05
Game 6& Moscow (9/24/72)
56 One Step Back .02 .05
Game 6 Statistics
57 Bobby Clarke .16 .40
58 Valeri Kharlamov .20 .50
59 Alexander Volchkov .06 .15
60 Standing Guard .06 .15
61 Stan Mikita .16 .40
62 One More To Go .02 .05
Game 7 Statistics
Moscow (9/26/72)
63 The Winner .02 .05
64 The Fans Go Wild .02 .05
65 Alexander Ragulin .06 .15
66 Jean Ratelle .06 .15
67 Gennady Tsygankov .06 .15
68 Valeri Vasiliev .16 .40
69 International Dialogue .02 .05
70 Series Stars .16 .40
Phil Esposito
Alexander Yakushev
71 Series Stars .16 .40
Paul Henderson
Vladislav Tretiak
72 No Solitudes .02 .05
Game 8& Moscow (9/28/72)
The Telegrams
73 2-2 .02 .05
Game 8& Moscow (9/28/72)
74 Rod Gilbert .06 .15
75 Yevgeny Mishokov .06 .15
76 Ron Ellis .02 .05
77 5-4 .02 .05
78 Different Games .02 .05
Game 8& Moscow (9/28/72)
Interlude
79 Bill Goldsworthy .02 .05
80 The Huddle .02 .05
81 The Moment .20 .50
82 Yvan Cournoyer .10 .25
83 Yuri Liapkin .02 .05
84 Phil Esposito .16 .40
85 Ken Dryden .20 .50
86 Peace .02 .05
Game 8 Statistics
87 Gary Bergman .02 .05
88 Brian Glennie .02 .05
89 Dennis Hull .02 .05
90 Vyacheslav Anisin .02 .05
91 Marcel Dionne .10 .25
92 Guy Lapointe .06 .15
93 Ed Johnston .04 .10
94 Harry Sinden GM .02 .05
95 Brad Park .10 .25
96 Tony Esposito .10 .25
97 Alexander Yakushev .16 .40
98 Paul Henderson .20 .50
99 J.P. Parise .02 .05
100 Valeri Kharlamov .20 .50
Alex Kharlamov on back
101 Checklist .06 .15

1992 Future Trends '76 Canada Cup

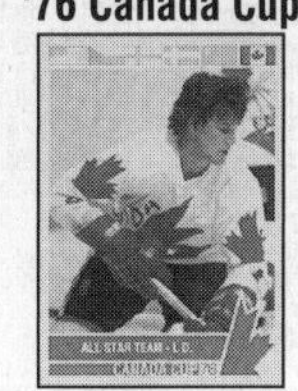

This 100-card, standard-size set was produced by The Future Trends Experience Ltd. and licensed by Hockey Canada. Commemorating the 1976 Canada Cup, the card numbering picked up where the '72 Team Canada set left off by tracing the growth of international hockey. According to the company the production run was 50,000 numbered display boxes. Randomly inserted in the packs were 3,750 gold-foil stamped signature cards; five players (Bobby Orr, Bobby Hull, Rogatien Vachon, Darryl Sittler, and Bobby Clarke) signed 750 cards each. These cards are valued generally 75 to 100 times the values below. A Tretiak card serial-numbered out of 1976 is also known to exist. The cards featured vertical and horizontal color action and posed player and team photos. Some shots were of game action with several players pictured. The bottom of each was accented by red and gold border stripes with a red Canada Cup logo in the right corner. Most cards were bordered in white, but some were bordered on the top by the national flags of the various teams in the set. The horizontal backs carried the same flag pattern ghosted behind information about the pictured player or team. A color photo of the players or player was displayed to the right of the copy. Red and gold border stripes similar to the front appeared below. Topical subsets featured are '72 Retrospective (102-106), 1974 Russian team vs. WHA (107-110), a 6-card training camp subset (111-116), MVPs (184-190), and the first ever Canada Cup All-Star team (195-200). The cards were numbered on the back. An 8 1/2" by 11" sheet was also issued; it has an artist's color painting of the players on the front and a checklist on its back.

COMPLETE SET (100) 3.20 8.00
102 Phil Esposito .16 .40
103 Vladislav Tretiak .20 .50
104 Bobby Orr .30 .75
105 Paul Henderson .06 .15
The Goal
106 Alexander Yakushev .06 .15
107 Bobby Hull .20 .50
108 Valeri Kharlamov .16 .40
109 Gerry Cheevers .10 .25
Vladislav Tretiak
110 Bobby Hull .20 .50
Vladislav Tretiak
111 Soviet on-ice workout .04 .10
112 Czech on-ice workout .02 .05
113 Finn on-ice workout .02 .05
114 Swedes take the ice .02 .05
115 USA on-ice workout .04 .10
116 Darryl Sittler .10 .25
117 Serge Savard .06 .15
118 Team Finland .02 .05
119 Team Sweden .02 .05
120 Team Czechoslavakia .02 .05
121 Soviets .06 .15
122 Team USA .06 .15
123 Team Canada .06 .15
124 The Opening Barrage .02 .05
125 Richard Martin .02 .05
126 Bobby Orr .30 .75
127 Sweden vs. USA .02 .05
128 Ivan Hlinka .02 .05
129 CSSR 5 - CCCP 3 .02 .05
130 Helmut Balderis .06 .15
131 Peter Stastny .08 .20
132 Valeri Vasiliev .06 .15
133 Out of Contention .02 .05
134 Standing Alone .02 .05
135 The Miracle On Ice .02 .05
136 Josef Augusta .02 .05
137 A Soviet Rout .02 .05
138 Vicktor Zhluktov .04 .10
139 Bobby Hull .16 .40
Phil Esposito
Marcel Dionne
140 Bob Gainey .06 .15
141 Anders Hedberg .06 .15
142 Bobby Hull .20 .50
143 Ulf Nilsson .06 .15
144 Sergei Kapustin .06 .15
145 Borje Salming .06 .15
146 Well Enough To Win .02 .05
147 Biggest Upset .02 .05
148 Matti Hagman .02 .05
149 Unbeatable .02 .05
150 Boris Alexandrov .06 .15
151 A Goal Tending Duel .04 .10
152 Vladimir Dzurilla .04 .10
153 Phil Esposito .16 .40
154 Rogatien Vachon .06 .15
155 Milan Novy .02 .05
156 Vladimir Martinec .04 .10
157 Good For Hockey .02 .05
158 Bill Nyrop .02 .05
159 Pride .02 .05
160 Another Summit .02 .05
161 Alexander Maltsev .06 .15
162 Gilbert Perreault .10 .25
163 Vladislav Tretiak .20 .50
163A Vladislav Tretiak AU
164 Vladimir Vikulov .04 .10
165 Canada Cup Final .02 .05
Game 1
166 Not There Yet .02 .05
167 Fast and Furious .02 .05
168 4 - 3 .02 .05
4 - 4
169 Bill Barber .06 .15
170 The Grapevine .04 .10
171 Guy Lapointe .06 .15
172 Reggie Leach .02 .05
173 Sittler's Goal .10 .25
174 Lanny McDonald .10 .25
175 Darryl Sittler .10 .25
176 The Canada Cup .06 .15
177 Bobby Clarke .10 .25
178 Last Time for No. 9 .10 .25
179 Marcel Dionne .10 .25
180 Peter Mahovlich .02 .05
181 Denis Potvin .10 .25
182 Larry Robinson .10 .25
183 Steve Shutt .06 .15
184 Bobby Orr .30 .75
Tournament MVP
185 Rogatien Vachon .06 .15
186 Milan Novy .04 .10
187 Matti Hagman .02 .05
188 Borje Salming .06 .15
189 Robbie Ftorek .02 .05
190 Alexander Maltsev .06 .15
191 Canada Final Series .02 .05
192 Canada Series Totals .02 .05
193 CSSR Final Series .02 .05
194 CSSR Series Totals .02 .05
195 Rogatien Vachon AS .06 .15
196 Bobby Orr AS .30 .75
197 Borje Salming AS .06 .15
198 Milan Novy AS .02 .05
199 Darryl Sittler AS .06 .15
200 Alexander Maltsev AS .06 .15
201 Canada Cup Checklist .04 .10
NNO Checklist Sheet .80 2.00
(8 1/2- by 11-; artist rendition on front)

1997 Gatorade Stickers

This set was issued as a promotional giveaway with the purchase of a Gatorade beverage in Canada. The stickers featured head shots and a brief note of interest about the player. They were distributed in six sheets, with four players appearing on each sheet.

COMPLETE SET (6) 8.00 20.00
1 Daniel Alfredsson .40 1.00
Vincent Damphousse
Bill Guerin
Jarome Iginla
2 Saku Koivu
Eric Lindros
Mark Messier
Mike Modano
3 Alexander Mogilny .60 1.50
Jose Theodore
Ron Tugnutt
Doug Weight
4 Joe Nieuwendyk .60 1.50
Chris Pronger
Mark Recchi
Luc Robitaille
5 Tie Domi 2.00 5.00
Grant Fuhr
Jaromir Jagr
Paul Kariya
6 Patrick Roy 4.00 10.00
Joe Sakic
Teemu Selanne
Mats Sundin

2006-07 Gatorade

COMPLETE SET (91) 60.00 100.00
1 Miikka Kiprusoff 1.50 4.00
2 Dion Phaneuf 2.00 5.00
3 Jarome Iginla 2.00 5.00
4 Alex Tanguay 1.25 3.00
5 Daymond Langkow .75 2.00
6 Matthew Lombardi .75 2.00
7 Chuck Kobasew .40 1.00
8 Kristian Huselius .40 1.00
9 Roman Hamrlik .40 1.00
10 Stephane Yelle .40 1.00
11 Tony Amonte .40 1.00
12 Robyn Regehr .40 1.00
13 Jeff Friesen .40 1.00
14 Marcus Nilson .40 1.00
15 Andrew Ference .40 1.00
16 Petr Sykora .40 1.00
17 Ales Hemsky 1.25 3.00
18 Joffrey Lupul .75 2.00
19 Dwayne Roloson .75 2.00
20 Ryan Smyth 1.25 3.00
21 Jarret Stoll .75 2.00
22 Patrick Thoresen .75 2.00
23 Raffi Torres .75 2.00
24 Fernando Pisani .75 2.00
25 Shawn Horcoff .75 2.00
26 Marc-Andre Bergeron .40 1.00
27 Jason Smith .40 1.00
28 Ladislav Smid .40 1.00
29 Steve Staios .40 1.00
30 Jussi Markkanen .60 1.50
31 Saku Koivu 2.00 5.00
32 Chris Higgins .75 2.00
33 Sheldon Souray .40 1.00
34 Andrei Markov .40 1.00
35 Michael Ryder .75 2.00
36 Cristobal Huet 1.50 4.00
37 David Aebischer .75 2.00
38 Alex Kovalev .40 1.00
39 Mike Johnson .40 1.00
40 Alexander Perezhogin .40 1.00
41 Guillaume Latendresse 2.00 5.00
42 Radek Bonk .40 1.00
43 Sergei Samsonov .75 2.00
44 Tomas Plekanec .75 2.00
45 Michael Komisarek .75 2.00
46 Jason Spezza 1.25 3.00
47 Dany Heatley 1.50 4.00
48 Joe Corvo .40 1.00
49 Daniel Alfredsson 1.25 3.00
50 Martin Gerber .75 2.00
51 Ray Emery 1.25 3.00
52 Antoine Vermette .40 1.00
53 Patrick Eaves .75 2.00
54 Dean McAmmond .40 1.00
55 Mike Fisher .75 2.00
56 Chris Neil .75 2.00
57 Wade Redden .75 2.00
58 Chris Phillips .75 2.00
59 Andrej Meszaros .75 2.00
60 Chris Kelly .40 1.00
61 Mats Sundin 1.25 3.00
62 Alexander Steen 1.25 3.00
63 Darcy Tucker 1.25 3.00
64 Kyle Wellwood .75 2.00
65 Andrew Raycroft .75 2.00
66 Bryan McCabe .75 2.00
67 Tomas Kaberle .75 2.00
68 Jeff O'Neill .40 1.00
69 Alexei Ponikarovsky .40 1.00
70 Ian White .40 1.00
71 Michael Peca .75 2.00
72 Chad Kilger .40 1.00
73 Hal Gill .40 1.00
74 Matt Stajan .75 2.00
75 Pavel Kubina .40 1.00
76 Markus Naslund .75 2.00
77 Roberto Luongo 2.00 5.00
78 Daniel Sedin .75 2.00
79 Henrik Sedin .75 2.00
80 Brendan Morrison .40 1.00
81 Sami Salo .40 1.00
82 Jan Bulis .40 1.00
83 Taylor Pyatt .40 1.00
84 Mattias Ohlund .40 1.00
85 Lukas Krajicek .40 1.00
86 Trevor Linden 1.25 3.00
87 Ryan Kesler .40 1.00
88 Matt Cooke .40 1.00
89 Willie Mitchell .40 1.00
90 Kevin Bieksa .75 2.00
91 Sidney Crosby SP 25.00 60.00

1967-68 General Mills

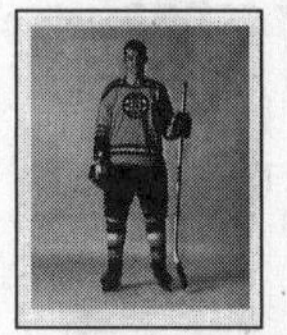

Little is known about this recently catalogued five-card set, save for it measured approximately 2 5/16" by 2 13/16" and featured color player photos in a white border. It appeared the cards were cut-outs from boxes of General Mills cereal, as a full box back picturing Harry Howell with a checklist listing these cards was known to exist. Further information would be appreciated. The backs are blank. The cards are unnumbered and checklisted below in alphabetical order.

COMPLETE SET (5) 500.00 1000.00
1 Jean Beliveau 75.00 150.00
2 Gordie Howe 150.00 300.00
3 Harry Howell 40.00 80.00
4 Stan Mikita 62.50 125.00
5 Bobby Orr 250.00 500.00

1991-92 Gillette

This 48-card standard-size set, sponsored by Gillette, featured players from the old four divisions of the NHL: Smythe (1-10), Norris (11-20), Adams (21-30), and Patrick (31-40). Each ten-card pack came with a trivia card and a checklist card. To receive one ten-card pack, collectors were required to send to Gillette of Canada one UPC symbol from any Canadian Gillette product, the dated receipt with purchase price circled, and 2.00 for shipping and handling. The entire set could be obtained by sending in three UPC symbols plus 5.00. Reportedly just 30,000 sets were produced, and the offer expired on August 28, 1992. On a black card face, the fronts carried a color action photo enclosed by a gold frame. The title "Gillette Series" appeared in gold lettering at the top, while the player's name appeared at the bottom between the 75th NHL Anniversary logo and the team logo. Some of the cards had the words "Rookie Card" in the bottom gold border (numbers 3, 10, 20, 30, 40). In a horizontal format, the backs had biography and statistics (1987-91) in English and French, as well as a color head shot. The player cards were numbered on the back. Although the backs of the four unnumbered checklist cards were identical (each one lists all 40 cards), a different division name appeared on the front of each checklist card: Smythe, Norris, Adams, and Patrick. The fronts of each of the four unnumbered trivia cards were identical, while their backs featured two different questions and answers.

COMPLETE SET (48) 10.00 25.00
1 Luc Robitaille .20 .50
2 Esa Tikkanen .10 .25
3 Pat Falloon .06 .15
4 Theo Fleury .30 .75
5 Trevor Linden .20 .50

1991-92 Gillette

6 Rob Blake .20 .50
7 Al MacInnis .20 .50
8 Bob Essensa .20 .50
9 Bill Ranford .20 .50
10 Pavel Bure .80 2.00
11 Wendel Clark .20 .50
12 Sergei Fedorov .60 1.50
13 Jeremy Roenick .30 .75
14 Brett Hull .40 1.00
15 Mike Modano .40 1.00
16 Chris Chelios .30 .75
17 Dave Ellett .06 .15
18 Ed Belfour .30 .75
19 Grant Fuhr .20 .50
20 Martin Lapointe .06 .15
21 Kirk Muller .10 .25
22 Joe Sakic .60 1.50
23 Pat LaFontaine .20 .50
24 Pat Verbeek .20 .50
25 Owen Nolan .20 .50
26 Ray Bourque .40 1.00
27 Eric Desjardins .10 .25
28 Patrick Roy 1.60 4.00
29 Andy Moog .20 .50
30 Valeri Kamensky .20 .50
31 Mark Messier .40 1.00
32 Mike Ricci .20 .50
33 Mario Lemieux 1.60 4.00
34 Jaromir Jagr 1.00 2.50
35 Pierre Turgeon .20 .50
36 Kevin Hatcher .06 .15
37 Paul Coffey .30 .75
38 Chris Terreri .10 .25
39 Mike Richter .30 .75
40 Kevin Todd .06 .15
NNO Adams Checklist .04 .10
NNO Smythe Checklist .04 .10
NNO Norris Trivia .04 .10
NNO Patrick Trivia .04 .10
NNO Norris Checklist .04 .10
NNO Smythe Trivia .04 .10
NNO Patrick Checklist .04 .10
NNO Adams Trivia .04 .10

2001-02 Greats of the Game

Released in mid-October 2001, this set carried an SRP of $5.99 for a 5-card pack. The 89-card set featured past greats of the NHL with color and black-and-white photos on white background card fronts.

COMPLETE SET (89) 15.00 30.00
1 Gordie Howe .75 2.00
2 Glenn Hall .25 .60
3 Jean Beliveau .25 .60
4 Bob Nystrom .12 .30
5 Phil Esposito .40 1.00
6 Dennis Maruk .12 .30
7 Bobby Hull .40 1.00
8 Guy Lafleur .30 .75
9 Gilbert Perreault .12 .30
10 John Davidson .20 .50
11 Peter Stastny .20 .50
12 Steve Shutt .12 .30
13 Henri Richard .25 .60
14 Johnny Bower .25 .60
15 Barry Beck .12 .30
16 Marcel Dionne .25 .60
17 Billy Smith .20 .50
18 Dale Hunter .12 .30
19 Tony Esposito .30 .75
20 Guy Lapointe .12 .30
21 Ed Giacomin .25 .60
22 Denis Savard .20 .50
23 Rod Gilbert .25 .60
24 Steve Larmer .12 .30
25 Yvan Cournoyer .25 .60
26 Ulf Nilsson .12 .30
27 Jean Ratelle .12 .30
28 Dino Ciccarelli .12 .30
29 Bryan Trottier .20 .50
30 Tim Horton .25 .60
31 Stan Mikita .30 .75
32 Glenn Anderson .12 .30
33 Bobby Clarke .25 .60
34 Wendel Clark .20 .50
35 Reggie Leach .12 .30
36 Terry Sawchuk .40 1.00
37 Bernie Geoffrion .25 .60
38 Bill Barber .12 .30
39 Tiger Williams .20 .50
40 Alex Delvecchio .25 .60
41 Bernie Parent .25 .60
42 Paul Henderson .12 .30
43 Norm Ullman .12 .30
44 Larry Robinson .20 .50
45 Dave Schultz .20 .50
46 John Ogrodnick .12 .30
47 Rick MacLeish .12 .30
48 Richard Brodeur .20 .50
49 Rick Martin .12 .30
50 Bobby Smith .12 .30
51 Denis Potvin .20 .50
52 Darryl Sittler .25 .60
53 Lanny McDonald .12 .30
54 Brian Bellows .12 .30
55 Frank Mahovlich .25 .60
56 Cam Neely .25 .60
57 Grant Fuhr .20 .50
58 Harry Howell .12 .30
59 Michel Goulet .12 .30
60 Gerry Cheevers .30 .75
61 Dave Taylor .12 .30
62 Clark Gillies .12 .30
63 Bernie Federko .12 .30
64 Chico Resch .20 .50
65 Andy Bathgate .25 .60
66 Jacques Lemaire .25 .60
67 Ken Hodge .12 .30
68 Rogie Vachon .25 .60
69 Brian Sutter .20 .50
70 Rick Middleton .12 .30
71 Neal Broten .12 .30
72 Mike Bossy .25 .60
73 Borje Salming .20 .50
74 Ted Lindsay .25 .60
75 Mike Gartner .12 .30
76 John Bucyk .12 .30
77 Brad Park .20 .50
78 Red Kelly .25 .60
79 Joe Mullen .12 .30
80 Terry O'Reilly .12 .30
81 Mario Lemieux 1.00 2.50
82 Butch Goring .20 .50
83 Mike Liut .20 .50
84 Marcel Pronovost .20 .50
85 Serge Savard .25 .60
86 Jari Kurri .20 .50
87 Rick Kehoe .12 .30
88 Gump Worsley .25 .60
89 Kent Nilsson .12 .30

2001-02 Greats of the Game Retro Collection

This 13-card set featured both color and vintage black-and-white action photos on the card fronts with colored foil at each top corner and along the card bottom. The players name was printed on the bottom of the card front, and the card backs carried a player bio and league stats.

COMPLETE SET (13) 15.00 30.00
1 Gordie Howe 2.50 6.00
2 Jean Beliveau 1.00 2.50
3 Phil Esposito 1.25 3.00
4 Bobby Hull 1.25 3.00
5 Guy LaFleur 1.00 2.50
6 Peter Stastny .60 1.50
7 Henri Richard .60 1.50
8 Marcel Dionne .75 2.00
9 Bryan Trottier .60 1.50
10 Bobby Clarke .75 2.00
11 Terry Sawchuk 1.25 3.00
12 Mario Lemieux 3.00 8.00
13 Tony Esposito 1.00 2.50

2001-02 Greats of the Game Autographs

Inserted at a rate of 1:12 hobby and 1:120 retail, this set paralleled the base set but the featured player's autograph on the front bottom of the card. Card backs carried a congratulatory message and a statement of authenticity. Cards #30, 36, and 88 were not produced. Most players signed between 400-475 cards except those marked as SP below. Short prints were reported to be less than 200 copies each.

1 Gordie Howe SP 75.00 200.00
2 Glenn Hall SP 25.00 60.00
3 Jean Beliveau SP 20.00 50.00
4 Bob Nystrom 8.00 20.00
5 Phil Esposito SP 25.00 60.00
6 Dennis Maruk 8.00 20.00
7 Bobby Hull SP 30.00 80.00
8 Guy Lafleur SP 20.00 50.00
9 Gilbert Perreault 8.00 20.00
10 John Davidson 8.00 20.00
11 Peter Stastny SP 20.00 50.00
12 Steve Shutt 8.00 20.00
13 Henri Richard SP 25.00 60.00
14 Johnny Bower 8.00 20.00
15 Barry Beck 8.00 20.00
16 Marcel Dionne SP 20.00 50.00
17 Billy Smith 8.00 20.00
18 Dale Hunter 8.00 20.00
19 Tony Esposito 12.00 30.00
20 Guy LaPointe 8.00 20.00
21 Ed Giacomin 15.00 40.00
22 Denis Savard 8.00 20.00
23 Rod Gilbert 8.00 20.00
24 Steve Larmer 8.00 20.00
25 Yvan Cournoyer 8.00 20.00
26 Ulf Nilsson 8.00 20.00
27 Jean Ratelle 8.00 20.00
28 Dino Ciccarelli 12.00 30.00
29 Bryan Trottier SP 15.00 40.00
31 Stan Mikita SP 25.00 60.00
32 Glenn Anderson 8.00 20.00
33 Bobby Clarke SP 25.00 60.00
34 Wendel Clark 15.00 40.00
35 Reggie Leach 8.00 20.00
37 Bernie Geoffrion 15.00 40.00
38 Bill Barber 8.00 20.00
39 Tiger Williams 8.00 20.00
40 Alex Delvecchio SP 15.00 40.00
41 Bernie Parent 12.00 30.00
42 Paul Henderson SP 30.00 80.00
43 Norm Ullman 8.00 20.00
44 Larry Robinson 8.00 20.00
45 Dave Schultz 8.00 20.00
46 John Ogrodnick 8.00 20.00
47 Rick MacLeish 8.00 20.00
48 Richard Brodeur 8.00 20.00
49 Rick Martin 8.00 20.00
50 Bobby Smith 8.00 20.00
51 Denis Potvin 8.00 20.00
52 Darryl Sittler 8.00 20.00
53 Lanny McDonald 8.00 20.00
54 Brian Bellows 8.00 20.00
55 Frank Mahovlich 8.00 20.00
56 Cam Neely SP 25.00 60.00
57 Grant Fuhr 12.00 30.00
58 Harry Howell 8.00 20.00
59 Michel Goulet 8.00 20.00
60 Gerry Cheevers 12.00 30.00
61 Dave Taylor 8.00 20.00
62 Clark Gillies 8.00 20.00
63 Bernie Federko 8.00 20.00
64 Chico Resch 8.00 20.00
65 Andy Bathgate 8.00 20.00
66 Jacques Lemaire 8.00 20.00
67 Ken Hodge 8.00 20.00
68 Rogie Vachon 8.00 20.00
69 Brian Sutter 8.00 20.00
70 Rick Middleton 8.00 20.00
71 Neal Broten 8.00 20.00
72 Mike Bossy SP 20.00 50.00
73 Borje Salming 8.00 20.00
74 Ted Lindsay SP 25.00 60.00
75 Mike Gartner SP 20.00 50.00
76 John Bucyk 12.00 30.00
77 Brad Park 8.00 20.00
78 Red Kelly 8.00 20.00
79 Joe Mullen 8.00 20.00
80 Terry O'Reilly 8.00 20.00
81 Mario Lemieux 50.00 125.00
82 Butch Goring 8.00 20.00
83 Mike Liut 8.00 20.00
84 Marcel Pronovost 8.00 20.00
85 Serge Savard 8.00 20.00
86 Jari Kurri 8.00 20.00
87 Rick Kehoe 8.00 20.00
89 Kent Nilsson 8.00 20.00
NNO Rod Langway 12.00 30.00

2001-02 Greats of the Game Board Certified

Inserted at a rate of 1:24 hobby and 1:17 retail packs, this 5-card set featured a swatch of the boards from Joe Louis Arena in Detroit. The card fronts carried a full color photo of the featured player and the board swatch. The card backs carried a congratulatory message and authenticity statement. Cards were not numbered and are listed below in alphabetical order.

1 Mike Bossy 3.00 8.00
2 Guy LaFleur 3.00 8.00
3 Mario Lemieux 10.00 25.00
4 Cam Neely 3.00 8.00
5 Peter Stastny 3.00 8.00

2001-02 Greats of the Game Jerseys

Inserted at a rate of 1:30 hobby packs, this 8-card set featured a swatch of game-worn jersey from the featured player on the card front accompanied by a full color photo of the player trimmed in the team's colors. Card backs carried a congratulatory message and a statement of authenticity. Cards were not numbered and are listed below in alphabetical order. The Patrick Roy, long believed to have been pulled from circulation, has shown up in large numbers recently as a result of the Fleer inventory liquidation. The prices are reflective of this widespread availability.

*MULT.COLOR SWATCH: .75X TO 2X HI
1 Dino Ciccarelli 6.00 15.00
2 Tony Esposito 8.00 20.00
3 Michel Goulet 6.00 15.00
4 Guy Lafleur 10.00 25.00
5 Larry Robinson 8.00 20.00
6 Borje Salming 6.00 15.00
7 Glen Sather 6.00 15.00
8 Denis Savard 6.00 15.00
9 Patrick Roy 12.00 30.00

2001-02 Greats of the Game Patches Gold

This 8-card set paralleled the basic jersey set but featured a patch swatch on the card front. Each card was serial-numbered out of 50. The card backs carried a congratulatory message and authenticity statement. These cards were hobby exclusive.

*GOLD PATCH: 1.25X TO 3X BASIC JERSEY CARD

2001-02 Greats of the Game Sticks

Inserted at a rate of 1:84 hobby and 1:400 retail, this 11-card set featured pieces of game-used sticks of the featured players on the card fronts. The card backs carried a congratulatory message and authenticity statement.

1 Marcel Dionne 10.00 25.00
2 Phil Esposito 12.50 30.00
3 Tony Esposito 15.00 40.00
4 Gordie Howe 25.00 60.00
5 Bobby Hull 15.00 40.00
6 Cam Neely 10.00 25.00
7 Willie O'Ree 12.50 30.00
8 Brad Park 10.00 25.00
9 Henri Richard 10.00 25.00
10 Terry Sawchuk 25.00 60.00
11 Darryl Sittler 10.00 25.00

1983 Hall of Fame Postcards

A1 Sid Abel .80 2.00
A2 Punch Broadbent .40 1.00
A3 Clarence Campbell .40 1.00
A4 Neil Colville .40 1.00
A5 Charlie Conacher 1.20 3.00
A6 Mervyn(Red) Dutton .40 1.00
A7 Foster Hewitt 1.20 3.00
A8 Fred Hume .40 1.00
A9 Mickey Ion .40 1.00
A10 Ernest(Moose) Johnson .40 1.00
A11 Bill Mosienko .40 1.00
A12 Maurice Richard 6.00 15.00
A13 Barney Stanley .40 1.00
A14 Lord Stanley .80 2.00
A15 Cyclone Taylor 1.00 2.50
A16 Tiny Thompson 1.20 3.00
B1 Dan Bain .40 1.00
B2 Hobey Baker .80 2.00
B3 Frank Calder .40 1.00
B4 Frank Foyston .40 1.00
B5 James Hendy .40 1.00
B6 Gordie Howe 6.00 15.00
B7 Harry Lumley 1.20 3.00
B8 Reg Noble .40 1.00
B9 Frank Patrick .40 1.00
B10 Harvey Pulford .40 1.00
B11 Ken Reardon .60 1.50
B12 Bullet Joe Simpson .60 1.50
B13 Conn Smythe .80 2.00
B14 Red Storey .40 1.00
B15 Lloyd Turner .40 1.00
B16 Georges Vezina 3.00 7.50
C1 Jean Beliveau 3.00 7.50
C2 Max Bentley .60 1.50
C3 King Clancy 1.20 3.00
C4 Babe Dye .40 1.00
C5 Ebbie Goodfellow .40 1.00
C6 Charles Hay .40 1.00
C7 Percy Lesueur .60 1.50
C8 Tommy Lockhart .40 1.00
C9 Jack Marshall .40 1.00
C10 Lester Patrick .80 2.00
C11 Bill Quackenbush .60 1.50
C12 Frank Selke .60 1.50
C13 Cooper Smeaton .40 1.00
C14 Hooley Smith .40 1.00
C15 Capt.J.T.Sutherland .40 1.00
C16 Fred Whitcroft .40 1.00
D1 Charles F. Adams .40 1.00
D2 Russell Bowie .40 1.00
D3 Frank Fredrickson .40 1.00
D4 Billy Gilmour .40 1.00
D5 Ching Johnson .60 1.50
D6 Tom Johnson .60 1.50
D7 Aurel Joliat 1.60 4.00
D8 Duke Keats .40 1.00
D9 Red Kelly 1.20 3.00
D10 Frank McGee .40 1.00
D11 James D. Norris .60 1.50
D12 Philip D. Ross .40 1.00
D13 Terry Sawchuk 3.00 7.50
D14 Babe Siebert .60 1.50
D15 Anatoli V. Tarasov .60 1.50
D16 Roy Worters .80 2.00
E1 T. Franklin Ahearn .40 1.00
E2 Harold E. Ballard .80 2.00
E3 Billy Burch .40 1.00
E4 Bill Chadwick .40 1.00
E5 Sprague Cleghorn .80 2.00
E6 Rusty Crawford .40 1.00
E7 Alex Delvecchio 1.20 3.00
E8 George S. Dudley .40 1.00
E9 Ted Kennedy .80 2.00
E10 Newsy Lalonde 1.00 2.50
E11 Billy McGimsie .40 1.00
E12 Frank Nighbor .60 1.50
E13 Bobby Orr 6.00 15.00
E14 Sen. Donat Raymond .40 1.00
E15 Art Ross 1.00 2.50
E16 Jack Walker .40 1.00
F1 Doug Bentley .60 1.50
F2 Walter A. Brown .40 1.00
F3 Dit Clapper 1.00 2.50
F4 Hap Day .40 1.00
F5 Frank Dilio .40 1.00
F6 Bobby Hewitson .40 1.00
F7 Harry Howell .40 1.00
F8 Paul Loicq .40 1.00
F9 Sylvio Mantha .60 1.50
F10 Jacques Plante 3.20 8.00
F11 George Richardson .40 1.00
F12 Nels Stewart .80 2.00
F13 Hod Stuart .40 1.00
F14 Harry Trihey .40 1.00
F15 Marty Walsh .40 1.00
F16 Arthur M. Wirtz .40 1.00
G1 Toe Blake 1.20 3.00
G2 Frank Boucher .60 1.50
G3 Turk Broda 1.60 4.00
G4 Harry Cameron .40 1.00
G5 Leo Dandurand .40 1.00
G6 Joe Hall .40 1.00
G7 George Hay .40 1.00
G8 William A. Hewitt .40 1.00
G9 Bouse Hutton .40 1.00
G10 Dick Irvin .80 2.00
G11 Henri Richard 1.20 3.00
G12 John Ross Robertson .40 1.00
G13 Frank D. Smith .40 1.00
G14 Allan Stanley .40 1.00
G15 Norm Ullman .40 1.00
G16 Harry Watson .40 1.00
H1 Clint Benedict 1.20 3.00
H2 Dickie Boon .40 1.00
H3 Gordie Drillon .60 1.50
H4 Bill Gadsby .40 1.00
H5 Rod Gilbert .40 1.00
H6 Moose Goheen .40 1.00
H7 Tommy Gorman .40 1.00
H8 Glenn Hall 1.20 3.00
H9 Red Horner .40 1.00
H10 Gen.J.R.Kilpatrick .40 1.00
H11 Robert Lebel .40 1.00
H12 Howie Morenz 3.00 7.50
H13 Fred Scanlan .40 1.00
H14 Tommy Smith .40 1.00
H15 Fred C. Waghorne .40 1.00
H16 Cooney Weiland .80 2.00
I1 Weston Adams .40 1.00
I2 Sir Montagu Allan .40 1.00
I3 Frank Brimsek 1.20 3.00
I4 Angus Campbell .40 1.00
I5 Bill Cook .80 2.00
I6 Tom Dunderdale .40 1.00
I7 Emile Francis .40 1.00
I8 Charlie Gardiner .60 1.50
I9 Elmer Lach .60 1.50
I10 Frank Mahovlich 1.20 3.00
I11 Didier Pitre .40 1.00
I12 Joe Primeau 1.20 3.00
I13 Frank Rankin .40 1.00
I14 Ernie Russell .40 1.00
I15 Thayer Tutt .40 1.00
I16 Harry Westwick .40 1.00
J1 Jack Adams .40 1.00
J2 Bunny Ahearne .40 1.00
J3 J.P. Bickell .40 1.00
J4 Johnny Bucyk .60 1.50
J5 Art Coulter .40 1.00
J6 C.G. Drinkwater .40 1.00
J7 George Hainsworth 1.20 3.00
J8 Tim Horton 2.00 5.00
J9 Maj. F. McLaughlin .40 1.00
J10 Dickie Moore .80 2.00
J11 Pierre Pilote .40 1.00
J12 Claude C. Robinson .40 1.00
J13 Sweeney Schriner .40 1.00
J14 Oliver Seibert .40 1.00
J15 Alfred Smith .40 1.00
J16 Phat Wilson .60 1.50
K1 Yvan Cournoyer .60 1.50
K2 Scotty Davidson .40 1.00
K3 Cy Denneny .60 1.50
K4 Bill Durnan 1.00 2.50
K5 Shorty Green .40 1.00
K6 Riley Hern .40 1.00
K7 Bryan Hextall .40 1.00
K8 Bill Jennings .40 1.00
K9 Gordon W. Juckes .40 1.00
K10 Paddy Moran .60 1.50
K11 James Norris .40 1.00
K12 Harry Oliver .40 1.00
K13 Sam Pollock .40 1.00
K14 Marcel Pronovost .40 1.00
K15 Jack Ruttan .40 1.00
K16 Earl Seibert .40 1.00
L1 Buck Boucher .40 1.00
L2 George V. Brown .40 1.00
L3 Arthur F. Farrell .40 1.00
L4 Herb Gardiner .40 1.00
L5 Si Griffis .40 1.00
L6 Hap Holmes .40 1.00
L7 Harry Hyland .40 1.00
L8 Tommy Ivan .40 1.00
L9 Jack Laviolette .40 1.00
L10 Ted Lindsay 1.20 3.00
L11 Francis Nelson .40 1.00
L12 William M. Northey .40 1.00
L13 Babe Pratt .40 1.00
L14 Chuck Rayner .80 2.00
L15 Milt Rodden .40 1.00
L16 Milt Schmidt 1.00 2.50
M1 Butch Bouchard .60 1.50
M2 Jack Butterfield .40 1.00
M3 Joseph Cattarinich .40 1.00
M4 Alex Connell .80 2.00
M5 Bill Cowley .60 1.50
M6 Chaucer Elliott .40 1.00
M7 Jimmy Gardner .40 1.00
M8 Boom Boom Geoffrion 1.60 4.00
M9 Tom Hooper .40 1.00
M10 Syd Howe .40 1.00
M11 Harvey(Busher)Jackson .60 1.50
M12 Al Leader .40 1.00
M13 Steamer Maxwell .40 1.00
M14 Blair Russell .40 1.00
M15 William W. Wirtz .40 1.00
M16 Gump Worsley 1.20 3.00
N1 George Armstrong .80 2.00
N2 Ace Bailey 1.20 3.00
N3 Jack Darragh .40 1.00
N4 Ken Dryden 3.20 8.00
N5 Eddie Gerard .40 1.00
N6 Jack Gibson .40 1.00
N7 Hugh Lehman .40 1.00
N8 Mickey MacKay .40 1.00
N9 Joe Malone 1.20 3.00
N10 Bruce A. Norris .40 1.00
N11 J. Ambrose O'Brien .40 1.00
N12 Lynn Patrick .60 1.50
N13 Tommy Phillips .40 1.00
N14 Allan W. Pickard .40 1.00
N15 Jack Stewart .40 1.00
N16 Frank Udvari .40 1.00
O1 Syl Apps .80 2.00
O2 John G. Ashley .40 1.00
O3 Marty Barry .40 1.00
O4 Andy Bathgate .60 1.50
O5 Johnny Bower 1.20 3.00
O6 Frank Buckland .40 1.00
O7 Jimmy Dunn .40 1.00
O8 Michael Grant .40 1.00
O9 Doug Harvey 1.20 3.00
O10 George McNamara .40 1.00
O11 Stan Mikita 1.20 3.00
O12 Sen.H.de M. Molson .40 1.00
O13 Gordon Roberts .40 1.00
O14 Eddie Shore 3.00 7.50
O15 Bruce Stuart .40 1.00
O16 Carl P. Voss .40 1.00
NNO Binder .40 1.00

1985-87 Hall of Fame

This 261-card standard-size set was basically two different sets but the second set was merely a reissue of the first Hall of Fame set done two years before, adding the new inductees since that time. The only difference in the first 240 cards in this later 1987 set and the prior set was the different copyright year at the bottom of each reverse in this set. Note however that the copyright line for the 1985 set confusingly showed a 1983 copyright date (apparently referring back to the post card set) vertically printed on the card back. One exception was Gordie Howe; his career was so long that his season-by-season statistics filled up the entire card back leaving no room for a copyright line. The set featured members of the Hockey Hall of Fame portrayed by the artwork of Carlton McDiarmid. Backs were written in both French and English. The set was originally sold in the Canadian Sears 1985 Christmas Catalog.

COMPLETE SET (261) 40.00 100.00
1 Maurice Richard 3.20 8.00
2 Sid Abel .30 .75
3 Punch Broadbent .16 .40
4 Clarence S. Campbell .16 .40
5 Neil Colville .16 .40
6 Charlie Conacher .40 1.00
7 Mervyn(Red) Dutton .16 .40
8 Foster W. Hewitt .40 1.00
9 Mickey Ion .16 .40
10 Ernest(Moose) Johnson .16 .40
11 Bill Mosienko .16 .40
12 Russell Stanley .16 .40
13 Lord Stanley .30 .75
14 Cyclone Taylor .30 .75
15 Tiny Thompson .30 .75
16 Gordie Howe 3.20 8.00
17 Hobey Baker .30 .75
18 Frank Calder .16 .40
19 Jim Hendy .16 .40
20 Frank Foyston .16 .40
21 Harry Lumley .40 1.00
22 Reg Noble .16 .40
23 Frank A. Patrick .16 .40
24 Harvey Pulford .16 .40
25 Ken Reardon .20 .50
26 Bullet Joe Simpson .20 .50
27 Conn Smythe .30 .75
28 Red Storey .16 .40
29 Lloyd Turner .16 .40
30 Georges Vezina 1.00 2.50
31 Jean Beliveau 1.00 2.50
32 Max Bentley .20 .50
33 King Clancy .40 1.00
34 Babe Dye .16 .40
35 Ebbie Goodfellow .16 .40
36 Charles Hay .16 .40
37 Percy Lesueur .20 .50
38 Tommy Lockhart .16 .40
39 Jack Marshall .16 .40
40 Lester Patrick .30 .75
41 Frank Selke .20 .50
42 J. Cooper Smeaton .16 .40
43 Hooley Smith .16 .40
44 Capt.J.T. Sutherland .16 .40
45 Fred Whitcroft .16 .40
46 Terry Sawchuk 1.60 4.00
47 Charles F. Adams .16 .40
48 Russell Bowie .16 .40
49 Frank Fredickson .16 .40
50 Billy Gilmour .16 .40
51 Ching Johnson .20 .50
52 Tom Johnson .30 .75
53 Aurel Joliat .60 1.50
54 Duke Keats .16 .40
55 Red Kelly .40 1.00
56 Frank McGee .16 .40
57 James D. Norris .16 .40
58 Philip D. Ross .16 .40
59 Babe Siebert .20 .50
60 Roy Worters .30
61 Bobby Orr 3.20
62 T. Franklin Ahearn .16
63 Harold E. Ballard .30
64 Billy Burch .16
65 Bill Chadwick .16
66 Sprague Cleghorn .30
67 Rusty Crawford .16
68 George S. Dudley .16
69 Teeder Kennedy .30
70 Newsy Lalonde .40
71 Billy McGimsie .16
72 Frank Nighbor .20
73 Sen. Donat Raymond .16
74 Art Ross .40
75 Jack Walker .16
76 Jacques Plante 1.60
77 Doug Bentley .20
78 Walter A. Brown .16
79 Dit Clapper .40
80 Hap Day .16
81 Frank Dilio .16
82 Bobby Hewitson .16
83 Harry Howell .16
84 Sylvio Mantha .20
85 George Richardson .16
86 Nels Stewart .30
87 Hod Stuart .16
88 Harry Trihey .16
89 Marty Walsh .16
90 Arthur M. Wirtz .16
91 Henri Richard .60
92 Toe Blake .40
93 Frank Boucher .20
94 Turk Broda .60
95 Harry Cameron .16
96 Leo J.V. Dandurand .16
97 Joe Hall .16
98 George W. Hay .16
99 William A. Hewitt .16
100 Bouse Hutton .16
101 Dick Irvin .20
102 John Ross Robertson .16
103 Frank D. Smith .16
104 Norm Ullman .16
105 Moose Watson .16
106 Howie Morenz 1.00
107 Clint Benedict .40
108 Dickie Boon .16
109 Gordon Drillon .20
110 Bill Gadsby .16
111 Rod Gilbert .16
112 Moose Goheen .16
113 Tommy Gorman .16
114 Glenn Hall .40
115 Red Horner .16
116 Gen.J.R. Kilpatrick .16
117 Robert Lebel .16
118 Fred Scanlan .16
119 Fred C. Waghorne .16
120 Cooney Weiland .30
121 Frank Mahovlich .40
122 Weston Adams Sr. .16
123 Sir Montagu Allan .16
124 Frank Brimsek .40
125 Angus D. Campbell .16
126 Bill Cook .30
127 Tom Dunderdale .16
128 Chuck Gardiner .16
129 Elmer Lach .20
130 Didier Pitre .16
131 Joe Primeau .40
132 Frank Rankin .16
133 Ernie Russell .16
134 W. Thayer Tutt .16
135 Harry Westwick .16
136 Yvan Cournoyer .20
137 Scotty Davidson .16
138 Cy Denneny .20
139 Bill Durnan .40
140 Shorty Green .16
141 Bryan Hextall .16
142 Bill Jennings .16
143 Gordon W. Juckes .16
144 Paddy Moran .20
145 James Norris .16
146 Harold Oliver .16
147 Sam Pollock .16
148 Marcel Pronovost .16
149 Jack Ruttan .16
150 Earl W. Seibert .16
151 Ted Lindsay .40
152 George V. Brown .16
153 Arthur F. Farrell .16
154 Herb Gardiner .16
155 Si Griffis .16
156 Hap Holmes .16
157 Harry Hyland .16
158 Tommy Ivan .16
159 Jack Laviolette .16
160 Francis Nelson .16
161 William M. Northey .16
162 Babe Pratt .16
163 Chuck Rayner .30
164 Mike Rodden .16
165 Milt Schmidt .40
166 Boom Boom Geoffrion .60
167 Jack Butterfield .16
168 Joseph Cattarinich .16
169 Alex Connell .30
170 Bill Cowley .20
171 Chaucer Eliott .16
172 Jimmy Gardner .16
173 Tom Hooper .16
174 Syd Howe .16
175 Harvey(Busher) Jackson .20
176 Al Leader .16
177 Steamer Maxwell .16
178 Blair Russell .16
179 William W. Wirtz .16
180 Gump Worsley .40
181 Johnny Bucyk .20
182 Jack Adams .16
183 Bunny Ahearne .16
184 J.P. Bickell .16
185 Art Coulter .16
186 C.G. Drinkwater .16
187 George Hainsworth .40
188 Tim Horton 1.00
189 Maj.F. McLaughlin .16
190 Dickie Moore .30

?ierre Pilote	.16	.40
?laude C. Robinson	.16	.40
?liver L. Seibert	.16	.40
?lfred E. Smith	.16	.40
?hat Wilson	.16	.40
?en Dryden	1.60	4.00
George Armstrong	.30	.75
?ce Bailey	.40	1.00
?ack Darragh	.16	.40
?ddie Gerard	.16	.40
?ack Gibson	.16	.40
?ugh Lehman	.16	.40
Mickey MacKay	.16	.40
?oe Malone	.30	.75
?ruce A. Norris	.16	.40
?.Ambrose O'Brien	.16	.40
?ynn Patrick	.20	.50
?ommy Phillips	.16	.40
?llan W. Pickard	.16	.40
?ack Stewart	.16	.40
Johnny Bower	.40	1.00
?yl Apps	.30	.75
?ohn G. Ashley	.16	.40
Marty Barry	.16	.40
Andy Bathgate	.20	.50
?rank Buckland	.16	.40
?immy Dunn	.16	.40
Michael Grant	.16	.40
?oug Harvey	.40	1.00
?eorge McNamara	.16	.40
?en.H.deM. Molson	.16	.40
?ordon Roberts	.16	.40
?ddie Shore	1.00	2.50
?ruce Stuart	.16	.40
?arl P. Voss	.16	.40
?tan Mikita	.40	1.00
?an Bain	.16	.40
?utch Bouchard	.20	.50
?uck Boucher	.16	.40
?lex Delvecchio	.40	1.00
?mile P. Francis	.16	.40
?iley Hern	.16	.40
?red J. Hume	.16	.40
?aul Loicq	.16	.40
?ill Quackenbush	.20	.50
?weeney Schriner	.16	.40
?ommy Smith	.16	.40
?llan Stanley	.16	.40
?natoli V. Tarasov	.20	.50
?rank Udvari	.16	.40
?arry Sinden	.30	.75
?obby Hull	1.60	4.00
?unch Imlach	.24	.60
?hil Esposito	.80	2.00
?acques Lemaire	.30	.75
?ernie Parent	.40	1.00
?udy Pilous	.24	.60
?ert Olmstead	.24	.60
?ean Ratelle	.40	1.00
?erry Cheevers	.40	1.00
?illiam Hanley	.24	.60
?eo Boivin	.24	.60
?ake Milford	.24	.60
John Mariucci	.24	.60
?ave Keon	.40	1.00
?erge Savard	.24	.60
?ohn A. Ziegler Jr.	.24	.60
?obby Clarke	.60	1.50
?d Giacomin	.40	1.00
?acques Laperriere	.24	.60
?att Pavelich	.24	.60

1992-93 Hall of Fame Legends

?ockey Hall of Fame in association with ?iamond Connection and the Sports ?y of Art produced this 18-card set as ?rst of three series to be released each Over a four year period, all members ?uilders of Hockey's Hall of Fame will been featured. Production was limited ?,000 numbered sets, and buyers ?ed exclusive rights to their assigned ?er throughout the duration of the ?t. Issued in a cardboard box, the cards ?ured approximately 3 1/2" by 5 1/2" ?eatured the work of noted sports artist ? West. The front displayed a color ?duction of the artist's original painting. ?ack had a parchment background with blue borders and included biographical ?mation, a player profile, career ?tics, each team played for, and the ? played. A registration form and an ?rship transfer form were included with set. The card number and set serial ?er are in the lower right corner.

?PLETE SET (36)	60.00	150.00
?rry Lumley	2.00	5.00
?nn Smythe CO	1.60	4.00
?urice Richard	6.00	15.00
?bby Orr	8.00	20.00
?nie Geoffrion	2.40	6.00
?bey Baker	2.00	5.00
?il Esposito	2.40	6.00
?g Clancy	2.40	6.00
?rdie Howe	6.00	15.00
?mile Francis	1.60	4.00
?acques Plante	3.20	8.00
?id Abel	1.60	4.00
?oster Hewitt	2.00	5.00
?harlie Conacher	2.00	5.00
?tan Mikita	2.40	6.00
?obby Clarke	2.00	5.00
?orm Ullman	1.60	4.00
?ord Stanley of Preston	2.00	5.00
19 Ted Lindsay	2.00	5.00
20 Duke Keats	1.60	4.00
21 Jack Adams	1.60	4.00
22 Bill Mosienko	1.60	4.00
23 Johnny Bower	2.00	5.00
24 Tim Horton	3.20	8.00
25 Punch Imlach	1.60	4.00
26 Georges Vezina	4.00	10.00
27 Earl Seibert	1.60	4.00
28 Bryan Hextall Sr.	1.60	4.00
29 Babe Pratt	1.60	4.00
30 Gump Worsley	2.00	5.00
31 Ed Giacomin	2.00	5.00
32 Ace Bailey	2.00	5.00
33 Harry Sinden	1.60	4.00
34 Lanny McDonald	2.00	5.00
35 Tommy Ivan	1.60	4.00
36 Frank Calder	1.60	4.00

1994 Hall of Fame Tickets

Measuring approximately 2 5/16" by 3 1/2", each of these tickets admitted one to the Hockey Hall of Fame in Toronto. Each ticket was printed on thin cardboard stock and featured a full-bleed photo on its front. On a background that shades from blue to white, the horizontal backs carried the Hall of Fame's street address, a description of the front picture, founding sponsors' logos, and a barcode. The tickets were numbered on the back.

COMPLETE SET (12)	18.00	45.00
1 Stanley Cup	1.60	4.00
2 O'Brien Trophy	1.20	3.00
3 Dan Bain Artifacts	1.20	3.00
4 Art Ross Artifacts	1.60	4.00
5 Ace Bailey Artifacts	1.60	4.00
6 Clint Benedict Artifacts	2.00	5.00
7 Howie Morenz Artifacts	3.20	8.00
8 Roy Worters Artifacts	1.60	4.00
9 Andy Bathgate Artifacts	1.20	3.00
10 Jacques Plante Artifacts	3.20	8.00
11 Terry Sawchuk Artifacts	3.20	8.00
12 Milt Schmidt Artifacts	1.60	4.00

1998 Hall of Fame Medallions

Issued only in Canada, these medallions were mounted on a clear plastic holder and featured statistical and biographical information on the back.

COMPLETE SET (2)	6.00	15.00
1 Michel Goulet	3.20	8.00
2 Peter Stastny	4.00	8.00

1914 Happy Christmas Postcard

Full color postcard that measures 3 1/2 x 5 1/2. Front featured a young lady with a hockey stick and the words Happy Christmas in the lower right-hand corner. Small print on card back said Series 259 F.

NNO Happy Christmas	10.00	20.00

1999 Hasbro Starting Lineup Cards

These cards were packaged along with plastic figurines in the Hasbro Starting Lineup product. Because these packages often were left intact, it could be difficult to obtain these singles. This set was produced by Upper Deck.

COMPLETE SET (17)	10.00	25.00
1 Mike Dunham	9.00	1.00
2 Peter Forsberg	7.00	1.50
3 Wayne Gretzky	12.00	5.00
4 Jeff Hackett	7.00	1.50
5 Dominik Hasek	9.00	1.50
6 Jaromir Jagr	9.00	1.50
7 Curtis Joseph	9.00	2.00
8 Paul Kariya	9.00	1.50
9 Nikolai Khabibulin	7.00	1.00
10 Olaf Kolzig	6.00	1.00
11 Nicklas Lidstrom	18.00	2.00
12 Eric Lindros	9.00	1.50
13 Mike Modano	10.00	1.00
14 Keith Primeau	12.00	1.00
15 Chris Pronger	12.00	1.00
16 Sergei Samsonov	15.00	2.00
17 Steve Yzerman	12.00	3.00

1975-76 Heroes Stand-Ups

These 31 "Hockey Heroes Autographed Pin-up/Stand-Up Sportrophies" featured NHL players from five different teams. The stand-ups came in two different sizes. The Bruins and Flyers stand-ups were approximately 15 1/2" by 8/3/4", while the Islanders stand-ups were approximately 13 1/2" by 7 1/2" and were issued three to a strip. The stand-ups were made of laminated cardboard, and the yellow frame is decorated with red stars. Each stand-up featured a color action shot of the player. A facsimile autograph was inscribed across the bottom of the stand-up. The stand-ups were unnumbered and checklisted below alphabetically according to and within teams as follows: Boston Bruins (1-7), Montreal Canadiens (8-13), New York Islanders (14-19), Philadelphia Flyers (20-25), and Toronto Maple Leafs (26-31).

COMPLETE SET (31)	125.00	250.00
1 Gerry Cheevers	6.00	12.00
2 Terry O'Reilly	3.00	6.00
3 Bobby Orr	25.00	50.00
4 Brad Park	4.00	8.00
5 Jean Ratelle	4.00	8.00
6 Andre Savard	2.50	5.00
7 Gregg Sheppard	2.50	5.00
8 Yvan Cournoyer	4.00	8.00
9 Guy Lafleur	10.00	20.00
10 Jacques Lemaire	4.00	8.00
11 Peter Mahovlich	2.50	5.00
12 Doug Risebrough	2.50	5.00
13 Larry Robinson	6.00	12.00
14 Billy Harris	2.50	5.00
15 Gerry Hart	2.50	5.00
16 Denis Potvin	6.00	12.00
17 Glenn Resch	4.00	8.00
18 Bryan Trottier	6.00	12.00
19 Ed Westfall	2.50	5.00
20 Bill Barber	4.00	8.00
21 Bobby Clarke	6.00	12.00
22 Reggie Leach	2.50	5.00
23 Rick MacLeish	2.50	5.00
24 Bernie Parent	6.00	12.00
25 Dave Schultz	4.00	8.00
26 Lanny McDonald	4.00	8.00
27 Borje Salming	3.00	6.00
28 Darryl Sittler	4.00	8.00
29 Wayne Thomas	3.00	6.00
30 Errol Thompson	2.50	5.00
31 Dave(Tiger) Williams	4.00	8.00

1992-93 High Liner Stanley Cup

National Sea Products Ltd., producer and manufacturer of High Liner brand fish products, produced a 28-card, standard-size set to celebrate the Centennial of the Stanley Cup (1893-1993). Specially marked packages of High Liner frozen fish products contained two cards. Collectors could also order additional cards by clipping the order form from the box, checking the cards desired, and sending it in with six UPC symbols from any High Liner brand product plus 3.99. The form limited requests to one card request per card number. The fronts featured full-bleed black-and-white and color team pictures of Stanley Cup champions. The pale blue, horizontal backs presented a French and English summary of the championship season and a list of the players pictured. A darker blue stripe across the top displayed the Stanley Cup logo and the set name in French and English. The team name and the year they won the Stanley Cup appeared in the lower left corner.

COMPLETE SET (28)	16.00	40.00
1 Montreal AAA	.40	1.00
2 Winnipeg Victorias	.40	1.00
3 Montreal Victorias	.40	1.00
4 Montreal Shamrocks	.40	1.00
5 Ottawa Silver Seven	.40	1.00
6 Kenora Thistles	.40	1.00
7 Montreal Wanderers	1.00	2.50
8 Quebec Bulldogs	.40	1.00
9 Toronto Blueshirts	1.00	2.50
10 Vancouver Millionaires	1.00	2.50
11 Seattle Metropolitans	1.00	2.50
12 Toronto Arenas	1.00	2.50
13 Toronto St. Patricks	1.00	2.50
14 Victoria Cougars	.40	1.00
15 Ottawa Senators	.40	1.00
16 Montreal Maroons	1.00	2.50
17 New York Rangers	.40	1.00
18 Detroit Red Wings	1.20	3.00
19 Montreal Canadiens	1.60	4.00
20 Chicago Blackhawks	.40	1.00
21 Toronto Maple Leafs	1.20	3.00
22 Boston Bruins	1.20	3.00
23 Philadelphia Flyers	.40	1.00
24 New York Islanders	.40	1.00
25 Edmonton Oilers	2.00	5.00
26 Calgary Flames	.40	1.00
27 Pittsburgh Penguins	1.00	2.50
28 Checklist Card	.40	1.00

1993-94 High Liner Greatest Goalies

National Sea Products Ltd., producer and manufacturer of High Liner brand fish products, produced a 15-card, standard-size set of the Greatest Goalies of the NHL, a follow-up to High Liner's 28-card 1992-93 Stanley Cup Centennial set. Specially marked packages of High Liner frozen fish products contained one card. Collectors could also order the complete set through a mail-in offer as outlined on the inside of the specially marked High Liner packages. The set was made from white card stock and was primarily devoted to goalies that have won the Vezina Trophy, the NHL's top annual award for goaltenders. The fronts featured white-bordered color player action shots, with the player's name, team and, season printed in white within a blue band at the bottom. The logo, with Greatest Goalies printed in French and English, appeared in the lower left. The white back had a color posed player head shot in the upper left, with the player's name in orange lettering alongside to the right. A biography, stat table, and career highlights were printed in English and French. The High Liner, NHLPA, and NHL logos on the bottom rounded out the card.

COMPLETE SET (15)	8.00	20.00
1 Patrick Roy	3.20	8.00
2 Ed Belfour	.60	1.50
3 Grant Fuhr	.40	1.00
4 Ron Hextall	.40	1.00
5 John Vanbiesbrouck	.40	1.00
6 Tom Barrasso	.40	1.00
7 Bernie Parent	.40	1.00
8 Tony Esposito	.60	1.50
9 Johnny Bower	.60	1.50
10 Jacques Plante	1.00	2.50
11 Terry Sawchuk	1.00	2.50
12 Bill Durnan	.40	1.00
13 Felix Potvin	.60	1.50
14 The Evolution of the Goalie Mask	1.00	2.50
15 Vezina Trophy Checklist	.40	1.00

1992 High-5 Previews

These six cards featured color action player photos with the player's name and position printed above the photo. The backs carried another color player photo, with the player's name and career highlights on a white panel. The words "Preview Sample" appeared in the top left corner. The cards were numbered on the back with a "P" prefix. Bourque and Belfour were produced in larger quantities. The cards were originally distributed as promo items at the 1992 National which led to extremely high values. In 1996, an additional supply of these cards was inserted into boxes of Collector's Edge Future Legends product in three-card sleeves. The additional quantities severely dampened demand. A signed version of the Belfour card also was included as a random insert in these packs, and as a promotional giveaway direct from Collector's Edge. This card was serially numbered out of 1500.

COMPLETE SET (6)	48.00	120.00
P1 Ray Bourque DP	2.00	5.00
P2 Mario Lemieux Pittsburgh	4.00	10.00
P3 Wayne Gretzky	20.00	50.00
P4 Mark Messier	4.00	10.00
P5 Mario Lemieux	16.00	40.00
P6 Ed Belfour DP	1.60	4.00
P6 Ed Belfour AU/1500	20.00	50.00

1997 Highland Mint Legends Mint-Cards

The Highland Mint Legends Mint-Card Collection featured NHL greats in a Highland Mint designed Mint-Card and was processed in the same way as the regular Highland Mint series. These standard-sized bronze ingots were enclosed in a plastic display holder case. Silver versions of these cards were produced as well. Since these cards are unnumbered, they are listed below in alphabetical order.

1 Gordie Howe 95/S/1000	175.00	225.00
2 Gordie Howe 95/B/5000	35.00	50.00
3 Bobby Orr 95/S/1000	175.00	225.00
4 Bobby Orr 95/B/5000	35.00	50.00

1997 Highland Mint Magnum Series Medallions

Measuring 2 1/2" in diameter and encased in a 6" by 5" velvet box, these larger medallions commemorated the Colorado Avalanche's Stanley Cup Championship. The relief on these medallions are 10 times greater than the regular medallions.

1 Colorado Avalanche S/250	150.00	200.00
2 Colorado Avalanche B/1000	45.00	60.00

1997 Highland Mint Mint-Cards Pinnacle/Score

These Highland Mint cards were exact replicas of Pinnacle or Score brand cards. The silver and bronze cards contained 4.25 ounces of metal; the gold cards were 24-karat gold-plated on silver. Each card was individually numbered, packaged in a Lucite display holder and accompanied by a certificate of authenticity. The production mintage according to Highland Mint is listed below.

1 Martin Brodeur 95/S/250	175.00	225.00
2 Martin Brodeur 95/B/1500	45.00	60.00
3 Alexandre Daigle 94/S/250	175.00	225.00
4 Alexandre Daigle 94/B/1500	35.00	50.00
5 Jaromir Jagr 94/S/500	175.00	225.00
6 Jaromir Jagr 94/B/2500	45.00	60.00
7 Paul Kariya 94/S/250	175.00	225.00
8 Paul Kariya 94/B/1500	45.00	60.00
9 Pat LaFontaine 93/S/250	175.00	225.00
10 Pat LaFontaine 93/B/1500	35.00	50.00
11 Cam Neely 95/S/250	175.00	225.00
12 Cam Neely 95/B/1500	35.00	50.00
13 Jeremy Roenick 94/S/500	175.00	225.00
14 Jeremy Roenick 94/B/2500	35.00	50.00

1997 Highland Mint Mint-Cards Topps

These cards, from the Highland Mint, measured 2 1/2" by 3 1/2", and were exact reproductions of Topps hockey cards. The cards were packaged in a Lucite display case within a numbered album. Each card came with a sequentially numbered Certificate of Authenticity. The cards featured future heroes, current, and past stars. When the Highland Mint/Topps relationship ended in 1994, the remaining unsold stock was destroyed; the final available mintage according to Highland Mint is listed below. The cards are checklisted below alphabetically.

1 Ray Bourque 80/S/128	200.00	250.00
2 Ray Bourque 80/B/634	50.00	65.00
3 Pavel Bure 92/S/414	175.00	225.00
4 Pavel Bure 92/B/1519	35.00	50.00
5 Sergei Fedorov 91/S/208	200.00	250.00
6 Sergei Fedorov 91/B/914	45.00	60.00
7 Doug Gilmour 85/S/101	200.00	250.00
8 Doug Gilmour 85/B/461	35.00	50.00
9 Wayne Gretzky 79/S/1000	375.00	500.00
10 Wayne Gretzky 79/B/5000	100.00	140.00
11 Bobby Hull 95/S/500	175.00	225.00
12 Bobby Hull 95/B/2500	35.00	50.00
13 Brett Hull 88/S/500	175.00	225.00
14 Brett Hull 88/B/1202	35.00	50.00
15 Mario Lemieux 85/S/999	250.00	325.00
16 Mario Lemieux 85/B/3557	45.00	60.00
17 Eric Lindros 92/S/694	200.00	250.00
18 Eric Lindros 92/B/2668	45.00	60.00
19 Mark Messier 84/S/280	175.00	225.00
20 Mark Messier 84/B/1034	35.00	50.00
21 Felix Potvin 92/S/210	175.00	225.00
22 Felix Potvin 92/B/902	35.00	50.00
23 Patrick Roy 86/S/500	200.00	250.00
24 Patrick Roy 86/B/1986	50.00	65.00
25 Teemu Selanne 92/S/131	175.00	225.00
26 Teemu Selanne 92/B/537	35.00	50.00
27 Steve Yzerman 84/S/233	175.00	225.00
28 Steve Yzerman 84/B/926	55.00	75.00

1997 Highland Mint Mint-Coins

Each medallion weighed one-troy ounce and was individually numbered. The fronts featured a player likeness as well as name, uniform number, and signature. The backs displayed the team logo and statistics. The suggested retail prices for silver ranged from $19.95 to $24.95. The medallions were packaged in a hard plastic capsule and a velvet jewelry box. The Gold-Signature series medallions were two-tone silver medallions with gold plating in selected areas. Packaged in a box with a special foil certificate of authenticity, the front featured the player's likeness, name, uniform number and signatures, while the back carried the NHLPA logo. The suggested retail price was $49.95.

1 Ray Bourque S/5000	15.00	20.00
2 Pavel Bure S/5000	15.00	20.00
3 Sergei Fedorov S/5000	20.00	25.00
4 Brett Hull S/5000	15.00	20.00
5 Jaromir Jagr S/5000	20.00	25.00
6 Mario Lemieux Gold Sig./1000	45.00	60.00
7 Mario Lemieux S/5000	20.00	25.00
8 Mario Lemieux B/25000	9.00	12.00
9 Eric Lindros Gold Sig./1000	45.00	60.00
10 Eric Lindros S/5000	20.00	25.00
11 Bobby Orr S/5000	20.00	25.00
12 B.Orr/R.Bourque S/500	35.00	50.00
13 Chris Osgood S/5000	15.00	20.00
14 Patrick Roy S/5000	20.00	25.00
15 Teemu Selanne S/5000	15.00	20.00
16 J.Vanbiesbrouck S/5000	20.00	25.00
17 Steve Yzerman S/5000	15.00	20.00

1997 Highland Mint Sandblast Mint-Cards

These Highland Mint cards were metal replicas of already issued Pinnacle cards. All these standard size replicas contained approximately 4.25 ounces of metal and featured a "sandblast" background that accents the shiny surface of the player's likeness. Suggested retail was 60.00 for bronze and 250.00 for silver. Each card included a certificate of authenticity, and was packaged in a numbered album and a three-piece Lucite display. The cards were checklisted below alphabetically; the final mintage figures for each card are also listed.

1 Mario Lemieux 96/S/250	200.00	250.00
2 Mario Lemieux 96/B/1500	50.00	65.00

1994 Hockey Wit

Seventh in a series of "WIT" trivia games, this Hockey Wit card set featured 108 standard-size cards and included hockey players of the past and present. The fronts featured full-bleed color action player photos, with the player's name inside a blue box with a gold-foil border and the words "Hockey Wit". On a white background, the backs carried a small color headshot, player biography and trivia questions and answers. Inserted in each master case of 72 games was a bonus card which collectors could redeem for one of 500 limited edition sets of uncut flat sheets. The production run was reportedly limited to 30,000 sets, and a portion of the proceeds from the sale benefited amateur hockey in Canada and the United States. The set included 21 Hall of Famers. The collector who answers all the questions on the backs achieved a perfect score of 801, the total number of goals scored in the NHL by Gordie Howe. The cards were numbered on the back at the lower right corner.

COMPLETE SET (108)	8.00	20.00
1 Mike Richter	.08	.20
2 Tony Amonte	.08	.20
3 Patrick Roy	1.20	3.00
4 Craig Janney	.04	.10
5 Adam Oates	.08	.20
6 Geoff Sanderson	.08	.20
7 Pavel Bure	.60	1.50
8 Steve Duchesne	.04	.10
9 Gordie Howe	.80	2.00
10 Brad Park	.08	.20
11 Brian Bellows	.04	.10
12 Chris Chelios	.20	.50
13 Bill Barber	.08	.20
14 Gump Worsley	.08	.20
15 The Stanley Cup	.08	.20
16 Maurice Richard	.20	.50
17 Kevin Hatcher	.04	.10
18 Ed Belfour	.20	.50
19 Kirk Muller	.08	.20
20 Kevin Stevens	.08	.20
21 Dave Taylor	.04	.10
22 Dale Hawerchuk	.10	.25
23 Jean Beliveau	.10	.25
24 Rogatien Vachon	.08	.20
25 Tom Barrasso	.08	.20
26 Rod Langway	.04	.10
27 Pierre Turgeon	.10	.25
28 Derek King	.04	.10
29 Brendan Shanahan	.40	1.00
30 Darren Turcotte	.04	.10
31 Chris Terreri	.04	.10
32 Tony Granato	.04	.10
33 Michel Goulet	.04	.10
34 Felix Potvin	.10	.25
35 Curtis Joseph	.30	.75
36 Cam Neely	.10	.25
37 Borje Salming	.08	.20
38 Denis Savard	.08	.20
39 Stan Mikita	.10	.25
40 Grant Fuhr	.08	.20
41 Gary Suter	.04	.10
42 Serge Savard	.04	.10
43 Steve Larmer	.08	.20
44 Bryan Trottier	.10	.25
45 Mike Vernon	.08	.20
46 Paul Coffey	.10	.25
47 Bernie Federko	.04	.10
48 Larry Murphy	.08	.20
49 Scotty Bowman CO	.10	.25
50 Glenn Anderson	.04	.10
51 Mats Sundin	.20	.50
52 Henri Richard	.10	.25
53 Ron Francis	.10	.25
54 Scott Niedermayer	.08	.20
55 Teemu Selanne	.40	1.00
56 Frank Mahovlich	.10	.25
57 Owen Nolan	.08	.20
58 Rick Tocchet	.08	.20
59 Rod Brind'Amour	.08	.20
60 Mike Modano	.10	.25
61 Doug Gilmour	.10	.25
62 Jimmy Carson	.04	.10
63 Mike Keane	.04	.10
64 Bernie Nicholls	.08	.20
65 Scott Stevens	.08	.20
66 Mario Lemieux Pittsburg	1.20	3.00
67 Keith Primeau	.10	.25
68 Bobby Carpenter	.04	.10
69 Sergei Fedorov	.40	1.00
70 Peter Stastny	.08	.20
71 Brian Leetch	.10	.25
72 Vincent Damphousse	.08	.20
73 Darryl Sitter	.08	.20
74 Al Iafrate	.08	.20
75 Alexander Mogilny	.08	.20
76 Bill Ranford	.10	.25
77 Ray Bourque	.30	.75
78 Joey Mullen	.04	.10
79 Mike Ricci	.08	.20
80 Bobby Clarke	.10	.25
81 Gerry Cheevers	.08	.20
82 Joe Nieuwendyk	.08	.20
83 Terry Sawchuk	.10	.25
84 Ray Ferraro	.04	.10
85 Lanny McDonald	.08	.20
86 Adam Graves	.08	.20
87 Tomas Sandstrom	.04	.10
88 Eric Lindros	.60	1.50
89 Jari Kurri	.10	.25
90 Al MacInnis	.08	.20
91 Alexandre Daigle	.04	.10
92 Larry Robinson	.10	.25
93 Kelly Hrudey	.08	.20
94 Theo Fleury	.10	.25
95 Billy Smith	.08	.20
96 Luc Robitaille	.10	.25
97 Brett Hull	.30	.75
98 Pat Falloon	.08	.20
99 Wayne Gretzky	1.60	4.00
100 Joe Sakic	.40	1.00
101 Phil Housley	.08	.20
102 Mark Messier	.20	.50
103 Jeremy Roenick	.10	.25
104 Mark Recchi	.10	.25
105 Pat LaFontaine	.10	.25
106 Trevor Linden	.08	.20
107 Jaromir Jagr	.80	2.00
108 Steve Yzerman	.80	2.00

1996-97 Hockey Greats Coins

This 25-coin set featured one coin and checklist card per pack. Each box -- with a suggested retail price of $149.95 contained 80 packs. The coins were silver in color, about the size of a half dollar and featured a bust of the player on the obverse. A Collectors Album also was available for $5.49. The Chris Chelios coin (#4) was believed to be short printed, and thus earns the sizable premium noted below. A gold parallel version of the set existed as well. These coins were inserted at a rate of 1:150 packs. The gold coins are valued at 15 to 25 times the prices below, except for the Chelios, which goes for 3 to 5 times.

COMPLETE SET (25)	30.00	75.00
*GOLD: 15X TO 25X BASIC COIN		
1 Ed Belfour	.60	1.50
2 Ray Bourque	.80	2.00
3 Pavel Bure	1.20	3.00
4 Chris Chelios	6.00	15.00
5 Vincent Damphousse	.40	1.00
6 Sergei Fedorov	1.20	3.00
7 Theo Fleury	.60	1.50
8 Doug Gilmour	.60	1.50
9 Wayne Gretzky	4.00	10.00
10 Brett Hull	.80	2.00
11 Jaromir Jagr	1.60	4.00
12 Paul Kariya	1.60	4.00
13 Mario Lemieux	3.20	8.00
14 Eric Lindros	1.20	3.00
15 Mark Messier	.80	2.00
16 Alexander Mogilny	.40	1.00
17 Jeremy Roenick	.60	1.50
18 Patrick Roy	3.20	8.00
19 Joe Sakic	1.20	3.00
20 Steve Yzerman	2.00	5.00
21 Sergei Berezin	.40	1.00
22 Jim Campbell	.20	.50
23 Jarome Iginla	.60	1.50
24 Rem Murray	.20	.50
25 David Wilkie	.20	.50
NNO Album	2.00	5.00

1924-25 Holland Creameries

The 1924-25 Holland Creameries set contained ten black and white cards measuring approximately 1 1/2" by 3". The front had a black and white head and shoulders shot of the player, in an oval-shaped black frame on white card stock. The words %%Holland Hockey Competition~ appeared above the picture, with the player's name and position below. The cards were numbered in the lower left corner on the front. The horizontally formatted card back had an offer to exchange one complete collection of ten players for either a brick of ice cream or three Holland Banquets. Supposedly the difficult card in the set was Connie Neil, marked as SP in the checklist below.

COMPLETE SET (10) 1000.00 1500.00
1 Wally Fridfinson 60.00 150.00
2 Harold McMunn 60.00 150.00
3 Art Somers 60.00 150.00
4 Frank Woodall 60.00 150.00
5 Frank Frederickson 125.00 300.00
6 Bobby Benson 60.00 150.00
7 Harry Neal 60.00 150.00
8 Wally Byron 60.00 150.00
9 Connie Neil SP 300.00 500.00
10 J. Austman 60.00 150.00

2005-06 Hot Prospects

COMPLETE SET w/o SPs (100) 8.00 20.00
UNIQUE SWATCHES MAY EARN SUBSTANTIAL PREMIUM
1 Joffrey Lupul .10 .25
2 Jean-Sebastien Giguere .15 .40
3 Teemu Selanne .20 .50
4 Marian Hossa .15 .40
5 Ilya Kovalchuk .25 .60
6 Kari Lehtonen .20 .50
7 Patrice Bergeron .20 .50
8 Brian Leetch .20 .50
9 Andrew Raycroft .15 .40
10 Glen Murray .10 .25
11 Ryan Miller .15 .40
12 Chris Drury .15 .40
13 Tim Connolly .10 .25
14 Jarome Iginla .25 .60
15 Miikka Kiprusoff .20 .50
16 Mark Recchi .15 .40
17 Eric Staal .15 .40
18 Martin Gerber .15 .40
19 Doug Weight .15 .40
20 Erik Cole .10 .25
21 Nikolai Khabibulin .20 .50
22 Tuomo Ruutu .10 .25
23 Joe Sakic .40 1.00
24 Marek Svatos .10 .25
25 Milan Hejduk .20 .50
26 Alex Tanguay .15 .40
27 Jose Theodore .25 .60
28 Sergei Fedorov .20 .50
29 Rick Nash .25 .60
30 Mike Modano .20 .50
31 Marty Turco .15 .40
32 Brenden Morrow .15 .40
33 Steve Yzerman .75 2.00
34 Brendan Shanahan .20 .50
35 Pavel Datsyuk .20 .50
36 Henrik Zetterberg .20 .50
37 Nicklas Lidstrom .20 .50
38 Chris Pronger .15 .40
39 Shawn Horcoff .10 .25
40 Ryan Smyth .15 .40
41 Ales Hemsky .10 .25
42 Olli Jokinen .15 .40
43 Roberto Luongo .25 .60
44 Nathan Horton .15 .40
45 Alexander Frolov .15 .40
46 Luc Robitaille .15 .40
47 Pavol Demitra .15 .40
48 Jeremy Roenick .25 .60
49 Marian Gaborik .40 1.00
50 Manny Fernandez .15 .40
51 David Aebischer .15 .40
52 Saku Koivu .20 .50
53 Michael Ryder .15 .40
54 Mike Ribeiro .10 .25
55 Paul Kariya .20 .50
56 Tomas Vokoun .15 .40
57 Steve Sullivan .10 .25
58 Martin Brodeur 1.00 2.50
59 Patrik Elias .15 .40
60 Brian Gionta .10 .25
61 Scott Gomez .15 .40
62 Alexei Yashin .10 .25
63 Rick DiPietro .15 .40
64 Miroslav Satan .10 .25
65 Jaromir Jagr .30 .75
66 Martin Straka .10 .25
67 Jason Spezza .20 .50
68 Dominik Hasek .40 1.00
69 Daniel Alfredsson .15 .40
70 Dany Heatley .25 .60
71 Peter Forsberg .30 .75
72 Simon Gagne .20 .50
73 Keith Primeau .10 .25
74 Antero Niittymaki .15 .40
75 Curtis Joseph .20 .50
76 Shane Doan .10 .25
77 Ladislav Nagy .10 .25
78 Mario Lemieux 1.25 3.00
79 Marc-Andre Fleury .15 .40
80 Sergei Gonchar .15 .40
81 Ryan Malone .10 .25
82 Joe Thornton .30 .75
83 Patrick Marleau .15 .40
84 Evgeni Nabokov .15 .40
85 Jonathan Cheechoo .20 .50
86 Barret Jackman .10 .25
87 Keith Tkachuk .20 .50
88 Vincent Lecavalier .20 .50
89 Brad Richards .15 .40
90 Vaclav Prospal .10 .25
91 Martin St. Louis .15 .40
92 Mats Sundin .20 .50
93 Ed Belfour .20 .50
94 Bryan McCabe .10 .25
95 Eric Lindros .20 .50
96 Markus Naslund .20 .50
97 Alexander Auld .10 .25
98 Todd Bertuzzi .20 .50
99 Brendan Morrison .10 .25
100 Olaf Kolzig .15 .40
101 Dustin Penner RC 3.00 8.00
102 Zenon Konopka RC 1.50 4.00
103 Michael Wall RC 2.00 5.00
104 Brian Eklund RC 2.00 5.00
105 Jay Leach RC 1.50 4.00
106 Eric Healey RC 1.50 4.00
107 Ben Guite RC 1.50 4.00
108 Nathan Paetsch RC 1.50 4.00
109 Jiri Novotny RC 1.50 4.00
110 Richie Regehr RC 1.50 4.00
111 Mark Giordano RC 1.50 4.00
112 Chad Larose RC 1.50 4.00
113 Keith Aucoin RC 1.50 4.00
114 David Gove RC 1.50 4.00
115 Cam Barker RC 2.50 6.00
116 Corey Crawford RC 2.00 5.00
117 Martin St. Pierre RC 1.50 4.00
118 Mark Cullen RC 1.50 4.00
119 James Wisniewski RC 1.50 4.00
120 Vitaly Kolesnik RC 2.00 5.00
121 Steven Goertzen RC 1.50 4.00
122 Joakim Lindstrom RC 1.50 4.00
123 Andrew Penner RC 1.50 4.00
124 Geoff Platt RC 1.50 4.00
125 Junior Lessard RC 1.50 4.00
126 Vojtech Polak RC 1.50 4.00
127 Kyle Brodziak RC 1.50 4.00
128 Matt Greene RC 1.50 4.00
129 Danny Syvret RC 1.50 4.00
130 Adam Hauser RC 2.50 6.00
131 Jean-Francois Jacques RC 1.50 4.00
132 Mathieu Roy RC 1.50 4.00
133 Petr Taticek RC 1.50 4.00
134 Greg Jacina RC 1.50 4.00
135 Rob Globke RC 1.50 4.00
136 Yanick Lehoux RC 1.50 4.00
137 Petr Kanko RC 2.00 5.00
138 Jeff Giuliano RC 1.50 4.00
139 Matt Ryan RC 1.50 4.00
140 Connor James RC 1.50 4.00
141 Richard Petiot RC 1.50 4.00
142 Jean-Philippe Cote RC 1.50 4.00
143 Mark Streit RC 1.50 4.00
144 Jonathan Ferland RC 1.50 4.00
145 Kevin Klein RC 1.50 4.00
146 Pekka Rinne RC 2.00 5.00
147 Greg Zanon RC 1.50 4.00
148 Jason Ryznar RC 1.50 4.00
149 Cam Janssen RC 1.50 4.00
150 Bruno Gervais RC 1.50 4.00
151 Kevin Colley RC 1.50 4.00
152 Petr Prucha RC 3.00 8.00
153 Brandon Bochenski RC 1.50 4.00
154 Brian McGrattan RC 1.50 4.00
155 Stefan Ruzicka RC 1.50 4.00
156 Wade Skolney RC 1.50 4.00
157 Ryan Ready RC 1.50 4.00
158 Josh Gratton RC 1.50 4.00
159 Alexandre Picard RC 1.50 4.00
160 Matt Jones RC 1.50 4.00
161 Colby Armstrong RC 4.00 10.00
162 Doug Murray RC 1.50 4.00
163 Grant Stevenson RC 1.50 4.00
164 Dennis Wideman RC 1.50 4.00
165 Andy Roach RC 1.50 4.00
166 Colin Hemingway RC 1.50 4.00
167 Chris Beckford-Tseu RC 2.50 6.00
168 Jon DiSalvatore RC 1.50 4.00
169 Mike Glumac RC 1.50 4.00
170 Gerald Coleman RC 2.00 5.00
171 Nick Tarnasky RC 1.50 4.00
172 Paul Ranger RC 1.50 4.00
173 Darren Reid RC 1.50 4.00
174 Doug O'Brien RC 1.50 4.00
175 Chris Holt RC 1.50 4.00
176 Jay Harrison RC 1.50 4.00
177 Staffan Kronwall RC 1.50 4.00
178 Tomas Mojzis RC 1.50 4.00
179 Rob McVicar RC 2.00 5.00
180 Rick Rypien RC 1.50 4.00
181 Alexandre Burrows RC 1.50 4.00
182 Prestin Ryan RC 1.50 4.00
183 Mike Green RC 1.50 4.00
184 David Steckel RC 1.50 4.00
185 Joey Tenute RC 1.50 4.00
186 Louis Robitaille RC 2.50 6.00
187 Jim Slater AU RC 4.00 10.00
188 Adam Berkhoel AU RC 4.00 10.00
189 Jordan Sigalet AU RC 4.00 10.00
190 Ben Walter AU RC 2.50 6.00
191 Chris Thorburn AU RC 2.50 6.00
192 Niklas Nordgren AU RC 2.50 6.00
193 Danny Richmond AU RC 2.50 6.00
194 Rene Bourque AU RC 2.50 6.00
195 Duncan Keith AU RC 4.00 10.00
196 Jaroslav Balastik AU RC 2.50 6.00
197 Ole-Kristian Tollefsen AU RC 2.50 6.00
198 Alexandre Picard AU RC 4.00 10.00
199 Brett Lebda AU RC 2.50 6.00
200 Kyle Quincey AU RC 2.50 6.00
201 George Parros AU RC 2.50 6.00
202 Matt Foy AU RC 2.50 6.00
203 Derek Boogaard AU RC 4.00 10.00
204 Maxim Lapierre AU RC 2.50 6.00
205 Chris Campoli AU RC 2.50 6.00
206 Ryan Hollweg AU RC 2.50 6.00
207 Patrick Eaves AU RC 6.00 15.00
208 Christoph Schubert AU RC 2.50 6.00
209 Erik Christensen AU RC 4.00 10.00
210 Dimitri Patzold AU RC 4.00 10.00
211 Josh Gorges AU RC 2.50 6.00
212 Ryane Clowe AU RC 3.00 8.00
213 Jay McClement AU RC 2.50 6.00
214 Lee Stempniak AU RC 4.00 10.00
215 Kevin Dallman AU RC 2.50 6.00
216 Andrew Wozniewski AU RC 2.50 6.00
217 Corey Perry JSY AU RC 30.00 80.00
218 Ryan Getzlaf JSY AU RC 50.00 125.00
219 Braydon Coburn JSY AU RC 12.00 30.00
220 Andrew Alberts JSY AU RC 10.00 25.00
221 Hannu Toivonen JSY AU RC 15.00 40.00
222 Milan Jurcina JSY AU RC 10.00 25.00
223 Daniel Paille JSY AU RC 12.00 30.00
224 Thomas Vanek JSY AU RC 50.00 150.00
225 Eric Nystrom JSY AU RC 10.00 25.00
226 Andrew Ladd JSY AU RC 12.00 30.00
227 Cam Ward JSY AU RC 25.00 60.00
228 Kevin Nastiuk JSY AU RC 12.00 30.00
229 Brent Seabrook JSY AU RC 15.00 40.00
230 Brad Richardson JSY AU RC 12.00 30.00
231 Peter Budaj JSY AU RC 15.00 40.00
232 Wojtek Wolski JSY AU RC 40.00 100.00
233 Gilbert Brule JSY AU RC 40.00 100.00
234 Jussi Jokinen JSY AU RC 15.00 40.00
235 Jim Howard JSY AU RC 15.00 40.00
236 Johan Franzen JSY AU RC 10.00 25.00
237 Valtteri Filppula AU RC 15.00 40.00
238 Brad Winchester JSY AU RC 10.00 25.00
239 Anthony Stewart JSY AU RC 12.00 30.00
240 Rostislav Olesz JSY AU RC 15.00 40.00
241 Jeff Tambellini JSY AU RC 10.00 25.00
242 Mikko Koivu JSY AU RC 20.00 50.00
243 Alexander Perezhogin JSY AU RC 10.00 25.00
244 Andrei Kostitsyn JSY AU RC 20.00 50.00
245 Yann Danis JSY AU RC 15.00 40.00
246 Raitis Ivanans JSY AU RC 15.00 40.00
247 Ryan Suter JSY AU RC 12.00 30.00
248 Barry Tallackson JSY AU RC 12.00 30.00
249 Zach Parise JSY AU RC 30.00 80.00
250 Jeremy Colliton JSY AU RC 10.00 25.00
251 Petteri Nokelainen JSY AU RC 10.00 25.00
252 Robert Nilsson JSY AU RC 10.00 25.00
253 Al Montoya JSY AU RC 15.00 40.00
254 Henrik Lundqvist JSY AU RC 75.00 200.00
255 Andrej Meszaros JSY AU RC 12.00 30.00
256 Ben Eager JSY AU RC 10.00 25.00
257 Jeff Carter JSY AU RC 40.00 100.00
258 Mike Richards JSY AU RC 20.00 50.00
259 R.J. Umberger JSY AU RC 12.00 30.00
260 David LeNeveu JSY AU RC 12.00 30.00
261 Keith Ballard JSY AU RC 10.00 25.00
262 Maxime Talbot JSY AU RC 12.00 30.00
263 Ryan Whitney JSY AU RC 20.00 50.00
264 Steve Bernier AU RC 10.00 25.00
265 Jeff Hoggan JSY AU RC 10.00 25.00
266 Jeff Woywitka JSY AU RC 12.00 30.00
267 Timo Helbling JSY AU RC 10.00 20.00
268 Evgeny Artyukhin JSY AU RC 12.00 30.00
269 Ryan Craig JSY AU RC 12.00 30.00
270 Alexander Steen JSY AU RC 30.00 80.00
271 Kevin Bieksa JSY AU RC 12.00 30.00
272 Jakub Klepis JSY AU RC 12.00 30.00
273 Tomas Fleischmann JSY AU RC 12.00 30.00
274 Dion Phaneuf JSY AU RC 75.00 200.00
275 Alexander Ovechkin JSY AU RC 175.00 350.00
276 Sidney Crosby JSY AU RC 700.00 1400.00

2005-06 Hot Prospects Autographed Patch Variation

STATED PRINT RUN 5 SETS
NOT PRICED DUE TO SCARCITY

2005-06 Hot Prospects Autographed Patch Variation Gold

STATED PRINT RUN 1/1
NOT PRICED DUE TO SCARCITY

2005-06 Hot Prospects En Fuego

STATED PRINT RUN 1/1
NOT PRICED DUE TO SCARCITY

2005-06 Hot Prospects Hot Materials

STATED ODDS 1:8
HMAA Andrew Alberts 2.00 5.00
HMAH Adam Hall 2.00 5.00
HMAK Andrei Kostitsyn 2.50 6.00
HMAL Andrew Ladd 2.50 6.00
HMAM Andrej Meszaros 2.00 5.00
HMAO Alexander Ovechkin 8.00 20.00
HMAP Alexander Perezhogin 2.50 6.00
HMAS Anthony Stewart 2.50 6.00
HMBC Braydon Coburn 2.50 6.00
HMBE Ben Eager 2.00 5.00
HMBG Bill Guerin 2.00 5.00
HMBI Kevin Bieksa 2.00 5.00
HMBR Brad Richardson 2.00 5.00
HMBS Brent Seabrook 2.00 5.00
HMBT Barry Tallackson 2.00 5.00
HMBW Brad Winchester 2.00 5.00
HMCA Carlo Colaiacovo 2.00 5.00
HMCC Chris Campoli 2.00 5.00
HMCO Jeremy Colliton 2.00 5.00
HMCP Corey Perry 3.00 8.00
HMCS Christoph Schubert 2.00 5.00
HMCT Chris Thorburn 2.00 5.00
HMCW Cam Ward 3.00 8.00
HMDB Derek Boogaard 2.50 6.00
HMDH Dan Hamhuis 2.00 5.00
HMDK Duncan Keith 2.50 6.00
HMDL David Legwand 2.50 6.00
HMDP Dimitri Patzold 2.50 6.00
HMDR Danny Richmond 2.00 5.00
HMEA Evgeny Artyukhin 2.00 5.00
HMEC Erik Christensen 2.50 6.00
HMEN Eric Nystrom 2.00 5.00
HMFP Fernando Pisani 2.00 5.00
HMGB Gilbert Brule 3.00 8.00
HMGP George Parros 2.50 6.00
HMHL Henrik Lundqvist 5.00 12.00
HMHT Hannu Toivonen 2.50 6.00
HMJB Jaroslav Balastik 2.00 5.00
HMJC Jeff Carter 3.00 8.00
HMJF Johan Franzen 2.00 5.00
HMJH Jim Howard 2.50 6.00
HMJJ Jussi Jokinen 2.50 6.00
HMJK Jakub Klepis 2.00 5.00
HMJS Jim Slater 2.50 6.00
HMJT Jeff Tambellini 2.00 5.00
HMJW Jeff Woywitka 2.00 5.00
HMKB Keith Ballard 2.00 5.00
HMKD Kevin Dallman 2.00 5.00
HMKI Jason King 2.00 5.00
HMKN Kevin Nastiuk 2.50 6.00
HMKQ Kyle Quincey 2.00 5.00
HMLE David Leneveu 2.50 6.00
HMLS Lee Stempniak 2.50 6.00
HMMC Mike Cammalleri 2.00 5.00
HMMF Matt Foy 2.00 5.00
HMMG Martin Gerber 2.50 6.00
HMMJ Milan Jurcina 2.00 5.00
HMMK Mikko Koivu 2.50 6.00
HMML Maxim Lapierre 2.00 5.00
HMMO Al Montoya 2.50 6.00
HMMR Mike Richards 2.50 6.00
HMMT Maxime Talbot 2.00 5.00
HMNN Niklas Nordgren 2.00 5.00
HMOT Ole-Kristian Tollefsen 2.00 5.00
HMPA Daniel Paille 2.00 5.00
HMPB Peter Budaj 2.50 6.00
HMPH Dion Phaneuf 5.00 12.00
HMPN Petteri Nokelainen 2.00 5.00
HMPS Patrik Stefan 2.00 5.00
HMRC Ryan Craig 2.00 5.00
HMRG Ryan Getzlaf 4.00 10.00
HMRI Raitis Ivanans 2.00 5.00
HMRN Robert Nilsson 2.50 6.00
HMRO Rostislav Olesz 2.50 6.00
HMRS Ryan Suter 2.50 6.00
HMRU R.J. Umberger 2.50 6.00
HMRW Ryan Whitney 2.00 5.00
HMSA Philippe Sauve 2.50 6.00
HMSB Steve Bernier 3.00 8.00
HMSC Sidney Crosby 20.00 50.00
HMSI Jordan Sigalet 2.50 6.00
HMST Alexander Steen 2.50 6.00
HMTF Tomas Fleischmann 2.00 5.00
HMTH Timo Helbling 2.00 5.00
HMTV Thomas Vanek 4.00 10.00
HMVF Valtteri Filppula 2.00 5.00
HMWI Brendan Witt 2.00 5.00
HMWW Wojtek Wolski 3.00 8.00
HMYD Yann Danis 2.50 6.00
HMZP Zach Parise 3.00 8.00

2005-06 Hot Prospects Red Hot

*RED: 5X TO 12X BASE HI
*RED RC/1999 : .75X TO 2X BASE HI
1-186 PRINT RUN: 100 SETS
217-276 PRINT RUN: 50 SETS
SKIP-NUMBERED SET
216 Andrew Wozniewski AU 8.00 20.00
217 Corey Perry JSY AU 25.00 60.00
218 Ryan Getzlaf JSY AU 40.00 100.00
219 Braydon Coburn JSY AU 8.00 20.00
220 Andrew Alberts JSY AU 8.00 20.00
221 Hannu Toivonen JSY AU 20.00 40.00
222 Milan Jurcina JSY AU 8.00 20.00
224 Thomas Vanek JSY AU 75.00 175.00
225 Eric Nystrom JSY AU 8.00 20.00
226 Andrew Ladd JSY AU 15.00 30.00
227 Cam Ward JSY AU 40.00 100.00
228 Kevin Nastiuk JSY AU 8.00 20.00
229 Brent Seabrook JSY AU 8.00 20.00
230 Brad Richardson JSY AU 8.00 20.00
231 Peter Budaj JSY AU 20.00 40.00
232 Wojtek Wolski JSY AU 50.00 100.00
234 Jussi Jokinen JSY AU 25.00 60.00
235 Jim Howard JSY AU 20.00 50.00
236 Johan Franzen JSY AU 8.00 20.00
238 Brad Winchester JSY AU 8.00 20.00
239 Anthony Stewart JSY AU 8.00 20.00
240 Rostislav Olesz JSY AU 10.00 25.00
241 Jeff Tambellini JSY AU 8.00 20.00
242 Mikko Koivu JSY AU 15.00 30.00
243 Alexander Perezhogin JSY AU 8.00 20.00
244 Andrei Kostitsyn JSY AU 20.00 40.00
245 Yann Danis JSY AU 10.00 25.00
246 Raitis Ivanans JSY AU 8.00 20.00
247 Ryan Suter JSY AU 10.00 25.00
248 Barry Tallackson JSY AU 8.00 20.00
249 Zach Parise JSY AU 30.00 80.00
250 Jeremy Colliton JSY AU 8.00 20.00
251 Petteri Nokelainen JSY AU 8.00 20.00
252 Robert Nilsson JSY AU 8.00 20.00
253 Al Montoya JSY AU 20.00 40.00
254 Henrik Lundqvist JSY AU 75.00 175.00
255 Andrej Meszaros JSY AU 8.00 20.00
256 Ben Eager JSY AU 8.00 20.00
257 Jeff Carter JSY AU 30.00 80.00
258 Mike Richards JSY AU 20.00 40.00
259 R.J. Umberger JSY AU 8.00 20.00
260 David Leneveu JSY AU 8.00 20.00
261 Keith Ballard JSY AU 15.00 30.00
262 Maxime Talbot JSY AU 8.00 20.00
263 Ryan Whitney JSY AU 20.00 40.00
265 Jeff Hoggan JSY AU 8.00 20.00
266 Jeff Woywitka JSY AU 8.00 20.00
267 Timo Helbling JSY AU 8.00 20.00
268 Evgeny Artyukhin JSY AU 8.00 20.00
269 Ryan Craig JSY AU 20.00 50.00
270 Alexander Steen JSY AU 30.00 60.00
271 Kevin Bieksa JSY AU 8.00 20.00
272 Jakub Klepis JSY AU 15.00 30.00
273 Tomas Fleischmann JSY AU 15.00 30.00
274 Dion Phaneuf JSY AU 75.00 175.00
275 Alexander Ovechkin JSY AU 150.00 300.00
276 Sidney Crosby JSY AU 600.00 1000.00

2005-06 Hot Prospects White Hot

STATED PRINT RUN: 10 SETS
NOT PRICED DUE TO SCARCITY

2006-07 Hot Prospects

1 Chris Pronger .25 .60
2 Jean-Sebastien Giguere .25 .60
3 Teemu Selanne .30 .75
4 Ilya Kovalchuk .40 1.00
5 Marian Hossa .25 .60
6 Kari Lehtonen .30 .75
7 Patrice Bergeron .30 .75
8 Hannu Toivonen .25 .60
9 Zdeno Chara .15 .40
10 Brad Boyes .15 .40
11 Ryan Miller .30 .75
12 Thomas Vanek .25 .60
13 Daniel Briere .25 .60
14 Maxim Afinogenov .15 .40
15 Jarome Iginla .40 1.00
16 Dion Phaneuf .40 1.00
17 Alex Tanguay .25 .60
18 Miikka Kiprusoff .30 .75
19 Eric Staal .30 .75
20 Cam Ward .30 .75
21 Rod Brind'Amour .25 .60
22 Tuomo Ruutu .15 .40
23 Nikolai Khabibulin .30 .75
24 Martin Havlat .25 .60
25 Joe Sakic .60 1.50
26 Jose Theodore .30 .75
27 Milan Hejduk .15 .40
28 Marek Svatos .15 .40
29 Rick Nash .30 .75
30 Sergei Fedorov .30 .75
31 Pascal LeClaire .25 .60
32 Nikolai Zherdev .15 .40
33 Mike Modano .30 .75
34 Eric Lindros .30 .75
35 Marty Turco .25 .60
36 Pavel Datsyuk .25 .60
37 Dominik Hasek .50 1.25
38 Nicklas Lidstrom .30 .75
39 Henrik Zetterberg .30 .75
40 Ryan Smyth .25 .60
41 Ales Hemsky .15 .40
42 Dwayne Roloson .30 .75
43 Ed Belfour .30 .75
44 Todd Bertuzzi .25 .60
45 Olli Jokinen .15 .40
46 Rob Blake .25 .60
47 Alexander Frolov .15 .40
48 Marian Gaborik .40 1.00
49 Manny Fernandez .25 .60
50 Pavol Demitra .15 .40
51 Saku Koivu .30 .75
52 Cristobal Huet .40 1.00
53 Michael Ryder .25 .60
54 David Aebischer .25 .60
55 Paul Kariya .30 .75
56 Tomas Vokoun .25 .60
57 Martin Brodeur 1.00 2.50
58 Patrik Elias .15 .40
59 Brian Gionta .15 .40
60 Rick DiPietro .25 .60
61 Alexei Yashin .15 .40
62 Miroslav Satan .15 .40
63 Jaromir Jagr .50 1.25
64 Brendan Shanahan .30 .75
65 Henrik Lundqvist .40 1.00
66 Daniel Alfredsson .25 .60
67 Jason Spezza .30 .75
68 Dany Heatley .40 1.00
69 Martin Gerber .25 .60
70 Peter Forsberg .50 1.25
71 Simon Gagne .30 .75
72 Jeff Carter .30 .75
73 Antero Niittymaki .25 .60
74 Shane Doan .15 .40
75 Jeremy Roenick .40 1.00
76 Curtis Joseph .30 .75
77 Sidney Crosby 2.50 6.00
78 Marc-Andre Fleury .30 .75
79 Mark Recchi .15 .40
80 Doug Weight .15 .40
81 Manny Legace .25 .60
82 Keith Tkachuk .25 .60
83 Joe Thornton .50 1.25
84 Jonathan Cheechoo .30 .75
85 Patrick Marleau .25 .60
86 Vesa Toskala .25 .60
87 Vincent Lecavalier .30 .75
88 Brad Richards .25 .60
89 Martin St. Louis .25 .60
90 Mats Sundin .30 .75
91 Andrew Raycroft .25 .60
92 Alexander Steen .25 .60
93 Darcy Tucker .15 .40
94 Roberto Luongo .40 1.00
95 Markus Naslund .30 .75
96 Daniel Sedin .15 .40
97 Henrik Sedin .15 .40
98 Alexander Ovechkin 1.25 3.00
99 Olaf Kolzig .30 .75
100 Alexander Semin .25 .60
101 Ryan Shannon JSY AU RC 10.00 25.00
102 Shane O'Brien JSY AU RC 10.00 25.00
103 Yan Stastny JSY AU RC 10.00 25.00
104 Mark Stuart JSY AU RC 10.00 25.00
105 Drew Stafford JSY AU RC 50.00 150.00
106 Dustin Boyd JSY AU RC 15.00 40.00
107 Dustin Byfuglien JSY AU RC 10.00 25.00
108 Paul Stastny JSY AU RC 30.00 80.00
109 Fredrik Norrena JSY AU RC 12.00 30.00
110 Filip Novak JSY AU RC 10.00 25.00
111 Loui Eriksson JSY AU RC 10.00 25.00
112 Tomas Kopecky JSY AU RC 12.00 30.00
113 M-A Pouliot JSY AU RC 15.00 40.00
114 Ladislav Smid JSY AU RC 10.00 25.00
115 Patrick Thoresen JSY AU RC 12.00 30.00
116 Patrick O'Sullivan JSY AU RC 12.00 30.00
117 Anze Kopitar JSY AU RC 30.00 80.00
118 K. Pushkaryov JSY AU RC 10.00 25.00
119 G. Latendresse JSY AU RC 40.00 100.00
120 Shea Weber JSY AU RC 12.00 30.00
121 Alexander Radulov JSY AU RC 30.00 80.00
122 Travis Zajac JSY AU RC 15.00 40.00
123 Jarkko Immonen JSY AU RC 8.00 20.00
124 Nigel Dawes JSY AU RC 10.00 25.00
125 Ryan Potulny JSY AU RC 12.00 30.00
126 Benoit Pouliot JSY AU RC 12.00 30.00
127 Keith Yandle JSY AU RC 10.00 25.00
128 Noah Welch JSY AU RC 10.00 25.00
129 Kristopher Letang JSY AU RC 12.00 30.00
130 Michel Ouellet JSY AU RC 15.00 40.00
131 Matt Carle JSY AU RC 12.00 30.00
132 M-E Vlasic JSY AU RC 12.00 30.00
133 Marek Schwarz JSY AU RC 15.00 40.00
134 Roman Polak JSY AU RC 10.00 25.00
135 Ben Ondrus JSY AU RC 10.00 25.00
136 Brendan Bell JSY AU RC 10.00 25.00
137 Ian White JSY AU RC 10.00 25.00
138 Jeremy Williams JSY AU RC 10.00 25.00
139 Eric Fehr JSY AU RC 15.00 40.00
140 Jordan Staal JSY/199 AU RC 100.00 300.00
141 Phil Kessel JSY/199 AU RC 60.00 150.00
142 Evgeni Malkin JSY/199 AU RC 125.00 300.00
143 David McKee RC 2.50 6.00
144 Mike Brown RC 1.50 4.00
145 Matt Lashoff RC 1.50 4.00
146 Nate Thompson RC 1.50 4.00
147 Mike Card RC 1.50 4.00
148 Adam Dennis RC 1.50 4.00
149 Michael Funk RC 1.50 4.00
150 Michael Ryan RC 1.50 4.00
151 Brandon Prust RC 1.50 4.00
152 Adam Burish RC 1.50 4.00
153 Michael Blunden RC 1.50 4.00
154 Dave Bolland RC 1.50 4.00
155 Stefan Liv RC 2.50 6.00
156 Alexei Mikhnov RC 1.50 4.00
157 Jan Hejda RC 1.50 4.00
158 Jeff Drouin-Deslauriers RC 1.50 4.00
159 Drew Larman RC 1.50 4.00
160 Janis Sprukts RC 1.50 4.00
161 David Booth RC 1.50 4.00
162 Peter Harrold RC 1.50 4.00
163 Benoit Pouliot RC 1.50 4.00
164 Niklas Backstrom RC 3.00 8.00
165 Miroslav Kopriva RC 1.50 4.00
166 Mikko Lehtonen RC 1.50 4.00
167 John Oduya RC 1.50 4.00
168 Alex Brooks RC 1.50 4.00
169 Kelly Guard RC 1.50 4.00
170 Martin Houle RC 1.50 4.00
171 Jussi Timonen RC 1.50 4.00
172 Lars Jonsson RC 1.50 4.00
173 Triston Grant RC 1.50 4.00
174 Bill Thomas RC 1.50 4.00
175 Patrick Fischer RC 1.50 4.00
176 Joe Pavelski RC 2.50 6.00
177 D.J. King RC 1.50 4.00
178 Blair Jones RC 1.50 4.00
179 Jean-Francois Racine RC 1.50 4.00
180 Nathan McIver RC 1.50 4.00
181 Alexander Edler RC 1.50 4.00
182 Luc Bourdon RC 2.50 6.00
183 Patrick Coulombe RC 1.50 4.00
184 Jesse Schultz RC 1.50 4.00
185 Kyle Cumiskey RC 1.50 4.00
186 David Backes RC 2.50 6.00
187 Mikhail Grabovski RC 1.50 4.00
188 Daren Machesney RC 1.50 4.00
189 Enver Lisin RC 1.50 4.00
190 Tim Brent RC 1.50 4.00
191 Blake Comeau RC 1.50 4.00
192 Barry Brust RC 1.50 4.00
193 Karri Ramo RC 1.50 4.00
194 Kris Newbury RC 1.50 4.00
195 Kamil Kreps RC 1.50 4.00
196 Derek Meech RC 1.50 4.00
197 Andrej Sekera RC 1.50 4.00
198 Clarke MacArthur RC 1.50 4.00
199 Josh Hennessy RC 1.50 4.00
200 Niklas Grossman RC 1.50 4.00
201 Joel Perrault RC 1.50 4.00
202 Troy Brouwer RC 2.50 6.00

2006-07 Hot Prospects Red Hot

*1-100: 5X TO 12X BASE HI
PRINT RUN 100 #'d SETS (1-100/143-180)
PRINT RUN 25 #'d SETS (101-142)
101-142 NOT PRICED DUE TO SCARCITY
AU RCs: 1.5X TO 3X BASE HI
NON-AU RCs: .75X TO 1.5X BASE HI
1 Chris Pronger JSY 3.00 8.00
2 Jean-Sebastien Giguere JSY 3.00 8.00
3 Teemu Selanne JSY 4.00 10.00
4 Ilya Kovalchuk JSY 5.00 12.00
5 Marian Hossa JSY 3.00 8.00
6 Kari Lehtonen JSY 4.00 10.00
7 Patrice Bergeron JSY 4.00 10.00
8 Hannu Toivonen JSY 3.00 8.00
9 Zdeno Chara JSY 2.00 5.00
10 Brad Boyes JSY 2.00 5.00
11 Ryan Miller JSY 4.00 10.00
13 Daniel Briere JSY 3.00 8.00
14 Maxim Afinogenov JSY 2.00 5.00
15 Jarome Iginla JSY 5.00 12.00
16 Dion Phaneuf JSY 5.00 12.00
17 Alex Tanguay JSY 3.00 8.00
18 Miikka Kiprusoff JSY 4.00 10.00
19 Eric Staal JSY 4.00 10.00
20 Cam Ward JSY 4.00 10.00
21 Rod Brind'Amour JSY 3.00 8.00
22 Tuomo Ruutu JSY 2.00 5.00
23 Nikolai Khabibulin JSY 4.00 10.00
24 Martin Havlat JSY 3.00 8.00
25 Joe Sakic JSY 8.00 20.00
26 Jose Theodore JSY 4.00 10.00
27 Milan Hejduk JSY 2.00 5.00
28 Marek Svatos JSY 2.00 5.00
29 Rick Nash JSY 4.00 10.00
30 Sergei Federov JSY 4.00 10.00
31 Pascal LeClaire JSY 3.00 8.00
32 Nikolai Zherdev JSY 2.00 5.00
33 Mike Modano JSY 4.00 10.00
34 Eric Lindros JSY 4.00 10.00
35 Marty Turco JSY 3.00 8.00
36 Pavel Datsyuk JSY 3.00 8.00
37 Dominik Hasek JSY 6.00 15.00
38 Nicklas Lidstrom JSY 4.00 10.00
39 Henrik Zetterberg JSY 4.00 10.00
40 Ryan Smyth JSY 3.00 8.00
41 Ales Hemsky JSY 2.00 5.00
42 Dwayne Roloson JSY 4.00 10.00
43 Ed Belfour JSY 4.00 10.00
44 Todd Bertuzzi JSY 3.00 8.00
45 Olli Jokinen JSY 2.00 5.00
46 Rob Blake JSY 3.00 8.00
47 Alexander Frolov JSY 2.00 5
48 Marian Gaborik JSY 5.00 12
49 Manny Fernandez JSY 3.00 8
50 Pavol Demitra JSY 2.00 5
51 Saku Koivu JSY 4.00 10
52 Cristobal Huet JSY 5.00 12
53 Michael Ryder JSY 3.00 8
54 David Aebischer JSY 3.00 8
55 Paul Kariya JSY 4.00 10
56 Tomas Vokoun JSY 3.00 8
57 Martin Brodeur JSY 12.00 30
58 Patrik Elias JSY 2.00 5
59 Brian Gionta JSY 2.00 5
60 Rick DiPietro JSY 3.00 8
61 Alexei Yashin JSY 2.00 5
62 Miroslav Satan JSY 2.00 5
63 Jaromir Jagr JSY 6.00 15
64 Brendan Shanahan JSY 4.00 10
65 Henrik Lundqvist JSY 5.00 12
66 Daniel Alfredsson JSY 3.00 8
67 Jason Spezza JSY 4.00 10
68 Dany Heatley JSY 5.00 12
69 Martin Gerber JSY 4.00 10
70 Peter Forsberg JSY 6.00 15
71 Simon Gagne JSY 4.00 10
72 Joni Pitkanen JSY 2.00 5
73 Antero Niittymaki JSY 3.00 8
74 Shane Doan JSY 2.00 5
75 Jeremy Roenick JSY 5.00 12
76 Curtis Joseph JSY 4.00 10
77 Sidney Crosby JSY 20.00 50
79 Mark Recchi JSY 2.00 5
80 Doug Weight JSY 2.00 5
81 Manny Legace JSY 3.00 8
82 Keith Tkachuk JSY 3.00 8
83 Joe Thornton JSY 6.00 15
84 Jonathan Cheechoo JSY 4.00 10
85 Patrick Marleau JSY 3.00 8
86 Evgeni Nabokov JSY 3.00 8
87 Vincent Lecavalier JSY 4.00 10
88 Brad Richards JSY 3.00 8
89 Martin St. Louis JSY 3.00 8
90 Mats Sundin JSY 4.00 10
91 Andrew Raycroft JSY 3.00 8
92 Alexander Steen JSY 3.00 8
93 Darcy Tucker JSY 2.00 5
94 Roberto Luongo JSY 5.00 12
95 Markus Naslund JSY 4.00 10
96 Daniel Sedin JSY 2.00 5
97 Henrik Sedin JSY 2.00 5
98 Alexander Ovechkin JSY 15.00 40
99 Olaf Kolzig JSY 4.00 10
101 Ryan Shannon JSY AU
102 Shane O'Brien JSY AU
103 Yan Stastny JSY AU
104 Mark Stuart JSY AU
105 Drew Stafford JSY AU
106 Dustin Boyd JSY AU
107 Dustin Byfuglien JSY AU
108 Paul Stastny JSY AU
109 Fredrik Norrena JSY AU
110 Filip Novak JSY AU
111 Loui Eriksson JSY AU
112 Tomas Kopecky JSY AU
113 Marc-Antoine Pouliot JSY AU
114 Ladislav Smid JSY AU
115 Patrick Thoresen JSY AU
116 Patrick O'Sullivan JSY AU
117 Anze Kopitar JSY AU
118 Konstantin Pushkaryov JSY AU
119 Guillaume Latendresse JSY AU
120 Shea Weber JSY AU
121 Alexander Radulov JSY AU
122 Travis Zajac JSY AU
123 Jarkko Immonen JSY AU
124 Nigel Dawes JSY AU
125 Ryan Potulny JSY AU
126 Benoit Pouliot JSY AU
127 Keith Yandle JSY AU
128 Noah Welch JSY AU
129 Kristopher Letang JSY AU
130 Michel Ouellet JSY AU
131 Matt Carle JSY AU
132 Marc-Edouard Vlasic JSY AU
133 Marek Schwarz JSY AU
134 Roman Polak JSY AU
135 Ben Ondrus JSY AU
136 Brendan Bell JSY AU
137 Ian White JSY AU
138 Jeremy Williams JSY AU
139 Eric Fehr JSY AU
140 Jordan Staal JSY AU
141 Phil Kessel JSY AU
142 Evgeni Malkin JSY AU
143 David McKee 4.00 10
144 Mike Brown AU 5.00 12
145 Matt Lashoff AU 6.00 15
146 Nate Thompson AU 5.00 12
147 Mike Card AU 5.00 12
148 Adam Dennis AU 6.00 15
149 Michael Funk 2.50 6
150 Michael Ryan 2.50 6
151 Brandon Prust AU 5.00 12
152 Adam Burish AU 5.00 12
153 Michael Blunden AU 5.00 12
154 Dave Bolland AU 5.00 12
155 Stefan Liv 4.00 10
157 Jan Hejda 2.50 6
158 Jeff Drouin-Deslauriers AU 5.00 12
159 Drew Larman AU 5.00 12
160 Janis Sprukts AU 5.00 12
161 David Booth 2.50 6.
162 Peter Harrold 2.50 6.
163 Shawn Belle 2.50 6.
164 Niklas Backstrom 5.00 12.
165 Miroslav Kopriva 2.50 6.
166 Mikko Lehtonen 2.50 6.
167 John Oduya 2.50 6.
168 Alex Brooks AU 5.00 12.
169 Kelly Guard AU 5.00 12.
170 Martin Houle 2.50 6.
171 Jussi Timonen 2.50 6.
172 Lars Jonsson 2.50 6.
173 Triston Grant 2.50 6.
174 Bill Thomas 2.50 6.
175 Patrick Fischer 2.50 6.
176 Joe Pavelski 5.00 12.
177 D.J. King 2.50 6.
178 Blair Jones 2.50 6.
179 Jean-Francois Racine AU 5.00 12.
180 Nathan McIver AU 5.00 12.

31 Alexander Edler AU 5.00 12.00
32 Luc Bourdon 5.00 12.00
33 Patrick Coulombe 2.50 6.00
34 Jesse Schultz 2.50 6.00

2006-07 Hot Prospects White Hot

PRINT RUN 10 #'d SETS (1-99, 143-184)
PRINT RUN 1/1 (101-142)
NOT PRICED DUE TO SCARCITY

2006-07 Hot Prospects Hot Materials

ODDS 1:8
MAE David Aebischer 2.50 6.00
MAK Anze Kopitar 4.00 10.00
MAO Alexander Ovechkin SP 8.00 20.00
MAS Alexander Steen SP 3.00 8.00
MBB Brandon Bochenski 2.00 5.00
MBE Brendan Bell 2.00 5.00
MBM Brenden Morrow 2.50 6.00
MBO Ben Ondrus 2.00 5.00
MBR Brad Boyes 2.00 5.00
MBS Brendan Shanahan 3.00 8.00
MBT Billy Thompson 1.50 4.00
MCD Chris Drury 2.00 5.00
MCJ Curtis Joseph 3.00 8.00
MCP Corey Perry 2.50 6.00
MCS Curtis Sanford 2.50 6.00
MCW Cam Ward 3.00 8.00
MDA Daniel Alfredsson 2.50 6.00
MDH Dominik Hasek SP 5.00 12.00
MDP Dion Phaneuf 4.00 10.00
MDS Drew Stafford 4.00 10.00
MEB Ed Belfour 3.00 8.00
MEF Eric Fehr 2.50 6.00
MEM Evgeni Malkin 8.00 20.00
MES Eric Staal 3.00 8.00
MGL Guillaume Latendresse 4.00 10.00
MGM Glen Murray 2.00 5.00
MGR Gary Roberts 2.00 5.00
MHA Martin Havlat 2.50 6.00
MHE Dany Heatley SP 4.00 10.00
MHJ Milan Hejduk 2.00 5.00
MHS Henrik Sedin 2.00 5.00
MHT Hannu Toivonen 2.50 6.00
MIG Jarome Iginla 4.00 10.00
MIK Ilya Kovalchuk 4.00 10.00
MIW Ian White 2.00 5.00
MJB Jay Bouwmeester 2.00 5.00
MJC Jeff Carter 3.00 8.00
MJD J.P. Dumont 2.00 5.00
MJI Jarkko Immonen 1.50 4.00
MJJ Jaromir Jagr 5.00 12.00
MJL Jere Lehtinen 2.00 5.00
MJP Joni Pitkanen 2.00 5.00
MJS Jarret Stoll 2.00 5.00
MJT Joe Thornton 5.00 12.00
MKL Kristopher Letang 2.50 6.00
MKP Konstantin Pushkaryov 2.00 5.00
MKY Keith Yandle 2.00 5.00
MLB Luc Bourdon 2.50 6.00
MLE Loui Eriksson 2.00 5.00
MLS Ladislav Smid 2.00 5.00
MLU Joffrey Lupul 2.00 5.00
MMB Martin Brodeur 8.00 20.00
MMC Matt Carle 2.50 6.00
MMG Marian Gaborik 4.00 10.00
MMH Marian Hossa 2.50 6.00
MMI Mike Grier 2.00 5.00
MML Mario Lemieux 10.00 25.00
MMM Mike Modano 3.00 8.00
MMN Markus Naslund 3.00 8.00
MMP Marc-Antoine Pouliot 2.50 6.00
MMR Mark Recchi 2.00 5.00
MMS Mark Stuart 2.00 5.00
MMV Marc-Edouard Vlasic 2.00 5.00
MND Nigel Dawes 2.00 5.00
MNL Nicklas Lidstrom 3.00 8.00
MNW Noah Welch 2.00 5.00
MOK Olaf Kolzig 3.00 8.00
MOS Patrick O'Sullivan 2.00 5.00
MPA Patrick Thoresen 2.50 6.00
MPB Patrice Bergeron 3.00 8.00
MPE Michael Peca 2.00 5.00
MPF Peter Forsberg 4.00 10.00
MPK Phil Kessel 4.00 10.00
MPM Patrick Marleau 2.50 6.00
MPR Patrick Roy 10.00 25.00
MPS Paul Stastny 3.00 8.00
MPT Pierre Turgeon 2.00 5.00
MRE Robert Esche 2.50 6.00
MRI Brad Richards 2.50 6.00
MRL Roberto Luongo 4.00 10.00
MRN Rick Nash 3.00 8.00
MRY Michael Ryder 2.50 6.00
MSA Joe Sakic 5.00 12.00
MSC Sidney Crosby SP 20.00 50.00
MSD Shane Doan 2.00 5.00
MSK Saku Koivu 3.00 8.00
MSO Shane O'Brien 2.00 5.00
MSP Jason Spezza 3.00 8.00
MSS Sergei Samsonov 2.50 6.00
MST Jordan Staal 10.00 25.00
MSU Mats Sundin 3.00 8.00
MSW Shea Weber 2.50 6.00
MTH Tomas Holmstrom 2.00 5.00
MTP Tom Poti 2.00 5.00
MTS Teemu Selanne 3.00 8.00
MTT Tim Thomas 2.50 6.00
MTV Tomas Vokoun 2.50 6.00
MTZ Travis Zajac 3.00 8.00
MZC Zdeno Chara 2.00 5.00

2006-07 Hot Prospects Hot Materials Red Hot

RED HOT: .6X TO 1.5X HOT MATERIALS
PRINT RUN 100 #'d SETS

2006-07 Hot Prospects Hot Materials White Hot

PRINT RUN 10 #'d SETS
NOT PRICED DUE TO SCARCITY

2006-07 Hot Prospects Hotagraphs

1 HOT PACK PER 180 PACKS
5 HOTAGRAPHS PER HOT PACK
HAF Alexander Frolov 4.00 10.00
HAK Anze Kopitar 15.00 40.00
HAR Andrew Raycroft 6.00 15.00
HBB Brendan Bell 3.00 8.00
HBE Patrice Bergeron 8.00 20.00
HBI Martin Biron 6.00 15.00
HBM Brenden Morrow 6.00 15.00
HBO Ben Ondrus 3.00 8.00
HBP Benoit Pouliot 6.00 15.00
HBR Brad Boyes 3.00 8.00
HBT Barry Tallackson 3.00 8.00
HCA Mike Cammalleri 3.00 8.00
HCH Chris Higgins 5.00 12.00
HCK Chris Kunitz 3.00 8.00
HCP Chris Phillips 3.00 8.00
HDA David Aebischer 6.00 15.00
HDK Duncan Keith 3.00 8.00
HDL David Leneveu 6.00 15.00
HDR Dwayne Roloson 8.00 20.00
HEF Eric Fehr 6.00 15.00
HEM Evgeni Malkin 75.00 150.00
HES Eric Staal 8.00 20.00
HFL Marc-Andre Fleury 10.00 25.00
HFN Filip Novak 3.00 8.00
HFP Fernando Pisani 3.00 8.00
HGB Gilbert Brule 8.00 20.00
HGL Guillaume Latendresse 20.00 50.00
HHA Martin Havlat 6.00 15.00
HHO Tomas Holmstrom 3.00 8.00
HHU Cristobal Huet 10.00 25.00
HIG Jarome Iginla 15.00 40.00
HIK Ilya Kovalchuk 10.00 25.00
HIW Ian White 3.00 8.00
HJB Jaroslav Balastik 3.00 8.00
HJC Jeff Carter 8.00 20.00
HJI Jarkko Immonen 4.00 10.00
HJL John-Michael Liles 3.00 8.00
HJO Jonathan Cheechoo 8.00 20.00
HJP Joni Pitkanen 3.00 8.00
HJS Jarret Stoll 3.00 8.00
HJT Joe Thornton 15.00 40.00
HJW Jeremy Williams 4.00 10.00
HKB Keith Ballard 3.00 8.00
HKC Kyle Calder 3.00 8.00
HKE Kevin Bieksa 3.00 8.00
HKL Kari Lehtonen 8.00 20.00
HKO Chuck Kobasew 3.00 8.00
HLE Loui Eriksson 3.00 8.00
HLN Ladislav Nagy 3.00 8.00
HLS Ladislav Smid 3.00 8.00
HMA Mark Stuart 3.00 8.00
HMB Martin Brodeur 30.00 80.00
HMC Matt Carle 6.00 15.00
HMF Matt Foy 4.00 10.00
HMH Marcel Hossa 4.00 10.00
HMI Michal Handzus 3.00 8.00
HML Mario Lemieux SP
HMM Masi Marjamaki 3.00 8.00
HMO Michel Ouellet 8.00 20.00
HMP Marc-Antoine Pouliot 6.00 15.00
HMR Michael Ryder 6.00 15.00
HMS Marek Svatos 3.00 8.00
HMV Mike Van Ryn 3.00 8.00
HND Nigel Dawes 3.00 8.00
HNW Noah Welch 3.00 8.00
HNZ Nikolai Zherdev 3.00 8.00
HOT Ole-Kristian Tollefsen 3.00 8.00
HPA Patrik Elias 3.00 8.00
HPB Pierre-Marc Bouchard 3.00 8.00
HPE Michael Peca 3.00 8.00
HPK Phil Kessel 12.00 30.00
HPM Paul Mara 3.00 8.00
HPO Patrick O'Sullivan 6.00 15.00
HPP Petr Prucha 4.00 10.00
HPR Paul Ranger 3.00 8.00
HPS Paul Stastny 15.00 40.00
HRA Alexander Radulov 15.00 40.00
HRB Keith Yandle 3.00 8.00
HRE Robert Esche 6.00 15.00
HRK Rostislav Klesla 3.00 8.00
HRL Roberto Luongo 12.00 30.00
HRM Ryan Malone 3.00 8.00
HRP Roman Polak 3.00 8.00
HRS Ryan Shannon 3.00 8.00
HRY Ryan Potulny 6.00 15.00
HSC Sidney Crosby 100.00 200.00
HSG Scott Gomez 3.00 8.00
HSO Shane O'Brien 3.00 8.00
HST Jordan Staal 40.00 100.00
HSW Shea Weber 6.00 15.00
HTH Trent Hunter 3.00 8.00
HTK Tomas Kopecky 6.00 15.00
HTZ Travis Zajac 8.00 20.00
HVF Valtteri Filppula 6.00 15.00
HVL Vincent Lecavalier 10.00 25.00
HYS Yan Stastny 3.00 8.00
HZC Zdeno Chara 4.00 10.00

1995-96 Hoyle Eastern Playing Cards

COMPLETE SET (54) 8.00 20.00
1 Eric Lindros .20 .50
2 Peter Bondra .20 .50
3 Radek Bonk .10 .25
4 Ray Bourque .40 1.00
5 Brian Bradley .10 .25
6 Rod Brind'Amour .20 .50
7 Martin Brodeur .75 2.00
8 Wendel Clark .40 1.00
9 Alexandre Daigle .10 .25
10 Vincent Damphousse .10 .25
11 Ray Ferraro .10 .25
12 Stephane Fiset .20 .50
13 Peter Forsberg .60 1.50
14 Joe Sakic .75 2.00
15 Mikael Renberg .10 .25
16 Stephane Richer .10 .25
17 Mike Richter .40 1.00
18 Luc Robitaille .40 1.00
19 Geoff Sanderson .10 .25
20 Bryan Smolinski .10 .25
21 Kevin Stevens .10 .25
22 Scott Stevens .10 .25
23 Steve Thomas .10 .25
24 Darren Turcotte .10 .25
25 John Vanbiesbrouck .20 .50
26 New Jersey Devils Cup Winners .10
.25
27 Patrick Roy 1.25 3.00
28 Chris Gratton .10 .25
29 Adam Graves .10 .25
30 Dominik Hasek .60 1.50
31 Ron Hextall .40 1.00
32 Jaromir Jagr .60 1.50
33 Joe Juneau .10 .25
34 Dimitri Khristich .10 .25
35 Petr Klima .10 .25
36 Bob Kudelski .10 .25
37 Scott Lachance .10 .25
38 Pat Lafontaine .10 .25
39 John Leclair .10 .25
40 Mark Messier .40 1.00
41 Brian Leetch .20 .50
42 Alexander Mogilny .20 .50
43 Kirk Muller .10 .25
44 Cam Neely .40 1.00
45 Rob Niedermayer .10 .25
46 Scott Niedermayer .20 .50
47 Owen Nolan .10 .25
48 Adam Oates .10 .25
49 Michal Pivonka .10 .25
50 Derek Plante .10 .25
51 Chris Pronger .20 .50
52 Mark Recchi .20 .50
53 Sergei Zubov .10 .25
54 Alexei Yashin .10 .25

1995-96 Hoyle Western Playing Cards

COMPLETE SET (54) 8.00 20.00
1 Jeremy Roenick .40 1.00
2 Dave Andreychuk .10 .25
3 Jason Arnott .10 .25
4 Ed Belfour .40 1.00
5 Rob Blake .20 .50
6 Jeff Brown .10 .25
7 Patrick Carnback .10 .25
8 Chris Chelios .30 .75
9 Tim Cheveldae .20 .50
10 Paul Coffey .30 .75
11 Shayne Corson .10 .25
12 Geoff Courtnall .10 .25
13 Russ Courtnall .10 .25
14 Wayne Gretzky 2.00 5.00
15 Joe Sacco .10 .25
16 Denis Savard .20 .50
17 Teemu Selanne .40 1.00
18 Brendan Shanahan .40 1.00
19 Ray Sheppard .10 .25
20 Mats Sundin .40 1.00
21 Esa Tikkanen .10 .25
22 German Titov .10 .25
23 Keith Tkachuk .20 .50
24 Rick Tocchet .10 .25
25 Doug Weight .10 .25
26 Detroit Red Wings Team Photo .10
.25
27 Sergei Fedorov .40 1.00
28 Ulf Dahlen .10 .25
29 Pat Falloon .10 .25
30 Theoren Fleury .20 .50
31 Doug Gilmour .40 1.00
32 Todd Harvey .10 .25
33 Kevin Hatcher .10 .25
34 Guy Hebert .20 .50
35 Phil Housley .10 .25
36 Brett Hull .60 1.50
37 Arturs Irbe .20 .50
38 Curtis Joseph .40 1.00
39 Paul Kariya .40 1.00
40 Pavel Bure .30 .75
41 Jari Kurri .30 .75
42 Igor Larionov .10 .25
43 Nicklas Lidstrom .20 .50
44 Trevor Linden .40 1.00
45 Marty McSorley .10 .25
46 Mike Modano .40 1.00
47 Bernie Nicholls .10 .25
48 Joe Nieuwendyk .20 .50
49 David Oliver .10 .25
50 Felix Potvin .40 1.00
51 Bill Ranford .20 .50
52 Gary Roberts .10 .25
53 Steve Yzerman 1.25 3.00
54 Alexei Zhamnov .10 .25

1975-76 Houston Aeros WHA

Little was known about this rare WHA issue. The checklist was confirmed and as the cards are unnumbered, they are listed below in alphabetical order. Any additional information can be forwarded to hockeymag@beckett.com.

COMPLETE SET (19) 40.00 80.00
1 Ron Grahame 2.00 4.00
2 Larry Hale 1.00 2.00
3 Murray Hall 1.50 3.00
4 Gordie Howe 15.00 30.00
5 Mark Howe 5.00 10.00
6 Marty Howe 4.00 8.00
7 Andre Hinse 1.00 2.00
8 Frank Hughes 1.00 2.00
9 Glen Irwin 1.00 2.00
10 Gord Labossiere 1.50 3.00
11 Don Larway 1.00 2.00
12 Larry Lund 1.50 3.00
13 Paul Popeil 1.50 3.00
14 Rich Preston 1.50 3.00
15 Terry Ruskowski 1.50 3.00
16 Wayne Rutledge 2.00 4.00
17 John Schella 1.00 2.00
18 Ted Taylor 1.00 2.00
19 John Tonelli 5.00 10.00

1992-93 Humpty Dumpty I

This 26-card set was sponsored by Humpty Dumpty Foods Ltd., a snack food company located in Eastern Canada and owned by Borden Inc. This promotion consisted of one cello-wrapped (approximately) 1 7/16" by 1 15/16" mini-hockey card, which was inserted into specially marked bags of Humpty Dumpty Chips and Snacks. Two series of cards were produced, and complete sets could be obtained only by collecting the cards through the promotion. The promotion lasted from October 1992 to March 1993. A total of 11,000,000 series I cards were produced, or 423,077 of each card, and they were evenly distributed between Ontario, Quebec, and the Atlantic provinces. The fronts displayed glossy color action photos, with the team logo superimposed toward the bottom of the picture. On a white panel framed by gray, the back presented 1991-92 season statistics and biography in French and English. The cards were unnumbered and checklisted below in alphabetical order.

COMPLETE SET (26) 8.00 20.00
1 Ray Bourque .40 1.00
2 Rod Brind'Amour .20 .50
3 Chris Chelios .30 .75
4 Wendel Clark .20 .50
5 Gilbert Dionne .10 .25
6 Pat Falloon .16 .40
7 Ray Ferraro .16 .40
8 Theo Fleury .30 .75
9 Grant Fuhr .20 .50
10 Wayne Gretzky 2.00 5.00
11 Kevin Hatcher .10 .25
12 Valeri Kamensky .20 .50
13 Mike Keane .10 .25
14 Brian Leetch .30 .75
15 Kirk McLean .20 .50
16 Alexander Mogilny .24 .60
17 Troy Murray .10 .25
18 Patrick Roy 1.60 4.00
19 Joe Sakic .60 1.50
20 Brendan Shanahan .60 1.50
21 Kevin Stevens .16 .40
22 Scott Stevens .20 .50
23 Mark Tinordi .10 .25
24 Steve Yzerman 1.00 2.50
25 Zarley Zalapski .10 .25
26 Checklist .20 .50

1992-93 Humpty Dumpty II

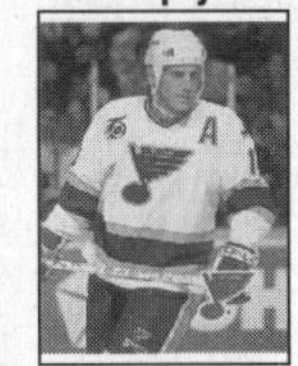

This 26-card set was sponsored by Humpty Dumpty Foods Ltd., a snack food company located in Eastern Canada and owned by Borden Inc. This promotion consisted of one cello-wrapped approximately 1 7/16" by 1 15/16" mini-hockey card randomly inserted into specially marked bags of Humpty Dumpty Chips and Snacks. Two series of cards were produced, and complete sets could be obtained only by collecting the cards through the promotion. The promotion lasted from October 1992 to March 1993. A total of 18,000,000 series II cards were produced, or 692,307 of each card, and they were evenly distributed between Ontario, Quebec, and the Atlantic provinces. The fronts displayed glossy color action photos, with the team logo superimposed toward the bottom of the picture. On a white panel framed by beige, the back presented 1991-92 season statistics and biography in French and English. The cards were unnumbered and checklisted below in alphabetical order.

COMPLETE SET (26) 8.00 20.00
1 Drake Berehowsky .10 .25
2 Shayne Corson .16 .40
3 Russ Courtnall .16 .40
4 Dave Ellett .10 .25
5 Sergei Fedorov .60 1.50
6 Dave Gagner .16 .40
7 Doug Gilmour .30 .75
8 Phil Housley .16 .40
9 Brett Hull .40 1.00
10 Jaromir Jagr 1.00 2.50
11 Pat LaFontaine .20 .50
12 Mario Lemieux 1.60 4.00
13 Trevor Linden .16 .40
14 Al MacInnis .20 .50
15 Mark Messier .40 1.00
16 Cam Neely .30 .75
17 Owen Nolan .20 .50
18 Bill Ranford .20 .50
19 Luc Robitaille .24 .60
20 Jeremy Roenick .30 .75
21 Mats Sundin .30 .75
22 Chris Terreri .16 .40
23 Steve Thomas .16 .40
24 Pat Verbeek .16 .40
25 Neil Wilkinson .10 .25
26 Checklist .20 .50

1997-98 Hurricanes Team Issue

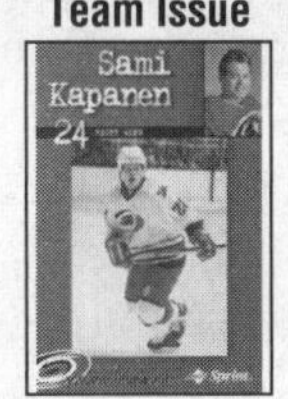

The set was issued by the team as a promotional giveaway. The cards were unnumbered and checklisted below in alphabetical order.

COMPLETE SET (28) 4.80 12.00
1 Jeff Brown .10 .25
2 Sean Burke .40 1.00
3 Adam Burt .10 .25
4 Steve Chiasson .10 .25
5 Enrico Ciccone .10 .25
6 Kevin Dineen .12 .30
7 Nelson Emerson .12 .30
8 Martin Gelinas .12 .30
9 Stu Grimson .12 .30
10 Steve Halko .10 .25
11 Kevin Haller .10 .25
12 Sean Hill .10 .25
13 Sami Kapanen 1.20 3.00
14 Trevor Kidd .40 1.00
15 Robert Kron .12 .30
16 Steve Leach .12 .30
17 Curtis Leschyshyn .10 .25
18 Kent Manderville .10 .25
19 Jeff O'Neill .10 .25
20 Nolan Pratt .10 .25
21 Keith Primeau .60 1.50
22 Paul Ranheim .10 .25
23 Steven Rice .12 .30
24 Gary Roberts .12 .30
25 Geoff Sanderson .20 .50
26 Glen Wesley .12 .30
27 Paul Maurice .08 .20
Tom Webster
Randy Ladouceur CO
28 Stormy the Mascot .04 .10

1998-99 Hurricanes Team Issue

This set featured the Hurricanes of the NHL. The postcard-sized singles were issued at autograph signings and other promotional ventures. Other singles may exist as well; information on these can be forwarded to hockeymag@beckett.com.

COMPLETE SET (25) 12.00 30.00
1 Arturs Irbe 1.20 2.00
2 Glen Wesley .40 1.00
3 Steve Chiasson .40 1.00
4 Nolan Pratt .40 1.00
5 Marek Malik .40 1.00
6 Adam Burt .40 1.00
7 Curtis Leschyshyn .40 1.00
8 Gary Roberts .40 1.00
9 Kevin Dineen .40 1.00
10 Bates Battaglia .40 1.50
11 Steven Halko .40 1.00
12 Byron Ritchie .40 1.00
13 Ron Francis 1.20 3.00
14 Sean Hill .40 1.00
15 Martin Gelinas .40 1.00
16 Sami Kapanen .80 2.00
17 Ray Sheppard .40 1.00
18 Paul Ranheim .40 1.00
19 Dave Karpa .40 1.00
20 Trevor Kidd .80 1.50
21 Kent Manderville .40 1.00
22 Mike Rucinski .40 1.00
23 Keith Primeau .80 1.50
24 Jeff O'Neill .80 2.00
25 Stormy MASCOT .10 .25

2002-03 Hurricanes Postcards

These 3X5 blank backed cards feature a photo, stats and player ID on the front. They were issued as promotional items at team events. The checklist is not complete -- if you can confirm others, please write us at hockeymag@beckett.com.

COMPLETE SET (?)
1 Rod Brind'Amour 1.50
2 Erik Cole 1.50
3 Ron Francis 1.50
4 Arturs Irbe 2.00
5 Jeff O'Neill 1.00
6 Kevin Weekes 1.50
7 Glen Wesley 1.00

2003-04 Hurricanes Postcards

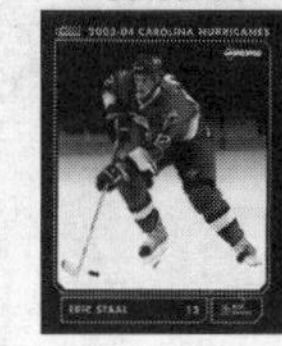

These oversized cards were issued by the team and sponsored by Pepsi.

COMPLETE SET (24) 10.00 25.00
1 Craig Adams .30 .75
2 Kevyn Adams .30 .75
3 Ryan Bayda .30 .75
4 Bob Boughner .30 .75
5 Jesse Boulerice .30 .75
6 Pavel Brendl .30 .75
7 Rod Brind'Amour .60 1.50
8 Erik Cole .40 1.00
9 Ron Francis .60 1.50
10 Bret Hedican .30 .75
11 Sean Hill .30 .75
12 Kevin McCarthy .30 .75
13 Marty Murray .30 .75
14 Jeff O'Neill .40 1.00
15 Eric Staal 2.00 5.00
16 Bruno St. Jacques .30 .75
17 Jamie Storr .40 1.00
18 Jaroslav Svoboda .30 .75
19 Josef Vasicek .30 .75
20 Radim Vrbata .30 .75
21 Niclas Wallin .30 .75
22 Aaron Ward .30 .75
23 Kevin Weekes .40 1.00
24 Glen Wesley .30 .75

2006-07 Hurricanes Postcards

COMPLETE SET (28) 15.00 25.00
1 Logo Card .10 .25
2 Craig Adams .40 1.00
3 Kevyn Adams .40 1.00
4 Anton Babchuk .40 1.00
5 Eric Belanger .40 1.00
6 Rod Brind'Amour .75 2.00
7 Erik Cole 1.00 2.50
8 Mike Commodore .40 1.00
9 Jeff Daniels ACO .10 .25
10 Tim Gleason .40 1.00
11 John Grahame .60 1.50
12 Bret Hedican .40 1.00
13 Andrew Hutchinson .40 1.00
14 Frantisek Kaberle .40 1.00
15 Andrew Ladd .40 1.00
16 Chad Larose .40 1.00
17 Peter Laviolette CO .20 .50
18 Trevor Letowski .40 1.00
19 Kevin McCarthy ACO .10 .25
20 Eric Staal 1.25 3.00
21 Cory Stillman .40 1.00
22 David Tanabe .40 1.00
23 Scott Walker .40 1.00
24 Niclas Wallin .40 1.00
25 Cam Ward .75 2.00
26 Glen Wesley .40 1.00
27 Ray Whitney .40 1.00
28 Justin Williams .75 2.00

1995-96 Imperial Stickers

This set of 136 stickers was released in five-sticker packs (plus one stick of tasty gum!) late in the 1995-96 season. The stickers measured the standard size and featured color player photos and name on the front, and playing information on the back. Collation of this product was extremely poor, making set building somewhat arduous.

COMPLETE SET (136) 14.00 35.00
1 Ducks Logo .20 .50
2 Paul Kariya .80 2.00
3 Chad Kilger .20 .50
4 Oleg Tverdovsky .20 .50
5 Bruins Logo .20 .50
6 Ray Bourque .60 1.50
7 Cam Neely .24 .60
8 Adam Oates .20 .50
9 Kevin Stevens .20 .50
10 Sabres Logo .20 .50
11 Pat LaFontaine .24 .60
12 Dominik Hasek .40 1.00
13 Alexei Zhitnik .02 .05
14 Flames Logo .20 .50
15 Theo Fleury .20 .50
16 Phil Housley .20 .50
17 Trevor Kidd .20 .50
18 Joe Nieuwendyk .20 .50
19 Zarley Zalapski .02 .05
20 Blackhawks Logo .20 .50
21 Jeremy Roenick .20 .50
22 Chris Chelios .20 .50
23 Ed Belfour .24 .60
24 Joe Murphy .20 .50
25 Patrick Poulin .02 .05
26 Avalanche Logo .20 .50
27 Joe Sakic .60 1.50
28 Peter Forsberg .60 1.50
29 Sandis Ozolinsh .20 .50
30 Mike Ricci .04 .10
31 Valeri Kamensky .20 .50
32 Stars Logo .20 .50
33 Mike Modano .30 .75
34 Kevin Hatcher .02 .05
35 Andy Moog .20 .50
36 Red Wings Logo .20 .50
37 Steve Yzerman 1.20 3.00
38 Sergei Fedorov .40 1.00
39 Paul Coffey .20 .50
40 Keith Primeau .04 .10
41 Nicklas Lidstrom .24 .60
42 Oilers Logo .20 .50
43 Doug Weight .20 .50
44 Jason Arnott .20 .50
45 Bill Ranford .20 .50
46 Panthers Logo .20 .50
47 John Vanbiesbrouck .20 .50
48 Stu Barnes .20 .50
49 Scott Mellanby .04 .10
50 Rob Niedermayer .20 .50
51 Whalers Logo .20 .50
52 Brendan Shanahan .40 1.00
53 Geoff Sanderson .20 .50
54 Sean Burke .04 .10
55 Jeff O'Neill .04 .10
56 Kings Logo .20 .50
57 Wayne Gretzky 2.00 5.00
58 Rob Blake .20 .50
59 Rick Tocchet .20 .50
60 Dimitri Khristich .02 .05
61 Kelly Hrudey .20 .50
62 Canadiens Logo .20 .50
63 Pierre Turgeon .20 .50
64 Mark Recchi .20 .50
65 Saku Koivu .20 .50
66 Patrick Roy 1.60 4.00
67 Vincent Damphousse .20 .50
68 Devils Logo .20 .50
69 Stephane Richer .02 .05
70 Martin Brodeur .60 1.50
71 Scott Niedermayer .20 .50
72 Scott Stevens .20 .50
73 Islander Logo .20 .50
74 Kirk Muller .04 .10
75 Mathieu Schneider .02 .05
76 Derek King .02 .05
77 Wendel Clark .02 .05
78 Ranger Logo .20 .50
79 Brian Leetch .20 .50
80 Mark Messier .30 .75
81 Alexei Kovalev .20 .50
82 Luc Robitaille .20 .50
83 Mike Richter .20 .50
84 Senators Logo .20 .50
85 Dan Quinn .02 .05
86 Alexandre Daigle .04 .10
87 Steve Duchesne .02 .05
88 Radek Bonk .04 .10
89 Flyers Logo .20 .50
90 Eric Lindros .80 2.00
91 Mikael Renberg .20 .50
92 John LeClair .40 1.00
93 Eric Desjardins .20 .50
94 Rod Brind'Amour .20 .50
95 Penguins Logo .20 .50
96 Jaromir Jagr .80 2.00
97 Mario Lemieux 1.60 4.00
98 Ron Francis .20 .50
99 Sergei Zubov .04 .10
100 Blues Logo .20 .50
101 Brett Hull .30 .75
102 Al MacInnis .20 .50
103 Dale Hawerchuk .20 .50
104 Chris Pronger .20 .50
105 Sharks Logo .20 .50
106 Craig Janney .04 .10
107 Pat Falloon .02 .05
108 Arturs Irbe .20 .50
109 Ulf Dahlen .02 .05
110 Owen Nolan .20 .50
111 Lightning Logo .20 .50
112 Roman Hamrlik .20 .50
113 Brian Bradley .20 .50
114 Chris Gratton .20 .50
115 Brian Bellows .02 .05
116 Maple Leafs Logo .20 .50
117 Doug Gilmour .20 .50
118 Mats Sundin .20 .50
119 Dave Andreychuk .20 .50
120 Felix Potvin .20 .50
121 Larry Murphy .20 .50
122 Canucks Logo .20 .50
123 Pavel Bure .60 1.50
124 Alexander Mogilny .20 .50
125 Trevor Linden .20 .50
126 Jeff Brown .02 .05
127 Kirk McLean .20 .50
128 Capitals Logo .20 .50
129 Joe Juneau .20 .50
130 Peter Bondra .20 .50
131 Jim Carey .20 .50
132 Calle Johansson .02 .05
133 Jets Logo .20 .50
134 Teemu Selanne .40 1.00
135 Alexei Zhamnov .20 .50
136 Keith Tkachuk .24 .60

1995-96 Imperial Stickers Die Cut Superstars

These die-cut stickers were randomly inserted in packs at indeterminate odds. They featured player images over a starburst background. Backs were blank.

COMPLETE SET (25) 12.00 30.00
1 Pierre Turgeon .20 .50
2 Patrick Roy 1.60 4.00
3 Pat LaFontaine .20 .50
4 Joe Sakic .60 1.50
5 Paul Coffey .30 .75
6 Ray Bourque .40 1.00
7 Brian Leetch .30 .75
8 Joe Juneau .16 .40
9 Jeremy Roenick .30 .75
10 Chris Chelios .30 .75
11 Brett Hull .40 1.00
12 Paul Kariya 1.20 3.00
13 Jason Arnott .16 .40
14 Pavel Bure .80 2.00

15 Steve Duchesne .20 .50
16 Martin Brodeur .80 2.00
17 Eric Lindros 1.00 2.50
18 Mikael Renberg .20 .50
19 Felix Potvin .24 .60
20 Roman Hamrlik .16 .40
21 Wayne Gretzky 2.00 5.00
22 Brendan Shanahan .60 1.50
23 Jaromir Jagr 1.00 2.50
24 Mario Lemieux 1.60 4.00
25 Steve Yzerman 1.00 2.50

1927 Imperial Tobacco

Card was black and white and measured approximately 1 1/2 x 2 1/2.
NNO Montreal Victorias 25.00 50.00

1929 Imperial Tobacco

Card is black and white and measured approximately 2 1/2 x 3.
NNO Ice Hockey 20.00 40.00

2003-04 ITG Action

ITG Action was the largest set of the year consisiting of 600 veteran cards found in packs and 74 update cards available via various redemptions. Cards 601-616 were available via redemption cards found in hobby boxes. Cards 617-624 were available only in factory sets and cards 625-674 were available via an online only purchase. Print runs for cards 601-624 are listed below.

COMP.SET w/o UPDATE (600) 75.00 150.00
1 Joe Thornton .50 1.25
2 Dany Heatley .40 1.00
3 Ales Kotalik .10 .25
4 Steve Montador .10 .25
5 Dan Bylsma .10 .25
6 Andrew Ference .10 .25
7 Andy Hilbert .10 .25
8 Andy McDonald .10 .25
9 Bob Boughner .10 .25
10 Brad Tapper .10 .25
11 Brian Campbell .10 .25
12 Brian Rolston .10 .25
13 Daniel Tjarnqvist .10 .25
14 Glen Murray .10 .25
15 Byron Dafoe .25 .60
16 Bryan Berard .10 .25
17 Alexei Zhitnik .10 .25
18 Craig Conroy .10 .25
19 Curtis Brown .10 .25
20 Dan McGillis .10 .25
21 Dan Snyder .10 .25
22 Daniel Briere .10 .25
23 Chris Clark .10 .25
24 Frantisek Kaberle .10 .25
25 Adam Oates .25 .60
26 Denis Gauthier .10 .25
27 Dimitri Kalinin .10 .25
28 Martin Lapointe .10 .25
29 Keith Carney .10 .25
30 Garnet Exelby .10 .25
31 Dean McAmmond .10 .25
32 Hal Gill .10 .25
33 Henrik Tallinder .10 .25
34 Ilya Kovalchuk .40 1.00
35 Ivan Huml .10 .25
36 J-P Dumont .10 .25
37 Alexei Smirnov .10 .25
38 Jarome Iginla .40 1.00
39 Jason Krog .10 .25
40 Jay McKee .10 .25
41 J-S Giguere .25 .60
42 Krzysztof Oliwa .10 .25
43 Jeff Odgers .10 .25
44 Jochen Hecht .10 .25
45 Joe DiPenta RC .30 .75
46 Adam Mair .10 .25
47 Jonathan Girard .10 .25
48 Jordan Leopold .10 .25
49 Andrew Raycroft .25 .60
50 Kamil Piros .10 .25
51 Eric Boulton .10 .25
52 Kurt Sauer .10 .25
53 Lubos Bartecko .10 .25
54 Marc Chouinard .10 .25
55 Marc Savard .10 .25
56 Martin Biron .25 .60
57 Martin Gelinas .10 .25
58 Martin Gerber .25 .60
59 Chuck Kobasew .10 .25
60 Martin Samuelsson .10 .25
61 Jamie McLennan .10 .25
62 Mika Noronen .10 .25
63 Mike Knuble .10 .25
64 Mike Leclerc .10 .25
65 Pasi Nurminen .25 .60
66 Miroslav Satan .10 .25
67 Nick Boynton .10 .25
68 Niclas Havelid .10 .25
69 Oleg Saprykin .10 .25
70 Milan Bartovic RC .30 .75
71 P.J. Stock .10 .25
72 Roman Turek .25 .60
73 Patrik Stefan .10 .25
74 Maxim Afinogenov .10 .25
75 Petr Sykora .10 .25
76 Rick Mrozik RC .10 .25
77 Rob Niedermayer .10 .25
78 Robyn Regehr .10 .25
79 P.J. Axelsson .10 .25
80 Ruslan Salei .10 .25
81 Ryan Miller .25 .60
82 Sandis Ozolinsh .10 .25
83 Blake Sloan .10 .25
84 Tim Connolly .10 .25
85 Shaone Morrisonn .10 .25
86 Shawn McEachern .10 .25
87 Shean Donovan .10 .25
88 Simon Gamache .10 .25
89 Stanislav Chistov .10 .25
90 Stephane Yelle .10 .25
91 Steve Rucchin .10 .25
92 Steve Shields .25 .60
93 Steve Thomas .10 .25
94 Taylor Pyatt .10 .25
95 Yannick Tremblay .10 .25
96 Toni Lydman .10 .25
97 Tony Hrkac .10 .25
98 Vitali Vishnevsky .10 .25
99 Slava Kozlov .10 .25
100 Sergei Samsonov .25 .60
101 Riku Hahl .10 .25
102 Tyler Wright .10 .25
103 Tyler Arnason .25 .60
104 Tomas Kurka .10 .25
105 Theo Fleury .10 .25
106 Stu Barnes .10 .25
107 Steve Sullivan .10 .25
108 Paul Kariya .30 .75
109 Steve Poapst .10 .25
110 Steve Ott .10 .25
111 Steve McCarthy .10 .25
112 Sergei Zubov .10 .25
113 Serge Aubin .10 .25
114 Niko Kapanen .10 .25
115 Pascal Leclaire .25 .60
116 Patrick Roy 1.50 4.00
117 Pavel Brendl .10 .25
118 Peter Forsberg .75 2.00
119 Philippe Boucher .10 .25
120 Radim Vrbata .10 .25
121 Ray Whitney .10 .25
122 Richard Matvichuk .10 .25
123 Rick Nash .40 1.00
124 Sami Helenius .10 .25
125 Rob Blake .25 .60
126 Rob DiMaio .10 .25
127 Rod Brind'Amour .25 .60
128 Chris McAllister .10 .25
129 Ron Tugnutt .25 .60
130 Rostislav Klesla .10 .25
131 Ryan Bayda .10 .25
132 Ryan VandenBussche .10 .25
133 Ron Francis .25 .60
134 Charlie Stephens .10 .25
135 Scott Young .10 .25
136 Sean Hill .10 .25
137 Sean Pronger .10 .25
138 Nathan Dempsey .10 .25
139 Jason Bacashihua .25 .60
140 Jason Strudwick .10 .25
141 Jeff O'Neill .10 .25
142 Jere Lehtinen .25 .60
143 Alexander Karpovtsev .10 .25
144 Jody Shelley .10 .25
145 Alex Tanguay .25 .60
146 John Erskine .10 .25
147 Jon Klemm .10 .25
148 Josef Vasicek .10 .25
149 Kent McDonell RC .30 .75
150 Kevyn Adams .10 .25
151 Kyle Calder .10 .25
152 Lasse Pirjeta .10 .25
153 Manny Malhotra .10 .25
154 Marc Denis .25 .60
155 Mark Bell .10 .25
156 Martin Skoula .10 .25
157 Marty Turco .25 .60
158 Matt Davidson .10 .25
159 Michael Leighton .25 .60
160 Kevin Weekes .25 .60
161 Luke Richardson .10 .25
162 Mike Keane .10 .25
163 Mike Modano .50 1.25
164 Scott Lachance .10 .25
165 Mike Zigomanis .10 .25
166 Milan Hejduk .30 .75
167 Jason Arnott .10 .25
168 Jaroslav Svoboda .10 .25
169 Jaroslav Spacek .10 .25
170 Aaron Ward .10 .25
171 Alexei Zhamnov .10 .25
172 Teemu Selanne .30 .75
173 Jan Hlavac .10 .25
174 Duvie Westcott .10 .25
175 Erik Cole .10 .25
176 Philippe Sauve .25 .60
177 Eric Daze .10 .25
178 Derrick Walser .10 .25
179 Aaron Downey .10 .25
180 Derek Morris .10 .25
181 David Vyborny .10 .25
182 Craig Andersson .10 .25
183 Patrick DesRochers .10 .25
184 David Aebischer .25 .60
185 Stephane Robidas .10 .25
186 Dan Hinote .10 .25
187 Craig Adams .10 .25
188 Burke Henry .10 .25
189 Bret Hedican .10 .25
190 Brenden Morrow .25 .60
191 Brad DeFauw .10 .25
192 Bill Guerin .25 .60
193 Bates Battaglia .10 .25
194 Andrew Cassels .10 .25
195 Adam Foote .10 .25
196 Geoff Sanderson .10 .25
197 Jocelyn Thibault .25 .60
198 Joe Sakic .60 1.50
199 Espen Knutsen .10 .25
200 Igor Radulov .10 .25
201 Jason Smith .10 .25
202 Dominik Hasek .60 1.50
203 Sean Avery .10 .25
204 Steve Staios .10 .25
205 Kirk Maltby .10 .25
206 Denis Shvidki .10 .25
207 Sergei Fedorov .50 1.25
208 Sergei Zholtok .10 .25
209 Shawn Horcoff .10 .25
210 Stephen Weiss .10 .25
211 Steve Yzerman 1.50 4.00
212 Brad Chartrand .10 .25
213 Brad Isbister .10 .25
214 Valeri Bure .10 .25
215 Brendan Shanahan .30 .75
216 Ryan Smyth .10 .25
217 Chris Chelios .30 .75
218 Cliff Ronning .10 .25
219 Curtis Joseph .30 .75
220 Darcy Hordichuk .10 .25
221 Darren McCarty .10 .25
222 Eric Brewer .10 .25
223 Derek Armstrong .10 .25
224 Dwayne Roloson .25 .60
225 Eric Belanger .10 .25
226 Brett Hull .40 1.00
227 Joe Corvo .10 .25
228 Ethan Moreau .10 .25
229 Felix Potvin .30 .75
230 Fernando Pisani .10 .25
231 Filip Kuba .10 .25
232 Georges Laraque .10 .25
233 Henrik Zetterberg .30 .75
234 Ian Laperriere .10 .25
235 Igor Larionov .10 .25
236 Mattias Norstrom .10 .25
237 Ivan Novoseltsev .10 .25
238 Jamie Storr .25 .60
239 Jani Hurme .25 .60
240 Jani Rita .10 .25
241 Willie Mitchell .10 .25
242 Jaroslav Bednar .10 .25
243 Jaroslav Modry .10 .25
244 Lubomir Sekeras .10 .25
245 Lubomir Visnovsky .10 .25
246 Manny Fernandez .25 .60
247 Jared Aulin .10 .25
248 Marcus Nilson .10 .25
249 Ales Hemsky .25 .60
250 Igor Ulanov .10 .25
251 Alexei Semenov .10 .25
252 Mathieu Schneider .10 .25
253 Matt Cullen .10 .25
254 Andrew Brunette .10 .25
255 Viktor Kozlov .10 .25
256 Mike Comrie .25 .60
257 Brad Bombardir .10 .25
258 Scott Ferguson .10 .25
259 Tomas Holmstrom .10 .25
260 Tomas Zizka .10 .25
261 Manny Legace .25 .60
262 Jon Sim .10 .25
263 Wes Walz .10 .25
264 Jay Bouwmeester .10 .25
265 Zigmund Palffy .25 .60
266 Andreas Lilja .10 .25
267 Pascal Dupuis .10 .25
268 Alexander Frolov .10 .25
269 Tommy Salo .25 .60
270 Antti Laaksonen .10 .25
271 Mike Cammalleri .10 .25
272 Bill Muckalt .10 .25
273 Mike York .10 .25
274 Nick Schultz .10 .25
275 Nicklas Lidstrom .30 .75
276 Andrei Zyuzin .10 .25
277 Adam Deadmarsh .10 .25
278 Olli Jokinen .25 .60
279 Pavel Datsyuk .30 .75
280 Jason Chimera .10 .25
281 Kristian Huselius .10 .25
282 Jarret Stoll .10 .25
283 Jason Allison .10 .25
284 Richard Park .10 .25
285 Marty Reasoner .10 .25
286 Mathieu Biron .25 .60
287 Jason Woolley .10 .25
288 Pavel Trnka .10 .25
289 Jim Dowd .10 .25
290 Kris Draper .10 .25
291 Peter Worrell .10 .25
292 P-M Bouchard .10 .25
293 Radek Dvorak .10 .25
294 Matt Johnson .10 .25
295 Aaron Miller .10 .25
296 Mathieu Dandenault .10 .25
297 Marian Gaborik .60 1.50
298 Roberto Luongo .40 1.00
299 Jason Williams .10 .25
300 Niklas Hagman .10 .25
301 Jamie Langenbrunner .10 .25
302 Greg Johnson .10 .25
303 Alexei Kovalev .25 .60
304 Ron Hainsey .10 .25
305 Ari Ahonen .10 .25
306 Mark Parrish .10 .25
307 Andrei Markov .10 .25
308 Jason York .10 .25
309 Jason Wiemer .10 .25
310 Mark Messier .30 .75
311 Joe Juneau .10 .25
312 Colin White .10 .25
313 Mike Dunham .25 .60
314 Brian Finley .25 .60
315 Jeff Friesen .10 .25
316 Boris Mironov .10 .25
317 Brian Rafalski .10 .25
318 Chad Kilger .10 .25
319 Arron Asham .10 .25
320 Corey Schwab .25 .60
321 Craig Rivet .10 .25
322 Dale Purinton .10 .25
323 John Madden .10 .25
324 Bill Houlder .10 .25
325 Denis Arkhipov .10 .25
326 Bobby Holik .10 .25
327 Jay Pandolfo .10 .25
328 Adam Hall .10 .25
329 Adrian Aucoin .10 .25
330 Michael Rupp .10 .25
331 Donald Audette .10 .25
332 Brian Gionta .10 .25
333 Jan Bulis .10 .25
334 Jamie Lundmark .10 .25
335 Jason Ward .10 .25
336 Anson Carter .25 .60
337 Grant Marshall .10 .25
338 Garth Snow .25 .60
339 Eric Lindros .30 .75
340 Dusan Salficky RC .30 .75
341 Darius Kasparaitis .10 .25
342 Patrik Elias .25 .60
343 David Legwand .25 .60
344 Brian Leetch .25 .60
345 Jason Blake .10 .25
346 Kimmo Timonen .10 .25
347 Dan Blackburn .25 .60
348 Jose Theodore .40 1.00
349 Justin Mapletoft .10 .25
350 Vernon Fiddler .10 .25
351 Ken Daneyko .10 .25
352 Martin Erat .10 .25
353 Janne Niinimaa .10 .25
354 Marcel Hossa .10 .25
355 Scott Niedermayer .10 .25
356 Petr Nedved .10 .25
357 Martin Brodeur .75 2.00
358 Rick DiPietro .25 .60
359 Mathieu Garon .25 .60
360 Vladimir Malakhov .10 .25
361 Mike Ribeiro .10 .25
362 Michael Peca .10 .25
363 Andreas Dackell .10 .25
364 Scott Stevens .25 .60
365 Dave Scatchard .10 .25
366 Mike Richter .30 .75
367 Niklas Sundstrom .10 .25
368 Oleg Petrov .10 .25
369 Alexei Yashin .10 .25
370 Darren Haydar .10 .25
371 Patrice Brisebois .10 .25
372 Scott Walker .10 .25
373 Pavel Bure .30 .75
374 Yanic Perreault .10 .25
375 Vladimir Orszagh .10 .25
376 Kenny Jonsson .10 .25
377 Vitali Yachmenev .10 .25
378 Turner Stevenson .10 .25
379 Trent Hunter .10 .25
380 Tomas Vokoun .25 .60
381 Tom Poti .10 .25
382 Shawn Bates .10 .25
383 Sergei Brylin .10 .25
384 Scottie Upshall .10 .25
385 Mattias Weinhandl .10 .25
386 Joe Nieuwendyk .25 .60
387 Mike Komisarek .10 .25
388 Matthew Barnaby .10 .25
389 Scott Gomez .10 .25
390 Sandy McCarthy .10 .25
391 Saku Koivu .30 .75
392 Ronald Petrovicky .10 .25
393 Scott Hartnell .10 .25
394 Roman Hamrlik .10 .25
395 Andreas Johansson .10 .25
396 Richard Zednik .10 .25
397 Rem Murray .10 .25
398 Randy Robitaille .10 .25
399 Randy McKay .10 .25
400 Oleg Kvasha .10 .25
401 Steve McKenna .10 .25
402 Radoslav Suchy .10 .25
403 Wayne Primeau .10 .25
404 Wade Redden .10 .25
405 Vincent Damphousse .10 .25
406 Sebastien Caron .25 .60
407 Vaclav Varada .10 .25
408 Tony Amonte .25 .60
409 Tomas Surovy .10 .25
410 Sami Kapanen .10 .25
411 Mike Ricci .10 .25
412 Alexei Morozov .10 .25
413 Miroslav Zalesak .10 .25
414 Mark Recchi .25 .60
415 Patrick Marleau .25 .60
416 Robert Esche .25 .60
417 Brooks Orpik .10 .25
418 Ville Nieminen .10 .25
419 Mike Rathje .10 .25
420 Michal Rozsival .10 .25
421 Todd Harvey .10 .25
422 Zdeno Chara .10 .25
423 Scott Hannan .10 .25
424 Rob Ray .10 .25
425 Zac Bierk .25 .60
426 Vesa Toskala .10 .25
427 Todd White .10 .25
428 Eric Meloche .10 .25
429 Niko Dimitrakos .10 .25
430 Patrick Lalime .25 .60
431 Simon Gagne .30 .75
432 Sean Burke .25 .60
433 John LeClair .30 .75
434 Petr Schastlivy .10 .25
435 Scott Thornton .10 .25
436 Radek Bonk .10 .25
437 Rico Fata .10 .25
438 Mike Johnson .10 .25
439 Mike Fisher .10 .25
440 Radovan Somik .10 .25
441 Peter Schaefer .10 .25
442 Michal Handzus .10 .25
443 Landon Wilson .10 .25
444 Jonathan Cheechoo .12 .30
445 Mario Lemieux 2.00 5.00
446 Martin Havlat .25 .60
447 Mark Smith .10 .25
448 Kris Beech .10 .25
449 Keith Primeau .25 .60
450 Marian Hossa .30 .75
451 Marcus Ragnarsson .10 .25
452 Martin Straka .10 .25
453 Kim Johnsson .10 .25
454 Milan Kraft .10 .25
455 Martin Prusek .10 .25
456 Krys Kolanos .10 .25
457 Kyle McLaren .10 .25
458 Ladislav Nagy .10 .25
459 Claude Lapointe .10 .25
460 Magnus Arvedson .10 .25
461 Marco Sturm .10 .25
462 Karel Rachunek .10 .25
463 Justin Williams .10 .25
464 Evgeni Nabokov .25 .60
465 Mathias Johansson .10 .25
466 Eric Desjardins .10 .25
467 Daniel Alfredsson .25 .60
468 Chris Therien .10 .25
469 Jeremy Roenick .40 1.00
470 Jeff Taffe .10 .25
471 Johan Hedberg .25 .60
472 Dimitri Yushkevich .10 .25
473 Shane Doan .10 .25
474 Paul Mara .10 .25
475 Eric Weinrich .10 .25
476 Jim Fahey .10 .25
477 Konstantin Koltsov .10 .25
478 Jason Jaspers .10 .25
479 Jason Spezza .30 .75
480 J-S Aubin .10 .25
481 Deron Quint .10 .25
482 Dennis Seidenberg .10 .25
483 Daymond Langkow .10 .25
484 Kelly Buchberger .10 .25
485 Michal Sivek .10 .25
486 Donald Brashear .10 .25
487 Chris Phillips .10 .25
488 Chris Gratton .10 .25
489 Bryan Smolinski .10 .25
490 Guillaume Lefebvre .10 .25
491 Brian Savage .10 .25
492 Alyn McCauley .10 .25
493 Andrei Nazarov .10 .25
494 Anton Volchenkov .10 .25
495 Brad Ference .10 .25
496 Brad Stuart .10 .25
497 Branko Radivojevic .10 .25
498 Brian Boucher .25 .60
499 Dick Tarnstrom .10 .25
500 Adam Graves .10 .25
501 Al MacInnis .25 .60
502 Scott Mellanby .10 .25
503 Matt Stajan RC 3.00 8.00
504 Andre Roy .10 .25
505 Alexander Mogilny .25 .60
506 Barret Jackman .25 .60
507 Nik Antropov .10 .25
508 Ben Clymer .10 .25
509 Maxime Ouellet .25 .60
510 Trevor Kidd .25 .60
511 Brad Richards .25 .60
512 Todd Bertuzzi .30 .75
513 Wade Belak .10 .25
514 Brian Sutherby .10 .25
515 Fedor Fedorov .10 .25
516 Cory Sarich .10 .25
517 Brent Sopel .10 .25
518 Chris Pronger .25 .60
519 Brendan Morrison .25 .60
520 Sebastien Charpentier .25 .60
521 Alexander Svitov .10 .25
522 Calle Johansson .10 .25
523 Bryan McCabe .10 .25
524 Bryan Allen .10 .25
525 Bryce Salvador .10 .25
526 Dainius Zubrus .10 .25
527 Dallas Drake .10 .25
528 Dan Boyle .10 .25
529 Dan Cloutier .25 .60
530 Ken Klee .10 .25
531 Keith Tkachuk .30 .75
532 Brandon Reid .10 .25
533 Sergei Berezin .10 .25
534 Alex Auld .10 .25
535 Jaromir Jagr .50 1.25
536 Markus Naslund .30 .75
537 Jamal Mayers .10 .25
538 Ivan Ciernik .10 .25
539 Marek Malik .10 .25
540 Karel Pilar .10 .25
541 Fredrik Modin .10 .25
542 Gary Roberts .10 .25
543 Eric Boguniecki .10 .25
544 Henrik Sedin .10 .25
545 Ed Belfour .30 .75
546 Doug Weight .25 .60
547 Carlo Colaiacovo .10 .25
548 Peter Sejna RC 2.00 5.00
549 Michael Nylander .10 .25
550 Daniel Sedin .10 .25
551 Kip Miller .10 .25
552 Robert Reichel .10 .25
553 Olaf Kolzig .25 .60
554 Reed Low .10 .25
555 Mikael Renberg .10 .25
556 Mike Grier .10 .25
557 Owen Nolan .25 .60
558 Nikolai Khabibulin .30 .75
559 Brad May .10 .25
560 Nikita Alexeev .10 .25
561 Sami Salo .10 .25
562 Martin St. Louis .25 .60
563 Brendan Witt .10 .25
564 Martin Rucinsky .10 .25
565 Mattias Ohlund .10 .25
566 Doug Gilmour .25 .60
567 Matt Cooke .10 .25
568 Dave Andreychuk .10 .25
569 Robert Lang .10 .25
570 Alexander Khavanov .10 .25
571 Tie Domi .25 .60
572 Ruslan Fedotenko .10 .25
573 Robert Svehla .10 .25
574 Tim Taylor .10 .25
575 Brent Johnson .25 .60
576 Brad Lukowich .10 .25
577 Sergei Gonchar .10 .25
578 Sheldon Keefe .10 .25
579 Steve Eminger .10 .25
580 Tomas Kaberle .10 .25
581 Steve Konowalchuk .10 .25
582 Chris Osgood .25 .60
583 Trevor Linden .10 .25
584 Travis Green .10 .25
585 Steve Martins .10 .25
586 John Grahame .25 .60
587 Darcy Tucker .10 .25
588 Jassen Cullimore .10 .25
589 Peter Bondra .25 .60
590 Pavol Demitra .25 .60
591 Nolan Pratt .10 .25
592 Jeff Halpern .10 .25
593 Vincent Lecavalier .30 .75
594 Petr Cajanek .10 .25
595 Chris Dingman .10 .25
596 Artem Chubarov .10 .25
597 Curtis Sanford .10 .25
598 Ed Jovanovski .25 .60
599 Mats Sundin .30 .75
600 Jarkko Ruutu .10 .25
601 Marc-Andre Fleury RC/321 20.00 50.00
602 Eric Staal RC/340 10.00 25.00
603 Tuomo Ruutu RC/299 6.00 15.00
604 Joni Pitkanen RC/316 6.00 15.00
605 Dustin Brown RC/287 4.00 10.00
606 Alexander Semin RC/291 10.00 25.00
607 Boyd Gordon RC/268 4.00 10.00
608 Pavel Vorobiev RC/203 4.00 10.00
609 Dan Hamhuis RC/286 6.00 15.00
610 Marek Zidlicky RC/308 4.00 10.00
611 Brent Burns RC/270 6.00 15.00
612 Cody McCormick RC/271 4.00 10.00
613 Antoine Vermette RC/280 4.00 10.00
614 Sean Bergenheim RC/291 4.00 10.00
615 Ryan Malone RC/310 8.00 20.00
616 Peter Sarno RC/284 4.00 10.00
617 Nathan Horton XRC/301 8.00 20.00
618 Joffrey Lupul XRC/306 8.00 20.00
619 Jordin Tootoo XRC/302 8.00 20.00
620 Patrice Bergeron XRC/299 10.00 25.00
621 Jiri Hudler XRC/291 8.00 20.00
622 Chris Higgins XRC/297 10.00 25.00
623 Maxim Kondratiev XRC/293 5.00 12.00
624 Brent Krahn XRC/283 5.00 12.00
625 Cover Card/Checklist .10 .25
626 Kari Lehtonen XRC 3.00 8.00
627 Dan Fritsche XRC .60 1.50
628 Tim Gleason XRC .60 1.50
629 Derek Roy XRC .60 1.50
630 Matthew Lombardi XRC .60 1.50
631 John-Michael Liles XRC .60 1.50
632 Brian Leetch .25 .60
633 Michael Ryder .10 .25
634 Karl Stewart XRC .60 1.50
635 Jed Ortmeyer XRC .60 1.50
636 Dominic Moore XRC .60 1.50
637 Andrew Allen XRC .60 1.50
638 Ryan Kesler XRC .60 1.50
639 Tony Salmelainen XRC .60 1.50
640 Mikhail Yakubov XRC .60 1.50
641 Nathan Robinson XRC .60 1.50
642 Chris Simon .10 .25
643 Jeff Hamilton XRC .60 1.50
644 Nikolai Zherdev XRC 2.00 5.00
645 Steve Sullivan .10 .25
646 Niklas Kronwall XRC 2.00 5.00
647 Joey MacDonald XRC .60 1.50
648 Antero Niittymaki XRC 4.00 10.00
649 Noah Clarke XRC .60 1.50
650 Tim Jackman XRC .60 1.50
651 Timofei Shishkanov XRC .60 1.50
652 Marek Svatos XRC 4.00 10.00
653 Sergei Fedorov .50 1.25
654 Aleksander Suglobov XRC .60 1.50
655 Darryl Bootland XRC 2.00 5.00
656 Andrew Peters XRC 2.00 5.00
657 Anton Babchuk XRC .60 1.50
658 Kyle Wellwood XRC 2.00 5.00
659 Chris Kunitz XRC .60 1.50
660 Jozef Balej XRC .60 1.50
661 Christian Ehrhoff XRC .60 1.50
662 Dan Ellis XRC .60 1.50
663 Robert Lang .10 .25
664 Thomas Pihlman XRC .60 1.50
665 Andy Chiodo XRC .60 1.50
666 Adam Munro XRC .60 1.50
667 Denis Grebeshkov XRC .60 1.50
668 Matt Underhill XRC .60 1.50
669 Brad Boyes XRC 2.50 6.00
670 Paul Martin XRC .60 1.50
671 Matthew Yeats XRC .60 1.50
672 Alexei Zhamnov .10 .25
673 Wade Dubielewicz XRC .60 1.50
674 Miikka Kiprusoff .25 .60

2003-04 ITG Action Center of Attention

COMPLETE SET (10) 20.00 40.00
STATED ODDS 1:46
CA1 Mario Lemieux 5.00 12.00
CA2 Steve Yzerman 4.00 10.00
CA3 Joe Sakic 2.50 6.00
CA4 Peter Forsberg 3.00 8.00
CA5 Todd Bertuzzi 1.25 3.00
CA6 Joe Thornton 2.00 5.00
CA7 Sergei Fedorov 1.50 4.00
CA8 Mike Modano 2.00 5.00
CA9 Jason Spezza 2.00 5.00
CA10 Mats Sundin 1.25 3.00

2003-04 ITG Action First Time All-Star

COMPLETE SET (10) 8.00 15.00
STATED ODDS 1:38
FT1 Marian Gaborik 2.00 5.00
FT2 Dany Heatley 1.25 3.00
FT3 Marty Turco .75 2.00
FT4 Todd Bertuzzi .75 2.00
FT5 Olli Jokinen .75 2.00
FT6 Vincent Lecavalier .75 2.00
FT7 Patrick Lalime .75 2.00
FT8 Glen Murray .75 2.00
FT9 Martin St-Louis .75 2.00
FT10 Jocelyn Thibault .75 2.00

2003-04 ITG Action Highlight Reel

COMPLETE SET (12) 20.00 40.00
STATED ODDS 1:38
HR1 J-S Giguere .75 2.00
HR2 Patrick Roy 3.00 8.00
HR3 Martin Brodeur 2.50 6.00
HR4 Mario Lemieux 4.00 10.00
HR5 Dany Heatley 1.00 2.50
HR6 Joe Sakic 2.00 5.00
HR7 Joe Nieuwendyk .75 2.00
HR8 Jaromir Jagr 1.25 3.00
HR9 Brett Hull 1.00 2.50
HR10 Rick Nash 1.00 2.50
HR11 Marty Turco .75 2.00
HR12 Marian Gaborik 1.50 4.00

2003-04 ITG Action Homeboys

COMPLETE SET (14) 15.00 30.00
STATED ODDS 1:24
HB1 Markus Naslund / Peter Forsberg 1.50 4.00
HB2 Ron Francis / Marty Turco .75 2.00
HB3 Z.Chara/M.Gaborik .75 2.00
HB4 Mike Comrie / Scott Niedermayer .75 2.00
HB5 Mark Messier / Jarome Iginla .75 2.00
HB6 Doug Gilmour / Kirk Muller .75 2.00
HB7 Eric Lindros / Joe Thornton 1.00 2.50
HB8 Nikolai Khabibulin / Alexei Yashin .75 2.00
HB9 Jani Hurme / Saku Koivu .75 2.00
HB10 M.Brodeur/M.Lemieux 5.00 12.00
HB11 Bates Battaglia / Chris Chelios .75 2.00
HB12 Stephen Weiss / Anson Carter .75 2.00
HB13 J-S Giguere / Roberto Luongo .75 2.00
HB14 Pavel Bure / Sergei Samsonov .75 2.00

2003-04 ITG Action Jerseys

This 270-card memorabilia set was tiered by color. Ruby cards (M1-M90) were serial-numbered to 500 each. Sapphire (M91-M120) were serial-numbered to 300 each. Emerald cards (M121-150) were serial-numbered to 200 sets. Bronze (M151-M180) were serial-numbered to 100. Silver (M181-M200) were serial-numbered to 50 each. Gold cards (M201-M220) were 1/1's and are not priced due to scarcity. Quad jerseys (M221-M240) were serial-numbered to 50 each. Cards M240-M270 were only available in factory sets and were limited to 100 each.

M1 Nik Antropov 4.00 10.00
M2 Jason Arnott 4.00 10.00
M3 Jared Aulin 4.00 10.00
M4 Mark Bell 4.00 10.00
M5 Bryan Berard 4.00 10.00
M6 Martin Biron 4.00 10.00
M7 Radek Bonk 4.00 10.00
M8 Nick Boynton 4.00 10.00
M9 Donald Brashear 4.00 10.00
M10 Eric Brewer 4.00 10.00
M11 Sergei Brylin 4.00 10.00
M12 Mike Cammalleri 4.00 10.00
M13 Dan Cloutier 4.00 10.00
M14 Carlo Colaiacovo 4.00 10.00
M15 Tim Connolly 4.00 10.00
M16 Byron Dafoe 4.00 10.00
M17 Adam Deadmarsh 4.00 10.00
M18 Shane Doan 4.00 10.00
M19 Tie Domi 4.00 10.00
M20 J-P Dumont 4.00 10.00
M21 Robert Esche 4.00 10.00
M22 Mike Fisher 4.00 10.00
M23 Adam Foote 4.00 10.00
M24 Martin Gerber 6.00 15.00
M25 Scott Gomez 4.00 10.00
M26 John Grahame 6.00 15.00

27 Jeff Hackett 6.00 15.00
28 Ron Hainsey 4.00 10.00
29 Scott Hartnell 4.00 10.00
30 Derian Hatcher 4.00 10.00
31 Bobby Holik 4.00 10.00
32 Marcel Hossa 4.00 10.00
33 Ivan Huml 4.00 10.00
34 Barret Jackman 6.00 15.00
35 Brent Johnson 6.00 15.00
36 Ed Jovanovski 6.00 15.00
37 Tomas Kaberle 4.00 10.00
38 Niko Kapanen 4.00 10.00
39 Sami Kapanen 4.00 10.00
40 Darius Kasparaitis 4.00 10.00
41 Rostislav Klesla 4.00 10.00
42 Chuck Kobasew 4.00 10.00
43 Vyacheslav Kozlov 4.00 10.00
44 Georges Laraque 6.00 15.00
45 Igor Larionov 4.00 10.00
46 Manny Legace 4.00 10.00
47 David Legwand 4.00 10.00
48 Jordan Leopold 4.00 10.00
49 Trevor Linden 4.00 10.00
50 John Madden 4.00 10.00
51 Patrick Marleau 6.00 15.00
52 Aleksey Morozov 4.00 10.00
53 Derek Morris 4.00 10.00
54 Brendan Morrison 6.00 15.00
55 Brenden Morrow 6.00 15.00
56 Rob Niedermayer 4.00 10.00
57 Scott Niedermayer 4.00 10.00
58 Joe Nieuwendyk 6.00 15.00
59 Mika Noronen 4.00 10.00
60 Pasi Nurminen 4.00 10.00
61 Sandis Ozolinsh 4.00 10.00
62 Yanic Perreault 4.00 10.00
63 Chris Phillips 4.00 10.00
64 Tom Poti 4.00 10.00
65 Keith Primeau 4.00 10.00
66 Branko Radivojevic 4.00 10.00
67 Brian Rafalski 4.00 10.00
68 Wade Redden 4.00 10.00
69 Brandon Reid 4.00 10.00
70 Steven Reinprecht 4.00 10.00
71 Mike Richter 8.00 20.00
72 Brian Rolston 4.00 10.00
73 Miroslav Satan 4.00 10.00
74 Kevin Sawyer 4.00 10.00
75 Nick Schultz 4.00 10.00
76 Daniel Sedin 4.00 10.00
77 Henrik Sedin 4.00 10.00
78 Alexei Smirnov 4.00 10.00
79 Ryan Smyth 4.00 10.00
80 Garth Snow 4.00 10.00
81 Radovan Somik 4.00 10.00
82 Martin Straka 4.00 10.00
83 Alexander Svitov 4.00 10.00
84 Darryl Sydor 4.00 10.00
85 Roman Turek 6.00 15.00
86 Pierre Turgeon 4.00 10.00
87 Scottie Upshall 4.00 10.00
88 Anton Volchenkov 4.00 10.00
89 Peter Worrell 4.00 10.00
90 Scott Young 5.00 10.00
91 David Aebischer 6.00 15.00
92 Jason Allison 6.00 15.00
93 Tyler Arnason 6.00 15.00
94 Dan Blackburn 6.00 15.00
95 Daniel Briere 6.00 15.00
96 Sean Burke 6.00 15.00
97 Roman Cechmanek 6.00 15.00
98 Erik Cole 6.00 15.00
99 Vincent Damphousse 6.00 15.00
100 Pavol Demitra 6.00 15.00
101 Marc Denis 6.00 15.00
102 Chris Drury 6.00 15.00
103 Mike Dunham 6.00 15.00
104 Manny Fernandez 6.00 15.00
105 Simon Gagne 10.00 25.00
106 Mathieu Garon 6.00 15.00
107 Sergei Gonchar 6.00 15.00
108 Johan Hedberg 6.00 15.00
109 Ales Hemsky 6.00 15.00
110 Kristian Huselius 6.00 15.00
111 Jamie Langenbrunner 6.00 15.00
112 Felix Potvin 10.00 25.00
113 Brad Richards 6.00 15.00
114 Dwayne Roloson 10.00 25.00
115 Patrik Stefan 6.00 15.00
116 Scott Stevens 6.00 15.00
117 Alex Tanguay 6.00 15.00
118 Kevin Weekes 6.00 15.00
119 Stephen Weiss 6.00 15.00
120 Sergei Zubov 6.00 15.00
121 Daniel Alfredsson 8.00 20.00
122 Tony Amonte 8.00 20.00
123 Peter Bondra 8.00 20.00
124 Chris Chelios 10.00 25.00
125 Stanislav Chistov 8.00 20.00
126 Pavel Datsyuk 12.50 30.00
127 Eric Daze 8.00 20.00
128 Patrik Elias 8.00 20.00
129 Alexander Frolov 8.00 20.00
130 Doug Gilmour 8.00 20.00
131 Martin Havlat 8.00 20.00
132 Olli Jokinen 8.00 20.00
133 Nikolai Khabibulin 10.00 25.00
134 Olaf Kolzig 8.00 20.00
135 Patrick Lalime 8.00 20.00
136 Vincent Lecavalier 10.00 25.00
137 Ryan Miller 8.00 20.00
138 Glen Murray 8.00 20.00
139 Evgeni Nabokov 8.00 20.00
140 Adam Oates 8.00 20.00
141 Zigmund Palffy 8.00 20.00
142 Mike Peca 8.00 20.00
143 Chris Pronger 8.00 20.00
144 Mark Recchi 8.00 20.00
145 Gary Roberts 8.00 20.00
146 Tommy Salo 8.00 20.00
147 Martin St-Louis 8.00 20.00
148 Keith Tkachuk 10.00 25.00
149 Doug Weight 8.00 20.00
150 Alexei Yashin 8.00 20.00
151 Ed Belfour 12.50 30.00
152 Todd Bertuzzi 12.50 30.00
153 Rob Blake 10.00 25.00
154 Jay Bouwmeester 10.00 25.00
155 Mike Comrie 10.00 25.00
156 Rick DiPietro 10.00 25.00
157 Ron Francis 10.00 25.00
M158 Bill Guerin 10.00 25.00
M159 Milan Hejduk 12.50 30.00
M160 Marian Hossa 12.50 30.00
M161 Jarome Iginla 15.00 40.00
M162 Saku Koivu 12.50 30.00
M163 John LeClair 12.50 30.00
M164 Brian Leetch 10.00 25.00
M165 Eric Lindros 12.50 30.00
M166 Roberto Luongo 15.00 40.00
M167 Al MacInnis 10.00 25.00
M168 Mark Messier 15.00 40.00
M169 Alexander Mogilny 10.00 25.00
M170 Rick Nash 12.00 30.00
M171 Markus Naslund 12.50 30.00
M172 Owen Nolan 10.00 25.00
M173 Luc Robitaille 10.00 25.00
M174 Jeremy Roenick 15.00 40.00
M175 Sergei Samsonov 12.50 30.00
M176 Brendan Shanahan 12.50 30.00
M177 Jason Spezza 12.50 30.00
M178 Mats Sundin 12.50 30.00
M179 Jocelyn Thibault 10.00 25.00
M180 Marty Turco 10.00 25.00
M181 Martin Brodeur 30.00 80.00
M182 Pavel Bure 12.50 30.00
M183 Sergei Fedorov 20.00 50.00
M184 Peter Forsberg 20.00 50.00
M185 Marian Gaborik 20.00 50.00
M186 J-S Giguere 12.50 30.00
M187 Dany Heatley 20.00 50.00
M188 Brett Hull 20.00 50.00
M189 Jaromir Jagr 20.00 50.00
M190 Paul Kariya 12.50 30.00
M191 Ilya Kovalchuk 20.00 50.00
M192 Mario Lemieux 30.00 80.00
M193 Nicklas Lidstrom 20.00 50.00
M194 Mike Modano 15.00 40.00
M195 Patrick Roy 25.00 60.00
M196 Joe Sakic 20.00 50.00
M197 Dominik Hasek 15.00 40.00
M198 Jose Theodore 20.00 50.00
M199 Joe Thornton 15.00 40.00
M200 Steve Yzerman 30.00 80.00
M201 Martin Brodeur
M202 Pavel Bure
M203 Sergei Fedorov
M204 Peter Forsberg
M205 Marian Gaborik
M206 J-S Giguere
M207 Dany Heatley
M208 Brett Hull
M209 Jaromir Jagr
M210 Paul Kariya
M211 Ilya Kovalchuk
M212 Mario Lemieux
M213 Nicklas Lidstrom
M214 Mike Modano
M215 Patrick Roy
M216 Joe Sakic
M217 Dominik Hasek
M218 Jose Theodore
M219 Joe Thornton
M220 Steve Yzerman
M221 Gig/Chistv/Kriya/Sykra 20.00 50.00
M222 Brdur/Elias/Stens/Maddn 20.00 50.00
M223 Belfr/Sndin/Mgilny/Noln 30.00 80.00
M224 LeClr/Rnick/Amnte/Ggne 40.00 100.00
M225 Berrd/Smsnv/Thrntn/Mrry 20.00 50.00
M226 Hull/Yze/Hasek/Fedrv 40.00 100.00
M227 Roy/Frsbrg/Sakic/Hduk 40.00 100.00
M228 Turco/Mdno/Guerin/Mrrow 20.00 50.00
M229 Blckbrn/Bure/Mess/Lndros 30.00 80.00
M230 Lalime/Hssa/Spzza/Hvlat 60.00 150.00
M231 Thiblt/Daze/Sllivn/Arnson 15.00 40.00
M232 Miller/Satn/Afingnv/Briere 25.00 60.00
M233 Salo/Comrie/Smith/Laraque 20.00 50.00
M234 Heat/Kvlchuk/Dfoe/Stfan 20.00 50.00
M235 Osgd/Jkmn/Prngr/McInns 20.00 50.00
M236 Klzig/Jagr/Bndra/Emnger 20.00 50.00
M237 Lmieux/Hdbrg/Strka/Mrzv 40.00 100.00
M238 Clotier/Brtzzi/Nslnd/Jovo 20.00 50.00
M239 Vkun/Hartnll/Lgwnd/Upshll 20.00 50.00
M240 Theodre/Koivu/Garn/Hnsy 30.00 80.00
M241 J-S Giguere 10.00 25.00
M242 Dany Heatley 12.50 30.00
M243 Joe Thornton 12.50 30.00
M244 Miroslav Satan 10.00 25.00
M245 Jarome Iginla 15.00 40.00
M246 Ron Francis 10.00 25.00
M247 Jocelyn Thibault 10.00 25.00
M248 Patrick Roy 25.00 60.00
M249 Rick Nash 12.00 30.00
M250 Mike Modano 12.50 30.00
M251 Steve Yzerman 30.00 80.00
M252 Mike Comrie 10.00 25.00
M253 Roberto Luongo 15.00 40.00
M254 Zigmund Palffy 10.00 25.00
M255 Marian Gaborik 15.00 40.00
M256 Jose Theodore 15.00 40.00
M257 David Legwand 10.00 25.00
M258 Martin Brodeur 30.00 80.00
M259 Alexei Yashin 10.00 25.00
M260 Pavel Bure 12.50 30.00
M261 Marian Hossa 12.50 30.00
M262 Jeremy Roenick 12.50 30.00
M263 Sean Burke 10.00 25.00
M264 Mario Lemieux 40.00 100.00
M265 Chris Pronger 10.00 25.00
M266 Evgeni Nabokov 10.00 25.00
M267 Vincent Lecavalier 12.50 30.00
M268 Mats Sundin 12.50 30.00
M269 Markus Naslund 12.50 30.00
M270 Jaromir Jagr 12.50 30.00

2003-04 ITG Action League Leaders

COMPLETE SET (10) 12.50 25.00
STATED ODDS 1:29
L1 Peter Forsberg 2.50 6.00
Milan Hejduk
L2 Milan Hejduk .60 1.50
L3 Peter Forsberg 2.00 5.00
L4 Peter Forsberg 2.00 5.00
L5 Marty Turco .60 1.50
L6 Henrik Zetterberg .60 1.50
L7 Martin Brodeur 1.50 4.00
L8 Martin Brodeur 1.50 4.00
L9 Markus Naslund .60 1.50
L10 Dany Heatley .75 2.00

2003-04 ITG Action Oh Canada

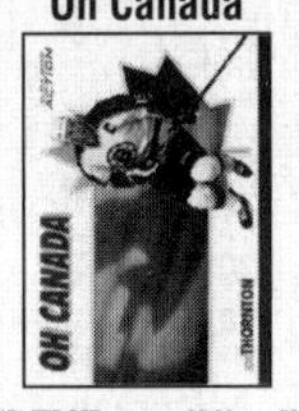

COMPLETE SET 25.00 50.00
STATED ODDS 1:21
OC1 Mario Lemieux 4.00 10.00
OC2 Patrick Roy 3.00 8.00
OC3 Steve Yzerman 3.00 8.00
OC4 Martin Brodeur 2.50 6.00
OC5 Paul Kariya .75 2.00
OC6 Joe Sakic 2.00 5.00
OC7 Mark Messier .75 2.00
OC8 J-S Giguere .75 2.00
OC9 Jason Spezza 1.00 2.50
OC10 Dany Heatley 1.00 2.50
OC11 Curtis Joseph .75 2.00
OC12 Ed Belfour .75 2.00
OC13 Brendan Shanahan .75 2.00
OC14 Joe Thornton 1.00 2.50

2003-04 ITG Action Trophy Winners

STATED ODDS 1:64
TW1 Peter Forsberg 3.00 8.00
TW2 Martin Brodeur 3.00 8.00
TW3 Nicklas Lidstrom 1.50 4.00
TW4 Barret Jackman 1.50 4.00
TW5 Markus Naslund 1.50 4.00
TW6 Peter Forsberg 3.00 8.00

2004 ITG NHL All-Star FANtasy All-Star History Jerseys

Available only in "Super Boxes" produced by ITG for the 2004 NHL All-Star FANtasy, this 54-card set featured jerseys of players who represented the All-Star game from 1947 to the present. Cards SB1-SB21 were limited to 10 copies each; cards SB22-SB41 were limited to 20 copies each and cards SB42-SB54 were limited to 30 copies each. Cards under 30 were not priced due to scarcity.

SB1 Turk Broda
SB2 Frank Brimsek
SB3 Ted Kennedy
SB4 Maurice Richard
SB5 Chuck Rayner
SB6 Bill Mosienko
SB7 Jean Beliveau
SB8 Doug Harvey
SB9 Ted Lindsay
SB10 Henri Richard
SB11 Jacques Plante
SB12 Glenn Hall
SB13 Terry Sawchuk
SB14 Bobby Hull
SB15 Johnny Bower
SB16 Tim Horton
SB17 John Bucyk
SB18 Stan Mikita
SB19 Bill Gadsby
SB20 Ed Giacomin
SB21 Bobby Orr
SB22 Bernie Parent
SB23 Bobby Clarke
SB24 Gilbert Perreault
SB25 Frank Mahovlich
SB26 Tony Esposito
SB27 Denis Potvin
SB28 Guy Lafleur
SB29 Bryan Trottier
SB30 Lanny McDonald
SB31 Marcel Dionne
SB32 Bill Barber
SB33 Mike Bossy
SB34 Mark Messier
SB35 Ray Bourque
SB36 Steve Yzerman
SB37 Mario Lemieux
SB38 Grant Fuhr
SB39 Patrick Roy
SB40 Brett Hull
SB41 Brian Leetch
SB42 Jeremy Roenick 12.50 30.00
SB43 Jaromir Jagr 12.50 30.00
SB44 Luc Robitaille 12.50 30.00
SB45 Joe Sakic 15.00 40.00
SB46 Eric Lindros 12.50 30.00
SB47 Paul Kariya 15.00 40.00
SB48 Mike Modano 12.50 30.00
SB49 Peter Forsberg 20.00 50.00
SB50 Pavel Bure 12.50 30.00
SB51 Milan Hejduk 12.50 30.00
SB52 Mats Sundin 12.50 30.00
SB53 Marian Gaborik 15.00 40.00
SB54 Ilya Kovalchuk 12.50 30.00

2004 ITG All-Star FANtasy Hail Minnesota

This 10-card set was only available in "Super Boxes" produced by ITG booth for the 2004 NHL All-Star Fantasy. Each card was limited to 100 copies each.

COMPLETE SET (10) 75.00 125.00
1 Mike Gartner 4.00 10.00
2 Derian Hatcher 4.00 10.00
3 Mike Modano 12.00 30.00
4 Jordan Leopold 4.00 10.00
5 Manny Fernandez 6.00 15.00
6 Dwayne Roloson 6.00 15.00
7 Marian Gaborik 20.00 50.00
8 Pierre-Marc Bouchard 6.00 15.00
9 Gump Worsley 12.00 30.00
10 Dino Ciccarelli 4.00 10.00

2004-05 ITG Franchises Canadian

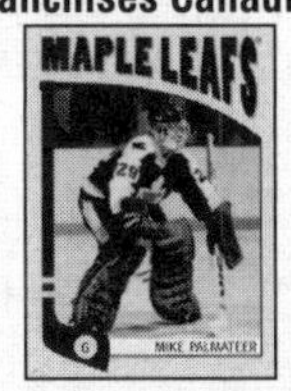

This 150-card set was the first release in the Franchise trio produced by In the Game. The set focused on vintage players from Canadian clubs.

COMPLETE SET (150) 20.00 40.00
1 Dan Bouchard .30 .75
2 Phil Housley .20 .50
3 Reggie Lemelin .30 .75
4 Hakan Loob .20 .50
5 Jamie Macoun .20 .50
6 Kent Nilsson .20 .50
7 Joel Otto .20 .50
8 Jim Peplinski .20 .50
9 Paul Ranheim .20 .50
10 Mark Hunter .20 .50
11 Doug Gilmour .30 .75
12 Joe Mullen .30 .75
13 Lanny McDonald .30 .75
14 Paul Reinhart .20 .50
15 Gary Suter .20 .50
16 Guy Chouinard .20 .50
17 Grant Fuhr .40 1.00
18 Bernie Nicholls .20 .50
19 Andy Moog .30 .75
20 Esa Tikkanen .20 .50
21 Dave Semenko .20 .50
22 Mark Napier .20 .50
23 Bill Ranford .30 .75
24 Paul Coffey .40 1.00
25 Glenn Anderson .20 .50
26 Kent Nilsson .20 .50
27 Jari Kurri .50 1.25
28 Randy Gregg .20 .50
29 Charlie Huddy .20 .50
30 Dave Hunter .20 .50
31 Mike Krushelnyski .20 .50
32 Ed Mio .30 .75
33 Garry Unger .20 .50
34 Lee Fogolin .20 .50
35 Billy Burch .20 .50
36 Goldie Prodgers .20 .50
37 Rocket Richard .75 2.00
38 Henri Richard .40 1.00
39 Jean Beliveau .50 1.25
40 Jacques Plante .60 1.50
41 Doug Harvey .30 .75
42 Howie Morenz .30 .75
43 Bernie Geoffrion .40 1.00
44 Georges Vezina .60 1.50
45 Gump Worsley .40 1.00
46 Rogie Vachon .40 1.00
47 John Ferguson .20 .50
48 Guy Lafleur .50 1.25
49 Dickie Moore .40 1.00
50 Larry Robinson .30 .75
51 Serge Savard .40 1.00
52 Yvan Cournoyer .40 1.00
53 Toe Blake .40 1.00
54 Butch Bouchard .30 .75
55 Steve Shutt .40 1.00
56 Jacques Lemaire .40 1.00
57 Frank Mahovlich .40 1.00
58 Georges Hainsworth .30 .75
59 Patrick Roy .75 2.00
60 Guy Lapointe .30 .75
61 Elmer Lach .20 .50
62 Jacques Laperriere .30 .75
63 Aurel Joliat .40 1.00
64 Bill Durnan .20 .50
65 Nels Stewart .20 .50
66 Clint Benedict .30 .75
67 Hooley Smith .20 .50
68 Art Ross .30 .75
69 Cy Denneny .20 .50
70 Frank Finnigan .20 .50
71 Joe Malone .30 .75
72 Harry Mummery RC .60 1.50
73 Andre Savard .20 .50
74 Marian Stastny .20 .50
75 Marc Tardif .20 .50
76 Peter Stastny .30 .75
77 Dan Bouchard .30 .75
78 Michel Goulet .30 .75
79 Dale Hunter .20 .50
80 Real Cloutier .20 .50
81 Robbie Ftorek .20 .50
82 Mike Hough .20 .50
83 Anton Stastny .20 .50
84 Jack Adams .30 .75
85 Reg Noble .20 .50
86 Ken Randall .20 .50
87 Red Kelly .40 1.00
88 Teeder Kennedy .20 .50
89 Frank Mahovlich .40 1.00
90 Dick Duff .30 .75
91 Bob Pulford .30 .75
92 Ace Bailey .30 .75
93 Sid Smith .20 .50
94 Johnny Bower .40 1.00
95 Bob Nevin .20 .50
96 Bob Baun .30 .75
97 Jim McKenny .20 .50
98 Mike Palmateer .30 .75
99 Frank McCool RC .60 1.50
100 Lanny McDonald .30 .75
101 Tiger Williams .30 .75
102 Darryl Sittler .40 1.00
103 Borje Salming .30 .75
104 Ian Turnbull .20 .50
105 King Clancy .30 .75
106 Joe Primeau .20 .50
107 Turk Broda .40 1.00
108 Howie Meeker .30 .75
109 Rick Vaive .20 .50
110 Tim Horton .40 1.00
111 Wendel Clark .30 .75
112 Doug Gilmour .30 .75
113 Bill Barilko RC 1.25 3.00
114 Red Horner .20 .50
115 Babe Dye .20 .50
116 Hap Day .30 .75
117 Tiger Williams .30 .75
118 Harold Snepsts .20 .50
119 Richard Brodeur .30 .75
120 Stan Smyl .20 .50
121 Cam Neely .40 1.00
122 Dennis Kearns .20 .50
123 Brian Bradley .20 .50
124 Jack McIlhargey .20 .50
125 Andre Boudrias .20 .50
126 Gary Smith .30 .75
127 Gino Odjick .20 .50
128 Kirk McLean .20 .50
129 Darcy Rota .20 .50
130 Garth Butcher .20 .50
131 Ron Delorme .20 .50
132 Thomas Gradin .20 .50
133 Dale Tallon .20 .50
134 Don Lever .20 .50
135 Bobby Hull .60 1.50
136 Laurie Boschman .20 .50
137 Bob Essensa .30 .75
138 Jimmy Mann .20 .50
139 Randy Carlyle .20 .50
140 Dale Hawerchuck .20 .50
141 Thomas Steen .20 .50
142 Darrin Shannon .20 .50
143 Doug Smail .20 .50
144 Mario Marois .20 .50
145 Morris Lukowich .20 .50
146 Jim Kyte .20 .50
147 Dave Ellet .20 .50
148 Dave Babych .20 .50
149 Tim Watters .20 .50
150 Paul MacLean .20 .50

2004-05 ITG Franchises Canadian Autographs

STATED ODDS 1:16
AM2 Andy Moog 8.00 20.00
AS2 Allan Stanley 15.00 40.00
BB2 Bobby Baun 15.00 40.00
BG Bernie Geoffrion 20.00 50.00
BH2 Bobby Hull SP 40.00 80.00
BN2 Bob Nevin 8.00 20.00
BR Bill Ranford 5.00 12.00
BS Borje Salming SP 25.00 60.00
CN2 Cam Neely SP 20.00 50.00
DB2 Dan Bouchard 8.00 20.00
Calgary
DB3 Dan Bouchard 8.00 20.00
Quebec
DD Dick Duff 15.00 40.00
DG2 Doug Gilmour 20.00 50.00
DK Dennis Kearns 5.00 12.00
DM2 Dickie Moore 15.00 40.00
DS2 Darryl Sittler SP 25.00 60.00
EL Elmer Lach SP 20.00 50.00
EM Ed Mio 5.00 12.00
FM2 Frank Mahovlich SP 25.00 60.00
Toronto
FM3 Frank Mahovlich SP 25.00 60.00
Montreal
GA Glenn Anderson 5.00 12.00
GB Garth Butcher 5.00 12.00
GF Grant Fuhr SP 20.00 50.00
GL Guy Lafleur SP 30.00 80.00
GO Gino Odjick 5.00 12.00
GS Gary Suter 5.00 12.00
GU2 Garry Unger 5.00 12.00
GW3 Gump Worsley 15.00 40.00
HM Howie Meeker 20.00 50.00
HR Henri Richard SP 12.00 30.00
HS Harold Snepsts 5.00 12.00
IT Ian Turnbull 5.00 12.00
JB Johnny Bower 20.00 50.00
JF John Ferguson 5.00 12.00
JK Jari Kurri SP 12.50 30.00
JL Jacques Laperriere 10.00 25.00
KN Kent Nilsson 5.00 12.00
LF Lee Fogolin 8.00 20.00
LM2 Lanny McDonald SP 25.00 60.00
Calgary
LM3 Lanny McDonald SP 25.00 60.00
Montreal
MG2 Michel Goulet 12.00 30.00
MM Mario Marois 5.00 12.00
MN Mark Napier 5.00 12.00
MP Mike Palmateer 25.00 60.00
MT Marc Tardiff 5.00 12.00
PC1 Paul Coffey SP 25.00 60.00
PH2 Phil Housley 5.00 12.00
PR2 Patrick Roy 100.00 250.00
RC2 Randy Carlyle 8.00 20.00
RD Ron Delorme 5.00 12.00
RV2 Rogie Vachon 12.00 30.00
TG Thomas Gradin 5.00 12.00
TK Teeder Kennedy 20.00 50.00
TW1 Tiger Williams 12.00 30.00
Toronto
TW2 Tiger Williams SP 12.00 30.00
Montreal
YC Yvan Cournoyer 12.00 30.00
ABO Andre Boudrias 5.00 12.00
ASV Andre Savard 5.00 12.00
BBO Butch Bouchard 12.00 30.00
BES Bob Essensa 5.00 12.00
BPL Bob Pulford 8.00 20.00
CHU Charlie Huddy 5.00 12.00
DBB Dave Babych 5.00 12.00
DEL Dave Ellett 5.00 12.00
DHA Dale Hawerchuk 20.00 50.00
DHU2 Dale Hunter 5.00 12.00
DLV Don Lever 15.00 40.00
DRO Darcy Rota 5.00 12.00
DSE Dave Semenko 8.00 20.00
DSH Darrin Shannon 5.00 12.00
DSM Doug Smail 5.00 12.00
DTL Dale Tallon 5.00 12.00
DVH Dave Hunter 5.00 12.00
GCH Guy Chouinard 5.00 12.00
GLP Guy Lapointe 8.00 20.00
JBE Jean Beliveau SP 25.00 60.00
JKY Jim Kyte 8.00 20.00
JLE Jacques Lemaire 8.00 20.00
JMC Jamie Macoun 5.00 12.00
JMI0 Jack McIlhargey 5.00 12.00
JMK Jim McKenny 5.00 12.00
JMN Jimmy Mann 5.00 12.00
JOT Joel Otto 5.00 12.00
JPE Jim Peplinski 5.00 12.00
KML Kirk McLean 5.00 12.00
LBH Laurie Boschman 5.00 12.00
MKR Mike Krushelnyski 5.00 12.00
MLU Morris Lukowich 5.00 12.00
MST Marian Stastny 5.00 12.00
PML Paul MacLean 5.00 12.00
PRA Paul Ranheim 5.00 12.00
PRE Paul Reinhart 5.00 12.00
RBR Richard Brodeur 8.00 20.00
RCL Real Cloutier 5.00 12.00
RFT Robbie Ftorek 5.00 12.00
RGR Randy Gregg 5.00 12.00
RHO Red Horner SP 75.00 150.00
RLM Reggie Lemelin 5.00 12.00
RVA Rick Vaive 15.00 40.00
SSH Steve Shutt 8.00 20.00
SSM Stan Smyl 5.00 12.00
SSV Serge Savard 5.00 12.00
TWA Tim Watters 5.00 12.00
WCL2 Wendel Clark 20.00 50.00

2004-05 ITG Franchises Canadian Barn Burners

PRINT RUN 50 SETS
GOLD PRINT RUN 20 SETS
GOLD NOT PRICED DUE TO SCARCITY
BB1 Lanny McDonald 12.50 30.00
BB2 Darryl Sittler 12.50 30.00
BB3 Jean Beliveau 15.00 40.00
BB4 Rick Vaive 12.50 30.00
BB5 Paul Coffey 15.00 40.00
BB6 Henri Richard 12.50 30.00
BB7 Jacques Plante 25.00 60.00
BB8 Rocket Richard 50.00 125.00

2004-05 ITG Franchises Canadian Boxtoppers

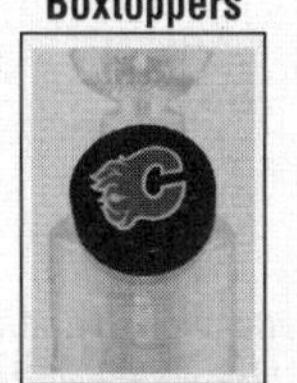

This 25-card set of jumbo boxtoppers were inserted at 1 per box and depicted the various Canadian clubs' logos through the years.

TH1 Calgary Flames/Original 2.00 5.00
TH2 Calgary Flames/Horse 2.00 5.00
TH3 Calgary Flames 2.00 5.00
TH4 Edmonton Oilers/Original 2.00 5.00
TH5 Edmonton Oilers 2.00 5.00
TH6 Edmonton Oilers/25th Ann. 2.00 5.00
TH7 Hamilton Tigers 2.00 5.00
TH8 Montreal Canadiens 2.00 5.00
TH9 Montreal Maroons 2.00 5.00
TH10 Montreal Wanderers 2.00 5.00
TH11 Ottawa Senators/Original 2.00 5.00
TH12 Ottawa Senators 2.00 5.00
TH13 Quebec Bulldogs 2.00 5.00
TH14 Quebec Nordiques 2.00 5.00
TH15 Toronto Arenas 2.00 5.00
TH16 Toronto Maple Leafs/Original 2.00 5.00
TH17 Toronto Maple Leafs/1950s 2.00 5.00
TH18 Toronto Maple Leafs/1960s 2.00 5.00
TH19 Toronto Maple Leafs 2.00 5.00
TH20 Toronto St. Patricks 2.00 5.00
TH21 Vancouver Canucks/original 2.00 5.00
TH22 Vancouver Canucks/1980s 2.00 5.00
TH23 Vancouver Canucks 2.00 5.00
TH24 Winnipeg Jets/1980s 2.00 5.00
TH25 Winnipeg Jets/1990s 2.00 5.00

2004-05 ITG Franchises Canadian Complete Jerseys

PRINT RUN 10 SETS
NOT PRICED DUE TO SCARCITY
GOLD 1/1'S EXIST
CJ1 Jacques Plante
CJ2 Jean Beliveau
CJ3 Patrick Roy
CJ4 Grant Fuhr
CJ5 Wendel Clark
CJ6 Glenn Anderson
CJ7 Richard Brodeur
CJ8 Phil Housley
CJ9 Paul Coffey
CJ10 Jari Kurri

2004-05 ITG Franchises Canadian Double Memorabilia

PRINT RUN 60 SETS
GOLD PRINT RUN 20 SETS
GOLD NOT PRICED DUE TO SCARCITY
DM1 George Hainsworth 25.00 60.00
DM2 Jean Beliveau 25.00 60.00
DM3 Johnny Bower 25.00 60.00
DM4 Georges Vezina 100.00 200.00
DM5 Patrick Roy 30.00 80.00
DM6 Aurel Joliat 30.00 80.00
DM7 Jacques Plante 30.00 80.00
DM8 Howie Morenz 60.00 125.00
DM9 Gump Worsley 15.00 40.00
DM10 Guy Lafleur 25.00 60.00
DM11 Wendel Clark 20.00 50.00
DM12 Grant Fuhr 15.00 40.00
DM13 Bernie Geoffrion 15.00 40.00
DM14 Tim Horton 40.00 100.00
DM15 Frank Mahovlich 15.00 40.00
DM16 Joe Mullen 15.00 40.00
DM17 Henri Richard 15.00 40.00
DM18 Jari Kurri 15.00 40.00
DM19 Glenn Anderson 15.00 40.00
DM20 Paul Coffey 15.00 40.00
DM21 Phil Housley 15.00 40.00
DM22 Doug Gilmour 15.00 40.00

2004-05 ITG Franchises Canadian Double Memorabilia Autographs

PRINT RUN 10 SETS
NOT PRICED DUE TO SCARCITY
DM2 Jean Beliveau
DM3 Johnny Bower
DM5 Patrick Roy
DM10 Guy Lafleur
DM11 Wendel Clark
DM12 Grant Fuhr
DM15 Frank Mahovlich
DM17 Henri Richard
DM18 Jari Kurri
DM20 Paul Coffey

2004-05 ITG Franchises Canadian Forever Rivals

PRINT RUN 50 SETS
GOLD PRINT RUN 20 SETS
GOLD NOT PRICED DUE TO SCARCITY
FR1 Johnny Bower 50.00 125.00
Jacques Plante
FR2 Red Kelly 30.00 80.00
Jean Beliveau
FR3 Grant Fuhr 20.00 50.00
Mike Vernon
FR4 B.Salming/G.Lafleur 25.00 60.00
FR5 Paul Coffey 15.00 40.00
Joe Mullen
FR6 Jari Kurri 25.00 60.00
Hakan Loob
FR7 Darryl Sittler 15.00 40.00
Larry Robinson
FR8 Wendel Clark 50.00 125.00
Patrick Roy
FR9 Tim Horton 40.00 100.00
Henri Richard
FR10 Lanny McDonald 15.00 40.00
Steve Shutt

2004-05 ITG Franchises Canadian Goalie Gear

PRINT RUN 70 SETS
GOLD PRINT RUN 20 SETS
GOLD NOT PRICED DUE TO SCARCITY
GG1 Bill Durnan 10.00 25.00
GG2 Johnny Bower 15.00 40.00
GG3 Patrick Roy 20.00 50.00
GG4 Grant Fuhr 15.00 40.00
GG5 Jacques Plante 20.00 50.00
GG6 Gump Worsley 15.00 40.00
GG7 Mike Vernon 15.00 40.00
GG8 Dan Bouchard 10.00 25.00
GG9 Bill Ranford 10.00 25.00
GG10 Richard Brodeur 12.50 30.00

2004-05 ITG Franchises Canadian Goalie Gear Autographs

PRINT RUN 10 SETS
NOT PRICED DUE TO SCARCITY
GG2 Johnny Bower
GG3 Patrick Roy
GG4 Grant Fuhr
GG6 Gump Worsley
GG9 Bill Ranford
GG10 Richard Brodeur

2004-05 ITG Franchises Canadian Memorabilia

PRINT RUN 70 SETS
GOLD PRINT RUN 20 SETS
GOLD NOT PRICED DUE TO SCARCITY
SM1 Jacques Plante 20.00 50.00
SM2 Henri Richard 12.50 30.00
SM3 Jean Beliveau 15.00 40.00
SM4 Larry Robinson 8.00 20.00
SM5 Patrick Roy 20.00 50.00
SM6 Paul Coffey 12.50 30.00
SM7 Grant Fuhr 12.50 30.00
SM8 Yvan Cournoyer 8.00 20.00
SM9 Lanny McDonald 8.00 20.00
SM10 Guy Lapointe 8.00 20.00
SM11 Serge Savard 8.00 20.00
SM12 Gump Worsley 8.00 20.00
SM13 Guy Lafleur 12.50 30.00
SM14 Borje Salming 8.00 20.00
SM15 Joe Mullen 8.00 20.00
SM17 Steve Shutt 8.00 20.00
SM18 Wendel Clark 12.50 30.00
SM19 Frank Mahovlich 12.50 30.00
SM20 Glenn Anderson 8.00 20.00
SM21 John Ferguson 8.00 20.00
SM22 Richard Brodeur 8.00 20.00
SM23 Tim Horton 20.00 50.00
SM24 Jari Kurri 12.50 30.00
SM25 Jacques Laperriere 8.00 20.00
SM26 Newsy Lalonde 15.00 40.00
SM27 Phil Housley 8.00 20.00
SM28 Bernie Geoffrion 12.50 30.00
SM29 Aurel Joliat 20.00 50.00
SM30 Doug Gilmour 12.50 30.00
SM31 Rick Vaive 8.00 20.00
SM32 Hakan Loob 8.00 20.00

2004-05 ITG Franchises Canadian Memorabilia Autographs

PRINT RUN 10 SETS
NOT PRICED DUE TO SCARCITY
SM2 Henri Richard
SM3 Jean Beliveau
SM5 Patrick Roy
SM6 Paul Coffey
SM7 Grant Fuhr
SM8 Yvan Cournoyer
SM9 Lanny McDonald
SM10 Guy Lapointe
SM11 Serge Savard
SM12 Gump Worsley
SM13 Guy Lafleur
SM14 Borje Salming
SM17 Steve Shutt
SM18 Wendel Clark
SM19 Frank Mahovlich
SM22 Richard Brodeur
SM24 Jari Kurri
SM30 Doug Gilmour

2004-05 ITG Franchises Canadian Original Sticks

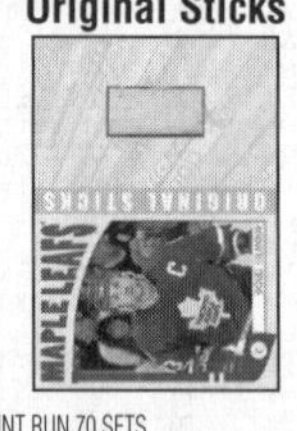

PRINT RUN 70 SETS
GOLD PRINT RUN 20 SETS
GOLD NOT PRICED DUE TO SCARCITY
OS1 Jean Beliveau 12.50 30.00
OS2 Paul Coffey 8.00 20.00
OS3 Guy Lafleur 12.50 30.00
OS4 Lanny McDonald 6.00 15.00
OS5 Guy Lapointe 6.00 15.00
OS6 Larry Robinson 6.00 15.00
OS7 Steve Shutt 6.00 15.00
OS8 Patrick Roy 15.00 40.00
OS9 Rogie Vachon 8.00 20.00
OS10 Denis Savard 6.00 15.00
OS11 Jacques Plante 15.00 40.00
OS12 Dale Hawerchuk 8.00 20.00
OS13 Phil Housley 6.00 15.00
OS14 Doug Gilmour 15.00 40.00
OS15 Jari Kurri 10.00 25.00
OS16 Glenn Anderson 6.00 15.00

2004-05 ITG Franchises Canadian Original Sticks Autographs

PRINT RUN 10 SETS
NOT PRICED DUE TO SCARCITY
OS1 Jean Beliveau
OS2 Paul Coffey
OS3 Guy Lafleur
OS4 Lanny McDonald
OS5 Guy Lapointe
OS7 Steve Shutt
OS8 Patrick Roy
OS12 Dale Hawerchuk

2004-05 ITG Franchises Canadian Teammates

PRINT RUN 60 SETS
GOLD PRINT RUN 20 SETS
GOLD NOT PRICED DUE TO SCARCITY
TM1 George Hainsworth 25.00 60.00
Aurel Joliat
TM2 Glenn Anderson 15.00 40.00
Jari Kurri
TM3 Mike Vernon 12.50 30.00
Phil Housley
TM4 Jean Beliveau 20.00 50.00
Jacques Plante
TM5 Lanny McDonald 20.00 50.00
Darryl Sittler
TM6 G.Fuhr/P.Coffey 15.00 40.00
TM7 Guy Lapointe 12.50 30.00
Larry Robinson
TM8 Patrick Roy 30.00 80.00
Denis Savard
TM9 Henri Richard 20.00 50.00
Gump Worsley
TM10 Doug Gilmour 20.00 50.00
Wendel Clark

2004-05 ITG Franchises Canadian Triple Memorabilia

PRINT RUN 20 SETS
GOLD PRINT RUN 5 SETS
NOT PRICED DUE TO SCARCITY
TM1 Patrick Roy
TM2 Maurice Richard
TM3 Guy Lafleur
TM4 Jacques Plante
TM5 Aurel Joliat
TM6 Tim Horton
TM7 Jean Beliveau
TM8 Grant Fuhr
TM9 Johnny Bower
TM10 Wendel Clark

2004-05 ITG Franchises Canadian Triple Memorabilia Autographs

PRINT RUN 10 SETS
NOT PRICED DUE TO SCARCITY
TM1 Patrick Roy
TM3 Guy Lafleur
TM7 Jean Beliveau
TM8 Grant Fuhr
TM9 Johnny Bower
TM10 Wendel Clark

2004-05 ITG Franchises Canadian Trophy Winners

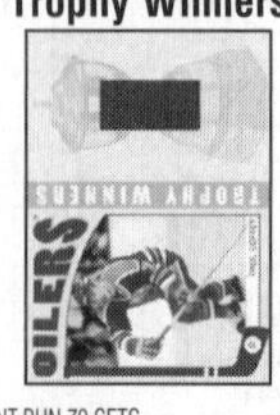

PRINT RUN 70 SETS
GOLD PRINT RUN 20 SETS
GOLD NOT PRICED DUE TO SCARCITY
TW1 Guy Lafleur 12.50 30.00
TW2 Jacques Plante 25.00 60.00
TW3 Gump Worsley 12.50 30.00
TW4 Patrick Roy 20.00 50.00
TW5 Larry Robinson 8.00 20.00
TW6 Paul Coffey 12.50 30.00
TW7 Bill Ranford 8.00 20.00
TW8 Jean Beliveau 15.00 40.00
TW9 Doug Gilmour 12.50 30.00
TW10 Henri Richard 12.50 30.00

2004-05 ITG Franchises He Shoots-He Scores Prizes

PRINT RUN 20 SER.#'d SETS
NOT PRICED DUE TO SCARCITY
1 Joe Mullen
2 Grant Fuhr
3 Jari Kurri
4 Rocket Richard
5 Henri Richard
6 Jean Beliveau
7 Jacques Plante
8 Gump Worsley
9 Guy Lafleur
10 Larry Robinson
11 Yvan Cournoyer
12 Patrick Roy
13 Frank Mahovlich
14 Johnny Bower
15 Lanny McDonald
16 Darryl Sittler
17 Richard Brodeur
18 Bobby Hull
19 Stan Mikita
20 Tony Esposito
21 Denis Savard
22 Patrick Roy
23 Ray Bourque
24 Ted Lindsay
25 Steve Yzerman
26 Alex Delvecchio
27 Marcel Dionne
28 Mario Lemieux
29 Glenn Hall
30 Michel Goulet
31 Roger Crozier
32 Rogie Vachon
33 Paul Coffey
34 Ray Bourque
35 John Bucyk
36 Gerry Cheevers
37 Phil Esposito
38 Ed Giacomin
39 Jean Ratelle
40 Bryan Trottier
41 Mike Bossy
42 Denis Potvin
43 Billy Smith
44 Bobby Clarke
45 Bill Barber
46 Bernie Parent
47 Gilbert Perreault
48 Cam Neely
49 Roy Worters
50 Pelle Lindbergh

2004-05 ITG Franchises Update

Available only online, this 50-card set rounded out the Franchises product run. Each update set contained included a memorabilia card or autograph card also.

COMPLETE SET (50) 12.00 25.00
451 Jari Kurri .40 1.00
452 Bill Quackenbush .20 .50
453 Jean Ratelle .40 1.00
454 Lionel Hitchman .20 .50
455 Terry Sawchuk .60 1.50
456 Grant Fuhr .40 1.00
457 Bill Clement .20 .50
458 Paul Coffey .40 1.00
459 Dick Irvin .20 .50
460 Pierre Pilote .40 1.00
461 Mike Karakas .20 .50
462 Tom Lysiak .20 .50
463 Andy Moog .30 .75
464 Marcel Dionne .40 1.00
465 Borje Salming .30 .75
466 Johnny Bucyk .40 1.00
467 Norm Smith .20 .50
468 Marty McSorley .20 .50
469 Dave Keon .20 .50
470 Rick MacLeish .20 .50
471 Steve Shutt .20 .50
472 Billy Smith .30 .75
473 Neal Broten .20 .50
474 Guy Carbonneau .30 .75
475 Peter Mahovlich .20 .50
476 Tony Esposito .40 1.00
477 Rod Langway .20 .50
478 Newsy Lalonde .50 1.25
479 Pat Verbeek .20 .50
480 Joe Simpson .20 .50
481 Wendel Clark .30 .75
482 Marcel Dionne .40 1.00
483 Frank Boucher .20 .50
484 Johnny Bower .40 1.00
485 Don Beaupre .20 .50
486 Brad Marsh .20 .50
487 Darryl Sittler .40 1.00
488 Barry Ashbee .20 .50
489 Michel Briere .20 .50
490 Guy Lafleur .50 1.25
491 Brian Sutter .20 .50
492 Denis Savard .40 1.00
493 Terry Sawchuk .60 1.50
494 Syl Apps .20 .50
495 Marcel Pronovost .30 .75
496 Dave Keon .20 .50
497 Garth Boesch .20 .50
498 Rick Vaive .20 .50
499 Dino Ciccarelli .20 .50
500 Serge Savard .40 1.00

2004-05 ITG Franchises Update Autographs

ONE AUTO OR MEM.CARD PER SET
AA Al Arbour 6.00 15.00
CK Cliff Koroll 6.00 15.00
DC2 Dino Ciccarelli 12.50 30.00
ET Esa Tikkanen 8.00 20.00
HL Hakan Loob 6.00 15.00
JG John Garrett 6.00 15.00
KW Ken Wregget 6.00 15.00
PF Pat Falloon 6.00 15.00
PV1 Pat Verbeek SP 8.00 20.00
TR Tom Reid 6.00 15.00
TS Thomas Steen 6.00 15.00
ALX Andre Lacroix 6.00 15.00
DKN1 Dave Keon Har. SP 40.00 100.00
DKN2 Dave Keon TML SP 50.00 125.00
JPA Jim Pappin 6.00 15.00
MBU Mike Bullard 6.00 15.00
PBR Pat Price 6.00 15.00
RBA Ralph Backstrom 6.00 15.00
RLY Rick Ley 6.00 15.00

2004-05 ITG Franchises Update Complete Jerseys

PRINT RUN 10 SETS
GOLD PRINT RUN 1 SET
NOT PRICED DUE TO SCARCITY
UCJ1 Larry Robinson
UCJ2 Dan Bouchard
UCJ3 Hakan Loob
UCJ4 Dino Ciccarelli
UCJ5 Dale Hawerchuk
UCJ6 Mike Bossy

2004-05 ITG Franchises Update Double Memorabilia

PRINT RUN 60 SETS
GOLD PRINT RUN 20 SETS
GOLD NOT PRICED DUE TO SCARCITY
UDM1 Pat Lafontaine 15.00 40.00
UDM2 Bill Durnan 20.00 50.00
UDM3 Frank Brimsek 15.00 40.00
UDM4 Billy Smith 12.50 30.00

2004-05 ITG Franchises Update Exceptions

PRINT RUN 25 SETS
GOLD PRINT RUN 5 SETS
GOLD NOT PRICED DUE TO SCARCITY
1 Howie Morenz

2004-05 ITG Franchises Update Goalie Gear

PRINT RUN 60 SETS
GOLD PRINT RUN 20 SETS
GOLD NOT PRICED DUE TO SCARCITY
UGG1 Jacques Plante 20.00 50.00
UGG2 Terry Sawchuk 15.00 40.00
UGG3 Mike Richter 12.50 30.00
UGG4 John Vanbiesbrouck 12.50 30.00

2004-05 ITG Franchises Update Linemates

PRINT RUN 10 SETS
GOLD PRINT RUN 1 SET
NOT PRICED DUE TO SCARCITY
ULI1 Joe Primeau/Charlie Conacher/Busher Jackson
ULI2 Elmer Lach/Toe Blake/Rocket Richard
ULI3 Clark Gillies/Bryan Trottier/Mike Bossy
ULI4 Guy Lafleur/Pete Mahovlich/Steve Shutt
ULI5 Moore/Geoffrion/Beliveau

2004-05 ITG Franchises Update Memorabilia

PRINT RUN 70 SETS
GOLD PRINT RUN 20 SETS
GOLD NOT PRICED DUE TO SCARCITY
USM1 Patrick Roy 15.00 40.00
USM2 Mario Lemieux 15.00 40.00
USM3 Steve Yzerman 12.50 30.00
USM4 Frank Brimsek 8.00 20.00
USM5 Gary Dornhoefer 8.00 20.00
USM6 Rick MacLeish 8.00 20.00
USM7 Pelle Lindbergh 25.00 60.00
USM8 Marcel Dionne 8.00 20.00

2004-05 ITG Franchises Update Memorabilia Autographs

PRINT RUN 10 SETS
NOT PRICED DUE TO SCARCITY
WSM-DC Dino Ciccarelli

2004-05 ITG Franchises Update Original Sticks

PRINT RUN 70 SETS
GOLD PRINT RUN 20 SETS
GOLD NOT PRICED DUE TO SCARCITY
UOS1 Doug Harvey 8.00 20.00
UOS2 Dave Keon 12.50 30.00
UOS3 Bill Durnan 6.00 15.00
UOS4 Terry Sawchuk 15.00 40.00
UOS5 Wayne Cashman 6.00 15.00
UOS6 Phil Esposito 12.50 30.00
UOS7 Mark Howe 6.00 15.00
UOS8 Clark Gillies 6.00 15.00
UOS9 Howie Morenz 15.00 40.00
UOS10 Bob Davidson 6.00 15.00

2004-05 ITG Franchises Update Original Sticks Autographs

PRINT RUN 10 SETS
NOT PRICED DUE TO SCARCITY
UOSDK Dave Keon

2004-05 ITG Franchises Update Teammates

PRINT RUN 60 SETS
GOLD PRINT RUN 20 SETS
GOLD NOT PRICED DUE TO SCARCITY
UTM1 Gilles Gilbert/Gerry Cheevers 15.00 40.00
UTM2 Marcel Dionne/Charlie Simmer 12.50 30.00
UTM3 Dave Keon/Red Kelly 15.00 40.00

2004-05 ITG Franchises Update Trophy Winners

PRINT RUN 70 SETS
GOLD PRINT RUN 20 SETS
GOLD NOT PRICED DUE TO SCARCITY
UTW1 Mario Lemieux 15.00 40.00
UTW2 Steve Yzerman 12.50 30.00
UTW3 Dave Keon 15.00 40.00
UTW4 John Vanbiesbrouck 8.00 20.00

2004-05 ITG Franchises US East

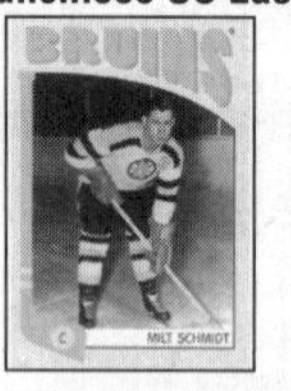

The last in the series issued in pack form, Franchises US East focused on the history of clubs from the eastern United States. Numbering picked up where US West left ended.

COMPLETE SET (150) 25.00 50.00
301 Tom Lysiak .20 .50
302 Bob MacMillan .20 .50
303 Guy Chouinard .20 .50
304 Pat Quinn .50 1.25
305 Eric Vail .20 .50
306 Dan Bouchard .30 .75
307 Curt Bennett .20 .50
308 Phil Myre .30 .75
309 Milt Schmidt .50 1.25
310 Woody Dumart .30 .75
311 Gerry Cheevers .60 1.50
312 Brad Park .30 .75
313 Jacques Plante .60 1.50
314 Johnny Bucyk .40 1.00
315 Terry O'Reilly .20 .50
316 Derek Sanderson .20 .50
317 Phil Esposito .75 2.00
318 Wayne Cashman .20 .50
319 Frank Brimsek .30 .75
320 Wayne Carleton .20 .50
321 Gilles Gilbert .30 .75
322 Bronco Horvath .20 .50
323 Eddie Shore .40 1.00
324 Bill Cowley .20 .50
325 Don Marcotte .20 .50
326 Cam Neely .40 1.00
327 Ray Bourque .75 2.00
328 Andy Moog .30 .75
329 Pete Peeters .20 .50
330 Bobby Bauer .20 .50
331 Tiny Thompson .30 .75
332 Don Awrey .20 .50
333 Rogie Vachon .40 1.00
334 Dit Clapper .30 .75
335 Rick Middleton .30 .75
336 Chuck Rayner .30 .75
337 Mel Hill .20 .50
338 Rick Martin .20 .50
339 Pat LaFontaine .20 .50
340 Sean McKenna RC .20 .50
341 Gilbert Perreault .40 1.00
342 Mike Foligno .20 .50
343 Don Edwards .30 .75
344 Danny Gare .20 .50
345 Phil Housley .20 .50
346 Larry Playfair .20 .50
347 Don Luce .20 .50
348 Tim Horton .40 1.00
349 Roger Crozier .30 .75
350 John Vanbiesbrouck .30 .75
351 Mike Hough .20 .50
352 Bobby Hull .75 2.00
353 Dave Babych .20 .50
354 Tiger Williams .30 .75
355 Mark Howe .20 .50
356 Mike Liut .20 .50
357 Chico Resch .30 .75
358 Bob Carpenter .20 .50
359 Doug Gilmour .40 1.00
360 Chris Terreri .30 .75
361 Kirk Muller .20 .50
362 John MacLean .20 .50
363 Don Lever .20 .50
364 Bruce Driver .20 .50
365 Red Dutton .20 .50
366 Ching Johnson .20 .50
367 Roy Worters .30 .75
368 Sweeney Schriner .20 .50
369 Mike Bossy .40 1.00
370 Billy Smith .30 .75
371 Denis Potvin .30 .75
372 Butch Goring .30 .75
373 Clark Gillies .20 .50
374 Bryan Trottier .30 .75
375 Chico Resch .30 .75
376 Pat LaFontaine .20 .50
377 Garry Howatt .20 .50
378 Bob Bourne .20 .50
379 Bob Nystrom .20 .50
380 J.P. Parise .20 .50
381 Edgar Laprade .20 .50
382 Nick Fotiu .20 .50
383 Rod Gilbert .40 1.00
384 Ed Giacomin .40 1.00
385 Brad Park .30 .75
386 Jean Ratelle .40 1.00
387 John Davidson .30 .75
388 Barry Beck .20 .50
389 Gump Worsley .40 1.00
390 Ron Duguay .20 .50
391 Andy Bathgate .40 1.00
392 Harry Howell .30 .75
393 Phil Esposito .75 2.00
394 Bob Nevin .20 .50
395 Bill Cook .20 .50
396 Allan Stanley .40 1.00
397 Bernie Geoffrion .40 1.00
398 Red Garrett RC .20 .50
399 Don Marshall .20 .50
400 Ron Greschner .20 .50
401 Mike Richter .40 1.00
402 Doug Harvey .20 .50
403 Don Murdoch .20 .50
404 Red Sullivan .20 .50
405 Camille Henry .20 .50
406 Terry Sawchuk .60 1.50
407 Fred Shero .20 .50
408 Red Berenson .20 .50
409 Jim Neilson .20 .50
410 Vic Hadfield .20 .50
411 Bobby Clarke .40 1.00
412 Dave Schultz .30 .75
413 Joe Watson .20 .50
414 Bernie Parent .40 1.00
415 Ron Hextall .30 .75
416 Reggie Leach .20 .50
417 Bill Barber .20 .50
418 Gary Dornhoefer .20 .50
419 Don Saleski .20 .50
420 Bill Clement .20 .50
421 Orest Kindrachuk .20 .50
422 Pelle Lindbergh .30 .75
423 Bobby Taylor .20 .50
424 Mark Howe .20 .50
425 Tom Bladon .20 .50
426 Doug Favell .30 .75
427 Mel Bridgman .20 .50
428 Andre Dupont .20 .50
429 Bob Kelly .20 .50
430 Tim Kerr .20 .50
431 Brad Marsh .20 .50
432 Brian Propp .20 .50
433 Rick MacLeish .20 .50
434 Paul Holmgren .20 .50
435 Keith Acton .20 .50
436 Syd Howe .20 .50
437 Brian Bradley .20 .50
438 Wendel Clark .30 .75
439 Dino Ciccarelli .20 .50
440 Daren Puppa .30 .75
441 Larry Murphy .20 .50
442 Bob Mason RC .30 .75
443 Yvon Labre .20 .50
444 Dennis Maruk .20 .50
445 Dale Hunter .20 .50
446 Al Iafrate .20 .50
447 Rod Langway .20 .50
448 Ryan Walter .20 .50
449 Mike Palmateer .20 .50
450 Don Beaupre .30 .75

2004-05 ITG Franchises US East Autographs

STATED ODDS 1:16
A-DGA Danny Gare 8.00 20.00
A-RMI Rick Middleton 5.00 12.00
A-BMM Bob MacMillan 5.00 12.00
A-RMA Rick Martin 5.00 12.00
A-JBU Johnny Bucyk 8.00 20.00
A-GHO Garry Howatt 5.00 12.00
A-TBL Tom Bladon 5.00 12.00
A-WCA Wayne Carleton 5.00 12.00
A-DOS Don Saleski 5.00 12.00
A-CBN Curt Bennett 5.00 12.00
A-BBN Bob Bourne 5.00 12.00
A-DMR Don Marshall 5.00 12.00
A-BBA Bill Barber 10.00 25.00
A-DMU Don Murdoch 5.00 12.00
A-BHV Bronco Horvath 8.00 20.00
A-DMA Don Marcotte 5.00 12.00
A-PHO Paul Holmgren 5.00 12.00
A-BSM Billy Smith 12.50 30.00
A-RLN Rod Langway 5.00 12.00
A-BCL Bill Clement 8.00 20.00
A-BBR Brian Bradley 5.00 12.00
A-TKR Tim Kerr 5.00 12.00
A-RGI Rod Gilbert 15.00 40.00
A-PMY Phil Myre 8.00 20.00
A-MHO Mike Hough 5.00 12.00
A-BNY Bob Nystrom 5.00 12.00
A-ADU Andre Dupont 5.00 12.00
A-BMS Bob Mason 5.00 12.00
A-TLY Tom Lysiak 5.00 12.00
A-BPA Bernie Parent 20.00 50.00
A-BCA Bobby Carpenter 5.00 12.00
A-MBO Mike Bossy 8.00 20.00
A-BDR Bruce Driver 5.00 12.00
A-DPU Daren Puppa 5.00 12.00
A-BPR Brian Propp 8.00 20.00
A-BTA Bobby Taylor 5.00 12.00
A-SMK Sean McKenna 5.00 12.00
A-DLU Don Luce 8.00 20.00
A-WCL Wendel Clark SP 20.00 50.00
A-JMA John MacLean 5.00 12.00
A-DBR Don Beaupre 5.00 12.00
A-RDU Ron Duguay 5.00 12.00
A-RSU Red Sullivan 5.00 12.00
A-DMK1 Dennis Maruk 5.00 12.00
A-DHU1 Dale Hunter 5.00 12.00
A-DSC1 Dave Schultz 12.50 30.00
A-BBK1 Barry Beck 5.00 12.00
A-PPE1 Pete Peeters 8.00 20.00
A-DSA1 Derek Sanderson 10.00 25.00
A-BGO2 Butch Goring 5.00 12.00
A-LMU2 Larry Murphy 8.00 20.00
A-PPE2 Pete Peeters 8.00 20.00
A-AB Andy Bathgate 8.00 20.00
A-AM1 Andy Moog 10.00 25.00
A-BC Bobby Clarke 15.00 40.00
A-BK Bob Kelly 8.00 20.00
A-BM Brad Marsh 5.00 12.00
A-BN1 Bob Nevin 10.00 25.00
A-BP1 Brad Park BOS SP 20.00 50.00
A-BP2 Brad Park NYR SP 15.00 40.00
A-BT Bryan Trottier 10.00 25.00
A-CG Clark Gillies 8.00 20.00
A-CN1 Cam Neely SP 25.00 60.00
A-CR2 Chico Resch 10.00 25.00
A-CR3 Chico Resch 8.00 20.00
A-CT Chris Terreri 5.00 12.00
A-DA Don Awrey 5.00 12.00
A-DB1 Dan Bouchard 10.00 25.00
A-DC1 Dino Ciccarelli SP
A-DE Don Edwards 8.00 20.00
A-DF1 Doug Favell 5.00 12.00
A-DP Denis Potvin 8.00 20.00
A-EG1 Ed Giacomin 15.00 40.00
A-EV Eric Vail 5.00 12.00
A-GC Gerry Cheevers SP 30.00 80.00
A-GD Gary Dornhoefer 5.00 12.00
A-GG Gilles Gilbert 10.00 25.00
A-GP Gilbert Perreault 15.00 40.00
A-GW1 Gump Worsley 15.00 40.00
A-HH Harry Howell 5.00 12.00
A-IA Al Iafrate 5.00 12.00
A-JD John Davidson 5.00 12.00
A-JN Jim Neilson 5.00 12.00
A-JR Jean Ratelle 8.00 20.00
A-JV John Vanbiesbrouck 5.00 12.00
A-JW1 Joe Watson 5.00 12.00
A-KM2 Kirk Muller 5.00 12.00
A-LA Lou Angotti 8.00 20.00
A-LP Larry Playfair 5.00 12.00
A-MF Mike Foligno 8.00 20.00
A-MH Mark Howe 5.00 12.00
A-NF Nick Fotiu 5.00 12.00
A-OK Orest Kindrachuk 5.00 12.00
A-PC2 Paul Coffey SP 25.00 60.00
A-PE1 Phil Esposito BOS SP 25.00 60.00
A-PE2 Phil Esposito NYR SP 20.00 50.00
A-PH1 Phil Housley 5.00 12.00
A-PL1 Pat LaFontaine BUF SP 40.00 100.00
A-PL2 Pat LaFontaine NYI SP 40.00 100.00
A-PQ Pat Quinn 8.00 20.00
A-PV2 Pat Verbeek 5.00 12.00
A-RB1 Ray Bourque SP 75.00 150.00
A-RG Ron Greschner 5.00 12.00
A-RH Ron Hextall 12.50 30.00
A-RL Reggie Leach 10.00 25.00
A-RM Rick MacLeish 8.00 20.00
A-RW Ryan Walter 5.00 12.00
A-TO Terry O'Reilly 8.00 20.00
A-WC Wayne Cashman 5.00 12.00
A-YL Yvon Labre 5.00 12.00

2004-05 ITG Franchises US East Barn Burners

INT RUN 50 SETS
LD PRINT RUN 20 SETS
LD NOT PRICED DUE TO SCARCITY
B1 Jean Ratelle 8.00 20.00
B2 Mike Bossy 8.00 20.00
B3 Denis Potvin 8.00 20.00
B4 Gerry Cheevers 12.50 30.00
B5 Reggie Leach 8.00 20.00
B6 Ray Bourque 15.00 40.00
B7 Billy Smith 8.00 20.00
B8 Cam Neely 20.00 50.00
B9 Pat LaFontaine 15.00 40.00
B10 Mike Richter 10.00 25.00

2004-05 ITG Franchises US East Boxtoppers

MPLETE SET (25) 40.00 80.00
E PER BOX
-51 Atlanta Flames 2.00 5.00
-52 Atlanta Thrashers 2.00 5.00
-53 Atlanta Thrashers Alt 2.00 5.00
-54 Boston Bruins Orig 2.00 5.00
-55 Boston Bruins 2.00 5.00
-56 Boston Bruins Alt 2.00 5.00
-57 Brooklyn Americans 2.00 5.00
-58 Buffalo Sabres Orig 2.00 5.00
-59 Buffalo Sabres 2.00 5.00
-60 Carolina Hurricanes 2.00 5.00
-61 Florida Panthers 2.00 5.00
-62 Hartford Whalers 2.00 5.00
-63 Nashville Predators 2.00 5.00
-64 Nashville Predators Alt 2.00 5.00
-65 New Jersey Devils 2.00 5.00
-66 New York Americans 2.00 5.00
-67 New York Islanders 2.00 5.00
-68 New York Islanders Fish 2.00 5.00
-69 New York Rangers 2.00 5.00
-70 New York Rangers Liberty 2.00 5.00
-71 Philadelphia Flyers 2.00 5.00
-72 Philadelphia Quakers 2.00 5.00
-73 Tampa Bay Lightning 2.00 5.00
-74 Washington Capitals Orig 2.00 5.00
-75 Washington Capitals 2.00 5.00

2004-05 ITG Franchises US East Complete Jerseys

INT RUN 10 SETS
T PRICED DUE TO SCARCITY
PRICED GOLD 1/1's EXIST
J1 Ray Bourque
J2 Paul Coffey
J3 Bill Barber
J4 Gilbert Perreault
J5 Cam Neely
J6 Brad Park
J7 Denis Potvin
J8 Dale Hawerchuk
J9 Terry O'Reilly
J10 Bobby Clarke

2004-05 ITG Franchises US East Double Memorabilia

INT RUN 60 SETS
LD PRINT RUN 20 SETS
LD NOT PRICED DUE TO SCARCITY
M1 Eddie Shore 20.00 50.00
M2 Bobby Clarke 12.50 30.00
M3 Gerry Cheevers 15.00 40.00
M4 Cam Neely 25.00 60.00
M5 Bernie Parent 20.00 50.00
M6 Tiny Thompson 20.00 50.00
M7 Ray Bourque 15.00 40.00
M8 Ron Hextall 30.00 80.00
M9 Ed Giacomin 25.00 60.00
M10 Gilles Gilbert 15.00 40.00
M11 Bryan Trottier 10.00 25.00
M12 Mike Bossy 10.00 25.00
M13 Gilbert Perreault 15.00 40.00
M14 Denis Potvin 10.00 25.00
M15 Bill Barber 10.00 25.00
M16 Terry O'Reilly 10.00 25.00
M17 Reggie Leach 10.00 25.00
M18 Bob Nystrom 10.00 25.00
M19 Pelle Lindbergh 30.00 80.00
M20 Phil Esposito 20.00 50.00
M21 Rick Middleton 12.50 30.00
M22 Mike Richter 12.50 30.00

2004-05 ITG Franchises US East Double Memorabilia Autographs

INT RUN 10 SETS
T PRICED DUE TO SCARCITY
M-RM Rick Middleton
M-GC Gerry Cheevers
M-GG Gilles Gilbert
M-DP Denis Potvin
M-MB Mike Bossy
M-RH Ron Hextall
M-RB Ray Bourque
M-BB Bill Barber
M-BT Bryan Trottier
M-CN Cam Neely
M-EG Ed Giacomin
M-TO Terry O'Reilly
M-BP Bernie Parent
M-BC Bobby Clarke
M-GP Gilbert Perreault
M-BN Bob Nystrom
M-PE Phil Esposito

2004-05 ITG Franchises US East Forever Rivals

PRINT RUN 50 SETS
GOLD PRINT RUN 20 SETS
GOLD NOT PRICED DUE TO SCARCITY
EFR1 Phil Esposito/Brad Park 15.00 40.00
EFR2 Mike Bossy/Rick Middleton 12.50 30.00
EFR3 G.Perreault/B. Clarke 12.50 30.00
EFR4 Cam Neely/Pat LaFontaine 15.00 40.00
EFR5 Gerry Cheevers/Bernie Parent 30.00 75.00
EFR6 Ray Bourque/Denis Potvin 15.00 40.00

2004-05 ITG Franchises US East Goalie Gear

GOLD PRINT RUN 20 SETS
GOLD NOT PRICED DUE TO SCARCITY
EGG1 Gerry Cheevers 12.50 30.00
EGG2 Billy Smith 12.50 30.00
EGG3 Tiny Thompson 15.00 40.00
EGG4 Bernie Parent 15.00 40.00
EGG5 Pelle Lindbergh 20.00 50.00
EGG6 Ed Giacomin 20.00 50.00
EGG7 Andy Moog 12.50 30.00
EGG8 Gilles Gilbert 12.50 30.00

2004-05 ITG Franchises US East Goalie Gear Autographs

PRINT RUN 10 SETS
NOT PRICED DUE TO SCARCITY
EGG-BS Billy Smith
EGG-BP Bernie Parent
EGG-EG Ed Giacomin
EGG-GC Gerry Cheevers
EGG-GG Gilles Gilbert

2004-05 ITG Franchises US East Memorabilia

PRINT RUN 70 SETS
GOLD PRINT RUN 20 SETS
GOLD NOT PRICED DUE TO SCARCITY
ESM1 Eddie Shore 15.00 40.00
ESM2 Bobby Clarke 8.00 20.00
ESM3 Ray Bourque 15.00 40.00
ESM4 Reggie Leach 8.00 20.00
ESM5 Gerry Cheevers 12.50 30.00
ESM6 Ron Hextall 20.00 50.00
ESM7 Paul Coffey 12.50 30.00
ESM8 Cam Neely 20.00 50.00
ESM9 Gilbert Perreault 12.50 30.00
ESM10 Brad Park 8.00 20.00
ESM11 Billy Smith 8.00 20.00
ESM12 Dave Schultz 15.00 40.00
ESM13 Denis Potvin 8.00 20.00
ESM14 Bill Barber 8.00 20.00
ESM15 Tiny Thompson 15.00 40.00
ESM16 Mike Bossy 8.00 20.00
ESM17 Bryan Trottier 8.00 20.00
ESM18 Gilles Gilbert 12.50 30.00
ESM19 Phil Esposito 15.00 40.00
ESM20 Roy Worters 12.50 30.00
ESM21 Ed Giacomin 20.00 50.00
ESM22 Terry O'Reilly 8.00 20.00
ESM23 Rick Middleton 10.00 25.00
ESM24 Doug Gilmour 8.00 20.00
ESM25 Dale Hawerchuk 12.50 30.00
ESM26 Kirk McLean 8.00 20.00
ESM27 Andy Moog 12.50 30.00
ESM28 Bob Nystrom 8.00 20.00
ESM29 Bernie Parent 15.00 40.00
ESM30 Jean Ratelle 8.00 20.00
ESM31 Pat Verbeek 8.00 20.00
ESM32 John Vanbiesbrouck 10.00 25.00
ESM33 Pat LaFontaine 15.00 40.00
ESM34 Mike Richter 10.00 25.00

2004-05 ITG Franchises US East Memorabilia Autographs

PRINT RUN 10 SETS
NOT PRICED DUE TO SCARCITY
ESM-JR Jean Ratelle
ESM-PL Pat LaFontaine
ESM-RM Rick Middleton
ESM-CN Cam Neely
ESM-PV Pat Verbeek
ESM-TO Terry O'Reilly
ESM-MB Mike Bossy
ESM-BP Bernie Parent
ESM-BC Bobby Clarke
ESM-PE Phil Esposito
ESM-DS Dave Schultz
ESM-GC Gerry Cheevers
ESM-GG Gilles Gilbert
ESM-EG Ed Giacomin
ESM-BT Bryan Trottier
ESM-BS Billy Smith
ESM-RH Ron Hextall
ESM-DP Denis Potvin
ESM-BB Bill Barber
ESM-BP Brad Park
ESM-BN Bob Nystrom
ESM-RB Ray Bourque
ESM-GP Gilbert Perreault

2004-05 ITG Franchises US East Original Sticks

PRINT RUN 70 SETS
GOLD PRINT RUN 20 SETS
GOLD NOT PRICED DUE TO SCARCITY
EOS1 Cam Neely 12.50 30.00
EOS2 Larry Murphy 6.00 15.00
EOS3 Bobby Clarke 6.00 15.00
EOS4 Ron Duguay 8.00 20.00
EOS5 Phil Esposito 12.50 30.00
EOS6 Vic Hadfield 6.00 15.00
EOS7 Reggie Leach 6.00 15.00
EOS8 Pelle Lindbergh 20.00 50.00
EOS9 Ray Bourque 12.50 30.00
EOS10 Bob Nystrom 6.00 15.00
EOS11 Terry O'Reilly 6.00 15.00
EOS12 Denis Potvin 6.00 15.00
EOS13 Bill Barber 6.00 15.00
EOS14 Ed Giacomin 15.00 40.00
EOS15 Ron Hextall 15.00 40.00
EOS16 Bernie Parent 12.50 30.00
EOS17 Gerry Cheevers 10.00 25.00
EOS18 Johnny Bucyk 6.00 15.00
EOS19 Rick Middleton 8.00 20.00
EOS20 John Davidson 6.00 15.00

2004-05 ITG Franchises US East Original Sticks Autographs

PRINT RUN 10 SETS
NOT PRICED DUE TO SCARCITY
EOS-CN Cam Neely
EOS-TO Terry O'Reilly
EOS-GC Gerry Cheevers
EOS-RM Rick Middleton
EOS-RH Ron Hextall
EOS-DP Denis Potvin
EOS-EG Ed Giacomin
EOS-RD Ron Duguay
EOS-JB John Bucyk
EOS-BB Bill Barber
EOS-PE Phil Esposito
EOS-BP Bernie Parent
EOS-BC Bobby Clarke
EOS-BN Bob Nystrom
EOS-RB Ray Bourque

2004-05 ITG Franchises US East Teammates

PRINT RUN 60 SETS
GOLD PRINT RUN 20 SETS
GOLD NOT PRICED DUE TO SCARCITY
ETM1 T.Thompson/E.Shore 30.00 80.00
ETM2 Mike Bossy/Bryan Trottier 15.00 40.00
ETM3 Bobby Clarke/Bill Barber 12.50 30.00
ETM4 Ray Bourque/Cam Neely 20.00 50.00
ETM5 Brad Park/Rick Middleton 12.50 30.00
ETM6 R.Leach/D.Schultz 15.00 40.00
ETM7 Bob Nystrom/Denis Potvin 12.50 30.00
ETM8 Gerry Cheevers/Terry O'Reilly 12.50 30.00

2004-05 ITG Franchises US East Triple Memorabilia

PRINT RUN 20 SETS
GOLD PRINT RUN 5 SETS
NOT PRICED DUE TO SCARCITY
ETM1 Gerry Cheevers
ETM2 Bernie Parent
ETM3 Eddie Shore
ETM4 Ray Bourque
ETM5 Cam Neely
ETM6 Ron Hextall
ETM7 Ed Giacomin

2004-05 ITG Franchises US East Triple Memorabilia Autographs

PRINT RUN 10 SETS
NOT PRICED DUE TO SCARCITY
ETM-RH Ron Hextall
ETM-EG Ed Giacomin
ETM-RB Ray Bourque
ETM-CN Cam Neely
ETM-GC Gerry Cheevers
ETP-BP Bernie Parent

2004-05 ITG Franchises US East Trophy Winners

PRINT RUN 70 SETS
GOLD PRINT RUN 10 SETS
GOLD NOT PRICED DUE TO SCARCITY
ETW1 Eddie Shore 12.50 30.00
ETW2 Bobby Clarke 8.00 20.00
ETW3 Mike Bossy 8.00 20.00
ETW4 Bryan Trottier 8.00 20.00
ETW5 Ray Bourque 15.00 40.00
ETW6 Reggie Leach 8.00 20.00
ETW7 Ron Hextall 20.00 50.00
ETW8 Denis Potvin 8.00 20.00
ETW9 Bernie Parent 15.00 40.00
ETW10 Pelle Lindbergh 20.00 50.00

2004-05 ITG Franchises US West

The second product of the series, Franchises US West focused on the history of clubs in the western United States. Numbering picked up where Franchises Canadian ended.

COMPLETE SET (150) 20.00 40.00
151 Guy Hebert .30 .75
152 Wayne Carleton .20 .50
153 Gary Sabourin .20 .50
154 Gilles Meloche .30 .75
155 Gary Smith .30 .75
156 Bob Stewart .20 .50
157 Reggie Leach .20 .50
158 Glenn Hall .40 1.00
159 Bobby Hull .60 1.50
160 Dennis Hull .30 .75
161 Stan Mikita .50 1.25
162 Bill White .20 .50
163 Tony Esposito .50 1.25
164 Pat Stapleton .20 .50
165 Moose Vasko .20 .50
166 Bill Mosienko .40 1.00
167 Michel Goulet .30 .75
168 Dirk Graham .20 .50
169 Doug Bentley .20 .50
170 Max Bentley .20 .50
171 Phil Esposito .75 2.00
172 Charlie Gardiner .30 .75
173 Lou Angotti .20 .50
174 Denis Savard .40 1.00
175 Murray Bannerman .30 .75
176 Cliff Koroll .20 .50
177 Johnny Gottselig .20 .50
178 Al MacAdam .20 .50
179 Dennis Maruk .20 .50
180 Greg Smith .20 .50
181 Dave Gardner .20 .50
182 Gilles Meloche .20 .50
183 Patrick Roy .75 2.00
184 Ray Bourque .60 1.50
185 Barry Beck .20 .50
186 Chico Resch .30 .75
187 Joe Watson .20 .50
188 Wilf Paiement .20 .50
189 Doug Favell .20 .50
190 Lanny McDonald .30 .75
191 Bob MacMillan .20 .50
192 Jack Valiquette .20 .50
193 Guy Carbonneau .30 .75
194 Kirk Muller .20 .50
195 Neal Broten .20 .50
196 Craig Ludwig .20 .50
197 Frank Foyston RC .50 1.25
198 Carson Cooper .20 .50
199 Ebbie Goodfellow .30 .75
200 Herb Lewis .20 .50
201 Frank Mahovlich .40 1.00
202 Peter Mahovlich .20 .50
203 Ted Lindsay .40 1.00
204 Red Kelly .40 1.00
205 Ed Giacomin .30 .75
206 Roger Crozier .30 .75
207 Henry Boucha .20 .50
208 Reed Larson .20 .50
209 Vladimir Konstantinov .20 .50
210 Steve Yzerman .75 2.00
211 Glenn Hall .40 1.00
212 Sid Abel .40 1.00
213 Terry Sawchuk .50 1.25
214 Alex Delvecchio .40 1.00
215 Mud Bruneteau .20 .50
216 Mark Howe .20 .50
217 Harry Lumley .30 .75
218 Bruce MacGregor .20 .50
219 Jack Stewart .20 .50
220 Darryl Sittler .40 1.00
221 John Ogrodnick .20 .50
222 Norm Ullman .20 .50
223 Alex Faulkner .20 .50
224 Marcel Pronovost .30 .75
225 Joe Kocur .20 .50
226 Wilf Paiement .20 .50
227 Dennis Herron .30 .75
228 Henry Boucha .20 .50
229 Gary Croteau .20 .50
230 Marcel Dionne .40 1.00
231 Charlie Simmer .20 .50
232 Dave Taylor .20 .50
233 Terry Sawchuk .50 1.25
234 Grant Fuhr .40 1.00
235 Rogie Vachon .40 1.00
236 Mike Murphy .20 .50
237 Bob Pulford .30 .75
238 Butch Goring .30 .75
239 Larry Robinson .30 .75
240 Jari Kurri .40 1.00
241 Bernie Nicholls .20 .50
242 Larry Murphy .20 .50
243 Bill Masterton RC 1.25 3.00
244 Bobby Smith .20 .50
245 J.P. Parise .20 .50
246 Gump Worsley .40 1.00
247 Cesare Maniago .30 .75
248 Keith Acton .20 .50
249 Fred Barrett .20 .50
250 Brian Bellows .20 .50
251 Don Beaupre .20 .50
252 Dino Ciccarelli .30 .75
253 Lou Nanne .20 .50
254 Dave Gagner .20 .50
255 Bill Goldsworthy .20 .50
256 Danny Grant .20 .50
257 Craig Hartsburg .20 .50
258 Basil McRae .20 .50
259 Bob Baun .30 .75
260 Bill Hicke .20 .50
261 Carol Vadnais .20 .50
262 Ted Hampson .20 .50
263 Charlie Hodge .20 .50
264 Kent Douglas .20 .50
265 Harry Howell .20 .50
266 Darrin Shannon .20 .50
267 Mario Lemieux 1.00 2.50
268 Greg Malone .20 .50
269 Rick Kehoe .20 .50
270 Les Binkley .30 .75
271 Randy Carlyle .20 .50
272 Lowell MacDonald .20 .50
273 Paul Coffey .40 1.00
274 Kevin Stevens .20 .50
275 Syl Apps Jr. .20 .50
276 Dave Schultz .20 .50
277 Pierre Larouche .20 .50
278 Tim Horton .40 1.00
279 Mike Bullard .20 .50
280 Lionel Conacher .20 .50
281 Odie Cleghorn .20 .50
282 Roy Worters .30 .75
283 Red Berenson .20 .50
284 Mark Hunter .20 .50
285 Glenn Hall .40 1.00
286 Dickie Moore .40 1.00
287 Derek Sanderson .20 .50
288 Wayne Babych .20 .50
289 Bernie Federko .30 .75
290 Doug Harvey .30 .75
291 Jacques Plante .50 1.25
292 Garry Unger .20 .50
293 Doug Gilmour .30 .75
294 Joe Mullen .30 .75
295 Mike Liut .30 .75
296 Frank Finnigan .20 .50
297 Syd Howe .20 .50
298 Brian Hayward .20 .50
299 Kelly Kisio .20 .50
300 Pat Falloon .20 .50

2004-05 ITG Franchises US West Autographs

STATED ODDS 1:16
A-PLA Pierre Larouche 5.00 12.00
A-GAS Gary Smith 10.00 25.00
A-DHE Denis Herron 5.00 12.00
A-GCR Gary Croteau 5.00 12.00
A-GMA Greg Malone 5.00 12.00
A-AMA Al MacAdam 5.00 12.00
A-BST Bob Stewart 5.00 12.00
A-BHA Brian Hayward 5.00 12.00
A-BMG Bruce MacGregor 5.00 12.00
A-BNI Bernie Nicholls 5.00 12.00
A-CLU Craig Ludwig 5.00 12.00
A-GRS Greg Smith 5.00 12.00
A-MHU Mark Hunter 5.00 12.00
A-RLA Reed Larson 5.00 12.00
A-JVA Jack Valiquette 5.00 12.00
A-BMC Basil McRae 5.00 12.00
A-GCA Guy Carbonneau 5.00 12.00
A-THA Ted Hampson 5.00 12.00
A-DGH Dirk Graham 5.00 12.00
A-RKE Rick Kehoe 5.00 12.00
A-BHI Bill Hicke 5.00 12.00
A-JKO Joey Kocur 5.00 12.00
A-DSV Denis Savard 15.00 40.00
A-GSB Gary Sabourin 5.00 12.00
A-DVG Dave Gardner 5.00 12.00
A-BBE Brian Bellows 5.00 12.00
A-DGG Dave Gagner 5.00 12.00
A-CHA Craig Hartsburg 5.00 12.00
A-DGR Danny Grant 5.00 12.00
A-DTA Dave Taylor 5.00 12.00
A-MPR Marcel Pronovost 10.00 25.00
A-JPP J.P. Parise 5.00 12.00
A-MLE Mario Lemieux 75.00 200.00
A-MIM Mike Murphy 5.00 12.00
A-BSH Bobby Smith 5.00 12.00
A-JOG John Ogrodnick 5.00 12.00
A-GHE Guy Hebert 10.00 25.00
A-LMD Lowell MacDonald 5.00 12.00
A-RBE Red Berenson 5.00 12.00
A-BGO1 Butch Goring 5.00 12.00
A-GME1 Gilles Meloche 10.00 25.00
A-LMU1 Larry Murphy 8.00 20.00
A-DMK2 Dennis Maruk 5.00 12.00
A-BBK2 Barry Beck 5.00 12.00
A-GME2 Gilles Meloche 10.00 25.00
A-AD Alex Delvecchio SP 30.00 80.00
A-AF Alex Faulkner 15.00 40.00
A-BB1 Bobby Baun 10.00 25.00
A-BF Bernie Federko 10.00 25.00
A-BH1 Bobby Hull SP 40.00 100.00
A-BW Bill White 5.00 12.00
A-CH Charlie Hodge 5.00 12.00
A-CM Cesare Maniago 10.00 25.00
A-CR1 Chico Resch 8.00 20.00
A-CS Charlie Simmer 5.00 12.00
A-CV Carol Vadnais 5.00 12.00
A-DF1 Doug Favell 5.00 12.00
A-DG1 Doug Gilmour SP 15.00 40.00
A-DH Dennis Hull 10.00 25.00
A-DM1 Dickie Moore 15.00 40.00
A-DS1 Darryl Sittler 20.00 50.00
A-EG2 Ed Giacomin SP 40.00 100.00
A-FB Fred Barrett 5.00 12.00
A-FM1 Frank Mahovlich SP 30.00 80.00
A-GH1 Glenn Hall SP 20.00 50.00
A-GH2 Glenn Hall SP 20.00 50.00
A-GH3 Glenn Hall SP 20.00 50.00
A-GU Garry Unger 5.00 12.00
A-GW2 Gump Worsley SP 20.00 50.00
A-HB Henry Boucha 5.00 12.00
A-JM2 Joe Mullen 10.00 25.00
A-KA Keith Acton 5.00 12.00
A-KD Kent Douglas 5.00 12.00
A-KK Kelly Kisio 5.00 12.00
A-KM1 Kirk Muller 5.00 12.00
A-KS Kevin Stevens 5.00 12.00
A-LB Les Binkley 10.00 25.00
A-LM1 Lanny McDonald SP 20.00 50.00
A-LN Lou Nanne 5.00 12.00
A-LR1 Larry Robinson 10.00 25.00
A-MBN Murray Bannerman 10.00 25.00
A-MD Marcel Dionne SP 15.00 40.00
A-MG1 Michel Goulet 10.00 25.00
A-ML Mike Liut 10.00 25.00
A-NB Neal Broten 5.00 12.00
A-NU Norm Ullman 5.00 12.00
A-PC3 Paul Coffey SP 40.00 100.00
A-PE3 Phil Esposito SP 30.00 80.00
A-PR1 Patrick Roy SP 125.00 250.00
A-PS Pat Stapleton 5.00 12.00
A-RB2 Ray Bourque SP 30.00 75.00
A-RC1 Randy Carlyle 10.00 25.00
A-RK Red Kelly 15.00 40.00
A-RV1 Rogie Vachon 15.00 40.00
A-SA Syl Apps Jr 5.00 12.00
A-SM Stan Mikita SP 15.00 40.00
A-SY Steve Yzerman SP 75.00 200.00
A-TE Tony Esposito SP 15.00 40.00
A-TL Ted Lindsay SP 15.00 40.00
A-WB Wayne Babych 5.00 12.00
A-WP1 Wilf Paiement 5.00 12.00
A-WP2 Wilf Paiement 5.00 12.00

2004-05 ITG Franchises US West Barn Burners

PRINT RUN 50 SETS
WBB1 Mario Lemieux 20.00 50.00
WBB2 Bill Mosienko 10.00 25.00
WBB3 Ray Bourque 15.00 40.00
WBB4 Garry Unger 10.00 25.00
WBB5 Patrick Roy 15.00 40.00
WBB6 Marcel Dionne 10.00 25.00
WBB7 Ted Lindsay 12.50 30.00
WBB8 Bobby Hull 12.50 30.00
WBB9 Steve Yzerman 20.00 50.00
WBB10 Glenn Hall 12.50 30.00

2004-05 ITG Franchises US West Boxtoppers

COMPLETE SET (25) 40.00 80.00
ONE PER BOX
TH26 Mighty Ducks of Anaheim 2.00 5.00
TH27 California Golden Seals 2.00 5.00
TH28 Chicago Blackhawks 2.00 5.00
1930's
TH29 Chicago Blackhawks 2.00 5.00
TH30 Cleveland Barons 2.00 5.00
TH31 Colorado Avalanche 2.00 5.00
TH32 Colorado Rockies 2.00 5.00
TH33 Columbus Blue Jackets 2.00 5.00
TH34 Dallas Stars 2.00 5.00
TH35 Detroit Cougars 2.00 5.00
TH36 Detroit Falcons 2.00 5.00
TH37 Detroit Red Wings 2.00 5.00
TH38 Kansas City Scouts 2.00 5.00
TH39 Los Angeles Kings 2.00 5.00
Original
TH40 Los Angeles Kings 2.00 5.00
TH41 Minnesota North Stars 2.00 5.00
TH42 Minnesota Wild 2.00 5.00
TH43 Oakland Seals 2.00 5.00
TH44 Phoenix Coyotes 2.00 5.00
TH45 Pittsburgh Penguins 2.00 5.00
Original
TH46 Pittsburgh Penguins 2.00 5.00
TH47 Pittsburgh Pirates 2.00 5.00
TH48 St. Louis Blues 2.00 5.00
TH49 St. Louis Eagles 2.00 5.00
TH50 San Jose Sharks 2.00 5.00

2004-05 ITG Franchises US West Complete Jerseys

PRINT RUN 10 SETS
NOT PRICED DUE TO SCARCITY
UNPRICED GOLD 1/1's EXIST
WCJ1 Ray Bourque
WCJ2 Jari Kurri
WCJ3 Paul Coffey
WCJ4 Stan Mikita
WCJ5 Steve Yzerman
WCJ6 Patrick Roy
WCJ7 Mario Lemieux
WCJ8 Norm Ullman

2004-05 ITG Franchises US West Double Memorabilia

PRINT RUN 60 SETS
GOLD PRINT RUN 20 SETS
GOLD NOT PRICED DUE TO SCARCITY
WDM1 Bill Mosienko 12.50 30.00
WDM2 Harry Lumley 15.00 40.00
WDM3 Dino Ciccarelli 12.50 30.00
WDM4 Marcel Dionne 12.50 30.00
WDM5 Frank Brimsek 12.50 30.00
WDM6 Patrick Roy 20.00 50.00
WDM7 Ray Bourque 15.00 40.00
WDM8 Glenn Hall 15.00 40.00
WDM9 Jari Kurri 12.50 30.00
WDM10 Mario Lemieux 30.00 80.00
WDM11 Stan Mikita 12.50 30.00
WDM12 Bobby Hull 12.50 30.00
WDM13 Steve Yzerman 20.00 50.00
WDM14 Tony Esposito 12.50 30.00
WDM15 Terry Sawchuk 20.00 50.00
WDM16 Norm Ullman 12.50 30.00
WDM17 Garry Unger 12.50 30.00
WDM18 Michel Goulet 12.50 30.00
WDM19 Roger Crozier 12.50 30.00

2004-05 ITG Franchises US West Double Memorabilia Autographs

PRINT RUN 10 SETS
NOT PRICED DUE TO SCARCITY
WDMBH Bobby Hull
WDMGH Glenn Hall
WDMMD Marcel Dionne
WDMML Mario Lemieux
WDMPR Patrick Roy
WDMRB Ray Bourque
WDMSM Stan Mikita
WDMSY Steve Yzerman
WDMTE Tony Esposito

2004-05 ITG Franchises US West Forever Rivals

PRINT RUN 50 SETS
WFR1 P.Roy/S.Yzerman 25.00 60.00
WFR2 Bill Mosienko/Sid Abel 12.50 30.00
WFR3 Ted Lindsay/Harry Lumley 15.00 40.00
WFR4 Alex Delvecchio/Stan Mikita 20.00 50.00
WFR5 B.Hull/T.Sawchuk 30.00 80.00

2004-05 ITG Franchises US West Goalie Gear

COMMON CARD (WGG1-WGG6) 10.00 25.00
PRINT RUN 60 SETS
WGG1 Roger Crozier 10.00 25.00
WGG2 Tony Esposito 12.50 30.00
WGG3 Charlie Gardiner 10.00 25.00
WGG4 Patrick Roy 15.00 40.00
WGG5 Frank Brimsek 12.50 30.00
WGG6 Glenn Hall 12.50 30.00

2004-05 ITG Franchises US West Memorabilia

PRINT RUN 70 SETS
WSM1 Bill Mosienko 8.00 20.00
WSM2 Roger Crozier 8.00 20.00
WSM3 Ted Lindsay 10.00 25.00
WSM4 Harry Lumley 10.00 25.00
WSM5 Dino Ciccarelli 8.00 20.00
WSM6 Alex Delvecchio 8.00 20.00
WSM7 Marcel Dionne 8.00 20.00
WSM8 Frank Brimsek 10.00 25.00
WSM9 Patrick Roy 15.00 40.00
WSM10 Ray Bourque 12.50 30.00
WSM11 Charlie Gardiner 10.00 25.00
WSM12 Glenn Hall 10.00 25.00
WSM13 Jari Kurri 12.50 30.00
WSM14 Mario Lemieux 12.50 30.00
WSM15 Stan Mikita 8.00 20.00
WSM16 Sid Abel 8.00 20.00
WSM17 Bobby Hull 12.50 30.00
WSM18 Craig Hartsburg 8.00 20.00
WSM19 Paul Coffey 8.00 20.00
WSM20 Grant Fuhr 10.00 25.00
WSM21 Steve Yzerman 12.50 30.00
WSM22 Tony Esposito 10.00 25.00
WSM23 Bill Gadsby 8.00 20.00
WSM24 Michel Goulet 8.00 20.00
WSM25 Dennis Hull 8.00 20.00
WSM26 Terry Sawchuk 15.00 40.00
WSM27 Norm Ullman 8.00 20.00
WSM28 Steve Yzerman 12.50 30.00
WSM29 Patrick Roy 15.00 40.00
WSM30 Mario Lemieux 15.00 40.00
WSM31 Garry Unger 8.00 20.00
WSM32 Larry Murphy 8.00 20.00
WSM33 Mike Vernon 12.50 30.00

2004-05 ITG Franchises US West Original Sticks

COMMON CARD (WOS1-WOS15) 6.00 15.00
PRINT RUN 70 SETS
WOS1 Patrick Roy 15.00 40.00
WOS2 Harry Lumley 10.00 25.00
WOS3 Steve Yzerman 12.50 30.00
WOS4 Glenn Hall 8.00 20.00
WOS5 Jari Kurri 10.00 25.00
WOS6 Garry Unger 6.00 15.00
WOS7 Stan Mikita 6.00 15.00
WOS8 Ray Bourque 12.50 30.00
WOS9 Roger Crozier 6.00 15.00
WOS10 Marcel Dionne 6.00 15.00
WOS11 Tony Esposito 8.00 20.00
WOS12 Denis Savard 6.00 15.00
WOS13 Mario Lemieux 15.00 40.00
WOS14 Cesare Maniago 6.00 15.00
WOS15 Charlie Simmer 6.00 15.00

2004-05 ITG Franchises US West Teammates

PRINT RUN 60 SETS
WTM1 Sid Abel/Ted Lindsay 20.00 50.00
WTM2 Stan Mikita/Bobby Hull 15.00 40.00
WTM3 Garry Unger/Glenn Hall 12.50 30.00
WTM4 Patrick Roy/Ray Bourque 20.00 50.00
WTM5 M.Lemieux/P.Coffey 20.00 50.00
WTM6 Bill Gadsby/Norm Ullman 12.50 30.00
WTM7 Michel Goulet/Denis Savard 12.50 30.00
WTM8 Steve Yzerman/
Dino Ciccarelli 20.00 50.00
WTM9 Tony Esposito/Dennis Hull 12.50 30.00
WTM10 Terry Sawchuk/
Alex Delvecchio 25.00 60.00

2004-05 ITG Franchises US West Triple Memorabilia

WTM1 Roger Crozier
WTM2 Harry Lumley
WTM3 Marcel Dionne
WTM4 Patrick Roy
WTM5 Ray Bourque
WTM6 Glenn Hall
WTM7 Steve Yzerman
WTM8 Mario Lemieux
WTM9 Stan Mikita
WTM10 Tony Esposito

2004-05 ITG Franchises US West Trophy Winners

PRINT RUN 70 SETS
WTW1 Stan Mikita 8.00 20.00
WTW2 Mario Lemieux 12.50 30.00
WTW3 Bobby Hull 10.00 25.00
WTW4 Ted Lindsay 10.00 25.00
WTW5 Marcel Dionne 8.00 20.00
WTW6 Roger Crozier 8.00 20.00
WTW7 Glenn Hall 8.00 20.00
WTW8 Patrick Roy 15.00 40.00
WTW9 Steve Yzerman 12.50 30.00
WTW10 Charlie Gardiner 12.50 30.00

2006 ITG Going For Gold

COMPLETE SET (25) 4.00 10.00
1 Charline Labonte .40 1.00
2 Kim St. Pierre .40 1.00
3 Gillian Ferrari .20 .50
4 Becky Kellar .20 .50
5 Carla MacLeod .20 .50
6 Caroline Ouellette .20 .50
7 Cheryl Pounder .20 .50
8 Colleen Sostorics .20 .50
9 Meghan Agosta .20 .50
10 Gillian Apps .20 .50
11 Jennifer Botterill .20 .50
12 Cassie Campbell .40 1.00
13 Danielle Goyette .20 .50
14 Jayna Hefford .40 1.00
15 Gina Kingsbury .20 .50
16 Cherie Piper .20 .50
17 Vicky Sunohara .20 .50
18 Sarah Vaillancourt .20 .50
19 Katie Weatherston .20 .50
20 Hayley Wickenheiser .75 2.00
21 Sami Jo Small .40 1.00
22 Delaney Collins .20 .50
23 France St. Louis .20 .50
24 Stacy Wilson .20 .50
25 Checklist .02 .10

2006 ITG Going For Gold Autographs

ONE AU OR GJ PER BOX SET
AA Meghan Agosta 12.00 30.00
AAP Gillian Apps 20.00 50.00
AB Jennifer Botterill 12.00 30.00
AC Cassie Campbell 25.00 60.00
ACO Delaney Collins 12.00 30.00
AF Gillian Ferrari 12.00 30.00
AG Danielle Goyette 12.00 30.00
AH Jayna Hefford 20.00 50.00
AK Becky Kellar 12.00 30.00
AKI Gina Kingsbury 12.00 30.00
AL Charline Labonte 20.00 50.00
AM Carla MacLeod 12.00 30.00
AO Caroline Ouellette 12.00 30.00
AP Cherie Piper 12.00 30.00
APO Cheryl Pounder 12.00 30.00
AS Colleen Sostorics 12.00 30.00
ASM Sami Jo Small 20.00 50.00
AST Kim St. Pierre 20.00 50.00
ASTL France St. Louis 12.00 30.00
ASU Vicky Sunohara 12.00 30.00
AV Sarah Vaillancourt 12.00 30.00
AW Katie Weatherston 12.00 30.00
AWI Hayley Wickenheiser 25.00 60.00
AWIL Stacy Wilson 12.00 30.00

2006 ITG Going For Gold Jerseys

ONE GJ OR AU PER BOXED SET
GUJ4 Becky Kellar 10.00 25.00
GUJ5 Carla MacLeod 10.00 25.00
GUJ6 Caroline Ouellette 10.00 25.00
GUJ12 Cassie Campbell 20.00 50.00
GUJ1 Charline Labonte 15.00 40.00
GUJ16 Cherie Piper 10.00 25.00
GUJ7 Cheryl Pounder 10.00 25.00
GUJ8 Colleen Sostorics 10.00 25.00
GUJ13 Danielle Goyette 10.00 25.00
GUJ22 Delaney Collins 10.00 25.00
GUJ10 Gillian Apps 10.00 25.00
GUJ3 Gillian Ferrari 10.00 25.00
GUJ15 Gina Kingsbury 10.00 25.00
GUJ20 Hayley Wickenheiser 15.00 40.00
GUJ14 Jayna Hefford 15.00 40.00
GUJ11 Jennifer Botterill 10.00 25.00
GUJ19 Katie Weatherston 10.00 25.00
GUJ2 Kim St. Pierre 12.00 30.00
GUJ9 Meghan Agosta 10.00 25.00
GUJ21 Sami Jo Small 15.00 40.00
GUJ18 Sarah Vaillancourt 10.00 25.00
GUJ17 Vicky Sunohara 10.00 25.00

2006-07 ITG International Ice

1 Vladislav Tretiak 2.00 5.00
2 Bobby Hull 1.50 4.00
3 Bobby Clarke 1.25 3.00
4 Raymond Bourque 2.00 5.00
5 Paul Coffey 1.00 2.50
6 Pat LaFontaine .75 2.00
7 Brett Hull 1.25 3.00
8 Steve Yzerman 4.00 10.00
9 Marek Schwarz 1.00 2.50
10 Sidney Crosby 6.00 15.00
11 Gerry Cheevers 1.00 2.50
12 Phil Esposito 1.25 3.00
13 Marcel Dionne 1.25 3.00
14 Grant Fuhr 2.00 5.00
15 Jaromir Jagr 2.50 6.00
16 Antero Niittymaki 1.00 2.50
17 Mario Lemieux 5.00 12.00
18 Henrik Lundqvist 2.00 5.00
19 Alexander Yakushev 1.00 2.50
20 Michel Goulet .75 2.00
21 Paul Coffey 1.00 2.50
22 Darryl Sittler 1.25 3.00
23 Stan Mikita 1.25 3.00
24 Borje Salming 1.00 2.50
25 Vladislav Tretiak 2.00 5.00
26 Steve Yzerman 4.00 10.00
27 Dale Hawerchuk .75 2.00
28 Martin Brodeur 3.00 8.00
29 Ilya Bryzgalov 1.25 3.00
30 Bobby Ryan 1.25 3.00
31 Tony Esposito 1.25 3.00
32 Jari Kurri 1.25 3.00
33 Larry Robinson 1.00 2.50
34 Doug Gilmour 1.25 3.00
35 Mike Richter 1.00 2.50
36 Brett Hull 1.50 4.00
37 Michael Frolik 1.25 3.00
38 Cristobal Huet 1.25 3.00
39 Phil Esposito 1.25 3.00
40 Valeri Vasilyev .75 2.00
41 Borje Salming 1.00 2.50
42 Glenn Anderson .75 2.00
43 Raymond Bourque 2.50 5.00
44 Luc Robitaille 1.00 2.50
45 Pat LaFontaine .75 2.00
46 Petr Prucha 1.25 3.00
47 Steve Shutt .75 2.00
48 Larry Robinson 1.00 2.50
49 Mats Naslund .75 2.00
50 Dale Hawerchuk .75 2.00
51 Pat LaFontaine .75 2.00
52 Jaromir Jagr 2.50 6.00
53 John Tavares 5.00 12.00
54 Tuukka Rask 2.00 5.00
55 Anders Hedberg .75 2.00
56 John Vanbiesbrouck 1.00 2.50
57 Larry Murphy .75 2.00
58 Jari Kurri 1.25 3.00
59 Alexander Ovechkin 3.00 8.00
60 Mike Bossy 1.00 2.50
61 Valeri Kharlamov 2.00 5.00
62 Rick Ley .75 2.00
63 Guy Lafleur 2.00 5.00
64 Tony Esposito 1.25 3.00
65 Kent Nilsson .75 2.00
66 Paul Coffey 1.00 2.50
67 Bill Ranford 1.25 3.00
68 Nicklas Lidstrom 1.25 3.00
69 Evgeni Malkin 4.00 10.00
70 Alexander Radulov 2.50 6.00
71 Borje Salming 1.00 2.50
72 Michel Goulet .75 2.00
73 Thomas Steen .75 2.00
74 Denis Potvin 1.00 2.50
75 Larry Robinson 1.00 2.50
76 Mark Howe .75 2.00
77 Wayne Cashman .75 2.00
78 Marcel Dionne 1.25 3.00
79 Neal Broten .75 2.00
80 Grant Fuhr 2.00 5.00
81 Jari Kurri 1.25 3.00
82 Brian Leetch 1.25 3.00
83 Jim Craig 1.25 3.00
84 Al Montoya 1.25 3.00
85 Mark Messier 1.25 3.00
86 Esa Tikkanen .75 2.00
87 Glenn Anderson .75 2.00
88 Brian Bellows .75 2.00
89 Ulf Nilsson .75 2.00
90 Gilbert Perreault 1.25 3.00
91 Peter Mahovlich .75 2.00
92 Peter Stastny .75 2.00
93 Igor Larionov .75 2.00
94 Mark Messier 1.25 3.00
95 Vladimir Krutov .75 2.00
96 Mats Naslund .75 2.00
97 Mike Richter 1.00 2.50
98 Martin Brodeur 3.00 8.00
99 Justin Pogge 1.50 4.00
100 Paul Coffey 1.00 2.50
101 Paul Henderson 1.25 3.00
102 Mark Messier 1.25 3.00
103 Gilbert Perreault 1.25 3.00
104 Pelle Lindbergh 1.25 3.00
105 Bill Barber .75 2.00
106 Andre Lacroix .75 2.00
107 J.P. Parise .75 2.00
108 Brad Park 1.00 2.50
109 Alex Auld 1.00 2.50
110 Phil Kessel 2.50 6.00
111 Yan Stastny 1.25 3.00
112 Steve Larmer .75 2.00
113 Mats Naslund .75 2.00
114 Rod Langway .75 2.00
115 Peter Stastny .75 2.00
116 Bryan Trottier 1.00 2.50
117 Bobby Hull 1.50 4.00
118 Frank Mahovlich 1.25 3.00
119 Guy Lapointe .75 2.00
120 Danny Gare .75 2.00
121 Guy Lafleur 1.50 4.00
122 Rick Middleton 1.00 2.50
123 Larry Murphy .75 2.00
124 Jeff Glass 1.00 2.50
125 Chris Chelios 1.00 2.50
126 Ryan Malone .75 2.00
127 Marc-Andre Fleury 1.50 4.00
128 Patrick Roy 5.00 12.00
129 Paul Henderson 1.25 3.00
130 Marcel Dionne 1.25 3.00
131 Serge Savard .75 2.00
132 Gilbert Perreault 1.25 3.00
133 Raymond Bourque 2.00 5.00
134 Phil Housley .75 2.00
135 Rogie Vachon 1.25 3.00
136 Vladimir Myshkin .75 2.00
137 Bobby Clarke 1.25 3.00
138 Robbie Schremp 1.25 3.00
139 Peter Mahovlich .75 2.00
140 Mike Bossy 1.00 2.50
141 Esa Tikkanen .75 2.00
142 Chris Chelios 1.00 2.50
143 Serge Savard .75 2.00
144 Lanny McDonald 1.00 2.50
145 Ilya Kovalchuk 2.00 5.00
146 Jason Spezza 1.25 3.00
147 Ryan Miller 1.50 4.00
148 Denis Potvin 1.00 2.50
149 Peter Mueller 1.25 3.00
150 Yvan Cournoyer 1.25 3.00
151 Ladislav Smid 1.00 2.50
152 Chris Bourque 1.00 2.50
153 Ralph Backstrom .75 2.00
154 Henrik Zetterberg 1.25 3.00
155 Angelo Esposito 3.00 8.00
156 Alexei Kasatonov .75 2.00
157 Ed Olczyk .75 2.00
158 Mark Messier 2.00 5.00
159 Andrei Markov .75 2.00
160

1993-94 OPC Premier Team Canada

1 Brett Lindros .75 2.00
2 Manny Legace .75 2.00
3 Adrian Aucoin .60 1.50
4 Ken Lovsin .60 1.50
5 Craig Woodcroft .60 1.50
6 Derek Mayer .60 1.50
7 Fabian Joseph .60 1.50
8 Todd Brost .60 1.50
9 Chris Therien .75 2.00
10 Brad Turner .60 1.50
11 Trevor Sim .60 1.50
12 Todd Hlushko .60 1.50
13 Dwayne Norris .60 1.50
14 Chris Kontos .60 1.50
15 Petr Nedved .75 2.00
16 Brian Savage .75 2.00
17 Paul Kariya 6.00 15.00
18 Corey Hirsch .75 2.00
19 Todd Warriner .75 2.00

1994-95 O-Pee-Chee Finest Inserts

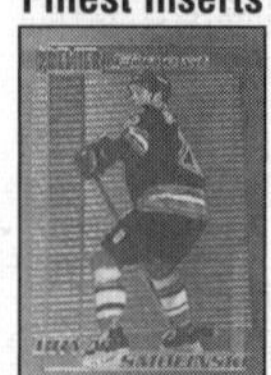

The 23 cards in this set were randomly inserted at a rate of 1:36 OPC Premier series 1 packs. The set includes top rookies of 1993-94. Cards feature an isolated player photo over a textured rainbow background. A reflective rainbow border is broken up by the player name. Premier Finest is written across the top of the card. Backs have a small player photo with brief personal information, and statistical breakdown. Cards are numbered "X of 23".

COMPLETE SET (23) 40.00 80.00
1 Patrik Carnback .60 1.50
2 Bryan Smolinski .60 1.50
3 Derek Plante .60 1.50
4 Alexander Karpovtsev .60 1.50
5 Trevor Kidd 1.25 3.00
6 Iain Fraser .60 1.50
7 Alexandre Daigle .60 1.50
8 Chris Osgood 8.00 20.00
9 Rob Niedermayer 1.50 3.00
10 Jason Arnott .60 1.50
11 Chris Pronger 4.00 10.00
12 Jesse Belanger .60 1.50
13 Oleg Petrov .60 1.50
14 Martin Brodeur 12.50 30.00
15 Alexei Yashin .60 1.50
16 Mikael Renberg 2.50 6.00
17 Boris Mironov .60 1.50
18 Damian Rhodes 2.50 6.00
19 Darren McCarty .60 1.50
20 Chris Gratton 1.25 3.00
21 Jamie McLennan 1.25 3.00
22 Nathan Lafayette .60 1.50
23 Jeff Shantz .60 1.50

1998-99 OPC Chrome

The 1998-99 OPC Chrome set was issue in one series by Topps totaling 242 cards and was distributed in four card packs with a suggested retail price of $3. The fronts feature color action photos of veteran players, 1998 NHL Draft Picks, and CHL All-Stars. The backs carry player information and career statistics.

COMPLETE SET (242) 40.00 100.00
1 Peter Forsberg 1.00 2.50
2 Petr Sykora .20 .50
3 Byron Dafoe .30 .75
4 Ron Francis .30 .75
5 Alexei Yashin .20 .50
6 Dave Ellett .20 .50
7 Jamie Langenbrunner .20 .50
8 Doug Weight .30 .75
9 Jason Woolley .20 .50
10 Paul Coffey .40 1.00
11 Uwe Krupp .20 .50
12 Tomas Sandstrom .20 .50
13 Scott Mellanby .20 .50
14 Vladimir Tsyplakov .20 .50
15 Martin Rucinsky .20 .50
16 Mikael Renberg .30 .75
17 Marco Sturm .20 .50
18 Eric Lindros .40 1.00
19 Sean Burke .30 .75
20 Martin Brodeur 1.25 3.00
21 Boyd Devereaux .20 .50
22 Kelly Buchberger .20 .50
23 Scott Stevens .30 .75
24 Jamie Storr .30 .75
25 Anders Eriksson .20 .50
26 Gary Suter .20 .50
27 Theo Fleury .20 .50
28 Steve Leach .20 .50
29 Felix Potvin .40 1.00
30 Brett Hull .60 1.50
31 Mike Grier .20 .50
32 Cale Hulse .20 .50
33 Larry Murphy .30 .75
34 Rick Tocchet .30 .75
35 Eric Desjardins .30 .75
36 Igor Kravchuk .20 .50
37 Rob Niedermayer .20 .50
38 Bryan Smolinski .20 .50
39 Valeri Kamensky .20 .50
40 Ryan Smyth .30 .75
41 Bruce Driver .20 .50
42 Mike Johnson .20 .50
43 Rob Zamuner .20 .50
44 Steve Duchesne .20 .50
45 Martin Straka .20 .50
46 Bill Houlder .20 .50
47 Craig Conroy .20 .50
48 Guy Hebert .30 .75
49 Colin Forbes .20 .50
50 Mike Modano .60 1.50
51 Jamie Pushor .20 .50
52 Jarome Iginla .75 2.00
53 Paul Kariya .40 1.00
54 Mattias Ohlund .30 .75
55 Sergei Berezin .30 .75
56 Peter Zezel .20 .50
57 Teppo Numminen .20 .50
58 Dale Hunter .20 .50
59 Sandy Moger .20 .50
60 John LeClair .40 1.00
61 Wade Redden .20 .50
62 Patrik Elias .30 .75
63 Rob Blake .30 .75
64 Todd Marchant .20 .50
65 Claude Lemieux .20 .50
66 Trevor Kidd .30 .75
67 Sergei Fedorov .60 1.50
68 Joe Sakic 1.00 2.50
69 Derek Morris .20 .50
70 Alexei Morozov .20 .50
71 Mats Sundin .40 1.00
72 Daymond Langkow .30 .75
73 Kevin Hatcher .20 .50
74 Damian Rhodes .30 .75
75 Brian Leetch .40 1.00
76 Saku Koivu .40 1.00
77 Rick Tabaracci .30 .75
78 Bernie Nicholls .30 .75
79 Alyn McCauley .30 .75
80 Patrice Brisebois .20 .50
81 Bret Hedican .20 .50
82 Sandy McCarthy .20 .50
83 Viktor Kozlov .20 .50
84 Derek King .20 .50
85 Alexander Selivanov .20 .50
86 Mike Vernon .30 .75
87 Jeff Beukeboom .20 .50
88 Tommy Salo .30 .75
89 Adam Graves .20 .50
90 Randy McKay .20 .50
91 Rich Pilon .20 .50
92 Richard Zednik .20 .50
93 Jeff Hackett .30 .75
94 Michael Peca .20 .50
95 Brent Gilchrist .20 .50
96 Stu Grimson .20 .50
97 Bob Probert .20 .50
98 Stu Barnes .20 .50
99 Ruslan Salei .20 .50
100 Al MacInnis .30 .75
101 Ken Daneyko .20 .50
102 Paul Ranheim .20 .50
103 Marty McInnis .20 .50
104 Marian Hossa .40 1.00
105 Darren McCarty .20 .50
106 Guy Carbonneau .20 .50
107 Dallas Drake .20 .50
108 Sergei Samsonov .30 .75
109 Teemu Selanne .40 1.00
110 Checklist .20 .50
111 Jaromir Jagr 1.00 2.50
112 Joe Thornton 1.00 2.50
113 Jon Klemm .20 .50
114 Grant Fuhr .30 .75
115 Nikolai Khabibulin .30 .75
116 Rod Brind'Amour .30 .75
117 Trevor Linden .30 .75
118 Vincent Damphousse .20 .50
119 Dino Ciccarelli .30 .75
120 Pat Verbeek .20 .50
121 Sandis Ozolinsh .20 .50
122 Garth Snow .30 .75
123 Ed Belfour .40 1.00
124 Keith Primeau .20 .50
125 Jason Allison .20 .50
126 Peter Bondra .30 .75
127 Ulf Samuelsson .20 .50
128 Jeff Friesen .20 .50
129 Jason Bonsignore .20 .50
130 Daniel Alfredsson .20 .50
131 Bobby Holik .30 .75
132 Jozef Stumpel .30 .75
133 Brian Bellows .20 .50
134 Chris Osgood .30 .75
135 Alexei Zhamnov .20 .50
136 Mattias Norstrom .20 .50
137 Drake Berehowsky .20 .50
138 Mark Messier .40 1.00
139 Geoff Courtnall .20 .50
140 Marc Bureau .20 .50
141 Don Sweeney .20 .50
142 Wendel Clark .20 .50
143 Scott Niedermayer .20 .50
144 Chris Therien .20 .50
145 Kirk Muller .20 .50
146 Wayne Primeau .20 .50
147 Tony Granato .20 .50
148 Derian Hatcher .20 .50
149 Daniel Briere .20 .50
150 Fredrik Olausson .20 .50
151 Joe Juneau .30 .75
152 Michal Grosek .20 .50
153 Janne Laukkanen .20 .50
154 Keith Tkachuk .40 1.00
155 Marty McSorley .20 .50
156 Owen Nolan .30 .75
157 Mark Tinordi .20 .50
158 Steve Washburn .20 .50
159 Luke Richardson .20 .50
160 Kris King .20 .50
161 Joe Nieuwendyk .30 .75
162 Travis Green .20 .50
163 Dominik Hasek 1.00 2.50
164 Dimitri Khristich .20 .50
165 Dave Manson .20 .50
166 Chris Chelios .40 1.00
167 Claude LaPointe .20 .50
168 Kris Draper .20 .50
169 Brad Isbister .20 .50
170 Patrick Marleau .20 .50
171 Jeremy Roenick .60 1.50
172 Darren Langdon .20 .50
173 Kevin Dineen .20 .50
174 Luc Robitaille .30 .75
175 Steve Yzerman 1.50 4.00
176 Sergei Zubov .20 .50
177 Ed Jovanovski .20 .50
178 Sami Kapanen .20 .50
179 Adam Oates .30 .75
180 Pavel Bure .40 1.00
181 Chris Pronger .30 .75
182 Pat Falloon .20 .50
183 Darcy Tucker .20 .50
184 Zigmund Palffy .30 .75
185 Curtis Brown .20 .50
186 Curtis Joseph .40 1.00
187 Valeri Zelepukin .20 .50
188 Russ Courtnall .20 .50
189 Adam Foote .20 .50
190 Patrick Roy 1.50 4.00
191 Cory Stillman .20 .50
192 Alexei Zhitnik .20 .50
193 Olaf Kolzig .30 .75
194 Mark Fitzpatrick .20 .50
195 Eric Daze .30 .75
196 Zarley Zalapski .20 .50
197 Niklas Sundstrom .20 .50
198 Bryan Berard .30 .75
199 Jason Arnott .20 .50
200 Mike Richter .40 1.00
201 Ken Baumgartner .20 .50
202 Jason Dawe .20 .50
203 Nicklas Lidstrom .40 1.00
204 Tony Amonte .30 .75
205 Kjell Samuelsson .20 .50
206 Ray Bourque .60 1.50
207 Alexander Mogilny .30 .75
208 Pierre Turgeon .30 .75
209 Tom Barrasso .30 .75
210 Richard Matvichuk .20 .50
211 Sergei Krivokrasov .20 .50
212 Ted Drury .20 .50
213 Matthew Barnaby .20 .50
214 Denis Pederson .20 .50
215 John Vanbiesbrouck .30 .75
216 Brendan Shanahan .40 1.00
217 Jocelyn Thibault .30 .75
218 Nelson Emerson .20 .50
219 Wayne Gretzky 2.00 5.00
220 Checklist .20 .50
221 Ramzi Abid RC .40 1.00
222 Mark Bell RC .75 2.00
223 Michael Henrich RC .40 1.00
224 Vincent Lecavalier .75 2.00
225 Rico Fata .40 1.00
226 Bryan Allen .40 1.00
227 Daniel Tkaczuk .40 1.00
228 Brad Stuart RC .75 2.00
229 Derrick Walser RC .40 1.00
230 Jonathan Cheechoo RC 4.00 10.00
231 Sergei Varlamov .40 1.00
232 Scott Gomez RC 1.50 4.00
233 Jeff Heerema RC .40 1.00
234 David Legwand .40 1.00
235 Manny Malhotra .40 1.00
236 Michael Rupp RC .40 1.00
237 Alex Tanguay .40 1.00
238 Mathieu Biron RC .40 1.00
239 Bujar Amidovski RC .40 1.00
240 Brian Finley RC .40 1.00
241 Philippe Sauve RC .40 1.00
242 Jiri Fischer RC .40 1.00
*232 S.Gomez Refractor 40.00 100.00

1998-99 OPC Chrome Refractors

Randomly inserted in packs at the rate of 1:12, this 242-card set is a refractive parallel version of the base set.

*STARS: 4X TO 10X BASE CARD HI
*ROOKIES: 1X TO 2X BASE CARD HI

1998-99 OPC Chrome Blast From the Past

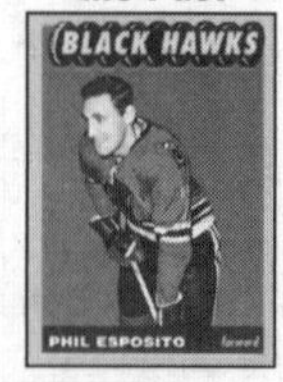

Randomly inserted into packs at the rate of 1:28, this 10-card set features reprints of the rookie cards of selected great retired as well as current stars. A refractor parallel version of this set was also produced with an insertion rate of 1:112.

COMPLETE SET (10) 40.00 80.00
*REFRACTORS: 1.5X TO 3X BASIC INSERTS
1 Wayne Gretzky 8.00 20.00
2 Mark Messier 3.00 8.00
3 Ray Bourque 5.00 12.00
4 Patrick Roy 6.00 15.00
5 Grant Fuhr 3.00 8.00
6 Brett Hull 3.00 8.00
7 Gordie Howe 8.00 20.00
8 Stan Mikita 4.00 10.00
9 Bobby Hull 5.00 12.00
10 Phil Esposito 4.00 10.00

1998-99 OPC Chrome Board Members

Randomly inserted into packs at the rate of 1:12, this 15-card set features color action photos of some of the great defensive superstars of the NHL. A refractor parallel version of this set was also produced with an insertion rate of 1:36.

COMPLETE SET (15) 30.00 60.00
*REFRACTORS: 1X TO 2X BASIC INSERTS
B1 Chris Pronger 2.00 5.00
B2 Chris Chelios 3.00 8.00
B3 Brian Leetch 2.00 5.00
B4 Ray Bourque 5.00 12.00
B5 Mattias Ohlund 2.00 5.00
B6 Nicklas Lidstrom 3.00 8.00
B7 Sergei Zubov 2.00 5.00
B8 Scott Niedermayer 1.25 3.00
B9 Larry Murphy 2.00 5.00
B10 Sandis Ozolinsh 1.25 3.00
B11 Rob Blake 2.00 5.00
B12 Scott Stevens 2.00 5.00
B13 Derian Hatcher 1.25 3.00
B14 Kevin Hatcher 1.25 3.00
B15 Wade Redden 1.25 3.00

1998-99 OPC Chrome Season's Best

Randomly inserted into packs at the rate of 1:8, this 30-card set features color action photos of top players in five distinct categories: Net Minders, the league's top goalies; Sharpshooters, the top scoring leaders; Puck Providers, assist leaders; Performers Plus, leaders in ice time by plus/minus ratio; and Ice Hot, powerful rookies. A refractor parallel version of this set was also produced with an insertion rate of 1:24.

COMPLETE SET (30) 30.00 60.00
*REFRACTORS: 1.25X TO 2.5X BASIC INSERTS
SB1 Dominik Hasek 2.00 5.00
SB2 Martin Brodeur 2.50 6.00
SB3 Ed Belfour 1.00 2.50
SB4 Curtis Joseph 1.00 2.50
SB5 Jeff Hackett .75 2.00
SB6 Tom Barrasso .75 2.00
SB7 Mike Johnson .40 1.00
SB8 Sergei Samsonov .75 2.00
SB9 Patrik Elias .75 2.00
SB10 Patrick Marleau .75 2.00
SB11 Mattias Ohlund .75 2.00
SB12 Marco Sturm .75 2.00
SB13 Teemu Selanne 1.00 2.50
SB14 Peter Bondra .75 2.00
SB15 Pavel Bure 1.00 2.50
SB16 John LeClair 1.00 2.50
SB17 Zigmund Palffy .75 2.00
SB18 Keith Tkachuk 1.00 2.50
SB19 Jaromir Jagr 1.50 4.00
SB20 Wayne Gretzky 6.00 15.00
SB21 Peter Forsberg 2.50 6.00
SB22 Ron Francis .40 1.00
SB23 Adam Oates .40 1.00
SB24 Jozef Stumpel .40 1.00
SB25 Chris Pronger .75 2.00
SB26 Larry Murphy .40 1.00
SB27 Jason Allison .40 1.00
SB28 John LeClair 1.00 2.50
SB29 Randy McKay .40 1.00
SB30 Dainius Zubrus .40 1.00

1999-00 O-Pee-Chee

This 286-card set parallels the Topps set of the same season. See the Topps listings for complete prices and checklists.

*OPC: 1X TO 1.5X TOPPS

2000-01 O-Pee-Chee

This 330-card set parallels the Topps set of the same season. See the Topps listing for complete prices and checklist.

COMPLETE SET (300)
*BASE CARDS SAME VALUE AS TOPPS

2001-02 O-Pee-Che

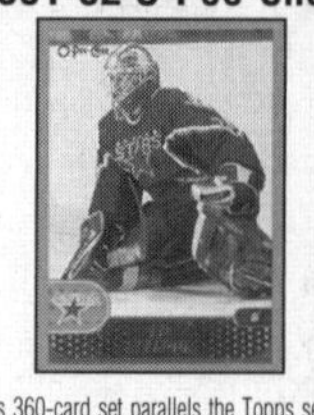

This 360-card set parallels the Topps set the same season. See the Topps listing complete prices and checklist. Pack S was $1.49 for a 10-card pack and there w 36 packs per box.

*BASE CARDS SAME VALUE AS TOPPS
*ROOKIES: .75X TO 2X

2001-02 O-Pee-Che Heritage Parallel

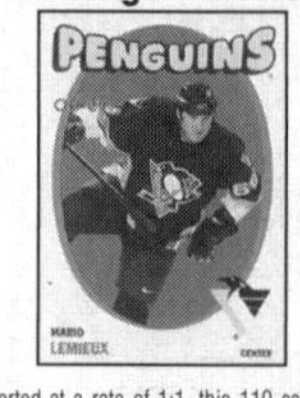

Inserted at a rate of 1:1, this 110-card parallels the first 110 cards of the O-Pe Chee base set. The card fronts carry t same photo as the base cards, but use t 1971-72 O-Pee-Chee design. Card bac are the same as the base set. A limit parallel to these inserts were also creat these parallels look the same but ca different colored foil and serial number out of 50.

*STARS: 1.25X TO 2.5X BASIC CARDS
*LIMITED: 40X TO 80X BASIC CARD

2001-02 O-Pee-Che Premier Parallel

This parallel to the base set was inserted 1:4 packs. Cards from this set were stamp with a OPC Premier silver foil stamp on t card fronts.

*STARS: 1.5X TO 4X BASIC CARDS

2001-02 O-Pee-Che Jumbos

Inserted in retail value boxes only as b toppers, very little is known about th eight oversized cards other than that th were numbered "X of 8".

1 Mario Lemieux 2.00 5.0
2 Steve Yzerman 2.00 5.0
3 Martin Brodeur .75 2.0
4 Paul Kariya 1.00 2.5
5 Patrick Roy 2.00 5.0
6 Curtis Joseph .75 2.0
7 Martin Havlat .75 2.0
8 Mike Comrie .40 1.0

2002-03 O-Pee-Che

Available in Canada only, this 341-card mirrors the Topps issue. Values for sing can be found by using the multipliers belo Cards 331-340 were available via mail redemption.

*BASE CARDS SAME VALUE AS TOPPS
*ROOKIES: .6X TO 1.5X

2002-03 O-Pee-Che Jumbos

Inserted as boxtoppers in OPC boxes, t 25-card set consists of jumbo-sized repri of 25 base cards.

COMPLETE SET (25) 60.0
1 Joe Thornton 5.0
2 Jarome Iginla 3.0
3 Roman Turek 2.0
4 Ron Francis 2.0
5 Patrick Roy 10.0
6 Joe Sakic 7.0
7 Steve Yzerman 10.0
8 Brendan Shanahan 5.0
9 Mike Comrie 3.0
10 Ryan Smyth 2.0
11 Paul Kariya 5.0
12 Jose Theodore 3.0
13 Saku Koivu 3.0
14 Martin Brodeur 5.0
15 Mike Peca 1.0
16 Daniel Alfredsson 1.0
17 Martin Havlat 3.0
18 Sean Burke 2.0
19 Mario Lemieux 10.0
20 Owen Nolan 2.0
21 Chris Pronger 2.0
22 Mats Sundin 3.0

Curtis Joseph 3.00
Markus Naslund 2.00
Todd Bertuzzi 2.00

2002-03 O-Pee-Chee Premier Blue Parallel

is set paralleled the base set but carried ue borders and blue foil accents. The OPC emier logo was stamped on the card fronts blue foil and each card was serial-mbered out of 500.

STARS: 3X TO 8X BASIC CARDS
ROOKIES: 1.25X TO 3X

2002-03 O-Pee-Chee Premier Red Parallel

is set paralleled the base set but carried d borders and red foil accents. The OPC emier logo was stamped on the card fronts red foil and each card was serial-mbered out of 100.

STARS: 8X TO 20X BASIC CARDS
ROOKIES: 4X TO 10X HI

2002-03 O-Pee-Chee Factory Set

OMPLETE FACTORY SET 30.00 60.00
STARS: .6X TO 1.5X REG.TOPPS
ROOKIES: 1X TO 2.5X REG.TOPPS

2002-03 O-Pee-Chee Factory Set Hometown Heroes

SAME VALUE AS REGULAR INSERTS

2003-04 O-Pee-Chee

eleased in late-August, this 340-card set nsisted of 330-base cards and a special -card rookie redemption subset. Rookie demption cards were seeded at 1:36.

OPC: .6X TO 1.5X TOPPS

2003-04 OPC Blue

is 330-card set paralleled the base set but rried blue glitter borders and the Topps go. These parallels were inserted at 1:5 d each card was serial numbered out of 0. The Rookie Redemption parallel card s inserted at 1:1562.

STARS: 5X TO 12X TOPPS BASE
ROOKIES: 1X TO 2.5X TOPPS

2003-04 OPC Gold

is 330-card set paralleled the base set but rried gold glitter borders and the Topps go. These parallels were inserted at 1:23 d each card was serial numbered out of . The Rookie Redemption parallel card s inserted at 1:7485.

STARS: 10X TO 25X TOPPS BASE
ROOKIES: 3X TO 8X TOPPS

2003-04 OPC Red

is 330-card set paralleled the base set but rried blue glitter borders and the Topps go. These parallels were inserted at 2:36 d each card was serial numbered out of 0. The Rookie Redemption parallel card s inserted at 1:5852.

STARS: 8X TO 20X TOPPS BASE
ROOKIES: 2.5X TO 6X TOPPS

2006-07 O-Pee-Chee

OMPLETE SET (700) 150.00 300.00
OMP. SET w/o SPs (500) 40.00 100.00
Chris Pronger .20 .50
Samuel Pahlsson .12 .30
Andy McDonald .12 .30
Todd Fedoruk .12 .30
Teemu Selanne .25 .60
Chris Kunitz .12 .30
Scott Niedermayer .12 .30
Corey Perry .20 .50
Sean O'Donnell .12 .30
Ryan Getzlaf .20 .50
Francois Beauchemin .12 .30
Dustin Penner .12 .30
Rob Niedermayer .12 .30
Todd Marchant .12 .30
Ilya Bryzgalov .20 .50
Stanislav Chistov .12 .30
Jean-Sebastien Giguere .20 .50
Andy Sutton .12 .30
Steve Rucchin .12 .30
Greg de Vries .12 .30
Vitaly Vishnevski .12 .30
Ilya Kovalchuk .30 .75
Scott Mellanby .12 .30
Jim Slater .12 .30
Kari Lehtonen .25 .60
Johan Hedberg .20 .50
Niclas Havelid .12 .30
Marian Hossa .20 .50
Bobby Holik .12 .30
Garnet Exelby .12 .30
Steve McCarthy .12 .30
Niko Kapanen .12 .30
Slava Kozlov .12 .30
P.J. Axelsson .12 .30
Hannu Toivonen .20 .50
Patrice Bergeron .25 .60
Tim Thomas .20 .50
Marc Savard .12 .30
Nathan Dempsey .12 .30
Glen Murray .12 .30
Brad Stuart .12 .30
Shean Donovan .12 .30
Marco Sturm .12 .30
Mark Mowers .12 .30
45 Paul Mara .12 .30
46 Andrew Alberts .12 .30
47 Brad Boyes .12 .30
48 Wayne Primeau .12 .30
49 Milan Jurcina .12 .30
50 Jason York .12 .30
51 Zdeno Chara .12 .30
52 Jiri Novotny .12 .30
53 Derek Roy .12 .30
54 Teppo Numminen .12 .30
55 Jason Pominville .12 .30
56 Henrik Tallinder .12 .30
57 Adam Mair .12 .30
58 Daniel Briere .20 .50
59 Chris Drury .12 .30
60 Ryan Miller .25 .60
61 Ales Kotalik .12 .30
62 Thomas Vanek .20 .50
63 Brian Campbell .12 .30
64 Paul Gaustad .12 .30
65 Jaroslav Spacek .12 .30
66 Jochen Hecht .12 .30
67 Maxim Afinogenov .12 .30
68 Martin Biron .20 .50
69 Robyn Regehr .12 .30
70 Dion Phaneuf .30 .75
71 Miikka Kiprusoff .25 .60
72 Jamie Lundmark .12 .30
73 Roman Hamrlik .12 .30
74 Kristian Huselius .12 .30
75 Darren McCarty .12 .30
76 Stephane Yelle .12 .30
77 Marcus Nilson .12 .30
78 Daymond Langkow .12 .30
79 Jamie McLennan .20 .50
80 Tony Amonte .12 .30
81 Chuck Kobasew .12 .30
82 Jarome Iginla .30 .75
83 Alex Tanguay .20 .50
84 Andrew Ference .12 .30
85 Matthew Lombardi .12 .30
86 Jeff Friesen .12 .30
87 Glen Wesley .12 .30
88 Cory Stillman .12 .30
89 John Grahame .20 .50
90 Erik Cole .12 .30
91 Chad Larose .12 .30
92 Andrew Ladd .12 .30
93 Craig Adams .12 .30
94 Eric Staal .25 .60
95 Rod Brind'Amour .20 .50
96 Mike Commodore .12 .30
97 Ray Whitney .12 .30
98 Justin Williams .12 .30
99 Kevyn Adams .12 .30
100 Cam Ward .25 .60
101 Eric Belanger .12 .30
102 Scott Walker .12 .30
103 Bret Hedican .12 .30
104 Tim Gleason .12 .30
105 Adrian Aucoin .12 .30
106 Nikolai Khabibulin .25 .60
107 Michal Handzus .12 .30
108 Tuomo Ruutu .12 .30
109 Martin Lapointe .12 .30
110 Jim Vandermeer .12 .30
111 Martin Havlat .20 .50
112 Bryan Smolinski .12 .30
113 Michael Holmqvist .12 .30
114 Rene Bourque .12 .30
115 Brandon Bochenski .12 .30
116 Patrick Sharp .12 .30
117 Brent Seabrook .12 .30
118 Duncan Keith .12 .30
119 Jeffrey Hamilton .12 .30
120 Radim Vrbata .12 .30
121 Joe Sakic .50 1.25
122 Peter Budaj .20 .50
123 Tyler Arnason .12 .30
124 Mark Rycroft .12 .30
125 John-Michael Liles .12 .30
126 Milan Hejduk .12 .30
127 Andrew Brunette .12 .30
128 Ian Laperriere .12 .30
129 Antti Laaksonen .12 .30
130 Marek Svatos .12 .30
131 Wojtek Wolski .12 .30
132 Patrice Brisebois .12 .30
133 Pierre Turgeon .12 .30
134 Brett McLean .12 .30
135 Karlis Skrastins .12 .30
136 Brad Richardson .12 .30
137 Brett Clark .12 .30
138 Jose Theodore .25 .60
139 Rick Nash .25 .60
140 Nikolai Zherdev .12 .30
141 Rostislav Klesla .12 .30
142 David Vyborny .12 .30
143 Anders Eriksson .12 .30
144 Adam Foote .12 .30
145 Jody Shelley .12 .30
146 Duvie Westcott .12 .30
147 Gilbert Brule .25 .60
148 Jason Chimera .12 .30
149 Pascal LeClaire .20 .50
150 Manny Malhotra .12 .30
151 Ron Hainsey .12 .30
152 Anson Carter .12 .30
153 Fredrik Modin .12 .30
154 Dan Fritsche .12 .30
155 Sergei Fedorov .25 .60
156 Marty Turco .20 .50
157 Jussi Jokinen .12 .30
158 Steve Ott .12 .30
159 Jaroslav Modry .12 .30
160 Patrik Stefan .12 .30
161 Matthew Barnaby .12 .30
162 Jeff Halpern .12 .30
163 Eric Lindros .25 .60
164 Sergei Zubov .12 .30
165 Darryl Sydor .12 .30
166 Brenden Morrow .20 .50
167 Antti Miettinen .12 .30
168 Jere Lehtinen .12 .30
169 Philippe Boucher .12 .30
170 Mike Ribeiro .12 .30
171 Stu Barnes .12 .30
172 Mike Modano .25 .60
173 Dominik Hasek .40 1.00
174 Tomas Holmstrom .12 .30
175 Johan Franzen .12 .30
176 Robert Lang .12 .30
177 Mathieu Schneider .12 .30
178 Nicklas Lidstrom .25 .60
179 Chris Osgood .20 .50
180 Jason Williams .12 .30
181 Mikael Samuelsson .12 .30
182 Chris Chelios .20 .50
183 Pavel Datsyuk .20 .50
184 Dan Cleary .12 .30
185 Kirk Maltby .12 .30
186 Kris Draper .12 .30
187 Andreas Lilja .12 .30
188 Brett Lebda .12 .30
189 Jiri Hudler .20 .50
190 Henrik Zetterberg .25 .60
191 Ales Hemsky .12 .30
192 Fernando Pisani .12 .30
193 Joffrey Lupul .12 .30
194 Dwayne Roloson .25 .60
195 Matt Greene .12 .30
196 Jason Smith .12 .30
197 Ethan Moreau .12 .30
198 Jarret Stoll .12 .30
199 Jussi Markkanen .20 .50
200 Brad Winchester .12 .30
201 Marc-Andre Bergeron .12 .30
202 Raffi Torres .12 .30
203 Petr Sykora .12 .30
204 Shawn Horcoff .12 .30
205 Steve Staios .12 .30
206 Ryan Smyth .20 .50
207 Jay Bouwmeester .12 .30
208 Ed Belfour .25 .60
209 Ruslan Salei .12 .30
210 Stephen Weiss .12 .30
211 Rostislav Olesz .12 .30
212 Mike Van Ryn .12 .30
213 Jozef Stumpel .12 .30
214 Nathan Horton .12 .30
215 Alexander Auld .20 .50
216 Juraj Kolnik .12 .30
217 Martin Gelinas .12 .30
218 Joe Nieuwendyk .20 .50
219 Gary Roberts .12 .30
220 Todd Bertuzzi .20 .50
221 Chris Gratton .12 .30
222 Bryan Allen .12 .30
223 Olli Jokinen .12 .30
224 Alexander Frolov .12 .30
225 Mathieu Garon .20 .50
226 Dustin Brown .12 .30
227 Lubomir Visnovsky .12 .30
228 Sean Avery .12 .30
229 Brent Sopel .12 .30
230 Craig Conroy .12 .30
231 Aaron Miller .12 .30
232 Scott Thornton .12 .30
233 Mattias Norstrom .12 .30
234 Dan Cloutier .20 .50
235 Mike Cammalleri .12 .30
236 Oleg Tverdovsky .12 .30
237 Derek Armstrong .12 .30
238 Tom Kostopoulos .12 .30
239 Rob Blake .20 .50
240 Marian Gaborik .30 .75
241 Derek Boogaard .12 .30
242 Brian Rolston .12 .30
243 Keith Carney .12 .30
244 Mark Parrish .12 .30
245 Wes Walz .12 .30
246 Todd White .12 .30
247 Pierre-Marc Bouchard .12 .30
248 Nick Schultz .12 .30
249 Kurtis Foster .12 .30
250 Pascal Dupuis .12 .30
251 Mikko Koivu .12 .30
252 Manny Fernandez .20 .50
253 Wyatt Smith .12 .30
254 Brent Burns .12 .30
255 Kim Johnsson .12 .30
256 Pavol Demitra .12 .30
257 Michael Ryder .20 .50
258 David Aebischer .20 .50
259 Andrei Markov .12 .30
260 Alexander Perezhogin .12 .30
261 Sheldon Souray .12 .30
262 Cristobal Huet .30 .75
263 Chris Higgins .12 .30
264 Steve Begin .12 .30
265 Radek Bonk .12 .30
266 Janne Niinimaa .12 .30
267 Mike Komisarek .12 .30
268 Tomas Plekanec .12 .30
269 Sergei Samsonov .20 .50
270 Alexei Kovalev .12 .30
271 Craig Rivet .12 .30
272 Mathieu Dandenault .12 .30
273 Mike Johnson .12 .30
274 Saku Koivu .25 .60
275 Tomas Vokoun .20 .50
276 Scott Hartnell .12 .30
277 Marek Zidlicky .12 .30
278 Josef Vasicek .12 .30
279 Jordin Tootoo .20 .50
280 Ryan Suter .12 .30
281 Martin Erat .12 .30
282 David Legwand .12 .30
283 Kimmo Timonen .12 .30
284 Chris Mason .20 .50
285 Steve Sullivan .12 .30
286 Jason Arnott .12 .30
287 Dan Hamhuis .12 .30
288 J.P. Dumont .12 .30
289 Darcy Hordichuk .12 .30
290 Paul Kariya .25 .60
291 Martin Brodeur 1.00 2.50
292 Brian Gionta .12 .30
293 Paul Martin .12 .30
294 John Madden .12 .30
295 Brian Rafalski .12 .30
296 Colin White .12 .30
297 Zach Parise .20 .50
298 Jay Pandolfo .12 .30
299 Jamie Langenbrunner .12 .30
300 Scott Gomez .12 .30
301 Sergei Brylin .12 .30
302 Scott Clemmensen .20 .50
303 Jim Fahey .12 .30
304 Erik Rasmussen .12 .30
305 Brad Lukowich .12 .30
306 Patrik Elias .12 .30
307 Rick DiPietro .20 .50
308 Jason Blake .12 .30
309 Tom Poti .12 .30
310 Trent Hunter .12 .30
311 Brendan Witt .12 .30
312 Chris Simon .12 .30
313 Arron Asham .12 .30
314 Alexei Yashin .12 .30
315 Mike Sillinger .12 .30
316 Alexei Zhitnik .12 .30
317 Jeff Tambellini .12 .30
318 Mike Dunham .20 .50
319 Mike York .12 .30
320 Shawn Bates .12 .30
321 Viktor Kozlov .12 .30
322 Miroslav Satan .12 .30
323 Henrik Lundqvist .30 .75
324 Fedor Tyutin .12 .30
325 Michal Rozsival .12 .30
326 Michael Nylander .12 .30
327 Sandis Ozolinsh .12 .30
328 Matt Cullen .12 .30
329 Brendan Shanahan .25 .60
330 Darius Kasparaitis .12 .30
331 Kevin Weekes .20 .50
332 Petr Prucha .12 .30
333 Martin Straka .12 .30
334 Aaron Ward .12 .30
335 Marek Malik .12 .30
336 Blair Betts .12 .30
337 Jason Ward .12 .30
338 Jaromir Jagr .40 1.00
339 Dany Heatley .30 .75
340 Wade Redden .12 .30
341 Peter Schaefer .12 .30
342 Mike Fisher .12 .30
343 Ray Emery .20 .50
344 Tom Preissing .12 .30
345 Patrick Eaves .12 .30
346 Daniel Alfredsson .20 .50
347 Chris Phillips .12 .30
348 Andrej Meszaros .12 .30
349 Martin Gerber .25 .60
350 Joe Corvo .12 .30
351 Antoine Vermette .12 .30
352 Chris Neil .12 .30
353 Anton Volchenkov .12 .30
354 Chris Kelly .12 .30
355 Jason Spezza .25 .60
356 Simon Gagne .25 .60
357 Antero Niittymaki .20 .50
358 Joni Pitkanen .12 .30
359 Jeff Carter .25 .60
360 Randy Jones .12 .30
361 R.J. Umberger .12 .30
362 Mike Knuble .12 .30
363 Derian Hatcher .12 .30
364 Sami Kapanen .12 .30
365 Fredrick Meyer .12 .30
366 Mike Richards .20 .50
367 Robert Esche .20 .50
368 Randy Robitaille .12 .30
369 Stefan Ruzicka .12 .30
370 Geoff Sanderson .12 .30
371 Kyle Calder .12 .30
372 Peter Forsberg .40 1.00
373 Curtis Joseph .25 .60
374 Ladislav Nagy .12 .30
375 Nick Boynton .12 .30
376 Dave Scatchard .12 .30
377 Derek Morris .12 .30
378 Mike Comrie .12 .30
379 Ed Jovanovski .12 .30
380 Georges Laraque .12 .30
381 Oleg Saprykin .12 .30
382 Keith Ballard .12 .30
383 Steven Reinprecht .12 .30
384 Jeremy Roenick .30 .75
385 Zbynek Michalek .12 .30
386 Owen Nolan .20 .50
387 Fredrik Sjostrom .12 .30
388 David Leneveu .20 .50
389 Shane Doan .12 .30
390 Marc-Andre Fleury .25 .60
391 Sergei Gonchar .12 .30
392 Dominic Moore .12 .30
393 Ryan Whitney .12 .30
394 Nils Ekman .12 .30
395 Brooks Orpik .12 .30
396 Mark Eaton .12 .30
397 Jocelyn Thibault .20 .50
398 Andre Roy .12 .30
399 Colby Armstrong .20 .50
400 Ryan Malone .12 .30
401 Jarkko Ruutu .12 .30
402 Mark Recchi .12 .30
403 John LeClair .20 .50
404 Josef Melichar .12 .30
405 Sidney Crosby 2.00 5.00
406 Jonathan Cheechoo .25 .60
407 Steve Bernier .12 .30
408 Evgeni Nabokov .20 .50
409 Marcel Goc .12 .30
410 Christian Ehrhoff .12 .30
411 Mark Bell .12 .30
412 Mike Grier .12 .30
413 Patrick Marleau .20 .50
414 Scott Hannan .12 .30
415 Mark Smith .12 .30
416 Milan Michalek .12 .30
417 Ville Nieminen .12 .30
418 Kyle McLaren .12 .30
419 Vesa Toskala .20 .50
420 Josh Gorges .12 .30
421 Joe Thornton .40 1.00
422 Keith Tkachuk .20 .50
423 Barret Jackman .12 .30
424 Lee Stempniak .12 .30
425 Jay McClement .12 .30
426 Dallas Drake .12 .30
427 Curtis Sanford .20 .50
428 Petr Cajanek .12 .30
429 Eric Brewer .12 .30
430 Bill Guerin .12 .30
431 Jamal Mayers .12 .30
432 Manny Legace .20 .50
433 Christian Backman .12 .30
434 Martin Rucinsky .12 .30
435 Dennis Wideman .12 .30
436 Jay McKee .12 .30
437 Doug Weight .12 .30
438 Brad Richards .20 .50
439 Ruslan Fedotenko .12 .30
440 Johan Holmqvist .20 .50
441 Filip Kuba .12 .30
442 Dimitry Afanasenkov .12 .30
443 Ryan Craig .12 .30
444 Dan Boyle .12 .30
445 Paul Ranger .12 .30
446 Marc Denis .20 .50
447 Vaclav Prospal .12 .30
448 Tim Taylor .12 .30
449 Martin St. Louis .20 .50
450 Cory Sarich .12 .30
451 Nikita Alexeev .12 .30
452 Nolan Pratt .12 .30
453 Vincent Lecavalier .25 .60
454 Mats Sundin .25 .60
455 Darcy Tucker .12 .30
456 Kyle Wellwood .12 .30
457 Nik Antropov .12 .30
458 Tomas Kaberle .12 .30
459 Hal Gill .12 .30
460 Jean-Sebastien Aubin .20 .50
461 Matt Stajan .12 .30
462 Alexander Steen .20 .50
463 Bryan McCabe .12 .30
464 Jeff O'Neill .12 .30
465 Wade Belak .12 .30
466 Michael Peca .12 .30
467 Carlo Colaiacovo .12 .30
468 Chad Kilger .12 .30
469 Alexei Ponikarovsky .12 .30
470 Andrew Raycroft .20 .50
471 Roberto Luongo .30 .75
472 Ryan Kesler .12 .30
473 Jan Bulis .12 .30
474 Matt Cooke .12 .30
475 Sami Salo .12 .30
476 Brendan Morrison .12 .30
477 Henrik Sedin .12 .30
478 Daniel Sedin .12 .30
479 Mattias Ohlund .12 .30
480 Willie Mitchell .12 .30
481 Dany Sabourin .20 .50
482 Lukas Krajicek .12 .30
483 Marc Chouinard .12 .30
484 Trevor Linden .12 .30
485 Taylor Pyatt .12 .30
486 Markus Naslund .25 .60
487 Olaf Kolzig .25 .60
488 Donald Brashear .12 .30
489 Chris Clark .12 .30
490 Dainius Zubrus .12 .30
491 Matt Pettinger .12 .30
492 Jamie Heward .12 .30
493 Bryan Muir .12 .30
494 Steve Eminger .12 .30
495 Brian Pothier .12 .30
496 Brian Sutherby .12 .30
497 Richard Zednik .12 .30
498 Brent Johnson .20 .50
499 Matt Bradley .12 .30
500 Alexander Ovechkin 1.00 2.50
501 Dustin Byfuglien RC .75 2.00
502 Yan Stastny RC .75 2.00
503 Mark Stuart RC .75 2.00
504 Eric Fehr RC 1.25 3.00
505 Bill Thomas RC .75 2.00
506 Joel Perrault RC .75 2.00
507 Frank Doyle RC 1.25 3.00
508 Carsen Germyn RC .75 2.00
509 Ryan Potulny RC 1.25 3.00
510 David Printz RC .75 2.00
511 Rob Collins RC .75 2.00
512 Steve Regier RC .75 2.00
513 Matt Koalska RC .75 2.00
514 Ryan Caldwell RC .75 2.00
515 Masi Marjamaki RC .75 2.00
516 Cole Jarrett RC .75 2.00
517 Konstantin Pushkaryov RC .75 2.00
518 Ben Ondrus RC .75 2.00
519 Brendan Bell RC .75 2.00
520 Ian White RC .75 2.00
521 Jeremy Williams RC .75 2.00
522 Marc-Antoine Pouliot RC 1.25 3.00
523 Noah Welch RC .75 2.00
524 Michel Ouellet RC 1.25 3.00
525 Shea Weber RC 1.00 2.50
526 Jarkko Immonen RC .75 2.00
527 David Liffiton RC .75 2.00
528 Tomas Kopecky RC 1.00 2.50
529 Billy Thompson RC .75 2.00
530 Filip Novak RC .75 2.00
531 Matt Carle RC 1.00 2.50
532 Dan Jancevski RC .75 2.00
533 Erik Reitz RC .75 2.00
534 Miroslav Kopriva RC .75 2.00
535 Jonas Johansson RC .75 2.00
536 Shane O'Brien RC .75 2.00
537 Ryan Shannon RC .75 2.00
538 Patrick O'Sullivan RC 1.00 2.50
539 Anze Kopitar RC 2.50 6.00
540 John Oduya RC .75 2.00
541 Travis Zajac RC 1.50 4.00
542 Fredrik Norrena RC .75 2.00
543 Phil Kessel RC 2.00 5.00
544 Guillaume Latendresse RC 2.50 6.00
545 Nigel Dawes RC .75 2.00
546 Jordan Staal RC 4.00 10.00
547 Kristopher Letang RC 1.25 3.00
548 Paul Stastny RC 2.50 6.00
549 Niklas Backstrom RC 1.50 4.00
550 D.J. King RC .75 2.00
551 Marc-Edouard Vlasic RC .75 2.00
552 Patrick Thoresen RC 1.25 3.00
553 Ladislav Smid RC .75 2.00
554 Loui Eriksson RC .75 2.00
555 Patrick Fischer RC .75 2.00
556 Mikko Lehtonen RC .75 2.00
557 Roman Polak RC .75 2.00
558 Luc Bourdon RC 1.25 3.00
559 Keith Yandle RC .75 2.00
560 Enver Lisin RC .75 2.00
561 Adam Burish RC .75 2.00
562 Alexei Kaigorodov RC .75 2.00
563 Alex Brooks RC .75 2.00
564 Evgeni Malkin RC 5.00 12.00
565 Nate Thompson RC .75 2.00
566 Janis Sprukts RC .75 2.00
567 Alexander Radulov RC 2.00 5.00
568 Alexei Mikhnov RC .75 2.00
569 Dave Bolland RC .75 2.00
570 Michael Blunden RC .75 2.00
571 Lars Jonsson RC .75 2.00
572 Triston Grant RC .75 2.00
573 Matt Lashoff RC .75 2.00
574 Dustin Boyd RC 1.25 3.00
575 Brandon Prust RC .75 2.00
576 Alexander Edler RC .75 2.00
577 Jan Hejda RC .75 2.00
578 Drew Stafford RC 2.00 5.00
579 Kelly Guard RC .75 2.00
580 Patrick Coulombe RC .75 2.00
581 Nathan McIver RC .75 2.00
582 Mike Brown RC .75 2.00
583 Jean-Francois Racine RC .75 2.00
584 Adam Dennis RC .75 2.00
585 Drew Larman RC .75 2.00
586 Mike Card RC .75 2.00
587 Michael Funk RC .75 2.00
588 Stefan Liv RC 1.25 3.00
589 David Booth RC .75 2.00
590 Blair Jones RC .75 2.00
591 Jussi Timonen RC .75 2.00
592 David McKee RC 1.25 3.00
593 Michael Ryan RC .75 2.00
594 Peter Harrold RC .75 2.00
595 Joe Pavelski RC 1.25 3.00
596 Karl Goehring RC 1.25 3.00
597 Benoit Pouliot RC 1.25 3.00
598 Jesse Schultz RC .75 2.00
599 Jeff Drouin-Deslauriers RC .75 2.00
600 Martin Houle RC .75 2.00
601 Joe Thornton .40 1.00
602 Jonathan Cheechoo .25 .60
603 Wade Redden .12 .30
604 Michal Rozsival .12 .30
605 Ilya Kovalchuk .30 .75
606 Marian Hossa .20 .50
607 Sean Avery .12 .30
608 Martin Brodeur 1.00 2.50
609 Miikka Kiprusoff .25 .60
610 Cristobal Huet .30 .75
611 Eric Staal .25 .60
612 Fernando Pisani .12 .30
613 Dwayne Roloson .25 .60
614 Ilya Bryzgalov .20 .50
615 Alexander Ovechkin 1.00 2.50
616 Patrick Eaves .75 2.00
Alexei Kaigorodov
617 Keith Ballard .75 2.00
Keith Yandle
618 Dion Phaneuf .75 2.00
Luc Bourdon
619 Jussi Jokinen .75 2.00
Loui Eriksson
620 Marek Svatos .75 2.00
Paul Stastny
621 Sidney Crosby 3.00 8.00
Evgeni Malkin
622 Chris Higgins .75 2.00
Guillaume Latendresse
623 Brad Boyes .75 2.00
Phil Kessel
624 Alexander Ovechkin 1.25 3.00
Evgeni Malkin
625 Petr Prucha .75 2.00
Nigel Dawes
626 Andrej Meszaros .75 2.00
Ladislav Smid
627 Jeff Carter .75 2.00
Patrick O'Sullivan
628 Zach Parise .75 2.00
Travis Zajac
629 Ryan Whitney .75 2.00
Noah Welch
630 Ryan Suter .75 2.00
Shea Weber
631 Josh Gorges .75 2.00
Matt Carle
632 Ryan Getzlaf .75 2.00
Ryan Shannon
633 Mike Richards .75 2.00
Ryan Potulny
634 Pascal LeClaire .75 2.00
Fredrik Norrena
635 Brad Winchester .75 2.00
Marc-Antoine Pouliot
636 Mikko Koivu .75 2.00
Anze Kopitar
637 Andrew Alberts .75 2.00
Mark Stuart
638 Thomas Vanek 1.00 2.50
Drew Stafford
639 Johan Franzen .75 2.00
Tomas Kopecky
640 Carlo Colaiacovo .75 2.00
Ian White
641 Francois Beauchemin .75 2.00
Shane O'Brien
642 Steve Bernier .75 2.00
Eric Fehr
643 Corey Perry 1.25 3.00
Jordan Staal
644 Alexander Steen .75 2.00
Patrick Thoresen
645 Brent Seabrook .75 2.00
Kristopher Letang
646 Teemu Selanne .25 .60
647 Joe Sakic .50 1.25
648 Mike Modano .25 .60
649 Eric Lindros .25 .60
650 Dominik Hasek .40 1.00
651 Nicklas Lidstrom .25 .60
652 Chris Chelios .20 .50
653 Joe Nieuwendyk .20 .50
654 Ed Belfour .25 .60
655 Rob Blake .20 .50
656 Saku Koivu .25 .60
657 Paul Kariya .25 .60
658 Martin Brodeur .75 2.00
659 Jaromir Jagr .40 1.00
660 Brendan Shanahan .25 .60
661 Daniel Alfredsson .20 .50
662 Peter Forsberg .40 1.00
663 Jeremy Roenick .30 .75
664 Curtis Joseph .25 .60
665 Sidney Crosby 2.00 5.00
666 Mark Recchi .12 .30
667 Doug Weight .12 .30
668 Keith Tkachuk .20 .50
669 Mats Sundin .25 .60
670 Markus Naslund .25 .60
671 Teemu Selanne .25 .60
672 Ilya Kovalchuk .30 .75
673 Patrice Bergeron .25 .60
674 Ryan Miller .25 .60
675 Miikka Kiprusoff .25 .60
676 Eric Staal .25 .60
677 Nikolai Khabibulin .25 .60
678 Rick Nash .25 .60
679 Joe Sakic .50 1.25
680 Mike Modano .25 .60
681 Nicklas Lidstrom .25 .60
682 Ryan Smyth .20 .50
683 Olli Jokinen .12 .30
684 Rob Blake .20 .50
685 Marian Gaborik .30 .75
686 Saku Koivu .25 .60
687 Martin Brodeur 1.00 2.50
688 Paul Kariya .25 .60
689 Miroslav Satan .12 .30
690 Jaromir Jagr .40 1.00
691 Daniel Alfredsson .20 .50
692 Peter Forsberg .40 1.00
693 Shane Doan .12 .30
694 Sidney Crosby 2.00 5.00
695 Patrick Marleau .20 .50
696 Keith Tkachuk .20 .50
697 Vincent Lecavalier .25 .60
698 Mats Sundin .25 .60
699 Markus Naslund .25 .60
700 Alexander Ovechkin 1.00 2.50

2006-07 O-Pee-Chee Rainbow

RAINBOW: 6X TO 15X BASE HI
PRINT RUN 100 #'d SETS
5 Teemu Selanne 15.00 40.00
121 Joe Sakic 12.00 30.00
173 Dominik Hasek 6.00 15.00
291 Martin Brodeur 8.00 20.00
405 Sidney Crosby 20.00 50.00
500 Alexander Ovechkin 20.00 50.00
539 Anze Kopitar 12.00 30.00
544 Guillaume Latendresse 12.00 30.00
546 Jordan Staal 15.00 40.00
548 Paul Stastny 10.00 25.00
564 Evgeni Malkin 15.00 40.00
567 Alexander Radulov 8.00 20.00
608 Martin Brodeur 10.00 25.00
615 Alexander Ovechkin 20.00 50.00
621 Sidney Crosby 25.00 60.00
Evgeni Malkin
624 Alexander Ovechkin 12.00 30.00
Evgeni Malkin
647 Joe Sakic 8.00 20.00
650 Dominik Hasek 6.00 15.00
658 Martin Brodeur 10.00 25.00
665 Sidney Crosby 20.00 50.00
679 Joe Sakic 8.00 20.00
687 Martin Brodeur 10.00 25.00
694 Sidney Crosby 20.00 50.00
700 Alexander Ovechkin 8.00 20.00

2006-07 O-Pee-Chee Autographs

ODDS 1:360
A-AH Ales Hemsky 6.00 15.00
A-AM Andy McDonald 10.00 25.00
A-AN Antero Niittymaki SP 20.00 50.00
A-AR Andrew Raycroft SP 20.00 50.00
A-BB Brad Boyes SP 20.00 50.00
A-BG Brian Gionta 6.00 15.00
A-BM Brendan Morrison 6.00 15.00
A-BO Bobby Orr SP 400.00 700.00
A-CC Chris Campoli 6.00 15.00
A-CH Cristobal Huet 12.00 30.00
A-CK Chris Kunitz 6.00 15.00
A-CS Cory Stillman 6.00 15.00
A-CW Cam Ward SP 40.00 100.00
A-DB Daniel Briere 15.00 30.00
A-DH Dany Heatley SP
A-DR Dwayne Roloson 15.00 40.00
A-EM Evgeni Malkin 125.00 200.00
A-GB Gilbert Brule SP 30.00 60.00
A-HA Dominik Hasek SP 40.00 80.00
A-HT Hannu Toivonen 10.00 25.00
A-IK Ilya Kovalchuk SP 30.00 80.00
A-JA Jason Arnott 6.00 15.00
A-JC Jeff Carter 15.00 30.00
A-JI Jarome Iginla SP 40.00 80.00
A-JL John-Michael Liles 6.00 15.00
A-JS Jordan Staal 30.00 80.00
A-JT Joe Thornton SP
A-KB Keith Ballard 6.00 15.00
A-KC Kyle Calder 12.00 30.00
A-KD Kris Draper SP
A-KO Mikko Koivu 6.00 15.00
A-MC Mike Cammalleri 10.00 25.00
A-MG Marian Gaborik SP 50.00 100.00
A-MP Marc-Antoine Pouliot 12.00 30.00
A-MR Mike Richards 12.00 30.00
A-MS Marek Svatos 6.00 15.00
A-NA Rick Nash 20.00 50.00
A-NH Nathan Horton 10.00 25.00
A-NL Nicklas Lidstrom SP 40.00 100.00
A-OJ Olli Jokinen SP
A-PB Pierre-Marc Bouchard 6.00 15.00
A-PK Phil Kessel SP 60.00 125.00
A-PP Petr Prucha 10.00 25.00
A-PS Paul Stastny 60.00 125.00
A-RB Rob Blake 15.00 40.00
A-RL Roberto Luongo SP 75.00 150.00
A-RM Ryan Malone 6.00 15.00
A-RN Robert Nilsson 6.00 15.00
A-RS Ryan Smyth 15.00 40.00
A-SB Steve Bernier 10.00 25.00
A-SW Stephen Weiss 6.00 15.00
A-WR Wade Redden 6.00 15.00
A-WW Wojtek Wolski 12.00 30.00

2006-07 O-Pee-Chee Swatches

STATED ODDS 1:24
S-AA Arron Asham 3.00 8.00
S-AE David Aebischer 5.00 12.00
S-AF Alexander Frolov 3.00 8.00
S-AH Ales Hemsky 3.00 8.00

S-AM Andrej Meszaros 3.00 8.00
S-AO Alexander Ovechkin 25.00 60.00
S-AS Alexander Steen 5.00 12.00
S-AT Alex Tanguay 5.00 12.00
S-AY Alexei Yashin 3.00 8.00
S-BB Brandon Bochenski 3.00 8.00
S-BM Brendan Morrison 3.00 8.00
S-BS Brad Stuart 3.00 8.00
S-CC Chris Chelios 5.00 12.00
S-CD Chris Drury 3.00 8.00
S-CH Jonathan Cheechoo 10.00 25.00
S-CK Chuck Kobasew 3.00 8.00
S-CP Chris Pronger 5.00 12.00
S-DA Daniel Alfredsson 5.00 12.00
S-DE Pavol Demitra 3.00 8.00
S-DH Dominik Hasek 10.00 25.00
S-DK Duncan Keith 3.00 8.00
S-DT Darcy Tucker 3.00 8.00
S-DW Doug Weight 3.00 8.00
S-EN Evgeni Nabokov 5.00 12.00
S-ES Eric Staal 6.00 15.00
S-FP Fernando Pisani 3.00 8.00
S-GA Mathieu Garon 5.00 12.00
S-GL Guy Lafleur SP 75.00 125.00
S-GM Glen Murray 3.00 8.00
S-GR Gary Roberts 3.00 8.00
S-HA Martin Havlat 5.00 12.00
S-HE Milan Hejduk 3.00 8.00
S-HO Shawn Horcoff 3.00 8.00
S-HS Henrik Sedin 3.00 8.00
S-HT Hannu Toivonen 5.00 12.00
S-JA Jason Arnott 3.00 8.00
S-JB Jay Bouwmeester 3.00 8.00
S-JC Jeff Carter 6.00 15.00
S-JG Jean-Sebastien Giguere 5.00 12.00
S-JI Jarome Iginla 8.00 20.00
S-JJ Jaromir Jagr 10.00 25.00
S-JL Jere Lehtinen 3.00 8.00
S-JP Joni Pitkanen 3.00 8.00
S-JR Jeremy Roenick 8.00 20.00
S-JS Jason Spezza 8.00 20.00
S-KL Kari Lehtonen 6.00 15.00
S-LE Jordan Leopold 3.00 8.00
S-LX Mario Lemieux SP 50.00 100.00
S-MA Maxim Afinogenov 3.00 8.00
S-MB Martin Brodeur 20.00 50.00
S-MC Mike Cammalleri 3.00 8.00
S-MD Marc Denis 5.00 12.00
S-MF Manny Fernandez 5.00 12.00
S-MG Marian Gaborik 8.00 20.00
S-MH Marian Hossa 5.00 12.00
S-MI Miroslav Satan 3.00 8.00
S-ML Manny Legace 5.00 12.00
S-MM Mike Modano 8.00 20.00
S-MN Markus Naslund 6.00 15.00
S-MR Mark Recchi 3.00 8.00
S-MS Martin St. Louis SP 5.00 12.00
S-MT Marty Turco 5.00 12.00
S-NL Nicklas Lidstrom 6.00 15.00
S-OJ Olli Jokinen 3.00 8.00
S-OT Steve Ott 8.00 20.00
S-PB Patrice Bergeron 6.00 15.00
S-PD Pavel Datsyuk 8.00 20.00
S-PF Peter Forsberg 8.00 20.00
S-PK Paul Kariya 10.00 25.00
S-PL Pascal LeClaire 5.00 12.00
S-PM Patrick Marleau 5.00 12.00
S-PR Patrick Roy 25.00 60.00
S-PS Peter Stastny 3.00 8.00
S-RB Rod Brind'Amour 5.00 12.00
S-RD Rick DiPietro 5.00 12.00
S-RE Robert Esche 5.00 12.00
S-RF Ruslan Fedotenko 3.00 8.00
S-RI Mike Ribeiro 3.00 8.00
S-RK Rostislav Klesla 3.00 8.00
S-RL Robert Lang 3.00 8.00
S-RM Ryan Miller 6.00 15.00
S-RN Rick Nash 8.00 20.00
S-RS Ryan Smyth 5.00 12.00
S-RY Michael Ryder 5.00 12.00
S-SA Joe Sakic 15.00 40.00
S-SB Steve Bernier 3.00 8.00
S-SC Sidney Crosby SP 75.00 150.00
S-SD Shane Doan 3.00 8.00
S-SF Sergei Fedorov 6.00 15.00
S-SG Scott Gomez 3.00 8.00
S-SH Brendan Shanahan 6.00 15.00
S-SO Sandis Ozolinsh 3.00 8.00
S-SS Sergei Samsonov 5.00 12.00
S-ST Martin Straka 3.00 8.00
S-SU Mats Sundin 6.00 15.00
S-TR Tuomo Ruutu 3.00 8.00
S-TS Teemu Selanne 8.00 20.00
S-TV Tomas Vokoun 5.00 12.00
S-VL Vincent Lecavalier 6.00 15.00
S-ZC Zdeno Chara 3.00 8.00

1976 Old Timers

This 18-card set of indeterminate origin measures approximately 2 1/2" by 3 5/8" and features black-and-white player photos in a white border. Members of the Red Wings, Maple Leafs and Blackhawks are pictured. The backs are blank. The cards are unnumbered and checklisted below in alphabetical order.

COMPLETE SET (18) 30.00 60.00
1 Gerry Abel 1.25 2.50
2 Sid Abel 4.00 8.00
3 Doug Barkley 1.25 2.50
4 Joe Carveth 1.25 2.50
5 Billy Dea 1.25 2.50
6 Alex Delvecchio 7.50 15.00
7 Bill Gadsby 1.25 2.50
8 Hal Jackson 1.25 2.50
9 Joe Klukay 1.25 2.50
10 Ted Lindsay 7.50 15.00
11 Jim Orlando 1.25 2.50
12 Marty Pavlich 1.25 2.50
13 Jim Peters 1.25 2.50
14 Marcel Pronovost 1.25 2.50
15 Marc Reaume 1.25 2.50
16 Leo Reise 1.25 2.50
17 Glen Skov 1.25 2.50
18 Jack Stewart 1.25 2.50

1999-00 Oscar Mayer Lunchables

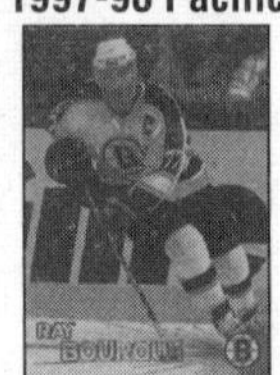

These cards were featured on the backs of Oscar Mayer Lunchables packages. Each package contained both a 3 x 5 player card and a postcard size artist rendition of the player as a comic book superhero. The inside of each package contained a checklist of the set, player stats, and one part of the twelve part comic series.

COMPLETE SET (12) 6.00 15.00
1 Ray Bourque .60 1.50
2 Pavel Bure .80 2.00
3 Dominik Hasek .60 1.50
4 Jaromir Jagr 1.00 2.50
5 Curtis Joseph .40 1.00
6 Paul Kariya 1.20 3.00
7 Saku Koivu .30 .75
8 Eric Lindros 1.00 2.50
9 Al MacInnis .20 .50
10 Mark Messier .40 1.00
11 Mats Sundin .40 1.00
12 Alexei Yashin .24 .60

1997-98 Pacific

The 1997-98 inaugural issue of the Pacific Crown Collection NHL Hockey cards was issued in one series totaling 350 cards and was distributed in eight-card packs. The fronts feature color action player photos with gold foil highlights. The backs carry player information. Pacific chose not to print a card #66, as a tribute to Mario Lemieux.

COMPLETE SET (350) 20.00 40.00
1 Ray Bourque .30 .75
2 Brian Leetch .20 .50
3 Claude Lemieux .05 .15
4 Mike Modano .30 .75
5 Zigmund Palffy .15 .40
6 Nikolai Khabibulin .15 .40
7 Chris Chelios .20 .50
8 Teemu Selanne .20 .50
9 Paul Kariya .20 .50
10 John LeClair .20 .50
11 Mark Messier .20 .50
12 Jarome Iginla .25 .60
13 Petr Nedved .05 .15
14 Brendan Shanahan .20 .50
15 Dino Ciccarelli .05 .15
16 Brett Hull .25 .60
17 Wendel Clark .05 .15
18 Peter Bondra .15 .40
19 Steve Yzerman 1.00 2.50
20 Ed Belfour .20 .50
21 Peter Forsberg .50 1.25
22 Mike Gartner .05 .15
23 Jim Carey .15 .40
24 Mike Vernon .15 .40
25 Vincent Damphousse .05 .15
26 Adam Graves .05 .15
27 Ron Hextall .15 .40
28 Keith Tkachuk .20 .50
29 Felix Potvin .20 .50
30 Martin Brodeur .50 1.25
31 Rod Brind'Amour .15 .40
32 Pierre Turgeon .15 .40
33 Patrick Roy 1.00 2.50
34 John Vanbiesbrouck .15 .40
35 Andy Moog .15 .40
36 Sergei Berezin .05 .15
37 Adam Oates .15 .40
38 Joe Sakic .40 1.00
39 Dominik Hasek .40 1.00
40 Patrick Lalime .15 .40
41 Bobby Dollas .05 .15
42 Kyle McLaren .05 .15
43 Wayne Primeau .05 .15
44 Stephane Richer .05 .15
45 Theo Fleury .05 .15
46 Kevin Miller .05 .15
47 Adam Deadmarsh .05 .15
48 Darryl Sydor .05 .15
49 Igor Larionov .05 .15
50 Radek Dvorak .05 .15
51 Andrei Kovalenko .05 .15
52 Keith Primeau .05 .15
53 Ray Ferraro .05 .15
54 David Wilkie .05 .15
55 Bobby Holik .05 .15
56 Tommy Salo .15 .40
57 Jeff Beukeboom .05 .15
58 Daniel Alfredsson .15 .40
59 Mikael Renberg .05 .15
60 Norm Maciver .05 .15
61 Darius Kasparaitis .05 .15
62 Geoff Courtnall .05 .15
63 Jeff Friesen .05 .15
64 Brian Bradley .05 .15
65 Tie Domi .15 .40
66 Martin Gelinas .05 .15
67 Martin Gelinas .05 .15
68 Jaromir Jagr .30 .75
69 Steve Konowalchuk .05 .15
70 Brian Bellows .05 .15
71 Jozef Stumpel .05 .15
72 Darryl Shannon .05 .15
73 Todd Simpson .05 .15
74 Ulf Dahlen .05 .15
75 Sandis Ozolinsh .05 .15
76 Sergei Zubov .05 .15
77 Paul Coffey .20 .50
78 Nicklas Lidstrom .20 .50
79 Jason Arnott .05 .15
80 Ray Sheppard .05 .15
81 Sean Burke .15 .40
82 Vladimir Tsyplakov .05 .15
83 Darcy Tucker .05 .15
84 Dave Andreychuk .05 .15
85 Scott Lachance .05 .15
86 Niklas Sundstrom .05 .15
87 Ron Tugnutt .15 .40
88 Eric Lindros .20 .50
89 Alexander Mogilny .15 .40
90 Kris King .05 .15
91 Sergei Fedorov .30 .75
92 Ed Olczyk .05 .15
93 Doug Gilmour .15 .40
94 Ryan Smyth .05 .15
95 Scott Pellerin .05 .15
96 Pavel Bure .20 .50
97 Jeremy Roenick .25 .60
98 Todd Gill .05 .15
99 Wayne Gretzky 1.25 3.00
100 Roman Hamrlik .05 .15
101 Rob Zettler .05 .15
102 Sergei Nemchinov .05 .15
103 Sergei Gonchar .05 .15
104 Steve Rucchin .05 .15
105 Landon Wilson .05 .15
106 Anatoli Semenov .05 .15
107 Corey Millen .05 .15
108 Eric Daze .15 .40
109 Mike Ricci .05 .15
110 Jamie Langenbrunner .05 .15
111 Slava Fetisov .05 .15
112 Rem Murray .05 .15
113 Tom Fitzgerald .05 .15
114 Robert Kron .05 .15
115 Kevin Stevens .05 .15
116 Valeri Bure .05 .15
117 Bill Guerin .15 .40
118 Bryan McCabe .05 .15
119 Alexei Kovalev .05 .15
120 Alexei Yashin .05 .15
121 Eric Desjardins .05 .15
122 Teppo Numminen .05 .15
123 Ron Francis .15 .40
124 Chris Pronger .15 .40
125 Viktor Kozlov .05 .15
126 Corey Schwab .15 .40
127 Fredrik Modin .05 .15
128 Markus Naslund .20 .50
129 Dale Hunter .05 .15
130 Warren Rychel .05 .15
131 Anson Carter .15 .40
132 Miroslav Satan .05 .15
133 Trevor Kidd .15 .40
134 Sergei Krivokrasov .05 .15
135 Adam Foote .05 .15
136 Brent Gilchrist .05 .15
137 Chris Osgood .15 .40
138 Doug Weight .15 .40
139 Martin Straka .05 .15
140 Jeff O'Neill .05 .15
141 Byron Dafoe .15 .40
142 Brian Savage .05 .15
143 Lyle Odelein .05 .15
144 Niklas Andersson .05 .15
145 Luc Robitaille .15 .40
146 Damian Rhodes .05 .15
147 Garth Snow .15 .40
148 Craig Janney .05 .15
149 Fredrik Olausson .05 .15
150 Joe Murphy .05 .15
151 Owen Nolan .15 .40
152 Shawn Burr .05 .15
153 Dimitri Yushkevich .05 .15
154 Trevor Linden .05 .15
155 Joe Juneau .05 .15
156 Sean Pronger .05 .15
157 Jeff Odgers .05 .15
158 Brian Holzinger .05 .15
159 Dave Gagner .05 .15
160 Jeff Hackett .15 .40
161 Eric Lacroix .05 .15
162 Pat Verbeek .05 .15
163 Darren McCarty .05 .15
164 Mike Grier .05 .15
165 Per Gustafsson .05 .15
166 Andrew Cassels .05 .15
167 Vitali Yachmenev .05 .15
168 Jocelyn Thibault .15 .40
169 John MacLean .05 .15
170 Travis Green .05 .15
171 Ulf Samuelsson .05 .15
172 Bruce Gardiner RC .05 .15
173 Janne Niinimaa .05 .15
174 Jim Johnson .05 .15
175 Stu Barnes .05 .15
176 Harry York .05 .15
177 Al Iafrate .05 .15
178 Paul Ysebaert .05 .15
179 Mathieu Schneider .05 .15
180 Corey Hirsch .15 .40
181 Mark Tinordi .05 .15
182 Kevin Todd .05 .15
183 Tim Sweeney .05 .15
184 Donald Audette .05 .15
185 Jonas Hoglund .05 .15
186 Brent Sutter .05 .15
187 Scott Young .05 .15
188 Arturs Irbe .15 .40
189 Vladimir Konstantinov .05 .15
190 Mats Lindgren .05 .15
191 David Nemirovsky .05 .15
192 Sami Kapanen .05 .15
193 Rob Blake .15 .40
194 Sebastien Bordeleau .05 .15
195 Steve Thomas .05 .15
196 Bryan Smolinski .05 .15
197 Mike Richter .20 .50
198 Randy Cunneyworth .05 .15
199 Pat Falloon .05 .15
200 Cliff Ronning .05 .15
201 Ken Wregget .05 .15
202 Al MacInnis .15 .40
203 Tony Granato .05 .15
204 Rob Zamuner .05 .15
205 Mats Sundin .20 .50
206 Mike Ridley .05 .15
207 Sylvain Cote .05 .15
208 Joe Sacco .05 .15
209 Ted Donato .05 .15
210 Matthew Barnaby .05 .15
211 Cory Stillman .05 .15
212 Gary Suter .05 .15
213 Valeri Kamensky .05 .15
214 Derian Hatcher .05 .15
215 Jamie Pushor .05 .15
216 Mariusz Czerkawski .05 .15
217 Kirk Muller .05 .15
218 Kevin Dineen .05 .15
219 Dimitri Khristich .05 .15
220 Martin Rucinsky .05 .15
221 Denis Pederson .05 .15
222 Bryan Berard .05 .15
223 Alexander Karpovtsev .05 .15
224 Shawn McEachern .05 .15
225 Dale Hawerchuk .05 .15
226 Bob Corkum .05 .15
227 Kevin Hatcher .05 .15
228 Grant Fuhr .15 .40
229 Darren Turcotte .05 .15
230 Patrick Poulin .05 .15
231 Jamie Macoun .05 .15
232 Jyrki Lumme .05 .15
233 Bill Ranford .05 .15
234 Dmitri Mironov .05 .15
235 Mattias Timander .05 .15
236 Alexei Zhitnik .05 .15
237 Hnat Domenichelli .05 .15
238 Murray Craven .05 .15
239 Mike Keane .05 .15
240 Benoit Hogue .05 .15
241 Martin Lapointe .05 .15
242 Curtis Joseph .20 .50
243 Robert Svehla .05 .15
244 Glen Wesley .05 .15
245 Stephane Fiset .05 .15
246 Shayne Corson .05 .15
247 Scott Niedermayer .05 .15
248 Steve Webb RC .05 .15
249 Esa Tikkanen .05 .15
250 Alexandre Daigle .05 .15
251 Trent Klatt .05 .15
252 Oleg Tverdovsky .05 .15
253 Dave Roche .05 .15
254 Tony Twist .05 .15
255 Bernie Nicholls .05 .15
256 Rick Tabaracci .05 .15
257 Todd Warriner .05 .15
258 Kirk McLean .05 .15
259 Phil Housley .05 .15
260 Guy Hebert .15 .40
261 Steve Heinze .05 .15
262 Derek Plante .05 .15
263 German Titov .05 .15
264 Tony Amonte .15 .40
265 Uwe Krupp .05 .15
266 Joe Nieuwendyk .15 .40
267 Vyacheslav Kozlov .05 .15
268 Kelly Buchberger .05 .15
269 Rob Niedermayer .05 .15
270 Geoff Sanderson .05 .15
271 Jan Vopat .05 .15
272 Saku Koivu .20 .50
273 Scott Stevens .15 .40
274 Eric Fichaud .05 .15
275 Russ Courtnall .05 .15
276 Wade Redden .05 .15
277 Petr Svoboda .05 .15
278 Andreas Dackell .05 .15
279 Jason Woolley .05 .15
280 Stephane Matteau .05 .15
281 Stephen Guolla RC .05 .15
282 John Cullen .05 .15
283 Steve Sullivan .05 .15
284 Bret Hedican .05 .15
285 Michal Pivonka .05 .15
286 Darren Van Impe .05 .15
287 Rob DiMaio .05 .15
288 Garry Galley .05 .15
289 Kent Manderville .05 .15
290 Bob Probert .05 .15
291 Keith Jones .05 .15
292 Guy Carbonneau .05 .15
293 Tomas Sandstrom .05 .15
294 Daniel McGillis RC .05 .15
295 Brian Skrudland .05 .15
296 Stu Grimson .05 .15
297 Doug Zmolek .05 .15
298 Mark Recchi .15 .40
299 Valeri Zelepukin .05 .15
300 Derek Armstrong .05 .15
301 Eric Cairns RC .05 .15
302 Steve Duchesne .05 .15
303 Dainius Zubrus .05 .15
304 Deron Quint .05 .15
305 Joe Dziedzic .05 .15
306 Mike Peluso .05 .15
307 Andrei Nazarov .05 .15
308 Chris Gratton .05 .15
309 Mike Craig .05 .15
310 Lonny Bohonos .05 .15
311 Rick Tocchet .05 .15
312 Ted Drury .05 .15
313 Jean-Yves Roy .05 .15
314 Jason Dawe .05 .15
315 Jamie Allison .05 .15
316 Alexei Zhamnov .05 .15
317 Aaron Miller .05 .15
318 Todd Krygier .05 .15
319 Tomas Holmstrom .05 .15
320 Todd Marchant .05 .15
321 Scott Mellanby .05 .15
322 Marek Malik .05 .15
323 Dan Bylsma RC .05 .15
324 Stephane Quintal .05 .15
325 Ken Daneyko .05 .15
326 Robert Reichel .05 .15
327 Daniel Goneau .05 .15
328 Sergei Zholtok .05 .15
329 Kjell Samuelsson .05 .15
330 Shane Doan .05 .15
331 Radek Bonk .05 .15
332 Jim Campbell .05 .15
333 Marty McSorley .05 .15
334 Brantt Myhres .05 .15
335 Mike Johnson RC .20 .50
336 Mike Sillinger .05 .15
337 Kelly Hrudey .05 .15
338 Joel Bouchard .05 .15
339 Brian Noonan .05 .15
340 Dean Chynoweth .05 .15
341 Michael Peca .05 .15
342 Jeff Toms RC .05 .15
343 Denis Savard .05 .15
344 Stephane Yelle .05 .15
345 Grant Ledyard .05 .15
346 Ronnie Stern .05 .15
347 Petr Klima .05 .15
348 Johan Garpenlov .05 .15
349 Nelson Emerson .05 .15
350 Matt Johnson .05 .15
351 Ken Belanger RC .05 .15
CM1 Mark Messier .20 .50

1997-98 Pacific Copper

*STARS: 3X TO 6X BASIC CARDS
STATED ODDS 1:1 HOBBY

1997-98 Pacific Emerald Green

*STARS: 4X TO 8X BASIC CARDS
STATED ODDS 1:1 CANADIAN ONLY

1997-98 Pacific Ice Blue

*STARS: 8X TO 15X BASIC CARDS
STATED ODDS 1:73
STATED PRINT RUN 67 SETS

1997-98 Pacific Red

*STARS: 6X TO 12X BASIC CARDS
STATED ODDS 1:1 TREAT PACKS

1997-98 Pacific Silver

*STARS: 3X TO 6X BASIC CARDS
STATED ODDS 1:1 RETAIL PACKS

1997-98 Pacific Card-Supials

Randomly inserted at a rate of 1:37 packs, this 20-card set features color action player photos of some of the great players in Hockey. A smaller card is made to pair with the regular size card of the same player. The backs carry a slot for insertion of the small card.

*MINIS: .3X TO .6X BASIC CARDS
1 Paul Kariya 1.50 4.00
2 Teemu Selanne 1.50 4.00
3 Jarome Iginla 2.00 5.00
4 Peter Forsberg 2.50 6.00
5 Mike Modano 2.00 5.00
6 Sergei Fedorov 2.00 5.00
7 Vladimir Konstantinov 1.00 2.50
8 Steve Yzerman 4.00 10.00
9 John Vanbiesbrouck 1.00 2.50
10 Martin Brodeur 3.00 8.00
11 Doug Gilmour 1.00 2.50
12 Wayne Gretzky 6.00 15.00
13 Mark Messier 1.50 4.00
14 John LeClair 1.00 2.50
15 Eric Lindros 1.50 4.00
16 Jeremy Roenick 1.50 4.00
17 Keith Tkachuk 1.00 2.50
18 Brett Hull 1.50 4.00
19 Felix Potvin 1.50 4.00
20 Pavel Bure 1.50 4.00

1997-98 Pacific Cramer's Choice

Randomly inserted in packs at the rate of 1:721, this 10-card set features top NHL Hockey players as chosen by Pacific President and CEO, Michael Cramer. The fronts display a color action player cut-out on a pyramid die-cut shaped background.

COMPLETE SET (10) 100.00 200.00
1 Paul Kariya 4.00 10.00
2 Dominik Hasek 8.00 20.00
3 Jarome Iginla 5.00 12.00
4 Peter Forsberg 10.00 25.00
5 Patrick Roy 20.00 50.00
6 Steve Yzerman 20.00 50.00
7 Wayne Gretzky 25.00 60.00
8 Mark Messier 4.00 10.00
9 Eric Lindros 4.00 10.00
10 Jaromir Jagr 6.00 15.00

1997-98 Pacific Gold Crown Die-Cuts

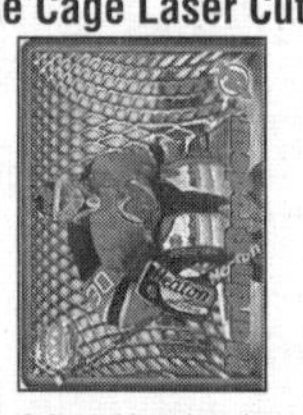

COMPLETE SET (20) 30.00 80.00
STATED ODDS 1:37
1 Paul Kariya 1.50 4.00
2 Teemu Selanne 1.25 3.00
3 Dominik Hasek 3.00 8.00
4 Michael Peca .75 2.00
5 Jarome Iginla 2.00 4.00
6 Chris Chelios .75 2.00
7 Peter Forsberg 2.00 5.00
8 Patrick Roy 8.00 20.00
9 Joe Sakic 3.00 8.00
10 Brendan Shanahan 1.50 4.00
11 Steve Yzerman 6.00 15.00
12 Ryan Smyth .75 2.00
13 John Vanbiesbrouck 1.25 3.00
14 Martin Brodeur 4.00 10.00
15 Wayne Gretzky 10.00 25.00
16 Mark Messier 1.50 4.00
17 Eric Lindros 1.25 3.00
18 Jaromir Jagr 2.00 5.00
19 Brett Hull 1.25 3.00
20 Pavel Bure 1.50 4.00

1997-98 Pacific In The Cage Laser Cuts

Randomly inserted in packs at the rate of 1:145, this 20-card set honors top goalies of the NHL. The laser-cut fronts feature color player photos with the net as the background. The backs carry player information.

COMPLETE SET (20) 40.00 100.00
1 Guy Hebert 2.00 5.00
2 Dominik Hasek 5.00 12.00
3 Trevor Kidd 2.00 5.00
4 Jeff Hackett 2.00 5.00
5 Patrick Roy 10.00 25.00
6 Andy Moog 2.00 5.00
7 Chris Osgood 2.00 5.00
8 Mike Vernon 2.00 5.00
9 Curtis Joseph 4.00 10.00
10 John Vanbiesbrouck 4.00 10.00
11 Jocelyn Thibault 2.00 5.00
12 Martin Brodeur 6.00 15.00
13 Mike Richter 4.00 10.00
14 Ron Hextall 4.00 10.00
15 Garth Snow 2.00 5.00
16 Nikolai Khabibulin 4.00 10.00
17 Patrick Lalime 2.00 5.00
18 Grant Fuhr 4.00 10.00
19 Ed Belfour 4.00 10.00
20 Felix Potvin 4.00 10.00

1997-98 Pacific Slap Shots Die-Cuts

Randomly inserted in packs at the rate of 1:73, this 36-card set features color player photos of top NHL players. Three cards of players from the same team were made to fit on top of each other to form a hockey stick on the cards' right sides with the words, "Pacific Trading Cards," printed on the middle section of the stick. The cards that go together have the same number with the letters, "A, B, or C" after the number to indicate where the cards should be placed to form the giant hockey stick.

COMPLETE SET (36) 50.00 125.00
1A Paul Kariya 2.00 5.00
1B Jari Kurri 1.50 4.00
1C Teemu Selanne 1.50 4.00
2A Peter Forsberg 3.00 8.00
2B Joe Sakic 4.00 10.00
2C Claude Lemieux 1.00 2.50
3A Brendan Shanahan 2.00 5.00
3B Sergei Fedorov 2.00 5.00
3C Steve Yzerman 6.00 15.00
4A Mark Recchi 1.00 2.50
4B Vincent Damphousse 1.00 2.50
4C Stephane Richer 1.00 2.50
5A Wayne Gretzky 10.00 25.0
5B Mark Messier 2.00 5.0
5C Brian Leetch 1.50 4.0
6A Rod Brind'Amour 1.00 2.5
6B Eric Lindros 2.00 5.0
6C John LeClair 1.00 2.5
7A Keith Tkachuk 1.00 2.5
7B Jeremy Roenick 2.00 5.0
7C Mike Gartner 1.00 2.5
8A Petr Nedved 1.00 2.5
8B Ron Francis 1.00 2.5
8C Jaromir Jagr 3.00 8.0
9A Geoff Courtnall 1.00 2.5
9B Pierre Turgeon 1.00 2.5
9C Brett Hull 2.00 5.0
10A Wendel Clark 1.50 4.0
10B Mats Sundin 1.50 4.0
10C Sergei Berezin 1.00 2.5
11A Pavel Bure 2.00 5.0
11B Trevor Linden 1.50 4.0
11C Alexander Mogilny 1.00 2.5
12A Joe Juneau 1.00, 2.5
12B Adam Oates 1.00 2.5
12C Peter Bondra 1.00 2.5

1997-98 Pacific Team Checklists

Randomly inserted in packs at the rate 1:73, this 26-card set features color play photos with the player's team logo in a circ next to the player's image. The backs car the checklist of the team the player plays or

COMPLETE SET (26) 50.00 125.0
1 Teemu Selanne 2.00 5.0
2 Ray Bourque 2.00 5.0
3 Dominik Hasek 4.00 10.0
4 Jarome Iginla 2.50 6.0
5 Keith Primeau .75 2.0
6 Chris Chelios 1.25 3.0
7 Patrick Roy 10.00 25.0
8 Mike Modano 2.00 5.0
9 Steve Yzerman 8.00 20.0
10 Curtis Joseph 1.25 3.0
11 John Vanbiesbrouck 1.25 3.0
12 Rob Blake .75 2.0
13 Stephane Richer .75 2.0
14 Martin Brodeur 6.00 15.0
15 Zigmund Palffy 1.25 3.0
16 Wayne Gretzky 12.00 30.0
17 Alexandre Daigle .75 2.0
18 Eric Lindros 1.25 3.0
19 Jeremy Roenick 2.00 5.0
20 Jaromir Jagr 3.00 8.0
21 Brett Hull 2.00 5.0
22 Owen Nolan .75 2.0
23 Dino Ciccarelli .75 2.0
24 Felix Potvin 1.25 3.0
25 Pavel Bure 2.00 5.0
26 Peter Bondra .75 2.0

1998-99 Pacific

The 1998-99 Pacific set was issued in o series totaling 450 cards and was distribute in 10-card packs. The fronts feature borderless action color player photos. Th backs carry player information and care statistics.

COMPLETE SET (450) 25.00 40.0
1 Damian Rhodes .05 .1
2 Mattias Ohlund .05 .1
3 Craig Ludwig .05 .1
4 Rob Blake .15 .4
5 Nicklas Lidstrom .20 .5
6 Calle Johansson .05 .1
7 Chris Chelios .20 .5
8 Teemu Selanne .20 .5
9 Paul Kariya .20 .5
10 Pavel Bure .20 .5
11 Mark Messier .20 .5
12 Peter Bondra .15 .4
13 Mats Sundin .20 .5
14 Brendan Shanahan .20 .5
15 Jamie Langenbrunner .05 .1
16 Brett Hull .25 .6
17 Rod Brind'Amour .15 .4
18 Adam Deadmarsh .05 .1
19 Steve Yzerman 1.00 2.5
20 Ed Belfour .20 .5
21 Peter Forsberg .50 1.2
22 Dino Ciccarelli .05 .1
23 Brian Bellows .05 .1
24 Janne Niinimaa .05 .1
25 Joe Nieuwendyk .15 .4
26 Patrik Elias .15 .4
27 Michael Peca .05 .1
28 Tie Domi .15 .4
29 Felix Potvin .20 .5
30 Martin Brodeur .50 1.2
31 Grant Fuhr .15 .4
32 Trevor Linden .05 .1
33 Patrick Roy 1.00 2.5
34 John Vanbiesbrouck .15 .4
35 Tom Barrasso .15 .4
36 Matthew Barnaby .05 .1

37 Olaf Kolzig .15 .40
38 Pavol Demitra .15 .40
39 Dominik Hasek .40 1.00
40 Chris Terreri .15 .40
41 Jason Allison .05 .15
42 Richard Smehlik .05 .15
43 Frank Banham .05 .15
44 Chris Pronger .15 .40
45 Matt Cullen .05 .15
46 Mike Rucinski RC .05 .15
47 Mike Crowley RC .15 .40
48 Scott Young .05 .15
49 Brian Savage .05 .15
50 Travis Green .05 .15
51 John LeClair .20 .50
52 Adam Foote .05 .15
53 Derek Morris .05 .15
54 Guy Hebert .15 .40
55 Chris Gratton .15 .40
56 Sergei Zubov .05 .15
57 Dave Karpa .05 .15
58 Sergei Varlamov .05 .15
59 Josef Marha .05 .15
60 Jason Marshall .05 .15
61 Jeff Nielsen RC .05 .15
62 Steve Rucchin .05 .15
63 Tomas Sandstrom .05 .15
64 Jason Bonsignore .05 .15
65 Mikhail Shtalenkov .05 .15
67 Tom Askey RC .05 .15
68 Jaromir Jagr .30 .75
69 Per Axelsson .05 .15
70 Ken Baumgartner .05 .15
71 Jiri Slegr .05 .15
72 Mathieu Schneider .05 .15
73 Anson Carter .15 .40
74 Byron Dafoe .15 .40
75 Rob DiMaio .05 .15
76 Ted Donato .05 .15
77 Ray Bourque .30 .75
78 Dave Ellett .05 .15
79 Steve Heinze .05 .15
80 Geoff Sanderson .15 .40
81 Miroslav Satan .15 .40
82 Martin Straka .05 .15
83 Dimitri Khristich .05 .15
84 Grant Ledyard .05 .15
85 Cameron Mann .05 .15
86 Kyle McLaren .05 .15
87 Sergei Samsonov .15 .40
88 Eric Lindros .20 .50
89 Alexander Mogilny .15 .40
90 Joe Juneau .05 .15
91 Sergei Fedorov .30 .75
92 Rick Tocchet .05 .15
93 Doug Gilmour .15 .40
94 Ryan Smyth .05 .15
95 Alexei Morozov .05 .15
96 Phil Housley .05 .15
97 Jeremy Roenick .25 .60
98 Jay More .05 .15
99 Wayne Gretzky 1.25 3.00
100 Robbie Tallas .05 .15
101 Tim Taylor .05 .15
102 Joe Thornton .30 .75
103 Donald Audette .05 .15
104 Curtis Brown .05 .15
105 Michal Grosek .05 .15
106 Brian Holzinger .05 .15
107 Derek Plante .05 .15
108 Rob Ray .05 .15
109 Darryl Shannon .05 .15
110 Steve Shields .15 .40
111 Vaclav Varada .05 .15
112 Dixon Ward .05 .15
113 Jason Woolley .05 .15
114 Alexei Zhitnik .05 .15
115 Andrew Cassels .05 .15
116 Hnat Domenichelli .05 .15
117 Theo Fleury .05 .15
118 Denis Gauthier .05 .15
119 Cale Hulse .05 .15
120 Jarome Iginla .25 .60
121 Marty McInnis .05 .15
122 Tyler Moss .05 .15
123 Michael Nylander .05 .15
124 Dwayne Roloson .05 .15
125 Cory Stillman .05 .15
126 Rick Tabaracci .05 .15
127 German Titov .05 .15
128 Jason Wiemer .05 .15
129 Steve Chiasson .05 .15
130 Kevin Dineen .05 .15
131 Nelson Emerson .05 .15
132 Martin Gelinas .05 .15
133 Stu Grimson .05 .15
134 Sami Kapanen .05 .15
135 Trevor Kidd .15 .40
136 Robert Kron .05 .15
137 Jeff O'Neill .05 .15
138 Keith Primeau .05 .15
139 Paul Ranheim .05 .15
140 Gary Roberts .05 .15
141 Glen Wesley .05 .15
142 Tony Amonte .15 .40
143 Eric Daze .15 .40
144 Jeff Hackett .15 .40
145 Greg Johnson .05 .15
146 Chad Kilger .05 .15
147 Sergei Krivokrasov .05 .15
148 Christian LaFlamme .05 .15
149 Jean-Yves Leroux .05 .15
150 Dmitri Nabokov .05 .15
151 Jeff Shantz .05 .15
152 Gary Suter .05 .15
153 Eric Weinrich .05 .15
154 Todd White RC .05 .15
155 Alexei Zhamnov .05 .15
156 Wade Belak .05 .15
157 Craig Billington .05 .15
158 Rene Corbet .05 .15
159 Shean Donovan .05 .15
160 Valeri Kamensky .05 .15
161 Uwe Krupp .05 .15
162 Jari Kurri .15 .40
163 Eric Lacroix .05 .15
164 Claude Lemieux .05 .15
165 Eric Messier .05 .15
166 Jeff Odgers .05 .15
167 Sandis Ozolinsh .05 .15
168 Warren Rychel .05 .15
169 Joe Sakic .40 1.00
170 Stephane Yelle .05 .15
171 Greg Adams .05 .15
172 Jason Botterill .05 .15
173 Guy Carbonneau .05 .15
174 Shawn Chambers .05 .15
175 Manny Fernandez .05 .15
176 Derian Hatcher .05 .15
177 Benoit Hogue .05 .15
178 Mike Keane .05 .15
179 Jere Lehtinen .05 .15
180 Juha Lind .05 .15
181 Mike Modano .30 .75
182 Brian Skrudland .05 .15
183 Darryl Sydor .05 .15
184 Roman Turek .15 .40
185 Pat Verbeek .05 .15
186 Jamie Wright .05 .15
187 Doug Brown .05 .15
188 Kris Draper .05 .15
189 Anders Eriksson .05 .15
190 Slava Fetisov .05 .15
191 Brent Gilchrist .05 .15
192 Kevin Hodson .05 .15
193 Tomas Holmstrom .05 .15
194 Michael Knuble .15 .40
195 Joey Kocur .05 .15
196 Vyacheslav Kozlov .15 .40
197 Martin Lapointe .05 .15
198 Igor Larionov .05 .15
199 Kirk Maltby .05 .15
200 Norm Maracle RC .30 .75
201 Darren McCarty .05 .15
202 Dmitri Mironov .05 .15
203 Larry Murphy .15 .40
204 Chris Osgood .15 .40
205 Kelly Buchberger .05 .15
206 Bob Essensa .15 .40
207 Scott Fraser .05 .15
208 Mike Grier .05 .15
209 Bill Guerin .15 .40
210 Tony Hrkac .05 .15
211 Curtis Joseph .20 .50
212 Mats Lindgren .05 .15
213 Todd Marchant .05 .15
214 Dean McAmmond .05 .15
215 Craig Millar .05 .15
216 Boris Mironov .05 .15
217 Doug Weight .15 .40
218 Valeri Zelepukin .05 .15
219 Roman Hamrlik .05 .15
220 Radek Dvorak .05 .15
221 Dave Gagner .05 .15
222 Ed Jovanovski .05 .15
223 Viktor Kozlov .05 .15
224 Paul Laus .05 .15
225 Kirk McLean .05 .15
226 Scott Mellanby .05 .15
227 Kirk Muller .05 .15
228 Robert Svehla .05 .15
229 Steve Washburn .05 .15
230 Kevin Weekes .15 .40
231 Ray Whitney .05 .15
232 Peter Worrell RC .25 .60
233 Russ Courtnall .05 .15
234 Stephane Fiset .15 .40
235 Garry Galley .05 .15
236 Craig Johnson .05 .15
237 Ian Laperriere .05 .15
238 Donald MacLean .05 .15
239 Steve McKenna .05 .15
240 Sandy Moger .05 .15
241 Glen Murray .05 .15
242 Sean O'Donnell .05 .15
243 Yanic Perreault .05 .15
244 Luc Robitaille .15 .40
245 Jamie Storr .15 .40
246 Jozef Stumpel .05 .15
247 Vladimir Tsyplakov .05 .15
248 Benoit Brunet .05 .15
249 Shayne Corson .05 .15
250 Vincent Damphousse .05 .15
251 Eric Houde RC .05 .15
252 Saku Koivu .20 .50
253 Vladimir Malakhov .05 .15
254 Dave Manson .05 .15
255 Andy Moog .15 .40
256 Mark Recchi .15 .40
257 Martin Rucinsky .05 .15
258 Jocelyn Thibault .15 .40
259 Mick Vukota .05 .15
260 Dave Andreychuk .15 .40
261 Jason Arnott .05 .15
262 Mike Dunham .15 .40
263 Bobby Holik .05 .15
264 Randy McKay .05 .15
265 Brendan Morrison .15 .40
266 Scott Niedermayer .05 .15
267 Lyle Odelein .05 .15
268 Krzysztof Oliwa .05 .15
269 Denis Pederson .05 .15
270 Brian Rolston .05 .15
271 Sheldon Souray RC .30 .75
272 Scott Stevens .15 .40
273 Petr Sykora .05 .15
274 Steve Thomas .05 .15
275 Bryan Berard .15 .40
276 Zdeno Chara .05 .15
277 Vladimir Chebaturkin RC .05 .15
278 Tom Chorske .05 .15
279 Mariusz Czerkawski .05 .15
280 Jason Dawe .05 .15
281 Wade Flaherty .15 .40
282 Kenny Jonsson .05 .15
283 Sergei Nemchinov .05 .15
284 Zigmund Palffy .15 .40
285 Rich Pilon .05 .15
286 Robert Reichel .05 .15
287 Joe Sacco .05 .15
288 Tommy Salo .15 .40
289 Bryan Smolinski .05 .15
290 Jeff Beukeboom .05 .15
291 Dan Cloutier .15 .40
292 Bruce Driver .05 .15
293 Adam Graves .05 .15
294 Alexei Kovalev .15 .40
295 Pat LaFontaine .20 .50
296 Darren Langdon .05 .15
297 Brian Leetch .20 .50
298 Mike Richter .20 .50
299 Ulf Samuelsson .05 .15
300 Marc Savard .05 .15
301 Kevin Stevens .05 .15
302 Niklas Sundstrom .05 .15
303 Tim Sweeney .05 .15
304 Vladimir Vorobiev .05 .15
305 Daniel Alfredsson .15 .40
306 Magnus Arvedson .05 .15
307 Radek Bonk .05 .15
308 Andreas Dackell .05 .15
309 Bruce Gardiner .05 .15
310 Igor Kravchuk .05 .15
311 Denny Lambert .05 .15
312 Janne Laukkanen .05 .15
313 Shawn McEachern .05 .15
314 Chris Phillips .05 .15
315 Wade Redden .05 .15
316 Ron Tugnutt .15 .40
317 Shaun Van Allen .05 .15
318 Alexei Yashin .05 .15
319 Jason York .05 .15
320 Sergei Zholtok .05 .15
321 Sean Burke .15 .40
322 Paul Coffey .20 .50
323 Alexandre Daigle .05 .15
324 Eric Desjardins .15 .40
325 Colin Forbes .05 .15
326 Ron Hextall .15 .40
327 Trent Klatt .05 .15
328 Dan McGillis .05 .15
329 Joel Otto .05 .15
330 Shjon Podein .05 .15
331 Mike Sillinger .05 .15
332 Chris Therien .05 .15
333 Dainius Zubrus .05 .15
334 Bob Corkum .05 .15
335 Jim Cummins .05 .15
336 Jason Doig .05 .15
337 Dallas Drake .05 .15
338 Mike Gartner .15 .40
339 Brad Isbister .05 .15
340 Craig Janney .05 .15
341 Nikolai Khabibulin .15 .40
342 Teppo Numminen .05 .15
343 Cliff Ronning .05 .15
344 Keith Tkachuk .20 .50
345 Oleg Tverdovsky .05 .15
346 Jim Waite .15 .40
347 Juha Ylonen .05 .15
348 Stu Barnes .05 .15
349 Rob Brown .05 .15
350 Robert Dome .05 .15
351 Ron Francis .15 .40
352 Kevin Hatcher .05 .15
353 Alex Hicks .05 .15
354 Darius Kasparaitis .05 .15
355 Robert Lang .05 .15
356 Fredrik Olausson .05 .15
357 Ed Olczyk .05 .15
358 Peter Skudra .05 .15
359 Chris Tamer .05 .15
360 Ken Wregget .05 .15
361 Blair Atcheynum .05 .15
362 Jim Campbell .05 .15
363 Kelly Chase .05 .15
364 Craig Conroy .05 .15
365 Geoff Courtnall .05 .15
366 Steve Duchesne .15 .40
367 Todd Gill .05 .15
368 Al MacInnis .15 .40
369 Jamie McLennan .05 .15
370 Scott Pellerin .05 .15
371 Pascal Rheaume .05 .15
372 Jamie Rivers .15 .40
373 Darren Turcotte .05 .15
374 Pierre Turgeon .15 .40
375 Tony Twist .05 .15
376 Terry Yake .05 .15
377 Richard Brennan .05 .15
378 Murray Craven .05 .15
379 Jeff Friesen .05 .15
380 Tony Granato .05 .15
381 Bill Houlder .05 .15
382 Kelly Hrudey .15 .40
383 Alexander Korolyuk .15 .40
384 John MacLean .05 .15
385 Bryan Marchment .05 .15
386 Patrick Marleau .15 .40
387 Stephane Matteau .05 .15
388 Marty McSorley .05 .15
389 Bernie Nicholls .05 .15
390 Owen Nolan .15 .40
391 Mike Ricci .15 .40
392 Marco Sturm .05 .15
393 Mike Vernon .15 .40
394 Andrei Zyuzin .05 .15
395 Mikael Andersson .05 .15
396 Zac Bierk RC .05 .15
397 Enrico Ciccone .05 .15
398 Louie DeBrusk .05 .15
399 Karl Dykhuis .05 .15
400 Daymond Langkow .15 .40
401 Mike McBain .05 .15
402 Sandy McCarthy .05 .15
403 Daren Puppa .15 .40
404 Mikael Renberg .15 .40
405 Stephane Richer .15 .40
406 Alexander Selivanov .05 .15
407 Darcy Tucker .05 .15
408 Paul Ysebaert .05 .15
409 Rob Zamuner .05 .15
410 Sergei Berezin .05 .15
411 Wendel Clark .05 .15
412 Sylvain Cote .05 .15
413 Mike Johnson .05 .15
414 Derek King .05 .15
415 Kris King .05 .15
416 Igor Korolev .05 .15
417 Daniil Markov RC .05 .15
418 Alyn McCauley .05 .15
419 Fredrik Modin .05 .15
420 Martin Prochazka .05 .15
421 Jason Smith .05 .15
422 Steve Sullivan .05 .15
423 Yannick Tremblay .05 .15
424 Todd Bertuzzi .20 .50
425 Donald Brashear .05 .15
426 Bret Hedican .05 .15
427 Arturs Irbe .15 .40
428 Jyrki Lumme .05 .15
429 Brad May .05 .15
430 Bryan McCabe .05 .15
431 Markus Naslund .20 .50
432 Brian Noonan .05 .15
433 Dave Scatchard .05 .15
434 Garth Snow .15 .40
435 Scott Walker RC .05 .15
436 Peter Zezel .05 .15
437 Craig Berube .05 .15
438 Jeff Brown .05 .15
439 Andrew Brunette .15 .40
440 Jan Bulis .05 .15
441 Sergei Gonchar .05 .15
442 Dale Hunter .15 .40
443 Steve Konowalchuk .05 .15
444 Kelly Miller .05 .15
445 Adam Oates .15 .40
446 Bill Ranford .15 .40
447 Jaroslav Svejkovsky .05 .15
448 Esa Tikkanen .05 .15
449 Mark Tinordi .05 .15
450 Brendan Witt .05 .15
451 Richard Zednik .05 .15
S181 Mike Modano SAMPLE .75 1.50

1998-99 Pacific Ice Blue

*STARS: 6X TO 15X BASIC CARD
*ROOKIES: 1.25X TO 3X BASIC CARD
STATED ODDS 1:73

1998-99 Pacific Red

*STARS: 4X TO 8X BASIC CARD
*ROOKIES: 2X TO 4X BASIC CARD
STATED ODDS 1:1 TREAT PACKS

1998-99 Pacific Cramer's Choice

Randomly inserted in packs at the rate of 1:721, this 10-card set features action color photos of players picked by President/CEO Michael Cramer and printed on die-cut trophy cards.

COMPLETE SET (10) 100.00 200.00
1 Sergei Samsonov 4.00 10.00
2 Dominik Hasek 10.00 25.00
3 Peter Forsberg 12.50 30.00
4 Patrick Roy 25.00 60.00
5 Mike Modano 8.00 20.00
6 Martin Brodeur 12.50 30.00
7 Wayne Gretzky 30.00 80.00
8 Eric Lindros 5.00 12.00
9 Jaromir Jagr 8.00 20.00
10 Pavel Bure 5.00 12.00

1998-99 Pacific Dynagon Ice Inserts

Randomly inserted in packs at the rate of 4:37, this 20-card set features color photos of some of the NHL's most exciting players printed on mirror-patterned full-foil cards. A titanium parallel was also created and randomly inserted in packs. Titanium Ice parallels were numbered to just 99.

COMPLETE SET (20) 30.00 60.00
*TITANIUM ICE: 5X TO 12X BASIC INSERTS
1 Paul Kariya .75 2.00
2 Teemu Selanne .75 2.00
3 Sergei Samsonov .60 1.50
4 Dominik Hasek 1.50 4.00
5 Peter Forsberg 2.00 5.00
6 Patrick Roy 4.00 10.00
7 Joe Sakic 1.50 4.00
8 Mike Modano 1.25 3.00
9 Sergei Fedorov 1.25 3.00
10 Steve Yzerman 4.00 10.00
11 Saku Koivu .75 2.00
12 Martin Brodeur 2.00 5.00
13 Wayne Gretzky 5.00 12.00
14 John LeClair .75 2.00
15 Eric Lindros .75 2.00
16 Jaromir Jagr 1.25 3.00
17 Pavel Bure .75 2.00
18 Mark Messier .75 2.00
19 Peter Bondra .60 1.50
20 Olaf Kolzig .60 1.50

1998-99 Pacific Gold Crown Die-Cuts

Randomly inserted in packs at the rate of 1:37, this 36-card set features color photos of top NHL stars printed on die-cut crown design 24-point card stock with laser cutting and dual foil.

COMPLETE SET (36) 75.00 150.00
1 Paul Kariya 2.00 5.00
2 Teemu Selanne 2.00 5.00
3 Sergei Samsonov 1.50 4.00
4 Dominik Hasek 4.00 10.00
5 Michael Peca .75 2.00
6 Theo Fleury .75 2.00
7 Chris Chelios .75 2.00
8 Peter Forsberg 5.00 12.00
9 Patrick Roy 10.00 25.00
10 Joe Sakic 4.00 10.00
11 Ed Belfour 2.00 5.00
12 Mike Modano 3.00 8.00
13 Sergei Fedorov 2.50 6.00
14 Chris Osgood 1.50 4.00
15 Brendan Shanahan 2.00 5.00
16 Steve Yzerman 10.00 25.00
17 Saku Koivu 2.00 5.00
18 Martin Brodeur 6.00 15.00
19 Patrik Elias .75 2.00
20 Doug Gilmour 1.50 4.00
21 Trevor Linden .75 2.00
22 Zigmund Palffy .75 2.00
23 Wayne Gretzky 12.00 30.00
24 John LeClair .75 2.00
25 Eric Lindros 2.00 5.00
26 Dainius Zubrus .75 2.00
27 Keith Tkachuk .75 2.00
28 Tom Barrasso 1.50 4.00
29 Jaromir Jagr 3.00 8.00
30 Brett Hull 2.50 6.00
31 Felix Potvin 2.00 5.00
32 Mats Sundin 2.00 5.00
33 Pavel Bure 2.00 5.00
34 Mark Messier 2.00 5.00
35 Peter Bondra .75 2.00
36 Olaf Kolzig 1.50 4.00

1998-99 Pacific Martin Brodeur Show Promo

This card was created by Pacific to honor its relationship with new spokesman Martin Brodeur. It was given away free at three shows in early 1999 to those who opened complete boxes of Pacific product at the company's booth. It was reported that 5,000 copies were produced, but few ever make their way onto market.

COMPLETE SET (1) 10.00
1 Martin Brodeur 10.00

1998-99 Pacific Team Checklists

COMPLETE SET (30) 15.00 30.00
STATED ODDS 2:37
1 Paul Kariya .40 1.00
2 Sergei Samsonov .30 .75
3 Dominik Hasek .75 2.00
4 Theo Fleury .10 .30
5 Keith Primeau .10 .30
6 Chris Chelios .40 1.00
7 Patrick Roy 2.00 5.00
8 Mike Modano .60 1.50
9 Steve Yzerman 2.00 5.00
10 Ryan Smyth .10 .30
11 John Vanbiesbrouck .30 .75
12 Jozef Stumpel .10 .30
13 Saku Koivu .40 1.00
14 Mike Dunham .30 .75
15 Martin Brodeur 1.00 2.50
16 Zigmund Palffy .30 .75
17 Wayne Gretzky 2.50 6.00
18 Alexei Yashin .10 .30
19 Eric Lindros .40 1.00
20 Keith Tkachuk .40 1.00
21 Jaromir Jagr .60 1.50
22 Brett Hull .50 1.25
23 Patrick Marleau .10 .30
24 Rob Zamuner .10 .30
25 Mats Sundin .40 1.00
26 Pavel Bure .40 1.00
27 Olaf Kolzig .30 .75
28 Atlanta Thrashers .40 1.00
29 Minnesota Wild .40 1.00
30 Columbus Blue Jackets .40 1.00

1998-99 Pacific Timelines

COMPLETE SET (20) 60.00 150.00
STATED ODDS 1:181
1 Teemu Selanne 3.00 8.00
2 Dominik Hasek 6.00 15.00
3 Peter Forsberg 6.00 15.00
4 Patrick Roy 12.00 30.00
5 Joe Sakic 6.00 15.00
6 Ed Belfour 3.00 8.00
7 Brendan Shanahan 3.00 8.00
8 Steve Yzerman 10.00 25.00
9 Mike Modano 4.00 10.00
10 Doug Gilmour 2.50 6.00
11 Wayne Gretzky 15.00 40.00
12 Pat LaFontaine 3.00 8.00
13 John LeClair 3.00 8.00
14 Eric Lindros 3.00 8.00
15 Keith Tkachuk 3.00 8.00
16 Jaromir Jagr 4.00 10.00
17 Brett Hull 4.00 10.00
18 Mats Sundin 3.00 8.00
19 Pavel Bure 3.00 8.00
20 Mark Messier 3.00 8.00

1998-99 Pacific Trophy Winners

COMPLETE SET (10) 10.00 20.00
STATED ODDS 1:37 CANADIAN PACKS
1 Martin Brodeur 2.50 6.00
2 Dominik Hasek 1.50 4.00
3 Jaromir Jagr 1.25 3.00
4 Sergei Samsonov .25 .60
5 Sergei Fedorov 1.00 2.50
6 Nicklas Lidstrom .75 2.00
7 Darren McCarty .25 .60
8 Chris Osgood .25 .60
9 Brendan Shanahan .75 2.00
10 Steve Yzerman 3.00 8.00

1999-00 Pacific

Among the first sets released during the 1999-00 hockey season, these cards featured near full bleed photography on the front, along with stars and biographical information on the back. Cards #451-466 were not found in packs. They were available only as part of an arena giveaway program. As such, they are not considered part of the base set. #461 does not exist.

COMPLETE SET (450) 40.00 80.00
1 Matt Cullen .05 .15
2 Johan Davidsson .05 .15
3 Scott Ferguson RC .05 .15
4 Travis Green .05 .15
5 Stu Grimson .05 .15
6 Kevin Haller .05 .15
7 Guy Hebert .15 .40
8 Paul Kariya .20 .50
9 Marty McInnis .05 .15
10 Jim McKenzie .05 .15
11 Fredrik Olausson .05 .15
12 Dominic Roussel .15 .40
13 Steve Rucchin .05 .15
14 Ruslan Salei .05 .15
15 Tomas Sandstrom .05 .15
16 Teemu Selanne .20 .50
17 Jason Allison .05 .15
18 P.J. Axelsson .05 .15
19 Shawn Bates .05 .15
20 Ray Bourque .30 .75
21 Anson Carter .15 .40
22 Byron Dafoe .15 .40
23 Hal Gill .05 .15
24 Steve Heinze .05 .15
25 Dmitri Khristich .05 .15
26 Cameron Mann .05 .15
27 Kyle McLaren .05 .15
28 Sergei Samsonov .15 .40
29 Robbie Tallas .15 .40
30 Joe Thornton .30 .75
31 Landon Wilson .05 .15
32 J.Girard/A.Savage RC .20 .50
33 Stu Barnes .05 .15
34 Martin Biron .05 .15
35 Curtis Brown .05 .15
36 Michal Grosek .05 .15
37 Dominik Hasek .40 1.00
38 Brian Holzinger .15 .40
39 Joe Juneau .15 .40
40 Jay McKee .05 .15
41 Michael Peca .15 .40
42 Erik Rasmussen .05 .15
43 Rob Ray .05 .15
44 Geoff Sanderson .15 .40
45 Miroslav Satan .15 .40
46 Darryl Shannon .05 .15
47 Vaclav Varada .05 .15
48 Dixon Ward .05 .15
49 Jason Woolley .05 .15
50 Alexei Zhitnik .05 .15
51 Fred Brathwaite .15 .40
52 Valeri Bure .05 .15
53 Andrew Cassels .05 .15
54 Rene Corbet .05 .15
55 J-S Giguere .15 .40
56 Phil Housley .05 .15
57 Jarome Iginla .25 .60
58 Derek Morris .05 .15
59 Andrei Nazarov .05 .15
60 Jeff Shantz .05 .15
61 Todd Simpson .05 .15
62 Cory Stillman .05 .15
63 Jason Wiemer .05 .15
64 Clarke Wilm .05 .15
65 Ken Wregget .15 .40
66 Rico Fata RC .05 .15
Tyrone Garner
67 Bates Battaglia .05 .15
68 Paul Coffey .20 .50
69 Kevin Dineen .05 .15
70 Ron Francis .15 .40
71 Martin Gelinas .05 .15
72 Arturs Irbe .15 .40
73 Sami Kapanen .05 .15
74 Trevor Kidd .05 .15
75 Andrei Kovalenko .05 .15
76 Robert Kron .05 .15
77 Kent Manderville .05 .15
78 Jeff O'Neill .05 .15
79 Keith Primeau .05 .15
80 Gary Roberts .05 .15
81 Ray Sheppard .15 .40
82 Glen Wesley .05 .15
83 Byron Ritchie RC .15 .40
Craig MacDonald
84 Tony Amonte .15 .40
85 Eric Daze .15 .40
86 J-P Dumont .15 .40
87 Anders Eriksson .05 .15
88 Mark Fitzpatrick .15 .40
89 Doug Gilmour .15 .40
90 J.Y. Leroux .05 .15
91 Dave Manson .05 .15
92 Josef Marha .05 .15
93 Dean McAmmond .05 .15
94 Boris Mironov .05 .15
95 Ed Olczyk .05 .15
96 Bob Probert .05 .15
97 Jocelyn Thibault .15 .40
98 Alexei Zhamnov .05 .15
99 Remi Royer .05 .15
Ty Jones
100 Craig Billington .15 .40
101 Adam Deadmarsh .05 .15
102 Chris Drury .15 .40
103 Theo Fleury .05 .15
104 Adam Foote .05 .15
105 Peter Forsberg .50 1.25
106 Milan Hejduk .20 .50
107 Dale Hunter .05 .15
108 Valeri Kamensky .15 .40
109 Sylvain Lefebvre .05 .15
110 Claude Lemieux .05 .15
111 Aaron Miller .05 .15
112 Jeff Odgers .05 .15
113 Sandis Ozolinsh .05 .15
114 Patrick Roy 1.00 2.50
115 Joe Sakic .40 1.00
116 Stephane Yelle .05 .15
117 Ed Belfour .20 .50
118 Derian Hatcher .05 .15
119 Benoit Hogue .05 .15
120 Brett Hull .25 .60
121 Mike Keane .05 .15
122 Jamie Langenbrunner .05 .15
123 Jere Lehtinen .15 .40
124 Brad Lukowich RC .05 .15
125 Grant Marshall .05 .15
126 Mike Modano .30 .75
127 Joe Nieuwendyk .15 .40
128 Derek Plante .05 .15
129 Darryl Sydor .05 .15
130 Roman Turek .15 .40
131 Pat Verbeek .05 .15
132 Sergei Zubov .15 .40
133 Jonathan Sim RC .20 .50
Blake Sloan
134 Doug Brown .05 .15
135 Chris Chelios .20 .50
136 Wendel Clark .15 .40
137 Kris Draper .05 .15
138 Sergei Fedorov .30 .75
139 Tomas Holmstrom .05 .15
140 Vyacheslav Kozlov .15 .40
141 Martin Lapointe .05 .15
142 Igor Larionov .05 .15
143 Nicklas Lidstrom .20 .50
144 Darren McCarty .05 .15
145 Larry Murphy .15 .40
146 Chris Osgood .15 .40
147 Bill Ranford .15 .40
148 Ulf Samuelsson .05 .15
149 Brendan Shanahan .20 .50
150 Aaron Ward .05 .15
151 Steve Yzerman 1.00 2.50
152 Josef Beranek .05 .15
153 Pat Falloon .05 .15
154 Mike Grier .05 .15
155 Bill Guerin .15 .40
156 Roman Hamrlik .05 .15
157 Chad Kilger .05 .15
158 Georges Laraque RC .25 .60
159 Todd Marchant .05 .15
160 Ethan Moreau .05 .15
161 Rem Murray .05 .15
162 Janne Niinimaa .05 .15
163 Tom Poti .05 .15

164 Tommy Salo .15 .40
165 Alexander Selivanov .05 .15
166 Ryan Smyth .15 .40
167 Doug Weight .15 .40
168 Steve Passmore RC .20 .50
169 Pavel Bure .20 .50
170 Sean Burke .15 .40
171 Dino Ciccarelli .15 .40
172 Radek Dvorak .05 .15
173 Viktor Kozlov .05 .15
174 Oleg Kvasha .05 .15
175 Paul Laus .05 .15
176 Bill Lindsay .05 .15
177 Kirk McLean .15 .40
178 Scott Mellanby .05 .15
179 Rob Niedermayer .05 .15
180 Mark Parrish .05 .15
181 Jaroslav Spacek .05 .15
182 Robert Svehla .05 .15
183 Ray Whitney .05 .15
184 Peter Worrell .05 .15
185 Dan Boyle RC .15 .40
Marcus Nilson
186 Donald Audette .05 .15
187 Rob Blake .15 .40
188 Russ Courtnall .05 .15
189 Ray Ferraro .05 .15
190 Stephane Fiset .15 .40
191 Craig Johnson .05 .15
192 Olli Jokinen .15 .40
193 Glen Murray .05 .15
194 Mattias Norstrom .05 .15
195 Sean O'Donnell .05 .15
196 Luc Robitaille .15 .40
197 Pavel Rosa .15 .40
198 Jamie Storr .15 .40
199 Jozef Stumpel .15 .40
200 Vladimir Tsyplakov .05 .15
201 Benoit Brunet .05 .15
202 Shayne Corson .05 .15
203 Jeff Hackett .15 .40
204 Matt Higgins .05 .15
205 Saku Koivu .20 .50
206 Vladimir Malakhov .05 .15
207 Patrick Poulin .05 .15
208 Stephane Quintal .05 .15
209 Martin Rucinsky .05 .15
210 Brian Savage .05 .15
211 Turner Stevenson .05 .15
212 Jose Theodore .25 .60
213 Eric Weinrich .05 .15
214 Sergei Zholtok .05 .15
215 Dainius Zubrus .15 .40
216 Terry Ryan .05 .15
Miloslav Guren
217 Drake Berehowsky .05 .15
218 Sebastien Bordeleau .05 .15
219 Bob Boughner .05 .15
220 Andrew Brunette .15 .40
221 Patrick Cote .05 .15
222 Mike Dunham .15 .40
223 Tom Fitzgerald .05 .15
224 Jamie Heward .05 .15
225 Greg Johnson .05 .15
226 Patric Kjellberg .05 .15
227 Sergei Krivokrasov .05 .15
228 Denny Lambert .05 .15
229 David Legwand .20 .50
230 Mark Mowers RC .15 .40
231 Cliff Ronning .05 .15
232 Tomas Vokoun .05 .15
233 Scott Walker .05 .15
234 Jason Arnott .05 .15
235 Martin Brodeur .50 1.25
236 Ken Daneyko .05 .15
237 Patrik Elias .15 .40
238 Bobby Holik .15 .40
239 John Madden RC .30 .75
240 Randy McKay .05 .15
241 Brendan Morrison .15 .40
242 Scott Niedermayer .05 .15
243 Lyle Odelein .05 .15
244 Krzysztof Oliwa .05 .15
245 Jay Pandolfo .05 .15
246 Brian Rolston .05 .15
247 Vadim Sharifijanov .05 .15
248 Petr Sykora .05 .15
249 Chris Terreri .15 .40
250 Scott Stevens .15 .40
251 Eric Brewer .15 .40
252 Zdeno Chara .05 .15
253 Mariusz Czerkawski .05 .15
254 Wade Flaherty .05 .15
255 Kenny Jonsson .05 .15
256 Claude Lapointe .05 .15
257 Mark Lawrence .05 .15
258 Trevor Linden .05 .15
259 Mats Lindgren .05 .15
260 Warren Luhning .05 .15
261 Zigmund Palffy .15 .40
262 Rich Pilon .05 .15
263 Felix Potvin .20 .50
264 Barry Richter .05 .15
265 Bryan Smolinski .05 .15
266 Mike Watt .05 .15
267 Dan Cloutier .05 .15
268 Brent Fedyk .05 .15
269 Adam Graves .05 .15
270 Todd Harvey .05 .15
271 Mike Knuble .05 .15
272 Brian Leetch .20 .50
273 John MacLean .05 .15
274 Manny Malhotra .15 .40
275 Rumun Ndur .05 .15
276 Petr Nedved .15 .40
277 Peter Popovic .05 .15
278 Mike Richter .20 .50
279 Marc Savard .05 .15
280 Mathieu Schneider .05 .15
281 Kevin Stevens .15 .40
282 Niklas Sundstrom .15 .40
283 Daniel Alfredsson .15 .40
284 Magnus Arvedson .05 .15
285 Radek Bonk .05 .15
286 Andreas Dackell .05 .15
287 Bruce Gardiner .05 .15
288 Marian Hossa .20 .50
289 Andreas Johansson .05 .15
290 Igor Kravchuk .05 .15
291 Shawn McEachern .05 .15
292 Vaclav Prospal .05 .15
293 Wade Redden .05 .15
294 Damian Rhodes .15 .40
295 Sami Salo .05 .15
296 Ron Tugnutt .15 .40
297 Alexei Yashin .15 .40
298 Jason York .05 .15
299 Rod Brind'Amour .15 .40
300 Adam Burt .05 .15
301 Eric Desjardins .15 .40
302 Ron Hextall .15 .40
303 Jody Hull .05 .15
304 Keith Jones .05 .15
305 Daymond Langkow .15 .40
306 John LeClair .20 .50
307 Eric Lindros .20 .50
308 Sandy McCarthy .05 .15
309 Dan McGillis .05 .15
310 Mark Recchi .15 .40
311 Mikael Renberg .15 .40
312 Chris Therien .05 .15
313 John Vanbiesbrouck .15 .40
314 Valeri Zelepukin .05 .15
315 Greg Adams .05 .15
316 Keith Carney .05 .15
317 Bob Corkum .05 .15
318 Jim Cummins .05 .15
319 Shane Doan .05 .15
320 Dallas Drake .05 .15
321 Nikolai Khabibulin .15 .40
322 Jyrki Lumme .05 .15
323 Teppo Numminen .05 .15
324 Robert Reichel .05 .15
325 Jeremy Roenick .25 .60
326 Mikhail Shtalenkov .05 .15
327 Mike Stapleton .05 .15
328 Keith Tkachuk .20 .50
329 Rick Tocchet .15 .40
330 Oleg Tverdovsky .05 .15
331 Juha Ylonen .05 .15
332 Robert Esche RC .05 .15
Scott Langkow
333 Matthew Barnaby .15 .40
334 Tom Barrasso .15 .40
335 Rob Brown .05 .15
336 Kevin Hatcher .05 .15
337 Jan Hrdina .05 .15
338 Jaromir Jagr .30 .75
339 Darius Kasparaitis .05 .15
340 Dan Kesa .05 .15
341 Alexei Kovalev .05 .15
342 Robert Lang .05 .15
343 Kip Miller .05 .15
344 Alexei Morozov .15 .40
345 Peter Skudra .05 .15
346 Jiri Slegr .05 .15
347 Martin Straka .05 .15
348 German Titov .05 .15
349 Brad Werenka .05 .15
350 J.S. Aubin RC .15 .40
Brian Bonin
351 Blair Atcheynum .05 .15
352 Lubos Bartecko .05 .15
353 Craig Conroy .05 .15
354 Geoff Courtnall .15 .40
355 Pavol Demitra .15 .40
356 Grant Fuhr .15 .40
357 Michal Handzus .15 .40
358 Al MacInnis .15 .40
359 Jamal Mayers .05 .15
360 Jamie McLennan .15 .40
361 Scott Pellerin .05 .15
362 Chris Pronger .15 .40
363 Pascal Rheaume .05 .15
364 Pierre Turgeon .15 .40
365 Tony Twist .15 .40
366 Scott Young .05 .15
367 Jochen Hecht RC .50 1.25
Brent Johnson
368 Tyson Nash RC .15 .40
Marty Reasoner
369 Vincent Damphousse .05 .15
370 Jeff Friesen .05 .15
371 Tony Granato .05 .15
372 Bill Houlder .05 .15
373 Alexander Korolyuk .05 .15
374 Bryan Marchment .05 .15
375 Patrick Marleau .15 .40
376 Stephane Matteau .05 .15
377 Joe Murphy .05 .15
378 Owen Nolan .15 .40
379 Mike Rathje .05 .15
380 Mike Ricci .05 .15
381 Steve Shields .15 .40
382 Ronnie Stern .05 .15
383 Marco Sturm .05 .15
384 Mike Vernon .15 .40
385 Scott Hannan RC .15 .40
Shawn Heins
386 Cory Cross .05 .15
387 Alexandre Daigle .05 .15
388 Colin Forbes .05 .15
389 Chris Gratton .05 .15
390 Kevin Hodson .15 .40
391 Pavel Kubina .05 .15
392 Vincent Lecavalier .20 .50
393 Michael Nylander .05 .15
394 Stephane Richer .15 .40
395 Corey Schwab .15 .40
396 Mike Sillinger .05 .15
397 Petr Svoboda .05 .15
398 Darcy Tucker .05 .15
399 Rob Zamuner .05 .15
400 Paul Mara RC .20 .50
Mario Larocque
401 Bryan Berard .15 .40
402 Sergei Berezin .15 .40
403 Lonny Bohonos .05 .15
404 Sylvain Cote .05 .15
405 Tie Domi .15 .40
406 Mike Johnson .05 .15
407 Curtis Joseph .20 .50
408 Tomas Kaberle .05 .15
409 Alexander Karpovtsev .05 .15
410 Derek King .05 .15
411 Igor Korolev .05 .15
412 Adam Mair RC .15 .40
413 Alyn McCauley .15 .40
414 Yanic Perreault .05 .15
415 Steve Sullivan .05 .15
416 Mats Sundin .20 .50
417 Steve Thomas .05 .15
418 Garry Valk .05 .15
419 Adrian Aucion .05 .15
420 Todd Bertuzzi .20 .50
421 Donald Brashear .05 .15
422 Dave Gagner .05 .15
423 Josh Holden .05 .15
424 Ed Jovanovski .05 .15
425 Bryan McCabe .15 .40
426 Mark Messier .20 .50
427 Alexander Mogilny .15 .40
428 Bill Muckalt .15 .40
429 Markus Naslund .20 .50
430 Mattias Ohlund .15 .40
431 Dave Scatchard .05 .15
432 Peter Schaefer .05 .15
433 Garth Snow .15 .40
434 Kevin Weekes .05 .15
435 Brian Bellows .05 .15
436 James Black .05 .15
437 Peter Bondra .15 .40
438 Jan Bulis .05 .15
439 Sergei Gonchar .05 .15
440 Benoit Gratton RC .05 .15
441 Calle Johansson .05 .15
442 Ken Klee .05 .15
443 Olaf Kolzig .15 .40
444 Steve Konowalchuk .05 .15
445 Andrei Nikolishin .05 .15
446 Adam Oates .15 .40
447 Jaroslav Svejkovsky .05 .15
448 Rick Tabaracci .15 .40
449 Richard Zednik .05 .15
450 Nolan Baumgartner RC .20 .50
Alexei Tezikov
451 Ladislav Kohn AG
452 Petr Buzek AG
453 Robyn Regehr AG
454 David Tanabe AG
455 Jiri Fischer AG
456 Paul Comrie AG
457 Brad Chartrand AG
458 Scott Gomez AG
459 Roberto Luongo AG
460 Mike York AG
462 Trevor Letowski AG
463 Brad Stuart AG
464 Ben Clymer AG
465 Nikolai Antropov AG
466 Jeff Halpern AG

1999-00 Pacific Copper

*STARS: 10X TO 25X BASIC CARD
*RC's: 6X TO 15X BASIC CARD
STATED PRINT RUN 99 SERIAL #'d SETS

1999-00 Pacific Emerald Green

*STARS: 6X TO 15X BASIC CARD
*RC's: 4X TO 10X BASIC CARD
STATED PRINT RUN 199 SERIAL #'d SETS

1999-00 Pacific Gold

*STARS: 8X TO 20X BASIC CARD
*RC's: 5X TO 12X BASIC CARD
STATED PRINT RUN 199 SER.#'d SETS

1999-00 Pacific Ice Blue

*STARS: 40X TO 100X BASIC CARDS
*ROOKIES: 10X TO 25X BASIC CARDS
STATED PRINT RUN 75 SERIAL #'d SETS

1999-00 Pacific Premiere Date

*STARS: 40X TO 100X BASIC CARDS
ROOKIES: 15X TO 30X BASIC CARDS
STATED PRINT RUN 46 SER.#'d SETS

1999-00 Pacific Red

*RED: 1X TO 1.5X BASIC CARDS
*RC's: .5X TO 1X BASIC CARDS

1999-00 Pacific Center Ice

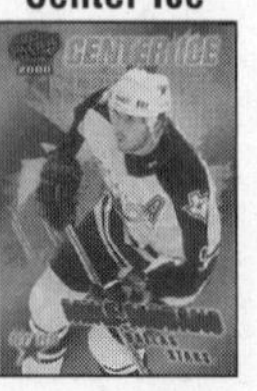

Randomly inserted in the 7-eleven pack release, this set identifies some of the NHL's top stars. A parallel proof version of this set was released also where cards are sequentially numbered to 10. Proofs are not priced due to scarcity.

COMPLETE SET (20) 20.00 40.00
1 Paul Kariya .75 2.00
2 Teemu Selanne .75 2.00
3 Dominik Hasek 1.50 4.00
4 Jarome Iginla 1.00 2.50
5 Theo Fleury .25 .60
6 Peter Forsberg 2.00 5.00
7 Patrick Roy 4.00 10.00
8 Joe Sakic 1.50 4.00
9 Mike Modano 1.25 3.00
10 Brendan Shanahan .75 2.00
11 Steve Yzerman 4.00 10.00
12 Doug Weight .60 1.50
13 Trevor Linden .25 .60
14 Martin Brodeur 2.00 5.00
15 Alexei Yashin .25 .60
16 Eric Lindros .75 2.00
17 Jaromir Jagr 1.25 3.00
18 Curtis Joseph .75 2.00
19 Mats Sundin .75 2.00
20 Mark Messier .75 2.00

1999-00 Pacific Cramer's Choice

Randomly inserted into packs, this set continues the tradition of the Cramer's Choice Awards. For the first time, these cards are serial numbered out of 299.

COMPLETE SET (10) 175.00 350.00
1 Paul Kariya 8.00 20.00
2 Dominik Hasek 15.00 40.00
3 Peter Forsberg 20.00 50.00
4 Patrick Roy 40.00 100.00
5 Joe Sakic 15.00 40.00
6 Mike Modano 12.50 30.00
7 Steve Yzerman 40.00 100.00
8 Eric Lindros 8.00 20.00
9 Jaromir Jagr 12.50 30.00
10 Curtis Joseph 8.00 20.00

1999-00 Pacific Gold Crown Die-Cuts

COMPLETE SET (36) 100.00 200.00
STATED ODDS 1:25
1 Paul Kariya 2.00 5.00
2 Teemu Selanne 2.00 5.00
3 Ray Bourque 3.00 8.00
4 Byron Dafoe 1.25 3.00
5 Dominik Hasek 4.00 10.00
6 Michael Peca 1.25 3.00
7 Chris Drury 1.25 3.00
8 Theo Fleury 1.25 3.00
9 Peter Forsberg 5.00 12.00
10 Milan Hejduk 1.25 3.00
11 Patrick Roy 10.00 25.00
12 Joe Sakic 4.00 10.00
13 Ed Belfour 2.00 5.00
14 Brett Hull 2.50 6.00
15 Mike Modano 3.00 8.00
16 Chris Chelios 1.25 3.00
17 Brendan Shanahan 2.00 5.00
18 Steve Yzerman 10.00 25.00
19 Pavel Bure 2.00 5.00
20 David Legwand 1.25 3.00
21 Martin Brodeur 6.00 15.00
22 Felix Potvin 2.00 5.00
23 Mike Richter 2.00 5.00
24 Alexei Yashin 1.25 3.00
25 John LeClair 1.25 3.00
26 Eric Lindros 2.00 5.00
27 Mark Recchi 1.25 3.00
28 John Vanbiesbrouck 1.25 3.00
29 Jeremy Roenick 2.50 6.00
30 Keith Tkachuk 1.25 3.00
31 Jaromir Jagr 3.00 8.00
32 Vincent Lecavalier 2.00 5.00
33 Sergei Berezin 1.25 3.00
34 Curtis Joseph 2.00 5.00
35 Mats Sundin 2.00 5.00
36 Mark Messier 2.00 5.00

1999-00 Pacific Home and Away

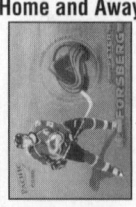

Inserted 2:25 packs, these cards feature players in both their Home and Away jerseys. Cards 1-10 can be found in retail packs, while cards 11-20 can be found in hobby packs.

COMPLETE SET (20) 50.00 100.00
1 Paul Kariya 1.25 3.00
2 Teemu Selanne 1.25 3.00
3 Dominik Hasek 2.50 6.00
4 Peter Forsberg 3.00 8.00
5 Patrick Roy 6.00 15.00
6 Mike Modano 2.00 5.00
7 Steve Yzerman 6.00 15.00
8 John LeClair 1.25 3.00
9 Eric Lindros 1.25 3.00
10 Jaromir Jagr 2.00 5.00
11 Paul Kariya 1.25 3.00
12 Teemu Selanne 1.25 3.00
13 Dominik Hasek 2.50 6.00
14 Peter Forsberg 3.00 8.00
15 Patrick Roy 6.00 15.00
16 Mike Modano 2.00 5.00
17 Steve Yzerman 6.00 15.00
18 John LeClair 1.25 3.00
19 Eric Lindros 1.25 3.00
20 Jaromir Jagr 2.00 5.00

1999-00 Pacific In the Cage Net-Fusions

Inserted 1:97 packs, these cards are die-cut and feature actual netting as the background. Cards are full color and feature goalie action shots.

COMPLETE SET (20) 50.00 100.00
1 Guy Hebert 2.00 5.00
2 Byron Dafoe 2.00 5.00
3 Dominik Hasek 5.00 12.00
4 Arturs Irbe 2.00 5.00
5 Patrick Roy 12.50 30.00
6 Ed Belfour 2.50 6.00
7 Chris Osgood 2.00 5.00
8 Tommy Salo 2.00 5.00
9 Jeff Hackett 2.00 5.00
10 Martin Brodeur 6.00 15.00
11 Felix Potvin 2.50 6.00
12 Mike Richter 2.50 6.00
13 Ron Tugnutt 2.00 5.00
14 John Vanbiesbrouck 2.00 5.00
15 Nikolai Khabibulin 2.00 5.00
16 Tom Barrasso 2.00 5.00
17 Grant Fuhr 2.00 5.00
18 Mike Vernon 2.00 5.00
19 Curtis Joseph 2.50 6.00
20 Olaf Kolzig 2.00 5.00

1999-00 Pacific Past and Present

A hobby only insert seeded 1:49 that features 20 of the NHL's top stars in both their old and current uniforms.

COMPLETE SET (20) 100.00 200.00
1 Paul Kariya 2.00 5.00
2 Teemu Selanne 2.00 5.00
3 Ray Bourque 3.00 8.00
4 Dominik Hasek 6.00 15.00
5 Theo Fleury 1.50 4.00
6 Peter Forsberg 8.00 20.00
7 Patrick Roy 12.00 30.00
8 Joe Sakic 6.00 15.00
9 Ed Belfour 2.00 5.00
10 Brett Hull 3.00 8.00
11 Mike Modano 3.00 8.00
12 Brendan Shanahan 2.00 5.00
13 Steve Yzerman 12.00 30.00
14 Pavel Bure 2.00 5.00
15 Martin Brodeur 8.00 20.00
16 John LeClair 1.50 4.00
17 Eric Lindros 2.00 5.00
18 John Vanbiesbrouck 1.50 4.00
19 Jaromir Jagr 4.00 10.00
20 Curtis Joseph 2.00 5.00

1999-00 Pacific Team Leaders

Randomly inserted in packs at the rate of 2:25, this set features 27 of the NHL's premier team leaders. Each card features holographic foil with a complete team checklist on the back.

COMPLETE SET (28) 30.00 60.00
1 Paul Kariya 1.00 2.50
2 Atlanta Thrashers .30 .75
3 Ray Bourque 1.50 4.00
4 Dominik Hasek 2.00 5.00
5 Jarome Iginla 1.25 3.00
6 Arturs Irbe .75 2.00
7 Doug Gilmour .75 2.00
8 Patrick Roy 5.00 12.00
9 Mike Modano 1.50 4.00
10 Steve Yzerman 5.00 12.00
11 Bill Guerin .75 2.00
12 Pavel Bure 1.00 2.50
13 Luc Robitaille .75 2.00
14 Saku Koivu 1.00 2.50
15 Mike Dunham .75 2.00
16 Martin Brodeur 2.50 6.00
17 Zigmund Palffy .75 2.00
18 Mike Richter 1.00 2.50
19 Alexei Yashin .30 .75
20 Eric Lindros 1.00 2.50
21 Keith Tkachuk 1.00 2.50
22 Jaromir Jagr 1.50 4.00
23 Grant Fuhr .75 2.00
24 Mike Vernon .75 2.00
25 Vincent Lecavalier 1.00 2.50
26 Curtis Joseph 1.00 2.50
27 Mark Messier 1.00 2.50
28 Peter Bondra .75 2.00

2000-01 Pacific

Released as a 450-card set, Pacific features full color action shots and cards enhanced with silver foil highlights. Pacific was packaged in 36-pack boxes with packs containing 12 cards each and carried a suggested retail price of $2.99.

COMPLETE SET (450) 30.00 60.00
1 Maxim Balmochnykh .15 .40
2 Matt Cullen .05 .15
3 Ted Donato .05 .15
4 Guy Hebert .15 .40
5 Paul Kariya .20 .50
6 Ladislav Kohn .05 .15
7 Marty McInnis .05 .15
8 Kip Miller .05 .15
9 Dominic Roussel .15 .40
10 Steve Rucchin .05 .15
11 Teemu Selanne .20 .50
12 Oleg Tverdovsky .05 .15
13 Vitali Vishnevski .05 .15
14 Donald Audette .05 .15
15 Andrew Brunette .15 .40
16 Petr Buzek .05 .15
17 Hnat Domenichelli .05 .15
18 Ray Ferraro .05 .15
19 Steve Guolla .05 .15
20 Denny Lambert .05 .15
21 Damian Rhodes .15 .40
22 Mike Stapleton .05 .15
23 Patrik Stefan .05 .15
24 Per Svartvadet .05 .15
25 Dean Sylvester .05 .15
26 Yannick Tremblay .05 .15
27 Bryan Adams .15 .40
Scott Fankhouser
28 Herbert Vasiljevs RC .20 .50
Sergei Vyshedkevich RC
29 Jason Allison .05 .15
30 Per Johan Axelsson .05 .15
31 Anson Carter .15 .40
32 Byron Dafoe .15 .40
33 Hal Gill .05 .15
34 John Grahame .15 .40
35 Steve Heinze .05 .15
36 Joe Hulbig .05 .15
37 Mike Knuble .05 .15
38 Kyle McLaren .05 .15
39 Eric Nickulas RC .05 .15
40 Brian Rolston .05 .15
41 Sergei Samsonov .15 .40
42 Andre Savage .05 .15
43 Joe Thornton .30 .75
44 Darren Van Impe .05 .15
45 Nick Boynton .15 .40
Johnathan Aitken
46 Maxim Afinogenov .05 .15
47 Stu Barnes .05 .15
48 Martin Biron .15 .40
49 Curtis Brown .05 .15
50 Doug Gilmour .15 .40
51 Chris Gratton .05 .15
52 Dominik Hasek .40 1.00
53 Michael Peca .15 .40
54 Erik Rasmussen .05 .15
55 Rob Ray .15 .40
56 Geoff Sanderson .05 .15
57 Miroslav Satan .15 .40
58 Vladimir Tsyplakov .05 .15
59 Vaclav Varada .05 .15
60 Jason Woolley .05 .15
61 Fred Brathwaite .15 .40
62 Valeri Bure .05 .15
63 Bobby Dollas .05 .15
64 J-S Giguere .05 .15
65 Phil Housley .05 .15
66 Jarome Iginla .25 .60
67 Andreas Johansson .05 .15
68 Sergei Krivokrasov .05 .15
69 Bill Lindsay .05 .15
70 Derek Morris .05 .15
71 Andrei Nazarov .05 .15
72 Oleg Saprykin .05 .15
73 Marc Savard .15 .40
74 Jeff Shantz .05 .15
75 Cory Stillman .05 .15
76 Jason Wiemer .05 .15
77 Chris Clark .05 .15
Sergei Varlamov
78 Bates Battaglia .05 .15
79 Rod Brind'Amour .15 .40
80 Paul Coffey .20 .50
81 Ron Francis .15 .40
82 Sean Hill .05 .15
83 Arturs Irbe .15 .40
84 Sami Kapanen .05 .15
85 Dave Karpa .05 .15
86 Andrei Kovalenko .05 .15
87 Robert Kron .05 .15
88 Jeff O'Neill .05 .15
89 Gary Roberts .05 .15
90 Dave Tanabe .15 .40
91 Tommy Westlund .05 .15
92 Tony Amonte .15 .40
93 Eric Daze .15 .40
94 Kevin Dean .05 .15
95 Michal Grosek .05 .15
96 Dean McAmmond .05 .15
97 Bryan McCabe .05 .15
98 Steven McCarthy .05 .15
99 Boris Mironov .05 .15
100 Michael Nylander .05 .15
101 Bob Probert .15 .40
102 Steve Sullivan .05 .15
103 Jocelyn Thibault .15 .40
104 Ryan Vandenbussche .05 .15
105 Alexei Zhamnov .15 .40
106 Dave Andreychuk .15 .40
107 Ray Bourque .40 1.00
108 Adam Deadmarsh .05 .15
109 Marc Denis .15 .40
110 Greg DeVries .05 .15
111 Chris Drury .15 .40
112 Adam Foote .05 .15
113 Peter Forsberg .50 1.25
114 Alexei Gusarov .05 .15
115 Milan Hejduk .20 .50
116 Eric Messier .05 .15
117 Sandis Ozolinsh .05 .15
118 Shjon Podein .05 .15
119 Dave Reid .05 .15
120 Patrick Roy 1.00 2.50
121 Joe Sakic .40 1.00
122 Martin Skoula .15 .40
123 Alex Tanguay .15 .40
124 Stephane Yelle .05 .15
125 Serge Aubin RC .75 2.00
Ville Nieminen RC
126 Ed Belfour .20 .50
127 Guy Carbonneau .05 .15
128 Sylvain Cote .05 .15
129 Manny Fernandez .15 .40
130 Derian Hatcher .05 .15
131 Brett Hull .25 .60
132 Mike Keane .05 .15
133 Jamie Langenbrunner .05 .15
134 Jere Lehtinen .15 .40
135 Dave Manson .05 .15
136 Richard Matvichuk .05 .15
137 Mike Modano .30 .75
138 Brenden Morrow .15 .40
139 Joe Nieuwendyk .15 .40
140 Blake Sloan .05 .15
141 Darryl Sydor .05 .15
142 Scott Thornton .05 .15
143 Sergei Zubov ERR .05 .15
Misnumbered 142
144 Doug Brown .05 .15
145 Chris Chelios .20 .50
146 Kris Draper .05 .15
147 Sergei Fedorov .30 .75
148 Tomas Holmstrom .05 .15
149 Vyacheslav Kozlov .05 .15
150 Darryl Laplante .05 .15
151 Martin Lapointe .05 .15
152 Igor Larionov .05 .15
153 Nicklas Lidstrom .20 .50
154 Kirk Maltby .05 .15
155 Darren McCarty .05 .15
156 Larry Murphy .15 .40
157 Chris Osgood .15 .40
158 Brendan Shanahan .20 .50
159 Pat Verbeek .05 .15
160 Jesse Wallin .05 .15
161 Ken Wregget .15 .40
162 Steve Yzerman 1.00 2.50
163 Boyd Devereaux .05 .15
164 Jim Dowd .05 .15
165 Mike Grier .05 .15
166 Bill Guerin .15 .40
167 Roman Hamrlik .15 .40
168 Georges Laraque .05 .15
169 Todd Marchant .05 .15
170 Ethan Moreau .05 .15
171 Tom Poti .05 .15
172 Tommy Salo .15 .40
173 Alexander Selivanov .05 .15
174 Ryan Smyth .15 .40
175 German Titov .05 .15
176 Doug Weight .15 .40
177 Pavel Bure .20 .50
178 Trevor Kidd .15 .40
179 Viktor Kozlov .15 .40
180 Oleg Kvasha .05 .15
181 Paul Laus .05 .15
182 Scott Mellanby .05 .15
183 Rob Niedermayer .05 .15
184 Ivan Novoseltsev .15 .40
185 Mark Parrish .05 .15
186 Mikhail Shtalenkov .05 .15
187 Robert Svehla .05 .15
188 Mike Vernon .15 .40
189 Ray Whitney .15 .40
190 Peter Worrell .05 .15
191 Erix Boguniecki .05 .15
Brad Ference
192 Aki Berg .05 .15
193 Rob Blake .15 .40
194 Kelly Buchberger .05 .15
195 Nelson Emerson .05 .15
196 Stephane Fiset .15 .40
197 Garry Galley .05 .15
198 Glen Murray .05 .15
199 Jan Nemecek .05 .15
200 Zigmund Palffy .15 .40
201 Luc Robitaille .15 .40
202 Bryan Smolinski .05 .15

203 Jamie Storr .15 .40
204 Jozef Stumpel .15 .40
205 Patrice Brisebois .05 .15
206 Benoit Brunet .05 .15
207 Shayne Corson .05 .15
208 Jeff Hackett .15 .40
209 Saku Koivu .20 .50
210 Trevor Linden .05 .15
211 Oleg Petrov .05 .15
212 Martin Rucinsky .05 .15
213 Brian Savage .05 .15
214 Sheldon Souray .05 .15
215 Jose Theodore .25 .60
216 Eric Weinrich .05 .15
217 Sergei Zholtok .05 .15
218 Dainius Zubrus .05 .15
219 Sebastien Bordeleau .05 .15
220 Mike Dunham .15 .40
221 Tom Fitzgerald .05 .15
222 Greg Johnson .05 .15
223 David Legwand .15 .40
224 Craig Millar .05 .15
225 Cliff Ronning .05 .15
226 Kimmo Timonen .05 .15
227 Tomas Vokoun .05 .15
228 Scott Walker .05 .15
229 Alexandre Boikov RC .15 .40
Marc Moro RC
230 David Gosselin .20 .50
Chris Mason
231 Jason Arnott .05 .15
232 Martin Brodeur .50 1.25
233 Patrik Elias .15 .40
234 Scott Gomez .05 .15
235 Bobby Holik .05 .15
236 Claude Lemieux .05 .15
237 John Madden .15 .40
238 Vladimir Malakhov .05 .15
239 Randy McKay .05 .15
240 Alexander Mogilny .15 .40
241 Scott Niedermayer .05 .15
242 Brian Rafalski .05 .15
243 Scott Stevens .15 .40
244 Petr Sykora .05 .15
245 Chris Terreri .15 .40
246 Willie Mitchell RC .15 .40
Colin White RC
247 Tim Connolly .05 .15
248 Mariusz Czerkawski .05 .15
249 Josh Green .05 .15
250 Brad Isbister .05 .15
251 Jason Krog .05 .15
252 Claude Lapointe .05 .15
253 Roberto Luongo .25 .60
254 Petr Mika RC .05 .15
255 Dave Scatchard .05 .15
256 Steve Valiquette RC .20 .50
257 Kevin Weekes .05 .15
258 Alexandre Daigle .05 .15
259 Radek Dvorak .05 .15
260 Theo Fleury .05 .15
261 Adam Graves .05 .15
262 Jan Hlavac .15 .40
263 Kim Johnsson .05 .15
264 Valeri Kamensky .15. .40
265 Brian Leetch .15 .40
266 John MacLean .05 .15
267 Kirk McLean .05 .15
268 Petr Nedved .15 .40
269 Mike Richter .20 .50
270 Mathieu Schneider .05 .15
271 Johan Witehall RC .05 .15
272 Mike York .05 .15
273 Daniel Alfredsson .15 .40
274 Magnus Arvedson .05 .15
275 Tom Barrasso .15 .40
276 Radek Bonk .05 .15
277 Mike Fisher .15 .40
278 Marian Hossa .20 .50
279 Jani Hurme RC .40 1.00
280 Joe Juneau .15 .40
281 Patrick Lalime .15 .40
282 Grant Ledyard .05 .15
283 Shawn McEachern .05 .15
284 Chris Phillips .05 .15
285 Vaclav Prospal .05 .15
286 Wade Redden .05 .15
287 Sami Salo .05 .15
288 Alexei Yashin .05 .15
289 Jason York .05 .15
290 Rob Zamuner .05 .15
291 Erich Goldmann RC .05 .15
Petr Schastlivy
292 Craig Berube .05 .15
293 Brian Boucher .20 .50
294 Andy Delmore .15 .40
295 Eric Desjardins .15 .40
296 Simon Gagne .20 .50
297 Jody Hull .05 .15
298 Keith Jones .05 .15
299 Daymond Langkow .15 .40
300 John LeClair .20 .50
301 Eric Lindros .20 .50
302 Kent Manderville .05 .15
303 Dan McGillis .05 .15
304 Gino Odjick .05 .15
305 Keith Primeau .05 .15
306 Mark Recchi .15 .40
307 Chris Therien .05 .15
308 Rick Tocchet .15 .40
309 John Vanbiesbrouck .15 .40
310 Valeri Zelepukin .05 .15
311 Sean Burke .05 .15
312 Keith Carney .05 .15
313 Louie DeBrusk .05 .15
314 Shane Doan .05 .15
315 Dallas Drake .05 .15
316 Travis Green .05 .15
317 Nikolai Khabibulin .20 .50
318 Trevor Letowski .05 .15
319 Jyrki Lumme .05 .15
320 Mikael Renberg .05 .15
321 Jeremy Roenick .25 .60
322 Keith Tkachuk .20 .50
323 Robert Esche .05 .15
Wyatt Smith
324 Jean-Sebastien Aubin .15 .40
325 Matthew Barnaby .05 .15
326 Pat Falloon .05 .15
327 Jan Hrdina .05 .15
328 Jaromir Jagr .30 .75
329 Darius Kasparaitis .05 .15
330 Alexei Kovalev .05 .15
331 Robert Lang .05 .15
332 Janne Laukkanen .05 .15
333 Stephen Leach .05 .15
334 Alexei Morozov .05 .15
335 Michal Rozsival .05 .15
336 Jiri Slegr .05 .15
337 Martin Straka .05 .15
338 Ron Tugnutt .15 .40
339 Lubos Bartecko .05 .15
340 Marc Bergevin .05 .15
341 Pavol Demitra .15 .40
342 Mike Eastwood .05 .15
343 Dave Ellett .05 .15
344 Michal Handzus .15 .40
345 Jochen Hecht .05 .15
346 Al MacInnis .15 .40
347 Jamie McLennan .15 .40
348 Tyson Nash .15 .40
349 Chris Pronger .15 .40
350 Marty Reasoner .15 .40
351 Stephane Richer .05 .15
352 Roman Turek .15 .40
353 Pierre Turgeon .15 .40
354 Scott Young .05 .15
355 Derek Bekar RC .15 .40
Ladislav Nagy
356 Vincent Damphousse .05 .15
357 Jeff Friesen .05 .15
358 Todd Harvey .05 .15
359 Alexander Korolyuk .05 .15
360 Patrick Marleau .15 .40
361 Stephane Matteau .05 .15
362 Evgeni Nabokov .15 .40
363 Owen Nolan .15 .40
364 Mike Ricci .15 .40
365 Steve Shields .15 .40
366 Brad Stuart .15 .40
367 Marco Sturm .05 .15
368 Gary Suter .05 .15
369 Dan Cloutier .15 .40
370 Stan Drulia .05 .15
371 Matt Elich RC .05 .15
372 Brian Holzinger .05 .15
373 Mike Johnson .05 .15
374 Ryan Johnson .05 .15
375 Dieter Kochan RC .20 .50
376 Pavel Kubina .05 .15
377 Vincent Lecavalier .20 .50
378 Fredrik Modin .05 .15
379 Wayne Primeau .05 .15
380 Cory Sarich .05 .15
381 Petr Svoboda .05 .15
382 Kaspars Astashenko RC .05 .15
Kyle Freadrich RC
383 Gordie Dwyer .05 .15
Marek Posmyk
384 Nikolai Antropov .05 .15
385 Sergei Berezin .05 .15
386 Wendel Clark .15 .40
387 Tie Domi .15 .40
388 Gerald Diduck .05 .15
389 Jeff Farkas .15 .40
390 Glenn Healy .05 .15
391 Jonas Hoglund .05 .15
392 Curtis Joseph .20 .50
393 Tomas Kaberle .05 .15
394 Alexander Karpovtsev .05 .15
395 Dimitri Khristich .05 .15
396 Igor Korolev .05 .15
397 Yanic Perreault .05 .15
398 DJ Smith .05 .15
399 Mats Sundin .20 .50
400 Steve Thomas .05 .15
401 Darcy Tucker .05 .15
402 Dimitri Yushkevich .05 .15
403 Adrian Aucoin .05 .15
404 Todd Bertuzzi .20 .50
405 Donald Brashear .05 .15
406 Andrew Cassels .05 .15
407 Harold Druken .05 .15
408 Ed Jovanovski .05 .15
409 Steve Kariya .05 .15
410 Trent Klatt .05 .15
411 Mark Messier .20 .50
412 Markus Naslund .20 .50
413 Mattias Ohlund .05 .15
414 Felix Potvin .20 .50
415 Peter Schaefer .05 .15
416 Garth Snow .15 .40
417 Alfie Michaud .05 .15
Jarkko Ruutu
418 Peter Bondra .20 .50
419 Martin Brochu RC .05 .15
420 Jan Bulis .05 .15
421 Sergei Gonchar .05 .15
422 Jeff Halpern .05 .15
423 Calle Johansson .05 .15
424 Ken Klee .05 .15
425 Olaf Kolzig .15 .40
426 Steve Konowalchuk .05 .15
427 Glen Metropolit .05 .15
428 Adam Oates .15 .40
429 Chris Simon .05 .15
430 Richard Zednik .05 .15
431 Jorgen Jonsson SF .05 .15
432 Teemu Selanne SF .15 .40
433 Sami Kapanen SF .05 .15
434 Peter Forsberg SF .20 .50
435 Jere Lehtinen SF .05 .15
436 Nicklas Lidstrom SF .05 .15
437 Janne Niinimaa SF .05 .15
438 Tommy Salo SF .05 .15
439 Saku Koivu SF .05 .15
440 Patric Kjellberg SF .05 .15
441 Olli Jokinen SF .15 .40
442 Kenny Jonsson SF .05 .15
443 Daniel Alfredsson SF .15 .40
444 Andreas Dackell SF .05 .15
445 Teppo Numminen SF .05 .15
446 Marcus Ragnarsson SF .05 .15
447 Niklas Sundstrom SF .05 .15
448 Mats Sundin SF .05 .15
449 Markus Naslund SF .20 .50
450 Ulf Dahlen SF .05 .15

2000-01 Pacific Copper

*STARS: 20X TO 50X BASIC CARDS
*ROOKIES: 8X TO 20X BASIC CARDS
STATED PRINT RUN 40 SERIAL #'d SETS
STATED ODDS 1:37 HOBBY

2000-01 Pacific Gold

*STARS: 20X TO 50X BASIC CARDS
*ROOKIES: 8X TO 20X BASIC CARDS
STATED ODDS 1:37 RETAIL
STATED PRINT RUN 50 SERIAL #'d SETS

2000-01 Pacific Ice Blue

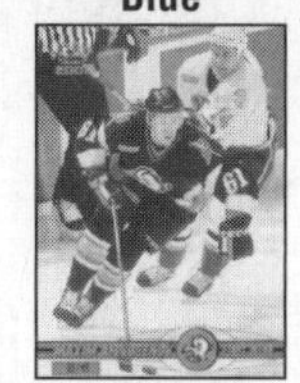

*STARS: 20X TO 50X BASIC CARDS
*ROOKIES: 8X TO 20X BASIC CARDS
STATED ODDS 1:73
STATED PRINT RUN 45 SERIAL #'d SETS

2000-01 Pacific Premiere Date

*STARS: 12X TO 30X BASIC CARDS
*ROOKIES: 8X TO 20X BASIC CARDS
STATED ODDS 1:37 HOBBY
STATED PRINT RUN 40 SERIAL #'d SETS

2000-01 Pacific 2001: Ice Odyssey

COMPLETE SET (20) 40.00 80.00
STATED ODDS 1:37
1 Paul Kariya 2.00 5.00
2 Teemu Selanne 2.00 5.00
3 Martin Biron 1.50 4.00
4 Jarome Iginla 2.50 6.00
5 Chris Drury 1.50 4.00
6 Peter Forsberg 5.00 12.00
7 Milan Hejduk 2.00 5.00
8 Patrick Roy 12.00 25.00
9 Steve Yzerman 10.00 25.00
10 Pavel Bure 2.50 6.00
11 Jose Theodore 2.50 6.00
12 Martin Brodeur 5.00 12.00
13 Patrik Elias 1.50 4.00
14 Scott Gomez 1.50 4.00
15 Roberto Luongo 2.50 6.00
16 Marian Hossa 2.00 5.00
17 Brian Boucher 2.00 5.00
18 Jaromir Jagr 3.00 8.00
19 Vincent Lecavalier 2.00 5.00
20 Mats Sundin 2.00 5.00

2000-01 Pacific Autographs

Randomly inserted in packs, this 20-card set utilizes the base card design and number. Each card is autographed by the featured player and contains a Pacific stamp of authenticity. This set is skip numbered. Card number 262 has recently been confirmed. It appears that they arrived to late to be inserted into packs and were held back at the Pacific offices. When the company folded, the cards were sold to Fairfield, a repackager, and only recently have begun to appear.Each card is serial numbered, and the totals are listed beside the player's name below.

57 Miroslav Satan/500 5.00 12.00
123 Alex Tanguay/250 15.00 30.00
126 Ed Belfour/250 6.00 15.00
137 Mike Modano/250 15.00 30.00
138 Brenden Morrow/500 5.00 12.00
169 Todd Marchant/250 5.00 12.00
172 Tommy Salo/500 5.00 12.00
215 Jose Theodore/250 10.00 25.00
223 David Legwand/250 5.00 12.00
233 Patrik Elias/500 5.00 12.00
234 Scott Gomez/500 5.00 12.00
251 Jason Krog/500 5.00 12.00
262 Jan Hlavac/500 6.00 15.00
272 Mike York/500 5.00 12.00
296 Simon Gagne/1000 6.00 15.00
300 John LeClair/250 12.50 30.00
352 Roman Turek/500 5.00 12.00
377 Vincent Lecavalier/1000 6.00 15.00
384 Nikolai Antropov/250 5.00 12.00

2000-01 Pacific Cramer's Choice

Randomly inserted in packs at the rate of 1:721, this 10-card set features a die-cut holographic foil card stock showcasing Michael Cramer's top player choices.

COMPLETE SET (10) 100.00 200.00
1 Paul Kariya 5.00 12.00
2 Teemu Selanne 5.00 12.00
3 Peter Forsberg 12.50 30.00
4 Patrick Roy 25.00 60.00
5 Steve Yzerman 25.00 60.00
6 Pavel Bure 5.00 12.00
7 Martin Brodeur 12.50 30.00
8 Scott Gomez 1.50 4.00
9 Jaromir Jagr 8.00 20.00
10 Mats Sundin 5.00 12.00

2000-01 Pacific Euro-Stars

COMPLETE SET (10) 30.00 60.00
STATED ODDS 1:37
1 Teemu Selanne 2.50 6.00
2 Dominik Hasek 5.00 12.00
3 Peter Forsberg 6.00 15.00
4 Sergei Fedorov 5.00 12.00
5 Pavel Bure 3.00 8.00
6 Jaromir Jagr 4.00 10.00
7 Pavol Demitra 2.00 5.00
8 Roman Turek 2.00 5.00
9 Mats Sundin 2.50 6.00
10 Olaf Kolzig 2.00 5.00

2000-01 Pacific Jerseys

RANDOM INSERTS IN PACKS
1 Ray Bourque 10.00 25.00
2 Eric Messier 4.00 10.00
3 Patrick Roy 12.50 30.00
4 Joe Sakic 10.00 25.00
5 Mike Modano 6.00 15.00
6 Darryl Sydor 4.00 10.00
7 Brendan Shanahan 4.00 10.00
8 Steve Yzerman 12.50 30.00
9 Pavel Bure 4.00 10.00
10 Eric Desjardins 4.00 10.00
11 Daymond Langkow 4.00 10.00
12 Shane Doan 4.00 10.00
13 Jaromir Jagr 10.00 25.00
14 Mark Messier 4.00 10.00
15 Olaf Kolzig 4.00 10.00

2000-01 Pacific Jersey Patches

Randomly inserted in packs, this 10-card set parallels the base Game-Worn Jersey insert set with cards containing premium jersey swatches of patches and numbers. Each card is sequentially numbered to 10.

NOT PRICED DUE TO SCARCITY

2000-01 Pacific Gold Crown Die Cuts

Randomly seeded in packs at the rate of 1:37, this 36-card set features top NHL players on a crown die-cut card with enhanced holofoil and gold foil stamping. Card number 12 was not released.

COMPLETE SET (36) 100.00 200.00
1 Paul Kariya 2.00 5.00
2 Teemu Selanne 2.00 5.00
3 Joe Thornton 3.00 8.00

4 Dominik Hasek 4.00 10.00
5 Valeri Bure 1.50 4.00
6 Tony Amonte 1.50 4.00
7 Ray Bourque 4.00 10.00
8A Peter Forsberg 5.00 12.00
8B Milan Hejduk 2.00 5.00
9 Joe Sakic 4.00 10.00
10 Patrick Roy 10.00 25.00
11 Brett Hull 2.50 6.00
13 Mike Modano 3.00 8.00
14 Brendan Shanahan 3.00 8.00
15 Steve Yzerman 10.00 25.00
16 Pavel Bure 2.50 6.00
17 Luc Robitaille 1.50 4.00
18 Martin Brodeur 5.00 12.00
19 Scott Gomez 1.50 4.00
20 Roberto Luongo 2.50 6.00
21 Marian Hossa 2.00 5.00
22 Brian Boucher 2.00 5.00
23 John LeClair 2.50 6.00
24 Eric Lindros 3.00 8.00
25 Mark Recchi 1.50 4.00
26 Keith Tkachuk 2.00 5.00
27 Jeremy Roenick 2.50 6.00
28 Jaromir Jagr 3.00 8.00
29 Chris Pronger 1.50 4.00
30 Roman Turek 1.50 4.00
31 Owen Nolan 1.50 4.00
32 Vincent Lecavalier 2.00 5.00
33 Mats Sundin 2.00 5.00
34 Curtis Joseph 2.00 5.00
35 Mark Messier 2.50 6.00
36 Olaf Kolzig 1.50 4.00

2000-01 Pacific In the Cage Net-Fusions

Inserted at 1:73 packs, these cards are die-cut and feature a goalie game action photograph where the goal itself has been die cut out and replaced with "netting."

COMPLETE SET (10) 30.00 60.00
1 Dominik Hasek 5.00 12.00
2 Fred Brathwaite 2.00 5.00
3 Patrick Roy 12.50 30.00
4 Mike Vernon 2.00 5.00
5 Stephane Fiset 2.00 5.00
6 Jeff Hackett 2.00 5.00
7 Martin Brodeur 6.00 15.00
8 Mike Richter 2.50 6.00
9 Brian Boucher 2.50 6.00
10 Curtis Joseph 2.50 6.00

2000-01 Pacific North American Stars

COMPLETE SET (10) 50.00 100.00
STATED ODDS 1:37
1 Paul Kariya 2.50 6.00
2 Joe Sakic 5.00 12.00
3 Patrick Roy 12.50 30.00
4 Mike Modano 4.00 10.00
5 Brendan Shanahan 4.00 10.00
6 Steve Yzerman 12.50 30.00
7 Martin Brodeur 6.00 15.00
8 Scott Gomez 2.50 6.00
9 John LeClair 3.00 8.00
10 Curtis Joseph 2.50 6.00

2000-01 Pacific Reflections

Randomly inserted in packs at the rate of 1:145, this 20-card set features a die cut base card in the shape of a helmet. Each helmet has an iridescent visor that shows the reflection of the featured player.

COMPLETE SET (20) 60.00 150.00
1 Paul Kariya 2.50 6.00
2 Teemu Selanne 2.50 6.00
3 Doug Gilmour 2.00 5.00
4 Ray Bourque 4.00 10.00
5 Peter Forsberg 8.00 20.00
6 Joe Sakic 6.00 15.00
7 Brett Hull 3.00 8.00
8 Mike Modano 4.00 10.00
9 Brendan Shanahan 3.00 8.00
10 Steve Yzerman 12.00 30.00
11 Pavel Bure 3.00 8.00
12 Zigmund Palffy 2.00 5.00
13 Scott Gomez 2.00 5.00
14 Marian Hossa 2.00 5.00
15 John LeClair 2.00 5.00
16 Eric Lindros 3.00 8.00
17 Jaromir Jagr 4.00 10.00
18 Vincent Lecavalier 2.50 6.00
19 Mats Sundin 2.50 6.00
20 Mark Messier 3.00 8.00

2000-01 Pacific 2001: Ice Odyssey Anaheim National

Given away by Pacific at the 21st National card convention in Anaheim, this 20-card set parallels the official base insert release of Pacific 2001: Ice Odyssey. Each card is enhanced with a special gold foil 21st National Anaheim stamp and is hand numbered out of 10.

COMPLETE SET (20)
1 Paul Kariya
2 Teemu Selanne
3 Martin Biron
4 Jarome Iginla
5 Chris Drury
6 Peter Forsberg
7 Milan Hejduk
8 Patrick Roy
9 Steve Yzerman
10 Pavel Bure
11 Jose Theodore
12 Martin Brodeur
13 Patrik Elias
14 Scott Gomez
15 Roberto Luongo
16 Marian Hossa
17 Brian Boucher
18 Jaromir Jagr
19 Vincent Lecavalier
20 Mats Sundin

2001-02 Pacific

Pacific was released as a 452-card set with the last 10 cards of the set available only by mail-in redemption. Cards 444-451 were issued as autographed cards numbered to 500 and card 452 had stated odds of 1 per case. The card front design had only 1 border, with the featured player's name and team, and it was highlighted with silver-foil. The 'Pacific 2002' logo was also done with silver-foil to let it stand out. The card backs had player stats by season and there was a brief synopsis of the career highlights.

COMPLETE SET w/o AU's (444) 40.0080.00
COMP.UPDATE SET (10) 25.00 50.00
1 Matt Cullen .08 .20
2 Jim Cummins .08 .20
3 Jeff Friesen .08 .20
4 J-S Giguere .20 .50
5 Tony Hrkac .08 .20
6 Paul Kariya .25 .60
7 Mike Leclerc .08 .20
8 Marty McInnis .08 .20
9 Steve Rucchin .08 .20
10 Ruslan Salei .08 .20
11 Steve Shields .20 .50
12 Oleg Tverdovsky .08 .20
13 Bob Wren RC .20 .50
14 Andrew Brunette .08 .20
15 Hnat Domenichelli .08 .20
16 Ray Ferraro .08 .20
17 Stephen Guolla .08 .20
18 Milan Hnilicka .20 .50
19 Tomi Kallio .08 .20
20 Norm Maracle .20 .50
21 Rumun Ndur .08 .20
22 Jeff Odgers .08 .20
23 Damian Rhodes .20 .50
24 Jiri Slegr .08 .20
25 Patrik Stefan .08 .20
26 J.P. Vigier .08 .20
27 Jason Allison .08 .20
28 P.J. Axelsson .08 .20
29 Byron Dafoe .20 .50
30 John Grahame .20 .50
31 Bill Guerin .20 .50
32 Mike Knuble .08 .20
33 Andrei Kovalenko .08 .20
34 Eric Manlow .08 .20
35 Andrei Nazarov .08 .20
36 Brian Rolston .08 .20
37 Sergei Samsonov .20 .50
38 Peter Skudra .08 .20
39 Don Sweeney .08 .20
40 Joe Thornton .40 1.00
41 Eric Weinrich .08 .20
42 Maxim Afinogenov .08 .20
43 Dave Andreychuk .20 .50
44 Donald Audette .08 .20
45 Stu Barnes .08 .20
46 Martin Biron .20 .50
47 J-P Dumont .08 .20
48 Doug Gilmour .20 .50
49 Chris Gratton .08 .20
50 Dominik Hasek .50 1.25
51 Steve Heinze .08 .20
52 Erik Rasmussen .08 .20
53 Rob Ray .08 .20
54 Miroslav Satan .20 .50
55 Alexei Zhitnik .08 .20
56 Tommy Albelin .08 .20
57 Fred Brathwaite .20 .50
58 Valeri Bure .08 .20
59 Craig Conroy .08 .20
60 Phil Housley .08 .20
61 Jarome Iginla .30 .75
62 Dave Lowry .08 .20
63 Derek Morris .08 .20
64 Oleg Saprykin .08 .20
65 Marc Savard .08 .20
66 Daniel Tkaczuk .08 .20
67 Mike Vernon .20 .50
68 Jason Wiemer .08 .20
69 Bates Battaglia .08 .20
70 Rod Brind'Amour .20 .50
71 Ron Francis .20 .50
72 Martin Gelinas .08 .20
73 Kevin Hatcher .08 .20
74 Arturs Irbe .20 .50
75 Sami Kapanen .08 .20
76 Dave Karpa .08 .20
77 Tyler Moss .08 .20
78 Jeff O'Neill .08 .20
79 Sandis Ozolinsh .08 .20
80 Scott Pellerin .08 .20
81 Shane Willis .08 .20
82 Tony Amonte .20 .50
83 Mark Bell .08 .20
84 Eric Daze .20 .50
85 Steve Dubinsky .08 .20
86 Chris Herperger .08 .20
87 Michel Larocque .08 .20
88 Michael Nylander .08 .20
89 Steve Passmore .08 .20
90 Bob Probert .08 .20
91 Stephane Quintal .08 .20
92 Steve Sullivan .08 .20
93 Jocelyn Thibault .20 .50
94 Alexei Zhamnov .08 .20
95 David Aebischer .20 .50
96 Rick Berry .08 .20
97 Rob Blake .20 .50
98 Ray Bourque .50 1.25
99 Chris Drury .20 .50
100 Adam Foote .08 .20
101 Peter Forsberg .60 1.50
102 Milan Hejduk .25 .60
103 Ville Nieminen .20 .50
104 Shjon Podein .08 .20
105 Steven Reinprecht .20 .50
106 Patrick Roy 1.25 3.00
107 Joe Sakic .50 1.25
108 Alex Tanguay .20 .50
109 Serge Aubin .20 .50
110 Mathieu Darche RC .08 .20
111 Matt Davidson RC .20 .50
112 Marc Denis .20 .50
113 Rostislav Klesla .20 .50
114 Espen Knutsen .08 .20
115 Chris Nielsen .08 .20
116 Geoff Sanderson .08 .20
117 Martin Spanhel RC .08 .20
118 Ron Tugnutt .20 .50
119 David Vyborny .08 .20
120 Ray Whitney .08 .20
121 Tyler Wright .08 .20
122 Ed Belfour .25 .60
123 Steve Gainey .20 .50
124 Derian Hatcher .08 .20
125 Sami Helenius .08 .20
126 Brett Hull .30 .75
127 Jamie Langenbrunner .08 .20
128 Jere Lehtinen .20 .50
129 Brad Lukowich .08 .20
130 Grant Marshall .08 .20
131 Mike Modano .40 1.00
132 Brenden Morrow .20 .50
133 Kirk Muller .08 .20
134 Joe Nieuwendyk .20 .50
135 Darryl Sydor .08 .20
136 Marty Turco .20 .50
137 Sergei Zubov .08 .20
138 Chris Chelios .25 .60
139 Sergei Fedorov .40 1.00
140 Todd Gill .08 .20
141 Tomas Holmstrom .08 .20
142 Slava Kozlov .08 .20
143 Martin Lapointe .08 .20
144 Igor Larionov .08 .20
145 Manny Legace .20 .50
146 Nicklas Lidstrom .25 .60
147 Darren McCarty .08 .20
148 Chris Osgood .20 .50
149 Brendan Shanahan .25 .60
150 Pat Verbeek .08 .20
151 Aaron Ward .08 .20
152 Steve Yzerman 1.25 3.00
153 Anson Carter .20 .50
154 Jason Chimera RC .20 .50
155 Daniel Cleary .08 .20
156 Mike Comrie .20 .50
157 Mike Grier .08 .20
158 Shawn Horcoff .20 .50
159 Georges Laraque .08 .20
160 Todd Marchant .08 .20
161 Rem Murray .08 .20
162 Janne Niinimaa .08 .20
163 Dominic Roussel .08 .20
164 Tommy Salo .20 .50

165 Jason Smith .08 .20
166 Ryan Smyth .08 .20
167 Doug Weight .20 .50
168 Kevyn Adams .08 .20
169 Pavel Bure .25 .60
170 Anders Eriksson .08 .20
171 Trevor Kidd .20 .50
172 Viktor Kozlov .08 .20
173 Roberto Luongo .30 .75
174 Rob Niedermayer .08 .20
175 Marcus Nilsson .08 .20
176 Andrej Podkonicky RC .08 .20
177 Robert Svehla .08 .20
178 Peter Worrell .08 .20
179 Eric Belanger .08 .20
180 Adam Deadmarsh .08 .20
181 Stu Grimson .08 .20
182 Andreas Lilja .08 .20
183 Glen Murray .08 .20
184 Zigmund Palffy .20 .50
185 Felix Potvin .25 .60
186 Luc Robitaille .20 .50
187 Mathieu Schneider .08 .20
188 Bryan Smolinski .08 .20
189 Jamie Storr .20 .50
190 Jozef Stumpel .08 .20
191 Lubomir Visnovsky .08 .20
192 Jim Dowd .08 .20
193 Manny Fernandez .20 .50
194 Marian Gaborik .50 1.25
195 Derek Gustafson .08 .20
196 Matt Johnson .08 .20
197 Filip Kuba .08 .20
198 Antti Laaksonen .08 .20
199 Jamie McLennan .08 .20
200 Lubomir Sekeras .08 .20
201 Wes Walz .08 .20
202 Francis Belanger RC .20 .50
203 Patrice Brisebois .08 .20
204 Jan Bulis .08 .20
205 Karl Dykhuis .08 .20
206 Mathieu Garon .20 .50
207 Jeff Hackett .20 .50
208 Chad Kilger .08 .20
209 Saku Koivu .25 .60
210 Oleg Petrov .08 .20
211 Martin Rucinsky .08 .20
212 Brian Savage .08 .20
213 Jose Theodore .30 .75
214 Richard Zednik .08 .20
215 Marian Cisar .08 .20
216 Mike Dunham .20 .50
217 Scott Hartnell .08 .20
218 Greg Johnson .08 .20
219 Patric Kjellberg .08 .20
220 David Legwand .20 .50
221 Cliff Ronning .08 .20
222 Tomas Vokoun .20 .50
223 Scott Walker .08 .20
224 Vitali Yachmenev .08 .20
225 Jason Arnott .08 .20
226 Jiri Bicek .08 .20
227 Martin Brodeur .60 1.50
228 Sergei Brylin .08 .20
229 Patrik Elias .20 .50
230 Scott Gomez .08 .20
231 Bobby Holik .08 .20
232 John Madden .08 .20
233 Randy McKay .08 .20
234 Jim McKenzie .08 .20
235 Alexander Mogilny .20 .50
236 Sergei Nemchinov .08 .20
237 Scott Niedermayer .08 .20
238 Scott Stevens .20 .50
239 Petr Sykora .08 .20
240 John Vanbiesbrouck .20 .50
241 Ed Ward .08 .20
242 Zdeno Chara .08 .20
243 Tim Connolly .08 .20
244 Mariusz Czerkawski .08 .20
245 Rick DiPietro .20 .50
246 Garry Galley .08 .20
247 Kevin Haller .08 .20
248 Roman Hamrlik .08 .20
249 Brad Isbister .08 .20
250 Kenny Jonsson .08 .20
251 Claude Lapointe .08 .20
252 Mark Parrish .08 .20
253 Dave Scatchard .08 .20
254 Chris Terreri .20 .50
255 Radek Dvorak .08 .20
256 Theo Fleury .08 .20
257 Adam Graves .08 .20
258 Guy Hebert .20 .50
259 Jan Hlavac .08 .20
260 Valeri Kamensky .08 .20
261 Brian Leetch .20 .50
262 Sylvain Lefebvre .08 .20
263 Sandy McCarthy .08 .20
264 Mark Messier .25 .60
265 Petr Nedved .08 .20
266 Rich Pilon .08 .20
267 Mike Richter .25 .60
268 Mike York .08 .20
269 Daniel Alfredsson .20 .50
270 Magnus Arvedson .08 .20
271 Radek Bonk .08 .20
272 Martin Havlat .20 .50
273 Marian Hossa .25 .60
274 Jani Hurme .20 .50
275 Patrick Lalime .20 .50
276 Shawn McEachern .08 .20
277 Chris Phillips .08 .20
278 Wade Redden .08 .20
279 Andre Roy .08 .20
280 Mike Sillinger .08 .20
281 Alexei Yashin .08 .20
282 Rob Zamuner .08 .20
283 Brian Boucher .20 .50
284 Roman Cechmanek .20 .50
285 Eric Desjardins .08 .20
286 Ruslan Fedotenko .20 .50
287 Simon Gagne .25 .60
288 Daymond Langkow .08 .20
289 John LeClair .25 .60
290 Eric Lindros .25 .60
291 Dan McGillis .08 .20
292 Keith Primeau .08 .20
293 Paul Ranheim .08 .20
294 Mark Recchi .20 .50
295 Rick Tocchet .08 .20
296 Justin Williams .20 .50
297 Joel Bouchard .08 .20
298 Daniel Briere .08 .20
299 Sean Burke .20 .50
300 Keith Carney .08 .20
301 Shane Doan .08 .20
302 Robert Esche .08 .20
303 Michal Handzus .08 .20
304 Mike Johnson .08 .20
305 Joe Juneau .08 .20
306 Claude Lemieux .08 .20
307 Teppo Numminen .08 .20
308 Jeremy Roenick .30 .75
309 Landon Wilson .08 .20
310 Jean-Sebastien Aubin .20 .50
311 Jan Hrdina .08 .20
312 Jaromir Jagr .40 1.00
313 Darius Kasparaitis .08 .20
314 Alexei Kovalev .20 .50
315 Robert Lang .08 .20
316 Mario Lemieux 1.50 4.00
317 Garth Snow .20 .50
318 Kevin Stevens .08 .20
319 Martin Straka .08 .20
320 Sebastien Bordeleau .08 .20
321 Pavol Demitra .20 .50
322 Dallas Drake .08 .20
323 Jochen Hecht .08 .20
324 Brent Johnson .20 .50
325 Reed Low .08 .20
326 Al MacInnis .20 .50
327 Scott Mellanby .08 .20
328 Jaroslav Obsut RC .20 .50
329 Chris Pronger .20 .50
330 Darren Rumble .08 .20
331 Cory Stillman .08 .20
332 Keith Tkachuk .25 .60
333 Roman Turek .20 .50
334 Pierre Turgeon .20 .50
335 Scott Young .08 .20
336 Vincent Damphousse .08 .20
337 Miikka Kiprusoff .20 .50
338 Bryan Marchment .08 .20
339 Patrick Marleau .20 .50
340 Evgeni Nabokov .20 .50
341 Owen Nolan .20 .50
342 Jeff Norton .08 .20
343 Mike Ricci .08 .20
344 Teemu Selanne .25 .60
345 Brad Stuart .08 .20
346 Marco Sturm .08 .20
347 Niklas Sundstrom .08 .20
348 Scott Thornton .08 .20
349 Matthew Barnaby .08 .20
350 Brian Holzinger .08 .20
351 Nikolai Khabibulin .25 .60
352 Alexander Kharitonov .20 .50
353 Pavel Kubina .08 .20
354 Kristian Kudroc .08 .20
355 Vincent Lecavalier .25 .60
356 Fredrik Modin .08 .20
357 Brad Richards .20 .50
358 Martin St. Louis .08 .20
359 Kevin Weekes .20 .50
360 Thomas Ziegler RC .20 .50
361 Sergei Berezin .08 .20
362 Shayne Corson .08 .20
363 Cory Cross .08 .20
364 Tie Domi .08 .20
365 Glenn Healy .20 .50
366 Jonas Hoglund .08 .20
367 Curtis Joseph .25 .60
368 Don MacLean .08 .20
369 Dave Manson .08 .20
370 Yanic Perreault .08 .20
371 Alexei Ponikarovsky .08 .20
372 Gary Roberts .08 .20
373 Mats Sundin .25 .60
374 Steve Thomas .08 .20
375 Darcy Tucker .08 .20
376 Murray Baron .08 .20
377 Todd Bertuzzi .25 .60
378 Donald Brashear .08 .20
379 Andrew Cassels .08 .20
380 Dan Cloutier .20 .50
381 Bob Essensa .08 .20
382 Ed Jovanovski .20 .50
383 Brendan Morrison .20 .50
384 Markus Naslund .25 .60
385 Mattias Ohlund .08 .20
386 Peter Schaefer .08 .20
387 Daniel Sedin .08 .20
388 Henrik Sedin .08 .20
389 Craig Billington .08 .20
390 Peter Bondra .25 .60
391 Ulf Dahlen .08 .20
392 Sergei Gonchar .08 .20
393 Jeff Halpern .08 .20
394 Dmitri Khristich .08 .20
395 Olaf Kolzig .20 .50
396 Steve Konowalchuk .08 .20
397 Trevor Linden .20 .50
398 Adam Oates .20 .50
399 Chris Simon .08 .20
400 Dainius Zubrus .08 .20
401 Paul Kariya .20 .50
Jim Cummins
402 Ray Ferraro .20 .50
Jeff Odgers
403 Jason Allison .20 .50
Ken Belanger
404 Jean-Pierre Dumont .20 .50
Rob Ray
405 Jarome Iginla .20 .50
Jason Wiemer
406 Ron Francis .20 .50
Darren Langdon
407 Steve Sullivan .20 .50
Bob Probert
408 Joe Sakic .20 .50
Scott Parker
409 Mike Modano .20 .50
Grant Marshall
410 Steve Yzerman .20 .50
Darren McCarty
411 Ryan Smyth .20 .50
Georges Laraque
412 Pavel Bure .20 .50
Peter Worrell
413 Ziggy Palffy .20 .50
Stu Grimson
414 Patrick Elias .20 .50
Colin White
415 Mariusz Czerkawski .20 .50
Zdeno Chara
416 Theoren Fleury .20 .50
Sandy McCarthy
417 Marian Hossa .20 .50
Andre Roy
418 Jeremy Roenick .20 .50
Louie DeBrusk
419 Mario Lemieux .20 .50
Krzysztof Oliwa
420 Pierre Turgeon .20 .50
Reed Low
421 Teemu Selanne .20 .50
Bryan Marchment
422 Vincent Lecavalier .20 .50
Matthew Barnaby
423 Mats Sundin .20 .50
Tie Domi
424 Markus Naslund .20 .50
Donald Brashear
425 Peter Bondra .20 .50
Chris Simon
426 Jason Allison .20 .50
Joe Thornton
427 Joe Sakic 1.25 3.00
Patrick Roy
428 M.Modano/B.Hull .20 .50
429 Sergei Fedorov .20 .50
Nicklas Lidstrom
430 Doug Weight .20 .50
Ryan Smyth
431 Pavel Bure .20 .50
Roberto Luongo
432 Luc Robitaille .20 .50
Ziggy Palffy
433 Patrik Elias .20 .50
Alexander Mogilny
434 Mariusz Czerkawski .20 .50
Rick DiPietro
435 Theoren Fleury .20 .50
Brian Leetch
436 Alexei Yashin .20 .50
Marian Hossa
437 Keith Primeau .20 .50
Roman Cechmanek
438 JeremyRoenick .20 .50
Sean Burke
439 Jaromir Jagr 1.50 4.00
Mario Lemieux
440 Pierre Turgeon .20 .50
Brent Johnson
441 Teemu Selanne .20 .50
Evgeni Nabokov
442 Mats Sundin .20 .50
Curtis Joseph
443 Adam Oates .20 .50
Peter Bondra
444 David Aebischer AU/500 10.00 25.00
445 Steven Reinprecht AU/500 10.0025.00
446 Marty Turco AU/500 10.00 25.00
447 Marian Gaborik AU/500 15.00 40.00
448 Martin Havlat AU/500 10.00 25.00
449 Brent Johnson AU/500 10.00 25.00
450 Evgeni Nabokov AU/500 10.00 25.00
451 Brad Richards AU/500 10.00 25.00
452 Johan Hedberg SP .20 .50
453 Timo Parssinen RC 2.00 5.00
454 Ilya Kovalchuk RC 10.00 25.00
455 Vaclav Nedorost RC 2.00 5.00
456 Kristian Huselius RC 2.50 6.00
457 Jaroslav Bednar RC 2.00 5.00
458 Dan Blackburn RC 2.00 5.00
459 Jiri Dopita RC 2.00 5.00
460 Krystofer Kolanos RC 2.00 5.00
461 Jeff Jillson RC 2.00 5.00
462 Nikita Alexeev RC 2.00 5.00

2001-02 Pacific Extreme LTD

Randomly inserted at 1 per hobby box or 1:2 retail boxes, this set parallels the base set except that the words "Extreme LTD" are embossed across the front of the card diagonally. These cards were limited to 49 serial-numbered sets.

*EXTREME: 12X TO 30X BASIC CARDS

2001-02 Pacific Gold

Randomly inserted in packs of 2001-02 Pacific, this 43-card set featured a gold version of the base set cards 401-443. Each card was serial numbered to 100, and featured 2 player on the cards.

*GOLD: 8X TO 20X BASIC CARDS

2001-02 Pacific Hobby LTD

Randomly inserted, this set parallels the base set except that the words "Hobby LTD" are embossed across the front of the card diagonally. These cards were limited to 99 serial-numbered sets.

*HOBBY LTD: 5X TO 12X BASIC CARDS

2001-02 Pacific Premiere Date

Randomly inserted in packs of 2001-02 Pacific, this 400-card set was parallel to the base set along with the 'Premiere Date' stamp on these and each card was serial numbered to 45.

*PREM.DATE: 12X TO 30X BASIC CARDS

2001-02 Pacific Retail LTD

Randomly inserted, this set parallels the base set except that the words "Retail LTD" are embossed across the front of the card diagonally. These cards were limited to 149 serial-numbered sets.

*RETAIL LTD: 8X TO 20X BASIC CARDS

2001-02 Pacific All-Stars

Randomly inserted in packs of 2001-02 Pacific at a rate of 1:37, this 20-card set featured 10 World All Stars and 10 North America All Stars. The cards were die-cut and featured silver-foil lettering and highlights.

COMPLETE SET (20) 60.00 125.00
W1 Dominik Hasek 3.00 8.00
W2 Peter Forsberg 4.00 10.00
W3 Sergei Fedorov 3.00 8.00
W4 Pavel Bure 2.00 5.00
W5 Zigmund Palffy 1.25 3.00
W6 Marian Hossa 1.50 4.00
W7 Roman Cechmanek 3.00 8.00
W8 Alexei Kovalev 1.50 4.00
W9 Evgeni Nabokov 3.00 8.00
W10 Mats Sundin 1.50 4.00
NA1 Paul Kariya 1.50 4.00
NA2 Bill Guerin 1.25 3.00
NA3 Ray Bourque 6.00 15.00
NA4 Patrick Roy 8.00 20.00
NA5 Joe Sakic 3.00 8.00
NA6 Brett Hull 2.00 5.00
NA7 Doug Weight 1.25 3.00
NA8 Luc Robitaille 1.25 3.00
NA9 Martin Brodeur 4.00 10.00
NA10 Mario Lemieux 10.00 25.00

2001-02 Pacific Cramer's Choice

Randomly inserted in packs of 2001-02 Pacific, this 10-card set was serial numbered to 49.

1 Paul Kariya 8.00 20.00
2 Ray Bourque 20.00 50.00
3 Patrick Roy 40.00 100.00
4 Joe Sakic 20.00 50.00
5 Steve Yzerman 30.00 80.00
6 Pavel Bure 15.00 40.00
7 Martin Brodeur 25.00 60.00
8 Jaromir Jagr 12.50 30.00
9 Mario Lemieux 40.00 100.00
10 Curtis Joseph 15.00 40.00

2001-02 Pacific Jerseys

*MULT.COLOR: 1X TO 1.5X
STATED ODDS 2:37 HOBBY/1:145 RETAIL
STATED PRINT RUNS LISTED BELOW
1 Andre Savage/510 2.50 6.00
2 Eric Weinrich/510 2.50 6.00
3 Jay McKee/1135 2.50 6.00
4 Fred Brathwaite/1135 3.00 8.00
5 Marc Savard/760 2.50 6.00
6 Tony Amonte/1135 3.00 8.00
7 Alexei Zhamnov/1135 2.50 6.00
8 Chris Dingman/510 2.50 6.00
9 Joe Sakic/510 6.00 15.00
10 Derian Hatcher/1135 2.50 6.00
11 Jamie Langenbrunner/1135 2.50 6.00
12 Sergei Zubov/760 3.00 8.00
13 Mathieu Dandenault/1135 2.50 6.00
14 Chris Osgood/760 3.00 8.00
15 Doug Weight/260 2.50 6.00
16 Aaron Miller/510 2.50 6.00
17 Cliff Ronning/510 2.50 6.00
18 Bobby Holik/760 2.50 6.00
19 Mariusz Czerkawski/510 2.50 6.00
20 Chris Terreri/1135 2.50 6.00
21 Guy Hebert/760 3.00 8.00
22 Mike Richter/760 3.00 8.00
23 Mika Alatalo/510 2.50 6.00
24 Shane Doan/310 2.50 6.00
25 Jyrki Lumme/1135 2.50 6.00
26 Jan Hrdina/510 2.50 6.00
27 Jaromir Jagr/210 6.00 15.00
28 Mario Lemieux/110 20.00 50.00
29 Kip Miller/1135 2.50 6.00
30 Ian Moran/1135 2.50 6.00
31 Martin Straka/110 2.50 6.00
32 Cory Stillman/1135 2.50 6.00
33 Vincent Damphousse/1010 2.50 6.00
34 Teemu Selanne/1135 3.00 8.00
35 Mats Sundin/760 3.00 8.00
36 Dainius Zubrus/760 2.50 6.00

2001-02 Pacific Gold Crown Die-Cuts

COMPLETE SET (20) 60.00 125.00
STATED ODDS 1:73
1 Paul Kariya 1.50 4.00
2 Joe Thornton 2.50 6.00
3 Dominik Hasek 4.00 10.00
4 Ray Bourque 3.00 8.00
5 Peter Forsberg 5.00 12.00
6 Patrick Roy 8.00 20.00
7 Joe Sakic 4.00 10.00
8 Mike Modano 2.50 6.00
9 Sergei Fedorov 2.50 6.00
10 Steve Yzerman 8.00 20.00
11 Pavel Bure 1.50 4.00
12 Martin Brodeur 6.00 15.00
13 Rick DiPietro 1.50 4.00
14 Mark Messier 2.50 6.00
15 Marian Hossa 1.50 4.00
16 Jaromir Jagr 3.00 8.00
17 Mario Lemieux 12.00 30.00
18 Keith Tkachuk 1.50 4.00
19 Evgeni Nabokov 2.50 6.00
20 Curtis Joseph 1.50 4.00

2001-02 Pacific Impact Zone

COMPLETE SET (20) 15.00 40.00
STATED ODDS 1:37
1 Paul Kariya 1.50 4.00
2 Byron Dafoe .75 2.00
3 Doug Gilmour .75 2.00
4 Dominik Hasek 3.00 8.00
5 Ron Francis .75 2.00
6 Ray Bourque 3.00 8.00
7 Patrick Roy 6.00 15.00
8 Ed Belfour 1.50 4.00
9 Derian Hatcher .40 1.00
10 Mike Modano 2.50 6.00
11 Chris Osgood .75 2.00
12 Martin Brodeur 4.00 10.00
13 Marian Hossa .75 2.00
14 Patrick Lalime .75 2.00
15 Roman Cechmanek .40 1.00
16 Chris Pronger .75 2.00
17 Tie Domi .40 1.00
18 Curtis Joseph 1.50 4.00
19 Mats Sundin 1.50 4.00
20 Andrew Cassels .40 1.00

2001-02 Pacific 97-98 Subset

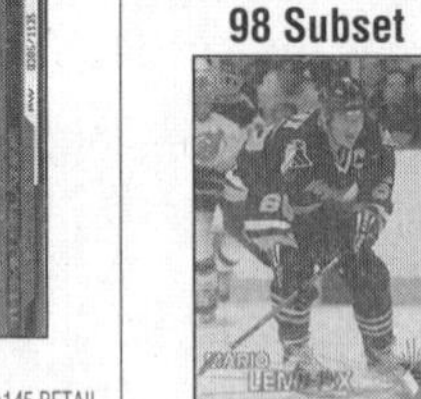

Randomly inserted in packs of 2001-02 Pacific, this 7-card set was issued as an update to the 1997-98 set. The cards featured a similar design as that of the original set and added 7 players who were not originally included in the set. There was also a gold version available in random retail packs. Gold cards were serial-numbered to 100.

COMPLETE SET (7) 10.00 20.00
*GOLD: 10X TO 20X BASIC CARDS
66 Mario Lemieux 2.50 6.00
352 Mike LeClerc 1.25 3.00
353 Sergei Samsonov 1.50 4.00
354 Joe Thornton 2.50 6.00
355 Steve Shields 1.25 3.00
356 Patrik Elias 1.25 3.00
357 Marian Hossa 1.50 4.00

2001-02 Pacific Steel Curtain

COMPLETE SET (20) 30.00 60.00
STATED ODDS 2:37
1 Steve Shields 1.00 2.50
2 Byron Dafoe 1.00 2.50
3 Dominik Hasek 2.50 6.00

4 Jocelyn Thibault 1.00 2.50
5 Patrick Roy 6.00 15.00
6 Ed Belfour 1.25 3.00
7 Manny Legace 1.00 2.50
8 Tommy Salo 1.00 2.50
9 Roberto Luongo 1.50 4.00
10 Jose Theodore 1.50 4.00
11 Martin Brodeur 3.00 8.00
12 Rick DiPietro 1.00 2.50
13 Mike Richter 1.25 3.00
14 Patrick Lalime 1.00 2.50
15 Roman Cechmanek 1.00 2.50
16 Sean Burke 1.00 2.50
17 Roman Turek 1.00 2.50
18 Evgeni Nabokov 1.00 2.50
19 Curtis Joseph 1.25 3.00
20 Olaf Kolzig 1.00 2.50

2001-02 Pacific Top Draft Picks

Randomly inserted in packs of 2001-02 Pacific at a rate of 1:37, this 10-card set featured some of the top draft picks from the last 20 years. These cards were identical to the Promos with the exception of gold-foil instead of silver, and these were not serial numbered.

COMPLETE SET (10) 10.00 25.00
1 Rick DiPietro .75 2.00
2 Patrik Stefan .40 1.00
3 Vincent Lecavalier 1.25 3.00
4 Joe Thornton 2.00 5.00
5 Eric Lindros 1.25 3.00
6 Owen Nolan .75 2.00
7 Mats Sundin 1.25 3.00
8 Mike Modano 2.00 5.00
9 Pierre Turgeon .75 2.00
10 Mario Lemieux 4.00 10.00

2001 Pacific Top Draft Picks Draft Day Promos

This 10-card set was given away at the 2001 NHL Draft. Collectors could obtain one card in exchange for a Titanium Draft Day wrapper, or combination of other Pacific wrappers. Although the cards mirror the inserts found in 2001-02 Pacific, these cards differ in that they are serial numbered to 499, and are highlighted by silver foil lettering. It is believed that far fewer than 499 sets were actually distributed.

COMPLETE SET (10) 40.00 100.00
1 Rick DiPietro 6.00 15.00
2 Patrik Stefan 2.00 5.00
3 Vincent LeCavalier 4.80 12.00
4 Joe Thornton 6.00 15.00
5 Eric Lindros 4.80 12.00
6 Owen Nolan 4.00 10.00
7 Mats Sundin 4.80 12.00
8 Mike Modano 6.00 15.00
9 Pierre Turgeon 4.00 10.00
10 Mario Lemieux 12.00 30.00

2002-03 Pacific

This 400-card set was released in late-July 2002 and carried an SRP of $2.99 for a 10-card pack. A red parallel of this set was also created and inserted 1:2 packs. Cards 401-410 were available as a mail-in redemption only and were serial-numbered out of 999.

COMPLETE SET (400) 50.00 100.00
*RED: .5X TO 1.25X BASIC CARD
1 Matt Cullen .08 .20
2 Jeff Friesen .08 .20
3 J-S Giguere .20 .50
4 Paul Kariya .25 .60
5 Mike Leclerc .08 .20
6 Andy McDonald .08 .20
7 Steve Rucchin .08 .20
8 Steve Shields .20 .50
9 German Titov .08 .20
10 Oleg Tverdovsky .08 .20
11 Jason York .08 .20
12 Lubos Bartecko .08 .20
13 Dany Heatley .30 .75
14 Milan Hnilicka .20 .50
15 Tony Hrkac .08 .20
16 Frantisek Kaberle .08 .20
17 Tomi Kallio .08 .20
18 Ilya Kovalchuk .30 .75
19 Jeff Odgers .08 .20
20 Damian Rhodes .20 .50
21 Patrik Stefan .08 .20
22 Daniel Tjarnqvist .08 .20
23 Nicholas Boynton .08 .20
24 Sean Brown .08 .20
25 Byron Dafoe .20 .50
26 Hal Gill .08 .20
27 John Grahame .20 .50
28 Bill Guerin .20 .50
29 Martin Lapointe .08 .20
30 Glen Murray .08 .20
31 Brian Rolston .08 .20
32 Sergei Samsonov .20 .50
33 P.J. Stock .08 .20
34 Jozef Stumpel .08 .20
35 Joe Thornton .40 1.00
36 Maxim Afinogenov .08 .20
37 Stu Barnes .08 .20
38 Martin Biron .20 .50
39 Curtis Brown .08 .20
40 Tim Connolly .08 .20
41 J-P Dumont .08 .20
42 Chris Gratton .08 .20
43 Ales Kotalik .08 .20
44 Slava Kozlov .08 .20
45 Jay McKee .08 .20
46 Mika Noronen .20 .50
47 Rob Ray .08 .20
48 Miroslav Satan .20 .50
49 Alexei Zhitnik .08 .20
50 Bob Boughner .08 .20
51 Chris Clark .08 .20
52 Craig Conroy .08 .20
53 Denis Gauthier .08 .20
54 Jarome Iginla .30 .75
55 Toni Lydman .08 .20
56 Dean McAmmond .08 .20
57 Derek Morris .08 .20
58 Rob Niedermayer .08 .20
59 Marc Savard .08 .20
60 Roman Turek .20 .50
61 Mike Vernon .20 .50
62 Bates Battaglia .08 .20
63 Rod Brind'Amour .20 .50
64 Erik Cole .08 .20
65 Ron Francis .20 .50
66 Bret Hedican .08 .20
67 Arturs Irbe .20 .50
68 Sami Kapanen .08 .20
69 Jeff O'Neill .08 .20
70 Dave Tanabe .08 .20
71 Josef Vasicek .08 .20
72 Kevin Weekes .20 .50
73 Tony Amonte .20 .50
74 Mark Bell .08 .20
75 Kyle Calder .08 .20
76 Eric Daze .20 .50
77 Phil Housley .08 .20
78 Jon Klemm .08 .20
79 Boris Mironov .08 .20
80 Steve Passmore .08 .20
81 Bob Probert .08 .20
82 Steve Sullivan .08 .20
83 Jocelyn Thibault .20 .50
84 Steve Thomas .08 .20
85 Alexei Zhamnov .08 .20
86 David Aebischer .20 .50
87 Rob Blake .20 .50
88 Chris Drury .20 .50
89 Adam Foote .08 .20
90 Peter Forsberg .60 1.50
91 Milan Hejduk .25 .60
92 Darius Kasparaitis .08 .20
93 Scott Parker .08 .20
94 Steven Reinprecht .08 .20
95 Patrick Roy 1.25 3.00
96 Joe Sakic .50 1.25
97 Alex Tanguay .20 .50
98 Radim Vrbata .08 .20
99 Marc Denis .20 .50
100 Rostislav Klesla .08 .20
101 Espen Knutsen .08 .20
102 Grant Marshall .08 .20
103 Deron Quint .08 .20
104 Geoff Sanderson .08 .20
105 Jody Shelley .08 .20
106 Mike Sillinger .08 .20
107 Ron Tugnutt .20 .50
108 David Vyborny .08 .20
109 Ray Whitney .08 .20
110 Jason Arnott .08 .20
111 Ed Belfour .25 .60
112 Derian Hatcher .08 .20
113 Jere Lehtinen .08 .20
114 Mike Modano .40 1.00
115 Brenden Morrow .20 .50
116 Kirk Muller .08 .20
117 Scott Pellerin .08 .20
118 Darryl Sydor .08 .20
119 Marty Turco .20 .50
120 Pierre Turgeon .20 .50
121 Pat Verbeek .08 .20
122 Sergei Zubov .08 .20
123 Chris Chelios .25 .60
124 Pavel Datsyuk .25 .60
125 Boyd Devereaux .08 .20
126 Kris Draper .08 .20
127 Sergei Fedorov .40 1.00
128 Dominik Hasek .50 1.25
129 Brett Hull .30 .75
130 Igor Larionov .08 .20
131 Manny Legace .20 .50
132 Nicklas Lidstrom .25 .60
133 Luc Robitaille .20 .50
134 Brendan Shanahan .25 .60
135 Jiri Slegr .08 .20
136 Jason Williams .08 .20
137 Steve Yzerman 1.25 3.00
138 Eric Brewer .08 .20
139 Anson Carter .20 .50
140 Daniel Cleary .08 .20
141 Mike Comrie .20 .50
142 Mike Grier .08 .20
143 Jochen Hecht .08 .20
144 Georges Laraque .08 .20
145 Todd Marchant .08 .20
146 Jussi Markkanen .20 .50
147 Janne Niinimaa .08 .20

148 Tommy Salo .20 .50
149 Ryan Smyth .08 .20
150 Mike York .08 .20
151 Eric Beaudoin .08 .20
152 Valeri Bure .08 .20
153 Niklas Hagman .08 .20
154 Kristian Huselius .08 .20
155 Trevor Kidd .20 .50
156 Roberto Luongo .30 .75
157 Marcus Nilsson .08 .20
158 Sandis Ozolinsh .08 .20
159 Nick Smith .08 .20
160 Robert Svehla .08 .20
161 Stephen Weiss .08 .20
162 Jason Wiemer .08 .20
163 Peter Worrell .08 .20
164 Jason Allison .08 .20
165 Adam Deadmarsh .08 .20
166 Steve Heinze .08 .20
167 Craig Johnson .08 .20
168 Ian Laperriere .08 .20
169 Aaron Miller .08 .20
170 Jaroslav Modry .08 .20
171 Zigmund Palffy .20 .50
172 Felix Potvin .25 .60
173 Cliff Ronning .08 .20
174 Mathieu Schneider .08 .20
175 Bryan Smolinski .08 .20
176 Jamie Storr .20 .50
177 Andrew Brunette .08 .20
178 Hnat Domenichelli .08 .20
179 Jim Dowd .08 .20
180 Pascal Dupuis .08 .20
181 Manny Fernandez .20 .50
182 Marian Gaborik .50 1.25
183 Darby Hendrickson .08 .20
184 Filip Kuba .08 .20
185 Antti Laaksonen .08 .20
186 Stacy Roest .08 .20
187 Dwayne Roloson .08 .20
188 Wes Walz .08 .20
189 Sergei Zholtok .08 .20
190 Donald Audette .08 .20
191 Sergei Berezin .08 .20
192 Patrice Brisebois .08 .20
193 Andreas Dackell .08 .20
194 Stephane Fiset .08 .20
195 Mathieu Garon .20 .50
196 Doug Gilmour .20 .50
197 Joe Juneau .08 .20
198 Saku Koivu .25 .60
199 Andrei Markov .08 .20
200 Yanic Perreault .08 .20
201 Oleg Petrov .08 .20
202 Mike Ribeiro .08 .20
203 Jose Theodore .30 .75
204 Richard Zednik .08 .20
205 Denis Arkhipov .08 .20
206 Andy Delmore .08 .20
207 Mike Dunham .20 .50
208 Martin Erat .08 .20
209 Stu Grimson .08 .20
210 Scott Hartnell .08 .20
211 Greg Johnson .08 .20
212 David Legwand .20 .50
213 Vladimir Orszagh .08 .20
214 Kimmo Timonen .08 .20
215 Tomas Vokoun .20 .50
216 Scott Walker .08 .20
217 Vitali Yachmenev .08 .20
218 Martin Brodeur .60 1.50
219 Sergei Brylin .08 .20
220 Patrik Elias .20 .50
221 Brian Gionta .08 .20
222 Scott Gomez .08 .20
223 Bobby Holik .08 .20
224 Jamie Langenbrunner .08 .20
225 John Madden .08 .20
226 Scott Niedermayer .08 .20
227 Joe Nieuwendyk .20 .50
228 Brian Rafalski .08 .20
229 Scott Stevens .20 .50
230 Petr Sykora .08 .20
231 John Vanbiesbrouck .20 .50
232 Adrian Aucoin .08 .20
233 Shawn Bates .08 .20
234 Mariusz Czerkawski .08 .20
235 Rick DiPietro .20 .50
236 Roman Hamrlik .08 .20
237 Brad Isbister .08 .20
238 Kenny Jonsson .08 .20
239 Kip Miller .08 .20
240 Chris Osgood .20 .50
241 Mark Parrish .08 .20
242 Michael Peca .08 .20
243 Garth Snow .20 .50
244 Raffi Torres .08 .20
245 Alexei Yashin .08 .20
246 Matthew Barnaby .08 .20
247 Bryan Berard .08 .20
248 Dan Blackburn .20 .50
249 Pavel Bure .25 .60
250 Radek Dvorak .08 .20
251 Theo Fleury .08 .20
252 Brian Leetch .20 .50
253 Eric Lindros .25 .60
254 Vladimir Malakhov .08 .20
255 Sandy McCarthy .08 .20
256 Mark Messier .25 .60
257 Petr Nedved .08 .20
258 Mike Richter .25 .60
259 Martin Rucinsky .08 .20
260 Daniel Alfredsson .20 .50
261 Magnus Arvedson .08 .20
262 Chris Bala .08 .20
263 Radek Bonk .08 .20
264 Zdeno Chara .08 .20
265 Mike Fisher .08 .20
266 Martin Havlat .20 .50
267 Marian Hossa .25 .60
268 Jani Hurme .20 .50
269 Patrick Lalime .20 .50
270 Shawn McEachern .08 .20
271 Chris Phillips .08 .20
272 Wade Redden .08 .20
273 Sami Salo .08 .20
274 Todd White .08 .20
275 Brian Boucher .20 .50
276 Donald Brashear .08 .20
277 Roman Cechmanek .20 .50
278 Eric Desjardins .08 .20
279 Jiri Dopita .08 .20
280 Simon Gagne .25 .60
281 Kim Johnsson .08 .20
282 John LeClair .25 .60
283 Neil Little .08 .20
284 Adam Oates .20 .50
285 Keith Primeau .08 .20
286 Mark Recchi .20 .50
287 Jeremy Roenick .30 .75
288 Bill Tibbetts .08 .20
289 Eric Weinrich .08 .20
290 Justin Williams .08 .20
291 Daniel Briere .08 .20
292 Sean Burke .20 .50
293 Shane Doan .08 .20
294 Robert Esche .08 .20
295 Michal Handzus .08 .20
296 Mike Johnson .08 .20
297 Krystofer Kolanos .08 .20
298 Daymond Langkow .08 .20
299 Claude Lemieux .08 .20
300 Daniil Markov .08 .20
301 Ladislav Nagy .08 .20
302 Andrei Nazarov .08 .20
303 Teppo Numminen .08 .20
304 Brian Savage .08 .20
305 J-S Aubin .08 .20
306 Kris Beech .08 .20
307 Johan Hedberg .20 .50
308 Jan Hrdina .08 .20
309 Alexei Kovalev .20 .50
310 Milan Kraft .08 .20
311 Robert Lang .08 .20
312 Mario Lemieux 1.50 4.00
313 Alexei Morozov .08 .20
314 Toby Peterson .08 .20
315 Wayne Primeau .08 .20
316 Randy Robitaille .08 .20
317 Michal Rozsival .08 .20
318 Martin Straka .08 .20
319 Fred Brathwaite .20 .50
320 Pavol Demitra .20 .50
321 Dallas Drake .08 .20
322 Ray Ferraro .08 .20
323 Brent Johnson .20 .50
324 Reed Low .08 .20
325 Al MacInnis .20 .50
326 Scott Mellanby .20 .50
327 Chris Pronger .20 .50
328 Cory Stillman .08 .20
329 Keith Tkachuk .25 .60
330 Doug Weight .20 .50
331 Scott Young .08 .20
332 Vincent Damphousse .08 .20
333 Adam Graves .08 .20
334 Jeff Jillson .08 .20
335 Bryan Marchment .08 .20
336 Patrick Marleau .20 .50
337 Evgeni Nabokov .20 .50
338 Owen Nolan .20 .50
339 Mike Ricci .08 .20
340 Teemu Selanne .25 .60
341 Brad Stuart .08 .20
342 Marco Sturm .08 .20
343 Gary Suter .08 .20
344 Scott Thornton .08 .20
345 Nikita Alexeev .08 .20
346 Dave Andreychuk .20 .50
347 Ben Clymer .08 .20
348 Nikolai Khabibulin .25 .60
349 Dieter Kochan .20 .50
350 Pavel Kubina .08 .20
351 Vincent Lecavalier .25 .60
352 Fredrik Modin .08 .20
353 Vaclav Prospal .08 .20
354 Brad Richards .20 .50
355 Martin St.Louis .20 .50
356 Shane Willis .08 .20
357 Tom Barrasso .20 .50
358 Shayne Corson .08 .20
359 Tie Domi .20 .50
360 Travis Green .08 .20
361 Curtis Joseph .25 .60
362 Tomas Kaberle .08 .20
363 Bryan McCabe .08 .20
364 Alyn McCauley .08 .20
365 Alexander Mogilny .20 .50
366 Robert Reichel .08 .20
367 Mikael Renberg .08 .20
368 Gary Roberts .08 .20
369 Corey Schwab .20 .50
370 Mats Sundin .25 .60
371 Darcy Tucker .08 .20
372 Dimitri Yushkevich .08 .20
373 Todd Bertuzzi .25 .60
374 Andrew Cassels .08 .20
375 Dan Cloutier .20 .50
376 Matt Cooke .08 .20
377 Jan Hlavac .08 .20
378 Ed Jovanovski .20 .50
379 Trevor Linden .20 .50
380 Brendan Morrison .20 .50
381 Markus Naslund .25 .60
382 Mattias Ohlund .08 .20
383 Daniel Sedin .08 .20
384 Henrik Sedin .08 .20
385 Peter Skudra .08 .20
386 Brent Sopel .08 .20
387 Craig Billington .08 .20
388 Peter Bondra .20 .50
389 Ulf Dahlen .08 .20
390 Sergei Gonchar .08 .20
391 Jeff Halpern .08 .20
392 Jaromir Jagr .40 1.00
393 Calle Johansson .08 .20
394 Dimitri Khristich .08 .20
395 Olaf Kolzig .20 .50
396 Steve Konowalchuk .08 .20
397 Andrei Nikolishin .08 .20
398 Stephen Peat .08 .20
399 Chris Simon .08 .20
400 Dainius Zubrus .08 .20
401 Stanislav Chistov RC 2.00 5.00
402 Alexei Smirnov RC 2.50 6.00
403 Chuck Kobasew RC 2.00 5.00
404 Rick Nash RC 8.00 20.00
405 Henrik Zetterberg RC 8.00 20.00
406 Ales Hemsky RC 5.00 12.00
407 Jay Bouwmeester RC 2.50 6.00
408 Alexander Frolov RC 3.00 8.00
409 P-M Bouchard RC 3.00 8.00
410 Alexander Svitov RC 2.50 6.00

2002-03 Pacific Blue

This 400-card set paralleled the base set but carried blue foil highlights in place of the silver foil on the base set. Cards in this set were serial-numbered out of 45.
*BLUE: 12X TO 30X BASIC CARD

2002-03 Pacific Cramer's Choice

This 10-card set was inserted at 1:732 packs. Each card was serial-numbered to just 95 copies.
1 Dany Heatley 6.00 15.00
2 Ilya Kovalchuk 6.00 15.00
3 Joe Thornton 6.00 15.00
4 Peter Forsberg 10.00 25.00
5 Patrick Roy 25.00 60.00
6 Dominik Hasek 8.00 20.00
7 Steve Yzerman 25.00 60.00
8 Martin Brodeur 15.00 40.00
9 Mario Lemieux 30.00 75.00
10 Mats Sundin 4.00 10.00

2002-03 Pacific Impact Zone

This 10-card set was inserted at 1:9 packs.
COMPLETE SET (10) 8.00 15.00
1 Paul Kariya .40 1.00
2 Ilya Kovalchuk .50 1.25
3 Joe Thornton .60 1.50
4 Jarome Iginla .50 1.25
5 Joe Sakic .75 2.00
6 Brendan Shanahan .60 1.50
7 Saku Koivu .40 1.00
8 Eric Lindros .40 1.00
9 Mario Lemieux 2.50 6.00
10 Teemu Selanne .40 1.00

2002-03 Pacific Jerseys

Inserted at 2:37, this 50-card set featured swatches of game-worn jerseys. The NNO card at the end of this set was inserted at a stated rate of 1:732 and each card was serial-numbered out of 500. A holo-silver hobby only parallel was also created and serial-numbered to 40 sets. The parallel had a silver foil border around the jersey swatch.
*HOLO-SILVER: 1X TO 2.5X BASIC JERSEY
1 Dany Heatley 5.00 12.00
2 Milan Hnilicka 3.00 8.00
3 Joe Thornton 6.00 15.00
4 Miroslav Satan 3.00 8.00
5 Roman Turek 3.00 8.00
6 Arturs Irbe 3.00 8.00
7 Tony Amonte 3.00 8.00
8 Steve Sullivan 3.00 8.00
9 Rob Blake 3.00 8.00
10 Chris Drury 3.00 8.00
11 Joe Sakic 8.00 20.00
12 Marc Denis 3.00 8.00
13 Ron Tugnutt 3.00 8.00
14 Jason Arnott 3.00 8.00
15 Mike Modano 6.00 15.00
16 Sergei Fedorov 5.00 12.00
17 Dominik Hasek 12.50 30.00
18 Jason Williams 3.00 8.00
19 Tommy Salo 3.00 8.00
20 Wade Flaherty 3.00 8.00
21 Jason Allison 3.00 8.00
22 Aaron Miller 3.00 8.00
23 Cliff Ronning 3.00 8.00
24 Manny Fernandez 3.00 8.00
25 Sergei Berezin 3.00 8.00
26 Yanic Perreault 3.00 8.00
27 Jose Theodore 5.00 12.00
28 Martin Erat 3.00 8.00
29 Jukka Hentunen 3.00 8.00
30 Jamie Langenbrunner SP 3.00 8.00
31 Joe Nieuwendyk SP 3.00 8.00
32 Michael Peca 3.00 8.00
33 Alexei Yashin 3.00 8.00
34 Pavel Bure 4.00 10.00
35 Theo Fleury 3.00 8.00
36 Mark Messier 4.00 10.00
37 Martin Havlat 3.00 8.00
38 Jiri Dopita 3.00 8.00
39 Simon Gagne 4.00 10.00
40 Adam Oates 3.00 8.00
41 Daymond Langkow 3.00 8.00
42 Mario Lemieux 12.50 30.00
43 Pavol Demitra 3.00 8.00
44 Ray Ferraro 3.00 8.00
45 Evgeni Nabokov 3.00 8.00
46 Fredrik Modin 3.00 8.00
47 Alexander Mogilny 3.00 8.00
48 Darcy Tucker 3.00 8.00
49 Dan Cloutier 3.00 8.00
50 Jaromir Jagr 6.00 15.00
NNO Ilya Kovalchuk 30.00 80.00
JSY/STK AU

2002-03 Pacific Lamplighters

This 14-card set was inserted at 1:20 packs.
COMPLETE SET (14) 25.00 50.00
1 Dany Heatley 1.00 2.50
2 Ilya Kovalchuk 1.00 2.50
3 Joe Thornton 1.25 3.00
4 Jarome Iginla 1.00 2.50
5 Peter Forsberg 2.00 5.00
6 Joe Sakic 1.50 4.00
7 Steve Yzerman 4.00 10.00
8 Alexei Yashin .75 2.00
9 Pavel Bure 1.25 3.00
10 Eric Lindros .75 2.00
11 Mario Lemieux 5.00 12.00
12 Mats Sundin .75 2.00
13 Todd Bertuzzi .75 2.00
14 Jaromir Jagr 1.25 3.00

2002-03 Pacific Main Attractions

This 20-card set was inserted at 1:12 packs.
COMPLETE SET (20) 15.00 30.00
1 Paul Kariya .40 1.00
2 Ilya Kovalchuk 1.50 4.00
3 Joe Thornton .60 1.50
4 Jarome Iginla .50 1.25
5 Patrick Roy 2.00 5.00
6 Mike Modano .60 1.50
7 Steve Yzerman 2.00 5.00
8 Mike Comrie .30 .75
9 Jason Allison .30 .75
10 Jose Theodore .50 1.25
11 Martin Brodeur 1.00 2.50
12 Alexei Yashin .30 .75
13 Pavel Bure .60 1.50
14 Daniel Alfredsson .30 .75
15 Jeremy Roenick .50 1.25
16 Mario Lemieux 2.50 6.00
17 Keith Tkachuk .40 1.00
18 Mats Sundin .40 1.00
19 Markus Naslund .40 1.00
20 Jaromir Jagr .60 1.50

2002-03 Pacific Maximum Impact

This 16-card set was inserted at 1:12 packs.
COMPLETE SET (16) 12.50 25.00
1 Roman Turek .30 .75
2 Patrick Roy 2.00 5.00
3 Dominik Hasek .75 2.00
4 Jose Theodore .50 1.25
5 Martin Brodeur 1.00 2.50
6 Sean Burke .30 .75
7 Evgeni Nabokov .30 .75
8 Curtis Joseph .40 1.00
9 Ilya Kovalchuk 1.50 4.00
10 Joe Thornton .60 1.50
11 Jarome Iginla .50 1.25
12 Joe Sakic .75 2.00
13 Steve Yzerman 2.00 5.00
14 Eric Lindros .40 1.00
15 Mario Lemieux 2.50 6.00
16 Mats Sundin .40 1.00

2002-03 Pacific Shining Moments

This 10-card set was inserted at 1:20 packs.
COMPLETE SET (10) 20.00 40.00
1 Dany Heatley 3.00 8.00
2 Ilya Kovalchuk 3.00 8.00

3 Erik Cole 1.50 4.00
4 Radim Vrbata 1.50 4.00
5 Pavel Datsyuk 2.50 6.00
6 Kristian Huselius 1.50 4.00
7 Stephen Weiss 1.50 4.00
8 Mike Ribeiro 1.50 4.00
9 Dan Blackburn 2.00 5.00
10 Krystofer Kolanos 1.50 4.00

2003-04 Pacific

Released in late July 2003, this 350-card set was the first of the 2003-04 season. Cards 351-360 were available only by a mail-in/internet redemption offer and cards 361-368 were available in packs of Pacific Calder.
351-360 PRINT RUN 999 SER.#'d SETS
361-368 PRINT RUN 1225 SER.#'d SETS
1 Stanislav Chistov .20 .50
2 Martin Gerber .20 .50
3 J-S Giguere .20 .50
4 Niclas Havelid .08 .20
5 Paul Kariya .25 .60
6 Mike Leclerc .08 .20
7 Adam Oates .20 .50
8 Sandis Ozolinsh .08 .20
9 Steve Rucchin .08 .20
10 Petr Sykora .08 .20
11 Steve Thomas .08 .20
12 Byron Dafoe .20 .50
13 Joe DiPenta RC .75 2.00
14 Dany Heatley .30 .75
15 Milan Hnilicka .20 .50
16 Ilya Kovalchuk .30 .75
17 Slava Kozlov .08 .20
18 Shawn McEachern .08 .20
19 Pasi Nurminen .20 .50
20 Jeff Odgers .08 .20
21 Marc Savard .08 .20
22 Patrik Stefan .08 .20
23 P.J. Axelsson .08 .20
24 Bryan Berard .08 .20
25 Nick Boynton .08 .20
26 Jeff Hackett .20 .50
27 Mike Knuble .08 .20
28 Glen Murray .08 .20
29 Brian Rolston .08 .20
30 Sergei Samsonov .20 .50
31 Steve Shields .20 .50
32 P.J. Stock .08 .20
33 Jozef Stumpel .08 .20
34 Joe Thornton .40 1.00
35 Milan Bartovic RC .75 2.00
36 Martin Biron .20 .50
37 Daniel Briere .08 .20
38 Curtis Brown .08 .20
39 Tim Connolly .08 .20
40 J-P Dumont .08 .20
41 Ales Kotalik .08 .20
42 Ryan Miller .20 .50
43 Mika Noronen .20 .50
44 Taylor Pyatt .08 .20
45 Miroslav Satan .08 .20
46 Alexei Zhitnik .08 .20
47 Craig Conroy .08 .20
48 Chris Drury .20 .50
49 Martin Gelinas .08 .20
50 Jarome Iginla .30 .75
51 Chuck Kobasew .08 .20
52 Jordan Leopold .08 .20
53 Toni Lydman .08 .20
54 Dean McAmmond .08 .20
55 Jamie McLennan .20 .50
56 Roman Turek .20 .50
57 Stephane Yelle .08 .20
58 Ryan Bayda .08 .20
59 Rod Brind'Amour .20 .50
60 Erik Cole .08 .20
61 Ron Francis .20 .50
62 Jeff Heerema .08 .20
63 Sean Hill .08 .20
64 Arturs Irbe .20 .50
65 Jeff O'Neill .08 .20
66 Radim Vrbata .08 .20
67 Kevin Weekes .20 .50
68 Craig Andersson .08 .20
69 Tyler Arnason .20 .50
70 Mark Bell .08 .20
71 Kyle Calder .08 .20
72 Eric Daze .20 .50
73 Theoren Fleury .08 .20
74 Steve Passmore .08 .20
75 Chris Simon .08 .20
76 Steve Sullivan .08 .20
77 Jocelyn Thibault .20 .50
78 Alexei Zhamnov .08 .20
79 David Aebischer .20 .50
80 Bates Battaglia .08 .20
81 Rob Blake .20 .50
82 Adam Foote .08 .20
83 Peter Forsberg .50 1.25
84 Milan Hejduk .25 .60
85 Derek Morris .08 .20
86 Vaclav Nedorost .08 .20
87 Steven Reinprecht .08 .20
88 Patrick Roy 1.25 3.00
89 Joe Sakic .50 1.25
90 Alex Tanguay .20 .50
91 Andrew Cassels .08 .20
92 Marc Denis .20 .50
93 Rostislav Klesla .08 .20
94 Pascal Leclaire .20 .50
95 Kent McDonell RC .75 2.00
96 Rick Nash .30 .75
97 Geoff Sanderson .08 .20
98 Mike Sillinger .08 .20
99 David Vyborny .08 .20
100 Ray Whitney .08 .20
101 Tyler Wright .08 .20
102 Jason Arnott .08 .20
103 Ulf Dahlen .08 .20
104 Bill Guerin .20 .50
105 Derian Hatcher .08 .20
106 Jere Lehtinen .20 .50
107 Mike Modano .40 1.00
108 Brenden Morrow .20 .50
109 Steve Ott .08 .20
110 Ron Tugnutt .20 .50
111 Marty Turco .20 .50
112 Pierre Turgeon .20 .50
113 Scott Young .08 .20
114 Sergei Zubov .08 .20
115 Chris Chelios .25 .60
116 Pavel Datsyuk .25 .60
117 Sergei Fedorov .40 1.00
118 Tomas Holmstrom .08 .20
119 Brett Hull .30 .75
120 Curtis Joseph .25 .60
121 Igor Larionov .08 .20
122 Manny Legace .20 .50
123 Nicklas Lidstrom .25 .60
124 Luc Robitaille .20 .50
125 Mathieu Schneider .08 .20
126 Brendan Shanahan .25 .60
127 Steve Yzerman 1.25 3.00
128 Henrik Zetterberg .25 .60
129 Eric Brewer .08 .20
130 Jason Chimera .08 .20
131 Mike Comrie .20 .50
132 Ales Hemsky .20 .50
133 Brad Isbister .08 .20
134 Georges Laraque .08 .20
135 Todd Marchant .08 .20
136 Jussi Markkanen .08 .20
137 Tommy Salo .20 .50
138 Ryan Smyth .08 .20
139 Mike York .08 .20
140 Jaroslav Bednar .08 .20
141 Jay Bouwmeester .08 .20
142 Matt Cullen .08 .20
143 Jani Hurme .20 .50
144 Kristian Huselius .08 .20
145 Olli Jokinen .20 .50
146 Viktor Kozlov .08 .20
147 Roberto Luongo .30 .75
148 Marcus Nilsson .08 .20
149 Stephen Weiss .08 .20
150 Peter Worrell .08 .20
151 Jason Allison .08 .20
152 Jared Aulin .08 .20
153 Michael Cammalleri .08 .20
154 Adam Deadmarsh .08 .20
155 Alexander Frolov .08 .20
156 Cristobal Huet .20 .50
157 Jaroslav Modry .08 .20
158 Zigmund Palffy .20 .50
159 Felix Potvin .25 .60
160 Jamie Storr .20 .50
161 Pierre-Marc Bouchard .08 .20
162 Andrew Brunette .08 .20
163 Pascal Dupuis .08 .20
164 Manny Fernandez .20 .50
165 Marian Gaborik .40 1.00
166 Filip Kuba .08 .20
167 Antti Laaksonen .08 .20
168 Richard Park .08 .20
169 Dwayne Roloson .20 .50
170 Cliff Ronning .08 .20
171 Wes Walz .08 .20
172 Sergei Zholtok .08 .20
173 Donald Audette .08 .20
174 Patrice Brisebois .08 .20
175 Jan Bulis .08 .20
176 Mathieu Garon .20 .50
177 Marcel Hossa .08 .20
178 Saku Koivu .25 .60
179 Andrei Markov .08 .20
180 Yanic Perreault .08 .20
181 Mike Ribeiro .08 .20
182 Niklas Sundstrom .08 .20
183 Jose Theodore .30 .75
184 Richard Zednik .08 .20
185 Denis Arkhipov .08 .20
186 Andy Delmore .08 .20
187 Adam Hall .08 .20
188 Scott Hartnell .08 .20
189 Andreas Johansson .08 .20
190 David Legwand .20 .50
191 Oleg Petrov .08 .20
192 Kimmo Timonen .08 .20
193 Scottie Upshall .20 .50
194 Tomas Vokoun .20 .50
195 Scott Walker .08 .20
196 Martin Brodeur .60 1.50
197 Patrik Elias .20 .50
198 Jeff Friesen .08 .20
199 Brian Gionta .08 .20
200 Scott Gomez .08 .20
201 Jamie Langenbrunner .08 .20
202 John Madden .08 .20
203 Scott Niedermayer .08 .20
204 Joe Nieuwendyk .20 .50
205 Brian Rafalski .08 .20
206 Scott Stevens .20 .50
207 Oleg Tverdovsky .08 .20
208 Arron Asham .08 .20
209 Shawn Bates .08 .20
210 Jason Blake .08 .20
211 Rick DiPietro .20 .50
212 Roman Hamrlik .08 .20
213 Mark Parrish .08 .20
214 Michael Peca .08 .20
215 Dave Scatchard .08 .20
216 Garth Snow .20 .50
217 Mattias Weinhandl .08 .20
218 Alexei Yashin .08 .20
219 Matthew Barnaby .08 .20
220 Dan Blackburn .20 .50
221 Pavel Bure .25 .60
222 Anson Carter .20 .50
223 Mike Dunham .20 .50
224 Bobby Holik .08 .20
225 Alex Kovalev .20 .50
226 Brian Leetch .20 .50
227 Eric Lindros .25 .60
228 Mark Messier .25 .60
229 Petr Nedved .08 .20
230 Tom Poti .08 .20
231 Mike Richter .25 .60
232 Daniel Alfredsson .20 .50
233 Magnus Arvedson .08 .20
234 Radek Bonk .08 .20
235 Zdeno Chara .08 .20
236 Mike Fisher .08 .20
237 Martin Havlat .20 .50
238 Marian Hossa .25 .60
239 Patrick Lalime .20 .50
240 Martin Prusek .20 .50
241 Wade Redden .08 .20
242 Bryan Smolinski .08 .20
243 Jason Spezza .25 .60
244 Vaclav Varada .08 .20
245 Todd White .08 .20
246 Tony Amonte .20 .50
247 Donald Brashear .08 .20
248 Roman Cechmanek .20 .50
249 Eric Desjardins .08 .20
250 Robert Esche .20 .50
251 Simon Gagne .25 .60
252 Michal Handzus .08 .20
253 Kim Johnsson .08 .20
254 John LeClair .25 .60
255 Keith Primeau .20 .50
256 Mark Recchi .20 .50
257 Jeremy Roenick .30 .75
258 Zac Bierk .20 .50
259 Brian Boucher .20 .50
260 Sean Burke .20 .50
261 Shane Doan .08 .20
262 Chris Gratton .08 .20
263 Jan Hrdina .08 .20
264 Mike Johnson .08 .20
265 Daymond Langkow .08 .20
266 Ladislav Nagy .08 .20
267 Teppo Numminen .08 .20
268 Jeff Taffe .08 .20
269 Ramzi Abid .08 .20
270 Rico Fata .08 .20
271 Johan Hedberg .20 .50
272 Brian Holzinger .08 .20
273 Mathias Johansson .08 .20
274 Mario Lemieux 1.50 4.00
275 Alexei Morozov .08 .20
276 Martin Straka .08 .20
277 Tomas Surovy .08 .20
278 Dick Tarnstrom .08 .20
279 Eric Boguniecki .08 .20
280 Pavol Demitra .20 .50
281 Dallas Drake .08 .20
282 Barret Jackman .20 .50
283 Brent Johnson .20 .50
284 Al MacInnis .20 .50
285 Scott Mellanby .08 .20
286 Chris Osgood .20 .50
287 Chris Pronger .20 .50
288 Peter Sejna RC .75 2.00
289 Cory Stillman .08 .20
290 Keith Tkachuk .25 .60
291 Doug Weight .20 .50
292 Jonathan Cheechoo .10 .25
293 Vincent Damphousse .08 .20
294 Niko Dimitrakos .08 .20
295 Miikka Kiprusoff .20 .50
296 Patrick Marleau .20 .50
297 Alyn McCauley .08 .20
298 Evgeni Nabokov .20 .50
299 Mike Ricci .08 .20
300 Teemu Selanne .25 .60
301 Marco Sturm .08 .20
302 Vesa Toskala .08 .20
303 Dave Andreychuk .08 .20
304 Dan Boyle .08 .20
305 Ruslan Fedotenko .08 .20
306 John Grahame .20 .50
307 Nikolai Khabibulin .25 .60
308 Vincent Lecavalier .25 .60
309 Fredrik Modin .08 .20
310 Vaclav Prospal .08 .20
311 Brad Richards .20 .50
312 Martin St. Louis .20 .50
313 Alexander Svitov .08 .20
314 Nik Antropov .08 .20
315 Ed Belfour .25 .60
316 Tie Domi .20 .50
317 Doug Gilmour .20 .50
318 Tomas Kaberle .08 .20
319 Trevor Kidd .20 .50
320 Alexander Mogilny .20 .50
321 Owen Nolan .20 .50
322 Gary Roberts .08 .20
323 Matt Stajan RC 1.50 4.00
324 Mats Sundin .25 .60
325 Robert Svehla .08 .20
326 Darcy Tucker .08 .20
327 Todd Bertuzzi .25 .60
328 Dan Cloutier .20 .50
329 Matt Cooke .08 .20
330 Ed Jovanovski .20 .50
331 Trent Klatt .08 .20
332 Trevor Linden .20 .50
333 Brendan Morrison .20 .50
334 Markus Naslund .25 .60
335 Daniel Sedin .08 .20
336 Henrik Sedin .08 .20
337 Peter Skudra .20 .50
338 Brent Sopel .08 .20
339 Sergei Berezin .08 .20
340 Peter Bondra .20 .50
341 Sebastien Charpentier .20 .50
342 Sergei Gonchar .08 .20
343 Mike Grier .08 .20
344 Jeff Halpern .08 .20
345 Jaromir Jagr .40 1.00
346 Olaf Kolzig .20 .50
347 Robert Lang .08 .20
348 Kip Miller .08 .20

349 Michael Nylander .08 .20
350 Dainius Zubrus .08 .20
351 Joffrey Lupul RC 1.25 3.00
352 Eric Staal RC 3.00 8.00
353 Tuomo Ruutu RC 2.00 5.00
354 Pavel Vorobiev RC .75 2.00
355 Nathan Horton RC 2.00 5.00
356 Dustin Brown RC .75 2.00
357 Jordin Tootoo RC 1.50 4.00
358 Marc-Andre Fleury RC 4.00 10.00
359 Milan Michalek RC 1.25 3.00
360 Boyd Gordon RC .75 2.00
361 Derek Roy RC 1.00 2.50
362 Matthew Lombardi RC .75 2.00
363 Nikolai Zherdev RC 2.00 5.00
364 Jiri Hudler RC 1.25 3.00
365 Niklas Kronwall RC .75 2.00
366 Fredrik Sjostrom RC .75 2.00
367 Ryan Malone RC 1.25 3.00
368 Ryan Kesler RC .75 2.00

2003-04 Pacific Blue

*STARS: 1.25X TO 3X BASIC CARDS
PRINT RUN 250 SER.#'d SETS

2003-04 Pacific Red

*STARS: .5X TO 1.25X BASIC CARDS
STATED ODDS: 1:3

2003-04 Pacific Cramer's Choice

STATED PRINT RUN 99 SER.#'d SETS
1 Peter Forsberg 12.00 30.00
2 Patrick Roy 25.00 60.00
3 Rick Nash 12.00 30.00
4 Mike Modano 8.00 20.00
5 Steve Yzerman 20.00 50.00
6 Henrik Zetterberg 10.00 25.00
7 Martin Brodeur 15.00 40.00
8 Mario Lemieux 30.00 80.00
9 Markus Naslund 4.00 10.00
10 Jaromir Jagr 10.00 25.00

2003-04 Pacific In the Crease

COMPLETE SET (12) 10.00 20.00
STATED ODDS 1:10
1 J-S Giguere .60 1.50
2 Jocelyn Thibault .60 1.50
3 Patrick Roy 1.50 4.00
4 Marty Turco .60 1.50
5 Curtis Joseph .75 2.00
6 Jose Theodore 1.00 2.50
7 Martin Brodeur 1.25 3.00
8 Patrick Lalime .60 1.50
9 Roman Cechmanek .60 1.50
10 Sean Burke .60 1.50
11 Ed Belfour .75 2.00
12 Dan Cloutier .60 1.50

2003-04 Pacific Jerseys

STATED ODDS 1:19
1 Paul Kariya 3.00 8.00
2 Dany Heatley 4.00 10.00
3 Milan Hnilicka 2.50 6.00
4 Ilya Kovalchuk 4.00 10.00
5 Joe Thornton 6.00 15.00
6 J-P Dumont 2.50 6.00
7 Chris Drury 2.50 6.00
8 Peter Forsberg 8.00 20.00
9 Patrick Roy 10.00 25.00
10 Joe Sakic 6.00 15.00
11 Alex Tanguay 2.50 6.00
12 Geoff Sanderson 2.50 6.00
13 Mike Modano 4.00 10.00
14 Marty Turco 2.50 6.00
15 Brendan Shanahan 3.00 8.00
16 Steve Yzerman 8.00 20.00
17 Ryan Smyth 2.50 6.00
18 Ziggy Palffy 2.50 6.00
19 Filip Kuba 2.50 6.00
20 Saku Koivu 3.00 8.00
21 Jose Theodore 4.00 10.00
22 Scott Walker 2.50 6.00
23 Martin Brodeur 10.00 25.00
24 Alexei Yashin 2.50 6.00
25 Pavel Bure 3.00 8.00
26 Eric Lindros 3.00 8.00
27 Daniel Alfredsson 2.50 6.00
28 Jason Spezza 6.00 15.00
29 Roman Cechmanek 2.50 6.00
30 Jeremy Roenick 4.00 10.00
31 Mario Lemieux 10.00 25.00
32 Brent Johnson 2.50 6.00
33 Keith Tkachuk 3.00 8.00
34 Miikka Kiprusoff 2.50 6.00
35 Vincent Lecavalier 2.50 6.00
36 Fredrik Modin 2.50 6.00
37 Ed Belfour 3.00 8.00
38 Todd Bertuzzi 3.00 8.00
39 Dan Cloutier 2.50 6.00
40 Jaromir Jagr 5.00 12.00

2003-04 Pacific Jerseys Gold

*GOLD: 1X TO 2.5X BASIC JERSEY
PRINT RUN 50 SER.#'d SETS

2003-04 Pacific Main Attractions

STATED ODDS 1:10
1 Paul Kariya .60 1.50
2 Ilya Kovalchuk .75 2.00
3 Joe Thornton .75 2.00
4 Peter Forsberg 1.25 3.00
5 Mike Modano .75 2.00
6 Steve Yzerman 1.50 4.00
7 Marian Gaborik 1.00 2.50
8 Saku Koivu .60 1.50
9 Pavel Bure .60 1.50
10 Marian Hossa .60 1.50
11 John LeClair .60 1.50
12 Mario Lemieux 2.00 5.00
13 Teemu Selanne .60 1.50
14 Mats Sundin .60 1.50
15 Markus Naslund .60 1.50
16 Jaromir Jagr .75 2.00

2003-04 Pacific Marty Turco

This 6-card set highlighted the young career of Marty Turco and was inserted at 1:37.
COMPLETE SET (6) 8.00 15.00
COMMON CARD (1-6) 1.25 3.00

2003-04 Pacific Marty Turco Autographs

This 6-card set paralleled the regular insert set but carried certified autographs. Cards #1-5 were serial-numbered to 99 and card #6 was serial-numbered to 35 copies.
COMMON AUTO/99 (1-5) 15.00 40.00
COMMON AUTO/35 (6) 40.00 100.00

2003-04 Pacific Maximum Impact

COMPLETE SET (10) 10.00 20.00
STATED ODDS 1:19
1 Joe Thornton 1.25 3.00
2 Jarome Iginla 1.00 2.50
3 Rick Nash 1.00 2.50
4 Brendan Shanahan .75 2.00
5 Michael Peca .60 1.50
6 Eric Lindros .75 2.00
7 Mark Messier .75 2.00
8 Jeremy Roenick 1.00 2.50
9 Owen Nolan .60 1.50
10 Todd Bertuzzi .75 2.00

2003-04 Pacific Milestones

COMPLETE SET (8) 10.00 20.00
STATED ODDS 1:19
1 Patrick Roy 2.50 6.00
2 Joe Sakic 1.50 4.00
3 Mike Modano 1.25 3.00
4 Marty Turco .60 1.50
5 Brett Hull 1.00 2.50
6 Joe Nieuwendyk .60 1.50
7 Mats Sundin .75 2.00
8 Jaromir Jagr 1.25 3.00

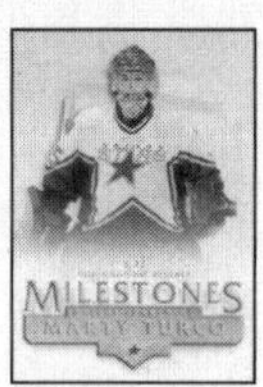

2003-04 Pacific View from the Crease

COMPLETE SET (8) 15.00 30.00
STATED ODDS 1:37
1 Paul Kariya 1.25 3.00
2 Joe Thornton 2.00 5.00
3 Joe Sakic 2.50 6.00
4 Mike Modano 2.00 5.00
5 Sergei Fedorov 1.50 4.00
6 Brett Hull 1.50 4.00
7 Marian Gaborik 2.50 6.00
8 Todd Bertuzzi 1.25 3.00

2004-05 Pacific

This 300-card set was issued in the summer of 2004 before the eventual NHL lockout. It was the last set produced by Pacific Trading Cards.
COMPLETE SET (300) 40.00 80.00
1 Stanislav Chistov .08 .20
2 Sergei Fedorov .40 1.00
3 Martin Gerber .20 .50
4 J-S Giguere .20 .50
5 Joffrey Lupul .08 .20
6 Vaclav Prospal .08 .20
7 Steve Rucchin .08 .20
8 Martin Skoula .08 .20
9 Petr Sykora .08 .20
10 Dany Heatley .30 .75
11 Ilya Kovalchuk .30 .75
12 Slava Kozlov .08 .20
13 Shawn McEachern .08 .20
14 Pasi Nurminen .20 .50
15 Ronald Petrovicky .08 .20
16 Randy Robitaille .08 .20
17 Marc Savard .08 .20
18 Patrik Stefan .08 .20
19 Patrice Bergeron .20 .50
20 Sergei Gonchar .08 .20
21 Mike Knuble .08 .20
22 Glen Murray .08 .20
23 Felix Potvin .25 .60
24 Andrew Raycroft .08 .20
25 Brian Rolston .08 .20
26 Sergei Samsonov .20 .50
27 Joe Thornton .40 1.00
28 Maxim Afinogenov .08 .20
29 Martin Biron .20 .50
30 Daniel Briere .08 .20
31 Chris Drury .20 .50
32 J-P Dumont .08 .20
33 Jochen Hecht .08 .20
34 Mika Noronen .20 .50
35 Derek Roy .08 .20
36 Miroslav Satan .20 .50
37 Craig Conroy .08 .20
38 Shean Donovan .08 .20
39 Martin Gelinas .08 .20
40 Jarome Iginla .30 .75
41 Miikka Kiprusoff .20 .50
42 Jordan Leopold .08 .20
43 Matthew Lombardi .08 .20
44 Steven Reinprecht .08 .20
45 Chris Simon .08 .20
46 Rod Brind'Amour .20 .50
47 Erik Cole .08 .20
48 Sean Hill .08 .20
49 Jeff O'Neill .08 .20
50 Eric Staal .08 .20
51 Josef Vasicek .08 .20
52 Radim Vrbata .08 .20
53 Kevin Weekes .20 .50
54 Justin Williams .08 .20
55 Craig Andersson .08 .20
56 Tyler Arnason .20 .50
57 Mark Bell .08 .20
58 Bryan Berard .08 .20
59 Kyle Calder .08 .20
60 Eric Daze .20 .50
61 Brett McLean .08 .20
62 Tuomo Ruutu .20 .50
63 Jocelyn Thibault .20 .50
64 David Aebischer .20 .50
65 Rob Blake .20 .50
66 Peter Forsberg .60 1.50
67 Milan Hejduk .25 .60
68 Paul Kariya .25 .60
69 Joe Sakic .50 1.25
70 Tommy Salo .20 .50
71 Teemu Selanne .25 .60
72 Alex Tanguay .20 .50
73 Andrew Cassels .08 .20
74 Marc Denis .20 .50
75 Anders Eriksson .08 .20
76 Trevor Letowski .08 .20
77 Manny Malhotra .08 .20
78 Todd Marchant .08 .20
79 Rick Nash .30 .75
80 David Vyborny .08 .20
81 Nikolai Zherdev .08 .20
82 Jason Arnott .08 .20
83 Valeri Bure .08 .20
84 Bill Guerin .20 .50
85 Jere Lehtinen .20 .50
86 Mike Modano .40 1.00
87 Brenden Morrow .20 .50
88 Marty Turco .20 .50
89 Pierre Turgeon .20 .50
90 Sergei Zubov .08 .20
91 Pavel Datsyuk .25 .60
92 Kris Draper .08 .20
93 Brett Hull .30 .75
94 Curtis Joseph .25 .60
95 Robert Lang .08 .20
96 Manny Legace .20 .50
97 Nicklas Lidstrom .25 .60
98 Brendan Shanahan .25 .60
99 Steve Yzerman 1.25 3.00
100 Ty Conklin .20 .50
101 Radek Dvorak .08 .20
102 Ales Hemsky .08 .20
103 Shawn Horcoff .08 .20
104 Ethan Moreau .08 .20
105 Petr Nedved .08 .20
106 Ryan Smyth .08 .20
107 Raffi Torres .08 .20
108 Mike York .08 .20
109 Jay Bouwmeester .08 .20
110 Niklas Hagman .08 .20
111 Nathan Horton .08 .20
112 Kristian Huselius .08 .20
113 Olli Jokinen .20 .50
114 Juraj Kolnik .08 .20
115 Roberto Luongo .30 .75
116 Mike Van Ryn .08 .20
117 Stephen Weiss .08 .20
118 Derek Armstrong .08 .20
119 Dustin Brown .08 .20
120 Roman Cechmanek .20 .50
121 Alexander Frolov .08 .20
122 Cristobal Huet .20 .50
123 Trent Klatt .08 .20
124 Ziggy Palffy .20 .50
125 Luc Robitaille .20 .50
126 Jozef Stumpel .08 .20
127 Andrew Brunette .08 .20
128 Brent Burns .08 .20
129 Alexandre Daigle .08 .20
130 Pascal Dupuis .08 .20
131 Manny Fernandez .20 .50
132 Marian Gaborik .50 1.25
133 Filip Kuba .08 .20
134 Antti Laaksonen .08 .20
135 Dwayne Roloson .20 .50
136 Patrice Brisebois .08 .20
137 Saku Koivu .25 .60
138 Alex Kovalev .08 .20
139 Yanic Perreault .08 .20
140 Mike Ribeiro .08 .20
141 Michael Ryder .08 .20
142 Sheldon Souray .08 .20
143 Jose Theodore .30 .75
144 Richard Zednik .08 .20
145 Martin Erat .08 .20
146 Adam Hall .08 .20
147 Scott Hartnell .08 .20
148 David Legwand .20 .50
149 Steve Sullivan .08 .20
150 Jordin Tootoo .08 .20
151 Tomas Vokoun .20 .50
152 Scott Walker .08 .20
153 Marek Zidlicky .08 .20
154 Martin Brodeur .60 1.50
155 Patrik Elias .20 .50
156 Jeff Friesen .08 .20
157 Brian Gionta .08 .20
158 Scott Gomez .08 .20
159 Jamie Langenbrunner .08 .20
160 John Madden .08 .20
161 Scott Niedermayer .08 .20
162 Scott Stevens .20 .50
163 Adrian Aucoin .08 .20
164 Jason Blake .08 .20
165 Mariusz Czerkawski .08 .20
166 Rick DiPietro .20 .50
167 Trent Hunter .08 .20
168 Oleg Kvasha .08 .20
169 Mark Parrish .08 .20
170 Michael Peca .08 .20
171 Alexei Yashin .20 .50
172 Mike Dunham .20 .50
173 Jan Hlavac .08 .20
174 Bobby Holik .08 .20
175 Jaromir Jagr .40 1.00
176 Eric Lindros .25 .60
177 Mark Messier .25 .60
178 Boris Mironov .08 .20
179 Tom Poti .08 .20
180 Fedor Tyutin .08 .20
181 Daniel Alfredsson .20 .50
182 Peter Bondra .20 .50
183 Zdeno Chara .08 .20
184 Martin Havlat .20 .50
185 Marian Hossa .25 .60
186 Patrick Lalime .20 .50
187 Wade Redden .08 .20
188 Bryan Smolinski .08 .20
189 Jason Spezza .25 .60
190 Tony Amonte .20 .50
191 Sean Burke .20 .50
192 Robert Esche .20 .50
193 Simon Gagne .25 .60
194 Michal Handzus .08 .20
195 John LeClair .25 .60
196 Joni Pitkanen .20 .50
197 Mark Recchi .20 .50
198 Jeremy Roenick .30 .75
199 Brian Boucher .20 .50
200 Mike Comrie .20 .50
201 Shane Doan .08 .20
202 Daymond Langkow .08 .20
203 Paul Mara .08 .20
204 Derek Morris .08 .20
205 Ladislav Nagy .08 .20
206 Fredrik Sjostrom .08 .20
207 Jeff Taffe .08 .20
208 Jean-Sebastien Aubin .08 .20
209 Rico Fata .08 .20
210 Marc-Andre Fleury .20 .50
211 Ric Jackman .08 .20
212 Milan Kraft .08 .20
213 Mario Lemieux 1.50 4.00
214 Ryan Malone .08 .20
215 Aleksey Morozov .08 .20
216 Dick Tarnstrom .08 .20
217 Pavol Demitra .08 .20
218 Dallas Drake .08 .20
219 Barret Jackman .20 .50
220 Al MacInnis .20 .50
221 Chris Osgood .20 .50
222 Chris Pronger .20 .50
223 Mark Rycroft .08 .20
224 Keith Tkachuk .25 .60
225 Doug Weight .20 .50
226 Jonathan Cheechoo .10 .25
227 Vincent Damphousse .08 .20
228 Nils Ekman .08 .20
229 Alex Korolyuk .08 .20
230 Patrick Marleau .20 .50
231 Alyn McCauley .08 .20
232 Evgeni Nabokov .20 .50
233 Marco Sturm .08 .20
234 Vesa Toskala .08 .20
235 Dave Andreychuk .08 .20
236 John Grahame .20 .50
237 Nikolai Khabibulin .25 .60
238 Pavel Kubina .08 .20
239 Vincent Lecavalier .25 .60
240 Fredrik Modin .08 .20
241 Brad Richards .20 .50
242 Martin St. Louis .20 .50
243 Cory Stillman .08 .20
244 Ed Belfour .25 .60
245 Brian Leetch .25 .60
246 Bryan McCabe .08 .20
247 Alexander Mogilny .20 .50
248 Joe Nieuwendyk .20 .50
249 Owen Nolan .20 .50
250 Gary Roberts .08 .20
251 Mats Sundin .25 .60
252 Darcy Tucker .08 .20
253 Todd Bertuzzi .25 .60
254 Dan Cloutier .20 .50
255 Ed Jovanovski .20 .50
256 Trevor Linden .08 .20
257 Brendan Morrison .20 .50
258 Markus Naslund .25 .60
259 Mattias Ohlund .08 .20
260 Daniel Sedin .08 .20
261 Henrik Sedin .08 .20
262 Sebastien Charpentier .20 .50
263 Jeff Halpern .08 .20
264 Olaf Kolzig .20 .50
265 Kip Miller .08 .20
266 Maxime Ouellet .20 .50
267 Matt Pettinger .08 .20
268 Brian Willsie .08 .20
269 Brendan Witt .08 .20
270 Dainius Zubrus .08 .20
271 Chris Kunitz .08 .20
272 Kari Lehtonen .20 .50
273 Brett Lysak .08 .20
274 Matt Keith .30 .75
275 Adam Munro .20 .50
276 Mikhail Kuleshov .08 .20
277 John-Michael Liles .08 .20
278 Marek Svatos .08 .20
279 Dan Fritsche .08 .20
280 Greg Mauldin .08 .20
281 Mike Pandolfo .08 .20
282 Dan Ellis .20 .50
283 Mike Bishai .08 .20
284 Lukas Krajicek .08 .20
285 Denis Grebeshkov .08 .20
286 Tomas Plekanec .08 .20
287 Timofei Shishkanov .08 .20
288 Scottie Upshall .08 .20
289 Thomas Pihlman .08 .20
290 Aleksander Suglobov .08 .20
291 Jozef Balej .08 .20
292 Bryce Lampman .08 .20
293 Randy Jones .08 .20
294 Antero Niittymaki .20 .50
295 Mike Stutzel .08 .20
296 Niko Dimitrakos .08 .20
297 Marcel Goc RC .25 .60
298 Matt Stajan .08 .20
299 Alexander Semin .08 .20
300 Roman Tvrdon .08 .20

2004-05 Pacific Blue

*STARS: 1.25X TO 3X BASIC CARDS
STATED PRINT RUN 250 SER.#'d SETS

2004-05 Pacific Red

*STARS: .5X TO 1.25X BASIC CARDS
STATED ODDS 1:3

2004-05 Pacific All-Stars

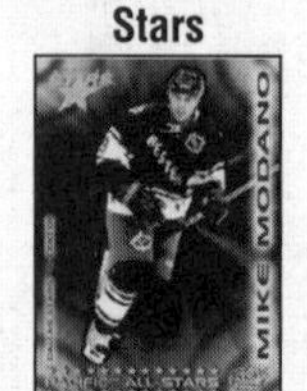

COMPLETE SET (12) 8.00 15.00
STATED ODDS 1:10
1 Ilya Kovalchuk .75 2.00
2 Joe Thornton .75 2.00
3 Joe Sakic 1.25 3.00
4 Rick Nash .75 2.00
5 Mike Modano 1.00 2.50
6 Marty Turco .50 1.25
7 Robert Lang .50 1.25
8 Nicklas Lidstrom .60 1.50
9 Jose Theodore .75 2.00
10 Martin Brodeur 1.50 4.00
11 Patrick Marleau .50 1.25
12 Martin St. Louis .50 1.25

2004-05 Pacific Cramer's Choice

STATED ODDS 1:721
PRINT RUN 99 SER.#'d SETS
1 Ilya Kovalchuk 12.00 30.00
2 Joe Thornton 12.00 30.00
3 Jarome Iginla 12.00 30.00
4 Joe Sakic 15.00 40.00
5 Rick Nash 12.00 30.00
6 Steve Yzerman 20.00 50.00
7 Martin Brodeur 15.00 40.00
8 Mario Lemieux 20.00 50.00
9 Martin St. Louis 8.00 20.00
10 Ed Belfour 8.00 20.00

2004-05 Pacific Global Connection

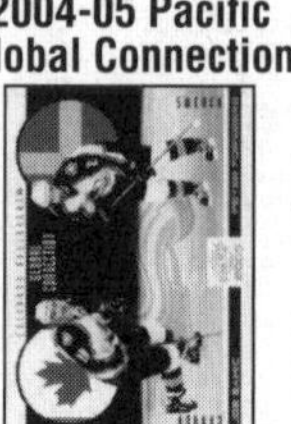

COMPLETE SET (8) 8.00 15.00
STATED ODDS 1:19
1 Dany Heatley / Ilya Kovalchuk 1.25 3.00
2 Sergei Samsonov / Joe Thornton 1.00 2.50
3 Peter Forsberg / Joe Sakic 1.50 4.00
4 Paul Kariya / Teemu Selanne 1.00 2.50
5 Pavel Datsyuk / Henrik Zetterberg 1.25 3.00
6 Brett Hull / Nicklas Lidstrom 1.00 2.50
7 Martin Havlat / Marian Hossa 1.00 2.50
8 Alexander Mogilny / Mats Sundin 1.00 2.50

2004-05 Pacific Gold Crown Die-Cuts

COMPLETE SET (8) 10.00 20.00
STATED ODDS 1:37
1 Ilya Kovalchuk 2.00 5.00
2 Andrew Raycroft 1.00 2.50
3 Eric Staal 1.25 3.00
4 Henrik Zetterberg 1.25 3.00
5 Michael Ryder 1.00 2.50
6 Jordin Tootoo 1.25 3.00
7 Jason Spezza 2.00 5.00
8 Jonathan Cheechoo 1.25 3.00

2004-05 Pacific In The Crease

COMPLETE SET (10) 8.00 15.00
STATED ODDS 1:19
1 Andrew Raycroft .75 2.00
2 Miikka Kiprusoff .75 2.00
3 David Aebischer .75 2.00
4 Marty Turco .75 2.00
5 Dominik Hasek 1.25 3.00
6 Roberto Luongo 1.25 3.00
7 Jose Theodore 1.25 3.00
8 Martin Brodeur 1.50 4.00
9 Nikolai Khabibulin 1.00 2.50
10 Ed Belfour 1.00 2.50

2004-05 Pacific Jerseys

Card #45 in this 45-card set featured the Richard Trophy winners for 2003-04. The card carried jersey swatches of both Ilya Kovlachuk and Jarome Iginla on front and a certified Rick Nash autograph on the back.
STAT.ODDS 2:36 HBBY/1:36 RETAIL
CARD#45 PRINT RUN 100 SER.#'d SETS
*GOLD: 1X TO 2X BASIC JERSEYS
1 Sergei Fedorov 4.00 10.00
2 Patrice Bergeron 3.00 8.00
3 Sergei Samsonov 3.00 8.00
4 Joe Thornton 5.00 12.00
5 Ales Kotalik 2.00 5.00
6 Mark Bell 2.00 5.00
7 Jocelyn Thibault 2.00 5.00
8 Peter Forsberg 8.00 20.00
9 Paul Kariya 4.00 10.00
10 Joe Sakic 6.00 15.00
11 Mike Modano 5.00 12.00
12 Derian Hatcher 2.00 5.00
13 Jason Williams 2.00 5.00
14 Steve Yzerman 10.00 25.00
15 Ryan Smyth 2.00 5.00
16 Roberto Luongo 3.00 8.00
17 Vaclav Nedorost 2.00 5.00
18 Jason Allison 2.00 5.00
19 Alex Kovalev 2.00 5.00
20 Martin Brodeur 10.00 25.00
21 Alexei Yashin 2.00 5.00
22 Pavel Bure 3.00 8.00
23 Eric Lindros 3.00 8.00
24 Daniel Alfredsson 3.00 8.00
25 Martin Havlat 3.00 8.00
26 Jeff Hackett 2.00 5.00
27 Joni Pitkanen 2.00 5.00
28 Jeremy Roenick 3.00 8.00
29 Brent Johnson 2.00 5.00
30 Krystofer Kolanos 2.00 5.00
31 Kris Beech 2.00 5.00
32 Mike Eastwood 2.00 5.00
33 Rico Fata 2.00 5.00
34 Mario Lemieux 12.00 30.00
35 Chris Osgood 2.00 5.00
36 Peter Sejna 2.00 5.00
37 Vincent Lecavalier 3.00 8.00
38 Ed Belfour 3.00 8.00
39 Matt Stajan 2.00 5.00
40 Mats Sundin 3.00 8.00
41 Todd Bertuzzi 3.00 8.00
42 Dan Cloutier 2.00 5.00
43 Brendan Morrison 2.00 5.00
44 Olaf Kolzig 3.00 8.00
45 Ilya Kovalchuk JSY/Jarome Iginla JSY/Rick Nash AU 75.00 200.00

2004-05 Pacific Milestones

COMPLETE SET (6) 10.00 20.00
STATED ODDS 1:37
1 Steve Yzerman 3.00 8.00
2 Martin Brodeur 3.00 8.00
3 Jaromir Jagr 1.50 4.00
4 Mark Messier 1.00 2.50
5 Mario Lemieux 4.00 10.00
6 Ed Belfour 1.00 2.50

2004-05 Pacific Philadelphia

COMPLETE SET (16) 12.50 25.00
STATED ODDS 1:10
1 Sergei Fedorov .75 2.00
2 Joe Sakic 1.25 3.00
3 Chris Chelios .60 1.50
4 Dominik Hasek 1.25 3.00
5 Brett Hull .75 2.00
6 Steve Yzerman 1.50 4.00
7 Luc Robitaille .50 1.25
8 Jaromir Jagr 1.00 2.50
9 Eric Lindros .60 1.50
10 Mark Messier .60 1.50
11 John LeClair .60 1.50
12 Jeremy Roenick .75 2.00
13 Mario Lemieux 2.00 5.00
14 Keith Tkachuk .60 1.50
15 Ron Francis .50 1.25
16 Brian Leetch .60 1.50

2001-02 Pacific Adrenaline

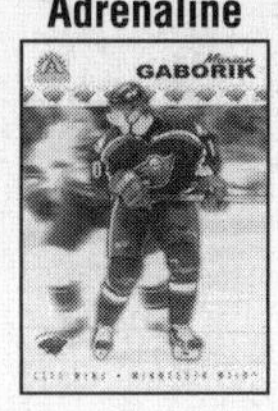

Released in December 2001, this 225-card set carried an SRP of $3.50 for a 5-card pack. Base cards carried full color action photos on white card fronts. Short printed rookies were serial-numbered out of 984, and the Kovalchuk autographed card was inserted at a rate of 1:721 hobby packs/1:1921 retail packs and serial-numbered to 500. The 500 Kovalchuk cards were inserted in both hobby and retail packs.

COMP.SET w/o SP's (200) 15.00 40.00
1 Jeff Friesen .10 .25
2 J-S Giguere .20 .50
3 Paul Kariya .30 .75
4 Marty McInnis .10 .25
5 Steve Shields .20 .50
6 Oleg Tverdovsky .10 .25
7 Ray Ferraro .10 .25
8 Milan Hnilicka .10 .25
9 Tomi Kallio .10 .25
10 Damian Rhodes .10 .25
11 Patrik Stefan .10 .25
12 Byron Dafoe .20 .50
13 Bill Guerin .20 .50
14 Martin Lapointe .10 .25
15 Sergei Samsonov .20 .50
16 Jozef Stumpel .10 .25
17 Joe Thornton .60 1.50
18 Stu Barnes .10 .25
19 Martin Biron .20 .50
20 Tim Connolly .10 .25
21 J-P Dumont .10 .25
22 Chris Gratton .10 .25
23 Slava Kozlov .10 .25
24 Miroslav Satan .20 .50
25 Jarome Iginla .60 1.50
26 Derek Morris .10 .25
27 Rob Niedermayer .10 .25
28 Marc Savard .10 .25
29 Roman Turek .20 .50
30 Mike Vernon .20 .50
31 Rod Brind'Amour .20 .50
32 Ron Francis .20 .50
33 Martin Gelinas .10 .25
34 Arturs Irbe .20 .50
35 Sami Kapanen .10 .25
36 Jeff O'Neill .10 .25
37 Shane Willis .10 .25
38 Tony Amonte .20 .50
39 Eric Daze .20 .50
40 Michael Nylander .10 .25
41 Steve Sullivan .10 .25
42 Jocelyn Thibault .20 .50
43 Alexei Zhamnov .10 .25
44 David Aebischer .20 .50
45 Rob Blake .20 .50
46 Chris Drury .20 .50
47 Peter Forsberg .60 1.50
48 Milan Hejduk .30 .75
49 Patrick Roy 1.50 4.00
50 Joe Sakic .75 2.00
51 Alex Tanguay .20 .50
52 Marc Denis .20 .50
53 Rostislav Klesla .10 .25
54 Espen Knutsen .10 .25
55 Geoff Sanderson .10 .25
56 Ron Tugnutt .20 .50
57 Donald Audette .10 .25
58 Ed Belfour .30 .75
59 Mike Modano .60 1.50
60 Joe Nieuwendyk .20 .50
61 Marty Turco .20 .50
62 Pierre Turgeon .20 .50
63 Chris Chelios .30 .75
64 Sergei Fedorov .40 1.00
65 Dominik Hasek .75 2.00
66 Brett Hull .40 1.00
67 Nicklas Lidstrom .30 .75
68 Luc Robitaille .20 .50
69 Brendan Shanahan .30 .75
70 Steve Yzerman 1.25 3.00
71 Eric Brewer .10 .25
72 Anson Carter .20 .50
73 Daniel Cleary .10 .25
74 Mike Comrie .20 .50
75 Mike Grier .10 .25
76 Jochen Hecht .10 .25
77 Tommy Salo .20 .50
78 Ryan Smyth .10 .25
79 Pavel Bure .30 .75
80 Valeri Bure .10 .25
81 Trevor Kidd .20 .50
82 Viktor Kozlov .10 .25
83 Roberto Luongo .60 1.50
84 Marcus Nilsson .10 .25
85 Jason Allison .10 .25
86 Adam Deadmarsh .10 .25
87 Zigmund Palffy .20 .50
88 Felix Potvin .30 .75
89 Mathieu Schneider .10 .25
90 Bryan Smolinski .10 .25
91 Manny Fernandez .20 .50
92 Marian Gaborik .60 1.50
93 Darby Hendrickson .10 .25
94 Lubomir Sekeras .10 .25
95 Wes Walz .10 .25
96 Joe Juneau .10 .25
97 Yanic Perreault .10 .25
98 Oleg Petrov .10 .25
99 Martin Rucinsky .10 .25
100 Brian Savage .10 .25
101 Jose Theodore .40 1.00
102 Richard Zednik .10 .25
103 Mike Dunham .20 .50
104 Scott Hartnell .10 .25
105 Patric Kjellberg .10 .25
106 David Legwand .20 .50
107 Cliff Ronning .10 .25
108 Tomas Vokoun .20 .50
109 Scott Walker .10 .25
110 Jason Arnott .10 .25
111 Martin Brodeur 1.00 2.50
112 Sergei Brylin .10 .25
113 Patrik Elias .20 .50
114 Scott Gomez .10 .25
115 John Madden .10 .25
116 Randy McKay .10 .25
117 Scott Stevens .20 .50
118 Mariusz Czerkawski .10 .25
119 Rick DiPietro .20 .50
120 Brad Isbister .10 .25
121 Chris Osgood .20 .50
122 Michael Peca .10 .25
123 Alexei Yashin .10 .25
124 Radek Dvorak .10 .25
125 Theo Fleury .10 .25
126 Brian Leetch .20 .50
127 Eric Lindros .30 .75
128 Mark Messier .30 .75
129 Petr Nedved .10 .25
130 Mike Richter .30 .75
131 Daniel Alfredsson .20 .50
132 Radek Bonk .10 .25
133 Martin Havlat .20 .50
134 Marian Hossa .30 .75
135 Patrick Lalime .20 .50
136 Shawn McEachern .10 .25
137 Wade Redden .10 .25
138 Roman Cechmanek .20 .50
139 Simon Gagne .30 .75
140 John LeClair .30 .75
141 Keith Primeau .10 .25
142 Mark Recchi .20 .50
143 Jeremy Roenick .40 1.00
144 Justin Williams .10 .25
145 Sergei Berezin .10 .25
146 Sean Burke .20 .50
147 Shane Doan .10 .25
148 Michal Handzus .10 .25
149 Daymond Langkow .10 .25
150 Claude Lemieux .10 .25
151 Johan Hedberg .20 .50
152 Jan Hrdina .10 .25
153 Alexei Kovalev .20 .50
154 Robert Lang .10 .25
155 Mario Lemieux 2.50 5.00
156 Martin Straka .10 .25
157 Fred Brathwaite .20 .50
158 Pavol Demitra .20 .50
159 Brent Johnson .10 .25
160 Al MacInnis .20 .50
161 Chris Pronger .20 .50
162 Cory Stillman .10 .25
163 Keith Tkachuk .30 .75
164 Doug Weight .20 .50
165 Miikka Kiprusoff .20 .50
166 Patrick Marleau .10 .25
167 Evgeni Nabokov .20 .50
168 Owen Nolan .20 .50
169 Mike Ricci .10 .25
170 Teemu Selanne .30 .75
171 Marco Sturm .10 .25
172 Brian Holzinger .10 .25
173 Nikolai Khabibulin .30 .75
174 Vincent Lecavalier .30 .75
175 Fredrik Modin .10 .25
176 Brad Richards .20 .50
177 Martin St. Louis .20 .50
178 Kevin Weekes .10 .25
179 Tie Domi .20 .50
180 Jonas Hoglund .10 .25
181 Curtis Joseph .30 .75
182 Tomas Kaberle .10 .25
183 Alexander Mogilny .20 .50
184 Gary Roberts .10 .25
185 Mats Sundin .30 .75
186 Darcy Tucker .10 .25
187 Todd Bertuzzi .30 .75
188 Andrew Cassels .10 .25
189 Dan Cloutier .20 .50
190 Brendan Morrison .20 .50
191 Markus Naslund .30 .75
192 Daniel Sedin .10 .25
193 Henrik Sedin .10 .25
194 Peter Bondra .30 .75
195 Sergei Gonchar .10 .25
196 Jeff Halpern .10 .25
197 Jaromir Jagr .60 1.50
198 Olaf Kolzig .20 .50
199 Steve Konowalchuk .10 .25
200 Adam Oates .20 .50
201 Ilja Bryzgalov RC 2.50 5.00
202 Timo Parssinen RC 2.50 5.00
203 Ilya Kovalchuk AU RC 30.00 80.00
204 Kamil Piros RC 2.50 5.00
205 Erik Cole RC 2.50 6.00
206 Vaclav Nedorost RC 2.50 5.00
207 Pavel Datsyuk RC 8.00 20.00
208 Ty Conklin RC 2.00 5.00
209 Niklas Hagman RC 2.00 5.00
210 Kristian Huselius RC 3.00 8.00
211 Jaroslav Bednar RC 2.00 5.00
212 Nick Schultz RC 2.00 5.00
213 Martin Erat RC 2.00 5.00
214 Scott Clemmensen RC 2.00 5.00
215 Andreas Salomonsson RC 2.00 5.00
216 Radek Martinek RC 2.00 5.00
217 Dan Blackburn RC 2.00 5.00
218 Chris Neil RC 2.50 6.00
219 Pavel Brendl SP 2.00 5.00
220 Jiri Dopita RC 2.00 5.00
221 Krystofer Kolanos RC 2.00 5.00
222 Mark Rycroft RC 2.00 5.00
223 Jeff Jillson RC 2.00 5.00
224 Nikita Alexeev RC 2.00 5.00
225 Brian Sutherby RC 2.00 5.00

2001-02 Pacific Adrenaline Blue

This 225-card set directly parallels the base set, with the only difference being a blue foil stamp rather than gold and serial numbering out of 62 on the card front. The cards were

inserted randomly in hobby packs at a rate of 1:25.
*STARS: 6X TO 15X BASIC CARD
*SP's: .5X TO 1.25X BASIC CARD

2001-02 Pacific Adrenaline Premiere Date

This 225-card set directly parallels the base set, with the only difference being a gold premiere date stamp and serial numbering out of 62 on the card front. The cards were inserted randomly in hobby packs at a rate of 1:25.
*STARS: 6X TO 15X BASIC CARD
*SP's: .5X TO 1.25X BASIC CARD

2001-02 Pacific Adrenaline Red

Randomly inserted into retail packs at a rate of one per box, this 225 card set paralleled the base set but carried red foil and was serial-numbered to 54 sets.
*STARS: 8X TO 20X BASIC CARD
*SP's: .6X TO 1.5X BASIC CARDS

2001-02 Pacific Adrenaline Retail

Though similar to the hobby version, the retail set had silver foil highlights and short prints were non-serial numbered. SP's were inserted at a rate of 4:25. There were two versions of the Kovalchuk card, a nonserial-numbered regular card and a serial-numbered out of 500 autographed card. Odds for the Kovalchuk auto card were 1:1921 for retail packs and the cards were inserted in both retail and hobby packs.
*RETAIL BASE SAME VALUE AS HOBBY
*RETAIL SPs: .15X TO .4X HOBBY CARDS
203 Ilya Kovalchuk RC 8.00 20.00
207 Pavel Datsyuk RC 6.00 15.00

2001-02 Pacific Adrenaline Blade Runners

Inserted into hobby packs at a rate of 1:481, this 10-card set featured a color action photo of the featured player on a blue and gold micro-chip design background. Borders were white with the same micro-chip design, and each card was serial-numbered out of 63.
1 Paul Kariya 15.00 40.00
2 Patrick Roy 30.00 80.00
3 Joe Sakic 12.50 30.00
4 Dominik Hasek 12.50 30.00
5 Steve Yzerman 30.00 80.00
6 Pavel Bure 8.00 20.00
7 Martin Brodeur 15.00 40.00
8 Eric Lindros 10.00 25.00
9 Mario Lemieux 40.00 100.00
10 Jaromir Jagr 10.00 25.00

2001-02 Pacific Adrenaline Creased Lightning

COMPLETE SET (20) 20.00 40.00
STATED ODDS 1:25
1 Martin Biron .60 1.50
2 Arturs Irbe .60 1.50
3 Jocelyn Thibault .60 1.50
4 Patrick Roy 4.00 10.00
5 Ed Belfour .75 2.00
6 Dominik Hasek 2.00 5.00
7 Tommy Salo .60 1.50
8 Roberto Luongo 1.00 2.50
9 Felix Potvin .60 1.50
10 Jose Theodore 1.00 2.50
11 Martin Brodeur 2.50 6.00
12 Rick DiPietro .60 1.50
13 Mike Richter .75 2.00
14 Patrick Lalime .60 1.50
15 Roman Cechmanek .60 1.50
16 Sean Burke .60 1.50
17 Johan Hedberg .60 1.50
18 Brent Johnson .60 1.50
19 Evgeni Nabokov .60 1.50
20 Curtis Joseph .75 2.00

2001-02 Pacific Adrenaline Jerseys

*MULT.COLOR SWATCH: 1X TO 1.5X
STATED ODDS 2:25 HOBBY/1:73 RETAIL
1 Oleg Tverdovsky 2.00 5.00
2 Sergei Samsonov 4.00 10.00
3 J-P Dumont 2.00 5.00
4 Jay McKee 2.00 5.00
5 Jarome Iginla 6.00 15.00
6 Roman Turek 2.00 5.00
7 Tony Amonte 4.00 10.00
8 Alexei Zhamnov 2.00 5.00
9 Patrick Roy 15.00 40.00
10 Joe Sakic 8.00 20.00
11 Ed Belfour 4.00 10.00
12 Derian Hatcher 2.00 5.00
13 Joe Nieuwendyk 4.00 10.00
14 Pierre Turgeon 4.00 10.00
15 Brett Hull 6.00 15.00
16 Steve Yzerman 12.00 30.00
17 Jochen Hecht 2.00 5.00
18 Valeri Bure 2.00 5.00
19 Robert Svehla 2.00 5.00
20 Felix Potvin 4.00 10.00
21 Jamie McLennan 2.00 5.00
22 Saku Koivu 4.00 10.00
23 Patric Kjellberg 2.00 5.00
24 Kimmo Timonen 2.00 5.00
25 Martin Brodeur 10.00 25.00
26 Petr Sykora 2.00 5.00
27 Chris Osgood 4.00 10.00
28 Eric Lindros 5.00 12.00
29 Petr Nedved 2.00 5.00
30 Mike Richter 4.00 10.00
31 Zdeno Chara 2.00 5.00
32 John LeClair 2.00 5.00
33 Shane Doan 2.00 5.00
34 Daymond Langkow 2.00 5.00
35 Alexei Kovalev 2.00 5.00
36 Milan Kraft 2.00 5.00
37 Robert Lang 2.00 5.00
38 Mario Lemieux 15.00 40.00
39 Fred Brathwaite 2.00 5.00
40 Cory Stillman 2.00 5.00
41 Doug Weight 4.00 10.00
42 Scott Young 2.00 5.00
43 Teemu Selanne 4.00 10.00
44 Nikolai Khabibulin 4.00 10.00
45 Vincent Lecavalier 5.00 12.00
46 Shayne Corson 2.00 5.00
47 Mats Sundin 5.00 12.00
48 Dimitri Yushkevich 2.00 5.00
49 Andrew Cassels 2.00 5.00
50 Jaromir Jagr 8.00 20.00

2001-02 Pacific Adrenaline Playmakers

COMPLETE SET (10) 10.00 25.00
STATED ODDS 1:49
1 Joe Thornton 2.50 6.00
2 Milan Hejduk .75 2.00
3 Mike Modano 2.50 6.00
4 Brett Hull 1.50 4.00
5 Mike Comrie .75 2.00
6 Marian Gaborik 2.50 6.00
7 Martin Havlat 1.25 3.00
8 Teemu Selanne 1.50 4.00
9 Daniel Sedin 1.25 3.00
10 Henrik Sedin 1.25 3.00

2001-02 Pacific Adrenaline Power Play

This 36-card set was inserted at a rate of 1:1. The cards were sponsored by Power Play magazine and the NHLPA. This set featured the top goalies of the league.
COMPLETE SET (36) 8.00 20.00
1 J-S Giguere .20 .50
2 Steve Shields .20 .50
3 Milan Hnilicka .20 .50
4 Byron DaFoe .20 .50

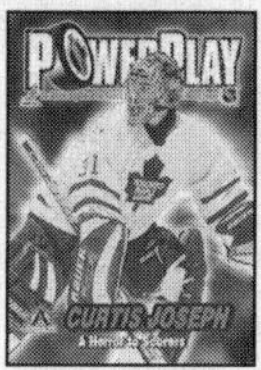

5 Martin Biron .20 .50
6 Roman Turek .20 .50
7 Arturs Irbe .20 .50
8 Jocelyn Thibault .20 .50
9 Patrick Roy 1.50 4.00
10 Marc Denis .20 .50
11 Ron Tugnutt .20 .50
12 Ed Belfour .30 .75
13 Marty Turco .30 .75
14 Dominik Hasek .60 1.50
15 Tommy Salo .20 .50
16 Trevor Kidd .20 .50
17 Roberto Luongo .40 1.00
18 Felix Potvin .30 .75
19 Manny Fernandez .20 .50
20 Jose Theodore .40 1.00
21 Mike Dunham .20 .50
22 Martin Brodeur .75 2.00
23 Rick DiPietro .30 .75
24 Mike Richter .30 .75
25 Patrick Lalime .20 .50
26 Roman Cechmanek .20 .50
27 Sean Burke .20 .50
28 Johan Hedberg .20 .50
29 Fred Brathwaite .20 .50
30 Brent Johnson .20 .50
31 Miikka Kiprusoff .40 1.00
32 Evgeni Nabokov .20 .50
33 Nikolai Khabibulin .30 .75
34 Curtis Joseph .30 .75
35 Dan Cloutier .20 .50
36 Olaf Kolzig .40 1.00

2001-02 Pacific Adrenaline Rookie Report

COMPLETE SET (20) 15.00 40.00
STATED ODDS 2:25
1 Ilja Bryzgalov 1.25 3.00
2 Dany Heatley 3.00 8.00
3 Ilya Kovalchuk 8.00 20.00
4 Erik Cole 1.25 3.00
5 Mark Bell .40 1.00
6 Vaclav Nedorost .40 1.00
7 Rostislav Klesla .40 1.00
8 Pavel Datsyuk 5.00 12.00
9 Kristian Huselius .40 1.00
10 Jaroslav Bednar .40 1.00
11 Rick DiPietro 2.00 5.00
12 Dan Blackburn .40 1.00
13 Pavel Brendl .40 1.00
14 Krystofer Kolanos .40 1.00
15 Kris Beech .40 1.00
16 Johan Hedberg .40 1.00
17 Jeff Jillson .40 1.00
18 Miikka Kiprusoff 2.00 5.00
19 Nikita Alexeev .40 1.00
20 Brian Sutherby .40 1.00

2001-02 Pacific Adrenaline World Beaters

COMPLETE SET (20) 25.00 50.00
STATED ODDS 3:25
1 Paul Kariya .75 2.00
2 Chris Drury .60 1.50
3 Joe Sakic 1.25 3.00
4 Mike Modano 1.00 2.50
5 Brett Hull .75 2.00
6 Steve Yzerman 3.00 8.00
7 Pavel Bure .75 2.00
8 Zigmund Palffy .60 1.50
9 Marian Gaborik 1.50 4.00
10 Patrik Elias .60 1.50
11 Alexei Yashin .60 1.50
12 Eric Lindros 1.00 2.50
13 Martin Havlat .60 1.50
14 John LeClair .75 2.00
15 Alexei Kovalev .60 1.50
16 Mario Lemieux 4.00 10.00
17 Keith Tkachuk .75 2.00
18 Teemu Selanne .75 2.00
19 Mats Sundin .75 2.00
20 Jaromir Jagr 1.00 2.50

2003 Pacific All-Star Game-Used Goal Net Cards

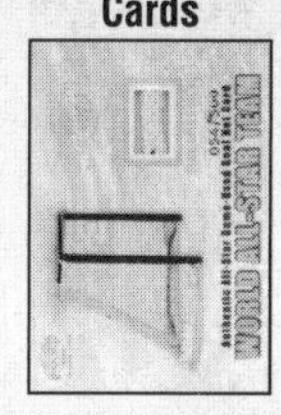

Given away exclusivley at the 2003 NHL All-Star block party as a wrapper redemption, this 2-card set featured swatches of the actual goal netting used during the 2002 NHL All-Star game. Each card was serial-numbered out of 500.
COMPLETE SET (2) 20.00 40.00
1 North American All-Star Team 20.0025.00
2 World All-Star Team 20.00 25.00

2003 Pacific Atlantic City National Convention

Available via wrapper redemption at the Pacific booth during the 2003 Atlantic City National Sports Collectors Convention, this 6-card dual player set was numbered to just 500 copies.
COMPLETE SET (6) 12.50 30.00
1 Rick Nash 3.00 8.00
John LeClair
2 Henrik Zetterberg 4.00 10.00
Ilya Kovalchuk
3 Ryan Miller 2.50 6.00
Martin Brodeur
4 Jay Bouwmeester 2.00 5.00
Scott Stevens
5 Jason Spezza 3.00 8.00
Jeremy Roenick
6 Stanislav Chistov 2.00 5.00
Paul Kariya

2002 Pacific Calder Collection All-Star Fantasy

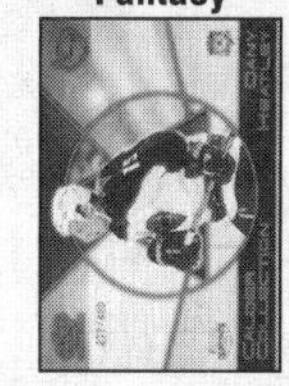

Available via wrapper redemption from the Pacific booth at the NHL All-Star Fantasy show, this 10-card set featured top rookies from the 2001-02 season. Each card was serial numbered out of 400.
COMPLETE SET (10) 20.00 50.00
1 Dany Heatley 3.20 8.00
2 Ilya Kovalchuk 8.00 20.00
3 Erik Cole 2.40 6.00
4 Vaclav Nedorost 2.40 6.00
5 Kristian Huselius 2.40 6.00
6 Jaroslav Bednar 1.20 3.00
7 Martin Erat 1.20 3.00
8 Dan Blackburn 3.20 8.00
9 Krys Kolanos 2.40 6.00
10 Jeff Jillson 1.60 4.00

2003 Pacific Calder Collection NHL All-Star Block Party

Given away as wrapper redemptions exclusively at the Pacific booth during the 2003 NHL All-Star block party, this 10-card set featured players eligible for Calder consideration. Each card was serial-numbered out of 500.
COMPLETE SET 25.00
1 Stanislav Chistov 2.40 1.00
2 Chuck Kobasew 1.60 2.00
3 Jordan Leopold .80 2.00
4 Rick Nash 4.00 10.00
5 Henrik Zetterberg 4.00 10.00
6 Jay Bouwmeester 2.40 6.00
7 Alexander Frolov 2.00 5.00
8 P-M Bouchard 2.40 5.00
9 Jason Spezza 3.20 8.00
10 Alexander Svitov 1.20 1.00

2003 Pacific Calder Contenders NHL Entry Draft

Distributed exclusively at the 2003 NHL Entry Draft, this 10-card set paralleled the regular Calder Contenders set in Pacific Quest for the Cup, but carried a foil Draft stamp and gold background. Each card was serial-numbered to just 500 copies.
COMPLETE SET 40.00
1 Stanislav Chistov 2.40 2.00
2 Ales Kotalik .80 1.00
3 Ryan Miller 2.00 3.00
4 Tyler Arnason .80 1.00
5 Pascal Leclaire 2.40 3.00
6 Rick Nash 4.00 10.00
7 Henrik Zetterberg 4.00 8.00
8 Ales Hemsky 2.40 2.00
9 Jay Bouwmeester 2.40 5.00
10 Jason Spezza 3.20 8.00

2002-03 Pacific Calder

Released in June, this 150-card set featured veteran players who were nominated for the Calder trophy and rookies. Rookie cards were serial-numbered to 825.
COMP.SET w/o SP'S (100) 30.00 60.00
1 Dany Heatley .40 1.00
2 Ilya Kovalchuk .40 1.00
3 Evgeni Nabokov .25 .60
4 Brad Richards .25 .60
5 Scott Gomez .10 .25
6 Brad Stuart .25 .60
7 Chris Drury .25 .60
8 Marian Hossa .30 .75
9 Sergei Samsonov .25 .60
10 Mattias Ohlund .10 .25
11 Bryan Berard .10 .25
12 Jarome Iginla .40 1.00
13 Daniel Alfredsson .25 .60
14 Eric Daze .25 .60
15 Peter Forsberg .75 2.00
16 Martin Brodeur .75 2.00
17 Jason Arnott .10 .25
18 Teemu Selanne .30 .75
19 Pavel Bure .30 .75
20 Nicklas Lidstrom .30 .75
21 Ed Belfour .30 .75
22 Sergei Fedorov .50 1.25
23 Mike Modano .50 1.25
24 Brian Leetch .25 .60
25 Joe Nieuwendyk .25 .60
26 Luc Robitaille .25 .60
27 Mario Lemieux 2.50 6.00
28 Chris Chelios .30 .75
29 Steve Yzerman 1.50 4.00
30 Paul Kariya .30 .75
31 Joe Thornton .50 1.25
32 Theoren Fleury .10 .25
33 Milan Hejduk .30 .75
34 Patrick Roy 1.50 4.00
35 Joe Sakic .60 1.50
36 Marty Turco .25 .60
37 Brett Hull .40 1.00
38 Curtis Joseph .30 .75
39 Brendan Shanahan .30 .75
40 Mike Comrie .25 .60
41 Marian Gaborik .60 1.50
42 Saku Koivu .30 .75
43 Jose Theodore .40 1.00
44 Alexei Yashin .10 .25
45 Alex Kovalev .25 .60
46 Eric Lindros .30 .75
47 Mark Messier .30 .75
48 Tony Amonte .25 .60
49 Vincent Lecavalier .30 .75
50 Mats Sundin .30 .75
51 Markus Naslund .30 .75
52 Jaromir Jagr .50 1.25
53 Dan Snyder .10 .25
54 Lee Goren .10 .25
55 Ivan Huml .10 .25
56 Andrew Raycroft .25 .60
57 Ales Kotalik .10 .25
58 Mika Noronen .10 .25
59 Henrik Tallinder .10 .25
60 Pavel Brendl .10 .25
61 Jeff Heerema .10 .25
62 Jaroslav Svoboda .10 .25
63 Tyler Arnason .25 .60
64 Riku Hahl .10 .25
65 Vaclav Nedorost .10 .25
66 Niko Kapanen .10 .25
67 Jesse Wallin .10 .25
68 Jason Chimera .10 .25
69 Jani Rita .10 .25
70 Raffi Torres .10 .25
71 Jaroslav Bednar .10 .25

72 Stephen Weiss .10 .25
73 Joe Corvo .10 .25
74 Kyle Wanvig .10 .25
75 Mathieu Garon .25 .60
76 Marcel Hossa .10 .25
77 Jan Lasak .10 .25
78 Christian Berglund .10 .25
79 Jiri Bicek .10 .25
80 Michael Rupp .10 .25
81 Rick DiPietro .25 .60
82 Justin Mapletoft .10 .25
83 Mattias Weinhandl .10 .25
84 Jamie Lundmark .10 .25
85 Ales Pisa .10 .25
86 Toni Dahlman .10 .25
87 Eric Chouinard .10 .25
88 Ramzi Abid .10 .25
89 Sebastien Caron .10 .25
90 Dan Focht .10 .25
91 Barret Jackman .25 .60
92 Justin Papineau .10 .25
93 Jonathan Cheechoo .12 .30
94 Miikka Kiprusoff .25 .60
95 Vesa Toskala .10 .25
96 Karel Pilar .10 .25
97 Fedor Fedorov .10 .25
98 Sebastien Charpentier .25 .60
99 Joel Kwiatkowski .10 .25
100 Brian Sutherby .10 .25
101 Stanislav Chistov RC 2.00 5.00
102 Kurt Sauer RC 2.00 5.00
103 Alexei Smirnov RC 2.00 5.00
104 Shaone Morrisonn RC 2.00 5.00
105 Kris Vernarsky RC 2.00 5.00
106 Ryan Miller RC 2.00 5.00
107 Chuck Kobasew RC 2.00 5.00
108 Jordan Leopold RC 2.00 5.00
109 Ryan Bayda RC 2.00 5.00
110 Igor Radulov RC 2.00 5.00
111 Pascal Leclaire RC 2.00 5.00
112 Rick Nash RC 8.00 20.00
112A Rick Nash AU/100 60.00 125.00
113 Jason Bacashihua RC 3.00 8.00
114 Steve Ott RC 2.00 5.00
115 Dmitri Bykov RC 2.00 5.00
116 Henrik Zetterberg RC 5.00 12.00
117 Ales Hemsky RC 3.00 8.00
118 Fernando Pisani RC 2.00 5.00
119 Jay Bouwmeester RC 2.00 5.00
120 Jared Aulin RC 2.00 5.00
121 Michael Cammalleri RC 2.00 5.00
122 Alexander Frolov RC 2.50 6.00
123 Cristobal Huet RC 4.00 10.00
124 P-M Bouchard RC 2.50 6.00
125 Stephane Veilleux RC 2.00 5.00
126 Ron Hainsey RC 2.00 5.00
127 Mike Komisarek RC 2.50 6.00
128 Vernon Fiddler RC 2.00 5.00
129 Adam Hall RC 2.00 5.00
130 Scottie Upshall RC 2.00 5.00
131 Eric Godard RC 2.00 5.00
132 Ray Emery RC 2.00 5.00
133 Jason Spezza RC 6.00 15.00
134 Anton Volchenkov RC 2.00 5.00
135 Dennis Seidenberg RC 2.00 5.00
136 Radovan Somik RC 2.00 5.00
137 Jim Vandermeer RC 2.00 5.00
138 Jeff Taffe RC 2.00 5.00
139 Brooks Orpik RC 2.00 5.00
140 Tomas Surovy RC 2.00 5.00
141 Curtis Sanford RC 2.00 5.00
142 Matt Walker RC 2.00 5.00
143 Niko Dimitrakos RC 2.00 5.00
144 Jim Fahey RC 2.00 5.00
145 Lynn Loyns RC 2.00 5.00
146 Alexander Svitov RC 2.00 5.00
147 Carlo Colaiacovo RC 2.00 5.00
148 Mikael Tellqvist RC 2.00 5.00
149 Steve Eminger RC 2.00 5.00
150 Alex Henry RC 2.00 5.00

2002-03 Pacific Calder Silver

*STARS: 1.25X TO 3X BASIC CARD
*SP's: .25X TO .75X
PRINT RUN 299 SER.#'d SETS

2002-03 Pacific Calder Chasing Glory

COMPLETE SET (10) 10.00 20.00
STATED ODDS 1:13
1 Joe Thornton 1.00 2.50
2 Peter Forsberg 1.50 4.00
3 Patrick Roy 2.50 6.00
4 Mike Modano 1.00 2.50
5 Marty Turco .60 1.50
6 Martin Brodeur 1.50 4.00
7 Marian Hossa .60 1.50
8 Mario Lemieux 3.00 8.00
9 Ed Belfour .60 1.50
10 Markus Naslund .60 1.50

2002-03 Pacific Calder Hardware Heroes

COMPLETE SET (12) 10.00 20.00
STATED ODDS 1:9
1 Dany Heatley .60 1.50
2 Patrick Roy 2.00 5.00
3 Joe Sakic 1.00 2.50
4 Brett Hull .60 1.50
5 Nicklas Lidstrom .50 1.25

6 Steve Yzerman 2.00 5.00
7 Jose Theodore .60 1.50
8 Eric Lindros .50 1.25
9 Mark Messier .50 1.25
10 Mario Lemieux 2.50 6.00
11 Ed Belfour .50 1.25
12 Jaromir Jagr .75 2.00

2002-03 Pacific Calder Hart Stoppers

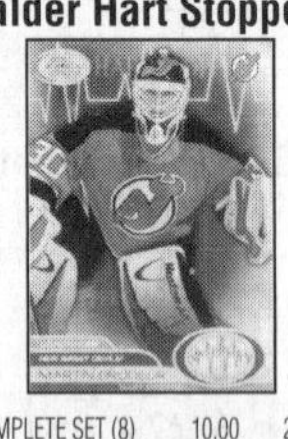

COMPLETE SET (8) 10.00 20.00
STATED ODDS 1:13
1 Joe Thornton 1.00 2.50
2 Peter Forsberg 1.50 4.00
3 Patrick Roy 2.50 6.00
4 Mike Modano 1.00 2.50
5 Marty Turco .60 1.50
6 Martin Brodeur 1.50 4.00
7 Marian Hossa .60 1.50
8 Markus Naslund .60 1.50

2002-03 Pacific Calder Jerseys

STATED ODDS 1:13
1 Dany Heatley 5.00 12.00
2 Patrik Stefan 3.00 8.00
3 Glen Murray 3.00 8.00
4 Joe Thornton 5.00 12.00
5 Miroslav Satan 3.00 8.00
6 Alexei Zhamnov 3.00 8.00
7 Peter Forsberg 8.00 20.00
8 Patrick Roy 10.00 25.00
9 Marty Turco 5.00 12.00
10 Luc Robitaille 3.00 8.00
11 Olli Jokinen 3.00 8.00
12 Yanic Perreault 3.00 8.00
13 Tomas Vokoun 3.00 8.00
14 Rick DiPietro 3.00 8.00
15 Daniel Alfredsson 3.00 8.00
16 Jason Spezza 6.00 15.00
17 Roman Cechmanek 3.00 8.00
18 Mario Lemieux 12.50 30.00
19 Valeri Bure 3.00 8.00
20 Doug Weight 3.00 8.00
21 Ed Belfour 4.00 10.00
22 Mats Sundin 4.00 10.00
23 Brendan Morrison 3.00 8.00
24 Markus Naslund 4.00 10.00
25 Jaromir Jagr 6.00 15.00

2002-03 Pacific Calder Reflections

COMPLETE SET (20) 12.00 30.00
STATED ODDS 1:5
1 Stanislav Chistov .60 1.50
2 Ivan Huml .60 1.50
3 Ales Kotalik .60 1.50
4 Ryan Miller 1.50 4.00
5 Jordan Leopold .60 1.50
6 Tyler Arnason .60 1.50
7 Pascal Leclaire 1.00 2.50
8 Rick Nash 2.00 5.00
9 Henrik Zetterberg 1.50 4.00
10 Ales Hemsky 1.25 3.00
11 Jay Bouwmeester .75 2.00
12 Stephen Weiss .75 2.00
13 Michael Cammalleri .75 2.00
14 Alexander Frolov 1.00 2.50
15 P-M Bouchard .75 2.00
16 Marcel Hossa .75 2.00
17 Rick DiPietro 1.00 2.50
18 Jason Spezza 1.50 4.00
19 Barret Jackman .60 1.50
20 Jonathan Cheechoo 1.25 3.00

2003-04 Pacific Calder

The last Pacific brand of the season, Calder focused on rookies and prospects. Cards 101-140 were serial-numbered to 775 copies each. Cards 141 through 175 were jersey cards.

JSY RC PRINT RUN 500 SER.#'d SETS
1 Sergei Fedorov .40 1.00
2 J-S Giguere .25 .60
3 Dany Heatley .40 1.00
4 Ilya Kovalchuk .40 1.00
5 Marc Savard .15 .40
6 Sergei Gonchar .15 .40
7 Glen Murray .15 .40
8 Andrew Raycroft .25 .60
9 Joe Thornton .50 1.25
10 Martin Biron .25 .60
11 Daniel Briere .15 .40
12 Mika Noronen .25 .60
13 Jarome Iginla .40 1.00
14 Miikka Kiprusoff .25 .60
15 Chuck Kobasew .15 .40
16 Erik Cole .15 .40
17 Josef Vasicek .15 .40
18 Justin Williams .15 .40
19 Tyler Arnason .25 .60
20 Mark Bell .15 .40
21 Kyle Calder .15 .40
22 Peter Forsberg .75 2.00
23 Milan Hejduk .30 .75
24 Paul Kariya .30 .75
25 Joe Sakic .60 1.50
26 Philippe Sauve .25 .60
27 Alex Tanguay .25 .60
28 Marc Denis .25 .60
29 Rick Nash .40 1.00
30 Valeri Bure .15 .40
31 Bill Guerin .25 .60
32 Mike Modano .50 1.25
33 Marty Turco .25 .60
34 Pavel Datsyuk .30 .75
35 Kris Draper .15 .40
36 Dominik Hasek .60 1.50
37 Brett Hull .40 1.00
38 Curtis Joseph .30 .75
39 Robert Lang .25 .60
40 Brendan Shanahan .30 .75
41 Steve Yzerman .75 2.00
42 Ryan Smyth .15 .40
43 Raffi Torres .15 .40
44 Mike York .15 .40
45 Jay Bouwmeester .15 .40
46 Olli Jokinen .25 .60
47 Roberto Luongo .40 1.00
48 Roman Cechmanek .25 .60
49 Alexander Frolov .15 .40
50 Ziggy Palffy .25 .60
51 Alexandre Daigle .15 .40
52 Marian Gaborik .60 1.50
53 Dwayne Roloson .25 .60
54 Saku Koivu .30 .75
55 Alex Kovalev .25 .60
56 Mike Ribeiro .15 .40
57 Michael Ryder .15 .40
58 Jose Theodore .40 1.00
59 Scott Hartnell .15 .40
60 Scottie Upshall .15 .40
61 Tomas Vokoun .25 .60
62 Martin Brodeur .75 2.00
63 Patrik Elias .25 .60
64 Jeff Friesen .15 .40
65 Rick DiPietro .25 .60
66 Trent Hunter .15 .40
67 Jaromir Jagr .50 1.25
68 Eric Lindros .30 .75
69 Mark Messier .30 .75
70 Daniel Alfredsson .25 .60
71 Martin Havlat .25 .60
72 Marian Hossa .30 .75
73 Jason Spezza .30 .75
74 Mark Recchi .25 .60
75 Jeremy Roenick .40 1.00
76 Brian Boucher .25 .60
77 Mike Comrie .25 .60
78 Shane Doan .15 .40
79 Ladislav Nagy .15 .40
80 Rico Fata .15 .40
81 Mario Lemieux 1.50 4.00
82 Pavol Demitra .15 .40
83 Chris Osgood .25 .60
84 Keith Tkachuk .30 .75
85 Doug Weight .25 .60
86 Jonathan Cheechoo .20 .50
87 Patrick Marleau .25 .60
88 Evgeni Nabokov .25 .60
89 Nikolai Khabibulin .30 .75
90 Vincent Lecavalier .30 .75
91 Martin St. Louis .25 .60
92 Ed Belfour .30 .75
93 Owen Nolan .25 .60
94 Gary Roberts .15 .40
95 Mats Sundin .30 .75
96 Todd Bertuzzi .30 .75
97 Dan Cloutier .25 .60
98 Jason King .15 .40
99 Brendan Morrison .25 .60
100 Markus Naslund .30 .75
101 Chris Kunitz RC 1.50 4.00
102 Kari Lehtonen RC 8.00 20.00
103 Jason Pominville RC 2.00 5.00
104 Derek Roy RC 1.50 4.00
105 Brent Krahn RC 1.50 4.00
106 Eric Staal RC 6.00 15.00
107 Adam Munro RC 1.50 4.00
108 Tuomo Ruutu RC 2.50 6.00
109 Pavel Vorobiev RC 1.50 4.00
110 Cody McCormick RC 1.50 4.00
111 Dan Fritsche RC 1.50 4.00
112 Tim Jackman RC 1.50 4.00
113 Nikolai Zherdev RC 3.00 8.00
114 Dan Ellis RC 1.50 4.00
115 Jiri Hudler RC 2.50 6.00
116 Niklas Kronwall RC 2.00 5.00
117 Nathan Robinson RC 1.50 4.00
118 Doug Lynch RC 1.50 4.00
119 Scott Barney 1.50 4.00
120 Noah Clarke RC 1.50 4.00
121 Brent Burns RC 1.50 4.00
122 Dan Hamhuis RC 2.00 5.00
123 Timofei Shishkanov RC 1.50 4.00
124 Marek Zidlicky RC 1.50 4.00
125 Tuomas Pihlman RC 1.50 4.00
126 Jozef Balej RC 2.00 5.00
127 Dominic Moore RC 1.50 4.00
128 Chad Wiseman 1.50 4.00
129 Fredrik Sjostrom RC 1.50 4.00
130 Marc-Andre Fleury RC 8.00 20.00
131 Ryan Malone RC 2.50 6.00
132 Matt Murley RC 1.50 4.00
133 John Pohl RC 1.50 4.00
134 Milan Michalek RC 2.00 5.00
135 Kyle Wellwood RC 4.00 10.00
136 Wade Brookbank RC 1.50 4.00
137 Ryan Kesler RC 1.50 4.00
138 Peter Sarno RC 1.50 4.00
139 Alexander Semin RC 3.00 8.00
140 Rastislav Stana RC 1.50 4.00
141 J-S Giguere 2.50 6.00
142 Ilya Kovalchuk 8.00 20.00
143 Joe Thornton 6.00 15.00
144 Jarome Iginla 6.00 15.00
145 Peter Forsberg 8.00 20.00
146 Milan Hejduk 3.00 8.00
147 Rick Nash 4.00 10.00
148 Marty Turco 6.00 15.00
149 Roman Cechmanek 2.50 6.00
150 Martin Brodeur 12.00 30.00
151 Jaromir Jagr 6.00 15.00
152 Daniel Alfredsson 2.50 6.00
153 Marian Hossa 3.00 8.00
154 Jeff Hackett 2.50 6.00
155 Mario Lemieux/66 15.00 40.00
156 Chris Osgood 2.50 6.00
157 Vincent Lecavalier .30 .75
158 Ed Belfour 3.00 8.00
159 Todd Bertuzzi 3.00 8.00
160 Brendan Morrison 2.50 6.00
161 Olaf Kolzig 2.50 6.00
162 Joffrey Lupul RC 4.00 10.00
163 Patrice Bergeron RC 8.00 20.00
164 Matthew Lombardi RC 3.00 8.00
165 Antti Miettinen RC 3.00 8.00
166 Nathan Horton RC 5.00 12.00
167 Dustin Brown RC 3.00 8.00
168 Chris Higgins RC 4.00 10.00
169 Jordin Tootoo RC 5.00 12.00
170 Sean Bergenheim RC 3.00 8.00
171 Antoine Vermette RC 3.00 8.00
172 Joni Pitkanen RC 4.00 10.00
173 Peter Sejna RC 3.00 8.00
174 Matt Stajan RC 4.00 10.00
175 Boyd Gordon RC 3.00 8.00
176 Andrew Raycroft AU/250 12.00 30.00

2003-04 Pacific Calder Silver

*STARS: 2X TO 5X BASIC CARDS
*ROOKIES: .25X TO .6X
PRINT RUN 575 SER.#'d SETS

2003-04 Pacific Calder Reflections

COMPLETE SET 15.00 30.00
STATED ODDS 1:13
1 Joffrey Lupul 2.00 5.00
2 Patrice Bergeron 3.00 8.00
3 Andrew Raycroft 3.00 8.00
4 Eric Staal 2.50 6.00
5 Michael Ryder 2.00 5.00
6 Trent Hunter 2.00 5.00
7 Marc-Andre Fleury 4.00 10.00
8 Ryan Malone 2.00 5.00

2002 Pacific Chicago National *

Available via a wrapper redemption at the Pacific booth during the 2002 Chicago National Convention, this 8-card set was serial-numbered to just 500 copies. Collectors had to open a box of 2002 Pacific football or 2001-02 Pacific hockey product to receive the set. Each card featured an NHL player and an NFL player on either side.

COMPLETE SET (8) 20.00 40.00
1 Ilya Kovalchuk 4.00 10.00
Michael Vick
2 Joe Thornton 2.50 6.00
Tom Brady
3 Eric Daze 2.00 5.00
Anthony Thomas
4 Peter Forsberg 2.50 6.00
Brian Griese
5 Mike Modano 2.50 6.00
Emmitt Smith
6 Steve Yzerman 4.00 10.00
Joey Harrington
7 Eric Lindros 2.50 6.00
Ron Dayne
8 Chris Pronger 2.00 5.00
Kurt Warner

2002-03 Pacific Complete

This 600-card super set was inserted into various Pacific products throughout the season. A red parallel set was also created and sold via an online offer.

*RED: 6X TO 15X BASIC CARDS
*RED ROOKIES: 3X TO 8X
RED PRINT RUN 99 SER.#'d SETS
1 Nicklas Lidstrom .15 .40
2 Mika Noronen .05 .15
3 Alexei Kovalev .12 .30
4 Jason Allison .05 .15
5 Erik Cole .05 .15
6 Sami Kapanen .05 .15
7 Marty Turco .12 .30
8 Brad Isbister .05 .15
9 Saku Koivu .15 .40
10 Jarome Iginla .20 .50
11 J-S Giguere .12 .30
12 Roman Turek .12 .30
13 Joe Sakic .30 .75
14 Peter Bondra .12 .30
15 Dany Heatley .20 .50
16 Vincent Lecavalier .15 .40
17 Manny Fernandez .12 .30
18 Simon Gagne .15 .40
19 Rick DiPietro .12 .30
20 Mark Recchi .12 .30
21 Mike Richter .15 .40
22 Daymond Langkow .05 .15
23 Pavel Datsyuk .15 .40
24 Mark Messier .15 .40
25 Ed Belfour .15 .40
26 Michael Peca .05 .15
27 Krystofer Kolanos .05 .15
28 Alexander Mogilny .12 .30
29 Martin Straka .05 .15
30 Shane Willis .05 .15
31 Alyn McCauley .05 .15
32 Ryan Smyth .05 .15
33 Tomi Kallio .05 .15
34 Doug Weight .12 .30
35 Nicholas Boynton .05 .15
36 Pascal Dupuis .05 .15
37 Jaroslav Svoboda .05 .15
38 Al MacInnis .12 .30
39 Peter Forsberg .40 1.00
40 Rostislav Klesla .05 .15
41 Kimmo Timonen .05 .15
42 Darren McCarty .05 .15
43 Brian Savage .05 .15
44 Ethan Moreau .05 .15
45 Peter Worrell .05 .15
46 Doug Gilmour .12 .30
47 David Aebischer .12 .30
48 Aaron Miller .05 .15
49 Nick Schultz .05 .15
50 Magnus Arvedson .05 .15
51 Cale Hulse .05 .15
52 Brian Gionta .05 .15
53 Trevor Linden .05 .15
54 Raffi Torres .05 .15
55 Jean-Sebastien Aubin .12 .30
56 Zdeno Chara .05 .15
57 Mattias Ohlund .05 .15
58 Travis Green .05 .15
59 Michael Nylander .05 .15
60 Andreas Dackell .05 .15
61 Craig Billington .05 .15
62 Chris Therien .05 .15
63 Eric Brewer .05 .15
64 Shayne Corson .05 .15
65 Patrice Brisebois .05 .15
66 Sean O'Donnell .05 .15
67 Sergei Varlamov .05 .15
68 Donald Brashear .05 .15
69 Vaclav Prospal .05 .15
70 Mike Ricci .05 .15
71 Fredrik Modin .05 .15
72 Stu Grimson .05 .15
73 Jeff Jillson .05 .15
74 Andre Roy .05 .15
75 Filip Kuba .05 .15
76 Martin Skoula .05 .15
77 Sandis Ozolinsh .05 .15
78 Robert Reichel .05 .15
79 Wes Walz .05 .15
80 Keith Carney .05 .15
81 Steve Kariya .05 .15
82 Dave Tanabe .05 .15
83 Robert Svehla .05 .15
84 Rob Ray .05 .15
85 Niklas Hagman .05 .15
86 Stu Barnes .05 .15
87 Scott Gomez .05 .15
88 Rob Niedermayer .05 .15
89 Dave Scatchard .05 .15
90 Petr Nedved .05 .15
91 Bob Probert .05 .15
92 Dallas Drake .05 .15
93 Mike Leclerc .05 .15
94 Janne Niinimaa .05 .15
95 Rob Zamuner .05 .15
96 Jim Dowd .05 .15
97 Richard Matvichuk .05 .15
98 Boyd Devereaux .05 .15
99 Jamie Storr .12 .30
100 Rem Murray .05 .15
101 Jaromir Jagr .25 .60
102 Todd Bertuzzi .15 .40
103 Mike Modano .25 .60
104 Sergei Fedorov .25 .60
105 Ilya Kovalchuk .20 .50
106 Patrik Elias .12 .30
107 Marian Hossa .15 .40
108 Paul Kariya .15 .40
109 Manny Legace .12 .30
110 Milan Hejduk .15 .40
111 Adam Deadmarsh .05 .15
112 Owen Nolan .12 .30
113 Patrick Marleau .12 .30
114 Adam Oates .12 .30
115 Donald Audette .05 .15
116 Steven Reinprecht .05 .15
117 Jere Lehtinen .12 .30
118 Joe Nieuwendyk .12 .30
119 Roman Cechmanek .12 .30
120 Brian Rolston .05 .15
121 Chris Drury .12 .30
122 J-P Dumont .05 .15
123 Denis Arkhipov .05 .15
124 Sergei Zubov .05 .15
125 Scott Hartnell .05 .15
126 Espen Knutsen .05 .15
127 Slava Kozlov .12 .30
128 Roberto Luongo .20 .50
129 John LeClair .15 .40
130 Daniel Sedin .05 .15
131 Justin Williams .05 .15
132 Kyle Calder .05 .15
133 Bryan Smolinski .05 .15
134 Scott Mellanby .05 .15
135 Martin Lapointe .05 .15
136 Dwayne Roloson .12 .30
137 Niklas Sundstrom .05 .15
138 Ladislav Nagy .05 .15
139 Mathieu Schneider .05 .15
140 Scott Walker .05 .15
141 Marcus Nilsson .05 .15
142 Steve Thomas .05 .15
143 Kevin Weekes .12 .30
144 Vladimir Orszagh .05 .15
145 Brad Stuart .05 .15
146 Shawn Bates .05 .15
147 Oleg Tverdovsky .05 .15
148 Andy Delmore .05 .15
149 Stanislav Neckar .05 .15
150 Phil Housley .05 .15
151 Matt Cooke .05 .15
152 Scott Niedermayer .05 .15
153 Jeff Hackett .12 .30
154 Ruslan Fedotenko .05 .15
155 Daniel Cleary .12 .30
156 Martin Prusek .05 .15
157 Matt Cullen .05 .15
158 Jason Woolley .05 .15
159 Fred Brathwaite .12 .30
160 Adam Graves .05 .15
161 Kenny Jonsson .05 .15
162 Todd Marchant .05 .15
163 Jason Williams .05 .15
164 Joe Juneau .05 .15
165 Patrick Roy .75 2.00
166 Tie Domi .12 .30
167 Adrian Aucoin .05 .15
168 Dan Blackburn .12 .30
169 Vitali Yachmenev .05 .15
170 Derian Hatcher .05 .15
171 Mike Ribeiro .05 .15
172 Mike Van Ryn .05 .15
173 Brian Willsie .05 .15
174 Chris Phillips .05 .15
175 Jason York .05 .15
176 Kris Draper .05 .15
177 Sean Burke .12 .30
178 Kevin Dineen .05 .15
179 Toni Lydman .05 .15
180 Artem Chubarov .05 .15
181 Trevor Letowski .05 .15
182 P.J. Axelsson .05 .15
183 Lubos Bartecko .05 .15
184 Mike Knuble .05 .15
185 Ossi Vaananen .05 .15
186 David Vyborny .05 .15
187 Kevyn Adams .05 .15
188 Johan Hedberg .12 .30
189 Brent Gilchrist .05 .15
190 Eric Boguniecki .05 .15
191 Marcus Ragnarsson .05 .15
192 Eric Weinrich .05 .15
193 Yannick Tremblay .05 .15
194 Mike Keane .05 .15
195 Chad Kilger .05 .15
196 Glen Metropolit .05 .15
197 Stephane Quintal .05 .15
198 Tyler Arnason .12 .30
199 Jan Bulis .05 .15
200 Patric Kjellberg .05 .15
201 Eric Lindros .15 .40
202 Markus Naslund .12 .30
203 Ziggy Palffy .15 .40
204 Brian Rafalski .05 .15
205 Miroslav Satan .12 .30
206 Marian Gaborik .30 .75
207 Tony Amonte .12 .30
208 Tomas Kaberle .05 .15
209 Ray Whitney .05 .15
210 Ron Francis .12 .30
211 Steve Sullivan .05 .15
212 Bryan Berard .05 .15
213 Mark Recchi .12 .30
214 Vincent Damphousse .05 .15
215 Richard Zednik .05 .15
216 Ed Jovanovski .12 .30
217 Valeri Bure .05 .15
218 Jozef Stumpel .05 .15
219 Alexei Zhamnov .05 .15
220 Mariusz Czerkawski .05 .15
221 John Grahame .12 .30
222 Mark Parrish .05 .15
223 Mike York .05 .15
224 Chris Osgood .12 .30
225 Scott Young .05 .15
226 Derek Morris .05 .15
227 Brendan Morrison .12 .30
228 Mike Sillinger .05 .15
229 Todd White .05 .15
230 Tom Poti .05 .15
231 Sergei Zholtok .05 .15
232 Kip Miller .05 .15
233 Pasi Nurminen .05 .15
234 Michal Handzus .05 .15
235 Henrik Sedin .05 .15
236 Phil Housley .05 .15
237 Jeff Halpern .05 .15
238 Stephen Weiss .05 .15
239 Pavel Kubina .05 .15
240 Luc Robitaille .12 .30
241 Michal Rozsival .05 .15
242 Martin Gelinas .05 .15
243 Curtis Brown .05 .15
244 Steve Passmore .05 .15
245 Tony Hrkac .05 .15
246 Alexei Yashin .05 .15
247 Richard Park .05 .15
248 Viktor Kozlov .05 .15
249 Andrei Markov .05 .15
250 Dan Boyle .05 .15
251 Paul Mara .05 .15
252 Jeremy Roenick .20 .50
253 Randy McKay .05 .15
254 Tommy Salo .12 .30
255 Jaroslav Spacek .05 .15
256 Adam Foote .12 .30
257 Martin Erat .05 .15
258 Jamal Mayers .05 .15
259 Chris Neil .05 .15
260 Mark Bell .05 .15
261 Matt Bradley .05 .15
262 Boris Mironov .05 .15
263 Trevor Kidd .12 .30
264 Dave Andreychuk .05 .15
265 Jaroslav Modry .05 .15
266 Vaclav Varada .05 .15
267 Marty Murray .05 .15
268 Ben Clymer .05 .15
269 Mikael Renberg .05 .15
270 Sean Hill .05 .15
271 Eric Belanger .05 .15
272 Andy McDonald .05 .15
273 Miikka Kiprusoff .12 .30
274 Brad May .05 .15
275 Dan LaCouture .05 .15
276 Andy Sutton .05 .15
277 Kirk Maltby .05 .15
278 Kirk Muller .05 .15
279 Alex Tanguay .12 .30
280 Bryan Marchment .05 .15
281 Jason Smith .05 .15
282 Dan Bylsma .05 .15
283 Jyrki Lumme .05 .15
284 Chris Gratton .05 .15
285 Chris Clark .05 .15
286 Scott Walker .05 .15
287 Alexander Khavanov .05 .15
288 Marc Chouinard .05 .15
289 Rob DiMaio .05 .15
290 Sean Avery .05 .15
291 Tommy Albelin .05 .15
292 Jean-Francois Fortin .05 .15
293 Matthew Barnaby .05 .15
294 Jan Hrdina .05 .15
295 Harold Druken .05 .15
296 Jody Hull .05 .15
297 Shjon Podein .05 .15
298 Jochen Hecht .05 .15
299 Glen Murray .05 .15
300 Sergei Brylin .05 .15
301 Pavel Bure .15 .40
302 Mike Comrie .12 .30
303 Mario Lemieux 1.00 2.50
304 Mats Sundin .15 .40
305 Jason Blake .05 .15
306 Robert Lang .05 .15
307 Bill Guerin .12 .30
308 Brad Richards .12 .30
309 Radek Bonk .05 .15
310 Craig Conroy .05 .15
311 Brett Hull .20 .50
312 Dainius Zubrus .05 .15
313 Petr Sykora .05 .15
314 Craig Rivet .05 .15
315 Andrew Brunette .05 .15
316 Kristian Huselius .05 .15
317 Rod Brind'Amour .12 .30
318 Tim Connolly .05 .15
319 Anson Carter .12 .30
320 Cory Stillman .05 .15
321 Teppo Numminen .05 .15
322 Jason Arnott .05 .15
323 Oleg Petrov .05 .15
324 Shawn McEachern .05 .15
325 Scott Thornton .05 .15
326 Oleg Kvasha .05 .15
327 Byron Dafoe .12 .30
328 Glen Wesley .05 .15
329 Eric Messier .05 .15
330 Brad Lukowich .05 .15
331 Jon Klemm .05 .15
332 Tomas Vokoun .12 .30
333 Scott Hannan .05 .15
334 Mike Eastwood .05 .15
335 Peter Skudra .05 .15
336 Roman Hamrlik .05 .15
337 Josef Vasicek .05 .15
338 Bryan McCabe .05 .15
339 Igor Larionov .05 .15
340 Darryl Sydor .05 .15
341 Mike Fisher .05 .15
342 Greg Johnson .05 .15
343 Danny Markov .05 .15
344 Frantisek Kaberle .05 .15
345 Michal Grosek .05 .15
346 Ivan Novoseltsev .05 .15
347 Marty McInnis .05 .15
348 Eric Desjardins .05 .15
349 Jason Wiemer .05 .15
350 Fredrik Olausson .05 .15
351 Bill Muckalt .05 .15
352 Ville Nieminen .05 .15
353 Taylor Pyatt .05 .15
354 Mike Rathje .05 .15
355 Trent Klatt .05 .15
356 Bret Hedican .05 .15

357 Tyler Wright .05 .15
358 Greg deVries .05 .15
359 Lubomir Sekeras .05 .15
360 Jonas Hoglund .05 .15
361 Mike Grier .05 .15
362 Wade Redden .05 .15
363 Nik Antropov .05 .15
364 Philippe Boucher .05 .15
365 Clarke Wilm .05 .15
366 Erik Rasmussen .05 .15
367 Per Svartvadet .05 .15
368 Felix Potvin .15 .40
369 Igor Korolev .05 .15
370 Vladimir Malakhov .05 .15
371 Mathieu Dandenault .05 .15
372 Brent Johnson .12 .30
373 Shaun Van Allen .05 .15
374 Scott Pellerin .05 .15
375 Radim Vrbata .05 .15
376 Mike Johnson .05 .15
377 Mikael Samuelsson .05 .15
378 Radek Martinek .05 .15
379 Curtis Joseph .15 .40
380 Craig Johnson .05 .15
381 Kelly Buchberger .05 .15
382 Todd Harvey .05 .15
383 Jason Chimera .05 .15
384 Claude Lapointe .05 .15
385 Marc Denis .12 .30
386 Lyle Odelein .05 .15
387 Dimitri Kalinin .05 .15
388 Scott Nichol .05 .15
389 Tom Fitzgerald .05 .15
390 Darius Kasparaitis .12 .30
391 Bryan Allen .05 .15
392 Jamie McLennan .05 .15
393 Martin St. Louis .12 .30
394 Landon Wilson .05 .15
395 Kim Johnsson .05 .15
396 Pavel Trnka .05 .15
397 P.J. Stock .05 .15
398 Alexandre Daigle .05 .15
399 Andrew Cassels .05 .15
400 Wayne Primeau .05 .15
401 Theo Fleury .05 .15
402 Cliff Ronning .05 .15
403 Sergei Samsonov .12 .30
404 Jean-Francois Labbe .12 .30
405 Darcy Tucker .05 .15
406 Daniel Briere .05 .15
407 Marc Savard .05 .15
408 Blake Sloan .05 .15
409 Sergei Berezin .05 .15
410 Ron Tugnutt .12 .30
411 Jocelyn Thibault .12 .30
412 Jose Theodore .20 .50
413 Sheldon Keefe .05 .15
414 Yanic Perreault .05 .15
415 Jason Krog .05 .15
416 John Madden .05 .15
417 Jonathan Girard .05 .15
418 Niclas Havelid .05 .15
419 Daniel Alfredsson .15 .40
420 Dean McAmmond .05 .15
421 Brenden Morrow .12 .30
422 Dimitri Yushkevich .05 .15
423 Alexei Zhitnik .05 .15
424 Jani Hurme .12 .30
425 Antti Laaksonen .05 .15
426 Corey Schwab .12 .30
427 Geoff Sanderson .05 .15
428 Brian Leetch .12 .30
429 Brad Tapper .05 .15
430 Derek Armstrong .05 .15
431 Evgeni Nabokov .12 .30
432 Jan Hlavac .05 .15
433 Bob Boughner .05 .15
434 Andreas Johansson .05 .15
435 Jeff Odgers .05 .15
436 Teemu Selanne .15 .40
437 Pavol Demitra .05 .15
438 Tomas Holmstrom .05 .15
439 Jeff Friesen .05 .15
440 Eric Boulton .05 .15
441 Oleg Saprykin .05 .15
442 Chris Chelios .15 .40
443 Stephane Yelle .05 .15
444 Martin Havlat .12 .30
445 Jeff O'Neill .05 .15
446 Dan Cloutier .12 .30
447 Nikolai Khabibulin .15 .40
448 Grant Marshall .05 .15
449 Pierre Turgeon .12 .30
450 Jamie Langenbrunner .12 .30
451 Steve Staios .05 .15
452 Alexei Morozov .05 .15
453 Shawn Horcoff .05 .15
454 Adam Mair .05 .15
455 Ruslan Salei .05 .15
456 Robert Esche .05 .15
457 Brent Sopel .05 .15
458 Aaron Ward .05 .15
459 Martin Biron .12 .30
460 Brian Boucher .12 .30
461 Richard Jackman .05 .15
462 Jarkko Ruutu .05 .15
463 Bates Battaglia .05 .15
464 Sergei Gonchar .05 .15
465 Martin Brodeur .40 1.00
466 Patrick Stefan .05 .15
467 Scott Stevens .12 .30
468 Gary Roberts .05 .15
469 Shane Doan .05 .15
470 Keith Tkachuk .15 .40
471 Brendan Witt .05 .15
472 Todd Fedoruk .05 .15
473 Patrick Lalime .12 .30
474 Mike Dunham .12 .30
475 Ulf Dahlen .05 .15
476 Olli Jokinen .12 .30
477 Garth Snow .05 .15
478 Sean Pronger .05 .15
479 Milan Kraft .05 .15
480 Aki Berg .05 .15
481 Steve Shields .12 .30
482 Sami Salo .05 .15
483 Brendan Shanahan .15 .40
484 Niclas Wallin .05 .15
485 Sandy McCarthy .05 .15
486 Olaf Kolzig .12 .30
487 Cory Sarich .05 .15
488 Zac Bierk .12 .30
489 Luke Richardson .05 .15
490 Colin White .05 .15
491 Reed Low .05 .15
492 Joe Thornton .25 .60
493 Rob Blake .12 .30
494 Bobby Holik .05 .15
495 Chris Simon .05 .15
496 Wade Belak .05 .15
497 Eric Daze .05 .15
498 Hal Gill .05 .15
499 Chris Pronger .12 .30
500 Steve Yzerman .75 2.00
501 Justin Papineau .05 .15
502 Alex Auld .05 .15
503 Niko Kapanen .05 .15
504 Michael Cammalleri .05 .15
505 Sebastien Charpentier .05 .15
506 Stanislav Chistov .50 1.25
507 Jiri Bicek .05 .15
508 Ryan Flinn .05 .15
509 Christian Berglund .05 .15
510 Vernon Fiddler .05 .15
511 Andrej Nedorost .05 .15
512 Lynn Loyns .05 .15
513 Niko Dimitrakos .05 .15
514 Ryan Bayda .05 .15
515 Curtis Sanford .05 .15
516 Pierre-Marc Bouchard .50 1.25
517 Sebastien Caron .12 .30
518 Steve Ott .30 .75
519 Dan Snyder .05 .15
520 Mattias Weinhandl .05 .15
521 Henrik Zetterberg .75 2.00
522 Tomas Surovy .05 .15
523 Ales Hemsky .75 2.00
524 Jamie Lundmark .05 .15
525 Barret Jackman .12 .30
526 Toni Dahlman .05 .15
527 Jaroslav Bednar .05 .15
528 Ales Pisa .05 .15
529 Joel Kwiatkowski .05 .15
530 Jan Lasak .05 .15
531 Jim Fahey .05 .15
532 Pavel Brendl .05 .15
533 Stephane Veilleux .05 .15
534 Vaclav Nedorost .05 .15
535 Tomas Malec .05 .15
536 Jeff Heerema .05 .15
537 Dmitri Bykov .05 .15
538 Dennis Seidenberg .05 .15
539 Jonathan Cheechoo .08 .20
540 Fernando Pisani .05 .15
541 Riku Hahl .05 .15
542 Jani Rita .05 .15
543 Jim Vandermeer .05 .15
544 Jordan Leopold .05 .15
545 Joe Corvo .05 .15
546 Ales Kotalik .05 .15
547 Ryan Miller .50 1.25
548 Tomas Kurka .05 .15
549 Arturs Irbe .12 .30
550 Radovan Somik .05 .15
551 Mathieu Garon .12 .30
552 Jesse Wallin .05 .15
553 Steve Eminger .05 .15
554 Jason Bacashihua .40 1.00
555 Ramzi Abid .05 .15
556 Marcel Hossa .05 .15
557 Rick Nash .75 2.00
558 Kris Vernarsky .05 .15
559 Brian Sutherby .05 .15
560 Adam Hall .05 .15
561 Eric Chouinard .05 .15
562 Henrik Tallinder .05 .15
563 Alexander Svitov .05 .15
564 Kurt Sauer .05 .15
565 Matt Walker .05 .15
566 Ray Emery .60 1.50
567 Eric Godard .05 .15
568 Jay Bouwmeester .60 1.50
569 Kip Brennan .05 .15
570 Mike Komisarek .05 .15
571 Alex Henry .05 .15
572 Scottie Upshall .30 .75
573 Chuck Kobasew .30 .75
574 Anton Volchenkov .05 .15
575 Carlo Colaiacovo .30 .75
576 Pascal Leclaire .50 1.25
577 Jason Spezza 1.00 2.50
578 Jeff Taffe .05 .15
579 Alexander Frolov .50 1.25
580 Shaone Morrisonn .05 .15
581 Ron Hainsey .05 .15
582 Alexei Smirnov .05 .15
583 Andrew Raycroft .05 .15
584 Brooks Orpik .05 .15
585 Dan Focht .05 .15
586 Fedor Fedorov .05 .15
587 Ivan Huml .05 .15
588 Jared Aulin .05 .15
589 Justin Mapletoft .05 .15
590 Karel Pilar .05 .15
591 Kyle Wanvig .05 .15
592 Lee Goren .05 .15
593 Cristobal Huet 1.00 2.50
594 Mikael Tellqvist .12 .30
595 Igor Radulov .05 .15
596 Kirill Safronov .05 .15
597 Jerred Smithson .05 .15
598 Vesa Toskala .05 .15
599 Dick Tarnstrom .05 .15
600 Martin Gerber .12 .30

2003-04 Pacific Complete

This 600-card super set was inserted into various Pacific products throughout the season. A red parallel set was also created and available randomly.

*RED: 6X TO 15X BASE HI
*RED ROOKIES: 3X TO 8X
RED PRINT RUN 99 SER.#'d SETS

1 Donald Brashear .05 .15
2 Chris Gratton .05 .15
3 Alyn McCauley .05 .15
4 Mats Sundin .15 .40
5 Brenden Morrow .12 .30
6 Jaroslav Modry .05 .15
7 Brian Rafalski .05 .15
8 Mike Grier .05 .15
9 Marco Sturm .05 .15
10 Mike Comrie .12 .30
11 Derek Morris .05 .15
12 Scott Niedermayer .05 .15
13 Dainius Zubrus .05 .15
14 Jason Krog .05 .15
15 Brian Rolston .05 .15
16 Dany Heatley .20 .50
17 Dean McAmmond .05 .15
18 Glen Murray .05 .15
19 Adam Mair .05 .15
20 Tony Amonte .12 .30
21 David Vyborny .05 .15
22 Tyler Wright .05 .15
23 Doug Gilmour .12 .30
24 Andy Sutton .05 .15
25 Ivan Huml .05 .15
26 Olli Jokinen .12 .30
27 Kimmo Timonen .05 .15
28 Donald Audette .05 .15
29 Martin St. Louis .12 .30
30 Martin Skoula .05 .15
31 Wade Redden .05 .15
32 Kyle Calder .05 .15
33 Shawn Bates .05 .15
34 Brendan Shanahan .05 .15
35 Martin Havlat .12 .30
36 Radim Vrbata .05 .15
37 Eric Daze .12 .30
38 J-P Dumont .05 .15
39 Scott Mellanby .05 .15
40 Brad Richards .12 .30
41 Jason Allison .05 .15
42 Rostislav Klesla .05 .15
43 Tyler Arnason .12 .30
44 Henrik Sedin .05 .15
45 Markus Naslund .15 .40
46 Daniel Sedin .05 .15
47 Niklas Sundstrom .05 .15
48 Rod Brind'Amour .12 .30
49 Martin Straka .05 .15
50 Craig Conroy .05 .15
51 Tomas Kaberle .05 .15
52 Robyn Regehr .05 .15
53 Scott Hartnell .05 .15
54 Sergei Zholtok .05 .15
55 Pierre Turgeon .12 .30
56 Mike Ricci .05 .15
57 Brad Tapper .05 .15
58 Martin Gelinas .05 .15
59 Philippe Boucher .05 .15
60 Alex Tanguay .12 .30
61 Niclas Havelid .05 .15
62 Kristian Huselius .05 .15
63 Dave Lowry .05 .15
64 Tim Connolly .12 .30
65 Robert Lang .05 .15
66 Taylor Pyatt .05 .15
67 Bryan Smolinski .05 .15
68 Keith Primeau .12 .30
69 Anson Carter .12 .30
70 Dallas Drake .05 .15
71 Curtis Brown .05 .15
72 Nik Antropov .05 .15
73 Aaron Ward .05 .15
74 Tie Domi .12 .30
75 Mike Leclerc .05 .15
76 Tom Poti .05 .15
77 Kris Draper .05 .15
78 Joe Juneau .05 .15
79 Milan Kraft .05 .15
80 Marty Reasoner .05 .15
81 Shaun Van Allen .05 .15
82 Kenny Jonsson .05 .15
83 Alexander Khavanov .05 .15
84 Pavel Kubina .05 .15
85 Vladimir Malakhov .05 .15
86 Willie Mitchell .05 .15
87 Jason Smith .05 .15
88 Radoslav Suchy .05 .15
89 Mattias Timander .05 .15
90 Eric Weinrich .05 .15
91 Andrei Zyuzin .05 .15
92 Christian Berglund .05 .15
93 Jamie Lundmark .05 .15
94 Kirk Maltby .05 .15
95 Brian Savage .05 .15
96 Petr Schastlivy .05 .15
97 Ian Laperriere .05 .15
98 Alexei Morozov .05 .15
99 Justin Williams .05 .15
100 Jason Chimera .05 .15
101 Patrick Marleau .12 .30
102 Ryan Smyth .05 .15
103 Michal Handzus .05 .15
104 Brett Hull .20 .50
105 Tom Fitzgerald .05 .15
106 Ben Clymer .05 .15
107 Rick Nash .20 .50
108 Scott Walker .05 .15
109 Rob Niedermayer .05 .15
110 Sergei Gonchar .05 .15
111 Chris Chelios .15 .40
112 Brian Leetch .12 .30
113 David Legwand .12 .30
114 Sean Hill .05 .15
115 Brad Isbister .05 .15
116 Pavel Datsyuk .15 .40
117 Alexei Yashin .05 .15
118 Jere Lehtinen .12 .30
119 Jason Spezza .15 .40
120 Daniel Briere .05 .15
121 Andreas Dackell .05 .15
122 Shane Doan .05 .15
123 Josef Vasicek .05 .15
124 Dan McGillis .05 .15
125 Geoff Sanderson .05 .15
126 Teemu Selanne .15 .40
127 Andreas Johansson .05 .15
128 Al MacInnis .12 .30
129 Ruslan Fedotenko .05 .15
130 Scott Stevens .12 .30
131 Frantisek Kaberle .05 .15
132 Toni Lydman .05 .15
133 Kip Miller .05 .15
134 Dan Hinote .05 .15
135 Mike Modano .25 .60
136 Scott Thornton .05 .15
137 Eric Lindros .15 .40
138 Grant Marshall .05 .15
139 Vincent Damphousse .05 .15
140 Mario Lemieux 1.00 2.50
141 Patrice Brisebois .05 .15
142 Sergei Samsonov .12 .30
143 Sergei Zubov .05 .15
144 Alexei Zhamnov .05 .15
145 Oleg Kvasha .05 .15
146 Brendan Morrison .12 .30
147 Jason York .05 .15
148 Eric Boguniecki .05 .15
149 Henrik Zetterberg .15 .40
150 Nick Boynton .05 .15
151 Trevor Linden .05 .15
152 Joe Nieuwendyk .12 .30
153 Filip Kuba .05 .15
154 Matthew Barnaby .05 .15
155 Ales Hemsky .12 .30
156 Jan Bulis .05 .15
157 Yannick Tremblay .05 .15
158 Andre Roy .05 .15
159 Jaroslav Bednar .05 .15
160 Stephane Yelle .05 .15
161 Paul Mara .05 .15
162 Sandis Ozolinsh .05 .15
163 Trent Klatt .05 .15
164 Brian Gionta .05 .15
165 Jaroslav Spacek .05 .15
166 Rob Blake .12 .30
167 Ziggy Palffy .12 .30
168 Chris Clark .05 .15
169 John LeClair .15 .40
170 Landon Wilson .05 .15
171 Mark Bell .05 .15
172 Simon Gagne .15 .40
173 Michael Nylander .05 .15
174 Andy McDonald .05 .15
175 Todd Bertuzzi .15 .40
176 Dick Tarnstrom .05 .15
177 Radek Dvorak .05 .15
178 Antti Laaksonen .05 .15
179 Steve Rucchin .05 .15
180 Steve Sullivan .05 .15
181 Viktor Kozlov .05 .15
182 Miroslav Satan .12 .30
183 Lubomir Visnovsky .05 .15
184 Stephen Weiss .05 .15
185 John Madden .05 .15
186 Mike Knuble .05 .15
187 Michael Peca .05 .15
188 Adam Foote .05 .15
189 Steve McKenna .05 .15
190 Adam Deadmarsh .05 .15
191 Barret Jackman .12 .30
192 Marian Gaborik .30 .75
193 Zdeno Chara .05 .15
194 Chris Drury .12 .30
195 Sami Salo .05 .15
196 Daniel Tjarnqvist .05 .15
197 Vaclav Varada .05 .15
198 Shawn McEachern .05 .15
199 Kevyn Adams .05 .15
200 Roman Hamrlik .05 .15
201 Keith Carney .05 .15
202 Scott Gomez .05 .15
203 Marcus Nilsson .05 .15
204 Tomas Surovy .05 .15
205 Vladimir Orszagh .05 .15
206 Owen Nolan .12 .30
207 Matt Cooke .05 .15
208 Jeremy Roenick .20 .50
209 Andrew Cassels .05 .15
210 Jim Dowd .05 .15
211 Todd Marchant .05 .15
212 Joe Sakic .30 .75
213 Krystofer Kolanos .05 .15
214 Chris Phillips .05 .15
215 Stanislav Chistov .05 .15
216 Steve Yzerman .75 2.00
217 Jamie Langenbrunner .05 .15
218 Daymond Langkow .12 .30
219 Jarome Iginla .20 .50
220 Darryl Sydor .05 .15
221 Mark Messier .15 .40
222 Richard Matvichuk .05 .15
223 Jay Bouwmeester .05 .15
224 Sheldon Souray .05 .15
225 Niklas Hagman .05 .15
226 Bill Lindsay .05 .15
227 Ray Whitney .05 .15
228 Jordan Leopold .05 .15
229 Daniel Alfredsson .12 .30
230 Kyle McLaren .05 .15
231 Vincent Lecavalier .15 .40
232 Bobby Holik .05 .15
233 Adam Hall .05 .15
234 Mark Recchi .05 .15
235 Alexander Mogilny .12 .30
236 Alexei Zhitnik .05 .15
237 Jay McKee .05 .15
238 Jaromir Jagr .25 .60
239 Ladislav Nagy .05 .15
240 Radek Bonk .12 .30
241 Mike Van Ryn .05 .15
242 Joe Thornton .20 .50
243 Peter Bondra .12 .30
244 Keith Tkachuk .15 .40
245 Luc Robitaille .12 .30
246 Alexandre Daigle .05 .15
247 Jason Blake .05 .15
248 Jonathan Cheechoo .08 .20
249 Alexander Frolov .05 .15
250 Danny Markov .05 .15
251 Oleg Saprykin .05 .15
252 Maxim Afinogenov .05 .15
253 Alexander Karpovtsev .05 .15
254 Peter Forsberg .60 1.50
255 Espen Knutsen .05 .15
256 Erik Cole .05 .15
257 Dan Boyle .05 .15
258 Marc Savard .05 .15
259 Adrian Aucoin .05 .15
260 Brian Holzinger .05 .15
261 Cory Stillman .05 .15
262 Mattias Ohlund .05 .15
263 Petr Sykora .12 .30
264 Jeff Halpern .05 .15
265 Patrik Stefan .05 .15
266 Jeff Jillson .05 .15
267 Mariusz Czerkawski .05 .15
268 Jeff O'Neill .05 .15
269 Brad Stuart .05 .15
270 Ron Francis .12 .30
271 Mike Johnson .05 .15
272 Richard Park .05 .15
273 Yanic Perreault .05 .15
274 Eric Belanger .05 .15
275 Stu Barnes .05 .15
276 Nathan Dempsey .05 .15
277 Bryan McCabe .05 .15
278 Andrew Brunette .05 .15
279 Ville Nieminen .05 .15
280 Greg Johnson .05 .15
281 Alex Kovalev .12 .30
282 Raffi Torres .05 .15
283 Drake Berehowsky .05 .15
284 Steve McCarthy .05 .15
285 Martin Erat .05 .15
286 Pavol Demitra .12 .30
287 Saku Koivu .15 .40
288 Milan Hejduk .15 .40
289 Sami Kapanen .12 .30
290 Nicklas Lidstrom .15 .40
291 Eric Brewer .05 .15
292 Martin Lapointe .05 .15
293 Andrei Markov .05 .15
294 Doug Weight .12 .30
295 Jason Arnott .12 .30
296 Mike York .05 .15
297 Jay Pandolfo .05 .15
298 Ed Jovanovski .12 .30
299 Bill Guerin .12 .30
300 Petr Cajanek .05 .15
301 Shawn Horcoff .05 .15
302 Ales Kotalik .05 .15
303 Chris Dingman .05 .15
304 Arron Asham .05 .15
305 Steve Staios .05 .15
306 Artem Chubarov .05 .15
307 Karlis Skrastins .05 .15
308 Nick Schultz .05 .15
309 Rico Fata .05 .15
310 Jan Hrdina .05 .15
311 Brendan Witt .05 .15
312 Lyle Odelein .05 .15
313 Pascal Dupuis .05 .15
314 Paul Kariya .15 .40
315 Petr Nedved .05 .15
316 Tim Taylor .05 .15
317 Ethan Moreau .05 .15
318 Shean Donovan .05 .15
319 Ruslan Salei .05 .15
320 Rem Murray .05 .15
321 Eric Nickulas .05 .15
322 Rob DiMaio .05 .15
323 Steven Reinprecht .05 .15
324 Cory Cross .05 .15
325 Kim Johnsson .05 .15
326 Chris Simon .05 .15
327 Gary Roberts .05 .15
328 Ken Klee .05 .15
329 Krzysztof Oliwa .05 .15
330 Marian Hossa .15 .40
331 Valeri Bure .05 .15
332 Bret Hedican .05 .15
333 Pavel Trnka .05 .15
334 Darcy Tucker .05 .15
335 Peter Schaefer .05 .15
336 Sergei Brylin .05 .15
337 Hal Gill .05 .15
338 Jason Woolley .05 .15
339 Mike Rathje .05 .15
340 Marty Murray .05 .15
341 Todd White .05 .15
342 Brent Sopel .05 .15
343 Glen Wesley .05 .15
344 Jozef Stumpel .05 .15
345 Scott Nichol .05 .15
346 Derrick Walser .05 .15
347 Marc Bergevin .05 .15
348 Richard Zednik .05 .15
349 Mike Ribeiro .05 .15
350 Mike Eastwood .05 .15
351 Trevor Letowski .05 .15
352 Fredrik Modin .05 .15
353 Mark Parrish .05 .15
354 Sandy McCarthy .05 .15
355 Tomas Holmstrom .05 .15
356 Dmitri Kalinin .05 .15
357 Janne Niinimaa .05 .15
358 Dave Andreychuk .12 .30
359 Boyd Devereaux .05 .15
360 Sergei Fedorov .20 .50
361 Josef Melichar .05 .15
362 Stephane Quintal .05 .15
363 Lasse Pirjeta .05 .15
364 Denis Arkhipov .05 .15
365 Matt Cullen .05 .15
366 Teppo Numminen .05 .15
367 Ilya Kovalchuk .20 .50
368 Reed Low .05 .15
369 Jochen Hecht .05 .15
370 Martin Rucinsky .05 .15
371 Mark Eaton .05 .15
372 Nils Ekman .05 .15
373 Slava Kozlov .05 .15
374 Scott Young .05 .15
375 Mathieu Schneider .05 .15
376 Scott Hannan .05 .15
377 Brad May .05 .15
378 Jeff Friesen .05 .15
379 P.J. Axelsson .05 .15
380 Brian Sutherby .05 .15
381 David Tanabe .05 .15
382 Pierre-Marc Bouchard .05 .15
383 Steve Konowalchuk .05 .15
384 Chris Pronger .12 .30
385 Craig Rivet .05 .15
386 Eric Desjardins .05 .15
387 Jody Shelley .05 .15
388 Vaclav Prospal .05 .15
389 Aaron Miller .05 .15
390 Deron Quint .05 .15
391 Joel Kwiatkowski .05 .15
392 Branko Radivojevic .05 .15
393 Niko Kapanen .05 .15
394 Wayne Primeau .05 .15
395 Patrik Elias .12 .30
396 Ronald Petrovicky .05 .15
397 Mike Cammalleri .05 .15
398 Bryan Berard .05 .15
399 Jason Doig .05 .15
400 Marcus Ragnarsson .05 .15
401 Aaron Downey .05 .15
402 Byron Dafoe .12 .30
403 J-S Giguere .12 .30
404 Dwayne Roloson .12 .30
405 Marc-Andre Fleury 2.50 6.00
406 Ray Emery .12 .30
407 Derek Armstrong .05 .15
408 Randy Robitaille .05 .15
409 Manny Fernandez .12 .30
410 Jeff Hackett .12 .30
411 Nikolai Khabibulin .15 .40
412 Tomas Vokoun .12 .30
413 Chris Neil .05 .15
414 Andrei Nikolishin .05 .15
415 Garth Snow .12 .30
416 Marty Turco .12 .30
417 Roberto Luongo .20 .50
418 Mikael Tellqvist .12 .30
419 Chris Osgood .12 .30
420 Jocelyn Thibault .12 .30
421 Olaf Kolzig .12 .30
422 Tommy Salo .12 .30
423 Corey Schwab .12 .30
424 Johan Hedberg .12 .30
425 Travis Green .05 .15
426 Pascal Leclaire .12 .30
427 Craig Andersson .12 .30
428 John Grahame .12 .30
429 Pasi Nurminen .12 .30
430 Trevor Kidd .12 .30
431 Scott Lachance .12 .30
432 Brent Johnson .12 .30
433 Jamie Storr .12 .30
434 Miikka Kiprusoff .12 .30
435 Cristobal Huet .12 .30
436 Jose Theodore .20 .50
437 Ty Conklin .12 .30
438 Curtis Joseph .15 .40
439 Jussi Markkanen .12 .30
440 Patrick Lalime .12 .30
441 Vesa Toskala .12 .30
442 Dan Cloutier .12 .30
443 Kevin Weekes .12 .30
444 Peter Worrell .05 .15
445 Zac Bierk .12 .30
446 Evgeni Nabokov .12 .30
447 Martin Biron .12 .30
448 Rick DiPietro .12 .30
449 Ed Belfour .15 .40
450 Martin Gerber .12 .30
451 Reinhard Divis .12 .30
452 Brian Finley .12 .30
453 Jason Bacashihua .12 .30
454 Mika Noronen .12 .30
455 Scott Clemmensen .12 .30
456 Brian Boucher .12 .30
457 Jason LaBarbera .12 .30
458 Mike Dunham .12 .30
459 Sean Burke .12 .30
460 Felix Potvin .15 .40
461 Martin Brodeur .75 2.00
462 Sebastien Caron .12 .30
463 Rob Zamuner .05 .15
464 Igor Larionov .05 .15
465 Andrew Raycroft .05 .15
466 Mathieu Garon .05 .15
467 Roman Turek .12 .30
468 Steve Passmore .12 .30
469 Chris Mason .05 .15
470 Jean-Sebastien Aubin .12 .30
471 Milan Hnilicka .12 .30
472 Steve Shields .12 .30
473 Arturs Irbe .12 .30
474 Ilja Bryzgalov .12 .30
475 Roman Cechmanek .12 .30
476 Steve Ott .05 .15
477 Mattias Weinhandl .05 .15
478 Brent Krahn .05 .15
479 Jamie McLennan .12 .30
480 Michael Leighton .12 .30
481 Ryan Miller .12 .30
482 Dominik Hasek .30 .75
483 Marc Denis .12 .30
484 Rastislav Stana .12 .30
485 Alex Auld .12 .30
486 Fred Brathwaite .12 .30
487 Martin Prusek .12 .30
488 Robert Esche .12 .30
489 Sebastien Charpentier .12 .30
490 David Aebischer .12 .30
491 Manny Legace .12 .30
492 Philippe Sauve .12 .30
493 Bob Boughner .05 .15
494 Maxime Ouellet .12 .30
495 Ron Tugnutt .12 .30
496 J.P. Vigier .05 .15
497 Steve Thomas .12 .30
498 Manny Malhotra .05 .15
499 Dany Sabourin .05 .15
500 Pavel Brendl .05 .15
501 Derek Roy .40 1.00
502 Lawrence Nycholat .20 .50
503 Simon Gamache .20 .50
504 Dan Fritsche .20 .50
505 Chris Higgins 1.25 3.00
506 Pierre Hedin .20 .50
507 Marc-Andre Fleury 2.50 6.00
508 Tony Salmelainen .20 .50
509 Ryan Kesler .40 1.00
510 John-Michael Liles .40 1.00
511 Zbynek Michalek .20 .50
512 Trent Hunter .20 .50
513 Matthew Lombardi .20 .50
514 Matt Stajan 1.00 2.50
515 Gregory Campbell .20 .50
516 Chad Wiseman .20 .50
517 Konstantin Koltsov .20 .50
518 Joffrey Lupul .60 1.50
519 Jeff MacMillan .20 .50
520 Wade Brookbank .20 .50
521 Timofei Shishkanov .20 .50
522 Eric Staal 2.00 5.00
523 Nathan Horton 1.00 2.50
524 Julien Vauclair .20 .50
525 Tom Preissing .20 .50
526 Kent McDonell .20 .50
527 Antoine Vermette .20 .50
528 Anton Babchuk .20 .50
529 Grant McNeill .20 .50
530 Chris Hajt .20 .50
531 Burke Henry .20 .50
532 Kyle Rossiter .20 .50
533 Joni Pitkanen .40 1.00
534 Maxim Kondratiev .20 .50
535 Peter Sejna .20 .50
536 Sergei Zinovjev .20 .50
537 Nathan Robinson .20 .50
538 Tuomas Pihlman .20 .50
539 Lasse Kukkonen .20 .50
540 Tomas Plekanec .20 .50
541 Alexander Semin 1.25 3.00
542 Fredrik Sjostrom .20 .50
543 Kari Lehtonen 3.00 8.00
544 Matt Murley .20 .50
545 Dustin Brown .30 .75
546 Tuomo Ruutu 1.25 3.00
547 Dominic Moore .20 .50
548 Garnet Exelby .20 .50
549 Dan Hamhuis .30 .75
550 Ryan Malone 1.00 2.50
551 Milan Michalek 1.00 2.50
552 Aaron Johnson .20 .50
553 Matthew Spiller .20 .50
554 Christian Ehrhoff .20 .50
555 Doug Lynch .20 .50
556 Andrew Peters .20 .50
557 Aleksander Suglobov .20 .50
558 Chuck Kobasew .20 .50
559 Sean Bergenheim .20 .50
560 Jason Pominville .60 1.50
561 Andrew Hutchinson .20 .50
562 Garrett Burnett .20 .50
563 Nikolai Zherdev 1.25 3.00
564 Tony Martensson .20 .50
565 Antti Miettinen .20 .50
566 Scott Barney .20 .50
567 Jordin Tootoo 1.25 3.00
568 Brad Leeb .20 .50
569 Peter Sarno .20 .50
570 Jed Ortmeyer .40 1.00
571 Kyle Wellwood 1.00 2.50
572 Brent Krahn .40 1.00
573 Dmitri Afanasenkov .20 .50
574 Jarret Stoll .20 .50
575 Marek Zidlicky .20 .50
576 Karl Stewart .20 .50
577 Darryl Bootland .20 .50
578 Niklas Kronwall .20 .50
579 Paul Martin .20 .50
580 Adam Munro .20 .50
581 Pat Leahy .20 .50
582 Cody McCormick .20 .50
583 Jozef Balej .20 .50
584 Boyd Gordon .20 .50
585 Jason King .20 .50
586 Trevor Daley .40 1.00
587 Robert Schnabel .20 .50
588 Chris Kunitz .40 1.00
589 Mike Danton .05 .15
590 Mikhail Yakubov .20 .50
591 John Pohl .40 1.00
592 Brent Burns .40 1.00
593 Patrice Bergeron 1.50 4.00
594 Jiri Hudler .75 2.00
595 David Hale .20 .50
596 Travis Moen .40 1.00
597 Michael Ryder .40 1.00
598 Tim Gleason .20 .50
599 Christian Backman .40 1.00
600 Pavel Vorobiev .20 .50

1997-98 Pacific Dynagon

The 1997-98 Pacific Dynagon set was issued in one series totaling 156 cards and was distributed in three-card packs with a suggested retail price of $2.49. The fronts feature color action player photos printed on fully foiled and double etched cards. The backs carry a small circular player head photo and player information.

COMPLETE SET (156) 25.00 60.00
1 Brian Bellows .20 .50
2 Guy Hebert .30 .75
3 Paul Kariya .40 1.00
4 Steve Rucchin .20 .50
5 Teemu Selanne .40 1.00
6 Jason Allison .20 .50
7 Ray Bourque .60 1.50
8 Jim Carey .20 .50
9 Jozef Stumpel .20 .50
10 Dominik Hasek 1.00 2.50
11 Brian Holzinger .20 .50
12 Michael Peca .20 .50
13 Derek Plante .20 .50
14 Miroslav Satan .20 .50
15 Theo Fleury .20 .50
16 Jonas Hoglund .20 .50
17 Jarome Iginla .60 1.50
18 Trevor Kidd .30 .75
19 German Titov .20 .50
20 Sean Burke .30 .75
21 Andrew Cassels .20 .50
22 Keith Primeau .20 .50

23 Geoff Sanderson .20 .50
24 Tony Amonte .30 .75
25 Chris Chelios .40 1.00
26 Eric Daze .20 .50
27 Jeff Hackett .30 .75
28 Ethan Moreau .20 .50
29 Peter Forsberg .75 2.00
30 Valeri Kamensky .20 .50
31 Claude Lemieux .20 .50
32 Sandis Ozolinsh .20 .50
33 Patrick Roy 1.50 4.00
34 Joe Sakic 1.00 2.50
35 Derian Hatcher .20 .50
36 Jamie Langenbrunner .20 .50
37 Mike Modano .60 1.50
38 Joe Nieuwendyk .30 .75
39 Darryl Sydor .20 .50
40 Sergei Zubov .20 .50
41 Sergei Fedorov .60 1.50
42 Vladimir Konstantinov .30 .75
43 Chris Osgood .30 .75
44 Brendan Shanahan .40 1.00
45 Mike Vernon .30 .75
46 Steve Yzerman 1.25 3.00
47 Kelly Buchberger .20 .50
48 Mike Grier .20 .50
49 Curtis Joseph .40 1.00
50 Rem Murray .20 .50
51 Ryan Smyth .30 .75
52 Doug Weight .30 .75
53 Ed Jovanovski .20 .50
54 Scott Mellanby .20 .50
55 Ray Sheppard .20 .50
56 Robert Svehla .20 .50
57 John Vanbiesbrouck .30 .75
58 Rob Blake .30 .75
59 Ray Ferraro .20 .50
60 Dimitri Khristich .20 .50
61 Vladimir Tsyplakov .20 .50
62 Vincent Damphousse .20 .50
63 Saku Koivu .40 1.00
64 Mark Recchi .30 .75
65 Stephane Richer .20 .50
66 Jocelyn Thibault .30 .75
67 Dave Andreychuk .20 .50
68 Martin Brodeur 1.25 3.00
69 Doug Gilmour .30 .75
70 Bobby Holik .20 .50
71 John MacLean .20 .50
72 Bryan Berard .20 .50
73 Travis Green .20 .50
74 Zigmund Palffy .30 .75
75 Tommy Salo .30 .75
76 Bryan Smolinski .20 .50
77 Adam Graves .20 .50
78 Wayne Gretzky 2.00 5.00
79 Alexei Kovalev .20 .50
80 Brian Leetch .40 1.00
81 Mark Messier .40 1.00
82 Mike Richter .40 1.00
83 Daniel Alfredsson .30 .75
84 Alexandre Daigle .20 .50
85 Wade Redden .20 .50
86 Damian Rhodes .20 .50
87 Alexei Yashin .20 .50
88 Rod Brind'Amour .30 .75
89 Ron Hextall .30 .75
90 John LeClair .30 .75
91 Eric Lindros .40 1.00
92 Janne Niinimaa .20 .50
93 Garth Snow .30 .75
94 Dainius Zubrus .20 .50
95 Mike Gartner .30 .75
96 Nikolai Khabibulin .30 .75
97 Jeremy Roenick .60 1.50
98 Keith Tkachuk .30 .75
99 Oleg Tverdovsky .20 .50
100 Ron Francis .30 .75
101 Kevin Hatcher .20 .50
102 Jaromir Jagr .75 2.00
103 Patrick Lalime .30 .75
104 Petr Nedved .20 .50
105 Jim Campbell .20 .50
106 Grant Fuhr .30 .75
107 Brett Hull .60 1.50
108 Pierre Turgeon .30 .75
109 Harry York .20 .50
110 Jeff Friesen .20 .50
111 Tony Granato .20 .50
112 Stephen Guolla RC .20 .50
113 Viktor Kozlov .20 .50
114 Owen Nolan .20 .50
115 Dino Ciccarelli .20 .50
116 John Cullen .20 .50
117 Chris Gratton .30 .75
118 Roman Hamrlik .20 .50
119 Daymond Langkow .20 .50
120 Sergei Berezin .20 .50
121 Wendel Clark .30 .75
122 Felix Potvin .40 1.00
123 Steve Sullivan .20 .50
124 Mats Sundin .40 1.00
125 Pavel Bure .40 1.00
126 Martin Gelinas .20 .50
127 Trevor Linden .30 .75
128 Kirk McLean .30 .75
129 Alexander Mogilny .30 .75
130 Peter Bondra .30 .75
131 Joe Juneau .30 .75
132 Steve Konowalchuk .20 .50
133 Adam Oates .30 .75
134 Bill Ranford .30 .75
135 P.Kariya/T.Selanne .40 1.00
136 D.Hasek/M.Peca .30 .75
137 Theo Fleury .60 1.50
Jarome Iginla
138 P.Forsberg/P.Roy 1.00 2.50
139 B.Shanahan/S.Yzerman 1.00 2.50
140 W.Gretzky/M.Messier 1.25 3.00
141 J.LeClair/E.Lindros .40 1.00
142 J.Jagr/P.Lalime .30 .75
143 J.Campbell/B.Hull .30 .75
144 S.Berezin/M.Sundin .30 .75
NNO Shawn Bates RC .30 .75
NNO Daniel Cleary .20 .50
NNO Marian Hossa RC 4.00 10.00
NNO Olli Jokinen RC 1.25 3.00
NNO Espen Knutsen RC .40 1.00
NNO Patrick Marleau .60 1.50
NNO Alyn McCauley .20 .50
NNO Mattias Ohlund .20 .50
NNO Chris Phillips .20 .50
NNO Erik Rasmussen .20 .50
NNO Sergei Samsonov .40 1.00
NNO Joe Thornton .75 2.00

1997-98 Pacific Dynagon Copper

Randomly inserted in hobby packs only at the rate of 2:37, this 156-card set is a parallel version of the base set and is distinguished by the copper foil enhancements.
*STARS: 4X TO 10X BASIC CARDS
*ROOKIES: 1.25X TO 3X BASIC CARDS

1997-98 Pacific Dynagon Dark Grey

Randomly inserted in hobby packs only at the rate of 2:37, this 156-card set is a parallel version of the base set and is distinguished by the gray foil enhancements.
*STARS: 4X TO 10X BASIC CARDS
*ROOKIES: 1.25X TO 3X BASIC CARDS

1997-98 Pacific Dynagon Emerald Green

Randomly inserted in Canadian packs only at the rate of 2:37, this 156-card set is a parallel version of the base set and is distinguished by the green foil enhancements.
*STARS: 5X TO 12X BASIC CARDS
*ROOKIES: 1.5X TO 4X BASIC CARDS

1997-98 Pacific Dynagon Ice Blue

Randomly inserted in packs at the rate of 1:73, this 156-card set is a parallel version of the base set and is distinguished by the blue foil enhancements.
*STARS: 12.5X TO 25X BASIC CARDS
*ROOKIES: 2.5X TO 6X BASIC CARDS

1997-98 Pacific Dynagon Red

Randomly inserted in packs at the rate of 2:37 Treat packs, this 156-card set is a parallel version of the base set and is distinguished by the red foil enhancements.
*STARS: 3X TO 6X BASIC CARDS
*ROOKIES: 1.5X TO 4X BASIC CARDS

1997-98 Pacific Dynagon Silver

Randomly inserted in retail packs only at the rate of 2:37, this 156-card set is a parallel version of the base set and is distinguished by the silver foil enhancements.
*STARS: 3X TO 6X BASIC CARDS
*ROOKIES: 1.5X TO 4X BASIC CARDS

1997-98 Pacific Dynagon Best Kept Secrets

Randomly inserted one per pack, this 110-card set features color action player photos of the top NHL players made to resemble a picture paper clipped to a file. A small slide-look version of the player's picture appears at the top. The backs carry player information and career statistics.

COMPLETE SET (110) 12.50 25.00
1 J.J. Daigneault .02 .10
2 Paul Kariya .15 .40
3 Dave Karpa .02 .10
4 Teemu Selanne .15 .40
5 Ray Bourque .25 .60
6 Jim Carey .08 .25
7 Davis Payne .02 .10
8 Paxton Schafer .02 .10
9 Bob Boughner .02 .10
10 Dominik Hasek .30 .75
11 Brad May .02 .10
12 Cale Hulse .02 .10
13 Jarome Iginla .20 .50
14 James Patrick .02 .10
15 Zarley Zalapski .02 .10
16 Jeff Brown .02 .10
17 Keith Primeau .08 .25
18 Steven Rice .02 .10
19 James Black .02 .10
20 Chris Chelios .15 .40
21 Steve Dubinsky .02 .10
22 Steve Smith .02 .10
23 Craig Billington .08 .25
24 Peter Forsberg .40 1.00
25 Jon Klemm .02 .10
26 Patrick Roy .75 2.00
27 Joe Sakic .30 .75
28 Neal Broten .02 .10
29 Richard Matvichuk .02 .10
30 Mike Modano .25 .60
31 Andy Moog .08 .25
32 Sergei Fedorov .30 .75
33 Kirk Maltby .02 .10
34 Brendan Shanahan .25 .60
35 Tim Taylor .02 .10
36 Steve Yzerman .75 2.00
37 Louie DeBrusk .02 .10
38 Joe Hulbig .02 .10
39 Ryan Smyth .08 .25
40 Mike Hough .02 .10
41 Jody Hull .02 .10
42 Paul Laus .08 .25
43 John Vanbiesbrouck .15 .40
44 Aki Berg .02 .10
45 Ray Ferraro .02 .10
46 Craig Johnson .02 .10
47 Ian Laperriere .02 .10
48 Vincent Damphousse .08 .25
49 Dave Manson .02 .10
50 Stephane Richer .08 .25
51 Craig Rivet .02 .10
52 Martin Brodeur .40 1.00
53 Jay Pandolfo .02 .10
54 Brian Rolston .02 .10
55 Doug Houda .02 .10
56 Brent Hughes .02 .10
57 Zigmund Palffy .15 .40
58 Adam Graves .08 .25
59 Wayne Gretzky 1.00 2.50
60 Chris Ferraro .02 .10
61 Glenn Healy .08 .25
62 Brian Leetch .15 .40
63 Mark Messier .20 .50
64 Radim Bicanek .02 .10
65 Philip Crowe .02 .10
66 Christer Olsson .02 .10
67 Jason York .02 .10
68 Rod Brind'Amour .08 .25
69 John Druce .02 .10
70 Daniel Lacroix .02 .10
71 John LeClair .20 .50
72 Eric Lindros .30 .75
73 Murray Baron .02 .10
74 Mike Gartner .08 .25
75 Brad McCrimmon .02 .10
76 Keith Tkachuk .15 .40
77 Jaromir Jagr .25 .60
78 Patrick Lalime .08 .25
79 Ian Moran .02 .10
80 Petr Nedved .08 .25
81 Brett Hull .20 .50
82 Robert Petrovicky .02 .10
83 Pierre Turgeon .08 .25
84 Trent Yawney .02 .10
85 Tim Hunter .02 .10
86 Marcus Ragnarsson .02 .10
87 Dody Wood .02 .10
88 Dino Ciccarelli .02 .10
89 Alexander Selivanov .02 .10
90 Jason Wiemer .02 .10
91 Sergei Berezin .08 .25
92 Felix Potvin .15 .40
93 Mats Sundin .15 .40
94 Craig Wolanin .02 .10
95 Pavel Bure .25 .60
96 Troy Crowder .02 .10
97 Dana Murzyn .02 .10
98 Gino Odjick .08 .25
99 Craig Berube .02 .10
100 Peter Bondra .15 .40
101 Mike Eagles .02 .10
102 Andrei Nikolishin .02 .10
103 Paul Kariya .15 .40
104 Dominik Hasek .30 .75
105 Michael Peca .02 .10
106 M.Brodeur/M.Dunham .20 .50
107 Bryan Berard .08 .25
108 Brian Leetch .15 .40
109 Tony Granato .02 .10
110 Trevor Linden .08 .25

1997-98 Pacific Dynagon Dynamic Duos

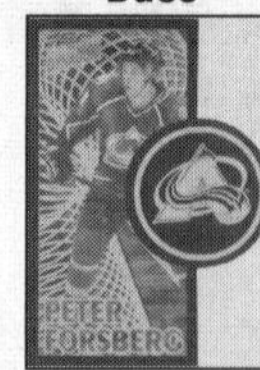

Randomly inserted in packs at the rate of 1:37, this 30-card set features color action images of the NHL's top teammates printed on a die-cut gold foil card and framed with a textured hockey puck border. When placed side by side, the matching cards are joined together by their team logo.

COMPLETE SET (30) 30.00 80.00
1A Paul Kariya 1.50 4.00
1B Teemu Selanne 1.50 4.00
2A Ray Bourque 2.00 5.00
2B Jim Carey .75 2.00
3A Dominik Hasek 3.00 8.00
3B Michael Peca .40 1.00
4A Theo Fleury .75 2.00
4B Jarome Iginla 2.00 5.00
5A Peter Forsberg 2.50 6.00
5B Claude Lemieux .40 1.00
6A Patrick Roy 8.00 20.00
6B Joe Sakic 3.00 8.00
7A Sergei Fedorov 1.50 4.00
7B Vladimir Konstantinov .75 2.00
8A Brendan Shanahan 1.50 4.00
8B Steve Yzerman 6.00 15.00
9A Bryan Berard .40 1.00
9B Zigmund Palffy .75 2.00
10A Wayne Gretzky 10.00 25.00
10B Mark Messier 1.50 4.00
11A Eric Lindros 1.50 4.00
11B Dainius Zubrus .40 1.00
12A Jeremy Roenick 2.00 5.00
12B Keith Tkachuk 1.25 3.00
13A Jaromir Jagr 2.50 6.00
13B Patrick Lalime .75 2.00
14A Jim Campbell .40 1.00
14B Brett Hull 1.50 4.00
15A Pavel Bure 1.50 4.00
15B Alexander Mogilny .75 2.00

1997-98 Pacific Dynagon Kings of the NHL

COMPLETE SET (10) 60.00 125.00
STATED ODDS 1:361
1 Paul Kariya 3.00 8.00
2 Peter Forsberg 8.00 20.00
3 Patrick Roy 15.00 40.00
4 Joe Sakic 6.00 15.00
5 John Vanbiesbrouck 2.50 6.00
6 Wayne Gretzky 20.00 50.00
7 Mark Messier 3.00 8.00
8 Eric Lindros 3.00 8.00
9 Jaromir Jagr 5.00 12.00
10 Pavel Bure 3.00 8.00

1997-98 Pacific Dynagon Stonewallers

COMPLETE SET (20) 25.00 60.00
STATED ODDS 1:73
1 Guy Hebert 1.25 3.00
2 Jim Carey 1.25 3.00
3 Dominik Hasek 4.00 10.00
4 Trevor Kidd 1.25 3.00
5 Jeff Hackett 1.25 3.00
6 Patrick Roy 10.00 25.00
7 Chris Osgood 1.25 3.00
8 Mike Vernon 1.50 4.00
9 Curtis Joseph 1.50 4.00
10 John Vanbiesbrouck 1.50 4.00
11 Jocelyn Thibault 1.25 3.00
12 Martin Brodeur 6.00 15.00
13 Tommy Salo 1.25 3.00
14 Mike Richter 1.50 4.00
15 Ron Hextall 1.50 4.00
16 Garth Snow 1.25 3.00
17 Nikolai Khabibulin 1.50 4.00
18 Patrick Lalime 1.25 3.00
19 Grant Fuhr 1.50 4.00
20 Felix Potvin 2.00 5.00

1997-98 Pacific Dynagon Tandems

Randomly inserted in packs at the rate of 1:37, this 72-card set features color player images printed on double front, holographic fully foiled, double etched cards.

1 Wayne Gretzky 10.00 25.00
Eric Lindros
2 Joe Sakic 4.00 10.00
Paul Kariya
3 Jarome Iginla 4.00 10.00
Mark Messier
4 Patrick Roy 8.00 20.00
Dominik Hasek
5 Peter Forsberg 4.00 10.00
Jaromir Jagr
6 Brendan Shanahan 1.25 3.00
Keith Tkachuk
7 Steve Yzerman 4.00 10.00
Teemu Selanne
8 Sergei Fedorov 4.00 10.00
Brett Hull
9 Danius Zubrus .40 1.00
Patrick Lalime
10 Sergei Berezin .40 1.00
Mike Grier
11 Zigmund Palffy .75 2.00
Curtis Joseph
12 Chris Osgood 4.00 10.00
Martin Brodeur
13 John Vanbiesbrouck .75 2.00
Jocelyn Thibault
14 Saku Koivu 2.00 5.00
Pavel Bure
15 John LeClair .75 2.00
Peter Bondra
16 Mats Sundin .75 2.00
Janne Niinimaa
17 Felix Potvin 1.25 3.00
Jim Carey
18 Grant Fuhr 2.00 5.00
Brett Hull
Jim Campbell
19 Wayne Gretzky 8.00 20.00
Mark Messier
Brian Leetch
20 Eric Lindros 2.00 5.00
John LeClair
Rod Brind'Amour
21 Dominik Hasek 2.00 5.00
Michael Peca
Miroslav Satan
22 Jaromir Jagr 2.00 5.00
Patrick Lalime
Petr Nedved
23 Jarome Iginla 2.00 5.00
Theo Fleury
Trevor Kidd
24 Paul Kariya 2.00 5.00
Teemu Selanne
Guy Hebert
25 Peter Forsberg 8.00 20.00
Patrick Roy
Claude Lemieux
26 Steve Yzerman 8.00 20.00
Brendand Shanahan
Vladimir Konstantinov
27 Mats Sundin 2.00 5.00
Sergei Berezin
Wendel Clark
28 Ray Bourque 2.00 5.00
Derek Plante
29 Brian Bellows .40 1.00
Jason Allison
30 Steve Rucchin .40 1.00
Keith Primeau
31 Jozef Stumpel .40 1.00
Eric Daze
32 Brian Holzinger .40 1.00
Jamie Langenbrunner
33 Michael Peca .40 1.00
Tony Amonte
34 German Titov .40 1.00
Darryl Sydor
35 Theo Fleury .75 2.00
Chris Chelios
36 Jonas Hoglund .40 1.00
Dimitri Khristich
37 Sean Burke .40 1.00
Dave Andreychuk
38 Geoff Sanderson .40 1.00
Derian Hatcher
39 Andrew Cassels .40 1.00
Jeff Hackett
40 Ethan Moreau .40 1.00
Ray Ferraro
41 Sandis Ozolinsh .75 2.00
Doug Gilmour
42 Valeri Kamensky 1.25 3.00
Mike Modano
43 Joe Nieuwendyk .40 1.00
Vladimir Tsyplakov
44 Sergei Zubov .40 1.00
Mike Vernon
45 Rob Blake .40 1.00
Bobby Holik
46 Vincent Damphousse .40 1.00
Doug Weight
47 Mark Recchi .75 2.00
Ryan Smyth
48 Stephane Richer .40 1.00
John MacLean
49 Kelly Buchberger .40 1.00
Ed Jovanovski
50 Rem Murray .40 1.00
Owen Nolan
51 Robert Svehla .40 1.00
Bill Ranford
52 Ray Sheppard .40 1.00
Steve Sullivan
53 Scott Mellanby .40 1.00
John Cullen
54 Garth Snow .40 1.00
Alexandre Daigle
55 Ron Hextall .75 2.00
Alexander Mogilny
56 Kirk McLean .75 2.00
Adam Oates
57 Joe Juneau .40 1.00
Dino Ciccarelli
58 Steve Konowalchuk .40 1.00
Jim Campbell
59 Trevor Linden .40 1.00
Pierre Turgeon
60 Martin Gelinas .40 1.00
Jeff Friesen
61 Roman Hamrlik .40 1.00
Harry York
62 Kevin Hatcher .40 1.00
Chris Gratton
63 Ron Francis 1.25 3.00
Jeremy Roenick
64 Nikolai Khabibulin .75 2.00
Viktor Kozlov
65 Daymond Langkow .40 1.00
Mike Gartner
66 Oleg Tverdovsky .40 1.00
Steve Guolla
67 Tony Granato .40 1.00
Tommy Salo
68 Bryan Smolinski .40 1.00
Wade Redden
69 Adam Graves .40 1.00
Damian Rhodes
70 Mike Richter .75 2.00
Alexei Yashin
71 Daniel Alfredsson .40 1.00
Bryan Berard
72 Travis Green .40 1.00
Alexei Kovalev

1998-99 Pacific Dynagon Ice

The 1998-99 Pacific Dynagon Ice set was issued in one series totaling 200 cards and was distributed in five-card packs with a suggested retail price of $2.49. The set features color action player photos printed on gold foil cards with player highlights and statistics displayed on the backs.

COMPLETE SET (200) 25.00 50.00
1 Travis Green .10 .25
2 Guy Hebert .25 .60
3 Paul Kariya .30 .75
4 Steve Rucchin .10 .25
5 Tomas Sandstrom .10 .25
6 Teemu Selanne .30 .75
7 Jason Allison .10 .25
8 Ray Bourque .50 1.25
9 Byron Dafoe .25 .60
10 Anson Carter .25 .60
11 Dimitri Khristich .10 .25
12 Antti Laaksonen RC .10 .25
13 Peter Nordstrom RC .10 .25
14 Sergei Samsonov .25 .60
15 Joe Thornton .50 1.25
16 Matthew Barnaby .10 .25
17 Michal Grosek .10 .25
18 Dominik Hasek .60 1.50
19 Brian Holzinger .10 .25
20 Michael Peca .10 .25
21 Miroslav Satan .25 .60
22 Vaclav Varada .10 .25
23 Andrew Cassels .10 .25
24 Rico Fata .10 .25
25 Theo Fleury .10 .25
26 Phil Housley .10 .25
27 Jarome Iginla .40 1.00
28 Martin St. Louis RC 2.00 5.00
29 Ken Wregget .25 .60
30 Kevin Dineen .10 .25
31 Ron Francis .25 .60
32 Martin Gelinas .10 .25
33 Arturs Irbe .25 .60
34 Sami Kapanen .10 .25
35 Trevor Kidd .25 .60
36 Robert Kron .10 .25
37 Keith Primeau .10 .25
38 Tony Amonte .25 .60
39 Chris Chelios .30 .75
40 Eric Daze .25 .60
41 Doug Gilmour .25 .60
42 Jeff Hackett .25 .60
43 Ty Jones .25 .60
44 Bob Probert .10 .25
45 Adam Deadmarsh .10 .25
46 Chris Drury .25 .60
47 Peter Forsberg .75 2.00
48 Milan Hejduk RC 1.25 3.00
49 Valeri Kamensky .10 .25
50 Claude Lemieux .10 .25
51 Patrick Roy 1.50 4.00
52 Joe Sakic .60 1.50
53 Ed Belfour .30 .75
54 Sergey Gusev RC .10 .25
55 Derian Hatcher .10 .25
56 Brett Hull .40 1.00
57 Jamie Langenbrunner .10 .25
58 Jere Lehtinen .10 .25
59 Mike Modano .50 1.25
60 Joe Nieuwendyk .25 .60
61 Sergei Zubov .10 .25
62 Sergei Fedorov .50 1.25
63 Vyacheslav Kozlov .25 .6
64 Uwe Krupp .10 .2
65 Nicklas Lidstrom .30 .7
66 Darren McCarty .10 .2
67 Chris Osgood .25 .6
68 Brendan Shanahan .30 .7
69 Steve Yzerman 1.50 4.0
70 Bob Essensa .25 .60
71 Mike Grier .10 .25
72 Bill Guerin .25 .60
73 Roman Hamrlik .10 .25
74 Janne Niinimaa .10 .25
75 Tom Poti .10 .25
76 Ryan Smyth .25 .60
77 Doug Weight .25 .60
78 Sean Burke .10 .25
79 Dino Ciccarelli .25 .60
80 Dave Gagner .10 .25
81 Ed Jovanovski .10 .25
82 Viktor Kozlov .10 .25
83 Oleg Kvasha RC .30 .75
84 Paul Laus .10 .25
85 Mark Parrish RC .40 1.00
86 Rob Blake .25 .60
87 Stephane Fiset .25 .60
88 Josh Green RC .10 .25
89 Yanic Perreault .10 .25
90 Luc Robitaille .25 .60
91 Jozef Stumpel .25 .60
92 Vladimir Tsyplakov .10 .25
93 Brad Brown .10 .25
94 Shayne Corson .25 .60
95 Vincent Damphousse .10 .25
96 Saku Koivu .30 .75
97 Mark Recchi .25 .60
98 Jocelyn Thibault .25 .60
99 Sergei Zholtok .10 .25
100 Andrew Brunette .25 .60
101 Mike Dunham .25 .60
102 Tom Fitzgerald .10 .25
103 Patrik Kjellberg .10 .25
104 Sergei Krivokrasov .10 .25
105 Darren Turcotte .10 .25
106 Dave Andreychuk .25 .60
107 Jason Arnott .10 .25
108 Martin Brodeur .75 2.00
109 Patrik Elias .25 .60
110 Bobby Holik .10 .25
111 Brendan Morrison .25 .60
112 Scott Stevens .25 .60
113 Bryan Berard .25 .60
114 Eric Brewer .10 .25
115 Trevor Linden .25 .60
116 Zigmund Palffy .25 .60
117 Robert Reichel .10 .25
118 Tommy Salo .25 .60
119 Bryan Smolinski .10 .25
120 Adam Graves .10 .25
121 Wayne Gretzky 2.00 5.00
122 Alexei Kovalev .10 .25
123 Brian Leetch .30 .75
124 Manny Malhotra .25 .60
125 Mike Richter .30 .75
126 Daniel Alfredsson .25 .60
127 Igor Kravchuk .10 .25
128 Shawn McEachern .10 .25
129 Vaclav Prospal .25 .60
130 Damian Rhodes .25 .60
131 Sami Salo RC .25 .60
132 Alexei Yashin .10 .25
133 Rod Brind'Amour .25 .60
134 Alexandre Daigle .10 .25
135 Chris Gratton .25 .60
136 Ron Hextall .25 .60
137 John LeClair .30 .75
138 Eric Lindros .30 .75
139 Mike Maneluk RC .10 .25
140 John Vanbiesbrouck .25 .60
141 Dainius Zubrus .10 .25
142 Brad Isbister .10 .25
143 Nikolai Khabibulin .25 .60
144 Jeremy Roenick .40 1.00
145 Keith Tkachuk .30 .75
146 Rick Tocchet .25 .60
147 Oleg Tverdovsky .10 .25
148 Tom Barrasso .25 .60
149 Kevin Hatcher .10 .25
150 Jan Hrdina RC .50 1.25
151 Jaromir Jagr .50 1.25
152 Alexei Morozov .10 .25
153 Jiri Slegr .10 .25
154 Martin Straka .10 .25
155 Jim Campbell .10 .25
156 Geoff Courtnall .10 .25
157 Grant Fuhr .25 .60
158 Michal Handzus RC .40 1.00
159 Al MacInnis .25 .60
160 Jamie McLennan .25 .60
161 Chris Pronger .25 .60
162 Marty Reasoner .25 .60
163 Pierre Turgeon .25 .60
164 Jeff Friesen .10 .25
165 Tony Granato .10 .25
166 Scott Hannan RC .25 .60
167 Patrick Marleau .10 .25
168 Owen Nolan .25 .60
169 Marco Sturm .10 .25
170 Mike Vernon .25 .60
171 Wendel Clark .25 .60
172 John Cullen .10 .25
173 Vincent Lecavalier 1.00 2.50
174 Stephane Richer .25 .60
175 Paul Ysebaert .10 .25
176 Rob Zamuner .10 .25
177 Sergei Berezin .25 .60
178 Tie Domi .25 .60
179 Mike Johnson .10 .25
180 Curtis Joseph .30 .75
181 Tomas Kaberle RC .40 1.00
182 Igor Korolev .10 .25
183 Alyn McCauley .10 .25
184 Mats Sundin .30 .75
185 Todd Bertuzzi .30 .75
186 Donald Brashear .10 .25
187 Pavel Bure .30 .75
188 Matt Cooke RC .10 .25
189 Mark Messier .30 .75
190 Alexander Mogilny .25 .60
191 Mattias Ohlund .10 .25
192 Garth Snow .25 .60
193 Peter Bondra .25 .60

194 Matthew Herr RC .10 .25
195 Calle Johansson .10 .25
196 Joe Juneau .25 .60
197 Olaf Kolzig .25 .60
198 Adam Oates .25 .60
199 Jaroslav Svejkovsky .10 .25
200 Richard Zednik .10 .25

1998-99 Pacific Dynagon Ice Blue

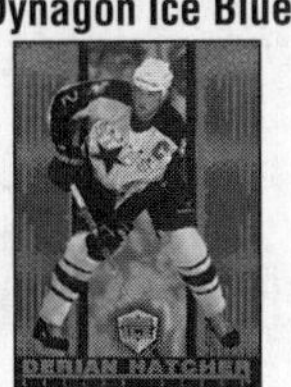

Randomly inserted into packs, this 200-card set is a blue foil parallel version of the base set. Only 67 serially numbered sets were made.
*STARS: 10X TO 25X BASE CARD
*ROOKIES: 4X TO 10X BASE CARD

1998-99 Pacific Dynagon Ice Red

Randomly inserted into Treat retail packs only at the rate of 4:37, this 200-card set is a red foil parallel version of the base set made especially for Treat Entertainment.
*STARS: 5X TO 10X BASE CARD
*ROOKIES: 2X TO 4X BASE CARD

1998-99 Pacific Dynagon Ice Adrenaline Rush Bronze

Randomly inserted into Canadian retail packs only at the rate of 1:37, this 10-card set is a Canadian insert to the Pacific Dynagon Ice base set. Four limited edition parallel sets were also made and inserted into packs: Bronze with only 180 sets made, Ice Blue with 10 sets made, Red with 79 sets made, and Silver with 120 sets made.
COMPLETE SET (10) 60.00 125.00
ICE BLUE NOT PRICED DUE TO SCARCITY
*REDS: .75X TO 2X BASIC INSERTS
*SILVERS: .5X TO 1.25X BASIC INSERTS
1 Paul Kariya 2.00 5.00
2 Teemu Selanne 10.00 25.00
3 Dominik Hasek 5.00 12.00
4 Peter Forsberg 6.00 15.00
5 Patrick Roy 12.50 30.00
6 Joe Sakic 5.00 12.00
7 Steve Yzerman 12.50 30.00
8 Wayne Gretzky 20.00 50.00
9 Eric Lindros 3.00 8.00
10 Jaromir Jagr 4.00 10.00

1998-99 Pacific Dynagon Ice Forward Thinking

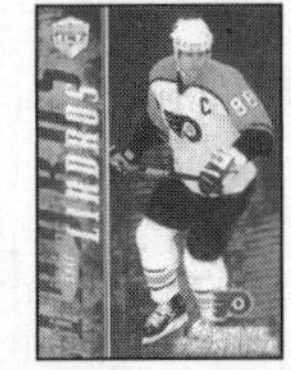

COMPLETE SET (20) 15.00 40.00
STATED ODDS 1:37
1 Paul Kariya 1.25 3.00
2 Teemu Selanne 1.25 3.00
3 Michael Peca .40 1.00
4 Doug Gilmour .75 2.00
5 Peter Forsberg 2.00 5.00
6 Joe Sakic 2.00 5.00
7 Brett Hull 1.50 4.00
8 Mike Modano 1.50 4.00
9 Sergei Fedorov 1.50 4.00
10 Brendan Shanahan 1.25 3.00
11 Steve Yzerman 3.00 8.00
12 Saku Koivu 1.25 3.00
13 Wayne Gretzky 4.00 10.00
14 John LeClair .40 1.00
15 Eric Lindros 1.25 3.00
16 Jaromir Jagr 2.00 5.00
17 Vincent Lecavalier 1.50 4.00
18 Mats Sundin 1.25 3.00
19 Mark Messier 1.25 3.00
20 Peter Bondra .75 2.00

1998-99 Pacific Dynagon Ice Watchmen

COMPLETE SET (10) 30.00 80.00
STATED ODDS 1:73
1 Dominik Hasek 6.00 15.00
2 Patrick Roy 12.00 30.00
3 Ed Belfour 2.00 5.00
4 Chris Osgood 2.00 5.00
5 Martin Brodeur 8.00 20.00
6 Mike Richter 2.00 5.00
7 John Vanbiesbrouck 2.00 5.00
8 Grant Fuhr 2.00 5.00
9 Curtis Joseph 3.00 8.00
10 Olaf Kolzig 2.00 5.00

1998-99 Pacific Dynagon Ice Preeminent Players

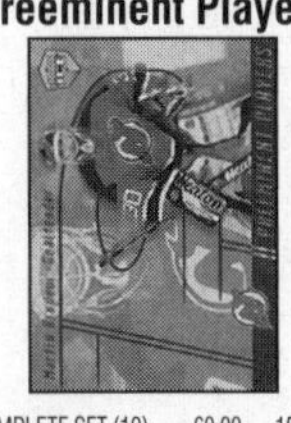

COMPLETE SET (10) 60.00 150.00
STATED ODDS 1:181
1 Paul Kariya 4.00 10.00
2 Dominik Hasek 8.00 20.00
3 Peter Forsberg 6.00 15.00
4 Patrick Roy 12.00 30.00
5 Mike Modano 5.00 12.00
6 Steve Yzerman 12.00 30.00
7 Martin Brodeur 10.00 25.00
8 Wayne Gretzky 15.00 40.00
9 Eric Lindros 4.00 10.00
10 Jaromir Jagr 6.00 15.00

1998-99 Pacific Dynagon Ice Rookies

COMPLETE SET (10) 20.00 40.00
STATED ODDS 1:73 HOBBY ONLY
1 Chris Drury 2.00 5.00
2 Milan Hejduk 2.00 5.00
3 Mark Parrish .75 2.00
4 Brendan Morrison 2.00 5.00
5 Mike Maneluk .75 2.00
6 Jan Hrdina .75 2.00
7 Marty Reasoner .75 2.00
8 Vincent Lecavalier 10.00 25.00
9 Tomas Kaberle .75 2.00
10 Bill Muckalt .75 2.00

1998-99 Pacific Dynagon Ice Team Checklists

STATED ODDS 2:37
1 Paul Kariya 1.25 3.00
2 Ray Bourque 1.25 3.00
3 Dominik Hasek 2.50 6.00
4 Theo Fleury .40 1.00
5 Keith Primeau .40 1.00
6 Chris Chelios .75 2.00
7 Patrick Roy 6.00 15.00
8 Mike Modano 1.50 4.00
9 Steve Yzerman 4.00 10.00
10 Ryan Smyth 1.00 2.00
11 Dino Ciccarelli .40 1.00
12 Rob Blake .75 2.00
13 Saku Koivu .75 2.00
14 Mike Dunham .75 2.00
15 Martin Brodeur 3.00 8.00
16 Trevor Linden .75 2.00
17 Wayne Gretzky 8.00 20.00
18 Alexei Yashin .40 1.00
19 Eric Lindros 1.25 3.00
20 Keith Tkachuk .75 2.00
21 Jaromir Jagr 2.00 5.00
22 Grant Fuhr .75 2.00
23 Mike Vernon .75 2.00
24 Vincent Lecavalier 2.00 5.00
25 Mats Sundin 1.25 3.00
26 Mark Messier 1.25 3.00
27 Peter Bondra 1.00 2.00

1999-00 Pacific Dynagon Ice

Released as a 206-card set, Dynagon Ice features base cards with full color action photography set against each respective player's team logo and feature silver foil highlights. Dynagon Ice was packaged in 36-pack boxes with packs containing five cards and carried a suggested retail price of $2.49.
COMPLETE SET (206) 50.00 100.00
COMP.SET w/o SP's (200) 35.00 70.00
1 Steve Kariya SP RC 2.00 4.00
2 Simon Gagne SP 3.00 6.00
3 Mike Fisher SP RC 2.50 6.00
4 Mike Ribeiro SP 2.00 4.00
5 Oleg Saprykin SP RC 4.00 10.00
6 Patrik Stefan SP RC 4.00 10.00
7 Ted Donato .10 .25
8 Niclas Havelid RC .30 .75
9 Guy Hebert .25 .60
10 Paul Kariya .30 .75
11 Steve Rucchin .10 .25
12 Teemu Selanne .30 .75
13 Oleg Tverdovsky .10 .25
14 Kelly Buchberger .10 .25
15 Nelson Emerson .10 .25
16 Ray Ferraro .10 .25
17 Norm Maracle .25 .60
18 Damian Rhodes .25 .60
19 Per Svartvadet RC .10 .25
20 Jason Allison .10 .25
21 Ray Bourque .50 1.25
22 Anson Carter .25 .60
23 Byron Dafoe .25 .60
24 John Grahame RC .60 1.50
25 Sergei Samsonov .25 .60
26 Joe Thornton .50 1.25
27 Stu Barnes .10 .25
28 Martin Biron .25 .60
29 Curtis Brown .10 .25
30 Michal Grosek .10 .25
31 Dominik Hasek .60 1.50
32 Michael Peca .25 .60
33 Miroslav Satan .25 .60
34 Valeri Bure .10 .25
35 Grant Fuhr .25 .60
36 Jarome Iginla .40 1.00
37 Derek Morris .10 .25
38 Marc Savard .10 .25
39 Cory Stillman .10 .25
40 Ron Francis .25 .60
41 Arturs Irbe .25 .60
42 Sami Kapanen .10 .25
43 Keith Primeau .10 .25
44 Dave Tanabe .10 .25
45 Tommy Westlund RC .25 .60
46 Tony Amonte .25 .60
47 Wendel Clark .10 .25
48 Eric Daze .25 .60
49 J-P Dumont .25 .60
50 Doug Gilmour .25 .60
51 Steve McCarthy .10 .25
52 Jocelyn Thibault .25 .60
53 Alexei Zhamnov .10 .25
54 Adam Deadmarsh .10 .25
55 Chris Drury .25 .60
56 Peter Forsberg .75 2.00
57 Milan Hejduk .30 .75
58 Dan Hinote RC .25 .60
59 Patrick Roy 1.50 4.00
60 Joe Sakic .60 1.50
61 Martin Skoula RC .75 2.00
62 Alex Tanguay .25 .60
63 Ed Belfour .30 .75
64 Derian Hatcher .10 .25
65 Brett Hull .40 1.00
66 Jamie Langenbrunner .10 .25
67 Jere Lehtinen .25 .60
68 Mike Modano .50 1.25
69 Joe Nieuwendyk .25 .60
70 Pavel Patera RC .10 .25
71 Yuri Butsayev RC .10 .25
72 Chris Chelios .30 .75
73 Sergei Fedorov .50 1.25
74 Vyacheslav Kozlov .10 .25
75 Nicklas Lidstrom .30 .75
76 Darren McCarty .10 .25
77 Chris Osgood .25 .60
78 Brendan Shanahan .30 .75
79 Steve Yzerman 1.50 4.00
80 Paul Comrie RC .25 .60
81 Mike Grier .10 .25
82 Tom Poti .10 .25
83 Bill Ranford .25 .60
84 Tommy Salo .25 .60
85 Ryan Smyth .25 .60
86 Doug Weight .25 .60
87 Pavel Bure .30 .75
88 Sean Burke .25 .60
89 Trevor Kidd .25 .60
90 Viktor Kozlov .10 .25
91 Ivan Novoseltsev RC .60 1.50
92 Mark Parrish .10 .25
93 Ray Whitney .10 .25
94 Jason Blake RC .25 .60
95 Rob Blake .25 .60
96 Stephane Fiset .25 .60
97 Zigmund Palffy .25 .60
98 Luc Robitaille .25 .60
99 Jozef Stumpel .25 .60
100 Shayne Corson .10 .25
101 Jeff Hackett .25 .60
102 Saku Koivu .30 .75
103 Trevor Linden .10 .25
104 Martin Rucinsky .10 .25
105 Brian Savage .10 .25
106 Mike Dunham .25 .60
107 Greg Johnson .10 .25
108 Sergei Krivokrasov .10 .25
109 David Legwand .25 .60
110 Ville Peltonen .10 .25
111 Cliff Ronning .10 .25
112 Scott Walker .10 .25
113 Jason Arnott .10 .25
114 Martin Brodeur .75 2.00
115 Patrik Elias .25 .60
116 Scott Gomez .10 .25
117 Bobby Holik .10 .25
118 Scott Niedermayer .10 .25
119 Brian Rafalski RC .60 1.50
120 Petr Sykora .10 .25
121 Mathieu Biron .25 .60
122 Tim Connolly .10 .25
123 Mariusz Czerkawski .10 .25
124 Olli Jokinen .25 .60
125 Jorgen Jonsson RC .10 .25
126 Kenny Jonsson .10 .25
127 Felix Potvin .30 .75
128 Theo Fleury .10 .25
129 Adam Graves .10 .25
130 Kim Johnsson RC .25 .60
131 Valeri Kamensky .25 .60
132 Brian Leetch .30 .75
133 Petr Nedved .25 .60
134 Mike Richter .30 .75
135 Mike York .10 .25
136 Daniel Alfredsson .25 .60
137 Magnus Arvedson .10 .25
138 Radek Bonk .10 .25
139 Marian Hossa .30 .75
140 Patrick Lalime .25 .60
141 Ron Tugnutt .25 .60
142 Alexei Yashin .10 .25
143 Rob Zamuner .10 .25
144 Brian Boucher .30 .75
145 Rod Brind'Amour .25 .60
146 Mark Eaton RC .30 .75
147 John LeClair .30 .75
148 Eric Lindros .30 .75
149 Mark Recchi .25 .60
150 John Vanbiesbrouck .25 .60
151 Travis Green .10 .25
152 Nikolai Khabibulin .25 .60
153 Jeremy Roenick .40 1.00
154 Mikhail Shtalenkov .25 .60
155 Keith Tkachuk .30 .75
156 Rick Tocchet .25 .60
157 Matthew Barnaby .10 .25
158 Tom Barrasso .25 .60
159 Jaromir Jagr .50 1.25
160 Alexei Kovalev .10 .25
161 Alexei Morozov .10 .25
162 Michal Rozsival RC .10 .25
163 Martin Straka .10 .25
164 German Titov .10 .25
165 Pavol Demitra .25 .60
166 Al MacInnis .25 .60
167 Chris Pronger .25 .60
168 Roman Turek .25 .60
169 Pierre Turgeon .25 .60
170 Scott Young .10 .25
171 Vincent Damphousse .10 .25
172 Jeff Friesen .10 .25
173 Patrick Marleau .30 .75
174 Owen Nolan .25 .60
175 Steve Shields .25 .60
176 Brad Stuart .25 .60
177 Niklas Sundstrom .10 .25
178 Mike Vernon .25 .60
179 Dan Cloutier .25 .60
180 Chris Gratton .10 .25
181 Vincent Lecavalier .30 .75
182 Fredrik Modin .10 .25
183 Darcy Tucker .10 .25
184 Nikolai Antropov RC .75 2.00
185 Sergei Berezin .10 .25
186 Tie Domi .25 .60
187 Jonas Hoglund .10 .25
188 Mike Johnson .10 .25
189 Curtis Joseph .30 .75
190 Mats Sundin .30 .75
191 Steve Thomas .10 .25
192 Andrew Cassels .10 .25
193 Artem Chubarov .10 .25
194 Mark Messier .30 .75
195 Alexander Mogilny .25 .60
196 Bill Muckalt .10 .25
197 Markus Naslund .30 .75
198 Kevin Weekes .25 .60
199 Peter Bondra .25 .60
200 Jan Bulis .10 .25
201 Jeff Halpern RC .75 2.00
202 Olaf Kolzig .25 .60
203 Adam Oates .25 .60
204 Chris Simon .10 .25
205 Alexander Volchkov RC .25 .60
206 Richard Zednik .10 .25
NNO Martin Brodeur SAMPLE 1.60 4.00

1999-00 Pacific Dynagon Ice Blue

Randomly inserted in packs, this 206-card set parallels the base Dynagon Ice set and is enhanced with blue foil highlights. Each card set sequentially numbered to 67.
*STARS: 15X TO 40X BASIC CARDS
*SP's: 2.5X TO 6X BASIC CARDS

1999-00 Pacific Dynagon Ice Copper

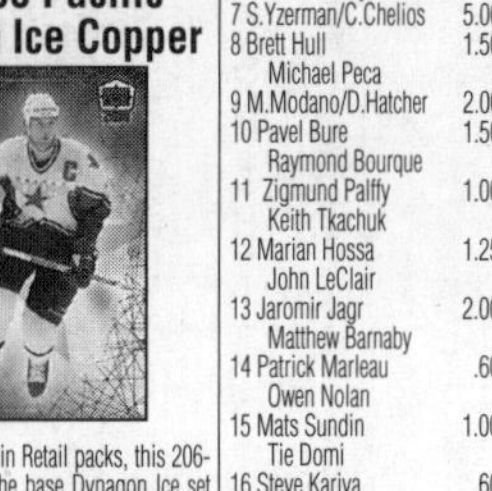

Randomly inserted in Retail packs, this 206-card set parallels the base Dynagon Ice set and is enhanced with copper foil highlights. Each card set sequentially numbered to 99.
*STARS: 10X TO 25X BASIC CARDS
*SP's: 1.5X TO 4X BASIC CARDS
STATED PRINT RUN 99 SER.#'d SETS

1999-00 Pacific Dynagon Ice Gold

Randomly inserted in Retail packs, this 206-card set parallels the base Dynagon Ice set and is enhanced with gold foil highlights. Each card set sequentially numbered to 199.
*STARS: 4X TO 10X BASIC CARDS
*SP's: .75X TO 2X BASIC CARDS
STATED PRINT RUN 199 SER.#'d SETS

1999-00 Pacific Dynagon Ice Premiere Date

Randomly inserted in packs, this 206-card set parallels the base Dynagon Ice set and is enhanced with a Premier Date stamp. Each card set sequentially numbered to 63.
*STARS: 15X TO 40X BASIC CARDS
*SP's: 2.5X TO 6X BASIC CARDS
STATED PRINT RUN 63 SER.#'d SETS

1999-00 Pacific Dynagon Ice 2000 All-Star Preview

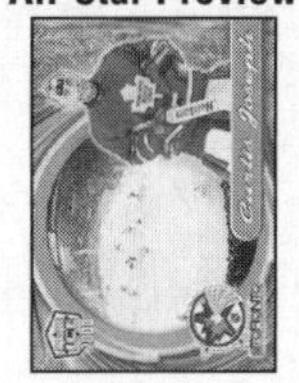

Randomly inserted in Hobby packs at the rate of 2:37, this 20-card set features color player photos set against a circular panoramic shot of a live hockey game and the 1999-2000 All-Star game logo in the lower left corner.
COMPLETE SET (20) 50.00 100.00
1 Paul Kariya 1.25 3.00
2 Teemu Selanne 1.25 3.00
3 Ray Bourque 2.00 5.00
4 Dominik Hasek 2.50 6.00
5 Patrick Roy 6.00 15.00
6 Joe Sakic 2.50 6.00
7 Nicklas Lidstrom 1.25 3.00
8 Steve Yzerman 6.00 15.00
9 Ed Belfour 1.25 3.00
10 Jere Lehtinen 1.00 2.50
11 Mike Modano 2.00 5.00
12 Pavel Bure 1.50 4.00
13 Martin Brodeur 3.00 8.00
14 John LeClair 1.50 4.00
15 Eric Lindros 2.00 5.00
16 Jaromir Jagr 2.00 5.00
17 Keith Tkachuk 1.25 3.00
18 Curtis Joseph 1.25 3.00
19 Mats Sundin 1.25 3.00
20 Peter Bondra 1.00 2.50

1999-00 Pacific Dynagon Ice Checkmates American

Randomly inserted in American packs at the rate of two in 37, this 30-card set pairs a top goal scorer on the card front and an enforcer on the card back for numbers 1-15, then switches to enforcer on the front and scorer on the back for card numbers 16-30.
COMPLETE SET (30) 40.00 100.00
1 Paul Kariya .60 1.50
Steve Kariya
2 Teemu Selanne .60 1.50
Brendan Shanahan
3 Patrik Stefan .60 1.50
Eric Lindros
4 Tony Amonte .60 1.50
Chris Pronger
5 Chris Drury 3.00 8.00
Peter Forsberg
6 Joe Sakic 2.50 6.00
Theo Fleury
7 S.Yzerman/C.Chelios 5.00 12.00
8 Brett Hull 1.50 4.00
Michael Peca
9 M.Modano/D.Hatcher 2.00 5.00
10 Pavel Bure 1.50 4.00
Raymond Bourque
11 Zigmund Palffy 1.00 2.50
Keith Tkachuk
12 Marian Hossa 1.25 3.00
John LeClair
13 Jaromir Jagr 2.00 5.00
Matthew Barnaby
14 Patrick Marleau .60 1.50
Owen Nolan
15 Mats Sundin 1.00 2.50
Tie Domi
16 Steve Kariya .60 1.50
Paul Kariya
17 Brendan Shanahan .60 1.50
Teemu Selanne
18 Eric Lindros 1.25 3.00
Patrik Stefan
19 Chris Pronger 1.00 2.50
Tony Amonte
20 Peter Forsberg 3.00 8.00
Chris Drury
21 Theo Fleury 2.50 6.00
Joe Sakic
22 C.Chelios/S.Yzerman 5.00 12.00
23 Michael Peca 1.50 4.00
Brett Hull
24 D.Hatcher/M.Modano 2.00 5.00
25 Raymond Bourque 1.50 4.00
Pavel Bure
26 Keith Tkachuk 1.00 2.50
Zigmund Palffy
27 John LeClair 1.25 3.00
Marian Hossa
28 Matthew Barnaby 2.00 5.00
Jaromir Jagr
29 Owen Nolan 1.25 3.00
Patrick Marleau
30 Tie Domi 1.25 3.00
Mats Sundin

1999-00 Pacific Dynagon Ice Checkmates Canadian

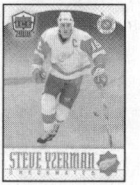

Randomly inserted in Canadian packs at a rate of 2:37, this 30-cards set features top NHL players in both their home and away jerseys.
COMPLETE SET (30) 40.00 80.00
1 Steve Kariya .60 1.50
2 Brendan Shanahan 2.00 5.00
3 Eric Lindros 2.00 5.00
4 Chris Pronger 1.00 2.50
5 Peter Forsberg 3.00 8.00
6 Theo Fleury .60 1.50
7 Chris Chelios 1.25 3.00
8 Michael Peca 1.00 2.50
9 Derian Hatcher .60 1.50
10 Ray Bourque 2.00 5.00
11 Keith Tkachuk 1.25 3.00
12 John LeClair 1.25 3.00
13 Matthew Barnaby .60 1.50
14 Owen Nolan 1.00 2.50
15 Tie Domi .60 1.50
16 Paul Kariya 1.25 3.00
17 Teemu Selanne 1.25 3.00
18 Patrik Stefan 1.00 2.50
19 Tony Amonte 1.00 2.50
20 Chris Drury 1.00 2.50
21 Joe Sakic 2.50 6.00
22 Steve Yzerman 5.00 12.00
23 Brett Hull 1.50 4.00
24 Mike Modano 2.00 5.00
25 Pavel Bure 1.50 4.00
26 Zigmund Palffy 1.00 2.50
27 Marian Hossa 1.25 3.00
28 Jaromir Jagr 2.00 5.00
29 Patrick Marleau 1.25 3.00
30 Mats Sundin 1.25 3.00

1999-00 Pacific Dynagon Ice Lamplighter Net-Fusions

Randomly inserted in packs at the rate of 1:73, this 10-card set features a laser cut background that has been filled in with actual "netting."
COMPLETE SET (10) 40.00 80.00
1 Paul Kariya 2.50 6.00
2 Teemu Selanne 2.50 6.00
3 Patrik Stefan 2.00 5.00
4 Joe Sakic 5.00 12.00
5 Steve Yzerman 12.50 30.00
6 Pavel Bure 3.00 8.00
7 Theo Fleury 2.50 6.00
8 John LeClair 3.00 8.00
9 Eric Lindros 4.00 10.00
10 Jaromir Jagr 4.00 10.00

1999-00 Pacific Dynagon Ice Lords of the Rink

COMPLETE SET (10) 100.00 200.00
STATED ODDS 1:181
1 Paul Kariya 15.00 40.00
2 Teemu Selanne 15.00 40.00
3 Dominik Hasek 8.00 20.00
4 Peter Forsberg 10.00 25.00
5 Patrick Roy 20.00 50.00
6 Joe Sakic 8.00 20.00
7 Steve Yzerman 20.00 50.00
8 Martin Brodeur 10.00 25.00
9 Eric Lindros 6.00 15.00
10 Jaromir Jagr 6.00 15.00

1999-00 Pacific Dynagon Ice Masks

Randomly inserted in packs at the rate of 1:37, this 10-card set showcases some of the NHL's to goalies' masks. Each card is enhanced with holographic foil stamping. Card numbers 1-5 are found only in hobby packs, and card numbers 6-10 are only found in retail packs.
COMPLETE SET (10) 20.00 40.00
1 Patrick Roy 6.00 15.00
2 Martin Brodeur 5.00 12.00
3 Mike Richter 1.00 2.50
4 John Vanbiesbrouck 1.00 2.50
5 Curtis Joseph 1.00 2.50
6 Patrick Roy 6.00 15.00
7 Martin Brodeur 3.00 8.00
8 Mike Richter 1.00 2.50
9 John Vanbiesbrouck 1.00 2.50
10 Curtis Joseph 1.00 2.50

1999-00 Pacific Dynagon Ice Masks Holographic Blue

Randomly inserted in packs, this 10-card set parallels the base Masks insert set on a holographic blue card. Each card is sequentially numbered to 67.
*STARS: 2X TO 4X BASIC INSERT

1999-00 Pacific Dynagon Ice Masks Holographic Gold

Randomly inserted in packs, this 10-card set parallels the base Masks insert set on a holographic gold card. Each card is sequentially numbered to 99.
*STARS: 1.5X TO 3X BASIC INSERT

1999-00 Pacific Dynagon Ice Masks Holographic Purple

Randomly inserted in packs, this 10-card set parallels the base Masks insert set on a holographic purple card. Each card is numbered one of one.
NOT PRICED DUE TO SCARCITY

2002 Pacific Entry Draft

Available as a wrapper redemption at the 2002 NHL Entry Draft, held in Toronto. Each card was serial-numbered on the back out of 500.
COMPLETE SET (10) 24.00 40.00
1 Ilya Kovalchuk 10.00 20.00
2 Erik Cole 3.20 5.00
3 Mark Bell 1.20 2.00
4 Marcel Hossa 2.00 3.00
5 Mike Ribeiro 1.20 2.00
6 Rick DiPietro 4.00 5.00
7 Raffi Torres 2.00 2.00
8 Dan Blackburn 4.00 5.00

9 Krys Kolanos 3.20 5.00
10 Jeff Jillson 2.00 3.00

2002-03 Pacific Exclusive

This 200-card set consisted of 175 veteran cards, 17 prospect cards and 8 autographed rookie cards shortprinted to 1000 copies each. A glitch during production caused two different versions of card #179 to be inserted into packs. Both Alex Henry and Jason Spezza cards were created and have been verified, they are labeled below with "A" and "B" suffixes for checklisting only.

COMP.SET w/o SP's (192) 100.00 200.00
1 J-S Giguere .40 1.00
2 Paul Kariya .50 1.25
3 Adam Oates .40 1.00
4 Petr Sykora .20 .50
5 Dany Heatley .60 1.50
6 Milan Hnilicka .40 1.00
7 Tomi Kallio .20 .50
8 Ilya Kovalchuk .60 1.50
9 Patrik Stefan .20 .50
10 Nick Boynton .20 .50
11 Glen Murray .20 .50
12 Brian Rolston .20 .50
13 Sergei Samsonov .40 1.00
14 Steve Shields .40 1.00
15 Joe Thornton .75 2.00
16 Martin Biron .40 1.00
17 Tim Connolly .20 .50
18 J-P Dumont .20 .50
19 Mika Noronen .20 .50
20 Miroslav Satan .40 1.00
21 Craig Conroy .20 .50
22 Chris Drury .40 1.00
23 Jarome Iginla .60 1.50
24 Roman Turek .40 1.00
25 Bates Battaglia .20 .50
26 Rod Brind'Amour .40 1.00
27 Erik Cole .20 .50
28 Ron Francis .40 1.00
29 Arturs Irbe .40 1.00
30 Sami Kapanen .20 .50
31 Jeff O'Neill .20 .50
32 Jaroslav Svoboda .20 .50
33 Josef Vasicek .20 .50
34 Mark Bell .20 .50
35 Eric Daze .40 1.00
36 Theo Fleury .20 .50
37 Jocelyn Thibault .40 1.00
38 Alexei Zhamnov .40 1.00
39 Rob Blake .40 1.00
40 Peter Forsberg 1.25 3.00
41 Milan Hejduk .50 1.25
42 Dean McAmmond .20 .50
43 Derek Morris .20 .50
44 Steven Reinprecht .20 .50
45 Patrick Roy 2.50 6.00
46 Joe Sakic 1.00 2.50
47 Alex Tanguay .40 1.00
48 Radim Vrbata .20 .50
49 Andrew Cassels .20 .50
50 Marc Denis .40 1.00
51 Rostislav Klesla .20 .50
52 Espen Knutsen .20 .50
53 Ray Whitney .20 .50
54 Jason Arnott .20 .50
55 Bill Guerin .40 1.00
56 Jere Lehtinen .40 1.00
57 Mike Modano .75 2.00
58 Marty Turco .40 1.00
59 Pierre Turgeon .40 1.00
60 Chris Chelios .50 1.25
61 Pavel Datsyuk .50 1.25
62 Sergei Fedorov .75 2.00
63 Brett Hull .60 1.50
64 Curtis Joseph .50 1.25
65 Nicklas Lidstrom .50 1.25
66 Luc Robitaille .40 1.00
67 Brendan Shanahan .50 1.25
68 Steve Yzerman 2.50 6.00
69 Anson Carter .40 1.00
70 Mike Comrie .40 1.00
71 Tommy Salo .40 1.00
72 Jason Smith .20 .50
73 Ryan Smyth .20 .50
74 Mike York .20 .50
75 Valeri Bure .20 .50
76 Kristian Huselius .20 .50
77 Roberto Luongo .60 1.50
78 Stephen Weiss .20 .50
79 Jason Allison .20 .50
80 Adam Deadmarsh .20 .50
81 Zigmund Palffy .40 1.00
82 Felix Potvin .50 1.25
83 Bryan Smolinski .20 .50
84 Andrew Brunette .20 .50
85 Pascal Dupuis .20 .50
86 Manny Fernandez .40 1.00
87 Marian Gaborik 1.00 2.50
88 Cliff Ronning .20 .50
89 Mariusz Czerkawski .20 .50
90 Marcel Hossa .20 .50
91 Saku Koivu .50 1.25
92 Yanic Perreault .20 .50
93 Oleg Petrov .20 .50
94 Jose Theodore .60 1.50
95 Richard Zednik .20 .50
96 Denis Arkhipov .20 .50
97 Mike Dunham .40 1.00
98 Scott Hartnell .20 .50
99 Greg Johnson .20 .50
100 David Legwand .40 1.00
101 Christian Berglund .20 .50
102 Martin Brodeur 1.25 3.00
103 Patrik Elias .40 1.00
104 Jeff Friesen .20 .50
105 Joe Nieuwendyk .40 1.00
106 Rick DiPietro .40 1.00
107 Brad Isbister .20 .50
108 Chris Osgood .40 1.00
109 Mark Parrish .20 .50
110 Michael Peca .20 .50
111 Alexei Yashin .20 .50
112 Dan Blackburn .40 1.00
113 Pavel Bure .50 1.25
114 Bobby Holik .20 .50
115 Brian Leetch .40 1.00
116 Eric Lindros .50 1.25
117 Mark Messier .50 1.25
118 Mike Richter .50 1.25
119 Daniel Alfredsson .40 1.00
120 Radek Bonk .20 .50
121 Martin Havlat .40 1.00
122 Marian Hossa .50 1.25
123 Patrick Lalime .40 1.00
124 Pavel Brendl .20 .50
125 Roman Cechmanek .40 1.00
126 Simon Gagne .50 1.25
127 John LeClair .50 1.25
128 Mark Recchi .40 1.00
129 Jeremy Roenick .60 1.50
130 Tony Amonte .40 1.00
131 Brian Boucher .40 1.00
132 Daniel Briere .20 .50
133 Sean Burke .40 1.00
134 Krystofer Kolanos .20 .50
135 Daymond Langkow .20 .50
136 Johan Hedberg .40 1.00
137 Alexei Kovalev .40 1.00
138 Mario Lemieux 3.00 8.00
139 Alexei Morozov .20 .50
140 Martin Straka .20 .50
141 Pavol Demitra .40 1.00
142 Barret Jackman .40 1.00
143 Brent Johnson .40 1.00
144 Al MacInnis .40 1.00
145 Chris Pronger .40 1.00
146 Keith Tkachuk .50 1.25
147 Doug Weight .40 1.00
148 Vincent Damphousse .20 .50
149 Patrick Marleau .40 1.00
150 Evgeni Nabokov .40 1.00
151 Owen Nolan .40 1.00
152 Teemu Selanne .50 1.25
153 Scott Thornton .20 .50
154 Dave Andreychuk .40 1.00
155 Nikolai Khabibulin .50 1.25
156 Vincent Lecavalier .50 1.25
157 Brad Richards .40 1.00
158 Shane Willis .20 .50
159 Ed Belfour .50 1.25
160 Alyn McCauley .20 .50
161 Alexander Mogilny .40 1.00
162 Gary Roberts .20 .50
163 Mats Sundin .50 1.25
164 Darcy Tucker .20 .50
165 Todd Bertuzzi .50 1.25
166 Dan Cloutier .40 1.00
167 Ed Jovanovski .40 1.00
168 Brendan Morrison .40 1.00
169 Markus Naslund .50 1.25
170 Peter Bondra .40 1.00
171 Sergei Gonchar .20 .50
172 Jaromir Jagr .75 2.00
173 Olaf Kolzig .40 1.00
174 Robert Lang .20 .50
175 Dainius Zubrus .20 .50
176 Martin Gerber RC 1.50 4.00
177 Dmitri Bykov RC 1.50 4.00
178 Ales Hemsky RC 4.00 10.00
179A Alex Henry RC 1.50 4.00
179B Jason Spezza SP RC 6.00 15.00
180 P-M Bouchard RC 4.00 10.00
181 Ron Hainsey RC 1.50 4.00
182 Adam Hall RC 1.50 4.00
183 Scottie Upshall RC 2.00 5.00
184 Mike Danton .20 .50
185 Jamie Lundmark .20 .50
186 Anton Volchenkov RC 1.50 4.00
187 Dennis Seidenberg RC 2.00 5.00
188 Patrick Sharp RC 1.50 4.00
189 Petr Cajanek .20 .50
190 Jonathan Cheechoo .03 .60
191 Fedor Fedorov .20 .50
192 Steve Eminger RC 1.50 4.00
193 Stanislav Chistov AU RC 6.00 15.00
194 Alexei Smirnov AU RC 5.00 12.00
195 Chuck Kobasew AU RC 6.00 15.00
196 Rick Nash AU RC 25.00 60.00
197 Henrik Zetterberg AU RC 20.00 50.00
198 Jay Bouwmeester AU RC 8.00 20.00
199 Alexander Frolov AU RC 10.00 25.00
200 Alexander Svitov AU RC 6.00 15.00

2002-03 Pacific Exclusive Blue

Inserted into hobby packs at a stated rate of 1:11, this 25-card set paralleled the last 25 cards of the base set but carried blue foil backgrounds on the card fronts. No cards in this parallel set were autographed. Each card was serial-numbered out of 699.

*NON-SP's: .3X TO .75X BASE HI
*SP's: .10X TO .25X BASE HI
179B Jason Spezza 6.00 15.00

2002-03 Pacific Exclusive Gold

This 200-card set was inserted at 1:1 hobby and 1:2 retail packs and directly paralleled the base set but card fronts carried a gold foil background. Cards 193-200 were not autographed as in the base set.

*STARS: .5X TO 1.25X BASE HI
*ROOKIE SP's: X TO X BASE HI

2002-03 Pacific Exclusive Retail

The only cards that were different in retail packs than hobby packs of 2002-03 Pacific Exclusive were cards 193-200. Those retail cards were unsigned and carried the same dot matrix pattern as the other players. All other players had the same card in both hobby and retail.

*STARS: SAME VALUE AS HOBBY
193 Stanislav Chistov RC 4.00 10.00
194 Alexei Smirnov RC 2.50 6.00
195 Chuck Kobasew RC 3.00 8.00
196 Rick Nash RC 8.00 20.00
197 Henrik Zetterberg RC 8.00 20.00
198 Jay Bouwmeester RC 5.00 12.00
199 Alexander Frolov RC 4.00 10.00
200 Alexander Svitov RC 2.00 5.00

2002-03 Pacific Exclusive Advantage

COMPLETE SET (15) 10.00 20.00
STATED ODDS 1:6 HOBBY/1:13 RETAIL
1 J-S Giguere .50 1.25
2 Roman Turek .50 1.25
3 Arturs Irbe .50 1.25
4 Patrick Roy 2.00 5.00
5 Marc Denis .50 1.25
6 Marty Turco .50 1.25
7 Curtis Joseph .60 1.50
8 Roberto Luongo .75 2.00
9 Felix Potvin .60 1.50
10 Jose Theodore .75 2.00
11 Martin Brodeur 1.00 2.50
12 Mike Richter .60 1.50
13 Brent Johnson .50 1.25
14 Evgeni Nabokov .50 1.25
15 Ed Belfour .60 1.50

2002-03 Pacific Exclusive Destined

COMPLETE SET (10) 6.00 15.00
STATED ODDS 1:11 HOBBY/1:25 RETAIL
1 Stanislav Chistov .60 1.50
2 Dany Heatley 1.25 3.00
3 Ilya Kovalchuk 1.50 4.00
4 Ivan Huml .60 1.50
5 Rick Nash 2.00 5.00
6 Pavel Datsyuk 1.25 3.00
7 Kristian Huselius .60 1.50
8 Stephen Weiss .60 1.50
9 Jamie Lundmark .60 1.50
10 Jonathan Cheechoo 1.25 3.00

2002-03 Pacific Exclusive Etched in Stone

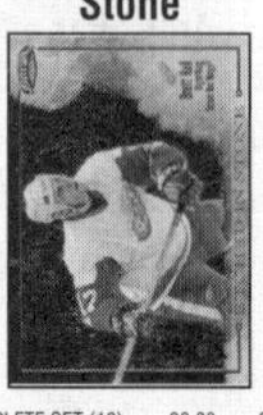

COMPLETE SET (10) 30.00 60.00
STATED ODDS 1:21 HOBBY/1:25 RETAIL
1 Paul Kariya .75 2.00
2 Ron Francis .75 2.00
3 Patrick Roy 5.00 12.00
4 Joe Sakic 2.00 5.00
5 Brett Hull 1.25 3.00
6 Steve Yzerman 5.00 12.00
7 Martin Brodeur 2.50 6.00
8 Eric Lindros .75 2.00
9 Mario Lemieux 6.00 15.00
10 Jaromir Jagr 1.50 4.00

2002-03 Pacific Exclusive Great Expectations

COMPLETE SET (15) 12.50 25.00
STATED ODDS 1:6 HOBBY/1:13 RETAIL
1 Dany Heatley 1.25 3.00
2 Ilya Kovalchuk 1.25 3.00
3 Ivan Huml .75 2.00
4 Erik Cole .75 2.00
5 Radim Vrbata .75 2.00
6 Pavel Datsyuk 1.00 2.50
7 Mike Comrie .75 2.00
8 Kristian Huselius .75 2.00
9 Stephen Weiss .75 2.00
10 Marian Gaborik 2.00 5.00
11 Marcel Hossa .75 2.00
12 Rick DiPietro .75 2.00
13 Dan Blackburn .75 2.00
14 Krystofer Kolanos .75 2.00
15 Barret Jackman .75 2.00

2002-03 Pacific Exclusive Jerseys

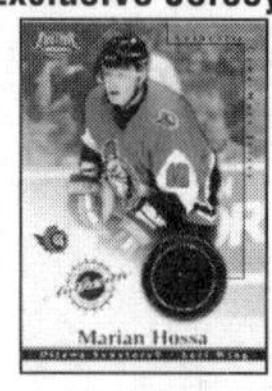

COMMON CARD (1-25) 3.00 8.00
*MULT.COLOR SWATCH: .5X TO 1.25X HI
STATED ODDS 2:21 HOBBY/1:49 RETAIL
1 Tomi Kallio 3.00 8.00
2 Joe Thornton 10.00 25.00
3 Miroslav Satan 5.00 12.00
4 Theo Fleury 3.00 8.00
5 Milan Hejduk 6.00 15.00
6 Pierre Turgeon 5.00 12.00
7 Sergei Fedorov 12.50 30.00
8 Nicklas Lidstrom 6.00 15.00
9 Tommy Salo 5.00 12.00
10 Kristian Huselius 3.00 8.00
11 Roberto Luongo 8.00 20.00
12 Bryan Smolinski 3.00 8.00
13 Manny Fernandez 5.00 12.00
14 Mariusz Czerkawski 3.00 8.00
15 David Legwand 5.00 12.00
16 Bobby Holik 3.00 8.00
17 Eric Lindros 6.00 15.00
18 Marian Hossa 6.00 15.00
19 Michal Handzus 3.00 8.00
20 Alexei Kovalev 5.00 12.00
21 Keith Tkachuk 6.00 15.00
22 Patrick Marleau 5.00 12.00
23 Brad Richards 5.00 12.00
24 Mats Sundin 6.00 15.00
25 Olaf Kolzig 5.00 12.00

2002-03 Pacific Exclusive Jerseys Gold

STATED PRINT RUN 25 SER.#'d SETS
NOT PRICED DUE TO SCARCITY

2002-03 Pacific Exclusive Maximum Overdrive

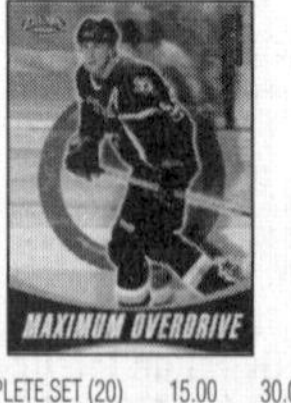

COMPLETE SET (20) 15.00 30.00
STATED ODDS 1:6 HOBBY/1:13 RETAIL
1 Paul Kariya .40 1.00
2 Dany Heatley .50 1.25
3 Ilya Kovalchuk .50 1.25
4 Joe Thornton .60 1.50
5 Jarome Iginla .50 1.25
6 Peter Forsberg 1.00 2.50
7 Joe Sakic .75 2.00
8 Mike Modano .60 1.50
9 Sergei Fedorov .75 2.00
10 Steve Yzerman 2.00 5.00
11 Saku Koivu .40 1.00
12 Patrik Elias .40 1.00
13 Alexei Yashin .40 1.00
14 Pavel Bure .50 1.25
15 Simon Gagne .40 1.00
16 Mario Lemieux 2.50 6.00
17 Teemu Selanne .40 1.00
18 Mats Sundin .40 1.00
19 Markus Naslund .40 1.00
20 Jaromir Jagr .60 1.50

2003-04 Pacific Exhibit

This 225-card set was released in eraly-October and consisted of four distinct subsets. Cards 1-150 were regular base cards, cards 151-200 were over-sized cards measuring approximatley 3.5" X 5"and cards 201-215 were over-sized jersey cards. Cards 216-225 made up the "Time Warp" subset, the cards were over-sized and contained a jersey swatch of a current player and an authentic autograph of a retired great, each serial-numbered out of 565. Cards 226-235 were available in packs of Pacific Calder.

COMP.SET w/o SP's (150) 30.00 60.00
COMP.SET w/o JSYS (200) 50.00 100.00
1 Stanislav Chistov .10 .25
2 Mike Leclerc .10 .25
3 Adam Oates .10 .25
4 Sandis Ozolinsh .10 .25
5 Vaclav Prospal .10 .25
6 Steve Rucchin .10 .25
7 Steve Thomas .10 .25
8 Byron Dafoe .20 .50
9 Joe DiPenta RC .20 .50
10 Slava Kozlov .10 .25
11 Patrik Stefan .10 .25
12 Bryan Berard .10 .25
13 Mike Knuble .10 .25
14 Glen Murray .10 .25
15 Brian Rolston .20 .50
16 Milan Bartovic RC .20 .50
17 Daniel Briere .10 .25
18 Chris Drury .20 .50
19 J-P Dumont .10 .25
20 Ales Kotalik .10 .25
21 Ryan Miller .20 .50
22 Miroslav Satan .20 .50
23 Craig Conroy .10 .25
24 Martin Gelinas .10 .25
25 Roman Turek .20 .50
26 Rod Brind'Amour .20 .50
27 Erik Cole .10 .25
28 Arturs Irbe .20 .50
29 Jeff O'Neill .10 .25
30 Tyler Arnason .20 .50
31 Kyle Calder .10 .25
32 Eric Daze .10 .25
33 Theoren Fleury .10 .25
34 Alexei Zhamnov .10 .25
35 David Aebischer .20 .50
36 Rob Blake .10 .25
37 Milan Hejduk .25 .60
38 Derek Morris .10 .25
39 Teemu Selanne .25 .60
40 Alex Tanguay .20 .50
41 Andrew Cassels .10 .25
42 Marc Denis .20 .50
43 Kent McDonell RC .20 .50
44 Geoff Sanderson .10 .25
45 Ray Whitney .10 .25
46 Jason Arnott .10 .25
47 Bill Guerin .20 .50
48 Jere Lehtinen .10 .25
49 Brenden Morrow .10 .25
50 Teppo Numminen .10 .25
51 Chris Chelios .25 .60
52 Pavel Datsyuk .25 .60
53 Derian Hatcher .10 .25
54 Nicklas Lidstrom .25 .60
55 Brendan Shanahan .25 .60
56 Henrik Zetterberg .25 .60
57 Mike Comrie .20 .50
58 Ales Hemsky .20 .50
59 Georges Laraque .10 .25
60 Tommy Salo .20 .50
61 Mike York .10 .25
62 Jay Bouwmeester .10 .25
63 Kristian Huselius .10 .25
64 Olli Jokinen .20 .50
65 Stephen Weiss .10 .25
66 Jason Allison .20 .50
67 Roman Cechmanek .20 .50
68 Adam Deadmarsh .10 .25
69 Alexander Frolov .10 .25
70 Felix Potvin .20 .50
71 Andrew Brunette .10 .25
72 Manny Fernandez .10 .25
73 Filip Kuba .10 .25
74 Dwayne Roloson .10 .25
75 Cliff Ronning .10 .25
76 Mathieu Garon .20 .50
77 Marcel Hossa .10 .25
78 Yanic Perreault .10 .25
79 Richard Zednik .10 .25
80 Scott Hartnell .10 .25
81 Andreas Johansson .10 .25
82 Tomas Vokoun .20 .50
83 Scott Walker .10 .25
84 Patrik Elias .20 .50
85 Jeff Friesen .10 .25
86 Scott Gomez .10 .25
87 Jamie Langenbrunner .10 .25
88 John Madden .10 .25
89 Joe Nieuwendyk .10 .25
90 Scott Stevens .20 .50
91 Jason Blake .10 .25
92 Rick DiPietro .20 .50
93 Roman Hamrlik .10 .25
94 Mark Parrish .10 .25
95 Dan Blackburn .10 .25
96 Anson Carter .10 .25
97 Mike Dunham .20 .50
98 Bobby Holik .10 .25
99 Alex Kovalev .20 .50
100 Tom Poti .10 .25
101 Daniel Alfredsson .20 .50
102 Zdeno Chara .10 .25
103 Mike Fisher .10 .25
104 Martin Havlat .20 .50
105 Bryan Smolinski .10 .25
106 Jason Spezza .25 .60
107 Todd White .10 .25
108 Tony Amonte .20 .50
109 Simon Gagne .25 .60
110 Jeff Hackett .20 .50
111 Keith Primeau .20 .50
112 Mark Recchi .20 .50
113 Shane Doan .10 .25
114 Chris Gratton .10 .25
115 Mike Johnson .10 .25
116 Daymond Langkow .10 .25
117 Johan Hedberg .20 .50
118 Aleksey Morozov .10 .25
119 Martin Straka .10 .25
120 Dick Tarnstrom .10 .25
121 Pavol Demitra .20 .50
122 Al MacInnis .20 .50
123 Chris Pronger .20 .50
124 Peter Sejna RC .20 .50
125 Keith Tkachuk .25 .60
126 Doug Weight .20 .50
127 Jonathan Cheechoo .12 .30
128 Vincent Damphousse .10 .25
129 Patrick Marleau .20 .50
130 Dave Andreychuk .10 .25
131 John Grahame .20 .50
132 Brad Richards .20 .50
133 Martin St. Louis .20 .50
134 Nik Antropov .10 .25
135 Tie Domi .20 .50
136 Doug Gilmour .20 .50
137 Alexander Mogilny .20 .50
138 Matt Stajan RC 1.00 2.50
139 Darcy Tucker .10 .25
140 Dan Cloutier .20 .50
141 Ed Jovanovski .20 .50
142 Trevor Linden .10 .25
143 Brendan Morrison .20 .50
144 Daniel Sedin .10 .25
145 Henrik Sedin .10 .25
146 Sergei Berezin .10 .25
147 Peter Bondra .20 .50
148 Sebastien Charpentier .20 .50
149 Sergei Gonchar .10 .25
150 Michael Nylander .10 .25
151 Sergei Fedorov .75 2.00
152 J-S Giguere .60 1.50
153 Dany Heatley .75 2.00
154 Ilya Kovalchuk .75 2.00
155 Joe Thornton .75 2.00
156 Martin Biron .60 1.50
157 Jarome Iginla .75 2.00
158 Ron Francis .60 1.50
159 Jocelyn Thibault .60 1.50
160 Peter Forsberg 1.50 4.00
161 Paul Kariya .10 .25
162 Patrick Roy 2.00 5.00
163 Joe Sakic 1.25 3.00
164 Rick Nash .75 2.00
165 Mike Modano 1.00 2.50
166 Marty Turco .60 1.50
167 Dominik Hasek 1.25 3.00
168 Brett Hull .75 2.00
169 Steve Yzerman 2.00 5.00
170 Ryan Smyth .60 1.50
171 Roberto Luongo .75 2.00
172 Ziggy Palffy .60 1.50
173 Marian Gaborik 1.25 3.00
174 Saku Koivu .60 1.50
175 Jose Theodore .75 2.00
176 David Legwand .60 1.50
177 Martin Brodeur 1.50 4.00
178 Michael Peca .60 1.50
179 Alexei Yashin .60 1.50
180 Pavel Bure .60 1.50
181 Eric Lindros .60 1.50
182 Mark Messier .60 1.50
183 Marian Hossa .60 1.50
184 Patrick Lalime .60 1.50
185 John LeClair .60 1.50
186 Jeremy Roenick .75 2.00
187 Sean Burke .60 1.50
188 Mario Lemieux 2.50 6.00
189 Barret Jackman .60 1.50
190 Chris Osgood .60 1.50
191 Evgeni Nabokov .60 1.50
192 Nikolai Khabibulin .60 1.50
193 Vincent Lecavalier .60 1.50
194 Ed Belfour .60 1.50
195 Owen Nolan .60 1.50
196 Mats Sundin .60 1.50
197 Todd Bertuzzi .60 1.50
198 Markus Naslund .60 1.50
199 Jaromir Jagr 1.00 2.50
200 Olaf Kolzig .60 1.50
201 Stanislav Chistov 6.00 15.00
202 Martin Biron 6.00 15.00
203 Eric Daze 6.00 15.00
204 Milan Hejduk 8.00 20.00
205 Bill Guerin 6.00 15.00
206 Marty Turco 6.00 15.00
207 Jason Allison 6.00 15.00
208 Roman Cechmanek 6.00 15.00
209 David Legwand 6.00 15.00
210 Patrick Lalime 6.00 15.00
211 Tony Amonte 6.00 15.00
212 Jeff Hackett 6.00 15.00
213 Sean Burke 6.00 15.00
214 Chris Osgood 6.00 15.00
215 Nikolai Khabibulin 8.00 20.00
216 B.Hull/B.Hull 20.00 50.00
217 S.Yzerman/T.Esposito 15.00 40.00
218 P.Roy/J.Beliveau 30.00 80.00
219 I.Kovalchuk/G.Lafleur 15.00 40.00
220 D.Heatley/G.Hall 15.00 40.00
221 M.Lemieux/J.Bower 30.00 80.00
222 J.Theodore/D.Sittler 15.00 40.00
223 P.Kariya/M.Dionne 15.00 40.00
224 M.Brodeur/F.Mahovlich 25.00 60.00
225 J.Sakic/B.Park 15.00 40.00
226 Joffrey Lupul RC 1.50 4.00
227 Patrice Bergeron RC 4.00 10.00
228 Matthew Lombardi RC 1.00 2.50
229 Eric Staal RC 3.00 8.00
230 Nikolai Zherdev RC 4.00 10.00
231 Nathan Horton RC 2.50 6.00
232 Brent Burns RC 1.00 2.50
233 Joni Pitkanen RC 1.50 4.00
234 Marc-Andre Fleury RC 6.00 15.00
235 Ryan Malone RC 2.00 5.00

2003-04 Pacific Exhibit Blue Backs

*CARDS 1-150: .75X TO 2X BASE HI
1-150 ODDS 1:10 HOBBY/1:13 RETAIL
1-150 PRINT RUN 275 SER.#'d SETS
*CARDS 151-200: 1X TO 2.5X
151-200 ODDS 1:15 HOBBY/1:25 RETAIL
151-200 PRINT RUN 425 SER.#'d SETS

2003-04 Pacific Exhibit Yellow Backs

*STARS: .5X TO 1.25X BASE HI
ONE PER HOBBY PACK

2003-04 Pacific Exhibit History Makers

COMPLETE SET (8) 12.50 25.00
STATED ODDS 1:29 HOBBY/1:25 RETAIL
1 Paul Kariya .60 1.50
2 Peter Forsberg 1.50 4.00
3 Joe Sakic 1.25 3.00
4 Brett Hull .75 2.00
5 Steve Yzerman 2.50 6.00
6 Mario Lemieux 3.00 8.00
7 Todd Bertuzzi .60 1.50
8 Markus Naslund .60 1.50

2003-04 Pacific Exhibit Pursuing Prominence

COMPLETE SET (12) 8.00 15.00
STATED ODDS 1:15 HOBBY/1:13 RETAIL
1 Dany Heatley 1.00 2.50
2 Ilya Kovalchuk 1.00 2.50
3 Joe Thornton 1.00 2.50
4 Rick Nash 1.00 2.50
5 Henrik Zetterberg 1.00 2.50
6 Ales Hemsky .50 1.25
7 Jay Bouwmeester .50 1.25
8 Marian Gaborik 2.00 5.00
9 Marian Hossa .50 1.25
10 Jason Spezza 1.00 2.50
11 Barret Jackman .50 1.25
12 Vincent Lecavalier .50 1.25

2003-04 Pacific Exhibit Standing on Tradition

COMPLETE SET (10) 10.00 20.00
STATED ODDS 1:29 HOBBY/1:25 RETAIL
1 J-S Giguere .60 1.50
2 Jocelyn Thibault .60 1.50
3 Patrick Roy 2.50 6.00
4 Marty Turco .60 1.50
5 Dominik Hasek 1.50 4.00
6 Roberto Luongo 1.00 2.50
7 Jose Theodore 1.00 2.50
8 Martin Brodeur 2.00 5.00
9 Patrick Lalime .60 1.50
10 Ed Belfour .75 2.00

2001-02 Pacific Heads-Up

Released in mid-November 2001, this 120-card set carried an SRP of $3.99 for a 5-card hobby pack with 18 packs per box. The set consisted of 100 veteran cards and 20 shortprinted rookie cards available in hobby packs only. Rookies were serial-numbered to 999 sets.

COM.SET w/o SP's (100) 20.00 50.00
1 Paul Kariya .30 .75
2 Steve Shields .10 .25
3 Ray Ferraro .10 .25
4 Milan Hnilicka .20 .50
5 Patrik Stefan .10 .25
6 Jason Allison .10 .25
7 Byron Dafoe .20 .50
8 Bill Guerin .20 .50
9 Sergei Samsonov .20 .50
10 Joe Thornton .60 1.50
11 J-P Dumont .10 .25
12 Jarome Iginla .60 1.50
13 Marc Savard .10 .25
14 Roman Turek .20 .50
15 Ron Francis .20 .50
16 Arturs Irbe .20 .50
17 Jeff O'Neill .10 .25
18 Tony Amonte .20 .50
19 Steve Sullivan .10 .25
20 Jocelyn Thibault .20 .50
21 Rob Blake .20 .50
22 Chris Drury .20 .50
23 Peter Forsberg .75 2.00
24 Milan Hejduk .20 .50
25 Patrick Roy 2.00 5.00
26 Joe Sakic .75 2.00
27 Marc Denis .20 .50
28 Geoff Sanderson .10 .25
29 Ed Belfour .30 .75
30 Brett Hull .40 1.00
31 Mike Modano .60 1.50
32 Joe Nieuwendyk .20 .50
33 Pierre Turgeon .20 .50
34 Sergei Fedorov .60 1.50
35 Dominik Hasek .75 2.00
36 Chris Osgood .20 .50
37 Luc Robitaille .20 .50
38 Brendan Shanahan .30 .75
39 Steve Yzerman 1.50 4.00
40 Mike Comrie .20 .50
41 Tommy Salo .20 .50
42 Ryan Smyth .10 .25
43 Pavel Bure .30 .75
44 Roberto Luongo .60 1.50
45 Steve Heinze .10 .25
46 Zigmund Palffy .20 .50
47 Felix Potvin .30 .75
48 Manny Fernandez .20 .50
49 Marian Gaborik .60 1.50
50 Saku Koivu .30 .75
51 Brian Savage .10 .25
52 Jose Theodore .40 1.00
53 Mike Dunham .20 .50
54 David Legwand .20 .50
55 Jason Arnott .10 .25
56 Martin Brodeur 1.00 2.50
57 Patrik Elias .20 .50
58 Scott Stevens .20 .50
59 Mariusz Czerkawski .10 .25
60 Rick DiPietro .20 .50
61 Mike Peca .10 .25
62 Alexei Yashin .10 .25
63 Theo Fleury .20 .50
64 Brian Leetch .20 .50
65 Mark Messier .30 .75
66 Mike Richter .30 .75
67 Daniel Alfredsson .20 .50
68 Martin Havlat .20 .50
69 Marian Hossa .30 .75
70 Patrick Lalime .20 .50
71 Roman Cechmanek .20 .50
72 John LeClair .20 .50
73 Mark Recchi .20 .50
74 Jeremy Roenick .40 1.00
75 Sean Burke .20 .50
76 Johan Hedberg .20 .50
77 Alexei Kovalev .20 .50
78 Mario Lemieux 2.00 5.00
79 Fred Brathwaite .20 .50
80 Chris Pronger .20 .50
81 Keith Tkachuk .20 .50
82 Doug Weight .20 .50
83 Patrick Marleau .20 .50
84 Evgeni Nabokov .20 .50
85 Teemu Selanne .30 .75
86 Nikolai Khabibulin .30 .75
87 Vincent Lecavalier .30 .75
88 Brad Richards .20 .50
89 Curtis Joseph .30 .75
90 Alexander Mogilny .20 .50
91 Gary Roberts .10 .25
92 Mats Sundin .30 .75
93 Dan Cloutier .20 .50
94 Markus Naslund .20 .50
95 Daniel Sedin .10 .25
96 Henrik Sedin .10 .25
97 Peter Bondra .20 .50
98 Jaromir Jagr .60 1.50
99 Olaf Kolzig .20 .50
100 Adam Oates .20 .50
101 Ilja Bryzgalov RC 3.00 8.00
102 Timo Parssinen RC 1.25 3.00
103 Ilya Kovalchuk RC 12.00 30.00
104 Erik Cole RC 3.00 8.00
105 Vaclav Nedorost RC 1.25 3.00
106 Pavel Datsyuk RC 8.00 20.00
107 Kristian Huselius RC 3.00 8.00
108 Jaroslav Bednar RC 1.25 3.00
109 Pascal Dupuis RC 1.25 3.00
110 Martin Erat RC 1.25 3.00
111 Scott Clemmensen RC 1.25 3.00
112 Dan Blackburn RC 3.00 8.00
113 Chris Neil RC 3.00 8.00
114 Pavel Brendl SP 1.25 3.00
115 Jiri Dopita RC 1.25 3.00
116 Krystofer Kolanos RC 1.25 3.00
117 Mark Rycroft RC 1.25 3.00
118 Jeff Jillson RC 1.25 3.00
119 Nikita Alexeev RC 1.25 3.00
120 Brian Sutherby RC 1.25 3.00

2001-02 Pacific Heads-Up Blue

Randomly inserted in packs at a rate of 1:37 hobby packs, This 100-card set paralleled the base set but featured full color action card fronts with a blue holographic background. Each card was serial-numbered to 55 on the card fronts.

*BLUE: 10X TO 25X BASIC CARD

2001-02 Pacific Heads-Up Premiere Date

Randomly inserted into hobby packs at the rate of one per box, this 100-card set paralleled the base set but was enhanced with a foil premiere date box on the card front. Each card was serial-numbered out of 105.

*STARS: 6X TO 15X BASIC CARD

2001-02 Pacific Heads-Up Red

Randomly inserted in retail packs at a rate of 2:25 , this 100 card set paralleled the base set but carried a red holographic background. Each card was serial-numbered to 165.

*RED: 5X TO 12X BASIC CARDS

2001-02 Pacific Heads-Up Silver

Randomly inserted into packs at 1:145 hobby and 1:241 retail, this 100-card set paralleled the base set but featured a silver holographic card front. Each card was serial-numbered to 27.

NOT PRICED DUE TO SCARCITY

2001-02 Pacific Heads-Up All-Star Net

Randomly inserted in packs at a rate of 1:1153 hobby and 1:2401 retail. This set featured 2 player action color photos on the card front along with a swatch of game-used NHL All-Star goal net located in a gold box at the bottom center of card. Cards were serial-numbered to 65.

1 Evgeni Nabokov 25.00 60.00
Roman Cechmanek
2 Martin Brodeur 50.00 125.00
Rob Blake
3 Bill Guerin 25.00 60.00
Doug Weight
4 Pavel Bure 25.00 60.00
Zigmund Palffy
5 Paul Kariya 25.00 60.00
Mats Sundin
6 Chris Pronger 25.00 60.00
Nicklas Lidstrom

2001-02 Pacific Heads-Up Bobble Heads

Randomly inserted in hobby boxes at a rate of 1 per box and in retail packs as redemption cards at 1:121, this 12-player ceramic bobble head doll set featured the Pacific logo on the base along with the Pacific Heads-Up logo with the last name of each player. Please note that the Comrie bobble head was not produced and was redeemable for another randomly chosen bobble head as a replacement. Collectors receiving a bobble head of Pacific president Mike Cramer also received a redemption card good for the entire set. Approximately 12 of these dolls were randomly inserted into boxes.

1 Paul Kariya 12.50 30.00
2 Patrick Roy 15.00 40.00
3 Joe Sakic 12.50 30.00
4 Dominik Hasek 12.50 30.00
5 Steve Yzerman 15.00 40.00
6 Exchange Card 12.50 30.00
7 Martin Brodeur 15.00 40.00
8 Mark Messier 12.50 30.00
9 Johan Hedberg 12.50 30.00
10 Mario Lemieux 20.00 50.00
11 Curtis Joseph 12.50 30.00
12 Jaromir Jagr 12.50 30.00

2001-02 Pacific Heads-Up Breaking the Glass

COMPLETE SET (20) 30.00 60.00
STAT.ODDS 1:19 HOBBY/1:25 RETAIL
1 Milan Hnilicka 1.25 3.00
2 Patrik Stefan 1.25 3.00
3 J-P Dumont 1.25 3.00
4 Shane Willis 1.25 3.00
5 David Aebischer 1.25 3.00
6 Chris Drury 1.25 3.00
7 Alex Tanguay 2.00 5.00
8 Marc Denis 1.25 3.00
9 Marty Turco 1.25 3.00
10 Mike Comrie 1.25 3.00
11 Roberto Luongo 1.50 4.00
12 Marian Gaborik 3.00 8.00
13 David Legwand 1.25 3.00
14 Rick DiPietro 1.25 3.00
15 Martin Havlat 1.25 3.00
16 Johan Hedberg 1.25 3.00
17 Evgeni Nabokov 1.25 3.00
18 Brad Richards 1.25 3.00
19 Daniel Sedin 1.25 3.00
20 Henrik Sedin 1.25 3.00

2001-02 Pacific Heads-Up HD NHL

Cards 1-10 in this 20-card set were only available in hobby packs at rate of 1:19. Cards 11-20 were only available in retail packs at an insertion rate of 1:25. Cards featured color player photos on silver metallic card stock.

COMPLETE SET (20) 25.00 50.00
1 Paul Kariya .75 2.00
2 Peter Forsberg 2.00 5.00
3 Joe Sakic 1.50 4.00
4 Mike Modano 1.25 3.00
5 Steve Yzerman 4.00 10.00
6 Pavel Bure 1.00 2.50
7 Mario Lemieux 5.00 12.00
8 Teemu Selanne .75 2.00
9 Mats Sundin .75 2.00
10 Jaromir Jagr 1.25 3.00
11 Roman Turek .60 1.50
12 Ed Belfour .75 2.00
13 Chris Osgood .60 1.50
14 Tommy Salo .60 1.50
15 Felix Potvin .75 2.00
16 Jose Theodore 1.00 2.50
17 Martin Brodeur 2.00 5.00
18 Mike Richter .60 1.50
19 Roman Cechmanek .60 1.50
20 Curtis Joseph .75 2.00

2001-02 Pacific Heads-Up Prime Picks

COMPLETE SET (10) 15.00 40.00
STAT.ODDS 1:73 HOBBY/1:121 RETAIL
1 Mike Comrie 1.50 4.00
2 Roberto Luongo 4.00 10.00
3 Marian Gaborik 4.00 10.00
4 Rick DiPietro 1.50 4.00
5 Martin Havlat 1.50 4.00
6 Johan Hedberg 1.50 4.00
7 Evgeni Nabokov 1.50 4.00
8 Brad Richards 1.50 4.00
9 Daniel Sedin 1.50 4.00
10 Henrik Sedin 1.50 4.00

2001-02 Pacific Heads-Up Quad Jerseys

Randomly inserted in packs at a rate of 2:19 hobby and 1:97 retail, this 29-card set featured color action photo's along with

game-used jersey swatches on both card front and back for a total of 4 per card.

1 J-S Giguere 6.00 15.00
Mike Leclerc
Teemu Selanne
Guy Hebert
2 Joe Thornton 8.00 20.00
Sergei Samsonov
Kyle McLaren
Byron Dafoe
3 Scott Niedermeyer 8.00 20.00
Bobby Holik
P.J. Axelsson
Don Sweeney
4 Dominik Hasek 6.00 15.00
Stu Barnes
Mariusz Czerkawski
Kenny Jonsson
5 Jarome Iginla 6.00 15.00
Valeri Bure
Marc Savard
Rico Fata
6 Tony Amonte 6.00 15.00
Eric Daze
Jocelyn Thibault
Kyle Calder
7 Steve Sullivan 6.00 15.00
Alexei Zhamnov
Michael Nylander
Boris Mironov
8 Peter Forsberg 10.00 25.00
Joe Sakic
Aaron Miller
Dave Reid
9 Patrick Roy 8.00 20.00
Chris Dingman
Greg deVries
Jon Klemm
10 Mike Modano 6.00 15.00
Joe Nieuwendyk
Darryl Sydor
Derian Hatcher
11 Brendan Shanahan 8.00 20.00
Chris Chelios
Mathieu Dandenault
Chris Osgood
12 Benoit Brunet 6.00 15.00
Sergei Zholtok
Dainius Zubrus
Ulf Dahlen
13 Mike Dunham 6.00 15.00
David Legwnd
Tom Fitzgerald
Scott Walker
14 Theo Fleury 6.00 15.00
Brian Leetch
Mike Richter
Petr Nedved
15 John LeClair 6.00 15.00
Eric Desjardins
Kevin Stevens
Kip Miller
16 Jeremy Roenick 6.00 15.00
Sean Burke
Mika Alatalo
Shane Doan
17 Mario Lemieux 15.00 40.00
Jaromir Jagr
Jan Hrdina
Darius Kasparaitis
18 Martin Straka 6.00 15.00
Alexei Kovalev
Jean-Sebastien Aubin
Rich Parent
19 Tie Domi 6.00 15.00
Glenn Healy
Daniel Alfredsson
Dan Cloutier
20 Patrick Roy 20.00 50.00
Curtis Joseph
Dominik Hasek
Mike Richter
21 Lemieux/Sakic/Moda./Bure 30.00 80.00
22 Doug Weight 10.00 25.00
Chris Chelios
Derian Hatcher
Brian Leetch
23 Alexei Zhitnik 6.00 15.00
Eric Rasmussen
Rob Ray
Richard Smehlik
24 Jere Lehtinen 6.00 15.00
Mike Keane
Benoit Hogue
Blake Sloan
25 Mike York 6.00 15.00
Adam Graves
Sylvain Lefebvre
Manny Malhotra
26 Sean Burke 6.00 15.00
Teppo Numminen
Radoslav Suchy
Jyrki Lumme
27 Vincent Lecavalier 6.00 15.00
Keith Primeau
Matthew Barnaby
Milan Kraft
28 Martin Straka 6.00 15.00
Alexei Morozov
Josef Beranek
Bob Boughner
29 Alexei Kovalev 6.00 15.00
Michal Rozsival
Rich Parent
Darius Kasparaitis

2001-02 Pacific Heads-Up Rink Immortals

Randomly inserted in packs at a rate of 1:289 packs, this 10-card set featured full color action shots with a grey silhouette background. Cards were serial numbered to 99 of each on the front of the card in lower right hand corner.

1 Paul Kariya 8.00 20.00
2 Patrick Roy 20.00 50.00
3 Joe Sakic 10.00 25.00
4 Brett Hull 8.00 20.00
5 Dominik Hasek 10.00 25.00
6 Steve Yzerman 15.00 40.00
7 Pavel Bure 6.00 15.00
8 Martin Brodeur 12.00 30.00
9 Mario Lemieux 25.00 60.00
10 Jaromir Jagr 10.00 25.00

2001-02 Pacific Heads-Up Showstoppers

COMPLETE SET (20) 20.00 40.00
STATED ODDS 2:19 HOBBY/2:25 RETAIL
1 Steve Shields .60 1.50
2 Byron Dafoe .60 1.50
3 Roman Turek .60 1.50
4 Patrick Roy 4.00 10.00
5 Ed Belfour .75 2.00
6 Dominik Hasek 1.50 4.00
7 Chris Osgood .60 1.50
8 Tommy Salo .60 1.50
9 Roberto Luongo 1.00 2.50
10 Felix Potvin .75 2.00
11 Jose Theodore 1.00 2.50
12 Martin Brodeur 2.00 5.00
13 Rick DiPietro .60 1.50
14 Mike Richter .60 1.50
15 Patrick Lalime .60 1.50
16 Roman Cechmanek .60 1.50
17 Johan Hedberg .60 1.50
18 Evgeni Nabokov .60 1.50
19 Curtis Joseph .75 2.00
20 Olaf Kolzig .60 1.50

2001-02 Pacific Heads-Up Stat Masters

COMPLETE SET (20) 25.00 50.00
STATED ODDS 2:19 HOBBY/2:25 RETAIL
1 Paul Kariya .60 1.50
2 Joe Thornton 1.00 2.50
3 Peter Forsberg 1.50 4.00
4 Joe Sakic 1.25 3.00
5 Brett Hull .75 2.00
6 Mike Modano 1.00 2.50
7 Steve Yzerman 3.00 8.00
8 Pavel Bure .75 2.00
9 Zigmund Palffy .50 1.25
10 Jason Arnott .50 1.25
11 Theo Fleury .50 1.25
12 Marian Hossa .60 1.50
13 Jeremy Roenick .75 2.00
14 Mario Lemieux 4.00 10.00
15 Keith Tkachuk .60 1.50
16 Teemu Selanne .60 1.50
17 Vincent Lecavalier .60 1.50
18 Brad Richards .50 1.25
19 Mats Sundin .60 1.50
20 Jaromir Jagr 1.00 2.50

2002-03 Pacific Heads-Up

This 125-card set contained 125 veteran cards and 20 shortprinted rookie cards. Rookies were serial-numbered to 1000 each and were only available via a mail in redemption card found in packs.

COMPLETE SET (145) 100.00 200.00
COMP.SET w/o SP's (125) 30.00 60.00
1 J-S Giguere .30 .75
2 Paul Kariya .40 1.00
3 Adam Oates .30 .75
4 Dany Heatley .50 1.25
5 Milan Hnilicka .30 .75
6 Ilya Kovalchuk .50 1.25
7 Byron Dafoe .30 .75
8 Glen Murray .12 .30
9 Brian Rolston .12 .30
10 Sergei Samsonov .30 .75
11 Joe Thornton .60 1.50
12 Martin Biron .30 .75
13 J-P Dumont .12 .30
14 Miroslav Satan .30 .75
15 Craig Conroy .12 .30
16 Jarome Iginla .50 1.25
17 Dean McAmmond .12 .30
18 Roman Turek .30 .75
19 Erik Cole .30 .75
20 Ron Francis .30 .75
21 Arturs Irbe .30 .75
22 Sami Kapanen .12 .30
23 Jeff O'Neill .12 .30
24 Tony Amonte .30 .75
25 Eric Daze .30 .75
26 Jocelyn Thibault .30 .75
27 Alexei Zhamnov .12 .30
28 Rob Blake .30 .75
29 Chris Drury .30 .75
30 Peter Forsberg 1.00 2.50
31 Milan Hejduk .40 1.00
32 Patrick Roy 2.00 5.00
33 Joe Sakic .75 2.00
34 Marc Denis .30 .75
35 Rostislav Klesla .12 .30
36 Ray Whitney .12 .30
37 Jason Arnott .12 .30
38 Bill Guerin .30 .75
39 Mike Modano .60 1.50
40 Marty Turco .30 .75
41 Sergei Fedorov .60 1.50
42 Dominik Hasek .75 2.00
43 Brett Hull .50 1.25
44 Curtis Joseph .40 1.00
45 Nicklas Lidstrom .40 1.00
46 Luc Robitaille .30 .75
47 Brendan Shanahan .40 1.00
48 Steve Yzerman 2.00 5.00
49 Mike Comrie .30 .75
50 Tommy Salo .30 .75
51 Ryan Smyth .12 .30
52 Kristian Huselius .12 .30
53 Roberto Luongo .50 1.25
54 Stephen Weiss .12 .30
55 Jason Allison .12 .30
56 Adam Deadmarsh .12 .30
57 Zigmund Palffy .30 .75
58 Felix Potvin .40 1.00
59 Andrew Brunette .12 .30
60 Manny Fernandez .30 .75
61 Marian Gaborik .75 2.00
62 Donald Audette .12 .30
63 Doug Gilmour .30 .75
64 Saku Koivu .40 1.00
65 Yanic Perreault .12 .30
66 Jose Theodore .50 1.25
67 Denis Arkhipov .12 .30
68 Scott Hartnell .12 .30
69 David Legwand .30 .75
70 Martin Brodeur 1.00 2.50
71 Patrik Elias .30 .75
72 Joe Nieuwendyk .30 .75
73 Chris Osgood .30 .75
74 Mark Parrish .12 .30
75 Michael Peca .12 .30
76 Alexei Yashin .12 .30
77 Daniel Blackburn .30 .75
78 Pavel Bure .40 1.00
79 Theo Fleury .12 .30
80 Bobby Holik .12 .30
81 Brian Leetch .30 .75
82 Eric Lindros .40 1.00
83 Mike Richter .40 1.00
84 Daniel Alfredsson .30 .75
85 Radek Bonk .12 .30
86 Martin Havlat .30 .75
87 Marian Hossa .40 1.00
88 Patrick Lalime .30 .75
89 Roman Cechmanek .30 .75
90 Simon Gagne .40 1.00
91 John LeClair .40 1.00
92 Mark Recchi .30 .75
93 Jeremy Roenick .50 1.25
94 Daniel Briere .12 .30
95 Sean Burke .30 .75
96 Krystofer Kolanos .12 .30
97 Daymond Langkow .12 .30
98 Johan Hedberg .30 .75
99 Alexei Kovalev .30 .75
100 Mario Lemieux 2.50 6.00
101 Alexei Morozov .12 .30
102 Pavol Demitra .30 .75
103 Brent Johnson .30 .75
104 Chris Pronger .30 .75
105 Keith Tkachuk .30 .75
106 Doug Weight .30 .75
107 Patrick Marleau .30 .75
108 Evgeni Nabokov .30 .75
109 Owen Nolan .30 .75
110 Teemu Selanne .40 1.00
111 Nikolai Khabibulin .40 1.00
112 Vincent Lecavalier .40 1.00
113 Brad Richards .30 .75
114 Ed Belfour .40 1.00
115 Alyn McCauley .12 .30
116 Alexander Mogilny .30 .75
117 Gary Roberts .12 .30
118 Mats Sundin .40 1.00
119 Todd Bertuzzi .40 1.00
120 Dan Cloutier .30 .75
121 Brendan Morrison .30 .75
122 Markus Naslund .40 1.00
123 Peter Bondra .30 .75
124 Jaromir Jagr .60 1.50
125 Olaf Kolzig .30 .75
126 Stanislav Chistov RC 1.50 4.00
127 Martin Gerber RC 2.50 6.00
128 Alexei Smirnov RC 1.50 4.00
129 Chuck Kobasew RC 2.50 6.00
130 Rick Nash RC 8.00 20.00
131 Dmitri Bykov RC 1.50 4.00
132 Henrik Zetterberg RC 6.00 15.00
133 Ales Hemsky RC 5.00 12.00
134 Jay Bouwmeester RC 3.00 8.00
135 Alexander Frolov RC 3.00 8.00
136 Sylvain Blouin RC 1.50 4.00
137 P-M Bouchard RC 3.00 8.00
138 Ron Hainsey RC 1.50 4.00
139 Scottie Upshall RC 1.50 4.00
140 Mike Danton SP 1.50 4.00
141 Ray Schultz RC 1.50 4.00
142 Anton Volchenkov RC 1.50 4.00
143 Dennis Seidenberg RC 1.50 4.00
144 Alexander Svitov RC 1.50 4.00
145 Steve Eminger RC 1.50 4.00

2002-03 Pacific Heads-Up Blue

*BLUE: 1.25X TO 3X BASIC CARDS
STATED PRINT RUN 240 SER.#'d SETS

2002-03 Pacific Heads-Up Purple

*PURPLE: 12X TO 30X BASIC CARDS
STATED ODDS 1:73
STATED PRINT RUN 30 SER.#'d SETS

2002-03 Pacific Heads-Up Red

*RED: 8X TO 20X BASIC CARDS
STATED ODDS 1:19 HOBBY PACKS
STATED PRINT RUN 80 SER.#'d SETS

2002-03 Pacific Heads-Up Bobble Heads

Randomly inserted on per hobby box, this 14-player ceramic bobble head doll set featured the Pacific logo on the base along with the Pacific Heads-Up logo with the last name of each player.

1 Jason Allison 10.00 25.00
2 Pavel Bure 10.00 25.00
3 Mike Comrie 10.00 25.00
4 Peter Forsberg 15.00 50.00
5 Jarome Iginla 15.00 40.00
6 Saku Koivu 10.00 25.00
7 Ilya Kovalchuk 15.00 40.00
8 Eric Lindros 10.00 25.00
9 Evgeni Nabokov 10.00 25.00
10 Brendan Shanahan 10.00 25.00
11 Mats Sundin 10.00 25.00
12 Jose Theodore 15.00 40.00
13 Joe Thornton 15.00 40.00
14 Alexei Yashin 10.00 25.00

2002-03 Pacific Heads-Up Etched in Time

This 15-card set was inserted at a rate of 1:289 and each card was serial-numbered to just 85 copies.

1 Paul Kariya 6.00 15.00
2 Ilya Kovalchuk 8.00 20.00
3 Joe Thornton 8.00 20.00
4 Jarome Iginla 8.00 20.00
5 Ron Francis 6.00 15.00
6 Peter Forsberg 15.00 40.00
7 Patrick Roy 20.00 50.00
8 Joe Sakic 12.50 30.00
9 Dominik Hasek 15.00 40.00
10 Steve Yzerman 20.00 50.00
11 Martin Brodeur 15.00 40.00
12 Eric Lindros 6.00 15.00
13 Mario Lemieux 25.00 60.00
14 Mats Sundin 6.00 15.00
15 Jaromir Jagr 10.00 25.00

2002-03 Pacific Heads-Up Head First

This 16-card set was inserted at a rate of 1:19.

COMPLETE SET (16) 20.00 40.00
1 Dany Heatley 1.50 4.00
2 Ilya Kovalchuk 2.00 5.00
3 Sergei Samsonov 1.00 2.50
4 Joe Thornton 2.00 5.00
5 Stephen Weiss 1.00 2.50
6 Marian Gaborik 2.50 6.00
7 Scott Hartnell 1.00 2.50
8 Rick DiPietro 1.00 2.50

9 Raffi Torres 1.00 2.50
10 Dan Blackburn 1.00 2.50
11 Martin Havlat 1.00 2.50
12 Simon Gagne 1.25 3.00
13 Krystofer Kolanos 1.00 2.50
14 Vincent Lecavalier 1.25 3.00
15 Daniel Sedin 1.00 2.50
16 Henrik Sedin 1.00 2.50

2002-03 Pacific Heads-Up Inside the Numbers

This 24-card set was inserted at a rate of 1:10.
COMPLETE SET (24) 30.00 60.00
1 Adam Oates .60 1.50
2 Dany Heatley 1.00 2.50
3 Ilya Kovalchuk 1.00 2.50
4 Joe Thornton 1.25 3.00
5 Jarome Iginla 1.00 2.50
6 Ron Francis .60 1.50
7 Patrick Roy 3.00 8.00
8 Joe Sakic 1.50 4.00
9 Mike Modano 1.25 3.00
10 Dominik Hasek 2.00 5.00
11 Brendan Shanahan 1.25 3.00
12 Jose Theodore 1.00 2.50
13 Martin Brodeur 2.50 6.00
14 Alexei Yashin .60 1.50
15 Eric Lindros .75 2.00
16 Daniel Alfredsson .60 1.50
17 Mario Lemieux 4.00 10.00
18 Pavol Demitra .60 1.50
19 Evgeni Nabokov .60 1.50
20 Nikolai Khabibulin .75 2.00
21 Mats Sundin .75 2.00
22 Todd Bertuzzi .75 2.00
23 Markus Naslund .75 2.00
24 Jaromir Jagr 1.25 3.00

2002-03 Pacific Heads-Up Postseason Picks

This 10-card set was inserted at a rate of 1:37.
COMPLETE SET (10) 20.00 40.00
1 Erik Cole .75 2.00
2 Ron Francis .75 2.00
3 Peter Forsberg 2.00 5.00
4 Patrick Roy 4.00 10.00
5 Joe Sakic 1.50 4.00
6 Dominik Hasek 1.50 4.00
7 Brendan Shanahan 1.25 3.00
8 Steve Yzerman 4.00 10.00
9 Jose Theodore 1.00 2.50
10 Mats Sundin .75 2.00

2002-03 Pacific Heads-Up Quad Jerseys

Inserted at 2:19, this 36-card set featured four swatches of game-used jerseys. Two swatches appeared on the card front and two on the card back.
1 Jeff Friesen 5.00 12.00
Oleg Tverdovsky
Jason Allison
Adam Deadmarsh
2 Ilya Kovalchuk 5.00 12.00
Patrik Stefan
Milan Hnilicka
Tomi Kallio
3 Sergei Samsonov 5.00 12.00
Joe Thornton
Kyle McLaren
Don Sweeney
4 J.P. Dumont 5.00 12.00
Martin Biron
Jay McKee
Miroslav Satan
5 Roman Turek 5.00 12.00
Marc Savard
Mike Comrie
Ryan Smyth
6 Franc/Irbe/Brdmour/O'Neill 12.50 30.00
7 Amonte/Daze/Bell/Sulli 5.00 12.00
8 Chris Drury 5.00 12.00
Milan Hejduk
Alex Tanguay
Vaclav Nedorost
9 Rob Blake 15.00 40.00
Joe Sakic
Luc Robitaille
Sergei Fedorov
10 Marc Denis 5.00 12.00
Ron Tugnutt
Rostislav Klesla
Geoff Sanderson
11 Belfour/Turco/Trgeon/Mdno 6.00 15.00
12 Dominik Hasek 10.00 25.00
Brett Hull
Nicklas Lidstrom
Jason Williams
13 Jason Allison 5.00 12.00
Ziggy Palffy
Felix Potvin
Bryan Smolinski
14 Gbrik/Kuba/McLnn/Ferndz 6.00 15.00
15 Jose Theodore 10.00 25.00
Yanic Perreault
Sergei Berezin
Saku Koivu
16 Martin Erat 5.00 12.00
David Legwand
Scott Walker
Jukka Hentunen
17 Martin Brodeur 12.50 30.00
Patrik Elias
Scott Gomez
Scott Stevens
18 Michael Peca 5.00 12.00
Alexei Yashin
Eric Lindros
Theoren Fleury
19 Daniel Alfredsson 10.00 25.00
Patrick Lalime
Martin Havlat
Marian Hossa
20 Adam Oates 5.00 12.00
Jeremy Roenick
Roman Cechmanek
Jiri Dopita
21 Krystofer Kolanos 5.00 12.00
Michal Handzus
Daymond Langkow
Shane Doan
22 Johan Hedberg 5.00 12.00
Robert Lang
Toby Petersen
Kris Beech
23 Chris Pronger 5.00 12.00
Keith Tkachuk
Pavol Demitra
Sergei Varlamov
24 Evgeni Nabokov 8.00 20.00
Owen Nolan
Miikka Kiprusoff
Patrick Marleau
25 Nikolai Khabibulin 10.00 25.00
Brad Richards
Valeri Bure
Roberto Luongo
26 Curtis Joseph 12.50 30.00
Gary Roberts
Alexander Mogilny
Darcy Tucker
27 Dan Cloutier 8.00 20.00
Todd Bertuzzi
Daniel Sedin
Henrik Sedin
28 Lemx/Prnger/Brodeur/Cujo 20.00 50.00
29 Guerin/Mdno/Hull/Leetch 12.50 30.00
30 Pavel Bure 15.00 40.00
Nikolai Khabibulin
Sergei Fedorov
Alexei Yashin
31 Mats Sundin 5.00 12.00
Daniel Alfredsson
Tommy Salo
Johan Hedberg
32 Jaromir Jagr 10.00 25.00
Dominik Hasek
Milan Hejduk
Patrik Elias
33 Teemu Selanne 5.00 12.00
Jere Lehtinen
Jyrki Lumme
Tomi Kallio
34 Bndra/Gbrik/Demitra/Plffy 8.00 20.00
35 Ilya Kovalchuk 15.00 40.00
Dany Heatley
Krystofer Kolanos
Erik Cole
36 Kristian Huselius 5.00 12.00
Jiri Dopita
Martin Erat
Jukka Hentunen

2002-03 Pacific Heads-Up Quad Jerseys Gold

*GOLD: 1X TO 2.5X BASIC JERSEYS
STATED PRINT RUN 30 SER.#'d SETS

2002-03 Pacific Heads-Up Showstoppers

This 20-card set was inserted at a rate of 1:10 and featured goalies only.
COMPLETE SET (20) 25.00 50.00
1 J-S Giguere .40 1.00
2 Byron Dafoe .40 1.00
3 Roman Turek .40 1.00
4 Arturs Irbe .40 1.00
5 Jocelyn Thibault .40 1.00
6 Patrick Roy 3.00 8.00
7 Marty Turco .40 1.00
8 Dominik Hasek 1.25 3.00
9 Curtis Joseph .60 1.50
10 Roberto Luongo .75 2.00
11 Felix Potvin .60 1.50
12 Jose Theodore .75 2.00
13 Martin Brodeur 1.50 4.00
14 Chris Osgood .40 1.00
15 Patrick Lalime .40 1.00
16 Sean Burke .40 1.00
17 Brent Johnson .40 1.00
18 Evgeni Nabokov .40 1.00
19 Nikolai Khabibulin .60 1.50
20 Dan Cloutier .40 1.00

2002-03 Pacific Heads-Up Stat Masters

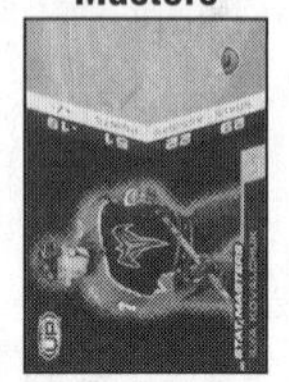

This 15-card set was inserted at a rate of 1:73.
COMPLETE SET (15) 40.00 80.00
1 Paul Kariya 1.25 3.00
2 Dany Heatley 1.50 4.00
3 Ilya Kovalchuk 1.50 4.00
4 Joe Thornton 2.00 5.00
5 Jarome Iginla 1.50 4.00
6 Ron Francis 1.25 3.00
7 Joe Sakic 2.50 6.00
8 Brett Hull 1.50 4.00
9 Steve Yzerman 6.00 15.00
10 Pavel Bure 1.50 4.00
11 Eric Lindros 1.25 3.00
12 Mario Lemieux 8.00 20.00
13 Mats Sundin 1.25 3.00
14 Todd Bertuzzi 1.25 3.00
15 Jaromir Jagr 2.00 5.00

2003-04 Pacific Heads-Up

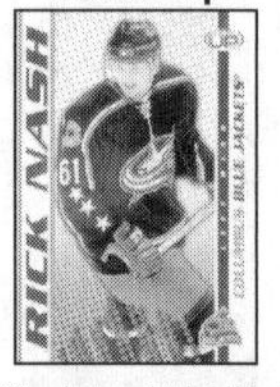

This 136-card set consisted of 100 veteran cards and 36 short-printed rookie cards (101-136). Rookie cards were serial-numbered to just 899 copies each.
COMPLETE SET (136) 75.00 150.00
COMP.SET w/o SP's (100) 15.00 30.00
1 Sergei Fedorov .50 1.25
2 J-S Giguere .30 .75
3 Steve Rucchin .12 .30
4 Ilya Kovalchuk .50 1.25
5 Shawn McEachern .12 .30
6 Pasi Nurminen .30 .75
7 Mike Knuble .12 .30
8 Andrew Raycroft .30 .75
9 Brian Rolston .30 .75
10 Joe Thornton .60 1.50
11 Martin Biron .30 .75
12 Daniel Briere .12 .30
13 J-P Dumont .12 .30
14 Jarome Iginla .50 1.25
15 Jamie McLennan .12 .30
16 Steven Reinprecht .12 .30
17 Ron Francis .30 .75
18 Josef Vasicek .12 .30
19 Kevin Weekes .30 .75
20 Mark Bell .12 .30
21 Michael Leighton .30 .75
22 Jocelyn Thibault UER .30 .75
Michael Leighton pictured on front
23 David Aebischer .30 .75
24 Peter Forsberg 1.00 2.50
25 Paul Kariya .30 .75
26 Joe Sakic .75 2.00
27 Alex Tanguay .30 .75
28 Marc Denis .30 .75
29 Rick Nash .50 1.25
30 David Vyborny .12 .30
31 Bill Guerin .30 .75
32 Mike Modano .60 1.50
33 Marty Turco .40 1.00
34 Pavel Datsyuk .40 1.00
35 Dominik Hasek .75 2.00
36 Brett Hull .50 1.25
37 Brendan Shanahan .40 1.00
38 Steve Yzerman 2.00 5.00
39 Henrik Zetterberg .40 1.00
40 Ty Conklin .30 .75
41 Ales Hemsky .12 .30
42 Ryan Smyth .12 .30
43 Jay Bouwmeester .12 .30
44 Olli Jokinen .30 .75
45 Roberto Luongo .50 1.25
46 Roman Cechmanek .30 .75
47 Cristobal Huet .30 .75
48 Ziggy Palffy .30 .75
49 Pierre-Marc Bouchard .12 .30
50 Marian Gaborik .75 2.00
51 Dwayne Roloson .30 .75
52 Saku Koivu .40 1.00
53 Mike Ribeiro .12 .30
54 Michael Ryder UER .12 .30
Front pictures Andrei Markov
55 Jose Theodore .50 1.25
56 Scott Hartnell .12 .30
57 David Legwand .30 .75
58 Martin Brodeur 1.00 2.50
59 Patrik Elias .30 .75
60 Jamie Langenbrunner .12 .30
61 Mariusz Czerkawski .12 .30
62 Rick DiPietro .30 .75
63 Trent Hunter .12 .30
64 Alexei Yashin .12 .30
65 Alex Kovalev .30 .75
66 Eric Lindros .40 1.00
67 Mark Messier .40 1.00
68 Daniel Alfredsson .30 .75
69 Marian Hossa .40 1.00
70 Patrick Lalime .30 .75
71 Jason Spezza .40 1.00
72 Tony Amonte .30 .75
73 Robert Esche .30 .75
74 Jeremy Roenick .50 1.25
75 Justin Williams .12 .30
76 Sean Burke .30 .75
77 Ladislav Nagy .12 .30
78 Rico Fata .12 .30
79 Mario Lemieux 2.50 6.00
80 Barret Jackman .12 .30
81 Chris Osgood .30 .75
82 Chris Pronger .30 .75
83 Patrick Marleau .30 .75
84 Alyn McCauley .12 .30
85 Marco Sturm .12 .30
86 Nikolai Khabibulin .40 1.00
87 Vincent Lecavalier .40 1.00
88 Martin St. Louis .30 .75
89 Cory Stillman .12 .30
90 Ed Belfour .40 1.00
91 Alexander Mogilny .30 .75
92 Owen Nolan .30 .75
93 Mats Sundin .40 1.00
94 Todd Bertuzzi .40 1.00
95 Dan Cloutier .30 .75
96 Jason King .12 .30
97 Brendan Morrison .12 .30
98 Markus Naslund .40 1.00
99 Jaromir Jagr .60 1.50
100 Robert Lang .12 .30
101 Joffrey Lupul RC 2.00 5.00
102 Patrice Bergeron RC 4.00 10.00
103 Pat Leahy RC 1.50 4.00
104 Brent Krahn RC 1.50 4.00
105 Matthew Lombardi RC 1.50 4.00
106 Eric Staal RC 6.00 15.00
107 Tuomo Ruutu RC 4.00 10.00
108 Mikhail Yakubov RC 1.50 4.00
109 Cody McCormick RC 1.50 4.00
110 Dan Fritsche RC 1.50 4.00
111 Nikolai Zherdev RC 2.50 6.00
112 Antti Miettinen RC 1.50 4.00
113 Darryl Bootland RC 1.50 4.00
114 Jiri Hudler RC 2.00 5.00
115 Nathan Robinson RC 1.50 4.00
116 Tony Salmelainen RC 1.50 4.00
117 Peter Sarno RC 1.50 4.00
118 Nathan Horton RC 3.00 8.00
119 Dustin Brown RC 1.50 4.00
120 Brent Burns RC 1.50 4.00
121 Christopher Higgins RC 4.00 10.00
122 Dan Hamhuis RC 1.50 4.00
123 Jordin Tootoo RC 3.00 8.00
124 Marek Zidlicky RC 1.50 4.00
125 Paul Martin RC 1.50 4.00
126 Dominic Moore RC 1.50 4.00
127 Antoine Vermette RC 1.50 4.00
128 Joni Pitkanen RC 1.50 4.00
129 Fredrik Sjostrom RC 1.50 4.00
130 Marc-Andre Fleury RC 6.00 15.00
131 John Pohl RC 1.50 4.00
132 Peter Sejna RC 1.50 4.00
133 Milan Michalek RC 1.50 4.00
134 Matt Stajan RC 3.00 8.00
135 Boyd Gordon RC 1.50 4.00
136 Alexander Semin RC 3.00 8.00

2003-04 Pacific Heads-Up Hobby LTD

*STARS: 2X TO 5X BASIC CARDS
1-100 PRINT RUN
*ROOKIES: .5X TO 1.25X
101-136 PRINT RUN 250 SER.#'d SETS

2003-04 Pacific Heads-Up Retail LTD

*STARS: .5X TO 1.25X
*ROOKIES: .25X TO .5X
STATED ODDS 1:2 RETAIL PACKS

2003-04 Pacific Heads-Up Fast Forwards

STATED ODDS 1:9
*LTD: .75X TO 2X
LTD PRINT RUN 175 SER.#'d SETS
1 Sergei Fedorov 1.00 2.50
2 Ilya Kovalchuk 1.00 2.50
3 Rick Nash 1.00 2.50
4 Mike Modano 1.25 3.00
5 Marian Gaborik 1.50 4.00
6 Marian Hossa .75 2.00
7 Jeremy Roenick 1.00 2.50

8 Alexander Mogilny .75 2.00
9 Markus Naslund .75 2.00

2003-04 Pacific Heads-Up In Focus

STATED ODDS 1:13
*LTD: .75X TO 2X
LTD PRINT RUN 175 SER.#'d SETS
1 Sergei Fedorov 1.00 2.50
2 Ilya Kovalchuk 1.00 2.50
3 Eric Staal 1.00 2.50
4 Joe Sakic 1.50 4.00
5 Alex Tanguay .75 2.00
6 Rick Nash 1.00 2.50
7 Henrik Zetterberg .75 2.00
8 Jay Bouwmeester .75 2.00
9 Jason Spezza .75 2.00
10 Todd Bertuzzi .75 2.00

2003-04 Pacific Heads-Up Jerseys

This 25-card memorabilia set was inserted at 2 per 24-pack box. Known SP's are noted below.
1 Joffrey Lupul 2.00 5.00
2 Ilya Kovalchuk SP 8.00 20.00
3 Joe Thornton SP 10.00 25.00
4 Ales Kotalik 2.00 5.00
5 Ryan Miller 3.00 8.00
6 Matthew Lombardi 2.00 5.00
7 David Aebischer 3.00 8.00
8 Peter Forsberg SP 10.00 25.00
9 Antti Miettinen 2.00 5.00
10 Steve Yzerman SP 12.50 30.00
11 Ales Hemsky 2.00 5.00
12 Jay Bouwmeester 2.00 5.00
13 Nathan Horton 3.00 8.00
14 Dustin Brown 2.00 5.00
15 Ziggy Palffy 3.00 8.00
16 Chris Higgins 4.00 10.00
17 Jordin Tootoo 6.00 15.00
18 Martin Brodeur 3.00 8.00
19 Rick DiPietro 3.00 8.00
20 Jason Spezza 6.00 15.00
21 Antoine Vermette 2.00 5.00
22 Mario Lemieux SP 15.00 40.00
23 Barret Jackman 2.00 5.00
24 Owen Nolan 2.00 5.00
25 Boyd Gordon 2.00 5.00

2003-04 Pacific Heads-Up Mini Sweaters

Inserted at one per hobby box, these small replica sweaters measured about 6" high.
1 Marc-Andre Fleury 12.00 30.00
2 Ilya Kovalchuk 12.00 30.00
3 Joe Thornton 12.00 30.00
4 Peter Forsberg 12.00 30.00
5 Steve Yzerman 15.00 40.00
6 Martin Brodeur 15.00 40.00
7 Marian Gaborik 12.00 30.00
8 Ed Belfour 8.00 20.00
9 Todd Bertuzzi 8.00 20.00

2003-04 Pacific Heads-Up Prime Prospects

COMPLETE SET (10) 10.00 20.00
STATED ODDS 1:7
*LTD: .6X TO 1.5X
LTD PRINT RUN 175 SER.#'d SETS
1 Joffrey Lupul .75 2.00
2 Patrice Bergeron 1.50 4.00
3 Ryan Miller 1.25 3.00
4 Matthew Lombardi .40 1.00
5 Eric Staal 2.00 5.00
6 Philippe Sauve .40 1.00
7 Nikolai Zherdev 1.25 3.00
8 Jiri Hudler .75 2.00
9 Nathan Horton .75 2.00
10 Dustin Brown .40 1.00
11 Brent Burns .40 1.00
12 Christopher Higgins 1.25 3.00
13 Michael Ryder 1.25 3.00
14 Jordin Tootoo 1.25 3.00
15 Antoine Vermette .40 1.00
16 Joni Pitkanen .75 2.00
17 Marc-Andre Fleury 2.00 5.00
18 Milan Michalek .75 2.00
19 Matt Stajan .75 2.00
20 Jason King .40 1.00

2003-04 Pacific Heads-Up Rink Immortals

STATED ODDS 1:13
*LTD: .75X TO 2X
LTD PRINT RUN 175 SER.#'d SETS
1 Joe Thornton 1.00 2.50
2 Peter Forsberg 2.00 5.00
3 Joe Sakic 1.50 4.00
4 Dominik Hasek 1.50 4.00
5 Brett Hull 1.00 2.50
6 Steve Yzerman 2.50 6.00
7 Martin Brodeur 2.50 6.00
8 Mark Messier 1.00 2.50
9 Mario Lemieux 3.00 8.00
10 Ed Belfour 1.00 2.50

2003-04 Pacific Heads-Up Stonewallers

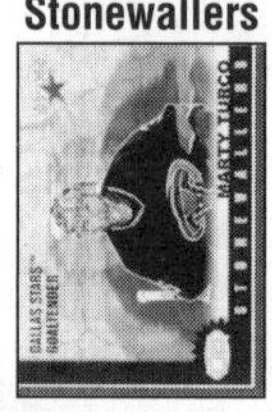

STATED ODDS 1:9
*LTD: .75X TO 2X
LTD.PRINT RUN 175 SER.#'d SETS
1 J-S Giguere .60 1.50
2 Pasi Nurminen .60 1.50
3 David Aebischer .60 1.50
4 Marty Turco .60 1.50
5 Dominik Hasek 1.50 4.00
6 Jose Theodore 1.00 2.50
7 Martin Brodeur 2.50 6.00
8 Rick DiPietro .60 1.50
9 Patrick Lalime .60 1.50
10 Nikolai Khabibulin .75 2.00
11 Ed Belfour .75 2.00
12 Dan Cloutier .60 1.50

2001-02 Pacific High Voltage

Available via a mail-in offer advertised in Powerplay magazine, this 10-card set featured hot rookies from the 2001-02 season. To receive a set, collectors had to send in wrappers from other Pacific products.
COMPLETE SET (10) 20.00 50.00
1 Dany Heatley 2.40 6.00
2 Ilya Kovalchuk 10.00 25.00
3 Erik Cole 2.40 6.00
4 Vaclav Nedorost 2.40 6.00
5 Kristian Huselius 3.20 8.00
6 Martin Erat .80 2.00
7 Dan Blackburn 1.00 2.50
8 Krystofer Kolanos 2.40 6.00
9 Jeff Jillson 1.60 4.00
10 Nikita Alexeev 1.60 4.00

1997-98 Pacific Invincible

The 1997-98 Pacific Invincible set was issued in one series totaling 150 cards and distributed in three-card packs. The fronts feature color action player images with gold foil background enhancements and a small player head photo in a clear, circular "window" at the bottom. The backs carry player information.
COMPLETE SET (150) 20.00 50.00
1 Brian Bellows .20 .50

2 Guy Hebert .30 .75
3 Paul Kariya .40 1.00
4 Teemu Selanne .40 1.00
5 Darren Van Impe .20 .50
6 Jason Allison .20 .50
7 Ray Bourque .40 1.00
8 Jim Carey .30 .75
9 Ted Donato .20 .50
10 Jozef Stumpel .20 .50
11 Jason Dawe .20 .50
12 Dominik Hasek 1.00 2.50
13 Michael Peca .20 .50
14 Derek Plante .20 .50
15 Miroslav Satan .20 .50
16 Theo Fleury .20 .50
17 Dave Gagner .20 .50
18 Jonas Hoglund .20 .50
19 Jarome Iginla .60 1.50
20 Trevor Kidd .30 .75
21 German Titov .20 .50
22 Sean Burke .30 .75
23 Andrew Cassels .20 .50
24 Derek King .20 .50
25 Keith Primeau .20 .50
26 Geoff Sanderson .20 .50
27 Tony Amonte .30 .75
28 Chris Chelios .30 .75
29 Eric Daze .20 .50
30 Jeff Hackett .30 .75
31 Ethan Moreau .20 .50
32 Alexei Zhamnov .20 .50
33 Adam Deadmarsh .20 .50
34 Peter Forsberg .60 1.50
35 Valeri Kamensky .20 .50
36 Claude Lemieux .20 .50
37 Sandis Ozolinsh .20 .50
38 Patrick Roy 1.50 4.00
39 Joe Sakic 1.00 2.50
40 Jamie Langenbrunner .20 .50
41 Mike Modano .40 1.00
42 Andy Moog .30 .75
43 Joe Nieuwendyk .30 .75
44 Pat Verbeek .20 .50
45 Sergei Zubov .20 .50
46 Sergei Fedorov .40 1.00
47 Vladimir Konstantinov .40 1.00
48 Vyacheslav Kozlov .20 .50
49 Nicklas Lidstrom .40 1.00
50 Chris Osgood .30 .75
51 Brendan Shanahan .40 1.00
52 Mike Vernon .20 .50
53 Steve Yzerman 1.25 3.00
54 Jason Arnott .20 .50
55 Mike Grier .20 .50
56 Curtis Joseph .40 1.00
57 Rem Murray .20 .50
58 Ryan Smyth .30 .75
59 Doug Weight .30 .75
60 Ed Jovanovski .30 .75
61 Scott Mellanby .20 .50
62 Kirk Muller .20 .50
63 Ray Sheppard .20 .50
64 John Vanbiesbrouck .40 1.00
65 Rob Blake .30 .75
66 Ray Ferraro .20 .50
67 Stephane Fiset .30 .75
68 Dimitri Khristich .20 .50
69 Vladimir Tsyplakov .20 .50
70 Vincent Damphousse .20 .50
71 Saku Koivu .40 1.00
72 Mark Recchi .30 .75
73 Stephane Richer .20 .50
74 Jocelyn Thibault .30 .75
75 Dave Andreychuk .20 .50
76 Martin Brodeur 1.25 3.00
77 Doug Gilmour .30 .75
78 Bobby Holik .20 .50
79 Denis Pederson .20 .50
80 Bryan Berard .20 .50
81 Travis Green .20 .50
82 Zigmund Palffy .30 .75
83 Tommy Salo .30 .75
84 Bryan Smolinski .20 .50
85 Adam Graves .20 .50
86 Wayne Gretzky 2.00 5.00
87 Alexei Kovalev .20 .50
88 Brian Leetch .30 .75
89 Mark Messier .40 1.00
90 Mike Richter .30 .75
91 Luc Robitaille .40 1.00
92 Daniel Alfredsson .40 1.00
93 Alexandre Daigle .20 .50
94 Steve Duchesne .20 .50
95 Wade Redden .20 .50
96 Ron Tugnutt .20 .50
97 Alexei Yashin .20 .50
98 Rod Brind'Amour .20 .50
99 Paul Coffey .30 .75
100 Ron Hextall .30 .75
101 John LeClair .30 .75
102 Eric Lindros .40 1.00
103 Janne Niinimaa .20 .50
104 Mikael Renberg .20 .50
105 Dainius Zubrus .20 .50
106 Mike Gartner .30 .75
107 Nikolai Khabibulin .30 .75
108 Jeremy Roenick .40 1.00
109 Keith Tkachuk .20 .50
110 Oleg Tverdovsky .20 .50
111 Ron Francis .30 .75
112 Kevin Hatcher .20 .50
113 Jaromir Jagr .60 1.50
114 Patrick Lalime .20 .50
115 Petr Nedved .20 .50
116 Ed Olczyk .20 .50
117 Jim Campbell .20 .50
118 Geoff Courtnall .20 .50
119 Grant Fuhr .30 .75

120 Brett Hull .40 1.00
121 Sergio Momesso .20 .50
122 Pierre Turgeon .30 .75
123 Ed Belfour .40 1.00
124 Jeff Friesen .20 .50
125 Tony Granato .20 .50
126 Stephen Guolla RC .20 .50
127 Bernie Nicholls .20 .50
128 Owen Nolan .30 .75
129 Dino Ciccarelli .20 .50
130 John Cullen .20 .50
131 Chris Gratton .20 .50
132 Roman Hamrlik .20 .50
133 Daymond Langkow .20 .50
134 Paul Ysebaert .20 .50
135 Sergei Berezin .20 .50
136 Wendel Clark .30 .75
137 Felix Potvin .40 1.00
138 Steve Sullivan .20 .50
139 Mats Sundin .40 1.00
140 Pavel Bure .40 1.00
141 Martin Gelinas .20 .50
142 Trevor Linden .30 .75
143 Kirk McLean .30 .75
144 Alexander Mogilny .30 .75
145 Peter Bondra .30 .75
146 Dale Hunter .20 .50
147 Joe Juneau .20 .50
148 Steve Konowalchuk .20 .50
149 Adam Oates .30 .75
150 Bill Ranford .30 .75

1997-98 Pacific Invincible Copper

Randomly inserted in U.S. hobby packs only at the rate of 2:37, this 150-card set is parallel to the regular gold foil base set only with copper foil enhancements.
*STARS: 2X TO 4X BASIC CARDS

1997-98 Pacific Invincible Emerald Green

Randomly inserted in Canadian packs only at the rate of 2:37, this 150-card set is parallel to the regular gold foil base set only with green foil enhancements.
*STARS: 2X TO 4X BASIC CARDS

1997-98 Pacific Invincible Ice Blue

Randomly inserted in packs at the rate of 1:73, this 150-card set is parallel to the regular gold foil base set only with blue foil enhancements.
*STARS: 10X TO 20X BASIC CARDS

1997-98 Pacific Invincible Red

Randomly inserted at the rate of 2:37 into special packs found only in Wal-Mart stores, this 150-card set is parallel to the regular gold foil base set only with red foil enhancements.
*STARS: 2.5X TO 6X BASIC CARDS

1997-98 Pacific Invincible Silver

Randomly inserted in U.S. retail packs only at the rate of 2:37, this 150-card set is parallel to the regular gold foil base set only with silver foil enhancements.
*STARS: 2.5X TO 6X BASIC CARDS

1997-98 Pacific Invincible Attack Zone

Randomly inserted in packs at the rate of 1:37, this 24-card set features color action player images on a bright, colorful background. The backs carry player information.
COMPLETE SET (24) 50.00 100.00
1 Paul Kariya 2.50 6.00
2 Teemu Selanne 2.50 6.00
3 Michael Peca 1.00 2.50
4 Jarome Iginla 3.00 8.00
5 Peter Forsberg 6.00 15.00
6 Claude Lemieux 1.00 2.50
7 Joe Sakic 5.00 12.00
8 Mike Modano 4.00 10.00
9 Sergei Fedorov 4.00 10.00
10 Brendan Shanahan 2.50 6.00
11 Steve Yzerman 12.50 30.00
12 Bryan Berard 2.00 5.00
13 Zigmund Palffy 2.00 5.00
14 Wayne Gretzky 15.00 40.00
15 Brian Leetch 2.50 6.00
16 Mark Messier 2.50 6.00
17 John LeClair 2.50 6.00
18 Eric Lindros 2.50 6.00
19 Ron Francis 2.00 5.00
20 Jaromir Jagr 4.00 10.00
21 Brett Hull 3.00 8.00
22 Dino Ciccarelli 1.00 2.50
23 Pavel Bure 2.50 6.00
24 Alexander Mogilny 2.00 5.00

1997-98 Pacific Invincible Feature Performers

Randomly inserted in packs at the rate of 2:37, this 36-card set features color action player made to look as if they are breaking through the ice.
COMPLETE SET (36) 30.00 80.00
1 Paul Kariya 1.25 3.00
2 Teemu Selanne 1.25 3.00
3 Ray Bourque 2.00 5.00
4 Dominik Hasek 3.00 8.00
5 Jarome Iginla 2.00 5.00
6 Chris Chelios 1.25 3.00
7 Peter Forsberg 2.50 6.00
8 Claude Lemieux .40 1.00
9 Patrick Roy 6.00 15.00
10 Joe Sakic 3.00 8.00
11 Mike Modano 1.50 4.00
12 Sergei Fedorov 1.25 3.00
13 Vladimir Konstantinov 1.25 3.00
14 Brendan Shanahan 1.25 3.00
15 Mike Vernon .75 2.00
16 Steve Yzerman 4.00 10.00
17 John Vanbiesbrouck .75 2.00
18 Saku Koivu 1.25 3.00
19 Martin Brodeur 4.00 10.00
20 Zigmund Palffy .75 2.00
21 Wayne Gretzky 8.00 20.00
22 Mark Messier 1.25 3.00
23 Alexandre Daigle .40 1.00
24 John LeClair .75 2.00
25 Eric Lindros 1.25 3.00
26 Janne Niinimaa .40 1.00
27 Jeremy Roenick 2.00 5.00
28 Jaromir Jagr 2.50 6.00
29 Patrick Lalime .75 2.00
30 Jim Campbell .40 1.00
31 Brett Hull 1.25 3.00
32 Sergei Berezin .40 1.00
33 Felix Potvin 1.25 3.00
34 Mats Sundin 1.25 3.00
35 Alexander Mogilny .75 2.00
36 Peter Bondra .75 2.00

1997-98 Pacific Invincible NHL Regime

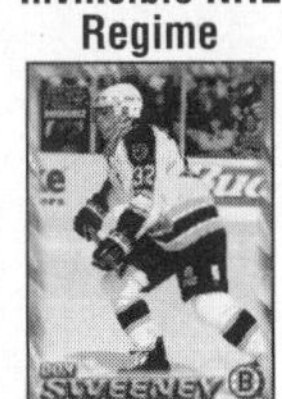

Randomly inserted one in every pack, this 220-card set features color action player photos with a faint lavender border. The backs carry player information.
COMPLETE SET (220) 8.00 20.00
1 Ken Baumgartner .05 .15
2 Mark Janssens .05 .15
3 Jean-Francois Jomphe .05 .15
4 Paul Kariya .10 .30
5 Jason Marshall .05 .15
6 Richard Park .05 .15
7 Teemu Selanne .10 .30
8 Mikhail Shtalenkov .05 .15
9 Bob Beers .05 .15
10 Ray Bourque .20 .50
11 Jim Carey .05 .15
12 Brett Harkins .05 .15
13 Sheldon Kennedy .05 .15
14 Troy Mallette .05 .15
15 Sandy Moger .05 .15
16 Jon Rohloff .05 .15
17 Don Sweeney .05 .15
18 Randy Burridge .05 .15
19 Michal Grosek .05 .15
20 Dominik Hasek .25 .60
21 Rob Ray .05 .15
22 Steve Shields .08 .25
23 Richard Smehlik .05 .15
24 Dixon Ward .05 .15
25 Mike Wilson .05 .15
26 Tommy Albelin .05 .15
27 Aaron Gavey .05 .15
28 Todd Hlushko .05 .15
29 Jarome Iginla .12 .40
30 Yves Racine .05 .15
31 Dwayne Roloson .10 .25
32 Mike Sullivan .05 .15
33 Ed Ward .05 .15
34 Adam Burt .05 .15
35 Nelson Emerson .05 .15
36 Kevin Haller .05 .15
37 Derek King .05 .15
38 Curtis Leschyshyn .05 .15
39 Chris Murray .05 .15
40 Jason Muzzatti .05 .15
41 Keith Carney .05 .15
42 Chris Chelios .10 .30
43 Enrico Ciccone .05 .15
44 Jim Cummins .05 .15
45 Cam Russell .05 .15
46 Jeff Shantz .05 .15
47 Michal Sykora .05 .15
48 Chris Terreri .08 .25
49 Eric Weinrich .05 .15
50 Rene Corbet .05 .15
51 Peter Forsberg .30 .75
52 Alexei Gusarov .05 .15
53 Uwe Krupp .05 .15
54 Sylvain Lefebvre .05 .15
55 Eric Messier .08 .25
56 Patrick Roy .60 1.50
57 Joe Sakic .25 .60
58 Brent Severyn .05 .15
59 Greg Adams .05 .15
60 Todd Harvey .05 .15
61 Jere Lehtinen .05 .15
62 Craig Ludwig .05 .15
63 Mike Modano .20 .50
64 Andy Moog .08 .25
65 Dave Reid .05 .15
66 Roman Turek .05 .15
67 Doug Brown .05 .15
68 Kris Draper .05 .15
69 Sergei Fedorov .20 .50
70 Joey Kocur .05 .15
71 Kirk Maltby .05 .15
72 Bob Rouse .05 .15
73 Brendan Shanahan .10 .30
74 Aaron Ward .05 .15
75 Steve Yzerman .60 1.50
76 Greg DeVries .05 .15
77 Bob Essensa .08 .25
78 Kevin Lowe .05 .15
79 Bryan Marchment .05 .15
80 Dean McAmmond .05 .15
81 Boris Mironov .05 .15
82 Luke Richardson .05 .15
83 Ryan Smyth .08 .25
84 Terry Carkner .05 .15
85 Ed Jovanovski .05 .15
86 Bill Lindsay .05 .15
87 Dave Lowry .05 .15
88 Gord Murphy .05 .15
89 John Vanbiesbrouck .08 .25
90 Steve Washburn .05 .15
91 Chris Wells .05 .15
92 Philippe Boucher .05 .15
93 Steven Finn .05 .15
94 Mattias Norstrom .05 .15
95 Kai Nurminen .05 .15
96 Sean O'Donnell .05 .15
97 Yanic Perreault .05 .15
98 Jeff Shevalier .05 .15
99 Brad Smyth .05 .15
100 Brad Brown RC .05 .15
101 Jassen Cullimore .05 .15
102 Vincent Damphousse .05 .15
103 Vladimir Malakhov .05 .15
104 Peter Popovic .05 .15
105 Stephane Richer .08 .25
106 Turner Stevenson .05 .15
107 Jose Theodore .12 .40
108 Martin Brodeur .30 .75
109 Bob Carpenter .05 .15
110 Mike Dunham .08 .25
111 Patrik Elias .08 .25
112 Dave Ellett .05 .15
113 Doug Gilmour .08 .25
114 Randy McKay .05 .15
115 Todd Bertuzzi .10 .30
116 Kenny Jonsson .05 .15
117 Paul Kruse .05 .15
118 Claude Lapointe .05 .15
119 Zigmund Palffy .08 .25
120 Rich Pilon .05 .15
121 Dan Plante .05 .15
122 Dennis Vaske .05 .15
123 Shane Churla .05 .15
124 Bruce Driver .05 .15
125 Mike Eastwood .05 .15
126 Patrick Flatley .05 .15
127 Adam Graves .05 .15
128 Wayne Gretzky .75 2.00
129 Brian Leetch .10 .30
130 Doug Lidster .05 .15
131 Mark Messier .10 .30
132 Tom Chorske .05 .15
133 Sean Hill .05 .15
134 Denny Lambert .05 .15
135 Janne Laukkanen .05 .15
136 Frank Musil .05 .15
137 Lance Pitlick .05 .15
138 Shaun Van Allen .05 .15
139 Rod Brind'Amour .08 .25
140 Paul Coffey .10 .30
141 Karl Dykhuis .05 .15
142 Dan Kordic .05 .15
143 Daniel Lacroix .05 .15
144 John LeClair .10 .30
145 Eric Lindros .10 .30
146 Joel Otto .05 .15
147 Shjon Podein .05 .15
148 Chris Therien .05 .15
149 Shane Doan .05 .15
150 Dallas Drake .05 .15
151 Jeff Finley .05 .15
152 Mike Gartner .08 .25
153 Nikolai Khabibulin .08 .25
154 Darrin Shannon .05 .15
155 Mike Stapleton .05 .15
156 Keith Tkachuk .10 .30
157 Tom Barrasso .08 .25
158 Josef Beranek .05 .15
159 Alex Hicks .05 .15
160 Jaromir Jagr .20 .50
161 Patrick Lalime .08 .25
162 Francois Leroux .05 .15
163 Petr Nedved .08 .25
164 Roman Oksiuta .05 .15
165 Chris Tamer .05 .15
166 Marc Bergevin .05 .15
167 Jon Casey .08 .25
168 Craig Conroy .05 .15
169 Brett Hull .15 .40
170 Igor Kravchuk .05 .15
171 Stephen Leach .05 .15
172 Ricard Persson .05 .15
173 Pierre Turgeon .08 .25
174 Ed Belfour .10 .30
175 Doug Bodger .05 .15
176 Shean Donovan .05 .15
177 Bob Errey .05 .15
178 Todd Ewen .05 .15
179 Wade Flaherty .05 .15
180 Mike Rathje .05 .15
181 Ron Sutter .05 .15
182 Mikael Andersson .05 .15
183 Dino Ciccarelli .05 .15
184 Cory Cross .05 .15
185 Jamie Huscroft .05 .15
186 Rudy Poeschek .05 .15
187 Daren Puppa .08 .25
188 David Shaw .05 .15
189 Jay Wells .05 .15
190 Jamie Baker .05 .15
191 Sergei Berezin .08 .25
192 Brandon Convery .05 .15
193 Darby Hendrickson .05 .15
194 Matt Martin .05 .15
195 Felix Potvin .10 .30
196 Jason Smith .05 .15
197 Craig Wolanin .05 .15
198 Adrian Aucoin .05 .15
199 Dave Babych .05 .15
200 Donald Brashear .05 .15
201 Pavel Bure .10 .30
202 Chris Joseph .05 .15
203 Alexander Mogilny .08 .25
204 David Roberts .05 .15
205 Scott Walker .05 .15
206 Peter Bondra .08 .25
207 Andrew Brunette .05 .15
208 Calle Johansson .05 .15
209 Ken Klee .05 .15
210 Olaf Kolzig .08 .25
211 Kelly Miller .05 .15
212 Joe Reekie .05 .15
213 Chris Simon .05 .15
214 Brendan Witt .05 .15
215 Paul Kariya TL .10 .30
216 Peter Forsberg TL .10 .30
217 Patrick Roy TL .10 .30
218 Wayne Gretzky TL .10 .30
219 Eric Lindros TL .10 .30
220 Jaromir Jagr TL .10 .30

1997-98 Pacific Invincible Off The Glass

Randomly inserted in packs at the rate of 1:73, this 20-card set features borderless color action photos of top hockey players with gold foil highlights.
COMPLETE SET (20) 25.00 60.00
1 Paul Kariya 1.25 3.00
2 Teemu Selanne 1.25 3.00
3 Michael Peca .75 2.00
4 Jarome Iginla 2.00 5.00
5 Peter Forsberg 3.00 8.00
6 Joe Sakic 4.00 10.00
7 Sergei Fedorov 1.50 4.00
8 Brendan Shanahan 1.25 3.00
9 Steve Yzerman 6.00 15.00
10 Mike Grier .75 2.00
11 Saku Koivu 1.25 3.00
12 Wayne Gretzky 10.00 25.00
13 Mark Messier 1.50 4.00
14 Eric Lindros 1.25 3.00
15 Dainius Zubrus .75 2.00
16 Keith Tkachuk 1.25 3.00
17 Jaromir Jagr 3.00 8.00
18 Brett Hull 1.50 4.00
19 Sergei Berezin .75 2.00
20 Pavel Bure 1.50 4.00

2003-04 Pacific Invincible

This 125-card set consisited of 100 veteran cards (1-100) and 25 shortprinted rookie cards (101-125). Rookies were serial-numbered to 799.
COMPLETE SET (125)
COMP.SET w/o SP's (100) 40.00 80.00
1 Stanislav Chistov .20 .50
2 Sergei Fedorov .50 1.25
3 J-S Giguere .30 .75
4 Dany Heatley .50 1.25
5 Ilya Kovalchuk .50 1.25
6 Glen Murray .20 .50
7 Sergei Samsonov .30 .75
8 Joe Thornton .60 1.50
9 Martin Biron .30 .75
10 Ryan Miller .30 .75
11 Miroslav Satan .30 .75
12 Craig Conroy .20 .50
13 Jarome Iginla .50 1.25
14 Roman Turek .30 .75
15 Ron Francis .30 .75
16 Jeff O'Neill .20 .50
17 Eric Daze .30 .75
18 Jocelyn Thibault .30 .75
19 Alexei Zhamnov .20 .50
20 David Aebischer .30 .75
21 Peter Forsberg 1.00 2.50
22 Milan Hejduk .40 1.00
23 Paul Kariya .40 1.00
24 Patrick Roy 2.00 5.00
25 Joe Sakic .75 2.00
26 Teemu Selanne .40 1.00
27 Marc Denis .30 .75
28 Rick Nash .50 1.25
29 Bill Guerin .30 .75
30 Mike Modano .60 1.50
31 Marty Turco .30 .75
32 Dominik Hasek .75 2.00
33 Brett Hull .50 1.25
34 Nicklas Lidstrom .40 1.00
35 Brendan Shanahan .40 1.00
36 Steve Yzerman 2.00 5.00
37 Henrik Zetterberg .40 1.00
38 Mike Comrie .30 .75
39 Ales Hemsky .30 .75
40 Ryan Smyth .20 .50
41 Jay Bouwmeester .20 .50
42 Olli Jokinen .30 .75
43 Roberto Luongo .50 1.25
44 Jason Allison .20 .50
45 Roman Cechmanek .30 .75
46 Zigmund Palffy .30 .75
47 Manny Fernandez .20 .50
48 Marian Gaborik .75 2.00
49 Marcel Hossa .20 .50
50 Saku Koivu .40 1.00
51 Jose Theodore .50 1.25
52 David Legwand .30 .75
53 Scottie Upshall .20 .50
54 Tomas Vokoun .30 .75
55 Martin Brodeur 1.00 2.50
56 Patrik Elias .30 .75
57 Jeff Friesen .20 .50
58 Jamie Langenbrunner .20 .50
59 Scott Stevens .30 .75
60 Rick DiPietro .30 .75
61 Mark Parrish .20 .50
62 Michael Peca .20 .50
63 Alexei Yashin .20 .50
64 Pavel Bure .40 1.00
65 Alex Kovalev .30 .75
66 Eric Lindros .40 1.00
67 Mark Messier .40 1.00
68 Daniel Alfredsson .30 .75
69 Marian Hossa .40 1.00
70 Patrick Lalime .30 .75
71 Jason Spezza .40 1.00
72 Tony Amonte .30 .75
73 Jeff Hackett .30 .75
74 John LeClair .40 1.00
75 Jeremy Roenick .40 1.00
76 Sean Burke .30 .75
77 Daymond Langkow .20 .50
78 Mario Lemieux 2.50 6.00
79 Pavol Demitra .30 .75
80 Barret Jackman .30 .75
81 Chris Osgood .30 .75
82 Doug Weight .30 .75
83 Patrick Marleau .30 .75
84 Evgeni Nabokov .30 .75
85 John Grahame .30 .75
86 Nikolai Khabibulin .40 1.00
87 Vincent Lecavalier .40 1.00
88 Martin St. Louis .30 .75
89 Ed Belfour .40 1.00
90 Alexander Mogilny .30 .75
91 Owen Nolan .30 .75
92 Mats Sundin .40 1.00
93 Todd Bertuzzi .40 1.00
94 Dan Cloutier .30 .75
95 Johan Hedberg .30 .75
96 Brendan Morrison .30 .75
97 Markus Naslund .40 1.00
98 Peter Bondra .30 .75
99 Jaromir Jagr .60 1.50
100 Olaf Kolzig .30 .75
101 Joffrey Lupul RC 2.00 5.00
102 Patrice Bergeron RC 6.00 15.00
103 Milan Bartovic RC 2.00 5.00
104 Matthew Lombardi RC 2.00 5.00
105 Eric Staal RC 6.00 15.00
106 Tuomo Ruutu RC 4.00 10.00
107 Pavel Vorobiev RC 2.00 5.00
108 Dan Fritsche RC 2.00 5.00
109 Kent McDonell RC 2.00 5.00
110 Antti Miettinen RC 2.00 5.00
111 Nathan Horton RC 4.00 10.00
112 Dustin Brown RC 2.00 5.00
113 Tim Gleason RC 2.00 5.00
114 Brent Burns RC 2.00 5.00
115 Christopher Higgins RC 4.00 10.00
116 Dan Hamhuis RC 2.00 5.00
117 Jordin Tootoo RC 4.00 10.00
118 Sean Bergenheim RC 2.00 5.00
119 Antoine Vermette RC 2.00 5.00
120 Joni Pitkanen RC 2.00 5.00
121 Marc-Andre Fleury RC 8.00 20.00
122 Peter Sejna RC 2.00 5.00
123 Milan Michalek RC 2.00 5.00
124 Matt Stajan RC 4.00 10.00
125 Boyd Gordon RC 2.00 5.00

2003-04 Pacific Invincible Blue

*STARS: 2X TO 5X BASIC CARDS
*ROOKIES: .5X TO 1.25X
STATED PRINT RUN 350 SER.#'d SETS

2003-04 Pacific Invincible Red

This retail only parallel carried a red foil logo and was serial-numbered out of 850.
*STARS: 1.25X TO 3X BASIC CARDS
*ROOKIES: .25X TO .75X

2003-04 Pacific Invincible Retail

*STARS: SAME VALUE HOBBY
*ROOKIES: .25X TO .75X

2003-04 Pacific Invincible Afterburners

STAT.ODDS 1:41 HBBY/1:49 RETAIL
1 Ilya Kovalchuk 1.25 3.00
2 Paul Kariya .75 2.00
3 Teemu Selanne .75 2.00
4 Mike Modano 1.50 4.00
5 Henrik Zetterberg .75 2.00
6 Marian Gaborik 2.00 5.00
7 Pavel Bure .75 2.00
8 Marian Hossa .75 2.00
9 Martin St. Louis .75 2.00
10 Markus Naslund .75 2.00

2003-04 Pacific Invincible Featured Performers

COMPLETE SET (30) 20.00 40.00
STAT.ODDS 1:11 HBBY/1:25 RETAIL
1 J-S Giguere .40 1.00
2 Dany Heatley .75 2.00
3 Joe Thornton 1.00 2.50
4 Miroslav Satan .40 1.00
5 Jarome Iginla .50 1.25
6 Ron Francis .40 1.00
7 Jocelyn Thibault .40 1.00
8 Peter Forsberg 1.50 4.00
9 Rick Nash .75 2.00
10 Mike Modano 1.00 2.50
11 Steve Yzerman 2.00 5.00
12 Ales Hemsky .40 1.00
13 Olli Jokinen .40 1.00
14 Ziggy Palffy .40 1.00
15 Marian Gaborik 1.25 3.00
16 Jose Theodore .50 1.25
17 David Legwand .40 1.00
18 Martin Brodeur 1.50 4.00
19 Michael Peca .40 1.00
20 Eric Lindros .40 1.00
21 Jason Spezza .75 2.00
22 Jeremy Roenick .50 1.25
23 Sean Burke .40 1.00
24 Mario Lemieux 2.50 6.00
25 Pavol Demitra .40 1.00
26 Patrick Marleau .40 1.00
27 Vincent Lecavalier .40 1.00
28 Mats Sundin .40 1.00
29 Todd Bertuzzi .40 1.00
30 Jaromir Jagr 1.00 2.50

2003-04 Pacific Invincible Freeze Frame

COMPLETE SET (24) 10.00 20.00
STAT.ODDS 1:11/1:25 RETAIL
1 J-S Giguere .30 .75
2 Ryan Miller .30 .75
3 Jocelyn Thibault .30 .75
4 Patrick Roy 2.50 6.00
5 Marc Denis .30 .75
6 Marty Turco .30 .75
7 Dominik Hasek 1.00 2.50
8 Roberto Luongo .50 1.25
9 Roman Cechmanek .30 .75
10 Jose Theodore .50 1.25
11 Tomas Vokoun .30 .75
12 Martin Brodeur 1.25 3.00
13 Rick DiPietro .30 .75
14 Garth Snow .30 .75
15 Mike Dunham .30 .75
16 Patrick Lalime .30 .75
17 Sean Burke .30 .75
18 Chris Osgood .30 .75
19 Evgeni Nabokov .30 .75
20 John Grahame .30 .75
21 Nikolai Khabibulin .40 1.00
22 Ed Belfour .40 1.00
23 Dan Cloutier .30 .75
24 Olaf Kolzig .30 .75

2003-04 Pacific Invincible Jerseys

Known SP's are noted below.
STAT.ODDS 1:11 HBBY/1:25 RETAIL
1 Byron Dafoe 3.00 8.00
2 Milan Hnilicka 3.00 8.00
3 Martin Biron 3.00 8.00
4 Jamie McLennan 3.00 8.00
5 Roman Turek 3.00 8.00
6 Patrick Roy SP 15.00 40.00
7 Fred Brathwaite SP 5.00 12.00
8 Marc Denis 3.00 8.00
9 Ron Tugnutt 3.00 8.00
10 Marty Turco 5.00 12.00
11 Dominik Hasek SP 10.00 25.00
12 Curtis Joseph 3.00 8.00
13 Roman Cechmanek 3.00 8.00
14 Felix Potvin 3.00 8.00
15 Manny Fernandez 3.00 8.00
16 Jose Theodore 4.00 10.00
17 Tomas Vokoun 5.00 12.00
18 Martin Brodeur 8.00 20.00
19 Rick DiPietro 5.00 12.00
20 Mike Richter 3.00 8.00
21 Patrick Lalime 3.00 8.00
22 Jeff Hackett 3.00 8.00
23 Sean Burke 3.00 8.00
24 Johan Hedberg 3.00 8.00
25 Brent Johnson 3.00 8.00
26 Chris Osgood 3.00 8.00
27 Miikka Kiprusoff 5.00 12.00
28 Evgeni Nabokov 5.00 12.00
29 Nikolai Khabibulin 3.00 8.00
30 Ed Belfour SP 6.00 15.00
31 Dan Cloutier 3.00 8.00
32 Olaf Kolzig 4.00 10.00

2003-04 Pacific Invincible New Sensations

STAT.ODDS 1:21 HBBY/1:49 RETAIL
1 Stanislav Chistov .60 1.50
2 Dany Heatley 1.25 3.00
3 Ilya Kovalchuk 1.25 3.00
4 Ales Kotalik .60 1.50
5 Ryan Miller .60 1.50
6 Chuck Kobasew .60 1.50
7 Jordan Leopold .60 1.50
8 Tyler Arnason .60 1.50
9 Rick Nash 1.00 2.50
10 Pavel Datsyuk .60 1.50
11 Henrik Zetterberg 1.00 2.50
12 Ales Hemsky .60 1.50
13 Jay Bouwmeester .60 1.50
14 Alexander Frolov .60 1.50
15 Marcel Hossa .60 1.50
16 Rick DiPietro .60 1.50
17 Mattias Weinhandl .60 1.50
18 Jason Spezza 1.00 2.50
19 Barret Jackman .60 1.50
20 Jonathan Cheechoo .75 2.00

2003-04 Pacific Invincible Top Line

STATED ODDS 1:41 HOBBY
1 Sergei Fedorov 1.50 3.00
2 Peter Forsberg 2.50 6.00
3 Paul Kariya 1.00 2.50
4 Joe Sakic 2.00 5.00
5 Brett Hull 1.25 3.00
6 Steve Yzerman 4.00 10.00
7 Marian Gaborik 2.00 5.00
8 Mario Lemieux 5.00 12.00
9 Markus Naslund 1.00 2.50
10 Jaromir Jagr 1.50 4.00

2002 Pacific Les Gardiens

This 7-card set was available via a wrapper redemption at the Pacific booth during the

Montreal show in October 2002. Each card was serial-numbered to just 199 copies. A gold parallel was also created and available randomly.

COMPLETE SET (7) 30.00
*GOLD: .6X TO 1.5X BASIC CARDS
GOLD PRINT RUN 99 SER.#'d SETS
1 J-S Giguere 2.00 5.00
2 Jocelyn Thibault 2.00 3.00
3 Patrick Roy 4.80 10.00
4 Roberto Luongo 2.00 5.00
5 Jose Theodore 3.20 5.00
6 Martin Brodeur 4.00 8.00
7 Patrick Lalime 2.00 3.00

2003-04 Pacific Luxury Suite

This mostly memorabilia set consisted of 23 veteran cards with up to 4 versions of each player; 25 dual-player cards with as many as 4 versions of each card; 30 short-printed rookie cards and 20 short-printed rookie cards that carried certified autographs and memorabilia swatches. Single player stick/blade cards were serial-numbered out of 20 and single player patch/blade cards were serial-numbered out of 10. Dual-player jerseys were serial-numbered out of 650 (unless otherwise noted below); dual-player patch cards were serial-numbered out of 100 (unless otherwise noted); dual-player blade cards were serial-numbered out of 10 and dual-player patch/blade cards were serial-numbered out of 10. Rookie cards #51-80 were serial-numbered out of 599 and rookie autograph/memorabilia cards #81-100 were serial-numbered out of 299.

PRINT RUNS UNDER 25 NOT
PRICED DUE TO SCARCITY
1A Sergei Fedorov J/S-150 12.50 30.00
1B Sergei Fedorov J/P-100 15.00 40.00
1C Sergei Fedorov S/B
1D Sergei Fedorov P/B
2A Ilya Kovalchuk J/S-300 12.50 30.00
2B Ilya Kovalchuk J/P-100 20.00 50.00
2C Ilya Kovalchuk S/B
2D Ilya Kovalchuk P/B
3A Jarome Iginla J/S-150 20.00 50.00
3B Jarome Iginla J/P-100 30.00 80.00
3C Jarome Iginla S/B
3D Jarome Iginla P/B
4A Ron Francis P/S-65 30.00 80.00
4B Ron Francis S/B
4C Ron Francis P/B
5A Peter Forsberg J/S-150 15.00 40.00
5B Peter Forsberg J/P-100 20.00 50.00
5C Peter Forsberg S/B
5D Peter Forsberg P/B
6A Joe Sakic J/S-300 15.00 30.00
6B Joe Sakic J/P-100 20.00 50.00
6C Joe Sakic S/B
6D Joe Sakic P/B
7A Marc Denis P/S-175 12.50 30.00
7B Marc Denis S/B
7C Marc Denis P/B
8A Mike Modano J/S-150 15.00 40.00
8B Mike Modano J/P-100 12.50 30.00
8C Mike Modano S/B
8D Mike Modano P/B
9A Dominik Hasek P/S-30
9B Dominik Hasek S/B
9C Dominik Hasek P/B
10A Steve Yzerman J/S-150 30.00 80.00
10B Steve Yzerman J/P-100 30.00 80.00
10C Steve Yzerman S/B
10D Steve Yzerman P/B
11A Ziggy Palffy J/S-150 8.00 20.00
11B Ziggy Palffy J/P-100 12.50 30.00
11C Ziggy Palffy S/B
11D Ziggy Palffy P/B
12A Jose Theodore J/S-300 15.00 40.00
12B Jose Theodore J/P-100 20.00 50.00
12C Jose Theodore S/B
12D Jose Theodore P/B
13A Martin Brodeur J/S-300 15.00 40.00
13B Martin Brodeur J/P-100 25.00 60.00
13C Martin Brodeur S/B
13D Martin Brodeur P/B
14A Jason Spezza J/S-300 10.00 25.00
14B Jason Spezza J/P-50 30.00 80.00
14C Jason Spezza S/B
14D Jason Spezza P/B
15A Mike Comrie J/S-300 6.00 15.00
15B Mike Comrie J/P-50 10.00 25.00
15C Mike Comrie S/B
15D Mike Comrie P/B
16A Mario Lemieux J/S-100 40.00 100.00
16B Mario Lemieux S/B
16C Mario Lemieux P/B
17A Nikolai Khabibulin J/S-150 12.50 30.00
17B Nikolai Khabibulin J/P-50 25.0060.00
17C Nikolai Khabibulin S/B
17D Nikolai Khabibulin P/B
18A Vincent Lecavalier J/S-100 15.0040.00
18B Vincent Lecavalier J/P-50 12.5030.00
18C Vincent Lecavalier S/B
18D Vincent Lecavalier P/B
19A Ed Belfour J/S-300 12.50 30.00
19B Ed Belfour J/P-50 15.00 40.00
19C Ed Belfour S/B
19D Ed Belfour P/B
20A Mats Sundin J/S-300 12.00 30.00
20B Mats Sundin J/P-50 15.00 40.00
20C Mats Sundin S/B
20D Mats Sundin P/B
21A Todd Bertuzzi J/S-300 12.50 30.00
21B Todd Bertuzzi J/P-50 20.00 50.00
21C Todd Bertuzzi S/B
21D Todd Bertuzzi P/B
22A Markus Naslund J/S-300 10.00 25.00
22B Markus Naslund J/P-50 15.00 40.00
22C Markus Naslund S/B
22D Markus Naslund P/B
23A Olaf Kolzig J/S-150 6.00 15.00
23B Olaf Kolzig J/P-50 15.00 40.00
23C Olaf Kolzig S/B
23D Olaf Kolzig P/B
24A Sergei Fedorov JSY 8.00 20.00
J-S Giguere JSY
24B Sergei Fedorov JSY 15.00 40.00
J-S Giguere JSY
24C Sergei Fedorov JSY
J-S Giguere JSY
25A Ilya Kovalchuk 10.00 25.00
Dany Heatley
25B Kovalchuk/Heatley P/P-50 30.0080.00
25C Kovalchuk/Heatley B/B
26A Joe Thornton 8.00 20.00
Sergei Samsonov
26B J.Thornton/S.Samsonov P/P 20.00 50.00
26C J.Thornton/S.Samsonov J/S 12.50 30.00
26D J.Thornton/S.Samsonov P/B
27A Ryan Miller 8.00 20.00
Ales Kotalik
27B R.Miller/A.Kotalik P/P 12.00 30.00
28A Peter Forsberg 12.50 30.00
Joe Sakic
28B P.Forsberg/J.Sakic P/P 40.00 100.00
28C P.Forsberg/J.Sakic B/B
29A Paul Kariya 5.00 12.00
Teemu Selanne
29B P.Kariya/T.Selanne P/P 25.00 60.00
29C P.Kariya/T.Selanne P/B
30A Paul Kariya 10.00 25.00
Milan Hejduk
30B P.Kariya/M.Hejduk P/P 20.00 50.00
30C P.Kariya/M.Hejduk P/B
31A Teemu Selanne 8.00 20.00
David Aebischer
31B T.Selanne/D.Aebischer P/P 15.00 40.00
32A M.Modano/M.Turco J/J 6.00 15.00
32B M.Modano/M.Turco P/P 20.00 50.00
32C M.Modano/M.Turco B/B
33A Brett Hull 8.00 20.00
Brendan Shanahan
33B B.Hull/B. Shanahan P/P 20.00 50.00
33C B.Hull/B. Shanahan P/B
34A Chris Chelios 20.00 50.00
Nicklas Lidstrom
34B C.Chelios/N.Lidstrom B/B
35A Ryan Smyth 6.00 15.00
Ales Hemsky
35B R.Smyth/A.Hemsky P/P 20.00 50.00
35C R.Smyth/A.Hemsky P/B
36A Jay Bouwmeester 6.00 15.00
Roberto Luongo
36B Bouwmeester/Luongo P/P 25.0060.00
37A Ziggy Palffy 5.00 12.00
Adam Deadmarsh
37B Palffy/Deadmarsh P/P 10.00 25.00
37C Palffy/Deadmarsh B/B 15.00 40.00
38A Saku Koivu 10.00 25.00
Jose Theodore
38B S.Koivu/J.Theodore P/P 25.00 60.00
38C S.Koivu/J.Theodore B/B
39A Tomas Vokoun 5.00 12.00
Scott Walker
39B Vokoun/Walker P/P 20.00 50.00
39C Vokoun/Walker J/S-100 8.00 20.00
39D T.Vokoun/S.Walker P/B
40A Martin Brodeur 8.00 20.00
Patrick Elias
40B M.Brodeur/P.Elias P/P 30.00 80.00
40C M.Brodeur/P.Elias P/B
41A Alexei Yashin 8.00 20.00
Rick DiPietro
41B A.Yashin/R.DiPietro P/P 20.00 50.00
42A Eric Lindros 8.00 20.00
Brian Leetch
42B Lindros/Leetch P/P-75 20.00 50.00
42C Lindros/Leetch B/B
43A Marian Hossa 6.00 15.00
Patrick Lalime
43B M. Hossa/P.Lalime P/P 20.00 50.00
43C M. Hossa/P.Lalime B/B
44A Jeremy Roenick 8.00 20.00
Jeff Hackett
44B J.Roenick/J.Hackett P/P 15.00 40.00
45A Barret Jackman 8.00 20.00
Chris Pronger
45B Jackman/Pronger P/P-50 20.00 50.00
46A Doug Weight 8.00 20.00
Chris Oagood
46B D.Weight/C.Osgood P/P 20.00 50.00
46C D.Weight/C.Osgood B/B
47A Nikolai Khabibulin 10.00 25.00
Vincent Lecavalier
47B N.Khabibulin/V.Lecavalier P/P 20.00 50.00
47C N.Khabibulin/V.Lecavalier B/B
48A Mats Sundin 6.00 15.00
Alexander Mogilny
48B Sundin/Mogilny P/P-25
48C Sundin/Mogilny B/B
49A Brendan Morrison 6.00 15.00
Dan Cloutier
49B B.Morrison/D.Cloutier P/P 15.0040.00
50A Jaromir Jagr 10.00 25.00
Peter Bondra
50B J.Jagr/P.Bondra P/P 25.00 60.00
50C J.Jagr/P.Bondra B/B
51 Garrett Burnett RC 4.00 10.00
52 Tony Martensson RC 4.00 10.00
53 Sergei Zinovjev RC 4.00 10.00
54 Andrew Peters RC 4.00 10.00
55 Matthew Lombardi RC 4.00 10.00
56 Travis Moen RC 4.00 10.00
57 Pavel Vorobiev RC 4.00 10.00
58 Mikhail Yakubov RC 4.00 10.00
59 Cody McCormick RC 4.00 10.00
60 Dan Fritsche RC 4.00 10.00
61 Kent McDonell RC 4.00 10.00
62 Nikolai Zherdev RC 8.00 20.00
63 Darryl Bootland RC 4.00 10.00
64 Nathan Robinson RC 4.00 10.00
65 Tony Salmelainen RC 4.00 10.00
66 Peter Sarno RC 4.00 10.00
67 Gregory Campbell RC 4.00 10.00
68 Dan Hamhuis RC 4.00 10.00
69 Marek Zidlicky RC 4.00 10.00
70 David Hale RC 4.00 10.00
71 Paul Martin RC 4.00 10.00
72 Dominic Moore RC 4.00 10.00
73 Fredrik Sjostrom RC 4.00 10.00
74 Matt Murley RC 4.00 10.00
75 John Pohl RC 4.00 10.00
76 Tom Preissing RC 4.00 10.00
77 Maxim Kondratiev RC 4.00 10.00
78 Ryan Kesler RC 4.00 10.00
79 Alexander Semin RC 8.00 20.00
80 Rastislav Stana RC 5.00 12.00
81 Joffrey Lupul JSY AU RC 12.00 30.00
82 Patrice Bergeron JSY AU RC 25.00 60.00
83 Brent Krahn PCK AU RC 8.00 20.00
84 Eric Staal PCK AU RC 40.00 100.00
85 Tuomo Ruutu PCK AU RC 12.00 30.00
86 Antti Miettinen JSY AU RC 8.00 20.00
87 Jiri Hudler PCK AU RC 12.00 30.00
88 Nathan Horton JSY AU RC 15.00 40.00
89 Dustin Brown JSY AU RC 10.00 25.00
90 Brent Burns PCK AU RC 10.00 25.00
91 Chris Higgins JSY AU RC 15.00 40.00
92 Jordin Tootoo JSY AU RC 15.00 40.00
93 S.Bergenheim PCK AU RC 8.00 20.00
94 Antoine Vermette JSY AU RC 10.00 25.00
95 Joni Pitkanen JSY AU RC 8.00 20.00
96 M-A Fleury PCK AU RC 50.00 125.00
97 Peter Sejna PCK AU RC 8.00 20.00
98 Milan Michalek PCK AU RC 15.0040.00
99 Matt Stajan PCK AU RC 12.50 30.00
100 Boyd Gordon JSY AU RC 10.00 25.00

2003-04 Pacific Luxury Suite Gold

STATED PRINT RUN 10 SER.#'d SETS
NOT PRICED DUE TO SCARCITY

2003 Pacific Montreal International

This set was issued at the Spring 2003 Montreal show as a wrapper redemption by Pacific. The cards feature members of the Montreal Canadiens on one side and Montreal Alouettes on the other.

COMPLETE SET (6) 15.00
1 Saku Koivu 5.00
Anthony Calvillo
2 Jose Theodore 5.00
Jermaine Copeland
3 Yanic Perreault 2.00
Ben Cahoon
4 Richard Zednik 2.00
Eric Lapointe
5 Jan Bulis 2.00
Bruno Heppell
6 Patrice Brisebois 2.00
Kevin Johnson

2003 Pacific Montreal Olympic Stadium Show

Serial-numbered to 299, this 8-card set was available via wrapper redemption at the Pacific booth during the 2003 Spring " Collections Sport et Jouet" in Montreal at the Olympic Stadium. A gold version was also created and numbered to 99. Values for gold parallels can be found by using the multipliers below.

COMPLETE SET (8) 40.00
*GOLD: .75X TO 2X BASIC CARDS
1 Stanislav Chistov 3.20 5.00
2 Pascal Leclaire 3.20 5.00
3 Rick Nash 4.80 15.00
4 Henrik Zetterberg 4.80 15.00
5 Jay Bouwmeester 3.20 8.00
6 Alexander Frolov 2.40 5.00
7 Ron Hainsey 2.40 5.00
8 Jason Spezza 4.00 12.00

2004 Pacific Montreal International

Available via redemption only at the 2004 Montreal International show, this 8-card set featured promising prospects.

COMPLETE SET (8) 15.00
STATED PRINT RUN 499 SER.#'d SETS
*GOLD: 2X TO 4X BASIC CARDS
GOLD PRINT RUN 99 SER.#'d SETS
1 Patrice Bergeron 4.00
2 Eric Staal 2.00
3 Nathan Horton 2.00
4 Chris Higgins 1.00
5 Jordin Tootoo 2.00
6 Antoine Vermette 1.00
7 Joni Pitkanen 2.00
8 Marc-Andre Fleury 4.00

2004 Pacific NHL All-Star FANtasy

This 10-card set was available via wrapper redemption at the Pacific booth during the 2004 NHL All-Star FANtasy. Cards were serial-numbered out of 499.

COMPLETE SET (10)
1 Joffrey Lupul 1.50
2 Patrice Bergeron 4.00
3 Eric Staal 2.00
4 Jiri Hudler 2.00
5 Brent Burns 1.50
6 Jordin Tootoo 2.00
7 Joni Pitkanen 2.00
8 Marc-Andre Fleury 4.00
9 Peter Sejna 1.00
10 Matt Stajan 2.50

2004 Pacific NHL All-Star Nets

These cards were available via redemption at the Pacific booth during the 2004 NHL All-Star FANtasy. Cards were serial-numbered out of 499. A gold parallel was also created and available randomly.

*GOLD: 1X TO 2.5X BASIC CARDS
GOLD PRINT RUN 99 SER.#'d SETS
1 Eastern Team 12.50 30.00
Joe Thornton
Martin Brodeur
Marian
2 Western Team 15.00 25.00
Mike Modano
Marty Turco
Marian Gab

2004 Pacific NHL Draft All-Star Nets

Available via wrapper redemption at the Pacific booth during the 2004 NHL Draft, this 3-card set features pieces of netting from the 2004 All-Star game. Each card was serial numbered out of 250.

COMPLETE SET (3) 60.00 125.00
1 I.Kovalchuk/R.Nash 20.00 50.00
2 Martin St. Louis 15.00 40.00
Joe Sakic
3 M.Turco/M.Brodeur 20.00 50.00

2004 Pacific NHL Draft Show Calder Reflections

COMPLETE SET (8)
1 Joffrey Lupul 2.00

2 Patrice Bergeron 4.00
3 Andrew Raycroft 3.00
4 Eric Staal 2.00
5 Michael Ryder 2.00
6 Trent Hunter 1.00
7 Marc-Andre Fleury 4.00
8 Ryan Malone 1.00

1997-98 Pacific Omega

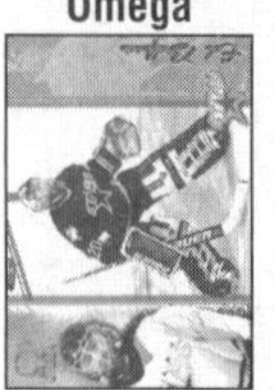

The 1997-98 Pacific Omega set was issued in one series totaling 250 cards and was distributed in six-card packs with a suggested retail price of $1.99. The fronts feature color action photos etched in foil of players who are popular with fans. The backs carry another photo and the player's accomplishments.

COMPLETE SET (250) 12.00 30.00
1 Matt Cullen RC .20 .50
2 Guy Hebert .10 .30
3 Paul Kariya .15 .40
4 Dmitri Mironov .05 .15
5 Steve Rucchin .05 .15
6 Tomas Sandstrom .05 .15
7 Teemu Selanne .15 .40
8 Mikhail Shtalenkov .05 .15
9 Pavel Trnka .05 .15
10 Jason Allison .05 .15
11 Per Axelsson .05 .15
12 Ray Bourque .25 .60
13 Anson Carter .10 .30
14 Byron Dafoe .10 .30
15 Ted Donato .05 .15
16 Hal Gill RC .05 .15
17 Dimitri Khristich .05 .15
18 Sergei Samsonov .10 .30
19 Joe Thornton .40 1.00
20 Jason Dawe .05 .15
21 Michal Grosek .05 .15
22 Dominik Hasek .30 .75
23 Brian Holzinger .05 .15
24 Michael Peca .05 .15
25 Derek Plante .05 .15
26 Miroslav Satan .05 .15
27 Steve Shields RC .25 .60
28 Andrew Cassels .05 .15
29 Theo Fleury .05 .15
30 Jarome Iginla .20 .50
31 Derek Morris RC .20 .50
32 Tyler Moss RC .05 .15
33 Michael Nylander .05 .15
34 Dwayne Roloson .10 .30
35 Cory Stillman .05 .15
36 Rick Tabaracci .10 .30
37 German Titov .05 .15
38 Bates Battaglia RC .05 .15
39 Nelson Emerson .05 .15
40 Martin Gelinas .05 .15
41 Sami Kapanen .05 .15
42 Trevor Kidd .10 .30
43 Kevin Dineen .05 .15
44 Keith Primeau .05 .15
45 Gary Roberts .05 .15
46 Tony Amonte .10 .30
47 Keith Carney .05 .15
48 Chris Chelios .15 .40
49 Eric Daze .10 .30
50 Brian Felsner .05 .15
51 Jeff Hackett .10 .30
52 Christian Laflamme RC .05 .15
53 Alexei Zhamnov .05 .15
54 Craig Billington .10 .30
55 Adam Deadmarsh .05 .15
56 Peter Forsberg .30 .75
57 Valeri Kamensky .10 .30
58 Uwe Krupp .05 .15
59 Jari Kurri .10 .30
60 Claude Lemieux .05 .15
61 Eric Messier RC .10 .30
62 Jeff Odgers .05 .15
63 Sandis Ozolinsh .05 .15
64 Patrick Roy .75 2.00
65 Joe Sakic .30 .75
66 Greg Adams .05 .15
67 Ed Belfour .15 .40
68 Manny Fernandez .05 .15
69 Derian Hatcher .05 .15
70 Jamie Langenbrunner .05 .15
71 Jere Lehtinen .05 .15
72 Juha Lind RC .05 .15
73 Mike Modano .20 .50
74 Joe Nieuwendyk .10 .30
75 Darryl Sydor .05 .15
76 Pat Verbeek .05 .15
77 Sergei Zubov .05 .15
78 Slava Fetisov .05 .15
79 Brent Gilchrist .05 .15
80 Kevin Hodson .10 .30
81 Vyacheslav Kozlov .05 .15
82 Igor Larionov .05 .15
83 Nicklas Lidstrom .15 .40
84 Darren McCarty .05 .15
85 Larry Murphy .05 .15
86 Chris Osgood .10 .30
87 Brendan Shanahan .15 .40
88 Steve Yzerman .60 1.50
89 Kelly Buchberger .05 .15
90 Mike Grier .05 .15
91 Bill Guerin .10 .30
92 Roman Hamrlik .05 .15
93 Curtis Joseph .15 .40
94 Boris Mironov .05 .15
95 Ryan Smyth .10 .30
96 Doug Weight .10 .30
97 Dino Ciccarelli .05 .15
98 Dave Gagner .05 .15
99 Ed Jovanovski .10 .30
100 Scott Mellanby .05 .15
101 Robert Svehla .05 .15
102 John Vanbiesbrouck .10 .30
103 Steve Washburn .05 .15
104 Kevin Weekes RC .40 1.00
105 Ray Whitney .05 .15
106 Rob Blake .10 .30
107 Stephane Fiset .10 .30
108 Garry Galley .05 .15
109 Steve McKenna RC .05 .15
110 Glen Murray .05 .15
111 Yanic Perreault .05 .15
112 Luc Robitaille .10 .30
113 Jamie Storr .10 .30
114 Jozef Stumpel .10 .30
115 Vladimir Tsyplakov .05 .15
116 Shayne Corson .05 .15
117 Vincent Damphousse .05 .15
118 Saku Koivu .15 .40
119 Vladimir Malakhov .05 .15
120 Andy Moog .10 .30
121 Mark Recchi .10 .30
122 Martin Rucinsky .05 .15
123 Brian Savage .05 .15
124 Jocelyn Thibault .10 .30
125 Jason Arnott .05 .15
126 Brad Bombardir RC .05 .15
127 Martin Brodeur .40 1.00
128 Patrik Elias RC 1.00 2.50
129 Doug Gilmour .10 .30
130 Bobby Holik .05 .15
131 Randy McKay .05 .15
132 Scott Niedermayer .05 .15
133 Krzysztof Oliwa RC .05 .15
134 Scott Stevens .10 .30
135 Petr Sykora .05 .15
136 Bryan Berard .05 .15
137 Travis Green .05 .15
138 Bryan McCabe .05 .15
139 Sergei Nemchinov .05 .15
140 Zigmund Palffy .10 .30
141 Robert Reichel .05 .15
142 Tommy Salo .10 .30
143 Bryan Smolinski .05 .15
144 Adam Graves .05 .15
145 Wayne Gretzky 1.00 2.50
146 Pat LaFontaine .15 .40
147 Brian Leetch .15 .40
148 Mike Richter .15 .40
149 Kevin Stevens .10 .30
150 Niklas Sundstrom .05 .15
151 Tim Sweeney .05 .15
152 Daniel Alfredsson .10 .30
153 Magnus Arvedson .05 .15
154 Andreas Dackell .05 .15
155 Igor Kravchuk .05 .15
156 Shawn McEachern .05 .15
157 Damian Rhodes .10 .30
158 Ron Tugnutt .10 .30
159 Alexei Yashin .05 .15
160 Rod Brind'Amour .10 .30
161 Paul Coffey .15 .40
162 Eric Desjardins .10 .30
163 Colin Forbes .05 .15
164 Chris Gratton .10 .30
165 Ron Hextall .10 .30
166 Trent Klatt .05 .15
167 John LeClair .15 .40
168 Eric Lindros .15 .40
169 Joel Otto .05 .15
170 Garth Snow .10 .30
171 Dainius Zubrus .15 .40
172 Dallas Drake .05 .15
173 Mike Gartner .10 .30
174 Nikolai Khabibulin .10 .30
175 Teppo Numminen .05 .15
176 Jeremy Roenick .20 .50
177 Keith Tkachuk .15 .40
178 Rick Tocchet .10 .30
179 Oleg Tverdovsky .05 .15
180 Juha Ylonen .05 .15
181 Stu Barnes .05 .15
182 Tom Barrasso .10 .30
183 Rob Brown .05 .15
184 Ron Francis .10 .30
185 Kevin Hatcher .05 .15
186 Jaromir Jagr .25 .60
187 Alexei Morozov .10 .30
188 Ed Olczyk .05 .15
189 Jim Campbell .05 .15
190 Geoff Courtnall .05 .15
191 Pavol Demitra .10 .30
192 Steve Duchesne .05 .15
193 Grant Fuhr .10 .30
194 Brett Hull .20 .50
195 Al MacInnis .10 .30
196 Chris Pronger .10 .30
197 Pascal Rheaume RC .05 .15
198 Jamie Rivers .05 .15
199 Pierre Turgeon .10 .30
200 Jeff Friesen .05 .15
201 Tony Granato .05 .15
202 John MacLean .05 .15
203 Patrick Marleau .25 .60
204 Marty McSorley .05 .15
205 Owen Nolan .10 .30
206 Marco Sturm RC .25 .60
207 Mike Vernon .10 .30
208 Andrei Zyuzin RC .05 .15
209 Karl Dykhuis .05 .15
210 Daymond Langkow .10 .30
211 Louie DeBrusk .05 .15
212 Daren Puppa .10 .30
213 Mikael Renberg .10 .30
214 Alexander Selivanov .05 .15
215 Paul Ysebaert .05 .15
216 Rob Zamuner .05 .15
217 Sergei Berezin .05 .15
218 Wendel Clark .10 .30
219 Marcel Cousineau .10 .30
220 Tie Domi .10 .30
221 Mike Johnson RC .15 .40
222 Igor Korolev .05 .15
223 Felix Potvin .15 .40
224 Mathieu Schneider .05 .15
225 Mats Sundin .15 .40
226 Yannick Tremblay RC .05 .15
227 Donald Brashear .05 .15
228 Pavel Bure .15 .40
229 Sean Burke .10 .30
230 Trevor Linden .10 .30
231 Mark Messier .15 .40
232 Alexander Mogilny .10 .30
233 Markus Naslund .15 .40
234 Mattias Ohlund .10 .30
235 Dave Scatchard RC .05 .15
236 Peter Bondra .10 .30
237 Andrew Brunette .10 .30
238 Phil Housley .05 .15
239 Dale Hunter .05 .15
240 Calle Johansson .05 .15
241 Joe Juneau .10 .30
242 Olaf Kolzig .10 .30
243 Adam Oates .10 .30
244 Richard Zednik .05 .15
245 Chris Chelios .15 .40
Keith Tkachuk
246 M.Modano/E.Belfour .15 .40
247 Teemu Selanne .15 .40
Saku Koivu
248 Eric Lindros .15 .40
Shayne Corson
249 Patrick Roy .40 1.00
Martin Brodeur
250 Wayne Gretzky .60 1.50
Mark Messier
S73 Mike Modano SAMPLE 1.00 2.00

1997-98 Pacific Omega Copper

Inserted one in every hobby pack, this 250-card set is parallel to the base set with copper foil highlights.

*STARS: 2X TO 4X BASIC CARDS
*ROOKIES: 1X TO 2X BASIC CARDS

1997-98 Pacific Omega Dark Gray

Inserted one in every Canadian retail pack, this 250-card set is parallel to the base set with dark gray foil highlights.

*STARS: 2.5X TO 5X BASIC CARDS
*ROOKIES: 1.5X TO 3X BASIC CARDS

1997-98 Pacific Omega Emerald Green

Inserted one in every Canadian pack only, this 250-card set is parallel to the base set with green foil highlights.

*STARS: 2X TO 4X BASIC CARDS
*ROOKIES: 1.25X TO 2.5X BASIC CARDS

1997-98 Pacific Omega Gold

Inserted one in every U.S. retail pack only, this 250-card set is parallel to the base set with gold foil highlights.

*STARS: 2.5X TO 5X BASIC CARDS
*ROOKIES: 1.5X TO 3X BASIC CARDS

1997-98 Pacific Omega Ice Blue

Randomly inserted in both Canadian and U.S. hobby and retail packs at the rate of 1:73, this 250-card set is parallel to the base set with blue foil highlights.

*STARS: 20X TO 50X BASIC CARDS

1997-98 Pacific Omega Game Face

Randomly inserted in hobby and retail packs at the rate of 1:37, this 20-card set features color photos of top goalies printed on die-cut helmet-shaped cards with a cel facemask. The backs carry player information and describe his talents as a goalie.

COMPLETE SET (20)	20.00	40.00
1 Paul Kariya	.60	1.50
2 Teemu Selanne	.60	1.50
3 Peter Forsberg	1.50	4.00
4 Joe Sakic	1.25	3.00
5 Mike Modano	1.00	2.50
6 Nicklas Lidstrom	.60	1.50
7 Brendan Shanahan	.60	1.50
8 Steve Yzerman	3.00	8.00
9 Ryan Smyth	.50	1.25
10 Saku Koivu	.60	1.50
11 Wayne Gretzky	4.00	10.00
12 John LeClair	.60	1.50
13 Eric Lindros	.60	1.50
14 Dainius Zubrus	.60	1.50
15 Keith Tkachuk	.60	1.50
16 Jaromir Jagr	1.00	2.50
17 Brett Hull	.75	2.00
18 Pavel Bure	.60	1.50
19 Mark Messier	.60	1.50
20 Peter Bondra	.50	1.25

1997-98 Pacific Omega No Scoring Zone

COMPLETE SET (10)	6.00	12.00
STATED ODDS 2:37		
1 Dominik Hasek	1.00	2.50
2 Patrick Roy	2.50	6.00
3 Ed Belfour	.50	1.25
4 Chris Osgood	.40	1.00
5 John Vanbiesbrouck	.40	1.00
6 Andy Moog	.40	1.00
7 Martin Brodeur	1.25	3.00
8 Mike Richter	.50	1.25
9 Ron Hextall	.40	1.00
10 Felix Potvin	.50	1.25

1997-98 Pacific Omega Silks

Randomly inserted in hobby and retail packs at the rate of 1:73, this 12-card set features color photos of top players printed on a silk-like fabric card stock.

COMPLETE SET (12)	30.00	60.00
1 Paul Kariya	1.25	3.00
2 Teemu Selanne	2.50	6.00
3 Peter Forsberg	3.00	8.00
4 Patrick Roy	6.00	15.00
5 Joe Sakic	2.50	6.00
6 Steve Yzerman	6.00	15.00
7 Martin Brodeur	3.00	8.00
8 Wayne Gretzky	8.00	20.00
9 Eric Lindros	1.25	3.00
10 Jaromir Jagr	2.00	5.00
11 Pavel Bure	1.25	3.00
12 Mark Messier	1.25	3.00

1997-98 Pacific Omega Stick Handle Laser Cuts

Randomly inserted in hobby and retail packs at the rate of 1:145, this 20-card set features color photos of popular players printed on full foil card stock with laser-cut hockey sticks crossing in the background. The backs carry a description of the player's accomplishments on ice.

COMPLETE SET (20)	60.00	125.00
1 Paul Kariya	5.00	12.00
2 Teemu Selanne	6.00	15.00
3 Theo Fleury	2.00	5.00
4 Chris Chelios	2.00	5.00
5 Peter Forsberg	6.00	15.00
6 Joe Sakic	4.00	10.00
7 Mike Modano	3.00	8.00
8 Brendan Shanahan	2.00	5.00
9 Steve Yzerman	12.50	30.00
10 Saku Koivu	2.00	5.00
11 Doug Gilmour	2.00	5.00
12 Zigmund Palffy	2.00	5.00
13 Wayne Gretzky	15.00	40.00
14 Pat LaFontaine	2.00	5.00
15 John LeClair	2.00	5.00
16 Eric Lindros	2.00	5.00
17 Jaromir Jagr	3.00	8.00
18 Mats Sundin	2.00	5.00
19 Pavel Bure	2.00	5.00
20 Mark Messier	2.00	5.00

1997-98 Pacific Omega Team Leaders

COMPLETE SET (20)	15.00	30.00
STATED ODDS 2:48 CANADIAN PACKS		
1 Paul Kariya	.50	1.25
2 Ray Bourque	.75	2.00
3 Theo Fleury	.20	.50
4 Patrick Roy	2.50	6.00
5 Joe Sakic	1.00	2.50
6 Ed Belfour	.50	1.25
7 Joe Nieuwendyk	.40	1.00
8 Brendan Shanahan	.50	1.25
9 Steve Yzerman	2.50	6.00
10 Ryan Smyth	.40	1.00
11 Shayne Corson	.20	.50
12 Mark Recchi	.40	1.00
13 Martin Brodeur	1.25	3.00
14 Wayne Gretzky	3.00	8.00
15 Rod Brind'Amour	.40	1.00
16 Eric Lindros	.50	1.25
17 Chris Pronger	.40	1.00
18 Felix Potvin	.50	1.25
19 Pavel Bure	.50	1.25
20 Mark Messier	.50	1.25

1998-99 Pacific Omega

The 1998-99 Pacific Omega set was issued in one series totaling 250 cards and was distributed in six-card packs with a suggested retail price of $1.99. The fronts feature color action photos of the NHL's greatest stars and most exciting rookies printed on etched silver foil cards. The backs carry player information and career statistics.

COMPLETE SET (252)	40.00	80.00
COMP.SET w/o SP's (1-250)	30.00	60.00
1 Travis Green	.05	.15
2 Stu Grimson	.05	.15
3 Guy Hebert	.10	.30
4 Paul Kariya	.15	.40
5 Marty McInnis	.05	.15
6 Fredrik Olausson	.05	.15
7 Steve Rucchin	.05	.15
8 Teemu Selanne	.15	.40
9 Johan Davidsson	.15	.40
Antti Aalto		
10 Jason Allison	.05	.15
11 Ken Belanger	.05	.15
12 Ray Bourque	.25	.60
13 Anson Carter	.10	.30
14 Byron Dafoe	.10	.30
15 Steve Heinze	.05	.15
16 Dimitri Khristich	.05	.15
17 Sergei Samsonov	.10	.30
18 Robbie Tallas	.10	.30
19 Joe Thornton	.20	.60
20 Matthew Barnaby	.10	.30
21 Curtis Brown	.05	.15
22 Michal Grosek	.05	.15
23 Dominik Hasek	.30	.75
24 Brian Holzinger	.10	.30
25 Micael Peca	.10	.30
26 Rob Ray	.05	.15
27 Geoff Sanderson	.10	.30
28 Miroslav Satan	.10	.30
29 Dixon Ward	.05	.15
30 Valeri Bure	.05	.15
31 Theo Fleury	.05	.15
32 J-S Giguere	.10	.30
33 Jarome Iginla	.20	.50
34 Tyler Moss	.05	.15
35 Cory Stillman	.05	.15
36 Jason Wiemer	.05	.15
37 Clarke Wilm RC	.05	.15
38 Martin St.Louis RC	2.00	5.00
Rico Fata		
39 Paul Coffey	.15	.40
40 Ron Francis	.10	.30
41 Martin Gelinas	.05	.15
42 Arturs Irbe	.10	.30
43 Sami Kapanen	.05	.15
44 Trevor Kidd	.10	.30
45 Keith Primeau	.05	.15
46 Gary Roberts	.05	.15
47 Ray Sheppard	.10	.30
48 Tony Amonte	.10	.30
49 Chris Chelios	.15	.40
50 Eric Daze	.10	.30
51 Nelson Emerson	.05	.15
52 Doug Gilmour	.10	.30
53 Mike Maneluk RC	.05	.15
54 Bob Probert	.05	.15
55 Jocelyn Thibault	.10	.30
56 Alexei Zhamnov	.05	.15
57 Todd White RC	.05	.15
Brad Brown		
58 Adam Deadmarsh	.05	.15
59 Marc Denis	.10	.30
60 Peter Forsberg	.40	1.00
61 Claude Lemieux	.05	.15
62 Jeff Odgers	.05	.15
63 Sandis Ozolinsh	.05	.15
64 Patrick Roy	.75	2.00
65 Joe Sakic	.30	.75
66 Wade Belak RC	.10	.30
Scott Parker		
67 Chris Drury RC	2.00	5.00
Milan Hejduk		
68 Ed Belfour	.15	.40
69 Derian Hatcher	.05	.15
70 Brett Hull	.20	.50
71 Jamie Langenbrunner	.05	.15
72 Jere Lehtinen	.10	.30
73 Mike Modano	.25	.60
74 Joe Nieuwendyk	.10	.30
75 Darryl Sydor	.05	.15
76 Roman Turek	.10	.30
77 Sergei Zubov	.05	.15
78 Sergei Gusev RC	.05	.15
Jamie Wright		
79 Sergei Fedorov	.25	.60
80 Joey Kocur	.05	.15
81 Martin LaPointe	.05	.15
82 Igor Larionov	.05	.15
83 Nicklas Lidstrom	.15	.40
84 Darren McCarty	.05	.15
85 Larry Murphy	.10	.30
86 Chris Osgood	.10	.30
87 Brendan Shanahan	.15	.40
88 Steve Yzerman	.75	2.00
89 Norm Maracle RC	.25	.60
Stacy Roest		
90 Josef Beranek	.05	.15
91 Sean Brown	.05	.15
92 Bill Guerin	.10	.30
93 Roman Hamrlik	.05	.15
94 Janne Niinimaa	.05	.15
95 Mikhail Shtalenkov	.05	.15
96 Ryan Smyth	.10	.30
97 Doug Weight	.10	.30
98 Tom Poti	.10	.30
Craig Millar		
99 Pavel Bure	.15	.40
100 Sean Burke	.10	.30
101 Dino Ciccarelli	.10	.30
102 Bret Hedican	.05	.15
103 Viktor Kozlov	.05	.15
104 Paul Laus	.05	.15
105 Rob Niedermayer	.05	.15
106 Mark Parrish RC	.10	.30
107 Ray Whitney	.05	.15
108 Oleg Kvasha RC	.20	.50
Peter Worrell		
109 Rob Blake	.10	.30
110 Stephane Fiset	.10	.30
111 Glen Murray	.05	.15
112 Luc Robitaille	.10	.30
113 Jamie Storr	.10	.30
114 Jozef Stumpel	.10	.30
115 Vladimir Tsyplakov	.05	.15
116 M.Visheau RC/J.Green RC	.05	.15
117 Olli Jokinen RC	.10	.30
Pavel Rosa		
118 Benoit Brunet	.05	.15
119 Shayne Corson	.10	.30
120 Vincent Damphousse	.05	.15
121 Jeff Hackett	.10	.30
122 Matt Higgins RC	.05	.15
123 Saku Koivu	.15	.40
124 Mark Recchi	.10	.30
125 Martin Rucinsky	.05	.15
126 Brian Savage	.05	.15
127 Andrew Brunette	.10	.30
128 Mike Dunham	.10	.30
129 Greg Johnson	.05	.15
130 Sergei Krivokrasov	.05	.15
131 Denny Lambert	.05	.15
132 Cliff Ronning	.05	.15
133 Tomas Vokoun	.05	.15
134 Patrick Cote	.10	.30
Kimmo Timonen		
135 Jason Arnott	.05	.15
136 Martin Brodeur	.40	1.00
137 Patrik Elias	.10	.30
138 Bobby Holik	.05	.15
139 Brendan Morrison	.10	.30
140 Krzysztof Oliwa	.05	.15
141 Brian Rolston	.05	.15
142 Vadim Sharifijanov	.05	.15
143 Scott Stevens	.10	.30
144 Petr Sykora	.05	.15
145 Ted Donato	.05	.15
146 Kenny Jonsson	.05	.15
147 Trevor Linden	.10	.30
148 Gino Odjick	.05	.15
149 Zigmund Palffy	.10	.30
150 Felix Potvin	.15	.40
151 Robert Reichel	.05	.15
152 Tommy Salo	.10	.30
153 Mike Watt	.10	.30
Eric Brewer		
154 Dan Cloutier	.10	.30
155 Adam Graves	.05	.15
156 Wayne Gretzky	1.00	2.50
157 Todd Harvey	.05	.15
158 Brian Leetch	.15	.40
159 Manny Malhotra	.10	.30
160 Petr Nedved	.10	.30
161 Mike Richter	.15	.40
162 Esa Tikkanen	.05	.15
163 Daniel Alfredsson	.10	.30
164 Marian Hossa	.15	.40
165 Andreas Johansson	.05	.15
166 Shawn McEachern	.05	.15
167 Wade Redden	.05	.15
168 Damian Rhodes	.10	.30
169 Ron Tugnutt	.10	.30
170 Alexei Yashin	.05	.15
171 Patrick Traverse RC	.05	.15
Sami Salo		
172 Rod Brind'Amour	.10	.30
173 Eric Desjardins	.10	.30
174 Ron Hextall	.10	.30
175 Keith Jones	.10	.30
176 John LeClair	.15	.40
177 Eric Lindros	.15	.40
178 Mikael Renberg	.10	.30
179 Dimitri Tertyshny RC	.05	.15
180 John Vanbiesbrouck	.10	.30
181 Dainius Zubrus	.05	.15
182 Daniel Briere	.05	.15
183 Dallas Drake	.05	.15
184 Nikolai Khabibulin	.10	.30
185 Jyrki Lumme	.05	.15
186 Teppo Numminen	.05	.15
187 Jeremy Roenick	.20	.50
188 Keith Tkachuk	.15	.40
189 Rick Tocchet	.10	.30
190 Oleg Tverdovsky	.05	.15
191 Jim Waite	.10	.30
192 Jean-Sebastien Aubin RC	.30	.75
193 Stu Barnes	.05	.15
194 Tom Barrasso	.10	.30
195 Jaromir Jagr	.25	.60
196 Alexei Kovalev	.05	.15
197 Robert Lang	.05	.15
198 Alexei Morozov	.05	.15
199 Martin Straka	.05	.15
200 Jan Hrdina RC	.25	.60
Maxim Galanov		
201 Pavol Demitra	.10	.30
202 Grant Fuhr	.10	.30
203 Al MacInnis	.10	.30
204 Jamie McLennan	.10	.30
205 Chris Pronger	.10	.30
206 Pierre Turgeon	.10	.30
207 Tony Twist	.05	.15
208 Marty Reasoner RC	.30	.75
Lubos Bartecko		
209 Jeff Friesen	.05	.15
210 Bryan Marchment	.05	.15
211 Patrick Marleau	.10	.30
212 Owen Nolan	.10	.30
213 Mike Ricci	.10	.30
214 Steve Shields	.10	.30
215 Marco Sturm	.10	.30
216 Mike Vernon	.10	.30
217 Wendel Clark	.10	.30
218 Chris Gratton	.05	.15
219 Vincent Lecavalier	.50	1.25
220 Sandy McCarthy	.05	.15
221 Stephane Richer	.10	.30
222 Darcy Tucker	.05	.15
223 Rob Zamuner	.05	.15
224 Pavel Kubina RC	.50	1.25
Zac Bierk		
225 Bryan Berard	.05	.15
226 Tie Domi	.10	.30
227 Mike Johnson	.10	.30
228 Curtis Joseph	.15	.40
229 Igor Korolev	.05	.15
230 Alyn McCauley	.05	.15
231 Mats Sundin	.15	.40
232 Steve Thomas	.05	.15
233 Tomas Kaberle RC	.20	.50
Daniil Markov		
234 Adrian Aucoin	.05	.15
235 Corey Hirsch	.10	.30
236 Mark Messier	.15	.40
237 Alexander Mogilny	.10	.30
238 Bill Muckalt RC	.05	.15
239 Markus Naslund	.15	.40
240 Mattias Ohlund	.10	.30
241 Garth Snow	.10	.30
242 Matt Cooke RC	.05	.15
Peter Schaefer		
243 Brian Bellows	.05	.15
244 Craig Berube	.05	.15
245 Peter Bondra	.10	.30
246 Matt Herr RC	.05	.15
247 Joe Juneau	.10	.30
248 Olaf Kolzig	.10	.30
249 Adam Oates	.10	.30
250 Richard Zednik	.05	.15
251 Last Game at MLG SP	2.00	5.00
252 First Game at ACC SP	2.00	5.00
S136 Martin Brodeur SAMPLE	.20	.50

1998-99 Pacific Omega Red

Found at a rate of 4:25 Treat packs, this tough insert features red foil on the front as its distinguishing mark.

*STARS: 5X TO 10X BASIC CARDS
*ROOKIES: .75X TO 2X BASIC CARDS

1998-99 Pacific Omega Opening Day Issue

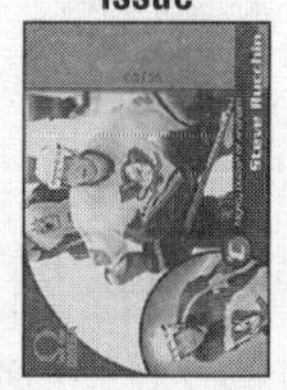

Randomly inserted into packs, this 250-card set is parallel to the base set. Only 56 serially numbered sets were made.

*STARS: 75X TO 150X BASIC CARDS
*ROOKIES: 25X TO 50X BASIC CARDS

1998-99 Pacific Omega Championship Spotlight

Randomly inserted in special packs at the rate of 1:49, this 10-card set features color action photos of top NHL players with player information on the backs. Three limited edition parallel sets were also produced to be inserted into Treat packs. Only 50 serially numbered Green parallel versions were made, 10 serially numbered Red parallel versions, and one Gold parallel version. Gold parallels not priced due to scarcity.

COMPLETE SET (10)	75.00	150.00
*GREENS: 4X TO 8X BASIC INSERTS		
1 Paul Kariya	4.00	10.00
2 Dominik Hasek	6.00	15.00
3 Patrick Roy	12.50	30.00
4 Steve Yzerman	12.50	30.00
5 Pavel Bure	4.00	10.00
6 Martin Brodeur	8.00	20.00
7 Wayne Gretzky	15.00	40.00
8 Eric Lindros	4.00	10.00
9 Jaromir Jagr	5.00	12.00
10 Curtis Joseph	4.00	10.00

1998-99 Pacific Omega EO Portraits

Randomly inserted into packs at the rate of 1:73, this 20-card set features color player images of some of hockey's biggest superstars printed using Electro-Optical technology to laser-cut the player image into every card. A special one of a kind Hobby only parallel set was also produced with "1/1" laser-cut into each card, they are not priced due to scarcity.

COMPLETE SET (20)	30.00	60.00
1 Paul Kariya	.75	2.00
2 Teemu Selanne	.75	2.00
3 Dominik Hasek	1.50	4.00
4 Peter Forsberg	2.00	5.00
5 Patrick Roy	4.00	10.00
6 Joe Sakic	1.50	4.00
7 Brett Hull	1.00	2.50
8 Mike Modano	1.25	3.00
9 Sergei Fedorov	1.25	3.00
10 Brendan Shanahan	.75	2.00
11 Steve Yzerman	4.00	10.00
12 Pavel Bure	.75	2.00
13 Martin Brodeur	2.00	5.00
14 Wayne Gretzky	5.00	12.00
15 John LeClair	.75	2.00
16 Eric Lindros	.75	2.00
17 Keith Tkachuk	.75	2.00
18 Jaromir Jagr	1.25	3.00
19 Mats Sundin	.75	2.00
20 Mark Messier	.75	2.00

1998-99 Pacific Omega Face to Face

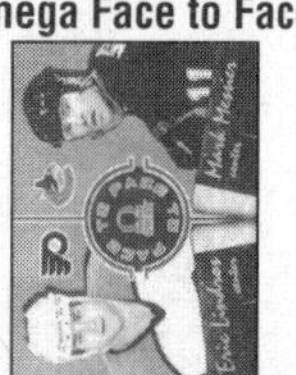

Randomly inserted into packs at the rate of 1:145, this 10-card set features color portraits of top NHL players printed on silver-foiled and etched cards. Two players are matched on every card creating an all-star face-off effect.

COMPLETE SET (10)	75.00	150.00
1 P.Roy/M.Brodeur	12.50	30.00
2 Wayne Gretzky	15.00	40.00
Paul Kariya		
3 Dominik Hasek	5.00	12.00
Jaromir Jagr		
4 Sergei Fedorov	5.00	12.00
Pavel Bure		
5 Keith Tkachuk	4.00	10.00
Brendan Shanahan		
6 Steve Yzerman	12.50	30.00
Joe Sakic		
7 Teemu Selanne	4.00	10.00
Saku Koivu		
8 Peter Forsberg	10.00	25.00
Mats Sundin		
9 Mike Modano	5.00	12.00
John LeClair		
10 Eric Lindros	4.00	10.00
Mark Messier		

1998-99 Pacific Omega Online

Randomly inserted into packs at the rate of 4:37, this 36-card set features color photos of NHL stars with interesting player facts on the backs. Each card invites fans to learn more about each player and team by logging on to their respective internet sites at www.nhlpa.com and www.nhl.com.

COMPLETE SET (36)	10.00	20.00
1 Paul Kariya	.20	.50
2 Teemu Selanne	.20	.50
3 Ray Bourque	.30	.75
4 Dominik Hasek	.20	.50
5 Theo Fleury	.10	.20
6 Chris Chelios	.20	.50
7 Doug Gilmour	.15	.40
8 Peter Forsberg	.50	1.25
9 Patrick Roy	1.00	2.50
10 Joe Sakic	.40	1.00
11 Ed Belfour	.20	.50
12 Brett Hull	.25	.60
13 Mike Modano	.30	.75
14 Sergei Fedorov	.30	.75
15 Brendan Shanahan	.20	.50
16 Steve Yzerman	1.00	2.50
17 Pavel Bure	.20	.50
18 Saku Koivu	.20	.50
19 Martin Brodeur	.50	1.25
20 Brendan Morrison	.15	.40
21 Zigmund Palffy	.15	.40
22 Felix Potvin	.20	.50
23 Wayne Gretzky	1.25	3.00
24 Alexei Yashin	.10	.20
25 John LeClair	.20	.50
26 Eric Lindros	.20	.50
27 John Vanbiesbrouck	.15	.40
28 Nikolai Khabibulin	.15	.40
29 Keith Tkachuk	.20	.50
30 Jaromir Jagr	.30	.75
31 Vincent Lecavalier	.60	1.50
32 Curtis Joseph	.20	.50
33 Mats Sundin	.20	.50
34 Mark Messier	.20	.50
35 Bill Muckalt	.10	.20
36 Peter Bondra	.15	.40

1998-99 Pacific Omega Planet Ice

Randomly inserted into hobby packs only with an insertion rate of 4:37, this 30-card set features action color photos of top NHL players. The backs carry player information.

COMPLETE SET (30)	8.00	15.00
1 Ray Bourque	.30	.75
2 Chris Chelios	.15	.40
3 Vincent Lecavalier	.10	.25
4 Mark Parrish	.10	.25
5 Felix Potvin	.15	.40
6 Alexei Yashin	.10	.25
7 Ed Belfour	.15	.40
8 Peter Bondra	.10	.25
9 Brett Hull	.25	.60
10 Mark Messier	.25	.60
11 Mats Sundin	.10	.25
12 John Vanbiesbrouck	.10	.25
13 Sergei Fedorov	.30	.75
14 Curtis Joseph	.15	.40
15 John LeClair	.15	.40
16 Mike Modano	.30	.75
17 Brendan Shanahan	.15	.40
18 Keith Tkachuk	.15	.40
19 Martin Brodeur	1.00	2.50
20 Pavel Bure	.15	.40
21 Dominik Hasek	.40	1.00
22 Joe Sakic	.40	1.00
23 Teemu Selanne	.15	.40
24 Steve Yzerman	1.00	2.50
25 Peter Forsberg	.50	1.25
26 Wayne Gretzky	1.25	3.00
27 Jaromir Jagr	.30	.75
28 Paul Kariya	.15	.40
29 Eric Lindros	.15	.40
30 Patrick Roy	1.00	2.50

1998-99 Pacific Omega Planet Ice Parallel

Randomly inserted into hobby packs only, this 30-card set is a parallel version of the regular Pacific Omega Planet Ice insert set. The set is spun off into five different tiers of six cards each. Each serially numbered tier is foiled in its own unique color with varying amounts of each tier produced. Tier 1 (1-6) is printed with blue foil and serially

numbered to 100. Tier 2 (7-12) is a red foil set and serially numbered to 75. Tier 3 (13-18) has green foil highlights and only 50 sets were made. Tier 4 (19-24) is printed in purple foil with a print run of 25 serially numbered sets. Tier 5 (25-30) is a gold foil set with only 1 of each card produced. Tier 5 cards not priced due to scarcity.

*TIER 1 (1-6): 6X TO 15X BASIC INSERTS
*TIER 2 (7-12): 8X TO 20X BASIC INSERTS
*TIER 3 (13-18): 12.5X TO 30X BASIC INSERTS
*TIER 4 (19-24): 25X TO 60X BASIC INSERTS

1998-99 Pacific Omega Prism

COMPLETE SET (20)	20.00	40.00
STATED ODDS 1:37		
1 Paul Kariya	.60	1.50
2 Teemu Selanne	.60	1.50
3 Dominik Hasek	.60	1.50
4 Peter Forsberg	1.50	4.00
5 Patrick Roy	3.00	8.00
6 Joe Sakic	1.25	3.00
7 Mike Modano	1.00	2.50
8 Sergei Fedorov	1.00	2.50
9 Brendan Shanahan	.60	1.50
10 Steve Yzerman	3.00	8.00
11 Pavel Bure	.60	1.50
12 Martin Brodeur	1.50	4.00
13 Wayne Gretzky	4.00	10.00
14 Alexei Yashin	.25	.60
15 John LeClair	.60	1.50
16 Eric Lindros	.60	1.50
17 Keith Tkachuk	.60	1.50
18 Jaromir Jagr	1.00	2.50
19 Mats Sundin	.60	1.50
20 Mark Messier	.60	1.50

1998-99 Pacific Omega Toronto Spring Expo

Available via wrapper redemption at the 1999 Toronto Spring Expo from the Pacific booth, these cards are stamped on the front in silver foil with the Expo logo. Each card was serial numbered to just 20. Although these cards have a secondary market interest, there is not enough data to accurately price them. The list below is partial, please forward any additional information to Beckett.com.

8 Teemu Selanne
31 Theo Fleury
65 Joe Sakic
88 Steve Yzerman
156 Wayne Gretzky
177 Eric Lindros
195 Jaromir Jagr

1999-00 Pacific Omega

The 1999-00 Pacific Omega set was released as a 250-card set. It is available in both hobby and retail version, limiting certain inserts to hobby only or retail only. The base card features full-color photography and a silver foil player portrait in the bottom right corner, while prospect cards contain two players in split screen format. Each pack contains 6 cards, and carries a suggested retail price of $1.99.

COMPLETE SET (250)	30.00	60.00
1 Matt Cullen	.05	.15
2 Guy Hebert	.10	.30
3 Paul Kariya	.15	.40
4 Marty McInnis	.05	.15

5 Steve Rucchin .05 .15
6 Teemu Selanne .15 .40
7 Pascal Trepanier .10 .30
8 Ladislav Kohn .10 .30
Vitaly Vishnevski
9 Andrew Brunette .10 .30
10 Nelson Emerson .05 .15
11 Ray Ferraro .05 .15
12 Damian Rhodes .10 .30
13 Patrik Stefan RC .30 .75
14 Dean Sylvester RC .30 .75
15 Petr Buzek RC .30 .75
Scott Fankhouser
16 Jason Allison .05 .15
17 Dave Andreychuk .10 .30
18 Ray Bourque .25 .60
19 Anson Carter .10 .30
20 Byron Dafoe .10 .30
21 Sergei Samsonov .10 .30
22 Joe Thornton .25 .60
23 J.GrahameRC/J.HendersonRC .30 .75
24 Maxim Afinogenov .05 .15
25 Martin Biron .10 .30
26 Curtis Brown .05 .15
27 Brian Campbell RC .30 .75
28 Dominik Hasek .30 .75
29 Dimitri Kalinin RC .30 .75
30 Michael Peca .05 .15
31 Miroslav Satan .10 .30
32 Rhett Warrener .05 .15
33 Jean-Luc Grand-Pierre RC .30 .75
David Moravec
34 Fred Brathwaite .05 .15
35 Valeri Bure .05 .15
36 Grant Fuhr .05 .15
37 Phil Housley .05 .15
38 Jarome Iginla .20 .50
39 Oleg Saprykin RC .60 1.50
40 Marc Savard .05 .15
41 Cory Stillman .05 .15
42 Travis Brigley RC .30 .75
Robyn Regehr
43 Ron Francis .10 .30
44 Sean Hill .05 .15
45 Arturs Irbe .10 .30
46 Sami Kapanen .05 .15
47 Curtis Leschyshyn .05 .15
48 Jeff O'Neill .05 .15
49 Gary Roberts .05 .15
50 D.Tanabe RC/T.Westlund .30 .75
51 Tony Amonte .10 .30
52 Eric Daze .10 .30
53 Doug Gilmour .10 .30
54 Michael Nylander .05 .15
55 Steve Sullivan .05 .15
56 Jocelyn Thibault .10 .30
57 Alexei Zhamnov .05 .15
58 J-P Dumont .30 .75
Marc Lamothe RC
59 Chris Harperger RC .30 .75
Steve McCarthy
60 Adam Deadmarsh .05 .15
61 Chris Drury .10 .30
62 Peter Forsberg .40 1.00
63 Milan Hejduk .15 .40
64 Sandis Ozolinsh .05 .15
65 Patrick Roy .75 2.00
66 Joe Sakic .30 .75
67 Alex Tanguay .10 .30
68 Marc Denis RC .30 .75
Martin Skoula
69 Sami Helenius RC .30 .75
Brian Willsie
70 Ed Belfour .15 .40
71 Manny Fernandez .10 .30
72 Brett Hull .20 .50
73 Jere Lehtinen .10 .30
74 Mike Modano .25 .60
75 Brenden Morrow .15 .40
76 Joe Nieuwendyk .10 .30
77 Sergei Zubov .05 .15
78 Ryan Christie RC .30 .75
Roman Lyashenko
79 R.Jackman/A.Letang RC .30 .75
80 Chris Chelios .15 .40
81 Sergei Fedorov .25 .60
82 Igor Larionov .05 .15
83 Nicklas Lidstrom .15 .40
84 Chris Osgood .10 .30
85 Brendan Shanahan .15 .40
86 Pat Verbeek .05 .15
87 Ken Wregget .10 .30
88 Steve Yzerman .75 2.00
89 Paul Comrie RC .05 .15
90 Bill Guerin .05 .15
91 Tom Poti .05 .15
92 Bert Robertsson RC .30 .75
93 Tommy Salo .10 .30
94 Alexander Selivanov .05 .15
95 Ryan Smyth .05 .15
96 Doug Weight .10 .30
97 Pavel Bure .15 .40
98 Viktor Kozlov .05 .15
99 Mark Parrish .05 .15
100 Mikhail Shtalenkov .05 .15
101 Robert Svehla .05 .15
102 Mike Vernon .10 .30
103 Ray Whitney .10 .30
104 Dave Duerden RC .30 .75
Ivan Novoseltsev
105 John Jakopin RC .30 .75
Filip Kuba
106 Rob Blake .10 .30
107 Stephane Fiset .10 .30
108 Jaroslav Modry .05 .15
109 Glen Murray .05 .15
110 Zigmund Palffy .10 .30
111 Luc Robitaille .10 .30
112 Bryan Smolinski .10 .30
113 Jamie Storr .10 .30
114 Marko Tuomainen .05 .15
115 Brad Chartrand RC .30 .75
Frantisek Kaberle
116 Shayne Corson .05 .15
117 Craig Darby .05 .15
118 Jeff Hackett .10 .30
119 Saku Koivu .15 .40
120 Trevor Linden .05 .15
121 Martin Rucinsky .10 .30
122 Brian Savage .05 .15
123 Jose Theodore .20 .50
124 Francis Bouillon RC .30 .75
Stephane Robidas
125 Mike Ribeiro .10 .30
Jason Ward
126 Mike Dunham .10 .30
127 Patric Kjellberg .05 .15
128 Cliff Ronning .10 .30
129 Tomas Vokoun .05 .15
130 David Legwand .10 .30
Randy Robitaille
131 Richard Lintner RC .30 .75
Karlis Skrastins
132 Jason Arnott .05 .15
133 Martin Brodeur .40 1.00
134 Patrik Elias .10 .30
135 Scott Gomez .05 .15
136 Bobby Holik .05 .15
137 Claude Lemieux .05 .15
138 Petr Sykora .05 .15
139 John Madden RC .30 .75
Brian Rafalski
140 Mariusz Czerkawski .05 .15
141 Brad Isbister .05 .15
142 Jorgen Jonsson RC .30 .75
143 Roberto Luongo .20 .50
144 Bill Muckalt .05 .15
145 Kevin Weekes .10 .30
146 Tim Connolly RC .30 .75
Evgeny Korolev
147 Alexandre Daigle .05 .15
148 Radek Dvorak .05 .15
149 Theo Fleury .05 .15
150 Adam Graves .05 .15
151 Brian Leetch .15 .40
152 Petr Nedved .10 .30
153 Mike Richter .15 .40
154 Michael York .05 .15
155 Jan Hlavac .30 .75
Kim Johnsson RC RC
156 Daniel Alfredsson .10 .30
157 Magnus Arvedson .05 .15
158 Radek Bonk .05 .15
159 Marian Hossa .15 .40
160 Patrick Lalime .10 .30
161 Shawn McEachern .10 .30
162 Petr Schastlivy RC .30 .75
163 Ron Tugnutt .10 .30
164 Shaun Van Allen .05 .15
165 Alexei Yashin .05 .15
166 Mike Fisher RC .30 .75
Andre Roy
167 Brian Boucher .15 .40
168 Eric Desjardins .10 .30
169 Simon Gagne .15 .40
170 Daymond Langkow .10 .30
171 John LeClair .15 .40
172 Eric Lindros .15 .40
173 Keith Primeau .05 .15
174 Mark Recchi .10 .30
175 Mikael Renberg .10 .30
176 John Vanbiesbrouck .10 .30
177 Andy Delmore RC .30 .75
Mark Eaton
178 Shane Doan .05 .15
179 Dallas Drake .05 .15
180 Robert Esche RC .10 .30
181 Travis Green .10 .30
182 Nikolai Khabibulin .10 .30
183 Teppo Numminen .05 .15
184 Jeremy Roenick .20 .50
185 Keith Tkachuk .15 .40
186 Trevor Letowski RC .30 .75
Radoslav Suchy
187 Jan Hrdina .05 .15
188 Jaromir Jagr .25 .60
189 Hans Jonsson RC .30 .75
190 Alexei Kovalev .10 .30
191 Martin Straka .05 .15
192 German Titov .05 .15
193 Tyler Wright .05 .15
194 Jean-Sebastien Aubin RC .30 .75
Michael Rozsival
195 Pavol Demitra .10 .30
196 Al MacInnis .10 .30
197 Jamie McLennan .10 .30
198 Tyson Nash RC .30 .75
199 Chris Pronger .10 .30
200 Todd Reirden RC .30 .75
201 Roman Turek .10 .30
202 Pierre Turgeon .10 .30
203 Jochen Hecht RC .75 2.00
Ladislav Nagy
204 Vincent Damphousse .05 .15
205 Jeff Friesen .05 .15
206 Todd Harvey .05 .15
207 Alexander Korolyuk .05 .15
208 Patrick Marleau .10 .30
209 Owen Nolan .10 .30
210 Steve Shields .10 .30
211 Gary Suter .05 .15
212 Evgeni Nabokov RC 2.00 5.00
Brad Stuart
213 Dan Cloutier .05 .15
214 Stan Drulia .05 .15
215 Chris Gratton .05 .15
216 Vincent Lecavalier .15 .40
217 Steve Martins RC .30 .75
218 Fredrik Modin .05 .15
219 Mike Sillinger .05 .15
220 Ben Clymer RC .30 .75
Nils Ekman
221 Nikolai Antropov RC .60 1.50
222 Sergei Berezin .10 .30
223 Tie Domi .10 .30
224 Jonas Hoglund .10 .30
225 Curtis Joseph .15 .40
226 Tomas Kaberle .05 .15
227 Dimitri Khristich .05 .15
228 Mats Sundin .15 .40
229 Steve Thomas .10 .30
230 Adam Mair RC .30 .75
Dmitri Yakushin
231 Todd Bertuzzi .15 .40
232 Andrew Cassels .05 .15
233 Steve Kariya RC .30 .75
234 Mark Messier .15 .40
235 Alexander Mogilny .10 .30
236 Markus Naslund .15 .40
237 Felix Potvin .15 .40
238 Ryan Bonni RC .30 .75
Zenith Komarniski
239 Harold Druken .05 .15
Peter Schaefer
240 Brad Leeb RC .30 .75
Alfie Michaud
241 Peter Bondra .10 .30
242 Jan Bulis .05 .15
243 Olaf Kolzig .10 .30
244 Steve Konowalchuk .05 .15
245 Adam Oates .10 .30
246 Jeff Halpern RC .30 .75
Glen Metropolit
247 Alexei Tezikov RC .30 .75
Alexandre Volchkov
248 North American All-Stars .10 .30
249 World All-Stars .10 .30
250 Pavel Bure .15 .40
Valeri Bure
NNO Martin Brodeur SAMPLE .40 1.00

1999-00 Pacific Omega Copper

Randomly inserted in packs, this 250-card Hobby Only set parallels the base set and enhances the base card design with copper foil on the text and on the player portrait in the bottom right front corner. Just above the player portrait is a box that contains each card's serial number. Each of the Copper parallel version cards are numbered out of 99.

*STARS: 15X TO 40X BASIC CARDS
*ROOKIES: 5X TO 12X BASIC CARDS

1999-00 Pacific Omega Gold

Randomly inserted in packs, this 250-card Retail Only set parallels the base set and enhances the base card design with gold foil on the text and on the player portrait in the bottom right front corner. Just above the player portrait is a box that contains each card's serial number. Each of the Gold parallel version cards are numbered out of 299.

*STARS: 6X TO 15X BASIC CARDS
*ROOKIES: 2X TO 5X BASIC CARDS

1999-00 Pacific Omega Ice Blue

Randomly inserted in packs, this 250-card set parallels the base set and enhances the base card design with blue foil on the text and on the player portrait in the bottom right front corner. Just above the player portrait is a box that contains each card's serial number. Each of the Ice Blue parallel version cards are numbered out of 75. This set was available in both Hobby and Retail packs.

*STARS: 25X TO 50X BASIC CARDS
*ROOKIES: 8X TO 20X BASIC CARDS

1999-00 Pacific Omega Premiere Date

Randomly inserted in packs at a rate of 1:37, this 250 card set paralleled the base set except for a gold foil stamp just above the player's name. The stamps carried a serial number out of 68. The date of the player's 'premiere' in the NHL is under the stamp.

*STARS: 25X TO 50X BASIC CARDS
*RC's: 8X TO 20X BASIC CARDS

1999-00 Pacific Omega Cup Contenders

COMPLETE SET (20) 50.00 100.00
STATED ODDS 1:37
1 Paul Kariya 1.50 4.00
2 Dominik Hasek 3.00 8.00
3 Peter Forsberg 4.00 10.00
4 Patrick Roy 8.00 20.00
5 Joe Sakic 3.00 8.00
6 Brett Hull 2.00 5.00
7 Mike Modano 2.50 6.00

8 Sergi Fedorov 3.00 8.00
9 Brendan Shanahan 2.50 6.00
10 Steve Yzerman 8.00 20.00
11 Pavel Bure 2.00 5.00
12 Martin Broedur 4.00 10.00
13 Theo Fleury 1.50 4.00
14 Mike Richter 1.50 4.00
15 John LeClair 2.00 5.00
16 Jeremy Roenick 2.00 5.00
17 Jaromir Jagr 2.50 6.00
18 Al MacInnis 1.25 3.00
19 Curtis Joseph 1.50 4.00
20 Mark Messier 2.00 5.00

1999-00 Pacific Omega EO Portraits

Randomly inserted in packs at 1:73, this 20-card set features laser-cut player images on one side and a full color photo on the other. Parallels numbered 1/1 also exist; they are not priced due to scarcity.

COMPLETE SET (20) 25.00 50.00
1 Paul Kariya .75 2.00
2 Teemu Selanne .75 2.00
3 Patrik Stefan .75 2.00
4 Dominik Hasek 1.50 4.00
5 Peter Forsberg 2.00 5.00
6 Patrick Roy 4.00 10.00
7 Mike Modano 1.25 3.00
8 Brendan Shanahan .75 2.00
9 Steve Yzerman 4.00 10.00
10 Pave Bure .75 2.00
11 Martin Brodeur 2.00 5.00
12 Scott Gomez .75 2.00
13 Eric Lindros .75 2.00
14 John Vanbiesbrouck .75 2.00
15 Keith Tkachuk .75 2.00
16 Jaromir Jagr 1.25 3.00
17 Vincent Lecavalier .75 2.00
18 Curtis Joseph .75 2.00
19 Mats Sundin .75 2.00
20 Mark Messier .75 2.00

1999-00 Pacific Omega Game-Used Jerseys

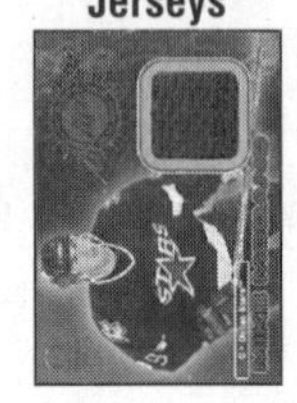

Randomly inserted in packs at 1:180, this 10-card set features a swatch of game used jersey on each card. This set was not announced in the initial release, and was a last minute addition.

1 Teemu Selanne 4.00 10.00
2 Mike Modano 4.00 10.00
3 Steve Yzerman 10.00 25.00
4 Martin Brodeur 8.00 20.00
5 Mike Richter 4.00 10.00
6 John LeClair 4.00 10.00
7 Eric Lindros 4.00 10.00
8 John Vanbiesbrouck 4.00 10.00
9 Jaromir Jagr 6.00 15.00
10 Mats Sundin 4.00 10.00

1999-00 Pacific Omega NHL Generations

Randomly seeded in packs at one in 1:145, this 10-card set features two players on each card. The left side pictures an NHL standout veteran paired with a top rated prospect on the right. The green background on each side contains a silhouette of both respective players.

COMPLETE SET (10) 50.00 125.00
1 Paul Kariya 6.00 15.00
Steve Kariya
2 Teemu Selanne 6.00 15.00
Milan Hejduk
3 Peter Forsberg 8.00 20.00
Chris Drury
4 Patrick Roy 15.00 40.00
Roberto Luongo
5 M.Modano/D.Legwand 6.00 15.00
6 Steve Yzerman 12.00 30.00
Scott Gomez
7 Pavel Bure 6.00 15.00
Marian Hossa
8 John LeClair 4.00 10.00
Simon Gagne
9 Eric Lindros 6.00 15.00
Vincent Lecavalier
10 Jaromir Jagr 8.00 20.00
Patrik Stefan

1999-00 Pacific Omega North American All-Stars

Randomly inserted in packs at 2:37, this 10-card die-cut set pictured some of North America's most dominating All-Stars set against the Toronto All-Star logo.

COMPLETE SET (10) 15.00 30.00
1 Paul Kariya 1.00 2.50
2 Ray Bourque 1.25 3.00
3 Joe Sakic 1.50 4.00
4 Mike Modano 1.25 3.00
5 Brendan Shanahan 1.25 3.00
6 Steve Yzerman 4.00 10.00
7 Martin Brodeur 2.00 5.00
8 Scott Gomez 1.00 2.50
9 Curtis Joseph 1.00 2.50
10 Mark Messier 1.00 2.50

1999-00 Pacific Omega 5 Star Talents

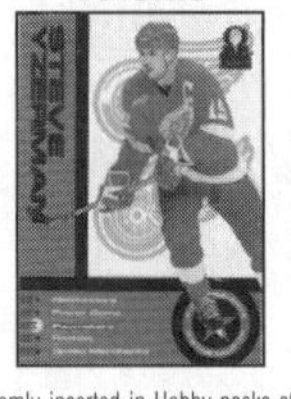

Randomly inserted in Hobby packs at the rate of 4:37, this 30-card set segments NHL players into five different groups of six cards each. Card #'s 1-6 are top prospects (Rookies), card #'s 7-12 are power players (Power Game), card #'s 13-18 are some of the NHL's quickest (Speed Merchants), card #'s 19-24 are some of the top set-up guys (Playmakers), and card #'s 25-30 are some of the NHL's most dominating goaltenders (Netminders). A five-tier serial #'d parallel of this set was released also.

COMPLETE SET (30) 20.00 40.00
1 Patrik Stefan .75 2.00
2 Alex Tanguay .40 1.00
3 David Legwand .40 1.00
4 Scott Gomez .40 1.00
5 Roberto Luongo .60 1.50
6 Steve Kariya .50 1.25
7 Brendan Shanahan .50 1.25
8 John LeClair .50 1.25
9 Eric Lindros .50 1.25
10 Keith Tkachuk .50 1.25
11 Owen Nolan .40 1.00
12 Mark Messier .50 1.25
13 Paul Kariya .50 1.25
14 Teemu Selanne .50 1.25
15 Pavel Bure .50 1.25
16 Theo Fleury .50 1.25
17 Marian Hossa .40 1.00
18 Jaromir Jagr .75 2.00
19 Peter Forsberg 1.25 3.00
20 Mike Modano .75 2.00
21 Steve Yzerman 2.50 6.00
22 Mark Recchi .40 1.00
23 Vincent Lecavalier .50 1.25
24 Mats Sundin .50 1.25
25 Dominik Hasek 1.00 2.50
26 Patrick Roy 2.50 6.00
27 Ed Belfour .50 1.25
28 Martin Brodeur 1.25 3.00
29 John Vanbiesbrouck .50 1.25
30 Curtis Joseph .50 1.25

1999-00 Pacific Omega 5 Star Talents Parallel

*TIER 1 (1-6): 10X TO 25X BASIC INSERTS
TIER 1 STATED PRINT RUN 100 SETS
*TIER 2 (7-12): 15X TO 40X BASIC INSERTS
TIER 2 STATED PRINT RUN 75 SETS
*TIER 3 (13-18): 25X TO 60X BASIC INSERTS
TIER 3 STATED PRINT RUN 50 SETS
*TIER 4 (19-24): 40X TO 100X BASIC INSERTS
TIER 4 STATED PRINT RUN 25 SETS
TIER 5 STATED PRINT RUN 1 SET
TIER 5 (25-30) NOT PRICED DUE TO SCARCITY

1999-00 Pacific Omega World All-Stars

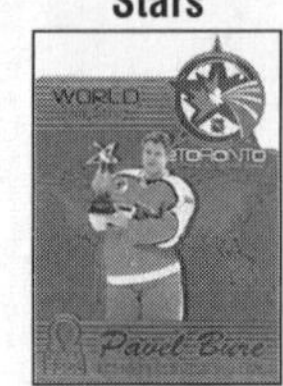

Randomly inserted in packs at 2:37, this 10-card die-cut set pictured some of the World's most dominating All-Stars set against the Toronto All-Star logo.

COMPLETE SET (10) 6.00 12.00
1 Teemu Selanne .60 1.50
2 Valeri Bure .60 1.50
3 Nicklas Lidstrom .60 1.50
4 Pavel Bure .60 1.50
5 Viktor Kozlov .60 1.50
6 Jaromir Jagr 1.25 3.00
7 Pavol Demitra .60 1.50
8 Roman Turek .60 1.50
9 Mats Sundin .75 2.00
10 Olaf Kolzig .60 1.50

1999-00 Pacific Prism

The 1999-00 Pacific Prism set was released in both hobby and retail versions as a 150-card set featuring both veterans and prospects. The base cards are printed on silver holo-foil, and the prospects are denoted by a red diamond in the lower front right corner. Prism was packaged in 20-pack boxes with three cards per pack.

COMPLETE SET (150) 30.00 60.00
1 Guy Hebert .15 .40
2 Paul Kariya .20 .50
3 Mike Leclerc .10 .30
4 Steve Rucchin .10 .30
5 Teemu Selanne .20 .50
6 Andrew Brunette .15 .40
7 Petr Buzek .15 .40
8 Damian Rhodes .10 .30
9 Patrik Stefan RC .75 2.00
10 Jason Allison .10 .30
11 Dave Andreychuk .15 .40
12 Ray Bourque .30 .75
13 Byron Dafoe .15 .40
14 Sergei Samsonov .15 .40
15 Joe Thornton .30 .75
16 Maxim Afinogenov .10 .30
17 Martin Biron .15 .40
18 Curtis Brown .10 .30
19 Dominik Hasek .40 1.00
20 Michael Peca .10 .30
21 Miroslav Satan .15 .40
22 Valeri Bure .15 .40
23 Grant Fuhr .15 .40
24 Jarome Iginla .25 .60
25 Oleg Saprykin RC .60 1.50
26 Cory Stillman .10 .30
27 Bates Battaglia .10 .30
28 Ron Francis .10 .30
29 Arturs Irbe .15 .40
30 Sami Kapanen .10 .30
31 Keith Primeau .10 .30
32 Tony Amonte .15 .40
33 J-P Dumont .15 .40
34 Doug Gilmour .15 .40
35 Jocelyn Thibault .15 .40
36 Alexei Zhamnov .10 .30
37 Chris Drury .15 .40
38 Peter Forsberg .50 1.25
39 Milan Hejduk .20 .50
40 Patrick Roy 1.00 2.50
41 Joe Sakic .40 1.00
42 Alex Tanguay .15 .40
43 Ed Belfour .20 .50
44 Brett Hull .25 .60
45 Roman Lyashenko .10 .30
46 Mike Modano .30 .75
47 Joe Nieuwendyk .15 .40
48 Brendan Shanahan .20 .50
49 Chris Chelios .20 .50
50 Sergei Fedorov .30 .75
51 Jiri Fischer .10 .30
52 Nicklas Lidstrom .20 .50
53 Chris Osgood .15 .40
54 Steve Yzerman 1.00 2.50
55 Bill Guerin .10 .30
56 Tommy Salo .15 .40
57 Alexander Selivanov .10 .30
58 Ryan Smyth .10 .30
59 Doug Weight .15 .40
60 Pavel Bure .20 .50
61 Trevor Kidd .10 .30
62 Viktor Kozlov .15 .40
63 Mark Parrish .10 .30
64 Ray Whitney .15 .40
65 Rob Blake .15 .40
66 Stephane Fiset .15 .40
67 Frantisek Kaberle .10 .30
68 Zigmund Palffy .15 .40
69 Luc Robitaille .15 .40
70 Francis Bouillon RC .10 .30
71 Jeff Hackett .15 .40
72 Saku Koivu .20 .50
73 Trevor Linden .15 .40
74 Brian Savage .10 .30
75 Mike Dunham .15 .40
76 David Legwand .20 .50
77 Cliff Ronning .15 .40
78 Rob Valicevic RC .10 .30
79 Martin Brodeur .50 1.25
80 Patrik Elias .15 .40
81 Scott Gomez .10 .30
82 Bobby Holik .10 .30
83 Claude Lemieux .10 .30
84 Petr Sykora .10 .30
85 Tim Connolly .10 .30
86 Mariusz Czerkawski .10 .30
87 Brad Isbister .10 .30
88 Roberto Luongo .25 .60
89 Theo Fleury .10 .30
90 Jan Hlavac .10 .30
91 Brian Leetch .20 .50
92 Mike Richter .20 .50
93 Mike York .10 .30
94 Daniel Alfredsson .15 .40
95 Radek Bonk .10 .30
96 Marian Hossa .20 .50
97 Shawn McEachern .10 .30
98 Ron Tugnutt .15 .40
99 Alexei Yashin .10 .30
100 Brian Boucher .20 .50
101 Simon Gagne .20 .50
102 John LeClair .20 .50
103 Eric Lindros .20 .50
104 Mark Recchi .15 .40
105 John Vanbiesbrouck .15 .40
106 Mike Alatalo RC .15 .40
107 Travis Green .10 .30
108 Nikolai Khabibulin .15 .40
109 Jeremy Roenick .25 .60
110 Keith Tkachuk .20 .50
111 Rick Tocchet .15 .40
112 Jean-Sebastien Aubin .15 .40
113 Andrew Ference .10 .30
114 Jaromir Jagr .30 .75
115 Alexei Kovalev .10 .30
116 Martin Straka .10 .30
117 Pavol Demitra .15 .40
118 Jochen Hecht RC .75 2.00
119 Al MacInnis .15 .40
120 Chris Pronger .15 .40
121 Roman Turek .15 .40
122 Pierre Turgeon .15 .40
123 Vincent Damphousse .10 .30
124 Jeff Friesen .10 .30
125 Patrick Marleau .15 .40
126 Owen Nolan .15 .40
127 Steve Shields .15 .40
128 Brad Stuart .15 .40
129 Dan Cloutier .10 .30
130 Ben Clymer RC .20 .50
131 Chris Gratton .10 .30
132 Vincent Lecavalier .20 .50
133 Darcy Tucker .10 .30
134 Nikolai Antropov RC 1.25 3.00
135 Sergei Berezin .10 .30
136 Tie Domi .15 .40
137 Curtis Joseph .20 .50
138 Dimitri Khristich .10 .30
139 Mats Sundin .20 .50
140 Steve Kariya RC .60 1.50
141 Mark Messier .20 .50
142 Alfie Michaud RC .40 1.00
143 Alexander Mogilny .15 .40
144 Jarkko Ruutu RC .20 .50
145 Peter Schaefer .15 .40
146 Peter Bondra .15 .40
147 Jan Bulis .15 .40
148 Olaf Kolzig .15 .40
149 Glen Metropolit RC .60 1.50
150 Adam Oates .15 .40
NNO Martin Brodeur SAMPLE .80 2.00

1999-00 Pacific Prism Holographic Blue

Randomly inserted in packs, this 150-card set parallels the base set in a holographic blue foil version. Each card is numbered out of 80 in the top left-hand corner.

*STARS: 6X TO 15X BASIC CARDS
*ROOKIES: 3X TO 8X BASIC CARDS

1999-00 Pacific Prism Holographic Gold

Randomly inserted in packs, this 150-card set parallels the base set in a holographic gold foil version. Each card is numbered out of 480 in the top left-hand corner.

*STARS: 1.25X TO 3X BASIC CARDS
*ROOKIES: .75X TO 2X BASIC CARDS

1999-00 Pacific Prism Holographic Mirror

Randomly inserted in packs, this 150-card set parallels the base set in a holographic silver rainbow foil version. Each card is numbered out of 160 in the top left-hand corner.

*STARS: 4X TO 10X BASIC CARDS
*ROOKIES: 2X TO 5X BASIC CARDS
STATED PRINT RUN 160 SER.#'d SETS

1999-00 Pacific Prism Holographic Purple

andomly inserted in hobby packs, this 150-ard set parallels the base set in a olographic purple foil version. Each card is umbered out of 99 in the top left-hand orner.
STARS: 5X TO 12X BASIC CARDS
ROOKIES: 2.5X TO 6X BASIC CARDS

1999-00 Pacific Prism Premiere Date

andomly inserted in packs, the 150-card et parallels the base set and is serial umbered in the upper-left front corner out f 69. The center of the cards also contains "premiere date" embossed stamp.
STARS: 8X TO 20X BASIC CARDS
ROOKIES: 4X TO 10X BASIC CARDS

1999-00 Pacific Prism Clear Advantage

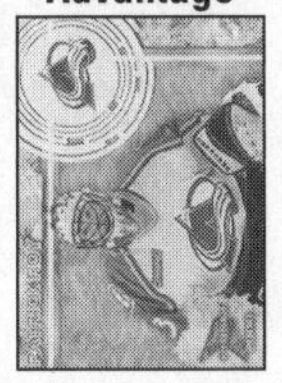

andomly seeded in packs at 2:25, this 20-ard set features 20 of hockey's most xciting players. Action player photos are et against an icy-looking blue background.

OMPLETE SET (20) 20.00 40.00
Paul Kariya .60 1.50
Teemu Selanne .60 1.50
Dominik Hasek 1.25 3.00
Peter Forsberg 1.50 4.00
Patrick Roy 3.00 8.00
Alex Tanguay .50 1.25
Brett Hull .75 2.00
Brendan Shanahan 1.00 2.50
Steve Yzerman 3.00 8.00
0 Pavel Bure .75 2.00
1 Zigmund Palffy .50 1.25
2 Martin Brodeur 1.50 4.00
3 Theo Fleury .50 1.25
4 Marian Hossa .60 1.50
5 John LeClair .75 2.00
6 Eric Lindros 1.00 2.50
7 Mark Recchi .50 1.25
8 Jaromir Jagr 1.00 2.50
9 Vincent Lecavalier .60 1.50
0 Mats Sundin .60 1.50

1999-00 Pacific Prism Ice Prospects

andomly inserted in hobby packs at 1:97, is 10-card set features some of hockey's p and coming prospects.

OMPLETE SET (10) 30.00 60.00
Patrik Stefan 3.00 8.00
Martin Biron 3.00 8.00
Alex Tanguay 3.00 8.00
David Legwand 3.00 8.00
Scott Gomez 3.00 8.00
Simon Gagne 3.00 8.00
Brad Stuart 3.00 8.00
Nikolai Antropov 3.00 8.00
Steve Kariya 3.00 8.00
0 Peter Schaefer 3.00 8.00

1999-00 Pacific Prism Dial-a-Stats

andomly inserted in packs at 1:193, this 0-card set showcases NHL superstars that oast impressive statistics. The card is cut

and fitted with a fastener in the middle to allow a wheel with stat numbers on it to be spun to display the player's career statistics versus the various NHL teams faced.

COMPLETE SET (10) 40.00 80.00
1 Paul Kariya 6.00 15.00
2 Teemu Selanne 6.00 15.00
3 Dominik Hasek 4.00 10.00
4 Peter Forsberg 5.00 12.00
5 Patrick Roy 10.00 25.00
6 Mike Modano 3.00 8.00
7 Steve Yzerman 10.00 25.00
8 Eric Lindros 3.00 8.00
9 Jaromir Jagr 3.00 8.00
10 Mark Messier 2.50 6.00

1999-00 Pacific Prism Sno-Globe Die-Cuts

Randomly seeded in packs at one in 1:25, this 20-card set features NHL greats on a full foil die-cut card shaped like a glass sno-globe.

COMPLETE SET (20) 20.00 40.00
1 Paul Kariya .60 1.50
2 Teemu Selanne .60 1.50
3 Ray Bourque 1.00 2.50
4 Dominik Hasek 1.25 3.00
5 Peter Forsberg 1.50 4.00
6 Patrick Roy 3.00 8.00
7 Joe Sakic 1.25 3.00
8 Ed Belfour .60 1.50
9 Mike Modano 1.00 2.50
10 Brendan Shanahan 1.00 2.50
11 Steve Yzerman 3.00 8.00
12 Pavel Bure .75 2.00
13 Martin Brodeur 1.50 4.00
14 Theo Fleury .60 1.50
15 John LeClair .75 2.00
16 Eric Lindros 1.00 2.50
17 John Vanbiesbrouck .60 1.50
18 Keith Tkachuk .60 1.50
19 Jaromir Jagr 1.00 2.50
20 Curtis Joseph .60 1.50

2003-04 Pacific Prism

Released in mid-August, this 150-card set consisted of 100 base cards and 50 jersey cards. Jersey cards were one per pack and were serial-numbered. Numbering for individual cards can be found below. Cards 151-160 were available only in packs of Pacific Calder.

COMP.SET w/o JSY's (100) 30.00 60.00
1 Stanislav Chistov .10 .25
2 J-S Giguere .25 .60
3 Adam Oates .25 .60
4 Petr Sykora .10 .25
5 Joe DiPenta RC 1.50 4.00
6 Slava Kozlov .10 .25
7 Marc Savard .10 .25
8 Patrik Stefan .10 .25
9 Jeff Hackett .25 .60
10 Mike Knuble .10 .25
11 Sergei Samsonov .25 .60
12 Steve Shields .25 .60
13 Milan Bartovic RC 1.50 4.00
14 Martin Biron .25 .60
15 Daniel Briere .10 .25
16 Ryan Miller .25 .60
17 Miroslav Satan .25 .60
18 Craig Conroy .10 .25
19 Roman Turek .25 .60
20 Ron Francis .25 .60
21 Arturs Irbe .25 .60
22 Jeff O'Neill .10 .25
23 Tyler Arnason .25 .60
24 Theo Fleury .10 .25
25 Jocelyn Thibault .25 .60
26 Alexei Zhamnov .10 .25
27 Rob Blake .25 .60
28 Alex Tanguay .25 .60
29 Marc Denis .25 .60
30 Kent McDonell RC .30 .75
31 Rick Nash .40 1.00
32 Geoff Sanderson .10 .25
33 Ray Whitney .10 .25
34 Jason Arnott .10 .25
35 Jere Lehtinen .25 .60
36 Pavel Datsyuk .30 .75
37 Brett Hull .40 1.00
38 Curtis Joseph .30 .75
39 Henrik Zetterberg .30 .75
40 Ales Hemsky .25 .60
41 Tommy Salo .25 .60
42 Ryan Smyth .10 .25
43 Jay Bouwmeester .10 .25
44 Olli Jokinen .25 .60
45 Roberto Luongo .40 1.00
46 Stephen Weiss .10 .25
47 Michael Cammalleri .10 .25
48 Adam Deadmarsh .10 .25
49 Alexander Frolov .10 .25
50 Felix Potvin .30 .75
51 Andrew Brunette .10 .25
52 Manny Fernandez .25 .60
53 Marian Gaborik .60 1.50
54 Dwayne Roloson .25 .60
55 Cliff Ronning .10 .25
56 Marcel Hossa .10 .25
57 Yanic Perreault .10 .25
58 Scottie Upshall .10 .25
59 Tomas Vokoun .25 .60
60 Scott Walker .10 .25
61 Patrik Elias .25 .60
62 Jamie Langenbrunner .10 .25
63 John Madden .10 .25
64 Joe Nieuwendyk .25 .60
65 Scott Stevens .25 .60
66 Jason Blake .10 .25
67 Rick DiPietro .25 .60
68 Mark Parrish .10 .25
69 Mike Dunham .25 .60
70 Alex Kovalev .25 .60
71 Brian Leetch .25 .60
72 Mark Messier .30 .75
73 Zdeno Chara .10 .25
74 Martin Havlat .25 .60
75 Todd White .10 .25
76 John LeClair .30 .75
77 Mark Recchi .25 .60
78 Shane Doan .10 .25
79 Mike Johnson .10 .25
80 Johan Hedberg .25 .60
81 Martin Straka .10 .25
82 Pavol Demitra .25 .60
83 Barret Jackman .25 .60
84 Al MacInnis .25 .60
85 Peter Sejna RC 1.50 4.00
86 Keith Tkachuk .30 .75
87 Patrick Marleau .25 .60
88 Evgeni Nabokov .25 .60
89 Teemu Selanne .30 .75
90 Dave Andreychuk .10 .25
91 Brad Richards .25 .60
92 Alexander Mogilny .25 .60
93 Owen Nolan .25 .60
94 Matt Stajan RC 1.50 4.00
95 Ed Jovanovski .25 .60
96 Daniel Sedin .10 .25
97 Henrik Sedin .10 .25
98 Peter Bondra .25 .60
99 Sergei Gonchar .10 .25
100 Olaf Kolzig .25 .60
101 Paul Kariya/935 4.00 10.00
102 Dany Heatley/924 5.00 12.00
103 Ilya Kovalchuk/935 5.00 12.00
104 Glen Murray/1185 3.00 8.00
105 Joe Thornton/674 5.00 12.00
106 Chris Drury/935 3.00 8.00
107 Jarome Iginla/1183 5.00 12.00
108 Eric Daze/1171 3.00 8.00
109 Milan Hejduk/1183 4.00 10.00
110 Peter Forsberg/685 5.00 12.00
111 Patrick Roy/185 12.50 30.00
112 Joe Sakic/935 6.00 15.00
113 Bill Guerin/1136 3.00 8.00
114 Mike Modano/935 4.00 10.00
115 Marty Turco/685 4.00 10.00
116 Sergei Fedorov/685 4.00 10.00
117 Brendan Shanahan/935 4.00 10.00
118 Steve Yzerman/185 15.00 40.00
119 Mike Comrie/935 3.00 8.00
120 Jason Allison/1176 3.00 8.00
121 Roman Cechmanek/1185 3.00 8.00
122 Zigmund Palffy/1060 3.00 8.00
123 Saku Koivu/935 4.00 10.00
124 Jose Theodore/1185 4.00 10.00
125 Richard Zednik/1185 3.00 8.00
126 David Legwand/1185 3.00 8.00
127 Martin Brodeur/685 8.00 20.00
128 Michael Peca/1185 3.00 8.00
129 Alexei Yashin/1185 3.00 8.00
130 Pavel Bure/935 4.00 10.00
131 Eric Lindros/935 4.00 10.00
132 Daniel Alfredsson/185 5.00 12.00
133 Marian Hossa/185 5.00 12.00
134 Jason Spezza/185 8.00 20.00
135 Tony Amonte/1163 3.00 8.00
136 Jeremy Roenick/1185 4.00 10.00
137 Sean Burke/1185 3.00 8.00
138 Mario Lemieux/305 12.50 30.00
139 Chris Osgood/1185 3.00 8.00
140 Doug Weight/1185 3.00 8.00
141 Nikolai Khabibulin/1125 4.00 10.00
142 Vincent Lecavalier/935 3.00 8.00
143 Martin St. Louis/1185 3.00 8.00
144 Ed Belfour/685 4.00 10.00
145 Mats Sundin/685 4.00 10.00
146 Todd Bertuzzi/935 4.00 10.00
147 Dan Cloutier/1185 3.00 8.00
148 Brendan Morrison/685 3.00 8.00
149 Markus Naslund/185 8.00 20.00
150 Jaromir Jagr/185 10.00 25.00
151 Joffrey Lupul RC 2.00 5.00
152 Patrice Bergeron RC 4.00 10.00
153 Matthew Lombardi RC 2.00 5.00
154 Eric Staal RC 5.00 12.00
155 Nikolai Zherdev RC 2.50 6.00
156 Jiri Hudler RC 2.00 5.00
157 Nathan Horton RC 3.00 8.00
158 Jordin Tootoo RC 3.00 8.00
159 Antoine Vermette RC 2.00 5.00
160 Marc-Andre Fleury RC 6.00 15.00

2003-04 Pacific Prism Blue

*STARS 1-100: .6X TO 1.5X BASE CARDS
*ROOKIES 1-100: .3X TO .75X
*CARDS 101-150: .75X TO 2X BASIC JERSEYS
1-100 ODDS: ONE PER U.S. PACK
1-100 PRINT RUN 325 SER.#'d SETS
101-150 PRINT RUN 90 SER.#'d SETS
U.S. PACKS ONLY

2003-04 Pacific Prism Gold

Inserted at a rate of 6 per retail box, this 100-card set paralleled the base cards of the regular set but carried gold foil highlights and serial-numbering out of 425.
*GOLD: .5X TO 1.25X BASIC CARDS
*ROOKIES: .3X TO .75X

2003-04 Pacific Prism Patches

*PATCHES: 1X TO 2.5X BASIC JERSEYS
118 Steve Yzerman SP 50.00 125.00

2003-04 Pacific Prism Red

*CARDS 1-100: .75X TO 2X BASE CARDS
*ROOKIES 1-100: .4X TO 1X
*JSYS 101-150: .75X TO 2X BASIC JERSEYS
CARDS 1-100: ONE PER CANADIAN PACK

1-100 PRINT RUN 260 SER.#'d SETS
101-150 PRINT RUN 75 SER.#'d SETS
CANADIAN PACKS ONLY

2003-04 Pacific Prism Retail

This 150-card set mirrored the hobby set but cards 101-150 carried silver foil highlights and were serial numbered out of 150.
*RETAIL JERSEYS: .6X TO 1.5X HOBBY

2003-04 Pacific Prism Crease Police

COMPLETE SET (8) 10.00 20.00
STATED ODDS 1:9
1 J-S Giguere 1.50 4.00
2 Patrick Roy 3.00 8.00
3 Marty Turco 1.50 4.00
4 Curtis Joseph 1.50 4.00
5 Jose Theodore 2.00 5.00
6 Martin Brodeur 2.50 6.00
7 Patrick Lalime 1.50 4.00
8 Ed Belfour 1.50 4.00

2003-04 Pacific Prism Paramount Prodigies

COMPLETE SET (20) 15.00 30.00
STATED ODDS 1:3
1 Stanislav Chistov .60 1.50
2 J-S Giguere .60 1.50
3 Dany Heatley 1.00 2.50
4 Ilya Kovalchuk 1.00 2.50
5 Tyler Arnason .60 1.50
6 Rick Nash 1.00 2.50
7 Pavel Datsyuk .75 2.00
8 Henrik Zetterberg 1.00 2.50
9 Mike Comrie .60 1.50
10 Ales Hemsky .60 1.50
11 Jay Bouwmeester .60 1.50
12 Stephen Weiss .60 1.50
13 Alexander Frolov .60 1.50
14 Marian Gaborik 1.25 3.00
15 David Legwand .60 1.50
16 Martin Havlat .60 1.50
17 Marian Hossa .75 2.00
18 Jason Spezza 1.00 2.50
19 Barret Jackman .60 1.50
20 Vincent Lecavalier .60 1.50

2003-04 Pacific Prism Rookie Revolution

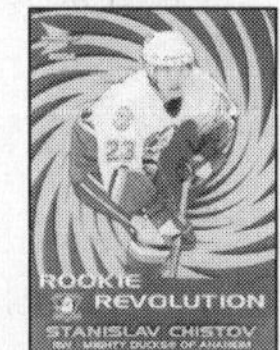

COMPLETE SET (12) 8.00 15.00
STATED ODDS 1:5
1 Stanislav Chistov .40 1.00
2 Ales Kotalik .40 1.00
3 Ryan Miller 1.00 2.50
4 Tyler Arnason .40 1.00
5 Rick Nash 1.00 2.50
6 Henrik Zetterberg .75 2.00
7 Ales Hemsky .75 2.00
8 Jay Bouwmeester .60 1.50
9 Alexander Frolov .60 1.50
10 Pierre-Marc Bouchard .60 1.50
11 Jason Spezza 1.00 2.50
12 Jonathan Cheechoo .75 2.00

2003-04 Pacific Prism Stat Masters

COMPLETE SET (10) 8.00 15.00
STATED ODDS 1:9
1 Paul Kariya .40 1.00
2 Joe Thornton .50 1.25
3 Peter Forsberg 1.00 2.50
4 Milan Hejduk .40 1.00
5 Mike Modano .60 1.50
6 Steve Yzerman 1.50 4.00
7 Mario Lemieux 2.00 5.00
8 Todd Bertuzzi .40 1.00
9 Markus Naslund .40 1.00
10 Jaromir Jagr .60 1.50

2002-03 Pacific Quest for the Cup

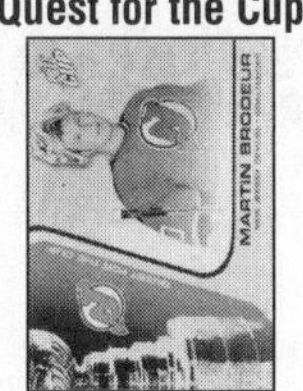

Released in May 2003, this 150-card set featured color player photos on the right side of the card fronts and a silver holographic image of the Stanley Cup on the left. Cards 151-150 were shortprinted to 950 and inserted at 1:5 hobby packs and 1:9 retail packs. Hobby packs contained 6 cards, and retail packs contained 4 cards.

COMP.SET w/o SP's (100) 20.00 40.00
1 J-S Giguere .25 .60
2 Paul Kariya .30 .75
3 Sandis Ozolinsh .10 .25
4 Dany Heatley .40 1.00
5 Ilya Kovalchuk .40 1.00
6 Jeff Hackett .25 .60
7 Glen Murray .10 .25
8 Joe Thornton .50 1.25
9 Martin Biron .25 .60
10 Miroslav Satan .25 .60
11 Chris Drury .25 .60
12 Jarome Iginla .40 1.00
13 Roman Turek .25 .60
14 Ron Francis .25 .60
15 Jeff O'Neill .10 .25
16 Eric Daze .25 .60
17 Theo Fleury .10 .25
18 Jocelyn Thibault .25 .60
19 Alexei Zhamnov .10 .25
20 Rob Blake .25 .60
21 Peter Forsberg .75 2.00
22 Milan Hejduk .30 .75
23 Patrick Roy 1.50 4.00
24 Joe Sakic .60 1.50
25 Marc Denis .25 .60
26 Ray Whitney .10 .25
27 Bill Guerin .25 .60
28 Jere Lehtinen .25 .60
29 Mike Modano .50 1.25
30 Marty Turco .25 .60
30AU Marty Turco AU/500 8.00 20.00
31 Pierre Turgeon .25 .60
32 Sergei Fedorov .50 1.25
33 Brett Hull .40 1.00
34 Curtis Joseph .30 .75
35 Nicklas Lidstrom .30 .75
36 Brendan Shanahan .30 .75
37 Steve Yzerman 1.50 4.00
38 Mike Comrie .25 .60
39 Tommy Salo .25 .60
40 Ryan Smyth .10 .25
41 Olli Jokinen .25 .60
42 Roberto Luongo .40 1.00
43 Jason Allison .10 .25
44 Zigmund Palffy .25 .60
45 Felix Potvin .30 .75
46 Pascal Dupuis .10 .25
47 Manny Fernandez .25 .60
48 Marian Gaborik .60 1.50
49 Cliff Ronning .10 .25
50 Saku Koivu .30 .75
51 Yanic Perreault .10 .25
52 Jose Theodore .40 1.00
53 Richard Zednik .10 .25
54 David Legwand .25 .60
55 Tomas Vokoun .25 .60
56 Martin Brodeur .75 2.00
57 Patrik Elias .25 .60
58 Jeff Friesen .10 .25
59 Jamie Langenbrunner .10 .25
60 Rick DiPietro .25 .60
61 Michael Peca .10 .25
62 Alexei Yashin .10 .25
63 Pavel Bure .30 .75
64 Anson Carter .25 .60
65 Alexei Kovalev .25 .60
66 Eric Lindros .30 .75
67 Mark Messier .30 .75
68 Daniel Alfredsson .25 .60
69 Radek Bonk .10 .25
70 Martin Havlat .25 .60
71 Marian Hossa .30 .75
72 Patrick Lalime .25 .60
73 Tony Amonte .25 .60
74 Roman Cechmanek .25 .60
75 Simon Gagne .30 .75
76 Sami Kapanen .10 .25
77 Jeremy Roenick .40 1.00
78 Sean Burke .25 .60
79 Johan Hedberg .25 .60
80 Mario Lemieux 2.50 6.00
81 Pavol Demitra .25 .60
82 Brent Johnson .25 .60
83 Cory Stillman .10 .25
84 Keith Tkachuk .30 .75
85 Doug Weight .25 .60
86 Evgeni Nabokov .25 .60
87 Teemu Selanne .30 .75
88 Nikolai Khabibulin .30 .75
89 Vincent Lecavalier .30 .75
90 Martin St. Louis .25 .60
91 Ed Belfour .30 .75
92 Alexander Mogilny .25 .60
93 Mats Sundin .30 .75
94 Todd Bertuzzi .30 .75
95 Dan Cloutier .25 .60
96 Brendan Morrison .25 .60
97 Markus Naslund .30 .75
98 Jaromir Jagr .50 1.25
99 Olaf Kolzig .25 .60
100 Michael Nylander .10 .25
101 Stanislav Chistov RC 1.50 4.00
102 Martin Gerber RC 2.00 5.00
103 Kurt Sauer RC 1.50 4.00
104 Alexei Smirnov RC 1.50 4.00
105 Shaone Morrisonn RC 1.50 4.00
106 Tim Thomas RC 2.00 5.00
107 Ryan Miller RC 4.00 10.00
108 Chuck Kobasew RC 2.00 5.00
109 Jordan Leopold RC 1.50 4.00
110 Ryan Bayda RC 1.50 4.00
111 Tomas Malec RC 1.50 4.00
112 Pascal Leclaire RC 2.00 5.00
113 Rick Nash RC 6.00 15.00
114 Jason Bacashihua RC 2.00 5.00
115 Steve Ott RC 2.00 5.00
116 Dmitri Bykov RC 1.50 4.00
117 Henrik Zetterberg RC 4.00 10.00
118 Ales Hemsky RC 5.00 12.00
119 Fernando Pisani RC 2.00 5.00
120 Jay Bouwmeester RC 3.00 8.00
121 Kip Brennan .10 .25
122 Michael Cammalleri RC 2.00 5.00
123 Alexander Frolov RC 3.00 8.00
124 P-M Bouchard RC 3.00 8.00
125 Stephane Veilleux RC 1.50 4.00
126 Ron Hainsey RC 1.50 4.00
127 Mike Komisarek RC 1.50 4.00
128 Vernon Fiddler RC 1.50 4.00
129 Adam Hall RC 1.50 4.00
130 Scottie Upshall RC 1.50 4.00
131 Eric Godard RC 1.50 4.00
132 Ray Emery RC 3.00 8.00
133 Jason Spezza RC 6.00 15.00
134 Anton Volchenkov RC 1.50 4.00
135 Dennis Seidenberg RC 1.50 4.00
136 Radovan Somik RC 1.50 4.00
137 Jim Vandermeer RC 1.50 4.00
138 Jeff Taffe RC 1.50 4.00
139 Brooks Orpik RC 1.50 4.00
140 Tomas Surovy RC 1.50 4.00
141 Dick Tarnstrom RC 1.50 4.00
142 Curtis Sanford RC 2.00 5.00
143 Matt Walker RC 1.50 4.00
144 Niko Dimitrakos RC 1.50 4.00
145 Jim Fahey RC 1.50 4.00
146 Lynn Loyns RC 1.50 4.00
147 Alexander Svitov RC 1.50 4.00
148 Carlo Colaiacovo RC 1.50 4.00
149 Mikael Tellqvist RC 2.00 5.00
150 Steve Eminger RC 1.50 4.00

2002-03 Pacific Quest for the Cup Gold

This 150-card set directly paralleled the base set but carried gold foil highlights on the card fronts. Each card was also serial-numbered out of 325 on the card back.
*STARS: 1.25X TO 3X BASIC CARD
*SP's: .25X TO .75X

2002-03 Pacific Quest For the Cup Calder Contenders

Inserted at 1:13 hobby and 1:25 retail, this 10-card set featured color player photos on gold foil backgrounds on the card fronts.

COMPLETE SET (10) 15.00 30.00
1 Stanislav Chistov 2.00 5.00
2 Ales Kotalik 1.00 2.50
3 Ryan Miller 1.50 4.00
4 Tyler Arnason 1.00 2.50
5 Pascal Leclaire 2.00 5.00
6 Rick Nash 2.50 6.00
7 Henrik Zetterberg 3.00 8.00
8 Ales Hemsky 1.50 4.00
9 Jay Bouwmeester 1.50 4.00
10 Jason Spezza 2.00 5.00

2002-03 Pacific Quest For the Cup Chasing the Cup

COMPLETE SET (20) 10.00 20.00
STATED ODDS 1:5 HOBBY/1:13 RETAIL
1 Paul Kariya .50 1.25
2 Dany Heatley .60 1.50
3 Ilya Kovalchuk .60 1.50
4 Joe Thornton .75 2.00
5 Marty Turco .40 1.00
6 Curtis Joseph .50 1.25
7 Marian Gaborik 1.00 2.50
8 Jose Theodore .60 1.50
9 Alexei Yashin .40 1.00
10 Pavel Bure .50 1.25
11 Eric Lindros .50 1.25
12 Daniel Alfredsson .40 1.00
13 Marian Hossa .50 1.25
14 Jeremy Roenick .60 1.50
15 Teemu Selanne .50 1.25
16 Owen Nolan .40 1.00
17 Mats Sundin .50 1.25
18 Todd Bertuzzi .50 1.25
19 Brendan Morrison .40 1.00
20 Markus Naslund .40 1.00

2002-03 Pacific Quest for the Cup Itech Masks

This insert set was pulled from production because of licensing issues, but a few random copies apparently made it into packs The only confirmed single to exist is the DiPietro card. Due to the scarcity of the card, it is not priced. If you know of other singles, please send information to hockeymag@beckett.com.
6 Rick DiPietro

2002-03 Pacific Quest for the Cup Jerseys

*MULT.COLOR SWATCH: .75X TO 1.5X
STATED ODDS 1:9 HOBBY/1:25 RETAIL
1 Dany Heatley 5.00 12.00
2 Glen Murray 3.00 8.00
3 Joe Thornton 6.00 15.00
4 Rob Blake 3.00 8.00
5 Peter Forsberg 8.00 20.00
6 Patrick Roy 12.50 30.00
7 Mike Modano 6.00 15.00
8 Marty Turco 5.00 12.00
9 Nicklas Lidstrom 4.00 10.00
10 Rick DiPietro 3.00 8.00
11 Mark Messier 4.00 10.00
12 Daniel Alfredsson 3.00 8.00
13 Marian Hossa 4.00 10.00
14 Jason Spezza 8.00 20.00
15 Roman Cechmanek 3.00 8.00
16 Jeremy Roenick 5.00 12.00
17 Mario Lemieux 12.50 30.00
18 Brent Johnson 3.00 8.00
19 Doug Weight 3.00 8.00
20 Martin St. Louis 3.00 8.00
21 Ed Belfour 4.00 10.00
22 Gary Roberts 3.00 8.00
23 Markus Naslund 4.00 10.00
24 Jaromir Jagr 6.00 15.00
25 Olaf Kolzig 3.00 8.00

2002-03 Pacific Quest For the Cup Raising the Cup

STATED ODDS 1:9 HOBBY/1:13 RETAIL
1 Peter Forsberg 1.50 4.00
2 Patrick Roy 2.50 6.00
3 Joe Sakic 1.25 3.00
4 Mike Modano 1.00 2.50
5 Sergei Fedorov 1.00 2.50
6 Brett Hull .75 2.00
7 Brendan Shanahan .60 1.50
8 Steve Yzerman 2.50 6.00

9 Martin Brodeur 1.50 4.00
10 Mark Messier .60 1.50
11 Mario Lemieux 3.00 8.00
12 Jaromir Jagr 1.00 2.50

2003-04 Pacific Quest for the Cup

This 140-card set consisted of 100 veteran cards and 40 rookie cards (101-140) that were serial-numbered out of 950.

COMP.SET w/o SP's 20.00 40.00
1 Sergei Fedorov .40 1.00
2 J-S Giguere .25 .60
3 Dany Heatley .40 1.00
4 Ilya Kovalchuk .40 1.00
5 Slava Kozlov .15 .40
6 Pasi Nurminen .25 .60
7 Mike Knuble .15 .40
8 Glen Murray .15 .40
9 Andrew Raycroft .25 .60
10 Joe Thornton .40 1.00
11 Daniel Briere .15 .40
12 Ales Kotalik .15 .40
13 Miroslav Satan .25 .60
14 Shean Donovan .15 .40
15 Jarome Iginla .40 1.00
16 Miikka Kiprusoff .25 .60
17 Erik Cole .15 .40
18 Ron Francis .25 .60
19 Tyler Arnason .25 .60
20 Mark Bell .15 .40
21 Kyle Calder .15 .40
22 David Aebischer .25 .60
23 Peter Forsberg .75 2.00
24 Milan Hejduk .30 .75
25 Paul Kariya .30 .75
26 Joe Sakic .60 1.50
27 Teemu Selanne .30 .75
28 Alex Tanguay .25 .60
29 Marc Denis .25 .60
30 Rick Nash .40 1.00
31 Bill Guerin .25 .60
32 Mike Modano .50 1.25
33 Marty Turco .25 .60
34 Pavel Datsyuk .30 .75
35 Kris Draper .15 .40
36 Dominik Hasek .60 1.50
37 Brett Hull .40 1.00
38 Curtis Joseph .30 .75
39 Robert Lang .25 .60
40 Brendan Shanahan .30 .75
41 Steve Yzerman 1.50 4.00
42 Ales Hemsky .25 .60
43 Ryan Smyth .15 .40
44 Raffi Torres .15 .40
45 Jay Bouwmeester .15 .40
46 Valeri Bure .15 .40
47 Olli Jokinen .25 .60
48 Roberto Luongo .40 1.00
49 Roman Cechmanek .25 .60
50 Alexander Frolov .15 .40
51 Ziggy Palffy .25 .60
52 Andrew Brunette .15 .40
53 Alexandre Daigle .15 .40
54 Marian Gaborik .60 1.50
55 Saku Koivu .30 .75
56 Mike Ribeiro .15 .40
57 Michael Ryder .15 .40
58 Sheldon Souray .15 .40
59 Jose Theodore .40 1.00
60 Martin Erat .15 .40
61 Scott Hartnell .15 .40
62 Tomas Vokoun .25 .60
63 Martin Brodeur .75 2.00
64 Patrik Elias .25 .60
65 Scott Stevens .25 .60
66 Rick DiPietro .25 .60
67 Trent Hunter .15 .40
68 Alexei Yashin .15 .40
69 Jaromir Jagr .50 1.25
70 Alex Kovalev .25 .60
71 Eric Lindros .30 .75
72 Daniel Alfredsson .25 .60
73 Peter Bondra .25 .60
74 Martin Havlat .25 .60
75 Marian Hossa .30 .75
76 Patrick Lalime .25 .60
77 Jason Spezza .30 .75
78 Tony Amonte .25 .60
79 Mark Recchi .25 .60
80 Jeremy Roenick .40 1.00
81 Shane Doan .15 .40
82 Ladislav Nagy .15 .40
83 Rico Fata .15 .40
84 Mario Lemieux 2.00 5.00
85 Pavol Demitra .25 .60
86 Keith Tkachuk .30 .75
87 Doug Weight .25 .60
88 Jonathan Cheechoo .20 .50
89 Patrick Marleau .25 .60
90 Evgeni Nabokov .25 .60
91 Nikolai Khabibulin .30 .75
92 Vincent Lecavalier .30 .75
93 Martin St. Louis .25 .60
94 Ed Belfour .30 .75
95 Owen Nolan .25 .60
96 Mats Sundin .30 .75
97 Todd Bertuzzi .30 .75
98 Jason King .15 .40
99 Brendan Morrison .25 .60
100 Markus Naslund .30 .75
101 Joffrey Lupul RC 1.25 3.00
102 Patrice Bergeron RC 4.00 10.00
103 Derek Roy RC 1.50 4.00
104 Brent Krahn RC 1.25 3.00
105 Matthew Lombardi RC 1.25 3.00
106 Eric Staal RC 5.00 12.00
107 Anton Babchuk RC 1.25 3.00
108 Tuomo Ruutu RC 2.50 6.00
109 Pavel Vorobiev RC 1.25 3.00
110 Mikhail Yakubov RC 1.25 3.00
111 Dan Fritsche RC 1.25 3.00
112 Nikolai Zherdev RC 2.50 6.00
113 Antti Miettinen RC 1.25 3.00
114 Darryl Bootland RC 1.25 3.00
115 Jiri Hudler RC 2.00 5.00
116 Nathan Robinson RC 1.25 3.00
117 Tony Salmelainen RC 1.25 3.00
118 Nathan Horton RC 3.00 8.00
119 Dustin Brown RC 1.25 3.00
120 Brent Burns RC 1.25 3.00
121 Christopher Higgins RC 3.00 8.00
122 Dan Hamhuis RC 1.25 3.00
123 Jordin Tootoo RC 3.00 8.00
124 Marek Zidlicky RC 1.25 3.00
125 David Hale RC 1.25 3.00
126 Paul Martin RC 1.25 3.00
127 Dominic Moore RC 1.25 3.00
128 Antoine Vermette RC 1.25 3.00
129 Joni Pitkanen RC 1.25 3.00
130 Fredrik Sjostrom RC 1.25 3.00
131 Marc-Andre Fleury RC 6.00 15.00
132 Ryan Malone RC 2.00 5.00
133 John Pohl RC 1.25 3.00
134 Peter Sejna RC 1.25 3.00
135 Milan Michalek RC 1.25 3.00
136 Matt Stajan RC 2.00 5.00
137 Ryan Kesler RC 1.25 3.00
138 Boyd Gordon RC 1.25 3.00
139 Alexander Semin RC 3.00 8.00
140 Rastislav Stana RC 1.25 3.00

2003-04 Pacific Quest for the Cup Blue

*STARS: 2X TO 5X BASE HI
STATED ODDS 1:25
STATED PRINT RUN 150 SER.#'d SETS

2003-04 Pacific Quest for the Cup Calder Contenders

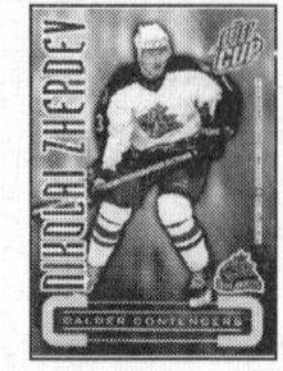

COMPLETE SET (20) 15.00 30.00
STATED ODDS 1:7
1 Patrice Bergeron 2.50 6.00
2 Andrew Raycroft 2.50 6.00
3 Matthew Lombardi 1.25 3.00
4 Eric Staal 2.00 5.00
5 Tuomo Ruutu 2.00 5.00
6 Philippe Sauve 1.25 3.00
7 Nikolai Zherdev 2.00 5.00
8 Jiri Hudler 1.25 3.00
9 Nathan Horton 1.50 4.00
10 Dustin Brown 1.25 3.00
11 Brent Burns 1.25 3.00
12 Michael Ryder 1.50 4.00
13 Jordin Tootoo 1.50 4.00
14 Trent Hunter 1.25 3.00
15 Antoine Vermette 1.25 3.00
16 Joni Pitkanen 1.25 3.00
17 Marc-Andre Fleury 3.00 8.00
18 Ryan Malone 1.25 3.00
19 Matt Stajan 1.50 4.00
20 Jason King 1.25 3.00

2003-04 Pacific Quest for the Cup Chasing the Cup

COMPLETE SET (9) 5.00 10.00
STATED ODDS 1:16
1 Dany Heatley 1.00 2.50
2 Ilya Kovalchuk 1.00 2.50
3 Joe Thornton 1.00 2.50
4 Paul Kariya .50 1.25
5 Rick Nash .60 1.50
6 Marty Turco .50 1.25
7 Jason Spezza .50 1.25
8 Mats Sundin .50 1.25
9 Todd Bertuzzi .50 1.25

2003-04 Pacific Quest for the Cup Connquest

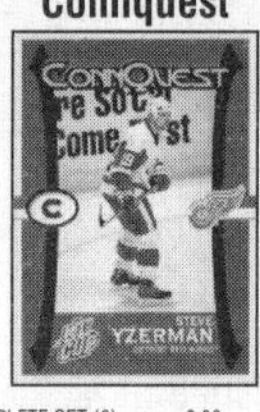

COMPLETE SET (6) 8.00 15.00
STATED ODDS 1:48
1 J-S Giguere .75 2.00
2 Joe Sakic 1.50 4.00
3 Nicklas Lidstrom .75 2.00
4 Steve Yzerman 2.50 6.00
5 Scott Stevens .75 2.00
6 Mario Lemieux 3.00 8.00

2003-04 Pacific Quest for the Cup Eternal Champions

This 2-card set featured certified player autographs from two retired great who partcipated in the 2003 Heritage Classic game. Due to unknown reasons, it is thought that the cards were pulled from production at the last minute and the mention of the cards was crossed off of packs. Since Pacific went out of business soon afterwards, there is no way to confirm the exact distribution of these cards as a handful have made their way onto the secondary market. The cards are not priced due to scarcity.

NOT PRICED DUE TO SCARCITY
1 Guy Lafleur
2 Grant Fuhr

2003-04 Pacific Quest for the Cup Jerseys

COMPLETE SET (19)
STATED ODDS 1:25
1 Ilya Kovalchuk SP 5.00 12.00
2 Joe Thornton 4.00 10.00
3 Jarome Iginla 3.00 8.00
4 Jocelyn Thibault 2.50 6.00
5 David Aebischer SP 4.00 10.00
6 Joe Sakic 5.00 12.00
7 Rick Nash 4.00 10.00
8 Marty Turco 2.50 6.00
9 Steve Yzerman SP 8.00 20.00
10 Ryan Smyth 2.50 6.00
11 Scott Walker 2.50 6.00
12 Patrik Elias 2.50 6.00
13 Jaromir Jagr 4.00 10.00
14 Martin Havlat 2.50 6.00
15 Jeff Hackett 2.50 6.00
16 Mario Lemieux SP 10.00 25.00
17 Nikolai Khabibulin 2.50 6.00
18 Ed Belfour SP 5.00 12.00
19 Dan Cloutier 2.50 6.00

2003-04 Pacific Quest for the Cup Raising the Cup

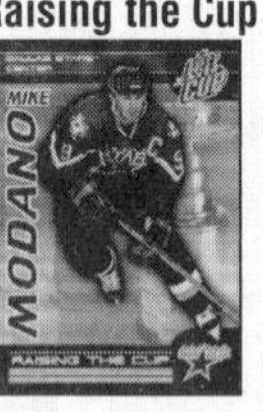

STATED ODDS 1:9
1 Sergei Fedorov .75 2.00
2 Rob Blake .60 1.50
3 Peter Forsberg 1.50 4.00
4 Milan Hejduk .60 1.50
5 Joe Sakic 1.25 3.00
6 Mike Modano 1.00 2.50
7 Dominik Hasek 1.25 3.00
8 Brett Hull .75 2.00
9 Nicklas Lidstrom .60 1.50
10 Brendan Shanahan .60 1.50
11 Steve Yzerman 2.00 5.00
12 Martin Brodeur 2.00 5.00
13 Scott Stevens .60 1.50
14 Mark Messier .60 1.50
15 Mario Lemieux 2.50 6.00

2003-04 Pacific Supreme

This 140-card set consisted of 100 veteran cards and 40 rookie cards (101-140) serial-numbered to 775 copies each. There were also 14 autographed parallels of rookie players that were seeded randomly and serial-numbered out of 375. These cards are noted below with a "A" suffix which does not

appear on the actual cards.

COMP. SET w/o SP's (100) 20.00 40.00
COMMON ROOKIE AUTO 6.00 15.00
ROOK.AUTO PRINT RUN 375 SER.#'d SETS
1 Sergei Fedorov .30 .75
2 J-S Giguere .20 .50
3 Petr Sykora .12 .30
4 Dany Heatley .30 .75
5 Ilya Kovalchuk .30 .75
6 Glen Murray .12 .30
7 Sergei Samsonov .20 .50
8 Joe Thornton .40 1.00
9 Daniel Briere .12 .30
10 Chris Drury .20 .50
11 Ales Kotalik .12 .30
12 Ryan Miller .20 .50
13 Jarome Iginla .30 .75
14 Chuck Kobasew .12 .30
15 Ron Francis .20 .50
16 Jeff O'Neill .12 .30
17 Radim Vrbata .12 .30
18 Tyler Arnason .20 .50
19 Steve Sullivan .12 .30
20 Jocelyn Thibault .20 .50
21 Peter Forsberg .60 1.50
22 Milan Hejduk .25 .60
23 Paul Kariya .25 .60
24 Patrick Roy 1.25 3.00
25 Joe Sakic .40 1.00
26 Marc Denis .20 .50
27 Rick Nash .30 .75
28 Geoff Sanderson .12 .30
29 Jason Arnott .20 .50
30 Mike Modano .50 1.25
31 Marty Turco .20 .50
32 Dominik Hasek .50 1.25
33 Brett Hull .30 .75
34 Ray Whitney .12 .30
35 Steve Yzerman 1.25 3.00
36 Henrik Zetterberg .25 .60
37 Mike Comrie .20 .50
38 Ales Hemsky .20 .50
39 Tommy Salo .20 .50
40 Ryan Smyth .12 .30
41 Jay Bouwmeester .12 .30
42 Olli Jokinen .20 .50
43 Roberto Luongo .30 .75
44 Roman Cechmanek .20 .50
45 Alexander Frolov .12 .30
46 Ziggy Palffy .20 .50
47 Pierre-Marc Bouchard .12 .30
48 Marian Gaborik .50 1.25
49 Dwayne Roloson .20 .50
50 Marcel Hossa .12 .30
51 Saku Koivu .25 .60
52 Jose Theodore .30 .75
53 Richard Zednik .12 .30
54 Andreas Johansson .12 .30
55 David Legwand .20 .50
56 Tomas Vokoun .20 .50
57 Martin Brodeur .60 1.50
58 Patrik Elias .20 .50
59 John Madden .12 .30
60 Jamie Langenbrunner .12 .30
61 Jason Blake .20 .50
62 Rick DiPietro .12 .30
63 Michael Peca .12 .30
64 Alexei Yashin .12 .30
65 Anson Carter .20 .50
66 Alex Kovalev .20 .50
67 Eric Lindros .25 .60
68 Petr Nedved .12 .30
69 Daniel Alfredsson .20 .50
70 Marian Hossa .25 .60
71 Patrick Lalime .20 .50
72 Jason Spezza .25 .60
73 Tony Amonte .20 .50
74 John LeClair .25 .60
75 Jeremy Roenick .30 .75
76 Sean Burke .20 .50
77 Mike Johnson .12 .30
78 Sebastien Caron .20 .50
79 Mario Lemieux 1.50 4.00
80 Pavol Demitra .20 .50
81 Barret Jackman .20 .50
82 Chris Pronger .20 .50
83 Keith Tkachuk .25 .60
84 Patrick Marleau .20 .50
85 Evgeni Nabokov .20 .50
86 Marco Sturm .12 .30
87 Nikolai Khabibulin .25 .60
88 Vincent Lecavalier .25 .60
89 Martin St. Louis .25 .60
90 Ed Belfour .25 .60
91 Alexander Mogilny .20 .50
92 Owen Nolan .20 .50
93 Mats Sundin .25 .60
94 Todd Bertuzzi .25 .60
95 Dan Cloutier .20 .50
96 Brendan Morrison .20 .50
97 Markus Naslund .25 .60
98 Peter Bondra .20 .50
99 Jaromir Jagr .40 1.00
100 Olaf Kolzig .20 .50
101 Garrett Burnett RC 2.00 5.00
102 Joffrey Lupul RC 3.00 8.00
102A Joffrey Lupul AU 8.00 20.00
103 Joe DiPenta RC 2.00 5.00
104 Patrice Bergeron RC 6.00 15.00
105 Milan Bartovic RC 2.00 5.00
106 Andrew Peters RC 2.00 5.00
107 Brent Krahn RC 2.00 5.00
108 Matthew Lombardi RC 2.00 5.00
109 Eric Staal RC 6.00 15.00
109A Eric Staal AU 20.00 50.00
110 Travis Moen RC 2.00 5.00
111 Tuomo Ruutu RC 3.00 8.00
111A Tuomo Ruutu AU 8.00 20.00
112 Pavel Vorobiev RC 2.00 5.00
113 Cody McCormick RC 2.00 5.00
114 Dan Fritsche RC 2.00 5.00
115 Kent McDonell RC 2.00 5.00
116 Antti Miettinen RC 2.00 5.00
117 Jiri Hudler RC 3.00 8.00
117A Jiri Hudler AU 8.00 20.00
118 Nathan Horton RC 4.00 10.00
118A Nathan Horton AU 10.00 25.00
119 Dustin Brown RC 2.00 5.00
119A Dustin Brown AU 6.00 15.00
120 Tim Gleason RC 2.00 5.00
121 Esa Pirnes RC 2.00 5.00
122 Brent Burns RC 2.00 5.00
123 Chris Higgins RC 4.00 10.00
123A Chris Higgins AU 12.00 30.00
124 Dan Hamhuis RC 2.00 5.00
125 Jordin Tootoo RC 4.00 10.00
125A Jordin Tootoo AU 10.00 25.00
126 Marek Zidlicky RC 2.00 5.00
127 David Hale RC 2.00 5.00
128 Paul Martin RC 2.00 5.00
129 Sean Bergenheim RC 2.00 5.00
130 Antoine Vermette RC 2.00 5.00
130A Antoine Vermette AU 6.00 15.00
131 Joni Pitkanen RC 2.00 5.00
131A Joni Pitkanen AU 8.00 20.00
132 Matthew Spiller RC 2.00 5.00
133 Marc-Andre Fleury RC 8.00 20.00
133A Marc-Andre Fleury AU 20.00 50.00
134 Matt Murley RC 2.00 5.00
135 Peter Sejna RC 2.00 5.00
135A Peter Sejna AU 4.00 10.00
136 Milan Michalek RC 3.00 8.00
136A Milan Michalek AU 10.00 25.00
137 Tom Preissing RC 2.00 5.00
138 Maxim Kondratiev RC 2.00 5.00
139 Matt Stajan RC 4.00 10.00
139A Matt Stajan AU 8.00 20.00
140 Boyd Gordon RC 2.00 5.00

2003-04 Pacific Supreme Blue

*STARS: 1.5X TO 4X BASIC CARDS
1-100 ODDS 1:2
*ROOKIES: .75X TO 2X
STATED PRINT RUN 250 SER.#'d SETS

2003-04 Pacific Supreme Red

*STARS: 1.5X TO 4X BASIC CARD
1-100 ODDS 1:3
*ROOKIES: .5X TO 1.25X
ROOKIE PRINT RUN 425 SER.#'d SETS

2003-04 Pacific Supreme Retail

This 140-card set mirrored the hobby version but carried silver foil highlights in place of the gold foil. Rookie cards were not serial-numbered and were inserted at 1:4.

*STARS: SAME VALUE AS HOBBY
*ROOKIES: .25X TO .75X HOBBY

2003-04 Pacific Supreme Generations

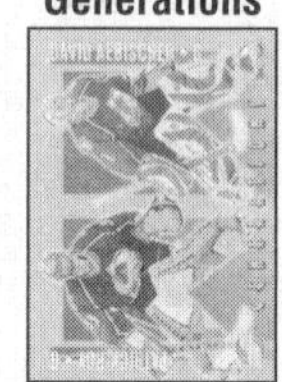

COMPLETE SET (24) 25.00 50.00
STATED ODDS 1:7
1 Ron Francis 1.50 4.00
Radim Vrbata
2 Patrick Roy 3.00 8.00
David Aebischer
3 Geoff Sanderson 1.50 4.00
Rick Nash
4 Steve Yzerman 4.00 10.00
Pavel Datsyuk
5 Brett Hull 3.00 8.00
Henrik Zetterberg
6 Daniel Alfredsson 2.50 6.00
Jason Spezza
7 Sean Burke 1.50 4.00
Zac Bierk
8 M.Lemieux/M-A Fleury 5.00 12.00
9 Al MacInnis 1.50 4.00
Barret Jackman
10 V.Damphousse/J.Cheechoo 1.50 4.00
11 Mats Sundin 1.50 4.00
Nik Antropov
12 Markus Naslund 1.50 4.00
Daniel Sedin

2003-04 Pacific Supreme Jerseys

STATED ODDS 2:10
1 Sergei Fedorov 4.00 10.00
2 Ilya Kovalchuk 4.00 10.00
3 Joe Thornton 5.00 12.00
4 Chris Drury 2.50 6.00
5 Miroslav Satan 2.50 6.00
6 Jarome Iginla 4.00 10.00
7 Eric Daze 2.50 6.00
8 Peter Forsberg SP 8.00 20.00
9 Paul Kariya 3.00 8.00
10 Patrick Roy 10.00 25.00
11 Brett Hull 4.00 10.00
12 Steve Yzerman SP 10.00 25.00
13 Mike Comrie 2.50 6.00
14 Ryan Smyth 2.50 6.00
15 Olli Jokinen 2.50 6.00
16 Jose Theodore 4.00 10.00
17 Pavel Bure 3.00 8.00
18 Eric Lindros 3.00 8.00
19 Tony Amonte 2.50 6.00
20 Jeremy Roenick 4.00 10.00
21 Mario Lemieux 10.00 25.00
22 Vincent Lecavalier 2.50 6.00
23 Mats Sundin 3.00 8.00
24 Markus Naslund 3.00 8.00
25 Jaromir Jagr 5.00 12.00

2003-04 Pacific Supreme Standing Guard

COMPLETE SET (12) 20.00 40.00
STATED ODDS 1:12
1 J-S Giguere 1.25 3.00
2 Jocelyn Thibault 1.25 3.00
3 Patrick Roy 3.00 8.00
4 Marc Denis 1.25 3.00
5 Marty Turco 1.25 3.00
6 Dominik Hasek 2.00 5.00
7 Roberto Luongo 2.00 5.00
8 Jose Theodore 2.00 5.00
9 Martin Brodeur 2.50 6.00
10 Patrick Lalime 1.25 3.00
11 Sean Burke 1.25 3.00
12 Ed Belfour 1.50 4.00

2003-04 Pacific Supreme Team

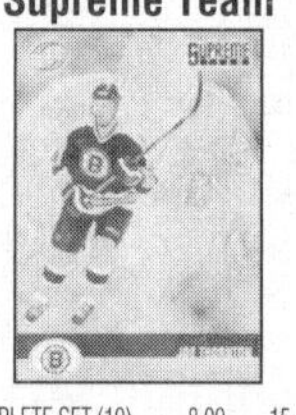

COMPLETE SET (10) 8.00 15.00
STATED ODDS 1:12
1 Joe Thornton .50 1.25
2 Peter Forsberg 1.00 2.50
3 Joe Sakic .60 1.50
4 Brett Hull .40 1.00
5 Steve Yzerman 2.00 5.00
6 Marian Gaborik .60 1.50
7 Mario Lemieux 2.50 6.00
8 Todd Bertuzzi .30 .75
9 Markus Naslund .30 .75
10 Jaromir Jagr .50 1.25

2002 Pacific Toronto Fall Expo

Available as a wrapper redemption at the 2002 Toronto Fall Expo, this 10-card set focused on goalies from around the league. One goalie was pictured on each side of the cards and each card was serial-numbered out of 500. A gold parallel was also created and available randomly.

COMPLETE SET (10) 25.00
*GOLD: 1.5X TO 4X
GOLD PRINT RUN 99 SER.#'d SETS
1 Ed Belfour 1.20 5.00
Curtis Joseph
2 Jose Theodore 1.60 10.00
Patrick Roy
3 Roman Turek 1.00
Tommy Salo
4 Patrick Lalime 1.00
Dan Cloutier
5 Roberto Luongo 3.00
Nikolai Khabibulin
6 Martin Brodeur 1.20 5.00
Mike Richter
7 J-S Giguere 5.00
Felix Potvin
8 Marty Turco 3.00
Sean Burke
9 Martin Biron 1.00
Jocelyn Thibault
10 Brent Johnson 1.00
Evgeni Nabokov

2002 Pacific Toronto Spring Expo Rookie Collection

Available as a wrapper redemption at the Pacific booth during the 2002 Spring Exp in Toronto, this 10-card set featured some c the hottest rookies of the year. Each card wa serial-numbered out of 500.

COMPLETE SET (10) 10.00 25.00
1 Dany Heatley 2.00 5.00
2 Ilya Kovalchuk 3.00 8.00
5 Rostislav Klesla 1.25 3.00
6 Pavel Datsyuk 3.00 8.00
9 Dan Blackburn 1.25 3.00

2003 Pacific Toronto Spring Expo

Serial-numbered to 499, this 8-card set wa available only via wrapper redemption at th Pacific booth during the Toronto Sprin Expo. A gold parallel numbered to 99 wa also available for the first 99 visitors to ope a Pacific box at the booth. Values for gol parallels can be found by using th multipliers below.

COMPLETE SET (8) 15.00 35.00
*GOLD: 1.5X TO 4X BASIC CARDS
1 Stanislav Chistov 2.40 3.00
2 Ryan Miller 2.00 5.00
3 Rick Nash 4.00 10.00
4 Henrik Zetterberg 4.00 10.00
5 Jay Bouwmeester 2.40 6.00
6 Mike Cammalleri 2.00 3.00
7 Jason Spezza 3.20 8.00
8 Carlo Colaiacovo 2.00 3.00

2003 Pacific Toronto Fall Expo

This 6-card set was part of a wrappe redemption during the 2003 Fall Expo Cards were serial-numbered out of 500 an featured a NHL player on the front and a CF player on the back.

COMPLETE SET (6) 10.00 20.00
1 Todd Bertuzzi 1.50 4.00
Dave Dickenson
2 Jarome Iginla 2.00 5.0
Marcus Crandell
3 Ryan Smyth 1.25 3.0
Ricky Ray
4 Jose Theodore 2.00 5.0
Anthony Calvillo
5 Marian Hossa 1.25 3.0
Josh Ranek
6 Ed Belfour 1.50 4.0
Damon Allen

2004 Pacific National Convention

These cards were intended to be issued a part of a wrapper redemption at the 200 National Sports Collectors Convention Cleveland, due to circumstances, Pacific d not attend the show and the entire lot wa sold on consignment. The cards are seri numbered out of 499. The full bleed borde make them susceptible to chipping.

COMPLETE SET (6) 8.00 20.00
1 Ilya Kovalchuk 2.00 5.00
2 Joe Thornton 2.00 5.00
3 Rick Nash 2.00 5.00
4 Rick DiPietro .75 2.0
5 Marc-Andre Fleury 1.50 4.00
6 Vincent Lecavalier 1.25 3.00

2004 Pacific Toronto Spring Expo

Available only via wrapper redemption at the 2004 Toronto Spring Expo, this 8-card se featured rookies from the 2003-04 seasor Each card was serial-numbered out of 499. gold parallel was also randomly available.

COMPLETE SET (8)
*GOLD: 1.5X TO 3X BASIC CARDS
GOLD PRINT RUN 99 SER.#'d SETS
1 Patrice Bergeron 4.0

2 Eric Staal 2.00
3 Nathan Horton 2.00
4 Dustin Brown 1.00
5 Jordin Tootoo 2.00
6 Antoine Vermette 1.00
7 Marc-Andre Fleury 4.00
8 Matt Stajan 2.00

2004 Pacific WHA Autographs

These two autographed cards were the only two WHA cards that Pacific produced before the company shut their doors in 2004. Each card was serial-numbered to 1972 and were available only via the Pacific website and various other online dealers for $25US.

1 Bobby Hull 25.00
2 Andre Lacroix 20.00

1987-88 Panini Stickers

This set of 396 hockey stickers was produced and distributed by Panini. The sticker number is only on the backing of the sticker. The stickers measure approximately 2 1/8" by 2 11/16". The team logos are foil stickers. On the inside back cover of the sticker album the company offered (via direct mail-order) up to 30 different stickers of your choice for either ten cents each or in trade one-for-one for your unwanted extra stickers plus 1.00 for postage and handling; this is one reason why the values of the most popular players in these sticker sets are somewhat depressed compared to traditional card prices.

COMPLETE SET (396) 14.00 35.00
1 Stanley Cup .04 .10
2 Bruins Action .02 .05
3 Bruins Emblem .02 .05
4 Doug Keans .02 .05
5 Bill Ranford .60 1.50
6 Ray Bourque .40 1.00
7 Reed Larson .02 .05
8 Mike Milbury .02 .05
9 Michael Thelven .02 .05
10 Cam Neely .20 .50
11 Charlie Simmer .02 .05
12 Rick Middleton .02 .05
13 Tom McCarthy .02 .05
14 Keith Crowder .02 .05
15 Steve Kasper .02 .05
16 Ken Linseman .02 .05
17 Dwight Foster .02 .05
18 Jay Miller .02 .05
19 Sabres Action .02 .05
20 Sabres Emblem .02 .05
21 Jacques Cloutier .04 .10
22 Tom Barrasso .04 .10
23 Daren Puppa .04 .10
24 Phil Housley .02 .05
25 Mike Ramsey .02 .05
26 Bill Hajt .02 .05
27 Dave Andreychuk .04 .10
28 Christian Ruuttu .02 .05
29 Mike Foligno .02 .05
30 John Tucker .02 .05
31 Adam Creighton .02 .05
32 Wilf Paiement .02 .05
33 Paul Cyr .02 .05
34 Clark Gillies .02 .05
35 Lindy Ruff .02 .05
36 Whalers Action .02 .05
37 Whalers Emblem .02 .05
38 Mike Liut .04 .10
39 Steve Weeks .02 .05
40 Dave Babych .02 .05
41 Ulf Samuelsson .20 .50
42 Dana Murzyn .02 .05
43 Ron Francis .04 .10
44 Kevin Dineen .02 .05
45 John Anderson .02 .05
46 Ray Ferraro .02 .05
47 Dean Evason .02 .05
48 Paul Lawless .02 .05
49 Stewart Gavin .02 .05
50 Sylvain Turgeon .02 .05
51 Dave Tippett .02 .05
52 Doug Jarvis .02 .05
53 Canadiens Action .02 .05
54 Canadiens Emblem .02 .05
55 Brian Hayward .04 .10
56 Patrick Roy 1.20 3.00
57 Larry Robinson .04 .10
58 Chris Chelios .30 .75
59 Craig Ludwig .02 .05
60 Rick Green .02 .05
61 Mats Naslund .02 .05
62 Bobby Smith .02 .05
63 Claude Lemieux .60 1.50
64 Guy Carbonneau .04 .10
65 Stephane Richer .30 .75
66 Mike McPhee .04 .10
67 Brian Skrudland .02 .05
68 Chris Nilan .02 .05
69 Bob Gainey .04 .10
70 Devils Action .02 .05
71 Devils Emblem .02 .05
72 Craig Billington .04 .10
73 Alain Chevrier .02 .05
74 Bruce Driver .02 .05
75 Joe Cirella .02 .05
76 Ken Daneyko .02 .05
77 Craig Wolanin .02 .05
78 Aaron Broten .02 .05
79 Kirk Muller .04 .10
80 John MacLean .02 .05
81 Pat Verbeek .02 .05
82 Doug Sulliman .02 .05
83 Mark Johnson .02 .05
84 Greg Adams .02 .05
85 Claude Loiselle .02 .05
86 Andy Brickley .02 .05
87 Islanders Action .02 .05
88 Islanders Emblem .02 .05
89 Billy Smith .04 .10
90 Kelly Hrudey .04 .10
91 Denis Potvin .02 .05
92 Tomas Jonsson .02 .05
93 Ken Leiter .02 .05
94 Ken Morrow .02 .05
95 Brian Curran .02 .05
96 Bryan Trottier .04 .10
97 Mike Bossy .20 .50
98 Pat LaFontaine .20 .50
99 Brent Sutter .02 .05
100 Mikko Makela .02 .05
101 Pat Flatley .02 .05
102 Duane Sutter .02 .05
103 Rich Kromm .02 .05
104 Rangers Action .02 .05
105 Rangers Emblem .02 .05
106 John Vanbiesbrouck .80 2.00
107 James Patrick .02 .05
108 Ron Greschner .02 .05
109 Willie Huber .02 .05
110 Curt Giles .02 .05
111 Larry Melnyk .02 .05
112 Walt Poddubny .02 .05
113 Marcel Dionne .20 .50
114 Tomas Sandstrom .02 .05
115 Kelly Kisio .02 .05
116 Pierre Larouche .02 .05
117 Don Maloney .02 .05
118 Tony McKegney .02 .05
119 Ron Duguay .02 .05
120 Jan Erixon .02 .05
121 Flyers Action .02 .05
122 Flyers Emblem .02 .05
123 Ron Hextall .40 1.00
124 Mark Howe .02 .05
125 Doug Crossman .02 .05
126 Brad McCrimmon .02 .05
127 Brad Marsh .02 .05
128 Tim Kerr .02 .05
129 Peter Zezel .02 .05
130 Dave Poulin .02 .05
131 Brian Propp .02 .05
132 Pelle Eklund .02 .05
133 Murray Craven .02 .05
134 Rick Tocchet .40 1.00
135 Derrick Smith .02 .05
136 Ilkka Sinisalo .02 .05
137 Ron Sutter .02 .05
138 Penguins Action .02 .05
139 Penguins Emblem .02 .05
140 Gilles Meloche .04 .10
141 Doug Bodger .02 .05
142 Moe Mantha .02 .05
143 Jim Johnson .02 .05
144 Rod Buskas .02 .05
145 Randy Hillier .02 .05
146 Mario Lemieux 1.20 3.00
147 Dan Quinn .02 .05
148 Randy Cunneyworth .02 .05
149 Craig Simpson .02 .05
150 Terry Ruskowski .02 .05
151 John Chabot .02 .05
152 Bob Errey .02 .05
153 Dan Frawley .02 .05
154 Dave Hannan .02 .05
155 Nordiques Action .02 .05
156 Nordiques Emblem .02 .05
157 Mario Gosselin .04 .10
158 Clint Malarchuk .04 .10
159 Risto Siltanen .02 .05
160 Robert Picard .02 .05
161 Normand Rochefort .02 .05
162 Randy Moller .02 .05
163 Michel Goulet .04 .10
164 Peter Stastny .04 .10
165 John Ogrodnick .02 .05
166 Anton Stastny .02 .05
167 Paul Gillis .02 .05
168 Dale Hunter .02 .05
169 Alain Cote .02 .05
170 Mike Eagles .02 .05
171 Jason Lafreniere .02 .05
172 Capitals Action .02 .05
173 Capitals Emblem .02 .05
174 Pete Peeters .04 .10
175 Bob Mason .04 .10
176 Larry Murphy .20 .50
177 Scott Stevens .04 .10
178 Rod Langway .02 .05
179 Kevin Hatcher .20 .50
180 Mike Gartner .20 .50
181 Mike Ridley .02 .05
182 Craig Laughlin .02 .05
183 Gaetan Duchesne .02 .05
184 Dave Christian .02 .05
185 Greg Adams .02 .05
186 Kelly Miller .02 .05
187 Alan Haworth .02 .05
188 Lou Franceschetti .02 .05
189 Stanley Cup (top half) .04 .10
190 Stanley Cup (bottom half) .04 .10
191 Ron Hextall .60 1.50
192 Wayne Gretzky 1.60 4.00
193 Brian Propp .02 .05
194 Mark Messier .40 1.00
195 Flyers/Oilers Action .02 .05
196 Flyers/Oilers Action .02 .05
197 Gretzky Holding Cup (upper left) .40 1.00
198 Gretzky Holding Cup (upper right) .40 1.00
199 Gretzky Holding Cup (lower left) .40 1.00
200 Gretzky Holding Cup (lower right) .40 1.00
201 Flames Action .02 .05
202 Flames Emblem .02 .05
203 Mike Vernon .60 1.50
204 Rejean Lemelin .04 .10
205 Al MacInnis .20 .50
206 Paul Reinhart .02 .05
207 Gary Suter .04 .10
208 Jamie Macoun .02 .05
209 Neil Sheehy .02 .05
210 Joe Mullen .04 .10
211 Carey Wilson .02 .05
212 Joel Otto .02 .05
213 Jim Peplinski .02 .05
214 Hakan Loob .02 .05
215 Lanny McDonald .02 .05
216 Tim Hunter .02 .05
217 Gary Roberts .04 .10
218 Blackhawks Action .02 .05
219 Blackhawks Emblem .02 .05
220 Bob Sauve .04 .10
221 Murray Bannerman .02 .05
222 Doug Wilson .02 .05
223 Bob Murray .02 .05
224 Gary Nylund .02 .05
225 Denis Savard .04 .10
226 Steve Larmer .04 .10
227 Troy Murray .02 .05
228 Wayne Presley .02 .05
229 Al Secord .02 .05
230 Ed Olczyk .02 .05
231 Curt Fraser .02 .05
232 Bill Watson .02 .05
233 Keith Brown .02 .05
234 Darryl Sutter .02 .05
235 Red Wings Action .02 .05
236 Red Wings Emblem .02 .05
237 Greg Stefan .02 .05
238 Glen Hanlon .04 .10
239 Darren Veitch .02 .05
240 Mike O'Connell .02 .05
241 Harold Snepsts .02 .05
242 Dave Lewis .02 .05
243 Steve Yzerman .80 2.00
244 Brent Ashton .02 .05
245 Gerard Gallant .02 .05
246 Petr Klima .02 .05
247 Shawn Burr .02 .05
248 Adam Oates .04 .10
249 Mel Bridgman .02 .05
250 Tim Higgins .02 .05
251 Joey Kocur .02 .05
252 Oilers Action .02 .05
253 Oilers Emblem .02 .05
254 Grant Fuhr .20 .50
255 Andy Moog .04 .10
256 Paul Coffey .20 .50
257 Kevin Lowe .04 .10
258 Craig Muni .02 .05
259 Steve Smith .02 .05
260 Charlie Huddy .02 .05
261 Wayne Gretzky 1.60 4.00
262 Jari Kurri .20 .50
263 Mark Messier .40 1.00
264 Esa Tikkanen .02 .05
265 Glenn Anderson .04 .10
266 Mike Krushelnyski .02 .05
267 Craig MacTavish .02 .05
268 Dave Hunter .02 .05
269 Kings Action .02 .05
270 Kings Emblem .02 .05
271 Roland Melanson .04 .10
272 Darren Eliot .02 .05
273 Grant Ledyard .02 .05
274 Jay Wells .02 .05
275 Mark Hardy .02 .05
276 Dean Kennedy .02 .05
277 Luc Robitaille 1.00 2.50
278 Bernie Nicholls .04 .10
279 Jimmy Carson .02 .05
280 Dave Taylor .02 .05
281 Jim Fox .02 .05
282 Bryan Erickson .02 .05
283 Dave(Tiger) Williams .02 .05
284 Sean McKenna .02 .05
285 Phil Sykes .02 .05
286 North Stars Action .02 .05
287 North Stars Emblem .02 .05
288 Kari Takko .04 .10
289 Don Beaupre .04 .10
290 Craig Hartsburg .02 .05
291 Ron Wilson .02 .05
292 Frantisek Musil .02 .05
293 Dino Ciccarelli .04 .10
294 Brian MacLellan .02 .05
295 Dirk Graham .02 .05
296 Brian Bellows .02 .05
297 Neal Broten .02 .05
298 Dennis Maruk .02 .05
299 Keith Acton .02 .05
300 Brian Lawton .02 .05
301 Bob Brooke .02 .05
302 Willi Plett .02 .05
303 Blues Action .02 .05
304 Blues Emblem .02 .05
305 Rick Wamsley .04 .10
306 Rob Ramage .02 .05
307 Ric Nattress .02 .05
308 Bruce Bell .02 .05
309 Charlie Bourgeois .02 .05
310 Jim Pavese .02 .05
311 Doug Gilmour .20 .50
312 Bernie Federko .02 .05
313 Mark Hunter .02 .05
314 Greg Paslawski .02 .05
315 Gino Cavallini .02 .05
316 Rick Meagher .02 .05
317 Ron Flockhart .02 .05
318 Doug Wickenheiser .02 .05
319 Jocelyn Lemieux .02 .05
320 Maple Leafs Action .02 .05
321 Maple Leafs Emblem .02 .05
322 Ken Wregget .04 .10
323 Allan Bester .04 .10
324 Todd Gill .02 .05
325 Al Iafrate .02 .05
326 Borje Salming .02 .05
327 Russ Courtnall .02 .05
328 Rick Vaive .02 .05
329 Steve Thomas .02 .05
330 Wendel Clark .30 .75
331 Gary Leeman .02 .05
332 Tom Fergus .02 .05
333 Vincent Damphousse .20 .50
334 Peter Ihnacak .02 .05
335 Brad Smith .02 .05
336 Miroslav Ihnacak .02 .05
337 Canucks Action .02 .05
338 Canucks Emblem .02 .05
339 Frank Caprice .02 .05
340 Richard Brodeur .02 .05
341 Doug Lidster .02 .05
342 Michel Petit .02 .05
343 Garth Butcher .02 .05
344 Dave Richter .02 .05
345 Tony Tanti .02 .05
346 Barry Pederson .02 .05
347 Petri Skriko .02 .05
348 Patrik Sundstrom .02 .05
349 Stan Smyl .02 .05
350 Rich Sutter .02 .05
351 Steve Tambellini .02 .05
352 Jim Sandlak .02 .05
353 Dave Lowry .02 .05
354 Jets Action .02 .05
355 Jets Emblem .02 .05
356 Daniel Berthiaume .04 .10
357 Pokey Reddick .04 .10
358 Dave Ellett .02 .05
359 Mario Marois .02 .05
360 Randy Carlyle .02 .05
361 Fredrick Olausson .02 .05
362 Jim Kyte .02 .05
363 Dale Hawerchuk .04 .10
364 Paul MacLean .02 .05
365 Thomas Steen .02 .05
366 Gilles Hamel .02 .05
367 Doug Smail .02 .05
368 Laurie Boschman .02 .05
369 Ray Neufeld .02 .05
370 Andrew McBain .02 .05
371 Wayne Gretzky 1.60 4.00
372 Hart Trophy .02 .05
373 Wayne Gretzky 1.60 4.00
374 Art Ross Trophy .02 .05
375 Jennings Trophy .02 .05
376A Brian Hayward .04 .10
376B Patrick Roy 1.20 3.00
377 Vezina Trophy .02 .05
378 Ron Hextall .20 .50
379 Luc Robitaille 1.00 2.50
380 Calder Trophy .02 .05
381 Ray Bourque .20 .50
382 Norris Trophy .02 .05
383 Lady Byng Trophy .02 .05
384 Joe Mullen .04 .10
385 Frank Selke Trophy .02 .05
386 Dave Poulin .02 .05
387 Doug Jarvis .02 .05
388 Masterton Trophy .02 .05
389 Wayne Gretzky 1.60 4.00
390 Emery Edge Award .02 .05
391 Flyers Team Photo (left half) .02 .05
392 Flyers Team Photo (right half) .02 .05
393 Prince of Wales Trophy .02 .05
394 Clarence S. Campbell Bowl .02 .05
395 Oilers Team Photo (left half) .02 .05
396 Oilers Team Photo (right half) .02 .05
xx Sticker Album 2.00 5.00

1988-89 Panini Stickers

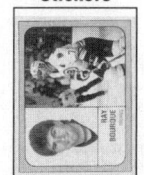

This set of 408 hockey stickers was produced and distributed by Panini. The sticker number is only on the backing of the sticker. The stickers measure approximately 2 1/8" by 2 11/16". The team picture cards are double stickers with each sticker showing half of the photo; in the checklist below these halves are denoted by LH (left half) and RH (right half). There was an album issued with the set for holding the stickers. On the inside back cover of the sticker album the company offered (via direct mail-order) up to 30 different stickers of your choice for either ten cents each or in trade one-for-one for your unwanted extra stickers plus 1.00 for postage and handling; this is one reason why the values of the most popular players in these sticker sets are somewhat depressed compared to traditional card prices.

COMPLETE SET (408) 12.00 30.00
1 Road to the Cup Stanley Cup Draw .02 .05
2 Flames Emblem .02 .05
3 Flames Uniform .02 .05
4 Mike Vernon .04 .10
5 Al MacInnis .04 .10
6 Brad McCrimmon .02 .05
7 Gary Suter .04 .10
8 Mike Bullard .02 .05
9 Hakan Loob .02 .05
10 Lanny McDonald .02 .05
11 Joe Mullen .04 .10
12 Joe Nieuwendyk .20 .50
13 Joel Otto .02 .05
14 Jim Peplinski .02 .05
15 Gary Roberts .04 .10
16 Flames Team LH .02 .05
17 Flames Team RH .02 .05
18 Blackhawks Emblem .02 .05
19 Blackhawks Uniform .02 .05
20 Bob Mason .04 .10
21 Darren Pang .04 .10
22 Bob Murray .02 .05
23 Gary Nylund .02 .05
24 Doug Wilson .02 .05
25 Dirk Graham .02 .05
26 Steve Larmer .04 .10
27 Troy Murray .02 .05
28 Brian Noonan .02 .05
29 Denis Savard .04 .10
30 Steve Thomas .02 .05
31 Rick Vaive .02 .05
32 Blackhawks Team LH .02 .05
33 Blackhawks Team RH .02 .05
34 Red Wings Emblem .02 .05
35 Red Wings Uniform .02 .05
36 Glen Hanlon .04 .10
37 Greg Stefan .04 .10
38 Jeff Sharples .02 .05
39 Darren Veitch .02 .05
40 Brent Ashton .02 .05
41 Shawn Burr .02 .05
42 John Chabot .02 .05
43 Gerard Gallant .02 .05
44 Petr Klima .02 .05
45 Adam Oates .04 .10
46 Bob Probert .04 .10
47 Steve Yzerman .60 1.50
48 Red Wings Team LH .02 .05
49 Red Wings Team RH .02 .05
50 Oilers Emblem .02 .05
51 Oilers Uniform .02 .05
52 Grant Fuhr .20 .50
53 Charlie Huddy .02 .05
54 Kevin Lowe .04 .10
55 Steve Smith .02 .05
56 Jeff Beukeboom .02 .05
57 Glenn Anderson .04 .10
58 Wayne Gretzky 1.00 2.50
59 Jari Kurri .20 .50
60 Craig MacTavish .02 .05
61 Mark Messier .30 .75
62 Craig Simpson .02 .05
63 Esa Tikkanen .04 .10
64 Oilers Team LH .02 .05
65 Oilers Team RH .02 .05
66 Kings Emblem .02 .05
67 Kings Uniform .02 .05
68 Glenn Healy .20 .50
69 Roland Melanson .04 .10
70 Steve Duchesne .20 .50
71 Tom Laidlaw .02 .05
72 Jay Wells .02 .05
73 Mike Allison .02 .05
74 Bob Carpenter .02 .05
75 Jimmy Carson .02 .05
76 Jim Fox .02 .05
77 Bernie Nicholls .04 .10
78 Luc Robitaille .20 .50
79 Dave Taylor .02 .05
80 Kings Team LH .02 .05
81 Kings Team RH .02 .05
82 North Stars Emblem .02 .05
83 North Stars Uniform .02 .05
84 Don Beaupre .04 .10
85 Kari Takko .04 .10
86 Craig Hartsburg .02 .05
87 Frantisek Musil .02 .05
88 Dave Archibald .02 .05
89 Brian Bellows .02 .05
90 Scott Bjugstad .02 .05
91 Bob Brooke .02 .05
92 Neal Broten .02 .05
93 Dino Ciccarelli .04 .10
94 Brian Lawton .02 .05
95 Brian MacLellan .02 .05
96 North Stars Team LH .02 .05
97 North Stars Team RH .02 .05
98 Blues Emblem .02 .05
99 Blues Uniform .02 .05
100 Greg Millen .04 .10
101 Brian Benning .02 .05
102 Gordie Roberts .02 .05
103 Gino Cavallini .02 .05
104 Bernie Federko .02 .05
105 Doug Gilmour .20 .50
106 Tony Hrkac .02 .05
107 Brett Hull .20 .50
108 Mark Hunter .02 .05
109 Tony McKegney .02 .05
110 Rick Meagher .02 .05
111 Brian Sutter .02 .05
112 Blues Team LH .02 .05
113 Blues Team RH .02 .05
114 Maple Leafs Emblem .02 .05
115 Maple Leafs Uniform .02 .05
116 Allan Bester .04 .10
117 Ken Wregget .04 .10
118 Al Iafrate .02 .05
119 Luke Richardson .02 .05
120 Borje Salming .02 .05
121 Wendel Clark .04 .10
122 Russ Courtnall .02 .05
123 Vincent Damphousse .04 .10
124 Dan Daoust .02 .05
125 Gary Leeman .02 .05
126 Ed Olczyk .02 .05
127 Mark Osborne .02 .05
128 Maple Leafs Team LH .02 .05
129 Maple Leafs Team RH .02 .05
130 Canucks Emblem .02 .05
131 Canucks Uniform .02 .05
132 Kirk McLean .04 .10
133 Jim Benning .02 .05
134 Garth Butcher .02 .05
135 Doug Lidster .02 .05
136 Greg Adams .02 .05
137 David Bruce .02 .05
138 Barry Pederson .02 .05
139 Jim Sandlak .02 .05
140 Petri Skriko .02 .05
141 Stan Smyl .02 .05
142 Rich Sutter .02 .05
143 Tony Tanti .02 .05
144 Canucks Team LH .02 .05
145 Canucks Team RH .02 .05
146 Jets Emblem .02 .05
147 Jets Uniform .02 .05
148 Daniel Berthiaume .04 .10
149 Randy Carlyle .02 .05
150 Dave Ellett .02 .05
151 Mario Marois .02 .05
152 Peter Taglianetti .02 .05
153 Laurie Boschman .02 .05
154 Iain Duncan .02 .05
155 Dale Hawerchuk .04 .10
156 Paul MacLean .02 .05
157 Andrew McBain .02 .05
158 Doug Smail .02 .05
159 Thomas Steen .02 .05
160 Jets Team LH .02 .05
161 Jets Team RH .02 .05
162 Prince of Wales Trophy .02 .05
163 Caps/Flyers Action .02 .05
164 Bruins/Canadiens Action .02 .05
165 Caps/Devils Action .02 .05
166 Bruins/Devils Action LH .02 .05
167 Bruins/Devils Action RH .02 .05
168 Flames/Kings Action .02 .05
169 Clarence S. Campbell Bowl .02 .05
170 Oilers/Flames Action .02 .05
171 Blues/Red Wings Action .02 .05
172 Oilers/Red Wings Action LH .02 .05
173 Oilers/Red Wings Action RH .02 .05
174 Oilers Celebrate .02 .05
175 Oilers/Bruins Action .02 .05
176 Stanley Cup (top half) .04 .10
177 Stanley Cup (bottom half) .04 .10
178 Bruins Action .02 .05
178 Wayne Gretzky 1.00 2.50
179 Oilers/Bruins Action RH .02 .05
180 Oilers/Bruins Action .02 .05
181 Wayne Gretzky 1.00 2.50
182 Conn Smythe Trophy .02 .05
183 Oilers Celebrate UL .02 .05
184 Oilers Celebrate UR .02 .05
185 Oilers Celebrate LL .02 .05
186 Oilers Celebrate LR .02 .05
187 Flames Action .02 .05
188 Grant Fuhr .20 .50
189 Devils Action .02 .05
190 Marcel Dionne .20 .50
191 Cam Neely .20 .50
192 Capitals Action .02 .05
193 Wayne Gretzky 1.00 2.50
194 Jets/Bruins Action .02 .05
195 Bruins/Canadiens Action .02 .05
196 Blues Action .02 .05
197 Caps/Flyers Action .02 .05
198 Islanders Action .02 .05
199 Flames Action .02 .05
200 Penguins Action .02 .05
201 Bruins Emblem .02 .05
202 Bruins Uniform .02 .05
203 Rejean Lemelin .04 .10
204 Ray Bourque .20 .50
205 Gord Kluzak .02 .05
206 Michael Thelven .02 .05
207 Glen Wesley .02 .05
208 Randy Burridge .02 .05
209 Keith Crowder .02 .05
210 Steve Kasper .02 .05
211 Ken Linseman .02 .05
212 Jay Miller .02 .05
214 Bob Sweeney .02 .05
215 Bruins Team LH .02 .05
216 Bruins Team RH .02 .05
217 Sabres Emblem .02 .05
218 Sabres Uniform .02 .05
219 Tom Barrasso .04 .10
220 Phil Housley .02 .05
221 Calle Johansson .02 .05
222 Mike Ramsey .02 .05
223 Dave Andreychuk .04 .10
224 Scott Arniel .02 .05
225 Adam Creighton .02 .05
226 Mike Foligno .02 .05
227 Christian Ruuttu .02 .05
228 Ray Sheppard .20 .50
229 John Tucker .02 .05
230 Pierre Turgeon .20 .50
231 Sabres Team LH .02 .05
232 Sabres Team RH .02 .05
233 Whalers Emblem .02 .05
234 Whalers Uniform .02 .05
235 Mike Liut .04 .10
236 Dave Babych .02 .05
237 Sylvain Cote .02 .05
238 Ulf Samuelsson .02 .05
239 John Anderson .02 .05
240 Kevin Dineen .02 .05
241 Ray Ferraro .02 .05
242 Ron Francis .04 .10
243 Paul MacDermid .02 .05
244 Dave Tippett .02 .05
245 Sylvain Turgeon .02 .05
246 Carey Wilson .02 .05
247 Whalers Team LH .02 .05
248 Whalers Team RH .02 .05
249 Canadiens Emblem .02 .05
250 Canadiens Uniform .02 .05
251 Brian Hayward .04 .10
252 Patrick Roy .80 2.00
253 Chris Chelios .20 .50
254 Craig Ludwig .02 .05
255 Petr Svoboda .02 .05
256 Guy Carbonneau .04 .10
257 Claude Lemieux .20 .50
258 Mike McPhee .02 .05
259 Mats Naslund .02 .05
260 Stephane Richer .04 .10
261 Bobby Smith .02 .05
262 Ryan Walter .02 .05
263 Canadiens Team LH .02 .05
264 Canadiens Team RH .02 .05
265 Devils Emblem .02 .05
266 Devils Uniform .02 .05
267 Sean Burke .20 .50
268 Joe Cirella .02 .05
269 Bruce Driver .02 .05
270 Craig Wolanin .02 .05
271 Aaron Broten .02 .05
272 Doug Brown .02 .05
273 Claude Loiselle .02 .05
274 John MacLean .02 .05
275 Kirk Muller .04 .10
276 Brendan Shanahan .20 .50
277 Patrik Sundstrom .02 .05
278 Pat Verbeek .02 .05
279 Devils Team LH .02 .05
280 Devils Team RH .02 .05
281 Islanders Emblem .02 .05
282 Islanders Uniform .02 .05
283 Kelly Hrudey .04 .10
284 Steve Konroyd .02 .05
285 Ken Morrow .02 .05
286 Pat Flatley .02 .05
287 Greg Gilbert .02 .05
288 Alan Kerr .02 .05
289 Derek King .02 .05
290 Pat LaFontaine .20 .50
291 Mikko Makela .02 .05
292 Brent Sutter .02 .05
293 Bryan Trottier .04 .10
294 Randy Wood .02 .05
295 Islanders Team .02 .05
296 Islanders Team .02 .05
297 Rangers Emblem .02 .05
298 Rangers Uniform .02 .05
299 Bob Froese .04 .10
300 John Vanbiesbrouck .20 .50
301 Brian Leetch .20 .50
302 Norm Maciver .02 .05
303 James Patrick .02 .05
304 Michel Petit .02 .05
305 Ulf Dahlen .02 .05
306 Jan Erixon .02 .05
307 Kelly Kisio .02 .05
308 Don Maloney .02 .05
309 Walt Poddubny .02 .05
310 Tomas Sandstrom .02 .05
311 Rangers Team LH .02 .05
312 Rangers Team RH .02 .05
313 Flyers Emblem .02 .05
314 Flyers Uniform .02 .05
315 Ron Hextall .04 .10
316 Mark Howe .02 .05
317 Kerry Huffman .02 .05
318 Kjell Samuelsson .02 .05
319 Dave Brown .02 .05
320 Murray Craven .02 .05
321 Tim Kerr .02 .05
322 Scott Mellanby .04 .10
323 Dave Poulin .02 .05
324 Brian Propp .02 .05
325 Ilkka Sinisalo .02 .05
326 Rick Tocchet .04 .10
327 Flyers Team LH .02 .05
328 Flyers Team RH .02 .05
329 Penguins Emblem .02 .05
330 Penguins Uniform .02 .05
331 Frank Pietrangelo .04 .10
332 Doug Bodger .02 .05
333 Paul Coffey .20 .50
334 Jim Johnson .02 .05
335 Ville Siren .02 .05
336 Rob Brown .02 .05
337 Randy Cunneyworth .02 .05
338 Dan Frawley .02 .05
339 Dave Hunter .02 .05
340 Mario Lemieux .80 2.00
341 Troy Loney .02 .05
342 Dan Quinn .02 .05
343 Penguins Team LH .02 .05
344 Penguins Team RH .02 .05
345 Nordiques Emblem .02 .05
346 Nordiques Uniform .02 .05
347 Mario Gosselin .04 .10
348 Tommy Albelin .02 .05
349 Jeff Brown .02 .05
350 Steven Finn .02 .05
351 Randy Moller .02 .05
352 Alain Cote .02 .05
353 Gaetan Duchesne .02 .05
354 Mike Eagles .02 .05
355 Michel Goulet .04 .10
356 Lane Lambert .02 .05
357 Anton Stastny .02 .05
358 Peter Stastny .04 .10
359 Nordiques Team LH .02 .05
360 Nordiques Team RH .02 .05
361 Capitals Emblem .02 .05
362 Capitals Uniform .02 .05
363 Clint Malarchuk .04 .10
364 Pete Peeters .04 .10
365 Kevin Hatcher .04 .10
366 Rod Langway .02 .05
367 Larry Murphy .04 .10
368 Scott Stevens .04 .10
369 Dave Christian .02 .05
370 Mike Gartner .20 .50
371 Bengt Gustafsson .02 .05
372 Dale Hunter .02 .05
373 Kelly Miller .02 .05
374 Mike Ridley .02 .05
375 Capitals Team LH .02 .05
376 Capitals Team RH .02 .05
377 Hockey Rink Schematic .02 .05
378 Hockey Rink Schematic .02 .05
379 Cross-checking .02 .05

380 Elbowing .02 .05
381 High-sticking .02 .05
382 Holding .02 .05
383 Hooking .02 .05
384 Interference .02 .05
385 Spearing .02 .05
386 Tripping .02 .05
387 Boarding .02 .05
388 Charging .02 .05
389 Delayed Calling of Penalty .02 .05
390 Kneeing .02 .05
391 Misconduct .02 .05
392 Roughing .02 .05
393 Slashing .02 .05
394 Unsportsmanlike Conduct .02 .05
395 Wash-out .02 .05
396 Icing .02 .05
397 Off-side .02 .05
398 Wash-out .02 .05
399 Bill Masterton Memorial Trophy Bob Bourne .02 .05
400 Hart Memorial Trophy Mario Lemieux .20 .50
401 Art Ross Trophy Mario Lemeiux .20 .50
402 William M. Jennings Trophy Brian Hayward and Patrick Roy .20 .50
403 Vezina Trophy Grant Fuhr .04 .10
404 Calder Memorial Trophy Joe Nieuwendyk .04 .10
405 James Norris Memorial Trophy Ray Bourque .20 .50
406 Lady Byng Trophy Mats Naslund .04 .10
407 Frank J. Selke Trophy Guy Carbonneau .04 .10
408 Emery Edge Award Brad McCrimmon .04 .10
xx Sticker Album 2.00 5.00

1989-90 Panini Stickers

This set of 384 hockey stickers was produced and distributed by Panini. The stickers are numbered on the back and measure 1 7/8" by 3". The stickers display color action shots of players, teams, arenas, and logos. Some team pictures consist of two stickers, each showing half of the photo; in the checklist below these halves are denoted by LH (left half) and RH (right half), and in the case of a four sticker picture, note the additional prefixes U (upper) and L (lower). A 52-page, full-color glossy album was issued with the set for holding the stickers. The album includes player information and statistics in English and French.

COMPLETE SET (384) 10.00 25.00
1 NHL Logo .02 .05
2 Playoff schedule .02 .05
3 Flames/Blackhawks action .02 .05
4 Flames/Canucks action .02 .05
5 Kings/Oilers action .02 .05
6 Vernon goal LH .02 .05
7 Vernon goal RH .02 .05
8 Bruins/Sabres action .02 .05
9 Canadiens/Bruins action .02 .05
10 Flyers score .02 .05
11 Canadiens/Flyers action LH .02 .05
12 Canadiens/Flyers action RH .02 .05
13 Canadiens/Flames action .02 .05
14 Canadiens celebration .02 .05
15 Canadiens/Flames action .02 .05
16 Canadiens/Flames action .02 .05
17 Flames celebration .02 .05
18 Flames/Canadiens action LH .02 .05
19 Flames/Canadiens action RH .02 .05
20 Al MacInnis Conn Smythe Trophy .04 .10
21 Stanley Cup/Flames UL .04 .10
22 Stanley Cup/Flames UR .04 .10
23 Stanley Cup/Flames LL .04 .10
24 Stanley Cup/Flames LR .04 .10
25 Stanley Cup .04 .10
26 Calgary Flames logo .02 .05
27 Joe Mullen .04 .10
28 Doug Gilmour .20 .50
29 Joe Nieuwendyk .04 .10
30 Gary Suter .04 .10
31 Flames team .02 .05
32 Al MacInnis .04 .10
33 Brad McCrimmon .02 .05
34 Mike Vernon .04 .10
35 Gary Roberts .04 .10
36 Colin Patterson .02 .05
37 Jim Peplinski .02 .05
38 Jamie Macoun .02 .05
39 Lanny McDonald .02 .05
40 Saddledome .02 .05
41 Chicago Blackhawks logo .02 .05
42 Darren Pang .04 .10
43 Steve Larmer .04 .10
44 Dirk Graham .02 .05
45 Doug Wilson .02 .05
46 Blackhawks/Oilers action (Ed Belfour shown) .02 .05
47 Dave Manson .02 .05
48 Troy Murray .02 .05
49 Denis Savard .04 .10
50 Steve Thomas .02 .05
51 Adam Creighton .02 .05
52 Wayne Presley .02 .05
53 Trent Yawney .02 .05
54 Alain Chevrier .02 .05
55 Chicago Stadium .02 .05
56 Detroit Red Wings logo .02 .05
57 Steve Yzerman .50 1.25
58 Gerard Gallant .02 .05
59 Greg Stefan .04 .10
60 Dave Barr .02 .05
61 Red Wings team .02 .05
62 Steve Chiasson .02 .05
63 Shawn Burr .02 .05
64 Rick Zombo .02 .05
65 Glen Hanlon .04 .10
66 Jeff Sharples .02 .05
67 Joey Kocur .02 .05
68 Lee Norwood .02 .05
69 Mike O'Connell .02 .05
70 Joe Louis Arena .02 .05
71 Edmonton Oilers logo .02 .05
72 Jimmy Carson .02 .05
73 Jari Kurri .20 .50
74 Mark Messier .20 .50
75 Craig Simpson .02 .05
76 Oilers/Flyers action .02 .05
77 Glenn Anderson .04 .10
78 Craig MacTavish .02 .05
79 Kevin Lowe .04 .10
80 Craig Muni .02 .05
81 Bill Ranford .04 .10
82 Charlie Huddy .02 .05
83 Steve Smith .02 .05
84 Normand Lacombe .02 .05
85 Northlands Coliseum .02 .05
86 L.A. Kings logo .02 .05
87 Wayne Gretzky 1.00 2.50
88 Bernie Nicholls .04 .10
89 Kelly Hrudey .04 .10
90 John Tonelli .02 .05
91 Oilers/Kings action .02 .05
92 Steve Kasper .02 .05
93 Steve Duchesne .02 .05
94 Mike Krushelnyski .02 .05
95 Luc Robitaille .20 .50
96 Ron Duguay .02 .05
97 Glenn Healy .04 .10
98 Dave Taylor .02 .05
99 Marty McSorley .02 .05
100 The Great Western Forum .02 .05
101 Minnesota North Stars logo .02 .05
102 Kari Takko .04 .10
103 Dave Gagner .02 .05
104 Mike Gartner .20 .50
105 Brian Bellows .02 .05
106 North Stars team .02 .05
107 Neal Broten .02 .05
108 Larry Murphy .04 .10
109 Basil McRae .02 .05
110 Perry Berezan .02 .05
111 Shawn Chambers .02 .05
112 Curt Giles .02 .05
113 Stewart Gavin .02 .05
114 Jon Casey .04 .10
115 Metropolitan Sports Center .02 .05
116 St. Louis Blues logo .02 .05
117 Brett Hull .20 .50
118 Peter Zezel .02 .05
119 Tony Hrkac .02 .05
120 Vincent Riendeau .04 .10
121 Blues/Islanders action .02 .05
122 Cliff Ronning .02 .05
123 Gino Cavallini .02 .05
124 Brian Benning .02 .05
125 Rick Meagher .02 .05
126 Steve Tuttle .02 .05
127 Paul Cavallini .02 .05
128 Tom Tilley .02 .05
129 Greg Millen .04 .10
130 St. Louis Arena .02 .05
131 Toronto Maple Leafs logo .02 .05
132 Ed Olczyk .02 .05
133 Gary Leeman .02 .05
134 Vincent Damphousse .04 .10
135 Tom Fergus .02 .05
136 Maple Leafs action .02 .05
137 Daniel Marois .02 .05
138 Mark Osborne .02 .05
139 Allan Bester .04 .10
140 Al Iafrate .02 .05
141 Brad Marsh .02 .05
142 Luke Richardson .02 .05
143 Todd Gill .02 .05
144 Wendel Clark .04 .10
145 Maple Leafs Gardens .02 .05
146 Vancouver Canucks logo .02 .05
147 Petri Skriko .02 .05
148 Trevor Linden .04 .10
149 Tony Tanti .02 .05
150 Steve Weeks .02 .05
151 Canucks/Islanders action .02 .05
152 Brian Bradley .02 .05
153 Barry Pederson .02 .05
154 Greg Adams .02 .05
155 Kirk McLean .04 .10
156 Jim Sandlak .02 .05
157 Rich Sutter .02 .05
158 Garth Butcher .02 .05
159 Stan Smyl .02 .05
160 Pacific Coliseum .02 .05
161 Winnipeg Jets logo .02 .05
162 Dale Hawerchuk .04 .10
163 Thomas Steen .02 .05
164 Brent Ashton .02 .05
165 Pat Elynuik .02 .05
166 Jets/Islanders action .02 .05
167 Dave Ellett .02 .05
168 Randy Carlyle .02 .05
169 Laurie Boschman .02 .05
170 Iain Duncan .02 .05
171 Doug Smail .02 .05
172 Teppo Numminen .02 .05
173 Bob Essensa .04 .10
174 Peter Taglianetti .02 .05
175 Winnipeg Arena .02 .05
176 Steve Duchesne AS .02 .05
177 Luc Robitaille AS .04 .10
178 Mike Vernon AS .04 .10
179 Wayne Gretzky AS .50 1.25
180 Kevin Lowe AS .04 .10
181 Jari Kurri AS .20 .50
182 Cam Neely AS .20 .50
183 Paul Coffey AS .20 .50
184 Mario Lemieux AS .40 1.00
185 Sean Burke AS .04 .10
186 Rob Brown AS .02 .05
187 Ray Bourque AS .20 .50
188 Boston Bruins logo .02 .05
189 Greg Hawgood .02 .05
190 Ken Linseman .02 .05
191 Andy Moog .04 .10
192 Cam Neely .20 .50
193 Bruins/Flyers action .02 .05
194 Andy Brickley .02 .05
195 Rejean Lemelin .04 .10
196 Bob Carpenter .02 .05
197 Randy Burridge .02 .05
198 Craig Janney .02 .05
199 Bob Joyce .02 .05
200 Glen Wesley .02 .05
201 Ray Bourque .20 .50
202 Boston Garden .02 .05
203 Buffalo Sabres logo .02 .05
204 Pierre Turgeon .04 .10
205 Phil Housley .02 .05
206 Rick Vaive .02 .05
207 Christian Ruuttu .02 .05
208 Flyers/Sabres action .02 .05
209 Doug Bodger .02 .05
210 Mike Foligno .02 .05
211 Ray Sheppard .02 .05
212 John Tucker .02 .05
213 Scott Arniel .02 .05
214 Daren Puppa .04 .10
215 Dave Andreychuk .04 .10
216 Uwe Krupp .02 .05
217 Memorial Auditorium .02 .05
218 Hartford Whalers logo .02 .05
219 Kevin Dineen .02 .05
220 Peter Sidorkiewicz .04 .10
221 Ron Francis .04 .10
222 Ray Ferraro .02 .05
223 Islanders/Whalers action .02 .05
224 Scott Young .02 .05
225 Dave Babych .02 .05
226 Dave Tippett .02 .05
227 Paul MacDermid .02 .05
228 Ulf Samuelsson .02 .05
229 Sylvain Cote .02 .05
230 Jody Hull .02 .05
231 Don Maloney .02 .05
232 Hartford Civic Center .02 .05
233 Montreal Canadiens logo .02 .05
234 Mats Naslund .02 .05
235 Patrick Roy .80 2.00
236 Bobby Smith .02 .05
237 Chris Chelios .20 .50
238 Flames/Canadiens action .02 .05
239 Stephane Richer .04 .10
240 Claude Lemieux .04 .10
241 Guy Carbonneau .04 .10
242 Shayne Corson .02 .05
243 Mike McPhee .02 .05
244 Petr Svoboda .02 .05
245 Larry Robinson .04 .10
246 Brian Hayward .04 .10
247 Montreal Forum .02 .05
248 New Jersey Devils logo .02 .05
249 John MacLean .02 .05
250 Patrik Sundstrom .02 .05
251 Kirk Muller .04 .10
252 Tom Kurvers .02 .05
253 Bruins/Devils action .02 .05
254 Aaron Broten .02 .05
255 Brendan Shanahan .20 .50
256 Sean Burke .02 .05
257 Tommy Albelin .02 .05
258 Ken Daneyko .02 .05
259 Randy Velischek .02 .05
260 Mark Johnson .02 .05
261 Jim Korn .02 .05
262 Brendan Byrne Arena .02 .05
263 New York Islanders logo .02 .05
264 Pat LaFontaine .04 .10
265 Mark Fitzpatrick .04 .10
266 Brent Sutter .02 .05
267 David Volek .04 .10
268 Islanders/Rangers action .02 .05
269 Bryan Trottier .04 .10
270 Mikko Makela .02 .05
271 Derek King .04 .10
272 Pat Flatley .02 .05
273 Jeff Norton .02 .05
274 Gerald Diduck .02 .05
275 Alan Kerr .02 .05
276 Jeff Hackett .04 .10
277 Nassau Veterans Memorial Coliseum .02 .05
278 New York Rangers logo .02 .05
279 Brian Leetch .20 .50
280 Carey Wilson .02 .05
281 Tomas Sandstrom .02 .05
282 John Vanbiesbrouck .20 .50
283 Oilers/Rangers action .02 .05
284 Bob Froese .04 .10
285 Tony Granato .02 .05
286 Brian Mullen .02 .05
287 Kelly Kisio .02 .05
288 Ulf Dahlen .02 .05
289 James Patrick .02 .05
290 John Ogrodnick .02 .05
291 Michel Petit .02 .05
292 Madison Square Garden .02 .05
293 Philadelphia Flyers logo .02 .05
294 Tim Kerr .02 .05
295 Rick Tocchet .04 .10
296 Pelle Eklund .02 .05
297 Terry Carkner .02 .05
298 Flyers/Canadiens action .02 .05
299 Ron Sutter .02 .05
300 Mark Howe .02 .05
301 Keith Acton .02 .05
302 Ron Hextall .04 .10
303 Gord Murphy .02 .05
304 Derrick Smith .02 .05
305 Dave Poulin .02 .05
306 Brian Propp .02 .05
307 The Spectrum .02 .05
308 Pittsburgh Penguins logo .02 .05
309 Mario Lemieux .80 2.00
310 Rob Brown .02 .05
311 Paul Coffey .20 .50
312 Tom Barrasso .04 .10
313 Penguins/Flyers action .02 .05
314 Dan Quinn .02 .05
315 Bob Errey .02 .05
316 John Cullen .02 .05
317 Phil Bourque .02 .05
318 Zarley Zalapski .02 .05
319 Troy Loney .02 .05
320 Jim Johnson .02 .05
321 Kevin Stevens .02 .05
322 Civic Arena .02 .05
323 Quebec Nordiques logo .02 .05
324 Peter Stastny .04 .10
325 Jeff Brown .02 .05
326 Michel Goulet .04 .10
327 Joe Sakic .20 .50
328 Flyers/Nordiques action .02 .05
329 Iiro Jarvi .02 .05
330 Paul Gillis .02 .05
331 Randy Moller .02 .05
332 Ron Tugnutt .04 .10
333 Robert Picard .02 .05
334 Curtis Leschyshyn .02 .05
335 Marc Fortier .02 .05
336 Mario Marois .02 .05
337 Le Colisee .02 .05
338 Washington Capitals logo .02 .05
339 Mike Ridley .02 .05
340 Geoff Courtnall .02 .05
341 Scott Stevens .04 .10
342 Dino Ciccarelli .04 .10
343 Capitals/Flames action .02 .05
344 Bob Mason .04 .10
345 Dave Christian .02 .05
346 Dale Hunter .02 .05
347 Kevin Hatcher .04 .10
348 Kelly Miller .02 .05
349 Stephen Leach .02 .05
350 Rod Langway .02 .05
351 Bob Rouse .02 .05
352 Capital Centre .02 .05
353 Calgary Flames logo .02 .05
354 Edmonton Oilers logo .02 .05
355 Winnipeg Jets logo .02 .05
356 Toronto Maple Leafs logo .02 .05
357 Buffalo Sabres logo .02 .05
358 Montreal Canadiens logo .02 .05
359 Quebec Nordiques logo .02 .05
360 New Jersey Devils logo .02 .05
361 Boston Bruins logo .02 .05
362 Hartford Whalers logo .02 .05
363 Vancouver Canucks logo .02 .05
364 Minnesota North Stars logo .02 .05
365 Los Angeles Kings logo .02 .05
366 St. Louis Blues logo .02 .05
367 Chicago Blackhawks logo .02 .05
368 Detroit Red Wings logo .02 .05
369 Pittsburgh Penguins logo .02 .05
370 Washington Capitals logo .02 .05
371 Philadelphia Flyers logo .02 .05
372 New York Rangers logo .02 .05
373 New York Islanders logo .02 .05
374 Wayne Gretzky 1.00 2.50
375 Mario Lemieux .80 2.00
376 Patrick Roy and Brian Hayward .30 .75
377 Tim Kerr .02 .05
378 Brian Leetch .20 .50
379 Chris Chelios .20 .50
380 Joe Mullen .04 .10
381 Guy Carbonneau .04 .10
382 Bryan Trottier .04 .10
383 Patrick Roy .80 2.00
384 Joe Mullen .04 .10
xx Sticker Album 1.00 2.50

1990-91 Panini Stickers

This set of 351 hockey stickers was produced and distributed by Panini. The stickers are numbered on the back and measure approximately 2 1/16" by 2 15/16". The fronts feature full color action photos of the players. Different color triangles (in one of the team's colors) overlay the upper left corner of the pictures, with the team name in white lettering. A variegated stripe appears below the player photos, with the player's name below. The team logo and conference stickers are in foil. The stickers are arranged according to alphabetical team order.

COMPLETE SET (351) 8.00 20.00
1 Prince of Wales Conference .02 .05
2 Clarence Campbell Conference .02 .05
3 Stanley Cup .04 .10
4 Dave Poulin .02 .05
5 Brian Propp .02 .05
6 Glen Wesley .02 .05
7 Bob Carpenter .02 .05
8 John Carter .02 .05
9 Cam Neely .20 .50
10 Greg Hawgood .02 .05
11 Andy Moog .04 .10
12 Boston Bruins logo .02 .05
13 Rejean Lemelin .04 .10
14 Craig Janney .02 .05
15 Bob Sweeney .02 .05
16 Andy Brickley .02 .05
17 Ray Bourque .20 .50
18 Dave Christian .02 .05
19 Dave Snuggerud .02 .05
20 Christian Ruuttu .02 .05
21 Phil Housley .02 .05
22 Uwe Krupp .02 .05
23 Rick Vaive .02 .05
24 Mike Ramsey .02 .05
25 Mike Foligno .02 .05
26 Clint Malarchuk .04 .10
27 Buffalo Sabres logo .02 .05
28 Pierre Turgeon .04 .10
29 Dave Andreychuk .04 .10
30 Scott Arniel .02 .05
31 Daren Puppa .04 .10
32 Mike Hartman .02 .05
33 Doug Bodger .02 .05
34 Scott Young .02 .05
35 Todd Krygier .02 .05
36 Pat Verbeek .04 .10
37 Dave Tippett .02 .05
38 Peter Sidorkiewicz .04 .10
39 Ron Francis .04 .10
40 Dave Babych .02 .05
41 Randy Ladouceur .02 .05
42 Hartford Whalers logo .02 .05
43 Kevin Dineen .02 .05
44 Dean Evason .02 .05
45 Ray Ferraro .02 .05
46 Mike Tomlak .04 .10
47 Mikael Andersson .02 .05
48 Brad Shaw .02 .05
49 Chris Chelios .20 .50
50 Petr Svoboda .02 .05
51 Patrick Roy .60 1.50
52 Bobby Smith .02 .05
53 Stephane Richer .04 .10
54 Shayne Corson .02 .05
55 Brian Skrudland .02 .05
56 Russ Courtnall .02 .05
57 Montreal Canadiens logo .02 .05
58 Guy Carbonneau .04 .10
59 Sylvain Lefebvre .02 .05
60 Mathieu Schneider .02 .05
61 Brian Hayward .04 .10
62 Mats Naslund .02 .05
63 Mike McPhee .02 .05
64 Brendan Shanahan .20 .50
65 Patrik Sundstrom .02 .05
66 Mark Johnson .02 .05
67 Doug Brown .02 .05
68 Chris Terreri .04 .10
69 Bruce Driver .02 .05
70 Peter Stastny .04 .10
71 Sylvain Turgeon .02 .05
72 New Jersey Devils logo .02 .05
73 Kirk Muller .04 .10
74 John MacLean .02 .05
75 Slava Fetisov .02 .05
76 Tommy Albelin .02 .05
77 Sean Burke .04 .10
78 Janne Ojanen .02 .05
79 Randy Wood .02 .05
80 Gary Nylund .02 .05
81 Pat LaFontaine .20 .50
82 Pat Flatley .02 .05
83 Bryan Trottier .04 .10
84 Don Maloney .02 .05
85 Gerald Diduck .02 .05
86 Mark Fitzpatrick .04 .10
87 New York Islanders logo .02 .05
88 Glenn Healy .04 .10
89 Alan Kerr .02 .05
90 Brent Sutter .02 .05
91 Doug Crossman .02 .05
92 Hubie McDonough .02 .05
93 Jeff Norton .02 .05
94 Kelly Kisio .02 .05
95 Brian Leetch .20 .50
96 Brian Mullen .02 .05
97 James Patrick .02 .05
98 Mike Richter .04 .10
99 John Ogrodnick .02 .05
100 Troy Mallette .02 .05
101 Mark Janssens .02 .05
102 New York Rangers logo .02 .05
103 Mike Gartner .20 .50
104 Jan Erixon .02 .05
105 Carey Wilson .02 .05
106 Bernie Nicholls .04 .10
107 Darren Turcotte .02 .05
108 John Vanbiesbrouck .20 .50
109 Ron Sutter .02 .05
110 Kjell Samuelsson .02 .05
111 Ken Linseman .02 .05
112 Ken Wregget .04 .10
113 Pelle Eklund .02 .05
114 Terry Carkner .02 .05
115 Gord Murphy .02 .05
116 Murray Craven .02 .05
117 Philadelphia Flyers logo .02 .05
118 Ron Hextall .04 .10
119 Mike Bullard .02 .05
120 Tim Kerr .02 .05
121 Rick Tocchet .04 .10
122 Mark Howe .02 .05
123 Ilkka Sinisalo .02 .05
124 Tony Tanti .02 .05
125 John Cullen .02 .05
126 Zarley Zalapski .02 .05
127 Wendell Young .04 .10
128 Rob Brown .02 .05
129 Phil Bourque .02 .05
130 Mark Recchi .20 .50
131 Kevin Stevens .02 .05
132 Pittsburgh Penguins logo .02 .05
133 Bob Errey .02 .05
134 Tom Barrasso .04 .10
135 Paul Coffey .20 .50
136 Mario Lemieux .60 1.50
137 Randy Hillier .02 .05
138 Troy Loney .02 .05
139 Joe Sakic .20 .50
140 Lucien DeBlois .02 .05
141 Joe Cirella .02 .05
142 Ron Tugnutt .04 .10
143 Paul Gillis .02 .05
144 Bryan Fogarty .02 .05
145 Guy Lafleur .04 .10
146 Tony Hrkac .02 .05
147 Quebec Nordiques logo .02 .05
148 Michel Petit .02 .05
149 Tony McKegney .02 .05
150 Curtis Leschyshyn .02 .05
151 Claude Loiselle .02 .05
152 Mario Brunetta .02 .05
153 Marc Fortier .02 .05
154 Michal Pivonka .02 .05
155 Scott Stevens .04 .10
156 Kelly Miller .02 .05
157 John Tucker .02 .05
158 Don Beaupre .04 .10
159 Geoff Courtnall .02 .05
160 Alan May .02 .05
161 Dino Ciccarelli .04 .10
162 Washington Capitals logo .02 .05
163 Mike Ridley .02 .05
164 Bob Rouse .02 .05
165 Mike Liut .04 .10
166 Stephen Leach .02 .05
167 Kevin Hatcher .04 .10
168 Dale Hunter .02 .05
169 Prince of Wales Trophy .02 .05
170 Clarence Campbell Trophy .02 .05
171 Stanley Cup Championship .04 .10
172 Doug Gilmour .20 .50
173 Brad McCrimmon .02 .05
174 Joe Nieuwendyk .04 .10
175 Mike Vernon .04 .10
176 Theo Fleury .20 .50
177 Gary Suter .04 .10
178 Jamie Macoun .02 .05
179 Gary Roberts .04 .10
180 Calgary Flames logo .02 .05
181 Paul Ranheim .02 .05
182 Jiri Hrdina .02 .05
183 Joe Mullen .04 .10
184 Sergei Makarov .02 .05
185 Al MacInnis .04 .10
186 Rick Wamsley .04 .10
187 Trent Yawney .02 .05
188 Greg Millen .04 .10
189 Doug Wilson .02 .05
190 Jocelyn Lemieux .02 .05
191 Dirk Graham .02 .05
192 Keith Brown .02 .05
193 Adam Creighton .02 .05
194 Steve Larmer .04 .10
195 Chicago Blackhawks logo .02 .05
196 Greg Gilbert .02 .05
197 Jacques Cloutier .04 .10
198 Denis Savard .04 .10
199 Dave Manson .02 .05
200 Troy Murray .02 .05
201 Jeremy Roenick .20 .50
202 Lee Norwood .02 .05
203 Glen Hanlon .04 .10
204 Marc Habscheid .02 .05
205 Gerard Gallant .02 .05
206 Rick Zombo .02 .05
207 Steve Chiasson .02 .05
208 Steve Yzerman .40 1.00
209 Bernie Federko .02 .05
210 Detroit Red Wings logo .02 .05
211 Joey Kocur .02 .05
212 Tim Cheveldae .04 .10
213 Shawn Burr .02 .05
214 Jimmy Carson .02 .05
215 Mike O'Connell .02 .05
216 John Chabot .02 .05
217 Craig Muni .02 .05
218 Bill Ranford .04 .10
219 Mark Messier .20 .50
220 Craig MacTavish .02 .05
221 Charlie Huddy .02 .05
222 Jari Kurri .20 .50
223 Esa Tikkanen .04 .10
224 Kevin Lowe .04 .10
225 Edmonton Oilers logo .02 .05
226 Steve Smith .02 .05
227 Glenn Anderson .04 .10
228 Petr Klima .02 .05
229 Craig Simpson .02 .05
230 Grant Fuhr .20 .50
231 Randy Gregg .02 .05
232 Bob Kudelski .02 .05
233 Luc Robitaille .04 .10
234 Marty McSorley .02 .05
235 John Tonelli .02 .05
236 Dave Taylor .02 .05
237 Mikko Makela .02 .05
238 Steve Kasper .02 .05
239 Tony Granato .02 .05
240 Los Angeles Kings logo .02 .05
241 Steve Duchesne .02 .05
242 Wayne Gretzky .80 2.00
243 Tomas Sandstrom .02 .05
244 Larry Robinson .04 .10
245 Mike Krushelnyski .02 .05
246 Kelly Hrudey .04 .10
247 Aaron Broten .02 .05
248 Dave Gagner .02 .05
249 Basil McRae .02 .05
250 Curt Giles .02 .05
251 Larry Murphy .04 .10
252 Shawn Chambers .02 .05
253 Mike Modano .20 .50
254 Jon Casey .04 .10
255 Minnesota North Stars logo .02 .05
256 Gaetan Duchesne .02 .05
257 Brian Bellows .02 .05
258 Frantisek Musil .02 .05
259 Don Barber .02 .05
260 Stewart Gavin .02 .05
261 Neal Broten .02 .05
262 Brett Hull .20 .50
263 Sergio Momesso .02 .05
264 Peter Zezel .02 .05
265 Gino Cavallini .02 .05
266 Rod Brind'Amour .20 .50
267 Mike Lalor .02 .05
268 Vincent Riendeau .04 .10
269 Gordie Roberts .02 .05
270 St. Louis Blues logo .02 .05
271 Paul MacLean .02 .05
272 Curtis Joseph .20 .50
273 Rick Meagher .02 .05
274 Jeff Brown .02 .05
275 Adam Oates .04 .10
276 Paul Cavallini .02 .05
277 Brad Marsh .02 .05
278 Mark Osborne .02 .05
279 Gary Leeman .02 .05
280 Rob Ramage .02 .05
281 Jeff Reese .04 .10
282 Tom Fergus .02 .05
283 Ed Olczyk .02 .05
284 Daniel Marois .02 .05
285 Toronto Maple Leafs logo .02 .05
286 Wendel Clark .04 .10
287 Tom Kurvers .02 .05
288 Gilles Thibaudeau .02 .05
289 Lou Franceschetti .02 .05
290 Al Iafrate .02 .05
291 Vincent Damphousse .04 .10
292 Stan Smyl .02 .05
293 Paul Reinhart .02 .05
294 Igor Larionov .02 .05
295 Doug Lidster .02 .05
296 Kirk McLean .04 .10
297 Andrew McBain .02 .05
298 Petri Skriko .02 .05
299 Trevor Linden .04 .10
300 Vancouver Canucks logo .02 .05
301 Steve Bozek .02 .05
302 Brian Bradley .02 .05
303 Greg Adams .02 .05
304 Vladimir Krutov .02 .05
305 Dan Quinn .02 .05
306 Jim Sandlak .02 .05
307 Teppo Numminen .02 .05
308 Doug Smail .02 .05
309 Greg Paslawski .02 .05
310 Dave Ellett .02 .05
311 Bob Essensa .04 .10
312 Pat Elynuik .02 .05
313 Paul Fenton .02 .05
314 Randy Carlyle .02 .05
315 Winnipeg Jets logo .02 .05
316 Thomas Steen .02 .05
317 Dale Hawerchuk .04 .10
318 Fredrik Olausson .02 .05
319 Dave McLlwain .02 .05
320 Laurie Boschman .02 .05
321 Brent Ashton .02 .05
322 Ray Bourque .20 .50
323 Patrick Roy .60 1.50
324 Paul Coffey .20 .50
325 Brian Propp .02 .05
326 Mario Lemieux .60 1.50
327 Cam Neely .20 .50
328 Al MacInnis .04 .10
329 Mike Vernon .04 .10
330 Kevin Lowe .04 .10
331 Luc Robitaille .04 .10
332 Wayne Gretzky .80 2.00
333 Brett Hull .20 .50
334 Sergei Makarov .02 .05
335 Alexei Kasatonov .02 .05
336 Igor Larionov .02 .05
337 Vladimir Krutov .02 .05
338 Alexander Mogilny .04 .10
339 Slava Fetisov .02 .05
340 Mike Modano .20 .50
341 Mark Recchi .20 .50
342 Paul Ranheim .02 .05
343 Rod Brind'Amour .02 .05
344 Brad Shaw .02 .05
345 Mike Richter .04 .10
346 Hart Trophy .02 .05

347 Art Ross Trophy .02 .05
348 Calder Memorial Trophy .02 .05
349 Lady Byng Trophy .02 .05
350 Norris Trophy .02 .05
351 Vezina Trophy .02 .05
xx Sticker Album 1.00 2.50

1991-92 Panini Stickers

This set of 344 stickers was produced by Panini. They measure approximately 1 7/8" by 2 7/8" and were to be pasted in a 8 1/4" by 10 1/2" bilingual sticker album. The fronts feature color action shots of the players. Pages 2-5 of the album picture highlights of the 1991 Stanley Cup playoffs and finals. Team pages have team colors that highlight player stickers. The NHL 75th Anniversary logo (3-4) and the circular-shaped team logos (148-169) are foil. The stickers are numbered on the back and checklisted below alphabetically according to team.

COMPLETE SET (344) 8.00 20.00
1 NHL Logo .02 .05
2 NHLPA Logo .02 .05
3 NHL Logo 75th Anniversary (Left) .02 .05
4 NHL Logo 75th Anniversary (Right) .02 .05
5 Clarence Campbell Conference Logo .02 .05
6 Prince of Wales Conference Logo .02 .05
7 Stanley Cup Championship Logo .04 .10
8 Steve Larmer .04 .10
9 Ed Belfour .20 .50
10 Chris Chelios .20 .50
11 Michel Goulet .04 .10
12 Jeremy Roenick .20 .50
13 Adam Creighton .02 .05
14 Steve Thomas .02 .05
15 Dave Manson .02 .05
16 Dirk Graham .02 .05
17 Troy Murray .02 .05
18 Doug Wilson .02 .05
19 Wayne Presley .02 .05
20 Jocelyn Lemieux .02 .05
21 Keith Brown .02 .05
22 Curtis Joseph .20 .50
23 Jeff Brown .02 .05
24 Gino Cavallini .02 .05
25 Brett Hull .20 .50
26 Scott Stevens .04 .10
27 Dan Quinn .02 .05
28 Garth Butcher .02 .05
29 Bob Bassen .02 .05
30 Rod Brind'Amour .02 .05
31 Adam Oates .04 .10
32 Dave Lowry .02 .05
33 Rich Sutter .02 .05
34 Ron Wilson .02 .05
35 Paul Cavallini .02 .05
36 Trevor Linden .04 .10
37 Troy Gamble .02 .05
38 Geoff Courtnall .02 .05
39 Greg Adams .02 .05
40 Doug Lidster .02 .05
41 Dave Capuano .02 .05
42 Igor Larionov .02 .05
43 Tom Kurvers .02 .05
44 Sergio Momesso .02 .05
45 Kirk McLean .04 .10
46 Cliff Ronning .02 .05
47 Robert Kron .02 .05
48 Steve Bozek .02 .05
49 Petr Nedved .04 .10
50 Al MacInnis .04 .10
51 Theo Fleury .20 .50
52 Gary Roberts .04 .10
53 Joe Nieuwendyk .04 .10
54 Paul Ranheim .02 .05
55 Mike Vernon .04 .10
56 Carey Wilson .02 .05
57 Gary Suter .04 .10
58 Sergei Makarov .02 .05
59 Doug Gilmour .20 .50
60 Joel Otto .02 .05
61 Jamie Macoun .02 .05
62 Stephane Matteau .02 .05
63 Robert Reichel .02 .05
64 Ed Olczyk .02 .05
65 Phil Housley .02 .05
66 Pat Elynuik .02 .05
67 Fredrik Olausson .02 .05
68 Thomas Steen .02 .05
69 Paul MacDermid .02 .05
70 Brent Ashton .02 .05
71 Teppo Numminen .02 .05
72 Danton Cole .02 .05
73 Dave McLlwain .02 .05
74 Scott Arniel .02 .05
75 Bob Essensa .04 .10
76 Randy Carlyle .02 .05
77 Mark Osborne .02 .05
78 Wayne Gretzky 1.20 3.00
79 Tomas Sandstrom .02 .05
80 Steve Duchesne .02 .05
81 Kelly Hrudey .04 .10
82 Larry Robinson .02 .05
83 Tony Granato .02 .05
84 Marty McSorley .02 .05
85 Todd Elik .02 .05
86 Rob Blake .04 .10
87 Bob Kudelski .02 .05
88 Steve Kasper .02 .05
89 Dave Taylor .02 .05
90 John Tonelli .02 .05
91 Luc Robitaille .04 .10
92 Vincent Damphousse .04 .10
93 Brian Bradley .02 .05
94 Dave Ellett .02 .05
95 Daniel Marois .02 .05
96 Rob Ramage .02 .05
97 Mike Krushelnyski .02 .05
98 Michel Petit .02 .05
99 Peter Ing .02 .05
100 Lucien DeBlois .02 .05
101 Bob Rouse .02 .05
102 Wendel Clark .04 .10
103 Peter Zezel .02 .05
104 David Reid .02 .05
105 Aaron Broten .02 .05
106 Brian Hayward .04 .10
107 Neal Broten .02 .05
108 Brian Bellows .02 .05
109 Mark Tinordi .02 .05
110 Ulf Dahlen .02 .05
111 Doug Smail .02 .05
112 Dave Gagner .02 .05
113 Bobby Smith .02 .05
114 Brian Glynn .02 .05
115 Brian Propp .02 .05
116 Mike Modano .04 .10
117 Gaetan Duchesne .02 .05
118 Jon Casey .04 .10
119 Basil McRae .02 .05
120 Glenn Anderson .04 .10
121 Steve Smith .02 .05
122 Adam Graves .04 .10
123 Esa Tikkanen .04 .10
124 Mark Messier .20 .50
125 Bill Ranford .04 .10
126 Petr Klima .02 .05
127 Anatoli Semenov .02 .05
128 Martin Gelinas .02 .05
129 Charlie Huddy .02 .05
130 Craig Simpson .02 .05
131 Kevin Lowe .04 .10
132 Craig MacTavish .02 .05
133 Craig Muni .02 .05
134 Steve Yzerman .60 1.50
135 Shawn Burr .02 .05
136 Tim Cheveldae .04 .10
137 Rick Zombo .02 .05
138 Marc Habscheid .02 .05
139 Jimmy Carson .02 .05
140 Brent Fedyk .02 .05
141 Yves Racine .02 .05
142 Gerard Gallant .02 .05
143 Steve Chiasson .02 .05
144 Johan Garpenlov .02 .05
145 Sergei Fedorov .20 .50
146 Bob Probert .04 .10
147 Rick Green .02 .05
148 Chicago Blackhawks Logo .02 .05
149 Detroit Red Wings Logo .02 .05
150 Minnesota North Stars Logo .02 .05
151 St. Louis Blues Logo .02 .05
152 Toronto Maple Leafs Logo .02 .05
153 Calgary Flames Logo .02 .05
154 Edmonton Oilers Logo .02 .05
155 Los Angeles Kings Logo .02 .05
156 San Jose Sharks Logo .02 .05
157 Vancouver Canucks Logo .02 .05
158 Winnipeg Jets Logo .02 .05
159 Boston Bruins Logo .02 .05
160 Buffalo Sabres Logo .02 .05
161 Hartford Whalers Logo .02 .05
162 Montreal Canadiens Logo .02 .05
163 Quebec Nordiques Logo .02 .05
164 New Jersey Devils Logo .02 .05
165 New York Islanders Logo .02 .05
166 New York Rangers Logo .02 .05
167 Philadelphia Flyers Logo .02 .05
168 Pittsburgh Penguins Logo .02 .05
169 Washington Capitals Logo .02 .05
170 Craig Janney .02 .05
171 Ray Bourque .20 .50
172 Rejean Lemelin .04 .10
173 Dave Christian .02 .05
174 Randy Burridge .02 .05
175 Garry Galley .02 .05
176 Cam Neely .20 .50
177 Bob Sweeney .02 .05
178 Ken Hodge Jr. .02 .05
179 Andy Moog .04 .10
180 Don Sweeney .02 .05
181 Bob Carpenter .02 .05
182 Glen Wesley .02 .05
183 Chris Nilan .02 .05
184 Patrick Roy 1.00 2.50
185 Petr Svoboda .02 .05
186 Russ Courtnall .02 .05
187 Denis Savard .04 .10
188 Mike McPhee .02 .05
189 Eric Desjardins .04 .10
190 Mike Keane .02 .05
191 Stephan Lebeau .02 .05
192 J.J. Daigneault .02 .05
193 Stephane Richer .04 .10
194 Brian Skrudland .02 .05
195 Mathieu Schneider .02 .05
196 Shayne Corson .02 .05
197 Guy Carbonneau .04 .10
198 Kevin Hatcher .04 .10
199 Mike Ridley .02 .05
200 John Druce .02 .05
201 Don Beaupre .02 .05
202 Kelly Miller .02 .05
203 Dale Hunter .02 .05
204 Nick Kypreos .02 .05
205 Calle Johansson .02 .05
206 Michal Pivonka .02 .05
207 Dino Ciccarelli .04 .10
208 Al Iafrate .02 .05
209 Rod Langway .02 .05
210 Mikhail Tatarinov .02 .05
211 Stephen Leach .02 .05
212 Sean Burke .04 .10
213 John MacLean .02 .05
214 Lee Norwood .02 .05
215 Laurie Boschman .02 .05
216 Alexei Kasatonov .02 .05
217 Patrik Sundstrom .02 .05
218 Ken Daneyko .02 .05
219 Kirk Muller .04 .10
220 Peter Stastny .04 .10
221 Chris Terreri .04 .10
222 Brendan Shanahan .20 .50
223 Eric Weinrich .02 .05
224 Claude Lemieux .04 .10
225 Bruce Driver .02 .05
226 Tim Kerr .02 .05
227 Ron Hextall .04 .10
228 Pelle Eklund .02 .05
229 Rick Tocchet .04 .10
230 Gord Murphy .02 .05
231 Mike Ricci .02 .05
232 Derrick Smith .02 .05
233 Ron Sutter .02 .05
234 Murray Craven .02 .05
235 Terry Carkner .02 .05
236 Ken Wregget .04 .10
237 Keith Acton .02 .05
238 Scott Mellanby .04 .10
239 Kjell Samuelsson .02 .05
240 Jeff Hackett .04 .10
241 David Volek .02 .05
242 Craig Ludwig .02 .05
243 Pat LaFontaine .20 .50
244 Randy Wood .02 .05
245 Pat Flatley .02 .05
246 Brent Sutter .02 .05
247 Derek King .02 .05
248 Jeff Norton .02 .05
249 Glenn Healy .04 .10
250 Ray Ferraro .02 .05
251 Gary Nylund .02 .05
252 Joe Reekie .02 .05
253 Dave Chyzowski .02 .05
254 Mike Hough .02 .05
255 Mats Sundin .20 .50
256 Curtis Leschyshyn .02 .05
257 Joe Sakic .20 .50
258 Stephane Fiset .04 .10
259 Bryan Fogarty .02 .05
260 Alexei Gusarov .02 .05
261 Steven Finn .02 .05
262 Everett Sanipass .02 .05
263 Stephane Morin .02 .05
264 Craig Wolanin .02 .05
265 Randy Velischek .02 .05
266 Owen Nolan .04 .10
267 Ron Tugnutt .04 .10
268 Mario Lemieux 1.00 2.50
269 Kevin Stevens .02 .05
270 Larry Murphy .04 .10
271 Tom Barrasso .04 .10
272 Phil Bourque .02 .05
273 Scott Young .02 .05
274 Paul Stanton .02 .05
275 Jaromir Jagr .20 .50
276 Paul Coffey .20 .50
277 Ulf Samuelsson .02 .05
278 Joe Mullen .04 .10
279 Bob Errey .02 .05
280 Mark Recchi .04 .10
281 Ron Francis .04 .10
282 John Vanbiesbrouck .20 .50
283 Jan Erixon .02 .05
284 Brian Leetch .20 .50
285 Darren Turcotte .04 .10
286 Ray Sheppard .02 .05
287 James Patrick .02 .05
288 Bernie Nicholls .04 .10
289 Brian Mullen .02 .05
290 Mike Richter .04 .10
291 Kelly Kisio .02 .05
292 Mike Gartner .20 .50
293 John Ogrodnick .02 .05
294 David Shaw .02 .05
295 Troy Mallette .02 .05
296 Dale Hawerchuk .04 .10
297 Rick Vaive .02 .05
298 Daren Puppa .04 .10
299 Mike Ramsey .02 .05
300 Benoit Hogue .02 .05
301 Clint Malarchuk .04 .10
302 Mikko Makela .02 .05
303 Pierre Turgeon .04 .10
304 Alexander Mogilny .04 .10
305 Uwe Krupp .02 .05
306 Christian Ruuttu .02 .05
307 Doug Bodger .02 .05
308 Dave Snuggerud .02 .05
309 Dave Andreychuk .04 .10
310 Peter Sidorkiewicz .04 .10
311 Brad Shaw .02 .05
312 Dean Evason .02 .05
313 Pat Verbeek .02 .05
314 John Cullen .02 .05
315 Rob Brown .02 .05
316 Bobby Holik .02 .05
317 Todd Krygier .02 .05
318 Adam Burt .02 .05
319 Mike Tomlak .02 .05
320 Randy Cunneyworth .02 .05
321 Paul Cyr .02 .05
322 Zarley Zalapski .02 .05
323 Kevin Dineen .02 .05
324 Luc Robitaille .04 .10
325 Brett Hull .20 .50
326 All-Star Game Logo .02 .05
327 Wayne Gretzky 1.20 3.00
328 Mike Vernon .04 .10
329 Chris Chelios .20 .50
330 Al MacInnis .04 .10
331 Rick Tocchet .04 .10
332 Cam Neely .20 .50
333 Patrick Roy 1.00 2.50
334 Joe Sakic .20 .50
335 Ray Bourque .20 .50
336 Paul Coffey .20 .50
337 Ed Belfour .20 .50
338 Mike Ricci .02 .05
339 Rob Blake .04 .10
340 Sergei Fedorov .50 1.25
341 Ken Hodge Jr. .02 .05
342 Bobby Holik .02 .05
343 Robert Reichel .02 .05
344 Jaromir Jagr .20 .50
xx Sticker Album .60 1.50

1992-93 Panini Stickers

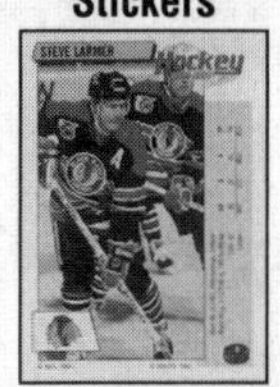

This set of 330 stickers was produced by Panini. They measure approximately 2 3/8" by 3 3/8" and were to be pasted in a 9" by 11" album. The fronts have action color player photos with statistics running down the right side in a colored bar. The player's name appears at the top. The team logo is superimposed on the photo at the lower left corner. The backs feature questions and answers that go with the Slap-shot game that is included in the album. The team logos scattered throughout the set are foil. The stickers are numbered on the front on a puck icon at the lower right corner. They are checklisted below alphabetically according to teams in the Campbell and Wales Conferences. Also included are subsets of the 1992 NHL's Top Rookies (270-275), the 1992 All-Star Game (276-289), the European Invasion (290-302), and The Trophies (303-308). Randomly inserted throughout the packs were 22 lettered "Ice-Breaker" stickers, each featuring a star player from each of the 22 NHL teams (minus the new expansion teams, the Tampa Bay Lightning and the Ottawa Senators.

COMPLETE SET (330) 14.00 35.00
*FRENCH: SAME VALUE
1 Stanley Cup .04 .10
2 Blackhawks logo .02 .05
3 Ed Belfour .20 .50
4 Jeremy Roenick .20 .50
5 Steve Larmer .02 .05
6 Michel Goulet .04 .10
7 Dirk Graham .02 .05
8 Jocelyn Lemieux .02 .05
9 Brian Noonan .02 .05
10 Rob Brown .02 .05
11 Chris Chelios .20 .50
12 Steve Smith .02 .05
13 Keith Brown .02 .05
14 St. Louis Blues .02 .05
15 Curtis Joseph .20 .50
16 Brett Hull .30 .75
17 Brendan Shanahan .50 1.25
18 Ron Wilson .02 .05
19 Rich Sutter .02 .05
20 Ron Sutter .02 .05
21 Dave Lowry .02 .05
22 Craig Janney .02 .05
23 Paul Cavallini .02 .05
24 Garth Butcher .02 .05
25 Jeff Brown .02 .05
26 Canucks Logo .02 .05
27 Kirk McLean .04 .10
28 Trevor Linden .04 .10
29 Geoff Courtnall .02 .05
30 Cliff Ronning .02 .05
31 Petr Nedved .04 .10
32 Igor Larionov .02 .05
33 Robert Kron .02 .05
34 Jim Sandlak .02 .05
35 Dave Babych .02 .05
36 Jyrki Lumme .02 .05
37 Doug Lidster .02 .05
38 Flames Logo .02 .05
39 Mike Vernon .04 .10
40 Joe Nieuwendyk .04 .10
41 Gary Leeman .02 .05
42 Robert Reichel .02 .05
43 Joel Otto .02 .05
44 Paul Ranheim .02 .05
45 Gary Roberts .04 .10
46 Theo Fleury .20 .50
47 Sergei Makarov .02 .05
48 Gary Suter .04 .10
49 Al MacInnis .04 .10
50 Jets Logo .02 .05
51 Bob Essensa .04 .10
52 Teppo Numminen .02 .05
53 Thomas Steen .02 .05
54 Pat Elynuik .02 .05
55 Ed Olczyk .02 .05
56 Danton Cole .02 .05
57 Troy Murray .02 .05
58 Darrin Shannon .02 .05
59 Russ Romaniuk .02 .05
60 Fredrik Olausson .02 .05
61 Phil Housley .02 .05
62 Kings Logo .02 .05
63 Kelly Hrudey .04 .10
64 Wayne Gretzky .80 2.00
65 Luc Robitaille .04 .10
66 Jari Kurri .04 .10
67 Tomas Sandstrom .02 .05
68 Tony Granato .02 .05
69 Bob Kudelski .02 .05
70 Corey Millen .02 .05
71 Rob Blake .04 .10
72 Paul Coffey .20 .50
73 Marty McSorley .02 .05
74 Maple Leafs Logo .02 .05
75 Grant Fuhr .04 .10
76 Glenn Anderson .04 .10
77 Doug Gilmour .20 .50
78 Mike Krushelnyski .02 .05
79 Wendel Clark .04 .10
80 Rob Pearson .02 .05
81 Peter Zezel .02 .05
82 Todd Gill .02 .05
83 Dave Ellett .02 .05
84 Mike Foligno .02 .05
85 Ken Baumgartner .02 .05
86 North Stars Logo .02 .05
87 Jon Casey .04 .10
88 Brian Bellows .02 .05
89 Neal Broten .02 .05
90 Dave Gagner .02 .05
91 Mike Modano .30 .75
92 Ulf Dahlen .02 .05
93 Brian Propp .02 .05
94 Jim Johnson .02 .05
95 Mike Craig .02 .05
96 Bobby Smith .02 .05
97 Mark Tinordi .02 .05
98 Oilers Logo .02 .05
99 Bill Ranford .04 .10
100 Joe Murphy .04 .10
101 Craig MacTavish .02 .05
102 Craig Simpson .02 .05
103 Esa Tikkanen .04 .10
104 Vincent Damphousse .04 .10
105 Petr Klima .02 .05
106 Martin Gelinas .02 .05
107 Kevin Lowe .04 .10
108 Dave Manson .02 .05
109 Bernie Nicholls .04 .10
110 Red Wings Logo .02 .05
111 Tim Cheveldae .04 .10
112 Steve Yzerman .80 2.00
113 Sergei Fedorov .50 1.25
114 Jimmy Carson .02 .05
115 Kevin Miller .02 .05
116 Gerard Gallant .02 .05
117 Keith Primeau .02 .05
118 Paul Ysebaert .02 .05
119 Yves Racine .02 .05
120 Steve Chiasson .02 .05
121 Ray Sheppard .02 .05
122 Sharks Logo .02 .05
123 Jeff Hackett .04 .10
124 Kelly Kisio .02 .05
125 Brian Mullen .02 .05
126 David Bruce .02 .05
127 Rob Zettler .02 .05
128 Neil Wilkinson .02 .05
129 Doug Wilson .02 .05
130 Jeff Odgers .02 .05
131 Dean Evason .02 .05
132 Brian Lawton .02 .05
133 Dale Craigwell .02 .05
134 Bruins Logo .02 .05
135 Andy Moog .04 .10
136 Adam Oates .04 .10
137 Dave Poulin .02 .05
138 Vladimir Ruzicka .02 .05
139 Jeff Lazaro .02 .05
140 Bob Carpenter .02 .05
141 Peter Douris .02 .05
142 Glen Murray .02 .05
143 Cam Neely .20 .50
144 Ray Bourque .30 .75
145 Glen Wesley .02 .05
146 Canadiens Logo .02 .05
147 Patrick Roy .60 1.50
148 Kirk Muller .04 .10
149 Guy Carbonneau .04 .10
150 Shayne Corson .02 .05
151 Stephan Lebeau .02 .05
152 Denis Savard .04 .10
153 Brent Gilchrist .02 .05
154 Russ Courtnall .02 .05
155 Patrice Brisebois .02 .05
156 Eric Desjardins .04 .10
157 Matt Schneider .02 .05
158 Capitals Logo .02 .05
159 Don Beaupre .04 .10
160 Dino Ciccarelli .04 .10
161 Michal Pivonka .02 .05
162 Mike Ridley .02 .05
163 Randy Burridge .02 .05
164 Peter Bondra .20 .50
165 Dale Hunter .02 .05
166 Kelly Miller .02 .05
167 Kevin Hatcher .04 .10
168 Al Iafrate .02 .05
169 Rod Langway .02 .05
170 Devils Logo .02 .05
171 Chris Terreri .04 .10
172 Claude Lemieux .04 .10
173 Stephane Richer .04 .10
174 Peter Stastny .04 .10
175 Zdeno Ciger .02 .05
176 Alexander Semak .02 .05
177 Valeri Zelepukin .02 .05
178 Bruce Driver .02 .05
179 Scott Niedermayer .02 .05
180 Alexei Kasatonov .02 .05
181 Scott Stevens .04 .10
182 Flyers Logo .02 .05
183 Dominic Roussel .04 .10
184 Mike Ricci .02 .05
185 Mark Recchi .04 .10
186 Kevin Dineen .02 .05
187 Rod Brind'Amour .02 .05
188 Mark Pederson .02 .05
189 Pelle Eklund .02 .05
190 Terry Carkner .02 .05
191 Mark Howe .02 .05
192 Steve Duchesne .02 .05
193 Andrei Lomakin .02 .05
194 Islanders Logo .02 .05
195 Mark Fitzpatrick .04 .10
196 Pierre Turgeon .04 .10
197 Benoit Hogue .02 .05
198 Ray Ferraro .02 .05
199 Derek King .02 .05
200 David Volek .02 .05
201 Patrick Flatley .02 .05
202 Uwe Krupp .02 .05
203 Steve Thomas .02 .05
204 Adam Creighton .02 .05
205 Jeff Norton .02 .05
206 Nordiques Logo .02 .05
207 Stephane Fiset .04 .10
208 Mikhail Tatarinov .02 .05
209 Joe Sakic .50 1.25
210 Owen Nolan .04 .10
211 Mike Hough .02 .05
212 Mats Sundin .20 .50
213 Claude Lapointe .02 .05
214 Stephane Morin .02 .05
215 Alexei Gusarov .02 .05
216 Steven Finn .02 .05
217 Curtis Leschyshyn .02 .05
218 Penguins Logo .02 .05
219 Tom Barrasso .04 .10
220 Mario Lemieux .60 1.50
221 Kevin Stevens .02 .05
222 Shawn McEachern .02 .05
223 Joe Mullen .04 .10
224 Ron Francis .04 .10
225 Phil Bourque .02 .05
226 Rick Tocchet .04 .10
227 Bryan Trottier .04 .10
228 Larry Murphy .04 .10
229 Ulf Samuelsson .02 .05
230 Rangers Logo .02 .05
231 Mike Richter .20 .50
232 John Vanbiesbrouck .20 .50
233 Mark Messier .30 .75
234 Sergei Nemchinov .02 .05
235 Darren Turcotte .04 .10
236 Doug Weight .04 .10
237 Mike Gartner .04 .10
238 Adam Graves .04 .10
239 Brian Leetch .20 .50
240 James Patrick .02 .05
241 Jan Erixon .02 .05
242 Sabres Logo .02 .05
243 Tom Draper .02 .05
244 Grant Ledyard .02 .05
245 Doug Bodger .02 .05
246 Pat LaFontaine .20 .50
247 Dale Hawerchuk .04 .10
248 Alexander Mogilny .04 .10
249 Dave Andreychuk .04 .10
250 Christian Ruuttu .02 .05
251 Randy Wood .02 .05
252 Brad May .04 .10
253 Mike Ramsey .02 .05
254 Whalers Logo .02 .05
255 Kay Whitmore .04 .10
256 Pat Verbeek .04 .10
257 John Cullen .02 .05
258 Mikael Andersson .02 .05
259 Yvon Corriveau .02 .05
260 Randy Cunneyworth .02 .05
261 Robert Holik .02 .05
262 Murray Craven .02 .05
263 Zarley Zalapski .02 .05
264 Adam Burt .02 .05
265 Brad Shaw .02 .05
266 Lightning Logo .02 .05
267 Lightning Jersey .02 .05
268 Senators Logo .02 .05
269 Senators Jersey .02 .05
270 Tony Amonte .04 .10
271 Pavel Bure .60 1.50
272 Gilbert Dionne .02 .05
273 Pat Falloon .02 .05
274 Nicklas Lidstrom .20 .50
275 Kevin Todd .02 .05
276 Prince of Wales Conference Logo .02 .05
277 Patrick Roy AS .60 1.50
278 Paul Coffey AS .20 .50
279 Ray Bourque AS .30 .75
280 Mario Lemieux AS .60 1.50
281 Kevin Stevens AS .02 .05
282 Jaromir Jagr AS .80 2.00
283 Clarence Campbell Conference Logo .02 .05
284 Ed Belfour AS .20 .50
285 Al MacInnis AS .04 .10
286 Chris Chelios AS .20 .50
287 Wayne Gretzky AS .80 2.00
288 Luc Robitaille AS .04 .10
289 Brett Hull AS .20 .50
290 Pavel Bure .60 1.50
291 Sergei Fedorov .50 1.25
292 Dominik Hasek .50 1.25
293 Robert Holik .02 .05
294 Jaromir Jagr .80 2.00
295 Valeri Kamensky .02 .05
296 Alexander Semak .02 .05
297 Igor Kravchuk .02 .05
298 Nicklas Lidstrom .20 .50
299 Alexander Mogilny .04 .10
300 Petr Nedved .04 .10
301 Robert Reichel .02 .05
302 Mats Sundin .20 .50
303 Calder Trophy .02 .05
304 Hart Trophy .02 .05
305 Lady Byng Trophy .02 .05
306 Norris Trophy .02 .05
307 Selke Trophy .02 .05
308 Vezina Trophy .02 .05
A Igor Kravchuk .16 .40
B Nelson Emerson .16 .40
C Pavel Bure 1.60 4.00
D Tomas Forsland .16 .40
E Luciano Borsato .16 .40
F Darryl Sydor .16 .40
G Felix Potvin .20 .50
H Derian Hatcher .16 .40
I Joseph Beranek .16 .40
J Nicklas Lidstrom .20 .50
K Pat Falloon .16 .40
L Joe Juneau .16 .40
M Gilbert Dionne .16 .40
N Dimitri Khristich .16 .40
O Kevin Todd .16 .40
P Eric Lindros 2.00 5.00
Q Scott Lachance .16 .40
R Valeri Kamensky .16 .40
S Jaromir Jagr 2.00 5.00
T Tony Amonte .16 .40
U Donald Audette .16 .40
V Geoff Sanderson .16 .40
xx Sticker Album .60 1.50

1993-94 Panini Stickers

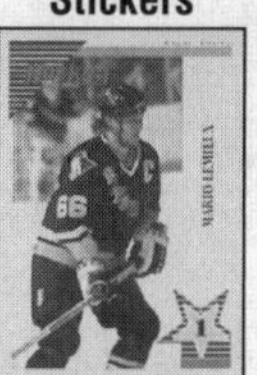

This set of 300 stickers was produced by Panini. They measure approximately 2 3/8" by 3 3/8" and were to be pasted in a 9" by 11" sticker album. The fronts have action color player photos with the player's name and the team name printed to the left side of the photo. The backs promote collecting Panini stickers. Also included are a subset Best of the Best (133-144), and a subset of 24 glitter stickers of Panini's superstars (A-X), one per team. The stickers are numbered on the back. The album also includes players' statistics and a Stanley Cup final review.

COMPLETE SET (300) 10.00 25.00
1 Bruins Logo .02 .05
2 Adam Oates .04 .10
3 Cam Neely .20 .50
4 Dave Poulin .02 .05
5 Steve Leach .02 .05
6 Glen Wesley .02 .05
7 Dmitri Kvartalnov .02 .05
8 Ted Donato .02 .05
9 Andy Moog .04 .10
10 Ray Bourque .40 1.00
11 Don Sweeney .02 .05
12 Canadiens Logo .02 .05
13 Vincent Damphousse .04 .10
14 Kirk Muller .04 .10
15 Brian Bellows .02 .05
16 Stephan Lebeau .02 .05
17 Denis Savard .04 .10
18 Gilbert Dionne .02 .05
19 Guy Carbonneau .04 .10
20 Benoit Brunet .02 .05
21 Eric Desjardins .04 .10
22 Mathieu Schneider .02 .05
23 Capitals Logo .02 .05
24 Peter Bondra .04 .10
25 Mike Ridley .02 .05
26 Dale Hunter .02 .05
27 Michal Pivonka .02 .05
28 Dimitri Khristich .04 .10
29 Pat Elynuik .02 .05
30 Kelly Miller .02 .05
31 Calle Johansson .02 .05
32 Al Iafrate .02 .05
33 Don Beaupre .04 .10
34 Devils Logo .02 .05
35 Claude Lemieux .04 .10
36 Alexander Semak .02 .05
37 Stephane Richer .04 .10
38 Valeri Zelepukin .02 .05
39 Bernie Nicholls .04 .10
40 John MacLean .02 .05
41 Peter Stastny .04 .10
42 Scott Niedermayer .02 .05
43 Scott Stevens .04 .10
44 Bruce Driver .02 .05
45 Flyers Logo .02 .05
46 Mark Recchi .04 .10
47 Rod Brind'Amour .04 .10
48 Brent Fedyk .02 .05
49 Kevin Dineen .02 .05
50 Keith Acton .02 .05
51 Pelle Eklund .02 .05
52 Andrei Lomakin .02 .05
53 Garry Galley .02 .05
54 Terry Carkner .02 .05
55 Tommy Soderstrom .02 .05
56 Islanders Logo .02 .05
57 Steve Thomas .02 .05
58 Derek King .02 .05
59 Benoit Hogue .02 .05
60 Patrick Flatley .02 .05
61 Brian Mullen .02 .05
62 Marty McInnis .02 .05
63 Scott Lachance .02 .05
64 Jeff Norton .02 .05
65 Glenn Healy .04 .10
66 Mark Fitzpatrick .04 .10
67 Nordiques Logo .02 .05
68 Mats Sundin .04 .10
69 Mike Ricci .02 .05
70 Owen Nolan .04 .10
71 Andrei Kovalenko .02 .05
72 Valeri Kamensky .02 .05
73 Scott Young .02 .05
74 Martin Rucinsky .02 .05
75 Steven Finn .02 .05
76 Steve Duchesne .02 .05
77 Ron Hextall .04 .10
78 Penguins Logo .02 .05
79 Kevin Stevens .02 .05
80 Rick Tocchet .04 .10
81 Ron Francis .04 .10
82 Jaromir Jagr .20 .50
83 Joe Mullen .04 .10
84 Shawn McEachern .02 .05
85 Dave Tippett .02 .05
86 Larry Murphy .04 .10
87 Ulf Samuelsson .02 .05
88 Tom Barrasso .04 .10
89 Rangers Logo .02 .05
90 Tony Amonte .04 .10
91 Mike Gartner .20 .50
92 Adam Graves .04 .10
93 Sergei Nemchinov .02 .05
94 Darren Turcotte .02 .05
95 Esa Tikkanen .04 .10
96 Brian Leetch .20 .50
97 Kevin Lowe .04 .10

98 John Vanbiesbrouck .20 .50
99 Mike Richter .04 .10
100 Sabres Logo .02 .05
101 Pat LaFontaine .20 .50
102 Dale Hawerchuk .04 .10
103 Donald Audette .04 .10
104 Bob Sweeney .02 .05
105 Randy Wood .02 .05
106 Yuri Khmylev .02 .05
107 Wayne Presley .02 .05
108 Grant Fuhr .20 .50
109 Doug Bodger .02 .05
110 Richard Smehlik .02 .05
111 Senators Logo .02 .05
112 Norm Maciver .02 .05
113 Jamie Baker .02 .05
114 Bob Kudelski .02 .05
115 Jody Hull .02 .05
116 Mike Peluso .02 .05
117 Mark Lamb .02 .05
118 Mark Freer .02 .05
119 Neil Brady .02 .05
120 Brad Shaw .02 .05
121 Peter Sidorkiewicz .04 .10
122 Whalers Logo .02 .05
123 Andrew Cassels .02 .05
124 Pat Verbeek .02 .05
125 Terry Yake .02 .05
126 Patrick Poulin .02 .05
127 Mark Janssens .02 .05
128 Michael Nylander .02 .05
129 Zarley Zalapski .02 .05
130 Eric Weinrich .02 .05
131 Sean Burke .04 .10
132 Frank Pietrangelo .04 .10
133 Phil Housley .02 .05
134 Paul Coffey .20 .50
135 Larry Murphy .04 .10
136 Mario Lemieux .60 1.50
137 Pat LaFontaine .20 .50
138 Adam Oates .04 .10
139 Felix Potvin .20 .50
140 Ed Belfour .20 .50
141 Tom Barrasso .04 .10
142 Teemu Selanne .30 .75
143 Joe Juneau .02 .05
144 Eric Lindros .20 .50
145 Blackhawks Logo .02 .05
146 Steve Larmer .04 .10
147 Dirk Graham .02 .05
148 Michel Goulet .04 .10
149 Brian Noonan .02 .05
150 Stephane Matteau .02 .05
151 Brent Sutter .02 .05
152 Jocelyn Lemieux .02 .05
153 Chris Chelios .20 .50
154 Steve Smith .02 .05
155 Ed Belfour .20 .50
156 Blues Logo .02 .05
157 Craig Janney .02 .05
158 Brendan Shanahan .20 .50
159 Nelson Emerson .02 .05
160 Rich Sutter .02 .05
161 Ron Sutter .02 .05
162 Ron Wilson .02 .05
163 Bob Bassen .02 .05
164 Garth Butcher .02 .05
165 Jeff Brown .02 .05
166 Curtis Joseph .04 .10
167 Canucks Logo .02 .05
168 Cliff Ronning .02 .05
169 Murray Craven .02 .05
170 Geoff Courtnall .02 .05
171 Petr Nedved .04 .10
172 Trevor Linden .04 .10
173 Greg Adams .02 .05
174 Anatoli Semenov .02 .05
175 Jyrki Lumme .02 .05
176 Doug Lidster .02 .05
177 Kirk McLean .04 .10
178 Flames Logo .02 .05
179 Theo Fleury .20 .50
180 Robert Reichel .02 .05
181 Gary Roberts .04 .10
182 Joe Nieuwendyk .04 .10
183 Sergei Makarov .02 .05
184 Paul Ranheim .02 .05
185 Joel Otto .02 .05
186 Gary Suter .04 .10
187 Jeff Reese .02 .05
188 Mike Vernon .04 .10
189 Jets Logo .02 .05
190 Alexei Zhamnov .02 .05
191 Thomas Steen .02 .05
192 Darrin Shannon .02 .05
193 Keith Tkachuk .20 .50
194 Evgeny Davydov .02 .05
195 Luciano Borsato .02 .05
196 Phil Housley .02 .05
197 Teppo Numminen .02 .05
198 Fredrik Olausson .02 .05
199 Bob Essensa .04 .10
200 Kings Logo .02 .05
201 Luc Robitaille .04 .10
202 Jari Kurri .20 .50
203 Tony Granato .02 .05
204 Jimmy Carson .02 .05
205 Tomas Sandstrom .02 .05
206 Dave Taylor .02 .05
207 Corey Millen .02 .05
208 Marty McSorley .02 .05
209 Rob Blake .04 .10
210 Kelly Hrudey .04 .10
211 Lightning Logo .02 .05
212 John Tucker .02 .05
213 Chris Kontos .02 .05
214 Rob Zamuner .02 .05
215 Adam Creighton .02 .05
216 Mikael Andersson .02 .05
217 Bob Beers .02 .05
218 Rob DiMaio .02 .05
219 Shawn Chambers .02 .05
220 J.C. Bergeron .02 .05
221 Wendell Young .04 .10
222 Maple Leafs Logo .02 .05
223 Dave Andreychuk .04 .10
224 Nikolai Borschevsky .02 .05
225 Glenn Anderson .04 .10
226 John Cullen .04 .10
227 Wendel Clark .04 .10
228 Mike Foligno .02 .05
229 Mike Krushelnyski .02 .05
230 James Macoun .02 .05
231 Dave Ellett .02 .05
232 Felix Potvin .20 .50
233 Oilers Logo .02 .05
234 Petr Klima .02 .05
235 Doug Weight .04 .10
236 Shayne Corson .02 .05
237 Craig Simpson .02 .05
238 Todd Elik .02 .05
239 Zdeno Ciger .02 .05
240 Craig MacTavish .02 .05
241 Kelly Buchberger .02 .05
242 Dave Manson .02 .05
243 Scott Mellanby .04 .10
244 Red Wings Logo .02 .05
245 Dino Ciccarelli .04 .10
246 Sergei Fedorov .20 .50
247 Ray Sheppard .02 .05
248 Paul Ysebaert .02 .05
249 Bob Probert .04 .10
250 Keith Primeau .02 .05
251 Steve Chiasson .02 .05
252 Paul Coffey .20 .50
253 Nicklas Lidstrom .20 .50
254 Tim Cheveldae .04 .10
255 Sharks Logo .02 .05
256 Kelly Kisio .02 .05
257 Johan Garpenlov .02 .05
258 Robert Gaudreau .02 .05
259 Dean Evason .02 .05
260 Jeff Odgers .02 .05
261 Ed Courtenay .02 .05
262 Mike Sullivan .02 .05
263 Doug Zmolek .02 .05
264 Doug Wilson .02 .05
265 Brian Hayward .04 .10
266 Stars Logo .02 .05
267 Brian Propp .02 .05
268 Russ Courtnall .02 .05
269 Dave Gagner .02 .05
270 Ulf Dahlen .02 .05
271 Mike Craig .02 .05
272 Neal Broten .02 .05
273 Gaetan Duchesne .02 .05
274 Derian Hatcher .02 .05
275 Mark Tinordi .02 .05
276 Jon Casey .04 .10
A Joe Juneau .16 .40
B Patrick Roy 1.20 3.00
C Kevin Hatcher .16 .40
D Chris Terreri .20 .50
E Eric Lindros .20 .50
F Pierre Turgeon .20 .50
G Joe Sakic .80 2.00
H Mario Lemieux 1.20 3.00
I Mark Messier .30 .75
J Alexander Mogilny .20 .50
K Sylvain Turgeon .16 .40
L Geoff Sanderson .16 .40
M Jeremy Roenick .20 .50
N Brett Hull .20 .50
O Pavel Bure .50 1.25
P Al MacInnis .16 .40
Q Teemu Selanne .60 1.50
R Wayne Gretzky 1.60 4.00
S Brian Bradley .16 .40
T Doug Gilmour .20 .50
U Bill Ranford .20 .50
V Steve Yzerman .80 2.00
W Pat Falloon .16 .40
X Mike Modano .20 .50

1995-96 Panini Stickers

This popular set of NHL player stickers was distributed primarily in Europe by Panini. The stickers -- which are about half the size of a regulation trading card -- feature action photos on the front, with the card number and licensing logos on the back.

COMPLETE SET (306) 32.00 80.00
1 Claude Lemieux .16 .40
2 Claude Lemieux .16 .40
3 Adam Oates .16 .40
4 Ted Donato .04 .10
5 Mariusz Czerkawski .04 .10
6 Sandy Moger .04 .10
7 Kevin Stevens .04 .10
8 Cam Neely .20 .50
9 Ray Bourque .40 1.00
10 Bruins Logo .04 .10
11 Don Sweeney .16 .40
12 Al Iafrate .16 .40
13 Blaine Lacher .16 .40
14 Brian Holzinger .16 .40
15 Pat LaFontaine .20 .50
16 Derek Plante .16 .40
17 Yuri Khmylev .04 .10
18 Jason Dawe .04 .10
19 Donald Audette .04 .10
20 Alexei Zhitnik .04 .10
21 Sabres Logo .04 .10
22 Richard Smehlik .04 .10
23 Garry Galley .04 .10
24 Dominik Hasek .40 1.00
25 Andrew Cassels .04 .10
26 Jimmy Carson .04 .10
27 Darren Turcotte .16 .40
28 Geoff Sanderson .16 .40
29 Andrei Nikolishin .04 .10
30 Kevin Smyth .04 .10
31 Brendan Shanahan .40 1.00
32 Whalers Logo .04 .10
33 Steven Rice .04 .10
34 Frantisek Kucera .04 .10
35 Sean Burke .16 .40
36 Brian Savage .04 .10
37 Pierre Turgeon .16 .40
38 Vincent Damphousse .16 .40
39 Benoit Brunet .04 .10
40 Mike Keane .04 .10
41 Mark Recchi .16 .40
42 Vladimir Malakhov .04 .10
43 Canadiens Logo .04 .10
44 Patrice Brisebois .04 .10
45 Stephane Quintal .04 .10
46 Patrick Roy 1.20 3.00
47 Alexandre Daigle .16 .40
48 Alexei Yashin .16 .40
49 Dan Quinn .04 .10
50 Radek Bonk .04 .10
51 Scott Levins .04 .10
52 Sylvain Turgeon .16 .40
53 Pavol Demitra .16 .40
54 Senators Logo .04 .10
55 Steve Larouche .04 .10
56 Sean Hill .04 .10
57 Don Beaupre .16 .40
58 Ron Francis .16 .40
59 Mario Lemieux 1.20 3.00
60 Bryan Smolinski .16 .40
61 Luc Robitaille .16 .40
62 Tomas Sandstrom .16 .40
63 Jaromir Jagr .60 1.50
64 Joe Mullen .16 .40
65 Penguins Logo .04 .10
66 Ulf Samuelsson .04 .10
67 Dmitri Mironov .04 .10
68 Ken Wregget .16 .40
69 Stu Barnes .04 .10
70 Jesse Belanger .04 .10
71 Rob Niedermayer .16 .40
72 Brian Skrudland .04 .10
73 Dave Lowry .04 .10
74 Jody Hull .04 .10
75 Scott Mellanby .04 .10
76 Panthers Logo .04 .10
77 Gord Murphy .04 .10
78 Magnus Svensson .04 .10
79 John Vanbiesbrouck .20 .50
80 Neal Broten .04 .10
81 Bill Guerin .16 .40
82 Claude Lemieux .16 .40
83 John Maclean .16 .40
84 Randy McKay .04 .10
85 Stephane Richer .16 .40
86 Shawn Chambers .04 .10
87 Devils Logo .04 .10
88 Scott Niedermayer .16 .40
89 Scott Stevens .16 .40
90 Martin Brodeur .50 1.25
91 Kirk Muller .04 .10
92 Derek King .04 .10
93 Patrick Flatley .04 .10
94 Brett Lindros .04 .10
95 Steve Thomas .04 .10
96 Darius Kasparaitis .16 .40
97 Scott Lachance .04 .10
98 Islanders Logo .04 .10
99 Mathieu Schneider .04 .10
100 Dennis Vaske .04 .10
101 Tommy Salo .16 .40
102 Mark Messier .24 .60
103 Ray Ferraro .04 .10
104 Petr Nedved .16 .40
105 Adam Graves .16 .40
106 Alexei Kovalev .16 .40
107 Steve Larmer .04 .10
108 Pat Verbeek .16 .40
109 Rangers Logo .04 .10
110 Brian Leetch .20 .50
111 Sergei Zubov .16 .40
112 Mike Richter .20 .50
113 Eric Lindros .60 1.50
114 Rod Brind'Amour .16 .40
115 Joel Otto .04 .10
116 John LeClair .30 .75
117 Mikael Renberg .16 .40
118 Chris Therien .04 .10
119 Eric Desjardins .16 .40
120 Flyers Logo .04 .10
121 Dimitri Yushkevich .04 .10
122 Karl Dykhuis .04 .10
123 Ron Hextall .16 .40
124 Brian Bradley .04 .10
125 John Tucker .04 .10
126 Chris Gratton .16 .40
127 Alexander Semak .04 .10
128 Brian Bellows .04 .10
129 Paul Ysebaert .04 .10
130 Petr Klima .04 .10
131 Lightning Logo .04 .10
132 Alexander Selivanov .04 .10
133 Roman Hamrlik .04 .10
134 Daren Puppa .16 .40
135 Dale Hunter .16 .40
136 Michal Pivonka .04 .10
137 Steve Konowalchuk .04 .10
138 Joe Juneau .16 .40
139 Peter Bondra .20 .50
140 Keith Jones .16 .40
141 Sergei Gonchar .16 .40
142 Capitals Logo .04 .10
143 Calle Johansson .04 .10
144 Mark Tinordi .04 .10
145 Jim Carey .04 .10
146 Eric Lindros AW .30 .75
147 Paul Coffey AW .10 .25
148 Peter Forsberg AW .24 .60
149 Dominik Hasek AW .20 .50
150 Jaromir Jagr AW .30 .75
151 Peter Bondra LL .10 .25
152 Ron francis LL .04 .10
153 Cam Neely LL .06 .15
154 Dominik Hasek LL .20 .50
155 Ian Laperriere LL .04 .10
156 Bernie Nicholls .04 .10
157 Jeremy Roenick .20 .50
158 Patrick Poulin .04 .10
159 Eric Daze .04 .10
160 Tony Amonte .16 .40
161 Sergei Krivokrasov .04 .10
162 Joe Murphy .04 .10
163 Blackhawks Logo .04 .10
164 Chris Chelios .20 .50
165 Gary Suter .04 .10
166 Ed Belfour .20 .50
167 Dave Gagner .04 .10
168 Mike Modano .24 .60
169 Todd Harvey .16 .40
170 Mike Donnelly .04 .10
171 Mike Kennedy .04 .10
172 Trent Klatt .04 .10
173 Derian Hatcher .04 .10
174 Stars Logo .04 .10
175 Kevin Hatcher .04 .10
176 Grant Ledyard .04 .10
177 Andy Moog .16 .40
178 Sergei Fedorov .40 1.00
179 Steve Yzerman .80 2.00
180 Vyacheslav Kozlov .16 .40
181 Keith Primeau .16 .40
182 Dino Ciccarelli .16 .40
183 Ray Sheppard .16 .40
184 Paul Coffey .20 .50
185 Red Wings Logo .04 .10
186 Nicklas Lidstrom .20 .50
187 Chris Osgood .20 .50
188 Mike Vernon .16 .40
189 Dale Hawerchuk .16 .40
190 Ian Laperriere .04 .10
191 David Roberts .04 .10
192 Esa Tikkanen .04 .10
193 Geoff Courtnall .04 .10
194 Brett Hull .24 .60
195 Steve Duchesne .16 .40
196 Blues Logo .04 .10
197 Al MacInnis .16 .40
198 Chris Pronger .16 .40
199 Jon Casey .16 .40
200 Doug Gilmour .20 .50
201 Mats Sundin .20 .50
202 Benoit Hogue .04 .10
203 Dave Andreychuk .16 .40
204 Mike Gartner .16 .40
205 Dave Ellett .04 .10
206 Todd Gill .04 .10
207 Maple Leafs Logo .04 .10
208 Kenny Jonsson .04 .10
209 Larry Murphy .16 .40
210 Felix Potvin .20 .50
211 Dallas Drake .04 .10
212 Alexei Zhamnov .16 .40
213 Mike Eastwood .04 .10
214 Keith Tkachuk .20 .50
215 Igor Korolev .04 .10
216 Nelson Emerson .04 .10
217 Teemu Selanne .40 1.00
218 Jets Logo .04 .10
219 Dave Manson .04 .10
220 Teppo Numminen .04 .10
221 Nikolai Khabibulin .16 .40
222 Steve Rucchin .04 .10
223 Shaun Van Allen .04 .10
224 Patrik Carnback .04 .10
225 Peter Douris .04 .10
226 Todd Krygier .04 .10
227 Paul Kariya .80 2.00
228 Bobby Dollas .04 .10
229 Ducks Logo .04 .10
230 Milos Holan .04 .10
231 Oleg Tverdovsky .16 .40
232 Guy Hebert .16 .40
233 Joe Nieuwendyk .16 .40
234 German Titov .04 .10
235 Paul Kruse .04 .10
236 Gary Roberts .04 .10
237 Theo Fleury .20 .50
238 Ronnie Stern .04 .10
239 Steve Chiasson .04 .10
240 Flames Logo .04 .10
241 Phil Housley .04 .10
242 Zarley Zalapski .04 .10
243 Trevor Kidd .04 .10
244 Peter Forsberg .50 1.25
245 Mike Ricci .16 .40
246 Joe Sakic .40 1.00
247 Wendel Clark .16 .40
248 Valeri Kamensky .04 .10
249 Owen Nolan .16 .40
250 Scott Young .04 .10
251 Avalanche Logo .04 .10
252 Uwe Krupp .04 .10
253 Curtis Leschyshyn .04 .10
254 Jocelyn Thibault .16 .40
255 Jason Arnott .16 .40
256 Jason Bonsignore .04 .10
257 Todd Marchant .04 .10
258 Scott Thornton .04 .10
259 Doug Weight .16 .40
260 Shayne Corson .16 .40
261 Kelly Buchberger .04 .10
262 Oilers Logo .04 .10
263 David Oliver .04 .10
264 Igor Kravchuk .04 .10
265 Curtis Joseph .24 .60
266 Wayne Gretzky 1.60 4.00
267 Tony Granato .16 .40
268 Dimitri Khristich .04 .10
269 John Druce .04 .10
270 Jari Kurri .04 .10
271 Rick Tocchet .16 .40
272 Rob Blake .16 .40
273 Kings Logo .04 .10
274 Marty McSorley .04 .10
275 Darryl Sydor .04 .10
276 Kelly Hrudey .16 .40
277 Craig Janney .16 .40
278 Jeff Friesen .16 .40
279 Viktor Kozlov .16 .40
280 Ray Whitney .04 .10
281 Ulf Dahlen .04 .10
282 Sergei Makarov .04 .10
283 Sandis Ozolinsh .16 .40
284 Sharks Logo .04 .10
285 Mike Rathje .04 .10
286 Michal Sykora .04 .10
287 Arturs Irbe .16 .40
288 Trevor Linden .16 .40
289 Mike Ridley .04 .10
290 Cliff Ronning .04 .10
291 Josef Beranek .16 .40
292 Roman Oksiuta .04 .10
293 Pavel Bure .50 1.25
294 Alexander Mogilny .16 .40
295 Canucks Logo .04 .10
296 Russ Courtnall .16 .40
297 Jeff Brown .04 .10
298 Kirk McLean .16 .40
299 Peter Forsberg .50 1.25
300 Paul Kariya .80 2.00
301 Chris Therien .04 .10
302 Blaine Lacher .04 .10
303 Jim Carey .16 .40
304 Jeff Friesen .16 .40
305 Ian Laperriere .04 .10
306 Kenny Jonsson .04 .10

1998-99 Panini Photocards

These postcard-like collectibles were issued in packs of five by Panini for sale primarily in Europe. The fronts featured a full-bleed action photo, while the backs carried the player's name and team. These issues were printed on very thin paper stock, which makes them somewhat condition sensitive.

COMPLETE SET (108) 20.00 40.00
1 Daniel Alfredsson .20 .50
2 Jason Allison .25 .60
3 Tony Amonte .30 .75
4 Jason Arnott .25 .60
5 Tom Barrasso .25 .60
6 Stu Barnes .20 .50
7 Ed Belfour .30 .75
8 Bryan Berard .20 .50
9 Rob Blake .25 .60
10 Peter Bondra .30 .75
11 Ray Bourque .60 1.50
12 Rod Brind'Amour .25 .60
13 Martin Brodeur .75 2.00
14 Andrew Brunette .20 .50
15 Pavel Bure .30 .75
16 Chris Chelios .30 .75
17 Vincent Damphousse .25 .60
18 Eric Daze .20 .50
19 Detroit Red Wings .20 .50
20 Mike Dunham .25 .60
21 Sergei Fedorov .50 1.25
22 Stephane Fiset .20 .50
23 Theo Fleury .30 .75
24 Peter Forsberg .75 2.00
25 Ron Francis .25 .60
26 Jeff Friesen .25 .60
27 Grant Fuhr .25 .60
28 Doug Gilmour .30 .75
29 Adam Graves .25 .60
30 Wayne Gretzky 2.00 5.00
31 Michal Grosek .20 .50
32 Dominik Hasek .60 1.50
33 Kevin Hatcher .20 .50
34 Brett Hull .40 1.00
35 Jaromir Jagr .75 2.00
36 Mike Johnson .20 .50
37 Curtis Joseph .40 1.00
38 Joe Juneau .20 .50
39 Paul Kariya 1.00 2.50
40 Nikolai Khabibulin .25 .60
41 Saku Koivu .25 .60
42 Olaf Kolzig .25 .60
43 Oleg Kvasha .20 .50
44 Vincent Lecavalier .50 1.25
45 John LeClair .40 1.00
46 Brian Leetch .25 .60
47 Claude Lemieux .20 .50
48 Trevor Linden .20 .50
49 Eric Lindros .30 .75
50 Al MacInnis .25 .60
51 Mark Messier .30 .75
52 Mike Modano .50 1.25
53 Alexander Mogilny .25 .60
54 Brendan Morrison .20 .50
55 Scott Niedermayer .25 .60
56 Joe Nieuwendyk .25 .60
57 Adam Oates .25 .60
58 Chris Osgood .30 .75
59 Zigmund Palffy .30 .75
60 Mark Parrish .20 .50
61 Michael Peca .20 .50
62 Yanic Perreault .20 .50
63 Felix Potvin .30 .75
64 Keith Primeau .25 .60
65 Chris Pronger .25 .60
66 Daren Puppa .20 .50
67 Mark Recchi .25 .60
68 Mike Richter .30 .75
69 Luc Robitaille .30 .75
70 Jeremy Roenick .30 .75
71 Patrick Roy 1.50 4.00
72 Joe Sakic .60 1.50
73 Tommy Salo .25 .60
74 Sergei Samsonov .25 .60
75 Geoff Sanderson .20 .50
76 Teemu Selanne .60 1.50
77 Brendan Shanahan .30 .75
78 Ryan Smyth .20 .50
79 Garth Snow .25 .60
80 Cory Stillman .20 .50
81 Mats Sundin .30 .75
82 Jocelyn Thibault .25 .60
83 Joe Thornton .30 .75
84 Keith Tkachuk .30 .75
85 Pierre Turgeon .25 .60
86 Oleg Tverdovsky .20 .50
87 John Vanbiesbrouck .30 .75
88 Mike Vernon .25 .60
89 Doug Weight .25 .60
90 Alexei Yashin .25 .60
91 Steve Yzerman 1.25 3.00
92 Steve Yzerman w/CUP 1.25 3.00
93 Rob Blake AW .25 .60
94 Martin Brodeur AW .75 2.00
95 Ron Francis AW .25 .60
96 Dominik Hasek AW .60 1.50
97 Jaromir Jagr AW .75 2.00
98 Sergei Samsonov AW .25 .60
99 Peter Bondra AS .30 .75
100 Ray Bourque AS .60 1.50
101 Peter Forsberg AS .75 2.00
102 Wayne Gretzky AS 2.00 5.00
103 Saku Koivu AS .25 .60
104 Eric Lindros AS .30 .75
105 Mark Messier AS .30 .75
106 Patrick Roy 1.50 4.00
107 Teemu Selanne AS .60 1.50
108 Mats Sundin AS .30 .75

1998-99 Panini Stickers

This set of undersized stickers were issued in packs of five, primarily in Europe. The fronts feature action photos, while the backs display card number and player name.

COMPLETE SET (248) 10.00 25.00
1 Teemu Selanne .60 1.50
2 Peter Bondra .30 .75
3 Wayne Gretzky 2.00 5.00
4 Jaromir Jagr .75 2.00
5 Chris Pronger .22 .56
6 Ed Belfour .30 .75
7 Bruins logo .20 .50
8 Dmitri Khristich .20 .50
9 PJ Axelsson .20 .50
10 Byron Dafoe .22 .56
11 Ted Donato .20 .50
12 Ray Bourque .60 1.50
13 Sergei Samsonov .22 .56
14 Jason Allison .22 .56
15 Sabres logo .20 .50
16 Miroslav Satan .22 .56
17 Donald Audette .22 .56
18 Michal Grosek .20 .50
19 Dominik Hasek .60 1.50
20 Richard Smehlik .20 .50
21 Mike Peca .20 .50
22 Alexei Zhitnik .20 .50
23 Hurricanes logo .22 .56
24 Trevor Kidd .22 .56
25 Nelson Emerson .20 .50
26 Curtis Leschyshyn .20 .50
27 Robert Kron .20 .50
28 Gary Roberts .22 .56
29 Sami Kapanen .20 .50
30 Keith Primeau .22 .56
31 Canadiens logo .20 .50
32 Saku Koivu .22 .56
33 Vladimir Malakhov .20 .50
34 Mark Recchi .22 .56
35 Jocelyn Thibault .22 .56
36 Peter Popovic .20 .50
37 Martin Rucinsky .20 .50
38 Jonas Hoglund .20 .50
39 Senators logo .20 .50
40 Damian Rhodes .22 .56
41 Radek Bonk .22 .56
42 Daniel Alfredsson .22 .56
43 Alexei Yashin .22 .56
44 Magnus Arvedson .20 .50
45 Janne Laukkanen .20 .50
46 Igor Kravchuk .20 .50
47 Penguins logo .20 .50
48 Jaromir Jagr .75 2.00
49 Ron Francis .22 .56
50 Darius Kasparaitis .20 .50
51 Tom Barrasso .22 .56
52 Martin Straka .22 .56
53 Alexei Morozov .20 .50
54 Fredrik Olausson .20 .50
55 Panthers logo .20 .50
56 Radek Dvorak .20 .50
57 Robert Svehla .20 .50
58 Ray Whitney .20 .50
59 Dave Gagner .20 .50
60 John Vanbiesbrouck .30 .75
61 Ed Jovanovski .22 .56
62 Viktor Kozlov .20 .50
63 Devils logo .20 .50
64 Petr Sykora .22 .56
65 Scott Niedermayer .22 .56
66 Dave Andreychuk .22 .56
67 Martin Brodeur .75 2.00
68 Bobby Holik .20 .50
69 Doug Gilmour .30 .75
70 Patrik Elias .30 .75
71 Islanders logo .22 .56
72 Tommy Salo .22 .56
73 Zigmund Palffy .30 .75
74 Bryan Smolinski .20 .50
75 Robert Reichel .20 .50
76 Sergei Nemchinov .20 .50
77 Kenny Jonsson .20 .50
78 Bryan Berard .20 .50
79 Rangers logo .20 .50
80 Wayne Gretzky 2.00 5.00
81 Adam Graves .22 .56
82 Mike Richter .30 .75
83 Brian Leetch .22 .56
84 Alexei Kovalev .20 .50
85 Ulf Samuelsson .20 .50
86 Niklas Sundstrom .20 .50
87 Flyers logo .20 .50
88 John LeClair .40 1.00
89 Petr Svoboda .20 .50
90 Rod Brind'Amour .22 .56
91 Sean Burke .22 .56
92 Dainius Zubrus .20 .50
93 Alexandre Daigle .20 .50
94 Eric Lindros .50 1.25
95 Lightning logo .20 .50
96 Mark Fitzpatrick .20 .50
97 Alexander Selivanov .20 .50
98 Mikael Renberg .20 .50
99 Rob Zamuner .20 .50
100 Karl Dykhuis .20 .50
101 Paul Ysebaert .20 .50
102 Mikael Andersson .20 .50
103 Capitals logo .20 .50
104 Peter Bondra .30 .75
105 Sergei Gonchar .60 1.50
106 Adam Oates .22 .56
107 Calle Johansson .20 .50
108 Olaf Kolzig .22 .56
109 Esa Tikkanen .20 .50
110 Andrei Nikolishin .20 .50
111 Blackhawks logo .20 .50
112 Alexei Zhamnov .20 .50
113 Eric Daze .20 .50
114 Chris Chelios .30 .75
115 Jeff Hackett .20 .50
116 Gary Suter .20 .50
117 Eric Weinrich .20 .50
118 Tony Amonte .30 .75
119 Stars logo .20 .50
120 Jere Lehtinen .22 .56
121 Joe Nieuwendyk .22 .56
122 Ed Belfour .30 .75
123 Mike Modano .50 1.25
124 Sergei Zubov .20 .50
125 Darryl Sydor .20 .50
126 Pat Verbeek .22 .56
127 Red Wings logo .20 .50
128 Chris Osgood .30 .75
129 Sergei Fedorov .60 1.50
130 Stanley Cup .20 .50
131 Igor Larionov .20 .50
132 Slava Kozlov .20 .50
133 Brendan Shanahan .50 1.25
134 Nicklas Lidstrom .30 .75
135 Steve Yzerman 1.25 3.00
136 Predators logo .20 .50
137 Jan Vopat .20 .50
138 Sergei Krivokrasov .20 .50
139 Darren Turcotte .20 .50
140 Tom Fitzgerald .20 .50
141 Joel Bouchard .20 .50
142 Scott Walker .20 .50
143 Coyotes logo .20 .50
144 Keith Tkachuk .30 .75
145 Craig Janney .20 .50
146 Oleg Tverdovsky .20 .50
147 Nikolai Khabibulin .22 .56
148 Teppo Numminen .20 .50
149 Cliff Ronning .20 .50
150 Jeremy Roenick .30 .75
151 Blues logo .20 .50
152 Brett Hull .40 1.00
153 Chris Pronger .22 .56
154 Pierre Turgeon .22 .56
155 Grant Fuhr .22 .56
156 Geoff Courtnall .20 .50
157 Pavol Demitra .22 .56
158 Steve Duchesne .20 .50
159 Maple Leafs logo .20 .50
160 Fredrik Modin .22 .56
161 Dimitri Yushkevich .20 .50
162 Tie Domi .22 .56
163 Igor Korolev .20 .50
164 Mats Sundin .30 .75
165 Felix Potvin .30 .75
166 Sergei Berezin .20 .50
167 Mighty Ducks logo .20 .50
168 Guy Hebert .22 .56
169 Teemu Selanne .60 1.50
170 Paul Kariya 1.00 2.50
171 Steve Rucchin .20 .50
172 Tomas Sandstrom .20 .50
173 Josef Marha .20 .50
174 Ruslan Salei .20 .50
175 Flames logo .20 .50
176 Theo Fleury .30 .75
177 Michael Nylander .20 .50
178 German Titov .20 .50
179 Rick Tabaracci .20 .50
180 Cory Stillman .20 .50
181 Jarome Iginla .22 .56
182 Tommy Albelin .20 .50
183 Avalanche logo .20 .50
184 Patrick Roy 1.50 4.00
185 Peter Forsberg .75 2.00
186 Alexei Gusarov .20 .50
187 Uwe Krupp .20 .50
188 Valeri Kamensky .22 .56
189 Joe Sakic .60 1.50
190 Sandis Ozolinsh .22 .56
191 Oilers logo .20 .50
192 Boris Mironov .20 .50
193 Mats Lindgren .20 .50
194 Andrei Kovalenko .20 .50
195 Curtis Joseph .40 1.00
196 Roman Hamrlik .20 .50
197 Doug Weight .22 .56
198 Janne Niinimaa .20 .50
199 Kings logo .20 .50
200 Stephane Fiset .20 .50
201 Jozef Stumpel .20 .50
202 Aki Berg .20 .50
203 Glenn Murray .20 .50
204 Vladimir Tsyplakov .20 .50
205 Rob Blake .22 .56
206 Mattias Norstrom .20 .50
207 Sharks logo .20 .50
208 Marcus Ragnarsson .20 .50
209 Jeff Friesen .22 .56
210 Owen Nolan .22 .56
211 Mike Vernon .22 .56
212 John MacLean .20 .50
213 Andrei Zyuzin .20 .50
214 Marco Sturm .20 .50
215 Canucks logo .20 .50
216 Pavel Bure .75 2.00
217 Alexander Mogilny .22 .56
218 Arturs Irbe .22 .56
219 Mark Messier .20 .50
220 Markus Naslund .30 .75
221 Mattias Ohlund .20 .50
222 Jyrki Lumme .20 .50
223 Dominik Hasek .60 1.50
224 Rob Blake .22 .56
225 Sergei Samsonov .22 .56
226 Jere Lehtinen .22 .56
227 Ron Francis .22 .56
228 Jamie McLennan .20 .50

2000-01 Panini Stickers

COMPLETE SET (212) 15.00 40.00
1 NHL logo .02 .10
2 NHLPA logo .02 .10
3 Atlanta logo .02 .10
4 Johan Garpenlov .08 .20
5 Patrick Stefan .08 .20
6 Andrew Brunette .08 .20
7 Andreas Karlsson .08 .20

8 Ray Ferraro .08 .20
9 Petr Buzek .08 .20
10 Boston logo .02 .10
11 Sergei Samsonov .20 .50
12 P.J. Axelsson .08 .20
13 Anson Carter .08 .20
14 Eric Nickulas .08 .20
15 Mikko Eloranta .08 .20
16 Joe Thornton .40 1.00
17 Buffalo logo .02 .10
18 Dominik Hasek .40 1.00
19 Curtis Brown .08 .20
20 Michael Peca .08 .20
21 Vaclav Varada .08 .20
22 Alexei Zhitnik .08 .20
23 Miroslav Satan .08 .20
24 Carolina logo .02 .10
25 Sami Kapanen .08 .20
26 Paul Coffey .20 .50
27 Marek Malik .08 .20
28 Andrei Kovalenko .08 .20
29 Arturs Irbe .20 .50
30 Ron Francis .20 .50
31 Florida logo .02 .10
32 Scott Mellanby .08 .20
33 Viktor Kozlov .08 .20
34 Jaroslav Spacek .08 .20
35 Ray Whitney .08 .20
36 Robert Svehla .08 .20
37 Pavel Bure .30 .75
38 Montreal logo .02 .10
39 Saku Koivu .20 .50
40 Trevor Linden .20 .50
41 Karl Dykhuis .08 .20
42 Sergei Zholtok .08 .20
43 Martin Rucinsky .08 .20
44 Dainius Zubrus .08 .20
45 New Jersey logo .02 .10
46 Alexander Mogilny .20 .50
47 Petr Sykora .08 .20
48 Martin Brodeur .75 2.00
49 Bobby Holik .08 .20
50 Scott Gomez .20 .50
51 Patrik Elias .08 .20
52 NY Islanders logo .02 .10
53 Brad Isbister .08 .20
54 Mariusz Czerkawski .08 .20
55 Mats Lindgren .08 .20
56 Tim Connolly .08 .20
57 Kenny Jonsson .08 .20
58 Olli Jokinen .08 .20
59 NY Rangers logo .02 .10
60 Brian Leetch .20 .50
61 Petr Nedved .08 .20
62 Radek Dvorak .08 .20
63 Valeri Kamensky .08 .20
64 Theo Fleury .20 .50
65 Jan Hlavac .08 .20
66 Ottawa logo .02 .10
67 Magnus Arvedson .08 .20
68 Igor Kravchuk .08 .20
69 Vaclav Prospal .08 .20
70 Daniel Alfredsson .20 .50
71 Shawn McEachern .08 .20
72 Radek Bonk .08 .20
73 Philadelphia logo .02 .10
74 John LeClair .08 .20
75 Eric Lindros .20 .50
76 Mark Recchi .20 .50
77 Daymond Langkow .08 .20
78 Ulf Samuelsson .08 .20
79 Valeri Zelepukin .08 .20
80 Pittsburgh logo .02 .10
81 Jaromir Jagr .60 1.50
82 Martin Straka .08 .20
83 Alexei Morozov .08 .20
84 Alexei Kovalev .08 .20
85 Robert Lang .08 .20
86 Darius Kasparaitis .08 .20
87 Tampa Bay logo .02 .10
88 Vincent Lecavalier .40 1.00
89 Fredrik Modin .08 .20
90 Jaroslav Svejkovsky .08 .20
91 Mike Johnson .08 .20
92 Pavel Kubina .08 .20
93 Petr Svoboda .08 .20
94 Toronto logo .02 .10
95 Mats Sundin .40 1.00
96 Darcy Tucker .08 .20
97 Steve Thomas .08 .20
98 Jonas Hoglund .08 .20
99 Igor Korolev .08 .20
100 Yanic Perreault .08 .20
101 Washington logo .02 .10
102 Peter Bondra .20 .50
103 Sergei Gonchar .08 .20
104 Joe Sacco .08 .20
105 Ulf Dahlen .08 .20
106 Adam Oates .20 .50
107 Calle Johansson .08 .20
108 Anaheim logo .02 .10
109 Paul Kariya .40 1.00
110 Guy Hebert .08 .20
111 Teemu Selanne .60 1.50
112 Ruslan Salei .08 .20
113 Vitali Vishnevsky .08 .20
114 Oleg Tverdovsky .08 .20
115 Calgary logo .02 .10
116 Valeri Bure .08 .20
117 Jarome Iginla .60 1.50
118 Marc Savard .08 .20
119 Andrei Nazarov .08 .20
120 Phil Housley .08 .20
121 Derek Morris .08 .20
122 Chicago logo .02 .10
123 Michael Nylander .08 .20
124 Boris Mironov .08 .20
125 Alexei Zhamnov .08 .20
126 Tony Amonte .20 .50
127 Michal Grosek .08 .20
128 Steve Sullivan .08 .20
129 Colorado logo .02 .10
130 Peter Forsberg .60 1.50
131 Patrick Roy 1.00 2.50
132 Joe Sakic .60 1.50
133 Stephane Yelle .08 .20
134 Sandis Ozolinsh .08 .20
135 Milan Hejduk .40 1.00
136 Columbus logo .02 .10
137 Geoff Sanderson .08 .20
138 Ron Tugnutt .08 .20
139 Radim Bicanek .08 .20
140 Mattias Timander .08 .20
141 Krzsystof Oliwa .08 .20
142 Espen Knutsen .08 .20
143 Dallas logo .02 .10
144 Mike Modano .40 1.00
145 Joe Nieuwendyk .40 1.00
146 Sergei Zubov .08 .20
147 Richard Matvichuk .08 .20
148 Brett Hull .40 1.00
149 Jamie Langenbrunner .08 .20
150 Detroit logo .02 .10
151 Sergei Fedorov .40 1.00
152 Brendan Shanahan .40 1.00
153 Nicklas Lidstrom .40 1.00
154 Slava Kozlov .08 .20
155 Igor Larionov .08 .20
156 Steve Yzerman .75 2.00
157 Edmonton logo .02 .10
158 Doug Weight .08 .20
159 German Titov .08 .20
160 Janne Niinimaa .08 .20
161 Roman Hamrlik .08 .20
162 Ryan Smyth .40 1.00
163 Alexander Selivanov .08 .20
164 Los Angeles logo .02 .10
165 Rob Blake .20 .50
166 Luc Robitaille .40 1.00
167 Ziggy Palffy .08 .20
168 Jozef Stumpel .08 .20
169 Glen Murray .20 .50
170 Mattias Norstrom .08 .20
171 Minnesota logo .02 .10
172 Curtis Leschyshyn .08 .20
173 Sergei Krivokrasov .08 .20
174 Antti Laaksonen .08 .20
175 Pavel Patera .08 .20
176 Sean O'Donnell .08 .20
177 Manny Fernandez .20 .50
178 Nashville logo .02 .10
179 Vitali Yachmenev .08 .20
180 Patric Kjellberg .08 .20
181 Ville Peltonen .08 .20
182 Cliff Ronning .08 .20
183 Greg Johnson .08 .20
184 Kimmo Timonen .08 .20
185 Phoenix logo .02 .10
186 Jeremy Roenick .40 1.00
187 Jyrki Lumme .08 .20
188 Travis Green .08 .20
189 Teppo Numminen .08 .20
190 Keith Tkachuk .20 .50
191 Radoslav Suchy .08 .20
192 St. Louis logo .02 .10
193 Chris Pronger .20 .50
194 Pierre Turgeon .08 .20
195 Pavol Demitra .08 .20
196 Roman Turek .08 .20
197 Michal Handzus .08 .20
198 Stephane Richer .08 .20
199 San Jose logo .02 .10
200 Vincent Damphousse .08 .20
201 Niklas Sundstrom .08 .20
202 Stephane Matteau .08 .20
203 Marcus Ragnarsson .08 .20
204 Owen Nolan .08 .20
205 Alexander Korolyuk .08 .20
206 Vancouver logo .02 .10
207 Andrew Cassels .08 .20
208 Artem Chubarov .08 .20
208 Mark Messier .40 1.00
210 Mattias Ohlund .08 .20
211 Todd Bertuzzi .20 .50
212 Markus Naslund .20 .50

2005-06 Panini Stickers

1 Sidney Crosby 4.00 10.00
2 Alexander Ovechkin 1.50 4.00
3 Mike Richards .40 1.00
4 Dion Phaneuf .75 2.00
5 Corey Perry .40 1.00
6 Henrik Lundqvist .75 2.00
7 Ilya Kovalchuk .60 1.50
8 Marian Hossa .20 .50
9 Bobby Holik .10 .25
10 Kari Lehtonen .20 .50
11 Marc Savard .10 .25
12 Jaroslav Modry .10 .25
13 Thrashers Team Logo .10 .25
14 Thrashers Action Shot A .10 .25
15 Thrashers Action Shot B .10 .25
16 Peter Bondra .10 .25
17 Slava Kozlov .10 .25
18 Patrik Stefan .10 .25
19 Joe Thornton .75 2.00
20 Brian Leetch .20 .50
21 Sergei Samsonov .10 .25
22 Patrice Bergeron .20 .50
23 Glen Murray .20 .50
24 Bruins Team Logo .10 .25
25 Bruins Action Shot A .10 .25
26 Bruins Action Shot B .10 .25
27 Andrew Raycroft .20 .50
28 Jiri Slegr .10 .25
29 Shawn McEachern .10 .25
30 P.J. Axelsson .10 .25
31 Sabres Action Shot A .10 .25
32 Sabres Action Shot B .10 .25
33 Chris Drury .20 .50
34 Daniel Briere .20 .50
35 Ryan Miller .40 1.00
36 Maxim Afinogenov .10 .25
37 J.P. Dumont .10 .25
38 Sabres Team Logo .10 .25
39 Jochen Hecht .10 .25
40 Thomas Vanek .75 2.00
41 Andrew Peters .10 .25
42 Teppo Numminen .10 .25
43 Rod Brind'Amour .10 .25
44 Eric Staal .40 1.00
45 Erik Cole .10 .25
46 Justin Williams .10 .25
47 Oleg Tverdovsky .10 .25
48 Hurricanes Action Shot A .10 .25
49 Hurricanes Action Shot B .10 .25
50 Hurricanes Team Logo .10 .25
51 Cory Stillman .10 .25
52 Ray Whitney .10 .25
53 Glen Wesley .10 .25
54 Martin Gerber .20 .50
55 Roberto Luongo .75 2.00
56 Olli Jokinen .10 .25
57 Gary Roberts .10 .25
58 Joe Nieuwendyk .20 .50
59 Jay Bouwmeester .20 .50
60 Panthers Action Shot A .10 .25
61 Panthers Action Shot B .10 .25
62 Panthers Team Logo .10 .25
63 Nathan Horton .20 .50
64 Stephen Weiss .10 .25
65 Kristian Huselius .10 .25
66 Jozef Stumpel .10 .25
67 Canadiens Action Shot A .10 .25
68 Canadiens Action Shot B .10 .25
69 Jose Theodore .40 1.00
70 Saku Koivu .40 1.00
71 Alex Kovalev .10 .25
72 Michael Ryder .20 .50
73 Canadiens Team Logo .10 .25
74 Mike Ribeiro .10 .25
75 Sheldon Souray .10 .25
76 Richard Zednik .10 .25
77 Mathieu Dandenault .10 .25
78 Radek Bonk .10 .25
79 Martin Brodeur .20 .50
80 Scott Gomez .20 .50
81 Alexander Mogilny .20 .50
82 Vladimir Malakhov .10 .25
83 Brian Rafalski .10 .25
84 Jamie Langenbrunner .10 .25
85 Devils Team Logo .10 .25
86 Devils Action Shot A .10 .25
87 Devils Action Shot B .10 .25
88 Brian Gionta .10 .25
89 John Madden .10 .25
90 Zach Parise .75 2.00
91 Alexei Yashin .10 .25
92 Rick DiPietro .40 1.00
93 Miroslav Satan .10 .25
94 Jason Blake .10 .25
95 Mark Parrish .10 .25
96 Islanders Action Shot A .10 .25
97 Islanders Action Shot B .10 .25
98 Islanders Team Logo .10 .25
99 Trent Hunter .10 .25
100 Mike York .10 .25
101 Alexei Zhitnik .10 .25
102 Garth Snow .20 .50
103 Jaromir Jagr .75 2.00
104 Michael Nylander .10 .25
105 Martin Straka .10 .25
106 Darius Kasparaitis .10 .25
107 Rangers Action Shot A .10 .25
108 Rangers Action Shot B .10 .25
109 Kevin Weekes .20 .50
110 Tom Poti .10 .25
111 Rangers Team Logo .10 .25
112 Martin Rucinsky .10 .25
113 Steve Rucchin .10 .25
114 Marek Malik .10 .25
115 Dany Heatley .60 1.50
116 Jason Spezza .40 1.00
117 Dominik Hasek .75 2.00
118 Daniel Alfredsson .30 .75
119 Senators Action Shot A .10 .25
120 Senators Action Shot B .10 .25
121 Zdeno Chara .10 .25
122 Martin Havlat .20 .50
123 Senators Team Logo .10 .25
124 Mike Fisher .10 .25
125 Wade Redden .10 .25
126 Chris Phillips .10 .25
127 Flyers Action Shot A .10 .25
128 Flyers Action Shot B .10 .25
129 Peter Forsberg .75 2.00
130 Keith Primeau .10 .25
131 Simon Gagne .20 .50
132 Robert Esche .20 .50
133 Joni Pitkanen .10 .25
134 Flyers Team Logo .10 .25
135 Derian Hatcher .10 .25
136 Mike Knuble .10 .25
137 Eric Desjardins .10 .25
138 Jeff Carter .75 2.00
139 Sidney Crosby 4.00 10.00
140 Mario Lemieux 1.25 3.00
141 Mark Recchi .10 .25
142 Zigmund Palffy .10 .25
143 Sergei Gonchar .10 .25
144 Penguins Action Shot A .10 .25
145 Penguins Action Shot B .10 .25
146 Penguins Team Logo .10 .25
147 Marc-Andre Fleury .40 1.00
148 John LeClair .10 .25
149 Ryan Malone .10 .25
150 Dick Tarnstrom .10 .25
151 Vincent Lecavalier .40 1.00
152 Brad Richards .20 .50
153 Martin St. Louis .20 .50
154 Lightning Action Shot A .10 .25
155 Lightning Action Shot B .10 .25
156 John Grahame .20 .50
157 Fredrik Modin .10 .25
158 Lightning Team Logo .10 .25
159 Ruslan Fedotenko .10 .25
160 Dan Boyle .10 .25
161 Pavel Kubina .10 .25
162 Dave Andreychuk .10 .25
163 Mats Sundin .40 1.00
164 Ed Belfour .40 1.00
165 Eric Lindros .40 1.00
166 Darcy Tucker .10 .25
167 Jeff O'Neill .10 .25
168 Bryan McCabe .10 .25
169 Maple Leafs Team Logo .10 .25
170 Maple Leafs Action Shot A .10 .25
171 Maple Leafs Action Shot B .10 .25
172 Tie Domi .20 .50
173 Tomas Kaberle .10 .25
174 Matt Stajan .20 .50
175 Alexander Ovechkin 1.50 4.00
176 Olaf Kolzig .40 1.00
177 Brian Sutherby .10 .25
178 Jeff Halpern .10 .25
179 Danius Zubrus .10 .25
180 Capitals Action Shot A .10 .25
181 Capitals Action Shot B .10 .25
182 Capitals Team Logo .10 .25
183 Brendan Witt .10 .25
184 Andrew Cassels .10 .25
185 Jeff Friesen .10 .25
186 Steve Eminger .10 .25
187 Jean Sebastien Giguere .40 1.00
188 Ruslan Salei .10 .25
189 Scott Niedermayer .20 .50
190 Rob Niedermayer .10 .25
191 Sandis Ozolinsh .10 .25
192 Teemu Selanne .40 1.00
193 Mighty Ducks Team Logo .10 .25
194 Mighty Ducks Action Shot A .10 .25
195 Mighty Ducks Action Shot B .10 .25
196 Joffrey Lupul .20 .50
197 Petr Sykora .10 .25
198 Ryan Getzlaf .75 2.00
199 Jarome Iginla .75 2.00
200 Miikka Kiprusoff .60 1.50
201 Shean Donovan .10 .25
202 Roman Hamrlik .10 .25
203 Daymond Langkow .10 .25
204 Steven Reinprecht .10 .25
205 Flames Team Logo .10 .25
206 Flames Action Shot A .10 .25
207 Flames Action Shot B .10 .25
208 Chuck Kobasew .10 .25
209 Jordan Leopold .10 .25
210 Tony Amonte .10 .25
211 Tuomo Ruutu .20 .50
212 Nikolai Khabibulin .20 .50
213 Jassen Cullimore .10 .25
214 Adrian Aucoin .10 .25
215 Tyler Arnason .10 .25
216 Blackhawks Team Logo .10 .25
217 Matthew Barnaby .10 .25
218 Blackhawks Action Shot A .10 .25
219 Blackhawks Action Shot B .10 .25
220 Mark Bell .10 .25
221 Kyle Calder .10 .25
222 Martin Lapointe .10 .25
223 Joe Sakic 1.25 3.00
224 Milan Hejduk .20 .50
225 Rob Blake .20 .50
226 Alex Tanguay .20 .50
227 David Aebischer .20 .50
228 John-Michael Liles .10 .25
229 Avalanche Team Logo .10 .25
230 Avalanche Action Shot A .10 .25
231 Avalanche Action Shot B .10 .25
232 Pierre Turgeon .10 .25
233 Andrew Brunette .10 .25
234 Steve Konowalchuk .10 .25
235 Rick Nash .60 1.50
236 Adam Foote .10 .25
237 Marc Denis .20 .50
238 Nikolai Zherdev .20 .50
239 Dan Fritsche .10 .25
240 Manny Malhotra .10 .25
241 Blue Jackets Team Logo .10 .25
242 Blue Jackets Action Shot A .10 .25
243 Blue Jackets Action Shot B .10 .25
244 Bryan Berard .10 .25
245 David Vyborny .10 .25
246 Sergei Federov .40 1.00
247 Mike Modano .40 1.00
248 Bill Guerin .20 .50
249 Sergei Zubov .10 .25
250 Jere Lehtinen .20 .50
251 Jason Arnott .10 .25
252 Stars Team Logo .10 .25
253 Brenden Morrow .20 .50
254 Stars Action Shot A .10 .25
255 Stars Action Shot B .10 .25
256 Stu Barnes .10 .25
257 Antti Miettinen .10 .25
258 Marty Turco .30 .75
259 Steve Yzerman 1.00 2.50
260 Brendan Shanahan .40 1.00
261 Nicklas Lidstrom .40 1.00
262 Kris Draper .10 .25
263 Robert Lang .10 .25
264 Pavel Datsyuk .40 1.00
265 Red Wings Team Logo .10 .25
266 Red Wings Action Shot A .10 .25
267 Red Wings Action Shot B .10 .25
268 Chris Osgood .20 .50
269 Chris Chelios .20 .50
270 Henrik Zetterberg .40 1.00
271 Ryan Smyth .20 .50
272 Chris Pronger .20 .50
273 Michael Peca .10 .25
274 Ty Conklin .20 .50
275 Georges Laraque .20 .50
276 Oilers Action Shot A .10 .25
277 Oilers Action Shot B .10 .25
278 Oilers Team Logo .10 .25
279 Ales Hemsky .20 .50
280 Jason Smith .10 .25
281 Steve Staios .10 .25
282 Radek Dvorak .10 .25
283 Luc Robitaille .40 1.00
284 Jeremy Roenick .75 2.00
285 Alexander Frolov .20 .50
286 Pavol Demitra .10 .25
287 Mattias Norstrom .10 .25
288 Kings Team Logo .10 .25
289 Kings Action Shot A .10 .25
290 Kings Action Shot B .10 .25
291 Lubomir Visnovsky .10 .25
292 Eric Belanger .10 .25
293 Mathieu Garon .20 .50
294 Mike Cammalleri .20 .50
295 Marian Gaborik .75 2.00
296 Dwayne Roloson .20 .50
297 Marc Chouinard .10 .25
298 Brian Rolston .10 .25
299 Pierre-Marc Bouchard .20 .50
300 Willie Mitchell .10 .25
301 Wild Team Logo .10 .25
302 Wild Action Shot A .10 .25
303 Wild Action Shot B .10 .25
304 Manny Fernandez .20 .50
305 Alexandre Daigle .10 .25
306 Wes Walz .10 .25
307 Paul Kariya .40 1.00
308 Steve Sullivan .10 .25
309 Tomas Vokoun .20 .50
310 Kimmo Timonen .10 .25
311 Marek Zidlicky .10 .25
312 Dan Hamuis .10 .25
313 David Legwand .10 .25
314 Predators Team Logo .10 .25
315 Scott Walker .10 .25
316 Predators Action Shot A .10 .25
317 Predators Action Shot B .10 .25
318 Greg Johnson .10 .25
319 Shane Doan .10 .25
320 Geoff Sanderson .10 .25
321 Mike Comrie .10 .25
322 Curtis Joseph .20 .50
323 Mike Ricci .10 .25
324 Paul Mara .10 .25
325 Coyotes Team Logo .10 .25
326 Coyotes Action Shot A .10 .25
327 Coyotes Action Shot B .10 .25
328 Oleg Saprykin .10 .25
329 Petr Nedved .10 .25
330 Derek Morris .10 .25
331 Blues Action Shot A .10 .25
332 Blues Action Shot B .10 .25
333 Doug Weight .10 .25
334 Keith Tkachuk .20 .50
335 Barret Jackman .10 .25
336 Eric Brewer .10 .25
337 Patrick Lalime .20 .50
338 Blues Team Logo .10 .25
339 Dallas Drake .10 .25
340 Scott Young .10 .25
341 Petr Cajanek .10 .25
342 Bryce Salvador .10 .25
343 Evgeni Nabokov .20 .50
344 Patrick Marleau .20 .50
345 Marco Sturm .10 .25
346 Brad Stuart .10 .25
347 Jonathan Cheechoo .20 .50
348 Scott Hannan .10 .25
349 Sharks Team Logo .10 .25
350 Sharks Action Shot A .10 .25
351 Sharks Action Shot B .10 .25
352 Alyn McCauley .10 .25
353 Niko Dimitrakos .10 .25
354 Wayne Primeau .10 .25
355 Markus Naslund .20 .50
356 Brendan Morrison .10 .25
357 Ed Jovanovski .10 .25
358 Todd Bertuzzi .20 .50
359 Dan Cloutier .20 .50
360 Canucks Action Shot A .10 .25
361 Canucks Action Shot B .10 .25
362 Canucks Team Logo .10 .25
363 Trevor Linden .20 .50
364 Daniel Sedin .20 .50
365 Henrik Sedin .20 .50
366 Mattias Ohlund .10 .25
367 Action Shot 1A .10 .25
368 Action Shot 1B .10 .25
369 Action Shot 2A .10 .25
370 Action Shot 2B .10 .25
371 Action Shot 3A .10 .25
372 Action Shot 3B .10 .25
373 Action Shot 4A .10 .25
374 Action Shot 4B .10 .25
375 Action Shot 5A .10 .25
376 Action Shot 5B .10 .25
377 Action Shot 6A .10 .25
378 Action Shot 6B .10 .25
379 Action Shot 7A .10 .25
380 Action Shot 7B .10 .25
381 Action Shot 8A .10 .25
382 Action Shot 8B .10 .25
383 Action Shot 9A .10 .25
384 Action Shot 9B .10 .25
385 Action Shot 10A .10 .25
386 Action Shot 10B .10 .25
387 Action Shot 11A .10 .25
388 Action Shot 11B .10 .25
389 Action Shot 12A .10 .25
390 Action Shot 12B .10 .25

2006-07 Panini Stickers

COMPLETE SET (360) 25.00 60.00
1 Atlanta Thrashers Puzzle Piece .07 .20
2 Atlanta Thrashers Puzzle Piece .07 .20
3 Atlanta Thrashers Team Logo .07 .20
4 Bobby Holik .15 .40
5 Marian Hossa .25 .60
6 Ilya Kovalchuk .40 1.00
7 Vyacheslav Kozlov .15 .40
8 Scott Mellanby .15 .40
9 Kari Lehtonen .30 .75
10 Niclas Havelid .15 .40
11 Steve Rucchin .15 .40
12 Andy Sutton .15 .40
13 Boston Bruins Puzzle Piece .07 .20
14 Boston Bruins Puzzle Piece .07 .20
15 Boston Bruins Team Logo .07 .20
16 P.J. Axelsson .15 .40
17 Patrice Bergeron .30 .75
18 Brad Boyes .15 .40
19 Glen Murray .15 .40
20 Marc Savard .15 .40
21 Marco Sturm .15 .40
22 Zdeno Chara .15 .40
23 Brad Stuart .15 .40
24 Paul Mara .15 .40
25 Buffalo Sabres Puzzle Piece .07 .20
26 Buffalo Sabres Puzzle Piece .07 .20
27 Buffalo Sabres Team Logo .07 .20
28 Ryan Miller .30 .75
29 Chris Drury .15 .40
30 Maxim Afinogenov .15 .40
31 Ales Kotalik .15 .40
32 Daniel Briere .25 .60
33 Thomas Vanek .25 .60
34 Derek Roy .15 .40
35 Brian Campbell .15 .40
36 Tim Connolly .15 .40
37 Carolina Hurricanes Puzzle Piece .07 .20
38 Carolina Hurricanes Puzzle Piece .07 .20
39 Carolina Hurricanes Team Logo .07 .20
40 Cam Ward .30 .75
41 Rod Brind'Amour .25 .60
42 Erik Cole .15 .40
43 Eric Staal .30 .75
44 Cory Stillman .15 .40
45 Ray Whitney .15 .40
46 Justin Williams .15 .40
47 Frantisek Kaberle .15 .40
48 Bret Hedican .15 .40
49 Florida Panthers Puzzle Piece .07 .20
50 Florida Panthers Puzzle Piece .07 .20
51 Florida Panthers Team Logo .07 .20
52 Todd Bertuzzi .25 .60
53 Nathan Horton .15 .40
54 Olli Jokinen .15 .40
55 Joe Nieuwendyk .25 .60
56 Rostislav Olesz .15 .40
57 Gary Roberts .15 .40
58 Josef Stumpel .15 .40
59 Jay Bouwmeester .15 .40
60 Ed Belfour .30 .75
61 Montreal Canadiens Puzzle Piece .07 .20
62 Montreal Canadiens Puzzle Piece .07 .20
63 Montreal Canadiens Team Logo .07 .20
64 Saku Koivu .30 .75
65 Alexei Kovalev .15 .40
66 Chris Higgins .15 .40
67 Mike Ribeiro .15 .40
68 Michael Ryder .25 .60
69 Sergei Samsonov .25 .60
70 Andrei Markov .15 .40
71 Sheldon Souray .15 .40
72 Cristobal Huet .40 1.00
73 New Jersey Devils Puzzle Piece .07 .20
74 New Jersey Devils Puzzle Piece .07 .20
75 New Jersey Devils Team Logo .07 .20
76 Martin Brodeur 1.00 2.50
77 Brian Gionta .15 .40
78 Patrik Elias .15 .40
79 Scott Gomez .15 .40
80 Brian Rafalski .15 .40
81 Colin White .15 .40
82 Jamie Langenbrunner .15 .40
83 John Madden .15 .40
84 Zach Parise .25 .60
85 New York Islanders Puzzle Piece .07 .20
86 New York Islanders Puzzle Piece .07 .20
87 New York Islanders Team Logo .07 .20
88 Rick DiPietro .25 .60
89 Miroslav Satan .15 .40
90 Alexei Yashin .15 .40
91 Mike York .15 .40
92 Jason Blake .15 .40
93 Brendan Witt .15 .40
94 Alexei Zhitnik .15 .40
95 Mike Sillinger .15 .40
96 Trent Hunter .15 .40
97 New York Rangers Puzzle Piece .07 .20
98 New York Rangers Puzzle Piece .07 .20
99 New York Rangers Team Logo .07 .20
100 Jaromir Jagr .50 1.25
101 Brendan Shanahan .30 .75
102 Henrik Lundqvist .40 1.00
103 Marek Malik .15 .40
104 Michal Rozsival .15 .40
105 Petr Prucha .15 .40
106 Martin Straka .15 .40
107 Michael Nylander .15 .40
108 Darius Kasparaitis .15 .40
109 Ottawa Senators Puzzle Piece .07 .20
110 Ottawa Senators Puzzle Piece .07 .20
111 Ottawa Senators Team Logo .07 .20
112 Daniel Alfredsson .25 .60
113 Jason Spezza .30 .75
114 Dany Heatley .40 1.00
115 Mike Fisher .15 .40
116 Patrick Eaves .15 .40
117 Chris Phillips .15 .40
118 Wade Redden .15 .40
119 Martin Gerber .30 .75
120 Ray Emery .25 .60
121 Philadelphia Flyers Puzzle Piece .07 .20
122 Philadelphia Flyers Puzzle Piece .07 .20
123 Philadelphia Flyers Team Logo .07 .20
124 Peter Forsberg .50 1.25
125 Kyle Calder .15 .40
126 Simon Gagne .30 .75
127 Petr Nedved .15 .40
128 Derian Hatcher .15 .40
129 Joni Pitkanen .15 .40
130 Robert Esche .25 .60
131 Mike Knuble .15 .40
132 Jeff Carter .30 .75
133 Pittsburgh Penguins Puzzle Piece .07 .20
134 Pittsburgh Penguins Puzzle Piece .07 .20
135 Pittsburgh Penguins Team Logo .07 .20
136 Sidney Crosby 2.50 6.00
137 Mark Recchi .15 .40
138 Marc-Andre Fleury .30 .75
139 Sergei Gonchar .15 .40
140 Ronald Petrovicky .15 .40
141 John LeClair .25 .60
142 Ryan Malone .15 .40
143 Ryan Whitney .15 .40
144 Nils Ekman .15 .40
145 Tampa Bay Lightning Puzzle Piece .07 .20
146 Tampa Bay Lightning Puzzle Piece .07 .20
147 Tampa Bay Lightning Team Logo .07 .20
148 Marc Denis .25 .60
149 Vincent Lecavalier .30 .75
150 Brad Richards .25 .60
151 Vaclav Prospal .15 .40
152 Dan Boyle .15 .40
153 Martin St. Louis .25 .60
154 Filip Kuba .15 .40
155 Ruslan Fedotenko .15 .40
156 Cory Sarich .15 .40
157 Toronto Maple Leafs Puzzle Piece .07 .20
158 Toronto Maple Leafs Puzzle Piece .07 .20
159 Toronto Maple Leafs Team Logo .07 .20
160 Andrew Raycroft .25 .60
161 Mats Sundin .30 .75
162 Pavel Kubina .15 .40
163 Michael Peca .15 .40
164 Darcy Tucker .15 .40
165 Tomas Kaberle .15 .40
166 Bryan McCabe .15 .40
167 Jeff O'Neill .15 .40
168 Alexander Steen .25 .60
169 Washington Capitals Puzzle Piece .07 .20
170 Washington Capitals Puzzle Piece .07 .20
171 Washington Capitals Team Logo .07 .20
172 Alexander Ovechkin 1.00 2.50
173 Richard Zednik .15 .40
174 Dainius Zubrus .15 .40
175 Olaf Kolzig .30 .75
176 Chris Clark .15 .40
177 Matt Pettinger .15 .40
178 Ben Clymer .15 .40
179 Brian Sutherby .15 .40
180 Brian Pothier .15 .40
181 Anaheim Ducks Puzzle Piece .07 .20
182 Anaheim Ducks Puzzle Piece .07 .20
183 Anaheim Ducks Team Logo .07 .20
184 Chris Pronger .25 .60
185 Scott Niedermayer .15 .40
186 Jean-Sebastien Giguere .25 .60
187 Teemu Selanne .30 .75
188 Andy McDonald .15 .40
189 Rob Niedermayer .15 .40
190 Ilya Bryzgalov .25 .60
191 Ryan Getzlaf .25 .60
192 Chris Kunitz .15 .40
193 Calgary Flames Puzzle Piece .07 .20
194 Calgary Flames Puzzle Piece .07 .20
195 Calgary Flames Team Logo .07 .20
196 Jarome Iginla .40 1.00
197 Miikka Kiprusoff .30 .75
198 Alex Tanguay .25 .60
199 Dion Phaneuf .40 1.00
200 Tony Amonte .15 .40
201 Robyn Regehr .15 .40
202 Rhett Warrener .15 .40
203 Daymond Langkow .15 .40
204 Kristian Huselius .15 .40
205 Chicago Blackhawks Puzzle Piece .07 .20
206 Chicago Blackhawks Puzzle Piece .07 .20
207 Chicago Blackhawks Team Logo .07 .20
208 Nikolai Khabibulin .30 .75
209 Martin Havlat .25 .60
210 Tuomo Ruutu .15 .40
211 Michal Handzus .15 .40
212 Radim Vrbata .15 .40
213 Bryan Smolinski .15 .40
214 Patrick Sharp .15 .40
215 Adrian Aucoin .15 .40
216 Martin Lapointe .15 .40
217 Colorado Avalanche Puzzle Piece .07 .20
218 Colorado Avalanche Puzzle Piece .07 .20
219 Colorado Avalanche Team Logo .07 .20
220 Jose Theodore .30 .75
221 Joe Sakic .60 1.50
222 Milan Hejduk .15 .40
223 Marek Svatos .15 .40
224 Pierre Turgeon .15 .40
225 Andrew Brunette .15 .40
226 Steve Konowalchuk .15 .40
227 John-Michael Liles .15 .40
228 Ian Laperriere .15 .40
229 Columbus Blue Jackets Puzzle Piece .07 .20
230 Columbus Blue Jackets Puzzle Piece .07 .20
231 Columbus Blue Jackets Team Logo .07 .20
232 Rick Nash .30 .75
233 Sergei Fedorov .30 .75
234 Fredrik Modin .15 .40
235 David Vyborny .15 .40
236 Adam Foote .15 .40
237 Rostislav Klesla .15 .40
238 Pascal Leclaire .25 .60
239 Nikolai Zherdev .15 .40
240 Jason Chimera .15 .40
241 Dallas Stars Puzzle Piece .07 .20
242 Dallas Stars Puzzle Piece .07 .20
243 Dallas Stars Team Logo .07 .20
244 Marty Turco .25 .60
245 Mike Modano .30 .75
246 Eric Lindros .30 .75
247 Sergei Zubov .15 .40
248 Jere Lehtinen .15 .40
249 Brenden Morrow .25 .60
250 Jaroslav Modry .15 .40
251 Stu Barnes .15 .40
252 Phillipe Boucher .15 .40
253 Detroit Red Wings Puzzle Piece .07 .20
254 Detroit Red Wings Puzzle Piece .07 .20
255 Detroit Red Wings Team Logo .07 .20
256 Dominik Hasek .50 1.25
257 Pavel Datsyuk .25 .60
258 Chris Chelios .25 .60
259 Nicklas Lidstrom .30 .75
260 Henrik Zetterberg .30 .75
261 Robert Lang .15 .40
262 Mathieu Schneider .15 .40
263 Kris Draper .15 .40
264 Tomas Holmstrom .15 .40
265 Edmonton Oilers Puzzle Piece .07 .20
266 Edmonton Oilers Puzzle Piece .07 .20
267 Edmonton Oilers Team Logo .07 .20
268 Dwayne Roloson .30 .75
269 Ryan Smyth .25 .60
270 Jason Smith .15 .40
271 Joffrey Lupul .15 .40
272 Ales Hemsky .15 .40
273 Fernando Pisani .15 .40
274 Raffi Torres .15 .40
275 Shawn Horcoff .15 .40
276 Jarret Stoll .15 .40
277 Los Angeles Kings Puzzle Piece .07 .20
278 Los Angeles Kings Puzzle Piece .07 .20
279 Los Angeles Kings Team Logo .07 .20
280 Alexander Frolov .15 .40
281 Rob Blake .25 .60
282 Dan Cloutier .25 .60
283 Mattias Norstrom .15 .40
284 Lubomir Visnovsky .15 .40
285 Craig Conroy .15 .40
286 Sean Avery .15 .40
287 Mike Cammalleri .15 .40
288 Dustin Brown .15 .40
289 Minnesota Wild Puzzle Piece .07 .20
290 Minnesota Wild Puzzle Piece .07 .20
291 Minnesota Wild Team Logo .07 .20
292 Manny Fernandez .25 .60
293 Marian Gaborik .40 1.00
294 Mark Parrish .15 .40
295 Pavol Demitra .15 .40
296 Brian Rolston .15 .40
297 Wes Walz .15 .40
298 Pierre-Marc Bouchard .15 .40
299 Todd White .15 .40
300 Martin Skoula .15 .40
301 Nashville Predators Puzzle Piece .07 .20
302 Nashville Predators Puzzle Piece .07 .20
303 Nashville Predators Team Logo .07 .20
304 Paul Kariya .30 .75
305 Jason Arnott .15 .40
306 Steve Sullivan .15 .40
307 Tomas Vokoun .25 .60
308 Marek Zidlicky .15 .40
309 David Legwand .15 .40

310 Martin Erat .15 .40
311 Kimmo Timonen .15 .40
312 Scott Hartnell .15 .40
313 Phoenix Coyotes Puzzle Piece .07 .20
314 Phoenix Coyotes Puzzle Piece .07 .20
315 Phoenix Coyotes Team Logo .07 .20
316 Ed Jovanovski .15 .40
317 Jeremy Roenick .40 1.00
318 Curtis Joseph .30 .75
319 Shane Doan .15 .40
320 Mike Comrie .15 .40
321 Ladislav Nagy .15 .40
322 Nick Boynton .15 .40
323 Derek Morris .15 .40
324 Steve Reinprecht .15 .40
325 San Jose Sharks Puzzle Piece .07 .20
326 San Jose Sharks Puzzle Piece .07 .20
327 San Jose Sharks Team Logo .07 .20
328 Vesa Toskala .25 .60
329 Evgeni Nabokov .25 .60
330 Joe Thornton .50 1.25
331 Jonathan Cheechoo .30 .75
332 Mark Bell .15 .40
333 Patrick Marleau .25 .60
334 Steve Bernier .15 .40
335 Scott Hannan .15 .40
336 Milan Michalek .15 .40
337 St. Louis Blues Puzzle Piece .07 .20
338 St. Louis Blues Puzzle Piece .07 .20
339 St. Louis Blues Team Logo .07 .20
340 Doug Weight .15 .40
341 Bill Guerin .15 .40
342 Martin Rucinsky .15 .40
343 Jay McKee .15 .40
344 Barret Jackman .15 .40
345 Eric Brewer .15 .40
346 Keith Tkachuk .25 .60
347 Manny Legace .25 .60
348 Petr Cajanek .15 .40
349 Vancouver Canucks Puzzle Piece .07 .20
350 Vancouver Canucks Puzzle Piece .07 .20
351 Vancouver Canucks Team Logo .07 .20
352 Roberto Luongo .60 1.50
353 Jan Bulis .15 .40
354 Markus Naslund .30 .75
355 Brendan Morrison .15 .40
356 Daniel Sedin .15 .40
357 Henrik Sedin .15 .40
358 Mattias Ohlund .15 .40
359 Sami Salo .15 .40
360 Matt Cooke .15 .40

1993-94 Panthers Team Issue

These eight blank-backed cards were printed on thin stock and measure approximately 3 3/4" by 7". They feature on their white-bordered fronts black-and-white action shots framed by a thin red line. The player's uniform number (in large red characters), his name and position, and the Panthers' logo are printed across the top. The cards are unnumbered and checklisted below in alphabetical order.

COMPLETE SET (8) 4.80 12.00
1 Joe Cirella .60 1.50
2 Tom Fitzgerald .60 1.50
3 Mike Foligno .60 1.50
4 Paul Laus .80 2.00
5 Bill Lindsay .60 1.50
6 Andrei Lomakin .60 1.50
7 Scott Mellanby .80 2.00
8 Brent Severyn .60 1.50

1994-95 Panthers Pop-ups

Issued by Health Plan of Florida, these cards measure 4" x 10". They were given away at five different home games throughout the season. Back has biographical information.

COMPLETE SET (5) 4.00 10.00
1 Brian Skrudland .60 1.50
2 John Vanbiesbrouck 1.20 3.00
3 Scott Mellanby .60 1.50
4 Stu Barnes .60 1.50
5 Jesse Belanger .60 1.50

2000-01 Panthers Team Issue

This set features the Panthers of the NHL. The cards were issued as a promotional giveaway. The perforated card sheets were stapled into a booklet with four cards per page.

COMPLETE SET (32) 10.00 25.00
1 Bill Torrey CO .04 .10
2 Chuck Fletcher GM .04 .10
3 Duane Sutter CO .10 .25
4 Panther MASCOT .04 .10
5 Slavomir Lener TR .04 .10
6 Billy Smith CO .40 1.00
7 Roberto Luongo 2.00 5.00
8 Lance Pitlick .20 .50
9 Paul Laus .40 1.00
10 Bret Hedican .20 .50
11 Mike Wilson .20 .50
12 Peter Worrell .60 1.50
13 Len Barrie .20 .50
14 Pavel Bure 2.00 5.00
15 Olli Jokinen .30 .75
16 Vaclav Prospal .20 .50
17 Ray Whitney .20 .50
18 John Jakopin .20 .50
19 Mike Sillinger .20 .50
20 Greg Adams .20 .50
21 Marcus Nilsson .20 .50
22 Serge Payer .20 .50
23 Todd Simpson .20 .50
24 Robert Svehla .20 .50
25 Viktor Kozlov .30 .75
26 Dan Boyle .20 .50
27 Scott Mellanby .20 .50
28 Anders Eriksson .20 .50
29 Trevor Kidd .30 .75
30 Ivan Novoseltsev .30 .75
31 Rob Niedermayer .20 .50
32 Lance Ward .20 .50

2003-04 Panthers Team Issue

These cards are oversized and were distributed by the team at club events. It's likely this checklist is incomplete. Additional information can be forwarded to hockeymag@beckett.com.

COMPLETE SET (18) 8.00 20.00
1 Mathieu Biron .20 .50
2 Jay Bouwmeester .40 1.00
3 Valeri Bure .20 .50
4 Matt Cullen .20 .50
5 Niklas Hagman .20 .50
6 Darcy Hordichuk .40 1.00
7 Nathan Horton 1.50 4.00
8 Kristian Huselius .30 .75
9 Olli Jokinen .40 1.00
10 Viktor Kozlov .20 .50
11 Roberto Luongo 1.25 3.00
12 Eric Messier .20 .50
13 Branislav Mezei .20 .50
14 Lyle Odelein .20 .50
15 Mikael Samuelsson .20 .50
16 Pavel Trnka .20 .50
17 Mike Van Ryn .20 .50
18 Stephen Weiss .40 1.00

1943-48 Parade Sportive *

These blank-backed photo sheets of sports figures from the Montreal area in the mid-1940s measure approximately 5" by 8 1/4". They were issued to promote a couple of Montreal radio stations that used to broadcast interviews with some of the pictured athletes. The sheets feature white-bordered black-and-white player photos, some of them crudely retouched. The player's name appears in the bottom white margin and also as a facsimile autograph across the photo. The sheets are unnumbered and are listed below in alphabetical order. It's possible that other example exist of hockey players, so any additions to this checklist are appreciated. Many players are known to appear on two versions of these cards, and those players with (2) following their name, have been found with additional cards. Photos on these cards are often the same, with only the correspondence address at the top being different. A complete checklist for this set, covering all sports, is found in the Beckett Almanac of Baseball Cards and Collectibles.

COMPLETE SET (97) 500.00 1000.00
1 George Allen 5.00 10.00
2 Aldrege Bastien 5.00 10.00
3 Bobby Bauer 12.50 25.00
Milt Schmidt
Bill Durnan
4 Joe Benoit 5.00 10.00
5 Paul Bibeault 5.00 10.00
6 Butch Bouchard 7.50 15.00
8 Toe Blake 12.50 25.00
9 Butch Bouchard (2) 7.50 15.00
10 Butch Bouchard (3) 7.50 15.00
11 Butch Bouchard 12.50 25.00
Leo Lamoureux
Bill Durnan
12 Lionel Bouvrette 5.00 10.00
13 Lionel Bouvrette (2) 5.00 10.00
14 Frank Brimsek 12.50 25.00
15 Turk Broda 12.50 25.00
16 Turk Broda (2) 12.50 25.00
17 Eddie Bruneteau 5.00 10.00
18 Modere Bruneteau 5.00 10.00
19 Modere (Mud) Bruneteau 5.00 10.00
20 J.C. Campeau 5.00 10.00
21 J.C. Campeau 5.00 10.00
22 Bob Carse 5.00 10.00
23 Joe Carveth 5.00 10.00
24 Denys Casavant 5.00 10.00
25 Denys Casavant (2) 5.00 10.00
26 Murph Chamberlain 5.00 10.00
27 Bill Cowley 10.00 20.00
28 Floyd Curry 5.00 10.00
29 Tony Demers 5.00 10.00
30 Tony Demers (2) 5.00 10.00
31 Connie Dion 5.00 10.00
32 Bill Durnan 12.50 25.00
33 Bill Durnan (2) 12.50 25.00
34 Normand Dussault 5.00 10.00
35 Normand Dussault (2) 5.00 10.00
36 Frank Eddolls 5.00 10.00
37 Bob Fillion 5.00 10.00
38 Bob Fillion (2) 5.00 10.00
39 Johnny Gagnon 5.00 10.00
40 Johnny Gagnon 17.50 35.00
Aurel Joliat
Howie Morenz
41 Armand Gaudreault 5.00 10.00
42 Armand Gaudreault (2) 5.00 10.00
43 Fernand Gauthier 5.00 10.00
44 Fernand Gauthier (2) 5.00 10.00
45 Fernand Gauthier 5.00 10.00
Buddy O'Connor
Dutch Hiller
46 Jean Gladu 5.00 10.00
47 Jean Gladu (2)
48 Leo Gravelle 5.00 10.00
49 Glen Harmon 5.00 10.00
50 Glen Harmon (2) 5.00 10.00
51 Glen Harmon (close up) 5.00 10.00
52 Doug Harvey 12.50 25.00
53 Jerry Heffernan 5.00 10.00
Buddy O'Connor
Pete Morin
54 Sugar Jim Henry 10.00 20.00
55 Dutch Hiller 7.50 15.00
56 Dutch Hiller (2) 7.50 15.00
57 Rosario Joanette 5.00 10.00
58 Michael Karakas 10.00 20.00
59 Mike Karakas 10.00 20.00
60 Elmer Lach 10.00 20.00
61 Ernest Laforce 5.00 10.00
62 Leo Lamoreaux 5.00 10.00
63 Edgar Laprade 7.50 15.00
64 Jerry Plamondon 5.00 10.00
65 Hal Laycoe 5.00 10.00
66 Paul Raymond 5.00 10.00
67 Billy Reay 7.50 15.00
68 Roger Leger 5.00 10.00
69 John Quilty 5.00 10.00
70 Jacques Locas 5.00 10.00
71 Jacques Locas (2) 5.00 10.00
72 Kenny Reardon 7.50 15.00
73 Maurice Richard 30.00 60.00
74 Harry Lumley 12.50 25.00
75 Maurice Richard (2) 30.00 60.00
76 Fernand Mageau 5.00 10.00
77 Maurice Richard 37.50 75.00
Elmer Lach
Toe Blake
78 Georges Mantha 10.00 20.00
79 Howie(Rip) Riopelle 5.00 10.00
80 Gaye Stewart 5.00 10.00
81 Georges Mantha (2) 5.00 10.00
82 Jean Marois 6.00 12.00
83 Phil Watson 5.00 10.00
84 Mike McMahon 5.00 10.00
85 Montreal Canadiens 10.00 20.00
Team Photo 1943-44
86 Montreal Canadiens
(Team Photo 1944-45
87 Montreal Canadiens
(Team Photo 1945-46
88 Montreal Canadiens
(Team Photo 1946-47
89 Gerry McNeil 12.50 25.00
90 Pierre(Pete) Morin 5.00 10.00
91 Ken Mosdell 5.00 10.00
92 Bill Mosienko 10.00 20.00
Max Bentley
Doug Bentley
93 Buddy O'Connor 5.00 10.00
94 Robert (Bob) Pepin 5.00 10.00
95 Jimmy Peters 5.00 10.00
96 Gerry Plamondon 5.00 10.00
97 Gerry Plamondon UER 5.00 10.00
(misspelled as Jerry

1997-98 Paramount

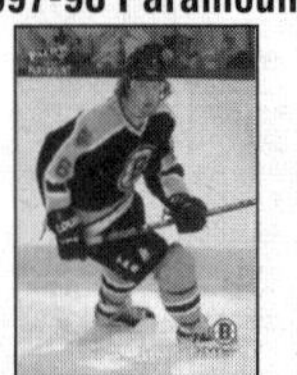

The 1997-98 Pacific Paramount set was issued in one series totaling 200 cards and distributed in five-card packs. The fronts feature color action player photos with holographic gold foil highlights. The backs carry another action player photo and player information.

COMPLETE SET (200) 10.00 25.00
1 Guy Hebert .08 .25
2 Paul Kariya .10 .30
3 Espen Knutsen RC .20 .50
4 Dmitri Mironov .02 .10
5 Steve Rucchin .02 .10
6 Tomas Sandstrom .02 .10
7 Teemu Selanne .10 .30
8 Scott Young .02 .10
9 Ray Bourque .20 .50
10 Jim Carey .08 .25
11 Anson Carter .08 .25
12 Ted Donato .02 .10
13 Dave Ellett .02 .10
14 Dmitri Khristich .02 .10
15 Sergei Samsonov .08 .25
16 Joe Thornton .25 .60
17 Matthew Barnaby .02 .10
18 Jason Dawe .02 .10
19 Dominik Hasek .25 .60
20 Brian Holzinger .02 .10
21 Michael Peca .02 .10
22 Derek Plante .02 .10
23 Erik Rasmussen .02 .10
24 Miroslav Satan .02 .10
25 Steve Begin RC .02 .10
26 Andrew Cassels .02 .10
27 Chris Dingman RC .02 .10
28 Theo Fleury .02 .10
29 Jonas Hoglund .02 .10
30 Jarome Iginla .12 .40
31 Rick Tabaracci .08 .25
32 German Titov .02 .10
33 Kevin Dineen .02 .10
34 Nelson Emerson .02 .10
35 Trevor Kidd .08 .25
36 Stephen Leach .02 .10
37 Keith Primeau .02 .10
38 Steven Rice .02 .10
39 Gary Roberts .02 .10
40 Tony Amonte .08 .25
41 Chris Chelios .10 .30
42 Daniel Cleary .08 .25
43 Eric Daze .08 .25
44 Jeff Hackett .08 .25
45 Sergei Krivokrasov .02 .10
46 Ethan Moreau .02 .10
47 Alexei Zhamnov .02 .10
48 Adam Deadmarsh .02 .10
49 Peter Forsberg .20 .50
50 Valeri Kamensky .08 .25
51 Jari Kurri .08 .25
52 Claude Lemieux .02 .10
53 Sandis Ozolinsh .02 .10
54 Patrick Roy .60 1.50
55 Joe Sakic .25 .60
56 Ed Belfour .10 .30
57 Derian Hatcher .02 .10
58 Jamie Langenbrunner .02 .10
59 Jere Lehtinen .02 .10
60 Mike Modano .20 .50
61 Joe Nieuwendyk .08 .25
62 Darryl Sydor .02 .10
63 Pat Verbeek .02 .10
64 Anders Eriksson .02 .10
65 Sergei Fedorov .15 .40
66 Vyacheslav Kozlov .02 .10
67 Nicklas Lidstrom .10 .30
68 Darren McCarty .02 .10
69 Chris Osgood .08 .25
70 Brendan Shanahan .10 .30
71 Steve Yzerman .40 1.00
72 Jason Arnott .02 .10
73 Boyd Devereaux .02 .10
74 Mike Grier .02 .10
75 Curtis Joseph .10 .30
76 Andrei Kovalenko .02 .10
77 Ryan Smyth .08 .25
78 Doug Weight .08 .25
79 Dave Gagner .02 .10
80 Ed Jovanovski .08 .25
81 Scott Mellanby .02 .10
82 Kirk Muller .02 .10
83 Rob Niedermayer .02 .10
84 Ray Sheppard .02 .10
85 Esa Tikkanen .02 .10
86 John Vanbiesbrouck .08 .25
87 Rob Blake .08 .25
88 Stephane Fiset .08 .25
89 Garry Galley .02 .10
90 Olli Jokinen RC .75 2.00
91 Luc Robitaille .08 .25
92 Jozef Stumpel .08 .25
93 Shayne Corson .02 .10
94 Vincent Damphousse .02 .10
95 Saku Koivu .10 .30
96 Andy Moog .08 .25
97 Mark Recchi .08 .25
98 Stephane Richer .02 .10
99 Brian Savage .02 .10
100 Dave Andreychuk .02 .10
101 Martin Brodeur .30 .75
102 Doug Gilmour .08 .25
103 Bobby Holik .02 .10
104 John MacLean .02 .10
105 Brian Rolston .02 .10
106 Bryan Berard .08 .25
107 Todd Bertuzzi .10 .30
108 Travis Green .02 .10
109 Zigmund Palffy .08 .25
110 Robert Reichel .02 .10
111 Tommy Salo .08 .25
112 Bryan Smolinski .02 .10
113 Christian Dube .02 .10
114 Adam Graves .02 .10
115 Wayne Gretzky .75 2.00
116 Alexei Kovalev .02 .10
117 Pat LaFontaine .10 .30
118 Brian Leetch .10 .30
119 Mike Richter .10 .30
120 Brian Skrudland .02 .10
121 Kevin Stevens .08 .25
122 Daniel Alfredsson .08 .25
123 Radek Bonk .02 .10
124 Alexandre Daigle .02 .10
125 Marian Hossa RC 1.25 3.00
126 Igor Kravchuk .02 .10
127 Chris Phillips .02 .10
128 Damian Rhodes .08 .25
129 Alexei Yashin .02 .10
130 Rod Brind'Amour .08 .25
131 Chris Gratton .08 .25
132 Ron Hextall .08 .25
133 John LeClair .10 .30
134 Eric Lindros .10 .30
135 Janne Niinimaa .08 .25
136 Vaclav Prospal RC .10 .30
137 Garth Snow .08 .25
138 Dainius Zubrus .10 .30
139 Mike Gartner .08 .25
140 Brad Isbister .02 .10
141 Nikolai Khabibulin .08 .25
142 Jeremy Roenick .15 .40
143 Cliff Ronning .02 .10
144 Keith Tkachuk .10 .30
145 Rick Tocchet .08 .25
146 Oleg Tverdovsky .02 .10
147 Tom Barrasso .08 .25
148 Ron Francis .08 .25
149 Kevin Hatcher .02 .10
150 Jaromir Jagr .20 .50
151 Darius Kasparaitis .02 .10
152 Alexei Morozov .08 .25
153 Petr Nedved .08 .25
154 Ed Olczyk .02 .10
155 Jim Campbell .02 .10
156 Kelly Chase .02 .10
157 Geoff Courtnall .02 .10
158 Grant Fuhr .08 .25
159 Brett Hull .15 .40
160 Joe Murphy .02 .10
161 Pierre Turgeon .08 .25
162 Tony Twist .08 .25
163 Shawn Burr .02 .10
164 Jeff Friesen .02 .10
165 Tony Granato .02 .10
166 Viktor Kozlov .02 .10
167 Patrick Marleau .15 .40
168 Stephane Matteau .02 .10
169 Owen Nolan .08 .25
170 Mike Vernon .08 .25
171 Dino Ciccarelli .08 .25
172 Karl Dykhuis .02 .10
173 Roman Hamrlik .02 .10
174 Daymond Langkow .08 .25
175 Mikael Renberg .08 .25
176 Alexander Selivanov .02 .10
177 Paul Ysebaert .02 .10
178 Sergei Berezin .02 .10
179 Wendel Clark .08 .25
180 Glenn Healy .08 .25
181 Derek King .02 .10
182 Alyn McCauley .08 .25
183 Felix Potvin .10 .30
184 Martin Prochazka RC .02 .10
185 Mats Sundin .10 .30
186 Pavel Bure .10 .30
187 Martin Gelinas .02 .10
188 Trevor Linden .08 .25
189 Kirk McLean .08 .25
190 Mark Messier .10 .30
191 Lubomir Vaic .02 .10
192 Mattias Ohlund .08 .25
193 Peter Bondra .08 .25
194 Dale Hunter .02 .10
195 Joe Juneau .08 .25
196 Olaf Kolzig .08 .25
197 Steve Konowalchuk .02 .10
198 Adam Oates .08 .25
199 Bill Ranford .08 .25
200 Jaroslav Svejkovsky .08 .25
P60 Mike Modano PROMO .40 1.00

1997-98 Paramount Copper

*STARS: 3X TO 6X BASIC CARDS
*ROOKIES: .6X TO 1.5X HI
STATED ODDS 1:1 HOBBY

1997-98 Paramount Dark Grey

*STARS: 3X TO 6X BASIC CARDS
*ROOKIES: .6X TO 1.5X HI
STATED ODDS 1:1 HOBBY

1997-98 Paramount Emerald Green

*STARS: 3X TO 6X BASIC CARDS
*ROOKIES: .6X TO 1.5X HI
STATED ODDS 1:1 CANADIAN PACKS

1997-98 Paramount Ice Blue

*STARS: 40X TO 80X BASIC CARDS
*ROOKIES: 8X TO 20X HI
STATED ODDS 1:73

1997-98 Paramount Red

*STARS: 6X TO 12X BASIC CARDS
*ROOKIES: .6X TO 1.5X HI
STATED ODDS 1:1 TREAT

1997-98 Paramount Silver

*STARS: 3X TO 6X BASIC CARDS
*ROOKIES: .6X TO 1.5X HI
STATED ODDS 1:1 RETAIL

1997-98 Paramount Big Numbers Die-Cuts

Randomly inserted in packs at the rate of 1:37, this 20-card set features die-cut textured cards in the shape of the players jersey number. The backs carry a small player head photo and player information in a newspaper story design.

COMPLETE SET (20) 25.00 50.00
1 Paul Kariya .75 2.00
2 Teemu Selanne .75 2.00
3 Joe Thornton 2.00 5.00
4 Dominik Hasek 1.50 4.00
5 Peter Forsberg 2.00 5.00
6 Patrick Roy 4.00 10.00
7 Joe Sakic 1.50 4.00
8 Sergei Fedorov 1.25 3.00
9 Brendan Shanahan .75 2.00
10 Steve Yzerman 4.00 10.00
11 John Vanbiesbrouck .60 1.50
12 Martin Brodeur 2.00 5.00
13 Doug Gilmour .60 1.50
14 Wayne Gretzky 5.00 12.00
15 Eric Lindros .75 2.00
16 Keith Tkachuk .75 2.00
17 Jaromir Jagr 1.25 3.00
18 Brett Hull 1.00 2.50
19 Pavel Bure .75 2.00
20 Mark Messier .75 2.00

1997-98 Paramount Canadian Greats

Randomly inserted at 2:48 Canadian retail packs only, this 12-card set features color photos of star players. The backs carry player information.

COMPLETE SET (12) 15.00 30.00
1 Paul Kariya .60 1.50
2 Joe Thornton 1.50 4.00
3 Jarome Iginla .75 2.00
4 Patrick Roy 3.00 8.00
5 Joe Sakic 1.25 3.00
6 Brendan Shanahan .60 1.50
7 Steve Yzerman 3.00 8.00
8 Ryan Smyth .50 1.25
9 Martin Brodeur 1.50 4.00
10 Wayne Gretzky 4.00 10.00
11 Eric Lindros .60 1.50
12 Mark Messier .60 1.50

1997-98 Paramount Glove Side Laser Cuts

Randomly inserted in packs at the rate of 1:73, this 20-card set features color photos of top goalies printed on a die-cut card in the shape of the goalie's glove.

COMPLETE SET (20) 50.00 100.00
1 Guy Hebert 2.00 5.00
2 Dominik Hasek 5.00 12.00
3 Trevor Kidd 2.00 5.00
4 Jeff Hackett 2.00 5.00
5 Patrick Roy 12.50 30.00
6 Ed Belfour 2.50 6.00
7 Chris Osgood 2.00 5.00
8 Curtis Joseph 2.50 6.00
9 John Vanbiesbrouck 2.00 5.00
10 Andy Moog 2.00 5.00
11 Martin Brodeur 6.00 15.00
12 Tommy Salo 2.00 5.00
13 Mike Richter 2.50 6.00
14 Ron Hextall 2.00 5.00
15 Garth Snow 2.00 5.00
16 Nikolai Khabibulin 2.00 5.00
17 Tom Barrasso 2.00 5.00
18 Grant Fuhr 2.00 5.00
19 Mike Vernon 2.00 5.00
20 Felix Potvin 2.50 6.00

1997-98 Paramount Photoengravings

Randomly inserted in packs at the rate of 2:37, this 20-card set features color images of top stars using photoengraving technology and printed with a textured paper stock finish.

COMPLETE SET (20) 20.00 40.00
1 Paul Kariya .60 1.50
2 Teemu Selanne .60 1.50
3 Joe Thornton 1.50 4.00
4 Dominik Hasek 1.25 3.00
5 Peter Forsberg 1.50 4.00
6 Patrick Roy 3.00 8.00
7 Joe Sakic 1.25 3.00
8 Mike Modano 1.00 2.50
9 Brendan Shanahan .60 1.50
10 Steve Yzerman 3.00 8.00
11 John Vanbiesbrouck .50 1.25
12 Saku Koivu .60 1.50
13 Wayne Gretzky 4.00 10.00
14 John LeClair .60 1.50
15 Eric Lindros .60 1.50
16 Keith Tkachuk .60 1.50
17 Jaromir Jagr 1.00 2.50
18 Brett Hull .75 2.00
19 Pavel Bure .60 1.50
20 Mark Messier .60 1.50

1998-99 Paramount

The 1998-99 Pacific Paramount set consists of 250 standard-size cards. The fronts feature full bleed action photos with the player's name and team logo on holographic gold foil. The flipside offers the player's statistics. Each pack contains six cards. The cards were released around October, 1998.

COMPLETE SET (250) 15.00 30.00
1 Travis Green .02 .10
2 Guy Hebert .08 .25
3 Paul Kariya .02 .10
4 Josef Marha .02 .10
5 Steve Rucchin .02 .10
6 Tomas Sandstrom .02 .10
7 Teemu Selanne .10 .30
8 Jason Allison .02 .10
9 Per Axelsson .02 .10
10 Ray Bourque .20 .50
11 Anson Carter .08 .25
12 Byron Dafoe .08 .25
13 Ted Donato .02 .10
14 Dave Ellett .02 .10
15 Dimitri Khristich .02 .10
16 Sergei Samsonov .08 .25
17 Matthew Barnaby .02 .10
18 Michal Grosek .02 .10
19 Dominik Hasek .25 .60
20 Brian Holzinger .02 .10
21 Michael Peca .02 .10
22 Miroslav Satan .08 .25
23 Vaclav Varada .02 .10
24 Dixon Ward .02 .10
25 Alexei Zhitnik .02 .10
26 Andrew Cassels .02 .10
27 Theo Fleury .02 .10
28 Jarome Iginla .15 .40
29 Marty McInnis .02 .10
30 Derek Morris .02 .10
31 Michael Nylander .02 .10
32 Cory Stillman .02 .10
33 Rick Tabaracci .02 .10
34 Kevin Dineen .02 .10
35 Nelson Emerson .02 .10
36 Martin Gelinas .02 .10
37 Sami Kapanen .02 .10
38 Trevor Kidd .08 .25
39 Robert Kron .02 .10
40 Jeff O'Neill .02 .10
41 Keith Primeau .02 .10
42 Gary Roberts .02 .10
43 Tony Amonte .08 .25
44 Chris Chelios .10 .30
45 Paul Coffey .10 .30
46 Eric Daze .08 .25
47 Doug Gilmour .08 .25
48 Jeff Hackett .08 .25
49 Jean-Yves Leroux .02 .10
50 Eric Weinrich .02 .10
51 Alexei Zhamnov .02 .10
52 Craig Billington .08 .25
53 Adam Deadmarsh .02 .10
54 Adam Foote .02 .10
55 Peter Forsberg .30 .75
56 Valeri Kamensky .08 .25
57 Claude Lemieux .02 .10
58 Eric Messier .02 .10
59 Sandis Ozolinsh .02 .10
60 Patrick Roy .60 1.50
61 Joe Sakic .25 .60
62 Ed Belfour .10 .30
63 Derian Hatcher .02 .10
64 Brett Hull .15 .40
65 Jamie Langenbrunner .02 .10
66 Jere Lehtinen .02 .10
67 Juha Lind .02 .10
68 Mike Modano .20 .50
69 Joe Nieuwendyk .08 .25
70 Darryl Sydor .02 .10
71 Roman Turek .08 .25
72 Sergei Zubov .02 .10
73 Anders Eriksson .02 .10
74 Sergei Fedorov .20 .50
75 Kevin Hodson .08 .25
76 Vyacheslav Kozlov .08 .25
77 Igor Larionov .02 .10
78 Nicklas Lidstrom .10 .30
79 Darren McCarty .02 .10
80 Larry Murphy .08 .25
81 Chris Osgood .08 .25
82 Brendan Shanahan .10 .30
83 Steve Yzerman .60 1.50
84 Kelly Buchberger .02 .10
85 Mike Grier .02 .10
86 Bill Guerin .08 .25
87 Roman Hamrlik .02 .10
88 Todd Marchant .02 .10
89 Dean McAmmond .02 .10
90 Boris Mironov .02 .10
91 Janne Niinimaa .02 .10
92 Ryan Smyth .08 .25
93 Doug Weight .08 .25
94 Dino Ciccarelli .08 .25
95 Dave Gagner .02 .10
96 Ed Jovanovski .02 .10
97 Viktor Kozlov .02 .10
98 Paul Laus .02 .10
99 Scott Mellanby .02 .10
100 Robert Svehla .02 .10
101 Ray Whitney .02 .10
102 Rob Blake .08 .25
103 Russ Courtnall .02 .10

04 Stephane Fiset .08 .25
05 Glen Murray .02 .10
06 Yanic Perreault .02 .10
07 Luc Robitaille .08 .25
08 Jamie Storr .08 .25
09 Jozef Stumpel .08 .25
10 Vladimir Tsyplakov .02 .10
11 Shayne Corson .02 .10
12 Vincent Damphousse .02 .10
13 Saku Koivu .10 .30
14 Vladimir Malakhov .02 .10
15 Dave Manson .02 .10
16 Mark Recchi .08 .25
17 Martin Rucinsky .02 .10
18 Brian Savage .02 .10
19 Jocelyn Thibault .08 .25
20 Blair Atcheynum .02 .10
21 Andrew Brunette .08 .25
22 Mike Dunham .08 .25
23 Tom Fitzgerald .02 .10
24 Sergei Krivokrasov .02 .10
25 Denny Lambert .02 .10
26 Jay More .02 .10
27 Mikhail Shtalenkov .02 .10
28 Darren Turcotte .02 .10
29 Scott Walker .02 .10
30 Dave Andreychuk .08 .25
31 Jason Arnott .02 .10
32 Martin Brodeur .30 .75
33 Patrik Elias .08 .25
34 Bobby Holik .02 .10
35 Randy McKay .02 .10
36 Scott Niedermayer .02 .10
37 Krzysztof Oliwa .02 .10
38 Sheldon Souray RC .40 1.00
39 Scott Stevens .08 .25
40 Bryan Berard .08 .25
41 Mariusz Czerkawski .02 .10
42 Jason Dawe .02 .10
43 Kenny Jonsson .02 .10
44 Trevor Linden .08 .25
45 Zigmund Palffy .08 .25
46 Rich Pilon .02 .10
47 Robert Reichel .02 .10
48 Tommy Salo .08 .25
49 Bryan Smolinski .02 .10
50 Dan Cloutier .02 .10
51 Adam Graves .02 .10
52 Wayne Gretzky .75 2.00
53 Alexei Kovalev .02 .10
54 Pat LaFontaine .10 .30
55 Brian Leetch .10 .30
56 Mike Richter .10 .30
57 Ulf Samuelsson .02 .10
58 Kevin Stevens .02 .10
59 Niklas Sundstrom .02 .10
60 Daniel Alfredsson .08 .25
61 Magnus Arvedson .02 .10
62 Andreas Dackell .02 .10
63 Igor Kravchuk .02 .10
64 Shawn McEachern .02 .10
65 Chris Phillips .02 .10
66 Damian Rhodes .08 .25
67 Ron Tugnutt .08 .25
68 Alexei Yashin .02 .10
69 Rod Brind'Amour .08 .25
70 Alexandre Daigle .02 .10
71 Eric Desjardins .08 .25
72 Colin Forbes .02 .10
73 Chris Gratton .08 .25
74 Ron Hextall .08 .25
75 Trent Klatt .02 .10
76 John LeClair .10 .30
77 Eric Lindros .10 .30
78 John Vanbiesbrouck .08 .25
79 Dainius Zubrus .02 .10
80 Dallas Drake .02 .10
81 Brad Isbister .02 .10
82 Nikolai Khabibulin .08 .25
83 Teppo Numminen .02 .10
84 Jeremy Roenick .15 .40
85 Cliff Ronning .02 .10
86 Keith Tkachuk .10 .30
87 Rick Tocchet .08 .25
88 Oleg Tverdovsky .02 .10
89 Stu Barnes .02 .10
90 Tom Barrasso .08 .25
91 Kevin Hatcher .02 .10
92 Jaromir Jagr .20 .50
93 Darius Kasparaitis .02 .10
94 Alexei Morozov .02 .10
95 Fredrik Olausson .02 .10
96 Jiri Slegr .02 .10
97 Martin Straka .02 .10
98 Jim Campbell .02 .10
99 Kelly Chase .02 .10
00 Craig Conroy .02 .10
01 Geoff Courtnall .02 .10
02 Pavol Demitra .08 .25
03 Grant Fuhr .08 .25
04 Al MacInnis .08 .25
05 Jamie McLennan .08 .25
06 Chris Pronger .08 .25
07 Pierre Turgeon .08 .25
08 Tony Twist .02 .10
09 Jeff Friesen .02 .10
0 Tony Granato .02 .10
1 Patrick Marleau .02 .10
2 Stephane Matteau .02 .10
3 Marty McSorley .02 .10
4 Owen Nolan .08 .25
5 Marco Sturm .08 .25
6 Mike Vernon .08 .25
7 Karl Dykhuis .02 .10
8 Sandy McCarty .02 .10
9 Mikael Renberg .08 .25
20 Stephane Richer .08 .25
21 Alexander Selivanov .02 .10
22 Paul Ysebaert .02 .10
23 Rob Zamuner .02 .10
24 Sergei Berezin .08 .25
25 Tie Domi .08 .25
26 Mike Johnson .02 .10
27 Curtis Joseph .10 .30
28 Derek King .02 .10
29 Igor Korolev .02 .10
30 Mathieu Schneider .02 .10
31 Mats Sundin .10 .30
32 Todd Bertuzzi .10 .30
33 Donald Brashear .02 .10
34 Pavel Bure .10 .30

235 Arturs Irbe .08 .25
236 Mark Messier .10 .30
237 Alexander Mogilny .08 .25
238 Mattias Ohlund .08 .25
239 Dave Scatchard .02 .10
240 Garth Snow .08 .25
241 Brian Bellows .02 .10
242 Peter Bondra .08 .25
243 Jeff Brown .02 .10
244 Sergei Gonchar .02 .10
245 Calle Johansson .02 .10
246 Joe Juneau .08 .25
247 Olaf Kolzig .08 .25
248 Steve Konowalchuk .02 .10
249 Adam Oates .08 .25
250 Richard Zednik .02 .10
NNO Martin Brodeur SAMPLE .75 1.50

1998-99 Paramount Copper

*STARS: 3X TO 6X BASIC CARD
STATED ODDS 1:1 US HOBBY

1998-99 Paramount Emerald Green

*STARS: 3X TO 6X BASIC CARD
STATED ODDS 1:1 CANADIAN HOBBY

1998-99 Paramount Holo-Electric

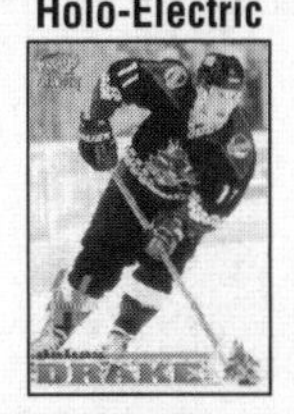

This 250-card parallel set carried a holographic silver foil and gold foil impression. Cards were numbered out of 99.
*STARS: 100X TO 200X BASIC CARDS

1998-99 Paramount Ice Blue

*STARS: 20X TO 40X BASIC CARD
STATED ODDS 1:73

1998-99 Paramount Silver

*STARS: 4X TO 8X BASIC CARD
STATED ODDS 1:1 RETAIL

1998-99 Paramount Glove Side Laser Cuts

The 1998-99 Pacific Paramount Glove Side Laser Cuts set consists of 20 cards and is an insert of the regular Pacific Paramount base set. The cards are randomly inserted in packs at a rate of 1:73. The cards feature 20 superstar goalies delivered on one of the most unique designs.

COMPLETE SET (20) 40.00 80.00
1 Guy Hebert 2.00 5.00
2 Byron Dafoe 2.00 5.00
3 Dominik Hasek 5.00 12.00
4 Trevor Kidd 2.00 5.00
5 Jeff Hackett 2.00 5.00
6 Patrick Roy 12.50 30.00
7 Ed Belfour 2.50 6.00
8 Chris Osgood 2.00 5.00
9 Mike Dunham 2.00 5.00
10 Martin Brodeur 6.00 15.00
11 Tommy Salo 2.00 5.00
12 Mike Richter 2.00 5.00
13 Damian Rhodes 2.00 5.00
14 Ron Hextall 2.00 5.00
15 Nikolai Khabibulin 2.00 5.00
16 Tom Barrasso 2.00 5.00
17 Grant Fuhr 2.00 5.00
18 Mike Vernon 2.00 5.00
19 Curtis Joseph 2.50 6.00
20 Olaf Kolzig 2.00 5.00

1998-99 Paramount Hall of Fame Bound

This 10-card set was inserted in packs at a rate of 1:361. The cards honor 10 NHL superstars on a fully foiled and etched card. A proof parallel was also created and randomly inserted in packs. Each parallel

card is limited to only 20 copies.

COMPLETE SET (10) 100.00 200.00
*PACIFIC PROOFS: 3X TO 6X BASIC INSERTS
1 Teemu Selanne 5.00 12.00
2 Dominik Hasek 8.00 20.00
3 Peter Forsberg 10.00 25.00
4 Patrick Roy 15.00 40.00
5 Steve Yzerman 15.00 40.00
6 Martin Brodeur 12.50 30.00
7 Wayne Gretzky 20.00 50.00
8 Eric Lindros 5.00 12.00
9 Jaromir Jagr 6.00 15.00
10 Mark Messier 5.00 12.00

1998-99 Paramount Ice Galaxy

Randomly inserted into Canadian retail packs only at a rate of 1:97, this 10-card set features action color player photos with bronze foil highlights. Only 140 sets were made. A silver foil parallel set was also produced. Only 50 of these sets were made. A very limited gold foil parallel set was produced with a print run of only 10 sets.

COMPLETE SET (10) 100.00 200.00
*SILVERS: 1X TO 2.5X BASIC INSERTS
GOLD NOT PRICED DUE TO SCARCITY
1 Paul Kariya 6.00 15.00
2 Peter Forsberg 8.00 20.00
3 Patrick Roy 15.00 40.00
4 Joe Sakic 6.00 15.00
5 Steve Yzerman 15.00 40.00
6 Martin Brodeur 8.00 20.00
7 Wayne Gretzky 20.00 50.00
8 Alexei Yashin 3.00 8.00
9 Eric Lindros 6.00 15.00
10 Curtis Joseph 6.00 15.00

1998-99 Paramount Special Delivery Die-Cuts

This 20-card set was inserted in packs at a rate of 1:37.

COMPLETE SET (20) 20.00 40.00
1 Paul Kariya .25 .60
2 Teemu Selanne .75 2.00
3 Sergei Samsonov .60 1.50
4 Peter Forsberg 2.00 5.00
5 Joe Sakic 1.50 4.00
6 Mike Modano 1.25 3.00
7 Sergei Fedorov 1.25 3.00
8 Brendan Shanahan .75 2.00
9 Steve Yzerman 4.00 10.00
10 Saku Koivu .75 2.00
11 Zigmund Palffy .60 1.50
12 Wayne Gretzky 5.00 12.00
13 John LeClair .75 2.00
14 Eric Lindros .75 2.00
15 Keith Tkachuk .75 2.00
16 Jaromir Jagr 1.25 3.00
17 Mats Sundin .75 2.00
18 Pavel Bure .75 2.00
19 Mark Messier .75 2.00
20 Peter Bondra .60 1.50

1998-99 Paramount Team Checklists Die-Cuts

This 27-card set was inserted in packs at a rate of 2:37. The set included the league's 1998-99 expansion franchise, the Nashville Predators.

COMPLETE SET (27) 20.00 40.00
1 Teemu Selanne .60 1.50
2 Sergei Samsonov .50 1.25
3 Dominik Hasek 1.25 3.00
4 Theo Fleury .20 .50
5 Keith Primeau .20 .50
6 Chris Chelios .60 1.50
7 Patrick Roy 3.00 8.00
8 Mike Modano 1.00 2.50
9 Steve Yzerman 3.00 8.00
10 Ryan Smyth .50 1.25
11 Dino Ciccarelli .50 1.25
12 Rob Blake .50 1.25
13 Saku Koivu .60 1.50
14 Tom Fitzgerald .20 .50
15 Martin Brodeur 1.50 4.00
16 Zigmund Palffy .50 1.25
17 Wayne Gretzky 4.00 10.00
18 Alexei Yashin .20 .50
19 Eric Lindros .60 1.50
20 Keith Tkachuk .60 1.50
21 Jaromir Jagr 1.00 2.50
22 Grant Fuhr .50 1.25
23 Patrick Marleau .20 .50
24 Rob Zamuner .20 .50
25 Mats Sundin .60 1.50
26 Mark Messier .60 1.50
27 Peter Bondra .50 1.25

1999-00 Paramount

Released as a 251-card set, Paramount featured white bordered base cards with color action photography and silver foil highlights. Paramount was packaged in 36-pack boxes with packs containing six cards and carried an SRP of $1.49. Cards #251-269 were not found in packs. They were available only as stadium giveaways as part of an NHL/NHLPA trading card promotion. They are not included in the complete set price and are not found in any of the parallel versions. #262 and #265 appear not to exist.

COMPLETE SET (251) 15.00 30.00
1 Matt Cullen .02 .10
2 Guy Hebert .08 .25
3 Paul Kariya .10 .30
4 Marty McInnis .02 .10
5 Fredrik Olausson .02 .10
6 Steve Rucchin .08 .25
7 Ruslan Salei .02 .10
8 Teemu Selanne .10 .30
9 Jason Botterill .02 .10
10 Andrew Brunette .08 .25
11 Kelly Buchberger .02 .10
12 Matt Johnson .02 .10
13 Norm Maracle .08 .25
14 Damian Rhodes .08 .25
15 Steve Staios .02 .10
16 Jason Allison .02 .10
17 Ray Bourque .20 .50
18 Anson Carter .08 .25
19 Byron Dafoe .08 .25
20 Jonathan Girard .02 .10
21 Steve Heinze .02 .10
22 Dimitri Khristich .02 .10
23 Sergei Samsonov .08 .25
24 Joe Thornton .20 .50
25 Stu Barnes .02 .10
26 Curtis Brown .02 .10
27 Michal Grosek .02 .10
28 Dominik Hasek .25 .60
29 Michael Peca .08 .25
30 Geoff Sanderson .08 .25
31 Miroslav Satan .08 .25
32 Dixon Ward .02 .10
33 Jason Woolley .02 .10
34 Alexei Zhitnik .02 .10
35 Valeri Bure .02 .10
36 Rene Corbet .02 .10
37 Rico Fata .02 .10
38 J-S Giguere .08 .25
39 Phil Housley .08 .25
40 Jarome Iginla .15 .40
41 Derek Morris .02 .10
42 Steve Smith .02 .10
43 Cory Stillman .02 .10
44 Ron Francis .08 .25
45 Martin Gelinas .02 .10
46 Arturs Irbe .08 .25
47 Sami Kapanen .02 .10
48 Jeff O'Neill .02 .10
49 Keith Primeau .02 .10
50 Gary Roberts .02 .10
51 Shane Willis .02 .10
52 Tony Amonte .08 .25
53 Eric Daze .08 .25
54 J-P Dumont .08 .25
55 Doug Gilmour .08 .25
56 Dean McAmmond .02 .10
57 Boris Mironov .02 .10
58 Jocelyn Thibault .08 .25
59 Alexei Zhamnov .08 .25
60 Adam Deadmarsh .02 .10
61 Marc Denis .08 .25
62 Chris Drury .08 .25
63 Peter Forsberg .30 .75
64 Milan Hejduk .10 .30
65 Claude Lemieux .02 .10
66 Sandis Ozolinsh .02 .10
67 Patrick Roy .60 1.50
68 Joe Sakic .25 .60
69 Ed Belfour .10 .30
70 Guy Carbonneau .02 .10
71 Derian Hatcher .02 .10
72 Brett Hull .15 .40
73 Jamie Langenbrunner .02 .10
74 Jere Lehtinen .08 .25
75 Mike Modano .20 .50
76 Joe Nieuwendyk .08 .25
77 Darryl Sydor .08 .25
78 Sergei Zubov .08 .25
79 Chris Chelios .10 .30
80 Sergei Fedorov .20 .50
81 Vyacheslav Kozlov .08 .25
82 Igor Larionov .02 .10
83 Nicklas Lidstrom .10 .30
84 Darren McCarty .02 .10
85 Larry Murphy .08 .25
86 Chris Osgood .08 .25
87 Brendan Shanahan .10 .30
88 Steve Yzerman .60 1.50
89 Josef Beranek .02 .10
90 Pat Falloon .02 .10
91 Mike Grier .08 .25
92 Bill Guerin .02 .10
93 Rem Murray .02 .10
94 Tom Poti .02 .10
95 Tommy Salo .08 .25
96 Ryan Smyth .08 .25
97 Doug Weight .08 .25
98 Pavel Bure .10 .30
99 Sean Burke .08 .25
100 Viktor Kozlov .02 .10
101 Oleg Kvasha .08 .25
102 Scott Mellanby .02 .10
103 Rob Niedermayer .02 .10
104 Marcus Nilsson .02 .10
105 Mark Parrish .02 .10
106 Ray Whitney .08 .25
107 Donald Audette .02 .10
108 Rob Blake .08 .25
109 Stephane Fiset .08 .25
110 Glen Murray .02 .10
111 Zigmund Palffy .08 .25
112 Jamie Storr .08 .25
113 Jozef Stumpel .08 .25
114 Benoit Brunet .02 .10
115 Shayne Corson .02 .10
116 Jeff Hackett .08 .25
117 Saku Koivu .10 .30
118 Trevor Linden .08 .25
119 Vladimir Malakhov .02 .10
120 Martin Rucinsky .02 .10
121 Igor Ulanov .02 .10
122 Dainius Zubrus .08 .25
123 Mike Dunham .08 .25
124 Tom Fitzgerald .02 .10
125 Greg Johnson .02 .10
126 Sergei Krivokrasov .02 .10
127 David Legwand .08 .25
128 Cliff Ronning .08 .25
129 Scott Walker .02 .10
130 Jason Arnott .02 .10
131 Martin Brodeur .30 .75
132 Patrik Elias .08 .25
133 Bobby Holik .02 .10
134 John Madden RC .25 .60
135 Randy McKay .02 .10
136 Brendan Morrison .08 .25
137 Scott Niedermayer .02 .10
138 Brian Rolston .02 .10
139 Petr Sykora .02 .10
140 Eric Brewer .02 .10
141 Mariusz Czerkawski .02 .10
142 Kenny Jonsson .02 .10
143 Claude Lapointe .02 .10
144 Mats Lindgren .02 .10
145 Vladimir Orszagh RC .02 .10
146 Felix Potvin .10 .30
147 Mike Watt .02 .10
148 Theo Fleury .02 .10
149 Adam Graves .02 .10
150 Todd Harvey .08 .25
151 Valeri Kamensky .08 .25
152 Brian Leetch .10 .30
153 John MacLean .02 .10
154 Manny Malhotra .08 .25
155 Petr Nedved .02 .10
156 Mike Richter .10 .30
157 Kevin Stevens .08 .25
158 Daniel Alfredsson .08 .25
159 Magnus Arvedson .02 .10
160 Radek Bonk .02 .10
161 Andreas Dackell .02 .10
162 Marian Hossa .10 .30
163 Shawn McEachern .02 .10
164 Wade Redden .02 .10
165 Sami Salo .08 .25
166 Ron Tugnutt .08 .25
167 Alexei Yashin .02 .10
168 Rod Brind'Amour .08 .25
169 Eric Desjardins .08 .25
170 Keith Jones .02 .10
171 Daymond Langkow .08 .25
172 John Leclair .10 .30
173 Eric Lindros .10 .30
174 Mark Recchi .02 .10
175 Mikael Renberg .02 .10
176 John Vanbiesbrouck .08 .25
177 Greg Adams .02 .10
178 Dallas Drake .02 .10
179 Nikolai Khabibulin .08 .25
180 Jyrki Lumme .02 .10
181 Teppo Numminen .08 .25
182 Jeremy Roenick .15 .40
183 Mike Sullivan .02 .10
184 Keith Tkachuk .10 .30
185 Rick Tocchet .08 .25
186 Matthew Barnaby .08 .25
187 Tom Barrasso .08 .25
188 Jan Hrdina .02 .10
189 Jaromir Jagr .20 .50
190 Alexei Kovalev .02 .10
191 Ian Moran .02 .10
192 Martin Straka .02 .10
193 German Titov .02 .10
194 Craig Conroy .02 .10
195 Pavol Demitra .08 .25
196 Grant Fuhr .08 .25
197 Jochen Hecht RC .50 1.25
198 Al MacInnis .08 .25
199 Ricard Persson .02 .10
200 Chris Pronger .08 .25
201 Pierre Turgeon .08 .25
202 Scott Young .02 .10
203 Vincent Damphousse .02 .10
204 Jeff Friesen .02 .10
205 Alexander Korolyuk .02 .10
206 Patrick Marleau .08 .25
207 Owen Nolan .08 .25
208 Mike Ricci .08 .25
209 Steve Shields .08 .25
210 Marco Sturm .08 .25
211 Ron Sutter .02 .10
212 Mike Vernon .08 .25
213 Karel Betik RC .02 .10
214 Dan Cloutier .08 .25
215 Jassen Cullimore .02 .10
216 Colin Forbes .02 .10
217 Chris Gratton .08 .25
218 Pavel Kubina .08 .25
219 Vincent Lecavalier .10 .30
220 Darcy Tucker .02 .10
221 Bryan Berard .08 .25
222 Sergei Berezin .08 .25
223 Tie Domi .08 .25
224 Mike Johnson .02 .10
225 Curtis Joseph .10 .30
226 Derek King .02 .10
227 Igor Korolev .02 .10
228 Yanic Perreault .02 .10
229 Steve Sullivan .02 .10
230 Mats Sundin .10 .30
231 Steve Thomas .02 .10
232 Adrian Aucoin .02 .10
233 Donald Brashear .08 .25
234 Ed Jovanovski .02 .10
235 Mark Messier .10 .30
236 Alexander Mogilny .08 .25
237 Bill Muckalt .08 .25
238 Markus Naslund .10 .30
239 Mattias Ohlund .08 .25
240 Garth Snow .08 .25
241 Brian Bellows .02 .10
242 Peter Bondra .08 .25
243 Jan Bulis .02 .10
244 Sergei Gonchar .02 .10
245 Olaf Kolzig .08 .25
246 Steve Konowalchuk .02 .10
247 Andrei Nikolishin .02 .10
248 Adam Oates .08 .25
249 Alexei Tezikov RC .02 .10
250 Richard Zednik .02 .10
251 Patrik Stefan RC 1.50 4.00
252 Jonathan Girard AG
253 Maxim Afinogenov AG
254 Byron Ritchie AG
255 Alex Tanguay AG
256 Brenden Morrow AG
257 Yuri Butsayev AG
258 Ivan Novoseltsev AG
259 Frantisek Kaberle AG
260 Richard Lintner AG
261 Tim Connolly AG
263 Jason Doig AG
264 Mike Fisher AG
266 Stan Neckar AG
267 Andrew Ference AG
268 Paul Mara AG
269 Steve Kariya AG

1999-00 Paramount Copper

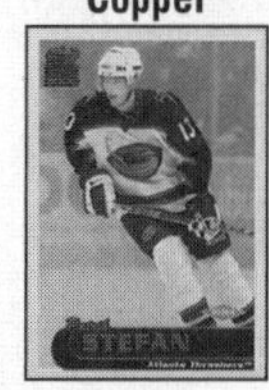

*STARS: 2X TO 5 BASIC CARDS
*ROOKIES: .75X TO 2X HI
STATED ODDS 1:1 HOBBY

1999-00 Paramount Emerald

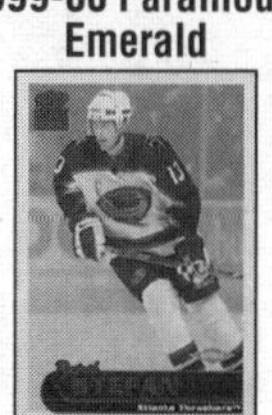

*STARS: 2X TO 5X BASIC CARDS
*ROOKIES: .75X TO 2X HI
STATED ODDS 1:1 CANADIAN

1999-00 Paramount Gold

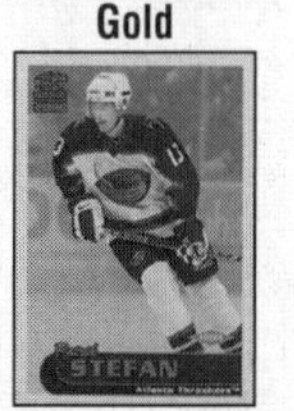

*STARS: 2.5X TO 6X BASIC CARDS
*ROOKIES: 1.25X TO 3X HI
STATED ODDS 1:1 RETAIL

1999-00 Paramount Holographic Emerald

Randomly inserted in Canadian 7-11 packs, this 251-card set parallels the base Paramount set and is enhanced with green foil highlights. Each card is serial numbered out of 99.
*STARS: 30X TO 80X BASIC CARDS
*ROOKIES: 3X TO 8X HI

1999-00 Paramount Holographic Gold

*STARS: 10X TO 25X BASIC CARDS
*ROOKIES: 1.5X TO 4X HI
STATED PRINT RUN 199 SERIAL #'d SETS
RANDOM INSERTS IN RETAIL PACKS

1999-00 Paramount Holographic Silver

*STARS: 30X TO 80X BASIC CARDS
*ROOKIES: 3X TO 8X HI
STATED PRINT RUN 99 SERIAL #'d SETS
RANDOM INSERTS IN HOBBY PACKS

1999-00 Paramount Ice Blue

*STARS: 25X TO 50X BASIC CARDS
*ROOKIES: 4X TO 10X HI
STATED ODDS 1:73

1999-00 Paramount Premiere Date

*STARS: 60X TO 150X BASIC CARDS
*ROOKIES: 5X TO 12X HI
PRINT RUN 50 SER.#'d SETS
STATED ODDS 1:37 HOBBY

1999-00 Paramount Red

Randomly inserted in Jewel Boxes, this 251-card set parallels the base Paramount set and is enhanced with red foil highlights.
*STARS: .6X TO 1.5X BASIC CARDS
*ROOKIES: .6X TO 1.5X HI

1999-00 Paramount Glove Side Net Fusions

Randomly inserted in packs at the rate of 1:73, this 20-card set features circular goalie portraits on a die cut card in the shape of a goalie's glove with actual netting.

COMPLETE SET (20) 50.00 100.00
1 Guy Hebert 2.00 5.00
2 Byron Dafoe 2.00 5.00
3 Dominik Hasek 5.00 12.00
4 Arturs Irbe 2.00 5.00
5 Jocelyn Thibault 2.00 5.00
6 Patrick Roy 12.50 30.00
7 Ed Belfour 2.50 6.00
8 Chris Osgood 2.00 5.00
9 Tommy Salo 2.00 5.00
10 Jeff Hackett 2.00 5.00
11 Martin Brodeur 6.00 15.00
12 Felix Potvin 2.50 6.00
13 Mike Richter 2.50 6.00
14 Ron Tugnutt 2.00 5.00
15 John Vanbiesbrouck 2.00 5.00
16 Nikolai Khabibulin 2.00 5.00
17 Tom Barrasso 2.00 5.00
18 Grant Fuhr 2.00 5.00
19 Curtis Joseph 2.50 6.00
20 Olaf Kolzig 2.00 5.00

1999-00 Paramount Hall of Fame Bound

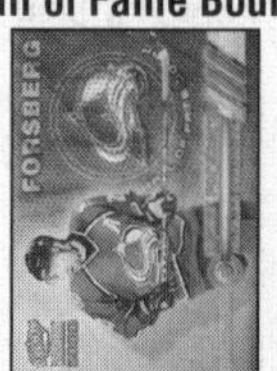

Randomly inserted in packs at the rate of 1:361, this 10-card set features future NHL hall of famers. Card fronts contain action player photos and the respective player's team logo on a "mesh jersey" card stock. A proof parallel was also created and inserted randomly. Proof were serial numbered to just 35 and their value can be determined by using the multiplier below.

COMPLETE SET (10) 75.00 150.00
*PROOFS: 1.25X TO 3X BASIC CARDS
1 Paul Kariya 5.00 12.00
2 Ray Bourque 8.00 20.00
3 Dominik Hasek 8.00 20.00
4 Peter Forsberg 10.00 25.00
5 Patrick Roy 15.00 40.00
6 Steve Yzerman 15.00 40.00
7 Martin Brodeur 12.50 30.00

8 Eric Lindros 5.00 12.00
9 Jaromir Jagr 6.00 15.00
10 Mark Messier 5.00 12.00

1999-00 Paramount Ice Advantage

Randomly inserted in Canadian packs at the rate of 2:25, this 20-card set featured top NHL players. A proof parallel was also created and randomly inserted Canadian 7-11 retail packs. Proofs were numbered to just 10 and are not priced due to scarcity.

COMPLETE SET (20) 20.00 40.00
1 Paul Kariya .60 1.50
2 Teemu Selanne .60 1.50
3 Dominik Hasek 1.25 3.00
4 Jarome Iginla .75 2.00
5 Peter Forsberg 1.50 4.00
6 Patrick Roy 3.00 8.00
7 Joe Sakic 1.25 3.00
8 Joe Nieuwendyk .50 1.25
9 Brendan Shanahan .60 1.50
10 Steve Yzerman 3.00 8.00
11 Doug Weight .50 1.25
12 Pavel Bure .60 1.50
13 Jeff Hackett .50 1.25
14 Martin Brodeur 1.50 4.00
15 Marian Hossa .60 1.50
16 Eric Lindros .60 1.50
17 Jaromir Jagr 1.00 2.50
18 Curtis Joseph .60 1.50
19 Mats Sundin .60 1.50
20 Mark Messier .60 1.50

1999-00 Paramount Ice Alliance

Randomly inserted in packs at the rate of 2:37, this 28-card set features NHL team leader portraits with their team's logo in gold foil.

COMPLETE SET (28) 20.00 40.00
1 Paul Kariya .60 1.50
2 Damian Rhodes .50 1.25
3 Ray Bourque 1.00 2.50
4 Dominik Hasek 1.50 4.00
5 Jarome Iginla .75 2.00
6 Keith Primeau .50 1.25
7 Tony Amonte .50 1.25
8 Patrick Roy 3.00 8.00
9 Mike Modano 1.00 2.50
10 Steve Yzerman 3.00 8.00
11 Bill Guerin .50 1.25
12 Pavel Bure .60 1.50
13 Luc Robitaille .50 1.25
14 Jeff Hackett .50 1.25
15 Cliff Ronning .50 1.25
16 Martin Brodeur 1.50 4.00
17 Felix Potvin .60 1.50
18 Brian Leetch .50 1.25
19 Alexei Yashin .50 1.25
20 Eric Lindros .60 1.50
21 Keith Tkachuk .60 1.50
22 Jaromir Jagr 1.00 2.50
23 Pierre Turgeon .50 1.25
24 Vincent Damphousse .50 1.25
25 Vincent Lecavalier .60 1.50
26 Curtis Joseph .60 1.50
27 Mark Messier .60 1.50
28 Peter Bondra .50 1.25

1999-00 Paramount Personal Best

Randomly inserted in packs at the rate of 1:37, this 36-card set features color portraits set against a blue background with silver foil highlights of some of the NHL's marquee players.

COMPLETE SET (36) 30.00 60.00
1 Paul Kariya .75 2.00
2 Teemu Selanne .75 2.00
3 Ray Bourque 1.25 3.00
4 Sergei Samsonov .40 1.00
5 Dominik Hasek 1.50 4.00
6 Michael Peca .40 1.00
7 Tony Amonte .40 1.00
8 Chris Drury .40 1.00
9 Peter Forsberg 2.00 5.00
10 Patrick Roy 4.00 10.00
11 Joe Sakic 1.50 4.00
12 Ed Belfour .75 2.00
13 Brett Hull 1.00 2.50
14 Mike Modano 1.25 3.00
15 Joe Nieuwendyk .40 1.00
16 Sergei Fedorov 1.50 4.00
17 Brendan Shanahan .75 2.00
18 Steve Yzerman 4.00 10.00
19 Pavel Bure .75 2.00
20 Saku Koivu .75 2.00
21 Martin Brodeur 2.00 5.00
22 Theo Fleury .40 1.00
23 Mike Richter .75 2.00
24 Alexei Yashin .40 1.00
25 John LeClair .75 2.00
26 Eric Lindros .75 2.00
27 Mark Recchi .40 1.00
28 John Vanbiesbrouck .40 1.00
29 Jeremy Roenick 1.00 2.50
30 Keith Tkachuk .75 2.00
31 Jaromir Jagr 1.25 3.00
32 Pavol Demitra .40 1.00
33 Vincent Lecavalier .75 2.00
34 Curtis Joseph .75 2.00
35 Mats Sundin .75 2.00
36 Mark Messier .75 2.00

2000-01 Paramount

Released as a 252-card set, Paramount features a white bordered card stock with full color player action photography centered on the card. The majority of the background is white, but in the areas directly around the player photo, the real life background can be seen. The featured player's team name is in gold and is overlaid with the player's name in silver foil. Paramount was packaged in 36-pack boxes with each pack containing six cards.

COMPLETE SET (252) 20.00 40.00
1 Antti Aalto .05 .15
2 Maxim Balmochnyk .15 .40
3 Matt Cullen .05 .15
4 Guy Hebert .15 .40
5 Paul Kariya .20 .50
6 Steve Rucchin .05 .15
7 Teemu Selanne .20 .50
8 Oleg Tverdovsky .05 .15
9 Donald Audette .05 .15
10 Andrew Brunette .05 .15
11 Shean Donovan .05 .15
12 Scott Fankhouser .05 .15
13 Ray Ferraro .05 .15
14 Damian Rhodes .05 .15
15 Patrik Stefan .05 .15
16 Jason Allison .05 .15
17 Anson Carter .15 .40
18 Byron Dafoe .15 .40
19 John Grahame .15 .40
20 Brian Rolston .15 .40
21 Sergei Samsonov .15 .40
22 Don Sweeney .05 .15
23 Joe Thornton .30 .75
24 Maxim Afinogenov .05 .15
25 Stu Barnes .05 .15
26 Martin Biron .15 .40
27 Curtis Brown .05 .15
28 Doug Gilmour .15 .40
29 Chris Gratton .05 .15
30 Dominik Hasek .40 1.00
31 Michael Peca .05 .15
32 Miroslav Satan .15 .40
33 Fred Brathwaite .15 .40
34 Valeri Bure .05 .15
35 Phil Housley .05 .15
36 Jarome Iginla .25 .60
37 Oleg Saprykin .05 .15
38 Marc Savard .05 .15
39 Cory Stillman .05 .15
40 Clarke Wilm .05 .15
41 Rod Brind'Amour .15 .40
42 Ron Francis .15 .40
43 Arturs Irbe .15 .40
44 Sami Kapanen .05 .15
45 Jeff O'Neill .05 .15
46 Dave Tanabe .05 .15
47 Glen Wesley .05 .15
48 Tony Amonte .15 .40
49 Michal Grosek .05 .15
50 Dean McAmmond .05 .15
51 Boris Mironov .05 .15
52 Michael Nylander .05 .15
53 Steve Sullivan .05 .15
54 Jocelyn Thibault .15 .40
55 Alexei Zhamnov .15 .40
56 Ray Bourque .40 1.00
57 Adam Deadmarsh .05 .15
58 Chris Drury .15 .40
59 Adam Foote .15 .40
60 Peter Forsberg .50 1.25
61 Milan Hejduk .20 .50
62 Patrick Roy 1.00 2.50
63 Joe Sakic .40 1.00
64 Martin Skoula .05 .15
65 Alex Tanguay .15 .40
66 Kevyn Adams .05 .15
67 Serge Aubin RC .20 .50
68 Marc Denis .15 .40
69 Ted Drury .05 .15
70 Steve Heinze .05 .15
71 Lyle Odelein .05 .15
72 Ron Tugnutt .15 .40
73 Ed Belfour .20 .50
74 Derian Hatcher .05 .15
75 Brett Hull .25 .60
76 Jamie Langenbrunner .05 .15
77 Jere Lehtinen .15 .40
78 Roman Lyashenko .05 .15
79 Mike Modano .30 .75
80 Brenden Morrow .15 .40
81 Joe Nieuwendyk .15 .40
82 Sergei Zubov .05 .15
83 Chris Chelios .20 .50
84 Mathieu Dandenault .05 .15
85 Sergei Fedorov .30 .75
86 Martin Lapointe .05 .15
87 Nicklas Lidstrom .20 .50
88 Chris Osgood .15 .40
89 Brendan Shanahan .20 .50
90 Pat Verbeek .05 .15
91 Jesse Wallin .05 .15
92 Ken Wregget .15 .40
93 Steve Yzerman 1.00 2.50
94 Mike Grier .15 .40
95 Bill Guerin .15 .40
96 Todd Marchant .05 .15
97 Tom Poti .05 .15
98 Tommy Salo .15 .40
99 Alexander Selivanov .15 .40
100 Ryan Smyth .15 .40
101 Doug Weight .15 .40
102 Pavel Bure .20 .50
103 Brad Ference .05 .15
104 Trevor Kidd .15 .40
105 Viktor Kozlov .15 .40
106 Scott Mellanby .05 .15
107 Ivan Novoseltsev .15 .40
108 Robert Svehla .05 .15
109 Ray Whitney .15 .40
110 Rob Blake .15 .40
111 Stephane Fiset .15 .40
112 Glen Murray .05 .15
113 Zigmund Palffy .15 .40
114 Luc Robitaille .15 .40
115 Bryan Smolinski .05 .15
116 Jamie Storr .15 .40
117 Jozef Stumpel .05 .15
118 Manny Fernandez .15 .40
119 Sergei Krivokrasov .05 .15
120 Jamie McLennan .15 .40
121 Jeff Nielsen .05 .15
122 Sean O'Donnell .05 .15
123 Jeff Odgers .05 .15
124 Scott Pellerin .05 .15
125 Jeff Hackett .15 .40
126 Saku Koivu .20 .50
127 Trevor Linden .15 .40
128 Patrick Poulin .05 .15
129 Mike Ribeiro .05 .15
130 Martin Rucinsky .05 .15
131 Brian Savage .05 .15
132 Jose Theodore .25 .60
133 Dainius Zubrus .05 .15
134 Mike Dunham .15 .40
135 Greg Johnson .05 .15
136 David Legwand .15 .40
137 Cliff Ronning .05 .15
138 Rob Valicevic .05 .15
139 Tomas Vokoun .05 .15
140 Vitali Yachmenev .05 .15
141 Jason Arnott .05 .15
142 Martin Brodeur .50 1.25
143 Patrik Elias .15 .40
144 Scott Gomez .05 .15
145 John Madden .05 .15
146 Alexander Mogilny .15 .40
147 Scott Niedermayer .05 .15
148 Brian Rafalski .05 .15
149 Scott Stevens .15 .40
150 Petr Sykora .05 .15
151 Colin White RC .15 .40
152 Tim Connolly .05 .15
153 Mariusz Czerkawski .05 .15
154 Brad Isbister .05 .15
155 Jason Krog .05 .15
156 Claude Lapointe .05 .15
157 Bill Muckalt .05 .15
158 Steve Valiquette RC .20 .50
159 Radek Dvorak .05 .15
160 Theo Fleury .05 .15
161 Adam Graves .05 .15
162 Jan Hlavac .15 .40
163 Brian Leetch .15 .40
164 Sylvain Lefebvre .05 .15
165 Mark Messier .20 .50
166 Petr Nedved .15 .40
167 Mike Richter .20 .50
168 Mike York .05 .15
169 Daniel Alfredsson .15 .40
170 Magnus Arvedson .05 .15
171 Radek Bonk .05 .15
172 Marian Hossa .20 .50
173 Jani Hurme RC 1.25 3.00
174 Patrick Lalime .15 .40
175 Shawn McEachern .05 .15
176 Vaclav Prospal .05 .15
177 Brian Boucher .20 .50
178 Andy Delmore .15 .40
179 Eric Desjardins .05 .15
180 Simon Gagne .20 .50
181 Daymond Langkow .15 .40
182 John LeClair .20 .50
183 Eric Lindros .20 .50
184 Keith Primeau .05 .15
185 Mark Recchi .15 .40
186 Rick Tocchet .15 .40
187 Shane Doan .05 .15
188 Robert Esche .05 .15
189 Travis Green .05 .15
190 Trevor Letowski .05 .15
191 Stanislav Neckar .05 .15
192 Teppo Numminen .05 .15
193 Jeremy Roenick .25 .60
194 Keith Tkachuk .20 .50
195 Jean-Sebastien Aubin .15 .40
196 Matthew Barnaby .05 .15
197 Jan Hrdina .05 .15
198 Jaromir Jagr .30 .75
199 Alexei Kovalev .15 .40
200 Robert Lang .05 .15
201 John Slaney .05 .15
202 Martin Straka .05 .15
203 Lubos Bartecko .05 .15
204 Pavol Demitra .15 .40
205 Michal Handzus .15 .40
206 Al MacInnis .15 .40
207 Jamal Mayers .05 .15
208 Chris Pronger .15 .40
209 Roman Turek .15 .40
210 Pierre Turgeon .15 .40
211 Scott Young .05 .15
212 Vincent Damphousse .05 .15
213 Jeff Friesen .05 .15
214 Patrick Marleau .15 .40
215 Owen Nolan .15 .40
216 Mike Ricci .15 .40
217 Steve Shields .15 .40
218 Brad Stuart .15 .40
219 Dan Cloutier .15 .40
220 Brian Holzinger .05 .15
221 Mike Johnson .05 .15
222 Vincent Lecavalier .20 .50
223 Fredrik Modin .05 .15
224 Petr Svoboda .05 .15
225 Todd Warriner .05 .15
226 Nikolai Antropov .05 .15
227 Sergei Berezin .05 .15
228 Tie Domi .15 .40
229 Jeff Farkas .05 .15
230 Curtis Joseph .20 .50
231 Tomas Kaberle .05 .15
232 Yanic Perreault .05 .15
233 Mats Sundin .20 .50
234 Steve Thomas .05 .15
235 Darcy Tucker .05 .15
236 Todd Bertuzzi .20 .50
237 Andrew Cassels .05 .15
238 Ed Jovanovski .05 .15
239 Steve Kariya .05 .15
240 Markus Naslund .20 .50
241 Mattias Ohlund .05 .15
242 Felix Potvin .20 .50
243 Peter Bondra .20 .50
244 Sergei Gonchar .05 .15
245 Jeff Halpern .05 .15
246 Olaf Kolzig .15 .40
247 Steve Konowalchuk .05 .15
248 Adam Oates .15 .40
249 Chris Simon .05 .15
250 Richard Zednik .05 .15
251 Daniel Sedin .05 .15
252 Henrik Sedin .05 .15

2000-01 Paramount Copper

*STARS: 1.5X TO 4X BASIC CARDS
*ROOKIES: 1X TO 2.5X BASIC CARDS
STATED ODDS 1:1 HOBBY

2000-01 Paramount Gold

*STARS: 2.5X TO 6X BASIC CARDS
*ROOKIES: 1.5X TO 4X BASIC CARDS
STATED ODDS 1:1 RETAIL

2000-01 Paramount Holo-Gold

Randomly inserted in Retail packs at the rate of 2:37, this 252-card set parallels the base set enhanced with a holographic gold foil shift from the base set silver on the player's name. Each card is sequentially numbered to 74.

*STARS: 10X TO 25X BASIC CARDS
*ROOKIES: 5X TO 12X

2000-01 Paramount Holo-Silver

Randomly inserted in Hobby packs, this 252-card set parallels the base set enhanced with a holographic silver foil shift from the base set silver on the player's name. Each card is sequentially numbered to 74.

*STARS: 12.5X TO 30X BASIC CARDS
*ROOKIES: 5X TO 12X BASIC CARDS

2000-01 Paramount Ice Blue

*STARS: 20X TO 50X BASIC CARDS
*ROOKIES: 8X TO 20X BASIC CARDS
STATED PRINT RUN 50 SER.#'d SETS
STATED ODDS 1:73 HOBBY

2000-01 Paramount Premiere Date

*STARS: 20X TO 50X BASIC CARDS
*ROOKIES: 8X TO 20X BASIC CARDS
STATED PRINT RUN 45 SER.#'d SETS
RANDOM INSERTS IN HOBBY PACKS

2000-01 Paramount Epic Scope

This 20-card set was inserted at a rate of 2:37.

COMPLETE SET (20) 30.00 60.00
1 Paul Kariya 1.00 2.50
2 Teemu Selanne 1.00 2.50
3 Dominik Hasek 2.00 5.00
4 Ray Bourque 2.00 5.00
5 Peter Forsberg 2.50 6.00
6 Patrick Roy 5.00 12.00
7 Joe Sakic 2.00 5.00
8 Brett Hull 1.25 3.00
9 Mike Modano 1.50 4.00
10 Brendan Shanahan 1.00 2.50
11 Steve Yzerman 5.00 12.00
12 Pavel Bure 1.00 2.50
13 Martin Brodeur 2.50 6.00
14 Scott Gomez .75 2.00
15 Brian Boucher .75 2.00
16 John LeClair 1.00 2.50
17 Jaromir Jagr 1.50 4.00
18 Vincent Lecavalier 1.00 2.50
19 Curtis Joseph 1.00 2.50
20 Mats Sundin 1.00 2.50

2000-01 Paramount Freeze Frame

Randomly inserted in packs at the rate of 1:37, this 36-card set features full color player action shots and a filmstrip border along the top and bottom of the card. Cards are highlighted with copper foil.

COMPLETE SET (36) 50.00 100.00
1 Paul Kariya 1.25 3.00
2 Teemu Selanne 1.25 3.00
3 Doug Gilmour 1.00 2.50
4 Dominik Hasek 2.50 6.00
5 Valeri Bure .40 1.00
6 Tony Amonte 1.00 2.50
7 Ray Bourque 2.50 6.00
8 Peter Forsberg 3.00 8.00
9 Joe Sakic 2.50 6.00
10 Patrick Roy 6.00 15.00
11 Ed Belfour 1.25 3.00
12 Brett Hull 1.50 4.00
13 Mike Modano 2.00 5.00
14 Sergei Fedorov 2.50 6.00
15 Brendan Shanahan 1.25 3.00
16 Steve Yzerman 6.00 15.00
17 Doug Weight 1.00 2.50
18 Pavel Bure 1.25 3.00
19 Luc Robitaille 1.00 2.50
20 Saku Koivu 1.25 3.00
21 Martin Brodeur 3.00 8.00
22 Scott Gomez .40 1.00
23 Tim Connolly .40 1.00
24 Marian Hossa 1.25 3.00
25 Brian Boucher 1.25 3.00
26 John LeClair 1.25 3.00
27 Mark Recchi 1.00 2.50
28 Jaromir Jagr 2.00 5.00
29 Jeremy Roenick 1.50 4.00
30 Chris Pronger 1.00 2.50
31 Roman Turek 1.00 2.50
32 Owen Nolan 1.00 2.50
33 Vincent Lecavalier 1.25 3.00
34 Mats Sundin 1.25 3.00
35 Curtis Joseph 1.25 3.00
36 Olaf Kolzig 1.00 2.50

2000-01 Paramount Game Used Sticks

Randomly inserted in packs, this 17-card set features player action photography on a horizontal design front coupled with an oval swatch of a game used stick. Each card is individually serial numbered in a gold foil box in the lower right hand corner of the card front.

1 Ron Francis/165 10.00 25.00
2 Ray Bourque/190 20.00 50.00
3 Adam Deadmarsh/200 10.00 25.00
4 Chris Drury/205 10.00 25.00
5 Joe Sakic/190 15.00 40.00
6 Martin Skoula/200 10.00 25.00
7 Alex Tanguay/200 10.00 25.00
8 Ed Belfour/205 15.00 40.00
9 Chris Chelios/165 12.50 30.00
10 Chris Osgood/205 10.00 25.00
11 Doug Weight/165 10.00 25.00
12 Luc Robitaille/185 10.00 25.00
13 Alexander Mogilny/155 10.00 25.00
14 Theo Fleury/190 10.00 25.00
15 Eric Lindros/150 12.50 30.00
16 Al MacInnis/165 10.00 25.00
17 Curtis Joseph/150 12.50 30.00

2000-01 Paramount Jersey and Patches

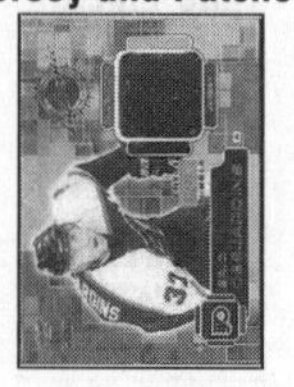

Randomly inserted in Hobby packs, this 10-card set features full color action photography coupled with a swatch of a game worn jersey on the card front and a game worn jersey patch on the back. Each card is sequentially numbered to 30.

1 Jarome Iginla 50.00 125.00
2 Tony Amonte 40.00 100.00
3 Ray Bourque 100.00 200.00
4 Joe Sakic 75.00 200.00
5 Darryl Sydor 40.00 100.00
6 Saku Koivu 40.00 100.00
7 John Vanbiesbrouck 40.00 100.00
8 Eric Desjardins 40.00 100.00
9 Shane Doan 40.00 100.00
10 Olaf Kolzig 40.00 100.00

2000-01 Paramount Glove Side Net Fusions

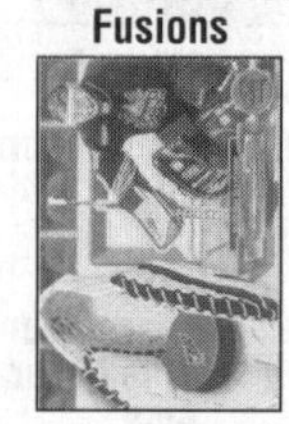

Randomly seeded in packs at the rate of 1:73, this 20-card set features a close-up of a goalie glove on the left side, player action shots on the right, and a die cut goal in the background with goal "netting." A platinum parallel numbered to just 25 was also created and inserted randomly.

COMPLETE SET (20) 50.00 100.00
*PLATINUM: 2.5X TO 6X BASIC CARDS
1 Byron Dafoe 2.00 5.00
2 Martin Biron 2.00 5.00
3 Dominik Hasek 5.00 12.00
4 Fred Brathwaite 2.00 5.00
5 Arturs Irbe 2.00 5.00
6 Jocelyn Thibault 2.00 5.00
7 Patrick Roy 12.50 30.00
8 Ed Belfour 2.50 6.00
9 Chris Osgood 2.00 5.00
10 Tommy Salo 2.00 5.00
11 Jose Theodore 3.00 8.00
12 Martin Brodeur 6.00 15.00
13 Mike Richter 2.50 6.00
14 Brian Boucher 2.00 5.00
15 Jean-Sebastien Aubin 2.00 5.00
16 Roman Turek 2.00 5.00
17 Steve Shields 2.00 5.00
18 Curtis Joseph 2.50 6.00
19 Felix Potvin 2.50 6.00
20 Olaf Kolzig 2.00 5.00

2000-01 Paramount Hall of Fame Bound

Randomly inserted in packs at the rate of 1:361, this 10-card set features embossed oval portraits of top NHL players and a banner bearing the line "Hall of Fame Bound." Two different proof parallels were also created. Regular proofs were randon inserted and numbered to just 25, canv proofs were randomly inserted a numbered 1/1. Canvas proofs not priced d to scarcity.

COMPLETE SET (10) 75.00 150.0
*PROOFS: 1.25X TO 3X BASIC CARDS
1 Paul Kariya 5.00 12.0
2 Dominik Hasek 8.00 20.0
3 Ray Bourque 8.00 20.0
4 Patrick Roy 15.00 40.0
5 Brett Hull 10.00 25.0
6 Steve Yzerman 15.00 40.0
7 Pavel Bure 5.00 12.0
8 Martin Brodeur 12.50 30.0
9 John LeClair 5.00 12.0
10 Jaromir Jagr 6.00 15.0

2000-01 Paramount Sub Zero

Randomly inserted in Canadian Retail pac at the rate of 1:49, this 10-card set featur top NHL players on a card enhanced wi silver foil highlights. Each card sequentially numbered to 159. A go parallel was also created and numbered 99. Red 1/1 parallels also were created, th are not priced due to scarcity.

*GOLD: 1X TO 2X BASIC CARDS
1 Paul Kariya 4.00 10.0
2 Peter Forsberg 6.00 15.0
3 Patrick Roy 20.00 50.0
4 Brendan Shanahan 4.00 10.0
5 Steve Yzerman 12.00 30.0
6 Pavel Bure 4.00 10.0
7 Martin Brodeur 10.00 25.0
8 Jaromir Jagr 6.00 15.0
9 Curtis Joseph 4.00 10.0
10 Mats Sundin 4.00 10.0

1951-52 Parkhurst

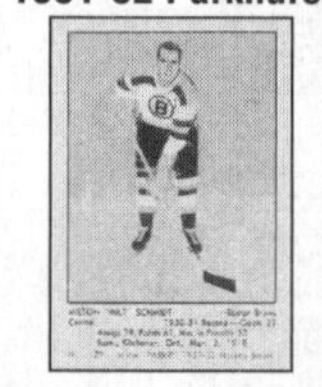

1 Elmer Lach 350.00 500.0
2 Paul Meger RC 40.00 60.0
3 Butch Bouchard RC 75.00 200.0
4 Maurice Richard RC 1200.00 1500.0
5 Bert Olmstead RC 60.00 100.0
6 Bud MacPherson RC 40.00 60.0
7 Tom Johnson RC 60.00 100.0
8 Paul Masnick RC 40.00 60.0
9 Calum Mackay RC 40.00 60.0
10 Doug Harvey RC 400.00 600.0
11 Ken Mosdell RC 50.00 80.0
12 Floyd(Busher) Curry RC 50.00 80.0
13 Billy Reay RC 50.00 80.0
14 Bernie Geoffrion RC 400.00 600.0
15 Gerry McNeil RC 175.00 300.0
16 Dick Gamble RC 50.00 80.0
17 Gerry Couture RC 40.00 60.0
18 Ross Robert Lowe RC 40.00 60.0
19 Jim Henry RC 90.00 150.0
20 Victor Ivan Lynn 40.00 60.0
21 Walter(Gus) Kyle RC 40.00 60.0
22 Ed Sandford RC 40.00 60.0
23 John Henderson RC 50.00 80.0
24 Dunc Fisher RC 40.00 60.0
25 Hal Laycoe RC 50.00 80.0
26 Bill Quackenbush RC 75.00 125.0
27 George Sullivan RC 50.00 80.0
28 Woody Dumart 50.00 100.0
29 Milt Schmidt 100.00 150.0
30 Adam Brown RC 40.00 60.0
31 Pentti Lund RC 50.00 80.0
32 Ray Barry RC 40.00 60.0
33 Ed Kryznowski UER 40.00 60.0
(Misspelled Kryzanowski on car
34 Johnny Peirson RC 50.00 80.0
35 Lorne Ferguson RC 40.00 60.0
36 Clare(Rags) Raglan 40.00 60.0
37 Bill Gadsby RC 60.00 100.0
38 Al Dewsbury RC 40.00 60.0
39 George Clare Martin RC 40.00 60.0
40 Gus Bodnar RC 50.00 80.0
41 Jim Peters RC 40.00 60.0
42 Bep Guidolin RC 50.00 80.0
43 George Gee RC 40.00 60.0
44 Jim McFadden RC 40.00 60.0
45 Fred Hucul RC 40.00 60.0
46 Lee Fogolin RC 40.00 60.0
47 Harry Lumley RC 90.00 150.0
48 Doug Bentley RC 60.00 100.0
49 Bill Mosienko RC 60.00 125.0
50 Roy Conacher 50.00 80.0
51 Pete Babando RC 40.00 60.0
52 The Winning Goal 300.00 500.0
(Bill Barilko against Gerry McNeil)
53 Jack Stewart 50.00 80.0
54 Marty Pavelich RC 40.00 60.0
55 Red Kelly RC 200.00 300.0
56 Ted Lindsay RC 200.00 300.0
57 Glen Skov RC 40.00 60.0
58 Benny Woit 40.00 60.0
59 Tony Leswick RC 50.00 80.0

60 Fred Glover RC 40.00 60.00
61 Terry Sawchuk RC 800.00 1200.00
62 Vic Stasiuk RC 50.00 80.00
63 Alex Delvecchio RC 275.00 400.00
64 Sid Abel 60.00 100.00
65 Metro Prystai RC 40.00 60.00
66 Gordie Howe RC 2000.00 3000.00
67 Bob Goldham RC 40.00 60.00
68 Marcel Pronovost RC 50.00 100.00
69 Leo Reise 40.00 60.00
70 Harry Watson RC 50.00 80.00
71 Danny Lewicki RC 40.00 60.00
72 Howie Meeker RC 90.00 150.00
73 Gus Mortson RC 50.00 80.00
74 Joe Klukay RC 40.00 60.00
75 Turk Broda 125.00 200.00
76 Al Rollins RC 75.00 150.00
77 Bill Juzda RC 40.00 60.00
78 Ray Timgren 40.00 60.00
79 Hugh Bolton RC 40.00 60.00
80 Fern Flaman RC 60.00 125.00
81 Max Bentley 60.00 100.00
82 Jim Thomson 40.00 60.00
83 Fleming Mackell RC 50.00 80.00
84 Sid Smith RC 50.00 100.00
85 Cal Gardner RC 50.00 80.00
86 Teeder Kennedy RC 175.00 275.00
87 Tod Sloan RC 50.00 80.00
88 Bob Solinger 40.00 60.00
89 Frank Eddolls RC 40.00 60.00
90 Jack Evans RC 50.00 100.00
91 Hy Buller RC 40.00 60.00
92 Steve Kraftcheck 40.00 60.00
93 Don Raleigh RC 40.00 60.00
94 Allan Stanley RC 90.00 150.00
95 Paul Ronty RC 40.00 60.00
96 Edgar Laprade RC 50.00 80.00
97 Nick Mickoski RC 40.00 60.00
98 Jack McLeod RC 40.00 60.00
99 Gaye Stewart 40.00 60.00
100 Wally Hergesheimer RC 50.00 80.00
101 Ed Kullman RC 40.00 60.00
102 Ed Slowinski RC 40.00 60.00
103 Reg Sinclair RC 40.00 60.00
104 Chuck Rayner RC 75.00 125.00
105 Jim Conacher RC 100.00 200.00

1952-53 Parkhurst

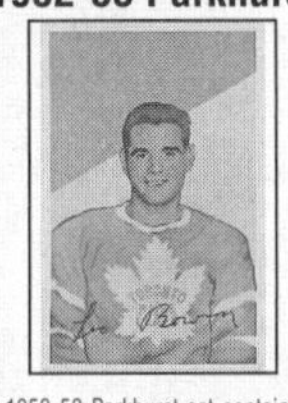

The 1952-53 Parkhurst set contains 105 color, line-drawing cards. Cards are approximately 1 15/16" by 2 15/16". The obverse contains a facsimile autograph of the player pictured while the backs contain a short biography in English and 1951-52 statistics. The backs also contain the card number and a special album (for holding a set of cards) offer. The cards feature players from each of the Original Six NHL teams. The set numbering is roughly according to teams, i.e., Montreal Canadiens (1-15, 52, 53), Boston Bruins (68-85), Chicago Blackhawks (16-17, 26-27, 29-33, 35-41, 55-56), Detroit Red Wings (53, 60-67, 86-92, 104), Toronto Maple Leafs (28, 34, 42-43, 50-51, 54, 58-59, 94-96, 105), and New York Rangers (18-25, 49, 57, 97-103). The key Rookie Cards in this set are George Armstrong, Tim Horton, and Dickie Moore.

COMPLETE SET (105) 4500.00 7000.00
1 Maurice Richard 800.00 1200.00
2 Billy Reay 25.00 40.00
3 Bernie Geoffrion 150.00 250.00
UER (Misspelled Gioffrion on back)
4 Paul Meger 18.00 30.00
5 Dick Gamble 25.00 40.00
6 Elmer Lach 50.00 80.00
7 Floyd(Busher) Curry 25.00 40.00
8 Ken Mosdell 25.00 40.00
9 Tom Johnson 25.00 40.00
10 Dickie Moore RC 150.00 250.00
11 Bud MacPherson 18.00 30.00
12 Gerry McNeil 60.00 100.00
13 Butch Bouchard 25.00 40.00
14 Doug Harvey 150.00 250.00
15 John McCormack 18.00 30.00
16 Pete Babando 18.00 30.00
17 Al Dewsbury 18.00 30.00
18 Ed Kullman 18.00 30.00
19 Ed Slowinski 18.00 30.00
20 Wally Hergesheimer 25.00 40.00
21 Allan Stanley 50.00 80.00
22 Chuck Rayner 40.00 60.00
23 Steve Kraftcheck 18.00 30.00
24 Paul Ronty 18.00 30.00
25 Gaye Stewart 18.00 30.00
26 Fred Hucul 18.00 30.00
27 Bill Mosienko 30.00 50.00
28 Jim Morrison RC 18.00 30.00
29 Ed Kryznowski 18.00 30.00
30 Cal Gardner 25.00 40.00
31 Al Rollins 40.00 60.00
32 Enio Sclisizzi RC 18.00 30.00
33 Pete Conacher RC 25.00 40.00
34 Leo Boivin RC 40.00 60.00
35 Jim Peters 18.00 30.00
36 George Gee 18.00 30.00
37 Gus Bodnar 25.00 40.00
38 Jim McFadden 18.00 30.00
39 Gus Mortson 25.00 40.00
40 Fred Glover 18.00 30.00
41 Gerry Couture 18.00 30.00
42 Howie Meeker 50.00 80.00
43 Jim Thomson 18.00 30.00
44 Teeder Kennedy 60.00 100.00
45 Sid Smith 25.00 40.00
46 Harry Watson 30.00 50.00
47 Fern Flaman 25.00 40.00
48 Tod Sloan 25.00 40.00
49 Leo Reise 18.00 30.00
50 Bob Solinger 18.00 30.00
51 George Armstrong RC 150.00 250.00
52 Dollard St.Laurent RC 25.00 40.00
53 Alex Delvecchio 90.00 150.00
54 Gord Hannigan RC 18.00 30.00
55 Lee Fogolin 18.00 30.00
56 Bill Gadsby 30.00 50.00
57 Herb Dickenson RC 18.00 30.00
58 Tim Horton RC 400.00 600.00
59 Harry Lumley 60.00 100.00
60 Metro Prystai 18.00 30.00
61 Marcel Pronovost 25.00 40.00
62 Benny Woit 18.00 30.00
63 Glen Skov 18.00 30.00
64 Bob Goldham 18.00 30.00
65 Tony Leswick 18.00 30.00
66 Marty Pavelich 18.00 30.00
67 Red Kelly 90.00 150.00
68 Bill Quackenbush 30.00 50.00
69 Ed Sandford 18.00 30.00
70 Milt Schmidt 40.00 60.00
71 Hal Laycoe 25.00 40.00
72 Woody Dumart 25.00 40.00
73 Zellio Toppazzini 18.00 30.00
74 Jim Henry 25.00 40.00
75 Joe Klukay 18.00 30.00
76 Dave Creighton RC 25.00 40.00
77 Jack McIntyre 18.00 30.00
78 Johnny Peirson 18.00 30.00
79 George Sullivan 25.00 40.00
80 Real Chevrefils RC 25.00 40.00
81 Leo Labine RC 30.00 50.00
82 Fleming Mackell 25.00 40.00
83 Pentti Lund 18.00 30.00
84 Bob Armstrong RC 18.00 30.00
85 Warren Godfrey RC 18.00 30.00
86 Terry Sawchuk 300.00 500.00
87 Ted Lindsay 90.00 150.00
88 Gordie Howe 600.00 1000.00
89 Johnny Wilson RC 18.00 30.00
90 Vic Stasiuk 25.00 40.00
91 Larry Zeidel 18.00 30.00
92 Larry Wilson RC 18.00 30.00
93 Bert Olmstead 25.00 40.00
94 Ron Stewart RC 25.00 40.00
95 Max Bentley 30.00 50.00
96 Rudy Migay RC 18.00 30.00
97 Jack Stoddard 18.00 30.00
98 Hy Buller 18.00 30.00
99 Don Raleigh 18.00 30.00
100 Edgar Laprade 25.00 40.00
101 Nick Mickoski 18.00 30.00
102 Jack McLeod UER 18.00 30.00
(Robert on back)
103 Jim Conacher 25.00 40.00
104 Reg Sinclair 18.00 30.00
105 Bob Hassard RC 75.00 125.00

1953-54 Parkhurst

The 1953-54 Parkhurst set contains 100 cards in full color. Cards measure approximately 2 1/2" by 3 5/8". The cards were sold in five-cent wax packs each containing four cards and gum. The size of the card increased from the previous year, and the picture and color show marked improvement. A facsimile autograph of the player is found on the front. The backs contain the card number, 1952-53 statistics, a short biography, and an album offer. The back data is presented in both English and French. The cards feature players from each of the six NHL teams. The set numbering is basically according to teams, i.e., Toronto Maple Leafs (1-17), Montreal Canadiens (18-35), Detroit Red Wings (36-52), New York Rangers (53-68), Chicago Blackhawks (69-84), and Boston Bruins (85-100). The key Rookie Cards in this set are Al Arbour, Andy Bathgate, Jean Beliveau, Harry Howell, and Gump Worsley.

COMPLETE SET (100) 3000.00 4500.00
1 Harry Lumley 150.00 250.00
2 Sid Smith 20.00 40.00
3 Gord Hannigan 20.00 40.00
4 Bob Hassard 20.00 40.00
5 Tod Sloan 20.00 40.00
6 Leo Boivin 20.00 40.00
7 Teeder Kennedy 35.00 70.00
8 Jim Thomson 20.00 40.00
9 Ron Stewart 20.00 40.00
10 Eric Nesterenko RC 40.00 80.00
11 George Armstrong 60.00 100.00
12 Harry Watson 30.00 60.00
13 Tim Horton 175.00 300.00
14 Fern Flaman 25.00 50.00
15 Jim Morrison 20.00 40.00
16 Bob Solinger 20.00 40.00
17 Rudy Migay 20.00 40.00
18 Dick Gamble 20.00 40.00
19 Bert Olmstead 25.00 50.00
20 Eddie Mazur RC 20.00 40.00
21 Paul Meger 20.00 40.00
22 Bud MacPherson 20.00 40.00
23 Dollard St.Laurent 20.00 40.00
24 Maurice Richard 300.00 500.00
25 Gerry McNeil 50.00 80.00
26 Doug Harvey 125.00 200.00
27 Jean Beliveau RC 450.00 600.00
28 Dickie Moore UER 75.00 125.00
(Photo actually Jean Beliveau)
29 Bernie Geoffrion 125.00 200.00
30 Lach/Richard 125.00 200.00
Elmer Lach and Maurice Richard
31 Elmer Lach 35.00 70.00
32 Butch Bouchard 25.00 50.00
33 Ken Mosdell 20.00 40.00
34 John McCormack 20.00 40.00
35 Floyd (Busher) Curry 20.00 40.00
36 Earl Reibel RC 20.00 40.00
37 Bill Dineen RC UER 40.00 80.00
(Photo actually Al Arbour)
38 Al Arbour RC UER 60.00 100.00
(Photo actually Bill Dineen)
39 Vic Stasiuk 20.00 40.00
40 Red Kelly 60.00 100.00
41 Marcel Pronovost 25.00 50.00
42 Metro Prystai 20.00 40.00
43 Tony Leswick 20.00 40.00
44 Marty Pavelich 20.00 40.00
45 Benny Woit 20.00 40.00
46 Terry Sawchuk 200.00 350.00
47 Alex Delvecchio 60.00 100.00
48 Glen Skov 20.00 40.00
49 Bob Goldham 20.00 40.00
50 Gordie Howe 500.00 800.00
51 Johnny Wilson 20.00 40.00
52 Ted Lindsay 60.00 100.00
53 Gump Worsley RC 275.00 400.00
54 Jack Evans 20.00 40.00
55 Max Bentley 30.00 60.00
56 Andy Bathgate RC 90.00 150.00
57 Harry Howell RC 90.00 150.00
58 Hy Buller 20.00 40.00
59 Chuck Rayner 25.00 50.00
60 Jack Stoddard 20.00 40.00
61 Ed Kullman 20.00 40.00
62 Nick Mickoski 20.00 40.00
63 Paul Ronty 20.00 40.00
64 Allan Stanley 30.00 60.00
65 Leo Reise 20.00 40.00
66 Aldo Guidolin RC 20.00 40.00
67 Wally Hergesheimer 20.00 40.00
68 Don Raleigh 20.00 40.00
69 Jim Peters 20.00 40.00
70 Pete Conacher 20.00 40.00
71 Fred Hucul 20.00 40.00
72 Lee Fogolin 20.00 40.00
73 Larry Zeidel 20.00 40.00
74 Larry Wilson 20.00 40.00
75 Gus Bodnar 20.00 40.00
76 Bill Gadsby 30.00 60.00
77 Jim McFadden 20.00 40.00
78 Al Dewsbury 20.00 40.00
79 Clare Raglan 20.00 40.00
80 Bill Mosienko 30.00 60.00
81 Gus Mortson 20.00 40.00
82 Al Rollins 25.00 50.00
83 George Gee 20.00 40.00
84 Gerry Couture 20.00 40.00
85 Dave Creighton 20.00 40.00
86 Jim Henry 25.00 50.00
87 Hal Laycoe 20.00 40.00
88 Johnny Peirson UER 25.00 50.00
(Misspelled Pierson on card back)
89 Real Chevrefils 20.00 40.00
90 Ed Sandford 20.00 40.00
91A Fleming Mackell ERR 25.00 50.00
(No bio)
91B Fleming Mackell COR 25.00 50.00
92 Milt Schmidt 35.00 70.00
93 Leo Labine 20.00 40.00
94 Joe Klukay 20.00 40.00
95 Warren Godfrey 20.00 40.00
96 Woody Dumart 25.00 50.00
97 Frank Martin RC 20.00 40.00
98 Jerry Toppazzini RC 20.00 40.00
99 Cal Gardner 20.00 40.00
100 Bill Quackenbush 75.00 150.00

1954-55 Parkhurst

The 1954-55 Parkhurst set contains 100 cards in full color with both the card number and a facsimile autograph on the fronts. Cards in the set measure approximately 2 1/2" by 3 5/8". Unopened wax packs consisted of four cards. The backs, in both English and French, contain 1953-54 statistics, a short player biography, and an album offer (contained only on cards 1-88). Cards 1-88 feature players from each of the six NHL teams and the remaining cards are action scenes. Cards 1-88 were available with either a stat or a premium back. The cards with the statistics on the back are more desirable but there is currently no price differential. The player/set numbering is basically according to teams, i.e., Montreal Canadiens (1-15), Toronto Maple Leafs (16-32), Detroit Red Wings (33-48), Boston Bruins (49-64), New York Rangers (65-76), and Chicago Blackhawks (77-88), and All-Star selections from the previous season are noted discreetly on the card front by a red star (first team selection) or blue star (second team). The key Rookie Card in this set is Johnny Bower, although there are several Action Scene cards featuring Jacques Plante in the year before his regular Rookie Card.

COMPLETE SET (100) 2500.00 4000.00
*PREM.BACKS 1-88: SAME VALUE
1 Gerry McNeil 75.00 125.00
2 Dickie Moore 50.00 80.00
3 Jean Beliveau 200.00 300.00
4 Eddie Mazur 15.00 25.00
5 Bert Olmstead 18.00 30.00
6 Butch Bouchard 18.00 30.00
7 Maurice Richard 275.00 400.00
8 Bernie Geoffrion 75.00 125.00
9 John McCormack 15.00 25.00
10 Tom Johnson 18.00 30.00
11 Calum Mackay 15.00 25.00
12 Ken Mosdell 15.00 25.00
13 Paul Masnick 15.00 25.00
14 Doug Harvey 75.00 125.00
15 Floyd(Busher) Curry 15.00 25.00
16 Harry Lumley 25.00 40.00
17 Harry Watson 25.00 40.00
18 Jim Morrison 15.00 25.00
19 Eric Nesterenko 15.00 25.00
20 Fern Flaman 18.00 30.00
21 Rudy Migay 15.00 25.00
22 Sid Smith 15.00 25.00
23 Ron Stewart 15.00 25.00
24 George Armstrong 50.00 80.00
25 Earl Balfour RC 15.00 25.00
26 Leo Boivin 15.00 25.00
27 Gord Hannigan 15.00 25.00
28 Bob Bailey RC 15.00 25.00
29 Teeder Kennedy 30.00 50.00
30 Tod Sloan 15.00 25.00
31 Tim Horton 150.00 250.00
32 Jim Thomson 15.00 25.00
33 Terry Sawchuk 150.00 250.00
34 Marcel Pronovost 18.00 30.00
35 Metro Prystai 15.00 25.00
36 Alex Delvecchio 50.00 80.00
37 Earl Reibel 15.00 25.00
38 Benny Woit 15.00 25.00
39 Bob Goldham 15.00 25.00
40 Glen Skov 15.00 25.00
41 Gordie Howe 400.00 600.00
42 Red Kelly 50.00 80.00
43 Marty Pavelich 15.00 25.00
44 Johnny Wilson 15.00 25.00
45 Tony Leswick 15.00 25.00
46 Ted Lindsay 50.00 00.00
47 Keith Allen RC 18.00 30.00
48 Bill Dineen 15.00 25.00
49 Jim Henry 25.00 40.00
50 Fleming Mackell 18.00 30.00
51 Bill Quackenbush 25.00 40.00
52 Hal Laycoe 15.00 25.00
53 Cal Gardner 15.00 25.00
54 Joe Klukay 15.00 25.00
55 Bob Armstrong 15.00 25.00
56 Warren Godfrey 15.00 25.00
57 Doug Mohns RC 25.00 40.00
58 Dave Creighton 15.00 25.00
59 Milt Schmidt 30.00 50.00
60 Johnny Peirson 15.00 25.00
61 Leo Labine 15.00 25.00
62 Gus Bodnar 15.00 25.00
63 Real Chevrefils 15.00 25.00
64 Ed Sandford 15.00 25.00
65 Johnny Bower RC UER 200.00 400.00
(Misspelled Bowers)
66 Paul Ronty 15.00 25.00
67 Leo Reise 15.00 25.00
68 Don Raleigh 15.00 25.00
69 Bob Chrystal 15.00 25.00
70 Harry Howell 35.00 60.00
71 Wally Hergesheimer 15.00 25.00
72 Jack Evans 15.00 25.00
73 Camille Henry RC 18.00 30.00
74 Dean Prentice RC 25.00 40.00
75 Nick Mickoski 15.00 25.00
76 Ron Murphy RC 15.00 25.00
77 Al Rollins 25.00 40.00
78 Al Dewsbury 15.00 25.00
79 Lou Jankowski 15.00 25.00
80 George Gee 15.00 25.00
81 Gus Mortson 15.00 25.00
82 Fred Saskamoose RC UER 75.00 125.00
(born on Dec. 25 on Whitefish Reserve)
83 Ike Hildebrand RC 15.00 25.00
84 Lee Fogolin 15.00 25.00
85 Larry Wilson 15.00 25.00
86 Pete Conacher 15.00 25.00
87 Bill Gadsby 25.00 40.00
88 Jack McIntyre 15.00 25.00
89 Busher Curry goes up and over 15.00 25.00
90 Delvecchio finds Leaf defense hard to crack 18.00 30.00
(Tim Horton)
91 Battle of All-Stars 25.00 40.00
(Red Kelly and Harry Lumley)
92 Lum stops Howe With help of Stewart's stick 60.00 100.00
93 Net-minders nightmare 15.00 25.00
(Harry Lumley and others)
94 Meger goes down and under 15.00 25.00
(Jim Morrison)
95 Harvey takes nosedive 30.00 50.00
(Eric Nesterenko)
96 Terry boots out Teeder's blast 60.00 100.00
(Terry Sawchuk and Teeder Kennedy)
97 Reibel tests Habs Rookie "Mr. Zero" 60.00 100.00
(Jacques Plante and Butch Bouchard)
98 Plante protects against slippery Sloan 60.00 100.00
(Doug Harvey)
99 Placid Plante foils tireless Teeder 60.00 100.00
100 Sawchuck stops Boom Boom 125.00 200.00

1955-56 Parkhurst

The 1955-56 Parkhurst set contains 79 cards in full color with the number and team insignia on the fronts. Cards in the set measure approximately 2 1/2" by 3 9/16". The set features players from Montreal and Toronto as well as Old-Time Greats. The Old-Time Great selections are numbers 21-32 and 55-66. The backs, printed in red ink, in both English and French, contain 1954-55 statistics, a short biography, a "Do You Know" information section, and an album offer. The key Rookie Card in this set is Jacques Plante. The same 79 cards can also be found with Quaker Oats backs, i.e., green printing on back. The Quaker Oats version is much tougher to locate. Using regular Parkhurst card values as a base, multipliers can be found in the header below to determine value for these. Reportedly, cards #1, 33 and 37 are extremely difficult to acquire in the Quaker Oats version, and can sell for much more than the suggested multipliers.

COMPLETE SET (79) 2800.00 5000.00
*QUAKER OATS: 2X TO 3X BASIC CARDS
1 Harry Lumley 200.00 300.00
2 Sid Smith 15.00 30.00
3 Tim Horton 150.00 250.00
4 George Armstrong 50.00 80.00
5 Ron Stewart 15.00 30.00
6 Joe Klukay 12.00 20.00
7 Marc Reaume 12.00 20.00
8 Jim Morrison 12.00 20.00
9 Parker MacDonald RC 12.00 20.00
10 Tod Sloan 12.00 20.00
11 Jim Thomson 12.00 20.00
12 Rudy Migay 12.00 20.00
13 Brian Cullen RC 12.00 20.00
14 Hugh Bolton 12.00 20.00
15 Eric Nesterenko 15.00 30.00
16 Larry Cahan RC 12.00 20.00
17 Willie Marshall 12.00 20.00
18 Dick Duff RC 50.00 100.00
19 Jack Caffery RC 12.00 20.00
20 Billy Harris RC 15.00 30.00
21 Lorne Chabot OTG 15.00 30.00
22 Busher Jackson OTG 30.00 50.00
23 Turk Broda OTG 60.00 100.00
24 Joe Primeau OTG 25.00 40.00
25 Gordie Drillon OTG 15.00 30.00
26 Chuck Conacher OTG 25.00 40.00
27 Sweeney Schriner OTG 15.00 30.00
28 Syl Apps OTG 25.00 40.00
29 Teeder Kennedy OTG 30.00 50.00
30 Ace Bailey OTG 40.00 60.00
31 Babe Pratt OTG 15.00 30.00
32 Harold Cotton OTG 15.00 30.00
33 King Clancy 60.00 100.00
34 Hap Day 15.00 30.00
35 Don Marshall RC 30.00 50.00
36 Jackie LeClair RC 15.00 30.00
37 Maurice Richard 275.00 400.00
38 Dickie Moore 50.00 80.00
39 Ken Mosdell 15.00 30.00
40 Floyd(Busher) Curry 12.00 20.00
41 Calum Mackay 12.00 20.00
42 Bert Olmstead 15.00 30.00
43 Bernie Geoffrion 75.00 125.00
44 Jean Beliveau 250.00 350.00
45 Doug Harvey 75.00 125.00
46 Butch Bouchard 15.00 30.00
47 Bud MacPherson 12.00 20.00
48 Dollard St.Laurent 12.00 20.00
49 Tom Johnson 15.00 30.00
50 Jacques Plante RC 600.00 800.00
51 Paul Meger 12.00 20.00
52 Gerry McNeil 25.00 40.00
53 Jean-Guy Talbot RC 15.00 30.00
54 Bob Turner 12.00 20.00
55 Newsy Lalonde OTG 40.00 60.00
56 Georges Vezina OTG 75.00 125.00
57 Howie Morenz OTG 60.00 100.00
58 Aurel Joliat OTG 40.00 60.00
59 Geo. Hainsworth OTG 60.00 100.00
60 Sylvio Mantha OTG 15.00 30.00
61 Battleship Leduc OTG 15.00 30.00
62 Babe Siebert OTG UER 18.00 40.00
(Misspelled Seibert on both sides)
63 Bill Durnan OTG RC 40.00 60.00
64 Ken Reardon OTG RC 40.00 60.00
65 Johnny Gagnon OTG 15.00 30.00
66 Billy Reay OTG 15.00 30.00
67 Toe Blake CO 30.00 50.00
68 Frank Selke MG 18.00 30.00
69 Hugh beats Hodge 18.00 30.00
(Hugh Bolton and Charlie Hodge)
70 Lum stops Boom Boom 40.00 60.00
(Harry Lumley)
71 Plante is protected 50.00 80.00
(Butch Bouchard and Tom Johnson)
72 Rocket roars through 50.00 80.00
(Maurice Richard)
73 Richard tests Lumley 50.00 80.00
(Maurice Richard)
74 Beliveau bats puck 40.00 60.00
(Harry Lumley)
75 Leaf speedsters attack 50.00 80.00
(Eric Nesterenko& Sid Smith& and Jacques Plante)
76 Curry scores again 15.00 30.00
(Harry Lumley and Jim Morrison)
77 Jammed on the boards 50.00 80.00
(Tod Sloan& Parker MacDonald& Doug Harvey& and Jean Beliveau)
78 The Montreal Forum 150.00 300.00
79 Maple Leaf Gardens 150.00 300.00

1957-58 Parkhurst

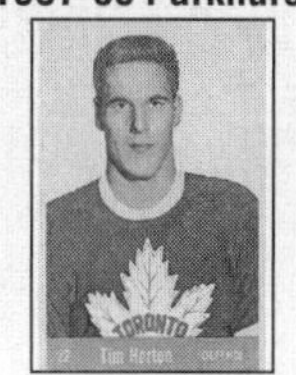

The 1957-58 Parkhurst set contains 50 color cards featuring Montreal and Toronto players. Cards are approximately 2 7/16" by 3 5/8". There are card numbers 1 to 25 for Montreal (M prefix in checklist) and card numbers 1 to 25 for Toronto (T prefix in checklist). The cards are numbered on the fronts and the backs feature resumes in both French and English. The card number, the player's name, and his position appear in a red rectangle on the front. The backs are printed in blue ink. The key Rookie Cards in this set are Frank Mahovlich and Henri Richard. There was no Parkhurst hockey set in 1956-57 reportedly due to market re-evaluation.

COMPLETE SET (50) 2000.00 3500.00
M1 Doug Harvey 150.00 275.00
M2 Bernie Geoffrion 75.00 125.00
M3 Jean Beliveau 200.00 300.00
M4 Henri Richard RC 400.00 600.00
M5 Maurice Richard 300.00 400.00
M6 Tom Johnson 15.00 25.00
M7 Andre Pronovost RC 20.00 40.00
M8 Don Marshall 12.00 20.00
M9 Jean-Guy Talbot 12.00 20.00
M10 Dollard St.Laurent 12.00 20.00
M11 Phil Goyette RC 25.00 40.00
M12 Claude Provost RC 25.00 40.00
M13 Bob Turner 12.00 20.00
M14 Dickie Moore 35.00 60.00
M15 Jacques Plante 250.00 400.00
M16 Toe Blake CO 25.00 40.00
M17 Charlie Hodge RC 50.00 80.00
M18 Marcel Bonin 12.00 20.00
M19 Bert Olmstead 15.00 25.00
M20 Floyd (Busher) Curry 12.00 20.00
M21 Canadiens on guard 25.00 40.00
(Len Broderick RC)
M22 Brian Cullen scores 12.00 20.00
M23 Puck and sticks high 25.00 40.00
(Len Broderick and Doug Harvey)
M24 Geoffrion side-steps Chadwick 30.00 50.00
M25 Olmstead beats Chadwick 18.00 30.00
T1 George Armstrong 60.00 100.00
T2 Ed Chadwick RC 75.00 125.00
T3 Dick Duff 15.00 25.00
T4 Bob Pulford RC 90.00 150.00
T5 Tod Sloan 15.00 25.00
T6 Rudy Migay
T7 Ron Stewart
T8 Gerry James RC 15.00 25.00
T9 Brian Cullen
T10 Sid Smith
T11 Jim Morrison
T12 Marc Reaume
T13 Hugh Bolton
T14 Pete Conacher
T15 Billy Harris
T16 Mike Nykoluk RC
T17 Frank Mahovlich RC 300.00 500.00
T18 Ken Girard RC
T19 Al MacNeil RC
T20 Bob Baun RC 60.00 100.00
T21 Barry Cullen RC
T22 Tim Horton 100.00 175.00
T23 Gary Collins RC
T24 Gary Aldcorn RC
T25 Billy Reay CO 18.00 30.00

1958-59 Parkhurst

The 1958-59 Parkhurst set contains 50 color cards of Montreal and Toronto players. Cards are approximately 2 7/16" by 3 5/8". In contrast to the 1957-58 Parkhurst set, the cards, numbered on the fronts, are numbered continuously from 1 to 50. Resumes on the backs of the cards are in both French and English. The player's name and the team logo appears in a yellow rectangle at the bottom on the front. The number, position, and (usually) a hockey stick appear on the front at the upper left. The backs are printed in black ink. The key Rookie Card in this set is Ralph Backstrom.

COMPLETE SET (50) 1200.00 1800.00
1 Pulford Comes Close 30.00 50.00
2 Henri Richard 125.00 200.00
3 Andre Pronovost 10.00 15.00
4 Billy Harris 12.00 18.00
5 Albert Langlois RC 10.00 15.00
6 Noel Price RC 10.00 15.00
7 Armstrong Breaks Through 15.00 25.00
(Tom Johnson)
8 Dickie Moore 25.00 40.00
9 Toe Blake CO 15.00 25.00
10 Tom Johnson 12.00 18.00
11 An Object of Interest 35.00 50.00
(Jacques Plante and George Armstrong)
12 Ed Chadwick 25.00 40.00
13 Bob Nevin RC 15.00 25.00
14 Ron Stewart 12.00 18.00
15 Bob Baun 25.00 40.00
16 Ralph Backstrom RC 30.00 50.00
17 Charlie Hodge 25.00 40.00
18 Gary Aldcorn 10.00 15.00
19 Willie Marshall 10.00 15.00
20 Marc Reaume 10.00 15.00
21 All Eyes on Puck 40.00 60.00
(Jacques Plante and others)
22 Jacques Plante 200.00 300.00
23 Allan Stanley 15.00 25.00
24 Ian Cushenan RC 10.00 15.00
25 Billy Reay CO 12.00 18.00
26 Plante Catches a Shot 40.00 60.00
27 Bert Olmstead 12.00 18.00
28 Bernie Geoffrion 50.00 80.00
29 Dick Duff 12.00 18.00
30 Ab McDonald RC 10.00 15.00
31 Barry Cullen 10.00 15.00
32 Marcel Bonin 10.00 15.00
33 Frank Mahovlich 125.00 200.00
34 Jean Beliveau 125.00 200.00
35 Canadiens on Guard 40.00 60.00
(Jacques Plante and others)
36 Brian Cullen Shoots 12.00 18.00
37 Steve Kraftcheck 10.00 15.00
38 Maurice Richard 200.00 300.00
39 Action Around the Net 40.00 60.00
(Jacques Plante and others)
40 Bob Turner 10.00 15.00
41 Jean-Guy Talbot 12.00 18.00
42 Tim Horton 75.00 125.00
43 Claude Provost 12.00 18.00
44 Don Marshall 12.00 18.00
45 Bob Pulford 18.00 30.00
46 Johnny Bower UER 90.00 150.00
(Misspelled Bowers on card front)
47 Phil Goyette 12.00 18.00
48 George Armstrong 25.00 40.00
49 Doug Harvey 50.00 80.00
50 Brian Cullen 20.00 40.00

1959-60 Parkhurst

The 1959-60 Parkhurst set contains 50 color cards of Montreal and Toronto players. Cards are approximately 2 7/16" by 3 5/8". The cards are numbered on the fronts. The backs, which contain 1958-59 statistics, a short biography, and a Hockey Gum contest ad, are written in both French and English. The key Rookie Cards in this set are Carl Brewer and Punch Imlach.

COMPLETE SET (50) 700.00 1400.00
1 Canadiens on Guard 75.00 125.00
(Versus Maple Leafs)
2 Maurice Richard 150.00 250.00
3 Carl Brewer RC 40.00 60.00
4 Phil Goyette 12.50 25.00
5 Ed Chadwick 15.00 30.00
6 Jean Beliveau 75.00 125.00
7 George Armstrong 15.00 30.00
8 Doug Harvey 40.00 60.00
9 Billy Harris 12.50 25.00
10 Tom Johnson 12.50 25.00
11 Marc Reaume 12.50 25.00
12 Marcel Bonin 12.50 25.00
13 Johnny Wilson 12.50 25.00
14 Dickie Moore 20.00 40.00
15 Punch Imlach CO/MG RC 25.00 40.00
16 Charlie Hodge 15.00 30.00
17 Larry Regan 12.50 25.00
18 Claude Provost 12.50 25.00
19 Gerry Ehman RC 12.50 25.00
20 Ab McDonald 12.50 25.00
21 Bob Baun 12.50 25.00
22 Ken Reardon VP 12.50 25.00
23 Tim Horton 65.00 100.00
24 Frank Mahovlich 75.00 125.00
25 Johnny Bower IA 25.00 40.00
26 Ron Stewart 12.50 25.00
27 Toe Blake CO 12.50 25.00
28 Bob Pulford 12.50 25.00
29 Ralph Backstrom 12.50 25.00
30 Action Around the Net 15.00 30.00
31 Bill Hicke RC 12.00 20.00
32 Johnny Bower 65.00 100.00
33 Bernie Geoffrion 40.00 60.00
34 Ted Hampson RC 12.50 25.00
35 Andre Pronovost 12.50 25.00
36 Stafford Smythe CHC 12.50 25.00
37 Don Marshall 12.50 25.00
38 Dick Duff 12.50 25.00
39 Henri Richard 75.00 125.00
40 Bert Olmstead 12.50 25.00
41 Jacques Plante 100.00 200.00
42 Noel Price 12.50 25.00
43 Bob Turner 12.50 25.00
44 Allan Stanley 20.00 40.00
45 Albert Langlois 12.50 25.00
46 Officials Intervene 12.50 25.00
47 Frank Selke MD 12.00 20.00
48 Gary Edmundson RC 12.50 25.00
49 Jean-Guy Talbot 12.50 25.00
50 King Clancy AGM 50.00 80.00

1960-61 Parkhurst

The 1960-61 Parkhurst set of 61 color cards, numbered on the fronts, contains players from Montreal, Toronto, and Detroit. The numbering of the players in the set is

basically by teams, i.e., Toronto Maple Leafs (1-19), Detroit Red Wings (20-37), and Montreal Canadiens (38-55). Cards in the set are 2 7/16" by 3 5/8". The backs, in both French and English, are printed in blue ink and contain NHL lifetime records, vital statistics, and biographical data of the player. This set contains the last card of Maurice "Rocket" Richard. The key Rookie Card in this set is John McKenzie.

COMPLETE SET (61)	1100.00	1700.00
1 Tim Horton	90.00	150.00
2 Frank Mahovlich	65.00	100.00
3 Johnny Bower	50.00	80.00
4 Bert Olmstead	10.00	18.00
5 Gary Edmundson	9.00	15.00
6 Ron Stewart	9.00	15.00
7 Gerry James	9.00	15.00
8 Gerry Ehman	9.00	15.00
9 Red Kelly	18.00	30.00
10 Dave Creighton	9.00	15.00
11 Bob Baun	10.00	18.00
12 Dick Duff	10.00	18.00
13 Larry Regan	9.00	15.00
14 Johnny Wilson	9.00	15.00
15 Billy Harris	9.00	15.00
16 Allan Stanley	12.00	20.00
17 George Armstrong	12.00	20.00
18 Carl Brewer	10.00	18.00
19 Bob Pulford	10.00	18.00
20 Gordie Howe	200.00	350.00
21 Val Fonteyne	9.00	15.00
22 Murray Oliver RC	12.00	20.00
23 Sid Abel CO	12.00	20.00
24 Jack McIntyre	9.00	15.00
25 Marc Reaume	9.00	15.00
26 Norm Ullman	30.00	50.00
27 Brian Smith	9.00	15.00
28 Gerry Melnyk UER (Misspelled Jerry on both sides	9.00	15.00
29 Marcel Pronovost	10.00	18.00
30 Warren Godfrey	9.00	15.00
31 Terry Sawchuk	75.00	150.00
32 Barry Cullen	9.00	15.00
33 Gary Aldcorn	9.00	15.00
34 Pete Goegan	9.00	15.00
35 Len Lunde	9.00	15.00
36 Alex Delvecchio	18.00	30.00
37 John McKenzie RC	15.00	25.00
38 Dickie Moore	15.00	25.00
39 Albert Langlois	9.00	15.00
40 Bill Hicke	9.00	15.00
41 Ralph Backstrom	9.00	15.00
42 Don Marshall	9.00	15.00
43 Bob Turner	9.00	15.00
44 Tom Johnson	10.00	18.00
45 Maurice Richard	100.00	200.00
46 Bernie Geoffrion	30.00	50.00
47 Henri Richard	65.00	100.00
48 Doug Harvey	30.00	50.00
49 Jean Beliveau	60.00	100.00
50 Phil Goyette	9.00	15.00
51 Marcel Bonin	9.00	15.00
52 Jean-Guy Talbot	10.00	18.00
53 Jacques Plante	125.00	200.00
54 Claude Provost	9.00	15.00
55 Andre Pronovost	9.00	15.00
56 Bill Hicke, Ab McDonald, Ralph Backstrom	12.00	20.00
57 Don Marshall, Dickie Moore, Henri Richard	30.00	50.00
58 Claude Provost, Jean Pronovost, Phil Goyette	12.00	20.00
59 Boom Boom Geoffrion, Don Marshall, Jean Beliveau	50.00	80.00
60 Ab McDonald	9.00	15.00
61 Jim Morrison	60.00	100.00

1961-62 Parkhurst

The 1961-62 Parkhurst set contains 51 cards in full color, numbered on the fronts. Cards are 2 7/16" by 3 5/8". The backs contain 1960-61 statistics and a cartoon; the punch line for which could be seen by rubbing the card with a coin. The cards contain players from Montreal, Toronto, and Detroit. The numbering of the players in the set is basically by teams, i.e., Toronto Maple Leafs (1-18), Detroit Red Wings (19-34), and Montreal Canadiens (35-51). The backs are in both French and English. The key Rookie Card in this set is Dave Keon.

COMPLETE SET (51)	1000.00	1600.00
1 Tim Horton	100.00	200.00
2 Frank Mahovlich	50.00	80.00
3 Johnny Bower	35.00	60.00
4 Bert Olmstead	10.00	18.00
5 Dave Keon RC	150.00	250.00
6 Ron Stewart	10.00	18.00
7 Eddie Shack	60.00	100.00
8 Bob Pulford	10.00	18.00
9 Red Kelly	15.00	25.00
10 Bob Nevin	10.00	18.00
11 Bob Baun	10.00	18.00
12 Dick Duff	10.00	18.00
13 Larry Keenan	9.00	15.00
14 Larry Hillman	10.00	18.00
15 Billy Harris	9.00	15.00
16 Allan Stanley	12.00	20.00
17 George Armstrong	12.00	20.00
18 Carl Brewer	10.00	18.00
19 Howie Glover	9.00	15.00
20 Gordie Howe	150.00	250.00
21 Val Fonteyne	9.00	15.00
22 Al Johnson	9.00	15.00
23 Pete Goegan	9.00	15.00
24 Len Lunde	9.00	15.00
25 Alex Delvecchio	15.00	25.00
26 Norm Ullman	25.00	40.00
27 Bill Gadsby	9.00	15.00
28 Ed Litzenberger	9.00	15.00
29 Marcel Pronovost	10.00	18.00
30 Warren Godfrey	9.00	15.00
31 Terry Sawchuk	75.00	125.00
32 Vic Stasiuk	9.00	15.00
33 Leo Labine	9.00	15.00
34 John McKenzie	12.00	20.00
35 Bernie Geoffrion	30.00	50.00
36 Dickie Moore	12.00	20.00
37 Albert Langlois	9.00	15.00
38 Bill Hicke	9.00	15.00
39 Ralph Backstrom	10.00	18.00
40 Don Marshall	10.00	18.00
41 Bob Turner	9.00	15.00
42 Tom Johnson	10.00	18.00
43 Henri Richard	50.00	80.00
44 Wayne Connelly RC UER (Misspelled Conolly on both sides)	12.00	20.00
45 Jean Beliveau	50.00	80.00
46 Phil Goyette	9.00	15.00
47 Marcel Bonin	9.00	15.00
48 Jean-Guy Talbot	10.00	18.00
49 Jacques Plante	100.00	175.00
50 Claude Provost	10.00	18.00
51 Andre Pronovost UER (Shown as Montreal& should be Boston)	25.00	40.00

1962-63 Parkhurst

The 1962-63 Parkhurst set contains 55 cards in full color, with the card number and, on some cards, a facsimile autograph on the front. There is also one unnumbered checklist which is part of the complete set price. An unnumbered game or tally card, which is also referred to as the "Zip" card, is not part of the set. Both of these are considered rather difficult to obtain. Cards are approximately 2 7/16" by 3 5/8". The backs, in both French and English, contain player lifetime statistics and player vital statistics in paragraph form. There are several different styles or designs within this set depending on card number, e.g., some cards have a giant puck as background for their photo on the front. Other cards have the player's team logo as background. The numbering of the players in the set is basically by teams, i.e., Toronto Maple Leafs (1-18), Detroit Red Wings (19-36), and Montreal Canadiens (37-54). The notable Rookie Cards in this set are Bobby Rousseau, Gilles Tremblay, and J.C.Tremblay.

COMPLETE SET (55)	1200.00	2000.00
1 Billy Harris	25.00	40.00
2 Dick Duff	9.00	15.00
3 Bob Baun	9.00	15.00
4 Frank Mahovlich	50.00	80.00
5 Red Kelly	18.00	30.00
6 Ron Stewart	7.00	12.00
7 Tim Horton	60.00	100.00
8 Carl Brewer	9.00	15.00
9 Allan Stanley	10.00	20.00
10 Bob Nevin	9.00	15.00
11 Bob Pulford	9.00	15.00
12 Ed Litzenberger	7.00	12.00
13 George Armstrong	10.00	20.00
14 Eddie Shack	35.00	60.00
15 Dave Keon	60.00	100.00
16 Johnny Bower	30.00	50.00
17 Larry Hillman	9.00	15.00
18 Frank Mahovlich	40.00	70.00
19 Hank Bassen	9.00	15.00
20 Gerry Odrowski	7.00	12.00
21 Norm Ullman	18.00	30.00
22 Vic Stasiuk	7.00	12.00
23 Bruce MacGregor	7.00	12.00
24 Claude Laforge	7.00	12.00
25 Bill Gadsby	7.00	12.00
26 Leo Labine	7.00	12.00
27 Val Fonteyne	7.00	12.00
28 Howie Glover	7.00	12.00
29 Marc Boileau	7.00	12.00
30 Gordie Howe	150.00	250.00
31 Gordie Howe	150.00	250.00
32 Alex Delvecchio	15.00	25.00
33 Marcel Pronovost	9.00	15.00
34 Sid Abel CO	9.00	15.00
35 Len Lunde	7.00	12.00
36 Warren Godfrey	7.00	12.00
37 Phil Goyette	7.00	12.00
38 Henri Richard	50.00	80.00
39 Jean Beliveau	50.00	80.00
40 Bill Hicke	7.00	12.00
41 Claude Provost	7.00	12.00
42 Dickie Moore	10.00	20.00
43 Don Marshall	9.00	15.00
44 Ralph Backstrom	9.00	15.00
45 Marcel Bonin	7.00	12.00
46 Gilles Tremblay RC	20.00	40.00
47 Bobby Rousseau RC	15.00	25.00
48 Bernie Geoffrion	25.00	40.00
49 Jacques Plante	75.00	125.00
50 Tom Johnson	9.00	15.00
51 Jean-Guy Talbot	9.00	15.00
52 Lou Fontinato	9.00	15.00
53 Bernie Geoffrion	25.00	40.00
54 J.C. Tremblay RC !	40.00	60.00
NNO1 Tally Game Card	125.00	250.00
NNO2 Checklist Card	250.00	400.00

1963-64 Parkhurst

The 1963-64 Parkhurst set contains 99 color cards. Cards measure approximately 2 7/16" by 3 5/8". The fronts of the cards feature the player with a varying background depending upon whether the player is on Detroit (American flag), Toronto (Canadian Red Ensign), or Montreal (multi-color striped background). The numbering of the players in the set is basically by teams, i.e., Toronto Maple Leafs (1-20 and 61-79), Detroit Red Wings (41-60), and Montreal Canadiens (21-40 and 80-99). The backs, in both French and English, contain the card number, player lifetime NHL statistics, player biography, and a Stanley Cup replica offer. The set includes two different cards of each Montreal and Toronto player and only one of each Detroit player (with the following exceptions, numbers 15, 20, and 75 (single card Maple Leafs). Each Toronto player's double is obtained by adding 60, e.g., 1 and 61, 2 and 62, 3 and 63, etc., are the same player. Each Montreal player's double is obtained by adding 59, e.g., 21 and 80, 22 and 81, 23 and 82, etc., are the same player. The key Rookie Cards in the set are Red Berenson, Alex Faulkner, John Ferguson, Jacques Laperriere, and Cesare Maniago. Maniago is the last card in the set and is not often found in top condition.

COMPLETE SET (99)	1500.00	2500.00
1 Allan Stanley	25.00	40.00
2 Don Simmons	9.00	15.00
3 Red Kelly	12.00	25.00
4 Dick Duff	9.00	15.00
5 Johnny Bower	30.00	50.00
6 Ed Litzenberger	7.00	12.00
7 Kent Douglas	7.00	12.00
8 Carl Brewer	9.00	15.00
9 Eddie Shack	40.00	80.00
10 Bob Nevin	9.00	15.00
11 Billy Harris	7.00	12.00
12 Bob Pulford	9.00	15.00
13 George Armstrong	10.00	20.00
14 Ron Stewart	7.00	12.00
15 John McMillan	7.00	12.00
16 Tim Horton	50.00	100.00
17 Frank Mahovlich	40.00	70.00
18 Bob Baun	9.00	15.00
19 Punch Imlach ACO/GM	12.00	25.00
20 King Clancy ACO	18.00	30.00
21 Gilles Tremblay	9.00	15.00
22 Jean-Guy Talbot	9.00	15.00
23 Henri Richard	40.00	70.00
24 Ralph Backstrom	9.00	15.00
25 Bill Hicke	7.00	12.00
26 Red Berenson RC	25.00	40.00
27 Jacques Laperriere RC	30.00	50.00
28 Jean Gauthier	7.00	12.00
29 Bernie Geoffrion	25.00	40.00
30 Jean Beliveau	45.00	75.00
31 J.C. Tremblay	9.00	15.00
32 Terry Harper RC	18.00	30.00
33 John Ferguson RC	50.00	80.00
34 Toe Blake CO	12.00	25.00
35 Bobby Rousseau	9.00	15.00
36 Claude Provost	7.00	12.00
37 Marc Reaume	7.00	12.00
38 Dave Balon	7.00	12.00
39 Gump Worsley	25.00	40.00
40 Cesare Maniago RC	25.00	50.00
41 Bruce MacGregor	7.00	12.00
42 Alex Faulkner RC	60.00	125.00
43 Pete Goegan	7.00	12.00
44 Parker MacDonald	7.00	12.00
45 Andre Pronovost	7.00	12.00
46 Marcel Pronovost	9.00	15.00
47 Bob Dillabough	7.00	12.00
48 Larry Jeffrey	7.00	12.00
49 Ian Cushenan	7.00	12.00
50 Alex Delvecchio	12.00	25.00
51 Hank Ciesla	7.00	12.00
52 Norm Ullman	18.00	30.00
53 Terry Sawchuk	70.00	110.00
54 Ron Ingram	7.00	12.00
55 Gordie Howe	300.00	450.00
56 Billy McNeil	7.00	12.00
57 Floyd Smith	7.00	12.00
58 Vic Stasiuk	7.00	12.00
59 Bill Gadsby	7.00	12.00
60 Doug Barkley	7.00	12.00
61 Allan Stanley	10.00	20.00
62 Don Simmons	9.00	15.00
63 Red Kelly	12.00	25.00
64 Dick Duff	9.00	15.00
65 Johnny Bower	30.00	50.00
66 Ed Litzenberger	7.00	12.00
67 Kent Douglas	7.00	12.00
68 Carl Brewer	9.00	15.00
69 Eddie Shack	30.00	50.00
70 Bob Nevin	9.00	15.00
71 Billy Harris	7.00	12.00
72 Bob Pulford	9.00	15.00
73 George Armstrong	10.00	20.00
74 Ron Stewart	7.00	12.00
75 Dave Keon	50.00	80.00
76 Tim Horton	50.00	80.00
77 Frank Mahovlich	40.00	70.00
78 Bob Baun	9.00	15.00
79 Punch Imlach ACO/GM	12.00	25.00
80 Gilles Tremblay	9.00	15.00
81 Jean-Guy Talbot	7.00	12.00
82 Henri Richard	40.00	70.00
83 Ralph Backstrom	9.00	15.00
84 Bill Hicke	7.00	12.00
85 Red Berenson RC	25.00	40.00
86 Jacques Laperriere RC	25.00	40.00
87 Jean Gauthier	7.00	12.00
88 Bernie Geoffrion	25.00	40.00
89 Jean Beliveau	50.00	80.00
90 J.C. Tremblay	9.00	15.00
91 Terry Harper RC	20.00	30.00
92 John Ferguson RC	50.00	80.00
93 Toe Blake CO	12.00	25.00
94 Bobby Rousseau	9.00	15.00
95 Claude Provost	7.00	12.00
96 Marc Reaume	7.00	12.00
97 Dave Balon	7.00	12.00
98 Gump Worsley	25.00	40.00
99 Cesare Maniago RC	100.00	175.00

1991-92 Parkhurst

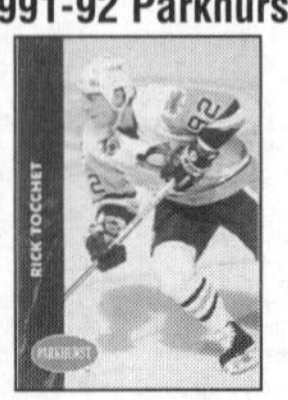

The 1991-92 Parkhurst hockey set marks Pro Set's resurrection of this venerable hockey card brand. The set was primarily released in two series. Both series contain 225 standard-size cards and five (four in the second series) special PHC collectible cards randomly inserted into foil packs. First and second series production quantities were each reported to be 15,000 numbered ten-box foil cases, including 2,500 cases that were translated into French and distributed predominantly to Quebec. The fronts feature full-bleed glossy color photos, bordered on the left by a dark brown marbled border stripe. The player's name appears in the stripe; Parkhurst's teal oval-shaped logo in the lower left corner rounds out the card face. The backs carry a color head shot, with biography, career statistics, and player profile all on a bronze background. The NNO Santa Claus card was randomly inserted in first series packs. A special promotion offer for a 25-card Final Update set was included on Parkhurst Series II packs. It is estimated that less than 15,000 of these sets exist.

COMPLETE SET (450)	10.00	20.00
COMPLETE SERIES 1 (225)	5.00	10.00
COMPLETE SERIES 2 (225)	5.00	10.00
COMP.FINAL UPD.SET (25)	30.00	60.00
*FRENCH: SAME VALUE		
1 Matt DelGuidice	.05	.15
2 Ken Hodge Jr.	.01	.05
3 Vladimir Ruzicka UER (Misspelled Vladimar Ruzika on card front)	.01	.05
4 Craig Janney	.05	.15
5 Glen Wesley	.01	.05
6 Stephen Leach	.01	.05
7 Garry Galley	.01	.05
8 Andy Moog	.08	.25
9 Ray Bourque	.15	.40
10 Brad May	.01	.05
11 Donald Audette	.01	.05
12 Alexander Mogilny	.08	.25
13 Randy Wood	.01	.05
14 Daren Puppa	.05	.15
15 Doug Bodger	.01	.05
16 Pat LaFontaine	.08	.25
17 Dave Andreychuk	.05	.15
18 Dale Hawerchuk	.05	.15
19 Mike Ramsey	.01	.05
20 Tomas Forslund RC UER (Misspelled Thomas on card back)	.01	.05
21 Robert Reichel	.01	.05
22 Theo Fleury	.01	.05
23 Joe Nieuwendyk	.05	.15
24 Gary Roberts	.05	.15
25 Gary Suter	.01	.05
26 Doug Gilmour	.05	.15
27 Mike Vernon	.05	.15
28 Al MacInnis	.05	.15
29 Jeremy Roenick	.08	.25
30 Ed Belfour	.08	.25
31 Steve Smith	.01	.05
32 Chris Chelios	.08	.25
33 Dirk Graham	.01	.05
34 Steve Larmer	.05	.15
35 Brent Sutter	.01	.05
36 Michel Goulet	.05	.15
37 Nicklas Lidstrom RC UER (Misspelled Niklas on card front)	.60	1.50
38 Sergei Fedorov	.15	.40
39 Tim Cheveldae	.05	.15
40 Kevin Miller	.01	.05
41 Ray Sheppard	.01	.05
42 Paul Ysebaert	.01	.05
43 Jimmy Carson	.01	.05
44 Steve Yzerman	.50	1.25
45 Shawn Burr	.01	.05
46 Vladimir Konstantinov RC	.30	.75
47 Josef Beranek RC	.01	.05
48 Vincent Damphousse	.01	.05
49 Dave Manson	.01	.05
50 Scott Mellanby	.01	.05
51 Kevin Lowe	.05	.15
52 Joe Murphy	.01	.05
53 Bill Ranford	.05	.15
54 Craig Simpson	.01	.05
55 Esa Tikkanen	.01	.05
56 Michel Picard RC	.01	.05
57 Geoff Sanderson RC	.08	.25
58 Kay Whitmore	.05	.15
59 John Cullen	.01	.05
60 Rob Brown	.01	.05
61 Zarley Zalapski	.01	.05
62 Brad Shaw	.01	.05
63 Mikael Andersson	.01	.05
64 Pat Verbeek	.01	.05
65 Peter Ahola RC	.01	.05
66 Tony Granato	.01	.05
67 Dave Taylor	.05	.15
68 Luc Robitaille	.05	.15
69 Marty McSorley	.01	.05
70 Tomas Sandstrom	.01	.05
71 Kelly Hrudey	.05	.15
72 Jari Kurri	.08	.25
73 Wayne Gretzky	.60	1.50
74 Larry Robinson	.05	.15
75 Derian Hatcher	.05	.15
76 Ulf Dahlen	.01	.05
77 Jon Casey	.05	.15
78 Dave Gagner	.01	.05
79 Brian Bellows	.01	.05
80 Neal Broten	.05	.15
81 Mike Modano	.20	.50
82 Brian Propp	.01	.05
83 Bobby Smith	.05	.15
84 John LeClair RC	.60	1.50
85 Eric Desjardins	.05	.15
86 Shayne Corson	.01	.05
87 Stephan Lebeau	.01	.05
88 Mathieu Schneider	.01	.05
89 Kirk Muller	.01	.05
90 Patrick Roy	.50	1.25
91 Sylvain Turgeon	.01	.05
92 Guy Carbonneau	.05	.15
93 Denis Savard	.05	.15
94 Scott Niedermayer	.01	.05
95 Tom Chorske	.01	.05
96 Slava Fetisov	.01	.05
97 Kevin Todd RC	.01	.05
98 Chris Terreri	.05	.15
99 David Maley	.01	.05
100 Stephane Richer	.05	.15
101 Claude Lemieux	.01	.05
102 Scott Stevens	.05	.15
103 Peter Stastny	.05	.15
104 David Volek	.01	.05
105 Steve Thomas	.01	.05
106 Pierre Turgeon	.05	.15
107 Glenn Healy	.05	.15
108 Derek King	.01	.05
109 Uwe Krupp	.01	.05
110 Ray Ferraro	.01	.05
111 Pat Flatley	.01	.05
112 Tom Kurvers	.01	.05
113 Adam Creighton	.01	.05
114 Tony Amonte RC UER (Back says shoots right)	.60	1.50
115 John Ogrodnick	.01	.05
116 Doug Weight RC	.50	1.25
117 Mike Richter	.08	.25
118 Darren Turcotte	.01	.05
119 Brian Leetch	.08	.25
120 James Patrick	.01	.05
121 Mark Messier	.08	.25
122 Mike Gartner	.05	.15
123 Mike Ricci	.08	.25
124 Rod Brind'Amour	.08	.25
125 Steve Duchesne	.01	.05
126 Ron Hextall	.05	.15
127 Brad Jones	.01	.05
128 Pelle Eklund	.01	.05
129 Rick Tocchet	.05	.15
130 Mark Howe	.01	.05
131 Andrei Lomakin	.01	.05
132 Jaromir Jagr	.15	.40
133 Jim Paek RC	.01	.05
134 Mark Recchi	.08	.25
135 Kevin Stevens	.01	.05
136 Phil Bourque	.01	.05
137 Mario Lemieux	.60	1.50
138 Bob Errey	.01	.05
139 Tom Barrasso	.05	.15
140 Paul Coffey	.08	.25
141 Joe Mullen	.05	.15
142 Kip Miller	.01	.05
143 Owen Nolan	.08	.25
144 Mats Sundin	.08	.25
145 Mikhail Tatarinov	.01	.05
146 Bryan Fogarty	.01	.05
147 Stephane Morin	.01	.05
148 Joe Sakic	.20	.50
149 Ron Tugnutt	.05	.15
150 Mike Hough	.01	.05
151 Nelson Emerson	.01	.05
152 Curtis Joseph	.08	.25
153 Brendan Shanahan	.08	.25
154 Paul Cavallini	.01	.05
155 Adam Oates	.05	.15
156 Jeff Brown	.01	.05
157 Brett Hull	.10	.30
158 Ron Sutter	.01	.05
159 Dave Christian	.01	.05
160 Pat Falloon	.01	.05
161 Pat MacLeod RC	.01	.05
162 Jarmo Myllys	.01	.05
163 Wayne Presley	.01	.05
164 Perry Anderson	.01	.05
165 Kelly Kisio	.01	.05
166 Brian Mullen	.01	.05
167 Brian Lawton	.01	.05
168 Doug Wilson	.05	.15
169 Rob Pearson RC	.01	.05
170 Wendel Clark	.05	.15
171 Brian Bradley	.01	.05
172 Dave Ellett	.01	.05
173 Gary Leeman	.01	.05
174 Peter Zezel	.01	.05
175 Grant Fuhr	.08	.25
176 Bob Rouse	.01	.05
177 Glenn Anderson	.05	.15
178 Petr Nedved	.05	.15
179 Trevor Linden	.05	.15
180 Jyrki Lumme	.01	.05
181 Kirk McLean	.05	.15
182 Cliff Ronning	.01	.05
183 Greg Adams	.01	.05
184 Doug Lidster	.01	.05
185 Sergio Momesso	.01	.05
186 Geoff Courtnall	.05	.15
187 Dave Babych	.01	.05
188 Peter Bondra	.05	.15
189 Dimitri Khristich	.01	.05
190 Randy Burridge	.01	.05
191 Kevin Hatcher	.05	.15
192 Mike Ridley	.01	.05
193 Dino Ciccarelli	.05	.15
194 Al Iafrate	.05	.15
195 Dale Hunter	.01	.05
196 Mike Liut	.05	.15
197 Rod Langway	.01	.05
198 Russell Romaniuk RC	.01	.05
199 Bob Essensa	.05	.15
200 Teppo Numminen	.01	.05
201 Darrin Shannon	.01	.05
202 Pat Elynuik	.01	.05
203 Fredrik Olausson	.01	.05
204 Ed Olczyk	.01	.05
205 Phil Housley	.05	.15
206 Troy Murray	.01	.05
207 Wayne Gretzky 1000	.40	1.00
208 Bryan Trottier 1000	.05	.15
209 Peter Stastny 1000	.05	.15
210 Jari Kurri 1000	.05	.15
211 Denis Savard 1000	.01	.05
212 Paul Coffey 1000	.05	.15
213 Mark Messier 1000	.08	.25
214 Dave Taylor 1000	.01	.05
215 Michel Goulet 1000	.01	.05
216 Dale Hawerchuk 1000	.01	.05
217 Bobby Smith 1000	.05	.15
218 Ed Belfour LL	.08	.25
219 Brett Hull LL	.08	.25
220 Patrick Roy AS	.30	.75
221 Ray Bourque AS	.08	.25
222 Wayne Gretzky AS	.30	.75
223 Jari Kurri AS	.05	.15
224 Luc Robitaille AS	.05	.15
225 Paul Coffey AS	.05	.15
226 Bob Carpenter	.01	.05
227 Gord Murphy	.01	.05
228 Don Sweeney	.01	.05
229 Glen Murray RC	.20	.50
230 Ted Donato RC	.01	.05
231 Jozef Stumpel RC	.20	.50
232 Stephen Heinze RC	.01	.05
233 Adam Oates	.05	.15
234 Joe Juneau RC	.30	.75
235 Gord Hynes RC	.01	.05
236 Tony Tanti	.01	.05
237 Petr Svoboda	.01	.05
238 Bob Corkum	.01	.05
239 Ken Sutton RC	.01	.05
240 Tom Draper RC	.05	.15
241 Grant Ledyard	.01	.05
242 Christian Ruuttu	.01	.05
243 Brad Miller	.01	.05
244 Clint Malarchuk	.05	.15
245 Trent Yawney	.01	.05
246 Craig Berube	.01	.05
247 Sergei Makarov	.01	.05
248 Alexander Godynyuk	.01	.05
249 Paul Ranheim	.01	.05
250 Jeff Reese	.01	.05
251 Chris Lindberg RC	.01	.05
252 Michel Petit	.01	.05
253 Joel Otto	.01	.05
254 Gary Leeman	.01	.05
255 Ray Leblanc RC	.05	.15
256 Jocelyn Lemieux	.01	.05
257 Igor Kravchuk RC	.01	.05
258 Rob Brown	.01	.05
259 Stephane Matteau	.01	.05
260 Mike Hudson	.01	.05
261 Keith Brown	.01	.05
262 Karl Dykhuis	.01	.05
263 Dominik Hasek RC	2.00	5.00
264 Brian Noonan	.01	.05
265 Yves Racine	.01	.05
266 Slava Kozlov RC	.20	.50
267 Martin Lapointe	.05	.15
268 Steve Chiasson	.01	.05
269 Gerard Gallant	.01	.05
270 Brent Fedyk	.01	.05
271 Brad McCrimmon	.01	.05
272 Bob Probert	.05	.15
273 Alan Kerr	.01	.05
274 Luke Richardson	.01	.05
275 Kelly Buchberger	.01	.05
276 Craig MacTavish	.01	.05
277 Ron Tugnutt	.05	.15
278 Bernie Nicholls	.05	.15
279 Anatoli Semenov	.01	.05
280 Petr Klima	.01	.05
281 Louie DeBrusk RC	.01	.05
282 Norm Maciver RC	.01	.05
283 Martin Gelinas	.01	.05
284 Randy Cunneyworth	.01	.05
285 Andrew Cassels	.01	.05
286 Peter Sidorkiewicz	.05	.15
287 Steve Konroyd	.01	.05
288 Murray Craven	.01	.05
289 Randy Ladouceur	.01	.05
290 Bobby Holik	.05	.15
291 Adam Burt	.01	.05
292 Corey Millen RC	.01	.05
293 Rob Blake	.05	.15
294 Mike Donnelly RC	.01	.05
295 Kyosti Karjalainen RC	.05	.15
296 John McIntyre	.01	.05
297 Paul Coffey	.08	.25
298 Charlie Huddy	.01	.05
299 Bob Kudelski	.01	.05
300 Todd Elik	.01	.05
301 Mike Craig	.01	.05
302 Marc Bureau	.01	.05
303 Jim Johnson	.01	.05
304 Mark Tinordi	.01	.05
305 Gaetan Duchesne	.01	.05
306 Darcy Wakaluk RC	.05	.15
307 Sylvain Lefebvre	.01	.05
308 Russ Courtnall	.01	.05
309 Patrice Brisebois	.01	.05
310 Mike McPhee	.01	.05
311 Mike Keane	.01	.05
312 J.J. Daigneault	.01	.05
313 Gilbert Dionne RC	.05	.15
314 Brian Skrudland	.01	.05
315 Brent Gilchrist	.01	.05
316 Laurie Boschman	.01	.05
317 Ken Daneyko	.01	.05
318 Eric Weinrich	.01	.05
319 Alexei Kasatonov	.01	.05
320 Craig Billington RC	.05	.15
321 Claude Vilgrain	.01	.05
322 Bruce Driver	.01	.05
323 Alexander Semak RC	.01	.05
324 Valeri Zelepukin RC	.01	.05
325 Rob DiMaio	.01	.05
326 Scott Lachance RC	.05	.15
327 Marty McInnis RC	.01	.05
328 Joe Reekie	.01	.05
329 Daniel Marois	.01	.05
330 Wayne McBean	.01	.05
331 Jeff Norton	.01	.05
332 Benoit Hogue	.01	.05
333 Tie Domi	.08	.25
334 Sergei Nemchinov	.01	.05
335 Randy Gilhen	.01	.05
336 Paul Broten	.01	.05
337 Kris King	.01	.05
338 John Vanbiesbrouck	.05	.15
339 Adam Graves	.05	.15
340 Joe Cirella	.01	.05
341 Jeff Beukeboom	.01	.05
342 Terry Carkner	.01	.05
343 Mark Freer RC	.01	.05
344 Corey Foster RC	.01	.05
345 Mark Pederson	.01	.05
346 Kimbi Daniels	.01	.05
347 Mark Recchi	.08	.25
348 Kevin Dineen	.01	.05
349 Kerry Huffman	.01	.05
350 Garry Galley	.01	.05
351 Dan Quinn	.01	.05
352 Troy Loney	.01	.05
353 Ron Francis	.05	.15
354 Rick Tocchet	.05	.15
355 Shawn McEachern RC	.20	.50
356 Kjell Samuelsson	.01	.05
357 Ken Wreggett	.05	.15
358 Larry Murphy	.05	.15
359 Ken Priestlay	.01	.05
360 Bryan Trottier	.08	.25
361 Ulf Samuelsson	.01	.05
362 Valeri Kamensky RC	.05	.15
363 Stephane Fiset	.05	.15
364 Alexei Gusarov RC	.05	.15
365 Greg Paslawski	.01	.05
366 Martin Rucinsky RC	.08	.25
367 Curtis Leschyshyn	.01	.05
368 Jacques Cloutier	.05	.15
369 Craig Wolanin	.01	.05
370 Claude Lapointe RC	.01	.05
371 Adam Foote RC	.15	.40
372 Rich Sutter	.01	.05
373 Lee Norwood	.01	.05
374 Garth Butcher	.01	.05
375 Philippe Bozon RC	.01	.05
376 Dave Lowry	.01	.05
377 Darin Kimble	.01	.05
378 Craig Janney	.05	.15
379 Bob Bassen	.01	.05
380 Rick Zombo	.01	.05
381 Perry Berezan	.01	.05
382 Neil Wilkinson	.01	.05
383 Mike Sullivan RC	.01	.05
384 David Bruce RC	.01	.05
385 Johan Garpenlov	.01	.05
386 Jeff Odgers RC	.01	.05
387 Jay More RC	.01	.05
388 Dean Evason	.01	.05
389 Dale Craigwell	.01	.05
390 Darryl Shannon RC	.01	.05
391 Dimitri Mironov	.05	.15
392 Kent Manderville	.01	.05
393 Todd Gill	.01	.05
394 Rick Wamsley	.05	.15
395 Joe Sacco RC	.01	.05
396 Doug Gilmour	.05	.15
397 Mike Bullard	.01	.05
398 Felix Potvin	.40	1.00
399 Guy Larose RC	.01	.05
400 Tom Fergus	.01	.05
401 Ryan Walter	.01	.05
402 Troy Gamble	.05	.15
403 Robert Dirk	.01	.05
404 Pavel Bure	.08	.25
405 Jim Sandlak	.01	.05
406 Igor Larionov	.01	.05
407 Gerald Diduck	.01	.05
408 Todd Krygier	.01	.05
409 Tim Bergland	.01	.05
410 Calle Johansson	.01	.05
411 Nick Kypreos	.01	.05
412 Michal Pivonka	.01	.05
413 Brad Schlegel RC	.01	.05
414 Kelly Miller	.01	.05
415 John Druce	.01	.05
416 Don Beaupre	.05	.15
417 Alan May	.01	.05
418 Randy Carlyle	.01	.05
419 Stu Barnes	.01	.05
420 Mike Eagles	.01	.05
421 Igor Ulanov RC	.05	.15
422 Evgeny Davydov RC	.01	.05
423 Shawn Cronin	.01	.05
424 Keith Tkachuk RC	1.00	2.50
425 Luciano Borsato RC	.01	.05
426 Stephane Beauregard	.05	.15
427 Mike Lalor	.01	.05
428 Michel Goulet 500	.01	.05
429 Wayne Gretzky 500	.40	1.00
430 Mike Gartner 500	.01	.05
431 Bryan Trottier 500	.05	.15
432 Brett Hull LL	.08	.25
433 Wayne Gretzky LL	.30	.75
434 Steve Yzerman LL	.25	.60
435 Paul Ysebaert LL	.01	.05
436 Gary Roberts LL	.01	.05
437 Dave Andreychuk LL	.01	.05
438 Brian Leetch LL	.05	.15
439 Jeremy Roenick LL	.08	.25
440 Kirk McLean LL	.01	.05

Tim Cheveldae LL .01 .05
Patrick Roy LL .30 .75
Tony Amonte RL .30 .75
Kevin Todd RL .01 .05
Nicklas Lidstrom RL .30 .75
Pavel Bure RL .08 .25
Gilbert Dionne RL .01 .05
Tom Draper RL .05 .15
Dominik Hasek RL .40 1.00
Dominic Roussel RL RC .05 .15
Header/Checklist .30 .75
Trent Klatt XRC .30 .75
Bill Guerin XRC 1.50 4.00
Ray Whitney XRC 1.00 2.50
Boston Bruins .30 .75
Adams Winner
Pittsburgh Penguins .30 .75
Patrick Winner
(Larry Murphy et al.)
Chicago Blackhawks .30 .75
Norris Winner
(Pile up in front of net)
Edmonton Oilers .30 .75
Smythe Winner
(Oiler celebrate win;
Joe Murphy/Petr Klima et al.)
Pittsburgh Penguins 1.50 3.00
Wales Winner
(Andy Moog with glove save;
Mario Lemieux in background)
Chicago Blackhawks .30 .75
Campbell Winner
(Brent Sutter and Craig Muni
in front of Bill Ranford)
Pittsburgh Penguins .30 .75
Stanley Cup Winner
(Igor Kravchuk checking Bryan Trottier)
Pavel Bure .08 .25
Calder Winner
Patrick Roy 5.00 12.00
Vezina Winner
Brian Leetch 1.25 3.00
Norris Winner
Wayne Gretzky 6.00 15.00
Lady Byng Winner
Guy Carbonneau 1.25 3.00
Selke Winner
Mario Lemieux AW 5.00 12.00
Mark Messier 2.50 6.00
Pearson Winner
Ray Bourque 2.50 6.00
Clancy Winner
Patrick Roy AS 5.00 12.00
Brian Leetch AS 1.00 2.50
Ray Bourque AS 2.50 6.00
Kevin Stevens AS 1.00 2.50
Brett Hull AS 2.00 5.00
Mark Messier AS .08 .25
Santa Claus .40 1.00
Robert Reichel PROMO .40 1.00
Doug Gilmour PROMO 1.00 2.50

1991-92 Parkhurst PHC

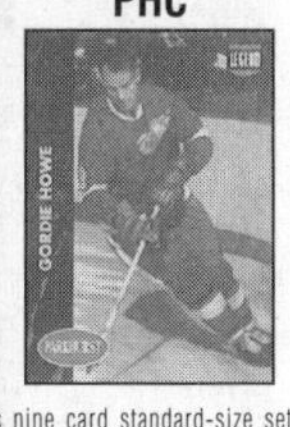

nine card standard-size set was domly inserted in packs of 1991-92 khurst hockey cards with cards 1-5 being the first series and 6-9 in the second es, which featured award winners. PHC ds for Parkhurst Collectibles. The cards numbered with a "PHC" prefix. A French ion of these cards exist and are valued same.

1 Gordie Howe 1.25 3.00
2 Alex Delvecchio .40 1.00
3 Ken Hodge Jr. .40 1.00
4 Robert Kron .40 1.00
5 Sergei Fedorov 1.00 2.50
6 Brett Hull .75 2.00
7 Mario Lemieux 2.50 6.00
8 New York Rangers .60 1.50
(Brian Leetch/Mark Messier/
Mike Gartner/John Ziegler)
9 Terry Sawchuk .60 1.50

1992-93 Parkhurst Previews

domly inserted in 1992-93 Pro Set foil s, these five preview standard-size cards e issued to show the design of the 1992- Parkhurst issue. The fronts feature color on player photos that are full-bleed ept for one edge that is bordered by a k blue-green marbleized stripe. The yer's name is printed vertically in this pe. The Parkhurst logo overlays the pe. The backs have a bluish-green ground and carry small close-up graphy, statistics, and career highlights French and English. The cards are bered on the back with a "PV" prefix.

1 Paul Ysebaert .60 1.50
2 Sean Burke .80 2.00
PV3 Gilbert Dionne .60 1.50
PV4 Ken Hammond .60 1.50
PV5 Grant Fuhr .80 2.00

1992-93 Parkhurst

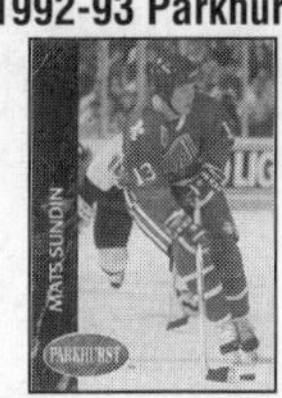

The 1992-93 Parkhurst set consists of 480 standard-size cards plus a 30-card update set. The set was released in two series of 240. The final 30 cards were issued in set form only and are slightly more difficult to obtain. The fronts feature color action player photos that are full-bleed except for one edge that is bordered by a dark blue-green marbleized stripe. The Parkhurst logo overlays the stripe. The backs have a bluish green background and carry small close-up shots, biographies, statistics, and career highlights in French and English. The second series featured traded players in their new uniforms as well as 35 Calder Candidates. The cards are checklisted alphabetically according to teams.

COMPLETE SET (480) 15.00 30.00
COMPLETE SERIES 1 (240) 9.00 18.00
COMPLETE SERIES 2 (240) 6.00 12.00
COMPLETE FINAL UPD. (30) 5.00 10.00
1 Ray Bourque .20 .50
2 Joe Juneau .02 .10
3 Andy Moog .08 .25
4 Adam Oates .02 .10
5 Vladimir Ruzicka .01 .05
6 Glen Wesley .01 .05
7 Dmitri Kvartalnov RC .01 .05
8 Ted Donato .01 .05
9 Glen Murray .01 .05
10 Dave Andreychuk .02 .10
11 Dale Hawerchuk .02 .10
12 Pat LaFontaine .08 .25
13 Alexander Mogilny .02 .10
14 Richard Smehlik RC .01 .05
15 Keith Carney RC .30 .75
16 Philippe Boucher .01 .05
17 Viktor Gordiouk RC .01 .05
18 Donald Audette .01 .05
19 Theo Fleury .01 .05
20 Al MacInnis .02 .10
21 Joe Nieuwendyk .02 .10
22 Gary Roberts .01 .05
23 Gary Suter .01 .05
24 Mike Vernon .02 .10
25 Sergei Makarov .01 .05
26 Robert Reichel .01 .05
27 Chris Lindberg .01 .05
28 Ed Belfour .08 .25
29 Chris Chelios .08 .25
30 Steve Larmer .02 .10
31 Jeremy Roenick .08 .25
32 Steve Smith .01 .05
33 Brent Sutter .01 .05
34 Christian Ruuttu .01 .05
35 Igor Kravchuk .01 .05
36 Sergei Krivokasov .01 .05
37 Tim Cheveldae .02 .10
38 Mike Sillinger .01 .05
39 Sergei Fedorov .15 .40
40 Viacheslav Kozlov .02 .10
41 Bob Probert .02 .10
42 Nicklas Lidstrom .08 .25
43 Paul Ysebaert .01 .05
44 Steve Yzerman .50 1.25
45 Dino Ciccarelli .02 .10
46 Esa Tikkanen .01 .05
47 Dave Manson .01 .05
48 Craig MacTavish .01 .05
49 Bernie Nicholls .02 .10
50 Bill Ranford .02 .10
51 Craig Simpson .01 .05
52 Scott Mellanby .01 .05
53 Shayne Corson .01 .05
54 Petr Klima .01 .05
55 Murray Craven .01 .05
56 Eric Weinrich .01 .05
57 Sean Burke .02 .10
58 Pat Verbeek .01 .05
59 Zarley Zalapski .01 .05
60 Patrick Poulin .01 .05
61 Robert Petrovicky RC UER .01 .05
(Assists total for 1990-91
reads 114)
62 Geoff Sanderson .02 .10
63 Paul Coffey .08 .25
64 Robert Lang RC .01 .05
65 Wayne Gretzky .60 1.50
66 Kelly Hrudey .02 .10
67 Jari Kurri .08 .25
68 Luc Robitaille .02 .10
69 Darryl Sydor .01 .05
70 Jim Hiller RC .01 .05
71 Alexei Zhitnik .01 .05
72 Derian Hatcher .01 .05
73 Jon Casey .02 .10
74 Richard Matvichuk RC .02 .10
75 Mike Modano .20 .50
76 Mark Tinordi .01 .05
77 Todd Elik .01 .05
78 Russ Courtnall .01 .05
79 Tommy Sjodin RC .01 .05
80 Eric Desjardins .01 .05
81 Gilbert Dionne .02 .10
82 Stephan Lebeau .01 .05
83 Kirk Muller .01 .05
84 Patrick Roy .50 1.25
85 Denis Savard .02 .10
86 Vincent Damphousse .01 .05
87 Brian Bellows .01 .05
88 Ed Ronan RC .01 .05
89 Claude Lemieux .01 .05
90 John MacLean .02 .10
91 Stephane Richer .02 .10
92 Scott Stevens .02 .10
93 Chris Terreri .02 .10
94 Kevin Todd .01 .05
95 Scott Niedermayer .01 .05
96 Bobby Holik .02 .10
97 Bill Guerin RC .30 .75
98 Ray Ferraro .01 .05
99 Mark Fitzpatrick .01 .05
100 Derek King .01 .05
101 Uwe Krupp .01 .05
102 Darius Kasparaitis .01 .05
103 Pierre Turgeon .02 .10
104 Benoit Hogue .01 .05
105 Scott Lachance .01 .05
106 Marty McInnis .01 .05
107 Tony Amonte .02 .10
108 Mike Gartner .02 .10
109 Alexei Kovalev .02 .10
110 Brian Leetch .08 .25
111 Mark Messier .08 .25
112 Mike Richter .08 .25
113 James Patrick .01 .05
114 Sergei Nemchinov .01 .05
115 Doug Weight .08 .25
116 Mark Lamb .01 .05
117 Norm Maciver .01 .05
118 Mike Peluso .01 .05
119 Jody Hull .01 .05
120 Peter Sidorkiewicz .02 .10
121 Sylvain Turgeon .01 .05
122 Laurie Boschman .01 .05
123 Brad Marsh .01 .05
124 Neil Brady .01 .05
125 Brian Benning .01 .05
126 Rod BrindAmour .02 .10
127 Kevin Dineen .01 .05
128 Eric Lindros .08 .25
129 Dominic Roussel .02 .10
130 Mark Recchi .02 .10
131 Brent Fedyk .01 .05
132 Greg Paslawski .01 .05
133 Dimitri Yushkevich RC .02 .10
134 Tom Barrasso .02 .10
135 Jaromir Jagr .15 .40
136 Mario Lemieux .50 1.25
137 Larry Murphy .02 .10
138 Kevin Stevens .01 .05
139 Rick Tocchet .02 .10
140 Martin Straka RC .40 1.00
141 Ron Francis .02 .10
142 Shawn McEachern .01 .05
143 Steve Duchesne .01 .05
144 Ron Hextall .02 .10
145 Owen Nolan .02 .10
146 Mike Ricci .02 .10
147 Joe Sakic .20 .50
148 Mats Sundin .08 .25
149 Martin Rucinsky .01 .05
150 Andrei Kovalenko RC .02 .10
151 Dave Karpa RC .01 .05
152 Nelson Emerson .01 .05
153 Brett Hull .15 .40
154 Craig Janney .02 .10
155 Curtis Joseph .08 .25
156 Brendan Shanahan .08 .25
157 Vitali Prokhorov RC .01 .05
158 Igor Korolev RC .02 .10
159 Philippe Bozon .01 .05
160 Ray Whitney RC .15 .40
161 Pat Falloon .01 .05
162 Jeff Hackett .02 .10
163 Brian Lawton .01 .05
164 Sandis Ozolinsh .01 .05
165 Neil Wilkinson .01 .05
166 Kelly Kisio .01 .05
167 Doug Wilson .02 .10
168 Dale Craigwell .01 .05
169 Mikael Andersson .01 .05
170 Wendell Young .02 .10
171 Rob Zamuner RC .02 .10
172 Adam Creighton .01 .05
173 Roman Hamrlik RC .15 .40
174 Brian Bradley .01 .05
175 Rob Ramage .01 .05
176 Chris Kontos RC .01 .05
177 Stan Drulia RC .01 .05
178 Glenn Anderson .02 .10
179 Wendel Clark .08 .25
180 John Cullen .01 .05
181 Dave Ellett .01 .05
182 Grant Fuhr .08 .25
183 Doug Gilmour .02 .10
184 Kent Manderville .01 .05
185 Joe Sacco .01 .05
186 Nikolai Borschevsky RC .01 .05
187 Felix Potvin .08 .25
188 Pavel Bure .08 .25
189 Geoff Courtnall .01 .05
190 Trevor Linden .02 .10
191 Jyrki Lumme .01 .05
192 Kirk McLean .02 .10
193 Cliff Ronning .01 .05
194 Dixon Ward RC .02 .10
195 Greg Adams .01 .05
196 Jiri Slegr .01 .05
197 Don Beaupre .02 .10
198 Kevin Hatcher .01 .05
199 Brad Schlegel .01 .05
200 Mike Ridley .01 .05
201 Calle Johansson .01 .05
202 Steve Konowalchuk RC .02 .10
203 Al Iafrate .02 .10
204 Peter Bondra .02 .10
205 Pat Elynuik .01 .05
206 Keith Tkachuk .08 .25
207 Bob Essensa .02 .10
208 Phil Housley .02 .10
209 Teemu Selanne .50 1.25
210 Alexei Zhamnov .02 .10
211 Evgeny Davydov .01 .05
212 Fredrik Olausson .01 .05
213 Ed Olczyk .01 .05
214 Thomas Steen .01 .05
215 Darius Kasparaitis .01 .05
216 Nikolai Borschevsky .01 .05
217 Teemu Selanne .25 .60
218 Alexander Mogilny .02 .10
219 Sergei Fedorov .08 .25
220 Jaromir Jagr .08 .25
221 Mats Sundin .02 .10
222 Dimitri Kvartalnov .01 .05
223 Andrei Kovalenko .01 .05
224 Tommy Sjodin .01 .05
225 Alexei Kovalev .02 .10
226 Evgeny Davydov .01 .05
227 Robert Lang .01 .05
228 Valeri Zelepukin .01 .05
229 Doug Weight .08 .25
230 Valeri Kamensky .01 .05
231 Donald Audette .01 .05
232 Nelson Emerson .01 .05
233 Pat Falloon .01 .05
234 Pavel Bure .08 .20
235 Tony Amonte .05 .12
236 Sergei Nemchinov .01 .05
237 Gilbert Dionne .01 .05
238 Kevin Todd .01 .05
239 Nicklas Lidstrom .02 .10
240 Brad May .01 .05
241 Stephen Leach .01 .05
242 Dave Poulin .01 .05
243 Grigori Panteleyev RC .01 .05
244 Don Sweeney .01 .05
245 John Blue RC .02 .10
246 C.J. Young RC .01 .05
247 Stephen Heinze .01 .05
248 Cam Neely .08 .25
249 David Reid .01 .05
250 Grant Fuhr .08 .25
251 Bob Sweeney .01 .05
252 Rob Ray .02 .10
253 Doug Bodger .01 .05
254 Ken Sutton .01 .05
255 Yuri Khmylev RC .01 .05
256 Mike Ramsey .01 .05
257 Brad May .01 .05
258 Brent Ashton .01 .05
259 Joel Otto .01 .05
260 Paul Ranheim .01 .05
261 Kevin Dahl RC .01 .05
262 Trent Yawney .01 .05
263 Roger Johansson .01 .05
264 Jeff Reese .01 .05
265 Ron Stern .01 .05
266 Brian Skrudland .01 .05
267 Bryan Marchment .01 .05
268 Stephane Matteau .01 .05
269 Frantisek Kucera .01 .05
270 Jim Waite .02 .10
271 Dirk Graham .01 .05
272 Michel Goulet .02 .10
273 Joe Murphy .01 .05
274 Keith Brown .01 .05
275 Jocelyn Lemieux .01 .05
276 Paul Coffey .08 .25
277 Keith Primeau .01 .05
278 Vincent Riendeau .02 .10
279 Mark Howe .01 .05
280 Ray Sheppard .01 .05
281 Jim Hiller .01 .05
282 Steve Chiasson .01 .05
283 Vladimir Konstantinov .08 .25
284 Brian Benning .01 .05
285 Kevin Todd .01 .05
286 Zdeno Ciger .01 .05
287 Brian Glynn .01 .05
288 Shaun Van Allen .01 .05
289 Brad Werenka RC .01 .05
290 Ron Tugnutt .02 .10
291 Igor Kravchuk .01 .05
292 Todd Elik .01 .05
293 Terry Yake .01 .05
294 Michael Nylander RC .02 .10
295 Yvon Corriveau .01 .05
296 Frank Pietrangelo .02 .10
297 Nick Kypreos .01 .05
298 Andrew Cassels .01 .05
299 Steve Konroyd .01 .05
300 Allen Pedersen .01 .05
301 Tony Granato .01 .05
302 Rob Blake .02 .10
303 Robb Stauber .02 .10
304 Marty McSorley .01 .05
305 Lonnie Loach RC .01 .05
306 Corey Millen .01 .05
307 Dave Taylor .02 .10
308 Jimmy Carson .01 .05
309 Warren Rychel RC .01 .05
310 Ulf Dahlen .01 .05
311 Dave Gagner .02 .10
312 Brad Berry RC .01 .05
313 Neal Broten .02 .10
314 Mike Craig .01 .05
315 Darcy Wakaluk .02 .10
316 Shane Churla .01 .05
317 Trent Klatt RC .02 .10
318 Mike Keane .01 .05
319 Mathieu Schneider .01 .05
320 Patrice Brisebois .01 .05
321 Andre Racicot .02 .10
322 Mario Roberge .01 .05
323 Gary Leeman .01 .05
324 Jean-Jacques .01 .05
Daigneault
325 Lyle Odelein .01 .05
326 John LeClair .20 .50
327 Valeri Zelepukin .01 .05
328 Bernie Nicholls .02 .10
329 Alexander Semak .01 .05
330 Craig Billington .02 .10
331 Randy McKay .01 .05
332 Ken Daneyko .01 .05
333 Bruce Driver .01 .05
334 Slava Fetisov .01 .05
335 Dennis Vaske .01 .05
336 Brad Dalgarno .01 .05
337 Jeff Norton .01 .05
338 Steve Thomas .02 .10
339 Vladimir Malakhov .01 .05
340 David Volek .01 .05
341 Glenn Healy .02 .10
342 Patrick Flatley .01 .05
343 Travis Green RC .25 .60
344 Corey Hirsch RC .08 .25
345 Darren Turcotte .01 .05
346 Adam Graves .01 .05
347 Steve King RC .01 .05
348 Kevin Lowe .02 .10
349 John Vanbiesbrouck .08 .25
350 Ed Olczyk .01 .05
351 Sergei Zubov RC .25 .60
352 Brad Shaw .01 .05
353 Jamie Baker .01 .05
354 Mark Freer .01 .05
355 Darcy Loewen .01 .05
356 Darren Rumble RC .01 .05
357 Bob Kudelski .01 .05
358 Ken Hammond .01 .05
359 Daniel Berthiaume .02 .10
360 Josef Beranek .01 .05
361 Greg Hawgood .01 .05
362 Terry Carkner .01 .05
363 Vyatcheslav Butsayev RC .01 .05
364 Garry Galley .01 .05
365 Andre Faust RC .01 .05
366 Ryan McGill RC .01 .05
367 Tommy Soderstrom RC .02 .10
368 Joe Mullen .02 .10
369 Ulf Samuelsson .01 .05
370 Mike Needham RC .01 .05
371 Ken Wregget .02 .10
372 Dave Tippett .01 .05
373 Kjell Samuelsson .01 .05
374 Bob Errey .01 .05
375 Jim Paek .01 .05
376 Bill Lindsay RC .01 .05
377 Valeri Kamensky .01 .05
378 Stephane Fiset .02 .10
379 Steven Finn .01 .05
380 Mike Hough .01 .05
381 Scott Pearson .01 .05
382 Kerry Huffman .01 .05
383 Scott Young .01 .05
384 Stephane Quintal .01 .05
385 Bret Hedican RC .02 .10
386 Guy Hebert RC .30 .75
387 Vitali Karamnov RC .01 .05
388 Doug Crossman .01 .05
389 Ron Sutter .01 .05
390 Garth Butcher .01 .05
391 Basil McRae .01 .05
392 Dean Evason .01 .05
393 Doug Zmolek RC .01 .05
394 Jay More .01 .05
395 Mike Sullivan .01 .05
396 Arturs Irbe .08 .25
397 Johan Garpenlov .01 .05
398 Jeff Odgers .01 .05
399 Jaroslav Otevrel RC .01 .05
400 Marc Bureau .01 .05
401 Bob Beers .01 .05
402 Rob DiMaio .01 .05
403 Steve Kasper .01 .05
404 Pat Jablonski .02 .10
405 John Tucker .01 .05
406 Shawn Chambers .01 .05
407 Mike Hartman .01 .05
408 Danton Cole .01 .05
409 Dave Andreychuk .02 .10
410 Peter Zezel .01 .05
411 Mike Krushelnyski .01 .05
412 Daren Puppa .02 .10
413 Ken Baumgartner .01 .05
414 Rob Pearson .01 .05
415 Mike Foligno .01 .05
416 Sylvain Lefebvre .01 .05
417 Dimitri Mironov .01 .05
418 Petr Nedved .02 .10
419 Gerald Diduck .01 .05
420 Anatoli Semenov .01 .05
421 Sergio Momesso .01 .05
422 Gino Odjick .01 .05
423 Kay Whitmore .02 .10
424 Dave Babych .01 .05
425 Robert Dirk .01 .05
426 Reggie Savage .01 .05
427 Keith Jones RC .08 .25
428 Dimitri Khristich .01 .05
429 Jason Woolley RC .01 .05
430 Jim Hrivnak .02 .10
431 Sylvain Cote .01 .05
432 Michal Pivonka .01 .05
433 Rod Langway .01 .05
434 Tie Domi .08 .25
435 Sergei Bautin RC .01 .05
436 Darrin Shannon .01 .05
437 John Druce .01 .05
438 Teppo Numminen .01 .05
439 Luciano Borsato .01 .05
440 Igor Ulanov .01 .05
441 Mike O'Neill RC .02 .10
442 Kris King .01 .05
443 Roman Hamrlik .02 .10
444 Steve Smith .01 .05
445 Jari Kurri .08 .25
446 Ulf Samuelsson .01 .05
447 Sergei Nemchinov .01 .05
448 Tommy Soderstrom .02 .10
449 Petr Nedved .02 .10
450 Peter Sidorkiewicz .02 .10
451 Nicklas Lidstrom .02 .10
452 Philippe Bozon .01 .05
453 Uwe Krupp .01 .05
454 Steve Thomas .02 .10
455 Owen Nolan .02 .10
456 Steve Yzerman .25 .60
457 Chris Schmidt .08 .25
458 Paul Coffey .08 .25
459 Brett Hull .08 .25
460 Pavel Bure .08 .20
461 Ed Belfour .02 .10
462 Mario Lemieux AS .25 .60
463 Patrick Roy .25 .60
464 Ray Bourque .08 .25
465 Jaromir Jagr .08 .25
466 Kevin Stevens .01 .05
467 Brian Leetch .02 .10
468 Bobby Clarke .02 .10
469 Bill Barber .02 .10
470 Bernie Parent .02 .10
471 Reggie Leach .01 .05
472 Rick MacLeish .01 .05
473 Dave Schultz .02 .10
474 Joe Watson .01 .05
475 Bobby Taylor .01 .05
476 Orest Kindrachuk .01 .05
477 Bob Kelly .01 .05
478 Bill Clement .02 .10
479 Ed Van Impe .01 .05
480 Fred Shero .02 .10
481 Bryan Smolinski RC .25 .60
482 Sergei Zholtok .10 .30
483 Matthew Barnaby RC .10 .30
484 Gary Shuchuk .10 .30
485 Guy Carbonneau .10 .30
486 Oleg Petrov RC .10 .30
487 Sean Hill RC .10 .30
488 Jesse Belanger RC .10 .30
489 Paul DiPietro .05 .15
490 Rich Pilon .05 .15
491 Greg Parks .10 .30
492 Jeff Daniels .10 .30
493 Denny Felsner RC .10 .30
494 Mike Eastwood RC .10 .30
495 Murray Craven .10 .30
496 Vincent Damphousse .05 .15
497 Grant Fuhr .25 .60
498 Mario Lemieux SCP 1.25 3.00
499 Ray Ferraro .05 .15
500 Teemu Selanne .75 2.00
501 Luc Robitaille .10 .30
502 Doug Gilmour .10 .30
503 Curtis Joseph .25 .60
504 Kirk Muller .05 .15
505 Glenn Healy .10 .30
506 Pavel Bure .08 .25
507 Felix Potvin .10 .30
508 Guy Carbonneau .10 .30
509 Wayne Gretzky 1.50 4.00
510 Patrick Roy 1.25 3.00

1992-93 Parkhurst Emerald Ice

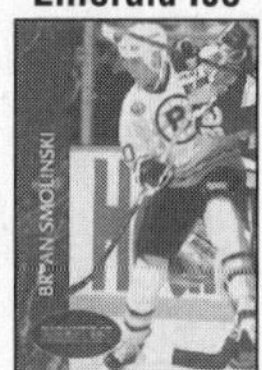

The '92-93 Parkhurst Emerald Ice set consists of 480 cards and a 30 card update set. This parallel set version can be differentiated from its basic set counterpart by the company's use of an "emerald green" embossed-foil Parkhurst logo on the lower left of the card. Cards 1-240 were inserted one per foil pack, two per jumbo pack in series one product; likewise for cards 241-480 in series two product. Cards 481-510 were available in set form only, and are slightly more difficult to obtain.

*STARS: 2X TO 5X BASIC CARDS
*ROOKIES: 1.25X TO 3X BASIC CARDS

1992-93 Parkhurst Cherry Picks

Randomly inserted in second series Parkhurst foil packs, this 21-card standard-size set features Don Cherry's "Cherry Picks" as selected by the ex-coach and host of "Coach's Corner" on Hockey Night in Canada. The cards feature full-bleed, color action player photos. The player's name is printed in gold foil near the bottom of the card along with the Cherry Picks logo. The backs have a dark blue-gray and black stripe background. Set at an angle on this background is a hockey arena graphic design that carries comments from Don Cherry in French and English. Overlapping the arena design is a small, action player photo. The cards are numbered on the backs with a "CP" prefix. The cover card carries a message from Don Cherry. The Doug Gilmour card (CP 1993) was randomly inserted in Final Update sets.

CP1 Doug Gilmour 1.00 2.50
CP2 Jeremy Roenick 2.50 6.00
CP3 Brent Sutter 1.00 2.50
CP4 Mark Messier 2.00 5.00
CP5 Kirk Muller 1.00 2.50
CP6 Eric Lindros 2.00 5.00
CP7 Dale Hunter 1.00 2.50
CP8 Gary Roberts 1.00 2.50
CP9 Bob Probert 1.00 2.50
CP10 Brendan Shanahan 2.00 5.00
CP11 Wendel Clark 1.00 2.50
CP12 Rick Tocchet 1.00 2.50
CP13 Owen Nolan 2.00 5.00
CP14 Cam Neely 2.00 5.00
CP15 Dave Manson 1.00 2.50
CP16 Chris Chelios 2.00 5.00
CP17 Marty McSorley 1.00 2.50
CP18 Scott Stevens 1.00 2.50
CP19 John Blue 1.00 2.50
CP20 Ron Hextall 1.00 2.50
CP1993 Doug Gilmour 6.00 15.00
Cherry Pick of the Year
NNO Don Cherry AU 40.00 100.00
NNO Don Cherry 8.00 20.00
Checklist back
NNO Don Cherry 4.00 10.00
Redemption

1992-93 Parkhurst Cherry Picks Sheet

This approximately 11" by 8 1/2" sheet displays the cards of the 1992-93 Parkhurst Cherry Picks insert set. The sheet could be

obtained by collectors in exchange for four Don Cherry redemption cards, which were randomly inserted in 1992-93 Parkhurst series II packs. The sheet pictures the fronts of the cards from the 1992-93 Cherry Picks set with Don Cherry's card in the middle. The words "1993 Cherry Picks Promo" are printed in a pink to purple shaded bar at the top of the sheet. The back is blank and the sheet is unnumbered.

1 Dale Hunter 5.00 10.00
Dave Manson
Doug Gilmour
Gary Roberts
Chris Chelios
Jeremy Roenick
Bob Probert
Marty McSorley
Brent Sutter
Brendan Shanahan
Don Cherry
Mark Messier
Wendel Clark
Kirk Muller
Rick Tocchet
Scott Stevens
Eric Lindros
Owen Nolan
John Blue
Ron Hextall

1992-93 Parkhurst Parkie Reprints

This set of 36 cards was issued in four separate series. The cards are reprints of cards from the 1950s. Capturing eight goalies from the 1950's Parkhurst collections, the first set was undercollated into first series 12-card foil packs. The second eight cards showcase defensemen; these cards were randomly inserted in series 1 jumbo packs. Forwards (17-24) were inserted in second series foil with the remaining forwards (25-32) inserted in second series jumbo packs. The cover cards, which reproduce Parkhurst wrappers on their fronts (1953-54 and 1955-56), have a checklist on their backs. The fronts vary in design but all carry a color shot of the featured player. The players' names are on the fronts, some in print, some in signature form. The backs carry the information from the original card. The print varies from red to black to a combination. The Turk Broda and Terry Sawchuk cards are blank on the back as the originals are. The cards are numbered on the back with a "PR" prefix. Only Canadian cases included a newly created 1954-55 Don Cherry Parkie 101 card. The Parkie Reprints set is considered complete without it.

COMPLETE SET (36) 75.00 150.00
PR1 Jacques Plante 3.00 8.00
PR2 Terry Sawchuk 3.00 8.00
PR3 Johnny Bower 2.00 5.00
PR4 Gump Worsley 2.00 5.00
PR5 Harry Lumley 2.00 5.00
PR6 Turk Broda 2.00 5.00
PR7 Jim Henry 2.00 5.00
PR8 Al Rollins 2.00 5.00
PR9 Bill Gadsby 2.00 5.00
PR10 Red Kelly 2.00 5.00
PR11 Allan Stanley 2.00 5.00
PR12 Bob Baun 2.00 5.00
PR13 Carl Brewer 2.00 5.00
PR14 Doug Harvey 2.00 5.00
PR15 Harry Howell 2.00 5.00
PR16 Tim Horton 2.00 5.00
PR17 George Armstrong 2.00 5.00
PR18 Ralph Backstrom 2.00 5.00
PR19 Alex Delvecchio 2.00 5.00
PR20 Bill Mosienko 2.00 5.00
PR21 Dave Keon 2.00 5.00
PR22 Andy Bathgate 2.00 5.00
PR23 Milt Schmidt 2.00 5.00
PR24 Dick Duff 2.00 5.00
PR25 Norm Ullman 2.00 5.00
PR26 Dickie Moore 2.00 5.00
PR27 Jerry Toppazzini 2.00 5.00
PR28 Henri Richard 2.00 5.00
PR29 Frank Mahovlich 2.00 5.00
PR30 Jean Beliveau 2.00 5.00
PR31 Ted Lindsay 2.00 5.00
PR32 Bernie Geoffrion 2.00 5.00
CL1 Parkies Checklist 1 2.00 5.00
(Repro of 1955-56
Parkie Wrapper)
CL2 Parkies Checklist 2 2.00 5.00
(Repro of 1953-54
Parkie Wrapper)
CL3 Parkies Checklist 3 2.00 5.00
(Repro of 1958-59
Parkie Wrapper)
CL4 Parkies Checklist 4 2.00 5.00
(Repro of 1954-55
Parkie Wrapper)
AU Don Cherry Parkie AU 40.00 100.00
NNO D.Cherry Parkie 101 6.00 15.00

1992-93 Parkhurst Arena Tour Sheets

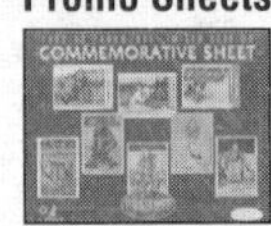

Each sheet in this set of eight measures approximately 11" by 8 1/2" and commemorates a stop on the Canadian Arena Tour. The fronts feature color photos of 1992-93 Parkhurst hockey cards against a blue-green background that shades from dark to light. A thin metallic gold line frames the cards, and the word "Commemorative" is printed in large white letters on this line at the top of the sheet. Near the center are the words "Canadian Arena Tour" and a specific arena name along with the date the sheet was distributed. The team logo is printed above this text. Each sheet carries a serial number and the production run (noted beside the dates below). The backs are blank. The sheets are unnumbered and checklisted below in chronological order. The Montreal sheet was not distributed at the Forum; reportedly because the sheet was not bilingual.

1 Calgary Flames 4.00 10.00
Olympic Saddledome
April 1 1993 (22,000)
Mike Vernon
Theoren Fleury
Trent Yawney
Brian Skrudland
Joel Otto
Al MacInnis
2 Edmonton Oilers 4.00 10.00
Northlands Coliseum
April 3 1993 (22,000)
Zdeno Ciger
Bill Ranford
Todd Elik
Igor Kravchuk
Craig MacTavish
Shayne Corson
3 Quebec Nordiques 4.00 10.00
Colisee de Quebec
April 6 1993 (22,000)
Bill Lindsay
Ron Hextall
Valeri Kamensky
Kerry Huffman
Mats Sundin
Joe Sakic
4 Vancouver Canucks 6.00 15.00
Pacific Coliseum
April 11 1993 (22,000)
Dave Babych
Pavel Bure
Petr Nedved
Anatoli Semenov
Kirk McLean
Trevor Linden
5 Montreal Canadiens 10.00 25.00
The Forum
April 12 1993 (22,000)
Denis Savard
Kirk Muller
J.J. Daigneault
Patrice Brisebois
Mathieu Schneider
Patrick Roy
6 Toronto Maple Leafs 8.00 20.00
Maple Leaf Gardens
April 13 1993 (22,000)
Felix Potvin
Dave Andreychuk
Wendel Clark
Peter Zezel
Doug Gilmour
Sylvain Lefebvre
7 Ottawa Senators 4.00 10.00
Ottawa Civic Centre
April 14 1993 (22,000)
Brad Marsh
Ken Hammond
Bob Kudelski
Peter Sidorkiewicz
Sylvain Turgeon
Mark Freer
8 Winnipeg Jets 4.00 10.00
Winnipeg Arena
April 15 1993 (22,000)
Phil Housley
John Druce
Sergei Bautin
Tie Domi
Evgeny Davydov
Teemu Selanne

1992-93 Parkhurst Parkie Sheets

These five commemorative sheets measure approximately 8 1/2" by 11". The sheets are individually numbered; the production quantities are listed in the checklist below. The sheets were distributed one per case as an insert with the various series of 1992-93 Parkhurst hockey cards. The players pictured are the players in that respective Parkie reprint series. The Stanley Cup Commemorative Update sheet was issued one per case of Final Update. These unnumbered sheets are numbered chronologically below for convenience in reference.

1 Goalies 8.00 20.00
(7000 sheets issued)
2 Defensemen 10.00 25.00
(3000 sheets issued)
3 Forwards/Wingers 8.00 20.00
(7000 sheets issued)
4 Forwards/Centers 12.00 30.00
(3000 sheets issued)
5 Stanley Cup Update 16.00 40.00
(1000 sheets issued)

1992-93 Parkhurst Promo Sheets

These 11" by 8 1/2" sheets were promos of the 1992-93 Parkhurst Limited Edition Commemorative Sheets. The fronts feature color photos of actual Parkhurst Parkies. The cards are set against a dark green marbleized background. A thin metallic gold line frames the cards. The words "Commemorative Sheet" are printed in white over the gold line near the top of the sheet. Above this, are the words "1992-93 Parkhurst Limited Edition" printed in metallic gold. A gold or white oval at the bottom right corner carries the word "Promo." The backs are blank. The sheets are unnumbered.

1 Toronto Maple Leafs 10.00 25.00
vs. Montreal Canadiens
Alumni Game
April 4& 1993
Maple Leaf Gardens
Johnny Bower
Harry Lumley
Jacques Plante
Dave Keon
Doug Harvey
Tim Horton
Ralph Backstrom
Frank Mahovlich
2 Dave Keon 6.00 15.00
Milt Schmidt
Dick Duff
Bill Mosienko
Alex Delvecchio
Ralph Backstrom
George Armstrong
Andy Bathgate

1993-94 Parkhurst

Issued in two series, these 540 standard-size cards feature color player action shots on their fronts. They are borderless, except on the right, where black and green stripes set off by a silver-foil line carry the player's name in white lettering; and at the lower left, where a black and green corner backs up the silver-foil-stamped Parkhurst logo. The player's team name appears near the right edge in vertical silver-foil lettering. The horizontal back carries another color player action shot on the right. On the left are the player's team name, position, biography, career highlights, and statistics. Card numbers 398 and 498 were not issued.

COMPLETE SET (540) 15.00 30.00
COMPLETE SERIES 1 (270) 7.50 15.00
COMPLETE SERIES 2 (270) 7.50 15.00
1 Steven King .02 .10
2 Sean Hill .02 .10
3 Anatoli Semenov .02 .10
4 Garry Valk .02 .10
5 Todd Ewen .02 .10
6 Bob Corkum .02 .10
7 Tim Sweeney .02 .10
8 Patrick Carnback RC .20 .50
9 Troy Loney .02 .10
10 Cam Neely .08 .25
11 Adam Oates .05 .15
12 Jon Casey .05 .15
13 Don Sweeney .02 .10
14 Ray Bourque .15 .40
15 Jozef Stumpel .02 .10
16 Glen Murray .02 .10
17 Glen Wesley .02 .10
18 Fred Knipscheer RC .20 .50
19 Craig Simpson .02 .10
20 Richard Smehlik .02 .10
21 Alexander Mogilny .05 .15
22 Grant Fuhr .05 .15
23 Dale Hawerchuk .05 .15
24 Philippe Boucher .02 .10
25 Scott Thomas RC .20 .50
26 Donald Audette .05 .15
27 Brad May .05 .15
28 Theo Fleury .05 .15
29 Andrei Trefilov .02 .10
30 Sandy McCarthy .02 .10
31 Joe Nieuwendyk .05 .15
32 Paul Ranheim .02 .10
33 Kelly Kisio .02 .10
34 Joel Otto .02 .10
35 Ted Drury .02 .10
36 Al MacInnis .05 .15
37 Kevin Todd .02 .10
38 Joe Murphy .02 .10
39 Christian Ruuttu .02 .10
40 Steve Dubinsky RC .20 .50
41 Stephane Matteau .02 .10
42 Ivan Droppa RC .20 .50
43 Jocelyn Lemieux .02 .10
44 Ed Belfour .08 .25
45 Chris Chelios .08 .25
46 Derian Hatcher .02 .10
47 Andy Moog .05 .15
48 Trent Klatt .02 .10
49 Mike Modano .15 .40
50 Paul Cavallini .02 .10
51 Mike McPhee .02 .10
52 Brent Gilchrist .02 .10
53 Russ Courtnall .02 .10
54 Neal Broten .05 .15
55 Steve Chiasson .02 .10
56 Paul Coffey .08 .25
57 Slava Kozlov .05 .15
58 Sergei Fedorov .15 .40
59 Tim Cheveldae .05 .15
60 Dino Ciccarelli .05 .15
61 Dallas Drake RC .20 .50
62 Nicklas Lidstrom .08 .25
63 Martin Lapointe .02 .10
64 Dean McAmmond .02 .10
65 Igor Kravchuk .02 .10
66 Shjon Podein RC .20 .50
67 Bill Ranford .05 .15
68 Brad Werenka .02 .10
69 Doug Weight .05 .15
70 Ian Herbers RC .20 .50
71 Todd Elik .02 .10
72 Steven Rice .02 .10
73 John Vanbiesbrouck .05 .15
74 Alexander Godynyuk .02 .10
75 Brian Skrudland .02 .10
76 Jody Hull .02 .10
77 Brent Severyn RC .20 .50
78 Evegny Davydov .02 .10
79 Dave Lowry .02 .10
80 Scott Levins RC .20 .50
81 Scott Mellanby .05 .15
82 Dan Keczmer .02 .10
83 Michael Nylander .02 .10
84 Jim Sandlak .02 .10
85 Brian Propp .02 .10
86 Geoff Sanderson .05 .15
87 Mike Lenarduzzi RC .20 .50
88 Zarley Zalapski .02 .10
89 Robert Petrovicky .02 .10
90 Robert Kron .02 .10
91 Luc Robitaille .05 .15
92 Alexei Zhitnik .02 .10
93 Tony Granato .02 .10
94 Rob Blake .05 .15
95 Gary Shuchuk .02 .10
96 Darryl Sydor .02 .10
97 Kelly Hrudey .05 .15
98 Warren Rychel .02 .10
99 Wayne Gretzky .60 1.50
100 Patrick Roy .50 1.25
101 Gilbert Dionne .02 .10
102 Eric Desjardins .05 .15
103 Peter Popovic RC .20 .50
104 Vincent Damphousse .02 .10
105 Patrice Brisebois .02 .10
106 Pierre Sevigny .02 .10
107 John LeClair .08 .25
108 Paul DiPietro .02 .10
109 Alexander Semak .02 .10
110 Claude Lemieux .02 .10
111 Scott Niedermayer .02 .10
112 Chris Terreri .05 .15
113 Stephane Richer .05 .15
114 Scott Stevens .05 .15
115 John MacLean .05 .15
116 Scott Pellerin RC .20 .50
117 Bernie Nicholls .02 .10
118 Ron Hextall .05 .15
119 Derek King .02 .10
120 Scott Lachance .02 .10
121 Scott Scissons .02 .10
122 Darius Kasparaitis .02 .10
123 Ray Ferraro .02 .10
124 Steve Thomas .02 .10
125 Vladimir Malakhov .02 .10
126 Travis Green .05 .15
127 Mark Messier .08 .25
128 Sergei Nemchinov .02 .10
129 Tony Amonte .08 .25
130 Alexei Kovalev .05 .15
131 Brian Leetch .08 .25
132 Mike Richter .08 .25
133 Sergei Zubov .02 .10
134 Adam Graves .02 .10
135 Esa Tikkanen .02 .10
136 Sylvain Turgeon .02 .10
137 Norm Maciver .02 .10
138 Craig Billington .05 .15
139 Dmitri Filiminov .02 .10
140 Pavel Demitra .05 .15
141 Brian Glynn .02 .10
142 Darrin Madeley RC .20 .50
143 Radek Hamr RC .20 .50
144 Robert Burakovsky RC .20 .50
145 Dmitri Yushkevich .02 .10
146 Claude Boivin .02 .10
147 Pelle Eklund .02 .10
148 Brent Fedyk .02 .10
149 Mark Recchi .05 .15
150 Tommy Soderstrom .05 .15
151 Vyacheslav Butsayev .02 .10
152 Rod Brind'Amour .05 .15
153 Josef Beranek .02 .10
154 Jaromir Jagr .15 .40
155 Ulf Samuelsson .02 .10
156 Martin Straka .02 .10
157 Tom Barrasso .05 .15
158 Kevin Stevens .02 .10
159 Joe Mullen .05 .15
160 Ron Francis .05 .15
161 Marty McSorley .02 .10
162 Larry Murphy .05 .15
163 Owen Nolan .05 .15
164 Stephane Fiset .05 .15
165 Dave Karpa .02 .10
166 Martin Gelinas .02 .10
167 Andrei Kovalenko .02 .10
168 Steve Duchesne .02 .10
169 Joe Sakic .20 .50
170 Martin Rucinsky .02 .10
171 Chris Simon RC .20 .50
172 Brendan Shanahan .08 .25
173 Jeff Brown .02 .10
174 Phil Housley .05 .15
175 Curtis Joseph .08 .25
176 Jim Montgomery RC .20 .50
177 Bret Hedican .02 .10
178 Kevin Miller .02 .10
179 Philippe Bozon .02 .10
180 Brett Hull .10 .30
181 Jimmy Waite .05 .15
182 Ray Whitney .02 .10
183 Pat Falloon .02 .10
184 Tom Pederson .02 .10
185 Igor Larionov .02 .10
186 Dody Wood RC .20 .50
187 Sandis Ozolinsh .02 .10
188 Sergei Makarov .02 .10
189 Rob Gaudreau RC .20 .50
190 Roman Hamrlik .05 .15
191 Stan Drulia .02 .10
192 Pat Jablonski .05 .15
193 Denis Savard .05 .15
194 Rob Zamuner .02 .10
195 Petr Klima .02 .10
196 Rob Dimiao .02 .10
197 Chris Kontos .02 .10
198 Mikael Andersson .02 .10
199 Drake Berehowsky .02 .10
200 Dave Andreychuk .05 .15
201 Glenn Anderson .05 .15
202 Felix Potvin .08 .25
203 Nikolai Borschevsky .02 .10
204 Kent Manderville .02 .10
205 Dave Ellett .02 .10
206 Peter Zezel .02 .10
207 Ken Baumgartner .02 .10
208 Murray Craven .02 .10
209 Dixon Ward .02 .10
210 Cliff Ronning .02 .10
211 Pavel Bure .08 .25
212 Sergio Momesso .02 .10
213 Kirk McLean .05 .15
214 Jiri Slegr .02 .10
215 Trevor Linden .05 .15
216 Geoff Courtnall .02 .10
217 Al Iafrate .02 .10
218 Mike Ridley .02 .10
219 Enrico Ciccone .02 .10
220 Dimitri Khristich .02 .10
221 Kevin Hatcher .02 .10
222 Peter Bondra .05 .15
223 Steve Konowalchuk .02 .10
224 Pat Elynuik .02 .10
225 Don Beaupre .05 .15
226 Stu Barnes .02 .10
227 Fredrik Olausson .02 .10
228 Keith Thachuk .08 .25
229 Mike Eagles .02 .10
230 Tie Domi .05 .15
231 Teppo Numminen .02 .10
232 Arto Blomsten .02 .10
233 Teemu Selanne .08 .25
234 Bob Essensa .05 .15
235 Teemu Selanne SPH .08 .25
236 Eric Lindros SPH .08 .25
237 Felix Potvin SPH .05 .15
238 Alexei Kovalev SPH .05 .15
239 Vladimir Malakhov SPH .02 .10
240 Scott Niedermayer SPH .02 .10
241 Joe Juneau SPH .05 .15
242 Shawn McEachern SPH .02 .10
243 Alexei Zhamnov SPH .05 .15
244 Alexandre Daigle PKP .02 .10
245 Markus Naslund PKP .08 .25
246 Rob Niedermayer PKP .05 .15
247 Jocelyn Thibault PKP RC .20 .50
248 Brent Gretzky PKP RC .20 .50
249 Chris Pronger PKP .10 .30
250 Chris Gratton PKP .05 .15
251 Mikael Renberg PKP .08 .25
252 Jarkko Varvio PKP .02 .10
253 Micah Aivazoff PKP RC .20 .50
254 Alexei Yashin PKP .02 .10
255 German Titov PKP RC .20 .50
256 Mattias Norstrom PKP RC .20 .50
257 Michal Sykora PKP RC .20 .50
258 Roman Oksiuta PKP RC .20 .50
259 Bryan Smolinski PKP .02 .10
260 Alexei Kudashov PKP RC .20 .50
261 Jason Arnott PKP RC .50 1.25
262 Aaron Ward PKP RC .20 .50
263 Vesa Viitakoski PKP RC .20 .50
264 Boris Mironov PKP .02 .10
265 Darren McCarty PKP RC .20 .50
266 Vlastimil Kroupa PKP RC .20 .50
267 Denny Felsner PKP .02 .10
268 Milos Holan PKP RC .20 .50
269 Alex. Karpovtsev PKP .02 .10
270 Greg Johnson PKP .02 .10
271 Terry Yake .02 .10
272 Bill Houlder .02 .10
273 Joe Sacco .02 .10
274 Myles O'Connor .02 .10
275 Mark Fenner RC .20 .50
276 Alexei Kasatanov .02 .10
277 Stu Grimson .02 .10
278 Shaun Van Allen .02 .10
279 Guy Hebert .05 .15
280 Joe Juneau .05 .15
281 Sergei Zholtok .02 .10
282 Daniel Marois .02 .10
283 Ted Donato .02 .10
284 Cam Stewart RC .20 .50
285 Stephen Leach .02 .10
286 Darren Banks .02 .10
287 Dmitri Kvartalnov .02 .10
288 Paul Stanton .02 .10
289 Pat LaFontaine .08 .25
290 Bob Sweeney .02 .10
291 Craig Muni .02 .10
292 Sergei Petrenko .02 .10
293 Derek Plante RC .20 .50
294 Wayne Presley .02 .10
295 Mark Astley RC .20 .50
296 Matthew Barnaby .05 .15
297 Randy Wood .02 .10
298 Kevin Dahl .02 .10
299 Gary Suter .02 .10
300 Robert Reichel .02 .10
301 Mike Vernon .05 .15
302 Gary Roberts .02 .10
303 Ronnie Stern .02 .10
304 Michel Petit .02 .10
305 Wes Walz .05 .15
306 Brad Miller RC .20 .50
307 Patrick Poulin .02 .10
308 Brent Sutter .02 .10
309 Jeremy Roenick .12 .30
310 Steve Smith .02 .10
311 Eric Weinrich .02 .10
312 Jeff Hackett .05 .15
313 Michel Goulet .05 .15
314 Jeff Shantz RC .20 .50
315 Neil Wilkinson .02 .10
316 Shane Churla .02 .10
317 Dave Gagner .05 .15
318 Chris Tancill .02 .10
319 Dean Evason .02 .10
320 Mark Tinordi .02 .10
321 Grant Ledyard .02 .10
322 Ulf Dahlen .02 .10
323 Mike Craig .02 .10
324 Paul Broten .02 .10
325 Vladimir Konstantinov .05 .15
326 Steve Yzerman .50 1.25
327 Keith Primeau .02 .10
328 Shawn Burr .02 .10
329 Chris Osgood RC .60 1.50
330 Ray Sheppard .05 .15
331 Mike Sillinger .02 .10
332 Terry Carkner .02 .10
333 Bob Probert .05 .15
334 Adam Bennett .02 .10
335 Dave Manson .02 .10
336 Zdeno Ciger .02 .10
337 Louie DeBrusk .02 .10
338 Shayne Corson .02 .10
339 Vladimir Vujtek .02 .10
340 Tyler Wright .02 .10
341 Ilya Byakin RC .02 .10
342 Craig MacTavish .02 .10
343 Brian Benning .02 .10
344 Mark Fitzpatrick .05 .15
345 Gord Murphy .02 .10
346 Jesse Belanger .02 .10
347 Joe Cirella .02 .10
348 Tom Fitzgerald .02 .10
349 Andrei Lomakin .02 .10
350 Bill Lindsay .02 .10
351 Len Barrie .02 .10
352 Frank Pietrangelo .05 .15
353 Pat Verbeek .02 .10
354 Jim Storm .02 .10
355 Mark Janssens .02 .10
356 Darren Turcotte .02 .10
357 Jim McKenzie .02 .10
358 Brad McCrimmon .02 .10
359 Andrew Cassels .02 .10
360 James Patrick .02 .10
361 Bob Jay RC .02 .10
362 Tomas Sandstrom .02 .10
363 Pat Conacher .02 .10
364 Shawn McEachern .02 .10
365 Jari Kurri .08 .25
366 Dominic Lavoie .02 .10
367 Dave Taylor .05 .15
368 Jimmy Carson .02 .10
369 Mike Donnelly .02 .10
370 Lyle Odelein .02 .10
371 Brian Bellows .02 .10
372 Guy Carbonneau .02 .10
373 Mathieu Schneider .02 .10
374 Stephan Lebeau .02 .10
375 Benoit Brunet .02 .10
376 Kevin Haller .02 .10
377 J.J. Daigneault .02 .10
378 Kirk Muller .02 .10
379 Jason Smith RC .20 .50
380 Martin Brodeur .30 .75
381 Corey Millen .02 .10
382 Bill Guerin .02 .10
383 Valeri Zelepukin .02 .10
384 Tom Chorske .02 .10
385 Bobby Holik .02 .10
386 Jaroslav Modry RC .20 .50
387 Ken Daneyko .02 .10
388 Uwe Krupp .02 .10
389 Pierre Turgeon .05 .15
390 Marty McInnis .02 .10
391 Patrick Flatley .02 .10
392 Tom Kurvers .02 .10
393 Brad Dalgarno .02 .10
394 Steve Junker RC .20 .50
395 David Volek .02 .10
396 Benoit Hogue .02 .10
397 Zigmund Palffy .05 .15
399 Joby Messier RC .20 .50
400 Mike Gartner .05 .15
401 Joey Kocur .02 .10
402 Ed Olczyk .02 .10
403 Doug Lidster .02 .10
404A Greg Gilbert .02 .10
404B Steve Larmer UER .05 .15
(Should be 398)
405 Glenn Healy .05 .15
406 Dennis Vial .02 .10
407 Darcy Loewen .02 .10
408 Bob Kudelski .02 .10
409 Hank Lammens RC .20 .50
410 Jarmo Kekalainen .02 .10
411 Darren Rumble .02 .10
412 Francois Leroux .02 .10
413 Troy Mallette .02 .10
414 Bill Huard RC .20 .50
415 Ryan McGill .02 .10
416 Eric Lindros .08 .25
417 Dominic Roussel .05 .15
418 Jason Bowen RC .20 .50
419 Andre Faust .02 .10
420 Stewart Malgunas RC .20 .50
421 Kevin Dineen .02 .10
422 Yves Racine .02 .10
423 Garry Galley .02 .10
424 Doug Brown .02 .10
425 Mario Lemieux .50 1.25
426 Ladislav Karabin RC .20 .50
427 Grant Jennings .02 .10
428 Rick Tocchet .05 .15
429 Jeff Daniels .02 .10
430 Peter Taglianetti .02 .10
431 Bryan Trottier .05 .15
432 Kjell Samuelsson .02 .10
433 Rene Corbet RC .20 .50
434 Iain Fraser RC .20 .50
435 Mats Sundin .08 .25
436 Curtis Leschyshyn .02 .10
437 Claude LaPointe .02 .10
438 Valeri Kamensky .05 .15
439 Mike Ricci .02 .10
440 Chris Lindberg .02 .10
441 Alexei Gusarov .02 .10
442 Tom Tilley .02 .10
443 Craig Janney .05 .15
444 Vitali Karamnov .02 .10
445 Bob Bassen .02 .10
446 Igor Korolev .02 .10
447 Kevin Miehm .02 .10
448 Tony Hrkac .02 .10
449 Garth Butcher .02 .10
450 Vitali Prokhorov .02 .10
451 Arturs Irbe .05 .15
452 Jay More .02 .10
453 Bob Errey .02 .10
454 Mike Sullivan .02 .10
455 Jeff Norton .02 .10
456 Gaeten Duchesne .02 .10
457 Doug Zmolek .02 .10
458 Mike Rathje .02 .10
459 Jamie Baker .02 .10
460 Joe Reekie .02 .10
461 Mark Bureau .02 .10
462 John Tucker .02 .10
463 Bill McDougall RC .20 .50
464 Danton Cole .02 .10
465 Brian Bradley .02 .10
466 Jason Lafreniere .02 .10
467 Donald Dufresne .02 .10
468 Daren Puppa .05 .15
469 Doug Gilmour .05 .15
470 Damian Rhodes RC .20 .50
471 Matt Martin RC .20 .50
472 Bill Berg .02 .10
473 John Cullen .02 .10
474 Rob Pearson .02 .10
475 Wendel Clark .05 .15
476 Mark Osborne .02 .10
477 Dmitri Mironov .02 .10
478A Kay Whitmore .05 .15
478B Kris King UER .02 .10
(Should be 498)
479 Shawn Antoski .02 .10
480 Greg Adams .02 .10
481 Dave Babych .02 .10
482 John McIntyre .02 .10
483 Jyrki Lumme .02 .10
484 Jose Charbonneau RC .20 .50
485 Gino Odjick .02 .10
486 Dana Murzyn .02 .10
487 Michal Pivonka .02 .10
488 Dave Poulin .02 .10
489 Sylvain Cote .02 .10
490 Jason Woolley .02 .10
491 Kelly Miller .02 .10
492 Randy Burridge .02 .10
493 Kevin Kaminski RC .20 .50
494 John Slaney .02 .10
495 Keith Jones .02 .10
496 Harijs Vitolinsh .02 .10
497 Nelson Emerson .02 .10
499 Darrin Shannon .02 .10
500 Stephane Quintal .02 .10
501 Luciano Borsato .02 .10
502 Thomas Steen .02 .10
503 Alexei Zhamnov .05 .15
504 Paul Ysebaert .02 .10
505 Jeff Friesen RC .60 1.50
506 Niklas Sundstrom .02 .10
507 Nick Stajduhar RC .20 .50
508 Jamie Storr RC .20 .50
509 Valeri Bure RC .20 .50
510 Jason Bonsignore RC .20 .50
511 Mats Lindgren RC .20 .50
512 Yannick Dube RC .20 .50
513 Todd Harvey RC .20 .50
514 Ladislav Prokupek RC .20 .50
515 Tomas Vlasak RC .20 .50
516 Josef Marha RC .20 .50
517 Tomas Blazek RC .20 .50
518 Zdenek Nedved RC .20 .50
519 Jaroslav Miklenda RC .20 .50
520 Janne Niinimaa RC .20 .50
521 Saku Koivu .08 .25
522 Tommi Miettinen RC .20 .50
523 Tuomas Gronman .02 .10
524 Jani Nikko RC .20 .50
525 Jouni Vauhkonen .02 .10
526 Nikolai Tsulygin .02 .10
527 Vadim Sharifjanov .05 .15
528 Valeri Bure RC .20 .50
529 Alexander Kharlamov RC .20 .50
530 Nikolai Zavarukhin RC .20 .50
531 Oleg Tverdovsky RC .20 .50
532 Sergei Kondrashkin RC .20 .50
533 Evgeni Ryabchikov RC .20 .50
534 Mats Lindgren RC .20 .50
535 Kenny Jonsson .02 .10
536 Edvin Frylen RC .20 .50
537 Mathias Johansson RC .20 .50
538 Johan Davidsson RC .20 .50
539 Mikael Hakansson RC .20 .50
540 Anders Eriksson RC .20 .50

1993-94 Parkhurst Emerald Ice

The 540 cards in this parallel set can be found one per foil pack and two per jumbo pack. The Parkhurst logo, team name, a vertical strip near the right edge of the c are adorned with green foil, as opposed the silver foil used for the basic card set.
*STARS: 2.5X TO 6X BASIC CARDS
*RCs: 1.5X TO 4X BASIC CARDS

1993-94 Parkhurst Calder Candidates

The silver trade card randomly insertec '93-94 Parkhurst packs was redeemable this Calder Candidates insert set.This was also randomly inserted in U.S. Serie retail packs. The gold trade card w redeemable for a gold foil-enhanced editi multipliers can be found below to determ values for these. The expiration date for b trade cards was July 31st, 1994.
*GOLD: 1X TO 1.5X BASIC CARDS
C1 Alexandre Daigle .40 1.
C2 Chris Pronger 1.50 4.
C3 Chris Gratton .40 1.
C4 Rob Niedermayer .40 1.
C5 Markus Naslund .40 1.
C6 Jason Arnott 1.00 2.
C7 Pierre Sevigny .40 1.
C8 Jarkko Varvio .40 1.
C9 Dean McAmmond .40 1.
C10 Alexei Yashin .40 1.
C11 Philippe Boucher .40 1.
C12 Mikael Renberg .40 1.
C13 Chris Simon .40 1.
C14 Brent Gretzky .40 1.
C15 Jesse Belanger .40 1.
C16 Jocelyn Thibault .75 2.
C17 Chris Osgood .40 1.
C18 Derek Plante .40 1.
C19 Iain Fraser .40 1.
C20 Vesa Viitakoski .40 1.
NNO Gold Trade Card 3.00 6.
NNO Silver Trade Card 1.50 4.

1993-94 Parkhurst Cherry's Playoff Heroes

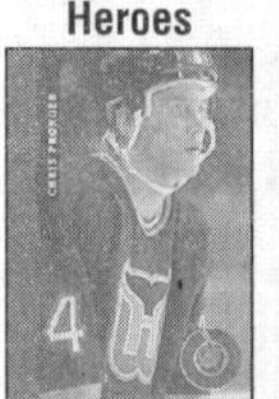

Randomly inserted in Canadian seco series foil packs, these twenty different ca feature color player action shots on th fronts and a photo of Machiavellian personality Don Cherry -- who chose players to be featured in this set based his unique set of standards -- on the ba The cards are numbered with a "D" prefix.
COMPLETE SET (20) 20.00 40.
D1 Wayne Gretzky 3.00 8.
D2 Mario Lemieux 2.50 6.
D3 Al MacInnis .40 1.
D4 Mark Messier .60 1.
D5 Dino Ciccarelli .40 1.
D6 Dale Hunter .40 1.
D7 Grant Fuhr .60 1.
D8 Paul Coffey .60 1.
D9 Doug Gilmour .50 1.
D10 Patrick Roy 2.50 6.
D11 Alexandre Daigle .40 1.
D12 Chris Gratton .40 1.
D13 Chris Pronger .50 1.
D14 Felix Potvin .60 1.
D15 Eric Lindros .60 1.
D16 Maurice Richard 2.50 6.
D17 Gordie Howe 2.00 5.
D18 Henri Richard .50 1.
D19 Reggie Leach .40 1.
D20 Checklist 1.00 2.
Don Cherry and Blue

1993-94 Parkhurst East/West Stars

Randomly inserted in U.S. second-se hobby packs, these cards feature cc player action shots on their fronts. The ten cards feature Eastern Conference st numbered with an "E" prefix, while the ten cards present Western Conference st numbered with a "W" prefix.
COMPLETE SET (20) 20.00 40.
E1 Eric Lindros .60 1.
E2 Mario Lemieux 4.00 6.
E3 Alexandre Daigle .30

4 Patrick Roy 4.00 6.00
5 Rob Niedermayer .50 .75
6 Chris Gratton .50 .75
7 Alexei Yashin .30 .50
8 Pat LaFontaine .40 1.00
9 Joe Sakic 1.50 2.50
10 Pierre Turgeon .50 .75
V1 Wayne Gretzky 5.00 8.00
V2 Pavel Bure .60 1.50
V3 Teemu Selanne .60 1.50
V4 Doug Gilmour .50 .75
V5 Steve Yzerman 4.00 6.00
V6 Jeremy Roenick 1.00 1.50
V7 Brett Hull 1.00 1.50
V8 Jason Arnott .60 1.50
V9 Felix Potvin .60 1.50
V10 Sergei Fedorov 1.25 2.00

1993-94 Parkhurst First Overall

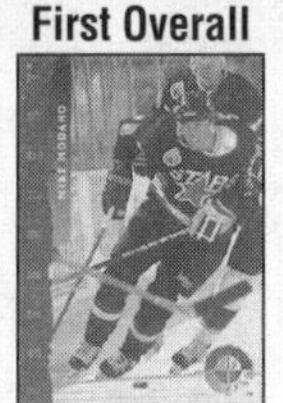

andomly inserted in Canadian Series I tail foil packs, this ten-card set featured olor action shots of players drafted first verall in the annual NHL Entry Draft over e past decade. The cards are numbered on e back with an "F" prefix.

OMPLETE SET (10) 30.00 60.00
1 Alexandre Daigle .30 .75
2 Roman Hamrlik .50 1.25
3 Eric Lindros .75 2.00
4 Owen Nolan .50 1.25
5 Mats Sundin .75 2.00
6 Mike Modano 1.25 3.00
7 Pierre Turgeon .50 1.25
8 Joe Murphy .30 .75
9 Wendel Clark .50 1.25
10 Mario Lemieux 4.00 10.00

1993-94 Parkhurst Parkie Reprints

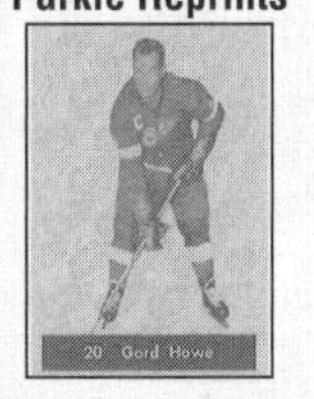

continuation of the '92-93 Parkie Reprints t, these 40 (numbered 33-68, plus four ecklists) cards measure the standard-size. e first ten cards (33-41, plus checklist (5) ere randomly inserted in '93-94 Parkhurst ries I foil packs. The second series (42-50, us checklist (6) were random inserts in rkhurst series one jumbo packs only. The rd series (51-59, plus checklist (7) were ndom inserts in all series two Parkhurst cks. The fourth Parkie Reprints series (60-, plus checklist (8) were random inserts in rkhurst series two jumbo packs. The nts are that of 1951-64 Parkhurst styles, t all carry a color player photo. The backs rry the information from the original card. e print varies from red to black to a mbination. The cards are numbered on the ck with a "PR" prefix. A hobby exclusive rkie Reprints bonus pack was included in ery series one and series two case.

OMPLETE SET (40) 25.00 60.00
R33 Gordie Howe 2.00 5.00
R34 Tim Horton 2.00 5.00
R35 Bill Barilko 2.00 5.00
R36 Elmer Lach .75 2.00
Maurice Richard
R37 Terry Sawchuk .75 2.00
R38 George Armstrong .75 2.00
R39 William Harris .75 2.00
R40 Doug Harvey .75 2.00
R41 Gump Worsley 2.00 5.00
R42 Gordie Howe 2.00 5.00
R43 Jacques Plante 2.00 5.00
R44 Frank Mahovlich 2.00 5.00
R45 Fern Flaman .75 2.00
R46 Bernie Geoffrion 2.00 5.00
R47 Toe Blake CO .75 2.00
R48 Maurice Richard 2.00 5.00
R49 Ted Lindsay .75 2.00
R50 Camille Henry .75 2.00
R51 Gordie Howe 2.00 5.00
R52 Jean-Guy Talbot .75 2.00
R53 Terry Sawchuk .75 2.00
R54 Warren Godfrey .75 2.00
R55 Tom Johnson .75 2.00
R56 Bert Olmstead .75 2.00
R57 Cal Gardner .75 2.00
R58 Red Kelly .75 2.00
R59 Phil Goyette .75 2.00
R60 Gordie Howe 2.00 5.00
R61 Lou Fontinato .75 2.00
R62 Bill Dineen .75 2.00
R63 Maurice Richard 2.00 5.00
R64 Vic Stasiuk .75 2.00
R65 Marcel Pronovost .75 2.00
R66 Ed Litzenberger .75 2.00
R67 Dave Keon 2.00 5.00
R68 Dollard St. Laurent .75 2.00
L5 Parkies Checklist 5 .75 2.00
L6 Parkies Checklist 6 .75 2.00
L7 Parkies Checklist 7 .75 2.00
L8 Parkies Checklist 8 .75 2.00

1993-94 Parkhurst Parkie Reprints Case Inserts

These sets were inserted one per hobby case. Cards 1-6 were found in series I cases, while 7-12 were inserted in series II cases. Parkhurst selected vintage cards from its past to reprint in this 12-card standard-size set. The cards are coated on both sides and are easily recognizable as reprints. The cards are numbered on the back with the prefix "DPR".

COMP.SERIES 1 SET (6) 12.00 30.00
1 Gordie Howe 6.00 15.00
2 Milt Schmidt 2.40 6.00
3 Tim Horton 3.20 8.00
4 Al Rollins 2.40 6.00
5 Maurice Richard 4.00 10.00
6 Harry Howell 2.40 6.00
7 Gordie Howe 6.00 15.00
8 Johnny Bower 4.00 10.00
9 Dean Prentice 2.40 6.00
10 Leo Labine 2.40 6.00
11 Harry Watson 2.80 7.00
12 Dickie Moore 2.80 7.00

1993-94 Parkhurst USA/Canada Gold

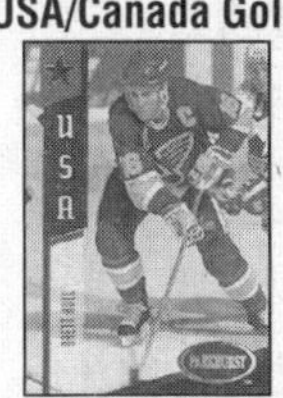

Randomly inserted at the rate of 1:30 U.S. Series I foil packs, this 10-card set depicted the 10 best NHL players form both the U.S. and Canada. Accordingly, cards 1-5 are USA Gold while cards 6-10 are Canadian Gold. The cards are numbered on the back with a "G" prefix.

COMPLETE SET (10) 25.00 50.00
G1 Wayne Gretzky 3.00 8.00
G2 Mario Lemieux 2.50 6.00
G3 Eric Lindros .50 1.25
G4 Brett Hull .60 1.50
G5 Rob Niedermayer .30 .75
G6 Alexandre Daigle .20 .50
G7 Pavel Bure .50 1.25
G8 Teemu Selanne .50 1.25
G9 Patrick Roy 2.50 6.00
G10 Doug Gilmour .30 .75

1994 Parkhurst Missing Link

This 180-card set attempts to capture what a Parkhurst set might have looked like had one been produced for the 1956-57 NHL campaign. Although the inclusion of all six original teams may seem somewhat anachronistic (keeping in mind that Parkhurst, at that time, issued cards featuring Canadian-based players only) the set does capture the old-time flavor. The simple design includes an isolated player photo (taken during the 1955-56 season) over a cream colored background. A black bar runs along the left side of the card front, and contains the player name and team logo. Card backs include stats for the 1955-56 season and biographical information in both French and English. Subsets include All-Stars (135-146), Trophy Winners (147-152), Action Shots (153-168), Team Leaders (169-174) and Playoffs (175-178). The set was issued in 10-card wax packs and production was limited to 1956 numbered cases for each of the Canadian and American markets.

COMPLETE SET (180) 20.00 35.00
COMMON CARD (1-180) .10 .10
CL (179/180) .10 .25
STARS .15 .40
HOF STARS .20 .50
1 Jerry Toppazzini .04 .10
2 Fern Flaman .16 .40
3 Fleming MacKell .04 .10
4 Leo Labine .08 .20
5 John Peirson .06 .15
6 Don McKenney .06 .15
7 Bob Armstrong .04 .10
8 Real Chevrefils .04 .10
9 Vic Stasiuk .06 .15
10 Cal Gardner .04 .10
11 Leo Boivin .16 .40
12 Jack Caffery .04 .10
13 Bob Beckett RC .04 .10
14 Jack Bionda .04 .10
15 Claude Pronovost RC .16 .40
16 Larry Regan .04 .10
17 Terry Sawchuk 1.00 2.50
18 Doug Mohns .08 .20
19 Marcel Bonin .06 .15
20 Allan Stanley .20 .50
21 Milt Schmidt CO .20 .50
22 Al Dewsbury .04 .10
23 Glen Skov .06 .15
24 Ed Litzenberger .06 .15
25 Nick Mickoski .04 .10
26 Wally Hergesheimer .04 .10
27 Jack McIntyre .04 .10
28 Al Rollins .20 .50
29 Hank Ciesla .04 .10
30 Gus Mortson .04 .10
31 Elmer Vasko .06 .15
32 Pierre Pilote .20 .50
33 Ron Ingram .04 .10
34 Frank Martin .04 .10
35 Forbes Kennedy .08 .20
36 Harry Watson .06 .15
37 Eddie Kachur RC .04 .10
38 Hec Lalande .04 .10
39 Eric Nesterenko .08 .20
40 Ben Woit .04 .10
41 Ken Mosdell .06 .15
42 Tommy Ivan CO RC .16 .40
43 Gordie Howe 2.00 4.00
44 Ted Lindsay .20 .50
45 Norm Ullman .20 .50
46 Glenn Hall .40 1.00
47 Billy Dea .04 .10
48 Bill McNeill .04 .10
49 Earl Reibel .06 .15
50 Bill Dineen .08 .20
51 Warren Godfrey .06 .15
52 Red Kelly .20 .50
53 Marty Pavelich .04 .10
54 Lorne Ferguson .04 .10
55 Larry Hillman .06 .15
56 John Bucyk .20 .50
57 Metro Prystai .04 .10
58 Marcel Pronovost .20 .50
59 Alex Delvecchio .20 .50
60 Murray Costello RC .04 .10
61 Al Arbour .20 .50
62 Bucky Hollingworth .04 .10
63 Jim Skinner CO RC .04 .10
64 Jean Beliveau .75 2.00
65 Maurice Richard 1.00 2.50
66 Henri Richard .20 .50
67 Doug Harvey .20 .50
68 Bernie Geoffrion .30 .75
69 Dollard St. Laurent .10 .25
70 Dickie Moore .20 .50
71 Bert Olmstead .10 .25
72 Jacques Plante 1.00 2.50
73 Claude Provost .16 .40
74 Phil Goyette .06 .15
75 Andre Pronovost .06 .15
76 Don Marshall .10 .25
77 Ralph Backstrom .08 .20
78 Floyd Curry .08 .20
79 Tom Johnson .20 .50
80 Jean Guy Talbot .08 .20
81 Bob Turner .04 .10
82 Connie Broden RC .04 .10
83 Jackie Leclair .04 .10
84 Toe Blake CO .30 .75
85 Frank Selke MD .20 .50
86 George Sullivan .04 .10
87 Larry Cahan .04 .10
88 Jean Guy Gendron .04 .10
89 Bill Gadsby .20 .50
90 Andy Bathgate .20 .50
91 Dean Prentice .04 .10
92 Gump Worsley .40 1.00
93 Lou Fontinato .06 .15
94 Gerry Foley .04 .10
95 Larry Popein .06 .15
96 Harry Howell .20 .50
97 Andy Hebenton .04 .10
98 Danny Lewicki .04 .10
99 Dave Creighton .04 .10
100 Camille Henry .04 .10
101 Jack Evans .04 .10
102 Ron Murphy .04 .10
103 Johnny Bower .30 .75
104 Parker MacDonald .04 .10
105 Bronco Horvath .08 .20
106 Bruce Cline RC .04 .10
107 Ivan Irwin .04 .10
108 Phil Watson CO .04 .10
109 Sid Smith .04 .10
110 Ron Stewart .04 .10
111 Rudy Migay .04 .10
112 Tod Sloan .06 .15
113 Bob Pulford .20 .50
114 Marc Reaume .06 .15
115 Jim Morrison .06 .15
116 Ted Kennedy .20 .50
117 Gerry James .08 .20
118 Brian Cullen .10 .25
119 Jim Thomson .04 .10
120 Barry Cullen .04 .10
121 Al MacNeil .06 .15
122 Gary Aldcorn .04 .10
123 Bob Baun .20 .50
124 Hugh Bolton .04 .10
125 George Armstrong .20 .50
126 Dick Duff .20 .50
127 Tim Horton .50 2.00
128 Ed Chadwick .20 .50
129 Billy Harris .16 .40
130 Mike Nykoluk .04 .10
131 Noel Price .04 .10
132 Ken Girard .04 .10
133 Howie Meeker .20 .50
134 Hap Day CO .10 .25
135 Jacques Plante AS .40 1.00
136 Doug Harvey AS .20 .50
137 Bill Gadsby AS .20 .50
138 Jean Beliveau AS .30 .75
139 Maurice Richard AS .40 1.00
140 Ted Lindsay AS .16 .40
141 Glenn Hall AS .20 .50
142 Red Kelly AS .20 .50
143 Tom Johnson AS .20 .50
144 Tod Sloan AS .06 .15
145 Gordie Howe AS .50 1.50
146 Bert Olmstead AS .10 .25
147 Earl Reibel AW .04 .10
Lady Byng
148 Doug Harvey AW .20 .50
Norris
149 Jean Beliveau AW .30 .75
Hart
150 Jean Beliveau AW .30 .75
Art Ross
151 Jacques Plante AW .40 1.00
Vezina
152 Glenn Hall AW .20 .50
Calder
153 Terry Sawchuk IA .40 1.00
154 Action Shot .10 .25
155 Action Shot .10 .25
156 Jean Beliveau IA .30 .75
157 Jean Beliveau IA .30 .75
158 Action Shot .10 .25
159 Action Shot .10 .25
160 Gordie Howe IA .50 1.50
161 Jacques Plante IA .40 1.00
162 Gordie Howe IA .50 1.50
163 Jacques Plante IA .40 1.00
164 Action Shot .10 .25
165 Action Shot .10 .25
166 Action Shot .10 .25
167 Terry Sawchuk IA .40 1.00
168 Terry Sawchuk IA .40 1.00
169 Vic Stasiuk SL .06 .15
170 George Sullivan SL .06 .15
171 Gordie Howe SL .50 1.50
172 Jean Beliveau SL .30 .75
173 Andy Bathgate SL .20 .50
174 Tod Sloan SL .06 .15
175 Stanley Cup .10 .25
176 Stanley Cup .10 .25
177 Stanley Cup .10 .25
178 Stanley Cup .10 .25
179 Checklist 1 .04 .10
180 Checklist 2 .04 .10

1994 Parkhurst Missing Link Autographs

The 1994 Parkhurst Missing Link Autograph set is comprised of six Hall of Famers. Randomly inserted in Missing Link packs, the cards are autographed on the front and numbered "X of 956" on the back. The cards are also numbered for set purposes A1-A6. The design is different from those found in the Missing Link issue. Card fronts are color, but do not contain the player's name (except for autograph) or team name. The backs provide a congratulatory note to the collector.

1 Gordie Howe 75.00 150.00
2 Maurice Richard 100.00 200.00
3 Bernie Geoffrion 40.00 80.00
4 Gump Worsley 40.00 100.00
5 Jean Beliveau 75.00 150.00
6 Frank Mahovlich 25.00 60.00

1994 Parkhurst Missing Link Future Stars

The six cards in this set were randomly inserted in both US and Canadian product and featured well-known players who had yet to make their mark in the league by the 1956-57 season, the year which is represented in this set. Cards are numbered with an "FS" prefix.

COMPLETE SET (6) 30.00 70.00
RANDOM INSERTS IN PACKS
FS1 Carl Brewer 3.00 8.00
FS2 Dave Keon 5.00 12.00
FS3 Stan Mikita 6.00 15.00
FS4 Eddie Shack 5.00 12.00
FS5 Frank Mahovlich 6.00 15.00
FS6 Charlie Hodge 5.00 12.00

1994 Parkhurst Missing Link Pop-Ups

These 12 die-cut cards were randomly inserted over two distribution channels: cards 1-6 in Canadian cases and 7-12 in American product. The cards feature the heroes of hockey's past in a design which approximates the style made famous by the 1936-37 O-Pee-Chee V304D set. The cards are created in such a way that they may be popped open for a 3-D effect; collectors are strongly urged not to follow this course of action unless you're not concerned about the

card's value. Card backs contain brief personal information, as well as a wrap-up of career statistics. The cards are numbered with a P prefix in the top left corner. Only 1,000 of each card were circulated.

COMPLETE SET (12) 200.00 350.00
RANDOM INSERTS IN US PACKS
P1 Howie Morenz 20.00 50.00
P2 George Hainsworth 12.00 30.00
P3 Georges Vezina 20.00 50.00
P4 King Clancy 18.00 35.00
P5 Syl Apps 12.00 30.00
P6 Turk Broda 12.00 30.00
P7 Eddie Shore 25.00 50.00
P8 Bill Cook 10.00 25.00
P9 Woody Dumart 10.00 25.00
P10 Lester Patrick 12.00 30.00
P11 Doug Bentley 10.00 25.00
P12 Earl Seibert 10.00 25.00

1994 Parkhurst Tall Boys

This 180-card set recreates what might have been had the Parkhurst company issued a set of NHL player cards for the 1964-65 season. As the title suggests, the card size matches that of the 1964-65 Topps Tall Boys set (2 1/2" by 4 11/16"). Announced production was 1,964 cases for each of the US and Canadian hobby markets.

COMPLETE SET (180) 10.00 12.00
1 John Bucyk .16 .40
2 Murray Oliver .04 .10
3 Ted Green .06 .15
4 Tom Williams .04 .10
5 Dean Prentice .04 .10
6 Ed Westfall .04 .10
7 Orland Kurtenbach .04 .10
8 Reg Fleming .04 .10
9 Leo Boivin .06 .15
10 Bob McCord .04 .10
11 Bob Leiter .04 .10
12 Tom Johnson .10 .25
13 Bob Woytowich .04 .10
14 Ab McDonald .04 .10
15 Ed Johnston .10 .25
16 Forbes Kennedy .06 .15
17 Murray Balfour .04 .10
18 Wayne Cashman .06 .15
19 Don Awrey .04 .10
20 Gary Dornhoefer .06 .15
21 Ron Schock .04 .10
22 Milt Schmidt .20 .50
23 Ken Wharram .06 .15
24 Chico Maki .04 .10
25 Bobby Hull 1.25 2.00
26 Stan Mikita .30 .75
27 Doug Mohns .06 .15
28 Denis DeJordy .08 .20
29 Phil Esposito .20 .50
30 Elmer Vasko .04 .10
31 Pierre Pilote .10 .25
32 Glenn Hall .30 .75
33 Eric Nesterenko .04 .10
34 Doug Robinson .04 .10
35 Matt Ravlich .04 .10
36 John McKenzie .06 .15
37 Fred Stanfield .04 .10
38 Doug Jarrett .04 .10
39 Dennis Hull .08 .20
40 Al MacNeil .04 .10
41 Wayne Hillman .04 .10
42 Bill Hay .04 .10
43 Billy Reay .04 .10
44 Parker MacDonald .04 .10
45 Floyd Smith .04 .10
46 Gordie Howe 1.25 2.50
47 Bruce MacGregor .04 .10
48 Ron Murphy .04 .10
49 Doug Barkley .04 .10
50 Paul Henderson .06 .15
51 Pit Martin .06 .15
52 Al Langlois .04 .10
53 Roger Crozier .10 .25
54 Bill Gadsby .10 .25
55 Marcel Pronovost .16 .40
56 Alex Delvecchio .16 .40
57 Gary Bergman .04 .10
58 Norm Ullman .16 .40
59 Larry Jeffrey .04 .10
60 Lowell MacDonald .04 .10
61 Pete Goegan .04 .10
62 Andre Pronovost .06 .15
63 Warren Godfrey .04 .10
64 Ted Lindsay .16 .40
65 Sid Abel .16 .40
66 John Ferguson .06 .15
67 Henri Richard .20 .50
68 Dave Balon .04 .10
69 Noel Picard .04 .10
70 Claude Provost .06 .15
71 Claude Larose .04 .10
72 Jacques Laperriere .10 .25
73 Ralph Backstrom .06 .15
74 J.C. Tremblay .06 .15
75 Yvan Cournoyer .16 .40
76 Jean-Guy Talbot .06 .15
77 Gilles Tremblay .04 .10
78 Ted Harris .04 .10
79 Jim Roberts .04 .10
80 Red Berenson .06 .15
81 Gump Worsley .30 .75
82 Charlie Hodge .10 .25
83 Terry Harper .04 .10
84 Bobby Rousseau .04 .10
85 Jean Beliveau .60 1.50
86 Bill Hicke .04 .10
87 Toe Blake .20 .50
88 Don Marshall .06 .15
89 Jean Ratelle .16 .40
90 Vic Hadfield .04 .10
91 Earl Ingarfield .04 .10
92 Harry Howell .16 .40
93 Rod Seiling .04 .10
94 Dave Richardson .04 .10
95 Val Fonteyne .04 .10
96 Lou Angotti .04 .10
97 Arnie Brown .04 .10
98 Don Johns .04 .10
99 Jim Mikol .04 .10
100 Jacques Plante .75 2.00
101 Marcel Paille .06 .15
102 Jim Neilson .04 .10
103 Bob Nevin .04 .10
104 Rod Gilbert .16 .40
105 Phil Goyette .04 .10
106 Dick Duff .10 .25
107 Camille Henry .04 .10
108 Red Sullivan .04 .10
109 Kent Douglas .04 .10
110 Bob Pulford .06 .15
111 Dave Keon .20 .50
112 Don McKenney .04 .10
113 Pete Stemkowski .04 .10
114 Carl Brewer .06 .15
115 Allan Stanley .10 .25
116 Dickie Moore .16 .40
117 Ed Shack .20 .50
118 Larry Hillman .04 .10
119 Terry Sawchuk .75 2.00
120 Bob Baun .10 .25
121 Brit Selby .04 .10
122 George Armstrong .20 .50
123 Jim Pappin .04 .10
124 Andy Bathgate .16 .40
125 Ron Ellis .04 .10
126 Billy Harris .04 .10
127 Red Kelly .08 .20
128 Ron Stewart .04 .10
129 Johnny Bower .20 .50
130 Frank Mahovlich .30 .50
131 Tim Horton .40 1.50
132 King Clancy .16 .40
133 Glenn Hall AS .15 .50
134 Pierre Pilote AS .10 .25
135 Tim Horton AS .20 .75
136 Bobby Hull AS .60 1.00
137 Ken Wharram AS .06 .15
138 Stan Mikita AS .15 .50
139 Charlie Hodge AS .06 .15
140 Jacques Laperriere AS .06 .15
141 Elmer Vasko AS .04 .10
142 Jean Beliveau AS .30 .75
143 Frank Mahovlich AS .15 .40
144 Gordie Howe AS .60 1.50
145 Pierre Pilote .10 .25
146 Jean Beliveau .30 .75
147 Stan Mikita .15 .40
148 Charlie Hodge .10 .25
149 Jacques Laperriere .10 .25
150 Ken Wharram .06 .15
151 1964 All Star Game .06 .15
152 Ratelle Invades Crease .10 .25
153 Center Ice Action .06 .15
154 Old Teammates Duel .60 1.50
155 All Eyes on the Puck .06 .15
156 Detroit Defense .40 1.00
Stands Tall
157 Crozier Makes The .06 .15
Stretch
158 Crozier Plays .10 .25
Center Field
159 Hawks Eye Beliveau .30 .75
160 Montreal's Speedy .06 .15
Rookie
161 Laperriere Wins Race .06 .15
162 Ellis Robbed by Habs .06 .15
163 Sawchuk Eyes .40 1.00
Bouncing Disc
164 Shack Entertains .16 .40
165 ~Mr. Goalie~ In .15 .50
Action
166 Hall Holds His .16 .40
Ground
167 Johnston Freezes .06 .15
Action
168 Ellis Robbed By .06 .15
Johnston
169 Murray Oliver LL .04 .10
170 Stan Mikita LL .15 .50
171 Gordie Howe LL .60 1.50
172 Jean Beliveau LL .30 .75
173 Phil Goyette LL .04 .10
174 Andy Bathgate LL .10 .25
175 Stanley Cup .04 .10
Semi-Finals
176 Stanley Cup .04 .10
Semi-Finals
177 Stanley Cup Finals .60 1.50
178 Stanley Cup .10 .25
179 Checklist 1 .04 .10
180 Checklist 2 .04 .10

1994 Parkhurst Tall Boys Autographs

This 6-card set was randomly inserted throughout the production run of 1994 Parkhurst Tall Boys. The player's autograph appears in a white, oblong box along the bottom. A congratulatory note appears on the back. The cards are serially numbered out of 964 on the back.

COMPLETE SET (6) 350.00 500.00

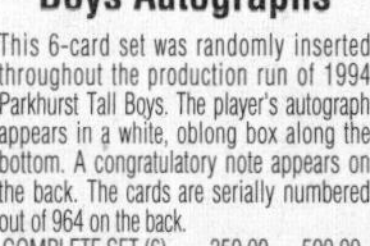

A1 Rod Gilbert 40.00 50.00
A2 Yvan Cournoyer 40.00 60.00
A3 Bobby Hull 40.00 100.00
A4 Phil Esposito 60.00 100.00
A5 Gordie Howe 75.00 150.00
A6 Dave Keon 50.00 80.00

1994 Parkhurst Tall Boys Future Stars

The six cards in this set were randomly inserted in both US and Canadian product and featured well-known players who had yet to make their mark in the league by the 1964-65 season, the year which is represented in this set. Card backs include 1963-64 amateur stats, a report on the player's prospects in both French and English, and a merchandise offer. Cards are numbered with an "FS" prefix.

COMPLETE SET (6) 40.00 80.00
FS1 Jacques Lemaire 7.50 15.00
FS2 Gerry Cheevers 12.00 25.00
FS3 Ken Hodge 4.00 10.00
FS4 Bernie Parent 9.00 18.00
FS5 Rogatien Vachon 7.50 15.00
FS6 Derek Sanderson 10.00 20.00

1994 Parkhurst Tall Boys Greats

The 12 cards in this set were split over two distribution channels: cards 1-6 were randomly inserted in Canadian wax, while 7-12 were inserted in American. The cards feature legendary greats from the game's past. These oddly designed cards were the same size as the regular Tall Boys if maintained intact. A large, beige border surrounded the "real card", which approximates the appearance and size of the smaller 1951-52 Parkhurst issue. Although the cards are scored so that they may be punched out from the larger background, collectors are strongly advised against doing this. Card backs are blank. 1,000 copies of each of these cards were circulated.

COMPLETE SET (12) 175.00 250.00
1 Ace Bailey 20.00 30.00
2 Alex Levinsky 6.00 15.00
3 Babe Pratt 6.00 15.00
4 Elmer Lach 6.00 15.00
5 Maurice Richard 25.00 40.00
6 Bill Durnan 18.00 30.00
7 Frank Brimsek 18.00 30.00
8 Dit Clapper 8.00 20.00
9 Tiny Thompson 18.00 30.00
10 Bun Cook 6.00 15.00
11 Ching Johnson 8.00 20.00
12 Lionel Conacher 15.00 30.00

1994 Parkhurst Tall Boys Mail-Ins

Available through a mail-in offer, the cards in these three six-card sets measure 2 1/2" by 4 3/4". To obtain one of the sets, the collector sent in 10 "Tall Boy" wrappers and a check or money order for 12.95. The fronts feature color action cutouts on team color-coded backgrounds. The information on the beige backs varies depending on the particular series. At the bottom, each card carries its serial number out of a total of 1,964. The cards are arranged below as follows: All-Stars, Scoring Leaders, and Trophy Winners.

COMPLETE SET (18) 20.00 50.00
AS1 Roger Crozier 1.00 2.50

AS2 Pierre Pilote .80 2.00
AS3 Jacques Laperriere .80 2.00
AS4 Norm Ullman 1.00 2.50
AS5 Bobby Hull 4.00 10.00
AS6 Claude Provost .40 1.00
SL1 John Bucyk 1.00 2.50
SL2 Stan Mikita 1.60 4.00
SL3 Norm Ullman 1.00 2.50
SL4 Claude Provost .40 1.00
SL5 Rod Gilbert 1.00 2.50
SL6 Frank Mahovlich 1.60 4.00
TW1 Pierre Pilote .80 2.00
TW2 Bobby Hull 4.00 10.00
TW3 Stan Mikita 1.60 4.00
TW4 Terry Sawchuk 3.20 8.00
Johnny Bower
TW5 Roger Crozier 1.00 2.50
TW6 Bobby Hull 4.00 10.00

1994-95 Parkhurst

This 315-card set was issued in one series. Due to the NHL lockout, series two was not released; therefore, this set does not have a comprehensive player selection. Ten card packs retailed for 99 cents in 36 pack boxes. Sixteen-card jumbo packs also were produced. The design features a nearly full-bleed front, broken only in the lower right corner where a small gray bar features a silver foil hockey player icon. The green Parkhurst logo appears in an upper corner with player name running down either side. Card backs are unique in that they have full career stats and a player photo. Subsets included Rookie Standouts (270-294) and Parkie's Best (295-315). This set is noteworthy for being the last product domestically released by Upper Deck using the Parkhurst name. Although no second series was domestically released, a European-only product - Parkhurst SE - appears to have been the remnants of that planned issue. Prices for that set appear elsewhere.

COMPLETE SET (315) 8.00 18.00
1 Anatoli Semenov .01 .05
2 Stephan Lebeau .01 .05
3 Stu Grimson .01 .05
4 Mikhail Shtalenkov RC .01 .05
5 Troy Loney .01 .05
6 Sean Hill UER .01 .05
('92-93 points total is 54 instead of 8 and career total is 81 instead of 35)
7 Patrik Carnback .01 .05
8 John Lilley .01 .05
9 Tim Sweeney .01 .05
10 Maxim Bets .01 .05
11 Cam Neely .07 .20
12 Bryan Smolinski .01 .05
13 Ray Bourque .10 .30
14 Vincent Riendeau .02 .10
15 Al Iafrate .01 .05
16 Andrew McKim RC .01 .05
17 Glen Wesley .01 .05
18 Daniel Marois .01 .05
19 Jozef Stumpel .01 .05
20 Mariusz Czerkawski RC .08 .25
21 Alexander Mogilny .02 .10
22 Yuri Khmylev .01 .05
23 Donald Audette .01 .05
24 Dominik Hasek .20 .50
25 Randy Wood .01 .05
26 Brad May .01 .05
27 Wayne Presley .01 .05
28 Richard Smehlik .01 .05
29 Dale Hawerchuk .02 .10
30 Rob Ray .01 .05
31 Zarley Zalapski .01 .05
32 Michael Nylander .01 .05
33 Joe Nieuwendyk .02 .10
34 Robert Reichel .01 .05
35 Al MacInnis .02 .10
36 Andrei Trefilov .01 .05
37 Leonard Esau .01 .05
38 Wes Walz .01 .05
39 Michel Petit .01 .05
40 James Patrick .01 .05
41 Ed Belfour .07 .20
42 Christian Ruuttu .01 .05
43 Eric Weinrich .01 .05
44 Joe Murphy .01 .05
45 Chris Chelios .07 .20
46 Jeff Shantz .01 .05
47 Gary Suter .01 .05
48 Paul Ysebaert .01 .05
49 Ivan Droppa .01 .05
50 Keith Carney .01 .05
51 Andy Moog .07 .20
52 Russ Courtnall .01 .05
53 Neal Broten .02 .10
54 Mike Craig .01 .05
55 Brent Gilchrist .01 .05
56 Pelle Eklund .01 .05
57 Richard Matvichuk .01 .05
58 Dave Gagner .02 .10
59 Mark Tinordi .01 .05
60 Paul Broten .01 .05
61 Nicklas Lidstrom .07 .20
62 Shawn Burr .01 .05
63 Paul Coffey .07 .20
64 Bob Essensa .02 .10
65 Dino Ciccarelli .02 .10
66 Slava Kozlov .02 .10
67 Keith Primeau .01 .05
68 Steve Chiasson .01 .05
69 Terry Carkner .01 .05
70 Martin Lapointe .01 .05
71 Bob Probert .02 .10
72 Bill Ranford .02 .10
73 Scott Thornton .01 .05
74 Doug Weight .02 .10
75 Shayne Corson .01 .05
76 Zdeno Ciger .01 .05
77 Adam Bennett .01 .05
78 Scott Pearson .01 .05
79 Brent Grieve RC .01 .05
80 Gordon Mark RC .01 .05
81 Shjon Podein .01 .05
82 Geoff Smith .01 .05
83 Bob Kudelski .01 .05
84 Andrei Lomakin .01 .05
85 Scott Mellanby .02 .10
86 Jesse Belanger .01 .05
87 Mark Fitzpatrick .02 .10
88 Peter Andersson .01 .05
89 Jody Hull .01 .05
90 Brent Severyn .01 .05
91 Jim Sandlak .01 .05
92 Pat Verbeek .01 .05
93 Ted Crowley .01 .05
94 Robert Petrovicky .01 .05
95 Geoff Sanderson .02 .10
96 Ted Drury .01 .05
97 Andrew Cassels .01 .05
98 Igor Chibirev .01 .05
99 Kevin Smyth .01 .05
100 Alexander Godynyuk .01 .05
101 Alexei Zhitnik .01 .05
102 Dixon Ward .01 .05
103 Wayne Gretzky .60 1.50
104 Jari Kurri .02 .10
105 Rob Blake .02 .10
106 Marty McSorley .01 .05
107 Pat Conacher .01 .05
108 Kevin Todd .01 .05
109 Robb Stauber .02 .10
110 Keith Redmond .01 .05
111 John LeClair .07 .20
112 Brian Bellows .01 .05
113 Patrick Roy .40 1.00
114 Les Kuntar RC .01 .05
115 Vincent Damphousse .01 .05
116 Patrice Brisebois .01 .05
117 Pierre Sevigny .01 .05
118 Eric Desjardins .02 .10
119 Oleg Petrov .01 .05
120 Kevin Haller .01 .05
121 Christian Proulx RC .01 .05
122 Corey Millen .01 .05
123 Jaroslav Modry .01 .05
124 Valeri Zelepukin .01 .05
125 John MacLean .02 .10
126 Martin Brodeur .20 .50
127 Bill Guerin .02 .10
128 Bobby Holik .01 .05
129 Claude Lemieux .01 .05
130 Jason Smith .01 .05
131 Ken Daneyko .01 .05
132 Derek King .01 .05
133 Darius Kasparaitis .01 .05
134 Ray Ferraro .01 .05
135 Pierre Turgeon .02 .10
136 Ron Hextall .02 .10
137 Travis Green .02 .10
138 Joe Day .01 .05
139 David Volek .01 .05
140 Scott Lachance .01 .05
141 Dennis Vaske .01 .05
142 Alexei Kovalev .01 .05
143 Brian Noonan .01 .05
144 Sergei Zubov .01 .05
145 Craig MacTavish .01 .05
146 Steve Larmer .02 .10
147 Adam Graves .01 .05
148 Jeff Beukeboom .01 .05
149 Corey Hirsch .02 .10
150 Stephane Matteau .01 .05
151 Brian Leetch .07 .20
152 Mattias Norstrom .02 .10
153 Sylvain Turgeon .01 .05
154 Norm Maciver .01 .05
155 Scott Levins .01 .05
156 Derek Mayer .01 .05
157 Dave McLlwain .01 .05
158 Craig Billington .02 .10
159 Claude Boivin .01 .05
160 Troy Mallette .01 .05
161 Evgeny Davydov .01 .05
162 Dmitri Filimonov .01 .05
163 Dimitri Yushkevich .01 .05
164 Rob Zettler .01 .05
165 Mark Recchi .02 .10
166 Josef Beranek .01 .05
167 Rod Brind'Amour .02 .10
168 Yves Racine .01 .05
169 Dominic Roussel .02 .10
170 Brent Fedyk .01 .05
171 Bob Wilkie RC .01 .05
172 Kevin Dineen .01 .05
173 Shawn McEachern .01 .05
174 Jaromir Jagr .12 .30
175 Tomas Sandstrom .01 .05
176 Ron Francis .02 .10
177 Kevin Stevens .01 .05
178 Jim McKenzie .01 .05
179 Larry Murphy .02 .10
180 Joe Mullen .02 .10
181 Greg Hawgood .01 .05
182 Tom Barrasso .02 .10
183 Ulf Samuelsson .01 .05
184 Bob Bassen .01 .05
185 Mats Sundin .07 .20
186 Mike Ricci .01 .05
187 Iain Fraser .01 .05
188 Garth Butcher .01 .05
189 Jocelyn Thibault .07 .20
190 Valeri Kamensky .02 .10
191 Martin Rucinsky .01 .05
192 Ron Sutter .01 .05
193 Rene Corbet .01 .05
194 Reggie Savage .01 .05
195 Alexei Kasatonov .01 .05
196 Brendan Shanahan .07 .20
197 Phil Housley .02 .10
198 Jim Montgomery .01 .05
199 Curtis Joseph .07 .20
200 Craig Janney .02 .10
201 David Roberts .01 .05
202 Dave Mackey .01 .05
203 Peter Stastny .02 .10
204 Terry Hollinger RC .01 .05
205 Steve Duchesne .01 .05
206 Vitali Prokhorov .01 .05
207 Rob Gaudreau .01 .05
208 Sandis Ozolinsh .01 .05
209 Johan Garpenlov .01 .05
210 Todd Elik .01 .05
211 Sergei Makarov .01 .05
212 Jean-Francois Quintin .01 .05
213 Vyacheslav Butsayev .01 .05
214 Jimmy Waite .02 .10
215 Ulf Dahlen .01 .05
216 Andrei Nazarov .01 .05
217 Denis Savard .02 .10
218 Brent Gretzky .01 .05
219 Petr Klima .01 .05
220 Chris Gratton .01 .05
221 Brian Bradley .01 .05
222 Adam Creighton .01 .05
223 Shawn Chambers .01 .05
224 Rob Zamuner .01 .05
225 Daren Puppa .02 .10
226 Mikael Andersson .01 .05
227 Dave Ellett .01 .05
228 Mike Gartner .02 .10
229 Felix Potvin .07 .20
230 Yanic Perreault .01 .05
231 Nikolai Borschevsky .01 .05
232 Dmitri Mironov .01 .05
233 Todd Gill .01 .05
234 Eric Lacroix RC .01 .05
235 Kent Manderville .01 .05
236 Chris Govedaris .01 .05
237 Frank Bialowas RC .01 .05
238 Kirk McLean .02 .10
239 Jimmy Carson .01 .05
240 Geoff Courtnall .01 .05
241 Trevor Linden .02 .10
242 Murray Craven .01 .05
243 Bret Hedican .01 .05
244 Jeff Brown .01 .05
245 Mike Peca .01 .05
246 Yevgeny Namestnikov .01 .05
247 Nathan Lafayette .01 .05
248 Shawn Antoski .01 .05
249 Sergio Momesso .01 .05
250 Mike Ridley .01 .05
251 Peter Bondra .02 .10
252 Dimitri Khristich .01 .05
253 Dave Poulin .01 .05
254 Dale Hunter .01 .05
255 Rick Tabaracci .02 .10
256 Kelly Miller .01 .05
257 John Slaney .01 .05
258 Todd Krygier .01 .05
259 Kevin Hatcher .01 .05
260 Alexei Zhamnov .02 .10
261 Dallas Drake .01 .05
262 Dave Manson .01 .05
263 Thomas Steen .01 .05
264 Keith Tkachuk .07 .20
265 Russ Romaniuk .01 .05
266 Michal Grosek RC .01 .05
267 Nelson Emerson .01 .05
268 Michael O'Neill RC .01 .05
269 Kris King .01 .05
270 Teppo Numminen .01 .05
271 Jason Arnott .01 .05
272 Mikael Renberg .02 .10
273 Alexei Yashin .01 .05
274 Chris Pronger .02 .10
275 Jocelyn Thibault .07 .20
276 Bryan Smolinski .01 .05
277 Derek Plante .01 .05
278 Martin Brodeur RS .07 .20
279 Jim Dowd .01 .05
280 Iain Fraser .01 .05
281 Pat Peake .01 .05
282 Chris Gratton .01 .05
283 Chris Osgood .02 .10
284 Jesse Belanger .01 .05
285 Alexandre Daigle .01 .05
286 Robert Lang .01 .05
287 Markus Naslund .07 .20
288 Trevor Kidd .02 .10
289 Jeff Shantz .01 .05
290 Jaroslav Modry .01 .05
291 Oleg Petrov .01 .05
292 Scott Levins .01 .05
293 Jozef Stumpel .01 .05
294 Rob Niedermayer .02 .10
295 Brent Gretzky .01 .05
296 Mario Lemieux PB .30 .75
297 Pavel Bure .07 .20
298 Brendan Shanahan .07 .20
299 Steve Yzerman .07 .20
300 Teemu Selanne .07 .20
301 Eric Lindros .07 .20
302 Jeremy Roenick .10 .25
303 Dave Andreychuk .02 .10
304 Ray Bourque .07 .20
305 Sergei Fedorov .07 .20
306 Wayne Gretzky .40 1.00
307 Adam Graves .01 .05
308 Mike Modano PB .15 .40
309 Brett Hull .07 .20
310 Pat LaFontaine .02 .10
311 Adam Oates .02 .10
312 Patrick Roy .30 .75
313 Doug Gilmour .02 .10
314 Jaromir Jagr .07 .20
315 Mark Recchi .02 .10

1994-95 Parkhurst Gold

The 315 cards in this parallel version of the '94-95 Parkhurst set were issued 1:47 packs. A gold foil hockey player icon and the addition of the word "Parkie", written in gold foil distinguish this set from the regular Parkhurst set. The Rookie Standout and Parkie's Best subset gold cards were made available for the European marketplace by means other than normal pack distribution, and a sufficient amount of product made its way back into the North American

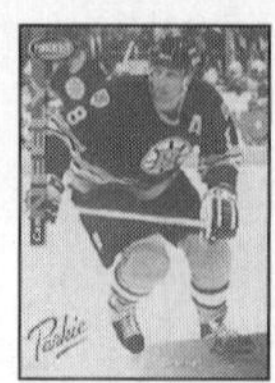

marketplace. With the hockey card market not having absorbed the saturation, multipliers for these subset cards are lower than other cards from this set.

COMPLETE SET (315) 400.00 900.00
*STARS: 20X TO 50X BASIC CARDS
*RC'S: 8X TO 20X BASIC CARDS

1994-95 Parkhurst Crash the Game Green

The 28 cards in this set were randomly inserted into Parkhurst product at a rate of 1:23 packs. There were three variations of each card in this set. Each of the three foil logo colors reflected the different distribution method. Red foil indicated Canadian packaging, blue foil U.S. retail and green foil U.S. hobby. The cards were numbered on the back with a corresponding prefix of C, R, or H. Since the cards were created to be used as an interactive game, the backs contain the rules in extremely fine-print legalese in both English and French, as well as two game dates. If the team featured on the front won on one or both of those dates, the card could be redeemed for a specially foiled set. Unfortunately, the NHL lockout of 1994 prevented the games from being played. As a result, Upper Deck declared all cards winners, enabling each to be redeemed for a 28-card gold-foil version of the set by mail. Because these gold foil versions are so plentiful, they are worth considerably less than their inserted counterparts. Furthermore, the gold version is more commonly seen in complete set form than the other versions, further dampening demand for this product. The prices below reflect green, red and blue versions. The expiration date for the exchange was June 30th, 1995.

COMPLETE SET (28) 20.00 40.00
*GOLD: .2X TO .5X BASIC CARDS
1 Stephan Lebeau .25 .60
2 Ray Bourque .60 1.50
3 Pat LaFontaine .40 1.00
4 Joe Nieuwendyk .30 .75
5 Jeremy Roenick .40 1.00
6 Mike Modano .50 1.25
7 Sergei Fedorov .75 2.00
8 Jason Arnott .30 .75
9 John Vanbiesbrouck .40 1.00
10 Geoff Sanderson .25 .60
11 Wayne Gretzky 2.50 6.00
12 Patrick Roy 2.00 5.00
13 Scott Stevens .30 .75
14 Pierre Turgeon .30 .75
15 Adam Graves .30 .75
16 Alexei Yashin .30 .75
17 Eric Lindros .75 2.00
18 Mario Lemieux 2.00 5.00
19 Joe Sakic .75 2.00
20 Brett Hull .50 1.25
21 Sandis Ozolinsh .30 .75
22 Chris Gratton .25 .60
23 Doug Gilmour .40 1.00
24 Pavel Bure 1.00 2.50
25 Joe Juneau .30 .75
26 Teemu Selanne .40 1.00
27 Mark Messier 1.25 3.00
Eastern Conference
28 Wayne Gretzky 4.00 10.00
Western Conference

1994-95 Parkhurst Vintage

The 90 cards in this set were included one per Parkhurst pack and two per jumbo pack. They are printed on heavy white card stock with a design that hearkens back to the style of Parkhurst issues of the '50s and '60s. The player photo is cut out and placed on a white and tan background. The player's name appears in a black bar on the lower portion of the card, alongside the set logo. The card backs are an unfinished cardboard and feature professional statistics, biography and a "Did You Know" section containing interesting trivia. This trivia did not apply to the player pictured. The cards were numbered with a "V" prefix.

COMPLETE SET (90) 15.00 30.00
V1 Dominik Hasek .60 1.50
V2 Mike Modano .40 1.00
V3 Shayne Corson .05 .15
V4 Kirk Muller .05 .15
V5 Mike Richter .20 .50
V6 Mario Lemieux 1.50 4.00
V7 Sandis Ozolinsh .05 .15
V8 Dave Ellett .05 .15
V9 Dave Manson .05 .15
V10 Terry Yake .05 .15
V11 Craig Simpson .05 .15
V12 Paul Cavallini .05 .15
V13 John Vanbiesbrouck .08 .25
V14 Gilbert Dionne .05 .15
V15 Brian Leetch .20 .50
V16 Martin Straka .05 .15
V17 Curtis Joseph .20 .50
V18 Pavel Bure .30 .75
V19 Garry Valk .05 .15
V20 Theo Fleury .08 .25
V21 Brent Gilchrist .05 .15
V22 Rob Niedermayer .05 .15
V23 Vincent Damphousse .05 .15
V24 Alexei Kovalev .05 .15
V25 Rick Tocchet .05 .15
V26 Steve Duchesne .05 .15
V27 Jiri Slegr .05 .15
V28 Patrick Carnback .05 .15
V29 Gary Roberts .05 .15
V30 Derian Hatcher .05 .15
V31 Jesse Belanger .05 .15
V32 Mathieu Schneider .05 .15
V33 Mark Messier .30 .75
V34 Joe Sakic .75 2.00
V35 Brett Hull .30 .75
V36 Martin Gelinas .05 .15
V37 Maxim Bets .05 .15
V38 Joel Otto .05 .15
V39 Sergei Fedorov .30 .75
V40 Chris Pronger .20 .50
V41 Scott Stevens .08 .25
V42 Alexandre Daigle .05 .15
V43 Owen Nolan .08 .25
V44 Petr Nedved .05 .15
V45 Jeff Brown .05 .15
V46 Adam Oates .08 .25
V47 Robert Reichel .05 .15
V48 Slava Kozlov .08 .25
V49 Geoff Sanderson .05 .15
V50 Stephane Richer .05 .15
V51 Sylvain Turgeon .05 .15
V52 Mike Ricci .08 .25
V53 Roman Hamrlik .05 .15
V54 Kevin Hatcher .05 .15
V55 Mariusz Czerkawski .05 .15
V56 Tony Amonte .08 .25
V57 Steve Yzerman 1.25 3.00
V58 Andrew Cassels .05 .15
V59 Claude Lemieux .05 .15
V60 Derek Mayer .05 .15
V61 Jocelyn Thibault .08 .25
V62 Brent Gretzky .05 .15
V63 Pat Peake .05 .15
V64 Cam Neely .30 .75
V65 Jeremy Roenick .30 .75
V66 Keith Primeau .05 .15
V67 Luc Robitaille .08 .25
V68 Steve Thomas .05 .15
V69 Eric Lindros .30 .75
V70 Pat Falloon .05 .15
V71 Brian Bradley .05 .15
V72 Kelly Miller .05 .15
V73 Pat LaFontaine .20 .50
V74 Gary Suter .05 .15
V75 Bill Ranford .08 .25
V76 Tony Granato .05 .15
V77 Vladimir Malakhov .05 .15
V78 Mikael Renberg .08 .25
V79 Arturs Irbe .08 .25
V80 Doug Gilmour .08 .25
V81 Teemu Selanne .30 .75
V82 Dale Hawerchuk .05 .15
V83 Eric Weinrich .05 .15
V84 Jason Arnott .05 .15
V85 Rob Blake .08 .25
V86 Ray Ferraro .05 .15
V87 Garry Galley .05 .15
V88 Igor Larionov .05 .15
V89 Dave Andreychuk .05 .15
V90 Dallas Drake .05 .15

1994-95 Parkhurst SE

This 270-card set apparently was designed to serve as the second series to the 1994-95 Parkhurst product. In the wake of the NHL lockout of that year, licensing regulations were relaxed, and Upper Deck chose to release the SP line instead. This product subsequently was issued in eleven European countries. However, large quantities eventually made their way to North America. The basic cards have the same design as Parkhurst. Although essentially a companion issue to Parkhurst, this set is numbered from 1-270, with an SE prefix. Subsets include World Junior Championships (206-250) and CAHA Program of Excellence (251-270). Although this set contains the first year cards of many players, they are not recognized as Rookie Cards because of the European-only distribution. A 4" X 6" blowup version of 1994-95 Upper Deck #226, which commemorates Wayne Gretzky's 802 career goals, is inserted at the top of each box.

COMPLETE SET (270) 15.00 30.00
SE1 Guy Hebert .05 .15
SE2 Bob Corkum .02 .10
SE3 Randy Ladouceur .02 .10
SE4 Tom Kurvers .02 .10
SE5 Joe Sacco .02 .10
SE6 Valeri Karpov .02 .10
SE7 Garry Valk .02 .10
SE8 Paul Kariya .10 .30
SE9 Alexei Kasatonov .02 .10
SE10 Sergei Zholtok .02 .10
SE11 Glen Murray .02 .10
SE12 David Reid .02 .10
SE13 Adam Oates .05 .15
SE14 Ted Donato .02 .10
SE15 Don Sweeney .02 .10
SE16 Philippe Boucher .02 .10
SE17 Bob Sweeney .02 .10
SE18 Pat LaFontaine .10 .30
SE19 Derek Plante .05 .15
SE20 Jason Dawe .02 .10
SE21 Petr Svoboda .02 .10
SE22 Craig Simpson .02 .10
SE23 Viktor Gordiouk .02 .10
SE24 Trevor Kidd .05 .15
SE25 Todd Hlushko .02 .10
SE26 German Titov .05 .15
SE27 Gary Roberts .02 .10
SE28 Theo Fleury .02 .10
SE29 Cory Stillman .05 .15
SE30 Phil Housley .05 .15
SE31 Joel Otto .02 .10
SE32 Patrick Poulin .02 .10
SE33 Christian Soucy .05 .15
SE34 Karl Dykhuis .02 .10
SE35 Jeremy Roenick .15 .40
SE36 Tony Amonte .05 .15
SE37 Sergei Krivokrasov .02 .10
SE38 Bernie Nicholls .05 .15
SE39 Todd Harvey .05 .15
SE40 Jarkko Varvio .02 .10
SE41 Shane Churla .02 .10
SE42 Paul Cavallini .02 .10
SE43 Trent Klatt .02 .10
SE44 Darcy Wakaluk .02 .10
SE45 Derian Hatcher .02 .10
SE46 Dean Evason .02 .10
SE47 Mike Modano .20 .50
SE48 Greg Johnson .02 .10
SE49 Ray Sheppard .05 .15
SE50 Sergei Fedorov .20 .50
SE51 Bob Rouse .02 .10
SE52 Mike Vernon .05 .15
SE53 Vladimir Konstantinov .05 .15
SE54 Chris Osgood .05 .15
SE55 Steve Yzerman .60 1.50
SE56 Jason York .05 .15
SE57 Boris Mironov .02 .10
SE58 Igor Kravchuk .02 .10
SE59 Jason Arnott .02 .10
SE60 David Oliver .05 .15
SE61 Todd Marchant .02 .10
SE62 Dean McAmmond .02 .10
SE63 Brian Skrudland .02 .10
SE64 Tom Fitzgerald .02 .10
SE65 Brian Benning .02 .10
SE66 Stu Barnes .02 .10
SE67 John Vanbiesbrouck .05 .15
SE68 Rob Niedermayer .05 .15
SE69 Jimmy Carson .02 .10
SE70 Mark Janssens .02 .10
SE71 Sean Burke .05 .15
SE72 Andrei Nikolishin .02 .10
SE73 Chris Pronger .10 .30
SE74 Jeff Reese .05 .15
SE75 Darren Turcotte .02 .10
SE76 Robert Kron .02 .10
SE77 Kevin Brown .02 .10
SE78 Robert Lang .02 .10
SE79 Rick Tocchet .05 .15
SE80 Jamie Storr .05 .15
SE81 Kelly Hrudey .05 .15
SE82 Darryl Sydor .02 .10
SE83 Tony Granato .02 .10
SE84 Warren Rychel .02 .10
SE85 Gary Shuchuk .02 .10
SE86 Peter Popovic .02 .10
SE87 Valeri Bure .02 .10
SE88 Kirk Muller .05 .15
SE89 Lyle Odelein .02 .10
SE90 Brian Savage .02 .10
SE91 Gilbert Dionne .02 .10
SE92 Mathieu Schneider .02 .10
SE93 Jim Montgomery .02 .10
SE94 Chris Terreri .05 .15
SE95 Scott Niedermayer .02 .10
SE96 Bob Carpenter .02 .10
SE97 Scott Stevens .05 .15
SE98 Jim Dowd .02 .10
SE99 Brian Rolston .02 .10
SE100 Stephane Richer .05 .15
SE101 Mick Vukota .02 .10
SE102 Steve Thomas .02 .10
SE103 Patrick Flatley .02 .10
SE104 Marty McInnis .02 .10
SE105 Rich Pilon .02 .10
SE106 Benoit Hogue .02 .10
SE107 Zigmund Palffy .05 .15
SE108 Vladimir Malakhov .02 .10
SE109 Brett Lindros .02 .10
SE110 Mike Richter .10 .30
SE111 Greg Gilbert .02 .10
SE112 Kevin Lowe .02 .10
SE113 Mark Messier .10 .30
SE114 Alexander Karpovtsev .02 .10
SE115 Sergei Nemchinov .02 .10
SE116 Petr Nedved .05 .15
SE117 Glenn Healy .05 .15
SE118 Dave Archibald .02 .10
SE119 Alexandre Daigle .02 .10
SE120 Darrin Madeley .02 .10
SE121 Pavol Demitra .05 .15
SE122 Brad Shaw .02 .10
SE123 Alexei Yashin .02 .10
SE124 Sean Hill .02 .10
SE125 Vladislav Boulin .02 .10
SE126 Kevin Haller .02 .10
SE127 Chris Therien .02 .10
SE128 Garry Galley .02 .10
SE129 Mikael Renberg .05 .15
SE130 Ron Hextall .05 .15
SE131 Eric Lindros .10 .30
SE132 Craig MacTavish .02 .10
SE133 Patrik Juhlin .05 .15
SE134 Martin Straka .02 .10
SE135 Doug Brown .02 .10
SE136 Markus Naslund .10 .30
SE137 Luc Robitaille .05 .15
SE138 Kjell Samuelsson .02 .10
SE139 Ken Wregget .05 .15
SE140 John Cullen .02 .10
SE141 Peter Taglianetti .02 .10
SE142 Janne Laukkanen .02 .10
SE143 Owen Nolan .05 .15
SE144 Adam Deadmarsh .02 .10
SE145 Dave Karpa .02 .10
SE146 Wendel Clark .05 .15
SE147 Joe Sakic .25 .60
SE148 Alexei Gusarov .02 .10
SE149 Peter Forsberg .50 1.25
SE150 Kevin Miller .02 .10
SE151 Denny Felsner .02 .10
SE152 Al MacInnis .05 .15
SE153 Philippe Bozon .02 .10
SE154 Brett Hull .15 .40
SE155 Guy Carbonneau .02 .10
SE156 Igor Korolev .02 .10
SE157 Esa Tikkanen .05 .15
SE158 Jon Casey .05 .15
SE159 Viktor Kozlov .05 .15
SE160 Mike Rathje .02 .10
SE161 Bob Errey .02 .10
SE162 Arturs Irbe .05 .15
SE163 Ray Whitney .02 .10
SE164 Igor Larionov .02 .10
SE165 Pat Falloon .02 .10
SE166 Jeff Friesen .02 .10
SE167 Vlastimil Kroupa .02 .10
SE168 Chris Joseph .02 .10
SE169 Danton Cole .02 .10
SE170 John Tucker .02 .10
SE171 Roman Hamrlik .05 .15
SE172 Jason Wiemer .02 .10
SE173 Kenny Jonsson .02 .10
SE174 Eric Fichaud XRC .15 .40
SE175 Mats Sundin .10 .30
SE176 Doug Gilmour .05 .15
SE177 Drake Berehowsky .02 .10
SE178 Mike Ridley .02 .10
SE179 Jamie Macoun .02 .10
SE180 Alexei Kudashov .02 .10
SE181 Bill Berg .02 .10
SE182 Dave Andreychuk .05 .15
SE183 Mike Eastwood .02 .10
SE184 Martin Gelinas .02 .10
SE185 Greg Adams .02 .10
SE186 Gino Odjick .02 .10
SE187 Pavel Bure .10 .30
SE188 Cliff Ronning .02 .10
SE189 Jiri Slegr .02 .10
SE190 Jyrki Lumme .02 .10
SE191 Jassen Cullimore .02 .10
SE192 Steve Konowalchuk .02 .10
SE193 Sylvain Cote .02 .10
SE194 Jason Allison .02 .10
SE195 Sergei Gonchar .02 .10
SE196 Pat Peake .02 .10
SE197 Calle Johansson .02 .10
SE198 Joe Juneau .05 .15
SE199 Jeff Nelson .02 .10
SE200 Luciano Borsato .02 .10
SE201 Teemu Selanne .10 .30
SE202 Tie Domi .05 .15
SE203 Tim Cheveldae .05 .15
SE204 Darrin Shannon .02 .10
SE205 Ravil Gusmanov .02 .10
SE206 Todd Harvey .02 .10
SE207 Ed Jovanovski XRC .15 .40
SE208 Jason Allison .02 .10
SE209 Bryan McCabe .02 .10
SE210 Dan Cloutier XRC .40 1.00
SE211 Ladislav Kohn XRC .15 .40
SE212 Marek Malik XRC .15 .40
SE213 Jan Hlavac XRC .15 .40
SE214 Petr Cajanek XRC .15 .40
SE215 Jussi Markkanen XRC .75 2.00
SE216 Jere Karalahti XRC .15 .40
SE217 Janne Niinimaa .10 .30
SE218 Kimmo Timonen .05 .15
SE219 Mikko Helisten XRC .15 .40
SE220 Niko Halttunen XRC .15 .40
SE221 Tommi Miettinen .05 .15
SE222 Veli-Pekka Nutikka XRC .15 .40
SE223 Timo Salonen XRC .15 .40
SE224 Tommi Sova XRC .15 .40
SE225 Jussi Tarvainen XRC .15 .40
SE226 Tommi Rajamaki XRC .15 .40
SE227 Antti Aalto XRC .15 .40
SE228 Alexander Korolyuk XRC .15 .40
SE229 Vitali Yachmenev .05 .15
SE230 Nikolai Zavarukhin .05 .15
SE231 Vadim Epantchinsev .05 .15
SE232 Dmitri Klevakin .05 .15
SE233 Anders Eriksson .05 .15
SE234 Anders Soderberg .05 .15
SE235 Per Svartvadet XRC .15 .40
SE236 Johan Davidsson .02 .10
SE237 Niklas Sundstrom .05 .15
SE238 J. Andersson-Junkka XRC .15 .40
SE239 Dick Tarnstrom XRC .15 .40
SE240 P.J. Axelsson XRC .05 .15
SE241 Frederik Johansson .05 .15
SE242 Peter Strom .05 .15
SE243 Mattias Ohlund .05 .15
SE244 Jesper Mattsson .05 .15
SE245 Jonas Forsberg .05 .15
SE246 Adam Deadmarsh .02 .10
SE247 Deron Quint .05 .15
SE248 Jamie Langenbrunner .02 .10
SE249 Richard Park .02 .10
SE250 Bryan Berard XRC .15 .40
SE251 David Belitski XRC .15 .40
SE252 Mike McBain XRC .15 .40
SE253 Hugh Hamilton XRC .15 .40
SE254 Jason Doig XRC .15 .40
SE255 Xavier Delisle XRC .15 .40
SE256 Wade Redden XRC .15 .40
SE257 Jeff Ware XRC .15 .40
SE258 Christian Dube XRC .15 .40
SE259 Louis-Phil.Sevigny XRC .15 .40

SE260 Jarome Iginla XRC 4.00 10.00
SE261 Daniel Briere XRC 3.00 8.00
SE262 Justin Kurtz XRC .15 .40
SE263 Marc Savard XRC .40 1.00
SE264 Alyn McCauley XRC .15 .40
SE265 Brad Mehalko XRC .15 .40
SE266 Jeffrey Ambrosio XRC.15 .40
SE267 Todd Norman XRC .15 .40
SE268 Brian Scott XRC .15 .40
SE269 Brad Larsen XRC .15 .40
SE270 J-S Giguere XRC 2.00 5.00
NNO Wayne Gretzky Large 1.50 4.00

1994-95 Parkhurst SE Gold

his 270-card set parallels the regular arkhurst SE issue. The distinguishing ature between the two is that the normally lver player icon on the card front is now old with the word "Parkie" printed ongside it in gold foil. Interestingly, these ards, which were inserted at a rate of one er pack, are significantly easier to find than e gold cards which paralleled the regular arkhurst set which were inserted 1:35 acks. The cards are grouped alphabetically thin teams and checklisted as in the gular set.

STARS: 1X TO 2.5X BASIC CARDS
ROOKIES: .75X to 2X

1994-95 Parkhurst SE Euro-Stars

he 20 cards in this set were randomly serted in Parkhurst SE product at an pproximate rate of 1:8 packs. The set has ome of the top European-born talent in the HL. The cards feature a horizontal design th an action photo on the right and set go and European map elements on the left. ard numbers have an "ES" prefix.

OMPLETE SET (20) 10.00 20.00
S1 Peter Forsberg 2.50 6.00
S2 Mats Sundin .60 1.50
S3 Mikael Renberg .30 .75
S4 Nicklas Lidstrom .60 1.50
S5 Mariusz Czerkawski .15 .40
S6 Ulf Dahlen .15 .40
S7 Kjell Samuelsson .15 .40
S8 Jyrki Lumme .15 .40
S9 Jari Kurri .30 .75
S10 Teppo Numminen .15 .40
S11 Esa Tikkanen .15 .40
S12 Christian Ruuttu .15 .40
S13 Teemu Selanne .60 1.50
S14 Alexander Mogilny .30 .75
S15 Pavel Bure .60 1.50
S16 Sergei Fedorov 1.00 2.50
S17 Arturs Irbe .30 .75
S18 Alexei Kovalev .15 .40
S19 Dominik Hasek 1.25 3.00
S20 Jaromir Jagr 1.00 2.50

1994-95 Parkhurst SE Vintage

is 45-card standard-size was inserted in arkhurst SE packs at approximately the rate 1:6. They are printed on heavy white card ock with a design that hearkens back to the yle of Parkhurst issues of the 1950s and 960s. The player photo is cut out and aced on a white-and-tan background. The ayer's name appears in a black bar on the wer portion of the card, alongside the set go. The card backs are an unfinished rdboard and feature professional statistics, ography and a "Did You Know" section ntaining interesting trivia, which did not ply to the player pictured. The cards were mbered with a "seV" prefix.

OMPLETE SET (45) 15.00 40.00
Paul Kariya .60 1.50
Dino Ciccarelli .10 .25
Patrick Roy 3.00 8.00
Markus Naslund .60 1.50
Trevor Linden .50 1.25
Valeri Karpov .10 .25
Pat Verbeek .10 .25
Martin Brodeur 1.50 4.00
9 Kevin Stevens .10 .25
10 Kirk McLean .50 1.25
11 Stephan Lebeau .10 .25
12 Scott Niedermayer .10 .25
13 Peter Bondra .50 1.25
14 Ed Belfour .60 1.50
15 Paul Coffey .60 1.50
16 Chris Gratton .10 .25
17 Joe Juneau .50 1.25
18 Ray Bourque .60 1.50
19 Sergei Krivokrasov .10 .25
20 Wayne Gretzky 4.00 10.00
21 Alexei Yashin .10 .25
22 Al Iafrate .10 .25
23 Doug Weight .50 1.25
24 Jari Kurri .10 .25
25 Rod Brind'Amour .50 1.25
26 Bryan Smolinski .10 .25
27 Darius Kasparaitis .10 .25
28 Mark Recchi .10 .25
29 Mike Gartner .50 1.25
30 Russ Courtnall .10 .25
31 Pierre Turgeon .50 1.25
32 Felix Potvin .60 1.50
33 Nelson Emerson .10 .25
34 Alexander Mogilny .50 1.25
35 Bob Kudelski .10 .25
36 Brett Lindros .10 .25
37 Mats Sundin .60 1.50
38 Keith Tkachuk .60 1.50
39 Derek Plante .10 .25
40 Oleg Petrov .10 .25
41 Adam Graves .10 .25
42 Jaromir Jagr 1.00 2.50
43 Viktor Kozlov .10 .25
44 Nathan Lafayette .10 .25
45 Alexei Zhamnov .50 1.25

1995-96 Parkhurst '66-67 Promos

This five-card set was issued to promote the third installment of the Missing Link trilogy. The cards mirror the corresponding regular versions, save for the word PROMO stamped on the back, and a statement which reveals these cards were limited to 1966 copies.

COMPLETE SET (5) 6.00 15.00
1 Gerry Cheevers 1.20 3.00
Boston Bruins
2 Bob Nevin .30 .75
New York Rangers
3 Jacques Laperriere .30 .75
Norris Trophy Winner
4 Jean Beliveau 1.60 4.00
Stan Mikita AS
5 Gordie Howe 4.00 10.00
Detroit Red Wings

1995-96 Parkhurst '66-67

This 150-card set lovingly speculates on what might have been had Parkhurst, the venerable Canadian card manufacturer, been active during Bobby Orr's rookie card season. 2500 numbered 16-box cases were produced of the eight-card packs. The cards utilized period photos and a design element consistent with the time. There were two five-card insert sets honoring "Super Rookie" Orr and "Mr. Hockey" Gordie Howe. Orr and Howe autographed 500 of each card in their respective sets. The five promo cards were issued in set form. They are identical to the regular versions of the cards, save for the bold notation on the back which proclaims them to be prototypes limited to 1966 copies.

COMPLETE SET (150) 15.00 25.00
1 Pit Martin .05 .12
2 Ron Stewart .05 .12
3 Joe Watson .02 .10
4 Ed Westfall .02 .10
5 John Bucyk .10 .25
6 Ted Green .05 .12
7 Bobby Orr 2.50 5.00
8 Bob Woytowich .02 .10
9 Murray Oliver .02 .10
10 John McKenzie .05 .12
11 Tom Williams .02 .10
12 Don Awrey .02 .10
13 Ron Schock .02 .10
14 Bernie Parent .40 1.00
15 Ron Murphy .02 .10
16 Gerry Cheevers .40 1.00
17 Gilles Marotte .02 .10
18 Ed Johnston .05 .12
19 Derek Sanderson .40 1.00
20 Wayne Connelly .02 .10
21 Bobby Hull 1.50 3.00
22 Matt Ravlich .02 .10
23 Ken Hodge .05 .12
24 Stan Mikita .60 1.50
25 Fred Stanfield .02 .10
26 Eric Nesterenko .05 .12
27 Doug Jarrett .05 .12
28 Lou Angotti .02 .10
29 Ken Wharram .02 .10
30 Bill Hay .02 .10
31 Glenn Hall .60 1.50
32 Chico Maki .02 .10
33 Phil Esposito .60 1.50
34 Pierre Pilote .10 .25
35 Doug Mohns .02 .10
36 Ed Van Impe .05 .12
37 Dennis Hull .05 .12
38 Pat Stapleton .02 .10
39 Denis DeJordy .02 .10
40 Paul Henderson .05 .12
41 Gary Bergman .02 .10
42 Gordie Howe 2.00 4.00
43 Bob McCord .02 .10
44 Andy Bathgate .10 .25
45 Norm Ullman .10 .25
46 Peter Mahovlich .05 .12
47 Ted Hampson .02 .10
48 Leo Boivin .10 .25
49 Bruce MacGregor .02 .10
50 Ab McDonald .05 .12
51 Dean Prentice .02 .10
52 Floyd Smith .02 .10
53 Alex Delvecchio .10 .25
54 Pete Goegan .02 .10
55 Parker MacDonald .02 .10
56 Roger Crozier .05 .12
57 Val Fonteyne .02 .10
58 Henri Richard .40 1.00
59 John Ferguson .05 .12
60 Yvan Cournoyer .10 .25
61 Claude Provost .05 .12
62 Dave Balon .02 .10
63 Ted Harris .02 .10
64 Ralph Backstrom .05 .12
65 Jacques Laperriere .10 .25
66 Terry Harper .05 .12
67 J.C. Tremblay .05 .12
68 Jean Guy Talbot .05 .12
69 Claude Larose .05 .12
70 Charlie Hodge .05 .12
71 Gilles Tremblay .05 .12
72 Jim Roberts .02 .10
73 Jean Beliveau .60 1.50
74 Serge Savard .10 .25
75 Rogatien Vachon .30 .75
76 Lorne Worsley .60 1.50
77 Bobby Rousseau .05 .12
78 Dick Duff .05 .12
79 Rod Gilbert .10 .25
80 Harry Howell .10 .25
81 Jim Neilson .02 .10
82 Don Marshall .02 .10
83 Reg Fleming .02 .10
84 Wayne Hillman .02 .10
85 Bob Nevin .02 .10
86 Arnie Brown .02 .10
87 Earl Ingarfield .02 .10
88 Jean Ratelle .10 .25
89 Bernie Geoffrion .40 1.00
90 Orland Kurtenbach .02 .10
91 Bill Hicke .02 .10
92 Red Berenson .05 .12
93 Ed Giacomin .10 .25
94 Al MacNeil .02 .10
95 Rod Seiling .02 .10
96 Doug Robinson .02 .10
97 Cesare Maniago .05 .12
98 Vic Hadfield .02 .10
99 Phil Goyette .02 .10
100 Dave Keon .10 .25
101 Mike Walton .02 .10
102 Frank Mahovlich .60 1.50
103 Tim Horton .60 1.50
104 Larry Hillman .02 .10
105 Kent Douglas .02 .10
106 Ron Ellis .02 .10
107 Jim Pappin .02 .10
108 Marcel Pronovost .10 .25
109 Red Kelly .10 .25
110 Allan Stanley .10 .25
111 Brit Selby .02 .10
112 Pete Stemkowski .02 .10
113 Eddie Shack .40 1.00
114 Bob Pulford .10 .25
115 Larry Jeffrey .02 .10
116 George Armstrong .10 .25
117 Bob Baun .05 .12
118 Bruce Gamble .05 .12
119 Johnny Bower .60 1.50
120 Terry Sawchuk .75 2.00
121 Hall/Worsley AS .30 .75
122 Laperriere/Stanley AS .05 .12
123 Pilote/Stapleton AS .05 .12
124 Hull/Mahovlich AS .40 1.00
125 Mikita/Beliveau AS .30 .75
126 Howe/Rousseau AS .60 1.50
127 Alex Delvecchio .05 .12
Lady Byng
128 Jacques Laperriere .05 .12
Norris
129 Bobby Hull .60 1.50
Hart
130 Bobby Hull .60 1.50
Art Ross
131 Worsley/Hodge .20 .50
Vezina
132 Brit Selby .02 .10
Calder
133 Action Card .05 .12
All-Star Game
134 Action Card .05 .12
135 Action Card .05 .12
136 Action Card .05 .12
137 Action Card .05 .12
138 Action Card .05 .12
139 Action Card .05 .12
140 Murray Oliver L .02 .10
141 Bobby Hull L .60 1.50
142 Gordie Howe L .75 2.00
143 Bobby Rousseau L .02 .10
144 Bob Nevin L .02 .10
145 Mahovlich/Pulford L .10 .25
146 Stanley Cup Playoffs .05 .12
Semifinals
147 Stanley Cup Playoffs .05 .12
Semifinals
148 Stanley Cup Playoffs Finals.05 .12
149 Checklist .02 .10
150 Checklist .02 .10
PR16 Gerry Cheevers promo.02 .10
PR42 Gordie Howe promo .02 .10
PR125 Stan Mikita/Jean Beliveau.02 .10
AS promo
PR128 Jacques Laperriere .02 .10
TW promo
PR144 Bob Nevin SL promo.02 .10
SR1 Bobby Orr 7.50 15.00
SR2 Bobby Orr 7.50 15.00
SR3 Bobby Orr 7.50 15.00
SR4 Bobby Orr 7.50 15.00
SR5 Bobby Orr 7.50 15.00
MHA1 Gordie Howe AU 50.00 100.00
MHA2 Gordie Howe AU 50.00 100.00
MHA3 Gordie Howe AU 50.00 100.00
MHA4 Gordie Howe AU 50.00 100.00
MHA5 Gordie Howe AU 50.00 100.00
MRH1 Gordie Howe 6.00 12.00
MRH2 Gordie Howe 6.00 12.00
MRH3 Gordie Howe 6.00 12.00
MRH4 Gordie Howe 6.00 12.00
MRH5 Gordie Howe 6.00 12.00
SRA1 Bobby Orr AU 125.00 250.00
SRA2 Bobby Orr AU 125.00 250.00
SRA3 Bobby Orr AU 125.00 250.00
SRA4 Bobby Orr AU 125.00 250.00
SRA5 Bobby Orr AU 125.00 250.00

1995-96 Parkhurst '66-67 Coins

In tip of the hat fashion, this 120-coin insert set recreates the popular Shirriff coins of the 1960s. The plastic coins were team color coded, and were inserted one per pack. The coins measure about 1 3/8" in diameter. They are numbered in identical fashion to the card set as the same players are featured. Several collectors and dealers have reported the Paul Henderson coin (#40) as being difficult to locate. Parkhurst officials, however, say no coin was printed in shorter quantity than any other. There also were five black coins randomly inserted honoring Bobby Orr and Gordie Howe.

COMPLETE SET (120) 90.00 175.00
1 Pit Martin .40 1.00
2 Ron Stewart .40 1.00
3 Joe Watson .25 .60
4 Ed Westfall .25 .60
5 John Bucyk .50 1.50
6 Ted Green .40 1.00
7 Bobby Orr 5.00 10.00
8 Bob Woytowich .25 .60
9 Murray Oliver .25 .60
10 John McKenzie .40 1.00
11 Tom Williams .25 .60
12 Don Awrey .25 .60
13 Ron Schock .25 .60
14 Bernie Parent 1.50 3.00
15 Ron Murphy .25 .60
16 Gerry Cheevers 1.50 3.00
17 Gilles Marotte .25 .60
18 Ed Johnston .40 1.00
19 Derek Sanderson 1.50 3.00
20 Wayne Connelly .25 .60
21 Bobby Hull 3.00 6.00
22 Matt Ravlich .25 .60
23 Ken Hodge .40 1.00
24 Stan Mikita 2.00 4.00
25 Fred Stanfield .25 .60
26 Eric Nesterenko .40 1.00
27 Doug Jarrett .25 .60
28 Lou Angotti .25 .60
29 Ken Wharram .25 .60
30 Bill Hay .25 .60
31 Glenn Hall 2.00 4.00
32 Chico Maki .25 .60
33 Phil Esposito 2.00 4.00
34 Pierre Pilote .50 1.50
35 Doug Mohns .25 .60
36 Ed Van Impe .25 .60
37 Dennis Hull .40 1.00
38 Pat Stapleton .25 .60
39 Denis DeJordy .25 .60
40 Paul Henderson 5.00 10.00
41 Gary Bergman .25 .60
42 Gordie Howe 4.00 8.00
43 Bob McCord .25 .60
44 Andy Bathgate .50 1.50
45 Norm Ullman .50 1.50
46 Peter Mahovlich .40 1.00
47 Ted Hampson .25 .60
48 Leo Boivin .50 1.50
49 Bruce MacGregor .25 .60
50 Ab McDonald .40 1.00
51 Dean Prentice .25 .60
52 Floyd Smith .25 .60
53 Alex Delvecchio .50 1.50
54 Pete Goegan .25 .60
55 Parker MacDonald .25 .60
56 Roger Crozier .40 1.00
57 Val Fonteyne .25 .60
58 Henri Richard 1.50 3.00
59 John Ferguson .40 1.00
60 Yvan Cournoyer .50 1.50
61 Claude Provost .40 1.00
62 Dave Balon .25 .60
63 Ted Harris .25 .60
64 Ralph Backstrom .40 1.00
65 Jacques Laperriere .50 1.50
66 Terry Harper .40 1.00
67 J.C. Tremblay .40 1.00
68 Jean Guy Talbot .40 1.00
69 Claude Larose .40 1.00
70 Charlie Hodge .40 1.00
71 Gilles Tremblay .25 .60
72 Jim Roberts .25 .60
73 Jean Beliveau 2.00 4.00
74 Serge Savard .50 1.50
75 Rogatien Vachon 1.50 3.00
76 Lorne Worsley 2.00 4.00
77 Bobby Rousseau .40 1.00
78 Dick Duff .40 1.00
79 Rod Gilbert .50 1.50
80 Harry Howell .50 1.50
81 Jim Neilson .25 .60
82 Don Marshall .25 .60
83 Reg Fleming .25 .60
84 Wayne Hillman .25 .60
85 Bob Nevin .25 .60
86 Arnie Brown .25 .60
87 Earl Ingarfield .25 .60
88 Jean Ratelle .50 1.50
89 Bernie Geoffrion 1.50 3.00
90 Orland Kurtenbach .25 .60
91 Bill Hicke .25 .60
92 Red Berenson .40 1.00
93 Ed Giacomin .50 1.50
94 Al MacNeil .25 .60
95 Rod Seiling .25 .60
96 Doug Robinson .25 .60
97 Cesare Maniago .40 1.00
98 Vic Hadfield .25 .60
99 Phil Goyette .25 .60
100 Dave Keon .50 1.50
101 Mike Walton .25 .60
102 Frank Mahovlich 2.00 4.00
103 Tim Horton 2.00 4.00
104 Larry Hillman .25 .60
105 Kent Douglas .25 .60
106 Ron Ellis .25 .60
107 Jim Pappin .25 .60
108 Marcel Pronovost .50 1.50
109 Red Kelly .50 1.50
110 Allan Stanley .50 1.50
111 Brit Selby .25 .60
112 Pete Stemkowski .25 .60
113 Eddie Shack 1.50 3.00
114 Bob Pulford .50 1.50
115 Larry Jeffrey .25 .60
116 George Armstrong .50 1.50
117 Bob Baun .40 1.00
118 Bruce Gamble .25 .60
119 Johnny Bower 2.00 4.00
120 Terry Sawchuk 2.50 5.00
BO1 Bobby Orr Black Coin 4.00 10.00
BO2 Bobby Orr Black Coin 4.00 10.00
BO3 Bobby Orr Black Coin 4.00 10.00
BO4 Bobby Orr Black Coin 4.00 10.00
BO5 Bobby Orr Black Coin 4.00 10.00
GH1 Gordie Howe Black Coin 3.20 8.00
GH2 Gordie Howe Black Coin 3.20 8.00
GH3 Gordie Howe Black Coin 3.20 8.00
GH4 Gordie Howe Black Coin 3.20 8.00
GH5 Gordie Howe Black Coin 3.20 8.00

1995-96 Parkhurst International

This two-series issue was produced by Parkhurst in Canada for release in eleven European countries. Interest in the cards, which featured NHL players and were licensed by both the NHL and NHLPA, was such that they became widely available throughout North America. The first series was produced in larger quantities than the second series, which by some estimates was limited to around 900 cases. Each box included 48 14-card packs. The second series is notable for including the first card of Wayne Gretzky in a St. Louis Blues uniform. Two different players autographed cards for insertion in each series: Teemu Selanne and Mikael Renberg each signed 2,500 cards for series 1, while Martin Brodeur and Saku Koivu inked up 2,500 each for series 2. One jumbo Saku Koivu card was inserted in each series 2 box; autographed copies of this jumbo card were randomly inserted as well.

COMPLETE SET (540) 15.00 40.00
COMPLETE SERIES 1 (270) 8.00 20.00
COMPLETE SERIES 2 (270) 8.00 20.00
1 Patrik Carnback .02 .10
2 Milos Holan .02 .10
3 Paul Kariya .08 .25
4 Guy Hebert .05 .15
5 Garry Valk .02 .10
6 Mikhail Shtalenkov .02 .10
7 Randy Ladouceur .02 .10
8 Shaun Van Allen .02 .10
9 Oleg Tverdovsky .02 .10
10 Kevin Stevens .02 .10
11 Ray Bourque .15 .40
12 Cam Neely .08 .25
13 Jozef Stumpel .02 .10
14 Blaine Lacher .05 .15
15 Alexei Kasatonov .02 .10
16 Adam Oates .05 .15
17 Ted Donato .02 .10
18 Mariusz Czerkawski .02 .10
19 Alexei Zhitnik .02 .10
20 Pat LaFontaine .08 .25
21 Garry Galley .02 .10
22 Scott Pearson .02 .10
23 Yuri Khmylev .02 .10
24 Jason Dawe .02 .10
25 Robb Stauber .05 .15
26 Wayne Primeau .02 .10
27 Brian Holzinger XRC .08 .25
28 German Titov .02 .10
29 Theo Fleury .08 .25
30 Phil Housley .05 .15
31 Zarley Zalapski .02 .10
32 Rick Tabaracci .05 .15
33 Joe Nieuwendyk .05 .15
34 Michael Nylander .02 .10
35 Trevor Kidd .05 .15
36 Dean Evason .02 .10
37 Bernie Nicholls .02 .10
38 Chris Chelios .08 .25
39 Gary Suter .02 .10
40 Denis Savard .05 .15
41 Ed Belfour .08 .25
42 Patrick Poulin .02 .10
43 Steve Smith .02 .10
44 Jeff Hackett .05 .15
45 Eric Daze .05 .15
46 Joe Sakic .20 .50
47 John Slaney .02 .10
48 Valeri Kamensky .05 .15
49 Owen Nolan .05 .15
50 Uwe Krupp .02 .10
51 Andrei Kovalenko .02 .10
52 Janne Laukkanen .02 .10
53 Jocelyn Thibault .08 .25
54 Adam Deadmarsh .02 .10
55 Mike Modano .15 .40
56 Kevin Hatcher .02 .10
57 Mike Donnelly .02 .10
58 Derian Hatcher .02 .10
59 Andy Moog .08 .25
60 Jamie Langenbrunner .05 .15
61 Shane Churla .05 .15
62 Todd Harvey .05 .15
63 Manny Fernandez .08 .25
64 Nicklas Lidstrom .08 .25
65 Vyacheslav Kozlov .05 .15
66 Paul Coffey .08 .25
67 Chris Osgood .05 .15
68 Slava Fetisov .02 .10
69 Vladimir Konstantinov .05 .15
70 Steve Yzerman .50 1.25
71 Aaron Ward .02 .10
72 Keith Primeau .02 .10
73 Jason Arnott .02 .10
74 Igor Kravchuk .02 .10
75 Boris Mironov .02 .10
76 David Oliver .02 .10
77 Kelly Buchberger .02 .10
78 Bill Ranford .05 .15
79 Zdeno Ciger .02 .10
80 Jason Bonsignore .02 .10
81 Louie DeBrusk .02 .10
82 Rob Niedermayer .05 .15
83 Magnus Svensson .02 .10
84 Robert Svehla .02 .10
85 John Vanbiesbrouck .05 .15
86 Stu Barnes .02 .10
87 Jesse Belanger .02 .10
88 Mark Fitzpatrick .05 .15
89 Jason Woolley .02 .10
90 Johan Garpenlov .02 .10
91 Geoff Sanderson .02 .10
92 Robert Kron .02 .10
93 Darren Turcotte .02 .10
94 Andrei Nikolishin .02 .10
95 Steven Rice .02 .10
96 Sean Burke .05 .15
97 Brendan Shanahan .08 .25
98 Glen Wesley .02 .10
99 Marek Malik .02 .10
100 Wayne Gretzky .75 2.00
101 Robert Lang .02 .10
102 Jari Kurri .08 .25
103 Kelly Hrudey .05 .15
104 Jamie Storr .05 .15
105 Marty McSorley .02 .10
106 Rob Blake .05 .15
107 Eric LaCroix .02 .10
108 Dimitri Khristich .02 .10
109 Pierre Turgeon .05 .15
110 Vincent Damphousse .02 .10
111 Peter Popovic .02 .10
112 Brian Savage .02 .10
113 Patrick Roy .50 1.25
114 Valeri Bure .02 .10
115 Vladimir Malakhov .02 .10
116 Benoit Brunet .02 .10
117 Stephane Quintal .02 .10
118 Stephane Richer .05 .15
119 Sergei Brylin .02 .10
120 Neal Broten .05 .15
121 Scott Stevens .05 .15
122 Martin Brodeur .25 .60
123 John MacLean .02 .10
124 Bill Guerin .05 .15
125 Bobby Holik .02 .10
126 Tommy Albelin .02 .10
127 Tommy Soderstrom .05 .15
128 Tommy Salo .05 .15
129 Kirk Muller .02 .10
130 Mathieu Schneider .02 .10
131 Zigmund Palffy .05 .15
132 Derek King .02 .10
133 Brett Lindros .02 .10
134 Marty McInnis .02 .10
135 Alexander Semak .02 .10
136 Mark Messier .08 .25
137 Adam Graves .02 .10
138 Mike Richter .08 .25
139 Alexei Kovalev .02 .10
140 Luc Robitaille .05 .15
141 Sergei Nemchinov .02 .10
142 Alexander Karpovtsev .02 .10
143 Mattias Norstrom .02 .10
144 Brian Leetch .05 .15
145 Martin Straka .02 .10
146 Sylvain Turgeon .02 .10
147 Radek Bonk .02 .10
148 Stanislav Neckar .02 .10
149 Pavol Demitra .08 .25
150 Alexandre Daigle .02 .10
151 Alexei Yashin .02 .10
152 Don Beaupre .05 .15
153 Steve Duchesne .02 .10
154 Eric Lindros .08 .25
155 Kjell Samuelsson .02 .10
156 Chris Therien .02 .10
157 John LeClair .08 .25
158 Rod Brind'Amour .05 .15
159 Ron Hextall .05 .15
160 Patrik Juhlin .02 .10
161 Mikael Renberg .02 .10
162 Joel Otto .02 .10
163 Markus Naslund .08 .25
164 Ron Francis .05 .15
165 Jaromir Jagr .15 .40
166 Tomas Sandstrom .02 .10
167 Ken Wregget .05 .15
168 Bryan Smolinski .02 .10
169 Richard Park .02 .10
170 Mario Lemieux .50 1.25
171 Norm Maciver .02 .10
172 Brett Hull .12 .30
173 Esa Tikkanen .02 .10
174 Shayne Corson .02 .10
175 Chris Pronger .08 .25
176 Ian Laperriere .02 .10
177 Jon Casey .05 .15
178 Al MacInnis .05 .15
179 David Roberts .02 .10
180 Dale Hawerchuk .08 .25
181 Michal Sykora .02 .10
182 Jeff Friesen .02 .10
183 Ray Whitney .05 .15
184 Igor Larionov .02 .10
185 Sandis Ozolinsh .02 .10
186 Andrei Nazarov .02 .10
187 Viktor Kozlov .05 .15
188 Arturs Irbe .05 .15
189 Wade Flaherty .05 .15
190 Brian Bradley .02 .10
191 Paul Ysebaert .02 .10
192 John Tucker .02 .10
193 Jason Wiemer .02 .10
194 Alexander Selivanov .02 .10
195 Daren Puppa .05 .15
196 Mikael Andersson .02 .10
197 Petr Klima .02 .10
198 Roman Hamrlik .05 .15
199 Doug Gilmour .05 .15
200 Damian Rhodes .05 .15
201 Mats Sundin .08 .25
202 Todd Gill .02 .10
203 Kenny Jonsson .02 .10
204 Felix Potvin .08 .25
205 Tie Domi .05 .15
206 Mike Gartner .05 .15
207 Larry Murphy .05 .15
208 Josef Beranek .02 .10
209 Trevor Linden .05 .15
210 Russ Courtnall .02 .10
211 Roman Oksiuta .02 .10
212 Alexander Mogilny .05 .15
213 Kirk McLean .05 .15
214 Mike Ridley .02 .10
215 Jyrki Lumme .02 .10
216 Bret Hedican .02 .10
217 Keith Jones .05 .15
218 Calle Johansson .02 .10
219 Kelly Miller .02 .10
220 Olaf Kolzig .05 .15
221 Joe Juneau .02 .10
222 Sylvain Cote .02 .10
223 Dale Hunter .05 .15
224 Mark Tinordi .02 .10
225 Sergei Gonchar .02 .10
226 Alexei Zhamnov .05 .15
227 Igor Korolev .02 .10
228 Teppo Numminen .02 .10
229 Craig Martin .02 .10
230 Nikolai Khabibulin .05 .15
231 Michal Grosek .02 .10
232 Teemu Selanne .08 .25
233 Dave Manson .02 .10
234 Tim Cheveldae .05 .15
235 Esa Tikkanen .02 .10
236 Dominik Hasek .08 .25
237 Peter Forsberg .10 .30
238 Sergei Fedorov .08 .25
239 Jari Kurri .08 .25
240 Tommy Soderstrom .05 .15
241 Alexei Zhamnov .05 .15
242 Alexei Yashin .02 .10
243 Mikael Renberg .05 .15
244 Jaromir Jagr .10 .25
245 Ulf Dahlen .02 .10
246 Alexander Mogilny .05 .15
247 Mats Sundin .05 .15
248 Pavel Bure .08 .25
249 Slava Fetisov .02 .10
250 Teemu Selanne .08 .25
251 Arturs Irbe .05 .15
252 Nicklas Lidstrom .08 .25
253 Aki-Petteri Berg .02 .10
254 Zdenek Nedved .02 .10
255 Chad Kilger .02 .10
256 Bryan McCabe .02 .10
257 Daniel Alfredsson XRC .60 1.50
258 Brendan Witt .02 .10
259 Jeff O'Neill .02 .10
260 Radek Dvorak .02 .10
261 Niklas Sundstrom .05 .15
262 Kyle McLaren .02 .10
263 Saku Koivu .08 .25
264 Todd Bertuzzi .08 .25
265 Jere Lehtinen .05 .15
266 Vitali Yachmenev .02 .10
267 Shane Doan .02 .10
268 Marko Kiprusoff .02 .10
269 Deron Quint .08 .25
270 Daymond Langkow XRC .20 .50
271 Alex Hicks .02 .10
272 Steve Rucchin .02 .10
273 David Karpa .02 .10
274 Mike Sillinger .02 .10
275 Teemu Selanne .08 .25
276 Todd Krygier .02 .10
277 Valeri Karpov .02 .10
278 Peter Douris .02 .10
279 Team Checklist .02 .10
280 Shawn McEachern .02 .10
281 Dave Reid .02 .10
282 Bill Ranford .05 .15
283 Don Sweeney .02 .10
284 Stephen Leach .02 .10
285 Craig Billington .05 .15
286 Clayton Beddoes .02 .10
287 Rick Tocchet .05 .15
288 Team Checklist .02 .10
289 Brad May .02 .10
290 Mike Peca .05 .15
291 Dominik Hasek .20 .50
292 Donald Audette .02 .10
293 Randy Burridge .02 .10
294 Derek Plante .02 .10
295 Martin Biron XRC 1.00 2.50
296 Andrei Trefilov .02 .10
297 Team Checklist .02 .10
298 Steve Chiasson .02 .10
299 Cory Stillman .02 .10
300 Mike Sullivan .02 .10
301 Gary Roberts .02 .10
302 Pavel Torgajev .02 .10
303 James Patrick .02 .10
304 Corey Millen .02 .10
305 Ed Ward .02 .10
306 Team Checklist .02 .10

307 Jeremy Roenick .12 .30
308 Mike Prokopec .02 .10
309 Joe Murphy .02 .10
310 Eric Weinrich .02 .10
311 Tony Amonte .05 .15
312 Bob Probert .05 .15
313 Murray Craven .02 .10
314 Sergei Krivokrasov .02 .10
315 Team Checklist .02 .10
316 Peter Forsberg .25 .60
317 Stephane Fiset .05 .15
318 Mike Ricci .05 .15
319 Claude Lemieux .02 .10
320 Sandis Ozolinsh .02 .10
321 Sylvain Lefebvre .02 .10
322 Scott Young .02 .10
323 Patrick Roy .50 1.25
324 Team Checklist .02 .10
325 Brent Fedyk .02 .10
326 Brent Gilchrist .02 .10
327 Greg Adams .02 .10
328 Richard Matvichuk .05 .15
329 Joe Nieuwendyk .05 .15
330 Benoit Hogue .02 .10
331 Darcy Wakaluk .05 .15
332 Guy Carbonneau .08 .25
333 Team Checklist .02 .10
334 Mike Vernon .05 .15
335 Mathieu Dandenault .02 .10
336 Igor Larionov .02 .10
337 Sergei Fedorov .15 .40
338 Greg Johnson .02 .10
339 Dino Ciccarelli .05 .15
340 Martin Lapointe .02 .10
341 Darren McCarty .02 .10
342 Team Checklist .02 .10
343 Joaquin Gage .02 .10
344 Jiri Slegr .02 .10
345 Mariusz Czerkawski .02 .10
346 Doug Weight .05 .15
347 Todd Marchant .02 .10
348 Miroslav Satan XRC .25 .60
349 Jeff Norton .02 .10
350 Curtis Joseph .08 .25
351 Team Checklist .02 .10
352 Tom Fitzgerald .02 .10
353 Jody Hull .02 .10
354 Terry Carkner .02 .10
355 Scott Mellanby .02 .10
356 Bill Lindsay .02 .10
357 Gord Murphy .02 .10
358 Brian Skrudland .02 .10
359 David Nemirovsky .02 .10
360 Team Checklist .02 .10
361 Paul Ranheim .02 .10
362 Jason Muzzatti .05 .15
363 Glen Featherstone .02 .10
364 Andrew Cassels .02 .10
365 Jeff Brown .02 .10
366 Kevin Dineen .02 .10
367 Nelson Emerson .02 .10
368 Gerald Diduck .02 .10
369 Team Checklist .02 .10
370 Kevin Stevens .02 .10
371 Darryl Sydor .05 .15
372 Yanic Perreault .02 .10
373 Arto Blomsten .02 .10
374 Kevin Todd .02 .10
375 Byron Dafoe .05 .15
376 Tony Granato .02 .10
377 Vladimir Tsyplakov XRC .02 .10
378 Team Checklist .02 .10
379 Martin Rucinsky .02 .10
380 Patrice Brisebois .02 .10
381 Lyle Odelein .02 .10
382 Andrei Kovalenko .02 .10
383 Mark Recchi .05 .15
384 Jocelyn Thibault .08 .25
385 Turner Stevenson .02 .10
386 Pat Jablonski .05 .15
387 Team Checklist .02 .10
388 Scott Niedermayer .02 .10
389 Corey Schwab XRC .05 .15
390 Steve Thomas .05 .15
391 Valeri Zelepukin .02 .10
392 Shawn Chambers .02 .10
393 Jocelyn Lemieux .02 .10
394 Brian Rolston .02 .10
395 Denis Pederson .02 .10
396 Team Checklist .02 .10
397 Martin Straka .02 .10
398 Niclas Andersson .02 .10
399 Wendel Clark .05 .15
400 Travis Green .05 .15
401 Chris Marinucci .02 .10
402 Darius Kasparaitis .02 .10
403 Patrick Flatley .02 .10
404 Jamie McLennan .05 .15
405 Team Checklist .02 .10
406 Glenn Healy .05 .15
407 Pat Verbeek .02 .10
408 Ian Laperriere .02 .10
409 Ray Ferraro .02 .10
410 Jeff Beukeboom .02 .10
411 Ulf Samuelsson .02 .10
412 Doug Lidster .02 .10
413 Bruce Driver .02 .10
414 Team Checklist .02 .10
415 Antti Tormanen .02 .10
416 Sean Hill .02 .10
417 Damian Rhodes .05 .15
418 Jaroslav Modry .02 .10
419 Mike Bales .02 .10
420 Trent McCleary .02 .10
421 Randy Cunneyworth .02 .10
422 Ted Drury .02 .10
423 Team Checklist .02 .10
424 Pat Falloon .02 .10
425 Garth Snow .05 .15
426 Shjon Podein .02 .10
427 Petr Svoboda .02 .10
428 Eric Desjardins .05 .15
429 Anatoli Semenov .02 .10
430 Kevin Haller .02 .10
431 Rob Dimaio .02 .10
432 Team Checklist .02 .10
433 Chris Joseph .02 .10
434 Sergei Zubov .02 .10
435 Tom Barrasso .05 .15
436 Chris Tamer .02 .10
437 Dmitri Mironov .02 .10
438 Petr Nedved .05 .15
439 Neil Wilkinson .02 .10
440 Glen Murray .02 .10
441 Team Checklist .02 .10
442 J.J. Daigneault .02 .10
443 Grant Fuhr .08 .25
444 Adam Creighton .02 .10
445 Brian Noonan .02 .10
446 Stephane Matteau .02 .10
447 Roman Vopat .02 .10
448 Geoff Courtnall .02 .10
449 Wayne Gretzky .75 2.00
450 Team Checklist .02 .10
451 Chris Terreri .05 .15
452 Ulf Dahlen .02 .10
453 Owen Nolan .05 .15
454 Doug Bodger .02 .10
455 Craig Janney .02 .10
456 Ville Peltonen .02 .10
457 Ray Sheppard .02 .10
458 Shean Donovan .02 .10
459 Team Checklist .02 .10
460 Jeff Reese .02 .10
461 Shawn Burr .02 .10
462 Chris Gratton .02 .10
463 John Cullen .02 .10
464 Bill Houlder .02 .10
465 J.C. Bergeron .02 .10
466 Brian Bellows .02 .10
467 Drew Bannister .02 .10
468 Team Checklist .02 .10
469 Dimitri Yushkevich .02 .10
470 Dave Andreychuk .05 .15
471 Dave Gagner .02 .10
472 Todd Warriner .02 .10
473 Sergio Momesso .02 .10
474 Kirk Muller .02 .10
475 Dave Ellett .02 .10
476 Ken Baumgartner .02 .10
477 Team Checklist .02 .10
478 Esa Tikkanen .02 .10
479 Cliff Ronning .02 .10
480 Martin Gelinas .02 .10
481 Brian Loney .02 .10
482 Pavel Bure .08 .25
483 Corey Hirsch .05 .15
484 Scott Walker .02 .10
485 Jim Dowd .02 .10
486 Team Checklist .02 .10
487 Michal Pivonka .02 .10
488 Pat Peake .02 .10
489 Martin Gendron .02 .10
490 Peter Bondra .05 .15
491 Nolan Baumgartner .02 .10
492 Jim Carey .05 .15
493 Steve Konowalchuk .02 .10
494 Jason Allison .02 .10
495 Team Checklist .02 .10
496 Oleg Tverdovsky .02 .10
497 Craig Mills .02 .10
498 Darren Turcotte .02 .10
499 Norm Maciver .02 .10
500 Chad Kilger .02 .10
501 Keith Tkachuk .08 .25
502 Kris King .02 .10
503 Dallas Drake .02 .10
504 Team Checklist .02 .10
505 Saku Koivu .08 .25
506 Vitali Yachmenev .02 .10
507 Daniel Alfredsson .05 .15
508 Radek Dvorak .02 .10
509 Miroslav Satan .08 .25
510 Aki Berg .02 .10
511 Valeri Bure .02 .10
512 Petr Sykora .02 .10
513 Andrei Vasilyev .02 .10
514 Niklas Sundstrom .05 .15
515 Viktor Kozlov .05 .15
516 Sami Kapanen .02 .10
517 Anders Myrvold .02 .10
518 Jere Lehtinen .05 .15
519 Marcus Ragnarsson XRC .05 .15
520 Stefan Ustorf .02 .10
521 Ville Peltonen .02 .10
522 Antti Tormanen .02 .10
523 Petr Sykora .02 .10
524 Scott Bailey .02 .10
525 Kevin Hodson XRC .20 .50
526 Landon Wilson .02 .10
527 Aaron Gavey .02 .10
528 Darren Langdon XRC .02 .10
529 Jason Doig .02 .10
530 Marty Murray .02 .10
531 Marcus Ragnarsson .02 .10
532 Peter Ferraro .02 .10
533 Grant Marshall .02 .10
534 Mike Wilson XRC .02 .10
535 Rory Fitzpatrick .02 .10
536 Ed Jovanovski .08 .25
537 Eric Fichaud .05 .15
538 Stefan Ustorf .02 .10
539 Stephane Yelle .02 .10
540 Ethan Moreau XRC .08 .25
NNO1 M.Renberg AU/2500 4.00 10.00
NNO2 T.Selanne AU/2500 12.50 30.00
NNO3 M.Brodeur AU/1500 30.00 80.00
NNO4 S.Koivu AU/1500 8.00 20.00
NNO5 Saku Koivu Jumbo .75 2.00
NNO6 Saku Koivu Jumbo AU 8.00 20.00

1995-96 Parkhurst International Emerald Ice

This 540-card set was issued as a parallel to the regular Parkhurst International series. The cards feature the standard card player photo superimposed on brilliant emerald green foil. The cards were inserted at a rate of 1:3 packs.
*SER.1 STARS: 7.5X TO 15X BASIC CARDS
*SER.2 STARS: 10X TO 20X BASIC CARDS

1995-96 Parkhurst International All-Stars

These six two-sided cards feature the best foreign-born stars in the NHL at each position. The cards were randomly inserted at a rate of 1:96 first series packs.
1 Dominik Hasek 1.00 2.50
Arturs Irbe
2 Nicklas Lidstrom 3.00 8.00
Sandis Ozolinsh
3 Sergei Zubov .40 1.00
Alexei Zhitnik
4 Sergei Fedorov 1.25 3.00
Peter Forsberg
5 Jaromir Jagr 1.00 2.50
Teemu Selanne
6 Mats Sundin 3.00 8.00
Mikael Renberg

1995-96 Parkhurst International Crown Collection Silver Series 1

This sixteen-card set features some of the most popular players in the game on an attractive silver etched foil background. The cards were inserted 1:16 series 1 packs. A gold parallel version of this set exists as well. These cards were significantly tougher, coming out of 1:96 series 1 packs.
COMPLETE SET (16) 15.00 30.00
*GOLD: 1.5X to 3X SILVER CARDS
1 Eric Lindros .50 1.25
2 Felix Potvin .50 1.25
3 Mario Lemieux 2.50 6.00
4 Paul Kariya .50 1.25
5 Pavel Bure .50 1.25
6 Wayne Gretzky 4.00 10.00
7 Mikael Renberg .30 .75
8 Paul Coffey .50 1.25
9 Teemu Selanne .50 1.25
10 Brett Hull .60 1.50
11 Martin Brodeur 1.25 3.00
12 Doug Gilmour .30 .75
13 Peter Forsberg 1.25 3.00
14 Sergei Fedorov .75 2.00
15 Saku Koivu .50 1.25
16 Jim Carey .30 .75

1995-96 Parkhurst International Crown Collection Silver Series 2

This 16-card set of the NHL's top stars was randomly inserted in series 2 packs. Although this set echoes the theme of the series 1 Crown Collection, the numbering again is 1-16. There also are several players who make return appearances in this set. As with series one, the silver version come 1:16 packs, while the gold are found 1:96 packs.
COMPLETE SET (16) 15.00 30.00
*GOLD: 1.5X TO 3X SILVER CARDS
1 Jaromir Jagr .75 2.00
2 Patrick Roy 2.50 6.00
3 Alexander Mogilny .30 .75
4 Paul Kariya .50 1.25
5 Dominik Hasek 1.00 2.50
6 Peter Forsberg 1.25 3.00
7 Mark Messier .50 1.25
8 Mats Sundin .50 1.25
9 Ray Bourque .75 2.00
10 Wayne Gretzky 4.00 10.00
11 Eric Lindros .50 1.25
12 John Vanbiesbrouck .30 .75
13 Chris Chelios .50 1.25
14 Brian Leetch .30 .75
15 Daniel Alfredsson 1.25 3.00
16 Eric Daze .30 .75

1995-96 Parkhurst International Goal Patrol

This 12-card, horizontally-oriented set salutes the top netminders in the NHL. The cards feature an embossed photo in the Action Packed style, and were inserted 1:24 series 1 packs.
COMPLETE SET (12) 15.00 30.00
1 Martin Brodeur 3.00 8.00

2 Felix Potvin 1.25 3.00
3 Patrick Roy 6.00 15.00
4 Dominik Hasek 2.50 6.00
5 Jim Carey .75 2.00
6 Ed Belfour 1.25 3.00
7 John Vanbiesbrouck .75 2.00
8 Trevor Kidd .75 2.00
9 Bill Ranford .75 2.00
10 Arturs Irbe .75 2.00
11 Kirk McLean .75 2.00
12 Mike Richter 1.25 3.00

1995-96 Parkhurst International NHL All-Stars

These six, two-sided cards feature the NHL's top players by position. The cards were randomly inserted in series 2 packs at a rate of 1:96.
COMPLETE SET (6) 12.00 25.00
1 M.Lemieux/W.Gretzky 4.00 10.00
2 Jaromir Jagr 1.25 3.00
Brett Hull
3 Brendan Shanahan 2.50 6.00
Pavel Bure
4 Scott Stevens 2.50 6.00
Chris Chelios
5 Ray Bourque 1.50 4.00
Paul Coffey
6 Martin Brodeur 2.00 5.00
Ed Belfour

1995-96 Parkhurst International Parkie's Trophy Picks

This 54-card set illustrates Parkhurst's choices for the key individual awards for the 1995-96 NHL season. The cards were noted as being one of 1,000 produced, but were not individually numbered. The odds of pulling one from a second series pack were 1:48.
COMPLETE SET (54) 30.00 80.00
PP1 Eric Lindros 1.00 2.50
PP2 Mario Lemieux 3.00 8.00
PP3 Sergei Fedorov 1.25 3.00
PP4 Peter Forsberg 1.50 4.00
PP5 John Vanbiesbrouck .60 1.50
PP6 Mark Messier 1.00 2.50
PP7 Jaromir Jagr 1.50 4.00
PP8 Joe Sakic 1.50 4.00
PP9 Grant Fuhr .60 1.50
PP10 Eric Lindros 1.00 2.50
PP11 Mario Lemieux 3.00 8.00
PP12 Mark Messier 1.00 2.50
PP13 Peter Forsberg 1.50 4.00
PP14 Jaromir Jagr 1.50 4.00
PP15 Paul Kariya 1.00 2.50
PP16 Joe Sakic .50 4.00
PP17 Teemu Selanne 1.00 2.50
PP18 Alexander Mogilny .60 1.50
PP19 Paul Coffey 1.00 2.50
PP20 Chris Chelios 1.00 2.50
PP21 Brian Leetch .60 1.50
PP22 Ray Bourque 1.00 2.50
PP23 Larry Murphy .40 1.00
PP24 Nicklas Lidstrom 1.00 2.50
PP25 Roman Hamrlik .40 1.00
PP26 Gary Suter .40 1.00
PP27 Sergei Zubov .40 1.00
PP28 Dominik Hasek 1.50 4.00
PP29 John Vanbiesbrouck .60 1.50
PP30 Chris Osgood .60 1.50
PP31 Mike Richter 1.00 2.50
PP32 Martin Brodeur 2.00 5.00
PP33 Ron Hextall .60 1.50
PP34 Grant Fuhr 1.00 2.50
PP35 Patrick Roy 3.00 8.00
PP36 Jim Carey .40 1.00
PP37 Vitali Yachmenev .40 1.00
PP38 Daniel Alfredsson .60 1.50
PP39 Saku Koivu 1.00 2.50
PP40 Eric Daze .40 1.00
PP41 Marcus Ragnarsson .40 1.00
PP42 Ed Jovanovski .40 1.00
PP43 Petr Sykora .40 1.00
PP44 Todd Bertuzzi 1.00 2.50
PP45 Radek Dvorak .40 1.00
PP46 Paul Kariya 1.00 2.50
PP47 Ron Francis .60 1.50
PP48 Alexander Mogilny .60 1.50
PP49 Pat LaFontaine 1.00 2.50
PP50 Pierre Turgeon .40 1.00
PP51 Teemu Selanne 1.00 2.50
PP52 Sergei Fedorov 1.25 3.00
PP53 Adam Oates .60 1.50
PP54 Brett Hull 1.25 3.00

1995-96 Parkhurst International Trophy Winners

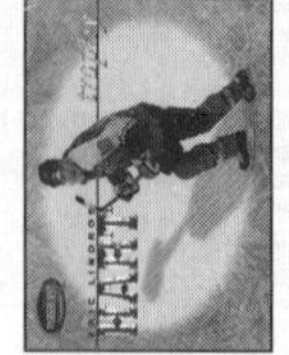

This six-card set recognizes the winners of the key individual trophies from the 1994-95 season. The cards were inserted at a rate of 1:24 series one packs.
COMPLETE SET (6) 4.00 8.00
1 Eric Lindros-Hart .50 1.25
2 Jaromir Jagr-Art Ross .75 2.00
3 Peter Forsberg-Calder 1.25 3.00
4 Paul Coffey-Norris .50 1.25
5 Dominik Hasek-Vezina 1.00 2.50
6 Ron Francis-Lady Byng .30 .75

1996 Parkhurst Beehive Promos

These cards were available as part of a card show wrapper redemption offer. The five Howe cards were available at the 1996 National in Anaheim in exchange for Parkhurst '66-67 wrappers. The Orr promos were available at several major shows.
COMMON BOBBY ORR 4.00 10.00
COMMON GORDIE HOWE 3.20 8.00

2001-02 Parkhurst

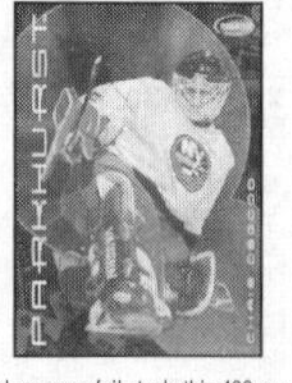

Printed on green foil stock, this 400-card set was originally released in late-November 2001 as a 300 card base set with 50 short prints. Cards 301-400 were available in packs of BAP Update. Cards 251-300 were serial-numbered to 500 copies each.
COMP.SER. 1 SET w/o SP's (250) 40.00 80.00
1 Paul Kariya .30 .75
2 Patrik Stefan .10 .25
3 Jeremy Roenick .40 1.00
4 Patrick Roy 1.50 4.00
5 Jarome Iginla .40 1.00
6 Jeff O'Neill .10 .25
7 Sergei Samsonov .25 .60
8 Peter Forsberg .75 2.00
9 Scott Gomez .10 .25
10 Mike Modano .50 1.25
11 Brendan Shanahan .30 .75
12 J-S Giguere .25 .60
13 Pavel Bure .30 .75
14 Zigmund Palffy .25 .60
15 Marian Gaborik .60 1.50
16 Pavol Demitra .25 .60
17 Alexei Kovalev .25 .60
18 Patrik Elias .25 .60
19 Keith Tkachuk .30 .75
20 Mats Sundin .30 .75
21 Marian Hossa .30 .75
22 Mark Recchi .25 .60
23 John Madden .10 .25
24 Mario Lemieux 2.00 5.00
25 Teemu Selanne .30 .75
26 Joe Sakic .60 1.50
27 Brad Richards .25 .60
28 Brian Leetch .25 .60
29 Markus Naslund .30 .75
30 Peter Bondra .30 .75
31 Steve Yzerman 1.50 4.00
32 Michael Peca .10 .25
33 Bill Guerin .25 .60
34 Jaromir Jagr .50 1.25
35 Alexei Yashin .10 .25
36 Theo Fleury .10 .25
37 Al MacInnis .25 .60
38 Milan Hejduk .30 .75
39 Martin Biron .25 .60
40 Brad Isbister .10 .25
41 Nicklas Lidstrom .30 .75
42 Rick DiPietro .25 .60
43 Roberto Luongo .40 1.00
44 Tim Connolly .10 .25
45 Manny Fernandez .25 .60
46 Scott Niedermayer .10 .25
47 David Legwand .25 .60
48 Petr Sykora .10 .25
49 Ryan Smyth .10 .25
50 Mark Messier .30 .75
51 Dave Tanabe .10 .25
52 Keith Primeau .10 .25
53 Teppo Numminen .10 .25
54 Milan Kraft .25 .60
55 Owen Nolan .25 .60
56 Alexander Mogilny .25 .60
57 Brent Johnson .25 .60
58 Curtis Joseph .30 .75
59 Felix Potvin .30 .75
60 Olaf Kolzig .25 .60
61 Eric Lindros .30 .75
62 Pierre Turgeon .25 .60
63 Martin Straka .10 .25
64 Maxim Afinogenov .10 .25
65 Oleg Saprykin .10 .25
66 Shane Willis .10 .25
67 Brett Hull .40 1.00
68 Alex Tanguay .25 .60
69 Marc Denis .25 .60
70 Ed Belfour .30 .75
71 Roman Cechmanek .25 .60
72 Tommy Salo .25 .60
73 Rob Blake .25 .60
74 Jose Theodore .40 1.00
75 Henrik Sedin .10 .25
76 Tony Amonte .25 .60
77 Scott Hartnell .10 .25
78 Brian Rafalski .10 .25
79 Joe Thornton .50 1.25
80 Patrick Marleau .25 .60
81 Daniel Alfredsson .25 .60
82 Simon Gagne .30 .75
83 Patrick Lalime .25 .60
84 Johan Hedberg .25 .60
85 Adam Oates .25 .60
86 Chris Pronger .25 .60
87 Vincent Lecavalier .30 .75
88 Tomas Kaberle .10 .25
89 Daniel Sedin .10 .25
90 Martin Lapointe .10 .25
91 Chris Drury .25 .60
92 Dominik Hasek .60 1.50
93 Evgeni Nabokov .25 .60
94 Ed Jovanovski .10 .25
95 John LeClair .30 .75
96 Sergei Fedorov .50 1.25
97 Martin Havlat .25 .60
98 Martin Brodeur .75 2.00
99 Jason Arnott .10 .25
100 Mike Comrie .25 .60
101 Petr Nedved .10 .25
102 Ray Ferraro .10 .25
103 Miroslav Satan .25 .60
104 Rod Brind'Amour .25 .60
105 Ron Tugnutt .25 .60
106 Oleg Tverdovsky .10 .25
107 Anson Carter .25 .60
108 Wes Walz .10 .25
109 Andrei Markov .10 .25
110 Mike Dunham .25 .60
111 Eric Desjardins .10 .25
112 Radek Dvorak .10 .25
113 Pavel Kubina .10 .25
114 Gary Roberts .10 .25
115 Andrew Cassels .10 .25
116 Vitali Vishnevski .10 .25
117 Byron Dafoe .25 .60
118 Chris Gratton .10 .25
119 Marc Savard .10 .25
120 Shawn McEachern .10 .25
121 Jocelyn Thibault .25 .60
122 Joe Nieuwendyk .25 .60
123 Janne Niinimaa .10 .25
124 Shane Doan .10 .25
125 Willie Mitchell .10 .25
126 Glen Murray .10 .25
127 Scott Walker .10 .25
128 Geoff Sanderson .10 .25
129 Kenny Jonsson .10 .25
130 Radek Bonk .10 .25
131 Brad Stuart .25 .60
132 Scott Young .10 .25
133 Brendan Morrison .25 .60
134 Sergei Gonchar .10 .25
135 Jonathan Girard .10 .25
136 Arturs Irbe .25 .60
137 Chris Herperger .10 .25
138 Brenden Morrow .25 .60
139 Sergei Zubov .10 .25
140 Lubomir Visnovsky .10 .25
141 Aaron Miller .10 .25
142 Ossi Vaananen .10 .25
143 Saku Koivu .30 .75
144 Sean Burke .25 .60
145 Darryl Sydor .10 .25
146 Chris Chelios .30 .75
147 Brian Savage .10 .25
148 Wade Redden .10 .25
149 Derian Hatcher .10 .25
150 Igor Larionov .10 .25
151 Steve Sullivan .10 .25
152 Michal Handzus .10 .25
153 Ron Francis .25 .60
154 David Vyborny .10 .25
155 Manny Legace .25 .60
156 Jeff Friesen .10 .25
157 Jeff Hackett .25 .60
158 Marian Cisar .10 .25
159 Mike York .10 .25
160 Nikolai Antropov .10 .25
161 Trevor Linden .10 .25
162 Bryan Smolinski .10 .25
163 Janne Laukkanen .10 .25
164 Dan Cloutier .25 .60
165 Scott Stevens .25 .60
166 Jani Hurme .25 .60
167 Fredrik Modin .10 .25
168 Steven Reinprecht .10 .25
169 Kevyn Adams .10 .25
170 Richard Zednik .10 .25
171 Viktor Kozlov .10 .25
172 Cliff Ronning .10 .25
173 Mariusz Czerkawski .10 .25
174 Todd Bertuzzi .30 .75
175 Vincent Damphousse .10 .25
176 Roman Hamrlik .10 .25
177 Sandis Ozolinsh .10 .25
178 Mike Richter .30 .75
179 Stu Barnes .10 .25
180 Patric Kjellberg .10 .25
181 Tomas Holmstrom .10 .25
182 Sergei Brylin .10 .25
183 Magnus Arvedson .10 .25
184 Sami Kapanen .10 .25
185 Niklas Sundstrom .10 .25
186 Todd Marchant .10 .25
187 Mark Parrish .10 .25
188 Adam Foote .10 .25
189 Peter Schaefer .10 .25
190 Mike Ricci .10 .25
191 Alexei Zhamnov .10 .25
192 Dainius Zubrus .10 .25
193 Espen Knutsen .10 .25
194 Shean Donovan .10 .25
195 Bobby Holik .10 .25
196 Tom Poti .10 .25
197 Marcus Ragnarsson .10 .25
198 Jozef Stumpel .10 .25
199 Martin Rucinsky .10 .25
200 Matt Davidson RC .30 .75
201 Jan Bulis .10 .25
202 Matt Pettinger .10 .25
203 Rob Zamuner .10 .25
204 Chris Osgood .25 .60
205 Dan Hinote .10 .25
206 Travis Green .10 .25
207 Joe Juneau .10 .25
208 Mikael Renberg .10 .25
209 Zdeno Ciger .10 .25
210 Jochen Hecht .10 .25
211 Jan Hlavac .10 .25
212 Jeff Halpern .10 .25
213 Tom Barrasso .10 .25
214 Bill Muckalt .10 .25
215 Luc Robitaille .25 .60
216 Jason Wiemer .10 .25
217 Deron Quint .10 .25
218 Jyrki Lumme .10 .25
219 Andreas Dackell .10 .25
220 Tomi Kallio .10 .25
221 Roman Turek .25 .60
222 Taylor Pyatt .10 .25
223 Richard Jackman .10 .25
224 Michael Nylander .10 .25
225 Brian Pothier RC .30 .75
226 Slava Kozlov .10 .25
227 Kim Johnsson .10 .25
228 J-P Dumont .10 .25
229 Marty Reasoner .10 .25
230 Dimitri Kalinin .10 .25
231 Damian Rhodes .10 .25
232 Jason Allison .10 .25
233 Doug Weight .25 .60
234 Yanic Perreault .10 .25
235 Eric Daze .25 .60
236 Brian Campbell .10 .25
237 Valeri Bure .10 .25
238 Adam Deadmarsh .10 .25
239 Robert Reichel .10 .25
240 Anders Eriksson .10 .25
241 Nikolai Khabibulin .30 .75
242 Sean O'Donnell .10 .25
243 Bob Essensa .10 .25
244 Josef Vasicek .10 .25
245 Donald Audette .10 .25
246 Steve Heinze .10 .25
247 Bryan Berard .10 .25
248 Ville Nieminen .10 .25
249 Eric Weinrich .10 .25
250 Adam Graves .10 .25
251 Jesse Boulerice SP 2.50 6.00
252 Marko Kiprusoff SP 2.50 6.00
253 Ivan Ciernik RC 3.00 8.00
254 Pavel Datsyuk RC 15.00 40.00
255 Jaroslav Bednar RC 3.00 8.00
256 Andreas Salomonsson RC 3.00 8.00
257 Mike Ribeiro SP 2.50 6.00
258 Darcy Hordichuk SP 2.50 6.00
259 Chris Neil RC 3.00 8.00
260 Rostislav Klesla SP 1.00 2.50
261 Kristian Huselius RC 4.00 10.00
262 Brian Sutherby RC 3.00 8.00
263 Jiri Dopita RC 3.00 8.00
264 Radek Martinek RC 3.00 8.00
265 Barrett Heisten SP 2.50 6.00
266 Krystofer Kolanos RC 3.00 8.00
267 Pascal Dupuis RC 3.00 8.00
268 Andreas Lilja SP 2.50 6.00
269 Chris Mason SP 2.50 6.00
270 Mathieu Garon SP 3.00 8.00
271 Andrew Raycroft SP 2.50 6.00
272 Jeff Jillson RC 3.00 8.00
273 Jiri Bicek SP 2.50 6.00
274 Niklas Hagman RC 3.00 8.00
275 Pavel Brendl SP 3.00 8.00
276 Stephen Peat SP 3.00 8.00
277 Sascha Goc SP 2.50 6.00
278 Nick Boynton SP 2.50 6.00
279 Timo Parssinen RC 3.00 8.00
280 Mika Noronen SP 2.50 6.00
281 Scott Clemmensen RC 3.00 8.00
282 Dan Blackburn RC 4.00 10.00
283 Nikita Alexeev RC 3.00 8.00
284 Vaclav Nedorost RC 3.00 8.00
285 Ilja Bryzgalov RC 3.00 8.00
286 Danny Heatley SP 4.00 10.00
287 Niko Kapanen RC 1.00 2.50
288 Rick Berry SP 2.50 6.00
289 Mark Bell SP 2.50 6.00
290 Kamil Piros RC 3.00 8.00
291 Maxime Ouellet SP 3.00 8.00
292 Kris Beech SP 2.50 6.00
293 Miikka Kiprusoff SP 4.00 10.00
294 Martti Jarventie SP 2.50 6.00
295 Ilya Kovalchuk RC 20.00 50.00
296 Nick Schultz RC 3.00 8.00
297 Bryan Allen SP 2.50 6.00
298 Josef Boumedienne RC 3.00 8.00
299 Jason Williams SP 3.00 8.00
300 Daniel Tjarnqvist SP 2.50 6.00
301 Frederic Cassivi RC .75 2.00
302 Mark Hartigan RC .75 2.00
303 Pasi Nurminen RC .75 2.00
304 Ivan Huml RC .75 2.00
305 Zdenek Kutlak RC .75 2.00

Card	Low	High
6 Ales Kotalik RC	1.00	2.50
7 Jukka Hentunen RC	.75	2.00
8 Erik Cole RC	3.00	8.00
9 Tyler Arnason RC	3.00	8.00
0 Jaroslav Obsut RC	.75	2.00
1 Riku Hahl RC	.75	2.00
2 Martin Spanhel RC	.75	2.00
3 Andrej Nedorost RC	.75	2.00
4 Ty Conklin RC	.75	2.00
5 Jason Chimera RC	.75	2.00
6 Kyle Rossiter RC	.75	2.00
7 Lukas Krajicek RC	.75	2.00
8 Stephen Weiss RC	4.00	10.00
9 Tony Virta RC	.75	2.00
0 Marcel Hossa RC	.75	2.00
1 Olivier Michaud RC	.75	2.00
2 Henrik Tallinder RC	.75	2.00
3 Martin Erat RC	.75	2.00
4 Nathan Perrott RC	.75	2.00
5 Pavel Skrbek RC	.75	2.00
6 Robert Schnabel RC	.75	2.00
7 Christian Berglund	.75	2.00
8 Stanislav Gron RC	.75	2.00
9 Raffi Torres RC	.75	2.00
0 Mikael Samuelsson RC	.75	2.00
1 Chris Bala RC	.75	2.00
2 Josh Langfeld RC	.75	2.00
3 Martin Prusek RC	.75	2.00
4 Sean Avery RC	.75	2.00
5 Neil Little RC	.75	2.00
6 Tomas Divisek RC	.75	2.00
7 Vaclav Pletka RC	.75	2.00
8 Guillaume Lefebvre RC	.75	2.00
9 Branko Radivojevic RC	.75	2.00
0 Trent Hunter RC	4.00	10.00
1 Jan Lasak RC	.75	2.00
2 Tom Kostopoulos RC	.75	2.00
3 Hannes Hyvonen RC	.75	2.00
4 Shane Endicott RC	.75	2.00
5 Evgeny Konstantinov RC	.75	2.00
6 Martin Cibak RC	.75	2.00
7 Karel Pilar RC	.75	2.00
8 Sebastien Centomo RC	.75	2.00
9 Mike Farrell RC	.75	2.00
0 Sebastien Charpentier RC	.75	2.00
1 Radim Vrbata	.10	.25
2 Andy McDonald	.10	.25
3 J.P. Vigier	.10	.25
4 Donald Brashear	.10	.25
5 Adrian Aucoin	.10	.25
6 Stephane Richer	.10	.25
7 Byron Ritchie	.10	.25
8 Sergei Berezin	.10	.25
9 Cliff Ronning	.10	.25
0 Tony Hrkac	.10	.25
1 Andre Roy	.10	.25
2 Shjon Podein	.10	.25
3 Andrei Nazarov	.10	.25
4 Marty McInnis	.10	.25
5 Petr Tenkrat	.10	.25
6 Trevor Letowski	.10	.25
7 Randy Robitaille	.10	.25
8 Kim Johnsson	.10	.25
9 Jozef Stumpel	.10	.25
0 P.J. Stock	.10	.25
1 Dean McAmmond	.10	.25
2 Steve Thomas	.10	.25
3 Darius Kasparaitis	.10	.25
4 Mike Sillinger	.10	.25
5 Jason Arnott	.10	.25
6 Alex Auld	.10	.25
7 Mike York	.10	.25
8 Pierre Dagenais	.10	.25
9 Andrew Brunette	.10	.25
0 Sergei Zholtok	.10	.25
1 Donald Audette	.10	.25
2 Doug Gilmour	.10	.25
3 Andy Delmore	.10	.25
4 Martin Rucinsky	.10	.25
5 Jamie Langenbrunner	.10	.25
6 Joe Nieuwendyk	.25	.60
7 John Vanbiesbrouck	.25	.60
8 Shawn Bates	.10	.25
9 Matthew Barnaby	.10	.25
0 Pavel Bure	.30	.75
1 Tom Poti	.10	.25
2 Zdeno Chara	.10	.25
3 Adam Oates	.25	.60
4 Marty Murray	.10	.25
5 Brian Savage	.10	.25
6 Daniil Markov	.10	.25
7 Tom Barrasso	.25	.60
8 Jan Hlavac	.10	.25
9 Trevor Linden	.10	.25
0 Ivan Ciernik	.10	.25

2001-02 Parkhurst Gold

s 300-card set paralleled the base 250 ds but carried gold foil in place of the er. Cards were numbered out of 50 on card backs.
OLD: 12.5X TO 30X BASIC CARD

Card	Low	High
Patrick Roy	25.00	60.00
Peter Forsberg	20.00	50.00
Mario Lemieux	25.00	60.00
Steve Yzerman	25.00	60.00

2001-02 Parkhurst Silver

s 300-card set paralleled the first 100 e cards but carried silver foil in place of silver. Cards were numbered out of 500 the card backs.
ILVER: 1.5X TO 4X BASIC CARD

2001-02 Parkhurst Autographs

This 59-card set featured autographs of retired greats. Each card was green in color with a full-color player photo in the center of the card. Underneath the photo was a light area that the featured player signed. Print runs are listed below for each card and cards with less than 25 copies are not priced due to scarcity. Cards PA41-PA59 were only available in BAP Update packs.

Card	Low	High
PA1 Frank Mahovlich/20		
PA2 Glenn Hall/90	15.00	40.00
PA3 Jean Beliveau/60	25.00	60.00
PA4 Frank Mahovlich/20		
PA5 Henri Richard/90	12.50	30.00
PA6 Jean Beliveau/60	25.00	60.00
PA7 Milt Schmidt/90	12.50	30.00
PA8 Elmer Lach/90	12.50	30.00
PA9 Woody Dumart/20		
PA10 Chuck Rayner/90	12.50	30.00
PA11 Henri Richard/90	15.00	40.00
PA12 Gordie Howe/20	75.00	200.00
PA13 Phil Esposito/60	20.00	50.00
PA14 Bernie Geoffrion/60	20.00	50.00
PA15 Dollard St.Laurent/90	12.50	30.00
PA16 Dickie Moore/90	20.00	50.00
PA17 Jean-Guy Talbot/90	12.50	30.00
PA18 Bill Gadsby/90	12.50	30.00
PA19 Lanny McDonald/80	12.50	30.00
PA20 Gilbert Perreault/60	20.00	50.00
PA21 Johnny Bucyk/90	12.50	30.00
PA22 Dale Hawerchuk/80	12.50	30.00
PA23 Mike Gartner/80	12.50	30.00
PA24 Johnny Bower/90	15.00	40.00
PA25 Butch Bouchard/90	15.00	40.00
PA26 Gordie Howe/20	75.00	200.00
PA27 Jean Beliveau/60	25.00	60.00
PA28 Guy Lafleur/60	40.00	100.00
PA29 Mike Bossy/80	12.50	30.00
PA30 Bryan Trottier/80	12.50	30.00
PA31 Marcel Dionne/60	12.50	30.00
PA32 Jari Kurri/80	30.00	80.00
PA33 Gerry Cheevers/90	15.00	40.00
PA34 Dino Ciccarelli/90	12.50	30.00
PA35 Stan Mikita/60	25.00	60.00
PA36 Gordie Howe/20	75.00	200.00
PA37 Tony Esposito/60	20.00	50.00
PA38 Gump Worsley/90	12.50	30.00
PA39 Ted Lindsay/90	12.50	30.00
PA40 Red Kelly/90	20.00	50.00
PA41 Joe Watson/90	12.50	30.00
PA42 Bobby Clarke/90	15.00	40.00
PA43 Dave Schultz/90	12.50	30.00
PA44 Tiger Williams/90	12.50	30.00
PA45 Serge Savard/90	12.50	30.00
PA46 Jacques Laperriere/90	12.50	30.00
PA47 Peter Mahovlich/90	12.50	30.00
PA48 Denis Potvin/90	12.50	30.00
PA49 Cam Neely/90	20.00	50.00
PA50 Ron Hextall/90	12.50	30.00
PA51 Steve Shutt/90	12.50	30.00
PA52 Yvan Cournoyer/90	20.00	50.00
PA53 Bill Barber/90	12.50	30.00
PA54 Reggie Leach/90	12.50	30.00
PA55 Dennis Hull/90	12.50	30.00
PA56 Bernie Parent/90	12.50	30.00
PA57 Bob Nystrom/90	12.50	30.00
PA58 Guy Lapointe/90	12.50	30.00
PA59 Larry Robinson/90	12.50	30.00

2001-02 Parkhurst 500 Goal Scorers

This 27-card set featured players who hit the milestone of 500 goals in their career. Each card featured an action photo of the given player alongside a game-worn swatch of his jersey on the card front. Print runs are listed below. The Shanahan and Francis cards were available in random packs of BAP Update only.

Card	Low	High
PGS1 Bobby Hull/30	40.00	100.00
PGS2 Gordie Howe/30	150.00	300.00
PGS3 Marcel Dionne/30	25.00	60.00
PGS4 Phil Esposito/30	25.00	60.00
PGS5 Mike Gartner/80	12.50	30.00
PGS6 Mark Messier/30	40.00	100.00
PGS7 Steve Yzerman/30	75.00	150.00
PGS8 Brett Hull/30	30.00	80.00
PGS9 Mario Lemieux/30	100.00	200.00
PGS10 Dino Ciccarelli/80	10.00	25.00
PGS11 Jari Kurri/80	10.00	25.00
PGS12 Luc Robitaille/30	25.00	60.00
PGS13 Mike Bossy/30	25.00	60.00
PGS14 Dave Andreychuk/80	10.00	25.00
PGS15 Guy Lafleur/30	30.00	80.00
PGS16 John Bucyk/80	10.00	25.00
PGS17 Maurice Richard/80	100.00	250.00
PGS18 Stan Mikita/80	10.00	25.00
PGS19 Frank Mahovlich/80	20.00	50.00
PGS20 Bryan Trottier/80	10.00	25.00
PGS21 Dale Hawerchuk/80	10.00	25.00
PGS22 Gilbert Perreault/80	10.00	25.00
PGS23 Jean Beliveau/80	40.00	100.00
PGS24 Pat Verbeek/80	10.00	25.00
PGS25 Michel Goulet/80	10.00	25.00
PGS26 Joe Mullen/80	10.00	25.00
PGS27 Lanny McDonald/80	10.00	25.00
NNO Brendan Shanahan/25	20.00	50.00
NNO Ron Francis/25	20.00	50.00

2001-02 Parkhurst He Shoots-He Scores Points

Inserted one per pack, these cards carried a value of 1, 2 or 3 points. The points could be redeemed for special memorabilia cards. The cards are unnumbered and are listed below in alphabetical order by point value. The redemption program ended November 31, 2002.

Card	Low	High
1 Jean Beliveau 1 pt.	.20	.50
2 Doug Harvey 1 pt.	.20	.50
3 Tim Horton 1 pt.	.20	.50
4 Bobby Hull 1 pt.	.20	.50
5 Ted Lindsay 1 pt.	.20	.50
6 Stan Mikita 1 pt.	.20	.50
7 Jacques Plante 1 pt.	.20	.50
8 Chris Pronger 1 pt.	.20	.50
9 Terry Sawchuk 1 pt.	.20	.50
10 Mats Sundin 1 pt.	.20	.50
11 Martin Brodeur 2 pt.	.20	.50
12 Peter Forsberg 2 pt.	.20	.50
13 Patrick Roy 2 pt.	.20	.50
14 Joe Sakic 2 pt.	.20	.50
15 Steve Yzerman 2 pt.	.20	.50
16 Paul Kariya 2 pt.	.20	.50
17 Pavel Bure 3 pt.	.20	.50
18 Gordie Howe 3 pt.	.20	.50
19 Mario Lemieux 3 pt.	.20	.50
20 Rocket Richard 3 pt.	.20	.50

2001-02 Parkhurst He Shoots-He Scores Prizes

Available only by redeeming 400 Parkhurst He Shoots-He Scores points, this 40-card set featured game-used swatches of jersey and a color photo of the player. Each card had a stated print run of 20 serial-numbered sets and each was encased in a clear plastic slab with a descriptive label at the top. This set is unpriced due to scarcity and volatility.

1 Paul Kariya
2 Patrick Roy
3 Jarome Iginla
4 Mike Modano
5 Brendan Shanahan
6 Pavel Bure
7 Mats Sundin
8 Mario Lemieux
9 Teemu Selanne
10 Joe Sakic
11 Denis Potvin
12 Markus Naslund
13 Steve Yzerman
14 John LeClair
15 Sergei Fedorov
16 Martin Brodeur
17 Milan Hejduk
18 Ilya Kovalchuk
19 Saku Koivu
20 Mark Messier
21 Curtis Joseph
22 Alex Tanguay
23 Ed Belfour
24 Rob Blake
25 Tony Amonte
26 Chris Drury
27 Doug Weight
28 Jaromir Jagr
29 Alexander Mogilny
30 Jeremy Roenick
31 Eric Lindros
32 Bobby Clarke
33 Tommy Salo
34 Dominik Hasek
35 Gordie Howe
36 Jacques Plante
37 Ted Lindsay
38 Bobby Hull
39 Terry Sawchuk
40 Jean Beliveau

2001-02 Parkhurst Heroes

This 16-card set featured game-worn jersey swatches of the two players featured on each card. Each card pictured both players, the modern player in color and the vintage player in opaque. Cards from this set were limited to 40 copies each.

Card	Low	High
H1 Jean Beliveau	15.00	40.00
Vincent Lecavalier		
H2 Gordie Howe	75.00	200.00
Steve Yzerman		
H3 Terry Sawchuk	125.00	300.00
Patrick Roy		
H4 Rocket Richard	40.00	100.00
Pavel Bure		
H5 Phil Esposito	15.00	40.00
Joe Thornton		
H6 Guy Lafleur	15.00	40.00
Paul Kariya		
H7 Doug Harvey	15.00	40.00
Brian Leetch		
H8 Stan Mikita	50.00	125.00
Joe Sakic		
H9 Jacques Plante	60.00	150.00
Martin Brodeur		
H10 Ted Lindsay	20.00	50.00
Owen Nolan		
H11 Vladislav Tretiak	60.00	150.00
Ed Belfour		
H12 Tim Horton	15.00	40.00
Scott Stevens		
H13 Bobby Hull	50.00	125.00
Brett Hull		
H14 Gilbert Perreault	30.00	80.00
Mario Lemieux		
H15 Henri Richard	15.00	40.00
Scott Gomez		
H16 Bill Gadsby	15.00	40.00
Chris Pronger		

2001-02 Parkhurst Jerseys

Cards from this 60-card set featured swatches of game-worn jersey from the featured player. Each card carried a player photo and the swatch on a multi-colored card front which included part of the background from the action photo. Cards in this set were limited to 90 copies each.
*MULT.COLOR SWATCH: .5X TO 1.5X

Card	Low	High
PJ1 Mario Lemieux	25.00	60.00
PJ2 Milan Hejduk	6.00	15.00
PJ3 Vincent Lecavalier	6.00	15.00
PJ4 Mats Sundin	8.00	20.00
PJ5 Mark Recchi	6.00	15.00
PJ6 Mark Messier	8.00	20.00
PJ7 Peter Bondra	8.00	20.00
PJ8 Jeff Friesen	6.00	15.00
PJ9 Scott Gomez	6.00	15.00
PJ10 Daniel Alfredsson	6.00	15.00
PJ11 Nicklas Lidstrom	8.00	20.00
PJ12 Daniel Sedin	6.00	15.00
PJ13 Peter Forsberg	12.00	30.00
PJ14 Ron Francis	6.00	15.00
PJ15 Joe Sakic	15.00	40.00
PJ16 Mike Modano	12.50	30.00
PJ17 Patrik Stefan	6.00	15.00
PJ18 Steve Yzerman	20.00	50.00
PJ19 Pavel Bure	8.00	20.00
PJ20 Al MacInnis	6.00	15.00
PJ21 Joe Thornton	12.50	30.00
PJ22 John LeClair	8.00	20.00
PJ23 Owen Nolan	6.00	15.00
PJ24 Paul Kariya	8.00	20.00
PJ25 Tony Amonte	6.00	15.00
PJ26 Zigmund Palffy	6.00	15.00
PJ27 Brian Leetch	6.00	15.00
PJ28 Scott Stevens	6.00	15.00
PJ29 Sergei Gonchar	6.00	15.00
PJ30 Chris Drury	6.00	15.00
PJ31 Fredrik Modin	6.00	15.00
PJ32 Alexei Zhamnov	6.00	15.00
PJ33 Curtis Joseph	6.00	15.00
PJ34 Patrik Elias	6.00	15.00
PJ35 Roberto Luongo	8.00	20.00
PJ36 Darren McCarty	6.00	15.00
PJ37 Saku Koivu	8.00	20.00
PJ38 Patrick Roy	25.00	60.00
PJ39 Brendan Shanahan	8.00	20.00
PJ40 Chris Pronger	6.00	15.00
PJ41 Martin Straka	6.00	15.00
PJ42 Chris Chelios	8.00	20.00
PJ43 Theo Fleury	6.00	15.00
PJ44 Roman Cechmanek	6.00	15.00
PJ45 Viktor Kozlov	6.00	15.00
PJ46 Martin Brodeur	20.00	50.00
PJ47 Radek Bonk	6.00	15.00
PJ48 Byron Dafoe	6.00	15.00
PJ49 Adam Foote	6.00	15.00
PJ50 Eric Daze	6.00	15.00
PJ51 Ed Belfour	8.00	20.00
PJ52 Milan Kraft	6.00	15.00
PJ53 Arturs Irbe	6.00	15.00
PJ54 Alex Tanguay	6.00	15.00
PJ55 Sergei Fedorov	8.00	20.00
PJ56 Mike Richter	8.00	20.00
PJ57 Marian Hossa	8.00	20.00
PJ58 Joe Nieuwendyk	6.00	15.00
PJ59 Keith Primeau	6.00	15.00
PJ60 Olaf Kolzig	6.00	15.00

2001-02 Parkhurst Jersey and Stick

This set partially paralleled the jersey set but each card carried a jersey swatch and a stick piece from the featured player. Cards in this set were limited to just 70 copies each.
*JSY/STK: .5X TO 1.25X JERSEY CARDS

2001-02 Parkhurst Milestones

This 56-card set featured players who hit the various milestones in their career. Each card featured an action photo of the given player alongside a game-worn swatch of his jersey on the card front. Cards M1-M22 were limited to just 50 cards each. Cards M19U-M52 were limited to just 90 copies each and were available in random BAP Update packs. Due to a printing error, card numbers M19-M22 were used for two different cards each, a "U" suffix is used below to denote the cards available in BAP Update packs.

Card	Low	High
M1 Chris Osgood	6.00	15.00
200 Wins		
M2 Martin Brodeur	15.00	40.00
M3 Jaromir Jagr	12.50	30.00
1000 Points		
M4 Jaromir Jagr	12.50	30.00
400 Goals		
M5 Ed Belfour	6.00	15.00
50 Shutouts		
M6 Brian Leetch	6.00	15.00
600 Assists		
M7 Luc Robitaille	6.00	15.00
600 Assists		
M8 Jaromir Jagr	12.50	30.00
600 Assists		
M9 Mark Recchi	6.00	15.00
Mark Recchi		
M10 Curtis Joseph	8.00	20.00
300 Wins		
M11 Dominik Hasek	15.00	40.00
50 Shutouts		
M12 Mark Messier	15.00	40.00
1500 Games		
M13 Scott Stevens	6.00	15.00
1400 Games		
M14 Steve Yzerman	20.00	50.00
1300 Games		
M15 Doug Gilmour	6.00	15.00
1300 Games		
M16 Martin Brodeur	15.00	40.00
M17 Steve Yzerman	20.00	50.00
1600 Points		
M18 Patrick Roy	20.00	50.00
50 Shutouts		
M19 Ray Bourque	12.00	30.00
1600 Games		
M19U Luc Robitaille	8.00	20.00
600 Goals		
M20 Mario Lemieux	20.00	50.00
M20U Brett Hull	8.00	20.00
650 Goals		
M21 Ray Bourque	12.00	30.00
400 Goals		
M21U Mario Lemieux	20.00	50.00
M22 Jeremy Roenick	10.00	25.00
400 Goals		
M22U Steve Yzerman	15.00	40.00
650 Goals		
M23 Joe Nieuwendyk	5.00	12.00
1000 Games		
M24 Ron Francis	5.00	12.00
500 Goals		
M25 Brendan Shanahan	8.00	20.00
500 Goals		
M26 Pavel Bure	8.00	20.00
400 Goals		
M27 Alexander Mogilny	5.00	12.00
400 Goals		
M28 Peter Bondra	5.00	12.00
400 Goals		
M29 Mats Sundin	5.00	12.00
400 Goals		
M30 Mark Recchi	5.00	12.00
400 Goals		
M31 Mike Modano	12.50	30.00
M32 Teemu Selanne	8.00	20.00
400 Goals		
M33 Steve Yzerman	15.00	40.00
1000 Assists		
M34 Adam Oates	5.00	12.00
1000 Assists		
M35 Mark Messier	8.00	20.00
1800 Points		
M36 Mario Lemieux	20.00	50.00
M37 Patrick Roy	20.00	50.00
500 Wins		
M38 Dominik Hasek	12.00	30.00
60 Shutouts		
M39 Patrick Roy	20.00	50.00
60 Shutouts		
M40 Ed Belfour	6.00	15.00
350 Wins		
M41 Curtis Joseph	8.00	20.00
350 Shutouts		
M42 Mike Richter	6.00	15.00
300 Wins		
M43 Martin Brodeur	20.00	50.00
M44 Ron Francis	5.00	12.00
1700 Points		
M45 Adam Oates	5.00	12.00
1300 Points		
M46 Brett Hull	8.00	20.00
1200 Points		
M47 Joe Sakic	15.00	40.00
1200 Points		
M48 Al MacInnis	5.00	12.00
1200 Points		
M49 Jaromir Jagr	12.50	30.00
1100 Points		
M50 Theo Fleury	5.00	12.00
1000 Points		
M51 Brendan Shanahan	6.00	15.00
1000 Points		
M52 Jeremy Roenick	8.00	20.00
1000 Points		

2001-02 Parkhurst Reprints

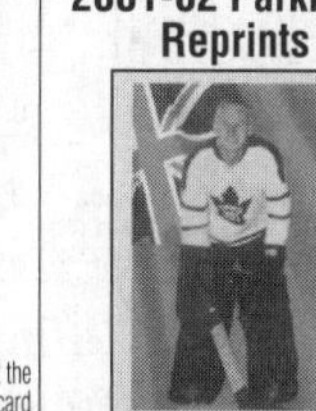

This 150-card set featured reprints of vintage Parkhurst cards. Of the 150 cards, 57 were printed with blank backs to form the Parkie Back Checking Contest. Collector's who received a blank back card had to answer a question from the BAP website that could be answered by reading the back of the original card, write the answer on the blank back card and send it to BAP. They would then receive the card back with a printed back. Cards #1, 18, 27, 36, 45, 54, 63, 72, 81, 90, 99, and 108 were originally produced as blank backs in 1951-52 and were not included in the contest.

Card	Low	High
PR1 Gordie Howe	1.00	5.00
PR2 Maurice Richard	1.00	5.00
PR3 Bernie Geoffrion	1.00	5.00
PR4 Bill Mosienko	1.00	5.00
PR5 Terry Sawchuk	1.00	5.00
PR6 Woody Dumart	1.00	5.00
PR7 Doug Harvey	1.00	5.00
PR8 Frank Mahovlich	1.00	5.00
PR9 Jean Beliveau	1.00	5.00
PR10 Jacques Plante	1.00	5.00
PR11 Jean-Guy Talbot	1.00	5.00
PR12 Gordie Howe	1.00	5.00
PR13 Terry Sawchuk	1.00	5.00
PR14 Maurice Richard	1.00	5.00
PR15 Harry Lumley	1.00	5.00
PR16 Jean Beliveau	1.00	5.00
PR17 Red Kelly	1.00	5.00
PR18 Bernie Geoffrion	1.00	5.00
PR19 Dickie Moore	1.00	5.00
PR20 Dollard St.Laurent	1.00	5.00
PR21 Terry Sawchuk	1.00	5.00
PR22 Harry Lumley	1.00	5.00
PR23 Woody Dumart	1.00	5.00
PR24 Tim Horton	1.00	5.00
PR25 George Hainsworth	1.00	5.00
PR26 Johnny Bower	1.00	5.00
PR27 Doug Harvey	1.00	5.00
PR28 Bill Gadsby	1.00	5.00
PR29 Dickie Moore	1.00	5.00
PR30 Gordie Howe	1.00	5.00
PR31 Red Kelly	1.00	5.00
PR32 Bernie Geoffrion	1.00	5.00
PR33 Jean Beliveau	1.00	5.00
PR34 Jacques Plante	1.00	5.00
PR35 Henri Richard	1.00	5.00
PR36 Chuck Rayner	1.00	5.00
PR37 Henri Richard	1.00	5.00
PR38 Frank Mahovlich	1.00	5.00
PR39 Bill Gadsby	1.00	5.00
PR40 Bernie Geoffrion	1.00	5.00
PR41 Doug Harvey	1.00	5.00
PR42 Maurice Richard	1.00	5.00
PR43 Georges Vezina	1.00	5.00
PR44 Jean-Guy Talbot	1.00	5.00
PR45 Terry Sawchuk	1.00	5.00
PR46 Terry Sawchuk	1.00	5.00
PR47 Jacques Plante	1.00	5.00
PR48 Frank Mahovlich	1.00	5.00
PR49 Bill Gadsby	1.00	5.00
PR50 Butch Bouchard	1.00	5.00
PR51 Bernie Geoffrion	1.00	5.00
PR52 Dollard St. Laurent	1.00	5.00
PR53 Red Kelly	1.00	5.00
PR54 Red Kelly	1.00	5.00
PR55 Johnny Bower	1.00	5.00
PR56 Henri Richard	1.00	5.00
PR57 Bernie Geoffrion	1.00	5.00
PR58 Howe/Lumley	1.00	5.00
PR59 Chuck Rayner	1.00	5.00
PR60 Red Kelly	1.00	5.00
PR61 Dickie Moore	1.00	5.00
PR62 Bernie Geoffrion	1.00	5.00
PR63 Butch Bouchard	1.00	5.00
PR64 Frank Mahovlich	1.00	5.00
PR65 Doug Harvey	1.00	5.00
PR66 Jacques Plante	1.00	5.00
PR67 Tim Horton	1.00	5.00
PR68 Dollard St. Laurent	1.00	5.00
PR69 Bernie Geoffrion	1.00	5.00
PR70 Butch Bouchard	1.00	5.00
PR71 Gordie Howe	1.00	5.00
PR72 Milt Schmidt	1.00	5.00
PR73 Butch Bouchard	1.00	5.00
PR74 Henri Richard	1.00	5.00
PR75 Tim Horton	1.00	5.00
PR76 Gordie Howe	1.00	5.00
PR77 Dickie Moore	1.00	5.00
PR78 Elmer Lach	1.00	5.00
PR79 Bernie Geoffrion	1.00	5.00
PR80 Jean Beliveau	1.00	5.00
PR81 Bill Gadsby	1.00	5.00
PR82 Jean Beliveau	1.00	5.00
PR83 Bill Gadsby	1.00	5.00
PR84 Henri Richard	1.00	5.00
PR85 Plante/Sloan	1.00	5.00
PR86 Frank Mahovlich	1.00	5.00
PR87 Terry Sawchuk	1.00	5.00
PR88 Maurice Richard	1.00	5.00
PR89 Tim Horton	1.00	5.00
PR90 Ted Lindsay	1.00	5.00
PR91 Johnny Bower	1.00	5.00
PR92 Maurice Richard	1.00	5.00
PR93 Red Kelly	1.00	5.00
PR94 Dickie Moore	1.00	5.00
PR95 Bill Gadsby	1.00	5.00
PR96 Ted Lindsay	1.00	5.00
PR97 Tim Horton	1.00	5.00
PR98 Bernie Geoffrion	1.00	5.00
PR99 Woody Dumart	1.00	5.00
PR100 Doug Harvey	1.00	5.00
PR101 Frank Mahovlich	1.00	5.00
PR102 Dickie Moore	1.00	5.00
PR103 Tim Horton	1.00	5.00
PR104 Harry Lumley	1.00	5.00
PR105 Butch Bouchard	1.00	5.00
PR106 Turk Broda	1.00	5.00
PR107 Jean Beliveau	1.00	5.00
PR108 Maurice Richard	1.00	5.00
PR109 Red Kelly	1.00	5.00
PR110 Jean Beliveau	1.00	5.00
PR111 Jean-Guy Talbot	1.00	5.00
PR112 Sawchuk/Geoffrion	1.00	5.00
PR113 Tim Horton	1.00	5.00
PR114 Dollard St. Laurent	1.00	5.00
PR115 Doug Harvey	1.00	5.00
PR116 Gump Worsley	1.00	5.00
PR117 Milt Schmidt	1.00	5.00
PR118 Jean Beliveau	1.00	5.00
PR119 Tim Horton	1.00	5.00
PR120 Dickie Moore	1.00	5.00
PR121 Doug Harvey	1.00	5.00
PR122 Henri Richard	1.00	5.00
PR123 Milt Schmidt	1.00	5.00
PR124 Frank Mahovlich	1.00	5.00
PR125 Johnny Bower	1.00	5.00
PR126 Ted Lindsay	1.00	5.00
PR127 Tim Horton	1.00	5.00
PR128 Jacques Plante	1.00	5.00
PR129 Jean-Guy Talbot	1.00	5.00
PR130 Jean Beliveau	1.00	5.00
PR131 Doug Harvey	1.00	5.00
PR132 Gump Worsley	1.00	5.00
PR133 Terry Sawchuk	1.00	5.00
PR134 Frank Mahovlich	1.00	5.00
PR135 Bill Mosienko	1.00	5.00
PR136 Jean Beliveau	1.00	5.00
PR137 Tim Horton	1.00	5.00
PR138 Jacques Plante	1.00	5.00
PR139 Johnny Bower	1.00	5.00
PR140 Gordie Howe	1.00	5.00
PR141 Chuck Rayner	1.00	5.00
PR142 Henri Richard	1.00	5.00
PR143 Gump Worsley	1.00	5.00
PR144 Red Kelly	1.00	5.00
PR145 Dickie Moore	1.00	5.00
PR146 Frank Mahovlich	1.00	5.00
PR147 Henri Richard	1.00	5.00
PR148 Johnny Bower	1.00	5.00
PR149 Red Kelly	1.00	5.00
PR150 Bill Gadsby	1.00	5.00

2001-02 Parkhurst Sticks

This 70-card set featured pieces of game-used sticks from the featured players alongside color player photos. Cards in this set were limited to 90 copies each.
*SINGLE COLOR SWATCH: .25X TO .75X HI

Card	Low	High
PS1 Mario Lemieux	30.00	80.00
PS2 Milan Hejduk	8.00	20.00
PS3 Vincent Lecavalier	8.00	20.00
PS4 Mats Sundin	8.00	20.00
PS5 Mark Recchi	6.00	15.00
PS6 Mark Messier	8.00	20.00
PS7 Peter Bondra	6.00	15.00
PS8 Jeff Friesen	6.00	15.00
PS9 Scott Gomez	6.00	15.00
PS10 Daniel Alfredsson	6.00	15.00
PS11 Nicklas Lidstrom	8.00	20.00
PS12 Daniel Sedin	6.00	15.00
PS13 Peter Forsberg	15.00	40.00
PS14 Ron Francis	6.00	15.00
PS15 Joe Sakic	15.00	40.00
PS16 Mike Modano	12.50	30.00
PS17 Patrik Stefan	6.00	15.00
PS18 Steve Yzerman	25.00	60.00
PS19 Pavel Bure	8.00	20.00
PS20 Al MacInnis	6.00	15.00
PS21 Joe Thornton	12.50	30.00
PS22 John LeClair	8.00	20.00
PS23 Owen Nolan	6.00	15.00
PS24 Paul Kariya	8.00	20.00
PS25 Tony Amonte	8.00	20.00
PS26 Zigmund Palffy	6.00	15.00
PS27 Brian Leetch	8.00	20.00
PS28 Scott Stevens	6.00	15.00
PS29 Sergei Gonchar	6.00	15.00
PS30 Chris Drury	6.00	15.00
PS31 Martin Brodeur	20.00	50.00
PS32 Chris Chelios	8.00	20.00
PS33 Rob Blake	6.00	15.00
PS34 Teemu Selanne	8.00	20.00

PS35 Pavol Demitra 6.00 15.00
PS36 Markus Naslund 8.00 20.00
PS37 Alex Tanguay 6.00 15.00
PS38 Keith Primeau 6.00 15.00
PS39 Olaf Kolzig 6.00 15.00
PS40 Sergei Fedorov 12.50 30.00
PS41 Brad Richards 6.00 15.00
PS42 Adam Oates 6.00 15.00
PS43 Darren McCarty 6.00 15.00
PS44 Adam Foote 6.00 15.00
PS45 Sandis Ozolinsh 6.00 15.00
PS46 Chris Pronger 6.00 15.00
PS47 Jason Arnott 6.00 15.00
PS48 Keith Tkachuk 8.00 20.00
PS49 Sergei Samsonov 6.00 15.00
PS50 Kenny Jonsson 6.00 15.00
PS51 Gary Roberts 6.00 15.00
PS52 Marian Hossa 8.00 20.00
PS53 Brendan Shanahan 8.00 20.00
PS54 Patrick Roy 25.00 60.00
PS55 Pierre Turgeon 6.00 15.00
PS56 Roman Turek 6.00 15.00
PS57 Doug Weight 6.00 15.00
PS58 Jaromir Jagr 12.50 30.00
PS59 Brett Hull 10.00 25.00
PS60 Dominik Hasek 15.00 40.00
PS61 Luc Robitaille 6.00 15.00
PS62 Eric Lindros 8.00 20.00
PS63 Stan Mikita 15.00 40.00
PS64 Guy Lafleur 15.00 40.00
PS65 Lanny McDonald 12.50 30.00
PS66 Jari Kurri 15.00 40.00
PS67 Jeremy Roenick 10.00 25.00
PS68 Rick DiPietro 6.00 15.00
PS69 Joe Nieuwendyk 6.00 15.00
PS70 Alexander Mogilny 6.00 15.00

2001-02 Parkhurst Teammates

Cards in this 28-card set featured three swatches of game-worn jerseys from the three teammates pictured on the card front. The cards were produced vertically, and the swatches were affixed parallel to a photo of each player. Cards T1-T18 were available in random packs of Parkhurst and were limited to 30 copies each. Cards T19-T28 were available in random packs of BAP Update and were limited to 80 copies each.

T1 Brendan Shanahan 75.00 200.00
Steve Yzerman
Nicklas Lidstrom
T2 Milan Kraft 60.00 150.00
Jean-Sebastien Aubin
Mario Lemieux
T3 Theo Fleury 20.00 50.00
Mark Messier
Brian Leetch
T4 Byron Dafoe 12.00 30.00
Joe Thornton
Jason Allison
T5 Adam Foote 20.00 50.00
Joe Sakic
Chris Drury
T6 Olaf Kolzig 20.00 50.00
Sergei Gonchar
Olaf Bondra
T7 Curtis Joseph 20.00 50.00
Mats Sundin
Tomas Kaberle
T8 Patrick Roy 60.00 150.00
Peter Forsberg
Milan Hejduk
T9 Jocelyn Thibault 10.00 25.00
Tony Amonte
Eric Daze
T10 Roberto Luongo 20.00 50.00
Pavel Bure
Viktor Kozlov
T11 Martin Biron 10.00 25.00
Miroslav Satan
Alexei Zhitnik
T12 Belfour/Modano/Sydor 20.00 50.00
T13 Roman Cechmanek 10.00 25.00
Mark Recchi
John LeClair
T14 Martin Brodeur 50.00 125.00
Scott Stevens
Patrik Elias
T15 Bobby Holik 10.00 25.00
Scott Gomez
Jason Arnott
T16 Marion Hossa 25.00
Daniel Alfredsson
Radek Bonk
T17 Daniel Sedin 20.00 50.00
Markus Naslund
Todd Bertuzzi
T18 Ron Francis 10.00 25.00
Arturs Irbe
Sandis Ozolinsh
T19 Sergei Samsonov 30.00 80.00
Joe Thornton
Bill Guerin
T20 Sandis Ozolinsh 12.50 30.00
Pavel Bure
Roberto Luongo
T21 Marty Turco 30.00 80.00
Mike Modano
Ed Belfour
T22 Joe Sakic 40.00 100.00
Patrick Roy
Chris Drury
T23 Steve Yzerman 30.00 80.00
Brendan Shanahan
Dominik Hasek
T24 Eric Lindros 15.00 40.00
Brian Leetch
Mark Messier
T25 Teemu Selanne 12.50 30.00
Jani Hurme
Sami Kapanen
T26 Mats Sundin 12.50 30.00
Tommy Salo
Markus Naslund
T27 Jaromir Jagr 25.00 60.00
Dominik Hasek
Tomas Kaberle
T28 Steve Yzerman 40.00 100.00
Mario Lemieux
Martin Brodeur

2001-02 Parkhurst Vintage Memorabilia

Cards from this 30-card set featured reprints of vintage Parkhurst cards with a piece of game-used memorabilia attached to the card front. Production quantities varied and are listed below beside the card descriptions. Cards with print runs less than 25 are not priced due to scarcity.

MULT.COLOR SWATCH: 1X TO 2X HI
PV1 Rocket Richard GJ/90 60.00 150.00
PV2 Rocket Richard Number/5
PV3 Rocket Richard Emblem/5
PV4 Jacques Plante GJ/90 30.00 80.00
PV5 Jacques Plante Glove/90 30.00 80.00
PV6 Jacques Plante Emblem/5
PV7 Jacques Plante Number/5
PV8 Jacques Plante Stick/90 30.00 80.00
PV9 Bill Gadsby Glove/90 15.00 40.00
PV10 Doug Harvey GJ/90 15.00 40.00
PV11 Doug Harvey Emblem/5
PV12 Doug Harvey Number/5
PV13 Gordie Howe GJ/40 75.00 200.00
PV14 Gordie Howe Emblem/5
PV15 Gordie Howe Number/5
PV16 Bill Mosienko Pants/90 15.00 40.00
PV17 Jean Beliveau GJ/90 20.00 50.00
PV18 Jean Beliveau Number/5
PV19 Jean Beliveau Emblem/5
PV20 Turk Broda Glove/90 25.00 60.00
PV21 Tim Horton 30.00 80.00
PV22 Henri Richard GJ/90 15.00 40.00
PV23 Henri Richard Emblem/5
PV24 Chuck Rayner Glove/90 40.00 100.00
PV25 T.Sawchuk Glove/90 30.00 80.00
PV26 Terry Sawchuk Pad/90 30.00 80.00
PV27 Terry Sawchuk GJ/90 30.00 80.00
PV28 Ted Lindsay GJ/90 15.00 40.00
PV29 Ted Lindsay Emblem/5
PV30 Johnny Bower Pad/90 15.00 40.00

2001-02 Parkhurst World Class Jerseys

This 8-card set featured player photos and game-worn jersey swatches over a background of the national flag of the given player. Each card in this set was limited to just 80 copies each.

WCJ1 Steve Yzerman 20.00 50.00
WCJ2 Teemu Selanne 10.00 25.00
WCJ3 Olaf Kolzig 10.00 25.00
WCJ4 Zigmund Palffy 10.00 25.00
WCJ5 Peter Forsberg 15.00 40.00
WCJ6 Mike Modano 12.50 30.00
WCJ7 Jaromir Jagr 15.00 40.00
WCJ8 Alexei Yashin 10.00 25.00

2001-02 Parkhurst World Class Emblems

This 8-card set paralleled the jersey set but featured swatches of emblems from the player's jersey. Each card was limited to just 20 copies each.

EMBLEMS NOT PRICED DUE TO SCARCITY

2001-02 Parkhurst World Class Numbers

This 8-card set paralleled the jersey set but featured swatches from the numbers on the player's jersey. Each card was limited to just 20 copies each.

NUMBERS NOT PRICED DUE TO SCARCITY

2001-02 Parkhurst Waving the Flag

Inspired by the 1963-64 Parkhurst Design, this set featured a portrait shot of the player with his native flag in the background. Card backs summarize each player's international experience in tournaments. The cards were

printed on 20-point foilboard stock and the print run was limited to 2,002 sets. Each set was accompanied by a sequentially-numbered header card to enhance collectibility. The set was available by mail via the Be a Player website.

1 Mario Lemieux 6.00 15.00
2 Joe Sakic 2.00 5.00
3 Steve Yzerman 5.00 12.00
4 Paul Kariya 1.00 2.50
5 Curtis Joseph 1.00 2.50
6 Martin Brodeur 2.50 6.00
7 Eric Lindros 1.00 2.50
8 Chris Pronger .75 2.00
9 Jaromir Jagr 1.50 4.00
10 Milan Hejduk 1.00 2.50
11 Dominik Hasek 2.00 5.00
12 Martin Havlat .75 2.00
13 Teemu Selanne 1.00 2.50
14 Jani Hurme .75 2.00
15 Miikka Kiprusoff .75 2.00
16 Sami Kapanen .75 2.00
17 Mats Sundin 1.00 2.50
18 Nicklas Lidstrom 1.00 2.50
19 Tommy Salo .75 2.00
20 Kristian Huselius .75 2.00
21 Jeremy Roenick 1.25 3.00
22 Doug Weight .75 2.00
23 Tony Amonte .75 2.00
24 Brian Leetch .75 2.00
25 Mike Modano 1.50 4.00
26 Brett Hull 1.25 3.00
27 John LeClair 1.00 2.50
28 Keith Tkachuk 1.00 2.50
29 Alexei Yashin .75 2.00
30 Pavel Bure 1.00 2.50
31 Nikolai Khabibulin 1.00 2.50
32 Darius Kasparaitis .75 2.00

2001-02 Parkhurst Beckett Promos

Inserted into issues of Beckett Hockey collector, this 50-card set paralleled the base Parkhurst set but carried a "Beckett" stamp on the card backs. There is very little secondary market information for these cards, therefore they are unpriced.

251 Jesse Boulerice
252 Marko Kiprusoff
253 Ivan Ciernik
254 Pavel Datsyuk
255 Jaroslav Bednar
256 Andreas Salomonsson
257 Mike Ribeiro
258 Darcy Hordichuk
259 Chris Neil
260 Rostislav Klesla
261 Kristian Huselius
262 Brian Sutherby
263 Jiri Dopita
264 Radek Martinek
265 Barrett Heisten
266 Krystofer Kolanos
267 Pascal Dupuis
268 Andreas Lilja
269 Chris Mason
270 Mathieu Garon
271 Andrew Raycroft
272 Jeff Jillson
273 Jiri Bicek
274 Niklas Hagman
275 Pavel Brendl
276 Stephen Peat
277 Sascha Goc
278 Nick Boynton
279 Timo Parssinen
280 Mika Noronen
281 Scott Clemmensen
282 Dan Blackburn
283 Nikita Alexeev
284 Vaclav Nedorost
285 Ilja Bryzgalov
286 Dany Heatley
287 Niko Kapanen
288 Rick Berry
289 Mark Bell
290 Kamil Piros
291 Maxime Ouellet
292 Kris Beech
293 Miikka Kiprusoff
294 Martti Jarventie
295 Ilya Kovalchuk
296 Nick Schultz
297 Bryan Allen
298 Josef Boumedienne
299 Jason Williams
300 Daniel Tjarnqvist

2002-03 Parkhurst

Released in late February, this 250-card set consisted of 200 veteran cards and 50 shortprinted rookie cards. Rookies were serial-numbered out of 500.

COMP.SET w/o SP's (200) 25.00 50.00
1 Rod Brind'Amour .25 .60
2 Alexei Kovalev .25 .60
3 Brad Richards .25 .60
4 Milan Hnilicka .25 .60
5 Arturs Irbe .25 .60
6 Al MacInnis .25 .60
7 Pavel Bure .30 .75
8 Patrick Lalime .25 .60
9 Vincent Damphousse .10 .25
10 Bates Battaglia .10 .25
11 Evgeni Nabokov .25 .60
12 Glen Murray .10 .25
13 Chris Osgood .25 .60
14 Pierre Turgeon .25 .60
15 Scott Stevens .25 .60
16 Daniel Briere .10 .25
17 Patrik Stefan .10 .25
18 Pavol Demitra .25 .60
19 Mark Parrish .10 .25
20 Jason Allison .10 .25
21 Jaromir Jagr .50 1.25
22 Mike Modano .50 1.25
23 Mark Messier .30 .75
24 Ilya Kovalchuk .40 1.00
25 Teemu Selanne .30 .75
26 Marty Turco .25 .60
27 Keith Tkachuk .30 .75
28 Simon Gagne .30 .75
29 Brent Johnson .25 .60
30 Anson Carter .25 .60
31 Jeff Jillson .10 .25
32 Gary Roberts .10 .25
33 Mike Richter .30 .75
34 Martin Lapointe .10 .25
35 Todd Bertuzzi .30 .75
36 Valeri Bure .10 .25
37 Marian Hossa .30 .75
38 Eric Daze .25 .60
39 Nikolai Khabibulin .30 .75
40 Miikka Kiprusoff .25 .60
41 Kevin Weekes .25 .60
42 Mark Recchi .25 .60
43 Dan Cloutier .25 .60
44 Keith Primeau .10 .25
45 Alex Tanguay .25 .60
46 Ed Jovanovski .25 .60
47 Roberto Luongo .40 1.00
48 Saku Koivu .30 .75
49 Chris Drury .25 .60
50 Olaf Kolzig .25 .60
51 Dan Blackburn .25 .60
52 Erik Cole .10 .25
53 Darcy Tucker .10 .25
54 Chris Chelios .30 .75
55 Pavel Datsyuk .30 .75
56 Mike Comrie .25 .60
57 Paul Kariya .30 .75
58 Eric Lindros .30 .75
59 Martin Havlat .25 .60
60 Scott Niedermayer .10 .25
61 Krys Kolanos .10 .25
62 Rostislav Klesla .10 .25
63 Jocelyn Thibault .25 .60
64 Mike Dunham .25 .60
65 Shane Doan .10 .25
66 John LeClair .30 .75
67 Tommy Salo .25 .60
68 Doug Gilmour .25 .60
69 Johan Hedberg .25 .60
70 Brett Hull .40 1.00
71 Alexander Mogilny .25 .60
72 Chris Pronger .25 .60
73 Sergei Fedorov .50 1.25
74 David Legwand .25 .60
75 Kristian Huselius .10 .25
76 Manny Fernandez .25 .60
77 Vincent Lecavalier .30 .75
78 Rick DiPietro .25 .60
79 Mike Peca .10 .25
80 Ryan Smyth .10 .25
81 Brian Rolston .25 .60
82 Brian Leetch .25 .60
83 Steve Sullivan .10 .25
84 Scott Gomez .10 .25
85 Adam Foote .10 .25
86 Scott Hartnell .10 .25
87 Alexei Zhamnov .10 .25
88 Marc Denis .25 .60
89 Joe Nieuwendyk .25 .60
90 Brad Stuart .10 .25
91 Patrik Elias .25 .60
92 Mats Sundin .30 .75
93 Jose Theodore .40 1.00
94 Brendan Shanahan .30 .75
95 Daniel Alfredsson .25 .60
96 Martin Brodeur .75 2.00
97 Jarome Iginla .40 1.00
98 Peter Bondra .25 .60
99 Peter Forsberg .60 1.50
100 Steve Yzerman 1.50 4.00
101 Alexei Yashin .10 .25
102 Patrick Roy 1.50 4.00
103 Markus Naslund .30 .75
104 Jeremy Roenick .30 .75
105 Darius Kasparaitis .10 .25
106 Curtis Joseph .30 .75
107 Marian Gaborik .60 1.50
108 Bill Guerin .25 .60
109 Joe Sakic .60 1.50
110 Adam Oates .25 .60
111 Owen Nolan .25 .60
112 Rob Blake .25 .60
113 Nicklas Lidstrom .30 .75
114 Joe Thornton .50 1.25
115 Mario Lemieux 2.00 5.00
116 Sergei Gonchar .10 .25
117 Bobby Holik .10 .25
118 Sandis Ozolinsh .10 .25
119 Steven Reinprecht .10 .25
120 Jeff O'Neill .10 .25
121 Radek Bonk .10 .25
122 Milan Hejduk .30 .75
123 Zigmund Palffy .25 .60
124 Luc Robitaille .25 .60
125 Dany Heatley .40 1.00
126 Doug Weight .25 .60
127 Fredrik Modin .10 .25
128 Ron Francis .25 .60
129 Roman Turek .25 .60
130 Adam Deadmarsh .10 .25
131 Sami Kapanen .10 .25
132 Sergei Samsonov .25 .60
133 Jeff Friesen .10 .25
134 Martin St. Louis .25 .60
135 Phil Housley .10 .25
136 Mark Bell .10 .25
137 Felix Potvin .30 .75
138 Ed Belfour .30 .75
139 Martin Biron .25 .60
140 Alyn McCauley .10 .25
141 Miroslav Satan .25 .60
142 Jan Hrdina .10 .25
143 Ron Tugnutt .25 .60
144 Steve Shields .25 .60
145 Cliff Ronning .10 .25
146 Wade Redden .10 .25
147 Patrick Marleau .25 .60
148 Tony Amonte .25 .60
149 Byron Dafoe .25 .60
150 Roman Cechmanek .25 .60
151 Martin Straka .10 .25
152 Sergei Zubov .10 .25
153 Maxim Afinogenov .10 .25
154 Brian Boucher .25 .60
155 Jason Arnott .10 .25
156 Oleg Tverdovsky .10 .25
157 Daymond Langkow .10 .25
158 Andrew Brunette .10 .25
159 Brian Rafalski .10 .25
160 Mike York .10 .25
161 Richard Zednik .10 .25
162 Radim Vrbata .10 .25
163 Tim Connolly .10 .25
164 Jamie Storr .25 .60
165 Henrik Sedin .10 .25
166 Sean Burke .25 .60
167 Daniel Sedin .10 .25
168 Jason Smith .10 .25
169 Stephen Weiss .10 .25
170 Bryan McCabe .10 .25
171 Theo Fleury .10 .25
172 J-S Giguere .25 .60
173 Espen Knutsen .10 .25
174 Mika Noronen .25 .60
175 Michael Nylander .10 .25
176 Yanic Perreault .10 .25
177 Donald Brashear .10 .25
178 Denis Arkhipov .10 .25
179 Adrian Aucoin .10 .25
180 Tie Domi .25 .60
181 Andrew Cassels .10 .25
182 Eric Brewer .10 .25
183 Trevor Linden .10 .25
184 Brendan Witt .10 .25
185 Robert Lang .10 .25
186 Brendan Morrison .25 .60
187 Mike Fisher .10 .25
188 Alexei Morozov .10 .25
189 Martin Erat .10 .25
190 Jeff Hackett .25 .60
191 Mariusz Czerkawski .10 .25
192 Olli Jokinen .25 .60
193 Brad Isbister .10 .25
194 Niklas Hagman .10 .25
195 Jere Lehtinen .25 .60
196 Igor Larionov .10 .25
197 Curtis Brown .10 .25
198 Ray Whitney .10 .25
199 Grant Marshall .10 .25
200 Craig Conroy .10 .25
201 P-M Bouchard RC 8.00 20.00
202 Rick Nash RC 15.00 40.00
203 Dennis Seidenberg RC 2.00 5.00
204 Jay Bouwmeester RC 6.00 15.00
205 Stanislav Chistov RC 2.00 5.00
206 Jared Aulin RC 2.00 5.00
207 Ivan Majesky RC 2.00 5.00
208 Chuck Kobasew RC 5.00 12.00
209 Jordan Leopold RC 4.00 10.00
210 Ryan Miller RC 12.00 30.00
211 Ales Hemsky RC 10.00 25.00
212 Patrick Sharp RC 2.00 5.00
213 Kari Haakana RC 2.00 5.00
214 Dmitri Bykov RC 2.00 5.00
215 Pascal Leclaire RC 6.00 15.00
216 Henrik Zetterberg RC 15.00 40.00
217 Alexander Frolov RC 8.00 20.00
218 Steve Eminger RC 2.00 5.00
219 Scottie Upshall RC 5.00 12.00
220 Tom Koivisto RC 2.00 5.00
221 Shaone Morrisonn RC 2.00 5.00
222 Ron Hainsey RC 2.00 5.00
223 Martin Gerber RC 6.00 15.00
224 Adam Hall RC 2.00 5.00
225 Lasse Pirjeta RC 2.00 5.00
226 Anton Volchenkov RC 2.00 5.00
227 Craig Andersson RC 2.00 5.00
228 Rickard Wallin RC 2.00 5.00
229 Alexander Svitov RC 2.00 5.00
230 Alexei Smirnov RC 2.00 5.00
231 Jeff Taffe RC 2.00 5.00
232 Mikael Tellqvist RC 5.00 12.00
233 Radovan Somik RC 2.00 5.00
234 Dick Tarnstrom RC 2.00 5.00
235 Steve Ott RC 5.00 12.00
236 Brooks Orpik RC 2.00 5.00
237 Eric Bertrand RC 2.00 5.00
238 Sylvain Blouin RC 2.00 5.00
239 Greg Koehler RC 2.00 5.00
240 Stephane Veilleux RC 2.00 5.00
241 Curtis Sanford RC 5.00 12.00
242 Carlo Colaiacovo RC 2.00 5.00
243 Patrick Boileau RC 2.00 5.00
244 Tim Thomas RC 5.00 12.00
245 Mike Cammalleri RC 5.00 12.00
246 Levente Szuper RC 2.00 5.00
247 Jason Spezza RC 15.00 40.00
248 Cody Rudkowsky RC 2.00 5.00
249 Eric Godard RC 2.00 5.00
250 Valeri Kharlamov RC 8.00 20.00

2002-03 Parkhurst Bronze

This 250-card parallel set was serial-numbered to just 100 sets.

*BRONZE: 4X TO 10X BASIC CARDS
*ROOKIES: .25X TO .75X

2002-03 Parkhurst Gold

This 250-card parallel set was serial-numbered to just 10 sets.

GOLD NOT PRICED DUE TO SCARCITY

2002-03 Parkhurst Silver

This 250-card parallel set was serial-numbered to just 50 sets.

*SILVER: 6X TO 15X BASIC CARDS
*ROOKIES: .5X TO 1.25X

2002-03 Parkhurst College Ranks

This 18-card set featured players who played in the NCAA. Cards were limited to 100 copies each.

CR1 Chris Drury 4.00 10.00
CR2 Erik Cole 3.00 8.00
CR3 Keith Tkachuk 4.00 10.00
CR4 Rick DiPietro 3.00 8.00
CR5 Rob Blake 3.00 8.00
CR6 Adam Oates 3.00 8.00
CR7 Chris Chelios 4.00 10.00
CR8 Brett Hull 5.00 12.00
CR9 Paul Kariya 4.00 10.00
CR10 Tony Amonte 3.00 8.00
CR11 Doug Weight 3.00 8.00
CR12 Dany Heatley 5.00 12.00
CR13 Steven Reinprecht 3.00 8.00
CR14 Curtis Joseph 4.00 10.00
CR15 Anson Carter 3.00 8.00
CR16 Mike Dunham 3.00 8.00
CR17 Mike Richter 4.00 10.00
CR18 Ed Belfour 4.00 10.00

2002-03 Parkhurst College Ranks Jerseys

This 18-card set paralleled the regular set with the addition of jersey swatches. Cards were limited to 60 copies each.

*MULT.COLOR SWATCH: .5X TO 1.25X
CRM1 Chris Drury 8.00 20.00
CRM2 Erik Cole 8.00 20.00
CRM3 Keith Tkachuk 8.00 20.00
CRM4 Rick DiPietro 8.00 20.00
CRM5 Rob Blake 8.00 20.00
CRM6 Adam Oates 8.00 20.00
CRM7 Chris Chelios 8.00 20.00
CRM8 Brett Hull 15.00 40.00
CRM9 Paul Kariya 8.00 20.00
CRM10 Tony Amonte 8.00 20.00
CRM11 Doug Weight 10.00 25.00
CRM12 Dany Heatley 12.50 30.00
CRM13 Steven Reinprecht 8.00 20.00
CRM14 Curtis Joseph 8.00 20.00
CRM15 Anson Carter 8.00 20.00
CRM16 Mike Dunham 10.00 25.00
CRM17 Mike Richter 8.00 20.00
CRM18 Ed Belfour 10.00 25.00

2002-03 Parkhurst Franchise Players

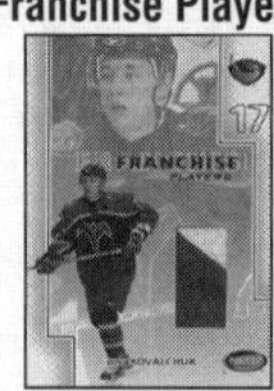

Limited to just 50 copies each, this 30-card set featured game jersey swatches from team leaders.

*MULT.COLOR SWATCH: .5X TO 1.25X
FP1 Paul Kariya 8.00 20.00
FP2 Ilya Kovalchuk 12.50 30.00
FP3 Joe Thornton 15.00 40.00
FP4 Miroslav Satan 8.00 20.00
FP5 Jarome Iginla 12.50 30.00
FP6 Jeff O'Neill 8.00 20.00
FP7 Eric Daze 8.00 20.00
FP8 Patrick Roy 25.00 60.00
FP9 Rostislav Klesla 8.00 20.00
FP10 Mike Modano 10.00 25.00
FP11 Steve Yzerman 20.00 50.00
FP12 Mike Comrie 8.00 20.00
FP13 Roberto Luongo 10.00 25.00
FP14 Zigmund Palffy 8.00 20.00
FP15 Marian Gaborik 15.00 40.00
FP16 Jose Theodore 15.00 40.00
FP17 Scott Hartnell 8.00 20.00
FP18 Martin Brodeur 20.00 50.0
FP19 Alexei Yashin 8.00 20.0
FP20 Pavel Bure 8.00 20.0
FP21 Marian Hossa 8.00 20.0
FP22 Simon Gagne 8.00 20.0
FP23 Daniel Briere 8.00 20.0
FP24 Mario Lemieux 25.00 60.0
FP25 Chris Pronger 8.00 20.0
FP26 Owen Nolan 8.00 20.0
FP27 Nikolai Khabibulin 8.00 20.0
FP28 Mats Sundin 8.00 20.0
FP29 Markus Naslund 8.00 20.0
FP30 Jaromir Jagr 12.50 30.0

2002-03 Parkhurst Hardware

These cards were part of a redempti program launched by BAP focusing on t annual NHL awards. Each trophy w represented by 9 hopefuls and a Wild Ca Collectors had the choice of keeping th redemption cards (numbered to just 1 copies each), or sending them in fo chance to win a memorabilia card number to just 10. Collectors had to send in the ca of the eventual trophy winner in order to eligible for the random drawing. Winr cards are not priced due to their scarci Numbers below correlate to the amount cards not redeemed.

COMMON CARD 4.00 10.0
A1 Eric Lindros/96 4.00 10.0
A2 Jarome Iginla/95 5.00 12.0
A3 Jaromir Jagr/98 4.00 10.0
A4 Joe Sakic/97 4.00 10.0
A5 Markus Naslund/82 4.00 10.0
A6 Pavel Bure/94 4.00 10.0
A7 Peter Forsberg/83 8.00 20.0
A8 Mario Lemieux/88 4.00 10.0
A9 Mats Sundin/98 4.00 10.0
A10 Wildcard/87 4.00 10.0
C1 Chuck Kobasew/95 4.00 10.0
C2 Henrik Zetterberg/78 8.00 20.0
C3 Alexander Svitov/94 4.00 10.0
C4 Jay Bouwmeester/92 4.00 10.0
C5 Jordan Leopold/95 4.00 10.0
C6 Ron Hainsey/96 4.00 10.0
C7 Rick Nash/81 8.00 20.0
C8 Stanislav Chistov/94 4.00 10.0
C9 Stephen Weiss/96 4.00 10.0
C10 Wildcard/85 4.00 10.0
H1 Eric Lindros/92 4.00 10.0
H2 Jarome Iginla/88 5.00 12.0
H3 Jaromir Jagr/85 4.00 10.0
H4 Joe Sakic/82 4.00 10.0
H5 Jose Theodore/91 5.00 12.0
H6 Markus Naslund/78 4.00 10.0
H7 Pavel Bure/91 4.00 10.0
H8 Peter Forsberg/73 8.00 20.0
H9 Mario Lemieux/92 4.00 10.0
H10 Wildcard/85 4.00 10.0
N1 Nicklas Lidstrom/85 6.00 15.0
N2 Sergei Gonchar/95 4.00 10.0
N3 Rob Blake/93 4.00 10.0
N4 Ed Jovanovski/96 4.00 10.0
N5 Brian Rafalski/99 4.00 10.0
N6 Bryan McCabe/98 4.00 10.0
N7 Chris Chelios/95 4.00 10.0
N8 Adrian Aucoin/97 4.00 10.0
N9 Brian Leetch/96 4.00 10.0
N10 Wildcard/77 4.00 10.0
P1 Eric Lindros/94 4.00 10.0
P2 Jarome Iginla/96 5.00 12.0
P3 Jaromir Jagr/88 4.00 10.0
P4 Joe Sakic/89 4.00 10.0
P5 Markus Naslund/79 6.00 15.0
P6 Pavel Bure/98 4.00 10.0
P7 Peter Forsberg/81 4.00 10.0
P8 Mario Lemieux/88 4.00 10.0
P9 Mats Sundin/93 4.00 10.0
P10 Wildcard/77 4.00 10.0
V1 Curtis Joseph/96 4.00 10.0
V2 Evgeni Nabokov/95 4.00 10.0
V3 Jose Theodore/95 5.00 12.0
V4 Martin Brodeur/72 8.00 20.0
V5 Mike Richter/97 4.00 10.0
V6 Patrick Lalime/93 4.00 10.0
V7 Patrick Roy/86 4.00 10.0
V8 Roberto Luongo/97 5.00 12.0
V9 Olaf Kolzig/98 4.00 10.0
V10 Wildcard/86 4.00 10.0
AW1 Peter Forsberg/Hart
AW2 Barret Jackman/Calder
AW3 Martin Brodeur/Vezina
AW4 Peter Forsberg/Art Ross
AW5 Nicklas Lidstrom/Norris
AW6 Markus Naslund/Pearson

2002-03 Parkhurst Heroes

Limited to 25 sets, this 12-card set featur swatches of game jerseys from modern players and their idols.

Ilya Kovalchuk 60.00 150.00
Valeri Kharlamov
J.Thornton/S.Yzerman 50.00 125.00
Jarome Iginla 30.00 80.00
Mark Messier
S.Yzerman/B.Trottier 60.00 150.00
S.Gagne/M.Lemieux 50.00 125.00
Eric Lindros 30.00 80.00
Mark Messier
M.Lemieux/G.Lafleur 60.00 150.00
R.Nash/M.Sundin 30.00 80.00
Chris Pronger 30.00 80.00
Al MacInnis
J.Bouwmeester/S.Yzerman 30.00 80.00
1 Dany Heatley 60.00 150.00
Brett Hull
2 Stephen Weiss 50.00 125.00
Peter Forsberg

002-03 Parkhurst He Shoots-He Scores Points

ted one per pack, these cards carried a of 1, 2 or 3 points. The points could be emed for special memorabilia cards. The s are unnumbered and are listed below phabetical order by point value. The mption program ended January 31,

artin Brodeur 1pt. .40 1.00
eter Forsberg 1pt. .40 1.00
ark Messier 1pt. .40 1.00
wen Nolan 1 pt. .40 1.00
remy Roenick 1 pt. .40 1.00
atrick Roy 1 pt. .40 1.00
e Sakic 1 pt. .40 1.00
endan Shanahan 1 pt. .40 1.00
ats Sundin 1 pt. .40 1.00
Jose Theodore 1 pt. .40 1.00
Joe Thornton 1 pt. .40 1.00
Pavel Bure 2 pt. .40 1.00
Jaromir Jagr 2 pt. .40 1.00
Paul Kariya 2 pt. .40 1.00
Eric Lindros 2 pt. .40 1.00
Mike Modano 2 pt. .40 1.00
Steve Yzerman 2 pt. .40 1.00
Jarome Iginla 3 pt. .40 1.00
Ilya Kovalchuk 3 pt. .40 1.00
Mario Lemieux 3 pt. .40 1.00

002-03 Parkhurst He Shoots-He Scores Prizes

able only by redeeming 400 Parkhurst hoots-He Scores points, this 30-card eatured game-used swatches of jersey a color photo of the player. Each card e stated print run of 20 serial-numbered and each was encased in a clear plastic with a descriptive label at the top. This s unpriced due to scarcity and volatility.
PRICED DUE TO SCARCITY

ario Lemieux
avel Bure
aromir Jagr
ic Lindros
aul Kariya
a Kovalchuk
ike Modano
e Thornton
ose Theodore
eremy Roenick
Martin Brodeur
Mats Sundin
Mark Messier
Steve Yzerman
Peter Forsberg
Patrick Roy
Jarome Iginla
Brendan Shanahan
Owen Nolan
Joe Sakic
Teemu Selanne
Nicklas Lidstrom
John LeClair
Dany Heatley
Luc Robitaille
Eric Daze
Keith Tkachuk
Brian Leetch
Milan Hejduk
Rob Blake

002-03 Parkhurst Jerseys

LT.COLOR SWATCH: .5X TO 1.25X
TED PRINT RUN 90 SETS
Mario Lemieux 20.00 50.00
Jose Theodore 10.00 25.00
Brian Leetch 6.00 15.00
Jaromir Jagr 10.00 25.00

GJ5 Steve Yzerman 20.00 50.00
GJ6 Eric Daze 6.00 15.00
GJ7 Saku Koivu 8.00 20.00
GJ8 John LeClair 8.00 20.00
GJ9 Jeff O'Neill 6.00 15.00
GJ10 Gary Roberts 6.00 15.00
GJ11 Al MacInnis 6.00 15.00
GJ12 Marian Gaborik 12.50 30.00
GJ13 Teemu Selanne 8.00 20.00
GJ14 Alexander Mogilny 6.00 15.00
GJ15 Eric Lindros 8.00 20.00
GJ16 Milan Hejduk 8.00 20.00
GJ17 Zigmund Palffy 8.00 20.00
GJ18 Luc Robitaille 6.00 15.00
GJ19 Ilya Kovalchuk 10.00 25.00
GJ20 Rostislav Klesla 6.00 15.00
GJ21 Mark Messier 8.00 20.00
GJ22 Ron Francis 6.00 15.00
GJ23 Chris Pronger 6.00 15.00
GJ24 Dany Heatley 10.00 25.00
GJ25 Mark Recchi 6.00 15.00
GJ26 Doug Weight 6.00 15.00
GJ27 Alex Tanguay 8.00 20.00
GJ28 Sergei Fedorov 10.00 25.00
GJ29 Todd Bertuzzi 8.00 20.00
GJ30 Sami Kapanen 6.00 15.00
GJ31 Sergei Samsonov 6.00 15.00
GJ32 Jeremy Roenick 10.00 25.00
GJ33 Mike Modano 10.00 25.00
GJ34 Joe Sakic 15.00 40.00
GJ35 Pavel Bure 8.00 20.00
GJ36 Paul Kariya 8.00 20.00
GJ37 Owen Nolan 6.00 15.00
GJ38 Rob Blake 6.00 15.00
GJ39 Nicklas Lidstrom 8.00 20.00
GJ40 Joe Thornton 12.50 30.00
GJ41 Brendan Shanahan 8.00 20.00
GJ42 Daniel Alfredsson 6.00 15.00
GJ43 Martin Brodeur 20.00 50.00
GJ44 Jarome Iginla 10.00 25.00
GJ45 Peter Bondra 6.00 15.00
GJ46 Peter Forsberg 12.00 30.00
GJ47 Mats Sundin 8.00 20.00
GJ48 Alexei Yashin 6.00 15.00
GJ49 Patrick Roy 20.00 50.00
GJ50 Markus Naslund 8.00 20.00
GJ51 Jay Bouwmeester 6.00 15.00
GJ52 Jason Spezza 12.50 30.00
GJ53 Stephen Weiss 6.00 15.00
GJ54 Ron Hainsey 6.00 15.00
GJ55 Jordan Leopold 6.00 15.00
GJ56 Chuck Kobasew 6.00 15.00
GJ57 Rick Nash 12.50 30.00
GJ58 Scottie Upshall 6.00 15.00

2002-03 Parkhurst Magnificent Inserts

This 10-card set featured game-used equipment from the career of Mario Lemieux. Cards MI1-MI5 had a print run of 40 copies each and cards MI6-MI10 were limited to just 10 copies each. Cards MI6-MI10 are not priced due to scarcity.
MI6-MI10 NOT PRICED DUE TO SCARCITY

MI1 2000-01 Season Jersey 30.00 80.00
MI2 1985-86 Season Jersey 30.00 80.00
MI3 2002 All-Star Game Jersey 30.0080.00
MI4 1987 Canada Cup Jersey 30.00 80.00
MI5 Dual Jersey 50.00 125.00
MI6 Number
MI7 Emblem
MI8 Triple Jersey
MI9 Quad Jersey
MI10 Complete Package

2002-03 Parkhurst Magnificent Inserts Autographs

This 10-card set paralleled the base Magnificent Inserts but carried certified autographs and each card was hand numbered. Cards MI1-MI5 were serial-numbered to 15 each and cards MI6-MI10 were serial numbered out of 5.
NOT PRICED DUE TO SCARCITY

2002-03 Parkhurst Mario's Mates

Limited to 25 sets, this 10-card set carried dual jersey swatches of Mario Lemieux and other top players.

MM1 M.Lemieux/P.Roy 75.00 200.00
MM2 M.Lemieux/S.Yzerman 60.00 150.00
MM3 M.Lemieux/J.Jagr 50.00 125.00
MM4 M.Lemieux/M.Brodeur 60.00 150.00
MM5 M.Lemieux/E.Lindros 40.00 100.00
MM6 M.Lemieux/R.Francis 30.00 80.00
MM7 M.Lemieux/M.Sundin 30.00 80.00
MM8 M.Lemieux/J.Sakic 60.00 150.00
MM9 M.Lemieux/P.Kariya 30.00 80.00
MM10 M.Lemieux/J.Theodore 40.00100.00

2002-03 Parkhurst Milestones

This 11-card set honored career highlights of several veteran players. Cards were limited to 60 copies each (except for the Roy card).
*MULT.COLOR SWATCH: .5X TO 1.25X

MS1 Jeremy Roenick 12.50 30.00
600 Assists
MS2 Martin Brodeur 20.00 50.00
MS3 Ed Belfour 10.00 25.00
60 Shutouts
MS4 Mike Richter 10.00 25.00
300 Wins
MS5 Jaromir Jagr 12.50 30.00
700 Assists
MS6 Vincent Damphousse 10.00 25.00
400 Goals
MS7 Ron Francis 10.00 25.00
1200 Assists
MS8 Mats Sundin 10.00 25.00
400 Goals
MS9 Peter Forsberg 20.00 50.00
600 Points
MS10 Pavel Bure 10.00 25.00
750 Points
MS11 Patrick Roy 30.00 80.00
1000 Games/33

2002-03 Parkhurst Patented Power

STATED PRINT RUN 20 SETS
NOT PRICED DUE TO SCARCITY
PP1 M.Lemieux/B.Shanahan
PP2 Steve Yzerman
Mats Sundin
PP3 Jaromir Jagr
Teemu Selanne
PP4 Paul Kariya
Jeremy Roenick
PP5 J.Sakic/M.Modano
PP6 Pavel Bure
Dany Heatley
PP7 Peter Forsberg
Sergei Fedorov
PP8 Eric Lindros
Todd Bertuzzi
PP9 Ilya Kovalchuk
Mark Messier
PP10 Brett Hull
Joe Thornton

2002-03 Parkhurst Reprints

This 150-card set of Parkhurst reprints picks up the numbering where the 2001-02 reprint set left off.

151 Floyd Curry 1.00 5.00
152 Billy Reay 1.00 5.00
153 Jim Henry 1.00 5.00
154 Ed Sandford 1.00 5.00
155 Pentti Lund 1.00 5.00
156 Al Dewsbury 1.00 5.00
157 Gerry McNeil 1.00 5.00
The Winning Goal
158 Jack Stewart 1.00 5.00
159 Alex Delvecchio 1.00 5.00
160 Sid Abel 1.00 5.00
161 Ray Timgren 1.00 5.00
162 Ed Kullman 1.00 5.00
163 Billy Reay 1.00 5.00
164 Floyd Curry 1.00 5.00
165 Al Dewsbury 1.00 5.00
166 Allan Stanley 1.00 5.00
167 Paul Ronty 1.00 5.00
168 Gaye Stewart 1.00 5.00
169 Al Rollins 1.00 5.00
170 Leo Boivin 1.00 5.00
171 George Gee 1.00 5.00
172 Ted Kennedy 1.00 5.00
173 Alex Delvecchio 1.00 5.00
174 Marcel Pronovost 1.00 5.00
175 Leo Boivin 1.00 5.00
176 Ted Kennedy 1.00 5.00
177 Ron Stewart 1.00 5.00
178 Bud MacPherson 1.00 5.00
179 Marcel Pronovost 1.00 5.00
180 Alex Delvecchio 1.00 5.00
181 Max Bentley 1.00 5.00
182 Andy Bathgate 1.00 5.00
183 Harry Howell 1.00 5.00
184 Allan Stanley 1.00 5.00
185 Ed Sandford 1.00 5.00
186 Bill Quackenbush 1.00 5.00
187 Eddie Mazur 1.00 5.00
188 Floyd Curry 1.00 5.00
189 Eric Nesterenko 1.00 5.00
190 Ron Stewart 1.00 5.00
191 Leo Boivin 1.00 5.00
192 Ted Kennedy 1.00 5.00
193 Alex Delvecchio 1.00 5.00
194 Bob Armstrong 1.00 5.00
195 Paul Ronty 1.00 5.00
196 Camille Henry 1.00 5.00
197 Al Rollins 1.00 5.00
198 Al Dewsbury 1.00 5.00
199 Netminders nightmare 1.00 5.00
200 Ron Stewart 1.00 5.00
201 Dick Duff 1.00 5.00
202 Lorne Chabot 1.00 5.00
203 Busher Jackson 1.00 5.00
204 Joe Primeau 1.00 5.00
205 Harold Cotton 1.00 5.00
206 King Clancy 1.00 5.00
207 Hap Day 1.00 5.00
208 Newsy Lalonde 1.00 5.00
209 Albert Leduc 1.00 5.00
210 Babe Siebert 1.00 5.00
211 Toe Blake 1.00 5.00
Coach
212 Claude Provost 1.00 5.00
213 Toe Blake 1.00 5.00
214 Charlie Hodge 1.00 5.00
215 Floyd Curry 1.00 5.00
216 Len Broderick 1.00 5.00
Canadiens on guard
217 Ed Chadwick 1.00 5.00
Geoffrion sidesteps Chadwick
218 George Armstrong 1.00 5.00
219 Dick Duff 1.00 5.00
220 Ron Stewart 1.00 5.00
221 Billy Harris 1.00 5.00
222 Bob Baun 1.00 5.00
223 Billy Reay 1.00 5.00
224 Billy Harris 1.00 5.00
225 Toe Blake 1.00 5.00
226 Bob Nevin 1.00 5.00
227 Bob Baun 1.00 5.00
228 Charlie Hodge 1.00 5.00
229 Allan Stanley 1.00 5.00
230 Billy Reay 1.00 5.00
231 Dick Duff 1.00 5.00
232 Marcel Bonin 1.00 5.00
233 Claude Provost 1.00 5.00
234 Canadiens on guard 1.00 5.00
235 E.Lach/R.Richard 1.00 5.00
236 Billy Harris 1.00 5.00
237 Punch Imlach 1.00 5.00
238 Charlie Hodge 1.00 5.00
239 Bob Baun 1.00 5.00
240 Ron Stewart 1.00 5.00
241 Toe Blake 1.00 5.00
242 Action around the net 1.00 5.00
243 Officials intervene 1.00 5.00
244 Frank Selke 1.00 5.00
General Manager
245 King Clancy 1.00 5.00
246 Ron Stewart 1.00 5.00
247 Bob Baun 1.00 5.00
248 Dick Duff 1.00 5.00
249 Billy Harris 1.00 5.00
250 Allan Stanley 1.00 5.00
251 Jacques Plante 1.00 5.00
252 Sid Abel 1.00 5.00
253 Norm Ullman 1.00 5.00
254 Marcel Pronovost 1.00 5.00
255 Alex Delvecchio 1.00 5.00
256 Marcel Bonin 1.00 5.00
257 Claude Provost 1.00 5.00
258 Ron Stewart 1.00 5.00
259 Bob Nevin 1.00 5.00
260 Bob Baun 1.00 5.00
261 Dick Duff 1.00 5.00
262 Billy Harris 1.00 5.00
263 Allan Stanley 1.00 5.00
264 Maurice Richard 1.00 5.00
265 Alex Delvecchio 1.00 5.00
266 Norm Ullman 1.00 5.00
267 Ed Litzenberger 1.00 5.00
268 Marcel Pronovost 1.00 5.00
269 Marcel Bonin 1.00 5.00
270 Billy Harris 1.00 5.00
271 Dick Duff 1.00 5.00
272 Bob Baun 1.00 5.00
273 Maurice Richard 1.00 5.00
274 Allan Stanley 1.00 5.00
275 Bob Nevin 1.00 5.00
276 Ed Litzenberger 1.00 5.00
277 Norm Ullman 1.00 5.00
278 Alex Delvecchio 1.00 5.00
279 Marcel Pronovost 1.00 5.00
280 Sid Abel 1.00 5.00
281 Claude Provost 1.00 5.00
282 J.C. Tremblay 1.00 5.00
283 Allan Stanley 1.00 5.00
284 Ed Litzenberger 1.00 5.00
285 Rocket Roars Through 1.00 5.00
286 Bob Nevin 1.00 5.00
287 Jacques Laperriere 1.00 5.00
288 J.C. Tremblay 1.00 5.00
289 John Ferguson 1.00 5.00
290 Toe Blake 1.00 5.00
291 Mael Pronovost 1.00 5.00
292 Alex Delvecchio 1.00 5.00
293 Allan Stanley 1.00 5.00
294 Dick Duff 1.00 5.00
295 Maurice Richard 1.00 5.00
296 Ron Stewart 1.00 5.00
297 J.C. Tremblay 1.00 5.00
298 John Ferguson 1.00 5.00
299 Toe Blake 1.00 5.00
300 Bill Quackenbush 1.00 5.00

2002-03 Parkhurst Stick and Jerseys

*STK/JSY: .5X TO 1.25X BASIC JERSEY
STATED PRINT RUN 90 SETS

2002-03 Parkhurst Teammates

This 20-card set featured three swatches of game jersey from players who were with the same club. Cards were limited to just 60 copies each.

TT1 Eric Lindros 12.50 30.00
Brian Leetch
Pavel Bure
TT2 John LeClair 12.50 30.00
Mark Recchi
Simon Gagne
TT3 Mats Sundin 12.50 30.00
Alexander Mogilny
Gary Roberts
TT4 Steve Yzerman 50.00 125.00
Brendan Shanahan
Sergei Fedorov
TT5 Brodeur/Stevens/Elias 20.00 50.00
TT6 Felix Potvin 12.50 30.00
Zigmund Palffy
Jason Allison
TT7 Saku Koivu 12.50 30.00
Jose Theodore
Craig Rivet
TT8 Joe Thornton 12.50 30.00
Sergei Samsonov
Kyle McLaren
TT9 Ilya Kovalchuk 20.00 50.00
Dany Heatley
Patrik Stefan
TT10 Mike Dunham 12.50 30.00
David Legwand
Scott Hartnell
TT11 Daniel Alfredsson 25.00 60.00
Marin Havlat
Marian Hossa
TT12 Miroslav Satan 12.50 30.00
Tim Connolly
J-P Dumont
TT13 Eric Daze 12.50 30.00
Jocelyn Thibault
Alexei Zhamnov
TT14 Mario Lemieux 30.00 80.00
Johan Hedberg
Alexei Kovalev
TT15 Owen Nolan 12.50 30.00
Teemu Selanne
Evgeni Nabokov
TT16 Chris Pronger 12.50 30.00
Al MacInnis
Doug Weight
TT17 Jaromir Jagr 12.50 30.00
Olaf Kolzig
Peter Bondra
TT18 Dan Cloutier 12.50 30.00
Todd Bertuzzi
Markus Naslund
TT19 Peter Forsberg 30.00 80.00
Joe Sakic
Patrick Roy
TT20 Sean Burke 12.50 30.00
Daniel Briere
Teppo Numminen

2002-03 Parkhurst Vintage Memorabilia

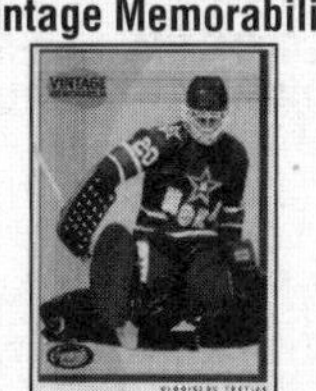

This 20-card set featured pieces of game-used equipment. Each card was limited to just 20 copies each. This set is not priced due to scarcity.

VM1 John Bucyk
VM2 Gilbert Perreault
VM3 Bobby Hull
VM4 Stan Mikita
VM5 Marcel Dionne
VM6 Jari Kurri
VM7 Jean Beliveau
VM8 Doug Harvey
VM9 Guy Lafleur
VM10 Frank Mahovlich
VM11 Henri Richard
VM12 Maurice Richard
VM13 Tiny Thompson
VM14 Bernie Parent
VM15 Tim Horton
VM16 Terry Sawchuk
VM17 Vladislav Tretiak
VM18 Gerry Cheevers
VM19 Ted Kennedy
VM20 Bill Gadsby

2002-03 Parkhurst Vintage Teammates

Limited to just 20 sets, this 20-card set featured dual game jersey swatches from retired greats who played for the same club. This set is not priced due to scarcity.

VT1 Brett Hull
Dennis Hull
VT2 Phil Esposito
Ed Giacomin
VT3 John Bucyk
Gerry Cheevers
VT4 Serge Savard
Larry Robinson
VT5 Tony Esposito
Stan Mikita
VT6 Terry Sawchuk
Sid Abel
VT7 Frank Mahovlich
Peter Mahovlich
VT8 Jean Beliveau
Doug Harvey
VT9 Guy Lafleur
Henri Richard
VT10 Bryan Trottier
Mike Bossy
VT11 Denis Potvin
Bob Nystrom
VT12 Bobby Clarke
Bill Barber
VT13 Bernie Parent
Dave Schultz
VT14 Tim Horton
Red Kelly
VT15 Valeri Kharlamov
Vladislav Tretiak
VT16 Bill Mosienko
Harry Lumley
VT17 Alex Delvecchio
Roger Crozier
VT18 Ace Bailey
King Clancy
VT19 Eddie Shore
Tiny Thompson
VT20 Lanny McDonald
Tiger Williams

2003-04 Parkhurst Toronto Spring Expo Rookie Preview

Inserted one in each "Super Box" available at the Toronto Spring Expo, this 20 -card set featured promising prospects and swatches of game-used jerseys.

PRP-1 Marc-Andre Fleury 30.00 80.00
PRP-2 Jordin Tootoo 15.00 40.00
PRP-3 Joni Pitkanen 12.50 30.00
PRP-4 Fedor Tyutin 8.00 20.00
PRP-5 Derek Roy 8.00 20.00
PRP-6 Nathan Horton 15.00 40.00
PRP-7 Eric Staal 20.00 50.00
PRP-8 Patrice Bergeron 25.00 60.00
PRP-9 Dustin Brown 10.00 25.00
PRP-10 Dan Hamhuis 10.00 25.00
PRP-11 Tim Gleason 8.00 20.00
PRP-12 Rastislav Stana 8.00 20.00
PRP-13 Matt Stajan 15.00 40.00
PRP-14 Matthew Lombardi 8.00 20.00
PRP-15 Nikolai Zherdev 25.00 60.00
PRP-16 Tuomo Ruutu 20.00 50.00
PRP-17 Ryan Malone 15.00 40.00
PRP-18 Antoine Vermette 8.00 20.00
PRP-19 Kari Lehtonen 30.00 80.00
PRP-20 Alexander Semin 40.00 80.00

2003-04 Parkhurst Original Six Boston

This 100-card set featured players from one of the Original Six teams in the NHL, Boston. The set was produced as a stand alone product.

COMPLETE SET (100) 25.00 50.00
1 P. J. Axelsson .15 .40
2 Michal Grosek .15 .40
3 Nick Boynton .15 .40
4 Jeff Jillson .15 .40

5 Felix Potvin .50 1.25
6 Patrick Leahy XRC .40 1.00
7 Joe Thornton .60 1.50
8 Ted Donato .15 .40
9 Hal Gill .15 .40
10 Jonathan Girard .15 .40
11 Rob Zamuner .15 .40
12 Shoane Morrisonn .15 .40
13 Martin Samuelsson .15 .40
14 Doug Doull XRC .15 .40
15 Ivan Huml .15 .40
16 Mike Knuble .15 .40
17 Kris Vernarsky .15 .40
18 Patrice Bergeron XRC 3.00 8.00
19 Sergei Zinovjev XRC .40 1.00
20 Martin Lapointe .15 .40
21 Dan McGillis .15 .40
22 Sandy McCarthy .15 .40
23 Glen Murray .15 .40
24 P.J. Stock .15 .40
25 Sean O'Donnell .15 .40
26 Andrew Raycroft .40 1.00
27 Brian Rolston .15 .40
28 Sergei Samsonov .40 1.00
29 Ian Moran .15 .40
30 Travis Green .15 .40
31 Adam Oates .40 1.00
32 Cam Neely .75 2.00
33 Jason Allison .15 .40
34 Dit Clapper .50 1.25
35 Fern Flaman .15 .40
36 John Bucyk .50 1.25
37 Milt Schmidt .50 1.25
38 Brad Park .50 1.25
39 Terry O'Reilly .50 1.25
40 Wayne Cashman .40 1.00
41 Ray Bourque .75 2.00
42 Allan Stanley .15 .40
43 Bernie Parent .60 1.50
44 Derek Sanderson .50 1.25
45 Bobby Orr 1.50 4.00
46 Tiny Thompson .60 1.50
47 Eddie Shore 1.00 2.50
48 Frank Brimsek .50 1.25
49 Jean Ratelle .50 1.25
50 Ken Hodge .40 1.00
51 Lionel Hitchman .15 .40
52 Phil Esposito .60 1.50
53 Rick Middleton .50 1.25
54 Terry Sawchuk .60 1.50
55 Woody Dumart .15 .40
56 Gerry Cheevers .60 1.50
57 Andy Moog .50 1.25
58 Byron Dafoe .40 1.00
59 Anson Carter .15 .40
60 Bill Guerin .40 1.00
61 Frank Brimsek .50 1.25
62 Bobby Orr 1.50 4.00
63 Eddie Shore 1.00 2.50
64 Dit Clapper .50 1.25
65 Cam Neely .75 2.00
66 Phil Esposito .60 1.50
67 Milt Schmidt .50 1.25
68 Johnny Bucyk .50 1.25
69 Woody Dumart .15 .40
70 Ray Bourque .75 2.00
71 Joe Thornton .60 1.50
72 Dit Clapper .50 1.25
73 Ray Bourque .75 2.00
74 Fern Flaman .15 .40
75 Johnny Bucyk .50 1.25
76 Milt Schmidt .50 1.25
77 Rick Middleton .50 1.25
78 Terry O'Reilly .50 1.25
79 Wayne Cashman .40 1.00
80 Lionel Hitchman .15 .40
81 Bobby Orr 1.50 4.00
82 Johnny Bucyk .50 1.25
83 Phil Esposito .60 1.50
84 Frank Brimsek .50 1.25
85 Fern Flaman .15 .40
86 Gerry Cheevers .60 1.50
87 Dit Clapper .50 1.25
88 Woody Dumart .15 .40
89 Eddie Shore 1.00 2.50
90 Milt Schmidt .50 1.25
91 Bobby Orr 1.50 4.00
92 Johnny Bucyk .50 1.25
93 Terry O'Reilly .50 1.25
94 Ray Bourque .75 2.00
95 Cam Neely .75 2.00
96 Phil Esposito .60 1.50
97 Bobby Orr 1.50 4.00
98 Cam Neely .75 2.00
99 Phil Esposito .60 1.50
100 Ray Bourque .75 2.00

2003-04 Parkhurst Original Six Boston Autographs

This 18-card set featured certified autographs of past Bruins greats. Print runs are listed below.

1 Ray Bourque/30 75.00 200.00
2 Johnny Bucyk/90 20.00 50.00
3 Wayne Cashman/85 20.00 50.00
4 Gerry Cheevers/90 30.00 80.00
5 Phil Esposito/55 50.00 125.00
6 Fern Flaman/85 25.00 60.00
7 Ken Hodge/90 20.00 50.00
8 Stan Jonathan/85 20.00 50.00
9 Rick Middleton/90 20.00 50.00
10 Andy Moog/90 25.00 60.00
11 Cam Neely/90 40.00 100.00
12 Terry O'Reilly/95 20.00 50.00
13 Bobby Orr/30 350.00 600.00
14 Bernie Parent/90 20.00 50.00
15 Brad Park/90 20.00 50.00
16 Jean Ratelle/90 25.00 60.00
17 Derek Sanderson/90 30.00 80.00
18 Milt Schmidt/85 30.00 80.00

2003-04 Parkhurst Original Six Boston Inserts

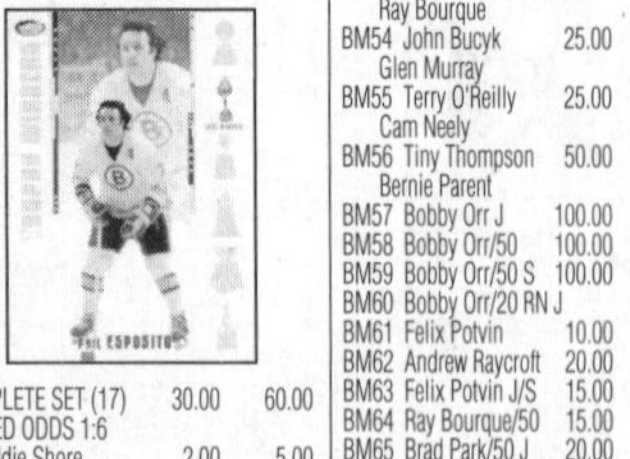

COMPLETE SET (17) 30.00 60.00
STATED ODDS 1:6
B1 Eddie Shore 2.00 5.00
B2 Milt Schmidt 1.50 4.00
B3 Dit Clapper 1.50 4.00
B4 Phil Esposito 2.00 5.00
B5 Johnny Bucyk 1.50 4.00
B6 Bobby Orr 3.00 8.00
B7 Eddie Shore 2.00 5.00
B8 Phil Esposito 2.00 5.00
B9 Milt Schmidt 1.50 4.00
B10 Phil Esposito 2.00 5.00
B11 Bobby Orr 3.00 8.00
B12 Ray Bourque 2.50 6.00
B13 Derek Sanderson 1.50 4.00
B14 Tiny Thompson 2.00 5.00
B15 Frank Brimsek 1.50 4.00
B16 Joe Thornton 2.00 5.00
B17 Ray Bourque 2.50 6.00

2003-04 Parkhurst Original Six Boston Memorabilia

This 67-card set featured memorabilia from past and present Bruins players. Cards BM1-13 and BM61-62 were single jerseys and were limited to 100 copies sets. Cards BM14-18 and BM63 were jersey/stick combos and were limited to 80 sets. Cards BM19-20 were game gear inserts and print runs are listed below. Cards BM21-26, BM58 and BM64 were vintage memorabilia cards and print runs are listed below. Cards BM27-34, BM57 and BM65-67 were vintage jersey cards and were limited to 50 copies each. Cards BM35-39 and BM59 were vintage stick cards and print runs are listed below. Cards BM39-40 and BM60 are retired numbers cards and were limited to 20 copies. Cards BM51-56 were grouped into a subset known as Original Six Shooters, players who have scored high career totals against original six teams. The shooters cards were limited to 100 copies each. Cards BM51-56 were dual-jersey cards and were limited to 100 copies each.

PRINT RUNS UNDER 25 NOT
PRICED DUE TO SCARCITY
BM1 Brian Rolston 10.00 25.00
BM2 Sergei Samsonov 6.00 15.00
BM3 Martin Lapointe 6.00 15.00
BM4 Don Sweeny 6.00 15.00
BM5 Nick Boynton 6.00 15.00
BM6 Joe Thornton 20.00 50.00
BM7 Jeff Hackett 6.00 15.00
BM8 Ivan Huml 6.00 15.00
BM9 Steve Shields 8.00 20.00
BM10 Glen Murray 6.00 15.00
BM11 Shaone Morrisonn 6.00 15.00
BM12 Bryan Berard 8.00 20.00
BM13 Mike Knuble 6.00 15.00
BM14 Bryan Berard J/S 15.00 40.00
BM15 Sergei Samsonov J/S 15.00 40.00
BM16 Joe Thornton J/S/50 30.00 80.00
BM17 Jeff Hackett J/S 10.00 25.00
BM18 Steve Shields J/S 12.50 30.00
BM19 Joe Thornton/20
BM20 S.Samsonov/50 Glove 15.00 40.00
BM21 Tiny Thompson/20
BM22 Gilles Gilbert/50 15.00 40.00
BM23 Gerry Cheevers/50 Pad 30.00 80.00
BM24 Eddie Shore/20 Glove
BM25 Eddie Shore/60 Pants 20.00 50.00
BM26 Frank Brimsek/20
BM27 John Bucyk J 20.00 50.00
BM28 Gerry Cheevers J 20.00 50.00
BM29 Andy Moog J 25.00 60.00
BM30 Gilles Gilbert J 20.00 50.00
BM31 Jason Allison J 20.00 50.00
BM32 Cam Neely J 30.00 80.00
BM33 Phil Esposito J 20.00 50.00
BM34 Adam Oates J 20.00 50.00
BM35 Phil Esposito/30 S 15.00 40.00
BM36 Ray Bourque/50 S 30.00 80.00
BM37 John Bucyk/20 S
BM38 Gerry Cheevers/50 S 15.00 40.00
BM39 Eddie Shore/20 RN J
BM40 Cam Neely/20 RN J
BM41 Mario Lemieux SS 15.00 40.00
BM42 Ron Francis SS 6.00 15.00
BM43 Joe Sakic SS 12.50 30.00
BM44 Brett Hull SS 8.00 20.00
BM45 Jaromir Jagr SS 8.00 20.00
BM46 Mike Modano SS 8.00 20.00
BM47 Teemu Selanne SS 6.00 15.00
BM48 Pavel Bure SS 6.00 15.00
BM49 Paul Kariya SS 8.00 20.00
BM50 Peter Forsberg SS 10.00 25.00
BM51 Gerry Cheevers 20.00 50.00
Felix Potvin
BM52 Phil Esposito 40.00 100.00
Joe Thornton
BM53 Bobby Orr 100.00 250.00
Ray Bourque
BM54 John Bucyk 25.00 60.00
Glen Murray
BM55 Terry O'Reilly 25.00 60.00
Cam Neely
BM56 Tiny Thompson 50.00 125.00
Bernie Parent
BM57 Bobby Orr J 100.00 250.00
BM58 Bobby Orr/50 100.00 250.00
BM59 Bobby Orr/50 S 100.00 250.00
BM60 Bobby Orr/20 RN J
BM61 Felix Potvin 10.00 25.00
BM62 Andrew Raycroft 20.00 50.00
BM63 Felix Potvin J/S 15.00 40.00
BM64 Ray Bourque/50 15.00 40.00
BM65 Brad Park/50 J 20.00 50.00
BM66 Ray Bourque/50 J 20.00 50.00
BM67 Terry O'Reilly/50 J 20.00 50.00

2003-04 Parkhurst Original Six Chicago

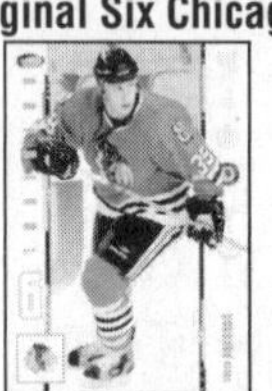

This 100-card set featured players from one of the Original Six teams in the NHL, Chicago. The set was produced as a stand alone product.

COMPLETE SET 25.00 50.00
1 Tyler Arnason .40 1.00
2 Mark Bell .15 .40
3 Deron Quint .15 .40
4 Kyle Calder .15 .40
5 Bryan Berard .15 .40
6 Eric Daze .40 1.00
7 Jason Strudwick .15 .40
8 Nathan Dempsey .15 .40
9 Jon Klemm .15 .40
10 Igor Korolev .15 .40
11 Pavel Vorobiev XRC 1.50 4.00
12 Scott Nichol .15 .40
13 Alexander Karpovtsev .15 .40
14 Tuomo Ruutu XRC 3.00 8.00
15 Ville Nieminen .15 .40
16 Steve McCarthy .15 .40
17 Igor Radulov .15 .40
18 Alexei Zhamnov .15 .40
19 Burke Henry .15 .40
20 Craig Andersson .15 .40
21 Steve Passmore .40 1.00
22 Lasse Kukkonen XRC 1.50 4.00
23 Steve Poapst .15 .40
24 Michael Leighton .40 1.00
25 Shawn Thornton .15 .40
26 Brett McLean .15 .40
27 Steve Sullivan .15 .40
28 Jocelyn Thibault .40 1.00
29 Travis Moen XRC 1.50 4.00
30 Ryan Vandenbussche .15 .40
31 Chris Chelios .50 1.25
32 Dominik Hasek .75 2.00
33 Jeremy Roenick .60 1.50
34 Ed Belfour .50 1.25
35 Doug Gilmour .40 1.00
36 Charlie Gardiner .40 1.00
37 Howie Morenz .75 2.00
38 Steve Larmer .15 .40
39 Dirk Graham .15 .40
40 Ken Wharram .40 1.00
41 Pat Stapleton .15 .40
42 Pierre Pilote .40 1.00
43 Bobby Hull 1.25 3.00
44 Tony Amonte .40 1.00
45 Stan Mikita .60 1.50
46 Dennis Hull .60 1.50
47 Denis Savard .75 2.00
48 Doug Wilson .15 .40
49 Bobby Orr 1.50 4.00
50 Glenn Hall .75 2.00
51 Harry Lumley .50 1.25
52 Bill Mosienko .50 1.25
53 Ken Hodge .40 1.00
54 Michel Goulet .50 1.25
55 Keith Magnuson .75 2.00
56 Ted Lindsay .50 1.25
57 Bill Gadsby .40 1.00
58 Darren Pang .50 1.25
59 Tony Esposito .75 2.00
60 Phil Esposito .60 1.50
61 Glenn Hall .75 2.00
62 Ed Belfour .50 1.25
63 Charlie Gardiner .40 1.00
64 Tony Esposito .75 2.00
65 Stan Mikita .60 1.50
66 Bobby Hull 1.25 3.00
67 Pierre Pilote .40 1.00
68 Doug Wilson .15 .40
69 Chris Chelios .50 1.25
70 Ken Wharram .40 1.00
71 Alexei Zhamnov .15 .40
72 Chris Chelios .50 1.25
73 Doug Gilmour .40 1.00
74 Bill Gadsby .40 1.00
75 Denis Savard .75 2.00
76 Tony Amonte .40 1.00
77 Dirk Graham .15 .40
78 Stan Mikita .60 1.50
79 Ed Litzenberger .60 1.50
80 Pierre Pilote .40 1.00
81 Denis Savard .75 2.00
82 Pierre Pilote .40 1.00
83 Stan Mikita .60 1.50
84 Bill Mosienko .50 1.25
85 Glenn Hall .75 2.00
86 Bobby Hull 1.25 3.00
87 Phil Esposito .60 1.50
88 Tony Esposito .75 2.00
89 Bill Gadsby .40 1.00
90 Michel Goulet .50 1.25
91 Bobby Hull MS 1.25 3.00
92 Stan Mikita .60 1.50
93 Stan Mikita .60 1.50
94 Tony Esposito .75 2.00
95 Bobby Hull 1.25 3.00
96 Denis Savard .75 2.00
97 Tony Esposito 1.25 3.00
98 Ed Belfour .50 1.25
99 Chris Chelios .50 1.25
100 Steve Larmer .75 2.00

2003-04 Parkhurst Original Six Chicago Autographs

This 18-card set featured certified autographs of past Blackhawks greats. Print runs are listed below.

STATED PRINT RUNS LISTED BELOW
1 Phil Esposito/55 50.00 125.00
2 Tony Esposito/85 30.00 80.00
3 Michel Goulet/90 20.00 50.00
4 Dirk Graham/90 15.00 40.00
5 Glenn Hall/85 60.00 150.00
6 Ken Hodge/89 20.00 50.00
7 Bobby Hull/75 60.00 150.00
8 Steve Larmer/85 40.00 80.00
9 Ted Lindsay/90 20.00 50.00
10 Eddie Litzenberger/90 20.00 50.00
11 Keith Magnuson/99 40.00 80.00
12 Stan Mikita/80 20.00 50.00
13 Darren Pang/99 15.00 40.00
14 Pierre Pilote/85 20.00 50.00
15 Denis Savard/90 25.00 60.00
16 Ken Wharram/90 30.00 80.00
17 Doug Wilson/90 25.00 60.00

2003-04 Parkhurst Original Six Chicago Inserts

COMPLETE SET (16) 30.00 60.00
C1 Stan Mikita 2.50 6.00
C2 Bobby Hull 2.50 6.00
C3 Tony Esposito 2.00 5.00
C4 Glenn Hall 1.50 4.00
C5 Denis Savard 2.00 5.00
C6 Bobby Hull 2.50 6.00
C7 Ed Belfour 1.50 4.00
C8 Tony Esposito 2.00 5.00
C9 Glenn Hall 1.50 4.00
C10 Tony Esposito 2.00 5.00
C11 Stan Mikita 2.50 6.00
C12 Bobby Hull 2.50 6.00
C13 Pierre Pilote 1.50 4.00
C14 Charlie Gardiner 1.50 4.00
C15 Jeremy Roenick 2.00 5.00
C16 Denis Savard 2.00 5.00

2003-04 Parkhurst Original Six Chicago Memorabilia

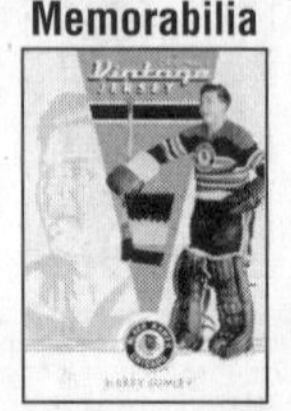

This 62-card set featured memorabilia from past and present Blackhawks players. Cards CM1-9 were single jerseys and were limited to 100 copies sets. Cards CM10-13 were jersey/stick combos and were limited to 80 sets. Cards CM15-18 were vintage memorabilia cards and were limited to 20 copies each. Cards CM19-30 and CM59-62 were vintage jersey cards and print runs are listed below. Cards CM31-36 were vintage stick cards and print runs are listed below. Cards CM37-40 were retired numbers cards and were limited to 20 copies. Cards CM41-50 were grouped into a subset known as Original Six Shooters; players who have scored high career totals against original six teams. The shooters cards were limited to 100 copies each. Cards CM51-58 were dual-jersey cards and were limited to 100 copies each.

PRINT RUNS UNDER 25 NOT
PRICED DUE TO SCARCITY
CM1 Jocelyn Thibault 10.00 25.00
CM2 Steve Sullivan 10.00 25.00
CM3 Eric Daze 6.00 15.00
CM4 Alexei Zhamnov 6.00 15.00
CM5 Mark Bell 6.00 15.00
CM6 Steve McCarthy 6.00 15.00
CM7 Tyler Arnason 6.00 15.00
CM8 Steve Passmore 10.00 25.00
CM9 Ryan Vandenbussche 6.00 15.00
CM10 Jocelyn Thibault J/S 20.00 50.00
CM11 Steve Sullivan J/S 20.00 50.00
CM12 Eric Daze J/S 12.50 30.00
CM13 Alexei Zhamnov J/S 12.50 30.00
CM14 Jocelyn Thibault/50 40.00 100.00
CM15 Tony Esposito
CM16 Bill Mosienko Pants
CM17 Chuck Gardiner Pad
CM18 Harry Lumley
CM19 Frank Brimsek/20 J
CM20 Ed Belfour/100 J 15.00 40.00
CM21 Jeremy Roenick/100 J 15.00 40.00
CM22 Tony Amonte/100 J 15.00 40.00
CM23 Bill Mosienko/60 J 25.00 60.00
CM24 Michel Goulet/100 J 15.00 40.00
CM25 Bobby Hull/50 J 25.00 60.00
CM26 Dennis Hull/60 J 15.00 40.00
CM27 Glenn Hall/50 J 20.00 50.00
CM28 Tony Esposito/50 J 25.00 60.00
CM29 Harry Lumley/50 J 20.00 50.00
CM30 Stan Mikita/50 J 25.00 60.00
CM31 Bobby Hull/50 S 30.00 80.00
CM32 Tony Esposito/60 S 25.00 60.00
CM33 Glenn Hall/60 S 15.00 40.00
CM34 Michel Goulet/70 S 10.00 25.00
CM35 Tony Amonte/70 S 10.00 25.00
CM36 Jeremy Roenick/70 S 10.00 25.00
CM37 Stan Mikita/20 RN
CM38 Bobby Hull/20 RN
CM39 Tony Esposito/20 RN
CM40 Glenn Hall/20 RN
CM41 Mario Lemieux SS 15.00 40.00
CM42 Ron Francis SS 6.00 15.00
CM43 Joe Sakic SS 10.00 25.00
CM44 Brett Hull SS 8.00 20.00
CM45 Jaromir Jagr SS 8.00 20.00
CM46 Mike Modano SS 8.00 20.00
CM47 Teemu Selanne SS 6.00 15.00
CM48 Pavel Bure SS 6.00 15.00
CM49 Paul Kariya SS 8.00 20.00
CM50 Peter Forsberg SS 10.00 25.00
CM51 Glenn Hall 12.50 30.00
Tony Esposito
CM52 Bobby Hull 25.00 60.00
Jeremy Roenick
CM53 Stan Mikita 15.00 40.00
Tony Amonte
CM54 Harry Lumley 12.50 30.00
Jocelyn Thibault
CM55 Michel Goulet 15.00 40.00
Eric Daze
CM56 Bill Mosienko 12.50 30.00
Steve Sullivan
CM57 Frank Brimsek 12.50 30.00
Ed Belfour
CM58 Dennis Hull 15.00 40.00
Alexei Zhamnov
CM59 Chris Chelios/100 J 15.00 40.00
CM60 Jeff Hackett/100 J 15.00 40.00
CM61 Bob Probert/100 J 20.00 50.00
CM62 Denis Savard/100 J 20.00 50.00

2003-04 Parkhurst Original Six Detroit

This 100-card set featured players from one of the Original Six teams in the NHL, Detroit. The set was produced as a stand alone product.

COMPLETE SET (100) 25.00 50.00
1 Mathieu Schneider .15 .40
2 Chris Chelios .40 1.00
3 Mathieu Dandenault .15 .40
4 Pavel Datsyuk .60 1.50
5 Boyd Devereaux .15 .40
6 Kris Draper .15 .40
7 Jason Woolley .15 .40
8 Mark Mowers .15 .40
9 Ray Whitney .15 .40
10 Jiri Fischer .15 .40
11 Tomas Holmstrom .15 .40
12 Brett Hull .60 1.50
13 Curtis Joseph .50 1.25
14 Jamie Rivers .15 .40
15 Dominik Hasek .75 2.00
16 Henrik Zetterberg .60 1.50
17 Steve Thomas .15 .40
18 Manny Legace .40 1.00
19 Nicklas Lidstrom .50 1.25
20 Kirk Maltby .15 .40
21 Darren McCarty .15 .40
22 Jiri Hudler XRC 2.00 5.00
23 Brendan Shanahan .50 1.25
24 Marc Lamothe .40 1.00
25 Derian Hatcher .15 .40
26 Jason Williams .15 .40
27 Steve Yzerman 2.00 4.00
28 Michel Picard .15 .40
29 Derek King .15 .40
30 Dmitri Bykov .15 .40
31 Bob Probert .15 .40
32 Chris Osgood .40 1.00
33 Mike Vernon .40 1.00
34 Adam Oates .40 1.00
35 Terry Sawchuk .50 1.25
36 Alex Delvecchio .50 1.25
37 Danny Gare .15 .40
38 Marcel Dionne .50 1.25
39 Mickey Redmond .40 1.00
40 Ted Lindsay .40 1.00
41 Sid Abel .40 1.00
42 Red Kelly .40 1.00
43 Reed Larson .15 .40
44 Ebbie Goodfellow .15 .40
45 Bill Gadsby .40 1.00
46 Dino Ciccarelli .40 1.00
47 Glenn Hall .50 1.25
48 John Bucyk .50 1.25
49 Brad Smith .40 1.00
50 Norm Ullman .40 1.00
51 Marcel Pronovost .15 .40
52 Roger Crozier .50 1.25
53 Brad Park .50 1.25
54 Keith Primeau .50 1.25
55 Adam Graves .40 1.00
56 Ed Giacomin .50 1.25
57 Pat Verbeek .40 1.00
58 Harry Lumley .40 1.00
59 Gary Bergman .15 .40
60 Gerard Gallant .15 .40
61 Terry Sawchuk AS .50 1.25
62 Glenn Hall AS .50 1.25
63 Red Kelly AS .40 1.00
64 Nicklas Lidstrom AS .50 1.25
65 Marcel Pronovost AS .15 .40
66 Ted Lindsay AS .40 1.00
67 Sid Abel AS .40 1.00
68 Steve Yzerman AS .75 2.00
69 Brendan Shanahan AS .50 1.25
70 Alex Delvecchio AS .50 1.25
71 Steve Yzerman C .75 2.00
72 Alex Delvecchio C .50 1.25
73 Danny Gare C .15 .40
74 Marcel Dionne C .50 1.25
75 Mickey Redmond C .40 1.00
76 Ted Lindsay C .40 1.00
77 Sid Abel C .40 1.00
78 Red Kelly C .40 1.00
79 Reed Larson C .15 .40
80 Ebbie Goodfellow C .15 .40
81 Sid Abel E .40 1.00
82 Alex Delvecchio E .50 1.25
83 Ed Giacomin E .50 1.25
84 Red Kelly E .40 1.00
85 Ted Lindsay E .40 1.00
86 Marcel Pronovost E .15 .40
87 Terry Sawchuk E .50 1.25
88 Norm Ullman E .40 1.00
89 Bill Gadsby E .40 1.00
90 Glenn Hall E .50 1.25
91 Steve Yzerman .75 2.00
goals in a season
92 Steve Yzerman .75 2.00
points in a season
93 Steve Yzerman .75 2.00
assists in a season
94 Terry Sawchuk .50 1.25
career wins
95 Terry Sawchuk .50 1.25
career shutouts
96 Steve Yzerman .75 2.00
career playoff points
97 Sergei Fedorov .30 .75
career playoff assists
98 Nicklas Lidstrom .50 1.25
career points by a defenseman
99 Marcel Dionne .50 1.25
rookie assists in a season
100 Alex Delvecchio .50 1.25
career games by a centerman

2003-04 Parkhurst Original Six Detroit Autographs

This 18-card set featured certified autographs of past Red Wings greats. Print runs are listed below.

PRINT RUNS LISTED BELOW
OS-GG Gerard Gallant/90 20.00 50.00
OS-DC Dino Ciccarelli/85 20.00 50.00
OS-RK Red Kelly/80 30.00 80.00
OS-BS Brad Smith/90 15.00 40.00
OS-RL Reed Larson/98 15.00 40.00
OS-MD Marcel Dionne/75 25.00 60.00
OS-NU Norm Ullman/85 15.00 40.00
OS-DG Danny Gare/90 15.00 40.00
OS-MP Marcel Pronovost/88 15.00 40.00
OS-TL Ted Lindsay/90 30.00 80.00
OS-JB John Bucyk/80 30.00 80.00
OS-BG Bill Gadsby/90 15.00 40.00
OS-AD Alex Delvecchio/90 30.00 80.00
OS-GH Glenn Hall/80 40.00 100.00

2003-04 Parkhurst Original Six Detroit Inserts

COMPLETE SET (18) 30.00 60.00
STATED ODDS 1:6

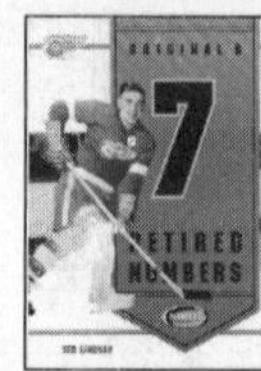

D-1 Terry Sawchuk 2.00 5.00
D-2 Ted Lindsay 1.50 4.00
D-3 Alex Delvecchio 2.00 5.00
D-4 Sid Abel 1.50 4.00
D-5 Ted Lindsay 1.50 4.00
D-6 Sid Abel 1.50 4.00
D-7 Terry Sawchuk 2.00 5.00
D-8 Red Kelly 1.50 4.00
D-9 Glenn Hall 2.00 5.00
D-10 Roger Crozier 2.00 5.00
D-11 Alex Delvecchio 2.00 5.00
D-12 Red Kelly 1.50 4.00
D-13 Nicklas Lidstrom 2.00 5.00
D-14 Steve Yzerman 3.00 8.00
D-15 Steve Yzerman 3.00 8.00
D-16 Keith Primeau 1.50 4.00
D-17 Marcel Dionne 2.00 5.00
D-18 Martin Lapointe 1.50 4.00

2003-04 Parkhurst Original Six Detroit Memorabilia

This 63-card set featured memorabilia from past and present Red Wings players. Cards DM1-13 and DM57-59 were single jerseys and were limited to 100 copies sets. Cards DM14-19 and DM60-62 were jersey/stick combos and were limited to 80 sets. Cards DM20-25 were memorabilia cards and were limited to 20 copies each. Cards DM26-33 were vintage jersey cards and print runs are listed below. Cards DM34-36 were vintage stick cards and print runs are listed below. Cards DM37-40 were retired numbers cards and were limited to 20 copies. Cards DM41-50 were grouped into a subset known as Original Six Shooters; players who have scored high career totals against original six teams. The shooters cards were limited to 100 copies each. Cards DM51-56 were dual-jersey cards and were limited to 100 copies each.

PRINT RUNS UNDER 25 NOT
PRICE DUE TO SCARCITY
DM1 Nicklas Lidstrom 10.00 25.00
DM2 Brendan Shanahan 10.00 25.00
DM3 Sergei Fedorov 15.00 40.00
DM4 Luc Robitaille 12.50 30.00
DM5 Steve Yzerman 20.00 50.00
DM6 Manny Legace 10.00 25.00
DM7 Mathieu Dandenault 6.00 15.00
DM8 Jiri Fischer 10.00 25.00
DM9 Darren McCarty 12.00 30.00
DM10 Pavel Datsyuk 15.00 40.00
DM11 Brett Hull 12.50 30.00
DM12 Igor Larionov 15.00 40.00
DM13 Chris Chelios 12.50 30.00
DM14 Nicklas Lidstrom J/S 15.00 40.00
DM15 Steve Yzerman J/S 40.00 80.00
DM16 Luc Robitaille J/S 15.00 40.00
DM17 Brendan Shanahan J/S 15.00 40.00
DM18 Sergei Fedorov J/S 20.00 50.00
DM19 Brett Hull J/S 15.00 40.00
DM20 Sergei Fedorov Glove
DM21 Henrik Zetterberg Skate
DM22 Pavel Datsyuk Skate
DM23 Bill Gadsby/50 Glove
DM24 Roger Crozier/20 Pad
DM25 Terry Sawchuk/20 Glove
DM26 Sid Abel/40 J 40.00 100.00
DM27 Dino Ciccarelli/60 J 20.00 50.00
DM28 Alex Delvecchio/60 J 20.00 50.00
DM29 Terry Sawchuk/20 J
DM30 Ted Lindsay/20 J
DM31 Chris Osgood/80 J 12.50 30.00
DM32 Keith Primeau/80 J 12.50 30.00
DM33 Roger Crozier/50 J
DM34 Terry Sawchuk/20 S
DM35 Dino Ciccarelli/60 S 12.50 30.00
DM36 Ed Giacomin/60 S 25.00 60.00
DM37 T.Sawchuk/20 RN J
DM38 A.Delvecchio/20 RN J
DM39 S.Abel/20 RN J
DM40 T.Lindsay/20 RN J
DM41 Mario Lemieux SS 15.00 40.00
DM42 Ron Francis SS 6.00 15.00
DM43 Joe Sakic SS 10.00 25.00
DM44 Brett Hull SS 10.00 25.00
DM45 Jaromir Jagr SS 8.00 20.00
DM46 Mike Modano SS 8.00 20.00
DM47 Teemu Selanne SS 6.00 15.00
DM48 Pavel Bure SS 6.00 15.00
DM49 Paul Kariya SS 8.00 20.00
DM50 Peter Forsberg SS 10.00 25.00
DM51 Lindsay/Hull 20.00 50.00
DM52 Sawchuk/Hasek 30.00 80.00
DM53 Abel/Yzerman 25.00 60.00
DM54 Delvecchio/Shanahan 20.00 50.00
DM55 Ciccarelli/Datsyuk 20.00 50.00
DM56 Crozier/Osgood 15.00 40.00
DM57 Henrik Zetterberg 15.00 40.00
DM58 Dominik Hasek 15.00 40.00
DM59 Manny Legace 15.00 40.00
DM60 Henrik Zetterberg J/S 30.00 80
DM61 Pavel Datsyuk J/S 25.00 60
DM62 Dominik Hasek J/S 20.00 50
DM63 Mike Vernon/100 J 15.00 40

2003-04 Parkhurs[t] Original Six He Shoots-He Scores Prizes

Available only by redeeming Parkh[urst] Original Six HSHS points, this 60-card featured dual-swatches of players, past present, who played for the same origina[l] team. The popularity of the program cau[sed] ITG to produce an extra 30 cards, diffe[rent] from the original 30 available. Those ac[...] cards are denoted by an "A" suffix below.

PRINT RUN 20 SETS
NOT PRICED DUE TO SCARCITY
1 E.Belfour/C.Joseph
1A E.Belfour/C.Joseph
2 M.Sundin/D.Sittler
2A M.Sundin/D.Sittler
3 A.Mogilny/L.McDonald
3A A.Mogilny/L.McDonald
4 O.Nolan/W.Clark
4A O.Nolan/W.Clark
5 B.McCabe/B.Salming
5A B.McCabe/B.Salming
6 T.Domi/T.Williams
6A T.Domi/T.Williams
7 M.Garon/G.Worsley
7A M.Garon/G.Worsley
8 S.Koivu/J.Beliveau
8A S.Koivu/J.Beliveau
9 J.Theodore/P.Roy
9A J.Theodore/P.Roy
10 S.Quintal/D.Harvey
10A S.Quintal/D.Harvey
11 G.Lafleur/M.Richard
11A G.Lafleur/M.Richard
12 P.Roy/J.Plante
12A P.Roy/J.Plante
13 J.Thornton/P.Esposito
13A J.Thornton/P.Esposito
14 A.Raycroft/G.Cheevers
14A A.Raycroft/G.Cheevers
15 S.Samsonov/C.Neely
15A S.Samsonov/C.Neely
16 B.Orr/E.Shore
16A B.Orr/E.Shore
17 R.Bourque/B.Orr
17A R.Bourque/B.Orr
18 P.Bergeron/C.Neely
18A P.Bergeron/C.Neely
19 J.Thibault/T.Esposito
19A J.Thibault/T.Esposito
20 T.Arnason/S.Mikita
20A T. Arnason/S.Mikita
21 E.Daze/Bo.Hull
21A E.Daze/Bo.Hull
22 M.Messier/P.Esposito
22A M.Messier/P.Esposito
23 E.Lindros/R.Gilbert
23A E.Lindros/R.Gilbert
24 A.Kovalev/J.Ratelle
24A A.Kovalev/J.Ratelle
25 Curtis Joseph
Roger Crozier
25A C.Joseph/R.Crozier
26 D.Hasek/T.Sawchuk
26A D.Hasek/T.Sawchuk
27 S.Yzerman/T.Lindsay
27A S.Yzerman/T.Lindsay
28 Br.Hull/A.Delvecchio
28A Br.Hull/A.Delvecchio
29 N.Lidstrom/B.Gadsby
29A N.Lidstrom/B.Gadsby
30 P.Datsyuk/S.Abel
30A P.Datsyuk/S.Abel

2003-04 Parkhurs[t] Original Six Montreal

This 100-card set featured players from[...] of the Original Six teams in the N[HL,] Montreal. The set was produced as a s[tand] alone product.

COMPLETE SET (100) 25.00 50[.00]
COMP. SET w/o SP's
1 Tomas Plekanec XRC .15
2 Jose Theodore .60 1
3 Ron Hainsey .15
4 Patrice Brisebois .15
5 Jan Bulis .15
6 Niklas Sundstrom .15
7 Steve Begin .15
8 Andreas Dackell .15
9 Karl Dykhuis .15
10 Michael Ryder .60 1
11 Jason Ward .15

12 Benoit Gratton .15 .40
13 Chistopher Higgins XRC .75 2.00
14 Craig Rivet .15 .40
15 Marcel Hossa .50 1.25
16 Joe Juneau .15 .40
17 Chad Kilger .15 .40
18 Saku Koivu .50 1.25
19 Sheldon Souray .15 .40
20 Andrei Markov .15 .40
21 Olivier Michaud .15 .40
22 Mathieu Garon .15 .40
23 Yanic Perreault .15 .40
24 Francis Bouillon .15 .40
25 Mike Ribeiro .15 .40
26 Stephane Quintal .15 .40
27 Richard Zednik .15 .40
28 Darren Langdon .15 .40
29 Mike Komisarek .15 .40
30 Pierre Dagenais .15 .40
31 Chris Chelios .50 1.25
32 John LeClair .50 1.25
33 Mark Recchi .40 1.00
34 Rejean Houle .15 .40
35 Howie Morenz .40 1.00
36 Jacques Laperriere .15 .40
37 Elmer Lach .40 1.00
38 Yvan Cournoyer .50 1.25
39 Larry Robinson .50 1.25
40 Serge Savard .50 1.25
41 Butch Bouchard .15 .40
42 Guy Lafleur 1.00 2.50
43 Henri Richard .50 1.25
44 Jean Beliveau .60 1.50
45 Maurice Richard 1.50 4.00
46 Toe Blake .50 1.25
47 Guy Lapointe .15 .40
48 Gump Worsley .75 2.00
49 Patrick Roy 1.50 4.00
50 Rogie Vachon .40 1.00
51 Bill Durnan .40 1.00
52 John Ferguson .40 1.00
53 Georges Vezina 1.25 3.00
54 Denis Savard .40 1.00
55 Dollard St-Laurent .15 .40
56 Jean-Guy Talbot .15 .40
57 Steve Shutt .40 1.00
58 Frank Mahovlich .50 1.25
59 Jacques Plante 1.00 2.50
60 Dickie Moore .40 1.00
61 Howie Morenz .40 1.00
62 Maurice Richard 1.50 4.00
63 Jean Beliveau .60 1.50
64 Elmer Lach .40 1.00
65 Henri Richard .50 1.25
66 Doug Harvey .50 1.25
67 Jacques Plante 1.00 2.50
68 Larry Robinson .50 1.25
69 Patrick Roy 1.50 4.00
70 Guy Lafleur 1.00 2.50
71 Saku Koivu .50 1.25
72 Butch Bouchard .15 .40
73 Vincent Damphousse .15 .40
74 Henri Richard .50 1.25
75 Jean Beliveau .60 1.50
76 Maurice Richard 1.50 4.00
77 Newsy Lalonde .15 .40
78 Yvan Cournoyer .50 1.25
79 Doug Harvey .50 1.25
80 Serge Savard .50 1.25
81 Howie Morenz .40 1.00
82 Georges Vezina 1.25 3.00
83 Elmer Lach .40 1.00
84 Maurice Richard 1.50 4.00
85 Jean Beliveau .60 1.50
86 Yvan Cournoyer .50 1.25
87 Doug Harvey .50 1.25
88 Guy Lafleur 1.00 2.50
89 Larry Robinson .50 1.25
90 Henri Richard .50 1.25
91 Henri Richard .50 1.25
92 Maurice Richard 1.50 4.00
93 Guy Lafleur 1.00 2.50
94 Guy Lafleur 1.00 2.50
95 Jacques Plante 1.00 2.50
96 Steve Shutt .40 1.00
97 Jean Beliveau .60 1.50
98 Larry Robinson .50 1.25
99 Patrick Roy 1.50 4.00
100 Maurice Richard 1.50 4.00

2003-04 Parkhurst Original Six Montreal Autographs

This 18-card set featured certified autographs of past Canadiens greats. Print runs are listed below.

PRINT RUNS LISTED BELOW
1 Jean Beliveau/85 30.00 80.00
2 Butch Bouchard/85 20.00 50.00
3 Yvan Cournoyer/85 25.00 60.00
4 John Ferguson/90 20.00 50.00
5 Charlie Hodge/85 20.00 50.00
6 Rejean Houle/85 20.00 50.00
7 Elmer Lach/90 25.00 60.00
8 Guy Lafleur/85 40.00 100.00
9 Jacques Laperriere/85 20.00 50.00
10 Frank Mahovlich/90 20.00 50.00
11 Dickie Moore/85 20.00 50.00
12 Henri Richard/85 25.00 60.00
13 Larry Robinson/85 30.00 80.00
14 Denis Savard/90 20.00 50.00
15 Serge Savard/85 25.00 60.00
16 Steve Shutt/85 20.00 50.00
17 Jean-Guy Talbot/85 20.00 50.00
18 Gump Worsley/40 75.00 150.00

2003-04 Parkhurst Original Six Montreal Inserts

COMPLETE SET (16) 25.00 50.00
STATED ODDS 1:6
M1 Jacques Plante 2.00 5.00
M2 Doug Harvey 1.50 4.00
M3 Jean Beliveau 1.50 4.00
M4 Maurice Richard 3.00 8.00
M5 Henri Richard 1.50 4.00
M6 Howie Morenz 1.50 4.00
M7 Guy Lafleur 2.00 5.00
M8 Jean Beliveau 2.00 5.00
M9 Jacques Plante 2.00 5.00
M10 Howie Morenz 1.50 4.00
M11 Doug Harvey 1.50 4.00
M12 Elmer Lach 1.50 4.00
M13 Bill Durnan 1.50 4.00
M14 Patrick Roy 3.00 8.00
M15 Saku Koivu 1.50 4.00
M16 Guy Lafleur 2.00 5.00

2003-04 Parkhurst Original Six Montreal Memorabilia

This 63-card set featured memorabilia from past and present Canadiens players. Cards MM1-10 and MM57-58 were single jerseys and were limited to 100 copies sets. Cards MM11-13 were jersey/stick combos and were limited to 80 sets. Cards MM15-21 were vintage memorabilia cards and print runs are listed below. Cards MM16-30 and MM59-63 were vintage jersey cards and print runs are listed below. Cards MM31-35 were vintage stick cards and print runs are listed below. Cards MM35-40 were retired numbers cards and were limited to 20 copies. Cards MM41-50 were grouped into a subset known as Original Six Shooters; players who have scored high career totals against original six teams. The shooters cards were limited to 100 copies each. Cards MM51-56 were dual-jersey cards and were limited to 100 copies each.

JSY PRINT RUN 100 SETS
JSY/STK PRINT RUN 80 SETS
VIN.MEM PRINT RUNS LISTED BELOW
VIN.JSY PRINT RUNS LISTED BELOW
VIN.STICK PRINT RUNS LISTED BELOW
RET.NMBRS PRINT RUN 20 SETS
SIX SHOOT.PRINT RUN 100 SETS
TIMELINE PRINT RUN 100 SETS
MM1 Jose Theodore 15.00 40.00
MM2 Niklas Sundstrom 6.00 15.00
MM3 Stephane Quintal 6.00 15.00
MM4 Jan Bulis 6.00 15.00
MM5 Saku Koivu 10.00 25.00
MM6 Craig Rivet 6.00 15.00
MM7 Mathieu Garon 10.00 25.00
MM8 Yanic Perreault 8.00 20.00
MM9 Chad Kilger 8.00 20.00
MM10 Marcel Hossa 10.00 25.00
MM11 Jose Theodore J/S 25.00 60.00
MM12 Stephane Quintal J/S 12.50 30.00
MM13 Saku Koivu J/S 25.00 60.00
MM14 Jose Theodore/80 20.00 50.00
MM15 Patrick Roy/80 Pad 30.00 80.00
MM16 Dickie Moore/70 J 30.00 80.00
MM17 Jacques Plante/20
MM18 Guy Lafleur/80 30.00 80.00
MM19 Doug Harvey/60 20.00 50.00
MM20 Charlie Hodge/50 Glove 20.0050.00
MM21 Newsy Lalonde/65 40.00 100.00
MM22 Aurel Joliat/50 J 40.00 100.00
MM23 Henri Richard/60 J 20.00 50.00
MM24 Jean Beliveau/60 J 20.00 50.00
MM25 Doug Harvey/60 J 20.00 50.00
MM26 Guy Lafleur/50 J 20.00 50.00
MM27 Gump Worsley/70 J 20.00 50.00
MM28 George Hainsworth/20 J
MM29 Maurice Richard/20 J
MM30 Patrick Roy/80 J 30.00 80.00
MM31 Maurice Richard/20 S
MM32 Jean Beliveau/60 S 25.00 60.00
MM33 Guy Lafleur/50 S 30.00 80.00
MM34 Jacques Plante/60 S 30.00 80.00
MM35 Georges Vezina/20 RN J
MM36 Jacques Plante/20 RN J
MM37 Maurice Richard/20 RN J
MM38 Jean Beliveau/20 RN J
MM39 Guy Lafleur/20 RN J
MM40 Doug Harvey/20 RN J
MM41 Mario Lemieux SS 15.00 40.00
MM42 Ron Francis SS 6.00 15.00
MM43 Joe Sakic SS 10.00 25.00
MM44 Brett Hull SS 10.00 25.00
MM45 Jaromir Jagr SS 8.00 20.00
MM46 Mike Modano SS 8.00 20.00
MM47 Teemu Selanne SS 6.00 15.00
MM48 Pavel Bure SS 6.00 15.00
MM49 Paul Kariya SS 8.00 20.00
MM50 Peter Forsberg SS 10.00 25.00
MM51 Jacques Plante 60.00 150.00
Patrick Roy
MM52 Henri Richard 30.00 80.00
Saku Koivu
MM53 Doug Harvey 15.00 40.00
Larry Robinson
MM54 Gump Worsley 40.00 100.00
Jose Theodore
MM55 Jean Beliveau 15.00 40.00
John LeClair
MM56 Aurel Joliat 40.00 100.00
Guy Lafleur
MM57 Mike Komisarek/100 J 10.00 25.00
MM58 Ron Hainsey/100 J 10.00 25.00
MM59 Guy Lapointe/80 J 20.00 50.00
MM60 Serge Savard/100 J 20.00 50.00
MM61 Steve Shutt/100 J 20.00 50.00
MM62 Peter Mahovlich/100 J 20.00 50.00
MM63 Jacques Plante/100 J 20.00 50.00

2003-04 Parkhurst Original Six New York

This 100-card set featured players from one of the Original Six teams in the NHL, New York. The set was produced as a stand alone product.

COMPLETE SET (100) 25.00 50.00
1 Matthew Barnaby .15 .40
2 Alex Kovalev .40 1.00
3 Dan Blackburn .40 1.00
4 Pavel Bure .50 1.25
5 Anson Carter .40 1.00
6 Jussi Markkanen .40 1.00
7 Jamie Lundmark .15 .40
8 Boris Mironov .15 .40
9 Joel Bouchard .15 .40
10 Dale Purinton .15 .40
11 Bobby Holik .15 .40
12 Dan Lacouture .15 .40
13 Mike Dunham .40 1.00
14 Greg de Vries .15 .40
15 Darius Kasparaitis .15 .40
16 Dominic Moore XRC .15 .40
17 Martin Rucinsky .15 .40
18 Brian Leetch .75 2.00
19 Pascal Rheaume .15 .40
20 Eric Lindros .50 1.25
21 Jan Hlavac .15 .40
22 Chris Simon .15 .40
23 Vladimir Malakhov .15 .40
24 Jed Ortmeyer XRC .15 .40
25 Mark Messier 1.50 4.00
26 Jason Labarbera .15 .40
27 Phil Osaer XRC .15 .40
28 Petr Nedved .15 .40
29 Tom Poti .15 .40
30 Jason MacDonald XRC .15 .40
31 Adam Graves .15 .40
32 Doug Weight .40 1.00
33 Tony Amonte .40 1.00
34 Ed Giacomin .60 1.50
35 Mike Gartner 1.50 3.00
36 Phil Esposito 1.50 4.00
37 Dan Cloutier .40 1.00
38 Ron Greschner .40 1.00
39 Luc Robitaille .40 1.00
40 Andy Bathgate .40 1.00
41 Frank Boucher .40 1.00
42 Brad Park .50 1.25
43 Ron Duguay .40 1.00
44 Bill Gadsby .40 1.00
45 Harry Howell .40 1.00
46 Ching Johnson .40 1.00
47 Doug Harvey .50 1.25
48 Guy Lafleur 1.50 3.00
49 John Davidson .60 1.50
50 Jean Ratelle .50 1.25
51 Mike Richter .75 2.00
52 John Vanbiesbrouck .40 1.00
53 Chuck Rayner .40 1.00
54 Lou Fontinato .15 .40
55 Rod Gilbert .50 1.25
56 Lester Patrick .50 1.25
57 Vic Hadfield .50 1.25
58 Walt Tkaczuk .15 .40
59 Gump Worsley .75 2.00
60 Bun Cook .40 1.00
61 Mark Messier 1.50 4.00
62 Brian Leetch .75 2.00
63 Phil Esposito 1.50 4.00
64 Ed Giacomin .60 1.50
65 Brad Park .50 1.25
66 Jean Ratelle .50 1.25
67 Pat Verbeek .15 .40
68 Barry Beck .15 .40
69 Rod Gilbert .50 1.25
70 Chuck Rayner .40 1.00
71 Mark Messier 1.50 4.00
72 Brian Leetch .75 2.00
73 Vic Hadfield .50 1.25
74 Phil Esposito 1.50 4.00
75 Ron Greschner .40 1.00
76 Walt Tkaczuk .15 .40
77 Harry Howell .40 1.00
78 Andy Bathgate .40 1.00
79 Barry Beck .15 .40
80 Brad Park .50 1.25
81 Brad Park .50 1.25
82 Ed Giacomin .60 1.50
83 Jean Ratelle .50 1.25
84 Phil Esposito 1.50 4.00
85 Rod Gilbert .50 1.25
86 Harry Howell .40 1.00
87 Chuck Rayner .40 1.00
88 Ching Johnson .40 1.00
89 Bill Cook .75 2.00
90 Andy Bathgate .40 1.00
91 Rod Gilbert .50 1.25
92 Harry Howell .40 1.00
93 Brian Leetch .75 2.00
94 Mike Richter .75 2.00
95 Ed Giacomin .60 1.50
96 Jean Ratelle .50 1.25
97 Brad Park .50 1.25
98 Mark Messier 1.50 4.00
99 Brian Leetch .75 2.00
100 Adam Graves .15 .40

2003-04 Parkhurst Original Six New York Autographs

This 18-card set featured certified autographs of past Rangers greats. Print runs are listed below.

PRINT RUNS LISTED BELOW
1 Andy Bathgate/80 25.00 60.00
2 John Davidson/90 15.00 40.00
3 Ron Duguay/90 15.00 40.00
4 Phil Esposito/55 30.00 80.00
5 Lou Fontinato/95 15.00 40.00
6 Ed Giacomin/90 30.00 80.00
7 Rod Gilbert/85 30.00 80.00
8 Ron Greschner/95 15.00 40.00
9 Vic Hadfield/90 15.00 40.00
10 Harry Howell/95 20.00 50.00
11 Guy Lafleur/90 30.00 80.00
12 Brad Park/90 20.00 50.00
13 Jean Ratelle/90 20.00 50.00
14 Allan Stanley/85 20.00 50.00
15 Walt Tkaczuk/90 15.00 40.00
16 Gump Worsley/80 25.00 60.00

2003-04 Parkhurst Original Six New York Inserts

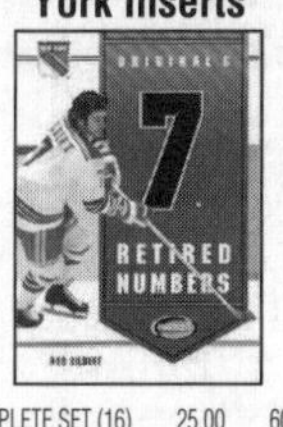

COMPLETE SET (16) 25.00 60.00
STATED ODDS 1:6
N1 Rod Gilbert 1.50 4.00
N2 Ed Giacomin 2.00 5.00
N3 Frank Boucher 1.50 4.00
N4 Rod Gilbert 1.50 4.00
N5 Phil Esposito 3.00 8.00
N6 Gump Worsley 2.00 5.00
N7 Ed Giacomin 2.00 5.00
N8 Doug Harvey 1.50 4.00
N9 Mark Messier 3.00 8.00
N10 Jean Ratelle 1.50 4.00
N11 Andy Bathgate 1.50 4.00
N12 Brian Leetch 2.00 5.00
N13 Chuck Rayner 1.50 4.00
N14 Brian Leetch 1.50 4.00
N15 Alex Kovalev 1.50 4.00
N16 Brad Park 1.50 4.00

2003-04 Parkhurst Original Six New York Memorabilia

This 63-card set featured memorabilia from past and present Rangers players. Cards NM1-12 and NM56-58 were single jerseys and were limited to 100 copies sets. Cards NM13-19 and NM57 were jersey/stick combos and were limited to 80 sets. Cards NM21-26 were vintage memorabilia cards and were limited to 20 copies each. Cards NM27-33 and NM62-63 were vintage jersey cards and print runs are listed below. Cards NM34-38 and NM59-61 were vintage stick cards and print runs are listed below. Cards NM39-40 were retired numbers cards and were limited to 20 copies. Cards NM411-50 were grouped into a subset known as Original Six Shooters; players who have scored high career totals against original six teams. The shooters cards were limited to 100 copies each. Cards NM51-55 were dual-jersey cards and were limited to 100 copies each.

JSY PRINT RUN 100 SETS
JSY/STK PRINT RUN 80 SETS
VIN.MEM PRINT RUN 20 SETS
VIN.STICK PRINT RUNS LISTED BELOW
RET.NMBRS PRINT RUN 20 SETS
SIX SHOOT.PRINT RUN 100 SETS
TIMELINE PRINT RUN 100 SETS
NM1 Mike Dunham 10.00 25.00
NM2 Brian Leetch 15.00 40.00
NM3 Eric Lindros 10.00 25.00
NM4 Mark Messier 10.00 25.00
NM5 Tom Poti 6.00 15.00
NM6 Pavel Bure 10.00 25.00
NM7 Mike Richter 12.50 30.00
NM8 Dan Blackburn 6.00 15.00
NM9 Darius Kasparaitis 6.00 15.00
NM10 Bobby Holik 6.00 15.00
NM11 Vladimir Malakhov 6.00 15.00
NM12 Jamie Lundmark 6.00 15.00
NM13 Brian Leetch J/S 15.00 40.00
NM14 Eric Lindros J/S 15.00 40.00
NM15 Mark Messier J/S 30.00 80.00
NM16 Mike Richter J/S 20.00 50.00
NM17 Pavel Bure J/S 15.00 40.00
NM18 Dan Blackburn J/S 12.50 30.00
NM19 Mike Dunham J/S 15.00 40.00
NM20 Eric Lindros/30 150.00 40.00
NM21 Terry Sawchuk/20
NM22 Jacques Plante/20
NM23 Bill Gadsby/20
NM24 Doug Harvey/20
NM25 Chuck Rayner/20
NM26 Ed Giacomin/20
NM27 Theo Fleury/50 J 10.00 25.00
NM28 Bryan Berard/60 J 10.00 25.00
NM29 Marcel Dionne/60 J 15.00 40.00
NM30 Ed Giacomin/50 J 40.00 100.00
NM31 Phil Esposito/50 J 15.00 40.00
NM32 Rod Gilbert/50 J 30.00 80.00
NM33 Jean Ratelle/50 J 30.00 80.00
NM34 Emile Francis/60 S 15.00 40.00
NM35 Gilles Villemure/60 S 20.00 50.00
NM36 Ed Giacomin/20 S
NM37 Phil Esposito/20 S
NM38 Johnny Bower/20 S
NM39 Ed Giacomin/20 RN
NM40 Rod Gilbert/20 RN
NM41 Mario Lemieux SS 15.00 40.00
NM42 Ron Francis SS 6.00 15.00
NM43 Joe Sakic SS 10.00 25.00
NM44 Brett Hull SS 8.00 20.00
NM45 Jaromir Jagr SS 8.00 20.00
NM46 Mike Modano SS 8.00 20.00
NM47 Teemu Selanne SS 6.00 15.00
NM48 Pavel Bure SS 6.00 15.00
NM49 Paul Kariya SS 8.00 20.00
NM50 Peter Forsberg SS 10.00 25.00
NM51 Ed Giacomin 40.00 100.00
Dan Blackburn
NM52 Phil Esposito 20.00 50.00
Eric Lindros
NM53 Marcel Dionne 12.50 30.00
Alex Kovalev
NM54 Jean Ratelle 50.00 125.00
Mark Messier
NM55 Rod Gilbert 12.50 30.00
Pavel Bure
NM56 Alex Kovalev/100 J 15.00 40.00
NM57 Alex Kovalev/100 J/S 20.00 50.00
NM58 Anson Carter/100 J 12.50 30.00
NM59 John Davidson/100 S 20.00 50.00
NM60 Marcel Dionne/100 S 15.00 40.00
NM61 Adam Graves/100 S 12.50 30.00
NM62 Sergei Zubov/100 J 12.50 30.00
NM63 Dan Cloutier/100 J 12.50 30.00

2003-04 Parkhurst Original Six Shooters

This ten card set paralleled the Shooters cards in each of the Original Six products, but each card carried the total number of points scored against all Original Six team in the player's career. Each card was limited to 10 copies each.

NOT PRICED DUE TO SCARCITY
OSM1 Mario Lemieux
OSM2 Ron Francis
OSM3 Joe Sakic
OSM4 Brett Hull
OSM5 Jaromir Jagr
OSM6 Mike Modano
OSM7 Teemu Selanne
OSM8 Pavel Bure
OSM9 Paul Kariya
OSM10 Peter Forsberg

2003-04 Parkhurst Original Six Toronto

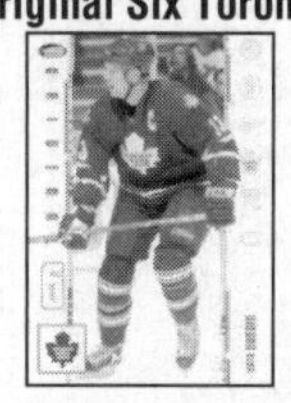

This 100-card set featured players from one of the Original Six teams in the NHL, Toronto. The set was produced as a stand alone product.

COMPLETE SET (100) 25.00 50.00
1 Nikolai Antropov .15 .40
2 Wade Belak .15 .40
3 Ed Belfour .50 1.25
4 Aki Berg .15 .40
5 Maxim Kondratiev XRC 2.00 5.00
6 Owen Nolan .40 1.00
7 Nathan Perrott .15 .40
8 Tie Domi .40 1.00
9 Matt Stajan XRC 4.00 10.00
10 Ken Klee .15 .40
11 Bryan Marchment .15 .40
12 Jamie Hodson .15 .40
13 Carlo Colaiacovo .15 .40
14 Tomas Kaberle .15 .40
15 Joe Nieuwendyk .40 1.00
16 Bryan McCabe .15 .40
17 Ric Jackman .15 .40
18 Alexander Mogilny .40 1.00
19 Karel Pilar .15 .40
20 Alexei Ponikarovsky .15 .40
21 Robert Reichel .15 .40
22 Mikael Renberg .15 .40
23 Gary Roberts .15 .40
24 Mats Sundin .50 1.25
25 Mikael Tellqvist .40 1.00
26 Darcy Tucker .15 .40
27 Aaron Gavey .15 .40
28 Josh Holden .15 .40
29 Trevor Kidd .40 1.00
30 Tom Fitzgerald .15 .40
31 Charlie Conacher .50 1.25
32 Doug Gilmour .40 1.00
33 Felix Potvin .50 1.25
34 Vincent Damphousse .40 1.00
35 Terry Sawchuk .75 2.00
36 Tiger Williams 1.00 2.50
37 Wendel Clark .75 2.00
38 Teeder Kennedy .50 1.25
39 Syl Apps .40 1.00
40 Hap Day .15 .40
41 Rick Vaive .15 .40
42 Curtis Joseph .50 1.25
43 Darryl Sittler .50 1.25
44 Bill Barilko XRC .60 1.50
45 Bobby Baun .40 1.00
46 Borje Salming .50 1.25
47 Harry Lumley .50 1.25
48 Dick Duff .40 1.00
49 Mike Palmateer 1.25 3.00
50 Norm Ullman .50 1.25
51 Frank Mahovlich .50 1.25
52 Red Kelly .50 1.25
53 Sid Smith .40 1.00
54 Mike Gartner 1.00 2.50
55 Dave Andreychuk .15 .40
56 Johnny Bower 2.00 5.00
57 Turk Broda .60 1.50
58 Tim Horton 1.50 4.00
59 King Clancy .50 1.25
60 Ace Bailey .60 1.50
61 Mats Sundin .50 1.25
62 Doug Gilmour .40 1.00
63 Borje Salming .50 1.25
64 Lanny McDonald .50 1.25
65 Darryl Sittler 1.00 2.50
66 King Clancy .50 1.25
67 Turk Broda .60 1.50
68 Felix Potvin .50 1.25
69 Tim Horton 1.50 4.00
70 Sid Smith .40 1.00
71 Mats Sundin .50 1.25
72 Doug Gilmour .40 1.00
73 Wendel Clark .75 2.00
74 Teeder Kennedy .50 1.25
75 Syl Apps .40 1.00
76 Hap Day .15 .40
77 Rick Vaive .15 .40
78 Charlie Conacher .50 1.25
79 Darryl Sittler 1.00 2.50
80 Sid Smith .40 1.00
81 Ace Bailey .60 1.50
82 Johnny Bower 2.00 5.00
83 Turk Broda .60 1.50
84 Tim Horton 1.50 4.00
85 Red Kelly .50 1.25
86 Frank Mahovlich .50 1.25
87 Borje Salming .50 1.25
88 Marcel Pronovost .75 2.00
89 King Clancy .50 1.25
90 Syl Apps .40 1.00
91 Darryl Sittler 1.00 2.50
92 Tim Horton 1.50 4.00
93 Darryl Sittler 1.00 2.50
94 Borje Salming .50 1.25
95 Turk Broda .60 1.50
96 Rick Vaive .15 .40
97 Doug Gilmour .40 1.00
98 Frank Mahovlich .50 1.25
99 Wendel Clark .75 2.00
100 Ed Belfour .50 1.25

2003-04 Parkhurst Original Six Toronto Autographs

This 18-card set featured certified autographs of past Maple Leafs greats. Print runs are listed below.

COMMON CARD (1-16) 20.00 50.00
1 Bobby Baun/85 30.00 80.00
2 Johnny Bower/90 30.00 80.00
3 Wendel Clark/90 40.00 100.00
4 Dick Duff/85 20.00 50.00
5 Red Kelly/90 25.00 60.00
6 Ted Kennedy/85 25.00 60.00
7 Frank Mahovlich/85 25.00 60.00
8 Eddie Shack/85 25.00 60.00
9 Darryl Sittler/95 40.00 80.00
10 Sid Smith/95 40.00 100.00
11 Ron Stewart/85 20.00 50.00
12 Rick Vaive/95 25.00 60.00
13 Tiger Williams/90 25.00 60.00
14 Mike Palmateer/85 40.00 80.00
15 Mike Kitchen/85 20.00 50.00
16 Borje Salming/85 40.00 80.00

2003-04 Parkhurst Original Six Toronto Inserts

COMPLETE SET (17) 30.00 60.00
STATED ODDS 1:6
T1 Bill Barilko 2.00 5.00
T2 Ace Bailey 2.00 5.00
T3 Tim Horton 3.00 8.00
T4 Syl Apps 1.50 4.00
T5 Ted Kennedy 2.00 5.00
T6 Frank Mahovlich 3.00 8.00
T7 Ted Kennedy 2.00 5.00
T8 Red Kelly 2.00 5.00
T9 Ace Bailey 2.00 5.00
T10 Charlie Conacher 2.00 5.00
T11 Syl Apps 1.50 4.00
T12 Turk Broda 2.00 5.00
T13 Terry Sawchuk 1.50 4.00
T14 Johnny Bower 2.50 6.00
T15 Darryl Sittler 1.50 4.00
T16 Wendel Clark 3.00 8.00
T17 Lanny McDonald 1.50 4.00

2003-04 Parkhurst Original Six Toronto Memorabilia

This 63-card set featured memorabilia from past and present Maple Leafs players. Cards TM1-13 were single jerseys and were limited to 100 copies sets. Cards TM14-19 were jersey/stick combos and were limited to 80 sets. Cards TM20-27 were vintage memorabilia cards and print runs are listed below. Cards TM28-32 and TM59-62 were vintage jersey cards and print runs are listed below. Cards TM33-35 and TM63 were vintage stick cards and print runs are listed below. Cards TM37-40 were retired numbers cards and were limited to 20 copies. Cards TM41-50 were grouped into a subset known as Original Six Shooters; players who have scored high career totals against original six teams. The shooters cards were limited to 100 copies each. Cards tM51-58 were dual-jersey cards and were limited to 100 copies each.

TM1 Mats Sundin 15.00 40.00
TM2 Gary Roberts 10.00 25.00
TM3 Bryan McCabe 8.00 20.00
TM4 Darcy Tucker 10.00 25.00
TM5 Nik Antropov 10.00 25.00
TM6 Tomas Kaberle 10.00 25.00
TM7 Alexander Mogilny 10.00 25.00
TM8 Tie Domi 10.00 25.00
TM9 Ed Belfour 12.50 30.00
TM10 Owen Nolan 8.00 20.00
TM11 Carlo Colaiacovo 6.00 15.00
TM12 Robert Svehla 6.00 15.00
TM13 Trevor Kidd 10.00 25.00
TM14 Mats Sundin J/S 15.00 40.00
TM15 Alexander Mogilny J/S 12.50 30.00
TM16 Darcy Tucker J/S 12.50 30.00
TM17 Bryan McCabe J/S 12.50 30.00
TM18 Tomas Kaberle J/S 20.00 50.00
TM19 Gary Roberts J/S 12.50 30.00
TM20 Johnny Bower/20 Glove
TM21 Terry Sawchuk/20 Glove
TM22 Ted Kennedy/20 Glove
TM23 Charlie Conacher/20
TM24 Tim Horton/60 Pants 40.00 100.00
TM25 Wendel Clark/30 20.00 50.00
TM26 Bill Barilko/20
TM27 Borje Salming/80 15.00 40.00
TM28 Tim Horton/20 J
TM29 Red Kelly/20 J
TM30 Lanny McDonald/60 J 25.00 60.00
TM31 Tiger Williams/60 J 15.00 40.00
TM32 Curtis Joseph/60 J 20.00 50.00
TM33 Frank Mahovlich/50 S 25.00 60.00
TM34 Johnny Bower/50 S 30.00 80.00
TM35 Turk Broda/20 S
TM36 Mats Sundin/50
TM37 Johnny Bower/20 RN J
TM38 T.Kennedy/20 RN Glove
TM39 Ace Bailey/20 RN Glove
TM40 Tim Horton/20 RN Pants
TM41 Mario Lemieux SS 15.00 40.00
TM42 Ron Francis SS 6.00 15.00
TM43 Joe Sakic SS 10.00 25.00
TM44 Brett Hull SS 8.00 20.00
TM45 Jaromir Jagr SS 8.00 20.00
TM46 Mike Modano SS 8.00 20.00
TM47 Teemu Selanne SS 6.00 15.00
TM48 Pavel Bure SS 6.00 15.00
TM49 Paul Kariya SS 8.00 20.00
TM50 Peter Forsberg SS 10.00 25.00
TM51 T.Horton/W.Clark 40.00 100.00
TM52 R.Kelly/O.Nolan 15.00 40.00
TM53 L.McDonald/A.Mogilny 15.00 40.00
TM54 T.Williams/T.Domi 25.00 60.00
TM55 D.Sittler/M.Sundin 30.00 80.00
TM56 M.Gartner/G.Roberts 15.00 40.00
TM57 B.Salming/B.McCabe 15.00 40.00
TM58 R.Vaive/D.Tucker 15.00 40.00
TM59 Felix Potvin/100 J 15.00 40.00
TM60 Wendel Clark/100 J 25.00 60.00
TM61 Mike Gartner/100 J 15.00 40.00
TM62 Rick Vaive/100 J 20.00 50.00
TM63 Mike Gartner/80 S 15.00 40.00

2005-06 Parkhurst

COMPLETE SET (700) 50.00 150.00
1 Andy McDonald .15 .40
2 Teemu Selanne .30 .75
3 Scott Niedermayer .15 .40

4 Joffrey Lupul .15 .40
5 Todd Marchant .15 .40
6 Chris Kunitz .15 .40
7 J-S Giguere .25 .60
8 Samuel Pahlsson .15 .40
9 Jonathan Hedstrom .15 .40
10 Ilja Bryzgalov .25 .60
11 Jeff Friesen .15 .40
12 Rob Niedermayer .15 .40
13 Francois Beauchemin .15 .40
14 Vitaly Vishnevski .15 .40
15 Ruslan Salei .15 .40
16 Todd Fedoruk .15 .40
17 Dustin Penner 1.50 4.00
18 Ilya Kovalchuk .40 1.00
19 Marc Savard .15 .40
20 Marian Hossa .25 .60
21 Vyacheslav Kozlov .15 .40
22 Peter Bondra .25 .60
23 Jaroslav Modry .15 .40
24 Greg de Vries .15 .40
25 Niclas Havelid .15 .40
26 Patrik Stefan .15 .40
27 Serge Aubin .15 .40
28 Andy Sutton .15 .40
29 Kari Lehtonen .30 .75
30 Garnet Exelby .15 .40
31 Michael Garnett .15 .40
32 Bobby Holik .15 .40
33 Scott Mellanby .15 .40
34 Patrice Bergeron .30 .75
35 Brad Boyes .15 .40
36 Tim Thomas .15 .40
37 Glen Murray .15 .40
38 Marco Sturm .15 .40
39 Wayne Primeau .15 .40
40 Brad Stuart .15 .40
41 Andrew Raycroft .25 .60
42 P.J. Axelsson .15 .40
43 Brian Leetch .30 .75
44 Travis Green .15 .40
45 David Tanabe .15 .40
46 Nick Boynton .15 .40
47 Hal Gill .15 .40
48 Josh Langfeld .15 .40
49 Tom Fitzgerald .15 .40
50 Ales Kotalik .15 .40
51 Maxim Afinogenov .15 .40
52 Chris Drury .25 .60
53 Tim Connolly .15 .40
54 Ryan Miller .25 .60
55 Brian Campbell .15 .40
56 Jochen Hecht .15 .40
57 Teppo Numminen .15 .40
58 Martin Biron .25 .60
59 Derek Roy .15 .40
60 Mike Grier .15 .40
61 Paul Gaustad .15 .40
62 Daniel Briere .15 .40
63 Jason Pominville .15 .40
64 Jay McKee .15 .40
65 J.P. Dumont .15 .40
66 Henrik Tallinder .15 .40
67 Jarome Iginla .40 1.00
68 Daymond Langkow .15 .40
69 Kristian Huselius .15 .40
70 Tony Amonte .25 .60
71 Andrew Ference .15 .40
72 Chuck Kobasew .15 .40
73 Miikka Kiprusoff .30 .75
74 Robyn Regehr .15 .40
75 Roman Hamrlik .15 .40
76 Darren McCarty .15 .40
77 Stephane Yelle .15 .40
78 Chris Simon .15 .40
79 Jordan Leopold .15 .40
80 Rhett Warrener .15 .40
81 Shean Donovan .15 .40
82 Marcus Nilson .15 .40
83 Mike LeClerc .15 .40
84 Eric Staal .25 .60
85 Cory Stillman .15 .40
86 Erik Cole .15 .40
87 Justin Williams .25 .60
88 Rod Brind`Amour .25 .60
89 Martin Gerber .25 .60
90 Doug Weight .25 .60
91 Ray Whitney .15 .40
92 Matt Cullen .15 .40
93 Frantisek Kaberle .15 .40
94 Bret Hedican .15 .40
95 Oleg Tverdovsky .15 .40
96 Kevyn Adams .15 .40
97 Aaron Ward .15 .40
98 Mark Recchi .25 .60
99 Glen Wesley .15 .40
100 Josef Vasicek .15 .40
101 Brandon Bochenski RC .75 2.00
102 Kyle Calder .15 .40
103 Mark Bell .15 .40
104 Martin Lapointe .15 .40
105 Pavel Vorobiev .15 .40
106 Nikolai Khabibulin .30 .75
107 Craig Anderson .15 .40
108 Matthew Barnaby .15 .40
109 Radim Vrbata .15 .40
110 Rene Bourque RC .75 2.00
111 Eric Daze .25 .60
112 Tuomo Ruutu .15 .40
113 Adrian Aucoin .15 .40
114 Jim Vandermeer .15 .40
115 Milan Bartovic .15 .40
116 Curtis Brown .15 .40
117 Alex Tanguay .25 .60
118 Joe Sakic .60 1.50
119 Marek Svatos .15 .40
120 Jose Theodore .40 1.00
121 Andrew Brunette .15 .40
122 Milan Hejduk .30 .75
123 John-Michael Liles .15 .40
124 Rob Blake .25 .60
125 Pierre Turgeon .15 .40
126 Ian Laperriere .15 .40
127 Antti Laaksonen .15 .40
128 Patrice Brisebois .15 .40
129 Brett Clark .15 .40
130 Karlis Skrastins .15 .40
131 Brett McLean .15 .40
132 Dan Hinote .15 .40
133 Steve Konowalchuk .15 .40
134 David Vyborny .15 .40
135 Nikolai Zherdev .25 .60
136 Bryan Berard .15 .40
137 Rick Nash .40 1.00
138 Sergei Fedorov .30 .75
139 Jan Hrdina .15 .40
140 Duvie Westcott .15 .40
141 Manny Malhotra .15 .40
142 Marc Denis .25 .60
143 Jason Chimera .15 .40
144 Trevor Letowski .15 .40
145 Adam Foote .15 .40
146 Rostislav Klesla .15 .40
147 Dan Fritsche .15 .40
148 Pascal LeClaire .25 .60
149 Jody Shelley .15 .40
150 Jaroslav Balastik RC .75 2.00
151 Johan Hedberg .25 .60
152 Trevor Daley .15 .40
153 Jon Klemm .15 .40
154 Willie Mitchell .15 .40
155 Steve Ott .15 .40
156 Antti Miettinen .15 .40
157 Niko Kapanen .15 .40
158 Stu Barnes .15 .40
159 Philippe Boucher .15 .40
160 Bill Guerin .15 .40
161 Jason Arnott .15 .40
162 Mike Modano .30 .75
163 Marty Turco .25 .60
164 Brenden Morrow .25 .60
165 Sergei Zubov .15 .40
166 Jere Lehtinen .25 .60
167 Pavel Datsyuk .30 .75
168 Henrik Zetterberg .30 .75
169 Manny Legace .30 .75
170 Nicklas Lidstrom .30 .75
171 Brendan Shanahan .30 .75
172 Jason Williams .15 .40
173 Steve Yzerman 1.25 3.00
174 Mathieu Schneider .15 .40
175 Robert Lang .15 .40
176 Tomas Holmstrom .15 .40
177 Mikael Samuelsson .15 .40
178 Chris Osgood .25 .60
179 Kris Draper .15 .40
180 Kirk Maltby .15 .40
181 Chris Chelios .30 .75
182 Johan Franzen RC 1.00 2.50
183 Brett Lebda RC .75 2.00
184 Jiri Fischer .15 .40
185 Shawn Horcoff .15 .40
186 Ty Conklin .25 .60
187 Ales Hemsky .15 .40
188 Jarret Stoll .15 .40
189 Ryan Smyth .25 .60
190 Chris Pronger .25 .60
191 Jaroslav Spacek .15 .40
192 Raffi Torres .15 .40
193 Jussi Markkanen .15 .40
194 Marc-Andre Bergeron .15 .40
195 Fernando Pisani .15 .40
196 Michael Peca .15 .40
197 Jason Smith .15 .40
198 Dwayne Roloson .25 .60
199 Georges Laraque .15 .40
200 Sergei Samsonov .25 .60
201 Olli Jokinen .25 .60
202 Roberto Luongo .40 1.00
203 Nathan Horton .15 .40
204 Joe Nieuwendyk .25 .60
205 Jozef Stumpel .15 .40
206 Jay Bouwmeester .15 .40
207 Gary Roberts .15 .40
208 Chris Gratton .15 .40
209 Martin Gelinas .15 .40
210 Stephen Weiss .15 .40
211 Mike Van Ryn .15 .40
212 Jamie McLennan .15 .40
213 Lukas Krajicek .15 .40
214 Jon Sim .15 .40
215 Sean Hill .15 .40
216 Juraj Kolnik .15 .40
217 Pavol Demitra .25 .60
218 Mathieu Garon .25 .60
219 Lubomir Visnovsky .15 .40
220 Craig Conroy .15 .40
221 Alexander Frolov .25 .60
222 Mike Cammalleri .15 .40
223 Derek Armstrong .15 .40
224 Joe Corvo .15 .40
225 Eric Belanger .15 .40
226 Sean Avery .15 .40
227 Luc Robitaille .25 .60
228 Dustin Brown .15 .40
229 Jeremy Roenick .40 1.00
230 Jason Labarbera .25 .60
231 Mattias Norstrom .15 .40
232 Mark Parrish .15 .40
233 Brian Rolston .15 .40
234 Pierre-Marc Bouchard .15 .40
235 Manny Fernandez .25 .60
236 Marian Gaborik .60 1.50
237 Randy Robitaille .15 .40
238 Todd White .15 .40
239 Alexandre Daigle .15 .40
240 Wes Walz .15 .40
241 Marc Chouinard .15 .40
242 Martin Skoula .15 .40
243 Filip Kuba .15 .40
244 Nick Schultz .15 .40
245 Kurtis Foster .15 .40
246 Derek Boogaard RC .75 2.00
247 Brent Burns .15 .40
248 Pascal Dupuis .15 .40
249 Saku Koivu .30 .75
250 David Aebischer .25 .60
251 Alex Kovalev .25 .60
252 Michael Ryder .25 .60
253 Mike Ribeiro .15 .40
254 Andrei Markov .15 .40
255 Jan Bulis .15 .40
256 Craig Rivet .15 .40
257 Steve Begin .15 .40
258 Sheldon Souray .15 .40
259 Tomas Plekanec .15 .40
260 Richard Zednik .15 .40
261 Cristobal Huet .25 .60
262 Francis Bouillon .15 .40
263 Chris Higgins .15 .40
264 Radek Bonk .15 .40
265 Niklas Sundstrom .15 .40
266 Pierre Dagenais .15 .40
267 Mathieu Dandenault .15 .40
268 Paul Kariya .30 .75
269 Tomas Vokoun .25 .60
270 Steve Sullivan .15 .40
271 Yanic Perreault .15 .40
272 Mike Sillinger .15 .40
273 Kimmo Timonen .15 .40
274 Marek Zidlicky .15 .40
275 Scott Hartnell .15 .40
276 Martin Erat .15 .40
277 Dan Hamhuis .15 .40
278 Adam Hall .15 .40
279 Scottie Upshall .15 .40
280 David Legwand .25 .60
281 Darcy Hordichuk .15 .40
282 Vernon Fiddler .15 .40
283 Scott Walker .15 .40
284 Brendan Witt .15 .40
285 Brian Gionta .15 .40
286 Scott Gomez .25 .60
287 Martin Brodeur 1.50 4.00
288 Jamie Langenbrunner .15 .40
289 Brian Rafalski .15 .40
290 Sergei Brylin .15 .40
291 Patrik Elias .25 .60
292 John Madden .15 .40
293 Viktor Kozlov .15 .40
294 Scott Clemmensen .25 .60
295 Grant Marshall .15 .40
296 Jay Pandolfo .15 .40
297 Richard Matvichuk .15 .40
298 Erik Rasmussen .15 .40
299 Colin White .15 .40
300 Paul Martin .15 .40
301 Alexei Yashin .15 .40
302 Miroslav Satan .15 .40
303 Mike York .15 .40
304 Jason Blake .15 .40
305 Robert Nilsson RC 1.00 2.50
306 Trent Hunter .15 .40
307 Alexei Zhitnik .15 .40
308 Eric Godard .15 .40
309 Rick DiPietro .25 .60
310 Arron Asham .15 .40
311 Denis Grebeshkov .15 .40
312 John Erskine .15 .40
313 Radek Martinek .15 .40
314 Garth Snow .25 .60
315 Shawn Bates .15 .40
316 Sean Bergenheim .15 .40
317 Jaromir Jagr .50 1.25
318 Martin Straka .15 .40
319 Michael Nylander .15 .40
320 Martin Rucinsky .15 .40
321 Kevin Weekes .25 .60
322 Petr Sykora .15 .40
323 Steve Rucchin .15 .40
324 Jason Ward .15 .40
325 Michal Rozsival .15 .40
326 Fedor Tyutin .15 .40
327 Marek Malik .15 .40
328 Tom Poti .15 .40
329 Dominic Moore .15 .40
330 Darius Kasparaitis .15 .40
331 Jed Ortmeyer .15 .40
332 Marcel Hossa .15 .40
333 Dominik Hasek .60 1.50
334 Daniel Alfredsson .25 .60
335 Dany Heatley .40 1.00
336 Jason Spezza .30 .75
337 Wade Redden .15 .40
338 Peter Schaefer .15 .40
339 Bryan Smolinski .15 .40
340 Mike Fisher .15 .40
341 Zdeno Chara .25 .60
342 Chris Neil .15 .40
343 Antoine Vermette .15 .40
344 Ray Emery .25 .60
345 Patrick Eaves RC 1.50 4.00
346 Vaclav Varada .15 .40
347 Martin Havlat .25 .60
348 Chris Phillips .15 .40
349 Tyler Arnason .15 .40
350 Antero Niittymaki .25 .60
351 Simon Gagne .30 .75
352 Peter Forsberg .50 1.25
353 Mike Knuble .15 .40
354 Michal Handzus .15 .40
355 Joni Pitkanen .15 .40
356 Sami Kapanen .15 .40
357 Kim Johnsson .15 .40
358 Mike Rathje .15 .40
359 Eric Desjardins .15 .40
360 Derian Hatcher .15 .40
361 Robert Esche .25 .60
362 Brian Savage .15 .40
363 Chris Therien .15 .40
364 Keith Primeau .15 .40
365 Petr Nedved .15 .40
366 Donald Brashear .15 .40
367 Curtis Joseph .30 .75
368 Ladislav Nagy .15 .40
369 Shane Doan .15 .40
370 Mike Comrie .25 .60
371 Mike Johnson .15 .40
372 Paul Mara .15 .40
373 Geoff Sanderson .15 .40
374 Steven Reinprecht .15 .40
375 Dave Scatchard .15 .40
376 Oleg Saprykin .15 .40
377 Zbynek Michalek .15 .40
378 Boyd Devereaux .15 .40
379 Fredrik Sjostrom .15 .40
380 Mike Ricci .15 .40
381 Tyson Nash .15 .40
382 Derek Morris .15 .40
383 Niklas Nordgren RC .75 2.00
384 Sergei Gonchar .15 .40
385 Marc-Andre Fleury .25 .60
386 John LeClair .30 .75
387 Richard Jackman .15 .40
388 Ryan Malone .15 .40
389 Sebastien Caron .15 .40
390 Mario Lemieux 2.00 5.00
391 Brooks Orpik .15 .40
392 Konstantin Koltsov .15 .40
393 Erik Christensen RC .75 2.00
394 Josef Melichar .15 .40
395 Jocelyn Thibault .25 .60
396 Tomas Surovy .15 .40
397 Andre Roy .15 .40
398 Jani Rita .15 .40
399 Vesa Toskala .25 .60
400 Joe Thornton .50 1.25
401 Patrick Marleau .25 .60
402 Jonathan Cheechoo .30 .75
403 Evgeni Nabokov .25 .60
404 Nils Ekman .15 .40
405 Tom Preissing .15 .40
406 Milan Michalek .15 .40
407 Alyn McCauley .15 .40
408 Scott Thornton .15 .40
409 Kyle McLaren .15 .40
410 Scott Hannan .15 .40
411 Marcel Goc .15 .40
412 Grant Stevenson RC .75 2.00
413 Christian Ehrhoff .15 .40
414 Mark Smith .15 .40
415 Scott Young .15 .40
416 Petr Cajanek .15 .40
417 Dean McAmmond .15 .40
418 Curtis Sanford .15 .40
419 Keith Tkachuk .30 .75
420 Dallas Drake .15 .40
421 Jamal Mayers .15 .40
422 Jeff Hoggan RC .75 2.00
423 Christian Backman .15 .40
424 Barret Jackman .15 .40
425 Mark Rycroft .15 .40
426 Jay McClement RC .75 2.00
427 Patrick Lalime .25 .60
428 Kevin Dallman RC .75 2.00
429 Dennis Wideman RC .75 2.00
430 Brad Richards .25 .60
431 Vaclav Prospal .15 .40
432 John Grahame .25 .60
433 Vincent Lecavalier .30 .75
434 Martin St. Louis .25 .60
435 Dan Boyle .15 .40
436 Fredrik Modin .15 .40
437 Ruslan Fedotenko .15 .40
438 Pavel Kubina .15 .40
439 Darryl Sydor .15 .40
440 Sean Burke .25 .60
441 Tim Taylor .15 .40
442 Cory Sarich .15 .40
443 Nolan Pratt .15 .40
444 Rob DiMaio .15 .40
445 Paul Ranger RC .75 2.00
446 Ryan Craig RC 1.25 3.00
447 Mats Sundin .30 .75
448 Ed Belfour .30 .75
449 Bryan McCabe .15 .40
450 Jason Allison .15 .40
451 Tomas Kaberle .15 .40
452 Darcy Tucker .15 .40
453 Kyle Wellwood .15 .40
454 Jeff O`Neill .15 .40
455 Alexei Ponikarovsky .15 .40
456 Eric Lindros .30 .75
457 Chad Kilger .15 .40
458 Mikael Tellqvist .25 .60
459 Staffan Kronwall RC .75 2.00
460 Nik Antropov .15 .40
461 Matt Stajan .15 .40
462 Tie Domi .25 .60
463 Luke Richardson .15 .40
464 Alexander Khavanov .15 .40
465 Markus Naslund .30 .75
466 Daniel Sedin .15 .40
467 Henrik Sedin .15 .40
468 Todd Bertuzzi .30 .75
469 Alexander Auld .15 .40
470 Brendan Morrison .15 .40
471 Anson Carter .25 .60
472 Sami Salo .15 .40
473 Ed Jovanovski .25 .60
474 Nolan Baumgartner .15 .40
475 Mattias Ohlund .15 .40
476 Dan Cloutier .25 .60
477 Jarkko Ruutu .15 .40
478 Bryan Allen .15 .40
479 Ryan Kesler .15 .40
480 Matt Cooke .15 .40
481 Trevor Linden .15 .40
482 Mika Noronen .25 .60
483 Brooks Laich .15 .40
484 Dainius Zubrus .15 .40
485 Olaf Kolzig .25 .60
486 Matt Pettinger .15 .40
487 Jeff Halpern .15 .40
488 Brian Willsie .15 .40
489 Brent Johnson .15 .40
490 Chris Clark .15 .40
491 Brian Sutherby .15 .40
492 Jamie Heward .15 .40
493 Ben Clymer .15 .40
494 Bryan Muir .15 .40
495 Mathieu Biron .15 .40
496 Shaone Morrisonn .15 .40
497 Matt Bradley .15 .40
498 Mike Green RC .75 2.00
499 Rico Fata .15 .40
500 Gordie Howe 1.50 4.00
501 Scott Niedermayer CPT .15 .40
502 Scott Mellanby CPT .15 .40
503 Vincent Lecavalier CPT .30 .75
504 Chris Drury CPT .25 .60
505 Jarome Iginla CPT .40 1.00
506 Rod Brind`Amour CPT .25 .60
507 Adrian Aucoin CPT .15 .40
508 Joe Sakic CPT .60 1.50
509 Adam Foote CPT .15 .40
510 Mike Modano CPT .30 .75
511 Steve Yzerman CPT 1.25 3.00
512 Jason Smith CPT .15 .40
513 Olli Jokinen CPT .25 .60
514 Mattias Norstrom CPT .15 .40
515 Saku Koivu CPT .30 .75
516 Greg Johnson CPT .15 .40
517 Alexei Yashin CPT .15 .40
518 Daniel Alfredsson CPT .25 .60
519 Keith Primeau CPT .15 .40
520 Shane Doan CPT .15 .40
521 Patrick Marleau CPT .25 .60
522 Dallas Drake CPT .15 .40
523 Mats Sundin CPT .30 .75
524 Markus Naslund CPT .30 .75
525 Jeff Halpern CPT .15 .40
526 Sidney Crosby CPT 2.50 6.00
527 Brian Leetch CPT .30 .75
528 Jaromir Jagr CPT .50 1.25
529 Wes Walz CPT .15 .40
530 Patrik Elias CPT .25 .60
531 Anaheim Mighty Ducks .15 .40
532 Atlanta Thrashers .15 .40
533 Boston Bruins .15 .40
534 Buffalo Sabres .15 .40
535 Calgary Flames .15 .40
536 Carolina Hurricanes .15 .40
537 Chicago Blackhawks .15 .40
538 Colorado Colorado Avalanche.15 .40
539 Columbus Blue Jackets .15 .40
540 Dallas Stars .15 .40
541 Detroit Red Wings .15 .40
542 Edmonton Oilers .15 .40
543 Florida Panthers .15 .40
544 Los Angeles Kings .15 .40
545 Minnesota Wild .15 .40
546 Montreal Canadiens .15 .40
547 Nashville Predators .15 .40
548 New Jersey Devils .15 .40
549 New York Islanders .15 .40
550 New York Rangers .15 .40
551 Ottawa Senators .15 .40
552 Philadelphia Flyers .15 .40
553 Phoenix Coyotes .15 .40
554 Pittsburgh Penguins .15 .40
555 San Jose Sharks .15 .40
556 St. Louis Blues .15 .40
557 Tampa Bay Lightning .15 .40
558 Toronto Maple Leafs .15 .40
559 Vancouver Canucks .15 .40
560 Washington Capitals .15 .40
561 Martin Brodeur NS 1.50 4.00
562 Roberto Luongo NS .40 1.00
563 Marty Turco NS .25 .60
564 Rob Blake NS .15 .40
565 Adam Foote NS .15 .40
566 Chris Pronger NS .15 .40
567 Wade Redden NS .15 .40
568 Robyn Regehr NS .15 .40
569 Todd Bertuzzi NS .15 .40
570 Shane Doan NS .15 .40
571 Kris Draper NS .15 .40
572 Simon Gagne NS .15 .40
573 Dany Heatley NS .40 1.00
574 Jarome Iginla NS .40 1.00
575 Vincent Lecavalier NS .30 .75
576 Rick Nash NS .40 1.00
577 Brad Richards NS .25 .60
578 Joe Sakic NS .60 1.50
579 Ryan Smyth NS .25 .60
580 Martin St. Louis NS .25 .60
581 Joe Thornton NS .50 1.25
582 Jay Bouwmeester NS .15 .40
583 Bryan McCabe NS .15 .40
584 Ed Jovanovski NS .25 .60
585 Scott Niedermayer NS .15 .40
586 Sidney Crosby HL 2.50 6.00
587 Sidney Crosby HL 2.50 6.00
588 Alexander Ovechkin HL 1.50 4.00
589 Ed Belfour HL .30 .75
590 Mario Lemieux HL 2.00 5.00
591 Joe Thornton HL .50 1.25
592 Teemu Selanne HL .30 .75
593 Sidney Crosby HL 2.50 6.00
594 Jaromir Jagr HL .50 1.25
595 Luc Robitaille HL .25 .60
596 Manny Legace HL .30 .75
597 Alexander Ovechkin HL 1.50 4.00
598 Daniel Alfredsson HL .25 .60
599 Henrik Lundqvist HL .60 1.50
600 Alexander Ovechkin HL 1.50 4.00
601 Ryan Getzlaf RC 2.50 6.00
602 Corey Perry RC 2.00 5.00
603 Braydon Coburn RC 1.50 4.00
604 Jim Slater RC 1.50 4.00
605 Andrew Alberts RC 1.00 2.50
606 Hannu Toivonen RC 1.50 4.00
607 Milan Jurcina RC 1.00 2.50
608 Jordan Sigalet RC 1.50 4.00
609 Ben Walter RC 1.00 2.50
610 Thomas Vanek RC 2.00 5.00
611 Daniel Paille RC 1.00 2.50
612 Dion Phaneuf RC 3.00 8.00
613 Eric Nystrom RC 1.50 4.00
614 Cam Ward RC 2.00 5.00
615 Andrew Ladd RC 1.50 4.00
616 Brent Seabrook RC 1.00 2.50
617 Cam Barker RC 1.50 4.00
618 Corey Crawford RC 1.50 4.00
619 Peter Budaj RC 1.50 4.00
620 Wojtek Wolski RC 2.00 5.00
621 Brad Richardson RC 1.00 2.50
622 Gilbert Brule RC 2.00 5.00
623 Alexandre Picard RC 1.50 4.00
624 Jussi Jokinen RC 1.50 4.00
625 Jim Howard RC 1.50 4.00
626 Kyle Quincey RC 1.00 2.50
627 Valtteri Filppula RC 1.00 2.50
628 Matt Greene RC .75 2.00
629 Jean-Francois Jacques RC 1.00 2.50
630 Rostislav Olesz RC 1.50 4.00
631 Anthony Stewart RC 1.50 4.00
632 Rob Globke RC 1.00 2.50
633 George Parros RC 1.00 2.50
634 Mikko Koivu RC 1.50 4.00
635 Yann Danis RC 1.50 4.00
636 Alexander Perezhogin RC 1.50 4.00
637 Maxim Lapierre RC 1.00 2.50
638 Andrei Kostitsyn RC 1.50 4.00
639 Ryan Suter RC 1.50 4.00
640 Zach Parise RC 2.00 5.00
641 Barry Tallackson RC 1.00 2.50
642 Jeff Tambellini RC 1.00 2.50
643 Chris Campoli RC 1.00 2.50
644 Jeremy Colliton RC 1.00 2.50
645 Bruno Gervais RC 1.00 2.50
646 Henrik Lundqvist RC 3.00 8.00
647 Petr Prucha RC 1.50 4.00
648 Al Montoya RC 1.50 4.00
649 Patrick Eaves RC 1.50 4.00
650 Andrej Meszaros RC 1.00 2.50
651 Christoph Schubert RC 1.00 2.50
652 Mike Richards RC 1.50 4.00
653 Jeff Carter RC 1.50 4.00
654 R.J. Umberger RC 1.50 4.00
655 Ben Eager RC 1.00 2.50
656 Keith Ballard RC 1.00 2.50
657 Sidney Crosby RC 20.00 40.00
658 Maxime Talbot RC 1.00 2.50
659 Ryan Whitney RC 1.00 2.50
660 Colby Armstrong RC 1.50 4.00
661 Ryane Clowe RC 1.00 2.50
662 Steve Bernier RC 1.50 4.00
663 Dimitri Patzold RC 1.00 2.50
664 Lee Stempniak RC 1.00 2.50
665 Evgeny Artyukhin RC 1.00 2.50
666 Jay Harrison RC 1.00 2.50
667 Alexander Steen RC 1.50 4.00
668 Kevin Bieksa RC 1.00 2.50
669 Alexander Ovechkin RC 6.00 15.00
670 Tomas Fleischmann RC 1.00 2.50
671 Jean-Sebastien Giguere TC .25 .60
672 Ilya Kovalchuk TC .40 1.00
673 Patrice Bergeron TC .30 .75
674 Ryan Miller TC .25 .60
675 Jarome Iginla TC .40 1.00
676 Eric Staal TC .25 .60
677 Nikolai Khabibulin TC .30 .75
678 Joe Sakic TC .60 1.50
679 Rick Nash TC .40 1.00
680 Mike Modano TC .30 .75
681 Steve Yzerman TC 1.25 3.00
682 Chris Pronger TC .25 .60
683 Roberto Luongo TC .40 1.00
684 Luc Robitaille TC .25 .60
685 Marian Gaborik TC .60 1.50
686 Saku Koivu TC .30 .75
687 Paul Kariya TC .30 .75
688 Martin Brodeur TC 1.50 4.00
689 Alexei Yashin TC .15 .40
690 Jaromir Jagr TC .50 1.25
691 Dominik Hasek TC .60 1.50
692 Peter Forsberg TC .50 1.25
693 Shane Doan TC .15 .40
694 Sidney Crosby TC 2.50 6.00
695 Joe Thornton TC .50 1.25
696 Keith Tkachuk TC .30 .75
697 Vincent Lecavalier TC .30 .75
698 Mats Sundin TC .30 .75
699 Markus Naslund TC .30 .75
700 Alexander Ovechkin TC 2.00 5.00

2005-06 Parkhurst Facsimile Auto Parallel

PRINT RUN 100 #'d SETS
657 Sidney Crosby 60.00 125.00

2005-06 Parkhurst Signatures

AL Andrew Alberts 5.00 12.00
AB Adam Berkhoel 5.00 12.00
AK Andrei Kostitsyn 6.00 15.00
AL Andrew Ladd 6.00 15.00
AM Andrei Meszaros 3.00 8.00
AM Al Montoya 8.00 20.00
AN Antero Niittymaki 8.00 20.00
AO Alexander Ovechkin SP 75.00 200.00
AP Alexandre Picard SP 10.00 25.00
BA Milan Bartovic 3.00 8.00
BB Brad Boyes 3.00 8.00
BC Braydon Coburn 5.00 12.00
BE Ben Eager 5.00 12.00
BL Brett Lebda 5.00 12.00
BO Brandon Bochenski 5.00 12.00
BS Brent Seabrook 5.00 12.00
BT Barry Tallackson 5.00 12.00
BU Peter Budaj 6.00 15.00
BW Ben Walter 3.00 8.00
CC Chris Campoli 3.00 8.00
CK Chuck Kobasew 3.00 8.00
CS Christoph Schubert 3.00 8.00
CT Chris Thorburn 3.00 8.00
DB Daniel Briere 8.00 20.00
DE Derek Boogaard 5.00 12.00
DK Duncan Keith 5.00 12.00
DL David Leneveu 5.00 12.00
DP Dimitri Patzold 5.00 12.00
DW Dwayne Roloson 6.00 15.00
EA Evgeny Artyukhin 3.00 8.00
FP Fernando Pisani 6.00 15.00
GP George Parros 3.00 8.00
HO Marcel Hossa SP 10.00 25.00
JF Johan Franzen 5.00 12.00
JH Jim Howard 10.00 25.00
JH Jeff Halpern 3.00 8.00
JI Jarome Iginla SP 40.00 80.00
JJ Jussi Jokinen SP 10.00 25.00
JL Jason Labarbera 3.00 8.00
JS Jordan Sigalet 6.00 15.00
JS Jim Slater 5.00 12.00
JT Jeff Tambellini 3.00 8.00
JV Josef Vasicek 3.00 8.00
JW Jeff Woywitka 3.00 8.00
KC Kyle Calder 3.00 8.00
KN Kevin Nastiuk 5.00 12.00
KO Mikko Koivu 8.00 20.00
KQ Kyle Quincey 3.00 8.00
IL Ian Laperriere 5.00 12.00
LI John-Michael Liles 6.00 15.00
LS Lee Stempniak SP 8.00 20.00
MA Maxim Afinogenov SP 12.00 30.00
MB Martin Biron 6.00 15.00
MC Mike Cammalleri 5.00 12.00
MG Marian Gaborik SP 40.00 80.00
MH Michal Handzus 8.00 20.00
MJ Milan Jurcina SP 8.00 20.00
ML Maxim Lapierre 6.00 15.00
MM Milan Michalek SP 8.00 20.00
MR Mike Richards SP 12.00 30.00
MS Marc Savard 3.00 8.00
MT Mikael Tellqvist 6.00 15.00
NA Nik Antropov SP 10.00 25.00
NN Niklas Nordgren 3.00 8.00
OJ Olli Jokinen SP 15.00 40.00
OK Ole-Kristian Tollefson 3.00 8.00
OK Olaf Kolzig 6.00 15.00
PB Pierre-Marc Bouchard 3.00 8.00
PE Patrick Eaves 6.00 15.00
PN Petteri Nokelainen 3.00 8.00
PP Petr Prucha SP 10.00 25.00
PS Philippe Sauve 3.00 8.00
RC Ryan Craig 5.00 12.00
RE Robert Esche SP 10.00 25.00
RF Ruslan Fedotenko 3.00 8.00
RG Ryan Getzlaf SP 20.00 50.00
RH Ryan Hollweg 5.00 12.00
RM Ryan Malone 5.00 12.00
RN Robert Nilsson 5.00 12.00
RO Rostislav Olesz 5.00 12.00
SB Steve Bernier 8.00 20.00
SC Sidney Crosby SP 400.00 600.00
SH Scott Hartnell 3.00 8.00
TB Todd Bertuzzi SP 25.00 50.00
TC Ty Conklin 3.00 8.00
TF Tomas Fleischmann 5.00 12.00
TG Tim Gleason 3.00 8.00
TS Timofei Shishkanov 3.00 8.00
WI Brad Winchester 5.00 12.00
YD Yann Danis 6.00 15.00
ZM Zbynek Michalek 3.00 8.00
ZP Zach Parise 10.00 25.00

2005-06 Parkhurst True Colors

STATED ODDS 1:432
TCANA Teemu Selanne 40.00 100.00
Rob Niedermayer
Scott Niedermayer
Sandis Ozolinsh
J-S Giguere
Joffrey Lupul
Corey Perry
Ryan Getzlaf
TCATL Peter Bondra 40.00 80.00
Marian Hossa
Marc Savard
Scott Mellanby
Bobby Holik
Patriik Stefan
Ilya Kovalchuk
Kari Lehtonen
TCBOS Brian Leetch 50.00 100.00
Sergei Samsonov
Glen Murray
Andrew Raycroft
Patrice Bergeron
Andrew Alberts
Hannu Toivonen
Milan Jurcina
TCBUF Jochen Hecht 50.00 100.00
Tim Connolly
Maxim Afinogenov
Chris Drury
Mike Grier
Derek Roy
Ryan Miller
Thomas Vanek
TCCAR Doug Weight 40.00 80.00
Cory Stillman
Justin Williams
Martin Gerber
Rod Brind`Amour
Eric Staal
Cam Ward
Andrew Ladd
TCCGY Tony Amonte 50.00 125.00
Jarome Iginla
Darren McCarty
Chuck Kobasew
Jordan Leopold
Miikka Kiprusoff
Matthew Lombardi
Dion Phaneuf
TCCHI Kyle Calder 50.00 100.00
Nikolai Khabibulin
Eric Daze
Adrian Aucoin
Tuomo Ruutu
Brent Seabrook
Rene Bourque
Cam Barker
TCCLB Sergei Fedorov 75.00 150.00
Adam Foote
Marc Denis
Rick Nash
Nikolai Zherdev
Jaroslav Balastik
Gilbert Brule
Alexandre Picard
TCCOL Pierre Turgeon 40.00 80.00
Joe Sakic
Rob Blake
Milan Hejduk
David Aebischer
Alex Tanguay
Marek Svatos
Peter Budaj
TCDAL Mike Modano 30.00 60.00
Sergei Zubov
Bill Guerin
Marty Turco
Brenden Morrow
Trevor Daley
Steve Ott
Jussi Jokinen
TCDET Brendan Shanahan 75.00 150.00
Steve Yzerman
Nicklas Lidstrom
Robert Lang

Manny Legace
Kris Draper
Pavel Datsyuk
Henrik Zetterberg
EDM Chris Pronger 60.00 125.00
Michael Peca
Ryan Smyth
Jason Smith
Shawn Horcoff
Ty Conklin
Fernando Pisani
Ales Hemsky
FLA Roberto Luongo 40.00 80.00
Joe Nieuwendyk
Olli Jokinen
Gary Roberts
Jay Bouwmeester
Stephen Weiss
Rostislav Olesz
Anthony Stewart
LAK Luc Robitaille 40.00 100.00
Pavol Demitra
Jeremy Roenick
Mathieu Garon
Alexander Frolov
Mike Cammalleri
Dustin Brown
George Parros
MIN Manny Fernandez 40.00 100.00
Brian Rolston
Marian Gaborik
Dwayne Roloson
Pierre-Marc Bouchard
Mikko Koivu
Matt Foy
Derek Boogaard
MTL Saku Koivu 60.00 125.00
Mike Ribeiro
Jose Theodore
Richard Zednik
Michael Ryder
Alexei Kovalev
Alexander Perezhogin
Yann Danis
NJD Scott Gomez 75.00 150.00
Martin Brodeur
Brian Rafalski
Patrik Elias
Viktor Kozlov
Brian Gionta
Zach Parise
Barry Tallackson
NSH Paul Kariya 30.00 80.00
Tomas Vokoun
David Legwand
Scott Hartnell
Dan Hamhuis
Adam Hall
Scott Upshall
Ryan Suter
NYI Mark Parrish 75.00 150.00
Miroslav Satan
Jason Blake
Alexei Yashin
Rick DiPietro
Trent Hunter
Chris Campoli
Jeremy Colliton SP
NYR Jaromir Jagr 40.00 80.00
Martin Straka
Petr Sykora
Tom Poti
Ville Nieminen
Marcel Hossa
Henrik Lundqvist
Dominic Moore
OTT Dominik Hasek 30.00 80.00
Daniel Alfredsson
Wade Redden
Martin Havlat
Jason Spezza
Zdeno Chara
Dany Heatley
Andrei Meszaros
PHI Keith Primeau 40.00 100.00
Peter Forsberg
Robert Esche
Simon Gagne
Derian Hatcher
Joni Pitkanen
Mike Richards
Jeff Carter
PHX Curtis Joseph 25.00 60.00
Mike Comrie
Ladislav Nagy
Shane Doan
Steven Reinprecht
Philippe Sauve
Keith Ballard
David Leneveu
PIT Mario Lemieux 125.00 225.00
Jocelyn Thibault
John LeClair
Mark Recchi
Erik Christensen
Sidney Crosby
Maxime Talbot
Ryan Whitney
SJS Patrick Marleau 40.00 80.00
Joe Thornton
Evgeni Nabokov
Jonathan Cheechoo
Milan Michalek
Ryane Clowe
Josh Gorges
Steve Bernier
STL Keith Tkachuk 25.00 60.00
Patrick Lalime
Barret Jackman
Jay McClement
Jeff Woywitka
Jeff Hoggan
Kevin Dallman
Lee Stempniak
TBL Vincent Lecavalier 50.00 100.00
Brad Richards
Vaclav Prospal
Sean Burke
Martin St. Louis
Ruslan Fedotenko
Ryan Craig
Evgeny Artyukhin
TCTOR Mats Sundin 40.00 80.00
Bryan McCabe
Jason Allison
Carlo Colaiacovo
Nik Antropov
Alexander Steen
Ed Belfour
Eric Lindros
TCVAN Dan Cloutier 50.00 100.00
Markus Naslund
Trevor Linden
Ed Jovanovski
Brendan Morrison
Todd Bertuzzi
Alex Auld
Kevin Bieksa
TCWAS Olaf Kolzig 75.00 150.00
Jeff Friesen
Jeff Halpern
Brendan Witt
Shaone Morrisonn
Alexander Ovechkin
Thomas Fleischmann
Jakub Klepis
TCCHDE Kyle Calder 50.00 100.00
Nicklas Lidstrom
Nikolai Khabibulin
Eric Daze
Manny Legace
Kris Draper
Pavel Datsyuk
Tuomo Ruutu
TCDECO Joe Sakic 75.00 125.00
Brendan Shanahan
Steve Yzerman
Rob Blake
Milan Hejduk
Alex Tanguay
Pavel Datsyuk#Henrik Zetterberg
TCEDCA Chris Pronger 40.00 100.00
Jarome Iginla
Ryan Smyth
Shawn Horcoff
Chuck Kobasew
Ales Hemsky
Miikka Kiprusoff
Dion Phaneuf
TCFLTB Vincent Lecavalier 40.00 100.00
Brad Richards
Vaclav Prospal
Roberto Luongo
Olli Jokinen
Martin St. Louis
Jay Bouwmeester
Stephen Weiss
TCMIDA Mike Modano 40.00 100.00
Bill Guerin
Manny Fernandez
Brian Rolston
Marian Gaborik
Marty Turco
Brenden Morrow
P-M Bouchard
TCMOBO Brian Leetch 40.00 100.00
Saku Koivu
Mike Ribeiro
Jose Theodore
Glen Murray
Andrew Raycroft
Michael Ryder
Patrice Bergeron
TCNJNY Jaromir Jagr 75.00 150.00
Scott Gomez
Martin Straka
Martin Brodeur
Brian Rafalski
Patrik Elias
Henrik Lundqvist
Dominic Moore
TCNYNY Jaromir Jagr 40.00 100.00
Martin Straka
Miroslav Satan
Jason Blake
Tom Poti
Alexei Yashin
Rick DiPietro
Henrik Lundqvist SP
TCOTTO Ed Belfour 40.00 100.00
Eric Lindros
Mats Sundin
Dominik Hasek
Daniel Alfredsson
Bryan McCabe
Jason Spezza
Dany Heatley
TCPHPI Mario Lemieux 100.00 200.00
Keith Primeau
John LeClair
Peter Forsberg
Simon Gagne
Erik Christensen
Joni Pitkanen
Sidney Crosby
TCSJLA Luc Robitaille 40.00 100.00
Pavol Demitra
Patrick Marleau
Jeremy Roenick
Joe Thornton
Evgeni Nabokov
Jonathan Cheechoo
Alexander Frolov
TCTOMO Ed Belfour 40.00 80.00
Mats Sundin
Saku Koivu
Jose Theodore
Jason Allison
Michael Ryder
Alexei Kovalev
Alexander Steen

2006-07 Parkhurst

COMPLETE SET w/ SPs (250) 100.00 200.00
COMPLETE SET (160) 15.00 40.00
ENFORCE/CAPT PRINT RUN 3999
1 Ron MacLean .40 1.00
2 John Anderson .20 .50
3 Al Arbour .20 .50
4 Lou Fontinato .20 .50
5 Grant Fuhr .40 1.00
6 Bill Gadsby .30 .75
7 Danny Gare .20 .50
8 Ed Giacomin .40 1.00
9 Andy Bathgate .30 .75
10 Bob Baun .30 .75
11 Don Beaupre .30 .75
12 Barry Beck .20 .50
13 Jean Beliveau .60 1.50
14 Rod Gilbert .30 .75
15 Clark Gillies .30 .75
16 Doug Gilmour .60 1.50
17 Danny Grant .20 .50
18 Ron Greschner .20 .50
19 Bob Bourne .20 .50
20 Mike Bossy .60 1.50
21 Johnny Bower .60 1.50
22 Scotty Bowman .60 1.50
23 Stu Grimson .20 .50
24 Richard Brodeur .30 .75
25 Aaron Broten .20 .50
26 Neal Broten .20 .50
27 Dale Hawerchuk .40 1.00
28 Johnny Bucyk .40 1.00
29 Paul Henderson .30 .75
30 Ron Hextall .60 1.50
31 Rejean Houle .20 .50
32 Harry Howell .30 .75
33 Gerry Cheevers .40 1.00
34 Don Cherry 1.25 3.00
35 Kelly Hrudey .30 .75
36 Bobby Hull .75 2.00
37 Dino Ciccarelli .30 .75
38 Wendel Clark .40 1.00
39 Bobby Clarke .40 1.00
40 Dale Hunter .20 .50
41 Dick Irvin .20 .50
42 Tom Johnson .30 .75
43 Mike Keenan .20 .50
44 J.P. Kelly .20 .50
45 Red Kelly .40 1.00
46 John Davidson .40 1.00
47 Kelly Kisio .20 .50
48 Marcel Dionne .40 1.00
49 Joey Kocur .20 .50
50 Kevin Dineen .20 .50
51 Jari Kurri .40 1.00
52 Elmer Lach .30 .75
53 Ron Duguay .20 .50
54 Ron Ellis .20 .50
55 Guy Lafleur .75 2.00
56 Phil Esposito .60 1.50
57 Tony Esposito .40 1.00
58 Bernie Federko .20 .50
59 Rod Langway .20 .50
60 Edgar Laprade .20 .50
61 Pierre Larouche .20 .50
62 Mike Foligno .20 .50
63 Reed Larson .20 .50
64 Reggie Leach .20 .50
65 Rejean Lemelin .30 .75
66 Ted Lindsay .40 1.00
67 Mike Liut .30 .75
68 Al MacInnis .30 .75
69 Clint Malarchuk .30 .75
70 Cesare Maniago .30 .75
71 Butch Bouchard .30 .75
72 Brian McFarlane .20 .50
73 Marty McSorley .20 .50
74 Howie Meeker .20 .50
75 Gilles Meloche .20 .50
76 Barry Melrose .20 .50
77 Ray Bourque .60 1.50
78 Brian Mullen .20 .50
79 Joe Mullen .20 .50
80 Cam Neely .60 1.50
81 Eric Nesterenko .20 .50
82 Bernie Nicholls .20 .50
83 Kent Nilsson .20 .50
84 Ulf Nilsson .20 .50
85 Adam Oates .30 .75
86 John Ogrodnick .20 .50
87 Willie O'Ree .40 1.00
88 Terry O'Reilly .40 1.00
89 Bobby Orr 2.00 5.00
90 Greg Millen .30 .75
91 Jim Pappin .20 .50
92 Bernie Parent .40 1.00
93 Brad Park .30 .75
94 Jim Peplinski .20 .50
95 Gilbert Perreault .30 .75
96 Pete Peeters .20 .50
97 Pierre Pilote .20 .50
98 Willi Plett .20 .50
99 Wayne Cashman .20 .50
100 Denis Potvin .30 .75
101 Bob Probert .40 1.00
102 Marcel Pronovost .20 .50
103 Rob Ramage .20 .50
104 Mike Krushelnyski .20 .50
105 Pokey Reddick .30 .75
106 Larry Robinson .30 .75
107 Reijo Ruotsalainen .20 .50
108 Jim Rutherford .20 .50
109 Borje Salming .40 1.00
110 Milt Schmidt .30 .75
111 Jim Schoenfeld .20 .50
112 Dave Schultz .30 .75
113 Dave Semenko .20 .50
114 Eddie Shack .30 .75
115 Claude Lemieux .20 .50
116 Darryl Sittler .40 1.00
117 Dickie Moore .20 .50
118 Bobby Smith .20 .50
119 Clint Smith .30 .75
120 Anton Stastny .20 .50
121 Marian Stastny .20 .50
122 Peter Stastny .30 .75
123 Thomas Steen .20 .50
124 Scott Stevens .20 .50
125 Brent Sutter .20 .50
126 Duane Sutter .20 .50
127 Darryl Sutter .20 .50
128 J.P. Parise .20 .50
129 Ron Sutter .20 .50
130 Brian Sutter .20 .50
131 Walt Tkaczuk .20 .50
132 Denis Savard .20 .50
133 Frank Udvari .20 .50
134 Gump Worsley .30 .75
135 Doug Jarvis .20 .50
136 Jacques Lemaire .20 .50
137 Peter McNab .20 .50
138 Rick Middleton .30 .75
139 Mike Rogers .20 .50
140 Mats Naslund .30 .75
141 Jim Neilson .20 .50
142 Don Metz .20 .50
143 Pat LaFontaine .30 .75
144 Gordie Howe .75 2.00
145 Patrick Roy 1.25 3.00
146 Garry Unger .20 .50
147 Larry Murphy .20 .50
148 Rick Vaive .20 .50
149 Tiger Williams .30 .75
150 Mario Lemieux 1.25 3.00
151 Michel Dion .30 .75
152 Bill Dineen .20 .50
153 Gary Dornhoefer .20 .50
154 Hakan Loob .20 .50
155 Craig MacTavish .20 .50
156 Allan Stanley .20 .50
157 Marc Tardif .20 .50
158 Ryan Walter .20 .50
159 Zigmund Palffy .30 .75
160 Wilf Paiement .20 .50
161 Milt Schmidt 1.25 3.00
162 Johnny Bucyk 1.25 3.00
163 Ray Bourque 1.50 4.00
164 Terry O'Reilly 1.25 3.00
165 Jim Schoenfeld 1.00 2.50
166 Danny Gare 1.00 2.50
167 Gilbert Perreault 1.25 3.00
168 Mike Foligno 1.00 2.50
169 Jim Peplinski 1.00 2.50
170 Pierre Pilote 1.00 2.50
171 Darryl Sutter 1.00 2.50
172 Denis Savard 1.00 2.50
173 Bill Gadsby 1.25 3.00
174 Marc Tardif 1.00 2.50
175 Peter Stastny 1.25 3.00
176 J.P. Parise 1.00 2.50
177 Ted Lindsay 1.25 3.00
178 Red Kelly 1.25 3.00
179 Gordie Howe 2.00 5.00
180 Danny Grant 1.00 2.50
181 Reed Larson 1.00 2.50
182 Wayne Cashman 1.00 2.50
183 Craig MacTavish 1.00 2.50
184 Doug Wilson 1.00 2.50
185 Marcel Dionne 1.25 3.00
186 Butch Bouchard 1.25 3.00
187 Jean Beliveau 1.50 4.00
188 Wilf Paiement 1.00 2.50
189 Scott Stevens 1.00 2.50
190 Clark Gillies 1.00 2.50
191 Denis Potvin 1.25 3.00
192 Brent Sutter 1.00 2.50
193 Allan Stanley 1.25 3.00
194 Andy Bathgate 1.25 3.00
195 Brad Park 1.25 3.00
196 Phil Esposito 1.50 4.00
197 Barry Beck 1.00 2.50
198 Ron Greschner 1.00 2.50
199 Kelly Kisio 1.00 2.50
200 Bobby Clarke 1.50 4.00
201 Ron Sutter 1.00 2.50
202 Dale Hawerchuk 1.50 4.00
203 Thomas Steen 1.00 2.50
204 Mario Lemieux 2.50 6.00
205 Al Arbour 1.00 2.50
206 Brian Sutter 1.00 2.50
207 Bernie Federko 1.00 2.50
208 Scott Stevens 1.00 2.50
209 Darryl Sittler 1.50 4.00
210 Rick Vaive 1.00 2.50
211 Rob Ramage 1.00 2.50
212 Wendel Clark 1.25 3.00
213 Doug Gilmour 1.50 4.00
214 Kevin Dineen 1.00 2.50
215 Rod Langway 1.00 2.50
216 Dale Hunter 1.00 2.50
217 Adam Oates 1.25 3.00
218 Walt Tkaczuk 1.00 2.50
219 Harry Howell 1.00 2.50
220 Rob Ramage 1.00 2.50
221 Clint Smith 1.25 3.00
222 Doug Gilmour 1.50 4.00
223 Mike Rogers 1.00 2.50
224 Pat LaFontaine 1.25 3.00
225 Neal Broten 1.00 2.50
226 Al MacInnis 1.25 3.00
227 Kevin Dineen 1.00 2.50
228 Joey Kocur 1.00 2.50
229 Tiger Williams 1.25 3.00
230 Tiger Williams 1.25 3.00
231 Dale Hunter 1.00 2.50
232 Marty McSorley 1.00 2.50
233 Bob Probert 1.50 4.00
234 Stu Grimson 1.00 2.50
235 Dave Schultz 1.25 3.00
236 Bill Gadsby 1.25 3.00
237 Lou Fontinato 1.00 2.50
238 Joey Kocur 1.00 2.50
239 Ted Lindsay 1.25 3.00
240 Dave Semenko 1.00 2.50
241 Gary Dornhoefer 1.00 2.50
242 Pierre Pilote 1.00 2.50
243 Clark Gillies 1.00 2.50
244 Terry O'Reilly 1.25 3.00
245 Wendel Clark 1.25 3.00
246 Willi Plett 1.00 2.50
247 Wilf Paiement 1.00 2.50
248 Tiger Williams 1.25 3.00
249 Marty McSorley 1.00 2.50
250 Bob Probert 1.50 4.00

2006-07 Parkhurst Autographs

STATED ODDS 1:6 PACKS
2 John Anderson 8.00 20.00
3 Al Arbour 8.00 20.00
4 Lou Fontinato 8.00 20.00
5 Grant Fuhr 10.00 25.00
6 Bill Gadsby 10.00 25.00
7 Danny Gare SP 10.00 25.00
8 Ed Giacomin 10.00 25.00
9 Andy Bathgate 4.00 10.00
10 Bob Baun 15.00 40.00
11 Don Beaupre 6.00 15.00
12 Barry Beck 4.00 10.00
13 Jean Beliveau SP
14 Rod Gilbert SP 60.00 100.00
15 Clark Gillies 4.00 10.00
16 Doug Gilmour 12.00 30.00
17 Danny Grant 6.00 15.00
18 Ron Greschner 4.00 10.00
19 Bob Bourne 4.00 10.00
20 Mike Bossy 15.00 40.00
21 Johnny Bower 8.00 20.00
22 Scotty Bowman SP 100.00 150.00
23 Stu Grimson 5.00 12.00
24 Richard Brodeur 4.00 10.00
25 Aaron Broten 4.00 10.00
26 Neal Broten 4.00 10.00
27 Dale Hawerchuk 10.00 25.00
28 Johnny Bucyk SP 30.00 80.00
29 Paul Henderson 8.00 20.00
30 Ron Hextall 8.00 20.00
31 Rejean Houle 10.00 25.00
32 Harry Howell 8.00 20.00
33 Gerry Cheevers 10.00 25.00
34 Don Cherry 30.00 60.00
35 Kelly Hrudey 6.00 15.00
36 Bobby Hull 25.00 60.00
37 Dino Ciccarelli 8.00 20.00
38 Wendel Clark 15.00 40.00
39 Bobby Clarke 12.00 30.00
40 Dale Hunter 6.00 15.00
41 Dick Irvin 10.00 25.00
42 Tom Johnson 15.00 40.00
43 Mike Keenan 6.00 15.00
44 J.P. Kelly 4.00 10.00
45 Red Kelly 6.00 15.00
46 John Davidson 4.00 10.00
47 Kelly Kisio 4.00 10.00
48 Marcel Dionne 10.00 25.00
49 Joey Kocur 6.00 15.00
50 Kevin Dineen 10.00 25.00
51 Jari Kurri 6.00 15.00
52 Elmer Lach 15.00 40.00
53 Ron Duguay 4.00 10.00
54 Ron Ellis 5.00 12.00
55 Guy Lafleur 15.00 40.00
56 Phil Esposito 12.00 30.00
57 Tony Esposito 10.00 25.00
58 Bernie Federko 5.00 12.00
59 Rod Langway 4.00 10.00
60 Edgar Laprade 20.00 50.00
61 Pierre Larouche 8.00 20.00
62 Mike Foligno 4.00 10.00
63 Reed Larson 4.00 10.00
64 Reggie Leach 8.00 20.00
66 Ted Lindsay 8.00 20.00
67 Mike Liut 8.00 20.00
68 Al MacInnis 8.00 20.00
69 Clint Malarchuk 8.00 20.00
70 Cesare Maniago 8.00 20.00
71 Butch Bouchard 30.00 80.00
72 Brian McFarlane 4.00 10.00
73 Marty McSorley 5.00 12.00
74 Howie Meeker 10.00 25.00
75 Gilles Meloche 8.00 20.00
76 Barry Melrose 8.00 20.00
77 Ray Bourque SP 60.00 100.00
78 Brian Mullen 4.00 10.00
79 Joe Mullen 4.00 10.00
80 Cam Neely 15.00 40.00
81 Eric Nesterenko 8.00 20.00
82 Bernie Nicholls 4.00 10.00
84 Ulf Nilsson 5.00 12.00
85 Adam Oates 6.00 15.00
86 John Ogrodnick 4.00 10.00
87 Willie O'Ree 10.00 25.00
88 Terry O'Reilly 8.00 20.00
89 Bobby Orr 175.00 250.00
90 Greg Millen 4.00 10.00
91 Jim Pappin 8.00 20.00
92 Bernie Parent 8.00 20.00
93 Brad Park 6.00 15.00
94 Jim Peplinski 4.00 10.00
95 Gilbert Perreault 6.00 15.00
96 Pete Peeters 8.00 20.00
97 Pierre Pilote 8.00 20.00
98 Willi Plett 4.00 10.00
100 Denis Potvin 5.00 12.00
101 Bob Probert 8.00 20.00
102 Marcel Pronovost 8.00 20.00
103 Rob Ramage 4.00 10.00
104 Mike Krushelnyski 4.00 10.00
106 Larry Robinson 10.00 25.00
107 Reijo Ruotsalainen 4.00 10.00
108 Jim Rutherford 12.00 30.00
109 Borje Salming 10.00 25.00
110 Milt Schmidt 6.00 15.00
111 Jim Schoenfeld 6.00 15.00
112 Dave Schultz 4.00 10.00
113 Dave Semenko 5.00 12.00
114 Eddie Shack 6.00 15.00
115 Claude Lemieux 5.00 12.00
116 Darryl Sittler 20.00 50.00
118 Bobby Smith 4.00 10.00
119 Clint Smith 40.00 80.00
120 Anton Stastny 5.00 12.00
121 Marian Stastny 4.00 10.00
122 Peter Stastny 10.00 25.00
123 Thomas Steen 4.00 10.00
124 Scott Stevens 15.00 40.00
125 Brent Sutter 4.00 10.00
126 Duane Sutter 5.00 12.00
127 Darryl Sutter 5.00 12.00
128 J.P. Parise 4.00 10.00
130 Brian Sutter 5.00 12.00
131 Walt Tkaczuk 6.00 15.00
132 Denis Savard SP 25.00 50.00
133 Frank Udvari 8.00 20.00
135 Doug Jarvis 10.00 25.00
136 Jacques Lemaire 8.00 20.00
137 Peter McNab 8.00 20.00
138 Rick Middleton 15.00 40.00
139 Mike Rogers 5.00 12.00
140 Mats Naslund 6.00 15.00
141 Jim Neilson 6.00 15.00
143 Pat LaFontaine 8.00 20.00
144 Gordie Howe 30.00 80.00
145 Patrick Roy SP
146 Garry Unger 4.00 10.00
148 Rick Vaive 8.00 20.00
149 Tiger Williams 12.00 30.00
150 Mario Lemieux SP
151 Michel Dion
152 Bill Dineen 15.00 40.00
153 Gary Dornhoefer 4.00 10.00
154 Hakan Loob 6.00 15.00
155 Craig MacTavish 4.00 10.00
156 Allan Stanley 8.00 20.00
157 Marc Tardif 8.00 20.00
158 Ryan Walter 4.00 10.00
160 Wilf Paiement 4.00 10.00
161 Milt Schmidt CAP 12.00 30.00
162 Johnny Bucyk CAP SP
163 Ray Bourque CAP SP
164 Terry O'Reilly CAP 10.00 25.00
165 Jim Schoenfeld CAP 8.00 20.00
166 Danny Gare CAP 4.00 10.00
167 Gilbert Perreault CAP 12.00 30.00
168 Mike Foligno CAP 4.00 10.00
169 Jim Peplinski CAP 15.00 30.00
170 Pierre Pilote CAP 12.00 30.00
171 Darryl Sutter CAP 6.00 15.00
172 Denis Savard CAP 50.00 100.00
173 Bill Gadsby CAP 10.00 25.00
174 Marc Tardif CAP 8.00 20.00
175 Peter Stastny CAP 15.00 40.00
176 J.P. Parise CAP 6.00 15.00
177 Ted Lindsay CAP 12.00 30.00
178 Red Kelly CAP 12.00 30.00
179 Gordie Howe CAP 60.00 125.00
180 Danny Grant CAP 8.00 20.00
181 Reed Larson CAP 6.00 15.00
183 Craig MacTavish CAP 4.00 10.00
185 Marcel Dionne CAP
186 Butch Bouchard CAP
187 Jean Beliveau CAP SP 25.00 50.00
188 Wilf Paiement CAP 4.00 10.00
189 Scott Stevens CAP 15.00 40.00
190 Clark Gillies CAP 10.00 25.00
191 Denis Potvin CAP 6.00 15.00
192 Brent Sutter CAP 4.00 10.00
193 Allan Stanley CAP 12.00 30.00
194 Andy Bathgate CAP 6.00 15.00
195 Brad Park CAP 6.00 15.00
196 Phil Esposito CAP 15.00 40.00
197 Barry Beck CAP 6.00 15.00
198 Ron Greschner CAP 6.00 15.00
199 Kelly Kisio CAP
200 Bobby Clarke CAP 25.00 60.00
202 Dale Hawerchuk CAP 12.00 30.00
203 Thomas Steen CAP 10.00 25.00
204 Mario Lemieux CAP SP
205 Al Arbour CAP 8.00 20.00
206 Brian Sutter CAP 6.00 15.00
207 Bernie Federko CAP 10.00 25.00
208 Scott Stevens CAP SP 25.00 60.00
209 Darryl Sittler CAP 25.00 60.00
210 Rick Vaive CAP
211 Rob Ramage CAP 10.00 25.00
212 Wendel Clark CAP 15.00 40.00
213 Doug Gilmour CAP 10.00 25.00
214 Kevin Dineen CAP
215 Rod Langway CAP 4.00 10.00
216 Dale Hunter CAP 8.00 20.00
217 Adam Oates CAP 8.00 20.00
219 Harry Howell CAP 15.00 40.00
220 Rob Ramage CAP
221 Clint Smith CAP 25.00 60.00
222 Doug Gilmour CAP EXCH 12.00 30.00
223 Mike Rogers CAP 20.00 50.00
224 Pat LaFontaine CAP
225 Neal Broten CAP 12.00 30.00
226 Al MacInnis CAP 8.00 20.00
227 Kevin Dineen CAP 10.00 25.00
228 Joey Kocur ENF 15.00 40.00
229 Tiger Williams ENF EXCH 12.00 30.00
230 Tiger Williams ENF 15.00 40.00
231 Dale Hunter ENF 8.00 20.00
232 Marty McSorley ENF 10.00 25.00
233 Bob Probert ENF 15.00 30.00
234 Stu Grimson ENF 10.00 25.00
235 Dave Schultz ENF 20.00 50.00
236 Bill Gadsby ENF 25.00 60.00
237 Lou Fontinato ENF
238 Joey Kocur ENF
239 Ted Lindsay ENF 10.00 25.00
240 Dave Semenko ENF 15.00 40.00
241 Gary Dornhoefer ENF 15.00 30.00
242 Pierre Pilote ENF 12.00 30.00
243 Clark Gillies ENF 4.00 10.00
244 Terry O'Reilly ENF 20.00 50.00
245 Wendel Clark ENF 12.00 30.00
246 Willi Plett ENF 4.00 10.00
247 Wilf Paiement ENF 4.00 10.00
248 Tiger Williams ENF
249 Marty McSorley ENF
250 Bob Probert ENF 15.00 30.00

2006-07 Parkhurst Autographs Dual

DAAB Al Arbour 60.00 100.00
Scotty Bowman
DABB Neal Broten 60.00 125.00
Aaron Broten
DABG Mike Bossy
Clark Gillies
DABL Butch Bouchard
Elmer Lach
DABM Jean Beliveau
Dickie Moore
DABO Gerry Cheevers
Brad Park
DACB Dino Ciccarelli
Neal Broten
DACL Bobby Clarke 90.00 150.00
Reggie Leach
DACP Bobby Clarke
Bernie Parent
DADN Marcel Dionne
Bernie Nicholls
DADR Denis Savard 30.00 60.00
Rick Vaive
DAEB Phil Esposito 60.00 125.00
Johnny Bucyk
DAEE Phil Esposito 30.00 80.00
Tony Esposito
DAES Ron Ellis 20.00 50.00
Eddie Shack
DAFG Lou Fontinato
Bill Gadsby
DAFM Bernie Federko 60.00 100.00
Joe Mullen
DAGB Ron Greschner 30.00 80.00
Barry Beck
DAGC Grant Fuhr
Craig MacTavish
DAHE Bobby Hull 50.00 125.00
Tony Esposito
DAHL Gordie Howe
Ted Lindsay
DAHP Bobby Hull 25.00 60.00
Jim Pappin
DAHS Dale Hawerchuk
Tomas Steen
DAIM Dick Irvin 15.00 40.00
Brian McFarlane
DALD Mike Liut
Kevin Dineen
DALK Ted Lindsay
Red Kelly
DALL Guy Lafleur
Jacques Lemaire
DALS Pat LaFontaine
Brent Sutter
DAMB Gilles Meloche 75.00 150.00
Don Beaupre
DAMM Joe Mullen
Brian Mullen
DAMP Marty McSorley
Bob Probert
DANO Cam Neely 75.00 150.00
Adam Oates
DAOB Bobby Orr 200.00 350.00
Ray Bourque
DAOE Bobby Orr
Phil Esposito
DAOL John Ogrodnick
Reed Larson
DAOM Terry O'Reilly
Peter McNab
DAPF Gilbert Perreault 50.00 100.00
Mike Foligno
DAPG Gilbert Perreault 100.00 150.00
Danny Gare
DAPK Bob Probert 30.00 60.00
Joey Kocur
DAPM Pete Peeters 50.00 100.00
Rick Middleton
DAPP Jim Peplinski 30.00 60.00
Willi Plett
DARP Larry Robinson
Denis Potvin
DASB Milt Schmidt
Johnny Bucyk
DASD Dave Schultz
Gary Dornhoefer
DASV Darryl Sittler 40.00 80.00
Rick Vaive
DATB Tiger Williams
Richard Brodeur
DAWS Tiger Williams 75.00 125.00
Dave Semenko
DAST1 Peter Stastny
Anton Stastny
DAST2 Peter Stastny
Marian Stastny
DASU1 Darryl Sutter 30.00 60.00
Duane Sutter
DASU2 Brent Sutter
Brian Sutter

2002-03 Parkhurst Retro

Released in mid-April, this 250-card set payed tribute to the look and feel of the 1951-52 Parkhurst set. Card backs were blank. The set consisted of 200 veterans and 50 shorprinted rookies. Rookie cards were serial-numbered to 300 copies each.

COMP.SET w/o SP's (200) 40.00 80.00
1 Mario Lemieux 2.00 5.00
2 Jarome Iginla .40 1.00
3 Jaromir Jagr .50 1.25
4 Alexei Kovalev .25 .60
5 Todd Bertuzzi .30 .75
6 Joe Thornton .50 1.25
7 Jason Allison .10 .25
8 Markus Naslund .30 .75
9 Eric Lindros .30 .75
10 Keith Tkachuk .30 .75
11 Adam Oates .25 .60
12 Mike Modano .50 1.25
13 Pavel Bure .30 .75
14 Ron Francis .25 .60
15 Joe Sakic .60 1.50
16 Brendan Shanahan .30 .75
17 Alexei Yashin .10 .25
18 Patrick Roy 1.50 4.00
19 Dwayne Roloson .25 .60
20 Pavol Demitra .25 .60
21 Sergei Samsonov .25 .60
22 Steve Yzerman 1.50 4.00
23 Mats Sundin .30 .75
24 Peter Bondra .25 .60
25 Daniel Alfredsson .25 .60
26 Jeremy Roenick .40 1.00
27 Zigmund Palffy .25 .60
28 Ray Whitney .10 .25
29 Sami Kapanen .10 .25
30 Alexei Zhamnov .10 .25
31 Radek Bonk .10 .25
32 Eric Daze .25 .60
33 Tommy Salo .25 .60
34 Marian Gaborik .60 1.50
35 Alexander Mogilny .25 .60
36 Glen Murray .10 .25
37 Patrik Elias .25 .60
38 Simon Gagne .30 .75
39 Ryan Smyth .10 .25

Card	Low	High
40 Bill Guerin	.25	.60
41 Jeff Oneill	.10	.25
42 Miroslav Satan	.25	.60
43 Adam Deadmarsh	.10	.25
44 Sergei Fedorov	.50	1.25
45 Owen Nolan	.25	.60
46 Tony Amonte	.25	.60
47 Doug Weight	.25	.60
48 Marian Hossa	.30	.75
49 Mark Parrish	.10	.25
50 Theo Fleury	.10	.25
51 Steven Reinprecht	.10	.25
52 Dany Heatley	.40	1.00
53 Sergei Gonchar	.10	.25
54 Ilya Kovalchuk	.40	1.00
55 Brett Hull	.40	1.00
56 Daniel Briere	.10	.25
57 Brad Richards	.25	.60
58 Brendan Morrison	.25	.60
59 Steve Sullivan	.10	.25
60 Mike York	.10	.25
61 Nicklas Lidstrom	.30	.75
62 Michael Peca	.10	.25
63 Mark Recchi	.25	.60
64 Daymond Langkow	.10	.25
65 Tyler Arnason	.25	.60
66 Rob Blake	.25	.60
67 Mike Comrie	.25	.60
68 Felix Potvin	.30	.75
69 Brian Rolston	.25	.60
70 Martin Brodeur	.75	2.00
71 Anson Carter	.25	.60
72 Roberto Luongo	.40	1.00
73 Joe Nieuwendyk	.25	.60
74 Dean McAmmond	.10	.25
75 Niko Kapanen	.10	.25
76 Jan Hrdina	.10	.25
77 Vincent Damphousse	.10	.25
78 Jozef Stumpel	.10	.25
79 Milan Hejduk	.30	.75
80 Stu Barnes	.10	.25
81 Pierre Turgeon	.25	.60
82 Marty Turco	.25	.60
83 Bryan McCabe	.10	.25
84 Gary Roberts	.10	.25
85 Martin Havlat	.25	.60
86 Kyle Calder	.10	.25
87 Paul Kariya	.30	.75
88 Martin Straka	.10	.25
89 Yanic Perreault	.10	.25
90 Brian Boucher	.25	.60
91 Darcy Tucker	.10	.25
92 Mike Ricci	.10	.25
93 Keith Primeau	.10	.25
94 Bobby Holik	.10	.25
95 Chris Osgood	.25	.60
96 Brian Leetch	.25	.60
97 Teemu Selanne	.30	.75
98 Alex Tanguay	.25	.60
99 Rod Brind'Amour	.25	.60
100 Petr Sykora	.10	.25
101 Jere Lehtinen	.25	.60
102 Kevin Weekes	.25	.60
103 Jason Arnott	.10	.25
104 Al MacInnis	.25	.60
105 Scott Gomez	.10	.25
106 Byron Dafoe	.25	.60
107 Evgeni Nabokov	.25	.60
108 Sandis Ozolinsh	.10	.25
109 John LeClair	.30	.75
110 Mike Dunham	.25	.60
111 Manny Fernandez	.25	.60
112 Johan Hedberg	.25	.60
113 Chris Pronger	.25	.60
114 Fredrik Modin	.10	.25
115 Rostislav Klesla	.10	.25
116 Manny Legace	.25	.60
117 Teppo Numminen	.10	.25
118 Shane Doan	.10	.25
119 Martin Biron	.25	.60
120 Luc Robitaille	.30	.75
121 Igor Larionov	.10	.25
122 Doug Gilmour	.25	.60
123 Roman Cechmanek	.25	.60
124 Marc Savard	.10	.25
125 Scott Stevens	.25	.60
126 Steve Rucchin	.10	.25
127 Olaf Kolzig	.25	.60
128 Ed Jovanovski	.25	.60
129 Petr Nedved	.10	.25
130 Valeri Bure	.10	.25
131 J-P Dumont	.10	.25
132 Jocelyn Thibault	.25	.60
133 Martin Lapointe	.10	.25
134 Tomas Kaberle	.10	.25
135 Jose Theodore	.40	1.00
136 Bates Battaglia	.10	.25
137 Chris Drury	.25	.60
138 Patrick Lalime	.25	.60
139 Derek Morris	.10	.25
140 Sean Burke	.25	.60
141 Radek Dvorak	.10	.25
142 Ladislav Nagy	.10	.25
143 Oleg Petrov	.10	.25
144 Kristian Huselius	.10	.25
145 Mark Messier	.30	.75
146 Curtis Joseph	.30	.75
147 Tim Connolly	.10	.25
148 Arturs Irbe	.25	.60
149 Espen Knutsen	.10	.25
150 Ed Belfour	.30	.75
151 Jaroslav Modry	.10	.25
152 Dan Cloutier	.25	.60
153 Jeff Friesen	.10	.25
154 Janne Niinimaa	.10	.25
155 Nikolai Khabibulin	.30	.75
156 Justin Williams	.10	.25
157 Kyle McLaren	.10	.25
158 Sergei Zubov	.10	.25
159 Brian Savage	.10	.25
160 Chris Chelios	.30	.75
161 Roman Hamrlik	.10	.25
162 Scott Niedermayer	.10	.25
163 Danny Markov	.10	.25
164 Marc Denis	.25	.60
165 Scott Hartnell	.10	.25
166 Roman Turek	.25	.60
167 Brenden Morrow	.25	.60
168 David Legwand	.25	.60
169 Henrik Sedin	.10	.25
170 Oleg Tverdovsky	.10	.25
171 Peter Forsberg	.75	2.00
172 Vincent Lecavalier	.30	.75
173 Pavel Datsyuk	.30	.75
174 Dan Blackburn	.25	.60
175 Adam Foote	.10	.25
176 Joe Juneau	.10	.25
177 Mike Richter	.25	.60
178 Shawn Bates	.10	.25
179 Erik Cole	.10	.25
180 J-S Giguere	.25	.60
181 Saku Koivu	.30	.75
182 Zdeno Chara	.10	.25
183 Stephen Weiss	.10	.25
184 Robert Svehla	.10	.25
185 Patrick Stefan	.10	.25
186 Robert Lang	.10	.25
187 Olli Jokinen	.25	.60
188 Pavel Brendl	.10	.25
189 Brent Johnson	.25	.60
190 Boris Mironov	.10	.25
191 Tomas Vokoun	.25	.60
192 Darius Kasparaitis	.10	.25
193 Martin St. Louis	.25	.60
194 Radim Vrbata	.10	.25
195 Jeff Hackett	.25	.60
196 Nik Antropov	.10	.25
197 Craig Conroy	.10	.25
198 Nick Boynton	.10	.25
199 Richard Zednik	.10	.25
200 Vaclav Prospal	.10	.25
201 P-M Bouchard RC	5.00	12.00
202 Rick Nash RC	25.00	50.00
203 Dennis Seidenberg RC	5.00	10.00
204 Jay Bouwmeester RC	8.00	20.00
205 Stanislav Chistov RC	4.00	10.00
206 Pascal Leclaire RC	5.00	12.00
207 Jared Aulin RC	4.00	10.00
208 Chuck Kobasew RC	5.00	12.00
209 Jordan Leopold RC	5.00	12.00
210 Steve Ott RC	5.00	12.00
211 Ales Hemsky RC	10.00	25.00
212 Matt Walker RC	4.00	10.00
213 Tomas Malec RC	4.00	10.00
214 Dmitri Bykov RC	4.00	10.00
215 Michael Leighton RC	4.00	10.00
216 Henrik Zetterberg RC	20.00	50.00
217 Alexander Frolov RC	10.00	25.00
218 Steve Eminger RC	4.00	10.00
219 Scottie Upshall RC	4.00	10.00
220 Rickard Wallin RC	4.00	10.00
221 Alexei Semenov RC	4.00	10.00
222 Ron Hainsey RC	4.00	10.00
223 Martin Gerber RC	5.00	12.00
224 Adam Hall RC	4.00	10.00
225 Ray Emery RC	10.00	25.00
226 Anton Volchenkov RC	4.00	10.00
227 Levente Szuper RC	4.00	10.00
228 Carlo Colaiacovo RC	4.00	10.00
229 Alexander Svitov RC	.10	.25
230 Alexei Smirnov RC	4.00	10.00
231 Jeff Taffe RC	4.00	10.00
232 Mikael Tellqvist RC	5.00	12.00
233 Ari Ahonen RC	4.00	10.00
234 Martin Samuelsson RC	4.00	10.00
235 Shaone Morrisonn RC	4.00	10.00
236 Craig Andersson RC	4.00	10.00
237 Jim Fahey RC	4.00	10.00
238 Brooks Orpik RC	4.00	10.00
239 Mike Komisarek RC	5.00	12.00
240 Frederic Cloutier RC	4.00	10.00
241 Curtis Sanford RC	5.00	12.00
242 Jim Vandermeer RC	4.00	10.00
243 Paul Manning RC	4.00	10.00
244 Kris Vernarsky RC	4.00	10.00
245 Dany Sabourin RC	4.00	10.00
246 Mike Cammalleri RC	6.00	15.00
247 Jason Spezza RC	25.00	60.00
248 Cristobal Huet RC	12.00	30.00
249 Ryan Miller RC	20.00	50.00
250 Dick Tarnstrom RC	4.00	10.00

2002-03 Parkhurst Retro Minis

A throwback to the 1951-52 Parkhurst cards, this 250-card set paralleled the base set on cards approximately 2 1/2" X 1 1/2". Cards 201-250 were shortprinted, but no print run was made public.

*STARS: 1.25X TO 3X BASE HI
*SP's (201-250): .2X TO .5X

2002-03 Parkhurst Retro Back In Time

This 15-card set put Mario Lemieux on cards fashioned after Parkhurst designs of the past. Cards carried a swatch of game jersey and were limited to 30 copies each.

*MULT.COLOR SWATCH: .5X TO 1.25X

Card	Low	High
1 1951-52 Parkhurst	25.00	60.00
2 1952-53 Parkhurst	25.00	60.00
3 1953-54 Parkhurst	25.00	60.00
4 1954-55 Parkhurst	25.00	60.00
5 1955-56 Parkhurst	25.00	60.00
6 1957-58 Parkhurst	25.00	60.00
7 1958-89 Parkhurst	25.00	60.00
8 1959-60 Parkhurst	25.00	60.00
9 1960-61 Parkhurst	25.00	60.00
10 1961-62 Parkhurst	25.00	60.00
11 1962-63 Parkhurst	25.00	60.00
12 1962-63 Parkhurst	25.00	60.00
13 1962-63 Parkhurst	25.00	60.00
14 1963-64 Parkhurst	25.00	60.00
15 1963-64 Parkhurst	25.00	60.00

2002-03 Parkhurst Retro Back In Time Autographs

This 15-card set paralleled the regular insert but included a certified autograph on each card. Cards were serial-numbered to just 10 copies each.

NOT PRICED DUE TO SCARCITY

2002-03 Parkhurst Retro Franchise Players

Limited to just 60 copies each, this 30-card set featured game jersey swatches from team leaders.

*MULT.COLOR SWATCH: .5X TO 1.25X

Card	Low	High
RF1 Paul Kariya	8.00	20.00
RF2 Dany Heatley	12.50	30.00
RF3 Joe Thornton	15.00	40.00
RF4 Miroslav Satan	8.00	20.00
RF5 Jarome Iginla	12.50	30.00
RF6 Ron Francis	8.00	20.00
RF7 Jocelyn Thibault	8.00	20.00
RF8 Rick Nash	15.00	40.00
RF9 Joe Sakic	15.00	40.00
RF10 Mike Modano	10.00	25.00
RF11 Steve Yzerman	20.00	50.00
RF12 Mike Comrie	8.00	20.00
RF13 Roberto Luongo	15.00	40.00
RF14 Jason Allison	8.00	20.00
RF15 Marian Gaborik	15.00	40.00
RF16 Jose Theodore	15.00	40.00
RF17 David Legwand	8.00	20.00
RF18 Martin Brodeur	20.00	50.00
RF19 Mike Peca	8.00	20.00
RF20 Pavel Bure	8.00	20.00
RF21 Marian Hossa	8.00	20.00
RF22 Jeremy Roenick	10.00	25.00
RF23 Daniel Briere	8.00	20.00
RF24 Mario Lemieux	30.00	80.00
RF25 Teemu Selanne	8.00	20.00
RF26 Chris Pronger	8.00	20.00
RF27 Vincent Lecavalier	8.00	20.00
RF28 Mats Sundin	8.00	20.00
RF29 Markus Naslund	8.00	20.00
RF30 Jaromir Jagr	12.50	30.00

2002-03 Parkhurst Retro He Shoots-He Scores Points

Inserted one per pack, these cards carried a value of 1, 2 or 3 points. The points could be redeemed for special memorabilia cards. The cards are unnumbered and are listed below in alphabetical order by point value. The redemption program ended March 31, 2004.

Card	Low	High
1 Marian Gaborik 1 pt.	.20	.50
2 Dany Heatley 1 pt.	.20	.50
3 Marian Hossa 1 pt.	.20	.50
4 Mike Modano 1 pt.	.20	.50
5 Rick Nash 1 pt.	.20	.50
6 Brendan Shanahan 1 pt.	.20	.50
7 Joe Thornton 1 pt.	.20	.50
8 Marty Turco 1 pt.	.20	.50
9 Ed Belfour 2 pts.	.20	.50
10 Martin Brodeur 2 pts.	.20	.50
11 Pavel Bure 2 pts.	.20	.50
12 Peter Forsberg 2 pts.	.20	.50
13 Jaromir Jagr 2 pts.	.20	.50
14 Paul Kariya 2 pts.	.20	.50
15 Ilya Kovalchuk 2 pts.	.20	.50
16 Eric Lindros 2 pts.	.20	.50
17 Joe Sakic 2 pts.	.20	.50
18 Mario Lemieux 3 pts.	.20	.50
19 Patrick Roy 3 pts.	.20	.50
20 Steve Yzerman 3 pts.	.20	.50

2002-03 Parkhurst Retro He Shoots-He Scores Prizes

Available only by redeeming 400 Parkhurst Retro He Shoots-He Scores points, this 30-card set featured game-used swatches of jersey and a color photo of the player. Each card had a stated print run of 20 serial-numbered sets and each was encased in a clear plastic slab with a descriptive label at the top. This set is unpriced due to scarcity and volatility.

1 Steve Yzerman
2 Mario Lemieux
3 Patrick Roy
4 Jaromir Jagr
5 Ilya Kovalchuk
6 Eric Lindros
7 Martin Brodeur
8 Ed Belfour
9 Joe Sakic
10 Peter Forsberg
11 Pavel Bure
12 Paul Kariya
13 Dany Heatley
14 Brendan Shanahan
15 Marian Gaborik
16 Joe Thornton
17 Rick Nash
18 Marian Hossa
19 Marty Turco
20 Mike Modano
21 Roberto Luongo
22 Jose Theodore
23 Todd Bertuzzi
24 Nicklas Lidstrom
25 Jarome Iginla
26 Mats Sundin
27 Markus Naslund
28 Sergei Fedorov
29 Milan Hejduk
30 Teemu Selanne

2002-03 Parkhurst Retro Hopefuls

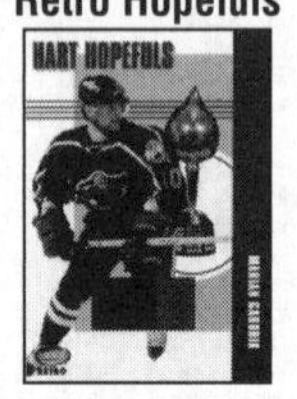

Limited to just 30 copies each, this 40-card set featured players who were considered contenders for the Calder, Hart, Norris, Richard, or Vezina awards. Each card carried a swatch of game jersey.

*MULT.COLOR SWATCH: .5X TO 1.25X

Card	Low	High
CH1 Tyler Arnason	12.50	30.00
CH2 Rick Nash	25.00	60.00
CH3 Ryan Miller	15.00	40.00
CH4 Niko Kapanen	10.00	25.00
CH5 Alexander Frolov	12.50	30.00
CH6 Stanislav Chistov	12.50	30.00
CH7 Barret Jackman	12.50	30.00
CH8 Jay Bouwmeester	12.50	30.00
HH1 Mario Lemieux	25.00	60.00
HH2 Joe Thornton	15.00	40.00
HH3 Markus Naslund	12.50	30.00
HH4 Marty Turco	12.50	30.00
HH5 Nicklas Lidstrom	12.50	30.00
HH6 Marian Gaborik	20.00	50.00
HH7 Marian Hossa	12.50	30.00
HH8 Jaromir Jagr	20.00	50.00
NH1 Nicklas Lidstrom	12.50	30.00
NH2 Rob Blake	12.50	30.00
NH3 Adam Foote	12.50	30.00
NH4 Al MacInnis	12.50	30.00
NH5 Sergei Zubov	12.50	25.00
NH6 Ed Jovanovski	12.50	25.00
NH7 Tomas Kaberle	12.50	25.00
NH8 Derian Hatcher	12.50	25.00
RR1 Jaromir Jagr	20.00	50.00
RR2 Marian Hossa	12.50	30.00
RR3 Mats Sundin	12.50	30.00
RR4 Marian Gaborik	20.00	50.00
RR5 Markus Naslund	12.50	30.00
RR6 Ilya Kovalchuk	25.00	60.00
RR7 Joe Thornton	15.00	40.00
RR8 Milan Hejduk	12.50	30.00
VH1 Ed Belfour	25.00	50.00
VH2 Marty Turco	12.50	30.00
VH3 Martin Brodeur	25.00	60.00
VH4 Patrick Lalime	12.50	30.00
VH5 J-S Giguere	12.50	30.00
VH6 Jocelyn Thibault	12.50	30.00
VH7 Patrick Roy	30.00	80.00
VH8 Nikolai Khabibulin	12.50	30.00

2002-03 Parkhurst Retro Jerseys

*MULT.COLOR SWATCH: .5X TO 1.25X

Card	Low	High
RJ1 Patrick Roy	20.00	50.00
RJ2 Mike Modano	10.00	25.00
RJ3 Peter Forsberg	12.50	30.00
RJ4 Mark Messier	8.00	20.00
RJ5 Brett Hull	12.50	30.00
RJ6 Martin Brodeur	15.00	40.00
RJ7 Joe Thornton	10.00	25.00
RJ8 Ed Belfour	8.00	20.00
RJ9 Pavel Bure	8.00	20.00
RJ10 Rick Nash	12.50	30.00
RJ11 Marty Turco	6.00	15.00
RJ12 Jay Bouwmeester	6.00	15.00
RJ13 Jason Spezza	12.50	30.00
RJ14 Jaromir Jagr	10.00	25.00
RJ15 Mario Lemieux	20.00	50.00
RJ16 Markus Naslund	8.00	20.00
RJ17 Brendan Shanahan	8.00	20.00
RJ18 Paul Kariya	8.00	20.00
RJ19 Roberto Luongo	10.00	25.00
RJ20 Joe Sakic	15.00	40.00
RJ21 Mats Sundin	8.00	20.00
RJ22 Steve Yzerman	15.00	40.00
RJ23 Dany Heatley	10.00	25.00
RJ24 Jose Theodore	10.00	25.00
RJ25 John LeClair	8.00	20.00
RJ26 Marian Hossa	8.00	20.00
RJ27 Eric Lindros	8.00	20.00
RJ28 Sergei Fedorov	10.00	25.00
RJ29 Todd Bertuzzi	8.00	20.00
RJ30 Sergei Samsonov	6.00	15.00
RJ31 Jeremy Roenick	10.00	25.00
RJ32 Nicklas Lidstrom	8.00	20.00
RJ33 Bill Guerin	6.00	15.00
RJ34 Chris Pronger	6.00	15.00
RJ35 Saku Koivu	8.00	20.00
RJ36 Marian Gaborik	12.50	30.00
RJ37 Ilya Kovalchuk	10.00	25.00
RJ38 Jocelyn Thibault	6.00	15.00
RJ39 Vincent Lecavalier	6.00	15.00
RJ40 Teemu Selanne	8.00	20.00

2002-03 Parkhurst Retro Jersey and Sticks

*JSY/STK: .6X TO 1.5X BASIC JERSEY
STATED PRINT RUN 60 SETS

2002-03 Parkhurst Retro Magnificent Inserts

This 10-card set featured game-used equipment from the career of Mario Lemieux. Cards MI1-MI5 had a print run of 40 copies each and cards MI6-MI10 were limited to just 10 copies each. Cards MI6-MI10 are not priced due to scarcity.

Card	Low	High
MI1 2000-01 Season	30.00	80.00
MI2 1985-86 Season	30.00	80.00
MI3 2002 All-Star	30.00	80.00
MI4 1987 Canada Cup	30.00	80.00
MI5 Dual Jersey	50.00	125.00
MI6 Number		
MI7 Emblem		
MI8 Triple Jersey		
MI9 Quad Jersey		
MI10 Complete Package		

2002-03 Parkhurst Retro Magnificent Inserts Autographs

This 10-card set paralleled the base Magnificent Inserts but carried certified autographs and each card was hand numbered. Cards MI1-MI5 were serial-numbered to 15 each and cards MI6-MI10 were serial numbered out of 5.

NOT PRICE DUE TO SCARCITY

2002-03 Parkhurst Retro Memorabilia

This 30-card set featured swatches of game-used equipment. Print runs for each card are listed below.

Card	Low	High
RM1 Mario Lemieux/50	20.00	50.00
RM2 Joe Sakic/50	15.00	40.00
RM3 Joe Thornton/60	15.00	40.00
RM4 Marian Hossa/50	10.00	25.00
RM5 Nicklas Lidstrom/50	10.00	25.00
RM6 Patrick Roy/50	20.00	50.00
RM7 Jose Theodore/50	12.50	30.00
RM8 Mario Lemieux/30	25.00	60.00
RM9 Martin Brodeur/50	20.00	50.00
RM10 Dany Heatley/50	12.50	30.00
RM11 Ilya Kovalchuk/60	12.50	30.00
RM12 Marty Turco/50	10.00	25.00
RM13 Sergei Fedorov/50	12.50	30.00
RM14 Steve Yzerman/50	20.00	50.00
RM15 Jason Spezza/60	10.00	25.00
RM16 Pavel Bure/50	10.00	25.00
RM17 Peter Forsberg/50	15.00	40.00
RM18 Brendan Shanahan/50	10.00	25.00
RM19 Joe Thornton/30	15.00	40.00
RM20 Mike Modano/60	12.50	30.00
RM21 Nikolai Khabibulin/30	10.00	25.00
RM22 Jaromir Jagr/60	12.50	30.00
RM23 Joe Sakic/50	15.00	40.00
RM24 Mats Sundin/50	10.00	25.00
RM25 Saku Koivu/60	10.00	25.00
RM26 Jay Bouwmeester/60	15.00	40.00
RM27 Paul Kariya/60	10.00	25.00
RM28 Rick Nash/50	12.50	30.00
RM29 Mario Lemieux/50	20.00	50.00
RM30 Brett Hull/30	15.00	40.00

2002-03 Parkhurst Retro Nicknames

This 30-card set featured game-used memorabilia swatches of the given player on the card fronts beside their "nickname". Individual print runs are listed below.

STAT.PRINT RUNS LISTED BELOW

Card	Low	High
RN1 Frank Brimsek/35	20.00	50.00
RN2 Henri Richard/40	20.00	50.00
RN3 Ed Giacomin/40	20.00	50.00
RN4 Bobby Hull/35	20.00	50.00
RN5 Bernie Geoffrion/20		
RN6 Gerry Cheevers/50	12.50	30.00
RN7 Johnny Bucyk/40	12.50	30.00
RN8 Johnny Bower/40	25.00	60.00
RN9 Gump Worsley/40	30.00	80.00
RN10 Glenn Hall/40	15.00	40.00
RN11 Red Kelly/40	15.00	40.00
RN12 Frank Mahovlich Pete Mahovlich	40.00	100.00
RN13 Ace Bailey/20		
RN14 King Clancy/20		
RN15 Roy Worters/20		
RN16 Stan Mikita/50	15.00	40.00
RN17 Rocket Richard/20		
RN18 Turk Broda/20		
RN19 Tony Esposito/35	25.00	60.00
RN20 Jean Beliveau/35	30.00	80.00
RN21 Jacques Plante/35	50.00	125.00
RN22 Steve Yzerman/65	20.00	50.00
RN23 Brett Hull/65	15.00	40.00
RN24 Patrick Roy/65	20.00	50.00
RN25 Felix Potvin/65	15.00	40.00
RN26 Teemu Selanne/65	12.50	30.00
RN27 Olaf Kolzig/65	12.50	30.00
RN28 Pavel Bure/65	12.50	30.00
RN29 Eric Lindros/65	12.50	30.00
RN30 Mario Lemieux/65	30.00	80.00

2003-04 Parkhurst Rookie

This 200-card set consisted of 60-vetaran cards; 18-dual prospect cards; 52-single prospect cards; 25-prospect jersey cards; 30-autographed prospect cards and 25 jersey/autograph prospect cards. Cards 61-130 were serial-numbered out of 500; cards 131-155 were numbered out of 180; cards 156-175 were numbered out of 120 and cards 176-200 were numbered to 100.

*MULT.COLOR SWATCH: .6X TO 1.5X

Card	Low	High
1 Steve Yzerman	5.00	12.00
2 Joe Sakic	3.00	8.00
3 Jeremy Roenick	2.00	5.00
4 Brian Leetch	1.50	4.00
5 Andrew Raycroft	1.25	3.00
6 Dan Cloutier	1.25	3.00
7 Marty Turco	1.25	3.00
8 Owen Nolan	1.25	3.00
9 Joe Thornton	2.00	5.00
10 Marian Gaborik	3.00	8.00
11 Mario Lemieux	6.00	15.00
12 Zigmund Palffy	1.25	3.00
13 Vincent Lecavalier	1.50	4.00
14 Sean Burke	1.25	3.00
15 Miikka Kiprusoff	1.25	3.00
16 Dominik Hasek	3.00	8.00
17 Nikolai Khabibulin	1.50	4.00
18 Ed Belfour	1.50	4.00
19 Ilya Kovalchuk	2.00	5.00
20 Marian Hossa	1.50	4.00
21 Tommy Salo	1.25	3.00
22 Keith Tkachuk	1.50	4.00
23 Alex Kovalev	1.25	3.00
24 Michael Ryder	.75	2.00
25 Steve Sullivan	.75	2.00
26 Martin St-Louis	1.25	3.00
27 Al MacInnis	1.25	3.00
28 Sergei Gonchar	.75	2.00
29 Jaromir Jagr	2.50	6.00
30 Ron Francis	1.25	3.0
31 Henrik Zetterberg	1.50	4.0
32 Paul Kariya	1.50	4.0
33 Robert Lang	.75	2.0
34 Nicklas Lidstrom	1.50	4.0
35 Sergei Fedorov	2.00	5.0
36 Jarome Iginla	2.00	5.0
37 Bill Guerin	1.25	3.0
38 Jose Theodore	2.00	5.0
39 Roberto Luongo	2.00	5.0
40 Alex Tanguay	1.25	3.0
41 Peter Forsberg	4.00	10.0
42 Mike Modano	2.00	5.0
43 Dwayne Roloson	1.25	3.0
44 Martin Brodeur	4.00	10.0
45 Dany Heatley	2.00	5.0
46 Rick Nash	2.00	5.0
47 Jason Spezza	1.50	4.0
48 Chris Pronger	1.25	3.0
49 Brett Hull	2.00	5.0
50 Markus Naslund	1.50	4.0
51 Curtis Joseph	1.50	4.0
52 Olaf Kolzig	1.25	3.0
53 Peter Bondra	1.25	3.0
54 Eric Lindros	1.50	4.0
55 Mats Sundin	1.50	4.0
56 Patrick Roy	5.00	12.0
57 Ray Bourque	3.00	8.0
58 Terry Sawchuk	3.00	8.0
59 Maurice Richard	5.00	12.0
60 Bobby Orr	6.00	15.0
61 M.Bartovic RC/J.Pominville RC	6.00	15.0
62 K.McDonell RC/A.Johnson RC	4.00	10.0
63 A.Hutchinson RC/L.Pivko RC	4.00	10.0
64 K.Gernander RC/P.Osaer RC	4.00	10.0
65 R.Mrozik RC/J.Pollock RC	4.00	10.0
66 S.Meyer RC/D.Verot RC	4.00	10.0
67 M.Yeats RC/D.Zinger RC	4.00	10.0
68 J.DiPenta RC/{J. Olson RC	4.00	10.0
69 A.Rourke RC/J.MacMillan RC	4.00	10.0
70 M.Underhill RC/D.Salficky RC	4.00	10.0
71 J.Vauclair RC/Z.Michalek RC	4.00	10.0
72 M.Hussey RC/M.Stutzel RC	4.00	10.0
73 B.Lampman RC/T.Pock RC	4.00	10.0
74 G.Mink RC/R.Tvrdon RC	4.00	10.0
75 J.MacDonald RC/M.Morrison RC	4.00	10.0
76 M.Pandolfo RC/G.Mauldin RC	4.00	10.0
77 J.Yablonski RC/C.Larose RC	4.00	10.0
78 C.Brandner RC/E.Perrin RC	4.00	10.0
79 Michal Barinka RC	3.00	8.0
80 Erik Westrum RC	3.00	8.0
81 Gavin Morgan RC	3.00	8.0
82 Matt Ellison RC	3.00	8.0
83 Seamus Kotyk RC	3.00	8.0
84 Andy Chiodo RC	3.00	8.0
85 Mikko Luoma RC	3.00	8.0
86 Jed Ortmeyer RC	3.00	8.0
87 Brad Boyes RC	6.00	15.0
88 Robert Scuderi RC	3.00	8.0
89 Nolan Schaefer RC	3.00	8.0
90 Colton Orr RC	3.00	8.0
91 Travis Moen RC	3.00	8.0
92 Fred Meyer RC	3.00	8.0
93 Joe Motzko RC	3.00	8.0
94 Ryan Barnes RC	3.00	8.0
95 Rob Skrlac RC	3.00	8.0
96 Quintin Laing RC	3.00	8.0
97 Mikhail Kuleshov RC	3.00	8.0
98 Adam Munro RC	3.00	8.0
99 Wade Dubielewicz RC	4.00	10.0
100 Matt Keith RC	3.00	8.0
101 Steve McLaren RC	3.00	8.0
102 Tim Jackman RC	3.00	8.0
103 Doug Doull RC	3.00	8.0
104 Lawrence Nycholat RC	3.00	8.0
105 Aleksander Suglobov RC	3.00	8.0
106 Martin Strbak RC	3.00	8.0
107 Lasse Kukkonen RC	3.00	8.0
108 Gregory Campbell RC	3.00	8.0
109 Tony Martensson RC	3.00	8.0
110 Carl Corazzini RC	3.00	8.0
111 Mike Green RC	3.00	8.0
112 Nathan Robinson RC	3.00	8.0
113 Brent Krahn RC	3.00	8.0
114 Mike Smith RC	4.00	10.0
115 Mike Stuart RC	3.00	8.0
116 Karl Stewart RC	3.00	8.0
117 Jason MacDonald RC	3.00	8.0
118 Brooks Laich RC	3.00	8.0
119 Tom Preissing RC	3.00	8.0
120 Mikhail Yakubov RC	3.00	8.0
121 Benoit Dusablon RC	3.00	8.0
122 Nathan Smith RC	3.00	8.0
123 Goran Bezina RC	3.00	8.0
124 Dan Ellis RC	4.00	10.0
125 Pat Rissmiller RC	3.00	8.0
126 Owen Fussey RC	3.00	8.0
127 Mike Bishai RC	3.00	8.0
128 Matt Murley RC	3.00	8.0
129 Wade Brookbank RC	3.00	8.0
130 Randy Jones RC	3.00	8.0
131 Fedor Tyutin JSY RC	10.00	25.0
132 Niklas Kronwall JSY RC	12.50	30.0
133 Boyd Kane JSY RC	8.00	20.0
134 Sergei Zinovjev JSY RC	8.00	20.0
135 Mark Popovic JSY RC	8.00	20.0
136 Sean Bergenheim JSY RC	8.00	20.0
137 Ryan Kesler JSY RC	8.00	20.0
138 Christian Ehrhoff JSY RC	8.00	20.0
139 Peter Sejna JSY RC	8.00	20.0
140 Denis Grebeshkov JSY RC	8.00	20.0
141 Tuomas Pihlman JSY RC	8.00	20.0
142 Antero Niittymaki JSY RC	20.00	50.0
143 Patrick Leahy JSY RC	8.00	20.0
144 Rastislav Stana JSY RC	8.00	20.0
145 Grant McNeill JSY RC	8.00	20.0
146 Cody McCormick JSY RC	8.00	20.0
147 Boyd Gordon JSY RC	8.00	20.0
148 Garth Murray JSY RC	8.00	20.0
149 Trevor Daley JSY RC	8.00	20.0
150 Marek Svatos JSY RC	25.00	60.0
151 Esa Pirnes JSY RC	8.00	20.0
152 Garrett Burnett JSY RC	8.00	20.0
153 Tony Salmelainen JSY RC	8.00	20.0
154 John Pohl JSY RC	8.00	20.0
155 Dominic Moore JSY RC	8.00	20.0
156 Fredrik Sjostrom AU RC	10.00	25.0
157 Jozef Balej AU RC	10.00	25.0
158 Jiri Hudler AU RC	15.00	40.0
159 Joffrey Lupul AU RC	20.00	50.0
160 Tomas Plekanec AU RC	10.00	25.0

61 Kyle Wellwood AU RC 25.00 60.00
62 Peter Sarno AU RC 10.00 25.00
63 Pavel Vorobiev AU RC 10.00 25.00
64 Andrew Peters AU RC 10.00 25.00
65 Jeff Hamilton AU RC 10.00 25.00
66 Darryl Bootland AU RC 10.00 25.00
67 Noah Clarke AU RC 10.00 25.00
68 Matthew Spiller AU RC 10.00 25.00
69 Milan Michalek AU RC 25.00 60.00
70 Doug Lynch AU RC 10.00 25.00
71 Timofei Shishkanov AU RC 10.0025.00
72 Maxim Kondratiev AU RC 10.00 25.00
73 Chris Kunitz AU RC 12.50 30.00
74 Jordin Tootoo AU RC 25.00 60.00
75 Anton Babchuk AU RC 10.00 25.00
76 Eric Staal JSY AU RC 75.00 200.00
77 Dan Fritsche JSY AU RC 20.00 50.00
78 Joni Pitkanen JSY AU RC 20.00 50.00
79 Tim Gleason JSY AU RC 15.00 40.00
80 Chris Higgins JSY AU RC 50.00100.00
81 Nathan Horton JSY AU RC 50.00 100.00
82 Marek Zidlicky JSY AU RC 20.0050.00
83 Antti Miettinen JSY AU RC 15.0040.00
84 Patrice Bergeron JSY AU RC 75.00150.00
85 Ryan Malone JSY AU RC 20.00 50.00
86 Matthew Lombardi JSY AU RC 20.00 50.00
87 Dan Hamhuis JSY AU RC 20.00 50.00
88 J-M Liles JSY AU RC 25.00 50.00
89 David Hale JSY AU RC 15.00 40.00
90 Tuomo Ruutu JSY AU RC 50.00100.00
91 Derek Roy JSY AU RC 25.00 60.00
92 Paul Martin JSY AU RC 15.00 40.00
93 Kari Lehtonen JSY AU RC 200.00 300.00
94 Dustin Brown JSY AU RC 20.00 50.00
95 Antoine Vermette JSY AU RC 20.00 50.00
96 Alexander Semin JSY AU RC 100.00200.00
97 Brent Burns JSY AU RC 15.00 40.00
98 Matt Stajan JSY AU RC 40.00 100.00
99 Nikolai Zherdev JSY AU RC 40.00 80.00
00 M-A Fleury JSY AU RC 150.00300.00

2003-04 Parkhurst Rookie All-Rookie

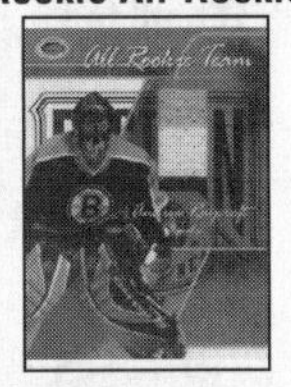

MULT.COLOR SWATCH: .6X TO 1.5X
RINT RUN 60 SETS
OLD PRINT RUN 10 SETS
OLD NOT PRICED DUE TO SCARCITY
RT-1 Andrew Raycroft 8.00 20.00
RT-2 Paul Martin 6.00 15.00
RT-3 Joni Pitkanen 6.00 15.00
RT-4 Eric Staal 12.00 30.00
RT-5 Michael Ryder 10.00 25.00
RT-6 Ryan Malone 6.00 15.00
RT-7 Philippe Sauve 6.00 15.00
RT-8 Dan Hamhuis 6.00 15.00
RT-9 John-Michael Liles 6.00 15.00
RT-10 Tuomo Ruutu 8.00 20.00
RT-11 Nikolai Zherdev 8.00 20.00
RT-12 Joffrey Lupul 6.00 15.00

2003-04 Parkhurst Rookie All-Rookie Autographs

RINT RUN 10 SETS
OT PRICED DUE TO SCARCITY
RT-AR Andrew Raycroft
RT-DH Dan Hamhuis
RT-ES Eric Staal
RT-JL John-Michael Liles
RT-JP Joni Pitkanen
RT-MR Michael Ryder
RT-PM Paul Martin
RT-TR Tuomo Ruutu
RT-JLU Joffrey Lupul

2003-04 Parkhurst Rookie Before the Mask

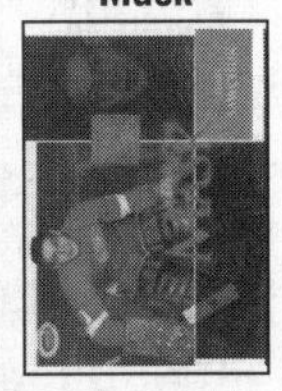

MULT.COLOR SWATCH: .6X TO 1.5X
RINT RUN 40 SETS
OLD PRINT RUN 10 SETS
OLD NOT PRICED DUE TO SCARCITY
TM-1 Roy Worters 12.50 30.00
TM-2 Frank Brimsek 12.50 30.00
TM-3 Harry Lumley 12.50 30.00
TM-4 Gump Worsley 12.50 30.00
TM-5 Johnny Bower 12.50 30.00
TM-6 Jacques Plante 25.00 60.00
TM-7 Tiny Thompson 12.50 30.00
TM-8 Charlie Gardiner 12.50 30.00
TM-9 Bill Durnan 12.50 30.00
TM-10 George Hainsworth 20.00 50.00
TM-11 Terry Sawchuk 20.00 50.00
TM-12 Glenn Hall 12.50 30.00
TM-13 Ed Giacomin 12.50 30.00
TM-14 Roger Crozier 12.50 30.00
TM-15 Chuck Rayner 12.50 30.00
TM-16 Turk Broda 12.50 30.00

2003-04 Parkhurst Rookie Calder Candidates

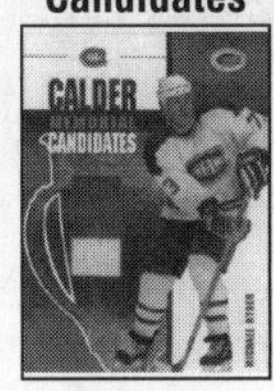

*MULT.COLOR SWATCH: .6X TO 1.5X
PRINT RUN 50 SETS
GOLD PRINT RUN 10 SETS
GOLD NOT PRICED DUE TO SCARCITY
CMC-1 Eric Staal 12.50 30.00
CMC-2 Michael Ryder 8.00 20.00
CMC-3 Marc-Andre Fleury 15.00 40.00
CMC-4 Patrice Bergeron 10.00 25.00
CMC-5 Ryan Malone 6.00 15.00
CMC-6 Joffrey Lupul 6.00 15.00
CMC-7 Andrew Raycroft 8.00 20.00
CMC-8 Mathew Lombardi 6.00 15.00
CMC-9 Joni Pitkanen 6.00 15.00
CMC-10 Nikolai Zherdev 8.00 20.00
CMC-11 Jordin Tootoo 10.00 25.00
CMC-12 Matt Stajan 8.00 20.00
CMC-13 Nathan Horton 10.00 25.00
CMC-14 Tuomo Ruutu 10.00 25.00
CMC-15 Derek Roy 6.00 15.00

2003-04 Parkhurst Rookie Calder Candidate Autographs

PRINT RUN 10 SETS
NOT PRICED DUE TO SCARCITY
CMC-AR Andrew Raycroft
CMC-DR Derek Roy
CMC-ES Eric Staal
CMC-JL Joffrey Lupul
CMC-MR Michael Ryder
CMC-MS Matt Stajan

2003-04 Parkhurst Rookie Emblems

PRINT RUN 9 SETS
NOT PRICED DUE TO SCARCITY
GUE-1 Pavel Datsyuk
GUE-2 Peter Forsberg
GUE-3 Rick Nash
GUE-4 Brian Leetch
GUE-5 Joe Sakic
GUE-6 Dany Heatley
GUE-7 Ray Bourque
GUE-8 Joe Thornton
GUE-9 Ilya Kovalchuk
GUE-10 Mario Lemieux

2003-04 Parkhurst Rookie Emblem Autographs

PRINT RUN 10 SETS
NOT PRICED DUE TO SCARCITY

2003-04 Parkhurst Rookie High Expectations

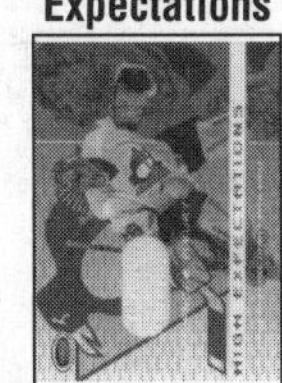

*MULT.COLOR SWATCH: .6X TO 1.5X
PRINT RUN 40 SETS
GOLD PRINT RUN 10 SETS
GOLD NOT PRICED DUE TO SCARCITY
HE-1 Ilya Kovalchuk 12.50 30.00
HE-2 Rick Nash 10.00 25.00
HE-3 Wendel Clark 15.00 40.00
HE-4 Mario Lemieux 20.00 50.00
HE-5 Guy Lafleur 10.00 25.00
HE-6 Gilbert Perreault 12.50 30.00
HE-7 Denis Potvin 8.00 20.00
HE-8 Mike Modano 12.50 30.00
HE-9 Mats Sundin 8.00 20.00
HE-10 Joe Thornton 15.00 40.00
HE-11 Rick DiPietro 8.00 20.00
HE-12 Marc-Andre Fleury 15.00 40.00
HE-13 Vincent Lecavalier 8.00 20.00
HE-14 Owen Nolan 8.00 20.00

2003-04 Parkhurst Rookie Jerseys

*MULT.COLOR SWATCH: .6X TO 1.5X
PRINT RUN 70 SETS

GOLD PRINT RUN 10 SETS
GOLD NOT PRICED DUE TO SCARCITY
GJ-1 Mario Lemieux 20.00 50.00
GJ-2 Ilya Kovalchuk 10.00 25.00
GJ-3 Joe Thornton 12.00 30.00
GJ-4 Bill Guerin 6.00 15.00
GJ-5 Jason Spezza 8.00 20.00
GJ-6 Peter Forsberg 10.00 25.00
GJ-7 Brian Leetch 8.00 20.00
GJ-8 Milan Hejduk 8.00 20.00
GJ-9 Evgeni Nabokov 6.00 15.00
GJ-10 Martin St. Louis 6.00 15.00
GJ-11 Rick Nash 10.00 25.00
GJ-12 Steve Yzerman 15.00 40.00
GJ-13 Pavel Datsyuk 8.00 20.00
GJ-14 Henrik Zetterberg 8.00 20.00
GJ-15 Joe Sakic 12.00 30.00
GJ-16 Jeremy Roenick 10.00 25.00
GJ-17 Martin Brodeur 15.00 40.00
GJ-18 Mats Sundin 8.00 20.00
GJ-19 Keith Tkachuk 8.00 20.00
GJ-20 Mike Modano 10.00 25.00
GJ-21 Dany Heatley 10.00 25.00
GJ-22 Roberto Luongo 10.00 25.00
GJ-23 Markus Naslund 8.00 20.00
GJ-24 Jose Theodore 10.00 25.00
GJ-25 Dominik Hasek 12.00 30.00
GJ-26 Paul Kariya 8.00 20.00
GJ-27 Teemu Selanne 8.00 20.00
GJ-28 Marian Hossa 8.00 20.00
GJ-29 Marian Gaborik 12.00 30.00
GJ-30 Sergei Fedorov 8.00 20.00
GJ-31 Mark Messier 15.00 40.00
GJ-32 Jarome Iginla 10.00 25.00
GJ-33 Brendan Shanahan 8.00 20.00
GJ-34 Ed Belfour 8.00 20.00
GJ-35 Curtis Joseph 8.00 20.00
GJ-36 Zdeno Chara 8.00 20.00
GJ-37 Vincent Lecavalier 8.00 20.00
GJ-38 Brett Hull 10.00 25.00
GJ-39 Nicklas Lidstrom 8.00 20.00
GJ-40 Marty Turco 6.00 15.00
GJ-41 Patrick Roy 20.00 50.00
GJ-42 Bobby Clarke 10.00 25.00
GJ-43 Lanny McDonald 6.00 15.00
GJ-44 Marcel Dionne 6.00 15.00
GJ-45 Gilbert Perreault 10.00 25.00
GJ-46 Ray Bourque 12.00 30.00
GJ-47 Mike Bossy 6.00 15.00
GJ-48 Vladislav Tretiak 25.00 60.00
GJ-49 Bobby Orr 50.00 125.00
GJ-50 Cam Neely 10.00 25.00

2003-04 Parkhurst Rookie Jersey Autographs

PRINT RUN 10 SETS
NOT PRICED DUE TO SCARCITY
GUJ-BG Bill Guerin
GUJ-BH Brett Hull
GUJ-CJ Curtis Joseph
GUJ-DH Dominik Hasek
GUJ-EN Evgeni Nabokov
GUJ-HZ Henrik Zetterberg
GUJ-JS Joe Sakic
GUJ-JS Jason Spezza
GUJ-JT Joe Thornton
GUJ-KT Keith Tkachuk
GUJ-ML Mario Lemieux
GUJ-MN Markus Naslund
GUJ-MS Mats Sundin
GUJ-PD Pavel Datsyuk
GUJ-RL Roberto Luongo
GUJ-RN Rick Nash
GUJ-SF Sergei Fedorov
GUJ-SY Steve Yzerman
GUJ-JTHE Jose Theodore

2003-04 Parkhurst Rookie Jersey and Sticks

*JSY/STKS: .6X TO 1.5X JSY
PRINT RUN 80 SETS
GOLD PRINT RUN 10 SETS
GOLD NOT PRICED DUE TO SCARCITY
SJ-6 Marc-Andre Fleury 20.00 50.00
SJ-7 Eric Lindros 12.50 30.00
SJ-15 Chris Pronger 10.00 25.00
SJ-21 Andrew Raycroft 12.50 30.00

2003-04 Parkhurst Rookie Records

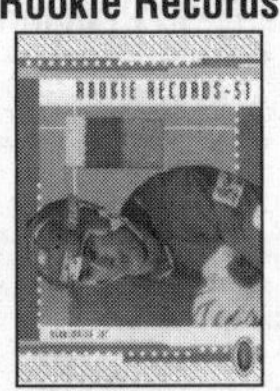

*MULT.COLOR SWATCH: .6X TO 1.5X
PRINT RUN 40 SETS
GOLD PRINT RUN 10 SETS
GOLD NOT PRICED DUE TO SCARCITY
RRE-1 Teemu Selanne 8.00 20.00
RRE-2 Teemu Selanne 8.00 20.00
RRE-3 Luc Robitaille 8.00 20.00
RRE-4 Joe Nieuwendyk 8.00 20.00
RRE-5 Brian Leetch 8.00 20.00
RRE-6 Tony Esposito 12.50 30.00
RRE-7 Patrick Lalime 15.00 40.00
RRE-8 Terry Sawchuk 20.00 50.00

2003-04 Parkhurst Rookie Retro Rookies

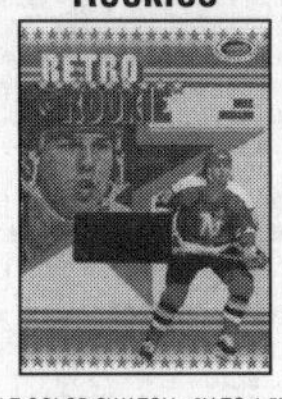

*MULT.COLOR SWATCH: .6X TO 1.5X
PRINT RUN 70 SETS
GOLD PRINT RUN 10 SETS
GOLD NOT PRICED DUE TO SCARCITY
RR-1 Mike Modano 10.00 25.00
RR-2 Peter Forsberg 15.00 40.00
RR-3 Joe Sakic 12.50 30.00
RR-4 Patrick Roy 20.00 50.00
RR-5 Jaromir Jagr 10.00 25.00
RR-6 Rob Blake 8.00 20.00
RR-7 Brett Hull 10.00 25.00
RR-8 Roberto Luongo 10.00 25.00
RR-9 Brian Leetch 8.00 20.00
RR-10 Jeremy Roenick 10.00 25.00
RR-11 Mats Sundin 8.00 20.00
RR-12 Ed Belfour 8.00 20.00
RR-13 Curtis Joseph 8.00 20.00
RR-14 Sergei Fedorov 10.00 25.00
RR-15 Paul Kariya 8.00 20.00
RR-16 Mark Messier 12.50 30.00
RR-17 Al MacInnis 8.00 20.00
RR-18 Felix Potvin 8.00 20.00
RR-19 Eric Lindros 8.00 20.00
RR-20 Teemu Selanne 8.00 20.00

2003-04 Parkhurst Rookie Retro Rookie Autographs

PRINT RUN 10 SETS
NOT PRICED DUE TO SCARCITY
RR-BH Brett Hull
RR-JJ Jaromir Jagr
RR-JS Joe Sakic
RR-MM Mike Modano
RR-PR Patrick Roy

2003-04 Parkhurst Rookie Road to the NHL

*MULT.COLOR SWATCH: .75X TO 2X
PRINT RUN 40 SETS
GOLD PRINT RUN 10 SETS
EMBLEM PRINT RUN 9 SETS
GOLD EMBLEM 1/1's EXIST
GOLD/EMBLM NOT PRICED DUE TO SCARCITY
RNJ-1 Nick Schultz 6.00 15.00
RNJ-2 Jason Spezza 12.50 30.00
RNJ-3 Rick Nash 15.00 40.00
RNJ-4 Dustin Brown 6.00 15.00
RNJ-5 Jay Bouwmeester 6.00 15.00
RNJ-6 Jose Theodore 12.00 30.00
RNJ-7 Barret Jackman 6.00 15.00
RNJ-8 Dany Heatley 15.00 40.00
RNJ-9 Eric Staal 15.00 40.00
RNJ-10 Scottie Upshall 6.00 15.00
RNJ-11 Derek Roy 6.00 15.00
RNJ-12 Dan Blackburn 6.00 15.00
RNJ-13 Tim Gleason 6.00 15.00
RNJ-14 Ron Hainsey 6.00 15.00
RNJ-15 Mathieu Garon 6.00 15.00
RNJ-16 Steve Ott 6.00 15.00
RNJ-17 Dan Hamhuis 6.00 15.00

2003-04 Parkhurst Rookie Road to the NHL Emblems

PRINT RUN 9 SETS
NOT PRICED DUE TO SCARCITY
GOLD 1/1's EXIST

2003-04 Parkhurst Rookie Rookie Emblems

This 50-card set paralleled the Rookie Jerseys set. Cards were limited to just 19 copies each and gold 1/1's were also created.
NOT PRICED DUE TO SCARCITY

2003-04 Parkhurst Rookie Rookie Emblem Autographs

PRINT RUN 10 SETS
NOT PRICED DUE TO SCARCITY
RE-AM Antti Miettinen
RE-AP Andrew Peters
RE-AR Andrew Raycroft
RE-AS Alexander Semin
RE-AV Antoine Vermette
RE-BB Brent Burns
RE-CH Chris Higgins
RE-DF Dan Fritsche
RE-DH Dan Hamhuis
RE-DR Derek Roy
RE-DHA David Hale
RE-ES Eric Staal
RE-JL Joffrey Lupul
RE-JP Joni Pitkanen
RE-JLI John-Michael Liles
RE-KL Kari Lehtonen
RE-MF Marc-Andre Fleury
RE-MR Michael Ryder
RE-MST Matt Stajan
RE-NH Nathan Horton
RE-NZ Nikolai Zherdev
RE-PB Patrice Bergeron
RE-PM Paul Martin
RE-RM Ryan Malone
RE-TR Tuomo Ruutu

2003-04 Parkhurst Rookie Rookie Jerseys

*MULT.COLOR SWATCH: .6X TO 1.5X
PRINT RUN 90 SETS
GOLD PRINT RUN 10 SETS
GOLD NOT PRICED DUE TO SCARCITY
RJ-1 Patrice Bergeron 12.00 30.00
RJ-2 Fedor Tyutin 6.00 15.00
RJ-3 Joffrey Lupul 6.00 15.00
RJ-4 Antti Miettinen 6.00 15.00
RJ-5 Nathan Horton 10.00 25.00
RJ-6 Dustin Brown 6.00 15.00
RJ-7 Tim Gleason 6.00 15.00
RJ-8 Chris Higgins 10.00 25.00
RJ-9 Jordin Tootoo 10.00 25.00
RJ-10 Dan Hamhuis 6.00 15.00
RJ-11 David Hale 6.00 15.00
RJ-12 Garth Murray 6.00 15.00
RJ-13 Paul Martin 6.00 15.00
RJ-14 Sean Bergenheim 6.00 15.00
RJ-15 Joni Pitkanen 6.00 15.00
RJ-16 John Pohl 6.00 15.00
RJ-17 Libor Pivko 6.00 15.00
RJ-18 Marek Svatos 10.00 25.00
RJ-19 Dan Fritsche 6.00 15.00
RJ-20 Denis Grebeshkov 6.00 15.00
RJ-21 Antero Niittymaki 8.00 20.00
RJ-22 Tuomo Ruutu 8.00 20.00
RJ-23 Kari Lehtonen 15.00 40.00
RJ-24 Dominic Moore 6.00 15.00
RJ-25 Tony Salmelainen 6.00 15.00
RJ-26 Christian Ehrhoff 6.00 15.00
RJ-27 Trevor Daley 6.00 15.00
RJ-28 Nikolai Zherdev 8.00 20.00
RJ-29 Mark Popovic 6.00 15.00
RJ-30 Peter Sejna 6.00 15.00
RJ-31 Derek Roy 8.00 20.00
RJ-32 Trent Hunter 6.00 15.00
RJ-33 Cody McCormick 6.00 15.00
RJ-34 John-Michael Liles 6.00 15.00
RJ-35 Matthew Lombardi 6.00 15.00
RJ-36 Marek Zidlicky 6.00 15.00
RJ-37 Ryan Malone 6.00 15.00
RJ-38 Niklas Kronwall 8.00 20.00
RJ-39 Rastislav Stana 6.00 15.00
RJ-40 Andrew Raycroft 8.00 20.00
RJ-41 Alexander Semin 10.00 25.00
RJ-42 Andrew Peters 6.00 15.00
RJ-43 Brent Burns 6.00 15.00
RJ-44 Matt Stajan 8.00 20.00
RJ-45 Antoine Vermette 6.00 15.00
RJ-46 Michael Ryder 10.00 25.00
RJ-47 Ryan Kesler 6.00 15.00
RJ-48 Eric Staal 12.00 30.00
RJ-49 Patrick Leahy 6.00 15.00
RJ-50 Marc-Andre Fleury 15.00 40.00

2003-04 Parkhurst Rookie Rookie Jersey Autographs

PRINT RUN 10 SETS
NOT PRICED DUE TO SCARCITY
RJ-AP Andrew Peters
RJ-AR Andrew Raycroft
RJ-AS Alexander Semin
RJ-AV Antoine Vermette
RJ-BB Brent Burns
RJ-CH Chris Higgins
RJ-DF Dan Fritsche
RJ-DH Dan Hamhuis
RJ-DR Derek Roy
RJ-DHA David Hale
RJ-ES Eric Staal
RJ-JL Joffrey Lupul
RJ-JP Joni Pitkanen
RJ-JLI John-Michael Liles
RJ-KL Kari Lehtonen
RJ-MF Marc-Andre Fleury
RJ-MR Michael Ryder
RJ-MST Matt Stajan
RJ-NH Nathan Horton
RJ-PB Patrice Bergeron
RJ-PM Paul Martin
RJ-RM Ryan Malone
RJ-TR Tuomo Ruutu

2003-04 Parkhurst Rookie Rookie Numbers

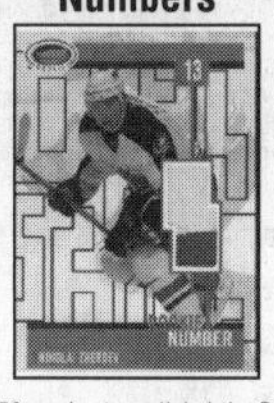

This 50-card set paralleled the Rookie Jerseys set. Cards were limited to just 19 copies each and gold 1/1's were also created.
NOT PRICED DUE TO SCARCITY

2003-04 Parkhurst Rookie Rookie Number Autographs

STATED PRINT RUN 10 SETS
NOT PRICED DUE TO SCARCITY
RN-AP Andrew Peters
RN-AR Andrew Raycroft
RN-AS Alexander Semin
RN-AV Antoine Vermette
RN-BB Brent Burns
RN-CH Chris Higgins
RN-DF Dan Fritsche
RN-DH Dan Hamhuis
RN-DR Derek Roy
RN-DHA David Hale
RN-ES Eric Staal
RN-JL Joffrey Lupul
RN-JP Joni Pitkanen
RN-JLI John-Michael Liles
RN-KL Kari Lehtonen
RN-MF Marc-Andre Fleury
RN-MR Michael Ryder
RN-MST Matt Stajan
RN-NH Nathan Horton
RN-PB Patrice Bergeron
RN-PM Paul Martin
RN-RM Ryan Malone
RN-TR Tuomo Ruutu

2003-04 Parkhurst Rookie ROYalty

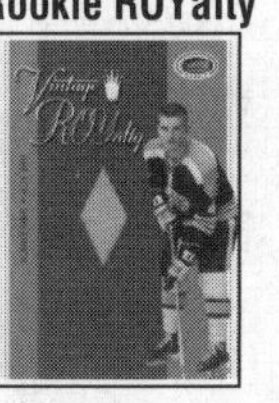

*MULT.COLOR SWATCH: .6X TO 1.5X
PRINT RUN 50 SETS
GOLD PRINT RUN 10 SETS
GOLD NOT PRICED DUE TO SCARCITY
VR-1 Dany Heatley 12.50 30.00
VR-2 Martin Brodeur 20.00 50.00
VR-3 Peter Forsberg 15.00 40.00
VR-4 Daniel Alfredsson 10.00 25.00
VR-5 Teemu Selanne 10.00 25.00
VR-6 Sergei Samsonov 10.00 25.00
VR-7 Ray Bourque 15.00 40.00
VR-8 Brian Leetch 10.00 25.00
VR-9 Mario Lemieux 30.00 80.00
VR-10 Bobby Orr 75.00 200.00
VR-11 Terry Sawchuk 15.00 40.00
VR-12 Jacques Laperriere 10.00 25.00
VR-13 Gilbert Perreault 12.50 30.00
VR-14 Bryan Trottier 10.00 25.00
VR-15 Denis Potvin 10.00 25.00
VR-16 Roger Crozier 10.00 25.00
VR-17 Pavel Bure 10.00 25.00
VR-18 Ed Belfour 10.00 25.00
VR-19 Glenn Hall 10.00 25.00
VR-20 Evgeni Nabokov 10.00 25.00
VR-21 Frank Brimsek 10.00 25.00
VR-22 Mike Bossy 12.50 30.00
VR-23 Luc Robitaille 10.00 25.00
VR-24 Scott Gomez 10.00 25.00
VR-25 Bernie Geoffrion 12.50 30.00
VR-26 Gump Worsley 10.00 25.00
VR-27 Joe Nieuwendyk 10.00 25.00
VR-28 Tony Esposito 15.00 40.00

2003-04 Parkhurst Rookie ROYalty Autographs

PRINT RUN 10 SETS
NOT PRICED DUE TO SCARCITY
VR-BL Brian Leetch
VR-BO Bobby Orr
VR-DH Dany Heatley
VR-GW Gump Worsley
VR-MB Martin Brodeur
VR-ML Mario Lemieux
VR-PF Peter Forsberg
VR-RB Ray Bourque
VR-TE Tony Esposito

2003-04 Parkhurst Rookie Teammates

*MULT.COLOR SWATCH: .6X TO 1.5X
PRINT RUN 60 SETS
GOLD PRINT RUN 10 SETS
GOLD NOT PRICED DUE TO SCARCITY
RT1 M.Lemieux/M.Fleury 25.00 60.00
RT2 Sergei Fedorov 15.00 40.00
Joffrey Lupul
RT3 Mats Sundin 15.00 40.00
Matt Stajan
RT4 R.Nash/N.Zherdev 15.00 40.00
RT5 Mike Modano 8.00 20.00
Trevor Daley
RT6 Jay Bouwmeester 10.00 25.00
Nathan Horton
RT7 Alexander Frolov 8.00 20.00
Dustin Brown
RT8 Jason Spezza 10.00 25.00
Antoine Vermette
RT9 Jeremy Roenick 8.00 20.00
{Joni Pitkanen
RT10 Joe Sakic 10.00 25.00
Cody McCormick
RT11 Joe Thornton 15.00 40.00
Patrice Bergeron
RT12 Peter Forsberg 20.00 50.00
Marek Svatos
RT13 David Legwand 12.50 30.00
Jordin Tootoo
RT14 Keith Tkachuk 8.00 20.00
Peter Sejna
RT15 Scott Stevens 8.00 20.00
{Paul Martin
RT16 Jose Theodore 15.00 40.00
Michael Ryder
RT17 Rob Blake 8.00 20.00
John-Michael Liles
RT18 Jarome Iginla 10.00 25.00
{Matthew Lombardi
RT19 Miroslav Satan 8.00 20.00
Derek Roy
RT20 Saku Koivu 8.00 20.00
Chris Higgins
RT21 Mark Messier 15.00 40.00
Dominic Moore
RT22 Joceylyn Thibault 10.00 25.00
{Tuomo Ruutu

1971-72 Penguins Postcards

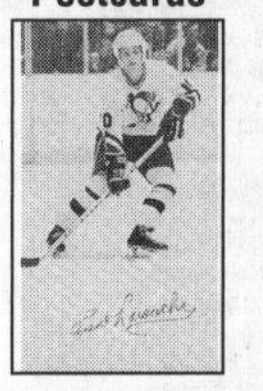

This 22-card set (measuring approximately 3 1/2" by 5 1/2") features full-bleed posed action color player photos. The cards originally came bound together in a flip book, but had perforations at the card top to allow them to be removed. The backs carry the player's name and biography in blue print on a white background. Only the Red Kelly card has a career summary on its back. The cards are unnumbered and checklisted below in alphabetical order. The set is dated by the inclusion of Roy Edwards, whose only season with the Penguins was 1971-72.

COMPLETE SET (22) 20.00 40.00
1 Syl Apps 1.25 2.50
2 Les Binkley 1.25 2.50
3 Dave Burrows 1.00 2.00
4 Darryl Edestrand .75 1.50
5 Roy Edwards 1.00 2.00
6 Val Fonteyne .75 1.50
7 Nick Harbaruk .75 1.50
8 Bryan Hextall 2.00 4.00
9 Sheldon Kannegiesser .75 1.50
10 Red Kelly CO 2.00 4.00
11 Bob Leiter .75 1.50
12 Keith McCreary .75 1.50
13 Joe Noris .75 1.50
14 Greg Polis .75 1.50
15 Jean Pronovost 2.00 4.00
16 Rene Robert 1.25 2.50
17 Jim Rutherford 1.25 2.50
18 Ken Schinkel .75 1.50
19 Ron Schock 1.00 2.00
20 Bryan Watson 1.00 2.00
21 Bob Woytowich .75 1.50
22 Title Card .75 1.50

1974-75 Penguins Postcards

This 22-card set features full-bleed black and white action pictures by photographer Paul Salva. The player's autograph is inscribed across the bottom of the picture. The cards are in the postcard format and measure approximately 3 1/2" by 5 1/2". The horizontal backs are blank. The cards are unnumbered and checklisted below in alphabetical order. The set is dated by the fact that Nelson Debenedet was only with the

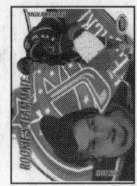

Penguins during the 1974-75 season. Pierre Larouche appears in this set prior to his Rookie Card appearance.

COMPLETE SET (22)	15.00	30.00
1 Syl Apps	1.25	2.50
2 Chuck Arnason	.75	1.50
3 Dave Burrows	1.00	2.00
4 Colin Campbell	1.25	2.50
5 Nelson Debenedet	.75	1.50
6 Steve Durbano	.75	1.50
7 Vic Hadfield	1.00	2.00
8 Gary Inness	1.00	2.00
9 Bob(B.J.) Johnson	.75	1.50
10 Rick Kehoe	1.25	2.50
11 Bob Kelly	.75	1.50
12 Jean-Guy Lagace	.75	1.50
13 Ron Lalonde	.75	1.50
14 Pierre Larouche	2.50	5.00
15 Lowell MacDonald	1.00	2.00
16 Dennis Owchar	.75	1.50
17 Bob Paradise	.75	1.50
18 Kelly Pratt	.75	1.50
19 Jean Pronovost	1.00	2.00
20 Ron Schock	1.00	2.00
21 Ron Stackhouse	1.00	2.00
22 Barry Williams	.75	1.50

1977-78 Penguins Puck Bucks

This 18-card set of Pittsburgh Penguins was sponsored by McDonald's restaurants, whose company logo appears at the top of the card face. The cards measure approximately 1 15/16" by 3 1/2" and are perforated so that the bottom tab (measuring 1 15/16" by 1") may be removed. The front of the top portion features a color head shot of the player, with a white border on a mustard-colored background. The back of the top portion has "Hockey Talk," in which a hockey term is explained. The front side of the tab portion shows a hockey puck on an orange background. Its back states that the "puck bucks" are coupons worth 1.00 toward the purchase of any 7.50 Penguins game ticket. These coupons had to be redeemed no later than December 31, 1977.

COMPLETE SET (18)	12.50	25.00
1 Denis Herron	1.50	3.00
2 Ron Stackhouse	1.00	2.00
4 Dave Burrows	.75	1.50
6 Colin Campbell	1.25	2.50
7 Russ Anderson	.75	1.50
9 Blair Chapman	.75	1.50
10 Pierre Larouche	1.50	3.00
12 Greg Malone	1.00	2.00
14 Wayne Bianchin	.75	1.50
17 Rick Kehoe	1.50	3.00
18 Lowell MacDonald	1.00	2.00
19 Jean Pronovost	1.25	2.50
23 Jim Hamilton	.75	1.50
25 Dennis Owchar	.75	1.50
26 Syl Apps	1.00	2.00
27 Mike Corrigan	.75	1.50
29 Dunc Wilson	1.00	2.00
NNO Johnny Wilson CO	.50	1.00

1983-84 Penguins Coke

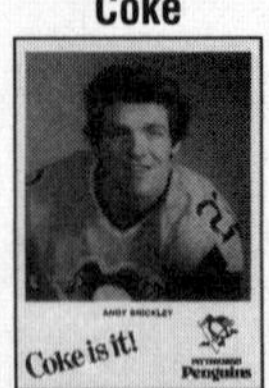

This 19-card set of the Pittsburgh Penguins measures approximately 5" by 7". The fronts feature black-and-white player portraits framed in white with the player's name, team name, team logo, and the words "Coke is it!" printed in black in the wide white bottom border. The backs are blank. The cards are unnumbered and checklisted below in alphabetical order. The card of Marty McSorley appears four years before his rookie card.

COMPLETE SET (19)	10.00	25.00
1 Pat Boutette	.60	1.50
2 Andy Brickley	.40	1.00
3 Mike Bullard	.80	2.00
4 Ted Bulley	.40	1.00
5 Rod Buskas	.40	1.00
6 Randy Carlyle	.80	2.00
7 Michel Dion	.80	2.00
8 Bob Errey	.80	2.00
9 Ron Flockhart	.60	1.50
10 Steve Gatzos	.40	1.00
11 Jim Hamilton	.40	1.00
12 Dave Hannan	.40	1.00
13 Denis Herron	1.00	2.50
14 Troy Loney	.40	1.00
15 Bryan Maxwell	.40	1.00
16 Marty McSorley	2.00	5.00
17 Norm Schmidt	.40	1.00
18 Mark Taylor	.40	1.00
19 Greg Tebbutt	.40	1.00

1983-84 Penguins Heinz Photos

This Pittsburgh Penguins "Photo Pak" was sponsored by Heinz. The cards are unnumbered and checklisted below in alphabetical order. They were giveaways at Pittsburgh Penguins home games. Each photo measures approximately 6" by 9" and they were produced on one large folded sheet.

COMPLETE SET (22)	10.00	25.00
1 Paul Baxter	.60	1.50
2 Pat Boutette	.60	1.50
3 Randy Boyd	.40	1.00
4 Mike Bullard	.80	2.00
5 Randy Carlyle	.80	2.00
6 Marc Chorney	.40	1.00
7 Michel Dion	.80	2.00
8 Bill Gardner	.40	1.00
9 Pat Graham	.40	1.00
10 Anders Hakansson	.40	1.00
11 Dave Hannan	.40	1.00
12 Denis Herron	1.00	2.50
13 Greg Hotham	.40	1.00
14 Stan Jonathan	.60	1.50
15 Rick Kehoe	1.00	2.50
16 Peter Lee	.80	2.00
17 Greg Malone	.60	1.50
18 Kevin McClelland	.40	1.00
19 Ron Meighan	.40	1.00
20 Doug Shedden	.40	1.00
21 Andre St. Laurent	.40	1.00
22 Rich Sutter	.60	1.50

1984-85 Penguins Heinz Photos

This Pittsburgh Penguins "Photo Pak" was sponsored by Heinz. The cards are unnumbered and checklisted below in alphabetical order. They were giveaways at Pittsburgh Penguins home games. Each photo measures approximately 6" by 9" and they were produced on one large folded sheet.

COMPLETE SET (22)	10.00	25.00
1 Pat Boutette	.60	1.50
2 Andy Brickley	.40	1.00
3 Mike Bullard	.80	2.00
4 Rod Buskas	.40	1.00
5 Randy Carlyle	.80	2.00
6 Michel Dion	.80	2.00
7 Bob Errey	.60	1.50
8 Ron Flockhart	.40	1.00
9 Greg Fox	.40	1.00
10 Steve Gatzos	.40	1.00
11 Denis Herron	1.00	2.50
12 Greg Hotham	.40	1.00
13 Rick Kehoe	.80	2.00
14 Bryan Maxwell	.60	1.50
15 Marty McSorley	2.00	5.00
16 Tom O'Regan	.40	1.00
17 Gary Rissling	.40	1.00
18 Roberto Romano	.60	1.50
19 Tom Roulston	.40	1.00
20 Rocky Saganiuk	.40	1.00
21 Doug Shedden	.60	1.50
22 Mark Taylor	.40	1.00

1986-87 Penguins Kodak

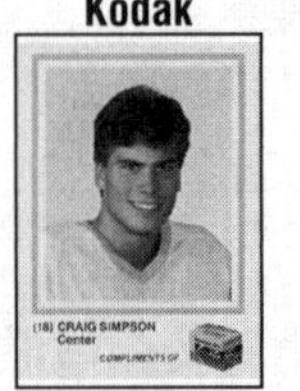

The 1986-87 Pittsburgh Penguins Team Photo Album was sponsored by Kodak and commemorates the team's 20 years in the NHL. It consists of three large sheets, each measuring approximately 11" by 8 1/4", joined together to form one continuous sheet. The first panel has a team photo of the 1967 Pittsburgh Penguins. The second panel presents three rows of five cards each. The third panel presents two rows of five cards, with five Kodak coupons completing the left over portion of the panel. After perforation, the cards measure approximately 2 3/16" by 2 1/2". They feature color posed photos bordered in yellow, with player information below the picture. A Kodak film box serving as a logo completes the card face. The back has biographical and statistical information in a horizontal format. We have checklisted the names below in alphabetical order, with the uniform number to the right of the name.

COMPLETE SET (26)	20.00	50.00
1 Bob Berry CO	.20	.50
2 Mike Blaisdell 26	.40	1.00
3 Doug Bodger 3	.40	1.00
4 Rod Buskas 7	.30	.75
5 John Chabot 9	.30	.75
6 Randy Cunneyworth 15	.30	.75
7 Ron Duguay 10	.40	1.00
8 Bob Errey 12	.40	1.00
9 Dan Frawley 28	.30	.75
10 Dave Hannan 32	.30	.75
11 Randy Hillier 23	.30	.75
12 Jim Johnson 6	.30	.75
13 Kevin Lavallee 16	.30	.75
14 Mario Lemieux 66	12.00	30.00
15 Willy Lindstrom 19	.30	.75
16 Moe Mantha 20	.30	.75
17 Gilles Meloche 27	.40	1.00
18 Dan Quinn 14	.40	1.00
19 Jim Roberts CO	.20	.50
20 Roberto Romano 30	.40	1.00
21 Terry Ruskowski 8	.40	1.00
22 Norm Schmidt 25	.30	.75
23 Craig Simpson 18	.60	1.50
24 Ville Siren 5	.30	.75
25 Warren Young 35	.40	1.00
NNO '67 Team Photo	.80	2.00

1987-88 Penguins Masks

These masks were issued by KDKA and Eagle Food Stores. Mask fronts show top of players head, and backs feature name, stats, and sponsors logos. These masks are unnumbered and checklisted below in alphabetical order.

COMPLETE SET (10)	8.00	20.00
1 Doug Bodger	.40	1.00
2 Randy Cunneyworth	.40	1.00
3 Bob Errey	.40	1.00
4 Dan Frawley	.40	1.00
5 Jim Johnson	.40	1.00
6 Mario Lemieux	4.00	10.00
7 Gilles Meloche	.80	2.00
8 Dan Quinn	.40	1.00
9 Craig Simpson	.80	2.00
10 Ville Siren	.40	1.00

1987-88 Penguins Kodak

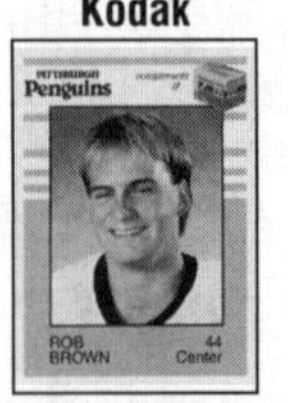

The 1987-88 Pittsburgh Penguins Team Photo Album was sponsored by Kodak. It consists of three large sheets, each measuring approximately 11" by 8 1/4", joined together to form one continuous sheet. The first panel has a team photo, with the players' names listed according to rows below the picture. The second panel presents three rows of five cards each. The third panel presents two rows of five cards, with five Kodak coupons completing the left over portion of the panel. After perforation, the cards measure approximately 2 3/16" by 2 1/2". A Kodak film box serves as a logo in the upper right hand corner of the card face. The front features a color head shot inside a thin black border. The picture is set on a Kodak "yellow" background, with white stripes traversing the top of the card. The player's name, number, and position are printed in black lettering below the picture. The back has biographical information and career statistics in a horizontal format. We have checklisted the cards below in alphabetical order, with the player's number to the right of his name.

COMPLETE SET (26)	14.00	35.00
1 Doug Bodger 3	.30	.75
2 Rob Brown 44	.40	1.00
3 Rod Buskas 7	.30	.75
4 Jock Callander 36	.30	.75
5 Paul Coffey 77	.80	2.00
6 Randy Cunneyworth 15	.30	.75
7 Chris Dahlquist 4	.30	.75
8 Bob Errey 12	.30	.75
9 Dan Frawley 28	.30	.75
10 Steve Guenette 30	.40	1.00
11 Randy Hillier 23	.30	.75
12 Dave Hunter 20	.30	.75
13 Jim Johnson 6	.30	.75
14 Mark Kachowski 26	.30	.75
15 Chris Kontos 14	.30	.75
16 Mario Lemieux 66	6.00	15.00
17 Troy Loney 24	.30	.75
18 Dwight Mathiasen 34	.30	.75
19 Dave McLlwain 19	.30	.75
20 Gilles Meloche 27	.40	1.00
21 Dan Quinn 10	.40	1.00
22 Pat Riggin 1	.40	1.00
23 Charlie Simmer 16	.40	1.00
24 Ville Siren 5	.30	.75
25 Wayne Van Dorp	.30	.75
NNO Large Team Photo	1.60	4.00

1989-90 Penguins Coke/Elby's

This set measures approximately 4" by 6" and features color action player photos bordered in white with player information at the top and sponsor logos in the bottom margin. The backs are blank except for a coupon for free burger and fries at participating Elby's Big Boy restaurants. The cards are unnumbered and checklisted below in alphabetical order.

COMPLETE SET (5)	4.80	12.00
1 Phil Bourque	.20	.50
2 Rob Brown	.30	.75
3 Mario Lemieux	4.00	10.00
4 Kevin Stevens	.80	2.00
5 Zarley Zalapski	.30	.75

1989-90 Penguins Foodland

This 15-card set was sponsored by Foodland in conjunction with the Pittsburgh Penguins and the Crime Prevention Officers of Western Pennsylvania. The Foodland company logo appears on the top and back of each card. The cards measure approximately 2 9/16" by 4 1/8" and could be collected from police officers. The front features a color action photo with a thin black border on white card stock. The player information below the picture is sandwiched between the Penguin and the Crime Dog McGruff logos. The back is dated and presents a Penguins tip and a safety tip (both illustrated with cartoons) in a horizontal format. There were two late issue cards distributed after trades. They are rather scarce and not typically considered part of the complete set.

COMPLETE SET (15)	8.00	20.00
1 Rob Brown	.30	.75
2 Jim Johnson	.20	.50
3 Zarley Zalapski	.30	.75
4 Paul Coffey	.80	2.00
5 Phil Bourque	.20	.50
6A Dan Quinn	.30	.75
6B Gilbert Delorme SP	.80	2.00
7 Kevin Stevens	.80	2.00
8 Bob Errey	.20	.50
9 John Cullen	.30	.75
10 Mario Lemieux	4.00	10.00
11 Randy Hillier	.20	.50
12 Jay Caufield	.20	.50
13A Andrew McBain	.20	.50
13B Troy Loney SP	.80	2.00
14 Wendell Young	.30	.75
15 Tom Barrasso	.40	1.00

1990-91 Penguins Foodland

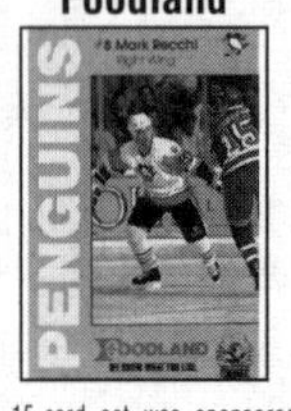

This 15-card set was sponsored by Foodland in conjunction with the Pittsburgh Penguins and the Crime Prevention Officers of Western Pennsylvania. The Foodland company logo appears at the bottom of the card front and the top of the horizontally oriented back. The cards measure approximately 2 11/16" by 4 1/8" and could be collected from police officers. The front features a color action photo with a thin black border surrounded by wide yellow margins on three sides. The team name is printed in white block lettering, running the length of the card on the left side of the picture. The back presents a Penguins tip and a safety tip (both illustrated with cartoons). The set features the appearance of three Penguins, Jaromir Jagr, Mark Recchi, and Kevin Stevens, in their Rookie Card year.

COMPLETE SET (15)	12.00	30.00
1 Phil Bourque 29	.10	.25
2 Paul Coffey 77	.40	1.00
3 Randy Hillier 23	.10	.25
4 Barry Pederson 10	.16	.40
5 Tom Barrasso 35	.30	.75
6 Mark Recchi 8	.80	2.00
7 Bob Johnson CO	.80	2.00
8 Joe Mullen 7	.30	.75
9 Kevin Stevens 25	.60	1.50
10 John Cullen 11	.16	.40
11 Jaromir Jagr 68	10.00	25.00
12 Zarley Zalapski 33	.16	.40
13 Mario Lemieux 66	3.20	8.00
14 Tony Tanti 9	.10	.25
15 Bryan Trottier 19	.30	.75

1991-92 Penguins Coke/Elby's

This 24-card set was sponsored by Cola-Cola in conjunction with Elby's Big Boy restaurants. The cards measure approximately 4" by 6" and are printed on thin card stock. The headline "1990-91 Stanley Cup Champions" adorns the top of each front. Immediately below appears the uniform number, player's name, and a twenty-fifth anniversary team logo. The color action player photos are bordered in white, with the two sponsor logos appearing in the bottom white border. The backs are blank. The cards are skip-numbered by uniform number and checklisted below accordingly.

COMPLETE SET (24)	10.00	25.00
1 Wendell Young	.30	.75
2 Jim Paek	.20	.50
3 Grant Jennings	.20	.50
5 Ulf Samuelsson	.40	1.00
7 Joe Mullen	.40	1.00
8 Mark Recchi	.80	2.00
10 Ron Francis	1.00	2.50
16 Jay Caufield	.20	.50
18 Ken Priestlay	.20	.50
19 Bryan Trottier	.40	1.00
20 Jamie Leach	.20	.50
22 Paul Stanton	.20	.50
24 Troy Loney	.20	.50
25 Kevin Stevens	.40	1.00
28 Gord Roberts	.20	.50
29 Phil Bourque	.20	.50
32 Peter Taglianetti	.20	.50
40 Frank Pietrangelo	.30	.75
43 Jeff Daniels	.20	.50
55 Larry Murphy	.40	1.00
66 Mario Lemieux	2.40	6.00
68 Jaromir Jagr	3.20	8.00
NNO Scotty Bowman CO	.40	1.00

1991-92 Penguins Foodland

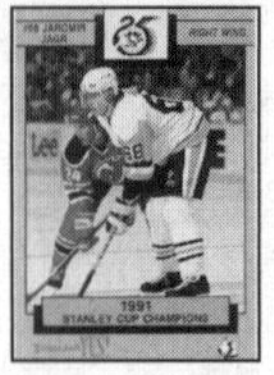

This 15-card standard-size set was sponsored by Foodland in conjunction with the Pittsburgh Penguins and the Crime Prevention Officers of Western Pennsylvania. The Foodland logo and McGruff the Crime Dog appear at the bottom of the card face, while a 25th year anniversary emblem appears at the top center. The fronts feature color action player photos on an orangish-yellow card face. The player's name, uniform number, and his position appear in the top silver stripe; the words "1991 Stanley Cup Champions" appears in another silver stripe beneath the picture. The horizontally oriented backs have a "Penguins Tip" and a "Safety Tip," each of which is illustrated by a cartoon.

COMPLETE SET (15)	8.00	20.00
1 Jim Paek	.20	.50
2 Ulf Samuelsson	.30	.75
3 Ron Francis	.80	2.00
4 Mario Lemieux	3.20	8.00
5 Rick Tocchet	.40	1.00
6 Joe Mullen	.40	1.00
7 Troy Loney	.20	.50
8 Kevin Stevens	.30	.75
9 Tom Barrasso	.40	1.00
10 Larry Murphy	.30	.75
11 Jaromir Jagr	3.20	8.00
12 Bryan Trottier	.40	1.00
13 Paul Stanton	.20	.50
14 Peter Taglianetti	.20	.50
15 Phil Bourque	.20	.50

1991-92 Penguins Foodland Coupon Stickers

This set of twelve stickers is the result of a unique cross-promotion with Topps and the Foodland stores of Pittsburgh. The stickers, issued in a 3-sticker sheet over a four week period, mimic the 1991-92 Topps card of a Penguin player on the front, with a coupon for Foodland on the peel-off backs. Most feature the player's regular card front; exceptions are Jaromir Jagr (Super Rookie), Mario Lemieux (Award Winner) and Kevin Stevens (All-Star). The stickers are unnumbered, but are listed below in issue of order, top to bottom, per week.

COMPLETE SET (12)	6.00	15.00
1 Bryan Trottier	.30	.75
2 Joe Mullen	.30	.75
3 Larry Murphy	.30	.75
4 Tom Barrasso	.30	.75
5 Ron Francis	.60	1.50
6 Ulf Samuelsson	.30	.75
7 Jaromir Jagr	2.40	6.00
8 Mario Lemieux	2.40	6.00
9 Kevin Stevens	.30	.75
10 Mark Recchi	.40	1.00
11 Paul Coffey	.60	1.50
12 Frank Pietrangelo	.30	.75

1992-93 Penguins Coke/Clark

This 26-card set was sponsored by Cola-Cola and Clark. These cards followed the same concept as Coke/Elby's sets of the previous years, i.e., large autograph cards issued to the players for use in personal appearances. The cards measure approximately 4" by 6" and were printed on thin card stock. The backs are blank. The cards are unnumbered and checklisted below in alphabetical order.

COMPLETE SET (26)	10.00	25.00
1 Tom Barrasso	.40	1.00
2 Scotty Bowman CO	.60	1.50
3 Jay Caufield	.20	.50
4 Jeff Daniels	.20	.50
5 Bob Errey	.20	.50
6 Bryan Fogarty	.20	.50
7 Ron Francis	.80	2.00
8 Jaromir Jagr	2.40	6.00
9 Grant Jennings	.20	.50
10 Mario Lemieux	2.40	6.00
11 Troy Loney	.20	.50
12 Shawn McEachern	.40	1.00
13 Joe Mullen	.40	1.00
14 Larry Murphy	.40	1.00
15 Mike Needham	.20	.50
16 Jim Paek	.20	.50
17 Kjell Samuelsson	.20	.50
18 Ulf Samuelsson	.30	.75
19 Paul Stanton	.20	.50
20 Mike Stapleton	.20	.50
21 Kevin Stevens	.30	.75
22 Martin Straka	.40	1.00
23 Dave Tippett	.20	.50
24 Rick Tocchet	.50	1.25
25 Ken Wregget	.50	1.25
26 Penguins Mascot	.10	.25

1992-93 Penguins Foodland

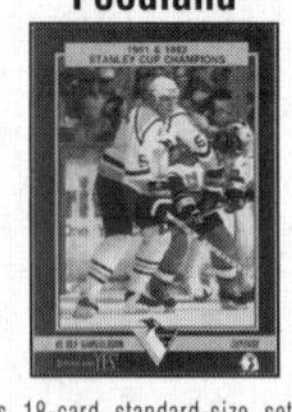

This 18-card standard-size set was sponsored by Foodland in conjunction with the Pittsburgh Penguins and the Crime Prevention Officers of Western Pennsylvania. The cards feature color action player photos with orange-yellow borders on a black card face. The player's name is printed in an orange-yellow stripe below the photo. The words "1991 and 1992 Stanley Cup Champions" are on an orange-yellow bar that overlaps the top of the picture. The Foodland logo and McGruff the Crime Dog appear at the bottom. The horizontal backs have a "Penguins Tip" and a "Safety Tip," each illustrated with a cartoon.

COMPLETE SET (18)	6.00	15.00
1 Mario Lemieux	2.00	5.00
2 Bob Errey	.20	.50
3 Jaromir Jagr	1.20	3.00
4 Rick Tocchet	.40	1.00
5 Tom Barrasso	.40	1.00
6 Joe Mullen	.30	.75
7 Ron Francis	.80	2.00
8 Troy Loney	.20	.50
9 Shawn McEachern	.20	.50
10 Larry Murphy	.30	.75
11 Jim Paek	.20	.50
12 Ulf Samuelsson	.20	.50
13 Paul Stanton	.20	.50
14 Kjell Samuelsson	.20	.50
15 Kevin Stevens	.30	.75
16 Dave Tippett	.20	.50
17 Martin Straka	.40	1.00
18 Penguins Mascot	.10	.25

1992-93 Penguins Foodland Coupon Stickers

Sponsored by Foodland and issued in four three-sticker vertical strips, this 12-sticker set features white-bordered color player action photos, with the peel-away backs doubling as manufacturer coupons for different products. Each sticker measures the standard size. The player's name and uniform number appear in a yellow bar under the photo and the words "Back to Back Champs" are printed in a bar alongside the left. The team logo also appears on the front. The strips are numbered as Week 1-4; the stickers themselves are unnumbered. The players are listed below in alphabetical order; W1 to W4 indicates the week the stickers were issued.

COMPLETE SET (12)	6.00	15.00
1 Tom Barrasso W2	.40	1.00
2 Ron Francis W1	.60	1.50
3 Jaromir Jagr W4	2.00	5.00
4 Mario Lemieux W2	2.40	6.00
5 Troy Loney W2	.20	.50
6 Shawn McEachern W4	.20	.50
7 Joe Mullen W3	.30	.75
8 Larry Murphy W4	.30	.75
9 Jim Paek W1	.20	.50
10 Ulf Samuelsson W3	.20	.50
11 Kevin Stevens W1	.30	.75
12 Rick Tocchet W3	.40	1.00

1993-94 Penguins Foodland

Sponsored by Foodland, this 25-card standard-size set features the 1993-94 Pittsburgh Penguins. The fronts have color action player photos with black borders on gray backgrounds. The team name appears in the top part of the card, while the player's name, number and position are printed under the photo. The Penguins logo on the bottom rounds out the front. The horizontal backs have a "Penguin Tip" and a "Safe Tip," each illustrated with a cartoon.

COMPLETE SET (25)	6.00	15.00
1 Mario Lemieux	1.60	4.00
2 Grant Jennings	.16	.40
3 Ulf Samuelsson	.20	.50
4 Rick Tocchet	.30	.75
5 Marty McSorley	.30	.75
6 Rick Kehoe ACO	.10	.25
7 Doug Brown	.16	.40
8 Martin Straka	.30	.75
9 Jim Paek	.16	.40
10 Ken Wregget	.30	.75
11 Jeff Daniels	.16	.40
12 Bryan Trottier	.20	.50
13 Larry Murphy	.20	.50
14 Ron Francis	.40	1.00
15 Mike Needham	.16	.40
16 Mike Ramsey	.16	.40
17 Kevin Stevens	.20	.50
18 Kjell Samuelsson	.16	.40
19 Ed Johnston CO	.10	.25
20 Markus Naslund	.20	.50
21 Mike Stapleton	.16	.40
22 Peter Taglianetti	.16	.40
23 Jaromir Jagr	.80	2.00
24 Tom Barrasso	.20	.50
25 Joe Mullen	.20	.50

1994-95 Penguins Foodland

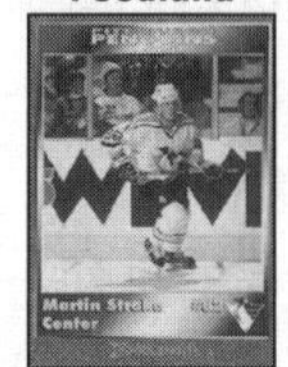

Sponsored by Foodland, this 25-ca standard-size set features the 1994-19 Pittsburgh Penguins. The fronts have col action player photos with gray borders marbleized gray backgrounds. The tea name across the top part of the card, whi the player's name, number, position, and t team logo are printed under the picture. T horizontal backs carry a "Penguin Tip" and "Safety Tip", each illustrated with a cartoon

COMPLETE SET (25)	4.80	12.00
1 Grant Jennings	.12	.30
2 Greg Hawgood	.12	.30
3 Shawn McEachern	.20	.50
4 Len Barrie	.12	.30
5 Ulf Samuelsson	.20	.50
6 Joe Mullen	.20	.50
7 John Cullen	.12	.30
8 Mike Hudson	.12	.30
9 Ron Francis	.40	1.00
10 Tomas Sandstrom	.20	.50
11 Eddie Johnston CO	.10	.25
12 Chris Tamer	.12	.30
13 Francois Leroux	.12	.30
14 Luc Robitaille	.40	1.00
15 Markus Naslund	.20	.50
16 Ken Wregget	.20	.50
17 Chris Joseph	.12	.30
18 Peter Taglianetti	.12	.30
19 Kevin Stevens	.20	.50
20 Jim McKenzie	.12	.30
21 Kjell Samuelsson	.12	.30
22 Tom Barrasso	.20	.50
23 Jaromir Jagr	1.60	4.00
24 Larry Murphy	.20	.50
25 Martin Straka	.12	.30

1995-96 Penguins Foodland

This 25-card set maintains the string issues released by Foodland, a Pittsburg area grocery chain, to honor the hometov Penguins. The cards feature action play photos surrounded by an icy blue border the front. The backs have two Penguin tip and the card number. Card number 2 erroneously pictures Ian Moran instead Bryan Smolinski. The error is not believed have been corrected.

COMPLETE SET (25)	4.00	10.00
1 Ron Francis	.40	1.00
2 Glen Murray	.10	.25
3 Chris Wells	.10	.25
4 Markus Naslund	.12	.30
5 Jaromir Jagr	1.20	3.00
6 Francois Leroux	.10	.25
7 Richard Park	.10	.25
8 Norm Maciver	.10	.25
9 Ken Wregget	.20	.50
10 Tom Barrasso	.20	.50
11 Rick Kehoe ACO	.10	.25
12 Sergei Zubov	.10	.25
13 Joe Dziedzic	.10	.25
14 Ed Patterson	.10	.25
15 Tomas Sandstrom	.12	.30
16 Dave Roche	.10	.25
17 Petr Nedved	.20	.50
18 Chris Tamer	.10	.25
19 Chris Joseph	.10	.25
20 Ian Moran	.10	.25
21 Iceburgh (Mascot)	.04	.10

22 Ed Johnston CO .10 .25
23 Mario Lemieux 1.60 4.00
24 Bryan Smolinski .12 .30
UER photo shown Chris Wells
25 Dmitri Mironov .12 .30

1996-97 Penguins Tribune-Review

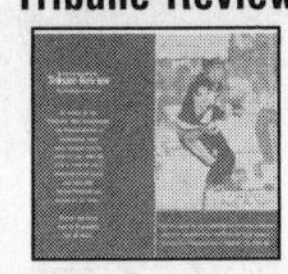

These oversized 5" x 7" thick stock cards were distributed as inserts in the Penguins game programs to honor the club's two Cup championships of the early '90s. As issued, the cards were folded in half, with the first two "pages" explaining the promotion, the third page actually containing the card/photo, and the fourth page offering biographical info and stats from one of the two seasons.

COMPLETE SET (8) 12.00 30.00
1 Ron Francis 1.60 4.00
2 Joe Mullen .80 2.00
3 Ulf Samuelsson .80 2.00
4 Bryan Trottier 1.20 3.00
5 Tom Barrasso .80 2.00
6 Kevin Stevens 1.20 3.00
7 Jaromir Jagr 3.20 8.00
8 Mario Lemieux 4.00 10.00

1997-98 Penguins USPS Lineup Cards

These oversized issues were inserted in Penguins programs and were sponsored by the post office. The front featured a glossy player photo, while the back listed that night's lineups. This obviously is not a complete listing. Anyone who can help fill it in is encouraged to write hockeymag@beckett.com.

COMPLETE SET (?) 3.20 8.00
NNO Darius Kasparaitis .80 2.00
NNO Ron Francis .80 2.00
NNO Jaromir Jagr 2.00 5.00

1980-81 Pepsi-Cola Caps

This set of 140 bottle caps features 20 players from each of the seven Canadian hockey teams. The bottle caps are written in French and English. There are two sizes of caps depending on whether the cap was from a small or large bottle. The top of the cap displays the Pepsi logo in the familiar red, white, and blue. The sides of the cap were done in blue and white lettering on a pink background. On the inside of the cap is a "black and aluminum" head shot of the player, with his name and the city (from which the team hails) below. We have checklisted the caps in alphabetical order of the teams as follows: Calgary Flames (1-20), Edmonton Oilers (21-40), Montreal Canadiens (41-60), Quebec Nordiques (61-80), Toronto Maple Leafs (81-100), Vancouver Canucks (101-120), and Winnipeg Jets (121-140). Also the players' names have been alphabetized within their teams. Also available through a mail-in offer -- in either English or French -- was a white plastic circular display plaque (approximately 24" by 24") for the caps. The French version sometimes sells for a slight premium. There also are reports that two different size variations exist: a 10 ounce and a 26 ounce size. There does not appear to be a premium on either size cap at this time.

COMPLETE SET (140) 100.00 200.00
1 Dan Bouchard 1.00 2.00
2 Guy Chouinard 1.00 2.00
3 Bill Clement 1.00 2.00
4 Randy Holt .75 1.50
5 Ken Houston .75 1.50
6 Kevin Lavallee .75 1.50
7 Don Lever .75 1.50
8 Bob MacMillan .75 1.50
9 Brad Marsh 1.25 2.50
10 Bob Murdoch .75 1.50
11 Kent Nilsson 1.00 2.00
12 Willi Plett 1.00 2.00
13 Jim Peplinski 1.00 2.00
14 Pekka Rautakillio .75 1.50
15 Paul Reinhart 1.00 2.00
16 Pat Riggin 1.00 2.00
17 Phil Russell .75 1.50
18 Brad Smith .75 1.50
19 Eric Vail .75 1.50
20 Bert Wilson .75 1.50
21 Glenn Anderson 2.00 4.00
22 Curt Brackenbury .75 1.50
23 Brett Callighen .75 1.50
24 Paul Coffey 7.50 15.00
25 Lee Fogolin .75 1.50
26 Matti Hagman .75 1.50
27 John Hughes .75 1.50
28 Dave Hunter .75 1.50
29 Jari Kurri 4.00 8.00
30 Ron Low 1.00 2.00
31 Kevin Lowe 1.25 2.50
32 Dave Lumley .75 1.50
33 Blair MacDonald .75 1.50
34 Mark Messier 12.50 25.00
35 Ed Mio 1.00 2.00
36 Don Murdoch .75 1.50
37 Pat Price .75 1.50
38 Dave Semenko 1.00 2.00
39 Risto Siltanen .75 1.50
40 Stan Weir .75 1.50
41 Keith Acton .75 1.50
42 Brian Engblom .75 1.50
43 Bob Gainey 1.50 3.00
44 Gaston Gingras .75 1.50
45 Denis Herron 1.00 2.00
46 Rejean Houle .75 1.50
47 Doug Jarvis .75 1.50
48 Yvon Lambert .75 1.50
49 Rod Langway 1.50 3.00
50 Guy Lapointe 1.00 2.00
51 Pierre Larouche 1.25 2.50
52 Pierre Mondou .75 1.50
53 Mark Napier 1.00 2.00
54 Chris Nilan 1.25 2.50
55 Doug Risebrough .75 1.50
56 Larry Robinson 2.00 4.00
57 Serge Savard 1.00 2.00
58 Steve Shutt 1.50 3.00
59 Mario Tremblay 1.00 2.00
60 Doug Wickenheiser .75 1.50
61 Serge Bernier .75 1.50
62 Kim Clackson .88 1.75
63 Real Cloutier .75 1.50
64 Andre Dupont .75 1.50
65 Robbie Ftorek 1.00 2.00
66 Michel Goulet 2.50 5.00
67 Jamie Hislop .75 1.50
68 Dale Hoganson .75 1.50
69 Dale Hunter 2.00 4.00
70 Pierre Lacroix .75 1.50
71 Garry Lariviere .75 1.50
72 Rich Leduc .75 1.50
73 John Paddock 1.00 2.00
74 Michel Plasse 1.00 2.00
75 Jacques Richard .75 1.50
76 Anton Stastny 1.00 2.00
77 Peter Stastny 3.00 6.00
78 Mark Tardif 1.00 2.00
79 Wally Weir .75 1.50
80 John Wensink 1.00 2.00
81 John Anderson .75 1.50
82 Laurie Boschman .75 1.50
83 Jiri Crha 1.00 2.00
84 Bill Derlago .75 1.50
85 Vitezslav Duris .75 1.50
86 Ron Ellis 1.00 2.00
87 Dave Farrish .75 1.50
88 Stewart Gavin 1.00 2.00
89 Pat Hickey .75 1.50
90 Dan Maloney 1.00 2.00
91 Terry Martin .75 1.50
92 Barry Melrose 1.00 2.00
93 Wilf Paiement 1.00 2.00
94 Robert Picard .75 1.50
95 Jim Rutherford 1.25 2.50
96 Rocky Saganiuk .75 1.50
97 Borje Salming 1.50 3.00
98 David Shand .75 1.50
99 Ian Turnbull 1.00 2.00
100 Rick Vaive 1.25 2.50
101 Brent Ashton .75 1.50
102 Ivan Boldirev .75 1.50
103 Per-Olov Brasar .75 1.50
104 Richard Brodeur 1.25 2.50
105 Jerry Butler .75 1.50
106 Colin Campbell 1.00 2.00
107 Curt Fraser .75 1.50
108 Thomas Gradin 1.00 2.00
109 Dennis Kearns .75 1.50
110 Rick Lanz .75 1.50
111 Lars Lindgren .75 1.50
112 Dave Logan .75 1.50
113 Mario Marois .75 1.50
114 Kevin McCarthy .75 1.50
115 Gerald Minor .75 1.50
116 Darcy Rota .75 1.50
117 Bobby Schmautz .75 1.50
118 Stan Smyl 1.00 2.00
119 Harold Snepsts 1.25 2.50
120 Dave(Tiger) Williams 1.25 2.50
121 Dave Babych 1.00 2.00
122 Al Cameron .75 1.50
123 Scott Campbell .75 1.50
124 Dave Christian 1.00 2.00
125 Jude Drouin .75 1.50
126 Norm Dupont .75 1.50
127 Dan Geoffrion .75 1.50
128 Pierre Hamel .75 1.50
129 Barry Legge .75 1.50
130 Willy Lindstrom .75 1.50
131 Barry Long .75 1.50
132 Kris Manery .75 1.50
133 Jimmy Mann .88 1.75
134 Moe Mantha .75 1.50
135 Markus Mattsson 1.00 2.00
136 Doug Smail 1.00 2.00
137 Don Spring .75 1.50
138 Anders Steen .75 1.50
139 Peter Sullivan .75 1.50
140 Ron Wilson .75 1.50
NNO Plastic Circular Display 40.00 80.00

1972-73 Philadelphia Blazers

These postcard-like issues feature the short-lived Blazers of the WHA. While we have confirmed just three cards, it is believed that many more exist. The cards are unnumbered and checklisted below in alphabetical order.

COMPLETE SET (3) 15.00 30.00
1 Danny Lawson 5.00 10.00
2 Bernie Parent 10.00 20.00
3 Ron Plumb 5.00 10.00

1974-75 Phoenix Roadrunners WHA Pins

These pins feature color head shots and measure 3 1/2" in diameter. Player name and team name are featured in a black rectangle at the bottom of the pin. Pins are checklisted below in alphabetical order.

COMPLETE SET (9) 20.00 40.00
1 Bob Barlow 2.00 4.00
2 Cam Connor 2.00 4.00
3 Michel Cormier 2.00 4.00
4 Robbie Ftorek 6.00 12.00
5 Dave Gorman 2.00 4.00
6 John Hughes 2.00 4.00
7 Murray Keogan 2.00 4.00
8 Dennis Sobchuk 2.00 4.00
9 Howie Young 2.00 4.00

1975-76 Phoenix Roadrunners WHA

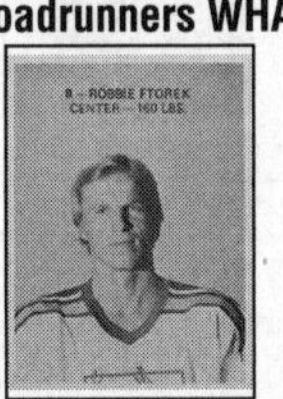

This 22-card set features players of the WHA Phoenix Roadrunners. The cards measure approximately 3" by 4" and the backs are blank. The front features a poor quality black and white head-and-shoulders shot of the player with a white border. The cards are numbered by the uniform number on the front and we have checklisted them below accordingly. The player's position and weight are also given.

COMPLETE SET (22) 25.00 50.00
1 Serge Beaudoin 1.00 2.00
2 Jim Boyd 1.00 2.00
3 Jim Clarke 1.00 2.00
4 Cam Connors 1.00 2.00
5 Michel Cormier 1.00 2.00
6 Barry Dean 1.00 2.00
7 Robbie Ftorek 7.50 15.00
8 Dave Gorman 1.50 3.00
9 John gray 1.00 2.00
10 Del Hall 1.00 2.00
11 Ron Huston 1.00 2.00
12 Murray Keogan 1.00 2.00
13 Gary Kurt 1.00 2.00
14 Garry Lariviere 1.00 2.00
15 Al McLeod 1.00 2.00
16 Peter McNamee 1.00 2.00
17 John Migneault 1.00 2.00
18 Lauri Mononen 1.00 2.00
19 Jim Niekamp 1.00 2.00
20 Jack Norris 1.00 2.00
21 Pekka Rautakallio 2.00 4.00
22 Ron Serafini 1.00 2.00

1976-77 Phoenix Roadrunners WHA

This 18-card set features players of the WHA Phoenix Roadrunners. Each card measures approximately 3 3/8" by 4 5/16". The front features a black and white head shot of the player, enframed by an aqua blue border on white card stock. The top and bottom inner borders are curved, creating space for the basic biographical information as well as the team and league logos that surround the picture. The backs are blank. The cards are unnumbered and we have checklisted them below in alphabetical order.

COMPLETE SET (18) 25.00 50.00
1 Serge Beaudoin 1.00 2.00
2 Michel Cormier 1.00 2.00
3 Robbie Ftorek 7.50 15.00
4 Del Hall 1.00 2.00
5 Clay Hebenton 1.00 2.00
6 Andre Hinse 1.00 2.00
7 Mike Hobin 1.00 2.00
8 Frank Hughes 1.00 2.00
9 Ron Huston 1.00 2.00
10 Gary Kurt 1.00 2.00
11 Garry Lariviere 1.00 2.00
12 Bob Liddington 1.00 2.00
13 Lauri Mononen 1.00 2.00
14 Jim Niekamp 1.00 2.00
15 Pekka Rautakallio 2.00 4.00
16 Seppo Repo 2.00 4.00
17 Jerry Rollins 1.00 2.00
18 Juhani Tamminen 2.00 4.00

1991-92 Pinnacle

The 1991-92 (Score) Pinnacle Hockey set was issued in English and French editions; each set consists of 420 standard-size cards. The front design of the veteran player cards features two color photos, an action photo and a head shot, on a black background with white borders. The card backs have a color action shot silhouetted against a black background. The rookie cards have the same design, except with green background on the front, and black-and-white head shots rather than action shots on the back. The backs of the veteran player cards include biography, player profile, and statistics, while those of the rookie cards only have a player profile. Rookie Cards include Tony Amonte, Valeri Kamensky, John LeClair, Nicklas Lidstrom, Geoff Sanderson and Doug Weight.

COMPLETE SET (420) 10.00 25.00
*FRENCH: SAME VALUE
1 Mario Lemieux .40 1.00
2 Trevor Linden .05 .15
3 Kirk Muller .02 .10
4 Phil Housley .05 .15
5 Mike Modano .30 .75
6 Adam Oates .05 .15
7 Tom Kurvers .02 .10
8 Doug Bodger .02 .10
9 Rod Brind'Amour .12 .30
10 Mats Sundin .12 .30
11 Gary Suter .02 .10
12 Glenn Anderson .05 .15
13 Doug Wilson .05 .15
14 Stephane Richer .05 .15
15 Ray Bourque .20 .50
16 Adam Graves .05 .15
17 Luc Robitaille .05 .15
18 Steve Smith .02 .10
19 Uwe Krupp .02 .10
20 Rick Tocchet .05 .15
21 Tim Cheveldae .05 .15
22 Kay Whitmore .05 .15
23 Kelly Miller .02 .10
24 Esa Tikkanen .02 .10
25 Pat LaFontaine .12 .30
26 James Patrick .02 .10
27 Daniel Marois .02 .10
28 Denis Savard .05 .15
29 Steve Larmer .05 .15
30 Pierre Turgeon .05 .15
31 Gary Leeman .02 .10
32 Mike Ricci .12 .30
33 Troy Murray .02 .10
34 Sergio Momesso .02 .10
35 Marty McSorley .02 .10
36 Paul Ysebaert .02 .10
37 Gary Roberts .05 .15
38 Mike Hudson .02 .10
39 Kelly Hrudey .05 .15
40 Dale Hunter .02 .10
41 Brendan Shanahan .12 .30
42 Steve Duchesne .02 .10
43 Pat Verbeek .02 .10
44 Tom Barrasso .05 .15
45 Scott Mellanby .05 .15
46 Stephen Leach .02 .10
47 Darren Turcotte .02 .10
48 Jari Kurri .12 .30
49 Michel Petit .02 .10
50 Mark Messier .12 .30
51 Terry Carkner .02 .10
52 Tim Kerr .02 .10
53 Jaromir Jagr .25 .60
54 Joe Nieuwendyk .05 .15
55 Randy Burridge .02 .10
56 Robert Reichel .02 .10
57 Craig Janney .05 .15
58 Chris Chelios .12 .30
59 Bryan Fogarty .02 .10
60 Christian Ruuttu .02 .10
61 Steve Bozek .02 .10
62 Dave Manson .02 .10
63 Bruce Driver .02 .10
64 Mike Ramsey .02 .10
65 Bobby Holik .05 .15
66 Bob Essensa .05 .15
67 Pat Flatley .02 .10
68 Wayne Presley .02 .10
69 Mike Bullard .02 .10
70 Claude Lemieux .02 .10
71 Dave Gagner .02 .10
72 Jeff Brown .02 .10
73 Eric Desjardins .05 .15
74 Fredrik Olausson .02 .10
75 Steve Yzerman .40 1.00
76 Tony Granato .02 .10
77 Adam Burt .02 .10
78 Cam Neely .12 .30
79 Brent Sutter .02 .10
80 Dale Hawerchuk .05 .15
81 Scott Stevens .05 .15
82 Adam Creighton .02 .10
83 Brian Hayward .02 .10
84 Dan Quinn .02 .10
85 Garth Butcher .02 .10
86 Shawn Burr .02 .10
87 Peter Bondra .05 .15
88 Brad Shaw .02 .10
89 Eric Weinrich .02 .10
90 Brian Bradley .02 .10
91 Vincent Damphousse .02 .10
92 Doug Gilmour .05 .15
93 Martin Gelinas .02 .10
94 Mike Ridley .02 .10
95 Ron Sutter .02 .10
96 Mark Osborne .02 .10
97 Mikhail Tatarinov .02 .10
98 Bob McGill .02 .10
99 Bob Carpenter .02 .10
100 Wayne Gretzky .60 1.50
101 Slava Fetisov .02 .10
102 Shayne Corson .02 .10
103 Clint Malarchuk .05 .15
104 Randy Wood .02 .10
105 Curtis Joseph .12 .30
106 Cliff Ronning .02 .10
107 Derek King .02 .10
108 Neil Wilkinson .02 .10
109 Michel Goulet .05 .15
110 Zarley Zalapski .02 .10
111 Dave Ellett .02 .10
112 Glen Wesley .02 .10
113 Bob Kudelski .02 .10
114 Jamie Macoun .02 .10
115 John MacLean .05 .15
116 Steve Thomas .05 .15
117 Pat Elynuik .02 .10
118 Ron Hextall .05 .15
119 Jeff Hackett .05 .15
120 Jeremy Roenick .12 .30
121 John Vanbiesbrouck .05 .15
122 Dave Andreychuk .05 .15
123 Ray Ferraro .02 .10
124 Ron Tugnutt .05 .15
125 John Cullen .02 .10
126 Andy Moog .12 .30
127 Ed Belfour .12 .30
128 Dino Ciccarelli .05 .15
129 Brian Bellows .02 .10
130 Guy Carbonneau .05 .15
131 Kevin Hatcher .05 .15
132 Mike Vernon .05 .15
133 Kevin Miller .02 .10
134 Pelle Eklund .02 .10
135 Brian Mullen .02 .10
136 Brian Leetch .12 .30
137 Daren Puppa .05 .15
138 Steven Finn .02 .10
139 Stephan Lebeau .02 .10
140 Gord Murphy .02 .10
141 Rob Brown .02 .10
142 Ken Daneyko .02 .10
143 Larry Murphy .05 .15
144 Jon Casey .05 .15
145 John Ogrodnick .02 .10
146 Benoit Hogue .02 .10
147 Mike McPhee .02 .10
148 Don Beaupre .05 .15
149 Kjell Samuelsson .02 .10
150 Joe Sakic .30 .75
151 Mark Recchi .12 .30
152 Ulf Dahlen .02 .10
153 Dean Evason .02 .10
154 Keith Brown .02 .10
155 Ray Sheppard .02 .10
156 Owen Nolan .12 .30
157 Sergei Fedorov .25 .60
158 Kirk McLean .05 .15
159 Petr Klima .02 .10
160 Brian Skrudland .02 .10
161 Neal Broten .05 .15
162 Dimitri Khristich .02 .10
163 Alexander Mogilny .12 .30
164 Mike Richter .12 .30
165 Daniel Berthiaume .05 .15
166 Teppo Numminen .02 .10
167 Ron Francis .05 .15
168 Grant Fuhr .12 .30
169 Mike Liut .05 .15
170 Bill Ranford .05 .15
171 Garry Galley .02 .10
172 Jeff Norton .02 .10
173 Jimmy Carson .02 .10
174 Peter Zezel .02 .10
175 Patrick Roy .40 1.00
176 Joe Mullen .05 .15
177 Murray Craven .02 .10
178 Tomas Sandstrom .02 .10
179 Joel Otto .02 .10
180 Steve Konroyd .02 .10
181 Vladimir Ruzicka .02 .10
182 Paul Cavallini .02 .10
183 Bob Probert .05 .15
184 Brian Propp .02 .10
185 Glenn Healy .05 .15
186 Paul Coffey .12 .30
187 Jan Erixon .02 .10
188 Kevin Lowe .05 .15
189 Doug Lidster .02 .10
190 Theo Fleury .05 .15
191 Kevin Stevens .02 .10
192 Petr Nedved .05 .15
193 Ed Olczyk .02 .10
194 Mike Hough .02 .10
195 Rod Langway .02 .10
196 Craig Simpson .02 .10
197 Petr Svoboda .02 .10
198 David Volek .02 .10
199 Mark Tinordi .02 .10
200 Brett Hull .20 .50
201 Rob Blake .05 .15
202 Mike Gartner .05 .15
203 Ken Hodge Jr. .02 .10
204 Murray Baron .02 .10
205 Gerard Gallant .02 .10
206 Joe Murphy .02 .10
207 Al Iafrate .05 .15
208 Larry Robinson .05 .15
209 Mathieu Schneider .02 .10
210 Bobby Smith .05 .15
211 Gerald Diduck .02 .10
212 Luke Richardson .02 .10
213 Rob Zettler .02 .10
214 Brad McCrimmon .02 .10
215 Craig MacTavish .02 .10
216 Gino Cavallini .02 .10
217 Craig Wolanin .02 .10
218 Greg Adams .02 .10
219 Mike Craig .02 .10
220 Al MacInnis .05 .15
221 Sylvain Cote .02 .10
222 Bob Sweeney .02 .10
223 Dave Snuggerud .02 .10
224 Randy Ladouceur .02 .10
225 Charlie Huddy .02 .10
226 Sylvain Turgeon .02 .10
227 Phil Bourque .02 .10
228 Rob Ramage .02 .10
229 Jeff Beukeboom .02 .10
230 Alexei Gusarov RC .05 .15
231 Kelly Kisio .02 .10
232 Calle Johansson .02 .10
233 Yves Racine .02 .10
234 Peter Sidorkiewicz .05 .15
235 Jim Johnson .02 .10
236 Brent Gilchrist .02 .10
237 Jyrki Lumme .02 .10
238 Randy Gilhen .02 .10
239 Ken Baumgartner .02 .10
240 Joey Kocur .05 .15
241 Bryan Trottier .12 .30
242 Todd Krygier .02 .10
243 Darrin Shannon .02 .10
244 Dave Christian .02 .10
245 Stephane Morin .02 .10
246 Kevin Dineen .02 .10
247 Chris Terreri .05 .15
248 Craig Ludwig .02 .10
249 Dave Taylor .05 .15
250 Wendel Clark .05 .15
251 David Shaw .02 .10
252 Paul Ranheim .02 .10
253 Mark Hunter .02 .10
254 Russ Courtnall .02 .10
255 Alexei Kasatonov .02 .10
256 Randy Moller .02 .10
257 Bob Errey .02 .10
258 Curtis Leschyshyn .02 .10
259 Rick Zombo .02 .10
260 Dana Murzyn .02 .10
261 Dirk Graham .02 .10
262 Craig Muni .02 .10
263 Geoff Courtnall .05 .15
264 Todd Elik .02 .10
265 Mike Keane .02 .10
266 Peter Stastny .05 .15
267 Ulf Samuelsson .02 .10
268 Rich Sutter .02 .10
269 Mike Krushelnyski .02 .10
270 Dave Babych .02 .10
271 Sergei Makarov .02 .10
272 David Maley .02 .10
273 Normand Rochefort .02 .10
274 Gordie Roberts .02 .10
275 Thomas Steen .02 .10
276 Dave Lowry .02 .10
277 Michal Pivonka .02 .10
278 Todd Gill .02 .10
279 Paul MacDermid .02 .10
280 Brent Ashton .02 .10
281 Randy Hillier .02 .10
282 Frank Musil .02 .10
283 Geoff Smith .02 .10
284 John Tonelli .02 .10
285 Joe Reekie .02 .10
286 Greg Paslawski .02 .10
287 Perry Berezan .02 .10
288 Randy Carlyle .02 .10
289 Chris Nilan .02 .10
290 Patrik Sundstrom .02 .10
291 Garry Valk .02 .10
292 Mike Foligno .02 .10
293 Igor Larionov .02 .10
294 Jim Sandlak .02 .10
295 Tom Chorske .02 .10
296 Claude Loiselle .02 .10
297 Mark Howe .02 .10
298 Steve Chiasson .02 .10
299 Mike Donnelly RC .02 .10
300 Bernie Nicholls .05 .15
301 Tony Amonte RC .40 1.00
302 Brad May .02 .10
303 Josef Beranek RC .02 .10
304 Rob Pearson RC .02 .10
305 Andrei Lomakin .02 .10
306 Kip Miller .02 .10
307 Kevin Haller RC .02 .10
308 Kevin Todd RC .02 .10
309 Geoff Sanderson RC .12 .30
310 Doug Weight RC .40 1.00
311 Vladimir Konstantinov RC .40 1.00
312 Peter Ahola RC .02 .10
313 Claude Lapointe RC .02 .10
314 Nelson Emerson .02 .10
315 Pavel Bure .12 .30
316 Jimmy Waite .05 .15
317 Sergei Nemchinov .02 .10
318 Alexander Godynyuk .02 .10
319 Stu Barnes .02 .10
320 Nicklas Lidstrom RC 1.00 2.50
321 Daryl Sydor .05 .15
322 John LeClair RC .40 1.00
323 Arturs Irbe .12 .30
324 Russ Romaniuk RC .02 .10
325 Ken Sutton RC .02 .10
326 Bob Beers .02 .10
327 Michel Picard RC .02 .10
328 Derian Hatcher .05 .15
329 Pat Falloon .02 .10
330 Donald Audette .05 .15
331 Pat Jablonski RC .05 .15
332 Corey Foster RC .02 .10
333 Tomas Forslund RC .02 .10
334 Steven Rice .02 .10
335 Marc Bureau .02 .10
336 Kimbi Daniels .02 .10
337 Adam Foote RC .12 .50
338 Dan Kordic RC .02 .10
339 Link Gaetz .02 .10
340 Valeri Kamensky RC .05 .15
341 Tom Draper RC .05 .15
342 Jay More RC .02 .10
343 Dominic Roussel RC .02 .10
344 Jim Paek RC .02 .10
345 Felix Potvin .30 .75
346 Dan Lambert RC .02 .10
347 Louie DeBrusk RC .02 .10
348 Jamie Baker RC .02 .10
349 Scott Niedermayer .02 .10
350 Paul Dipietro RC .02 .10
351 Chris Winnes RC .02 .10
352 Mark Greig .02 .10
353 Luciano Borsato RC .02 .10
354 Valeri Zelepukin RC .02 .10
355 Martin Lapointe .05 .15
356 Brett Hull GW .12 .30
357 Steve Larmer GW .05 .15
358 Theo Fleury GW .02 .10
359 Jeremy Roenick GW .12 .30
360 Mark Recchi GW .12 .30
361 Brad Marsh .02 .10
362 Kris King .02 .10
363 Doug Brown .02 .10
364 Carey Wilson .02 .10
365 Eric Lindros .12 .30
366 Kevin Dineen GG .02 .10
367 John Vanbiesbrouck GG .05 .15
368 Ray Bourque GG .12 .30
369 Doug Wilson GG .02 .10
370 Keith Brown GG .02 .10
371 Kevin Lowe GG .05 .15
372 Kelly Miller GG .02 .10
373 Dave Taylor GG .05 .15
374 Guy Carbonneau GG .05 .15
375 Tim Hunter GG .02 .10
376 Brett Hull TECH .12 .30
377 Paul Coffey TECH .12 .30
378 Adam Oates TECH .05 .15
379 Andy Moog TECH .05 .15
380 Mario Lemieux TECH .40 1.00
381 Joe Sakic IDOL .40 1.00
(Wayne Gretzky)
382 Rob Blake IDOL .12 .30
(Larry Robinson)
383 Doug Weight IDOL .40 1.00
(Steve Yzerman)
384 Mike Richter IDOL .12 .30
(Bernie Parent)
385 Luc Robitaille IDOL .05 .15
(Marcel Dionne)
386 Ed Olczyk IDOL .02 .10
(Bobby Clarke)
387 Patrick Roy IDOL .40 1.00
(Rogatien Vachon)
388 Ed Belfour IDOL .12 .30
(Tony Esposito)
389 Mats Sundin IDOL .12 .30
(Mats Naslund)
390 Tony Amonte IDOL .05 .15
(Mark Messier)
391 John Cullen IDOL .02 .10
(Ray Cullen)
392 Gary Suter IDOL .30 .75
(Bobby Orr)
393 Rick Zombo IDOL .02 .10
(Glenn Resch)
394 Todd Krygier IDOL .05 .15
(Gilbert Perreault)
395 John Druce IDOL .02 .10
(Bob Gainey)
396 Bob Carpenter SL .02 .10
397 Clint Malarchuk SL .02 .10
398 Jim Kyte SL .02 .10
399 Al MacInnis SL .05 .15
400 Ed Belfour SL .12 .30
401 Brad Marsh SL .02 .10
402 Brian Benning SL .02 .10
403 Larry Robinson SL .05 .15
404 Craig Ludwig SL .02 .10
405 Pat Flatley SL .02 .10
406 Gary Nylund SL .02 .10
407 Kjell Samuelsson SL .02 .10
408 Dan Quinn SL .02 .10
409 Garth Butcher SL .02 .10
410 Rick Zombo SL .02 .10
411 Paul Cavallini SL .02 .10
412 Link Gaetz SL .02 .10
413 Dave Hannan SL .02 .10
414 Peter Zezel SL .02 .10
415 Randy Gregg SL .02 .10
416 Pat Elynuik SL .02 .10
417 Rod Buskas SL .02 .10
418 Mark Howe SL .02 .10
419 Don Sweeney .02 .10
420 Mark Hardy .02 .10

1991-92 Pinnacle B

This 12-card standard-size set presents the starting lineup from the 1991 All-Star Game. It features six players each from the Wales Conference (B1-B6) and the Campbell Conference (B7-B12). The cards were inserted into Pinnacle French and English foil packs. The French version has a red name plate, while the English version has a blue name plate. The fronts feature black-and-white head shots, with black borders on three sides and a thicker white border at the bottom. The words "Team Pinnacle" appear in the top black border, while the player's name and team affiliation are listed in the bottom white border. The border design on the back is similar and frames a player profile. The cards are numbered on the back with a "B" prefix.

COMPLETE SET (12) 60.00 125.00
*FRENCH: SAME VALUE
B1 Patrick Roy 20.00 50.00
B2 Ray Bourque 6.00 15.00
B3 Brian Leetch 4.00 10.00
B4 Kevin Stevens 1.00 2.50
B5 Mario Lemieux 20.00 50.00
B6 Cam Neely 4.00 10.00
B7 Bill Ranford 3.00 8.00
B8 Al MacInnis 3.00 8.00
B9 Chris Chelios 4.00 10.00
B10 Luc Robitaille 3.00 8.00
B11 Wayne Gretzky 25.00 60.00
B12 Brett Hull 5.00 12.00

1992-93 Pinnacle American Promo Panel

This promo sheet features six standard-size cards and was issued to promote the U.S. edition of Pinnacle hockey cards. The cards feature color action photos with the players extending beyond the picture background. The card face is black and a thin white line forms a frame around the picture. The player's name appears in a gradated bar at the bottom that matches the team colors. The horizontal backs feature the player's name in

a gradated turquoise bar at the top. Close-up player photos are surrounded by biography, statistics, and career highlights on a black background. The backs have white borders. This sheet was intended to remain uncut and the disclaimers "Not For Resale" and "For Promotional Use Only" are printed in the white borders between the rows of cards. The cards are numbered on the back and listed as they appear on the sheet from left to right.

1 Promo Sheet 1.20 3.00
91 Andy Moog
36 Nelson Emerson
61 Denis Savard
6 Owen Nolan
22 Michel Goulet
88 Eric Lindros

1992-93 Pinnacle Canadian Promo Panels

These three promo panels were issued to preview the design of the Canadian version of the 1992-93 Pinnacle hockey series. Measuring approximately 5" by 7", each panel consists of four standard-size cards. The fronts display glossy color action photos framed by black borders. The horizontal backs feature the player's name in a gradated burgundy bar at the top. Close-up photos are surrounded by biography, statistics, and career highlights on a black background. The sheet was intended to remain uncut and the disclaimers "Not For Resale" and "For Promotional Use Only" are printed in the white borders between the rows of cards. The cards on the panels are listed below alphabetically according to player's last name.

COMPLETE SET (3) 2.40 6.00
1 Promo Panel 1.20 3.00
Pavel Bure
Al Iafrate
Mark Recchi
Scott Stevens
2 Promo Panel .80 2.00
Brian Bradley
Kirk Muller
Kevin Stevens
Pierre Turgeon
3 Promo Panel .80 2.00
Doug Gilmour
Alexander Mogilny
Luc Robitaille
Teemu Selanne

1992-93 Pinnacle

The 1992-93 Pinnacle Hockey set was issued in U.S. and Canadian bilingual editions; each set consists of 420 cards. While card numbers 1-220 and 271-390 have different front photography in the U.S. and Canadian versions, the subset cards (221-270) depict the same photos. Rookie Cards in the set include Roman Hamrlik, Andrei Kovalenko, and Martin Straka.

COMPLETE SET (420) 15.00 30.00
*FRENCH: 1X TO 1.25X BASIC CARDS
1 Mark Messier .10 .30
2 Ray Bourque .25 .60
3 Gary Roberts .02 .10
4 Bill Ranford .07 .20
5 Gilbert Dionne .02 .10
6 Owen Nolan .07 .20
7 Pat LaFontaine .10 .30
8 Nicklas Lidstrom .10 .30
9 Pat Falloon .02 .10
10 Jeremy Roenick .15 .40
11 Kevin Hatcher .02 .10
12 Cliff Ronning .02 .10
13 Jeff Brown .02 .10
14 Kevin Dineen .02 .10
15 Brian Leetch .10 .30
16 Eric Desjardins .07 .20
17 Derek King .02 .10
18 Mark Tinordi .02 .10
19 Kelly Hrudey .02 .10
20 Sergei Fedorov .20 .50
21 Mike Ramsey .02 .10
22 Michel Goulet .07 .20
23 Joe Murphy .02 .10
24 Mark Fitzpatrick .07 .20
25 Cam Neely .10 .30
26 Rod Brind'Amour .07 .20
27 Neil Wilkinson .02 .10
28 Greg Adams .02 .10
29 Thomas Steen .02 .10
30 Calle Johansson .02 .10
31 Joe Nieuwendyk .07 .20
32 Rob Blake .07 .20
33 Darren Turcotte .02 .10
34 Derian Hatcher .02 .10
35 Mikhail Tatarinov .02 .10
36 Nelson Emerson .02 .10
37 Tim Cheveldae .07 .20
38 Donald Audette .02 .10
39 Brent Sutter .02 .10
40 Adam Oates .07 .20
41 Luke Richardson .02 .10
42 Jon Casey .07 .20
43 Guy Carbonneau .07 .20
44 Patrick Flatley .02 .10
45 Brian Benning .02 .10
46 Curtis Leschyshyn .02 .10
47 Trevor Linden .07 .20
48 Don Beaupre .07 .20
49 Troy Murray .02 .10
50 Paul Coffey .10 .30
51 Frank Musil .02 .10
52 Doug Wilson .07 .20
53 Pat Elynuik .02 .10
54 Curtis Joseph .10 .30
55 Tony Amonte .07 .20
56 Bob Probert .07 .20
57 Steve Smith .02 .10
58 Dave Andreychuk .07 .20
59 Vladimir Ruzicka .02 .10
60 Jari Kurri .10 .30
61 Denis Savard .07 .20
62 Benoit Hogue .02 .10
63 Terry Carkner .02 .10
64 Valeri Kamensky .02 .10
65 Jyrki Lumme .02 .10
66 Al Iafrate .07 .20
67 Paul Ranheim .02 .10
68 Ulf Dahlen .02 .10
69 Tony Granato .02 .10
70 Phil Housley .07 .20
71 Brian Lawton .02 .10
72 Garth Butcher .02 .10
73 Steve Leach .02 .10
74 Steve Larmer .07 .20
75 Mike Richter .10 .30
76 Vladimir Konstantinov .10 .30
77 Alexander Mogilny .07 .20
78 Craig MacTavish .02 .10
79 Mathieu Schneider .02 .10
80 Mark Recchi .07 .20
81 Gerald Diduck .02 .10
82 Peter Bondra .07 .20
83 Al MacInnis .07 .20
84 Bob Kudelski .02 .10
85 Dave Gagner .07 .20
86 Uwe Krupp .02 .10
87 Randy Carlyle .02 .10
88 Eric Lindros .10 .30
89 Rob Zettler .02 .10
90 Mats Sundin .10 .30
91 Andy Moog .10 .30
92 Keith Brown .02 .10
93 Paul Ysebaert .02 .10
94 Mike Gartner .07 .20
95 Kelly Buchberger .02 .10
96 Dominic Roussel .07 .20
97 Doug Bodger .02 .10
98 Mike Donnelly .02 .10
99 Mike Craig .02 .10
100 Brett Hull .20 .50
101 Robert Reichel .02 .10
102 Jeff Norton .02 .10
103 Garry Galley .02 .10
104 Dale Hunter .07 .20
105 Jeff Hackett .07 .20
106 Darrin Shannon .02 .10
107 Craig Wolanin .02 .10
108 Adam Graves .02 .10
109 Chris Chelios .10 .30
110 Pavel Bure .10 .30
111 Kirk Muller .02 .10
112 Jeff Beukeboom .02 .10
113 Mike Hough .02 .10
114 Brendan Shanahan .10 .30
115 Randy Burridge .02 .10
116 Dave Poulin .02 .10
117 Petr Svoboda .02 .10
118 Ed Belfour .10 .30
119 Ray Sheppard .02 .10
120 Bernie Nicholls .07 .20
121 Glenn Healy .07 .20
122 Johan Garpenlov .02 .10
123 Mike Lalor .02 .10
124 Brad McCrimmon .02 .10
125 Theo Fleury .02 .10
126 Randy Gilhen .02 .10
127 Petr Nedved .07 .20
128 Steve Thomas .07 .20
129 Rick Zombo .02 .10
130 Patrick Roy .60 1.50
131 Rod Langway .02 .10
132 Gord Murphy .02 .10
133 Randy Wood .02 .10
134 Mike Hudson .02 .10
135 Gerard Gallant .02 .10
136 Brian Glynn .02 .10
137 Jim Johnson .02 .10
138 Corey Millen .02 .10
139 Daniel Marois .02 .10
140 James Patrick .02 .10
141 Claude Lapointe .02 .10
142 Bobby Smith .07 .20
143 Charlie Huddy .02 .10
144 Murray Baron .02 .10
145 Ed Olczyk .02 .10
146 Dimitri Khristich .02 .10
147 Doug Lidster .02 .10
148 Perry Berezan .02 .10
149 Pelle Eklund .02 .10
150 Joe Sakic .25 .60
151 Michal Pivonka .02 .10
152 Joey Kocur .07 .20
153 Patrice Brisebois .02 .10
154 Ray Ferraro .02 .10
155 Mike Modano .20 .50
156 Marty McSorley .02 .10
157 Norm Maciver .02 .10
158 Sergei Nemchinov .02 .10
159 David Bruce .02 .10
160 Kelly Miller .02 .10
161 Alexei Gusarov .02 .10
162 Andrei Lomakin .02 .10
163 Sergio Momesso .02 .10
164 Mike Keane .02 .10
165 Pierre Turgeon .07 .20
166 Martin Gelinas .02 .10
167 Chris Dahlquist .02 .10
168 Kris King .02 .10
169 Dean Evason .02 .10
170 Mike Ridley .02 .10
171 Shawn Burr .02 .10
172 Dana Murzyn .02 .10
173 Dirk Graham .02 .10
174 Trent Yawney .02 .10
175 Luc Robitaille .07 .20
176 Randy Moller .02 .10
177 Vincent Riendeau .07 .20
178 Brian Propp .02 .10
179 Don Sweeney .02 .10
180 Stephane Matteau .02 .10
181 Garry Valk .02 .10
182 Sylvain Cote .02 .10
183 Dave Snuggerud .02 .10
184 Gary Leeman .02 .10
185 John Druce .02 .10
186 John Vanbiesbrouck .07 .20
187 Geoff Courtnall .02 .10
188 David Volek .02 .10
189 Doug Weight .10 .30
190 Bob Essensa .07 .20
191 Jan Erixon .02 .10
192 Geoff Smith .02 .10
193 Dave Christian .02 .10
194 Brian Noonan .02 .10
195 Gary Suter .02 .10
196 Craig Janney .07 .20
197 Brad May .02 .10
198 Gaetan Duchesne .02 .10
199 Adam Creighton .02 .10
200 Wayne Gretzky .75 2.00
201 Dave Babych .02 .10
202 Fredrik Olausson .02 .10
203 Bob Bassen .02 .10
204 Todd Krygier .02 .10
205 Grant Ledyard .02 .10
206 Michel Petit .02 .10
207 Todd Elik .02 .10
208 Josef Beranek .02 .10
209 Neal Broten .07 .20
210 Jim Sandlak .02 .10
211 Kevin Haller .02 .10
212 Paul Broten .02 .10
213 Mark Pederson .02 .10
214 John McIntyre .02 .10
215 Teppo Numminen .02 .10
216 Ken Sutton .02 .10
217 Ronnie Stern .02 .10
218 Luciano Borsato .02 .10
219 Claude Loiselle .02 .10
220 Mark Hardy .02 .10
221 Joe Juneau RK .07 .20
222 Keith Tkachuk RK .10 .30
223 Scott Lachance RK .02 .10
224 Glen Murray RK .02 .10
225 Igor Kravchuk RK .02 .10
226 Evgeny Davydov RK .02 .10
227 Ray Whitney RK RC .20 .50
228 Bret Hedican RK RC .07 .20
229 Keith Carney RK RC .40 1.00
230 Slava Kozlov RK .07 .20
231 Drake Berehowsky RK .02 .10
232 Cam Neely SL .07 .20
233 Al Iafrate SL .02 .10
234 Randy Wood SL .02 .10
235 Luke Richardson SL .02 .10
236 Eric Lindros SL .10 .30
237 Dale Hunter SL .02 .10
238 Pat Falloon SL .02 .10
239 Dean Kennedy SL .02 .10
240 Uwe Krupp SL .02 .10
241 Scott Niedermayer IDOL .30 .75
(Steve Yzerman)
242 Gary Roberts IDOL .07 .20
(Lanny McDonald)
243 Peter Ahola IDOL .10 .30
(Jari Kurri)
244 Scott Lachance IDOL .07 .20
(Mark Howe)
245 Rob Pearson IDOL .15 .40
(Mike Bossy)
246 Kirk McLean IDOL .10 .30
(Bernie Parent)
247 Dmitri Mironov IDOL .07 .20
(Viacheslav Fetisov)
248 Brendan Shanahan IDOL .07 .20
(Darryl Sittler)
249 Petr Nedved IDOL .40 1.00
(Wayne Gretzky)
250 Todd Ewen IDOL .02 .10
(Clark Gillies)
251 Luc Robitaille GG .07 .20
252 Mark Tinordi GG .02 .10
253 Kris King GG .02 .10
254 Pat LaFontaine GG .07 .20
255 Ryan Walter GG .02 .10
256 Jeremy Roenick GW .15 .40
257 Brett Hull GW .10 .25
258 Steve Yzerman GW .30 .75
259 Claude Lemieux GW .02 .10
260 Mike Modano GW .12 .30
261 Vincent Damphousse GW .02 .10
262 Tony Granato GW .02 .10
263 Andy Moog MASK 1.50 3.00
264 Curtis Joseph MASK 2.00 4.00
265 Ed Belfour MASK 2.00 4.00
266 Brian Hayward MASK .75 2.00
267 Grant Fuhr MASK 1.50 3.00
268 Don Beaupre MASK .75 2.00
269 Tim Cheveldae MASK .75 2.00
270 Mike Richter MASK 1.50 3.00
271 Zarley Zalapski .02 .10
272 Kevin Todd .02 .10
273 Dave Ellett .02 .10
274 Chris Terreri .07 .20
275 Jaromir Jagr .20 .50
276 Wendel Clark .07 .20
277 Bobby Holik .07 .20
278 Bruce Driver .02 .10
279 Doug Gilmour .07 .20
280 Scott Stevens .07 .20
281 Murray Craven .02 .10
282 Rick Tocchet .07 .20
283 Peter Zezel .02 .10
284 Claude Lemieux .02 .10
285 John Cullen .02 .10
286 Valeri Zelepukin .02 .10
287 Rob Pearson .02 .10
288 Kevin Stevens .02 .10
289 Alexei Kasatonov .02 .10
290 Todd Gill .02 .10
291 Randy Ladouceur .02 .10
292 Larry Murphy .07 .20
293 Tom Chorske .02 .10
294 Jamie Macoun .02 .10
295 Sean Burke .07 .20
296 Ulf Samuelsson .02 .10
297 Eric Weinrich .02 .10
298 Tom Barrasso .07 .20
299 Slava Fetisov .02 .10
300 Mario Lemieux .60 1.50
301 Grant Fuhr .10 .30
302 Zdeno Ciger .02 .10
303 Ron Francis .07 .20
304 Scott Niedermayer .02 .10
305 Mark Osborne .02 .10
306 Kjell Samuelsson .02 .10
307 Geoff Sanderson .07 .20
308 Paul Stanton .02 .10
309 Frank Pietrangelo .07 .20
310 Bob Errey .02 .10
311 Dino Ciccarelli .07 .20
312 Gordie Roberts .02 .10
313 Kevin Miller .02 .10
314 Mike Ricci .07 .20
315 Bob Carpenter .02 .10
316 Dale Hawerchuk .07 .20
317 Christian Ruuttu .02 .10
318 Mike Vernon .07 .20
319 Paul Cavallini .02 .10
320 Steve Duchesne .02 .10
321 Craig Simpson .02 .10
322 Mark Howe .02 .10
323 Shayne Corson .02 .10
324 Tom Kurvers .02 .10
325 Brian Bellows .02 .10
326 Glen Wesley .02 .10
327 Daren Puppa .07 .20
328 Joel Otto .02 .10
329 Jimmy Carson .02 .10
330 Kirk McLean .07 .20
331 Rob Brown .02 .10
332 Yves Racine .02 .10
333 Brian Mullen .02 .10
334 Dave Manson .02 .10
335 Sergei Makarov .02 .10
336 Esa Tikkanen .02 .10
337 Russ Courtnall .02 .10
338 Kevin Lowe .07 .20
339 Steve Chiasson .02 .10
340 Ron Hextall .07 .20
341 Stephen Lebeau .02 .10
342 Mike McPhee .02 .10
343 David Shaw .02 .10
344 Petr Klima .02 .10
345 Tomas Sandstrom .07 .20
346 Scott Mellanby .02 .10
347 Brian Skrudland .02 .10
348 Pat Verbeek .02 .10
349 Vincent Damphousse .02 .10
350 Steve Yzerman .60 1.50
351 John MacLean .07 .20
352 Steve Konroyd .02 .10
353 Phil Bourque .02 .10
354 Ken Daneyko .02 .10
355 Glenn Anderson .07 .20
356 Ken Wregget .07 .20
357 Brent Gilchrist .02 .10
358 Bob Rouse .02 .10
359 Peter Stastny .07 .20
360 Joe Mullen .07 .20
361 Stephane Richer .07 .20
362 Kelly Kisio .02 .10
363 Keith Acton .02 .10
364 Felix Potvin .10 .30
365 Martin Lapointe .07 .20
366 Ron Tugnutt .07 .20
367 Dave Taylor .07 .20
368 Tim Kerr .02 .10
369 Carey Wilson .02 .10
370 Greg Paslawski .02 .10
371 Peter Sidorkiewicz .07 .20
372 Brad Shaw .02 .10
373 Sylvain Turgeon .02 .10
374 Mark Lamb .02 .10
375 Laurie Boschman .02 .10
376 Mark Osiecki .02 .10
377 Doug Smail .02 .10
378 Brad Marsh .02 .10
379 Mike Peluso .02 .10
380 Steve Weeks .07 .20
381 Wendell Young .07 .20
382 Joe Reekie .02 .10
383 Peter Taglianetti .02 .10
384 Mikael Andersson .02 .10
385 Marc Bergevin .02 .10
386 Anatoli Semenov .02 .10
387 Brian Bradley .02 .10
388 Michel Mongeau .02 .10
389 Rob Ramage .02 .10
390 Ken Hodge Jr. .02 .10
391 Richard Matvichuk RC .15 .40
392 Alexei Zhitnik UER .02 .10
(Drafted in fourth round, not third as bio indicates)
393 Dallas Drake RC .02 .10
394 Dimitri Yushkevich RC .07 .20
395 Andrei Kovalenko RC .07 .20
396 Vladimir Vujtek RC .02 .10
397 Nikolai Borschevsky RC .02 .10
398 Vitali Karamnov RC .02 .10
399 Jim Hiller RC .02 .10
400 Michael Nylander RC .07 .20
401 Tommy Sjodin RC .02 .10
402 Martin Straka RC .02 .10
403 Alexei Kovalev .07 .20
404 Vitali Prokhorov RC .02 .10
405 Dmitri Kvartalnov RC .02 .10
406 Teemu Selanne .60 1.50
407 Darius Kasparaitis .02 .10
408 Roman Hamrlik RC .20 .50
409 Vladimir Malakhov .02 .10
410 Sergei Krivokrasov .02 .10
411 Robert Lang RC .02 .10
412 Jozef Stumpel .02 .10
413 Denny Felsner RC .07 .20
414 Rob Zamuner RC .07 .20
415 Jason Woolley RC .02 .10
416 Alexei Zhamnov .07 .20
417 Igor Korolev RC .07 .20
418 Patrick Poulin .02 .10
419 Dmitri Mironov .02 .10
420 Shawn McEachern .02 .10

1992-93 Pinnacle Team 2000

Inserted two per 27-card super pack, these 30 standard-size cards feature players who Pinnacle predicts will be stars in the NHL in the year 2000. The U.S. version features glossy color action photos that are full-bleed on the top and right and edged by black wedged-shaped borders on the left and bottom. In a gold-foil edged circle, the team logo appears in the lower left corner at the intersection of these two stripes. In gold-foil lettering, the words "Team 2000" are printed vertically in the left stripe while the player's name appears in the bottom stripe. The Canadian version offers different player photos and has a maple leaf following the Team 2000 insignia. The horizontal backs have a black panel with bilingual player profile on the left half and a full-bleed color close-up photo on the right.

*FRENCH: 1X TO 1.25X BASIC CARDS
1 Eric Lindros .50 1.25
2 Mike Modano .75 2.00
3 Nicklas Lidstrom .50 1.25
4 Tony Amonte .30 .75
5 Felix Potvin .50 1.25
6 Scott Lachance .15 .40
7 Mats Sundin .50 1.25
8 Pavel Bure .50 1.25
9 Eric Desjardins .30 .75
10 Owen Nolan .30 .75
11 Dominic Roussel .30 .75
12 Scott Niedermayer .15 .40
13 Slava Kozlov .30 .75
14 Patrick Poulin .15 .40
15 Jaromir Jagr .75 2.00
16 Rob Blake .30 .75
17 Pierre Turgeon .30 .75
18 Rod Brind'Amour .30 .75
19 Joe Juneau .30 .75
20 Tim Cheveldae .30 .75
21 Joe Sakic 1.00 2.50
22 Kevin Todd .15 .40
23 Rob Pearson .15 .40
24 Trevor Linden .30 .75
25 Dimitri Khristich .15 .40
26 Pat Falloon .15 .40
27 Jeremy Roenick .60 1.50
28 Alexander Mogilny .30 .75
29 Gilbert Dionne .15 .40
30 Sergei Fedorov .75 2.00

1992-93 Pinnacle Team Pinnacle

Randomly inserted in 1992-93 Pinnacle foil packs, these six double-sided cards feature a top player from the Campbell Conference with his Wales Conference counterpart on the other side. According to Score, the odds of finding a card are not less than 1:125 packs. Painted by Score artist Christopher Greco, the pictures are full-bleed on three sides but edged on the bottom by a gold-foil stripe that features the player's name and position. A black stripe immediately below completes the card face. The words "Team Pinnacle" are printed in turquoise (pink in the Canadian version) vertically near the left edge of both sides of the card, and the conference logo appears below it. The backs of these cards may be distinguished from the fronts by the card number in the lower right corner.

*FRENCH: 1X TO 1.25X BASIC CARDS
1 Mike Richter 2.00 5.00
Ed Belfour
2 Ray Bourque 2.00 5.00
Chris Chelios
3 Brian Leetch 2.00 5.00
Paul Coffey
4 Kevin Stevens 2.00 5.00
Pavel Bure
5 Eric Lindros 8.00 20.00
Wayne Gretzky
6 Jaromir Jagr 5.00 12.00
Brett Hull

1992-93 Pinnacle Eric Lindros

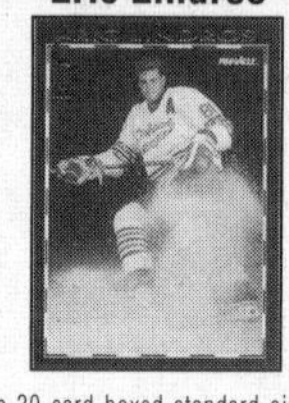

This 30-card boxed standard-size set features posed and action color photos of Eric Lindros as he has progressed from the junior leagues to the NHL. The set begins when Eric Lindros first received attention as a 14-year-old with the St. Michael's Buzzers and ends with his playing for the Philadelphia Flyers. According to Pinnacle, 3,750 numbered cases were produced. The cards have black borders, and his name is printed in gold foil at the top. The backs display a vertical, color photo and Eric's comments about a particular phase of his career.

COMPLETE SET (30) 4.80 12.00
1 St. Michael's Buzzers .30 .75
2 Detroit Compuware .20 .50
3 Oshawa Generals .20 .50
4 Oshawa Generals .20 .50
5 Oshawa Generals .20 .50
6 Oshawa Generals .20 .50
7 Memorial Cup .20 .50
8 World Junior Championship .20 .50
9 World Junior Championship .20 .50
10 World Junior Championship .40 1.00
11 Canada Cup .40 1.00
12 Canada Cup .20 .50
13 Canadian National .40 1.00
14 Canadian National .40 1.00
15 Canadian National .20 .50
16 Canadian National .20 .50
17 First-Round Draft Pick .20 .50
18 Trade To Philadelphia .20 .50
19 Happy Flyer .20 .50
20 Preseason Action .20 .50
21 Preseason Action .20 .50
22 Regular Season Debut .20 .50
23 First NHL Goal .20 .50
24 Winning Home Debut .20 .50
25 First NHL Hat Trick .20 .50
26 Playing Golf .20 .50
27 Backyard Fun .20 .50
28 Fan Favorite .20 .50
29 Welcome To Philly .20 .50
30 Philly Hero .40 1.00
NNO You're A Winner .60 1.50
(Lindros Instant Winner Game)

1993-94 Pinnacle I Samples

These six cards were distributed to dealers and media during the summer of 1993 to show the style of the upcoming Pinnacle hockey cards for the 1993-94 season. The cards can be differentiated from regular issues by the presence of dashes rather than stats in the tables on the reverse.

COMPLETE SET (6) 1.60 4.00
1 Tony Amonte .12 .30
2 Tom Barrasso .04 .10
3 Joe Juneau .10 .25
4 Eric Lindros .80 2.00
5 Teemu Selanne .60 1.50
6 Mats Sundin .20 .50

1993-94 Pinnacle II Samples

This 11-card hobby sample set was enclosed in a cello pack. With the exception of the Mogilny "Nifty 50" card, the top right corners of each card have been cut off, apparently to indicate that these are promo cards. The disclaimer "SAMPLE" is stamped across the photo on the back of the Mogilny, WJC card, and the Lindros redemption card.

COMPLETE SEALED SET (11) 4.00 10.00
275 Brian Leetch .02 .05
280 Guy Carbonneau .02 .05
300 Pat LaFontaine .02 .05
320 Pavel Bure .10 .25
340 Terry Yake .02 .05
341 Brian Benning .02 .05
0 World Jr. Championship .30 .75
NF9 Alexander Mogilny 1.20 3.00
SR1 Alexandre Daigle .20 .50
NNO Ad Card .20 .50

1993-94 Pinnacle

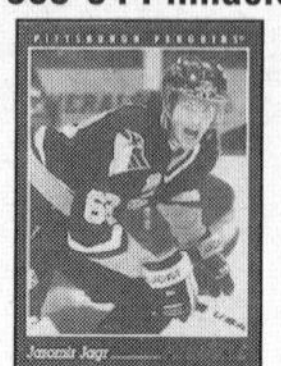

Issued in two series of 236 and 275 cards respectively, the 1993-94 Pinnacle hockey set consists of 511 standard-size cards. On a black background with a thin white border the fronts feature color action player photos. Both series were offered in both a U.S. version as well as a Canadian, bilingual version. Former prospect Brett Lindros is featured on a pair of cards with his talented brother Eric. Inserted at a rate of 1:100 packs, the cards are similar, but feature different photos for the U.S. and Canadian versions; the Canadian card also features bilingual text. A card honoring Wayne Gretzky's 802nd career goal was included in second series jumbo packs. Because of its distribution, the card (No. 512) is not considered part of the set. Rookie Cards include Jason Arnott, Jeff Friesen, Todd Harvey, Chris Osgood, Jamie Storr, Jocelyn Thibault and Oleg Tverdovsky.

COMPLETE SET (511) 15.00 35.00
COMPLETE SERIES 1 (236) 7.50 15.00
COMPLETE SERIES 2 (275) 8.00 20.00
*US AND CDN: SAME VALUE
1 Eric Lindros .10 .30
2 Mats Sundin .10 .30
3 Tom Barrasso .05 .15
4 Teemu Selanne .10 .30
5 Joe Juneau .05 .15
6 Tony Amonte .05 .15
7 Bob Probert .05 .15
8 Chris Kontos .02 .10
9 Geoff Sanderson .05 .15
10 Alexander Mogilny .05 .15
11 Kevin Lowe .02 .10
12 Nikolai Borschevsky .02 .10
13 Dale Hunter .02 .10
14 Gary Suter .02 .10
15 Curtis Joseph .10 .30
16 Mark Tinordi .02 .10
17 Doug Weight .05 .15
18 Benoit Hogue .02 .10
19 Tommy Soderstrom .05 .15
20 Pat Falloon .02 .10
21 Jyrki Lumme .02 .10
22 Brian Bellows .02 .10
23 Alexei Zhitnik .02 .10
24 Dirk Graham .02 .10
25 Scott Stevens .05 .15
26 Adam Foote .02 .10
27 Mike Gartner .05 .15
28 Dallas Drake RC .02 .10
29 Ulf Samuelsson .02 .10
30 Cam Neely .10 .30
31 Sean Burke .05 .15
32 Petr Svoboda .02 .10
33 Keith Tkachuk .10 .30
34 Roman Hamrlik .05 .15
35 Robert Reichel .02 .10
36 Igor Kravchuk .02 .10
37 Mathieu Schneider .02 .10
38 Bob Kudelski .02 .10
39 Jeff Brown .02 .10
40 Mike Modano .20 .50
41 Rob Gaudreau RC .02 .10
42 Dave Andreychuk .05 .15
43 Trevor Linden .05 .15
44 Dimitri Khristich .02 .10
45 Joe Murphy .02 .10
46 Rob Blake .05 .15
47 Alexander Semak .02 .10
48 Ray Ferraro .02 .10
49 Curtis Leschyshyn .02 .10
50 Mark Recchi .05 .15
51 Sergei Nemchinov .02 .10
52 Larry Murphy .05 .15
53 Steve Heinze .02 .10
54 Sergei Fedorov .20 .50
55 Gary Roberts .02 .10
56 Alexei Zhamnov .05 .15
57 Derian Hatcher .02 .10
58 Kelly Buchberger .02 .10
59 Eric Desjardins .05 .15
60 Brian Bradley .02 .10
61 Patrick Poulin .02 .10
62 Scott Lachance .02 .10
63 Johan Garpenlov .02 .10
64 Sylvain Turgeon .02 .10
65 Grant Fuhr .05 .15
66 Garth Butcher .02 .10
67 Michal Pivonka .02 .10
68 Todd Gill .02 .10
69 Cliff Ronning .02 .10
70 Steve Smith .02 .10
71 Bobby Holik .02 .10
72 Garry Galley .02 .10
73 Steve Leach .02 .10
74 Ron Francis .05 .15
75 Jari Kurri .10 .30
76 Alexei Kovalev .05 .15
77 Dave Gagner .05 .15
78 Steve Duchesne .02 .10
79 Theo Fleury .02 .10

80 Paul Coffey .10 .30
81 Bill Ranford .05 .15
82 Doug Bodger .02 .10
83 Nick Kypreos .02 .10
84 Darius Kasparaitis .02 .10
85 Vincent Damphousse .02 .10
86 Arturs Irbe .05 .15
87 Shawn Chambers .02 .10
88 Murray Craven .02 .10
89 Rob Pearson .02 .10
90 Kevin Hatcher .02 .10
91 Brent Sutter .02 .10
92 Teppo Numminen .02 .10
93 Shawn Burr .02 .10
94 Valeri Zelepukin .02 .10
95 Ron Sutter .02 .10
96 Craig MacTavish .02 .10
97 Dominic Roussel .05 .15
98 Nicklas Lidstrom .10 .30
99 Adam Graves .02 .10
100 Doug Gilmour .05 .15
101 Frank Musil .02 .10
102 Ted Donato .02 .10
103 Andrew Cassels .02 .10
104 Vladimir Malakhov .02 .10
105 Shawn McEachern .02 .10
106 Petr Nedved .05 .15
107 Calle Johansson .02 .10
108 Rich Sutter .02 .10
109 Evgeny Davydov .02 .10
110 Mike Ricci .02 .10
111 Scott Niedermayer .02 .10
112 John LeClair .10 .30
113 Darryl Sydor .02 .10
114 Paul DiPietro .02 .10
115 Stephane Fiset .05 .15
116 Christian Ruuttu .02 .10
117 Doug Zmolek .02 .10
118 Bob Sweeney .02 .10
119 Brent Fedyk .02 .10
120 Norm Maciver .02 .10
121 Rob Zamuner .02 .10
122 Brian Mullen .02 .10
123 Trent Yawney .02 .10
124 David Shaw .02 .10
125 Mark Messier .10 .30
126 Kevin Miller .02 .10
127 Dino Ciccarelli .05 .15
128 Derek King .02 .10
129 Scott Young .02 .10
130 Craig Janney .05 .15
131 Jamie Macoun .02 .10
132 Geoff Courtnall .02 .10
133 Bob Essensa .05 .15
134 Ken Daneyko .02 .10
135 Mike Ridley .02 .10
136 Stephan Lebeau .02 .10
137 Tony Granato .02 .10
138 Kay Whitmore .05 .15
139 Luke Richardson .02 .10
140 Jeremy Roenick .15 .40
141 Brad May .05 .15
142 Sandis Ozolinsh .02 .10
143 Stephane Richer .05 .15
144 John Tucker .02 .10
145 Luc Robitaille .05 .15
146 Dimitri Yushkevich .02 .10
147 Sean Hill .02 .10
148 John Vanbiesbrouck .05 .15
149 Kevin Stevens .02 .10
150 Patrick Roy .60 1.50
151 Owen Nolan .05 .15
152 Richard Smehlik .02 .10
153 Ray Sheppard .05 .15
154 Ed Olczyk .02 .10
155 Al MacInnis .05 .15
156 Sergei Zubov .02 .10
157 Wendel Clark .05 .15
158 Kirk McLean .05 .15
159 Thomas Steen .02 .10
160 Pierre Turgeon .05 .15
161 Dmitri Kvartalnov .02 .10
162 Brian Noonan .02 .10
163 Mike McPhee .02 .10
164 Peter Bondra .05 .15
165 Bernie Nicholls .02 .10
166 Michael Nylander .02 .10
167 Guy Hebert .05 .15
168 Scott Mellanby .05 .15
169 Bob Bassen .02 .10
170 Rod Brind'Amour .05 .15
171 Andrei Kovalenko .02 .10
172 Mike Donnelly .02 .10
173 Steve Thomas .02 .10
174 Rick Tocchet .05 .15
175 Steve Yzerman .60 1.50
176 Dixon Ward .02 .10
177 Randy Wood .02 .10
178 Dean Kennedy .02 .10
179 Joel Otto .02 .10
180 Kirk Muller .02 .10
181 Chris Chelios .10 .30
182 Richard Matvichuk .02 .10
183 John MacLean .05 .15
184 Joe Kocur .02 .10
185 Adam Oates .05 .15
186 Bob Beers .02 .10
187 Ron Tugnutt .05 .15
188 Brian Skrudland .02 .10
189 Al Iafrate .02 .10
190 Felix Potvin .10 .30
191 David Reid .02 .10
192 Jim Johnson .02 .10
193 Kevin Haller .02 .10
194 Steve Chiasson .02 .10
195 Jaromir Jagr .20 .50
196 Martin Rucinsky .02 .10
197 Sergei Bautin .02 .10
198 Joe Nieuwendyk .05 .15
199 Gilbert Dionne .02 .10
200 Brett Hull .15 .40
201 Yuri Khmylev .02 .10
202 Todd Elik .02 .10
203 Patrick Flatley .02 .10
204 Martin Straka .02 .10
205 Brendan Shanahan .10 .30
206 Mark Beaufait RC .02 .10
207 Mike Lenarduzzi RC .02 .10
208 Chris LiPuma .02 .10
209 Andre Faust .02 .10
210 Ben Hankinson RC .02 .10
211 Darrin Madeley RC .02 .10
212 Oleg Petrov .02 .10
213 Philippe Boucher .02 .10
214 Tyler Wright .02 .10
215 Jason Bowen RC .02 .10
216 Matthew Barnaby .05 .15
217 Bryan Smolinski .02 .10
218 Dan Keczmer .02 .10
219 Chris Simon RC .30 .75
220 Corey Hirsch AW .05 .15
221 Mario Lemieux AW .10 .30
222 Teemu Selanne AW .10 .30
223 Chris Chelios AW .05 .15
224 Ed Belfour AW .05 .15
225 Pierre Turgeon AW .05 .15
226 Doug Gilmour AW .05 .15
227 Ed Belfour AW .10 .30
228 Patrick Roy AW .10 .30
229 Dave Poulin AW .02 .10
230 Mario Lemieux AW .10 .30
231 Mike Vernon HH .05 .15
232 Vincent Damphousse HH .02 .10
233 Chris Chelios HH .05 .15
234 Cliff Ronning HH .02 .10
235 Mark Howe HH .02 .10
236 Alexandre Daigle .02 .10
237 Wayne Gretzky .10 .30
238 Mark Messier .10 .30
239 Dino Ciccarelli .05 .15
240 Joe Mullen .05 .15
241 Mike Gartner .05 .15
242 Mike Richter .10 .30
243 Pat Verbeek .02 .10
244 Valeri Kamensky .05 .15
245 Nelson Emerson .02 .10
246 James Patrick .02 .10
247 Greg Adams .02 .10
248 Ulf Dahlen .02 .10
249 Shayne Corson .02 .10
250 Ray Bourque .20 .50
251 Claude Lemieux .02 .10
252 Kelly Hrudey .05 .15
253 Patrice Brisebois .02 .10
254 Mark Howe .02 .10
255 Ed Belfour .10 .30
256 Pelle Eklund .02 .10
257 Zarley Zalapski .02 .10
258 Sylvain Cote .02 .10
259 Uwe Krupp .02 .10
260 Dale Hawerchuk .05 .15
261 Alexei Gusarov .02 .10
262 Dave Ellett .02 .10
263 Tomas Sandstrom .02 .10
264 Vladimir Konstantinov .05 .15
265 Paul Ranheim .02 .10
266 Darrin Shannon .02 .10
267 Chris Terreri .05 .15
268 Russ Courtnall .02 .10
269 Don Sweeney .02 .10
270 Kevin Todd .02 .10
271 Brad Shaw .02 .10
272 Adam Creighton .02 .10
273 Dana Murzyn .02 .10
274 Donald Audette .02 .10
275 Brian Leetch .10 .30
276 Kevin Dineen .02 .10
277 Bruce Driver .02 .10
278 Jim Paek .02 .10
279 Esa Tikkanen .02 .10
280 Guy Carbonneau .02 .10
281 Eric Weinrich .02 .10
282 Tim Cheveldae .05 .15
283 Bryan Marchment .02 .10
284 Kelly Miller .02 .10
285 Jimmy Carson .02 .10
286 Terry Carkner .02 .10
287 Mike Sullivan .02 .10
288 Joe Reekie .02 .10
289 Bob Rouse .02 .10
290 Joe Sakic .25 .60
291 Gerald Diduck .02 .10
292 Don Beaupre .05 .15
293 Kjell Samuelsson .02 .10
294 Claude Lapointe .02 .10
295 Tie Domi .05 .15
296 Charlie Huddy .02 .10
297 Peter Zezel .02 .10
298 Craig Muni .02 .10
299 Rick Tabaracci .05 .15
300 Pat LaFontaine .10 .30
301 Lyle Odelein .02 .10
302 Jocelyn Lemieux .02 .10
303 Craig Ludwig .02 .10
304 Marc Bergevin .02 .10
305 Bill Guerin .02 .10
306 Rick Zombo .02 .10
307 Steven Finn .02 .10
308 Gino Odjick .02 .10
309 Jeff Beukeboom .02 .10
310 Mario Lemieux .60 1.50
311 J.J. Daigneault .02 .10
312 Vincent Riendeau .05 .15
313 Adam Burt .02 .10
314 Mike Craig .02 .10
315 Bret Hedican .02 .10
316 Kris King .02 .10
317 Sylvain Lefebvre .02 .10
318 Troy Murray .02 .10
319 Gordie Roberts .02 .10
320 Pavel Bure .10 .30
321 Marc Bureau .02 .10
322 Randy McKay .02 .10
323 Mark Lamb .02 .10
324 Brian Mullen .02 .10
325 Ken Wregget .05 .15
326 Stephane Quintal .02 .10
327 Robert Dirk .02 .10
328 Mike Krushelnyski .02 .10
329 Mikael Andersson .02 .10
330 Paul Stanton .02 .10
331 Phil Bourque .02 .10
332 Andre Racicot .05 .15
333 Brad Dalgarno .02 .10
334 Neal Broten .05 .15
335 John Blue .05 .15
336 Ken Sutton .02 .10
337 Greg Paslawski .02 .10
338 Robb Stauber .05 .15
339 Mike Keane .02 .10
340 Terry Yake .02 .10
341 Brian Benning .02 .10
342 Brian Propp .02 .10
343 Frank Pietrangelo .05 .15
344 Stephane Matteau .02 .10
345 Steven King .02 .10
346 Joe Cirella .02 .10
347 Andy Moog .05 .15
348 Paul Ysebaert .02 .10
349 Petr Klima .02 .10
350 Corey Millen .02 .10
351 Phil Housley .05 .15
352 Craig Billington .05 .15
353 Jeff Norton .02 .10
354 Neil Wilkinson .02 .10
355 Doug Lidster .02 .10
356 Steve Larmer .05 .15
357 Jon Casey .05 .15
358 Brad McCrimmon .02 .10
359 Alexei Kasatonov .02 .10
360 Andrei Lomakin .02 .10
361 Daren Puppa .05 .15
362 Sergei Makarov .05 .15
363 Dave Manson .02 .10
364 Jim Sandlak .02 .10
365 Glenn Healy .05 .15
366 Martin Gelinas .02 .10
367 Igor Larionov .02 .10
368 Anatoli Semenov .02 .10
369 Mark Fitzpatrick .05 .15
370 Paul Cavallini .02 .10
371 Jimmy Waite .05 .15
372 Yves Racine .02 .10
373 Jeff Hackett .05 .15
374 Marty McSorley .02 .10
375 Scott Pearson .02 .10
376 Ron Hextall .05 .15
377 Gaetan Duchesne .02 .10
378 Jamie Baker .02 .10
379 Troy Loney .02 .10
380 Gord Murphy .02 .10
381 Peter Sidorkiewicz .05 .15
382 Pat Elynuik .02 .10
383 Glen Wesley .02 .10
384 Dean Evason .02 .10
385 Mike Peluso .02 .10
386 Darren Turcotte .02 .10
387 Dave Poulin .02 .10
388 John Cullen .02 .10
389 Randy Ladouceur .02 .10
390 Tom Fitzgerald .02 .10
391 Denis Savard .05 .15
392 Fredrik Olausson .02 .10
393 Sergio Momesso .02 .10
394 Mike Ramsey .02 .10
395 Kelly Kisio .02 .10
396 Craig Simpson .02 .10
397 Slava Fetisov .02 .10
398 Glenn Anderson .05 .15
399 Michel Goulet .05 .15
400 Wayne Gretzky .75 2.00
401 Stu Grimson .02 .10
402 Mike Hough .02 .10
403 Dominik Hasek .40 1.00
404 Gerard Gallant .02 .10
405 Greg Gilbert .02 .10
406 Vladimir Ruzicka .02 .10
407 Jim Hrivnak .05 .15
408 Dave Lowry .02 .10
409 Todd Ewen .02 .10
410 Bob Errey .02 .10
411 Bryan Trottier .05 .15
412 Dave Taylor .05 .15
413 Grant Ledyard .02 .10
414 Chris Dahlquist .02 .10
415 Brent Gilchrist .02 .10
416 Geoff Smith .02 .10
417 Jiri Slegr .02 .10
418 Randy Burridge .02 .10
419 Sergei Krivokrasov .02 .10
420 Keith Primeau .02 .10
421 Robert Kron .02 .10
422 Keith Brown .02 .10
423 David Volek .02 .10
424 Josef Beranek .02 .10
425 Wayne Presley .02 .10
426 Stu Barnes .02 .10
427 Milos Holan RC .02 .10
428 Jeff Shantz .02 .10
429 Brent Gretzky RC .02 .10
430 Jarkko Varvio .02 .10
431 Chris Osgood RC .60 1.50
432 Aaron Ward RC .02 .10
433 Jason Smith RC .02 .10
434 Cam Stewart RC .02 .10
435 Derek Plante RC .02 .10
436 Pat Peake .02 .10
437 Alexander Karpovtsev .02 .10
438 Jim Montgomery RC .02 .10
439 Rob Niedermayer .05 .15
440 Jocelyn Thibault RC .40 1.00
441 Jason Arnott RC .60 1.50
442 Mike Rathje .02 .10
443 Chris Gratton .05 .15
444 Vesa Vitakoski RC .02 .10
445 Alexei Kudashov RC .02 .10
446 Pavol Demitra .05 .15
447 Ted Drury .02 .10
448 Rene Corbet RC .02 .10
449 Markus Naslund .10 .30
450 Dmitri Filimonov .02 .10
451 Roman Oksiuta RC .02 .10
452 Michal Sykora RC .02 .10
453 Greg Johnson .02 .10
454 Mikael Renberg .10 .30
455 Alexei Yashin .10 .30
456 Chris Pronger .15 .40
457 Manny Fernandez RC .40 1.00
458 Jamie Storr RC .25 .60
459 Chris Armstrong RC .02 .10
460 Drew Bannister RC .02 .10
461 Joel Bouchard RC .02 .10
462 Bryan McCabe RC .10 .30
463 Nick Stajduhar RC .02 .10
464 Brent Tully .02 .10
465 Brendan Witt RC .02 .10
466 Jason Allison RC .60 1.50
467 Jason Botterill RC .02 .10
468 Curtis Bowen RC .02 .10
469 Anson Carter RC .30 .75
470 Brandon Convery RC .02 .10
471 Yanick Dube RC .02 .10
472 Jeff Friesen RC .60 1.50
473 Aaron Gavey RC .02 .10
474 Martin Gendron RC .02 .10
475 Rick Girard RC .02 .10
476 Todd Harvey RC .02 .10
477 Marty Murray RC .02 .10
478 Mike Peca RC .40 1.00
479 Aaron Ellis RC .02 .10
480 Toby Kvalevog RC .02 .10
481 Jon Coleman RC .02 .10
482 Ashlin Halfnight RC .02 .10
483 Jason McBain RC .02 .10
484 Chris O'Sullivan RC .02 .10
485 Deron Quint RC .10 .30
486 Blake Sloan RC .05 .15
487 David Wilkie RC .02 .10
488 Kevyn Adams RC .02 .10
489 Jason Bonsignore RC .02 .10
490 Andy Brink RC .02 .10
491 Adam Deadmarsh .02 .10
492 John Emmons .02 .10
493 Kevin Hilton RC .02 .10
494 Jason Karmanos RC .02 .10
495 Bob Lachance RC .02 .10
496 Jamie Langenbrunner RC .40 1.00
497 Jay Pandolfo RC .02 .10
498 Richard Park RC .02 .10
499 Ryan Sittler .02 .10
500 John Varga RC .02 .10
501 Valeri Bure RC .40 1.00
502 Maxim Bets RC .02 .10
503 Vadim Sharifjanov .05 .15
504 Alexander Kharlamov RC .02 .10
505 Pavel Desyatkov RC .02 .10
506 Oleg Tverdovsky RC .25 .60
507 Nikolai Tsulygin .02 .10
508 Evgeni Ryabchikov RC .02 .10
509 Sergei Brylin RC .02 .10
510 Maxim Sushinski RC .05 .15
511 Sergei Kondrashkin RC .02 .10
512 Wayne Gretzky HL SP 3.00 8.00
AU1 Alexandre Daigle 6.00 15.00
Autographed card
AU2 Eric Lindros 15.00 40.00
Autographed card
NNO Eric Lindros .10 .30
Brett Lindros
Canadian version
NNO Eric Lindros .10 .30
Brett Lindros
U.S. version
NNO Eric Lindros .10 .30
Expired Redemption

1993-94 Pinnacle All-Stars

One bonus Pinnacle All-Star card was inserted in every U.S. and Canadian pack of '93-94 Score series 1 hockey cards. The wrappers from those packs carried a mail-away offer for cards 46-50. These cards feature on their fronts color action shots of players in their All-Star uniforms. The photos of Canadian and U.S. cards differ, but there is no way of discerning the two.

COMPLETE INSERT SET (45) 5.00 10.00
1 Craig Billington .10 .25
2 Zarley Zalapski .05 .15
3 Kevin Lowe .05 .15
4 Scott Stevens .10 .25
5 Pierre Turgeon .10 .25
6 Mark Recchi .10 .25
7 Kirk Muller .05 .15
8 Mike Gartner .10 .25
9 Adam Oates .10 .25
10 Brad Marsh .05 .15
11 Pat LaFontaine .10 .25
12 Peter Bondra .10 .25
13 Joe Sakic .20 .50
14 Rick Tocchet .10 .25
15 Kevin Stevens .10 .25
16 Steve Duchesne .05 .15
17 Peter Sidorkiewicz .05 .15
18 Patrick Roy .50 1.25
19 Al Iafrate .05 .15
20 Jaromir Jagr .15 .40
21 Ray Bourque .10 .25
22 Alexander Mogilny .10 .25
23 Steve Chiasson .05 .15
24 Garth Butcher .05 .15
25 Phil Housley .05 .15
26 Chris Chelios .10 .25
27 Randy Carlyle .05 .15
28 Mike Modano .15 .40
29 Gary Roberts .05 .15
30 Kelly Kisio .05 .15
31 Pavel Bure .10 .25
32 Teemu Selanne .10 .25
33 Brian Bradley .05 .15
34 Brett Hull .10 .30
35 Jari Kurri .10 .25
36 Steve Yzerman .50 1.25
37 Luc Robitaille .10 .25
38 Dave Manson .05 .15
39 Jeremy Roenick .12 .30
40 Mike Vernon .10 .25
41 Jon Casey .10 .25
42 Ed Belfour .10 .25
43 Paul Coffey .10 .25
44 Doug Gilmour .10 .25
45 Wayne Gretzky .60 1.50
46 Mike Gartner 1.50 4.00
47 Al Iafrate 1.50 4.00
48 Ray Bourque 6.00 15.00
49 Jon Casey 1.50 4.00
50 Campbell Conf. 2.00 5.00

1993-94 Pinnacle Captains

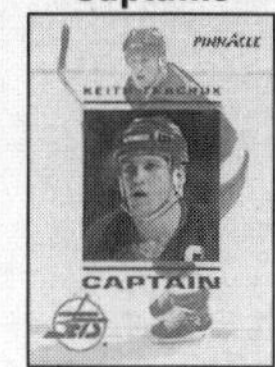

Randomly inserted in second-series jumbo packs at a rate of 1:4, these 27 standard-size cards feature on their fronts two photos of each NHL team captain. The photos of the Canadian and U.S. versions differ. The large borderless photo is a ghosted colour action shot; the smaller image in the center overlays the larger and is a full-contrast color head shot. The player's name in gold-foil lettering appears above the smaller photo. The grayish back carries a color action cutout on the left and a player profile in English (bilingual for the Canadian version) on the right. The cards are numbered on the back with a "CA" prefix.

COMPLETE SET (27) 40.00 100.00
*U.S. AND CDN: SAME VALUE
1 Troy Loney .75 2.00
2 Ray Bourque 3.00 8.00
3 Pat LaFontaine 1.25 3.00
4 Joe Nieuwendyk 1.25 3.00
5 Dirk Graham .75 2.00
6 Mark Tinordi .75 2.00
7 Steve Yzerman 8.00 20.00
8 Craig MacTavish .75 2.00
9 Brian Skrudland .75 2.00
10 Pat Verbeek .75 2.00
11 Wayne Gretzky 12.00 30.00
12 Guy Carbonneau .75 2.00
13 Scott Stevens .75 2.00
14 Pat Flatley .75 2.00
15 Mark Messier 2.50 6.00
16 Mark Lamb .75 2.00
Brad Shaw
17 Kevin Dineen .75 2.00
18 Mario Lemieux 10.00 25.00
19 Joe Sakic 5.00 12.00
20 Brett Hull 2.50 6.00
21 Bob Errey .75 2.00
22 Marc Bergevin .75 2.00
Denis Savard
John Tucker
23 Wendel Clark 1.25 3.00
24 Trevor Linden 1.25 3.00
25 Kevin Hatcher .75 2.00
26 Keith Tkachuk 1.25 3.00
27 Checklist 4.00 10.00

1993-94 Pinnacle Expansion

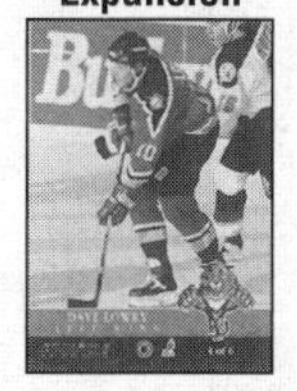

Inserted one per series 1 hobby box, this six-card set measures the standard size. One side features a color action shot of a player from the Anaheim Mighty Ducks; the other, his counterpart at that position from the Florida Panthers. Each player's name and position, along with his team's logo, appear in a team color-coded bar below the photo. The cards are numbered on both sides as "X of 6."

COMPLETE SET (6) 5.00 10.00
1 John Vanbiesbrouck 1.25 3.00
Guy Hebert
2 Gord Murphy .75 2.00
Randy Ladouceur
3 Joe Cirella .75 2.00
Sean Hill
4 Dave Lowry .75 2.00
Troy Loney
5 Brian Skrudland .75 2.00
Terry Yake
6 Scott Mellanby .75 2.00
Steven King

1993-94 Pinnacle Masks

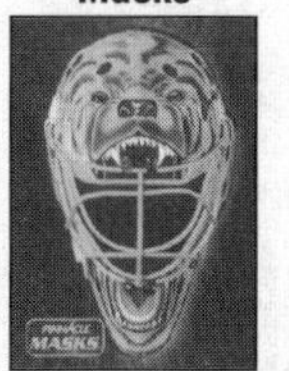

Randomly inserted in first-series packs at a rate of 1:24 packs, this 10-card standard-size set showcases some of the elaborate masks NHL goalies wear. The cards are numbered on the back as "X of 10."

COMPLETE SET (10) 40.00 80.00
1 Grant Fuhr 4.00 10.00
2 Mike Vernon 4.00 10.00
3 Robb Stauber 4.00 10.00
4 Dominic Roussel 4.00 10.00
5 Pat Jablonski 4.00 10.00
6 Stephane Fiset 4.00 10.00
7 Wendell Young 4.00 10.00
8 Ron Hextall 4.00 10.00
9 John Vanbiesbrouck 4.00 10.00
10 Peter Sidorkiewicz 4.00 10.00

1993-94 Pinnacle Nifty Fifty

Randomly inserted in second-series foil packs at a rate of 1:36 and featuring Pinnacle's Dufex process, this 15-card standard-size set spotlights players who scored 50 or more goals. The borderless fronts feature metallic color head shots with a gold-foil Nifty Fifty logo at the lower left. The cards are numbered on the back as "X of 15."

1 Introductory CL Card 2.50 6.00
2 Alexander Mogilny .50 1.25
3 Teemu Selanne 1.00 2.50
4 Mario Lemieux 5.00 12.00
5 Luc Robitaille .50 1.25
6 Pavel Bure 1.00 2.50
7 Pierre Turgeon .50 1.25
8 Steve Yzerman 5.00 12.00
9 Kevin Stevens .30 .75
10 Brett Hull 1.25 3.00
11 Dave Andreychuk .50 1.25
12 Pat LaFontaine 1.00 2.50
13 Mark Recchi .50 1.25
14 Brendan Shanahan 1.00 2.50
15 Jeremy Roenick 1.25 3.00

1993-94 Pinnacle Super Rookies

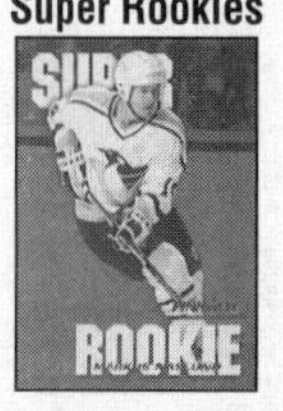

Randomly inserted in second-series hobby foil packs at a rate of 1:36, this nine-card standard-size set spotlights players who were rookies in 1993-94. The fronts feature color action player shots on darkened backgrounds. The player's name in gold-foil lettering appears at the lower right. On a dark red background, the horizontal backs carry a color player cutout on the left, with career highlights to the right. The set was issued in Canadian and U.S. versions. Each version carries its own front photos and the backs of the Canadian cards are bilingual. The cards are numbered on the back with an "SR" prefix.

COMPLETE SET (9) 2.00 5.00
*U.S. AND CDN: SAME VALUE
1 Alexandre Daigle .20 .50
2 Chris Pronger .60 1.50
3 Chris Gratton .20 .50
4 Rob Niedermayer .20 .50
5 Alexei Yashin .20 .50
6 Mikael Renberg .20 .50
7 Jason Arnott .60 1.50
8 Markus Naslund .40 1.00
9 Pat Peake .20 .50

1993-94 Pinnacle Team Pinnacle

Randomly inserted in packs at a rate of 1:90, this 12-card set measures the standard size. On the U.S. version, one side features a black-bordered color drawing of a player from the Eastern Conference, the other, one of a player from the Western Conference. The Canadian version carries color photos instead of color drawings. The cards are numbered on both sides as "X of 12."

*CANADIAN: .5X TO 1.25X BASIC CARDS
1 Patrick Roy 8.00 20.00
Ed Belfour
2 Brian Leetch 8.00 20.00
Chris Chelios
3 Scott Stevens 4.00 10.00
Al MacInnis
4 Kevin Stevens 4.00 10.00
Luc Robitaille
5 Mario Lemieux 10.00 25.00
Wayne Gretzky
6 Jaromir Jagr 5.00 12.00
Brett Hull
7 Tom Barrasso 4.00 10.00
Kirk McLean
8 Ray Bourque 4.00 10.00
Paul Coffey
9 Al Iafrate 4.00 10.00
Phil Housley
10 Vincent Damphousse 4.00 10.00
Pavel Bure
11 Eric Lindros 4.00 10.00
Jeremy Roenick
12 Alexander Mogilny 4.00 10.00
Teemu Selanne

1993-94 Pinnacle Team 2001

Inserted one per first-series jumbo pack, this 30-card set measures the standard size. The fronts feature color action player photos. The words "Team 2001" are printed in gold foil inside a black bar on the left, while the player's name in gold foil appears in a black bar on the bottom, along with the team logo. The horizontal backs carry a color head shot on the right. On a black background to the left of the photo are the player's name in gold foil and career highlights. The Canadian version carries color player drawings instead of photos. The cards are numbered on the back as "X of 30."

COMPLETE SET (30) 12.00 30.00
*CANADIAN: 5X TO 12X U.S. VERSION
CDN VERSION: .75X TO 1.5X HI COLUMN
1 Eric Lindros .75 2.00
2 Alexander Mogilny .40 1.00
3 Pavel Bure .75 2.00
4 Joe Juneau .40 1.00
5 Felix Potvin .75 2.00
6 Nicklas Lidstrom .75 2.00
7 Alexei Kovalev .40 1.00
8 Patrick Poulin .20 .50
9 Shawn McEachern .20 .50
10 Teemu Selanne .75 2.00
11 Rod Brind'Amour .40 1.00
12 Jaromir Jagr 1.50 4.00
13 Pierre Turgeon .40 1.00
14 Scott Niedermayer .20 .50
15 Mats Sundin .75 2.00
16 Trevor Linden .40 1.00
17 Mike Modano 1.25 3.00
18 Roman Hamrlik .20 .50
19 Tony Amonte .40 1.00
20 Jeremy Roenick 1.25 3.00
21 Scott Lachance .20 .50
22 Mike Ricci .20 .50
23 Dimitri Khristich .20 .50
24 Sergei Fedorov 1.25 3.00
25 Joe Sakic 2.00 5.00
26 Pat Falloon .20 .50
27 Mathieu Schneider .20 .50
28 Owen Nolan .40 1.00
29 Brendan Shanahan .75 2.00
30 Mark Recchi .40 1.00

1993-94 Pinnacle Daigle Entry Draft

To commemorate Daigle's signing with Score as a spokesperson, Score issued this standard-size card and distributed it to the news media and others who attended the 1993 NHL Draft in Quebec on June 26. The card was also distributed to media at the 1993 National Sports Collectors Convention in Chicago. The front features a color close-up photo with white borders. Daigle is pictured wearing a jersey with "Score" emblazoned across it. The back has a full-bleed action shot with Daigle wearing a "Pinnacle" jersey. A black stripe at the bottom carries the player's name and the anti-counterfeiting device. The card is unnumbered.

1 Alexandre Daigle 4.00 10.00

1994-95 Pinnacle I Hobby Samples

These standard-size cards were issued in a sealed ten-card pack to preview the 1994-95 Pinnacle I regular series. They are identical to the regular issue counterparts, except that the upper right corner has been cut off, and the printing of the names on front is done in the style of Rink Collection, rather than regular, cards. The cards are numbered on the back.

COMPLETE SEALED SET (10) 1.00 2.50
1 Eric Lindros .40 1.00
2 Alexandre Daigle .08 .20
3 Mike Modano .20 .50
Dallas Star
4 Vincent Damphousse .04 .10
5 Dave Andreychuk .04 .10
6 Curtis Joseph .12 .30
7 Joe Juneau .04 .10
246 Mariusz Czerkawski .02 .05
BR1 Al Iafrate .10 .25
(Boomers insert set)
NNO Title Card .20 .50

1994-95 Pinnacle

This 540-card standard-size set was issued in two series of 270 cards. Cards were distributed in 14-card U.S. and Canadian packs, and 17-card jumbo packs. Series 1 packs had exclusive Canadian and U.S. inserts, series 2 did not. Members of the St. Louis Blues and Calgary Flames are posed in front of a locker which displays their newly designed sweaters. Rookie Cards include Mariusz Czerkawski, Eric Daze, Eric Fichaud, Ed Jovanovski, Jeff O'Neill and Wade Redden. A one-per-case (360 packs) insert card was produced for Canadian, and U.S. series 1 packs. Pavel Bure is numbered MVPC, while Dominik Hasek is MVPU. Both cards have MVP printed at top front and utilize a silver Dufex design. The backs feature dual photos over a silver reflective background.

COMPLETE SET (540) 12.50 25.00
COMPLETE SERIES 1 (270) 7.50 15.00
COMPLETE SERIES 2 (270) 5.00 10.00
1 Eric Lindros .10 .30
2 Alexandre Daigle .02 .10
3 Mike Modano .20 .50
4 Vincent Damphousse .02 .10
5 Dave Andreychuk .05 .15
6 Curtis Joseph .10 .30
7 Joe Juneau .05 .15
8 Trevor Linden .05 .15
9 Rob Blake .05 .15
10 Mike Richter .10 .30
11 Chris Pronger .10 .30
12 Robert Reichel .02 .10
13 Bryan Smolinski .02 .10
14 Ray Sheppard .05 .15
15 Guy Hebert .05 .15
16 Tony Amonte .05 .15
17 Richard Smehlik .02 .10
18 Doug Weight .05 .15
19 Chris Gratton .02 .10
20 Tom Barrasso .05 .15
21 Brian Skrudland .02 .10
22 Sandis Ozolinsh .02 .10
23 Bill Guerin .05 .15
24 Curtis Leschyshyn .02 .10
25 Teemu Selanne .10 .30
26 Darius Kasparaitis .02 .10
27 Garry Galley .02 .10
28 Alexei Yashin .02 .10
29 Mark Tinordi .02 .10
30 Patrick Roy .60 1.50
31 Mike Gartner .05 .15
32 Brendan Shanahan .10 .30
33 Sylvain Cote .02 .10
34 Jeff Brown .02 .10
35 Jari Kurri .05 .15
36 Sergei Zubov .02 .10
37 Pat Verbeek .02 .10
38 Theo Fleury .02 .10
39 Al Iafrate .02 .10
40 Keith Primeau .02 .10
41 Bobby Dollas .02 .10
42 Ed Belfour .10 .30
43 Dale Hawerchuk .05 .15
44 Shayne Corson .02 .10
45 Danton Cole .02 .10
46 Ulf Samuelsson .02 .10
47 Stu Barnes .02 .10
48 Ulf Dahlen .02 .10
49 Valeri Zelepukin .02 .10
50 Joe Sakic .25 .60
51 Dave Manson .02 .10
52 Steve Thomas .02 .10
53 Mark Recchi .05 .15
54 Dave McLlwain .02 .10
55 Derian Hatcher .02 .10
56 Mathieu Schneider .02 .10
57 Bill Berg .02 .10
58 Petr Nedved .05 .15
59 Dimitri Khristich .02 .10
60 Kirk McLean .05 .15
61 Marty McSorley .02 .10
62 Adam Graves .02 .10
63 Geoff Sanderson .05 .15
64 Frank Musil .02 .10
65 Cam Neely .10 .30
66 Nicklas Lidstrom .10 .30
67 Stephan Lebeau .02 .10
68 Joe Murphy .02 .10
69 Yuri Khmylev .02 .10
70 Zdeno Ciger .02 .10
71 Daren Puppa .05 .15
72 Ron Francis .05 .15
73 Scott Mellanby .05 .15
74 Igor Larionov .02 .10
75 Scott Niedermayer .02 .10
76 Owen Nolan .05 .15
77 Teppo Numminen .02 .10
78 Pierre Turgeon .05 .15
79 Mikael Renberg .05 .15
80 Norm Maciver .02 .10
81 Paul Cavallini .02 .10
82 Kirk Muller .02 .10
83 Felix Potvin .10 .30
84 Craig Janney .05 .15
85 Dale Hunter .02 .10
86 Jyrki Lumme .02 .10
87 Alexei Zhitnik .02 .10
88 Steve Larmer .05 .15
89 Jocelyn Lemieux .02 .10
90 Joe Nieuwendyk .05 .15
91 Don Sweeney .02 .10
92 Slava Kozlov .05 .15
93 Tim Sweeney .02 .10
94 Chris Chelios .10 .30
95 Derek Plante .02 .10
96 Igor Kravchuk .02 .10
97 Shawn Chambers .02 .10
98 Jaromir Jagr .20 .50
99 Jeff Norton .02 .10
100 John Vanbiesbrouck .05 .15
101 John MacLean .05 .15
102 Stephane Fiset .05 .15
103 Keith Tkachuk .10 .30
104 Vladimir Malakhov .02 .10
105 Mike McPhee .02 .10
106 Eric Desjardins .05 .15
107 Alexei Kovalev .02 .10
108 Steve Duchesne .02 .10
109 Peter Zezel .02 .10
110 Randy Burridge .02 .10
111 Jason Bowen .02 .10
112 Phil Bourque .02 .10
113 Cliff Ronning .02 .10
114 Sean Burke .05 .15
115 Gary Roberts .02 .10
116 Vladimir Konstantinov .05 .15
117 Brent Sutter .02 .10
118 Tony Granato .02 .10
119 Garry Valk .02 .10
120 Adam Oates .05 .15
121 Arturs Irbe .05 .15
122 Jesse Belanger .02 .10
123 Roman Hamrlik .05 .15
124 Jason Arnott .02 .10
125 Alexander Mogilny .05 .15
126 Bruce Driver .02 .10
127 Shawn McEachern .02 .10
128 Andrei Kovalenko .02 .10
129 Benoit Hogue .02 .10
130 Tim Cheveldae .05 .15
131 Brian Noonan .02 .10
132 Lyle Odelein .02 .10
133 Russ Courtnall .02 .10
134 Peter Stastny .05 .15
135 Doug Gilmour .05 .15
136 Pat Peake .02 .10
137 Gary Suter .02 .10
138 Paul Ranheim .02 .10
139 Troy Murray .02 .10
140 Pavel Bure .10 .30
141 Gord Murphy .02 .10
142 Michael Nylander .02 .10
143 Craig Muni .02 .10
144 Bob Corkum .02 .10
145 Martin Brodeur .30 .75
146 Ted Donato .02 .10
147 Alexei Zhamnov .05 .15
148 Josef Beranek .02 .10
149 Joe Mullen .05 .15
150 Sergei Fedorov .20 .50
151 Mike Keane .02 .10
152 Sergei Makarov .02 .10
153 Marty McInnis .02 .10
154 Steven Rice .02 .10
155 Brian Leetch .10 .30
156 Chris Joseph .02 .10
157 Darcy Wakaluk .05 .15
158 Kelly Miller .02 .10
159 Jim Montgomery .02 .10
160 Nikolai Borschevsky .02 .10
161 Darren Turcotte .02 .10
162 Brad Shaw .02 .10
163 Mark Lamb .02 .10
164 Alexei Gusarov .02 .10
165 Jeremy Roenick .15 .40
166 Stephane Richer .05 .15
167 German Titov .02 .10
168 Rob Niedermayer .05 .15
169 Glen Murray .02 .10
170 Mario Lemieux .60 1.50
171 Thomas Steen .02 .10
172 Ron Tugnutt .05 .15
173 Pat Falloon .02 .10
174 Esa Tikkanen .02 .10
175 Dominik Hasek .30 .75
176 Patrick Flatley .02 .10
177 Gino Odjick .02 .10
178 Charlie Huddy .02 .10
179 Dave Poulin .02 .10
180 Darren McCarty .02 .10
181 Todd Gill .02 .10
182 Tom Chorske .02 .10
183 Marc Bergevin .02 .10
184 Dave Lowry .02 .10
185 Brent Gilchrist .02 .10
186 Eric Weinrich .02 .10
187 Ted Drury .02 .10
188 Boris Mironov .02 .10
189 Patrik Carnback .02 .10
190 Ray Bourque .20 .50
191 Patrice Brisebois .02 .10
192 Bob Errey .02 .10
193 Scott Lachance .02 .10
194 Brad May .02 .10
195 Jeff Beukeboom .02 .10
196 James Patrick .02 .10
197 Doug Brown .02 .10
198 Dana Murzyn .02 .10
199 Chris Osgood .20 .50
200 Wayne Gretzky .75 2.00
201 Bob Carpenter .02 .10
202 Evgeny Davydov .02 .10
203 Oleg Petrov .02 .10
204 Grant Ledyard .02 .10
205 Jocelyn Thibault .10 .30
206 Bill Houlder .02 .10
207 Tom Fitzgerald .02 .10
208 Dominic Roussel .05 .15
209 Dave Ellett .02 .10
210 Frank Kucera .02 .10
211 Steve Smith .02 .10
212 Vincent Riendeau .05 .15
213 Scott Pearson .02 .10
214 John Slaney .02 .10
215 Larry Murphy .05 .15
216 Travis Green .05 .15
217 Joel Otto .02 .10
218 Randy Wood .02 .10
219 Gaetan Duchesne .02 .10
220 Sergei Nemchinov .02 .10
221 Terry Carkner .02 .10
222 Randy McKay .02 .10
223 Mike Donnelly .05 .15
224 J.J. Daigneault .02 .10
225 Dallas Drake .02 .10
226 John Tucker .02 .10
227 Dimitri Yushkevich .02 .10
228 Mike Stapleton RC .12 .30
229 Dmitri Mironov .02 .10
230 Ken Wregget .05 .15
231 Claude Lapointe .02 .10
232 Joe Sacco .02 .10
233 Craig Ludwig .02 .10
234 David Reid .02 .10
235 Rich Sutter .02 .10
236 Mark Fitzpatrick .05 .15
237 Jim Storm .02 .10
238 Brad Dalgarno .02 .10
239 Dixon Ward .02 .10
240 Greg Adams .02 .10
241 Dino Ciccarelli .05 .15
242 Vlastimil Kroupa .02 .10
243 Joe Kocur .02 .10
244 Donald Audette .02 .10
245 Trent Yawney .02 .10
246 Mariusz Czerkawski RC .12 .30
247 Jason Allison .02 .10
248 Brian Savage .02 .10
249 Fred Knipscheer .02 .10
250 Jamie McLennan .05 .15
251 Aaron Gavey .02 .10
252 Jeff Friesen .02 .10
253 Adam Deadmarsh .02 .10
254 Jamie Storr .05 .15
255 Brian Rolston .02 .10
256 Zigmund Palffy .05 .15
257 Brett Lindros .02 .10
258 Denis Tsygurov RC .12 .30
259 Chris Tamer RC .12 .30
260 Mike Peca .02 .10
261 Oleg Tverdovsky .05 .15
262 Todd Harvey .02 .10
263 Yan Kaminsky .02 .10
264 Kenny Jonsson .02 .10
265 Paul Kariya .10 .30
266 Peter Forsberg .40 1.00
267 Atlantic Division .02 .10
Checklist
268 Northeast Division .02 .10
Checklist
269 Central Division .02 .10
Checklist
270 Pacific Division .02 .10
Checklist
271 Steve Yzerman .60 1.50
272 John LeClair .10 .30
273 Rod Brind'Amour .05 .15
274 Ron Hextall .05 .15
275 Todd Elik .02 .10
276 Geoff Courtnall .02 .10
277 Kjell Samuelsson .02 .10
278 Brian Bradley .02 .10
279 Darrin Shannon .02 .10
280 Mike Ricci .02 .10
281 Peter Bondra .05 .15
282 Terry Yake .02 .10
283 Patrick Poulin .02 .10
284 Bob Kudelski .02 .10
285 Bill Ranford .05 .15
286 Alexander Godynyuk .02 .10
287 Claude Lemieux .02 .10
288 Sylvain Turgeon .02 .10
289 Kevin Miller .02 .10
290 Brian Bellows .02 .10
291 Murray Craven .02 .10
292 Kelly Hrudey .05 .15
293 Neal Broten .05 .15
294 Craig Simpson .02 .10
295 Mark Howe .02 .10
296 Johan Garpenlov .02 .10
297 Jamie Macoun .02 .10
298 Steve Leach .02 .10
299 Kevin Stevens .02 .10
300 Mark Messier .10 .30
301 Paul Ysebaert .02 .10
302 Derek King .02 .10
303 Fredrik Olausson .02 .10
304 John Druce .02 .10
305 Calle Johansson .02 .10
306 Kelly Kisio .02 .10
307 Sergio Momesso .02 .10
308 Joe Cirella .02 .10
309 Tommy Soderstrom .05 .15
310 Scott Stevens .05 .15
311 Petr Klima .02 .10
312 Steven Finn .02 .10
313 Tomas Sandstrom .02 .10
314 Ray Ferraro .02 .10
315 Andy Moog .10 .30
316 Ray Whitney .02 .10
317 Dirk Graham .02 .10
318 Shawn Burr .02 .10
319 Andrew Cassels .02 .10
320 Craig Billington .05 .15
321 Wayne Presley .02 .10
322 Anatoli Semenov .02 .10
323 Michal Pivonka .02 .10
324 Martin Gelinas .02 .10
325 Nelson Emerson .02 .10
326 Brent Fedyk .02 .10
327 Bob Bassen .02 .10
328 Darryl Sydor .02 .10
329 Stephane Matteau .02 .10
330 Ken Daneyko .02 .10
331 Mikhail Shtalenkov RC .12 .30
332 Kelly Buchberger .02 .10
333 Mike Hough .02 .10
334 Dave Gagner .05 .15
335 Chris Terreri .05 .15
336 Robert Kron .02 .10
337 Andrei Lomakin .02 .10
338 Kevin Lowe .02 .10
339 Steve Konroyd .02 .10
340 Denis Savard .05 .15
341 Steve Heinze .02 .10
342 Zarley Zalapski .02 .10
343 Valeri Kamensky .05 .15
344 Tie Domi .05 .15
345 Kevin Hatcher .02 .10
346 Dean Evason .02 .10
347 Bobby Holik .02 .10
348 Steve Konowalchuk .02 .10
349 Rob Gaudreau .02 .10
350 Pat LaFontaine .10 .30
351 Joe Reekie .02 .10
352 Martin Straka .02 .10
353 Dave Babych .02 .10
354 Geoff Smith .02 .10
355 Don Beaupre .05 .15
356 Adam Burt .02 .10
357 Doug Bodger .02 .10
358 Dean McAmmond .02 .10
359 Gerald Diduck .02 .10
360 Rob DiMaio .02 .10
361 Scott Young .02 .10
362 Alexander Semak .02 .10
363 Mike Rathje .02 .10
364 Alexander Karpovtsev .02 .10
365 Trevor Kidd .05 .15
366 Jason Dawe .02 .10
367 Vitali Prokhorov .02 .10
368 Keith Brown .02 .10
369 Bret Hedican .02 .10
370 Markus Naslund .10 .30
371 Rick Tocchet .05 .15
372 Guy Carbonneau .02 .10
373 Kevin Haller .02 .10
374 Bob Rouse .02 .10
375 Rob Pearson .02 .10
376 Steve Chiasson .02 .10
377 Mike Vernon .05 .15
378 Keith Jones .02 .10
379 Sylvain Lefebvre .02 .10
380 Tom Kurvers .02 .10
381 Pat Elynuik .02 .10
382 Uwe Krupp .02 .10
383 Ron Sutter .02 .10
384 Mike Ridley .02 .10
385 Wendel Clark .05 .15
386 Mats Sundin .10 .30
387 Al MacInnis .05 .15
388 Glen Wesley .02 .10
389 Jim Paek .02 .10
390 Rudy Poeschek .02 .10
391 Yves Racine .02 .10
392 Craig MacTavish .02 .10
393 Jon Casey .05 .15
394 Garth Butcher .02 .10
395 Sean Hill .02 .10
396 Troy Loney .02 .10
397 John Cullen .02 .10
398 Alexei Kasatonov .02 .10
399 Mike Craig .02 .10
400 Luc Robitaille .05 .15
401 Randy Moller .02 .10
402 Chris Dahlquist .02 .10
403 Pat Conacher .02 .10
404 Bob Probert .05 .15
405 Robert Dirk .02 .10
406 Randy Cunneyworth .02 .10
407 Bryan Marchment .02 .10
408 Nick Kypreos .02 .10
409 Doug Lidster .02 .10
410 Phil Housley .05 .15
411 Bob Sweeney .02 .10
412 Mike Ramsey .02 .10
413 Robert Lang .02 .10
414 Brian Benning .02 .10
415 Greg Gilbert .02 .10
416 Martin Rucinsky .02 .10
417 Jason Smith .02 .10
418 Jozef Stumpel .02 .10
419 Bob Beers .02 .10
420 Ed Olczyk .02 .10
421 Grant Fuhr .05 .15
422 Gilbert Dionne .02 .10
423 Mike Peluso .02 .10
424 Petr Svoboda .02 .10
425 Corey Millen .02 .10
426 Kevin Dineen .02 .10
427 Brad McCrimmon .02 .10
428 Bob Essensa .05 .15
429 Paul Coffey .10 .30
430 Glenn Healy .05 .15
431 Luke Richardson .02 .10
432 Adam Foote .05 .15
433 Paul Broten .02 .10
434 Christian Ruuttu .02 .10
435 David Shaw .02 .10
436 Jimmy Carson .02 .10
437 Ken Sutton .02 .10
438 Kay Whitmore .05 .15
439 Jim Dowd .02 .10
440 Jim Johnson .02 .10
441 Kirk Maltby .02 .10
442 Trent Klatt .02 .10
443 Paul DiPietro .02 .10
444 Rick Tabaracci .05 .15
445 Craig Wolanin .02 .10
446 Dave Hannan .02 .10
447 Rick Zombo .02 .10
448 Tom Pederson .02 .10
449 Martin Lapointe .02 .10
450 Brett Hull .15 .40
451 Mikael Andersson .02 .10
452 Benoit Brunet .02 .10
453 Nathan Lafayette .02 .10
454 Kent Manderville .02 .10
455 Todd Krygier .02 .10
456 Dennis Vaske .02 .10
457 Peter Popovic .02 .10
458 Jeff Shantz .02 .10
459 Darrin Madeley .02 .10
460 Rene Corbet .02 .10
461 Alexander Daigle IB .02 .10
462 Mikael Renberg IB .02 .10
463 Jason Arnott IB .02 .10
464 Mikael Renberg IB .05 .15
465 Alexei Yashin IB .02 .10
466 Chris Pronger IB .05 .15
467 Mariusz Czerkawski IB .02 .10
468 Chris Gratton IB .02 .10
469 Rob Niedermayer IB .05 .15
470 Bryan Smolinski IB .02 .10
471 Chris Osgood IB .20 .50
472 Derek Plante IB .02 .10
473 Brian Rolston IB .02 .10
474 Jason Allison IB .02 .10
475 Jamie Storr IB .05 .15
476 Kenny Jonsson IB .02 .10
477 Viktor Kozlov IB .02 .10
478 Brett Lindros IB .02 .10
479 Peter Forsberg IB .40 1.00
480 Paul Kariya IB .10 .30
481 Viktor Kozlov .02 .10
482 Michal Grosek RC .12 .30
483 Maxim Bets .02 .10
484 Jason Wiemer RC .12 .30
485 Janne Laukkanen .02 .10
486 Valeri Karpov RC .12 .30
487 Andrei Nikolishin .02 .10
488 Dan Plante RC .12 .30
489 Mattias Norstrom .02 .10
490 David Oliver RC .12 .30
491 Todd Simon RC .12 .30
492 Valeri Bure .02 .10
493 Eric Fichaud RC .12 .30
494 Cory Stillman RC .12 .30
495 Chris Therien .02 .10
496 Matt Johnson RC .12 .30
497 Joby Messier .02 .10
498 Slava Butsayev .02 .10
499 Bernie Nicholls .05 .15
500 Mark Osborne .02 .10
501 Stephane Quintal .02 .10
502 Jamie Baker .02 .10
503 Todd Ewen .02 .10
504 Dan Quinn .02 .10
505 Peter Taglianetti .02 .10
506 Chris Simon .02 .10
507 Jay Wells .02 .10
508 Tommy Albelin .02 .10
509 Warren Rychel .02 .10
510 Brent Hughes .02 .10
511 Greg Johnson .02 .10
512 Stu Grimson .02 .10
513 Iain Fraser .02 .10
514 Rob Ray .02 .10
515 Craig Berube .02 .10
516 Shane Churla .02 .10
517 Checklist .02 .10
518 Checklist .02 .10
519 Checklist .02 .10
520 Checklist .02 .10
521 Jamie Storr .05 .15
522 Dan Cloutier RC .50 1.25
523 Bryan McCabe .02 .10
524 Ed Jovanovski RC .12 .30
525 Nolan Baumgartner RC .12 .30
526 Jamie Rivers RC .12 .30
527 Wade Redden RC .12 .30
528 Lee Sorochan RC .12 .30
529 Eric Daze RC .50 1.25
530 Jason Allison .02 .10
531 Alexandre Daigle .05 .15
532 Jeff Friesen .02 .10
533 Todd Harvey .02 .10
534 Jeff O'Neill RC .12 .30
535 Ryan Smyth RC .50 1.25
536 Marty Murray .02 .10
537 Darcy Tucker RC .12 .30
538 Denis Pederson RC .12 .30
539 Shean Donovan RC .12 .30
540 Larry Courville RC .12 .30
MVPC Pavel Bure .10 .30
MVPU Dominik Hasek 10.00 25.00

1994-95 Pinnacle Artist's Proofs

This set is a parallel version of the standard set. The difference is a reflective gold foil Artist's Proof logo on the front. Series 1 cards also featured an Artist's Proof logo on the back; this logo did not appear on series 2 card backs. The Pinnacle and player name bearing icon, which is gold on normal cards, is printed with a more reflective gold foil on these inserts. Series two production made this feature more bold than in series 1. Cards were inserted at a rate of 1:36 packs in both series 1 and 2, 14 card packs. There are no Artist's Proof versions of the first series checklists, however, there is an Artist's Proof version of the second series checklists. Estimated production of these cards varies; one press release suggests "less than 700 sets", while wrappers state "less than 500".

*STARS: 12X TO 30X BASIC CARDS
*ROOKIES: 4X TO 10X BASIC CARDS
200 Wayne Gretzky 100.00 250.00

1994-95 Pinnacle Rink Collection

This set is a parallel to the Pinnacle set. The cards were inserted in packs at a rate of 1:4. The fronts have a full-color action photo with the player's last name on the left surrounded by the chain for a gold medallion at the bottom. The background consists of silver-foil sunrays. The backs have a color photo with player information and statistics. The bottom has the words "Rink Collection" and the Pinnacle emblem.

*STARS: 4X TO 10X BASIC CARDS
*ROOKIES: 2X TO 5X

1994-95 Pinnacle Boomers

This 18-card set could be found randomly inserted at a rate of 1:24 U.S. series 1 hobby packs. These horizontally-oriented cards are notable for their design, which utilizes two-thirds of the space for an action shot of the featured player shooting the puck. The remaining third featured a ghosted goalie image. The player's last name is printed in gold foil down the left side of the card. "Boomers" is written in blue and red on the bottom left portion. The backs are occupied mostly with a player photo, while text assumes the remaining third. Cards are numbered with a "BR" prefix.

COMPLETE SET (18) 25.00 50.00
BR1 Al Iafrate .60 1.50
BR2 Vladimir Malakhov .60 1.50
BR3 Al MacInnis 1.00 2.50
BR4 Chris Chelios 2.00 5.00
BR5 Mike Modano 3.00 8.00
BR6 Brendan Shanahan 2.00 5.00
BR7 Ray Bourque 3.00 8.00
BR8 Geoff Sanderson 1.00 2.50
BR9 Brett Hull 2.50 6.00
BR10 Rob Blake 1.00 2.50
BR11 Steve Thomas .60 1.50
BR12 Cam Neely 2.00 5.00
BR13 Pavel Bure 2.00 5.00
BR14 Stephane Richer 1.00 2.50
BR15 Teemu Selanne 2.00 5.00
BR16 Eric Lindros 2.00 5.00
BR17 Alexander Mogilny 1.00 2.50
BR18 Rick Tocchet 1.00 2.50

1994-95 Pinnacle Gamers

This 18-card set was randomly inserted 1:18 packs of all Pinnacle series 2 product. The cards are enhanced by the Dufex printing technology. Each card is color-coded to the team colors of the player. The player is pictured inside a shape which approximates the design of his team's emblem. The backs are reflective colored, with a photo and paragraph of information. Cards are numbered with a "GR" prefix.

COMPLETE SET (18) 40.00 80.00
GR1 Teemu Selanne 2.50 6.00
GR2 Pat LaFontaine 2.50 6.00
GR3 Sergei Fedorov 4.00 10.00
GR4 Pavel Bure 2.50 6.00
GR5 Jaromir Jagr 4.00 10.00
GR6 Alexandre Daigle .75 2.00
GR7 Kirk Muller .75 2.00
GR8 Mike Modano 4.00 10.00
GR9 Mark Messier 2.50 6.00
GR10 Brendan Shanahan 2.50 6.00
GR11 Doug Gilmour 1.25 3.00
GR12 Rick Tocchet 1.25 3.00
GR13 Wendel Clark 1.25 3.00
GR14 Jeremy Roenick 3.00 8.00
GR15 Adam Graves .75 2.00
GR16 Eric Lindros 2.50 6.00
GR17 Cam Neely 2.50 6.00
GR18 Keith Tkachuk 2.50 6.00

1994-95 Pinnacle Goaltending Greats

Any one of the 18 cards in this set could be found randomly inserted at a rate of 1:9 Pinnacle series 2 jumbo packs. This horizontal set has a full-bleed photo design, with the set logo and player name in gold foil on the left side of the card. Vertical backs have a crowded design, with a small player photo on the lower left, personal information and statistics. Cards are numbered with a "GT" prefix.

COMPLETE SET (18) 40.00 80.00
GT1 Dominik Hasek 5.00 10.00
GT2 Mike Richter 2.50 6.00
GT3 John Vanbiesbrouck 1.50 4.00
GT4 Ed Belfour 3.00 8.00
GT5 Patrick Roy 8.00 20.00
GT6 Bill Ranford 1.50 4.00
GT7 Martin Brodeur 5.00 12.00
GT8 Felix Potvin 3.00 8.00
GT9 Arturs Irbe 1.50 4.00
GT10 Mike Vernon 1.50 4.00
GT11 Kirk McLean 1.50 4.00
GT12 Sean Burke 1.50 4.00
GT13 Curtis Joseph 2.50 6.00
GT14 Andy Moog 1.50 4.00
GT15 Daren Puppa 1.50 4.00
GT16 Chris Osgood 1.50 4.00
GT17 Tom Barrasso 1.50 4.00
GT18 Jocelyn Thibault 1.50 4.00

1994-95 Pinnacle Masks

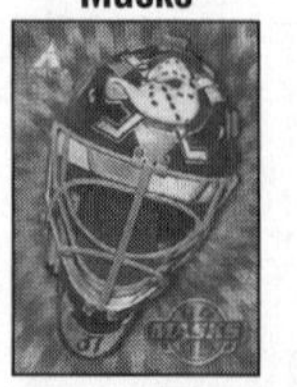

This popular ten-card insert set was inserted in Canadian series 1 product at the rate of 1:90 packs. The cards feature a photo of a goaltender's mask over a metallic blue Dufex background. No team or player name appears on the front. Backs feature dual photos on a mirror finish and the player and team names. Cards are numbered with an "MA" prefix.

COMPLETE SET (10) 100.00 200.00
MA1 Patrick Roy 25.00 50.00
MA2 John Vanbiesbrouck 10.00 25.00
MA3 Kelly Hrudey 10.00 25.00
MA4 Guy Hebert 8.00 20.00
MA5 Rick Tabaracci 8.00 20.00
MA6 Ron Hextall 10.00 25.00
MA7 Trevor Kidd 8.00 20.00
MA8 Andy Moog 10.00 25.00
MA9 Jimmy Waite 8.00 20.00
MA10 Curtis Joseph 10.00 25.00

1994-95 Pinnacle Northern Lights

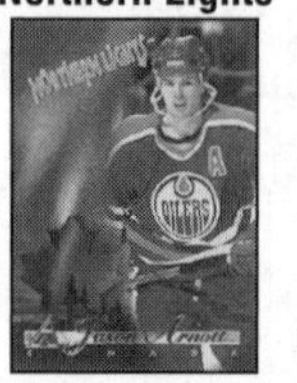

This 18-card insert set was randomly inserted 1:24 Canadian series 1 hobby packs. The series highlights the top players from Canadian-based teams. The fronts have a player photo which fades into a sky design with a northern lights image on the left side. The player name is stamped in gold foil above the word "Canada", written in yellow. The horizontal backs have a photo on the left, with some personal information printed over another interpretation of the famous northern lights. Cards are numbered with an "NL" prefix in a red maple leaf.

COMPLETE SET (18) 20.00 50.00
NL1 Patrick Roy 6.00 15.00
NL2 Kirk Muller .75 2.00
NL3 Vincent Damphousse .75 2.00
NL4 Joe Sakic 2.50 6.00
NL5 Wendel Clark 1.25 3.00
NL6 Alexandre Daigle .75 2.00
NL7 Alexei Yashin .75 2.00
NL8 Doug Gilmour 1.25 3.00
NL9 Felix Potvin 1.50 4.00
NL10 Mats Sundin 1.50 4.00
NL11 Teemu Selanne 1.50 4.00
NL12 Keith Tkachuk 1.25 3.00
NL13 Bill Ranford 1.25 3.00
NL14 Jason Arnott .75 2.00
NL15 Theo Fleury .75 2.00
NL16 Gary Roberts .75 2.00
NL17 Pavel Bure 1.50 4.00
NL18 Trevor Linden 1.25 3.00

1994-95 Pinnacle Rookie Team Pinnacle

The 12 cards in this set, featuring a player from each conference on either side, were inserted in Pinnacle series two product at the rate of 1:90 packs. The set focuses on 24 top rookies in the league. Cards are printed using the Gold-line foil technology; either side could be found with the Gold-line foil finish. The cards feature a cutout player photo on a striped background of reds and yellows. The player name is printed on a black border on the top of the card. One side has the card number with an "RTP" prefix and the Pinnacle anti-counterfeiting device.

COMPLETE SET (12) 30.00 75.00
1 Corey Hirsch 2.00 5.00
Jamie Storr
2 Mattias Norstrom 2.00 5.00
Oleg Tverdovsky
3 Denis Tsygurov 2.00 5.00
Janne Laukkanen
4 Chris Tamer 2.00 5.00
Kenny Jonsson
5 Zigmund Palffy 3.00 8.00
Viktor Kozlov
6 Rene Corbet 2.00 5.00
Maxim Bets
7 Jason Allison 3.00 8.00
Jeff Friesen
8 Brian Rolston 3.00 8.00
Michael Peca
9 Peter Forsberg 10.00 25.00
Paul Kariya
10 Brian Savage 2.00 5.00
Todd Harvey
11 Brett Lindros 2.00 5.00
Valeri Karpov
12 Mariusz Czerkawski 2.00 5.00
Sergei Krivokrasov

1994-95 Pinnacle Team Pinnacle

This 12-card set features 24 top players in the league, 12 per conference (one player on either side of the card). These were inserted in series 1 U.S. product at the rate of 1:90 packs. Cards have full-bleed photos on each side. Either side could be found with the Dufex technology, while the other has a mirror finish. The Dufexing of one particular side could have an effect on the value, depending upon the player and regional premium demands. The words "Team Pinnacle '94-95" are printed in gold on both sides. The player's last name is printed in an ovoid sphere along the bottom. Cards are numbered on one side with a "TP" prefix.

COMPLETE SET (12) 80.00 150.00
TP1 Felix Potvin 8.00 20.00
Patrick Roy
TP2 Curtis Joseph 5.00 12.00
Mike Richter
TP3 Ray Bourque 4.00 10.00
Chris Chelios
TP4 Brian Leetch 8.00 20.00
Rob Blake
TP5 Scott Stevens 8.00 20.00
Paul Coffey
TP6 Adam Graves 10.00 25.00
Brendan Shanahan
TP7 Kevin Stevens 4.00 10.00
Luc Robitaille
TP8 Eric Lindros 8.00 20.00
Sergei Fedorov
TP9 Wayne Gretzky 10.00 25.00
Mark Messier
TP10 Doug Gilmour 8.00 20.00
Mario Lemieux
TP11 Jaromir Jagr 5.00 12.00
Brett Hull
TP12 Pavel Bure 4.00 10.00
Cam Neely

1994-95 Pinnacle World Edition

The 18 cards in this set were randomly inserted at a rate of 1:18 Pinnacle series 2 hobby packs. The cards feature a player photo with his native country's flag as a background. The World Edition logo is stamped in gold foil on the upper left corner. Horizontal backs have a small player photo on the left and a paragraph of information. The cards are numbered with a "WE" prefix. The Pinnacle anti-counterfeiting device also appears on the back.

COMPLETE SET (18) 25.00 50.00
WE1 Teemu Selanne 1.25 3.00
WE2 Doug Gilmour .60 1.50
WE3 Jeremy Roenick 1.50 4.00
WE4 Ulf Dahlen .40 1.00
WE5 Sergei Fedorov 2.00 5.00
WE6 Dominik Hasek 3.00 8.00
WE7 Jari Kurri .60 1.50
WE8 Mario Lemieux 6.00 15.00
WE9 Mike Modano 2.00 5.00
WE10 Mikael Renberg .60 1.50
WE11 Sandis Ozolinsh .40 1.00
WE12 Alexei Kovalev .40 1.00
WE13 Robert Reichel .40 1.00
WE14 Eric Lindros 1.25 3.00
WE15 Brian Leetch 1.25 3.00
WE16 Nicklas Lidstrom 1.25 3.00
WE17 Alexei Yashin .40 1.00
WE18 Petr Nedved .60 1.50

1995-96 Pinnacle

This single-series issue of 225 cards was left incomplete when Pinnacle decided to release the Summit brand in the place of Pinnacle series 2. Nevertheless, most major stars are included. The highlight of the set is a large rookies subset, extending from card #201-220. However, there are no key Rookie Cards in this set.

COMPLETE SET (225) 5.00 12.00
1 Pavel Bure .10 .30
2 Paul Kariya .10 .30
3 Adam Oates .05 .15
4 Garry Galley .02 .10
5 Mark Messier .10 .30
6 Theo Fleury .02 .10
7 Alexandre Daigle .02 .10
8 Joe Murphy .02 .10
9 Eric Lindros .10 .30
10 Kevin Hatcher .02 .10
11 Jaromir Jagr .20 .50
12 Owen Nolan .05 .15
13 Ulf Dahlen .02 .10
14 Paul Coffey .10 .30
15 Brett Hull .15 .40
16 Jason Arnott .02 .10
17 Paul Ysebaert .02 .10
18 Jesse Belanger .02 .10
19 Mats Sundin .10 .30
20 Darren Turcotte .02 .10
21 Dale Hunter .05 .15
22 Jari Kurri .10 .30
23 Alexei Zhamnov .05 .15
24 Mark Recchi .05 .15
25 Dallas Drake .02 .10
26 John MacLean .05 .15
27 Keith Jones .05 .15
28 Mathieu Schneider .02 .10
29 Jeff Brown .02 .10
30 Patrick Flatley .02 .10
31 Dave Andreychuk .05 .15
32 Bill Guerin .05 .15
33 Chris Gratton .02 .10
34 Pierre Turgeon .05 .15
35 Stephane Richer .05 .15
36 Marty McSorley .02 .10
37 Craig Janney .02 .10
38 Geoff Sanderson .02 .10
39 Ron Francis .05 .15
40 Stu Barnes .02 .10
41 Mikael Renberg .05 .15
42 David Oliver .02 .10
43 Radek Bonk .02 .10
44 Sergei Fedorov .20 .50
45 Adam Graves .02 .10
46 Uwe Krupp .02 .10
47 Mike Richter .10 .30
48 Todd Harvey .05 .15
49 Stanislav Neckar .02 .10
50 Chris Chelios .10 .30
51 John LeClair .10 .30
52 German Titov .02 .10
53 Garth Butcher .02 .10
54 Pat LaFontaine .10 .30
55 Jeff Friesen .02 .10
56 Ray Bourque .20 .50
57 Esa Tikkanen .02 .10
58 Steve Rucchin .05 .15
59 Roman Hamrlik .05 .15
60 Oleg Tverdovsky .05 .15
61 Doug Gilmour .05 .15
62 Jocelyn Lemieux .02 .10
63 Roman Oksiuta .02 .10
64 Alexei Zhitnik .02 .10
65 Sylvain Cote .02 .10
66 Paul Kruse .02 .10
67 Teppo Numminen .02 .10
68 Gary Suter .02 .10
69 Darrin Shannon .02 .10
70 Derian Hatcher .02 .10
71 Sergei Gonchar .02 .10
72 Adam Deadmarsh .02 .10
73 Jyrki Lumme .02 .10
74 Dino Ciccarelli .05 .15
75 Mike Gartner .05 .15
76 Todd Marchant .02 .10
77 Jason Wiemer .02 .10
78 Scott Mellanby .05 .15
79 Al MacInnis .05 .15
80 Glen Wesley .02 .10
81 Igor Larionov .02 .10
82 Eric Lacroix .02 .10
83 Mike Keane .02 .10
84 Vincent Damphousse .02 .10
85 Robert Kron .02 .10
86 Scott Stevens .05 .15
87 Don Beaupre .05 .15
88 Zigmund Palffy .05 .15
89 Kevin Lowe .05 .15
90 Tommy Soderstrom .05 .15
91 Glenn Healy .05 .15
92 Randy McKay .02 .10
93 Sean Hill .02 .10
94 Brian Savage .02 .10
95 Ron Hextall .05 .15
96 Darryl Sydor .05 .15
97 Tom Barrasso .05 .15
98 Andrei Nikolishin .02 .10
99 Viktor Kozlov .05 .15
100 Rob Niedermayer .05 .15
101 Wayne Gretzky .75 2.00
102 Shaun Van Allen .02 .10
103 Dave Manson .02 .10
104 Donald Audette .02 .10
105 Daren Puppa .05 .15
106 Jeremy Roenick .15 .40
107 Ken Wregget .05 .15
108 Mike Modano .20 .50
109 Rod Brind'Amour .05 .15
110 Eric Desjardins .05 .15
111 Pat Verbeek .02 .10
112 Jeff Beukeboom .02 .10
113 John Druce .02 .10
114 Andy Moog .10 .30
115 Turner Stevenson .02 .10
116 Alexander Selivanov .02 .10
117 Neal Broten .05 .15
118 Nikolai Khabibulin .05 .15
119 Claude Lemieux .02 .10
120 Sergei Brylin .02 .10
121 Bob Corkum .02 .10
122 Kelly Hrudey .05 .15
123 Jason Dawe .02 .10
124 Sean Burke .05 .15
125 Dave Gagner .02 .10
126 Kirk Maltby .05 .15
127 Ian Laperriere .02 .10
128 Slava Kozlov .05 .15
129 Vladimir Konstantinov .05 .15
130 Kenny Jonsson .02 .10
131 Sylvain Lefebvre .02 .10
132 Kirk McLean .05 .15
133 Brian Leetch .05 .15
134 Olaf Kolzig .05 .15
135 Patrick Poulin .02 .10
136 Tim Cheveldae .05 .15
137 Gary Roberts .02 .10
138 Jim Carey .05 .15
139 Dominik Hasek .25 .60
140 Josef Beranek .02 .10
141 Don Sweeney .02 .10
142 Felix Potvin .10 .30
143 Guy Hebert .05 .15
144 Guy Carbonneau .10 .30
145 Mikhail Shtalenkov .02 .10
146 Kevin Miller .02 .10
147 Blaine Lacher .05 .15
148 Craig MacTavish .05 .15
149 Derek Plante .02 .10
150 Kevin Dineen .02 .10
151 Trevor Kidd .05 .15
152 Sergei Nemchinov .02 .10
153 Ed Belfour .10 .30
154 Sergei Krivokrasov .02 .10
155 Mike Rathje .02 .10
156 Mike Donnelly .02 .10
157 David Roberts .02 .10
158 Jocelyn Thibault .10 .30
159 Tie Domi .05 .15
160 Chris Osgood .05 .15
161 Martin Gelinas .02 .10
162 Scott Thornton .02 .10
163 Bob Rouse .02 .10
164 Randy Wood .02 .10
165 Chris Therien .02 .10
166 Steven Rice .02 .10
167 Scott Lachance .02 .10
168 Petr Svoboda .02 .10
169 Patrick Roy .60 1.50
170 Norm Maciver .02 .10
171 Todd Gill .02 .10
172 Brian Rolston .02 .10
173 Wade Flaherty RC .05 .15
174 Valeri Bure .02 .10
175 Mark Fitzpatrick .05 .15
176 Darren McCarty .02 .10
177 Ken Daneyko .02 .10
178 Yves Racine .02 .10
179 Murray Craven .02 .10
180 Nicklas Lidstrom .10 .30
181 Gord Murphy .02 .10
182 Eric Weinrich .02 .10
183 Todd Krygier .02 .10
184 Cliff Ronning .02 .10
185 Mariusz Czerkawski .02 .10
186 Benoit Hogue .02 .10
187 Richard Smehlik .02 .10
188 Jeff Norton .02 .10
189 Steve Chiasson .02 .10
190 Andrei Nazarov .02 .10
191 Steve Smith .02 .10
192 Mario Lemieux .60 1.50
193 Trent Klatt .02 .10
194 Valeri Zelepukin .02 .10
195 Adam Foote .05 .15
196 Lyle Odelein .02 .10
197 Keith Primeau .02 .10
198 Rob Blake .05 .15
199 Dave Lowry .02 .10
200 Adam Burt .02 .10
201 Martin Gendron .02 .10
202 Tommy Salo RC .40 1.00
203 Eric Daze .05 .15
204 Ryan Smyth .05 .15
205 Brian Holzinger RC .10 .30
206 Chris Marinucci RC .02 .10
207 Jason Bonsignore .02 .10
208 Craig Johnson RC .02 .10
209 Steve Larouche RC .02 .10
210 Chris McAlpine RC .02 .10
211 Shean Donovan .02 .10
212 Cory Stillman RC .02 .10
213 Craig Darby RC .02 .10
214 Philippe DeRouville .02 .10
215 Kevin Brown .02 .10
216 Manny Fernandez .10 .30
217 Radim Bicanek .02 .10
218 Craig Conroy RC .02 .10
219 Todd Warriner RC .02 .10
220 Richard Park .02 .10
221 Checklist .02 .10
222 Checklist .02 .10
223 Checklist .02 .10
224 Checklist .02 .10
225 Checklist .02 .10

1995-96 Pinnacle Artist's Proofs

This 225-card set is a high-end parallel of the standard Pinnacle issue. The cards utilize the same Dufex technology as the Rink Collection cards, but have the Artist's Proof logo embossed on, typically in the lower right corner. On some cards, this can be very difficult to detect: collectors should double check all dufexed cards before buying or selling to ensure which type they are. These cards were inserted at a rate of 1:48 packs.

*STARS: 12X TO 30X BASIC CARDS
*ROOKIES: 4X TO 10X

1995-96 Pinnacle Rink Collection

These 225 cards form a low-end parallel version of the Pinnacle set. The cards, which utilize the Dufex process, are difficult to distinguish from the very similar, but much more expensive Artist's Proof cards. Collectors are advised to carefully look for the embossed AP symbol in the lower right corner before buying or selling the 1995-96 Dufexed cards. The Rink Collection cards were inserted at a rate of 1:4 packs.

*STARS: 4X TO 10X BASIC CARDS
*RCs: 2X TO 5X BASIC CARDS

1995-96 Pinnacle Clear Shots

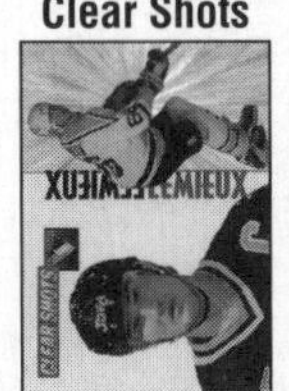

Fifteen veteran superstars are recognized in this set which is distinguished by its use of a clear plastic rainbow holographic printing technology. The cards were inserted at a rate of 1:60 hobby and retail packs.

COMPLETE SET (15) 15.00 30.00
1 Martin Brodeur 2.00 5.00
2 Brett Hull .60 1.50
3 Paul Kariya .50 1.25
4 Eric Lindros .50 1.25
5 Cam Neely .50 1.25
6 Doug Gilmour .25 .60
7 Sergei Fedorov .75 2.00
8 Peter Forsberg 2.00 5.00
9 Wayne Gretzky 3.00 8.00
10 Patrick Roy 2.50 6.00
11 Jaromir Jagr .75 2.00
12 Pavel Bure .50 1.25
13 Mario Lemieux 2.50 6.00
14 Pierre Turgeon .25 .60
15 Dominik Hasek 1.00 2.50

1995-96 Pinnacle First Strike

This 15-card set focusing on game breaking players is enhanced by the use of spot micro-etch technology. The cards were randomly inserted at a rate of 1:24 retail packs only.

COMPLETE SET (15) 10.00 20.00
1 Mark Messier .40 1.00
2 Wayne Gretzky 2.50 6.00
3 Doug Gilmour .20 .50
4 Patrick Roy 2.00 5.00
5 Cam Neely .40 1.00
6 Brian Leetch .20 .50
7 Ed Belfour .40 1.00
8 Wendel Clark .20 .50
9 Chris Chelios .40 1.00
10 Claude Lemieux .15 .30
11 Peter Forsberg .75 2.00
12 Brett Hull .50 1.25
13 Mario Lemieux 2.00 5.00
14 Dominik Hasek .75 2.00
15 Theo Fleury .15 .30

1995-96 Pinnacle Full Contact

This 12-card set used the spot micro-etch technology to bring out the best of the NHL's top bangers and bruisers. The cards were randomly inserted 1:9 retail jumbo packs.

COMPLETE SET (12) 2.50 5.00
RANDOM INSERTS IN HOBBY PACKS
1 Cam Neely .30 .75
2 Scott Stevens .15 .40
3 Owen Nolan .15 .40
4 Jeremy Roenick .40 1.00
5 Brendan Shanahan .10 .25
6 Chris Chelios .30 .75
7 Brett Lindros .10 .25
8 Jason Arnott .10 .25
9 Tie Domi .15 .40
10 Mark Tinordi .10 .25
11 Keith Tkachuk .30 .75
12 Mark Messier .30 .75

1995-96 Pinnacle Global Gold

These 25 cards were randomly inserted into Pinnacle International boxes at a rate of 1:6 packs. These cards are identical to the ones found in the Pinnacle U.S. basic set, save for the circular gold-foil stamp on the front that reads, "Global Gold", and the numbering on the back reading "X of 25" instead of the regular card number.

1 Pavel Bure 2.40 6.00
2 Jaromir Jagr 3.20 8.00
3 Mats Sundin 1.00 2.50
4 Jari Kurri .80 2.00
5 Mikael Renberg .80 2.00
6 Radek Bonk .20 .50
7 Sergei Fedorov 2.00 5.00
8 Uwe Krupp .20 .50
9 German Titov .20 .50
10 Esa Tikkanen .80 2.00
11 Oleg Tverdovsky .20 .50
12 Teppo Numminen .20 .50
13 Jyrki Lumme .20 .50
14 Zigmund Palffy 1.00 2.50
15 Tommy Soderstrom .80 2.00
16 Viktor Kozlov .80 2.00
17 Alexander Selivanov .20 .50
18 Sergei Brylin .20 .50
19 Dominik Hasek 2.00 5.00
20 Sergei Nemchinov .20 .50
21 Petr Svoboda .20 .50
22 Valeri Bure .80 2.00
23 Nicklas Lidstrom 1.00 2.50
24 Mariusz Czerkawski .80 2.00
25 Valeri Zelepukin .20 .50

1995-96 Pinnacle Masks

This popular Dufex set returns for the third year to spotlight the unique and colorful world of protection NHL style. No team or player names appear on the front. The cards were randomly inserted at the rate of 1:90 retail and hobby packs.

COMPLETE SET (10) 60.00 125.00
STATED ODDS 1:90 HOBBY/RETAIL
1 Blaine Lacher 6.00 15.00
2 Martin Brodeur 15.00 40.00
3 Jim Carey 6.00 15.00
4 Felix Potvin 10.00 25.00
5 Andy Moog 6.00 15.00
6 Mike Vernon 6.00 15.00
7 Mark Fitzpatrick 6.00 15.00
8 Ron Hextall 6.00 15.00
9 Sean Burke 6.00 15.00
10 Jocelyn Thibault 10.00 25.00

1995-96 Pinnacle Roaring 20s

This 20-card set highlights the young guns of the NHL. The cards benefit from the use of the spot micro-etch technology and were randomly inserted in 1:19 hobby packs.

COMPLETE SET (20) 25.00 50.00
1 Eric Lindros 1.25 3.00
2 Paul Kariya 1.25 3.00
3 Martin Brodeur 3.00 8.00
4 Jeremy Roenick 1.50 4.00
5 Mike Modano 2.00 5.00
6 Sergei Fedorov 2.00 5.00
7 Mats Sundin 1.25 3.00
8 Pavel Bure 1.25 3.00
9 Jim Carey .60 1.50
10 Felix Potvin 1.25 3.00
11 Alexei Zhamnov .60 1.50
12 Mikael Renberg .60 1.50
13 Jaromir Jagr 2.00 5.00
14 Peter Bondra 1.25 3.00
15 Peter Forsberg 3.00 8.00
16 John LeClair 1.25 3.00
17 Joe Sakic 2.50 6.00
18 Brendan Shanahan 1.25 3.00
19 Teemu Selanne 1.25 3.00
20 Pierre Turgeon .60 1.50

1995-96 Pinnacle FANtasy

This 30-card set was distributed as a promotional item at the 1996 All-Star FanFest in Boston and features players from that game as well as four extra Boston Bruins. The cards were available in 2-card packs, free for the asking. Pinnacle later handed out remaining packs at several large sports card conventions in Canada and the U.S. Card #31 features Bobby Orr and injured collegiate player Travis Roy. This tribute card was short printed, and the set is considered complete without it.

COMPLETE SET (30) 18.00 45.00
1 Cam Neely .40 1.00
2 Ray Bourque 1.20 3.00
3 Alexandre Daigle .10 .25
4 Mariusz Czerkawski .10 .25
5 Adam Oates .40 1.00
6 Brendan Shanahan .80 2.00
7 Arturs Irbe .40 1.00
8 Mario Lemieux 3.20 8.00
9 Theo Fleury .40 1.00
10 Patrick Roy 3.20 8.00
11 Roman Hamrlik .20 .50
12 Pavel Bure 1.20 3.00
13 Wayne Gretzky 4.00 10.00
14 Mike Modano .80 2.00
15 Teemu Selanne .80 2.00
16 John Vanbiesbrouck .40 1.00
17 Dominik Hasek .80 2.00
18 Mark Messier .80 2.00
19 Martin Brodeur 1.20 3.00
20 Jim Carey .20 .50
21 Wendel Clark .20 .50
22 Jason Arnott .20 .50
23 Jeremy Roenick .60 1.50
24 Brett Hull .80 2.00
25 Peter Forsberg 1.20 3.00
26 Paul Kariya 2.00 5.00
27 Eric Lindros 1.20 3.00
28 Kevin Stevens .10 .25
29 Felix Potvin .40 1.00
30 Sergei Fedorov .80 2.00
31 Travis Roy 8.00 20.00
Bobby Orr SP

1996-97 Pinnacle

This 250-card set was distributed in 10-card packs with a suggested retail price of $2.49. The set featured color action player photos with player statistics and included a rookie subset plus three numerical checklist cards. Rookies of note include Ethan Moreau and Kevin Hodson.

COMPLETE SET (250) 10.00 20.00
1 Wayne Gretzky 1.25 3.00
2 Mark Messier .15 .40
3 Kevin Hatcher .02 .10
4 Scott Stevens .08 .25
5 Derek Plante .02 .10
6 Theo Fleury .02 .10
7 Brian Rolston .02 .10
8 Teppo Numminen .02 .10
9 Adam Graves .02 .10
10 Jason Dawe .02 .10
11 Sergei Nemchinov .02 .10
12 Jeff Brown .02 .10
13 Alexei Zhamnov .08 .25
14 Paul Coffey .15 .40
15 Kevin Miller .02 .10
16 Mike Vernon .08 .25
17 Brian Bradley .02 .10
18 Jeff Friesen .02 .10
19 Phil Housley .02 .10
20 Ray Whitney .02 .10
21 Sergei Fedorov .20 .50
22 Pierre Turgeon .08 .25
23 Rick Tocchet .08 .25
24 Uwe Krupp .02 .10
25 Steve Yzerman .75 2.00
26 Tom Chorske .02 .10
27 Pat LaFontaine .15 .40
28 Nicklas Lidstrom .15 .40
29 Ray Ferraro .02 .10
30 Brian Noonan .02 .10
31 Dino Ciccarelli .08 .25
32 Rob Niedermayer .08 .25
33 Stephane Richer .08 .25
34 Chris Chelios .15 .40
35 Mike Gartner .08 .25
36 German Titov .02 .10
37 Sean Burke .08 .25
38 Robert Svehla .02 .10
39 Dave Gagner .08 .25
40 Sergei Gonchar .02 .10
41 Bernie Nicholls .02 .10
42 Yanic Perreault .02 .10
43 Adam Deadmarsh .02 .10
44 Dale Hawerchuk .08 .25
45 Alexei Kovalev .02 .10
46 Esa Tikkanen .02 .10
47 Valeri Kamensky .08 .25
48 Craig Janney .08 .25
49 John LeClair .15 .40
50 Radek Bonk .02 .10
51 David Oliver .02 .10
52 Todd Harvey .02 .10
53 Steve Thomas .02 .10
54 Tony Amonte .08 .25
55 Mikael Renberg .08 .25
56 Brendan Shanahan .15 .40
57 Tom Fitzgerald .02 .10
58 Chris Pronger .08 .25
59 Donald Audette .02 .10
60 Nelson Emerson .02 .10
61 Joe Mullen .08 .25
62 Marty McInnis .02 .10
63 Martin Rucinsky .02 .10
64 Mark Recchi .08 .25
65 Vladimir Konstantinov .08 .25
66 Rick Tabaracci .08 .25
67 Marty McSorley .02 .10
68 Pat Verbeek .02 .10
69 Garry Galley .02 .10
70 Travis Green .08 .25
71 Chris Tancill .02 .10
72 Vincent Damphousse .02 .10
73 Benoit Hogue .02 .10
74 Igor Larionov .02 .10
75 Russ Courtnall .02 .10
76 Mike Hough .02 .10
77 Alexander Selivanov .02 .10
78 Peter Forsberg .40 1.00
79 Petr Klima .02 .10
80 Adam Creighton .02 .10
81 Dave Lowry .02 .10
82 Andrew Cassels .02 .10
83 Martin Gelinas .02 .10
84 Bob Probert .08 .25
85 Calle Johansson .02 .10
86 Mario Lemieux .75 2.00
87 Alexander Mogilny .08 .25
88 Guy Hebert .08 .25
89 Bill Ranford .08 .25
90 Kirk McLean .08 .25
91 Kenny Jonsson .02 .10
92 Martin Brodeur .40 1.00
93 Keith Jones .02 .10
94 Ed Belfour .15 .40
95 Tom Barrasso .08 .25
96 Felix Potvin .15 .40
97 Daren Puppa .08 .25
98 Jeremy Roenick .20 .50
99 Chris Osgood UER .08 .25
{Kevin Hodson pictured on back
100 Zigmund Palffy .08 .25
101 Ron Hextall .08 .25
102 Jaromir Jagr .25 .60
103 Chris Terreri .08 .25
104 Shayne Corson .02 .10
105 Jim Carey .15 .40
106 Dominik Hasek .30 .75
107 Eric Lindros .15 .40
108 Petr Nedved .08 .25
109 Peter Bondra .08 .25
110 Jeff Hackett .08 .25
111 Trevor Linden .08 .25
112 Mike Richter .15 .40
113 Claude Lemieux .02 .10
114 Keith Tkachuk .15 .40
115 Pat Falloon .02 .10
116 Brent Fedyk .02 .10
117 Todd Marchant .02 .10
118 Jason Arnott .02 .10
119 Zarley Zalapski .02 .10
120 Kelly Hrudey .08 .25
121 Alexei Yashin .02 .10
122 Sergei Zubov .02 .10
123 Rod Brind'Amour .08 .25
124 Mathieu Schneider .02 .10
125 Bryan Smolinski .02 .10
126 Scott Mellanby .08 .25
127 Doug Gilmour .08 .25
128 Brett Hull .20 .50
129 Vyacheslav Kozlov .02 .10
130 Adam Oates .08 .25
131 Steve Konowalchuk .02 .10
132 Robert Kron .02 .10
133 Alexandre Daigle .02 .10
134 Brian Savage .02 .10
135 Stu Barnes .02 .10
136 Cam Neely .15 .40
137 Steve Rucchin .02 .10
138 Patrick Roy .75 2.00
139 Roman Oksiuta .02 .10
140 Greg Johnson .02 .10
141 Chris Gratton .08 .25
142 Jocelyn Thibault .15 .40
143 Ron Francis .08 .25
144 Mats Sundin .15 .40
145 Oleg Tverdovsky .08 .25
146 Geoff Courtnall .02 .10
147 Kirk Muller .02 .10
148 Zdeno Ciger .02 .10
149 John MacLean .08 .25
150 Damian Rhodes .08 .25
151 Michael Nylander .02 .10
152 Andrei Kovalenko .02 .10
153 Al MacInnis .08 .25
154 Mike Modano .25 .60
155 Teemu Selanne .15 .40
156 Tomas Sandstrom .02 .10
157 Bobby Dollas .02 .10
158 Doug Weight .08 .25
159 Sandis Ozolinsh .02 .10
160 Joe Juneau .02 .10
161 Nikolai Khabibulin .08 .25
162 Murray Craven .02 .10
163 Cliff Ronning .02 .10
164 Curtis Joseph .15 .40
165 Darren Turcotte .02 .10
166 Andy Moog .08 .25
167 Mariusz Czerkawski .02 .10
168 Keith Primeau .02 .10

169 Eric Desjardins .08 .25
170 Bill Guerin .02 .10
171 Glenn Anderson .08 .25
172 Mike Ridley .02 .10
173 Michal Pivonka .02 .10
174 Trevor Kidd .08 .25
175 Pavel Bure .15 .40
176 Todd Gill .02 .10
177 Dave Andreychuk .08 .25
178 Roman Hamrlik .08 .25
179 Andrei Nikolishin .02 .10
180 Alexei Zhitnik .02 .10
181 Grant Fuhr .08 .25
182 Dave Reid .02 .10
183 Joe Nieuwendyk .08 .25
184 Paul Kariya .15 .40
185 Jyrki Lumme .02 .10
186 Owen Nolan .08 .25
187 Geoff Sanderson .08 .25
188 Alexander Semak .02 .10
189 Larry Murphy .08 .25
190 Dimitri Khristich .02 .10
191 Shane Churla .02 .10
192 Bill Lindsay .02 .10
193 Brian Leetch .15 .40
194 Greg Adams .02 .10
195 Gary Suter .02 .10
196 Wendel Clark .08 .25
197 Scott Young .02 .10
198 Randy Burridge .02 .10
199 Ray Bourque .25 .60
200 Joe Murphy .02 .10
201 Joe Sakic .30 .75
202 Saku Koivu .15 .40
203 John Vanbiesbrouck .08 .25
204 Ed Jovanovski .08 .25
205 Daniel Alfredsson .08 .25
206 Vitali Yachmenev .02 .10
207 Marcus Ragnarsson .02 .10
208 Todd Bertuzzi .15 .40
209 Valeri Bure .02 .10
210 Jeff O'Neill .02 .10
211 Corey Hirsch .08 .25
212 Eric Daze .08 .25
213 David Sacco .02 .10
214 Jan Vopat .02 .10
215 Scott Bailey .02 .10
216 Jamie Rivers .02 .10
217 Jose Theodore .20 .50
218 Peter Ferraro .02 .10
219 Anders Eriksson .02 .10
220 Wayne Primeau .02 .10
221 Denis Pederson .02 .10
222 Jay McKee RC .02 .10
223 Sean Pronger .02 .10
224 Martin Biron RC 1.25 3.00
225 Marek Malik .02 .10
226 Steve Sullivan RC .20 .50
227 Curtis Brown .02 .10
228 Eric Fichaud .08 .25
229 Jan Caloun RC .02 .10
230 Niklas Sundblad .02 .10
231 Steve Staios RC .02 .10
232 Steve Washburn RC .02 .10
233 Chris Ferraro .02 .10
234 Marko Kiprusoff .02 .10
235 Larry Courville .02 .10
236 David Nemirovsky .02 .10
237 Ralph Intranuovo .02 .10
238 Kevin Hodson RC .15 .40
239 Ethan Moreau RC .15 .40
240 Daymond Langkow .08 .25
241 Brandon Convery .02 .10
242 Cale Hulse .02 .10
243 Zdenek Nedved .02 .10
244 Tommy Salo .08 .25
245 Nolan Baumgartner .02 .10
246 Patrick Labrecque RC .02 .10
247 Jamie Langenbrunner .02 .10
248 Pavel Bure CL (1-126) .15 .40
249 Peter Forsberg CL (127-250) .15 .40
250 Teemu Selanne CL (inserts) .15 .40

1996-97 Pinnacle Artist's Proofs

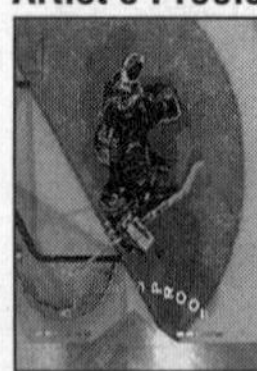

Randomly inserted in packs at a rate of 1:47 hobby packs and 1:67 magazine packs, this 250-card parallel set was distinguishable from the regular set by the inclusion of a special holographic foil-stamped Artist's Proof logo.
*STARS: 12X TO 30X BASIC CARDS
*ROOKIES: 4X TO 10X

1996-97 Pinnacle Foil

Randomly inserted in retail packs, this set parallels the base set with special foil highlights.
*STARS: 1X to 1.25X BASIC CARDS
*ROOKIES: .25X to .5X BASIC CARDS

1996-97 Pinnacle Premium Stock

This set parallels the base Pinnacle issue of that season, but unlike most parallels, this was a stand-alone brand, rather than an insert. As the name suggests, the cards were printed on thicker paper than the base brand and utilized additional foil to distinguish them from the other parallels from that season.
*STARS: 1.5X TO 3X BASIC CARDS
*ROOKIES: .5X to 1X BASIC CARDS

1996-97 Pinnacle Rink Collection

Randomly inserted in packs at a rate of 1:7, this 250-card parallel set was distinguished from the regular set through the use of the all-foil Dufex print technology. A Rink Collection logo is also found on the back of each card.
*STARS: 4X TO 10X BASIC CARDS
*ROOKIES: 2X TO 5X BASIC CARDS

1996-97 Pinnacle By The Numbers

Randomly inserted in packs at a rate of 1:23, this 15-card, die-cut set honored the league's top statistical standouts. The etched metal, Dufex insert pictured the player with a likeness of his jersey serving as the background. The backs carried the reason for his selection to this insert set. The three confirmed promos were not die-cut like the rest of the set. This design mirrored that which would later be used in the Premium Stock parallel version of this issue inserted at a rate of 1:8 premium stock packs. They are notable for the word PROMO written on the back. These three are all that have been confirmed so far, but it is believed others may exist as well. If you can confirm, please contact us with scan at hockeymag@beckett.com
COMPLETE SET (15) 25.00 50.00
*PRM.STOCK: 1.25X TO 2.5X BASIC INSERTS
1 Teemu Selanne 1.50 4.00
2 Brendan Shanahan 1.50 4.00
3 Sergei Fedorov 2.00 5.00
4 Ed Jovanovski 1.00 2.50
5 Doug Weight 1.00 2.50
6 Brett Hull 2.00 5.00
7 Doug Gilmour 1.00 2.50
8 Jaromir Jagr 2.50 6.00
9 Wayne Gretzky 12.50 30.00
10 Daniel Alfredsson 1.00 2.50
11 Eric Daze 1.00 2.50
12 Mark Messier 1.50 4.00
13 Jocelyn Thibault 1.50 4.00
14 Eric Lindros 1.50 4.00
15 Pavel Bure 1.50 4.00
P1 Teemu Selanne PROMO 1.50 4.00
P11 Eric Daze PROMO
P16 Brett Hull PROMO 2.00 5.00

1996-97 Pinnacle Masks

Randomly inserted in packs at a rate of 1:90, this 10-card set spotlighted the most colorful protective headgear worn in the NHL. A die-cut parallel was also created and inserted at a rate of 1:300 hobby packs.
COMPLETE SET (10) 60.00 125.00
*DIE CUTS: .75X TO 1.5X BASIC INSERTS
1 Patrick Roy 20.00 50.00
2 Jim Carey 4.00 10.00
3 John Vanbiesbrouck 6.00 15.00
4 Martin Brodeur 12.00 30.00
5 Jocelyn Thibault 4.00 10.00
6 Ron Hextall 6.00 15.00
7 Nikolai Khabibulin 6.00 15.00
8 Stephane Fiset 4.00 10.00
9 Mike Richter 6.00 15.00
10 Kelly Hrudey 4.00 10.00

1996-97 Pinnacle Team Pinnacle

Randomly inserted in packs at a rate of 1:90 hobby packs and 1:127 magazine packs, this 10-card set featured a double-front card design which showcased top players by position from both the Eastern and Western Conferences, back to back. One player from each conference was displayed on opposite sides of the cards, with one side also being enhanced with Dufex technology. Although a small premium might be attached to the card depending upon which side was Dufexed, this premium was not universally applied.
1 Wayne Gretzky 8.00 20.00
Joe Sakic
2 M.Lemieux/P.Forsberg 6.00 15.00
3 Eric Lindros 4.00 10.00
Jeremy Roenick
4 Mark Messier 4.00 10.00
Doug Weight
5 Brendan Shanahan 4.00 10.00
Paul Kariya
6 Jaromir Jagr 5.00 12.00
Brett Hull
7 Ed Jovanovski 4.00 10.00
Paul Coffey
8 John Vanbiesbrouck 6.00 15.00
Patrick Roy
9 Martin Brodeur 5.00 12.00
Chris Osgood
10 Saku Koivu 4.00 10.00
Eric Daze

1996-97 Pinnacle Trophies

Randomly inserted only in prepriced magazine packs at a rate of 1:33, this 10-card set featured NHL trophies with the previous season's winners on the card backs. Card fronts were printed with Dufex technology and featured the trophy itself. The card backs featured the recipients.
1 Mario Lemieux 15.00 40.00
2 Paul Kariya 4.00 10.00
3 Sergei Fedorov 4.00 10.00
4 Daniel Alfredsson 2.00 5.00
5 Jim Carey 1.00 2.50
6 Chris Osgood 4.00 10.00
Mike Vernon
7 Kris King 1.00 2.50
8 Chris Chelios 2.00 5.00
9 Joe Sakic 8.00 20.00
10 Colorado Avalanche 4.00 10.00

1997 Pinnacle Lemieux 600 Goals Commemorative

1 Mario Lemieux

1997-98 Pinnacle

The 1997-98 Pinnacle set was issued in one series totaling 200 cards and was distributed in packs and collectible Mask tins. The fronts feature color action player photos. The backs carry player information.
COMPLETE SET (200) 12.50 25.00
1 Espen Knutsen RC .20 .50
2 Juha Lind RC .02 .10
3 Erik Rasmussen .02 .10
4 Olli Jokinen RC .75 2.00
5 Chris Phillips .02 .10
6 Alexei Morozov .10 .30
7 Chris Dingman RC .02 .10
8 Mattias Ohlund .10 .30
9 Sergei Samsonov .10 .30
10 Daniel Cleary .10 .30
11 Terry Ryan .02 .10
12 Patrick Marleau .25 .60
13 Boyd Devereaux .02 .10
14 Donald MacLean .02 .10
15 Marc Savard .10 .30
16 Magnus Arvedson .02 .10
17 Marian Hossa RC 1.25 3.00
18 Alyn McCauley .10 .30
19 Vaclav Prospal RC .15 .40
20 Brad Isbister .02 .10
21 Robert Dome RC .02 .10
22 Kevyn Adams .02 .10
23 Joe Thornton .40 1.00
24 Jan Bulis RC .02 .10
25 Jaroslav Svejkovsky .10 .30
26 Saku Koivu .15 .40
27 Mark Messier .15 .40
28 Dominik Hasek .30 .75
29 Patrick Roy .75 2.00
30 Jaromir Jagr .25 .60
31 Jarome Iginla .20 .50
32 Joe Sakic .30 .75
33 Jeremy Roenick .20 .50
34 Chris Osgood .20 .50
35 Brett Hull .20 .50
36 Mike Vernon .10 .30
37 John Vanbiesbrouck .10 .30
38 Ray Bourque .25 .60
39 Doug Gilmour .10 .30
40 Keith Tkachuk .15 .40
41 Pavel Bure .15 .40
42 Sean Burke .10 .30
43 Martin Brodeur .40 1.00
44 Damian Rhodes .10 .30
45 Geoff Sanderson .10 .30
46 Bill Ranford .10 .30
47 Kevin Hodson .10 .30
48 Eric Lindros .15 .40
49 Owen Nolan .10 .30
50 Mats Sundin .15 .40
51 Ed Belfour .15 .40
52 Stephane Fiset .10 .30
53 Paul Kariya .15 .40
54 Doug Weight .10 .30
55 Mike Richter .15 .40
56 Zigmund Palffy .10 .30
57 John LeClair .15 .40
58 Alexander Mogilny .10 .30
59 Tommy Salo .10 .30
60 Trevor Kidd .10 .30
61 Jason Arnott .02 .10
62 Adam Oates .10 .30
63 Garth Snow .10 .30
64 Rob Blake .10 .30
65 Chris Chelios .15 .40
66 Eric Fichaud .10 .30
67 Wayne Gretzky 1.00 2.50
68 Dino Ciccarelli .02 .10
69 Pat LaFontaine .15 .40
70 Andy Moog .10 .30
71 Steve Yzerman .75 2.00
72 Jeff Hackett .10 .30
73 Peter Forsberg .40 1.00
74 Arturs Irbe .10 .30
75 Pierre Turgeon .10 .30
76 Tom Barrasso .10 .30
77 Sergei Fedorov .25 .60
78 Ron Francis .10 .30
79 Mike Dunham .10 .30
80 Brendan Shanahan .15 .40
81 Grant Fuhr .10 .30
82 Jamie Storr .10 .30
83 Jim Carey .10 .30
84 Daren Puppa .10 .30
85 Vincent Damphousse .02 .10
86 Teemu Selanne .15 .40
87 Dwayne Roloson .10 .30
88 Kirk McLean .10 .30
89 Olaf Kolzig .10 .30
90 Guy Hebert .10 .30
91 Mike Modano .25 .60
92 Brian Leetch .15 .40
93 Curtis Joseph .15 .40
94 Nikolai Khabibulin .10 .30
95 Felix Potvin .15 .40
96 Ken Wregget .10 .30
97 Steve Shields RC .25 .60
98 Jocelyn Thibault .10 .30
99 Ron Tugnutt .10 .30
100 Ron Hextall .10 .30
101 Mike Peca .02 .10
102 Donald Audette .02 .10
103 Theo Fleury .02 .10
104 Mark Recchi .10 .30
105 Dainius Zubrus .15 .40
106 Trevor Linden .10 .30
107 Joe Juneau .10 .30
108 Matthew Barnaby .02 .10
109 Keith Primeau .02 .10
110 Joe Nieuwendyk .10 .30
111 Rod Brind'Amour .10 .30
112 Daymond Langkow .02 .10
113 Ed Jovanovski .10 .30
114 Adam Deadmarsh .02 .10
115 Scott Niedermayer .02 .10
116 Al MacInnis .10 .30
117 Slava Kozlov .02 .10
118 Jere Lehtinen .02 .10
119 Jeff Friesen .02 .10
120 Alexei Kovalev .02 .10
121 Eric Daze .10 .30
122 Mariusz Czerkawski .02 .10
123 Alexei Zhamnov .02 .10
124 Petr Nedved .10 .30
125 Dmitri Mironov .02 .10
126 Alexei Yashin .02 .10
127 Todd Marchant .02 .10
128 Sandis Ozolinsh .02 .10
129 Igor Larionov .02 .10
130 Jim Campbell .02 .10
131 Dave Andreychuk .02 .10
132 Glen Wesley .02 .10
133 Rem Murray .02 .10
134 Steve Sullivan .02 .10
135 Miroslav Satan .02 .10
136 Bill Guerin .10 .30
137 Mike Gartner .10 .30
138 Jozef Stumpel .10 .30
139 Darryl Sydor .02 .10
140 Darcy Tucker .02 .10
141 Robert Svehla .02 .10
142 Steve Duchesne .02 .10
143 Kevin Stevens .02 .10
144 Mikael Renberg .10 .30
145 Bryan Berard .10 .30
146 Ray Ferraro .02 .10
147 Jason Allison .02 .10
148 Tony Amonte .10 .30
149 Luc Robitaille .10 .30
150 Mathieu Schneider .02 .10
151 Steve Rucchin .02 .10
152 Brian Savage .02 .10
153 Paul Coffey .15 .40
154 Jeff O'Neill .02 .10
155 Daniel Alfredsson .10 .30
156 Dave Gagner .02 .10
157 Rob Niedermayer .02 .10
158 Scott Stevens .10 .30
159 Alexandre Daigle .02 .10
160 Stephane Richer .02 .10
161 Harry York .02 .10
162 Sergei Berezin .02 .10
163 Claude Lemieux .02 .10
164 Ray Sheppard .02 .10
165 Bernie Nicholls .02 .10
166 Oleg Tverdovsky .02 .10
167 Travis Green .02 .10
168 Martin Gelinas .02 .10
169 Derek Plante .02 .10
170 Gary Roberts .02 .10
171 Kevin Hatcher .02 .10
172 Martin Rucinsky .02 .10
173 Pat Verbeek .02 .10
174 Adam Graves .02 .10
175 Roman Hamrlik .02 .10
176 Darren McCarty .02 .10
177 Mike Grier .02 .10
178 Andrew Cassels .02 .10
179 Dimitri Khristich .02 .10
180 Tomas Sandstrom .02 .10
181 Peter Bondra .10 .30
182 Derian Hatcher .02 .10
183 Chris Gratton .10 .30
184 John MacLean .02 .10
185 Wendel Clark .10 .30
186 Valeri Kamensky .10 .30
187 Tony Granato .02 .10
188 Vladimir Vorobiev RC .02 .10
189 Ethan Moreau .02 .10
190 Kirk Muller .02 .10
191 Peter Forsberg SM .15 .40
192 Wayne Gretzky SM .15 .40
193 Jaromir Jagr SM .10 .30
194 Mark Messier SM .15 .40
195 Brian Leetch SM .15 .40
196 John LeClair SM .10 .30
197 Jeremy Roenick SM .10 .30
198 Checklist .02 .10
199 Checklist .02 .10
200 Checklist .02 .10
NNO Paul Kariya 3x5 PROMO .15 .40
NNO J.Vanbiesbrouck 3x5 PROMO .15 .40

1997-98 Pinnacle Artist's Proofs

Randomly inserted in packs at the rate of 1:39 and in tins at the rate of one in 13, this 100-card set is a partial parallel version of the base set. The fronts display the "Artist's Proof" seal.
*STARS: 20X TO 50X BASIC CARDS
*ROOKIES: 4X TO 10X BASIC CARDS

1997-98 Pinnacle Rink Collection

Randomly inserted in packs at the rate of 1:7, this 100-card set is a partial parallel version of the 1997-98 Pinnacle base set printed using Dufex Technology.
*STARS: 4X TO 10X BASIC CARDS
*ROOKIES: 2X TO 5X

1997-98 Pinnacle Epix Game Orange

This 24-card set was inserted in various Pinnacle products at the following odds: Certified 1:15; Score 1:121; Pinnacle 1:21 and Zenith 1:11. The set was printed in progressively-scarce three color versions: orange, purple, and emerald and prices for those parallels can be found by using the multipliers below.
CARDS 1-6 FOUND IN SCORE PACKS
CARDS 7-12 FOUND IN PIN.CERT.PACKS
CARDS 13-18 FOUND IN ZENITH PACKS
CARDS 19-24 FOUND IN PINNACLE PACKS
ONLY ORANGE CARDS LISTED BELOW
*PURPLE: .75X TO 1.5X BASIC INSERTS
*EMERALD: 1.5X TO 3X BASIC INSERTS
1 Wayne Gretzky 8.00 20.00
2 John Vanbiesbrouck .75 2.00
3 Joe Sakic 2.00 5.00
4 Alexei Yashin .75 2.00
5 Sergei Fedorov 1.50 4.00
6 Keith Tkachuk .75 2.00
7 Patrick Roy 6.00 15.00
8 Martin Brodeur 3.00 8.00
9 Steve Yzerman 6.00 15.00
10 Saku Koivu .75 2.00
11 Felix Potvin .75 2.00
12 Mark Messier 1.25 3.00
13 Eric Lindros 1.25 3.00
14 Peter Forsberg 2.50 6.00
15 Teemu Selanne 1.25 3.00
16 Brendan Shanahan 1.25 3.00
17 Curtis Joseph 1.25 3.00
18 Brett Hull 1.50 4.00
19 Paul Kariya 1.25 3.00
20 Jaromir Jagr 2.00 5.00
21 Pavel Bure 1.25 3.00
22 Dominik Hasek 2.00 5.00
23 John LeClair .75 2.00
24 Doug Gilmour .75 2.00

1997-98 Pinnacle Epix Moment Orange

This 24-card set was inserted in various Pinnacle products at the following odds: Certified 1:15; Score 1:121; Pinnacle 1:21 and Zenith 1:11. The set was printed in progressively-scarce three color versions: orange, purple, and emerald and prices for those parallels can be found by using the multipliers below.
CARDS 1-6 FOUND IN ZENITH PACKS
CARDS 7-12 FOUND IN PINNACLE PACKS
CARDS 13-18 FOUND IN SCORE PACKS
CARDS 19-24 FOUND IN PIN.CERT.PACKS
ONLY ORANGE CARDS LISTED BELOW
*PURPLE: .75X TO 1.5X BASIC INSERTS
*EMERALD: 1.5X TO 3X BASIC INSERTS
PURPLE STATED ODDS 1:19
LESS THAN 30 MOMENT EMERALD EXIST
1 Wayne Gretzky 20.00 50.00
2 John Vanbiesbrouck 2.00 5.00
3 Joe Sakic 6.00 15.00
4 Alexei Yashin 2.00 5.00
5 Sergei Fedorov 4.00 10.00
6 Keith Tkachuk 2.00 5.00
7 Patrick Roy 15.00 40.00
8 Martin Brodeur 10.00 25.00
9 Steve Yzerman 15.00 40.00
10 Saku Koivu 3.00 8.00
11 Felix Potvin 3.00 8.00
12 Mark Messier 3.00 8.00
13 Eric Lindros 3.00 8.00
14 Peter Forsberg 8.00 20.00
15 Teemu Selanne 3.00 8.00
16 Brendan Shanahan 3.00 8.00
17 Curtis Joseph 3.00 8.00
18 Brett Hull 4.00 10.00
19 Paul Kariya 3.00 8.00
20 Jaromir Jagr 5.00 12.00
21 Pavel Bure 3.00 8.00
22 Dominik Hasek 6.00 15.00
23 John LeClair 2.00 5.00
24 Doug Gilmour 2.00 5.00

1997-98 Pinnacle Epix Play Orange

This 24-card set was inserted in various Pinnacle products at the following odds: Certified 1:15; Score 1:121; Pinnacle 1:21 and Zenith 1:11. The set was printed in progressively-scarce three color versions: orange, purple, and emerald and prices for those parallels can be found by using the multipliers below.
CARDS 1-6 FOUND IN PIN.CERT.PACKS
CARDS 7-12 FOUND IN ZENITH PACKS
CARDS 13-18 FOUND IN PINNACLE PACKS
CARDS 19-24 FOUND IN SCORE PACKS
*PURPLE: .75X TO 1.5X BASIC INSERTS
*EMERALD: 1.5X TO 3X BASIC INSERTS
PURPLE/EMERALD OVERALL ODDS 1:19
1 Wayne Gretzky 8.00 20.00
2 John Vanbiesbrouck .60 1.50
3 Joe Sakic 1.50 4.00
4 Alexei Yashin .60 1.50
5 Sergei Fedorov 1.25 3.00
6 Keith Tkachuk .75 2.00
7 Patrick Roy 4.00 10.00
8 Martin Brodeur 2.00 5.00
9 Steve Yzerman 4.00 10.00
10 Saku Koivu .75 2.00
11 Felix Potvin .75 2.00
12 Mark Messier .75 2.00
13 Eric Lindros .75 2.00
14 Peter Forsberg 2.00 5.00
15 Teemu Selanne .75 2.00
16 Brendan Shanahan .75 2.00
17 Curtis Joseph .75 2.00
18 Brett Hull 1.00 2.50
19 Paul Kariya .75 2.00
20 Jaromir Jagr 1.25 3.00
21 Pavel Bure .75 2.00
22 Dominik Hasek 1.50 4.00
23 John LeClair .75 2.00
24 Doug Gilmour .60 1.50

1997-98 Pinnacle Epix Season Orange

This 24-card set was inserted in various Pinnacle products at the following odds: Certified 1:15; Score 1:121; Pinnacle 1:21 and Zenith 1:11. The set was printed in progressively-scarce three color versions: orange, purple, and emerald and prices for those parallels can be found by using the multipliers below.

CARDS 1-6 FOUND IN PINNACLE PACKS
CARDS 7-12 FOUND IN SCORE PACKS
CARDS 13-18 FOUND IN PIN.CERT.PACKS
CARDS 19-24 FOUND IN ZENITH PACKS
*PURPLE: .75X TO 1.5X BASIC INSERTS
*EMERALD: 1.5X TO 3X BASIC INSERTS
LESS THAN 50 SEASON EMERALD EXIST
1 Wayne Gretzky 12.00 30.00
2 John Vanbiesbrouck 1.50 4.00
3 Joe Sakic 5.00 12.00
4 Alexei Yashin 1.50 4.00
5 Sergei Fedorov 3.00 8.00
6 Keith Tkachuk 1.50 4.00
7 Patrick Roy 10.00 25.00
8 Martin Brodeur 8.00 15.00
9 Steve Yzerman 10.00 25.00
10 Saku Koivu 2.50 6.00
11 Felix Potvin 2.50 6.00
12 Mark Messier 2.50 6.00
13 Eric Lindros 2.50 6.00
14 Peter Forsberg 6.00 15.00
15 Teemu Selanne 2.50 6.00
16 Brendan Shanahan 2.50 6.00
17 Curtis Joseph 2.50 6.00
18 Brett Hull 3.00 8.00
19 Paul Kariya 2.50 6.00
20 Jaromir Jagr 4.00 10.00
21 Pavel Bure 3.00 8.00
22 Dominik Hasek 5.00 12.00
23 John LeClair 1.50 4.00
24 Doug Gilmour 1.50 4.00

1997-98 Pinnacle Masks

Randomly inserted in packs at the rate of 1:89 and in tins at the rate of 1:30, this ten-card set features color photos of masks worn by the NHL's elite goalies printed on Dufex technology. A die-cut parallel was also produced and inserted at a rate of 1:299 packs and 1:100 tins.
*DIE CUTS: .5X TO 1.25X BASIC INSERTS
1 John Vanbiesbrouck 4.00 10.00
2 Mike Richter 4.00 10.00
3 Martin Brodeur 10.00 25.00
4 Curtis Joseph 4.00 10.00
5 Patrick Roy 20.00 50.00
6 Guy Hebert 4.00 10.00
7 Jeff Hackett 4.00 10.00
8 Garth Snow 4.00 10.00
9 Nikolai Khabibulin 4.00 10.00
10 Grant Fuhr 4.00 10.00

1997-98 Pinnacle Masks Jumbos

These cards featured the same design as the Pinnacle Masks insert set and were issued one per large pack.
COMPLETE SET (10) 32.00 80.00
COMMON CARD (1-10) 4.00 10.00

1997-98 Pinnacle Masks Promos

Produced as promotional material, this set paralleled the basic cards except that they carry the word 'promo' on the back.
COMPLETE SET (10) 16.00 40.00
1 John Vanbiesbrouck 1.60 4.00
2 Mike Richter 1.60 4.00
3 Martin Brodeur 2.40 6.00
4 Curtis Joseph 2.40 6.00
5 Patrick Roy 3.20 8.00
6 Guy Hebert 1.20 3.00
7 Jeff Hackett 1.20 3.00
8 Garth Snow 1.20 3.00
9 Nikolai Khabibulin 1.20 3.00

1997-98 Pinnacle Team Pinnacle

Randomly inserted in packs at the rate of 1:99 and in tins at the rate of 1:33, this 10-card set features color action photos of the game's biggest stars as voted by Hockey fans and printed on double-sided cards with mirror-Mylar technology. A mirror parallel was also created and inserted randomly.

COMPLETE SET (10) 40.00 80.00
*MIRRORS: 3X TO 8X BASIC CARDS
WHITE/SILVER FRONT: SAME VALUE
1 M.Brodeur/P.Roy 8.00 20.00
2 Dominik Hasek 4.00 10.00
Curtis Joseph
3 Brian Leetch 5.00 12.00
Chris Chelios
4 Wayne Gretzky 8.00 20.00
Paul Kariya
5 Eric Lindros 5.00 12.00
Mark Messier
6 Jaromir Jagr 5.00 12.00
Keith Tkachuk
7 Saku Koivu 4.00 10.00
Peter Forsberg
8 John LeClair 2.50 6.00
Brendan Shanahan
9 Doug Gilmour 6.00 15.00
Steve Yzerman
10 John Vanbiesbrouck 5.00 12.00
Chris Osgood

1997-98 Pinnacle Tins

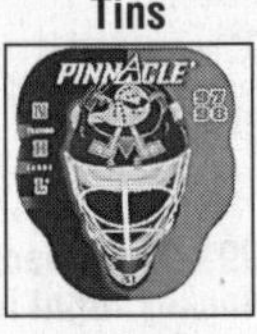

This set features photos of some of the most distinctive goalie masks in the game printed on collectible tins. Each tin contains 30 cards from the 1997-98 Pinnacle Hockey base set as well as insert sets. The tins are unnumbered and checklisted below in alphabetical order.

COMPLETE SET (10) 6.00 15.00
1 Martin Brodeur 1.25 3.00
2 Grant Fuhr .40 1.00
3 Jeff Hackett .40 1.00
4 Guy Hebert .40 1.00
5 Curtis Joseph .40 1.00
6 Nikolai Khabibulin .40 1.00
7 Mike Richter .50 1.25
8 Patrick Roy 2.00 5.00
9 Garth Snow .40 1.00
10 John Vanbiesbrouck .75 2.00

1997-98 Pinnacle Certified

The 1997-98 Pinnacle Certified set was issued in one series totaling 130 cards and was distributed in five-card hobby packs only with a suggested retail price of $4.99. The fronts feature borderless color action player photos. The backs carry player information.

COMPLETE SET (130) 20.00 40.00
1 Dominik Hasek .60 1.50
2 Patrick Roy 1.50 4.00
3 Martin Brodeur .75 2.00
4 Chris Osgood .20 .50
5 Andy Moog .20 .50
6 John Vanbiesbrouck .20 .50
7 Steve Shields RC .50 1.25
8 Mike Vernon .20 .50
9 Ed Belfour .30 .75
10 Grant Fuhr .20 .50
11 Felix Potvin .30 .75
12 Bill Ranford .20 .50
13 Mike Richter .30 .75
14 Stephane Fiset .20 .50
15 Jim Carey .20 .50
16 Nikolai Khabibulin .20 .50
17 Ken Wregget .20 .50
18 Curtis Joseph .30 .75
19 Guy Hebert .20 .50
20 Damian Rhodes .20 .50
21 Trevor Kidd .20 .50
22 Daren Puppa .20 .50
23 Patrick Lalime .20 .50
24 Tommy Salo .20 .50
25 Sean Burke .20 .50
26 Jocelyn Thibault .20 .50
27 Kirk McLean .20 .50
28 Garth Snow .20 .50
29 Ron Tugnutt .20 .50
30 Jeff Hackett .20 .50
31 Eric Lindros .30 .75
32 Peter Forsberg .75 2.00
33 Mike Modano .50 1.25
34 Paul Kariya .30 .75
35 Jaromir Jagr .50 1.25
36 Brian Leetch .30 .75
37 Keith Tkachuk .30 .75
38 Steve Yzerman 1.50 4.00
39 Teemu Selanne .30 .75
40 Bryan Berard .20 .50
41 Ray Bourque .50 1.25
42 Theo Fleury .07 .20
43 Mark Messier .30 .75
44 Saku Koivu .30 .75
45 Pavel Bure .30 .75
46 Peter Bondra .20 .50
47 Dave Gagner .07 .20
48 Ed Jovanovski .20 .50
49 Adam Oates .20 .50
50 Joe Sakic .60 1.50
51 Doug Gilmour .20 .50
52 Jim Campbell .07 .20
53 Mats Sundin .30 .75
54 Derian Hatcher .07 .20
55 Jarome Iginla .40 1.00
56 Sergei Fedorov .50 1.25
57 Keith Primeau .07 .20
58 Mark Recchi .20 .50
59 Owen Nolan .20 .50
60 Alexander Mogilny .20 .50
61 Brendan Shanahan .30 .75
62 Pierre Turgeon .20 .50
63 Joe Juneau .20 .50
64 Steve Rucchin .07 .20
65 Jeremy Roenick .40 1.00
66 Doug Weight .20 .50
67 Valeri Kamensky .20 .50
68 Tony Amonte .20 .50
69 Dave Andreychuk .07 .20
70 Brett Hull .40 1.00
71 Wendel Clark .20 .50
72 Vincent Damphousse .07 .20
73 Mike Grier .07 .20
74 Chris Chelios .30 .75
75 Nicklas Lidstrom .30 .75
76 Joe Nieuwendyk .20 .50
77 Rob Blake .20 .50
78 Alexei Yashin .07 .20
79 Ryan Smyth .20 .50
80 Pat LaFontaine .30 .75
81 Jeff Friesen .07 .20
82 Ray Ferraro .07 .20
83 Steve Sullivan .07 .20
84 Chris Gratton .20 .50
85 Mike Gartner .20 .50
86 Kevin Hatcher .07 .20
87 Ted Donato .07 .20
88 German Titov .07 .20
89 Sandis Ozolinsh .07 .20
90 Ray Sheppard .07 .20
91 John MacLean .07 .20
92 Luc Robitaille .20 .50
93 Rod Brind'Amour .20 .50
94 Zigmund Palffy .20 .50
95 Petr Nedved .20 .50
96 Adam Graves .07 .20
97 Jozef Stumpel .20 .50
98 Alexandre Daigle .07 .20
99 Mike Peca .07 .20
100 Wayne Gretzky 2.00 5.00
101 Alexei Zhamnov .07 .20
102 Paul Coffey .30 .75
103 Oleg Tverdovsky .07 .20
104 Trevor Linden .20 .50
105 Dino Ciccarelli .07 .20
106 Andrei Kovalenko .07 .20
107 Scott Mellanby .07 .20
108 Bryan Smolinski .07 .20
109 Bernie Nicholls .07 .20
110 Derek Plante .07 .20
111 Pat Verbeek .07 .20
112 Adam Deadmarsh .07 .20
113 Martin Gelinas .07 .20
114 Daniel Alfredsson .20 .50
115 Scott Stevens .20 .50
116 Dainius Zubrus .30 .75
117 Kirk Muller .07 .20
118 Brian Holzinger .07 .20
119 John LeClair .30 .75
120 Al MacInnis .20 .50
121 Ron Francis .20 .50
122 Eric Daze .20 .50
123 Travis Green .07 .20
124 Jason Arnott .07 .20
125 Geoff Sanderson .20 .50
126 Dimitri Khristich .07 .20
127 Sergei Berezin .07 .20
128 Jeff O'Neill .07 .20
129 Claude Lemieux .07 .20
130 Andrew Cassels .07 .20

1997-98 Pinnacle Certified Red

Randomly inserted in packs at the rate of 1:5, this 130-card set is parallel to the Pinnacle Certified base set and is distinguished by the red treatment of the mirror Mylar regular cards.
*STARS: 1.25X TO 3X BASIC CARDS

1997-98 Pinnacle Certified Mirror Blue

Randomly inserted in packs at the rate of 1:199, this 130-card set is parallel to the Pinnacle Certified base set. The difference is found in the blue-design element on holographic foil.
*STARS: 10X TO 25X BASIC CARDS

1997-98 Pinnacle Certified Mirror Gold

Randomly inserted in packs at the rate of 1:299, this 130-card set is parallel to the Pinnacle Certified base set. The difference is found in the golden holographic mirror Mylar highlights of the set.
*STARS: 20X TO 50X BASIC CARDS
100 Wayne Gretzky 75.00 150.00

1997-98 Pinnacle Certified Mirror Red

Randomly inserted in packs at the rate of 1:99, this 130-card set is parallel to the Pinnacle Certified base set. The difference is found in the holographic red foil design of the set.
*STARS: 4X TO 10X BASIC CARDS

1997-98 Pinnacle Certified Team

Randomly inserted in packs at the rate of 1:19, this 20-card set features color action photos of 10 Eastern Conference megastars matched with 10 Western Conference superstar counterparts and printed on mirror Mylar all-foil card stock. A gold parallel was also created and randomly inserted at a rate of 1:129. These parallels are distinctive because of the added gold accents and foil stamping. Only 300 of this set were produced and are sequentially numbered.

COMPLETE SET (20) 75.00 150.00
*GOLD TEAM: 2.5X TO 5X BASIC INSERTS
1 Martin Brodeur 5.00 12.00
2 Patrick Roy 10.00 25.00
3 John Vanbiesbrouck 1.25 3.00
4 Dominik Hasek 4.00 10.00
5 Chris Chelios 2.00 5.00
6 Brian Leetch 2.00 5.00
7 Wayne Gretzky 12.50 30.00
8 Eric Lindros 2.00 5.00
9 Paul Kariya 2.00 5.00
10 Peter Forsberg 5.00 12.00
11 Keith Tkachuk 2.00 5.00
12 Mark Messier 2.00 5.00
13 Steve Yzerman 10.00 25.00
14 Jaromir Jagr 3.00 8.00
15 Mats Sundin 2.00 5.00
16 Teemu Selanne 2.00 5.00
17 Brendan Shanahan 2.00 5.00
18 Saku Koivu 2.00 5.00
19 Brett Hull 2.50 6.00
20 John LeClair 2.00 5.00

1997-98 Pinnacle Certified Gold Team Promo

Produced as promotional material, this set paralleled the basic cards except that they carry the word 'promo' on the back.

COMPLETE SET (20) 32.00 80.00
1 Martin Brodeur 2.40 6.00
2 Patrick Roy 5.00 12.50
3 John Vanbiesbrouck 1.00 2.50
4 Dominik Hasek 2.00 5.00
5 Chris Chelios 1.00 2.50
6 Brian Leetch 1.00 2.50
7 Wayne Gretzky 6.00 15.00
8 Eric Lindros 1.60 4.00
9 Paul Kariya 3.20 8.00
10 Peter Forsberg 2.40 6.00
11 Keith Tkachuk 1.00 2.50
12 Mark Messier 1.20 3.00
13 Steve Yzerman 4.00 10.00
14 Jaromir Jagr 2.40 6.00
15 Mats Sundin 1.00 2.50
16 Teemu Selanne 2.00 5.00
17 Brendan Shanahan 1.60 4.00
18 Saku Koivu 1.00 2.50
19 Brett Hull 1.20 3.00
20 John LeClair 1.20 3.00

1997-98 Pinnacle Certified Rookie Redemption

Randomly inserted in packs at the rate of 1:19, this 12-card set was obtained through the mail with the redemption card and features color action player photos printed on super-premium 24-point card stock with an exclusive authenticator bar to protect the set from counterfeiting. Gold and Mirror Gold versions of these cards were also available via redemption. Gold parallels were inserted at a rate of 1:259 and were limited to 250 sets.

COMPLETE SET (12) 25.00 50.00
*GOLDS: 2.5X TO 5X BASIC INSERTS
*MIRROR GOLDS: 10X TO 20X BASIC INS.
A Joe Thornton 5.00 12.00
B Chris Phillips 2.00 4.00
C Patrick Marleau 4.00 10.00
D Sergei Samsonov 2.00 4.00
E Daniel Cleary 2.00 4.00
F Olli Jokinen 2.00 4.00
G Alyn McCauley 2.00 4.00
H Alexei Morozov 2.00 4.00
I Brad Isbister 2.00 4.00
J Boyd Devereaux 2.00 4.00
K Espen Knutsen 2.00 4.00
L Marc Savard 2.00 4.00

1997-98 Pinnacle Certified Summit Silver

Randomly inserted in packs at the rate of 1:29, this five card set features color action renditions of Paul Henderson by artist Daniel Parry printed on mirror Mylar. The set commemorates Paul Henderson's winning goal at the 1972 Canada-Russia Summit Series. Only 1,000 of each card were produced.

COMMON CARD (1-5) 4.00 10.00
NNO Paul Henderson 40.00 100.00
Silver AU/200
NNO Paul Henderson 20.00 50.00
Black AU/700
NNO Paul Henderson 75.00 200.00
Gold AU/100

1996-97 Pinnacle Fantasy

This 20-card set was made available to attendees of the All-Star FanFest held in San Jose in January, 1997. The cards were distributed in three-card packs, and featured an action photo with a blue foil shark bite design along the top. A 21st card featuring Sharks netminder Kelly Hrudey was available through a redemption card which was randomly inserted in packs. The card had to be redeemed at a San Jose-area card shop. There were, in fact, two variations of the Hrudey card, the more difficult of which featured a refractor-like gloss. Collectors may also run across what appears to be a non-gloss parallel version of this set. The cards are smaller and are in playing card form, with black along the top and a uniform black back with a Pinnacle logo. These were used for a promotion at the show and were not licensed by the NHL or NHLPA. Therefore, these cards will not be listed in the annual.

FC1 Ray Bourque 1.00 2.50
FC2 Paul Coffey .40 1.00
FC3 Eric Lindros 1.60 4.00
FC4 Mario Lemieux 3.20 8.00
FC5 Wayne Gretzky 4.00 10.00
FC6 Mark Messier 1.00 2.50
FC7 Jaromir Jagr 1.60 4.00
FC8 Brendan Shanahan 1.60 4.00
FC9 John Vanbiesbrouck .60 1.50
FC10 Mike Richter .60 1.50
FC11 Chris Chelios .60 1.50
FC12 Nicklas Lidstrom .20 .50
FC13 Sergei Fedorov 1.60 4.00
FC14 Pavel Bure 1.60 4.00
FC15 Peter Forsberg 2.40 6.00
FC16 Brett Hull 1.00 2.50
FC17 Joe Sakic 1.60 4.00
FC18 Owen Nolan .40 1.00
FC19 Patrick Roy 3.20 8.00
FC20 Ed Belfour .60 1.50
NNO1 Kelly Hrudey 10.00 25.00
NNO2 Kelly Hrudey FOIL 14.00 35.00
NNO3 Kelly Hrudey Offer Card 4.00 10.00

1997-98 Pinnacle Inside

The 1997-98 Pinnacle Inside set was issued in one series totaling 190 cards and was distributed inside 24 different collectible player cans with ten cards to a can. The fronts feature color action player photos printed on 20 pt. card stock. The backs carry player information.

COMPLETE SET (190) 20.00 40.00
1 Brendan Shanahan .25 .60
2 Dominik Hasek .50 1.25
3 Wayne Gretzky 1.50 4.00
4 Eric Lindros .25 .60
5 Keith Tkachuk .25 .60
6 Jaromir Jagr .40 1.00
7 Martin Brodeur .60 1.50
8 Peter Forsberg .60 1.50
9 Chris Osgood .20 .50
10 Paul Kariya .25 .60
11 Pavel Bure .25 .60
12 Brett Hull .30 .75
13 Saku Koivu .25 .60
14 Zigmund Palffy .20 .50
15 Mike Modano .40 1.00
16 Ray Bourque .40 1.00
17 Jarome Iginla .30 .75
18 Chris Chelios .25 .60
19 John Vanbiesbrouck .20 .50
20 Brian Leetch .25 .60
21 Mats Sundin .25 .60
22 Ron Hextall .20 .50
23 Stephane Fiset .20 .50
24 Steve Yzerman 1.25 3.00
25 Curtis Joseph .25 .60
26 Daniel Alfredsson .25 .60
27 Owen Nolan .20 .50
28 Adam Oates .20 .50
29 Corey Hirsch .20 .50
30 Sean Burke .20 .50
31 Eric Fichaud .20 .50
32 Ken Wregget .20 .50
33 Dainius Zubrus .25 .60
34 Alexander Mogilny .20 .50
35 Bill Ranford .20 .50
36 Vincent Damphousse .08 .20
37 Patrick Roy 1.25 3.00
38 Teemu Selanne .25 .60
39 Pat LaFontaine .25 .60
40 Theo Fleury .08 .20
41 Jeff Hackett .20 .50
42 Sergei Fedorov .40 1.00
43 Jocelyn Thibault .20 .50
44 Nikolai Khabibulin .20 .50
45 Daren Puppa .20 .50
46 Felix Potvin .25 .60
47 Andy Moog .20 .50
48 Doug Weight .20 .50
49 Tommy Salo .20 .50
50 Mark Messier .25 .60
51 Grant Fuhr .20 .50
52 Ron Francis .20 .50
53 Tony Amonte .20 .50
54 Joe Sakic .50 1.25
55 Jason Arnott .08 .20
56 Jose Theodore .30 .75
57 Alexei Yashin .08 .20
58 John LeClair .25 .60
59 Jeremy Roenick .30 .75
60 Kirk McLean .20 .50
61 Arturs Irbe .20 .50
62 Jim Carey .20 .50
63 J-S Giguere .20 .50
64 Marc Denis .20 .50
65 Damian Rhodes .20 .50
66 Jim Campbell .08 .20
67 Patrick Lalime .20 .50
68 Garth Snow .20 .50
69 Marcel Cousineau .20 .50
70 Guy Hebert .20 .50
71 Rob Blake .20 .50
72 Tomas Vokoun RC .60 1.50
73 Doug Gilmour .20 .50
74 Ed Belfour .25 .60
75 Parris Duffus RC .08 .20
76 Mike Fountain .08 .20
77 Steve Shields RC .25 .60
78 Geoff Sanderson .20 .50
79 Roman Turek .20 .50
80 Bryan Berard .20 .50
81 Mike Richter .25 .60
82 Ron Tugnutt .20 .50
83 Peter Bondra .20 .50
84 Mike Vernon .20 .50
85 Mike Grier .08 .20
86 Ed Jovanovski .20 .50
87 Trevor Kidd .20 .50
88 Eric Daze .20 .50
89 Wendel Clark .20 .50
90 Checklist (1-190) .08 .20
91 Nicklas Lidstrom .25 .60
92 Rod Brind'Amour .20 .50
93 Hnat Domenichelli .08 .20
94 Rem Murray .08 .20
95 Scott Niedermayer .08 .20
96 Martin Rucinsky .08 .20
97 Mike Gartner .20 .50
98 Kevin Hatcher .08 .20
99 Daymond Langkow .08 .20
100 Jamie Langenbrunner .08 .20
101 Ted Donato .08 .20
102 Steve Sullivan .08 .20
103 Martin Gelinas .08 .20
104 Adam Graves .08 .20
105 Donald Audette .08 .20
106 Andrew Cassels .08 .20
107 Alexei Zhamnov .08 .20
108 Kirk Muller .08 .20
109 Alexandre Daigle .08 .20
110 Chris Gratton .20 .50
111 Andrew Brunette .08 .20
112 Mark Recchi .20 .50
113 Jari Kurri .20 .50
114 Valeri Kamensky .20 .50
115 Joe Nieuwendyk .20 .50
116 Slava Kozlov .08 .20
117 Steve Kelly .08 .20
118 Dave Andreychuk .08 .20
119 Mikael Renberg .20 .50
120 Sergei Berezin .08 .20
121 Jeff Friesen .08 .20
122 Pierre Turgeon .20 .50
123 Vladimir Vorobiev RC .08 .20
124 Dimitri Khristich .08 .20
125 Jaroslav Svejkovsky .20 .50
126 Vladimir Konstantinov .20 .50
127 Jozef Stumpel .20 .50
128 Mike Peca .08 .20
129 Jonas Hoglund .08 .20
130 Travis Green .08 .20
131 Bill Guerin .20 .50
132 Oleg Tverdovsky .08 .20
133 Petr Nedved .08 .20
134 Dino Ciccarelli .08 .20
135 Brian Savage .08 .20
136 Steve Duchesne .08 .20
137 Sandis Ozolinsh .08 .20
138 Derian Hatcher .08 .20
139 Ray Sheppard .08 .20
140 Brian Bellows .08 .20
141 Paul Brousseau .08 .20
142 Tony Granato .08 .20
143 Vaclav Prospal RC .25 .60
144 Vitali Yachmenev .08 .20
145 John MacLean .08 .20
146 Igor Larionov .08 .20
147 Jason Allison .08 .20
148 Derek Plante .08 .20
149 Jeff O'Neill .08 .20
150 Trevor Linden .20 .50
151 Joe Juneau .20 .50
152 Brandon Convery .08 .20
153 Kevin Stevens .08 .20
154 Scott Stevens .08 .20
155 Niklas Sundstrom .08 .20
156 Claude Lemieux .08 .20
157 Pat Verbeek .08 .20
158 Mariusz Czerkawski .08 .20
159 Robert Svehla .08 .20
160 Paul Coffey .25 .60
161 Al MacInnis .20 .50
162 Roman Hamrlik .20 .50
163 Brian Holzinger .08 .20
164 Cory Stillman .08 .20
165 Scott Mellanby .08 .20
166 Todd Warriner .08 .20
167 Terry Ryan .08 .20
168 Luc Robitaille .20 .50
169 Ed Olczyk .08 .20
170 Adam Deadmarsh .08 .20
171 Anson Carter .20 .50
172 Mike Knuble RC .08 .20
173 Cliff Ronning .08 .20
174 Rick Tocchet .20 .50
175 Chris Pronger .20 .50
176 Matthew Barnaby .08 .20
177 Andrei Kovalenko .08 .20
178 Bryan Smolinski .08 .20
179 Janne Niinimaa .20 .50
180 Ray Ferraro .08 .20
181 Dave Gagner .08 .20
182 Rob Niedermayer .08 .20
183 Vadim Sharifijanov .08 .20
184 Ethan Moreau .08 .20
185 Bernie Nicholls .08 .20
186 Jean-Yves Leroux RC .08 .20
187 Jere Lehtinen .08 .20
188 Steve Rucchin .08 .20
189 Keith Primeau .08 .20
190 Red Wings Stanley .20 .50
Cup Champs CL (inserts)

1997-98 Pinnacle Inside Coach's Collection

Randomly inserted in cans at the rate of 1:7, this 90-card set is a partial parallel version of the base set and highlights some of the NHL's top impact players. The cards are printed entirely on silver foil with bronze foil stamped accents.
*STARS: 3X TO 8X HI COLUMN
*ROOKIES: 2X TO 5X HI

1997-98 Pinnacle Inside Executive Collection

Randomly inserted in cans at the rate of 1:57, this 90-card set is a partial parallel version of the base set printed on full prismatic foil with foil stamped treatments and an external die-cut card design.
*STARS: 8X TO 20X BASIC CARDS
*ROOKIES: 5X TO 12X BASIC CARDS

1997-98 Pinnacle Inside Stand Up Guys

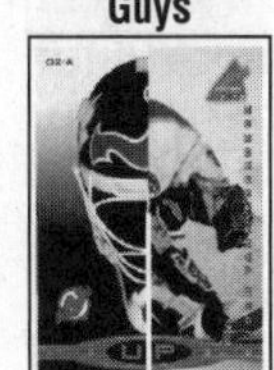

Inserted one per mask can, this 20-card set features color action photos of top goalies on one side with close-up photos of their masks on the flipsides.

1A/B Mike Vernon .60 1.50
Tom Barasso
1C/D M.Vernon/T.Barasso .60 1.50
2A/B John Vanbiesbrouck 2.00 5.00
Martin Brodeur
2C/D J.Vanbiesbrck/M.Brodeur 2.00 5.00
3A/B Jocelyn Thibault .60 1.50
Jim Carey
3C/D J.Thibault/J.Carey .60 1.50
4A/B Garth Snow .60 1.50
Marcel Cousineau
4C/D G.Snow/M.Cousineau .60 1.50
5A/B Patrick Roy 4.00 10.00
Eric Fichaud
5C/D P.Roy/E.Fichaud 4.00 10.00
6A/B Patrick Lalime .60 1.50
Grant Fuhr
6C/D P.Lalime/G.Fuhr .60 1.50
7A/B Olaf Kolzig .60 1.50
Jeff Hackett
7C/D O.Kolzig/J.Hackett .60 1.50
8A/B Trevor Kidd .60 1.50
Guy Hebert
8C/D T.Kidd/G.Hebert .60 1.50
9A/B Nikolai Khabibulin .60 1.50
Corey Hirsch
9C/D N.Khabibulin/C.Hirsch .60 1.50
10A/B Curtis Joseph .60 1.50
Kelly Hrudey
10C/D C.Joseph/K.Hrudey .60 1.50

1997-98 Pinnacle Inside Stand Up Guys Promos

Produced as promotional material, this set paralleled the basic cards except that they carry the word 'promo' on the back.

COMPLETE SET (20) 20.00 50.00
1A/B Mike Vernon .60 1.50
Tom Barasso
1C/D M.Vernon/T.Barasso .60 1.50
2A/B John Vanbiesbrouck 2.00 5.00
Martin Brodeur
2C/D J.Vanbiesbrck/M.Brodeur 2.00 5.00
3A/B Jocelyn Thibault .60 1.50
Jim Carey
3C/D J.Thibault/J.Carey .60 1.50
4A/B Garth Snow .60 1.50
Marcel Cousineau
4C/D G.Snow/M.Cousineau .60 1.50
5A/B Patrick Roy 4.00 10.00
Eric Fichaud
5C/D P.Roy/E.Fichaud 2.00 5.00
6A/B Patrick Lalime .60 1.50
Grant Fuhr
6C/D P.Lalime/G.Fuhr .60 1.50
7A/B Olaf Kolzig .60 1.50
Jeff Hackett
7C/D O.Kolzig/J.Hackett .60 1.50
8A/B Trevor Kidd .60 1.50
Guy Hebert
8C/D T.Kidd/G.Hebert .60 1.50
9A/B Nikolai Khabibulin .60 1.50
Corey Hirsch
9C/D N.Khabibulin/C.Hirsch .60 1.50
10A/B Curtis Joseph 1.00 2.50
Kelly Hrudey
10C/D C.Joseph/K.Hrudey 1.00 2.50

1997-98 Pinnacle Inside Stoppers

Randomly inserted in cans at the rate of 1:7, this 24-card set features color action photos of the NHL's top goal tenders printed on circular die-cut card stock in 3-D.

COMPLETE SET (24) 30.00 60.00
1 Patrick Roy 8.00 20.00
2 John Vanbiesbrouck 1.00 2.50
3 Dominik Hasek 3.00 8.00
4 Martin Brodeur 4.00 10.00
5 Mike Richter 1.50 4.00
6 Guy Hebert 1.00 2.50
7 Jim Carey 1.00 2.50
8 Jeff Hackett 1.00 2.50
9 Roman Turek 1.00 2.50
10 Kevin Hodson 1.00 2.50
11 Mike Vernon 1.00 2.50
12 Curtis Joseph 1.50 4.00
13 J-S Giguere 1.00 2.50
14 Jose Theodore 2.00 5.00
15 Jocelyn Thibault 1.00 2.50
16 Nikolai Khabibulin 1.00 2.50
17 Garth Snow 1.00 2.50
18 Ron Hextall 1.00 2.50
19 Steve Shields 1.00 2.50
20 Grant Fuhr 1.00 2.50
21 Felix Potvin 1.50 4.00
22 Marcel Cousineau 1.00 2.50
23 Bill Ranford 1.00 2.50
24 Ed Belfour 1.50 4.00

1997-98 Pinnacle Inside Track

Randomly inserted in cans at the rate of 1:19, this 30-card set features color action photos of some of the game's elite stars with information as to how they became the best players in the NHL.

COMPLETE SET (30) 75.00 200.00
1 Wayne Gretzky 15.00 40.00
2 Patrick Roy 10.00 25.00
3 Eric Lindros 3.00 8.00
4 Paul Kariya 3.00 8.00
5 Peter Forsberg 4.00 10.00
6 Martin Brodeur 6.00 15.00
7 John Vanbiesbrouck 2.00 5.00
8 Joe Sakic 5.00 12.00
9 Steve Yzerman 10.00 25.00
10 Jaromir Jagr 4.00 10.00
11 Teemu Selanne 3.00 8.00
12 Pavel Bure 3.00 8.00
13 Sergei Fedorov 3.00 8.00
14 Brendan Shanahan 3.00 8.00
15 Dominik Hasek 5.00 12.00
16 Saku Koivu 2.00 5.00
17 Jocelyn Thibault 1.00 2.50
18 Mark Messier 2.00 5.00
19 Brett Hull 4.00 10.00
20 Felix Potvin 3.00 8.00
21 Curtis Joseph 3.00 8.00

22 Zigmund Palffy 2.00 5.00
23 Mats Sundin 3.00 8.00
24 Keith Tkachuk 3.00 8.00
25 John LeClair 3.00 8.00
26 Mike Richter 3.00 8.00
27 Alexander Mogilny 2.00 5.00
28 Jarome Iginla 4.00 10.00
29 Mike Grier 1.00 2.50
30 Dainius Zubrus 1.00 2.50

1997-98 Pinnacle Inside Cans

This 24-can set features eight of the most distinctive goalie masks in the game and photos of 16 of the hottest superstars reproduced on the can labels and painted directly on the metal.

*GOLD CANS: 3X TO 6X BASIC CAN
1 Brendan Shanahan .15 .40
2 Jaromir Jagr .30 .75
3 Saku Koivu .15 .40
4 Mats Sundin .15 .40
5 Mike Vernon .20 .50
6 John LeClair .15 .40
7 Keith Tkachuk .15 .40
8 Joe Sakic .30 .75
9 Steve Yzerman .60 1.50
10 Eric Lindros .15 .40
11 Guy Hebert .20 .50
12 Patrick Roy .75 2.00
13 Pavel Bure .15 .40
14 Jocelyn Thibault .20 .50
15 Paul Kariya .40 1.00
16 Peter Forsberg .40 1.00
17 Martin Brodeur .40 1.00
18 Wayne Gretzky 1.00 2.50
19 Teemu Selanne .30 .75
20 John Vanbiesbrouck .20 .50
21 Mark Messier .15 .40
22 Mike Richter .15 .40
23 Brett Hull .20 .50
24 Curtis Joseph .15 .40

1997-98 Pinnacle Inside Promos

COMPLETE SET
1 Brendan Shanahan PROMO .40 1.00
7 Martin Brodeur/250 .75 2.00
8 Peter Forsberg PROMO .75 2.00
10 Paul Kariya/250 .75 2.00
70 Guy Hebert PROMO .40 1.00
84 Mike Vernon PROMO .40 1.00

1997 Pinnacle Mario's Moments

The Pinnacle Mario Lemieux "Moments" set was issued in one series totaling 18 cards. The set was a Pittsburgh area regional set and was sold over a period of six weeks in three-card packs at Giant Eagle grocery stores. A folder to hold the set, which pictured Lemieux, was available for 99 cents during the first week of the promotion. A gold parallel version of the set also can be found. These cards, issued at a rate of one per ten packs, featured gold foil lettering of Lemieux's name. Authentic autographed cards also were randomly inserted into packs. Reports from the manufacturer suggest approximately 700 of these were available.

COMPLETE SET (18) 10.00 25.00
COMMON CARD (1-18) .60 1.50
*GOLD: 2X to 5X BASIC CARDS
NNO Mario Lemieux AUTO 60.00 120.00

1996-97 Pinnacle Mint

The 1996-97 Pinnacle Mint set was issued in one series totaling 30 cards and was distributed in packs of three cards and two coins for a suggested retail price of $3.99. The challenge was to fit the coins with the die-cut cards that pictured the same player on the minted coin. The fronts feature color action player images on a sepia player portrait background with a cut-out area for the matching coin. Eric Lindros was featured on two promo cards, issued to dealers along with their ordering forms. The cards are identical to the regular die-cut and bronze cards except for the word "promo" written on the right hand side of the card back.

1 Mario Lemieux .75 2.00
2 Dominik Hasek .30 .75
3 Eric Lindros .50 1.00
4 Jaromir Jagr .50 1.25
5 Paul Kariya .60 1.50
6 Peter Forsberg .40 1.00
7 Pavel Bure .40 1.00
8 Sergei Fedorov .30 .75
9 Saku Koivu .25 .40
10 Daniel Alfredsson .15 .30
11 Joe Sakic .30 .75
12 Steve Yzerman .50 1.25
13 Teemu Selanne .30 .75
14 Brett Hull .20 .50
15 Jeremy Roenick .15 .40
16 Mark Messier .20 .50
17 Mats Sundin .15 .40
18 Brendan Shanahan .30 .60
19 Keith Tkachuk .20 .40
20 Paul Coffey .15 .40
21 Patrick Roy .75 2.00
22 Chris Chelios .15 .40
23 Martin Brodeur .40 1.00
24 Felix Potvin .20 .30
25 Chris Osgood .20 .40
26 John Vanbiesbrouck .25 .40
27 Jocelyn Thibault .20 .30
28 Jim Carey .20 .30
29 Jarome Iginla .20 .30
30 Jim Campbell .10 .30
P3A Eric Lindros Bronze Promo 1.20 3.00
P3B Eric Lindros Die-Cut Promo .40 1.00

1996-97 Pinnacle Mint Bronze

This 30-card version of the 1996-97 Pinnacle Mint set features color action player images on a sepia player portrait background with a bronze foil stamp instead of the die-cut area.

*BRONZE: 1X TO 2X BASIC CARDS

1996-97 Pinnacle Mint Gold

Randomly inserted in packs at a rate of 1:48 (and 1:72 magazine packs), this 30-card set parallels the regular issue version and is distinguished by the use of full Gold-foil Dufex print technologies.

*GOLD: 8X TO 20X BASIC CARDS

1996-97 Pinnacle Mint Silver

Randomly inserted in packs at a rate of 1:15 (and 1:23 magazine packs), this 30-card set is a parallel to the 1996-97 Pinnacle Mint set and features color action player images on a sepia player portrait background with a silver foil stamp instead of the die-cut area.

*SILVER: 4X TO10X BASIC CARDS

1996-97 Pinnacle Mint Coins Brass

This 30-coin set features embossed brass coins designed to be inserted into a die-cut card of the player who is pictured on the coin. Additional quantities of the Eric Lindros coin were mailed out to dealers with their order forms.

1 Mario Lemieux 2.50 4.00
2 Dominik Hasek 1.00 1.50
3 Eric Lindros 1.50 2.00
4 Jaromir Jagr 1.50 2.50
5 Paul Kariya 2.00 3.00
6 Peter Forsberg 1.25 2.00
7 Pavel Bure 1.25 2.00
8 Sergei Fedorov 1.00 1.50
9 Saku Koivu .75 .75
10 Daniel Alfredsson .50 .60
11 Joe Sakic 1.00 1.50
12 Steve Yzerman 1.50 2.50
13 Teemu Selanne 1.00 1.50
14 Brett Hull .60 1.00
15 Jeremy Roenick .50 .75
16 Mark Messier .60 1.00
17 Mats Sundin .50 .75
18 Brendan Shanahan 1.00 1.25
19 Keith Tkachuk .60 .75
20 Paul Coffey .50 .75
21 Patrick Roy 2.50 4.00
22 Chris Chelios .50 .75
23 Martin Brodeur 1.25 2.00
24 Felix Potvin .50 .75
25 Chris Osgood .60 .75
26 John Vanbiesbrouck .75 .75
27 Jocelyn Thibault .60 .60
28 Jim Carey .60 .60
29 Jarome Iginla .60 .60
30 Jim Campbell .40 .60

1996-97 Pinnacle Mint Coins Solid Gold

A 24kt. Gold redemption card was randomly inserted in packs at a rate of 1:29,959 and in magazine packs at a rate of 1:59,917. This card entitled the collector to obtain a coin from this set which was minted in genuine 24kt. gold. Due to scarcity no pricing is available.

NOT PRICED DUE TO SCARCITY

1996-97 Pinnacle Mint Coins Gold Plated

Randomly inserted in retail packs only at a rate of 1:72, this set is parallel to the regular brass coin set and features 24kt.gold plated coins with embossed player heads.

*GOLD PLATED: 4X TO 10X BRASS COINS

1996-97 Pinnacle Mint Coins Nickel

Randomly inserted in retail packs only at a rate of 1:30, this set is parallel to the regular brass coin set and features minted Nickel-Silver coins with embossed player heads.

*NICKEL: 2.5X TO 5X BRASS COINS

1996-97 Pinnacle Mint Coins Silver

Randomly inserted in packs at a rate of 1:2,945 and in magazine packs at a rate of 1:5,890, this set is parallel to the regular brass coin set and features solid silver coins with embossed player heads. Due to scarcity no pricing is available.

NOT PRICED DUE TO SCARCITY

1996 Pinnacle Bobby Orr Autograph

This extremely rare card was produced as a giveaway at a Dallas golf tournament run by Pinnacle. It is believed that fewer than 25 copies of this card exist. The card is an all gold foil laser-etched design using the basic card design from 1996-97 Pinnacle.

NNO Bobby Orr 75.00 200.00

1997-98 Pinnacle Mint

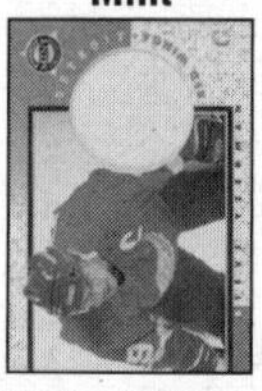

The 1997-98 Pinnacle Mint set was issued in one series totaling 30 cards and was distributed in packs of three cards and two coins with a suggested retail price of $3.99. The challenge was to fit the coins with the die-cut cards that pictured the same player on the minted coin. The fronts feature color player photos with a cut-out area for the matching coin.

1 Eric Lindros .15 .40
2 Paul Kariya .15 .40
3 Peter Forsberg .40 1.00
4 John Vanbiesbrouck .12 .30
5 Steve Yzerman .75 2.00
6 Brendan Shanahan .15 .40
7 Teemu Selanne .15 .40
8 Dominik Hasek .30 .75
9 Jarome Iginla .20 .50
10 Mats Sundin .15 .40
11 Patrick Roy .75 2.00
12 Joe Sakic .30 .75
13 Mark Messier .15 .40
14 Sergei Fedorov .25 .60
15 Saku Koivu .15 .40
16 Martin Brodeur .40 1.00
17 Pavel Bure .15 .40
18 Wayne Gretzky 1.00 2.50
19 Brian Leetch .12 .30
20 John LeClair .15 .40
21 Keith Tkachuk .15 .40
22 Jaromir Jagr .25 .60
23 Brett Hull .20 .50
24 Curtis Joseph .15 .40
25 Jaroslav Svejkovsky .08 .20
26 Sergei Samsonov .12 .30
27 Alexei Morozov .08 .20
28 Alyn McCauley .08 .20
29 Joe Thornton .25 .60
30 Vaclav Prospal RC .20 .50
P3 Peter Forsberg PROMO 3.00 8.00

1997-98 Pinnacle Mint Bronze

This 30-card set is parallel to the base set and is similar in design. The difference is found in the bronze foil stamp instead of the die-cut area. They were inserted at 1:1 hobby and 2:1 retail.

*BRONZE: 1X TO 2X BASIC CARDS

1997-98 Pinnacle Mint Gold Team

Randomly inserted in packs, this 30-card set is parallel version of the Pinnacle Mint base set printed on full gold foil card stock. They were inserted at 1:31 hobby and 1:71 retail.

*GOLD TEAM: 12.5X TO 25X BASIC CARDS

1997-98 Pinnacle Mint Silver Team

Randomly inserted in packs, this 30-card set is parallel version of the Pinnacle Mint base set printed on full silver foil card stock. They were inserted at 1:15 hobby and 1:23 retail.

*SILVER TEAM: 6X TO 12X BASIC CARDS

1997-98 Pinnacle Mint Coins Brass

Randomly inserted in packs at 2:1 hobby and 1:1 retail, this 30-card set features embossed brass coins designed to be inserted into a die-cut card of the player who is pictured on the coin. Artist proof parallels were also created and inserted randomly. These cards were limited to 500 sets.

*BRASS AP's: 7.5X TO 15X BASIC COINS
1 Eric Lindros 1.25 2.00
2 Paul Kariya 1.50 3.00
3 Peter Forsberg 1.00 2.00
4 John Vanbiesbrouck .60 .75
5 Steve Yzerman 1.25 2.50
6 Brendan Shanahan .75 1.25
7 Teemu Selanne .75 1.50
8 Dominik Hasek .75 1.50
9 Jarome Iginla .30 .60
10 Mats Sundin .40 .75
11 Patrick Roy 2.00 4.00
12 Joe Sakic .75 1.50
13 Mark Messier .50 1.00
14 Sergei Fedorov .75 1.50
15 Saku Koivu .60 .75
16 Martin Brodeur 1.00 2.00
17 Pavel Bure 1.00 2.00
18 Wayne Gretzky 2.50 5.00
19 Brian Leetch .40 .75
20 John LeClair .60 1.25
21 Keith Tkachuk .50 .75
22 Jaromir Jagr 1.25 2.50
23 Brett Hull .50 1.00
24 Curtis Joseph .40 1.00
25 Jaroslav Svejkovsky .30 .60
26 Sergei Samsonov .75 .75
27 Alexei Morozov .25 .60
28 Alyn McCauley .25 .60
29 Joe Thornton .75 .75
30 Vaclav Prospal .40 .60

1997-98 Pinnacle Mint Coins Gold Plated

Randomly inserted in packs at a rate of 1:199, this 30-coin set is parallel to the regular brass coin set and features 24 kt. gold plated coins with embossed player heads. Artist's proof parallels of the gold plated set were also created and limited to 100 sets.

*GOLD: 12.5X TO 25X BRASS
*GOLD AP's: 30X TO 60X BRASS

1997-98 Pinnacle Mint Coins Nickel Silver

Randomly inserted in packs at a rate of 1:41, this 30-coin set is parallel to the regular brass coin set and features nickel-silver coins with embossed player heads. Artist proof parallels of the nickel silver set were also created and limited to 250 sets.

*NICKEL: 2.5X TO 5X BRASS
*NICKEL AP's: 12.5X TO 25X BRASS

1997-98 Pinnacle Mint Coins Solid Gold

Randomly inserted in packs, this 30-coin set is a solid gold parallel version of the base set. The set was obtained through redemption cards. Only one coin for each player was produced.

NOT PRICED DUE TO SCARCITY

1997-98 Pinnacle Mint Coins Solid Silver

Randomly inserted in packs, this 30-coin set is parallel to the base coin set and features solid silver coins with embossed player heads.

NOT PRICED DUE TO SCARCITY

1997-98 Pinnacle Mint Minternational

Randomly inserted in hobby packs at the rate of 1:31 and retail packs at the rate of 1:47, this six-card set commemorates the Winter Olympic games with color photos of one player from each nation printed on full silver foil card stock.

COMPLETE SET (6) 15.00 30.00
1 Eric Lindros 6.00 15.00
2 Peter Forsberg 4.00 10.00
3 Brett Hull 2.00 5.00
4 Teemu Selanne 2.50 6.00
5 Dominik Hasek 3.00 8.00
6 Pavel Bure 2.50 6.00

1997-98 Pinnacle Mint Minternational Coins

Randomly inserted in hobby packs only at the rate of 1:31, this six-coin set is parallel to the 1997-98 Pinnacle Mint Minternational set and features the six players on double-sized embossed coins.

1 Eric Lindros 8.00 20.00
2 Peter Forsberg 6.00 20.00
3 Brett Hull 3.00 8.00
4 Teemu Selanne 5.00 12.00
5 Dominik Hasek 5.00 12.00
6 Pavel Bure 6.00 12.00

1997-98 Pinnacle Power Pack Blow-Ups

Randomly inserted in packs, this 24-card set features color action photos of some of the hottest players in the NHL printed on 3" X 5" cards.

1 Eric Lindros 1.00 2.50
2 Paul Kariya 1.20 3.00
3 Joe Thornton .40 1.00
4 Dominik Hasek .60 1.50
5 Patrick Roy 1.60 4.00
6 Keith Tkachuk .30 .75
7 Martin Brodeur .80 2.00
8 Brett Hull .40 1.00
9 Mark Messier .40 1.00
10 Saku Koivu .30 .75
11 Jaromir Jagr 1.00 2.50
12 Joe Sakic .60 1.50
13 John Vanbiesbrouck .30 .75
14 Pavel Bure .80 2.00
15 Jarome Iginla .24 .60
16 Mats Sundin .30 .75
17 Wayne Gretzky 2.00 5.00
18 Steve Yzerman 1.00 2.50
19 Peter Forsberg .80 2.00
20 Brendan Shanahan .60 1.50
21 Sergei Fedorov .60 1.50
22 Curtis Joseph .40 1.00
23 John LeClair .50 1.25
24 Teemu Selanne .60 1.50
P2 Paul Kariya PROMO 1.20 3.00
P13 John Vanbiesbrouck PROMO .60 1.50

1997-98 Pinnacle Totally Certified Platinum Blue

Inserted one in every pack, this 130-card set is parallel to the Totally Certified Platinum Gold and Platinum Red sets. The difference is found in the platinum blue micro-etched holographic foil and foil stamping. Only 2599 goalie cards and 3099 skater cards were printed.

*STARS: .75X TO 2X BASIC CARDS

1997-98 Pinnacle Totally Certified Platinum Gold

Randomly inserted in packs at the rate of 1:79, this 130-card set is parallel to the Totally Certified Platinum Blue and Platinum Red sets. The difference is found in the platinum gold micro-etched holographic foil and foil stamping. Only 59 serially numbered goalie cards and 69 serially numbered skater cards were printed. A mirror gold parallel to the gold set was also created and randomly inserted.

*SKATERS: 15X TO 30X BASIC CARDS
*MIRROR PLAT.GOLD STARS: 1.5X TO 2.5X GOLD

1997-98 Pinnacle Totally Certified Platinum Red

Inserted in packs at the rate of two to a pack, this 130-card set was distributed in three card packs with a suggested retail price of $7.99 and featured color player photos printed on 24 pt. card stock with micro-etched holographic foil and platinum red foil stamping. Only 4299 goalie cards and 6199 skater cards were printed and serially numbered.

COMPLETE SET (130) 100.00 250.00
1 Dominik Hasek 5.00 10.00
2 Patrick Roy 12.50 25.00
3 Martin Brodeur 6.00 12.00
4 Chris Osgood 1.50 4.00
5 Andy Moog 1.50 4.00
6 John Vanbiesbrouck 1.50 4.00
7 Steve Shields RC 2.00 5.00
8 Mike Vernon 1.50 4.00
9 Ed Belfour 2.00 5.00
10 Grant Fuhr 1.50 4.00
11 Felix Potvin 2.00 5.00
12 Bill Ranford 1.50 4.00
13 Mike Richter 2.00 5.00
14 Stephane Fiset
15 Jim Carey 1.50 4.00
16 Nikolai Khabibulin 1.50 4.00
17 Ken Wregget
18 Curtis Joseph 2.00 5.00
19 Guy Hebert 1.50 4.00
20 Damian Rhodes 1.50 4.00
21 Trevor Kidd 1.50 4.00
22 Daren Puppa
23 Patrick Lalime 1.50 4.00
24 Tommy Salo 1.50 4.00
25 Sean Burke
26 Jocelyn Thibault 1.50 4.00
27 Kirk McLean 1.50 4.00
28 Garth Snow 1.50 4.00
29 Ron Tugnutt 1.50 4.00
30 Jeff Hackett
31 Eric Lindros 1.50 4.00
32 Peter Forsberg 5.00 10.00
33 Mike Modano 3.00 6.00
34 Paul Kariya 1.50 4.00
35 Jaromir Jagr 2.50 6.00
36 Brian Leetch 1.50 4.00
37 Keith Tkachuk 1.50 4.00
38 Steve Yzerman 10.00 20.00
39 Teemu Selanne 1.50 4.00
40 Bryan Berard 1.25 3.00
41 Ray Bourque 2.50 5.00
42 Theo Fleury .75 2.00
43 Mark Messier 2.00 5.00
44 Saku Koivu 1.50 4.00
45 Pavel Bure 2.00 5.00
46 Peter Bondra 1.25 3.00
47 Dave Gagner .75 2.00
48 Ed Jovanovski 1.25 3.00
49 Adam Oates 1.25 3.00
50 Joe Sakic 4.00 8.00
51 Doug Gilmour 1.25 3.00
52 Jim Campbell .75 2.00
53 Mats Sundin 1.50 4.00
54 Derian Hatcher .75 2.00
55 Jarome Iginla 2.00 5.00
56 Sergei Fedorov 2.50 6.00
57 Keith Primeau .75 2.00
58 Mark Recchi 1.25 3.00
59 Owen Nolan 1.25 3.00
60 Alexander Mogilny 1.25 3.00
61 Brendan Shanahan 2.00 5.00
62 Pierre Turgeon 1.25 3.00
63 Joe Juneau 1.25 3.00
64 Steve Rucchin .75 2.00
65 Jeremy Roenick 2.00 5.00
66 Doug Weight 1.25 3.00
67 Valeri Kamensky 1.25 3.00
68 Tony Amonte 1.25 3.00
69 Dave Andreychuk .75 2.00
70 Brett Hull 2.50 5.00
71 Wendel Clark 1.25 3.00
72 Vincent Damphousse .75 2.00
73 Mike Grier .75 2.00
74 Chris Chelios 1.50 4.00
75 Nicklas Lidstrom 1.50 4.00
76 Joe Nieuwendyk 1.25 3.00
77 Rob Blake 1.25 3.00
78 Alexei Yashin .75 2.00
79 Ryan Smyth .75 2.00
80 Pat Lafontaine 1.50 4.00
81 Jeff Friesen .75 2.00
82 Ray Ferraro .75 2.00
83 Steve Sullivan .75 2.00
84 Chris Gratton 1.25 3.00
85 Mike Gartner 1.25 3.00
86 Kevin Hatcher .75 2.00
87 Ted Donato .75 2.00
88 German Titov .75 2.00
89 Sandis Ozolinsh .75 2.00
90 Ray Sheppard .75 2.00
91 John MacLean .75 2.00
92 Luc Robitaille 1.25 3.00
93 Rod Brind'Amour 1.25 3.00
94 Zigmund Palffy 1.25 3.00
95 Petr Nedved 1.25 3.00
96 Adam Graves .75 2.00
97 Jozef Stumpel 1.25 3.00
98 Alexandre Daigle .75 2.00
99 Mike Peca .75 2.00
100 Wayne Gretzky 12.50 25.00
101 Alexei Zhamnov .75 2.00
102 Paul Coffey 1.50 4.00
103 Oleg Tverdovsky .75 2.00
104 Trevor Linden 1.25 3.00
105 Dino Ciccarelli .75 2.00
106 Andrei Kovalenko .75 2.00
107 Scott Mellanby .75 2.00
108 Bryan Smolinski .75 2.00
109 Bernie Nicholls .75 2.00
110 Derek Plante .75 2.00
111 Pat Verbeek .75 2.00
112 Adam Deadmarsh .75 2.00
113 Martin Gelinas .75 2.00
114 Daniel Alfredsson 1.25 3.00
115 Scott Stevens .75 2.00
116 Dainius Zubrus 1.50 4.00
117 Kirk Muller .75 2.00
118 Brian Holzinger .75 2.00
119 John LeClair 2.00 5.00
120 Al MacInnis 1.25 3.00
121 Ron Francis 1.25 3.00
122 Eric Daze 1.25 3.00
123 Travis Green .75 2.00
124 Jason Arnott .75 2.00
125 Geoff Sanderson 1.25 3.00
126 Dimitri Khristich .75 2.00
127 Sergei Berezin .75 2.00
128 Jeff O'Neill .75 2.00
129 Claude Lemieux .75 2.00
130 Andrew Cassels .75 2.00

1997-98 Pinnacle Hockey Night in Canada

These cards feature the top on-air personalities from the only hockey broadcast that matters. The cards were produced by Pinnacle, and were given away at autograph signings and other personal appearances.

COMPLETE SET (13) 30.00 75.00
1 Steve Armitage 1.20 3.00
2 Don Cherry 20.00 50.00
3 Bob Cole 2.00 5.00
4 Chris Cuthbert 1.20 3.00
5 John Garrett 2.00 5.00
6 Dick Irvin, Jr. 4.00 10.00
7 Ron Maclean 4.00 10.00
8 Greg Millen 1.20 3.00
9 Harry Neale 2.00 5.00
10 Scott Oake 1.20 3.00
11 Scott Russell 1.20 3.00
12 John Shannon .80 2.00
13 Don Whittman 1.20 3.00

1995-96 Playoff One on One

The 1995-96 Playoff One on One Hockey Challenge is a set of 330 cards which can be used to play a fantasy game. The cards could be found in four different card types: Common (1-110), Uncommon (111-220), Rare, Ultra Rare (found in Booster Packs) and Ultra Rare (found in Starter Packs). The scarcer the card, the higher the point values that can be used during the game. Fifty-card starter decks, including three dice and a rule book, were available for $9.95 ea. Game players could add to the power of their decks by purchasing booster packs for $2.50 ea. Ultra rare cards are designated with suffixes below. URS cards were found in starter packs, while URB were hidden in booster packs.

COMPLETE SET (330) 100.00 250.00
1 Guy Hebert .08 .20
2 Paul Kariya .60 1.50
3 Mike Sillinger .04 .10
4 Oleg Tverdovsky .04 .10
5 Ray Bourque .40 1.00
6 Alexei Kasatonov .04 .10
7 Blaine Lacher .04 .10
8 Cam Neely .08 .20
9 Adam Oates .08 .20
10 Kevin Stevens .04 .10
11 Donald Audette .04 .10
12 Dominik Hasek .30 .75
13 Pat LaFontaine .08 .20
14 Alexei Zhitnik .04 .10
15 Steve Chiasson .04 .10
16 Theo Fleury .20 .50
17 Phil Housley .04 .10
18 Joe Nieuwendyk .08 .20
19 Gary Roberts .04 .10
20 German Titov .04 .10
21 Ed Belfour .20 .50
22 Chris Chelios .20 .50
23 Bernie Nicholls .04 .10
24 Jeremy Roenick .20 .50
25 Peter Forsberg .40 1.00
26 Sylvain Lefebvre .04 .10
27 Owen Nolan .08 .20
28 Joe Sakic .40 1.00
29 Jocelyn Thibault .10 .25
30 Dave Gagner .04 .10
31 Mike Modano .30 .75
32 Andy Moog .08 .20
33 Paul Coffey .08 .20
34 Sergei Fedorov .30 .75
35 Keith Primeau .04 .10
36 Ray Sheppard .04 .10
37 Jason Arnott .04 .10
38 David Oliver .04 .10
39 Mike Stapleton .04 .10

40 Jesse Belanger	.04	.10
41 Paul Laus	.04	.10
42 Rob Niedermayer	.04	.10
43 Brian Skrudland	.04	.10
44 John Vanbiesbrouck	.20	.50
45 Sean Burke	.04	.10
46 Andrew Cassels	.04	.10
47 Brendan Shanahan	.30	.75
48 Rob Blake	.04	.10
49 Tony Granato	.04	.10
50 Wayne Gretzky	2.00	5.00
51 Marty McSorley	.04	.10
52 Jamie Storr	.10	.25
53 Vincent Damphousse	.08	.20
54 Mark Recchi	.08	.20
55 Patrick Roy	1.40	3.50
56 Pierre Turgeon	.08	.20
57 Martin Brodeur	.40	1.00
58 Bill Guerin	.04	.10
59 Scott Niedermayer	.04	.10
60 Stephane Richer	.04	.10
61 Scott Stevens	.04	.10
62 Patrick Flatley	.04	.10
63 Brett Lindros	.04	.10
64 Mathieu Schneider	.04	.10
65 Kirk Muller	.04	.10
66 Adam Graves	.04	.10
67 Alexei Kovalev	.04	.10
68 Brian Leetch	.20	.50
69 Mike Richter	.20	.50
70 Pat Verbeek	.04	.10
71 Luc Robitaille	.08	.20
72 Radek Bonk	.04	.10
73 Alexandre Daigle	.04	.10
74 Alexei Yashin	.10	.25
75 Eric Desjardins	.06	.15
76 Eric Lindros	.30	.75
77 Ron Francis	.08	.20
78 Jaromir Jagr	.60	1.50
79 Mario Lemieux	1.40	3.50
80 Ken Wregget	.04	.10
81 Francois Leroux	.04	.10
82 Pat Falloon	.04	.10
83 Jeff Friesen	.04	.10
84 Arturs Irbe	.08	.20
85 Igor Larionov	.04	.10
86 Shayne Corson	.04	.10
87 Geoff Courtnall	.04	.10
88 Steve Duchesne	.04	.10
89 Brett Hull	.30	.75
90 Al MacInnis	.04	.10
91 Brian Bellows	.04	.10
92 Chris Gratton	.04	.10
93 Dave Andreychuk	.08	.20
94 Tie Domi	.16	.40
95 Mike Gartner	.04	.10
96 Doug Gilmour	.20	.50
97 Larry Murphy	.04	.10
98 Felix Potvin	.20	.50
99 Mats Sundin	.20	.50
100 Pavel Bure	.40	1.00
101 Kirk McLean	.04	.10
102 Alexander Mogilny	.06	.15
103 Christian Ruuttu	.04	.10
104 Jim Carey	.06	.15
105 Joe Juneau	.04	.10
106 Jason Allison	.06	.15
107 Teppo Numminen	.04	.10
108 Teemu Selanne	.30	.75
109 Keith Tkachuk	.20	.50
110 Alexei Zhamnov	.04	.10
111 Patrik Carnback	.04	.10
112 Bobby Dollas	.04	.10
113 Guy Hebert	.20	.50
114 Paul Kariya	.60	1.50
115 Shaun Van Allen	.04	.10
116 Ray Bourque	.40	1.00
117 Mariusz Czerkawski	.04	.10
118 Todd Elik	.04	.10
119 Blaine Lacher	.06	.15
120 Cam Neely	.20	.50
121 Adam Oates	.10	.25
122 Dave Reid	.04	.10
123 Kevin Stevens	.04	.10
124 Garry Galley	.04	.10
125 Dominik Hasek	.40	1.00
126 Brian Holzinger	.06	.15
127 Pat LaFontaine	.10	.25
128 Mike Peca	.20	.50
129 Phil Housley	.06	.15
130 Paul Kruse	.04	.10
131 Ronnie Stern	.04	.10
132 Zarley Zalapski	.04	.10
133 Patrick Poulin	.04	.10
134 Bob Probert	.06	.15
135 Jeremy Roenick	.20	.50
136 Adam Deadmarsh	.10	.25
137 Peter Forsberg	.80	2.00
138 Andrei Kovalenko	.04	.10
139 Joe Sakic	.40	1.00
140 Derian Hatcher	.04	.10
141 Grant Ledyard	.04	.10
142 Mike Modano	.30	.75
143 Paul Coffey	.10	.25
144 Sergei Fedorov	.40	1.00
145 Vladimir Konstantinov	.20	.50
146 Nicklas Lidstrom	.16	.40
147 Steve Yzerman	1.40	3.50
148 Igor Kravchuk	.04	.10
149 Kirk Maltby	.04	.10
150 Boris Mironov	.04	.10
151 Bill Ranford	.10	.25
152 Stu Barnes	.04	.10
153 Jesse Belanger	.04	.10
154 Scott Mellanby	.04	.10
155 Adam Burt	.04	.10
156 Steven Rice	.04	.10
157 Brendan Shanahan	.30	.75
158 Glen Wesley	.04	.10
159 Wayne Gretzky	2.00	5.00
160 Darryl Sydor	.04	.10
161 Rick Tocchet	.06	.15
162 Benoit Brunet	.04	.10
163 J.J. Daigneault	.04	.10
164 Saku Koivu	.20	.50
165 Lyle Odelein	.04	.10
166 Patrick Roy	1.40	3.50
167 Scott Stevens	.06	.15
168 Valeri Zelepukin	.04	.10
169 Steve Thomas	.08	.20
170 Dennis Vaske	.04	.10
171 Brett Lindros	.04	.10
172 Zigmund Palffy	.10	.25
173 Ray Ferraro	.04	.10
174 Brian Leetch	.10	.25
175 Mark Messier	.30	.75
176 Ulf Samuelsson	.04	.10
177 Don Beaupre	.06	.15
178 Alexandre Daigle	.04	.10
179 Steve Larouche	.04	.10
180 Scott Levins	.04	.10
181 Ron Hextall	.10	.25
182 Eric Lindros	.40	1.00
183 Mikael Renberg	.10	.25
184 Kjell Samuelsson	.04	.10
185 Jaromir Jagr	.60	1.50
186 Mario Lemieux	1.40	3.50
187 Sergei Zubov	.04	.10
188 Bryan Smolinski	.04	.10
189 Dmitri Mironov	.04	.10
190 Ulf Dahlen	.04	.10
191 Arturs Irbe	.20	.50
192 Craig Janney	.04	.10
193 Sandis Ozolinsh	.06	.15
194 Jon Casey	.06	.15
195 Brett Hull	.30	.75
196 Esa Tikkanen	.06	.15
197 Brian Bradley	.04	.10
198 Daren Puppa	.06	.15
199 Alexander Selivanov	.04	.10
200 Rob Zamuner	.04	.10
201 Ken Baumgartner	.04	.10
202 Doug Gilmour	.10	.25
203 Kenny Jonsson	.04	.10
204 Felix Potvin	.10	.25
205 Randy Wood	.04	.10
206 Jeff Brown	.06	.15
207 Pavel Bure	.40	1.00
208 Trevor Linden	.06	.15
209 Alexander Mogilny	.10	.25
210 Roman Oksiuta	.04	.10
211 Cliff Ronning	.04	.10
212 Peter Bondra	.10	.25
213 Jim Carey	.10	.25
214 Pat Peake	.04	.10
215 Mark Tinordi	.04	.10
216 Mike Eastwood	.04	.10
217 Nelson Emerson	.04	.10
218 Dave Manson	.04	.10
219 Teemu Selanne	.40	1.00
220 Keith Tkachuk	.20	.50
221 Bob Corkum R	.04	.10
222 Peter Douris R	.10	.25
223 Paul Kariya URB	10.00	25.00
224 Todd Krygier URS	.40	1.00
225 Mike Sillinger R	.10	.25
226 Ray Bourque URB	6.00	15.00
227 Fred Knipscheer R	.10	.25
228 Cam Neely URB	3.20	8.00
229 Adam Oates URB	2.00	5.00
230 Jason Dawe R	.10	.25
231 Yuri Khmylev R	.10	.25
232 Bob Sweeney URS	.40	1.00
233 Trevor Kidd R	.20	.50
234 Eric Daze R	.30	.75
235 Tony Amonte R	.30	.75
236 Jeremy Roenick URB	4.00	10.00
237 Denis Savard R	.20	.50
238 Gary Suter R	.10	.25
239 Peter Forsberg URS	8.00	20.00
240 Curtis Leschyshyn R	.10	.25
241 Owen Nolan URB	2.00	5.00
242 Joe Sakic URS	8.00	20.00
243 Valeri Kamensky R	.20	.50
244 Claude Lemieux R	.20	.50
245 Bob Bassen R	.10	.25
246 Shane Churla R	.10	.25
247 Todd Harvey R	.10	.25
248 Kevin Hatcher URS	.40	1.00
249 Richard Matvichuk R	.10	.25
250 Mike Modano URB	3.20	8.00
251 Dino Ciccarelli R	.10	.25
252 Paul Coffey URS	3.20	8.00
253 Sergei Fedorov URS	6.00	15.00
254 Vyacheslav Kozlov R	.10	.25
255 Mike Vernon R	.20	.50
256 Jason Bonsignore R	.10	.25
257 Dean McAmmond R	.10	.25
258 Bill Ranford R	.10	.25
259 Doug Weight URB	2.00	5.00
260 Bob Kudelski R	.10	.25
261 Dave Lowry R	.10	.25
262 Gord Murphy R	.10	.25
263 Rob Niedermayer URS	2.00	5.00
264 Frantisek Kucera R	.10	.25
265 Paul Ranheim R	.10	.25
266 Geoff Sanderson URS	.80	2.00
267 Darren Turcotte R	.10	.25
268 Pat Conacher R	.10	.25
269 Wayne Gretzky URB	20.00	50.00
270 Kelly Hrudey R	.20	.50
271 Jari Kurri R	.20	.50
272 Patrice Brisebois R	.10	.25
273 Vladimir Malakhov R	.10	.25
274 Patrick Roy URB	14.00	35.00
275 Martin Brodeur URB	8.00	20.00
276 Neal Broten R	.10	.25
277 Sergei Brylin R	.10	.25
278 John MacLean R	.10	.25
279 Wendel Clark R	.20	.50
280 Travis Green R	.10	.25
281 Scott Lachance URS	.40	1.00
282 Tommy Salo R	.20	.50
283 Brian Leetch URB	3.20	8.00
284 Mark Messier URB	4.00	10.00
285 Sergei Nemchinov R	.10	.25
286 Luc Robitaille URS	3.20	8.00
287 Sean Hill R	.10	.25
288 Jim Paek URS	.40	1.00
289 Martin Straka R	.20	.50
290 Sylvain Turgeon R	.10	.25
291 Rod Brind'Amour URS	2.00	5.00
292 Kevin Haller R	.10	.25
293 John LeClair R	.40	1.00
294 Eric Lindros URB	6.00	15.00
295 Joel Otto R	.10	.25
296 Chris Therien R	.10	.25
297 Jaromir Jagr URS	10.00	25.00
298 Mario Lemieux URB	14.00	35.00
299 Glen Murray R	.20	.50
300 Petr Nedved R	.10	.25
301 Jamie Baker R	.10	.25
302 Arturs Irbe URB	2.00	5.00
303 Jayson More R	.10	.25
304 Ray Whitney R	.10	.25
305 Geoff Courtnall URS	.40	1.00
306 Dale Hawerchuk R	.20	.50
307 Brett Hull URB	4.00	10.00
308 Ian Laperriere R	.10	.25
309 Chris Pronger R	.20	.50
310 Roman Hamrlik R	.20	.50
311 Petr Klima URS	.40	1.00
312 John Tucker R	.10	.25
313 Paul Ysebaert URB	.40	1.00
314 Ken Baumgartner R	.10	.25
315 Doug Gilmour URB	2.00	5.00
316 Pavel Bure URB	8.00	20.00
317 Bret Hedican R	.10	.25
318 Alexander Mogilny URS	2.00	5.00
319 Mike Ridley R	.10	.25
320 Peter Bondra R	.40	1.00
321 Sylvain Cote R	.10	.25
322 Dale Hunter R	.10	.25
323 Keith Jones URS	.40	1.00
324 Kelly Miller R	.10	.25
325 Tim Cheveldae R	.10	.25
326 Dallas Drake R	.10	.25
327 Igor Korolev R	.10	.25
328 Teppo Numminen R	.10	.25
329 Teemu Selanne URB	6.00	15.00
330 Alexei Zhamnov URS	.40	1.00

1996-97 Playoff One on One

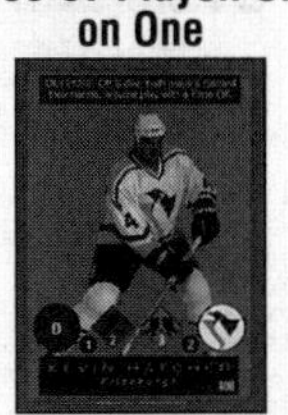

This 110-card set serves as a follow-up to the '95-96 game set of the same name, allowing collectors/players to expand their playing experience. As with the previous set, the cards were available in varying degrees of difficulty. The suffixes below indicate how difficult each is to obtain: C is common, UC is uncommon, R is rare and UR is ultra rare. The cards can also be differentiated quickly be referring to the background color: commons are green, uncommons are violet, rares are silver and ultra rares are gold.

COMPLETE SET (110)	80.00	200.00
331 Mike Sillinger C	.04	.10
332 Oleg Tverdovsky C	.08	.20
333 Kevin Stevens C	.04	.10
334 Joe Nieuwendyk C	.08	.20
335 Owen Nolan C	.10	.25
336 Jocelyn Thibault C	.08	.20
337 Dave Gagner C	.04	.10
338 Ray Sheppard C	.04	.10
339 Jesse Belanger C	.04	.10
340 Tony Granato C	.04	.10
341 Daniel Alfredsson C	.08	.20
342 Stephane Richer C	.04	.10
343 Mathieu Schneider C	.04	.10
344 Kirk Muller C	.04	.10
345 Arturs Irbe C	.10	.25
346 Igor Larionov C	.04	.10
347 Steve Duchesne C	.04	.10
348 Dave Andreychuk C	.04	.10
349 Mike Gartner C	.08	.20
350 Teppo Numminen C	.04	.10
351 Keith Tkachuk C	.20	.50
352 Mike Modano C	.20	.50
353 Paul Kariya C	.30	.75
354 German Titov C	.04	.10
355 Bernie Nicholls C	.04	.10
356 Doug Gilmour C	.20	.50
357 Peter Forsberg C	.30	.75
358 David Oliver C	.04	.10
359 Pat Verbeek C	.04	.10
360 Ron Francis C	.08	.20
361 Pat Falloon C	.04	.10
362 Jeff Friesen C	.08	.20
363 Todd Krygier C	.04	.10
364 Felix Potvin C	.20	.50
365 Shane Churla C	.04	.10
366 Steve Yzerman C	.40	1.00
367 Kelly Hrudey C	.04	.10
368 Mariusz Czerkawski U	.08	.20
369 Patrick Poulin U	.06	.15
370 Chris Chelios U	.10	.25
371 Ray Bourque U	.80	2.00
372 Igor Kravchuk U	.06	.15
373 Kirk Maltby U	.06	.15
374 Bill Ranford U	.08	.20
375 Darryl Sydor U	.06	.15
376 Rick Tocchet U	.08	.20
377 J.J. Daigneault U	.06	.15
378 Chris Osgood U	.40	1.00
379 Zigmund Palffy U	.20	.50
380 Ray Ferraro U	.06	.15
381 Don Beaupre U	.08	.20
382 Andy Moog U	.20	.50
383 Sergei Zubov U	.08	.20
384 Craig Janney U	.06	.15
385 Sandis Ozolinsh U	.08	.20
386 Dave Reid U	.06	.15
387 Scott Mellanby U	.08	.20
388 Saku Koivu U	.40	1.00
389 Bryan Smolinski U	.06	.15
390 Alexander Selivanov U	.06	.15
391 Peter Bondra U	.20	.50
392 Esa Tikkanen U	.08	.20
393 Ken Baumgartner U	.06	.15
394 Ed Belfour U	.40	1.00
395 Randy Wood U	.06	.15
396 Jeff Brown U	.06	.15
397 Roman Oksiuta U	.06	.15
398 Cliff Ronning U	.06	.15
399 Mike Eastwood U	.06	.15
400 Nelson Emerson U	.06	.15
401 Dave Manson U	.06	.15
402 Jamie Baker U	.06	.15
403 Ian Laperriere U	.06	.15
404 Petr Klima U	.06	.15
405 Dallas Drake R	.08	.20
406 Tim Cheveldae R	.20	.50
407 Igor Korolev R	.08	.20
408 Kevin Hatcher R	.08	.20
409 Dale Hawerchuk R	.40	1.00
410 Martin Straka R	.30	.75
411 Wendel Clark R	.80	2.00
412 Jari Kurri R	.80	2.00
413 Darren Turcotte R	.08	.20
414 Yuri Khmylev R	.08	.20
415 Bob Corkum R	.08	.20
416 Roman Hamrlik R	.30	.75
417 Jayson More R	.08	.20
418 Travis Green R	.30	.75
419 Dean McAmmond R	.08	.20
420 Valeri Kamensky R	.20	.50
421 Jason Dawe R	.08	.20
422 Alexander Mogilny R	.80	2.00
423 Keith Jones R	.08	.20
424 Mark Messier R	3.20	8.00
425 John Vanbiesbrouck R	2.00	5.00
426 Jim Carey R	.40	1.00
427 Brett Hull R	4.00	10.00
428 Teemu Selanne UR	6.00	15.00
429 Phil Housley UR	2.00	5.00
430 Wayne Gretzky UR	20.00	50.00
431 Patrick Roy UR	14.00	35.00
432 Joe Sakic UR	8.00	20.00
433 Jaromir Jagr UR	8.00	20.00
434 Doug Weight UR	2.00	5.00
435 Rob Niedermayer UR	2.00	5.00
436 Mario Lemieux UR	14.00	35.00
437 Sergei Fedorov UR	6.00	15.00
438 Pavel Bure UR	6.00	15.00
439 Eric Lindros UR	6.00	15.00
440 Martin Brodeur UR	8.00	20.00

1975-76 Popsicle

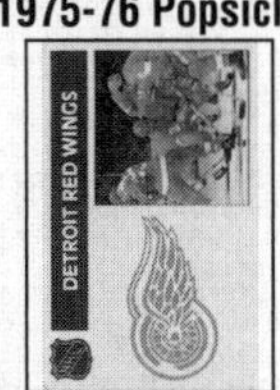

This 18-card set presents the teams of the NHL. The cards measure approximately 3 3/8" by 2 1/8" and are printed in the "credit card format", only slightly thinner than an actual credit card. The front has the NHL logo in the upper left hand corner, and the city and team names in the black bar across the top. A colorful team logo appears on the left side of the card face, while a color action shot of the teams' players appears on the right side. The back provides a brief history of the team. The set was issued in two versions (English and bilingual). We have checklisted the cards below in alphabetical order of the team nicknames.

COMPLETE SET (18)	15.00	30.00
1 Chicago Blackhawks	1.50	3.00
2 St. Louis Blues	1.00	2.00
3 Boston Bruins	1.50	3.00
4 Montreal Canadiens	1.50	3.00
5 Vancouver Canucks	1.00	2.00
6 Washington Capitals	1.00	2.00
7 Atlanta Flames	1.00	2.00
8 Philadelphia Flyers	1.00	2.00
9 California Golden Seals	1.50	3.00
10 New York Islanders	1.00	2.00
11 Los Angeles Kings	1.00	2.00
12 Toronto Maple Leafs	1.50	3.00
13 Minnesota North Stars	1.00	2.00
14 Pittsburgh Penguins	1.00	2.00
15 New York Rangers	1.50	3.00
16 Detroit Red Wings	1.50	3.00
17 Buffalo Sabres	1.00	2.00
18 Kansas City Scouts	1.50	3.00

1976-77 Popsicle

This 18-card set presents the teams of the NHL. The cards measure approximately 3 3/8" by 2 1/8" and are printed in the "credit card format", only slightly thinner than an actual credit card. The front has the NHL logo in the upper left hand corner, and the city and team names in the black bar across the top. A colorful team logo appears on the left side of the card face, while a color action shot of the teams' players appears on the right side. The back provides a brief history of the team. The set was issued in two versions (English and bilingual); a bilingual membership card is known to exist. We have checklisted the cards below in alphabetical order of the team nicknames.

COMPLETE SET (19)	20.00	40.00
1 Cleveland Barons	1.50	3.00
2 Chicago Blackhawks	1.50	3.00
3 St. Louis Blues	1.00	2.00
4 Boston Bruins	1.50	3.00
5 Montreal Canadiens	1.50	3.00
6 Vancouver Canucks	1.00	2.00
7 Washington Capitals	1.00	2.00
8 Atlanta Flames	1.50	3.00
9 Philadelphia Flyers	1.00	2.00
10 New York Islanders	1.00	2.00
11 Los Angeles Kings	1.00	2.00
12 Toronto Maple Leafs	1.50	3.00
13 Minnesota North Stars	1.00	2.00
14 Pittsburgh Penguins	1.00	2.00
15 New York Rangers	1.50	3.00
16 Detroit Red Wings	1.50	3.00
17 Colorado Rockies	1.50	3.00
18 Buffalo Sabres	1.00	2.00
19 Membership Card	1.50	3.00

1966-67 Post Cereal Box Backs

These three box backs seem to vary from the 1967-68 set, so we have listed them seperately. The backs picture Pulford and Hall in All-Star uniforms and Worsley in his Canadiens uniform with a notation that Montreal won the Stanley Cup in 1965-66. A "hockey tip" was printed below the pictures in both English and French, though often the picture was cut from the box without the writing underneath. If anyone has any further information about this set, please forward it to hockeymag@beckett.com.

1 Gump Worsley	40.00
2 Bob Pulford	40.00
3 Glenn Hall	40.00

1967-68 Post Cereal Box Backs

These photo premiums were issued on the back of Post cereal boxes. They measure approximately 6 1/2 by 7 1/2 and are blank backed. They are unnumbered and so are listed below in alphabetical order.

COMPLETE SET (13)		
1 Gordie Howe (net in background	25.00	50.00
2 Gordie Howe (no net	25.00	50.00
3 Harry Howell (passing	10.00	20.00
4 Harry Howell (kneeling	10.00	20.00
5 Jacques Laperriere (net in background	10.00	20.00
6 Jacques Laperriere (no net	10.00	20.00
7 Stan Mikita (red jersey	15.00	30.00
8 Stan Mikita (white jersey	15.00	30.00
9 Bobby Orr (posed	25.00	50.00
10 Bobby Orr (in action	25.00	50.00
11 Henri Richard (with puck	12.50	25.00
12 Henri Richard (no puck	12.50	25.00
13 checklist	25.00	50.00

1967-68 Post Flip Books

This 1967-68 Post set consists of 12 flip books. They display a Montreal player on one side of the page and a Toronto player on the other side. In the listing below, the Montreal player is listed first.

COMPLETE SET (12)	100.00	200.00
1 Gump Worsley / Johnny Bower	15.00	30.00
2 Rogatien Vachon / Johnny Bower	17.50	35.00
3 J.C. Tremblay / Tim Horton	12.50	25.00
4 Jacques Laperriere / Marcel Pronovost	7.50	15.00
5 Henri Richard / Frank Mahovlich	12.50	25.00
6 Dick Duff / Dave Keon	10.00	20.00
7 Jean Beliveau / Jim Pappin	15.00	30.00
8 Jean Beliveau / Ron Ellis	15.00	30.00
9 Gilles Tremblay / George Armstrong	10.00	20.00
10 J.C. Tremblay / Pete Stemkowski	5.00	10.00
11 Ralph Backstrom / Bob Pulford	7.50	15.00
12 Bobby Rousseau / Wayne Hillman	5.00	10.00

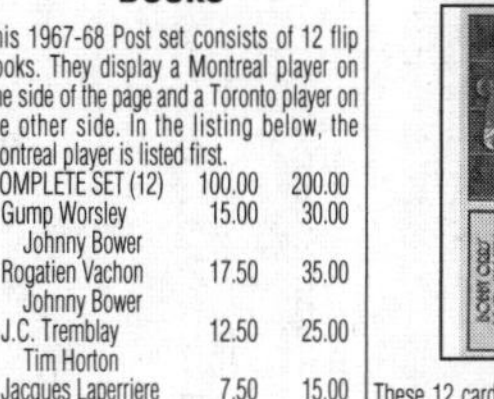

1968-69 Post Marbles

This set of 30 marbles was issued by Post Cereal in Canada and features players of the Montreal Canadiens (MC) and the Toronto Maple Leafs (TML). Also produced was an attractive game board which is rather difficult to find and not included in the complete set price below.

COMPLETE SET (30)	250.00	500.00
1 Ralph Backstrom MC	4.00	8.00
2 Jean Beliveau MC	20.00	40.00
3 Johnny Bower TML	7.50	15.00
4 Wayne Carleton TML	4.00	8.00
5 Yvan Cournoyer MC	10.00	20.00
6 Ron Ellis TML	4.00	8.00
7 John Ferguson MC	4.00	8.00
8 Bruce Gamble TML	4.00	8.00
9 Terry Harper MC	4.00	8.00
10 Ted Harris MC	4.00	8.00
11 Paul Henderson TML	5.00	10.00
12 Tim Horton TML	20.00	40.00
13 Dave Keon TML	12.50	25.00
14 Jacques Laperriere MC	5.00	10.00
15 Jacques Lemaire MC	12.50	25.00
16 Murray Oliver TML	4.00	8.00
17 Mike Pelyk TML	4.00	8.00
18 Pierre Pilote TML	5.00	10.00
19 Marcel Pronovost TML	5.00	10.00
20 Bob Pulford TML	5.00	10.00
21 Henri Richard MC	10.00	20.00
22 Bobby Rousseau MC	4.00	8.00
23 Serge Savard MC	5.00	10.00
24 Floyd Smith TML	4.00	8.00
25 Gilles Tremblay MC	4.00	8.00
26 J.C. Tremblay MC	4.00	8.00
27 Norm Ullman TML	5.00	10.00
28 Rogatien Vachon MC	15.00	30.00
29 Mike Walton TML	4.00	8.00
30 Gump Worsley MC	10.00	20.00
xx Game Board	87.50	175.00

1970-71 Post Shooters

This set of 16 shooters was intended to be used with the hockey game that Post had advertised as a premium. The shooter consists of a plastic figure with a colorful adhesive decal sheet, with stickers that could be applied to the shooter for identification. All players come with home and away, i.e., red or blue shoulders. The figures measure approximately 3 1/2" by 4 1/2". Players are featured in their NHLPA uniform. They are unnumbered and hence are listed below in alphabetical order.

COMPLETE SET (16)	150.00	300.00
1 Johnny Bucyk	7.50	15.00
2 Ron Ellis	5.00	10.00
3 Ed Giacomin	10.00	20.00
4 Paul Henderson	7.50	15.00
5 Ken Hodge	6.25	12.50
6 Dennis Hull	6.25	12.50
7 Orland Kurtenbach	5.00	10.00
8 Jacques Laperriere	6.25	12.50
9 Jacques Lemaire	7.50	15.00
10 Frank Mahovlich	7.50	15.00
11 Peter Mahovlich	6.25	12.50
12 Bobby Orr	50.00	100.00
13 Jacques Plante	20.00	40.00
14 Jean Ratelle	7.50	15.00
15 Dale Tallon	5.00	10.00
16 J.C. Tremblay	6.25	12.50

1972-73 Post Action Transfers

These 12 cards feature two players on each transfer. Each card depicts an important facet of the game. We are listing the players first and then the English title of the card afterwards.

COMPLETE SET (12)	125.00	250.00
1 Garry Unger / Bobby Orr / Defense	30.00	60.00
2 Red Berenson / Dale Tallon / In the Corner	7.50	15.00
3 Gary Dornhoefer / Wayne Cashman / Face Off	7.50	15.00
4 Jim McKenny / Ed Giacomin / Power Save	10.00	20.00
5 Pat Quinn / Keith Magnuson / Power Play Goal	7.50	15.00
6 Paul Shmyr / Rod Seiling / Break Away	7.50	15.00
7 Danny Grant / Jacques Plante / Slap Shot	10.00	20.00
8 Syl Apps Jr. / Serge Savard / Rebound	10.00	20.00
9 Gump Worsley / Gary Bergman / Wrist Shot	12.50	25.00
10 Roger Crozier / Ed Westfall / Last Minute	10.00	20.00
11 Dennis Hull / Orland Kurtenbach / Goalmouth Scramble	7.50	15.00
12 Rogatien Vachon / Yvan Cournoyer / Chest Save	15.00	30.00

1981-82 Post Standups

Each thick card in this 28-card set measures approximately 2 13/16" by 3 3/4" and consists of three panels joined together at one end. The front of the first panel has the logos of Post, the NHL, the NHLPA, and a NHL team, with the title NHL Stars in Action in English and French. The back of the first panel has a full color action photo of a player from the NHL team featured on the card. The second panel is blank backed and features a standup of the player, with his signature at the bottom of the standup. The front of the third panel has the player's name and statistics (from the 1980-81 regular season) in English and French for that player as well as for his entire team, with instructions on the card back in both languages for creating the standup. These three dimensional cards were issued in cellophane packs with one card per specially marked box of Post Sugar-Crisp, Honeycomb, or Alpha-Bits. The set is composed of two players from each Canadian team and one player from each American NHL team. The promotion included a mail-in offer for an official NHL fact chart, which featured the new NHL divisional alignment. Also available, but hard to find, is a two-piece display box; the cover has logos of all NHL teams with two slots inside for cards and space to display one "opened" card.

COMPLETE SET (28)	20.00	50.00
1 Ray Bourque	3.20	8.00
2 Gilbert Perreault	1.00	2.50
3 Denis Savard	1.60	4.00
4 Dale McCourt	.40	1.00
5 Bobby Smith	.60	1.50
6 Mike Bossy	2.40	6.00
7 Bobby Clarke	1.60	4.00
8 Randy Carlyle	.40	1.00
9 Mike Palmateer	.80	2.00
10 Dave(Tiger) Williams	.60	1.50
11 Mark Howe	.80	2.00
12 Marcel Dionne	1.20	3.00
13 Mike Liut	.60	1.50
14 Barry Beck	.40	1.00
15 Mark Messier	4.80	12.00
16 Larry Robinson	1.20	3.00
17 Real Cloutier	.40	1.00
18 Borje Salming	.80	2.00
19 Morris Lukowich	.40	1.00
20 Brett Callighen	.40	1.00
21 Rob Ramage	.60	1.50
22 Wilf Paiement	.40	1.00
23 Mario Tremblay	.60	1.50
24 Robbie Ftorek	.40	1.00
25 Stan Smyl	.60	1.50
26 Dave Babych	.40	1.00
27 Willi Plett	.40	1.00
28 Kent Nilsson	.80	2.00
xx Display Box	8.00	20.00

1982-83 Post Cereal

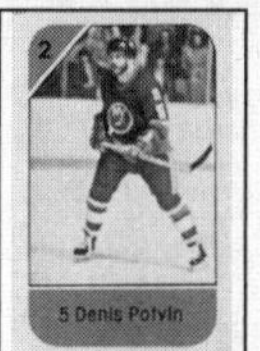

This set is composed of panels of 16 mini playing cards, each measuring approximately 1 1/4" by 2" after perforation. The cards were issued in panel form in a cellophane wrapper inside specially marked packages of Post Cereal. The front of each individual card has an action color photo of the player, with uniform number in the upper left-hand corner, and the player's name and uniform number beneath the picture. The back is done in the team's colors and includes the logos of the team, the sponsor (Post), the NHL, and the NHLPA. There were 21 panels produced, one for each NHL team. Game instructions were included in each box so that one could play Shut-out, Face Off, or Hockey Match with the set of 16 hockey playing cards. By mailing in the UPC code or a reasonable hand drawn facsimile, one could enter the sweepstakes for the grand prize of a trip for two to a Stanley Cup Final playoff game. The complete set was available for a limited time through a mail-in offer. Apparently, a salesman's promo kit was produced in conjunction with this offer, which included six oversized sample cards (Dale Hawerchuk, Real Cloutier, Kent Nilsson, Glenn Anderson, Bob Gainey and Rick Vaive). Not enough is known about this kit at this time to assign a value to it or the singles.

COMPLETE SET (21)	30.00	75.00
1 Boston Bruins	2.00	5.00
1 Rogie Vachon		
7 Ray Bourque		
8 Peter McNab		
11 Steve Kasper		
12 Wayne Cashman		
14 Mike Gillis		
16 Rick Middleton		
17 Stan Jonathan		
20 Mike O'Connell		
22 Brad Park		
24 Terry O'Reilly		
26 Mike Milbury		
28 Tom Fergus		

29 Brad McCrimmon
32 Bruce Crowder
33 Larry Melynk
2 Buffalo Sabres 1.40 3.50
1 Don Edwards
3 Richie Dunn
4 John Van Boxmeer
5 Mike Ramsey
7 Dale McCourt
8 Tony McKegney
10 Craig Ramsay
11 Gilbert Perreault
12 Andre Savard
15 Yvon Lambert
16 Ric Seiling
17 Mike Foligno
21 J. Francois Sauve
22 Lindy Ruff
24 Bill Hait
27 Larry Playfair
3 Calgary Flames 1.40 3.50
1 Pat Riggin
4 Pekka Rautakallio
5 Phil Russell
6 Ken Houston
9 Lanny McDonald
12 Dennis Cyr
14 Kent Nilsson
15 Kevin Lavalle
16 Guy Chouinard
17 Jamie Hislop
20 Bob Murdoch
23 Paul Reinhart
24 Jim Peplinski
25 Willi Plett
26 Mel Bridgeman
28 Gary McAdam
4 Chicago Blackhawks 2.00 5.00
2 Greg Fox
5 Dave Hutchison
8 Terry Ruskowski
10 Reg Kerr
12 Tom Lysiak
14 Bill Gardner
15 Tim Higgins
16 Rich Preston
18 Denis Savard
20 Al Secord
22 Grant Mulvey
23 Doug Crossman
24 Doug Wilson
26 Rick Paterson
29 Ted Bulley
35 Tony Esposito
5 Detroit Red Wings 1.00 2.50
2 Jim Schoenfeld
3 John Barrett
5 Greg Smith
7 Willie Huber
11 Walt McKechnie
15 Paul Woods
16 Mark Kirton
18 Danny Gare
20 Vaclav Nedomansky
21 Mike Blaisdell
22 Greg Joly
23 Mark Osborne
24 Derrek Smith
25 John Ogrodnick
Reed Larson
31 Bob Sauve
6 Edmonton Oilers 8.00 20.00
1 Grant Fuhr
2 Lee Fogolin
4 Kevin Lowe
6 Garry Lariviere
7 Paul Coffey
8 Risto Siltanen
9 Glenn Anderson
10 Matti Hagman
11 Mark Messier
12 Dave Hunter
16 Pat Hughes
17 Jari Kurri
18 Brett Callighen
20 Dave Lumley
27 Dave Semenko
99 Wayne Gretzky
7 Hartford Whalers 1.40 3.50
3 Paul Shmyr
4 Ron Francis
5 Mark Howe
6 Blake Wesley
8 Garry Howatt
11 Jordy Douglas
14 Dave Keon
16 George Lyle
21 Blaine Stoughton
22 Doug Sulliman
24 Chris Kotsopoulos
26 Don Nachbaur
27 Warren Miller
28 Pierre Larouche
30 Greg Millen
8 Los Angeles Kings 1.40 3.50
1 Mario Lessard
2 Rick Chartraw
4 Jerry Korab
5 Larry Murphy
11 Charlie Simmer
12 Dean Hopkins
16 Marcel Dionne
17 John P. Kelly
18 Dave Taylor
19 Jim Fox
20 Mark Hardy
22 Steve Jensen
23 Doug Smith
24 Jay Wells
25 Dave Lewis
26 Steve Bozek
9 Minnesota North Stars 1.00 2.50
2 Curt Giles
3 Fred Barrett
4 Craig Hartsburg
5 Brad Maxwell
8 K.E. Anderson
10 Gord Roberts
11 Tom McCarthy
14 Brad Palmer
15 Bobby Smith
17 Tim Young
20 Dino Ciccarelli
22 Gary Sargent
25 Al MacAdam
26 Steve Payne
27 Gilles Meloche
28 Steve Christoff
10 Montreal Canadiens 3.00 7.50
3 Brian Engblom
6 Pierre Mondou
8 Doug Risebrough
10 Guy Lafleur
12 Keith Acton
14 Mario Tremblay
17 Rod Langway
19 Larry Robinson
20 Mark Hunter
21 Doug Jarvis
22 Steve Shutt
23 Bob Gainey
24 Robert Picard
26 Craig Laughlin
31 Mark Napier
33 Richard Sevigny
11 New Jersey Devils 1.00 2.50
(Colorado Rockies)
1 Glenn Resch
2 Joe Cirella
4 Bob Lorimer
5 Rob Ramage
6 Joe Micheletti
9 Don Lever
10 Dave Cameron
12 Bob MacMillan
14 Steve Tambellini
15 Brent Ashton
16 Merlin Malinowski
18 Bobby Miller
20 Dwight Fostet
21 Kevin Maxwell
26 Mike Kitchen
27 John Wensink
12 New York Islanders 3.00 7.50
2 Mike McEwen
3 Tomas Jonsson
5 Denis Potvin
6 Ken Morrow
7 Stefan Persson
9 Clark Gillies
11 Wayne Merrick
14 Bob Bourne
19 Bryan Trottier
22 Mike Bossy
23 Bob Nystrom
26 Dave Langevin
27 John Tonelli
28 Anders Kallur
31 Billy Smith
91 Butch Goring
13 New York Rangers 1.00 2.50
2 Tom Laidlaw
3 Barry Beck
4 Ron Greschner
8 Steve Vickers
10 Ron Duguay
12 Don Maloney
14 Mike Allison
17 Ed Johnstone
22 Nick Fotiu
26 Dave Maloney
27 Mike Rogers
29 Reijo Ruotsalainen
31 Steve Weeks
33 Andre Dore
38 Robbie Ftorek
40 Mark Pavelich
14 Philadelphia Flyers 2.00 5.00
3 Behn Wilson
6 Fred Arthur
7 Bill Barber
8 Brad Marsh
9 Reid Bailey
9 Darryl Sittler
12 Tim Kerr
14 Kenny Linseman
16 Bobby Clarke
17 Paul Holmgren
20 Jimmy Watson
23 Ilkka Sinisalo
26 Brian Propp
27 Reggie Leach
29 Glen Cochrane
33 Pete Peeters
15 Pittsburgh Penguins 1.00 2.50
2 Pat Price
3 Ron Stackhouse
4 Paul Baxter
10 Peter Lee
11 George Ferguson
12 Greg Malone
14 Doug Shedden
15 Pat Boutette
16 Marc Chorney
17 Rick Kehoe
19 Gregg Sheppard
20 Paul Gardner
22 Mike Bullard
24 Pat Graham
25 Randy Cartyle
29 Michel Dion
16 Quebec Nordiques 1.40 3.50
1 John Garrett
2 Wally Weir
5 Normand Rochefort
8 Marc Tardif
9 Real Cloutier
12 Jere Gillis
16 Michel Goulet
18 Marion Stastny
19 Alain Cote
20 Anton Stastny
22 Mario Marois
23 Jacques Richard
26 Peter Stastny
27 Wilf Paiement
28 Andre Dupont
32 Dale Hunter
17 St. Louis Blues 1.00 2.50
1 Mike Liut
5 Guy Lapointe
6 Larry Patey
9 Perry Turnbull
10 Wayne Babych
11 Brian Sutter
16 Jack Brownschidle
17 Ed Kea
18 Rick Lapointe
19 Blake Dunlop
21 Mike Zuke
22 Jorgen Pettersson
24 Bernie Federko
25 Bill Baker
26 Mike Crombeen
35 Jim Payese
18 Toronto Maple Leafs 1.40 3.50
1 Michel Larocque
3 Bob Manno
4 Bob McGill
7 Rocky Saganiuk
10 John Anderson
11 Fred Boimistruck
12 Walt Poddubny
14 Miroslav Frycer
15 Jim Benning
17 Stewart Gavin
19 Bill Derlago
21 Borje Salming
22 Rick Vaive
24 Normand Aubin
25 Terry Martin
26 Barry Melrose
19 Vancouver Canucks 1.00 2.50
2 Doug Halward
7 Gary Lupul
9 Ivan Boldirev
12 Stan Smyl
13 Lars Lindgren
18 Darcy Rota
19 Ron Delorme
21 Ivan Hlinka
22 Dave(Tiger) Williams
23 Thomas Gradin
24 Curt Fraser
25 Kevin McCarthy
26 Lars Molin
27 Harold Snepsts
28 Marc Crawford
35 Richard Brodeur
20 Washington Capitals 1.40 3.50
2 Doug Hicks
4 Randy Holt
5 Rick Green
6 Darren Veitch
9 Ryan Walter
10 Bob Carpenter
11 Mike Gartner
12 Glen Currie
14 Gaetan Duchesne
16 Bengt Gustafsson
20 Greg Theberge
21 Dennis Maruk
23 Bob Gould
25 Terry Murray
28 Chris Valentine
35 Al Jensen
21 Winnipeg Jets 1.40 3.50
3 Bryan Maxwell
7 Tim Watters
10 Dale Hawerchuk
11 Scott Arniel
12 Morris Lukowich
13 Dave Christian
14 Tim Trimper
15 Paul MacLean
18 Serge Savard
20 Willy Lindstrom
22 Bengt Lundholm
23 Lucien DeBlois
27 Don Spring
28 Norm Dupont
31 Ed Staniowski
44 Dave Babych

1994-95 Post Box Backs

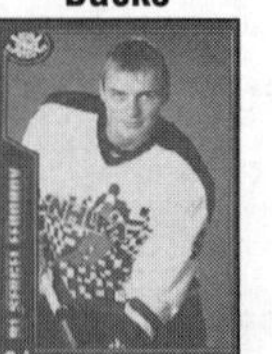

This set of 25 jumbo player cards was issued one per box on the backs of Post Honeycomb and Sugar-Crisp and Alpha-Bits cereals sold in Canada. Each jumbo card measures 8 3/4" by 12 1/4". Inside the box was information on a mail-in offer whereby the collector could receive a complete set by mailing in 4 UPC symbols and 8.00. The offer was valid while supplies lasted, and in no event extended beyond September 30, 1995. The fronts feature posed color photos framed by a black-and-red border design. The player's name and his number are printed vertically along the lower left edge, while the team's city is printed beneath the picture. On a ghosted version of the front photo, the bilingual backs present biography, statistics, and player profile. The prices below are for cut backs; complete, unopened cereal boxes sell for a premium of about two times the prices listed below. The box backs are unnumbered and checklisted below in alphabetical order.

COMPLETE SET (25) 16.00 40.00
1 Tony Amonte .80 2.00
2 Jason Arnott .60 1.50
3 Ray Bourque 1.20 3.00
4 Martin Brodeur 1.20 3.00
New Jers
5 Pavel Bure 1.20 3.00
6 Chris Chelios .80 2.00
7 Geoff Courtnall .60 1.50
8 Russ Courtnall .60 1.50
9 Steve Duchesne .60 1.50
10 Sergei Fedorov 1.20 3.00
11 Theo Fleury .80 2.00
12 Doug Gilmour .80 2.00
13 Wayne Gretzky 4.00 10.00
14 Jari Kurri .60 1.50
15 Eric Lindros 1.20 3.00
16 Marty McSorley .60 1.50
17 Alexander Mogilny .60 1.50
18 Kirk Muller .60 1.50
19 Rob Niedermayer .60 1.50
20 Felix Potvin .80 2.00
21 Luc Robitaille .80 2.00
22 Joe Sakic 1.60 4.00
23 Teemu Selanne 1.20 3.00
24 Alexei Yashin .60 1.50
25 Title Card .40 1.00

1995-96 Post Upper Deck

This 24-card set features color action photos on the front with the player's name in a black bar at the top. The backs carry a color player portrait, biographical information, and statistics. The cards were inserted one per specially marked box of Post cereals in Canada. Collectors also could get the cards through the mail in complete set form with proofs of purchase and a small charge. These factory sets included the NNO title and checklist cards. Cards still in the original cellophane wrapper from the cereal boxes are somewhat more desirable and can carry a slight premium of up to 1.5X the basic card. There were only 500 copies of the Wayne Gretzky autographed cards randomly inserted into Post cereal boxes. Lucky collectors who found this card could call a toll-free number to have their find certified by Upper Deck. The set is considered complete without the signed card.

COMPLETE FACTORY SET (26) 14.0035.00
COMPLETE CELLO. BOX SET (24) 20.00 50.00
1 Ray Bourque .80 2.00
2 Martin Brodeur 1.60 4.00
3 Steve Duchesne .10 .25
4 Vincent Damphousse .20 .50
5 Eric Desjardins .10 .25
6 Eric Lindros 2.00 5.00
7 Joe Juneau .20 .50
8 Luc Robitaille .20 .50
9 Mark Recchi .20 .50
10 Patrick Roy 3.20 8.00
11 Brendan Shanahan 1.20 3.00
12 Scott Stevens .10 .25
13 Jason Arnott .20 .50
14 Trevor Linden .10 .25
15 Chris Chelios .60 1.50
16 Paul Coffey .60 1.50
17 Wayne Gretzky 4.00 10.00
18 Doug Gilmour .60 1.50
19 Kelly Hrudey .10 .25
20 Paul Kariya 2.40 6.00
21 Larry Murphy .10 .25
22 Felix Potvin .50 1.25
23 Keith Tkachuk .60 1.50
24 Rob Blake .10 .25
AU17 W.Gretzky AU (500) 175.00 450.00
NNO Title card .10 .25
NNO Checklist .10 .25

1996-97 Post Upper Deck

This 24-card set marks the third consecutive season for Post's collaboration with the NHLPA, and second with Upper Deck. The cards feature action photography on the fronts, with all players pictured in NHLPA togs. The cards were issued one per specially marked box of Post Cereals during the mid-part of the '96-97 season. Unlike the '95-96 product, these cards were actually inserted into the cereal bag itself, making theft from stores more difficult. Because this factor was negated, fewer complete sets hit the market, hence the slightly higher values. The player's name and the logos of Upper Deck and Post also are prominently featured, the latter in the blue or purple border which defines the right side of the card. The backs are noteworthy for including a childhood photo of the player, as well as '95-96 and career totals. The cards are unnumbered, and are listed below in alphabetical order.

COMPLETE SET (24) 18.00 45.00
1 Ray Bourque .80 2.00
2 Chris Chelios .60 1.50
3 Paul Coffey .60 1.50
4 Vincent Damphousse .20 .50
5 Steve Duchesne .12 .30
6 Theo Fleury .60 1.50
7 Doug Gilmour .60 1.50
8 Wayne Gretzky 4.00 10.00
9 Curtis Joseph .80 2.00
10 Ed Jovanovski .20 .50
11 Paul Kariya 1.60 4.00
12 Eric Lindros 1.60 4.00
13 Al MacInnis .40 1.00
14 Felix Potvin .60 1.50
15 Mark Recchi .40 1.00
16 Luc Robitaille .40 1.00
17 Jeremy Roenick .60 1.50
18 Patrick Roy 3.20 8.00
19 Joe Sakic 1.20 3.00
20 Mathieu Schneider .20 .50
21 Brendan Shanahan 1.20 3.00
22 Scott Stevens .12 .30
23 John Vanbiesbrouck .60 1.50
24 Alexei Yashin .40 1.00

1997 Post Pinnacle

Card fronts feature full color photos on the front with jersey number and a Canadian flag also prominently displayed. Backs feature biographical information and 96-97 season stats.

COMPLETE SET (24) 12.00 30.00
1 Eric Lindros 1.00 2.50
2 Patrick Roy 1.60 4.00
3 Joe Sakic .60 1.50
4 Brian Leetch .30 .75
5 Mark Messier .40 1.00
6 Jason Arnott .24 .60
7 Paul Kariya 1.20 3.00
8 Martin Brodeur .80 2.00
9 Vincent Damphousse .24 .60
10 Steve Yzerman 1.00 2.50
11 Brett Hull .40 1.00
12 Chris Chelios .30 .75
13 Sergei Fedorov .60 1.50
14 Nicklas Lidstrom .24 .60
15 Sergei Berezin .16 .40
16 Dominik Hasek .60 1.50
17 Pavel Bure .80 2.00
18 Saku Koivu .30 .75
19 Teemu Selanne .60 1.50
20 Peter Forsberg .80 2.00
21 Jaromir Jagr 1.00 2.50
22 Peter Bondra .30 .75
23 Alexei Yashin .16 .40
24 Slava Fetisov .16 .40

1998-99 Post

1 Wayne Gretzky 2.00 5.00
2 Martin Brodeur .75 2.00
3 Joe Nieuwendyk .20 .50
4 Rick Tocchet .20 .50
5 Theoren Fleury .20 .50
6 Adam Oates .20 .50
7 Mark Recchi .20 .50
8 Eric Lindros .30 .75
9 Steve Yzerman 1.00 2.50
10 Wade Redden .20 .50
11 Glen Murray .20 .50
12 Mike Johnson .20 .50
13 Kelly Buchberger .20 .50
14 Joe Sakic .75 2.00
15 Mark Messier .40 1.00
16 Keith Primeau .20 .50
17 Mike Vernon .20 .50
18 Chris Pronger .20 .50
19 Mike Peca .20 .50
20 Dave Gagner .20 .50
21 Rob Zamuner .20 .50
22 Doug Gilmour .40 1.00
G1 Wayne Gretzky 2.00 5.00
G2 Wayne Gretzky 2.00 5.00
G3 Wayne Gretzky 2.00 5.00
G4 Wayne Gretzky 2.00 5.00
G5 Wayne Gretzky 2.00 5.00
G6 Wayne Gretzky 2.00 5.00

1999-00 Post Wayne Gretzky

These cards were included one per specially marked box of Post Cereals in Canada. The cards were wrapped in cellophane and often sell for slightly less if removed from that original packaging.

COMPLETE SET (14) 12.00 30.00
COMMON CARD (1-14) 1.20 3.00

1993-94 PowerPlay

This 520-card set measures 2 1/2" by 4 3/4". The fronts feature color action shots set within a blended team-colored border. The team name and the player's name appear in team-colored lettering below the photo. The backs carry color player photos at the upper left. The player's name appears above; his number, position, and a short biography are displayed alongside. Statistics are shown below. The cards are checklisted alphabetically according to teams. Rookie Cards include Jason Arnott, Chris Osgood, Damian Rhodes, and Jocelyn Thibault.

COMPLETE SET (520) 30.00 60.00
COMPLETE SERIES 1 (280) 15.00 30.00
COMPLETE SERIES 2 (240) 15.00 30.00
1 Stu Grimson .02 .10
2 Guy Hebert .08 .25
3 Sean Hill .02 .10
4 Bill Houlder .02 .10
5 Alexei Kasatonov .02 .10
6 Steven King .02 .10
7 Lonnie Loach .02 .10
8 Troy Loney .02 .10
9 Joe Sacco .02 .10
10 Anatoli Semenov .02 .10
11 Jarrod Skalde .02 .10
12 Tim Sweeney .02 .10
13 Ron Tugnutt .08 .25
14 Terry Yake .02 .10
15 Shaun Van Allen .02 .10
16 Ray Bourque .30 .75
17 Jon Casey .08 .25
18 Ted Donato .02 .10
19 Joe Juneau .08 .25
20 Dmitri Kvartalnov .02 .10
21 Steve Leach .02 .10
22 Cam Neely .20 .50
23 Adam Oates .08 .25
24 Don Sweeney .02 .10
25 Glen Wesley .02 .10
26 Doug Bodger .02 .10
27 Grant Fuhr .08 .25
28 Viktor Gordiouk .02 .10
29 Dale Hawerchuk .08 .25
30 Yuri Khmylev .02 .10
31 Pat LaFontaine .20 .50
32 Alexander Mogilny .08 .25
33 Richard Smehlik .02 .10
34 Bob Sweeney .02 .10
35 Randy Wood .02 .10
36 Theo Fleury .02 .10
37 Kelly Kisio .02 .10
38 Al MacInnis .08 .25
39 Joe Nieuwendyk .08 .25
40 Joel Otto .02 .10
41 Robert Reichel .02 .10
42 Gary Roberts .02 .10
43 Ronnie Stern .02 .10
44 Gary Suter .02 .10
45 Mike Vernon .08 .25
46 Ed Belfour .20 .50
47 Chris Chelios .20 .50
48 Karl Dykhuis .02 .10
49 Michel Goulet .08 .25
50 Dirk Graham .02 .10
51 Sergei Krivokrasov .02 .10
52 Steve Larmer .08 .25
53 Joe Murphy .02 .10
54 Jeremy Roenick .25 .60
55 Steve Smith .02 .10
56 Brent Sutter .02 .10
57 Neal Broten .08 .25
58 Russ Courtnall .02 .10
59 Ulf Dahlen .02 .10
60 Dave Gagner .08 .25
61 Derian Hatcher .02 .10
62 Trent Klatt .02 .10
63 Mike Modano .30 .75
64 Andy Moog .08 .25
65 Tommy Sjodin .02 .10
66 Mark Tinordi .02 .10
67 Tim Cheveldae .08 .25
68 Steve Chiasson .02 .10
69 Dino Ciccarelli .08 .25
70 Paul Coffey .20 .50
71 Dallas Drake RC .02 .10
72 Sergei Fedorov .30 .75
73 Vladimir Konstantinov .08 .25
74 Nicklas Lidstrom .20 .50
75 Keith Primeau .02 .10
76 Ray Sheppard .08 .25
77 Steve Yzerman 1.00 2.50
78 Zdeno Ciger .02 .10
79 Shayne Corson .02 .10
80 Todd Elik .02 .10
81 Igor Kravchuk .02 .10
82 Craig MacTavish .02 .10
83 Dave Manson .02 .10
84 Shjon Podein RC .02 .10
85 Bill Ranford .08 .25
86 Steven Rice .02 .10
87 Doug Weight .08 .25
88 Doug Barrault RC .02 .10
89 Jesse Belanger .02 .10
90 Brian Benning .02 .10
91 Joe Cirella .02 .10
92 Mark Fitzpatrick .08 .25
93 Randy Gilhen .02 .10
94 Mike Hough .02 .10
95 Bill Lindsay .02 .10
96 Andrei Lomakin .02 .10
97 Dave Lowry .02 .10
98 Scott Mellanby .08 .25
99 Gord Murphy .02 .10
100 Brian Skrudland .02 .10
101 Milan Tichy RC .02 .10
102 John Vanbiesbrouck .08 .25
103 Sean Burke .08 .25
104 Andrew Cassels .02 .10
105 Nick Kypreos .02 .10
106 Michael Nylander .02 .10
107 Robert Petrovicky .02 .10
108 Patrick Poulin .02 .10
109 Geoff Sanderson .08 .25
110 Pat Verbeek .02 .10
111 Eric Weinrich .02 .10
112 Zarley Zalapski .02 .10
113 Rob Blake .08 .25
114 Jimmy Carson .02 .10
115 Tony Granato .02 .10
116 Wayne Gretzky 1.25 3.00
117 Kelly Hrudey .08 .25
118 Jari Kurri .20 .50
119 Shawn McEachern .02 .10
120 Luc Robitaille .08 .25
121 Tomas Sandstrom .02 .10
122 Darryl Sydor .02 .10
123 Alexei Zhitnik .02 .10
124 Brian Bellows .02 .10
125 Patrice Brisebois .02 .10
126 Guy Carbonneau .02 .10
127 Vincent Damphousse .02 .10
128 Eric Desjardins .08 .25
129 Mike Keane .02 .10
130 Stephan Lebeau .02 .10
131 Kirk Muller .02 .10
132 Lyle Odelein .02 .10
133 Patrick Roy 1.00 2.50
134 Mathieu Schneider .02 .10
135 Bruce Driver .02 .10
136 Slava Fetisov .02 .10
137 Claude Lemieux .02 .10
138 John MacLean .08 .25
139 Bernie Nicholls .02 .10
140 Scott Niedermayer .02 .10
141 Stephane Richer .08 .25
142 Alexander Semak .02 .10
143 Scott Stevens .08 .25
144 Chris Terreri .08 .25
145 Valeri Zelepukin .02 .10
146 Patrick Flatley .02 .10
147 Ron Hextall .08 .25
148 Benoit Hogue .02 .10
149 Darius Kasparaitis .02 .10
150 Derek King .02 .10
151 Uwe Krupp .02 .10
152 Scott Lachance .02 .10
153 Vladimir Malakhov .02 .10
154 Steve Thomas .02 .10
155 Pierre Turgeon .08 .25
156 Tony Amonte .08 .25
157 Mike Gartner .08 .25
158 Adam Graves .02 .10
159 Alexei Kovalev .08 .25
160 Brian Leetch .20 .50
161 Joby Messier RC .02 .10
162 Mark Messier .20 .50
163 Sergei Nemchinov .02 .10
164 James Patrick .02 .10
165 Mike Richter .20 .50
166 Darren Turcotte .02 .10
167 Sergei Zubov .02 .10
168 Dave Archibald .02 .10
169 Craig Billington .08 .25
170 Bob Kudelski .02 .10
171 Mark Lamb .02 .10
172 Norm Maciver .02 .10
173 Darren Rumble .02 .10
174 Vladimir Ruzicka .02 .10
175 Brad Shaw .02 .10
176 Sylvain Turgeon .02 .10
177 Josef Beranek .02 .10
178 Rod Brind'Amour .08 .25
179 Kevin Dineen .02 .10
180 Pelle Eklund .02 .10
181 Brent Fedyk .02 .10
182 Garry Galley .02 .10
183 Eric Lindros .20 .50
184 Mark Recchi .08 .25
185 Tommy Soderstrom .08 .25
186 Dimitri Yushkevich .02 .10
187 Tom Barrasso .08 .25
188 Ron Francis .08 .25
189 Jaromir Jagr .30 .75
190 Mario Lemieux 1.00 2.50
191 Marty McSorley .02 .10
192 Joe Mullen .08 .25
193 Larry Murphy .08 .25
194 Ulf Samuelsson .02 .10
195 Kevin Stevens .02 .10
196 Rick Tocchet .08 .25
197 Steve Duchesne .02 .10
198 Stephane Fiset .08 .25
199 Valeri Kamensky .08 .25
200 Andrei Kovalenko .02 .10
201 Owen Nolan .08 .25
202 Mike Ricci .02 .10
203 Martin Rucinsky .02 .10
204 Joe Sakic .40 1.00
205 Mats Sundin .20 .50
206 Scott Young .02 .10
207 Jeff Brown .02 .10
208 Garth Butcher .02 .10
209 Nelson Emerson .02 .10
210 Bret Hedican .02 .10
211 Brett Hull .25 .60
212 Craig Janney .08 .25
213 Curtis Joseph .20 .50
214 Igor Korolev .02 .10
215 Kevin Miller .02 .10
216 Brendan Shanahan .20 .50
217 Ed Courtenay .02 .10
218 Pat Falloon .02 .10
219 Johan Garpenlov .02 .10
220 Rob Gaudreau RC .02 .10
221 Artus Irbe .08 .25
222 Sergei Makarov .02 .10
223 Jeff Norton .02 .10
224 Jeff Odgers .02 .10
225 Sandis Ozolinsh .02 .10
226 Tom Pederson .02 .10
227 Bob Beers .02 .10
228 Brian Bradley .02 .10
229 Shawn Chambers .02 .10
230 Gerard Gallant .02 .10
231 Roman Hamrlik .08 .25
232 Petr Klima .02 .10
233 Chris Kontos .02 .10
234 Daren Puppa .08 .25
235 John Tucker .02 .10
236 Rob Zamuner .02 .10
237 Glenn Anderson .08 .25
238 Dave Andreychuk .08 .25
239 Drake Berehowsky .02 .10
240 Nikolai Borschevsky .02 .10
241 Wendel Clark .08 .25
242 John Cullen .02 .10
243 Dave Ellett .02 .10
244 Doug Gilmour .08 .25
245 Dimitri Mironov .02 .10
246 Felix Potvin .20 .50
247 Greg Adams .02 .10
248 Pavel Bure .20 .50
249 Geoff Courtnall .02 .10
250 Gerald Diduck .02 .10
251 Trevor Linden .08 .25
252 Jyrki Lumme .02 .10
253 Kirk McLean .08 .25
254 Petr Nedved .08 .25
255 Cliff Ronning .02 .10
256 Jiri Slegr .02 .10
257 Dixon Ward .02 .10

258 Peter Bondra .08 .25
259 Sylvain Cote .02 .10
260 Pat Elynuik .02 .10
261 Kevin Hatcher .02 .10
262 Dale Hunter .02 .10
263 Al Iafrate .02 .10
264 Dimitri Khristich .02 .10
265 Michal Pivonka .02 .10
266 Mike Ridley .02 .10
267 Rick Tabaracci .08 .25
268 Sergei Bautin .02 .10
269 Evgeny Davydov .02 .10
270 Bob Essensa .08 .25
271 Phil Housley .08 .25
272 Teppo Numminen .02 .10
273 Fredrik Olausson .02 .10
274 Teemu Selanne .20 .50
275 Thomas Steen .02 .10
276 Keith Tkachuk .20 .50
277 Paul Ysebaert .02 .10
278 Alexei Zhamnov .08 .25
279 Checklist .02 .10
280 Checklist .02 .10
281 Patrick Carnback RC .02 .10
282 Bob Corkum .02 .10
283 Bobby Dollas .02 .10
284 Peter Douris .02 .10
285 Todd Ewen .02 .10
286 Garry Valk .02 .10
287 John Blue .08 .25
288 Glen Featherstone .02 .10
289 Steve Heinze .02 .10
290 David Reid .02 .10
291 Bryan Smolinski .02 .10
292 Cam Stewart RC .02 .10
293 Jozef Stumpel .02 .10
294 Sergei Zholtok .02 .10
295 Donald Audette .02 .10
296 Philippe Boucher .02 .10
297 Dominik Hasek .40 1.00
298 Brad May .08 .25
299 Craig Muni .02 .10
300 Derek Plante RC .02 .10
301 Craig Simpson .02 .10
302 Scott Thomas RC .02 .10
303 Ted Drury .02 .10
304 Dan Keczmer RC .02 .10
305 Trevor Kidd .08 .25
306 Sandy McCarthy .02 .10
307 Frank Musil .02 .10
308 Michel Petit .02 .10
309 Paul Ranheim .02 .10
310 German Titov RC .02 .10
311 Andrei Trefilov .02 .10
312 Jeff Hackett .08 .25
313 Stephane Matteau .02 .10
314 Brian Noonan .02 .10
315 Patrick Poulin .02 .10
316 Jeff Shantz RC .02 .10
317 Rich Sutter .02 .10
318 Kevin Todd .02 .10
319 Eric Weinrich .02 .10
320 Dave Barr .02 .10
321 Paul Cavallini .02 .10
322 Mike Craig .02 .10
323 Dean Evason .02 .10
324 Brent Gilchrist .02 .10
325 Grant Ledyard .02 .10
326 Mike McPhee .02 .10
327 Darcy Wakaluk .08 .25
328 Terry Carkner .02 .10
329 Mark Howe .02 .10
330 Greg Johnson .02 .10
331 Slava Kozlov .08 .25
332 Martin Lapointe .02 .10
333 Darren McCarty RC .25 .60
334 Chris Osgood RC 1.25 3.00
335 Bob Probert .08 .25
336 Mike Sillinger .02 .10
337 Jason Arnott RC .75 2.00
338 Bob Beers .02 .10
339 Fred Brathwaite RC .30 .75
340 Kelly Buchberger .02 .10
341 Ilya Byakin RC .02 .10
342 Fredrik Olausson .02 .10
343 Vladimir Vujtek .02 .10
344 Peter White RC .02 .10
345 Stu Barnes .02 .10
346 Mike Foligno .02 .10
347 Greg Hawgood .02 .10
348 Bob Kudelski .02 .10
349 Rob Niedermayer .08 .25
350 Igor Chibirev RC .02 .10
351 Robert Kron .02 .10
352 Bryan Marchment .02 .10
353 James Patrick .02 .10
354 Chris Pronger .25 .60
355 Jeff Reese .02 .10
356 Jim Storm RC .02 .10
357 Darren Turcotte .02 .10
358 Pat Conacher .02 .10
359 Mike Donnelly .02 .10
360 John Druce .02 .10
361 Charlie Huddy .02 .10
362 Warren Rychel .02 .10
363 Robb Stauber .08 .25
364 Dave Taylor .08 .25
365 Dixon Ward .02 .10
366 Benoit Brunet .02 .10
367 J.J. Daigneault .02 .10
368 Gilbert Dionne .02 .10
369 Paul DiPietro .02 .10
370 Kevin Haller .02 .10
371 Oleg Petrov .02 .10
372 Peter Popovic RC .02 .10
373 Ron Wilson .02 .10
374 Martin Brodeur .40 1.00
375 Tom Chorske .02 .10
376 Jim Dowd RC .02 .10
377 David Emma .02 .10
378 Bobby Holik .02 .10
379 Corey Millen .02 .10
380 Jaroslav Modry RC .02 .10
381 Jason Smith RC .02 .10
382 Ray Ferraro .02 .10
383 Travis Green .08 .25
384 Tom Kurvers .02 .10
385 Marty McInnis .02 .10
386 Jamie McLennan RC .08 .25
387 Dennis Vaske .02 .10
388 Dave Volek .02 .10
389 Jeff Beukeboom .02 .10
390 Glenn Healy .08 .25
391 Alexander Karpovtsev .02 .10
392 Steve Larmer .08 .25
393 Kevin Lowe .02 .10
394 Ed Olczyk .02 .10
395 Esa Tikkanen .02 .10
396 Alexandre Daigle .02 .10
397 Evgeny Davydov .02 .10
398 Dmitri Filimonov .02 .10
399 Brian Glynn .02 .10
400 Darrin Madeley RC .02 .10
401 Troy Mallette .02 .10
402 Dave McLlwain .02 .10
403 Alexei Yashin .02 .10
404 Jason Bowen RC .02 .10
405 Jeff Finley .02 .10
406 Yves Racine .02 .10
407 Rob Ramage .02 .10
408 Mikael Renberg .20 .50
409 Dominic Roussel .08 .25
410 Dave Tippett .02 .10
411 Doug Brown .02 .10
412 Markus Naslund .20 .50
413 Pat Neaton RC .02 .10
414 Kjell Samuelsson .02 .10
415 Martin Straka .02 .10
416 Bryan Trottier .08 .25
417 Ken Wregget .08 .25
418 Adam Foote .02 .10
419 Iain Fraser RC .02 .10
420 Alexei Gusarov .02 .10
421 Dave Karpa .02 .10
422 Claude Lapointe .02 .10
423 Curtis Leschyshyn .02 .10
424 Mike McKee RC .02 .10
425 Garth Snow RC .15 .40
426 Jocelyn Thibault RC .50 1.25
427 Phil Housley .08 .25
428 Jim Hrivnak .08 .25
429 Vitali Karamnov .02 .10
430 Basil McRae .02 .10
431 Jim Montgomery RC .02 .10
432 Vitali Prokhorov .02 .10
433 Gaetan Duchesne .02 .10
434 Todd Elik .02 .10
435 Bob Errey .02 .10
436 Igor Larionov .02 .10
437 Mike Rathje .02 .10
438 Jim Waite .08 .25
439 Ray Whitney .02 .10
440 Mikael Anderson .02 .10
441 Danton Cole .02 .10
442 Pat Elynuik .02 .10
443 Chris Gratton .08 .25
444 Pat Jablonski .08 .25
445 Chris Joseph .02 .10
446 Chris LiPuma RC .02 .10
447 Denis Savard .08 .25
448 Ken Baumgartner .02 .10
449 Todd Gill .02 .10
450 Sylvain Lefebvre .02 .10
451 Jamie Macoun .02 .10
452 Mark Osborne .02 .10
453 Rob Pearson .02 .10
454 Damian Rhodes RC .08 .25
455 Peter Zezel .02 .10
456 Dave Babych .02 .10
457 Jose Charbonneau RC .02 .10
458 Murray Craven .02 .10
459 Neil Eisenhut RC .02 .10
460 Dan Kesa RC .02 .10
461 Gino Odjick .02 .10
462 Kay Whitmore .08 .25
463 Don Beaupre .08 .25
464 Randy Burridge .02 .10
465 Calle Johansson .02 .10
466 Keith Jones .02 .10
467 Todd Krygier .02 .10
468 Kelly Miller .02 .10
469 Pat Peake .02 .10
470 Dave Poulin .02 .10
471 Luciano Borsato .02 .10
472 Nelson Emerson .02 .10
473 Randy Gilhen .02 .10
474 Boris Mironov .02 .10
475 Stephane Quintal .02 .10
476 Thomas Steen .02 .10
477 Igor Ulanov .02 .10
478 Adrian Aucoin RC .20 .50
479 Todd Brost RC .02 .10
480 Martin Gendron RC .02 .10
481 David Harlock .02 .10
482 Corey Hirsch .08 .25
483 Todd Hlushko RC .02 .10
484 Fabian Joseph RC .02 .10
485 Paul Kariya 2.00 5.00
486 Brett Lindros RC .02 .10
487 Ken Lovsin RC .02 .10
488 Jason Marshall .02 .10
489 Derek Mayer RC .02 .10
490 Petr Nedved .08 .25
491 Dwayne Norris RC .02 .10
492 Russ Romaniuk .02 .10
493 Brian Savage RC .20 .50
494 Trevor Sim RC .02 .10
495 Chris Therien RC .02 .10
496 Todd Warriner RC .02 .10
497 Craig Woodcroft RC .02 .10
498 Mark Beaufait RC .02 .10
499 Jim Campbell .02 .10
500 Ted Crowley RC .02 .10
501 Mike Dunham .08 .25
502 Chris Ferraro RC .02 .10
503 Peter Ferraro .02 .10
504 Brett Hauer RC .02 .10
505 Darby Hendrickson RC .02 .10
506 Chris Imes RC .02 .10
507 Craig Johnson RC .02 .10
508 Peter Laviolette RC .02 .10
509 Jeff Lazaro .02 .10
510 John Lilley RC .02 .10
511 Todd Marchant .02 .10
512 Ian Moran RC .02 .10
513 Travis Richards RC .08 .25
514 Barry Richter RC .02 .10
515 David Roberts RC .02 .10
516 Brian Rolston .02 .10
517 David Sacco RC .02 .10
518 Checklist .02 .10
519 Checklist .02 .10
520 Checklist .02 .10

1993-94 PowerPlay Gamebreakers

Randomly inserted in series two packs at 1:4, this ten-card set measures 2 1/2" by 4 3/4". The fronts feature color action cutouts on a borderless marbleized background. The player's name in gold foil appears at the lower right, while the word "Gamebreakers" is printed vertically in pastel-colored lettering on the left side. On the same marbleized background, the backs carry another color photo, with the player's name displayed above and career highlights shown below. The cards are numbered on the back as "X of 10."

COMPLETE SET (10) 10.00 20.00
1 Sergei Fedorov .60 1.50
2 Doug Gilmour .20 .50
3 Wayne Gretzky 2.50 6.00
4 Curtis Joseph .40 1.00
5 Mario Lemieux 2.00 5.00
6 Eric Lindros .40 1.00
7 Felix Potvin .40 1.00
8 Jeremy Roenick .50 1.25
9 Patrick Roy 2.00 5.00
10 Steve Yzerman 2.00 5.00

1993-94 PowerPlay Global Greats

Randomly inserted in series two packs at 1:4, this 10-card set measures 2 1/2" by 4 3/4". The borderless fronts feature color action cutouts superimposed on the player's national flag. The player's name and the Global Greats logo in gold foil appear at the bottom. On the same national flag background, the backs carry another color photo with the player's name above and career highlights below. The cards are numbered on the back as "X of 10."

COMPLETE SET (10) 6.00 12.00
1 Pavel Bure .50 1.25
2 Sergei Fedorov .50 1.25
3 Jaromir Jagr .75 2.00
4 Jari Kurri .40 1.00
5 Alexander Mogilny .25 .60
6 Mikael Renberg .10 .25
7 Teemu Selanne .50 1.25
8 Mats Sundin .50 1.25
9 Esa Tikkanen .10 .25
10 Alexei Yashin .10 .25

1993-94 PowerPlay Netminders

Randomly inserted at a rate of 1:8 series one packs, this eight-card set measures 2 1/2" by 4 3/4". On a blue marbleized background, the fronts feature color action photos with the goalie's name in blue-foil lettering under the photo.

COMPLETE SET (8) 15.00 30.00
1 Tom Barrasso .75 2.00
2 Ed Belfour 1.50 4.00
3 Grant Fuhr .75 2.00
4 Curtis Joseph 1.50 4.00
5 Felix Potvin 1.25 3.00
6 Bill Ranford .75 2.00
7 Patrick Roy 4.00 10.00
8 Tommy Soderstrom .75 2.00

1993-94 PowerPlay Point Leaders

Randomly inserted at a rate of 1:2 series one packs, this 20-card set measures 2 1/2" by 4 3/4". The yellow-bordered fronts feature color action cutouts against a yellow-tinted background. The player's name in silver foil appears under the photo. On a yellow background, the backs carry another color photo with the player's name in silver foil above the photo, and career highlights below. The cards are numbered on the back as "X of 20."

COMPLETE SET (20) 12.50 25.00
1 Pavel Bure .40 1.00
2 Doug Gilmour .20 .50
3 Wayne Gretzky 2.00 5.00
4 Brett Hull .50 1.25
5 Jaromir Jagr .60 1.50
6 Joe Juneau .10 .20
7 Pat LaFontaine .20 .50
8 Mario Lemieux 1.50 4.00
9 Mark Messier .40 1.00
10 Alexander Mogilny .20 .50
11 Adam Oates .20 .50
12 Mark Recchi .20 .50
13 Luc Robitaille .20 .50
14 Jeremy Roenick .50 1.25
15 Joe Sakic .75 2.00
16 Teemu Selanne .40 1.00
17 Kevin Stevens .10 .20
18 Mats Sundin .40 1.00
19 Pierre Turgeon .20 .50
20 Steve Yzerman 1.50 4.00

1993-94 PowerPlay Rising Stars

Randomly inserted in series two packs at 1:10, this ten-card set measures 2 1/2" by 4 3/4". Each borderless front features a color action cutout, highlighted with a yellow "aura" and yellow radial lines, set on a stellar background. The player's name and the words "Rising Star" in silver foil appear in a top corner. On a similar background, the borderless horizontal back carries another color cutout on the left, with the player's name and career highlights to the right. The cards are numbered on the back as "X of 10."

COMPLETE SET (10) 8.00 15.00
1 Arturs Irbe .30 .75
2 Slava Kozlov .30 .75
3 Felix Potvin 1.50 4.00
4 Keith Primeau .30 .75
5 Robert Reichel .30 .75
6 Geoff Sanderson .30 .75
7 Martin Straka .30 .75
8 Keith Tkachuk .75 2.00
9 Alexei Zhamnov .30 .75
10 Sergei Zubov .30 .75

1993-94 PowerPlay Rookie Standouts

Randomly inserted in series two packs at 1:5, this 16-card set measures 2 1/2" by 4 3/4". The borderless fronts feature color player action shots on grainy and ghosted backgrounds. The player's name and the words "Rookie Standouts" in gold foil are printed atop ghosted bars to the right of the player. The cards are numbered on the back as "X of 16."

COMPLETE SET (16) 4.00 10.00
1 Jason Arnott .60 1.50
2 Jesse Belanger .15 .30
3 Alexandre Daigle .15 .30
4 Iain Fraser .15 .30
5 Chris Gratton .15 .30
6 Boris Mironov .15 .30
7 Jaroslav Modry .15 .30
8 Rob Niedermayer .30 .75
9 Chris Osgood 1.25 3.00
10 Pat Peake .15 .30
11 Derek Plante .15 .30
12 Chris Pronger 1.25 3.00
13 Mikael Renberg .15 .30
14 Bryan Smolinski .15 .30
15 Jocelyn Thibault .60 1.50
16 Alexei Yashin .15 .30

1993-94 PowerPlay Second Year Stars

Randomly inserted at a rate of 1:3 series one packs, this 12-card set measures 2 1/2" by 4 3/4". The fronts feature color action photos with light blue metallic borders. The player's name in gold foil appears on the bottom, while the words "2nd Year Stars" are printed in gold foil in an upper corner. The cards are numbered on the back as "X of 12."

COMPLETE SET (12) 2.50 5.00
1 Rob Gaudreau .10 .20

2 Joe Juneau .20 .50
3 Darius Kasparaitis .10 .20
4 Dmitri Kvartalnov .10 .20
5 Eric Lindros .40 1.00
6 Vladimir Malakhov .10 .20
7 Shawn McEachern .10 .20
8 Felix Potvin .40 1.00
9 Patrick Poulin .10 .20
10 Teemu Selanne .40 1.00
11 Tommy Soderstrom .20 .50
12 Alexei Zhamnov .20 .50

1993-94 PowerPlay Slapshot Artists

Randomly inserted in series two packs at 1:10, this ten-card set measures 2 1/2" by 4 3/4". On a team-colored tinted background, the fronts feature color action cutouts with a smaller tinted head shot in an upper corner. The player's name and the Slapshot Artist logo in gold foil appear at the bottom. The cards are numbered on the back as "X of 10."

COMPLETE SET (10) 8.00 20.00
1 Dave Andreychuk .40 1.00
2 Ray Bourque 1.50 4.00
3 Sergei Fedorov 1.25 3.00
4 Brett Hull 1.25 3.00
5 Al Iafrate .40 1.00
6 Brian Leetch .60 1.50
7 Al MacInnis .60 1.50
8 Mike Modano 1.50 4.00
9 Teemu Selanne 1.25 3.00
10 Brendan Shanahan 1.25 3.00

1998-99 Predators Team Issue

This set features the Predators of the NHL. The cards were issued on six card sheets at Nashville-area Wendy's restaurants. Each sheet featured five cards and one ad card.

COMPLETE SET (25) 8.00 20.00
1 Blair Atcheynum .30 .75
2 Drake Berehowsky .30 .75
3 Sebastien Bordeleau .30 .75
4 Joel Bouchard .30 .75
5 Bob Boughner .40 1.00
6 Andrew Brunette .40 1.00
7 Patrick Cote .40 1.00
8 Mike Dunham .80 2.00
9 Eric Fichaud .40 1.00
10 Tom Fitzgerald .30 .75
11 Jamie Heward .30 .75
12 Greg Johnson .30 .75
13 Patric Kjellberg .30 .75
14 Sergei Krivokrasov .30 .75
15 Denny Lambert .30 .75
16 Jayson More .30 .75
17 Ville Peltonen .40 1.00
18 Cliff Ronning .40 1.00
19 John Slaney .30 .75
20 Kimmo Timonen .30 .75
21 Darren Turcotte .30 .75
22 Tomas Vokoun .80 1.50
23 Jan Vopat .30 .75
24 Scott Walker .30 1.00
25 Vitali Yachmenev .30 .75

2002-03 Predators Team Issue

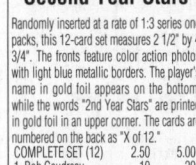

These oversized (8X10) blank-backed collectibles were issued by the Predators. It's believed they may have been offered as game program inserts, but that has not been confirmed. We have only listed the cards we have physically confirmed below. Any additional information regarding distribution or checklist should be sent to hockeymag@beckett.com.

COMPLETE SET (?)
1 Brent Gilchrist 3.00
2 Scott Hartnell 6.00
3 Greg Johnson 4.00
4 Domenic Pittis 3.00
5 Kimmo Timonen 4.00
6 Vitali Yachmenev 3.00

2000-01 Private Stock

Released in mid January 2001 as a 152-card set, Pacific Private Stock features 101 base card and 51 Short Prints, card numbers 101-151. Base cards feature a white background with gold highlights. SP's are sequentially numbered to 155. Private Stock came packaged with one memorabilia card per pack and carried a suggested retail price of $14.99.

COMP.SET w/o SP's (101) 25.00 50.00
SP STAT.ODDS 1:10 HOB, 1:49 RET
1 Guy Hebert .25 .60
2 Paul Kariya .30 .75
3 Teemu Selanne .30 .75
4 Ray Ferraro .10 .25
5 Damian Rhodes .10 .25
6 Patrik Stefan .10 .25
7 Byron Dafoe .10 .25
8 Sergei Samsonov .25 .60
9 Joe Thornton .50 1.25
10 Maxim Afinogenov .10 .25
11 Doug Gilmour .25 .60
12 Dominik Hasek .60 1.50
13 Miroslav Satan .25 .60
14 Fred Brathwaite .25 .60
15 Valeri Bure .10 .25
16 Ron Francis .25 .60
17 Arturs Irbe .25 .60
18 Sami Kapanen .10 .25
19 Tony Amonte .25 .60
20 Jocelyn Thibault .25 .60
21 Alexei Zhamnov .10 .25
22 Ray Bourque .50 1.25
23 Peter Forsberg .75 2.00
24 Milan Hejduk .30 .75
25 Patrick Roy 1.50 4.00
26 Joe Sakic .60 1.50
27 Marc Denis .25 .60
28 Ted Drury .10 .25
29 Geoff Sanderson .10 .25
30 Ed Belfour .30 .75
31 Brett Hull .40 1.00
32 Mike Modano .50 1.25
33 Brenden Morrow .25 .60
34 Joe Nieuwendyk .25 .60
35 Sergei Fedorov .50 1.25
36 Chris Osgood .25 .60
37 Brendan Shanahan .30 .75
38 Steve Yzerman 1.50 4.00
39 Tommy Salo .25 .60
40 Ryan Smyth .10 .25
41 Doug Weight .25 .60
42 Pavel Bure .30 .75
43 Trevor Kidd .25 .60
44 Viktor Kozlov .25 .60
45 Stephane Fiset .10 .25
46 Zigmund Palffy .25 .60
47 Luc Robitaille .25 .60
48 Manny Fernandez .25 .60
49 Sergei Krivokrasov .10 .25
50 Stacy Roest .10 .25
51 Saku Koivu .30 .75
52 Trevor Linden .25 .60
53 Jose Theodore .40 1.00
54 Mike Dunham .10 .25
55 David Legwand .25 .60
56 Jason Arnott .10 .25
57 Martin Brodeur .75 2.00
58 Patrik Elias .25 .60
59 Scott Gomez .10 .25
60 Petr Sykora .10 .25
61 Tim Connolly .10 .25
62 Mariusz Czerkawski .10 .25
63 John Vanbiesbrouck .25 .60
64 Theo Fleury .10 .25
65 Brian Leetch .25 .60
66 Mark Messier .30 .75
67 Mike Richter .30 .75
68 Daniel Alfredsson .25 .60
69 Radek Bonk .10 .25
70 Marian Hossa .30 .75
71 Brian Boucher .30 .75
72 Simon Gagne .30 .75
73 John LeClair .30 .75
74 Eric Lindros .30 .75
75 Nikolai Khabibulin .30 .75
76 Jeremy Roenick .40 1.00
77 Keith Tkachuk .30 .75
78 Jean-Sebastien Aubin .25 .60
79 Jan Hrdina .10 .25
80 Jaromir Jagr .50 1.25
81 Martin Straka .10 .25
82 Pavol Demitra .25 .60
83 Al MacInnis .25 .60
84 Chris Pronger .25 .60
85 Roman Turek .25 .60
86 Pierre Turgeon .25 .60
87 Vincent Damphousse .10 .25
88 Jeff Friesen .10 .25
89 Owen Nolan .25 .60
90 Dan Cloutier .10 .25
91 Vincent Lecavalier .30 .75
92 Nikolai Antropov .10 .25
93 Curtis Joseph .30 .75
94 Mats Sundin .30 .75
95 Steve Kariya .10 .25
96 Markus Naslund .30 .75
97 Felix Potvin .30 .75
98 Jeff Halpern .10 .25
99 Olaf Kolzig .25 .60
100 Adam Oates .25 .60
101 Jonas Ronnqvist SP RC 8.00 20.00
102 Samuel Pahlsson SP .75 2.00
103 Andrew Raycroft SP RC 15.00 40.00
104 Eric Boulton SP RC 8.00 20.00
105 Dimitri Kalinin SP .75 2.00
106 Mika Noronen SP .75 2.00
107 Oleg Saprykin SP .75 2.00
108 Josef Vasicek SP RC 8.00 20.00
109 Shane Willis SP .75 2.00
110 Steven McCarthy SP .75 2.00
111 David Aebischer SP RC 20.00 50.00
112 Serge Aubin SP RC 8.00 20.00
113 Rostislav Klesla SP RC 8.00 20.00
114 David Vyborny SP .75 2.00
115 Tyler Bouck SP RC 8.00 20.00
116 Richard Jackman SP .75 2.00
117 Marty Turco SP RC 40.00 100.00
118 Dan Lacouture SP .75 2.00
119 Brian Swanson SP RC 8.00 20.00
120 Denis Shvidki SP .75 2.00
121 Eric Belanger SP RC 8.00 20.00
122 Steven Reinprecht SP RC 8.00 20.00
123 Lubomir Visnovsky SP RC 8.00 20.00
124 Manny Fernandez SP .75 2.00
125 Marian Gaborik RC 125.00 250.00
126 Filip Kuba SP .75 2.00
127 Maxim Sushinski SP .75 2.00
128 Andrei Markov SP .75 2.00
129 Scott Hartnell SP RC 12.00 30.00
130 Colin White SP RC 8.00 20.00
131 Taylor Pyatt SP .75 2.00
132 Martin Havlat SP RC 40.00 100.00
133 Jani Hurme SP RC 8.00 20.00
134 Karel Rachunek SP .75 2.00
135 Maxime Ouellet SP .75 2.00
136 Justin Williams SP RC 15.00 40.00
137 Robert Esche SP .75 2.00
138 Wyatt Smith SP .75 2.00
139 Ossi Vaananen SP RC 8.00 20.00
140 Brent Johnson SP .75 2.00
141 Ladislav Nagy SP .75 2.00
142 Mike Van Ryn SP .75 2.00
143 Bryce Salvador SP RC 8.00 20.00
144 Evgeni Nabokov SP 6.00 15.00
145 Alexander Kharitonov SP RC 8.00 20.00
146 Brad Richards SP 6.00 15.00
147 Petr Svoboda SP RC 8.00 20.00
148 Daniel Sedin SP .10 .25
149 Henrik Sedin SP .10 .25
150 Kris Beech SP .75 2.00
151 Rick DiPietro SP RC 30.00 80.00
152 Mario Lemieux 3.00 8.00

2000-01 Private Stock Gold

Randomly inserted in Hobby packs, this 152-card set parallels the base set enhanced with a gold border and gold foil highlights. Each card is sequentially numbered to 75.

*STARS: 6X TO 15X BASIC CARDS
*SP's: .75X TO 2X BASIC CARDS
*ROOKIE SP's: .4X TO .8X BASIC CARDS

2000-01 Private Stock Premiere Date

Randomly inserted in Hobby packs at the rate of 2:21, this 152-card set parallels the base Private Stock Set enhanced with a foil premiere date box in which cards are sequentially numbered to 60.

*STARS: 8X TO 20X BASIC CARDS
* SP's: 6X TO 15X BASIC CARDS
*ROOKIE SP's: .5X TO 1X BASIC CARDS

2000-01 Private Stock Retail

This 152-card retail set mirrored the hobby set except that base cards featured silver highlights. SP's were sequentially numbered to 230 and were inserted at a rate of 1:49. Retail packs did not contain memorabilia cards in every pack, and carried an SRP of $2.99.

*NON-SP'S: SAME VALUE AS HOBBY
*SP's: .2X TO .5X HOBBY
125 Marian Gaborik RC 50.00 125.00
132 Martin Havlat RC 25.00 60.00

2000-01 Private Stock Silver

Randomly inserted in Retail packs at the rate of three in 25, this 152-card set parallels the main set enhanced with silver borders and silver foil highlights. Each card is sequentially numbered to 120.

*STARS: 4X TO 10X BASIC CARDS
*SP's: 3X TO 8X BASIC CARDS
*ROOKIE SP's: .25X TO .5X BASIC CARDS

2000-01 Private Stock Artist's Canvas

Randomly inserted in Hobby packs at the rate of 1:21 and retail packs at the rate of

1:49, this 20-card set features base card artwork on a card printed on canvas stock. Parallels numbered 1/1 also were created, they are not priced due to scarcity.
COMPLETE SET (20) 50.00 100.00
1 Paul Kariya 2.00 5.00
2 Teemu Selanne 2.00 5.00
3 Joe Thornton 3.00 8.00
4 Maxim Afinogenov 1.50 4.00
5 Dominik Hasek 4.00 10.00
6 Peter Forsberg 5.00 12.00
7 Patrick Roy 10.00 25.00
8 Joe Sakic 4.00 10.00
9 Brett Hull 2.50 6.00
10 Mike Modano 3.00 8.00
11 Brendan Shanahan 3.00 8.00
12 Steve Yzerman 10.00 25.00
13 Pavel Bure 2.00 5.00
14 Martin Brodeur 5.00 12.00
15 Mark Messier 2.50 6.00
16 John LeClair 2.50 6.00
17 Jeremy Roenick 2.50 6.00
18 Jaromir Jagr 3.00 8.00
19 Vincent Lecavalier 2.00 5.00
20 Curtis Joseph 2.00 5.00

2000-01 Private Stock Extreme Action

Randomly inserted in packs at the rate of 2:21, this 20-card set features full color panoramic photography of game action. Cards are enhanced with a colored border along the bottom of the card containing the featured player's name with gold foil highlights.
COMPLETE SET (20) 20.00 40.00
1 Paul Kariya .75 2.00
2 Teemu Selanne .75 2.00
3 Dominik Hasek 1.50 4.00
4 Patrick Roy 4.00 10.00
5 Joe Sakic 1.50 4.00
6 Ed Belfour .75 2.00
7 Brett Hull 1.00 2.50
8 Mike Modano 1.25 3.00
9 Steve Yzerman 4.00 10.00
10 Luc Robitaille .60 1.50
11 Trevor Linden .50 1.25
12 Petr Sykora .50 1.25
13 Martin Brodeur 2.00 5.00
14 Tim Connolly .50 1.25
15 John LeClair 1.00 2.50
16 Eric Lindros 1.25 3.00
17 Jeremy Roenick 1.00 2.50
18 Jaromir Jagr 1.25 3.00
19 Vincent Lecavalier .75 2.00
20 Curtis Joseph .75 2.00

2000-01 Private Stock Game Gear

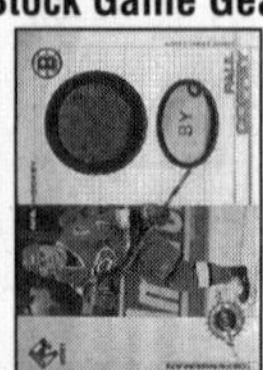

Inserted one per hobby and 1:49 retail packs, this 105-card set features one or two swatches of game used memorabilia. Included on cards are jersey swatches, stick swatches, or jersey/stick combos. Cards feature a full color action photograph and a circular memorabilia swatch.
*MULT.COLOR SWATCH: 1X TO 2X
1 Guy Hebert J 4.00 10.00
2 Marty McInnis J 2.00 5.00
3 Teemu Selanne J 5.00 12.00
4 Shawn Bates J 2.00 5.00
5 Paul Coffey S 8.00 20.00
6 Paul Coffey J/S 20.00 50.00
7 Bill Guerin S 6.00 15.00
8 Sergei Samsonov J 4.00 10.00
9 Dominik Hasek S 20.00 50.00
10 Jay McKee J 2.00 5.00
11 Jarome Iginla J 6.00 15.00
12 Rod Brind'Amour S 6.00 15.00
13 Kevin Hatcher S 4.00 10.00
14 Sandis Ozolinsh S 4.00 10.00
15 Tony Amonte J 4.00 10.00
16 Eric Daze J 2.00 5.00
17 Alexei Zhamnov J 2.00 5.00
18 Ray Bourque J 15.00 40.00
19 Ray Bourque S 20.00 50.00
20 Greg DeVries J 2.00 5.00
21 Chris Dingman J 2.00 5.00
22 Chris Drury S 6.00 15.00
23 Adam Foote S 4.00 10.00
24 Peter Forsberg S 15.00 40.00
25 Peter Forsberg J/S 15.00 40.00
26 Eric Messier J 2.00 5.00
27 Aaron Miller J 2.00 5.00
28 Patrick Roy S 20.00 50.00
29 Joe Sakic J/S 15.00 40.00
30 Joe Sakic J 10.00 25.00
31 Martin Skoula S 4.00 10.00
32 Alex Tanguay S 6.00 15.00
33 Marc Denis S 6.00 15.00
34 Ed Belfour S 8.00 20.00
35 Derian Hatcher J 2.00 5.00
36 Derian Hatcher J 2.00 5.00
37 Jamie Langenbrunner J 2.00 5.00
38 Jere Lehtinen J 2.00 5.00
39 Mike Modano J 8.00 20.00
40 Darryl Sydor J 2.00 5.00
41 Darryl Sydor J 2.00 5.00
42 Sergei Zubov J 2.00 5.00
43 Chris Chelios S 8.00 20.00
44 Sergei Fedorov J 8.00 20.00
45 Nicklas Lidstrom J 4.00 10.00
46 Chris Osgood J 4.00 10.00
47 Brendan Shanahan J 5.00 12.00
48 Anson Carter J 2.00 5.00
49 Tommy Salo S 4.00 10.00
50 Doug Weight J 4.00 10.00
51 Olli Jokinen S 4.00 10.00
52 Roberto Luongo J 6.00 15.00
53 Scott Mellanby S 4.00 10.00
54 Rob Blake S 6.00 15.00
55 Zigmund Palffy S 6.00 15.00
56 Jeff Hackett J 4.00 10.00
57 Saku Koivu J 5.00 12.00
58 Trevor Linden S 5.00 12.00
59 Brian Savage S 4.00 10.00
60 Eric Weinrich S 4.00 10.00
61 Dainius Zubrus J 2.00 5.00
62 Cliff Ronning S 4.00 10.00
63 Bobby Holik J 2.00 5.00
64 Scott Niedermayer J 2.00 5.00
65 Petr Sykora J 2.00 5.00
66 Chris Terreri J 4.00 10.00
67 Zdeno Chara J 2.00 5.00
68 Tim Connolly S 4.00 10.00
69 Mariusz Czerkawski J 2.00 5.00
70 Claude LaPointe J 2.00 5.00
71 Mats Lindgren J 2.00 5.00
72 John Vanbiesbrouck J 4.00 10.00
73 Adam Graves S 4.00 10.00
74 Valeri Kamensky S 4.00 10.00
75 Brian Leetch J 4.00 10.00
76 Brian Leetch J/S 20.00 50.00
77 Mark Messier J 5.00 12.00
78 Mike Richter J 5.00 12.00
79 Mike Richter S 5.00 12.00
80 Andreas Dackell J 2.00 5.00
81 Eric Desjardins J 2.00 5.00
82 Daymond Langkow J 2.00 5.00
83 John LeClair J 4.00 10.00
84 Eric Lindros J 5.00 12.00
85 Eric Lindros S 8.00 20.00
86 Rick Tocchet S 6.00 15.00
87 Shane Doan J 2.00 5.00
88 Radoslav Suchy J 2.00 5.00
89 Jaromir Jagr J 6.00 15.00
90 Dallas Drake J 2.00 5.00
91 Vincent Damphousse J 2.00 5.00
92 Vincent Damphousse J/S 15.00 40.00
93 Vincent Lecavalier S 8.00 20.00
94 Petr Svoboda J 2.00 5.00
95 Shayne Corson J 2.00 5.00
96 Curtis Joseph S 5.00 12.00
97 Yanic Perreault S 4.00 10.00
98 Gary Roberts S 4.00 10.00
99 Mats Sundin J 5.00 12.00
100 Craig Berube S 4.00 10.00
101 Peter Bondra J 5.00 12.00
102 Sylvain Cote S 4.00 10.00
103 Ulf Dahlen J 2.00 5.00
104 Olaf Kolzig J/S 15.00 40.00
105 Adam Oates S 6.00 15.00

2000-01 Private Stock Game Gear Patches

Randomly inserted in packs, this 62-card set parallels only the jersey portion of the Game Gear insert set. Cards is sequentially numbered and contains a premium swatch of a game jersey emblem or numbers. Card 81 is not priced due to scarcity.
1 Guy Hebert/164 12.50 30.00
2 Marty McInnis/156 10.00 25.00
3 Teemu Selanne/202 15.00 40.00
4 Shawn Bates/156 10.00 25.00
8 Sergei Samsonov/101 15.00 40.00
10 Jay McKee/161 10.00 25.00
11 Jarome Iginla/94 20.00 50.00
15 Tony Amonte/134 12.50 30.00
16 Eric Daze/177 12.50 30.00
17 Alexei Zhamnov/142 10.00 25.00
18 Ray Bourque/39 75.00 200.00
20 Greg DeVries/184 10.00 25.00
21 Chris Dingman/163 10.00 25.00
26 Eric Messier/121 10.00 25.00
27 Aaron Miller/202 10.00 25.00
35 Derian Hatcher/172 10.00 25.00
36 Derian Hatcher/184 10.00 25.00
37 Jamie Langenbrunner/178 10.00 25.00
38 Jere Lehtinen/151 10.00 25.00
39 Mike Modano/417 20.00 50.00
40 Darryl Sydor/90 12.50 30.00
41 Darryl Sydor/88 12.50 30.00
42 Sergei Zubov/220 10.00 25.00
44 Sergei Fedorov/175 20.00 50.00
45 Nicklas Lidstrom/193 15.00 40.00
46 Chris Osgood/143 12.50 30.00
47 Brendan Shanahan/17 150.00 300.00
48 Anson Carter/190 10.00 25.00
50 Doug Weight/162 12.50 30.00
52 Roberto Luongo/183 20.00 50.00
56 Jeff Hackett/149 10.00 25.00
57 Saku Koivu/28 90.00 150.00
61 Dainius Zubrus/172 10.00 25.00
63 Bobby Holik/144 10.00 25.00
64 Scott Niedermayer/119 10.00 25.00
65 Petr Sykora/247 10.00 25.00
66 Chris Terreri/149 10.00 25.00
67 Zdeno Chara/149 10.00 25.00
69 Mariusz Czerkawski/169 10.00 25.00
70 Claude LaPointe/137 10.00 25.00
71 Mats Lindgren/166 10.00 25.00
72 John Vanbiesbrouck/108 12.50 30.00
75 Brian Leetch/122 12.50 30.00
77 Mark Messier/67 15.00 40.00
78 Mike Richter/184 15.00 40.00
79 Mike Richter/193 15.00 40.00
80 Andreas Dackell/175 10.00 25.00
81 Eric Desjardins/20
82 Daymond Langkow/77 12.50 30.00
83 John LeClair/158 15.00 40.00
84 Eric Lindros 15.00 40.00
87 Shane Doan/92 10.00 25.00
88 Radoslav Suchy/125 10.00 25.00
89 Jaromir Jagr/388 20.00 50.00
90 Dallas Drake/180 10.00 25.00
94 Petr Svoboda/227 10.00 25.00
95 Shayne Corson/165 10.00 25.00
99 Mats Sundin/103 15.00 40.00
101 Peter Bondra/190 15.00 40.00
103 Ulf Dahlen/183 10.00 25.00

2000-01 Private Stock PS-2001 Action

Inserted two per pack, this 60-mini card set features top NHL players in action where cards are enhanced with gold foil highlights.
COMPLETE SET (60) 15.00 30.00
1 Paul Kariya .40 1.00
2 Teemu Selanne .40 1.00
3 Sergei Samsonov .30 .75
4 Joe Thornton .60 1.50
5 Maxim Afinogenov .30 .75
6 Doug Gilmour .30 .75
7 Dominik Hasek .75 2.00
8 Ray Bourque .75 2.00
9 Chris Drury .30 .75
10 Peter Forsberg 1.00 2.50
11 Milan Hejduk .40 1.00
12 Patrick Roy 2.00 5.00
13 Joe Sakic .75 2.00
14 Alex Tanguay .30 .75
15 Marc Denis .30 .75
16 Ed Belfour .40 1.00
17 Brett Hull .50 1.25
18 Mike Modano .60 1.50
19 Chris Chelios .40 1.00
20 Sergei Fedorov .75 2.00
21 Chris Osgood .30 .75
22 Brendan Shanahan .60 1.50
23 Steve Yzerman 2.00 5.00
24 Doug Weight .30 .75
25 Pavel Bure .50 1.25
26 Zigmund Palffy .30 .75
27 Luc Robitaille .30 .75
28 Saku Koivu .40 1.00
29 Jose Theodore .50 1.25
30 David Legwand .30 .75
31 Martin Brodeur 1.00 2.50
32 Patrik Elias .30 .75
33 Scott Gomez .30 .75
34 Petr Sykora .30 .75
35 Tim Connolly .30 .75
36 Theo Fleury .30 .75
37 Brian Leetch .30 .75
38 Mark Messier .50 1.25
39 Mike Richter .40 1.00
40 Marian Hossa .40 1.00
41 Brian Boucher .40 1.00
42 John LeClair .50 1.25
43 Eric Lindros .60 1.50
44 Jeremy Roenick .50 1.25
45 Keith Tkachuk .40 1.00
46 Jan Hrdina .30 .75
47 Jaromir Jagr .60 1.50
48 Martin Straka .30 .75
49 Jeff Friesen .30 .75
50 Owen Nolan .30 .75
51 Pavol Demitra .30 .75
52 Chris Pronger .30 .75
53 Pierre Turgeon .30 .75
54 Vincent Lecavalier .40 1.00
55 Curtis Joseph .40 1.00
56 Mats Sundin .40 1.00
57 Steve Kariya .30 .75
58 Markus Naslund .40 1.00
59 Peter Bondra .40 1.00
60 Olaf Kolzig .30 .75

2000-01 Private Stock PS-2001 New Wave

Randomly inserted at the rate of 2 per Hobby case and 1 per Retail case, this 25-card set features mini player cards with player action photograph and bronze foil highlights. Each card is sequentially numbered to 70.
COMPLETE SET (26) 60.00 150.00
1 Patrik Stefan 2.00 5.00
2 Joe Thornton 8.00 20.00
3 Maxim Afinogenov 4.00 10.00
4 Sami Kapanen 2.00 5.00
5 Valeri Bure 2.00 5.00
6 Oleg Saprykin 2.00 5.00
7 Jocelyn Thibault 2.00 5.00
8 Milan Hejduk 4.00 10.00
9 Marc Denis 4.00 10.00
10 Brenden Morrow 4.00 10.00
11 Jose Theodore 8.00 15.00
12 David Legwand 2.00 5.00
13 Patrik Elias 4.00 10.00
14 Scott Gomez 4.00 10.00
15 Tim Connolly 2.00 5.00
16 Marian Hossa 6.00 15.00
17 Brian Boucher 2.00 5.00
18 Simon Gagne 6.00 15.00
19 Jean-Sebastien Aubin 2.00 5.00
20 Roman Turek 2.00 5.00
21 Jeff Friesen 2.00 5.00
22 Dan Cloutier 2.00 5.00
23 Vincent Lecavalier 6.00 15.00
24 Nikolai Antropov 2.00 5.00
25 Steve Kariya 2.00 5.00
26 Rick DiPietro 10.00 25.00

2000-01 Private Stock PS-2001 Rookies

Randomly inserted in packs at the rate of one per Hobby and Retail cases, this 26-card set is comprised of mini cards that feature some of the NHL's brightest prospects. Cards are enhanced with silver foil highlights and are sequentially numbered to 45
1 Samuel Pahlsson 3.00 8.00
2 Andrew Raycroft 12.00 30.00
3 Dimitri Kalinin 3.00 8.00
4 Oleg Saprykin 6.00 15.00
5 Josef Vasicek 6.00 15.00
6 David Aebischer 15.00 40.00
7 David Vyborny 6.00 15.00
8 Marty Turco 20.00 50.00
9 Eric Belanger 3.00 8.00
10 Steven Reinprecht 6.00 15.00
11 Marian Gaborik 30.00 80.00
12 Andrei Markov 6.00 15.00
13 Colin White 3.00 8.00
14 Martin Havlat 20.00 50.00
15 Maxime Ouellet 6.00 15.00
16 Justin Williams 15.00 40.00
17 Wyatt Smith 3.00 8.00
18 Ossi Vaananen 3.00 8.00
19 Brent Johnson 6.00 15.00
20 Ladislav Nagy 6.00 15.00
21 Evegeni Nabokov 15.00 40.00
22 Alexander Kharitonov 3.00 8.00
23 Brad Richards 12.00 30.00
24 Daniel Sedin 15.00 40.00
25 Henrik Sedin 15.00 40.00
26 Rick DiPietro 20.00 50.00

2000-01 Private Stock PS-2001 Stars

Randomly inserted in packs at the rate of three per Hobby case and two per Retail case, this 25-card set features mini cards. Each card is features a portrait style photograph and cards are sequentially numbered to 105.
COMPLETE SET (25) 150.00 250.00
1 Paul Kariya 3.00 8.00
2 Teemu Selanne 3.00 8.00
3 Sergei Samsonov 2.50 6.00
4 Dominik Hasek 8.00 20.00
5 Ray Bourque 8.00 20.00
6 Peter Forsberg 10.00 25.00
7 Patrick Roy 15.00 40.00
8 Joe Sakic 8.00 20.00
9 Brett Hull 4.00 10.00
10 Mike Modano 5.00 12.00
11 Sergei Fedorov 8.00 20.00
12 Brendan Shanahan 6.00 15.00
13 Steve Yzerman 20.00 50.00
14 Pavel Bure 5.00 12.00
15 Luc Robitaille 2.50 6.00
16 Saku Koivu 3.00 8.00
17 Martin Brodeur 10.00 25.00
18 Mark Messier 4.00 10.00
19 John LeClair 5.00 12.00
20 Eric Lindros 5.00 12.00
21 Jeremy Roenick 4.00 10.00
22 Jaromir Jagr 6.00 15.00
23 Pierre Turgeon 2.50 6.00
24 Curtis Joseph 3.00 8.00
25 Mats Sundin 3.00 8.00

2000-01 Private Stock Reserve

Randomly inserted in Hobby packs at the rate of 1:21, this 20-card set features a framed oval portrait style photos of players accented with gold foil highlights.
COMPLETE SET (20) 40.00 80.00
1 Paul Kariya 1.50 4.00
2 Teemu Selanne 1.50 4.00
3 Patrik Stefan 1.25 3.00
4 Dominik Hasek 3.00 8.00
5 Peter Forsberg 4.00 10.00
6 Patrick Roy 8.00 20.00
7 Joe Sakic 3.00 8.00
8 Mike Modano 2.50 6.00
9 Brendan Shanahan 2.50 6.00
10 Steve Yzerman 8.00 20.00
11 Pavel Bure 1.50 4.00
12 Saku Koivu 1.50 4.00
13 Scott Gomez 1.25 3.00
14 Martin Brodeur 4.00 10.00
15 Mark Messier 2.00 5.00
16 John LeClair 2.00 5.00
17 Eric Lindros 2.50 6.00
18 Jaromir Jagr 2.50 6.00
19 Vincent Lecavalier 1.50 4.00
20 Curtis Joseph 1.50 4.00

2001-02 Private Stock

This 140-card set featured player action photos on mat-like finish card fronts with red foil highlights and white borders. Cards were 101-117 were short-printed and inserted at a rate of 1:17, while cards 111-140 were serial-numbered to 414 copies each.
COMP.SET w/o SP's 30.00 60.00
1 Jeff Friesen .10 .25
2 Paul Kariya .30 .75
3 Milan Hnilicka .25 .60
4 Patrik Stefan .10 .25
5 Bill Guerin .25 .60
6 Sergei Samsonov .25 .60
7 Joe Thornton .50 1.25
8 Martin Biron .25 .60
9 Tim Connolly .10 .25
10 J-P Dumont .10 .25
11 Jarome Iginla .40 1.00
12 Marc Savard .10 .25
13 Roman Turek .25 .60
14 Ron Francis .25 .60
15 Arturs Irbe .25 .60
16 Jeff O'Neill .10 .25
17 Tony Amonte .25 .60
18 Steve Sullivan .10 .25
19 Jocelyn Thibault .25 .60
20 Rob Blake .25 .60
21 Chris Drury .25 .60
22 Milan Hejduk .30 .75
23 Patrick Roy 1.50 4.00
24 Joe Sakic .60 1.50
25 Alex Tanguay .25 .60
26 Espen Knutsen .10 .25
27 Ron Tugnutt .25 .60
28 Ed Belfour .30 .75
29 Mike Modano .50 1.25
30 Joe Nieuwendyk .25 .60
31 Pierre Turgeon .25 .60
32 Sergei Fedorov .50 1.25
33 Dominik Hasek .60 1.50
34 Brett Hull .40 1.00
35 Nicklas Lidstrom .30 .75
36 Luc Robitaille .25 .60
37 Brendan Shanahan .30 .75
38 Steve Yzerman 1.50 4.00
39 Mike Comrie .25 .60
40 Tommy Salo .25 .60
41 Ryan Smyth .25 .60
42 Pavel Bure .30 .75
43 Roberto Luongo .40 1.00
44 Jason Allison .10 .25
45 Zigmund Palffy .25 .60
46 Felix Potvin .30 .75
47 Manny Fernandez .25 .60
48 Marian Gaborik .60 1.50
49 Yanic Perreault .10 .25
50 Brian Savage .10 .25
51 Jose Theodore .40 1.00
52 Mike Dunham .25 .60
53 David Legwand .25 .60
54 Jason Arnott .10 .25
55 Martin Brodeur .75 2.00
56 Patrik Elias .25 .60
57 Scott Gomez .10 .25
58 Chris Osgood .25 .60
59 Michael Peca .10 .25
60 Alexei Yashin .10 .25
61 Theo Fleury .10 .25
62 Brian Leetch .10 .25
63 Eric Lindros .30 .75
64 Mark Messier .30 .75
65 Mike Richter .30 .75
66 Daniel Alfredsson .25 .60
67 Martin Havlat .25 .60
68 Marian Hossa .30 .75
69 Patrick Lalime .25 .60
70 Roman Cechmanek .25 .60
71 Simon Gagne .30 .75
72 John LeClair .30 .75
73 Mark Recchi .25 .60
74 Jeremy Roenick .40 1.00
75 Sean Burke .25 .60
76 Daymond Langkow .25 .60
77 Alexei Kovalev .25 .60
78 Mario Lemieux 3.00 8.00
79 Martin Straka .10 .25
80 Brent Johnson .25 .60
81 Chris Pronger .25 .60
82 Keith Tkachuk .30 .75
83 Doug Weight .25 .60
84 Patrick Marleau .25 .60
85 Evgeni Nabokov .25 .60
86 Owen Nolan .25 .60
87 Teemu Selanne .30 .75
88 Vincent Lecavalier .30 .75
89 Brad Richards .25 .60
90 Curtis Joseph .30 .75
91 Alexander Mogilny .25 .60
92 Mats Sundin .30 .75
93 Dan Cloutier .25 .60
94 Markus Naslund .30 .75
95 Daniel Sedin .10 .25
96 Henrik Sedin .10 .25
97 Peter Bondra .30 .75
98 Jaromir Jagr .50 1.25
99 Olaf Kolzig .25 .60
100 Adam Oates .25 .60
101 Dany Heatley SP 6.00 15.00
102 Mark Bell SP 2.50 6.00
103 Rostislav Klesla SP 4.00 10.00
104 Jason Williams SP 2.50 6.00
105 Rick DiPietro SP 3.00 8.00
106 Pavel Brendl SP 2.50 6.00
107 Kris Beech SP 2.50 6.00
108 Johan Hedberg SP 2.50 6.00
109 Miikka Kiprusoff SP 2.50 6.00
110 Bryan Allen SP 2.50 6.00
111 Ilja Bryzgalov RC 4.00 10.00
112 Timo Parssinen RC 4.00 10.00
113 Ilya Kovalchuk RC 25.00 60.00
114 Kamil Piros RC 4.00 10.00
115 Brian Pothier RC 4.00 10.00
116 Jukka Hentunen RC 4.00 10.00
117 Erik Cole RC 4.00 10.00
118 Vaclav Nedorost RC 4.00 10.00
119 Niko Kapanen RC 4.00 10.00
120 Pavel Datsyuk RC 12.00 30.00
121 Jason Chimera RC 4.00 10.00
122 Niklas Hagman RC 4.00 10.00
123 Kristian Huselius RC 4.00 10.00
124 Jaroslav Bednar RC 4.00 10.00
125 Pascal Dupuis RC 4.00 10.00
126 Nick Schultz RC 4.00 10.00
127 Francis Belanger RC 4.00 10.00
128 Martin Erat RC 4.00 10.00
129 Scott Clemmensen RC 4.00 10.00
130 Radek Martinek RC 4.00 10.00
131 Dan Blackburn RC 4.00 10.00
132 Peter Smrek RC 4.00 10.00
133 Chris Neil RC 4.00 10.00
134 Jiri Dopita RC 4.00 10.00
135 David Cullen RC 4.00 10.00
136 Krystofer Kolanos RC 4.00 10.00
137 Jeff Jillson RC 4.00 10.00
138 Mark Rycroft RC 4.00 10.00
139 Nikita Alexeev RC 4.00 10.00
140 Brian Sutherby RC 4.00 10.00

2001-02 Private Stock Gold

This 140-card hobby only set paralleled the base set but featured gold foil highlights in place of the red. Cards were serial-numbered out of 106.
*GOLD: 5X TO 12X BASIC CARD
*GOLD SP's: 1X TO 3X BASIC CARD
*GOLD ROOKIES: .4X TO .8X BASIC CARD

2001-02 Private Stock Premiere Date

This 140-card hobby only set paralleled the base set but featured a premiere date stamp on the card front. Cards were serial-numbered on the card front out of 100.
*PREM.DATE: 5X TO 12X BASIC CARD
*PREM.DATE SP's: 1X TO 3X BASIC CARD
*PREM.DATE ROOKIES: .4X TO .8X BASIC CARD

2001-02 Private Stock Retail

This 140-card retail set mirrored the hobby set but featured blue foil highlights in place of the red. Cards 111-140 were serial numbered to 450.
*NON-SP's: SAME VALUE AS HOBBY
*SP's: .25X TO .75X HOBBY
*RC'S: SAME VALUE AS HOBBY
113 Ilya Kovalchuk RC 15.00 40.00

2001-02 Private Stock Silver

This 140-card retail only set paralleled the base set but featured silver foil highlights in place of the red. Cards were serial-numbered on the card front out of 108.
*SILVER: 5X TO 12X BASIC CARD
*SILVER SP's: 1X TO 3X BASIC CARD
*SILVER ROOKIES: .4X TO .8X BASIC CARD

2001-02 Private Stock Game Gear

Inserted at one per pack hobby and four per case retail, this 100-card set featured pieces of game-used jerseys or sticks. Stick cards were serial-numbered out of 200. Cards with significantly shorter print runs are noted below with an SP tag. Please note that cards

#58, 65 and 72 were not prodcued in jersey form.
*MULT.COLOR SWATCH: .75X TO 1.5X HI
1 J-S Giguere 5.00 12.00
2 Paul Kariya 5.00 12.00
3 Mike Leclerc SP 3.00 8.00
4 Steve Rucchin 3.00 8.00
5 Oleg Tverdovsky 3.00 8.00
6 Ilya Kovalchuk STK 15.00 40.00
7 P.J. Axelsson 3.00 8.00
8 Byron Dafoe 5.00 12.00
9 Stu Barnes SP 3.00 8.00
10 J-P Dumont 3.00 8.00
11 Jay McKee SP 3.00 8.00
12 Rob Ray 3.00 8.00
13 Richard Smehlik SP 3.00 8.00
14 Craig Conroy 3.00 8.00
15 Jarome Iginla 6.00 15.00
16 Marc Savard 3.00 8.00
17 Roman Turek 5.00 12.00
18 Rod Brind'Amour STK 10.00 25.00
19 Jeff O'Neill STK 10.00 25.00
20 Tony Amonte 5.00 12.00
21 Kyle Calder 3.00 8.00
22 Eric Daze SP 3.00 8.00
23 Boris Mironov 3.00 8.00
24 Michael Nylander 3.00 8.00
25 Steve Sullivan 3.00 8.00
26 Jocelyn Thibault 5.00 12.00
27 Alexei Zhamnov 3.00 8.00
28 Chris Drury STK 10.00 25.00
29 Peter Forsberg SP 15.00 40.00
30 Patrick Roy SP 15.00 40.00
31 Joe Sakic 10.00 25.00
32 Grant Marshall SP 3.00 8.00
33 Blake Sloan SP 3.00 8.00
34 Ed Belfour 5.00 12.00
35 Derian Hatcher 3.00 8.00
36 Jamie Langenbrunner 3.00 8.00
37 Mike Modano 8.00 20.00
38 Joe Nieuwendyk 5.00 12.00
39 Darryl Sydor 3.00 8.00
40 Pierre Turgeon 5.00 12.00
41 Sergei Zubov 3.00 8.00
42 Dominik Hasek SP 12.50 30.00
43 Brett Hull SP 10.00 25.00
44 Brendan Shanahan 5.00 12.00
45 Steve Yzerman 12.50 30.00
46 Anson Carter SP 5.00 12.00
47 Jochen Hecht 3.00 8.00
48 Ryan Smyth SP 3.00 8.00
49 Valeri Bure SP 3.00 8.00
50 Robert Svehla 3.00 8.00
51 Aaron Miller 3.00 8.00
52 Felix Potvin SP 5.00 12.00
53 Jamie McLennan 3.00 8.00
54 Saku Koivu SP 5.00 12.00
55 Jose Theodore 6.00 15.00
56 Mike Dunham 5.00 12.00
57 Tom Fitzgerald 3.00 8.00
59 Cliff Ronning 3.00 8.00
60 Bobby Holik 3.00 8.00
61 Shawn Bates 3.00 8.00
62 Mariusz Czerkawski 3.00 8.00
63 Kenny Jonsson SP 3.00 8.00
64 Chris Osgood 5.00 12.00
66 Rico Fata 3.00 8.00
67 Eric Lindros SP 5.00 12.00
68 Petr Nedved 5.00 12.00
69 Mike Richter 5.00 12.00
70 Pavel Brendl 5.00 12.00
71 John LeClair SP 5.00 12.00
73 Sean Burke 5.00 12.00
74 Shane Doan 3.00 8.00
75 Jean-Sebastien Aubin 5.00 12.00
76 Jan Hrdina 3.00 8.00
77 Alexei Kovalev 5.00 12.00
78 Milan Kraft 5.00 12.00
79 Mario Lemieux SP 20.00 50.00
80 Ian Moran 3.00 8.00
81 Alexei Morozov 3.00 8.00
82 Wayne Primeau SP 3.00 8.00
83 Michal Rozsival 3.00 8.00
84 Kevin Stevens 3.00 8.00
85 Martin Straka 3.00 8.00
86 Fred Brathwaite 5.00 12.00
87 Mike Eastwood 3.00 8.00
88 Cory Stillman 3.00 8.00
89 Doug Weight SP 5.00 12.00
90 Scott Young 3.00 8.00
91 Vincent Damphousse SP 3.00 8.00
92 Teemu Selanne 5.00 12.00
93 Vincent Lecavalier SP 5.00 12.00
94 Tie Domi 5.00 12.00
95 Curtis Joseph SP 8.00 20.00
96 Robert Reichel STK 10.00 25.00
97 Mats Sundin 5.00 12.00
98 Andrew Cassels 3.00 8.00
99 Peter Bondra 5.00 12.00
100 Jaromir Jagr 8.00 20.00

2001-02 Private Stock Game Gear Patches

This 88-card set paralleled the jerseys in the Game Gear set but carried swatches of patches. The set was skip numbered.
*PATCHES: .75X TO 1.5X JERSEY HI
58 David Legwand 10.00 20.00
65 Alexei Yashin 6.00 12.00
72 Jeremy Roenick 12.50 25.00

2001-02 Private Stock Moments in Time

This 10-card hobby only set featured a color action photo combined with a larger silhouette and a blurred effect on the card front. Each card was serial-numbered out of 85.
1 Dany Heatley 15.00 40.00
2 Ilya Kovalchuk 25.00 60.00
3 Vaclav Nedorost 15.00 40.00
4 Rostislav Klesla 10.00 25.00
5 Jaroslav Bednar 10.00 25.00
6 Rick DiPietro 10.00 25.00
7 Dan Blackburn 6.00 15.00
8 Pavel Brendl 10.00 25.00
9 Krystofer Kolanos 10.00 25.00
10 Johan Hedberg 10.00 25.00

2001-02 Private Stock PS-2002

This 102-card set featured small retro styled mini-cards. Card fronts carried a player photo, name, and birthplace. Card backs resembled vintage "tobacco" cards with single color printing. Cards 1-92 were inserted at 2 per pack and cards 93-102 were serial numbered out of 50 and inserted into hobby packs only. Cards 1-92 had red backs and cards 93-102 had blue backs.
1 Paul Kariya .40 1.00
2 Steve Shields .20 .50
3 Ray Ferraro .20 .50
4 Jason Allison .20 .50
5 Byron DaFoe .30 .75
6 Joe Thornton .60 1.50
7 Stu Barnes .20 .50
8 Martin Biron .30 .75
9 Miroslav Satan .30 .75
10 Jarome Iginla .50 1.25
11 Derek Morris .20 .50
12 Sami Kapanen .20 .50
13 Jeff O'Neill .20 .50
14 Eric Daze .30 .75
15 Jocelyn Thibault .30 .75
16 David Aebischer .30 .75
17 Chris Drury .30 .75
18 Peter Forsberg 1.00 2.50
19 Patrick Roy 2.00 5.00
20 Joe Sakic .75 2.00
21 Marc Denis .30 .75
22 Geoff Sanderson .20 .50
23 Ed Belfour .40 1.00
24 Mike Modano .60 1.50
25 Marty Turco .30 .75
26 Pat Verbeek .20 .50
27 Dominik Hasek .75 2.00
28 Brett Hull .50 1.25
29 Brendan Shanahan .60 1.50
30 Steve Yzerman 2.00 5.00
31 Mike Comrie .30 .75
32 Tommy Salo .30 .75
33 Ryan Smyth .20 .50
34 Pavel Bure .60 1.50
35 Roberto Luongo .50 1.25
36 Zigmund Palffy .30 .75
37 Felix Potvin .40 1.00
38 Marian Gaborik .75 2.00
39 Doug Gilmour .30 .75
40 Jeff Hackett .30 .75
41 Joe Juneau .20 .50
42 Cliff Ronning .20 .50
43 Jason Arnott .20 .50
44 Martin Brodeur 1.00 2.50
45 Michael Peca .20 .50
46 Alexei Yashin .20 .50
47 Zdeno Ciger .20 .50
48 Eric Lindros .60 1.50
49 Mark Messier .50 1.25
50 Petr Nedved .20 .50
51 Radek Bonk .20 .50
52 Martin Havlat .30 .75
53 Roman Cechmanek .30 .75
54 John LeClair .50 1.25
55 Jeremy Roenick .50 1.25
56 Sean Burke .30 .75
57 Shane Doan .20 .50
58 Robert Lang .20 .50
59 Mario Lemieux 2.50 6.00
60 Fred Brathwaite .30 .75
61 Chris Pronger .30 .75
62 Keith Tkachuk .40 1.00
63 Doug Weight .30 .75
64 Evgeni Nabokov .30 .75
65 Owen Nolan .30 .75
66 Teemu Selanne .40 1.00
67 Nikolai Khabibulin .40 1.00
68 Vincent Lecavalier .40 1.00
69 Brad Richards .30 .75
70 Curtis Joseph .40 1.00
71 Mats Sundin .40 1.00
72 Andrew Cassels .20 .50
73 Brendan Morrison .30 .75
74 Peter Bondra .40 1.00
75 Jaromir Jagr .60 1.50
76 Ilja Bryzgalov .30 .75
77 Timo Parssinen .20 .50
78 Erik Cole .20 .50
79 Mark Bell .20 .50
80 Pavel Datsyuk 8.00 20.00
81 Jason Williams .20 .50
82 Jaroslav Bednar .20 .50
83 Scott Clemmensen .30 .75
84 Pavel Brendl .30 .75
85 Jiri Dopita .20 .50
86 Kris Beech .20 .50
87 Mark Rycroft .20 .50
88 Jeff Jillson .20 .50
89 Miikka Kiprusoff .30 .75
90 Nikita Alexeev .20 .50
91 Bryan Allen .20 .50
92 Brian Sutherby .20 .50
93 Dany Heatley SP 12.50 30.00
94 Ilya Kovalchuk SP 25.00 60.00
95 Vaclav Nedorost SP 12.50 30.00
96 Rostislav Klesla SP 12.50 30.00
97 Kristian Huselius SP 12.50 30.00
98 Martin Erat SP 12.50 30.00
99 Rick DiPietro SP 12.50 30.00
100 Dan Blackburn SP 12.50 30.00
101 Krystofer Kolanos SP 12.50 30.00
102 Johan Hedberg SP 12.50 30.00

2001-02 Private Stock Reserve

This 40-card set consisted of 3 different subsets; goalies, superstars, and rookies. Goalies and rookies were inserted into packs at a rate of 1:4 boxes for hobby and 1:8 boxes for retail. Superstar cards were inserted at 1:2 boxes for hobby and 1:4 boxes retail. The prefix before each number below is for checklisting only, the letters do not appear on the cards themselves.
G1 Martin Biron .75 2.00
G2 Patrick Roy 8.00 20.00
G3 Ed Belfour 2.00 5.00
G4 Dominik Hasek 4.00 10.00
G5 Tommy Salo .75 2.00
G6 Roberto Luongo 3.00 8.00
G7 Martin Brodeur 5.00 12.00
G8 Roman Cechmanek .75 2.00
G9 Evgeni Nabokov .75 2.00
G10 Curtis Joseph 2.00 5.00
R1 Dany Heatley 6.00 15.00
R2 Ilya Kovalchuk 12.00 30.00
R3 Vaclav Nedorost 1.50 4.00
R4 Pavel Datsyuk 8.00 20.00
R5 Jaroslav Bednar 1.50 4.00
R6 Dan Blackburn 1.50 4.00
R7 Pavel Brendl 1.50 4.00
R8 Krys Kolanos 1.50 4.00
R9 Kris Beech 1.50 4.00
R10 Nikita Alexeev 1.50 4.00
S1 Paul Kariya 2.00 5.00
S2 Joe Thornton 3.00 8.00
S3 Joe Sakic 4.00 10.00
S4 Brendan Shanahan 2.00 5.00
S5 Steve Yzerman 8.00 20.00
S6 Mike Comrie .75 2.00
S7 Pavel Bure 2.50 6.00
S8 Zigmund Palffy .75 2.00
S9 Marian Gaborik 3.00 8.00
S10 Alexei Yashin .75 2.00
S11 Eric Lindros 2.00 5.00
S12 Martin Havlat .75 2.00
S13 John LeClair .75 2.00
S14 Jeremy Roenick 2.50 6.00
S15 Mario Lemieux 12.00 30.00
S16 Keith Tkachuk .75 2.00
S17 Teemu Selanne 2.00 5.00
S18 Vincent Lecavalier 2.00 5.00
S19 Mats Sundin 2.00 5.00
S20 Jaromir Jagr 3.00 8.00

2002-03 Private Stock Reserve

This 185-card set featured full-color player photos on white borderless card fronts accented with gold foil highlights. Cards 101-150 also carried swatches of game-worn jerseys on the card fronts. Cards 151-185 were serial-numbered to just 99 copies each.
COMP.SET w/o SP's (100) 20.00 40.00
1 J-S Giguere .25 .60
2 Paul Kariya .30 .75
3 Petr Sykora .10 .25
4 Milan Hnilicka .25 .60
5 Patrik Stefan .10 .25
6 Glen Murray .10 .25
7 Brian Rolston .10 .25
8 Sergei Samsonov .25 .60
9 Steve Shields .25 .60
10 Martin Biron .25 .60
11 Tim Connolly .10 .25
12 J-P Dumont .10 .25
13 Craig Conroy .10 .25
14 Chris Drury .25 .60
15 Rod Brind'Amour .25 .60
16 Erik Cole .10 .25
17 Arturs Irbe .25 .60
18 Jeff O'Neill .10 .25
19 Mark Bell .10 .25
20 Eric Daze .25 .60
21 Jocelyn Thibault .25 .60
22 Alexei Zhamnov .10 .25
23 Rob Blake .25 .60
24 Peter Forsberg .75 2.00
25 Milan Hejduk .30 .75
26 Dean McAmmond .10 .25
27 Steven Reinprecht .10 .25
28 Alex Tanguay .25 .60
29 Radim Vrbata .10 .25
30 Andrew Cassels .10 .25
31 Espen Knutsen .10 .25
32 Ray Whitney .10 .25
33 Marty Turco .25 .60
34 Pierre Turgeon .25 .60
35 Chris Chelios .30 .75
36 Brett Hull .40 1.00
37 Brendan Shanahan .30 .75
38 Anson Carter .25 .60
39 Ryan Smyth .10 .25
40 Mike York .10 .25
41 Valeri Bure .10 .25
42 Kristian Huselius .10 .25
43 Stephen Weiss .10 .25
44 Jason Allison .10 .25
45 Adam Deadmarsh .10 .25
46 Zigmund Palffy .25 .60
47 Bryan Smolinski .10 .25
48 Andrew Brunette .10 .25
49 Manny Fernandez .25 .60
50 Cliff Ronning .10 .25
51 Mariusz Czerkawski .10 .25
52 Marcel Hossa .10 .25
53 Saku Koivu .30 .75
54 Yanic Perreault .10 .25
55 Richard Zednik .10 .25
56 Denis Arkhipov .10 .25
57 Mike Dunham .25 .60
58 Scott Hartnell .10 .25
59 Greg Johnson .10 .25
60 Christian Berglund .10 .25
61 Jeff Friesen .10 .25
62 Joe Nieuwendyk .25 .60
63 Chris Osgood .25 .60
64 Mark Parrish .10 .25
65 Dan Blackburn .25 .60
66 Pavel Bure .30 .75
67 Bobby Holik .10 .25
68 Brian Leetch .25 .60
69 Mike Richter .30 .75
70 Daniel Alfredsson .25 .60
71 Radek Bonk .10 .25
72 Martin Havlat .25 .60
73 Patrick Lalime .25 .60
74 John LeClair .30 .75
75 Jeremy Roenick .40 1.00
76 Tony Amonte .25 .60
77 Daniel Briere .10 .25
78 Sean Burke .25 .60
79 Johan Hedberg .25 .60
80 Alexei Kovalev .25 .60
81 Alexei Morozov .10 .25
82 Pavol Demitra .25 .60
83 Barret Jackman .25 .60
84 Brent Johnson .25 .60
85 Doug Weight .25 .60
86 Vincent Damphousse .10 .25
87 Patrick Marleau .25 .60
88 Teemu Selanne .30 .75
89 Scott Thornton .10 .25
90 Dave Andreychuk .10 .25
91 Vincent Lecavalier .30 .75
92 Alexander Mogilny .25 .60
93 Gary Roberts .10 .25
94 Darcy Tucker .10 .25
95 Dan Cloutier .25 .60
96 Brendan Morrison .25 .60
97 Markus Naslund .30 .75
98 Sergei Gonchar .10 .25
99 Olaf Kolzig .25 .60
100 Dainius Zubrus .10 .25
101 Adam Oates J 4.00 10.00
102 Dany Heatley J 6.00 15.00
103 Ilya Kovalchuk J SP 8.00 20.00
104 Joe Thornton J 6.00 15.00
105 Miroslav Satan J 4.00 10.00
106 Jarome Iginla J SP 40.00 100.00
107 Roman Turek J 4.00 10.00
108 Ron Francis J 4.00 10.00
109 Theo Fleury J 4.00 10.00
110 Patrick Roy J SP 15.00 40.00
111 Joe Sakic J 10.00 25.00
112 Marc Denis J 4.00 10.00
113 Jason Arnott J 4.00 10.00
114 Bill Guerin J SP 4.00 10.00
115 Mike Modano J 8.00 20.00
116 Sergei Fedorov J 8.00 20.00
117 Dominik Hasek J 8.00 20.00
118 Curtis Joseph J 5.00 12.00
119 Nicklas Lidstrom J 5.00 12.00
120 Luc Robitaille J 4.00 10.00
121 Steve Yzerman J SP 12.50 30.00
122 Mike Comrie J 4.00 10.00
123 Tommy Salo J 4.00 10.00
124 Roberto Luongo J 6.00 15.00
125 Felix Potvin J 5.00 12.00
126 Marian Gaborik J 12.50 30.00
127 Jose Theodore J 6.00 15.00
128 David Legwand J 4.00 10.00
129 Martin Brodeur J 12.50 30.00
130 Patrik Elias J 4.00 10.00
131 Michael Peca J 4.00 10.00
132 Alexei Yashin J 4.00 10.00
133 Eric Lindros J 5.00 12.00
134 Marian Hossa J 5.00 12.00
135 Roman Cechmanek J 4.00 10.00
136 Simon Gagne J 5.00 12.00
137 Daymond Langkow J 4.00 10.00
138 Mario Lemieux J SP 15.00 40.00
139 Chris Pronger J 4.00 10.00
140 Keith Tkachuk J 5.00 12.00
141 Evgeni Nabokov J 4.00 10.00
142 Owen Nolan J 4.00 10.00
143 Nikolai Khabibulin J 5.00 12.00
144 Brad Richards J 4.00 10.00
145 Ed Belfour J SP 5.00 12.00
146 Mats Sundin J 5.00 12.00
147 Todd Bertuzzi J 5.00 12.00
148 Peter Bondra J 5.00 12.00
149 Jaromir Jagr J 10.00 25.00
150 Robert Lang J 4.00 10.00
151 Stanislav Chistov RC 12.00 30.00
152 Martin Gerber RC 12.00 30.00
153 Alexei Smirnov RC 10.00 25.00
154 Tim Thomas RC 12.00 30.00
155 Chuck Kobasew RC 12.00 30.00
156 Jordan Leopold RC 12.00 30.00
157 Rick Nash RC 125.00 250.00
158 Lasse Pirjeta RC 10.00 25.00
159 Dmitri Bykov RC 10.00 25.00
160 Henrik Zetterberg RC 75.00 200.00
161 Kari Haakana RC 10.00 25.00
162 Ales Hemsky RC 30.00 80.00
163 Jay Bouwmeester RC 20.00 50.00
164 Alexander Frolov RC 30.00 80.00
165 P-M Bouchard RC 20.00 50.00
166 Stephane Veilleux RC 12.50 30.00
167 Sylvain Blouin RC 10.00 25.00
168 Ron Hainsey RC 10.00 25.00
169 Adam Hall RC 10.00 25.00
170 Scottie Upshall RC 12.50 30.00
171 Ray Schultz RC 10.00 25.00
172 Mattias Weinhandl SP 10.00 25.00
173 Jason Spezza RC 125.00 300.00
174 Anton Volchenkov RC 12.50 30.00
175 Dennis Seidenberg RC 10.00 25.00
176 Patrick Sharp RC 10.00 25.00
177 Radovan Somik RC 10.00 25.00
178 Jeff Taffe RC 10.00 25.00
179 Dick Tarnstrom RC 10.00 25.00
180 Tom Koivisto RC 10.00 25.00
181 Curtis Sanford RC 12.50 30.00
182 Alexander Svitov RC 10.00 25.00
183 Carlo Colaiacovo RC 12.50 30.00
184 Steve Eminger RC 12.50 30.00
185 Alex Henry RC 10.00 25.00

2002-03 Private Stock Reserve Blue

This 135-card set paralleled the base set without the jersey card subset. Each card carried blue foil highlights. Cards 1-100 were serial-numbered to 499 and cards 151-185 were serial-numbered to 250.
*STARS: .75X TO 2X BASIC CARDS
*SP's: .10X TO .25X

2002-03 Private Stock Reserve Red

This hobby-only set paralled the base set but was accented with red foil. Cards were serial-numbered to just 50.
*STARS: 8X TO 20X BASIC CARDS
*JERSEYS: .75X TO 2X
*SP's: .15X TO .4X

2002-03 Private Stock Reserve Retail

This 185-card set mirrored the hobby version but with silver foil highlights. Shortprints (151-185) were serial-numbered to 1550.
*BASE/JSY CARDS SAME VALUE
*SP's: .05X TO .12X HBBY HI
157 Rick Nash RC 15.00 40.00
160 Henrik Zetterberg RC 15.00 40.00
173 Jason Spezza RC 12.50 30.00

2002-03 Private Stock Reserve Class Act

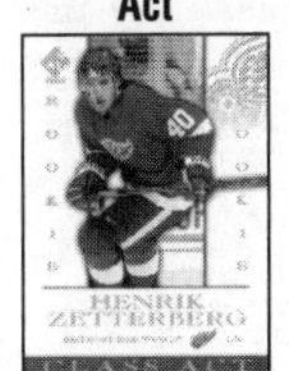

COMPLETE SET (10) 30.00 60.00
STATED ODDS 1:9 HBBY/1:49 RETAIL
1 Stanislav Chistov 4.00 10.00
2 Alexei Smirnov 2.50 6.00
3 Ivan Huml 1.50 4.00
4 Chuck Kobasew 3.00 8.00
5 Tyler Arnason 1.50 4.00
6 Rick Nash 6.00 15.00
7 Henrik Zetterberg 6.00 15.00
8 Jay Bouwmeester 5.00 12.00
9 Stephen Weiss 2.00 5.00
10 Barret Jackman 1.50 4.00

2002-03 Private Stock Reserve Elite

COMPLETE SET (6) 30.00 60.00
STATED ODDS 1:17 HBBY/1:49 RETAIL
1 Ilya Kovalchuk 2.50 6.00
2 Peter Forsberg 4.00 10.00
3 Patrick Roy 8.00 20.00
4 Steve Yzerman 8.00 20.00
5 Mario Lemieux 10.00 25.00
6 Jaromir Jagr 2.50 6.00

2002-03 Private Stock Reserve InCrease Security

COMPLETE SET (20) 15.00 30.00
STATED ODDS 1:3 HBBY/1:25 RETAIL
1 J-S Giguere .75 2.00
2 Roman Turek .75 2.00
3 Arturs Irbe .75 2.00
4 Jocelyn Thibault .75 2.00
5 Patrick Roy 3.00 8.00
6 Marc Denis .75 2.00
7 Marty Turco .75 2.00
8 Curtis Joseph 1.50 4.00
9 Tommy Salo .75 2.00
10 Roberto Luongo 2.00 5.00
11 Felix Potvin .75 2.00
12 Jose Theodore 2.00 5.00
13 Martin Brodeur 2.50 6.00
14 Chris Osgood .75 2.00
15 Mike Richter 1.50 4.00
16 Roman Cechmanek .75 2.00
17 Sean Burke .75 2.00
18 Brent Johnson .75 2.00
19 Evgeni Nabokov .75 2.00
20 Ed Belfour 1.50 4.00

2002-03 Private Stock Reserve Moments in Time

COMPLETE SET (8) 20.00 40.00
STATED ODDS 1:9 HBBY/1:49 RETAIL
1 Chuck Kobasew 3.00 8.00
2 Rick Nash 6.00 15.00
3 Jay Bouwmeester 5.00 12.00
4 Stephen Weiss 2.00 5.00
5 Alexander Frolov 4.00 10.00
6 Jamie Lundmark 1.50 4.00
7 Barret Jackman 1.50 4.00
8 Alexander Svitov 2.50 6.00

2002-03 Private Stock Reserve Patches

This 39-card hobby only set partially paralleled the jersey cards in the base set but were affixed with jersey patches. Each card was serial-numbered individually. Lower print runs are not priced due to scarcity.
102 Dany Heatley/50 20.00 50.00
103 Ilya Kovalchuk/50 25.00 60.00
104 Joe Thornton/275 15.00 40.00
105 Miroslav Satan/275 10.00 25.00
106 Jarome Iginla/70 20.00 50.00
107 Roman Turek/90 10.00 25.00
109 Theo Fleury/275 10.00 25.00
112 Marc Denis/250 10.00 25.00
113 Jason Arnott/250 10.00 25.00
114 Bill Guerin/100 10.00 25.00
115 Mike Modano/150 20.00 50.00
116 Sergei Fedorov/150 20.00 50.00
119 Nicklas Lidstrom/275 12.50 30.00
121 Steve Yzerman/15
122 Mike Comrie/125 10.00 25.00
123 Tommy Salo/275 10.00 25.00
124 Roberto Luongo/150 15.00 40.00
125 Felix Potvin/250 12.50 30.00
126 Marian Gaborik/100 30.00 80.00
127 Jose Theodore/50 15.00 40.00
128 David Legwand/250 10.00 25.00
129 Martin Brodeur/150 25.00 60.00
130 Patrik Elias/150 10.00 25.00
131 Michael Peca/250 10.00 25.00
133 Eric Lindros/250 12.50 30.00
134 Marian Hossa/250 12.50 30.00
135 Roman Cechmanek/250 10.00 25.00
136 Simon Gagne/200 12.50 30.00
137 Daymond Langkow/150 10.00 25.00
139 Chris Pronger/250 10.00 25.00
140 Keith Tkachuk/150 12.50 30.00
141 Evgeni Nabokov/200 10.00 25.00
142 Owen Nolan/250 10.00 25.00
143 Nikolai Khabibulin/275 12.50 30.00
144 Brad Richards/275 10.00 25.00
145 Ed Belfour/245 12.50 30.00
147 Todd Bertuzzi/275 12.50 30.00
148 Peter Bondra/275 12.50 30.00
150 Robert Lang/250 10.00 25.00

2003-04 Private Stock Reserve

This 212-card set was released in late-January and consisted of 100 base veteran cards; 40 short-printed rookie cards (numbered to 99) and 72 jersey cards with varying print runs. Jersey cards with substantially lower print runs are noted below. Jerseys were one per pack.
COMP.SET w/o SP's (100) 40.00 80.00
*MULT.COLOR SWATCH: .75X TO 2X
1 Stanislav Chistov .10 .25
2 J-S Giguere .25 .60
3 Vaclav Prospal .10 .25
4 Petr Sykora .10 .25
5 Byron Dafoe .25 .60
6 Slava Kozlov .10 .25
7 Pasi Nurminen .25 .60
8 Marc Savard .10 .25
9 Mike Knuble .10 .25
10 Felix Potvin .30 .75
11 Sergei Samsonov .25 .60
12 Daniel Briere .10 .25
13 Ales Kotalik .10 .25
14 Ryan Miller .25 .60
15 Blair Betts .10 .25
16 Chuck Kobasew .10 .25
17 Jordan Leopold .10 .25
18 Ron Francis .25 .60
19 Jeff O'Neill .25 .60
20 Kevin Weekes .25 .60
21 Igor Radulov .10 .25
22 Jocelyn Thibault .25 .60
23 Alexei Zhamnov .10 .25
24 David Aebischer .25 .60
25 Rob Blake .25 .60
26 Andrew Cassels .10 .25
27 Rick Nash .40 1.00
28 Geoff Sanderson .10 .25
29 Niko Kapanen .10 .25
30 Jere Lehtinen .25 .60
31 Steve Ott .10 .25
32 Pavel Datsyuk .30 .75
33 Nicklas Lidstrom .30 .75
34 Dominik Hasek .60 1.50
35 Henrik Zetterberg .30 .75
36 Ales Hemsky .25 .60
37 Georges Laraque .10 .25
38 Tommy Salo .25 .60
39 Mike York .10 .25
40 Jay Bouwmeester .10 .25
41 Valeri Bure .10 .25
42 Viktor Kozlov .10 .25
43 Roberto Luongo .40 1.00
44 Stephen Weiss .10 .25
45 Roman Cechmanek .25 .60
46 Adam Deadmarsh .10 .25
47 Alexander Frolov .10 .25
48 Pierre-Marc Bouchard .10 .25
49 Andrew Brunette .10 .25
50 Marian Gaborik .60 1.50
51 Dwayne Roloson .25 .60
52 Mathieu Garon .10 .25
53 Marcel Hossa .10 .25
54 Yanic Perreault .10 .25
55 Mike Ribeiro .10 .25
56 Andreas Johansson .10 .25
57 Scottie Upshall .10 .25
58 Scott Walker .10 .25
59 Patrik Elias .25 .60
60 Jeff Friesen .10 .25
61 Jamie Langenbrunner .10 .25
62 Scott Stevens .25 .60
63 Jason Blake .10 .25
64 Oleg Kvasha .10 .25
65 Mark Parrish .10 .25
66 Garth Snow .25 .60
67 Mattias Weinhandl .10 .25
68 Mike Dunham .25 .60
69 Alex Kovalev .25 .60
70 Brian Leetch .25 .60
71 Mark Messier .30 .75
72 Radek Bonk .25 .60
73 Vaclav Varada .10 .25
74 Todd White .10 .25
75 Simon Gagne .30 .75
76 John LeClair .30 .75
77 Mark Recchi .25 .60
78 Shane Doan .10 .25
79 Mike Johnson .10 .25
80 Daymond Langkow .25 .60
81 Ladislav Nagy .10 .25
82 Sebastien Caron .25 .60
83 Alexei Morozov .10 .25
84 Brent Johnson .25 .60
85 Al MacInnis .25 .60
86 Chris Pronger .25 .60
87 Keith Tkachuk .30 .75
88 Jonathan Cheechoo .12 .30
89 Vincent Damphousse .10 .25
90 Patrick Marleau .10 .25
91 Evgeni Nabokov .25 .60
92 Dave Andreychuk .10 .25
93 Dan Boyle .10 .25
94 Alexander Mogilny .25 .60
95 Owen Nolan .25 .60
96 Darcy Tucker .10 .25
97 Ed Jovanovski .25 .60
98 Trevor Linden .10 .25
99 Sergei Gonchar .10 .25
100 Olaf Kolzig .25 .60
101 Garrett Burnett RC 8.00 20.00
102 Joffrey Lupul RC 12.00 30.00
103 Joe DiPenta RC 8.00 20.00
104 Patrice Bergeron RC 40.00 80.00
105 Milan Bartovic RC 8.00 20.00
106 Andrew Peters RC 8.00 20.00
107 Brent Krahn RC 8.00 20.00
108 Eric Staal RC 60.00 125.00
109 Lasse Kukkonen RC 8.00 20.00
110 Travis Moen RC 8.00 20.00
111 Tuomo Ruutu RC 25.00 60.00
112 Pavel Vorobiev RC 8.00 20.00
113 Cody McCormick RC 8.00 20.00
114 Dan Fritsche RC 8.00 20.00
115 Kent McDonell RC 8.00 20.00
116 Trevor Daley RC 8.00 20.00
117 Antti Miettinen RC 8.00 20.00
118 Jiri Hudler RC 20.00 50.00
119 Nathan Horton RC 25.00 60.00
120 Dustin Brown RC 12.00 30.00
121 Tim Gleason RC 12.00 30.00
122 Esa Pirnes RC 8.00 20.00
123 Brent Burns RC 12.00 30.00
124 Chris Higgins RC 20.00 50.00
125 Dan Hamhuis RC 12.00 30.00
126 Jordin Tootoo RC 30.00 80.00
127 Marek Zidlicky RC 12.00 30.00
128 David Hale RC 8.00 20.00
129 Paul Martin RC 8.00 20.00
130 Sean Bergenheim RC 8.00 20.00
131 Antoine Vermette RC 12.00 30.00
132 Joni Pitkanen RC 12.00 30.00
133 Matthew Spiller RC 8.00 20.00
134 Marc-Andre Fleury RC 75.00 150.00
135 Matt Murley RC 8.00 20.00
136 Peter Sejna RC 8.00 20.00
137 Milan Michalek RC 20.00 50.00
138 Maxim Kondratiev RC 8.00 20.00
139 Matt Stajan RC 20.00 50.00
140 Boyd Gordon RC 8.00 20.00
141 Sergei Fedorov 5.00 12.00
142 Dany Heatley 5.00 12.00
143 Ilya Kovalchuk 5.00 12.00
144 Glen Murray 3.00 8.00
145 Joe Thornton 6.00 15.00
146 Martin Biron 5.00 12.00
147 Chris Drury 5.00 12.00
148 Miroslav Satan 5.00 12.00
149 Craig Conroy 3.00 8.00
150 Jarome Iginla 5.00 12.00
151 Erik Cole 3.00 8.00
152 Eric Daze 5.00 12.00
153 Theo Fleury 3.00 8.00
154 Peter Forsberg 6.00 15.00
155 Milan Hejduk 4.00 10.00
156 Paul Kariya 4.00 10.00
157 Patrick Roy SP 25.00 60.00
158 Joe Sakic 8.00 20.00
159 Teemu Selanne 4.00 10.00
160 Marc Denis 5.00 12.00
161 Rostislav Klesla 3.00 8.00
162 Bill Guerin 5.00 12.00
163 Mike Modano 5.00 12.00
164 Marty Turco 5.00 12.00
165 Brett Hull 5.00 12.00
166 Steve Yzerman 10.00 25.00
167 Mike Comrie 5.00 12.00
168 Ryan Smyth 3.00 8.00
169 Olli Jokinen 5.00 12.00
170 Jason Allison 3.00 8.00
171 Zigmund Palffy 5.00 12.00
172 Filip Kuba SP 8.00 20.00
173 Saku Koivu 4.00 10.00
174 Jose Theodore 5.00 12.00
175 Richard Zednik 3.00 8.00
176 David Legwand 5.00 12.00
177 Tomas Vokoun 5.00 12.00
178 Martin Brodeur 10.00 25.00
179 Rick DiPietro 5.00 12.00
180 Michael Peca 3.00 8.00
181 Alexei Yashin 3.00 8.00
182 Pavel Bure 4.00 10.00
183 Eric Lindros 4.00 10.00
184 Mike Richter SP
185 Daniel Alfredsson 5.00 12.00
186 Marian Hossa 4.00 10.00
187 Patrick Lalime 5.00 12.00
188 Bryan Smolinski 3.00 8.00
189 Jason Spezza 4.00 10.00
190 Tony Amonte 5.00 12.00
191 Jeff Hackett 5.00 12.00
192 Jeremy Roenick 5.00 12.00
193 Sean Burke 5.00 12.00
194 Mario Lemieux 12.50 30.00
195 Martin Straka 3.00 8.00
196 Pavol Demitra 5.00 12.00
197 Chris Osgood 5.00 12.00
198 Doug Weight 5.00 12.00
199 Nikolai Khabibulin 4.00 10.00
200 Vincent Lecavalier 4.00 10.00
201 Fredrik Modin 5.00 12.00
202 Brad Richards 5.00 12.00
203 Martin St. Louis 5.00 12.00
204 Cory Stillman SP 8.00 20.00
205 Ed Belfour 4.00 10.00
206 Mats Sundin 4.00 10.00
207 Todd Bertuzzi 4.00 10.00
208 Dan Cloutier 5.00 12.00
209 Brendan Morrison 5.00 12.00
210 Markus Naslund 4.00 10.00
211 Jaromir Jagr 6.00 15.00
212 Robert Lang 3.00 8.00

2003-04 Private Stock Reserve Blue

*STARS: .75X TO 2X BASIC CARDS
1-100 PRINT RUN 350 SER.#'d SETS
*ROOKIES: .06X TO .15X
ROOKIE PRINT RUN 250 SER.#'d SETS
*JERSEYS: 1.25X TO 3X
JERSEY PRINT RUN 25 SER.#'d SETS

2003-04 Private Stock Reserve Patches

This 68-card set paralleled the jerseys of the base set but included patch swatches. Please note that cards #151,159 and 161 do not exist. Cards with print runs under 25 were not priced due to scarcity. Known shortprints are listed below.
*PATCHES: 1.25X TO 3X BASE JSY
142 Dany Heatley/50 15.00 40.00

143 Ilya Kovalchuk/25 100.00 200.00
145 Joe Thornton/50 20.00 50.00
154 Peter Forsberg/70 20.00 50.00
157 Patrick Roy 20.00 50.00
164 Marty Turco/50 15.00 40.00
166 Steve Yzerman/19
167 Mike Comrie/25 50.00 100.00
168 Ryan Smyth/25 15.00 40.00
172 Filip Kuba 12.50 30.00
188 Bryan Smolinski/20
189 Jason Spezza/25
193 Sean Burke/65 15.00 40.00
202 Brad Richards/25 25.00 60.00
204 Cory Stillman 8.00 20.00
206 Mats Sundin/50 12.50 30.00
210 Markus Naslund/75 12.50 30.00

2003-04 Private Stock Reserve Red

*STARS: 1.25X TO 3X BASE HI
1-100 PRINT RUN 199 SER.#'d SETS
*ROOKIES: .06X TO .15X
ROOKIE PRINT RUN 225 SER.#'d SETS
*JERSEYS: .75X TO 2X BASE HI
JERSEY PRINT RUN 50 SER.#'d SETS

2003-04 Private Stock Reserve Retail

The retail version of this set carried silver foil highlights. Rookies were serial-numbered out of 1299.
*BASE CARDS SAME VALUE AS HOBBY
*RC: .03X TO .075X BASE HI
*JERSEYS: .6X TO 1.5X
108 Eric Staal 12.50 30.00

2003-04 Private Stock Reserve Class Act

COMPLETE SET (12) 15.00 30.00
STATED ODDS 1:9
1 Joffrey Lupul .75 2.00
2 Eric Staal 1.50 4.00
3 Tuomo Ruutu 1.00 2.50
4 Nathan Horton 1.25 3.00
5 Dustin Brown .50 1.25
6 Chris Higgins 1.00 2.50
7 Jordin Tootoo 1.25 3.00
8 Joni Pitkanen .75 2.00
9 Marc-Andre Fleury 2.00 5.00
10 Peter Sejna .50 1.25
11 Milan Michalek .50 1.25
12 Matt Stajan 1.00 2.50

2003-04 Private Stock Reserve Increase Security

COMPLETE SET (16) 15.00 30.00
STATED ODDS 1:5
1 J-S Giguere .75 2.00
2 Felix Potvin 1.00 2.50
3 Ryan Miller .75 2.00
4 Jocelyn Thibault .75 2.00
5 David Aebischer .75 2.00
6 Marty Turco .75 2.00
7 Dominik Hasek 2.00 5.00
8 Jose Theodore 1.25 3.00
9 Martin Brodeur 3.00 8.00
10 Rick DiPietro .75 2.00
11 Patrick Lalime .75 2.00
12 Sean Burke .75 2.00
13 Marc-Andre Fleury 3.00 8.00
14 Evgeni Nabokov .75 2.00
15 Nikolai Khabibulin 1.00 2.50
16 Ed Belfour 1.00 2.50

2003-04 Private Stock Reserve Moments in Time

COMPLETE SET (10) 20.00 40.00
STATED ODDS 1:17
1 Sergei Fedorov 1.00 2.50
2 Joe Thornton 1.25 3.00
3 Peter Forsberg 2.00 5.00
4 Paul Kariya 2.00 5.00
5 Joe Sakic 1.50 4.00
6 Mike Modano 1.25 3.00
7 Brett Hull 1.00 2.50
8 Steve Yzerman 2.50 6.00
9 Mario Lemieux 3.00 8.00
10 Todd Bertuzzi .75 2.00

2003-04 Private Stock Reserve Rising Stock

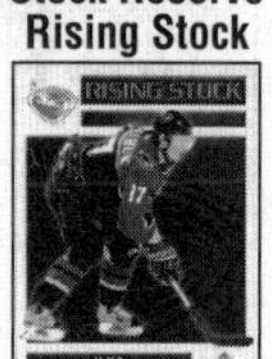

COMPLETE SET (12) 10.00 20.00
STATED ODDS 1:9
1 Ilya Kovalchuk 1.25 3.00
2 Ales Kotalik .40 1.00
3 Ryan Miller .40 1.00
4 Chuck Kobasew .40 1.00
5 Rick Nash .75 2.00
6 Henrik Zetterberg .75 2.00
7 Ales Hemsky .40 1.00
8 Jay Bouwmeester .40 1.00
9 Pierre-Marc Bouchard .40 1.00
10 Marcel Hossa .40 1.00
11 Jason Spezza .75 2.00
12 Barret Jackman .40 1.00

1995-96 Pro Magnets

This set of 130 magnets was produced by Chris Martin Enterprises. Each magnet featured a color photo of the player on front, along with his name and team. The backs were simply a black magnetic surface. The checklist to this set mirrors that of the NHL Pro Stamps.

COMPLETE SET (130) 30.00 75.00
1 Stephane Fiset .24 .60
2 Peter Forsberg .80 2.00
3 Claude Lemieux .20 .50
4 Mike Ricci .20 .50
5 Joe Sakic .80 2.00
6 Ed Belfour .40 1.00
7 Chris Chelios .40 1.00
8 Joe Murphy .20 .50
9 Bernie Nicholls .20 .50
10 Jeremy Roenick .40 1.00
11 Geoff Courtnall .20 .50
12 Brett Hull .40 1.00
13 Al MacInnis .20 .50
14 Chris Pronger .20 .50
15 Esa Tikkanen .20 .50
16 Ray Bourque .80 2.00
17 Blaine Lacher .24 .60
18 Cam Neely .30 .75
19 Adam Oates .20 .50
20 Kevin Stevens .20 .50
21 Valeri Bure .20 .50
22 Vincent Damphousse .24 .60
23 Mark Recchi .30 .75
24 Patrick Roy 1.60 4.00
25 Pierre Turgeon .24 .60
26 Pavel Bure .80 2.00
27 Trevor Linden .24 .60
28 Kirk McLean .24 .60
29 Alexander Mogilny .24 .60
30 Cliff Ronning .20 .50
31 Jason Allison .20 .50
32 Jim Carey .24 .60
33 Dale Hunter .20 .50
34 Joe Juneau .20 .50
35 Brendan Witt .20 .50
36 Martin Brodeur .80 2.00
37 John MacLean .20 .50
38 Scott Niedermayer .20 .50
39 Stephane Richer .20 .50
40 Scott Stevens .20 .50
41 Patrik Carnback .20 .50
42 Guy Hebert .24 .60
43 Paul Kariya 1.20 3.00
44 Oleg Tverdovsky .20 .50
45 Garry Valk .20 .50
46 Theo Fleury .24 .60
47 Trevor Kidd .24 .60
48 Joe Nieuwendyk .20 .50
49 Gary Roberts .20 .50
50 German Titov .20 .50
51 Rod Brind'Amour .20 .50
52 Ron Hextall .20 .50
53 John LeClair .40 1.00
54 Eric Lindros .80 2.00
55 Mikael Renberg .24 .60
56 Brett Lindros .20 .50
57 Wendel Clark .20 .50
58 Patrick Flatley .20 .50
59 Kirk Muller .20 .50
60 Mathieu Schneider .20 .50
61 Tim Cheveldae .24 .60
62 Dallas Drake .20 .50
63 Teemu Selanne .60 1.50
64 Keith Tkachuk .30 .75
65 Alexei Zhamnov .20 .50
66 Rob Blake .30 .75
67 Wayne Gretzky 2.00 5.00
68 Jari Kurri .20 .50
69 Jamie Storr .24 .60
70 Rick Tocchet .20 .50
71 Brian Bradley .20 .50
72 Chris Gratton .20 .50
73 Roman Hamrlik .20 .50
74 Paul Ysebaert .20 .50
75 Rob Zamuner .20 .50
76 Dave Andreychuk .20 .50
77 Doug Gilmour .24 .60
78 Kenny Jonsson .20 .50
79 Felix Potvin .40 1.00
80 Mats Sundin .30 .75
81 Jason Arnott .24 .60
82 Jason Bonsignore .20 .50
83 Todd Marchant .20 .50
84 Bill Ranford .24 .60
85 Doug Weight .24 .60
86 Jody Hull .20 .50
87 Bob Kudelski .20 .50
88 Scott Mellanby .20 .50
89 Rob Niedermayer .20 .50
90 John Vanbiesbrouck .30 .75
91 Ron Francis .24 .60
92 Jaromir Jagr .80 2.00
93 Mario Lemieux 1.60 4.00
94 Bryan Smolinski .20 .50
95 Sergei Zubov .20 .50
96 Adam Graves .20 .50
97 Brian Leetch .30 .75
98 Mark Messier .40 1.00
99 Mike Richter .30 .75
100 Luc Robitaille .24 .60
101 Paul Coffey .24 .60
102 Sergei Fedorov .60 1.50
103 Nicklas Lidstrom .30 .75
104 Ray Sheppard .20 .50
105 Steve Yzerman 1.60 4.00
106 Donald Audette .20 .50
107 Dominik Hasek .60 1.50
108 Yuri Khmylev .20 .50
109 Pat LaFontaine .20 .50
110 Alexei Zhitnik .20 .50
111 Radek Bonk .20 .50
112 Randy Cunneyworth .20 .50
113 Alexandre Daigle .20 .50
114 Steve Larouche .20 .50
115 Martin Straka .20 .50
116 Ulf Dahlen .20 .50
117 Pat Falloon .20 .50
118 Jeff Friesen .20 .50
119 Arturs Irbe .24 .60
120 Craig Janney .20 .50
121 Shane Churla .20 .50
122 Todd Harvey .20 .50
123 Derian Hatcher .20 .50
124 Mike Modano .40 1.00
125 Andy Moog .24 .60
126 Sean Burke .24 .60
127 Andrew Cassels .20 .50
128 Geoff Sanderson .20 .50
129 Brendan Shanahan .60 1.50
130 Darren Turcotte .20 .50

1995-96 Pro Magnets Iron Curtain Insert

1 Ed Belfour
2 Martin Brodeur
3 Arturs Irbe
4 Mike Richter
5 Mike Vernon
6 Ron Hextall

1990-91 Pro Set

The inaugural Pro Set issue contains 705 cards measuring the standard size, with the first series containing 405 cards followed by a 300 card second series. The fronts feature a color action photo, banded above and below in the team's colors. The horizontally oriented backs have a head shot of each player and player information sandwiched between color stripes in the team's colors. Many grammatical, statistical and factual errors punctuated this issue.

COMPLETE SET (705) 6.00 15.00
COMPLETE SERIES 1 (405) 3.00 8.00
COMPLETE SERIES 2 (300) 3.00 8.00
1A Brett Hull Promo UER 1.00 2.50
(Born 9/9/64& 85 games in '87-88, height 6-0, TM under Pro Set logos, aqua blue team color)
1B Ray Bourque ERR .12 .30
(Misspelled Borque on card front)
1C Ray Bourque COR .12 .30
2 Randy Burridge .01 .05
3 Lyndon Byers .01 .05
4 Bob Carpenter .01 .05
5 John Carter .01 .05
6 Dave Christian UER .01 .05
(28 games with Washington& 50 with Boston)
7A Garry Galley ERR .01 .05
7B Garry Galley COR .01 .05
8 Craig Janney .02 .10
9 Rejean Lemelin UER .02 .10
(Wrong headings, not for goalie; '89-90 stats are Andy Moog's)
10 Andy Moog UER .02 .10
('89-90 stats are Reggie Lemelin's; he was 3rd, not 2nd in Vezina voting)
11 Cam Neely UER .05 .15
(Bruins not capitalized in text)
12 Allen Pedersen .01 .05
13 Dave Poulin UER .01 .05
(Flyers' stats missing from '89-90)
14 Brian Propp .01 .05
15 Bob Sweeney .01 .05
16 Glen Wesley .01 .05
17A Dave Andreychuk ERR .02 .10
(Photo actually Scott Arniel on back)
17B Dave Andreychuk COR .02 .10
18A Scott Arniel ERR .01 .05
(Photo actually Dave Andreychuk on back)
18B Scott Arniel COR .01 .05
19 Doug Bodger .01 .05
20 Mike Foligno .01 .05
21A Phil Housley ERR .02 .10
21B Phil Housley COR .02 .10
22 Dean Kennedy .01 .05
23 Uwe Krupp .01 .05
24 Grant Ledyard .01 .05
25 Clint Malarchuk UER .02 .10
(Back in action 11 days after hurt& not 2 as said on card)
26 Alexander Mogilny RC .20 .50
27 Daren Puppa .02 .10
28 Mike Ramsey .01 .05
29 Christian Ruuttu .01 .05
30 Dave Snuggerud .01 .05
31 Pierre Turgeon .02 .10
32 Rick Vaive .01 .05
33 Theo Fleury .02 .10
34 Doug Gilmour .02 .10
35 Al MacInnis UER .02 .10
(Misspelled Allan on card back)
36 Brian MacLellan .01 .05
37 Jamie Macoun .01 .05
38 Sergei Makarov RC .01 .05
39A Brad McCrimmon ERR .01 .05
39B Brad McCrimmon COR .01 .05
40A Joe Mullen ERR .02 .10
40B Joe Mullen COR .02 .10
41 Dana Murzyn .01 .05
42A Joe Nieuwendyk ERR .02 .10
(Misspelled Niewendyk on card front)
42B Joe Nieuwendyk COR .02 .10
43 Joel Otto .01 .05
44 Paul Ranheim RC UER .01 .05
(Front LW& Back C)
45 Gary Roberts .01 .05
46 Gary Suter .01 .05
47 Mike Vernon .02 .10
48 Rick Wamsley .02 .10
(Misspelled Rich in bio on card back)
49 Keith Brown .01 .05
50 Adam Creighton .01 .05
51 Dirk Graham UER .01 .05
(Sparking& should be sparkling; season was '88-89& not '89-90)
52 Steve Konroyd .01 .05
53A Steve Larmer ERR .02 .10
(Position and sweater number in white& should be black)
53B Steve Larmer COR .02 .10
54A Dave Manson ERR .01 .05
(Both photos actually Steve Konroyd)
54B Dave Manson COR .01 .05
55A Bob McGill ERR .01 .05
55B Bob McGill COR .01 .05
56 Greg Millen .02 .10
57A Troy Murray .01 .05
(Position and sweater number are white)
57B Troy Murray .01 .05
(Position and sweater number are black)
58 Jeremy Roenick RC .25 .60
59A Denis Savard .02 .10
(No traded stripe; played 70 games in '86-87)
59B Denis Savard .02 .10
(Traded stripe; played 70 games in '86-87)
60A Al Secord .01 .05
60B Al Secord .01 .05
61A Duane Sutter ERR .01 .05
61B Duane Sutter COR .01 .05
62 Steve Thomas .01 .05
63A Doug Wilson .02 .10
(Position and sweater number are white)
63B Doug Wilson .02 .10
(Position and sweater number are black)
64 Trent Yawney .01 .05
65 Dave Barr .01 .05
66 Shawn Burr .01 .05
67 Jimmy Carson .01 .05
68 John Chabot .01 .05
69 Steve Chiasson .01 .05
70 Bernie Federko UER .02 .10
(Says only player from Foam Lake& but Elynuik was too)
71 Gerard Gallant .01 .05
72 Glen Hanlon .02 .10
73 Joey Kocur RC .12 .30
74 Lee Norwood .01 .05
75 Mike O'Connell .01 .05
76 Bob Probert .02 .10
77 Torrie Robertson .01 .05
78 Daniel Shank .01 .05
79 Steve Yzerman .25 .60
80 Rick Zombo .01 .05
81 Glenn Anderson .02 .10
82 Grant Fuhr .02 .10
83 Martin Gelinas RC UER .01 .05
(Back photo actually Joe Murphy)
84 Adam Graves RC UER .08 .25
(Stats missing '89-90 Detroit info)
85 Charlie Huddy UER .01 .05
(No accent in 1st e in Defenseur)
86 Petr Klima UER .01 .05
(Born Chomulov& should be Chaomutov)
87A Jari Kurri ERR .02 .10
87B Jari Kurri COR .02 .10
88 Mark Lamb .01 .05
89 Kevin Lowe .01 .05
90 Craig MacTavish .01 .05
91 Mark Messier .05 .15
92 Craig Muni .01 .05
93 Joe Murphy RC .01 .05
94 Bill Ranford .02 .10
95 Craig Simpson .01 .05
96 Steve Smith UER .01 .05
(No accent in 1st e in Defenseur)
97 Esa Tikkanen .01 .05
98 Mikael Andersson .01 .05
99 Dave Babych UER .01 .05
(Extra space included after Forum)
100 Yvon Corriveau .01 .05
101 Randy Cunneyworth .01 .05
102 Kevin Dineen .01 .05
103 Dean Evason .01 .05
104 Ray Ferraro .01 .05
105 Ron Francis .02 .10
106 Grant Jennings .01 .05
107 Todd Krygier .01 .05
108 Randy Ladouceur .01 .05
109 Ulf Samuelsson .01 .05
110 Brad Shaw .01 .05
111 Dave Tippett .01 .05
112 Pat Verbeek .01 .05
113 Scott Young .01 .05
114 Brian Benning UER .01 .05
(St.Louis and Los Angeles stats not separate)
115 Steve Duchesne .01 .05
116 Todd Elik RC .01 .05
117 Tony Granato UER .01 .05
(Plays RW& not C)
118 Wayne Gretzky .30 .75
119 Kelly Hrudey .02 .10
120 Steve Kasper .01 .05
121A Mike Kushelnyski ERR .01 .05
(No position and number on card front)
121B Mike Kushelnyski COR .01 .05
122 Bob Kudelski RC UER .01 .05
(Born Springfield& not Feeding Hills)
123 Tom Laidlaw .01 .05
124 Marty McSorley .01 .05
125 Larry Robinson .02 .10
126 Luc Robitaille UER .02 .10
(Kings, should be Kings')
127 Tomas Sandstrom UER .01 .05
('89-90 Rangers stats not printed)
128 Dave Taylor .02 .10
129A John Tonelli ERR .01 .05
(Misspelled Tonnelli on card front)
129B John Tonelli COR .01 .05
130A Brian Bellows ERR .01 .05
(Back photo actually Dave Gagner; front LW, back RW)
130B Brian Bellows COR/ERR .01 .05
(Back photo correct, facing forward; front LW, back RW)
131 Aaron Broten UER .01 .05
(New Jersey and Minnesota stats not separate)
132 Neal Broten .02 .10
133 Jon Casey .02 .10
134 Shawn Chambers .01 .05
135 Shane Churla RC .01 .05
136 Ulf Dahlen UER .01 .05
(Rangers and Minnesota stats not separate)
137 Gaetan Duchesne .01 .05
138 Dave Gagner .02 .10
139 Stewart Gavin .01 .05
140 Curt Giles .01 .05
141 Basil McRae .01 .05
142 Mike Modano RC .30 .75
143 Larry Murphy .02 .10
144 Ville Siren .01 .05
145 Mark Tinordi RC .01 .05
146 Guy Carbonneau UER .02 .10
(Sep Iles should be Sept-Iles)
147A Chris Chelios ERR .05 .15
147B Chris Chelios COR .05 .15
148 Shayne Corson .01 .05
149 Russ Courtnall .01 .05
150 Brian Hayward .02 .10
151 Mike Keane RC .01 .05
152 Stephan Lebeau RC .01 .05
153 Claude Lemieux UER .01 .05
(Reason is misspelled as reson)
154 Craig Ludwig .01 .05
155 Mike McPhee .01 .05
156 Stephane Richer .02 .10
157 Patrick Roy .25 .60
158 Mathieu Schneider RC .01 .05
159 Brian Skrudland .01 .05
160 Bobby Smith UER .02 .10
(No mention of trade from Montreal to Minnesota)
161 Petr Svoboda .01 .05
162 Tommy Albelin .01 .05
163 Doug Brown .01 .05
164 Sean Burke .02 .10
165 Ken Daneyko .01 .05
166 Bruce Driver .01 .05
167A Slava Fetisov RC .01 .05
ERR (Misspelled Vlacheslav on front)
167B Slava Fetisov RC .01 .05
COR
168 Mark Johnson .01 .05
169 Alexei Kasatonov RC UER .01 .05
(Stats should indicate either Soviet or NHL)
170 John MacLean UER .02 .10
(Should have apostrophe after Devils)
171A David Maley ERR .01 .05
171B David Maley COR .01 .05
172 Kirk Muller .01 .05
173 Janne Ojanen .01 .05
174 Brendan Shanahan .05 .15
175A Peter Stastny ERR .02 .10
(Front photo actually Patrik Sundstrom)
175B Peter Stastny COR .02 .10
176A Patrik Sundstrom ERR .01 .05
(Front photo actually Peter Stastny)
176B Patrik Sundstrom COR .01 .05
177 Sylvain Turgeon .01 .05
178 Ken Baumgartner .01 .05
179 Doug Crossman .01 .05
180 Gerald Diduck .01 .05
181 Mark Fitzpatrick RC .02 .10
182 Pat Flatley .01 .05
183 Glen Healy RC UER .02 .10
(Misspelled Glenn on card back)
184 Alan Kerr .01 .05
185 Derek King .01 .05
186 Pat LaFontaine .05 .15
187 Don Maloney .01 .05
188 Hubie McDonough .01 .05
189 Jeff Norton UER .01 .05
(Born Cambridge& Mass. not Acton)
190 Gary Nylund .01 .05
191 Brent Sutter .01 .05
192 Bryan Trottier UER .02 .10
(Finish the season& not finished)
193 David Volek .01 .05
194 Randy Wood .01 .05
195 Jan Erixon .01 .05
196 Mike Gartner UER .02 .10
(Minnesota and Rangers stats not separate)
197 Ron Greschner .01 .05
198A Miloslav Horava ERR .01 .05
198B Miloslav Horava COR .01 .05
199 Mark Janssens .01 .05
200 Kelly Kisio .01 .05
201 Brian Leetch .05 .15
202 Randy Moller .01 .05
203 Brian Mullen .01 .05
204 Bernie Nicholls UER .02 .10
(Kings and Rangers stats not separate)
205A Chris Nilan ERR .01 .05
205B Chris Nilan COR .01 .05
206 John Ogrodnick .01 .05
207 James Patrick .01 .05
208 Darren Turcotte RC UER .01 .05
(GP total says 97, should be 96)
209 John Vanbiesbrouck UER .02 .10
(Front C& back G)
210 Carey Wilson .01 .05
211 Mike Bullard .01 .05
212 Terry Carkner .01 .05
213 Jeff Chychrun .01 .05
214 Murray Craven .01 .05
215 Pelle Eklund UER .01 .05
(Centre and previous, not Center and previously)
216 Ron Hextall .02 .10
217 Mark Howe .01 .05
218 Tim Kerr .01 .05
219 Ken Linseman UER .01 .05
(Bruins and Flyers stats not separate)
220 Scott Mellanby .02 .10
221 Gord Murphy .01 .05
222 Kjell Samuelsson UER .01 .05
(Born 10/18/58, not 10/18/56)
223 Ilkka Sinisalo .01 .05
224 Ron Sutter .01 .05
225 Rick Tocchet .02 .10
226 Ken Wregget .02 .10
227 Tom Barrasso .02 .10
228A Phil Bourque ERR .01 .05
(Misspelled Borque on both sides)
228B Phil Bourque COR .01 .05
229 Rob Brown UER .01 .05
(Front RW, back C; actual position is LW)
230 Alain Chevrier UER .02 .10
(Chicago and Pittsburgh stats not separate)
231 Paul Coffey .05 .15
232 John Cullen .01 .05
233 Gord Dineen .01 .05
234 Bob Errey .01 .05
235 Jim Johnson .01 .05
236 Mario Lemieux .35 .75
237 Troy Loney .01 .05
238 Barry Pederson .01 .05
239 Mark Recchi RC .30 .75
240 Kevin Stevens RC UER .01 .05
(Front LW, back C)
241 Tony Tanti .01 .05
242 Zarley Zalapski UER .01 .05
(Pittsburgh misspelled as Pittsburg)
243 Joe Cirella .01 .05
244 Lucien DeBlois UER .01 .05
(Front C, back RW; misspelled Deblois in bio on card back)
245A Marc Fortier ERR .01 .05
245B Marc Fortier COR .01 .05
246 Paul Gillis .01 .05
247 Mike Hough .01 .05
248 Tony Hrkac UER .01 .05
(Blues and Nordiques stats not separate)
249 Jeff Jackson .01 .05
250 Guy Lafleur .05 .15
251 Curtis Leschyshyn RC .01 .05
252 Claude Loiselle .01 .05
253 Mario Marois .01 .05
254 Tony McKegney UER .01 .05
(Red Wings and Nordiques stats not separate)
255 Ken McRae .01 .05
256A Michel Petit ERR .01 .05
256B Michel Petit COR .01 .05
257 Joe Sakic UER .15 .40
(Front 88, back 19)
258 Ron Tugnutt .02 .10
259 Rod Brind'Amour RC UER .15 .40
(Misspelled Rob on card back)
260 Jeff Brown UER .01 .05
(Nordiques and Blues stats not separate)
261 Gino Cavallini UER .01 .05
(On back Meagher is misspelled as Meager)
262 Paul Cavallini .01 .05
263 Brett Hull .10 .30
264 Mike Lalor .01 .05
265 Dave Lowry .01 .05
266 Paul MacLean .01 .05
267 Rick Meagher .01 .05
268 Sergio Momesso RC UER .01 .05
(Text has 55 pts. in '89-90& stats 56)
269 Adam Oates .02 .10
270 Vincent Riendeau RC .02 .10
271 Gordie Roberts .01 .05
272 Rich Sutter UER .01 .05
(Canucks and Blues stats not separate)
273 Steve Tuttle .01 .05
274 Peter Zezel .01 .05
275A Allan Bester ERR .02 .10
275B Allan Bester COR .02 .10
276 Wendel Clark .02 .10
277 Brian Curran .01 .05
278 Vincent Damphousse .01 .05
(Name not listed on one line)
279A Tom Fergus ERR .01 .05
(Fourth line in bio has TI& should be that)
279B Tom Fergus COR .01 .05
280 Lou Franceschetti .01 .05
281 Al Iafrate .02 .10
282 Tom Kurvers UER .01 .05
(Played for Toronto in 71& not 70)
283 Gary Leeman .01 .05
284 Daniel Marois .01 .05
285 Brad Marsh .01 .05
286 Ed Olczyk .01 .05
287 Mark Osborne .01 .05
288 Rob Ramage .01 .05
289 Luke Richardson .01 .05
290 Gilles Thibaudeau .01 .05
291 Greg Adams .01 .05
292 Jim Benning .01 .05
293 Steve Bozek .01 .05
294 Brian Bradley .01 .05
295 Garth Butcher .01 .05
296 Vladimir Krutov .02 .10
297 Igor Larionov RC UER .01 .05
(Stats should indicate either Soviet or NHL)
298 Doug Lidster .01 .05
299 Trevor Linden .02 .10
300 Jyrki Lumme RC UER .01 .05
('89-90 Canadiens and Canucks stats not separate)
301A Andrew McBain ERR .01 .05
(Back photo actually Jim Sandlak)
301B Andrew McBain COR .01 .05
302 Kirk McLean UER .02 .10
(Career GAA should be 3.46, not 6.50)
303 Dan Quinn UER .01 .05
(Penguins and Canucks stats not separate)
304 Paul Reinhart .01 .05
305 Jim Sandlak .01 .05
306 Petri Skriko .01 .05
307 Don Beaupre .02 .10
308 Dino Ciccarelli .02 .10
309 Geoff Courtnall .01 .05
310 John Druce .01 .05
311 Kevin Hatcher .01 .05
312 Dale Hunter UER .01 .05
(Text has rougish& should be roguish)
313 Calle Johansson UER .01 .05
(No accent in first e in Defenseur)
314 Rod Langway .01 .05
315 Stephen Leach .01 .05
316 Mike Liut UER .02 .10
(Capitals and Whalers stats not separate)
317 Alan May .01 .05
318 Kelly Miller .01 .05
319 Michal Pivonka RC UER .01 .05
(1988-89 Goals should be 8, not 38)
320A Mike Ridley ERR .01 .05
320B Mike Ridley COR .01 .05
321 Scott Stevens UER .02 .10
(No accent in first e in Defenseur; 1987-886)
322 John Tucker UER .01 .05
(1989-90 Buffalo Sabres team affiliation and stats missing 8 games; Ottawa misspelled Ottowa)
323 Brent Ashton .01 .05
324 Laurie Boschman .01 .05
325 Randy Carlyle .01 .05
326 Dave Ellett .01 .05
327 Pat Elynuik .01 .05
328 Bob Essensa RC .08 .25
329 Paul Fenton .01 .05
330A Dale Hawerchuk .02 .10
(No traded stripe;

19089-90; Center
should be Centre)
330B Dale Hawerchuk .02 .10
(Traded stripe on
front; 19089-90; Center
should be Centre)
331 Paul MacDermid .01 .05
332 Moe Mantha .01 .05
333 Dave McLlwain .01 .05
334 Teppo Numminen RC .01 .05
335A Fredrik Olausson ERR .01 .05
(Misspelled Frederik
on both sides)
335B Fredrik Olausson COR .01 .05
336 Greg Paslawski .01 .05
(TM after Jets is larger
than other TM symbols)
337 Al MacInnis AS .02 .10
338 Mike Vernon AS .02 .10
339 Kevin Lowe AS .01 .05
340 Wayne Gretzky AS .05 .15
341 Luc Robitaille AS UER .02 .10
(Fewest shots by Eastern
AS's, not Boston)
342 Brett Hull AS .05 .15
343 Joe Mullen AS .02 .10
344 Joe Nieuwendyk AS .02 .10
345 Steve Larmer AS .02 .10
346 Doug Wilson AS .02 .10
347 Steve Yzerman AS .05 .15
348A Jari Kurri AS ERR .02 .10
348B Jari Kurri AS COR .02 .10
349 Mark Messier AS .05 .15
350 Steve Duchesne AS UER .01 .05
(Shot record held by
Boston, not East)
351 Mike Gartner AS .02 .10
352 Bernie Nicholls AS .02 .10
353 Paul Cavallini AS .01 .05
354 Al Iafrate AS .02 .10
355 Kirk McLean AS .02 .10
356 Thomas Steen AS .01 .05
357 Ray Bourque AS .05 .15
358 Cam Neely AS .02 .10
359 Patrick Roy AS .05 .15
360 Brian Propp AS .01 .05
361 Paul Coffey AS .05 .15
362 Mario Lemieux AS .05 .15
363 Dave Andreychuk AS .02 .10
364 Phil Housley AS .02 .10
365 Daren Puppa AS .02 .10
366 Pierre Turgeon AS .02 .10
367 Ron Francis AS .02 .10
368 Chris Chelios AS .05 .15
369A Shayne Corson AS ERR .01 .05
369B Shayne Corson AS COR .01 .05
370 Stephane Richer AS .02 .10
371 Kirk Muller AS .01 .05
372 Pat LaFontaine AS .02 .10
373 Brian Leetch AS .05 .15
374 Rick Tocchet AS .02 .10
375 Joe Sakic AS .05 .15
376 Kevin Hatcher AS .01 .05
377 Bob Murdoch Adams UER .01 .05
(One tie in 1989-90,
should be 11 ties)
378 Brett Hull Byng UER .05 .15
(Should be Lady Byng
Memorial Trophy)
379 Sergei Makarov Calder .01 .05
380 Kevin Lowe Clancy .01 .05
381 Mark Messier Hart .05 .15
382 Moog/Lemelin Jennings .01 .05
383 Gord Kluzak Mast UER .01 .05
(Should be Bill Masterton
Memorial Trophy)
384 Ray Bourque Norris .05 .15
385A Len Ceglarski Patrick ERR .01 .05
385B Len Ceglarski Patrick COR .01 .05
386 Mark Messier Pearson .05 .15
387 Boston Bruins .01 .05
388 Wayne Gretzky Ross UER .05 .15
(Gretzky has won eight
Art Ross Trophies)
389 Rick Meagher Selke .01 .05
390 Bill Ranford Smythe .02 .10
391 Patrick Roy Vezina .05 .15
392 Edmonton Oilers UER .01 .05
(Should be Clarence
S. Campbell Bowl)
393 Boston Bruins .01 .05
394 Wayne Gretzky LL UER .05 .15
(Lemieux and Dionne,
should read Lemieux only)
395 Brett Hull LL UER .05 .15
(Born 8/9/64,
not 9/9/64)
396 Sergei Makarov ROY .01 .05
397 Mark Messier MVP .05 .15
398 Mike Richter RLL UER .05 .15
(Plays, not lays)
399 Patrick Roy LL .05 .15
400 Darren Turcotte RLL .01 .05
UER (Front RW, back C)
401 Owen Nolan FDP RC .25 .60
402 Petr Nedved FDP RC .10 .30
403 Phil Esposito HOF .02 .10
404 Darryl Sittler HOF UER .02 .10
(Career: 15 seasons,
not stats)
405 Stan Mikita HOF .02 .10
406 Andy Brickley .01 .05
407 Peter Douris .01 .05
408 Nevin Markwart .01 .05
409 Chris Nilan .01 .05
410 Stephane Quintal RC .01 .05
411 Bruce Shoebottom .01 .05
412 Don Sweeney .01 .05
413 Jim Wiemer .01 .05
414 Mike Hartman .01 .05
415 Dale Hawerchuk .02 .10
416 Benoit Hogue .01 .05
417 Bill Houlder RC .01 .05
418 Mikko Makela .01 .05
419 Robert Ray RC .10 .25
420 John Tucker .01 .05
421 Jiri Hrdina .01 .05
422 Mark Hunter .01 .05
423 Tim Hunter RC .01 .05
424 Roger Johansson .01 .05
425 Frank Musil .01 .05
426 Ric Nattress .01 .05
427 Chris Chelios .05 .15
428 Jacques Cloutier .02 .10
429 Greg Gilbert .01 .05
430 Michel Goulet .02 .10
(White position and num-
ber on front, not black)
431 Mike Hudson .01 .05
432 Jocelyn Lemieux .01 .05
433 Brian Noonan .01 .05
434 Wayne Presley .01 .05
435 Brent Fedyk RC .01 .05
436 Rick Green .01 .05
437 Marc Habscheid .01 .05
438 Brad McCrimmon .01 .05
439 Jeff Beukeboom RC .01 .05
440 Dave Brown RC .01 .05
441 Kelly Buchberger .01 .05
442 Greg Hawgood .01 .05
443 Chris Joseph .01 .05
444 Ken Linseman .01 .05
445 Eldon Reddick .02 .10
446 Geoff Smith .01 .05
447 Adam Burt RC .01 .05
448 Sylvain Cote .01 .05
449 Paul Cyr .01 .05
450 Ed Kastelic .01 .05
451 Peter Sidorkiewicz .02 .10
452 Mike Tomlak .01 .05
453 Carey Wilson .01 .05
454 Daniel Berthiaume .02 .10
455 Scott Bjugstad .01 .05
456 Rod Buskas .01 .05
457 John McIntyre .01 .05
458 Tim Watters .01 .05
459 Perry Berezan .01 .05
460 Brian Propp .01 .05
461 Ilkka Sinisalo .01 .05
462 Doug Smail .01 .05
463 Bobby Smith .02 .10
464 Chris Dahlquist .01 .05
465 Neil Wilkinson .01 .05
466 J.J. Daigneault .01 .05
467 Eric Desjardins RC .15 .40
468 Gerald Diduck .01 .05
469 Donald Dufresne .01 .05
470A Todd Ewen ERR .01 .05
470B Todd Ewen COR .01 .05
471 Brent Gilchrist RC .01 .05
472 Sylvain Lefebvre .01 .05
473 Denis Savard .02 .10
474 Sylvain Turgeon .01 .05
475 Ryan Walter .01 .05
476 Laurie Boschman .01 .05
477 Pat Conacher RC .01 .05
478 Claude Lemieux .01 .05
479 Walt Poddubny .01 .05
480 Alan Stewart .01 .05
481 Chris Terreri RC .02 .10
482 Brad Dalgarno .01 .05
483 Dave Chyzowski .01 .05
484 Craig Ludwig .01 .05
485 Wayne McBean .01 .05
486 Rich Pilon RC .01 .05
487 Joe Reekie .01 .05
488 Mick Vukota .01 .05
489 Mark Hardy .01 .05
490 Jody Hull .01 .05
491 Kris King .01 .05
492 Troy Mallette .01 .05
493 Kevin Miller RC .01 .05
494 Normand Rochefort .01 .05
495 David Shaw .01 .05
496 Ray Sheppard .02 .10
497 Keith Acton .01 .05
498 Craig Berube .01 .05
499 Tony Horacek .01 .05
500 Normand Lacombe .01 .05
501 Jiri Latal .01 .05
502 Pete Peeters .02 .10
503 Derrick Smith .01 .05
504 Jay Caufield .01 .05
505 Peter Taglianetti .01 .05
506 Randy Gilhen .01 .05
507 Randy Hillier .01 .05
508 Joe Mullen .02 .10
509 Frank Pietrangelo .02 .10
510 Gordie Roberts .01 .05
511 Bryan Trottier .02 .10
512 Wendell Young .02 .10
513 Shawn Anderson .01 .05
514 Steven Finn .01 .05
515 Bryan Fogarty .01 .05
516 Mike Hough .01 .05
517 Darin Kimble .01 .05
518 Randy Velischek .01 .05
519 Craig Wolanin .01 .05
520 Bob Bassen .01 .05
521 Geoff Courtnall .01 .05
522 Robert Dirk .01 .05
523 Glen Featherstone .01 .05
524 Mario Marois .01 .05
525 Herb Raglan .01 .05
526 Cliff Ronning .01 .05
527 Harold Snepsts .01 .05
528 Scott Stevens .02 .10
529 Ron Wilson .01 .05
530 Aaron Broten .01 .05
531 Lucien DeBlois .01 .05
532 Dave Ellett .01 .05
533A Paul Fenton ERR .01 .05
(Trademark on front
next to name)
533B Paul Fenton COR .01 .05
534 Todd Gill RC .01 .05
535 Dave Hannan .01 .05
536 John Kordic .01 .05
537 Mike Krushelnyski .01 .05
538 Kevin Maguire .01 .05
539 Michel Petit .01 .05
540 Jeff Reese .01 .05
541 David Reid .01 .05
542 Doug Shedden .01 .05
543 Dave Capuano .01 .05
544 Craig Coxe .01 .05
545 Kevan Guy .01 .05
546 Rob Murphy .01 .05
547 Robert Nordmark .01 .05
548 Stan Smyl .01 .05
549 Ronnie Stern .01 .05
550 Tim Bergland .01 .05
551 Nick Kypreos .01 .05
552 Mike Lalor .01 .05
553 Rob Murray .01 .05
554 Bob Rouse .01 .05
555 Dave Tippett .01 .05
556 Peter Zezel UER .01 .05
(Card says number 25,
sweater shows 9)
557 Scott Arniel .01 .05
558 Don Barber .01 .05
559 Shawn Cronin .01 .05
560 Gord Donnelly .01 .05
561 Doug Evans .01 .05
562 Phil Housley .02 .10
563 Ed Olczyk .01 .05
564 Mark Osborne .01 .05
565 Thomas Steen .01 .05
566 Boston Bruins Logo .01 .05
567 Buffalo Sabres Logo .01 .05
568 Calgary Flames Logo .01 .05
569 Chicago Blackhawks Logo .01 .05
570 Detroit Red Wings Logo .01 .05
571 Edmonton Oilers Logo .01 .05
572 Hartford Whalers Logo .01 .05
573A Los Angeles Kings .01 .05
Logo ERR
(Registration mark
missing from Kings
on card front)
573B Los Angeles Kings Logo COR .01 .05
574 Minn. North Stars Logo .01 .05
575 Montreal Canadiens Logo .01 .05
576 New Jersey Devils Logo .01 .05
577 New York Islanders Logo .01 .05
578 New York Rangers Logo .01 .05
579 Philadelphia Flyers Logo .01 .05
580 Pittsburgh Penguins Logo .01 .05
581 Quebec Nordiques Logo .01 .05
582 St. Louis Blues Logo .01 .05
583 Toronto Maple Leafs Logo .01 .05
584 Vancouver Canucks Logo .01 .05
585 Washington Capitals Logo .01 .05
586 Winnipeg Jets Logo .01 .05
587 Ken Hodge Jr. RC .01 .05
588 Vladimir Ruzicka RC .01 .05
589 Wes Walz RC .01 .05
590 Greg Brown .01 .05
591 Brad Miller .01 .05
592 Darrin Shannon RC .01 .05
593 Stephane Matteau RC UER .01 .05
(Front RW&, back LW)
594 Sergei Priakin .01 .05
595 Robert Reichel RC .07 .20
596 Ken Sabourin .01 .05
597 Tim Sweeney .01 .05
598 Ed Belfour RC UER .50 1.25
(Born Carmen&
should be Carman)
599 Frantisek Kucera .01 .05
600 Mike McNeil .01 .05
601 Mike Peluso RC .01 .05
602 Tim Cheveldae RC .02 .10
603 Per Djoos .01 .05
604 Sergei Fedorov RC .30 .75
605 Johan Garpenlov RC .01 .05
606 Keith Primeau RC .01 .05
607 Paul Ysebaert RC .01 .05
608 Anatoli Semenov RC .01 .05
609 Bobby Holik RC .07 .20
610 Kay Whitmore RC .02 .10
611 Rob Blake RC .12 .30
612 Francois Breault .01 .05
613 Mike Craig RC UER .01 .05
(Wearing 50&
card says 20)
614 J.C. Bergeron RC UER .01 .05
(Front J.C.&
back Jean Claude)
615 Andrew Cassels .01 .05
616 Tom Chorske .01 .05
617 Lyle Odelein RC .01 .05
618 Mark Pederson .01 .05
619 Zdeno Ciger .01 .05
620 Troy Crowder RC .01 .05
621 Jon Morris .01 .05
622 Eric Weinrich .01 .05
623 David Marcinyshyn .01 .05
624 Jeff Hackett RC .02 .10
625 Rob DiMaio .01 .05
626 Steven Rice RC .01 .05
627 Mike Richter RC .20 .50
628 Dennis Vial .01 .05
629 Martin Hostak .01 .05
630 Pat Murray .01 .05
631 Mike Ricci RC UER .08 .20
(Born October,
not November)
632 Jaromir Jagr RC ERR .50 1.25
(Stat header not lined
up with stats on back)
632B Jaromir Jagr RC COR .05 .15
(Stat header lined
up with stats on back)
633 Paul Stanton .01 .05
634 Scott Gordon .01 .05
635 Owen Nolan .02 .10
636 Mats Sundin RC .25 .60
637 John Tanner .01 .05
638 Curtis Joseph RC .30 .75
639 Peter Ing .02 .10
640 Scott Thornton .01 .05
641 Troy Gamble .02 .10
642 Robert Kron .01 .05
643 Petr Nedved .01 .05
644 Adrien Plavsic .01 .05
645 Peter Bondra RC .20 .50
646 Jim Hrivnak RC .01 .05
647 Mikhail Tatarinov RC .01 .05
648 Stephane Beauregard RC .02 .10
649 Rick Tabaracci .02 .10
650 Mike Bossy CPL .02 .10
651 Bobby Clarke CPL .02 .10
652 Alex Delvecchio CPL .02 .10
653 Marcel Dionne CPL .02 .10
654 Gordie Howe CPL .08 .25
655 Stan Mikita CPL .02 .10
656 Denis Potvin CPL .02 .10
657 Bobby Clarke HOF .02 .10
658 Alex Delvecchio HOF .02 .10
659 Tony Esposito HOF .02 .10
660 Gordie Howe HOF .08 .25
661 Mike Milbury CO .01 .05
662 Rick Dudley CO .01 .05
663 Doug Risebrough CO .01 .05
664 Bryan Murray CO .01 .05
665 John Muckler CO .01 .05
666 Rick Ley CO .01 .05
667 Tom Webster CO .01 .05
668 Bob Gainey CO UER .01 .05
(Stats and bio are
Bob McCammon's)
669 Pat Burns CO .01 .05
670 John Cunniff CO .01 .05
671 Al Arbour CO .01 .05
672 Roger Neilson CO .01 .05
673 Paul Holmgren CO .01 .05
674 Bob Johnson CO RC .01 .05
675 Dave Chambers CO .01 .05
676 Brian Sutter CO UER .01 .05
(Coaching totals say
0-69-21& should
be 70-69-21)
677 Tom Watt CO .01 .05
678 Bob McCammon CO UER .01 .05
(Stats and bio are
Bob Gainey's)
679 Terry Murray CO .01 .05
680 Bob Murdoch CO .01 .05
681 Ron Asselstine REF .01 .05
682 Wayne Bonney REF .01 .05
683 Kevin Collins REF .01 .05
684 Pat Dapuzzo REF .01 .05
685 Ron Finn REF .01 .05
686 Kerry Fraser REF .01 .05
687 Gerard Gauthier REF .01 .05
688 Terry Gregson REF .01 .05
689 Bob Hodges REF .01 .05
690 Ron Hoggarth REF .01 .05
691 Don Koharski REF .01 .05
692 Dan Marouelli REF .01 .05
693 Danny McCourt REF .01 .05
694 Bill McCreary REF .01 .05
695 Denis Morel REF .01 .05
696 Jerry Pateman REF .01 .05
697 Ray Scapinello REF .01 .05
698 Rob Shick REF .01 .05
699 Paul Stewart REF .01 .05
700 Leon Stickle REF .01 .05
701 Andy van Hellemond REF .01 .05
702 Mark Vines REF .01 .05
703 Wayne Gretzky 2000th .05 .15
(2.33 goals per game&
should be points) UER
704 Stanley Cup Champs .01 .05
705 The Puck-La Rondelle .01 .05
NNO Stanley Cup Hologram 20.00 50.00

1990-91 Pro Set Player of the Month

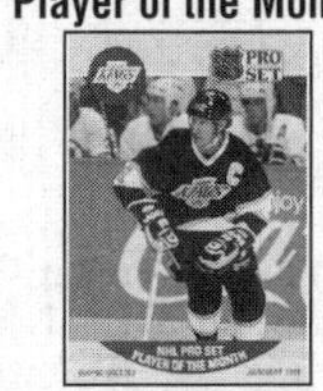

This four-card set features the NHL player of the month for four consecutive months (the month for which the player won the award is listed below his name). All cards feature the basic 1990-91 Pro Set design, and say NHL Pro Set Player of the Month and the date at the bottom of each obverse. The cards are numbered on the back; note that the Peeters card has no number. The cards were issued in the home rink of the winner each month after announcement of the winner. Pro Set sponsored the Player of the Week/Month/Year Awards for the NHL. Reportedly less than 25,000 of each POM card were produced.

COMPLETE SET (4) 8.00 20.00
P1 Tom Barrasso 1.60 4.00
POM December 1990
P2 Wayne Gretzky 4.00 10.00
POM January 1991
P3 Brett Hull 2.40 6.00
POM February 1991
NNO Pete Peeters 1.60 4.00
POM November 1990

1991-92 Pro Set Preview

This six-card standard-size set was given to dealers to show what the 1991-92 Pro Set hockey set would look like. There is really not that much interest in the set due to the egregiously poor player selection, i.e., no superstars in the set. The setup of the text on the card backs of these preview cards is different from the regular issue cards; cards are labeled "Promo" on the back where the card number is in the regular issue cards. The David Reid card has an entirely different photo. Even though the cards are unnumbered, they are assigned reference numbers below according to their numbers in the 1991-92 Pro Set regular issue.

COMPLETE SET (6) .60 1.50
151 Randy Wood NNO .10 .25
171 Gord Murphy NNO .10 .25
203 Craig Wolanin NNO .10 .25
229 David Reid NNO .10 .25
266 Bob Essensa NNO .10 .25
NNO Title Card .04 .10

1991-92 Pro Set

The Pro Set hockey issue contains 615 numbered cards. The set was released in two series of 345 and 270 cards, respectively. Pro Set also issued a French version which carries the same value. French wax boxes contained randomly inserted Patrick Roy personally autographed cards signed and numbered on the back; 1,000 of card number 125 (first series) and 1,000 of card number 599 numbered 1001 to 2000 (second series). Roy also signed 500 cards for distribution in Canadian collector's kits. Randomly inserted in U.S. packs were a limited quantity of Kirk McLean autographed cards. Ten thousand hand-numbered 3-D hologram cards were inserted in second series foil packs to commemorate the NHL's Diamond Anniversary.

COMPLETE SET (615) 7.50 15.00
COMPLETE SERIES 1 (345) 4.00 8.00
COMPLETE SERIES 2 (270) 4.00 8.00
*FRENCH VERSION: SAME VALUE
1 Glen Wesley .01 .05
2 Craig Janney .02 .10
3 Ken Hodge Jr. .01 .05
4 Randy Burridge .01 .05
5 Cam Neely .05 .15
6 Bob Sweeney .01 .05
7 Garry Galley .01 .05
8 Petri Skriko .01 .05
9 Ray Bourque .12 .30
10 Andy Moog UER .02 .10
(4.0 record
should be 4-0)
11 Dave Christian .01 .05
12 Dave Poulin .01 .05
13 Jeff Lazaro .01 .05
14 Darrin Shannon .01 .05
15 Pierre Turgeon UER .02 .10
(Born 8/29 not 8/28)
16 Alexander Mogilny .05 .15
17 Benoit Hogue UER .01 .05
(Stats show two seasons
with Winnipeg& should
say Buffalo)
18 Dave Snuggerud .01 .05
19 Doug Bodger UER .01 .05
(Second highest offens-
ive total of his career&
should say third highest)
20 Uwe Krupp .01 .05
21 Daren Puppa .02 .10
22 Christian Ruuttu .01 .05
23 Dave Andreychuk .02 .10
24 Dale Hawerchuk .02 .10
25 Mike Ramsey .01 .05
26 Rick Vaive .01 .05
27 Stephane Matteau .01 .05
28 Theo Fleury .01 .05
29 Joe Nieuwendyk .02 .10
30 Gary Roberts .01 .05
31 Paul Ranheim .01 .05
32 Gary Suter .01 .05
33 Al MacInnis .02 .10
34 Doug Gilmour .02 .10
35 Mike Vernon .02 .10
36 Carey Wilson .01 .05
37 Joel Otto .01 .05
38 Jamie Macoun .01 .05
39 Sergei Makarov .01 .05
40 Jeremy Roenick .10 .25
41 Dave Manson .01 .05
42 Adam Creighton .01 .05
43 Ed Belfour .10 .30
44 Wayne Presley .01 .05
45 Steve Thomas .01 .05
46 Troy Murray .01 .05
47 Bob McGill .01 .05
48 Chris Chelios .05 .15
49 Steve Larmer .02 .10
50 Michel Goulet .02 .10
51 Dirk Graham .01 .05
52 Doug Wilson .02 .10
53 Sergei Fedorov .08 .25
54 Yves Racine .01 .05
55 Jimmy Carson .01 .05
56 Johan Garpenlov .01 .05
57 Tim Cheveldae .02 .10
58 Shawn Burr .01 .05
59 Paul Ysebaert .01 .05
60 Kevin Miller .01 .05
61 Bob Probert .02 .10
62 Steve Yzerman .25 .60
63 Gerard Gallant .01 .05
64 Rick Zombo .01 .05
65 Dave Barr .01 .05
66 Martin Gelinas .01 .05
67 Adam Graves UER .02 .10
(Kid Line included
Gelinas not Simpson)
68 Joe Murphy .01 .05
69 Craig Simpson .01 .05
70 Bill Ranford .02 .10
71 Esa Tikkanen .01 .05
72 Petr Klima .01 .05
73 Steve Smith .01 .05
74 Mark Messier .05 .15
75 Glenn Anderson .02 .10
76 Kevin Lowe .02 .10
77 Craig MacTavish .01 .05
78 Grant Fuhr .05 .15
79 Bobby Holik .02 .10
80 Rob Brown .01 .05
81 Doug Houda .01 .05
82 Sylvain Cote .01 .05
83 Todd Krygier .01 .05
84 Dean Evason .01 .05
85 John Cullen .01 .05
86 Pat Verbeek .01 .05
87 Brad Shaw .01 .05
88 Paul Cyr UER .01 .05
(Stats show New York,
should say NY Rangers)
89 Kevin Dineen .01 .05
90 Peter Sidorkiewicz .02 .10
91 Zarley Zalapski .01 .05
92 Rob Blake .02 .10
93 Jari Kurri UER .05 .15
(No transaction
line on front, al-
though back says Kings)
94 Todd Elik .01 .05
95 Luc Robitaille .02 .10
96 Steve Duchesne .01 .05
97 Tomas Sandstrom .01 .05
98 Tony Granato .01 .05
99 Bob Kudelski .01 .05
100 Marty McSorley .01 .05
101 Wayne Gretzky .30 .75
102 Kelly Hrudey .02 .10
103 Dave Taylor .02 .10
104 Larry Robinson .02 .10
105 Mike Modano .10 .30
106 Ulf Dahlen .01 .05
107 Mark Tinordi .01 .05
108 Dave Gagner .01 .05
109 Brian Bellows .01 .05
110 Gaetan Duchesne .01 .05
111 Jon Casey .02 .10
112 Neal Broten .02 .10
113 Brian Propp .01 .05
114 Curt Giles .01 .05
115 Bobby Smith .02 .10
116 Jim Johnson .01 .05
117 Doug Smail .01 .05
118 Eric Desjardins .02 .10
119 Mathieu Schneider .01 .05
120 Stephan Lebeau .01 .05
121 Mike Keane .01 .05
122 Stephane Richer .02 .10
123 Petr Svoboda .01 .05
124 J.J. Daigneault .01 .05
125 Patrick Roy .25 .60
126 Russ Courtnall .01 .05
127 Brian Skrudland .01 .05
128 Denis Savard .02 .10
129 Mike McPhee .01 .05
130 Guy Carbonneau .02 .10
131 Brendan Shanahan .05 .15
132 Sean Burke .02 .10
133 Eric Weinrich .01 .05
134 Kirk Muller .01 .05
135 Claude Lemieux .01 .05
136 John MacLean .02 .10
137 Chris Terreri .02 .10
138 Doug Brown .01 .05
139 Ken Daneyko .01 .05
140 Bruce Driver .01 .05
141 Patrik Sundstrom .01 .05
142 Slava Fetisov .01 .05
143 Peter Stastny .02 .10
144 Wayne McBean .01 .05
145 Bill Berg .01 .05
146 Derek King .01 .05
147 David Volek .01 .05
148 Jeff Norton .01 .05
149 Pat LaFontaine .05 .15
150 Gary Nylund .01 .05
151 Randy Wood .01 .05
152 Pat Flatley .01 .05
153 Glenn Healy .02 .10
154 Brent Sutter .01 .05
155 Craig Ludwig .01 .05
156 Ray Ferraro .01 .05
157 Troy Mallette .01 .05
158 Mark Janssens .01 .05
159 Brian Leetch UER .05 .15
(Career points total
329 should be 229)
160 Darren Turcotte .01 .05
161 Mike Richter .05 .15
162 Ray Sheppard .01 .05
163 Randy Moller .01 .05
164 James Patrick .01 .05
165 Brian Mullen UER .01 .05
(Transaction says
drafted by San Jose&
was actually traded)
166 Bernie Nicholls .02 .10
167 Mike Gartner .02 .10
168 Kelly Kisio UER .01 .05
(Transaction says
drafted by Minnesota,
was actually traded
to San Jose)
169 John Ogrodnick .01 .05
170 Mike Ricci .05 .15
171 Gord Murphy .01 .05
172 Scott Mellanby .01 .05
173 Terry Carkner .01 .05
174 Derrick Smith .01 .05
175 Murray Craven .01 .05
176 Ron Hextall .02 .10
177 Rick Tocchet .02 .10
178 Ron Sutter .01 .05
179 Pelle Eklund .01 .05
180 Tim Kerr UER .01 .05
(Only transaction
line to show a date)
181 Kjell Samuelsson .01 .05
182 Mark Howe .01 .05
183 Jaromir Jagr .10 .25
184 Mark Recchi .05 .15
185 Kevin Stevens .01 .05
186 Tom Barrasso .02 .10
187 Bob Errey .01 .05
188 Ron Francis .02 .10
189 Phil Bourque .01 .05
190 Paul Coffey .05 .15
191 Joe Mullen .02 .10
192 Bryan Trottier .05 .15
193 Larry Murphy .02 .10
194 Mario Lemieux .25 .60
195 Scott Young .01 .05
196 Owen Nolan .05 .15
197 Mats Sundin .02 .10
198 Curtis Leschyshyn .01 .05
199 Joe Sakic .10 .30
200 Bryan Fogarty .01 .05
201 Stephane Morin .01 .05
202 Ron Tugnutt .02 .10
203 Craig Wolanin .01 .05
204 Steven Finn .01 .05
205 Tony Hrkac .01 .05
206 Randy Velischek .01 .05
207 Alexei Gusarov RC .02 .10
208 Scott Pearson .01 .05
209 Dan Quinn .01 .05
210 Garth Butcher .01 .05
211 Rod Brind'Amour UER .05 .15
(Type in stat box is
smaller than others)
212 Jeff Brown .01 .05
213 Vincent Riendeau .02 .10
214 Paul Cavallini .01 .05
215 Brett Hull .08 .25
216 Scott Stevens .02 .10
217 Rich Sutter .01 .05
218 Gino Cavallini .01 .05
219 Adam Oates UER .02 .10
(Stats are off-line
from top to bottom)
220 Ron Wilson .01 .05
221 Bob Bassen .01 .05
222 Peter Ing .02 .10
223 Daniel Marois .01 .05
224 Vincent Damphousse .01 .05
225 Wendel Clark UER .02 .10
(Connecticut not cap-
italized in last line)
226 Todd Gill .01 .05
227 Peter Zezel .01 .05
228 Bob Rouse .01 .05
229 David Reid .01 .05
230 Dave Ellett .01 .05
231 Gary Leeman .01 .05
232 Rob Ramage .01 .05
233 Mike Krushelnyski .01 .05
234 Tom Fergus .01 .05
235 Petr Nedved .02 .10
236 Trevor Linden .02 .10
237 Dave Capuano .01 .05
238 Troy Gamble .02 .10
239 Robert Kron UER .01 .05
(Type in stat box is
smaller than others)
240 Jyrki Lumme .01 .05
241 Cliff Ronning .01 .05
242 Sergio Momesso .01 .05
243 Greg Adams .01 .05
244 Tom Kurvers .01 .05
245 Geoff Courtnall .02 .10
246 Igor Larionov .02 .10
247 Doug Lidster UER .01 .05
(No space between 51
and assist in last
line of text)
248 Calle Johansson .01 .05
249 Kevin Hatcher .02 .10
250 Al Iafrate .02 .10
251 John Druce .01 .05
252 Michal Pivonka .01 .05
253 Stephen Leach .01 .05
254 Mike Ridley .01 .05
255 Mike Lalor .01 .05
256 Kelly Miller .01 .05
257 Don Beaupre .02 .10
258 Dino Ciccarelli .02 .10
259 Rod Langway .01 .05
260 Dimitri Khristich .01 .05
261 Teppo Numminen .01 .05
262 Pat Elynuik .01 .05
263 Danton Cole .01 .05
264 Fredrik Olausson UER .01 .05
(Fifth line of text&
the word the is missing
between in and 10th)
265 Ed Olczyk .01 .05
266 Bob Essensa .02 .10
267 Phil Housley .02 .10
268 Shawn Cronin .01 .05
269 Paul MacDermid .01 .05
270 Mark Osborne .01 .05
271 Thomas Steen .01 .05
272 Brent Ashton .01 .05
273 Randy Carlyle .01 .05
274 Theo Fleury AS .01 .05
275 Al MacInnis AS .01 .05
276 Gary Suter AS .01 .05
277 Mike Vernon AS .02 .10
278 Chris Chelios AS .02 .10
279 Steve Larmer AS .01 .05
280 Jeremy Roenick AS .05 .15
281 Steve Yzerman AS .12 .30
282 Mark Messier AS .05 .15
283 Bill Ranford AS .02 .10
284 Steve Smith AS .01 .05
285 Wayne Gretzky AS .12 .30
286 Luc Robitaille AS .02 .10
287 Tomas Sandstrom AS .01 .05
288 Dave Gagner AS .01 .05
289 Bobby Smith AS .01 .05
290 Brett Hull AS .05 .15
291 Adam Oates AS .01 .05
292 Scott Stevens AS .01 .05
293 Vincent Damphousse AS .01 .05
294 Trevor Linden AS .01 .05
295 Phil Housley AS .01 .05
296 Ray Bourque AS .05 .15
297 Dave Christian AS .01 .05
298 Garry Galley AS .01 .05
299 Andy Moog AS .02 .10
300 Cam Neely AS .02 .10
301 Uwe Krupp AS .01 .05
302 John Cullen AS .01 .05
303 Pat Verbeek AS .01 .05
304 Patrick Roy AS .10 .30
305 Denis Savard AS .01 .05
306 Brian Skrudland AS .01 .05
307 John MacLean AS .01 .05
308 Pat LaFontaine AS .02 .10
309 Brian Leetch AS .02 .10
310 Darren Turcotte AS .01 .05

311 Rick Tocchet AS .01 .05
312 Paul Coffey AS .02 .10
313 Mark Recchi AS .02 .10
314 Kevin Stevens AS .01 .05
315 Joe Sakic AS .05 .15
316 Kevin Hatcher AS .01 .05
317 Guy Lafleur AS .05 .15
318 Mario Lemieux Smythe .10 .30
319 Pittsburgh Penguins .01 .05
Stanley Cup Champs UER
(On fourth line says
won in 5 games& should
say 6 games)
320 Brett Hull .05 .15
Hart Trophy
321 Ed Belfour .05 .15
Vezina/Jennings
322 Ray Bourque .05 .15
Norris
323 Dirk Graham .01 .05
Selke
324 Wayne Gretzky .12 .30
Ross/Lady Byng
325 Dave Taylor .01 .05
King Clancy Trophy
326 Brett Hull .05 .15
PS Player of the Year
327 Brian Hayward .02 .10
328 Neil Wilkinson UER .01 .05
(Born Manitoba
not Minnesota)
329 Craig Coxe .01 .05
330 Rob Zettler .01 .05
331 Jeff Hackett .02 .10
332 Joe Malone .01 .05
333 Georges Vezina .05 .15
334 The Modern Arena .01 .05
335 Ace Bailey Benefit .05 .15
336 Howie Morenz .02 .10
337 The Punch Line .01 .05
338 The Kid Line .01 .05
339 Before the Zamboni .05 .15
340 Bill Barilko .02 .10
341 Jacques Plante .05 .15
342 Arena Designs .01 .05
343 Terry Sawchuk .05 .15
344 Gordie Howe .08 .25
345 Guy Carbonneau .02 .10
Play Smart
346 Stephen Leach .01 .05
347 Peter Douris .01 .05
348 David Reid .01 .05
349 Bob Carpenter .01 .05
350 Stephane Quintal .01 .05
351 Barry Pederson .01 .05
352 Brent Ashton .01 .05
353 Vladimir Ruzicka .01 .05
354 Brad Miller .01 .05
355 Robert Ray .01 .05
356 Colin Patterson .01 .05
357 Gord Donnelly .01 .05
358 Pat LaFontaine .05 .15
359 Randy Wood .01 .05
360 Randy Hillier .01 .05
361 Robert Reichel .01 .05
362 Ronnie Stern .01 .05
363 Ric Nattress .01 .05
364 Tim Sweeney .01 .05
365 Marc Habscheid .01 .05
366 Tim Hunter .01 .05
367 Rick Wamsley .02 .10
368 Frank Musil .01 .05
369 Mike Hudson .01 .05
370 Steve Smith .01 .05
371 Keith Brown .01 .05
372 Greg Gilbert .01 .05
373 John Tonelli .01 .05
374 Brent Sutter .01 .05
375 Brad Lauer .01 .05
376 Alan Kerr .01 .05
377 Brad McCrimmon .01 .05
378 Brad Marsh .01 .05
379 Brent Fedyk .01 .05
380 Ray Sheppard .01 .05
381 Vincent Damphousse .01 .05
382 Craig Muni .01 .05
383 Scott Mellanby .01 .05
384 Geoff Smith .01 .05
385 Kelly Buchberger .01 .05
386 Bernie Nicholls .02 .10
387 Luke Richardson .01 .05
388 Peter Ing .02 .10
389 Dave Manson .01 .05
390 Mark Hunter .01 .05
391 Jim McKenzie .01 .05
392 Randy Cunneyworth .01 .05
393 Murray Craven .01 .05
394 Mikael Andersson .01 .05
395 Andrew Cassels .01 .05
396 Randy Ladouceur .01 .05
397 Marc Bergevin .01 .05
398 Brian Benning .01 .05
399 Mike Donnelly RC .01 .05
400 Charlie Huddy .01 .05
401 John McIntyre .01 .05
402 Jay Miller .01 .05
403 Randy Gilhen .01 .05
404 Stewart Gavin .01 .05
405 Mike Craig .01 .05
406 Brian Glynn .01 .05
407 Rob Ramage .01 .05
408 Chris Dahlquist .01 .05
409 Basil McRae .01 .05
410 Todd Elik .01 .05
411 Craig Ludwig .01 .05
412 Kirk Muller .01 .05
413 Shayne Corson .01 .05
414 Brent Gilchrist .01 .05
415 Mario Roberge .01 .05
416 Sylvain Turgeon .01 .05
417 Alain Cote .01 .05
418 Donald Dufresne .01 .05
419 Todd Ewen .01 .05
420 Stephane Richer .02 .10
421 David Maley .01 .05
422 Randy McKay .01 .05
423 Scott Stevens .02 .10
424 Jon Morris .01 .05
425 Claude Vilgrain .01 .05
426 Laurie Boschman .01 .05
427 Pat Conacher .01 .05
428 Tom Kurvers .01 .05
429 Joe Reekie .01 .05
430 Rob DiMaio .01 .05
431 Tom Fitzgerald .01 .05
432 Ken Baumgartner .01 .05
433 Pierre Turgeon .02 .10
434 Dave McLlwain .01 .05
435 Benoit Hogue .01 .05
436 Uwe Krupp .01 .05
437 Adam Creighton .01 .05
438 Steve Thomas .01 .05
439 Mark Messier .05 .15
440 Tie Domi .05 .15
441 Sergei Nemchinov .01 .05
442 Mark Hardy .01 .05
443 Adam Graves .02 .10
444 Jeff Beukeboom .01 .05
445 Kris King .01 .05
446 Tim Kerr .01 .05
447 John Vanbiesbrouck .02 .10
448 Steve Duchesne .01 .05
449 Steve Kasper .01 .05
450 Ken Wregget .02 .10
451 Kevin Dineen .01 .05
452 Dave Brown .01 .05
453 Rod Brind'Amour .05 .15
454 Jiri Latal .01 .05
455 Tony Horacek .01 .05
456 Brad Jones .01 .05
457 Paul Stanton .01 .05
458 Gordie Roberts .01 .05
459 Ulf Samuelsson .01 .05
460 Ken Priestlay .01 .05
461 Jiri Hrdina .01 .05
462 Mikhail Tatarinov .01 .05
463 Mike Hough .01 .05
464 Don Barber .01 .05
465 Greg Smyth RC .01 .05
466 Doug Smail .01 .05
467 Mike McNeill .01 .05
468 John Kordic .01 .05
469 Greg Paslawski .01 .05
470 Herb Raglan .01 .05
471 Dave Christian .01 .05
472 Murray Baron .01 .05
473 Curtis Joseph .05 .15
474 Rick Zombo .01 .05
475 Brendan Shanahan .05 .15
476 Ron Sutter .01 .05
477 Mario Marois .01 .05
478 Doug Wilson .02 .10
479 Kelly Kisio .01 .05
480 Bob McGill .01 .05
481 Perry Anderson .01 .05
482 Brian Lawton .01 .05
483 Neil Wilkinson .01 .05
484 Ken Hammond RC .01 .05
485 David Bruce RC .01 .05
486 Steve Bozek .01 .05
487 Perry Berezan .01 .05
488 Wayne Presley .01 .05
489 Brian Bradley .01 .05
490 Darryl Shannon .01 .05
491 Lucien DeBlois .01 .05
492 Michel Petit .01 .05
493 Claude Loiselle .01 .05
494 Grant Fuhr .05 .15
495 Craig Berube .01 .05
496 Mike Bullard .01 .05
497 Jim Sandlak .01 .05
498 Dana Murzyn .01 .05
499 Garry Valk .01 .05
500 Andrew McBain .01 .05
501 Kirk McLean .02 .10
502 Gerald Diduck .01 .05
503 Dave Babych .01 .05
504 Ryan Walter .01 .05
505 Gino Odjick .01 .05
506 Dale Hunter .01 .05
507 Tim Bergland .01 .05
508 Alan May .01 .05
509 Jim Hrivnak .02 .10
510 Randy Burridge .01 .05
511 Peter Bondra .02 .10
512 Sylvain Cote .01 .05
513 Nick Kypreos .01 .05
514 Troy Murray .01 .05
515 Darrin Shannon .01 .05
516 Bryan Erickson .01 .05
517 Petri Skriko .01 .05
518 Mike Eagles .01 .05
519 Mike Hartman .01 .05
520 Bob Beers .01 .05
521 Matt DelGuidice .01 .05
522 Chris Winnes .01 .05
523 Brad May .01 .05
524 Donald Audette .01 .05
525 Kevin Haller RC .01 .05
526 Martin Simard .01 .05
527 Tomas Forslund RC .01 .05
528 Mark Osiecki .01 .05
529 Dominik Hasek RC .60 1.50
530 Jimmy Waite .02 .10
531 Nicklas Lidstrom RC UER.30 .75
(Misspelled Niklas
on card front)
532 Martin Lapointe .02 .10
533 Vladimir Konstantinov RC.15 .40
534 Josef Beranek RC .01 .05
535 Louie DeBrusk RC .01 .05
536 Geoff Sanderson RC .02 .10
537 Mark Greig .01 .05
538 Michel Picard RC .01 .05
539 Chris Tancill RC .01 .05
540 Peter Ahola RC .01 .05
541 Francois Breault .01 .05
542 Darryl Sydor .02 .10
543 Derian Hatcher .02 .10
544 Marc Bureau .01 .05
545 John LeClair RC .30 .75
546 Paul Dipietro RC .01 .05
547 Scott Niedermayer UER .01 .05
(Misspelled on front
as Neidermayer)
548 Kevin Todd RC .01 .05
549 Doug Weight RC .25 .60
550 Tony Amonte RC .30 .75
551 Corey Foster RC .01 .05
552 Dominic Roussel RC .02 .10
553 Dan Kordic RC .01 .05
554 Jim Paek RC .01 .05
555 Kip Miller .01 .05
556 Claude Lapointe RC .01 .05
557 Nelson Emerson .01 .05
558 Pat Falloon .01 .05
559 Pat MacLeod RC .01 .05
560 Rick Lessard .01 .05
561 Link Gaetz .01 .05
562 Rob Pearson RC .01 .05
563 Alexander Godynyuk .01 .05
564 Pavel Bure .05 .15
565 Russell Romaniuk RC .01 .05
566 Stu Barnes .01 .05
567 Ray Bourque CAP .05 .15
568 Mike Ramsey CAP .01 .05
569 Joe Nieuwendyk CAP .01 .05
570 Dirk Graham CAP .01 .05
571 Steve Yzerman CAP .12 .30
572 Kevin Lowe CAP .01 .05
573 Randy Ladouceur CAP .01 .05
574 Wayne Gretzky CAP .12 .30
575 Mark Tinordi CAP .01 .05
576 Guy Carbonneau CAP .02 .10
577 Bruce Driver CAP .01 .05
578 Pat Flatley CAP .01 .05
579 Mark Messier CAP .05 .15
580 Rick Tocchet CAP .01 .05
581 Mario Lemieux CAP .10 .30
582 Mike Hough CAP .01 .05
583 Garth Butcher CAP .01 .05
584 Doug Wilson CAP .01 .05
585 Wendel Clark CAP .02 .10
586 Trevor Linden CAP .01 .05
587 Rod Langway CAP .01 .05
588 Troy Murray CAP .01 .05
589 Practicing Outdoors .01 .05
590 Shape Up .01 .05
591 Boston Bruins Cartoon .01 .05
592 Opening Night .01 .05
593 Rod Gilbert .01 .05
594 Phil Esposito .05 .15
595 Dale Tallon .01 .05
596 Gilbert Perreault .01 .05
597 Bernie Federko .01 .05
598 All-Star Game .02 .10
599 Patrick Roy LL .10 .30
600 Ed Belfour LL .05 .15
601 Don Beaupre LL .01 .05
602 Bob Essensa LL .01 .05
603 Kirk McLean UER LL .02 .10
(Leader logo shows
PPG should be GAA)
604 Mike Gartner LL .01 .05
605 Jeremy Roenick LL .05 .15
606 Rob Brown LL .01 .05
607 Ulf Dahlen LL .01 .05
608 Paul Ysebaert LL .01 .05
609 Brad McCrimmon LL .01 .05
610 Nicklas Lidstrom LL .12 .30
611 Kelly Miller LL .01 .05
612 Jim Kyte SMART .01 .05
613 Patrick Roy SMART .10 .30
614 Alan May SMART .01 .05
615 Kelly Miller SMART .01 .05
AU125 Patrick Roy AU 100.00 200.00
(Certified autograph)
AU501 Kirk McLean AU 15.00 30.00
(Certified autograph)
AU599 Patrick Roy AU 50.00 125.00
(Certified autograph)
NNO 75th Anniversary 20.00 50.00
Hologram

1991-92 Pro Set CC

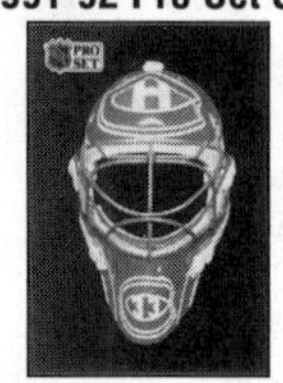

These standard-size cards were issued as random inserts in French and English Pro Set 15-card foil packs. The first four were in the first series and the last five were inserted in with the second series. The Pat Falloon and Scott Niedermayer cards were withdrawn early in the first series print run. This was due to the cards being released prior to the players having appeared in an NHL game; a contravention of licensing regulations. The cards are numbered on the back with a "CC" prefix.

COMPLETE SET (9) 6.00 15.00
*FRENCH VERSION: 1X TO 1.25X
CC1 Entry Draft .40 1.00
CC2 The Mask 1.00 2.50
CC3 Pat Falloon UER SP 1.25 3.00
(Born Birtle&
not Foxwarren)
CC4 Scott Niedermeyer SP 2.00 5.00
CC5 Wayne Gretzky 2.00 5.00
CC6 Brett Hull .60 1.50
CC7 Adam Oates .50 1.25
CC8 Mark Recchi .60 1.50
CC9 John Cullen .40 1.00

1991-92 Pro Set Gazette

These standard-size cards were issued in cello packs.The front of card number 2 had the words "Pro Set Gazette" in the upper left corner and the player's name in a blue stripe near the bottom of the card. The SC1 Roy card has his name appearing in a red stripe at the bottom with the words "Goalie of the Year" in a blue stripe. The card is numbered "Special Collectible 1" on the back.

COMPLETE SET (2) 2.00 5.00
2 Patrick Roy 1.20 3.00
(Gazette Collectible)
SC1 Patrick Roy 1.20 3.00
(Special Collectible 1)

1991-92 Pro Set HOF Induction

This 14-card set was issued by Pro Set to commemorate the 1991 Hockey Hall of Fame Induction Dinner and Ceremonies in September, 1991 held in Ottawa. The standard-size cards feature borderless glossy sepia-toned player or team photos on the fronts. A colorful insignia with the words "Hockey Hall of Fame and Museum" appears on the front of each card. The team cards represent the past Ottawa Stanley Cup winning teams.

COMPLETE SET (14) 30.00 75.00
1 Mike Bossy 6.00 15.00
1991 HOF Inductee
2 Denis Potvin 4.80 12.00
1991 HOF Inductee
3 Bob Pulford 3.20 8.00
1991 HOF Inductee
4 William Scott Bowman 6.00 15.00
1991 HOF Inductee
5 Neil P. Armstrong 2.40 6.00
1991 HOF Inductee
6 Clint Smith 2.40 6.00
1991 HOF Inductee
7 1903-04 Ottawa Silver 2.00 5.00
Seven
8 1905 Ottawa Silver 2.00 5.00
Seven
9 1909 Ottawa Senators 2.00 5.00
10 1911 Ottawa Senators 2.00 5.00
11 1920-21 Ottawa 2.00 5.00
Senators
12 1923 Ottawa Senators 2.00 5.00
13 1927 Ottawa Senators 2.00 5.00
14 Title Card 2.00 5.00
1991 Hockey Hall of Fame
Dinner and Ceremonies

1991-92 Pro Set Awards Special

This 17-card standard-size set features NHL players who were All-Stars, nominees, or winners of prestigious trophies. The fronts feature a borderless color action photo, with the team logo in the lower left corner, and the player's name in the black wedge below the logo. The backs present player information and the award which the player won or was nominated for, on a white and gray hockey puck background. The cards are numbered on the back and also have a star logo with the words "A Celebration of Excellence". The cards have the 1991-92 Pro Set style of design.

AC1 Ed Belfour 12.00 30.00
AC2 Mike Richter 12.00 30.00
AC3 Patrick Roy 75.00 200.00
AC4 Wayne Gretzky 125.00 300.00
AC5 Joe Sakic 30.00 75.00
AC6 Brett Hull 25.00 60.00
AC7 Ray Bourque 25.00 60.00
AC8 Al MacInnis 6.00 15.00
AC9 Luc Robitaille 10.00 25.00
AC10 Sergei Fedorov 40.00 100.00
AC11 Ken Hodge Jr. .75 2.00
AC12 Dirk Graham .75 2.00
AC13 Steve Larmer 2.00 5.00
AC14 Esa Tikkanen 4.00 10.00
AC15 Chris Chelios 15.00 40.00
AC16 Dave Taylor 1.50 4.00
NNO Title Card .40 1.00

1991-92 Pro Set NHL Sponsor Awards

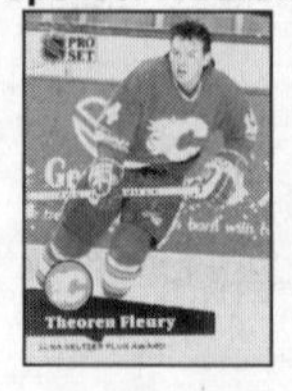

This eight-card standard-size set is numbered as an extension of the 1991-92 Pro Set NHL Awards Special. The cards feature the same glossy color player photos as does the regular issue. The fronts differ in having the name of the award inscribed across the bottom of the card face. Also the backs differ in that they omit the head and shoulders photo and have only a player profile. The cards were distributed at The Hockey News Sponsor Awards luncheon in Toronto on June 6, 1991.

AC17 Kevin Dineen 2.40 6.00
Bud Light/NHL Man
of the Year Award
AC18 Brett Hull 24.00 60.00
NHL Pro Set Player
of the Year Award
AC19 Ed Belfour 10.00 25.00
Trico Goaltender Award
AC20 Theo Fleury 10.00 25.00
Alka-Seltzer
Plus Award
AC21 Marty McSorley 2.40 6.00
Alka-Seltzer
Plus Award
AC22 Mike Ilitch 1.60 4.00
Detroit Red Wings OWN
Lester Patrick Award
AC23 Rod Gilbert 2.40 6.00
Lester Patrick Award
NNO Title Card .40 1.00
1990-91 NHL
Sponsor Awards

1991-92 Pro Set Opening Night

This six-card promo set was issued by Pro Set to commemorate the opening night of the 1991-92 NHL season. The standard-size player cards are the same as the regular issue, with borderless glossy color player photos on the fronts, and a color headshot and player information on the backs. Four (different each time) regular issue cards were included in each promo pack.

COMPLETE SET (2) 3.20 8.00
NNO NHL 75th Anniversary 1.60 4.00
Opening Night
NNO 1991-92 Opening Night 1.60 4.00

1991-92 Pro Set Platinum PC

The 1991-92 Pro Set Platinum PC set consists of 20 standard size cards randomly inserted in Platinum foil packs. The first series inserts were a ten-card Platinum Collectibles subset featuring Players of the Month (PC1-PC6) and Sensational Sophomores (PC7-PC10). The second series inserts were subtitled Platinum Milestones (PC11-PC20).

COMPLETE SET (20) 12.50 25.00
PC1 John Vanbiesbrouck .50 1.25
PC2 Pete Peeters .25 .60
PC3 Tom Barrasso .25 .60
PC4 Wayne Gretzky 2.00 5.00
PC5 Brett Hull .75 2.00
PC6 Kelly Hrudey .25 .60
PC7 Sergei Fedorov .75 2.00
PC8 Rob Blake .25 .60
PC9 Ken Hodge Jr. .15 .30
PC10 Eric Weinrich .15 .30
PC11 Mike Gartner .25 .60
PC12 Paul Coffey .50 1.25
PC13 Bobby Smith .25 .60
PC14 Wayne Gretzky 2.00 5.00
PC15 Michel Goulet .40 1.00
PC16 Mike Liut .25 .60
PC17 Brian Propp .15 .30
PC18 Denis Savard .25 .60
PC19 Bryan Trottier .40 1.00
PC20 Mark Messier .60 1.50

1991-92 Pro Set Platinum HOF 75th

This eight-card standard-size set was issued in a cello pack to pay tribute to the NHL's 75th Anniversary. The set includes the Original Six team cards (indistinguishable from cards 145-150 in the regular set) from the 1991-92 Pro Set Platinum hockey set and two special cards. The Hockey Hall of Fame Collectible features on the front a full-bleed sepia-toned picture of Exhibition Place, where the Hockey Hall of Fame has been located since 1961. In addition to commentary, the back features a small color picture of BCE Place, its new location beginning in the fall of 1992. On a black background, the title card features the Hockey Hall of Fame and Museum logo at the top as well as the NHL and Pro Set logos at the bottom. The title card has a blank back. The actual numbering of the cards is reflected in the listing below.

COMPLETE SET (8) 3.20 8.00
145 Boston Bruins .04 .10
146 Chicago Blackhawks .04 .10
147 Detroit Red Wings .04 .10
148 Montreal Canadiens .04 .10
149 New York Rangers .04 .10
150 Toronto Maple Leafs .04 .10
NNO Title Card 1.20 3.00
(Blank back)
HHOF1 Hockey Hall of Fame 2.00 5.00
Collectible; Excellence,
Education, Entertainment
(Pictures the opening
of the Hall of Fame
in 1961 in Toronto)

1991-92 Pro Set Player of the Month

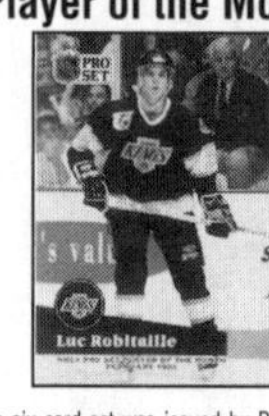

This six-card set was issued by Pro Set to honor hockey players for their outstanding performances during the season. The cards were distributed to all ticket holders at home games the evening of the presentation. Another feature of the presentation was a $1200 donation on behalf of the winning player to the youth hockey organization of his choice. Measuring the standard 2 1/2" by 3 1/2", card fronts feature borderless four-color action photographs. The player's team emblem appears in the lower left corner while the player's name is reversed-out white in a black wedge. On a screened hockey puck design, the horizontally oriented backs have a head shot in a circular format, biography, career statistics, and a summary of the outstanding achievement. The card number and team position appears in the upper right corner.

COMPLETE SET (6) 28.00 70.00
P1 Kirk McLean 2.00 5.00
POM October 1991
(Issued 11/19/91)
P2 Kevin Stevens 2.00 5.00
POM November 1991
(Issued 12/26/91)
P3 Mario Lemieux 12.00 30.00
Pittsburg
P4 Andy Moog 4.00 10.00
POM January 1991
P5 Pat LaFontaine 4.00 10.00
POM January 1991
P6 Luc Robitaille 4.00 10.00
POM February 1991

1991-92 Pro Set Puck Candy Promos

This set of three standard-size hockey cards was distributed in a cello pack to show the design of the upcoming Puck cards. The fronts of the promos are identical to the regular issue. Their backs differ in two respects: 1) instead of a card number, the promos have the words "Prototype For Review Only" in an aqua box; and 2) The "Puck Note" on the promos differs from that found on the regular cards. The cards are unnumbered and checklisted below in alphabetical order.

COMPLETE SET (3) 1.60 4.00
1 Kirk McLean .40 1.00
2 Andy Moog .80 2.00
3 Pat Verbeek .40 1.00

1991-92 Pro Set Puck Candy

This set of thirty standard-size hockey cards was created for a new product, the NHL Pro Set Puck, a combination chocolate, peanut vanilla nougat, and caramel confection. This test product was available in all U.S. NHL and Northeast markets, and each candy package contained three Puck hockey cards. The fronts feature a borderless four-color action player photo with the Pro Set logo and player's name in the bottom border. The

horizontally oriented backs have a head shot, biography, and a "Puck Note" that consists of personal information about the player. Pro Set advertised this 30-card set as Series 1; however no Series 2 was ever issued.

COMPLETE SET (30) 16.00 40.00
1 Ray Bourque .80 2.00
2 Andy Moog .30 .75
3 Doug Bodger .16 .40
4 Theo Fleury .30 .75
5 Al MacInnis .30 .75
6 Jeremy Roenick .60 1.50
7 Tim Cheveldae .16 .40
8 Steve Yzerman 1.60 4.00
9 Craig Simpson .16 .40
10 Pat Verbeek .16 .40
11 Wayne Gretzky 16.00 40.00
12 Luc Robitaille .30 .75
13 Brian Bellows .16 .40
14 Patrick Roy 3.20 8.00
15 Guy Carbonneau .16 .40
16 Peter Stastny .30 .75
17 Adam Creighton .16 .40
18 Glenn Healy .30 .75
19 Mark Messier .80 2.00
20 Rod Brind'Amour .30 .75
21 Paul Coffey .60 1.50
22 Tom Barasso .30 .75
23 Joe Sakic 1.20 3.00
24 Brett Hull .80 2.00
25 Adam Oates .30 .75
26 Kelly Kisio .16 .40
27 Grant Fuhr .30 .75
28 Kirk McLean .30 .75
29 Kevin Hatcher .16 .40
30 Phil Housley .16 .40

1991-92 Pro Set Rink Rat

These standard-size cards were produced by Pro Set to promote education. On card number 2 the front cartoon portrays the Rink Rat shooting the puck through a defenseman's legs right toward the viewer of the card; on a screen design with miniature hockey pucks, the horizontally oriented back has another circular-shaped cartoon picture of the Rink Rat reading and a "stay in school/study hard" message.

COMPLETE SET (2) 3.20 8.00
RR1 Rink Rat 1.60 4.00
(Holding stick over
head; copyright 1991)
RR2 Rink Rat 1.60 4.00
(Shooting puck)

1991-92 Pro Set St. Louis Midwest

This four-card standard-size set was available at the Midwest Sports Collectors Show in St. Louis in November 1991. The cards were a special issue for the card show; in fact, Pro Set did not even issue a Meagher card in its regular set. All four cards show explicitly on the front that they were a special issue from this show. The fronts of these cards differ from the regular issue in two respects: 1) a royal blue border stripe runs the length of the card on the right side; and 2) the cards are numbered in the stripe "X of Four Midwest Collectors Show". The card backs are the same as the regular issue cards.

COMPLETE SET (4) 4.00 10.00
1 Adam Oates 1.20 3.00
2 Paul Cavallini .40 1.00
3 Rick Meagher .40 1.00
4 Brett Hull 3.20 8.00

1992-93 Pro Set

The 1992-93 Pro Set hockey set consists of 270 cards. The production run was 8,000 numbered 20-box foil cases and 2,000 20-box jumbo cases. One thousand Kirk McLean autographed cards were randomly inserted. The McLean cards have No. 239 on the back; his regular card is #193. The most noteworthy Rookie Card in the set is Bill Guerin.

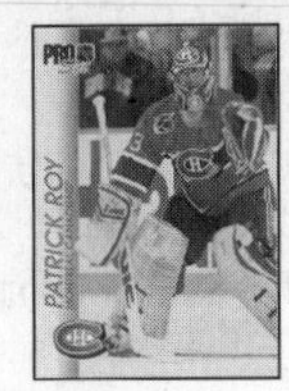

COMPLETE SET (270) 7.50 15.00
1 Mario Lemieux PS-POY .20 .50
2 Patrick Roy .20 .50
Hockey News POY
3 Adam Oates .02 .10
4 Ray Bourque .15 .40
5 Vladimir Ruzicka .01 .05
6 Stephen Leach .01 .05
7 Andy Moog .08 .25
8 Cam Neely .08 .25
9 Dave Poulin .01 .05
10 Glen Wesley .01 .05
11 Gord Murphy .01 .05
12 Dale Hawerchuk .02 .10
13 Pat LaFontaine .08 .25
14 Tom Draper .01 .05
15 Dave Andreychuk .02 .10
16 Petr Svoboda .01 .05
17 Doug Bodger .01 .05
18 Donald Audette .01 .05
19 Alexander Mogilny .02 .10
20 Randy Wood .01 .05
21 Gary Roberts .01 .05
22 Al MacInnis .02 .10
23 Theo Fleury .01 .05
24 Sergei Makarov .01 .05
25 Mike Vernon .02 .10
26 Joe Nieuwendyk .02 .10
27 Gary Suter .01 .05
28 Joel Otto .01 .05
29 Paul Ranheim .01 .05
30 Jeremy Roenick .12 .30
31 Steve Larmer .02 .10
32 Michel Goulet .02 .10
33 Ed Belfour .08 .25
34 Chris Chelios .08 .25
35 Igor Kravchuk .01 .05
36 Brent Sutter .01 .05
37 Steve Smith .01 .05
38 Dirk Graham .01 .05
39 Steve Yzerman .40 1.00
40 Sergei Fedorov .12 .30
41 Paul Ysebaert .01 .05
42 Nicklas Lidstrom .08 .25
43 Tim Cheveldae .02 .10
44 Vladimir Konstantinov .08 .25
45 Shawn Burr .01 .05
46 Bob Probert .02 .10
47 Ray Sheppard .01 .05
48 Kelly Buchberger .01 .05
49 Joe Murphy .01 .05
50 Norm Maciver .01 .05
51 Bill Ranford .02 .10
52 Bernie Nicholls .02 .10
53 Esa Tikkanen .01 .05
54 Scott Mellanby .01 .05
55 Dave Manson .01 .05
56 Craig Simpson .01 .05
57 John Cullen .01 .05
58 Pat Verbeek .01 .05
59 Zarley Zalapski .01 .05
60 Murray Craven .01 .05
61 Bobby Holik .02 .10
62 Steve Konroyd .01 .05
63 Geoff Sanderson .02 .10
64 Frank Pietrangelo .02 .10
65 Mikael Andersson UER .01 .05
66 Wayne Gretzky .50 1.25
67 Rob Blake .02 .10
68 Jari Kurri .08 .25
69 Marty McSorley .01 .05
70 Kelly Hrudey .02 .10
71 Paul Coffey .08 .25
72 Luc Robitaille .02 .10
73 Peter Ahola .01 .05
74 Tony Granato .01 .05
75 Derian Hatcher .01 .05
76 Mike Modano .15 .40
77 Dave Gagner .02 .10
78 Mark Tinordi .01 .05
79 Craig Ludwig .01 .05
80 Ulf Dahlen .01 .05
81 Bobby Smith .02 .10
82 Jon Casey .02 .10
83 Jim Johnson .01 .05
84 Denis Savard .02 .10
85 Patrick Roy .40 1.00
86 Eric Desjardins .02 .10
87 Kirk Muller .01 .05
88 Guy Carbonneau .02 .10
89 Shayne Corson .01 .05
90 Brent Gilchrist .01 .05
91 Mathieu Schneider UER .01 .05
92 Gilbert Dionne .01 .05
93 Stephane Richer .02 .10
94 Kevin Todd .01 .05
95 Scott Stevens .02 .10
96 Slava Fetisov .01 .05
97 Chris Terreri .02 .10
98 Claude Lemieux .01 .05
99 Bruce Driver .01 .05
100 Peter Stastny .02 .10
101 Alexei Kasatonov .01 .05
102 Patrick Flatley .01 .05
103 Adam Creighton UER .01 .05
104 Pierre Turgeon .02 .10
105 Ray Ferraro .01 .05
106 Steve Thomas .02 .10
107 Mark Fitzpatrick .02 .10
108 Benoit Hogue .01 .05
109 Uwe Krupp .01 .05
110 Derek King .01 .05
111 Mark Messier .08 .25
112 Brian Leetch .08 .25
113 Mike Gartner .02 .10
114 Darren Turcotte .01 .05
115 Adam Graves .01 .05
116 Mike Richter .08 .25
117 Sergei Nemchinov .01 .05
118 Tony Amonte .02 .10
119 James Patrick .01 .05
120 Andrew McBain .01 .05
121 Rob Murphy .01 .05
122 Mike Peluso .01 .05
123 Sylvain Turgeon .01 .05
124 Brad Shaw .01 .05
125 Peter Sidorkiewicz .02 .10
126 Brad Marsh .01 .05
127 Mark Freer .01 .05
128 Marc Fortier .01 .05
129 Ron Hextall .02 .10
130 Claude Boivin .01 .05
131 Mark Recchi .02 .10
132 Rod Brind'Amour .02 .10
133 Mike Ricci .02 .10
134 Kevin Dineen .01 .05
135 Brian Benning .01 .05
136 Kerry Huffman .01 .05
137 Steve Duchesne .01 .05
138 Rick Tocchet .02 .10
139 Mario Lemieux .40 1.00
140 Kevin Stevens .01 .05
141 Jaromir Jagr .12 .30
142 Joe Mullen .02 .10
143 Ulf Samuelsson .01 .05
144 Ron Francis .02 .10
145 Tom Barrasso .02 .10
146 Larry Murphy .02 .10
147 Alexei Gusarov .01 .05
148 Valeri Kamensky .01 .05
149 Mats Sundin .08 .25
150 Joe Sakic .15 .40
151 Claude Lapointe .01 .05
152 Stephane Fiset .02 .10
153 Owen Nolan .02 .10
154 Mike Hough .01 .05
155 Greg Paslawski .01 .05
156 Brett Hull .10 .30
157 Craig Janney .02 .10
158 Jeff Brown .01 .05
159 Paul Cavallini .01 .05
160 Garth Butcher .01 .05
161 Nelson Emerson .01 .05
162 Ron Sutter .01 .05
163 Brendan Shanahan .08 .25
164 Curtis Joseph .08 .25
165 Doug Wilson .02 .10
166 Pat Falloon .01 .05
167 Kelly Kisio .01 .05
168 Neil Wilkinson .01 .05
169 Jay More .01 .05
170 David Bruce .01 .05
171 Jeff Hackett .02 .10
172 David Williams RC .01 .05
173 Brian Lawton .01 .05
174 Brian Bradley .01 .05
175 Jock Callander RC .01 .05
176 Basil McRae .01 .05
177 Rob Ramage .01 .05
178 Pat Jablonski .02 .10
179 Joe Reekie .01 .05
180 Doug Crossman .01 .05
181 Jim Benning .01 .05
182 Ken Hodge Jr. .01 .05
183 Grant Fuhr .08 .25
184 Doug Gilmour .02 .10
185 Glenn Anderson .02 .10
186 Dave Ellett .01 .05
187 Peter Zezel .01 .05
188 Jamie Macoun .01 .05
189 Wendel Clark .02 .10
190 Bob Halkidis .01 .05
191 Rob Pearson .01 .05
192 Pavel Bure .08 .25
193 Kirk McLean .02 .10
194 Sergio Momesso .01 .05
195 Cliff Ronning .01 .05
196 Jyrki Lumme .01 .05
197 Trevor Linden .02 .10
198 Geoff Courtnall .01 .05
199 Doug Lidster .01 .05
200 Dave Babych .01 .05
201 Michal Pivonka .01 .05
202 Dale Hunter .02 .10
203 Calle Johansson .01 .05
204 Kevin Hatcher .01 .05
205 Al Iafrate .02 .10
206 Don Beaupre .02 .10
207 Randy Burridge .01 .05
208 Dimitri Khristich .01 .05
209 Peter Bondra .02 .10
210 Teppo Numminen .01 .05
211 Bob Essensa .02 .10
212 Phil Housley .02 .10
213 Ed Olczyk .01 .05
214 Pat Elynuik .01 .05
215 Troy Murray .01 .05
216 Igor Ulanov .01 .05
217 Thomas Steen .01 .05
218 Darrin Shannon .01 .05
219 Joe Juneau .02 .10
220 Stephen Heinze .01 .05
221 Ted Donato .01 .05
222 Glen Murray .01 .05
223 Keith Carney RC .30 .75
224 Dean McAmmond RC .01 .05
225 Slava Kozlov .02 .10
226 Martin Lapointe .02 .10
227 Patrick Poulin .01 .05
228 Darryl Sydor .01 .05
229 Trent Klatt RC .02 .10
230 Bill Guerin RC .12 .30
231 Jarrod Skalde .01 .05
232 Scott Niedermayer .01 .05
233 Marty McInnis .01 .05
234 Scott LaChance .01 .05
235 Dominic Roussel .02 .10
236 Eric Lindros .08 .25
237 Shawn McEachern .01 .05
238 Martin Rucinsky .01 .05
239 Bill Lindsay RC .01 .05
240 Bret Hedican RC .02 .10
241 Ray Whitney RC .15 .40
242 Felix Potvin .08 .25
243 Keith Tkachuk .08 .25
244 Evgeny Davydov .01 .05
245 Brett Hull SL .08 .25
246 Wayne Gretzky SL .25 .60
247 Steve Yzerman SL .20 .50
248 Paul Ysebaert SL .01 .05
249 Dave Andreychuk SL .01 .05
250 Kirk McLean SL .01 .05
251 Tim Cheveldae SL .01 .05
252 Jeremy Roenick SL .12 .30
253 NHL Pro Set NR .01 .05
Youth Parade
254 NHL Pro Set NR .01 .05
Youth Clinics
255 NHL Pro Set NR .01 .05
All-Time Team
256 Mike Gartner MS .01 .05
257 Brian Propp MS .01 .05
258 Dave Taylor MS .02 .10
259 Bobby Smith MS .02 .10
260 Denis Savard MS .01 .05
261 Ray Bourque MS .08 .20
262 Joe Mullen MS .01 .05
263 John Tonelli MS .01 .05
264 Brad Marsh MS .01 .05
265 Randy Carlyle MS .01 .05
266 Mike Hough PS .01 .05
Power
267 Bob Essensa PS .02 .10
Achieve
268 Mike Lalor PS .01 .05
Motivate
269 Terry Carkner PS .01 .05
Attitude
270 Todd Krygier PS .01 .05
Responsibility
AU239 Kirk McLean AU 20.00 40.00

1992-93 Pro Set Award Winners

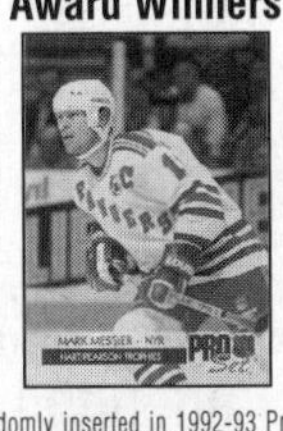

Randomly inserted in 1992-93 Pro Set packs, these five standard-size cards capture five NHL players who were honored with trophies for their outstanding play. The fronts feature full-bleed color action player photos. A gold-foil stamped "Award Winner" emblem is superimposed at the upper right corner. The player's name, team name, and trophy awarded appear in two bars toward the bottom of the picture. The backs carry a color headshot and a career summary.

COMPLETE SET (5) 8.00 15.00
CC1 Mark Messier 1.00 2.50
Hart/Pearson Trophies
CC2 Patrick Roy 4.00 10.00
Vezina/Jennings Trophies
CC3 Pavel Bure 1.00 2.50
Calder Trophy
CC4 Brian Leetch 1.00 2.50
Norris Trophy
CC5 Guy Carbonneau .40 1.00
Selke Trophy

1992-93 Pro Set Gold Team Leaders

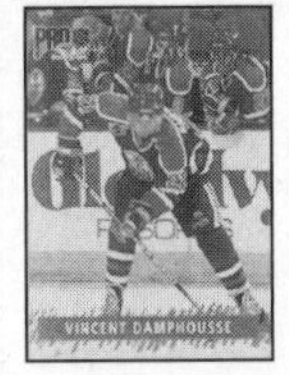

Inserted one per jumbo pack, this 15-card standard-size set spotlights team scoring leaders from the Campbell Conference. The color action player photos on the fronts are full-bleed with "1991-92 Team Leader" gold foil stamped on the picture at the upper right corner. Toward the bottom of the picture the player's name appears on a rust-colored bar that overlays a jagged design. Bordered by a dark brown screened background with Campbell Conference logos, the back carries career summary on a rust-colored panel. The cards are numbered on the back "X of 15."

1 Gary Roberts .20 .50
2 Jeremy Roenick 1.25 3.00
3 Steve Yzerman 2.00 5.00
4 Nicklas Lidstrom 1.00 2.50
5 Vincent Damphousse .40 1.00
6 Wayne Gretzky 3.00 8.00
7 Mike Modano 1.25 3.00
8 Brett Hull 1.25 3.00
9 Nelson Emerson .20 .50
10 Pat Falloon .20 .50
11 Doug Gilmour .40 1.00
12 Trevor Linden .40 1.00
13 Pavel Bure 1.00 2.50
14 Phil Housley .40 1.00
15 Luciano Borsato .20 .50

1992-93 Pro Set Rookie Goal Leaders

This 12-card Rookie Goal Leader standard-size set features the top rookie goal scorers from the 1991-92 season. The cards were randomly inserted in 1992-93 Pro Set packs. On a variegated purple card face, the fronts display color action player photos that are accented by gold drop borders. The player's name appears in a white bar above the picture, while the words "1991-92 Rookie Goal Leader" are gold foil-stamped across the bottom of the picture. On the same variegated purple background as the fronts, the backs present career summary.

1 Tony Amonte .40 1.00
2 Pavel Bure 1.25 3.00
3 Donald Audette .20 .50
4 Pat Falloon .20 .50
5 Nelson Emerson .20 .50
6 Gilbert Dionne .20 .50
7 Kevin Todd .20 .50
8 Luciano Borsato .20 .50
9 Rob Pearson .20 .50
10 Valeri Zelepukin .20 .50
11 Geoff Sanderson 4.00 1.00
12 Claude Lapointe .20 .50

1987 Pro-Sport All-Stars

Issued in Canadian retail packs that included an LCD quartz watch, each of these red, white, and blue oversized cards measures approximately 11 3/4" by 10 1/2" when unfolded and features a color player action shot at the lower right. The player's name, along with his career highlights in English and French, are shown at the lower left. A middle section is cut away to accommodate the watch. The cards are numbered on the front with a "CW" prefix. These cards are priced below without the watches. Number 4 was apparently not issued.

COMPLETE SET (17) 20.00 50.00
1 Larry Robinson 1.20 3.00
2 Guy Carbonneau .80 2.00
3 Chris Chelios 2.00 5.00
5 Mario Lemieux 6.00 15.00
Pittsburg
6 Mike Bossy 1.60 4.00
7 Dale Hawerchuk 1.20 3.00
8 Joe Mullen 1.20 3.00
9 Rick Vaive .80 2.00
10 Wendel Clark 1.60 4.00
11 Michel Goulet 1.20 3.00
12 Peter Stastny 1.20 3.00
13 Mark Messier 2.40 6.00
14 Paul Coffey 2.00 5.00
15 Tony Tanti .80 2.00
16 Borje Salming 1.20 3.00
17 Chris Nilan .80 2.00
18 Mats Naslund 1.20 3.00

1983-84 Puffy Stickers

This set of 150 puffy stickers was issued in panels of six stickers each. The panels measure approximately 3 1/2" by 6". There are 21 player panels and four logo panels. The NHL and NHLPA logos appear in the center of each panel. The stickers are oval-shaped and measure approximately 1 1/4" by 1 3/4". In the top portion of the oval they feature a color head shot of the player, with the team name above the head and the player name below the picture in a white box. The sticker background is wood-grain in design. The 21 player panels are numbered and we have checklisted them below accordingly. The logo panels are unnumbered and they are listed after the player panels. The backs are blank. There was also an album produced for this set; the album is not included in the complete set price below.

COMPLETE SET (25) 30.00 75.00
1 Doug Risebrough 6.00 15.00
Wayne Gretzky
Mats Naslund
Bill Derlago
Richard Brodeur
Dave Babych
2 Glenn Anderson 1.60 4.00
Larry Robinson
Rick Vaive
Stan Smyl
Scott Arniel
Don Edwards
3 Ryan Walter 1.20 3.00
Peter Ihnacak
Thomas Gradin
Morris Lukowich
Kent Nilsson
Paul Coffey
4 John Anderson 2.40 6.00
Dave(Tiger) Williams
Brian Mullen
Steve Tambellini
Mark Messier
Guy Lafleur
5 Darcy Rota 1.20 3.00
Dale Hawerchuk
Paul Reinhart
Jari Kurri
Mario Tremblay
Mike Palmateer
6 Paul MacLean 1.60 4.00
Lanny McDonald
Ken Linseman
Steve Shutt
Borje Salming
Kevin McCarthy
7 Barry Pederson 1.20 3.00
Mike Foligno
Jim Fox
Don Lever
Bobby Clarke
Greg Malone
8 Gilbert Perreault 1.20 3.00
Charlie Simmer
Hector Marini
Mark Howe
Rick Kehoe
Jim Schoenfeld
9 Larry Murphy 1.20 3.00
Phil Russell
Bill Barber
Mike Bullard
Pete Peeters
John Van Boxmeer
10 Tapio Levo 1.60 4.00
Darryl Sittler
Paul Gardner
Rick Middleton
Real Cloutier
Bernie Nicholls
11 Brian Propp 1.60 4.00
Michel Dion
Ray Bourque
Dale McCourt
Marcel Dionne
Bob MacMillan
12 Randy Carlyle 1.20 3.00
Terry O'Reilly
Phil Housley
Dave Taylor
Glenn Resch
Behn Wilson
13 Tony Esposito 1.60 4.00
Ron Duguay
Pierre Larouche
Neal Broten
Peter Stastny
Blake Dunlop
14 Walt McKechnie 1.00 2.50
Risto Siltanen
Bobby Smith
Anton Stastny
Mike Liut
Doug Wilson
15 Blaine Stoughton 1.20 3.00
Dino Ciccarelli
Michel Goulet
Jorgen Pettersson
Tom Lysiak
Brad Park
16 Craig Hartsburg 1.00 2.50
Marian Stastny
Rob Ramage
Al Secord
John Ogrodnick
Greg Millen
17 Tony McKegney 1.00 2.50
Brian Sutter
Steve Larmer
Danny Gare
Mark Johnson
Brian Bellows
18 Bernie Federko 1.20 3.00
Denis Savard
Reed Larson
Ron Francis
Dennis Maruk
Dan Bouchard
19 Mike Bossy 1.60 4.00
Anders Hedberg
Rod Langway
Billy Smith
Reijo Ruotsalainen
Milan Novy
20 Barry Beck 1.20 3.00
Bob Carpenter
Clark Gillies
Rob McClanahan
Brian Engblom
Denis Potvin
21 Mike Gartner 1.60 4.00
John Tonelli
Willie Huber
Pat Riggin
Bryan Trottier
Don Maloney
22 Norris Division 2.00 5.00
Blackhawks logo
Red Wings logo
North Stars logo
Blues logo
Maple Leafs logo
NHL logo
23 Patrick Division 2.00 5.00
Devils logo
Islanders logo
Rangers logo
Flyers logo
Penguins logo
Capitals logo
24 Adams Division 2.00 5.00
Bruins logo
Sabres logo
Whalers logo
Canadiens logo
Nordiques logo
NHL logo
25 Smythe Division 2.00 5.00
Flames logo
Oilers logo
Kings logo
Canucks logo
Jets logo
NHL logo
xx Album 10.00 25.00

1938-39 Quaker Oats Photos

This 30-card set of Toronto Maple Leafs and Montreal Canadiens was sponsored by Quaker Oats. The photos were obtainable by mail with the redemption of proofs of purchase. These oversized cards (approximately 6 1/4" by 7 3/8") are unnumbered and hence are listed below alphabetically. Facsimile autographs are printed in white on the fronts of these blank-backed cards.

COMPLETE SET (30) 750.00 1500.00
1 Syl Apps 62.50 125.00
2 Toe Blake 125.00 250.00
3 Buzz Boll 25.00 50.00
4 Turk Broda 87.50 175.00
5 Walter Buswell 25.00 50.00
6 Herb Cain 30.00 60.00
7 Murph Chamberlain 25.00 50.00
8 Wilf Cude 30.00 60.00
9 Bob Davidson 25.00 50.00
10 Gordie Drillon 50.00 100.00
11 Paul Drouin 25.00 50.00
12 Stew Evans 25.00 50.00
13 James Fowler 25.00 50.00
14 Johnny Gagnon 25.00 50.00
15 Robert Gracie 25.00 50.00
16 Reg Hamilton 25.00 50.00
17 Paul Haynes 25.00 50.00
18 Foster Hewitt 50.00 100.00
19 Red Horner 50.00 100.00
20 Harvey(Busher) Jackson 62.50 125.00
21 Bingo Kampman 25.00 50.00
22 Pep Kelly 25.00 50.00
23 Rod Lorrain 25.00 50.00
24 Georges Mantha 25.00 50.00
25 Nick Metz 25.00 50.00
26 George Parsons 25.00 50.00
27 Babe Siebert 50.00 100.00
28 Bill Thoms 25.00 50.00
29 James Ward 25.00 50.00
30 Cy Wentworth 30.00 60.00

1945-54 Quaker Oats Photos

Quaker Oats of Canada continued its tradition of redeeming proofs of purchase for photos of Montreal Canadiens and Toronto Maple Leafs in this nine-year series. Many players are featured in multiple versions, as their photos were updated over the years. The photos themselves are black and white with a thin white border and measure 8" X 10". Because of the numerous variations and the potential for more to be unearthed, no complete set price is listed below. Currently, 113 players are featured on 200 different photos. Anyone with information regarding other photos or variations is encouraged to contact Beckett Publications. The photos are blank-backed and unnumbered and are listed below in alphabetical order within their team (Toronto first, then Montreal).

1A Syl Apps 15.00 30.00
Home Still, CJS Apps auto.
1B Syl Apps 12.50 25.00
Home Still, Syl Apps auto.
1C Syl Apps 75.00 150.00
Away With Stanley Cup
2 George Armstrong 12.50 25.00
Home Action
3 Doug Baldwin 50.00 100.00
Home Still
4A Bill Barilko 12.50 25.00
Home Action
auto. 1/4" from border
4B Bill Barilko 12.50 25.00
Home Action
auto. 3/4" from border
4C Bill Barilko 12.50 25.00
Away Action
5 Baz Bastien 62.50 125.00
Home Still
6 Gordon Bell 62.50 125.00
Home Still
7A Max Bentley 10.00 20.00
Home Still
7B Max Bentley 75.00 150.00
Home Dressing Room
7C Max Bentley 10.00 20.00
Away Action
8 Gus Bodnar 20.00 40.00
Home Still
9A Garth Boesch 7.50 15.00
Home Still, closed B in auto.
9B Garth Boesch 7.50 15.00
Home Still, open B in auto.
9C Garth Boesch 50.00 100.00
Away Action
10 Hugh Bolton 6.00 12.00
Home Action
11 Leo Boivin 15.00 30.00
Home Action
12A Turk Broda 25.00 50.00
Away Splits, W.E. auto.
12B Turk Broda 20.00 40.00
Away Splits, Turk auto.
12C Turk Broda 20.00 40.00
Away Action
13 Lorne Carr 15.00 30.00
Home Still
14 Les Costello 15.00 30.00
Home Still
15 Bob Davidson 12.50 25.00
Home Still
16A Bill Ezinicki 10.00 20.00
cropped William auto., blue tint
16B Bill Ezinicki 6.00 12.00
entire William auto.
16C Bill Ezinicki 6.00 12.00
Home Still, Bill auto.
16D Bill Ezinicki 6.00 12.00
Away Action
17 Fernie Flaman 7.50 15.00
Home Action
18A Cal Gardner 6.00 12.00
Home Still
18B Cal Gardner 6.00 12.00
Away Action
19A Bob Goldham 6.00 12.00
sweeping G in auto.
19B Bob Goldham 6.00 12.00
normal G, entire blade
19C Bob Goldham 75.00 150.00
normal G, blade cropped
20 Gord Hannigan 15.00 30.00
Home Action
21 Bob Hassard 25.00 50.00
Away Action
22 Mel Hill 40.00 80.00
Home Still
23 Tim Horton 50.00 100.00
Home Action
24A Bill Judza 6.00 12.00
Home Still
24B Bill Judza 6.00 12.00
Away Action
25A Ted Kennedy 25.00 50.00
Home Still, blade in corner
25B Ted Kennedy 25.00 50.00
Home Still, large image
blade cropped, b&w tint
25C Ted Kennedy 50.00 100.00
Home Still, large image
blade cropped, blue tint
25D Ted Kennedy 10.00 20.00
Home Still, C on jersey
25E Ted Kennedy 87.50 175.00
Home With Stanley Cup
25F Ted Kennedy 10.00 20.00
Away Action
26A Joe Klukay 6.00 12.00
Home Still
26B Joe Klukay 6.00 12.00
Away Action
27 Danny Lewicki 7.50 15.00
Home Action
28 Harry Lumley 30.00 60.00
Home Action
29A Vic Lynn 6.00 12.00
Home Still,
head 3/8" from border
29B Vic Lynn 15.00 30.00
Home Still
head 1/8" from border
29C Vic Lynn 6.00 12.00
Away Action
30A Fleming Mackell 6.00 12.00
Home Still
30B Fleming Mackell 7.50 15.00
Away Action
31 Phil Maloney 40.00 80.00
Home Action
32 Frank Mathers 20.00 40.00
Home Still
33 Frank McCool 62.50 125.00
Home Still
34 John McCormick 15.00 30.00
Away Action
35A Howie Meeker 10.00 20.00
Home Still, large image
35B Howie Meeker 10.00 20.00
Home Still, small image
35C Howie Meeker 10.00 20.00
Away Action
36A Don Metz 6.00 12.00
Home, posed to right
36B Don Metz 12.50 25.00
Home, center pose, b&w tint
36C Don Metz 40.00 80.00
Home, center pose, blue tint
37A Nick Metz 6.00 12.00
Home Still, original stick
37B Nick Metz 12.50 25.00
Home Still, stick retouched
3/8" from border
37C Nick Metz 25.00 50.00
Home Still, stick retouched
1/8" from border
38 Rudy Migay 30.00 60.00
Home Action
39 Elwyn Morris 40.00 80.00
Home Still
40 Jim Morrison 6.00 12.00
Home Action
41A Gus Mortson 6.00 12.00
Home Still
41B Gus Mortson 6.00 12.00
Away Action
42 Eric Nesterenko 40.00 80.00
Home Action
43 Bud Poile 15.00 30.00
Home Still
44 Babe Pratt 50.00 100.00
Home Still
45 Al Rollins 12.50 25.00
Home Action
46 Dave Schriner 30.00 60.00
Home Still
47A Tod Sloan 12.50 25.00
Home Still
47B Tod Sloan 6.00 12.00
Away Action
48A Sid Smith 12.50 25.00
Home Still
48B Sid Smith 6.00 12.00
Away Action
49 Bob Solinger 15.00 30.00
50A Wally Stanowski 12.50 25.00
Home Still, entire blade

50B Wally Stanowski 6.00 12.00
Home Still, blade cropped
51A Gaye Stewart 50.00 100.00
Home Still
51B Gaye Stewart 6.00 12.00
Home Still, blue tint
52 Ron Stewart 50.00 100.00
Home Action
53 Harry Taylor 7.50 15.00
Home Still
54 Billy Taylor 25.00 50.00
Home Still
55 Cy Thomas 25.00 50.00
Home Still
56A Jim Thomson 30.00 60.00
Home Still, stick cropped
56B Jim Thomson 6.00 12.00
Home Still
stick touching border
56C Jim Thomson 30.00 60.00
Home Still
stick away from border
56D Jim Thomson 6.00 12.00
Away Action
57A Ray Timgren 7.50 15.00
Home Still
57B Ray Timgren 6.00 12.00
Away Action
58A Harry Watson 6.00 12.00
Home Still, tape on stick
58B Harry Watson 6.00 12.00
Home Still, no tape visible
58C Harry Watson 6.00 12.00
Away Action
59 1947-9 Toronto Maple Leafs 30.00 60.00
60A Leafs Attack McNeil 87.50 175.00
60B Gardner attacks Harvey 100.00 200.00
60C Rollins, Judza stop Curry 100.00 200.00
60D McNeil Saves on Gardner 100.00 200.00
61 George Allen 6.00 12.00
Home Still
62 Jean Beliveau 87.50 175.00
Home Action
63 Joe Benoit 10.00 20.00
Home Still
64A Toe Blake 75.00 150.00
Hector Toe Blake auto.
64B Toe Blake 10.00 20.00
Toe Blake auto. above skates
64C Toe Blake 10.00 20.00
Toe Blake auto. below skate
65A Butch Bouchard 6.00 12.00
Home Still, entire skate
65B Butch Bouchard 6.00 12.00
Home Still, skate cropped
65C Butch Bouchard 7.50 15.00
Home Action
66 Todd Campeau 6.00 12.00
Home Still
67 Bob Carse 6.00 12.00
Home Still
68 Joe Carveth 6.00 12.00
Home Portrait
69A Murph Chamberlain 10.00 20.00
facing sideways, entire skates
69B Murph Chamberlain 10.00 20.00
facing sideways, skates cropped
69C Murph Chamberlain 15.00 30.00
Home Still, facing forward
70 Gerry Couture 6.00 12.00
Home Action
71A Floyd Curry 62.50 125.00
Home Still
71B Floyd Curry 6.00 12.00
Home Action
72 Ed Dorohoy 6.00 12.00
Home Action
73A Bill Durnan 12.50 25.00
Home Still
stick handle cropped
73B Bill Durnan 25.00 50.00
Home Still
stick handle touching border
73C Bill Durnan 87.50 175.00
Home Still
stick handle away from border
73D Bill Durnan 15.00 30.00
Home Action
74A Norm Dussault 6.00 12.00
Home Portrait
74B Norm Dussault 15.00 30.00
Home Action
75 Frank Eddolls 10.00 20.00
Home Still
76A Bob Fillion 25.00 50.00
Home Still
small image
76B Bob Fillion 6.00 12.00
Home Still
large image, screen background
76C Bob Fillion 12.50 25.00
Home Still
large image
air brushed background
76D Bob Fillion 6.00 12.00
Home Action
77 Dick Gamble 10.00 20.00
Away Action
78 Bernie Geoffrion 15.00 30.00
Home Action
79A Leo Gravelle 6.00 12.00
Home Still
79B Leo Gravelle 25.00 50.00
Away Still
79C Leo Gravelle 6.00 12.00
Home Action
80A Glen Harmon 6.00 12.00
Home Still, entire puck
80B Glen Harmon 6.00 12.00
Home Still, no puck
80C Glen Harmon 12.50 25.00
Home Action
81A Doug Harvey 12.50 25.00
Home Still
81B Doug Harvey 10.00 20.00
Home Action
82 Dutch Hiller 10.00 20.00
Home Action
83 Bert Hirschfeld 10.00 20.00
Home Action
84 Tom Johnson 10.00 20.00
Home Action
85 Vern Kaiser 10.00 20.00
Home Action
86A Elmer Lach 10.00 20.00
Home Still, stick in corner
86B Elmer Lach 10.00 20.00
Home Still, stick cropped
86C Elmer Lach 40.00 80.00
Home Still
stick 1/2" up from corner
86D Elmer Lach 10.00 20.00
Home Action
87A Leo Lamoureaux 12.50 25.00
Home Still, entire blade
87B Leo Lamoureaux 10.00 20.00
Home Still, blade cropped
88A Hal Laycoe 50.00 100.00
Home Portrait
88B Hal Laycoe 6.00 12.00
Home Action
89A Roger Leger 6.00 12.00
Home Still
light background
89B Roger Leger 6.00 12.00
Home Still
dark background
89C Roger Leger 25.00 50.00
Home Action
90 Jacques Locas 10.00 20.00
Home Still
91 Ross Lowe 10.00 20.00
Away Action
92 Calum MacKay 6.00 12.00
Home Action
93 Murdo MacKay 6.00 12.00
Home Portrait
94 James MacPherson 6.00 12.00
Home Action
95 Paul Masnick 6.00 12.00
Home Action
96A John McCormick 50.00 100.00
Home Action, vertical
96B John McCormick 30.00 60.00
Home Action, horizontal
97 Mike McMahon 50.00 100.00
Home Still
98 Gerry McNeil 12.50 25.00
Home Action
99 Paul Meger 7.50 15.00
Home Action
100 Dickie Moore 15.00 30.00
Home Action
101A Ken Mosdell 6.00 12.00
Home Still, small image
101B Ken Mosdell 25.00 50.00
Home Still, large image
auto. cropped
101C Ken Mosdell 25.00 50.00
Home Still, large image
auto. not cropped
101D Ken Mosdell 6.00 12.00
Home Action
102A Buddy O'Connor 20.00 40.00
Home Still, entire blade
102B Buddy O'Connor 10.00 20.00
Home Still, blade cropped
103 Bert Olmstead 12.50 25.00
Home Action
104A Jim Peters 6.00 12.00
Home Still, large image
104B Jim Peters 6.00 12.00
Home Still, small image
105 Gerry Plamondon 7.50 15.00
Home Action
106 Johnny Quilty 7.50 15.00
Home Portrait
107A Ken Reardon 10.00 20.00
Home Still, large image
107B Ken Reardon 15.00 30.00
Home Still, small image
107C Kenny Reardon 10.00 20.00
Home Action
108A Billy Reay 6.00 12.00
Home Still, large image
stick touching border
108B Billy Reay 6.00 12.00
Home Still, large image
stick away from border
108C Billy Reay 62.50 125.00
Home Still, small image
108D Billy Reay 6.00 12.00
Home Action
109A Maurice Richard 150.00 300.00
Home, screen background
109B Maurice Richard 15.00 30.00
Home, large image
auto. cropped
109C Maurice Richard 15.00 30.00
Home, large image
entire auto.
109D Maurice Richard 30.00 60.00
Home Action
110A Howie Riopelle 10.00 20.00
Home Still
110B Howie Riopelle 10.00 20.00
Home Action
111 George Robertson 20.00 40.00
Home Action
112 Dollard St. Laurent 30.00 60.00
Home Action
113 Grant Warwick 40.00 80.00
Home Action

1973-74 Quaker Oats WHA

This set of 50 cards features players of the World Hockey Association. The cards were issued in strips (panels) of five in Quaker Oats products. The cards measure approximately 2 1/4" by 3 1/4" and are numbered on the back. The information on the card backs is written in English and French. The value of unseparated panels would be approximately 20 percent greater than the sum of the individual values listed below.

COMPLETE SET (50) 137.50 275.00
1 Jim Wiste 2.50 5.00
2 Al Smith 3.00 6.00
3 Rosaire Paiement 2.50 5.00
4 Ted Hampson 2.00 4.00
5 Gavin Kirk 2.00 4.00
6 Andre Lacroix 3.00 6.00
7 John Schella 2.00 4.00
8 Gerry Cheevers 10.00 20.00
9 Norm Beaudin 2.00 4.00
10 Jim Harrison 2.00 4.00
11 Gerry Pinder 2.50 5.00
12 Bob Sicinski 2.00 4.00
13 Bryan Campbell 2.00 4.00
14 Murray Hall 2.00 4.00
15 Chris Bordeleau 2.50 5.00
16 Al Hamilton 3.00 6.00
17 Jimmy McLeod 2.00 4.00
18 Larry Pleau 2.50 5.00
19 Larry Lund 2.00 4.00
20 Bobby Sheehan 2.50 5.00
21 Jan Popiel 2.00 4.00
22 Andre Gaudette 2.00 4.00
23 Bob Charlebois 2.00 4.00
24 Gene Peacosh 2.00 4.00
25 Rick Ley 2.50 5.00
26 Larry Hornung 2.00 4.00
27 Gary Jarrett 2.00 4.00
28 Ted Taylor 2.00 4.00
29 Pete Donnelly 2.00 4.00
30 J.C. Tremblay 3.00 6.00
31 Jim Cardiff 2.00 4.00
32 Gary Veneruzzo 2.00 4.00
33 John French 2.00 4.00
34 Ron Ward 2.50 5.00
35 Wayne Connelly 2.50 5.00
36 Ron Buchanan 2.00 4.00
37 Ken Block 2.00 4.00
38 Alain Caron 2.00 4.00
39 Brit Selby 2.50 5.00
40 Guy Trottier 2.00 4.00
41 Ernie Wakely 3.00 6.00
42 J.P. LeBlanc 2.00 4.00
43 Michel Parizeau 2.00 4.00
44 Wayne Rivers 2.00 4.00
45 Reg Fleming 2.50 5.00
46 Don Herriman 2.00 4.00
47 Jim Dorey 2.00 4.00
48 Danny Lawson 3.00 6.00
49 Dick Paradise 2.00 4.00
50 Bobby Hull 30.00 60.00

1989-90 Rangers Marine Midland Bank

This 30-card set of New York Rangers was sponsored by Marine Midland Bank; the card backs have the bank's logo and name at the bottom. The cards measure approximately 2 5/8" by 3 5/8". The fronts feature color action photos of the players, with a thin red border on the left and bottom of the picture. Outside the red border appears a blue margin, with the player's name, position, and jersey number printed at right angles to one another. The Rangers' logo in the lower right hand corner completes the face of the card. The back has biographical information and career statistics. The cards have been listed below according to sweater number. The key cards in the set are early cards of Brian Leetch and Mike Richter.

COMPLETE SET (30) 14.00 35.00
2 Brian Leetch 3.20 8.00
3 James Patrick .30 .75
4 Ron Greschner .40 1.00
5 Normand Rochefort .20 .50
6 Miloslav Horava .20 .50
8 Darren Turcotte .30 .75
9 Bernie Nicholls .40 1.00
11 Kelly Kisio .30 .75
12 Kris King .40 1.00
14 Mark Hardy .20 .50
15 Mark Janssens .20 .50
16 Ulf Dahlen .30 .75
17 Carey Wilson .20 .50
19 Brian Mullen .30 .75
20 Jan Erixon .20 .50
21 David Shaw .20 .50
23 Corey Millen .20 .50
24 Randy Moller .20 .50
25 John Ogrodnick .40 1.00
26 Troy Mallette .20 .50
29 Rudy Poeschek .40 1.00
30 Chris Nilan .40 1.00
33 Bob Froese .40 1.00
34 John Vanbiesbrouck 1.60 4.00
35 Mike Richter 3.20 8.00
37 Paul Broten .20 .50
38 Jeff Bloemberg .20 .50
44 Lindy Ruff .20 .50
NNO Roger Neilson CO .20 .50
NNO Rangers MasterCard .04 .10

2002-03 Rangers Team Issue

This unusual team issue features two different sizes. The player cards measure 6 X 9.5, while the coach cards measure approx. 5 X 6. The fronts feature different designs, but the backs are similar. Information on distribution and any additional cards in the checklist can be forwarded to hockeymag@beckett.com.

COMPLETE SET (?)
1 Matthew Barnaby .60 1.50
2 Dan Blackburn .60 1.50
3 Pavel Bure 2.00 5.00
4 Ted Green ACO .20 .50
5 Bobby Holik .40 1.00
6 Dave Karpa .40 1.00
7 Darius Kasparaitis .40 1.00
8 Sylvain Lefebvre .40 1.00
9 Vladimir Malakhov .40 1.00
10 Sandy McCarthy .60 1.50
11 Mark Messier 2.00 5.00
12 Terry O'Reilly ACO .40 1.00
13 Mike Richter .75 2.00
14 Jim Schoenfeld ACO .20 .50

2003-04 Rangers Team Issue

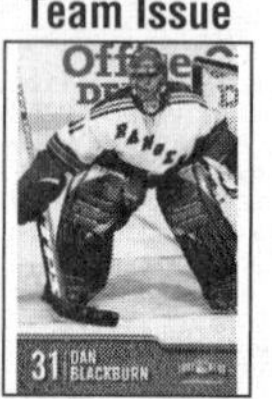

These oversized cards measure 6x9 and were available only at team events. This checklist is possibly incomplete. Please forward additional information to hockeymag@beckett.com.

COMPLETE SET (24) 15.00 30.00
1 Matthew Barnaby .75 2.00
2 Dan Blackburn .60 1.50
3 Anson Carter .60 1.50
4 Greg deVries .40 1.00
5 Mike Dunham .60 1.50
6 Jan Hlavac .40 1.00
7 Bobby Holik .40 1.00
8 Darius Kasparaitis .40 1.00
9 Alexei Kovalev .40 1.00
10 Dan Lacouture .40 1.00
11 Brian Leetch .75 2.00
12 Eric Lindros 1.25 3.00
13 Jamie Lundmark .40 1.00
14 Vladimir Malakhov .40 1.00
15 Jussi Markkanen .75 2.00
16 Mark Messier .75 2.00
17 Boris Mironov .40 1.00
18 Petr Nedved .40 1.00
19 Tom Poti .40 1.00
20 Dale Purinton .75 2.00
21 Martin Rucinsky .40 1.00
22 Glen Sather HCO .20 .50
23 Chris Simon .60 1.50
24 Glen Sather .20 .50
Tom Renney
Terry O'Reilly
Ted Green

1970-71 Red Wings Marathon

This 11-card (artistic) portrait set of Detroit Red Wings was part of a (Pro Star Portraits) promotion by Marathon Oil. The cards measure approximately 7 1/2" by 14"; the bottom portion, which measures 7 1/2" by 4 1/16", was a tear-off postcard in the form of a credit card application. The front features a full color portrait by Nicholas Volpe, with a facsimile autograph of the player inscribed across the bottom of the painting. The back included an offer for other sports memorabilia on the upper portion.

COMPLETE SET (11) 40.00 80.00
1 Gary Bergman 2.50 5.00
2 Wayne Connelly 2.00 4.00
3 Alex Delvecchio 5.00 10.00
4 Roy Edwards 2.50 5.00
5 Gordie Howe 25.00 50.00
6 Bruce MacGregor 2.00 4.00
7 Frank Mahovlich 6.00 12.00
8 Dale Rolfe 2.00 4.00
9 Jim Rutherford 3.00 6.00
10 Garry Unger 2.50 5.00
11 Tom Webster 2.50 5.00

1971 Red Wings Citgo Tumblers

These tumblers were available at Citgo gas stations and measure approximately 8" high. Tumblers feature color head shots, a facsimile autograph, and a color artwork action shot. They are made by Cinemac Inc, and feature a copyright of 1971.

COMPLETE SET 100.00 200.00
1 Wayne Connelly 12.50 25.00
2 Alex Delvecchio 20.00 40.00
3 Don Edwards 10.00 20.00
4 Garry Unger 10.00 20.00
5 Gordie Howe 37.50 75.00
6 Frank Mahovlich 15.00 30.00

1973-74 Red Wings Team Issue

Cards measure 8 3/4" x 10 3/4". Fronts feature color photos, and backs are blank. Cards are unnumbered and checklisted below in alphabetical order.

COMPLETE SET (18) 50.00 100.00
1 Ace Bailey 2.50 5.00
2 Red Berenson 4.00 8.00
3 Gary Bergman 2.50 5.00
4 Thommie Bergman 4.00 8.00
5 Guy Charron 2.50 5.00
6 Bill Collins 2.50 5.00
7 Denis Dejordy 4.00 8.00
8 Alex Delvecchio 7.50 15.00
9 Marcel Dionne 7.50 15.00
10 Gary Doak 2.50 5.00
11 Tim Ecclestone 2.50 5.00
12 Larry Johnston 2.50 5.00
13 Al Karlander 2.50 5.00
14 Brian Lavender 2.50 5.00
15 Nick Libett 2.50 5.00
16 Ken Murphy 2.50 5.00
17 Mickey Redmond 7.50 15.00
18 Ron Stackhouse 2.50 5.00

1973-75 Red Wings McCarthy Postcards

Measuring approximately 3 1/4" by 5 1/2", these postcards display color posed action shots on their fronts. The backs are blank. Since there is no Marcel Dionne or Alex Delvecchio (the latter played 11 games in 1973-74 before coaching), it is doubtful that this is a complete set. The date is established by two players: Brent Hughes (1973-74 was his only season with the Red Wings) and Tom Mellor (1974-75). The cards are unnumbered and checklisted below in alphabetical order. The photos and cards were produced by noted photographer J.D. McCarthy.

COMPLETE SET (15) 12.50 25.00
1 Garnet Bailey 1.00 2.00
2 Thommie Bergman 1.00 2.00
3 Henry Boucha 1.25 2.50
4 Guy Charron 1.00 2.00
5 Bill Collins 1.00 2.00
6 Doug Grant 1.00 2.00
7 Ted Harris 1.00 2.00
8 Bill Hogaboam 1.00 2.00
9 Brent Hughes 1.00 2.00
10 Pierre Jarry 1.00 2.00
11 Larry Johnston 1.00 2.00
12 Nick Libett 1.00 2.00
13 Tom Mellor 1.00 2.00
14 Doug Roberts 1.00 2.00
15 Ron Stackhouse 1.00 2.00

1979 Red Wings Postcards

This set features borderless color fronts and was issued by the Red Wings during the 1979 season.

COMPLETE SET (18) 7.50 15.00
1 Thommie Bergman .38 .75
2 Dan Bolduc .38 .75
3 Mike Foligno .38 .75
4 Jean Hamel .38 .75
5 Glen Hicks .38 .75
6 Greg Joly .38 .75
7 Willie Huber .38 .75
8 Jim Korn .38 .75
9 Dan Labraaten .38 .75
10 Barry Long .38 .75
11 Reed Larson .38 .75
12 Dale McCourt .38 .75
13 Vaclav Nedomansky .38 .75
14 Jim Rutherford .38 .75
15 Dennis Polonich .38 .75
16 Errol Thompson .38 .75
17 Rogie Vachon .38 .75
18 Paul Woods .38 .75

1981-82 Red Wings Oldtimers

This set of slightly undersized cards features black and white head shots of former players with the Detroit Red Wings. The backs are blank. It is not known how these were distributed. Any additional information can be forwarded to hockeymag@beckett.com.

COMPLETE SET (24) 10.00 25.00
1 Bob Johnson .40 1.00
2 Ed Giacomin .80 2.00
3 Gary Bergman .40 1.00
4 Bill Gadsby .40 1.00
5 Larry Johnston .40 1.00
6 Jim Peters .40 1.00
7 Bobby Kromm .40 1.00
8 Marcel Pronovost .80 2.00
9 Gerry Abel .40 1.00
10 Bill Collins .40 1.00
11 Billy Dea .40 1.00
12 Nelson DeBenedet .40 1.00
13 Alex Delvecchio .80 2.00
14 Dennis Hextall .60 1.50
15 Nick Libett .40 1.00
16 Mickey Redmond 1.20 3.00
17 John Wilson .40 1.00
18 Joe Klukay .40 1.00
19 Art Skov .40 1.00
20 Art Bouge .40 1.00
21 Rollie Roulston .40 1.00
22 Gordie Howe 2.00 5.00
23 Dr.C Boone .40 1.00
24 Checklist .40 1.00

1987-88 Red Wings Little Caesars

This 30-card set was sponsored by Little Caesars Pizza and measures approximately 3 3/4" by 6". The fronts have color action player photos with white borders. The player's name appears below the photo, along with the team and sponsor logos. The backs are blank. The cards are unnumbered and checklisted below in alphabetical order.

COMPLETE SET (30) 18.00 45.00
1 Brent Ashton .40 1.00
2 Dave Barr .40 1.00
3 Mel Bridgman .40 1.00
4 Shawn Burr .40 1.00
5 John Chabot .40 1.00
6 Steve Chiasson .60 1.50
7 Gilbert Delorme .40 1.00
8 Jacques Demers CO .80 2.00
9 Ron Duguay .40 1.00
10 Dwight Foster .40 1.00
11 Gerard Gallant .40 1.00
12 Adam Graves 1.60 4.00
13 Doug Halward .40 1.00
14 Glen Hanlon .60 1.50
15 Tim Higgins .40 1.00
16 Petr Klima .60 1.50
17 Joe Kocur .80 2.00
18 Lane Lambert .40 1.00
19 Joe Murphy .40 1.00
20 Lee Norwood .40 1.00
21 Adam Oates 4.00 10.00
22 Mike O'Connell .40 1.00
23 John Ogrodnick .60 1.50
24 Bob Probert 1.60 4.00
25 Jeff Sharples .40 1.00
26 Greg Smith .40 1.00
27 Greg Stefan .60 1.50
28 Darren Veitch .40 1.00
29 Steve Yzerman 4.80 12.00
30 Rick Zombo .40 1.00

1988-89 Red Wings Little Caesars

Set features color action photos with a white border. Players name and team logo are also visible on the front. Cards are blank backed and checklisted below in alphabetical order.

COMPLETE SET (24) 10.00 25.00
1 David Barr .40 1.00
2 Shawn Burr .40 1.00
3 John Chabot .40 1.00
4 Steve Chiasson .80 2.00
5 Gilbert Delorme .40 1.00
6 Jacques Demers .40 1.00
7 Gerard Gallant .40 1.00
8 Adam Graves .80 2.00
9 Doug Houda .40 1.00
10 Glen Hanlon .60 1.50
11 Kris King .40 1.00
12 Petr Klima .40 1.00
13 Joe Kocur .60 1.50
14 Paul Maclean .40 1.00
15 Jim Nill .40 1.00
16 Lee Norwood .40 1.00
17 Adam Oates 1.20 3.00
18 Mike O'Connell .40 1.00
19 Jim Pavese .40 1.00
20 Bob Probert .80 2.00
21 Jeff Sharples .40 1.00
22 Greg Stefan .60 1.50
23 Steve Yzerman 2.40 6.00
24 Rick Zombo .40 1.00

1989-90 Red Wings Little Caesars

This elongated postcard-sized set features color action photos with a white border. Players name and team logo are also visible on the front. Cards are blank backed and are checklisted below in alphabetical order, save for the recently confirmed team personnel cards that are lumped in at the end.

COMPLETE SET (24) 10.00 25.00
1 Dave Barr .40 1.00
2 Shawn Burr .40 1.00
3 Jim Carson .40 1.00
4 John Chabot .40 1.00
5 Steve Chiasson .40 1.00
6 Bernie Federko .40 1.00
7 Gerard Gallant .40 1.00
8 Marc Habscheid .40 1.00
9 Glen Hanlon .40 1.00
10 Doug Houda .40 1.00
11 Joey Kocur .40 1.00
12 Kevin McLelland .40 1.00
13 Lee Norwood .40 1.00
14 Mike O'Connell .40 1.00
15 Borje Salming .40 1.00
16 Greg Stefan .40 1.00
17 Steve Yzerman .40 1.00
18 Rick Zombo .40 1.00
19 Jacques Demers CO .40 1.00
20 Team Photo .40 1.00
21 Mickey Redmond .20 .50
22 Dave Lewis .20 .50
Phil Myre
Jacques Demers
Colin Campbell
23 Bruce Martin .20 .50
Paul Woods
24 Dave Strader .20 .50
Mickey Redmond

1990-91 Red Wings Little Caesars

Set features color action photos with a white border. Players name and team logo are also visible on the front. Cards are blank backed and checklisted below in alphabetical order.

COMPLETE SET (20) 16.00 40.00
1 Dave Barr .40 1.00
2 Shawn Burr .40 1.00
3 John Chabot .40 1.00
4 Tim Cheveldae .60 1.50
5 Per Djoos .40 1.00
6 Bobby Dollas .40 1.00
7 Sergei Fedorov 4.00 10.00
8 Brent Fedyk .40 1.00
9 Johan Garpenlov .40 1.00
10 Rick Green .40 1.00
11 Sheldon Kennedy .80 2.00
12 Kevin McClelland .40 1.00
13 Brad McCrimmon .40 1.00
14 Randy McKay .40 1.00
15 Keith Primeau 1.60 4.00
16 Bob Probert 1.20 3.00
17 Steve Yzerman 2.00 5.00
18 Rick Zombo .40 1.00
19 Bryan Murray CO .40 1.00
20 Team Photo .80 2.00

1991-92 Red Wings Little Caesars

Sponsored by Little Caesars, this 19-card set measures approximately 8 1/2" by 3 5/8" and features a color, action player photo on the left half of the card. The right half displays the player's name, position, biographical information, early career history, and jersey number, along with a close-up player photo. The backs are blank. The cards are unnumbered and checklisted below in alphabetical order.

COMPLETE SET (19) 16.00 40.00
1 Shawn Burr .40 1.00
2 Jimmy Carson .40 1.00
3 Steve Chiasson .40 1.00
4 Sergei Fedorov 3.20 8.00
5 Gerard Gallant .40 1.00
6 Johan Garpenlov .40 1.00
7 Rick Green .40 1.00
8 Marc Habscheid .40 1.00
9 Sheldon Kennedy .40 1.00
10 Martin Lapointe .80 2.00
11 Nicklas Lidstrom 1.20 3.00
12 Brad McCrimmon .40 1.00
13 Bryan Murray CO/MG .20 .50
14 Keith Primeau .60 1.50
15 Bob Probert 1.20 3.00
16 Dennis Vial .40 1.00
17 Paul Ysebaert .40 1.00
18 Steve Yzerman 4.00 10.00
19 Team Card .80 2.00

1996-97 Red Wings Detroit News/Free Press

These five posters were issued one per week in the Sunday editions of the Detroit News/Free Press. They measure approximately 12 by 18 inches and feature a full color photo on the front. The backs feature an ad for the issuing paper.

COMPLETE SET (5) 8.00 20.00
1 Darren McCarty 1.60 4.00
Kris Draper
Kirk Maltby
Joe Kocur
2 Sergei Fedorov 2.40 6.00
3 Mike Vernon 1.60 4.00
4 Mike Vernon 1.60 4.00
5 Sergei Fedorov 2.40 6.00

1932 Reemstma Olympia

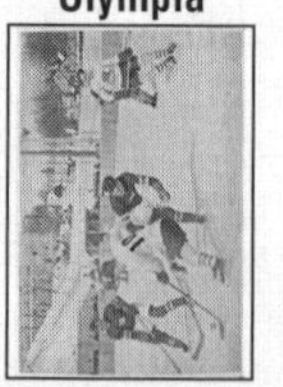

This colorful set was produced by Reemstma for the 1932 winter Olympics. Cards measure approximately 6 3/4 by 4 3/4 and are in full color. Backs are in German. Smaller versions of the cards also exist and are in black and white.

188 Dutch hockey player 10.00 20.00
191 USA vs. Canada 25.00 50.00

1936 Reemstma Olympia

This group of cards may or may not make up a complete set of Reemstma Olympia. These undersized issues picture international hockey players and matches from the early 1930s. It is believed they were issued as some sort of premium -- perhaps with cigarettes -- and it's likely that they were issued in Germany.

30 Team Canada 20.00 40.00
(6 3/4 x 4 3/4
31 Ice Hockey Spectators 20.00 40.00
32 Hockey Action Photo 20.00 40.00
33 Goalie making sliding save 20.00 40.00
34 Hockey Action Photo 20.00 40.00
35 Hockey Action Photo 20.00 40.00
Canada player in crease
36 Team Canada Photo 20.00 40.00
37 Team USA Photo 20.00 40.00
38 Gustav Jaenecke 20.00 40.00
39 Teiji Homna 20.00 40.00
Japan Goalie
40 Clearing the Ice 20.00 40.00

1997-98 Revolution

The 1997-98 Pacific Revolution set was issued in one series totaling 150 cards and distributed in three-card packs. The fronts feature color player images printed with etched gold and holographic silver foils on the circular design background. The backs carry another player photo and career statistics.

COMPLETE SET (150) 30.00 60.00
1 Guy Hebert .30 .75
2 Paul Kariya .40 1.00
3 Dmitri Mironov .20 .50
4 Ruslan Salei .20 .50
5 Teemu Selanne .40 1.00
6 Jason Allison .20 .50
7 Ray Bourque .75 2.00
8 Byron Dafoe .30 .75
9 Ted Donato .20 .50
10 Dimitri Khristich .20 .50
11 Joe Thornton .60 1.50
12 Matthew Barnaby .20 .50
13 Jason Dawe .20 .50
14 Dominik Hasek .75 2.00
15 Michael Peca .20 .50
16 Miroslav Satan .20 .50
17 Theo Fleury .20 .50
18 Jarome Iginla .50 1.25
19 Marty McInnis .20 .50
20 Cory Stillman .20 .50
21 Rick Tabaracci .30 .75
22 Martin Gelinas .20 .50
23 Sami Kapanen .20 .50
24 Trevor Kidd .30 .75
25 Keith Primeau .20 .50
26 Gary Roberts .20 .50
27 Tony Amonte .30 .75
28 Chris Chelios .40 1.00
29 Eric Daze .30 .75
30 Jeff Hackett .30 .75
31 Dmitri Nabokov .20 .50
32 Peter Forsberg 1.00 2.50
33 Valeri Kamensky .30 .75
34 Jari Kurri .30 .75
35 Claude Lemieux .20 .50
36 Eric Messier RC .30 .75
37 Sandis Ozolinsh .20 .50
38 Patrick Roy 1.50 4.00
39 Joe Sakic .75 2.00
40 Ed Belfour .40 1.00
41 Jamie Langenbrunner .20 .50
42 Jere Lehtinen .20 .50
43 Mike Modano .60 1.50
44 Joe Nieuwendyk .30 .75
45 Sergei Zubov .20 .50
46 Slava Fetisov .20 .50
47 Nicklas Lidstrom .40 1.00
48 Darren McCarty .20 .50
49 Larry Murphy .20 .50
50 Chris Osgood .30 .75
51 Brendan Shanahan .40 1.00
52 Steve Yzerman 1.50 4.00
53 Roman Hamrlik .30 .75
54 Bill Guerin .30 .75
55 Curtis Joseph .40 1.00
56 Ryan Smyth .30 .75
57 Doug Weight .30 .75
58 Dino Ciccarelli .20 .50
59 Dave Gagner .20 .50
60 Ed Jovanovski .30 .75
61 Paul Laus .20 .50
62 John Vanbiesbrouck .30 .75
63 Ray Whitney .20 .50
64 Russ Courtnall .20 .50
65 Yanic Perreault .20 .50
66 Luc Robitaille .30 .75
67 Jozef Stumpel .30 .75
68 Vladimir Tsyplakov .20 .50
69 Shayne Corson .20 .50
70 Vincent Damphousse .20 .50
71 Saku Koivu .40 1.00
72 Andy Moog .30 .75
73 Mark Recchi .30 .75
74 Jocelyn Thibault .30 .75
75 Martin Brodeur 1.00 2.50
76 Patrik Elias RC 2.00 5.00
77 Doug Gilmour .30 .75
78 Bobby Holik .20 .50
79 Scott Niedermayer .20 .50
80 Bryan Berard .30 .75
81 Travis Green .20 .50
82 Zigmund Palffy .30 .75
83 Robert Reichel .20 .50
84 Tommy Salo .30 .75
85 Dan Cloutier .20 .50
86 Adam Graves .20 .50
87 Wayne Gretzky 2.00 5.00
88 Pat LaFontaine .40 1.00
89 Brian Leetch .40 1.00
90 Mike Richter .40 1.00
91 Kevin Stevens .30 .75
92 Daniel Alfredsson .30 .75
93 Shawn McEachern .20 .50
94 Damian Rhodes .30 .75
95 Ron Tugnutt .30 .75
96 Alexei Yashin .20 .50
97 Rod Brind'Amour .30 .75
98 Paul Coffey .40 1.00
99 Alexandre Daigle .20 .50
100 Chris Gratton .30 .75
101 Ron Hextall .30 .75
102 John LeClair .40 1.00
103 Eric Lindros .40 1.00
104 Dainius Zubrus .40 1.00
105 Mike Gartner .30 .75
106 Craig Janney .20 .50
107 Nikolai Khabibulin .30 .75
108 Jeremy Roenick .50 1.25
109 Keith Tkachuk .40 1.00
110 Stu Barnes .20 .50
111 Tom Barrasso .30 .75
112 Ron Francis .30 .75
113 Jaromir Jagr .60 1.50
114 Peter Skudra RC .20 .50
115 Martin Straka .20 .50
116 Blair Atcheynum RC .20 .50
117 Jim Campbell .20 .50
118 Geoff Courtnall .20 .50
119 Steve Duchesne .20 .50
120 Grant Fuhr .30 .75
121 Brett Hull .50 1.25
122 Pierre Turgeon .30 .75
123 Jeff Friesen .20 .50
124 John MacLean .20 .50
125 Patrick Marleau .30 .75
126 Owen Nolan .30 .75
127 Marco Sturm RC 1.00 2.50
128 Mike Vernon .30 .75
129 Daren Puppa .30 .75
130 Mikael Renberg .30 .75
131 Paul Ysebaert .20 .50
132 Rob Zamuner .20 .50
133 Wendel Clark .30 .75
134 Tie Domi .30 .75
135 Igor Korolev .20 .50
136 Felix Potvin .40 1.00
137 Mats Sundin .40 1.00
138 Donald Brashear .20 .50
139 Pavel Bure .40 1.00
140 Sean Burke .30 .75
141 Trevor Linden .30 .75
142 Mark Messier .40 1.00
143 Alexander Mogilny .30 .75
144 Mattias Ohlund .30 .75
145 Peter Bondra .30 .75
146 Phil Housley .20 .50
147 Dale Hunter .20 .50
148 Joe Juneau .30 .75
149 Olaf Kolzig .30 .75
150 Adam Oates .30 .75

1997-98 Revolution Copper

*STARS: 4X TO 8X BASIC CARDS
*ROOKIES: 2X TO 4X HI
STATED ODDS 2:25 HOBBY

1997-98 Revolution Emerald

*STARS: 4X TO 8X BASIC CARDS
*ROOKIES: 2X TO 4X
STATED ODDS 2:25 CANADIAN

1997-98 Revolution Ice Blue

*STARS: 12.5X TO 25X BASIC CARDS
*ROOKIES: 2X TO 4X
STATED ODDS 1:49

1997-98 Revolution Silver

*STARS: 4X TO 8X BASIC CARDS
*ROOKIES: 2X TO 4X
STATED ODDS 2:25 RETAIL

1997-98 Revolution 1998 All-Star Game Die-Cuts

Randomly inserted in packs at the rate of 1:49, this 20-card set features color photos of the hottest players named to the 1998 NHL All-Star game printed on a die-cut star-background card and appearing in their All-Star uniform from the game in Vancouver.

COMPLETE SET (20) 40.00 80.00
1 Teemu Selanne 1.50 4.00
2 Ray Bourque 3.00 8.00
3 Dominik Hasek 3.00 8.00
4 Theo Fleury .75 2.00
5 Chris Chelios 1.50 4.00
6 Peter Forsberg 4.00 10.00
7 Patrick Roy 6.00 15.00
8 Joe Sakic 3.00 8.00
9 Ed Belfour 1.50 4.00
10 Mike Modano 2.50 6.00
11 Brendan Shanahan 1.50 4.00
12 Saku Koivu 1.50 4.00
13 Martin Brodeur 4.00 10.00
14 Wayne Gretzky 8.00 20.00
15 John LeClair 1.50 4.00
16 Eric Lindros 1.50 4.00
17 Jaromir Jagr 2.50 6.00
18 Pavel Bure 1.50 4.00
19 Mark Messier 1.50 4.00
20 Peter Bondra 1.25 3.00

1997-98 Revolution NHL Icons

Randomly inserted in packs at the rate of 1:121, this 10-card set features color photos of today's living legends of hockey printed on a die-cut card.

COMPLETE SET (10) 30.00 60.00
1 Paul Kariya 1.50 4.00
2 Teemu Selanne 1.50 4.00
3 Peter Forsberg 4.00 10.00
4 Patrick Roy 6.00 15.00
5 Steve Yzerman 6.00 15.00
6 Martin Brodeur 4.00 10.00
7 Wayne Gretzky 8.00 20.00
8 Eric Lindros 1.50 4.00
9 Jaromir Jagr 2.50 6.00
10 Pavel Bure 1.50 4.00

1997-98 Revolution Return to Sender Die-Cuts

Randomly inserted in packs at the rate of 1:25, this 20-card set features color photos of the top goalies printed on a postage stamp shaped die-cut card.

COMPLETE SET (20) 20.00 40.00
1 Guy Hebert 1.00 2.50
2 Byron Dafoe 1.00 2.50
3 Dominik Hasek 2.50 6.00
4 Jeff Hackett 1.00 2.50
5 Patrick Roy 5.00 12.00
6 Ed Belfour 1.25 3.00
7 Chris Osgood 1.00 2.50
8 Curtis Joseph 1.25 3.00
9 John Vanbiesbrouck 1.00 2.50
10 Andy Moog 1.00 2.50
11 Martin Brodeur 3.00 8.00
12 Tommy Salo 1.00 2.50
13 Mike Richter 1.25 3.00
14 Ron Hextall 1.00 2.50
15 Nikolai Khabibulin 1.00 2.50
16 Tom Barrasso 1.00 2.50
17 Grant Fuhr 1.00 2.50
18 Mike Vernon 1.00 2.50
19 Felix Potvin 1.25 3.00
20 Olaf Kolzig 1.00 2.50

1997-98 Revolution Team Checklist Laser Cuts

Randomly inserted in packs at the rate of 1:25, this 26-card set features color action photos of top players with his laser-cut team logo beside the player image. The backs carry a Revolution main set checklist.

COMPLETE SET (26) 40.00 80.00
1 Paul Kariya 1.25 3.00
2 Joe Thornton 2.00 5.00
3 Michael Peca .60 1.50
4 Theo Fleury .60 1.50
5 Keith Primeau .60 1.50
6 Chris Chelios 1.25 3.00
7 Patrick Roy 5.00 12.00
8 Mike Modano 2.00 5.00
9 Steve Yzerman 5.00 12.00
10 Ryan Smyth 1.00 2.50
11 John Vanbiesbrouck 1.00 2.50
12 Jozef Stumpel 1.00 2.50
13 Saku Koivu 1.25 3.00
14 Martin Brodeur 3.00 8.00
15 Zigmund Palffy 1.00 2.50
16 Wayne Gretzky 6.00 15.00
17 Daniel Alfredsson 1.00 2.50
18 Eric Lindros 1.25 3.00
19 Keith Tkachuk 1.25 3.00
20 Jaromir Jagr 2.00 5.00
21 Brett Hull 1.50 4.00
22 Mike Vernon 1.00 2.50
23 Rob Zamuner .60 1.50
24 Mats Sundin 1.25 3.00
25 Pavel Bure 1.25 3.00
26 Peter Bondra 1.00 2.50

1998-99 Revolution

The 1998-99 Pacific Revolution set was issued in one series totaling 150 cards and distributed in three-card packs with a suggested retail price of $3.99. The set features color action player photos on dual-foiled, etched and embossed cards. The backs carry another player photos, biographical information, and career statistics.

COMPLETE SET (150) 50.00 100.00
1 Guy Hebert .30 .75
2 Paul Kariya .40 1.00
3 Marty McInnis .20 .50
4 Steve Rucchin .20 .50
5 Teemu Selanne .40 1.00
6 Jason Allison .20 .50
7 Ray Bourque .75 2.00
8 Anson Carter .30 .75
9 Byron Dafoe .30 .75
10 Dimitri Khristich .20 .50
11 Sergei Samsonov .30 .75
12 Matthew Barnaby .20 .50
13 Michal Grosek .20 .50
14 Dominik Hasek .75 2.00
15 Michael Peca .20 .50
16 Miroslav Satan .20 .50
17 Dixon Ward .20 .50
18 Theo Fleury .20 .50
19 J-S Giguere .20 .50
20 Jarome Iginla .50 1.25
21 Tyler Moss .20 .50
22 Cory Stillman .20 .50
23 Ron Francis .30 .75
24 Arturs Irbe .30 .75
25 Trevor Kidd .30 .75
26 Keith Primeau .20 .50
27 Ray Sheppard .20 .50
28 Tony Amonte .30 .75
29 Chris Chelios .40 1.00
30 Eric Daze .30 .75
31 Doug Gilmour .30 .75
32 Jocelyn Thibault .30 .75
33 Adam Deadmarsh .20 .50
34 Chris Drury .30 .75
35 Peter Forsberg 1.00 2.50
36 Milan Hejduk RC 2.00 5.00
37 Claude Lemieux .20 .50
38 Patrick Roy 1.50 4.00
39 Joe Sakic .75 2.00
40 Ed Belfour .40 1.00
41 Brett Hull .50 1.25
42 Jamie Langenbrunner .20 .50
43 Jere Lehtinen .20 .50
44 Mike Modano .60 1.50
45 Joe Nieuwendyk .30 .75
46 Darryl Sydor .20 .50
47 Sergei Fedorov .50 1.25
48 Nicklas Lidstrom .40 1.00
49 Norm Maracle RC .75 2.00
50 Darren McCarty .20 .50
51 Chris Osgood .30 .75
52 Brendan Shanahan .40 1.00
53 Steve Yzerman 1.50 4.00
54 Bill Guerin .30 .75
55 Andrei Kovalenko .20 .50
56 Mikhail Shtalenkov .20 .50
57 Ryan Smyth .30 .75
58 Doug Weight .30 .75
59 Pavel Bure .40 1.00
60 Sean Burke .30 .75
61 Dino Ciccarelli .30 .75
62 Viktor Kozlov .20 .50
63 Rob Niedermayer .20 .50
64 Mark Parrish RC .50 1.25
65 Rob Blake .30 .75
66 Stephane Fiset .30 .75
67 Olli Jokinen .30 .75
68 Luc Robitaille .30 .75
69 Pavel Rosa RC .20 .50
70 Jozef Stumpel .30 .75
71 Shayne Corson .20 .50
72 Vincent Damphousse .20 .50
73 Jeff Hackett .30 .75
74 Saku Koivu .40 1.00
75 Mark Recchi .30 .75
76 Brian Savage .20 .50
77 Andrew Brunette .20 .50
78 Mike Dunham .30 .75
79 Sergei Krivokrasov .20 .50
80 Cliff Ronning .20 .50
81 Tomas Vokoun .20 .50
82 Jason Arnott .20 .50
83 Martin Brodeur 1.00 2.50
84 Patrik Elias .30 .75
85 Bobby Holik .20 .50
86 Brendan Morrison .30 .75
87 Kenny Jonsson .20 .50
88 Trevor Linden .30 .75
89 Zigmund Palffy .30 .75
90 Tommy Salo .30 .75
91 Mike Watt .20 .50
92 Wayne Gretzky 2.00 5.00
93 Todd Harvey .20 .50
94 Brian Leetch .40 1.00
95 Manny Malhotra .30 .75
96 Petr Nedved .20 .50
97 Mike Richter .40 1.00
98 Daniel Alfredsson .30 .75
99 Marian Hossa .40 1.00
100 Shawn McEachern .20 .50
101 Damian Rhodes .20 .50
102 Alexei Yashin .20 .50
103 Rod Brind'Amour .30 .75
104 Ron Hextall .30 .75
105 John LeClair .40 1.00
106 Eric Lindros .40 1.00
107 John Vanbiesbrouck .30 .75
108 Dainius Zubrus .20 .50
109 Daniel Briere .20 .50
110 Nikolai Khabibulin .30 .75
111 Jeremy Roenick .50 1.25
112 Keith Tkachuk .40 1.00
113 Rick Tocchet .30 .75
114 Jim Waite .30 .75
115 Jean-Sebastien Aubin RC 1.00 2.50
116 Stu Barnes .20 .50
117 Tom Barrasso .30 .75
118 Jaromir Jagr .60 1.50
119 Alexei Kovalev .20 .50
120 Martin Straka .20 .50
121 Pavol Demitra .30 .75
122 Grant Fuhr .30 .75
123 Al MacInnis .30 .75
124 Chris Pronger .30 .75
125 Pierre Turgeon .30 .75
126 Jeff Friesen .20 .50
127 Patrick Marleau .20 .50
128 Owen Nolan .30 .75
129 Marco Sturm .20 .50
130 Mike Vernon .30 .75
131 Wendel Clark .30 .75
132 Darren Puppa .30 .75
133 Vincent Lecavalier .40 1.00
134 Stephane Richer .30 .75
135 Rob Zamuner .20 .50
136 Tie Domi .30 .75
137 Mike Johnson .20 .50
138 Curtis Joseph .40 1.00
139 Tomas Kaberle RC .75 2.00
140 Mats Sundin .40 1.00
141 Mark Messier .40 1.00
142 Alexander Mogilny .30 .75
143 Bill Muckalt RC .20 .50
144 Mattias Ohlund .30 .75
145 Garth Snow .30 .75
146 Peter Bondra .30 .75
147 Joe Juneau .30 .75
148 Olaf Kolzig .30 .75
149 Adam Oates .30 .75
150 Richard Zednik .20 .50
S83 Martin Brodeur SAMPLE .20 .50

1998-99 Revolution Ice Shadow

Randomly inserted into hobby packs only, this 150-card set is a limited blue foil hobby parallel version of the base set. Only 99 serial-numbered sets were made.

*STARS: 8X TO 15X BASIC CARDS
*ROOKIES: 2X TO 4X

1998-99 Revolution Red

*STARS: 3X TO 6X BASIC CARDS
*ROOKIES: 2X TO 4X
STATED PRINT RUN 299 SERIAL #'d SETS

1998-99 Revolution All-Star Die Cuts

Randomly inserted in packs at the rate of 1:25, this 30-card set features color images of players from the 1999 World and North America All-Star teams printed on full-foil die-cut cards with a jagged star design at the top.

COMPLETE SET (30) 40.00 80.00
1 Tony Amonte .75 2.00
2 Ed Belfour 1.25 3.00
3 Peter Bondra .75 2.00
4 Ray Bourque 2.00 5.00
5 Martin Brodeur 3.00 8.00
6 Theo Fleury .75 2.00
7 Peter Forsberg 2.50 6.00
8 Wayne Gretzky 6.00 15.00
9 Dominik Hasek 2.50 6.00
10 Bobby Holik .40 1.00
11 Arturs Irbe .75 2.00
12 Jaromir Jagr 2.00 5.00
13 Paul Kariya 1.25 3.00
14 Nikolai Khabibulin 1.00 3.00
15 Sergei Krivokrasov .40 1.00
16 John LeClair .40 1.00
17 Nicklas Lidstrom .75 2.00
18 Eric Lindros 1.25 3.00
19 Al MacInnis .75 2.00
20 Mike Modano 2.00 5.00
21 Mattias Ohlund .40 1.00
22 Keith Primeau .75 2.00
23 Chris Pronger .75 2.00
24 Mark Recchi .75 2.00
25 Jeremy Roenick 1.50 4.00
26 Teemu Selanne 1.25 3.00
27 Brendan Shanahan 1.25 3.00
28 Mats Sundin 1.25 3.00
29 Keith Tkachuk .75 2.00
30 Alexei Yashin .40 1.00

1998-99 Revolution Chalk Talk Laser-Cuts

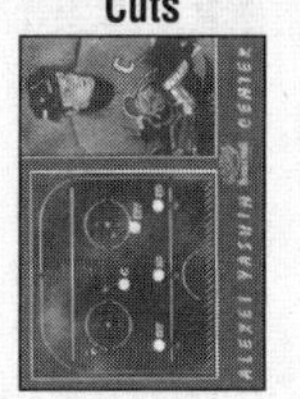

Randomly inserted into packs at the rate of 1:49, this 20-card set features color action player photos printed on full-foil horizontal cards alongside plays diagramed on a laser cut chalkboard.

COMPLETE SET (20) 40.00 80.00
1 Paul Kariya 1.50 4.00
2 Teemu Selanne 1.50 4.00
3 Theo Fleury .75 2.00
4 Peter Forsberg 4.00 10.00
5 Joe Sakic 3.00 8.00
6 Brett Hull 2.00 5.00
7 Mike Modano 2.50 6.00
8 Sergei Fedorov 2.00 5.00
9 Brendan Shanahan 1.50 4.00
10 Steve Yzerman 6.00 15.00
11 Wayne Gretzky 8.00 20.00
12 Alexei Yashin .75 2.00
13 John LeClair 1.50 4.00
14 Eric Lindros 1.50 4.00
15 Keith Tkachuk 1.50 4.00
16 Jaromir Jagr 2.50 6.00
17 Vincent Lecavalier 1.50 4.00
18 Mats Sundin 1.50 4.00
19 Mark Messier 1.50 4.00
20 Peter Bondra 1.25 3.00

1998-99 Revolution NHL Icons

Randomly inserted into packs at the rate of 1:121, this 10-card set features color images of some of the most renown players in hockey printed on die-cut silver foil cards.

COMPLETE SET (10) 30.00 60.00
1 Paul Kariya 1.50 4.00
2 Dominik Hasek 3.00 8.00
3 Peter Forsberg 4.00 10.00
4 Patrick Roy 6.00 15.00
5 Mike Modano 2.50 6.00
6 Steve Yzerman 6.00 15.00
7 Martin Brodeur 4.00 10.00
8 Wayne Gretzky 8.00 20.00
9 Eric Lindros 1.50 4.00
10 Jaromir Jagr 2.50 6.00

1998-99 Revolution Showstoppers

Randomly inserted into packs at the rate of 2:25, this 36-card set features color action photos of players known for their game-winning heroics printed on holographic silver foil cards.

COMPLETE SET (36) 20.00 50.00
1 Paul Kariya 1.00 2.50
2 Teemu Selanne 1.00 2.50
3 Ray Bourque 1.25 3.00
4 Dominik Hasek 2.00 5.00
5 Michael Peca .40 1.00
6 Theo Fleury .40 1.00
7 Tony Amonte .60 1.50
8 Chris Chelios .60 1.50
9 Doug Gilmour .60 1.50
10 Peter Forsberg 1.50 4.00
11 Patrick Roy 3.00 8.00
12 Joe Sakic 2.00 5.00
13 Ed Belfour 1.00 2.50
14 Brett Hull 1.25 3.00
15 Mike Modano 1.25 3.00
16 Sergei Fedorov 1.25 3.00
17 Brendan Shanahan 1.00 2.50
18 Steve Yzerman 3.00 8.00
19 Mark Parrish 1.00 2.50
20 Saku Koivu 1.00 2.50
21 Martin Brodeur 2.50 6.00
22 Zigmund Palffy .60 1.50
23 Wayne Gretzky 4.00 10.00
24 Alexei Yashin .40 1.00
25 John LeClair .60 1.50
26 Eric Lindros 1.00 2.50
27 John Vanbiesbrouck .60 1.50
28 Nikolai Khabibulin .60 1.50
29 Jeremy Roenick 1.25 3.00
30 Keith Tkachuk .60 1.50
31 Jaromir Jagr 1.50 4.00
32 Vincent Lecavalier 1.00 2.50
33 Curtis Joseph 1.00 2.50
34 Mats Sundin 1.00 2.50
35 Mark Messier 1.25 3.00
36 Peter Bondra .60 1.50

1998-99 Revolution Three Pronged Attack

Randomly inserted into hobby packs only at the rate of 4:25, this 30-card set features color action photos of some of the NHL's top players. A parallel version of this set was also produced and inserted only in hobby packs. The parallel consists of three separate tiers of 10 cards each with each tier serially numbered in varying amounts. Only 99 serial-numbered Tier 1 (cards #1-10) sets were made; 199 Tier 2 (11-20) serial-numbered sets were made; and 299 serial-numbered Tier 3 (21-30) sets were produced.

COMPLETE SET (30) 15.00 30.00
*TIER 1: 12.5X TO 25X BASIC INSERTS
*TIER 2 : 6X TO 12X BASIC INSERTS
*TIER 3: 4X TO 8X BASIC INSERTS
1 Matthew Barnaby .30 .75
2 Theo Fleury .30 .75
3 Chris Chelios .50 1.25
4 Darren McCarty .30 .75
5 Brendan Shanahan .50 1.25
6 Eric Lindros .50 1.25
7 Keith Tkachuk .50 1.25
8 Tony Twist .30 .75
9 Tie Domi .30 .75
10 Donald Brashear .30 .75
11 Dominik Hasek .75 2.00
12 Patrick Roy 1.25 3.00
13 Ed Belfour .50 1.25
14 Chris Osgood .40 1.00
15 Martin Brodeur 1.00 2.50
16 Mike Richter .50 1.25
17 John Vanbiesbrouck .40 1.00
18 Nikolai Khabibulin .40 1.00
19 Curtis Joseph .50 1.25
20 Olaf Kolzig .40 1.00
21 Paul Kariya .50 1.25
22 Teemu Selanne .50 1.25
23 Peter Forsberg 1.00 2.50
24 Joe Sakic .75 2.00
25 Mike Modano .30 .75
26 Steve Yzerman 1.25 3.00
27 Wayne Gretzky 1.50 4.00
28 John LeClair .50 1.25
29 Jaromir Jagr .60 1.50
30 Pavel Bure .50 1.25

1999-00 Revolution

Released as a 150-card set, Revolution features holographic foil base cards with gold foil highlights. Packaged in 24-pack boxes, each pack contained three cards and carried a suggested retail price of $3.99.

COMPLETE SET (150) 40.00 80.00
1 Guy Hebert .30 .75
2 Paul Kariya .40 1.00
3 Marty McInnis .20 .50
4 Teemu Selanne .40 1.00
5 Steve Rucchin .30 .75
6 Kelly Buchberger .20 .50
7 Ray Ferraro .20 .50
8 Damian Rhodes .20 .50
9 Johan Garpenlov .20 .50
10 Jason Allison .20 .50
11 Ray Bourque .75 2.00
12 Anson Carter .30 .75
13 Byron Dafoe .30 .75
14 Sergei Samsonov .30 .75
15 Joe Thornton .60 1.50
16 Martin Biron .30 .75
17 Curtis Brown .20 .50
18 Dominik Hasek .75 2.00
19 Michael Peca .30 .75
20 Miroslav Satan .30 .75
21 Dixon Ward .20 .50

22 Valeri Bure .20 .50
23 Fred Brathwaite .30 .75
24 Phil Housley .30 .75
25 Jarome Iginla .50 1.25
26 Cory Stillman .20 .50
27 Ron Francis .30 .75
28 Arturs Irbe .30 .75
29 Sami Kapanen .20 .50
30 Keith Primeau .20 .50
31 Gary Roberts .20 .50
32 Tony Amonte .30 .75
33 J-P Dumont .30 .75
34 Doug Gilmour .30 .75
35 Jocelyn Thibault .30 .75
36 Alexei Zhamnov .20 .50
37 Adam Deadmarsh .20 .50
38 Chris Drury .30 .75
39 Peter Forsberg 1.00 2.50
40 Milan Hejduk .40 1.00
41 Claude Lemieux .20 .50
42 Patrick Roy 1.50 4.00
43 Joe Sakic .75 2.00
44 Ed Belfour .40 1.00
45 Brett Hull .50 1.25
46 Jamie Langenbrunner .20 .50
47 Jere Lehtinen .30 .75
48 Mike Modano .60 1.50
49 Joe Nieuwendyk .30 .75
50 Chris Chelios .40 1.00
51 Sergei Fedorov .50 1.25
52 Vyacheslav Kozlov .30 .75
53 Nicklas Lidstrom .40 1.00
54 Chris Osgood .30 .75
55 Brendan Shanahan .40 1.00
56 Steve Yzerman 1.50 4.00
57 Mike Grier .30 .75
58 Bill Guerin .20 .50
59 Tommy Salo .30 .75
60 Ryan Smyth .30 .75
61 Doug Weight .30 .75
62 Pavel Bure .40 1.00
63 Sean Burke .30 .75
64 Viktor Kozlov .20 .50
65 Mark Parrish .20 .50
66 Ray Whitney .30 .75
67 Donald Audette .20 .50
68 Rob Blake .30 .75
69 Stephane Fiset .30 .75
70 Zigmund Palffy .30 .75
71 Luc Robitaille .30 .75
72 Jamie Storr .30 .75
73 Shayne Corson .20 .50
74 Jeff Hackett .30 .75
75 Saku Koivu .40 1.00
76 Vladimir Malakhov .20 .50
77 Martin Rucinsky .20 .50
78 Mike Dunham .30 .75
79 Greg Johnson .20 .50
80 Sergei Krivokrasov .20 .50
81 Cliff Ronning .30 .75
82 Scott Walker .20 .50
83 Jason Arnott .20 .50
84 Martin Brodeur 1.00 2.50
85 Patrik Elias .30 .75
86 Bobby Holik .20 .50
87 Brendan Morrison .30 .75
88 Scott Niedermayer .20 .50
89 Petr Sykora .20 .50
90 Mariusz Czerkawski .20 .50
91 Kenny Jonsson .20 .50
92 Mats Lindgren .20 .50
93 Felix Potvin .40 1.00
94 Mike Watt .20 .50
95 Theo Fleury .20 .50
96 Adam Graves .20 .50
97 Brian Leetch .40 1.00
98 John MacLean .20 .50
99 Petr Nedved .30 .75
100 Mike Richter .40 1.00
101 Magnus Arvedson .20 .50
102 Marian Hossa .40 1.00
103 Shawn McEachern .20 .50
104 Ron Tugnutt .30 .75
105 Alexei Yashin .20 .50
106 Rod Brind'Amour .30 .75
107 Eric Lindros .40 1.00
108 John LeClair .40 1.00
109 Mark Recchi .30 .75
110 John Vanbiesbrouck .30 .75
111 Nikolai Khabibulin .30 .75
112 Teppo Numminen .20 .50
113 Jeremy Roenick .50 1.25
114 Keith Tkachuk .40 1.00
115 Rick Tocchet .30 .75
116 Tom Barrasso .30 .75
117 Jan Hrdina .20 .50
118 Jaromir Jagr .60 1.50
119 Alexei Kovalev .20 .50
120 Martin Straka .20 .50
121 Pavol Demitra .30 .75
122 Jochen Hecht RC .75 2.00
123 Al MacInnis .30 .75
124 Chris Pronger .30 .75
125 Pierre Turgeon .30 .75
126 Vincent Damphousse .20 .50
127 Jeff Friesen .20 .50
128 Patrick Marleau .30 .75
129 Steve Shields .30 .75
130 Mike Vernon .30 .75
131 Chris Gratton .20 .50
132 Colin Forbes .20 .50
133 Vincent Lecavalier .40 1.00
134 Darcy Tucker .20 .50
135 Sergei Berezin .30 .75
136 Tie Domi .30 .75
137 Mike Johnson .30 .75
138 Curtis Joseph .40 1.00
139 Derek King .20 .50
140 Mats Sundin .40 1.00
141 Steve Thomas .20 .50
142 Mark Messier .40 1.00
143 Bill Muckalt .30 .75
144 Markus Naslund .40 1.00
145 Mattias Ohlund .30 .75
146 Garth Snow .30 .75
147 Peter Bondra .30 .75
148 Sergei Gonchar .20 .50
149 Olaf Kolzig .30 .75
150 Adam Oates .30 .75

1999-00 Revolution Premiere Date

Randomly inserted in Hobby packs at 1:25, this 150-card set parallels the base Revolution set with a foil Premier Date stamp. Each card is sequentially numbered to 42.
*STARS: 15X TO 40X BASIC CARDS

1999-00 Revolution Red

Randomly inserted in retail packs, this 150-card set parallels the base Revolution set in a red foil version. Each card is sequentially numbered to 299.
*STARS: 4X TO 10X BASIC CARDS

1999-00 Revolution Shadow Series

Randomly inserted in Hobby packs, this 150-card set parallels the base Revolution set. Each card has a Shadow Series stamp and is sequentially numbered to 99.
*STARS; 10X TO 25X BASIC CARDS

1999-00 Revolution Ice Sculptures

Randomly inserted in packs at the rate of 1:49, this 10-card set features top NHL players on an embossed silver foil card giving the effect of an ice carving.
COMPLETE SET (10) 50.00 100.00
1 Paul Kariya 2.00 5.00
2 Dominik Hasek 4.00 10.00
3 Patrick Roy 10.00 25.00
4 Joe Sakic 4.00 10.00
5 Steve Yzerman 10.00 25.00
6 Pavel Bure 2.50 6.00
7 Martin Brodeur 5.00 12.00
8 Theo Fleury 2.00 5.00
9 Eric Lindros 3.00 8.00
10 Jaromir Jagr 3.00 8.00

1999-00 Revolution NHL Icons

Randomly inserted in packs at the rate of 1:121, this 20-card set features close up action photography on a die cut card stock.
COMPLETE SET (20) 30.00 80.00
1 Teemu Selanne 1.50 4.00
2 Ray Bourque 3.00 8.00
3 Dominik Hasek 3.00 8.00
4 Doug Gilmour 1.25 3.00
5 Peter Forsberg 4.00 10.00
6 Patrick Roy 6.00 15.00
7 Joe Sakic 3.00 8.00
8 Brett Hull 2.00 5.00
9 Mike Modano 2.50 6.00
10 Brendan Shanahan 1.50 4.00
11 Steve Yzerman 6.00 15.00
12 Martin Brodeur 4.00 10.00
13 John LeClair 1.50 4.00
14 Eric Lindros 1.50 4.00
15 John Vanbiesbrouck 1.25 3.00
16 Keith Tkachuk 1.50 4.00
17 Jaromir Jagr 2.50 6.00
18 Curtis Joseph 1.50 4.00
19 Mats Sundin 1.50 4.00
20 Mark Messier 1.50 4.00

1999-00 Revolution Ornaments

Randomly seeded in packs at the rate of 1:25, this 20-card set features color player photos on a die-cut Christmas tree ornament.
COMPLETE SET (20) 40.00 80.00
1 Paul Kariya 1.25 3.00
2 Teemu Selanne 1.25 3.00
3 Sergei Samsonov 1.00 2.50
4 Dominik Hasek 2.50 6.00
5 Jarome Iginla 1.50 4.00
6 Peter Forsberg 3.00 8.00
7 Patrick Roy 5.00 12.00
8 Ed Belfour 1.25 3.00
9 Mike Modano 2.00 5.00
10 Brendan Shanahan 1.25 3.00
11 Steve Yzerman 5.00 12.00
12 Pavel Bure 1.25 3.00
13 Martin Brodeur 3.00 8.00
14 John LeClair 1.25 3.00
15 Eric Lindros 1.25 3.00
16 Jaromir Jagr 2.00 5.00
17 Vincent Lecavalier 1.25 3.00
18 Curtis Joseph 1.25 3.00
19 Mats Sundin 1.25 3.00
20 Mark Messier 1.25 3.00

1999-00 Revolution Showstoppers

Randomly seeded in packs at the rate of 2:25, this 36-card set features top NHL players on an all foil insert card.
COMPLETE SET (36) 40.00 80.00
1 Paul Kariya 1.00 2.50
2 Teemu Selanne 1.00 2.50
3 Ray Bourque 2.00 5.00
4 Byron Dafoe .75 2.00
5 Dominik Hasek 2.00 5.00
6 Michael Peca .75 2.00
7 Tony Amonte .75 2.00
8 Chris Drury .75 2.00
9 Peter Forsberg 2.50 6.00
10 Patrick Roy 4.00 10.00
11 Joe Sakic 2.00 5.00
12 Ed Belfour 1.00 2.50
13 Brett Hull 1.25 3.00
14 Mike Modano 1.50 4.00
15 Joe Nieuwendyk .75 2.00
16 Sergei Fedorov 1.25 3.00
17 Brendan Shanahan 1.00 2.50
18 Doug Weight .75 2.00
19 Pavel Bure 1.00 2.50
20 Mark Parrish .50 1.25
21 Martin Brodeur 2.50 6.00
22 Felix Potvin 1.00 2.50
23 Mike Richter 1.00 2.50
24 Marian Hossa 1.00 2.50
25 Alexei Yashin .50 1.25
26 John LeClair 1.00 2.50
27 John Vanbiesbrouck .75 2.00
28 Jeremy Roenick 1.25 3.00
29 Keith Tkachuk 1.00 2.50
30 Pavol Demitra .75 2.00
31 Patrick Marleau .75 2.00
32 Vincent Lecavalier 1.00 2.50
33 Curtis Joseph 1.00 2.50
34 Mats Sundin 1.00 2.50
35 Mark Messier 1.00 2.50
36 Peter Bondra .75 2.00

1999-00 Revolution Top of the Line

Randomly inserted in packs, this 30-card set was released as a three tier issue. Card numbers 1-10 are serial numbered out of 99, card numbers 11-20 are serial numbered out of 199, and card numbers 21-30 are serial numbered out of 299.
1 Paul Kariya/99 12.00 30.00
2 Sergei Samsonov/99 10.00 25.00
3 Brendan Shanahan/99 12.00 30.00
4 Pavel Bure/99 12.00 30.00
5 Luc Robitaille/99 10.00 25.00
6 Marian Hossa/99 10.00 25.00
7 John LeClair/99 8.00 20.00
8 Keith Tkachuk/99 12.00 30.00
9 Pavol Demitra/99 8.00 20.00
10 Jeff Friesen/99 8.00 20.00
11 Chris Drury/199 4.00 10.00
12 Peter Forsberg/199 12.00 30.00
13 Joe Sakic/199 12.00 30.00
14 Steve Yzerman/199 25.00 60.00
15 Mike Modano/199 10.00 25.00
16 Joe Nieuwendyk/199 6.00 15.00
17 Alexei Yashin/199 4.00 10.00
18 Eric Lindros/199 5.00 12.00
19 Mats Sundin/199 6.00 15.00
20 Mark Messier/199 6.00 15.00
21 Teemu Selanne/299 4.00 10.00
22 Miroslav Satan/299 3.00 8.00
23 Jarome Iginla/299 6.00 15.00
24 Tony Amonte/299 3.00 8.00
25 Milan Hejduk/299 3.00 8.00
26 Brett Hull/299 6.00 15.00
27 Theo Fleury/299 3.00 8.00
28 Mark Recchi/299 3.00 8.00
29 Jaromir Jagr/299 8.00 20.00
30 Peter Bondra/299 3.00 8.00

1999-00 Revolution Copper

Randomly inserted in packs, this 75-card set is skip numbered and parallels half of the base set with cards sequentially numbered to 10. This set is not priced due to scarcity.
NOT PRICED DUE TO SCARCITY

1999-00 Revolution Gold

Randomly inserted in packs, this 75-card set is skip numbered and parallels half of the base set with cards numbered one of one. The checklist parallels the copper set. This set not priced due to scarcity.
NOT PRICED DUE TO SCARCITY

2000-01 Revolution

Released as a 150-card set in late September 2000, Revolution base cards featured a centered player action photo set against holographic and gold foil accented blue card stock. Revolution was packaged in 24-pack boxes with each pack contained three cards.
COMPLETE SET (150) 50.00 100.00
1 Guy Hebert .50 1.25
2 Paul Kariya .60 1.50
3 Steve Rucchin .20 .50
4 Teemu Selanne .60 1.50
5 Andrew Brunette .50 1.25
6 Ray Ferraro .20 .50
7 Damian Rhodes .50 1.25
8 Patrik Stefan .20 .50
9 Anson Carter .50 1.25
10 Byron Dafoe .50 1.25
11 John Grahame .50 1.25
12 Sergei Samsonov .50 1.25
13 Joe Thornton 1.00 2.50
14 Maxim Afinogenov .20 .50
15 Martin Biron .50 1.25
16 Doug Gilmour .50 1.25
17 Dominik Hasek 1.25 3.00
18 Michael Peca .50 1.25
19 Miroslav Satan .50 1.25
20 Fred Brathwaite .50 1.25
21 Valeri Bure .20 .50
22 Phil Housley .50 1.25
23 Jarome Iginla .75 2.00
24 Oleg Saprykin .20 .50
25 Rod Brind'Amour .50 1.25
26 Ron Francis .50 1.25
27 Arturs Irbe .50 1.25
28 Sami Kapanen .20 .50
29 Tony Amonte .50 1.25
30 Michal Grosek .20 .50
31 Steve Sullivan .20 .50
32 Jocelyn Thibault .50 1.25
33 Alexei Zhamnov .50 1.25
34 Ray Bourque 1.25 3.00
35 Chris Drury .50 1.25
36 Peter Forsberg 1.50 4.00
37 Milan Hejduk .60 1.50
38 Patrick Roy 3.00 8.00
39 Joe Sakic 1.25 3.00
40 Alex Tanguay .50 1.25
41 Kevyn Adams .20 .50
42 Marc Denis .50 1.25
43 Krzysztof Oliwa .20 .50
44 Geoff Sanderson .20 .50
45 Ed Belfour .60 1.50
46 Brett Hull .75 2.00
47 Mike Modano 1.00 2.50
48 Brenden Morrow .50 1.25
49 Joe Nieuwendyk .50 1.25
50 Chris Chelios .60 1.50
51 Sergei Fedorov 1.00 2.50
52 Nicklas Lidstrom .60 1.50
53 Chris Osgood .50 1.25
54 Brendan Shanahan .60 1.50
55 Steve Yzerman 3.00 8.00
56 Bill Guerin .50 1.25
57 Todd Marchant .20 .50
58 Tommy Salo .50 1.25
59 Ryan Smyth .50 1.25
60 Doug Weight .50 1.25
61 Pavel Bure .60 1.50
62 Trevor Kidd .50 1.25
63 Viktor Kozlov .50 1.25
64 Scott Mellanby .20 .50
65 Ray Whitney .50 1.25
66 Rob Blake .50 1.25
67 Stephane Fiset .50 1.25
68 Zigmund Palffy .50 1.25
69 Luc Robitaille .50 1.25
70 Jamie Storr .50 1.25
71 Manny Fernandez .50 1.25
72 Jamie McLennan .50 1.25
73 Sean O'Donnell .20 .50
74 Stacy Roest .20 .50
75 Jeff Hackett .50 1.25
76 Saku Koivu .60 1.50
77 Trevor Linden .50 1.25
78 Martin Rucinsky .20 .50
79 Jose Theodore .75 2.00
80 Mike Dunham .50 1.25
81 David Gosselin RC .60 1.50
82 David Legwand .50 1.25
83 Cliff Ronning .20 .50
84 Jason Arnott .20 .50
85 Martin Brodeur 1.50 4.00
86 Patrik Elias .50 1.25
87 Scott Gomez .20 .50
88 Scott Stevens .50 1.25
89 Petr Sykora .20 .50
90 Tim Connolly .20 .50
91 Mariusz Czerkawski .20 .50
92 Brad Isbister .20 .50
93 Steve Valiquette RC .60 1.50
94 Theo Fleury .20 .50
95 Adam Graves .20 .50
96 Brian Leetch .50 1.25
97 Mark Messier .60 1.50
98 Petr Nedved .50 1.25
99 Mike Richter .60 1.50
100 Mike York .20 .50
101 Daniel Alfredsson .50 1.25
102 Radek Bonk .20 .50
103 Marian Hossa .60 1.50
104 Patrick Lalime .50 1.25
105 Shawn McEachern .20 .50
106 Brian Boucher .60 1.50
107 Eric Desjardins .50 1.25
108 Simon Gagne .60 1.50
109 John LeClair .60 1.50
110 Eric Lindros .60 1.50
111 Mark Recchi .50 1.25
112 Shane Doan .50 1.25
113 Nikolai Khabibulin .60 1.50
114 Jeremy Roenick .75 2.00
115 Keith Tkachuk .60 1.50
116 Jean-Sebastien Aubin .50 1.25
117 Jan Hrdina .20 .50
118 Jaromir Jagr 1.00 2.50
119 Alexei Kovalev .50 1.25
120 Martin Straka .20 .50
121 Pavol Demitra .50 1.25
122 Michal Handzus .50 1.25
123 Al MacInnis .50 1.25
124 Chris Pronger .50 1.25
125 Roman Turek .50 1.25
126 Pierre Turgeon .50 1.25
127 Vincent Damphousse .20 .50
128 Jeff Friesen .20 .50
129 Patrick Marleau .50 1.25
130 Owen Nolan .50 1.25
131 Steve Shields .50 1.25
132 Dan Cloutier .50 1.25
133 Mike Johnson .20 .50
134 Dieter Kochan RC .50 1.25
135 Vincent Lecavalier .60 1.50
136 Nikolai Antropov .20 .50
137 Tie Domi .50 1.25
138 Jeff Farkas .50 1.25
139 Curtis Joseph .60 1.50
140 Mats Sundin .60 1.50
141 Darcy Tucker .20 .50
142 Todd Bertuzzi .60 1.50
143 Steve Kariya .20 .50
144 Markus Naslund .60 1.50
145 Felix Potvin .60 1.50
146 Peter Bondra .60 1.50
147 Jeff Halpern .50 1.25
148 Olaf Kolzig .50 1.25
149 Adam Oates .50 1.25
150 Chris Simon .20 .50

2000-01 Revolution Blue

Randomly inserted in Hobby packs, this 150-card set parallels the base set with an embossed stamp in the middle of the card, and each card is sequentially numbered to 85.
*STARS: 6X TO 15X BASIC CARDS
*ROOKIES: 3X TO 8X BASIC CARDS

2000-01 Revolution Premiere Date

Randomly inserted in Hobby packs, this 150-card set parallels the base set where each card is sequentially numbered to 60.
*STARS: 8X TO 20X BASIC CARDS
*ROOKIES: 4X TO 10X BASIC CARDS

2000-01 Revolution Red

Randomly inserted in Retail packs, this 150-card set parallels the base set enhanced with red highlights where each card is sequentially numbered to 99.
*STARS: 4X TO 10X BASIC CARDS
*ROOKIES: 2.5X TO 6X BASIC CARDS

2000-01 Revolution Game-Worn Jerseys

Randomly inserted in packs, this 10-card set features a player action photo on the right side of the card front with circular swatches of game worn jerseys on the left. A gold foil serial number box appears right below the

jersey swatch, and each card is sequentially numbered to 400.
1 Marty McInnis 4.00 10.00
2 Anson Carter 6.00 15.00
3 Jarome Iginla 10.00 25.00
4 Tony Amonte 6.00 15.00
5 Jamie Langenbrunner 4.00 10.00
6 Saku Koivu 8.00 20.00
7 Zdeno Chara 6.00 15.00
8 Brian Leetch 6.00 15.00
9 Andreas Dackell 4.00 10.00
10 Petr Svoboda 4.00 10.00

2000-01 Revolution Game-Worn Jersey Patches

Randomly inserted in packs, this 10-card set parallels the base Game Worn Jerseys insert with premium swatches of game worn jerseys. Each card is sequentially numbered to 50.
*PATCHES: 1.25X TO 3X JERSEY CARD

2000-01 Revolution HD NHL

This 36-card set was randomly inserted in packs at the rate of 2:25.
COMPLETE SET (36) 30.00 60.00
1 Paul Kariya 1.00 2.50
2 Teemu Selanne 1.00 2.50
3 Patrik Stefan .30 .75
4 Joe Thornton 1.50 4.00
5 Dominik Hasek 2.00 5.00
6 Jarome Iginla 1.25 3.00
7 Tony Amonte .75 2.00
8 Peter Forsberg 2.50 6.00
9 Milan Hejduk 1.00 2.50
10 Joe Sakic 2.00 5.00
11 Patrick Roy 5.00 12.00
12 Ed Belfour 1.00 2.50
13 Brett Hull 1.25 3.00
14 Sergei Fedorov 1.50 4.00
15 Brendan Shanahan 1.00 2.50
16 Pavel Bure 1.00 2.50
17 Zigmund Palffy .75 2.00
18 Luc Robitaille .75 2.00
19 Saku Koivu 1.00 2.50
20 Martin Brodeur 2.50 6.00
21 Patrik Elias .75 2.00
22 Scott Gomez .30 .75
23 Marian Hossa 1.00 2.50
24 Brian Boucher 1.00 2.50
25 John LeClair 1.00 2.50
26 Mark Recchi .75 2.00
27 Jeremy Roenick 1.25 3.00
28 Keith Tkachuk 1.00 2.50
29 Chris Pronger .75 2.00
30 Roman Turek .75 2.00
31 Owen Nolan .75 2.00
32 Vincent Lecavalier 1.00 2.50
33 Nikolai Antropov .30 .75
34 Mats Sundin 1.00 2.50
35 Curtis Joseph 1.00 2.50
36 Olaf Kolzig .75 2.00

2000-01 Revolution Ice Immortals

Randomly inserted in packs at the rate of 1:25, this 20-card set features gray borders and a "snow" effect in front of player action photography on a blue and white background.
COMPLETE SET (20) 30.00 60.00
1 Paul Kariya 1.25 3.00
2 Teemu Selanne 1.25 3.00
3 Dominik Hasek 2.50 6.00
4 Ray Bourque 2.50 6.00
5 Peter Forsberg 3.00 8.00
6 Patrick Roy 6.00 15.00
7 Ed Belfour 1.25 3.00
8 Brett Hull 1.50 4.00
9 Mike Modano 2.00 5.00
10 Brendan Shanahan 1.25 3.00
11 Steve Yzerman 6.00 15.00
12 Pavel Bure 1.25 3.00
13 Martin Brodeur 3.00 8.00
14 Scott Gomez .40 1.00
15 John LeClair 1.25 3.00
16 Mark Recchi 1.00 2.50
17 Jeremy Roenick 1.50 4.00
18 Jaromir Jagr 2.00 5.00
19 Curtis Joseph 1.25 3.00
20 Olaf Kolzig 1.00 2.50

2000-01 Revolution NHL Game Gear

Randomly inserted in packs, this 10-card set features swatches of game worn jerseys and game used sticks. A player photo appears on the right side of the card front while two circular swatches of memorabilia, jersey on top and stick on bottom are separated by a gold serial number box. Each card is sequentially numbered to 200.
1 Peter Forsberg 15.00 40.00
2 Joe Sakic 15.00 40.00
3 Mike Modano 12.50 30.00
4 Sergei Fedorov 12.50 30.00
5 Nicklas Lidstrom 8.00 20.00
6 Steve Yzerman 20.00 50.00
7 Mark Messier 8.00 20.00
8 Nikolai Khabibulin 8.00 20.00
9 Jaromir Jagr 12.50 30.00
10 Peter Bondra 6.00 15.00

2000-01 Revolution NHL Icons

Randomly inserted in packs at the rate of 1:121, this 20-card set features a die-cut card stock in the shape of the NHL logo. Each card features gray borders around full color player photography.
COMPLETE SET (20) 50.00 100.00
1 Paul Kariya 1.50 4.00
2 Teemu Selanne 1.50 4.00
3 Doug Gilmour 1.25 3.00
4 Dominik Hasek 3.00 8.00
5 Ray Bourque 3.00 8.00
6 Peter Forsberg 4.00 10.00
7 Patrick Roy 8.00 20.00
8 Joe Sakic 3.00 8.00
9 Brett Hull 2.00 5.00
10 Mike Modano 2.50 6.00
11 Brendan Shanahan 1.50 4.00
12 Steve Yzerman 8.00 20.00
13 Pavel Bure 1.50 4.00
14 Luc Robitaille 1.25 3.00
15 Martin Brodeur 4.00 10.00
16 John LeClair 1.50 4.00
17 Jaromir Jagr 2.50 6.00
18 Curtis Joseph 1.50 4.00
19 Mats Sundin 1.50 4.00
20 Olaf Kolzig 1.25 3.00

2000-01 Revolution Stat Masters

Randomly inserted in packs, this 30-card set is a three tier issue. Tier one features top goal scorers and cards are sequentially numbered to 99, tier two features the NHL's leaders in shutouts and cards are sequentially numbered to 199, and tier three features assist leaders and cards are sequentially numbered to 299.
COMPLETE SET (30) 100.00 200.00
1 Teemu Selanne/99 6.00 15.00
2 Tony Amonte/99 5.00 12.00
3 Milan Hejduk/99 5.00 12.00
4 Brett Hull/99 6.00 15.00
5 Brendan Shanahan/99 5.00 12.00
6 Pavel Bure/99 5.00 12.00
7 Luc Robitaille/99 5.00 12.00
8 John LeClair/99 5.00 12.00
9 Jaromir Jagr/99 10.00 25.00
10 Owen Nolan/99 5.00 12.00
11 Martin Biron/199 2.50 6.00
12 Dominik Hasek/199 6.00 15.00
13 Patrick Roy/199 10.00 25.00
14 Ed Belfour/199 2.50 6.00
15 Jose Theodore/199 3.00 8.00
16 Martin Brodeur/199 6.00 15.00
17 Brian Boucher/199 2.50 6.00
18 Roman Turek/199 2.50 6.00
19 Curtis Joseph/199 2.50 6.00
20 Olaf Kolzig/199 2.50 6.00
21 Paul Kariya/299 5.00 12.00
22 Doug Gilmour/299 2.00 5.00

23 Ray Bourque/299 4.00 10.00
24 Joe Sakic/299 4.00 10.00
25 Mike Modano/299 3.00 8.00
26 Steve Yzerman/299 8.00 20.00
27 Scott Gomez/299 2.00 5.00
28 Mark Recchi/299 2.00 5.00
29 Mats Sundin/299 2.00 5.00
30 Adam Oates/299 2.00 5.00

2006-07 Rochester Americans

COMPLETE SET (25) 10.00 18.00
1 Craig Anderson .30 .75
2 David Booth .20 .50
3 Mike Card .20 .50
4 Adam Dennis .40 1.00
5 Mike Funk .20 .50
6 Rob Globke .40 1.00
7 Dylan Hunter .40 1.00
8 Greg Jacina .20 .50
9 Patrick Kaleta .20 .50
10 Kamil Kreps .20 .50
11 Drew Larman .20 .50
12 Martin Lojek .20 .50
13 Clarke MacArthur .40 1.00
14 Mark Mancari .40 1.00
15 Stefan Meyer .20 .50
16 Daniel Paille .40 1.00
17 Michael Ryan .40 1.00
18 Andrej Sekera .20 .50
19 Brandon Smith .20 .50
20 Janis Sprukts .20 .50
21 Drew Stafford .75 2.00
22 Anthony Stewart .30 .75
23 Marek Zagrapan .30 .75
24 Coaches .10 .25
NNO Cover Card .01 .01

1976-77 Rockies Puck Bucks

This 20-card set measures approximately 2 9/16" by 2 1/8" (after perforation) and features members of the then-expansion Colorado Rockies team. The set was issued in the Greater Denver area as part of a regional promotion for the Rockies. The cards feature a horizontal format on the front which has the player's photo. The cards were issued two to a panel (they could be separated, but then one couldn't compete in contest). Left side and right side in the rules refers to the two different cards that were joined: an action scene on the left side and a posed head shot in a circle on the right side). If the same player appeared in the action scene and in the circle, and if the ticket values and the color bars below both pictures matched, the contestant became an instant winner of two Colorado Rockies' hockey tickets, whose value is shown in the color bar. One could also save all player pictures until one had the same player appearing in the action scene and in the circle both with matching ticket values and matching color bars. The color bars at the bottom appeared in four different colors (yellow, blue, green, or orange). The cards feature either a "Play Puck Bucks" logo on the back, which also features a skeletal-like picture of a player, or a rules definition. Winners had to claim prizes by February 20, 1977. Since there is no numerical designation for the cards, they are checklisted alphabetically below.

COMPLETE SET (20) 37.50 75.00
1 Ron Andruff 2.00 4.00
2 Chuck Arnason 2.00 4.00
3 Henry Boucha 2.50 5.00
4 Colin Campbell 3.00 6.00
5 Gary Croteau 2.00 4.00
6 Guy Delparte 2.00 4.00
7 Steve Durbano 2.50 5.00
8 Tom Edur 2.00 4.00
9 Doug Favell 3.00 6.00
10 Dave Hudson 2.00 4.00
11 Bryan Lefley 2.00 4.00
12 Roger Lemelin 2.00 4.00
13 Simon Nolet 2.00 4.00
14 Wilf Paiement 2.50 5.00
15 Michel Plasse 3.00 6.00
16 Tracy Pratt 2.00 4.00
17 Nelson Pyatt 2.00 4.00
18 Phil Roberto 2.00 4.00
19 Sean Shanahan 2.00 4.00
20 Larry Skinner 2.00 4.00

1979-80 Rockies Team Issue

This 23-card set of the Colorado Rockies measures approximately 4" by 6". The fronts feature black-and-white action player photos. The backs are blank. The cards are unnumbered and checklisted below in alphabetical order.

COMPLETE SET (23) 20.00 40.00
1 Hardy Astrom 1.50 3.00
2 Doug Berry .75 1.50
3 Nick Beverley 1.00 2.00
4 Mike Christie .75 1.50
5 Gary Croteau 1.00 2.00
6 Lucien Deblois 1.00 2.00
7 Ron Delorme .75 1.50
8 Mike Gillis .75 1.50
9 Trevor Johansen .75 1.50
10 Mike Kitchen .75 1.50
11 Lanny McDonald 2.50 5.00
12 Mike McEwen .75 1.50
13 Bill McKenzie .75 1.50
14 Kevin Morrison .75 1.50
15 Bill Olesehuk .75 1.50
16 Randy Pierce .75 1.50
17 Michel Plasse 1.50 3.00
18 Joel Quenneville 1.00 2.00
19 Rob Ramage 2.50 5.00
20 Rene Robert 1.00 2.00
21 Don Saleski 1.00 2.00
22 Barry Smith 1.00 2.00
23 Jack Valiquette .75 1.50

1981-82 Rockies Postcards

This 30-card postcard set measures 3 1/2" by 5 1/2" and features borderless black-and-white action player photos of the Colorado Rockies. The backs have the standard white postcard design with the player's name and biographical information in the upper left corner. The team emblem is printed in light gray on the left side. The cards are unnumbered and checklisted below in alphabetical order.

COMPLETE SET (30) 14.00 35.00
1 Brent Ashton .80 2.00
2 Aaron Broten .40 1.00
3 Dave Cameron .40 1.00
4 Joe Cirella .80 2.00
5 Dwight Foster .40 1.00
6 Paul Gagne .40 1.00
7 Marshall Johnston CO .40 1.00
8 Veli-Pekka Ketola .60 1.50
9 Mike Kitchen .40 1.00
10 Rick Laferriere .40 1.00
11 Don Lever .60 1.50
12 Tapio Levo .40 1.00
13 Bob Lorimer .40 1.00
14 Bill MacMillan .40 1.00
15 Bob MacMillan VP .60 1.50
16 Merlin Malinowski .60 1.50
17 Bert Marshall GM .40 1.00
18 Kevin Maxwell .40 1.00
19 Joe Micheletti .80 2.00
20 Bobby Miller .40 1.00
21 Phil Myre .80 2.00
22 Graeme Nicolson .40 1.00
23 Jukka Porvari .40 1.00
24 Joel Quenneville .60 1.50
25 Rob Ramage 1.20 3.00
26 Glenn Resch 1.20 3.00
27 Steve Tambellini .60 1.50
28 Yvon Vautour .40 1.00
29 John Wensink .60 1.50
30 Title Card .80 2.00
(Team logo)

1952 Royal Desserts

The 1952 Royal Desserts Hockey set contains eight cards. The cards measure approximately 2 5/8" by 3 1/4". The set is cataloged as F219-2. The cards formed the backs of Royal Desserts packages of the period; consequently many cards are found with uneven edges stemming from the method of cutting the cards off the box. Each card has its number and the statement "Royal Stars of Hockey" in a red rectangle at the top. The blue tinted picture also features a facsimile autograph of the player. An album was presumably available as it is advertised on the card. The exact year (or years) of issue of these cards is not verified at this time.

COMPLETE SET (8) 6500.00 13000.00
1 Tony Leswick 250.00 500.00
2 Chuck Rayner 400.00 800.00
3 Edgar Laprade 300.00 600.00
4 Sid Abel 600.00 1200.00
5 Ted Lindsay 600.00 1200.00
6 Leo Reise 250.00 500.00
7 Red Kelly 600.00 1200.00
8 Gordie Howe 3750.00 7500.00

1971-72 Sabres Postcards

These standard-sized postcards feature borderless color photos. The backs feature player name, position, uniform number, and biographical information. These postcards were issued in bound form, with perforated top edges so as to be separated if necessary. The postcards are numbered in a long code format (for example, Punch Imlach is 82269-C). For space reasons, the 822 prefix and -C suffix have been deleted in the checklist below. Thanks to collector Edward Morse for updating the information seen below.

COMPLETE SET (22) 15.00 30.00
69 Punch Imlach CO 1.00 2.00
70 Roger Crozier 1.50 3.00
71 Jim Watson .50 1.00
72 Mike Robitaille .50 1.00
73 Tracy Pratt .50 1.00
74 Doug Barrie .50 1.00
75 Al Hamilton .50 1.00
76 Richard Martin 1.50 3.00
77 Dick Duff .75 1.50
78 Danny Lawson .50 1.00
79 Phil Goyette .50 1.00
80 Gil Perreault 4.00 8.00
81 Rod Zaine .50 1.00
82 Gerry Meehan .75 1.50
83 Ron Anderson .50 1.00
84 Floyd Smith .75 1.50
85 Kevin O'Shea .50 1.00
86 Steve Atkinson .50 1.00
87 Don Luce
88 Ray McKay .50 1.00
89 Eddie Shack 1.00 2.00
90 Dave Dryden 1.50 3.00

1972-73 Sabres Pepsi Pinback Buttons

These smallish buttons were apparently given away with the purchase of Pepsi products in the Buffalo area. The photos are black and white and feature early heroes of the Sabres history.

COMPLETE SET (9) 25.00 50.00
1 Roger Crozier 2.50 5.00
2 Don Luce 2.00 4.00
3 Rick Martin (action) 2.50 5.00
4 Rick Martin (head) 2.50 5.00
5 Gilbert Perreault (action) 5.00 10.00
6 Gilbert Perreault (head) 5.00 10.00
7 Rene Robert 2.50 5.00
8 Jim Schoenfeld 2.50 5.00
9 French Connection 5.00 10.00

1972-73 Sabres Postcards

This set of color postcards was issued by the team in response to autograph requests. It is not known whether they were actually sold in set form at any point, but given the difficulty in completing a set, it seems unlikely.

COMPLETE SET (20) 30.00 60.00
1 Steve Atkinson 1.00 2.00
2 Larry Carriere 1.00 2.00
3 Roger Crozier 4.00 8.00
4 Butch Deadmarsh 1.00 2.00
5 Dave Dryden 1.50 3.00
6 Larry Hillman 1.00 2.00
7 Tim Horton 5.00 10.00
8 Jim Lorentz 1.00 2.00
9 Don Luce 1.50 3.00
10 Richard Martin 3.00 6.00
11 Gerry Meehan 1.50 3.00
12 Larry Mickey 1.00 2.00
13 Gilbert Perreault 5.00 10.00
14 Tracy Pratt 1.50 3.00
15 Craig Ramsay 1.50 3.00
16 Rene Robert 1.50 3.00
17 Mike Robitaille 1.00 2.00
18 Jim Schoenfeld 3.00 6.00
19 Paul Terbenche 1.00 2.00
20 Randy Wyrozub 1.00 2.00

1973-74 Sabres Bells

This set of four photos of Buffalo Sabres players was sponsored by Bells Markets. The photos measure approximately 3 15/16" by 5 1/2" and were sold for 10 cents each. The front has a color action photo. These blank-backed cards are unnumbered and listed alphabetically in the checklist below. The team card was issued and cost 50 cents apiece.

COMPLETE SET (4) 15.00 30.00
1 Roger Crozier 4.00 8.00
2 Jim Lorentz 2.50 5.00
3 Richard Martin 4.00 8.00
4 Gilbert Perreault 6.00 12.00
5 Team Photo

1973-74 Sabres Postcards

This 13-card set was published by Robert B. Shaver of Kenmore, New York. The cards are in the postcard format and measure approximately 3 1/2" by 5 1/2". The fronts feature a black-and-white action shot with white borders. The backs carry the player's name, position, and team name at the upper left and are divided in the middle. The set is dated by the inclusion of Joe Norris, who played with the Sabres only during the 1973-74 season. The cards are unnumbered and checklisted below in alphabetical order.

COMPLETE SET (13) 20.00 40.00
1 Roger Crozier 2.00 4.00
2 Dave Dryden 2.00 4.00
3 Tim Horton 5.00 10.00
4 Jim Lorentz 1.00 2.00
5 Don Luce 1.25 2.50
6 Rick Martin 2.00 4.00
7 Gerry Meehan 1.50 3.00
8 Larry Mickey 1.00 2.00
9 Joe Noris 1.00 2.00
10 Gilbert Perreault 4.00 8.00
11 Mike Robitaille 1.00 2.00
12 Jim Schoenfeld 2.00 4.00
13 Paul Terbenche 1.00 2.00

1974-75 Sabres Postcards

This set of color postcards was issued by the team in response to autograph requests. It is not known whether they were actually sold in set form at any point, but given the difficulty in completing a set, it seems unlikely.

COMPLETE SET (21) 30.00 60.00
1 Gary Bromley 2.00 4.00
2 Larry Carriere 1.00 2.00
3 Roger Crozier 4.00 8.00
4 Rick Dudley 2.00 4.00
5 Rocky Farr 1.00 2.00
6 Lee Fogolin 2.00 4.00
7 Danny Gare 2.00 4.00
8 Norm Gratton 1.00 2.00
9 Jocelyn Guevremont 1.00 2.00
10 Bill Hajt 1.00 2.00
11 Jerry Korab 2.00 4.00
12 Jim Lorentz 1.00 2.00
13 Don Luce 1.25 2.50
14 Richard Martin 2.00 4.00
15 Peter McNab 1.25 2.50
16 Larry Mickey 1.00 2.00
17 Gilbert Perreault 4.00 8.00
18 Craig Ramsay 1.50 3.00
19 Rene Robert 1.50 3.00
20 Jim Schoenfeld 2.00 4.00
21 Brian Spencer 2.50 5.00

1975-76 Sabres Linnett

Produced by Linnett Studios, this 12-card set featured Buffalos Sabres players ftom the 1975-76 season.

COMPLETE SET (12) 15.00 30.00
1 Roger Crozier 2.00 4.00
2 Gerry Desjardins 1.50 3.00
3 Dave Dryden 1.50 3.00
4 Jim Lorentz 1.00 2.00
5 Don Luce 1.25 2.50
6 Richard Martin 2.00 4.00
7 Peter McNab 1.25 2.50
8 Gerry Meehan 1.00 2.00
9 Gilbert Perreault 4.00 8.00
10 Rene Robert 1.50 3.00
11 Jim Schoenfeld 2.00 4.00
12 Fred Stanfield 1.50 3.00

1976-77 Sabres Glasses

Glasses feature a black and white portrait of the player. Glasses were available at Your Host restaurants.

COMPLETE SET (4) 12.50 25.00
1 Jerry Korab 3.00 6.00
2 Rick Martin 3.00 6.00
3 Gilbert Perreault 3.00 6.00
4 Jim Schoenfeld 3.00 6.00

1979-80 Sabres Bells

This set of nine photos of Buffalo Sabres players was sponsored by Bells Markets. The photos measure approximately 7 5/8" by 10". The front has a color action photo, with the player's name and team name in the white border at the lower right hand corner. The back is printed in blue and has the Sabres' logo, a head shot of the player, biographical information, and career statistics.

COMPLETE SET (9) 10.00 20.00
1 Don Edwards 2.00 4.00
2 Danny Gare 1.25 2.50
3 Jerry Korab 1.00 2.00
4 Richard Martin 2.00 4.00
5 Tony McKegney 1.25 2.50
6 Craig Ramsay 1.00 2.00
7 Bob Sauve 2.00 4.00
8 Jim Schoenfeld 1.50 3.00
9 John Van Boxmeer 1.00 2.00

1979-80 Sabres Milk Panels

This set of four confirmed panels feature singles that are approximately 3 1/2 by 1 1/2. The top portion features a blue-toned head shot, while the bottom includes player bio information. The backs are blank.

COMPLETE SET (4) 3.00 6.00
1 Don Edwards .50 1.00
2 Ric Seiling .50 1.00
3 Jerry Korab .50 1.00
4 Gil Perreault .50 1.00

1980-81 Sabres Milk Panels

This set of Buffalo Sabres was issued on the side of half gallon milk cartons. After cutting, the panels measure approximately 3 3/4" by 7 1/2", with two players per panel. The picture and text of the player panels are printed in red; the set can also be found in blue print. The top of the panel reads "Kids, Collect a Complete Set of Buffalo Sabres Players". Arranged alongside each other, the

panel features for each player a head shot, biographical information, and player profile. The panels are subtly dated and numbered below the photo area in the following way, Perreault/Seiling is M325-80-4H (M325 is the product code, the number 80 gives the last two digits of the year, and 4 is the card number perhaps also indicating release week).

COMPLETE SET (2) 15.00 30.00
4 Gilbert Perreault and Ric Seiling 10.00 20.00
8 Bob Sauve and Richard Martin 6.00 12.00

1981-82 Sabres Milk Panels

This sixteen-panel set of Buffalo Sabres was issued by Wilson Farms Dairy on the side of 2 percent milk fat and homogenized Vitamin D half gallon milk cartons. After cutting, the panels measure approximately 3 3/4" by 7 1/2". Although the 2 percent milk fat cartons have some lime green lettering and a lime green stripe, the picture and text of the player panels are printed in red on both cartons. The top of the panel reads "Kids, Collect Action Photos of the 1981-82 Buffalo Sabres." Inside a red broken border, the panel has a action player photo, with player information and career summary beneath the picture. The panels are subtly dated and numbered below the photo area in the following way, Gilbert Perreault is M325-81-4H (M325 is the product code, the number 81 gives the last two digits of year, and 4 is the card number perhaps also indicating release week). The set can also be found in blue print.

COMPLETE SET (17) 60.00 150.00
1 Craig Ramsay 4.00 10.00
2 John Van Boxmeer 4.00 10.00
3 Don Edwards 4.80 12.00
4 Gilbert Perreault 8.00 20.00
5 Alan Haworth 4.00 10.00
6 Jim Schoenfeld 6.00 15.00
7 Richie Dunn 4.00 10.00
8 Bob Sauve 4.80 12.00
9 Bill Hajt 4.00 10.00
10 Larry Playfair 4.00 10.00
11 Tony McKegney 4.80 12.00
12 Mike Ramsey 4.80 12.00
13 Andre Savard 4.00 10.00
14 Derek Smith 4.00 10.00
15 Ric Seiling 4.00 10.00
16 Yvon Lambert 4.00 10.00
17 Dale McCourt 4.00 10.00

1982-83 Sabres Milk Panels

This seventeen-panel set of Buffalo Sabres was issued on the side of half gallon milk cartons. After cutting, the panels measure approximately 3 3/4" by 7 1/2". The picture and text of the player panels are printed in blue. The top of the panel reads "Kids, Clip and Save Exciting Tips and Pictures of Buffalo Sabres." Inside a blue broken border, the panel has a posed head and shoulders shot, with the player's name, position, and a hockey tip beneath the picture. The panels are subtly dated and numbered below the photo area in the following way, Gilbert Perreault is M325-82-7H. Phil Housley's card predates his Rookie Card.

COMPLETE SET (17) 60.00 150.00
2 1982-83 Home Schedule 6.00 15.00
3 Craig Ramsay 4.00 10.00
4 John Van Boxmeer 4.00 10.00
5 Lindy Ruff 4.00 10.00
6 Bob Sauve 4.80 12.00
7 Gilbert Perreault 8.00 20.00
8 Ric Seiling 4.00 10.00
9 Jacques Cloutier 4.80 12.00
10 Larry Playfair 4.00 10.00
11 Phil Housley 8.00 20.00
12 Mike Foligno 4.80 12.00
13 Tony McKegney 4.80 12.00
14 Dale McCourt 4.00 10.00
15 Mike Ramsey 4.00 10.00
16 Hannu Virta 4.00 10.00
17 Brent Peterson 4.00 10.00
18 Scott Bowman GM 8.00 20.00

1984-85 Sabres Blue Shield

This 21-card set was issued by the Buffalo Sabres in conjunction with Blue Shield of Western New York. The cards measure approximately 2 1/2" by 3 3/4". It has been reported that only 500 sets were printed as a test for future issues. The fronts feature a head and shoulders color photo with player information below the picture. The card backs have the Blue Shield logo and the words "The Caring Card -- The Blue Shield of Western New York, Inc." We have checklisted the cards below in alphabetical order. Dave Andreychuk and Tom Barrasso appear in their Rookie Card year.

COMPLETE SET (21) 40.00 100.00
1 Dave Andreychuk 8.00 20.00
2 Tom Barrasso 8.00 20.00
3 Adam Creighton 2.00 5.00
4 Paul Cyr 1.20 3.00
5 Malcolm Davis 1.20 3.00
6 Mike Foligno 2.00 5.00
7 Bill Hajt 1.20 3.00
8 Gilles Hamel 1.20 3.00
9 Phil Housley 4.00 10.00
10 Sean McKenna 1.20 3.00
11 Mike Moller 1.20 3.00
12 Gilbert Perreault 6.00 15.00
13 Brent Peterson 1.20 3.00
14 Larry Playfair 1.20 3.00
15 Craig Ramsay 2.00 5.00
16 Mike Ramsey 2.00 5.00
17 Lindy Ruff 2.00 5.00
18 Bob Sauve 2.00 5.00
19 Ric Seiling 1.20 3.00
20 John Tucker 2.00 5.00
21 Hannu Virta 1.20 3.00

1985-86 Sabres Blue Shield

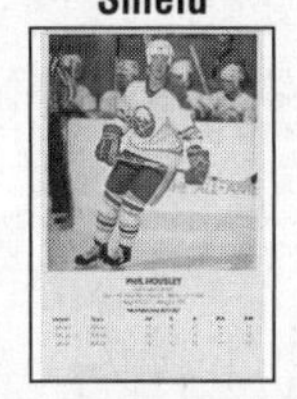

This 28-card set was issued by the Buffalo Sabres in conjunction with Blue Shield of Western New York. The cards were printed in two different sizes: large (4" by 6" with postcard backs) and small (2 1/2" by 3 1/2"). Both sizes have the Blue Shield logo on the backs. Though both sizes are scarce, the small cards are considered harder to obtain. The front of the large card features a color action photo of the player, with his name as well as biographical and statistical information below the picture. The front of the small card is identical except for the omission of the statistical information. The firing of Sabres' coach Jim Schoenfeld at the time the cards were issued makes his card rare as he was removed from the set. The set is priced below as complete without the Schoenfeld card. Daren Puppa's card predates his Rookie Card by three years.

COMPLETE SET (27) 16.00 40.00
1 Mikael Andersson .40 1.00
2 Dave Andreychuk 2.00 5.00
3 Tom Barrasso 1.20 3.00
4 Adam Creighton .40 1.00
5 Paul Cyr .40 1.00
6 Malcolm Davis .40 1.00
7 Steve Dykstra .40 1.00
8 Dave Fenyves .40 1.00
9 Mike Foligno .40 1.00
10 Bill Hajt .40 1.00
11 Bob Halkidis .40 1.00
12 Gilles Hamel .40 1.00
13 Phil Housley 1.20 3.00
14 Pat Hughes .40 1.00
15 Normand Lacombe .40 1.00
16 Chris Langevin .40 1.00
17 Sean McKenna .40 1.00
18 Gates Orlando .80 2.00
19 Gilbert Perreault 2.00 5.00
20 Larry Playfair .40 1.00
21 Daren Puppa 1.00 2.50
22 Craig Ramsay ACO .20 .50
23 Mike Ramsey .40 1.00
24 Lindy Ruff .40 1.00
25 Jim Schoenfeld CO SP 6.00 15.00
26 Ric Seiling .40 1.00
27 John Tucker .60 1.50
28 Hannu Virta .40 1.00

1985-86 Sabres Blue Shield Small

This set is the same as the regular Sabres Blue Shield set, only in a smaller format.

COMPLETE SET (27) 16.00 40.00
1 Mikael Andersson .40 1.00
2 Dave Andreychuk 1.60 4.00
3 Tom Barrasso .80 2.00
4 Adam Creighton .40 1.00
5 Paul Cyr .40 1.00
6 Malcolm Davis .40 1.00
7 Steve Dykstra .40 1.00
8 Dave Fenyves .40 1.00
9 Mike Foligno .40 1.00
10 Bill Hajt .40 1.00
11 Bob Halkidis .40 1.00
12 Gilles Hamel .40 1.00
13 Phil Housley .80 2.00
14 Pat Hughes .40 1.00
15 Normand Lacombe .40 1.00
16 Chris Langevin .40 1.00
17 Sean McKenna .40 1.00
18 Gates Orlando .60 1.50
19 Gilbert Perreault 1.60 4.00
20 Larry Playfair .40 1.00
21 Daren Puppa .80 2.00
22 Craig Ramsay ACO .20 .50
23 Mike Ramsey .40 1.00
24 Lindy Ruff .40 1.00
25 Jim Schoenfeld CO SP 4.00 10.00
26 Ric Seiling .40 1.00
27 John Tucker .60 1.50
28 Hannu Virta .40 1.00

1986-87 Sabres Blue Shield

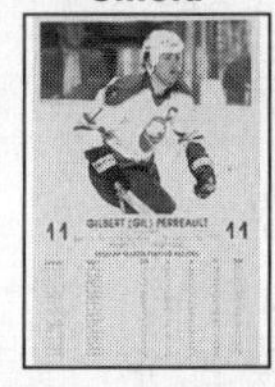

This 28-card set was issued by the Buffalo Sabres in conjunction with Blue Shield of Western New York. In contrast to the previous year's issue, the cards were printed only in one size, the approximately 4" by 6" postcard type with the Blue Shield logo on the backs. The front of the cards can be distinguished from the previous year's issue by the addition of the player's uniform number (inadvertently omitted on the Creighton and Fenyves cards) and updated statistics.

COMPLETE SET (28) 12.00 30.00
1 Shawn Anderson .30 .75
2 Dave Andreychuk 2.40 6.00
3 Scott Arniel .30 .75
4 Tom Barrasso 1.20 3.00
5 Jacques Cloutier .40 1.00
6 Adam Creighton .40 1.00
7 Paul Cyr .30 .75
8 Steve Dykstra .30 .75
9 Dave Fenyves .30 .75
10 Mike Foligno .60 1.50
11 Clark Gillies .80 2.00
12 Bill Hajt .30 .75
13 Bob Halkidis .30 .75
14 Jim Hofford .30 .75
15 Phil Housley 1.00 2.50
16 Jim Korn .30 .75
17 Uwe Krupp .60 1.50
18 Tom Kurvers .30 .75
19 Norm Lacombe .30 .75
20 Gates Orlando .30 .75
21 Wilf Paiement .40 1.00
22 Gilbert Perreault 2.00 5.00
23 Daren Puppa 1.20 3.00
24 Mike Ramsey .40 1.00
25 Lindy Ruff .30 .75
26 Christian Ruuttu .30 .75
27 Doug Smith .30 .75
28 John Tucker .40 1.00

1986-87 Sabres Blue Shield Small

Same as the regular Sabres Shield set only in a smaller format.

COMPLETE SET (28) 14.00 35.00
1 Shawn Anderson .30 .75
2 Dave Andreychuk 2.40 6.00
3 Scott Arniel .30 .75
4 Tom Barrasso 1.20 3.00
5 Jacques Cloutier .40 1.00
6 Adam Creighton .40 1.00
7 Paul Cyr .30 .75
8 Steve Dykstra .30 .75
9 Dave Fenyves .30 .75
10 Mike Foligno .60 1.50
11 Clark Gillies .80 2.00
12 Bill Hajt .30 .75
13 Bob Halkidis .30 .75
14 Jim Hofford .30 .75
15 Phil Housley 1.20 3.00
16 Jim Korn .30 .75
17 Uwe Krupp .60 1.50
18 Tom Kurvers .30 .75
19 Norm Lacombe .30 .75
20 Gates Orlando .30 .75
21 Wilf Paiement .40 1.00
22 Gilbert Perreault 2.00 5.00
23 Daren Puppa 1.20 3.00
24 Mike Ramsey .40 1.00
25 Lindy Ruff .30 .75
26 Christian Ruuttu .30 .75
27 Doug Smith .30 .75
28 John Tucker .40 1.00

1987-88 Sabres Blue Shield

This 28-card set was issued by the Buffalo Sabres in conjunction with Blue Shield of Western New York. In contrast to the previous year's issue, the cards are a different size, approximately 4" by 5", again in the postcard format with the Blue Shield logo on the backs. The front of the cards feature a color action photo of the player, with the player's name, team name, and team logo in a yellow stripe at the top. The player's number and a facsimile autograph appear in blue at the bottom on the front. Supposedly there exists a rare variation on the Phil Housley card which has his last name misspelled "Housley". The card of Pierre Turgeon predates his Rookie Card by one year.

COMPLETE SET (28)	10.00	25.00
1 Mikael Andersson 14	.30	.75
2 Dave Andreychuk 25	1.20	3.00
3 Scott Arniel 9	.30	.75
4 Tom Barrasso 30	.60	1.50
5 Jacques Cloutier 1	.40	1.00
6 Adam Creighton 38	.40	1.00
7 Mike Donnelly 16	.30	.75
8 Mike Foligno 17	.40	1.00
9 Clark Gillies 90	.40	1.00
10 Bob Halkidis 18	.30	.75
11 Mike Hartman 20	.30	.75
12 Ed Hospodar 24	.30	.75
13 Phil Housley 6	.60	1.50
14 Calle Johansson 3	.40	1.00
15 Uwe Krupp 40	.40	1.00
16 Jan Ludvig 36	.30	.75
17 Kevin Maguire 19	.30	.75
18 Mark Napier 65	.30	.75
19 Ken Priestlay 12	.30	.75
20 Daren Puppa 35	.60	1.50
21 Mike Ramsey 5	.40	1.00
22 Joe Reekie 27	.30	.75
23 Lindy Ruff 22	.30	.75
24 Christian Ruuttu 21	.40	1.00
25 Ray Sheppard 23	1.20	3.00
26 Doug Smith 15	.30	.75
27 John Tucker 7	.40	1.00
28 Pierre Turgeon 77	4.00	10.00

1987-88 Sabres Wonder Bread/Hostess

The 1987-88 Buffalo Sabres Team Photo Album was sponsored by Wonder Bread and Hostess Cakes. It consists of three large sheets, each measuring approximately 13 1/2" by 10 1/4" and joined together to form one continuous sheet. The first panel has a team photo of the Buffalo Sabres. The second and third panels present three rows of five cards each. After perforation, the cards measure approximately 2 5/8" by 3 3/8". They feature color posed photos bordered in various color dots, with player information below the picture sandwiched between the Sabres' and sponsors' logos. The back has biographical and statistical information in a horizontal format. We have checklisted the names below in alphabetical order, with the uniform number to the right of the name. The set features an early card of Pierre Turgeon pre-dating his Rookie Cards by one year.

COMPLETE SET (31)	8.00	20.00
1 Mikael Andersson 14	.20	.50
2 Shawn Anderson 37	.20	.50
3 Dave Andreychuk 25	1.00	2.50
4 Scott Arniel 9	.20	.50
5 Tom Barrasso 30	.80	2.00
6 Jacques Cloutier 1	.30	.75
7 Adam Creighton 38	.30	.75
8 Steve Dykstra 4	.20	.50
9 Mike Foligno 17	.30	.75
10 Clark Gillies 90	.30	.75
11 Ed Hospodar 24	.20	.50
12 Phil Housley 6	.50	1.25
13 Calle Johansson 3	.30	.75
14 Uwe Krupp 40	.30	.75
15 Don Lever CO	.20	.50
16 Bob Logan 26	.20	.50
17 Jan Ludvig 36	.20	.50
18 Kevin Maguire 19	.20	.50
19 Mark Napier 65	.30	.75
20 Daren Puppa 31	.60	1.50
21 Mike Ramsey 5	.30	.75
22 Joe Reekie 27	.30	.75
23 Lindy Ruff 22	.20	.50
24 Christian Ruuttu 21	.30	.75
25 Ted Sator CO	.20	.50
26 Ray Sheppard 23	.80	2.00
27 Barry Smith CO	.20	.50
28 Doug Smith 15	.20	.50
29 John Tucker 7	.30	.75
30 Pierre Turgeon 77	3.20	8.00
NNO Large Team Photo	1.20	3.00

1988-89 Sabres Blue Shield

This 28-card set was issued by the Buffalo Sabres in conjunction with Blue Shield of Western New York. The cards measure approximately 4" by 6" and are in the postcard format, with the Blue Shield logo on the backs. The fronts feature a color action photo of the player. The picture is sandwiched between yellow stripes, with team logo and player's name above, and player information below. The cards are unnumbered and we have checklisted them below in alphabetical order, with the uniform number next to the player's name. The cards of Benoit Hogue, Jan Ludvig, Mark Napier, and Joe Reekie were apparently late additions to the set; they are marked as SP in the checklist below.

COMPLETE SET (28)	10.00	25.00
1 Mikael Andersson 14	.20	.50
2 Dave Andreychuk 25	.60	1.50
3 Scott Arniel 9	.10	.25
4 Doug Bodger 8	.30	.75
5 Jacques Cloutier 1	.30	.75
6 Mike Donnelly 16	.20	.50
7 Mike Foligno 17	.30	.75
8 Bob Halkidis 18	.10	.25
9 Mike Hartman 20	.10	.25
10 Benoit Hogue 33 SP	1.20	3.00
11 Phil Housley 6	.40	1.00
12 Calle Johansson 3	.30	.75
13 Uwe Krupp 4	.30	.75
14 Jan Ludvig 36 SP	.80	2.00
15 Kevin Maguire 19	.10	.25
16 Mark Napier 65 SP	.80	2.00
17 Jeff Parker 29	.10	.25
18 Larry Playfair 27	.10	.25
19 Daren Puppa 31	.80	2.00
20 Mike Ramsey 5	.20	.50
21 Joe Reekie 55 SP	.80	2.00
22 Lindy Ruff 22	.10	.25
23 Christian Ruuttu 21	.20	.50
24 Sabretooth Mascot	.10	.25
25 Ray Sheppard 23	.60	1.50
26 John Tucker 7	.20	.50
27 Pierre Turgeon 77	2.40	6.00
28 Rick Vaive 12	.30	.75

1988-89 Sabres Wonder Bread/Hostess

The 1988-89 Buffalo Sabres Team Photo Album was sponsored by Wonder Bread and Hostess Cakes. It consists of three large sheets, each measuring approximately 13 1/2" by 10 1/4" and joined together to form one continuous sheet. The first panel has a team photo of the Sabres in civilian clothing. The second and third panels present three rows of five cards each. After perforation, the cards measure approximately 2 5/8" by 3 3/8". They feature color posed photos on white card stock. The top half has thin diagonal blue lines traversing the white background. Player information appears below the picture, between the Sabres' and sponsors' logos. The back has biographical and statistical information in a horizontal format. The cards are unnumbered and we have checklisted them below in alphabetical order, with the uniform number to the right of the player's name.

COMPLETE SET (31)	8.00	20.00
1 Mikael Andersson 14	.20	.50
2 Dave Andreychuk 25	.60	1.50
3 Scott Arniel 9	.20	.50
4 Doug Bodger 8	.30	.75
5 Jacques Cloutier 1	.30	.75
6 Adam Creighton 38	.24	.60
7 Mike Foligno 17	.30	.75
8 Bob Halkidis 18	.20	.50
9 Mike Hartman 20	.20	.50
10 Benoit Hogue 33	.40	1.00
11 Phil Housley 6	.40	1.00
12 Calle Johansson 3	.30	.75
13 Uwe Krupp 4	.30	.75
14 Don Lever CO	.20	.50
15 Jan Ludvig 36	.20	.50
16 Kevin Maguire 19	.20	.50
17 Brad Miller 44	.20	.50
18 Mark Napier 65	.20	.50
19 Jeff Parker 29	.20	.50
20 Larry Playfair 27	.20	.50
21 Daren Puppa 31	.80	2.00
22 Mike Ramsey 5	.20	.50
23 Joe Reekie 55	.20	.50
24 Lindy Ruff 22	.20	.50
25 Christian Ruuttu 21	.20	.50
26 Ted Sator CO	.20	.50
27 Ray Sheppard 23	.60	1.50
28 Barry Smith CO	.20	.50
29 John Tucker 7	.20	.50
30 Pierre Turgeon 77	2.40	6.00
xx Large Team Photo	.40	1.00

1989-90 Sabres Blue Shield

This 24-card set was issued by the Buffalo Sabres in conjunction with Blue Shield of Western New York. The cards measure approximately 4" by 6" and are in the postcard format, with the Blue Shield logo on the backs. The fronts feature a color action photo of the player. The picture is sandwiched between yellow stripes, with team logo and player's name above, and player information below. The cards are unnumbered and we have checklisted them below in alphabetical order, with the uniform number next to the player's name. The card of Alexander Mogilny predates his Rookie Card by one year.

COMPLETE SET (24)	8.00	20.00
1 Dave Andreychuk 25	.60	1.50
2 Scott Arniel 9	.20	.50
3 Doug Bodger 8	.20	.50
4 Mike Foligno 17	.30	.75
5 Mike Hartman 20	.20	.50
6 Benoit Hogue 33	.40	1.00
7 Phil Housley 6	.40	1.00
8 Dean Kennedy 26	.20	.50
9 Uwe Krupp 4	.30	.75
10 Grant Ledyard 3	.20	.50
11 Kevin Maguire 19	.20	.50
12 Clint Malarchuk 30	.30	.75
13 Alexander Mogilny 89	2.00	5.00
14 Jeff Parker 29	.20	.50
15 Larry Playfair 27	.20	.50
16 Ken Priestlay 56	.20	.50
17 Daren Puppa 31	.60	1.50
18 Mike Ramsey 5	.20	.50
19 Christian Ruuttu 21	.20	.50
20 Ray Sheppard 23	.40	1.00
21 Dave Snuggerud 18	.20	.50
22 Sabretooth Mascot	.10	.25
23 Pierre Turgeon 77	1.20	3.00
24 Rick Vaive 22	.30	.75

1989-90 Sabres Campbell's

The 1989-90 Buffalo Sabres Team Photo Album was sponsored by Campbell's and commemorates 20 years in the NHL. It consists of three large sheets (the first two measuring approximately 10" by 13 1/2" and the third smaller), all joined together to form one continuous sheet. The first panel has three color action shots superimposed on a large black and white picture of the Sabres. While the second panel presents four rows of four cards each (16 player cards), the third panel presents four rows of three cards each (11 player cards and a 20th year card). After perforation, the cards measure approximately 2 1/2" by 3 3/8". They feature color posed photos bordered in yellow (on three sides), on a dark blue background interspersed with Sabres' logos in light blue. Player information appears below the picture in a yellow diamond, sandwiched between the Sabres' and the Franco-American logos. The back has biographical and statistical information in a horizontal format. We have checklisted the names below in alphabetical order, with the uniform number to the right of the name. The card of Alexander Mogilny predates his Rookie Card by one year.

COMPLETE SET (28)	8.00	20.00
1 Shawn Anderson 37	.20	.50
2 Dave Andreychuk 25	.60	1.50
3 Scott Arniel 9	.20	.50
4 Doug Bodger 8	.20	.50
5 Rick Dudley CO	.30	.75
6 Mike Foligno 17	.30	.75
7 Mike Hartman 20	.20	.50
8 Benoit Hogue 33	.40	1.00
9 Phil Housley 6	.40	1.00
10 Dean Kennedy 26	.20	.50
11 Uwe Krupp 4	.30	.75
12 Grant Ledyard 3	.20	.50
13 Kevin Maguire 19	.20	.50
14 Clint Malarchuk 39	.30	.75
15 Alexander Mogilny 89	2.00	5.00
16 Mark Napier 65	.20	.50
17 Jeff Parker 29	.20	.50
18 Larry Playfair 27	.20	.50
19 Daren Puppa 31	.60	1.50
20 Mike Ramsey 5	.20	.50
21 Robert Ray 32	.40	1.00
22 Christian Ruuttu 21	.20	.50
23 Ray Sheppard 23	.40	1.00
24 Dave Snuggerud 18	.20	.50
25 John Tortorella CO	.20	.50
26 Pierre Turgeon 77	1.20	3.00
27 Rick Vaive 22	.30	.75
xx Large Team Photo	.40	1.00

1990-91 Sabres Blue Shield

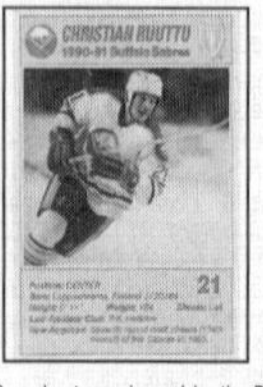

This 26-card set was issued by the Buffalo Sabres in conjunction with Blue Shield of Western New York. The cards measure approximately 4" by 6" and are in the postcard format, with the Blue Shield logo on the backs. The fronts feature a color action photo of the player. The picture is sandwiched between yellow stripes, with team logo and player's name above, and player information below. These cards may be distinguished from the previous year's issue by the "medical shield logo" in the upper right corner. The cards are unnumbered and we have checklisted them below in alphabetical order, with the uniform number next to the player's name.

COMPLETE SET (26)	6.00	15.00
1 Dave Andreychuk 25	.30	.75
2 Donald Audette 28	.40	1.00
3 Doug Bodger 8	.20	.50
4 Greg Brown 9	.20	.50
5 Brian Curran 39	.20	.50
6 Lou Franceschetti 15	.20	.50
7 Mike Hartman 20	.20	.50
8 Dale Hawerchuk 10	.40	1.00
9 Benoit Hogue 33	.24	.60
10 Dean Kennedy 26	.20	.50
11 Uwe Krupp 4	.30	.75
12 Grant Ledyard 3	.20	.50
13 Mikko Makela 42	.20	.50
14 Clint Malarchuk 30	.30	.75
15 Alexander Mogilny 89	1.20	3.00
16 Daren Puppa 31	.40	1.00
17 Mike Ramsey 5	.20	.50
18 Robert Ray 32	.30	.75
19 Christian Ruuttu 21	.20	.50
20 Sabretooth Mascot	.10	.25
21 Jiri Sejba 23	.20	.50
22 Dave Snuggerud 18	.20	.50
23 John Tucker 7	.20	.50
24 Pierre Turgeon 77	.60	1.50
25 Rick Vaive 22	.20	.50
26 Jay Wells 24	.20	.50

1990-91 Sabres Campbell's

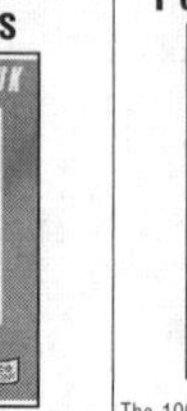

The 1990-91 Buffalo Sabres Team Photo Album was sponsored by Campbell's. It consists of three large sheets, each measuring approximately 10" by 13 1/2" and joined together to form one continuous sheet. The first panel has a team photo of the Sabres in street clothing. The second and third panels present four rows of four cards each (31 player cards plus a Sabres' logo card). After perforation, the cards measure approximately 2 1/2" by 3 3/8". They feature color posed photos bordered in white, on a dark blue background. The player's name is given above the picture, with the Sabres' logo, uniform number, and Franco-American logo below the picture. The back has biographical and statistical information in a horizontal format. We have checklisted the names below in alphabetical order, with the uniform number to the right of the name.

COMPLETE SET (32)	6.00	15.00
1 Dave Andreychuk 25	.30	.75
2 Donald Audette 28	.40	1.00
3 Doug Bodger 8	.20	.50
4 Greg Brown 9	.20	.50
5 Bob Corkum 19	.20	.50
6 Rick Dudley CO	.10	.25
7 Mike Foligno 17	.30	.75
8 Mike Hartman 20	.20	.50
9 Dale Hawerchuk 10	.40	1.00
10 Benoit Hogue 33	.24	.60
11 Dean Kennedy 26	.20	.50
12 Uwe Krupp 4	.30	.75
13 Grant Ledyard 3	.20	.50
14 Darcy Loewen 36	.20	.50
15 Mikko Makela 42	.20	.50
16 Clint Malarchuk 30	.30	.75
17 Brad Miller 44	.20	.50
18 Alexander Mogilny 89	1.20	3.00
19 Daren Puppa 31	.40	1.00
20 Mike Ramsey 5	.20	.50
21 Robert Ray 32	.30	.75
22 Christian Ruuttu 21	.20	.50
23 Jiri Sejba 23	.20	.50
24 Darrin Shannon 16	.20	.50
25 Dave Snuggerud 18	.20	.50
26 John Tortorella CO	.10	.25
27 John Tucker 7	.20	.50
28 Pierre Turgeon 77	.60	1.50
29 Rick Vaive 22	.20	.50
30 John Van Boxmeer CO	.10	.25
31 Jay Wells 24	.20	.50
xx Large Team Photo (In street clothes)	.40	1.00

1991-92 Sabres Blue Shield

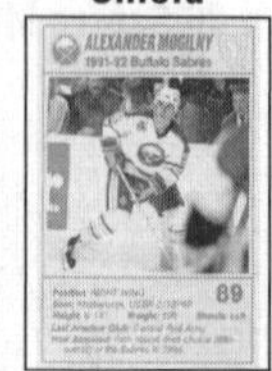

This 26-card postcard set of Buffalo Sabres measuring approximately 4" by 6" features an action photograph enclosed in white and blue borders. The player's name, date, and team name appear in blue lettering on a gold background and are flanked on the right and left by the team logo and Blue Shield of Western New York's logo. Biographical information and the player's jersey number appear in blue over gold within a blue border at the bottom. Card backs carry a large Blue Shield logo and motto on the left side. The cards are unnumbered and checklisted below in alphabetical order, with the jersey number to the right of the name.

COMPLETE SET (26)	6.00	15.00
1 Dave Andreychuk 25	.40	1.00
2 Donald Audette 28	.30	.75
3 Doug Bodger 8	.24	.60
4 Gord Donnelly 34	.20	.50
5 Tom Draper 35	.24	.60
6 Kevin Haller 7	.20	.50
7 Dale Hawerchuk 10	.60	1.50
8 Randy Hillier 23	.20	.50
9 Pat LaFontaine 16	1.20	3.00
10 Grant Ledyard 3	.20	.50
11 Clint Malarchuk 30	.30	.75
12 Brad May 27	.40	1.00
13 Brad Miller 44	.20	.50
14 Alexander Mogilny 89	.80	2.00
15 Colin Patterson 17	.20	.50
16 Daren Puppa 31	.40	1.00
17 Mike Ramsey 5	.20	.50
18 Robert Ray 32	.30	.75
19 Christian Ruuttu 21	.20	.50
20 Dave Snuggerud 18	.20	.50
21 Ken Sutton 41	.20	.50
22 Tony Tanti 19	.20	.50
23 Rick Vaive 22	.24	.60
24 Jay Wells 24	.20	.50
25 Randy Wood 15	.20	.50
26 Sabretooth (Mascot)	.10	.25

1991-92 Sabres Pepsi/Campbell's

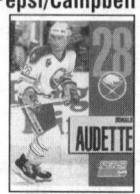

The 1991-92 Buffalo Sabres Team Photo Album was sponsored in two different varieties. One version was sponsored by Pepsi in conjunction with the Sheriff's Office of Erie County. The Pepsi logo appears on both sides of each card. A second version was sponsored by Campbell's; the card fronts have the Campbell's Chunky soup logo and the flipside carries the Franco-American emblem. The set consists of three large sheets, joined together to form one continuous sheet. The first panel has a team photo of the Sabres in street clothing, superimposed over lightning streaks on the left side. The second (10" by 13") and third (7 1/2" by 13") panels present 28 cards; after perforation, the cards measure 2 1/2" by 3 1/4". The color action photos are full-bleed on three sides; the blue border running down their right side carries the jersey number, team logo, player's name (on a gold band which jets out into the photo), and the Pepsi logo. The backs list biographical and statistical information. The cards are unnumbered and checklisted below in alphabetical order, with the jersey number to the right of the name.

COMPLETE SET (29)	6.00	15.00
1 Dave Andreychuk 25	.40	1.00
2 Donald Audette 28	.30	.75
3 Doug Bodger 8	.24	.60
4 Gord Donnelly 34	.20	.50
5 Tom Draper 35	.24	.60
6 Kevin Haller 7	.20	.50
7 Dale Hawerchuk 10	.60	1.50
8 Randy Hillier 23	.20	.50
9 Pat LaFontaine 16	.80	2.00
10 Grant Ledyard 3	.20	.50
11 Clint Malarchuk 30	.30	.75
12 Brad May 27	.40	1.00
13 Brad Miller 44	.20	.50
14 Alexander Mogilny 89	1.20	3.00
15 Colin Patterson 17	.20	.50
16 Daren Puppa 31	.40	1.00
17 Mike Ramsey 5	.20	.50
18 Robert Ray 32	.30	.75
19 Christian Ruuttu 21	.20	.50
20 Dave Snuggerud 18	.20	.50
21 Ken Sutton 41	.20	.50
22 Tony Tanti 19	.20	.50
23 Rick Vaive 22	.20	.50
24 Jay Wells 24	.20	.50
25 Randy Wood 15	.20	.50
26 Sabretooth (Mascot)	.10	.25
27 Team Logo	.10	.25
28 NHL Logo	.10	.25
xx Large Team Photo (In street clothes)	.40	1.00

1992-93 Sabres Blue Shield

Sponsored by Blue Shield of Western New York, this 26-card postcard set measures approximately 4" by 6" and features color action player photos. In a mustard-colored box at the top are printed the player's name, the year and team name, and the team and sponsor logos. In a mustard-colored box at the bottom is biographical information. These boxes and the photo are outlined by a thin royal blue line. The horizontal backs have a light blue postcard design with the sponsor logo and a "Wellness Goal." The cards are unnumbered and checklisted below in alphabetical order.

COMPLETE SET (26)	6.00	15.00
1 Dave Andreychuk	.30	.75
2 Donald Audette	.30	.75
3 Doug Bodger	.16	.40
4 Bob Corkum	.16	.40
5 Gord Donnelly	.16	.40
6 Dave Hannan	.16	.40
7 Dominik Hasek	2.40	6.00
8 Dale Hawerchuk	.40	1.00
9 Yuri Khmylev	.16	.40
10 Pat LaFontaine	.60	1.50
11 Grant Ledyard	.16	.40
12 Brad May	.20	.50
13 Alexander Mogilny	.60	1.50
14 Randy Moller	.16	.40
15 John Muckler CO	.16	.40
16 Colin Patterson	.16	.40
17 Wayne Presley	.16	.40
18 Daren Puppa	.30	.75
19 Mike Ramsey	.16	.40
20 Rob Ray	.30	.75
21 Richard Smehlik	.16	.40
22 Ken Sutton	.16	.40
23 Petr Svoboda	.20	.50
24 Bob Sweeney	.16	.40
25 Randy Wood	.16	.40
26 Sabretooth (Mascot)	.04	.10

1992-93 Sabres Jubilee Foods

Printed on thin white stock, the cards of this set, which are subtitled "Junior Fan Club," measure approximately 4" by 7" and feature color action shots of Sabres players on their fronts. These photos are borderless, except across the bottom, where a half-inch wide, mustard-colored stripe carries the sponsor's name. A thin blue stripe edges the card at the very bottom. The player's name appears vertically in blue lettering down one side. The Junior Fan Club logo in the lower left straddles the bottom of the photo and the two stripes. The backs have the player's name and biography in the upper left and the Sabres logo in the upper right. Beneath are highlights and stats from the 1991-92 season. The Stanley Cup logo at the bottom rounds out the card. The cards are unnumbered and checklisted below in alphabetical order.

COMPLETE SET (16)	4.80	12.00
1 Dave Andreychuk	.30	.75
2 Doug Bodger	.16	.40
3 Gord Donnelly Rob Ray	.40	1.00
4 Dominik Hasek Daren Puppa	2.40	6.00
5 Dale Hawerchuk	.40	1.00
6 Yuri Khmylev Viktor Gordijuk	.16	.40
7 Pat LaFontaine	.60	1.50
8 Brad May	.30	.75
9 Alexander Mogilny	.60	1.50
10 Randy Moller Ken Sutton	.16	.40
11 Wayne Presley Donald Audette	.30	.75
12 Mike Ramsey	.16	.40
13 Richard Smehlik Bob Corkum	.16	.40
14 Petr Svoboda	.20	.50
15 Bob Sweeney	.16	.40
16 Randy Wood	.16	.40

1993-94 Sabres Limited Edition Team Issue

Given out one per fan at a Sabres home game during the 93-94 season, these blank back cards with color action photos on the front are limited to 5,000 sets. There is a yellow stripe at the bottom of the card with the players name, and Sabres logo. Cards are unnumbered and checklisted below in alphabetical order.

COMPLETE SET (4)	4.00	10.00
1 Doug Bodger	.40	1.00
2 Dominik Hasek	2.00	5.00
3 Dale Hawerchuk	.80	2.00
4 Alexander Mogilny	1.20	3.00

1993-94 Sabres Noco

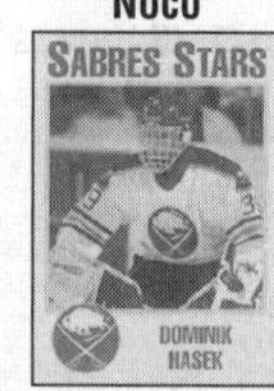

Subtitled Sabres Stars and issued in five-card perforated strips, these 20 standard-size cards feature on their fronts white-bordered color player action shots framed by a yellow line. The player's name and the team logo appear in the white margin below the photo. The white back carries the player's name and number at the top followed below by statistics and career highlights. The logo for the set's sponsor, Noco Express Shop, rounds out the card at the bottom. The cards are unnumbered and checklisted below in alphabetical order.

COMPLETE SET (20)	4.80	12.00
1 Roger Crozier	.24	.60
2 Rick Dudley	.20	.50
3 Mike Foligno	.20	.50
4 Grant Fuhr	.40	1.00
5 Danny Gare	.20	.50
6 Dominik Hasek	2.00	5.00
7 Dale Hawerchuk	.30	.75
8 Tim Horton	.80	2.00
9 Pat LaFontaine	.50	1.25
10 Don Luce	.20	.50
11 Rick Martin	.30	.75
12 Brad May	.24	.60
13 Alexander Mogilny	.50	1.25
14 Gilbert Perreault	.40	1.00
15 Craig Ramsay	.20	.50
16 Mike Ramsey	.20	.50
17 Rene Robert	.24	.60
18 Sabretooth Mascot	.16	.40
19 Jim Schoenfeld	.30	.75
20 Knoxes Unveil Sabres Uniform Northrup Knox Punch Imlach Seymour Knox	.16	.40

2002-03 Sabres Team Issue

This oversized (5X7) set features action photos on the front and blank backs. It was printed on very thin stock. The cards likely were handed out as promotional items at signing appearances. It's possible the checklist is not complete. Internal documents revealed that just 500 copies were printed for Mair, Hecht, Noronen, Patrick and Campbell. 1,000 copies of each were printed of the remaining players.

COMPLETE SET (14)	10.00	20.00
1 Stu Barnes	.75	2.00
2 Martin Biron	.75	2.00
3 Eric Boulton	.75	2.00
4 Brian Campbell	.75	2.00
5 Tim Connolly	.40	1.00
6 Jochen Hecht	.75	2.00
7 Dmitri Kalinin	.40	1.00
8 Adam Mair	.75	2.00
9 Jay McKee	.40	1.00
10 Mika Noronen	.75	2.00
11 James Patrick	.75	2.00
12 Taylor Pyatt	.40	1.00
13 Rob Ray	.75	2.00
14 Rhett Warrener	.40	1.00

1974-75 San Diego Mariners WHA

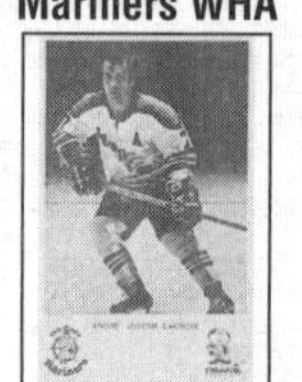

Sponsored by Dean's Photo Service Inc., this set of seven photos measures approximately 5 3/8" by 8 1/2" and features black-and-white action pictures against a white background on thin paper stock. The player's name appeared in the white margin below the photo along with the team and sponsor logos. The backs featured biographical information, career highlights and statistics. The cards came in a light blue paper "picture pack" with the team and sponsor logos and game dates suggested for acquiring autographs. The cards were unnumbered and checklisted below in alphabetical order. This set may be incomplete; additions to the checklist would be welcome.

COMPLETE SET (7)	20.00	40.00
1 Andre Lacroix	5.00	10.00
2 Mike Laughton	2.50	5.00
3 Brian Morenz	2.50	5.00
4 Kevin Morrison	2.50	5.00
5 Gene Peacosh	2.50	5.00
6 Ron Plumb	4.00	8.00
7 Craig Reichmuth	2.50	5.00

1976-77 San Diego Mariners WHA

These cards measure 5" x 8" and were issued in two sheets of seven players each. Card fronts feature black and white photos with a white border. Backs feature player statistics. Cards are unnumbered and checklisted below alphabetically. Prices below are for individual cards.

COMPLETE SET (14)	20.00	40.00
1 Kevin Devine	1.25	2.50

2 Bob Dubek 1.25 2.50
3 Norm Ferguson 1.25 2.50
4 Brent Hughes 1.25 2.50
5 Randy Legge 1.25 2.50
6 Ken Lockett 1.25 2.50
7 Kevin Morrison 1.25 2.50
8 Joe Norris 1.25 2.50
9 Gerry Pinder 2.00 4.00
10 Brad Rhiness 1.25 2.50
11 Wayne Rivers 2.00 4.00
12 Paul Shmyr 1.50 3.00
13 Gary Veneruzzo 1.50 3.00
14 Ernie Wakely 2.50 5.00

1994 Santa Fe Hotel and Casino Manon Rheaume Postcard

Card is full color, and measures 3" x 5". Was given out as promotional piece for the Santa Fe Hotel and Casino in Las Vegas. Item is limited to 10,000 pieces.

NNO Manon Rheaume 2.00 5.00

1970-71 Sargent Promotions Stamps

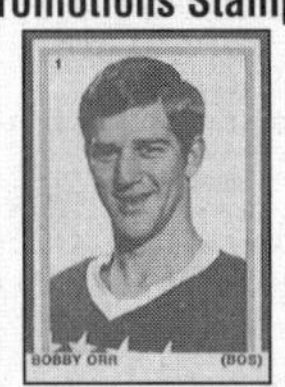

This set consists of 224 total stamps, 16 for each NHL team. Individual stamps measure approximately 2" by 2 1/2". The set could be put into a album featuring Bobby Orr on the cover. Stamp fronts feature a full-color head shot of the player, player's name, and team. The stamp number is located in the upper left corner. The 1970-71 set features one-time appearances in Eddie Sargent Promotions sets by Hall of Famers Gordie Howe, Jean Beliveau, Andy Bathgate. The set also features first appearances of Gil Perreault, Brad Park, and Bobby Clarke. The three have Rookie Cards in both Topps and O-Pee-Chee for the same year.

COMPLETE SET (224) 325.00 650.00
1 Bobby Orr 62.50 125.00
2 Don Awrey .50 1.00
3 Derek Sanderson 5.00 10.00
4 Ted Green .63 1.25
5 Eddie Johnston 1.25 2.50
6 Wayne Carleton .50 1.00
7 Ed Westfall .75 1.50
8 Johnny Bucyk 2.50 5.00
9 John McKenzie .50 1.00
10 Ken Hodge 1.00 2.00
11 Rick Smith .50 1.00
12 Fred Stanfield .50 1.00
13 Garnet Bailey .50 1.00
14 Phil Esposito 10.00 20.00
15 Gerry Cheevers 5.00 10.00
16 Dallas Smith .50 1.00
17 Joe Daley 1.00 2.00
18 Ron Anderson .50 1.00
19 Tracy Pratt .50 1.00
20 Gerry Meehan .75 1.50
21 Reg Fleming .50 1.00
22 Al Hamilton .63 1.25
23 Gil Perreault 12.50 25.00
24 Skip Krake .50 1.00
25 Kevin O'Shea .50 1.00
26 Roger Crozier 1.50 3.00
27 Bill Inglis .50 1.00
28 Mike McMahon .50 1.00
29 Cliff Schmautz .50 1.00
30 Floyd Smith .50 1.00
31 Randy Wyrozub .50 1.00
32 Jim Watson .50 1.00
33 Tony Esposito 15.00 30.00
34 Doug Jarrett .50 1.00
35 Keith Magnuson .63 1.25
36 Dennis Hull 1.00 2.00
37 Cliff Koroll .50 1.00
38 Eric Nesterenko .75 1.50
39 Pit Martin .63 1.25
40 Lou Angotti .50 1.00
41 Jim Pappin .63 1.25
42 Gerry Pinder .63 1.25
43 Bobby Hull 25.00 50.00
44 Pat Stapleton .63 1.25
45 Gerry Desjardins 1.00 2.00
46 Chico Maki .63 1.25
47 Doug Mohns .63 1.25
48 Stan Mikita 10.00 20.00
49 Gary Bergman .63 1.25
50 Pete Stemkowski .63 1.25
51 Bruce MacGregor .50 1.00
52 Ron Harris .50 1.00
53 Billy Dea .50 1.00
54 Wayne Connelly .50 1.00
55 Dale Rolfe .50 1.00
56 Gordie Howe 40.00 80.00
57 Tom Webster .63 1.25
58 Al Karlander .50 1.00
59 Alex Delvecchio 2.50 5.00
60 Nick Libett .63 1.25
61 Garry Unger 1.00 2.00
62 Roy Edwards 1.00 2.00
63 Frank Mahovlich 5.00 10.00
64 Bob Baun 1.25 2.50
65 Dick Duff 1.00 2.00
66 Ross Lonsberry .50 1.00
67 Ed Joyal .50 1.00
68 Dale Hoganson .50 1.00
69 Eddie Shack 2.50 5.00
70 Real Lemieux .50 1.00
71 Matt Ravlich .50 1.00
72 Bob Pulford 1.50 3.00
73 Denis DeJordy 1.25 2.50
74 Larry Mickey .50 1.00
75 Bill Flett .50 1.00
76 Juha Widing .75 1.50
77 Jim Peters .63 1.25
78 Gilles Marotte .63 1.25
79 Larry Cahan .50 1.00
80 Howie Hughes .50 1.00
81 Cesare Maniago 1.25 2.50
82 Ted Harris .50 1.00
83 Tom Williams .50 1.00
84 Gump Worsley 5.00 10.00
85 Tom Reid .50 1.00
86 Murray Oliver .50 1.00
87 Charlie Burns .50 1.00
88 Jude Drouin .50 1.00
89 Walt McKechnie .50 1.00
90 Danny O'Shea .50 1.00
91 Barry Gibbs .50 1.00
92 Danny Grant .63 1.25
93 Bob Barlow .50 1.00
94 J.P. Parise .63 1.25
95 Bill Goldsworthy .75 1.50
96 Bobby Rousseau .63 1.25
97 Jacques Laperriere 1.00 2.00
98 Henri Richard 5.00 10.00
99 J.C. Tremblay .75 1.50
100 Rogie Vachon 4.00 8.00
101 Claude Larose .50 1.00
102 Pete Mahovlich .75 1.50
103 Jacques Lemaire 4.00 8.00
104 Bill Collins .50 1.00
105 Guy Lapointe 1.50 3.00
106 Mickey Redmond 2.50 5.00
107 Larry Pleau .63 1.25
108 Jean Beliveau 12.50 25.00
109 Yvan Cournoyer 4.00 8.00
110 Serge Savard 4.00 8.00
111 Terry Harper .63 1.25
112 Phil Myre 1.00 2.00
113 Syl Apps .63 1.25
114 Ted Irvine .50 1.00
115 Ed Giacomin 5.00 10.00
116 Arnie Brown .50 1.00
117 Walt Tkaczuk .63 1.25
118 Jean Ratelle 2.50 5.00
119 Dave Balon .50 1.00
120 Ron Stewart .50 1.00
121 Jim Neilson .50 1.00
122 Rod Gilbert 2.50 5.00
123 Bill Fairbairn .50 1.00
124 Brad Park 10.00 20.00
125 Tim Horton 7.50 15.00
126 Vic Hadfield .75 1.50
127 Bob Nevin .50 1.00
128 Rod Seiling .50 1.00
129 Gary Smith 1.25 2.50
130 Carol Vadnais .50 1.00
131 Bert Marshall .50 1.00
132 Earl Ingarfield .50 1.00
133 Dennis Hextall .63 1.25
134 Harry Howell 1.50 3.00
135 Wayne Muloin .50 1.00
136 Mike Laughton .50 1.00
137 Ted Hampson .50 1.00
138 Doug Roberts .50 1.00
139 Dick Mattiussi .50 1.00
140 Gary Jarrett .50 1.00
141 Gary Croteau .50 1.00
142 Norm Ferguson .50 1.00
143 Bill Hicke .50 1.00
144 Gerry Ehman .50 1.00
145 Ralph McSweyn .50 1.00
146 Bernie Parent 7.50 15.00
147 Brent Hughes .50 1.00
148 Bobby Clarke 20.00 40.00
149 Gary Dornhoefer .63 1.25
150 Simon Nolet .50 1.00
151 Garry Peters .50 1.00
152 Doug Favell 1.25 2.50
153 Jim Johnson .50 1.00
154 Andre Lacroix .75 1.50
155 Larry Hale .50 1.00
156 Joe Watson .50 1.00
157 Jean-Guy Gendron .50 1.00
158 Larry Hillman .50 1.00
159 Ed Van Impe .50 1.00
160 Wayne Hillman .50 1.00
161 Al Smith 1.00 2.00
162 Jean Pronovost .63 1.25
163 Bob Woytowich .50 1.00
164 Bryan Watson .63 1.25
165 Dean Prentice .75 1.50
166 Duane Rupp .50 1.00
167 Glen Sather 1.00 2.00
168 Keith McCreary .50 1.00
169 Jim Morrison .50 1.00
170 Ron Schock .50 1.00
171 Wally Boyer .50 1.00
172 Nick Harbaruk .50 1.00
173 Andy Bathgate 2.50 5.00
174 Ken Schinkel .50 1.00
175 Les Binkley 1.00 2.00
176 Val Fonteyne .50 1.00
177 Red Berenson .75 1.50
178 Ab McDonald .50 1.00
179 Jim Roberts .50 1.00
180 Frank St. Marseille .50 1.00
181 Ernie Wakely 1.25 2.50
182 Terry Crisp .63 1.25
183 Bob Plager .75 1.50
184 Barclay Plager .75 1.50
185 Chris Bordeleau .50 1.00
186 Gary Sabourin .50 1.00
187 Bill Plager .63 1.25
188 Tim Ecclestone .50 1.00
189 Jean-Guy Talbot .75 1.50
190 Noel Picard .50 1.00
191 Bob Wall .50 1.00
192 Jim Lorentz .50 1.00
193 Bruce Gamble 1.50 3.00
194 Jim Harrison .50 1.00
195 Paul Henderson 1.50 3.00
196 Brian Glennie .50 1.00
197 Jim Dorey .50 1.00
198 Rick Ley .63 1.25
199 Jacques Plante 12.50 25.00
200 Ron Ellis .75 1.50
201 Jim McKenny .50 1.00
202 Brit Selby .50 1.00
203 Mike Pelyk .50 1.00
204 Norm Ullman 2.50 5.00
205 Bill MacMillan .50 1.00
206 Mike Walton .63 1.25
207 Garry Monahan .50 1.00
208 Dave Keon 2.50 5.00
209 Pat Quinn 1.00 2.00
210 Wayne Maki .50 1.00
211 Charlie Hodge 1.25 2.50
212 Orland Kurtenbach .63 1.25
213 Paul Popiel .63 1.25
214 Dan Johnson .50 1.00
215 Dale Tallon .63 1.25
216 Ray Cullen .63 1.25
217 Bob Dillabough .50 1.00
218 Gary Doak .50 1.00
219 Andre Boudrias .75 1.50
220 Rosaire Paiement .63 1.25
221 Darryl Sly .50 1.00
222 George Gardner .50 1.00
223 Jim Wiste .50 1.00
224 Murray Hall .50 1.00
xx Stamp Album 17.50 35.00
(Bobby Orr on cover)

1971-72 Sargent Promotions Stamps

Issued by Eddie Sargent Promotions in a series of 16 ten-cent sheets of 14 NHL players each, this 224-stamp set featured posed color photos of players in their NHLPA jerseys. The pictures are framed on their tops and sides in different color borders with the players' names and teams appearing along the bottom. Each sheet measured approximately 7 7/8" by 10" and was divided into four rows, with four 2" by 2 1/2" stamps per row. Two of these 16 sections gave the series number (e.g., Series 1), resulting in a total of 14 players per sheet. The stamps are perforated and the backs are blank. There was a stamp album (approximately 9 1/2" by 13") which featured information on the team history and individual players. The stamps are numbered in the upper left corner and they are grouped into 14 teams of 16 players each as follows: Boston Bruins (1-16), Buffalo Sabres (17-32), Chicago Blackhawks (33-48), Detroit Red Wings (49-64), Los Angeles Kings (65-80), Minnesota North Stars (81-96), Montreal Canadiens (97-112), New York Rangers (113-128), California Golden Seals (129-144), Philadelphia Flyers (145-160), Pittsburgh Penguins (161-176), St. Louis Blues (177-192), Toronto Maple Leafs (193-208), and Vancouver Canucks (209-224).

COMPLETE SET (224) 225.00 450.00
1 Fred Stanfield .50 1.00
2 Ed Westfall .75 1.50
3 John McKenzie .50 1.00
4 Derek Sanderson 4.00 8.00
5 Rick Smith .50 1.00
6 Teddy Green .63 1.25
7 Phil Esposito 7.50 15.00
8 Ken Hodge 1.00 2.00
9 Johnny Bucyk 4.00 8.00
10 Bobby Orr 50.00 100.00
11 Dallas Smith .50 1.00
12 Mike Walton .63 1.25
13 Don Awrey .50 1.00
14 Unknown .50 1.00
15 Eddie Johnston 1.00 2.00
16 Gerry Cheevers 4.00 8.00
17 Gerry Meehan .75 1.50
18 Ron Anderson .50 1.00
19 Gilbert Perreault 6.00 12.00
20 Eddie Shack 2.00 4.00
21 Jim Watson .50 1.00
22 Kevin O'Shea .50 1.00
23 Al Hamilton .50 1.00
24 Dick Duff .75 1.50
25 Tracy Pratt .50 1.00
26 Don Luce .50 1.00
27 Roger Crozier 1.00 2.00
28 Doug Barrie .50 1.00
29 Mike Robitaille .50 1.00
30 Phil Goyette .50 1.00
31 Larry Keenan .50 1.00
32 Dave Dryden 1.00 2.00
33 Stan Mikita 6.00 12.00
34 Bobby Hull 20.00 40.00
35 Cliff Koroll .50 1.00
36 Chico Maki .63 1.25
37 Danny O'Shea .50 1.00
38 Lou Angotti .50 1.00
39 Andre Lacroix .63 1.25
40 Jim Pappin .50 1.00
41 Doug Jarrett .50 1.00
42 Pit Martin .63 1.25
43 Gary Smith 1.00 2.00
44 Tony Esposito 7.50 15.00
45 Pat Stapleton .63 1.25
46 Dennis Hull 1.00 2.00
47 Bill White .50 1.00
48 Keith Magnuson .63 1.25
49 Bill Collins .50 1.00
50 Bob Wall .50 1.00
51 Red Berenson .75 1.50
52 Mickey Redmond 1.50 3.00
53 Nick Libett .50 1.00
54 Gary Bergman .63 1.25
55 Alex Delvecchio 2.50 5.00
56 Tim Ecclestone .50 1.00
57 Arnie Brown .50 1.00
58 Ron Harris .50 1.00
59 Ab McDonald .50 1.00
60 Guy Charron .63 1.25
61 Al Smith 1.00 2.00
62 Joe Daley 1.00 2.00
63 Leon Rochefort .50 1.00
64 Ron Stackhouse .50 1.00
65A Larry Johnston .75 1.50
65B Juha Widing .50 1.00
66 Bob Pulford 1.00 2.00
67 Bill Flett .50 1.00
68 Rogie Vachon 2.50 5.00
69 Ross Lonsberry .50 1.00
70 Gilles Marotte .50 1.00
71 Harry Howell 1.00 2.00
72 Real Lemieux .50 1.00
73 Butch Goring .50 1.00
74 Ed Joyal .50 1.00
75 Larry Hillman .50 1.00
76 Lucien Grenier .50 1.00
77 Paul Curtis .50 1.00
78 Unknown .50 1.00
79 Unknown .50 1.00
80 Unknown .50 1.00
81 Jude Drouin .50 1.00
82 Tom Reid .50 1.00
83 J.P. Parise .63 1.25
84 Doug Mohns .63 1.25
85 Danny Grant .63 1.25
86 Bill Goldsworthy .75 1.50
87 Charlie Burns .50 1.00
88 Murray Oliver .50 1.00
89 Dean Prentice .75 1.50
90 Bob Nevin .63 1.25
91 Ted Harris .63 1.25
92 Cesare Maniago 1.00 2.00
93 Lou Nanne .63 1.25
94 Ted Hampton .50 1.00
95 Barry Gibbs .50 1.00
96 Gump Worsley 4.00 8.00
97 J.C. Tremblay .75 1.50
98 Guy Lapointe 1.00 2.00
99 Pete Mahovlich .75 1.50
100 Larry Pleau .63 1.25
101 Phil Myre 1.00 2.00
102 Yvan Cournoyer 2.50 5.00
103 Henri Richard 5.00 10.00
104 Frank Mahovlich 5.00 10.00
105 Jacques Lemaire 2.00 4.00
106 Claude Larose .50 1.00
107 Terry Harper .63 1.25
108 Jacques Laperriere 1.00 2.00
109 Phil Roberto .50 1.00
110 Serge Savard 2.00 4.00
111 Marc Tardif .63 1.25
112 Pierre Bouchard .63 1.25
113 Rod Gilbert 2.50 5.00
114 Jean Ratelle 2.50 5.00
115 Pete Stemkowski .50 1.00
116 Brad Park 4.00 8.00
117 Bobby Rousseau .50 1.00
118 Dale Rolfe .50 1.00
119 Rod Seiling .50 1.00
120 Walt Tkaczuk .50 1.00
121 Vic Hadfield .63 1.25
122 Jim Neilson .50 1.00
123 Bill Fairbairn .50 1.00
124 Bruce MacGregor .50 1.00
125 Dave Balon .50 1.00
126 Ted Irvine .50 1.00
127 Gilles Villemure 1.00 2.00
128 Ed Giacomin 4.00 8.00
129 Walt McKechnie .50 1.00
130 Tom Williams .50 1.00
131 Wayne Carleton .63 1.25
132 Gerry Pinder .50 1.00
133 Gary Croteau .50 1.00
134 Bert Marshall .50 1.00
135 Tom Webster .50 1.00
136 Norm Ferguson .50 1.00
137 Carol Vadnais .50 1.00
138 Gary Jarrett .50 1.00
139 Ernie Hicke .50 1.00
140 Paul Shmyr .50 1.00
141 Marshall Johnston .50 1.00
142 Don O'Donoghue .50 1.00
143 Joey Johnston .50 1.00
144 Dick Redmond .50 1.00
145 Simon Nolet .50 1.00
146 Wayne Hillman .50 1.00
147 Brent Hughes .50 1.00
148 Jim Johnson .50 1.00
149 Larry Mickey .50 1.00
150 Ed Van Impe .50 1.00
151 Gary Dornhoefer .63 1.25
152 Bobby Clarke 12.50 25.00
153 Jean-Guy Gendron .50 1.00
154 Larry Hale .50 1.00
155 Serge Bernier .50 1.00
156 Doug Favell 1.00 2.00
157 Bob Kelly .50 1.00
158 Joe Watson .50 1.00
159 Larry Brown .50 1.00
160 Bruce Gamble 1.00 2.00
161 Syl Apps .63 1.25
162 Ken Schinkel .50 1.00
163 Val Fonteyne .50 1.00
164 Bryan Watson .75 1.50
165 Bob Woytowich .50 1.00
166 Les Binkley 1.00 2.00
167 Roy Edwards 1.00 2.00
168 Jean Pronovost .63 1.25
169 Tim Horton 6.00 12.00
170 Ron Schock .50 1.00
171 Nick Harbaruk .50 1.00
172 Greg Polis .50 1.00
173 Bryan Hextall .63 1.25
174 Keith McCreary .50 1.00
175 Bill Hicke .50 1.00
176 Jim Rutherford 1.00 2.00
177 Gary Sabourin .50 1.00
178 Garry Unger 1.00 2.00
179 Terry Crisp .63 1.25
180 Noel Picard .50 1.00
181 Jim Roberts .50 1.00
182 Barclay Plager .75 1.50
183 Brit Selby .50 1.00
184 Frank St. Marseille .50 1.00
185 Ernie Wakely 1.00 2.00
186 Wayne Connelly .50 1.00
187 Chris Bordeleau .50 1.00
188 Bill Sutherland .50 1.00
189 Bob Plager .75 1.50
190 Bill Plager .63 1.25
191 George Morrison .50 1.00
192 Jim Lorentz .50 1.00
193 Norm Ullman 2.50 5.00
194 Jim McKenny .50 1.00
195 Rick Ley .50 1.00
196 Bob Baun 1.00 2.00
197 Mike Pelyk .50 1.00
198 Bill MacMillan .50 1.00
199 Garry Monahan .50 1.00
200 Paul Henderson 1.50 3.00
201 Jim Dorey .50 1.00
202 Jim Harrison .50 1.00
203 Ron Ellis .75 1.50
204 Darryl Sittler 3.00 6.00
205 Bernie Parent 2.50 5.00
206 Dave Keon 2.50 5.00
207 Brad Selwood .50 1.00
208 Don Marshall .50 1.00
209 Dale Tallon .63 1.25
210 Dan Johnson .50 1.00
211 Murray Hall .50 1.00
212 Paul Popiel .63 1.25
213 George Gardner .50 1.00
214 Gary Doak .50 1.00
215 Andre Boudrias .63 1.25
216 Orland Kurtenbach .63 1.25
217 Wayne Maki .50 1.00
218 Rosaire Paiement .63 1.25
219 Pat Quinn 1.00 2.00
220 Fred Speck .50 1.00
221 Barry Wilkins .50 1.00
222 Dunc Wilson 1.00 2.00
223 Ted Taylor .50 1.00
224 Mike Corrigan .50 1.00
xx Stamp Album 12.50 25.00
(Bobby Orr on cover)

1972-73 Sargent Promotions Stamps

During the 1972-73 hockey season, Eddie Sargent Promotions produced a set of 224 stamps. They were issued in cello packages in a series of 16 sheets and, at that time, sold for ten cents per sheet with one sheet being available each week of the promotion. Each sheet measures approximately 7 7/8" by 10" and was divided into four rows, with four 2" by 2 1/2" sections per row. Since two of the 16 sections gave the series number (e.g., Series 1), color photos of fourteen NHL players were featured in each series. The set features 224 players from sixteen NHL teams. The pictures were numbered in the upper left hand corner and are checklisted below accordingly. The pictures are framed on their top and sides in different color borders, with the player's name and the team's city name given below. There are two sticker albums (approximately 11 1/4" by 12") available for the set, both of which are bilingual. After a general introduction, the album is divided into team sections, with two pages devoted to each team. A brief history of each team is presented, followed by 14 numbered sticker slots. Biographical information and career summary appear below each stamp slot on the page itself. The typically found album has Bobby Orr on the cover. Another album is the more difficult Paul Henderson Team Canada cover. The toughest of the three is the Richard Martin cover. The stamps are numbered on the front and checklisted below alphabetically according to teams as follows: Atlanta Flames (1-14), Boston Bruins (15-28), Buffalo Sabres (29-42), California Seals (43-56), Chicago Blackhawks (57-70), Detroit Red Wings (71-84), Los Angeles Kings (85-98), Minnesota North Stars (99-112), Montreal Canadiens (113-126), New York Islanders (127-140), New York Rangers (141-154), Philadelphia Flyers (155-168), Pittsburgh Penguins (169-182), St. Louis Blues (183-196), Toronto Maple Leafs (197-210), and Vancouver Canucks (211-224).

COMPLETE SET (224) 112.50 225.00
1 Lucien Grenier .25 .50
2 Phil Myre .50 1.00
3 Ernie Hicke .25 .50
4 Keith McCreary .25 .50
5 Bill MacMillan .25 .50
6 Pat Quinn .50 1.00
7 Bill Plager .38 .75
8 Noel Price .25 .50
9 Bob Leiter .25 .50
10 Randy Manery .25 .50
11 Bob Paradise .25 .50
12 Larry Romanchych .25 .50
13 Lew Morrison .25 .50
14 Dan Bouchard .50 1.00
15 Fred Stanfield .25 .50
16 Johnny Bucyk 1.50 3.00
17 Bobby Orr 20.00 40.00
18 Wayne Cashman .38 .75
19 Dallas Smith .25 .50
20 Ed Johnston .75 1.50
21 Phil Esposito 5.00 10.00
22 Ken Hodge .50 1.00
23 Don Awrey .25 .50
24 Mike Walton .25 .50
25 Carol Vadnais .25 .50
26 Doug Roberts .25 .50
27 Don Marcotte .25 .50
28 Garnet Bailey .25 .50
29 Gerry Meehan .25 .50
30 Tracy Pratt .25 .50
31 Gilbert Perreault 2.00 4.00
32 Roger Crozier 1.00 2.00
33 Don Luce .25 .50
34 Dave Dryden .50 1.00
35 Richard Martin .50 1.00
36 Jim Lorentz .25 .50
37 Tim Horton 4.00 8.00
38 Craig Ramsay .25 .50
39 Larry Hillman .25 .50
40 Steve Atkinson .25 .50
41 Jim Schoenfeld .38 .75
42 Rene Robert .38 .75
43 Walt McKechnie .25 .50
44 Marshall Johnston .25 .50
45 Joey Johnston .25 .50
46 Dick Redmond .25 .50
47 Bert Marshall .25 .50
48 Gary Croteau .25 .50
49 Marv Edwards .50 1.00
50 Gilles Meloche .50 1.00
51 Ivan Boldirev .25 .50
52 Stan Gilbertson .25 .50
53 Peter Laframboise .25 .50
54 Reggie Leach .50 1.00
55 Craig Patrick .50 1.00
56 Bob Stewart .25 .50
57 Keith Magnuson .38 .75
58 Doug Jarrett .25 .50
59 Cliff Koroll .25 .50
60 Chico Maki .25 .50
61 Gary Smith .50 1.00
62 Bill White .25 .50
63 Stan Mikita 3.00 6.00
64 Jim Pappin .25 .50
65 Lou Angotti .25 .50
66 Tony Esposito 4.00 8.00
67 Dennis Hull .50 1.00
68 Pit Martin .25 .50
69 Pat Stapleton .25 .50
70 Dan Maloney .25 .50
71 Bill Collins .25 .50
72 Arnie Brown .25 .50
73 Red Berenson .38 .75
74 Mickey Redmond 1.00 2.00
75 Nick Libett .25 .50
76 Alex Delvecchio 1.25 2.50
77 Ron Stackhouse .25 .50
78 Tim Ecclestone .25 .50
79 Gary Bergman .25 .50
80 Guy Charron .25 .50
81 Leon Rochefort .25 .50
82 Larry Johnston .25 .50
83 Andy Brown .25 .50
84 Henry Boucha .38 .75
85 Paul Curtis .25 .50
86 Jim Stanfield .25 .50
87 Rogatien Vachon 1.50 3.00
88 Ralph Backstrom .38 .75
89 Gilles Marotte .25 .50
90 Harry Howell .75 1.50
91 Real Lemieux .25 .50
92 Butch Goring .38 .75
93 Juha Widing .25 .50
94 Mike Corrigan .25 .50
95 Larry Brown .25 .50
96 Terry Harper .38 .75
97 Serge Bernier .25 .50
98 Bob Berry .25 .50
99 Tom Reid .25 .50
100 Jude Drouin .25 .50
101 Jean-Paul Parise .38 .75
102 Doug Mohns .38 .75
103 Danny Grant .38 .75
104 Bill Goldsworthy .50 1.00
105 Gump Worsley 2.50 5.00
106 Charlie Burns .25 .50
107 Murray Oliver .25 .50
108 Barry Gibbs .25 .50
109 Ted Harris .25 .50
110 Cesare Maniago 1.00 2.00
111 Lou Nanne .38 .75
112 Bob Nevin .25 .50
113 Guy Lapointe .75 1.50
114 Pete Mahovlich .38 .75
115 Jacques Lemaire 1.00 2.00
116 Pierre Bouchard .25 .50
117 Yvan Cournoyer 1.25 2.50
118 Marc Tardif .25 .50
119 Henri Richard 2.50 5.00
120 Frank Mahovlich 2.50 5.00
121 Jacques Laperriere .75 1.50
122 Claude Larose .25 .50
123 Serge Savard 1.00 2.00
124 Ken Dryden 10.00 20.00
125 Rejean Houle .38 .75
126 Jim Roberts .25 .50
127 Ed Westfall .25 .50
128 Terry Crisp .38 .75
129 Gerry Desjardins .50 1.00
130 Denis DeJordy .75 1.50
131 Billy Harris .25 .50
132 Brian Spencer .50 1.00
133 Germaine Gagnon UER .25 .50
134 David Hedson .25 .50
135 Lorne Henning .25 .50
136 Brian Marchinko .25 .50
137 Tom Miller .25 .50
138 Gerry Hart .25 .50
139 Bryan Lefley .25 .50
140 James Mair .25 .50
141 Rod Gilbert 1.25 2.50
142 Jean Ratelle 1.25 2.50
143 Pete Stemkowski .25 .50
144 Brad Park 1.50 3.00
145 Bobby Rousseau .25 .50
146 Dale Rolfe .25 .50
147 Ed Giacomin 1.50 3.00
148 Rod Seiling .25 .50
149 Walt Tkaczuk .25 .50
150 Bill Fairbairn .25 .50
151 Vic Hadfield .38 .75
152 Ted Irvine .25 .50
153 Bruce MacGregor .25 .50
154 Jim Neilson .25 .50
155 Brent Hughes .25 .50
156 Wayne Hillman .25 .50
157 Doug Favell .75 1.50
158 Simon Nolet .25 .50
159 Joe Watson .25 .50
160 Ed Van Impe .25 .50
161 Gary Dornhoefer .38 .75
162 Bobby Clarke 5.00 10.00
163 Bob Kelly .25 .50
164 Bill Flett .25 .50
165 Rick Foley .25 .50
166 Ross Lonsberry .25 .50
167 Rick MacLeish .50 1.00
168 Bill Clement .50 1.00
169 Syl Apps .38 .75
170 Ken Schinkel .25 .50
171 Nick Harbaruk .25 .50
172 Bryan Watson .38 .75
173 Bryan Hextall .38 .75
174 Roy Edwards .50 1.00
175 Jim Rutherford .75 1.50
176 Jean Pronovost .38 .75
177 Rick Kessell .25 .50
178 Greg Polis .25 .50
179 Ron Schock .25 .50
180 Duane Rupp .25 .50
181 Darryl Edestrand .25 .50
182 Dave Burrows .25 .50
183 Gary Sabourin .25 .50
184 Garry Unger .50 1.00
185 Noel Picard .25 .50
186 Bob Plager .38 .75
187 Barclay Plager .38 .75
188 Frank St. Marseille .25 .50
189 Danny O'Shea .25 .50
190 Kevin O'Shea .25 .50
191 Wayne Stephenson .50 1.00
192 Chris Evans .25 .50
193 Jacques Caron .25 .50
194 Andre Dupont .25 .50
195 Mike Murphy .25 .50
196 Jack Egers .25 .50
197 Norm Ullman 1.25 2.50
198 Jim McKenny .25 .50
199 Bob Baun .50 1.00
200 Mike Pelyk .25 .50
201 Ron Ellis .38 .75
202 Garry Monahan .25 .50
203 Paul Henderson 1.00 2.00
204 Darryl Sittler 1.75 3.50
205 Brian Glennie .25 .50
206 Dave Keon 1.25 2.50
207 Jacques Plante 5.00 10.00
208 Pierre Jarry .25 .50
209 Rick Kehoe .38 .75
210 Denis Dupere .25 .50
211 Dale Tallon .38 .75
212 Murray Hall .25 .50
213 Dunc Wilson .50 1.00
214 Andre Boudrias .38 .75
215 Orland Kurtenbach .38 .75
216 Wayne Maki .25 .50
217 Barry Wilkins .25 .50
218 Richard Lemieux .25 .50
219 Bobby Schmautz .25 .50
220 Dave Balon .25 .50
221 Robert Lalonde .25 .50
222 Jocelyn Guevremont .25 .50
223 Gregg Boddy .25 .50
224 Dennis Kearns .25 .50
XX Stamp Album 25.00 50.00
Richard Martin
xx Stamp Album 10.00 20.00
(Bobby Orr on cover)
xx Stamp Album 17.50 35.00
(Paul Henderson on cover)

1990-91 Score Promos

The 1990-91 Score Promo set contains six different player standard-size cards. The promos were issued in both a Canadian and an American version. Three (10 Patrick Roy, 40 Gary Leeman, and 100 Mark Messier) were distributed as Canadian promos and the other three were given to U.S. card dealer accounts. Though all these promo versions have the same numbering as the regular issues, several of them are easily distinguished from their regular issue counterparts. The Roy and Messier promos have different player photos on their fronts (Roy promo also has a different photo on its back). The photo on the front of the Roenick promo is cropped differently, and the blurb on its back is also slightly different. Even for those promos that appear to be otherwise identical with the regular cards, close inspection reveals the following distinguishing marks: 1) on the backs, the promos have the registered mark (circle R) by the Score logo, whereas the regular issues have instead the trademark (TM); and 2) on the back, the NHL logo is slightly larger on the promos and the text around it is only in English (the regular issues also have a French translation).

1A Wayne Gretzky ERR 24.00 60.00
(Catches Left)
1B Wayne Gretzky COR 10.00 25.00
(Shoots Left)
10 Patrick Roy 8.00 20.00
40 Gary Leeman .30 .75
100A Mark Messier ERR 6.00 15.00
(Won Smythe in 1990)
100B Mark Messier COR 2.40 6.00
(Won Smythe in 1984)
179 Jeremy Roenick 2.00 5.00
200 Ray Bourque 2.40 6.00

1990-91 Score

The 1990-91 Score hockey set contains 440 standard-size cards. The fronts feature a color action photo, superimposed over blue and red stripes on a white background. The

team logo appears in the upper left hand corner, while an image of a hockey player (in various colors) appears in the lower right hand corner. The backs are outlined in a blue border and show a head shot of the player on the upper half. The career statistics and highlights on the lower half are printed on a pale yellow background. The complete factory set price includes the five Eric Lindros bonus cards (B1-B5) that were only available in the factory sets sold to hobby dealers. The few card numbers that are different in the Canadian and U.S. versions are labeled with an A (American) or C (Canadian) suffix after the card number.

COMPLETE SET (440) 7.00 14.00
COMP.FACT.SET (445) 9.00 18.00
*CDN: SAME VALUE UNLESS NOTED
1 Wayne Gretzky .50 1.25
2 Mario Lemieux .60 1.25
3 Steve Yzerman .40 1.00
4 Cam Neely .08 .25
5 Al MacInnis .02 .10
6 Paul Coffey .08 .25
7 Brian Bellows .01 .05
8 Joe Sakic .25 .60
9 Bernie Nicholls .02 .10
10 Patrick Roy .40 1.00
11 Doug Houda .01 .05
12 David Volek .01 .05
13 Esa Tikkanen .01 .05
14 Thomas Steen .01 .05
15 Chris Chelios .08 .25
16 Bob Carpenter .01 .05
17 Dirk Graham .01 .05
18 Garth Butcher .01 .05
19 Patrik Sundstrom .01 .05
20 Rod Langway .01 .05
21 Scott Young .01 .05
22 Ulf Dahlen .01 .05
23 Mike Ramsey .01 .05
24 Peter Zezel .01 .05
25 Ron Hextall .02 .10
26 Steve Duchesne .01 .05
27 Allan Bester .02 .10
28 Everett Sanipass .01 .05
29 Steve Konroyd .01 .05
30A Joe Nieuwendyk ERR .02 .10
30B Joe Nieuwendyk COR .02 .10
31A Brent Ashton ERR .01 .05
31B Brent Ashton COR .01 .05
32 Trevor Linden .02 .10
33 Mike Ridley .01 .05
34 Sean Burke .02 .10
35 Pat Verbeek .01 .05
36 Rob Ramage .01 .05
37 Kelly Kisio .01 .05
38A Craig Muni ERR .01 .05
38B Craig Muni COR .01 .05
39 Brent Sutter .01 .05
40 Gary Leeman .01 .05
41 Jeff Brown .01 .05
42 Greg Millen .02 .10
43 Alexander Mogilny RC .30 .75
44 Dale Hunter .01 .05
45 Randy Moller .01 .05
46 Peter Sidorkiewicz .02 .10
47 Terry Carkner .01 .05
48 Tony Granato .01 .05
49 Shawn Burr .01 .05
50 Dale Hawerchuk .02 .10
51A Don Sweeney ERR .01 .05
51B Don Sweeney COR .01 .05
52 Mike Vernon UER .02 .10
53 Kevin Stevens RC .01 .05
54 Bryan Fogarty .01 .05
55 Dan Quinn .01 .05
56 Murray Craven .01 .05
57 Shawn Chambers .01 .05
58 Craig Simpson .01 .05
59 Doug Crossman .01 .05
60 Daren Puppa .02 .10
61 Bobby Smith .02 .10
62 Slava Fetisov RC .01 .05
63 Gino Cavallini .01 .05
64 Jimmy Carson .01 .05
65 Dave Ellett .01 .05
66 Steve Thomas .01 .05
67 Mike Lalor .01 .05
68 Mike Liut .02 .10
69 Tom Laidlaw .01 .05
70 Ron Francis .02 .10
71 Sergei Makarov RC .01 .05
72 Randy Burridge .01 .05
73 Doug Lidster .01 .05
74 Mike Richter RC .40 1.00
75 Stephane Richer .02 .10
76 Randy Hillier .01 .05
77 Christian Ruuttu .01 .05
78 Marc Fortier .01 .05
79 Bill Ranford .02 .10
80 Rick Tocchet .02 .10
81 Fredrik Olausson .01 .05
82 Adam Creighton .01 .05
83 Sylvain Cote .01 .05
84 Brian Mullen .01 .05
85 Adam Oates .02 .10
86 Gary Nylund .01 .05
87 Tim Cheveldae RC .02 .10
88 Gary Suter .01 .05
89 John Tonelli .01 .05
90 Kevin Hatcher .01 .05
91 Guy Carbonneau .02 .10
92 Curtis Leschyshyn RC .01 .05
93 Kirk McLean .02 .10
94 Curt Giles .01 .05
95 Vincent Damphousse .01 .05
96 Peter Stastny .02 .10
97 Glen Wesley .01 .05
98 David Shaw .01 .05
99 Brad Shaw .01 .05
100 Mark Messier .08 .25
101 Rick Zombo .01 .05
102A Mark Fitzpatrick RC ERR.02 .10
102B Mark Fitzpatrick RC COR.02 .10
103 Rick Vaive .01 .05
104 Mark Osborne .01 .05
105 Rob Brown .01 .05
106 Gary Roberts .01 .05
107 Vincent Riendeau RC .02 .10
108 Dave Gagner .02 .10
109 Bruce Driver .01 .05
110 Pierre Turgeon .02 .10
111 Claude Lemieux .01 .05
112 Bob Essensa RC .15 .40
113 John Ogrodnick .01 .05
114 Glenn Anderson .02 .10
115 Kelly Hrudey .02 .10
116 Sylvain Turgeon .01 .05
117 Gord Murphy RC .01 .05
118 Craig Janney .02 .10
119 Randy Wood .01 .05
120 Mike Modano RC .50 1.25
121 Tom Barrasso .02 .10
122 Daniel Marois .01 .05
123 Igor Larionov RC .15 .40
124 Geoff Courtnall .01 .05
125 Denis Savard .02 .10
126 Ron Tugnutt .02 .10
127 Mathieu Schneider RC .01 .05
128 Joel Otto .01 .05
129 Steve Smith .01 .05
130 Mike Gartner .02 .10
131 Rod Brind'Amour RC .30 .75
132 Jyrki Lumme RC .01 .05
133 Mike Foligno .01 .05
134 Ray Ferraro .01 .05
135 Steve Larmer .02 .10
136 Randy Carlyle .01 .05
137 Tony Tanti .01 .05
138 Jeff Chychrun .01 .05
139 Gerald Diduck .01 .05
140 Andy Moog .02 .10
141 Paul Gillis .01 .05
142 Tom Kurvers .01 .05
143 Bob Probert .02 .10
144 Neal Broten .02 .10
145 Phil Housley .02 .10
146 Brendan Shanahan .08 .25
147 Bob Rouse .01 .05
148 Russ Courtnall .01 .05
149 Normand Rochefort .01 .05
150 Luc Robitaille .02 .10
151 Curtis Joseph RC .60 1.50
152 Ulf Samuelsson .01 .05
153 Ron Sutter .01 .05
154 Petri Skriko .01 .05
155 Doug Gilmour .02 .10
156 Paul Fenton .01 .05
157 Jeff Norton .01 .05
158 Jari Kurri .02 .10
159 Rejean Lemelin .02 .10
160 Kirk Muller .01 .05
161 Keith Brown .01 .05
162 Aaron Broten .01 .05
163 Adam Graves RC .15 .40
164 John Cullen .01 .05
165 Craig Ludwig .01 .05
166 Dave Taylor .02 .10
167 Craig Wolanin .01 .05
168 Kelly Miller .01 .05
169 Uwe Krupp .01 .05
170 Kevin Lowe .01 .05
171 Wendel Clark .02 .10
172 Dave Babych .01 .05
173 Paul Reinhart .01 .05
174 Pat Flatley .01 .05
175 John Vanbiesbrouck .02 .10
176 Teppo Numminen RC .01 .05
177 Tim Kerr .01 .05
178 Ken Daneyko .01 .05
179 Jeremy Roenick RC .40 1.00
180 Gerard Gallant .01 .05
181 Allen Pederson .01 .05
182 Jon Casey .02 .10
183 Tomas Sandstrom .01 .05
184 Brad McCrimmon .01 .05
185 Paul Cavallini .01 .05
186 Mark Recchi RC .40 1.00
187 Michel Petit .01 .05
188 Scott Stevens .02 .10
189 Dave Andreychuk .02 .10
190 John MacLean .02 .10
191 Petr Svoboda .01 .05
192 Dave Tippett .01 .05
193 Dave Manson .01 .05
194 James Patrick .01 .05
195 Al Iafrate .02 .10
196 Doug Smail .01 .05
197 Kjell Samuelsson .01 .05
198 Brian Bradley .01 .05
199 Charlie Huddy .01 .05
200 Ray Bourque .15 .40
201 Joey Kocur RC .15 .40
202 Jim Johnson .01 .05
203 Paul MacLean .01 .05
204 Tim Watters .01 .05
205 Pat Elynuik .01 .05
206 Larry Murphy .02 .10
207 Claude Loiselle .01 .05
208 Joe Mullen .02 .10
209 Alexei Kasatonov RC .01 .05
210 Ed Olczyk .01 .05
211 Doug Bodger .01 .05
212 Kevin Dineen .01 .05
213 Shayne Corson .01 .05
214 Steve Chiasson .01 .05
215 Don Beaupre .02 .10
216 Jamie Macoun .01 .05
217 Dave Poulin .01 .05
218 Zarley Zalapski .01 .05
219 Brad Marsh .01 .05
220 Mark Howe .01 .05
221 Michel Goulet .02 .10
222 Hubie McDonough .01 .05
223 Frank Musil .01 .05
224 Sergio Momesso RC .01 .05
225 Brian Leetch .10 .30
226 Theo Fleury .01 .05
227 Mike Krushelnyski .01 .05
228 Glen Hanlon .02 .10
229 Mario Marois .01 .05
230 Dino Ciccarelli .02 .10
231A Dave McLlwain ERR .01 .05
231B Dave McLlwain COR .01 .05
232 Petr Klima .01 .05
233 Grant Ledyard .01 .05
234 Phil Bourque .01 .05
235 Rob Sweeney .01 .05
236 Luke Richardson .01 .05
237 Todd Krygier .01 .05
238 Brian Skrudland .01 .05
239 Chris Terreri RC .02 .10
240 Greg Adams .01 .05
241 Darren Turcotte RC .01 .05
242 Scott Mellanby .02 .10
243 Troy Murray .01 .05
244 Stewart Gavin .01 .05
245 Gordie Roberts .01 .05
246 John Druce .01 .05
247 Steve Kasper .01 .05
248 Paul Ranheim RC .01 .05
249 Greg Paslawski .01 .05
250 Pat LaFontaine .08 .25
251 Scott Arniel .01 .05
252 Bernie Federko .02 .10
253 Garry Galley RC .01 .05
254 Carey Wilson .01 .05
255 Bob Errey .01 .05
256 Tony Hrkac .01 .05
257 Andrew McBain .01 .05
258 Craig MacTavish .01 .05
259A Dean Evason ERR .01 .05
259B Dean Evason COR .01 .05
260 Larry Robinson .02 .10
261 Basil McRae .01 .05
262 Stephan Lebeau RC .01 .05
263 Ken Wregget .02 .10
264 Greg Gilbert .01 .05
265 Ken Baumgartner .01 .05
266 Lou Franceschetti .01 .05
267 Rick Meagher .01 .05
268 Michal Pivonka RC .01 .05
269 Brian Propp .01 .05
270 Bryan Trottier .02 .10
271 Marty McSorley .01 .05
272 Jan Erixon .01 .05
273 Vladimir Krutov .02 .10
274 Dana Murzyn .01 .05
275 Grant Fuhr .02 .10
276 Randy Cunneyworth .01 .05
277 John Chabot .01 .05
278 Walt Poddubny .01 .05
279 Stephen Leach .01 .05
280 Doug Wilson .02 .10
281 Rich Sutter .01 .05
282 Stephane Beauregard .02 .10
283 John Carter .01 .05
284 Don Barber .01 .05
285 Tom Fergus .01 .05
286 Ilkka Sinisalo .01 .05
287 Kevin McClelland .01 .05
288 Troy Mallette .01 .05
289 Clint Malarchuk .02 .10
290 Guy Lafleur .08 .25
291 Bob Joyce .01 .05
292 Trent Yawney .01 .05
293 Joe Murphy RC .01 .05
294 Glenn Healy RC .02 .10
295 Dave Christian .01 .05
296 Paul MacDermid .01 .05
297 Todd Elik RC .01 .05
298 Wendell Young .02 .10
299 Dean Kennedy .01 .05
300 Brett Hull .20 .50
301A Keith Acton .01 .05
301C Martin Gelinas RC .08 .25
302A Yvon Corriveau .01 .05
302C Ric Nattress .01 .05
303A Don Maloney .01 .05
303C Jim Sandlak .01 .05
304A Mark Tinordi RC .01 .05
304C Brian Hayward .02 .10
305A Bob Kudelski RC .01 .05
305C Joe Cirella .01 .05
306A Brian Benning .01 .05
306C Randy Gregg .01 .05
307A Alan Kerr .01 .05
307C Sylvain Lefebvre .01 .05
308A Pelle Eklund .01 .05
308C Mark Lamb .01 .05
309A Calle Johansson .01 .05
309C Rick Wamsley .02 .10
310A David Maley .01 .05
310C Moe Mantha .01 .05
311A Chris Nilan .01 .05
311C Tony McKegney .01 .05
312 Patrick Roy AS1 .10 .30
313 Ray Bourque AS1 .08 .25
314 Al MacInnis AS1 .02 .10
315 Mark Messier AS1 .08 .25
316 Luc Robitaille AS1 .02 .10
317 Brett Hull AS1 .08 .25
318 Daren Puppa AS2 .02 .10
319 Paul Coffey AS2 .08 .25
320 Doug Wilson AS2 .02 .10
321 Wayne Gretzky AS2 .15 .40
322 Brian Bellows AS2 .01 .05
323 Cam Neely AS2 .02 .10
324 Bob Essensa ART .02 .10
325 Brad Shaw ART .01 .05
326 Geoff Smith ART .01 .05
327 Mike Modano ART .02 .10
328 Rod Brind'Amour ART .02 .10
329 Sergei Makarov ART .01 .05
330A Kip Miller Hobey RC ERR.01 .05
330B Kip Miller Hobey RC COR.01 .05
330C Memorial Cup .20 .50
331 Edmonton Oilers Champs.01 .05
332 Paul Coffey Speed .08 .25
333 Mike Gartner Speed .02 .10
334 Al Iafrate Blaster .02 .10
335 Al MacInnis Blaster .02 .10
336 Wayne Gretzky Sniper .15 .40
337 Mario Lemieux Sniper .20 .50
338 Wayne Gretzky Magic .15 .40
339 Steve Yzerman Magic .08 .25
340 Cam Neely Banger .02 .10
341 Scott Stevens Banger .02 .10
342 Esa Tikkanen Shadow .01 .05
343 Jan Erixon Shadow .01 .05
344 Patrick Roy Stopper .10 .30
345 Bill Ranford Stopper .02 .10
346 Brett Hull RB .08 .25
347 Wayne Gretzky RB .15 .40
348 Jari Kurri LL .02 .10
349 Paul Cavallini LL .01 .05
350 Sergei Makarov RLL .01 .05
351 Brett Hull LL .08 .25
352 Wayne Gretzky LL .15 .40
353 Wayne Gretzky LL .15 .40
354 P.Roy/Liut LL .10 .30
355 Gilbert Perreault HOF .01 .05
356 Bill Barber HOF .01 .05
357 Fern Flaman HOF .01 .05
358 Bill Ranford Smythe .02 .10
359 Rick Meagher Selke .01 .05
360 Mark Messier Hart .08 .25
361 Wayne Gretzky Ross .15 .40
362 Sergei Makarov Calder .01 .05
363 Ray Bourque Norris .08 .25
364 Patrick Roy Vezina .10 .30
365 Moog/Lemelin Jennings.01 .05
366 Brett Hull Byng .08 .25
367 Gord Kluzak Mast .01 .05
368 Boston/Washington .01 .05
369 Edmonton/Chicago .01 .05
370 Adam Burt RC .01 .05
371 Troy Loney .01 .05
372 Dave Chyzowski .01 .05
373 Geoff Smith .01 .05
374 Stan Smyl .01 .05
375 Gaetan Duchesne .01 .05
376 Bob Murray .01 .05
377 Daniel Shank .01 .05
378 Tommy Albelin .01 .05
379 Perry Berezan .01 .05
380 Ken Linseman .01 .05
381 Stephane Matteau RC .01 .05
382 Mario Thyer .01 .05
383 Nelson Emerson RC .01 .05
384 Kory Kocur .01 .05
385 Bob Beers RC .01 .05
386 Jim Hrivnak RC .02 .10
387 Mark Pederson .01 .05
388 Jeff Hackett RC .15 .40
389 Eric Weinrich RC .01 .05
390 Steven Rice RC .01 .05
391 Stu Barnes RC .01 .05
392 Olaf Kolzig RC .40 1.00
393 Francois Leroux .01 .05
394 Adrien Plavsic .01 .05
395 Michel Mongeau RC .01 .05
396 Rick Corriveau .01 .05
397 Wayne Doucet .01 .05
398 Mats Sundin RC .40 1.00
399 Murray Baron .01 .05
400 Rick Bennett .01 .05
401 Jon Morris .01 .05
402 Kay Whitmore RC .02 .10
403 Peter Lappin .01 .05
404 Kris Draper RC .15 .40
405 Shayne Stevenson RC .01 .05
406 Paul Ysebaert RC .01 .05
407A Jimmy Waite RC ERR .02 .10
407B Jimmy Waite RC COR.02 .10
408 Cam Russell .01 .05
409 Kim Issel .01 .05
410 Darrin Shannon RC .01 .05
411 Link Gaetz RC .01 .05
412 Craig Fisher .01 .05
413 Bruce Hoffort .01 .05
414 Peter Ing .02 .10
415 Stephane Fiset RC .15 .40
416 Dominic Lavoie .01 .05
417 Steve Maltais .01 .05
418 Wes Walz RC .01 .05
419 Terry Yake RC .01 .05
420 Jamie Leach .01 .05
421 Rob Blake RC .20 .50
422 Andrew Cassels RC .01 .05
423 Marc Bureau .01 .05
424 Scott Allison .01 .05
425 Darryl Sydor RC .15 .40
426 Turner Stevenson RC .01 .05
427 Brad May RC .02 .10
428 Jaromir Jagr RC .75 2.00
429 Shawn Antoski RC .01 .05
430 Derian Hatcher RC .15 .40
431 Mark Greig RC .01 .05
432 Scott Scissons RC .01 .05
433 Mike Ricci RC .12 .30
434 Drake Berehowsky RC .01 .05
435 Owen Nolan RC .40 1.00
436 Keith Primeau RC .30 .75
437 Karl Dykhuis RC .01 .05
438 Trevor Kidd RC .25 .60
439 Martin Brodeur RC 4.00 10.00
440A Eric Lindros RC 1.25 3.00
440C Eric Lindros RC 2.00 5.00
B1 Eric Lindros .40 1.00
B2 Eric Lindros .40 1.00
B3 Eric Lindros .40 1.00
B4 Eric Lindros .40 1.00
B5 Eric Lindros .40 1.00

1990-91 Score Hottest/Rising Stars

This 100-card standard-size set was released along with a special book. The book provided further information about the players. The fronts of the cards have the same photos as the regular Score issue but the numbers are different on the back.

COMP.FACT SET (100) 6.00 15.00
1 Wayne Gretzky 2.00 5.00
2 Craig Simpson .04 .10
3 Brian Bellows .04 .10
4 Steve Yzerman 1.00 2.50
5 Bernie Nicholls .04 .10
6 Esa Tikkanen .04 .10
7 Joe Sakic .60 2.00
8 Thomas Steen .04 .10
9 Chris Chelios .30 .75
10 Patrik Sundstrom .04 .10
11 Rod Langway .04 .10
12 Scott Young .04 .10
13 Mike Ramsey .04 .10
14 Ron Hextall .20 .50
15 Steve Duchesne .10 .25
16 Trevor Linden .20 .50
17 Sean Burke .20 .50
18 Pat Verbeek .10 .25
19 Brent Sutter .04 .10
20 Gary Leeman .04 .10
21 Shawn Burr .04 .10
22 Dale Hawerchuk .10 .25
23 Mike Vernon .10 .25
24 Dan Quinn .04 .10
25 Patrick Roy 1.60 4.00
26 Daren Puppa .20 .25
27 Gino Cavallini .04 .10
28 Jimmy Carson .04 .10
29 Dave Ellett .04 .10
30 Steve Thomas .04 .10
31 Jeremy Roenick .80 2.00
32 Mike Liut .04 .10
33 Mark Messier .40 1.00
34 Mario Lemieux 1.60 4.00
35 Ray Bourque .40 1.00
36 Al MacInnis .20 .50
37 Ron Francis .20 .50
38 Stephane Richer .20 .50
39 Bill Ranford .20 .50
40 Rick Tocchet .10 .25
41 Adam Oates .20 .50
42 Kevin Hatcher .04 .10
43 Guy Carbonneau .04 .10
44 Curtis Leschyshyn .04 .10
45 Joe Nieuwendyk .20 .50
46 Kirk McLean .20 .50
47 Vincent Damphousse .20 .50
48 Peter Stastny .10 .25
49 Rick Zombo .04 .10
50 Mark Fitzpatrick .20 .25
51 Rob Brown .04 .10
52 Dave Gagner .04 .10
53 Pierre Turgeon .20 .50
54 Glenn Anderson .04 .10
55 Kelly Hrudey .20 .50
56 Gord Murphy .04 .10
57 Glen Wesley .04 .10
58 Craig Janney .10 .25
59 Denis Savard .10 .25
60 Mike Gartner .20 .50
61 Steve Larmer .04 .10
62 Andy Moog .20 .50
63 Phil Housley .04 .10
64 Ulf Samuelsson .04 .10
65 Paul Coffey .30 .75
66 Luc Robitaille .20 .50
67 Cam Neely .20 .75
68 Doug Wilson .04 .10
69 Doug Gilmour .30 .75
70 Jeff Norton .04 .10
71 Kirk Muller .04 .10
72 Aaron Broten .04 .10
73 John Cullen .04 .10
74 Craig Ludwig .04 .10
75 Kevin Lowe .04 .10
76 John Vanbiesbrouck .30 .75
77 Tim Kerr .04 .10
78 Gerard Gallant .04 .10
79 Tomas Sandstrom .04 .10
80 Jon Casey .20 .50
81 Mark Recchi .80 1.00
82 Scott Stevens .10 .25
83 John MacLean .04 .10
84 James Patrick .04 .10
85 Al Iafrate .04 .10
86 Pat Elyniuk .04 .10
87 Dave Andreychuk .04 .10
88 Joe Mullen .04 .10
89 Ed Olczyk .04 .10
90 Kevin Dineen .04 .10
91 Shayne Corson .10 .25
92 Mark Howe .04 .10
93 Brian Leetch .30 .50
94 Dino Ciccarelli .10 .25
95 Pat LaFontaine .20 .50
96 Guy Lafleur .20 .50
97 Mike Modano .80 2.00
98 Rod Brind'Amour .40 1.00
99 Sergei Makarov .10 .25
100 Brett Hull .40 1.00

1990-91 Score Rookie/Traded

The 1990-91 Score Rookie and Traded hockey set contains 110 standard-size cards. The cards were issued as a complete set in a factory box. The fronts feature a color action photo, superimposed over blue and red stripes on a white background. The team logo appears in the upper left hand corner, while an image of a hockey player (in various colors) appears in the lower right hand corner. Yellow strips appear at the top and bottom of the card front. The backs are outlined in a yellow border and show a head shot of the player on the upper half. The career statistics and highlights on the lower half are printed on a pale yellow background. Rookie Cards include Ed Belfour, Peter Bondra, Sergei Fedorov, Petr Nedved and Robert Reichel. The back of the set's custom box contains the set checklist. The cards are numbered with a "T" suffix.

COMP. FACT SET (110) 4.00 10.00
1T Denis Savard .05 .15
2T Dale Hawerchuk .05 .15
3T Phil Housley .01 .05
4T Chris Chelios .15 .40
5T Geoff Courtnall .01 .05
6T Peter Zezel .01 .05
7T Joe Mullen .05 .15
8T Craig Ludwig .01 .05
9T Claude Lemieux .01 .05
10T Bobby Holik RC .10 .30
11T Peter Ing .05 .15
12T Rod Buskas .01 .05
13T Tim Sweeney RC .01 .05
14T Don Barber .01 .05
15T Ray Ferraro .01 .05
16T Peter Taglianetti .01 .05
17T Johan Garpenlov RC .01 .05
18T Kevin Miller RC .01 .05
19T Frank Musil .01 .05
20T Sergei Fedorov RC .60 1.50
21T Aaron Broten .01 .05
22T Chris Nilan .01 .05
23T Gerald Diduck .01 .05
24T Marc Habscheid .01 .05
25T Glen Featherstone .01 .05
26T Mikko Makela .01 .05
27T Paul Stanton .01 .05
28T Mark Osborne .01 .05
29T Dave Tippett .01 .05
30T Robert Reichel RC .05 .15
31T Grant Jennings .01 .05
32T Troy Gamble .05 .15
33T Mark Janssens .01 .05
34T Brian Propp .01 .05
35T Donald Dufresne .01 .05
36T Martin Hostak .01 .05
37T Brad McCrimmon .01 .05
38T Dave Lowry RC .01 .05
39T Anatoli Semenov RC .01 .05
40T Scott Stevens .05 .15
41T Paul Broten .01 .05
42T Carey Wilson .01 .05
43T Troy Crowder RC .01 .05
44T Vladimir Ruzicka RC .01 .05
45T Rich Pilon .01 .05
46T John McIntyre RC .01 .05
47T Mike Krushelnyski .01 .05
48T Dave Snuggerud .01 .05
49T Bob McGill .01 .05
50T Petr Nedved RC .25 .60
51T Ed Olczyk .01 .05
52T Doug Crossman .01 .05
53T Mikhail Tatarinov RC .01 .05
54T Michel Petit .01 .05
55T Frank Pietrangelo .05 .15
56T Brian MacLellan .01 .05
57T Paul Fenton .01 .05
58T Eric Desjardins RC .25 .60
59T Mike Craig RC .01 .05
60T Mike Ricci .05 .15
61T Harold Snepsts .01 .05
62T John Byce .01 .05
63T Laurie Boschman .01 .05
64T Randy Velischek .01 .05
65T Robert Kron .01 .05
66T Jocelyn Lemieux .01 .05
67T Dave Ellett .01 .05
68T Scott Arniel .01 .05
69T Doug Smail .01 .05
70T Jaromir Jagr .75 2.00
71T Peter Bondra RC .30 .75
72T Paul Cyr .01 .05
73T Daniel Berthiaume .05 .15
74T Lee Norwood .01 .05
75T Bobby Smith .05 .15
76T Kris King .01 .05
77T Mark Hunter .01 .05
78T Brian Hayward .05 .15
79T Greg Hawgood .01 .05
80T Owen Nolan .40 1.00
81T Cliff Ronning .05 .15
82T Zdeno Ciger RC .01 .05
83T Gordie Roberts .01 .05
84T Rick Green .01 .05
85T Ken Hodge Jr. RC .01 .05
86T Derek King .01 .05
87T Brent Gilchrist RC .01 .05
88T Eric Lindros .75 2.00
89T Steve Bozek .01 .05
90T Keith Primeau .15 .40
91T Roger Johansson .01 .05
92T Wayne Presley .01 .05
93T Ilkka Sinisalo .01 .05
94T Mario Marois .01 .05
95T Ken Linseman .01 .05
96T Greg Brown .01 .05
97T Ray Sheppard .05 .15
98T Mike Lalor .01 .05
99T Normand Lacombe .01 .05
100T Mats Sundin .40 1.00
101T Jergus Baca .01 .05
102T Mike Keane RC .01 .05
103T Ed Belfour RC 1.00 2.50
104T Mark Hardy .01 .05
105T Dave Capuano .01 .05
106T Bryan Trottier .05 .15
107T Per Djoos .01 .05
108T Sylvain Turgeon .01 .05
109T David Reid .01 .05
110T Gretzky's 2000th Point .40 1.00

1990-91 Score Young Superstars

This 40-card standard-size set was issued by Score to honor some of the leading young players active in hockey. The set has a glossy sheen to it with an action shot of the player, while the back of the card has a portrait color shot on the back along with biographical and statistical information. The set was available only in this special box format. The set was also available direct to collectors through an offer detailed on certain wax wrappers.

COMP.FACT SET (40) 8.00 20.00
1 Pierre Turgeon .30 .75
2 Brian Leetch .40 1.00
3 Daniel Marois .04 .10
4 Peter Sidorkiewicz .20 .50
5 Rob Brown .04 .10
6 Theo Fleury .40 1.00
7 Mats Sundin 1.20 3.00
8 Glen Wesley .04 .10
9 Sergei Fedorov 1.20 3.00
10 Joe Sakic .80 2.00
11 Sean Burke .20 .50
12 Dave Chyzowski .04 .10
13 Gord Murphy .04 .10
14 Scott Young .04 .10
15 Curtis Joseph 1.20 3.00
16 Darren Turcotte .20 .50
17 Kevin Stevens .20 .50
18 Mathieu Schneider .04 .10
19 Trevor Linden .20 .50
20 Mike Modano 1.20 3.00
21 Martin Gelinas .04 .10
22 Stephane Fiset .20 .50
23 Brendan Shanahan .80 2.00
24 Jeremy Roenick 1.20 3.00
25 John Druce .04 .10
26 Alexander Mogilny .40 1.00
27 Mike Richter 1.20 3.00
28 Pat Elyniuk .04 .10
29 Robert Reichel .04 .10
30 Craig Janney .04 .10
31 Rod Brind'Amour .60 1.50
32 Mark Fitzpatrick .20 .50
33 Tony Granato .04 .10
34 Bobby Holik .04 .10
35 Mark Recchi .80 2.00
36 Owen Nolan .80 2.00
37 Petr Nedved .60 1.50
38 Keith Primeau .60 1.50
39 Mike Ricci .40 1.00
40 Eric Lindros 2.00 5.00

1991 Score National

This ten-card standard-size set features outstanding hockey players. The cards were given out as a cello-wrapped complete set by Score at the National Sports Collectors Convention in Anaheim, at the Fanfest in Toronto, and at the National Candy Wholesalers Convention in St. Louis. Some dealers have reported selling the cards with the NCWA imprint and no imprint (FanFest) for a premium above the prices listed below. The front has an action photo of the player, bounded by diagonal green borders above and below the picture. The player's name and team name appear in the top green border. The light blue background shows through above and below the green borders, and it is decorated with hockey pucks and player icons. The back presents player information and career summary in a diagonal format similar to the design of the front. Some dealers have reported getting premiums of 2-3 times the values below for the Toronto FanFest versions.

COMPLETE SET (10) 12.00 30.00
1 Wayne Gretzky 4.00 10.00
2 Brett Hull .80 2.00
3 Ray Bourque .80 2.00
4 Al MacInnis .50 1.25
5 Luc Robitaille .50 1.25
6 Ed Belfour .60 1.50
7 Steve Yzerman 2.00 5.00
8 Cam Neely .50 1.25
9 Paul Coffey .60 1.50
10 Patrick Roy 3.20 8.00

1991-92 Score American

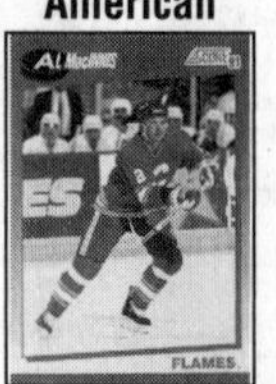

The 1991-92 Score American hockey set features 440 standard-size cards. As one moves down the card face, the fronts shade from purple to white. The color action player photo is enclosed by an thin red border, with a shadow border on the right and below. At the card top, the player's name is written over a hockey puck, and the team name is printed below the picture in the lower right corner. A purple border stripe at the bottom completes the front. In a horizontal format, the backs have biography, statistics, player profile, and a color close-up photo.

COMPLETE SET (440) 4.00 10.00
COMP.FACT.SET (440) 4.00 10.00
1 Brett Hull .08 .25
2 Al MacInnis .02 .10
3 Luc Robitaille .02 .10
4 Pierre Turgeon .02 .10
5 Brian Leetch .07 .20
6 Cam Neely .07 .20
7 John Cullen .01 .05
8 Trevor Linden .02 .10

9 Rick Tocchet .02 .10
10 John Vanbiesbrouck .02 .10
11 Steve Smith .01 .05
12 Doug Smail .01 .05
13 Craig Ludwig .01 .05
14 Paul Fenton .01 .05
15 Dirk Graham .01 .05
16 Brad McCrimmon .01 .05
17 Dean Evason .01 .05
18 Fredrik Olausson .01 .05
19 Guy Carbonneau .02 .10
20 Kevin Hatcher .02 .10
21 Paul Ranheim .01 .05
22 Claude Lemieux .01 .05
23 Vincent Riendeau .02 .10
24 Garth Butcher .01 .05
25 Joe Sakic .15 .40
26 Rick Vaive .01 .05
27 Rob Blake .02 .10
28 Mike Ricci .07 .20
29 Pat Flatley .01 .05
30 Bill Ranford .02 .10
31 Larry Murphy .02 .10
32 Bobby Smith .02 .10
33 Mike Krushelnyski .01 .05
34 Gerard Gallant .01 .05
35 Doug Wilson .02 .10
36 John Ogrodnick .01 .05
37 Mikhail Tatarinov .01 .05
38 Doug Crossman .01 .05
39 Mark Osborne .01 .05
40 Scott Stevens .02 .10
41 Ron Tugnutt .02 .10
42 Russ Courtnall .01 .05
43 Gord Murphy .01 .05
44 Greg Adams .01 .05
45 Christian Ruuttu .01 .05
46 Ken Daneyko .01 .05
47 Glenn Anderson .02 .10
48 Ray Ferraro .01 .05
49 Tony Tanti .01 .05
50 Ray Bourque .10 .30
51 Sergei Makarov .01 .05
52 Jim Johnson .01 .05
53 Troy Murray .01 .05
54 Shawn Burr .01 .05
55 Peter Ing .02 .10
56 Dale Hunter .01 .05
57 Tony Granato .01 .05
58 Curtis Leschyshyn .01 .05
59 Brian Mullen .01 .05
60 Ed Olczyk .01 .05
61 Mike Ramsey .01 .05
62 Dan Quinn .01 .05
63 Rich Sutter .01 .05
64 Terry Carkner .01 .05
65 Shayne Corson .01 .05
66 Peter Stastny .02 .10
67 Craig Muni .01 .05
68 Glenn Healy .02 .10
69 Phil Bourque .01 .05
70 Pat Verbeek .01 .05
71 Garry Galley .01 .05
72 Dave Gagner .01 .05
73 Bob Probert .02 .10
74 Craig Wolanin .01 .05
75 Patrick Roy .40 1.00
76 Keith Brown .01 .05
77 Gary Leeman .01 .05
78 Brent Ashton .01 .05
79 Randy Moller .01 .05
80 Mike Vernon .02 .10
81 Kelly Miller .01 .05
82 Ulf Samuelsson .01 .05
83 Todd Elik .01 .05
84 Uwe Krupp .01 .05
85 Rod Brind'Amour .07 .20
86 Dave Capuano .01 .05
87 Geoff Smith .01 .05
88 David Volek .01 .05
89 Bruce Driver .01 .05
90 Andy Moog .07 .20
91 Pelle Eklund .01 .05
92 Joey Kocur .02 .10
93 Mark Tinordi .01 .05
94 Steve Thomas .01 .05
95 Petr Svoboda .01 .05
96 Joel Otto .01 .05
97 Todd Krygier .01 .05
98 Jaromir Jagr .12 .30
99 Mike Liut .02 .10
100 Wayne Gretzky .50 1.25
101 Teppo Numminen .01 .05
102 Randy Burridge .01 .05
103 Michel Petit .01 .05
104 Tony McKegney .01 .05
105 Mathieu Schneider .01 .05
106 Daren Puppa .02 .10
107 Paul Cavallini .01 .05
108 Tim Kerr .01 .05
109 Kevin Lowe .02 .10
110 Kirk Muller .01 .05
111 Zarley Zalapski .01 .05
112 Mike Hough .01 .05
113 Ken Hodge Jr. .01 .05
114 Grant Fuhr .07 .20
115 Paul Coffey .07 .20
116 Wendel Clark .02 .10
117 Patrik Sundstrom .01 .05
118 Kevin Dineen .01 .05
119 Eric Desjardins .02 .10
120 Mike Richter .07 .20
121 Sergio Momesso .01 .05
122 Tony Hrkac .01 .05
123 Joe Reekie .01 .05
124 Petr Nedved .02 .10
125 Randy Carlyle .01 .05
126 Kevin Miller .01 .05
127 Rejean Lemelin .02 .10
128 Dino Ciccarelli .02 .10
129 Sylvain Cote .01 .05
130 Mats Sundin .07 .20
131 Eric Weinrich .01 .05
132 Daniel Berthiaume .02 .10
133 Keith Acton .01 .05
134 Benoit Hogue .01 .05
135 Mike Gartner .02 .10
136 Petr Klima .01 .05
137 Curt Giles .01 .05
138 Scott Pearson .01 .05
139 Luke Richardson .01 .05
140 Steve Larmer .02 .10
141 Ken Wregget .02 .10
142 Frank Musil .01 .05
143 Owen Nolan .07 .20
144 Keith Primeau .01 .05
145 Mark Recchi .07 .20
146 Don Sweeney .01 .05
147 Mike McPhee .01 .05
148 Ken Baumgartner .01 .05
149 Dave Lowry .01 .05
150 Geoff Courtnall .02 .10
151 Chris Terreri .02 .10
152 Dave Manson .01 .05
153 Bobby Holik .02 .10
154 Bob Kudelski .01 .05
155 Calle Johansson .01 .05
156 Mark Hunter .01 .05
157 Randy Gilhen .01 .05
158 Yves Racine .01 .05
159 Martin Gelinas .01 .05
160 Brian Bellows .01 .05
161 David Shaw .01 .05
162 Bob Carpenter .01 .05
163 Doug Brown .01 .05
164 Ulf Dahlen .01 .05
165 Denis Savard .02 .10
166 Paul Ysebaert .01 .05
167 Derek King .01 .05
168 Igor Larionov .01 .05
169 Bob Errey .01 .05
170 Joe Nieuwendyk .02 .10
171 Normand Rochefort .01 .05
172 John Tonelli .01 .05
173 David Reid .01 .05
174 Tom Kurvers .01 .05
175 Dimitri Khristich .01 .05
176 Bob Sweeney .01 .05
177 Rick Zombo .01 .05
178 Troy Mallette .01 .05
179 Bob Bassen .01 .05
180 John Druce .01 .05
181 Mike Craig .01 .05
182 John McIntyre .01 .05
183 Murray Baron .01 .05
184 Slava Fetisov .01 .05
185 Don Beaupre .02 .10
186 Brian Benning .01 .05
187 Dave Barr .01 .05
188 Petri Skriko .01 .05
189 Steve Konroyd .01 .05
190 Steve Yzerman .30 .75
191 Jon Casey .02 .10
192 Gary Nylund .01 .05
193 Michal Pivonka .01 .05
194 Alexei Kasatonov .01 .05
195 Garry Valk .01 .05
196 Darren Turcotte .01 .05
197 Chris Nilan .01 .05
198 Thomas Steen .01 .05
199 Gary Roberts .02 .10
200 Mario Lemieux .50 1.25
201 Michel Goulet .02 .10
202 Craig MacTavish .01 .05
203 Peter Sidorkiewicz .02 .10
204 Johan Garpenlov .01 .05
205 Steve Duchesne .01 .05
206 Dave Snuggerud .01 .05
207 Kjell Samuelsson .01 .05
208 Sylvain Turgeon .01 .05
209 Al Iafrate .02 .10
210 John MacLean .02 .10
211 Brian Hayward .02 .10
212 Cliff Ronning .01 .05
213 Ray Sheppard .01 .05
214 Dave Taylor .02 .10
215 Doug Lidster .01 .05
216 Peter Bondra .02 .10
217 Marty McSorley .01 .05
218 Doug Gilmour .02 .10
219 Paul MacDermid .01 .05
220 Jeremy Roenick .10 .25
221 Wayne Presley .01 .05
222 Jeff Norton .01 .05
223 Brian Propp .01 .05
224 Jimmy Carson .01 .05
225 Tom Barrasso .02 .10
226 Theo Fleury .01 .05
227 Carey Wilson .01 .05
228 Rod Langway .01 .05
229 Bryan Trottier .07 .20
230 James Patrick .01 .05
231 Kelly Hrudey .02 .10
232 Dave Poulin .01 .05
233 Rob Ramage .01 .05
234 Stephane Richer .02 .10
235 Chris Chelios .07 .20
236 Alexander Mogilny .07 .20
237 Bryan Fogarty .01 .05
238 Adam Oates .02 .10
239 Ron Hextall .02 .10
240 Bernie Nicholls .02 .10
241 Esa Tikkanen .01 .05
242 Jyrki Lumme .01 .05
243 Brent Sutter .01 .05
244 Gary Suter .01 .05
245 Sean Burke .02 .10
246 Rob Brown .01 .05
247 Mike Modano .15 .40
248 Kevin Stevens .01 .05
249 Mike Lalor .01 .05
250 Sergei Fedorov .12 .30
251 Bob Essensa .02 .10
252 Mark Howe .01 .05
253 Craig Janney .02 .10
254 Daniel Marois .01 .05
255 Craig Simpson .01 .05
256 Steve Kasper .01 .05
257 Randy Velischek .01 .05
258 Gino Cavallini .01 .05
259 Dale Hawerchuk .02 .10
260 Pat LaFontaine .07 .20
261 Kirk McLean .07 .20
262 Murray Craven .01 .05
263 Robert Reichel .02 .10
264 Jan Erixon .01 .05
265 Adam Creighton .01 .05
266 Mark Fitzpatrick .02 .10
267 Ron Francis .02 .10
268 Joe Mullen .02 .10
269 Peter Zezel .01 .05
270 Tomas Sandstrom .01 .05
271 Phil Housley .02 .10
272 Tim Cheveldae .02 .10
273 Glen Wesley .01 .05
274 Stephan Lebeau .01 .05
275 Dave Ellett .01 .05
276 Jeff Brown .01 .05
277 Dave Andreychuk .02 .10
278 Steven Finn .01 .05
279 Scott Mellanby .01 .05
280 Neal Broten .02 .10
281 Randy Wood .01 .05
282 Troy Gamble .02 .10
283 Mike Ridley .01 .05
284 Jamie Macoun .01 .05
285 Mark Messier .07 .20
286 Brendan Shanahan .07 .20
287 Scott Young .01 .05
288 Kelly Kisio .01 .05
289 Brad Shaw .01 .05
290 Ed Belfour .07 .20
291 Larry Robinson .02 .10
292 Dave Christian .01 .05
293 Steve Chiasson .01 .05
294 Brian Skrudland .01 .05
295 Pat Elynuik .01 .05
296 Curtis Joseph .07 .20
297 Doug Bodger .01 .05
298 Ron Sutter .01 .05
299 Joe Murphy .01 .05
300 Vincent Damphousse .01 .05
301 Cam Neely CC .02 .10
302 Rick Tocchet CC .01 .05
303 Scott Stevens CC .01 .05
304 Ulf Samuelsson CC .01 .05
305 Jeremy Roenick CC .10 .25
306 The Hunter Brothers .01 .05
Dale Hunter
Mark Hunter
307 The Broten Brothers .01 .05
Aaron Broten
Neal Broten
308 The Cavallini Brothers .01 .05
Gino Cavallini
Paul Cavallini
309 The Miller Brothers .01 .05
Kelly Miller
Kevin Miller
310 Dennis Vaske TP .01 .05
311 Rob Pearson TP RC .01 .05
312 Jason Miller TP .01 .05
313 John LeClair TP RC .50 1.25
314 Bryan Marchment TP RC .02 .10
315 Gary Shuchuk TP .01 .05
316 Dominik Hasek TP RC UER 1.50 4.00
(Misspelled Dominic
on both sides)
317 Michel Picard TP RC .01 .05
318 Corey Millen TP RC .01 .05
319 Joe Sacco TP RC .01 .05
320 Reggie Savage TP RC .01 .05
321 Pat Murray TP .01 .05
322 Myles O'Connor TP .01 .05
323 Shawn Antoski TP .01 .05
324 Geoff Sanderson TP RC .02 .10
325 Chris Govedaris TP .01 .05
326 Alexei Gusarov TP RC .02 .10
327 Mike Sillinger TP .01 .05
328 Bob Wilkie TP .01 .05
329 Pat Jablonski TP RC .02 .10
330 David Emma RC .01 .05
Hobey Baker Award
331 Kirk Muller FP .01 .05
332 Pat LaFontaine FP .02 .10
333 Brian Leetch FP .02 .10
334 Rick Tocchet FP .01 .05
335 Mario Lemieux FP .10 .30
336 Joe Sakic FP .07 .20
337 Brett Hull FP .07 .20
338 Vincent Damphousse FP .01 .05
339 Trevor Linden FP .01 .05
340 Kevin Hatcher FP .01 .05
341 Pat Elynuik FP .01 .05
342 Patrick Roy DT .10 .30
343 Brian Leetch DT .02 .10
344 Ray Bourque DT .07 .20
345 Luc Robitaille DT .02 .10
346 Wayne Gretzky DT .20 .50
347 Brett Hull DT .07 .20
348 Ed Belfour ART .07 .20
349 Rob Blake ART .01 .05
350 Eric Weinrich ART .01 .05
351 Jaromir Jagr ART .07 .20
352 Sergei Fedorov ART .07 .20
353 Ken Hodge Jr. ART .01 .05
354 Eric Lindros Art .07 .20
355 Eric Lindros .07 .20
Awards and Honors
356 Eric Lindros .07 .20
'91 1st Rd Draft Choice
357 Dana Murzyn .01 .05
358 Adam Graves .02 .10
359 Ken Linseman .01 .05
360 Mike Keane .01 .05
361 Stephane Morin .01 .05
362 Grant Ledyard .01 .05
363 Kris King .01 .05
364 Paul Gillis .01 .05
365 Chris Dahlquist .01 .05
366 Paul Stanton .01 .05
367 Jeff Hackett .02 .10
368 Bob McGill .01 .05
369 Neil Wilkinson .01 .05
370 Rob Zettler .01 .05
371 Brett Hull MOY .07 .20
372 Paul Coffey 1000 .07 .20
373 Mark Messier 1000 .07 .20
374 Dave Taylor 1000 .01 .05
375 Michel Goulet 1000 .01 .05
376 Dale Hawerchuk 1000 .01 .05
377 The Turgeon Brothers .02 .10
Pierre Turgeon
Sylvain Turgeon
378 The Sutter Brothers .01 .05
Rich Sutter
Brian Sutter
Ron Sutter
379 The Mullen Brothers .02 .10
Brian Mullen
Joe Mullen
380 The Courtnall Brothers .01 .05
Geoff Courtnall
Russ Courtnall
381 Trevor Kidd TP .02 .10
382 Patrice Brisebois TP .01 .05
383 Mark Greig TP .01 .05
384 Kip Miller TP .01 .05
385 Drake Berehowsky TP .01 .05
386 Kevin Haller TP RC .01 .05
387 Dave Gagnon TP .01 .05
388 Jason Marshall TP .01 .05
389 Donald Audette TP .01 .05
390 Patrick Lebeau TP RC .01 .05
391 Alexander Godynyuk TP .01 .05
392 Jarrod Skalde TP RC .01 .05
393 Ken Sutton TP RC .01 .05
394 Sergei Kharin TP .01 .05
395 Andre Racicot TP RC .02 .10
396 Doug Weight TP RC .30 .75
397 Kevin Todd TP RC .01 .05
398 Tony Amonte TP RC .50 1.25
399 Kimbi Daniels TP .01 .05
400 Jeff Daniels TP .01 .05
401 Guy Lafleur .07 .20
Speed and Grace
402 Guy Lafleur .07 .20
Awards and Achievements
403 Guy Lafleur .07 .20
A Hall of Famer
404 Brett Hull SL .07 .20
405 Wayne Gretzky SL .20 .50
406 Wayne Gretzky SL .20 .50
407 Theo Fleury SL and .01 .05
Marty McSorley SL
408 Sergei Fedorov SL .07 .20
409 Al MacInnis SL .01 .05
410 Ed Belfour SL .07 .20
411 Ed Belfour SL .07 .20
412 Brett Hull HL .07 .20
(50 goals in 50 games)
413 Wayne Gretzky HL .20 .50
(700th goal)
414 San Jose Sharks .01 .05
415 Ray Bourque FP .07 .20
416 Pierre Turgeon FP .01 .05
417 Al MacInnis FP .01 .05
418 Jeremy Roenick FP .10 .25
419 Steve Yzerman FP .10 .30
420 Mark Messier FP .07 .20
421 John Cullen FP .01 .05
422 Wayne Gretzky FP .20 .50
423 Mike Modano FP .07 .20
424 Patrick Roy FP .10 .30
425 Stanley Cup Champs .02 .10
426 Mario Lemieux Smythe .10 .30
427 Wayne Gretzky .20 .50
Art Ross Trophy
428 Brett Hull .07 .20
Hart Memorial Trophy
429 Ray Bourque .07 .20
Norris Trophy
430 Ed Belfour .07 .20
Calder Trophy
431 Ed Belfour .07 .20
Vezina Trophy
432 Dirk Graham .01 .05
Frank J. Selke Trophy
433 Ed Belfour .07 .20
Jennings Trophy
434 Wayne Gretzky .20 .50
Lady Byng Trophy
435 Dave Taylor .01 .05
Bill Masterton Trophy
436 Randy Ladouceur .01 .05
437 Dave Tippett .01 .05
438 Clint Malarchuk .02 .10
439 Gordie Roberts .01 .05
440 Frank Pietrangelo .01 .05

1991-92 Score Canadian Bilingual

The 1991-92 Score Canadian hockey set features 660 standard-size cards. The set was released in two series of 330 cards each. The borders on the front of first series cards shade from red to white, top to bottom. The fronts of the second series cards shade from bright blue to white. The two series also differ in that first series cards have the player enclosed by a thin purple border and second series cards have a red border. At the top, the player's name is written over a hockey puck and the team name is printed below the picture in the lower right corner. A red border stripe at the bottom completes the front. In a horizontal format, the bilingual backs have biography, statistics, player profile, and a color close-up photo. An identical version (Score Canadian-English) to this set exists, with the difference being that the text on each card is strictly in English. There is no difference in card values for this version.

COMPLETE SET (660) 5.00 12.00
COMP.FACT.SET (660) 5.00 12.00
COMPLETE SERIES 1 (330) 2.50 6.00
COMPLETE SERIES 2 (330) 2.50 6.00
1 Brett Hull .08 .25
2 Al MacInnis .02 .10
3 Luc Robitaille .02 .10
4 Pierre Turgeon .02 .10
5 Brian Leetch .07 .20
6 Cam Neely .07 .20
7 John Cullen .01 .05
8 Trevor Linden .02 .10
9 Rick Tocchet .02 .10
10 John Vanbiesbrouck .02 .10
11 Steve Smith .01 .05
12 Doug Smail .01 .05
13 Craig Ludwig .01 .05
14 Paul Fenton .01 .05
15 Dirk Graham .01 .05
16 Brad McCrimmon .01 .05
17 Dean Evason .01 .05
18 Fredrik Olausson .01 .05
19 Guy Carbonneau .02 .10
20 Kevin Hatcher .02 .10
21 Paul Ranheim .01 .05
22 Claude Lemieux .01 .05
23 Vincent Riendeau .02 .10
24 Garth Butcher .01 .05
25 Joe Sakic .15 .40
26 Rick Vaive .01 .05
27 Rob Blake .02 .10
28 Mike Ricci .07 .20
29 Pat Flatley .01 .05
30 Bill Ranford .02 .10
31 Larry Murphy .02 .10
32 Bobby Smith .02 .10
33 Mike Krushelnyski .01 .05
34 Gerard Gallant .01 .05
35 Doug Wilson .02 .10
36 John Ogrodnick .01 .05
37 Mikhail Tatarinov .01 .05
38 Doug Crossman .01 .05
39 Mark Osborne .01 .05
40 Scott Stevens .02 .10
41 Ron Tugnutt .02 .10
42 Russ Courtnall .01 .05
43 Gord Murphy .01 .05
44 Greg Adams .01 .05
45 Christian Ruuttu .01 .05
46 Ken Daneyko .01 .05
47 Glenn Anderson .02 .10
48 Ray Ferraro .01 .05
49 Tony Tanti .01 .05
50 Ray Bourque .10 .30
51 Sergei Makarov .01 .05
52 Jim Johnson .01 .05
53 Troy Murray .01 .05
54 Shawn Burr .01 .05
55 Peter Ing .02 .10
56 Dale Hunter .01 .05
57 Tony Granato .01 .05
58 Curtis Leschyshyn .01 .05
59 Brian Mullen .01 .05
60 Ed Olczyk .01 .05
61 Mike Ramsey .01 .05
62 Dan Quinn .01 .05
63 Rich Sutter .01 .05
64 Terry Carkner .01 .05
65 Shayne Corson .01 .05
66 Peter Stastny .02 .10
67 Craig Muni .01 .05
68 Glenn Healy .02 .10
69 Phil Bourque .01 .05
70 Pat Verbeek .01 .05
71 Garry Galley .01 .05
72 Dave Gagner .01 .05
73 Bob Probert .02 .10
74 Craig Wolanin .01 .05
75 Patrick Roy .40 1.00
76 Keith Brown .01 .05
77 Gary Leeman .01 .05
78 Brent Ashton .01 .05
79 Randy Moller .01 .05
80 Mike Vernon .02 .10
81 Kelly Miller .01 .05
82 Ulf Samuelsson .01 .05
83 Todd Elik .01 .05
84 Uwe Krupp .01 .05
85 Rod Brind'Amour .07 .20
86 Dave Capuano .01 .05
87 Geoff Smith .01 .05
88 David Volek .01 .05
89 Bruce Driver .01 .05
90 Andy Moog .07 .20
91 Pelle Eklund .01 .05
92 Joey Kocur .02 .10
93 Mark Tinordi .01 .05
94 Steve Thomas .01 .05
95 Petr Svoboda .01 .05
96 Joel Otto .01 .05
97 Todd Krygier .01 .05
98 Jaromir Jagr .12 .30
99 Mike Liut .02 .10
100 Wayne Gretzky .50 1.25
101 Teppo Numminen .01 .05
102 Randy Burridge .01 .05
103 Michel Petit .01 .05
104 Tony McKegney .01 .05
105 Mathieu Schneider .01 .05
106 Daren Puppa .02 .10
107 Paul Cavallini .01 .05
108 Tim Kerr .01 .05
109 Kevin Lowe .02 .10
110 Kirk Muller .01 .05
111 Zarley Zalapski .01 .05
112 Mike Hough .01 .05
113 Ken Hodge Jr. .01 .05
114 Grant Fuhr .07 .20
115 Paul Coffey .07 .20
116 Wendel Clark .02 .10
117 Patrik Sundstrom .01 .05
118 Kevin Dineen .01 .05
119 Eric Desjardins .02 .10
120 Mike Richter .07 .20
121 Sergio Momesso .01 .05
122 Tony Hrkac .01 .05
123 Joe Reekie .01 .05
124 Petr Nedved .02 .10
125 Randy Carlyle .01 .05
126 Kevin Miller .01 .05
127 Rejean Lemelin .02 .10
128 Dino Ciccarelli .02 .10
129 Sylvain Cote .01 .05
130 Mats Sundin .07 .20
131 Eric Weinrich .01 .05
132 Daniel Berthiaume .02 .10
133 Keith Acton .01 .05
134 Benoit Hogue .01 .05
135 Mike Gartner .02 .10
136 Petr Klima .01 .05
137 Curt Giles .01 .05
138 Scott Pearson .01 .05
139 Luke Richardson .01 .05
140 Steve Larmer .02 .10
141 Ken Wregget .02 .10
142 Frank Musil .01 .05
143 Owen Nolan .07 .20
144 Keith Primeau .01 .05
145 Mark Recchi .07 .20
146 Don Sweeney .01 .05
147 Mike McPhee .01 .05
148 Ken Baumgartner .01 .05
149 Dave Lowry .01 .05
150 Geoff Courtnall .02 .10
151 Chris Terreri .02 .10
152 Dave Manson .01 .05
153 Bobby Holik .02 .10
154 Bob Kudelski .01 .05
155 Calle Johansson .01 .05
156 Mark Hunter .01 .05
157 Randy Gilhen .01 .05
158 Yves Racine .01 .05
159 Martin Gelinas .01 .05
160 Brian Bellows .01 .05
161 David Shaw .01 .05
162 Bob Carpenter .01 .05
163 Doug Brown .01 .05
164 Ulf Dahlen .01 .05
165 Denis Savard .02 .10
166 Paul Ysebaert .01 .05
167 Derek King .01 .05
168 Igor Larionov .01 .05
169 Bob Errey .01 .05
170 Joe Nieuwendyk .02 .10
171 Normand Rochefort .01 .05
172 John Tonelli .01 .05
173 David Reid .01 .05
174 Tom Kurvers .01 .05
175 Dimitri Khristich .01 .05
176 Bob Sweeney .01 .05
177 Rick Zombo .01 .05
178 Troy Mallette .01 .05
179 Bob Bassen .01 .05
180 John Druce .01 .05
181 Mike Craig .01 .05
182 John McIntyre .01 .05
183 Murray Baron .01 .05
184 Slava Fetisov .01 .05
185 Don Beaupre .02 .10
186 Brian Benning .01 .05
187 Dave Barr .01 .05
188 Petri Skriko .01 .05
189 Steve Konroyd .01 .05
190 Steve Yzerman .30 .75
191 Jon Casey .02 .10
192 Gary Nylund .01 .05
193 Michal Pivonka .01 .05
194 Alexei Kasatonov .01 .05
195 Garry Valk .01 .05
196 Darren Turcotte .01 .05
197 Chris Nilan .01 .05
198 Thomas Steen .01 .05
199 Gary Roberts .02 .10
200 Mario Lemieux .50 1.25
201 Michel Goulet .02 .10
202 Craig MacTavish .01 .05
203 Peter Sidorkiewicz .02 .10
204 Johan Garpenlov .01 .05
205 Steve Duchesne .01 .05
206 Dave Snuggerud .01 .05
207 Kjell Samuelsson .01 .05
208 Sylvain Turgeon .01 .05
209 Al Iafrate .02 .10
210 John MacLean .02 .10
211 Brian Hayward .02 .10
212 Cliff Ronning .01 .05
213 Ray Sheppard .01 .05
214 Dave Taylor .02 .10
215 Doug Lidster .01 .05
216 Peter Bondra .02 .10
217 Marty McSorley .01 .05
218 Doug Gilmour .02 .10
219 Paul MacDermid .01 .05
220 Jeremy Roenick .12 .30
221 Wayne Presley .01 .05
222 Jeff Norton .01 .05
223 Brian Propp .01 .05
224 Jimmy Carson .01 .05
225 Tom Barrasso .02 .10
226 Theo Fleury .01 .05
227 Carey Wilson .01 .05
228 Rod Langway .01 .05
229 Bryan Trottier .07 .20
230 James Patrick .01 .05
231 Dana Murzyn .01 .05
232 Rick Wamsley .02 .10
233 Dave McLlwain .01 .05
234 Tom Fergus .01 .05
235 Adam Graves .02 .10
236 Jacques Cloutier .02 .10
237 Gino Odjick .01 .05
238 Andrew Cassels .01 .05
239 Ken Linseman .01 .05
240 Danton Cole .01 .05
241 Dave Hannan .01 .05
242 Stephane Matteau .01 .05
243 Gerald Diduck .01 .05
244 Rick Tabaracci .02 .10
245 Sylvain Lefebvre .01 .05
246 Bob Rouse .01 .05
247 Charlie Huddy .01 .05
248 Mike Foligno .01 .05
249 Ric Nattress .01 .05
250 Aaron Broten .01 .05
251 Mike Keane .01 .05
252 Steve Bozek .01 .05
253 Jeff Beukeboom .01 .05
254 Stephane Morin .01 .05
255 Brian Bradley .01 .05
256 Scott Arniel .01 .05
257 Robert Kron .01 .05
258 Anatoli Semenov .01 .05
259 Brent Gilchrist .01 .05
260 Jim Sandlak .01 .05
261 Brett Hull (Man of Year) .07 .20
262 Paul Coffey 1000 PTS .02 .10
263 Mark Messier 1000 PTS .07 .20
264 Dave Taylor 1000 PTS .01 .05
265 Michel Goulet 1000 PTS .01 .05
266 Dale Hawerchuk 1000 PTS .01 .05
267 The Turgeon Brothers .02 .10
Pierre Turgeon
Sylvain Turgeon
268 The Sutter Brothers .01 .05
Rich Sutter
Brian Sutter
Ron Sutter
269 The Mullen Brothers .02 .10
Brian Mullen
Joe Mullen
270 The Courtnall Brothers .01 .05
Geoff Courtnall
Russ Courtnall
271 Trevor Kidd TP .02 .10
272 Patrice Brisebois TP .01 .05
273 Mark Greig TP .01 .05
274 Kip Miller TP .01 .05
275 Drake Berehowsky TP .01 .05
276 Kevin Haller TP RC .01 .05
277 Dave Gagnon TP .01 .05
278 Jason Marshall TP .01 .05
279 Donald Audette TP .01 .05
280 Patrick Lebeau TP RC .01 .05
281 Alexander Godynyuk TP .01 .05
282 Jarrod Skalde TP RC .01 .05
283 Ken Sutton TP RC .01 .05
284 Sergei Kharin TP .01 .05
285 Andre Racicot TP RC .02 .10
286 Doug Weight TP RC .30 .75
287 Kevin Todd TP RC .01 .05
288 Tony Amonte TP RC .50 1.25
289 Kimbi Daniels TP .01 .05
290 Jeff Daniels TP .01 .05
291 Guy Lafleur .07 .20
Speed and Grace
292 Guy Lafleur .07 .20
Awards and Achievements
293 Guy Lafleur .07 .20
A Hall of Famer
294 Brett Hull SL .07 .20
295 Wayne Gretzky SL .20 .50
296 Wayne Gretzky SL .20 .50
297 Theo Fleury and .01 .05
Marty McSorley SL
298 Sergei Fedorov SL .07 .20
299 Al MacInnis SL .01 .05
300 Ed Belfour SL .07 .20
301 Ed Belfour SL .07 .20
302 Brett Hull 50/50 .07 .20
303 Wayne Gretzky .20 .50
700th Career Goal
304 San Jose Sharks Logo .01 .05
305 Cam Neely Crunch .02 .10
306 Rick Tocchet Crunch .01 .05
307 Scott Stevens Crunch .01 .05
308 Ulf Samuelsson Crunch .01 .05
309 Jeremy Roenick Crunch .10 .25
310 Mark Messier FRAN .07 .20
311 John Cullen FRAN .01 .05
312 Wayne Gretzky FRAN .20 .50
313 Mike Modano FRAN .07 .20
314 Patrick Roy FRAN .10 .30
315 Stanley Cup Champs .02 .10
316 Mario Lemieux Smythe .10 .30
317 Wayne Gretzky .20 .50
Art Ross Trophy
318 Brett Hull .07 .20
Hart Memorial Trophy
319 Ray Bourque .07 .20
Norris Trophy
320 Ed Belfour .07 .20
Calder Trophy
321 Ed Belfour .07 .20
Vezina Trophy
322 Dirk Graham .01 .05
Frank J. Selke Trophy
323 Ed Belfour .07 .20
Jennings Trophy
324 Wayne Gretzky .20 .50
Lady Byng Trophy
325 Dave Taylor .01 .05
Bill Masterton Trophy
326 Jeff Hackett .02 .10
327 Bob McGill .01 .05
328 Neil Wilkinson .01 .05
329 Eric Lindros .07 .20
1st Rd Draft Choice
330 Eric Lindros .07 .20
Awards and Honors
331 Ray Bourque FP .07 .20
332 Pierre Turgeon FP .01 .05
333 Al MacInnis FP .01 .05
334 Jeremy Roenick FP .10 .25
335 Steve Yzerman FP .12 .30
336 The Hunter Brothers .01 .05
Dale Hunter
Mark Hunter
337 The Broten Brothers .01 .05
Neal Broten
Aaron Broten
338 The Cavallini Brothers .01 .05
Gino Cavallini
Paul Cavallini
339 The Miller Brothers .01 .05
Kelly Miller
Kevin Miller
340 Dennis Vaske TP .01 .05
341 Rob Pearson TP RC .01 .05
342 Jason Miller TP .01 .05
343 John LeClair TP RC .50 1.25
344 Bryan Marchment TP RC .02 .10
345 Gary Shuchuk TP .01 .05
346 Dominik Hasek TP RC .75 2.00
347 Michel Picard TP RC .01 .05
348 Corey Millen TP RC .01 .05
349 Joe Sacco TP RC .01 .05
350 Reggie Savage TP RC .01 .05
351 Pat Murray TP .01 .05
352 Myles O'Connor TP .01 .05
353 Shawn Antoski TP .01 .05
354 Geoff Sanderson TP RC .08 .25
355 Chris Govedaris TP .01 .05
356 Alexei Gusarov TP RC .02 .10
357 Mike Sillinger TP .01 .05
358 Bob Wilkie TP .01 .05
359 Pat Jablonski TP RC .02 .10
360 Memorial Cup .01 .05
Spokane Chiefs
361 Kirk Muller FP .01 .05
362 Pat LaFontaine FP .02 .10
363 Brian Leetch FP .02 .10
364 Rick Tocchet FP .01 .05
365 Mario Lemieux FP .10 .30
366 Joe Sakic FP .07 .20
367 Brett Hull FP .07 .20
368 Vincent Damphousse FP .01 .05
369 Trevor Linden FP .01 .05
370 Kevin Hatcher FP .01 .05
371 Pat Elynuik FP .01 .05

372 Patrick Roy DT .10 .30
373 Brian Leetch DT .02 .10
374 Ray Bourque DT .07 .20
375 Luc Robitaille DT .02 .10
376 Wayne Gretzky DT .20 .50
377 Brett Hull DT .07 .20
378 Ed Belfour ART .07 .20
379 Rob Blake ART .01 .05
380 Eric Weinrich ART .01 .05
381 Jaromir Jagr ART .07 .20
382 Sergei Fedorov ART .07 .20
383 Ken Hodge Jr. ART .01 .05
384 Eric Lindros Art .07 .20
385 Eric Lindros .07 .20
with Rob Pearson
386 Ottawa/Tampa Bay .07 .20
Logo Card
387 Mick Vukota .01 .05
388 Lou Franceschetti .01 .05
389 Mike Hudson .01 .05
390 Frantisek Kucera .01 .05
391 Basil McRae .01 .05
392 Donald Dufresne .01 .05
393 Tommy Albelin .01 .05
394 Normand Lacombe .01 .05
395 Lucien DeBlois .01 .05
396 Tony Twist RC .07 .20
397 Rob Murphy .01 .05
398 Ken Sabourin .01 .05
399 Doug Evans .01 .05
400 Walt Poddubny .01 .05
401 Grant Ledyard .01 .05
402 Kris King .01 .05
403 Paul Gillis .01 .05
404 Chris Dahlquist .01 .05
405 Zdeno Ciger .01 .05
406 Paul Stanton .01 .05
407 Randy Ladouceur .01 .05
408 Ronnie Stern .01 .05
409 Dave Tippett .01 .05
410 Jeff Reese .01 .05
411 Vladimir Ruzicka .01 .05
412 Brent Fedyk .01 .05
413 Paul Cyr .01 .05
414 Mike Eagles .01 .05
415 Chris Joseph .01 .05
416 Brad Marsh .01 .05
417 Rich Pilon .01 .05
418 Jiri Hrdina .01 .05
419 Clint Malarchuk .02 .10
420 Steven Rice .01 .05
421 Mark Janssens .01 .05
422 Gordie Roberts .01 .05
423 Shawn Cronin .01 .05
424 Randy Cunneyworth .01 .05
425 Frank Pietrangelo .01 .05
426 David Maley .01 .05
427 Rod Buskas .01 .05
428 Dennis Vial .01 .05
429 Kelly Buchberger .01 .05
430 Wes Walz .01 .05
431 Dean Kennedy .01 .05
432 Nick Kypreos .01 .05
433 Stewart Gavin .01 .05
434 Norm Maciver RC .01 .05
435 Mark Pederson .01 .05
436 Laurie Boschman .01 .05
437 Stephane Quintal .01 .05
438 Darrin Shannon .01 .05
439 Trent Yawney .01 .05
440 Gaetan Duchesne .01 .05
441 Joe Cirella .01 .05
442 Doug Houda .01 .05
443 Dave Chyzowski .01 .05
444 Derrick Smith .01 .05
445 Jeff Lazaro .01 .05
446 Brian Glynn .01 .05
447 Jocelyn Lemieux .01 .05
448 Peter Taglianetti .01 .05
449 Adam Burt .01 .05
450 Hubie McDonough .01 .05
451 Kelly Hrudey .02 .10
452 Dave Poulin .01 .05
453 Mark Hardy .01 .05
454 Mike Hartman .01 .05
455 Chris Chelios .07 .20
456 Alexander Mogilny .07 .20
457 Bryan Fogarty .01 .05
458 Adam Oates .02 .10
459 Ron Hextall .02 .10
460 Bernie Nicholls .02 .10
461 Esa Tikkanen .01 .05
462 Jyrki Lumme .01 .05
463 Brent Sutter .01 .05
464 Gary Suter .01 .05
465 Sean Burke .02 .10
466 Rob Brown .01 .05
467 Mike Modano .15 .40
468 Kevin Stevens .01 .05
469 Mike Lalor .01 .05
470 Sergei Fedorov .12 .30
471 Bob Essensa .02 .10
472 Mark Howe .01 .05
473 Craig Janney .02 .10
474 Daniel Marois .01 .05
475 Craig Simpson .01 .05
476 Marc Bureau .01 .05
477 Randy Velischek .01 .05
478 Gino Cavallini .01 .05
479 Dale Hawerchuk .02 .10
480 Pat LaFontaine .07 .20
481 Kirk McLean .02 .10
482 Murray Craven .01 .05
483 Robert Reichel .01 .05
484 Jan Erixon .01 .05
485 Adam Creighton .01 .05
486 Mark Fitzpatrick .02 .10
487 Ron Francis .02 .10
488 Joe Mullen .02 .10
489 Peter Zezel .01 .05
490 Tomas Sandstrom .01 .05
491 Phil Housley .02 .10
492 Tim Cheveldae .02 .10
493 Glen Wesley .01 .05
494 Stephan Lebeau .01 .05
495 Dave Ellett .01 .05
496 Jeff Brown .01 .05
497 Dave Andreychuk .02 .10
498 Steven Finn .01 .05
499 Mike Donnelly RC .01 .05
500 Neal Broten .02 .10
501 Randy Wood .01 .05
502 Troy Gamble .02 .10
503 Mike Ridley .01 .05
504 Jamie Macoun .01 .05
505 Mark Messier .07 .20
506 Moe Mantha .01 .05
507 Scott Young .01 .05
508 Robert Dirk .01 .05
509 Brad Shaw .01 .05
510 Ed Belfour .07 .20
511 Larry Robinson .02 .10
512 Dale Kushner .01 .05
513 Steve Chiasson .01 .05
514 Brian Skrudland .01 .05
515 Pat Elynuik .01 .05
516 Curtis Joseph .07 .20
517 Doug Bodger .01 .05
518 Greg Brown .01 .05
519 Joe Murphy .01 .05
520 J.J. Daigneault .01 .05
521 Todd Gill .01 .05
522 Troy Loney .01 .05
523 Tim Watters .01 .05
524 Jody Hull .01 .05
525 Colin Patterson .01 .05
526 Darin Kimble .01 .05
527 Perry Berezan .01 .05
528 Lee Norwood .01 .05
529 Mike Peluso .01 .05
530 Wayne McBean .01 .05
531 Grant Jennings .01 .05
532 Claude Loiselle .01 .05
533 Ron Wilson .01 .05
534 Phil Sykes .01 .05
535 Jim Wiemer .01 .05
536 Herb Raglan .01 .05
537 Tim Hunter .01 .05
538 Mike Tomlak .01 .05
539 Greg Gilbert .01 .05
540 Jiri Latal .01 .05
541 Bill Berg .01 .05
542 Shane Churla .01 .05
543 Jay Miller .01 .05
544 Pete Peeters .02 .10
545 Alan May .01 .05
546 Mario Marois .01 .05
547 Jim Kyte .01 .05
548 Jon Morris .01 .05
549 Mikko Makela .01 .05
550 Nelson Emerson .01 .05
551 Doug Wilson .02 .10
552 Brian Mullen .01 .05
553 Kelly Kisio .01 .05
554 Brian Hayward .02 .10
555 Tony Hrkac .01 .05
556 Steve Bozek .01 .05
557 John Carter .01 .05
558 Neil Wilkinson .01 .05
559 Wayne Presley .01 .05
560 Bob McGill .01 .05
561 Craig Ludwig .01 .05
562 Mikhail Tatarinov .01 .05
563 Todd Elik .01 .05
564 Randy Burridge .01 .05
565 Tim Kerr .01 .05
566 Randy Gilhen .01 .05
567 John Tonelli .01 .05
568 Tom Kurvers .01 .05
569 Steve Duchesne .01 .05
570 Charlie Huddy .01 .05
571 Alan Kerr .01 .05
572 Shawn Chambers .01 .05
573 Rob Ramage .01 .05
574 Steve Kasper .01 .05
575 Scott Mellanby .01 .05
576 Stephen Leach .01 .05
577 Scott Niedermayer .01 .05
578 Craig Berube .01 .05
579 Greg Paslawski .01 .05
580 Randy Hillier .01 .05
581 Stephane Richer .02 .10
582 Brian MacLellan .01 .05
583 Marc Habscheid .01 .05
584 Dave Babych .01 .05
585 Troy Murray .01 .05
586 Ray Sheppard .01 .05
587 Glen Featherstone .01 .05
588 Brendan Shanahan .07 .20
589 Dave Christian .01 .05
590 Mike Bullard .01 .05
591 Ryan Walter .01 .05
592 Doug Smail .01 .05
593 Paul Fenton .01 .05
594 Adam Graves .02 .10
595 Scott Stevens .02 .10
596 Sylvain Cote .01 .05
597 Dave Barr .01 .05
598 Randy Gregg .01 .05
599 Allen Pedersen .01 .05
600 Jari Kurri .07 .20
601 Troy Mallette .01 .05
602 Troy Crowder .01 .05
603 Brad Jones .01 .05
604 Randy McKay .01 .05
605 Scott Thornton .01 .05
606 Bryan Marchment RC .02 .10
607 Andrew Cassels .01 .05
608 Grant Fuhr .07 .20
609 Vincent Damphousse .01 .05
610 Robert Ray .01 .05
611 Glenn Anderson .02 .10
612 Peter Ing .02 .10
613 Tom Chorske .01 .05
614 Kirk Muller .01 .05
615 Dan Quinn .01 .05
616 Murray Baron .01 .05
617 Sergei Nemchinov .01 .05
618 Rod Brind'Amour .07 .20
619 Ron Sutter .01 .05
620 Luke Richardson .01 .05
621 Nicklas Lidstrom RC .40 1.00
622 Ken Linseman .01 .05
623 Steve Smith .01 .05
624 Dave Manson .01 .05
625 Kay Whitmore .02 .10
626 Jeff Chychrun .01 .05
627 Russ Romaniuk RC .01 .05
628 Brad May .01 .05
629 Tomas Forslund RC .01 .05
630 Stu Barnes .01 .05
631 Darryl Sydor .02 .10
632 Jimmy Waite .02 .10
633 Peter Douris .01 .05
634 Dave Brown .01 .05
635 Mark Messier .07 .20
636 Neil Sheehy .01 .05
637 Todd Krygier .01 .05
638 Stephane Beauregard .02 .10
639 Barry Pederson .01 .05
640 Pat Falloon .01 .05
641 Dean Evason .01 .05
642 Jeff Hackett .02 .10
643 Rob Zettler .01 .05
644 David Bruce RC .01 .05
645 Pat MacLeod RC .01 .05
646 Craig Coxe .01 .05
647 Ken Hammond RC .01 .05
648 Brian Lawton .01 .05
649 Perry Anderson .01 .05
650 Kevin Evans .01 .05
651 Mike McHugh .01 .05
652 Mark Lamb .01 .05
653 Darcy Wakaluk RC .02 .10
654 Pat Conacher .01 .05
655 Martin Lapointe .02 .10
656 Derian Hatcher .02 .10
657 Bryan Erickson .01 .05
658 Ken Priestlay .01 .05
659 Vladimir Konstantinov RC .20 .50
660 Andrei Lomakin .01 .05

1991-92 Score Bobby Orr

This six-card standard-size set highlights the career of Bobby Orr, one of hockey's all-time greats. The cards were inserted in 1991-92 Score hockey poly packs. Cards 1 and 2 were inserted in both American and Canadian editions. Cards 3 and 4 were inserted in Canadian packs, while cards 5 and 6 were inserted in American packs. On a black card face, the fronts feature color player photos enclosed by a thin red border and accented by yellow borders on three sides. The backs carry a close-up color photo and biographical comments on Orr's career. The cards are not numbered on the back. It is claimed that 270,000 of these Orr cards were produced, and that Orr personally signed 2,500 of each of these cards. The personally autographed cards are autographed on the card back. They are slightly different in design.

COMMON ORR (1-6) 3.00 8.00
AU Bobby Orr AU 125.00 250.00
(Autographed card)

1991-92 Score Eric Lindros

This three-card standard-size set was produced by Score and distributed in a cello pack with the first printing of Eric Lindros' autobiography "Fire on Ice". The cards feature on the fronts color photos that capture three different moments in Lindros' life (childhood, adolescence, and NHL Entry Draft). The pictures are bordered on all sides by light blue, with the player's name in block lettering between two red stripes at the card top. A red stripe at the bottom separates the picture from its title line. The backs have relevant biographical comments as well as a second color photo. The cards are unnumbered and checklisted below in chronological order.

COMPLETE SET (3) 6.00 15.00
COMMON LINDROS (1-3) 2.00 5.00

1991-92 Score Hot Cards

The 1991-92 Score Hot cards were inserted in American and Canadian English 100-card blister packs at a rate of one per pack. The standard size cards feature on the fronts color action player photos bordered in bright red. Thin yellow stripes accent the photos, and the player's name appears beneath the picture in a purple stripe. The back design reflects the same three colors as the front and features a color head shot, team logo, and player profile. The cards are numbered on the back. Hot Cards differ in design, photos, and text from the regular issues.

COMPLETE SET (10) 8.00 20.00
1 Eric Lindros .75 2.00
2 Wayne Gretzky 3.00 8.00
3 Brett Hull 1.00 2.50
4 Sergei Fedorov 1.25 3.00
5 Mario Lemieux 4.00 10.00
6 Adam Oates .40 1.00
7 Theo Fleury .20 .50
8 Jaromir Jagr 1.25 3.00
9 Ed Belfour .75 2.00
10 Jeremy Roenick 1.00 2.50

1991-92 Score Rookie/Traded

The 1991-92 Score Rookie and Traded hockey set contains 110 standard-size cards. It was issued only as a factory set. As one moves down the card face, the fronts shade from dark green to white. The color action player photo is enclosed by an thin red border, with a shadow border on the right and below. At the card top, the player's name is written over a hockey puck, and the team name is printed below the picture in the lower right corner. A dark green border stripe at the bottom rounds out the front. In a horizontal format, the backs present biography, statistics, player profile, and a color close-up photo. The cards are numbered on the back with a "T" suffix. The set includes Eric Lindros pictured in his World Junior uniform. The back of the set's custom box contains the set checklist. The key Rookie Cards in this set are Valeri Kamensky and Nicklas Lidstrom.

COMP. FACT SET (110) 1.50 4.00
1T Doug Wilson .02 .10
2T Brian Mullen .01 .05
3T Kelly Kisio .01 .05
4T Brian Hayward .02 .10
5T Tony Hrkac .01 .05
6T Steve Bozek .01 .05
7T John Carter .01 .05
8T Neil Wilkinson .01 .05
9T Wayne Presley .01 .05
10T Bob McGill .01 .05
11T Craig Ludwig .01 .05
12T Mikhail Tatarinov .01 .05
13T Todd Elik .01 .05
14T Randy Burridge .01 .05
15T Tim Kerr .01 .05
16T Randy Gilhen .01 .05
17T John Tonelli .01 .05
18T Tom Kurvers .01 .05
19T Steve Duchesne .01 .05
20T Charlie Huddy .01 .05
21T Adam Creighton .01 .05
22T Brent Ashton .01 .05
23T Rob Ramage .01 .05
24T Steve Kasper .01 .05
25T Scott Mellanby .01 .05
26T Stephen Leach .01 .05
27T Scott Niedermayer .01 .05
28T Craig Berube .01 .05
29T Greg Paslawski .01 .05
30T Randy Hillier .01 .05
31T Stephane Richer .02 .10
32T Brian MacLellan .01 .05
33T Marc Habscheid .01 .05
34T Dave Babych .01 .05
35T Troy Murray .01 .05
36T Ray Sheppard .01 .05
37T Glen Featherstone .01 .05
38T Brendan Shanahan .08 .25
39T Dave Christian .01 .05
40T Mike Bullard .01 .05
41T Ryan Walter .01 .05
42T Randy Wood .01 .05
43T Vincent Riendeau .02 .10
44T Adam Graves .02 .10
45T Scott Stevens .02 .10
46T Sylvain Cote .01 .05
47T Dave Barr .01 .05
48T Randy Gregg .01 .05
49T Pavel Bure .08 .25
50T Jari Kurri .08 .25
51T Steve Thomas .01 .05
52T Troy Crowder .01 .05
53T Brad Jones .01 .05
54T Randy McKay .01 .05
55T Scott Thornton .01 .05
56T Bryan Marchment .02 .10
57T Andrew Cassels .01 .05
58T Grant Fuhr .08 .25
59T Vincent Damphousse .01 .05
60T Rick Zombo .01 .05
61T Glenn Anderson .02 .10
62T Peter Ing .02 .10
63T Tom Chorske .01 .05
64T Kirk Muller .01 .05
65T Dan Quinn .01 .05
66T Murray Baron .01 .05
67T Sergei Nemchinov .01 .05
68T Rod Brind'Amour .08 .25
69T Ron Sutter .01 .05
70T Luke Richardson .01 .05
71T Nicklas Lidstrom RC .40 1.00
72T Petri Skriko .01 .05
73T Steve Smith .01 .05
74T Dave Manson .01 .05
75T Kay Whitmore .02 .10
76T Valeri Kamensky RC .02 .10
77T Russ Romaniuk RC .01 .05
78T Brad May .01 .05
79T Tomas Forslund RC .01 .05
80T Stu Barnes .01 .05
81T Darryl Sydor .02 .10
82T Jimmy Waite .02 .10
83T Vladimir Ruzicka .01 .05
84T Dave Brown .01 .05
85T Mark Messier .08 .25
86T Neil Sheehy .01 .05
87T Todd Krygier .01 .05
88T Eric Lindros .08 .25
89T Nelson Emerson .01 .05
90T Pat Falloon .01 .05
91T Dean Evason .01 .05
92T Jeff Hackett .02 .10
93T Rob Zettler .01 .05
94T Perry Berezan .01 .05
95T Pat MacLeod RC .01 .05
96T Craig Coxe .01 .05
97T Ken Hammond RC .01 .05
98T Brian Lawton .01 .05
99T Perry Anderson .01 .05
100T Pat LaFontaine .08 .25
101T Pierre Turgeon .02 .10
102T Dave McLlwain .01 .05
103T Brent Sutter .01 .05
104T Uwe Krupp .01 .05
105T Martin Lapointe .02 .10
106T Derian Hatcher .02 .10
107T Darrin Shannon .01 .05
108T Benoit Hogue .01 .05
109T Vladimir Konstantinov RC .20 .50
110T Andrei Lomakin .01 .05

1991-92 Score Kellogg's

This 24-card standard-size set was produced by Score as a promotion for Kellogg's Canada. Two-card foil packs were inserted in specially marked 675-gram Kellogg's Corn Flakes cereals. The side panel of the cereal boxes presented a mail-in offer for the complete set and a card binder for 5.99 plus three proof of purchase tokens (one token featured per side panel). Card fronts have player action photos enclosed in a small red border, player's name in white reverse-out lettering, and team logo in bottom portion of the purple border. Card backs, also in purple, red, and white, carry the card number, Kellogg's Limited Edition Collector's Set logo, biography, statistics, and player profile in English and French.

COMPLETE SET (24) 14.00 35.00
1 Patrick Roy 3.20 8.00
2 Rick Tocchet .40 1.00
3 Wendel Clark .40 1.00
4 Mike Modano .80 2.00
5 Jeremy Roenick .60 1.50
6 Pierre Turgeon .40 1.00
7 Kevin Hatcher .20 .50
8 Brian Leetch .60 1.50
9 Mark Recchi .40 1.00
10 Andy Moog .40 1.00
11 Kevin Dineen .20 .50
12 Joe Sakic 1.20 3.00
13 John MacLean .20 .50
14 Steve Yzerman 2.00 5.00
15 Pat LaFontaine .40 1.00
16 Al MacInnis .40 1.00
17 Petr Klima .20 .50
18 Ed Olczyk .20 .50
19 Doug Wilson .20 .50
20 Trevor Linden .20 .50
21 Brett Hull .80 2.00
22 Rob Blake .20 .50
23 Dave Ellett .20 .50
24 Cornelius Rooster SP .80 2.00
Kellogg's mascot
NNO Card Binder 2.00 5.00

1991-92 Score Young Superstars

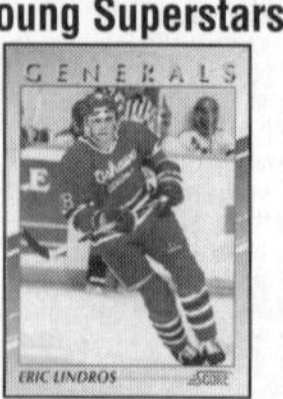

This 40-card standard-size set was issued by Score to showcase some of the leading young hockey players. The color action player photos on the fronts are framed in green on a card face consisting of blended diagonal taupe stripes. In a horizontal format, the backs have a color head shot on the left half while the right half carries biography, "Rink Report," and career statistics.

COMP. FACT SET (40) 4.00 10.00
1 Sergei Fedorov .60 1.50
2 Mike Richter .30 .75
3 Mats Sundin .30 .75
4 Theo Fleury .30 .75
5 John Cullen .06 .15
6 Dimitri Khristich .06 .15
7 Stephan Lebeau .06 .15
8 Rob Blake .30 .75
9 Ken Hodge Jr. .06 .15
10 Mike Ricci .16 .40
11 Trevor Linden .16 .40
12 Peter Ing .16 .40
13 Alexander Mogilny .16 .40
14 Martin Gelinas .06 .15
15 Chris Terreri .16 .40
16 Jeff Norton .06 .15
17 Bob Essensa .16 .40
18 Mark Tinordi .06 .15
19 Curtis Joseph .30 .75
20 Joe Sakic .60 1.50
21 Jeremy Roenick .30 .75
22 Mark Recchi .16 .40
23 Eric Desjardins .16 .40
24 Robert Reichel .06 .15
25 Tim Cheveldae .16 .40
26 Eric Weinrich .06 .15
27 Murray Baron .06 .15
28 Darren Turcotte .06 .15
29 Troy Gamble .16 .40
30 Eric Lindros 1.00 2.50
31 Benoit Hogue .06 .15
32 Ed Belfour .30 .75
33 Ron Tugnutt .16 .40
34 Pat Elynuik .06 .15
35 Mike Modano .30 .75
36 Bobby Holik .16 .40
37 Yves Racine .06 .15
38 Jaromir Jagr 1.00 2.50
39 Stephane Morin .06 .15
40 Kevin Miller .06 .15

1992-93 Score Canadian Promo Sheets

These two 5" by 7" promotional sheets each feature four uncut cards. If the cards were cut, they would measure the standard size. The fronts feature color action player photos bordered at the top and bottom by black stripes containing the player's name and position. The outer borders are metallic-blue with diagonal stripes formed by an alternating matte and glossy finish. The backs have the disclaimers "For Promotional Purposes Only" and "Not For Resale" overprinted in magenta. They show a white background with a narrow color player photo running along the left edge. Biography and career highlights are contained in a graded blue panel with black borders. Statistical information appears at the bottom. The cards are numbered on the back and are listed below as the appear on the sheets from left to right starting with the top row.

COMPLETE SET (2) 2.00 5.00
1 Promo Sheet 1 .80 2.00
6 Pat LaFontaine
25 Kevin Stevens
2 Chris Chelios
16 Esa Tikkanen
2 Promo Sheet 2 1.60 4.00
5 Mike Richter
14 Pavel Bure
6 Pat LaFontaine
25 Kevin Stevens

1992-93 Score

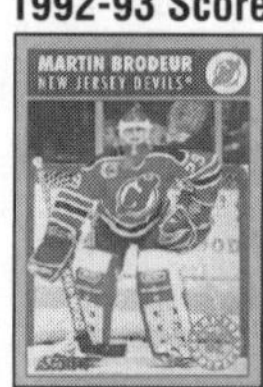

The 1992-93 Score hockey set contains 550 standard-size cards. The American and Canadian sets are identical in terms of player selection (except for card numbers 548-549) but feature different insert subsets (USA Greats in the American and Canadian Olympic Heroes in the Canadian). Moreover, the player photos and card design differ in each set. In the American set, the color action photos on the fronts have two-toned borders on three sides (icy gray diagonal stripes accented by either red, blue, or black); in the Canadian, the front borders are metallic blue with diagonally varnished stripes. The American backs are horizontally oriented and include biography, statistics, career summary, and a close-up photo; the Canadian backs are vertically oriented, bilingual, and have the same features in a different layout. A special Eric Lindros card, unnumbered and featuring his first photo in a Philadelphia Flyers uniform, was randomly inserted into packs. Reportedly more than 500 of these special Lindros "Press Conference" cards were given away to news media, members of the Flyers organization, and other guests attending the July 15 news conference which marked Lindros' signing with the Flyers. It is claimed that the odds of finding one of these cards are no less than one in 500 packs. Rookie Cards include Guy Hebert and Yanic Perrault.

COMPLETE SET (550) 7.50 15.00
*US AND CDN: SAME VALUE
1 Wayne Gretzky .50 1.25
2 Chris Chelios .08 .25
3 Joe Mullen .02 .10
4 Russ Courtnall .01 .05
5 Mike Richter .08 .25
6 Pat LaFontaine .08 .25
7 Mark Tinordi .01 .05
8 Claude Lemieux .01 .05
9 Jimmy Carson .01 .05
10 Cam Neely .08 .25
11 Al Iafrate .02 .10
12 Steve Thomas .02 .10
13 Fredrik Olausson .01 .05
14 Pavel Bure .08 .25
15 Doug Wilson .02 .10
16 Esa Tikkanen .01 .05
17 Gary Suter .01 .05
18 Murray Craven .01 .05
19 Garry Galley .01 .05
20 Grant Fuhr .08 .25
21 Craig Wolanin .01 .05
22 Paul Cavallini .01 .05
23 Eric Desjardins .02 .10
24 Joey Kocur .02 .10
25 Kevin Stevens .01 .05
26 Marty McSorley .01 .05
27 Dirk Graham .01 .05
28 Mike Ramsey .01 .05
29 Gord Murphy .01 .05
30 John MacLean .02 .10
31 Vladimir Konstantinov .08 .25
32 Neal Broten .02 .10
33 Dimitri Khristich .01 .05
34 Gerald Diduck .01 .05
35 Ken Baumgartner .01 .05
36 Darrin Shannon .01 .05
37 Steve Bozek .01 .05
38 Michel Petit .01 .05
39 Kevin Lowe .02 .10
40 Doug Gilmour .02 .10
41 Peter Sidorkiewicz .02 .10
42 Gino Cavallini .01 .05
43 Dan Quinn .02 .10
44 Steven Finn .01 .05
45 Larry Murphy .02 .10
46 Brent Gilchrist .01 .05
47 Daren Puppa .02 .10
48 Steve Smith .01 .05
49 Dave Taylor .02 .10
50 Mike Gartner .02 .10
51 Derian Hatcher .01 .05
52 Bob Probert .02 .10
53 Ken Daneyko .01 .05
54 Steve Leach .01 .05
55 Kelly Miller .01 .05
56 Jeff Norton .01 .05
57 Kelly Kisio .01 .05
58 Igor Larionov .01 .05
59 Paul MacDermid .01 .05
60 Mike Vernon .02 .10
61 Randy Ladouceur .01 .05
62 Luke Richardson .01 .05
63 Daniel Marois .01 .05
64 Mike Hough .01 .05
65 Garth Butcher .01 .05
66 Terry Carkner .01 .05
67 Mike Donnelly .01 .05
68 Keith Brown .01 .05
69 Mathieu Schneider .01 .05
70 Tom Barrasso .02 .10
71 Adam Graves .01 .05
72 Brian Propp .01 .05
73 Randy Wood .01 .05
74 Yves Racine .01 .05
75 Scott Stevens .02 .10
76 Chris Nilan .01 .05
77 Uwe Krupp .01 .05
78 Sylvain Cote .01 .05
79 Sergio Momesso .01 .05
80 Thomas Steen .01 .05
81 Craig Muni .01 .05
82 Jeff Hackett .02 .10
83 Frank Musil .01 .05
84 Mike Ricci .02 .10
85 Brad Shaw .01 .05
86 Ron Sutter .01 .05
87 Curtis Leschyshyn .01 .05
88 Jamie Macoun .01 .05
89 Brian Noonan .01 .05
90 Ulf Samuelsson .01 .05
91 Mike McPhee .01 .05
92 Charlie Huddy .01 .05
93 Tim Kerr .01 .05
94 Craig Ludwig .01 .05
95 Paul Ysebaert .01 .05
96 Brad May .01 .05
97 Slava Fetisov .01 .05
98 Todd Krygier .01 .05
99 Patrick Flatley .01 .05
100 Ray Bourque .15 .40
101 Petr Nedved .02 .10
102 Teppo Numminen .01 .05
103 Dean Evason .01 .05
104 Ron Hextall .02 .10
105 Josef Beranek .01 .05
106 Robert Reichel .01 .05
107 Mikhail Tatarinov .01 .05
108 Geoff Sanderson .02 .10
109 Dave Lowry .01 .05
110 Wendel Clark .02 .10
111 Corey Millen UER .01 .05
(Mike Donnelly pictured on front)
112 Brent Sutter .01 .05
113 Jaromir Jagr .12 .30
114 Petr Svoboda .01 .05
115 Sergei Nemchinov .01 .05
116 Tony Tanti .01 .05
117 Stewart Gavin .01 .05
118 Doug Brown .01 .05
119 Gerard Gallant .01 .05
120 Andy Moog .08 .25
121 John Druce .01 .05
122 Dave McLlwain .01 .05
123 Bob Essensa .02 .10
124 Doug Lidster .01 .05
125 Pat Falloon .01 .05
126 Kelly Buchberger .01 .05
127 Carey Wilson .01 .05
128 Bobby Holik .02 .10
129 Andrei Lomakin .01 .05
130 Bob Rouse .01 .05
131 Adam Foote .02 .10
132 Bob Bassen .01 .05

133 Brian Benning .01 .05
134 Greg Gilbert .01 .05
135 Paul Stanton .01 .05
136 Brian Skrudland .01 .05
137 Jeff Beukeboom .01 .05
138 Clint Malarchuk .02 .10
139 Mike Modano .12 .30
140 Stephane Richer .02 .10
141 Brad McCrimmon .01 .05
142 Bob Carpenter .01 .05
143 Rod Langway .01 .05
144 Adam Creighton .01 .05
145 Ed Olczyk .01 .05
146 Greg Adams .01 .05
147 Jay More .01 .05
148 Scott Mellanby .01 .05
149 Paul Ranheim .01 .05
150 John Cullen .01 .05
151 Steve Duchesne .01 .05
152 Dave Ellett .01 .05
153 Mats Sundin .08 .25
154 Rick Zombo .01 .05
155 Kelly Hrudey .02 .10
156 Mike Hudson .01 .05
157 Bryan Trottier .02 .10
158 Shayne Corson .01 .05
159 Kevin Haller .01 .05
160 John Vanbiesbrouck .02 .10
161 Jim Johnson .01 .05
162 Kevin Todd .01 .05
163 Ray Sheppard .01 .05
164 Brent Ashton .01 .05
165 Peter Bondra .02 .10
166 David Volek .01 .05
167 Randy Carlyle .01 .05
168 Dana Murzyn .01 .05
169 Perry Berezan .01 .05
170 Vincent Damphousse .01 .05
171 Gary Leeman .01 .05
172 Steve Konroyd .01 .05
173 Pelle Eklund .01 .05
174 Peter Zezel .01 .05
175 Greg Paslawski .01 .05
176 Murray Baron .01 .05
177 Rob Blake .02 .10
178 Ed Belfour .08 .25
179 Mike Keane .01 .05
180 Mark Recchi .02 .10
181 Kris King .01 .05
182 Dave Snuggerud .01 .05
183 David Shaw .01 .05
184 Tom Chorske .01 .05
185 Steve Chiasson .01 .05
186 Don Sweeney .01 .05
187 Mike Ridley .01 .05
188 Glenn Healy .02 .10
189 Troy Murray .01 .05
190 Tom Fergus .01 .05
191 Rob Zettler .01 .05
192 Geoff Smith .01 .05
193 Joe Nieuwendyk .02 .10
194 Mark Hunter .01 .05
195 Kjell Samuelsson .01 .05
196 Todd Gill .01 .05
197 Doug Smail .01 .05
198 Dave Christian .01 .05
199 Tomas Sandstrom .02 .10
200 Jeremy Roenick .12 .30
201 Gordie Roberts .01 .05
202 Denis Savard .02 .10
203 James Patrick .01 .05
204 Dave Andreychuk .02 .10
205 Bobby Smith .02 .10
206 Valeri Zelepukin .01 .05
207 Shawn Burr .01 .05
208 Vladimir Ruzicka .01 .05
209 Calle Johansson .01 .05
210 Mark Fitzpatrick .02 .10
211 Dean Kennedy .01 .05
212 Dave Babych .01 .05
213 Wayne Presley .01 .05
214 Dave Manson .01 .05
215 Mikael Andersson .01 .05
216 Trent Yawney .01 .05
217 Mark Howe .01 .05
218 Mike Bullard .01 .05
219 Claude Lapointe .01 .05
220 Jeff Brown .01 .05
221 Bob Kudelski .01 .05
222 Michel Goulet .02 .10
223 Phil Bourque .01 .05
224 Darren Turcotte .01 .05
225 Kirk Muller .01 .05
226 Doug Bodger .01 .05
227 Dave Gagner .02 .10
228 Craig Billington .02 .10
229 Kevin Miller .01 .05
230 Glen Wesley .01 .05
231 Dale Hunter .02 .10
232 Tom Kurvers .01 .05
233 Pat Elynuik .01 .05
234 Geoff Courtnall .01 .05
235 Neil Wilkinson .01 .05
236 Bill Ranford .02 .10
237 Ronnie Stern .01 .05
238 Zarley Zalapski .01 .05
239 Kerry Huffman .01 .05
240 Joe Sakic .15 .40
241 Glenn Anderson .02 .10
242 Stephane Quintal .01 .05
243 Tony Granato .01 .05
244 Rob Brown .01 .05
245 Rick Tocchet .02 .10
246 Stephan Lebeau .01 .05
247 Mark Hardy .01 .05
248 Alexander Mogilny .02 .10
249 Jon Casey .02 .10
250 Adam Oates .02 .10
251 Bruce Driver .01 .05
252 Sergei Fedorov .12 .30
253 Michal Pivonka .01 .05
254 Cliff Ronning .01 .05
255 Derek King .01 .05
256 Luciano Borsato .01 .05
257 Paul Fenton .01 .05
258 Craig Berube .01 .05
259 Brian Bradley .01 .05
260 Craig Simpson .01 .05
261 Adam Burt .01 .05
262 Curtis Joseph .08 .25
263 Mark Pederson .01 .05
264 Alexei Gusarov .01 .05
265 Paul Coffey .08 .25
266 Steve Larmer .02 .10
267 Ron Francis .02 .10
268 Randy Gilhen .01 .05
269 Guy Carbonneau .02 .10
270 Chris Terreri .02 .10
271 Mike Craig .01 .05
272 Dale Hawerchuk .02 .10
273 Kevin Hatcher .01 .05
274 Ken Hodge Jr. .01 .05
275 Tim Cheveldae .02 .10
276 Benoit Hogue .01 .05
277 Mark Osborne .01 .05
278 Brian Mullen .01 .05
279 Robert Dirk .01 .05
280 Theo Fleury .01 .05
281 Martin Gelinas .01 .05
282 Pat Verbeek .01 .05
283 Mike Krushelnyski .01 .05
284 Kevin Dineen .01 .05
285 Craig Janney .02 .10
286 Owen Nolan .02 .10
287 Bob Errey .01 .05
288 Bryan Marchment .01 .05
289 Randy Moller .01 .05
290 Luc Robitaille .02 .10
291 Peter Stastny .02 .10
292 Ken Sutton .01 .05
293 Brad Marsh .01 .05
294 Chris Dahlquist .01 .05
295 Patrick Roy .40 1.00
296 Andy Brickley .01 .05
297 Randy Burridge .01 .05
298 Ray Ferraro .01 .05
299 Phil Housley .02 .10
300 Mark Messier .08 .25
301 David Bruce .01 .05
302 Al MacInnis .02 .10
303 Craig MacTavish .01 .05
304 Kay Whitmore .02 .10
305 Trevor Linden .02 .10
306 Steve Kasper .01 .05
307 Todd Elik .01 .05
308 Eric Weinrich .01 .05
309 Jocelyn Lemieux .01 .05
310 Peter Ahola .01 .05
311 J.J. Daigneault .01 .05
312 Colin Patterson .01 .05
313 Darcy Wakaluk .02 .10
314 Doug Weight .08 .25
315 Dave Barr .01 .05
316 Keith Primeau .01 .05
317 Bob Sweeney .01 .05
318 Jyrki Lumme .01 .05
319 Stu Barnes .01 .05
320 Don Beaupre .02 .10
321 Joe Murphy .01 .05
322 Gary Roberts .01 .05
323 Andrew Cassels .01 .05
324 Rod Brind'Amour .02 .10
325 Pierre Turgeon .02 .10
326 Claude Vilgrain .01 .05
327 Rich Sutter .01 .05
328 Claude Loiselle .01 .05
329 John Ogrodnick .01 .05
330 Ulf Dahlen .01 .05
331 Gilbert Dionne .01 .05
332 Joel Otto .01 .05
333 Rob Pearson .01 .05
334 Christian Ruuttu .01 .05
335 Brian Bellows .01 .05
336 Anatoli Semenov .01 .05
337 Brent Fedyk .01 .05
338 Gaetan Duchesne .01 .05
339 Randy McKay .01 .05
340 Bernie Nicholls .02 .10
341 Keith Acton .01 .05
342 John Tonelli .01 .05
343 Brian Lawton .01 .05
344 Ric Nattress .01 .05
345 Mike Eagles .01 .05
346 Frantisek Kucera .01 .05
347 John McIntyre .01 .05
348 Troy Loney .01 .05
349 Norm Maciver .01 .05
350 Brett Hull .10 .30
351 Rob Ramage .01 .05
352 Claude Boivin .01 .05
353 Paul Broten .01 .05
354 Stephane Fiset .02 .10
355 Gary Valk .01 .05
356 Basil McRae .01 .05
357 Alan May .01 .05
358 Grant Ledyard .01 .05
359 Dave Poulin .01 .05
360 Valeri Kamensky .01 .05
361 Brian Glynn .01 .05
362 Jan Erixon .01 .05
363 Mike Lalor .01 .05
364 Jeff Chychrun .01 .05
365 Ron Wilson .01 .05
366 Shawn Cronin .01 .05
367 Sylvain Turgeon .01 .05
368 Mike Liut .02 .10
369 Joe Cirella .01 .05
370 David Maley .01 .05
371 Lucien Deblois .01 .05
372 Per Djoos .01 .05
373 Dominik Hasek .30 .75
374 Laurie Boschman .01 .05
375 Brian Leetch .08 .25
376 Nelson Emerson .01 .05
377 Normand Rochefort .01 .05
378 Jacques Cloutier .02 .10
379 Jim Sandlak .01 .05
380 David Reid .01 .05
381 Gary Nylund .01 .05
382 Sergei Makarov .01 .05
383 Petr Klima .01 .05
384 Peter Douris .01 .05
385 Kirk McLean .02 .10
386 Bob McGill .01 .05
387 Ron Tugnutt .02 .10
388 Patrice Brisebois .01 .05
389 Tony Amonte .02 .10
390 Mario Lemieux .40 1.00
391 Nicklas Lidstrom .08 .25
392 Brendan Shanahan .08 .25
393 Donald Audette .01 .05
394 Alexei Kasatonov .01 .05
395 Dino Ciccarelli .02 .10
396 Vincent Riendeau .02 .10
397 Joe Reekie .01 .05
398 Jari Kurri .08 .25
399 Ken Wregget .02 .10
400 Steve Yzerman .40 1.00
401 Scott Niedermayer .01 .05
402 Stephane Beauregard .02 .10
403 Tim Hunter .01 .05
404 Marc Bergevin .01 .05
405 Sylvain Lefebvre .01 .05
406 Johan Garpenlov .01 .05
407 Tony Hrkac .01 .05
408 Tie Domi .08 .25
409 Martin Lapointe .02 .10
410 Darryl Sydor .01 .05
411 Brett Hull SL .08 .25
412 Wayne Gretzky SL .25 .60
413 Mario Lemieux SL .20 .50
414 Paul Ysebaert SL .01 .05
415 Tony Amonte SL .02 .10
416 Brian Leetch SL .02 .10
417 Tim Cheveldae SL .01 .05
Kirk McLean SL
418 Patrick Roy SL .20 .50
419 Ray Bourque FP .08 .20
420 Pat LaFontaine FP .02 .10
421 Al MacInnis FP .01 .05
422 Jeremy Roenick FP .02 .10
423 Steve Yzerman FP .20 .50
424 Bill Ranford FP .01 .05
425 John Cullen FP .01 .05
426 Wayne Gretzky FP .25 .60
427 Mike Modano FP .02 .10
428 Patrick Roy FP .20 .50
429 Scott Stevens FP .01 .05
430 Pierre Turgeon FP .01 .05
431 Mark Messier FP .05 .15
432 Eric Lindros FP .08 .25
433 Mario Lemieux FP .20 .50
434 Joe Sakic FP .08 .25
435 Brett Hull FP .08 .25
436 Pat Falloon FP .01 .05
437 Grant Fuhr FP .02 .10
438 Trevor Linden FP .01 .05
439 Kevin Hatcher FP .01 .05
440 Phil Housley FP .01 .05
441 Paul Coffey SH .02 .10
442 Brett Hull SH .08 .25
443 Mike Gartner SH .01 .05
444 Michel Goulet SH .01 .05
445 Mike Gartner SH .01 .05
446 Bobby Smith SH .02 .10
447 Ray Bourque SH .08 .20
448 Mario Lemieux HL .20 .50
449 Scott Lachance TP .01 .05
450 Keith Tkaczuk TP .08 .25
451 Alexander Semak TP .01 .05
452 John Tanner TP .01 .05
453 Joe Juneau TP .01 .05
454 Igor Kravchuk TP .01 .05
455 Brent Thompson TP .01 .05
456 Evgeny Davydov TP .01 .05
457 Arturs Irbe TP .02 .10
458 Kent Manderville TP .01 .05
459 Shawn McEachern TP .01 .05
460 Guy Hebert TP RC .25 .60
461 Keith Carney TP RC .30 .75
462 Karl Dykhuis TP .01 .05
463 Bill Lindsay TP RC .01 .05
464 Dominic Roussel TP .01 .05
465 Marty McInnis TP .01 .05
466 Dale Craigwell TP .01 .05
467 Igor Ulanov TP .01 .05
468 Dimitri Mironov TP .01 .05
469 Dean McAmmond TP RC .01 .05
470 Bill Guerin TP RC .50 1.25
471 Bret Hedican TP RC .02 .10
472 Felix Potvin TP .08 .25
473 Slava Kozlov TP .01 .05
474 Martin Rucinsky TP .01 .05
475 Ray Whitney TP RC .15 .40
476 Stephen Heinze TP .01 .05
477 Brad Schlegel TP .01 .05
478 Patrick Poulin TP .01 .05
479 Ted Donato TP .01 .05
480 Martin Brodeur .30 .75
481 Denny Felsner TP RC .02 .10
482 Trent Klatt TP RC .02 .10
483 Gord Hynes TP .01 .05
484 Glen Murray TP .01 .05
485 Chris Lindberg TP .01 .05
486 Ray LeBlanc TP .01 .05
487 Yanic Perreault TP RC .12 .30
488 J.F. Quintin TP RC .01 .05
489 Patrick Roy DT .20 .50
490 Ray Bourque DT .08 .20
491 Brian Leetch DT .02 .10
492 Kevin Stevens DT .01 .05
493 Mark Messier DT .05 .15
494 Jaromir Jagr DT .08 .25
495 Bill Ranford DT .01 .05
496 Al MacInnis DT .01 .05
497 Chris Chelios DT .08 .25
498 Luc Robitaille DT .02 .10
499 Jeremy Roenick DT .05 .15
500 Brett Hull DT .08 .25
501 Felix Potvin RDT .02 .10
502 Nicklas Lidstrom RDT .02 .10
503 Vladimir Konstantinov .08 .25
RDT
504 Pavel Bure RDT .05 .15
505 Nelson Emerson RDT .01 .05
506 Tony Amonte RDT .02 .10
507 Tampa Bay Lightning .01 .05
Logo
508 Shawn Chambers .01 .05
509 Basil McRae .01 .05
510 Joe Reekie .01 .05
511 Wendell Young .02 .10
512 Ottawa Senators Logo .08 .25
513 Laurie Boschman .01 .05
514 Mark Lamb .01 .05
515 Peter Sidorkiewicz .02 .10
516 Sylvain Turgeon .01 .05
517 Bill Dineen .01 .05
Kevin Dineen
518 Stanley Cup .02 .10
Champions
519 Mario Lemieux AW .20 .50
520 Ray Bourque AW .08 .20
King Clancy
521 Mark Messier AW .05 .15
Hart Trophy
522 Brian Leetch AW .02 .10
Norris Trophy
523 Pavel Bure AW .05 .15
Calder Trophy
524 Guy Carbonneau AW .02 .10
Selke Trophy
525 Wayne Gretzky AW .25 .60
Lady Byng Trophy
526 Mark Fitzpatrick AW .02 .10
Masterton Trophy
527 Patrick Roy AW .20 .50
Vezina Trophy
528 Memorial Cup .01 .05
Kamloops Blazers
529 Rick Tabaracci .02 .10
530 Tom Draper .01 .05
531 Adrien Plavsic .01 .05
532 Joe Sacco .01 .05
533 Mike Sullivan .01 .05
534 Zdeno Ciger .01 .05
535 Frank Pietrangelo .02 .10
536 Mike Peluso .01 .05
537 Jim Paek .01 .05
538 Dave Hannan .01 .05
539 David Williams RC .01 .05
540 Gino Odjick .01 .05
541 Yvon Corriveau .01 .05
542 Grant Jennings .01 .05
543 Stephane Matteau .01 .05
544 Pat Conacher .01 .05
545 Steven Rice .01 .05
546 Marc Habscheid .01 .05
547 Steve Weeks .02 .10
548A Jay Wells USA .01 .05
548C Maurice Richard CAN .08 .25
549A Mick Vukota USA .01 .05
549C Maurice Richard CAN .08 .25
550 Eric Lindros UER .08 .25
(Acquired 6-30-92&
not 6-20-92)
NNO Eric Lindros 4.00 10.00
(Press Conference Card

1992-93 Score Canadian Olympians

This 13-card standard-size set showcases Canadian hockey players who participated in the '92 Olympics in Albertville, France. The cards were randomly inserted at the rate of 1:24 '92-93 Score Canadian hockey packs. The color action photos on the fronts are highlighted by a red border with a diagonal white stripe. The year appears in a maple leaf at the upper left. The player's name and position are printed in the borders above and below the picture respectively. The backs feature the same red border design as the front with a player profile printed on a ghosted photo of the Canadian flag. The cards are numbered on the back. Not part of the set, but inserted in Canadian foil packs are two Maurice Richard cards and one autographed card of The Rocket.

COMPLETE SET (13) 20.00 40.00
1 Eric Lindros 2.50 5.00
2 Joe Juneau 1.00 2.50
3 Dave Archibald 1.00 2.50
4 Randy Smith 1.00 2.50
5 Gord Hynes 1.00 2.50
6 Chris Lindberg 1.00 2.50
7 Jason Woolley 1.00 2.50
8 Fabian Joseph 1.00 2.50
9 Brad Schlegel 1.00 2.50
10 Kent Manderville 1.00 2.50
11 Adrien Plavsic 1.00 2.50
12 Trevor Kidd 1.00 2.50
13 Sean Burke 1.00 2.50
NNO1 Maurice Richard 2.00 5.00
The Rocket
NNO2 Maurice Richard 2.00 5.00
Stanley Cup Hero
AU1 Maurice Richard 75.00 150.00
((Certified autograph)

1992-93 Score Sharpshooters

This 30-card standard-size set showcases the most accurate shooters during the 1991-92 season. Two cards were inserted in each 1992-93 Score jumbo pack. The cards feature full-bleed color action photos. A black border at the bottom contains the player's name in red and the words "Sharp Shooters" in gold foil lettering. A puck and target icon fills out the card front at the lower left corner. The horizontal backs carry close-up player photos with statistics and the team logo on either side against a gray background. A black border, nearly identical to the front, runs across the bottom. The cards are numbered on the back and arranged in descending order of 1991-92 shooting percentage ranking.

COMPLETE SET (30) 5.00 12.00
*US AND CDN: SAME VALUE
1 Gary Roberts .08 .25
2 Sergei Makarov .08 .25
3 Ray Ferraro .08 .25
4 Dale Hunter .40 1.00
5 Sergei Nemchinov .08 .25
6 Mike Ridley .08 .25
7 Gilbert Dionne .08 .25
8 Pat LaFontaine .50 1.25
9 Jimmy Carson .08 .25
10 Jeremy Roenick .60 1.50
11 Kelly Buchberger .08 .25
12 Owen Nolan .40 1.00
13 Igor Larionov .08 .25
14 Claude Vilgrain .08 .25
15 Derek King .08 .25
16 Greg Paslawski .08 .25
17 Bob Probert .40 1.00
18 Mark Recchi .40 1.00
19 Donald Audette .08 .25
20 Ray Sheppard .08 .25
21 Benoit Hogue .08 .25
22 Rob Brown .08 .25
23 Pat Elyniuk .08 .25
24 Petr Klima .08 .25
25 Pierre Turgeon .40 1.00
26 Corey Millen .08 .25
27 Dimitri Khristich .08 .25
28 Anatoli Semenov .08 .25
29 Kirk Muller .08 .25
30 Craig Simpson .08 .25

1992-93 Score USA Greats

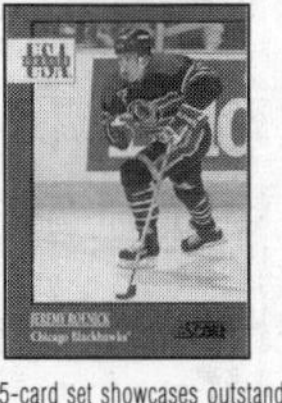

This 15-card set showcases outstanding United States-born players. The standard-size cards were randomly inserted at the rate of 1:24 '92-93 Score American hockey packs. The color action photos on the fronts are full-bleed on the right side only and framed on the other three sides by a red foil stripe and a blue outer border. The backs feature a close-up photo and a player profile.

COMPLETE SET (15) 15.00 40.00
1 Pat LaFontaine 1.50 4.00
2 Chris Chelios 1.50 4.00
3 Jeremy Roenick 1.50 4.00
4 Tony Granato 1.00 2.50
5 Mike Modano 2.00 5.00
6 Mike Richter 1.50 4.00
7 John Vanbiesbrouck 1.50 4.00
8 Brian Leetch 1.50 4.00
9 Joe Mullen 1.00 2.50
10 Kevin Stevens 1.00 2.50
11 Craig Janney 1.00 2.50
12 Brian Mullen 1.00 2.50
13 Kevin Hatcher 1.00 2.50
14 Kelly Miller 1.00 2.50
15 Ed Olczyk 1.00 2.50

1992-93 Score Young Superstars

This 40-card, boxed standard-size set was issued to showcase some of the leading young hockey players. The fronts feature glossy color player photos with white and bluish-gray streaked borders. The player's team name is printed in the top border, while the player's name is printed in the bottom border. The horizontal backs carry a close-up color photo, biography, "Rink Report," and statistics.

COMP.FACT SET (40) 3.20 8.00
1 Eric Lindros 1.00 2.50
2 Tony Amonte .12 .30
3 Mats Sundin .20 .50
4 Jaromir Jagr 1.00 2.50
5 Sergei Fedorov .60 1.50
6 Gilbert Dionne .04 .10
7 Mark Recchi .12 .30
8 Alexander Mogilny .12 .30
9 Mike Richter .20 .50
10 Jeremy Roenick .20 .50
11 Nicklas Lidstrom .20 .50
12 Scott Lachance .04 .10
13 Nelson Emerson .04 .10
14 Pat Falloon .04 .10
15 Dimitri Khristich .04 .10
16 Trevor Linden .12 .30
17 Curtis Joseph .40 1.00
18 Rob Pearson .04 .10
19 Kevin Todd .04 .10
20 Joe Sakic .60 1.50
21 Tim Cheveldae .12 .30
22 Joe Juneau .12 .30
23 Vladimir Konstantinov .12 .30
24 Valeri Kamensky .12 .30
25 Ed Belfour .20 .50
26 Rod Brind'Amour .12 .30
27 Pierre Turgeon .12 .30
28 Eric Desjardins .12 .30
29 Keith Tkachuk .20 .50
30 Pavel Bure .80 2.00
31 Patrick Poulin .04 .10
32 Viacheslav Kozlov .12 .30
33 Scott Niedermayer .12 .30
34 Jyrki Lumme .04 .10
35 Paul Ysebaert .04 .10
36 Dominic Roussel .12 .30
37 Owen Nolan .12 .30
38 Rob Blake .12 .30
39 Felix Potvin .20 .50
40 Mike Modano .20 .50

1993-94 Score Promo Panel

This promo panel was issued to promote the second series of the 1993-94 Score hockey series. Measuring approximately 5" by 2 1/2", the panel is actually the size of two standard-size cards. The left front features a Gold Rush version of the Alexandre Daigle card. On a purple foil background, the right front presents an advertisement for the second series. The reverse of the left front is the expected card back as with a regular card; the reverse of the right front is the front of the regular issue Daigle card.

587 Alexandre Daigle .80 2.00

1993-94 Score Samples

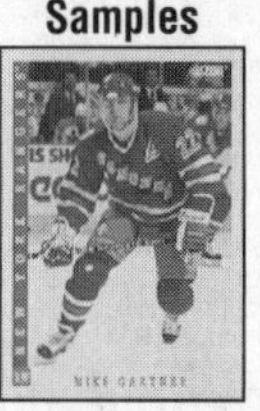

This six-card standard-size set was issued by Score as a preview of the design of the 1993-94 Score hockey set. The fronts display color action shots within a white border. The team name is printed on a team color-coded stripe along the left side. The player's position and name is printed across the bottom of the picture. The backs have team color-coded backgrounds with a head shot on the upper half and biography, statistics, and player profile. The words "sample card" are printed in the lower right corner.

COMPLETE SET (6) 1.60 4.00
1 Eric Lindros .80 2.00
2 Mike Gartner .20 .50
3 Steve Larmer .10 .25
4 Brian Bellows .10 .25
5 Felix Potvin .40 1.00
6 Pierre Turgeon .30 .75

1993-94 Score

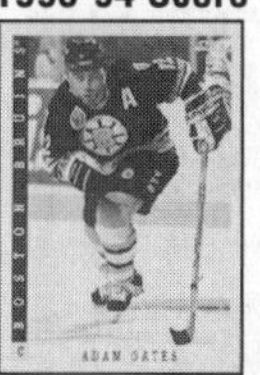

The 1993-94 Score hockey set consists of 661 standard-size cards. The first series contains 495 cards and the second series 166. The fronts of the first series feature white-bordered color player action shots. The player's name and position appear at the bottom, with his team name displayed vertically on the left within a team color-coded stripe. The second series was redesigned and consists of traded players in new uniforms, rookies and individual highlights. Blue borders surround the card with player name and team logo at the bottom. Card 496, Alexandre Daigle, is the card received after mailing in the unnumbered Daigle redemption card. The set is considered complete without it. The redemption card was randomly inserted in first series packs. An Eric Lindros All-Star card was the SP insert in series two, at a rate of 1:360 packs.

COMPLETE SET (661) 8.00 20.00
COMPLETE SERIES 1 (495) 6.00 15.00
COMPLETE SERIES 2 (166) 2.00 5.00
1 Eric Lindros .07 .20
2 Mike Gartner .02 .10
3 Steve Larmer .02 .10
4 Brian Bellows .01 .05
5 Felix Potvin .07 .20
6 Pierre Turgeon .07 .20
7 Joe Mullen .02 .10
8 Craig MacTavish .01 .05
9 Mats Sundin .07 .20
10 Pat Verbeek .01 .05
11 Andy Moog .02 .10
12 Dirk Graham .01 .05
13 Gary Suter .01 .05
14 Brent Fedyk .01 .05
15 Brad Shaw .01 .05
16 Benoit Hogue .01 .05
17 Cliff Ronning .01 .05
18 Mathieu Schneider .01 .05
19 Bernie Nicholls .01 .05
20 Vladimir Konstantinov .02 .10
21 Doug Bodger .01 .05
22 Peter Stastny .02 .10
23 Larry Murphy .02 .10
24 Darren Turcotte .01 .05
25 Doug Crossman .01 .05
26 Bob Essensa .02 .10
27 Kelly Kisio .01 .05
28 Nelson Emerson .01 .05
29 Ray Bourque .10 .30
30 Kelly Miller .01 .05
31 Peter Zezel .01 .05
32 Owen Nolan .02 .10
33 Sergei Makarov .01 .05
34 Stephane Richer .02 .10
35 Adam Graves .01 .05
36 Rob Ramage .01 .05
37 Ed Olczyk .01 .05
38 Jeff Hackett .02 .10
39 Ron Sutter .01 .05
40 Dale Hunter .01 .05
41 Nikolai Borschevsky .01 .05
42 Curtis Leschyshyn .01 .05
43 Mike Vernon .02 .10
44 Brent Sutter .01 .05
45 Rod Brind'Amour .02 .10
46 Sylvain Turgeon .01 .05
47 Kirk McLean .02 .10
48 Derek King .01 .05
49 Murray Craven .01 .05
50 Jaromir Jagr .12 .30
51 Guy Carbonneau .01 .05
52 Tony Granato .01 .05
53 Mark Tinordi .01 .05
54 Brad McCrimmon .01 .05
55 Randy Wood .01 .05
56 Scott Young .01 .05
57 Jamie Baker .01 .05
58 Don Beaupre .02 .10
59 Bob Probert .02 .10
60 Ray Ferraro .01 .05
61 Alexei Kasatonov .01 .05
62 Corey Millen .01 .05
63 Scott Mellanby .02 .10
64 Brian Benning .01 .05
65 Doug Lidster .01 .05
66 Doug Gilmour .02 .10
67 Shawn McEachern .01 .05
68 Tim Cheveldae .02 .10
69 Jeff Norton .01 .05
70 Ed Belfour .07 .20
71 Thomas Steen .01 .05
72 Stephan Lebeau .01 .05
73 James Patrick .01 .05
74 Joel Otto .01 .05
75 Grant Fuhr .02 .10
76 Calle Johansson .01 .05
77 Donald Audette .01 .05
78 Geoff Courtnall .01 .05
79 Fredrik Olausson .01 .05
80 Dimitri Khristich .01 .05
81 John MacLean .02 .10
82 Dominic Roussel .02 .10
83 Ray Sheppard .02 .10
84 Christian Ruuttu .01 .05
85 Mike McPhee .01 .05
86 Adam Creighton .01 .05
87 Uwe Krupp .01 .05
88 Steve Leach .01 .05
89 Kevin Miller .01 .05
90 Charlie Huddy .01 .05
91 Mark Howe .01 .05
92 Sylvain Cote .01 .05
93 Anatoli Semenov .01 .05
94 Jeff Beukeboom .01 .05
95 Gord Murphy .01 .05
96 Rob Pearson .01 .05
97 Esa Tikkanen .01 .05
98 Dave Gagner .02 .10
99 Mike Richter .07 .20
100 Jari Kurri .07 .20
101 Chris Chelios .07 .20
102 Peter Sidorkiewicz .02 .10
103 Scott Lachance .01 .05
104 Zarley Zalapski .01 .05
105 Denis Savard .02 .10
106 Paul Coffey .07 .20
107 Ulf Dahlen .01 .05
108 Shayne Corson .01 .05
109 Jimmy Carson .01 .05
110 Petr Svoboda .01 .05
111 Scott Stevens .02 .10
112 Kevin Lowe .01 .05
113 Chris Kontos .01 .05
114 Evgeny Davydov .01 .05
115 Doug Wilson .02 .10
116 Curtis Joseph .07 .20
117 Trevor Linden .02 .10
118 Michal Pivonka .01 .05
119 Dave Ellett .01 .05
120 Mike Ricci .01 .05
121 Al MacInnis .02 .10
122 Kevin Dineen .01 .05
123 Norm Maciver .01 .05
124 Darius Kasparaitis .01 .05
125 Adam Oates .02 .10
126 Sean Burke .02 .10
127 Dave Manson .01 .05
128 Eric Desjardins .02 .10
129 Tomas Sandstrom .01 .05
130 Russ Courtnall .01 .05
131 Roman Hamrlik .02 .10
132 Teppo Numminen .01 .05
133 Pat Falloon .01 .05
134 Jyrki Lumme .01 .05
135 Joe Sakic .15 .40
136 Kevin Hatcher .01 .05
137 Wendel Clark .01 .05
138 Neil Wilkinson .01 .05
139 Craig Simpson .01 .05
140 Kelly Hrudey .02 .10
141 Steve Thomas .01 .05
142 Mike Modano .12 .30

143 Garry Galley .01 .05
144 Jim Johnson .01 .05
145 Rod Langway .01 .05
146 Bob Sweeney .01 .05
147 Gary Leeman .01 .05
148 Alexei Zhitnik .01 .05
149 Adam Foote .01 .05
150 Mark Recchi .02 .10
151 Ron Francis .02 .10
152 Ron Hextall .02 .10
153 Michel Goulet .02 .10
154 Vladimir Ruzicka .01 .05
155 Bill Ranford .02 .10
156 Mike Craig .01 .05
157 Vladimir Malakhov .01 .05
158 Nicklas Lidstrom .07 .20
159 Dale Hawerchuk .02 .10
160 Claude Lemieux .01 .05
161 Ulf Samuelsson .01 .05
162 John Vanbiesbrouck .02 .10
163 Patrice Brisebois .01 .05
164 Andrew Cassels .01 .05
165 Paul Ranheim .01 .05
166 Neal Broten .02 .10
167 Joe Reekie .01 .05
168 Derian Hatcher .01 .05
169 Don Sweeney .01 .05
170 Mike Keane .01 .05
171 Mark Fitzpatrick .02 .10
172 Paul Cavallini .01 .05
173 Garth Butcher .01 .05
174 Andrei Kovalenko .01 .05
175 Shawn Burr .01 .05
176 Mike Donnelly .01 .05
177 Glenn Healy .02 .10
178 Gilbert Dionne .01 .05
179 Mike Ramsey .01 .05
180 Glenn Anderson .02 .10
181 Pelle Eklund .01 .05
182 Kerry Huffman .01 .05
183 Johan Garpenlov .01 .05
184 Kjell Samuelsson .01 .05
185 Todd Elik .01 .05
186 Craig Janney .02 .10
187 Dmitri Kvartalnov .01 .05
188 Al Iafrate .01 .05
189 John Cullen .01 .05
190 Steve Duchesne .01 .05
191 Theo Fleury .01 .05
192 Steve Smith .01 .05
193 Jon Casey .02 .10
194 Jeff Brown .01 .05
195 Keith Tkachuk .07 .20
196 Greg Adams .01 .05
197 Mike Ridley .01 .05
198 Bobby Holik .01 .05
199 Joe Nieuwendyk .02 .10
200 Mark Messier .07 .20
201 Jim Hrivnak .02 .10
202 Patrick Poulin .01 .05
203 Alexei Kovalev .02 .10
204 Robert Reichel .01 .05
205 David Shaw .01 .05
206 Brent Gilchrist .01 .05
207 Craig Billington .02 .10
208 Bob Errey .01 .05
209 Dmitri Mironov .01 .05
210 Dixon Ward .01 .05
211 Rick Zombo .01 .05
212 Marty McSorley .01 .05
213 Geoff Sanderson .02 .10
214 Dino Ciccarelli .02 .10
215 Tony Amonte .02 .10
216 Dimitri Yushkevich .01 .05
217 Scott Niedermayer .01 .05
218 Sergei Nemchinov .01 .05
219 Steve Konroyd .01 .05
220 Patrick Flatley .01 .05
221 Steve Chiasson .01 .05
222 Alexander Mogilny .02 .10
223 Pat Elynuik .01 .05
224 Jamie Macoun .01 .05
225 Tom Barrasso .02 .10
226 Gaetan Duchesne .01 .05
227 Eric Weinrich .01 .05
228 Dave Poulin .01 .05
229 Slava Fetisov .01 .05
230 Brian Bradley .01 .05
231 Petr Nedved .02 .10
232 Phil Housley .02 .10
233 Terry Carkner .01 .05
234 Kirk Muller .01 .05
235 Brian Leetch .07 .20
236 Rob Blake .02 .10
237 Chris Terreri .02 .10
238 Brendan Shanahan .07 .20
239 Paul Ysebaert .01 .05
240 Jeremy Roenick .10 .25
241 Gary Roberts .01 .05
242 Petr Klima .01 .05
243 Glen Wesley .01 .05
244 Vincent Damphousse .01 .05
245 Luc Robitaille .02 .10
246 Dallas Drake RC .01 .05
247 Rob Gaudreau RC .01 .05
248 Tommy Sjodin .01 .05
249 Richard Smehlik .01 .05
250 Sergei Fedorov .12 .30
251 Steve Heinze .01 .05
252 Luke Richardson .01 .05
253 Doug Weight .02 .10
254 Martin Rucinsky .01 .05
255 Sergio Momesso .01 .05
256 Alexei Zhamnov .02 .10
257 Bob Kudelski .01 .05
258 Brian Skrudland .01 .05
259 Terry Yake .01 .05
260 Alexei Gusarov .01 .05
261 Sandis Ozolinsh .01 .05
262 Ted Donato .01 .05
263 Bruce Driver .01 .05
264 Yves Racine .01 .05
265 Mike Peluso .01 .05
266 Craig Muni .01 .05
267 Bob Carpenter .01 .05
268 Kevin Haller .01 .05
269 Brad May .02 .10
270 Joe Kocur .01 .05
271 Igor Korolev .01 .05
272 Troy Murray .01 .05
273 Daren Puppa .02 .10
274 Gordie Roberts .01 .05
275 Michel Petit .01 .05
276 Vincent Riendeau .02 .10
277 Robert Petrovicky .01 .05
278 Valeri Zelepukin .01 .05
279 Bob Bassen .01 .05
280 Darrin Shannon .01 .05
281 Dominik Hasek .20 .50
282 Craig Ludwig .01 .05
283 Lyle Odelein .01 .05
284 Alexander Semak .01 .05
285 Richard Matvichuk .01 .05
286 Ken Daneyko .01 .05
287 Jan Erixon .01 .05
288 Robert Dirk .01 .05
289 Laurie Boschman .01 .05
290 Greg Paslawski .01 .05
291 Rob Zamuner .01 .05
292 Todd Gill .01 .05
293 Neil Brady .01 .05
294 Murray Baron .01 .05
295 Peter Taglianetti .01 .05
296 Wayne Presley .01 .05
297 Paul Broten .01 .05
298 Dana Murzyn .01 .05
299 J.J. Daigneault .01 .05
300 Wayne Gretzky .50 1.25
301 Keith Acton .01 .05
302 Yuri Khmylev .01 .05
303 Frank Musil .01 .05
304 Bob Rouse .01 .05
305 Greg Gilbert .01 .05
306 Geoff Smith .01 .05
307 Adam Burt .01 .05
308 Phil Bourque .01 .05
309 Igor Kravchuk .01 .05
310 Steve Yzerman .40 1.00
311 Darryl Sydor .01 .05
312 Tie Domi .02 .10
313 Sergei Zubov .01 .05
314 Chris Dahlquist .01 .05
315 Patrick Roy .40 1.00
316 Mark Osborne .01 .05
317 Kelly Buchberger .01 .05
318 John LeClair .07 .20
319 Randy McKay .01 .05
320 Jody Hull .01 .05
321 Paul Stanton .01 .05
322 Steven Finn .01 .05
323 Rich Sutter .01 .05
324 Ray Whitney .01 .05
325 Kevin Stevens .01 .05
326 Valeri Kamensky .02 .10
327 Doug Zmolek .01 .05
328 Mikhail Tatarinov .01 .05
329 Ken Wregget .02 .10
330 Joe Juneau .02 .10
331 Teemu Selanne .07 .20
332 Trent Yawney .01 .05
333 Pavel Bure .07 .20
334 Jim Paek .01 .05
335 Brett Hull .08 .25
336 Tommy Soderstrom .02 .10
337 Grigori Panteleyev .01 .05
338 Kevin Todd .01 .05
339 Mark Janssens .01 .05
340 Rick Tocchet .02 .10
341 Wendell Young .02 .10
342 Cam Neely .07 .20
343 Dave Andreychuk .02 .10
344 Peter Bondra .02 .10
345 Pat LaFontaine .07 .20
346 Robb Stauber .02 .10
347 Brian Mullen .01 .05
348 Joe Murphy .01 .05
349 Pat Jablonski .02 .10
350 Mario Lemieux .40 1.00
351 Sergei Bautin .01 .05
352 Claude Lapointe .01 .05
353 Dean Evason .01 .05
354 John Tucker .01 .05
355 Drake Berehowsky .01 .05
356 Gerald Diduck .01 .05
357 Todd Krygier .01 .05
358 Adrien Plavsic .01 .05
359 Sylvain Lefebvre .01 .05
360 Kay Whitmore .02 .10
361 Sheldon Kennedy .01 .05
362 Kris King .01 .05
363 Marc Bergevin .01 .05
364 Keith Primeau .01 .05
365 Jimmy Waite .02 .10
366 Dean Kennedy .01 .05
367 Mike Krushelnyski .01 .05
368 Ron Tugnutt .02 .10
369 Bob Beers .01 .05
370 Randy Burridge .01 .05
371 David Reid .01 .05
372 Frantisek Kucera .01 .05
373 Scott Pellerin RC .01 .05
374 Brad Dalgarno .01 .05
375 Martin Straka .01 .05
376 Scott Pearson .01 .05
377 Arturs Irbe .02 .10
378 Jiri Slegr .01 .05
379 Stephane Fiset .02 .10
380 Stu Barnes .01 .05
381 Ric Nattress .01 .05
382 Steven King .01 .05
383 Michael Nylander .01 .05
384 Keith Brown .01 .05
385 Gino Odjick .01 .05
386 Bryan Marchment .01 .05
387 Mike Foligno .01 .05
388 Zdeno Ciger .01 .05
389 Dave Taylor .02 .10
390 Mike Sullivan .01 .05
391 Shawn Chambers .01 .05
392 Brad Marsh .01 .05
393 Mike Hough .01 .05
394 Jeff Reese .01 .05
395 Bill Guerin .01 .05
396 Greg Hawgood .01 .05
397 Jim Sandlak .01 .05
398 Stephane Matteau .01 .05
399 John Blue .02 .10
400 Tony Twist .01 .05
401 Luciano Borsato .01 .05
402 Gerard Gallant .01 .05
403 Rick Tabaracci .02 .10
404 Nick Kypreos .01 .05
405 Marty McInnis .01 .05
406 Craig Wolanin .01 .05
407 Mark Lamb .01 .05
408 Martin Gelinas .01 .05
409 Ronnie Stern .01 .05
410 Ken Sutton .01 .05
411 Brian Noonan .01 .05
412 Stephane Quintal .01 .05
413 Rob Zettler .01 .05
414 Gino Cavallini .01 .05
415 Mark Hardy .01 .05
416 Jay Wells .01 .05
417 Keith Jones .01 .05
418 Dave McLlwain .01 .05
419 Frank Pietrangelo .02 .10
420 Jocelyn Lemieux .01 .05
421 Slava Kozlov .02 .10
422 Randy Moller .01 .05
423 Kevin Dahl .01 .05
424 Shjon Podein RC .01 .05
425 Shane Churla .01 .05
426 Guy Hebert .02 .10
427 Mikael Andersson .01 .05
428 Robert Kron .01 .05
429 Mike Eagles .01 .05
430 Alan May .01 .05
431 Ron Wilson .01 .05
432 Darcy Wakaluk .02 .10
433 Rob Ray .01 .05
434 Brent Ashton .01 .05
435 Jason Woolley .01 .05
436 Basil McRae .01 .05
437 Andre Racicot .02 .10
438 Brad Werenka .01 .05
439 Josef Beranek .01 .05
440 Dave Christian .01 .05
441 Theo Fleury LBM .01 .05
442 Mark Recchi LBM .02 .10
443 Cliff Ronning LBM .01 .05
444 Tony Granato LBM .01 .05
445 John Vanbiesbrouck LBM .02 .10
446 Jari Kurri HL .02 .10
500th goal
447 Mike Gartner HL .02 .10
14th Straight
30-goal season
448 Steve Yzerman HL .07 .20
1,000th Point
449 Glenn Anderson HL .02 .10
1,000th Point
450 Washington Caps HL .01 .05
Al Iafrate
Sylvain Cote
Kevin Hatcher
Highest Scoring Defense
in NHL History
451 Luc Robitaille HL .02 .10
Most Goals by
left winger
452 Pittsburgh Penguins HL .01 .05
17-Game Winning Streak
453 Corey Hirsch .02 .10
454 Jesse Belanger .01 .05
455 Philippe Boucher .01 .05
456 Robert Lang .01 .05
457 Doug Barrault RC .01 .05
458 Steve Konowalchuk .01 .05
459 Oleg Petrov .01 .05
460 Niclas Andersson .01 .05
461 Milan Tichy RC .01 .05
462 Darrin Madeley RC .01 .05
463 Tyler Wright .01 .05
464 Sergei Krivokrasov .01 .05
465 Vladimir Vujtek .01 .05
466 Rick Knickle RC .02 .10
467 Gord Kruppke RC .01 .05
468 David Emma .01 .05
469 Scott Thomas RC .01 .05
470 Shawn Rivers RC .01 .05
471 Jason Bowen RC .01 .05
472 Bryan Smolinski .01 .05
473 Chris Simon RC .20 .50
474 Peter Ciavaglia RC .01 .05
475 Sergei Zholtok .01 .05
476 Radek Hamr RC .01 .05
477 Teemu Selanne .07 .20
(Alexander Mogilny
SL Goals
478 Adam Oates SL .02 .10
Assists
479 Mario Lemieux SL .20 .50
480 Mario Lemieux SL .20 .50
481 Dave Andreychuk SL .02 .10
Power-Play Goals
482 Phil Housley SL .02 .10
Defenseman Scoring
483 Tom Barrasso SL .02 .10
Wins
484 Felix Potvin SL .07 .20
GAA
485 Ed Belfour SL .07 .20
486 Sault Ste. Marie .02 .10
Greyhounds
Memorial Cup Champions
487 Montreal Canadiens .02 .10
Stanley Cup Champions
488 Anaheim Mighty Ducks .07 .20
Logo
489 Guy Hebert .02 .10
490 Sean Hill .01 .05
491 Florida Panthers Logo .07 .20
492 John Vanbiesbrouck .07 .20
493 Tom Fitzgerald .01 .05
494 Paul DiPietro .01 .05
495 David Volek .01 .05
496 Alexandre Daigle .40 1.00
(Mail-in)
497 Shawn McEachern .01 .05
498 Rich Sutter .01 .05
499 Evgeny Davydov .01 .05
500 Sean Hill .01 .05
501 John Vanbiesbrouck .02 .10
502 Guy Hebert .02 .10
503 Scott Mellanby .02 .10
504 Ron Tugnutt .02 .10
505 Brian Skrudland .01 .05
506 Nelson Emerson .01 .05
507 Kevin Todd .01 .05
508 Terry Carkner .01 .05
509 Stephane Quintal .01 .05
510 Paul Stanton .01 .05
511 Terry Yake .01 .05
512 Brian Benning .01 .05
513 Brian Propp .01 .05
514 Steven King .01 .05
515 Joe Cirella .01 .05
516 Andy Moog .02 .10
517 Paul Ysebaert .01 .05
518 Petr Klima .01 .05
519 Corey Millen .01 .05
520 Phil Housley .02 .10
521 Craig Billington .02 .10
522 Jeff Norton .01 .05
523 Neil Wilkinson .01 .05
524 Doug Lidster .01 .05
525 Steve Larmer .02 .10
526 Jon Casey .02 .10
527 Brad McCrimmon .01 .05
528 Alexei Kasatonov .01 .05
529 Andrei Lomakin .01 .05
530 Daren Puppa .02 .10
531 Sergei Makarov .01 .05
532 Jim Sandlak .01 .05
533 Glenn Healy .02 .10
534 Martin Gelinas .01 .05
535 Igor Larionov .01 .05
536 Anatoli Semenov .01 .05
537 Mark Fitzpatrick .02 .10
538 Paul Cavallini .01 .05
539 Jimmy Waite .02 .10
540 Yves Racine .01 .05
541 Jeff Hackett .02 .10
542 Marty McSorley .01 .05
543 Scott Pearson .01 .05
544 Ron Hextall .02 .10
545 Gaetan Duchesne .01 .05
546 Jamie Baker .01 .05
547 Troy Loney .01 .05
548 Gord Murphy .01 .05
549 Bob Kudelski .01 .05
550 Dean Evason .01 .05
551 Mike Peluso .01 .05
552 Dave Poulin .01 .05
553 Randy Ladouceur .01 .05
554 Tom Fitzgerald .01 .05
555 Denis Savard .02 .10
556 Kelly Kisio .01 .05
557 Craig Simpson .01 .05
558 Stu Grimson .01 .05
559 Mike Hough .01 .05
560 Gerard Gallant .01 .05
561 Greg Gilbert .01 .05
562 Vladimir Ruzicka .01 .05
563 Jim Hrivnak .02 .10
564 Dave Lowry .01 .05
565 Todd Ewen .01 .05
566 Bob Errey .01 .05
567 Bryan Trottier .02 .10
568 Grant Ledyard .01 .05
569 Keith Brown .01 .05
570 Darren Turcotte .01 .05
571 Patrick Poulin .01 .05
572 Jimmy Carson .01 .05
573 Eric Weinrich .01 .05
574 James Patrick .01 .05
575 Bob Beers .01 .05
576 Chris Joseph .01 .05
577 Bryan Marchment .01 .05
578 Bob Carpenter .01 .05
579 Craig Muni .01 .05
580 Pat Elynuik .01 .05
581 Todd Elik .01 .05
582 Doug Brown .01 .05
583 Dave McLlwain .01 .05
584 Dave Tippett .01 .05
585 Jesse Belanger .01 .05
586 Chris Pronger .08 .25
587 Alexandre Daigle .01 .05
588 Cam Stewart RC .01 .05
589 Derek Plante RC .01 .05
590 Pat Peake .01 .05
591 Alexander Karpovtsev .01 .05
592 Rob Niedermayer .02 .10
593 Jocelyn Thibault RC .25 .60
594 Jason Arnott RC .40 1.00
595 Mike Rathje .01 .05
596 Chris Gratton .02 .10
597 Markus Naslund .07 .20
598 Dmitri Filimonov .01 .05
599 Andrei Trefilov .01 .05
600 Michal Sykora RC .01 .05
601 Greg Johnson .01 .05
602 Mikael Renberg .07 .20
603 Alexei Yashin .07 .20
604 Damian Rhodes RC .02 .10
605 Jeff Shantz RC .01 .05
606 Brent Gretzky RC .01 .05
607 Boris Mironov .01 .05
608 Ted Drury .01 .05
609 Chris Osgood RC .60 1.50
610 Jim Storm RC .01 .05
611 Dave Karpa .01 .05
612 Stewart Malgunas RC .01 .05
613 Jason Smith RC .01 .05
614 German Titov RC .01 .05
615 Patrick Carnback RC .01 .05
616 Jaroslav Modry RC .01 .05
617 Scott Levins RC .01 .05
618 Fred Brathwaite RC .10 .30
619 Ilya Byakin RC .01 .05
620 Jarkko Varvio .01 .05
621 Jim Montgomery RC .01 .05
622 Vesa Viitakoski RC .01 .05
623 Alexei Kudashov RC .01 .05
624 Pavol Demitra .02 .10
625 Iain Fraser RC .01 .05
626 Peter Popovic RC .01 .05
627 Kirk Maltby RC .01 .05
628 Garth Snow RC .02 .10
629 Peter White RC .01 .05
630 Mike McKee RC .01 .05
631 Darren McCarty RC .15 .40
632 Pat Neaton RC .01 .05
633 Sandy McCarthy .01 .05
634 Pierre Sevigny .01 .05
635 Matt Martin RC .01 .05
636 John Slaney .01 .05
637 Bob Corkum .01 .05
638 Mike Stapleton .01 .05
639 Bill Houlder .01 .05
640 Warren Rychel .01 .05
641 Garry Valk .01 .05
642 Greg Hawgood .01 .05
643 Randy Gilhen .01 .05
644 Stu Barnes .01 .05
645 Fredrik Olausson .01 .05
646 Geoff Smith .01 .05
647 Mike Foligno .01 .05
648 Martin Brodeur .20 .50
649 Ryan McGill .01 .05
650 Jeff Reese .01 .05
651 Mike Sillinger .01 .05
652 Brent Severyn RC .01 .05
653 Rob Ramage .01 .05
654 Dixon Ward .01 .05
655 Danton Cole .01 .05
656 Viacheslav Butsayev .01 .05
657 Ron Wilson .01 .05
658 Paul Broten .01 .05
659 Mike Hudson .01 .05
660 Trevor Kidd .02 .10
661 Travis Green .02 .10
662 Wayne Gretzky 1.00 2.50
NNO Alexandre Daigle .20 .50
Redemption card
NNO Eric Lindros AS SP .07 .20

1993-94 Score Gold

The 1993-94 Score Gold Rush set consists of 166 standard-size cards. The fronts are identical in design with the regular second-series Score cards, except for the metallic finish and gold marbleized borders. The backs are nearly identical to the regular issue cards, the Gold Rush logo at the top being the only difference. No Gold Rush parallels were produced for first series cards.
*STARS: 2.5X TO 6X BASIC CARDS
*RCs: 1.25X TO 3X BASIC CARDS

1993-94 Score Dream Team

Randomly inserted at the rate of 1:24 first series Canadian packs, this 24 card standard-size set features Score's Dream Team selections. Horizontal fronts feature an action photo and a head shot at lower right. The player's name and position appear in beneath the large photo. The backs contain career highlights and are numbered "X of 24".

1 Tom Barrasso .75 2.00
2 Patrick Roy 8.00 20.00
3 Chris Chelios 1.50 4.00
4 Al MacInnis .75 2.00
5 Scott Stevens .75 2.00
6 Brian Leetch 1.50 4.00
7 Ray Bourque 2.50 6.00
8 Paul Coffey 1.50 4.00
9 Al Iafrate .40 1.00
10 Mario Lemieux 8.00 20.00
11 Wayne Gretzky 10.00 25.00
12 Eric Lindros 1.50 4.00
13 Pat LaFontaine 1.50 4.00
14 Joe Sakic 3.00 8.00
15 Pierre Turgeon .75 2.00
16 Steve Yzerman 8.00 20.00
17 Adam Oates .75 2.00
18 Brett Hull 2.00 5.00
19 Pavel Bure 1.50 4.00
20 Alexander Mogilny .75 2.00
21 Teemu Selanne 1.50 4.00
22 Steve Larmer .75 2.00
23 Kevin Stevens .40 1.00
24 Luc Robitaille .75 2.00

1993-94 Score Dynamic Duos Canadian

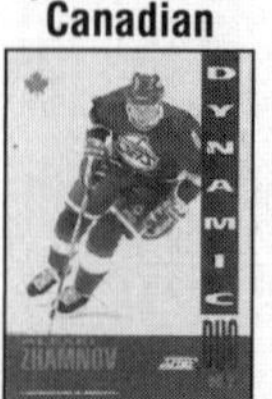

Randomly inserted at a rate of 1:48 Canadian second-series packs, this nine-card standard-size set highlights two team members on each card. Both the front and back of each card features a color player action shot. The player's name appears in red lettering within the team-colored bottom margin. The words "Dynamic Duos" appears in gold foil along the right side. A red maple leaf is placed at the upper left. The cards are numbered on the back with a "DD" prefix.
COMPLETE SET (9) 20.00 50.00
1 Doug Gilmour 2.00 5.00
Dave Andreychuk
2 Teemu Selanne 2.00 5.00
Alexei Zhamnov
3 Alexandre Daigle 1.50 4.00
Alexei Yashin
4 Gary Roberts 1.50 4.00
Joe Nieuwendyk
5 Joe Sakic 6.00 15.00
Mats Sundin
6 Brian Bellows 1.50 4.00
Kirk Muller
7 Shayne Corson 1.50 4.00
Jason Arnott
8 Mario Lemieux 10.00 25.00
Kevin Stevens
9 Pierre Turgeon 1.50 4.00
Derek King

1993-94 Score Dynamic Duos U.S.

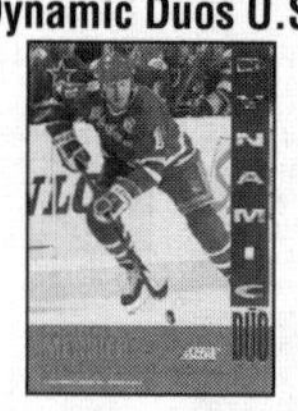

Randomly inserted at a rate of 1:48 U.S. second series packs, this nine-card standard-size set highlights two team members on each card. Both the front and back of each card features a color player action shot. The player's name appears in red lettering within the team-colored bottom margin. The words "Dynamic Duos" appear in gold foil along the right side. A blue star is placed at the upper left. The cards are numbered on the back with a "DD" prefix.
COMPLETE SET (9) 25.00 60.00
1 Mark Recchi 2.00 5.00
Eric Lindros
2 Pat LaFontaine 2.00 5.00
Alexander Mogilny
3 Adam Oates 2.00 5.00
Joe Juneau
4 Brett Hull 3.00 8.00
Craig Janney
5 Mark Messier 3.00 8.00
Adam Graves
6 Jeremy Roenick 2.00 5.00
Joe Murphy
7 Jari Kurri 10.00 25.00
Wayne Gretzky
8 Sergei Makarov 1.50 4.00
Igor Larionov
9 Steve Yzerman 8.00 20.00
Sergei Fedorov

1993-94 Score Franchise

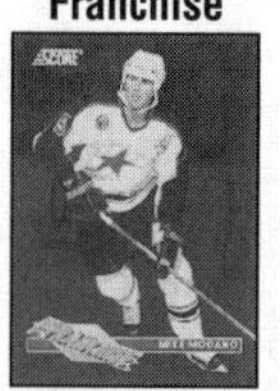

Randomly inserted at a rate of 1:24 U.S. first series packs, this 24-card set features borderless color player action shots on the fronts, the backgrounds of which are ghosted and darkened. The cards are numbered "X of 24" on the back.
1 Ray Bourque 2.50 6.00
2 Pat LaFontaine 1.50 4.00
3 Al MacInnis .75 2.00
4 Jeremy Roenick 2.00 5.00
5 Mike Modano 2.00 5.00
6 Steve Yzerman 5.00 12.00
7 Bill Ranford .75 2.00
8 Sean Burke .75 2.00
9 Wayne Gretzky 8.00 20.00
10 Patrick Roy 6.00 15.00
11 Scott Stevens .75 2.00
12 Pierre Turgeon .75 2.00
13 Brian Leetch 1.50 4.00
14 Peter Sidorkiewicz .75 2.00
15 Eric Lindros 1.50 4.00
16 Mario Lemieux 6.00 15.00
17 Joe Sakic 3.00 8.00
18 Brett Hull 2.00 5.00
19 Pat Falloon .40 1.00
20 Brian Bradley .40 1.00
21 Doug Gilmour .75 2.00
22 Pavel Bure 1.50 4.00
23 Kevin Hatcher .40 1.00
24 Teemu Selanne 1.50 4.00

1993-94 Score International Stars

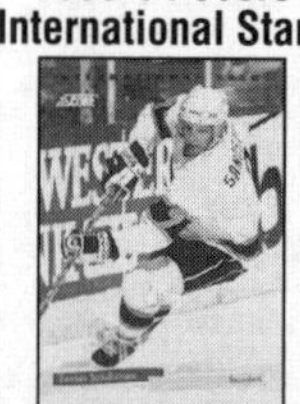

Inserted one per series one jumbo pack, this 22-card standard-size set highlights some of the NHL's hottest international stars. The fronts feature full-bleed color action shots, with the player's name and nationality appearing in a banner at the bottom that bears the colors of his national flag. The words "International Stars" in gold foil are printed at the top. On purplish backgrounds, the backs carry a color headshot at the upper left, with the player's national flag to the right and his name and country in his flag's colors below. Career highlights at the bottom round out the card. The cards are numbered on the back as "X of 22." Multipliers to determine values for the French version can be found in the header below.
COMPLETE SET (22) 8.00 20.00
*CDN VERSION:1X TO 1.25X U.S. VERSION

1 Pavel Bure 1.00 2.50
2 Teemu Selanne 1.00 2.50
3 Sergei Fedorov 1.50 4.00
4 Peter Bondra .40 1.00
5 Tommy Soderstrom .20 .50
6 Robert Reichel .20 .50
7 Jari Kurri 1.00 2.50
8 Alexander Mogilny .40 1.00
9 Jaromir Jagr 1.50 4.00
10 Mats Sundin 1.00 2.50
11 Uwe Krupp .20 .50
12 Nikolai Borschevsky .20 .50
13 Ulf Dahlen .20 .50
14 Alexander Semak .20 .50
15 Michal Pivonka .20 .50
16 Sergei Nemchinov .20 .50
17 Darius Kasparaitis .20 .50
18 Sandis Ozolinsh .20 .50
19 Alexei Kovalev .40 1.00
20 Dimitri Khristich .20 .50
21 Tomas Sandstrom .20 .50
22 Petr Nedved .20 .50

1994-95 Score Samples

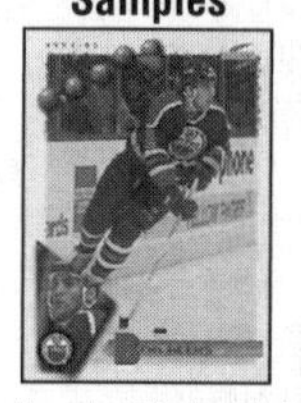

Issued in packs of 12, the 1994 Score hockey Hobby Sample cards measure the standard-size and preview the 1994 Score hockey issue. The top right and left corners have been cut off of some cards. The fronts feature color action player photos with white borders, and a small headshot in the left bottom corner. The player's name appears in colorful letters at the bottom of the picture. The horizontal backs carry another player photo on the left, along with the player's name, biography, career highlights and stats on the right.
COMPLETE SEALED SET (12) 1.60 4.00
1 Eric Lindros .20 .50
2 Pat LaFontaine .02 .05
3 Wendel Clark .02 .05
4 Cam Neely .02 .05
5 Larry Murphy .02 .05
6 Patrick Poulin .02 .05
7 Bob Beers .02 .05
254 Jason Arnott .04 .10
C13 Darius Kasparaitis .80 2.00
Check-It
TF16 Alexandre Daigle .40 1.00
The Franchise
NNO Pro Debut Rookie .20 .50
Redemption Card
NNO Title Card .02 .05

1994-95 Score

This 275-card standard-size set was issued in one series and does not have a comprehensive player selection. Due to the NHL lock-out, series two was replaced on the production schedule by Select; therefore many stars such as Patrick Roy and Wayne Gretzky were not featured in this set. The unique design features a full color player photo, surrounded by a white border. The Score logo appears in the top right corner, while a player head shot and team logo dominate the lower left. The upper right corner displays five globes; player name appears in a multi-hued strip along the card bottom. Cards were issued in 14-card U.S. and Canadian packs that included one Gold Line parallel card. Retail jumbo packs contained 30 cards and two Gold Line cards for $1.79. Subsets include World Junior Championships (201-215), Season Highlights (241-247), Young Stars (248-262), and Team Checklists (263-275). The only Rookie Card of note in the set is Mariusz Czerkawski.
COMPLETE SET (275) 5.00 12.00
1 Eric Lindros .07 .20
2 Pat LaFontaine .07 .20
3 Wendel Clark .02 .10
4 Cam Neely .07 .20

5 Larry Murphy .02 .10
6 Patrick Poulin .01 .05
7 Bob Beers .01 .05
8 James Patrick .01 .05
9 Gino Odjick .01 .05
10 Arturs Irbe .02 .10
11 Darius Kasparaitis .01 .05
12 Peter Bondra .02 .10
13 Garth Butcher .01 .05
14 Sergei Nemchinov .01 .05
15 Doug Brown .01 .05
16 Anatoli Semenov .01 .05
17 Mike McPhee .01 .05
18 Joel Otto .01 .05
19 Dino Ciccarelli .02 .10
20 Marty McSorley .01 .05
21 Ron Tugnutt .02 .10
22 Scott Niedermayer .01 .05
23 John Tucker .01 .05
24 Norm Maciver .01 .05
25 Kevin Miller .01 .05
26 Garry Galley .01 .05
27 Ted Donato .01 .05
28 Bob Kudelski .01 .05
29 Craig Muni .01 .05
30 Nikolai Borschevsky .01 .05
31 Tom Barrasso .02 .10
32 Brent Sutter .01 .05
33 Igor Kravchuk .01 .05
34 Andrew Cassels .01 .05
35 Jyrki Lumme .01 .05
36 Sandis Ozolinsh .01 .05
37 Steve Thomas .01 .05
38 Dave Poulin .01 .05
39 Andrei Kovalenko .01 .05
40 Steve Larmer .02 .10
41 Nelson Emerson .01 .05
42 Guy Hebert .02 .10
43 Russ Courtnall .01 .05
44 Gary Suter .01 .05
45 Steve Chiasson .01 .05
46 Guy Carbonneau .01 .05
47 Rob Blake .02 .10
48 Roman Hamrlik .02 .10
49 Valeri Zelepukin .01 .05
50 Mark Recchi .02 .10
51 Darrin Madeley .01 .05
52 Steve Duchesne .01 .05
53 Brian Skrudland .01 .05
54 Craig Simpson .01 .05
55 Todd Gill .01 .05
56 Dirk Graham .01 .05
57 Joe Mullen .02 .10
58 Doug Weight .02 .10
59 Michael Nylander .01 .05
60 Kirk McLean .02 .10
61 Igor Larionov .01 .05
62 Vladimir Malakhov .01 .05
63 Kelly Miller .01 .05
64 Curtis Leschyshyn .01 .05
65 Thomas Steen .01 .05
66 Jeff Beukeboom .01 .05
67 Troy Loney .01 .05
68 Mark Tinordi .01 .05
69 Theo Fleury .02 .10
70 Slava Kozlov .02 .10
71 Tony Granato .01 .05
72 Daren Puppa .02 .10
73 Brian Bellows .01 .05
74 Bernie Nicholls .02 .10
75 Rick Zombo .01 .05
76 Brad Shaw .01 .05
77 Josef Beranek .01 .05
78 Dominik Hasek .10 .25
79 Steve Leach .01 .05
80 David Reid .01 .05
81 Dave Lowry .01 .05
82 Martin Straka .01 .05
83 Dave Ellett .01 .05
84 Sean Burke .02 .10
85 Craig MacTavish .01 .05
86 Cliff Ronning .01 .05
87 Bob Errey .01 .05
88 Marty McInnis .01 .05
89 Mats Sundin .07 .20
90 Randy Burridge .01 .05
91 Teppo Numminen .01 .05
92 Tony Amonte .02 .10
93 Terry Yake .01 .05
94 Paul Cavallini .01 .05
95 German Titov .01 .05
96 Vladimir Konstantinov .02 .10
97 Darryl Sydor .01 .05
98 Chris Joseph .01 .05
99 Corey Millen .01 .05
100 Brett Hull .10 .30
101 Don Sweeney .01 .05
102 Scott Mellanby .01 .05
103 Mathieu Schneider .01 .05
104 Brad May .01 .05
105 Dominic Roussel .02 .10
106 Jamie Macoun .01 .05
107 Bryan Marchment .01 .05
108 Shawn McEachern .01 .05
109 Murray Craven .01 .05
110 Eric Desjardins .02 .10
111 Jon Casey .02 .10
112 Mike Gartner .02 .10
113 Neal Broten .02 .10
114 Jari Kurri .02 .10
115 Bruce Driver .01 .05
116 Patrick Flatley .01 .05
117 Gord Murphy .01 .05
118 Dimitri Khristich .01 .05
119 Nicklas Lidstrom .07 .20
120 Al MacInnis .02 .10
121 Steve Smith .01 .05
122 Zdeno Ciger .01 .05
123 Tie Domi .02 .10
124 Joe Juneau .02 .10
125 Todd Elik .01 .05
126 Stephane Fiset .02 .10
127 Craig Janney .02 .10
128 Stephan Lebeau .01 .05
129 Richard Smehlik .01 .05
130 Mike Richter .07 .20
131 Danton Cole .01 .05
132 Rod Brind'Amour .02 .10
133 Dave Archibald .01 .05
134 Dana Murzyn .01 .05
135 Jaromir Jagr .12 .30
136 Esa Tikkanen .01 .05
137 Rob Pearson .01 .05
138 Stu Barnes .01 .05
139 Frank Musil .01 .05
140 Ron Hextall .02 .10
141 Adam Oates .02 .10
142 Ken Daneyko .01 .05
143 Dale Hunter .01 .05
144 Geoff Sanderson .02 .10
145 Kelly Hrudey .02 .10
146 Kirk Muller .01 .05
147 Fredrik Olausson .01 .05
148 Derian Hatcher .01 .05
149 Ed Belfour .07 .20
150 Steve Yzerman .40 1.00
151 Adam Foote .01 .05
152 Pat Falloon .01 .05
153 Shawn Chambers .01 .05
154 Alexei Zhamnov .02 .10
155 Brendan Shanahan .07 .20
156 Ulf Samuelsson .01 .05
157 Donald Audette .01 .05
158 Bob Corkum .01 .05
159 Joe Nieuwendyk .02 .10
160 Felix Potvin .07 .20
161 Geoff Courtnall .01 .05
162 Yves Racine .01 .05
163 Tom Fitzgerald .01 .05
164 Adam Graves .01 .05
165 Vincent Damphousse .01 .05
166 Pierre Turgeon .02 .10
167 Craig Billington .02 .10
168 Al Iafrate .01 .05
169 Darren Turcotte .01 .05
170 Joe Murphy .01 .05
171 Alexei Zhitnik .01 .05
172 John MacLean .02 .10
173 Andy Moog .07 .20
174 Shayne Corson .01 .05
175 Ray Sheppard .02 .10
176 Johan Garpenlov .01 .05
177 Ron Sutter .01 .05
178 Teemu Selanne .07 .20
179 Brian Bradley .01 .05
180 Ray Bourque .15 .40
181 Curtis Joseph .07 .20
182 Kevin Stevens .01 .05
183 Alexei Kasatonov .01 .05
184 Brian Leetch .07 .20
185 Doug Gilmour .02 .10
186 Gary Roberts .01 .05
187 Mike Keane .01 .05
188 Mike Modano .15 .40
189 Chris Chelios .07 .20
190 Pavel Bure .07 .20
191 Bob Essensa .02 .10
192 Dale Hawerchuk .02 .10
193 Scott Stevens .02 .10
194 Claude Lapointe .01 .05
195 Scott Lachance .01 .05
196 Gaetan Duchesne .01 .05
197 Kevin Dineen .01 .05
198 Doug Bodger .01 .05
199 Mike Ridley .01 .05
200 Alexander Mogilny .02 .10
201 Jamie Storr .02 .10
202 Jason Botterill .01 .05
203 Jeff Friesen .02 .10
204 Todd Harvey .01 .05
205 Brendan Witt .01 .05
206 Jason Allison .01 .05
207 Aaron Gavey .01 .05
208 Deron Quint .01 .05
209 Jason Bonsignore .01 .05
210 Richard Park .01 .05
211 Jamie Langenbrunner .01 .05
212 Vadim Sharifjanov .02 .10
213 Alexander Kharlamov .01 .05
214 Oleg Tverdovsky .02 .10
215 Valeri Bure .01 .05
216 Dane Jackson RC .01 .05
217 Josef Cierny RC .01 .05
218 Yevgeny Namestnikov .01 .05
219 Dan Laperriere RC .01 .05
220 Fred Knipscheer .01 .05
221 Yan Kaminsky .01 .05
222 David Roberts .01 .05
223 Derek Mayer .01 .05
224 Jamie McLennan .02 .10
225 Kevin Smyth .01 .05
226 Todd Marchant .01 .05
227 Mariusz Czerkawski RC .08 .25
228 John Lilley .01 .05
229 Aaron Ward .01 .05
230 Brian Savage .01 .05
231 Jason Allison .01 .05
232 Maxim Bets .01 .05
233 Ted Crowley .01 .05
234 Todd Simon RC .01 .05
235 Zigmund Palffy .02 .10
236 Rene Corbet .01 .05
237 Mike Peca .01 .05
238 Dwayne Norris .01 .05
239 Andrei Nazarov .01 .05
240 David Sacco .01 .05
241 Wayne Gretzky .40 1.00
242 Mike Gartner .02 .10
243 Dino Ciccarelli .02 .10
244 Ron Francis .02 .10
245 Bernie Nicholls .02 .10
246 Dino Ciccarelli .02 .10
247 Brian Propp .01 .05
248 Alexandre Daigle .01 .05
249 Mikael Renberg .02 .10
250 Jocelyn Thibault .07 .20
251 Derek Plante .01 .05
252 Chris Pronger .02 .10
253 Alexei Yashin .01 .05
254 Jason Arnott .01 .05
255 Boris Mironov .01 .05
256 Chris Osgood .10 .30
257 Jesse Belanger .01 .05
258 Darren McCarty .01 .05
259 Trevor Kidd .02 .10
260 Oleg Petrov .01 .05
261 Mike Rathje .01 .05
262 John Slaney .01 .05
263 Anaheim Mighty Ducks .01 .05
Boston Bruins CL
264 Buffalo Sabres .01 .05
Calgary Flames CL
265 Chicago Blackhawks .01 .05
Dallas Stars CL
266 Detroit Red Wings .01 .05
Edmonton Oilers CL
267 Florida Panthers .01 .05
Hartford Whalers CL
268 Los Angeles Kings .01 .05
Montreal Canadiens CL
269 New Jersey Devils .01 .05
New York Islanders CL
270 New York Rangers .01 .05
Ottawa Senators CL
271 Philadelphia Flyers .01 .05
Pittsburgh Penguins CL
272 Quebec Nordiques .01 .05
St.Louis Blues CL
273 San Jose Sharks .01 .05
Tampa Bay Lightning CL
274 Toronto Maple Leafs .01 .05
Vancouver Canucks CL
275 Washington Capitals .01 .05
Winnipeg Jets CL

1994-95 Score Gold

These parallel cards were issued one per regular or jumbo pack. These differ from the basic cards through the usage of a gold foil coating. In a unique offer designed to promote set building, Score offered collectors who submitted complete team sets a limited Platinum foil team set in return. Redeemed gold cards were returned with a Pinnacle brand logo hole-punched through them. Hole-punched gold cards have a value of roughly 2X to 3X that of the basic cards.

*STARS: 4X TO 10X BASIC CARDS
*RC's: 2.5X TO 6X BASIC CARDS

1994-95 Score Platinum

This set was a partial parallel set to Score. Platinum cards could only be obtained through a mail-in offer via the trading of complete Score Gold Line team sets. The cards feature a platinum reflective mirror finish. Because the cards are almost invariably traded in complete team set form, that is how they are listed below. Score reportedly made 1,994 of each team set available for redemption. Pinnacle officials report very few sets were redeemed.

*STARS: 20X TO 40X BASIC CARDS
*YOUNG STARS: 12.5X TO 25X BASIC CARDS

COMPLETE BLACKHAWKS (9) 15.00 30.00
COMPLETE BLUES (10) 15.00 30.00
COMPLETE BRUINS (11) 12.50 25.00
COMPLETE CANADIENS (10) 12.50 25.00
COMPLETE CANUCKS (11) 20.00 40.00
COMPLETE CAPITALS (10) 7.50 15.00
COMPLETE DEVILS (9) 7.50 15.00
COMPLETE FLAMES (10) 12.50 25.00
COMPLETE FLYERS (9) 30.00 60.00
COMPLETE ISLANDERS (11) 7.50 15.00
COMPLETE JETS (6) 12.50 25.00
COMPLETE KINGS (8) 50.00 75.00
COMPLETE LIGHTNING (7) 7.50 15.00
COMPLETE MAPLE LEAFS (11) 15.00 30.00
COMPLETE MIGHTY DUCKS (8) 7.50 15.00
COMPLETE NORDIQUES (11) 15.00 30.00
COMPLETE OILERS (10) 12.50 25.00
COMPLETE PANTHERS (8) 7.50 15.00
COMPLETE PENGUINS (10) 17.50 35.00
COMPLETE RANGERS (8) 15.00 30.00
COMPLETE RED WINGS (13) 20.00 40.00
COMPLETE SABRES (12) 10.00 20.00
COMPLETE SENATORS (8) 7.50 15.00
COMPLETE SHARKS (10) 10.00 20.00
COMPLETE STARS (8) 7.50 15.00
COMPLETE WHALERS (9) 7.50 15.00

1994-95 Score Check It

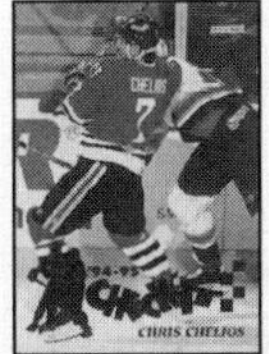

The 18 cards in this set were randomly inserted into Score Canadian hobby product at the rate of 1:72 packs.

COMPLETE SET (18) 40.00 100.00
CI1 Eric Lindros 6.00 10.00
CI2 Scott Stevens 1.50 4.00
CI3 Darius Kasparaitis 1.50 4.00
CI4 Kevin Stevens 1.50 4.00
CI5 Brendan Shanahan 6.00 15.00
CI6 Jeremy Roenick 6.00 15.00
CI7 Ulf Samuelsson 1.50 4.00
CI8 Cam Neely 6.00 15.00
CI9 Adam Graves 1.50 4.00
CI10 Kirk Muller 1.50 4.00
CI11 Rick Tocchet 1.50 4.00
CI12 Gary Roberts 1.50 4.00
CI13 Wendel Clark 3.00 8.00
CI14 Keith Tkachuk 3.00 8.00
CI15 Theo Fleury 1.50 4.00
CI16 Claude Lemieux 1.50 4.00
CI17 Chris Chelios 3.00 8.00
CI18 Pat Verbeek 1.50 4.00

1994-95 Score Dream Team

The 24 cards in this set were randomly inserted into all Score U.S. product at the rate of 1:36 packs. The cards feature a holographic image on the front which must be angled properly in the light, along with player name and the 1994 Dream Team logo. A full color photo and player information appear on the back. The cards are numbered with an "DT" prefix.

COMPLETE SET (24) 50.00 100.00
DT1 Patrick Roy 6.00 15.00
DT2 Felix Potvin 2.00 5.00
DT3 Ray Bourque 2.50 6.00
DT4 Brian Leetch 2.00 5.00
DT5 Scott Stevens 1.50 4.00
DT6 Paul Coffey 2.00 5.00
DT7 Al MacInnis 1.50 4.00
DT8 Chris Chelios 2.00 5.00
DT9 Adam Graves 1.00 2.50
DT10 Luc Robitaille 1.00 2.50
DT11 Dave Andreychuk 1.00 2.50
DT12 Sergei Fedorov 2.50 6.00
DT13 Doug Gilmour 1.50 4.00
DT14 Wayne Gretzky 10.00 25.00
DT15 Mario Lemieux 6.00 15.00
DT16 Mark Messier 2.00 5.00
DT17 Mike Modano 2.50 6.00
DT18 Jeremy Roenick 2.50 6.00
DT19 Eric Lindros 2.00 5.00
DT20 Steve Yzerman 5.00 12.00
DT21 Alexandre Daigle 1.00 2.50
DT22 Brett Hull 2.50 6.00
DT23 Cam Neely 2.00 5.00
DT24 Pavel Bure 2.00 5.00

1994-95 Score Franchise

The 26 cards in this set were randomly inserted into Score U.S. hobby product at the rate of 1:72 packs. The cards feature red printing and gold foil on the card face. A largely black and white action shot, with the player's head and torso punched out in full color, dominates the card front. Cards are numbered with a TF prefix on the back. The backs also feature a color photo with text information.

COMPLETE SET (26) 100.00 200.00
TF1 Guy Hebert 2.00 5.00
TF2 Cam Neely 4.00 10.00
TF3 Pat LaFontaine 4.00 10.00
TF4 Theo Fleury 2.00 5.00
TF5 Jeremy Roenick 5.00 12.00
TF6 Mike Modano 6.00 15.00
TF7 Sergei Fedorov 6.00 15.00
TF8 Jason Arnott 2.00 5.00
TF9 John Vanbiesbrouck 2.00 5.00
TF10 Geoff Sanderson 2.00 5.00
TF11 Wayne Gretzky 20.00 50.00
TF12 Patrick Roy 15.00 40.00
TF13 Scott Stevens 2.00 5.00
TF14 Pierre Turgeon 2.00 5.00
TF15 Mark Messier 4.00 10.00
TF16 Alexandre Daigle 2.00 5.00
TF17 Eric Lindros 5.00 12.00
TF18 Mario Lemieux 15.00 40.00
TF19 Joe Sakic 8.00 20.00
TF20 Brett Hull 5.00 12.00
TF21 Arturs Irbe 2.00 5.00
TF22 Daren Puppa 2.00 5.00
TF23 Doug Gilmour 2.00 5.00
TF24 Pavel Bure 5.00 12.00
TF25 Joe Juneau 2.00 5.00
TF26 Teemu Selanne 4.00 10.00

1994-95 Score 90 Plus Club

The 21 cards in this set were randomly inserted into Score retail jumbo packs at the rate of 1:4. The set features all players who tallied more than 90 points in the previous season. The cards have a full tan border. A

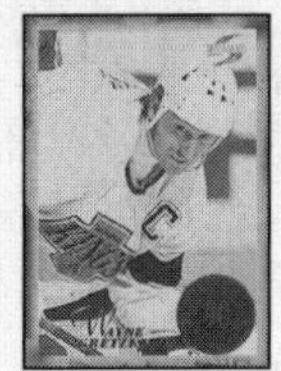

simple round set logo is on the lower portion of the card. The player name is in gold foil. The backs are team color coordinated, with a player photo, and short text information. The cards are numbered with an "NP" prefix.

COMPLETE SET (21) 30.00 60.00
1 Wayne Gretzky 12.50 30.00
2 Sergei Fedorov 3.00 8.00
3 Adam Oates 1.00 2.50
4 Doug Gilmour 1.00 2.50
5 Pavel Bure 2.00 5.00
6 Jeremy Roenick 2.50 6.00
7 Mark Recchi 1.00 2.50
8 Brendan Shanahan 2.00 5.00
9 Jaromir Jagr 3.00 8.00
10 Dave Andreychuk .40 1.00
11 Brett Hull 2.50 6.00
12 Eric Lindros 2.00 5.00
13 Rod Brind'Amour 1.00 2.50
14 Pierre Turgeon 1.00 2.50
15 Ray Sheppard 1.00 2.50
16 Mike Modano 3.00 8.00
17 Robert Reichel .40 1.00
18 Ron Francis 1.00 2.50
19 Joe Sakic 4.00 10.00
20 Vincent Damphousse .40 1.00
21 Ray Bourque 3.00 8.00

1994-95 Score Team Canada

The 24 cards in this set were randomly inserted into Score Canadian retail and hobby product at the rate of 1:36 packs. The cards feature a holographic player photo front with a background that reads Lillehammer. The set highlights players from the Canadian Olympic team which took home the silver in the 1994 Games. Although included in this set, Brett Lindros actually did not play in Norway due to an injury. The backs have a full color player portrait over a maple leaf background. The cards are numbered with a CT prefix.

COMPLETE SET (24) 30.00 60.00
CT1 Paul Kariya 5.00 12.00
CT2 Petr Nedved 1.50 4.00
CT3 Todd Warriner 1.50 4.00
CT4 Corey Hirsch 1.50 4.00
CT5 Greg Johnson 1.25 3.00
CT6 Chris Kontos 1.25 3.00
CT7 Dwayne Norris 1.25 3.00
CT8 Brian Savage 1.50 4.00
CT9 Todd Hlushko 1.25 3.00
CT10 Fabian Joseph 1.25 3.00
CT11 Greg Parks 1.25 3.00
CT12 Jean-Yves Roy 1.25 3.00
CT13 Mark Astley 1.25 3.00
CT14 Adrian Aucoin 1.25 3.00
CT15 David Harlock 1.25 3.00
CT16 Ken Lovsin 1.25 3.00
CT17 Derek Mayer 1.25 3.00
CT18 Brad Schlegel 1.25 3.00
CT19 Chris Therien 1.50 4.00
CT20 Manny Legace 2.00 5.00
CT21 Brad Werenka 1.25 3.00
CT22 Wally Schreiber 1.25 3.00
CT23 Allain Roy 1.25 3.00
CT24 Brett Lindros 1.25 3.00

1994-95 Score Top Rookie Redemption

The 10 cards in this set were available only through a redemption card offer. Redemption cards were inserted at the rate of 1:48 Score packs. The redemption cards were individually numbered 1-10, but do not mention the player for whom they are redeemable. The mail-in offer expired April 1, 1995. These redemption cards are priced in the header below. Top Rookie redeemed cards have a cut-out photo of the player over a silver foil background. The Top Rookie logo runs down the right side of the card; the player name, position and team logo are on the bottom of the card. The back has a color photo with text information and is numbered with a "TR" prefix.

COMPLETE SET (10) 20.00 40.00
1 Paul Kariya 8.00 20.00
2 Peter Forsberg 8.00 20.00
3 Brett Lindros 1.25 3.00
4 Oleg Tverdovsky 1.25 3.00
5 Jamie Storr 1.25 3.00
6 Kenny Jonsson 1.25 3.00
7 Brian Rolston 1.25 3.00
8 Jeff Friesen 1.25 3.00
9 Todd Harvey 1.25 3.00
10 Victor Kozlov 1.25 3.00

1995-96 Score Promos

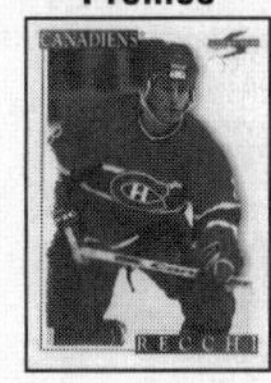

Enclosed in a cello pack, this nine-card standard-size set was issued to preview the 1995-96 Score hockey series. The cards are identical in design to their regular issue counterparts, save for the way the player's name is presented on the back and the hole punched into the upper right corner. On the promos, it is last name only, while the regular cards include Christian name as well.

COMPLETE SEALED SET (9) .80 2.00
3 Chris Chelios .10 .25
8 Jason Arnott .04 .10
10 Mark Recchi .06 .15
19 Trevor Kidd .06 .15
25 Martin Brodeur .20 .50
33 Keith Tkachuk .16 .40
313 Jamie Linden .02 .05
3 Cam Neely .40 1.00
Border Battle
NNO Ad Card .02 .05

1995-96 Score

This 330-card standard-size set was issued in one series in packs of 12-card hobby, 12-card retail and 24-card retail jumbo. Canadian packs of 5-cards each also were available. These packs also held chase cards, but because of the pack size, the odds were considerably more difficult. The fronts feature a full-color action photo on a white background with the player's last name at the bottom and the team name at the top both in team colors. The backs have a color photo with the player's name at the top. Player information, statistics and the team emblem are also on the back of the card. Subsets are Rookies (291-315) and Stoppers (316-325). The Ron Hextall Contest Winner card (#AD4) was awarded to collectors who correctly spotted four errors in a photograph in a contest sponsored by Score. The card back approximates the standard Score issue, but the front uses a silver prismatic foil background.

COMPLETE SET (330) 5.00 15.00
1 Jaromir Jagr .12 .30
2 Adam Graves .01 .05
3 Chris Chelios .07 .20
4 Felix Potvin .07 .20
5 Joe Sakic .15 .40
6 Chris Pronger .07 .20
7 Teemu Selanne .07 .20
8 Jason Arnott .01 .05
9 John LeClair .07 .20
10 Mark Recchi .02 .10
11 Rob Blake .02 .10
12 Kevin Hatcher .01 .05
13 Shawn Burr .01 .05
14 Brett Lindros .01 .05
15 Craig Janney .01 .05
16 Oleg Tverdovsky .01 .05
17 Blaine Lacher .02 .10
18 Alexandre Daigle .01 .05
19 Trevor Kidd .02 .10
20 Brendan Shanahan .07 .20
21 Alexander Mogilny .02 .10
22 Stu Barnes .01 .05
23 Jeff Brown .01 .05
24 Paul Coffey .07 .20
25 Martin Brodeur .20 .50
26 Darryl Sydor .02 .10
27 Steve Smith .01 .05
28 Ted Donato .01 .05
29 Bernie Nicholls .01 .05
30 Kenny Jonsson .01 .05
31 Peter Forsberg .20 .50
32 Sean Burke .02 .10
33 Keith Tkachuk .07 .20
34 Todd Marchant .01 .05
35 Mikael Renberg .02 .10
36 Vincent Damphousse .01 .05
37 Rick Tocchet .02 .10
38 Todd Harvey .01 .05
39 Chris Gratton .01 .05
40 Darius Kasparaitis .01 .05
41 Sergei Nemchinov .01 .05
42 Bob Corkum .01 .05
43 Bryan Smolinski .01 .05
44 Kevin Stevens .01 .05
45 Phil Housley .02 .10
46 Al MacInnis .02 .10
47 Alexei Zhitnik .01 .05
48 Rob Niedermayer .02 .10
49 Kirk McLean .02 .10
50 Mark Messier .07 .20
51 Nicklas Lidstrom .07 .20
52 Scott Niedermayer .01 .05
53 Peter Bondra .02 .10
54 Luc Robitaille .02 .10
55 Jeremy Roenick .10 .25
56 Mats Sundin .07 .20
57 Wendel Clark .02 .10
58 Todd Elik .01 .05
59 Dave Manson .01 .05
60 David Oliver .01 .05
61 Yuri Khmylev .01 .05
62 Sergei Krivokrasov .01 .05
63 Randy Wood .01 .05
64 Andy Moog .07 .20
65 Petr Klima .01 .05
66 Ray Ferraro .01 .05
67 Sandis Ozolinsh .01 .05
68 Joe Sacco .01 .05
69 Zarley Zalapski .01 .05
70 Ron Tugnutt .07 .20
71 German Titov .01 .05
72 Ian Laperriere .01 .05
73 Doug Gilmour .02 .10
74 Brian Skrudland .01 .05
75 Cliff Ronning .01 .05
76 Brian Savage .01 .05
77 John MacLean .02 .10
78 Jim Carey .02 .10
79 Alexei Kovalev .01 .05
80 Brian Rolston .01 .05
81 Shawn McEachern .01 .05
82 Gary Suter .01 .05
83 Owen Nolan .02 .10
84 Ray Whitney .02 .10
85 Alexei Zhamnov .02 .10
86 Shawn Chambers .01 .05
87 Ed Belfour .07 .20
88 Patrice Tardif .01 .05
89 Greg Adams .01 .05
90 Pierre Turgeon .02 .10
91 Jeff Friesen .01 .05
92 Marty McSorley .01 .05
93 Dave Gagner .01 .05
94 Guy Hebert .02 .10
95 Keith Jones .02 .10
96 Kirk Muller .01 .05
97 Gary Roberts .01 .05
98 Chris Therien .01 .05
99 Steve Duchesne .01 .05
100 Sergei Fedorov .12 .30
101 Donald Audette .01 .05
102 Jyrki Lumme .01 .05
103 Darrin Shannon .01 .05
104 Gord Murphy .01 .05
105 John Cullen .01 .05
106 Bill Guerin .02 .10
107 Dale Hunter .02 .10
108 Uwe Krupp .01 .05
109 Dave Andreychuk .02 .10
110 Joe Murphy .01 .05
111 Geoff Sanderson .02 .10
112 Garry Galley .01 .05
113 Ron Sutter .01 .05
114 Viktor Kozlov .02 .10
115 Jari Kurri .07 .20
116 Paul Ysebaert .01 .05
117 Vladimir Malakhov .01 .05
118 Josef Beranek .01 .05
119 Adam Oates .02 .10
120 Mike Modano .12 .30
121 Theo Fleury .01 .05
122 Pat Verbeek .01 .05
123 Esa Tikkanen .01 .05
124 Brian Leetch .02 .10
125 Paul Kariya .07 .20
126 Ken Wregget .02 .10
127 Ray Sheppard .02 .10
128 Jason Allison .01 .05
129 Dave Ellett .01 .05
130 Stephane Richer .02 .10
131 Jocelyn Thibault .07 .20
132 Martin Straka .01 .05
133 Tony Amonte .02 .10
134 Scott Mellanby .01 .05
135 Pavel Bure .07 .20
136 Andrew Cassels .01 .05
137 Ulf Dahlen .01 .05
138 Valeri Bure .01 .05
139 Teppo Numminen .01 .05
140 Mike Richter .07 .20
141 Rob Gaudreau .01 .05
142 Nikolai Khabibulin .02 .10
143 Mariusz Czerkawski .01 .05
144 Mark Tinordi .01 .05
145 Patrick Roy .40 1.00
146 Steve Chiasson .01 .05
147 Mike Donnelly .01 .05
148 Patrice Brisebois .01 .05
149 Jason Wiemer .01 .05
150 Eric Lindros .07 .20
151 Dimitri Khristich .01 .05
152 Tom Barrasso .02 .10
153 Curtis Leschyshyn .01 .05
154 Robert Kron .01 .05
155 Jesse Belanger .01 .05
156 Brian Noonan .01 .05
157 Mike Peca .02 .10
158 Patrick Poulin .01 .05
159 Sergei Makarov .01 .05
160 Scott Stevens .02 .10
161 Sergio Momesso .01 .05
162 Todd Gill .01 .05
163 Don Sweeney .01 .05
164 Randy Burridge .01 .05
165 Slava Kozlov .02 .10
166 Shaun Van Allen .01 .05
167 Steven Rice .01 .05
168 Adam Deadmarsh .01 .05
169 Andrei Nikolishin .01 .05
170 Valeri Karpov .01 .05
171 Doug Bodger .01 .05
172 Corey Millen .01 .05
173 Mark Fitzpatrick .02 .10
174 Bob Errey .01 .05
175 Dan Quinn .01 .05
176 Vladimir Konstantinov .02 .10
177 Scott Lachance .01 .05

1995-96 Score

178 Jeff Norton .01 .05
179 Valeri Zelepukin .01 .05
180 Dmitri Mironov .01 .05
181 Pat Peake .01 .05
182 Dominic Roussel .02 .10
183 Sylvain Cote .01 .05
184 Pat Falloon .01 .05
185 Roman Hamrlik .02 .10
186 Joel Otto .01 .05
187 Ron Francis .02 .10
188 Sergei Zubov .01 .05
189 Arturs Irbe .02 .10
190 Radek Bonk .01 .05
191 John Tucker .01 .05
192 Sylvain Lefebvre .01 .05
193 Doug Brown .01 .05
194 Glen Wesley .01 .05
195 Ron Hextall .02 .10
196 Patrick Flatley .01 .05
197 Darcy Wakaluk .02 .10
198 Kelly Hrudey .02 .10
199 Ray Bourque .10 .30
200 Dominik Hasek .15 .40
201 Pat LaFontaine .07 .20
202 Chris Osgood .08 .25
203 Ulf Samuelsson .01 .05
204 Mike Gartner .02 .10
205 Stephane Fiset .02 .10
206 Mathieu Schneider .01 .05
207 Eric Desjardins .02 .10
208 Trevor Linden .02 .10
209 Cam Neely .07 .20
210 Daren Puppa .02 .10
211 Steve Larmer .02 .10
212 Tim Cheveldae .02 .10
213 Derek Plante .01 .05
214 Murray Craven .01 .05
215 Tommy Soderstrom .02 .10
216 Bob Bassen .01 .05
217 Marty McInnis .01 .05
218 Dave Lowry .01 .05
219 Mike Vernon .02 .10
220 Petr Nedved .02 .10
221 Yves Racine .01 .05
222 Dale Hawerchuk .07 .20
223 Wayne Presley .01 .05
224 Darren Turcotte .01 .05
225 Derian Hatcher .01 .05
226 Steve Thomas .02 .10
227 Stephane Matteau .01 .05
228 Grant Fuhr .07 .20
229 Joe Nieuwendyk .02 .10
230 Alexei Yashin .01 .05
231 Brian Bellows .01 .05
232 Brian Bradley .01 .05
233 Tony Granato .01 .05
234 Mike Ricci .02 .10
235 Brett Hull .08 .25
236 Mike Ridley .01 .05
237 Al Iafrate .02 .10
238 Derek King .01 .05
239 Bill Ranford .02 .10
240 Steve Yzerman .40 1.00
241 John Vanbiesbrouck .02 .10
242 Russ Courtnall .01 .05
243 Chris Terreri .02 .10
244 Rod Brind'Amour .02 .10
245 Shayne Corson .01 .05
246 Don Beaupre .02 .10
247 Dino Ciccarelli .02 .10
248 Kevin Lowe .02 .10
249 Craig MacTavish .02 .10
250 Wayne Gretzky .50 1.25
251 Curtis Joseph .07 .20
252 Joe Mullen .02 .10
253 Andrei Kovalenko .01 .05
254 Igor Larionov .01 .05
255 Geoff Courtnall .01 .05
256 Joe Juneau .01 .05
257 Bruce Driver .01 .05
258 Michal Pivonka .01 .05
259 Nelson Emerson .01 .05
260 Larry Murphy .02 .10
261 Brent Gilchrist .01 .05
262 Benoit Hogue .01 .05
263 Doug Weight .02 .10
264 Keith Primeau .01 .05
265 Neal Broten .02 .10
266 Mike Keane .01 .05
267 Zigmund Palffy .02 .10
268 Valeri Kamensky .02 .10
269 Claude Lemieux .01 .05
270 Bryan Marchment .01 .05
271 Kelly Miller .01 .05
272 Brent Sutter .01 .05
273 Glenn Healy .02 .10
274 Sergei Brylin .01 .05
275 Tie Domi .02 .10
276 Norm Maciver .01 .05
277 Kevin Dineen .01 .05
278 Scott Young .01 .05
279 Tomas Sandstrom .01 .05
280 Guy Carbonneau .07 .20
281 Denis Savard .02 .10
282 Ed Olczyk .01 .05
283 Adam Creighton .01 .05
284 Tom Chorske .01 .05
285 Roman Oksiuta .01 .05
286 David Roberts .01 .05
287 Petr Svoboda .01 .05
288 Brad May .01 .05
289 Michael Nylander .01 .05
290 Jon Casey UER .01 .05
(back photo depicts Curtis Joseph)
291 Philippe DeRouville .01 .05
292 Craig Johnson .01 .05
293 Chris McAlpine RC .01 .05
294 Ralph Intranuovo .01 .05
295 Richard Park .01 .05
296 Todd Warriner .01 .05
297 Craig Conroy RC .01 .05
298 Marek Malik .01 .05
299 Manny Fernandez .07 .20
300 Cory Stillman .01 .05
301 Kevin Brown .01 .05
302 Steve Larouche RC .01 .05
303 Chris Taylor .01 .05
304 Ryan Smyth .02 .10
305 Craig Darby RC .01 .05
306 Radim Bicanek .01 .05
307 Shean Donovan .01 .05
308 Jason Bonsignore .01 .05
309 Chris Marinucci RC .01 .05
310 Brian Holzinger RC .07 .20
311 Mike Torchia RC .02 .10
312 Eric Daze .02 .10
313 Jamie Linden .01 .05
314 Tommy Salo RC .30 .75
315 Martin Gendron .01 .05
316 Felix Potvin ST .02 .10
317 Jim Carey ST .01 .05
318 Ed Belfour ST .07 .20
319 Mike Vernon ST .02 .10
320 Sean Burke ST .02 .10
321 Mike Richter ST .07 .20
322 John Vanbiesbrouck ST .02 .10
323 Martin Brodeur ST .07 .20
324 Patrick Roy ST .20 .50
325 Dominik Hasek ST .07 .20
326 Checklist .01 .05
Pacific Division
327 Checklist .01 .05
Central Division
328 Checklist .01 .05
Atlantic Division
329 Checklist .01 .05
Northeast Division
330 Checklist - Chase .01 .05
AD4 Ron Hextall Contest Winner 2.50 5.00

1995-96 Score Black Ice Artist's Proofs

This 330-card set is a high-end parallel of the basic Score issue. The cards can be differentiated from the standard issue by a black foil background with the words "Artist's Proof" written throughout. The cards were randomly inserted 1:36 packs.
*STARS: 40X TO 100X BASIC CARDS

1995-96 Score Black Ice

This 330-card set is a parallel version of the basic set. Card fronts differ in that they feature a silver, metallic background surrounded by a grayish border. The words "Black Ice" are stamped on the back in a gray block. They were inserted one in every three packs.
*STARS: 5X TO 10X BASIC CARDS

1995-96 Score Border Battle

This 15-card standard-size set was inserted in 12-card hobby and retail packs at a rate of one in 12 and retail jumbos at a rate of one in 9. The set features the top players from different countries. The fronts have a color action photo with the background in the color of the player's home country. The left side of the card has a gold foil triangle jutting out with a red circle in it that has the words "Border Battle" and the country's flag. The backs have a color head shot and an action photo tinted in the color of the player's country. The backs also state the player's home country and have information on him. The cards are numbered "X of 15" at the bottom.
COMPLETE SET (15) 10.00 20.00
1 Pierre Turgeon .25 .60
2 Wayne Gretzky 3.00 8.00
3 Cam Neely .50 1.25
4 Joe Sakic 1.00 2.50
5 Doug Gilmour .25 .60
6 Brett Hull .60 1.50
7 Pat LaFontaine .50 1.25
8 Joe Mullen .25 .60
9 Mike Modano .75 2.00
10 Jeremy Roenick .60 1.50
11 Pavel Bure .50 1.25
12 Alexei Zhamnov .25 .60
13 Sergei Fedorov UER .75 2.00
14 Jaromir Jagr .75 2.00
15 Mats Sundin .50 1.25

1995-96 Score Check It

This 12-card standard-size set was inserted in 12-card retail packs at a rate of 1:36, and

in 1:86 Canadian packs. Cards were numbered "X of 12" at the topof the card backs.
COMPLETE SET (12) 15.00 40.00
1 Eric Lindros 4.00 10.00
2 Owen Nolan .75 2.00
3 Brett Lindros .75 2.00
4 Chris Gratton .75 2.00
5 Chris Pronger 2.00 5.00
6 Adam Deadmarsh .75 2.00
7 Peter Forsberg 6.00 15.00
8 Derian Hatcher .75 2.00
9 Rob Blake .75 2.00
10 Jeff Friesen .75 2.00
11 Keith Tkachuk 1.50 4.00
12 Mike Ricci .75 2.00

1995-96 Score Dream Team

This 12-card standard-size set was inserted in 12-card hobby and retail packs at a rate of 1:72. The cards are numbered "X of 12" at the top.
COMPLETE SET (12) 30.00 60.00
1 Wayne Gretzky 12.50 30.00
2 Sergei Fedorov 1.25 3.00
3 Eric Lindros 1.00 2.50
4 Mark Messier 1.25 3.00
5 Peter Forsberg 3.00 8.00
6 Doug Gilmour .60 1.50
7 Paul Kariya 1.00 2.50
8 Jaromir Jagr 2.00 5.00
9 Brett Hull 1.25 3.00
10 Pavel Bure 1.00 2.50
11 Patrick Roy 6.00 15.00
12 Jim Carey .40 1.00

1995-96 Score Golden Blades

This 20-card set was randomly inserted in 1:18 retail jumbo packs. The cards, which feature the fastest skaters in the game, are printed on gold prismatic foil.
COMPLETE SET (20) 25.00 50.00
1 Joe Sakic 3.00 8.00
2 Teemu Selanne 1.50 4.00
3 Alexander Mogilny .40 1.00
4 Peter Bondra .40 1.00
5 Paul Coffey .75 2.00
6 Mike Modano 2.00 5.00
7 Alexei Yashin .40 1.00
8 Pat LaFontaine .75 2.00
9 Paul Kariya 2.00 5.00
10 Peter Forsberg 3.00 8.00
11 Jeff Friesen .40 1.00
12 Steve Yzerman 5.00 12.00
13 Theo Fleury .75 2.00
14 Stephane Richer .40 1.00
15 Mark Messier 2.00 5.00
16 Mats Sundin 1.50 4.00
17 Brendan Shanahan 1.50 4.00
18 Mark Recchi .75 2.00
19 Jeremy Roenick 1.50 4.00
20 Jason Arnott .40 1.00

1995-96 Score Lamplighters

This 15-card standard-size set was inserted in 12-card hobby packs at a rate of 1:36. The cards, which feature the top goal scorers in the game, are printed on a silver prismatic foil card stock.
COMPLETE SET (15) 25.00 50.00
1 Wayne Gretzky 8.00 20.00
2 Pavel Bure 1.25 3.00
3 Cam Neely 1.25 3.00
4 Owen Nolan .60 1.50
5 Sergei Fedorov 1.25 3.00
6 Pierre Turgeon .60 1.50
7 Peter Bondra .60 1.50
8 Mikael Renberg .60 1.50
9 Luc Robitaille .60 1.50
10 Alexei Zhamnov .60 1.50
11 Brett Hull 1.25 3.00
12 Jaromir Jagr 2.00 5.00
13 Theo Fleury .60 1.50
14 Teemu Selanne 1.25 3.00
15 Eric Lindros 1.25 3.00

1996-97 Score Samples

This eight-card set features samples of the 1996-97 Score hockey issue. Interestingly, all samples mirror the linen-stock Golden Blades parallel set rather than the basic issue. The cards are identical in design to their regular counterparts with the exception of the word "sample" printed on the backs at the bottom. The cards are listed below according to their regular issue numbers.
COMPLETE SET (8) 2.80 7.00
1 Patrick Roy 1.00 2.50
10 Martin Brodeur WINNER .50 1.25
10 Martin Brodeur .50 1.25
10 Martin Brodeur .50 1.25
(Golden Blades WINNER
16 Alexander Mogilny .20 .50
19 Brett Hull .24 .60
63 John Vanbiesbrouck .30 .75
77 Sergei Fedorov .40 1.00
236 Eric Daze .20 .50
238 Saku Koivu .20 .50

1996-97 Score

The 1996-97 Score set -- the first release of that season -- was issued in one series totaling 275 cards. The 10-card packs retailed for $.99 each. The cards featured action photography on the front complemented by simple white borders, while the backs were highlighted by another photograph and complete career stats. The only rookie of note is Ethan Moreau.
COMPLETE SET (275) 5.00 10.00
1 Patrick Roy .50 1.25
2 Brendan Shanahan .08 .25
3 Rob Niedermayer .02 .10
4 Jeff Friesen .01 .05
5 Teppo Numminen .01 .05
6 Mario Lemieux .50 1.25
7 Eric Lindros .08 .25
8 Paul Kariya .08 .25
9 Joe Sakic .20 .50
10 Martin Brodeur .25 .60
11 Mark Tinordi .01 .05
12 Theo Fleury .01 .05
13 Guy Hebert .02 .10
14 Dave Gagner .02 .10
15 Travis Green .02 .10
16 Alexander Mogilny .02 .10
17 Stephane Fiset .02 .10
18 Dominik Hasek .20 .50
19 Brett Hull .10 .30
20 Zdeno Ciger .01 .05
21 Pat Falloon .01 .05
22 Jyrki Lumme .01 .05
23 Rick Tabaracci .02 .10
24 Mark Messier .08 .25
25 Yanic Perreault .01 .05
26 Mark Recchi .02 .10
27 Alexander Selivanov .01 .05
28 Chris Terreri .02 .10
29 Jaromir Jagr .15 .40
30 Ted Donato .01 .05
31 Scott Mellanby .02 .10
32 Geoff Courtnall .01 .05
33 Michal Pivonka .01 .05
34 Glenn Healy .02 .10
35 Pavel Bure .08 .25
36 Chris Chelios .08 .25
37 Nelson Emerson .01 .05
38 Petr Nedved .02 .10
39 Greg Adams .01 .05
40 Bill Ranford .02 .10
41 Wayne Gretzky .60 1.50
42 Wendel Clark .02 .10
43 Sandis Ozolinsh .01 .05
44 Dave Andreychuk .02 .10
45 Brian Bradley .01 .05
46 Sean Burke .02 .10
47 Keith Tkachuk .08 .25
48 Brad May .02 .10
49 Brent Gilchrist .01 .05
50 Vincent Damphousse .02 .10
51 Dale Hawerchuk .02 .10
52 Randy Burridge .01 .05
53 Ray Bourque .15 .40
54 Keith Primeau .01 .05
55 Jason Arnott .01 .05
56 Ron Francis .02 .10
57 Craig Janney .02 .10
58 Trevor Kidd .02 .10
59 Jason Dawe .01 .05
60 Steve Yzerman .50 1.25
61 Alexei Kovalev .01 .05
62 Steve Duchesne .01 .05
63 John Vanbiesbrouck .02 .10
64 Steve Thomas .01 .05
65 Bernie Nicholls .01 .05
66 Alexandre Daigle .01 .05
67 Pat Peake .01 .05
68 Kelly Hrudey .02 .10
69 Owen Nolan .02 .10
70 Alexei Zhitnik .01 .05
71 Pierre Turgeon .02 .10
72 Mike Modano .15 .40
73 Slava Fetisov .01 .05
74 Jim Carey .08 .25
75 Larry Murphy .02 .10
76 Roman Oksiuta .01 .05
77 Sergei Fedorov .12 .30
78 Shayne Corson .01 .05
79 Michael Nylander .01 .05
80 Ron Hextall .02 .10
81 Adam Graves .01 .05
82 Tommy Soderstrom .02 .10
83 Robert Svehla .01 .05
84 Vladimir Konstantinov .02 .10
85 Jeff Hackett .02 .10
86 Todd Harvey .01 .05
87 Jeff Brown .01 .05
88 Bryan Smolinski .01 .05
89 Oleg Tverdovsky .02 .10
90 Curtis Joseph .08 .25
91 Grant Fuhr .02 .10
92 Rick Tocchet .02 .10
93 Adam Deadmarsh .02 .10
94 Pat Verbeek .01 .05
95 Doug Gilmour .02 .10
96 Jocelyn Thibault .08 .25
97 Radek Bonk .01 .05
98 Martin Gelinas .01 .05
99 Peter Forsberg .25 .60
100 Joe Murphy .01 .05
101 Dino Ciccarelli .02 .10
102 Rod Brind'Amour .02 .10
103 Kirk Muller .01 .05
104 Andy Moog .02 .10
105 Nikolai Khabibulin .02 .10
106 Mike Ricci .01 .05
107 Ray Ferraro .01 .05
108 Scott Niedermayer .01 .05
109 Russ Courtnall .01 .05
110 Dale Hunter .01 .05
111 Cam Neely .08 .25
112 Ray Sheppard .02 .10
113 Luc Robitaille .02 .10
114 Al MacInnis .02 .10
115 Mathieu Schneider .01 .05
116 Claude Lemieux .01 .05
117 Kevin Hatcher .01 .05
118 Daren Puppa .02 .10
119 Geoff Sanderson .02 .10
120 Zigmund Palffy .02 .10
121 Denis Savard .02 .10
122 Dimitri Khristich .01 .05
123 Ed Belfour .08 .25
124 Tom Barrasso .02 .10
125 Bob Rouse .01 .05
126 Tomas Sandstrom .01 .05
127 Roman Hamrlik .02 .10
128 Alexei Zhamnov .02 .10
129 Chris Osgood .08 .25
130 Rob Blake .02 .10
131 Garry Galley .01 .05
132 Greg Johnson .01 .05
133 Brian Skrudland .01 .05
134 Martin Rucinsky .01 .05
135 Steve Konowalchuk .01 .05
136 Damian Rhodes .02 .10
137 Jeremy Roenick .12 .30
138 Scott Stevens .02 .10
139 Pat LaFontaine .08 .25
140 Scott Young .01 .05
141 Benoit Hogue .01 .05
142 Paul Coffey .08 .25
143 John MacLean .02 .10
144 Joe Juneau .02 .10
145 Teemu Selanne .08 .25
146 Andrew Cassels .01 .05
147 Brian Savage .01 .05
148 Chris Gratton .02 .10
149 Corey Hirsch .02 .10
150 Mike Richter .08 .25
151 Shawn McEachern .01 .05
152 Joe Nieuwendyk .02 .10
153 Phil Housley .02 .10
154 Mike Gartner .02 .10
155 Kirk McLean .02 .10
156 Bob Probert .02 .10
157 Valeri Kamensky .02 .10
158 Vyacheslav Kozlov .02 .10
159 Eric Desjardins .02 .10
160 Mats Sundin .08 .25
161 John LeClair .08 .25
162 Adam Oates .02 .10
163 Cliff Ronning .01 .05
164 Mike Vernon .02 .10
165 German Titov .01 .05
166 Chris Pronger .02 .10
167 Norm MacIver .01 .05
168 Kenny Jonsson .01 .05
169 Tony Amonte .02 .10
170 Doug Weight .02 .10
171 Sergei Zubov .01 .05
172 Felix Potvin .08 .25
173 Trevor Linden .02 .10
174 Derek Plante .01 .05
175 Uwe Krupp .01 .05
176 Nicklas Lidstrom .08 .25
177 Mikael Renberg .02 .10
178 Igor Larionov .01 .05
179 Brian Leetch .08 .25
180 Stu Barnes .01 .05
181 Alexei Yashin .01 .05
182 Gary Suter .01 .05
183 Ken Wregget .02 .10
184 Mike Ridley .01 .05
185 Peter Bondra .02 .10
186 Steve Rucchin .01 .05
187 Jozef Stumpel .01 .05
188 Matthew Barnaby .02 .10
189 James Patrick .01 .05
190 Chris Simon .01 .05
191 Brent Fedyk .01 .05
192 Kris Draper .01 .05
193 David Oliver .01 .05
194 Dave Lowry .01 .05
195 Robert Kron .01 .05
196 Andrei Kovalenko .01 .05
197 Bill Guerin .01 .05
198 Ed Olczyk .01 .05
199 Yuri Khmylev .01 .05
200 Rob Ray .01 .05
201 Joe Mullen .02 .10
202 Petr Klima .01 .05
203 Todd Krygier .01 .05
204 Garth Snow .02 .10
205 Zarley Zalapski .01 .05
206 Ken Baumgartner .01 .05
207 Tony Twist .01 .05
208 Todd Gill .01 .05
209 Mike Peca .01 .05
210 Darcy Wakaluk .02 .10
211 Milos Holan .01 .05
212 Alexander Semak .01 .05
213 Jeff Reese .01 .05
214 Jon Casey .02 .10
215 Sandy McCarthy .01 .05
216 Curtis Leschyshyn .01 .05
217 Todd Marchant .01 .05
218 Bob Bassen .01 .05
219 Darren Turcotte .01 .05
220 David Reid .01 .05
221 Brian Bellows .01 .05
222 Jesse Belanger .01 .05
223 Bill Lindsay .01 .05
224 Lyle Odelein .01 .05
225 Keith Jones .01 .05
226 Sylvain Lefebvre .01 .05
227 Shaun Van Allen .01 .05
228 Dan Quinn .01 .05
229 Richard Matvichuk .01 .05
230 Craig MacTavish .01 .05
231 Craig Billington .02 .10
232 Stephane Richer .02 .10
233 Donald Audette .01 .05
234 Ulf Dahlen .01 .05
235 Steve Chiasson .01 .05
236 Eric Daze .02 .10
237 Petr Sykora .01 .05
238 Saku Koivu .08 .25
239 Ed Jovanovski .02 .10
240 Daniel Alfredsson .02 .10
241 Vitali Yachmenev .01 .05
242 Marcus Ragnarsson .01 .05
243 Cory Stillman .01 .05
244 Todd Bertuzzi .08 .25
245 Valeri Bure .01 .05
246 Jere Lehtinen .01 .05
247 Radek Dvorak .01 .05
248 Niclas Andersson .01 .05
249 Miroslav Satan .01 .05
250 Jeff O'Neill .01 .05
251 Nolan Baumgartner .01 .05
252 Roman Vopat .01 .05
253 Bryan McCabe .01 .05
254 Jamie Langenbrunner .01 .05
255 Chad Kilger .01 .05
256 Eric Fichaud .02 .10
257 Landon Wilson .01 .05
258 Kyle McLaren .01 .05
259 Aaron Gavey .01 .05
260 Byron Dafoe .02 .10
261 Grant Marshall .01 .05
262 Shane Doan .01 .05
263 Ralph Intranuovo .01 .05
264 Aki Berg .01 .05
265 Antti Tormanen .01 .05
266 Brian Holzinger .02 .10
267 Jose Theodore .12 .30
268 Ethan Moreau RC .08 .25
269 Niklas Sundstrom .01 .05
270 Brendan Witt .01 .05
271 Checklist (1-70) .01 .05
272 Checklist (71-140) .01 .05
273 Checklist (141-210) .01 .05
274 Checklist (211-275) .01 .05
275 Checklist (Chase Program) .01 .05

1996-97 Score Artist's Proofs

This 275-card parallel of the 1996-97 Score set could be differentiated from the regular cards by the bronze foil circular Artist's Proof logo on the card front. These chase cards were inserted 1:55 hobby and retail packs, and 1:27 magazine packs.
*STARS: 30X TO 80X BASIC CARDS

1996-97 Score Dealer's Choice Artist's Proofs

Another parallel to the Score set, these cards were sent to dealers whose customers pulled winning Golden Blades cards. The dealer mailed in the winning card and was given two cards in exchange. The customer received the Special Artist Proof while the dealer received this version. Identical to regular Artist Proofs, only the words 'Dealers Choice' were added around the circular AP logo.
*STARS: 75X TO 150X BASIC CARDS

1996-97 Score Special Artist's Proofs

A parallel to the Score set, these cards wer redemptions of winning Golden Blade cards, which had blacked out boxes readabl only with a special lens available at hobb shops. Customers received a Special Artis Proof card while the dealers who sent in th cards for the customers received simila versions called Dealer's Choice Artis Proofs. The only difference is on the Artis Proof logo, which adds the word 'Special' o these versions.
*STARS: 60X TO 120X BASIC CARDS

1996-97 Score Check It

Randomly inserted in magazine packs at rate of 1:35, this 16-card set features som of the toughest hitters in the game.
COMPLETE SET (16) 5.00 10.00
1 Eric Lindros .30 .75
2 Peter Forsberg 2.00 5.00
3 Keith Tkachuk .30 .75
4 Cam Neely .30 .75
5 Jeremy Roenick .40 1.00
6 Brendan Shanahan .30 .75
7 Wendel Clark .20 .50
8 Owen Nolan .20 .50
9 Doug Gilmour .20 .50
10 Trevor Linden .20 .50
11 Saku Koivu .30 .75
12 Ed Jovanovski .30 .75
13 Theo Fleury .20 .50
14 Doug Weight .20 .50
15 Chris Chelios .30 .75
16 Eric Daze .20 .50

1996-97 Score Golden Blades

This 275-card set was a parallel to the basi issue. The cards were inserted at rates of 1: hobby and retail packs, and 1:3 magazin packs. The cards were printed on line stock and featured the Golden Blades log superimposed over the stat package on th card backs. Each Golden Blades card has rectangular box within the player's pictur on the back which to the naked eye resembles television snow. But placing special Pinnacle device over the rectangl revealed (for one out of every eight Golde Blades) the words "Special Artist's Proof" These cards were eligible to be redeemed fo two more parallel cards: a Special Artist's Proof for the collector and a Dealer's Choic Artist Proof for the redeeming hobby stor owner. These SAP winner cards wer inserted at approximately the same rate a standard Artist Proof cards, but because o the limited redemption period, are i somewhat shorter supply.
COMPLETE SET (275) 100.00 200.00
*STARS: 6X TO 12X BASIC CARDS

1996-97 Score Dream Team

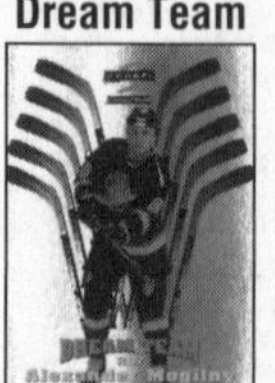

Randomly inserted in packs at a rate of 1:7 hobby and retail packs, this 12-card se features the top players at each position i the NHL today on an all-rainbow holographic foil card stock.
COMPLETE SET (12) 12.00 25.00
1 Eric Lindros .60 1.50
2 Paul Kariya .60 1.50
3 Joe Sakic 1.25 3.00
4 Peter Forsberg 1.50 4.00
5 Mark Messier .60 1.50
6 Mario Lemieux 3.00 8.00
7 Jaromir Jagr 1.00 2.50
8 Wayne Gretzky 4.00 10.00
9 Alexander Mogilny .25 .60
10 Pavel Bure .60 1.50
11 Sergei Fedorov .75 2.00
12 Patrick Roy 3.00 8.00

1996-97 Score Net Worth

nserted exclusively into retail packs at a rate 1:35, these cards feature the top etminders in the NHL today. Two photos race the front of each card, with one being a lack and silver metallic image.

COMPLETE SET (18) 10.00 20.00
1 Patrick Roy 2.00 5.00
2 Martin Brodeur 2.00 5.00
3 Jim Carey .40 1.00
4 Dominik Hasek 1.25 3.00
5 Ed Belfour .40 1.00
6 Chris Osgood .40 1.00
7 Curtis Joseph .40 1.00
8 John Vanbiesbrouck .40 1.00
9 Jocelyn Thibault .40 1.00
10 Stephane Fiset .40 1.00
11 Ron Hextall .40 1.00
12 Tom Barrasso .40 1.00
13 Daren Puppa .40 1.00
14 Mike Vernon .40 1.00
15 Bill Ranford .40 1.00
16 Corey Hirsch .40 1.00
17 Damian Rhodes .40 1.00
18 Nikolai Khabibulin .40 1.00

1996-97 Score Sudden Death

andomly inserted in hobby packs only at a ate of 1:35, this 15-card holofoil set eatures two action photos simulating natchups of some of the deadliest snipers gainst the stingiest netminders.

OMPLETE SET (15) 12.00 25.00
1 Martin Brodeur .75 2.00
Pierre Turgeon
2 Jim Carey 1.00 2.50
Steve Yzerman
3 Dominik Hasek .40 1.00
Brendan Shanahan
4 Ed Belfour .40 1.00
Brett Hull
5 Chris Osgood .40 1.00
Jeremy Roenick
6 Curtis Joseph .40 1.00
Pavel Bure
7 John Vanbiesbrouck 3.00 8.00
Mario Lemieux
8 Jocelyn Thibault .40 1.00
Alexander Mogilny
9 Mike Richter .40 1.00
Jaromir Jagr
10 Tom Barrasso .40 1.00
Mark Messier
11 Darren Puppa .75 2.00
Joe Sakic
12 Felix Potvin 3.00 8.00
Wayne Gretzky
13 Corey Hirsch .40 1.00
Paul Kariya
14 Ron Hextall .40 1.00
Sergei Fedorov
15 Nikolai Khabibulin .40 1.00
Teemu Selanne

1996-97 Score Superstitions

he 13-cards in this set (note the foolhardy se of this unlucky number!) highlight some f the unusual pre-game rituals and euroses of some of the NHL's most uccessful players. The cards were randomly nserted 1:19 hobby and retail packs and :10 magazine packs.

OMPLETE SET (13) 4.00 8.00
1 Teemu Selanne .30 .75
2 Doug Weight .25 .60
3 Mats Sundin .30 .75
4 Mike Modano .40 1.00
5 Felix Potvin .30 .75
6 Paul Coffey .30 .75
7 Ray Bourque .50 1.25
8 Chris Chelios .30 .75
9 Ron Hextall .25 .60
10 Alexander Selivanov .25 .60
11 Brett Hull .40 1.00
12 Mike Richter .30 .75
13 Scott Mellanby .25 .60

1997-98 Score

The 1997-98 Score set was issued in one series totaling 270 cards and was distributed in packs with a suggested retail price of $.99. The fronts feature color player photos in white borders. The backs carry player information.

COMPLETE SET (270) 7.50 15.00
1 Sean Burke .05 .15
2 Chris Osgood .05 .15
3 Garth Snow .05 .15
4 Mike Vernon .05 .15
5 Grant Fuhr .05 .15
6 Guy Hebert .05 .15
7 Arturs Irbe .05 .15
8 Andy Moog .05 .15
9 Tommy Salo .05 .15
10 Nikolai Khabibulin .05 .15
11 Mike Richter .10 .25
12 Corey Hirsch .05 .15
13 Bill Ranford .05 .15
14 Jim Carey .05 .15
15 Jeff Hackett .05 .15
16 Damian Rhodes .05 .15
17 Tom Barrasso .05 .15
18 Daren Puppa .05 .15
19 Craig Billington .05 .15
20 Ed Belfour .10 .25
21 Mikhail Shtalenkov .01 .05
22 Glenn Healy .05 .15
23 Marcel Cousineau .05 .15
24 Kevin Hodson .05 .15
25 Olaf Kolzig .05 .15
26 Eric Fichaud .05 .15
27 Ron Hextall .05 .15
28 Rick Tabaracci .05 .15
29 Felix Potvin .10 .25
30 Martin Brodeur .25 .60
31 Curtis Joseph .10 .25
32 Ken Wregget .05 .15
33 Patrick Roy .50 1.25
34 John Vanbiesbrouck .05 .15
35 Stephane Fiset .05 .15
36 Roman Turek .05 .15
37 Trevor Kidd .05 .15
38 Dwayne Roloson .01 .05
39 Dominik Hasek .20 .50
40 Patrick Lalime .05 .15
41 Jocelyn Thibault .05 .15
42 Jose Theodore .12 .30
43 Kirk McLean .05 .15
44 Steve Shields RC .15 .40
45 Mike Dunham .05 .15
46 Jamie Storr .05 .15
47 Byron Dafoe .05 .15
48 Chris Terreri .05 .15
49 Ron Tugnutt .05 .15
50 Kelly Hrudey .05 .15
51 Vaclav Prospal RC .10 .25
52 Alyn McCauley .05 .15
53 Jaroslav Svejkovsky .05 .15
54 Steve Shields .25 .60
55 Chris Dingman RC .01 .05
56 Vadim Sharifijanov .01 .05
57 Larry Courville .01 .05
58 Erik Rasmussen .01 .05
59 Sergei Samsonov .05 .15
60 Kevyn Adams .01 .05
61 Daniel Cleary .05 .15
62 Martin Prochazka RC .01 .05
63 Mattias Ohlund .05 .15
64 Juha Lind RC .01 .05
65 Olli Jokinen RC .30 .75
66 Espen Knutsen RC .20 .50
67 Marc Savard .05 .15
68 Hnat Domenichelli .01 .05
69 Warren Luhning RC .01 .05
70 Magnus Arvedson RC .01 .05
71 Chris Phillips .01 .05
72 Brad Isbister .01 .05
73 Boyd Devereaux .01 .05
74 Alexei Morozov .05 .15
75 Vladimir Vorobiev RC .01 .05
76 Steven Rice .01 .05
77 Tony Granato .01 .05
78 Lonny Bohonos .01 .05
79 Dave Gagner .01 .05
80 Brendan Shanahan .10 .25
81 Brett Hull .10 .30
82 Jaromir Jagr .15 .40
83 Peter Forsberg .25 .60
84 Paul Kariya .10 .25
85 Mark Messier .10 .25
86 Steve Yzerman .50 1.25
87 Keith Tkachuk .10 .25
88 Eric Lindros .10 .25
89 Ray Bourque .15 .40
90 Chris Chelios .10 .25
91 Sergei Fedorov .15 .40
92 Mike Modano .15 .40
93 Doug Gilmour .05 .15
94 Saku Koivu .10 .25
95 Mats Sundin .10 .25
96 Pavel Bure .10 .25
97 Theo Fleury .01 .05
98 Keith Primeau .01 .05
99 Wayne Gretzky .60 1.50
100 Doug Weight .05 .15
101 Alexander Daigle .01 .05
102 Owen Nolan .05 .15
103 Peter Bondra .05 .15
104 Pat LaFontaine .10 .25
105 Kirk Muller .01 .05
106 Zigmund Palffy .05 .15
107 Jeremy Roenick .15 .30
108 John LeClair .10 .25
109 Derek Plante .01 .05
110 Geoff Sanderson .05 .15
111 Dimitri Khristich .01 .05
112 Vincent Damphousse .01 .05
113 Teemu Selanne .10 .25
114 Tony Amonte .05 .15
115 Dave Andreychuk .01 .05
116 Alexei Yashin .01 .05
117 Adam Oates .05 .15
118 Pierre Turgeon .05 .15
119 Dino Ciccarelli .01 .05
120 Ryan Smyth .05 .15
121 Ray Sheppard .01 .05
122 Jozef Stumpel .05 .15
123 Jarome Iginla .12 .30
124 Pat Verbeek .01 .05
125 Joe Sakic .20 .50
126 Brian Leetch .10 .25
127 Rod Brind'Amour .05 .15
128 Wendel Clark .05 .15
129 Alexander Mogilny .05 .15
130 Mark Recchi .05 .15
131 Daniel Alfredsson .05 .15
132 Ron Francis .05 .15
133 Martin Gelinas .01 .05
134 Andrew Cassels .01 .05
135 Joe Nieuwendyk .05 .15
136 Jason Arnott .01 .05
137 Bryan Berard .05 .15
138 Mikael Renberg .05 .15
139 Mike Gartner .05 .15
140 Joe Juneau .05 .15
141 John MacLean .01 .05
142 Adam Graves .05 .15
143 Petr Nedved .05 .15
144 Trevor Linden .05 .15
145 Sergei Berezin .01 .05
146 Adam Deadmarsh .01 .05
147 Jeff O'Neill .01 .05
148 Rob Blake .05 .15
149 Luc Robitaille .05 .15
150 Markus Naslund .10 .25
151 Ethan Moreau .01 .05
152 Martin Rucinsky .01 .05
UER front Ruckinski
153 Mike Grier .01 .05
154 Craig Janney .01 .05
155 John Cullen .01 .05
156 Alexei Kovalev .01 .05
157 Tony Twist .05 .15
158 Claude Lemieux .01 .05
159 Kevin Stevens .05 .15
160 Mathieu Schneider .01 .05
161 Randy Cunneyworth .01 .05
162 Darius Kasparaitis .01 .05
163 Joe Murphy .01 .05
164 Brandon Convery .01 .05
165 Janne Niinimaa .05 .15
166 Paul Coffey .10 .25
167 Daymond Langkow .05 .15
168 Chris Gratton .05 .15
169 Ray Ferraro .01 .05
170 Jeff Friesen .01 .05
171 Ted Donato .01 .05
172 Brian Holzinger .01 .05
173 Travis Green .01 .05
174 Sandis Ozolinsh .01 .05
175 Alexei Zhamnov .01 .05
176 Steve Rucchin .01 .05
177 Scott Mellanby .01 .05
178 Andrei Kovalenko .01 .05
179 Donald Audette .01 .05
180 Bernie Nicholls .01 .05
181 Jonas Hoglund .01 .05
182 Nicklas Lidstrom .10 .25
183 Bobby Holik .01 .05
184 Geoff Courtnall .01 .05
185 Steve Sullivan .01 .05
186 Valeri Kamensky .05 .15
187 Mike Peca .01 .05
188 Jere Lehtinen .01 .05
189 Robert Svehla .01 .05
190 Darren McCarty .01 .05
191 Brian Savage .01 .05
192 Harry York .01 .05
193 Eric Daze .05 .15
194 Niklas Sundstrom .01 .05
195 Oleg Tverdovsky .01 .05
196 Eric Desjardins .05 .15
197 German Titov .01 .05
198 Derian Hatcher .01 .05
199 Bill Guerin .05 .15
200 Rob Zamuner .01 .05
201 Dale Hunter .01 .05
202 Darcy Tucker .01 .05
203 Andreas Dackell .01 .05
204 Jason Dawe .01 .05
205 Brian Rolston .01 .05
206 Ed Olczyk .01 .05
207 Todd Warriner .01 .05
208 Mariusz Czerkawski .01 .05
209 Slava Kozlov .01 .05
210 Marty McInnis .01 .05
211 Jamie Langenbrunner .01 .05
212 Vitali Yachmenev .01 .05
213 Stephane Richer .01 .05
214 Roman Hamrlik .05 .15
215 Jim Campbell .01 .05
216 Matthew Barnaby .01 .05
217 Benoit Hogue .01 .05
218 Robert Reichel .01 .05
219 Tie Domi .05 .15
220 Steve Konowalchuk .01 .05
221 Radek Dvorak .01 .05
222 Kevin Hatcher .01 .05
223 Viktor Kozlov .01 .05
224 Scott Stevens .05 .15
225 Cory Stillman .01 .05
226 Anson Carter .05 .15
227 Rem Murray .01 .05
228 Vladimir Konstantinov .05 .15
229 Scott Niedermayer .01 .05
230 Steve Duchesne .01 .05
231 Valeri Bure .01 .05
232 Miroslav Satan .01 .05
233 Jason Allison .01 .05
234 Mark Fitzpatrick .05 .15
235 Ed Jovanovski .05 .15
236 Esa Tikkanen .01 .05
237 Stu Barnes .01 .05
238 Darryl Sydor .01 .05
239 Ulf Samuelsson .01 .05
240 Dmitri Mironov .01 .05
241 Bryan Smolinski .01 .05
242 Rob Ray .01 .05
243 Todd Marchant .01 .05
244 Cliff Ronning .01 .05
245 Alexander Selivanov .01 .05
246 Rick Tocchet .05 .15
247 Vladimir Malakhov .01 .05
248 Al MacInnis .05 .15
249 Dainius Zubrus .10 .25
250 Keith Jones .01 .05
251 Darren Turcotte .01 .05
252 Ulf Dahlen .01 .05
253 Rob Niedermayer .01 .05
254 J.J. Daigneault .01 .05
255 Michal Grosek .01 .05
256 Chris Therien .01 .05
257 Adam Foote .01 .05
258 Tomas Sandstrom .01 .05
259 Scott Lachance .01 .05
260 Paul Kariya SM .10 .25
261 Pavel Bure SM .10 .25
262 Mike Modano SM .10 .25
263 Steve Yzerman SM .10 .25
264 Sergei Fedorov SM .10 .25
265 Eric Lindros SM .10 .25
266 Dominik Hasek CL (1-66) .05 .15
267 Bryan Berard CL (67-132) .01 .05
268 Mike Peca CL (133-201) .01 .05
269 Martin Brodeur .01 .05
Mike Dunham CL (202-270)
270 Paul Kariya CL (inserts) .10 .25
PR82 Jaromir Jagr PROMO 1.00 2.50
PR83 Peter Forsberg PROMO 1.25 3.00
PR84 Paul Kariya PROMO 1.50 4.00
PR86 Steve Yzerman PROMO 1.50 4.00

1997-98 Score Artist's Proofs

Randomly inserted in packs at the rate of 1:35, this 160-card set is a partial parallel version of the base set and is printed on prismatic foil board with the "Artist's Proof" seal on the front.

*STARS: 30X TO 60X BASIC CARDS

1997-98 Score Golden Blades

Randomly inserted in packs at the rate of 1:7, this 160-card set is a partial parallel version of the base set printed on silver gloss foil board.

*STARS: 5X TO 10X BASIC CARDS

1997-98 Score Check It

Randomly inserted in packs at the rate of 1:18, this 18-card set features action color photos of some of the toughest hitters in the game.

COMPLETE SET (18) 3.00 6.00
1 Eric Lindros .30 .75
2 Mark Recchi .20 .50
3 Brendan Shanahan .30 .75
4 Keith Tkachuk .30 .75
5 John LeClair .30 .75
6 Doug Gilmour .20 .50
7 Jarome Iginla .40 1.00
8 Ryan Smyth .20 .50
9 Chris Chelios .30 .75
10 Mike Grier .05 .15
11 Vincent Damphousse .05 .15
12 Bryan Berard .20 .50
13 Jaromir Jagr .50 1.25
14 Mike Peca .05 .15
15 Dino Ciccarelli .05 .15
16 Rod Brind'Amour .20 .50
17 Owen Nolan .20 .50
18 Pat Verbeek .05 .15

1997-98 Score Net Worth

Randomly inserted in packs at the rate of 1:35, this 18-card set features color action photos of the NHL's best goalies.

COMPLETE SET (18) 8.00 15.00
1 Guy Hebert .25 .60
2 Jim Carey .25 .60
3 Trevor Kidd .25 .60
4 Chris Osgood .25 .60
5 Curtis Joseph .40 1.00
6 Mike Richter .40 1.00
7 Damian Rhodes .25 .60
8 Garth Snow .25 .60
9 Nikolai Khabibulin .25 .60
10 Grant Fuhr .25 .60
11 Jocelyn Thibault .25 .60
12 Tommy Salo .25 .60
13 Patrick Roy 2.00 5.00
14 Martin Brodeur 1.00 2.50
15 John Vanbiesbrouck .25 .60
16 Felix Potvin .40 1.00
17 Dominik Hasek .75 2.00
18 Ed Belfour .40 1.00

1997-98 Score Avalanche

This 20-card team set of the Colorado Avalanche was produced by Pinnacle and features bordered color action player photos. The backs carry player information.

COMPLETE SET (20) 4.00 10.00
*PLATINUM: 3X BASIC CARDS
*PREMIER: 8X BASIC CARDS
1 Patrick Roy 1.60 4.00
2 Craig Billington .24 .60
3 Marc Denis .24 .60
4 Peter Forsberg 1.00 2.50
5 Jari Kurri .24 .60
6 Sandis Ozolinsh .24 .60
7 Valeri Kamensky .24 .60
8 Adam Deadmarsh .24 .60
9 Keith Jones .12 .30
10 Josef Marha .10 .25
11 Claude Lemieux .24 .60
12 Adam Foote .12 .30
13 Eric Lacroix .10 .25
14 Rene Corbet .10 .25
15 Uwe Krupp .10 .25
16 Sylvain Lefebvre .10 .25
17 Mike Ricci .24 .60
18 Joe Sakic .80 2.00
19 Stephane Yelle .10 .25
20 Yves Sarault .10 .25

1997-98 Score Blues

This 20-card team set of the St. Louis Blues was produced by Pinnacle and features bordered color action player photos. The backs carry player information.

COMPLETE SET (20) 3.20 8.00
*PLATINUM: 3X BASIC CARDS
*PREMIER: 8X BASIC CARDS
1 Brett Hull .40 1.00
2 Pierre Turgeon .24 .60
3 Joe Murphy .10 .25
4 Jim Campbell .10 .25
5 Harry York .10 .25
6 Al MacInnis .24 .60
7 Chris Pronger .24 .60
8 Darren Turcotte .10 .25
9 Robert Petrovicky .10 .25
10 Tony Twist .30 .75
11 Grant Fuhr .24 .60
12 Scott Pellerin .10 .25
13 Jamie Rivers .10 .25
14 Chris McAlpine .10 .25
15 Geoff Courtnall .24 .60
16 Steve Duchesne .20 .50
17 Libor Zabransky .10 .25
18 Pavol Demitra .24 .60
19 Marc Bergevin .10 .25
20 Jamie McLennan .10 .25

1997-98 Score Bruins

This 20-card team set of the Boston Bruins was produced by Pinnacle and features bordered color action player photos. The backs carry player information.

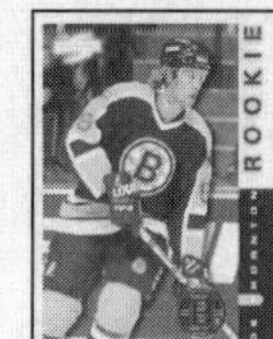

COMPLETE SET (20) 2.40 6.00
*PLATINUM: 3X BASIC CARDS
*PREMIER: 8X BASIC CARDS
1 Shawn Bates .10 .25
2 Jim Carey .16 .40
3 Rob Tallas .10 .25
4 Ray Bourque .30 .75
5 Dimitri Khristich .10 .25
6 Ted Donato .10 .25
7 Jason Allison .24 .60
8 Anson Carter .16 .40
9 Rob Dimaio .10 .25
10 Steve Heinze .10 .25
11 Jean Yves Roy .10 .25
12 Randy Robitaille .10 .25
13 Byron Dafoe .30 .75
14 Sergei Samsonov .80 2.00
15 Ken Baumgartner .10 .25
16 Dave Ellett .10 .25
17 Joe Thornton .80 2.00
18 Jeff Odgers .10 .25
19 Kyle McLaren .10 .25
20 Don Sweeney .10 .25

1997-98 Score Canadiens

This 20-card team set of the Montreal Canadiens was produced by Pinnacle and features bordered color action player photos. The backs carry player information.

COMPLETE SET (20) 3.20 8.00
*PLATINUM: 3X BASIC CARDS
*PREMIER: 8X BASIC CARDS
1 Andy Moog .24 .60
2 Jocelyn Thibault .24 .60
3 Jose Theodore .24 .60
4 Vincent Damphousse .24 .60
5 Mark Recchi .24 .60
6 Brian Savage .10 .25
7 Saku Koivu .60 1.50
8 Stephane Richer .24 .60
9 Martin Rucinsky .10 .25
10 Valeri Bure .10 .25
11 Vladimir Malakhov .10 .25
12 Shayne Corson .24 .60
13 Darcy Tucker .10 .25
14 Sebastien Bordeleau .10 .25
15 Terry Ryan .10 .25
16 David Ling .10 .25
17 Dave Manson .10 .25
18 Benoit Brunet .10 .25
19 Marc Bureau .10 .25
20 Patrice Brisebois .10 .25

1997-98 Score Canucks

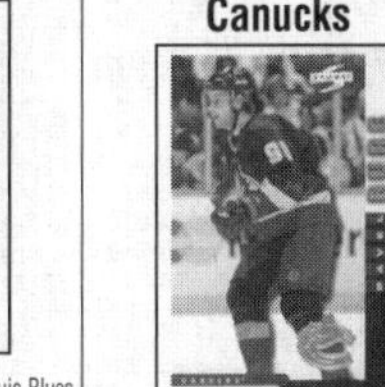

This 20-card team set of the Vancouver Canucks was produced by Pinnacle and features bordered color action player photos. The backs carry player information.

COMPLETE SET (20) 3.20 8.00
*PLATINUM: 3X BASIC CARDS
*PREMIER: 8X BASIC CARDS
1 Pavel Bure .60 1.50
2 Alexander Mogilny .24 .60
3 Mark Messier .40 1.00
4 Trevor Linden .24 .60
5 Martin Gelinas .10 .25
6 Mattias Ohlund .16 .40
7 Markus Naslund .10 .25
8 Jyrki Lumme .10 .25
9 Lonny Bohonos .10 .25
10 Kirk McLean .24 .60
11 Corey Hirsch .24 .60
12 Arturs Irbe .24 .60
13 Larry Courville .10 .25
14 Adrian Aucoin .10 .25
15 Grant Ledyard .10 .25
16 Gino Odjick .10 .25
17 Donald Brashear .10 .25
18 Brian Noonan .10 .25
19 David Roberts .10 .25
20 Dave Babych .10 .25

1997-98 Score Devils

This 20-card team set of the New Jersey Devils was produced by Pinnacle and features bordered color action player photos. The backs carry player information.

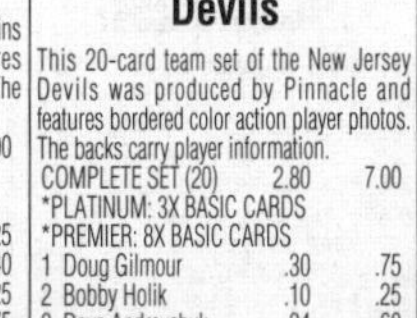

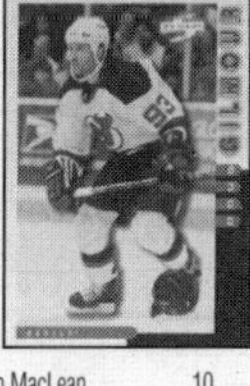

COMPLETE SET (20) 2.80 7.00
*PLATINUM: 3X BASIC CARDS
*PREMIER: 8X BASIC CARDS
1 Doug Gilmour .30 .75
2 Bobby Holik .10 .25
3 Dave Andreychuk .24 .60
4 John MacLean .10 .25
5 Bill Guerin .10 .25
6 Brian Rolston .10 .25
7 Scott Niedermayer .10 .25
8 Scott Stevens .10 .25
9 Valeri Zelepukin .10 .25
10 Steve Thomas .10 .25
11 Denis Pederson .10 .25
12 Randy McKay .10 .25
13 Mike Dunham .24 .60
14 Petr Sykora .16 .40
15 Lyle Odelein .10 .25
16 Martin Brodeur .80 2.00
17 Vadim Sharifijanov .10 .25
18 Bob Carpenter .10 .25
19 Sergei Brylin .10 .25
20 Ken Daneyko .10 .25

1997-98 Score Flyers

This 20-card team set of the Philadelphia Flyers was produced by Pinnacle and features bordered color action player photos. The backs carry player information.

COMPLETE SET (20) 4.00 10.00
*PLATINUM: 3X BASIC CARDS
*PREMIER: 8X BASIC CARDS
1 Ron Hextall .24 .60
2 Garth Snow .24 .60
3 Eric Lindros 1.20 3.00
4 John LeClair .60 1.50
5 Rod Brind'Amour .24 .60
6 Chris Gratton .16 .40
7 Eric Desjardins .10 .25
8 Trent Klatt .10 .25
9 Janne Niinimaa .24 .60
10 Luke Richardson .10 .25
11 Paul Coffey .30 .75
12 Dainius Zubrus .30 .75
13 Shjon Podein .10 .25
14 Joel Otto .10 .25
15 Chris Therien .10 .25
16 Pat Falloon .10 .25
17 Petr Svoboda .10 .25
18 Vaclav Prospal .30 .75
19 John Druce .10 .25
20 Daniel Lacroix .10 .25

1997-98 Score Maple Leafs

This 20-card team set of the Toronto Maple Leafs was produced by Pinnacle and features bordered color action player photos. The backs carry player information.

COMPLETE SET (20) 2.80 7.00
*PLATINUM: 3X BASIC CARDS
*PREMIER: 8X BASIC CARDS
1 Felix Potvin .30 .75
2 Glenn Healy .24 .60
3 Marcel Cousineau .24 .60
4 Mats Sundin .30 .75
5 Wendel Clark .24 .60
6 Sergei Berezin .24 .60
7 Steve Sullivan .10 .25
8 Tie Domi .12 .30
9 Todd Warriner .10 .25
10 Mathieu Schneider .10 .25
11 Mike Craig .10 .25
12 Darby Hendrickson .10 .25
13 Fredrik Modin .10 .25
14 Brandon Convery .10 .25
15 Kevyn Adams .10 .25
16 Dimitri Yushkevich .10 .25
17 Alyn McCauley .10 .25
18 Derek King .10 .25
19 Jamie Baker .10 .25
20 Martin Prochazka .10 .25

1997-98 Score Mighty Ducks

This 20-card team set of the Mighty Ducks of Anaheim was produced by Pinnacle and features bordered color action player photos. The backs carry player information.

COMPLETE SET (20) 4.00 10.00
*PLATINUM: 3X BASIC CARDS
*PREMIER: 8X BASIC CARDS
1 Paul Kariya 1.20 3.00
2 Teemu Selanne .70 1.75

3 Steve Rucchin .10 .25
4 Dmitri Mironov .10 .25
5 Matt Cullen .10 .25
6 Kevin Todd .10 .25
7 Joe Sacco .10 .25
8 J.J. Daigneault .10 .25
9 Darren Van Impe .10 .25
10 Scott Young .10 .25
11 Ted Drury .10 .25
12 Tomas Sandstrom .10 .25
13 Warren Rychel .10 .25
14 Guy Hebert .24 .60
15 Shawn Antoski .10 .25
16 Mikhail Shtalenkov .24 .60
17 Peter Leboutillier .10 .25
18 Sean Pronger .10 .25
19 Dave Karpa .10 .25
20 Espen Knutsen .20 .50

1997-98 Score Penguins

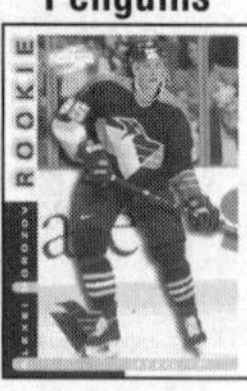

This 20-card team set of the Pittsburgh Penguins was produced by Pinnacle and features bordered color action player photos. The backs carry player information.

COMPLETE SET (20) 3.60 9.00
*PLATINUM: 3X BASIC CARDS
*PREMIER: 8X BASIC CARDS
1 Tom Barrasso .10 .25
2 Ken Wregget .24 .60
3 Patrick Lalime .24 .60
4 Jaromir Jagr 1.00 2.50
5 Ron Francis .24 .60
6 Petr Nedved .24 .60
7 Ed Olczyk .10 .25
8 Kevin Hatcher .10 .25
9 Stu Barnes .10 .25
10 Darius Kasparaitis .10 .25
11 Greg Johnson .10 .25
12 Garry Valk .10 .25
13 Roman Oksiuta .10 .25
14 Dan Quinn .10 .25
15 Alex Hicks .10 .25
16 Robert Dome .10 .25
17 Dave Roche .10 .25
18 Alexei Morozov .24 .60
19 Rob Brown .10 .25
20 Domenic Pittis .10 .25

1997-98 Score Rangers

This 20-card team set of the New York Rangers was produced by Pinnacle and features bordered color action player photos. The backs carry player information.

COMPLETE SET (20) 4.00 10.00
*PLATINUM: 3X BASIC CARDS
*PREMIER: 8X BASIC CARDS
1 Wayne Gretzky 2.00 5.00
2 Brian Leetch .30 .75
3 Mike Keane .10 .25
4 Adam Graves .24 .60
5 Niklas Sundstrom .10 .25
6 Kevin Stevens .10 .25
7 Alexei Kovalev .10 .25
8 Alexander Karpovtsev .10 .25
9 Bill Berg .10 .25
10 Pat Lafontaine .24 .60
11 Bruce Driver .10 .25
12 Pat Flatley .10 .25
13 Vladimir Vorobiev .10 .25
14 Christian Dube .10 .25
15 Ulf Samuelsson .10 .25
16 Mike Richter .30 .75
17 Jason Muzzatti .10 .25
18 Daniel Goneau .10 .25
19 Marc Savard .10 .25
20 Jeff Beukeboom .10 .25

1997-98 Score Red Wings

This 20-card team set of the Detroit Red Wings was produced by Pinnacle and features bordered color action player photos. The backs carry player information.

COMPLETE SET (20) 4.00 10.00
*PLATINUM: 3X BASIC CARDS
*PREMIER: 8X BASIC CARDS
1 Brendan Shanahan .60 1.50

2 Steve Yzerman 1.00 2.50
3 Sergei Fedorov .60 1.50
4 Nicklas Lidstrom .24 .60
5 Igor Larionov .16 .40
6 Darren McCarty .24 .60
7 Slava Kozlov .24 .60
8 Larry Murphy .24 .60
9 Vladimir Konstantinov .24 .60
10 Martin Lapointe .12 .30
11 Slava Fetisov .12 .30
12 Kris Draper .12 .30
13 Doug Brown .10 .25
14 Brent Gilchrist .10 .25
15 Kirk Maltby .10 .25
16 Tomas Holmstrom .10 .25
17 Chris Osgood .30 .75
18 Kevin Hodson .30 .75
19 Jamie Pushor .10 .25
20 Mike Knuble .24 .60

1997-98 Score Sabres

This 20-card team set of the Buffalo Sabres was produced by Pinnacle and features bordered color action player photos. The backs carry player information.

COMPLETE SET (20) 2.80 7.00
*PLATINUM: 3X BASIC CARDS
*PREMIER: 8X BASIC CARDS
1 Dominik Hasek .70 1.75
2 Steve Shields .24 .60
3 Dixon Ward .10 .25
4 Donald Audette .10 .25
5 Matthew Barnaby .10 .25
6 Randy Burridge .10 .25
7 Jason Dawe .10 .25
8 Michael Grosek .10 .25
9 Brian Holzinger .24 .60
10 Brad May .10 .25
11 Mike Peca .30 .75
12 Derek Plante .10 .25
13 Wayne Primeau .10 .25
14 Rob Ray .24 .60
15 Miroslav Satan .24 .60
16 Erik Rasmussen .10 .25
17 Jason Wooley .10 .25
18 Alexei Zhitnik .10 .25
19 Darryl Shannon .10 .25
20 Mike Wilson .10 .25

1967-68 Seals Team Issue

Produced as a first year team issue of the expansion Oakland Seals, this 19-piece set features 8x10 individual player cards on thin cardboard stock. They are not numbered and are listed below in alphabetical order.

1 Bobby Baun 10.00 20.00
2 Ron Boehm 2.00 4.00
3 Wally Boyer 3.00 6.00
4 Charlie Burns 4.00 8.00
5 Larry Cahan 2.00 4.00
6 Alain Caron 2.00 4.00
7 Terry Clancy 2.00 4.00
8 Kent Douglas 4.00 8.00
9 Gerry Ehman 3.00 6.00
10 Autry Erickson 3.00 6.00
11 Billy Harris 3.00 6.00
12 Ron Harris 3.00 6.00
13 Bill Hicke 3.00 6.00
14 Charlie Hodge 7.50 15.00
15 Mike Laughton 2.00 4.00
16 Bob Lemieux 2.00 4.00
17 Gary Smith 6.00 12.00
18 George Swarbrick 3.00 6.00
19 Joe Szura 3.00 6.00

1992-93 Seasons Patches

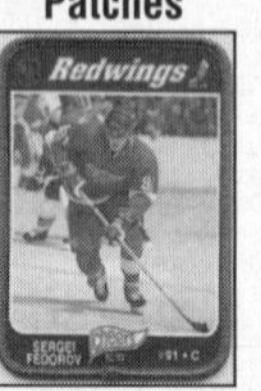

Each measuring approximately 3 1/8" by 4 1/4", these 70 patches were licensed by the NHL/NHLPA and feature color action player photos on black fabric. The player's team appears above the photo and his name, position, and sweater number are below. An embroidered border in the team color edges the patch. The patches come in a poly-wrap sleeve attached to a teal cardboard rack display. These displays were pegged on team customized counter display easels, showcasing four different players (six patches per player), for a total of 24 patches per team display. Two versions are available. The bilingual version has both French and English printed on the package. The other version is printed in English only. A checklist of 71 patches is printed on the back of the display. In the checklist, patch 22, an unnamed prototype, features ex-NHL star and Seasons President Grant Mulvey. Mulvey's patch was only available through him as a handout and could not be purchased by the public; it is not considered part of the complete set.

COMPLETE SET (70) 60.00 150.00
1 Jeremy Roenick 1.20 3.00
2 Steve Larmer 1.00 2.50
3 Ed Belfour 1.20 3.00
4 Chris Chelios 1.20 3.00
5 Sergei Fedorov 1.20 3.00
6 Steve Yzerman 2.00 5.00
7 Tim Cheveldae .40 1.00
8 Bob Probert 1.00 2.50
9 Wayne Gretzky 4.00 10.00
10 Luc Robitaille 1.00 2.50
11 Tony Granato .40 1.00
12 Kelly Hrudey 1.00 2.50
13 Brett Hull 1.20 3.00
14 Curtis Joseph 1.20 3.00
15 Brendan Shanahan 1.20 3.00
16 Nelson Emerson .40 1.00
17 Ray Bourque 1.20 3.00
18 Joe Juneau 1.00 2.50
19 Andy Moog 1.00 2.50
20 Adam Oates 1.00 2.50
21 Patrick Roy 3.20 8.00
22 Grant Mulvey (Prototype) 8.00 20.00
23 Denis Savard 1.00 2.50
24 Gilbert Dionne .40 1.00
25 Kirk Muller 1.00 2.50
26 Mark Messier 1.20 3.00
27 Tony Amonte 1.00 2.50
28 Brian Leetch 1.20 3.00
29 Mike Richter 1.20 3.00
30 Trevor Linden 1.00 2.50
31 Pavel Bure 1.20 3.00
32 Cliff Ronning .40 1.00
33 Russ Courtnall .40 1.00
34 Mario Lemieux 3.20 8.00
35 Jaromir Jagr 2.00 5.00
36 Tom Barrasso 1.00 2.50
37 Rick Tocchet 1.00 2.50
38 Eric Lindros 2.00 5.00
39 Rod Brind'Amour 1.00 2.50
40 Dominic Roussel .40 1.00
41 Mark Recchi 1.00 2.50
42 Pat LaFontaine 1.00 2.50
43 Donald Audette .40 1.00
44 Pat Verbeek 1.00 2.50
45 John Cullen .40 1.00
46 Owen Nolan 1.00 2.50
47 Joe Sakic 1.20 3.00
48 Kevin Hatcher .40 1.00
49 Don Beaupre .40 1.00
50 Scott Stevens 1.00 2.50
51 Chris Terreri .40 1.00
52 Scott Lachance .40 1.00
53 Pierre Turgeon 1.00 2.50
54 Grant Fuhr 1.00 2.50
55 Doug Gilmour 1.20 3.00
56 Dave Manson .40 1.00
57 Bill Ranford 1.00 2.50
58 Troy Murray .40 1.00
59 Phil Housley .40 1.00
60 Al MacInnis 1.00 2.50
61 Mike Vernon 1.00 2.50
62 Pat Falloon .40 1.00
63 Doug Wilson 1.00 2.50
64 Jon Casey .40 1.00
65 Mike Modano 1.20 3.00
66 Kevin Stevens .40 1.00
67 Al Iafrate .40 1.00
68 Dale Hawerchuk 1.00 2.50
69 Igor Kravchuk .40 1.00
70 Wendel Clark 1.00 2.50
71 Kirk McLean 1.00 2.50

1993-94 Seasons Patches

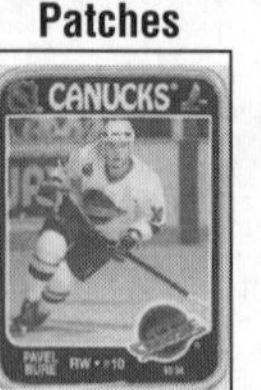

Each measuring approximately 3 1/8" by 4 1/4", these 20 patches were licensed by the NHL/NHLPA and feature color action player photos on black fabric. The player's team appears above the photo and his name, position, and jersey number are below. An embroidered border in the team color edges the patch. The team logo and year of issue in the lower right corner round out the front. The patches were encased in a hard plastic sleeve attached to a black cardboard rack display. A checklist was printed on the back of the display. The patches are unnumbered but are checklisted below according to the numbering of the checklist card.

COMPLETE SET (20) 24.00 60.00
1 Ed Belfour .60 1.50
2 Pavel Bure 1.20 3.00
3 Paul Coffey .60 1.50
4 Doug Gilmour .60 1.50
5 Wayne Gretzky 4.00 10.00
6 Brett Hull .80 2.00
7 Jaromir Jagr 2.00 5.00
8 Joe Juneau .40 1.00
9 Mario Lemieux 3.20 8.00
10 Eric Lindros 2.00 5.00
11 Shawn McEachern .40 1.00
12 Alexander Mogilny .50 1.25
13 Adam Oates .50 1.25
14 Felix Potvin .60 1.50
15 Jeremy Roenick .60 1.50
16 Patrick Roy 3.20 8.00
17 Joe Sakic 1.20 3.00
18 Teemu Selanne 1.20 3.00
19 Kevin Stevens .40 1.00
20 Steve Yzerman 2.00 5.00

1994-95 Select Promos

These nine standard-size cards were issued to herald the release of the 1994-95 Select hockey series. The fronts feature borderless color action player photos. The player's last name and position, the team logo and a small, sepia-toned player portrait appear on gold-foil background in the lower left corner. The backs carry another color action player photo with player biography, profile and stats next to it. The top right corner of these cards has been cut off to mark them as sample cards. The Jamie Storr YE1 card is a sample of the Youth Explosion insert set.

COMPLETE SEALED SET (9) .40 1.00
7 John Vanbiesbrouck .06 .15
90 Felix Potvin .06 .15
108 Stephane Richer .02 .05
118 Dino Ciccarelli .02 .05
128 Sylvain Cote .02 .05
142 Kevin Dineen .02 .05
194 Mattias Norstrom .02 .05
YE1 Jamie Storr .40 1.00
NNO Title Card .04 .10

1994-95 Select

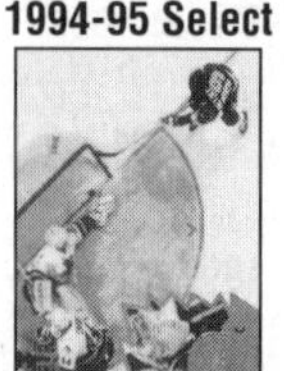

This 200-card set had an announced print run of 3,950, 24-box hobby-only cases. The design resembled a modernized version of the 1984-85 OPC set with a main action shot complemented by a corner head shot. The set is notable for the inclusion of 20 cards of players who competed in the 1994 Mexico Cup for 17-year-olds. One 4" by 6" bonus Mike Modano card featuring Sportflics technology was included in every box.

COMPLETE SET (200) 15.00 30.00
1 Mark Messier .08 .25
2 Rick Tocchet .05 .15
3 Alexandre Daigle .02 .10
4 Owen Nolan .05 .15
5 Bill Ranford .05 .15
6 Dave Gagner .05 .15
7 John Vanbiesbrouck .05 .15
8 Sergei Makarov .02 .10
9 Derek King .02 .10
10 Sergei Fedorov .20 .50
11 Trevor Linden .05 .15
12 Don Beaupre .05 .15
13 Dave Manson .02 .10
14 Sergei Zubov .02 .10
15 Keith Primeau .02 .10
16 Joe Mullen .05 .15
17 Bernie Nicholls .05 .15
18 Ray Bourque .20 .50
19 Mike Ridley .02 .10
20 Wendel Clark .05 .15
21 Mats Sundin .08 .25
22 Alexander Mogilny .05 .15
23 Mathieu Schneider .02 .10
24 Brian Leetch .08 .25
25 Rob Niedermayer .05 .15
26 Donald Audette .02 .10
27 Doug Weight .05 .15
28 Al MacInnis .05 .15
29 Jeremy Roenick .15 .40
30 Mark Recchi .05 .15
31 Chris Chelios .08 .25
32 Luc Robitaille .05 .15
33 Dale Hunter .02 .10
34 Kelly Hrudey .05 .15
35 Steve Yzerman .50 1.25
36 Martin Straka .02 .10
37 Arturs Irbe .05 .15
38 Mike Modano .20 .50
39 Cam Neely .08 .25
40 Igor Larionov .02 .10
41 Ray Ferraro .02 .10
42 Dale Hawerchuk .05 .15
43 Brian Bradley .02 .10
44 Joe Murphy .02 .10
45 Daren Puppa .05 .15
46 Pierre Turgeon .05 .15
47 Shayne Corson .02 .10
48 Adam Graves .02 .10
49 Craig Billington .05 .15
50 Derian Hatcher .02 .10
51 Alexei Zhamnov .05 .15
52 Dominik Hasek .25 .60
53 Ed Belfour .08 .25
54 Mike Vernon .05 .15
55 Bob Kudelski .02 .10
56 Ray Sheppard .05 .15
57 Pat LaFontaine .08 .25
58 Adam Oates .05 .15
59 Vincent Damphousse .02 .10
60 Jaromir Jagr .20 .50
61 Mikael Renberg .05 .15
62 Joe Sakic .25 .60
63 Sandis Ozolinsh .02 .10
64 Kirk McLean .05 .15
65 Stephan Lebeau .02 .10
66 Alexei Kovalev .02 .10
67 Ron Hextall .05 .15
68 Geoff Sanderson .05 .15
69 Doug Gilmour .05 .15
70 Russ Courtnall .02 .10
71 Jari Kurri .05 .15
72 Paul Coffey .08 .25
73 Claude Lemieux .02 .10
74 Teemu Selanne .08 .25
75 Keith Tkachuk .08 .25
76 Pat Verbeek .02 .10
77 Chris Gratton .02 .10
78 Martin Brodeur .30 .75
79 Guy Hebert .05 .15
80 Al Iafrate .02 .10
81 Glen Wesley .02 .10
82 Scott Stevens .05 .15
83 Wayne Gretzky .75 2.00
84 Ron Francis .05 .15
85 Scott Mellanby .05 .15
86 Joe Juneau .05 .15
87 Jason Arnott .02 .10
88 Tom Barrasso .05 .15
89 Peter Bondra .05 .15
90 Felix Potvin .08 .25
91 Brian Bellows .02 .10
92 Pavel Bure .08 .25
93 Grant Fuhr .05 .15
94 Andy Moog .08 .25
95 Mike Gartner .05 .15
96 Patrick Roy .60 1.50
97 Brett Hull .15 .40
98 Rob Blake .05 .15
99 Dave Andreychuk .05 .15
100 Eric Lindros .08 .25
101 Scott Niedermayer .02 .10
102 Tim Cheveldae .05 .15
103 Slava Kozlov .05 .15
104 Dimitri Khristich .02 .10
105 Steve Thomas .02 .10
106 Kevin Stevens .02 .10
107 Kirk Muller .02 .10
108 Stephane Richer .05 .15
109 Theo Fleury .02 .10
110 Jeff Brown .02 .10
111 Chris Pronger .08 .25
112 Steve Larmer .05 .15
113 Eric Desjardins .05 .15
114 Mike Ricci .02 .10
115 Tony Amonte .05 .15
116 Pat Falloon .02 .10
117 Garry Galley .02 .10
118 Dino Ciccarelli .05 .15
119 Rod Brind'Amour .05 .15
120 Petr Nedved .05 .15
121 Curtis Joseph .08 .25
122 Cliff Ronning .02 .10
123 Ulf Dahlen .02 .10
124 Marty McSorley .02 .10
125 Nelson Emerson .02 .10
126 Brian Skrudland .02 .10
127 Sean Burke .05 .15
128 Sylvain Cote .02 .10
129 Brendan Shanahan .08 .25
130 Benoit Hogue .02 .10
131 Joe Nieuwendyk .05 .15
132 Bryan Smolinski .02 .10
133 Mike Richter .08 .25
134 Nicklas Lidstrom .08 .25
135 Alexei Yashin .02 .10
136 John MacLean .05 .15
137 Geoff Courtnall .02 .10
138 Robert Reichel .02 .10
139 Craig Janney .05 .15
140 Zarley Zalapski .02 .10
141 Andrew Cassels .02 .10
142 Kevin Dineen .02 .10
143 Larry Murphy .05 .15
144 Valeri Kamensky .05 .15
145 Steve Duchesne .02 .10
146 Phil Housley .05 .15
147 Gary Roberts .02 .10
148 Kevin Hatcher .02 .10
149 Bryan Berard RC .30 .75
150 Marty Reasoner RC .25 .60
151 Andrew Berenzweig RC .02 .10
152 Erik Rasmussen RC .25 .60
153 Luke Curtin RC .02 .10
154 Dan Lacouture RC .02 .10
155 Brian Boucher RC 1.25 3.00
156 Wyatt Smith RC .10 .30
157 Maxim Kuznetsov RC .05 .15
158 Alexei Morozov RC .60 1.50
159 Dmitri Nabokov RC .02 .10
160 Wade Redden RC .20 .50
161 Jason Doig RC .02 .10
162 Alyn McCauley RC .20 .50
163 Jeff Ware RC .05 .15
164 Brad Larsen RC .02 .10
165 Jarome Iginla RC 3.00 8.00
166 Christian Dube RC .05 .15
167 Mike McBain RC .02 .10
168 Todd Norman RC .02 .10
169 Oleg Tverdovsky .08 .25
170 Jamie Storr .08 .25
171 Jason Wiemer RC .08 .25
172 Kenny Jonsson .02 .10
173 Paul Kariya .08 .25
174 Viktor Kozlov .08 .25
175 Peter Forsberg .50 1.25
176 Jeff Friesen .02 .10
177 Brian Rolston .08 .25
178 Brett Lindros .05 .15
179 Adam Deadmarsh .02 .10
180 Aaron Gavey .02 .10
181 Janne Laukkanen .02 .10
182 Todd Harvey .02 .10
183 Valeri Karpov RC .05 .15
184 Andrei Nikolishin .02 .10
185 Pavol Demitra .08 .25
186 Radek Bonk RC .30 .75
187 Valeri Bure .02 .10
188 Eric Fichaud RC .05 .15
189 Jamie McLennan .05 .15
190 Mariusz Czerkawski RC .12 .30
191 John Lilley .02 .10
192 Brian Savage .02 .10
193 Jason Allison .05 .30
194 Mattias Norstrom .02 .10
195 Todd Simon RC .02 .10
196 Zigmund Palffy .05 .15
197 Rene Corbet .02 .10
198 Mike Peca .02 .10
199 Checklist (1-100) .02 .10
200 Checklist (101-198) .02 .10
NNO Mike Modano Large 1.00 2.50

1994-95 Select Gold

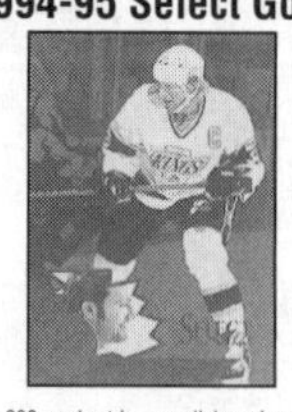

This 200-card set is a parallel version of the regular Select issue. These cards feature a gold foil printing process on the front, as well as a Certified Gold logo printed on the back. These were inserted at a rate of 1:3 packs.

*STARS: 1X TO 2.5X BASIC CARDS
*ROOKIES: .75X TO 2X BASIC CARDS
155 Brian Boucher 2.50 6.00

1994-95 Select First Line

The 12 cards in this set utilize the Dufex printing technology and were inserted at a rate of 1:48 packs. The player's name, team affiliation and "1st Line" logo appear along the left card front. Cards are numbered with an "FL" prefix.

FL1 Patrick Roy 5.00 12.00
FL2 Ray Bourque 1.50 4.00
FL3 Brian Leetch .75 2.00
FL4 Brendan Shanahan .75 2.00
FL5 Eric Lindros .75 2.00
FL6 Pavel Bure .75 2.00
FL7 Mike Richter .75 2.00
FL8 Scott Stevens .50 1.25
FL9 Chris Chelios .75 2.00
FL10 Luc Robitaille .50 1.25
FL11 Wayne Gretzky 6.00 15.00
FL12 Brett Hull 1.25 3.00

1994-95 Select Youth Explosion

The 12 cards in this set were randomly inserted in Select product at the rate of 1:24 packs. The striking design benefits from the use of a special holographic silver foil printing. The borders are blue and silver with player name and position above the set title located near the bottom. The cards are numbered with a "YE" prefix.

COMPLETE SET (12) 8.00 15.00
YE1 Jamie Storr .50 1.25
YE2 Oleg Tverdovsky .50 1.25
YE3 Janne Laukkanen .20 .50
YE4 Kenny Jonsson .20 .50
YE5 Paul Kariya .50 1.25
YE6 Viktor Kozlov .50 1.25
YE7 Peter Forsberg 2.50 6.00
YE8 Jason Allison .60 1.50
YE9 Jeff Friesen .20 .50
YE10 Brian Rolston .50 1.25
YE11 Mariusz Czerkawski .60 1.50
YE12 Brett Lindros .30 .75

1995-96 Select Certified Promos

These cards are samples of the 1995-9 Select Certified series. Their description i the same as the regular series with th exception of the word "Sample" printed o the back of each one. The cards are liste below according to their number in the regular series. The Pavel Bure card is fror the Gold Team insert series. It is identical t the expensive insert save for the wor "sample" written on the card back.

COMPLETE SET (9) 12.00 30.00
5 Pavel Bure Gold Team 6.00 15.00
12 Jim Carey .60 1.50
13 Paul Kariya 4.00 10.00
17 Mike Modano 1.20 3.00
19 Owen Nolan .80 2.00
43 Alexander Mogilny .80 2.00
68 Peter Forsberg 3.20 8.00
69 Felix Potvin .80 2.00
NNO Title Card .10 .25

1995-96 Select Certified

The 1995-96 Select Certified set was issue in one series totaling 144 cards. The 6-car packs retailed for $4.99. The cards featured smart, silver mirror finish, which wa protected from routine scratching by "Pinnacle Peel", which collectors coul remove if they so wished. Althoug collectors are free to do so, cards without th foil may be slightly harder to resell, althoug they will be more sightly. The card stock wa 24-point, double that of a normal carc Rookie Cards in this set include Danie Alfredsson and Petr Sykora.

COMPLETE SET (144) 25.00 50.00
1 Mario Lemieux 2.50 6.00
2 Chris Chelios .40 1.00
3 Scott Mellanby .08 .25
4 Brett Hull .60 1.50
5 Theo Fleury .08 .25
6 Alexei Zhamnov .20 .50
7 Mats Sundin .40 1.00
8 Mathieu Schneider .08 .25
9 Jason Arnott .08 .25
10 Mark Recchi .20 .50
11 Adam Oates .20 .50
12 Jim Carey .20 .50
13 Paul Kariya .40 1.00
14 Mark Messier .40 1.00
15 Eric Lindros .40 1.00
16 Pavel Bure .40 1.00
17 Mike Modano .75 1.50
18 Pat LaFontaine .40 1.00
19 Owen Nolan .20 .50
20 Roman Hamrlik .20 .50
21 Paul Coffey .40 1.00
22 Alexandre Daigle .08 .25
23 Wayne Gretzky 3.00 8.00
24 Martin Brodeur 1.25 3.00
25 Ulf Dahlen .08 .25
26 Geoff Sanderson .08 .25
27 Brian Leetch .20 .50
28 Dave Andreychuk .20 .50
29 Sergei Fedorov .60 1.50
30 Jocelyn Thibault .40 1.00
31 Mikael Renberg .20 .50
32 Joe Nieuwendyk .20 .50
33 Craig Janney .08 .25
34 Ray Bourque .75 2.00
35 Jari Kurri .40 1.00
36 Alexei Yashin .08 .25
37 Keith Tkachuk .40 1.00
38 Jaromir Jagr .75 2.00
39 Stephane Richer .20 .50
40 Trevor Kidd .20 .50
41 Kevin Hatcher .08 .25
42 Mike Vernon .20 .50
43 Alexander Mogilny .20 .50
44 John LeClair .40 1.00
45 Joe Sakic 1.00 2.50
46 Kevin Stevens .08 .25
47 Adam Graves .08 .25
48 Doug Gilmour .20 .50
49 Pierre Turgeon .20 .50
50 Joe Murphy .08 .25
51 Peter Bondra .20 .50
52 Ron Francis .20 .50
53 Luc Robitaille .20 .50
54 Mike Gartner .20 .50
55 Bill Ranford .20 .50
56 Jeff Friesen .08 .25
57 Cam Neely .40 1.00
58 Daren Puppa .20 .50
59 Rod Brind'Amour .20 .50
60 Jeremy Roenick .50 1.25
61 Brett Lindros .08 .25
62 Todd Harvey .20 .50
63 Kirk McLean .20 .50
64 Brendan Shanahan .40 1.00
65 Kelly Hrudey .20 .50
66 Scott Stevens .20 .50
67 Sergei Zubov .08 .25
68 Peter Forsberg 1.25 3.00
69 Felix Potvin .40 1.00
70 Scott Niedermayer .08 .25
71 Keith Primeau .08 .25
72 Al MacInnis .20 .50
73 Mike Richter .40 1.00
74 Rob Blake .20 .50
75 Vincent Damphousse .08 .25
76 Teemu Selanne .40 1.00
77 Andy Moog .40 1.00
78 Ron Hextall .20 .50
79 Oleg Tverdovsky .08 .25
80 Joe Juneau .08 .25

Patrick Roy 2.50 6.00
Wendel Clark .20 .50
Brian Bradley .08 .25
Curtis Joseph .40 1.00
John Vanbiesbrouck .20 .50
Phil Housley .20 .50
Trevor Linden .20 .50
Alexei Kovalev .08 .25
Dominik Hasek 1.00 2.50
Larry Murphy .20 .50
Arturs Irbe .20 .50
John MacLean .20 .50
Ed Belfour .40 1.00
Steve Yzerman 2.50 6.00
Tom Barrasso .20 .50
Rob Niedermayer .20 .50
Dale Hawerchuk .40 1.00
Rick Tocchet .20 .50
Claude Lemieux .08 .25
0 Sean Burke .20 .50
1 Shayne Corson .08 .25
2 Dino Ciccarelli .20 .50
3 Kirk Muller .08 .25
4 Don Beaupre .20 .50
5 Valeri Kamensky .20 .50
6 Markus Naslund .40 1.00
7 Tomas Sandstrom .08 .25
8 Pat Verbeek .08 .25
9 Doug Weight .20 .50
0 Brian Holzinger RC .40 1.00
1 Antti Tormanen .08 .25
2 Tommy Salo RC 1.50 4.00
3 Jason Bonsignore .08 .25
4 Shane Doan RC 1.25 3.00
5 Robert Svehla RC .08 .25
6 Chad Kilger RC .08 .25
7 Saku Koivu .40 1.00
8 Jeff O'Neill .08 .25
9 Brendan Witt .08 .25
0 Byron Dafoe .20 .50
1 Ryan Smyth .20 .50
2 Daniel Alfredsson RC 1.25 3.00
3 Todd Bertuzzi RC 1.50 4.00
4 Daymond Langkow RC .60 1.50
5 Miroslav Satan RC 1.25 3.00
6 Bryan McCabe .08 .25
7 Aki-Petteri Berg RC .20 .50
8 Cory Stillman .08 .25
9 Deron Quint .08 .25
0 Vitali Yachmenev .08 .25
1 Valeri Bure .08 .25
2 Eric Daze .20 .50
3 Radek Dvorak RC .60 1.50
4 Landon Wilson RC .08 .25
5 Niklas Sundstrom .20 .50
6 Jamie Storr .20 .50
7 Ed Jovanovski .40 1.00
8 Marcus Ragnarsson RC .20 .50
9 Kyle McLaren RC .08 .25
0 Sandy Moger .08 .25
1 Marty Murray .08 .25
2 Darby Hendrickson .08 .25
3 Corey Hirsch .20 .50
4 Petr Sykora RC 1.25 3.00

1995-96 Select Certified Mirror Gold

e cards from this high-end parallel set of e base Select Certified issue were ndomly inserted 1:5 packs. Instead of the pical silver finish, these, as the title ggests, had a golden background.
TARS: 2X TO 5X BASIC CARDS
OOKIES: .75X TO 2X

1995-96 Select Certified Double Strike

ndomly inserted in packs at a rate of 1:32, s 20-card set shines the spotlight on ayers whose abilities make them an posing threat both offensively and fensively. The cards feature a rainbow ver foil background on the front, while the cks contain a note stating that no more an 1,975 complete sets were produced. ere also was a Gold version of this set, th singles issued in black packs as inserts roughly every 3.5 boxes. The fronts are sentially the same, save for the use of a ld foil background. The backs contain a nall box reading "Case Chase" and "No ore than 903 sets produced."
OMPLETE SET (20) 15.00 40.00
GOLDS: 1.5X TO 2.5X BASIC INSERTS
Doug Gilmour .75 2.00
Ron Francis .75 2.00
Ray Bourque 1.50 4.00
Chris Chelios 1.25 3.00
Adam Oates .75 2.00
Mike Ricci .75 2.00
Jeremy Roenick 1.25 3.00
Jason Arnott .75 2.00
Brendan Shanahan 1.25 3.00
) Joe Nieuwendyk .75 2.00
Trevor Linden .75 2.00
Mikael Renberg .75 2.00
3 Theo Fleury .75 2.00
4 Sergei Fedorov 1.50 4.00
5 Mark Messier 1.50 4.00
6 Keith Primeau .75 2.00
7 Keith Tkachuk 1.25 3.00
8 Scott Stevens .75 2.00
9 Claude Lemieux .75 2.00
0 Alexei Zhamnov .75 2.00

1995-96 Select Certified Future

Randomly inserted in packs at a rate of 1:19, this 10-card set features some of the league's brightest future stars in silver rainbow holographic foil print technology.
COMPLETE SET (10) 15.00 30.00
1 Peter Forsberg 6.00 15.00
2 Jim Carey .75 2.00
3 Paul Kariya 2.00 5.00
4 Jocelyn Thibault 1.25 3.00
5 Saku Koivu 2.00 5.00
6 Brian Holzinger .75 2.00
7 Todd Harvey .75 2.00
8 Jeff O'Neill .75 2.00
9 Oleg Tverdovsky .75 2.00
10 Ed Jovanovski .75 2.00

1995-96 Select Certified Gold Team

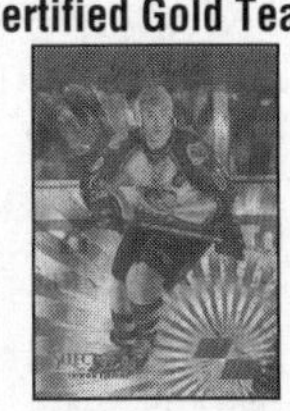

Randomly inserted in packs at a rate of 1:41, this 10-card set honors some of the league's top players, bestowing best-of-the-best honors with a Dufexed gold-foil design element. The presence of a Pavel Bure Gold Team sample card in the Promo set led to some softening of demand for the insert version of the card found in this set.
COMPLETE SET (10) 50.00 125.00
1 Eric Lindros 3.00 8.00
2 Wayne Gretzky 15.00 40.00
3 Mario Lemieux 10.00 25.00
4 Jaromir Jagr 4.00 10.00
5 Pavel Bure 3.00 8.00
6 Brett Hull 3.00 8.00
7 Cam Neely 3.00 8.00
8 Joe Sakic 6.00 15.00
9 Martin Brodeur 6.00 15.00
10 Patrick Roy 10.00 25.00

1996-97 Select Certified

The 1996-97 Select Certified set was issued in one series totaling 120 cards. The cards featured a silver mirror-like background with player names scripted horizontally in gold foil on the front and complete stats on the reverse against each opposing team.
COMPLETE SET (120) 15.00 40.00
1 Eric Lindros .30 .75
2 Mike Modano .50 1.25
3 Jocelyn Thibault .30 .75
4 Wayne Gretzky 2.00 5.00
5 Ray Bourque .50 1.25
6 Martin Brodeur .75 2.00
7 Rob Niedermayer .15 .40
8 Stephane Fiset .15 .40
9 Pat LaFontaine .30 .75
10 Mario Lemieux 1.50 4.00
11 Ed Belfour .30 .75
12 Ron Francis .15 .40
13 Luc Robitaille .15 .40
14 Paul Kariya .30 .75
15 Doug Gilmour .15 .40
16 Joe Sakic .60 1.50
17 Nikolai Khabibulin .15 .40
18 Valeri Bure .07 .20
19 Brett Hull .40 1.00
20 Chris Osgood .15 .40
21 Trevor Kidd .15 .40
22 Kirk McLean .15 .40
23 Zigmund Palffy .15 .40
24 Keith Tkachuk .30 .75
25 Andy Moog .15 .40
26 Bill Guerin .07 .20
27 Chris Chelios .30 .75
28 Damian Rhodes .15 .40
29 Jim Carey .30 .75
30 Ed Jovanovski .15 .40
31 Felix Potvin .30 .75
32 Teemu Selanne .30 .75
33 John LeClair .30 .75
34 Pavel Bure .30 .75
35 Grant Fuhr .15 .40
36 Mark Messier .30 .75
37 Vincent Damphousse .07 .20
38 Jason Arnott .07 .20
39 Mike Richter .30 .75
40 Keith Primeau .07 .20
41 Steve Yzerman 1.50 4.00
42 Trevor Linden .15 .40
43 Jaromir Jagr .50 1.25
44 Sean Burke .15 .40
45 Alexei Zhitnik .07 .20
46 Dimitri Khristich .07 .20
47 Daniel Alfredsson .15 .40
48 Roman Hamrlik .15 .40
49 Pat Verbeek .07 .20
50 Doug Weight .15 .40
51 Adam Graves .07 .20
52 Michal Pivonka .07 .20
53 Claude Lemieux .07 .20
54 Scott Stevens .15 .40
55 Sergei Fedorov .50 1.25
56 Owen Nolan .15 .40
57 Niklas Andersson .07 .20
58 Cory Stillman .07 .20
59 John Vanbiesbrouck .15 .40
60 Craig Janney .15 .40
61 Jeff Friesen .07 .20
62 Igor Larionov .07 .20
63 Ron Hextall .15 .40
64 Saku Koivu .30 .75
65 Wendel Clark .15 .40
66 Curtis Joseph .30 .75
67 Valeri Kamensky .15 .40
68 Adam Oates .15 .40
69 Daren Puppa .15 .40
70 Alexander Mogilny .15 .40
71 Corey Hirsch .15 .40
72 Brendan Shanahan .30 .75
73 Shayne Corson .07 .20
74 Dominik Hasek .60 1.50
75 Theo Fleury .30 .75
76 Brian Leetch .30 .75
77 Jeremy Roenick .40 1.00
78 Peter Bondra .15 .40
79 Eric Daze .15 .40
80 Todd Bertuzzi .30 .75
81 Patrick Roy 1.50 4.00
82 Pierre Turgeon .15 .40
83 Alexei Yashin .07 .20
84 Scott Mellanby .15 .40
85 Mats Sundin .30 .75
86 Jari Kurri .50 1.25
87 Kelly Hrudey .15 .40
88 Joe Nieuwendyk .15 .40
89 Paul Coffey .30 .75
90 Jeff O'Neill .07 .20
91 Kai Nurminen RC .07 .20
92 Anders Eriksson .07 .20
93 Jarome Iginla .40 1.00
94 Anson Carter .15 .40
95 Christian Dube .07 .20
96 Harry York RC .30 .75
97 Tomas Holmstrom RC .50 1.25
98 Sergei Berezin RC .60 1.50
99 Mattias Timander RC .07 .20
100 Wade Redden .07 .20
101 Mike Grier RC .60 1.50
102 Jonas Hoglund .07 .20
103 Eric Fichaud .15 .40
104 Janne Niinimaa .30 .75
105 Tuomas Gronman .07 .20
106 Jim Campbell .07 .20
107 Daniel Goneau RC .15 .40
108 Patrick Lalime RC 1.50 4.00
109 Ruslan Salei RC .07 .20
110 Richard Zednik RC .40 1.00
111 Chris O'Sullivan .07 .20
112 Fredrik Modin RC .40 1.00
113 Brad Smyth RC .07 .20
114 Bryan Berard .30 .75
115 Jamie Langenbrunner .07 .20
116 Ethan Moreau RC .30 .75
117 Daymond Langkow .15 .40
118 Andreas Dackell RC .07 .20
119 Rem Murray RC .15 .40
120 Dainius Zubrus RC .50 1.25
P60 Craig Janney PROMO .40 .80
P65 Wendel Clark PROMO .40 .80

1996-97 Select Certified Artist's Proofs

Inserted 1:48 packs, this insert parallels the base set. The cards can be distinguished by an Artist Proof logo stamped on the front of the card. Although the cards suggest that 500 were printed, there were, in fact, just 150 of each card made.
*STARS: 25X TO 50X BASIC CARDS
*ROOKIES: 6X TO 15X BASIC CARD

1996-97 Select Certified Blue

Inserted at 1:50 packs, these cards can be differentiated from the base cards by the blue foil background on the front of the card.
*STARS: 15X TO 40X BASIC CARDS
*ROOKIES: 6X TO 15X BASIC CARD

1996-97 Select Certified Mirror Blue

Inserted at 1:200 packs, these cards are differentiated by a blue holographic foil background on the front of the card and the words 'Mirror Blue' on the reverse. Though the actual number of cards printed is not known, sources estimate that only 36 copies of each Mirror Blue card exists.
*STARS: 25X TO 60X BASIC CARDS
*ROOKIES:20X TO 50X BASIC CARDS

1996-97 Select Certified Mirror Gold

Inserted at 1:300, this 120-card parallel set could be differentiated from the base set by a gold holographic foil background on the front of the card and the words 'Mirror Gold' on the reverse. Though the actual number of cards printed is not known, sources estimate that only 24 copies of each Mirror Gold card exists.
*STARS: 40X TO 100X BASIC CARDS
*ROOKIES: 25X TO 60X BASIC CARDS
4 Wayne Gretzky 100.00 200.00
6 Martin Brodeur 30.00 80.00
10 Mario Lemieux 75.00 150.00
41 Steve Yzerman 30.00 80.00
81 Patrick Roy 30.00 80.00

1996-97 Select Certified Mirror Red

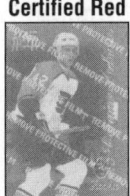

Inserted at 1:100 packs, these cards can be differentiated from the base set by a red holographic foil background on the front of the card and the words 'Mirror Red' on the reverse. Though the actual number of cards printed is not known, sources estimate that just 72 copies of each Mirror Red card exists.
*STARS: 15X TO 40X BASIC CARDS
*ROOKIES: 10X TO 25X BASIC CARDS

1996-97 Select Certified Red

A 1:8 pack parallel insert, these cards are differentiated from those in the base set by a red foil background on the front of the card.
*STARS: 2.5X TO 6X BASIC CARDS
*ROOKIES: 1.5X TO 3X BASIC CARD

1996-97 Select Certified Cornerstones

Randomly inserted in packs at a rate of 1:38, these cards feature a player photo framed in silver and black etched metal Dufex foil. The text on the card backs describe why each of the 15 players is considered his team's cornerstone player.
1 Eric Lindros 2.50 6.00
2 Mario Lemieux 8.00 20.00
3 Jaromir Jagr 4.00 10.00
4 Wayne Gretzky 10.00 25.00
5 Mark Messier 2.50 6.00
6 Brett Hull 2.50 6.00
7 Pavel Bure 2.50 6.00
8 Saku Koivu 2.00 5.00
9 Joe Sakic 4.00 10.00
10 Keith Tkachuk 2.00 5.00
11 Paul Kariya 2.50 6.00
12 Teemu Selanne 2.50 6.00
13 Sergei Fedorov 2.50 6.00
14 Steve Yzerman 6.00 15.00
15 Peter Forsberg 5.00 12.00

1996-97 Select Certified Freezers

Randomly inserted in packs at a rate of 1:41, this set features silver holofoil cards of 15 highly regarded NHL goaltenders.
COMPLETE SET (15) 50.00 100.00
1 Martin Brodeur 6.00 15.00
2 Patrick Roy 10.00 25.00
3 Jim Carey 2.00 5.00
4 John Vanbiesbrouck 2.50 6.00
5 Dominik Hasek 4.00 10.00
6 Ed Belfour 2.50 6.00
7 Curtis Joseph 2.50 6.00
8 Felix Potvin 2.50 6.00
9 Daren Puppa 2.00 5.00
10 Chris Osgood 2.50 6.00
11 Mike Richter 2.50 6.00
12 Jocelyn Thibault 2.00 5.00
13 Ron Hextall 2.00 5.00
14 Nikolai Khabibulin 2.00 5.00
15 Damian Rhodes 2.00 5.00

1992-93 Senators Team Issue

This 15-postcard set commemorates the inaugural season of the Ottawa Senators. The postcards feature full-bleed action photography, along with the logos of the set's two sponsors, CFRA Radio and Colonial Furniture. There is no indication of the player's identity anywhere on the card, so knowledge of obscure expansion draft-caliber players is a must to truly appreciate this set. The backs are blank. The cards are unnumbered, and are listed below alphabetically.
COMPLETE SET (15) 6.00 15.00
1 Jamie Baker .40 1.00
2 Daniel Berthiaume .60 1.50
3 Neil Brady .40 1.00
4 Ken Hammond .40 1.00
5 Dave Hannan .40 1.00
6 Jody Hull .40 1.00
7 Mark Lamb .40 1.00
8 Darcy Loewen .40 1.00
9 Norm Maciver .40 1.00
10 Brad Marsh .60 1.50
11 Andrew McBain .40 1.00
12 Mike Peluso .50 1.25
13 Darren Rumble .40 1.00
14 Brad Shaw .40 1.00
15 Sylvain Turgeon .40 1.00

1993-94 Senators Kraft Sheets

These 27 blank-backed photo sheets of the 1993-94 Ottawa Senators measure approximately 8 1/2" by 11" and feature color player action shots bordered in team colors (red, white, and gold). The player's name and uniform number, along with the Senators' logo, appear near the top. The logo for Kraft appears at the lower right; the logo for Loeb appears at the lower left. The production number out of the total produced for each sheet is shown within the white rectangle immediately above the Kraft logo. The sheets were produced in differing quantities. These production figures are shown in the checklist below. A special storage album was also available for the sheets. The sheets are unnumbered and checklisted below in alphabetical order.
COMPLETE SET (27) 60.00 150.00
1 Dave Archibald 3,500 2.00 5.00
2 Craig Billington 6,500 2.40 6.00
3 Rick Bowness CO 6,500 2.00 5.00
4 Robert Burakovsky 1,500 2.80 7.00
5 Alexandre Daigle 6,500 2.00 5.00
6 Pavol Demitra 1,500 4.00 10.00
7 Gord Dineen 3,500 2.00 5.00
8 Dmitri Filimonov 1,500 2.80 7.00
9 Brian Glynn 1,500 2.80 7.00
10 Bill Huard 1,500 2.80 7.00
11 Jarmo Kekalainen 1,500 2.80 7.00
12 Bob Kudelski 1,500 2.80 7.00
13 Mark Lamb 1,500 2.80 7.00
14 Darcy Loewen 3,500 2.00 5.00
15 Norm Maciver 3,500 2.00 5.00
16 Darrin Madeley 1,500 2.80 7.00
17 Troy Mallette 3,500 2.00 5.00
18 Brad Marsh 6,500 2.80 7.00
19 Dave McLlwain 3,500 2.00 5.00
20 Darren Rumble 1,500 2.80 7.00
21 Vladimir Ruzicka 1,500 2.80 7.00
22 Brad Shaw 6,500 2.00 5.00
23 Graeme Townshend 1,500 2.80 7.00
24 Sylvain Turgeon 6,500 2.40 6.00
25 Dennis Vial 1,500 2.80 7.00
26 Alexei Yashin 6,500 2.00 5.00
27 Team Photo 12,500 2.00 5.00
xx Album 6.00 15.00
NNO Team Photo 2.00 5.00

1994-95 Senators Team Issue

Sponsored by Bell Mobility, this 28-card sets measures approximately 4" by 6" and features members of the 1994-95 Ottawa Senators. The fronts have full-bleed color action player photos with a fading team color-coded inside border. The player's name appears alongside the left, while his uniform number is on the bottom. The team logo in the upper right corner and sponsor logos in English and French on the bottom round out the card face. The backs are blank. The cards are unnumbered and checklisted below in alphabetical order.
COMPLETE SET (28) 6.00 15.00
1 Dave Archibald .20 .50
2 Don Beaupre .30 .75
3 Radim Bicanek .20 .50
4 Craig Billington .30 .75
5 Claude Boivin .20 .50
6 Radek Bonk .40 1.00
7 Phil Bourque .20 .50
8 Rick Bowness CO .20 .50
9 Randy Cunneyworth .20 .50
10 Chris Dahlquist .20 .50
11 Alexandre Daigle .40 1.00
12 Pat Elynuik .20 .50
13 Rob Gaudreau .20 .50
14 Sean Hill .20 .50
15 Bill Huard .20 .50
16 Kerry Huffman .20 .50
17 Scott Levins .20 .50
18 Norm Maciver .20 .50
19 Darrin Madeley .30 .75
20 Troy Mallette .20 .50
21 Brad Marsh CO .30 .75
22 Dave McLlwain .20 .50
23 Troy Murray .20 .50
24 Stanislav Neckar .24 .60
25 Jim Paek .20 .50
26 Sylvain Turgeon .20 .50
27 Dennis Vial .20 .50
28 Alexei Yashin .80 2.00

1995-96 Senators Team Issue

This 24-postcard set was produced by the Senators as a promotional giveaway. The cards feature full-bleed action photography with the club's name in both English and French inscribed along three borders. The fourth border displays the player's name. The backs are blank. As the cards are unnumbered, they are listed below in alphabetical order.
COMPLETE SET (24) 6.00 15.00
1 Daniel Alfredsson 1.20 3.00
2 Dave Archibald .20 .50
3 Mike Bales .24 .60
4 Don Beaupre .30 .75
5 Radek Bonk .24 .60
6 Tom Chorske .20 .50
7 Randy Cunneyworth .20 .50
8 Alexandre Daigle .20 .50
9 Ted Drury .20 .50
10 Steve Duchesne .24 .60
11 Rob Gaudreau .20 .50
12 Sean Hill .20 .50
13 Kerry Huffman .20 .50
14 Scott Levins .20 .50
15 Troy Mallette .20 .50
16 Brad Marsh .40 1.00
17 Trent McCleary .20 .50
18 Jaroslav Modry .20 .50
19 Frank Musil .20 .50
20 Stan Neckar .24 .60
21 Martin Straka .40 1.00
22 Antti Tormanen .20 .50
23 Dennis Vial .20 .50
24 Alexei Yashin .40 1.00

1996-97 Senators Pizza Hut

This 30-card set of the Ottawa Senators was produced in conjunction with Pizza Hut as a promotional giveaway. This standard postcard size set features glossy fronts and full-bleed action photography, with the player's name on the right side, and the Pizza Hut Canada logo in the bottom left corner. The backs are blank. As the cards are unnumbered, they are listed below in alphabetical order.
COMPLETE SET (32) 6.00 15.00
1 Daniel Alfredsson .80 2.00
2 Radek Bonk .30 .75
3 Tom Chorske .20 .50
4 Randy Cunneyworth .20 .50
5 Andreas Dackell .20 .50
6 Alexandre Daigle .20 .50
7 Steve Duchesne .30 .75
8 Bruce Gardiner .20 .50
9 Dave Hannan .20 .50
10 Sean Hill .20 .50
11 Denny Lambert .20 .50
12 Janne Laukkanen .30 .75
13 Jacques Martin CO .10 .25
14 Shawn Mceachern .20 .50
15 Frank Musil .20 .50
16 Phil Myre ACO .20 .50
17 Stan Neckar .20 .50
18 Christer Olsson .20 .50
19 Perry Pearn ACO .10 .25
20 Lance Pitlick .20 .50
21 Craig Ramsay .20 .50
22 Wade Redden .40 1.00
23 Damian Rhodes .40 1.00
24 Ron Tugnutt .40 1.00
25 Shaun Van Allen .20 .50
26 Dennis Vial .20 .50
27 Alexei Yashin .40 1.00
28 Jason York .20 .50
29 Jason Zent .20 .50
30 Sergei Zholtok .20 .50

1998-99 Senators Team Issue

This set features the Senators of the NHL. These oversized cards were sold in set form by the team at home games. The backs are blank and the cards unnumbered. Therefore, they are listed in alphabetical order.
COMPLETE SET (26) 6.00 15.00
1 Daniel Alfredsson .40 1.00
2 Magnus Arvedson .20 .50
3 Bill Berg .20 .50
4 Radek Bonk .20 .50
5 Andreas Dackell .20 .50
6 Bruce Gardiner .20 .50
7 Marian Hossa .80 2.00
8 Andreas Johansson .20 .50
9 Igor Kravchuk .20 .50
10 Janne Laukkanen .20 .50
11 Jacques Martin CO .20 .50
12 Steve Martins .20 .50
13 Shawn McEachern .20 .50
14 Chris Murray .20 .50
15 Chris Phillips .20 .50
16 Lance Pitlick .20 .50
17 Vaclav Prospal .20 .50
18 Wade Redden .30 1.00
19 Damian Rhodes .30 .75
20 Sami Salo .20 .50
21 Patrick Traverse .20 .50
22 Ron Tugnutt .40 1.00
23 Shaun Van Allen .20 .50
24 Alexei Yashin .30 .50
25 Ottawa Senators .20 .50
26 Spartacat MASCOT .10 .25

1999-00 Senators Team Issue

This team-issued set measures approximately 4 1/2" x 8 1/2". The cards carry an action photo of each player on the front accompanied by their jersey number, the CCM logo and the team logo. The back of each card carries the Senators 1999-00 game schedule. The card are not numbered and are listed below in alphabetical order.
COMPLETE SET (26) 8.00 20.00
1 Daniel Alfredsson .40 1.00
2 Magnus Arvedson .20 .50
3 Radek Bonk .30 .75
4 Andreas Dackell .20 .50
5 Kevin Dineen .20 .50
6 Mike Fisher .30 1.00
7 Bruce Gardiner .20 .50
8 Marian Hossa 2.00 5.00
9 Joe Juneau .20 .50
10 Igor Kravchuk .20 .50
11 Patrick Lalime .60 1.50
12 Janne Laukkanen .20 .50
13 Shawn McEachern .30 .75
14 Chris Phillips .30 .75
15 Vaclav Prospal .20 .50

16 Wade Redden .30 1.00
17 Andre Roy .20 .50
18 Sami Salo .20 .50
19 Patrick Traverse .20 .50
20 Ron Tugnutt .40 1.00
21 Shaun Van Allen .20 .50
22 Jason York .20 .50
23 Rob Zamuner .20 .50
24 Jacques Martin HCO .10 .25
25 Spartacat MASCOT .04 .10
26 Team Photo .20 .50

2000-01 Senators Team Issue

This set features the Senators of the NHL. The slightly oversized cards were issued as a promotional giveaway early in the season. The cards feature an action photo on the front and a complete season schedule on the back.

COMPLETE SET (26)
1 Daniel Alfredsson .40 1.00
2 Magnus Arvedson .20 .50
3 Radek Bonk .30 .75
4 Andreas Dackell .20 .50
5 Mike Fisher .30 .75
6 Colin Forbes .20 .50
7 Martin Havlat 1.60 4.00
8 Marian Hossa 2.00 5.00
9 Jani Hurme .60 1.50
10 Patrick Lalime .60 1.50
11 Jacques Martin CO .10 .25
12 Shawn McEachern .20 .50
13 Roger Neilson ACO .10 .25
14 Perry Pearn ACO .10 .25
15 Ricard Persson .20 .50
16 Chris Phillips .20 .50
17 Vaclav Prospal .20 .50
18 Karel Rachunek .20 .50
19 Wade Redden .30 .75
20 Jamie Rivers .20 .50
21 Andre Roy .30 .75
22 Sami Salo .20 .50
23 Spartacat MASCOT .04 .10
24 Alexei Yashin .40 1.00
25 Jason York .20 .50
26 Rob Zamuner .20 .50
27 Team Photo

2001-02 Senators Team Issue

This 29-card set was issued by the NHL Senators. The cards measure and oversized 3 X 5 inches, and feature a stylized color photo on the front, with a black and white team schedule on the back. It is not known how they were distributed, but evidence suggests they were a giveaway of some kind. The cards are not numbered, so are listed below alphabetically. Note: the autograph card is not signed: it is a blank front with room for autographs.

COMPLETE SET (29)
1 Daniel Alfredsson .62 1.56
2 Magnus Arvedson .20 .50
3 Radek Bonk .20 .50
4 Zdeno Chara .20 .50
5 Ivan Ciernik .31 .78
6 Mike Fisher .31 .78
7 Martin Havlat 1.20 3.00
8 Chris Herperger .20 .50
9 Shane Hnidy .20 .50
10 Marian Hossa .80 2.00
11 Jani Hurme .62 1.56
12 Don Jackson ACO .04 .11
13 Patrick Lalime .40 1.00
14 Curtis Leschyshyn .20 .50
15 Jacques Martin CO .04 .11
16 Shawn McEachern .20 .50
17 Bill Muckalt .20 .50
18 Chris Neil .40 1.00
19 Roger Neilson ACO .04 .11
20 Perry Pearn ACO .04 .11
21 Ricard Persson .20 .50
22 Chris Phillips .20 .50
23 Karel Rachunek .20 .50
24 Wade Redden .31 .78
25 Andre Roy .31 .78
26 Sami Salo .20 .50
27 Todd White .20 .50
28 SpartaCat .04 .11
29 Autograph Card .04 .11

2002-03 Senators Team Issue

This 15-card set was issued by the team and given away as promotions. The cards measured approximately 3 1/2" X 4 1/2". Card backs carried the 02-03 schedule.

COMPLETE SET (15) 12.00 20.00
1 Daniel Alfredsson .75 2.00
2 Magnus Arvedsson .40 1.00
3 Radek Bonk .40 1.00
4 Zdeno Chara .60 1.50
5 Mike Fisher .60 1.50
6 Martin Havlat 1.25 3.00
7 Marian Hossa 1.25 3.00
8 Jody Hull .40 1.00
9 Patrick Lalime .60 1.50
10 Curtis Leschyshyn .40 1.00
11 Chris Neil .40 1.00
12 Chris Phillips .40 1.00
13 Martin Prusek .60 1.50
14 Wade Redden .60 1.50
15 Anton Volchenkov .40 1.00

2003-04 Senators Postcards

COMPLETE SET (28) 10.00 20.00
1 Brian Pothier .20 .50
2 Zdeno Chara .40 1.00
3 Chris Phillips .20 .50
4 Wade Redden .40 1.00
5 Curtis Leschyshyn .20 .50
6 Martin Havlat .60 1.50
7 Daniel Alfredsson .75 2.00
8 Mike Fisher .40 1.00
9 Radek Bonk .20 .50
10 Peter Schaefer .20 .50
11 Jody Hull .20 .50
12 Marian Hossa .60 1.50
13 Petr Schastlivy .20 .50
14 Bryan Smolinski .20 .50
15 Shaun Van Allen .20 .50
16 Karel Rachunek .20 .50
17 Anton Volchenkov .20 .50
18 Chris Neil .20 .50
19 Vaclav Varada .20 .50
20 Todd White .20 .50
21 Martin Prusek .30 .75
22 Shane Hnidy .20 .50
23 Jason Spezza 1.25 3.00
24 Patrick Lalime .40 1.00
25 Jacques Martin CO .10 .25
26 Don Jackson ACO .10 .25
27 Perry Pearn ACO .10 .25
28 Spartacat MASCOT .02 .10

2006-07 Senators Postcards

This listing is believed to be incomplete. If you can confirm other singles within this set, please email us at hockeymag@beckett.com.

3 Daniel Alfredsson 1.25 3.00
4 Joe Corvo .40 1.00
5 Denis Hamel .40 1.00
6 Dany Heatley 1.25 3.00
7 Chris Kelly .40 1.00
8 Brian McGrattan .75 2.00
9 Andrei Meszaros .40 1.00
10 Chris Phillips .40 1.00
11 Jason Spezza 1.25 3.00
12 Peter Schaefer .40 1.00
13 Christoph Schubert .40 1.00
14 Wade Redden .75 2.00
15 Logo Card .10 .25

1972-73 7-Eleven Slurpee Cups WHA

This 20-cup set features a color head shot and facsimile autograph on the front, and a 7-11 logo, team logo, players name, and biographical information on the back. Cups are unnumbered and checklisted below alphabetically.

COMPLETE SET (20) 125.00 250.00
1 Norm Beaudin 5.00 10.00
2 Chris Bordeleau 5.00 10.00
3 Carl Brewer 5.00 10.00
4 Wayne Carleton 6.00 12.00
5 Gerry Cheevers 12.50 25.00
6 Wayne Connelly 7.50 15.00
7 Jean-Guy Gendron 5.00 10.00
8 Ted Green 5.00 10.00
9 Al Hamilton 5.00 10.00
10 Jim Harrison 5.00 10.00
11 Bobby Hull 25.00 50.00
12 Andre Lacroix 6.00 12.00
13 Danny Lawson 5.00 10.00
14 John McKenzie 5.00 10.00
15 Jim Mcleod 5.00 10.00
16 Jack Norris 5.00 10.00
17 John Schella 5.00 10.00
18 J.C. Tremblay 7.50 15.00
19 Ron Ward 5.00 10.00
20 Jim Watson 5.00 10.00

1984-85 7-Eleven Discs

This set of 60 discs was sponsored by 7-Eleven. Each disc or coin measures approximately 2" in diameter and features an alternating portrait of the player and the team's logo. The coins are quite colorful and have adhesive backing. We have checklisted the coins below in alphabetical order of team name. Also the player's names have been alphabetized within their teams, and their uniform numbers placed to the right of their names. In addition, 7-Eleven also issued a large 4 1/2" diameter Wayne Gretzky disc which is not considered an essential part of the complete set. There is also a paper checklist sheet produced which pictured (in red, white, and blue) some of the coins and listed the players in the set.

COMPLETE SET (60) 50.00 125.00
1 Ray Bourque 7 2.00 5.00
2 Rick Middleton 16 .60 1.50
3 Tom Barrasso 30 1.00 2.50
4 Gilbert Perreault 11 .80 2.00
5 Rejean Lemelin 31 .60 1.50
6 Lanny McDonald 9 1.00 2.50
7 Paul Reinhart 23 .40 1.00
8 Doug Risebrough 8 .40 1.00
9 Denis Savard 18 1.00 2.50
10 Al Secord 20 .40 1.00
11 Steve Yzerman 19 6.00 15.00
12 Dave(Tiger) Williams 55 .60 1.50
13 Glenn Anderson 9 .80 2.00
14 Paul Coffey 7 2.00 5.00
15 Michel Goulet 16 .80 2.00
16 Wayne Gretzky 99 8.00 20.00
17 Charlie Huddy 22 .40 1.00
18 Pat Hughes 16 .40 1.00
19 Jari Kurri 17 1.20 3.00
20 Kevin Lowe 4 .40 1.00
21 Mark Messier 11 3.20 8.00
22 Ron Francis 10 1.60 4.00
23 Sylvain Turgeon 16 .40 1.00
24 Marcel Dionne 16 .80 2.00
25 Dave Taylor 18 .60 1.50
26 Brian Bellows 23 .40 1.00
27 Dino Ciccarelli 20 .60 1.50
28 Harold Snepsts 28 .60 1.50
29 Bob Gainey 23 .80 2.00
30 Larry Robinson 19 1.00 2.50
31 Mel Bridgman 18 .40 1.00
32 Chico Resch 1 .60 1.50
33 Mike Bossy 22 1.20 3.00
34 Bryan Trottier 19 1.00 2.50
35 Barry Beck 5 .40 1.00
36 Don Maloney 12 .40 1.00
37 Tim Kerr 12 .60 1.50
38 Darryl Sittler 27 1.00 2.50
39 Mike Bullard 22 .40 1.00
40 Rick Kehoe 17 .60 1.50
41 Peter Stastny 26 1.20 3.00
42 Bernie Federko 24 .60 1.50
43 Rob Ramage 5 .40 1.00
44 John Anderson 10 .40 1.00
45 Bill Derlago 19 .40 1.00
46 Gary Nylund 2 .40 1.00
47 Rick Vaive 22 .40 1.00
48 Richard Brodeur 35 .60 1.50
49 Gary Lupul 7 .40 1.00
50 Darcy Rota 18 .40 1.00
51 Stan Smyl 12 .60 1.50
52 Tony Tanti 9 .40 1.00
53 Mike Gartner 11 1.20 3.00
54 Rod Langway 5 .40 1.00
55 Scott Arniel 11 .40 1.00
56 Dave Babych 44 .40 1.00
57 Laurie Boschman 16 .40 1.00
58 Dale Hawerchuk 10 1.00 2.50
59 Paul MacLean 15 .40 1.00
60 Brian Mullen 19 .40 1.00
NNO Wayne Gretzky Large 10.00 25.00
NNO Paper Checklist Sheet 2.00 5.00

1985-86 7-Eleven Credit Cards

This 25-card set was sponsored by 7-Eleven. The cards measure approximately 3 3/8" by 2 1/8" and were issued in the "credit card" format. The front features color head and shoulder shots of two players from the same NHL team. These pictures are enframed by a black background, with the player's name, position, and uniform number in blue lettering below the photo. The information on the card back is framed in red boxes. In the smaller box on the left appears the 7-Eleven logo, card number, and the team logo. The right-hand box gives a brief history of the team. The key card in the set is Mario Lemieux, shown during his Rookie Card year.

COMPLETE SET (25) 14.00 35.00
1 Ray Bourque and Rick Middleton .80 2.00
2 Tom Barrasso and Gilbert Perreault .60 1.50
3 Paul Reinhart and Lanny McDonald .40 1.00
4 Denis Savard and Doug Wilson .60 1.50
5 Ron Duguay and Steve Yzerman 3.20 8.00
6 Paul Coffey and Jari Kurri 1.00 2.50
7 Ron Francis and Mike Liut .80 2.00
8 Marcel Dionne and Dave Taylor .50 1.25
9 Brian Bellows and Dino Ciccarelli .60 1.50
10 Larry Robinson and Guy Carbonneau .60 1.50
11 Mel Bridgman and Chico Resch .30 .75
12 Mike Bossy and Bryan Trottier 1.00 2.50
13 Reijo Ruotsalainen and Barry Beck .30 .75
14 Tim Kerr and Mark Howe .30 .75
15 Mario Lemieux and Mike Bullard 8.00 20.00
16 Peter Stastny and Michel Goulet 1.00 2.50
17 Rob Ramage and Brian Sutter .30 .75
18 Rick Vaive and Borje Salming .40 1.00
19 Patrik Sundstrom and Stan Smyl .30 .75
20 Rod Langway and Mike Gartner .50 1.25
21 Dale Hawerchuk and Paul MacLean .40 1.00
22 Stanley Cup Winners .30 .75
23 Prince of Wales Trophy Winners .30 .75
24 Clarence S. Campbell Bowl Winners .30 .75
25 Title Card .10 .25

1991-92 Sharks Sports Action

This 22-card standard-size set was issued by Sports Action and features members of the 1991-92 San Jose Sharks. The cards are printed on thin card stock. The fronts feature full-bleed glossy color action photos. The backs carry brief biography, career summary, and the team logo. The cards are unnumbered and checklisted below in alphabetical order.

COMPLETE SET (22) 4.00 10.00
1 Perry Anderson .20 .50
2 Perry Berezan .20 .50
3 Steve Bozek .20 .50
4 Dean Evason .20 .50
5 Pat Falloon .30 .75
6 Paul Fenton .20 .50
7 Link Gaetz .20 .50
8 Jeff Hackett .40 1.00
9 Ken Hammond .20 .50
10 Brian Hayward .30 .75
11 Tony Hrkac .20 .50
12 Kelly Kisio .24 .60
13 Brian Lawton .20 .50
14 Pat MacLeod .20 .50
15 Bob McGill .20 .50
16 Brian Mullen .20 .50
17 Jarmo Myllys .24 .60
18 Wayne Presley .20 .50
19 Neil Wilkinson .24 .60
20 Doug Wilson .40 1.00
21 Rob Zettler .20 .50
22 San Jose Sharks Game action .30 .75

1997 Sharks Fleer All-Star Sheet

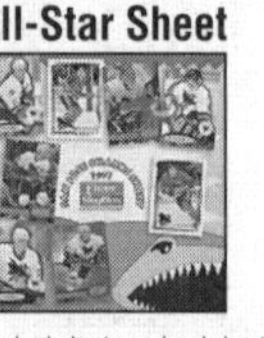

This odd-sized sheet was handed out to attendees of the '97 NHL All-Star Game to promote the '96-97 line of Fleer hockey products. The sheet also was available at the All-Star Fanfest card show. It features eight members of the hometown San Jose Sharks on three different types of Fleer cards; the brand pictured is listed after each player's name.

1 Sharks Sheet 1.60 4.00
Doug Bodger Fleer Picks
Kelly Hrudey Metal Universe
Al Iafrate Metal Universe
Bernie Nicholls Metal Universe
Owen Nolan Fleer
Marcus Ragnarsson Fleer
Chris Terreri Fleer
Alexei Yegorov Fleer Picks

2001-02 Sharks Postcards

This set was given away by the team during the 2001-02 season. The checklist below is not believed to be complete. Please forward any info to hockeymag@beckett.com. Special thanks to Sgt. Randy Garcia of the Humboldt County Sheriff's Dept. for the checklist and image.

1 Adam Graves .75 2.00
2 Vincent Damphousse .40 1.00
3 Matt Bradley .40 1.00
4 Brad Stuart .40 1.00
5 Owen Nolan .75 2.00
6 Patrick Marleau .75 2.00
7 Gary Suter .40 1.00
8 Niklas Sundstrom .40 1.00
9 Marco Sturm .40 1.00
10 Mike Ricci .40 1.00
11 Marcus Ragnarsson .40 1.00
12 Scott Thornton .40 1.00
13 Scott Hannan .40 1.00
14 Todd Harvey .40 1.00
15 Bryan Marchment .40 1.00
16 Teemu Selanne 1.25 3.00

2002-03 Sharks Team Issue

These 4X 7 blank backs were issued by the team at promotional events. It's likely more exist in the set. If you can confirm this, please contact us at hockeymag@beckett.com.

COMPLETE SET (?)
1 Vincent Damphousse 1.00
2 Adam Graves 1.00
3 Patrick Marleau 1.00
4 Evgeni Nabokov 2.00
5 Mike Rathje 1.00
6 Mike Ricci 1.00
7 Teemu Selanne 3.00
8 Marco Sturm 1.00

2003-04 Sharks Postcards

The checklist is likely incomplete. Please send additional info to hockeymag@beckett.com.

COMPLETE SET (?)
1 Jonathan Cheechoo 1.25 3.00
2 Vincent Damphousse .40 1.00
3 Rob Davidson .40 1.00
4 Nils Ekman .40 1.00
5 Jim Fahey .40 1.00
6 Scott Hannan .40 1.00
7 Todd Harvey .40 1.00
8 Alexander Korolyuk .40 1.00
9 Patrick Marleau .75 2.00
10 Alyn McCauley .40 1.00
11 Kyle McLaren .40 1.00
12 Evgeni Nabokov .75 2.00
13 Tom Preissing .40 1.00
14 Wayne Primeau .40 1.00
15 Mike Rathje .40 1.00
16 Mike Ricci .40 1.00
17 Brad Stuart .40 1.00
18 Marco Sturm .40 1.00
19 Scott Thornton .40 1.00

1960-61 Shirriff Coins

This set of 120 coins (each measuring approximately 1 3/8" in diameter) features players from all six NHL teams. These plastic coins are in color and numbered on the front. The coins are checklisted below according to teams as follows: Toronto Maple Leafs (1-20), Montreal Canadiens (21-40), Detroit Red Wings (41-60), Chicago Blackhawks (61-80), New York Rangers (81-100), and Boston Bruins (101-120). The set was also issued on a limited basis as a factory set in a black presentation box.

COMPLETE SET (120) 250.00 500.00
1 Johnny Bower 5.00 10.00
2 Dick Duff 2.50 5.00
3 Carl Brewer 2.50 5.00
4 Red Kelly 5.00 10.00
5 Tim Horton 7.50 15.00
6 Allan Stanley 2.50 5.00
7 Bob Baun 2.50 5.00
8 Billy Harris 1.50 3.00
9 George Armstrong 3.00 6.00
10 Ron Stewart 1.50 3.00
11 Bert Olmstead 2.50 5.00
12 Frank Mahovlich 7.50 15.00
13 Bob Pulford 2.50 5.00
14 Gary Edmundson 1.50 3.00
15 Johnny Wilson 1.50 3.00
16 Larry Regan 1.50 3.00
17 Gerry James 2.00 4.00
18 Rudy Migay 1.50 3.00
19 Gerry Ehman 1.50 3.00
20 Punch Imlach CO 2.00 4.00
21 Jacques Plante 12.50 25.00
22 Dickie Moore 3.00 6.00
23 Don Marshall 1.50 3.00
24 Albert Langlois 1.50 3.00
25 Tom Johnson 2.50 5.00
26 Doug Harvey 5.00 10.00
27 Phil Goyette 1.50 3.00
28 Boom Boom Geoffrion 6.00 12.00
29 Marcel Bonin 1.50 3.00
30 Jean Beliveau 10.00 20.00
31 Ralph Backstrom 2.00 4.00
32 Andre Pronovost 1.50 3.00
33 Claude Provost 2.00 4.00
34 Henri Richard 7.50 15.00
35 Jean-Guy Talbot 2.00 4.00
36 J.C. Tremblay 2.00 4.00
37 Bob Turner 1.50 3.00
38 Bill Hicke 1.50 3.00
39 Charlie Hodge 4.00 8.00
40 Toe Blake CO 2.50 5.00
41 Terry Sawchuk 10.00 20.00
42 Gordie Howe 25.00 50.00
43 John McKenzie 1.50 3.00
44 Alex Delvecchio 5.00 10.00
45 Norm Ullman 3.00 6.00
46 Jack McIntyre 1.50 3.00
47 Barry Cullen 2.00 4.00
48 Val Fonteyne 1.50 3.00
49 Warren Godfrey 1.50 3.00
50 Pete Goegan 1.50 3.00
51 Gerry Melnyk 1.50 3.00
52 Marc Reaume 1.50 3.00
53 Gary Aldcorn 1.50 3.00
54 Len Lunde 1.50 3.00
55 Murray Oliver 1.50 3.00
56 Marcel Pronovost 2.50 5.00
57 Howie Glover 1.50 3.00
58 Gerry Odrowski 1.50 3.00
59 Parker MacDonald 1.50 3.00
60 Sid Abel CO 2.50 5.00
61 Glenn Hall 6.00 12.00
62 Ed Litzenberger 2.00 4.00
63 Bobby Hull 20.00 40.00
64 Tod Sloan 1.50 3.00
65 Murray Balfour 1.50 3.00
66 Pierre Pilote 2.50 5.00
67 Al Arbour 2.50 5.00
68 Earl Balfour 1.50 3.00
69 Eric Nesterenko 2.00 4.00
70 Ken Wharram 2.50 5.00
71 Stan Mikita 12.50 25.00
72 Ab McDonald 1.50 3.00
73 Elmer Vasko 2.00 4.00
74 Dollard St.Laurent 2.00 4.00
75 Ron Murphy 1.50 3.00
76 Jack Evans 1.50 3.00
77 Bill(Red) Hay 1.50 3.00
78 Reg Fleming 2.00 4.00
79 Cecil Hoekstra 1.50 3.00
80 Tommy Ivan CO 2.00 4.00
81 Jack McCartan 4.00 8.00
82 Red Sullivan 1.50 3.00
83 Camille Henry 2.00 4.00
84 Larry Popein 1.50 3.00
85 John Hanna 1.50 3.00
86 Harry Howell 2.50 5.00
87 Eddie Shack 5.00 10.00
88 Irv Spencer 1.50 3.00
89 Andy Bathgate 3.00 6.00
90 Bill Gadsby 2.50 5.00
91 Andy Hebenton 1.50 3.00
92 Earl Ingarfield 1.50 3.00
93 Don Johns 1.50 3.00
94 Dave Balon 1.50 3.00
95 Jim Morrison 1.50 3.00
96 Ken Schinkel 1.50 3.00
97 Lou Fontinato 1.50 3.00
98 Ted Hampson 1.50 3.00
99 Brian Cullen 2.00 4.00
100 Alf Pike CO 1.50 3.00
101 Don Simmons 2.50 5.00
102 Fern Flaman 2.50 5.00
103 Vic Stasiuk 2.00 4.00
104 Johnny Bucyk 5.00 10.00
105 Bronco Horvath 2.00 4.00
106 Doug Mohns 4.00 8.00
107 Leo Boivin 2.50 5.00
108 Don McKenney 1.50 3.00
109 Jean-Guy Gendron 1.50 3.00
110 Jerry Toppazzini 1.50 3.00
111 Dick Meissner 1.50 3.00
112 Autry Erickson 1.50 3.00
113 Jim Bartlett 1.50 3.00
114 Orval Tessier 2.00 4.00
115 Billy Carter 1.50 3.00
116 Dallas Smith 2.00 4.00
117 Leo Labine 1.50 3.00
118 Bob Armstrong 1.50 3.00
119 Bruce Gamble 2.50 5.00
120 Milt Schmidt CO 3.00 6.00

1961-62 Shirriff/Salada Coins

This set of 120 coins (each measuring approximately 1 3/8" in diameter) features players of the NHL, all six teams. These plastic coins are in color and numbered on the front. The coins are numbered according to teams as follows: Boston Bruins (1-20), Chicago Blackhawks (21-40), Toronto Maple Leafs (41-60), Detroit Red Wings (61-80), New York Rangers (81-100), and Montreal Canadiens (101-120). The coins were also produced in identical fashion for Salada with a Salada imprint; the Salada version has the same values as listed below. This was the only year of Shirriff coins where collectors could obtain plastic shields for displaying their collection. These shields are not considered part of the complete set.

COMPLETE SET (120) 200.00 400.00
1 Cliff Pennington 1.25 2.50
2 Dallas Smith 2.00 4.00
3 Andre Pronovost 1.25 2.50
4 Charlie Burns 1.25 2.50
5 Leo Boivin 2.50 5.00
6 Don McKenney 1.25 2.50
7 Johnny Bucyk 4.00 8.00
8 Murray Oliver 1.25 2.50
9 Jerry Toppazzini 1.25 2.50
10 Doug Mohns 2.00 4.00
11 Don Head 2.00 4.00
12 Bob Armstrong 1.25 2.50
13 Pat Stapleton 2.00 4.00
14 Orland Kurtenbach 2.00 4.00
15 Dick Meissner 1.25 2.50
16 Ted Green 2.00 4.00
17 Tom Williams 1.25 2.50
18 Autry Erickson 1.25 2.50
19 Phil Watson CO 2.50 5.00
20 Ed Chadwick 2.50 5.00
21 Wayne Hillman 5.00 10.00
22 Stan Mikita 6.00 12.00
23 Eric Nesterenko 2.00 4.00
24 Reg Fleming 1.25 2.50
25 Bobby Hull 12.50 25.0
26 Elmer Vasko 1.25 2.5
27 Pierre Pilote 2.50 5.0
28 Chico Maki 2.00 4.0
29 Glenn Hall 5.00 10.0
30 Murray Balfour 1.25 2.5
31 Bronco Horvath 1.50 3.0
32 Ken Wharram 2.00 4.0
33 Ab McDonald 1.25 2.5
34 Bill(Red) Hay 1.25 2.5
35 Dollard St.Laurent 2.00 4.0
36 Ron Murphy 1.25 2.5
37 Bob Turner 1.25 2.5
38 Gerry Melnyk 1.25 2.5
39 Jack Evans 1.25 2.5
40 Rudy Pilous CO 2.50 5.0
41 Johnny Bower 5.00 10.0
42 Allan Stanley 3.00 6.0
43 Frank Mahovlich 5.00 10.0
44 Tim Horton 7.50 15.0
45 Carl Brewer 2.00 4.0
46 Bob Pulford 2.50 5.0
47 Bob Nevin 2.00 4.0
48 Eddie Shack 4.00 8.0
49 Red Kelly 4.00 8.0
50 Bob Baun 2.00 4.0
51 George Armstrong 3.00 6.0
52 Bert Olmstead 2.50 5.0
53 Dick Duff 2.00 4.0
54 Billy Harris 2.00 4.0
55 Larry Keenan 1.25 2.5
56 Johnny MacMillan 1.25 2.5
57 Punch Imlach CO 2.00 4.0
58 Dave Keon 7.50 15.0
59 Larry Hillman 1.25 2.5
60 Al Arbour 2.50 5.0
61 Sid Abel CO 2.50 5.0
62 Warren Godfrey 1.25 2.5
63 Vic Stasiuk 1.25 2.5
64 Leo Labine 1.25 2.5
65 Howie Glover 1.25 2.5
66 Gordie Howe 20.00 40.0
67 Val Fonteyne 1.25 2.5
68 Marcel Pronovost 2.50 5.0
69 Parker MacDonald 1.25 2.5
70 Alex Delvecchio 4.00 8.0
71 Ed Litzenberger 1.25 2.5
72 Al Johnson 1.25 2.5
73 Bruce MacGregor 1.25 2.5
74 Howie Young 1.25 2.5
75 Pete Goegan 1.25 2.5
76 Norm Ullman 3.00 6.0
77 Terry Sawchuk 12.50 25.0
78 Gerry Odrowski 1.25 2.5
79 Bill Gadsby 2.50 5.0
80 Hank Bassen 2.00 4.0
81 Doug Harvey 4.00 8.0
82 Earl Ingarfield 1.25 2.5
83 Pat Hannigan 1.25 2.5
84 Dean Prentice 2.00 4.0
85 Gump Worsley 5.00 10.0
86 Irv Spencer 1.25 2.5
87 Camille Henry 2.00 4.0
88 Andy Bathgate 3.00 6.0
89 Harry Howell 2.50 5.0
90 Andy Hebenton 1.25 2.5
91 Red Sullivan 1.25 2.5
92 Ted Hampson 1.25 2.5
93 Jean-Guy Gendron 1.25 2.5
94 Albert Langlois 1.25 2.5
95 Larry Cahan 1.25 2.5
96 Bob Cunningham 1.25 2.5
97 Vic Hadfield 2.00 4.0
98 Jean Ratelle 5.00 10.0
99 Ken Schinkel 1.25 2.5
100 Johnny Wilson 1.25 2.5
101 Toe Blake CO 2.50 5.0
102 Jean Beliveau 10.00 20.0
103 Don Marshall 1.25 2.5
104 Boom Boom Geoffrion 6.00 12.0
105 Claude Provost 2.00 4.0
106 Tom Johnson 2.50 5.0
107 Dickie Moore 4.00 8.0
108 Bill Hicke 1.25 2.5
109 Jean-Guy Talbot 2.00 4.0
110 Henri Richard 5.00 10.0
111 Lou Fontinato 1.50 3.0
112 Gilles Tremblay 1.25 2.5
113 Jacques Plante 10.00 20.0
114 Ralph Backstrom 2.00 4.0
115 Marcel Bonin 1.25 2.5
116 Phil Goyette 1.25 2.5
117 Bobby Rousseau 2.00 4.0
118 J.C. Tremblay 2.00 4.0
119 Al MacNeil 1.25 2.5
120 Jean Gauthier 1.25 2.5
S1 Boston Bruins Shield 30.00 60.0
S2 Chicago Blackhawks Shield 30.00 60.0
S3 Detroit Red Wings Shield 30.00 60.0
S4 Montreal Canadiens Shield 30.00 60.0
S5 New York Rangers Shield 30.00 60.0
S6 Toronto Maple Leafs Shield 30.00 60.0

1962-63 Shirriff Coins

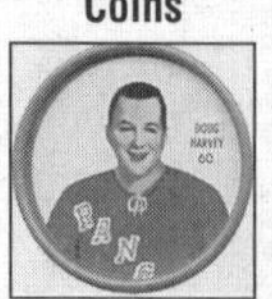

This set of 60 coins (each measuri approximately 1 1/2" in diameter) featu 12 All-Stars, six Trophy winners, a players from Montreal (20) and Toror (22). The four American teams in the N were not included in this set except whe they appeared as All-Stars or Trop winners. These metal coins are in color a numbered on the front. The backs are writ

French and English.
OMPLETE SET (60) 200.00 400.00
Johnny Bower 5.00 10.00
Allan Stanley 4.00 8.00
Frank Mahovlich 10.00 20.00
Tim Horton 10.00 20.00
Carl Brewer 2.50 5.00
Bob Pulford 4.00 8.00
Bob Nevin 2.50 5.00
Eddie Shack 4.00 8.00
Red Kelly 4.00 8.00
0 George Armstrong 4.00 8.00
1 Bert Olmstead 3.00 6.00
2 Dick Duff 2.50 5.00
3 Billy Harris 2.00 4.00
4 Johnny MacMillan 2.00 4.00
5 Punch Imlach CO 2.50 5.00
6 Dave Keon 7.50 15.00
7 Larry Hillman 2.00 4.00
8 Ed Litzenberger 2.00 4.00
9 Bob Baun 3.00 6.00
0 Al Arbour 4.00 8.00
1 Ron Stewart 2.00 4.00
2 Don Simmons 3.00 6.00
3 Lou Fontinato 2.00 4.00
4 Gilles Tremblay 2.00 4.00
5 Jacques Plante 12.50 25.00
6 Ralph Backstrom 2.50 5.00
7 Marcel Bonin 2.00 4.00
8 Phil Goyette 2.00 4.00
9 Bobby Rousseau 2.50 5.00
0 J.C. Tremblay 2.50 5.00
1 Toe Blake CO 4.00 8.00
2 Jean Beliveau 10.00 20.00
3 Don Marshall 2.00 4.00
4 Boom Boom Geoffrion 6.00 12.00
5 Claude Provost 2.50 5.00
6 Tom Johnson 3.00 6.00
7 Dickie Moore 5.00 10.00
8 Bill Hicke 2.00 4.00
9 Jean-Guy Talbot 2.50 5.00
0 Al MacNeil 2.50 5.00
1 Henri Richard 7.50 15.00
2 Red Berenson 2.50 5.00
3 Jacques Plante AS 12.50 25.00
4 Jean-Guy Talbot AS 2.50 5.00
5 Doug Harvey AS 5.00 10.00
6 Stan Mikita AS 5.00 10.00
7 Bobby Hull AS 12.50 25.00
8 Andy Bathgate AS 4.00 8.00
9 Glenn Hall AS 5.00 10.00
0 Pierre Pilote AS 4.00 8.00
1 Carl Brewer AS 2.50 5.00
2 Dave Keon AS 7.50 15.00
3 Frank Mahovlich AS 7.50 15.00
4 Gordie Howe AS 20.00 40.00
5 Dave Keon Byng 7.50 15.00
6 Bobby Rousseau Calder 2.50 5.00
7 Bobby Hull Ross 12.50 25.00
8 Jacques Plante Vezina 12.50 25.00
9 Jacques Plante Hart 12.50 25.00
0 Doug Harvey Norris 5.00 10.00

1968-69 Shirriff Coins

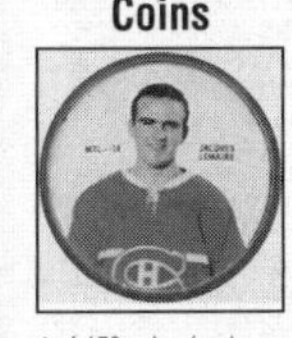

his set of 176 coins (each measuring pproximately 1 3/8" in diameter) features ayers from all of the teams in the NHL. hese plastic coins are in color and umbered on the front. However the coins e numbered by Shirriff within each team nd not for the whole set. The orrespondence between the actual coin umbers and the numbers assigned below hould be apparent. For those few situations here two coins from the same team have e same number, that number is listed in e checklist below next to the name. The oins are checklisted below according to eams as follows: Boston Bruins (1-16), hicago Blackhawks (17-33), Detroit Red ings (34-49), Los Angeles Kings (50-61), innesota North Stars (62-74), Montreal anadiens (75-92), New York Rangers (93-08), Oakland Seals (109-121), Philadelphia yers (122-134), Pittsburgh Penguins (135-46), St. Louis Blues (147-158), and oronto Maple Leafs (159-176). Some of the oins are quite challenging to find. It seems e higher numbers within each team and the oins from the players on the expansion eams are more difficult to find; these are arked by SP in the list below.

OMPLETE SET (176) 3000.00 6000.00
Eddie Shack 5.00 10.00
Ed Westfall 2.50 5.00
Don Awrey 2.00 4.00
Gerry Cheevers 6.00 12.00
Bobby Orr 50.00 100.00
Johnny Bucyk 5.00 10.00
Derek Sanderson 10.00 20.00
Phil Esposito 10.00 20.00
Fred Stanfield 2.00 4.00
0 Ken Hodge 3.00 6.00
1 John McKenzie 2.00 4.00
2 Ted Green 2.50 5.00
3 Dallas Smith SP 50.00 100.00
4 Gary Doak SP 50.00 100.00
5 Glen Sather SP 50.00 100.00
6 Tom Williams SP 37.50 75.00
7 Bobby Hull 25.00 50.00
8 Pat Stapleton 2.00 4.00
9 Wayne Maki 2.00 4.00
20 Denis DeJordy 4.00 8.00
21 Ken Wharram 2.50 5.00
22 Pit Martin 2.00 4.00
23 Chico Maki 2.00 4.00
24 Doug Mohns 2.50 5.00
25 Stan Mikita 7.50 15.00
26 Doug Jarrett 2.00 4.00
27 Dennis Hull 11 SP 50.00 100.00
(small portrait)
28 Dennis Hull 11 12.50 25.00
(large portrait)
29 Matt Ravlich 2.00 4.00
30 Dave Dryden SP 40.00 80.00
31 Eric Nesterenko SP 40.00 80.00
32 Gilles Marotte SP 40.00 80.00
33 Jim Pappin SP 40.00 80.00
34 Gary Bergman 2.00 4.00
35 Roger Crozier 4.00 8.00
36 Peter Mahovlich 3.00 6.00
37 Alex Delvecchio 4.00 8.00
38 Dean Prentice 2.50 5.00
39 Kent Douglas 2.00 4.00
40 Roy Edwards 3.00 6.00
41 Bruce MacGregor 2.00 4.00
42 Garry Unger 3.00 6.00
43 Pete Stemkowski 2.00 4.00
44 Gordie Howe 40.00 80.00
45 Frank Mahovlich 6.00 12.00
46 Bob Baun SP 40.00 80.00
47 Brian Conacher SP 40.00 80.00
48 Jim Watson SP 40.00 80.00
49 Nick Libett SP 40.00 80.00
50 Real Lemieux 2.50 5.00
51 Ted Irvine 2.50 5.00
52 Bob Wall 2.50 5.00
53 Bill White 2.50 5.00
54 Gord Labossiere 2.50 5.00
55 Eddie Joyal 2.00 4.00
56 Lowell MacDonald 2.50 5.00
57 Bill Flett 2.50 5.00
58 Wayne Rutledge 3.00 6.00
59 Dave Amadio 2.00 4.00
60 Skip Krake SP 25.00 50.00
61 Doug Robinson SP 25.00 50.00
62 Wayne Connelly 2.50 5.00
63 Bob Woytowich 2.50 5.00
64 Andre Boudrias 2.50 5.00
65 Bill Goldsworthy 3.00 6.00
66 Cesare Maniago 4.00 8.00
67 Milan Marcetta 2.50 5.00
68 Bill Collins SP 7 25.00 50.00
69 Claude Larose SP 7 50.00 100.00
70 Parker MacDonald 2.50 5.00
71 Ray Cullen 2.50 5.00
72 Mike McMahon 2.50 5.00
73 Bob McCord SP 25.00 50.00
74 Larry Hillman SP 25.00 50.00
75 Gump Worsley 5.00 10.00
76 Rogatien Vachon 7.50 15.00
77 Ted Harris 2.00 4.00
78 Jacques Laperriere 3.00 6.00
79 J.C. Tremblay 2.50 5.00
80 Jean Beliveau 15.00 30.00
81 Gilles Tremblay 2.00 4.00
82 Ralph Backstrom 2.50 5.00
83 Bobby Rousseau 2.00 4.00
84 John Ferguson 3.00 6.00
85 Dick Duff 3.00 6.00
86 Terry Harper 3.00 6.00
87 Yvan Cournoyer 4.00 8.00
88 Jacques Lemaire 6.00 12.00
89 Henri Richard 6.00 12.00
90 Claude Provost SP 50.00 100.00
91 Serge Savard SP 75.00 150.00
92 Mickey Redmond SP 75.00 150.00
93 Rod Seiling 2.00 4.00
94 Jean Ratelle 4.00 8.00
95 Ed Giacomin 7.50 15.00
96 Reg Fleming 2.00 4.00
97 Phil Goyette 2.00 4.00
98 Arnie Brown 2.00 4.00
99 Don Marshall 2.00 4.00
100 Orland Kurtenbach 3.00 6.00
101 Bob Nevin 2.00 4.00
102 Rod Gilbert 4.00 8.00
103 Harry Howell 3.00 6.00
104 Jim Neilson 2.00 4.00
105 Vic Hadfield SP 75.00 150.00
106 Larry Jeffrey SP 125.00 250.00
107 Dave Balon SP 75.00 150.00
108 Ron Stewart SP 75.00 150.00
109 Gerry Ehman 2.00 4.00
110 John Brenneman 2.50 5.00
111 Ted Hampson 2.50 5.00
112 Billy Harris 2.50 5.00
113 George Swarbrick SP 5 50.00 100.00
114 Carol Vadnais SP 5 250.00 500.00
115 Gary Smith 4.00 8.00
116 Charlie Hodge 4.00 8.00
117 Bert Marshall 2.50 5.00
118 Bill Hicke 2.50 5.00
119 Tracy Pratt 2.50 5.00
120 Gary Jarrett SP 250.00 500.00
121 Howie Young SP 250.00 500.00
122 Bernie Parent 20.00 40.00
123 John Miszuk 2.50 5.00
124 Ed Hoekstra SP 3 50.00 100.00
125 Allan Stanley SP 3 50.00 100.00
126 Gary Dornhoefer 3.00 6.00
127 Doug Favell 4.00 8.00
128 Andre Lacroix 2.50 5.00
129 Brit Selby 2.50 5.00
130 Don Blackburn 2.50 5.00
131 Leon Rochefort 2.50 5.00
132 Forbes Kennedy 2.50 5.00
133 Claude Laforge SP 40.00 80.00
134 Pat Hannigan SP 40.00 80.00
135 Ken Schinkel 2.50 5.00
136 Earl Ingarfield 2.50 5.00
137 Val Fonteyne 2.00 4.00
138 Noel Price 2.00 4.00
139 Andy Bathgate 4.00 8.00
140 Les Binkley 4.00 8.00
141 Leo Boivin 2.50 5.00
142 Paul Andrea 2.00 4.00
143 Dunc McCallum 3.00 6.00
144 Keith McCreary 2.50 5.00
145 Lou Angotti SP 40.00 80.00
146 Wally Boyer SP 40.00 80.00
147 Ron Schock 2.50 5.00
148 Bob Plager 3.00 6.00
149 Al Arbour 4.00 8.00
150 Red Berenson 3.00 6.00
151 Glenn Hall 7.50 15.00
152 Jim Roberts 2.50 5.00
153 Noel Picard 2.50 5.00
154 Barclay Plager 3.00 6.00
155 Larry Keenan 2.50 5.00
156 Terry Crisp 3.00 6.00
157 Gary Sabourin SP 40.00 80.00
158 Ab McDonald SP 40.00 80.00
159 George Armstrong 4.00 8.00
160 Wayne Carleton 2.00 4.00
161 Paul Henderson 3.00 6.00
162 Bob Pulford 3.00 6.00
163 Mike Walton 2.50 5.00
164 Johnny Bower 4.00 8.00
165 Ron Ellis 2.50 5.00
166 Mike Pelyk 2.00 4.00
167 Murray Oliver 2.00 4.00
168 Norm Ullman 4.00 8.00
169 Dave Keon 4.00 8.00
170 Floyd Smith 2.00 4.00
171 Marcel Pronovost 3.00 6.00
172 Tim Horton 7.50 15.00
173 Bruce Gamble 3.00 6.00
174 Jim McKenny SP 50.00 100.00
175 Mike Byers SP 50.00 100.00
176 Pierre Pilote SP 75.00 150.00

1995-96 SkyBox Impact Promo Panel

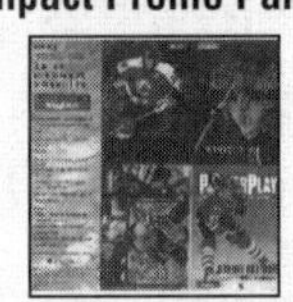

Measuring 7" by 7", this perforated promo panel was issued by SkyBox to celebrate the inaugural edition of the SkyBox Impact hockey series. The left strip consists of ad copy, with four standard-size player cards filling out the rest of the panel. As indicated in the listing below, Blaine Lacher is featured on two cards: a regular card as well as a Deflector insert card. The only difference from their regular issue counterparts is that these cards have the word "SAMPLE" on a black rectangle in place of card number.

1 Theo Fleury .40 1.00
Blaine Lacher
Blaine Lacher
Jeremy Roenick

1995-96 SkyBox Impact

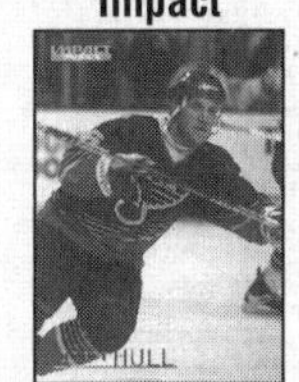

The 1996 Skybox Impact set was issued in one series totaling 250 cards. The 10-card packs retailed for $1.29. Each pack included an NHL on Fox Slapshot Instant Win Game Card, offering a chance at more than 20,000 prizes. The unused game cards sell for about ten cents. The Blaine Lacher SkyMotion exchange card was randomly inserted at a rate of 1:360 packs. The exchange deadline for the Lacher SkyMotion card was December 31st, 1996. Prices for the expired card and the redeemed card are listed below.

COMPLETE SET (250) 6.00 15.00
1 Bobby Dollas .01 .05
2 Guy Hebert .02 .10
3 Paul Kariya .07 .20
4 Todd Krygier .01 .05
5 Oleg Tverdovsky .01 .05
6 Shaun Van Allen .01 .05
7 Ray Bourque .10 .30
8 Al Iafrate .02 .10
9 Blaine Lacher .02 .10
10 Joe Mullen .02 .10
11 Cam Neely .07 .20
12 Adam Oates .02 .10
13 Kevin Stevens .01 .05
14 Donald Audette .01 .05
15 Garry Galley .01 .05
16 Dominik Hasek .15 .40
17 Pat LaFontaine .07 .20
18 Derek Plante .01 .05
19 Alexei Zhitnik .01 .05
20 Steve Chiasson .01 .05
21 Theo Fleury .01 .05
22 Phil Housley .02 .10
23 Trevor Kidd .02 .10
24 Joe Nieuwendyk .02 .10
25 German Titov .01 .05
26 Zarley Zalapski .01 .05
27 Ed Belfour .07 .20
28 Chris Chelios .07 .20
29 Sergei Krivokrasov .01 .05
30 Joe Murphy .01 .05
31 Bernie Nicholls .01 .05
32 Patrick Poulin .01 .05
33 Jeremy Roenick .10 .25
34 Gary Suter .01 .05
35 Peter Forsberg .20 .50
36 Valeri Kamensky .02 .10
37 Claude Lemieux .01 .05
38 Curtis Leschyshyn .01 .05
39 Sandis Ozolinsh .01 .05
40 Mike Ricci .02 .10
41 Joe Sakic .15 .40
42 Jocelyn Thibault .07 .20
43 Bob Bassen .01 .05
44 Dave Gagner .01 .05
45 Todd Harvey .02 .10
46 Derian Hatcher .01 .05
47 Kevin Hatcher .01 .05
48 Mike Modano .12 .30
49 Andy Moog .07 .20
50 Dino Ciccarelli .02 .10
51 Paul Coffey .07 .20
52 Sergei Fedorov .12 .30
53 Vladimir Konstantinov .02 .10
54 Slava Kozlov .02 .10
55 Nicklas Lidstrom .07 .20
56 Chris Osgood .02 .10
57 Keith Primeau .01 .05
58 Steve Yzerman .40 1.00
59 Jason Arnott .01 .05
60 Curtis Joseph .07 .20
61 Igor Kravchuk .01 .05
62 Todd Marchant .01 .05
63 David Oliver .01 .05
64 Bill Ranford .02 .10
65 Doug Weight .02 .10
66 Stu Barnes .01 .05
67 Jesse Belanger .01 .05
68 Gord Murphy .01 .05
69 Magnus Svensson .01 .05
70 John Vanbiesbrouck .02 .10
71 Sean Burke .02 .10
72 Andrew Cassels .01 .05
73 Nelson Emerson .01 .05
74 Andrei Nikolishin .01 .05
75 Geoff Sanderson .01 .05
76 Brendan Shanahan .07 .20
77 Glen Wesley .01 .05
78 Rob Blake .02 .10
79 Wayne Gretzky .60 1.50
80 Dimitri Khristich .01 .05
81 Jari Kurri .07 .20
82 Darryl Sydor .02 .10
83 Rick Tocchet .02 .10
84 Vincent Damphousse .01 .05
85 Vladimir Malakhov .01 .05
86 Mark Recchi .02 .10
87 Patrick Roy .40 1.00
88 Brian Savage .01 .05
89 Pierre Turgeon .02 .10
90 Martin Brodeur .20 .50
91 Neal Broten .02 .10
92 Shawn Chambers .01 .05
93 John MacLean .02 .10
94 Randy McKay .01 .05
95 Scott Niedermayer .01 .05
96 Stephane Richer .02 .10
97 Scott Stevens .02 .10
98 Steve Thomas .02 .10
99 Wendel Clark .02 .10
100 Patrick Flatley .01 .05
101 Scott Lachance .01 .05
102 Brett Lindros .01 .05
103 Kirk Muller .01 .05
104 Tommy Salo RC .30 .75
105 Mathieu Schneider .01 .05
106 Dennis Vaske .01 .05
107 Ray Ferraro .01 .05
108 Adam Graves .01 .05
109 Alexei Kovalev .01 .05
110 Brian Leetch .02 .10
111 Mark Messier .07 .20
112 Mike Richter .07 .20
113 Luc Robitaille .02 .10
114 Ulf Samuelsson .01 .05
115 Pat Verbeek .01 .05
116 Don Beaupre .02 .10
117 Radek Bonk .01 .05
118 Alexandre Daigle .01 .05
119 Steve Duchesne .01 .05
120 Dan Quinn .01 .05
121 Martin Straka .01 .05
122 Alexei Yashin .01 .05
123 Rod Brind'Amour .02 .10
124 Eric Desjardins .02 .10
125 Ron Hextall .02 .10
126 John LeClair .07 .20
127 Eric Lindros .07 .20
128 Mikael Renberg .02 .10
129 Chris Therien .01 .05
130 Ron Francis .02 .10
131 Jaromir Jagr .12 .30
132 Mario Lemieux .40 1.00
133 Petr Nedved .02 .10
134 Tomas Sandstrom .01 .05
135 Bryan Smolinski .01 .05
136 Ken Wregget .02 .10
137 Sergei Zubov .01 .05
138 Shayne Corson .01 .05
139 Geoff Courtnall .01 .05
140 Dale Hawerchuk .07 .20
141 Brett Hull .10 .25
142 Ian Laperriere .01 .05
143 Al MacInnis .02 .10
144 Chris Pronger .07 .20
145 Esa Tikkanen .01 .05
146 Ulf Dahlen .01 .05
147 Jeff Friesen .01 .05
148 Arturs Irbe .02 .10
149 Craig Janney .01 .05
150 Owen Nolan .02 .10
151 Mike Rathje .01 .05
152 Ray Sheppard .01 .05
153 Brian Bradley .01 .05
154 Chris Gratton .01 .05
155 Roman Hamrlik .02 .10
156 Petr Klima .01 .05
157 Daren Puppa .02 .10
158 Dave Andreychuk .02 .10
159 Mike Gartner .02 .10
160 Todd Gill .01 .05
161 Doug Gilmour .02 .10
162 Kenny Jonsson .01 .05
163 Larry Murphy .02 .10
164 Felix Potvin .07 .20
165 Mats Sundin .07 .20
166 Jeff Brown .01 .05
167 Pavel Bure .07 .20
168 Russ Courtnall .01 .05
169 Trevor Linden .02 .10
170 Kirk McLean .02 .10
171 Alexander Mogilny .02 .10
172 Roman Oksiuta .01 .05
173 Mike Ridley .01 .05
174 Peter Bondra .02 .10
175 Jim Carey .02 .10
176 Sergei Gonchar .01 .05
177 Dale Hunter .02 .10
178 Calle Johansson .01 .05
179 Joe Juneau .01 .05
180 Michal Pivonka .01 .05
181 Nikolai Khabibulin .02 .10
182 Dave Manson .01 .05
183 Teppo Numminen .01 .05
184 Teemu Selanne .07 .20
185 Keith Tkachuk .07 .20
186 Darren Turcotte .01 .05
187 Alexei Zhamnov .02 .10
188 Chad Kilger RC .01 .05
189 Kyle McLaren RC .01 .05
190 Brian Holzinger RC .07 .20
191 Wayne Primeau RC .01 .05
192 Marty Murray RC .01 .05
193 Eric Daze .02 .10
194 Jon Klemm RC .01 .05
195 Jere Lehtinen .01 .05
196 Jason Bonsignore RC .01 .05
197 Miroslav Satan RC .30 .75
198 Ryan Smyth .02 .10
199 Tyler Wright RC .01 .05
200 Radek Dvorak RC .15 .40
201 Ed Jovanovski .07 .20
202 Jeff O'Neill .01 .05
203 Aki-Petteri Berg RC .02 .10
204 Jamie Storr .02 .10
205 Vitali Yachmenov .01 .05
206 Saku Koivu .07 .20
207 Denis Pederson RC .01 .05
208 Todd Bertuzzi RC .50 1.25
209 Bryan McCabe RC .01 .05
210 Dan Plante RC .10 .25
211 Peter Ferraro .01 .05
212 Darren Langdon RC .01 .05
213 Niklas Sundstrom .01 .05
214 Daniel Alfredsson RC .30 .75
215 Garth Snow RC .02 .10
216 Ian Moran RC .01 .05
217 Richard Park RC .01 .05
218 Jamie Rivers RC .01 .05
219 Roman Vopat RC .01 .05
220 Marcus Ragnarsson RC .02 .10
221 Aaron Gavey .01 .05
222 Daymond Langkow RC .15 .40
223 Darby Hendrickson RC .01 .05
224 Martin Gendron RC .01 .05
225 Brendan Witt .01 .05
226 Shane Doan RC .25 .60
227 Deron Quint RC .01 .05
228 Jim Carey HH .01 .05
229 Peter Forsberg HH .10 .30
230 Paul Kariya HH .07 .20
231 David Oliver HH .01 .05
232 Blaine Lacher HH .02 .10
233 Todd Harvey HH .01 .05
234 Todd Marchant HH .01 .05
235 Jeff Friesen HH .01 .05
236 Oleg Tverdovsky HH .01 .05
237 Jason Arnott HH .01 .05
238 Cam Neely PP .02 .10
239 Keith Tkachuk PP .07 .20
240 Owen Nolan PP .02 .10
241 Keith Primeau PP .01 .05
242 Peter Bondra PP .02 .10
243 Jeremy Roenick PP .10 .25
244 John LeClair PP .07 .20
245 Mikael Renberg PP .02 .10
246 Dave Andreychuk PP .02 .10
247 Rick Tocchet PP .02 .10
NNO Blaine Lacher 4.00 10.00
SkyMotion card
NNO Blaine Lacher .02 .10
Exchange card

1995-96 SkyBox Impact Deflectors

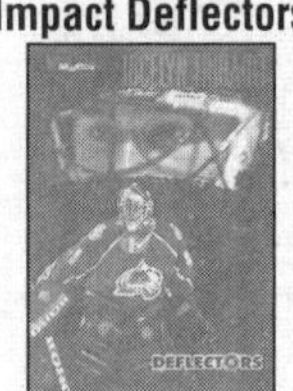

Randomly inserted in packs at a rate of 1:10, this 12-card set features top NHL goalies.

COMPLETE SET (12) 4.00 8.00
1 Dominik Hasek .50 1.25
2 Jim Carey .15 .30
3 Felix Potvin .25 .60
4 Sean Burke .15 .30
5 Blaine Lacher .15 .30
6 John Vanbiesbrouck .15 .30
7 Jocelyn Thibault .25 .60
8 Patrick Roy 1.25 3.00
9 Ed Belfour .25 .60
10 Trevor Kidd .15 .30
11 Martin Brodeur .60 1.50
12 Kirk McLean .15 .30

1995-96 SkyBox Impact Countdown to Impact

Randomly inserted in hobby packs only at a rate of 1:60, this set features nine explosive stars whose names can be found on the backs of many fans jerseys at NHL arenas across North America. The card fronts also point to statistical milestones that are within range for that player.

COMPLETE SET (9) 12.00 30.00
1 Eric Lindros 1.50 4.00
2 Jaromir Jagr 2.50 5.00
3 Mario Lemieux 4.00 10.00
4 Wayne Gretzky 6.00 15.00
5 Mark Messier 1.50 4.00
6 Sergei Fedorov 1.50 4.00
7 Paul Kariya 1.50 4.00
8 Doug Gilmour 1.00 2.50
9 Pavel Bure 1.50 4.00

1995-96 SkyBox Impact Ice Quake

Randomly inserted in packs at a rate of 1:20, this 15-card set delivers the rumble that goalies feel when the NHL's best forwards have the puck on their sticks and start skating towards the net.

COMPLETE SET (15) 15.00 40.00
1 Jaromir Jagr 2.50 6.00
2 Brett Hull 1.50 4.00
3 Pavel Bure 1.00 2.50
4 Eric Lindros 1.00 2.50
5 Mark Messier 1.50 4.00
6 Wayne Gretzky 6.00 15.00
7 Mario Lemieux 5.00 12.00
8 Peter Forsberg 2.50 6.00
9 Sergei Fedorov 1.50 4.00
10 Cam Neely 1.00 2.50
11 Owen Nolan .40 1.00
12 Alexei Zhamnov .40 1.00
13 Theo Fleury .40 1.00
14 Luc Robitaille .40 1.00
15 Teemu Selanne 1.00 2.50

1995-96 SkyBox Impact NHL On Fox

Randomly inserted in packs at a rate of 1:3, this 18-card set showcases both bright young stars and the company's strong affiliation with the NHL broadcasts on the Fox television network in the States.

COMPLETE SET (18) 2.00 5.00
1 Mariusz Czerkawski .20 .50
2 Roman Oksiuta .20 .50
3 David Oliver .20 .50
4 Adam Deadmarsh .20 .50
5 Denis Chasse .20 .50
6 Sergei Krivokrasov .20 .50
7 Ian Laperriere .20 .50
8 Chris Therien .20 .50
9 Brian Savage .20 .50
10 Todd Marchant .20 .50
11 Jeff O'Neill .20 .50
12 Brett Lindros .20 .50
13 Kenny Jonsson .20 .50
14 Manny Fernandez .40 1.00
15 Brian Holzinger .20 .50
16 Niklas Sundstrom .20 .50
17 Eric Daze .20 .50
18 Chad Kilger .20 .50

1996-97 SkyBox Impact

This 175-card set featured color action player photos of 118 seasoned stars plus a 20-card Rookies subset (#119-#138) and a 10-card Power Play subset (#139-#148). These ten Power Play cards had front designs that actually looked like miniature magazine covers. A special Stanley Cup logo appeared on all Colorado Avalanche player cards. The backs carried player stats, bio information, and a statement about the player as written by hockey HOF and Fox broadcaster Denis Potvin. A "John LeClair SkyPin Exchange" card, inserted at the rate of one in every 180 packs, entitled the collector to send for a John LeClair "preview card" from the proposed -- but never materialized -- SkyPin trading card line. One "SkyBox/Fox Game" card was inserted in every pack which enabled the holder to win big prizes from SkyBox, Fox, and the NHL.

COMPLETE SET (175) 5.00 12.00
1 Guy Hebert .05 .15
2 Paul Kariya .08 .25
3 Roman Oksiuta .02 .10
4 Teemu Selanne .08 .25
5 Ray Bourque .15 .40
6 Kyle McLaren .02 .10
7 Adam Oates .05 .15
8 Bill Ranford .05 .15
9 Rick Tocchet .05 .15
10 Dominik Hasek .20 .50
11 Pat LaFontaine .08 .25
12 Mike Peca .02 .10
13 Theo Fleury .02 .10
14 Trevor Kidd .05 .15
15 German Titov .02 .10
16 Tony Amonte .05 .15
17 Ed Belfour .08 .25
18 Chris Chelios .08 .25
19 Eric Daze .05 .15
20 Gary Suter .02 .10
21 Alexei Zhamnov .05 .15
22 Peter Forsberg .25 .60
23 Valeri Kamensky .05 .15
24 Uwe Krupp .02 .10
25 Claude Lemieux .02 .10
26 Sandis Ozolinsh .02 .10
27 Patrick Roy .50 1.25
28 Joe Sakic .20 .50
29 Derian Hatcher .02 .10
30 Mike Modano .15 .40
31 Joe Nieuwendyk .05 .15
32 Sergei Zubov .02 .10
33 Paul Coffey .08 .25
34 Sergei Fedorov .15 .40
35 Vladimir Konstantinov .05 .15
36 Slava Kozlov .05 .15
37 Nicklas Lidstrom .08 .25
38 Chris Osgood .05 .15
39 Keith Primeau .02 .10
40 Steve Yzerman .50 1.25
41 Jason Arnott .02 .10
42 Curtis Joseph .08 .25
43 Doug Weight .05 .15
44 Radek Dvorak .02 .10
45 Ed Jovanovski .05 .15
46 Scott Mellanby .05 .15
47 Rob Niedermayer .05 .15
48 Ray Sheppard .05 .15
49 Robert Svehla .02 .10
50 John Vanbiesbrouck .05 .15
51 Jeff Brown .02 .10
52 Sean Burke .05 .15
53 Andrew Cassels .02 .10
54 Geoff Sanderson .05 .15
55 Brendan Shanahan .08 .25
56 Byron Dafoe .05 .15
57 Ray Ferraro .02 .10
58 Dimitri Khristich .02 .10
59 Vitali Yachmenev .02 .10
60 Valeri Bure .02 .10
61 Vincent Damphousse .02 .10
62 Saku Koivu .08 .25
63 Mark Recchi .05 .15
64 Martin Rucinsky .02 .10
65 Jocelyn Thibault .08 .25
66 Pierre Turgeon .05 .15
67 Dave Andreychuk .05 .15
68 Martin Brodeur .25 .60
69 Bill Guerin .02 .10
70 Scott Niedermayer .02 .10
71 Scott Stevens .05 .15
72 Petr Sykora .02 .10
73 Steve Thomas .02 .10
74 Todd Bertuzzi .08 .25
75 Travis Green .05 .15
76 Kenny Jonsson .02 .10
77 Zigmund Palffy .05 .15
78 Adam Graves .02 .10
79 Wayne Gretzky .60 1.50
80 Alexei Kovalev .02 .10
81 Brian Leetch .08 .25
82 Mark Messier .08 .25
83 Mike Richter .08 .25
84 Ulf Samuelsson .02 .10
85 Niklas Sundstrom .02 .10
86 Daniel Alfredsson .05 .15
87 Radek Bonk .02 .10
88 Alexandre Daigle .02 .10
89 Steve Duchesne .02 .10
90 Damian Rhodes .05 .15
91 Alexei Yashin .02 .10
92 Rod Brind'Amour .05 .15
93 Eric Desjardins .05 .15
94 Dale Hawerchuk .05 .15
95 Ron Hextall .05 .15
96 John LeClair .08 .25
97 Eric Lindros .08 .25
98 Mikael Renberg .05 .15
99 Tom Barrasso .05 .15
100 Ron Francis .05 .15
101 Jaromir Jagr .15 .40
102 Mario Lemieux .50 1.25
103 Petr Nedved .05 .15
104 Bryan Smolinski .02 .10
105 Nikolai Khabibulin .05 .15
106 Teppo Numminen .02 .10
107 Keith Tkachuk .08 .25
108 Jeremy Roenick .12 .30
109 Oleg Tverdovsky .05 .15
110 Shayne Corson .02 .10
111 Geoff Courtnall .02 .10
112 Grant Fuhr .05 .15
113 Brett Hull .10 .30
114 Al MacInnis .05 .15
115 Chris Pronger .05 .15
116 Jeff Friesen .02 .10
117 Owen Nolan .05 .15
118 Marcus Ragnarsson .02 .10
119 Chris Terreri .05 .15
120 Brian Bradley .02 .10
121 Chris Gratton .05 .15
122 Roman Hamrlik .05 .15
123 Daren Puppa .05 .15
124 Alexander Selivanov .02 .10
125 Wendel Clark .05 .15
126 Doug Gilmour .05 .15
127 Kirk Muller .02 .10
128 Larry Murphy .05 .15
129 Felix Potvin .08 .25
130 Mats Sundin .08 .25
131 Pavel Bure .08 .25
132 Russ Courtnall .02 .10
133 Trevor Linden .05 .15
134 Kirk McLean .05 .15
135 Alexander Mogilny .05 .15
136 Peter Bondra .05 .15
137 Jim Carey .08 .25
138 Sylvain Cote .02 .10

139 Sergei Gonchar .02 .10
140 Phil Housley .05 .15
141 Joe Juneau .02 .10
142 Michal Pivonka .02 .10
143 Brendan Witt .02 .10
144 Nolan Baumgartner .02 .10
145 Martin Biron RC .60 1.50
146 Jason Bonsignore .02 .10
147 Andrew Brunette RC .15 .40
148 Jason Doig .02 .10
149 Peter Ferraro .02 .10
150 Eric Fichaud .05 .15
151 Ladislav Kohn .02 .10
152 Jamie Langenbrunner .02 .10
153 Daymond Langkow .05 .15
154 Jay McKee RC .02 .10
155 Marty Murray .02 .10
156 Wayne Primeau .02 .10
157 Jamie Pushor .02 .10
158 Jamie Rivers .02 .10
159 Jamie Storr .05 .15
160 Steve Sullivan RC .15 .40
161 Jose Theodore .12 .30
162 Roman Vppat .02 .10
163 Alexei Yegorov RC .02 .10
164 Daniel Alfredsson PP .05 .15
165 Niklas Andersson PP .02 .10
166 Todd Bertuzzi PP .08 .25
167 Valeri Bure PP .02 .10
168 Eric Daze PP .05 .15
169 Saku Koivu PP .08 .25
170 Miroslav Satan PP .02 .10
171 Petr Sykora PP .02 .10
172 Cory Stillman PP .02 .10
173 Vitali Yachmenev PP .02 .10
174 Checklist 1 .02 .10
175 Checklist 2 UER .02 .10
Pavel Bure misidentified as Paul
Palffy misspelled with one F
Lafontaine, not Lafontanine
Selanne, not Selanna
S1 John LeClair PROMO .15 .30
NNO SkyPin EXCH .02 .10
NNO John Leclair SkyPin .08 .25

1996-97 SkyBox Impact BladeRunners

Randomly inserted at the rate of 1:3 packs, this 25-card set featured some of the fastest hockey players on ice. The fronts carried a color action player photo while the backs displayed player information.

COMPLETE SET (25) 15.00 40.00
1 Brian Bradley .40 .75
2 Chris Chelios 1.00 2.00
3 Peter Forsberg 2.50 5.00
4 Ron Francis .60 1.25
5 Mike Gartner .60 1.25
6 Doug Gilmour .60 1.25
7 Phil Housley .60 1.25
8 Brett Hull 1.25 2.50
9 Valeri Kamensky .60 1.25
10 Pat LaFontaine 1.00 2.00
11 John LeClair 1.00 2.00
12 Claude Lemieux .40 .75
13 Nicklas Lidstrom 1.00 2.00
14 Mark Messier 1.00 2.00
15 Alexander Mogilny .60 1.25
16 Petr Nedved .60 1.25
17 Adam Oates .60 1.25
18 Zigmund Palffy .60 1.25
19 Jeremy Roenick 1.25 2.50
20 Teemu Selanne 1.00 2.00
21 Brendan Shanahan 1.00 2.00
22 Keith Tkachuk 1.00 2.00
23 Pierre Turgeon .60 1.25
24 Doug Weight .60 1.25
25 Steve Yzerman 5.00 10.00

1996-97 SkyBox Impact Countdown to Impact

Randomly inserted in hobby packs only at the rate of 1:30, this 10-card insert set focused on the true superstars of the game. The fronts displayed color player photos while the backs carried player information.

COMPLETE SET (10) 20.00 50.00
1 Pavel Bure 1.25 3.00
2 Sergei Fedorov 1.25 3.00
3 Wayne Gretzky 8.00 20.00
4 Jaromir Jagr 2.00 5.00
5 Ed Jovanovski .75 2.00
6 Paul Kariya 1.25 3.00
7 Mario Lemieux 6.00 15.00
8 Eric Lindros 1.25 3.00
9 Patrick Roy 6.00 15.00
10 Joe Sakic 3.00 8.00

1996-97 SkyBox Impact NHL on Fox

Randomly inserted at the rate of 1:10 packs, this 20-card set was a joint venture with Fox TV.

COMPLETE SET (20) 5.00 12.00
1 Daniel Alfredsson .40 1.00
2 Todd Bertuzzi .40 1.00
3 Ray Bourque 1.25 3.00
4 Valeri Bure .20 .50
5 Chris Chelios .75 2.00
6 Paul Coffey .75 2.00
7 Eric Daze .20 .50
8 Eric Desjardins .20 .50
9 Sergei Gonchar .20 .50
10 Phil Housley .20 .50
11 Ed Jovanovski .20 .50
12 Vladimir Konstantinov .75 2.00
13 Saku Koivu .75 2.00
14 Brian Leetch .40 1.00
15 Larry Murphy .20 .50
16 Teppo Numminen .20 .50
17 Sandis Ozolinsh .20 .50
18 Marcus Ragnarsson .20 .50
19 Petr Sykora .20 .50
20 Vitali Yachmenev .20 .50

1996-97 SkyBox Impact VersaTeam

Randomly inserted at the rate of 1:120 packs, this 10-card set featured the NHL's best multi-skilled players. The fronts displayed color player photos while the backs carried player information.

COMPLETE SET (10) 40.00 100.00
1 Pavel Bure 2.50 6.00
2 Sergei Fedorov 2.50 6.00
3 Peter Forsberg 4.00 10.00
4 Wayne Gretzky 15.00 40.00
5 Jaromir Jagr 4.00 10.00
6 Paul Kariya 2.50 6.00
7 Mario Lemieux 12.00 30.00
8 Eric Lindros 2.50 6.00
9 Joe Sakic 6.00 15.00
10 Teemu Selanne 2.50 6.00

1996-97 SkyBox Impact Zero Heroes

Randomly inserted in retail packs only at the rate of 1:30, this 10-card set featured the stingiest goaltenders in the league. The fronts displayed color player photos while the backs carried player information.

COMPLETE SET (10) 20.00 50.00
1 Ed Belfour 2.50 6.00
2 Sean Burke 1.00 2.50
3 Jim Carey 1.00 2.50
4 Dominik Hasek 4.00 10.00
5 Ron Hextall 2.50 6.00
6 Chris Osgood 2.50 6.00
7 Felix Potvin 2.50 6.00
8 Daren Puppa 1.00 2.50
9 Patrick Roy 10.00 25.00
10 John Vanbiesbrouck 2.50 6.00

1995-96 Slapshot

The 1995-96 Slapshot set features the players of the OHL and was issued in foil packs in one series totaling 440 cards. Randomly inserted into packs were promo cards and an autographed card of Zac Bierk. The set is notable for the inclusion of several top prospects, including Alexandre Volchkov, Boyd Devereaux, Joe Thornton, Daniel Cleary and Rico Fata.

COMPLETE SET (440) 20.00 50.00
1 Checklist .02 .05
2 Checklist .02 .05
3 Checklist .02 .05
4 Checklist .02 .05
5 David E. Branch .02 .05
6 Bert Templeton .02 .05
7 Chris George .02 .05
8 Chris Thompson .10 .25
9 Quade Lightbody .02 .05
10 Shane Delaronde .02 .05
11 Justin Robinson .02 .05
12 Shawn Frappier .02 .05
13 Lucio Nasato .10 .25
14 Jason Payne .02 .05
15 Jason Cannon .02 .05
16 Alexandre Volchkov .10 .25
17 Daniel Tkaczuk .40 .50
18 Gerry Lanigan .02 .05
19 Darrell Woodley .02 .05
20 Brian Barker .02 .05
21 Mauricio Alvarez .02 .05
22 Brock Boucher .02 .05
23 Jeff Cowan .14 .35
24 Jan Bulis .20 .50
25 Jeff Tetzlaff .02 .05
26 Caleb Ward .06 .15
27 Mike White .02 .05
28 Jeremy Miculinic .02 .05
29 Andrew Morrison .02 .05
30 Robert Dubois .02 .05
31 Kory Cooper .10 .25
32 Jason Gaggi .10 .25
33 Mike Van Volsen .02 .05
34 Paul McInness .02 .05
35 Harkie Stingh .02 .05
36 Robin Lacour .02 .05
37 Jamie Sokolsky .02 .05
38 Marc Dupuis .02 .05
39 Daniel Cleary .40 .50
40 David Peca .02 .05
41 Adam Robbins .02 .05
42 Steve Tracze .02 .05
43 James Boyd .02 .05
44 Jake Irsag .02 .05
45 Ryan Ready .02 .05
46 Walker McDonald .02 .05
47 Rob Guinn .02 .05
48 Rob Fitzgerald .02 .05
49 Joe Coombs .02 .05
50 Daniel Reja .02 .05
51 Joe Van Volsen .04 .10
52 Craig Mills .10 .25
53 Murray Hogg .02 .05
54 Andrei Shurupov .10 .25
55 Andrew Williamson .02 .05
56 Mike Minard .10 .25
57 Robert Esche .60 2.00
58 Lee Jinman .10 .25
59 Corey Neilson .08 .20
60 Troy Smith .02 .05
61 Mike Rucinski .08 .20
62 Colin Beardsmore .02 .05
63 Dan Pawlacyzk .02 .05
64 Scott Blair .02 .05
65 Mike Morrone .02 .05
66 Matt Ball .02 .05
67 Steve Dumonski .02 .05
68 Murray Sheehan .02 .05
69 Sean Haggerty .10 .25
70 Andrew Taylor .02 .05
71 Steve Wasylko .04 .10
72 Jan Vodrazka .02 .05
73 Dan Preston .02 .05
74 Jesse Boulerice .14 .50
75 Bryan Berard .30 .75
76 Nicolas Beaudoin .10 .25
77 Tom Buckley .04 .10
78 Mark Cadotte .08 .20
79 Greg Stephan .02 .05
80 Peter DeBoer .04 .10
81 Regan Stocco .02 .05
82 Andy Adams .10 .25
83 Brett Thompson .10 .25
84 Darryl McArthur .02 .05
85 Ryan Risidore .08 .20
86 Joel Cort .04 .10
87 Chris Hajt .10 .25
88 Bryan McKinney .02 .05
89 Dwayne Hay .20 .50
90 Andrew Clark .02 .05
91 Ryan Robichaud .02 .05
92 Mike Vellinga .02 .05
93 Jamie Wright .02 .05
94 Herbert Vasilijevs .02 .05
95 Dan Cloutier .80 2.00
96 Brian Wesenberg .10 .25
97 Michael Pittman .02 .05
98 Jeff Williams .02 .05
99 Todd Norman .10 .25
100 Brian Willsie .02 .05
101 Jason Jackman .08 .20
102 Mike Lankshear .06 .15
103 Andrew Long .08 .20
104 Nick Bootland .04 .10
105 E.J. McGuire .02 .05
106 Bujar Amidovski .20 .50
107 John Hultberg .10 .25
108 Eric Olsen .02 .05
109 Chris Allen .20 .50
110 Michael Tilson .02 .05
111 Jeff DaCosta .02 .05
112 Gord Walsh .02 .05
113 Matt Bradley .02 .05
114 Robert Mailloux .02 .05
115 Justin Davis .02 .05
116 Marc Moro .14 .35
117 Cail MacLean .02 .05
118 Jason Sands .02 .05
119 Matt Price .02 .05
120 Zdenek Skorepa .04 .10
121 Jason Morgan .02 .05
122 Mike Oliveira .10 .25
123 Colin Chaulk .02 .05
124 Dylan Taylor .02 .05
125 Kurt Johnston .02 .05
126 Bill Minkhorst .02 .05
127 Wes Swinson .10 .25
128 Adam Fleming .02 .05
129 Chris MacDonald .02 .05
130 Gary Agnew .02 .05
131 David Belitski .10 .25
132 Jarrett Rose .02 .05
133 Ryan Mougenel .02 .05
134 Rob Stanfield .02 .05
135 Duncan Fader .02 .05
136 Rob Maric .02 .05
137 Mark McMahon .02 .05
138 Serge Payer .02 .05
139 Paul Traynor .02 .05
140 Bogdan Rudenko .02 .05
141 Robert DeCiantis .06 .15
142 Andrew Dale .10 .25
143 Jeff Ambrosio .04 .10
144 Paul Doyle .08 .20
145 Bryan Duce .02 .05
146 Jason Byrnes .02 .05
147 Ryan Pepperall .10 .25
148 Wes Vander Wal .02 .05
149 Boyd Devereaux .40 .50
150 Keith Walsh .02 .05
151 Joe Birch .02 .05
152 Craig Nelson .02 .05
153 Brian Hayden .02 .05
154 Matt O'Dette .02 .05
155 Geoff Ward .02 .05
156 Frank Ivankovic .10 .25
157 Eoin McInerney .10 .50
158 Joel Dezainde .02 .05
159 Duncan Dalmao .02 .05
160 Brandon Sugden .02 .50
161 Jamie Wentzell .02 .05
162 Ryan Burgoyne .02 .05
163 Todd Crane .02 .05
164 Chad Cavanagh .02 .05
165 Andrew Fagan .02 .05
166 Ryan Gardner .02 .05
167 Kevin Boyd .02 .05
168 Kevin Barry .02 .05
169 Richard Pitirri .02 .05
170 Adam Colagiacomo .20 .50
171 Jason Brooks .02 .05
172 Justin McPolin .02 .05
173 Travis Riggin .02 .05
174 Steve Lowe .02 .05
175 Todd St. Louis .02 .05
176 Kevin Slota .02 .05
177 Ryan McKie .02 .05
178 Corey Isen .02 .05
179 Sasha Cucuz .02 .05
180 Tom Barrett .02 .05
181 Ken Carroll .02 .05
182 Ryan Penney .10 .25
183 Jay McKee .30 .75
184 Ryan Taylor .02 .05
185 Jeff Paul .02 .05
186 Jason Ward .20 .50
187 Jesse Black .04 .10
188 Steve Nimigon .08 .20
189 Chris Haskett .02 .05
190 Geoff Peters .10 .25
191 Ryan Cirillo .02 .05
192 David Froh .02 .05
193 Jeff Johnstone .02 .05
194 Shane Nash .08 .20
195 Jason Robinson .02 .05
196 Rich Vrataric .02 .05
197 Colin Pepperall .02 .05
198 Craig Jalbert .02 .05
199 Andrew Williamson .02 .05
200 Greg Tymchuk .02 .05
201 Chester Gallant .02 .05
202 Mike Perna .02 .05
203 Adam Nitel .02 .50
204 Dave Burkholder .02 .05
205 Chris Johnstone .02 .05
206 Elliott Faust .10 .25
207 Scott Roche .10 .25
208 Kam White .02 .05
209 Scott Atkins .02 .05
210 Luc Belliveau .02 .05
211 Jamie Vossen .02 .05
212 Ryan MacDonald .02 .05
213 Jim Midgley .02 .05
214 Steven Carpenter .02 .05
215 Jake Martel .02 .05
216 Alex Matvichuk .02 .05
217 Trevor Gallant .10 .25
218 Ryan Gillis .02 .05
219 Kris Cantu .02 .05
220 Mark Provenzano .02 .05
221 Brian Whitley .02 .05
222 Dustin Virag .02 .05
223 Lee Jinman .10 .25
224 Peter McCague .02 .05
225 Herb Bonvie .02 .05
226 Philippe Poirier .02 .05
227 Greg Labanski .02 .05
228 Milan Kostolny .10 .25
229 Ryan Power .02 .05
230 Shane Parker .02 .05
231 Travis Scott .10 .25
232 Tyrone Garner .10 .25
233 Marty Wilford .10 .25
234 Ole Anderson .02 .05
235 Ryan Tocher .02 .05
236 Nathan Perrott .20 .75
237 Brandon Coalter .02 .05
238 John Tripp .10 .25
239 Jay Legault .20 .50
240 Wayne Primeau .20 .50
241 Trevor Edgar .02 .05
242 Peter Hogan .02 .05
243 Warren Holmes .02 .05
244 Jason Metcalfe .02 .05
245 Mike Zanutto .02 .05
246 Jeff Ware .10 .25
247 Ian MacNeil .02 .05
248 Jan Snopek .08 .20
249 Kurt Walsh .02 .05
250 Marc Savard .30 .75
251 Darcy O'Shea .02 .05
252 Jason Sweitzer .02 .05
253 Ryan Lindsay .02 .05
254 Scott Seiling .02 .05
255 Stan Butler .10 .25
256 Tim Keyes .10 .25
257 Craig Hillier .10 .25
258 Craig Whynot .02 .05
259 David Bell .02 .05
260 Rich Bronila .02 .05
261 Roy Gray .02 .05
262 Nick Boynton .40 1.00
263 Mike Sim .10 .25
264 B.J. Johnston .02 .05
265 Niall Maynard .02 .05
266 Dan Tudin .10 .25
267 Jure Kovacavic .02 .05
268 Ben Gustavson .02 .05
269 Steve Zaryk .02 .05
270 Darren Debrie .02 .05
271 Troy Stonier .02 .05
272 David Nemirovsky .10 .25
273 Joel Trottier .10 .25
274 Mike Lavell .02 .05
275 Brian Campbell .20 .50
276 Chris Despatis .02 .05
277 Sean Blanchard .10 .25
278 Alyn McCauley .30 .75
279 Chris Pittman .08 .20
280 Daryl Rivers .02 .05
281 Brent Johnson .80 2.00
282 Shaun Gallant .02 .05
283 Shane Kenny .02 .05
284 Chris Biagini .02 .05
285 Jim Ensom .04 .10
286 Marek Babic .02 .05
287 Oleg Tsyrkunov .02 .05
288 Mike Loach .02 .05
289 Peter MacKellar .02 .05
290 Ryan Davis .02 .05
291 John Argiropoulos .02 .05
292 Jason Campbell .02 .05
293 Ryan Christie .20 .50
294 Dan Snyder .02 1.00
295 Steve Gallace .02 .05
296 Scott Seiling .02 .05
297 Jeremy Rebek .02 .05
298 Adam Mair .20 .50
299 Matt Osborne .02 .05
300 Mike Gelati .02 .05
301 Wayne Primeau .20 .50
302 Chris Wismer .02 .05
303 Larry Paleczny .10 .25
304 Kurt Walsh .02 .05
305 John Lovell .02 .05
306 Allan Hitchen .10 .25
307 Zac Bierk .20 .50
308 Mike Martone .02 .05
309 Jonathan Murphy .02 .05
310 Adrian Murray .02 .05
311 Rob Giffin .02 .05
312 Corey Crocker .10 .25
313 Cameron Mann .20 .50
314 Ryan Pawluk .02 .05
315 Jason MacMillan .02 .05
316 Shawn Thornton .02 1.00
317 Wade Dawe .02 .05
318 Eric Landry .02 .05
319 Steve Hogg .02 .05
320 Kevin Bolibruck .02 .05
321 Dave Duerden .10 .25
322 Mike Williams .02 .05
323 Andy Johnson .02 .05
324 Jaret Nixon .02 .05
325 Evgeny Korolev .10 .25
326 Matthew Lahey .02 .05
327 Ryan Schmidt .02 .05
328 Scott Barney .10 .25
329 Steve Jones .02 .05
330 Dave McQueen .02 .05
331 Jeff Salajko .10 .25
332 Patrick DesRochers .20 .50
333 Gerald Moriarity .02 .05
334 Allan Carr .02 .05
335 Tom Brown .02 .05
336 Andy Delmore .30 .50
337 Darren Mortier .02 .05
338 Aaron Brand .10 .25
339 Eric Boulton .02 1.00
340 Jonathan Sim .20 .50
341 Trevor Letowski .80 .50
342 Michael Hanson .02 .05
343 Todd Miller .02 .05
344 Brendan Yarema .02 .05
345 Brad Simms .02 .05
346 David Nemirovsky .10 .25
347 Jeff Brown .10 .25
348 Andrew Proskurnicki .02 .05
349 Wes Mason .10 .25
350 Scott Corbett .02 .05
351 Dave Bourque .02 .05
352 Sean Brown .20 .50
353 Marcin Snita .02 .05
354 Rich Brown .02 .05
355 Mark Hunter .02 .05
356 Michal Podolka .10 .25
357 Dan Cloutier .80 2.00
358 Cory Murphy .02 .05
359 Kevin Murnaghan .02 .05
360 Andre Payette .02 .05
361 Richard Uniacke .08 .20
362 Joe Seroski .06 .15
363 Joe Thornton 4.00 10.00
364 Ben Schust .02 .05
365 Peter Cava .02 .05
366 Darryl Green .02 .05
367 Trevor Tokarczyk .02 .05
368 Jeff Gies .02 .05
369 Rico Fata .20 .50
370 Brian Secord .02 .05
371 Scott Cherrey .06 .15
372 Brian Stacey .02 .05
373 Lee Cole .02 .05
374 Richard Jackman .20 .50
375 Jason Doyle .10 .25
376 Brian Stewart .04 .10
377 Blaine Fitzpatrick .02 .05
378 Robert Mulick .02 .05
379 Andy Adams .10 .25
380 Joe Paterson .02 .05
381 Dave MacDonald .10 .25
382 Stephan Valiquette .40 1.00
383 Tim Swartz .02 .05
384 Gregg Lalonde .02 .05
385 Tyson Flinn .02 .05
386 Ryan Sly .02 .05
387 Neal Martin .02 .05
388 Kevin Hansen .02 .05
389 Joe Lombardo .02 .05
390 Darryl Moxam .02 .05
391 Jeremy Adduono .06 .15
392 Ryan Shanahan .02 .05
393 Sean Venedam .06 .15
394 Andrew Dale .10 .25
395 Rob Butler .02 .05
396 Brian Scott .02 .05
397 Liam MacEachern .02 .05
398 Luc Gagne .02 .05
399 Richard Rochefort .02 .05
400 Noel Burkitt .02 .05
401 Simon Sherry .02 .05
402 Brad Domonsky .10 .25
403 Ron Newhook .14 .35
404 Serge Dunphy .02 .05
405 Todd Lalonde .02 .05
406 Ryan Gelinas .10 .25
407 Terry Joss .08 .20
408 Mike Martin .08 .20
409 Chris Van Dyk .08 .20
410 D.J. Smith .10 .50
411 Glenn Crawford .08 .20
412 Robert Blain .02 .05
413 Matt Masterson .02 .05
414 Adam Young .02 .05
415 Matt Cooke .40 1.00
416 Jeff Zehr .10 .50
417 Wes Ward .08 .20
418 Matt Elich .14 .35
419 Rob Shearer .14 .35
420 Dean Mando .02 .05
421 Chris Kerr .02 .05
422 Vladimir Kretchine .02 .05
423 Jeff Martin .02 .05
424 Valeri Svoboda .02 .05
425 Dave Geris .08 .20
426 Ryan Pawluk .02 .05
427 Ryan Shaver .02 .05
428 Cameron Kincaid .02 .05
429 Tim Findlay .10 .25
430 Tim Bryan .02 .05
431 Alexandre Volchkov .20 .50
432 Boyd Devereaux .40 1.00
433 Chris Allen .10 .25
434 Paul Doyle .08 .20
435 Wes Mason .10 .25
436 Chris Hajt .10 .25
437 Kurt Walsh .02 .05
438 Glenn Crawford .08 .20
439 Jeff Brown .10 .25
440 Geoff Peters .10 .25
NNO Zac Bierk autograph 2.00 5.00
NNO Nick Boynton promo .40 1.00
NNO Jay McKee promo .20 .50
NNO Zac Bierk promo .20 .50
NNO Cameron Mann promo .20 .50
NNO Sean Haggerty promo .20 .50
NNO Mike Martin promo .20 .50
NNO Adam Colagiacomo promo .20
.50
NNO Scott Roche promo .20 .50
NNO Ryan Pepperall promo .20 .50

1994-95 SP

Wayne Gretzky's card number 54 was released as a promo. The only discernible difference between the two versions is that the foil on the promo is a brighter gold than the regular issue card. A special Wayne Gretzky 2500 point card was inserted one per case. This card is designed horizontally with die-cutting of the top corners. Wayne appears on a gold background with "2500" in block numbers on the front of the card.

COMPLETE SET (195) 10.00 25.00
1 Paul Kariya .25 .60
2 Oleg Tverdovsky .05 .15
3 Stephan Lebeau .06 .15
4 Bob Corkum .05 .15
5 Guy Hebert .10 .30
6 Ray Bourque .40 1.00
7 Blaine Lacher RC .10 .30
8 Adam Oates .10 .30
9 Cam Neely .25 .60
10 Mariusz Czerkawski RC .30 .75
11 Bryan Smolinski .05 .15
12 Pat LaFontaine .25 .60
13 Alexander Mogilny .10 .30
14 Dominik Hasek .50 1.25
15 Dale Hawerchuk .10 .30
16 Alexei Zhitnik .05 .15
17 Theo Fleury .05 .15
18 German Titov .05 .15
19 Phil Housley .10 .30
20 Joe Nieuwendyk .10 .30
21 Trevor Kidd .10 .30
22 Jeremy Roenick .30 .75
23 Chris Chelios .25 .60
24 Ed Belfour .25 .60
25 Bernie Nicholls .05 .15
26 Tony Amonte .10 .30
27 Joe Murphy .05 .15
28 Mike Modano .40 1.00
29 Trent Klatt .05 .15
30 Dave Gagner .05 .15
31 Kevin Hatcher .05 .15
32 Andy Moog .25 .60
33 Sergei Fedorov .40 1.00
34 Steve Yzerman 1.25 3.00
35 Slava Kozlov .05 .15
36 Paul Coffey .25 .60
37 Keith Primeau .05 .15
38 Ray Sheppard .05 .15
39 Doug Weight .10 .30
40 Jason Arnott .05 .15
41 Bill Ranford .10 .30
42 Shayne Corson .05 .15
43 Stu Barnes .05 .15
44 John Vanbiesbrouck .10 .30
45 Johan Garpenlov .05 .15
46 Bob Kudelski .05 .15
47 Scott Mellanby .05 .1
48 Chris Pronger .25 .6
49 Darren Turcotte .05 .1
50 Andrew Cassels .05 .1
51 Sean Burke .10 .3
52 Geoff Sanderson .05 .1
53 Rob Blake .10 .3
54A Wayne Gretzky 1.50 4.0
54B Wayne Gretzky PROMO 4.00 5.0
55 Rick Tocchet .10 .3
56 Tony Granato .05 .1
57 Jari Kurri .25 .6
58 Vincent Damphousse .05 .1
59 Patrick Roy 1.25 3.0
60 Vladimir Malakhov .05 .1
61 Pierre Turgeon .10 .3
62 Mark Recchi .10 .3
63 Martin Brodeur .60 1.5
64 Stephane Richer .10 .3
65 John MacLean .05 .1
66 Scott Stevens .10 .3
67 Scott Niedermayer .05 .1
68 Kirk Muller .05 .1
69 Ray Ferraro .05 .1
70 Brett Lindros .05 .1
71 Steve Thomas .05 .1
72 Pat Verbeek .05 .1
73 Mark Messier .25 .6
74 Brian Leetch .10 .3
75 Mike Richter .25 .6
76 Alexei Kovalev .05 .1
77 Adam Graves .05 .1
78 Sergei Zubov .05 .1
79 Alexei Yashin .05 .1
80 Radek Bonk RC .30 .7
81 Alexandre Daigle .05 .1
82 Don Beaupre .10 .3
83 Mikael Renberg .05 .1
84 Eric Lindros .25 .6
85 John LeClair .25 .6
86 Rod Brind'Amour .10 .3
87 Ron Hextall .10 .3
88 Ken Wregget .10 .3
89 Jaromir Jagr .40 1.0
90 Tomas Sandstrom .05 .1
91 John Cullen .05 .1
92 Ron Francis .10 .3
93 Luc Robitaille .10 .3
94 Joe Sakic .50 1.2
95 Owen Nolan .10 .3
96 Peter Forsberg 1.00 2.5
97 Wendel Clark .10 .3
98 Mike Ricci .05 .1
99 Stephane Fiset .10 .3
100 Brett Hull .30 .7
101 Brendan Shanahan .25 .6
102 Curtis Joseph .25 .6
103 Esa Tikkanen .05 .1
104 Al MacInnis .10 .3
105 Arturs Irbe .10 .3
106 Ray Whitney .05 .1
107 Sergei Makarov .05 .1
108 Sandis Ozolinsh .05 .1
109 Craig Janney .05 .1
110 Petr Klima .05 .1
111 Chris Gratton .05 .1
112 Roman Hamrlik .10 .3
113 Alexander Selivanov RC .25 .6
114 Brian Bradley .05 .1
115 Doug Gilmour .10 .3
116 Mats Sundin .25 .6
117 Felix Potvin .25 .6
118 Mike Ridley .05 .1
119 Dave Andreychuk .10 .3
120 Dmitri Mironov .05 .1
121 Pavel Bure .25 .6
122 Trevor Linden .10 .3
123 Jeff Brown .05 .1
124 Kirk McLean .10 .3
125 Geoff Courtnall .05 .1
126 Joe Juneau .05 .1
127 Dale Hunter .05 .1
128 Jim Carey RC .25 .6
129 Peter Bondra .10 .3
130 Dimitri Khristich .05 .1
131 Teemu Selanne .25 .6
132 Keith Tkachuk .25 .6
133 Alexei Zhamnov .10 .3
134 Dave Manson .05 .1
135 Nelson Emerson .05 .1
136 Alexandre Daigle .05 .1
137 Jamie Storr .10 .3
138 Todd Harvey .05 .1
139 Wade Redden RC .30 .7
140 Ed Jovanovski RC .30 .7
141 Jamie Rivers RC .05 .1
142 Ryan Smyth RC .50 1.5
143 Jason Botterill .05 .1
144 Denis Pederson RC .05 .1
145 Jeff Friesen .05 .1
146 Dan Cloutier RC .30 .7
147 Lee Sorochan RC .05 .1
148 Marty Murray .05 .1
149 Shean Donovan RC .05 .1
150 Larry Courville RC .05 .1
151 Jason Allison .05 .1
152 Jeff O'Neill RC .30 .7
153 Bryan McCabe .05 .1
154 Miloslav Guren RC .10 .3
155 Petr Buzek RC .20 .5
156 Tomas Blazek .05 .1
157 Josef Marha .05 .1
158 Jan Hlavac RC .30 .7
159 Veli-Pekka Nutikka RC .10 .3
160 Kimmo Timonen .10 .3
161 Antti Aalto RC .10 .3
162 Janne Niinimaa .10 .3
163 Nikolai Zavarukhin .05 .1
164 Vadim Epantchinsev RC .10 .3
165 Alexander Korolyuk RC .40 1.0
166 Dmitri Klevakin RC .10 .3
167 Vitali Yachmenev RC .05 .1
168 Niklas Sundstrom .05 .1
169 Anders Soderberg RC .10 .3
170 Anders Eriksson .10 .3
171 Jesper Mattsson RC .10 .3
172 Mattias Ohlund RC .40 1.0
173 Jason Bonsignore .05 .1
174 Bryan Berard RC .30 1.0
175 Richard Park .05 .1
176 Mike McBain RC .05 .1

177 Jason Doig RC .05 .15
178 Xavier Delisle RC .10 .30
179 Christian Dube RC .25 .60
180 Louis-Philippe Sevigny RC .05 .15
181 Jarome Iginla RC 4.00 10.00
182 Marc Savard RC .40 1.00
183 Alyn McCauley RC .30 1.25
184 Brad Mehalko RC .10 .30
185 Todd Norman RC .05 .15
186 Brian Scott RC .05 .15
187 Brad Larsen RC .05 .15
188 Jeffrey Ware RC .25 .60
189 Sergei Samsonov RC 1.25 3.00
190 Andrei Petrunin RC .25 .60
191 Sean Haggerty RC .10 .30
192 Rory Fitzpatrick RC .05 .15
193 Deron Quint .05 .15
194 Jamie Langenbrunner .25 .60
195 Jeff Mitchell RC .05 .15
SP1 Wayne Gretzky 2500 10.00 25.00

1994-95 SP Die Cuts

his 195-card set is a parallel version of the egular issue. These were inserted at a rate f one per pack. They are distinguished by ne die-cutting of the top and bottom right orners of the card, and the use of a silver nstead of gold hologram. The numbering of ne cards is consistent with the regular ssue.
*STARS: .75X TO 2X BASIC CARDS
*ROOKIES: .75X to 2X BASIC CARDS

1994-95 SP Premier

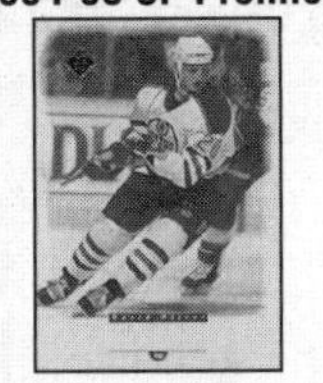

he 30 cards in this set were randomly nserted in SP at the rate of 1:9 packs. The ards are printed on white paper stock and ave a full white border. The action photo as a ghosted background, making the icture look slightly out of focus. The set ame is embossed on the lower card front. layer name and position are printed above nd below the set name. Player photo and mited text are the back. A gold rectangular ologram is used on this version.
COMPLETE SET (30) 20.00 40.00
*DIE CUTS: 4X TO 10X BASE CARD HI
1 Paul Kariya .60 1.50
2 Peter Forsberg 2.50 6.00
3 Viktor Kozlov .30 .75
4 Todd Marchant .30 .75
5 Oleg Tverdovsky .15 .40
6 Todd Harvey .15 .40
7 Kenny Jonsson .30 .75
8 Blaine Lacher .30 .75
9 Radek Bonk .75 2.00
10 Brett Lindros .15 .40
11 Valeri Bure .30 .75
12 Brian Rolston .15 .40
13 David Oliver .15 .40
14 Ian Laperriere .15 .40
15 Adam Deadmarsh .30 .75
16 Pavel Bure .60 1.50
17 Wayne Gretzky 4.00 10.00
18 Jeremy Roenick .75 2.00
19 Dominik Hasek 1.25 3.00
20 Ray Bourque 1.00 2.50
21 Doug Gilmour .30 .75
22 Teemu Selanne .60 1.50
23 Cam Neely .60 1.50
24 Sergei Fedorov 1.00 2.50
25 Bernie Nicholls .15 .40
26 Jaromir Jagr 1.00 2.50
27 Joe Sakic 1.25 3.00
28 Mark Messier .60 1.50
29 Brett Hull .75 2.00
30 Eric Lindros .60 1.50

1995-96 SP

The 1995-96 Upper Deck SP set was issued n one series totaling 188 cards. The 8-card packs had an SRP of $4.39 each. The Great Connections inserts (GC1and GC2), were randomly inserted at the rate of 1:381 packs. There are two versions of card number 66. The first features Wayne Gretzky in an All-Star sweater. This was used as a promotional card and was issued with the dealer solicitation. The second is the regular number 66 found in packs and features Craig Johnson, a player acquired by the Kings in the Gretzky trade.
COMPLETE SET (188) 20.00 40.00
1 Paul Kariya .25 .60
2 Teemu Selanne .25 .60
3 Guy Hebert .10 .30
4 Steve Rucchin .10 .30
5 Ray Bourque .40 1.00
6 Cam Neely .25 .60
7 Adam Oates .10 .30
8 Kyle McLaren RC .05 .15
9 Bill Ranford .10 .30
10 Shawn McEachern .05 .15
11 Don Sweeney .05 .15
12 Pat LaFontaine .25 .60
13 Dominik Hasek .50 1.25
14 Brian Holzinger RC .25 .60
15 Alexei Zhitnik .05 .15
16 Theo Fleury .05 .15
17 Cory Stillman .05 .15
18 German Titov .05 .15
19 Phil Housley .10 .30
20 Michael Nylander .05 .15
21 Trevor Kidd .10 .30
22 Eric Daze .10 .30
23 Chris Chelios .25 .60
24 Jeremy Roenick .30 .75
25 Gary Suter .05 .15
26 Bernie Nicholls .05 .15
27 Ed Belfour .25 .60
28 Tony Amonte .10 .30
29 Peter Forsberg .60 1.50
30 Patrick Roy 1.25 3.00
31 Joe Sakic .50 1.25
32 Sandis Ozolinsh .05 .15
33 Adam Deadmarsh .05 .15
34 Stephane Fiset .10 .30
35 Claude Lemieux .05 .15
36 Mike Modano .40 1.00
37 Kevin Hatcher .05 .15
38 Joe Nieuwendyk .10 .30
39 Todd Harvey .10 .30
40 Derian Hatcher .05 .15
41 Jere Lehtinen .10 .30
42 Nicklas Lidstrom .25 .60
43 Mathieu Dandenault .05 .15
44 Sergei Fedorov .40 1.00
45 Paul Coffey .25 .60
46 Steve Yzerman 1.25 3.00
47 Keith Primeau .05 .15
48 Chris Osgood .10 .30
49 Vyacheslav Kozlov .10 .30
50 Doug Weight .10 .30
51 Jason Arnott .05 .15
52 Miroslav Satan RC 1.00 2.50
53 Zdeno Ciger .05 .15
54 Curtis Joseph .25 .60
55 Scott Mellanby .05 .15
56 John Vanbiesbrouck .10 .30
57 Jody Hull .05 .15
58 Ed Jovanovski .25 .60
59 Radek Dvorak RC .40 1.00
60 Rob Niedermayer .10 .30
61 Andrew Cassels .05 .15
62 Brendan Shanahan .25 .60
63 Nelson Emerson .05 .15
64 Jeff O'Neill .05 .15
65 Sean Burke .10 .30
66A Wayne Gretzky promo card 4.00 10.00
66B Craig Johnson .05 .15
67 Dimitri Khristich .05 .15
68 Vitali Yachmenev .05 .15
69 Aki Berg RC .10 .30
70 Byron Dafoe .10 .30
71 Pierre Turgeon .10 .30
72 Mark Recchi .10 .30
73 Saku Koivu .25 .60
74 Valeri Bure .05 .15
75 Vincent Damphousse .05 .15
76 Jocelyn Thibault .25 .60
77 Patrice Brisebois .05 .15
78 John MacLean .10 .30
79 Martin Brodeur .60 1.50
80 Steve Thomas .10 .30
81 Scott Stevens .10 .30
82 Bill Guerin .10 .30
83 Petr Sykora RC 1.00 2.50
84 Scott Niedermayer .05 .15
85 Stephane Richer .10 .30
86 Zigmund Palffy .10 .30
87 Travis Green .10 .30
88 Todd Bertuzzi RC 2.00 5.00
89 Mathieu Schneider .05 .15
90 Eric Fichaud .10 .30
91 Bryan McCabe .05 .15
92 Mark Messier .25 .60
93 Pat Verbeek .05 .15
94 Brian Leetch .10 .30
95 Mike Richter .25 .60
96 Niklas Sundstrom .10 .30
97 Luc Robitaille .10 .30
98 Adam Graves .05 .15
99 Alexei Kovalev .05 .15
100 Daniel Alfredsson RC 2.00 5.00
101 Alexei Yashin .05 .15
102 Radek Bonk .05 .15
103 Alexandre Daigle .05 .15
104 Damian Rhodes .10 .30
105 Antti Tormanen .05 .15
106 Eric Lindros .25 .60
107 Mikael Renberg .10 .30
108 John LeClair .25 .60
109 Ron Hextall .10 .30
110 Rod Brind'Amour .10 .30
111 Joel Otto .05 .15
112 Eric Desjardins .10 .30
113 Mario Lemieux 1.25 3.00
114 Jaromir Jagr .40 1.00
115 Ron Francis .10 .30
116 Markus Naslund .25 .60
117 Sergei Zubov .05 .15
118 Tomas Sandstrom .05 .15
119 Tom Barrasso .10 .30
120 Richard Park .05 .15
121 Brett Hull .30 .75
122 Shayne Corson .05 .15
123 Dale Hawerchuk .25 .60
124 Chris Pronger .25 .60
125 Al MacInnis .10 .30
126 Grant Fuhr .25 .60
127 Wayne Gretzky 1.50 4.00
128 Geoff Courtnall .05 .15
129 Owen Nolan .10 .30
130 Ray Sheppard .05 .15
131 Chris Terreri .10 .30
132 Marcus Ragnarsson RC .10 .30
133 Jeff Friesen .05 .15
134 Doug Bodger .05 .15
135 Roman Hamrlik .10 .30
136 Petr Klima .05 .15
137 Daren Puppa .10 .30
138 Aaron Gavey .05 .15
139 Daymond Langkow RC .40 1.00
140 Alexander Selivanov .05 .15
141 Mats Sundin .25 .60
142 Kirk Muller .05 .15
143 Larry Murphy .10 .30
144 Doug Gilmour .10 .30
145 Darby Hendrickson .05 .15
146 Felix Potvin .25 .60
147 Kenny Jonsson .05 .15
148 Alexander Mogilny .10 .30
149 Pavel Bure .25 .60
150 Trevor Linden .10 .30
151 Corey Hirsch .10 .30
152 Kirk McLean .10 .30
153 Esa Tikkanen .05 .15
154 Cliff Ronning .05 .15
155 Peter Bondra .10 .30
156 Jim Carey .10 .30
157 Michal Pivonka .05 .15
158 Joe Juneau .05 .15
159 Dale Hunter .10 .30
160 Steve Konowalchuk .05 .15
161 Stefan Ustorf .05 .15
162 Brendan Witt .05 .15
163 Chad Kilger RC .05 .15
164 Keith Tkachuk .25 .60
165 Deron Quint .05 .15
166 Oleg Tverdovsky .05 .15
167 Alexei Zhamnov .10 .30
168 Igor Korolev .05 .15
169 Wade Redden .05 .15
170 Jarome Iginla .30 .75
171 Christian Dube .05 .15
172 Jason Podollan .05 .15
173 Alyn McCauley .10 .30
174 Nolan Baumgartner .05 .15
175 Jason Botterill .05 .15
176 Chris Phillips RC .30 .75
177 Dmitri Nabokov .10 .30
178 Andrei Petrunin .05 .15
179 Alexander Korolyuk .10 .30
180 Sergei Samsonov .60 1.50
181 Ilja Gorokhov RC .10 .30
182 Alexei Kolkunov RC .10 .30
183 Samuel Pahlsson RC .05 .15
184 Mattias Ohlund .05 .15
185 Marcus Nilsson RC .20 .50
186 Daniel Tjarnqvist RC .05 .15
187 Per Anton Lundstrom .05 .15
188 Fredrik Loven .05 .15
GC1 Wayne Gretzky 15.00 40.00
GC2 Sergei Samsonov 8.00 20.00

1995-96 SP Holoviews

Randomly inserted in packs at a rate of 1:5, this 20-card set utilizes UD's Holoview technology to great effect. There also exists a die-cut parallel version of this set (known as Special FX), issued 1:75 packs. Special FX cards are enhanced by rainbow foil, as well as the die-cutting. Multipliers to determine the value of these cards are listed below.
COMPLETE SET (20) 25.00 50.00
*SPECIAL FX: 1.25X TO 3X BASIC INSERTS
FX1 Teemu Selanne .60 1.50
FX2 Paul Kariya .60 1.50
FX3 Chris Chelios .60 1.50
FX4 Peter Forsberg 1.50 4.00
FX5 Sergei Fedorov 1.00 2.50
FX6 Paul Coffey .60 1.50
FX7 Steve Yzerman 3.00 8.00
FX8 Jason Arnott .15 .40
FX9 Doug Weight .30 .75
FX10 Wayne Gretzky 4.00 10.00
FX11 Vitali Yachmenev .15 .40
FX12 Martin Brodeur 1.50 4.00
FX13 Scott Stevens .30 .75
FX14 Mark Messier .60 1.50
FX15 Daniel Alfredsson 6.00 15.00
FX16 Eric Lindros .60 1.50
FX17 Mario Lemieux 3.00 8.00
FX18 Jaromir Jagr 1.00 2.50
FX19 Shayne Corson .15 .40
FX20 Pavel Bure .60 1.50

1995-96 SP Stars/Etoiles

Randomly inserted in packs at a rate of 1:3, this 30-card set uses a double die-cut design to highlight the top athletes in the NHL. This version uses silver foil as it's primary element. There also is a gold foil parallel version, which is significantly tougher to pull. These cards were randomly inserted 1:61 packs.
COMPLETE SET (30) 25.00 50.00
*GOLD: 3X TO 8X BASIC INSERTS
E1 Paul Kariya .50 1.25
E2 Teemu Selanne .50 1.25
E3 Ray Bourque .75 2.00
E4 Cam Neely .50 1.25
E5 Pat LaFontaine .50 1.25
E6 Theo Fleury .10 .30
E7 Jeremy Roenick .60 1.50
E8 Joe Sakic 1.00 2.50
E9 Patrick Roy 2.50 6.00
E10 Peter Forsberg 1.25 3.00
E11 Mike Modano .75 2.00
E12 Sergei Fedorov .75 2.00
E13 Paul Coffey .50 1.25
E14 Steve Yzerman 2.50 6.00
E15 Pierre Turgeon .25 .60
E16 Brendan Shanahan .50 1.25
E17 Wayne Gretzky 3.00 8.00
E18 Martin Brodeur 1.25 3.00
E19 Mark Messier .50 1.25
E20 Brian Leetch .25 .60
E21 Eric Lindros .50 1.25
E22 Mario Lemieux 2.50 6.00
E23 Jaromir Jagr .75 2.00
E24 Brett Hull .60 1.50
E25 Roman Hamrlik .25 .60
E26 Mats Sundin .50 1.25
E27 Felix Potvin .50 1.25
E28 Alexander Mogilny .25 .60
E29 Pavel Bure .50 1.25
E30 Keith Tkachuk .50 1.25

1996-97 SP

The 1996-97 SP set was issued in one series totaling 188 cards. The eight-card packs had a suggested retail price of $3.49 each. Printed on 20 pt. card stock, this set featured color action photos of 168 regular players from all 26 NHL teams and included a subset of 20 premier prospects. The backs carried player information and statistics. The Gretzky promo was distributed to dealers; it mirrored the regular issue save for the word SAMPLE written across the back.
COMPLETE SET (188) 30.00 50.00
1 Paul Kariya .30 .75
2 Teemu Selanne .30 .75
3 Jari Kurri .15 .40
4 Darren Van Impe .07 .20
5 Guy Hebert .15 .40
6 Steve Rucchin .07 .20
7 Ray Bourque .50 1.25
8 Kyle McLaren .07 .20
9 Bill Ranford .15 .40
10 Don Sweeney .07 .20
11 Adam Oates .15 .40
12 Rick Tocchet .15 .40
13 Ted Donato .07 .20
14 Curtis Brown .07 .20
15 Pat LaFontaine .30 .75
16 Derek Plante .07 .20
17 Dominik Hasek .60 1.50
18 Brian Holzinger .15 .40
19 Alexei Zhitnik .07 .20
20 Theo Fleury .07 .20
21 Trevor Kidd .15 .40
22 Steve Chiasson .07 .20
23 Jarome Iginla .40 1.00
24 German Titov .07 .20
25 Zarley Zalapski .07 .20
26 Eric Daze .15 .40
27 Chris Chelios .30 .75
28 Ed Belfour .30 .75
29 Gary Suter .07 .20
30 Alexei Zhamnov .15 .40
31 Ethan Moreau RC .30 .75
32 Tony Amonte .15 .40
33 Peter Forsberg .75 2.00
34 Joe Sakic .60 1.50
35 Patrick Roy 1.50 4.00
36 Adam Deadmarsh .07 .20
37 Mike Ricci .07 .20
38 Adam Foote .07 .20
39 Claude Lemieux .07 .20
40 Mike Modano .50 1.25
41 Pat Verbeek .07 .20
42 Todd Harvey .07 .20
43 Sergei Zubov .07 .20
44 Andy Moog .15 .40
45 Derian Hatcher .07 .20
46 Jamie Langenbrunner .07 .20
47 Steve Yzerman 1.50 4.00
48 Sergei Fedorov .50 1.25
49 Slava Kozlov .15 .40
50 Brendan Shanahan .30 .75
51 Chris Osgood .15 .40
52 Nicklas Lidstrom .30 .75
53 Vladimir Konstantinov .15 .40
54 Curtis Joseph .30 .75
55 Jason Arnott .07 .20
56 Ryan Smyth .30 .75
57 Doug Weight .15 .40
58 Andrei Kovalenko .07 .20
59 Mariusz Czerkawski .07 .20
60 Ed Jovanovski .15 .40
61 John Vanbiesbrouck .15 .40
62 Rob Niedermayer .15 .40
63 Robert Svehla .07 .20
64 Brian Skrudland .07 .20
65 Scott Mellanby .15 .40
66 Ray Sheppard .15 .40
67 Jeff O'Neill .07 .20
68 Keith Primeau .07 .20
69 Geoff Sanderson .15 .40
70 Sean Burke .15 .40
71 Kevin Dineen .07 .20
72 Andrew Cassels .07 .20
73 Kevin Stevens .07 .20
74 Rob Blake .15 .40
75 Ed Olczyk .07 .20
76 Mattias Norstrom .07 .20
77 Stephane Fiset .15 .40
78 Vitali Yachmenev .07 .20
79 Saku Koivu .30 .75
80 Valeri Bure .07 .20
81 Jocelyn Thibault .30 .75
82 David Wilkie .07 .20
83 Stephane Richer .15 .40
84 Shayne Corson .07 .20
85 Mark Recchi .15 .40
86 Martin Brodeur .75 2.00
87 Bobby Holik .07 .20
88 Petr Sykora .07 .20
89 Scott Stevens .15 .40
90 Scott Niedermayer .07 .20
91 Bill Guerin .07 .20
92 Eric Fichaud .15 .40
93 Kenny Jonsson .07 .20
94 Travis Green .15 .40
95 Derek King .07 .20
96 Todd Bertuzzi .30 .75
97 Zigmund Palffy .15 .40
98 Mark Messier .30 .75
99 Wayne Gretzky 2.00 5.00
100 Mike Richter .30 .75
101 Brian Leetch .30 .75
102 Luc Robitaille .15 .40
103 Adam Graves .07 .20
104 Alexei Kovalev .07 .20
105 Radek Bonk .07 .20
106 Alexandre Daigle .07 .20
107 Daniel Alfredsson .15 .40
108 Alexei Yashin .07 .20
109 Andreas Dackell RC .07 .20
110 Damian Rhodes .15 .40
111 Petr Svoboda .07 .20
112 John LeClair .30 .75
113 Eric Desjardins .15 .40
114 Eric Lindros .30 .75
115 Mikael Renberg .15 .40
116 Ron Hextall .15 .40
117 Dainius Zubrus RC .60 1.50
118 Keith Tkachuk .30 .75
119 Jeremy Roenick .40 1.00
120 Nikolai Khabibulin .15 .40
121 Oleg Tverdovsky .15 .40
122 Teppo Numminen .07 .20
123 Mike Gartner .15 .40
124 Cliff Ronning .07 .20
125 Mario Lemieux 1.50 4.00
126 Jaromir Jagr .50 1.25
127 Ron Francis .15 .40
128 Petr Nedved .15 .40
129 Darius Kasparaitis .07 .20
130 Kevin Hatcher .07 .20
131 Joe Mullen .15 .40
132 Joe Murphy .07 .20
133 Grant Fuhr .15 .40
134 Harry York RC .30 .75
135 Chris Pronger .15 .40
136 Brett Hull .40 1.00
137 Pierre Turgeon .15 .40
138 Owen Nolan .15 .40
139 Bernie Nicholls .07 .20
140 Tony Granato .07 .20
141 Kelly Hrudey .15 .40
142 Darren Turcotte .07 .20
143 Jeff Friesen .07 .20
144 Roman Hamrlik .15 .40
145 Chris Gratton .15 .40
146 Daymond Langkow .15 .40
147 Dino Ciccarelli .15 .40
148 Alexander Selivanov .07 .20
149 Brian Bradley .07 .20
150 Wendel Clark .15 .40
151 Mats Sundin .30 .75
152 Doug Gilmour .15 .40
153 Felix Potvin .30 .75
154 Larry Murphy .15 .40
155 Mathieu Schneider .07 .20
156 Kirk Muller .07 .20
157 Pavel Bure .30 .75
158 Alexander Mogilny .15 .40
159 Corey Hirsch .15 .40
160 Jyrki Lumme .07 .20
161 Russ Courtnall .07 .20
162 Mike Fountain RC .07 .20
163 Peter Bondra .15 .40
164 Jim Carey .30 .75
165 Sergei Gonchar .07 .20
166 Joe Juneau .07 .20
167 Phil Housley .15 .40
168 Jason Allison .07 .20
169 Ruslan Salei RC .07 .20
170 Mattias Timander RC .07 .20
171 Vaclav Varada RC .15 .40
172 Jonas Hoglund .07 .20
173 Jason Podollan .15 .40
174 Jose Theodore .40 1.00
175 Roman Turek RC 1.50 4.00
176 Anders Eriksson .07 .20
177 Mike Grier RC .60 1.50
178 Rem Murray RC .15 .40
179 Per Gustafsson RC .07 .20
180 Jay Pandolfo UER .07 .20
181 Kai Nurminen RC .07 .20
182 Bryan Berard .30 .75
183 Christian Dube .07 .20
184 Daniel Goneau RC .15 .40
185 Wade Redden .07 .20
186 Janne Niinimaa .30 .75
187 Jim Campbell .07 .20
188 Sergei Berezin RC 1.25 3.00
P99 Wayne Gretzky PROMO .07 .20

1996-97 SP Clearcut Winner

Randomly inserted in packs at a rate of 1:91, this 20-card set featured color player images in a chiseled-out ice block, die-cut card displaying a full body transparent Hologram.
CW1 Wayne Gretzky 15.00 40.00
CW2 Saku Koivu 2.50 6.00
CW3 Mario Lemieux 12.00 30.00
CW4 Sergei Fedorov 4.00 10.00
CW5 Paul Kariya 2.50 6.00
CW6 Patrick Roy 12.00 30.00
CW7 Jeremy Roenick 4.00 10.00
CW8 Brendan Shanahan 2.50 6.00
CW9 John Vanbiesbrouck 2.00 5.00
CW10 Doug Weight 2.00 5.00
CW11 Mark Messier 2.50 6.00
CW12 Mats Sundin 2.50 6.00
CW13 Paul Coffey 2.00 5.00
CW14 Theo Fleury 1.00 2.50
CW15 Steve Yzerman 10.00 25.00
CW16 Pavel Bure 2.50 6.00
CW17 Adam Deadmarsh 1.00 2.50
CW18 Chris Chelios 2.00 5.00
CW19 Joe Sakic 6.00 15.00
CW20 Eric Daze 1.00 2.50

1996-97 SP Holoview Collection

Randomly inserted in packs at a rate of 1:9, this 30-card set featured color player photos of some of the NHL's most elite stars printed on an all new design Holoview die-cut card.
COMPLETE SET (30) 30.00 60.00
HC1 Wayne Gretzky 6.00 15.00
HC2 Eric Daze .75 2.00
HC3 Doug Gilmour .75 2.00
HC4 Jason Arnott .75 2.00
HC5 Sergei Fedorov 2.00 5.00
HC6 Chris Chelios 1.00 2.50
HC7 Alexei Kovalev .75 2.00
HC8 Pat LaFontaine .25 .60
HC9 Daniel Alfredsson .75 2.00
HC10 Chris Pronger .75 2.00
HC11 Jocelyn Thibault .75 2.00
HC12 Chris Gratton .75 2.00
HC13 Alexei Yashin .25 .60
HC14 Peter Bondra .75 2.00
HC15 Saku Koivu 1.00 2.50
HC16 Valeri Bure .25 .60
HC17 Joe Juneau .25 .60
HC18 Tony Amonte 1.00 2.50
HC19 Brian Holzinger .25 .60
HC20 Mats Sundin 1.00 2.50
HC21 Chris Osgood .75 2.00
HC22 Roman Hamrlik .25 .60
HC23 Ray Bourque 2.00 5.00
HC24 Doug Weight .75 2.00
HC25 Mike Modano 1.50 4.00
HC26 Niklas Sundstrom .25 .60
HC27 Mike Richter 1.00 2.50
HC28 Zigmund Palffy .75 2.00
HC29 Adam Oates .75 2.00
HC30 Dominik Hasek 2.00 5.00

1996-97 SP Inside Info

Inserted at the rate of one per box, this eight-card set featured color action player photos with a special pull-out panel that displayed another photo of the same player and statistics. A gold version was also available and was seeded one in every two cases. Values for these cards can be determined by using the multipliers listed below.
COMPLETE SET (8) 20.00 50.00
*GOLDS: 2X TO 5X BASIC INSERTS
IN1 Wayne Gretzky 8.00 20.00
IN2 Keith Tkachuk 2.00 5.00
IN3 Brendan Shanahan 2.00 5.00
IN4 Teemu Selanne 2.00 5.00
IN5 Ray Bourque 3.00 8.00
IN6 Joe Sakic 4.00 10.00
IN7 Felix Potvin 2.00 5.00
IN8 Steve Yzerman 5.00 12.00

1996-97 SP Game Film

Randomly inserted in packs at a rate of 1:30, this 20-card set carried actual game photography featuring film footage of favorite NHL players.
COMPLETE SET (20) 75.00 150.00
GF1 Wayne Gretzky 20.00 50.00
GF2 Peter Forsberg 8.00 20.00
GF3 Patrick Roy 15.00 40.00
GF4 Brett Hull 3.00 8.00
GF5 Keith Tkachuk 2.00 5.00
GF6 Eric Lindros 3.00 8.00
GF7 Felix Potvin 3.00 8.00
GF8 John Vanbiesbrouck 2.00 5.00
GF9 Paul Kariya 3.00 8.00
GF10 Mark Messier 3.00 8.00
GF11 Ed Belfour 3.00 8.00
GF12 Alexander Mogilny 2.00 5.00
GF13 Jim Carey 4.00 10.00
GF14 Ed Jovanovski 2.00 5.00
GF15 Theo Fleury 1.00 2.50
GF16 Doug Gilmour 2.00 5.00
GF17 John LeClair 2.00 5.00
GF18 Pat LaFontaine 1.00 2.50
GF19 Paul Coffey 2.00 5.00
GF20 Daniel Alfredsson 2.00 5.00

1996-97 SP SPx Force

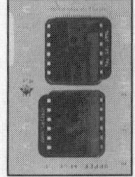

Randomly inserted in packs at a rate of 1:360, this five-card set featured top NHL players on a multi-image Holoview card. Each of the first four cards displayed a center, winger, goalie and rookie. The last card carried the top player from each of the previous cards.
COMPLETE SET (5) 60.00 150.00
1 Eric Lindros 25.00 60.00
Mario Lemieux
Peter Forsberg
Wayne Gretzky
2 Brett Hull 12.00 30.00
Jaromir Jagr
Pavel Bure
Teemu Selanne
3 Chris Osgood 12.00 30.00
Dominik Hasek
Martin Brodeur
Mike Richter
4 Anders Eriksson 8.00 20.00
Bryan Berard
Jarome Iginla
Sergei Berezin
5 Jarome Iginla 20.00 50.00
Jaromir Jagr
Wayne Gretzky
Martin Brodeur

1996-97 SP SPx Force Autographs

These four different autograph cards were randomly inserted one in 2,500 packs of 1996-97 SP. Besides the player's signature, the cards are parallel to the more common, unsigned SPx Force inserts. Only 100 cards were signed by each player.
1 Wayne Gretzky AU 200.00 400.00
2 Jaromir Jagr AU 50.00 125.00
3 Martin Brodeur AU 60.00 150.00
4 Jarome Iginla AU 30.00 80.00

1997-98 SP Authentic

The 1997-98 SP Authentic set was issued in one series totaling 198 cards and was distributed in five-card packs with a suggested retail price of $4.99. The fronts features color player photos printed on 24 pt. card stock. The backs carry player information. The set contains the topical subset: Future Watch (169-198).
COMPLETE SET (198) 30.00 60.00
1 Teemu Selanne .30 .75
2 Sean Pronger .10 .25
3 Joe Sacco .10 .25
4 Tomas Sandstrom .10 .25
5 Steve Rucchin .10 .25
6 Paul Kariya .30 .75
7 Ted Donato .10 .25
8 Ray Bourque .50 1.25
9 Tim Taylor .10 .25
10 Jason Allison .10 .25
11 Kyle McLaren .10 .25
12 Dimitri Khristich .10 .25
13 Jason Dawe .10 .25
14 Dominik Hasek .60 1.50

15 Miroslav Satan .10 .25
16 Brian Holzinger .10 .25
17 Alexei Zhitnik .10 .25
18 Theo Fleury .10 .25
19 Cory Stillman .10 .25
20 Jarome Iginla .40 1.00
21 Sandy McCarthy .10 .25
22 German Titov .10 .25
23 Glen Wesley .10 .25
24 Keith Primeau .10 .25
25 Geoff Sanderson .25 .60
26 Gary Roberts .10 .25
27 Sami Kapanen .10 .25
28 Jeff O'Neill .10 .25
29 Tony Amonte .25 .60
30 Chris Chelios .30 .75
31 Eric Daze .25 .60
32 Alexei Zhamnov .10 .25
33 Chris Terreri .25 .60
34 Sergei Krivokrasov .10 .25
35 Joe Sakic .60 1.50
36 Peter Forsberg .75 2.00
37 Patrick Roy 1.50 4.00
38 Claude Lemieux .10 .25
39 Valeri Kamensky .25 .60
40 Adam Deadmarsh .10 .25
41 Sandis Ozolinsh .10 .25
42 Jari Kurri .25 .60
43 Mike Modano .50 1.25
44 Ed Belfour .30 .75
45 Derian Hatcher .10 .25
46 Sergei Zubov .10 .25
47 Jamie Langenbrunner .10 .25
48 Jere Lehtinen .10 .25
49 Joe Nieuwendyk .25 .60
50 Vyacheslav Kozlov .10 .25
51 Chris Osgood .25 .60
52 Steve Yzerman 1.50 4.00
53 Nicklas Lidstrom .30 .75
54 Igor Larionov .10 .25
55 Brendan Shanahan .30 .75
56 Anders Eriksson .10 .25
57 Darren McCarty .10 .25
58 Doug Weight .25 .60
59 Jason Arnott .10 .25
60 Curtis Joseph .30 .75
61 Ryan Smyth .25 .60
62 Dean McAmmond .10 .25
63 Mike Grier .10 .25
64 Kelly Buchberger .10 .25
65 Ed Jovanovski .25 .60
66 Ray Whitney .10 .25
67 Rob Niedermayer .10 .25
68 Scott Mellanby .10 .25
69 John Vanbiesbrouck .25 .60
70 Viktor Kozlov .10 .25
71 Jozef Stumpel .25 .60
72 Rob Blake .25 .60
73 Garry Galley .10 .25
74 Vladimir Tsyplakov .10 .25
75 Yanic Perreault .10 .25
76 Stephane Fiset .25 .60
77 Luc Robitaille .25 .60
78 Valeri Bure .10 .25
79 Mark Recchi .25 .60
80 Saku Koivu .30 .75
81 Andy Moog .25 .60
82 Vincent Damphousse .10 .25
83 Vladimir Malakhov .10 .25
84 Shayne Corson .10 .25
85 Scott Stevens .25 .60
86 Bill Guerin .25 .60
87 Martin Brodeur .75 2.00
88 Doug Gilmour .25 .60
89 Bobby Holik .10 .25
90 Petr Sykora .10 .25
91 Zigmund Palffy .25 .60
92 Bryan Berard .25 .60
93 Tommy Salo .25 .60
94 Travis Green .10 .25
95 Kenny Jonsson .10 .25
96 Todd Bertuzzi .30 .75
97 Robert Reichel .10 .25
98 Pat LaFontaine .30 .75
99 Wayne Gretzky 2.00 5.00
100 Brian Leetch .30 .75
101 Mike Richter .30 .75
102 Alexei Kovalev .10 .25
103 Adam Graves .10 .25
104 Niklas Sundstrom .10 .25
105 Alexei Yashin .10 .25
106 Daniel Alfredsson .25 .60
107 Alexandre Daigle .10 .25
108 Wade Redden .10 .25
109 Andreas Dackell .10 .25
110 Shawn McEachern .10 .25
111 Eric Lindros .30 .75
112 Chris Gratton .25 .60
113 Paul Coffey .30 .75
114 John LeClair .30 .75
115 Rod Brind'Amour .25 .60
116 Ron Hextall .25 .60
117 Dainius Zubrus .30 .75
118 Jeremy Roenick .40 1.00
119 Keith Tkachuk .30 .75
120 Nikolai Khabibulin .25 .60
121 Rick Tocchet .25 .60
122 Teppo Numminen .10 .25
123 Craig Janney .10 .25
124 Mike Gartner .25 .60
125 Jaromir Jagr .50 1.25
126 Ron Francis .25 .60
127 Kevin Hatcher .10 .25
128 Robert Dome RC .10 .25
129 Martin Straka .10 .25
130 Peter Skudra RC .10 .25
131 Owen Nolan .25 .60
132 Bernie Nicholls .10 .25
133 Mike Vernon .25 .60
134 Jeff Friesen .10 .25
135 Tony Granato .10 .25
136 Mike Ricci .10 .25
137 Jim Campbell .10 .25
138 Brett Hull .40 1.00
139 Chris Pronger .25 .60
140 Al MacInnis .25 .60
141 Pierre Turgeon .25 .60
142 Pavol Demitra .25 .60
143 Grant Fuhr .25 .60
144 Steve Duchesne .10 .25
145 Daymond Langkow .25 .60
146 Alexander Selivanov .10 .25
147 Daren Puppa .25 .60
148 Dino Ciccarelli .10 .25
149 Roman Hamrlik .25 .60
150 Mats Sundin .30 .75
151 Felix Potvin .30 .75
152 Wendel Clark .25 .60
153 Sergei Berezin .10 .25
154 Steve Sullivan .10 .25
155 Alexander Mogilny .25 .60
156 Pavel Bure .30 .75
157 Mark Messier .30 .75
158 Bret Hedican .10 .25
159 Kirk McLean .25 .60
160 Trevor Linden .25 .60
161 Dave Scatchard RC .10 .25
162 Adam Oates .25 .60
163 Joe Juneau .25 .60
164 Peter Bondra .25 .60
165 Bill Ranford .25 .60
166 Sergei Gonchar .10 .25
167 Calle Johansson .10 .25
168 Phil Housley .10 .25
169 Espen Knutsen RC .75 2.00
170 Pavel Trnka RC .25 .60
171 Joe Thornton 1.00 2.50
172 Sergei Samsonov .40 1.00
173 Erik Rasmussen .25 .60
174 Tyler Moss RC .25 .60
175 Derek Morris RC .40 1.00
176 Craig Mills .25 .60
177 Daniel Cleary .25 .60
178 Eric Messier RC .30 .75
179 Kevin Hodson .25 .60
180 Mike Knuble RC .25 .60
181 Boyd Deveraux .25 .60
182 Craig Millar RC .10 .25
183 Kevin Weekes RC 2.00 5.00
184 Donald MacLean .25 .60
185 Patrik Elias RC 3.00 8.00
186 Zdeno Chara RC 2.00 5.00
187 Chris Phillips .25 .60
188 Vaclav Prospal RC .30 .75
189 Brad Isbister .25 .60
190 Alexei Morozov .25 .60
191 Patrick Marleau .60 1.50
192 Marco Sturm RC .50 1.25
193 Brendan Morrison RC 1.25 3.00
194 Mike Johnson RC .30 .75
195 Alyn McCauley .25 .60
196 Mattias Ohlund .25 .60
197 Richard Zednik .25 .60
198 Jan Bulis RC .25 .60

1997-98 SP Authentic Authentics

Randomly inserted in packs at the rate of 1:288, these special "trade" cards could be redeemed for an assortment of Wayne Gretzky's signed memorabilia from Upper Deck Authenticated such as autographed jerseys, pucks, sticks and other items. Only three "SP Authentics Collection" cards were produced that could be redeemed for Wayne Gretzky's entire collection of autographed memorabilia. We have listed and priced only the autographed trading card below.

10 W.Gretzky 802 Card (184) 25.00 50.00

1997-98 SP Authentic Icons

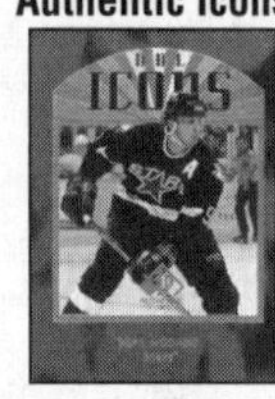

Randomly inserted in packs at the rate of 1:5, this 40-card set features color action photos of the most respected players of the NHL. Embossed and die cut parallels were also created and inserted randomly.

COMPLETE SET (40) 40.00 80.00
*EMBOSSED: .75X TO 2X BASIC INSERTS
*DIE CUTS: 4X TO 10X BASIC INSERTS
I1 Pat LaFontaine .75 2.00
I2 Brett Hull 1.00 2.50
I3 Chris Chelios .75 2.00
I4 Joe Sakic 1.50 4.00
I5 John Vanbiesbrouck .60 1.50
I6 Patrik Elias .75 2.00
I7 Eric Lindros .75 2.00
I8 Jaromir Jagr 1.25 3.00
I9 Joe Thornton 1.50 4.00
I10 Brendan Shanahan .75 2.00
I11 Paul Kariya .75 2.00
I12 Peter Forsberg 2.00 5.00
I13 Ed Belfour .75 2.00
I14 Martin Brodeur 2.00 5.00
I15 Alexei Morozov .60 1.50
I16 Mark Messier .75 2.00
I17 John LeClair .75 2.00
I18 Luc Robitaille .60 1.50
I19 Teemu Selanne .75 2.00
I20 Theo Fleury .25 .60
I21 Steve Yzerman 2.00 5.00
I22 Chris Phillips .25 .60
I23 Keith Tkachuk .75 2.00
I24 Patrick Roy 2.00 5.00
I25 Mark Recchi .60 1.50
I26 Wayne Gretzky 3.00 8.00
I27 Dino Ciccarelli .25 .60
I28 Ray Bourque 1.25 3.00
I29 Tony Amonte .60 1.50
I30 Daniel Alfredsson .60 1.50
I31 Saku Koivu .75 2.00
I32 Doug Weight .60 1.50
I33 Mats Sundin .75 2.00
I34 Dominik Hasek 1.50 4.00
I35 Scott Stevens .60 1.50
I36 Pavel Bure .75 2.00
I37 Mike Modano 1.25 3.00
I38 Zigmund Palffy .60 1.50
I39 Brian Leetch .75 2.00
I40 Marco Sturm .75 2.00

1997-98 SP Authentic Mark of a Legend

Randomly inserted in packs at the rate of 1:198, this six-card set features autographed color portraits of six of the NHL's greatest all-time players.

M1 Gordie Howe/112 100.00 250.00
M2 Billy Smith/560 10.00 25.00
M3 Cam Neely/560 15.00 40.00
M4 Bryan Trottier/560 12.50 30.00
M5 Bobby Hull/560 25.00 60.00
M6 Wayne Gretzky/560 75.00 200.00

1997-98 SP Authentic Sign of the Times

Randomly inserted in packs at the rate of 1:23, this 29-card set features autographed color action photos of top players in the NHL. Exchange card expired 3/16/99.

BB Bryan Berard 4.00 10.00
BH Brett Hull 10.00 25.00
BH Brian Holzinger 4.00 10.00
CC Chris Chelios 6.00 15.00
DM Darren McCarty 6.00 15.00
DW Doug Weight 5.00 12.00
DZ Dainius Zubrus 4.00 10.00
GF Grant Fuhr 5.00 12.00
GH Guy Hebert 4.00 10.00
JI Jarome Iginla 10.00 25.00
JS Jaroslav Svejkovsky 4.00 10.00
JLA Jamie Langenbrunner 4.00 10.00
JT Joe Thornton 10.00 25.00
JTH Jose Theodore 10.00 25.00
MB Martin Brodeur 40.00 100.00
MG Mike Grier 4.00 10.00
MS Mats Sundin 8.00 20.00
NK Nikolai Khabibulin 6.00 15.00
NL Nicklas Lidstrom 8.00 20.00
PB Peter Bondra 4.00 10.00
PR Patrick Roy 60.00 150.00
RB Ray Bourque 20.00 50.00
RN Rob Niedermayer 4.00 10.00
SB Sergei Berezin 4.00 10.00
SS Sergei Samsonov 5.00 12.00
SY Steve Yzerman 50.00 125.00
TA Tony Amonte 5.00 12.00
WG Wayne Gretzky 75.00 200.00
YP Yanic Perreault 4.00 10.00

1997-98 SP Authentic Tradition

Randomly inserted in packs at the rate of 1:340, this six-card set features color action dual photos and autographs of a current star and an NHL legend.

T1 Wayne Gretzky 200.00 500.00
Gordie Howe
T2 Patrick Roy 40.00 100.00
Billy Smith/333
T3 Joe Thornton 25.00 60.00
Cam Neely/352
T4 Bryan Berard 8.00 20.00
Bryan Trottier/352
T5 Brett Hull 40.00 100.00
Bobby Hull/352
T6 Ray Bourque 50.00 125.00
Cam Neely/140

1998-99 SP Authentic

The 1998-99 SP Authentic set was issued in one series totaling 135 cards and was distributed in five-card packs with a suggested retail price of $4.99. The set features action color photos of 90 superstars of the NHL (1-90) and 45 top prospects (91-135) which are numbered to just 2000.

COMPLETE SET (135) 125.00 300.00
COMP.SET w/o SP's (90) 10.00 25.00
1 Paul Kariya .30 .75
2 Teemu Selanne .30 .75

3 Guy Hebert .25 .60
4 Sergei Samsonov .25 .60
5 Joe Thornton .50 1.25
6 Jason Allison .10 .25
7 Ray Bourque .50 1.25
8 Dominik Hasek .60 1.50
9 Michael Peca .10 .25
10 Michal Grosek .10 .25
11 Derek Morris .10 .25
12 Theo Fleury .10 .25
13 Jarome Iginla .40 1.00
14 Ron Francis .25 .60
15 Keith Primeau .10 .25
16 Sami Kapanen .10 .25
17 Tony Amonte .25 .60
18 Doug Gilmour .25 .60
19 Chris Chelios .30 .75
20 Peter Forsberg .75 2.00
21 Patrick Roy 1.50 4.00
22 Joe Sakic .60 1.50
23 Adam Deadmarsh .10 .25
24 Brett Hull .40 1.00
25 Mike Modano .50 1.25
26 Ed Belfour .30 .75
27 Jere Lehtinen .10 .25
28 Sergei Fedorov .50 1.25
29 Brendan Shanahan .30 .75
30 Chris Osgood .25 .60
31 Steve Yzerman 1.50 4.00
32 Nicklas Lidstrom .30 .75
33 Doug Weight .25 .60
34 Bill Guerin .25 .60
35 Tom Poti .10 .25
36 Rob Niedermayer .10 .25
37 Ed Jovanovski .10 .25
38 Luc Robitaille .25 .60
39 Rob Blake .25 .60
40 Glen Murray .10 .25
41 Saku Koivu .30 .75
42 Mark Recchi .25 .60
43 Vincent Damphousse .10 .25
44 Mike Dunham .25 .60
45 Sergei Krivokrasov .10 .25
46 Andrew Brunette .25 .60
47 Brendan Morrison .25 .60
48 Martin Brodeur .75 2.00
49 Scott Stevens .25 .60
50 Patrik Elias .25 .60
51 Trevor Linden .25 .60
52 Zigmund Palffy .25 .60
53 Bryan Berard .10 .25
54 Robert Reichel .10 .25
55 Mike Richter .30 .75
56 Wayne Gretzky 2.00 5.00
57 Brian Leetch .25 .60
58 Wade Redden .25 .60
59 Alexei Yashin .10 .25
60 Daniel Alfredsson .25 .60
61 Eric Lindros .30 .75
62 John Vanbiesbrouck .25 .60
63 John LeClair .30 .75
64 Rod Brind'Amour .25 .60
65 Jeremy Roenick .40 1.00
66 Keith Tkachuk .30 .75
67 Nikolai Khabibulin .25 .60
68 German Titov .10 .25
69 Martin Straka .10 .25
70 Jaromir Jagr .50 1.25
71 Chris Pronger .25 .60
72 Al MacInnis .25 .60
73 Pierre Turgeon .25 .60
74 Pavol Demitra .25 .60
75 Patrick Marleau .10 .25
76 Jeff Friesen .10 .25
77 Owen Nolan .10 .25
78 Bill Ranford .10 .25
79 Wendel Clark .25 .60
80 Craig Janney .10 .25
81 Mike Johnson .10 .25
82 Curtis Joseph .30 .75
83 Mats Sundin .30 .75
84 Mattias Ohlund .25 .60
85 Mark Messier .30 .75
86 Pavel Bure .30 .75
87 Olaf Kolzig .25 .60
88 Peter Bondra .25 .60
89 Joe Juneau .25 .60
90 Adam Oates .25 .60
91 Johan Davidsson 1.50 4.00
92 Rico Fata 1.50 4.00
93 Mike Maneluk RC 2.50 5.00
94 J-P Dumont 1.50 4.00
95 Milan Hejduk RC 15.00 40.00
96 Chris Drury 1.50 4.00
97 Mark Parrish RC 4.00 10.00
98 Oleg Kvasha RC 2.00 5.00
99 Josh Green RC 2.00 5.00
100 Olli Jokinen 1.50 4.00
101 Manny Malhotra 1.50 4.00
102 Eric Brewer 1.50 4.00
103 Mike Watt 1.50 4.00
104 Daniel Briere 8.00 20.00
105 Jean-Sebastien Aubin RC 4.00 10.00
106 Jan Hrdina RC 2.00 5.00
107 Marty Reasoner 1.50 4.00
108 Michal Handzus RC 4.00 10.00
109 Vincent Lecavalier 4.00 10.00
110 Tomas Kaberle RC 4.00 10.00
111 Bill Muckalt RC 2.00 5.00
112 Josh Holden 1.50 4.00
113 Matt Herr RC 2.00 5.00
114 Brian Finley RC 3.00 8.00
115 Maxime Ouellet RC 2.00 5.00
116 Kurtis Foster RC 2.00 5.00
117 Barret Jackman RC 4.00 10.00
118 Ross Lupaschuk RC 2.00 5.00
119 Steven McCarthy RC 2.00 5.00
120 Peter Reynolds RC 2.00 5.00
121 Bart Rushmer RC 2.00 5.00
122 Jonathon Zion RC 2.00 5.00
123 Kris Beech RC 3.00 8.00
124 Brandin Cote RC 2.00 5.00
125 Scott Kelman RC 2.00 5.00
126 Jamie Lundmark RC 3.00 8.00
127 Derek MacKenzie RC 2.00 5.00
128 Rory McDade RC 2.00 5.00
129 David Morisset RC 2.00 5.00
130 Mirko Murovic RC 2.00 5.00
131 Taylor Pyatt RC 4.00 10.00
132 Charlie Stephens 2.00 5.00
133 Kyle Wanvig RC 2.00 5.00
134 Krzystof Wieckowski RC 2.00 5.00
135 Michael Zigomanis RC 2.00 5.00

1998-99 SP Authentic Power Shift

Randomly inserted into packs, this 135-card set is parallel to the base set. Only 500 sets were made.

*STARS: 5X TO 10X BASIC CARDS
*SP's: .5X TO 1X BASIC CARDS
95 Milan Hejduk 40.00 100.00

1998-99 SP Authentic Authentics

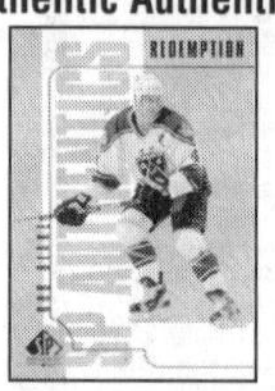

Randomly inserted into packs at the rate of 1:697, this set features hand numbered redemption cards for autographed merchandise and game used memorabilia. We have listed and priced only the autographed trading cards. The number of each item available is indicated below. The cards expired on February 23, 2000.

15 S.Yzerman Card/50 50.00 100.00
16 S.Yzerman 2-card 75.00 150.00
17 S.Yzerman '98 BD Card/50 75.00 150.00

1998-99 SP Authentic Sign of the Times

Randomly inserted into packs at the rate of 1:23, this 50-card set features autographed color photos of top players and future stars of the NHL. Some of the autographs were obtained through redemption cards.

AD Adam Deadmarsh 3.00 5.00
AM Alexander Mogilny 5.00 10.00
AS Alex Selivanov 3.00 8.00
BB Bates Battaglia 3.00 5.00
BD Byron Dafoe 5.00 10.00
BF Brian Finley 3.00 5.00
BH Brett Hull 12.50 30.00
BJ Barret Jackman 10.00 20.00
CJ Curtis Joseph 8.00 20.00
CS Charlie Stephens 3.00 5.00
DA Daniel Alfredsson 5.00 10.00
DM David Morisset 3.00 5.00
(unconfirmed)
DW Doug Weight 5.00 12.00
EJ Ed Jovanovski 3.00 10.00
JA Jason Allison 3.00 5.00
JJ Joe Juneau 5.00 10.00
JS Jozef Stumpel 3.00 5.00
JT Joe Thornton 10.00 25.00
KB Kris Beech 3.00 5.00
KF Kurtis Foster 3.00 8.00
KT Keith Tkachuk 8.00 20.00
MB Matthew Barnaby 3.00 5.00
MH Marian Hossa 8.00 20.00
MM Manny Malhotra 5.00 10.00
MO Mattias Ohlund 3.00 5.00
MS Mats Sundin 8.00 20.00
MZ Michael Zigomanis 3.00 5.00
NL Nicklas Lidstrom 8.00 20.00
ON Owen Nolan 5.00 10.00
PR Patrick Roy 40.00 80.00
RB Rob Blake 5.00 10.00
RL Ross Lupaschuk 3.00 5.00
RM Rory McDade 3.00 5.00
RN Rumun Ndur 3.00 5.00
RS Ryan Smyth 3.00 10.00
SG Sergei Gonchar 3.00 5.00
SK Scott Kelman 3.00 8.00
SM Steven McCarthy 3.00 5.00
SY Steve Yzerman 40.00 80.00
TH Tomas Holmstrom 3.00 10.00
TP Taylor Pyatt 5.00 12.00
VL Vincent Lecavalier 8.00 20.00
WG Wayne Gretzky 75.00 200.00
DMA Derek Mackenzie 3.00 5.00
MAO Maxime Ouellet 3.00 5.00
MIM Mirko Murovic 3.00 5.00
MMC Marty McSorley 3.00 10.00
PBO Peter Bondra 5.00 10.00
PRE Peter Reynolds 3.00 5.00
PB Pavel Bure 8.00 20.00

1998-99 SP Authentic Sign of the Times Gold

Randomly inserted into packs, this set is a parallel version of the regular SP Authentic Sign of the Times insert set with each card hand-numbered to the pictured player's jersey number. These numbers follow the player's name in the checklist below. Cards with print runs less than 25 are not priced due to scarcity.

AD Adam Deadmarsh/18
AM A.Mogilny/89 25.00 50.00
AS Alex Selivanov/29 12.50 25.00
BB Bates Battaglia/13
BD Byron Dafoe/34 20.00 50.00
BF Brian Finley/100 10.00 25.00
BH Brett Hull/22
BJ Barret Jackman/100 25.00 50.00
CJ Curtis Joseph/31 50.00 125.00
CS Charlie Stephens/100 6.00 15.00
DA Daniel Alfredsson/11
DM David Morisset/100 6.00 15.00
DW Doug Weight/39 25.00 50.00
EJ E.Jovanovski/55 25.00 50.00
JA Jason Allison/41 12.50 25.00
JJ Joe Juneau/49 12.50 25.00
JS Jozef Stumpel/16
JT Joe Thornton/10
KB Kris Beech/100 6.00 15.00
KF Kurtis Foster/100 6.00 15.00
KT Keith Tkachuk/10
MB Matthew Barnaby/36 12.50 25.00
MH Marian Hossa/18
MM Manny Malhotra/10
MO Mattias Ohlund/10
MS Mats Sundin/13
MZ Michael Zigomanis/100 8.00 20.00
NL Nicklas Lidstrom/10
ON Owen Nolan/11
PR Patrick Roy/33 150.00 300.00
RB Rob Blake/10
RL Ross Lupaschuk/100 6.00 15.00
RM Rory McDade/100 6.00 15.00
RN Rumun Ndur/40 12.50 25.00
RS Ryan Smyth/94 12.50 30.00
SG Sergei Gonchar/55 12.50 25.00
SK Scott Kelman/100 6.00 15.00
SM Steven McCarthy/100 6.00 15.00
SY Steve Yzerman/19
TH Tomas Holmstrom/96 12.50 25.00
TP Taylor Pyatt/100 15.00 30.00
VL Vincent Lecavalier/14
WG Wayne Gretzky/99 150.00 300.00
DMA Derek Mackenzie/100 6.00 15.00
MAO Maxime Ouellet/100 10.00 25.00
MIM Mirko Murovic/100 6.00 15.00
MMC Marty McSorley/33 12.50 25.00
PBO Peter Bondra/12
PRE Peter Reynolds/100 6.00 15.00
PB Pavel Bure/10

1998-99 SP Authentic Snapshots

Randomly inserted in packs at the rate of 1:11, this 30-card set features unique images of the NHL's most exciting players. The backs carry player information.

COMPLETE SET (30) 30.00 60.00
SS1 Wayne Gretzky 4.00 10.00
SS2 Patrick Roy 3.00 8.00
SS3 Steve Yzerman 3.00 8.00
SS4 Brett Hull .75 2.00
SS5 Jaromir Jagr 1.00 2.50
SS6 Peter Forsberg 1.50 4.00
SS7 Dominik Hasek 1.25 3.00
SS8 Paul Kariya .60 1.50
SS9 Eric Lindros .60 1.50
SS10 Teemu Selanne .60 1.50
SS11 John LeClair .60 1.50
SS12 Mike Modano 1.00 2.50
SS13 Martin Brodeur 1.50 4.00
SS14 Brendan Shanahan .60 1.50
SS15 Ray Bourque 1.00 2.50
SS16 John Vanbiesbrouck .50 1.25
SS17 Brian Leetch .50 1.25
SS18 Vincent Lecavalier 4.00 10.00
SS19 Joe Sakic 1.25 3.00
SS20 Chris Drury .75 2.00
SS21 Eric Brewer 1.00 2.50
SS22 Jeremy Roenick .75 2.00
SS23 Mats Sundin .60 1.50
SS24 Zigmund Palffy .50 1.25
SS25 Keith Tkachuk .60 1.50
SS26 Sergei Samsonov .50 1.25
SS27 Curtis Joseph .60 1.50
SS28 Peter Bondra .50 1.25
SS29 Sergei Fedorov 1.00 2.50
SS30 Doug Gilmour .50 1.25

1998-99 SP Authentic Stat Masters

Randomly inserted into packs, this 30-card set features color photos of the NHL's best players printed on sequentially numbered cards based on the achievements of the player featured. Each player's card is sequentially numbered to the player's key accomplishment. These numbers follow the player's name in the checklist below.

COMPLETE SET (30) 200.00 400.00
S1 Brendan Shanahan/400 2.50 6.00
S2 Brett Hull/1000 3.00 8.00
S3 Dominik Hasek/200 10.00 25.00
S4 Doug Gilmour/1200 2.50 6.00
S5 Doug Weight/500 2.50 6.00
S6 Eric Lindros/115 8.00 20.00
S7 Jaromir Jagr/301 6.00 15.00
S8 Joe Sakic/900 3.00 8.00
S9 John LeClair/500 3.00 8.00
S10 John Vanbiesbrouck/306 2.50 6.00
S11 Keith Tkachuk/250 2.50 6.00
S12 Mark Messier/600 2.50 6.00
S13 Martin Brodeur/200 12.50 30.00
S14 Mike Modano/650 3.00 8.00
S15 Patrick Roy/400 10.00 25.00
S16 Paul Kariya/108 15.00 40.00
S17 Pavel Bure/500 2.50 6.00
S18 Peter Bondra/300 2.50 6.00
S19 Peter Forsberg/400 5.00 12.00
S20 Ray Bourque/1500 3.00 8.00
S21 Ron Francis/1500 2.50 6.00
S22 Sergei Fedorov/600 3.00 8.00
S23 Steve Yzerman/1500 5.00 12.00
S24 Steve Yzerman/900 6.00 15.00
S25 Steve Yzerman/500 10.00 25.00
S26 Teemu Selanne/300 2.50 6.00
S27 Vincent Lecavalier/1998 2.50 6.00
S28 Wayne Gretzky/92 75.00 200.00
S29 Wayne Gretzky/900 5.00 12.00
S30 Wayne Gretzky/2000 3.00 8.00

1999-00 SP Authentic

Released as a 135-card set, the 1999-00 SP Authentic base set is composed of 90 regular issue cards and 45-short printed Future Watch cards which are serial numbered out of 2000. This subset features some of the NHL's most promising prospects. Base cards have a white border and are enhanced by an embossed SP Authentic logo towards the bottom, and embossed framing along the top and bottom. The Future Watch subset contains a foil SP Authentic logo in the lower left front corner and players are set against a green grid-line background. SP Authentic was released as 24-pack boxes containing 5-card packs that carried a suggested retail price of $4.99.

COMPLETE SET (135) 150.00 300.00
COMP.SET w/o SP's (90) 15.00 40.00
1 Paul Kariya .30 .75
2 Teemu Selanne .30 .75
3 Guy Hebert .25 .60
4 Ray Ferraro .10 .25
5 Andrew Brunette .25 .60
6 Joe Thornton .50 1.25
7 Ray Bourque .50 1.25
8 Sergei Samsonov .25 .60
9 Michael Peca .10 .25
10 Dominik Hasek .60 1.50
11 Miroslav Satan .10 .25
12 Maxim Afinogenov .10 .25
13 Valeri Bure .10 .25
14 Marc Savard .25 .60
15 Fred Brathwaite .25 .60
16 Ron Francis .25 .60
17 Arturs Irbe .25 .60
18 Sami Kapanen .10 .25
19 Tony Amonte .25 .60
20 Steve Passmore RC .40 1.00
21 Doug Gilmour .25 .60
22 Milan Hejduk .30 .75
23 Joe Sakic .60 1.50
24 Patrick Roy 1.50 4.00
25 Chris Drury .25 .60
26 Peter Forsberg .75 2.00
27 Mike Modano .50 1.25
28 Brett Hull .40 1.00
29 Ed Belfour .30 .75
30 Steve Yzerman 1.50 4.00
31 Chris Osgood .25 .60
32 Brendan Shanahan .30 .75
33 Sergei Fedorov .50 1.25
34 Doug Weight .25 .60
35 Bill Guerin .10 .25
36 Alexander Selivanov .10 .25
37 Pavel Bure .30 .75
38 Trevor Kidd .25 .60
39 Viktor Kozlov .10 .25

0 Luc Robitaille .25 .60
1 Zigmund Palffy .25 .60
2 Rob Blake .25 .60
3 Saku Koivu .30 .75
4 Mike Ribeiro .25 .60
5 Jose Theodore .40 1.00
6 David Legwand .25 .60
7 Mike Dunham .25 .60
8 Robert Valicevic RC .10 .25
9 Martin Brodeur .75 2.00
0 Claude Lemieux .10 .25
1 Scott Gomez .10 .25
2 Tim Connolly .10 .25
3 Roberto Luongo .40 1.00
4 Kenny Jonsson .10 .25
5 Mike Richter .30 .75
6 Theo Fleury .10 .25
7 Mike York .10 .25
8 Brian Leetch .30 .75
9 Radek Bonk .10 .25
0 Marian Hossa .30 .75
1 Patrick Lalime .25 .60
2 Keith Primeau .10 .25
3 Eric Lindros .30 .75
4 John LeClair .30 .75
5 Trevor Letowski .10 .25
6 Keith Tkachuk .30 .75
7 Jeremy Roenick .40 1.00
8 Jaromir Jagr .50 1.25
9 Alexei Kovalev .10 .25
0 Martin Straka .10 .25
1 Brad Stuart .10 .25
2 Steve Shields .25 .60
3 Owen Nolan .25 .60
4 Jeff Friesen .10 .25
5 Pavol Demitra .25 .60
6 Roman Turek .25 .60
7 Pierre Turgeon .25 .60
8 Vincent Lecavalier .30 .75
9 Dan Cloutier .25 .60
0 Chris Gratton .25 .60
1 Mats Sundin .30 .75
2 Bryan Berard .25 .60
3 Curtis Joseph .30 .75
4 Jonas Hoglund .10 .25
5 Mark Messier .30 .75
6 Peter Schaefer .10 .25
7 Alexander Mogilny .25 .60
8 Olaf Kolzig .25 .60
9 Adam Oates .25 .60
0 Peter Bondra .25 .60
1 Patrik Stefan RC 3.00 8.00
2 Dean Sylvester RC 2.00 5.00
3 Scott Fankhouser RC 2.00 5.00
4 Brian Campbell RC 2.00 5.00
5 Byron Ritchie RC 2.00 5.00
6 John Grahame RC 3.00 8.00
7 Andre Savage RC 2.00 5.00
8 Oleg Saprykin RC 3.00 8.00
9 Kyle Calder RC 3.00 8.00
00 Dan Hinote RC 3.00 8.00
01 Jonathan Sim RC 2.00 5.00
02 Marc Rodgers RC 2.00 5.00
03 Paul Comrie RC 2.00 5.00
04 Ivan Novoseltsev RC 2.00 5.00
05 Jason Blake RC 2.00 5.00
06 Brian Rafalski RC 3.00 8.00
07 John Madden RC 3.00 8.00
08 Jason Krog RC 3.00 8.00
09 Jorgen Jonsson RC 2.00 5.00
10 Kim Johnsson RC 2.00 5.00
11 Mike Fisher RC 3.00 8.00
12 Michal Rozsival RC 2.00 5.00
13 Mika Alatalo RC 2.00 5.00
14 Tyson Nash RC 2.00 5.00
15 Ladislav Nagy RC 6.00 15.00
16 Jochen Hecht RC 3.00 8.00
17 Adam Mair RC 2.00 5.00
18 Nikolai Antropov RC 4.00 10.00
19 Steve Kariya RC 2.00 5.00
20 Jeff Halpern RC 2.00 5.00
21 Alexandre Volchkov RC 2.00 5.00
22 Pavel Brendl RC 2.00 5.00
23 Sheldon Keefe RC 2.00 5.00
24 Branislav Mezei RC 2.00 5.00
25 Milan Kraft RC 2.00 5.00
26 Kristian Kudroc RC 2.00 5.00
27 Jaroslav Kristek RC 2.00 5.00
28 Alexander Buturlin RC 2.00 5.00
29 Andrei Shefer RC 2.00 5.00
30 Brad Moran RC 2.00 5.00
31 Ryan Jardine RC 2.00 5.00
32 Brett Lysak RC 2.00 5.00
33 Michal Sivek RC 2.00 5.00
34 Luke Sellars RC 2.00 5.00
35 Brad Ralph RC 2.00 5.00

1999-00 SP Authentic Buyback Signatures

Randomly inserted in packs at 1:287, this 6-card set features some of the NHL's most sought after autographs on Upper Deck and Upper Deck SP (Authentic) dating back to 1993-94. Each card is serial numbered out of how many were signed. Lower print runs are unpriced due to scarcity.

1 P.Bure 94SP/65 30.00 80.00
2 P.Bure 94SPDC/4
3 P.Bure 94UDSPI/60 30.00 80.00
4 P.Bure 94UDSPIDC/2
5 P.Bure 94SP/1
6 P.Bure 95SP/3
7 P.Bure 95SPHol/1
8 P.Bure 96SP/16
9 P.Bure 97SPAlcon/3
10 P.Bure 98SPA/30 100.00 200.00
11 W.Gretzky 94SP/56 150.00 400.00
12 W.Gretzky 94SPDC/1
13 W.Gretzky 94UDSPI/16
14 W.Gretzky 94UDSPIDC/5
15 W.Gretzky 95SP/1
16 W.Gretzky 95SPPromo/2
17 W.Gretzky 96SP/13
18 W.Gretzky 97SPAlcon/2
19 W.Gretzky 98SPA/101 200.00 300.00
21 B.Hull 94SP/92
22 B.Hull 94UDSPI/17
23 B.Hull 94UDSPIDC/3
24 B.Hull 95SP/2
25 B.Hull 95SPStars/4
26 B.Hull 97SPA/4
27 B.Hull 97SPAlcon/1
28 B.Hull 98SPA/100 25.00 60.00
30 M.Johnson 97SPA/25
31 M.Johnson 98SPA/300 5.00 12.00
32 C.Joseph 94SP/65 15.00 40.00
33 C.Joseph 94SPDC/9
34 C.Joseph 94UDSPI/34
35 C.Joseph 94UDSPIDC/4
36 C.Joseph 96SP/29 15.00 40.00
37 C.Joseph 98SPA/200 12.50 30.00
39 J.LeClair 94SP/150 12.50 30.00
40 J.LeClair 94SPDC/10
41 J.LeClair 96SP/130 15.00 40.00
42 J.LeClair 98SPA/100 20.00 50.00
43 Z.Palffy 94UDSPI/75 20.00 50.00
44 Z.Palffy 94UDSPI/10
45 Z.Palffy 96SP/33 20.00 50.00
46 Z.Palffy 97SPA/3
47 Z.Palffy 98SPA/100 12.50 30.00
48 L.Robitaille 93SPI/16
49 L.Robitaille 94SP/20
50 L.Robitaille 94SPDC/19 40.00 100.00
51 L.Robitaille 94UDSPI/60 20.00 50.00
52 L.Robitaille 94UDSPIDC/9
53 L.Robitaille 98SPA/65 20.00 50.00
54 J.Roenick 93SPI/11
55 J.Roenick 94SP/70 25.00 60.00
56 J.Roenick 94SPDC/14
57 J.Roenick 94UDSPI/40
58 J.Roenick 94UDSPIDC/13
59 J.Roenick 95SP/3
60 J.Roenick 96SP/32 60.00 120.00
61 J.Roenick 98SPA/97 25.00 60.00
62 S.Samsonov 94SP/65 30.00 80.00
63 S.Samsonov 94SPDC/15
64 S.Samsonov 95SP/10
65 S.Samsonov 98SPA/255 10.00 25.00
66 S.Yzerman 93SPI/3
67 S.Yzerman 94SP/65 60.00 150.00
68 S.Yzerman 96SP/21
69 S.Yzerman 98SPA/77 60.00 150.00

1999-00 SP Authentic Honor Roll

Randomly seeded in packs at 1:24, this 6-card set places some of hockey's most dominating on a grey card with a centered foil background. Card backs carry an "HR" prefix.

COMPLETE SET (6) 15.00 30.00
HR1 Paul Kariya 2.50 6.00
HR2 Patrick Roy 5.00 12.00
HR3 Steve Yzerman 5.00 12.00
HR4 Martin Brodeur 2.50 6.00
HR5 Eric Lindros 1.50 4.00
HR6 Jaromir Jagr 1.50 4.00

1999-00 SP Authentic Legendary Heroes

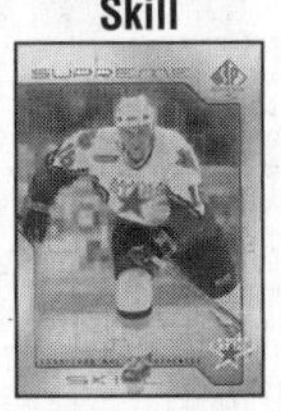

Randomly inserted in packs at 1:72, this 5-card set pays homage to the NHL's past superstars. Card backs carry an "LH" prefix.

COMPLETE SET (5) 20.00 40.00
LH1 Wayne Gretzky 5.00 12.00
LH2 Bobby Orr 5.00 12.00
LH3 Gordie Howe 4.00 10.00
LH4 Maurice Richard 4.00 10.00
LH5 Bobby Hull 3.00 8.00

1999-00 SP Authentic Sign of the Times

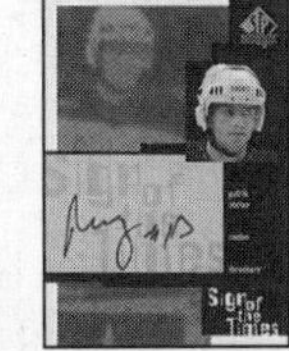

Randomly seeded in packs at 1:23, this 32-card set features autographs from past superstars, current veteran players, and top prospects. Each card is set with a white box in the middle containing the player's autograph.

AT Alex Tanguay 5.00 12.00
BC Brian Campbell 3.00 8.00
BH Bobby Hull 15.00 40.00
BM Bill Muckalt 3.00 8.00
BO Bobby Orr 75.00 200.00
BS Brad Stuart 3.00 8.00
CJ Curtis Joseph 8.00 20.00
DL David Legwand 3.00 8.00
DT Dave Tanabe 3.00 8.00
HG Gordie Howe 30.00 80.00
JH Jochen Hecht 3.00 8.00
JL John LeClair 5.00 12.00
JR Jeremy Roenick 8.00 20.00
LR Luc Robitaille 5.00 12.00
MH Marian Hossa 6.00 15.00
OS Oleg Saprykin 3.00 8.00
PB Pavel Bure 6.00 15.00
PM Paul Mara 3.00 8.00
PS Patrik Stefan 3.00 8.00
SF Sergei Fedorov 12.50 30.00
SG Simon Gagne 5.00 12.00
SS Sergei Samsonov 5.00 12.00
SY Steve Yzerman 30.00 80.00
TC Tim Connolly 3.00 8.00
TF Theo Fleury 5.00 12.00
WG Wayne Gretzky 75.00 200.00
ZP Zigmund Palffy 5.00 12.00
BHU Brett Hull 12.50 30.00
JST Jozef Stumpel 3.00 8.00
MRC Maurice Richard 150.00 300.00
MRI Mike Ribeiro 3.00 8.00
SGO Scott Gomez 3.00 8.00

1999-00 SP Authentic Sign of the Times Gold

Randomly inserted in packs, this 32-card set parallels the base Sign of the Times insert set. Each card is serial numbered out of 25. Cards # CJ, PM, and WG were inserted in packs as redemption cards.

*GOLD: 3X TO 6X BASIC INSERTS

1999-00 SP Authentic Special Forces

Randomly inserted in packs at 1:12, this 10-card set showcases top players set against an all foil true-life background. Card backs carry an "SF" prefix.

COMPLETE SET (10) 12.00 25.00
SF1 Paul Kariya .60 1.50
SF2 Joe Sakic 1.25 3.00
SF3 Patrick Roy 3.00 8.00
SF4 Steve Yzerman 3.00 8.00
SF5 Mike Modano 1.00 2.50
SF6 Pavel Bure .75 2.00
SF7 Jaromir Jagr 1.00 2.50
SF8 Eric Lindros 1.00 2.50
SF9 Curtis Joseph .60 1.50
SF10 Steve Kariya .60 1.50

1999-00 SP Authentic Supreme Skill

Randomly seeded in packs at 1:4, this 11-card set places NHL's most dominating against an all-foil true to life background. Card backs carry an "SS" prefix.

COMPLETE SET (11) 6.00 12.00
SS1 Paul Kariya .40 1.00
SS2 Teemu Selanne .40 1.00
SS3 Peter Forsberg 1.00 2.50
SS4 Brett Hull .50 1.25
SS5 Sergei Fedorov .75 2.00
SS6 Pavel Bure .50 1.25
SS7 Martin Brodeur 1.00 2.50
SS8 Theo Fleury .40 1.00
SS9 John LeClair .50 1.25
SS10 Keith Tkachuk .40 1.00
SS11 Jaromir Jagr .60 1.50

1999-00 SP Authentic Tomorrow's Headliners

Randomly inserted in packs at 1:10, this 10-card set features top prospects and young stars on an all-foil background. Card backs carry a "TH" prefix and contain a brief blurb about each player's standout skills.

COMPLETE SET (10) 10.00 20.00
TH1 Patrik Stefan 1.00 2.50
TH2 Joe Thornton 1.50 4.00
TH3 Maxim Afinogenov 1.00 2.50
TH4 Milan Hejduk 1.00 2.50
TH5 David Legwand 1.00 2.50
TH6 Scott Gomez 1.00 2.50
TH7 Marian Hossa 1.00 2.50
TH8 Jochen Hecht 1.00 2.50
TH9 Vincent Lecavalier 1.50 4.00
TH10 Steve Kariya 1.00 2.50

2000-01 SP Authentic

SP Authentic released these cards as a 165-card set with 75 short-printed rookies. The bas set design had white with blue and grey borders. The card fronts were highlighted with silver-foil lettering and logo. The card backs had a short summary about the player along with his statistics and a small photo. The short-printed rookies were serial numbered to 900.

COMPLETE SET w/o SP's 15.00 30.00
1 Paul Kariya .30 .75
2 J-S Giguere .25 .60
3 Oleg Tverdovsky .10 .25
4 Patrik Stefan .10 .25
5 Donald Audette .10 .25
6 Damian Rhodes .10 .25
7 Joe Thornton .50 1.25
8 Jason Allison .10 .25
9 Bill Guerin .25 .60
10 Dominik Hasek .60 1.50
11 Maxim Afinogenov .10 .25
12 Doug Gilmour .25 .60
13 Valeri Bure .10 .25
14 Marc Savard .10 .25
15 Jarome Iginla .40 1.00
16 Ron Francis .25 .60
17 Jeff O'Neill .10 .25
18 Sandis Ozolinsh .10 .25
19 Steve Sullivan .10 .25
20 Tony Amonte .25 .60
21 Rob Blake .25 .60
22 Ray Bourque .50 1.25
23 Patrick Roy 1.50 4.00
24 Peter Forsberg .60 1.50
25 Joe Sakic .60 1.50
26 Ron Tugnutt .25 .60
27 Geoff Sanderson .10 .25
28 Ed Belfour .30 .75
29 Mike Modano .50 1.25
30 Brett Hull .40 1.00
31 Steve Yzerman 1.50 4.00
32 Brendan Shanahan .30 .75
33 Nicklas Lidstrom .30 .75
34 Sergei Fedorov .50 1.25
35 Doug Weight .25 .60
36 Ryan Smyth .10 .25
37 Tommy Salo .25 .60
38 Pavel Bure .30 .75
39 Ray Whitney .10 .25
40 Ivan Novoseltsev .10 .25
41 Adam Deadmarsh .10 .25
42 Zigmund Palffy .25 .60
43 Luc Robitaille .25 .60
44 Darby Hendrickson .10 .25
45 Manny Fernandez .25 .60
46 Jose Theodore .40 1.00
47 Andrei Markov .10 .25
48 Trevor Linden .25 .60
49 David Legwand .25 .60
50 Mike Dunham .25 .60
51 Cliff Ronning .10 .25
52 Scott Gomez .10 .25
53 Martin Brodeur .75 2.00
54 Jason Arnott .10 .25
55 Mark Messier .30 .75
56 Theo Fleury .10 .25
57 Brian Leetch .25 .60
58 Tim Connolly .10 .25
59 Brad Isbister .10 .25
60 Taylor Pyatt .10 .25
61 Alexei Yashin .10 .25
62 Marian Hossa .30 .75
63 Patrick Lalime .25 .60
64 John LeClair .30 .75
65 Simon Gagne .30 .75
66 Mark Recchi .25 .60
67 Jeremy Roenick .40 1.00
68 Keith Tkachuk .30 .75
69 Shane Doan .10 .25
70 Jaromir Jagr .50 1.25
71 Alexei Kovalev .25 .60
72 Mario Lemieux 2.00 5.00
73 Owen Nolan .25 .60
74 Patrick Marleau .25 .60
75 Evgeni Nabokov 1.25 3.00
76 Pierre Turgeon .25 .60
77 Chris Pronger .25 .60
78 Roman Turek .25 .60
79 Brad Richards .25 .60
80 Vincent Lecavalier .30 .75
81 Fredrik Modin .10 .25
82 Mats Sundin .30 .75
83 Curtis Joseph .30 .75
84 Gary Roberts .10 .25
85 Daniel Sedin .10 .25
86 Henrik Sedin .10 .25
87 Markus Naslund .30 .75
88 Peter Bondra .30 .75
89 Olaf Kolzig .25 .60
90 Adam Oates .25 .60
91 Petr Tenkrat RC 2.00 5.00
92 Andy McDonald RC 8.00 20.00
93 Brad Tapper RC 2.00 5.00
94 Andrew Raycroft RC 10.00 25.00
95 Lee Goren RC 2.00 5.00
96 Josef Vasicek RC 2.00 5.00
97 Reto Von Arx RC 2.00 5.00
98 David Aebischer RC 10.00 25.00
99 Ville Nieminen RC 2.00 5.00
100 Serge Aubin RC 2.00 5.00
101 Rostislav Klesla RC 3.00 8.00
102 Marty Turco RC 20.00 50.00
103 Tyler Bouck RC 2.00 5.00
104 Jason Williams RC 3.00 8.00
105 Shawn Horcoff RC 4.00 10.00
106 Mike Comrie RC 10.00 25.00
107 Eric Belanger RC 2.00 5.00
108 Steven Reinprecht RC 3.00 8.00
109 Lubomir Visnovsky RC 2.00 5.00
110 Marian Gaborik RC 60.00 125.00
111 Peter Bartos RC 2.00 5.00
112 Scott Hartnell RC 5.00 12.00
113 Chris Mason RC 8.00 20.00
114 Rick DiPietro RC 12.00 30.00
115 Martin Havlat RC 20.00 50.00
116 Jani Hurme RC 2.00 5.00
117 Petr Hubacek RC 2.00 5.00
118 Justin Williams RC 6.00 15.00
119 Roman Cechmanek RC 2.00 5.00
120 Ruslan Fedotenko RC 2.00 5.00
121 Roman Simicek RC 2.00 5.00
122 Mark Smith RC 2.00 5.00
123 Alexander Kharitonov RC 2.00 5.00
124 Alexei Ponikarovsky RC 2.00 5.00
125 Matt Pettinger RC 2.00 5.00
126 Zdenek Blatny RC 2.00 5.00
127 Damian Surma RC 2.00 5.00
128 Marc-Andre Thinel RC 2.00 5.00
129 Fedor Fedorov RC 2.00 5.00
130 Jason Jaspers RC 2.00 5.00
131 Jordan Krestanovich RC 2.00 5.00
132 Jeff Bateman RC 2.00 5.00
133 Marc Chouinard RC 2.00 5.00
134 Darcy Hordichuk RC 2.00 5.00
135 Bryan Adams RC 2.00 5.00
136 Jarno Kultanen RC 2.00 5.00
137 Eric Boulton RC 2.00 5.00
138 Ronald Petrovicky RC 2.00 5.00
139 Martin Brochu RC 2.00 5.00
140 Craig Adams RC 2.00 5.00
141 Chris Nielsen RC 2.00 5.00
142 Petteri Nummelin RC 2.00 5.00
143 Brian Swanson RC 2.00 5.00
144 Michel Riesen RC 2.00 5.00
145 Lance Ward RC 2.00 5.00
146 Travis Scott RC 2.00 5.00
147 Lubomir Sekeras RC 2.00 5.00
148 Eric Landry RC 2.00 5.00
149 Greg Classen RC 2.00 5.00
150 Sascha Goc RC 2.00 5.00
151 Mike Commodore RC 2.00 5.00
152 Johan Holmqvist RC 3.00 8.00
153 Vitali Yeremeyev RC 2.00 5.00
154 Tomas Kloucek RC 2.00 5.00
155 Dale Purinton RC 2.00 5.00
156 Shane Hnidy RC 2.00 5.00
157 Todd Fedoruk RC 2.00 5.00
158 Jean-Guy Trudel RC 2.00 5.00
159 Ossi Vaananen RC 2.00 5.00
160 Greg Andrusak RC 2.00 5.00
161 Alexander Khavanov RC 2.00 5.00
162 Bryce Salvador RC 2.00 5.00
163 Reed Low RC 2.00 5.00
164 Petr Svoboda RC 2.00 5.00
165 Brent Sopel RC 2.00 5.00

2000-01 SP Authentic BuyBacks

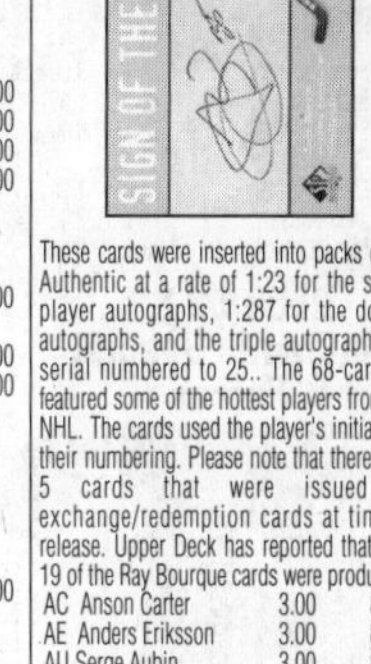

Randomly inserted in packs of 2000-01 SP Authentic at a rate of 1:144, this 114 card set featured original SP cards that were purchased from the secondary market and autographed. Cards with lower print runs are unpriced due to scarcity.

1 B.Orr 99SPALH/49 150.00 300.00
2 S.Samsonov 94SP/3
3 S.Samsonov 95SP/2
4 S.Samsonov 97SPA/3
5 S.Samsonov 98SPA/20
6 S.Samsonov 99SPA/184 8.00 20.00
7 B.Dafoe 95SP/7
8 M.Satan 95SP/4
9 M.Satan 97SPA/3
10 M.Satan 99SPA/145 20.00 40.00
11 P.Brendl 99SPA/3
12 Bo.Hull 99SPALH/98 25.00 60.00
13 M.Hejduk 99SPA/200 10.00 25.00
14 M.Hejduk 99SPATH/143 12.50 30.00
15 R.Bourque 98SPASS/1
16 R.Bourque 98SPA/24 75.00 200.00
17 R.Bourque 99SPA/122 40.00 80.00
18 M.Modano 94SP/61 20.00 50.00
19 M.Modano 95SP/10
20 M.Modano 96SP/5
21 M.Modano 97SPA/2
22 M.Modano 97SPASM/1
23 M.Modano 98SPA/40 25.00 60.00
24 M.Modano 99SPA/168 12.50 30.00
25 M.Modano 99SPASF/155 12.50 30.00
26 N.Lidstrom 94SP/6
27 N.Lidstrom 95SP/11
28 N.Lidstrom 96SP/14
29 N.Lidstrom 97SPA/1
30 N.Lidstrom 98SPA/19
31 Br.Hull 94SPDC/1
32 Br.Hull 94SP/7
33 Br.Hull 97SPA/3
34 Br.Hull 97SPAIC/2
35 Br.Hull 98SPA/16
36 Br.Hull 99SPA/119 20.00 50.00
37 T.Salo 97SPA/12
38 P.Bure 94SP/2
39 P.Bure 96SP/16
40 P.Bure 97SPA/6
41 P.Bure 97SPAIC/2
42 P.Bure 98SPA/1
43 P.Bure 99SPA/225 10.00 25.00
44 P.Bure 99SPASF/154 15.00 40.00
45 P.Bure 99SPASS/69 20.00 50.00
46 I.Novoseltsev 99SPA/1
47 L.Robitaille 94SP/36 25.00 60.00
48 L.Robitaille 94SPPRE/8
49 L.Robitaille 95SP/1
50 L.Robitaille 97SPA/6
51 L.Robitaille 97SPAIC/6
52 L.Robitaille 99SPA/97 15.00 40.00
53 M.Ribeiro 99SPA/117 12.50 30.00
54 D.Legwand 99SPA/214 6.00 15.00
55 D.Legwand 99SPATH/130 12.50 25.00
56 S.Gomez 99SPA/243 10.00 25.00
57 S.Gomez 99SPATH/157 12.50 30.00
58 P.Elias 97SPA/1
59 P.Elias 98SPA/43 15.00 40.00
60 M.Brodeur 94SPDC/3
61 M.Brodeur 95SP/11
62 M.Brodeur 96SP/21
63 M.Brodeur 98SPA/5
64 W.Gretzky 94SP/4
65 W.Gretzky 94SPDC/1
66 W.Gretzky 96SP/2
67 W.Gretzky 98SPA/4
68 W.Gretzky 99SPALH/9
69 M.Messier 94SP/50 60.00 125.00
70 M.Messier 95SP/9
71 M.Messier 96SP/3
72 M.Messier 97SPA/10
73 M.Messier 98SPA/26 60.00 125.00
74 M.Messier 99SPA/147 40.00 100.00
75 M.Richter 94SP/5
76 M.Richter 94SPPRE/8
77 M.Richter 95SP/21
78 M.Richter 96SP/21
79 M.Richter 97SPA/8
80 M.Richter 98SPA/48 15.00 30.00
81 M.Richter 99SPA/214 8.00 20.00
82 M.York 99SPA/212 8.00 20.00
83 J.LeClair 94SP/12
84 J.LeClair 95SP/24
85 J.LeClair 96SP/14
86 J.LeClair 97SPA/10
87 J.LeClair 97SPAIC/6
88 J.LeClair 98SPA/100 8.00 20.00
89 J.LeClair 99SPA/207 8.00 20.00
90 J.LeClair 99SPASS/116 15.00 40.00
91 J.Roenick 99SPA/98 15.00 40.00
92 M.Lemieux 95SP/19
93 M.Lemieux 96SP/1
94 M.Kraft 99SPA/3
95 S.Shields 99SPA/195 6.00 15.00
96 C.Joseph 98SPA/14
97 C.Joseph 99SPA/187 20.00 40.00
98 C.Joseph 99SPASF/135 20.00 40.00
99 F.Potvin 95SP/10
100 F.Potvin 96SP/2
101 F.Potvin 97SPA/5
102 S.Yzerman 93UDSP/3
103 S.Yzerman 94SP/22
104 S.Yzerman 94SPDC/2
105 S.Yzerman 94SPPRE/34 50.00 125.00
106 S.Yzerman 94SPPREDC/4
107 S.Yzerman 95SPHOL/1
108 S.Yzerman 95SP/2
109 S.Yzerman 96SP/9
110 S.Yzerman 98SPASS/1
111 S.Yzerman 98SPA/5
112 S.Yzerman 99SPA/152 30.00 80.00
113 S.Yzerman 99SPASF/35 50.00 125.00

2000-01 SP Authentic Honor

These cards were inserted into packs of SP Authentic at a rate of 1:24. The 7-card set featured the hottest players from the NHL. The cards carried a 'SP' prefix for their numbering.

COMPLETE SET (7) 12.00 25.00
SP1 Paul Kariya .75 2.00
SP2 Patrick Roy 3.00 8.00
SP3 Pavel Bure .75 2.00
SP4 Martin Brodeur 1.50 4.00
SP5 Mark Messier .75 2.00
SP6 Mario Lemieux 4.00 10.00
SP7 Jaromir Jagr 1.00 2.50

2000-01 SP Authentic Parents' Scrapbook

These cards were inserted into packs of SP Authentic at a rate of 1:24. The 7-card set featured the hottest players from the NHL. The cards carried a 'PS' prefix for their numbering.

COMPLETE SET (7) 5.00 10.00
PS1 Paul Kariya .50 1.25
PS2 Joe Thornton .75 2.00
PS3 Mike Modano .75 2.00
PS4 Scott Gomez .50 1.25
PS5 Martin Brodeur 1.25 3.00
PS6 John LeClair .36 1.50
PS7 Vincent Lecavalier .50 1.25

2000-01 SP Authentic Power Skaters

These cards were inserted into packs of SP Authentic at a rate of 1:24. The 7-card set featured Hall of Famers from the NHL. The cards carried a 'P' prefix for their numbering.

COMPLETE SET (7) 20.00 40.00
P1 Bobby Orr 3.00 8.00
P2 Bobby Hull 2.50 6.00
P3 Gordie Howe 2.50 6.00
P4 Wayne Gretzky 3.00 8.00
P5 Wayne Gretzky 3.00 8.00
P6 Wayne Gretzky 3.00 8.00
P7 Wayne Gretzky 3.00 8.00

2000-01 SP Authentic Sign of the Times

These cards were inserted into packs of SP Authentic at a rate of 1:23 for the single player autographs, 1:287 for the double autographs, and the triple autographs are serial numbered to 25.. The 68-card set featured some of the hottest players from the NHL. The cards used the player's initials for their numbering. Please note that there were 5 cards that were issued as exchange/redemption cards at time of release. Upper Deck has reported that only 19 of the Ray Bourque cards were produced.

AC Anson Carter 3.00 8.00
AE Anders Eriksson 3.00 8.00
AU Serge Aubin 3.00 8.00
BD Byron Dafoe 3.00 8.00
BH Bobby Hull 25.00 60.00
BI Martin Biron 3.00 8.00
BO Bobby Orr SP 125.00 250.00
BR Pavel Brendl 3.00 8.00
CJ Curtis Joseph 8.00 20.00
DG David Gosselin 3.00 8.00
DL David Legwand 3.00 8.00
DS Daniel Sedin 4.00 10.00
FP Felix Potvin 8.00 20.00
GH Gordie Howe 75.00 150.00
HA Martin Havlat 6.00 15.00
HS Henrik Sedin 4.00 10.00
IN Ivan Novoseltsev 3.00 8.00
JA Jean-Sebastien Aubin 3.00 8.00
JH Jani Hurme 3.00 8.00
JL John LeClair 8.00 20.00
JT Jose Theodore 10.00 25.00
LB Lubos Bartecko 3.00 8.00
LR Luc Robitaille 6.00 15.00
MB Martin Brodeur 30.00 80.00
MD Marc Denis 3.00 8.00
MG Marian Gaborik 12.00 30.00
MH Milan Hejduk SP 40.00 100.00
MK Milan Kraft 3.00 8.00
ML Mario Lemieux SP 150.00 300.00
MM Mark Messier SP 150.00 250.00
MO Mike Modano 10.00 25.00
MR Mike Richter 10.00 25.00
MS Miroslav Satan 3.00 8.00
MT Marty Turco 8.00 20.00
MY Mike York 3.00 8.00
NL Nicklas Lidstrom 8.00 20.00
PB Pavel Bure 8.00 20.00
PE Patrik Elias 3.00 8.00
PS Petr Sykora 3.00 8.00
RB Ray Bourque SP 200.00 400.00
RD Rick DiPietro 8.00 20.00
RI Michel Riesen 3.00 8.00
RK Rostislav Klesla 3.00 8.00
RO Mike Ribeiro 3.00 8.00
RT Ron Tugnutt 3.00 8.00
SA Sergei Samsonov 6.00 15.00
SG Scott Gomez 3.00 8.00
SH Scott Hartnell 3.00 8.00
SR Steven Reinprecht 3.00 8.00
SS Steve Shields 3.00 8.00

SY Steve Yzerman 50.00 125.00
TS Tommy Salo 3.00 8.00
WG Wayne Gretzky SP 250.00 500.00
B/S Martin Brodeur 40.00 80.00
Petr Sykora
B/N Pavel Bure 10.00 25.00
Ivan Novoseltsev
B/Y Pavel Brendl 8.00 20.00
Mike York
E/G Patrik Elias 10.00 25.00
Scott Gomez
H/G Gordie Howe 300.00 600.00
Wayne Gretzky
H/H Brett Hull 60.00 150.00
Bobby Hull
L/K Mario Lemieux 75.00 200.00
Milan Kraft
M/G Mark Messier 300.00 600.00
Wayne Gretzky
O/B Bobby Orr 200.00 500.00
Ray Bourque
S/S Daniel Sedin 12.00 30.00
Henrik Sedin
Y/L Steve Yzerman 100.00 200.00
Nicklas Lidstrom
BGE Martin Brodeur 100.00 200.00
Scott Gomez
Patrik Elias
GMF Wayne Gretzky 500.00 1200.00
Mark Messier
Grant Fuhr
HLY Hull/Lemieux/Yzerman 300.00 600.00
HOG Gordie Howe 1200.00 2500.00
Wayne Gretzky
Bobby Orr
LMB John LeClair 50.00 100.00
Mike Modano
Pavel Bure

2000-01 SP Authentic Significant Stars

These cards were inserted into packs of SP Authentic at a rate of 1:24. The 7-card set featured the hottest players from the NHL. The cards carried a 'ST' prefix for their numbering.
COMPLETE SET (7) 8.00 15.00
ST1 Peter Forsberg 1.25 3.00
ST2 Brett Hull .60 1.50
ST3 Steve Yzerman 2.50 6.00
ST4 Pavel Bure .60 1.50
ST5 Mark Messier .60 1.50
ST6 Jaromir Jagr .75 2.00
ST7 Mario Lemieux 3.00 8.00

2000-01 SP Authentic Special Forces

These cards were inserted into packs of SP Authentic at a rate of 1:24. The 7-card set featured the hottest players from the NHL. The cards carried a 'SF' prefix for their numbering.
COMPLETE SET (7) 4.00 8.00
SF1 Teemu Selanne .50 1.25
SF2 Mike Modano .75 2.00
SF3 Brendan Shanahan .50 1.25
SF4 Pavel Bure .50 1.25
SF5 John LeClair .50 1.25
SF6 Keith Tkachuk .50 1.25
SF7 Jaromir Jagr .75 2.00

2000-01 SP Authentic Super Stoppers

These cards were inserted into packs of SP Authentic at a rate of 1:24. The 7-card set featured the to the goalies from the NHL. The cards carried a 'SS' prefix for their numbering.
COMPLETE SET (7) 4.00 8.00
SS1 Dominik Hasek 1.00 2.50
SS2 Patrick Roy 2.50 6.00
SS3 Ed Belfour .50 1.25
SS4 Martin Brodeur 1.25 3.00
SS5 Roman Turek .40 1.00
SS6 Curtis Joseph .50 1.25
SS7 Olaf Kolzig .40 1.00

2001-02 SP Authentic

This 180-card set was released in mid-February with an SRP of $4.99 for a 5-card pack. The set consisted of 90 base cards, 50 Future Watch subset rookie cards (6 of which were autographed), 20 Future Greats subset cards and 20 All-Time Greats subset cards. Future Greats and All-Time Greats were serial-numbered out of 3500 while the Future Watch cards were serial-numbered to 900.
COMP.SET w/o SP's (90) 20.00 40.00
1 Jeff Friesen .10 .30
2 Paul Kariya .30 .75
3 Dany Heatley .40 1.00
4 Milan Hnilicka .25 .60
5 Bill Guerin .25 .60
6 Joe Thornton .50 1.25
7 Sergei Samsonov .25 .60
8 Miroslav Satan .25 .60
9 Martin Biron .25 .60
10 J-P Dumont .10 .30
11 Jarome Iginla .40 1.00
12 Roman Turek .25 .60
13 Craig Conroy .10 .30
14 Tony Amonte .25 .60
15 Steve Sullivan .10 .30
16 Joe Sakic .60 1.50
17 Milan Hejduk .30 .75
18 Patrick Roy 1.50 4.00
19 Rob Blake .25 .60
20 Chris Drury .25 .60
21 Ron Tugnutt .25 .60
22 Geoff Sanderson .10 .30
23 Mike Modano .50 1.25
24 Ed Belfour .30 .75
25 Pierre Turgeon .25 .60
26 Brett Hull .40 1.00
27 Dominik Hasek .60 1.50
28 Steve Yzerman 1.50 4.00
29 Sergei Fedorov .50 1.25
30 Luc Robitaille .25 .60
31 Brendan Shanahan .30 .75
32 Tommy Salo .25 .60
33 Ryan Smyth .10 .30
34 Mike Comrie .25 .60
35 Pavel Bure .30 .75
36 Valeri Bure .10 .30
37 Roberto Luongo .40 1.00
38 Jason Allison .10 .30
39 Zigmund Palffy .25 .60
40 Felix Potvin .30 .75
41 Manny Fernandez .25 .60
42 Marian Gaborik .60 1.50
43 Jose Theodore .40 1.00
44 Brian Savage .10 .30
45 David Legwand .25 .60
46 Mike Dunham .25 .60
47 Patrik Elias .25 .60
48 Martin Brodeur .75 2.00
49 Jason Arnott .10 .30
50 Scott Stevens .25 .60
51 Chris Osgood .25 .60
52 Alexei Yashin .10 .30
53 Mark Parrish .10 .30
54 Mark Messier .30 .75
55 Eric Lindros .30 .75
56 Petr Nedved .10 .30
57 Marian Hossa .30 .75
58 Radek Bonk .10 .30
59 Daniel Alfredsson .25 .60
60 Jeremy Roenick .40 1.00
61 John LeClair .30 .75
62 Keith Primeau .10 .30
63 Mark Recchi .25 .60
64 Roman Cechmanek .25 .60
65 Sean Burke .25 .60
66 Michal Handzus .10 .30
67 Shane Doan .10 .30
68 Mario Lemieux 2.00 5.00
69 Alexei Kovalev .25 .60
70 Johan Hedberg .25 .60
71 Teemu Selanne .30 .75
72 Owen Nolan .25 .60
73 Evgeni Nabokov .25 .60
74 Vincent Damphousse .10 .30
75 Pavol Demitra .25 .60
76 Doug Weight .25 .60
77 Keith Tkachuk .30 .75
78 Chris Pronger .25 .60
79 Brad Richards .25 .60
80 Vincent Lecavalier .30 .75
81 Nikolai Khabibulin .30 .75
82 Curtis Joseph .30 .75
83 Mats Sundin .30 .75
84 Alexander Mogilny .25 .60
85 Markus Naslund .30 .75
86 Daniel Sedin .10 .30
87 Henrik Sedin .10 .30
88 Peter Bondra .30 .75
89 Olaf Kolzig .25 .60
90 Jaromir Jagr .50 1.25
91 Paul Kariya ATG 1.25 3.00
92 Ray Bourque ATG 2.50 6.00
93 Patrick Roy ATG 5.00 12.00
94 Joe Sakic ATG 2.50 6.00
95 Mike Modano ATG 2.00 5.00
96 Ed Belfour ATG 1.25 3.00
97 Steve Yzerman ATG 5.00 12.00
98 Dominik Hasek ATG 2.50 6.00
99 Gordie Howe ATG 5.00 12.00
100 Brett Hull ATG 1.50 4.00
101 Wayne Gretzky ATG 6.00 15.00
102 Martin Brodeur ATG 3.00 8.00
103 Mark Messier ATG 1.50 4.00
104 John LeClair ATG 1.50 4.00
105 Jeremy Roenick ATG 1.50 4.00
106 Mario Lemieux ATG 5.00 12.00
107 Teemu Selanne ATG 1.25 3.00
108 Al MacInnis ATG 1.00 2.50
109 Curtis Joseph ATG 1.25 3.00
110 Jaromir Jagr ATG 2.00 5.00
111 Dany Heatley FG 2.50 6.00
112 Mike Comrie FG 1.00 2.50
113 David Legwand FG 1.00 2.50
114 Justin Williams FG .75 2.00
115 Mike Van Ryn FG .75 2.00
116 Alex Tanguay FG 3.00 8.00
117 Manny Fernandez FG 1.00 2.50
118 Martin Havlat FG 1.00 2.50
119 Kris Beech FG .75 2.00
120 Nikolai Antropov FG .75 2.00
121 Patrik Stefan FG .75 2.00
122 Steven Reinprecht FG .75 2.00
123 Marian Gaborik FG 4.00 10.00
124 Pavel Brendl FG 1.00 2.50
125 Brad Stuart FG .75 2.00
126 Martin Biron FG 1.00 2.50
127 Eric Belanger FG .75 2.00
128 Rick DiPietro FG 1.00 2.50
129 Ladislav Nagy FG .75 2.00
130 Brad Richards FG 1.00 2.50
131 Ilja Bryzgalov RC 4.00 10.00
132 Timo Parssinen RC 2.00 5.00
133 Kevin Sawyer RC 2.00 5.00
134 Brian Pothier RC 2.00 5.00
135 Kamil Piros RC 2.00 5.00
136 Ivan Huml RC .10 .30
137 Scott Nichol RC 2.00 5.00
138 Jukka Hentunen RC 2.00 5.00
139 Erik Cole RC 4.00 10.00
140 Casey Hankinson RC 2.00 5.00
141 Jaroslav Obsut RC 2.00 5.00
142 Jody Shelley RC 2.00 5.00
143 Matt Davidson RC 2.00 5.00
144 Niko Kapanen RC 2.00 5.00
145 Pavel Datsyuk RC 25.00 60.00
146 Ty Conklin RC 2.00 5.00
147 Sean Selmser RC 2.00 5.00
148 Jason Chimera RC 2.00 5.00
149 Andrej Podkonicky RC 2.00 5.00
150 Niklas Hagman RC 2.00 5.00
151 Jaroslav Bednar RC 2.00 5.00
152 Mike Matteucci RC 2.00 5.00
153 Pascal Dupuis RC 2.00 5.00
154 Francis Belanger RC 2.00 5.00
155 Martti Jarventie SP 2.00 5.00
156 Pavel Skrbek RC 2.00 5.00
157 Martin Erat RC 2.00 5.00
158 Andreas Salomonsson RC 2.00 5.00
159 Scott Clemmensen RC 2.00 5.00
160 Josef Boumedienne RC 2.00 5.00
161 Peter Smrek RC 2.00 5.00
162 Mikael Samuelsson RC 2.00 5.00
163 Radek Martinek RC 2.00 5.00
164 Joel Kwiatkowski RC 2.00 5.00
165 Ivan Ciernik RC 2.00 5.00
166 Chris Neil RC 2.00 5.00
167 Jiri Dopita RC 2.00 5.00
168 Vaclav Pletka RC 2.00 5.00
169 David Cullen RC 2.00 5.00
170 Jeff Jillson RC 2.00 5.00
171 Mark Rycroft RC 2.00 5.00
172 Nikita Alexeev RC 2.00 5.00
173 Ryan Tobler RC 2.00 5.00
174 Bob Wren RC 2.00 5.00
175 Ilya Kovalchuk AU RC 125.00 250.00
176 Vaclav Nedorost RC AU 6.00 15.00
177 Kristian Huselius AU RC 12.50 30.00
178 Dan Blackburn AU RC 6.00 15.00
179 Krys Kolanos AU RC 5.00 12.00
180 Raffi Torres 15.00 40.00
NNO Pavel Bure SAMPLE 1.00 2.50

2001-02 SP Authentic Limited

This 150-card set paralleled the base set but each cards was serial-numbered out of 150.
*LIMITED: 1.5X TO 4X BASIC CARD
*LTD SP's: .75X TO 2X BASIC CARD
*LTD ROOKIES: .3X TO .75X BASIC CARD
175 Ilya Kovalchuk AU 200.00 400.00
176 Vaclav Nedorost AU 6.00 15.00
177 Kristian Huselius AU 10.00 25.00
178 Dan Blackburn AU 8.00 20.00
179 Krys Kolanos AU 5.00 12.00
180 Raffi Torres AU 12.50 30.00

2001-02 SP Authentic Limited Gold

This 150-card set paralleled the base set but each card was serial-numbered out of 25.
*LTD.GOLD: 10X TO 25X BASIC CARD
*SP's: 6X TO 15X
*ROOKIES: .75X TO 2X
*ROOKIE AU: .5X TO 1.25X
175 Ilya Kovalchuk AU 400.00 550.00

2001-02 SP Authentic Buybacks

Randomly inserted into packs, this 41-card set featured original Upper Deck cards that were purchased from the secondary market and autographed. Print runs for each card are listed below. Cards with a stated print

run of less than 20 are not priced due to scarcity.
1 A.Irbe 00SPGU/8
2 B.Orr 98UDCL/2
3 B.Orr 99UDR/4
4 C.Joseph 00BDGG/4
5 C.Joseph 99WGTOG/3
6 C.Joseph 99UDMVPSC/31 40.00 100.00
7 D.Heatley 00UD/50 200.00 400.00
8 G.Howe 00UDLGJ/9
9 D.Weight 91UD/20
10 G.Howe 98UDCL/3
11 J.LeClair 00UDGJ/5
12 J.LeClair 99UDLJ/10
13 M.Biron 00BDGG/41 25.00 60.00
14 M.Brodeur 00UDLGJ/30 60.00 150.00
15 M.Comrie 00SPA/1
16 M.Comrie 00BD/37 30.00 80.00
17 M.Gaborik 00UD/32 50.00 125.00
18 M.Havlat 00UD/37 60.00 150.00
19 M.Modano 00UDLGJ/9
20 M.Modano 90UD/75 20.00 50.00
21 M.Turco 00UD/37 30.00 80.00
22 O.Kolzig 00BDGG/20
23 P.Bondra 90UD/10
24 P.Bure 90UD/6
25 R.Blake 90UD/4
26 R.Bourque 99MVPSCGS/20
27 R.Bourque 00UDLGJ/7
28 R.DiPietro 00UD/31 25.00 60.00
29 R.Brind'Amour 90UD/95 12.50 30.00
30 R.Klesla 00UD/46 25.00 60.00
31 S.Hartnell 00UD/84 15.00 40.00
32 S.Yzerman 99UDGJ/1
33 S.Yzerman 99UDGJP/1
34 S.Yzerman 99MVPSCGS/7
35 T.Salo 00BDGG/5
36 T.Salo 00BDGG/8
37 T.Selanne 00UDGJ/8
38 T.Selanne BDGG/3
39 Teemu Selanne 99MVPSCGS/13
40 W.Gretzky 00UDGJ/3
41 W.Gretzky 98UDCL/1

2001-02 SP Authentic Jerseys

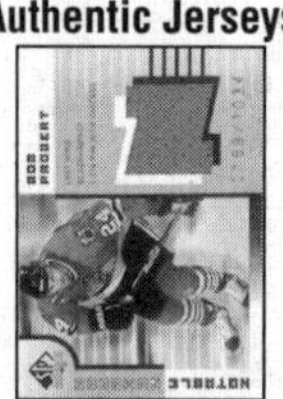

This 30-card set featured game-worn jersey swatches and were divided between two different subsets: Notable Numbers and Personal Prolifics. Each card was serial-numbered to an individual statistic for the featured player. All print runs are listed below.
*MULT.COLOR SWATCH: .75X TO 1.5X HI
NNBP Bob Probert/1034 8.00 20.00
NNBS Brendan Shanahan/955 4.00 10.00
NNCC Chris Chelios/1181 4.00 10.00
NNEL Eric Lindros/659 4.00 10.00
NNJK Jari Kurri/601 12.50 30.00
NNJL John LeClair/627 4.00 10.00
NNJS Joe Sakic/1178 12.50 30.00
NNKP Keith Primeau/496 4.00 10.00
NNMC Sandy McCarthy/1252 4.00 10.00
NNMG Mike Gartner/102 12.50 30.00
NNML Mario Lemieux/648 10.00 25.00
NNMM Mark Messier/651 4.00 10.00
NNMO Mike Modano/900 5.00 12.00
NNMR Mark Recchi/1010 4.00 10.00
NNPK Paul Kariya/531 4.00 10.00
NNRB Ray Bourque/1169 6.00 15.00
NNRT Rick Tocchet/950 4.00 10.00
NNSS Scott Stevens/1434 4.00 10.00
NNSY Steve Yzerman/1614 8.00 20.00
NNTD Tie Domi/1620 4.00 10.00
PPBH Brett Hull/86 20.00 50.00
PPJJ Jaromir Jagr/87 20.00 50.00
PPJS Joe Sakic/54 30.00 80.00
PPLR Luc Robitaille/63 15.00 40.00
PPMB Martin Brodeur/43 40.00 100.00
PPML Mario Lemieux/38 75.00 200.00
PPPR Patrick Roy/52 40.00 100.00
PPRB Ray Bourque/77 30.00 80.00
PPTS Teemu Selanne/76 25.00 60.00
PPWG Wayne Gretzky/92 60.00 150.00

2001-02 SP Authentic Sign of the Times

Randomly inserted into packs at overall odds of 1:24, this 82-card set featured autographs of one, two or three NHL players. Two player cards were serial-numbered out of 150 and triple player cards were serial-numbered to 25.
AI Arturs Irbe 6.00 15.00
AK Alexei Kovalev 4.00 10.00
AM Al MacInnis 6.00 15.00
BG Bill Guerin 4.00 10.00
BO Bobby Orr 100.00 250.00
BR Martin Brodeur 40.00 100.00
BS Brent Sopel 4.00 10.00
CJ Curtis Joseph 8.00 20.00
DH Dany Heatley 12.00 30.00
DS Daniel Sedin 6.00 15.00
DW Doug Weight 4.00 10.00
EB Ed Belfour 10.00 25.00
FP Felix Potvin 8.00 20.00
GH Gordie Howe 75.00 150.00
HA Martin Havlat 4.00 10.00
HE Johan Hedberg 4.00 10.00
HO Marian Hossa 6.00 15.00
HS Henrik Sedin 6.00 15.00
IK Ilya Kovalchuk 20.00 50.00
JA Jason Allison 4.00 10.00
JH Jochen Hecht 4.00 10.00
JI Jarome Iginla 10.00 25.00
JL John LeClair 8.00 20.00
JN Jeff O'Neill 4.00 10.00
JT Joe Thornton 12.50 30.00
KP Keith Primeau 4.00 10.00
MB Martin Biron 4.00 10.00
MC Mike Comrie 4.00 10.00
MF Manny Fernandez 6.00 15.00
MG Marian Gaborik 15.00 40.00
MH Milan Hejduk 8.00 20.00
MK Milan Kraft 4.00 10.00
MM Mike Modano 10.00 25.00
MN Markus Naslund 10.00 25.00
MR Mike Ribeiro 4.00 10.00
OK Olaf Kolzig 5.00 20.00
PB Pavel Bure 8.00 20.00
PR Patrick Roy/33 100.00 250.00
PS Patrik Stefan 4.00 10.00
RB Rob Blake 4.00 10.00
RB Rod Brind'Amour 4.00 10.00
RD Rick DiPietro 6.00 15.00
RK Rostislav Klesla 4.00 10.00
RL Roberto Luongo 20.00 50.00
SG Simon Gagne 8.00 20.00
SH Scott Hartnell 4.00 10.00
SY Steve Yzerman 30.00 80.00
TA Tony Amonte 4.00 10.00
TS Tommy Salo 4.00 10.00
TS Teemu Selanne 8.00 20.00
VL Vincent Lecavalier 8.00 20.00
WG Wayne Gretzky 125.00 250.00
ZP Zigmund Palffy 6.00 15.00
TRL Trevor Letowski 4.00 10.00
BB Martin Brodeur 40.00 100.00
Ed Belfour
BL Pavel Bure 12.50 30.00
Roberto Luongo
CH Mike Comrie 10.00 25.00
Jochen Hecht
DL Rick DiPietro 20.00 50.00
Roberto Luongo
ET Phil Esposito 30.00 80.00
Joe Thornton
FG Manny Fernandez 20.00 50.00
Marian Gaborik
GO Gordie Howe 200.00 400.00
Bobby Orr
HH Martin Havlat 15.00 40.00
Marian Hossa
HS Johan Hedberg 12.50 30.00
Tommy Salo
HT Marian Hossa 20.00 50.00
Joe Thornton
HY Gordie Howe 125.00 300.00
Steve Yzerman
IH Jarome Iginla 25.00 60.00
Milan Hejduk
LR John LeClair 10.00 25.00
Mark Recchi
PP Zigmund Palffy 12.50 30.00
Felix Potvin
SS Daniel Sedin 15.00 40.00
Henrik Sedin
TL Joe Thornton 25.00 60.00
Vincent Lecavalier
WM Doug Weight 10.00 25.00
Al MacInnis
YA S.Yzerman/J.Allison 30.00 80.00
BKK Pavel Bure 100.00 250.00
Ilya Kovalchuk
Alexei Kovalev
BOB Ray Bourque 250.00 450.00
Bobby Orr
Rob Blake
GWA Bill Guerin 40.00 100.00
Doug Weight
Tony Amonte
HBB Milan Hejduk 100.00 250.00
Ray Bourque
Rob Blake
HGY Gordie Howe 700.00 1500.00
Wayne Gretzky
Steve Yzerman
HHS Martin Havlat 40.00 100.00
Milan Hejduk
Petr Sykora
JBB Curtis Joseph 125.00 250.00
Martin Brodeur
Ed Belfour
PHG Zigmund Palffy 60.00 150.00
Marian Hossa
Marian Gaborik
SDP Tommy Salo 40.00 100.00
Rick DiPietro
Felix Potvin
SSN Daniel Sedin 40.00 100.00
Henrik Sedin
Markus Naslund

2002-03 SP Authentic

Released in late February, this 219-card set consisted of 90 veteran base cards, 15 shortprinted "Hat Trick" subset cards (serial-numbered to 1499), 30 shortprinted "Future Great" subset cards (serial numbered to 2003), 60 shortprinted rookies (serial-numbered to 900) and 20 shortprinted rookie autographs (serial-numbered to 999). Cards 202-218 were available only in packs of UD Rookie Update.
COMP.SET w/o SP's (90) 25.00 50.00
1 J-S Giguere .25 .60
2 Paul Kariya .30 .75
3 Adam Oates .25 .60
4 Dany Heatley .40 1.00
5 Ilya Kovalchuk .40 1.00
6 Joe Thornton .50 1.25
7 Sergei Samsonov .25 .60
8 Steve Shields .25 .60
9 Martin Biron .25 .60
10 Miroslav Satan .25 .60
11 Tim Connolly .10 .30
12 Jarome Iginla .40 1.00
13 Roman Turek .25 .60
14 Arturs Irbe .25 .60
15 Rod Brind'Amour .25 .60
16 Ron Francis .25 .60
17 Alexei Zhamnov .10 .30
18 Eric Daze .25 .60
19 Jocelyn Thibault .25 .60
20 Chris Drury .25 .60
21 Joe Sakic .60 1.50
22 Patrick Roy 1.50 4.00
23 Peter Forsberg .75 2.00
24 Rob Blake .25 .60
25 Ray Whitney .10 .30
26 Marc Denis .25 .60
27 Rostislav Klesla .10 .30
28 Bill Guerin .25 .60
29 Marty Turco .25 .60
30 Mike Modano .50 1.25
31 Brendan Shanahan .30 .75
32 Brett Hull .40 1.00
33 Curtis Joseph .30 .75
34 Nicklas Lidstrom .30 .75
35 Sergei Fedorov .50 1.25
36 Steve Yzerman 1.50 4.00
37 Mike Comrie .25 .60
38 Tommy Salo .25 .60
39 Anson Carter .25 .60
40 Roberto Luongo .40 1.00
41 Olli Jokinen .25 .60
42 Felix Potvin .30 .75
43 Zigmund Palffy .25 .60
44 Jason Allison .10 .30
45 Manny Fernandez .25 .60
46 Marian Gaborik .60 1.50
47 Jose Theodore .40 1.00
48 Saku Koivu .30 .75
49 Yanic Perreault .10 .30
50 Tomas Vokoun .25 .60
51 David Legwand .25 .60
52 Scott Hartnell .10 .30
53 Martin Brodeur .75 2.00
54 Patrik Elias .25 .60
55 Jeff Friesen .10 .30
56 Alexei Yashin .10 .30
57 Chris Osgood .25 .60
58 Michael Peca .10 .30
59 Eric Lindros .30 .75
60 Bobby Holik .10 .30
61 Pavel Bure .30 .75
62 Daniel Alfredsson .25 .60
63 Marian Hossa .30 .75
64 Patrick Lalime .25 .60
65 Jeremy Roenick .30 .75
66 Roman Cechmanek .25 .60
67 Simon Gagne .30 .75
68 John LeClair .30 .75
69 Sean Burke .25 .60
70 Tony Amonte .25 .60
71 Daniel Briere .10 .30
72 Alexei Kovalev .25 .60
73 Mario Lemieux 2.00 5.00
74 Evgeni Nabokov .25 .60
75 Owen Nolan .25 .60
76 Teemu Selanne .30 .75
77 Doug Weight .25 .60
78 Pavol Demitra .10 .30
79 Keith Tkachuk .30 .75
80 Nikolai Khabibulin .30 .75
81 Vincent Lecavalier .30 .75
82 Alexander Mogilny .25 .60
83 Ed Belfour .30 .75
84 Mats Sundin .30 .75
85 Markus Naslund .30 .75
86 Ed Jovanovski .25 .60
87 Todd Bertuzzi .30 .75
88 Jaromir Jagr .50 1.25
89 Olaf Kolzig .25 .60
90 Peter Bondra .25 .60
91 Paul Kariya HT 1.25 3.00
92 Joe Thornton HT 2.00 5.00
93 Jarome Iginla HT 1.50 4.00
94 Joe Sakic HT 2.50 6.00
95 Peter Forsberg HT 3.00 8.00
96 Steve Yzerman HT 6.00 15.00
97 Brendan Shanahan HT 2.00 5.00
98 Brett Hull HT 1.50 4.00
99 Wayne Gretzky HT 6.00 15.00
100 Eric Lindros HT 2.00 5.00
101 Pavel Bure HT 1.50 4.00
102 Mario Lemieux HT 8.00 20.00
103 Keith Tkachuk HT 1.25 3.00
104 Todd Bertuzzi HT 1.00 2.5
105 Peter Bondra HT 1.00 2.5
106 Andy McDonald FG 1.50 4.0
107 Dany Heatley FG 2.50 6.0
108 Ilya Kovalchuk FG 2.00 5.0
109 Ivan Huml FG 1.50 4.0
110 Maxim Afinogenov FG 1.50 4.0
111 Jaroslav Svoboda FG 1.50 4.0
112 Kyle Calder FG 1.50 4.0
113 Radim Vrbata FG 1.50 4.0
114 Rostislav Klesla FG 1.50 4.0
115 Pavel Datsyuk FG 2.50 6.0
116 Mike Comrie FG 2.00 5.0
117 Marcus Nilsson FG 1.50 4.0
118 Kristian Huselius FG 1.50 4.0
119 Marian Gaborik FG 2.00 5.0
120 Mike Ribeiro FG 1.50 4.0
121 Scott Hartnell FG 1.50 4.0
122 Brian Gionta FG 1.50 4.0
123 Raffi Torres FG 1.50 4.0
124 Dan Blackburn FG 2.00 5.0
125 Tom Poti FG 1.50 4.0
126 Petr Schastlivy FG 1.50 4.0
127 Pavel Brendl FG 1.50 4.0
128 Brian Boucher FG 2.00 5.0
129 Ville Nieminen FG 1.50 4.0
130 Jeff Jillson FG 1.50 4.0
131 Justin Papineau FG 1.50 4.0
132 Brad Richards FG 2.00 5.0
133 Nikita Alexeev FG 1.50 4.0
134 Nikolai Antropov FG 1.50 4.0
135 Matt Pettinger FG 1.50 4.0
136 Martin Gerber RC 6.00 15.0
137 Tim Thomas RC 6.00 15.0
138 Micki Dupont RC 2.00 5.0
139 Shawn Thornton RC 2.00 5.0
140 Matt Henderson RC 2.00 5.0
141 Jeff Paul RC 2.00 5.0
142 Lasse Pirjeta RC 2.00 5.0
143 Dmitri Bykov RC 2.00 5.0
144 Alex Henry RC 2.00 5.0
145 Kari Haakana RC 2.00 5.0
146 Ivan Majesky RC 2.00 5.0
147 Sylvain Blouin RC 2.00 5.0
148 Stephane Veilleux RC 2.00 5.0
149 Greg Koehler RC 2.00 5.0
150 Ray Schultz RC 2.00 5.0
151 Tomi Pettinen RC 2.00 5.0
152 Eric Godard RC 2.00 5.0
153 Dennis Seidenberg RC 2.00 5.0
154 Radovan Somik RC 2.00 5.0
155 Patrick Sharp RC 2.00 5.0
156 Lynn Loyns RC 2.00 5.0
157 Tom Koivisto RC 2.00 5.0
158 Curtis Sanford RC 5.00 12.0
159 Cody Rudkowsky RC 2.00 5.0
160 Steve Eminger RC 2.00 5.0
161 Shaone Morrisonn RC 2.00 5.0
162 Anton Volchenkov RC 2.00 5.0
163 Carlo Colaiacovo RC 2.00 5.0
164 Rickard Wallin RC 2.00 5.0
165 Matt Walker RC 2.00 5.0
166 Ryan Miller RC 25.00 60.0
167 Levente Szuper RC 2.00 5.0
168 Tomas Malec RC 2.00 5.0
169 Jim Fahey RC 2.00 5.0
170 Jonathan Hedstrom RC 2.00 5.0
171 Michael Leighton RC 2.00 5.0
172 Dany Sabourin RC 2.00 5.0
173 Mike Cammalleri RC 8.00 20.0
174 Craig Andersson RC 2.00 5.0
175 Darren Haydar RC 3.00 8.0
176 Vernon Fiddler RC 2.00 5.0
177 Curtis Murphy RC 2.00 5.0
178 Jared Aulin RC 2.00 5.0
179 Ian MacNeil RC 2.00 5.0
180 Dick Tarnstrom RC 2.00 5.0
181 Alexei Smirnov AU RC 6.00 15.0
182 Stanislav Chistov AU RC 6.00 15.0
183 Chuck Kobasew AU RC 8.00 20.0
184 Rick Nash AU RC 50.00 100.0
185 Pascal LeClaire AU RC 10.00 25.0
186 Henrik Zetterberg AU RC 40.00 100.0
187 Jay Bouwmeester AU RC 12.00 30.0
188 Alexander Frolov AU RC 15.00 40.0
189 Ron Hainsey AU RC 6.00 15.0
190 Adam Hall AU RC 6.00 15.0
191 Jason Spezza AU RC 75.00 150.0
192 Jeff Taffe AU RC 6.00 15.0
193 Kurt Sauer AU RC 6.00 15.0
194 Alexander Svitov AU RC 6.00 15.0
195 Mikael Tellqvist AU RC 10.00 25.0
196 Jordan Leopold AU RC 6.00 15.0
197 Ales Hemsky AU RC 15.00 40.0
198 P-M Bouchard AU RC 8.00 20.0
199 Scottie Upshall AU RC 8.00 20.0
200 Brooks Orpik AU RC 6.00 15.0
201 Steve Ott AU RC 6.00 15.0
202 Igor Radulov RC 2.00 5.0
203 Alexei Semenov RC 2.00 5.0
204 Mike Komisarek RC 5.00 12.0
205 Tomas Surovy RC 2.00 5.0
206 Jason Bacashihua RC 5.00 12.0
207 Ray Emery RC 8.00 20.0
208 Fernando Pisani RC 6.00 15.0
209 Simon Gamache RC 3.00 8.0
210 Ari Ahonen RC 3.00 8.0
211 Brandon Reid RC 3.00 8.0
212 Ryan Bayda RC 2.00 5.0
213 Niko Dimitrakos RC 3.00 8.0
214 Rob Davison RC 2.00 5.0
215 Konstantin Koltsov RC 6.00 15.00
216 Jarret Stoll RC 6.00 15.00
217 Cristobal Huet RC 12.00 30.00
218 Jason King RC 3.00 5.00
219 Tomas Kurka RC 2.00 5.00

2002-03 SP Authentic Beckett Promos

Inserted into copies of the April 2003 issue of Beckett Hockey Collector, this 90-card se parallels the base SP Authentic set bu carried a silver foil "UD Promo" stamp across the card fronts. Due to the type o distribution and the wide range of prices realized by these cards in the secondary market, they are not priced.
NOT PRICED DUE TO SCARCITY

2002-03 SP Authentic Legendary Cuts

s three card set featured cut autographs some of the pioneers of the sport. Only card was produced of Brimsek and two e produced of Abel and Adams. Please e that there is some controversy rounding the authenticity of one of the k Adams cuts. These cards are not priced to scarcity.

FB Frank Brimsek/1
JA Jack Adams/2
SA Sid Abel/2

2002-03 SP Authentic Sign of the Times

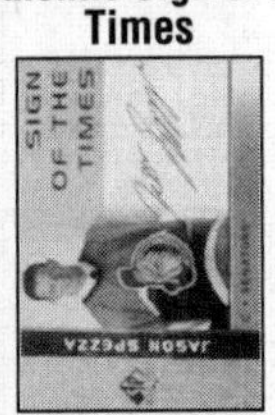

s 33-card set carried authentic player ographs of one, two or three NHL players. gle autographs were inserted at 1:96 cks, Dual autographs were serial-nbered to 99 sets and triple autographs e serial-numbered to 25 sets.

Alexander Frolov 15.00 40.00
Pavel Brendl 5.00 12.00
Bobby Orr SP 100.00 200.00
Curtis Joseph SP 15.00 40.00
Dany Heatley 15.00 40.00
Erik Cole 5.00 12.00
Evgeni Nabokov SP 5.00 12.00
Gordie Howe 60.00 150.00
Ales Hemsky 12.00 30.00
Henrik Zetterberg 20.00 50.00
Jay Bouwmeester 15.00 40.00
Jarome Iginla 10.00 25.00
John LeClair 6.00 15.00
Joe Thornton 12.50 30.00
Justin Williams 5.00 12.00
Maxim Afinogenov 5.00 12.00
Martin Brodeur SP 75.00 200.00
Mike Comrie EXCH 8.00 20.00
Manny Fernandez 5.00 12.00
Martin Havlat 5.00 12.00
Milan Kraft 5.00 12.00
Markus Naslund 8.00 20.00
Nikolai Khabibulin SP 20.00 50.00
Pavel Bure 6.00 15.00
Patrick Roy 75.00 200.00
Ray Bourque 20.00 50.00
Rick Nash SP 40.00 100.00
Simon Gagne 6.00 15.00
Jason Spezza 25.00 60.00
Sergei Samsonov 5.00 12.00
Steve Yzerman 30.00 80.00
Teemu Selanne 6.00 15.00
Wayne Gretzky 125.00 250.00
Bobby Orr 75.00 200.00
Jay Bouwmeester
Patrick Roy 75.00 200.00
Ray Bourque
Mike Comrie 15.00 40.00
Jarome Iginla
Simon Gagne 12.50 30.00
Pavel Brendl
Wayne Gretzky 100.00 200.00
Mike Comrie
Simon Gagne 20.00 50.00
John LeClair
Wayne Gretzky 300.00 600.00
Gordie Howe
Ilya Kovalchuk 15.00 40.00
Maxim Afinogenov
Ilya Kovalchuk 40.00 100.00
Dany Heatley
Evgeni Nabokov 15.00 40.00
Nikolai Khabibulin
John Leclair 12.50 30.00
Justin Williams
Martin Brodeur 30.00 80.00
Maxime Ouellet
Bobby Orr 175.00 350.00
Ray Bourque
Teemu Selanne 12.50 30.00
Evgeni Nabokov
Joe Thornton 12.50 30.00
Sergei Samsonov
Jason Spezza 60.00 125.00
Henrik Zetterberg
S.Yzerman/G.Howe 150.00 300.00
S.Yzerman/H.Zetterberg 75.00 200.00
O Wayne Gretzky 1000.00 1500.00
Gordie Howe
Bobby Orr
CI Dany Heatley 75.00 200.00
Mike Comrie
Jarome Iginla
BT Bobby Orr 200.00 500.00
Ray Bourque
Joe Thornton
ZB Jason Spezza 125.00 250.00
Henrik Zetterberg
Jason Bouwmeester
TSB Joe Thornton 100.00 250.00
Sergei Samsonov
Ray Bourque

2002-03 SP Authentic Signed Patches

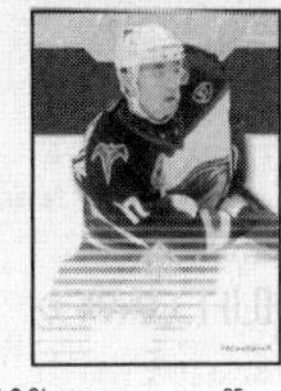

Limited to just 100 copies each, this 15-card set featured swatches of game jersey patches and authentic polayer autographs from some of the hottest rookies of the year.

*SINGLE COLOR: .25X TO .75X HI
PAF Alexander Frolov 75.00 200.00
PAH Ales Hemsky 75.00 200.00
PAS Alexander Svitov 30.00 80.00
PCK Chuck Kobasew 40.00 100.00
PHA Adam Hall 30.00 80.00
PHZ Henrik Zetterberg 150.00 300.00
PJB Jay Bouwmeester 75.00 150.00
PJL Jordan Leopold 30.00 80.00
PJS Jason Spezza 200.00 400.00
PPB P-M Bouchard 50.00 125.00
PRH Ron Hainsey 30.00 80.00
PRN Rick Nash 150.00 350.00
PSC Stanislav Chistov 30.00 80.00
PSM Alexei Smirnov 30.00 80.00
PSU Scottie Upshall 60.00 150.00

2002-03 SP Authentic Super Premiums

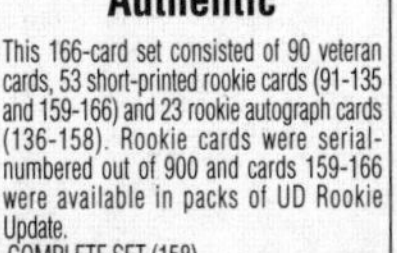

Randomly inserted, this memorabilia card set featured single, double or triple swatches of game used jerseys. Singles cards were serial-numbered to 599, doubles were numbered to 299 and triples were numbered to just 15. Triples are not priced due to scarcity.

SPAM Alexei Morozov 3.00 8.00
SPBG Bill Guerin 3.00 8.00
SPBI Martin Biron 3.00 8.00
SPBL Brian Leetch 3.00 8.00
SPBS Brendan Shanahan 5.00 12.00
SPDB Daniel Briere 3.00 8.00
SPDH Dan Hinote 3.00 8.00
SPEJ Ed Jovanovski 3.00 8.00
SPJA Jason Allison 3.00 8.00
SPJI Jarome Iginla 6.00 15.00
SPJJ Jaromir Jagr 6.00 15.00
SPJR Jeremy Roenick 6.00 15.00
SPJS Joe Sakic 8.00 20.00
SPJT Joe Thornton 6.00 15.00
SPMB Martin Brodeur 10.00 25.00
SPMD Marc Denis 3.00 8.00
SPML Mario Lemieux 10.00 25.00
SPMM Mike Modano 6.00 15.00
SPMN Markus Naslund 5.00 12.00
SPMS Mats Sundin 5.00 12.00
SPOK Olaf Kolzig 3.00 8.00
SPPF Peter Forsberg 6.00 15.00
SPPK Paul Kariya 5.00 12.00
SPPR Patrick Roy 10.00 25.00
SPSF Sergei Fedorov 6.00 15.00
SPSG Simon Gagne 5.00 12.00
SPSS Sergei Samsonov 3.00 8.00
SPSY Steve Yzerman 10.00 25.00
SPTH Jose Theodore 6.00 15.00
SPZP Zigmund Palffy 3.00 8.00
DPDS Chris Drury 6.00 15.00
Joe Sakic
DPFR Peter Forsberg 15.00 40.00
Patrick Roy
DPGL M.Lemieux/W.Gretzky 40.00 100.00
DPKJ Olaf Kolzig 8.00 20.00
Jaromir Jagr
DPMG M.Modano/B.Guerin 6.00 15.00
DPRG Jeremy Roenick 8.00 20.00
Simon Gagne
DPST Sergei Samsonov 10.00 25.00
Joe Thornton
DPTK Jose Theodore 12.50 30.00
Saku Koivu
DPYS S.Yzerman/B.Shanahan 15.00 40.00
TPGLY Lemieux/Gretzky/Yzerman
TPRBB Roy/Brodeur/Belfour
TPTBN Joe Thornton
Ray Bourque
Cam Neely

2003-04 SP Authentic

This 166-card set consisted of 90 veteran cards, 53 short-printed rookie cards (91-135 and 159-166) and 23 rookie autograph cards (136-158). Rookie cards were serial-numbered out of 900 and cards 159-166 were available in packs of UD Rookie Update.

COMPLETE SET (158)
COMP.SET w/o SP's (90) 15.00 30.00

1 J-S Giguere .25 .60
2 Sergei Fedorov .40 1.00
3 Stanislav Chistov .12 .30
4 Dany Heatley .40 1.00
5 Ilya Kovalchuk .40 1.00
6 Felix Potvin .30 .75
7 Joe Thornton .50 1.25
8 Sergei Samsonov .25 .60
9 Chris Drury .25 .60
10 Daniel Briere .12 .30
11 Martin Biron .25 .60
12 Jarome Iginla .40 1.00
13 Roman Turek .25 .60
14 Jamie Storr .25 .60
15 Ron Francis .25 .60
16 Alexei Zhamnov .12 .30
17 Jocelyn Thibault .25 .60
18 Tyler Arnason .25 .60
19 David Aebischer .25 .60
20 Joe Sakic .60 1.50
21 Paul Kariya .30 .75
22 Peter Forsberg .60 1.50
23 Marc Denis .25 .60
24 Rick Nash .40 1.00
25 Todd Marchant .12 .30
26 Bill Guerin .25 .60
27 Marty Turco .25 .60
28 Mike Modano .50 1.25
29 Dominik Hasek .60 1.50
30 Henrik Zetterberg .30 .75
31 Steve Yzerman 1.50 4.00
32 Ales Hemsky .25 .60
33 Raffi Torres .12 .30
34 Adam Oates .25 .60
35 Tommy Salo .25 .60
36 Jay Bouwmeester .12 .30
37 Olli Jokinen .25 .60
38 Roberto Luongo .40 1.00
39 Luc Robitaille .25 .60
40 Roman Cechmanek .25 .60
41 Zigmund Palffy .25 .60
42 Manny Fernandez .25 .60
43 Marian Gaborik .60 1.50
44 Pierre-Marc Bouchard .12 .30
45 Jose Theodore .40 1.00
46 Marcel Hossa .12 .30
47 Michael Ryder .40 1.00
48 Saku Koivu .25 .60
49 David Legwand .25 .60
50 Tomas Vokoun .25 .60
51 Martin Brodeur .75 2.00
52 Patrik Elias .25 .60
53 Scott Gomez .12 .30
54 Scott Stevens .25 .60
55 Alexei Yashin .12 .30
56 Michael Peca .12 .30
57 Rick DiPietro .25 .60
58 Eric Lindros .30 .75
59 Mark Messier .30 .75
60 Mike Dunham .25 .60
61 Jason Spezza .30 .75
62 Marian Hossa .30 .75
63 Patrick Lalime .25 .60
64 Jeff Hackett .25 .60
65 Jeremy Roenick .30 .75
66 Simon Gagne .30 .75
67 Mike Johnson .12 .30
68 Sean Burke .25 .60
69 Mario Lemieux 2.00 5.00
70 Martin Straka .12 .30
71 Evgeni Nabokov .25 .60
72 Patrick Marleau .25 .60
73 Vincent Damphousse .12 .30
74 Chris Osgood .25 .60
75 Doug Weight .25 .60
76 Keith Tkachuk .30 .75
77 Pavol Demitra .25 .60
78 Nikolai Khabibulin .30 .75
79 Vincent Lecavalier .30 .75
80 Alexander Mogilny .25 .60
81 Ed Belfour .30 .75
82 Mats Sundin .30 .75
83 Owen Nolan .25 .60
84 Ed Jovanovski .25 .60
85 Jason King .12 .30
86 Markus Naslund .30 .75
87 Todd Bertuzzi .30 .75
88 Jaromir Jagr .60 1.50
89 Olaf Kolzig .25 .60
90 Peter Bondra .25 .60
91 Andrew Hutchinson RC 2.00 5.00
92 Phil Osaer RC 2.00 5.00
93 Boyd Kane RC 2.00 5.00
94 Brent Krahn RC 4.00 10.00
95 Cody McCormick RC 2.00 5.00
96 Christoph Brandner RC 2.00 5.00
97 Dan Fritsche RC 2.00 5.00
98 David Hale RC 2.00 5.00
99 Esa Pirnes RC 2.00 5.00
100 Libor Pivko RC 2.00 5.00
101 Greg Campbell RC 2.00 5.00
102 John-Michael Liles RC 4.00 10.00
103 Mikhail Yakubov RC 2.00 5.00
104 Marek Svatos RC 12.00 30.00
105 Marek Zidlicky RC 4.00 10.00
106 Nathan Robinson RC 2.00 5.00
107 Matthew Lombardi RC 4.00 10.00
108 Matthew Spiller RC 2.00 5.00
109 Matt Murley RC 2.00 5.00
110 Maxim Kondratiev RC 2.00 5.00
111 Ryan Kesler RC 6.00 15.00
112 Paul Martin RC 2.00 5.00
113 Ryan Malone RC 8.00 20.00
114 Tim Gleason RC 2.00 5.00
115 Tom Preissing RC 2.00 5.00
116 Fredrik Sjostrom RC 2.00 5.00
117 Tony Martensson RC 2.00 5.00
118 Aaron Johnson RC 2.00 5.00
119 Seamus Kotyk RC 2.00 5.00
120 Pat Rissmiller RC 2.00 5.00
121 Jeff Hamilton RC 2.00 5.00
122 Sergei Zinovjev RC 2.00 5.00
123 Julien Vauclair RC 2.00 5.00
124 Nikolai Zherdev RC 8.00 20.00
125 Brent Burns RC 4.00 10.00
126 John Pohl RC 4.00 10.00
127 Dominic Moore RC 2.00 5.00
128 Rastislav Stana RC 2.00 5.00
129 Gavin Morgan RC 2.00 5.00
130 Darryl Bootland RC 2.00 5.00
131 Trevor Daley RC 2.00 5.00
132 Peter Sarno RC 2.00 5.00
133 Jed Ortmeyer RC 2.00 5.00
134 Nathan Smith RC 2.00 5.00
135 Grant McNeill RC 2.00 5.00
136 Joffrey Lupul AU RC 10.00 25.00
137 Eric Staal AU RC 50.00 100.00
138 Pavel Vorobiev AU RC 6.00 15.00
139 Tuomo Ruutu AU RC 12.00 30.00
140 Antoine Vermette AU RC 8.00 20.00
141 Antti Miettinen AU RC 6.00 15.00
142 Boyd Gordon AU RC 6.00 15.00
143 Nathan Horton AU RC 20.00 50.00
144 Tony Salmelainen AU RC 6.00 15.00
145 Christian Ehrhoff AU RC 6.00 15.00
146 Patrice Bergeron AU RC 25.00 60.00
147 Dan Hamhuis AU RC 6.00 15.00
148 Jordin Tootoo AU RC 12.00 30.00
149 Joni Pitkanen AU RC 8.00 20.00
150 Dustin Brown AU RC 8.00 20.00
151 Chris Higgins AU RC 15.00 40.00
152 Sean Bergenheim AU RC 6.00 15.00
153 Marc-Andre Fleury AU RC 60.00 125.00
154 Jiri Hudler AU RC 10.00 25.00
155 Milan Michalek AU RC 15.00 40.00
156 Peter Sejna AU RC 6.00 15.00
157 Matt Stajan AU RC 15.00 40.00
158 Alexander Semin AU RC 25.00 60.00
159 Niklas Kronwall RC 6.00 15.00
160 Derek Roy RC 8.00 20.00
161 Kyle Wellwood RC 8.00 20.00
162 Brad Boyes RC 6.00 15.00
163 Timofei Shishkanov RC 2.00 5.00
164 Jason Pominville RC 10.00 25.00
165 Aleksander Suglobov RC 2.00 5.00
166 Carl Corazzini RC 2.00 5.00

2003-04 SP Authentic Limited

*STARS: 4X TO 10X BASE HI
PRINT RUN 99 SER.#'d SETS
*ROOKIES: .75X TO 2X
*ROOKIE AUTOS: .6X TO 1.5X
ROOKIE PRINT RUN 50 SER.#'d SETS

2003-04 SP Authentic 10th Anniversary

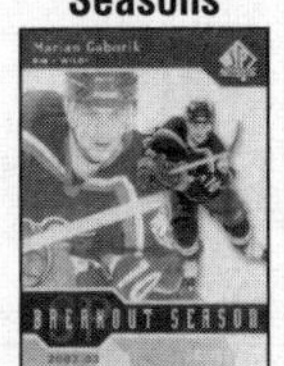

COMPLETE SET (20) 10.00 20.00
PRINT RUN 1994 SER.#'d SETS
*LIMITED: 1X TO 2.5X BASIC INSERTS
LTD PRINT RUN 99 SER.#'d SETS
SP1 Wayne Gretzky 2.50 6.00
SP2 Patrick Roy 1.50 4.00
SP3 Steve Yzerman 1.50 4.00
SP4 Mario Lemieux 2.00 5.00
SP5 Teemu Selanne .50 1.25
SP6 Joe Sakic 1.00 2.50
SP7 Jaromir Jagr .75 2.00
SP8 Sergei Fedorov .60 1.50
SP9 Mike Modano .75 2.00
SP10 Brett Hull .60 1.50
SP11 Jason Spezza .50 1.25
SP12 Joe Thornton .75 2.00
SP13 Rick Nash .60 1.50
SP14 Marian Gaborik 1.00 2.50
SP15 Ales Hemsky .40 1.00
SP16 Marian Hossa .50 1.25
SP17 J-S Giguere .40 1.00
SP18 Martin Brodeur 1.25 3.00
SP19 Todd Bertuzzi .50 1.25
SP20 Markus Naslund .50 1.25

2003-04 SP Authentic Breakout Seasons

PRINT RUN 500 SER.#'d SETS
*LIMITED: .75X TO 2X BASIC INSERTS
LTD PRINT RUN 99 SER.#'d SETS
B1 Steve Yzerman 5.00 12.00
B2 Martin Brodeur 5.00 12.00
B3 Nicklas Lidstrom 1.00 2.50
B4 Joe Thornton 1.50 4.00
B5 Jeremy Roenick 1.25 3.00
B6 Todd Bertuzzi 1.00 2.50
B7 Markus Naslund 1.00 2.50
B8 Sergei Fedorov 1.25 3.00
B9 Chris Pronger .75 2.00
B10 Zigmund Palffy .75 2.00
B11 Marian Gaborik 2.50 6.00
B12 Jose Theodore 1.25 3.00
B13 Mike Modano 1.50 4.00
B14 Vincent Lecavalier 1.00 2.50
B15 J-S Giguere .75 2.00
B16 Keith Tkachuk 1.00 2.50
B17 Mats Sundin 1.00 2.50
B18 Paul Kariya 1.00 2.50
B19 Jarome Iginla 1.25 3.00
B20 Jaromir Jagr 1.50 4.00
B21 Dominik Hasek 2.00 5.00
B22 Teemu Selanne 1.00 2.50
B23 Jocelyn Thibault .75 2.00
B24 Alexei Yashin .75 2.00
B25 Ilya Kovalchuk 1.25 3.00
B26 Marian Hossa 1.00 2.50
B27 Ed Belfour 1.00 2.50
B28 Peter Forsberg 3.00 8.00
B29 Mario Lemieux 6.00 15.00
B30 Saku Koivu 1.00 2.50

2003-04 SP Authentic Foundations

PRINT RUN 250 SER.#'d SETS
*LIMITED: .6X TO 1.5X BASIC INSERTS
LTD PRINT RUN 99 SER.#'d SETS
F1 S.Fedorov/J.Giguere 3.00 8.00
F2 J.Thornton/S.Samsonov 2.50 6.00
F3 P.Kariya/T.Selanne 2.50 6.00
F4 P.Forsberg/J.Sakic 5.00 12.00
F5 S.Yzerman/D.Hasek 3.00 8.00
F6 T.Bertuzzi/M.Naslund 2.50 6.00
F7 M.Modano/M.Turco 2.50 6.00
F8 M.Brodeur/S.Stevens 3.00 8.00
F9 M.Sundin/E.Belfour 4.00 10.00
F10 S.Koivu/J.Theodore 2.50 6.00

2003-04 SP Authentic Honors

PRINT RUN 900 SER.#'d SETS
*LIMITED: 1X TO 2.5X BASIC INSERTS
LTD PRINT RUN 99 SER.#'d SETS
H1 Wayne Gretzky 5.00 12.00
H2 Wayne Gretzky 5.00 12.00
H3 Wayne Gretzky 5.00 12.00
H4 Gordie Howe 4.00 10.00
H5 Gordie Howe 4.00 10.00
H6 Gordie Howe 4.00 10.00
H7 Scotty Bowman 1.00 2.50
H8 Scotty Bowman 1.00 2.50
H9 Scotty Bowman 1.00 2.50
H10 Don Cherry .60 1.50
H11 Don Cherry .60 1.50
H12 Patrick Roy 4.00 10.00
H13 Patrick Roy 4.00 10.00
H14 Bobby Clarke .60 1.50
H15 Marcel Dionne .60 1.50
H16 Guy Lafleur .60 1.50
H17 Mario Lemieux 5.00 12.00
H18 Jason Spezza .75 2.00
H19 J-S Giguere .60 1.50
H20 Mike Modano 1.25 3.00
H21 Rick Nash 1.00 2.50
H22 Todd Bertuzzi .75 2.00
H23 Marian Gaborik 1.50 4.00
H24 Martin Brodeur 2.00 5.00
H25 Joe Thornton 1.25 3.00
H26 Ed Belfour .75 2.00
H27 Saku Koivu .75 2.00
H28 Steve Yzerman 4.00 10.00
H29 Markus Naslund .75 2.00
H30 Marian Hossa .75 2.00

2003-04 SP Authentic Sign of the Times

This 77-card set featured certified autographs. Overall odds were stated at 1:24. Single player autos were inserted at 1:26, dual player autos were serial-numbered to 99 copies and triple player autos were serial-numbered to 25.

AF Alexander Frolov 6.00 15.00
AH Adam Hall 4.00 10.00
AS Alexei Smirnov 4.00 10.00
BC Bobby Clarke SP 25.00 60.00
BO Bobby Orr 75.00 200.00
CK Chuck Kobasew 4.00 10.00
DA David Aebischer 4.00 10.00
DC Don Cherry 15.00 40.00
EL Eric Lindros SP 20.00 50.00
GL Guy Lafleur SP 20.00 50.00
HZ Henrik Zetterberg 10.00 25.00
IK Ilya Kovalchuk 10.00 25.00
JI Jarome Iginla 12.50 30.00
JK Jari Kurri 8.00 20.00
JL Jordan Leopold 4.00 10.00
JN Joe Nieuwendyk 4.00 10.00
JP Joni Pitkanen 4.00 10.00
JR Jeremy Roenick 10.00 25.00
JS Jason Spezza 12.50 30.00
JT Jose Theodore 10.00 25.00
KL Eric Staal SP 25.00 60.00
LM Lanny McDonald 10.00 25.00
MB Martin Brodeur 50.00 125.00
MC Mike Comrie 4.00 10.00
MG Marian Gaborik 10.00 25.00
MH Gordie Howe 40.00 80.00
MT Marty Turco 5.00 12.00
MT Mikael Tellqvist SP 15.00 40.00
PE Phil Esposito SP 30.00 80.00
PL Pascal Leclaire 4.00 10.00
PR Patrick Roy SP 75.00 150.00
RN Rick Nash 15.00 40.00
SB Scotty Bowman SP 25.00 60.00
SC Stanislav Chistov 4.00 10.00
SF Sergei Fedorov 10.00 25.00
SG Curtis Joseph 6.00 15.00
SH Scott Hartnell 4.00 10.00
SK Saku Koivu SP 30.00 80.00
SM Stan Mikita 15.00 40.00
SS Sergei Samsonov 4.00 10.00
TB Todd Bertuzzi 8.00 20.00
TR Tuomo Ruutu 8.00 20.00
WG Wayne Gretzky 75.00 200.00
ZP Zigmund Palffy 5.00 12.00
AHY Ales Hemsky 5.00 12.00
JLC John LeClair 4.00 10.00
JSG J-S Giguere 5.00 12.00
JTH Joe Thornton 12.50 30.00
MAF Marc-Andre Fleury 25.00 60.00
MHA Marian Hossa 6.00 15.00
BL P.Bure/E.Lindros 15.00 40.00
CF S.Chistov/S.Fedorov 15.00 40.00
CH M.Comrie/A.Hemsky 10.00 25.00
CR B.Clarke/J.Roenick 20.00 50.00
ET P.Esposito/J.Thornton 30.00 80.00
FG S.Fedorov/J.Giguere 20.00 50.00
FS E.Staal/M.Fleury 60.00 150.00
GK W.Gretzky/J.Kurri 125.00 250.00
GR J.Giguere/P.Roy 50.00 125.00
HS M.Hossa/J.Spezza 25.00 60.00
IM J.Iginla/L.McDonald 20.00 50.00
NB M.Naslund/T.Bertuzzi 20.00 50.00
NL R.Nash/P.Leclaire 25.00 60.00
TK J.Theodore/S.Koivu 20.00 50.00
BCY S.Bowman/D.Cherry 75.00 150.00
BTG Bossy/Trottier/Gillies 100.00 250.00
CRG Clarke/Roenick/Gagne 75.00 200.00
GCF Giggy/Chistov/Fedrv 75.00 150.00
GKF Gretzky/Kurri/Fuhr 500.00 750.00
GMM Howe/Howe/Howe 250.00 400.00
GTS Gretzky/Thornton/Spezza 250.00 500.00
LFR Staal/Fleury/Ruutu 150.00 300.00
NSZ Nash/Spezza/Zetterberg 150.00 250.00
PAF Palffy/Aulin/Frolov 60.00 150.00
RGB Roy/Giguere/Brodeur 250.00 500.00

2003-04 SP Authentic Signed Patches

This 18-card set featured autographs as well as jersey patches from some of the hottest rookies of the 2003-04 season. Each card was serial-numbered to 100.

*SINGLE COLOR: .25X TO .75X
AM Antti Miettinen 25.00 60.00
AS Alexander Semin 100.00 200.00
CH Chris Higgins 60.00 150.00
DB Dustin Brown 50.00 125.00
DH Dan Hamhuis 40.00 100.00
ES Eric Staal 125.00 350.00
JH Jiri Hudler 50.00 125.00
JL Joffrey Lupul 40.00 100.00
JP Joni Pitkanen 40.00 100.00
JT Jordin Tootoo 75.00 200.00
MF Marc-Andre Fleury 200.00 450.00
MS Matt Stajan 60.00 150.00
NH Nathan Horton 60.00 150.00
PB Patrice Bergeron 100.00 250.00
PS Peter Sejna 25.00 60.00
SB Sean Bergenheim 25.00 60.00
TR Tuomo Ruutu 60.00 125.00
TS Tony Salmelainen 25.00 60.00

2003-04 SP Authentic Special Cuts

This 5-card set featured cut signatures of legendary players. Each card was serial-numbered 1/1.

NOT PRICED DUE TO SCARCITY
AC Alex Connell
AR Art Ross
HL Harry Lumley
TB Turk Broda
PROD Lindsay/Abel/Howe

2004-05 SP Authentic

This 150-card set was released in late May 2005, it consisted of 90 veteran player cards, 6 rookie cards and 54 All-World subset cards which were inserted at one per pack.

COMPLETE SET (150) 30.00 80.00
COMP.SET w/o SP's (90) 8.00 20.00
1 J-S Giguere .25 .60
2 Joffrey Lupul .12 .30
3 Sergei Fedorov .40 1.00
4 Dany Heatley .40 1.00
5 Ilya Kovalchuk .40 1.00
6 Kari Lehtonen .25 .60
7 Andrew Raycroft .25 .60
8 Joe Thornton .50 1.25
9 Patrice Bergeron .25 .60
10 Glen Murray .12 .30
11 Mika Noronen .25 .60
12 Miroslav Satan .25 .60
13 Maxim Afinogenov .12 .30
14 Jarome Iginla .40 1.00
15 Matthew Lombardi .12 .30
16 Miikka Kiprusoff .25 .60
17 Eric Staal .12 .30
18 Erik Cole .12 .30
19 Tyler Arnason .25 .60
20 Tuomo Ruutu .25 .60
21 David Aebischer .25 .60
22 Joe Sakic .60 1.50
23 Peter Forsberg .60 1.50
24 Milan Hejduk .30 .75
25 Alex Tanguay .25 .60
26 Rick Nash .40 1.00
27 Nikolai Zherdev .12 .30
28 Mike Modano .50 1.25
29 Bill Guerin .25 .60
30 Marty Turco .25 .60
31 Manny Legace .25 .60
32 Pavel Datsyuk .30 .75
33 Brendan Shanahan .30 .75
34 Steve Yzerman 1.25 3.00
35 Henrik Zetterberg .30 .75
36 Jason Smith .12 .30
37 Ryan Smyth .12 .30
38 Ty Conklin .25 .60
39 Nathan Horton .12 .30
40 Roberto Luongo .40 1.00
41 Olli Jokinen .25 .60
42 Alexander Frolov .12 .30
43 Zigmund Palffy .25 .60
44 Marian Gaborik .50 1.25
45 Manny Fernandez .25 .60
46 Michael Ryder .12 .30
47 Jose Theodore .30 .75
48 Saku Koivu .30 .75
49 Steve Sullivan .12 .30
50 Jordin Tootoo .12 .30
51 Tomas Vokoun .25 .60
52 Martin Brodeur .75 2.00
53 Patrik Elias .25 .60
54 Scott Stevens .25 .60
55 Eric Lindros .30 .75
56 Mark Messier .30 .75
57 Jaromir Jagr .50 1.25
58 Michael Peca .12 .30
59 Rick DiPietro .25 .60
60 Daniel Alfredsson .25 .60
61 Marian Hossa .30 .75
62 Jason Spezza .30 .75
63 Martin Havlat .25 .60
64 Dominik Hasek .60 1.50
65 Jeremy Roenick .40 1.00
66 Robert Esche .25 .60
67 Simon Gagne .30 .75
68 Brett Hull .40 1.00
69 Mike Comrie .25 .60
70 Shane Doan .12 .30
71 Marc-Andre Fleury .25 .60
72 Mario Lemieux 2.00 5.00
73 Mark Recchi .25 .60
74 Evgeni Nabokov .25 .60
75 Patrick Marleau .25 .60
76 Chris Pronger .25 .60
77 Doug Weight .25 .60
78 Keith Tkachuk .30 .75
79 Brad Richards .25 .60
80 Nikolai Khabibulin .30 .75
81 Martin St. Louis .25 .60
82 Vincent Lecavalier .30 .75
83 Owen Nolan .25 .60
84 Ed Belfour .30 .75
85 Mats Sundin .30 .75
86 Gary Roberts .12 .30
87 Ed Jovanovski .12 .30
88 Markus Naslund .30 .75
89 Trevor Linden .12 .30
90 Olaf Kolzig .25 .60
91 Brad Fast RC 1.25 3.00
92 Brennan Evans RC 1.25 3.00
93 Layne Ulmer RC 1.25 3.00
94 Mel Angelstad RC 1.25 3.00
95 Garret Stroshein RC 1.25 3.00
96 Marcel Goc RC 1.50 4.00
97 Sergei Fedorov AW 1.00 2.50
98 Dany Heatley AW 1.00 2.50
99 Joe Thornton AW 1.25 3.00
100 Glen Murray AW .60 1.50
101 Ilya Kovalchuk AW 1.00 2.50
102 Miroslav Satan AW .60 1.50
103 Jarome Iginla AW 1.00 2.50
104 Eric Daze AW .60 1.50
105 Paul Kariya AW .75 2.00
106 Peter Forsberg AW 1.25 3.00
107 Joe Sakic AW 1.50 4.00
108 Patrick Roy AW 3.00 8.00

2004-05 SP Authentic

109 Milan Hejduk AW .75 2.00
110 Mike Modano AW 1.25 3.00
111 Bill Guerin AW .60 1.50
112 Nicklas Lidstrom AW .75 2.00
113 Steve Yzerman AW 2.50 6.00
114 Brendan Shanahan AW .75 2.00
115 Martin St. Louis AW .60 1.50
116 Roberto Luongo AW 1.00 2.50
117 Zigmund Palffy AW .60 1.50
118 Luc Robitaille AW .60 1.50
119 Marian Gaborik AW 1.25 3.00
120 Saku Koivu AW .75 2.00
121 Jose Theodore AW .75 2.00
122 Martin Brodeur AW 1.50 4.00
123 Scott Niedermayer AW .60 1.50
124 Scott Stevens AW .60 1.50
125 Patrik Elias AW .60 1.50
126 Alexei Yashin AW .60 1.50
127 Pavel Bure AW .75 2.00
128 Jaromir Jagr AW 1.25 3.00
129 Wayne Gretzky AW 4.00 10.00
130 Dominik Hasek AW 1.25 3.00
131 Marian Hossa AW .75 2.00
132 Daniel Alfredsson AW .60 1.50
133 Jeremy Roenick AW 1.00 2.50
134 Keith Primeau AW .60 1.50
135 John LeClair AW .75 2.00
136 Tony Amonte AW .60 1.50
137 Brett Hull AW 1.00 2.50
138 Mario Lemieux AW 3.00 8.00
139 Vincent Damphousse AW.60 1.50
140 Keith Tkachuk AW .75 2.00
141 Doug Weight AW .60 1.50
142 Chris Pronger AW .60 1.50
143 Vincent Lecavalier AW .75 2.00
144 Nikolai Khabibulin AW .75 2.00
145 Mats Sundin AW .75 2.00
146 Ed Belfour AW .75 2.00
147 Joe Nieuwendyk AW .60 1.50
148 Brian Leetch AW .75 2.00
149 Markus Naslund AW .75 2.00
150 Olaf Kolzig AW .60 1.50

2004-05 SP Authentic Limited

This skip-numbered parallel set featured certified autographs. Cards 1-90 were serial-numbered out of 10 and cards 97-150 were serial-numbered out of 25.

1-90 NOT PRICED DUE TO SCARCITY
1 J-S Giguere
2 Joffrey Lupul
4 Dany Heatley
5 Ilya Kovalchuk
6 Kari Lehtonen
7 Andrew Raycroft
8 Joe Thornton
9 Patrice Bergeron
11 Mika Noronen
13 Maxim Afinogenov
14 Jarome Iginla
15 Matthew Lombardi
17 Eric Staal
18 Erik Cole
19 Tyler Arnason
20 Tuomo Ruutu
21 David Aebischer
24 Milan Hejduk
25 Alex Tanguay
26 Rick Nash
27 Nikolai Zherdev
30 Marty Turco
31 Manny Legace
35 Henrik Zetterberg
37 Ryan Smyth
39 Nathan Horton
40 Roberto Luongo
42 Alexander Frolov
43 Zigmund Palffy
44 Marian Gaborik
46 Michael Ryder
47 Jose Theodore
49 Steve Sullivan
52 Martin Brodeur
58 Michael Peca
60 Daniel Alfredsson
61 Marian Hossa
62 Jason Spezza
63 Martin Havlat
64 Dominik Hasek
65 Jeremy Roenick
66 Robert Esche
67 Simon Gagne
70 Shane Doan
71 Marc-Andre Fleury
74 Evgeni Nabokov
76 Chris Pronger
77 Doug Weight
79 Brad Richards
80 Nikolai Khabibulin
81 Martin St. Louis
82 Vincent Lecavalier
84 Ed Belfour
87 Ed Jovanovski
88 Markus Naslund
98 Dany Heatley AW 20.00 50.00
99 Joe Thornton AW 30.00 80.00
101 Ilya Kovalchuk AW 25.00 60.00
103 Jarome Iginla AW 30.00 80.00
109 Milan Hejduk AW 20.00 50.00
115 Martin St. Louis AW 20.00 50.00
116 Roberto Luongo AW 30.00 80.00
117 Zigmund Palffy AW 20.00 50.00
118 Luc Robitaille AW 20.00 50.00
119 Marian Gaborik AW 30.00 80.00
120 Saku Koivu AW 25.00 60.00
121 Jose Theodore AW 30.00 80.00
129 Wayne Gretzky AW 200.00 400.00
130 Dominik Hasek AW 60.00 150.00
131 Marian Hossa AW 20.00 50.00
132 Daniel Alfredsson AW
133 Jeremy Roenick AW 25.00 60.00
134 Keith Primeau AW 20.00 50.00
141 Doug Weight AW 20.00 50.00
142 Chris Pronger AW 20.00 50.00
144 Nikolai Khabibulin AW 20.00 50.00
146 Ed Belfour AW 25.00 60.00
148 Brian Leetch AW 20.00 50.00
149 Markus Naslund AW 20.00 50.00

2004-05 SP Authentic Buybacks

This 201-card set followed the historical notion of "Buybacks" as being previously issued cards that were bought back by Upper Deck, autographed by the player and then serial-numbered for inclusion into SP Authentic. For 2004-05 SP Authentic, Upper Deck also bought back rookie cards and previously signed cards for inclusion in packs. Since those cards were not altered from their previous form, they are not listed seperately.

PRINT RUNS UNDER 25 NOT PRICED DUE TO SCARCITY
1 Ales Hemsky
03UD Ice/2
2 Ales Hemsky
03UD Rookie Update/32
3 Ales Hemsky
03SPx/1
4 Alex Tanguay
01UD Classic Portraits Starring Cast/2
5 Alex Tanguay
02SP Game Used Authentic Fabrics/4
6 Alex Tanguay
02SP Game Used Authentic Fabrics/7
7 Alex Tanguay
02SP Game Used First Rounders/4
8 Alex Tanguay
02SP Game Used Future Fabrics/8
9 Alex Tanguay
03Black Diamond Threads/10
10 Alexander Frolov
03Black Diamond Threads/12
11 Alexander Frolov
03SPx/1
12 Andrew Raycroft
03UD Ice/2
13 Andrew Raycroft 12.50 30.00
03UD Rookie Update/51
14 Bobby Clarke
99UD Century Legends Jerseys of the Century/3
15 Bobby Hull 25.00 60.00
04UD Legendary Signatures/38
16 Brian Leetch
02SP Authentic Super Premium/11
17 Brian Leetch
02SP Game Used Authentic Fabrics/6
18 Brian Leetch
02SP Game Used First Rounders/2
19 Brian Leetch
02UD Specialists/8
20 Brian Leetch
03UD Ice Icons/1
21 Chris Drury
01UD Classic Portraits Classic Stitches/16
22 Chris Drury
02SP Game Used Authentic Fabrics/11
23 Chris Drury
02SP Game Used Piece of History/7
24 Chris Drury
02SP Game Used Piece of History/4
25 Chris Drury
03UD Ice/2
26 Chris Drury
03UD Rookie Update/23
27 Daniel Briere
02SP Authentic Super Premium/16
28 Daniel Briere
02SP Game Used First Rounders/1
29 Daniel Briere
02SP Game Used Future Fabrics/10
30 Daniel Briere
02UD CHL Graduates/11
31 Daniel Briere
02UD Hot Spot/8
32 Daniel Briere
02UD Speed Demon/18
33 Daniel Briere
03Black Diamond Threads/12
34 Daniel Briere
03UD Ice/5
35 Daniel Briere 15.00 40.00
03UD Rookie Update/48
36 Dany Heatley
03UD Rookie Update/15
37 David Aebischer
02SP Game Used Future Fabrics/9
38 David Aebischer
03Beehive Red Sticks/5
39 David Aebischer
03Black Diamond Threads/9
40 David Aebischer
03UD Ice/5
41 David Aebischer 12.50 30.00
03UD Rookie Update/52
42 David Aebischer
03SP Game Used Authentic Fabrics/16
43 Dominik Hasek
01SP Game Used Authentic Fabrics/1
44 Doug Weight
03Beehive Game Jerseys/23
45 Doug Weight
03Black Diamond Threads/12
46 Doug Weight
03UD Ice/1
47 Doug Weight
03UD Rookie Update/39
48 Ed Belfour
01SP Game Used Authentic Fabrics/1
49 Ed Belfour
03UD Rookie Update/6
50 Ed Jovanovski
02SP Authentic Super Premium/21
51 Ed Jovanovski
02UD All Stars/7
52 Ed Jovanovski
03Beehive Beige Sticks/8
53 Ed Jovanovski
03Black Diamond Threads/10
54 Ed Jovanovski
03UD Ice/5
55 Ed Jovanovski 10.00 25.00
03UD Rookie Update/55
56 Evgeni Nabokov
03UD Ice/1
57 Evgeni Nabokov
03SPx/1
58 Gerry Cheevers 20.00 50.00
04UD Legendary Signatures/45
59 Gilbert Perreault
04UD Legendary Signatures/22
60 Glenn Hall
04UD Legendary Signatures/19
61 Gordie Howe
01SP Authentic All Stars/7
62 Grant Fuhr
04UD Legendary Signatures/16
63 Henrik Zetterberg
03UD Ice/1
64 Henrik Zetterberg 15.00 40.00
03UD Rookie Update/40
65 Henrik Zetterberg
03SP Game Used Jsy/18
66 Henrik Zetterberg
03SPx/1
67 Ilya Kovalchuk
02SP Game Used Authentic Fabrics/5
68 Ilya Kovalchuk
02SP Game Used First Rounders/2
69 Ilya Kovalchuk
03UD Rookie Update/17
70 Jari Kurri
01SP Authentic Notable Numbers/7
71 Jarome Iginla
02SP Authentic Super Premium/8
72 Jarome Iginla
03UD Rookie Update/12
73 Jason Spezza
03Black Diamond Threads/7
74 Jason Spezza
03UD Ice/2
75 Jason Spezza
03UD Rookie Update/39
76 Jason Spezza
03SPx/1
77 Jason Spezza
03UD Highlight Heroes/1
78 Jay Bouwmeester
03Black Diamond Threads/7
79 Jay Bouwmeester
03UD Ice/4
80 Jay Bouwmeester 10.00 25.00
03UD Rookie Update/48
81 Jay Bouwmeester
03SPx/1
82 Jean Beliveau
03UD Trilogy/12
83 Jean Beliveau
03UD Trilogy Crest Variations/1
84 Jean Beliveau 20.00 50.00
04UD Legendary Signatures/49
85 J-S Giguere
02SP Game Used Authentic Fabrics/14
86 J-S Giguere
02SP Game Used Authentic Fabrics/3
87 J-S Giguere
02SP Game Used Future Fabrics/8
88 J-S Giguere
03Beehive Blue Sticks/2
89 J-S Giguere
03UD Ice/2
90 J-S Giguere
03UD Rookie Update/19
91 Jeremy Roenick
02SP Game Used First Rounders/4
92 Jeremy Roenick
02SP Game Used Tools of the Game/7
93 Jeremy Roenick
03UD Rookie Update/20
94 Joe Thornton
01UD Classic Portraits Classic Stitches/13
95 Joe Thornton
02SP Authentic Super Premium/15
96 Joe Thornton
02SP Game Used Authentic Fabrics/6
97 Joe Thornton
03UD Rookie Update/19
98 Johnny Bucyk
03UD Trilogy/14
99 Johnny Bucyk
03UD Trilogy Crest Variations/1
100 Jose Theodore 30.00 80.00
03UD Rookie Update/29
101 Keith Primeau
01SP Authentic Notable Numbers/7
102 Ladislav Nagy
03UD Ice/3
103 Lanny McDonald
03UD Trilogy/14
104 Lanny McDonald 15.00 40.00
04UD Legendary Signatures/48
105 Luc Robitaille
03Beehive Beige Sticks/3
106 Marcel Dionne
03Beehive Beige Sticks/3
107 Marcel Dionne
03Beehive Red Sticks/8
108 Marcel Dionne
03UD Trilogy Crest Variations/1
109 Marcel Dionne
03UD Trilogy/13
110 Marcel Hossa
03SPx Prospects/1
111 Marcel Hossa
03UD Classic Portraits Hockey Headliners/16
112 Marian Hossa
03Black Diamond Threads/11
113 Marian Hossa
03UD Ice/2
114 Marian Hossa
03UD Rookie Update/18
115 Markus Naslund
03UD Rookie Update/19
116 Markus Naslund
01UD Classic Portraits Starring Cast/8
117 Markus Naslund
01SP Game Used Authentic Fabrics/2
118 Markus Naslund
02SP Authentic Super Premium/15
119 Markus Naslund
02SP Game Used Authentic Fabrics/5
120 Markus Naslund
02SP Game Used Authentic Fabrics/5
121 Markus Naslund
02SP Game Used First Rounders/1
122 Markus Naslund
02UD All Stars/9
123 Markus Naslund
03Beehive Game Jerseys/9
124 Markus Naslund
03Black Diamond Threads/11
125 Markus Naslund
03UD Ice/4
126 Markus Naslund
03SPx/1
127 Martin Biron
01SP Authentic All Stars/2
128 Martin Biron
02SP Game Used Authentic Fabrics/6
129 Martin Biron
02SP Game Used First Rounders/4
130 Martin Biron
02SP Game Used Piece of History/3
131 Martin Biron
02UD Saviours/12
132 Martin Biron
03SP Game Used Authentic Fabrics/19
133 M.Brodeur 03Rookie Upd/3
134 Martin St. Louis
03SP Game Used Authentic Fabrics/17
135 Marty Turco
02SP Game Used Future Fabrics/5
136 Marty Turco
03Beehive Game Jerseys/12
137 Marty Turco
03Black Diamond Threads/11
138 Marty Turco
03UD Ice/3
139 Marty Turco 15.00 40.00
03UD Rookie Update/35
140 Marty Turco
03SP Game Used Authentic Fabrics/12
141 Maxim Afinogenov
01SP Game Used Authentic Fabrics Gold/1
142 Maxim Afinogenov
02SP Game Used Future Fabrics/6
143 Maxim Afinogenov
03Black Diamond Threads/11
144 Maxim Afinogenov
03UD Classic Portraits Classic Stitches/16
145 Michael Peca
03SPx/1
146 Mika Noronen
02SP Game Used First Rounders/4
147 Mika Noronen 10.00 25.00
03UD Rookie Update/35
148 Mika Noronen
01SP Game Used Authentic Fabrics/2
149 Mika Noronen
03Beehive Beige Sticks/15
150 Mika Noronen
03UD Ice/2
151 Mike Bossy
03SPx/1
152 Mike Bossy
99UD Century Legends Jerseys of the Century/4
153 Mike Bossy 12.50 30.00
04UD Legendary Signatures/47
154 Mike Ribeiro
02SP Game Used Future Fabrics/10
155 Mike Ribeiro
03UD Ice/2
156 Mike Ribeiro 10.00 25.00
03UD Rookie Update/53
157 Milan Hejduk
02SP Game Used Authentic Fabrics/7
158 Milan Hejduk
03Beehive Beige Sticks/2
159 Milan Hejduk
03SP Game Used Authentic Fabrics/17
160 Nikolai Khabibulin
03UD Ice/1
161 Nikolai Khabibulin 25.00 60.00
03UD Rookie Update/26
162 Phil Esposito
04UD Legendary Signatures/17
163 Ray Bourque
99UD Century Legends Jerseys of the Century/5
164 Reggie Leach
04UD Legendary Signatures/24
165 Rene Robert
04UD Legendary Signatures/24
166 R.Nash 03Beehive Jsy/11
167 R.Nash 03Blk Diam Threads/10
168 R.Nash 03Ice/2
169 R.Nash 03Rookie Upd/41 25.00 60.00
170 R.Nash 03UD Highlight Heroes/1
171 Roberto Luongo
03Black Diamond Threads/11
172 Roberto Luongo
03UD Ice/2
173 Roberto Luongo 15.00 40.00
03UD Rookie Update/45
174 Ryan Smyth
03Beehive Game Jerseys/20
175 Saku Koivu
03UD Rookie Update/11
176 Scotty Bowman
03UD Trilogy/4
177 Shane Doan
02SP Game Used Authentic Fabrics/6
178 Shane Doan
02SP Game Used Authentic Fabrics Gold/4
179 Shane Doan
02SP Game Used First Rounders/2
180 Shane Doan
02UD Hot Spots/8
181 Simon Gagne
01Honor Roll Grade A Jerseys/2
182 Simon Gagne
02SP Authentic Super Premium/13
183 Simon Gagne
02SP Game Used First Rounders/4
184 Simon Gagne
02SP Game Used Future Fabrics/7
185 Stan Mikita
03UD Trilogy/14
186 Stan Mikita
03UD Trilogy Crest Variations/1
187 Stan Mikita 10.00 25.00
04UD Legendary Signatures/30
188 Stanislav Chistov
03SPx/1
189 Stephen Weiss
03SPx/1
190 Steve Sullivan
02SP Game Used Authentic Fabrics/15
191 Steve Sullivan
02UD CHL Graduates/6
192 Steve Sullivan
02UD Speed Demon/20
193 Steve Sullivan 10.00 25.00
03UD Rookie Update/26
194 Tony Esposito
04UD Legendary Signatures/18
195 Trent Hunter
03UD Ice/4
196 Trent Hunter
03UD Rookie Update/7
197 Vincent Lecavalier
03UD Ice/1
198 Zigmund Palffy
01SP Game Used Authentic FabricsGold/1
199 Zigmund Palffy
02SP Authentic Super Premium/17
200 Zigmund Palffy 10.00 25.00
03UD Rookie Update/32

2004-05 SP Authentic Octographs

A first in the hockey market, this insert set featured certified autographs of eight different players. Four autographs were placed on the card fronts and four on the backs. This set was serial-numbered out of 5 and not priced due to scarcity.

PRINT RUN 5 SER.#'d SETS
NOT PRICED DUE TO SCARCITY
OS-ROK Fleury/Staal/Horton/Zherdev/Nash/Lehtonen/J-Bo/Pitkanen
OS-GOA Roy/Hall/T.Espo/Cheevers/Brodeur/Theodore/Luongo/Lehtonen
OS-CAP Wayne Gretzky/Bryan Trottier/Bobby Clarke/Phil Esposito/Jarome Iginla/Joe Thornton/Markus Naslund/Saku Koivu
OS-CUP Jarome Iginla/Matthew Lombardi/Robyn Regehr/Chuck Kobasew/Brad Richards/Martin St. Louis/Vincent Lecavalier/Nikolai Khabibulin
OS-ART Wayne Gretzky/Gordie Howe/Guy Lafleur/Jarome Iginla/Stan Mikita/Marcel Dionne/Bryan Trottier/Martin St. Louis

2004-05 SP Authentic Rookie Redemptions

This 51-card set was issued in packs as redemption cards redeemable for rookies who first skated in the 2005-06 season. Cards RR1-RR30 are team specific and cards RR31-RR51 were "Wild" cards. Print run was limited to 399 copies each. Please note that due to a printing error, cards 41 and 42 have a "PP" prefix.

RR1 Corey Perry 12.00 30.00
RR2 Braydon Coburn 4.00 10.00
RR3 Hannu Toivonen 8.00 20.00
RR4 Thomas Vanek 20.00 50.00
RR5 Dion Phaneuf 25.00 60.00
RR6 Cam Ward 12.00 30.00
RR7 Brent Seabrook 4.00 10.00
RR8 Wojtek Wolski 12.00 30.00
RR9 Gilbert Brule 12.00 30.00
RR10 Jussi Jokinen 8.00 20.00
RR11 Jim Howard 8.00 20.00
RR12 Brad Winchester 4.00 10.00
RR13 Rostislav Olesz 4.00 10.00
RR14 George Parros 4.00 10.00
RR15 Matt Foy 4.00 10.00
RR16 Alexander Perezhogin 8.00 20.00
RR17 Ryan Suter 4.00 10.00
RR18 Zach Parise 12.00 30.00
RR19 Robert Nilsson 4.00 10.00
RR20 Henrik Lundqvist 25.00 60.00
RR21 Andrej Meszaros 4.00 10.00
RR22 Jeff Carter 15.00 40.00
RR23 David Leneveu 4.00 10.00
RR24 Sidney Crosby 300.00 500.00
RR25 Ryane Clowe 4.00 10.00
RR26 Jeff Woywitka 4.00 10.00
RR27 Evgeny Artyukhin 4.00 10.00
RR28 Alexander Steen 12.00 30.00
RR29 Rob McVicar 4.00 10.00
RR30 Alexander Ovechkin 75.00 150.00
RR31 Peter Budaj 8.00 20.00
RR32 Rene Bourque 4.00 10.00
RR33 Duncan Keith 4.00 10.00
RR34 Lee Stempniak 4.00 10.00
RR35 Andrew Alberts 4.00 10.00
RR36 Milan Jurcina 4.00 10.00
RR37 Yann Danis 4.00 10.00
RR38 Keith Ballard 4.00 10.00
RR39 Eric Nystrom 4.00 10.00
RR40 Mike Richards 8.00 20.00
PP41 Kevin Nastiuk 4.00 10.00
PP42 Petteri Nokelainen 4.00 10.00
RR43 Chris Campoli 4.00 10.00
RR44 Andrew Wozniewski 4.00 10.00
RR45 Ryan Getzlaf 15.00 40.00
RR46 Maxime Talbot 4.00 10.00
RR47 Petr Prucha 8.00 20.00
RR48 Johan Franzen 4.00 10.00
RR49 Brandon Bochenski 4.00 10.00
RR50 Patrick Eaves 8.00 20.00
RR51 Jim Slater 4.00 10.00

2004-05 SP Authentic Rookie Review

This 42-card set featured certified player autographs along with jersey patch swatches. Each card was serial-numbered out of 100.

PRINT RUN 100 SER.#'d SETS
RR-WG Wayne Gretzky/12
RR-ZC Zdeno Chara 20.00 50.00
RR-MH Marcel Hossa 15.00 40.00
RR-JK Jari Kurri 40.00 100.00
RR-KL Kari Lehtonen 40.00 100.00
RR-MP Mark Parrish 20.00 50.00
RR-MR Michael Ryder 30.00 80.00
RR-HZ Henrik Zetterberg 30.00 80.00
RR-SC Stanislav Chistov 15.00 40.00
RR-RE Robert Esche 15.00 40.00
RR-HE Milan Hejduk 25.00 60.00
RR-KP Keith Primeau 15.00 40.00
RR-RL Roberto Luongo 30.00 80.00
RR-MA Maxim Afinogenov 15.00 40.00
RR-AB David Aebischer 20.00 50.00
RR-DW Doug Weight 15.00 40.00
RR-SP Jason Spezza 40.00 100.00
RR-RN Rick Nash 40.00 100.00
RR-EJ Ed Jovanovski 15.00 40.00
RR-IG Jarome Iginla 50.00 125.00
RR-AF Alexander Frolov 25.00 60.00
RR-MT Marty Turco 25.00 60.00
RR-HV Martin Havlat 25.00 60.00
RR-SG Simon Gagne 15.00 40.00
RR-PS Philippe Sauve 15.00 40.00
RR-MN Markus Naslund 25.00 60.00
RR-JL Joffrey Lupul 20.00 50.00
RR-NS Nathan Smith 15.00 40.00
RR-IK Ilya Kovalchuk 60.00 150.00
RR-CD Chris Drury 20.00 50.00
RR-RS Ryan Smyth 15.00 40.00
RR-MG Marian Gaborik 50.00 125.00
RR-DB Dustin Brown 15.00 40.00
RR-JR Jeremy Roenick 20.00 50.00
RR-PB Patrice Bergeron/90 40.00 80.00
RR-SW Stephen Weiss 15.00 40.00
RR-JB Jay Bouwmeester 20.00 50.00
RR-DA Daniel Briere 25.00 60.00
RR-DL David Legwand 15.00 40.00
RR-BR Martin Brodeur 75.00 200.00
RR-JT Joe Thornton 50.00 125.00

2004-05 SP Authentic Sign of the Times

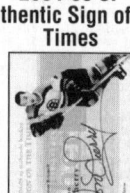

For 2004-05, the Sign of the Times set featured autograph cards carrying 1, 2, 3, 4, 5 and 6 player autographs. Single autographs were inserted at 1:20. Dual-player autos were serial-numbered to 100 (unless otherwise noted below). Triple-player autos were serial-numbered out of 25. Quad-player autos were serial-numbered out of 20. Five player-autos were serial numbered out of 15 and six player-autos were serial-numbered to just 10 copies each. Please note that card #SS-AWS contained two autographs of each of the three players depicted and was a 1/1.

UNDER 25 NOT PRICED DUE TO SCARCITY
ST-AB David Aebischer 6.00 15.00
ST-AF Maxim Afinogenov 20.00 50.00
ST-AH Ales Hemsky 6.00 15.00
ST-AR Andrew Raycroft 8.00 20.00
ST-AT Alex Tanguay 6.00 15.00
ST-BA Milan Bartovic 4.00 10.00
ST-BB Brad Boyes 6.00 15.00
ST-BI Martin Biron 6.00 15.00
ST-BL Brian Leetch SP 30.00 80.00
ST-BM Brenden Morrow 6.00 15.00
ST-BO Scotty Bowman SP 30.00 80.00
ST-BR Brad Richards 8.00 20.00
ST-CD Chris Drury 4.00 10.00
ST-CH Chris Higgins 8.00 20.00
ST-CP Chris Pronger 6.00 15.00
ST-DB Daniel Briere 6.00 15.00
ST-DC Don Cherry 15.00 40.00
ST-DH Dany Heatley SP 15.00 40.00
ST-DL David Legwand 4.00 10.00
ST-DR Dwayne Roloson 6.00 15.00
ST-DU Dustin Brown 4.00 10.00
ST-DW Doug Weight SP 12.50 30.00
ST-EC Erik Cole 4.00 10.00
ST-EJ Ed Jovanovski 4.00 10.00
ST-ES Eric Staal 15.00 40.00
ST-FL Marc-Andre Fleury 12.00 30.00

ST-FM Frank Mahovlich SP 30.00 80.
ST-FR Alexander Frolov 4.00 10.
ST-FS Fredrik Sjostrom 4.00 10.
ST-GA Marian Gaborik 12.50 30.
ST-GE Georges Laraque 4.00 10.
ST-GH Gordie Howe 40.00 80.
ST-GI Gilbert Perreault SP 30.00 80.
ST-GL Guy Lafleur SP 75.00 150.
ST-HA Dominik Hasek SP 20.00 50.
ST-HO Nathan Horton 4.00 10.
ST-HZ Henrik Zetterberg 8.00 20.
ST-IK Ilya Kovalchuk 15.00 40.
ST-JB Jay Bouwmeester 4.00 10.
ST-JG J-S Giguere 6.00 15.
ST-JI Jarome Iginla 15.00 40.
ST-JL Joffrey Lupul 6.00 15.
ST-JO Jose Theodore SP 25.00 60.
ST-JR Jeremy Roenick 10.00 25.
ST-JT Joe Thornton 12.50 30.
ST-KL Kari Lehtonen 12.50 30.
ST-KU Jari Kurri 10.00 25.
ST-LE Manny Legace 4.00 10.
ST-LM Lanny McDonald 8.00 20.
ST-LN Ladislav Nagy 4.00 10.
ST-LO Matthew Lombardi 4.00 10.
ST-MA Marcel Hossa 4.00 10.
ST-MB Martin Brodeur SP 75.00 200.
ST-MH Milan Hejduk 8.00 20.
ST-MJ Matt Stajan 6.00 15.
ST-ML John-Michael Liles 4.00 10.
ST-MN Markus Naslund 8.00 20.
ST-MO Brendan Morrison 4.00 10.
ST-MP Michael Peca 4.00 10.
ST-MT Marty Turco 6.00 15.
ST-NK Nikolai Khabibulin 12.00 30.
ST-NS Nathan Smith 4.00 10.
ST-NZ Nikolai Zherdev 6.00 15.
ST-PA Mark Parrish 4.00 10.
ST-PB Patrice Bergeron 8.00 20.
ST-PR Patrick Roy SP 300.00 400.
ST-PS Philippe Sauve 4.00 10.
ST-PW Peter Worrell 4.00 10.
ST-RE Robert Esche 4.00 10.
ST-RL Roberto Luongo 12.50 30.
ST-RN Rick Nash 15.00 40.
ST-RR Robyn Regehr 4.00 10.
ST-RS Ryan Smyth 6.00 15.
ST-RY Michael Ryder 6.00 15.
ST-SC Stanislav Chistov 4.00 10.
ST-SD Shane Doan 4.00 10.
ST-SG Simon Gagne 8.00 20.
ST-SK Saku Koivu 10.00 25.
ST-SP Jason Spezza SP 30.00 80.
ST-ST Martin St. Louis 8.00 20.
ST-SU Steve Sullivan 4.00 10.
ST-SW Stephen Weiss 4.00 10.
ST-TA Tyler Arnason 4.00 10.
ST-TH Trent Hunter 4.00 10.
ST-TU Tuomo Ruutu 6.00 15.
ST-VL Vincent Lecavalier SP 250.00400
ST-WG Wayne Gretzky SP 200.00 400.
ST-ZC Zdeno Chara 6.00 15.
DS-PR Perreault/Robert/25 25.00 60.
DS-AH D.Alfredsson/M.Hossa 15.00 40.
DS-BC Bowman/Cherry/25 75.00 150.
DS-BD M.Biron/C.Drury 12.50 30.
DS-BR Brodeur/Roy/25 300.00 450.
DS-BT Bossy/Trottier/25 50.00 125.
DS-CR R.Esche/J.Roenick 12.50 30.
DS-DS S.Doan/F.Sjostrom 12.00 30.
DS-EE T.Espo/P.Espo/25 75.00 125.
DS-FH G.Fuhr/G.Hall/25 50.00 100.
DS-HG Howe/Gretzky/25 400.00 650.
DS-HH M.Hossa/M.Hossa 15.00 40.
DS-HS D.Hasek/J.Spezza 40.00 100.
DS-IR J.Iginla/R.Regehr 20.00 50.
DS-KL N.Khabibulin/R.Luongo 25.0060.
DS-KN I.Kovalchuk/K.Lehtonen 50.00 100.
DS-LB B.Leetch/E.Belfour 25.00 60.
DS-LK M.St.Louis/I.Kovalchuk 40.00100.
DS-LL St. Louis/Lecavalier/25 60.00125.
DS-LW G.Laraque/P.Worrell 15.00 40.
DS-MJ M.Ryder/J.Theodore 25.00 60.
DS-MT B.Morrow/M.Turco 15.00 40.
DS-MZ M.Naslund/H.Zetterberg 15.0040.
DS-NH C.Neely/G.Howe/25 50.00 125.
DS-NJ M.Naslund/E.Jovanvski 15.0040.
DS-NK E.Nabokov/N.Khabablin 20.0050.
DS-NZ R.Nash/N.Zherdev 30.00 80.
DS-PH M.Peca/T.Hunter 12.50 30.
DS-PM P.Bergeron/M.Ryder 15.00 40.
DS-PW C.Pronger/D.Weight 12.50 30.
DS-RA R.Smyth/A.Hemsky 15.00 40.
DS-RL A.Raycroft/K.Lehtonen 20.00 50.
DS-RP R.Bourque/C.Neely 40.00 100.
DS-RR M.Ryder/M.Ribeiro 15.00 40.
DS-RT A.Raycroft/J.Thornton 20.00 50.
DS-SH J.Spezza/M.Havlat 20.00 50.
DS-ST E.Staal/J.Thornton 25.00 60.
DS-TN J.Thornton/C.Neely 30.00 80.
DS-WL S.Weiss/R.Luongo 15.00 40.
TS-BNT Bourque/Neely/Thornton 100.00 200.
TS-BTG Bossy/Trottier/Gillies 50.00125.
TS-CLR Clarke/Leach/Roenick 75.00150.
TS-GKF Gretzky/Kurri/Fuhr 400.00 700.
TS-GRE Gagne/Roenick/Esche 50.00125.
TS-HLK Heatly/Lehtnen/Kovlchk 100.00 200.
TS-HTA Hejduk/Tanguay/Aebischer 40.00 80.
TS-IKN Iginla/Kovalchuk/Nash 100.00 250.
TS-ILN Iginla/St. Louis/Nash 100.00250.
TS-KLL Khabiblin/Luongo/Lehtnen 50.00 125.
TS-LPJ Leetch/Pronger/Jovo 40.00100.
TS-LRZ Lupul/Ruutu/Zherdev 30.00 80.
TS-LWH Luongo/Weiss/Horton 60.00 150.
TS-NSS Nash/Spezza/Staal 150.00 300.
TS-PBF Palffy/Brown/Frolov 30.00 80.
TS-RBT Raycroft/Belfour/Turco 75.00 200.
TS-RKR Ribeiro/Koivu/Ryder 50.00 100.
TS-RLB Roy/Luongo/Brodeur 250.00500.
TS-SHZ Staal/Horton/Zherdev 60.00150.
TS-TRB Thorntn/Raycrft/Bergern 75.00 150.
QS-HRBG Bo.Hull/Robitaille/Bucyk/Gillie
QS-BBLK Patrice Bergeron/Dustin Brown/Joffrey Lupul/Ryan Kesler
QS-BDPB Jean Beliveau/Marcel Dionne/Gilbert Perreault/Mike Bossy
QS-BPBP Ray Bourque/Chris Pronger/Ja Bouwmeester/Joni Pitkanen
QS-BTCR Johnny Bucyk/Joe Thornton/Gerry Cheevers/Andrew Raycroft
QS-FBRE Grant Fuhr/Martin

Brodeur/Patrick Roy/Tony Esposito
QS-FSHZ Marc-Andre Fleury/Eric
Staal/Nathan Horton/Nikolai Zherdev
QS-GPRE Simon Gagne/Keith
Primeau/Jeremy Roenick/Robert Esche
QS-GTDC Wayne Gretzky/Joe
Thornton/Marcel Dionne/Bobby Clarke
QS-HINS Hejduk/Iginla/Nash/St. Louis
QS-IKHL Jarome Iginla/Chuck
Kobasew/Milan Hejduk/Jon-Michael Liles
QS-LKSN Martin St. Louis/Ilya
Kovalchuk/Marian Hossa/Markus Naslund
QS-LRLK Martin St. Louis/Brad
Richards/Vincent Lecavalier/Nikolai
Khabibulin
QS-MHCL Stan Mikita/Bobby Hull/Bobby
Clarke/Reggie Leach
QS-NHKS
Nash/Heatley/Kovalchuk/Bergeron
QS-TAHS Alex Tanguay/David
Aebischer/Milan Hejduk/Philippe Sauve
QS-TPLS Thornton/Primeau/Lecavalier/Eric
Staal
QS-VANC Markus Naslund/Brendan
Morrison/Ed Jovanovski/Ryan Kesler
FS-BOS Johnny Bucyk/Cam Neely/Ray
Bourque/Joe Thornton/Andrew Raycroft
FS-CTR Phil Esposito/Marcel
Dionne/Gilbert Perreault/Johnny
Bucyk/Brian Trottier
FS-GOL Marc-Andre Fleury/Kari
Lehtonen/Martin Brodeur/David
Aebischer/Jose Theodore
FS-MON Marcel Hossa/Guy Lafleur/Jose
Theodore/Michael Ryder/Jean Beliveau
FS-NED Brad Boyes/Michael Ryder/Jason
Spezza/Chris Drury/Matt Stajan
FS-PAC Alexander Frolov/Dustin
Brown/Shane Doan/Joffrey Lupul/Brendan
Morrow
FS-RGT Markus Naslund/Simon
Gagne/Dany Heatley/Milan Hejduk/Daniel
Alfredsson
FS-SEN Marian Hossa/Daniel
Alfredsson/Jason Spezza/Martin
Havlat/Dominik Hasek
FS-SES Ilya Kovalchuk/Dany Heatley/Kari
Lehtonen/Roberto Luongo/Stephen Weiss
FS-VAN Markus Naslund/Ryan Kesler/Ed
Jovanovski/Brendan Morrison/Nathan Smith
SS-AWS Wayne Gretzky/Jari Kurri/Luc
Robitaille/Wayne Gretzky/Jari Kurri/Luc
Robitaille/1
SS-ALS Gordie Howe/Guy Lafleur/Joe
Thornton/Patrick Roy/Grant Fuhr/Martin
Brodeur
SS-CAN Jarome Iginla/Ed Belfour/Martin
St. Louis/J-S Giguere/Jose
Theodore/Manny Legace
SS-CNP
Smyth/Spezza/Ribeiro/Iginla/Brodeur/Jovan
ovski
SS-DEE Ray Bourque/Chris Pronger/Jay
Bouwmeester/Brian Leetch/Joni Pitkanen/Ed
Jovanovski
SS-FIN Kari Lehtonen/Joni Pitkanen/Jari
Kurri/Mika Noronen/Tuomo Ruutu/Saku
Koivu
SS-ORG Gordie Howe/Wayne
Gretzky/Frank Mahovlich/Guy Lafleur/Phil
Esposito/Bobby Hull
SS-RLW Gordie Howe/Mike Bossy/Jari
Kurri/Bobby Hull/Luc Robitaille/Johnny
Bucyk
SS-USA Jeremy Roenick/Brian
Leetch/Robert Esche/Chris Drury/Doug
Weight/David Legwand

2005-06 SP Authentic

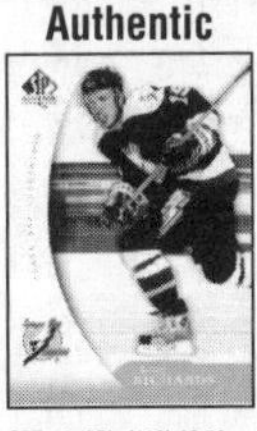

COMP.SET w/o SP's (100) 12.50 30.00
101-130 PRINT RUN 999 SER. #'d SETS
131-220 PRINT RUN 999 SER. #'d SETS
221-287 PRINT RUN 1,999 SER. #'d SETS
288-290 ONLY IN ROOKIE UPD. PACKS

1 J-S Giguere	.25	.60
2 Joffrey Lupul	.15	.40
3 Teemu Selanne	.30	.75
4 Scott Niedermayer	.15	.40
5 Ilya Kovalchuk	.40	1.00
6 Kari Lehtonen	.30	.75
7 Marian Hossa	.25	.60
8 Sergei Samsonov	.25	.60
9 Brian Leetch	.30	.75
10 Andrew Raycroft	.25	.60
11 Patrice Bergeron	.25	.60
12 Glen Murray	.15	.40
13 Chris Drury	.25	.60
14 Martin Biron	.25	.60
15 Daniel Briere	.15	.40
16 Jarome Iginla	.40	1.00
17 Miikka Kiprusoff	.30	.75
18 Doug Weight	.25	.60
19 Martin Gerber	.25	.60
20 Eric Staal	.25	.60
21 Nikolai Khabibulin	.30	.75
22 Tuomo Ruutu	.15	.40
23 Eric Daze	.25	.60
24 Joe Sakic	.60	1.50
25 Alex Tanguay	.25	.60
26 Milan Hejduk	.30	.75
27 David Aebischer	.25	.60
28 Rob Blake	.25	.60
29 Rick Nash	.40	1.00
30 Sergei Fedorov	.40	1.00
31 Mike Modano	.30	.75
32 Marty Turco	.25	.60
33 Bill Guerin	.15	.40
34 Brendan Shanahan	.30	.75
35 Steve Yzerman	1.25	3.00
36 Henrik Zetterberg	.30	.75
37 Pavel Datsyuk	.30	.75
38 Gordie Howe	1.50	4.00
39 Chris Pronger	.25	.60
40 Michael Peca	.15	.40
41 Ryan Smyth	.15	.40
42 Wayne Gretzky	2.00	5.00
43 Roberto Luongo	.40	1.00
44 Olli Jokinen	.25	.60
45 Luc Robitaille	.25	.60
46 Jeremy Roenick	.40	1.00
47 Alexander Frolov	.25	.60
48 Pavol Demitra	.25	.60
49 Marian Gaborik	.60	1.50
50 Dwayne Roloson	.25	.60
51 Jose Theodore	.40	1.00
52 Saku Koivu	.30	.75
53 Mike Ribeiro	.15	.40
54 Michael Ryder	.25	.60
55 Paul Kariya	.30	.75
56 Tomas Vokoun	.25	.60
57 Martin Brodeur	1.50	4.00
58 Patrik Elias	.25	.60
59 Scott Gomez	.25	.60
60 Brian Gionta	.15	.40
61 Miroslav Satan	.15	.40
62 Alexei Yashin	.15	.40
63 Rick DiPietro	.25	.60
64 Mark Parrish	.15	.40
65 Jaromir Jagr	.50	1.25
66 Martin Straka	.15	.40
67 Dominik Hasek	.60	1.50
68 Dany Heatley	.40	1.00
69 Wade Redden	.15	.40
70 Martin Havlat	.25	.60
71 Daniel Alfredsson	.25	.60
72 Jason Spezza	.30	.75
73 Peter Forsberg	.50	1.25
74 Keith Primeau	.15	.40
75 Simon Gagne	.30	.75
76 Robert Esche	.25	.60
77 Shane Doan	.15	.40
78 Curtis Joseph	.30	.75
79 Mario Lemieux	2.00	5.00
80 Zigmund Palffy	.25	.60
81 Mark Recchi	.25	.60
82 Jonathan Cheechoo	.30	.75
83 Evgeni Nabokov	.25	.60
84 Patrick Marleau	.25	.60
85 Joe Thornton	.50	1.25
86 Barret Jackman	.15	.40
87 Keith Tkachuk	.30	.75
88 Martin St. Louis	.25	.60
89 Vincent Lecavalier	.30	.75
90 Brad Richards	.25	.60
91 Sean Burke	.25	.60
92 Eric Lindros	.30	.75
93 Mats Sundin	.30	.75
94 Ed Belfour	.30	.75
95 Matt Stajan	.15	.40
96 Jason Allison	.15	.40
97 Todd Bertuzzi	.30	.75
98 Markus Naslund	.30	.75
99 Brendan Morrison	.15	.40
100 Olaf Kolzig	.25	.60
101 Mario Lemieux 999	5.00	12.00
102 Joe Sakic 999	5.00	12.00
103 Jaromir Jagr 999	4.00	10.00
104 Mike Modano 999	2.00	5.00
105 Dominik Hasek 999	4.00	10.00
106 Ilya Kovalchuk 999	3.00	8.00
107 Steve Yzerman 999	5.00	12.00
108 Nikolai Khabibulin 999	2.50	6.00
109 Joe Thornton 999	4.00	10.00
110 Jarome Iginla 999	3.00	8.00
111 Martin St. Louis 999	2.00	5.00
112 Paul Kariya 999	2.50	6.00
113 Martin Brodeur 999	5.00	12.00
114 Mats Sundin 999	2.50	6.00
115 Peter Forsberg 999	3.00	8.00
116 J-S Giguere 999	2.00	5.00
117 Marian Hossa 999	2.00	5.00
118 Alex Tanguay 999	2.00	5.00
119 Rick Nash 999	2.50	6.00
120 Jeremy Roenick 999	3.00	8.00
121 Dany Heatley 999	3.00	8.00
122 Brendan Shanahan 999	2.50	6.00
123 Jose Theodore 999	2.50	6.00
124 Patrik Elias 999	2.00	5.00
125 Curtis Joseph 999	2.50	6.00
126 Evgeni Nabokov 999	2.00	5.00
127 Vincent Lecavalier 999	2.50	6.00
128 Markus Naslund 999	2.50	6.00
129 Olaf Kolzig 999	2.00	5.00
130 Doug Weight 999	2.00	5.00
131 Ryan Getzlaf AU RC/999	30.00	60.00
132 Corey Perry AU RC/999	15.00	40.00
133 Braydon Coburn AU RC/999	5.00	12.00
134 Jim Slater AU RC/999	4.00	10.00
135 Hannu Toivonen AU RC/999	10.00	25.00
136 Andrew Alberts AU RC/999	4.00	10.00
137 Milan Jurcina AU RC/999	4.00	10.00
138 Kevin Dallman AU RC/999	4.00	10.00
139 Thomas Vanek AU RC/999	30.00	80.00
140 Dion Phaneuf AU RC/999	40.00	100.00
141 Eric Nystrom AU RC/999	5.00	12.00
142 Cam Ward AU RC/999	15.00	40.00
143 Kevin Nastiuk AU RC/999	4.00	10.00
144 Niklas Nordgren AU RC/999	4.00	10.00
145 Brent Seabrook AU RC/999	5.00	12.00
146 Cam Barker AU RC/999	8.00	20.00
147 Duncan Keith AU RC/999	4.00	10.00
148 Rene Bourque AU RC/999	4.00	10.00
149 Wojtek Wolski AU RC/999	15.00	40.00
150 Peter Budaj AU RC/999	8.00	20.00
151 Gilbert Brule AU RC/999	15.00	40.00
152 Jaroslav Balastik AU RC/999	4.00	10.00
153 Jussi Jokinen AU RC/999	10.00	25.00
154 Johan Franzen AU RC/999	5.00	12.00
155 Jim Howard AU RC/999	10.00	25.00
156 Brett Lebda AU RC/999	5.00	12.00
157 Brad Winchester AU RC/999	4.00	10.00
158 Rostislav Olesz AU RC/999	6.00	15.00
159 Anthony Stewart AU RC/999	4.00	10.00
160 George Parros AU RC/999	4.00	10.00
161 Matt Foy AU RC/999	4.00	10.00
162 Derek Boogaard AU RC/999	4.00	10.00
163 Alexander Perezhogin AU RC/999	6.00	15.00
164 Yann Danis AU RC/999	5.00	12.00
165 Raitis Ivanans AU RC/999	4.00	10.00
166 Ryan Suter AU RC/999	6.00	15.00
167 Zach Parise AU RC/999	20.00	50.00
168 Robert Nilsson AU RC/999	5.00	12.00
169 Petteri Nokelainen AU RC/999	4.00	10.00
170 Al Montoya AU RC/999	10.00	25.00
171 Henrik Lundqvist AU RC/999	40.00	100.00
172 Petr Prucha AU RC/999	10.00	25.00
173 Ryan Hollweg AU RC/999	5.00	12.00
174 Patrick Eaves AU RC/999	10.00	25.00
175 Brandon Bochenski AU RC/999	5.00	12.00
176 Andrej Meszaros AU RC/999	8.00	20.00
177 Jeff Carter AU RC/999	12.00	30.00
178 Mike Richards AU RC/999	12.00	30.00
179 David Leneveu AU RC/999	5.00	12.00
180 Keith Ballard AU RC/999	5.00	12.00
181 Sidney Crosby AU RC/999	600.00	800.00
182 Maxime Talbot AU RC/999	5.00	12.00
183 Josh Gorges AU RC/999	4.00	10.00
184 Ryane Clowe AU RC/999	5.00	12.00
185 Jay McClement AU RC/999	4.00	10.00
186 Jeff Hoggan AU RC/999	4.00	10.00
187 Jeff Woywitka AU RC/999	4.00	10.00
188 Alexander Steen AU RC/999	12.00	30.00
189 Andy Wozniewski AU RC/999	4.00	10.00
190 Alexander Ovechkin AU RC/999	150.00	250.00
191 Ryan Whitney AU RC/999	8.00	20.00
192 R.J. Umberger AU RC/999	6.00	15.00
193 Mikko Koivu AU RC/999	8.00	20.00
194 Steve Bernier AU RC/999	8.00	20.00
195 Timo Helbling AU RC/999	4.00	10.00
196 Ryan Craig AU RC/999	4.00	10.00
197 Valtteri Filppula AU RC/999	10.00	25.00
198 Daniel Paille AU RC/999	5.00	12.00
199 Danny Richmond AU RC/999	4.00	10.00
200 Maxim Lapierre AU RC/999	8.00	20.00
201 Barry Tallackson AU RC/999	5.00	12.00
202 Chris Campoli AU RC/999	4.00	10.00
203 Jeremy Colliton AU RC/999	4.00	10.00
204 Christoph Schubert AU RC/999	4.00	10.00
205 Kevin Bieksa AU RC/999	6.00	15.00
206 Jordan Sigalet AU RC/999	6.00	15.00
207 Adam Berkhoel AU RC/999	4.00	10.00
208 Erik Christensen AU RC/999	8.00	20.00
209 Ole-Kristian Tollefsen AU RC/999	4.00	10.00
210 Dimitri Patzold AU RC/999	4.00	10.00
211 Brad Richardson AU RC/999	4.00	10.00
212 Lee Stempniak AU RC/999	6.00	15.00
213 Andrei Kostitsyn AU RC/999	8.00	20.00
214 Evgeny Artyukhin AU RC/999	4.00	10.00
215 Ben Eager AU RC/999	4.00	10.00
216 Andrew Ladd AU RC/999	6.00	15.00
217 Jeff Tambellini AU RC/999	5.00	12.00
218 Kyle Quincey AU RC/999	6.00	15.00
219 Tomas Fleischmann AU RC/999	4.00	10.00
220 Jakub Klepis AU RC/999	6.00	12.00
221 Michael Wall RC/1999	2.00	5.00
222 Zenon Konopka RC/1999	2.00	5.00
223 Vojtech Polak RC/1999	2.00	5.00
224 Martin St. Pierre RC/1999	2.00	5.00
225 Steve Goertzen RC	2.00	5.00
226 Andrew Penner RC/1999	2.00	5.00
227 Danny Syvret RC/1999	2.00	5.00
228 Jeff Giuliano RC/1999	2.00	5.00
229 Adam Hauser RC/1999	2.00	5.00
230 Kyle Brodziak RC/1999	2.00	5.00
231 Cam Janssen RC/1999	2.00	5.00
232 Kevin Colley RC/1999	2.00	5.00
233 Chris Holt RC/1999	2.00	5.00
234 Greg Jacina RC/1999	2.00	5.00
235 Yanick Lehoux RC/1999	2.00	5.00
236 Brian McGrattan RC/1999	2.00	5.00
237 Colin Hemingway RC/1999	2.00	5.00
238 Paul Ranger RC/1999	2.00	5.00
239 Gerald Coleman RC/1999	2.00	5.00
240 Dennis Wideman RC/1999	2.00	5.00
241 Junior Lessard RC/1999	2.00	5.00
242 Matt Jones RC/1999	2.00	5.00
243 Brian Eklund RC/1999	2.00	5.00
244 Nick Tarnasky RC/1999	2.00	5.00
245 Bruno Gervais RC/1999	2.00	5.00
246 Staffan Kronwall RC/1999	2.00	5.00
247 Dustin Penner RC/1999	4.00	10.00
248 Kevin Klein RC/1999	2.00	5.00
249 Rob McVicar RC/1999	2.00	5.00
250 Eric Healey RC/1999	2.00	5.00
251 Ben Guite RC/1999	2.00	5.00
252 Nathan Paetsch RC/1999	2.00	5.00
253 Jiri Novotny RC/1999	2.00	5.00
254 Richie Regehr RC/1999	2.00	5.00
255 Mark Giordano RC/1999	2.00	5.00
256 Chad Larose RC/1999	2.00	5.00
257 Corey Crawford RC/1999	2.00	5.00
258 Vitaly Kolesnik RC/1999	2.00	5.00
259 Geoff Platt RC/1999	2.00	5.00
260 Matt Greene RC/1999	2.00	5.00
261 Jean-Francois Jacques RC/1999	2.00	5.00
262 Rob Globke RC	2.00	5.00
263 Petr Taticek RC/1999	2.00	5.00
264 Petr Kanko RC/1999	2.00	5.00
265 Matt Ryan RC/1999	2.00	5.00
266 Connor James RC/1999	2.00	5.00
267 Richard Petiot RC/1999	2.00	5.00
268 Mark Streit RC/1999	2.00	5.00
269 Jean-Philippe Cote RC/1999	2.00	5.00
270 Jonathan Ferland RC/1999	2.00	5.00
271 Pekka Rinne RC/1999	2.00	5.00
272 Jason Ryznar RC/1999	2.00	5.00
273 Josh Gratton RC/1999	2.00	5.00
274 Alexandre Picard RC/1999	2.00	5.00
275 Colby Armstrong RC/1999	4.00	10.00
276 Grant Stevenson RC/1999	2.00	5.00
277 Doug Murray RC/1999	2.00	5.00
278 Chris Beckford-Tseu RC/1999	3.00	8.00
279 Jon DiSalvatore RC/1999	2.00	5.00
280 Mike Glumac RC/1999	2.00	5.00
281 Darren Reid RC/1999	2.00	5.00
282 Doug O'Brien RC/1999	2.00	5.00
283 Jay Harrison RC/1999	2.00	5.00
284 Rick Rypien RC/1999	2.00	5.00
285 Alexandre Burrows RC/1999	2.00	5.00
286 David Steckel RC/1999	2.00	5.00
287 Mike Green RC/1999	2.00	5.00
288 Ben Walter AU RC	4.00	10.00
289 Alexandre Picard AU RC	6.00	15.00
290 Chris Thorburn AU RC	4.00	10.00

2005-06 SP Authentic Limited

COMMON LIMITED (1-100) 1.50 4.00
STARS 5X TO 12X BASE HI

131 Ryan Getzlaf	100.00	250.00
132 Corey Perry	60.00	150.00
133 Braydon Coburn	25.00	60.00
134 Jim Slater	50.00	125.00
135 Hannu Toivonen	40.00	100.00
136 Andrew Alberts	25.00	60.00
137 Milan Jurcina	25.00	60.00
138 Kevin Dallman	25.00	60.00
139 Thomas Vanek	100.00	250.00
140 Dion Phaneuf	150.00	400.00
141 Eric Nystrom	40.00	100.00
142 Cam Ward	75.00	200.00
143 Kevin Nastiuk	30.00	80.00
144 Niklas Nordgren	25.00	60.00
145 Brent Seabrook	50.00	125.00
146 Cam Barker	50.00	150.00
147 Duncan Keith	50.00	150.00
148 Rene Bourque	50.00	150.00
149 Wojtek Wolski	75.00	200.00
150 Peter Budaj	40.00	100.00
151 Gilbert Brule	100.00	250.00
152 Jaroslav Balastik	50.00	125.00
153 Jussi Jokinen	40.00	100.00
154 Johan Franzen	50.00	125.00
155 Jim Howard	50.00	125.00
156 Brett Lebda	25.00	60.00
157 Brad Winchester	40.00	100.00
158 Rostislav Olesz	50.00	125.00
159 Anthony Stewart	40.00	100.00
160 George Parros	25.00	60.00
161 Matt Foy	25.00	60.00
162 Derek Boogaard	30.00	80.00
163 Alexander Perezhogin	50.00	125.00
164 Yann Danis	40.00	100.00
165 Raitis Ivanans	25.00	60.00
166 Ryan Suter	50.00	125.00
167 Zach Parise	75.00	200.00
168 Robert Nilsson	40.00	100.00
169 Petteri Nokelainen	25.00	60.00
170 Alvaro Montoya	50.00	150.00
171 Henrik Lundqvist	125.00	300.00
172 Petr Prucha	50.00	150.00
173 Ryan Hollweg	25.00	60.00
174 Patrick Eaves	40.00	100.00
175 Brandon Bochenski	30.00	80.00
176 Andrej Meszaros	50.00	125.00
177 Jeff Carter	75.00	200.00
178 Mike Richards	50.00	125.00
179 David Leneveu	40.00	100.00
180 Keith Ballard	25.00	60.00
181 Sidney Crosby	800.00	1600.00
182 Maxime Talbot	40.00	100.00
183 Josh Gorges	25.00	60.00
184 Ryane Clowe	25.00	60.00
185 Jay McClement	25.00	60.00
186 Jeff Hoggan	30.00	80.00
187 Jeff Woywitka	25.00	60.00
188 Alexander Steen	50.00	125.00
189 Andy Wozniewski	25.00	60.00
190 Alexander Ovechkin	350.00	700.00
192 R.J. Umberger	25.00	60.00
193 Mikko Koivu	50.00	125.00
194 Steve Bernier	100.00	250.00
195 Timo Helbling	25.00	60.00
201 Barry Tallackson		
202 Chris Campoli	25.00	60.00
204 Christoph Schubert		
206 Jordan Sigalet		
210 Dimitri Patzold		
211 Brad Richardson	25.00	60.00
212 Lee Stempniak	30.00	80.00
214 Evgeny Artyukhin		
216 Andrew Ladd	25.00	60.00
217 Jeff Tambellini		
219 Tomas Fleischmann		
220 Jakub Klepis		

2005-06 SP Authentic Chirography

PRINT RUN 50 SER. #'d SETS

SPAR Andrew Raycroft	10.00	25.00
SPAT Alex Tanguay	10.00	25.00

SPAY Alexei Yashin	8.00	20.00
SPCP Chris Pronger	12.00	30.00
SPDH Dany Heatley	20.00	50.00
SPEB Ed Belfour	10.00	25.00
SPEN Evgeni Nabokov	10.00	25.00
SPHK Dominik Hasek	25.00	60.00
SPHV Martin Havlat	10.00	25.00
SPIK Ilya Kovalchuk	20.00	50.00
SPJG J-S Giguere	10.00	25.00
SPJI Jarome Iginla	20.00	50.00
SPJO Joe Thornton	25.00	50.00
SPJR Jeremy Roenick	20.00	50.00
SPJT Jose Theodore	15.00	40.00
SPMB Martin Brodeur	75.00	125.00
SPMG Marian Gaborik	20.00	50.00
SPMH Milan Hejduk	8.00	20.00
SPML Manny Legace	8.00	20.00
SPMM Mike Modano	15.00	40.00
SPMN Markus Naslund	10.00	25.00
SPOK Olaf Kolzig	15.00	40.00
SPPB Patrice Bergeron	12.00	30.00
SPRL Roberto Luongo	25.00	60.00
SPRN Rick Nash	15.00	40.00
SPSL Martin St. Louis	10.00	25.00
SPTV Tomas Vokoun	12.00	30.00
SPVL Vincent Lecavalier	25.00	60.00

2005-06 SP Authentic Exquisite Endorsements

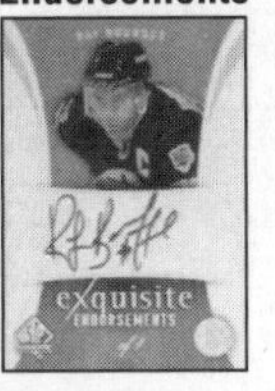

EEAO Alexander Ovechkin
EEAP Alexander Perezhogin
EEAR Andrew Raycroft
EEAS Alexander Steen
EEBH Bobby Hull
EEBS Borje Salming
EEBT Bryan Trottier
EECN Cam Neely
EECP Corey Perry
EEDH Dany Heatley
EEDS Darryl Sittler
EEDT Dave Taylor
EEEB Ed Belfour
EEGB Gilbert Brule
EEGC Gerry Cheevers
EEGF Grant Fuhr
EEGH Gordie Howe
EEGL Guy Lapointe
EEHK Dominik Hasek
EEHL Henrik Lundqvist
EEHT Hannu Toivonen
EEIK Ilya Kovalchuk
EEJC Jeff Carter
EEJG J-S Giguere
EEJI Jarome Iginla
EEJK Jari Kurri
EEJO Joe Thornton
EEJR Jeremy Roenick
EEJS Jason Spezza
EEJT Jose Theodore
EEKL Kari Lehtonen
EELF Guy Lafleur
EELU Luc Robitaille
EEMB Mike Bossy
EEMD Marcel Dionne
EEMK Mikko Koivu
EEMM Mike Modano
EEMS Mats Sundin
EEPB Patrice Bergeron
EEPR Patrick Roy
EERB Ray Bourque
EERL Roberto Luongo
EESC Sidney Crosby
EESK Saku Koivu
EESL Martin St. Louis
EETE Tony Esposito
EETV Thomas Vanek
EEVL Vincent Lecavalier
EEWC Wayne Cashman
EEWG Wayne Gretzky

2005-06 SP Authentic Immortal Inks

PRINT RUN 10 SER.#'d SETS
NOT PRICED DUE TO SCARCITY
IIBT Bryan Trottier
IICN Cam Neely
IIFM Frank Mahovlich
IIGI Gordie Howe
IIGL Guy Lafleur
IIMB Mike Bossy
IIPR Patrick Roy
IIRB Ray Bourque
IIWG Wayne Gretzky

2005-06 SP Authentic Marks of Distinction

COMMON CARD	8.00	20.00
PRINT RUN 25 SERIAL #'d SETS		
MDAO Alexander Ovechkin	250.00	350.00
MDAR Andrew Raycroft	15.00	40.00
MDAT Alex Tanguay	20.00	50.00
MDAY Alexei Yashin	8.00	20.00
MDBL Brian Leetch	20.00	50.00
MDBO Ray Bourque	50.00	100.00
MDBR Brad Richards	25.00	60.00
MDCP Chris Pronger	20.00	50.00
MDDH Dany Heatley	30.00	80.00
MDDW Doug Weight		
MDEB Ed Belfour	50.00	100.00
MDGH Gordie Howe	100.00	200.00
MDGL Guy Lafleur	75.00	125.00
MDHV Martin Havlat	20.00	50.00
MDIK Ilya Kovalchuk	50.00	100.00
MDJC Jonathan Cheechoo	30.00	60.00
MDJG J-S Giguere	20.00	40.00
MDJI Jarome Iginla	50.00	100.00
MDJO Joe Thornton		
MDJR Jeremy Roenick	30.00	60.00
MDJS Jason Spezza	30.00	60.00
MDJT Jose Theodore	40.00	80.00
MDKL Kari Lehtonen	40.00	80.00
MDKP Keith Primeau	8.00	20.00
MDMD Marcel Dionne		
MDMH Milan Hejduk	12.00	30.00
MDMM Mike Modano	50.00	100.00
MDMN Markus Naslund	20.00	50.00
MDMS Mats Sundin		
MDPB Patrice Bergeron	30.00	60.00
MDPE Phil Esposito	30.00	60.00
MDPR Patrick Roy	150.00	250.00
MDRB Rob Blake	12.00	30.00
MDRL Roberto Luongo	50.00	100.00
MDRN Rick Nash	75.00	150.00
MDSC Sidney Crosby	700.00	900.00
MDSG Simon Gagne	12.00	30.00
MDSK Saku Koivu	40.00	80.00
MDSL Martin St. Louis	20.00	50.00
MDSN Scott Niedermayer	12.00	30.00
MDVL Vincent Lecavalier	40.00	80.00

2005-06 SP Authentic Octographs

PRINT RUN 3 SER. #'d SETS
NOT PRICED DUE TO SCARCITY
OF Jarome Iginla
Martin St. Louis
Rick Nash
Dany Heatley
Ilya Kovalchuk
Patrice Bergeron
Marion Hossa
Markus Naslund
OG Patrick Roy
Dominik Hasek
Martin Brodeur
Ed Belfour
Olaf Kolzig
Jose Theodore
J-S Giguere
Evgeni Nabokov
OH Gordie Howe
Wayne Gretzky
Marcel Dionne
Guy Lafleur
Bryan Trottier
Bobby Hull
Phil Esposito
Mike Bossy
OR Dion Phaneuf
Alexander Ovechkin
Corey Perry
Jeff Carter
Gilbert Brule
Thomas Vanek
Alexander Steen
Alexander Perezhogin

2005-06 SP Authentic Prestigious Pairings

PPAH Daniel Alfredsson/Dany Heatley/100	20.00	50.00
PPBN Ray Bourque/Cam Neely/50	40.00	80.00
PPBP Rob Blake/Chris Pronger/100	15.00	40.00
PPBS Ed Belfour/Mats Sundin/50		
PPCE Gerry Cheevers/Phil Esposito/50		
PPCR Jeff Carter/Mike Richards/100	12.00	30.00
PPDT Marcel Dionne/Dave Taylor/100	40.00	80.00
PPEP Robert Esche/Joni Pitkanen/100	5.00	12.00
PPFK Grant Fuhr/Jarri Kurri/50	30.00	60.00
PPGR Marian Gaborik/Dwayne Roloson/100	12.00	30.00
PPGS Guy Lafleur/Saku Koivu/50	40.00	80.00
PPHB Nathan Horton/Jay Bouwmeester/100		
PPHE Bobby Hull/Tony Esposito/50		
PPHG Gordie Howe/Wayne Gretzky/50	300.00	400.00
PPHV Dominik Hasek/Tomas Vokoun/100	15.00	40.00
PPIS Jarome Iginla/Martin St. Louis/50	20.00	50.00
PPKN Nikolai Khabibulin/Evgeni Nabokov/100	8.00	20.00
PPLH Manny Legace/Jim Howard/100	15.00	40.00
PPLK Kari Lehtonen/Ilya Kovalchuk/100	15.00	40.00
PPLM Henrik Lundqvist/Alvaro Montoya/100	25.00	60.00
PPLR Vincent Lecavalier/Brad Richards/100	30.00	60.00
PPMB Ryan Miller/Martin Biron/100	20.00	50.00
PPNL Markus Naslund/Trevor Linden/100	25.00	60.00
PPNZ Rick Nash/Nikolai Zherdev/100	15.00	40.00
PPOS Rostislav Olesz/Anthony Stewart/100	5.00	12.00
PPPG Corey Perry/Ryan Getzlaf/100	25.00	60.00
PPPH Mark Parrish/Trent Hunter/100	5.00	12.00
PPPN Dion Phaneuf/Eric Nystrom/100	30.00	80.00
PPPO Dion Phaneuf/Alexander Ovechkin/50	75.00	150.00
PPPV Gilbert Perreault/Thomas Vanek/100	20.00	50.00
PPRA Tuomo Ruutu/Tyler Arnason/100	5.00	12.00
PPRB Patrick Roy/Martin Brodeur/50	150.00	250.00
PPRP Mark Recchi/Zigmund Palffy/100		
PPRR Michael Ryder/Mike Ribeiro/100		
PPTB Bryan Trottier/Mike Bossy/50	15.00	40.00
PPTC Joe Thornton/Jonathan Cheechoo/100	25.00	60.00
PPTF Jocelyn Thibault/Marc-Andre Fleury/100	20.00	50.00
PPTW Keith Tkachuk/Doug Weight/100		
PPTZ Marty Turco/Sergei Zubov/100	8.00	20.00

2005-06 SP Authentic Rarefied Rookies

PRINT RUN 1 SER.#'d SET
NOT PRICED DUE TO SCARCITY
RRAA Andrew Alberts
RRAL Alexander Steen
RRAM Andrej Meszaros
RRAO Alexander Ovechkin
RRAP Alexander Perezhogin
RRAS Anthony Stewart
RRAW Andrew Wozniewski
RRBC Braydon Coburn
RRBS Brent Seabrook
RRBW Brad Winchester
RRCB Cam Barker
RRCP Corey Perry
RRCW Cam Ward
RRDL David Leneveu
RRDP Dion Phaneuf
RREN Eric Nystrom
RRGB Gilbert Brule
RRHL Henrik Lundqvist
RRHT Hannu Toivonen
RRJC Jeff Carter
RRJF Johan Franzen
RRJH Jim Howard
RRJJ Jussi Jokinen
RRJM Jay McClement
RRJS Jim Slater
RRJW Jeff Woywitka
RRKB Keith Ballard
RRMF Matt Foy
RRMJ Milan Jurcina
RRMK Mikko Koivu
RRMO Al Montoya
RRMR Mike Richards
RRMT Maxime Talbot
RRPB Peter Budaj
RRPE Patrick Eaves
RRPP Petr Prucha
RRRB Rene Bourque

2005-06 SP Authentic Rarefied Rookies

RRRC Ryane Clowe
RRRG Ryan Getzlaf
RRRJ R.J. Umberger
RRRN Robert Nilsson
RRRO Rostislav Olesz
RRRS Ryan Suter
RRRW Ryan Whitney
RRSB Steve Bernier
RRSC Sidney Crosby
RRTV Thomas Vanek
RRWW Wojtek Wolski
RRYD Yann Danis
RRZP Zach Parise

2005-06 SP Authentic Rookie Authentics

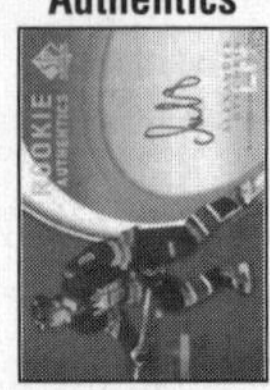

PRINT RUN 250 SER.#'d SETS
RAAM Andrej Meszaros 8.00 20.00
RAAO Alexander Ovechkin 40.00 100.00
RAAP Alexander Perezhogin 8.00 20.00
RAAS Alexander Steen 10.00 25.00
RABC Braydon Coburn 8.00 20.00
RABS Brent Seabrook 8.00 20.00
RABW Brad Winchester 8.00 20.00
RACB Cam Barker
RACP Corey Perry 12.00 30.00
RACW Cam Ward 12.00 30.00
RADP Dion Phaneuf
RAEN Eric Nystrom 8.00 20.00
RAGB Gilbert Brule 10.00 25.00
RAHL Henrik Lundqvist 20.00 50.00
RAHT Hannu Toivonen 12.00 30.00
RAJC Jeff Carter 12.00 30.00
RAJH Jim Howard 10.00 25.00
RAJJ Jussi Jokinen 8.00 20.00
RAJW Jeff Woywitka 8.00 20.00
RAKB Keith Ballard 8.00 20.00
RAMR Mike Richards 8.00 20.00
RARG Ryan Getzlaf 15.00 40.00
RARN Robert Nilsson 8.00 20.00
RARO Rostislav Olesz 10.00 25.00
RARS Ryan Suter 8.00 20.00
RAST Anthony Stewart 8.00 20.00
RATV Thomas Vanek 15.00 40.00
RAWW Wojtek Wolski 10.00 25.00
RAYD Yann Danis 8.00 20.00
RAZP Zach Parise 15.00 40.00

2005-06 SP Authentic Scripts to Success

PRINT RUN 100 SER.#'d SETS
SSAF Alexander Frolov 6.00 15.00
SSAH Ales Hemsky 6.00 15.00
SSAR Andrew Raycroft 6.00 15.00
SSCB Christian Backman 4.00 10.00
SSCC Carlo Colaiacovo 4.00 10.00
SSDB Dustin Brown 4.00 10.00
SSDF Dan Fritsche 4.00 10.00
SSES Eric Staal 12.00 30.00
SSFT Fedor Tjutin 4.00 10.00
SSHZ Henrik Zetterberg 10.00 25.00
SSJB Jay Bouwmeester 6.00 15.00
SSJC Jonathan Cheechoo 8.00 20.00
SSJL Jamie Lundmark 4.00 10.00
SSJM John-Michael Liles 4.00 10.00
SSJP Joni Pitkanen 4.00 10.00
SSJR Jani Rita 4.00 10.00
SSKL Kari Lehtonen 12.00 30.00
SSLU Joffrey Lupul 4.00 10.00
SSMF Marc-Andre Fleury 15.00 40.00
SSMH Marcel Hossa 4.00 10.00
SSMR Mike Ribeiro 4.00 10.00
SSMS Matt Stajan 6.00 15.00
SSPB Patrice Bergeron 12.00 30.00
SSPL Pascal Leclaire 4.00 10.00
SSPS Philippe Sauve 4.00 10.00
SSRK Ryan Kesler 4.00 10.00
SSRM Ryan Miller 12.00 30.00
SSRY Michael Ryder 10.00 25.00
SSTA Tyler Arnason 4.00 10.00
SSTR Tuomo Ruutu 10.00 25.00

2005-06 SP Authentic Sign of the Times

COMMON CARD 5.00 12.00
STATED ODDS 1:24
AF Alexander Frolov 4.00 10.00
AR Andrew Raycroft 6.00 15.00
AT Jason Arnott 4.00 10.00
AY Alexei Yashin 4.00 10.00
BL Brett Lebda 4.00 10.00
BO Derek Boogaard 4.00 10.00
BR Brian Rafalski 4.00 10.00
BW Jay Bouwmeester 4.00 10.00
CB Christian Backman 4.00 10.00
CC Carlo Colaiacovo 4.00 10.00
CO Craig Conroy 4.00 10.00
CP Chris Pronger SP 8.00 20.00
DB Dustin Brown 4.00 10.00
DC Dan Cloutier 4.00 10.00
DF Dan Fritsche 4.00 10.00
DH Dany Heatley SP 15.00 40.00
DK Duncan Keith 4.00 10.00
DW Doug Weight 4.00 10.00
ED Eric Daze 4.00 10.00
ES Eric Staal 10.00 25.00
FT Fedor Tjutin 4.00 10.00
GL Georges Laraque 4.00 10.00
GM Glen Murray SP 15.00 40.00
GP George Parros 4.00 10.00
HE Timo Helbling 4.00 10.00
HG Jeff Hoggan 4.00 10.00
HO Marcel Hossa 4.00 10.00
HV Martin Havlat 6.00 15.00
HZ Henrik Zetterberg 8.00 20.00
IL Ian Laperriere 4.00 10.00
JA Jani Rita 4.00 10.00
JB Jaroslav Balastik 4.00 10.00
JH Jochen Hecht 4.00 10.00
JI Jarome Iginla SP 25.00 60.00
JL Jamie Lundmark 4.00 10.00
JM John-Michael Liles 4.00 10.00
JO Jeff O'Neill 4.00 10.00
JP Joni Pitkanen 4.00 10.00
JR Jeremy Roenick SP 20.00 50.00
JS Jim Slater 4.00 10.00
KD Kris Draper 4.00 10.00
KE Kevin Dallman 4.00 10.00
KH Kristian Huselius 4.00 10.00
KL Kari Lehtonen 4.00 10.00
KP Keith Primeau 4.00 10.00
KW Kevin Weekes 6.00 15.00
LU Joffrey Lupul 4.00 10.00
MA Marc-Andre Fleury 10.00 25.00
MG Martin Gerber 4.00 10.00
MR Mike Ribeiro 4.00 10.00
MS Matt Stajan
MT Maxime Talbot 4.00 10.00
MW Brenden Morrow 4.00 10.00
NN Niklas Nordgren 4.00 10.00
NY Michael Nylander 4.00 10.00
OS Chris Osgood 4.00 10.00
PB Patrice Bergeron 6.00 15.00
PL Pascal Leclaire 4.00 10.00
PM Pierre-Marc Bouchard 4.00 10.00
PS Philippe Sauve 4.00 10.00
RA Raitis Ivanans 4.00 10.00
RH Ryan Hollweg 4.00 10.00
RI Brad Richards
RK Ryan Kesler 4.00 10.00
RL Roberto Luongo SP 20.00 50.00
RM Ryan Miller 10.00 25.00
RN Rob Niedermayer 4.00 10.00
RO Dwayne Roloson 6.00 15.00
RS Ryan Smith 6.00 15.00
RY Michael Ryder 6.00 15.00
SA Miroslav Satan 4.00 10.00
SB Sean Burke 4.00 10.00
SC Sidney Crosby 200.00 350.00
SL Martin St. Louis SP 15.00 40.00
SN Scott Niedermayer 4.00 10.00
SP Jason Spezza 10.00 25.00
SS Sheldon Souray 4.00 10.00
ST Marco Sturm 4.00 10.00
SZ Sergei Zubov 4.00 10.00
TA Tyler Arnason 4.00 10.00
TG Tim Gleason 4.00 10.00
TH Trent Hunter 4.00 10.00
TL Trevor Linden 6.00 15.00
TP Tom Poti 4.00 10.00
TU Tuomo Ruutu 6.00 15.00
VL Vincent Lecavalier 12.00 30.00
VP Vaclav Prospal 4.00 10.00
WG Wayne Gretzky/15 SP 350.00 500.00

2005-06 SP Authentic Sign of the Times Duals

STATED ODDS 1:288
DAS Nik Antropov 6.00 15.00
Matt Stajan
DBM Patrice Bergeron 8.00 20.00
Glen Murray
DBR Martin Brodeur 12.00 30.00
Brian Rafalski
DBS Cam Barker 10.00 25.00
Brent Seabrook
DCS Erik Cole 10.00 25.00
Eric Staal
DDV Chris Drury 12.00 30.00
Thomas Vanek
DGW Martin Gerber 10.00 25.00
Cam Ward
DHK Marian Hossa 12.00 30.00
Ilya Kovalchuk
DKO Olaf Kolzig 40.00 80.00
Alexander Ovechkin
DKP Saku Koivu 12.00 30.00
Alexander Perezhogin
DLO Manny Legace 6.00 15.00
Chris Osgood
DLP Joffrey Lupul 8.00 20.00
Corey Perry
DMA Mike Modano 12.00 30.00
Jason Arnott
DMC Brendan Morrison 6.00 15.00
Dan Cloutier
DNB Rick Nash 40.00 80.00
Gilbert Brule
DNC Evgeni Nabokov 12.00 30.00
Jonathan Cheechoo
DNN Scott Niedermayer 12.00 30.00
Rob Niedermayer
DPH Michael Peca 6.00 15.00
Ales Hemsky
DPR Keith Primeau 10.00 25.00
Mike Richards
DPS Chris Pronger 12.00 30.00
Ryan Smyth
DRR Jeremy Roenick 20.00 50.00
Luc Robitaille
DRT Andrew Raycroft 8.00 20.00
Hannu Toivonen
DSH Jason Spezza 40.00 100.00
Dany Heatley
DSL Martin St. Louis 20.00 50.00
Vincent Lecavalier
DSO Mats Sundin 15.00 40.00
Jeff O'Neill
DSS Thomas Steen 10.00 25.00
Alexander Steen
DTD Jose Theodore 10.00 25.00
Yann Danis
DWL Kevin Weekes 10.00 25.00
Henrik Lundqvist
DYS Alexei Yashin 6.00 15.00
Miroslav Satan
DZF Henrik Zetterberg 12.00 30.00
Johan Franzen

2005-06 SP Authentic Sign of the Times Triples

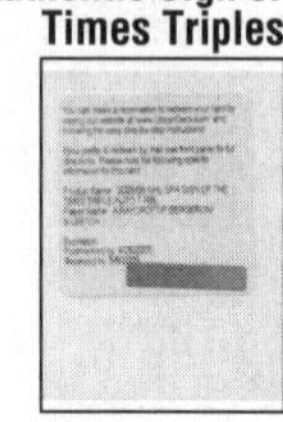

PRINT RUN 15 SER.#'d SETS
NOT PRICED DUE TO SCARCITY
TBSO Ed Belfour
Mats Sundin
Jeff O'Neill
TDBV Chris Drury
Daniel Briere
Thomas Vanek
THAS Dany Heatley
Daniel Alfredsson
Jason Spezza
THHC Dominik Hasek
Martin Havlat
Zdeno Chara
TIPN Jarome Iginla
Dion Phaneuf
Eric Nystrom
TKHL Ilya Kovalchuk
Marian Hossa
Kari Lehtonen
TKRB Nikolai Khabibulin
Tuomo Ruutu
Cam Barker
TLOH Manny Legace
Chris Osgood
Jim Howard
TLPG Joffrey Lupul
Corey Perry
Ryan Getzlaf
TNMB Markus Naslund
Brendan Morrison
Todd Bertuzzi
TPGC Keith Primeau
Simon Gagne
Jeff Carter
TRBL Andrew Raycroft
Patrice Bergeron
Brian Leetch
TRRP Michael Ryder
Mike Ribeiro
Alexander Perezhogin
TRTD Patrick Roy
Jose Theodore
Yann Danis
TSAS Matt Stajan
Nik Antropov
Alexander Steen
TSLR Martin St. Louis
Vincent Lecavalier
Brad Richards
TSOC Alexander Steen
Alexander Ovechkin
Jeff Carter
TTHW Alex Tanguay
Milan Hejduk
Wojtek Wolski
TYPN Alexei Yashin
Mark Parrish
Robert Nilsson
TZFD Henrik Zetterberg
Johan Franzen
Kris Draper

2005-06 SP Authentic Sign of the Times Quads

PRINT RUN 10 SER.#'d SETS
NOT PRICED DUE TO SCARCITY
QCECS Gerry Cheevers
Phil Esposito
Wayne Cashman
Derek Sanderson
QGTVD Wayne Gretzky
Dave Taylor
Rogie Vachon
Marcel Dionne
QPSCW Chris Pronger
Ryan Smyth
Ty Conklin
Brad Winchester
QRCEB Patrick Roy
Gerry Cheevers
Tony Esposito
Martin Brodeur
QSHAH Jason Spezza
Dany Heatley
Daniel Alfredsson
Martin Havlat
QSOPC Alexander Steen
Alexander Ovechkin
Corey Perry
Jeff Carter
QSSOS Mats Sundin
Matt Stajan
Jeff O'Neill
Alexander Steen
QTBNP Bryan Trottier
Mike Bossy
Bob Nystrom
Denis Potvin
QTNBB Joe Thornton
Cam Neely
Patrice Bergeron
Ray Bourque
QTRRK Jose Theodore
Michael Ryder
Mike Ribeiro
Saku Koivu

2005-06 SP Authentic Sign of the Times Fives

PRINT RUN 6 SER.#'d SETS
NOT PRICED DUE TO SCARCITY
ISNKN Jarome Iginla
Martin St. Louis
Rick Nash
Ilya Kovalchuk
Markus Naslund
LRMMG Guy Lafleur
Patrick Roy
Frank Mahovlich
Dickie Moore
Bernie Geoffrion
MMZTJ Mike Modano
Brenden Morrow
Sergei Zubov
Marty Turco
Jussi Jokinen
PEGCR Keith Primeau
Robert Esche
Simon Gagne
Jeff Carter
Mike Richards
POCLS Dion Phaneuf
Alexander Ovechkin
Jeff Carter
Henrik Lundqvist
Alexander
SMSMK Darryl Sittler
Frank Mahovlich
Borje Salming
Lanny McDonald
Red Kelly
TNCMC Joe Thornton
Evgeni Nabokov
Jonathan Cheechoo
Patrick Marleau
Ryane Clo
TWLDH Hannu Toivonen
Cam Ward
Henrik Lundqvist
Yann Danis
Jim Howard

2005-06 SP Authentic Six Star Signatures

PRINT RUN 5 SER.#'d SETS
NOT PRICED DUE TO SCARCITY
SSBO Gerry Cheevers
Ray Bourque
Cam Neely
Wayne Cashman
Phil Esposito
Johnny Bucyk
SSGO Patrick Roy
Martin Brodeur
Jose Theodore
Roberto Luongo
J-S Giguere
Yann Danis
SSHF Wayne Gretzky
Gordie Howe
Marcel Dionne
Guy Lafleur
Bryan Trottier
Bobby Hull
SSMO Bernie Geoffrion
Guy Lafleur
Guy Lapointe
Steve Shutt
Frank Mahovlich
Dickie Moore
SSRO Dion Phaneuf
Alexander Ovechkin
Corey Perry
Jeff Carter
Gilbert Brule
Thomas Vanek
SSTO Darryl Sittler
Lanny McDonald
Red Kelly
Borje Salming
Frank Mahovlich
Mats Sundin

2006-07 SP Authentic

NOTABLE PRINT RUN 999 #'d SETS
RC PRINT RUN 999 #'d SETS
1 Alexander Ovechkin 1.00 2.50
2 Olaf Kolzig .30 .75
3 Markus Naslund .30 .75
4 Roberto Luongo .40 1.00
5 Brendan Morrison .15 .40
6 Mats Sundin .30 .75
7 Michael Peca .15 .40
8 Alexander Steen .25 .60
9 Andrew Raycroft .25 .60
10 Vincent Lecavalier .30 .75
11 Martin St. Louis .25 .60
12 Brad Richards .25 .60
13 Doug Weight .15 .40
14 Keith Tkachuk .25 .60
15 Manny Legace .25 .60
16 Joe Thornton .50 1.25
17 Patrick Marleau .25 .60
18 Jonathan Cheechoo .30 .75
19 Vesa Toskala .25 .60
20 Sidney Crosby 2.00 5.00
21 Marc-Andre Fleury .30 .75
22 Mark Recchi .15 .40
23 Mario Lemieux 1.25 3.00
24 Shane Doan .15 .40
25 Jeremy Roenick .40 1.00
26 Owen Nolan .25 .60
27 Curtis Joseph .30 .75
28 Peter Forsberg .50 1.25
29 Simon Gagne .30 .75
30 Jeff Carter .30 .75
31 Mike Richards .25 .60
32 Jason Spezza .30 .75
33 Daniel Alfredsson .25 .60
34 Dany Heatley .40 1.00
35 Martin Gerber .30 .75
36 Jaromir Jagr .50 1.25
37 Brendan Shanahan .30 .75
38 Henrik Lundqvist .40 1.00
39 Petr Prucha .15 .40
40 Miroslav Satan .15 .40
41 Rick DiPietro .25 .60
42 Alexei Yashin .15 .40
43 Martin Brodeur 1.00 2.50
44 Patrik Elias .15 .40
45 Brian Gionta .15 .40
46 Paul Kariya .30 .75
47 Tomas Vokoun .25 .60
48 Saku Koivu .30 .75
49 Michael Ryder .25 .60
50 Cristobal Huet .30 .75
51 Chris Higgins .15 .40
52 Pavol Demitra .15 .40
53 Marian Gaborik .40 1.00
54 Manny Fernandez .25 .60
55 Wayne Gretzky 1.50 4.00
56 Rob Blake .25 .60
57 Alexander Frolov .15 .40
58 Ed Belfour .30 .75
59 Olli Jokinen .15 .40
60 Todd Bertuzzi .25 .60
61 Ryan Smyth .25 .60
62 Ales Hemsky .15 .40
63 Joffrey Lupul .15 .40
64 Gordie Howe .75 2.00
65 Henrik Zetterberg .30 .75
66 Dominik Hasek .50 1.25
67 Pavel Datsyuk .25 .60
68 Nicklas Lidstrom .30 .75
69 Marty Turco .25 .60
70 Mike Modano .30 .75
71 Eric Lindros .30 .75
72 Rick Nash .30 .75
73 Pascal LeClaire .25 .60
74 Sergei Fedorov .30 .75
75 Joe Sakic .60 1.50
76 Jose Theodore .30 .75
77 Milan Hejduk .15 .40
78 Marek Svatos .15 .40
79 Martin Havlat .25 .60
80 Tuomo Ruutu .15 .40
81 Nikolai Khabibulin .30 .75
82 Eric Staal .30 .75
83 Cam Ward .30 .75
84 Rod Brind'Amour .25 .60
85 Miikka Kiprusoff .30 .75
86 Alex Tanguay .25 .60
87 Jarome Iginla .40 1.00
88 Dion Phaneuf .40 1.00
89 Ryan Miller .30 .75
90 Chris Drury .15 .40
91 Daniel Briere .25 .60
92 Patrice Bergeron .30 .75
93 Brad Boyes .15 .40
94 Zdeno Chara .15 .40
95 Bobby Orr 1.25 3.00
96 Marian Hossa .25 .60
97 Kari Lehtonen .30 .75
98 Ilya Kovalchuk .40 1.00
99 Chris Pronger .25 .60
100 Teemu Selanne .30 .75
101 Ales Hemsky 1.25 3.00
102 Alexander Frolov 1.25 3.00
103 Alexander Ovechkin 2.50 6.00
104 Alexander Steen 2.00 5.00
105 Bobby Orr 3.00 8.00
106 Brendan Shanahan 2.00 5.00
107 Cam Ward 2.00 5.00
108 Dany Heatley 2.50 6.00
109 Dion Phaneuf 2.50 6.00
110 Dominik Hasek 2.50 6.00
111 Doug Weight 1.25 3.00
112 Ed Belfour 2.00 5.00
113 Eric Staal 2.50 6.00
114 Gordie Howe 2.50 6.00
115 Henrik Lundqvist 2.50 6.00
116 Henrik Zetterberg 2.00 5.00
117 Ilya Kovalchuk 2.50 6.00
118 Jarome Iginla 2.50 6.00
119 Jaromir Jagr 2.50 6.00
120 Larry Robinson 2.00 5.00
121 Jason Spezza 2.50 6.00
122 Jay Bouwmeester 1.25 3.00
123 Jeremy Roenick 2.50 6.00
124 Joe Sakic 3.00 8.00
125 Joe Thornton 2.50 6.00
126 Jonathan Cheechoo 1.50 4.00
127 Jose Theodore 1.50 4.00
128 Kari Lehtonen 1.50 4.00
129 Marc-Andre Fleury 1.50 4.00
130 Marian Gaborik 2.50 6.00
131 Mario Lemieux 4.00 10.00
132 Markus Naslund 1.50 4.00
133 Martin Brodeur 3.00 8.00
134 Scott Stevens 1.25 3.00
135 Martin Havlat 2.00 5.00
136 Martin St. Louis 2.00 5.00
137 Mats Sundin 2.00 5.00
138 Michael Ryder 2.00 5.00
139 Miikka Kiprusoff 2.00 5.00
140 Mike Modano 2.00 5.00
141 Milan Hejduk 1.25 3.00
142 Nicklas Lidstrom 2.00 5.00
143 Patrice Bergeron 2.00 5.00
144 Patrick Roy 4.00 10.00
145 Paul Kariya 2.00 5.00
146 Peter Forsberg 2.50 6.00
147 Bobby Clarke 2.00 5.00
148 Ray Bourque 2.50 6.00
149 Rick Nash 2.50 6.00
150 Rob Blake 2.00 5.00
151 Roberto Luongo 2.50 6.00
152 Ryan Miller 2.00 5.00
153 Saku Koivu 2.00 5.00
154 Shane Doan 1.25 3.00
155 Sidney Crosby 8.00 20.00
156 Simon Gagne 2.00 5.00
157 Teemu Selanne 2.50 6.00
158 Tomas Vokoun 2.00 5.00
159 Vincent Lecavalier 2.00 5.00
160 Wayne Gretzky 6.00 15.00
161 Ryan Shannon AU RC 5.00 12.00
162 Shane O'Brien AU RC 5.00 12.00
163 Phil Kessel AU RC 20.00 50.00
164 Mark Stuart AU RC 5.00 12.00
165 Matt Lashoff AU RC 5.00 12.00
166 Yan Stastny AU RC 5.00 12.00
167 Nate Thompson AU RC 5.00 12.00
168 Drew Stafford AU RC 15.00 40.00
169 Dustin Boyd AU RC 8.00 20.00
170 Brandon Prust AU RC 5.00 12.00
171 Dave Bolland AU RC 5.00 12.00
172 Michael Blunden AU RC 5.00 12.00
173 Dustin Byfuglien AU RC 5.00 12.00
174 Paul Stastny AU RC 25.00 60.00
175 Karri Ramo AU RC 5.00 12.00
176 Loui Eriksson AU RC 5.00 12.00
177 Tomas Kopecky AU RC 8.00 20.00
178 Ladislav Smid AU RC 5.00 12.00
179 Marc-Antoine Pouliot AU RC 8.00 20.00
180 Niklas Grossman AU RC 5.00 12.00
181 Patrick Thoresen AU RC 8.00 20.00
182 Janis Sprukts AU RC 5.00 12.00
183 Patrick O'Sullivan AU RC 10.00 25.00
184 Anze Kopitar AU RC 25.00 60.00
185 Konstantin Pushkaryov AU RC 5.00 12.00
186 Guillaume Latendresse AU RC 20.00 50.00
187 Shea Weber AU RC 8.00 20.00
188 Alexander Radulov AU RC 20.00 50.00
189 Travis Zajac AU RC 10.00 25.00
190 Jarkko Immonen AU RC 5.00 12.00
191 Nigel Dawes AU RC 5.00 12.00
192 Kelly Guard AU RC 5.00 12.00
193 Ryan Potulny AU RC 8.00 20.00
194 Benoit Pouliot AU RC 8.00 20.00
195 Keith Yandle AU RC 5.00 12.00
196 Evgeni Malkin AU RC 100.00 200.00
197 Noah Welch AU RC 5.00 12.00
198 Jordan Staal AU RC 75.00 150.00
199 Michel Ouellet AU RC 6.00 15.00
200 Kristopher Letang AU RC 8.00 20.00
201 Matt Carle AU RC 8.00 20.00
202 Marc-Edouard Vlasic AU RC 5.00 12.00
203 Roman Polak AU RC 5.00 12.00
204 Jeremy Williams AU RC 5.00 12.00
205 Ian White AU RC 5.00 12.00
206 Jesse Schultz AU RC 5.00 12.00
207 Brendan Bell AU RC 5.00 12.00
208 Luc Bourdon AU RC 8.00 20.00
209 Alexander Edler AU RC 5.00 12.00
210 Eric Fehr AU RC 8.00 20.00
211 Daren Machesney RC 2.00 5.00
212 Nathan McIver RC 2.00 5.00
213 Patrick Coulombe RC 2.00 5.00
214 Alexei Mikhnov RC 2.00 5.00
215 Kris Newbury RC 2.00 5.00
216 Blair Jones RC 2.00 5.00
217 Marek Schwarz RC 5.00 12.00
218 David Backes RC 4.00 10.00
219 Joe Pavelski RC 6.00 15.00
220 Patrick Fischer RC 2.00 5.00
221 Bill Thomas RC 2.00 5.00
222 Triston Grant RC 2.00 5.00
223 Lars Jonsson RC 2.00 5.00
224 David Printz RC 2.00 5.00
225 Jussi Timonen RC 2.00 5.00
226 Martin Houle RC 2.00 5.00
227 Josh Hennessy RC 2.00 5.00
228 Blake Comeau RC 2.00 5.00
229 Masi Marjamaki RC 2.00 5.00
230 Ben Ondrus RC 2.00 5.00
231 Fredrik Norrena RC 3.00 8.00
232 Johnny Oduya RC 2.00 5.00
233 Enver Lisin RC 2.00 5.00
234 Mikhail Grabovski RC 2.00 5.00
235 Mikko Lehtonen RC 2.00 5.00
236 Niklas Backstrom RC 4.00 10.00
237 Miroslav Kopriva RC 2.50 6.00
238 Benoit Pouliot RC 4.00 10.00
239 Peter Harrold RC 2.00 5.00
240 David Booth RC 2.00 5.00
241 Drew Larman RC 2.00 5.00
242 Jan Hejda RC 2.00 5.00
243 Jeff Deslauriers RC 2.00 5.00
244 Stefan Liv RC 3.00 8.00
245 Adam Burish RC 2.00 5.00
246 Michael Funk RC 2.00 5.00
247 Mike Card RC 2.00 5.00
248 Adam Dennis RC 2.00 5.00
249 Clarke MacArthur RC 2.00 5.00
250 David McKee RC 3.00 8.00

2006-07 SP Authentic Chirography

STATED PRINT RUN 75 #'d SETS
AF Alexander Frolov 8.00 20.00
AH Ales Hemsky 6.00 15.00
AK Anze Kopitar 20.00 50.00
BB Brad Boyes 4.00 10.00
CP Corey Perry 6.00 15.00
DH Dany Heatley 12.00 30.00
DR Dwayne Roloson 4.00 10.00
DT Darcy Tucker 8.00 20.00
EM Evgeni Malkin 30.00 80.00
ES Eric Staal 6.00 15.00
GE Martin Gerber 8.00 20.00
HA Dominik Hasek 20.00 50.00
HE Milan Hejduk 6.00 15.00
JC Jonathan Cheechoo 8.00 20.00
JI Jarome Iginla 20.00 50.00
JS Jordan Staal 30.00 80.00
KD Kris Draper 6.00 15.00
MC Mike Cammalleri 8.00 20.00
MF Marc-Andre Fleury 15.00 40.00
MH Martin Havlat 6.00 15.00
MM Mike Modano 8.00 20.00
MP Michael Peca 8.00 20.00
MS Marek Svatos 6.00 15.00
MT Marty Turco 8.00 20.00
NL Nicklas Lidstrom 15.00 30.00
PE Patrik Elias 6.00 15.00
PM Patrick Marleau 8.00 20.00
PO Patrick O'Sullivan 12.00 30.00
PP Petr Prucha 4.00 10.00
RM Ryan Miller 12.00 30.00
RN Rick Nash 15.00 40.00
RS Matt Carle 6.00 15.00
SC Sidney Crosby 125.00 200.00
TV Tomas Vokoun 8.00 20.00

2006-07 SP Authentic Limited

*LIMITED: 4X TO 10X BASE HI
STATED PRINT RUN 100 #'d SETS
1 Alexander Ovechkin 8.00 20.00
2 Olaf Kolzig 2.50 6.00
3 Markus Naslund 2.50 6.00
4 Roberto Luongo 4.00 10.00
5 Brendan Morrison 1.50 4.00
6 Mats Sundin 3.00 8.00
7 Michael Peca 1.50 4.00
8 Alexander Steen 2.50 6.00
9 Andrew Raycroft 2.50 6.00
10 Vincent Lecavalier 3.00 8.00
11 Martin St. Louis 2.50 6.00
12 Brad Richards 2.50 6.00
13 Doug Weight 1.50 4.00
14 Keith Tkachuk 2.50 6.00
15 Manny Legace 2.50 6.00
16 Joe Thornton 4.00 10.00
17 Patrick Marleau 2.50 6.00
18 Jonathan Cheechoo 3.00 8.00
19 Vesa Toskala 2.50 6.00
20 Sidney Crosby 15.00 40.00
21 Marc-Andre Fleury 3.00 8.00
22 Mark Recchi 1.50 4.00
23 Mario Lemieux 12.00 30.00
24 Shane Doan 1.50 4.00
25 Jeremy Roenick 4.00 10.00
26 Owen Nolan 2.50 6.00
27 Curtis Joseph 3.00 8.00
28 Peter Forsberg 4.00 10.00
29 Simon Gagne 3.00 8.00
30 Jeff Carter 3.00 8.00
31 Mike Richards 2.50 6.00
32 Jason Spezza 3.00 8.00
33 Daniel Alfredsson 2.50 6.00
34 Dany Heatley 4.00 10.00
35 Martin Gerber 3.00 8.00
36 Jaromir Jagr 4.00 10.00
37 Brendan Shanahan 3.00 8.00
38 Henrik Lundqvist 4.00 10.00
39 Petr Prucha 1.50 4.00
40 Miroslav Satan 1.50 4.00
41 Rick DiPietro 2.50 6.00
42 Alexei Yashin 1.50 4.00
43 Martin Brodeur 6.00 15.00
44 Patrik Elias 1.50 4.00
45 Brian Gionta 1.50 4.00
46 Paul Kariya 3.00 8.00
47 Tomas Vokoun 2.50 6.00
48 Saku Koivu 3.00 8.00
49 Michael Ryder 2.50 6.00
50 Cristobal Huet 3.00 8.00
51 Chris Higgins 2.50 6.00
52 Pavol Demitra 1.50 4.00
53 Marian Gaborik 4.00 10.00
54 Manny Fernandez 2.50 6.00
55 Wayne Gretzky 12.00 30.00
56 Rob Blake 2.50 6.00
57 Alexander Frolov 1.50 4.00
58 Ed Belfour 3.00 8.00
59 Olli Jokinen 1.50 4.00
60 Todd Bertuzzi 2.50 6.00
61 Ryan Smyth 2.50 6.00
62 Ales Hemsky 1.50 4.00
63 Joffrey Lupul 1.50 4.00
64 Gordie Howe 4.00 10.00
65 Henrik Zetterberg 3.00 8.00
66 Dominik Hasek 4.00 10.00
67 Pavel Datsyuk 2.50 6.00
68 Nicklas Lidstrom 3.00 8.00
69 Marty Turco 2.50 6.00
70 Mike Modano 4.00 10.00
71 Eric Lindros 3.00 8.00
72 Rick Nash 3.00 8.00
73 Pascal LeClaire 2.50 6.00
74 Sergei Fedorov 3.00 8.00
75 Joe Sakic 5.00 12.00
76 Jose Theodore 3.00 8.00
77 Milan Hejduk 1.50 4.00

78 Marek Svatos 1.50 4.00
79 Martin Havlat 2.50 6.00
80 Tuomo Ruutu 1.50 4.00
81 Nikolai Khabibulin 3.00 8.00
82 Eric Staal 3.00 8.00
83 Cam Ward 3.00 8.00
84 Rod Brind'Amour 2.50 6.00
85 Miikka Kiprusoff 3.00 8.00
86 Alex Tanguay 2.50 6.00
87 Jarome Iginla 4.00 10.00
88 Dion Phaneuf 4.00 10.00
89 Ryan Miller 3.00 8.00
90 Chris Drury 1.50 4.00
91 Daniel Briere 2.50 6.00
92 Patrice Bergeron 3.00 8.00
93 Brad Boyes 1.50 4.00
94 Zdeno Chara 1.50 4.00
95 Bobby Orr 10.00 25.00
96 Marian Hossa 2.50 6.00
97 Kari Lehtonen 3.00 8.00
98 Ilya Kovalchuk 4.00 10.00
99 Chris Pronger 2.50 6.00
100 Teemu Selanne 3.00 8.00
101 Ales Hemsky 1.50 4.00
102 Alexander Frolov 1.50 4.00
103 Alexander Ovechkin 8.00 20.00
104 Alexander Steen 2.50 6.00
105 Bobby Orr 10.00 25.00
106 Brendan Shanahan 3.00 8.00
107 Cam Ward 3.00 8.00
108 Dany Heatley 4.00 10.00
109 Dion Phaneuf 4.00 10.00
110 Dominik Hasek 4.00 10.00
111 Doug Weight 1.50 4.00
112 Ed Belfour 3.00 8.00
113 Eric Staal 3.00 8.00
114 Gordie Howe 4.00 10.00
115 Henrik Lundqvist 4.00 10.00
116 Henrik Zetterberg 3.00 8.00
117 Ilya Kovalchuk 4.00 10.00
118 Jarome Iginla 4.00 10.00
119 Jaromir Jagr 5.00 12.00
120 Larry Robinson 2.50 6.00
121 Jason Spezza 3.00 8.00
122 Jay Bouwmeester 1.50 4.00
123 Jeremy Roenick 4.00 10.00
124 Joe Sakic 5.00 12.00
125 Joe Thornton 5.00 12.00
126 Jonathan Cheechoo 3.00 8.00
127 Jose Theodore 3.00 8.00
128 Kari Lehtonen 3.00 8.00
129 Marc-Andre Fleury 3.00 8.00
130 Marian Gaborik 4.00 10.00
131 Mario Lemieux 12.00 30.00
132 Markus Naslund 3.00 8.00
133 Martin Brodeur 8.00 20.00
134 Scott Stevens 1.50 4.00
135 Martin Havlat 2.50 6.00
136 Martin St. Louis 2.50 6.00
137 Mats Sundin 3.00 8.00
138 Michael Ryder 2.50 6.00
139 Miikka Kiprusoff 3.00 8.00
140 Mike Modano 3.00 8.00
141 Milan Hejduk 1.50 4.00
142 Nicklas Lidstrom 3.00 8.00
143 Patrice Bergeron 3.00 8.00
144 Patrick Roy 12.00 30.00
145 Paul Kariya 3.00 8.00
146 Peter Forsberg 5.00 12.00
147 Bobby Clarke 3.00 8.00
148 Ray Bourque 5.00 12.00
149 Rick Nash 3.00 8.00
150 Rob Blake 2.50 6.00
151 Roberto Luongo 4.00 10.00
152 Ryan Miller 3.00 8.00
153 Saku Koivu 3.00 8.00
154 Shane Doan 1.50 4.00
155 Sidney Crosby 15.00 40.00
156 Simon Gagne 3.00 8.00
157 Teemu Selanne 3.00 8.00
158 Tomas Vokoun 2.50 6.00
159 Vincent Lecavalier 3.00 8.00
160 Wayne Gretzky 12.00 30.00
161 Ryan Shannon 25.00 60.00
162 Shane O'Brien 20.00 50.00
163 Phil Kessel 60.00 175.00
164 Mark Stuart 20.00 50.00
165 Matt Lashoff 25.00 60.00
166 Yan Stastny 25.00 60.00
167 Nate Thompson
168 Drew Stafford 60.00 175.00
169 Dustin Boyd 30.00 80.00
170 Brandon Prust 25.00 60.00
171 Dave Bolland 25.00 60.00
172 Michael Blunden 20.00 50.00
173 Dustin Byfuglien 25.00 60.00
174 Paul Stastny 100.00 250.00
175 Karri Ramo 25.00 60.00
176 Loui Eriksson 30.00 80.00
177 Tomas Kopecky 30.00 80.00
178 Ladislav Smid 25.00 60.00
179 Marc-Antoine Pouliot 25.00 60.00
180 Niklas Grossman 20.00 50.00
181 Patrick Thoresen 20.00 50.00
182 Janis Sprukts 20.00 50.00
183 Patrick O'Sullivan 40.00 100.00
184 Anze Kopitar 100.00 250.00
185 Konstantin Pushkaryov 20.00 50.00
186 Guillaume Latendresse 60.00 150.00
187 Shea Weber 30.00 80.00
188 Alexander Radulov 50.00 150.00
189 Travis Zajac 30.00 80.00
190 Jarkko Immonen 25.00 60.00
191 Nigel Dawes 20.00 50.00
192 Kelly Guard
193 Ryan Potulny 30.00 80.00
194 Benoit Pouliot 30.00 80.00
195 Keith Yandle 20.00 50.00
196 Evgeni Malkin 250.00 500.00
197 Noah Welch 20.00 50.00
198 Jordan Staal 150.00 350.00
199 Michel Ouellet 25.00 60.00
200 Kristopher Letang 30.00 80.00
201 Matt Carle 25.00 60.00
202 Marc-Edouard Vlasic 40.00 80.00
203 Roman Polak 15.00 40.00
204 Jeremy Williams 25.00 60.00
205 Ian White 15.00 40.00
206 Jesse Schultz 25.00 60.00
207 Brendan Bell 15.00 40.00
208 Luc Bourdon 40.00 100.00
209 Alexander Edler 30.00 80.00
210 Eric Fehr 30.00 80.00
211 Daren Machesney 3.00 8.00
212 Nathan McIver 3.00 8.00
213 Patrick Coulombe 3.00 8.00
214 Alexei Mikhnov 3.00 8.00
215 Kris Newbury 3.00 8.00
216 Blair Jones 3.00 8.00
217 Marek Schwarz 6.00 15.00
218 David Backes 5.00 12.00
219 Joe Pavelski 8.00 20.00
220 Patrick Fischer 3.00 8.00
221 Bill Thomas 3.00 8.00
222 Triston Grant 3.00 8.00
223 Lars Jonsson 3.00 8.00
224 David Printz 3.00 8.00
225 Jussi Timonen 3.00 8.00
226 Martin Houle 3.00 8.00
227 Josh Hennessy 3.00 8.00
228 Blake Comeau 3.00 8.00
229 Masi Marjamaki 3.00 8.00
230 Ben Ondrus 3.00 8.00
231 Fredrik Norrena 5.00 12.00
232 Johnny Oduya 3.00 8.00
233 Enver Lisin 3.00 8.00
234 Mikhail Grabovski 3.00 8.00
235 Mikko Lehtonen 3.00 8.00
236 Niklas Backstrom 6.00 15.00
237 Miroslav Kopriva 3.00 8.00
238 Benoit Pouliot 5.00 12.00
239 Peter Harrold 3.00 8.00
240 David Booth 3.00 8.00
241 Drew Larman 3.00 8.00
242 Jan Hejda 3.00 8.00
243 Jeff Deslauriers 3.00 8.00
244 Stefan Liv 5.00 12.00
245 Adam Burish 3.00 8.00
246 Michael Funk 3.00 8.00
247 Mike Card 3.00 8.00
248 Adam Dennis 3.00 8.00
249 Clarke MacArthur 3.00 8.00
250 David McKee 5.00 12.00

2006-07 SP Authentic Sign of the Times

The Phaneuf single was not part of the original checklist and may not have been issued in packs. However, a handful of copies were circulated, apparently by company employees, and thus it is included in this listing but without a price.

STATED ODDS 1:24
STAF Alexander Frolov 4.00 10.00
STAH Ales Hemsky 4.00 10.00
STAR Andrew Raycroft 6.00 15.00
STBG Brian Gionta 4.00 10.00
STBH Bobby Hull SP 20.00 50.00
STBO Bobby Orr 125.00 200.00
STBU Johnny Bucyk 6.00 15.00
STCA Colby Armstrong SP 10.00 25.00
STCP Corey Perry 8.00 20.00
STCW Cam Ward 8.00 20.00
STDC Don Cherry 12.00 30.00
STDH Dominik Hasek 15.00 40.00
STDR Dwayne Roloson 4.00 10.00
STDS Denis Savard 6.00 15.00
STEL Patrik Elias 4.00 10.00
STEM Evgeni Malkin 40.00 100.00
STES Eric Staal 8.00 20.00
STGB Gilbert Brule 8.00 20.00
STGE Martin Gerber SP 6.00 15.00
STGH Gordie Howe 50.00 100.00
STGO Scott Gomez 4.00 10.00
STHE Dany Heatley 10.00 25.00
STHJ Milan Hejduk 4.00 10.00
STIB Ray Bourque SP 40.00 80.00
STJB Jean Beliveau SP 40.00 100.00
STJC Jonathan Cheechoo 6.00 15.00
STJE Jeff Carter 4.00 10.00
STJG Jean-Sebastien Giguere 6.00 15.00
STJI Jarome Iginla 10.00 25.00
STJK Jari Kurri 8.00 20.00
STJM Joe Mullen 4.00 10.00
STJS Jarret Stoll 4.00 10.00
STJT Jose Theodore 6.00 15.00
STJW Justin Williams 4.00 10.00
STKD Kris Draper 4.00 10.00
STLR Luc Robitaille SP 125.00 200.00
STMA Matt Carle 4.00 10.00
STMB Martin Brodeur 40.00 80.00
STMF Marc-Andre Fleury 10.00 25.00
STMH Martin Havlat 6.00 15.00
STMI Ryan Miller 8.00 20.00
STML Mario Lemieux SP 100.00 250.00
STMM Mike Modano 8.00 20.00
STMO Brenden Morrow 6.00 15.00
STMT Marty Turco 6.00 15.00
STNL Nicklas Lidstrom 6.00 15.00
STPB Pierre-Marc Bouchard SP 4.00 10.00
STPE Michael Peca 4.00 10.00
STPK Phil Kessel 8.00 20.00
STPM Patrick Marleau SP 6.00 15.00
STPP Petr Prucha SP 15.00 40.00
STRN Rick Nash 10.00 25.00
STRY Michael Ryder 6.00 15.00
STSC Sidney Crosby 100.00 200.00
STSK Saku Koivu SP 12.00 30.00
STSV Marek Svatos 4.00 10.00
STTE Tony Esposito 15.00 40.00
STTV Tomas Vokoun 6.00 15.00
STVT Vesa Toskala 6.00 15.00
STWC Wendel Clark 10.00 25.00
STWG Wayne Gretzky 125.00 250.00
STWO Willie O'Ree SP 20.00 40.00

2006-07 SP Authentic Sign of the Times Duals

STAS Glenn Anderson 20.00 50.00
Ryan Smyth
STBE Ron Ellis 15.00 40.00
Johnny Bower
STBG Mike Bossy 15.00 40.00
Clark Gillies
STBM Rob Blake 10.00 25.00
Larry Murphy
STBW Martin Brodeur 50.00 100.00
Cam Ward
STCB Jonathan Cheechoo 10.00 25.00
Steve Bernier
STCC Bobby Clarke 20.00 50.00
Jeff Carter
STCT Gerry Cheevers 20.00 50.00
Hannu Toivonen
STDS Saku Koivu 20.00 50.00
Denis Savard
STDV Marcel Dionne 15.00 40.00
Rogie Vachon
STEG Patrik Elias 12.00 30.00
Brian Gionta
STET Tony Esposito 20.00 50.00
Marty Turco
STFK Alexander Frolov 15.00 40.00
Anze Kopitar
STFM Bernie Federko 8.00 20.00
Joe Mullen
STGL Mario Lemieux 400.00 600.00
Wayne Gretzky SP
STGR Grant Fuhr 25.00 60.00
Ryan Miller
STHA David Aebischer 20.00 50.00
Cristobal Huet
STHE Dany Heatley 12.00 30.00
Patrick Eaves
STHK Martin Havlat 12.00 30.00
Nikolai Khabibulin
STHO Bobby Orr 200.00 300.00
Gordie Howe
STHS Milan Hejduk 8.00 20.00
Marek Svatos
STIT Jarome Iginla 25.00 60.00
Alex Tanguay
STKB Patrice Bergeron 15.00 40.00
Phil Kessel
STKL Ilya Kovalchuk 20.00 40.00
Kari Lehtonen
STLB Roberto Luongo 40.00 100.00
Richard Brodeur
STLG Simon Gagne 12.00 30.00
Reggie Leach
STLM Mario Lemieux 150.00 250.00
Evgeni Malkin SP
STLR Guy Lafleur 20.00 50.00
Michael Ryder
STLS Nicklas Lidstrom 20.00 50.00
Borje Salming
STLT Vincent Lecavalier 30.00 80.00
Joe Thornton
STMC Guy Lafleur 20.00 50.00
Larry Robinson
STMM Mike Modano 12.00 30.00
Brenden Morrow
STMR Mike Modano 15.00 40.00
Mike Ribeiro
STNB Rick Nash 12.00 30.00
Gilbert Brule
STNK Cam Neely 30.00 80.00
Phil Kessel
STOB Bobby Orr 200.00 350.00
Ray Bourque
STPJ Patrick Marleau 12.00 30.00
Jonathan Cheechoo
STPP Zach Parise 25.00 60.00
J.P. Parise
STQC Peter Stastny 30.00 80.00
Paul Stastny
STRB Patrick Roy
Martin Brodeur SP
STRL Michael Ryder 25.00 60.00
Guillaume Latendresse
STRP Denis Potvin 10.00 25.00
Larry Robinson
STRR Dwayne Roloson 10.00 25.00
Bill Ranford
STRT Luc Robitaille 15.00 40.00
Dave Taylor
STSA Colby Armstrong 30.00 80.00
Jordan Staal
STSS Eric Staal 60.00 125.00
Jordan Staal
STSW Jarret Stoll 25.00 60.00
Cam Ward
STVA Tomas Vokoun 8.00 20.00
Jason Arnott
STVH Tomas Vokoun 20.00 50.00
Dominik Hasek
STWR Shea Weber 20.00 50.00
Alexander Radulov

2006-07 SP Authentic Sign of the Times Triples

STATED PRINT RUN 25 #'d SETS
ST3BBK Brad Boyes 60.00 125.00
Patrice Bergeron
Phil Kessel
ST3BEK Ron Ellis 50.00 100.00
Johnny Bower
Red Kelly
ST3COS Gerry Cheevers
Terry O'Reilly
Derek Sanderson
ST3DBM Chris Drury 60.00 125.00
Daniel Briere
Ryan Miller
ST3HNS Dany Heatley 100.00 175.00
Rick Nash
Eric Staal
ST3HTS Milan Hejduk 30.00 80.00
Jose Theodore
Marek Svatos
ST3ITK Jarome Iginla 50.00 100.00
Alex Tanguay
Miikka Kiprusoff
ST3LFM Mario Lemieux 250.00 400.00
Marc-Andre Fleury
Evgeni Malkin
ST3LGH Mario Lemieux 600.00 900.00
Wayne Gretzky
Gordie Howe
ST3LHZ Nicklas Lidstrom
Tomas Holmstrom
Henrik Zetterberg
ST3LRS Guy Lafleur
Steve Shutt
Larry Robinson
ST3MTC Patrick Marleau 60.00 125.00
Joe Thornton
Jonathan Cheechoo
ST3MTM Mike Modano 50.00 100.00
Marty Turco
Brenden Morrow
ST3NLM Markus Naslund 50.00 100.00
Roberto Luongo
Brendan Morrison
ST3OBE Phil Esposito
Bobby Orr
Ray Bourque
ST3PGB Mark Parrish 60.00 125.00
Marian Gaborik
Pierre-Marc Bouchard
ST3RBW Patrick Roy 250.00 350.00
Martin Brodeur
Cam Ward
ST3RHG Wade Redden
Dany Heatley
Martin Gerber
ST3RKH Chris Higgins 50.00 100.00
Saku Koivu
Michael Ryder
ST3SSH Ryan Smyth 30.00 80.00
Jarret Stoll
Ales Hemsky
ST3SSS Peter Stastny
Yan Stastny
Paul Stastny
ST3WSW Justin Williams 50.00 125.00
Eric Staal
Cam Ward
ST3SUT1 Brent Sutter 30.00 80.00
Darryl Sutter
Duane Sutter
ST3SUT2 Brian Sutter 30.00 80.00
Rich Sutter
Ron Sutter

2006-07 SP Authentic Sign of the Times Quads

PRINT RUN 10 #'d SETS
NOT PRICED DUE TO SCARCITY
ST4BCTS Mike Bossy
Bobby Clarke
Dave Taylor
Darryl Sittler
ST4BLSR Guy Lafleur
Steve Shutt
Scotty Bowman
Larry Robinson
ST4EBOC Phil Esposito
Johnny Bucyk
Bobby Orr
Don Cherry
ST4ECVP Tony Esposito
Gerry Cheevers
Rogie Vachon
Bernie Parent
ST4EHSW Tony Esposito
Bobby Hull
Denis Savard
Doug Wilson
ST4IKPT Jarome Iginla
Alex Tanguay
Miikka Kiprusoff
Dion Phaneuf
ST4LOGH Mario Lemieux
Bobby Orr
Wayne Gretzky
Gordie Howe
ST4MKSL Evgeni Malkin
Phil Kessel
Jordan Staal
Guillaume Latendresse
ST4RBLF Patrick Roy
Martin Brodeur
Roberto Luongo
Marc-Andre Fleury
ST4SSSS Peter Stastny
Anton Stastny
Yan Stastny
Paul Stastny

2000-01 SP Game Used

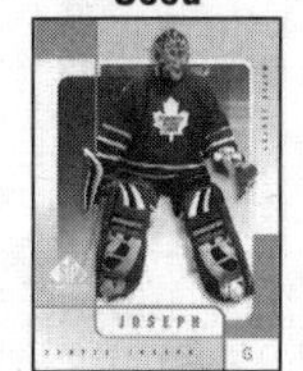

The SP Game-Used set was released as a 90-card set with 30 short-printed rookies, serial numbered to 900. The card fronts featured a full color photo of the featured player. The card design had grey and white boarders, along with silver-foil highlights. The card backs had a small color photo of the featured player along with his statistics and a brief summary of his 2000-01 season.

COMP.SET w/o SP's (60) 75.00 150.00
1 Paul Kariya 1.25 3.00
2 Teemu Selanne 1.25 3.00
3 Patrik Stefan .40 1.00
4 Byron Dafoe 1.00 2.50
5 Joe Thornton 2.00 5.00
6 Dominik Hasek 2.50 6.00
7 Maxim Afinogenov .40 1.00
8 Valeri Bure .40 1.00
9 Ron Francis 1.00 2.50
10 Arturs Irbe 1.00 2.50
11 Tony Amonte 1.00 2.50
12 Steve Sullivan .40 1.00
13 Patrick Roy 6.00 15.00
14 Joe Sakic 2.50 6.00
15 Peter Forsberg 3.00 8.00
16 Ray Bourque 2.50 6.00
17 Ron Tugnutt 1.00 2.50
18 Mike Modano 2.00 5.00
19 Brett Hull 1.50 4.00
20 Ed Belfour 1.25 3.00
21 Steve Yzerman 5.00 12.00
22 Brendan Shanahan 1.25 3.00
23 Sergei Fedorov 2.00 5.00
24 Nicklas Lidstrom 1.25 3.00
25 Doug Weight 1.00 2.50
26 Tommy Salo 1.00 2.50
27 Pavel Bure 1.25 3.00
28 Trevor Kidd 1.00 2.50
29 Luc Robitaille 1.00 2.50
30 Zigmund Palffy 1.00 2.50
31 Manny Fernandez 1.00 2.50
32 Jose Theodore 1.50 4.00
33 Trevor Linden 1.00 2.50
34 Mike Dunham .40 1.00
35 David Legwand 1.00 2.50
36 Martin Brodeur 3.00 8.00
37 Scott Gomez .40 1.00
38 Tim Connolly .40 1.00
39 John Vanbiesbrouck 1.00 2.50
40 Mike Richter 1.25 3.00
41 Mark Messier 1.25 3.00
42 Marian Hossa 1.25 3.00
43 Alexei Yashin .40 1.00
44 Brian Boucher 1.25 3.00
45 John LeClair 1.25 3.00
46 Jeremy Roenick 1.50 4.00
47 Keith Tkachuk 1.25 3.00
48 Jaromir Jagr 2.00 5.00
49 Mario Lemieux 6.00 15.00
50 Steve Shields 1.00 2.50
51 Owen Nolan 1.00 2.50
52 Roman Turek 1.00 2.50
53 Pavol Demitra 1.00 2.50
54 Vincent Lecavalier 1.25 3.00
55 Curtis Joseph 1.25 3.00
56 Mats Sundin 1.25 3.00
57 Daniel Sedin .40 1.00
58 Henrik Sedin .40 1.00
59 Olaf Kolzig 1.00 2.50
60 Chris Simon .40 1.00
61 Jonas Ronnqvist RC 2.50 6.00
62 Andy McDonald RC 4.00 10.00
63 Andrew Raycroft RC 6.00 15.00
64 Josef Vasicek RC 2.50 6.00
65 David Aebischer RC 6.00 15.00
66 Rostislav Klesla RC 3.00 8.00
67 Marty Turco RC 10.00 25.00
68 Tyler Bouck RC 2.50 6.00
69 Steven Reinprecht RC 2.50 6.00
70 Marian Gaborik RC 20.00 50.00
71 Scott Hartnell RC 4.00 10.00
72 Greg Classen RC 2.50 6.00
73 Rick DiPietro RC 10.00 25.00
74 Jason LaBarbera RC 3.00 8.00
75 Martin Havlat RC 10.00 25.00
76 Jani Hurme RC 2.50 6.00
77 Roman Cechmanek RC 2.50 6.00
78 Ruslan Fedotenko RC 2.50 6.00
79 Justin Williams RC 5.00 12.00
80 Roman Simicek RC 2.50 6.00
81 Mark Smith RC 2.50 6.00
82 Matt Elich RC 2.50 6.00
83 Alexander Kharitonov RC 2.50 6.00
84 Fedor Fedorov RC 2.50 6.00
85 Marc-Andre Thinel RC 2.50 6.00
86 Zdenek Blatny RC 2.50 6.00
87 Jeff Bateman RC 2.50 6.00
88 Jason Jaspers RC 2.50 6.00
89 Jordan Krestanovich RC 2.50 6.00
90 Damian Surma RC 2.50 6.00

2000-01 SP Game Used Patch Cards

Randomly inserted in SP Game-Used Edition packs, the 29-card set featured jersey patch swatches. The set had 5 combo player swatches. The card numbers carried a 'P' prefix and a 'D' prefix on the combo cards. The cards were serial numbered to 50.

D-FR Peter Forsberg 75.00 200.00
Patrick Roy
D-JL Jaromir Jagr 150.00 400.00
Mario Lemieux
D-KG Paul Kariya 200.00 500.00
Wayne Gretzky
D-MG Mark Messier 200.00 500.00
Wayne Gretzky
D-OB Bobby Orr 200.00 500.00
Ray Bourque
P-BB Brian Boucher 20.00 50.00
P-BH Brett Hull 30.00 80.00
P-BO Bobby Orr 150.00 400.00
P-GH Gordie Howe 125.00 300.00
P-JJ Jaromir Jagr 40.00 100.00
P-JL John LeClair 25.00 60.00
P-JR Jeremy Roenick 40.00 100.00
P-JS Joe Sakic 40.00 100.00
P-KT Keith Tkachuk 25.00 60.00
P-MB Martin Brodeur 60.00 150.00
P-ML Mario Lemieux 150.00 400.00
P-MM Mark Messier 60.00 150.00
P-MO Mike Modano 40.00 100.00
P-MS Mats Sundin 25.00 60.00
P-PB Pavel Bure 25.00 60.00
P-PF Peter Forsberg 60.00 150.00
P-PK Paul Kariya 25.00 60.00
P-PR Patrick Roy 75.00 200.00
P-RB Ray Bourque 50.00 125.00
P-SF Sergei Fedorov 25.00 60.00
P-SY Steve Yzerman 75.00 200.00
P-TA Tony Amonte 20.00 50.00
P-TS Teemu Selanne 25.00 60.00
P-WG Wayne Gretzky 150.00 400.00

2000-01 SP Game Used Tools of the Game

Randomly inserted in SP Game-Used Edition packs, the 38-card set featured game-used jersey swatches. The card numbers had the player's initials in place of the number. The cards were serial numbered to 350.

*MULT.COLOR SWATCH 1.5X TO 2X HI
*EXCL.STARS: 1X TO 1.5X HI COLUMN
EXCL.STAT.PRINT RUN 350 SER.#'d SETS
AM Al MacInnis 3.00 8.00
BB Brian Boucher 3.00 8.00
BD Byron Dafoe 3.00 8.00
BH Brett Hull 5.00 12.00
BL Brian Leetch 4.00 10.00
CO Chris Osgood 3.00 8.00
DL David Legwand 3.00 8.00
EL Eric Lindros 4.00 10.00
GH Gordie Howe 20.00 40.00
JJ Jaromir Jagr 5.00 12.00
JL John LeClair 4.00 10.00
JN Joe Nieuwendyk 3.00 8.00
JR Jeremy Roenick 5.00 12.00
JS Joe Sakic 8.00 20.00
KT Keith Tkachuk 4.00 10.00
MB Martin Brodeur 12.50 30.00
MH Michal Handzus 3.00 8.00
ML Mario Lemieux 12.50 30.00
MM Mark Messier 4.00 10.00
MO Mike Modano 5.00 12.00
MP Michael Peca 3.00 8.00
MR Mike Richter 6.00 15.00
MS Mats Sundin 4.00 10.00
NL Nicklas Lidstrom 4.00 10.00
PB Pavel Bure 4.00 10.00
PD Pavol Demitra 3.00 8.00
PF Peter Forsberg 6.00 15.00
PK Paul Kariya 4.00 10.00
PM Patrick Marleau 3.00 8.00
PR Patrick Roy 12.50 30.00
RB Ray Bourque 8.00 20.00
SF Sergei Fedorov 6.00 15.00
SO Sandis Ozolinsh 3.00 8.00
SS Sergei Samsonov 3.00 8.00
SY Steve Yzerman 10.00 25.00
TA Tony Amonte 3.00 8.00
TS Teemu Selanne 4.00 10.00
WG Wayne Gretzky 30.00 80.00

2000-01 SP Game Used Tools of the Game Combos

Randomly inserted in SP Game-Used Edition packs, the 21-card set featured combo game-used jersey swatches. The cards were serial numbered to 100.

C-BF Pavel Bure 20.00 50.00
Sergei Fedorov
C-BR Martin Brodeur 25.00 60.00
Mike Richter
C-DM Pavol Demitra 15.00 40.00
Al MacInnis
C-GS Doug Gilmour 20.00 50.00
Mats Sundin
C-GY Scott Gomez 15.00 40.00
Mike York
C-HB Brett Hull 15.00 40.00
Ed Belfour
C-HG Gordie Howe 75.00 200.00
Wayne Gretzky
C-HP Dominik Hasek 15.00 40.00
Michael Peca
C-KS Paul Kariya 15.00 40.00
Teemu Selanne
C-LB Brian Boucher 15.00 40.00
John LeClair
C-LG M.Lemieux/W.Gretzky 125.00 300.00
C-LJ Mario Lemieux 75.00 200.00
Jaromir Jagr
C-MG Mark Messier 125.00 300.00
Wayne Gretzky
C-MN Mike Modano 15.00 40.00
Joe Nieuwendyk
C-OL Chris Osgood 15.00 40.00
Nicklas Lidstrom
C-RF Patrick Roy 30.00 80.00
Peter Forsberg
C-RT Jeremy Roenick 15.00 40.00
Keith Tkachuk
C-SD Byron Dafoe 15.00 40.00
Sergei Samsonov
C-SH Brendan Shanahan 50.00 125.00
Gordie Howe
C-SS Joe Sakic 40.00 100.00
Joe Sakic
C-YH Steve Yzerman 100.00 250.00
Gordie Howe

2000-01 SP Game Used Tools of the Game Autographed Bronze

Randomly inserted in SP Game-Used Edition packs, the 8-card set featured game-used jersey swatches and the individual player's autograph. The cards were serial numbered to 300.

*SILVER: .5X TO 1.25X HI
SILV.STAT.PRINT RUN 100 SER.#'d SETS
*GOLD: .75X TO 2X HI
GOLD STAT.PRINT RUN 25 SER.#'d SETS
A-BR Brett Hull 20.00 50.00
A-JL John LeClair 12.50 30.00
A-PB Pavel Bure 12.50 30.00
A-RB Ray Bourque 30.00 80.00
A-RL Roberto Luongo 20.00 50.00
A-SG Scott Gomez 12.50 30.00
A-SY Steve Yzerman 50.00 125.00
A-WG Wayne Gretzky 100.00 250.00

2001-02 SP Game Used

Released in mid January 2001, this 100-card set carried an SRP of $29.99 per pack. Each pack contained 3 cards with a game-used insert card in every pack. The base set consisted of 60 veteran player cards and 40 rookie cards which were numbered to 499.

1 Paul Kariya 1.25 3.00
2 Dany Heatley 1.00 2.50
3 Joe Thornton 2.00 5.00
4 Bill Guerin 1.00 2.50
5 Miroslav Satan 1.00 2.50
6 Roman Turek 1.00 2.50
7 Jeff O'Neill .60 1.50
8 Tony Amonte 1.00 2.50
9 Rob Blake 1.00 2.50
10 Joe Sakic 2.00 5.00
11 Chris Drury 1.00 2.50
12 Patrick Roy 6.00 15.00
13 Ron Tugnutt 1.00 2.50
14 Mike Modano 2.00 5.00
15 Ed Belfour 1.25 3.00
16 Pierre Turgeon 1.00 2.50
17 Brendan Shanahan 1.25 3.00
18 Steve Yzerman 6.00 15.00
19 Brett Hull 2.00 5.00
20 Dominik Hasek 2.00 5.00
21 Luc Robitaille 1.00 2.50
22 Mike Comrie 1.00 2.50
23 Pavel Bure 1.25 3.00
24 Valeri Bure .60 1.50
25 Adam Deadmarsh .60 1.50
26 Zigmund Palffy 1.00 2.50
27 Marian Gaborik 2.00 5.00
28 Jose Theodore 1.00 2.50
29 Mike Dunham 1.00 2.50
30 Patrik Elias 1.00 2.50
31 Martin Brodeur 3.00 5.00
32 Rick DiPietro 1.00 2.50
33 Alexei Yashin .60 1.50
34 Eric Lindros 1.25 3.00
35 Mark Messier 1.25 3.00
36 Marian Hossa 1.25 3.00
37 Radek Bonk .60 1.50
38 John LeClair 1.00 2.50
39 Jeremy Roenick 2.00 2.50
40 Pavel Brendl .60 1.50
41 Roman Cechmanek .60 1.50
42 Sean Burke 1.00 2.50
43 Mario Lemieux 8.00 20.00
44 Johan Hedberg 1.00 2.50
45 Alexei Kovalev 1.00 2.50
46 Teemu Selanne 1.25 3.00
47 Evgeni Nabokov 1.00 2.50
48 Keith Tkachuk 1.00 2.50
49 Chris Pronger 1.00 2.50
50 Pavol Demitra 1.00 2.50
51 Doug Weight 1.00 2.50
52 Vincent Lecavalier 1.25 3.00
53 Curtis Joseph 1.25 3.00
54 Alexander Mogilny 1.00 2.50
55 Mats Sundin 1.25 3.00
56 Markus Naslund 1.25 3.00
57 Daniel Sedin .60 1.50
58 Jaromir Jagr 2.00 5.00
59 Olaf Kolzig 1.00 2.50
60 Peter Bondra 1.00 2.50
61 Ilja Bryzgalov RC 4.00 10.00
62 Timo Parssinen RC 2.00 5.00
63 Kevin Sawyer RC 2.00 5.00
64 Brian Pothier RC 2.00 5.00
65 Kamil Piros RC 2.00 5.00
66 Ilya Kovalchuk RC 30.00 80.00
67 Zdenek Kutlak RC 2.00 5.00
68 Scott Nichol RC 2.00 5.00
69 Erik Cole RC 4.00 10.00
70 Jaroslav Obsut RC 2.00 5.00
71 Vaclav Nedorost RC 2.00 5.00
72 Mathieu Darche RC 2.00 5.00

73 Matt Davidson RC 2.00 5.00
74 Niko Kapanen RC 2.00 5.00
75 Pavel Datsyuk RC 20.00 50.00
76 Ty Conklin RC 4.00 10.00
77 Jason Chimera RC 2.00 5.00
78 Niklas Hagman RC 2.00 5.00
79 Kristian Huselius RC 5.00 12.00
80 Jaroslav Bednar RC 2.00 5.00
81 Nick Schultz RC 2.00 5.00
82 Travis Roche RC 2.00 5.00
83 Martin Erat RC 2.00 5.00
84 Scott Clemmensen RC 2.00 5.00
85 Josef Boumedienne RC 2.00 5.00
86 Raffi Torres RC 5.00 12.00
87 Radek Martinek RC 2.00 5.00
88 Dan Blackburn RC 3.00 8.00
89 Peter Smrek RC 2.00 5.00
90 Ivan Ciernik RC 2.00 5.00
91 Chris Neil RC 2.00 5.00
92 Vaclav Pletka RC 2.00 5.00
93 Jiri Dopita RC 2.00 5.00
94 Krys Kolanos RC 2.00 5.00
95 Jeff Jillson RC 2.00 5.00
96 Mark Rycroft RC 2.00 5.00
97 Ryan Tobler RC 2.00 5.00
98 Nikita Alexeev RC 2.00 5.00
99 Chris Corrinet RC 2.00 5.00
100 Brian Sutherby RC 2.00 5.00

2001-02 SP Game Used Authentic Fabric

Inserted on per pack, this 77-card set featured game-worn jersey swatches from one, two, three or four players. Dual player cards were serial-numbered to 100 each, triple player cards were serial-numbered to 25, and quadruple player cards were serial-numbered to 10. Quadruple player cards are not priced due to scarcity.
*MULT.COLOR SWATCH: 1X TO 1.5X HI

AFAK Alexei Kovalev 3.00 8.00
AFBB Brian Boucher 3.00 8.00
AFBG Bill Guerin 3.00 8.00
AFBJ Brent Johnson 3.00 8.00
AFBN Radek Bonk 3.00 8.00
AFBS Brendan Shanahan 4.00 10.00
AFBU Pavel Bure SP 10.00 25.00
AFCO Chris Osgood 3.00 8.00
AFDH Dominik Hasek 6.00 15.00
AFEB Ed Belfour 4.00 10.00
AFFP Felix Potvin 4.00 10.00
AFGE Wayne Gretzky SP 20.00 50.00
AFGH Gordie Howe 15.00 40.00
AFGR Wayne Gretzky SP 20.00 50.00
AFJB Jaroslav Bednar 3.00 8.00
AFJD J-P Dumont 3.00 8.00
AFJH Jan Hlavac 3.00 8.00
AFJI Jarome Iginla 6.00 15.00
AFJJ Jaromir Jagr SP 12.50 30.00
AFJL John LeClair 4.00 10.00
AFJN Joe Nieuwendyk 3.00 8.00
AFJO Jose Theodore 6.00 15.00
AFJS Joe Sakic 6.00 15.00
AFJT Joe Thornton 10.00 25.00
AFKA Paul Kariya SP 15.00 40.00
AFKP Keith Primeau 3.00 8.00
AFLR Luc Robitaille 3.00 8.00
AFMA Maxim Afinogenov 3.00 8.00
AFMB Martin Brodeur 10.00 25.00
AFML Mario Lemieux 15.00 40.00
AFMM Mike Modano 5.00 12.00
AFMN Markus Naslund 4.00 10.00
AFMN Mika Noronen 3.00 8.00
AFMO Mike Modano SP 10.00 25.00
AFMR Mark Recchi 3.00 8.00
AFMS Miroslav Satan 3.00 8.00
AFMY Mike York 3.00 8.00
AFON Owen Nolan 3.00 8.00
AFPB Peter Bondra 4.00 10.00
AFPD Pavol Demitra 3.00 8.00
AFPF Peter Forsberg 6.00 15.00
AFPK Paul Kariya 4.00 10.00
AFPM Patrick Marleau 3.00 8.00
AFPR Patrick Roy 12.50 30.00
AFRB Ray Bourque 6.00 15.00
AFRD Radek Dvorak 3.00 8.00
AFRF Rico Fata 3.00 8.00
AFRF Ruslan Fedotenko 3.00 8.00
AFRL Robert Lang 3.00 8.00
AFSA Joe Sakic SP 12.50 30.00
AFSF Sergei Fedorov 5.00 12.00
AFSK Saku Koivu 4.00 10.00
AFSS Scott Stevens SP 10.00 25.00
AFSV Marc Savard 3.00 8.00
AFSY Steve Yzerman 10.00 25.00
AFTF Theo Fleury 3.00 8.00
AFTS Teemu Selanne SP 4.00 10.00
AFWG Wayne Gretzky SP 20.00 50.00
AFZP Zigmund Palffy 3.00 8.00
DFAB Maxim Afinogenov 10.00 25.00
Martin Biron
DFBR M.Brodeur/P.Roy 30.00 80.00
DFDS J-P Dumont/M.Satan 10.00 25.00
DFFD Theo Fleury 10.00 25.00
Radek Dvorak
DFFS Sergei Fedorov 25.00 60.00
Brendan Shanahan
DFFS Peter Forsberg 40.00 100.00
Joe Sakic
DFIS Jarome Iginla 10.00 25.00
Marc Savard
DFLB John LeClair 10.00 25.00
Brian Boucher
DFLG M.Lemieux/W.Gretzky 75.00 200.00
DFLK Mario Lemieux 25.00 60.00
Alexei Kovalev
DFMB Mike Modano 25.00 60.00
Ed Belfour
DFNB Markus Naslund 10.00 25.00
Peter Bondra
DFPK Paul Kariya 10.00 25.00
Paul Kariya
DFPL Keith Primeau 10.00 25.00
John LeClair
DFPP Zigmund Palffy 10.00 25.00
Felix Potvin
DFPT Felix Potvin 20.00 50.00
Jose Theodore
DFRF Mark Recchi 10.00 25.00
Ruslan Fedotenko
DFTG Joe Thornton 20.00 50.00
Bill Guerin
DFYO Steve Yzerman 30.00 80.00
Chris Osgood
TFFSR Peter Forsberg 125.00 250.00
Joe Sakic
Patrick Roy
TFLKL Mario Lemieux 125.00 300.00
Alexei Kovalev
Robert LangA
TFLRP John LeClair 60.00 150.00
Mark Recchi
Keith Primeau
TFMNB Mike Modano 40.00 100.00
Joe Nieuwendyk
Ed Belfour
TFYSF Steve Yzerman 125.00 250.00
Brendan Shanahan
Sergei Fedorov
FSRB Peter Forsberg
Joe Sakic
Patrick Roy
Ray Bourque
GYSL Gretz./Yze./Sakic/Lemieux
HGBL Howe/Gretz./Bour./Lem.
YSFO Steve Yzerman
Brendan Shanahan
Sergei Fedorov
Chris Osgood

2001-02 SP Game Used Authentic Fabric Gold

This 55-card set paralleled the single-player cards of the base jersey set but were gold on the card fronts. Cards denoted as short prints in the base set were serial-numbered out of 50 in this parallel. All other cards in this set were serial-numbered out of 300.
*GOLD NON-SP's: .5X TO 1.25X BASIC CARDS
*GOLD SP's: .6X TO 1.5X BASIC CARDS

2001-02 SP Game Used Inked Sweaters

Randomly inserted, this 40-card set featured swatches of game-worn jerseys and player autographs. Single player cards were serial-numbered to 100 unless otherwise noted below. Dual player cards were serial-numbered to just 10 and are not priced due to scarcity.

SCJ Curtis Joseph/50 30.00 80.00
SEB Ed Belfour/50 30.00 80.00
SGA Simon Gagne/50 25.00 60.00
SGH Gordie Howe/50 75.00 150.00
SJL John LeClair/50 15.00 40.00
SMB Martin Brodeur/50 60.00 150.00
SRB Ray Bourque/50 60.00 150.00
SSY Steve Yzerman/50 75.00 200.00
SWG Wayne Gretzky/50 150.00 400.00
ISAK Alexei Kovalev 10.00 25.00
ISCJ Curtis Joseph 15.00 40.00
ISHS Henrik Sedin 10.00 25.00
ISJI Jarome Iginla 25.00 60.00
ISJL John LeClair 15.00 40.00
ISJT Joe Thornton 30.00 80.00
ISMB Martin Brodeur 75.00 200.00
ISMB Martin Biron 10.00 25.00
ISMH Marian Hossa 15.00 40.00
ISMM Mike Modano 40.00 100.00
ISOK Olaf Kolzig 10.00 25.00
ISRB Ray Bourque 40.00 100.00
ISSG Simon Gagne 15.00 40.00
ISSY Steve Yzerman 75.00 200.00
ISVL Vincent Lecavalier 15.00 40.00
ISZP Zigmund Palffy 10.00 25.00
DSBH Ray Bourque
Milan Hejduk
DSBO Martin Biron
Maxime Ouellet
DSGO Simon Gagne
Maxime Ouellet
DSGP Wayne Gretzky
Zigmund Palffy
DSHG Gordie Howe
Wayne Gretzky
DSIG Jarome Iginla
Simon Gagne
DSJT Curtis Joseph
Jose Theodore
DSKB Olaf Kolzig
Peter Bondra
DSLG John LeClair
Simon Gagne
DSLK John LeClair
Alexei Kovalev
DSMA M.Modano/T.Amonte EXCH
DSPB Zigmund Palffy
Peter Bondra
DSST Sergei Samsonov
Joe Thornton
DSWM Doug Weight
Al MacInnis
DSYH Gordie Howe
Steve Yzerman

2001-02 SP Game Used Patches

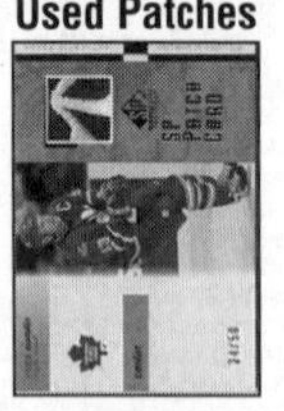

Randomly inserted, this 55-card set featured patch swatches from one, two or three different players' jerseys. Single player cards were serial-numbered out of 50, dual player cards were serial-numbered out of 25, and triple player cards were serial numbered to just 10 copies each. Triple player cards are not priced due to scarcity.

PBI Martin Biron 10.00 25.00
PBO Peter Bondra 10.00 25.00
PBS Brendan Shanahan 15.00 40.00
PCJ Curtis Joseph 25.00 60.00
PEB Ed Belfour 20.00 50.00
PJH Jani Hurme 10.00 25.00
PJI Jarome Iginla 20.00 50.00
PJJ Jaromir Jagr 25.00 60.00
PJL John LeClair 10.00 25.00
PJS Joe Sakic 30.00 80.00
PJT Joe Thornton 30.00 80.00
PKP Keith Primeau 10.00 25.00
PMB Martin Brodeur 40.00 100.00
PMH Marian Hossa 15.00 40.00
PML Mario Lemieux 60.00 150.00
PMM Mike Modano 20.00 50.00
PMS Mats Sundin 15.00 40.00
POK Olaf Kolzig 15.00 40.00
PPB Pavel Bure 15.00 40.00
PPF Peter Forsberg 25.00 60.00
PPK Paul Kariya 15.00 40.00
PPR Patrick Roy 60.00 150.00
PPS Patrik Stefan 10.00 25.00
PSA Miroslav Satan 15.00 40.00
PSF Sergei Fedorov 20.00 50.00
PSG Simon Gagne 15.00 40.00
PSS Sergei Samsonov 15.00 40.00
PSY Steve Yzerman 40.00 100.00
PTA Tony Amonte 15.00 40.00
PWG Wayne Gretzky 75.00 200.00
CPAI Tony Amonte 30.00 80.00
Jarome Iginla
CPBA Peter Bondra 20.00 50.00
Tony Amonte
CPBJ Martin Brodeur 75.00 200.00
Curtis Joseph
CPGK Simon Gagne 15.00 40.00
Paul Kariya
CPHB Jani Hurme 60.00 150.00
Martin Brodeur
CPHH Jani Hurme 25.00 60.00
Marian Hossa
CPHL Marian Hossa 25.00 60.00
John LeClair
CPJB Jaromir Jagr 50.00 100.00
Peter Bondra
CPKB Olaf Kolzig 30.00 80.00
Peter Bondra
CPKR Olaf Kolzig 75.00 200.00
Patrick Roy
CPKS Paul Kariya 30.00 80.00
Sergei Samsonov
CPLJ Mario Lemieux 150.00 400.00
Jaromir Jagr
CPLP John LeClair 25.00 60.00
Keith Primeau
CPPG Keith Primeau 30.00 80.00
Simon Gagne
CPSB Brendan Shanahan 30.00 80.00
Pavel Bure
CPSJ Mats Sundin 15.00 40.00
Curtis Joseph
CPSK Miroslav Satan 15.00 40.00
Paul Kariya
CPSR Joe Sakic 150.00 400.00
Patrick Roy
CPSY Brendan Shanahan 100.00 250.00
Steve Yzerman
CPYF Steve Yzerman 75.00 200.00
Sergei Fedorov
TPJBB Curtis Joseph
Martin Brodeur
Ed Belfour
TPKYB Paul Kariya
Steve Yzerman
Pavel Bure
TPLGY Lemieux/Gretzky/Yzerman
TPSLS Sergei Samsonov
John LeClair
Brendan Shanahan
TPSPP Patrik Stefan
Joe Sakic
Keith Primeau

2001-02 SP Game Used Patches Signed

This 20-card set partially paralleled the regular patch set, but included authentic autographs of the featured player(s). Single player cards were serial-numbered out of 50 and dual player cards were serial-numbered to just 10 copies each. Dual player cards are not priced due to scarcity. Please note that not all cards in this set have a parent card in the base patches set.

SPCJ Curtis Joseph 60.00 150.00
SPEB Ed Belfour 40.00 100.00
SPJI Jarome Iginla 40.00 100.00
SPJL John LeClair 30.00 80.00
SPJT Joe Thornton 60.00 150.00
SPKP Keith Primeau 30.00 80.00
SPMB Martin Brodeur 100.00 250.00
SPMB Martin Biron 30.00 80.00
SPMH Marian Hossa 30.00 80.00
SPOK Olaf Kolzig 30.00 80.00
SPPB Peter Bondra 30.00 80.00
SPPB Pavel Bure 30.00 80.00
SPPS Patrik Stefan 30.00 80.00
SPSG Simon Gagne 30.00 80.00
SPSS Sergei Samsonov 30.00 80.00
SPSY Steve Yzerman 75.00 200.00
SPTA Tony Amonte 30.00 80.00
SPTH Jose Theodore 40.00 100.00
SPTS Teemu Selanne 40.00 100.00
SPWG Wayne Gretzky 300.00 600.00
DSPAB Peter Bondra
Tony Amonte
DSPBJ Martin Brodeur
Curtis Joseph
DSPBK Olaf Kolzig
Martin Biron
DSPBL Pavel Bure
John LeClair
DSPGB Wayne Gretzky
Pavel Bure
DSPGP Simon Gagne
Keith Primeau
DSPHI Marian Hossa
Jarome Iginla
DSPKB Olaf Kolzig
Ed Belfour
DSPKBO Olaf Kolzig
Peter Bondra
DSPTB Joe Thornton
Martin Biron

2001-02 SP Game Used Signs of Tradition

This 5-card ultra short printed set featured "cut" autographs from legendary figures in hockey's history. Actual print runs for each card are listed below and this set is not priced due to scarcity.

LCCC Clarence Campbell/2
LCDH Doug Harvey/2
LCLS Lord Stanley/1
LCSA Sid Abel/2
LCTH Tim Horton/2

2001-02 SP Game Used Tools of the Game

Randomly inserted, this 52-card set featured one, two or three swatches of game-used gear from the player(s) featured. Single player cards were serial-numbered out of 100 (unless otherwise noted below), dual player cards were serial-numbered out of 50 and triple player cards were serial numbered out of 35. As of press time, not all cards have been verified.
*MULT.COLOR SWATCH: .5X TO 1.25X HI

TAC Anson Carter 12.50 30.00
TBB Brian Boucher 12.50 30.00
TBD Byron Dafoe 12.50 30.00
TCO Chris Osgood 12.50 30.00
TDA Byron Dafoe 12.50 30.00
TDF Byron Dafoe 12.50 30.00
TGF Grant Fuhr 15.00 40.00
TGP Gilbert Perreault/92 20.00 50.00
TJA Jaromir Jagr 15.00 40.00
TJF Jeff Friesen 8.00 20.00
TJH Johan Hedberg 8.00 20.00
TJJ Jaromir Jagr 15.00 40.00
TJT Joe Thornton/36 40.00 100.00
TLE John LeClair 10.00 25.00
TMM Mark Messier 12.50 30.00
TOK Olaf Kolzig 12.50 30.00
TPR Patrick Roy 30.00 80.00
TRA Bill Ranford 8.00 20.00
TRC Roman Cechmanek 12.50 30.00
TRD Rick DiPietro EXISTS?
TSA Sergei Samsonov/83 12.50 30.00
TSF Sergei Fedorov 12.50 30.00
TSS Sergei Samsonov 12.50 30.00
TSY Steve Yzerman/30 100.00 250.00
TTE Tony Esposito 30.00 80.00
TTH Jose Theodore 25.00 60.00
TWG Wayne Gretzky/71 100.00 250.00
CTCB Roman Cechmanek 20.00 50.00
Brian Boucher
CTCH Roman Cechmanek 20.00 50.00
Johan Hedberg
CTCS Anson Carter 20.00 50.00
Sergei Samsonov
CTDB Byron Dafoe 20.00 50.00
Brian Boucher
CTDC Byron Dafoe 20.00 50.00
Gerry Cheevers
CTEC Tony Esposito 25.00 60.00
Gerry Cheevers
CTFC Grant Fuhr 20.00 50.00
Roman Cechmanek
CTFF Sergei Fedorov 20.00 50.00
Jeff Friesen
CTFR Sergei Fedorov 25.00 60.00
Patrick Roy
CTHD Johan Hedberg 20.00 50.00
Byron Dafoe
CTKB Olaf Kolzig 20.00 50.00
Brian Boucher
CTKT Olaf Kolzig 20.00 50.00
Jose Theodore
CTLJ John LeClair 30.00 80.00
Jaromir Jagr
CTRC Patrick Roy 25.00 60.00
Roman Cechmanek
CTRF Bill Ranford 20.00 50.00
Grant Fuhr
CTRF Patrick Roy 30.00 80.00
Grant Fuhr
CTSF Sergei Samsonov 20.00 50.00
Sergei Fedorov
CTTD Jose Theodore 20.00 50.00
Byron Dafoe
TTDER Byron Dafoe 125.00 300.00
Tony Esposito
Patrick Roy
TTFCF Jeff Friesen 30.00 80.00
Anson Carter
Sergei Fedorov
TTFSL Sergei Fedorov 60.00 150.00
Sergei Samsonov
John LeClair
TTHCR Johan Hedberg 60.00 150.00
Gerry Cheevers
Patrick Roy
TTKCH Olaf Kolzig 40.00 100.00
Roman Cechmanek
Johan Hedberg
TTRBK Patrick Roy 75.00 200.00
Brian Boucher
Olaf Kolzig
TTRFE Bill Ranford 60.00 150.00
Grant Fuhr
Tony Esposito

2001-02 SP Game Used Tools of the Game Signed

This 22-card set featured swatches of game-worn gear as well as authentic player autographs of the player(s) featured. Single player cards were serial-numbered out of 100 while dual player cards were serial-numbered out of 35.

STBR Bill Ranford 40.00 80.00
STGF Grant Fuhr 40.00 80.00
STGP Gilbert Perrault 40.00 100.00
STJH Johan Hedberg 15.00 40.00
STJL John LeClair 20.00 50.00
STJT Joe Thornton 25.00 60.00
STJT Jose Theodore 40.00 100.00
STKP Keith Primeau 20.00 50.00
STLE John LeClair 20.00 50.00
STPB Peter Bondra 25.00 60.00
STRB Ray Bourque 40.00 100.00
STSA Sergei Samsonov 25.00 60.00
STSM Sergei Samsonov 25.00 60.00
STSY Steve Yzerman 75.00 200.00
STTS Teemu Selanne 20.00 50.00
SCBS Ray Bourque 100.00 200.00
Sergei Samsonov
SCLT John LeClair 75.00 200.00
Joe Thornton
SCPS Keith Primeau 25.00 60.00
Sergei Samsonov
SCPY Keith Primeau 60.00 150.00
Steve Yzerman
SCRF Bill Ranford 40.00 100.00
Grant Fuhr
SCRH Bill Ranford 40.00 100.00
Johan Hedberg
SCTY J.Thornton/S.Yzerman 125.00250.00

2002-03 SP Game Used

Released in March of 2003, this 103-card set carried an SRP of $29.99. There were two subsets; All-Star Flashbacks (51-65) and New Grooves (66-103). The All-Star Flashbacks were serial-numbered out of 999 and the New Grooves rookie cards were serial-numbered out of 750.

COMP.SET w/o SP's (50) 60.00 125.00
1 Paul Kariya 1.00 2.50
2 Ilya Kovalchuk 1.25 3.00
3 Dany Heatley 1.25 3.00
4 Joe Thornton 1.50 4.00
5 Sergei Samsonov .75 2.00
6 Martin Biron .75 2.00
7 Jarome Iginla 1.25 3.00
8 Jeff O'Neill .75 2.00
9 Ron Francis .75 2.00
10 Eric Daze .75 2.00
11 Peter Forsberg 2.00 5.00
12 Joe Sakic 2.00 5.00
13 Patrick Roy 5.00 12.00
14 Marc Denis .75 2.00
15 Bill Guerin .75 2.00
16 Mike Modano 1.50 4.00
17 Steve Yzerman 5.00 12.00
18 Brendan Shanahan 1.00 2.50
19 Curtis Joseph 1.00 2.50
20 Mike Comrie .75 2.00
21 Roberto Luongo 1.25 3.00
22 Felix Potvin 1.00 2.50
23 Zigmund Palffy 1.00 2.50
24 Marian Gaborik 2.00 5.00
25 Jose Theodore 1.25 3.00
26 Saku Koivu 1.00 2.50
27 Mike Dunham .75 2.00
28 Martin Brodeur 2.50 6.00
29 Patrik Elias .75 2.00
30 Mike Peca .75 2.00
31 Alexei Yashin .75 2.00
32 Eric Lindros 1.00 2.50
33 Pavel Bure 1.00 2.50
34 Martin Havlat .75 2.00
35 Daniel Alfredsson .75 2.00
36 Simon Gagne 1.00 2.50
37 Jeremy Roenick 1.25 3.00
38 Sean Burke .75 2.00
39 Tony Amonte .75 2.00
40 Mario Lemieux 6.00 15.00
41 Owen Nolan .75 2.00
42 Evgeni Nabokov .75 2.00
43 Chris Pronger .75 2.00
44 Keith Tkachuk 1.00 2.50
45 Vincent Lecavalier 1.00 2.50
46 Mats Sundin 1.00 2.50
47 Ed Belfour 1.00 2.50
48 Markus Naslund 1.00 2.50
49 Olaf Kolzig .75 2.00
50 Jaromir Jagr 1.50 4.00
51 Gordie Howe AF 6.00 15.00
52 Mario Lemieux AF 8.00 20.00
53 Wayne Gretzky AF 12.50 30.00
54 Mario Lemieux AF 8.00 20.00
55 Wayne Gretzky AF 8.00 20.00
56 Vincent Damphousse AF 2.00 5.00
57 Brett Hull AF 3.00 8.00
58 Mike Richter AF 2.00 5.00
59 Ray Bourque AF 5.00 12.00
60 Mark Recchi AF 2.00 5.00
61 Teemu Selanne AF 2.00 5.00
62 Wayne Gretzky AF 8.00 20.00
63 Pavel Bure AF 2.00 5.00
64 Bill Guerin AF 2.00 5.00
65 Eric Daze AF 2.00 5.00
66 Alexei Smirnov RC 2.00 5.00
67 Stanislav Chistov RC 4.00 10.00
68 Martin Gerber RC 4.00 10.00
69 Kurt Sauer RC 2.00 5.00
70 Chuck Kobasew RC 5.00 12.00
71 Jordan Leopold RC 2.00 5.00
72 Jeff Paul RC 2.00 5.00
73 Rick Nash RC 15.00 40.00
74 Lasse Pirjeta RC 2.00 5.00
75 Henrik Zetterberg RC 12.50 30.00
76 Dmitri Bykov RC 2.00 5.00
77 Ales Hemsky RC 8.00 20.00
78 Jay Bouwmeester RC 6.00 15.00
79 Alexander Frolov RC 8.00 20.00
80 Sylvain Blouin RC 2.00 5.00
81 P-M Bouchard RC 6.00 15.00
82 Jason Spezza RC 15.00 40.00
83 Ron Hainsey RC 2.00 5.00
84 Adam Hall RC 2.00 5.00
85 Scottie Upshall RC 4.00 10.00
86 Anton Volchenkov RC 2.00 5.00
87 Dennis Seidenberg RC 2.00 5.00
88 Patrick Sharp RC 2.00 5.00
89 Jeff Taffe RC 2.00 5.00
90 Cody Rudkowsky RC 2.00 5.00
91 Tom Koivisto RC 2.00 5.00
92 Curtis Sanford RC 4.00 10.00
93 Alexander Svitov RC 2.00 5.00
94 Carlo Colaiacovo RC 2.00 5.00
95 Steve Eminger RC 2.00 5.00
96 Shaone Morrisonn RC 2.00 5.00
97 Ryan Miller RC 15.00 30.00
98 Levente Szuper RC 2.00 5.00
99 Mike Cammalleri RC 4.00 10.00
100 Stephane Veilleux RC 2.00 5.00
101 Darren Haydar RC 2.00 5.00
102 Lynn Loyns RC 2.00 5.00
103 Mikael Tellqvist RC 4.00 10.00

2002-03 SP Game Used Authentic Fabrics

Randomly inserted, this 102-card set featured single or dual swatches of game-worn jerseys on the card fronts. Each card was serial-numbered in silver foil out of 225.

AFAM Tony Amonte 3.00 8.00
AFAT Alex Tanguay 3.00 8.00
AFAY Alexei Yashin 3.00 8.00
AFBB Brian Boucher 3.00 8.00
AFBD Peter Bondra 3.00 8.00
AFBG Bill Guerin 3.00 8.00
AFBH Brett Hull 6.00 15.00
AFBI Martin Biron 3.00 8.00
AFBL Brian Leetch 3.00 8.00
AFBO Peter Bondra 3.00 8.00
AFBQ Ray Bourque 8.00 20.00
AFBS Brendan Shanahan 4.00 10.00
AFCD Chris Drury 3.00 8.00
AFCK Roman Cechmanek 3.00 8.00
AFDA Eric Daze 3.00 8.00
AFDB Donald Brashear 3.00 8.00
AFDR Chris Drury 3.00 8.00
AFED Eric Daze 3.00 8.00
AFFO Peter Forsberg 8.00 20.00
AFFP Felix Potvin 4.00 10.00
AFFV Sergei Fedorov 5.00 12.00
AFGI J-S Giguere 3.00 8.00
AFGM Glen Murray 3.00 8.00
AFGU Bill Guerin 3.00 8.00
AFGY Wayne Gretzky 25.00 60.00
AFHE Milan Hejduk 4.00 10.00
AFHO Marian Hossa 4.00 10.00
AFHU Brett Hull 5.00 12.00
AFIK Ilya Kovalchuk 8.00 20.00
AFJA Jason Allison 3.00 8.00
AFJF Jeff Friesen 3.00 8.00
AFJG J-S Giguere 3.00 8.00
AFJI Jarome Iginla 8.00 20.00
AFJJ Jaromir Jagr 6.00 15.00
AFJL John LeClair 4.00 10.00
AFJR Jeremy Roenick 6.00 15.00
AFJS Joe Sakic 8.00 20.00
AFJT Joe Thornton 6.00 15.00
AFJW Justin Williams 3.00 8.00
AFKA Paul Kariya 4.00 10.00
AFKK Ilya Kovalchuk 8.00 20.00
AFKO Alexei Kovalev 3.00 8.00
AFKP Keith Primeau 3.00 8.00
AFKV Alexei Kovalev 3.00 8.00
AFMB Martin Brodeur 15.00 40.00
AFMD Marc Denis 3.00 8.00
AFMH Marian Hossa 4.00 10.00
AFML Mario Lemieux 15.00 40.00
AFMM Mike Modano 5.00 12.00
AFMN Markus Naslund 4.00 10.00
AFMO Mike Modano 8.00 20.00
AFMR Mark Recchi 3.00 8.00
AFMS Mats Sundin 4.00 10.00
AFMT Mats Sundin 4.00 10.00
AFNA Markus Naslund 4.00 10.00
AFOK Olaf Kolzig 3.00 8.00
AFPB Pavel Bure 4.00 10.00
AFPD Pavol Demitra 3.00 8.00
AFPK Paul Kariya 4.00 10.00
AFPM Patrick Marleau 3.00 8.00
AFPR Patrick Roy 15.00 40.00
AFPU Keith Primeau 3.00 8.00
AFRB Ray Bourque 6.00 15.00
AFRC Roman Cechmanek 3.00 8.00
AFRO Jeremy Roenick 6.00 15.00
AFRW Ray Whitney 3.00 8.00
AFRY Patrick Roy 15.00 40.00
AFSA Miroslav Satan 3.00 8.00
AFSC Joe Sakic 10.00 25.00
AFSD Shane Doan 3.00 8.00
AFSF Sergei Fedorov 8.00 20.00
AFSH Steve Shields 3.00 8.00
AFSK Saku Koivu 4.00 10.00
AFSN Brendan Shanahan 4.00 10.00
AFSS Sergei Samsonov 3.00 8.00
AFSU Steve Sullivan 3.00 8.00
AFSV Sergei Samsonov 3.00 8.00
AFSY Steve Yzerman 15.00 40.00
AFTA Alex Tanguay 3.00 8.00
AFTH Jose Theodore 8.00 20.00
AFTT Jocelyn Thibault 3.00 8.00
AFWG Wayne Gretzky 25.00 60.00
AFZP Zigmund Palffy 4.00 10.00
CFCS T.Connolly/M.Satan 6.00 15.00
CFDT P.Demitra/K.Tkachuk 6.00 15.00
CFFD Peter Forsberg Dual 20.00 50.00
CFFP Felix Potvin Dual 6.00 15.00
CFGR Wayne Gretzky Dual 30.00 80.00
CFJB J.Jagr/P.Bondra 6.00 15.00
CFJJ Jaromir Jagr Dual 10.00 25.00
CFJS Joe Sakic Dual 12.50 30.00
CFLK M.Lemieux/P.Kariya 15.00 40.00
CFMO Mike Modano Dual 8.00 20.00
CFNB J.Nieuwendyk/M.Brodeur 10.00 25.00
CFSH B.Shanahan/B.Hull 6.00 15.00
CFTB J.Thibault/M.Brodeur 10.00 25.00
CFTK J.Theodore/S.Koivu 12.50 30.00
CFTL K.Tkachuk/J.LeClair 6.00 15.00
CFTS J.Thornton/S.Samsonov 6.00 15.00
CFWD D.Weight/P.Demitra 6.00 15.00
CFWG Wayne Gretzky Dual 50.00 125.00
CFYR S.Yzerman/L.Robitaille 10.00 25.00

2002-03 SP Game Used Authentic Fabrics Gold

This 83-card set paralleled the basic insert set but each card was serial-numbered in gold foil to just 99 copies.
*GOLD: .5X TO 1.25X BASIC JERSEYS
GOLD PRINT RUN 99 SER.#'d SETS

2002-03 SP Game Used Authentic Fabrics Rainbow

This 83-card set paralleled the basic insert set but each card was serial-numbered in rainbow foi to just ten copies.
NOT PRICED DUE TO SCARCITY

2002-03 SP Game Used First Rounder Patches

Randomly inserted, this 58-card set featured swatches of game-worn jersey patches from the featured player. Each card was serial-numbered out of 30 on the card front and carried a "PC" prefix on the card back.

AD Adam Deadmarsh 15.00 40.00
AK Alexei Kovalev 15.00 40.00
AL Jason Allison 15.00 40.00

T Alex Tanguay 15.00 40.00
Y Alexei Yashin 15.00 40.00
B Brian Boucher 15.00 40.00
G Bill Guerin 15.00 40.00
I Martin Biron 15.00 40.00
S Brendan Shanahan 25.00 60.00
P Chris Pronger 15.00 40.00
B Daniel Briere 15.00 40.00
L David Legwand 15.00 40.00
L Eric Lindros 25.00 60.00
O Sergei Gonchar 15.00 40.00
K Ilya Kovalchuk 30.00 80.00
A Jason Arnott 15.00 40.00
D J-P Dumont 15.00 40.00
G J-S Giguere 15.00 40.00
Jarome Iginla 30.00 80.00
J Jaromir Jagr 30.00 80.00
R Jeremy Roenick 30.00 80.00
S Joe Sakic 40.00 100.00
T Joe Thornton 30.00 80.00
W Justin Williams 15.00 40.00
K Krys Kolanos 15.00 40.00
P Keith Primeau 15.00 40.00
T Keith Tkachuk 25.00 60.00
A Manny Malhotra 15.00 40.00
B Martin Brodeur 40.00 100.00
D Marc Denis 15.00 40.00
L Mario Lemieux 60.00 150.00
M Mike Modano 30.00 80.00
N Markus Naslund 25.00 60.00
S Mats Sundin 25.00 60.00
O Mika Noronen 15.00 40.00
K Olaf Kolzig 15.00 40.00
N Owen Nolan 15.00 40.00
F Peter Forsberg 30.00 80.00
K Paul Kariya 25.00 60.00
M Patrick Marleau 15.00 40.00
S Patrik Stefan 15.00 40.00
B Ray Bourque 40.00 100.00
K Rostislav Klesla 15.00 40.00
L Roberto Luongo 30.00 80.00
T Raffi Torres 15.00 40.00
D Shane Doan 15.00 40.00
G Simon Gagne 15.00 40.00
H Scott Hartnell 15.00 40.00
K Saku Koivu 25.00 60.00
S Sergei Samsonov 15.00 40.00
Y Steve Yzerman 60.00 150.00
C Tim Connolly 15.00 40.00
L Trevor Linden 15.00 40.00
P Taylor Pyatt 15.00 40.00
S Teemu Selanne 25.00 60.00
L Vincent Lecavalier 25.00 60.00
A Dan Blackburn 15.00 40.00
LE Brian Leetch 25.00 60.00

2002-03 SP Game Used Future Fabrics

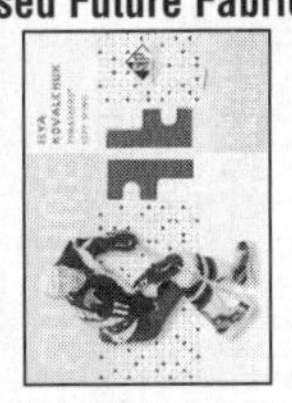

andomly inserted, this 31-card set featured watches of game-worn jerseys on the card onts. Each card was serial-numbered in lver foil out of 225.

FAE David Aebischer 3.00 8.00
FAT Alex Tanguay 3.00 8.00
FBJ Brent Johnson 3.00 8.00
FBM Brenden Morrow 3.00 8.00
FCA Kyle Calder 3.00 8.00
FDA Denis Arkhipov 3.00 8.00
FDB Daniel Briere 3.00 8.00
FEB Eric Belanger 3.00 8.00
FHA Jeff Halpern 3.00 8.00
FIB Ilja Bryzgalov 4.00 10.00
FIK Ilya Kovalchuk 8.00 20.00
FJG J-S Giguere 3.00 8.00
FJH Jeff Halpern 3.00 8.00
FKC Kyle Calder 3.00 8.00
FKO Ilya Kovalchuk 8.00 20.00
FMA Maxim Afinogenov 3.00 8.00
FMB Mark Bell 3.00 8.00
FME Martin Erat 3.00 8.00
FMM Manny Malhotra 3.00 8.00
FMP Matt Pettinger 3.00 8.00
FMR Mike Ribeiro 3.00 8.00
FMT Marty Turco 3.00 8.00
FPB Pavel Brendl 3.00 8.00
FRI Mike Ribeiro 3.00 8.00
FRK Rostislav Klesla 3.00 8.00
FSG Simon Gagne 3.00 8.00
FSH Scott Hartnell 3.00 8.00
FSR Steven Reinprecht 3.00 8.00
FTC Tim Connolly 3.00 8.00
FTP Taylor Pyatt 3.00 8.00
FVN Ville Nieminen 3.00 8.00

2002-03 SP Game Used Future Fabrics Gold

is 31-card set paralleled the basic insert et but each card was serial-numbered in old foil to just 99 copies.
*GOLD: .5X TO 1.25X BASIC JERSEY

2002-03 SP Game Used Future Fabrics Rainbow

This 31-card set paralleled the basic insert set but each card was serial-numbered in holographic rainbow foil to just 10 copies.
NOT PRICED DUE TO SCARCITY

2002-03 SP Game Used Piece of History

Randomly inserted, this 87-card set featured swatches of game-worn jerseys on the card fronts. Each card was serial-numbered in silver foil out of 225.

PHAD Adam Deadmarsh 6.00 15.00
PHAL Jason Allison 6.00 15.00
PHAM Tony Amonte 6.00 15.00
PHAT Alex Tanguay 6.00 15.00
PHAY Alexei Yashin 6.00 15.00
PHAZ Alexei Zhamnov 6.00 15.00
PHBD Peter Bondra 6.00 15.00
PHBH Brett Hull 8.00 20.00
PHBI Martin Biron 6.00 15.00
PHBL Brian Leetch 6.00 15.00
PHBO Peter Bondra 6.00 15.00
PHBQ Ray Bourque 8.00 20.00
PHBS Brendan Shanahan 6.00 15.00
PHCC Chris Chelios 6.00 15.00
PHCD Chris Drury 6.00 15.00
PHCJ Curtis Joseph 6.00 15.00
PHCK Roman Cechmanek 6.00 15.00
PHCL Claude Lemieux 6.00 15.00
PHDL David Legwand 6.00 15.00
PHDR Chris Drury 6.00 15.00
PHDU Mike Dunham 6.00 15.00
PHED Eric Daze 6.00 15.00
PHEK Espen Knutsen 6.00 15.00
PHEL Eric Lindros 6.00 15.00
PHFO Peter Forsberg 10.00 25.00
PHFP Felix Potvin 6.00 15.00
PHFV Sergei Fedorov 8.00 20.00
PHGO Sergei Gonchar 6.00 15.00
PHGU Bill Guerin 6.00 15.00
PHGY Wayne Gretzky 30.00 80.00
PHJA Jason Allison 6.00 15.00
PHJD J.P. Dumont 6.00 15.00
PHJG Jaromir Jagr 8.00 20.00
PHJI Jarome Iginla 8.00 20.00
PHJJ Jaromir Jagr 8.00 20.00
PHJL Joe LeClair 6.00 15.00
PHJN Joe Nieuwendyk 6.00 15.00
PHJO Jocelyn Thibault 6.00 15.00
PHJR Jeremy Roenick 8.00 20.00
PHJS Joe Sakic 10.00 25.00
PHJT Joe Thornton 8.00 20.00
PHKA Paul Kariya 6.00 15.00
PHKK Ilya Kovalchuk 8.00 20.00
PHKO Steve Konowalchuk 6.00 15.00
PHKP Keith Primeau 6.00 15.00
PHKU Saku Koivu 6.00 15.00
PHLM Nicklas Lidstrom 6.00 15.00
PHMB Martin Brodeur 12.50 30.00
PHMD Marc Denis 6.00 15.00
PHMH Milan Hejduk 6.00 15.00
PHML Mario Lemieux 15.00 40.00
PHMM Mike Modano 8.00 20.00
PHMN Markus Naslund 6.00 15.00
PHMO Mike Modano 10.00 25.00
PHMR Mark Recchi 6.00 15.00
PHMS Mats Sundin 6.00 15.00
PHMY Mike York 6.00 15.00
PHNA Markus Naslund 6.00 15.00
PHNL Nicklas Lidstrom 6.00 15.00
PHPB Pavel Bure 6.00 15.00
PHPF Peter Forsberg 10.00 25.00
PHPK Paul Kariya 6.00 15.00
PHPM Patrick Marleau 6.00 15.00
PHPR Patrick Roy 15.00 40.00
PHRB Ray Bourque 8.00 20.00
PHRC Roman Cechmanek 6.00 15.00
PHRK Jeremy Roenick 8.00 20.00
PHRO Rob Blake 6.00 15.00
PHRT Roman Turek 6.00 15.00
PHRY Patrick Roy 15.00 40.00
PHSA Marc Savard 6.00 15.00
PHSB Sean Burke 6.00 15.00
PHSC Joe Sakic 10.00 25.00
PHSF Sergei Fedorov 8.00 20.00
PHSG Simon Gagne 6.00 15.00
PHSH Brendan Shanahan 6.00 15.00
PHSK Saku Koivu 6.00 15.00
PHSS Sergei Samsonov 6.00 15.00
PHSU Mats Sundin 6.00 15.00
PHSV Sergei Samsonov 6.00 15.00
PHSY Steve Yzerman 15.00 40.00
PHTA Alex Tanguay 6.00 15.00
PHTC Tim Connolly 6.00 15.00
PHTH Jose Theodore 8.00 20.00
PHTS Teemu Selanne 6.00 15.00
PHTT Jocelyn Thibault 6.00 15.00
PHZP Zigmund Palffy 6.00 15.00

2002-03 SP Game Used Piece of History Gold

This 87-card set paralleled the basic insert set but each card was serial-numbered in gold foil to just 99 copies.
*GOLD: .5X TO 1.25X BASIC JERSEYS

2002-03 SP Game Used Piece of History Rainbow

This 87-card set paralleled the basic insert set but each card was serial-numbered in a rainbow foil to just ten copies.
NOT PRICED DUE TO SCARCITY

2002-03 SP Game Used Signature Style

Inserted at 1:12, this 32-card set featured authentic player autographs. Each card carried a "SS" prefix on the card backs.

AF Alexander Frolov 10.00 25.00
BO Bobby Orr 125.00 250.00
BR Pavel Brendl 6.00 15.00
CJ Curtis Joseph 12.00 30.00
DH Dany Heatley 10.00 25.00
EB Ed Belfour 15.00 40.00
EC Erik Cole 6.00 15.00
GH Gordie Howe 50.00 125.00
IK Ilya Kovalchuk 12.00 30.00
JI Jarome Iginla 10.00 25.00
JL John LeClair 6.00 15.00
JT Joe Thornton 12.00 30.00
JW Justin Williams 6.00 15.00
KH Kristian Huselius 6.00 15.00
MA Maxim Afinogenov 6.00 15.00
MB Martin Brodeur 40.00 100.00
MC Mike Comrie 6.00 15.00
MFO Manny Fernandez 6.00 15.00
MH Martin Havlat 6.00 15.00
MK Milan Kraft 6.00 15.00
NK Nikolai Khabibulin 10.00 25.00
PB Pavel Bure 8.00 20.00
PR Patrick Roy 60.00 150.00
RB Ray Bourque 20.00 50.00
SC Stanislav Chistov 10.00 25.00
SG Simon Gagne 6.00 15.00
SH Scott Hartnell 6.00 15.00
SP Jason Spezza 20.00 50.00
SS Sergei Samsonov 6.00 15.00
SY Steve Yzerman 30.00 80.00
TS Teemu Selanne 6.00 15.00
WG Wayne Gretzky 125.00 300.00

2002-03 SP Game Used Tools of the Game

Randomly inserted, this 30-card set featured swatches of game-worn gloves or goalie leg pads on the card fronts. Each card was serial-numbered in silver foil out of 99. Cards carried a "TG" prefix on the card backs.

AK Alexei Kovalev G 10.00 25.00
AM Alexander Mogilny G 10.00 25.00
BB Brian Boucher P 10.00 25.00
BD Byron Dafoe P 10.00 25.00
BE Ed Belfour P 12.50 30.00
BH Brett Hull G 15.00 40.00
BS Brendan Shanahan G 12.50 30.00
DH Dominik Hasek P 15.00 40.00
EB Ed Belfour G 12.50 30.00
JF Jeff Friesen G 10.00 25.00
JJ Jaromir Jagr G 15.00 40.00
JL John LeClair G 12.50 30.00
JR Jeremy Roenick G 15.00 40.00
JT Joe Thornton G 15.00 40.00
KP Keith Primeau G 10.00 25.00
KT Keith Tkachuk G 12.50 30.00
MD Marc Denis P 10.00 25.00
MS Mats Sundin G 12.50 30.00
OK Olaf Kolzig P 10.00 25.00
PB Peter Bondra G 10.00 25.00
PR Patrick Roy P 20.00 50.00
RC Roman Cechmanek P 10.00 25.00
RD Rick DiPietro P 10.00 25.00
RF Ron Francis G 10.00 25.00
RL Roberto Luongo P 15.00 40.00
SF Sergei Fedorov G 12.50 30.00
SH Steve Shields P 10.00 25.00
SS Sergei Samsonov G 10.00 25.00
TH Jose Theodore P 15.00 40.00
TS Teemu Selanne G 12.50 30.00

2003-04 SP Game Used

This 130-card set consisted of 50 veteran cards; Tier 1 rookie cards (51-82 and 123-130) serial-numbered to 600; Tier 2 rookies (83-92) serial-numbered to 99 and veteran jersey cards (93-122). Cards 123-130 were only available in packs of UD Rookie Update and were serial-numbered out of 600.

COMP.SET w/o SP's (50) 25.00 60.00
1 J-S Giguere .50 1.25
2 Sergei Fedorov 1.25 3.00
3 Dany Heatley 1.25 3.00
4 Ilya Kovalchuk 1.25 3.00
5 Joe Thornton 1.50 4.00
6 Sergei Samsonov .50 1.25
7 Chris Drury .50 1.25
8 Jarome Iginla 1.00 2.50
9 Ron Francis .50 1.25
10 Jocelyn Thibault .50 1.25
11 Joe Sakic 2.00 5.00
12 Peter Forsberg 2.50 6.00
13 Paul Kariya .75 2.00
14 Rick Nash 1.00 2.50
15 Marty Turco .50 1.25
16 Mike Modano 1.50 4.00
17 Steve Yzerman 5.00 12.00
18 Dominik Hasek 2.00 5.00
19 Ales Hemsky .50 1.25
20 Mike Comrie .50 1.25
21 Roberto Luongo 1.00 2.50
22 Zigmund Palffy .50 1.25
23 Marian Gaborik 2.00 5.00
24 Jose Theodore 1.00 2.50
25 Saku Koivu .75 2.00
26 Tomas Vokoun .50 1.25
27 Martin Brodeur 2.50 6.00
28 Alexei Yashin .40 1.00
29 Eric Lindros .75 2.00
30 Pavel Bure .75 2.00
31 Patrick Lalime .50 1.25
32 Marian Hossa .75 2.00
33 Jason Spezza .75 2.00
34 Simon Gagne .75 2.00
35 Jeremy Roenick 1.25 3.00
36 Sean Burke .50 1.25
37 Mario Lemieux 6.00 15.00
38 Niko Dimitrakos .40 1.00
39 Evgeni Nabokov .50 1.25
40 Al MacInnis .50 1.25
41 Keith Tkachuk .75 2.00
42 Chris Pronger .50 1.25
43 Nikolai Khabibulin .75 2.00
44 Vincent Lecavalier .75 2.00
45 Owen Nolan .50 1.25
46 Ed Belfour .75 2.00
47 Mats Sundin .75 2.00
48 Markus Naslund .75 2.00
49 Todd Bertuzzi .75 2.00
50 Jaromir Jagr 1.50 4.00
51 Jiri Hudler RC 4.00 10.00
52 Patrice Bergeron RC 10.00 25.00
53 Milan Bartovic RC 2.00 5.00
54 Matthew Lombardi RC 3.00 8.00
55 Lasse Kukkonen RC 2.00 5.00
56 Travis Moen RC 3.00 8.00
57 Marek Svatos RC 6.00 15.00
58 John-Michael Liles RC 3.00 8.00
59 Cody McCormick RC 2.00 5.00
60 Dan Fritsche RC 2.00 5.00
61 Antti Miettinen RC 2.00 5.00
62 Esa Pirnes RC 2.00 5.00
63 Tim Gleason RC 2.00 5.00
64 Brent Burns RC 3.00 8.00
65 Christoph Brandner RC 2.00 5.00
66 Chris Higgins RC 10.00 25.00
67 Dan Hamhuis RC 3.00 8.00
68 Marek Zidlicky RC 2.00 5.00
69 Wade Brookbank RC 2.00 5.00
70 David Hale RC 2.00 5.00
71 Paul Martin RC 2.00 5.00
72 Sean Bergenheim RC 2.00 5.00
73 Antoine Vermette RC 3.00 8.00
74 Matthew Spiller RC 2.00 5.00
75 Matt Murley RC 2.00 5.00
76 Christian Ehrhoff RC 2.00 5.00
77 Alexander Semin RC 10.00 25.00
78 Tom Preissing RC 2.00 5.00
79 Peter Sejna RC 2.00 5.00
80 Maxim Kondratiev RC 2.00 5.00
81 Matt Stajan RC 8.00 20.00
82 Boyd Gordon RC 3.00 8.00
83 Joffrey Lupul RC 15.00 40.00
84 Eric Staal RC 50.00 125.00
85 Tuomo Ruutu RC 25.00 50.00
86 Pavel Vorobiev RC 10.00 25.00
87 Nathan Horton RC 25.00 60.00
88 Dustin Brown RC 10.00 25.00
89 Jordin Tootoo RC 20.00 50.00
90 Joni Pitkanen RC 12.00 30.00
91 Marc-Andre Fleury RC 60.00 150.00
92 Milan Michalek RC 25.00 60.00
93 Joe Thornton 10.00 25.00
94 Jason Blake 4.00 10.00
95 Pavol Demitra 4.00 10.00
96 Martin St. Louis 4.00 10.00
97 Zigmund Palffy 4.00 10.00
98 Sean Burke 4.00 10.00
99 Todd Marchant 4.00 10.00
100 Jarome Iginla 8.00 20.00
101 Doug Weight 4.00 10.00
102 Henrik Zetterberg 10.00 25.00
103 Ilya Kovalchuk 10.00 25.00
104 Alexei Yashin 4.00 10.00
105 Mario Lemieux 12.50 30.00
106 Milan Hejduk 6.00 15.00
107 Martin Biron 4.00 10.00
108 Tomas Vokoun 4.00 10.00
109 Tommy Salo 4.00 10.00
110 Anson Carter 4.00 10.00
111 Nikolai Khabibulin 5.00 12.00
112 Keith Tkachuk 5.00 12.00
113 Martin Brodeur 15.00 40.00
114 Steve Yzerman 12.50 30.00
115 Jeremy Roenick 6.00 15.00
116 Mike Modano 10.00 25.00
117 Marian Hossa 5.00 12.00
118 Paul Kariya 5.00 12.00
119 Marty Turco 4.00 10.00
120 Peter Forsberg 8.00 20.00
121 Todd Bertuzzi 5.00 12.00
122 David Aebischer 4.00 10.00
123 Fedor Tyutin RC 2.00 5.00
124 John Pohl RC 2.00 5.00
125 Ryan Kesler RC 2.00 5.00
126 Fredrik Sjostrom RC 2.00 5.00
127 Aaron Johnson RC 2.00 5.00
128 Brad Boyes RC 4.00 10.00
129 Nikolai Zherdev RC 6.00 15.00
130 Tomas Plekanec RC 2.00 5.00

2003-04 SP Game Used Gold

*STARS: 4X TO 10X BASE HI
*TIER 1 ROOKIES: .75X TO 2X
1-82 PRINT RUN 40 SER.#'d SETS
*TIER 2 ROOKIES: .5X TO 1.25X
TIER 2 PRINT RUN 25 SER.#'d SETS
*JERSEYS: 1X TO 2.5X
JERSEY PRINT RUN 30 SER.#'d SETS

2003-04 SP Game Used Authentic Fabrics

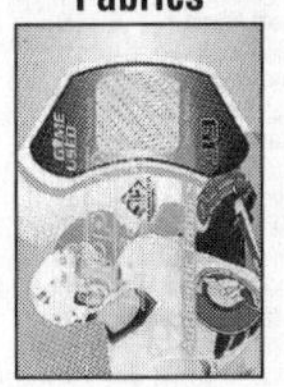

This 72-card set featured single, dual or quad jersey swatches. Single and dual swatch cards were serial-numbered to 99 while quad swatch cards were serial-numbered out of 55.

AFAF Alexander Frolov 5.00 12.00
AFEL Eric Lindros 6.00 15.00
AFHA Marcel Hossa 3.00 8.00
AFJG J-S Giguere 5.00 12.00
AFJI Jarome Iginla 10.00 25.00
AFJJ Jaromir Jagr 10.00 25.00
AFJR Jeremy Roenick 10.00 25.00
AFJS Jason Spezza 8.00 20.00
AFJT Joe Thornton 10.00 25.00
AFMH Marian Hossa 6.00 15.00
AFML Mario Lemieux 15.00 40.00
AFON Owen Nolan 5.00 12.00
AFPR Patrick Roy 15.00 40.00
AFPS Peter Sejna 3.00 8.00
AFRL Roberto Luongo 8.00 20.00
AFRN Rick Nash 12.50 30.00
AFSF Sergei Fedorov 10.00 25.00
AFSG Simon Gagne 6.00 15.00
AFSK Saku Koivu 6.00 15.00
AFTB Todd Bertuzzi 6.00 15.00
AFWG Wayne Gretzky 40.00 100.00
AFZP Zigmund Palffy 5.00 12.00
DFBJ R.Blake/E.Jovanovski 8.00 20.00
DFBL J.Bouwmeester/R.Luongo 15.00 40.00
DFBP M.Brodeur/P.Leclaire 15.00 40.00
DFBR M.Brodeur/P.Roy 25.00 60.00
DFBT Z.Palffy/A.Frolov 8.00 20.00
DFCM C.Drury/M.Satan 6.00 15.00
DFDS T.Domi/J.Shelley 8.00 20.00
DFFS P.Forsberg/J.Sakic 15.00 40.00
DFGR J.Giguere/P.Roy 20.00 50.00
DFGS W.Gretzky/J.Spezza 50.00 125.00
DFHC A.Hemsky/M.Comrie 8.00 20.00
DFHG G.Howe/W.Gretzky 50.00 125.00
DFHH M.Hossa/M.Hossa 10.00 25.00
DFHK D.Heatley/I.Kovalchuk 15.00 40.00
DFHL D.Hasek/N.Lidstrom 10.00 25.00
DFHY B.Hull/S.Yzerman 15.00 40.00
DFJB J.Jagr/P.Bondra 8.00 20.00
DFKF P.Kariya/P.Forsberg 12.00 30.00
DFKH S.Koivu/M.Hossa 8.00 20.00
DFKS P.Kariya/T.Selanne 8.00 20.00
DFLG M.Lemieux/W.Gretzky 50.00 125.00
DFLK G.Lafleur/S.Koivu 8.00 20.00
DFLP B.Leetch/T.Poti 8.00 20.00
DFMT M.Modano/M.Turco 15.00 40.00
DFNB M.Naslund/T.Bertuzzi 12.00 30.00
DFND R.Nash/M.Denis 8.00 20.00
DFNM R.Nash/T.Marchant 8.00 20.00
DFPC Z.Palffy/R.Cechmanek 6.00 15.00
DFRG J.Roenick/S.Gagne 8.00 20.00
DFSG S.Bowman/G.Lafleur 15.00 40.00
DFSH J.Spezza/M.Hossa 15.00 40.00
DFTK J.Theodore/S.Koivu 12.50 30.00
DFTM J.Thornton/G.Murray 8.00 20.00
DFVN V.Lecavalier/N.Khabibulin 8.00 20.00
DFWT D.Weight/K.Tkachuk 6.00 15.00
DFYH S.Yzerman/G.Howe 30.00 80.00
DFYP A.Yashin/M.Peca 6.00 15.00
DFZH H.Zetterberg/B.Hull 15.00 40.00
DFZT A.Zhamnov/J.Thibault 6.00 15.00
QARGL Amonte/Roen/Gags/LeC 25.00 60.00
QFSKS Frsbrg/Selnne/Karya/Sakic 40.00 100.00
QKTHK Koivu/Thedre/Hossa/Kmlsrek 50.00 120.00
QLGHL Lem/Gretz/Howe/Lafleur 150.00 350.00
QMGTM Mike Modano 25.00 60.00
Bill Guerin
Marty Turco
Brenden Morrow
QNBJM Naslund/Bert/Jov/Morr 30.00 80.00
QRGBT Roy/Giggy/Brodeur/Turco 60.00 150.00
QSAHL Spza/Alfdsn/Hossa/Lalm 25.00 60.00
QSNBM Sndin/Nolan/Bltour/Mogilny 25.00 60.00
QSNZH Spza/Nash/Zettrbrg/Hemsky 60.00 150.00
QYBHH Yzrmn/Bowmn/Hull/Hasek 75.00 200.00

2003-04 SP Game Used Authentic Fabrics Gold

This 72-card set paralleled the basic inserts set but with gold foil highlights and serial-numbering to 21 copies each. Some cards were autographed by the player(s) featured. Please note that there have been some inconsistencies in this checklist regarding the autographs, any additional info can be sent to hockeymag@beckett.com.

PRINT RUN 21 SER.#'d SETS
NOT PRICED DUE TO SCARCITY

2003-04 SP Game Used Authentic Patches

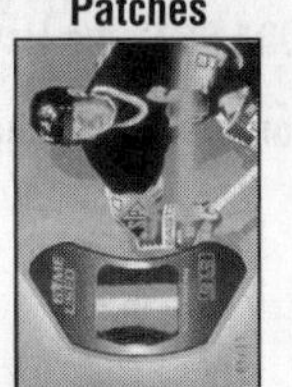

PRINT RUN 15 SERIAL #'d SETS
NOT PRICED DUE TO SCARCITY

APG1 Wayne Gretzky
APJTH Jose Theodore
APJSG J-S Giguere
APAH Ales Hemsky
APAY Alexei Yashin
APBG Bill Guerin
APCD Chris Drury
APDH Dominik Hasek
APEB Ed Belfour
APEL Eric Lindros
APHZ Henrik Zetterberg
APIK Ilya Kovalchuk
APJI Jarome Iginla
APJR Jeremy Roenick
APJT Joe Thornton
APMB Martin Brodeur
APMH Marcel Hossa
APML Mario Lemieux
APMM Mike Modano
APMN Markus Naslund
APMS Miroslav Satan
APON Owen Nolan
APPF Peter Forsberg
APPL Patrick Lalime
APPR Patrick Roy
APRN Rick Nash
APSF Sergei Fedorov
APTA Tony Amonte
APVL Vincent Lecavalier
APWG Wayne Gretzky

2003-04 SP Game Used Double Threads

This 27-card set featured dual-patch swatches of the featured players. Each card was serial-numbered out of 60.

DTAR D.Aebischer/P.Roy 60.00 150.00
DTBL J.Bouwmeester/R.Luongo 30.00 80.00
DTBR M.Brodeur/P.Roy 60.00 150.00
DTDS C.Drury/M.Satan 20.00 50.00
DTFS P.Forsberg/J.Sakic 30.00 80.00
DTKH S.Koivu/M.Hossa 20.00 50.00
DTKS P.Kariya/T.Selanne 20.00 50.00
DTLG M.Lemieux/W.Gretzky 75.00 200.00
DTLK V.Lecavalier/N.Khabibulin 30.00 80.00
DTLS V.Lecavalier/M.St. Louis 20.00 50.00
DTMG M.Modano/B.Guerin 25.00 60.00
DTMT M.Modano/M.Turco 30.00 80.00
DTNB M.Naslund/T.Bertuzzi 30.00 80.00
DTND R.Nash/M.Denis 30.00 80.00
DTNN R.Niedermayer/S.Niedermayer 25.00 60.00
DTPF Zigmund Palffy 20.00 50.00
Alexander Frolov
DTPK P.Kariya/P.Kariya 20.00 50.00
DTRA J.Roenick/T.Amonte 20.00 50.00
DTSB M.Sundin/E.Belfour 25.00 60.00
DTSF S.Fedorov/S.Fedorov 40.00 100.00
DTSH J.Spezza/M.Hossa 30.00 80.00
DTSN M.Sundin/O.Nolan 25.00 60.00
DTTM J.Thornton/G.Murray 20.00 50.00
DTTS J.Thornton/S.Samsonov 20.00 50.00
DTWG W.Gretzky/W.Gretzky 150.00 400.00
DTYZ S.Yzerman/H.Zetterberg 30.00 80.00
DTZT A.Zhamnov/J.Thibault 20.00 50.00

2003-04 SP Game Used Game Gear

PRINT RUN 99 SERIAL #'d SETS

GGBB Brian Boucher 6.00 15.00
GGBD Byron Dafoe 6.00 15.00
GGCJ Curtis Joseph 8.00 20.00
GGCO Chris Osgood 6.00 15.00
GGDH Dominik Hasek 12.50 30.00
GGGF Grant Fuhr 15.00 40.00
GGJF Jeff Friesen 6.00 15.00
GGJGR Jaromir Jagr 12.50 30.00
GGJH Johan Hedberg/36 6.00 15.00
GGJJ Jaromir Jagr 12.50 30.00
GGJT Jose Theodore 12.50 30.00
GGMB Martin Brodeur 15.00 40.00
GGMD Marc Denis 6.00 15.00
GGMS Mats Sundin 8.00 20.00
GGMT Marty Turco 6.00 15.00
GGOK Olaf Kolzig 6.00 15.00
GGPL Patrick Lalime 6.00 15.00
GGPR Patrick Roy 15.00 40.00
GGRC Roman Cechmanek 6.00 15.00
GGRD Rick DiPietro 6.00 15.00
GGRL Roberto Luongo 12.50 30.00
GGSAM Sergei Samsonov 6.00 15.00
GGSS Steve Shields 6.00 15.00
GGTS Teemu Selanne 8.00 20.00
GGTSA Tommy Salo 6.00 15.00

2003-04 SP Game Used Game Gear Combo

*COMBO: .5X TO 1.5X BASIC GEAR
PRINT RUN 85 SERIAL #'d SETS

2003-04 SP Game Used Limited Threads

PRINT RUN 75 SERIAL #'d SETS
GOLD PRINT RUN 21 SER.#'d SETS
GOLD NOT PRICED DUE TO SCARCITY

LTG1 Wayne Gretzky 50.00 100.00
LTWGR Wayne Gretzky 50.00 100.00
LTJBU Johnny Bucyk 6.00 15.00
LTMHO Marian Hossa 8.00 20.00
LTDHA Dominik Hasek 12.50 30.00
LTJSG J-S Giguere 6.00 15.00
LTJTH Jocelyn Thibault 6.00 15.00
LTAH Ales Hemsky 6.00 15.00
LTAK Ales Kotalik 6.00 15.00
LTAY Alexei Yashin 6.00 15.00
LTBG Bill Guerin 6.00 15.00
LTBL Brian Leetch 6.00 15.00
LTCD Chris Drury 6.00 15.00
LTDH Dany Heatley 10.00 25.00
LTGL Guy Lafleur 12.50 30.00
LTIK Ilya Kovalchuk 10.00 25.00
LTJB Jay Bouwmeester 6.00 15.00
LTJJ Jaromir Jagr 10.00 25.00
LTJS Jason Spezza 10.00 25.00
LTJT Joe Thornton 12.50 30.00
LTLM Lanny McDonald 6.00 15.00
LTMB Mike Bossy 6.00 15.00
LTMH Gordie Howe 25.00 60.00
LTMM Mike Modano 10.00 25.00
LTMN Markus Naslund 8.00 20.00
LTMS Mats Sundin 8.00 20.00
LTMT Marty Turco 6.00 15.00
LTPD Pavel Datsyuk 10.00 25.00
LTPF Peter Forsberg 15.00 40.00
LTPK Paul Kariya 8.00 20.00
LTPR Patrick Roy 30.00 80.00
LTRL Roberto Luongo 10.00 25.00
LTRN Rick Nash 10.00 25.00
LTSB Scotty Bowman 20.00 50.00
LTSF Sergei Fedorov 10.00 25.00
LTSU Scottie Upshall 6.00 15.00
LTSY Steve Yzerman 15.00 40.00
LTTA Tony Amonte 6.00 15.00
LTTB Todd Bertuzzi 8.00 20.00
LTTS Teemu Selanne 8.00 20.00
LTVL Vincent Lecavalier 8.00 20.00
LTWG Wayne Gretzky 50.00 100.00

2003-04 SP Game Used Premium Patches

PRINT RUN 6 SER.#'d SETS
NOT PRICED DUE TO SCARCITY

PPJSG J-S Giguere
PPJSA Joe Sakic
PPDH Dany Heatley
PPGL Guy Lafleur
PPJJ Jaromir Jagr
PPJR Jeremy Roenick
PPJS Jason Spezza
PPJT Jocelyn Thibault
PPMB Martin Brodeur
PPMC Mike Comrie
PPMH Marian Hossa
PPML Mario Lemieux
PPMS Mats Sundin
PPMT Marty Turco
PPPB Pavel Bure
PPPK Paul Kariya
PPPR Patrick Roy
PPRL Roberto Luongo
PPRN Rick Nash
PPSF Sergei Fedorov
PPSY Steve Yzerman
PPTB Todd Bertuzzi
PPTH Joe Thornton
PPTS Teemu Selanne
PPWG Wayne Gretzky

2003-04 SP Game Used Rookie Exclusives

PRINT RUN 100 SERIAL #'d SETS
RE1 Patrice Bergeron 20.00 50.00
RE2 Dustin Brown 10.00 25.00
RE3 Marc-Andre Fleury 30.00 80.00
RE4 Nathan Horton 15.00 40.00
RE5 Jiri Hudler 10.00 25.00
RE6 Jeffrey Lupul 10.00 25.00
RE7 Joni Pitkanen 10.00 25.00
RE8 Tuomo Ruutu 15.00 40.00
RE9 Eric Staal 30.00 80.00
RE10 Jordin Tootoo 15.00 40.00

2003-04 SP Game Used Signers

STATED ODDS 1:7
SPSBO Bobby Orr 75.00 200.00
SPSCJ Curtis Joseph 6.00 15.00
SPSDA David Aebischer 6.00 15.00
SPSEL Eric Lindros 12.50 30.00
SPSGH Gordie Howe 30.00 80.00
SPSHA Marian Hossa 6.00 15.00
SPSHV Martin Havlat 6.00 15.00
SPSHZ Henrik Zetterberg 10.00 25.00
SPSJB Jaromir Jagr SP 20.00 50.00
SPSJI Jarome Iginla 10.00 25.00
SPSJR Jeremy Roenick 8.00 20.00
SPSJS Jason Spezza 8.00 20.00
SPSJT Joe Thornton 10.00 25.00
SPSMG Marian Gaborik 12.50 30.00
SPSMH Marcel Hossa 6.00 15.00
SPSMT Marty Turco 6.00 15.00
SPSPB Pavel Bure 6.00 15.00
SPSPR Patrick Roy SP 60.00 150.00
SPSRB Ray Bourque 15.00 40.00
SPSRL Roberto Luongo 12.50 30.00
SPSRN Rick Nash 12.50 30.00
SPSSF Sergei Fedorov 12.50 30.00
SPSTB Todd Bertuzzi 6.00 15.00
SPSWG Wayne Gretzky SP 75.00 200.00
SSJSG J-S Giguere 6.00 15.00

2003-04 SP Game Used Team Threads

This 17-card set featured patch swatches from three teammates. Each card was serial-numbered out of 10.
NOT PRICED DUE TO SCARCITY
TTARL Amonte/Roenick/LeClair
TTBLK Bure/Lindros/Kovalev
TTBSG Brodeur/Stevens/Gomez
TTDSS Domi/Shelley/Brashear
TTFGC Fedorov/Giguere/Chistov
TTFSK Forsberg/Selanne/Kariya
TTHSC Hemsky/Salo/Comrie
TTKHK Kovalchuk/Heatley/Kozlov
TTKTH Koivu/Theodore/Hossa
TTLBF Lemieux/Bowman/Francis
TTLGH Lemieux/Gretzky/Howe
TTMGT Modano/Guerin/Turco
TTNBJ Naslund/Bertuzzi/Jovanovski
TTSHL Spezza/Hossa/Lalime
TTSNB Sundin/Nolan/Belfour
TTTMS Thornton/Murray/Samsonov
TTYZH Yzerman/Zetterberg/Hasek

2003-04 SP Game Used Top Threads

This 6-card set featured patch swatches from four star players. Each card was serial-numbered out of 6 and cards carried a "TP" prefix on the card back.
NOT PRICED DUE TO SCARCITY
ARGL Amnte/Rnick/Gagne/LeClair
FSKS Forsbrg/Selne/Krya/Sakic
LGHL Lemux/Gretz/Howe/Lafleur
NBJM Naslnd/Bertzi/Jovo/Morrson
SAHL Spezz/Alfrdsn/Hossa/Lalime
YZHH Yzemn/Zettbrg/Hull/Hasek

2004 SP Game Used Hawaii Trade Conference Patches

*

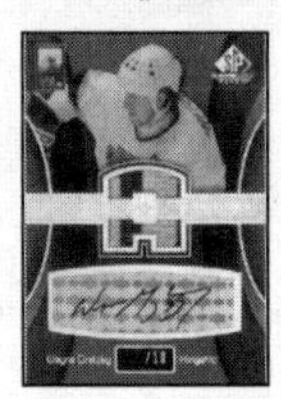

These eight cards were part of a larger set of multi-sport cards given away as promotional items during the 2004 Kit Young Hawaii Trade Conference. The cards are unpriced to due to scarcity, though sales of unsigned versions have been reported in the $300-400 range.
COMPLETE SET (8)
PP11 Joe Thornton/10
PP19 Mario Lemieux/10
PP22 Mike Modano/10
PP24 Peter Forsberg/10
PP30 Steve Yzerman/10
PP33 Wayne Gretzky/10
PPA6 Gordie Howe AU/10
PPA8 Wayne Gretzky AU/10

2005-06 SP Game Used

COMP.SET w/o SP's (100) 40.00 100.00
RC PRINT RUN 999 SER.#'d SETS
1 J-S Giguere .50 1.25
2 Teemu Selanne .60 1.50
3 Scott Niedermayer .30 .75
4 Ilya Kovalchuk .75 2.00
5 Kari Lehtonen .60 1.50
6 Marian Hossa .50 1.25
7 Peter Bondra .50 1.25
8 Glen Murray .30 .75
9 Brian Leetch .60 1.50
10 Andrew Raycroft .50 1.25
11 Patrice Bergeron .60 1.50
12 Chris Drury .50 1.25
13 Martin Biron .50 1.25
14 Maxim Afinogenov .30 .75
15 Jarome Iginla .75 2.00
16 Miikka Kiprusoff .60 1.50
17 Tony Amonte .50 1.25
18 Erik Cole .30 .75
19 Eric Staal .50 1.25
20 Nikolai Khabibulin .60 1.50
21 Tuomo Ruutu .30 .75
22 Tyler Arnason .30 .75
23 Joe Sakic 1.25 3.00
24 Milan Hejduk .60 1.50
25 Alex Tanguay .50 1.25
26 David Aebischer .50 1.25
27 Rob Blake .50 1.25
28 Rick Nash .75 2.00
29 Nikolai Zherdev .50 1.25
30 Sergei Fedorov .75 2.00
31 Mike Modano .60 1.50
32 Bill Guerin .50 1.25
33 Marty Turco .60 1.50
34 Brendan Shanahan .60 1.50
35 Steve Yzerman 2.50 6.00
36 Pavel Datsyuk .60 1.50
37 Henrik Zetterberg .60 1.50
38 Manny Legace .60 1.50
39 Ryan Smyth .30 .75
40 Chris Pronger .50 1.25
41 Ty Conklin .50 1.25
42 Stephen Weiss .30 .75
43 Joe Nieuwendyk .50 1.25
44 Roberto Luongo .75 2.00
45 Jeremy Roenick .75 2.00
46 Luc Robitaille .50 1.25
47 Pavol Demitra .50 1.25
48 Alexander Frolov .50 1.25
49 Marian Gaborik 1.25 3.00
50 Dwayne Roloson .50 1.25
51 Mike Ribeiro .30 .75
52 Jose Theodore .75 2.00
53 Michael Ryder .50 1.25
54 Saku Koivu .60 1.50
55 Paul Kariya .60 1.50
56 Steve Sullivan .30 .75
57 Tomas Vokoun .50 1.25
58 Martin Brodeur 2.00 5.00
59 Patrik Elias .50 1.25
60 Scott Gomez .50 1.25
61 Alexander Mogilny .50 1.25
62 Alexei Yashin .30 .75
63 Miroslav Satan .50 1.25
64 Rick DiPietro .50 1.25
65 Mark Parrish .30 .75
66 Kevin Weekes .50 1.25
67 Jaromir Jagr 1.00 2.50
68 Dany Heatley .75 2.00
69 Dominik Hasek 1.25 3.00
70 Jason Spezza .60 1.50
71 Martin Havlat .50 1.25
72 Peter Forsberg 1.00 2.50
73 Keith Primeau .30 .75
74 Simon Gagne .60 1.50
75 Robert Esche .50 1.25
76 Shane Doan .30 .75
77 Curtis Joseph .60 1.50
78 John LeClair .60 1.50
79 Mario Lemieux 4.00 10.00
80 Zigmund Palffy .50 1.25
81 Joe Thornton 1.00 2.50
82 Jonathan Cheechoo .60 1.50
83 Evgeni Nabokov .50 1.25
84 Patrick Marleau .50 1.25
85 Keith Tkachuk .60 1.50
86 Doug Weight .50 1.25
87 Martin St. Louis .50 1.25
88 Vincent Lecavalier .60 1.50
89 Brad Richards .50 1.25
90 Sean Burke .50 1.25
91 Mats Sundin .60 1.50
92 Ed Belfour .60 1.50
93 Eric Lindros .60 1.50
94 Jason Allison .30 .75
95 Nik Antropov .30 .75
96 Markus Naslund .60 1.50
97 Brendan Morrison .30 .75
98 Todd Bertuzzi .60 1.50
99 Olaf Kolzig .50 1.25
100 Brendan Witt .30 .75
101 Sidney Crosby RC 125.00 225.00
102 Brandon Bochenski RC 2.00 5.00
103 Rostislav Olesz RC 3.00 8.00
104 Jeff Hoggan RC 2.00 5.00
105 Brett Lebda RC 2.00 5.00
106 Brad Winchester RC 2.00 5.00
107 Wojtek Wolski RC 6.00 15.00
108 Patrick Eaves RC 4.00 10.00
109 Braydon Coburn RC 3.00 8.00
110 Yann Danis RC 3.00 8.00
111 Alexander Ovechkin RC 30.00 80.00
112 Peter Budaj RC 3.00 8.00
113 Jeff Carter RC 6.00 15.00
114 Duncan Keith RC 2.00 5.00
115 Mike Richards RC 4.00 10.00
116 Rene Bourque RC 2.00 5.00
117 Keith Ballard RC 2.00 5.00
118 Thomas Vanek RC 10.00 25.00
119 Robert Nilsson RC 3.00 8.00
120 Kevin Nastiuk RC 3.00 8.00
121 Jaroslav Balastik RC 2.00 5.00
122 Brent Seabrook RC 2.00 5.00
123 Maxime Talbot RC 2.00 5.00
124 Niklas Nordgren RC 2.00 5.00
125 David Leneveu RC 3.00 8.00
126 Eric Nystrom RC 3.00 8.00
127 Timo Helbling RC 2.00 5.00
128 George Parros RC 2.00 5.00
129 Lee Stempniak RC 3.00 8.00
130 Dion Phaneuf RC 12.00 30.00
131 Henrik Lundqvist RC 12.00 30.00
132 Cam Ward RC 6.00 15.00
133 Ryan Hollweg RC 2.00 5.00
134 Corey Perry RC 6.00 15.00
135 Matt Foy RC 2.00 5.00
136 Alexander Steen RC 4.00 10.00
137 Jim Slater RC 2.00 5.00
138 Ryan Suter RC 3.00 8.00
139 Gilbert Brule RC 5.00 12.00
140 Andrej Meszaros RC 2.00 5.00
141 Andrew Alberts RC 2.00 5.00
142 Zach Parise RC 4.00 10.00
143 Kevin Dallman RC 2.00 5.00
144 Chris Campoli RC 2.00 5.00
145 Johan Franzen RC 2.00 5.00
146 Jay McClement RC 2.00 5.00
147 Ryan Getzlaf RC 8.00 20.00
148 Alexander Perezhogin RC 3.00 8.00
149 Andrew Wozniewski RC 2.00 5.00
150 Jim Howard RC 4.00 10.00
151 Jeff Woywitka RC 2.00 5.00
152 Hannu Toivonen RC 4.00 10.00
153 Petteri Nokelainen RC 2.00 5.00
154 Jussi Jokinen RC 4.00 10.00
155 Ryane Clowe RC 2.00 5.00
156 Milan Jurcina RC 2.00 5.00
157 Mark Streit RC 2.00 5.00
158 Raitis Ivanans RC 2.00 5.00
159 Petr Prucha RC 4.00 10.00
160 Josh Gorges RC 2.00 5.00
161 Anthony Stewart RC 2.00 5.00
162 Alvaro Montoya RC 4.00 10.00
163 Paul Ranger RC 2.00 5.00
164 Chris Holt RC 2.00 5.00
165 Wade Skolney RC 2.00 5.00
166 Cam Barker RC 4.00 10.00
167 Adam Berkhoel RC 2.00 5.00
168 Kyle Brodziak RC 2.00 5.00
169 Brian McGrattan RC 2.00 5.00
170 Mikko Koivu RC 3.00 8.00
171 Derek Boogaard RC 3.00 8.00
172 Nick Tarnasky RC 2.00 5.00
173 Evgeny Artyukhin RC 2.00 5.00
174 Colin Hemingway RC 2.00 5.00
175 Michael Wall RC 2.00 5.00
176 Steve Goertzen RC 2.00 5.00
177 Junior Lessard RC 2.00 5.00
178 Vojtech Polak RC 2.00 5.00
179 Jakub Klepis RC 2.00 5.00
180 Jordan Sigalet RC 3.00 8.00
181 Steve Bernier RC 4.00 10.00
182 Dimitri Patzold RC 3.00 8.00
183 R.J. Umberger RC 3.00 8.00
184 Christoph Schubert RC 2.00 5.00
185 Staffan Kronwall RC 2.00 5.00
186 Ryan Whitney RC 3.00 8.00
187 Erik Christensen RC 3.00 8.00
188 Brian Eklund RC 2.00 5.00
189 Rob McVicar RC 2.00 5.00
190 Tomas Fleischmann RC 2.00 5.00
191 Zenon Konopka RC 2.00 5.00
192 Dustin Penner RC 4.00 10.00
193 Ben Walter RC 2.00 5.00
194 Daniel Paille RC 2.00 5.00
195 Chris Thorburn RC 2.00 5.00
196 Richie Regehr RC 2.00 5.00
197 Andrew Ladd RC 3.00 8.00
198 Chad Larose RC 2.00 5.00
199 Danny Richmond RC 2.00 5.00
200 Martin St. Pierre RC 2.00 5.00
201 Corey Crawford RC 2.00 5.00
202 Brad Richardson RC 2.00 5.00
203 Vitaly Kolesnik RC 2.00 5.00
204 Alexandre Picard RC 2.00 5.00
205 Ole-Kristian Tollefsen RC 2.00 5.00
206 Joakim Lindstrom RC 2.00 5.00
207 Kyle Quincey RC 2.00 5.00
208 Valtteri Filppula RC 2.00 5.00
209 Danny Syvret RC 2.00 5.00
210 Matt Greene RC 2.00 5.00
211 J-F Jacques RC 2.00 5.00
212 Greg Jacina RC 2.00 5.00
213 Rob Globke RC 2.00 5.00
214 Yanick Lehoux RC 2.00 5.00
215 Jeff Tambellini RC 2.00 5.00
216 Petr Kanko RC 2.00 5.00
217 Maxim Lapierre RC 2.00 5.00
218 J-P Cote RC 2.00 5.00
219 Andrei Kostitsyn RC 4.00 10.00
220 Kevin Klein RC 2.00 5.00
221 Pekka Rinne RC 3.00 8.00
222 Barry Tallackson RC 2.00 5.00
223 Jason Ryznar RC 2.00 5.00
224 Jeremy Colliton RC 2.00 5.00
225 Bruno Gervais RC 2.00 5.00
226 Stefan Ruzicka RC 2.00 5.00
227 Ben Eager RC 2.00 5.00
228 Alexandre Picard RC 2.00 5.00
229 Matt Jones RC 2.00 5.00
230 Colby Armstrong RC 4.00 10.00
231 Doug Murray RC 2.00 5.00
232 Grant Stevenson RC 2.00 5.00
233 Dennis Wideman RC 2.00 5.00
234 Doug O'Brien RC 2.00 5.00
235 Darren Reid RC 2.00 5.00
236 Ryan Craig RC 3.00 5.00
237 Jay Harrison RC 2.00 5.00
238 Tomas Mojzis RC 2.00 5.00
239 Kevin Bieksa RC 2.00 5.00
240 Mike Green RC 2.00 5.00

2005-06 SP Game Used Autographs

PRINT RUN 5 SER.#'d SETS
NOT PRICED DUE TO SCARCITY

2005-06 SP Game Used Gold

COMMON CARD (1-100) 2.50 6.00
*STARS: 4X TO 10X BASE HI
1-100 PRINT RUN 100 SER.#'d SETS
*ROOKIES: 1X TO 2.5X
ROOKIE PRINT RUN 25 SER.#'d SETS
35 Steve Yzerman 10.00 25.00
58 Martin Brodeur 12.00 30.00
72 Peter Forsberg 4.00 10.00
79 Mario Lemieux 15.00 40.00
101 Sidney Crosby 350.00 600.00
111 Alexander Ovechkin 200.00 300.00

2005-06 SP Game Used Authentic Fabrics

OVERALL MEM. ODDS 1:1
AF-AE David Aebischer 3.00 8.00
AF-AF Alexander Frolov 3.00 8.00
AF-AR Andrew Raycroft 3.00 8.00
AF-AT Alex Tanguay 3.00 8.00
AF-AY Alexei Yashin 2.50 6.00
AF-BE Daniel Briere 2.50 6.00
AF-BG Bill Guerin 2.00 5.00
AF-BL Rob Blake 3.00 8.00
AF-BM Brendan Morrison 3.00 8.00
AF-BO Mike Bossy 6.00 15.00
AF-BR Martin Brodeur 8.00 20.00
AF-BS Brendan Shanahan 4.00 10.00
AF-CD Chris Drury 3.00 8.00
AF-CJ Curtis Joseph 4.00 10.00
AF-CN Cam Neely 5.00 12.00
AF-CP Chris Pronger 3.00 8.00
AF-DA Daniel Alfredsson 3.00 8.00
AF-DB Dustin Brown 2.50 6.00
AF-DC Dan Cloutier 3.00 8.00
AF-DE Pavol Demitra 3.00 8.00
AF-DH Dany Heatley 5.00 12.00
AF-DW Doug Weight 3.00 8.00
AF-EB Ed Belfour 4.00 10.00
AF-GM Glen Murray 2.50 6.00
AF-GO Scott Gomez 4.00 10.00
AF-HA Dominik Hasek 6.00 15.00
AF-HJ Milan Hejduk 4.00 10.00
AF-HO Marian Hossa 3.00 8.00
AF-HU Trent Hunter 2.00 5.00
AF-HV Martin Havlat 3.00 8.00
AF-HZ Henrik Zetterberg 4.00 10.00
AF-IK Ilya Kovalchuk 5.00 12.00
AF-JB Jay Bouwmeester 2.00 5.00
AF-JC Jonathan Cheechoo 4.00 10.00
AF-JF Jeff Friesen 2.50 6.00
AF-JG J-S Giguere 3.00 8.00
AF-JI Jarome Iginla 5.00 12.00
AF-JJ Jaromir Jagr 6.00 15.00
AF-JR Jeremy Roenick 5.00 12.00
AF-JS Joe Sakic 6.00 15.00
AF-JT Joe Thornton 5.00 12.00
AF-KD Kris Draper 2.00 5.00
AF-KL Kari Lehtonen 4.00 10.00
AF-KP Keith Primeau 2.00 5.00
AF-KT Keith Tkachuk 4.00 10.00
AF-LE Manny Legace 4.00 10.00
AF-MB Martin Biron 3.00 8.00
AF-MD Marcel Dionne SP 6.00 15.00
AF-MG Marian Gaborik 5.00 12.00
AF-MI Mike Ribeiro 2.00 5.00
AF-ML Mario Lemieux 10.00 25.00
AF-MM Mike Modano 5.00 12.00
AF-MN Markus Naslund 4.00 10.00
AF-MP Mark Parrish 2.50 6.00
AF-MR Mark Recchi 3.00 8.00
AF-MT Marty Turco 3.00 8.00
AF-MW Brenden Morrow 3.00 8.00
AF-NH Nathan Horton 2.50 6.00
AF-NK Nikolai Khabibulin 4.00 10.00
AF-NL Nicklas Lidstrom 4.00 10.00
AF-NZ Nikolai Zherdev 3.00 8.00
AF-OK Olaf Kolzig 3.00 8.00
AF-PB Patrice Bergeron 3.00 8.00
AF-PD Pavel Datsyuk 4.00 10.00
AF-PE Patrik Elias 3.00 8.00
AF-PF Peter Forsberg 5.00 12.00
AF-PK Paul Kariya 4.00 10.00
AF-PM Patrick Marleau 3.00 8.00
AF-PR Patrick Roy 10.00 25.00
AF-RB Ray Bourque 5.00 12.00
AF-RD Rick DiPietro 3.00 8.00
AF-RE Robert Esche 3.00 8.00
AF-RI Brad Richards 3.00 8.00
AF-RL Roberto Luongo 5.00 12.00
AF-RN Rick Nash 5.00 12.00
AF-RS Ryan Smyth 3.00 8.00
AF-RY Michael Ryder 3.00 8.00
AF-SA Miroslav Satan 3.00 8.00
AF-SD Shane Doan 2.50 6.00
AF-SF Sergei Fedorov 4.00 10.00
AF-SG Simon Gagne 4.00 10.00
AF-SK Saku Koivu 4.00 10.00
AF-SP Jason Spezza 4.00 10.00
AF-ST Matt Stajan 2.50 6.00
AF-SU Mats Sundin 4.00 10.00
AF-SW Stephen Weiss 2.00 5.00
AF-SY Steve Yzerman 8.00 20.00
AF-TB Todd Bertuzzi 4.00 10.00
AF-TC Ty Conklin 3.00 8.00
AF-TH Jose Theodore 5.00 12.00
AF-TP Tom Poti 2.00 5.00
AF-TR Tuomo Ruutu 2.50 6.00
AF-TV Tomas Vokoun 3.00 8.00
AF-VL Vincent Lecavalier 4.00 10.00
AF-ZC Zdeno Chara 4.00 10.00
AF-ZP Zigmund Palffy 3.00 8.00

2005-06 SP Game Used Authentic Fabrics Autographs

*STARS: 1.5X TO 4X BASIC JERSEY
PRINT RUN 75 SER.#'d SETS
AAF-JC Jonathan Cheechoo 25.00 60.00
AAF-WG Wayne Gretzky 150.00 300.00

2005-06 SP Game Used Authentic Fabrics Dual

PRINT RUN 100 SER.#'d SETS
AH Daniel Alfredsson 10.00 25.00
Dany Heatley
BB Martin Biron 8.00 20.00
Daniel Briere
BF Dustin Brown 8.00 20.00
Alexander Frolov
BM Ed Belfour 8.00 20.00
Bryan McCabe
BN Martin Biron 8.00 20.00
Mika Noronen
CO Patrick Roy 12.50 30.00
Ray Bourque
DH Shane Doan 8.00 20.00
Brett Hull
DJ Dany Heatley 10.00 25.00
Jason Spezza
EB Patrik Elias 12.50 30.00
Martin Brodeur
ER Robert Esche 8.00 20.00
Peter Forsberg
GH Wayne Gretzky 50.00 100.00
Gordie Howe
GK Wayne Gretzky 50.00 100.00
Jari Kurri
GS Jean-Sebastien Giguere 8.00 20.00
Teemu Selanne
HH Dominik Hasek 10.00 25.00
Martin Havlat
HK Marian Hossa 8.00 20.00
Ilya Kovalchuk
HL Adam Hall 8.00 20.00
David Legwand
HS Trent Hunter 8.00 20.00
Miroslav Satan
IK Jarome Iginla 12.50 30.00
Miikka Kiprusoff
IS Jarome Iginla 8.00 20.00
Martin St.Louis
KK Nikolai Khabibulin 8.00 20.00
Miikka Kiprusoff
KT Saku Koivu 8.00 20.00
Jose Theodore
KV Paul Kariya 10.00 25.00
Tomas Vokoun
LN Kari Lehtonen 8.00 20.00
Mika Noronen
LS Vincent Lecavalier 10.00 25.00
Martin St. Louis
MC Patrick Marleau 8.00 20.00
Jonathan Cheechoo
MO Mats Sundin 8.00 20.00
Owen Nolan
MT Markus Naslund 8.00 20.00
Todd Bertuzzi
NB Cam Neely 10.00 25.00
Ray Bourque
NT Rick Nash 10.00 25.00
Joe Thornton
NY Bryan Trottier 8.00 20.00
Mike Bossy
PB Joe Thornton 8.00 20.00
Patrice Bergeron
PC Chris Pronger 8.00 20.00
Ty Conklin
PE Joni Pitkanen 8.00 20.00
Robert Esche
PG Keith Primeau 8.00 20.00
Simon Gagne
RA Raffi Torres 8.00 20.00
Ales Hemsky
RB Mike Ribeiro 6.00 15.00
Patrice Bergeron
RF Dwayne Roloson 8.00 20.00
Manny Fernandez
RR Michael Ryder 8.00 20.00
Mike Ribeiro
SA Jason Spezza 10.00 25.00
Daniel Alfredsson
SB Joe Sakic 8.00 20.00
Rob Blake
SC Ryan Smyth 8.00 20.00
Ty Conklin
SP Darryl Sittler 10.00 25.00
Gilbert Perreault
SR Philipe Sauve 8.00 20.00
Andrew Raycroft
SS Matt Stajan 8.00 20.00
Eric Staal
TH Alex Tanguay 8.00 20.00
Milan Hejduk
TM Marty Turco 8.00 20.00
Mike Modano
WB Peter Worrell 8.00 20.00
Donald Brashear
WH Stephen Weiss 8.00 20.00
Nathan Horton
WT Doug Weight 8.00 20.00
Keith Tkachuk
YS Steve Yzerman 12.50 30.00
Brendan Shanahan
ZD Henrik Zetterberg 8.00 20.00
Kris Draper

2005-06 SP Game Used Authentic Fabrics Dual Autographs

PRINT RUN 25 SER.#'d SETS
AH Daniel Alfredsson
Dany Heatley
BB Martin Biron 20.00 50.00
Daniel Briere
CO Patrick Roy 125.00 250.00
Ray Bourque
DJ Dany Heatley 40.00 100.00
Jason Spezza
DT Marcel Dionne 20.00 50.00
Bryan Trottier
GH Wayne Gretzky 300.00 500.00
Gordie Howe
HH Dominik Hasek 40.00 100.00
Martin Havlat
HK Marian Hossa 30.00 80.00
Ilya Kovalchuk
HS Trent Hunter 15.00 40.00
Miroslav Satan
IS Jarome Iginla 25.00 60.00
Martin St.Louis
KT Saku Koivu 40.00 100.00
Jose Theodore
LD Guy Lafleur 60.00 125.00
Marcel Dionne
LN Kari Lehtonen 25.00 60.00
Mika Noronen
LS Vincent Lecavalier 40.00 100.00
Martin St. Louis
MO Mats Sundin 30.00 80.00
Owen Nolan
MT Markus Naslund 20.00 50.00
Todd Bertuzzi
NB Cam Neely 75.00 200.00
Ray Bourque
NT Rick Nash 50.00 125.00
Joe Thornton
PB Joe Thornton 30.00 80.00
Patrice Bergeron
PC Chris Pronger 20.00 50.00
Ty Conklin
PE Joni Pitkanen 15.00 40.00
Robert Esche
PG Keith Primeau 15.00 40.00
Simon Gagne
RB Mike Ribeiro 20.00 50.00
Patrice Bergeron
RR Michael Ryder 20.00 50.00
Mike Ribeiro
SA Jason Spezza
Daniel Alfredsson
SR Philipe Sauve 15.00 40.00
Andrew Raycroft
SS Matt Stajan 30.00 80.00
Eric Staal
TH Alex Tanguay 25.00 60.00
Milan Hejduk
TM Marty Turco 30.00 80.00
Mike Modano
WH Stephen Weiss 15.00 40.00
Nathan Horton

2005-06 SP Game Used Authentic Fabrics Gold

*STARS: .75X TO 2X
PRINT RUN 100 SER.#'d SETS
AF-WG Wayne Gretzky 40.00 100.00

2005-06 SP Game Used Authentic Fabrics Quad

PRINT RUN 10 SER.#'d SETS
NOT PRICED DUE TO SCARCITY
BADS Martin Biron
Maxim Afinogenov
Chris Drury
Daniel Briere
BEGK Martin Brodeur
Patrick Elias
Scott Gomez
Viktor Kozlov
BLSR Sean Burke
Vincent Lecavalier
Martin St.Louis
Brad Richards
DLBN Tie Domi
Eric Lindros
Ed Belfour
Owen Nolan
EMMR Patrik Elias
Paul Martin
Alexander Mogilny
Brian Rafalski
FRRG Alexander Frolov
Jeremy Roenick
Luc Robitaille
Matheiu Garon
GFEP Simon Gagne
Peter Forsberg
Robert Esche
Keith Primeau
GFRB Marian Gaborik
Manny Fernandez
Dwayne Roloson
Pierre-Marc Bouchard
GMCF Wayne Gretzky
Mark Messier
Jari Kurri
Grant Fuhr
HLBJ Nathan Horton
Roberto Luongo
Jay Bouwmeester
Olli Jokinen
IAKL Jarome Iginla
Tony Amonte
Miikka Kiprusoff
Matthew Lombardi
KBJL Ryan Kesler
Todd Bertuzzi
Ed Jovanovski
Trevor Linden
KHLS Ilya Kovalchuk
Marian Hossa
Kari Lehtonen
Patrik Stefan
KLHV Paul Kariya
David Legwand
Adam Hall
Tomas Vokoun
LZDC Nicklas Lidstrom
Henrik Zetterberg
Pavel Datsyuk
Chris Chelios
MLYS Mark Messier
Mario Lemieux
Steve Yzerman
Joe Sakic
MNDB Ryan Miller
Mika Noronen
J.P Dumont
Daniel Briere
MTGA Mike Modano
Marty Turco
Bill Guerin
Jason Arnott
NSZB Rick Nash
Jason Spezza
Henrik Zetterberg
Jay Bouwmeester
NZDF Rick Nash
Nikolai Zherdev
Marc Denis
Sergei Fedorov
RBBF Patrick Roy
Rob Blake
Ray Bourque
Adam Foote
RBLT Patrick Roy
Martin Brodeur
Roberto Luongo
Jose Theodore
SAHH Jason Spezza
Daniel Alfredsson
Martin Havlat
Dany Heatley
SATH Joe Sakic
David Aebischer
Alex Tanguay
Milan Hejduk
SDYH Miroslav Satan
Rick Dipietro
Alexei Yashin
Trent Hunter
SGLC Teemu Selanne
J-S Giguere
Joffrey Lupul
Stanislav Chistov
SNSA Matt Stajan
Owen Nolan
Mats Sundin
Nikolai Antropov
TBYS Bryan Trottier
Mike Bossy
Alexei Yashin
Miroslav Satan
TRGL Keith Tkachuk
Jeremy Roenick
Bill Guerin
John LeClair
TRRK Jose Theodore
Michael Ryder
Mike Ribeiro
Saku Koivu
TRSB Joe Thornton
Andrew Raycroft
Sergei Samsonov
Patrice Bergeron
YDSL Steve Yzerman
Kris Draper
Brendan Shanahan
Manny Legace
SCPTB Ryan Smyth
Ty Conklin

Chris Pronger
Eric Brewer

2005-06 SP Game Used Authentic Patches Quad

PRINT RUN 5 SER.#'d SETS
NOT PRICED DUE TO SCARCITY

2005-06 SP Game Used Authentic Fabrics Triple

PRINT RUN 25 SER.#'d SETS
ARS Daniel Alfredsson 40.00 80.00
Brad Richards
Martin St.Louis
BBP Ray Bourque 20.00 50.00
Rob Blake
Chris Pronger
BBT Martin Brodeur 50.00 100.00
Ed Belfour
Marty Turco
BIS Martin Brodeur 60.00 125.00
Jarome Iginla
Martin St.Louis
BTR Martin Brodeur 100.00 200.00
Jose Theodore
Patrick Roy
CEA Ty Conklin 30.00 60.00
Robert Esche
David Aebischer
CNP Zdeno Chara 30.00 60.00
Scott Niedermeyar
Chris Pronger
CRH Zdeno Chara 30.00 60.00
Wade Redden
Dominik Hasek
DBS Tie Domi 20.00 50.00
Donald Brashear
Chris Simon
DKF Pavel Datsyuk 75.00 150.00
Ilya Kovalchuk
Sergei Fedorov
DLP Kris Draper 30.00 60.00
Jere Lehtinen
Michael Peca
GLY Wayne Gretzky 200.00 350.00
Mario Lemieux
Steve Yzerman
GNP Sergei Gonchar 20.00 50.00
Scott Niedermayer
Chris Pronger
HJH Dominik Hasek 50.00 100.00
Jaromir Jagr
Martin Havlat
HND Brett Hull 20.00 50.00
Ladislav Nagy
Shane Doan
INK Jarome Iginla 40.00 80.00
Rick Nash
Ilya Kovalchuk
ISL Jarome Iginla 40.00 80.00
Brendan Shanahan
Trevor Linden
KNS Ilya Kovalchuk 30.00 60.00
Markus Naslund
Cory Stillman
KRT Miikka Kiprusoff 40.00 80.00
Dwayne Roloson
Marty Turco
KSK Jari Kurri 60.00 125.00
Teemu Selanne
Saku Koivu
MLR Mike Modano 30.00 80.00
Trevor Linden
Jeremy Roenick
NKL Mika Noronen 40.00 80.00
Miikka Kiprusoff
Kari Lehtonen
NPJ Owen Nolan 30.00 60.00
Keith Primeau
Jaromir Jagr
NSL Owen Nolan 20.00 50.00
Mats Sundin
Eric Lindros
PCS Chris Pronger 20.00 50.00
Ty Conklin
Ryan Smyth
RLA Andrew Raycroft 50.00 100.00
Kari Lehtonen
David Aebischer
SEL Joe Sakic 30.00 60.00
Patrik Elias
Robert Lang
SFI Martin St.Louis 30.00 60.00
Peter Forsberg
Jarome Iginla
SFN Mats Sundin 40.00 80.00
Peter Forsberg
Markus Naslund
SHA Martin St. Louis
Marian Hossa
Daniel Alfredsson
SNI Martin St.Louis 40.00 80.00
Markus Naslund
Jarome Iginla
TBM Joe Thornton 30.00 60.00
Patrice Bergeron
Glen Murray
TSY Joe Thornton 50.00 100.00
Joe Sakic
Steve Yzerman
VKL Tomas Vokoun 20.00 50.00
Paul Kariya
David Legwand
YSP Alexei Yashin 40.00 80.00
Miroslav Satan
Mark Parrish

2005-06 SP Game Used Authentic Patches

*SINGLE COLORS: .2X TO .5X HI
*3+ COLORS: 1X TO 2X HI
PRINT RUN 75 SER.#'d SETS
AP-AE David Aebischer 10.00 25.00
AP-AF Alexander Frolov 10.00 25.00
AP-AR Andrew Raycroft 10.00 25.00
AP-AT Alex Tanguay 10.00 25.00
AP-AY Alexei Yashin 6.00 15.00
AP-BE Daniel Briere 10.00 25.00
AP-BG Bill Guerin 10.00 25.00
AP-BL Rob Blake 10.00 25.00
AP-BM Brendan Morrison 10.00 25.00
AP-BO Mike Bossy 12.00 30.00
AP-BR Martin Brodeur 25.00 60.00
AP-BS Brendan Shanahan 12.00 30.00
AP-CD Chris Drury 10.00 25.00
AP-CJ Curtis Joseph 12.00 30.00
AP-CN Cam Neely 12.00 30.00
AP-CP Chris Pronger 10.00 25.00
AP-DA Daniel Alfredsson 10.00 25.00
AP-DB Dustin Brown 6.00 15.00
AP-DC Dan Cloutier 10.00 25.00
AP-DE Pavol Demitra 10.00 25.00
AP-DH Dany Heatley 15.00 40.00
AP-DW Doug Weight 10.00 25.00
AP-EB Ed Belfour 12.00 30.00
AP-GM Glen Murray 6.00 15.00
AP-GO Scott Gomez 10.00 25.00
AP-HA Dominik Hasek 20.00 50.00
AP-HJ Milan Hejduk 12.00 30.00
AP-HO Marian Hossa 12.00 30.00
AP-HU Trent Hunter 6.00 15.00
AP-HV Martin Havlat 10.00 25.00
AP-HZ Henrik Zetterberg 12.00 30.00
AP-IK Ilya Kovalchuk 20.00 50.00
AP-JB Jay Bouwmeester 6.00 15.00
AP-JC Jonathan Cheechoo 20.00 50.00
AP-JF Jeff Friesen 6.00 15.00
AP-JG J-S Giguere 10.00 25.00
AP-JI Jarome Iginla 20.00 50.00
AP-JJ Jaromir Jagr 20.00 50.00
AP-JR Jeremy Roenick 15.00 40.00
AP-JS Joe Sakic 20.00 50.00
AP-JT Joe Thornton 20.00 50.00
AP-KD Kris Draper 6.00 15.00
AP-KL Kari Lehtonen 15.00 40.00
AP-KP Keith Primeau 6.00 15.00
AP-KT Keith Tkachuk 12.00 30.00
AP-LE Manny Legace 12.00 30.00
AP-MB Martin Biron 10.00 25.00
AP-MD Marcel Dionne 12.00 30.00
AP-MG Marian Gaborik 20.00 50.00
AP-MI Mike Ribeiro 6.00 15.00
AP-ML Mario Lemieux 30.00 80.00
AP-MM Mike Modano 15.00 40.00
AP-MN Markus Naslund 12.00 30.00
AP-MP Mark Parrish 6.00 15.00
AP-MR Mark Recchi 10.00 25.00
AP-MS Martin St. Louis 10.00 25.00
AP-MT Marty Turco 10.00 25.00
AP-MW Brenden Morrow 10.00 25.00
AP-NH Nathan Horton 6.00 15.00
AP-NK Nikolai Khabibulin 12.00 30.00
AP-NL Nicklas Lidstrom 12.00 30.00
AP-NZ Nikolai Zherdev 10.00 25.00
AP-OK Olaf Kolzig 10.00 25.00
AP-PB Patrice Bergeron 10.00 25.00
AP-PD Pavel Datsyuk 12.00 30.00
AP-PE Patrik Elias 10.00 25.00
AP-PF Peter Forsberg 20.00 50.00
AP-PK Paul Kariya 12.00 30.00
AP-PM Patrick Marleau 10.00 25.00
AP-PR Patrick Roy 30.00 80.00
AP-RB Ray Bourque 20.00 50.00
AP-RD Rick DiPietro 15.00 40.00
AP-RE Robert Esche 10.00 25.00
AP-RI Brad Richards 10.00 25.00
AP-RL Roberto Luongo 20.00 50.00
AP-RN Rick Nash 15.00 40.00
AP-RS Ryan Smyth 12.00 30.00
AP-RY Michael Ryder 10.00 25.00
AP-SA Miroslav Satan 10.00 25.00
AP-SD Shane Doan 6.00 15.00
AP-SF Sergei Fedorov 15.00 40.00
AP-SG Simon Gagne 12.00 30.00
AP-SK Saku Koivu 12.00 30.00
AP-SP Jason Spezza 15.00 40.00
AP-ST Matt Stajan 6.00 15.00
AP-SU Mats Sundin 12.00 30.00
AP-SW Stephen Weiss 6.00 15.00
AP-SY Steve Yzerman 30.00 80.00
AP-TB Todd Bertuzzi 12.00 30.00
AP-TC Ty Conklin 10.00 25.00
AP-TH Jose Theodore 15.00 40.00
AP-TP Tom Poti 6.00 15.00
AP-TR Tuomo Ruutu 6.00 15.00
AP-TV Tomas Vokoun 10.00 25.00
AP-VL Vincent Lecavalier 12.00 30.00
AP-WG Wayne Gretzky 50.00 125.00
AP-ZC Zdeno Chara 10.00 24.00
AP-ZP Zigmund Palffy 10.00 25.00

2005-06 SP Game Used Authentic Patches Autographs

*STARS: .75X TO 2X BASE PATCH
PRINT RUN 50 SER.#'d SETS

2005-06 SP Game Used Authentic Patches Dual

*DUAL PATCH: 1X TO 2.5X DUAL JSY
PRINT RUN 35 SER.#'d SETS
CO Patrick Roy 60.00 150.00
Ray Bourque
GH Wayne Gretzky 200.00 400.00
Gordie Howe
GK Wayne Gretzky 100.00 250.00
Jari Kurri
GL Wayne Gretzky 150.00 300.00
Mario Lemieux
LD Guy Lafleur 30.00 80.00
Marcel Dionne
MC Patrick Marleau 40.00 100.00
Jonathan Cheechoo
NT Rick Nash 75.00 200.00
Joe Thornton

2005-06 SP Game Used Authentic Patches Dual Autographs

PRINT RUN 10 SER.#'d SETS
NOT PRICED DUE TO SCARCITY

2005-06 SP Game Used Authentic Patches Triple

PRINT RUN 10 SER.#'d SETS
NOT PRICED DUE TO SCARCITY

2005-06 SP Game Used Auto Draft

PRINT RUNS LISTED BELOW
UNDER 24 NOT PRICED DUE TO SCARCITY
AD-AF Alexander Frolov/20
AD-AL Daniel Alfredsson/133 6.00 15.00
AD-AM Alvaro Montoya/29 30.00 60.00
AD-AO Alexander Ovechkin/1
AD-AP Alexander Perezhogin/25 25.00 50.00
AD-AS Alexander Steen/24 25.00 50.00
AD-BL Brian Leetch/9
AD-BO Ray Bourque/8
AD-BR Brad Richards/64 10.00 25.00
AD-BU Peter Budaj/63 15.00 40.00
AD-BW Brad Winchester/35 8.00 20.00
AD-BY Matthew Barnaby/83 6.00 15.00
AD-CA Michael Cammalleri/49 10.00 25.00
AD-CC Craig Conroy/123 6.00 15.00
AD-CD Chris Drury/72 10.00 25.00
AD-CN Cam Neely/9
AD-CP Corey Perry/28 25.00 60.00
AD-CW Cam Ward/25 30.00 75.00
AD-DA David Aebischer/161 6.00 15.00
AD-DB Daniel Briere/24 25.00 60.00
AD-DC Dan Cloutier/26 12.00 30.00
AD-DF Dan Fritsche/46 6.00 15.00
AD-DK Duncan Keith/54 6.00 15.00
AD-DL David Leneveu/46 15.00 40.00
AD-DM Darren McCarty/46 10.00 25.00
AD-DP Dion Phaneuf/9
AD-EC Erik Cole/71 8.00 20.00
AD-ED Eric Daze/90 6.00 15.00
AD-FT Fedor Tjutin/40 12.50 30.00
AD-GB Gilbert Brule/6
AD-GL Georges Laraque/31 15.00 40.00
AD-GU Guy Lafleur/1
AD-HE Jochen Hecht/49 10.00 25.00
AD-HT Hannu Toivonen/29 25.00 50.00
AD-HV Martin Havlat/26 25.00 60.00
AD-JA Jason Arnott/7
AD-JC Jonathan Cheechoo/29 30.00 75.00
AD-JE Jeff Carter/11
AD-JF Johan Franzen/97 8.00 20.00
AD-JH Jim Howard/64 15.00 40.00
AD-JI Jarome Iginla/11
AD-JJ Jussi Jokinen/192 8.00 20.00
AD-JK Jari Kurri/69 20.00 50.00
AD-JO Joe Thornton/1
AD-JS Jim Slater/30 10.00 25.00
AD-JT Jose Theodore/44 15.00 40.00
AD-JV Josef Vasicek/91 6.00 15.00
AD-JW Justin Williams/28 15.00 40.00
AD-KD Kris Draper/62 10.00 25.00
AD-KH Kristian Huselius/47 6.00 15.00
AD-KW Kevin Weekes/41 8.00 20.00
AD-LR Luc Robitaille/171 15.00 40.00
AD-MA Maxim Afinogenov/69 8.00 20.00
AD-MB Martin Brodeur/20 60.00 150.00
AD-MC Jay McClement/57 8.00 20.00
AD-MF Matt Foy/175 6.00 15.00
AD-MG Marian Gaborik/3
AD-MH Milan Hejduk/87 8.00 20.00
AD-MI Milan Bartovic/35 8.00 20.00
AD-MJ Milan Jurcina/241
AD-MM Mike Modano/1
AD-MN Markus Naslund/16 15.00 40.00
AD-MR Mike Ribeiro/45 6.00 15.00
AD-MS Matt Stajan/57 15.00 40.00
AD-MW Brenden Morrow/25 12.00 30.00
AD-NK Nikolai Khabibulin/204 6.00 15.00
AD-NO Mika Noronen/21
AD-NY Michael Nylander/59 8.00 20.00
AD-PB Patrice Bergeron/45 20.00 50.00
AD-PE Patrick Eaves/29 15.00 40.00
AD-PR Patrick Roy/51 75.00 150.00
AD-PS Philippe Sauve/38 8.00 20.00
AD-RB Rob Blake/70 8.00 20.00
AD-RC Mark Recchi/67
AD-RE Robert Esche/139 6.00 15.00
AD-RG Ryan Getzlaf/19 50.00 100.00
AD-RI Mike Richards/24 30.00 75.00
AD-RK Ryan Kesler/23 10.00 25.00
AD-RN Rick Nash/1
AD-SB Sean Burke/24 10.00 25.00
AD-SC Sidney Crosby/1
AD-SG Simon Gagne/22 30.00 60.00
AD-SH Sheldon Souray/71 6.00 15.00
AD-SK Saku Koivu/21 25.00 60.00
AD-SN Scott Niedermayer/3
AD-SP Jason Spezza/2
AD-SS Steve Sullivan/233 6.00 15.00
AD-SU Mats Sundin/1
AD-SV Marc Savard/91
AD-SZ Sergei Zubov/85 6.00 15.00
AD-TA Tyler Arnason/183 6.00 15.00
AD-TB Todd Bertuzzi/23
AD-TG Tim Gleason/23 10.00 25.00
AD-TH Trent Hunter/150 6.00 15.00
AD-TP Tom Poti/59 6.00 15.00
AD-TS Timofei Shishkanov/33 8.00 20.00
AD-TV Thomas Vanek/5
AD-VL Vincent Lecavalier/1
AD-VP Vaclav Prospal/71 6.00 15.00
AD-ZC Zdeno Chara/56 8.00 20.00

2005-06 SP Game Used Awesome Authentics

PRINT RUN 100 SER.#'d SETS
AA-AF Alexander Frolov
AA-AH Ales Hemsky 6.00 15.00
AA-AR Andrew Raycroft 6.00 15.00
AA-AT Alex Tanguay 6.00 15.00
AA-AY Alexei Yashin 6.00 15.00
AA-BG Bill Guerin 6.00 15.00
AA-BI Martin Biron 6.00 15.00
AA-BM Bryan McCabe 6.00 15.00
AA-BR Brad Richards 6.00 15.00
AA-BS Brendan Shanahan 8.00 20.00
AA-CD Chris Drury 6.00 15.00
AA-CJ Curtis Joseph 8.00 20.00
AA-CP Chris Pronger 6.00 15.00
AA-DA Daniel Alfredsson 6.00 15.00
AA-DB Daniel Briere 6.00 15.00
AA-DC Dan Cloutier 6.00 15.00
AA-DH Dany Heatley 10.00 25.00
AA-DL David Legwand 6.00 15.00
AA-DU Dustin Brown 6.00 15.00
AA-DW Doug Weight 6.00 15.00
AA-EB Ed Belfour 8.00 20.00
AA-EL Eric Lindros 8.00 20.00
AA-ES Eric Staal 8.00 20.00
AA-GM Glen Murray 6.00 15.00
AA-HJ Milan Hejduk 8.00 20.00
AA-HK Dominik Hasek/75 15.00 40.00
AA-HV Martin Havlat 6.00 15.00
AA-HZ Henrik Zetterberg 8.00 20.00
AA-IK Ilya Kovalchuk 10.00 25.00
AA-JB Jay Bouwmeester 6.00 15.00
AA-JG J-S Giguere 6.00 15.00
AA-JI Jarome Iginla 10.00 25.00
AA-JJ Jaromir Jagr 15.00 40.00
AA-JL John LeClair 8.00 20.00
AA-JO Joe Thornton 12.00 30.00
AA-JR Jeremy Roenick 10.00 25.00
AA-JS Jason Spezza 10.00 25.00
AA-JT Jocelyn Thibault 6.00 15.00
AA-JW Justin Williams 6.00 15.00
AA-KP Keith Primeau 4.00 10.00
AA-KT Keith Tkachuk 8.00 20.00
AA-LN Ladislav Nagy 6.00 15.00
AA-LU Joffrey Lupul 6.00 15.00
AA-LX Mario Lemieux 40.00 100.00
AA-MB Martin Brodeur 30.00 80.00
AA-MF Manny Fernandez 6.00 15.00
AA-MG Marian Gaborik 12.00 30.00
AA-MK Miikka Kiprusoff 8.00 20.00
AA-ML Manny Legace 8.00 20.00
AA-MM Mike Modano 12.00 30.00
AA-MN Markus Naslund 8.00 20.00
AA-MO Brendan Morrison 6.00 15.00
AA-MP Mark Parrish 6.00 15.00
AA-MS Matt Stajan 6.00 15.00
AA-MT Marty Turco 6.00 15.00
AA-MW Brenden Morrow 6.00 15.00
AA-NH Nathan Horton 6.00 15.00
AA-NK Nikolai Khabibulin 8.00 20.00
AA-NL Nicklas Lidstrom 8.00 20.00
AA-NZ Nikolai Zherdev 6.00 15.00
AA-OK Olaf Kolzig 6.00 15.00
AA-PB Patrice Bergeron 6.00 15.00
AA-PE Patrik Elias 6.00 15.00
AA-PF Peter Forsberg 15.00 40.00
AA-PK Paul Kariya 8.00 20.00
AA-RA Brian Rafalski 6.00 15.00
AA-RB Rob Blake 6.00 15.00
AA-RD Rick DiPietro 6.00 15.00
AA-RE Mark Recchi 6.00 15.00
AA-RF Ruslan Fedotenko 6.00 15.00
AA-RL Roberto Luongo 10.00 25.00
AA-RN Rick Nash 10.00 25.00
AA-RO Robert Esche 6.00 15.00
AA-RS Ryan Smyth 6.00 15.00
AA-RY Michael Ryder 6.00 15.00
AA-RZ Richard Zednik 6.00 15.00
AA-SA Joe Sakic 15.00 40.00
AA-SD Shane Doan 6.00 15.00
AA-SF Sergei Fedorov/75 10.00 25.00
AA-SG Simon Gagne 8.00 20.00
AA-SK Saku Koivu 8.00 20.00
AA-SL Martin St. Louis 6.00 15.00
AA-SU Mats Sundin 8.00 20.00
AA-SY Steve Yzerman 25.00 60.00
AA-TC Ty Conklin 6.00 15.00
AA-TH Jose Theodore 10.00 25.00
AA-TR Tuomo Ruutu 6.00 15.00
AA-TS Teemu Selanne 8.00 20.00
AA-TV Tomas Vokoun 6.00 15.00
AA-VL Vincent Lecavalier 8.00 20.00
AA-WR Wade Redden 6.00 15.00
AA-ZP Zigmund Palffy 6.00 15.00

2005-06 SP Game Used Awesome Authentics Gold

*GOLD: .6X TO 1.5X BASE JSY
PRINT RUN 25 SER.#'d SETS

2005-06 SP Game Used By the Letter

PRINT RUNS VARY
NOT PRICED DUE TO SCARCITY
LM-AK Alexei Kovalev/7
LM-BS Brendan Shanahan/8
LM-EB Ed Belfour /7
LM-EJ Ed Jovanovski/10
LM-HZ Henrik Zetterberg/10
LM-IK Ilya Kovalchuk/9
LM-JI Jarome Iginla/6
LM-ML Mario Lemieux/7
LM-MT Marty Turco/5
LM-PB Patrice Bergeron/8
LM-PR Patrick Roy/3
LM-RB Ray Bourque/7
LM-SF Sergei Fedorov/7
LM-SP Jason Spezza/6
LM-SY Steve Yzerman/7

2005-06 SP Game Used Endorsed Equipment

PRINT RUN 5 SER.#'d SETS
NOT PRICED DUE TO SCARCITY
EE-EB Ed Belfour
EE-GF Grant Fuhr
EE-JT Jose Theodore
EE-MF Marc-Andre Fleury
EE-MT Marty Turco
EE-OK Olaf Kolzig
EE-PR Patrick Roy
EE-TE Tony Esposito

2005-06 SP Game Used Game Gear

PRINT RUN 100 SER.#'d SETS
UNLESS OTHERWISE NOTED
GG-AF Maxim Afinogenov 4.00 10.00
GG-AK Alexei Kovalev 5.00 12.00
GG-AM Alexander Mogilny 5.00 12.00
GG-AO Alexander Ovechkin 30.00 80.00
GG-AP Alexander Perezhogin 4.00 10.00
GG-AR Andrew Raycroft 5.00 12.00
GG-AS Alexander Steen 6.00 15.00
GG-AT Alex Tanguay/45 10.00 25.00
GG-BA Rod Brind'Amour 5.00 12.00
GG-BE Patrice Bergeron 5.00 12.00
GG-BG Bill Guerin 4.00 10.00
GG-BL Rob Blake 5.00 12.00
GG-BO Ray Bourque 10.00 25.00
GG-BR Martin Brodeur 12.00 30.00
GG-BS Billy Smith 5.00 12.00
GG-BT Bryan Trottier 5.00 12.00
GG-CB Cam Barker 5.00 12.00
GG-CD Chris Drury 5.00 12.00
GG-CE Christian Ehrhoff 4.00 10.00
GG-CH Jonathan Cheechoo 6.00 15.00
GG-CN Cam Neely 6.00 15.00
GG-CP Chris Pronger 5.00 12.00
GG-DB Daniel Briere 4.00 10.00
GG-DH Dany Heatley 8.00 20.00
GG-DL David Legwand 5.00 12.00
GG-DP Dion Phaneuf 15.00 40.00
GG-EN Eric Nystrom 4.00 10.00
GG-ES Eric Staal 5.00 12.00
GG-GB Gilbert Brule 8.00 20.00
GG-GL Guy Lafleur 10.00 25.00
GG-HA Dominik Hasek 12.00 30.00
GG-HL Henrik Lundqvist 15.00 40.00
GG-HT Hannu Toivonen 6.00 15.00
GG-HZ Henrik Zetterberg 6.00 15.00
GG-IK Ilya Kovalchuk 8.00 20.00
GG-JB Jean Beliveau 10.00 25.00
GG-JC Jeff Carter 6.00 15.00
GG-JF Jeff Friesen 4.00 10.00
GG-JG J-S Giguere 5.00 12.00
GG-JH Jim Howard 6.00 15.00
GG-JI Jarome Iginla 8.00 20.00
GG-JJ Jaromir Jagr 12.00 30.00
GG-JO Joe Thornton 10.00 25.00
GG-JP Joni Pitkanen 4.00 10.00
GG-JR Jeremy Roenick 8.00 20.00
GG-JS Jason Spezza 6.00 15.00
GG-KP Keith Primeau 3.00 8.00
GG-KT Keith Tkachuk 6.00 15.00
GG-MA Paul Martin 4.00 10.00
GG-MB Mike Bossy 6.00 15.00
GG-ML Mario Lemieux 20.00 50.00
GG-MM Mike Modano 5.00 12.00
GG-MR Mike Ribeiro 4.00 10.00
GG-MT Marty Turco 5.00 12.00
GG-OK Olaf Kolzig 5.00 12.00
GG-OR Brooks Orpik 4.00 10.00
GG-PB Peter Bondra 5.00 12.00
GG-PE Corey Perry 6.00 15.00
GG-PF Peter Forsberg 10.00 25.00
GG-PK Paul Kariya 6.00 15.00
GG-PM Pierre-Marc Bouchard 4.00 10.00
GG-PS Philippe Sauve 5.00 12.00
GG-RB Ray Bourque 10.00 25.00
GG-RF Ruslan Fedotenko 4.00 10.00
GG-RG Ryan Getzlaf 8.00 20.00
GG-RI Mike Richards 6.00 15.00
GG-RK Rostislav Klesla 4.00 10.00
GG-RM Ryan Malone 4.00 10.00
GG-RN Rick Nash 8.00 20.00
GG-RT Raffi Torres 4.00 10.00
GG-RY Michael Ryder 5.00 12.00
GG-SA Joe Sakic 10.00 25.00
GG-SC Sidney Crosby 50.00 125.00
GG-SG Simon Gagne 6.00 15.00
GG-SH Brendan Shanahan 6.00 15.00
GG-SK Saku Koivu 6.00 15.00
GG-ST Anthony Stewart 4.00 10.00
GG-SU Mats Sundin 6.00 15.00
GG-SY Steve Yzerman 15.00 40.00
GG-TH Trent Hunter 4.00 10.00
GG-TV Thomas Vanek 12.00 30.00
GG-WW Wojtek Wolski 8.00 20.00
GG-YD Yann Danis 4.00 10.00
GG-ZP Zach Parise 8.00 20.00
GG-BH2 Bobby Hull 12.00 30.00
GG-GH1 Gordie Howe 12.00 30.00
GG-GH2 Gordie Howe 12.00 30.00
GG-PR1 Patrick Roy 20.00 50.00
GG-PR2 Patrick Roy 20.00 50.00

2005-06 SP Game Used Game Gear Autographs

PRINT RUN 10 SER.#'d SETS
NOT PRICED DUE TO SCARCITY

2005-06 SP Game Used Heritage Classic

PRINT RUN 100 SER.#'d SETS
HC-BR Bill Ranford 8.00 20.00
HC-BS Borje Salming 6.00 15.00
HC-DG Doug Gilmour 8.00 20.00
HC-DS Darryl Sittler 6.00 15.00
HC-DW Tiger Williams 6.00 15.00
HC-GF Grant Fuhr 6.00 15.00
HC-KM Kirk Muller 6.00 15.00
HC-LM Larry Murphy 6.00 15.00
HC-MC Lanny McDonald 6.00 15.00
HC-MK Mike Krushelnyski 6.00 15.00
HC-PS Peter Stastny 6.00 15.00
HC-RB Ray Bourque 8.00 20.00
HC-RE Ron Ellis 6.00 15.00
HC-RL Rod Langway 6.00 15.00
HC-RV Rick Vaive 6.00 15.00
HC-SS Steve Shutt 6.00 15.00
HC-WC Wendel Clark 8.00 20.00

2005-06 SP Game Used Heritage Classic Autographs

*AUTO: 1X TO 2.5X BASE JSY
PRINT RUN 100 SER.#'d SETS

2005-06 SP Game Used Heritage Classic Patches

*PATCH: .75X TO 2X BASE JSY
PRINT RUN 25 SER.#'d SETS

2005-06 SP Game Used Heritage Classic Patches Autographed

PRINT RUN 10 SER.#'d SETS
NOT PRICED DUE TO SCARCITY

2005-06 SP Game Used Oldtimer's Challenge

PRINT RUN 100 SER.#'d SETS
OC-BB Bob Bourne 4.00 10.00
OC-BR Ray Bourque 10.00 25.00
OC-BP Bob Probert 4.00 10.00
OC-DB Doug Bodger 4.00 10.00
OC-DG Doug Gilmour 10.00 25.00
OC-DS Darryl Sittler 6.00 15.00
OC-DW Tiger Williams 4.00 10.00
OC-GA Glenn Anderson 4.00 10.00
OC-GF Grant Fuhr 6.00 15.00
OC-GL Guy Lafleur 5.00 12.00
OC-GP Gilbert Perreault 4.00 10.00
OC-KM Kirk Muller 4.00 10.00
OC-MC Lanny McDonald 6.00 15.00
OC-RB Richard Brodeur 4.00 10.00
OC-SS Steve Shutt 4.00 10.00

2005-06 SP Game Used Oldtimer's Challenge Autographs

PRINT RUN 100 SER.#'d SETS
OCA-BB Bob Bourne 10.00 25.00
OCA-BO Ray Bourque 20.00 50.00
OCA-BP Bob Probert 12.00 30.00
OCA-DB Doug Bodger 10.00 25.00
OCA-DG Doug Gilmour 20.00 50.00
OCA-DS Darryl Sittler 15.00 40.00
OCA-DW Tiger Williams 10.00 25.00
OCA-GA Glenn Anderson 10.00 25.00
OCA-GF Grant Fuhr 15.00 40.00
OCA-GL Guy Lafleur 20.00 50.00
OCA-GP Gilbert Perreault 10.00 25.00
OCA-KM Kirk Muller 10.00 25.00
OCA-MC Lanny McDonald 15.00 40.00
OCA-RB Richard Brodeur 10.00 25.00
OCA-SS Steve Shutt 10.00 25.00

2005-06 SP Game Used Oldtimer's Challenge Patches Autographed

PRINT RUN 10 SER.#'d SETS
NOT PRICED DUE TO SCARCITY

2005-06 SP Game Used Rookie Exclusives

PRINT RUN 100 SER.#'d SETS
AA Andrew Alberts 4.00 10.00
AL Al Montoya 8.00 20.00
AM Andrej Meszaros 4.00 10.00
AO Alexander Ovechkin 75.00 150.00
AP Alexander Perezhogin 6.00 15.00
AS Alexander Steen 12.00 30.00
AW Andrew Wozniewski 4.00 10.00
BB Brandon Bochenski 4.00 10.00
BC Braydon Coburn 4.00 10.00
BL Brett Lebda 4.00 10.00
BS Brent Seabrook 4.00 10.00
BW Brad Winchester 4.00 10.00
CB Cam Barker 8.00 20.00
Error-G.Brule autograph
CC Chris Campoli 4.00 10.00
CP Corey Perry 15.00 40.00
CW Cam Ward 15.00 40.00
DK Duncan Keith 4.00 10.00
DL David Leneveu 4.00 10.00
DP Dion Phaneuf 50.00 100.00
EN Eric Nystrom 4.00 10.00
GB Gilbert Brule 12.00 30.00
GP George Parros 4.00 10.00
HL Henrik Lundqvist 50.00 100.00
HT Hannu Toivonen 8.00 20.00
JB Jaroslav Balastik 4.00 10.00
JC Jeff Carter 15.00 40.00
JF Johan Franzen 4.00 10.00
JG Josh Gorges 4.00 10.00
JH Jim Howard 10.00 25.00
JJ Jussi Jokinen 6.00 15.00
JM Jay McClement 4.00 10.00
JS Jim Slater 4.00 10.00
JW Jeff Woywitka 4.00 10.00
KB Keith Ballard 4.00 10.00
KD Kevin Dallman 4.00 10.00
KN Kevin Nastiuk 4.00 10.00
LS Lee Stempniak 4.00 10.00
MF Matt Foy 4.00 10.00
MJ Milan Jurcina 4.00 10.00
MR Mike Richards 12.00 30.00
MT Maxime Talbot 4.00 10.00
NN Niklas Nordgren 4.00 10.00
PB Peter Budaj 6.00 15.00
PE Patrick Eaves 6.00 15.00
PN Petteri Nokelainen 4.00 10.00
PP Petr Prucha 8.00 20.00
RB Rene Bourque 4.00 10.00
RC Ryane Clowe 4.00 10.00
RG Ryan Getzlaf 25.00 60.00
RH Ryan Hollweg 4.00 10.00
RI Raitis Ivanans 4.00 10.00
RN Robert Nilsson 4.00 10.00
RO Rostislav Olesz 6.00 15.00
RS Ryan Suter 6.00 15.00
SC Sidney Crosby 250.00 400.00
ST Anthony Stewart 4.00 10.00
TV Thomas Vanek 25.00 60.00
WW Wojtek Wolski 15.00 40.00
YD Yann Danis 6.00 15.00
ZP Zach Parise 15.00 40.00

2005-06 SP Game Used Rookie Exclusives Silver

PRINT RUN 5 SER.#'d SETS
NOT PRICED DUE TO SCARCITY

2005-06 SP Game Used Signature Sticks

PRINT RUN 5 SER.#'d SETS
NOT PRICED DUE TO SCARCITY
SS-AR Andrew Raycroft
SS-AT Alex Tanguay
SS-BT Bryan Trottier
SS-CD Chris Drury
SS-DB Daniel Briere
SS-DL David Legwand
SS-ES Eric Staal
SS-JB Jean Beliveau
SS-JC Jonathan Cheechoo
SS-JP Joni Pitkanen
SS-KP Keith Primeau
SS-MA Maxim Afinogenov
SS-MB Mike Bossy
SS-MR Michael Ryder
SS-OK Olaf Kolzig
SS-PB Patrice Bergeron
SS-PS Philippe Sauve
SS-RB Rob Blake
SS-RF Ruslan Fedotenko
SS-TE Tony Esposito
SS-TH Trent Hunter
SS-BH1 Bobby Hull
SS-BH2 Bobby Hull
SS-GH1 Gordie Howe
SS-GH2 Gordie Howe

2005-06 SP Game Used SIGnificance

PRINT RUN 100 SER.#'d SETS
AF Alexander Frolov 6.00 15.00
AL Daniel Alfredsson 6.00 15.00
AY Alexei Yashin 6.00 15.00
BM Brendan Morrison 6.00 15.00
BR Brad Richards 10.00 25.00
CD Chris Drury 6.00 15.00
CO Chris Osgood 6.00 15.00
CP Chris Pronger 6.00 15.00
CS Cory Stillman 6.00 15.00
DA David Aebischer 6.00 15.00
DB Dustin Brown 6.00 15.00
DC Dan Cloutier 6.00 15.00
DH Dany Heatley 12.50 30.00
DL David Legwand 6.00 15.00
DM Darren McCarty 6.00 15.00
DR Dwayne Roloson 6.00 15.00
EC Erik Cole 6.00 15.00
ED Eric Daze 6.00 15.00
EJ Ed Jovanovski 6.00 15.00
EN Evgeni Nabokov 6.00 15.00
ES Eric Staal 12.00 30.00
GH Gordie Howe 40.00 80.00
GM Glen Murray 6.00 15.00
HO Marian Hossa 6.00 15.00
HZ Henrik Zetterberg 10.00 25.00
IK Ilya Kovalchuk 20.00 50.00
JA Jason Arnott 6.00 15.00
JB Jay Bouwmeester 6.00 15.00
JC Jonathan Cheechoo 10.00 25.00
JI Jarome Iginla 15.00 40.00
JL Joffrey Lupul 6.00 15.00
JN Jocelyn Thibault 6.00 15.00
JO Jeff O'Neill 6.00 15.00
JP Joni Pitkanen 6.00 15.00
JR Jeremy Roenick 10.00 25.00
JS Jason Spezza 12.00 30.00
JT Joe Thornton 20.00 50.00
KD Kris Draper 6.00 15.00
KP Keith Primeau 6.00 15.00
MB Martin Brodeur 30.00 80.00
MC Mike Cammalleri 6.00 15.00
MH Martin Havlat 6.00 15.00
ML Manny Legace 6.00 15.00
MN Markus Naslund 6.00 15.00
MP Mark Parrish 6.00 15.00
MR Michael Ryder 6.00 15.00
MS Miroslav Satan 6.00 15.00
MT Marty Turco 6.00 15.00
MW Brenden Morrow 6.00 15.00
NY Michael Nylander 6.00 15.00
NZ Nikolai Zherdev 6.00 15.00
OK Olaf Kolzig 10.00 25.00
PB Patrice Bergeron 10.00 25.00
PM Pierre-Marc Bouchard 6.00 15.00

PR Patrick Roy 60.00 125.00
PS Philippe Sauve 6.00 15.00
RA Brian Rafalski 6.00 15.00
RB Rob Blake 6.00 15.00
RE Robert Esche 6.00 15.00
RF Ruslan Fedotenko 6.00 15.00
RL Roberto Luongo 10.00 25.00
RM Ryan Miller 10.00 25.00
RN Rick Nash 12.50 30.00
RO Rob Niedermayer 6.00 15.00
RS Ryan Smyth 6.00 15.00
SB Sean Burke 6.00 15.00
SD Shane Doan 6.00 15.00
SL Martin St. Louis 6.00 15.00
SN Scott Niedermayer 6.00 15.00
SS Sheldon Souray 6.00 15.00
SU Mats Sundin 10.00 25.00
SW Stephen Weiss 6.00 15.00
SZ Sergei Zubov 6.00 15.00
TA Tyler Arnason 6.00 15.00
TH Trent Hunter 6.00 15.00
TL Trevor Linden 10.00 25.00
VL Vincent Lecavalier 10.00 25.00
VP Vaclav Prospal 6.00 15.00
ZC Zdeno Chara 6.00 15.00

2005-06 SP Game Used SIGnificance Gold

PRINT RUN 25 SER.#'d SETS

2005-06 SP Game Used SIGnificance Extra

PRINT RUN 25 SER.#'d SETS
BL Martin Brodeur 100.00 200.00
Roberto Luongo
CR Jonathan Cheechoo 20.00 50.00
Michael Ryder
FB Alex Frolov 12.50 30.00
Dustin Brown
GH Gordie Howe 300.00 500.00
Wayne Gretzky
HH Dany Heatley 25.00 60.00
Martin Havlat
HK Marian Hossa 25.00 60.00
Ilya Kovalchuk
HP Trent Hunter
Mark Parrish
IH Jarome Iginla 20.00 50.00
Milan Hejduk
MS Ryan Miller 12.50 30.00
Philippe Sauve
MT Brenden Morrow 12.50 30.00
Marty Turco
NM Markus Naslund 20.00 50.00
Brendan Morrison
PE Keith Primeau 12.50 30.00
Robert Esche
RR Michael Ryder 15.00 40.00
Mike Ribeiro
SA Mats Sundin 20.00 50.00
Nik Antropov
SC Ryan Smyth 15.00 40.00
Ty Conklin
SF Martin St. Louis 15.00 40.00
Ruslan Fedotenko
TA Marty Turco 20.00 50.00
David Aebischer
TB Joe Thornton
Patrice Bergeron
WH Stephen Weiss 20.00 50.00
Nathan Horton
ZN Nikolai Zherdev 20.00 50.00
Rick Nash

2005-06 SP Game Used SIGnificance Extra Gold

PRINT RUN 10 SER.#'d SETS
NOT PRICED DUE TO SCARCITY

2005-06 SP Game Used Significant Numbers

PRINT RUNS LISTED BELOW
UNDER 24 NOT PRICED DUE TO SCARCITY
SN-AF Alexander Frolov/24 15.00 30.00
SN-AL Daniel Alfredsson/11
SN-AM Alvaro Montoya/29 25.00 60.00
SN-AO Alexander Ovechkin/8
SN-AP Alexander Perezhogin/42 15.00 40.00
SN-AS Alexander Steen/10
SN-AY Alexei Yashin/79 8.00 20.00
SN-BL Rob Blake/4
SN-BM Brendan Morrison/7
SN-BR Brian Rafalski/28 15.00 40.00
SN-BS Brent Seabrook/7
SN-BU Peter Budaj/31 30.00 60.00
SN-BY Mike Bossy/22
SN-CB Cam Barker/25 25.00 60.00
Error-G.Brule autograph
SN-CO Corey Perry/61 15.00 40.00
SN-CP Chris Pronger/44 10.00 25.00
SN-CW Cam Ward/30 40.00 80.00
SN-DB Dustin Brown/23
SN-DC Dan Cloutier/39 12.00 30.00
SN-DH Dany Heatley/15
SN-DL David Leneveu/30 20.00 50.00
SN-DP Dion Phaneuf/3
SN-DW Doug Weight/39 10.00 25.00
SN-EA Patrick Eaves/44 15.00 40.00
SN-EB Ed Belfour/20 50.00 100.00
SN-ED Eric Daze/55 8.00 20.00
SN-EJ Ed Jovanovski/55 8.00 20.00
SN-EN Eric Nystrom/23
SN-GB Gilbert Brule/17
SN-GH Gordie Howe/9
SN-GM Glen Murray/27 20.00 50.00
SN-GP George Parros/57 8.00 20.00
SN-HK Dominik Hasek/39 50.00 125.00
SN-HL Henrik Lundqvist/30 75.00 200.00
SN-HO Marian Hossa/18
SN-HT Hannu Toivonen/33 20.00 50.00
SN-HV Martin Havlat/9
SN-HZ Henrik Zetterberg/40 30.00 80.00
SN-IK Ilya Kovalchuk/17
SN-JC Jeff Carter/17
SN-JF Johan Franzen/39 12.00 30.00
SN-JH Jim Howard/35 60.00
SN-JI Jarome Iginla/12
SN-JJ Jussi Jokinen/36 15.00 40.00
SN-JK Jari Kurri/17
SN-JO Joe Thornton/19
SN-JP Joni Pitkanen/44 12.00 30.00
SN-JR Jeremy Roenick/97 10.00 25.00
SN-JS Jason Spezza/19
SN-JT Jose Theodore/61 20.00 50.00
SN-JW Jeff Woywitka/29
SN-KD Kris Draper/33 10.00 25.00
SN-KL Kari Lehtonen/32 30.00 80.00
SN-KP Keith Primeau/25 10.00 25.00
SN-LR Luc Robitaille/20
SN-MB Martin Brodeur/30 75.00 200.00
SN-MG Marian Gaborik/10
SN-MH Milan Hejduk/23
SN-MJ Milan Jurcina/62 8.00 20.00
SN-MM Mike Modano/9
SN-MN Markus Naslund/19
SN-MP Michael Peca/37 10.00 25.00
SN-MR Mike Richards/18
SN-MS Miroslav Satan/81 8.00 20.00
SN-MT Marty Turco/35 15.00 40.00
SN-MW Brenden Morrow/10
SN-NA Nik Antropov/80 8.00 20.00
SN-NH Nathan Horton/16
SN-NI Robert Nilsson/21
SN-NK Nikolai Khabibulin/53 15.00 40.00
SN-NZ Nikolai Zherdev/13
SN-ON Jeff O'Neill/92 8.00 20.00
SN-PB Patrice Bergeron/37 30.00 60.00
SN-PE Phil Esposito/77 30.00 80.00
SN-PM Pierre-Marc Bouchard/96 8.00 20.00
SN-PR Patrick Roy/33 125.00 250.00
SN-RB Ray Bourque/77 25.00 60.00
SN-RF Ruslan Fedotenko/17
SN-RG Ryan Getzlaf/51 20.00 50.00
SN-RL Roberto Luongo/1
SN-RN Rick Nash/61 20.00 50.00
SN-RO Rostislav Olesz/85 6.00 15.00
SN-RS Ryan Smyth/94 8.00 20.00
SN-RT Raffi Torres/14
SN-RY Michael Ryder/73 12.00 30.00
SN-SC Sidney Crosby/87 300.00 450.00
SN-SD Shane Doan/19
SN-SG Simon Gagne/12
SN-SL Martin St. Louis/26 15.00 40.00
SN-SM Ryan Suter/20
SN-SN Scott Niedermayer/27 12.50 30.00
SN-ST Anthony Stewart/57 8.00 20.00
SN-SU Mats Sundin/13
SN-TB Todd Bertuzzi/44 15.00 40.00
SN-TV Thomas Vanek/26 50.00 125.00
SN-VL Vincent Lecavalier/4
SN-YD Yann Danis/75 10.00 25.00
SN-ZP Zach Parise/9

2005-06 SP Game Used Statscriptions

PRINT RUNS LISTED BELOW
UNDER 24 NOT PRICED DUE TO SCARCITY
ST-AF Alexander Frolov/79 10.00 25.00
ST-AH Ales Hemsky/64 10.00 25.00
ST-AR Andrew Raycroft/29 15.00 40.00
ST-AY Alexei Yashin/44 10.00 25.00
ST-BA Matthew Barnaby/43 8.00 20.00
ST-BG Bernie Geoffrion/50 30.00 80.00
ST-BH Bobby Hull/58 20.00 50.00
ST-BM Bryan McCabe/63 10.00 25.00
ST-BP Brad Park/57 8.00 20.00
ST-BR Brendan Morrison/71 6.00 15.00
ST-BT Bryan Trottier/50 6.00 15.00
ST-CB Christian Backman/18
ST-CC Craig Conroy/69 6.00 15.00
ST-CD Chris Drury/50 8.00 20.00
ST-CO Chris Osgood/45 8.00 20.00
ST-DA Daniel Alfredsson/37 15.00 40.00
ST-DB Dustin Brown/31 8.00 20.00
ST-DC Dan Cloutier/33 10.00 25.00
ST-DH Dany Heatley/41 15.00 40.00
ST-DL David Legwand/48 8.00 20.00
ST-DT Dave Taylor/47 6.00 15.00
ST-DW Doug Weight/79 10.00 25.00
ST-ED Eric Daze/38 8.00 20.00
ST-ES Eric Staal/81 12.50 30.00
ST-FT Fedor Tjutin/25 10.00 25.00
ST-GL Guy Lafleur/60 15.00 40.00
ST-GM Glen Murray/44 8.00 20.00
ST-HO Marcel Hossa/59 10.00 25.00
ST-HV Martin Havlat/31 20.00 50.00
ST-HZ Henrik Zetterberg/44 20.00 50.00
ST-IL Ian Laperriere/78 10.00 25.00
ST-JA Jason Arnott/68 6.00 15.00
ST-JB Jay Bouwmeester/82 6.00 15.00
ST-JC Jonathan Cheechoo/63 15.00 40.00
ST-JH Jochen Hecht/52 10.00 25.00
ST-JI Jarome Iginla/52 20.00 50.00
ST-JL Jamie Lundmark/29 6.00 15.00
ST-JM John-Michael Liles/79 6.00 15.00
ST-JO Jeff O'Neill/41 8.00 20.00
ST-JP Joni Pitkanen/71 8.00 20.00
ST-JS Jason Spezza/55 15.00 40.00
ST-JT Jocelyn Thibault/36 10.00 25.00
ST-JV Josef Vasicek/45 8.00 20.00
ST-KD Kris Draper/40 8.00 20.00
ST-KH Kristian Huselius/45 6.00 15.00
ST-KL Kari Lehtonen/31 20.00 50.00
ST-KP Keith Primeau/57 8.00 20.00
ST-KT Kimmo Timonen/55 8.00 20.00
ST-KW Kevin Weekes/66 8.00 20.00
ST-LM Larry Murphy/63 6.00 15.00
ST-LU Roberto Luongo/25 30.00 80.00
ST-LU Joffrey Lupul/34 10.00 25.00
ST-MA Marc-Andre Fleury/46 40.00 80.00
ST-MB Mike Bossy/69 10.00 25.00
ST-MD Marcel Dionne/59 12.00 30.00
ST-MG Martin Gerber/54 15.00 40.00
ST-MN Michael Nylander/64 8.00 20.00
ST-MR Mike Ribeiro/65 6.00 15.00
ST-MS Matt Stajan/27 20.00 50.00
ST-MT Marty Turco/37 15.00 40.00
ST-MW Brenden Morrow/48 6.00 15.00
ST-NA Nik Antropov/45 6.00 15.00
ST-NH Nathan Horton/55 6.00 15.00
ST-NZ Nikolai Zherdev/34 10.00 25.00
ST-OK Olaf Kolzig/41 25.00 60.00
ST-PB Patrice Bergeron/39 25.00 50.00
ST-PC Grant Fuhr/40 25.00 60.00
ST-PL Pascal Leclaire/62 8.00 20.00
ST-PM Pierre-Marc Bouchard/42 8.00 20.00
ST-PS Peter Stastny/47 10.00 25.00
ST-RA Brian Rafalski/52 10.00 25.00
ST-RB Rob Blake/68 8.00 20.00
ST-RE Robert Esche/11
ST-RF Ruslan Fedotenko/39 8.00 20.00
ST-RK Ryan Kesler/28 10.00 25.00
ST-RL Reggie Leach/61 8.00 20.00
ST-RM Ryan Miller/18
ST-RN Rob Niedermayer/61 8.00 20.00
ST-RS Ryan Smyth/39 12.00 30.00
ST-RV Rogie Vachon/33 15.00 40.00
ST-RY Michael Ryder/63 10.00 25.00
ST-RZ Richard Zednik/50 6.00 15.00
ST-SA Philippe Sauve/27 8.00 20.00
ST-SB Sean Burke/35 8.00 20.00
ST-SD Shane Doan/68 6.00 15.00
ST-SG Simon Gagne/66 10.00 25.00
ST-SL Martin St. Louis/38 12.00 30.00
ST-SN Scott Niedermayer/57 8.00 20.00
ST-ST Marco Sturm/48 12.50 30.00
ST-SZ Sergei Zubov/79 6.00 15.00
ST-TA Tyler Arnason/55 8.00 20.00
ST-TE Tony Esposito/35 15.00 40.00
ST-TH Trent Hunter/51 8.00 20.00
ST-TL Trevor Linden/25 40.00 100.00
ST-TP Tom Poti/48 6.00 15.00
ST-TR Tuomo Ruutu/44 12.50 30.00
ST-VL Vincent Lecavalier/33 30.00 80.00
ST-VR Mike Van Ryn/37 10.00 25.00
ST-WC Wayne Cashman/30 8.00 20.00
ST-WG Wayne Gretzky/9

2006-07 SP Game Used

COMPLETE SET w/o SPs (100) 50.00 100.00
RC PRINT RUN 999 #'d SETS
1 Chris Pronger .50 1.25
2 Teemu Selanne .60 1.50
3 Jean-Sebastien Giguere .50 1.25
4 Ilya Kovalchuk .75 2.00
5 Kari Lehtonen .60 1.50
6 Marian Hossa .50 1.25
7 Patrice Bergeron .60 1.50
8 Brad Boyes .30 .75
9 Hannu Toivonen .60 1.50
10 Bobby Orr 2.00 5.00
11 Ryan Miller .60 1.50
12 Chris Drury .30 .75
13 Jarome Iginla .75 2.00
14 Miikka Kiprusoff .60 1.50
15 Alex Tanguay .50 1.25
16 Dion Phaneuf .75 2.00
17 Eric Staal .60 1.50
18 Cam Ward .60 1.50
19 Erik Cole .30 .75
20 Rod Brind'Amour .50 1.25
21 Nikolai Khabibulin .60 1.50
22 Martin Havlat .50 1.25
23 Tuomo Ruutu .30 .75
24 Joe Sakic 1.25 3.00
25 Jose Theodore .60 1.50
26 Milan Hejduk .30 .75
27 Marek Svatos .30 .75
28 Rick Nash .60 1.50
29 Sergei Fedorov .60 1.50
30 Pascal LeClaire .50 1.25
31 Mike Modano .60 1.50
32 Marty Turco .50 1.25
33 Eric Lindros .60 1.50
34 Gordie Howe 1.50 4.00
35 Henrik Zetterberg .60 1.50
36 Pavel Datsyuk .60 1.50
37 Dominik Hasek 1.00 2.50
38 Nicklas Lidstrom .60 1.50
39 Ales Hemsky .30 .75
40 Ryan Smyth .50 1.25
41 Joffrey Lupul .30 .75
42 Ed Belfour .60 1.50
43 Jay Bouwmeester .30 .75
44 Todd Bertuzzi .50 1.25
45 Olli Jokinen .30 .75
46 Wayne Gretzky 3.00 8.00
47 Alexander Frolov .30 .75
48 Rob Blake .50 1.25
49 Marian Gaborik .75 2.00
50 Manny Fernandez .50 1.25
51 Pavol Demitra .30 .75
52 Cristobal Huet .75 2.00
53 Patrick Roy 2.00 5.00
54 Michael Ryder .50 1.25
55 Saku Koivu .60 1.50
56 Alexei Kovalev .30 .75
57 Paul Kariya .60 1.50
58 Tomas Vokoun .50 1.25
59 Jason Arnott .30 .75
60 Martin Brodeur 1.50 4.00
61 Brian Gionta .30 .75
62 Patrik Elias .30 .75
63 Alexei Yashin .30 .75
64 Miroslav Satan .30 .75
65 Brendan Shanahan .60 1.50
66 Jaromir Jagr 1.00 2.50
67 Henrik Lundqvist .75 2.00
68 Dany Heatley .75 2.00
69 Martin Gerber .60 1.50
70 Daniel Alfredsson .50 1.25
71 Jason Spezza .60 1.50
72 Simon Gagne .60 1.50
73 Peter Forsberg 1.00 2.50
74 Jeff Carter .30 .75
75 Joni Pitkanen .30 .75
76 Shane Doan .30 .75
77 Jeremy Roenick .75 2.00
78 Owen Nolan .50 1.25
79 Curtis Joseph .60 1.50
80 Sidney Crosby 4.00 10.00
81 Mario Lemieux 2.00 5.00
82 Marc-Andre Fleury .60 1.50
83 Mark Recchi .30 .75
84 Joe Thornton 1.00 2.50
85 Patrick Marleau .50 1.25
86 Jonathan Cheechoo .60 1.50
87 Doug Weight .30 .75
88 Keith Tkachuk .50 1.25
89 Vincent Lecavalier .60 1.50
90 Martin St. Louis .50 1.25
91 Brad Richards .50 1.25
92 Alexander Steen .50 1.25
93 Mats Sundin .60 1.50
94 Andrew Raycroft .50 1.25
95 Michael Peca .30 .75
96 Markus Naslund .60 1.50
97 Roberto Luongo .75 2.00
98 Brendan Morrison .30 .75
99 Alexander Ovechkin 1.50 4.00
100 Olaf Kolzig .60 1.50
101 Shane O'Brien RC 2.00 5.00
102 Ryan Shannon RC 2.00 5.00
103 Yan Stastny RC 2.00 5.00
104 Mark Stuart RC 2.00 5.00
105 Nate Thompson RC 2.00 5.00
106 Phil Kessel RC 5.00 12.00
107 Matt Lashoff RC 2.00 5.00
108 Dave Bolland RC 2.00 5.00
109 Michael Blunden RC 2.00 5.00
110 Dustin Byfuglien RC 2.00 5.00
111 Paul Stastny RC 6.00 15.00
112 Fredrik Norrena RC 3.00 8.00
113 Loui Eriksson RC 2.00 5.00
114 Tomas Kopecky RC 3.00 8.00
115 Alexei Mikhnov RC 2.00 5.00
116 Marc-Antoine Pouliot RC 3.00 8.00
117 Patrick Thoresen RC 3.00 8.00
118 Ladislav Smid RC 2.00 5.00
119 Janis Sprukts RC 2.00 5.00
120 Konstantin Pushkaryov RC 2.00 5.00
121 Patrick O'Sullivan RC 3.00 8.00
122 Anze Kopitar RC 6.00 15.00
123 Benoit Pouliot RC 3.00 8.00
124 Miroslav Kopriva RC 2.00 5.00
125 Niklas Backstrom RC 3.00 8.00
126 Guillaume Latendresse RC 6.00 15.00
127 Alexander Radulov RC 5.00 12.00
128 Shea Weber RC 2.00 5.00
129 Mikko Lehtonen RC 2.00 5.00
130 Alex Brooks RC 2.00 5.00
131 John Oduya RC 2.00 5.00
132 Travis Zajac RC 3.00 8.00
133 Drew Stafford RC 5.00 12.00
134 Masi Marjamaki RC 2.00 5.00
135 Jarkko Immonen RC 2.00 5.00
136 Nigel Dawes RC 2.00 5.00
137 Alexei Kaigorodov RC 2.00 5.00
138 Lars Jonsson RC 2.00 5.00
139 Ryan Potulny RC 3.00 8.00
140 Triston Grant RC 2.00 5.00
141 Enver Lisin RC 2.00 5.00
142 Brandon Prust RC 2.00 5.00
143 Keith Yandle RC 2.00 5.00
144 Patrick Fischer RC 2.00 5.00
145 Noah Welch RC 2.00 5.00
146 Michel Ouellet RC 3.00 8.00
147 Jordan Staal RC 20.00 40.00
148 Kristopher Letang RC 3.00 8.00
149 Evgeni Malkin RC 25.00 60.00
150 Matt Carle RC 3.00 8.00
151 Marc-Edouard Vlasic RC 2.00 5.00
152 D.J. King RC 2.00 5.00
153 Roman Polak RC 2.00 5.00
154 Ben Ondrus RC 2.00 5.00
155 Brendan Bell RC 2.00 5.00
156 Ian White RC 2.00 5.00
157 Dustin Boyd RC 3.00 8.00
158 Luc Bourdon RC 3.00 8.00
159 Eric Fehr RC 3.00 8.00
160 Jonas Johansson RC 2.00 5.00

2006-07 SP Game Used Gold

GOLD: 2X to 5X BASE HI
RCs: .5 to 1.5X BASE HI
PRINT RUN 100 #'d SETS
1 Chris Pronger 2.50 6.00
2 Teemu Selanne 3.00 8.00
3 Jean-Sebastien Giguere 2.50 6.00
4 Ilya Kovalchuk 4.00 10.00
5 Kari Lehtonen 3.00 8.00
6 Marian Hossa 2.50 6.00
7 Patrice Bergeron 3.00 8.00
8 Brad Boyes 1.50 4.00
9 Hannu Toivonen 3.00 8.00
10 Bobby Orr 12.00 30.00
11 Ryan Miller 3.00 8.00
12 Chris Drury 1.50 4.00
13 Jarome Iginla 4.00 10.00
14 Miikka Kiprusoff 3.00 8.00
15 Alex Tanguay 2.50 6.00
16 Dion Phaneuf 4.00 10.00
17 Eric Staal 3.00 8.00
18 Cam Ward 3.00 8.00
19 Erik Cole 1.50 4.00
20 Rod Brind'Amour 2.50 6.00
21 Nikolai Khabibulin 3.00 8.00
22 Martin Havlat 2.50 6.00
23 Tuomo Ruutu 1.50 4.00
24 Joe Sakic 5.00 12.00
25 Jose Theodore 3.00 8.00
26 Milan Hejduk 1.50 4.00
27 Marek Svatos 1.50 4.00
28 Rick Nash 3.00 8.00
29 Sergei Fedorov 3.00 8.00
30 Pascal LeClaire 2.50 6.00
31 Mike Modano 3.00 8.00
32 Marty Turco 2.50 6.00
33 Eric Lindros 3.00 8.00
34 Gordie Howe 6.00 15.00
35 Henrik Zetterberg 3.00 8.00
36 Pavel Datsyuk 2.50 6.00
37 Dominik Hasek 4.00 10.00
38 Nicklas Lidstrom 3.00 8.00
39 Ales Hemsky 1.50 4.00
40 Ryan Smyth 2.50 6.00
41 Joffrey Lupul 1.50 4.00
42 Ed Belfour 3.00 8.00
43 Jay Bouwmeester 1.50 4.00
44 Todd Bertuzzi 2.50 6.00
45 Olli Jokinen 1.50 4.00
46 Wayne Gretzky 15.00 40.00
47 Alexander Frolov 1.50 4.00
48 Rob Blake 2.50 6.00
49 Marian Gaborik 4.00 10.00
50 Manny Fernandez 2.50 6.00
51 Pavol Demitra 1.50 4.00
52 Cristobal Huet 4.00 10.00
53 Patrick Roy 12.00 30.00
54 Michael Ryder 2.50 6.00
55 Saku Koivu 3.00 8.00
56 Alexei Kovalev 1.50 4.00
57 Paul Kariya 3.00 8.00
58 Tomas Vokoun 2.50 6.00
59 Jason Arnott 1.50 4.00
60 Martin Brodeur 6.00 15.00
61 Brian Gionta 1.50 4.00
62 Patrik Elias 1.50 4.00
63 Alexei Yashin 1.50 4.00
64 Miroslav Satan 1.50 4.00
65 Brendan Shanahan 3.00 8.00
66 Jaromir Jagr 5.00 12.00
67 Henrik Lundqvist 4.00 10.00
68 Dany Heatley 4.00 10.00
69 Martin Gerber 3.00 8.00
70 Daniel Alfredsson 1.50 4.00
71 Jason Spezza 3.00 8.00
72 Simon Gagne 3.00 8.00
73 Peter Forsberg 5.00 12.00
74 Jeff Carter 3.00 8.00
75 Joni Pitkanen 1.50 4.00
76 Shane Doan 1.50 4.00
77 Jeremy Roenick 4.00 10.00
78 Owen Nolan 2.50 6.00
79 Curtis Joseph 3.00 8.00
80 Sidney Crosby 30.00 80.00
81 Mario Lemieux 12.00 30.00
82 Marc-Andre Fleury 3.00 8.00
83 Mark Recchi 1.50 4.00
84 Joe Thornton 5.00 12.00
85 Patrick Marleau 2.50 6.00
86 Jonathan Cheechoo 3.00 8.00
87 Doug Weight 1.50 4.00
88 Keith Tkachuk 2.50 6.00
89 Vincent Lecavalier 3.00 8.00
90 Martin St. Louis 2.50 6.00
91 Brad Richards 2.50 6.00
92 Alexander Steen 2.50 6.00
93 Mats Sundin 3.00 8.00
94 Andrew Raycroft 2.50 6.00
95 Michael Peca 1.50 4.00
96 Markus Naslund 3.00 8.00
97 Roberto Luongo 4.00 10.00
98 Brendan Morrison 1.50 4.00
99 Alexander Ovechkin 8.00 20.00
100 Olaf Kolzig 3.00 8.00
101 Shane O'Brien 4.00 10.00
102 Ryan Shannon 4.00 10.00
103 Yan Stastny 4.00 10.00
104 Mark Stuart 4.00 10.00
105 Nate Thompson 4.00 10.00
106 Phil Kessel 12.00 30.00
107 Matt Lashoff 4.00 10.00
108 Dave Bolland 4.00 10.00
109 Michael Blunden 4.00 10.00
110 Dustin Byfuglien 4.00 10.00
111 Paul Stastny 15.00 40.00
112 Fredrik Norrena 6.00 15.00
113 Loui Eriksson 4.00 10.00
114 Tomas Kopecky 6.00 15.00
115 Alexei Mikhnov 4.00 10.00
116 Marc-Antoine Pouliot 6.00 15.00
117 Patrick Thoresen 6.00 15.00
118 Ladislav Smid 4.00 10.00
119 Janis Sprukts 4.00 10.00
120 Konstantin Pushkaryov 4.00 10.00
121 Patrick O'Sullivan 6.00 15.00
122 Anze Kopitar 12.00 30.00
123 Benoit Pouliot 6.00 15.00
124 Miroslav Kopriva 4.00 10.00
125 Niklas Backstrom 8.00 20.00
126 Guillaume Latendresse 15.00 40.00
127 Alexander Radulov 12.00 30.00
128 Shea Weber 6.00 15.00
129 Mikko Lehtonen 4.00 10.00
130 Alex Brooks 4.00 10.00
131 John Oduya 4.00 10.00
132 Travis Zajac 8.00 20.00
133 Drew Stafford 12.00 30.00
134 Masi Marjamaki 4.00 10.00
135 Jarkko Immonen 4.00 10.00
136 Nigel Dawes 4.00 10.00
137 Alexei Kaigorodov 4.00 10.00
138 Lars Jonsson 4.00 10.00
139 Ryan Potulny 6.00 15.00
140 Triston Grant 4.00 10.00
141 Enver Lisin 4.00 10.00
142 Brandon Prust 4.00 10.00
143 Keith Yandle 4.00 10.00
144 Patrick Fischer 4.00 10.00
145 Noah Welch 4.00 10.00
146 Michel Ouellet 8.00 20.00
147 Jordan Staal 25.00 60.00
148 Kristopher Letang 6.00 15.00
149 Evgeni Malkin 40.00 100.00
150 Matt Carle 6.00 15.00
151 Marc-Edouard Vlasic 4.00 10.00
152 D.J. King 4.00 10.00
153 Roman Polak 4.00 10.00
154 Ben Ondrus 4.00 10.00
155 Brendan Bell 4.00 10.00
156 Ian White 4.00 10.00
157 Dustin Boyd 6.00 15.00
158 Luc Bourdon 6.00 15.00
159 Eric Fehr 6.00 15.00
160 Jonas Johansson 4.00 10.00

2006-07 SP Game Used Rainbow

PRINT RUN 25 #'d SETS
NOT PRICED DUE TO SCARCITY

2006-07 SP Game Used Authentic Fabrics

OVERALL MEM. ODDS 1:1
AFAF Alexander Frolov 2.00 5.00
AFAH Ales Hemsky 2.00 5.00
AFAL Daniel Alfredsson 3.00 8.00
AFAO Alexander Ovechkin SP 10.00 25.00
AFAS Alexander Steen 3.00 8.00
AFAT Alex Tanguay 3.00 8.00
AFAY Alexei Yashin 2.00 5.00
AFBB Brad Boyes 2.00 5.00
AFBG Brian Gionta 2.00 5.00
AFBL Brian Leetch 4.00 10.00
AFBM Brenden Morrow 3.00 8.00
AFBO Pierre-Marc Bouchard 2.00 5.00
AFBR Brad Richards 3.00 8.00
AFBS Brendan Shanahan 4.00 10.00
AFCD Chris Drury 2.00 5.00
AFCJ Curtis Joseph 4.00 10.00
AFCS Curtis Sanford 3.00 8.00
AFCW Cam Ward 4.00 10.00
AFDA David Aebischer 3.00 8.00
AFDE Pavol Demitra 2.00 5.00
AFDH Dominik Hasek 5.00 12.00
AFDP Dion Phaneuf 4.00 10.00
AFDR Dwayne Roloson 4.00 10.00
AFDS Daniel Sedin 2.00 5.00
AFDW Doug Weight 2.00 5.00
AFEB Ed Belfour 4.00 10.00
AFEJ Ed Jovanovski 2.00 5.00
AFES Eric Staal 4.00 10.00
AFGA Simon Gagne 4.00 10.00
AFGR Gary Roberts 2.00 5.00
AFHE Dany Heatley 5.00 12.00
AFHL Henrik Lundqvist 5.00 12.00
AFHS Henrik Sedin 2.00 5.00
AFHT Hannu Toivonen 3.00 8.00
AFHZ Henrik Zetterberg 4.00 10.00
AFIK Ilya Kovalchuk SP 6.00 15.00
AFJB Jay Bouwmeester 2.00 5.00
AFJC Jeff Carter 4.00 10.00
AFJD J.P. Dumont 2.00 5.00
AFJI Jarome Iginla 5.00 12.00
AFJJ Jaromir Jagr SP 6.00 15.00
AFJL Jere Lehtinen 2.00 5.00
AFJN Joe Nieuwendyk 3.00 8.00
AFJP Joni Pitkanen 3.00 8.00
AFJS Joe Sakic 6.00 15.00
AFJT Joe Thornton 5.00 12.00
AFJW Jason Williams 2.00 5.00
AFLU Joffrey Lupul 2.00 5.00
AFMA Mark Recchi 2.00 5.00
AFMB Martin Brodeur SP 6.00 15.00
AFMC Mike Cammalleri 2.00 5.00
AFME Martin Erat 2.00 5.00
AFMF Manny Fernandez 3.00 8.00
AFMG Marian Gaborik 5.00 12.00
AFMH Milan Hejduk 4.00 10.00
AFMI Miroslav Satan 2.00 5.00
AFMM Mike Modano 4.00 10.00
AFMN Markus Naslund 4.00 10.00
AFMO Brendan Morrison 2.00 5.00
AFMP Michael Peca 2.00 5.00
AFMR Michael Ryder 3.00 8.00
AFMS Mats Sundin 4.00 10.00
AFNH Nathan Horton 2.00 5.00
AFNL Nicklas Lidstrom 4.00 10.00
AFOK Olaf Kolzig 4.00 10.00
AFPB Patrice Bergeron 4.00 10.00
AFPD Pavel Datsyuk 3.00 8.00
AFPE Patrik Elias 3.00 8.00
AFPF Peter Forsberg 5.00 12.00
AFPK Paul Kariya 4.00 10.00
AFPL Pascal LeClaire 3.00 8.00
AFPM Patrick Marleau 3.00 8.00
AFPS Patrik Stefan 2.00 5.00
AFPT Pierre Turgeon 2.00 5.00
AFRB Rob Blake 3.00 8.00
AFRD Rick DiPietro 3.00 8.00
AFRE Robert Esche 3.00 8.00
AFRF Ruslan Fedotenko 2.00 5.00
AFRG Ryan Getzlaf 3.00 8.00
AFRL Roberto Luongo 5.00 12.00
AFRM Ryan Malone 2.00 5.00
AFRN Rick Nash 4.00 10.00
AFRS Ryan Smyth 3.00 8.00
AFSC Sidney Crosby SP 40.00 80.00
AFSF Sergei Fedorov 4.00 10.00
AFSG Scott Gomez 3.00 8.00
AFSJ Matt Stajan 2.00 5.00
AFSK Saku Koivu 4.00 10.00
AFSM Martin St. Louis 3.00 8.00
AFSN Scott Niedermayer 2.00 5.00
AFSP Jason Spezza 4.00 10.00
AFSS Sergei Samsonov 2.00 5.00
AFST Jarret Stoll 2.00 5.00
AFSU Steve Sullivan 2.00 5.00
AFTA Tony Amonte 2.00 5.00
AFTH Tomas Holmstrom 2.00 5.00
AFTS Teemu Selanne 4.00 10.00
AFTT Tim Thomas 3.00 8.00
AFTV Tomas Vokoun 3.00 8.00
AFVL Vincent Lecavalier 4.00 10.00

2006-07 SP Game Used Authentic Fabrics Parallel

PARALLEL 1X to 1.25X
PRINT RUN 100 #'d SETS
AFAF Alexander Frolov 3.00 8.00
AFAH Ales Hemsky
AFAL Daniel Alfredsson 4.00 10.00
AFAO Alexander Ovechkin 15.00 40.00
AFAS Alexander Steen 4.00 10.00
AFAT Alex Tanguay 4.00 10.00
AFAY Alexei Yashin 3.00 8.00
AFBB Brad Boyes 3.00 8.00
AFBG Brian Gionta 3.00 8.00
AFBL Brian Leetch 5.00 12.00
AFBM Brenden Morrow
AFBO Pierre-Marc Bouchard 3.00 8.00
AFBR Brad Richards 4.00 10.00
AFBS Brendan Shanahan 5.00 12.00
AFCD Chris Drury 3.00 8.00
AFCJ Curtis Joseph 5.00 12.00
AFCS Curtis Sanford 4.00 10.00
AFCW Cam Ward 5.00 12.00
AFDA David Aebischer 4.00 10.00
AFDE Pavol Demitra 3.00 8.00
AFDH Dominik Hasek 8.00 20.00
AFDP Dion Phaneuf 6.00 15.00
AFDR Dwayne Roloson
AFDS Daniel Sedin 3.00 8.00
AFDW Doug Weight 3.00 8.00
AFEB Ed Belfour 5.00 12.00
AFEJ Ed Jovanovski 3.00 8.00
AFES Eric Staal
AFGA Simon Gagne 5.00 12.00
AFGR Gary Roberts
AFHE Dany Heatley 6.00 15.00
AFHL Henrik Lundqvist 6.00 15.00
AFHS Henrik Sedin 3.00 8.00
AFHT Hannu Toivonen 4.00 10.00
AFHZ Henrik Zetterberg 5.00 12.00
AFIK Ilya Kovalchuk 6.00 15.00
AFJB Jay Bouwmeester 3.00 8.00
AFJC Jeff Carter
AFJD J.P. Dumont
AFJI Jarome Iginla 6.00 15.00
AFJJ Jaromir Jagr 8.00 20.00
AFJL Jere Lehtinen 3.00 8.00
AFJN Joe Nieuwendyk 4.00 10.00
AFJP Joni Pitkanen 3.00 8.00
AFJS Joe Sakic 10.00 25.00
AFJT Joe Thornton 8.00 20.00
AFJW Jason Williams
AFLU Joffrey Lupul 3.00 8.00
AFMA Mark Recchi 3.00 8.00
AFMB Martin Brodeur 12.00 30.00
AFMC Mike Cammalleri 3.00 8.00
AFME Martin Erat 3.00 8.00
AFMF Manny Fernandez 4.00 10.00
AFMG Marian Gaborik
AFMH Milan Hejduk 3.00 8.00
AFMI Miroslav Satan 3.00 8.00
AFMM Mike Modano 5.00 12.00
AFMN Markus Naslund 5.00 12.00
AFMO Brendan Morrison 3.00 8.00
AFMP Michael Peca 3.00 8.00
AFMR Michael Ryder 4.00 10.00
AFMS Mats Sundin 5.00 12.00
AFNH Nathan Horton 3.00 8.00
AFNL Nicklas Lidstrom 5.00 12.00
AFOK Olaf Kolzig 5.00 12.00
AFPB Patrice Bergeron 5.00 12.00
AFPD Pavel Datsyuk 4.00 10.00
AFPE Patrik Elias 3.00 8.00
AFPF Peter Forsberg
AFPK Paul Kariya 5.00 12.00
AFPL Pascal LeClaire 4.00 10.00
AFPM Patrick Marleau 4.00 10.00
AFPS Patrik Stefan
AFPT Pierre Turgeon 3.00 8.00
AFRB Rob Blake 4.00 10.00
AFRD Rick DiPietro 4.00 10.00
AFRE Robert Esche 4.00 10.00
AFRF Ruslan Fedotenko 3.00 8.00
AFRG Ryan Getzlaf 4.00 10.00
AFRL Roberto Luongo 6.00 15.00
AFRM Ryan Malone 4.00 10.00
AFRN Rick Nash 5.00 12.00
AFRS Ryan Smyth 4.00 10.00
AFSC Sidney Crosby
AFSF Sergei Fedorov 5.00 12.00
AFSG Scott Gomez 3.00 8.00
AFSJ Matt Stajan 3.00 8.00
AFSK Saku Koivu 5.00 12.00
AFSM Martin St. Louis 4.00 10.00
AFSN Scott Niedermayer 3.00 8.00
AFSP Jason Spezza 5.00 12.00
AFSS Sergei Samsonov
AFST Jarret Stoll 3.00 8.00
AFSU Steve Sullivan 3.00 8.00
AFTA Tony Amonte
AFTH Tomas Holmstrom 3.00 8.00
AFTS Teemu Selanne 5.00 12.00
AFTT Tim Thomas 4.00 10.00
AFTV Tomas Vokoun 4.00 10.00
AFVL Vincent Lecavalier 5.00 12.00

2006-07 SP Game Used Authentic Fabrics Patches

PATCHES: 2X to 4X HI BASE JERSEYS
PRINT RUN 50 SER. #'d SETS
AFAF Alexander Frolov 8.00 20.00
AFAH Ales Hemsky 8.00 20.00
AFAL Daniel Alfredsson 12.00 30.00
AFAO Alexander Ovechkin 40.00 100.00
AFAS Alexander Steen 12.00 30.00
AFAT Alex Tanguay 12.00 30.00
AFAY Alexei Yashin 8.00 20.00
AFBB Brad Boyes 8.00 20.00
AFBG Brian Gionta 8.00 20.00
AFBL Brian Leetch 15.00 40.00
AFBM Brenden Morrow 12.00 30.00
AFBO Pierre-Marc Bouchard 8.00 20.00
AFBR Brad Richards 12.00 30.00
AFBS Brendan Shanahan 15.00 40.00
AFCD Chris Drury 8.00 20.00
AFCJ Curtis Joseph 15.00 40.00
AFCS Curtis Sanford 12.00 30.00
AFCW Cam Ward 15.00 40.00
AFDA David Aebischer 12.00 30.00
AFDE Pavol Demitra 8.00 20.00
AFDH Dominik Hasek 20.00 50.00
AFDP Dion Phaneuf 15.00 40.00
AFDR Dwayne Roloson 15.00 40.00
AFDS Daniel Sedin 8.00 20.00
AFDW Doug Weight 8.00 20.00
AFEB Ed Belfour 15.00 40.00
AFEJ Ed Jovanovski 8.00 20.00
AFES Eric Staal 15.00 40.00
AFGA Simon Gagne 15.00 40.00
AFGR Gary Roberts 8.00 20.00
AFHE Dany Heatley 20.00 50.00
AFHL Henrik Lundqvist 20.00 50.00
AFHS Henrik Sedin 8.00 20.00
AFHT Hannu Toivonen 12.00 30.00
AFHZ Henrik Zetterberg 15.00 40.00
AFIK Ilya Kovalchuk 15.00 40.00
AFJB Jay Bouwmeester 8.00 20.00
AFJC Jeff Carter 15.00 40.00
AFJD J.P. Dumont 8.00 20.00
AFJI Jarome Iginla 20.00 50.00
AFJJ Jaromir Jagr 20.00 50.00
AFJL Jere Lehtinen 8.00 20.00
AFJN Joe Nieuwendyk 12.00 30.00
AFJP Joni Pitkanen 8.00 20.00
AFJS Joe Sakic 25.00 60.00
AFJT Joe Thornton 20.00 50.00
AFJW Jason Williams 8.00 20.00
AFLU Joffrey Lupul 8.00 20.00
AFMA Mark Recchi 8.00 20.00
AFMB Martin Brodeur 25.00 60.00
AFMC Mike Cammalleri 8.00 20.00
AFME Martin Erat 8.00 20.00

AFMF Manny Fernandez 12.00 30.00
AFMG Marian Gaborik 20.00 50.00
AFMH Milan Hejduk 8.00 20.00
AFMI Miroslav Satan 8.00 20.00
AFMM Mike Modano 12.00 30.00
AFMN Markus Naslund 15.00 40.00
AFMO Brendan Morrison 8.00 20.00
AFMP Michael Peca 8.00 20.00
AFMR Michael Ryder 12.00 30.00
AFMS Mats Sundin 15.00 40.00
AFNH Nathan Horton 8.00 20.00
AFNL Nicklas Lidstrom 15.00 40.00
AFOK Olaf Kolzig 15.00 40.00
AFPB Patrice Bergeron 15.00 40.00
AFPD Pavel Datsyuk 12.00 30.00
AFPE Patrik Elias 8.00 20.00
AFPF Peter Forsberg 20.00 50.00
AFPK Paul Kariya 15.00 40.00
AFPL Pascal LeClaire 12.00 30.00
AFPM Patrick Marleau 12.00 30.00
AFPS Patrick Stefan 8.00 20.00
AFPT Pierre Turgeon 8.00 20.00
AFRB Rob Blake 12.00 30.00
AFRD Rick DiPietro 12.00 30.00
AFRE Robert Esche 12.00 30.00
AFRF Ruslan Fedotenko 8.00 20.00
AFRG Ryan Getzlaf 12.00 30.00
AFRL Roberto Luongo 20.00 50.00
AFRM Ryan Malone 8.00 20.00
AFRN Rick Nash 15.00 40.00
AFRS Ryan Smyth 12.00 30.00
AFSC Sidney Crosby 60.00 150.00
AFSF Sergei Fedorov 15.00 40.00
AFSG Scott Gomez 8.00 20.00
AFSJ Matt Stajan 8.00 20.00
AFSK Saku Koivu 15.00 40.00
AFSM Martin St. Louis 12.00 30.00
AFSN Scott Niedermayer 8.00 20.00
AFSP Jason Spezza 15.00 40.00
AFSS Sergei Samsonov 12.00 30.00
AFST Jarret Stoll 8.00 20.00
AFSU Steve Sullivan 8.00 20.00
AFTA Tony Amonte 8.00 20.00
AFTH Tomas Holmstrom 8.00 20.00
AFTS Teemu Selanne 15.00 40.00
AFTT Tim Thomas 12.00 30.00
AFTV Tomas Vokoun 12.00 30.00
AFVL Vincent Lecavalier 15.00 40.00

2006-07 SP Game Used Authentic Fabrics Dual

COMMONS 3.00 8.00
STATED PRINT RUN 100 #'d SETS
AF2AB Maxim Afinogenov 6.00 15.00
Daniel Briere
AF2AH David Aebischer 10.00 25.00
Cristobal Huet
AF2AS Jason Arnott 3.00 8.00
Steve Sullivan
AF2BF Rob Blake 4.00 10.00
Alexander Frolov
AF2BG Martin Brodeur 10.00 25.00
Brian Gionta
AF2BH Jay Bouwmeester 3.00 8.00
Nathan Horton
AF2DG Pavol Demitra 6.00 15.00
Marian Gaborik
AF2DM Chris Drury 6.00 15.00
Ryan Miller
AF2FC Peter Forsberg 8.00 20.00
Jeff Carter
AF2HK Martin Havlat 6.00 15.00
Nikolai Khabibulin
AF2HL Ales Hemsky 3.00 8.00
Joffrey Lupul
AF2HO Dominik Hasek 10.00 25.00
Chris Osgood
AF2HS Milan Hejduk 3.00 8.00
Marek Svatos
AF2HZ Tomas Holmstrom 8.00 20.00
Henrik Zetterberg
AF2IK Jarome Iginla 10.00 25.00
Miikka Kiprusoff
AF2JL Jaromir Jagr 10.00 25.00
Henrik Lundqvist
AF2KG Sami Kapanen 3.00 8.00
Simon Gagne
AF2KH Marian Hossa 6.00 15.00
Ilya Kovalchuk
AF2KO Olaf Kolzig 12.00 30.00
Alexander Ovechkin
AF2KR Saku Koivu 4.00 10.00
Michael Ryder
AF2KV Paul Kariya 6.00 15.00
Tomas Vokoun
AF2LC Pascal LeClaire 3.00 8.00
Ty Conklin
AF2LJ Jere Lehtinen 3.00 8.00
Jussi Jokinen
AF2LR Vincent Lecavalier 8.00 20.00
Brad Richards
AF2ML Mike Modano 6.00 15.00
Eric Lindros
AF2MT Patrick Marleau 8.00 20.00
Joe Thornton
AF2ND Owen Nolan 4.00 10.00
Shane Doan
AF2NF Rick Nash 8.00 20.00
Sergei Fedorov
AF2NL Markus Naslund 6.00 15.00
Roberto Luongo
AF2PB Mark Parrish 3.00 8.00
Pierre-Marc Bouchard
AF2PT Michael Peca 4.00 10.00
Darcy Tucker
AF2RC Mark Recchi 20.00 50.00
Sidney Crosby
AF2RL Guy Lapointe 4.00 15.00
Larry Robinson
AF2SB Marc Savard 6.00 15.00
Patrice Bergeron
AF2SC Brad Stuart 3.00 8.00
Zdeno Chara
AF2SD Miroslav Satan 4.00 10.00
Rick DiPietro
AF2SH Jason Spezza 8.00 20.00
Dany Heatley
AF2SJ Brendan Shanahan 10.00 25.00
Jaromir Jagr
AF2SP Teemu Selanne 6.00 15.00
Corey Perry
AF2SS Mats Sundin 8.00 20.00
Alexander Steen
AF2SW Eric Staal 6.00 15.00
Cam Ward
AF2TK Alex Tanguay 4.00 10.00
Chuck Kobasew
AF2TM Marty Turco 4.00 10.00
Brenden Morrow
AF2TP Raffi Torres 3.00 8.00
Fernando Pisani
AF2TS Pierre Turgeon 8.00 20.00
Joe Sakic
AF2TT Hannu Toivonen 4.00 10.00
Tim Thomas
AF2WB Justin Williams 3.00 8.00
Rod Brind'Amour
AF2WG Doug Weight 3.00 8.00
Bill Guerin

2006-07 SP Game Used Authentic Fabrics Dual Patches

PATCHES: 2X to 4X DUAL JSY HI
PRINT RUN 25 #'d SETS
AF2AB Maxim Afinogenov 25.00 60.00
Daniel Briere
AF2AH David Aebischer 40.00 100.00
Cristobal Huet
AF2AS Jason Arnott 20.00 40.00
Steve Sullivan
AF2BF Rob Blake 25.00 60.00
Alexander Frolov
AF2BG Martin Brodeur 50.00 125.00
Brian Gionta
AF2BH Jay Bouwmeester 20.00 40.00
Nathan Horton
AF2DG Pavol Demitra 25.00 60.00
Marian Gaborik
AF2DM Chris Drury 25.00 60.00
Ryan Miller
AF2FC Peter Forsberg 30.00 80.00
Jeff Carter
AF2HK Martin Havlat 25.00 60.00
Nikolai Khabibulin
AF2HL Ales Hemsky 20.00 40.00
Joffrey Lupul
AF2HO Dominik Hasek 50.00 125.00
Chris Osgood
AF2HS Milan Hejduk 20.00 40.00
Marek Svatos
AF2HZ Tomas Holmstrom 30.00 80.00
Henrik Zetterberg
AF2IK Jarome Iginla 40.00 100.00
Miikka Kiprusoff
AF2JL Jaromir Jagr 50.00 125.00
Henrik Lundqvist
AF2KG Sami Kapanen 20.00 40.00
Simon Gagne
AF2KH Marian Hossa 30.00 80.00
Ilya Kovalchuk
AF2KO Olaf Kolzig 40.00 100.00
Alexander Ovechkin
AF2KR Saku Koivu 25.00 60.00
Michael Ryder
AF2KV Paul Kariya 25.00 60.00
Tomas Vokoun
AF2LC Pascal LeClaire 20.00 40.00
Ty Conklin
AF2LJ Jere Lehtinen 20.00 40.00
Jussi Jokinen
AF2LR Vincent Lecavalier 30.00 80.00
Brad Richards
AF2ML Mike Modano 25.00 60.00
Eric Lindros
AF2MT Patrick Marleau 30.00 80.00
Joe Thornton
AF2ND Owen Nolan 20.00 40.00
Shane Doan
AF2NF Rick Nash 30.00 80.00
Sergei Fedorov
AF2NL Markus Naslund 25.00 60.00
Roberto Luongo
AF2PB Mark Parrish 20.00 40.00
Pierre-Marc Bouchard
AF2PT Michael Peca 20.00 40.00
Darcy Tucker
AF2RC Mark Recchi 100.00 200.00
Sidney Crosby
AF2RL Guy Lapointe 25.00 60.00
Larry Robinson
AF2SB Marc Savard 25.00 60.00
Patrice Bergeron
AF2SC Brad Stuart 20.00 40.00
Zdeno Chara
AF2SD Miroslav Satan 20.00 40.00
Rick DiPietro
AF2SH Jason Spezza 30.00 80.00
Dany Heatley
AF2SJ Brendan Shanahan 40.00 100.00
Jaromir Jagr
AF2SP Teemu Selanne 25.00 60.00
Corey Perry
AF2SS Mats Sundin 30.00 80.00
Alexander Steen
AF2SW Eric Staal 25.00 60.00
Cam Ward
AF2TK Alex Tanguay 20.00 40.00
Chuck Kobasew
AF2TM Marty Turco 20.00 40.00
Brenden Morrow
AF2TP Raffi Torres 20.00 40.00
Fernando Pisani
AF2TS Pierre Turgeon 30.00 80.00
Joe Sakic
AF2TT Hannu Toivonen 20.00 40.00
Tim Thomas
AF2WB Justin Williams 20.00 40.00
Rod Brind'Amour
AF2WG Doug Weight 20.00 40.00
Bill Guerin

2006-07 SP Game Used Authentic Fabrics Triple

PRINT RUN 25 #'d SETS
AF3ANA Teemu Selanne 20.00 50.00
Chris Pronger
Scott Niedermayer
AF3ATL Marian Hossa 25.00 60.00
Ilya Kovalchuk
Kari Lehtonen
AF3BOS Brad Boyes 20.00 50.00
Zdeno Chara
Patrice Bergeron
AF3BUF Chris Drury 25.00 60.00
Daniel Briere
Ryan Miller
AF3CAR Rod Brind'Amour 20.00 50.00
Eric Staal
Cam Ward
AF3CGY Jarome Iginla 30.00 80.00
Alex Tanguay
Miikka Kiprusoff
AF3CHI Martin Havlat 20.00 50.00
Tuomo Ruutu
Nikolai Khabibulin
AF3CLB Pascal LeClaire 25.00 60.00
Rick Nash
Sergei Fedorov
AF3COL Joe Sakic 40.00 100.00
Milan Hejduk
Jose Theodore
AF3DAL Mike Modano 25.00 60.00
Eric Lindros
Marty Turco
AF3DET Dominik Hasek 40.00 100.00
Nicklas Lidstrom
Henrik Zetterberg
AF3EDM Ryan Smyth 15.00 40.00
Dwayne Roloson
Ales Hemsky
AF3FLA Ed Belfour 20.00 50.00
Todd Bertuzzi
Jay Bouwmeester
AF3LAK Rob Blake 15.00 40.00
Alexander Frolov
Mike Cammalleri
AF3MIN Pavol Demitra 20.00 50.00
Marian Gaborik
Pierre-Marc Bouchard
AF3MTL Sergei Samsonov 30.00 80.00
Saku Koivu
Michael Ryder
AF3NAS Paul Kariya 20.00 50.00
Tomas Vokoun
Jason Arnott
AF3NJD Martin Brodeur 30.00 80.00
Patrik Elias
Brian Gionta
AF3NYI Miroslav Satan 20.00 50.00
Alexei Yashin
Rick DiPietro
AF3NYR Brendan Shanahan 50.00 100.00
Jaromir Jagr
Henrik Lundqvist
AF3OTT Daniel Alfredsson 25.00 60.00
Jason Spezza
Dany Heatley
AF3PHI Peter Forsberg 20.00 50.00
Robert Esche
Simon Gagne
AF3PHX Curtis Joseph 15.00 40.00
Jeremy Roenick
Shane Doan
AF3PIT Mark Recchi 75.00 150.00
Ryan Malone
Sidney Crosby
AF3SJS Patrick Marleau 30.00 80.00
Joe Thornton
Jonathan Cheechoo
AF3STL Doug Weight 15.00 40.00
Keith Tkachuk
Manny Legace
AF3TBL Vincent Lecavalier 30.00 80.00
Brad Richards
Martin St. Louis
AF3TOR Mats Sundin 25.00 60.00
Andrew Raycroft
Alexander Steen
AF3VAN Markus Naslund 25.00 60.00
Henrik Sedin
Daniel Sedin
AF3WAS Alexander Ovechkin 30.00 80.00
Olaf Kolzig
Richard Zednik

2006-07 SP Game Used Authentic Fabrics Triple Patches

PRINT RUN 10 #'d SETS
NOT PRICED DUE TO SCARCITY
AF3ANA Teemu Selanne
Chris Pronger
Scott Niedermayer
AF3ATL Marian Hossa
Ilya Kovalchuk
Kari Lehtonen
AF3BOS Brad Boyes
Zdeno Chara
Patrice Bergeron
AF3BUF Chris Drury
Daniel Briere
Ryan Miller
AF3CAR Rod Brind'Amour
Eric Staal
Cam Ward
AF3CGY Jarome Iginla
Alex Tanguay
Miikka Kiprusoff
AF3CHI Martin Havlat
Tuomo Ruutu
Nikolai Khabibulin
AF3CLB Pascal LeClaire
Rick Nash
Sergei Fedorov
AF3COL Joe Sakic
Milan Hejduk
Jose Theodore
AF3DAL Mike Modano
Eric Lindros
Marty Turco
AF3DET Dominik Hasek
Nicklas Lidstrom
Henrik Zetterberg
AF3EDM Ryan Smyth
Dwayne Roloson
Ales Hemsky
AF3FLA Ed Belfour
Todd Bertuzzi
Jay Bouwmeester
AF3LAK Rob Blake
Alexander Frolov
Mike Cammalleri
AF3MIN Pavol Demitra
Marian Gaborik
Pierre-Marc Bouchard
AF3MTL Sergei Samsonov
Saku Koivu
Michael Ryder
AF3NAS Paul Kariya
Tomas Vokoun
Jason Arnott
AF3NJD Martin Brodeur
Patrik Elias
Brian Gionta
AF3NYI Miroslav Satan
Alexei Yashin
Rick DiPietro
AF3NYR Brendan Shanahan
Jaromir Jagr
Henrik Lundqvist
AF3OTT Daniel Alfredsson
Jason Spezza
Dany Heatley
AF3PHI Peter Forsberg
Robert Esche
Simon Gagne
AF3PHX Curtis Joseph
Jeremy Roenick
Shane Doan
AF3PIT Mark Recchi
Ryan Malone
Sidney Crosby
AF3SJS Patrick Marleau
Joe Thornton
Jonathan Cheechoo
AF3STL Doug Weight
Keith Tkachuk
Manny Legace
AF3TBL Vincent Lecavalier
Brad Richards
Martin St. Louis
AF3TOR Mats Sundin
Andrew Raycroft
Alexander Steen
AF3VAN Markus Naslund
Henrik Sedin
Daniel Sedin
AF3WAS Olaf Kolzig
Richard Zednik
Alexander Ovechkin

2006-07 SP Game Used Authentic Fabrics Quads

PRINT RUN 10 #'d SETS
NOT PRICED DUE TO SCARCITY
AF4BJTW Ed Belfour
Curtis Joseph
Marty Turco
Cam Ward
AF4BPJM Rob Blake
Chris Pronger
Ed Jovanovski
Bryan McCabe
AF4FCSW Tony Esposito
Rogie Vachon
Billy Smith
Gump Worsley
AF4IDCH Jarome Iginla
Shane Doan
Jonathan Cheechoo
Dany Heatley
AF4JHEG Jaromir Jagr
Marian Hossa
Patrik Elias
Marian Gaborik
AF4LMSB Vincent Lecavalier
Patrick Marleau
Jason Spezza
Patrice Bergeron
AF4MWGD Mike Modano
Doug Weight
Scott Gomez
Chris Drury
AF4NMBT Cam Neely
Mike Bossy
Dave Taylor
Darryl Sittler
AF4RBTL Jose Theodore
Roberto Luongo
Patrick Roy
Martin Brodeur
AF4SFSZ Mats Sundin
Peter Forsberg
Henrik Sedin
Henrik Zetterberg
AF4SKGN Brendan Shanahan
Paul Kariya
Simon Gagne
Rick Nash
AF4STSC Joe Sakic
Joe Thornton
Eric Staal
Sidney Crosby

2006-07 SP Game Used Authentic Fabrics Quads Patches

PRINT RUN 5 #'d SETS
NOT PRICED DUE TO SCARCITY
AF4BJTW Ed Belfour
Curtis Joseph
Marty Turco
Cam Ward
AF4BPJM Rob Blake
Chris Pronger
Ed Jovanovski
Bryan McCabe
AF4FCSW Tony Esposito
Rogie Vachon
Billy Smith
Gump Worsley
AF4IDCH Jarome Iginla
Shane Doan
Jonathan Cheechoo
Dany Heatley
AF4JHEG Jaromir Jagr
Marian Hossa
Patrik Elias
Marian Gaborik
AF4LMSB Vincent Lecavalier
Patrick Marleau
Jason Spezza
Patrice Bergeron
AF4MWGD Mike Modano
Doug Weight
Scott Gomez
Chris Drury
AF4NMBT Cam Neely
Mike Bossy
Dave Taylor
Darryl Sittler
AF4RBTL Patrick Roy
Martin Brodeur
Jose Theodore
Roberto Luongo
AF4SFSZ Mats Sundin
Peter Forsberg
Henrik Sedin
Henrik Zetterberg
AF4SKGN Brendan Shanahan
Paul Kariya
Simon Gagne
Rick Nash
AF4STSC Joe Sakic
Joe Thornton
Eric Staal
Sidney Crosby

2006-07 SP Game Used Authentic Fabrics Fives

PRINT RUN 10 #'d SETS
NOT PRICED DUE TO SCARCITY
AF51ST Rick DiPietro
Ilya Kovalchuk
Rick Nash
Sidney Crosby
Alexander Ovechkin
AF550G Jaromir Jagr
Ilya Kovalchuk
Jonathan Cheechoo
Dany Heatley
Alexander Ovechkin
AF5ASG Joe Sakic
Teemu Selanne
Bill Guerin
Mark Recchi
Dany Heatley
AF5AST Jaromir Jagr
Brad Richards
Joe Thornton
Marc Savard
Jason Spezza
AF5DPT Sergei Zubov
Chris Pronger
Nicklas Lidstrom
Scott Niedermayer
Bryan McCabe
AF5GAA Dominik Hasek
Manny Legace
Henrik Lundqvist
Cristobal Huet
Miikka Kiprusoff
AF5GWG Olli Jokinen
Brian Gionta
Jonathan Cheechoo
Henrik Zetterberg
Marek Svatos
AP5PTS Jaromir Jagr
Joe Thornton
Daniel Alfredsson
Dany Heatley
Alexander Ovechkin
AP5RPT Brad Boyes
Marek Svatos
Sidney Crosby
Alexander Ovechkin
Jussi Jokinen
AP5SCP Chris Pronger
Cory Stillman
Daniel Briere
Shawn Horcoff
Eric Staal

2006-07 SP Game Used Authentic Fabrics Fives Patches

PRINT RUN 5 #'d SETS
NOT PRICED DUE TO SCARCITY
AF51ST Rick DiPietro
Ilya Kovalchuk
Rick Nash
Sidney Crosby
Alexander Ovechkin
AF550G Jaromir Jagr
Ilya Kovalchuk
Jonathan Cheechoo
Dany Heatley
Alexander Ovechkin
AF5ASG Joe Sakic
Teemu Selanne
Bill Guerin
Mark Recchi
Dany Heatley
AF5AST Jaromir Jagr
Brad Richards
Joe Thornton
Marc Savard
Jason Spezza
AF5DPT Sergei Zubov
Chris Pronger
Nicklas Lidstrom
Scott Niedermayer
Bryan McCabe
AF5GAA Dominik Hasek
Manny Legace
Henrik Lundqvist
Cristobal Huet
Miikka Kiprusoff
AF5GWG Olli Jokinen
Brian Gionta
Jonathan Cheechoo
Henrik Zetterberg
Marek Svatos
AP5PTS Jaromir Jagr
Joe Thornton
Daniel Alfredsson
Dany Heatley
Alexander Ovechkin
AP5RPT Brad Boyes
Marek Svatos
Sidney Crosby
Alexander Ovechkin
Jussi Jokinen
AP5SCP Chris Pronger
Cory Stillman
Daniel Briere
Shawn Horcoff
Eric Staal

2006-07 SP Game Used Authentic Fabrics Sixes

PRINT RUN 7 #'d SETS
NOT PRICED DUE TO SCARCITY
AF6500 Pierre Turgeon
Joe Sakic
Brendan Shanahan
Jaromir Jagr
Mats Sundin
Joe Nieuwendyk
AF6BYN Joe Sakic
Paul Kariya
Pavol Demitra
Brad Richards
Pavel Datsyuk
Wayne Gretzky
AF6JEN Patrick Roy
Ed Belfour
Martin Brodeur
Dominik Hasek
Robert Esche
Miikka Kiprusoff
AF6MAS Mario Lemieux
Teemu Selanne
Saku Koivu
Bryan Berard
Cam Neely
Gary Roberts
AF6MRT Teemu Selanne
Milan Hejduk
Jonathan Cheechoo
Rick Nash
Jarome Iginla
Ilya Kovalchuk
AF6NOR Chris Chelios
Rob Blake
Chris Pronger
Nicklas Lidstrom
Scott Niedermayer
Ray Bourque
AF6SEL Jere Lehtinen
Michael Peca
Kris Draper
Rod Brind'Amour
Sergei Fedorov
Doug Gilmour
AF6WIN Patrick Roy
Ed Belfour
Curtis Joseph
Martin Brodeur
Dominik Hasek
Grant Fuhr

2006-07 SP Game Used Authentic Fabrics Sixes Patches

PRINT RUN 3 #'d SETS
NOT PRICED DUE TO SCARCITY
AF6500 Pierre Turgeon
Joe Sakic
Mats Sundin
Joe Nieuwendyk
Brendan Shanahan
Jaromir Jagr
AF6BYN Joe Sakic
Paul Kariya
Pavol Demitra
Brad Richards
Pavel Datsyuk
Wayne Gretzky
AF6JEN Patrick Roy
Ed Belfour
Martin Brodeur
Dominik Hasek
Robert Esche
Miikka Kiprusoff
AF6MAS Mario Lemieux
Teemu Selanne
Saku Koivu
Bryan Berard
Cam Neely
Gary Roberts
AF6MRT Teemu Selanne
Milan Hejduk
Jarome Iginla
Ilya Kovalchuk
Jonathan Cheechoo
Rick Nash
AF6NOR Chris Chelios
Rob Blake
Chris Pronger
Nicklas Lidstrom
Scott Niedermayer
Ray Bourque
AF6SEL Jere Lehtinen
Michael Peca
Kris Draper
Rod Brind'Amour
Sergei Fedorov
Doug Gilmour
AF6WIN Patrick Roy
Ed Belfour
Curtis Joseph
Martin Brodeur
Dominik Hasek
Grant Fuhr

2006-07 SP Game Used Authentic Fabrics Sevens

PRINT RUN 5 #'d SETS
NOT PRICED DUE TO SCARCITY
AF7ART Mario Lemieux
Jaromir Jagr
Joe Thornton
Peter Forsberg
Jarome Iginla
Martin St. Louis
Wayne Gretzky
AF7CAL Scott Gomez
Chris Drury
Barret Jackman
Evgeni Nabokov
Andrew Raycroft
Dany Heatley
Alexander Ovechkin
AF7CON Patrick Roy
Mario Lemieux
Joe Sakic
Brad Richards
Nicklas Lidstrom
Jean-Sebastien Giguere
Cam Ward
AF7LBP Mario Lemieux
Joe Sakic
Jaromir Jagr
Dominik Hasek
Markus Naslund
Jarome Iginla
Martin St. Louis
AF7MVP Joe Thornton
Peter Forsberg
Jose Theodore
Martin St. Louis
Joe Sakic
Jaromir Jagr
Chris Pronger
AF7VEZ Patrick Roy
Ed Belfour
Olaf Kolzig
Martin Brodeur
Dominik Hasek
Jose Theodore
Miikka Kiprusoff

2006-07 SP Game Used Authentic Fabrics Sevens Patches

PRINT RUN 2 #'d SETS
NOT PRICED DUE TO SCARCITY
AF7ART Mario Lemieux
Jaromir Jagr
Joe Thornton
Peter Forsberg
Jarome Iginla
Martin St. Louis
Wayne Gretzky
AF7CAL Scott Gomez
Chris Drury
Barret Jackman
Evgeni Nabokov
Andrew Raycroft
Dany Heatley
Alexander Ovechkin
AF7CON Patrick Roy
Mario Lemieux
Joe Sakic
Brad Richards
Nicklas Lidstrom
Jean-Sebastien Giguere
Cam Ward
AF7LBP Mario Lemieux
Joe Sakic
Jaromir Jagr
Dominik Hasek
Markus Naslund
Jarome Iginla
Martin St. Louis
AF7MVP Joe Sakic
Jaromir Jagr
Chris Pronger
Joe Thornton
Peter Forsberg
Jose Theodore
Martin St. Louis
AF7VEZ Patrick Roy
Ed Belfour
Olaf Kolzig
Martin Brodeur
Dominik Hasek
Jose Theodore
Miikka Kiprusoff

2006-07 SP Game Used Authentic Fabrics Eights

PRINT RUN 3 #'d SETS
NOT PRICED DUE TO SCARCITY
AF8CAN Joe Sakic
Brendan Shanahan
Paul Kariya
Vincent Lecavalier

Martin Brodeur
Joe Thornton
Roberto Luongo
Jarome Iginla
AF8CEN Jason Spezza
Patrice Bergeron
Mike Ribeiro
Jarret Stoll
Eric Staal
Sidney Crosby
Alexander Steen
Jeff Carter
AF8FIN Teemu Selanne
Jere Lehtinen
Saku Koivu
Olli Jokinen
Miikka Kiprusoff
Joni Pitkanen
Kari Lehtonen
Jussi Jokinen
AF8HOF Patrick Roy
Mario Lemieux
Phil Esposito
Mike Bossy
Guy Lafleur
Wayne Gretzky
Gordie Howe
Ray Bourque
AF8RUS Sergei Zubov
Evgeni Nabokov
Pavel Datsyuk
Ilya Kovalchuk
Alexei Kovalev
Nikolai Khabibulin
Sergei Federov
Alexander Ovechkin
AF8SWE Mats Sundin
Markus Naslund
Nicklas Lidstrom
Peter Forsberg
Daniel Alfredsson
Tomas Holmstrom
Henrik Zetterberg
Henrik Lundqvist

2006-07 SP Game Used Authentic Fabrics Eights Patches

PRINT RUN 1/1
NOT PRICED DUE TO SCARCITY
AF8CAN Joe Sakic
Brendan Shanahan
Martin Brodeur
Joe Thornton
Roberto Luongo
Jarome Iginla
Paul Kariya
Vincent Lecavalier
AF8CEN Mike Ribeiro
Jarret Stoll
Jason Spezza
Patrice Bergeron
Eric Staal
Sidney Crosby
Alexander Steen
Jeff Carter
AF8FIN Teemu Selanne
Jere Lehtinen
Saku Koivu
Olli Jokinen
Miikka Kiprusoff
Joni Pitkanen
Kari Lehtonen
Jussi Jokinen
AF8HOF Patrick Roy
Mario Lemieux
Phil Esposito
Mike Bossy
Guy Lafleur
Wayne Gretzky
Gordie Howe
Ray Bourque
AF8RUS Sergei Zubov
Evgeni Nabokov
Pavel Datsyuk
Ilya Kovalchuk
Alexei Kovalev
Nikolai Khabibulin
Sergei Federov
Alexander Ovechkin
AF8SWE Mats Sundin
Markus Naslund
Nicklas Lidstrom
Peter Forsberg
Daniel Alfredsson
Tomas Holmstrom
Henrik Zetterberg
Henrik Lundqvist

2006-07 SP Game Used Autographs

PRINT RUN 10 #'d SETS
NOT PRICED DUE TO SCARCITY
4 Ilya Kovalchuk
5 Kari Lehtonen
8 Brad Boyes
9 Hannu Toivonen
10 Bobby Orr
11 Ryan Miller
13 Jarome Iginla
16 Dion Phaneuf
17 Eric Staal
19 Erik Cole
21 Nikolai Khabibulin
22 Martin Havlat
23 Tuomo Ruutu
25 Jose Theodore
26 Milan Hejduk
27 Marek Svatos
28 Rick Nash
31 Mike Modano
32 Marty Turco
34 Gordie Howe
35 Henrik Zetterberg
37 Dominik Hasek
38 Nicklas Lidstrom
39 Ales Hemsky
40 Ryan Smyth
43 Jay Bouwmeester
44 Todd Bertuzzi
46 Wayne Gretzky
47 Alexander Frolov
49 Marian Gaborik
52 Cristobal Huet
54 Michael Ryder
55 Saku Koivu
58 Tomas Vokoun
59 Jason Arnott
60 Martin Brodeur
61 Brian Gionta
62 Patrik Elias
63 Alexei Yashin
64 Miroslav Satan
68 Dany Heatley
69 Martin Gerber
74 Jeff Carter
75 Joni Pitkanen
76 Shane Doan
77 Jeremy Roenick
80 Sidney Crosby
82 Marc-Andre Fleury
85 Patrick Marleau
86 Jonathan Cheechoo
90 Martin St. Louis
94 Andrew Raycroft
95 Michael Peca
97 Roberto Luongo
101 Shane O'Brien
102 Ryan Shannon
103 Yan Stastny
104 Mark Stuart
106 Phil Kessel
107 Matt Lashoff
109 Michael Blunden
110 Dustin Byfuglien
111 Paul Stastny
112 Fredrik Norrena
113 Loui Eriksson
116 Marc-Antoine Pouliot
117 Patrick Thoresen
118 Ladislav Smid
119 Janis Sprukts
120 Konstantin Pushkaryov
121 Patrick O'Sullivan
122 Anze Kopitar
126 Guillaume Latendresse
127 Alexander Radulov
128 Shea Weber
130 Alex Brooks
132 Travis Zajac
133 Drew Stafford
135 Jarkko Immonen
136 Nigel Dawes
139 Ryan Potulny
143 Keith Yandle
145 Noah Welch
146 Michel Ouellet
147 Jordan Staal
149 Evgeni Malkin
150 Matt Carle
151 Marc-Edouard Vlasic
154 Ben Ondrus
155 Brendan Bell
156 Ian White
157 Dustin Boyd
159 Eric Fehr

2006-07 SP Game Used By The Letter

PRINT RUNS VARY FROM 3 - 10
NOT PRICED DUE TO SCARCITY
BLAM Maxim Afinogenov/10
BLAO Alexander Ovechkin/8
BLBO Mike Bossy/5
BLDH Dany Heatley/7
BLES Eric Staal/5
BLHA Dominik Hasek/5
BLHE Milan Hejduk/6
BLJJ Jaromir Jagr/4
BLJO Joe Sakic/5
BLJP Joni Pitkanen/8
BLJT Joe Thornton/8
BLKD Kris Draper/6
BLKL Kari Lehtonen/8
BLKT Keith Tkachuk/7
BLLC John LeClair/7
BLLE Jordan Leopold/7
BLLR Luc Robitaille/10
BLMA Mats Sundin/6
BLMB Martin Brodeur/7
BLMF Manny Fernandez/5
BLMH Martin Havlat/6
BLMI Miroslav Satan/5
BLMK Miikka Kiprusoff/8
BLML Mario Lemieux/7
BLMM Mike Modano/6
BLMN Markus Naslund/7
BLMP Michael Peca/4
BLMR Mark Recchi/6
BLMS Martin St. Louis/7
BLMT Marty Turco/5
BLNL Nicklas Lidstrom/8
BLOK Olaf Kolzig/6
BLPB Patrice Bergeron/8
BLPD Pavel Datsyuk/7
BLPE Patrik Elias/5
BLPF Peter Forsberg/8
BLPK Paul Kariya/6
BLPM Patrick Marleau/7
BLPR Patrick Roy/3
BLPS Peter Stastny/7
BLRB Ray Bourque/7
BLRD Rick DiPietro/8
BLRH Ron Hextall/7
BLRI Mike Ribeiro/7
BLRL Roberto Luongo/6
BLRM Ryan Miller/6
BLRN Rick Nash/4
BLRS Ryan Smyth/5
BLRY Michael Ryder/5
BLSC Sidney Crosby/6
BLSD Shane Doan/4
BLSF Sergei Fedorov/7
BLSK Saku Koivu/5
BLTB Todd Bertuzzi/8
BLTH Jose Theodore/8
BLTS Teemu Selanne/7
BLTV Tomas Vokoun/6
BLVL Vincent Lecavalier/10
BLWG Wayne Gretzky/7

2006-07 SP Game Used Inked Sweaters

PRINT RUN 100 #'d SETS
SP PRINT RUN 25 #'d SETS
ISAF Alexander Frolov 6.00 15.00
ISAH Ales Hemsky 8.00 20.00
ISAN Antero Niittymaki 12.00 30.00
ISAO Alexander Ovechkin SP 75.00 150.00
ISAR Andrew Raycroft 15.00 40.00
ISAY Alexei Yashin 6.00 15.00
ISBB Brad Boyes 6.00 15.00
ISBG Brian Gionta 6.00 15.00
ISBM Bryan McCabe 6.00 15.00
ISBS Borje Salming SP
ISCA Matt Carle 10.00 25.00
ISCH Chris Higgins 10.00 25.00
ISCN Cam Neely SP 20.00 50.00
ISCP Chris Pronger SP 15.00 40.00
ISCW Cam Ward 8.00 20.00
ISDA Dany Heatley 15.00 40.00
ISDB Daniel Briere 15.00 40.00
ISDH Dominik Hasek SP 40.00 80.00
ISDI Dion Phaneuf SP 25.00 60.00
ISDR Dwayne Roloson 10.00 25.00
ISDS Denis Savard SP 15.00 40.00
ISDT Darcy Tucker 10.00 25.00
ISEF Eric Fehr 6.00 15.00
ISEL Patrik Elias 8.00 20.00
ISES Eric Staal 12.00 30.00
ISFP Fernando Pisani 6.00 15.00
ISGE Martin Gerber 8.00 20.00
ISGH Gordie Howe SP
ISHA Martin Havlat 12.00 30.00
ISHE Milan Hejduk 8.00 20.00
ISHO Tomas Holmstrom 8.00 20.00
ISHT Hannu Toivonen 10.00 25.00
ISHU Cristobal Huet 12.00 30.00
ISIK Ilya Kovalchuk SP 20.00 50.00
ISIM Jarkko Immonen 8.00 20.00
ISJA Jason Arnott 6.00 15.00
ISJI Jarome Iginla SP 25.00 60.00
ISJL Joffrey Lupul 6.00 15.00
ISJP Joni Pitkanen 6.00 15.00
ISJS Jarret Stoll 6.00 15.00
ISJT Joe Thornton SP 25.00 60.00
ISJW Justin Williams 6.00 15.00
ISKD Kris Draper 6.00 15.00
ISKL Kari Lehtonen 10.00 25.00
ISKO Mikko Koivu 10.00 25.00
ISLN Ladislav Nagy 6.00 15.00
ISLR Luc Robitaille SP
ISMA Al MacInnis SP 20.00 50.00
ISMB Martin Brodeur SP 60.00 150.00
ISMC Mike Cammalleri 8.00 20.00
ISMG Marian Gaborik 15.00 40.00
ISMI Ryan Miller 12.00 30.00
ISML Mario Lemieux SP 100.00 200.00
ISMM Milan Michalek 6.00 15.00
ISMO Mike Modano SP 20.00 50.00
ISMP Mark Parrish 6.00 15.00
ISMR Mike Ribeiro 6.00 15.00
ISMT Marty Turco 10.00 25.00
ISNL Nicklas Lidstrom SP 20.00 50.00
ISNZ Nikolai Zherdev 6.00 15.00
ISPB Pierre-Marc Bouchard 6.00 15.00
ISPE Michael Peca 6.00 15.00
ISPM Patrick Marleau 8.00 20.00
ISPO Marc-Antoine Pouliot 8.00 20.00
ISPP Petr Prucha 10.00 25.00
ISPR Patrick Roy SP 125.00 250.00
ISRG Ryan Getzlaf 10.00 25.00
ISRH Ron Hextall SP
ISRI Mike Richards 8.00 20.00
ISRN Rick Nash SP 25.00 60.00
ISRS Ryan Smyth 10.00 25.00
ISSA Marc Savard 8.00 20.00
ISSB Steve Bernier 8.00 20.00
ISSC Sidney Crosby 125.00 225.00
ISSG Scott Gomez 8.00 20.00
ISSK Saku Koivu SP 20.00 50.00
ISSV Marek Svatos 8.00 20.00
ISSW Shea Weber 10.00 25.00
ISTV Tomas Vokoun 10.00 25.00
ISVL Vincent Lecavalier SP 20.00 50.00
ISVT Vesa Toskala 10.00 25.00
ISWG Wayne Gretzky SP 200.00 300.00
ISWR Wade Redden 6.00 15.00
ISZC Zdeno Chara 6.00 15.00

2006-07 SP Game Used Inked Sweaters Patches

PATCHES: 1.25X to 2X JSY HI
PRINT RUN 25 #'d SETS
SPs PRINT RUN 10 #'d SETS
SPs NOT PRICED DUE TO SCARCITY
ISAF Alexander Frolov 12.00 30.00
ISAH Ales Hemsky 15.00 40.00
ISAN Antero Niittymaki 25.00 60.00
ISAO Alexander Ovechkin SP 200.00 350.00
ISAR Andrew Raycroft 30.00 80.00
ISAY Alexei Yashin 12.00 30.00
ISBB Brad Boyes 12.00 30.00
ISBG Brian Gionta 12.00 30.00
ISBM Bryan McCabe 12.00 30.00
ISBS Borje Salming SP
ISCA Matt Carle 20.00 50.00
ISCH Chris Higgins 20.00 50.00
ISCN Cam Neely SP
ISCP Chris Pronger SP
ISCW Cam Ward 20.00 50.00
ISDA Dany Heatley 30.00 80.00
ISDB Daniel Briere 25.00 60.00
ISDH Dominik Hasek SP
ISDI Dion Phaneuf SP
ISDR Dwayne Roloson 20.00 50.00
ISDS Denis Savard SP
ISDT Darcy Tucker 20.00 50.00
ISEF Eric Fehr 12.00 30.00
ISEL Patrik Elias 15.00 40.00
ISES Eric Staal 20.00 50.00
ISFP Fernando Pisani 12.00 30.00
ISGE Martin Gerber 15.00 40.00
ISHA Martin Havlat 25.00 60.00
ISHE Milan Hejduk 15.00 40.00
ISHO Tomas Holmstrom 15.00 40.00
ISHT Hannu Toivonen 20.00 50.00
ISHU Cristobal Huet 30.00 80.00
ISIK Ilya Kovalchuk SP 60.00 100.00
ISIM Jarkko Immonen 15.00 40.00
ISJA Jason Arnott 12.00 30.00
ISJI Jarome Iginla SP 125.00 200.00
ISJL Joffrey Lupul 12.00 30.00
ISJP Joni Pitkanen 12.00 30.00
ISJS Jarret Stoll 12.00 30.00
ISJT Joe Thornton SP 125.00 200.00
ISJW Justin Williams 12.00 30.00
ISKD Kris Draper 15.00 40.00
ISKL Kari Lehtonen 20.00 50.00
ISKO Mikko Koivu 20.00 50.00
ISLN Ladislav Nagy 12.00 30.00
ISLR Luc Robitaille SP
ISMA Al MacInnis SP
ISMB Martin Brodeur SP
ISMC Mike Cammalleri 15.00 40.00
ISMG Marian Gaborik 30.00 80.00
ISMI Ryan Miller 25.00 60.00
ISML Mario Lemieux SP
ISMM Milan Michalek 12.00 30.00
ISMO Mike Modano SP
ISMP Mark Parrish 12.00 30.00
ISMR Mike Ribeiro 12.00 30.00
ISMT Marty Turco 20.00 50.00
ISNL Nicklas Lidstrom SP
ISNZ Nikolai Zherdev 12.00 30.00
ISPB Pierre-Marc Bouchard 12.00 30.00
ISPE Michael Peca
ISPM Patrick Marleau 15.00 40.00
ISPO Marc-Antoine Pouliot 15.00 40.00
ISPP Petr Prucha 20.00 50.00
ISPR Patrick Roy SP
ISRG Ryan Getzlaf 20.00 50.00
ISRH Ron Hextall SP
ISRI Mike Richards 15.00 40.00
ISRN Rick Nash SP
ISRS Ryan Smyth 20.00 50.00
ISSA Marc Savard 15.00 40.00
ISSB Steve Bernier 15.00 40.00
ISSC Sidney Crosby 400.00 600.00
ISSG Scott Gomez 15.00 40.00
ISSK Saku Koivu SP
ISSV Marek Svatos 15.00 40.00
ISSW Shea Weber 20.00 50.00
ISTH Jose Theodore SP
ISTV Tomas Vokoun 15.00 40.00
ISVL Vincent Lecavalier SP 75.00 150.00
ISVT Vesa Toskala 25.00 60.00
ISWG Wayne Gretzky SP
ISWR Wade Redden 12.00 30.00
ISZC Zdeno Chara 12.00 30.00

2006-07 SP Game Used Inked Sweaters Dual

PRINT RUN 50 #'d SETS
SP PRINT RUN 10 #'d SETS
IS2AS Jason Arnott 8.00 20.00
Steve Sullivan
IS2BB Brad Boyes 15.00 40.00
Patrice Bergeron
IS2BL Martin Brodeur 200.00 300.00
Roberto Luongo SP
IS2BP Denis Potvin 100.00 175.00
Ray Bourque SP
IS2CL Bobby Clarke
Guy Lafleur SP
IS2CP Gerry Cheevers 20.00 50.00
Brad Park
IS2DM Chris Drury 15.00 40.00
Ryan Miller
IS2EG Patrik Elias 10.00 25.00
Brian Gionta
IS2EP Robert Esche 8.00 20.00
Joni Pitkanen
IS2FC Alexander Frolov 10.00 25.00
Mike Cammalleri
IS2FR Grant Fuhr 20.00 50.00
Bill Ranford
IS2GB Marian Gaborik 20.00 50.00
Pierre-Marc Bouchard
IS2GC Simon Gagne
Jeff Carter
IS2GL Mario Lemieux
Wayne Gretzky SP
IS2HA David Aebischer 15.00 40.00
Cristobal Huet
IS2HH Michal Handzus 8.00 20.00
Martin Havlat
IS2HO Dominik Hasek 25.00 60.00
Chris Osgood
IS2HS Jarret Stoll 8.00 20.00
Ales Hemsky
IS2HT Milan Hejduk 12.00 30.00
Jose Theodore
IS2HV Tomas Vokoun 75.00 125.00
Dominik Hasek SP
IS2IT Jarome Iginla 15.00 40.00
Alex Tanguay
IS2KL Ilya Kovalchuk 25.00 60.00
Kari Lehtonen
IS2KR Saku Koivu 12.00 30.00
Michael Ryder
IS2LP Henrik Lundqvist 25.00 60.00
Petr Prucha
IS2LS Nicklas Lidstrom 20.00 50.00
Borje Salming
IS2MC Patrick Marleau 15.00 40.00
Jonathan Cheechoo
IS2MM Joe Mullen 12.00 30.00
Al MacInnis
IS2MS Marc Savard 10.00 25.00
Glen Murray
IS2MT Mike Modano 15.00 40.00
Marty Turco
IS2NH Dany Heatley 20.00 50.00
Rick Nash
IS2NM Markus Naslund 15.00 40.00
Brendan Morrison
IS2OJ Olli Jokinen 8.00 20.00
Jay Bouwmeester
IS2OK Ilya Kovalchuk 125.00 200.00
Alexander Ovechkin SP
IS2PT Michael Peca 15.00 40.00
Darcy Tucker
IS2RB Patrick Roy 200.00 300.00
Ray Bourque SP
IS2RD Jeremy Roenick 10.00 25.00
Shane Doan
IS2RG Wade Redden 10.00 25.00
Martin Gerber
IS2RS Andrew Raycroft 15.00 40.00
Alexander Steen
IS2RT Luc Robitaille 25.00 60.00
Dave Taylor
IS2SD Martin St. Louis 12.00 30.00
Marc Denis
IS2SR Ryan Smyth 12.00 30.00
Dwayne Roloson
IS2SS Jason Spezza 50.00 125.00
Eric Staal SP
IS2SW Justin Williams 10.00 25.00
Eric Staal
IS2SY Miroslav Satan 8.00 20.00
Alexei Yashin
IS2VW Tomas Vokoun 12.00 30.00
Shea Weber
IS2WP Dave Williams 12.00 30.00
Bob Probert
IS2WR Dwayne Roloson 12.00 30.00
Cam Ward
IS2ZH Tomas Holmstrom 20.00 50.00
Henrik Zetterberg
IS2HH2 Bobby Hull 150.00 225.00
Gordie Howe SP

2006-07 SP Game Used Inked Sweaters Dual Patches

PRINT RUN 15 #'d SETS
SP PRINT RUN 5 #'d SETS
NOT PRICED DUE TO SCARCITY
IS2AS Jason Arnott
Steve Sullivan
IS2BB Brad Boyes
Patrice Bergeron
IS2BL Martin Brodeur
Roberto Luongo SP
IS2BP Denis Potvin
Ray Bourque SP
IS2CL Bobby Clarke
Guy Lafleur SP
IS2CP Gerry Cheevers
Brad Park
IS2DM Chris Drury
Ryan Miller
IS2EG Patrik Elias
Brian Gionta
IS2EP Robert Esche
Joni Pitkanen
IS2FC Alexander Frolov
Mike Cammalleri
IS2GB Marian Gaborik
Pierre-Marc Bouchard
IS2GC Simon Gagne
Jeff Carter
IS2GL Mario Lemieux
Wayne Gretzky SP
IS2HA David Aebischer
Cristobal Huet
IS2HO Dominik Hasek
Chris Osgood
IS2HS Jarret Stoll
Ales Hemsky
IS2HT Milan Hejduk
Jose Theodore
IS2HV Tomas Vokoun
Dominik Hasek SP
IS2IT Jarome Iginla
Alex Tanguay
IS2KL Ilya Kovalchuk
Kari Lehtonen
IS2KR Saku Koivu
Michael Ryder
IS2LP Henrik Lundqvist
Petr Prucha
IS2LS Nicklas Lidstrom
Borje Salming
IS2MC Patrick Marleau
Jonathan Cheechoo
IS2MM Joe Mullen
Al MacInnis
IS2MS Marc Savard
Glen Murray
IS2MT Mike Modano
Marty Turco
IS2NH Dany Heatley
Rick Nash
IS2NM Markus Naslund
Brendan Morrison
IS2OJ Olli Jokinen
Jay Bouwmeester
IS2OK Ilya Kovalchuk
Alexander Ovechkin SP
IS2PT Michael Peca
Darcy Tucker
IS2RB Patrick Roy
Ray Bourque SP
IS2RD Jeremy Roenick
Shane Doan
IS2RG Wade Redden
Martin Gerber
IS2RS Andrew Raycroft
Alexander Steen
IS2RT Luc Robitaille
Dave Taylor
IS2SD Martin St. Louis
Marc Denis
IS2SR Ryan Smyth
Dwayne Roloson
IS2SS Jason Spezza
Eric Staal SP
IS2SW Justin Williams
Eric Staal
IS2SY Miroslav Satan
Alexei Yashin
IS2VW Tomas Vokoun
Shea Weber
IS2WP Dave Williams
Bob Probert
IS2WR Dwayne Roloson
Cam Ward
IS2ZH Tomas Holmstrom
Henrik Zetterberg
IS2HH2 Bobby Hull
Gordie Howe SP

2006-07 SP Game Used Legendary Fabrics

LFBC Bobby Clarke/100 6.00 15.00
LFGH Gordie Howe/25 20.00 50.00
LFGL Guy Lafleur/100 10.00 25.00
LFJB Jean Beliveau/100 12.00 30.00
LFMB Mike Bossy/100 6.00 15.00
LFML Mario Lemieux/25 30.00 80.00
LFPE Phil Esposito/25 12.00 30.00
LFPR Patrick Roy/25 40.00 100.00
LFRB Ray Bourque/25 20.00 50.00
LFWG Wayne Gretzky/25 75.00 150.00

2006-07 SP Game Used Legendary Fabrics Autographs

PRINT RUN 100 #'d SETS
LFBC Bobby Clarke 15.00 40.00
LFGH Gordie Howe 50.00 100.00
LFGL Guy Lafleur 20.00 50.00
LFJB Jean Beliveau 25.00 60.00
LFMB Mike Bossy 15.00 40.00
LFML Mario Lemieux SP
LFPE Phil Esposito SP 25.00 60.00
LFPR Patrick Roy SP
LFRB Ray Bourque SP 50.00 100.00
LFWG Wayne Gretzky SP 250.00 400.00

2006-07 SP Game Used Letter Marks

PRINT RUN 50 #'d SETS
LMAF Alexander Frolov 40.00 100.00
LMAK Andrei Kostitsyn 30.00 80.00
LMAL Andrew Ladd 25.00 60.00
LMAN Antero Niittymaki 30.00 80.00
LMBB Brad Boyes 30.00 60.00
LMBG Brian Gionta 40.00 80.00
LMBM Brenden Morrow 40.00 100.00
LMBP Bernie Parent 30.00 60.00
LMBQ Ray Bourque 75.00 150.00
LMBR Bill Ranford 40.00 80.00
LMCG Clark Gillies 30.00 80.00
LMCH Cristobal Huet 40.00 100.00
LMCK Chuck Kobasew 25.00 60.00
LMCN Cam Neely 60.00 125.00
LMCW Cam Ward 30.00 80.00
LMDC Dino Ciccarelli 25.00 60.00
LMDP Denis Potvin 30.00 80.00
LMDR Dwayne Roloson 30.00 80.00
LMDS Denis Savard 50.00 125.00
LMDW Dave Williams 25.00 60.00
LMEC Erik Cole 25.00 60.00
LMEL Patrik Elias 40.00 100.00
LMEM Evgeni Malkin
LMES Eric Staal 40.00 100.00
LMFP Fernando Pisani 25.00 60.00
LMGC Gerry Cheevers 40.00 80.00
LMGL Guillaume Latendresse 60.00 100.00
LMHA Dominik Hasek 60.00 100.00
LMHE Milan Hejduk 40.00 80.00
LMHO Gordie Howe 100.00 200.00
LMIK Ilya Kovalchuk 60.00 100.00
LMJA Jason Arnott 25.00 60.00
LMJC Jeff Carter 30.00 80.00
LMJI Jarome Iginla 75.00 200.00
LMJJ Jussi Jokinen 40.00 80.00
LMJL Joffrey Lupul 25.00 60.00
LMJP Joni Pitkanen 25.00 60.00
LMJT Jose Theodore 30.00 80.00
LMKD Kris Draper 30.00 80.00
LMLR Luc Robitaille 40.00 100.00
LMLU Roberto Luongo 100.00 200.00
LMMA Matt Carle 30.00 60.00
LMMB Martin Brodeur 100.00 250.00
LMMF Marc-Andre Fleury 75.00 175.00
LMMG Marian Gaborik 60.00 150.00
LMMI Mike Cammalleri 30.00 80.00
LMMM Mike Modano 75.00 200.00
LMMN Markus Naslund 50.00 125.00
LMMR Michael Ryder 30.00 80.00
LMMT Marty Turco 50.00 100.00
LMNL Nicklas Lidstrom 40.00 100.00
LMOJ Olli Jokinen 25.00 60.00
LMOR Bobby Orr 400.00 600.00
LMPE Michael Peca 30.00 80.00
LMPI Pierre-Marc Bouchard 25.00 60.00
LMPK Phil Kessel 40.00 80.00
LMPM Patrick Marleau 30.00 80.00
LMPO Ryan Potulny 25.00 60.00
LMPP Petr Prucha 100.00 200.00
LMRH Ron Hextall 60.00 150.00
LMRI Mike Ribeiro 25.00 60.00
LMRL Reggie Leach 25.00 60.00
LMRM Mike Richards 30.00 80.00
LMRV Rogie Vachon 30.00 80.00
LMRY Ryan Miller 75.00 175.00
LMSB Steve Bernier 50.00 100.00
LMSC Sidney Crosby 450.00 750.00
LMSK Saku Koivu 40.00 150.00
LMSM Ryan Smyth 50.00 125.00
LMSV Marek Svatos 30.00 80.00
LMTH Tomas Holmstrom 30.00 60.00
LMTL Ted Lindsay 30.00 80.00
LMTO Terry O'Reilly 30.00 80.00
LMVA Thomas Vanek 60.00 150.00
LMWG Wayne Gretzky 400.00 600.00
LMZC Zdeno Chara 25.00 60.00

2006-07 SP Game Used Rookie Exclusives Autographs

PRINT RUN 100 #'d SETS
REAB Adam Burish 3.00 8.00
REAE Alexander Edler 3.00 8.00
REAK Anze Kopitar 25.00 60.00
REAL Alex Brooks 3.00 8.00
REAR Alexander Radulov 25.00 60.00
REBB Brendan Bell 3.00 8.00
REBO Ben Ondrus 3.00 8.00
REBR Mike Brown 3.00 8.00
RECA Mike Card 3.00 8.00
REDB Dustin Byfuglien 3.00 8.00
REDL Drew Larman 3.00 8.00
REDS Drew Stafford 20.00 50.00
REDU Dustin Boyd 8.00 20.00
REEF Eric Fehr 5.00 12.00
REEM Evgeni Malkin 100.00 175.00
REGL Guillaume Latendresse 25.00 60.00
REIW Ian White 3.00 8.00
REJF Jean-Francois Racine 3.00 8.00
REJI Jarkko Immonen 3.00 8.00
REJS Jordan Staal 60.00 125.00
REJW Jeremy Williams 3.00 8.00
REKP Konstantin Pushkaryov 3.00 8.00
REKY Keith Yandle 3.00 8.00
RELE Loui Eriksson 3.00 8.00
RELS Ladislav Smid 3.00 8.00
REMB Michael Blunden 3.00 8.00
REMC Matt Carle 5.00 12.00
REMM Masi Marjamaki 3.00 8.00
REMO Michel Ouellet 8.00 20.00
REMP Marc-Antoine Pouliot 8.00 20.00
REMS Mark Stuart 3.00 8.00
REMV Marc-Edouard Vlasic 6.00 15.00
REND Nigel Dawes 3.00 8.00
RENM Nathan McIver 3.00 8.00
RENO Fredrik Norrena 5.00 12.00
RENW Noah Welch 3.00 8.00
REPO Patrick O'Sullivan 5.00 12.00
REPK Phil Kessel 20.00 50.00
REPO Ryan Potulny 5.00 12.00
REPS Paul Stastny 40.00 100.00
REPT Patrick Thoresen 8.00 20.00
RERS Ryan Shannon 3.00 8.00
RESO Shane O'Brien 3.00 8.00
RESP Janis Sprukts 3.00 8.00
RESW Shea Weber 5.00 12.00
RETK Tomas Kopecky 5.00 12.00
RETZ Travis Zajac 8.00 20.00
REYS Yan Stastny 3.00 8.00

2006-07 SP Game Used SIGnificance

PRINT RUN 50 #'d SETS
SAF Alexander Frolov 8.00 20.00
SAH Ales Hemsky 8.00 20.00
SAK Andrei Kostitsyn 6.00 15.00
SAL Andrew Ladd 8.00 20.00
SAM Al Montoya 10.00 25.00
SAN Antero Niittymaki 8.00 20.00
SBG Brian Gionta 8.00 20.00
SBM Bryan McCabe 10.00 25.00
SBN Bob Nystrom 6.00 15.00
SBR Daniel Briere 15.00 40.00
SCB Cam Barker 8.00 20.00
SCH Cristobal Huet 20.00 50.00
SCK Chuck Kobasew 6.00 15.00
SCN Cam Neely 12.00 30.00
SCW Cam Ward 10.00 25.00
SDB Dustin Brown 10.00 25.00
SDC Don Cherry 20.00 50.00
SDE Denis Savard 10.00 25.00
SDK Duncan Keith 6.00 15.00
SDP Denis Potvin 6.00 15.00
SDR Dwayne Roloson 6.00 15.00
SDS Derek Sanderson 12.00 30.00
SDT Dave Taylor 8.00 20.00
SEC Erik Cole 6.00 15.00
SEM Evgeni Malkin 75.00 150.00
SEN Eric Nystrom 6.00 15.00
SES Eric Staal 10.00 25.00
SFP Fernando Pisani 6.00 15.00
SGA Marian Gaborik 12.00 30.00
SGH Gordie Howe 30.00 80.00
SGL Guillaume Latendresse 30.00 80.00
SHI Chris Higgins 10.00 25.00
SHO Marcel Hossa 5.00 12.00
SHT Hannu Toivonen 8.00 20.00
SHZ Henrik Zetterberg 15.00 40.00
SIK Ilya Kovalchuk 15.00 40.00
SJA Jason Arnott 8.00 20.00
SJB Jay Bouwmeester 6.00 15.00
SJC Jeff Carter 10.00 25.00
SJP Joni Pitkanen 6.00 15.00
SJS Jarret Stoll 8.00 20.00
SKB Keith Ballard 6.00 15.00
SKD Kris Draper 8.00 20.00
SKL Kari Lehtonen 10.00 25.00
SKO Mikko Koivu 8.00 20.00
SLE Reggie Leach 6.00 15.00
SLN Ladislav Nagy 5.00 12.00
SMA Ryan Malone 8.00 20.00
SMB Martin Brodeur 60.00 100.00
SMC Mike Cammalleri 10.00 25.00
SMD Andy McDonald 6.00 15.00
SMG Martin Gerber 15.00 40.00
SMH Michal Handzus 5.00 12.00
SMM Milan Michalek 6.00 15.00
SMP Michael Peca 8.00 20.00
SMR Mike Richards 8.00 20.00
SMT Marty Turco 8.00 20.00
SNH Nathan Horton 8.00 20.00
SNZ Nikolai Zherdev 5.00 12.00
SPA Mark Parrish 5.00 12.00
SPB Pierre-Marc Bouchard 6.00 15.00
SPH Chris Phillips 5.00 12.00
SPP Petr Prucha 6.00 15.00
SRB Richard Brodeur 8.00 20.00
SRE Robert Esche 8.00 20.00
SRF Ruslan Fedotenko 5.00 12.00
SRH Ron Hextall 15.00 40.00
SRI Mike Ribeiro 5.00 12.00
SRK Rostislav Klesla 5.00 12.00
SRM Ryan Miller 20.00 50.00
SRN Rick Nash 10.00 25.00
SRS Ryan Smyth 6.00 15.00
SRV Rogie Vachon 15.00 40.00
SRW Ryan Whitney 5.00 12.00
SRY Michael Ryder 8.00 20.00
SSA Marc Savard 6.00 15.00
SSB Steve Bernier 6.00 15.00
SSC Sidney Crosby 150.00 300.00
SSV Marek Svatos 6.00 15.00
SSW Stephen Weiss 6.00 15.00
STH Tomas Holmstrom 6.00 15.00

STL Ted Lindsay	8.00	20.00
STO Terry O'Reilly	10.00	25.00
STU Darcy Tucker	10.00	25.00
STV Tomas Vokoun	6.00	15.00
SVA Thomas Vanek	12.00	30.00
SVF Valtteri Filppula	10.00	25.00
SVT Vesa Toskala	10.00	25.00
SWR Wade Redden	5.00	12.00
SZC Zdeno Chara	6.00	15.00

1933 Sport Kings R338 *

This multi-sport set from legendary manufacturer Goudey features 48 of the world's greatest athletes. The cards measure 2 3/8 by 2 7/8". The cards feature color artwork on the front, with b/w text on the back. We have listed the four hockey players in the set below.

19 Eddie Shore	400.00	800.00
24 Howie Morenz	500.00	1000.00
29 Ace Bailey	200.00	400.00
30 Ching Johnson	200.00	400.00

1935 Sporting Events and Stars

Cards measure approximately 2" x 3". Cards feature black and white fronts, along with informative backs. Set features 96 cards and was issued by various cigarette makers including Senior Service, Junior Member, and Illingworth's.

31 Ice Hockey	20.00	40.00

2006-07 Springfield Falcons

COMPLETE SET (28)	8.00	15.00
1 Sean Burke	.40	1.00
2 Doug O'Brien	.20	.50
3 Dan Cavanaugh	.20	.50
4 Andy Delmore	.20	.50
5 Eric Healey	.20	.50
6 Blair Jones	.20	.50
7 Sylvain Dufresne	.20	.50
8 Mitch Fritz	.30	.75
9 Jay Rosehill	.20	.50
10 Karri Ramo	.40	1.00
11 Zdenek Blatny	.20	.50
12 Justin Keller	.20	.50
13 Mike Egener	.30	.75
14 Darren Reid	.20	.50
15 David Spina	.20	.50
16 Marek Kvapil	.20	.50
17 Norm Milley	.20	.50
18 Andy Rogers	.20	.50
19 Matt Smaby	.40	1.00
20 Jonathan Boutin	.40	1.00
21 Zbynek Hrdel	.20	.50
22 Steve Stirling HC	.10	.25
23 Darren Rumble CO	.10	.25
24 Jared Aulin	.20	.50
25 Andre Deveaux	.20	.50
26 Adam Henrich	.20	.50
27 Geoff Waugh	.20	.50
28 Screech MASCOT	.02	.10

1996-97 SPx

The 1996-97 SPx set was issued in one series totaling 50 cards. The one-card packs retailed for $3.49 each. Each die-cut card features a full-motion hologram. Two special cards of Wayne Gretzky were randomly inserted, including a tribute (found 1:95), and an autographed tribute (found just one in 1297 packs). An additional special insert is the Great Futures card, which includes holoview images of four young stars (Eric Daze, Daniel Alfredsson, Vitali Yachmenev, and Saku Koivu) and was randomly inserted at a rate of 1:75 packs.

COMPLETE SET (50)	30.00	60.00
1 Paul Kariya	.60	1.50
2 Teemu Selanne	.60	1.50
3 Ray Bourque	1.00	2.50
4 Cam Neely	.60	1.50
5 Theo Fleury	.40	1.00
6 Chris Chelios	.60	1.50
7 Jeremy Roenick	.75	2.00
8 Peter Forsberg	1.50	4.00
9 Joe Sakic	1.25	3.00
10 Patrick Roy	3.00	8.00
11 Mike Modano	1.00	2.50
12 Joe Nieuwendyk	.50	1.25
13 Sergei Fedorov	1.00	2.50
14 Steve Yzerman	3.00	8.00
15 Paul Coffey	.60	1.50
16 Chris Osgood	.50	1.25
17 Doug Weight	.50	1.25
18 Pat LaFontaine	.60	1.50
19 Brendan Shanahan	.60	1.50
20 Vitali Yachmenev	.40	1.00
21 Saku Koivu	.60	1.50
22 Pierre Turgeon	.50	1.25
23 Petr Sykora	.40	1.00
24 Scott Stevens	.50	1.25
25 Martin Brodeur	1.50	4.00
26 Brian Leetch	.60	1.50
27 Mark Messier	.60	1.50
28 Mike Richter	.60	1.50
29 Zigmund Palffy	.50	1.25
30 Todd Bertuzzi	.60	1.50
31 Alexei Yashin	.40	1.00
32 Daniel Alfredsson	.50	1.25
33 Eric Lindros	.60	1.50
34 John LeClair	.60	1.50
35 Keith Tkachuk	.60	1.50
36 Alexei Zhamnov	.50	1.25
37 Mario Lemieux	3.00	8.00
38 Jaromir Jagr	1.00	2.50
39 Wayne Gretzky	4.00	10.00
40 Brett Hull	.75	2.00
41 Owen Nolan	.50	1.25
42 Roman Hamrlik	.50	1.25
43 Mats Sundin	.60	1.50
44 Felix Potvin	.60	1.50
45 Doug Gilmour	.50	1.25
46 Pavel Bure	.60	1.50
47 Alexander Mogilny	.50	1.25
48 Jim Carey	.60	1.50
49 Peter Bondra	.50	1.25
50 Eric Daze	.50	1.25
P39 Wayne Gretzky PROMO	.40	1.00
GF1 Wayne Gretzky Daniel Alfredsson Eric Daze Saku Koivu Vitali Yachmenev	5.00	12.00
GS1 W.Gretzky Tribute AU	75.00	200.00
GT1 Wayne Gretzky Tribute	8.00	20.00

1996-97 SPx Gold

A parallel to SPx, these cards feature gold foil stock and were inserted 1:7 packs.
*GOLDS: 1.25X TO 3X BASIC CARDS

1996-97 SPx Holoview Heroes

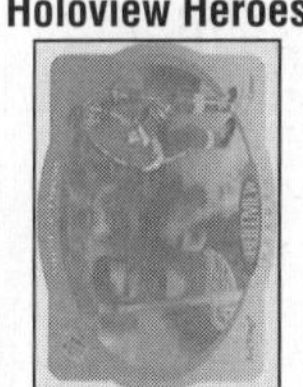

Randomly inserted in packs at a rate of 1:24, this 10-card set also was die-cut with a full-motion hologram.

COMPLETE SET (10)	50.00	100.00
HH1 Ray Bourque	4.00	10.00
HH2 Patrick Roy	12.50	30.00
HH3 Steve Yzerman	12.50	30.00
HH4 Paul Coffey	2.50	6.00
HH5 Mark Messier	2.50	6.00
HH6 Mario Lemieux	12.50	30.00
HH7 Wayne Gretzky	15.00	40.00
HH8 Brett Hull	3.00	8.00
HH9 Doug Gilmour	2.00	5.00
HH10 Grant Fuhr	2.00	5.00

1997-98 SPx

The 1997-98 SPx set was issued in one series totaling 50 cards and was distributed in three-card packs with a suggested retail price of $5.99. The fronts features color action player photos printed on 32-point card stock utilizing decorative foil on the exclusive Light F/X/Holoview cards.

COMPLETE SET (50)	25.00	50.00
1 Paul Kariya	.40	1.00
2 Teemu Selanne	.40	1.00
3 Ray Bourque	.60	1.50
4 Dominik Hasek	.75	2.00
5 Pat LaFontaine	.40	1.00
6 Theo Fleury	.20	.50
7 Jarome Iginla	.50	1.25
8 Tony Amonte	.30	.75
9 Chris Chelios	.40	1.00
10 Patrick Roy	2.00	5.00
11 Peter Forsberg	1.00	2.50
12 Joe Sakic	.75	2.00
13 Mike Modano	.60	1.50
14 Steve Yzerman	2.00	5.00
15 Sergei Fedorov	.60	1.50
16 Brendan Shanahan	.60	1.50
17 Doug Weight	.30	.75
18 Jason Arnott	.20	.50
19 Curtis Joseph	.40	1.00
20 John Vanbiesbrouck	.30	.75
21 Ed Jovanovski	.30	.75
22 Geoff Sanderson	.30	.75
23 Rob Blake	.30	.75
24 Saku Koivu	.40	1.00
25 Doug Gilmour	.30	.75
26 Scott Stevens	.30	.75
27 Martin Brodeur	1.50	4.00
28 Zigmund Palffy	.30	.75
29 Bryan Berard	.30	.75
30 Wayne Gretzky	2.50	6.00
30S Wayne Gretzky SAMPLE	.40	1.00
31 Mike Richter	.40	1.00
32 Mark Messier	.40	1.00
33 Brian Leetch	.40	1.00
34 Daniel Alfredsson	.30	.75
35 Alexei Yashin	.20	.50
36 Eric Lindros	.40	1.00
37 Janne Niinimaa	.30	.75
38 John LeClair	.40	1.00
39 Jeremy Roenick	.50	1.25
40 Keith Tkachuk	.40	1.00
41 Ron Francis	.30	.75
42 Jaromir Jagr	.60	1.50
43 Brett Hull	.50	1.25
44 Owen Nolan	.30	.75
45 Chris Gratton	.30	.75
46 Mats Sundin	.40	1.00
47 Pavel Bure	.40	1.00
48 Adam Oates	.30	.75
49 Joe Juneau	.30	.75
50 Peter Bondra	.30	.75

1997-98 SPx Bronze

Randomly inserted in packs at the rate of 1:3, this 50-card set is parallel to the base set and is similar in design. The difference is found in the bronze foil enhancements of the cards.
*STARS: 1.5X TO 3X BASIC CARDS

1997-98 SPx Gold

Randomly inserted in packs at the rate of 1:17, this 50-card set is parallel to the base set and is similar in design. The difference is found in the gold foil enhancements of the cards.
*STARS: 5X TO 10X BASIC CARDS

1997-98 SPx Silver

Randomly inserted in packs at the rate of 1:6, this 50-card set is parallel to the base set and is similar in design. The difference is found in the silver foil enhancements of the cards.
*STARS: 2X TO 4X BASIC CARDS

1997-98 SPx Steel

Inserted one in every pack, this 50-card set is parallel to the base set and is similar in design. The difference is found in the gray foil enhancements of the cards.
*STARS: 1X TO 2X BASIC CARDS

1997-98 SPx Dimension

Randomly inserted in packs at the rate of 1:54, this 20-card set features color action player photos printed with a rainbow Light F/X and Litho combination.

COMPLETE SET (20)	150.00	300.00
SPX1 Wayne Gretzky	30.00	80.00
SPX2 Jeremy Roenick	8.00	20.00
SPX3 Mark Messier	6.00	15.00
SPX4 Eric Lindros	6.00	15.00
SPX5 Doug Gilmour	4.00	10.00
SPX6 Pavel Bure	6.00	15.00
SPX7 Brendan Shanahan	6.00	15.00
SPX8 Bryan Berard	2.00	5.00
SPX9 Curtis Joseph	6.00	15.00
SPX10 Chris Chelios	4.00	10.00
SPX11 Sergei Fedorov	8.00	20.00
SPX12 Adam Oates	2.00	5.00
SPX13 Zigmund Palffy	4.00	10.00
SPX14 Theo Fleury	2.00	5.00
SPX15 Keith Tkachuk	2.00	5.00
SPX16 Peter Forsberg	15.00	40.00
SPX17 Mats Sundin	6.00	15.00
SPX18 Teemu Selanne	6.00	15.00
SPX19 Paul Kariya	6.00	15.00
SPX20 Brett Hull	8.00	20.00

1997-98 SPx DuoView

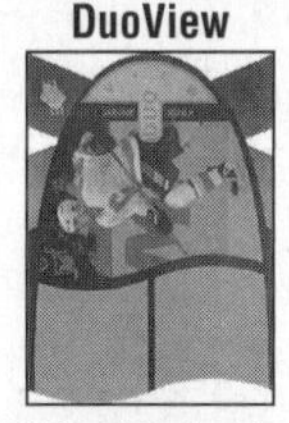

Randomly inserted in packs at the rate of 1:252, this 10-card set features two different holoview images of the player depicted on the card front in a unique silver and gold combination printed on Light F/X holoview cards.

COMPLETE SET (10)	125.00	250.00
1 Wayne Gretzky	30.00	80.00
2 Jaromir Jagr	8.00	20.00
3 Martin Brodeur	20.00	50.00
4 Jarome Iginla	6.00	15.00
5 Steve Yzerman	25.00	60.00
6 Patrick Roy	25.00	60.00
7 Doug Weight	4.00	10.00
8 John Vanbiesbrouck	4.00	10.00
9 Dominik Hasek	10.00	25.00
10 Joe Sakic	10.00	25.00

1997-98 SPx DuoView Autographs

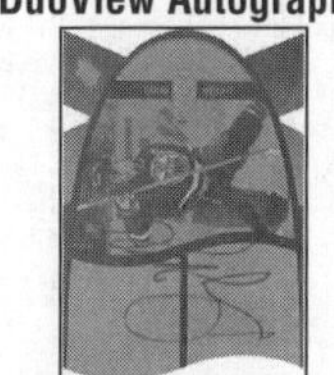

Randomly inserted in packs, this six-card set is a partial parallel version of the DuoView insert set featuring gold foil enhancements and the pictured player's autograph. Only 100 of each card was produced and are sequentially hand numbered.

1 Wayne Gretzky	150.00	300.00
2 Jaromir Jagr	25.00	60.00
3 Martin Brodeur	50.00	125.00
4 Jarome Iginla	15.00	40.00
5 Patrick Roy	75.00	200.00
6 Doug Weight	12.50	30.00

1997-98 SPx Grand Finale

Randomly inserted in packs, this 50-card set is parallel to the base set and is similar in design. The difference is found in the gold foil enhancements and gold Holoview/Hologram on the cards. Only 50 of each card of this set was produced.
*STARS: 60X TO 120X BASIC CARDS

1999-00 SPx

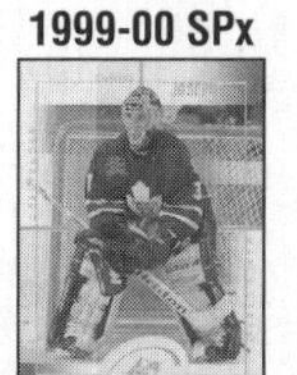

The 1999-00 Upper Deck SPx set was released as a 180-card set consisting of both veteran cards and prospect cards. Card numbers 162-180 are short printed, and the majority of them are autographed. The base card is printed on a rainbow holofoil card stock and enhanced with gold foil. Packaged in 18-pack boxes with three card packs, SPx carried a suggested retail price of $5.99. Each box also contained a 4-card pack of Wayne Gretzky exclusive cards.

COMPLETE SET (180)	125.00	250.00
COMP.SET w/o SP's (162)	40.00	80.00
COMMON SP AU's (163-180)	6.00	15.00
1 Damian Rhodes	.25	.60
2 Nelson Emerson	.10	.30
3 Ray Ferraro	.10	.30
4 Paul Kariya	.30	.75
5 Steve Rucchin	.25	.60
6 Guy Hebert	.25	.60
7 Oleg Tverdovsky	.10	.30
8 Ted Donato	.10	.30
9 Ray Bourque	.50	1.25
10 Sergei Samsonov	.25	.60
11 Joe Thornton	.50	1.25
12 Jason Allison	.10	.30
13 Byron Dafoe	.25	.60
14 Jonathan Girard	.10	.30
15 Dominik Hasek	.60	1.50
16 Alexei Zhitnik	.10	.30
17 Michael Peca	.25	.60
18 Cory Sarich	.25	.60
19 Martin Biron	.25	.60
20 Miroslav Satan	.25	.60
21 Valeri Bure	.10	.30
22 Derek Morris	.10	.30
23 Phil Housley	.25	.60
24 Jarome Iginla	.40	1.00
25 Rico Fata	.10	.30
26 J-S Giguere	.25	.60
27 Marc Savard	.10	.30
28 Arturs Irbe	.25	.60
29 Keith Primeau	.10	.30
30 Sami Kapanen	.10	.30
31 Ron Francis	.10	.30
32 Wendel Clark	.25	.60
33 J-P Dumont	.25	.60
34 Ty Jones	.10	.30
35 Tony Amonte	.25	.60
36 Jocelyn Thibault	.25	.60
37 Doug Gilmour	.25	.60
38 Bryan McCabe	.10	.30
39 Joe Sakic	.60	1.50
40 Peter Forsberg	.75	2.00
41 Alex Tanguay	.25	.60
42 Chris Drury	.25	.60
43 Patrick Roy	1.50	4.00
44 Sandis Ozolinsh	.10	.30
45 Adam Deadmarsh	.10	.30
46 Milan Hejduk	.30	.75
47 Mike Modano	.50	1.25
48 Brett Hull	.40	1.00
49 Darryl Sydor	.25	.60
50 Ed Belfour	.30	.75
51 Jere Lehtinen	.25	.60
52 Jamie Langenbrunner	.10	.30
53 Joe Nieuwendyk	.25	.60
54 Sergei Fedorov	.50	1.25
55 Steve Yzerman	1.50	4.00
56 Brendan Shanahan	.30	.75
57 Chris Osgood	.25	.60
58 Nicklas Lidstrom	.30	.75
59 Igor Larionov	.10	.30
60 Chris Chelios	.30	.75
61 Bill Guerin	.10	.30
62 Doug Weight	.25	.60
63 Mike Grier	.10	.30
64 Tommy Salo	.25	.60
65 Bill Ranford	.25	.60
66 Tom Poti	.10	.30
67 Daniel Cleary	.10	.30
68 Mark Parrish	.10	.30
69 Pavel Bure	.30	.75
70 Oleg Kvasha	.10	.30
71 Viktor Kozlov	.25	.60
72 Trevor Kidd	.25	.60
73 Rob Blake	.25	.60
74 Pavel Rosa	.10	.30
75 Luc Robitaille	.25	.60
76 Zigmund Palffy	.25	.60
77 Aki Berg	.10	.30
78 Saku Koivu	.30	.75
79 Jeff Hackett	.25	.60
80 Trevor Linden	.25	.60
81 Cliff Ronning	.25	.60
82 David Legwand	.25	.60
83 Mike Dunham	.25	.60
84 Scott Stevens	.25	.60
85 Martin Brodeur	.75	2.00
86 Patrik Elias	.25	.60
87 Brendan Morrison	.25	.60
88 Scott Niedermayer	.10	.30
89 Vadim Sharifijanov	.10	.30
90 Mike Watt	.10	.30
91 Felix Potvin	.30	.75
92 Eric Brewer	.10	.30
93 Jorgen Jonsson RC	.25	.60
94 Kenny Jonsson	.10	.30
95 Olli Jokinen	.25	.60
96 Theo Fleury	.10	.30
97 Brian Leetch	.25	.60
98 Mike Richter	.30	.75
99 Petr Nedved	.25	.60
100 Adam Graves	.10	.30
101 Manny Malhotra	.25	.60
102 Alexei Yashin	.25	.60
103 Daniel Alfredsson	.25	.60
104 Ron Tugnutt	.25	.60
105 Magnus Arvedson	.10	.30
106 Sami Salo	.10	.30
107 Marian Hossa	.30	.75
108 Eric Lindros	.30	.75
109 John Vanbiesbrouck	.25	.60
110 John LeClair	.30	.75
111 Rod Brind'Amour	.25	.60
112 Mark Recchi	.25	.60
113 Eric Desjardins	.25	.60
114 Jeremy Roenick	.40	1.00
115 Keith Tkachuk	.30	.75
116 Rick Tocchet	.25	.60
117 Robert Esche RC	1.00	2.50
118 Nikolai Khabibulin	.25	.60
119 Teppo Numminen	.10	.30
120 Jaromir Jagr	.50	1.25
121 Martin Straka	.10	.30
122 Jan Hrdina	.10	.30
123 German Titov	.10	.30
124 Alexei Kovalev	.25	.60
125 Matthew Barnaby	.25	.60
126 Vincent Damphousse	.10	.30
127 Owen Nolan	.25	.60
128 Jeff Friesen	.10	.30
129 Patrick Marleau	.25	.60
130 Marco Sturm	.25	.60
131 Mike Vernon	.25	.60
132 Pavol Demitra	.25	.60
133 Al MacInnis	.25	.60
134 Pierre Turgeon	.25	.60
135 Chris Pronger	.25	.60
136 Jochen Hecht RC	1.00	2.50
137 Vincent Lecavalier	.30	.75
138 Paul Mara	.25	.60
139 Dan Cloutier	.25	.60
140 Andrei Zyuzin	.10	.30
141 Pavel Kubina	.10	.30
142 Kevin Hodson	.25	.60
143 Mats Sundin	.30	.75
144 Curtis Joseph	.30	.75
145 Sergei Berezin	.25	.60
146 Bryan Berard	.10	.30
147 Tomas Kaberle	.10	.30
148 Daniil Markov	.10	.30
149 Mark Messier	.30	.75
150 Bill Muckalt	.25	.60
151 Markus Naslund	.30	.75
152 Mattias Ohlund	.25	.60
153 Ed Jovanovski	.10	.30
154 Steve Kariya RC	1.00	2.50
155 Josh Holden	.10	.30
156 Richard Zednik	.10	.30
157 Jaroslav Svejkovsky	.10	.30
158 Adam Oates	.25	.60
159 Peter Bondra	.25	.60
160 Sergei Gonchar	.10	.30
161 Olaf Kolzig	.25	.60
162 Jan Bulis	.10	.30
163 Patrik Stefan RC	8.00	20.00
164 Daniel Sedin AU	6.00	15.00
165 Henrik Sedin AU	6.00	15.00
166 Pavel Brendl AU RC	10.00	25.00
167 Brian Finley AU	6.00	15.00
168 Taylor Pyatt AU	8.00	20.00
169 Jamie Lundmark AU	6.00	15.00
170 Denis Shvidki	2.50	6.00
171 Jani Rita	2.50	6.00
172 Oleg Saprykin RC	6.00	15.00
173 Nick Boynton	2.50	6.00
174 Tim Connolly AU	6.00	15.00
175 Kris Beech AU	6.00	15.00
176 Roberto Luongo	4.00	10.00
177 David Legwand	3.00	8.00
178 Dave Tanabe	2.50	6.00
179 Barret Jackman	2.50	6.00
180 Maxime Ouellet	4.00	10.00

1999-00 SPx Radiance

Randomly inserted in packs, this 135-card set parallels the base SPx set. Cards are enhanced with green foil, and each card is serial numbered out of 100.
*STARS: 20X TO 50X BASIC CARDS
*SP's: 1X TO 3X BASIC CARDS
*SP AU's: 1X TO 1.25X BASIC CARDS

166 Pavel Brendl	40.00	100.00

1999-00 SPx Spectrum

Randomly inserted in packs, this 135-card set parallels the base SPx set. Cards are enhanced with red foil, and each is numbered one of one.
NOT PRICED DUE TO SCARCITY

1999-00 SPx 99 Cheers

Randomly inserted in packs at 1:17, this 15-card set pays tribute to Wayne Gretzky by capturing some of his most magical moments. Card backs carry a "CH" prefix.

COMPLETE SET (15)	30.00	60.00
COMMON GRETZKY (CH1-15)	2.50	6.00

1999-00 SPx Highlight Heroes

Randomly seeded in packs at 1:9, this 10-card set focuses on 10 of the NHL's top superstars. Action photos are set against a rainbow holo-foil checkered background. Card backs carry an "HH" prefix.

COMPLETE SET (10)	15.00	30.00
HH1 Wayne Gretzky	4.00	10.00
HH2 Sergei Samsonov	.60	1.50
HH3 Dominik Hasek	1.25	3.00
HH4 Jaromir Jagr	1.00	2.50
HH5 Patrick Roy	3.00	8.00
HH6 Paul Kariya	1.00	2.50
HH7 Pavel Bure	.75	2.00
HH8 Peter Forsberg	1.50	4.00
HH9 Eric Lindros	1.50	4.00
HH10 Teemu Selanne	1.00	2.50

1999-00 SPx Prolifics

Randomly seeded in packs at 1:17, this 15-card set highlights the 15 most collectible defensive players in the NHL. Card backs carry a "P" prefix.

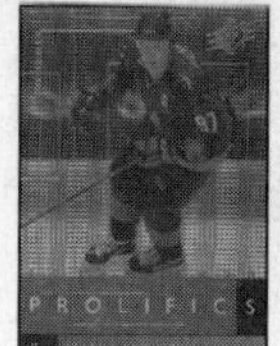

COMPLETE SET (15)	25.00	50.00
P1 Paul Kariya	1.00	2.50
P2 Jaromir Jagr	1.50	4.00
P3 Brett Hull	1.25	3.00
P4 Joe Sakic	2.00	5.00
P5 Sergei Samsonov	.75	2.00
P6 Keith Tkachuk	1.00	2.50
P7 Brendan Shanahan	1.50	4.00
P8 Vincent Lecavalier	1.00	2.50
P9 Steve Yzerman	5.00	12.00
P10 Jeremy Roenick	1.25	3.00
P11 Mike Modano	1.50	4.00
P12 John LeClair	1.25	3.00
P13 Peter Forsberg	2.50	6.00
P14 Ray Bourque	1.50	4.00
P15 David Legwand	.75	2.00

1999-00 SPx SPXcitement

Randomly seeded in packs at 1:3, this 20-card set features the most exciting NHL players on a holographic Light F/X background. Card backs carry an "X" prefix.

COMPLETE SET (20)	20.00	40.00
X1 Wayne Gretzky	3.00	8.00
X2 Patrick Roy	2.50	6.00
X3 Pavel Bure	.60	1.50
X4 Steve Yzerman	2.50	6.00
X5 David Legwand	.40	1.00
X6 Dominik Hasek	1.00	2.50
X7 Sergei Samsonov	.40	1.00
X8 Patrik Stefan	1.00	2.50
X9 Eric Lindros	.75	2.00
X10 Brett Hull	.60	1.50
X11 Steve Kariya	.50	1.25
X12 Keith Tkachuk	.50	1.25
X13 Alex Tanguay	.40	1.00
X14 Peter Forsberg	1.25	3.00
X15 Jaromir Jagr	.75	2.00
X16 Paul Kariya	.50	1.25
X17 Brendan Shanahan	.75	2.00
X18 Mike Modano	.75	2.00
X19 John LeClair	.60	1.50
X20 Teemu Selanne	.50	1.25

1999-00 SPx SPXtreme

Randomly inserted in packs at 1:6, this 20-card set showcases some of the most popular players in the NHL. Action shots are set against a holographic Light F/X background. Card backs carry an "XT" prefix.

COMPLETE SET (20)	20.00	40.00
XT1 Al MacInnis	.50	1.25
XT2 Keith Tkachuk	.60	1.50
XT3 Peter Forsberg	1.50	4.00
XT4 Teemu Selanne	.60	1.50
XT5 Patrick Roy	3.00	8.00
XT6 Sergei Samsonov	.50	1.25
XT7 Brendan Shanahan	1.00	2.50
XT8 Mike Modano	1.00	2.50
XT9 Eric Lindros	1.00	2.50
XT10 Paul Kariya	.60	1.50
XT11 Jaromir Jagr	1.00	2.50
XT12 Brett Hull	.75	2.00
XT13 Mats Sundin	.60	1.50
XT14 Dominik Hasek	1.25	3.00
XT15 Ray Bourque	1.00	2.50
XT16 Curtis Joseph	.60	1.50
XT17 John LeClair	.75	2.00
XT18 Ed Belfour	.60	1.50
XT19 David Legwand	.50	1.25
XT20 Wayne Gretzky	4.00	10.00

1999-00 SPx Starscape

Randomly inserted in packs at 1:9, this 10-card set places NHL's hottest in action over a holographic foil backdrop. Card backs carry an "S" prefix.

COMPLETE SET (10) 12.00 25.00
S1 Brett Hull .75 2.00
S2 Jaromir Jagr 1.00 2.50
S3 Pavel Bure .75 2.00
S4 Dominik Hasek 1.25 3.00
S5 Eric Lindros 1.00 2.50
S6 Paul Kariya .60 1.50
S7 Peter Forsberg 1.50 4.00
S8 Teemu Selanne .60 1.50
S9 Patrick Roy 3.00 8.00
S10 Keith Tkachuk .60 1.50

1999-00 SPx Winning Materials

Randomly inserted in packs at 1:252, this 12-card set features players with a swatch of a game-used jersey and puck. Also released with the set were autographed versions of Brett Hull and Wayne Gretzky.

WM1 Mike Modano 15.00 40.00
WM2 Martin Brodeur 25.00 60.00
WM3 Steve Yzerman 25.00 60.00
WM4 Jaromir Jagr 20.00 50.00
WM5 Dominik Hasek 25.00 60.00
WM6 Brett Hull 15.00 40.00
WM7 Patrick Roy 25.00 60.00
WM8 Ray Bourque 20.00 50.00
WM9 Eric Lindros 10.00 25.00
WM10 Wayne Gretzky 50.00 125.00
WM-A1 W.Gretzky AU/25 500.00 800.00
WM-A2 B.Hull AU/25 125.00 300.00

2000-01 SPx

SPx originally issued the set of 130 cards with 30 short-printed rookies, and 10 short-printed jersey cards. SPx later released an update set of 57 cards, which included 35 short-printed rookies. The card front design used silver-foil and added rainbow-holofoil for the SPx logo. The jersey cards were available in packs of 2000-01 SPx at a rate of 1:13.

COMPLETE SET (130) 250.00 500.00
COMP.SET w/o SP's (90) 20.00 40.00
1 Paul Kariya .30 .75
2 Teemu Selanne .30 .75
3 Patrik Stefan .10 .30
4 Jason Allison .10 .30
5 Sergei Samsonov .25 .60
6 Dominik Hasek .60 1.50
7 Miroslav Satan .25 .60
8 Fred Brathwaite .25 .60
9 Valeri Bure .10 .30
10 Ron Francis .25 .60
11 Arturs Irbe .25 .60
12 Tony Amonte .25 .60
13 Joe Sakic .60 1.50
14 Milan Hejduk .30 .75
15 Patrick Roy 1.50 4.00
16 Peter Forsberg .75 2.00
17 Ray Bourque .60 1.50
18 Ron Tugnutt .25 .60
19 Brett Hull .40 1.00
20 Ed Belfour .30 .75
21 Mike Modano .50 1.25
22 Sergei Fedorov .50 1.25
23 Brendan Shanahan .30 .75
24 Chris Osgood .25 .60
25 Steve Yzerman 1.50 4.00
26 Doug Weight .25 .60
27 Tommy Salo .25 .60
28 Pavel Bure .30 .75
29 Trevor Kidd .25 .60
30 Viktor Kozlov .25 .60
31 Rob Blake .25 .60
32 Zigmund Palffy .25 .60
33 Luc Robitaille .25 .60
34 Manny Fernandez .25 .60
35 Saku Koivu .30 .75
36 David Legwand .25 .60
37 Martin Brodeur .75 2.00
38 Patrik Elias .25 .60
39 Scott Gomez .10 .30
40 Scott Stevens .25 .60
41 Mariusz Czerkawski .25 .60
42 Tim Connolly .10 .30
43 Mark Messier .30 .75
44 Mike York .10 .30
45 Theo Fleury .10 .30
46 Marian Hossa .30 .75
47 Radek Bonk .10 .30
48 Simon Gagne .30 .75
49 Brian Boucher .30 .75
50 Rick Tocchet .25 .60
51 John LeClair .30 .75
52 Jeremy Roenick .40 1.00
53 Keith Tkachuk .30 .75
54 Jaromir Jagr .50 1.25
55 Jean-Sebastien Aubin .25 .60
56 Jeff Friesen .10 .30
57 Steve Shields .25 .60
58 Brad Stuart .25 .60
59 Chris Pronger .25 .60
60 Pavol Demitra .25 .60
61 Roman Turek .25 .60
62 Dan Cloutier .25 .60
63 Vincent Lecavalier .30 .75
64 Nikolai Antropov .10 .30
65 Curtis Joseph .30 .75
66 Mats Sundin .30 .75
67 Felix Potvin .30 .75
68 Markus Naslund .30 .75
69 Adam Oates .25 .60
70 Olaf Kolzig .25 .60
71 Peter Forsberg XE 1.00 2.50
72 Brendan Shanahan XE .60 1.50
73 Scott Stevens XE .30 .75
74 Mark Messier XE .50 1.25
75 John LeClair XE .50 1.25
76 Keith Primeau XE .40 1.00
77 Keith Tkachuk XE .40 1.00
78 Jeremy Roenick XE .50 1.25
79 Owen Nolan XE .40 1.00
80 Chris Pronger XE .40 1.00
81 Paul Kariya PRO .30 .75
82 Dominik Hasek PRO .75 2.00
83 Patrick Roy PRO 2.00 5.00
84 Ray Bourque PRO .75 2.00
85 Mike Modano PRO .60 1.50
86 Steve Yzerman PRO 2.00 5.00
87 Pavel Bure PRO .50 1.25
88 Martin Brodeur PRO 1.00 2.50
89 John LeClair PRO .50 1.25
90 Jaromir Jagr PRO .60 1.50
91 Herbert Vasiljevs RC 2.00 5.00
92 Eric Nickulas RC 2.00 5.00
93 Brandon Smith RC 2.00 5.00
94 Jeff Cowan RC 2.00 5.00
95 Serge Aubin RC 2.00 5.00
96 Mike Minard RC 2.00 5.00
97 Steven Reinprecht RC 2.00 5.00
98 David Gosselin RC 2.00 5.00
99 Colin White RC 2.00 5.00
100 Willie Mitchell RC 2.00 5.00
101 Steve Brule RC 2.00 5.00
102 Steve Valiquette RC 2.00 5.00
103 Petr Mika RC 2.00 5.00
104 Chris Kenady RC 2.00 5.00
105 Johan Witehall RC 2.00 5.00
106 Jani Hurme RC 2.50 6.00
107 Jean-Guy Trudel RC 2.00 5.00
108 Dale Rominski RC 2.00 5.00
109 Greg Andrusak RC 2.00 5.00
110 Martin Havlat RC 10.00 25.00
111 Jeremy Stevenson RC 2.00 5.00
112 Sergei Vyshedkevich RC 2.00 5.00
113 Johnathan Aitken RC 2.00 5.00
114 Keith Aldridge RC 2.00 5.00
115 Rich Parent RC 2.00 5.00
116 Kaspars Astashenko RC 2.00 5.00
117 Matt Elich RC 2.00 5.00
118 Dieter Kochan RC 2.00 5.00
119 Kyle Freadrich RC 2.00 5.00
120 Justin Williams RC 4.00 10.00
121 Andrew Raycroft RC 6.00 15.00
122 Zdenek Blatny RC 3.00 8.00
123 Pavel Brendl 3.00 8.00
124 Jason Jaspers RC 3.00 8.00
125 Fedor Fedorov RC 3.00 8.00
126 Jordan Krestanovich RC 3.00 8.00
127 Marc-Andre Thinel RC 3.00 8.00
128 Damian Surma RC 3.00 8.00
129 Jeff Bateman RC 3.00 8.00
130 Sheldon Keefe 3.00 8.00
131 Ray Ferraro .10 .30
132 Bill Guerin .25 .60
133 Ronald Petrovicky RC .75 2.00
134 Shane Willis .10 .30
135 Chris Nielsen RC .75 2.00
136 Petteri Nummelin RC .75 2.00
137 Igor Larionov .10 .30
138 Shawn Horcoff RC 3.00 8.00
139 Lance Ward RC .75 2.00
140 Manny Fernandez .25 .60
141 Scott Niedermayer .10 .30
142 Alexei Yashin .10 .30
143 Claude Lemieux .10 .30
144 Mario Lemieux 2.00 5.00
145 Milan Kraft .10 .30
146 Evgeni Nabokov .25 .60
147 Keith Tkachuk .30 .75
148 Gary Roberts .10 .30
149 Daniel Sedin .10 .30
150 Henrik Sedin .10 .30
151 Kris Beech .10 .30
152 Lee Goren RC 2.00 5.00
153 Pavel Kolarik RC 2.00 5.00
154 Greg Kuznik RC 2.00 5.00
155 Josef Vasicek RC 2.00 5.00
156 Rick Berry RC 2.00 5.00
157 David Aebischer RC 6.00 15.00
158 Rostislav Klesla RC 3.00 8.00
159 Marty Turco RC 10.00 25.00
160 Tyler Bouck RC 2.00 5.00
161 Mike Comrie RC 3.00 8.00
162 Eric Belanger RC 2.00 5.00
163 Marian Gaborik RC 15.00 40.00
164 Scott Hartnell RC 3.00 8.00
165 Jason Labarbera RC 3.00 8.00
166 Rick DiPietro RC 8.00 20.00
167 Ruslan Fedotenko RC 2.00 5.00
168 Petr Hubacek RC 2.00 5.00
169 Roman Cechmanek RC 2.50 6.00
170 Roman Simicek RC 2.00 5.00
171 Mark Smith RC 2.00 5.00
172 Jakub Cutta RC 2.00 5.00
173 Marc Chouinard RC 2.00 5.00
174 Darcy Hordichuk RC 2.00 5.00
175 Bryan Adams RC 2.00 5.00
176 Jarno Kultanen RC 2.00 5.00
177 Eric Boulton RC 2.00 5.00
178 Brian Swanson RC 2.00 5.00
179 Lubomir Sekeras RC 2.00 5.00
180 Eric Landry RC 2.00 5.00
181 Mike Commodore RC 2.00 5.00
182 Johan Holmqvist RC 2.00 5.00
183 Jeff Ulmer RC 2.00 5.00
184 Ossi Vaananen RC 2.00 5.00
185 Alexander Khavanov RC 2.00 5.00
186 Bryce Salvador RC 2.00 5.00
187 Reed Low RC 2.00 5.00

2000-01 SPx Spectrum

Randomly inserted in packs, this 130-card set parallels the base SPx set enhanced and sequentially numbered to 50.

*STARS: 25X TO 60X BASIC CARDS
*SP's: 1X TO 1.5X BASIC CARDS
*JERSEYS: 1X TO 1.5X BASIC CARDS

2000-01 SPx Highlight Heroes

Randomly inserted in packs at the rate of 1:7, this 14-card set features full color action photography with the words highlight heroes appearing as part of the background. Along the bottom of the card, the player's name and the words Highlight Heroes appear in silver foil.

COMPLETE SET (14) 10.00 20.00
HH1 Paul Kariya .60 1.50
HH2 Patrik Stefan .50 1.25
HH3 Joe Thornton 1.00 2.50
HH4 Valeri Bure .50 1.25
HH5 Milan Hejduk .60 1.50
HH6 Brett Hull .75 2.00
HH7 Brendan Shanahan 1.00 2.50
HH8 Pavel Bure .75 2.00
HH9 Marian Hossa .60 1.50
HH10 Brian Boucher .60 1.50
HH11 Jeremy Roenick .75 2.00
HH12 Jaromir Jagr 1.00 2.50
HH13 Chris Pronger .50 1.25
HH14 Curtis Joseph .60 1.50

2000-01 SPx Prolifics

Randomly inserted in packs at the rate of 1:14, this seven card set features an action photograph on the left side of the card front and a portrait style photo on the right. These two photos are separated by a silver foil line and the word Prolifics.

COMPLETE SET (7) 8.00 15.00
P1 Dominik Hasek 1.25 3.00
P2 Ray Bourque 1.25 3.00
P3 Brett Hull .75 2.00
P4 Steve Yzerman 3.00 8.00
P5 Mark Messier .75 2.00
P6 John LeClair .75 2.00
P7 Jaromir Jagr 1.00 2.50

2000-01 SPx Rookie Redemption

Randomly inserted in packs, this 30-card set was issued as team specific redemption cards that were redeemable for rookies who made their NHL debut in the 2001-02 season. Exchange cards expired 5/2002.

RR1 Ilja Bryzgalov 3.00 8.00
RR2 Ilya Kovalchuk 12.50 30.00
RR3 Ivan Huml 2.00 5.00
RR4 Ales Kotalik 3.00 8.00
RR5 Scott Nichol 2.00 5.00
RR6 Erik Cole 3.00 8.00
RR7 Casey Hankinson 2.00 5.00
RR8 Vaclav Nedorost 2.00 5.00
RR9 Martin Spanhel 2.00 52.00
RR10 Niko Kapanen 2.00 5.00
RR11 Pavel Datsyuk 8.00 20.00
RR12 Ty Conklin 3.00 8.00
RR13 Kristian Huselius 3.00 8.00
RR14 Jaroslav Bednar 2.00 5.00
RR15 Nick Schultz 2.00 5.00
RR16 Martti Jarventie 2.00 5.00
RR17 Martin Erat 3.00 8.00
RR18 Andreas Salomonsson 2.00 5.00
RR19 Raffi Torres 3.00 8.00
RR20 Dan Blackburn 3.00 8.00
RR21 Ivan Ciernik 2.00 5.00
RR22 Jiri Dopita 2.00 5.00
RR23 Krys Kolanos 2.00 5.00
RR24 Billy Tibbetts 2.00 5.00
RR25 Jeff Jillson 2.00 5.00
RR26 Mark Rycroft 2.00 5.00
RR27 Nikita Alexeev 2.00 5.00
RR28 Bob Wren 2.00 5.00
RR29 Pat Kavanagh 2.00 5.00
RR30 Brian Sutherby 3.00 8.00

2000-01 SPx SPXcitement

COMPLETE SET (14) 10.00 20.00
STATED ODDS 1:7
X1 Teemu Selanne .60 1.50
X2 Sergei Samsonov .50 1.25
X3 Tony Amonte .50 1.25
X4 Joe Sakic 1.25 3.00
X5 Mike Modano 1.00 2.50
X6 Sergei Fedorov 1.25 3.00
X7 Pavel Bure .75 2.00
X8 Martin Brodeur 1.50 4.00
X9 Simon Gagne .50 1.25
X10 Jaromir Jagr 1.00 2.50
X11 Jeff Friesen .50 1.25
X12 Roman Turek .50 1.25
X13 Vincent Lecavalier .60 1.50
X14 Mats Sundin .60 1.50

2000-01 SPx SPXtreme

COMPLETE SET (7) 8.00 15.00
STATED ODDS 1:14
S1 Paul Kariya .75 2.00
S2 Peter Forsberg 1.50 4.00
S3 Mike Modano 1.00 2.50
S4 Martin Brodeur 1.50 4.00
S5 Mark Messier .75 2.00
S6 John LeClair .75 2.00
S7 Jaromir Jagr 1.00 2.50

2000-01 SPx Winning Materials

Randomly seeded in SPx packs at the rate of 1:14 and UD Update packs at 1:60, this 48-card set features a player action photo and a swatch of a game worn jersey as well as a game used stick. Update cards are marked below.

*MULT.COLOR SWATCH/STICK: 1X TO 2X
AC Anson Carter SP 15.00 40.00
BH Brett Hull SP 12.50 30.00
BS Brendan Shanahan 6.00 15.00
CJ Curtis Joseph 8.00 20.00
CO Chris Osgood 5.00 12.00
DH Dominik Hasek 10.00 25.00
FP Felix Potvin 6.00 15.00
JJ Jaromir Jagr 8.00 20.00
JL John LeClair 6.00 15.00
JR Jeremy Roenick 8.00 20.00
JS Joe Sakic 12.50 30.00
KJ Kenny Jonsson 4.00 10.00
KT Keith Tkachuk 6.00 15.00
MB Martin Brodeur SP 20.00 50.00
ML Mario Lemieux 20.00 50.00
MM Mike Modano SP 20.00 50.00
NL Nicklas Lidstrom 6.00 15.00
PD Pavol Demitra SP 5.00 12.00
PF Peter Forsberg 12.50 30.00
PK Paul Kariya SP 12.50 30.00
PR Patrick Roy 15.00 40.00
RB Ray Bourque 12.50 30.00
SF Sergei Fedorov 8.00 20.00
SY Steve Yzerman 20.00 50.00
TO Tony Amonte 5.00 12.00
TS Teemu Selanne 6.00 15.00
WG Wayne Gretzky 40.00 80.00
PBO Peter Bondra SP 8.00 20.00
WBC Brian Boucher Upd 5.00 12.00
WBE Ed Belfour Upd 6.00 15.00
WBI Martin Biron Upd 5.00 12.00
WBO Ray Bourque Upd 15.00 40.00
WBU Valeri Bure Upd 4.00 10.00
WFE Sergei Fedorov Upd 10.00 25.00
WGR Wayne Gretzky Upd 40.00 80.00
WJJ Jaromir Jagr Upd 8.00 20.00
WKA Paul Kariya Upd 6.00 15.00
WLE John LeClair Upd 6.00 15.00
WLU Roberto Luongo Upd 8.00 20.00
WRE Jeremy Roenick Upd 8.00 20.00
WRO Patrick Roy Upd 20.00 50.00
WSA Miroslav Satan Upd 5.00 12.00
WSE Teemu Selanne Upd 6.00 15.00
WSU Mats Sundin Upd 6.00 15.00
WTB Jocelyn Thibault Upd 5.00 12.00
WTH Joe Thornton Upd 12.50 30.00
WTK Keith Tkachuk Upd 6.00 15.00
WYZ Steve Yzerman Upd 20.00 50.00

2000-01 SPx Winning Materials Autographs

Randomly inserted in packs, this 10-card set parallels the SPx Winning Materials set but adds an authentic player autograph. These cards were limited to 25 serial-numbered sets and are not priced due to scarcity and volatility.

NOT PRICED DUE TO SCARCITY
SBH Brett Hull
SCJ Curtis Joseph
SFP Felix Potvin
SJL John LeClair
SKT Keith Tkachuk
SMB Martin Brodeur
SML Mario Lemieux
SRB Ray Bourque
SSY Steve Yzerman
SWG Wayne Gretzky

2001-02 SPx

Released in mid-December 2001, this set originally consisted of 170 cards including 70 base cards, 42 rookie cards (91-132) short printed to 999, and 38 rookie threads cards (133-151) short printed to either 800 or 1500. The rookie threads subset had two versions, home and away, for each player. Cards 197-216 were available in random packs of UD Rookie Update and were serial-numbered to 999.

COMP.SET w/o SP's (155) 40.00 80.00
1 Paul Kariya .30 .75
2 Patrik Stefan .10 .30
3 Sergei Samsonov .25 .60
4 Joe Thornton .50 1.25
5 Bill Guerin .25 .60
6 Martin Biron .25 .60
7 Miroslav Satan .25 .60
8 Jarome Iginla .40 1.00
9 Marc Savard .10 .30
10 Arturs Irbe .25 .60
11 Tony Amonte .25 .60
12 Steve Sullivan .10 .30
13 Joe Sakic .60 1.50
14 Peter Forsberg .75 2.00
15 Ray Bourque .60 1.50
16 Milan Hejduk .30 .75
17 Patrick Roy 1.50 4.00
18 Ron Tugnutt .25 .60
19 Mike Modano .50 1.25
20 Ed Belfour .30 .75
21 Pierre Turgeon .25 .60
22 Steve Yzerman 1.50 4.00
23 Brendan Shanahan .30 .75
24 Sergei Fedorov .50 1.25
25 Luc Robitaille .25 .60
26 Dominik Hasek .60 1.50
27 Tommy Salo .25 .60
28 Mike Comrie .25 .60
29 Pavel Bure .30 .75
30 Zigmund Palffy .25 .60
31 Felix Potvin .30 .75
32 Adam Deadmarsh .10 .30
33 Marian Gaborik .60 1.50
34 Saku Koivu .30 .75
35 David Legwand .25 .60
36 Mike Dunham .25 .60
37 Martin Brodeur .75 2.00
38 Patrik Elias .25 .60
39 Jason Arnott .10 .30
40 Michael Peca .10 .30
41 Rick DiPietro .25 .60
42 Mark Messier .30 .75
43 Theo Fleury .10 .30
44 Marian Hossa .30 .75
45 Radek Bonk .10 .30
46 Jeremy Roenick .40 1.00
47 Roman Cechmanek .25 .60
48 Keith Primeau .10 .30
49 John LeClair .40 1.00
50 Sean Burke .25 .60
51 Alexei Kovalev .25 .60
52 Mario Lemieux 2.00 5.00
53 Johan Hedberg .25 .60
54 Robert Lang .10 .30
55 Evgeni Nabokov .25 .60
56 Teemu Selanne .30 .75
57 Owen Nolan .25 .60
58 Chris Pronger .25 .60
59 Keith Tkachuk .30 .75
60 Doug Weight .25 .60
61 Pavol Demitra .25 .60
62 Brad Richards .25 .60
63 Vincent Lecavalier .30 .75
64 Curtis Joseph .30 .75
65 Mats Sundin .30 .75
66 Markus Naslund .30 .75
67 Daniel Sedin .10 .30
68 Jaromir Jagr .50 1.25
69 Peter Bondra .30 .75
70 Olaf Kolzig .25 .60
71 Paul Kariya .30 .75
72 Peter Forsberg 1.00 2.50
73 Mike Modano .60 1.50
74 Sergei Fedorov .75 2.00
75 Steve Yzerman 2.00 5.00
76 Pavel Bure .50 1.25
77 Zigmund Palffy .25 .60
78 Mario Lemieux 2.50 6.00
79 Vincent Lecavalier .30 .75
80 Markus Naslund .30 .75
81 Joe Sakic .75 2.00
82 Chris Drury .25 .60
83 Patrick Roy 2.00 5.00
84 Mike Modano .60 1.50
85 Steve Yzerman 2.00 5.00
86 Pavel Bure .50 1.25
87 Martin Brodeur 1.00 2.50
88 John LeClair .40 1.00
89 Mario Lemieux 2.50 6.00
90 Chris Pronger .25 .60
91 Timo Parssinen RC 2.50 6.00
92 Ilja Bryzgalov RC 4.00 10.00
93 Kevin Sawyer RC 2.50 6.00
94 Dany Heatley SP 8.00 20.00
95 Zdenek Kutlak RC 2.50 6.00
96 Greg Crozier RC 2.50 6.00
97 Mika Noronen SP 4.00 10.00
98 Scott Nichol RC 2.50 6.00
99 Erik Cole RC 8.00 20.00
100 Casey Hankinson RC 2.50 6.00
101 Vaclav Nedorost RC 2.50 6.00
102 Jaroslav Obsut RC 2.50 6.00
103 Niko Kapanen RC 4.00 10.00
104 Pavel Datsyuk RC 12.00 30.00
105 Niklas Hagman RC 2.50 6.00
106 Kristian Huselius RC 8.00 20.00
107 Andrej Podkonicky RC 2.50 6.00
108 Francis Belanger RC 2.50 6.00
109 Martin Erat RC 2.50 6.00
110 Bill Bowler RC 2.50 6.00
111 Scott Clemmensen RC 2.50 6.00
112 Josef Boumedienne RC 2.50 6.00
113 Andreas Salomonsson RC 2.50 6.00
114 Mike Jefferson RC 2.50 6.00
115 Stanislav Gron RC 2.50 6.00
116 Radek Martinek RC 2.50 6.00
117 Dan Blackburn RC 4.00 10.00
118 Chris Neil RC 2.50 6.00
119 Ivan Ciernik RC 2.50 6.00
120 Pavel Brendl SP 2.50 6.00
121 David Cullen RC 2.50 6.00
122 Billy Tibbetts RC 2.50 6.00
123 Miikka Kiprusoff SP 6.00 15.00
124 Jeff Jillson RC 2.50 6.00
125 Michel Larocque RC 2.50 6.00
126 Mark Rycroft RC 2.50 6.00
127 Thomas Ziegler RC 2.50 6.00
128 Nikita Alexeev RC 2.50 6.00
129 Bob Wren RC 2.50 6.00
130 Mike Brown SP 2.50 6.00
131 Pat Kavanagh RC 2.50 6.00
132 Brian Sutherby RC 2.50 6.00
133 Brian Pothier AW RC/800 4.00 10.00
133 Brian Pothier HM RC/800 4.00 10.00
134 Dan Snyder HM RC/1500 4.00 10.00
134 Dan Snyder AW RC/1500 4.00 10.00
135 Jody Shelley AW RC/1500 4.00 10.00
135 Jody Shelley HM RC/1500 4.00 10.00
136 Martin Spanhel HM RC/1500 4.00 10.00
136 Martin Spanhel AW RC/1500 4.00 10.00
137 Mathieu Darche AW RC/1500 4.00 10.00
137 Mathieu Darche HM RC/1500 4.00 10.00
138 Matt Davidson HM RC/1500 4.00 10.00
138 Matt Davidson AW RC/1500 4.00 10.00
139 Sean Selmser AW RC/1500 4.00 10.00
139 Sean Selmser HM RC/1500 4.00 10.00
140 Jason Chimera AW RC/800 4.00 10.00
140 Jason Chimera HM RC/800 4.00 10.00
141 Mike Matteucci HM RC/1500 4.00 10.00
141 Mike Matteucci AW RC/1500 4.00 10.00
142 Pascal Dupuis AW RC/800 4.00 10.00
142 Pascal Dupuis HM RC/800 4.00 10.00
143 Peter Smrek HM RC/800 4.00 10.00
143 Peter Smrek AW RC/800 4.00 10.00
144 M.Samuelsson AW RC/1500 4.00 10.00
144 M.Samuelsson HM RC/1500 4.00 10.00
145 J.Kwiatkowski HM RC/1500 4.00 10.00
145 J.Kwiatkowski AW RC/1500 4.00 10.00
146 Kirby Law HM RC/1500 4.00 10.00
146 Kirby Law AW RC/1500 4.00 10.00
147 Tomas Divisek HM RC/1500 4.00 10.00
147 Tomas Divisek AW RC/1500 4.00 10.00
148 Ilya Kovalchuk RC 20.00 50.00
148 Ilya Kovalchuk AW RC 20.00 50.00
149 Jaroslav Bednar HM RC/800 4.00 10.00
149 Jaroslav Bednar AW RC/800 4.00 10.00
150 Jiri Dopita AW RC/800 4.00 10.00
150 Jiri Dopita HM RC/800 4.00 10.00
151 Krys Kolanos HM RC/800 4.00 10.00
151 Krys Kolanos AW RC/800 4.00 10.00
152 Jeff Friesen .10 .30
153 J-S Giguere .25 .60
154 Dany Heatley .40 1.00
155 Pascal Rheaume .10 .30
156 Andy Hilbert .10 .30
157 Jozef Stumpel .10 .30
158 Glen Murray .10 .30
159 Maxim Afinogenov .10 .30
160 Roman Turek .25 .60
161 Craig Conroy .10 .30
162 Jeff O'Neill .10 .30
163 Sami Kapanen .10 .30
164 Jocelyn Thibault .25 .60
165 Mark Bell .10 .30
166 Kyle Calder .10 .30
167 Alex Tanguay .25 .60
168 Darius Kasparaitis .10 .30
169 Chris Drury .25 .60
170 Radim Vrbata .10 .30
171 Rostislav Klesla .10 .30
172 Brett Hull .40 1.00
173 Jani Rita .10 .30
174 Mike York .10 .30
175 Roberto Luongo .40 1.00
176 Jason Allison .10 .30
177 Andrew Brunette .10 .30
178 Sergei Berezin .25 .60
179 Donald Audette .10 .30
180 Brian Gionta .10 .30
181 Alexei Yashin .10 .30
182 Chris Osgood .25 .60
183 Pavel Bure .30 .75
184 Tom Poti .10 .30
185 Eric Lindros .30 .75
186 Patrick Lalime .25 .60
187 Martin Havlat .25 .60
188 Brian Boucher .25 .60
189 Simon Gagne .30 .75
190 Brian Savage .10 .30
191 Brent Johnson .25 .60
192 Gordie Dwyer .10 .30
193 Nikolai Khabibulin .30 .75
194 Alexander Mogilny .25 .60
195 Brendan Morrison .25 .60
196 Trevor Linden .10 .30
197 Pasi Nurminen RC 2.50 6.00
198 Ivan Huml RC 2.50 6.00
199 Ales Kotalik RC 4.00 10.00
200 Mike Peluso RC 2.50 6.00
201 Riku Hahl RC 2.50 6.00
202 Kelly Fairchild RC 2.50 6.00
203 Blake Bellefeuille RC 2.50 6.00
204 Sean Avery RC 4.00 10.00
205 Brad Norton RC 2.50 6.00
206 Marcel Hossa RC 4.00 10.00
207 Olivier Michaud RC 2.50 6.00
208 Robert Schnabel RC 2.50 6.00
209 Christian Berglund RC 2.50 6.00
210 Raffi Torres RC 4.00 10.00
211 Toni Dahlman RC 2.50 6.00
212 Branko Radivojevic RC 4.00 10.00
213 Shane Endicott RC 2.50 6.00
214 Tom Kostopoulos RC 2.50 6.00
215 Sebastien Centomo RC 2.50 6.00
216 Karel Pilar RC 2.50 6.00
NNO Steve Yzerman SAMPLE 2.00 5.00

2001-02 SPx Hidden Treasures

Available in random packs of UD Rookie Update, this 22-card set featured swatches of game-used jerseys from two or three different NHL players. Dual jerseys were inserted at a rate of 1:45 while triple jerseys were inserted at 1:90.

DTAD Maxim Afinogenov / J-P Dumont 8.00 20.00
DTBJ Peter Bondra / Jaromir Jagr 10.00 25.00
DTBN Rob Blake / Ville Nieminen 8.00 20.00
DTFC Ruslan Fedotenko / Tim Connolly 8.00 20.00
DTGW Simon Gagne / Justin Williams 8.00 20.00
DTHB Milan Hejduk / Rob Blake 8.00 20.00
DTJD Jason Allison / Adam Deadmarsh 8.00 20.00
DTPS Zigmund Palffy / Miroslav Satan 8.00 20.00
DTSF Mats Sundin / Peter Forsberg 10.00 25.00
DTSG Steve Sullivan / Simon Gagne 8.00 20.00
DTTD Tony Amonte / Chris Drury 8.00 20.00
DTTP Jocelyn Thibault / Felix Potvin 10.00 25.00
DTTT Jocelyn Thibault / Jose Theodore 8.00 20.00
DTYL Mike York / Brian Leetch 8.00 20.00
TTBSS Peter Bondra / Teemu Selanne / Mats Sundin 12.50 30.00
TTBTT Martin Brodeur / Jocelyn Thibault / Jose Theodore 25.00 60.00
TTDBA J-P Dumont / Martin Biron / Maxim Afinogenov 12.50 30.00
TTDSA Eric Daze / Steve Sullivan / Tony Amonte 12.50 30.00
TTFSD Peter Forsberg / Brendan Shanahan / Adam Deadmarsh 15.00 40.00
TTKBL Rostislav Klesla / Rob Blake / Nicklas Lidstrom 12.50 30.00
TTTHN Alex Tanguay / Dan Hinote / Ville Nieminen 12.50 30.00
TTYLS Yzerman/Lemieux/Sakic 100.00 200.00

2001-02 SPx Hockey Treasures

Inserted at a rate of 1:19, this 19-card set featured swatches of game-used jerseys and sticks of the featured players. Cards were silver in color and the swatches were aligned parallel to one another with a color photo of the given player on the right side of the card front.

HTBH Brett Hull 6.00 15.00
HTCJ Curtis Joseph 5.00 12.00
HTDH Dominik Hasek 8.00 20.00
HTHU Brett Hull 6.00 15.00
HTJI Jarome Iginla 6.00 15.00
HTJL John LeClair 5.00 12.00
HTJN Joe Nieuwendyk 6.00 15.00
HTKP Keith Primeau 5.00 12.00
HTLE John LeClair 5.00 12.00
HTMB Martin Brodeur 10.00 25.00
HTML Mario Lemieux 15.00 40.00

HTMM Mike Modano 8.00 20.00
HTMO Mike Modano 6.00 15.00
HTPR Patrick Roy 12.50 30.00
HTRC Roman Cechmanek 5.00 12.00
HTSF Sergei Fedorov 6.00 15.00
HTSS Sergei Samsonov 5.00 12.00
HTSY Steve Yzerman 12.50 30.00
HTTS Teemu Selanne 5.00 12.00

2001-02 SPx Hockey Treasures Autographed

This set partially paralleled the base hockey treasures set but also carried authentic player autographs. Each card was serial-numbered out of 50. Please not that not all cards listed below have a parent card in the base hockey treasures set.

STBO Ray Bourque 75.00 200.00
STCJ Curtis Joseph 25.00 60.00
STJI Jarome Iginla 30.00 80.00
STJL John LeClair 25.00 60.00
STKE Keith Primeau 25.00 60.00
STKP Keith Primeau 25.00 60.00
STLE John LeClair 25.00 60.00
STRB Ray Bourque 75.00 200.00
STSY Steve Yzerman 75.00 200.00
STTU Marty Turco 40.00 100.00

2001-02 SPx Rookie Redemption

Randomly inserted into packs of UD Rookie Update, this 30-card set of redemption cards represented each team in the NHL. Redemption cards were redeemable for rookies who make their debut in the 2002/03 season. Cards were serial-numbered out of 1250. Redemption cards expire 4/30/2005.

R1 Stanislav Chistov 2.00 5.00
R2 Mark Hartigan 2.00 5.00
R3 Tim Thomas 5.00 12.00
R4 Henrik Tallinder 2.00 5.00
R5 Chuck Kobasew 4.00 10.00
R6 Jaroslav Svoboda 2.00 5.00
R7 Shawn Thornton 2.00 5.00
R8 Jeff Paul 2.00 5.00
R9 Rick Nash 10.00 25.00
R10 John Erskine 2.00 5.00
R11 Henrik Zetterberg 10.00 25.00
R12 Ales Hemsky 6.00 15.00
R13 Jay Bouwmeester 4.00 10.00
R14 Alexander Frolov 5.00 12.00
R15 P-M Bouchard 4.00 10.00
R16 Ron Hainsey 2.00 5.00
R17 Scottie Upshall 5.00 12.00
R18 Steve Ott 4.00 10.00
R19 Eric Godard 2.00 5.00
R20 Jamie Lundmark 2.00 5.00
R21 Jason Spezza 8.00 20.00
R22 Radovan Somik 2.00 5.00
R23 Jeff Taffe 2.00 5.00
R24 Shane Endicott 2.00 5.00
R25 Lynn Loyns 2.00 5.00
R26 Curtis Sanford 2.00 5.00
R27 Alexander Svitov 2.00 5.00
R28 Carlo Colaiacovo 2.00 5.00
R29 Fedor Fedorov 2.00 5.00
R30 Steve Eminger 2.00 5.00

2001-02 SPx Rookie Treasures

Available in random packs of UD Rookie Update at a rate of 1:20, this 20-card set resembled the hockey treasures design but focused on rookies and prospects. Each card carried a swatch of game-worn jersey as well as game-used stick.

RTBP Brian Pothier 4.00 10.00
RTDA Mathieu Darche 4.00 10.00
RTDS Dan Snyder 6.00 15.00
RTIK Ilya Kovalchuk 15.00 40.00
RTJB Jaroslav Bednar 4.00 10.00
RTJC Jason Chimera 4.00 10.00
RTJD Jiri Dopita 4.00 10.00
RTJK Joel Kwiatkowski 4.00 10.00
RTJS Jody Shelley 6.00 15.00
RTKK Krys Kolanos 4.00 10.00
RTKL Kirby Law 4.00 10.00
RTMD Matt Davidson 4.00 10.00
RTMM Mike Matteucci 4.00 10.00
RTMS Martin Spanhel 4.00 10.00
RTMS Mikael Samuelsson 4.00 10.00
RTPD Pascal Dupuis 4.00 10.00
RTPS Peter Smrek 4.00 10.00
RTRT Raffi Torres 4.00 10.00
RTSS Sean Selmser 4.00 10.00
RTTD Tomas Divisek 4.00 10.00

2001-02 SPx Signs of Xcellence

Inserted at 1:279, this 9-card set featured authentic player autographs. Card fronts were gold toned and displayed a large signing area with a smaller player photo off to the side of the card and a silhouette of the player in the background.

BO Bobby Orr 200.00 300.00
DW Doug Weight 10.00 25.00
GH Gordie Howe 100.00 250.00
JL John LeClair 10.00 25.00
MC Mike Comrie 5.00 12.00
MM Mark Messier 150.00 250.00
SG Simon Gagne 10.00 25.00
TL Trevor Letowski 5.00 12.00
WG Wayne Gretzky 200.00 300.00

2001-02 SPx Yzerman Tribute

This 26-card set paid homage to the long-time captain of the Detroit Red Wings. Steve Yzerman. Cards 1-19 carried authentic autographs and were serial-numbered out of 19 each. Autograph cards were gold toned on the card fronts and each card carried a different small photo of Yzerman. Cards 20-26 were inserted at 1:140 and carried either one or two large pieces of game-used jersey and/or equipment. Cards 20-26 were blue toned in color and each carried a different small photo of Yzerman.

COMMON AUTO (1-19) 150.00 250.00
COMMON SINGLE MEM. (25-26) 10.00 25.00
COMMON DBL.MEM. (20-24) 15.00 40.00

2002-03 SPx

Released in December 2002, this 193-card set consisted of 60 base veteran cards (1-60), 40 "Spxitement" subset cards (#61-100), 25 "SPx Prospects" cards numbered to 999 (#101-125), 20 "Career Achievement" cards (#126-145), 15 rookie jersey/autograph cards (#146-159 and #175), 15 rookie jersey cards numbered to 999 (#160-174) and 17 shortprinted rookie cards numbered to 999 (#176-193). Cards 176-193 were available only in packs of UD Rookie Update. Individual print runs for cards 126-159 and card 175 are listed below.

COMP.SET w/o SP's (100) 50.00 100.00
*MULT.COLOR JSY: .75X TO 2X
1 Paul Kariya .30 .75
2 J-S Giguere .25 .60
3 Ilya Kovalchuk .40 1.00
4 Dany Heatley .40 1.00
5 Joe Thornton .50 1.25
6 Sergei Samsonov .25 .60
7 Miroslav Satan .25 .60
8 Martin Biron .25 .60
9 Roman Turek .25 .60
10 Jarome Iginla .40 1.00
11 Jeff O'Neill .10 .30
12 Ron Francis .25 .60
13 Arturs Irbe .25 .60
14 Eric Daze .25 .60
15 Jocelyn Thibault .25 .60
16 Patrick Roy 1.50 4.00
17 Chris Drury .25 .60
18 Joe Sakic .60 1.50
19 Peter Forsberg .75 2.00
20 Rob Blake .25 .60
21 Rostislav Klesla .10 .30
22 Marc Denis .25 .60
23 Mike Modano .50 1.25
24 Marty Turco .25 .60
25 Bill Guerin .25 .60
26 Steve Yzerman 1.50 4.00
27 Sergei Fedorov .50 1.25
28 Nicklas Lidstrom .30 .75
29 Brett Hull .40 1.00
30 Curtis Joseph .30 .75
31 Brendan Shanahan .30 .75
32 Mike Comrie .25 .60
33 Tommy Salo .25 .60
34 Roberto Luongo .40 1.00
35 Kristian Huselius .10 .30
36 Felix Potvin .30 .75
37 Zigmund Palffy .25 .60
38 Marian Gaborik .60 1.50
39 Manny Fernandez .25 .60
40 Jose Theodore .40 1.00
41 Saku Koivu .30 .75
42 Patrik Elias .25 .60
43 Martin Brodeur .75 2.00
44 Scott Hartnell .10 .30
45 Mike Dunham .25 .60
46 Alexei Yashin .10 .30
47 Chris Osgood .25 .60
48 Michael Peca .10 .30
49 Eric Lindros .30 .75
50 Mike Richter .25 .60
51 Pavel Bure .30 .75
52 Patrick Lalime .25 .60
53 Marian Hossa .30 .75
54 Daniel Alfredsson .25 .60
55 Jeremy Roenick .40 1.00
56 Simon Gagne .30 .75
57 Roman Cechmanek .25 .60
58 Sean Burke .25 .60
59 Tony Amonte .25 .60
60 Alexei Kovalev .25 .60
61 Mario Lemieux 2.00 5.00
62 Owen Nolan .25 .60
63 Evgeni Nabokov .25 .60
64 Keith Tkachuk .30 .75
65 Chris Pronger .25 .60
66 Brent Johnson .25 .60
67 Nikolai Khabibulin .30 .75
68 Vincent Lecavalier .30 .75
69 Alexander Mogilny .25 .60
70 Mats Sundin .30 .75
71 Ed Belfour .30 .75
72 Todd Bertuzzi .30 .75
73 Markus Naslund .30 .75
74 Olaf Kolzig .25 .60
75 Jaromir Jagr .50 1.25
76 Paul Kariya .30 .75
77 Adam Oates .25 .60
78 Sergei Samsonov .25 .60
79 Bobby Orr 2.00 5.00
80 Joe Thornton .50 1.25
81 Jeff O'Neill .10 .30
82 Ron Francis .25 .60
83 Joe Sakic .60 1.50
84 Patrick Roy 1.50 4.00
85 Peter Forsberg .75 2.00
86 Bill Guerin .25 .60
87 Mike Modano .50 1.25
88 Curtis Joseph .30 .75
89 Gordie Howe 1.50 4.00
90 Steve Yzerman 1.50 4.00
91 Mike Comrie .25 .60
92 Jose Theodore .40 1.00
93 Martin Brodeur .75 2.00
94 Pavel Bure .40 1.00
95 Wayne Gretzky 2.00 5.00
96 John LeClair .40 1.00
97 Mario Lemieux 2.00 5.00
98 Evgeni Nabokov .25 .60
99 Mats Sundin .30 .75
100 Jaromir Jagr .50 1.25
101 Pasi Nurminen SP 2.50 5.00
102 Mark Hartigan SP 2.50 5.00
103 Andy Hilbert SP 2.50 5.00
104 Henrik Tallinder SP 2.50 5.00
105 Jaroslav Svoboda SP 2.50 5.00
106 Riku Hahl SP 2.50 5.00
107 Jordan Krestanovich SP 2.50 5.00
108 Andrej Nedorost SP 2.50 5.00
109 Sean Avery SP 4.00 10.00
110 Jani Rita SP 2.50 5.00
111 Stephen Weiss SP 2.50 6.00
112 Lukas Krajicek SP 2.50 5.00
113 Tony Virta SP 2.50 5.00
114 Marcel Hossa SP 2.50 5.00
115 Jan Lasak SP 2.50 5.00
116 Jonas Andersson SP 2.50 5.00
117 Trent Hunter SP 2.50 5.00
118 Martin Prusek SP 2.50 5.00
119 Bruno St. Jacques SP 2.50 5.00
120 Branko Radivojevic SP 2.50 5.00
121 Shane Endicott SP 2.50 5.00
122 Justin Papineau SP 2.50 5.00
123 Sebastien Centomo SP 2.50 5.00
124 Karel Pilar SP 2.50 5.00
125 Sebastien Charpentier SP 2.50 5.00
126 Mark Messier/1804 1.50 4.00
127 Ron Francis/1701 1.50 4.00
128 Steve Yzerman/1662 3.00 8.00
129 Mario Lemieux/1601 4.00 10.00
130 Luc Robitaille/1288 1.50 4.00
131 Joe Sakic/1257 2.50 6.00
132 Brett Hull/1246 2.00 5.00
133 Al MacInnis/1204 1.50 4.00
134 Pierre Turgeon/1192 1.50 4.00
135 Jaromir Jagr/1158 1.50 4.00
136 Mark Recchi/1074 1.50 4.00
137 Brendan Shanahan/1030 1.50 4.00
138 Jeremy Roenick/1014 1.50 4.00
139 Mike Modano/977 2.00 5.00
140 Mats Sundin/942 1.50 4.00
141 Sergei Fedorov/871 2.00 5.00
142 Teemu Selanne/855 1.50 4.00
143 Pavel Bure/749 1.50 4.00
144 Peter Bondra/734 1.50 4.00
145 Eric Lindros/732 1.50 4.00
146 Alexei Smirnov 6.00 15.00
JSY AU/1250 RC
147 Kurt Sauer 6.00 15.00
JSY AU/1250 RC
148 Chuck Kobasew 10.00 25.00
JSY AU/1250 RC
149 R.Nash JSY AU/500 RC 75.00 200.00
150 Jay Bouwmeester 20.00 50.00
JSY AU/500 RC
151 Henrik Zetterberg 60.00 125.00
JSY AU/1250 RC
152 Pierre-Marc Bouchard 8.00 20.00
JSY AU/1250 RC
153 R.Hainsey JSY AU/1250 RC 6.00 15.00
154 Adam Hall 6.00 15.00
JSY AU/1250 RC
155 S.Upshall JSY AU/1250 RC 8.00 20.00
156 S.Chistov JSY AU/500 RC 6.00 15.00
157 Jeff Taffe 6.00 15.00
JSY AU/1250 RC
158 Mikael Tellqvist 10.00 25.00
JSY AU/1250 RC
159 Alexander Svitov 6.00 15.00
JSY AU/1250 RC
160 Ales Hemsky JSY RC 8.00 20.00
161 Alexander Frolov JSY RC 10.00 25.00
162 Steve Eminger JSY RC 6.00 15.00
163 Anton Volchenkov JSY RC 6.00 15.00
164 Sylvain Blouin JSY RC 6.00 15.00
165 Greg Koehler JSY RC 6.00 15.00
166 Martin Gerber JSY RC 10.00 25.00
167 Micki Dupont JSY RC 6.00 15.00
168 Jordan Leopold JSY RC 6.00 15.00
169 Tomi Pettinen JSY RC 6.00 15.00
170 Lynn Loyns JSY RC 6.00 15.00
171 Matt Henderson JSY RC 6.00 15.00
172 Radovan Somik JSY RC 6.00 15.00
173 Patrick Sharp RC 6.00 15.00
174 Jeff Paul JSY RC 6.00 15.00
175 Jason Spezza 100.00 200.00
JSY AU/500 RC
176 Pascal LeClaire RC 4.00 10.00
177 Steve Ott RC 4.00 10.00
178 Brooks Orpik RC 3.00 5.00
179 Jared Aulin RC 3.00 5.00
180 Brandon Reid RC 3.00 5.00
181 Ray Emery RC 6.00 15.00
182 Ari Ahonen RC 2.00 5.00
183 Niko Dimitrakos RC 3.00 5.00
184 Jarret Stoll RC 5.00 12.00
185 Cristobal Huet RC 10.00 25.00
186 Mike Komisarek RC 4.00 10.00
187 Ryan Miller RC 15.00 40.00
188 Jason Bacashihua RC 4.00 10.00
189 Carlo Colaiacovo RC 3.00 5.00
190 Mike Cammalleri RC 4.00 10.00
191 Fernando Pisani RC 4.00 10.00
192 Alexei Semenov RC 3.00 5.00
193 Konstantin Koltsov RC 3.00 5.00

2002-03 SPx Spectrum Gold

STATED PRINT RUN 10 SER.#'d SETS
NOT PRICED DUE TO SCARCITY

2002-03 SPx Spectrum Silver

*STARS: 2X TO 5X BASIC CARDS
STATED PRINT RUN 199 SER.#'d SETS

2002-03 SPx Milestones

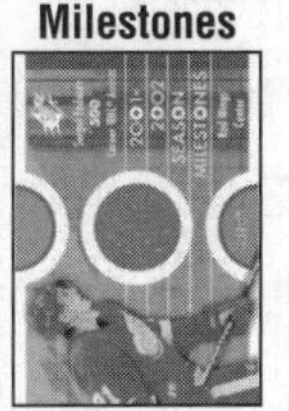

This 15-card set featured game jersey swatches. Cards were serial-numbered out of 99.

*MULT.COLOR SWATCH: .5X TO 1.25X HI
MBL Brian Leetch 6.00 15.00
MBO Peter Bondra 6.00 15.00
MBS Brendan Shanahan 6.00 15.00
MJR Jeremy Roenick 8.00 20.00
MJS Joe Sakic 10.00 25.00
MMB Martin Brodeur 12.50 30.00
MML Mario Lemieux 15.00 40.00
MMM Mike Modano 8.00 20.00
MMR Mark Recchi 6.00 15.00
MPB Pavel Bure 6.00 15.00
MPR Patrick Roy 15.00 40.00
MSF Sergei Fedorov 8.00 20.00
MSH Brendan Shanahan 6.00 15.00
MSY Steve Yzerman 15.00 40.00
MTS Teemu Selanne 6.00 15.00

2002-03 SPx Milestones Gold

This 15-card set paralleled the base insert set but each card was serial-numbered out of 15 in gold foil on the card front. All cards carried a "M" prefix on the card backs. This set is not priced due to scarcity.
NOT PRICED DUE TO SCARCITY

2002-03 SPx Milestones Silver

This 15-card set paralleled the base insert set but each card was serial-numbered out of 50 in silver foil on the card front. All cards carried a "M" prefix on the card backs.
*STARS: .75X TO 2X BASIC CARDS

2002-03 SPx Rookie Redemption

These 30 redemption cards were randomly inserted into packs and were redeemable for players making their debut in 2003-04. Cards R194-R214 were serial-numbered to 1500 and cards R215-223 were serial-numbered to 500.

R194 Matthew Lombardi 3.00 8.00
R195 Pavel Vorobiev 3.00 8.00
R196 Marek Svatos 4.00 10.00
R197 Cody McCormick 3.00 8.00

R198 John-Michael Liles 3.00 8.00
R199 Antti Miettinen 3.00 8.00
R200 Brent Burns 3.00 8.00
R201 Christoph Brandner 3.00 8.00
R202 Chris Higgins 4.00 10.00
R203 Dan Hamhuis 3.00 8.00
R204 Marek Zidlicky 3.00 8.00
R205 Paul Martin 3.00 8.00
R206 Sean Bergenheim 3.00 8.00
R207 Antoine Vermette 4.00 10.00
R208 Matthew Spiller 3.00 8.00
R209 Christian Ehrhoff 3.00 8.00
R210 Peter Sejna 3.00 8.00
R211 Maxim Kondratiev 3.00 8.00
R212 Matt Stajan 4.00 10.00
R213 Boyd Gordon 3.00 8.00
R214 Joffrey Lupul 4.00 10.00
R215 Patrice Bergeron 10.00 25.00
R216 Eric Staal 12.00 30.00
R217 Tuomo Ruutu 6.00 15.00
R218 Nathan Horton 6.00 15.00
R219 Dustin Brown 4.00 10.00
R220 Jordin Tootoo 4.00 10.00
R221 Joni Pitkanen 4.00 10.00
R222 Marc-Andre Fleury 15.00 40.00
R223 Milan Michalek 6.00 15.00

2002-03 SPx Smooth Skaters

This 17-card set featured game jersey swatches. Cards were serial-numbered out of 99.

*MULT.COLOR SWATCH: .5X TO 1.25X HI
ALL CARDS CARRY SS PREFIX
ED Eric Daze 6.00 15.00
JI Jarome Iginla 8.00 20.00
JJ Jaromir Jagr 8.00 20.00
JS Joe Sakic 10.00 25.00
JT Joe Thornton 10.00 25.00
ML Mario Lemieux 15.00 40.00
MM Mike Modano 8.00 20.00
MN Markus Naslund 6.00 15.00
MS Mats Sundin 6.00 15.00
PB Peter Bondra 6.00 15.00
PK Paul Kariya 6.00 15.00
SA Miroslav Satan 6.00 15.00
SG Simon Gagne 6.00 15.00
SS Sergei Samsonov 6.00 15.00
SU Steve Sullivan 6.00 15.00
SY Steve Yzerman 12.50 30.00
WG Wayne Gretzky 20.00 50.00

2002-03 SPx Smooth Skaters Gold

This 17-card set paralleled the base insert set but each card was serial-numbered out of 15 in gold foil on the card front. All cards carried a "SS" prefix on the card backs. This set is not priced due to scarcity.
NOT PRICED DUE TO SCARCITY

2002-03 SPx Smooth Skaters Silver

This 17-card set paralleled the base insert set but each card was serial-numbered out of 50 in silver foil on the card front. All cards carried a "SS" prefix on the card backs.
*STARS: .75X TO 2 X BASIC CARDS

2002-03 SPx Winning Materials

This 35-card memorabilia set had a stated print run of 99 serial-numbered copies each.

*MULT.COLOR SWATCH: .5X TO 1.25X HI
WMAY Alexei Yashin 6.00 15.00
WMBI Martin Biron 8.00 20.00
WMBL Brian Leetch 8.00 20.00
WMBO Ray Bourque 15.00 40.00
Colorado
WMCJ Curtis Joseph 8.00 20.00
WMDH Dominik Hasek 20.00 50.00
WMDL David Legwand 8.00 20.00
WMDU J-P Dumont 6.00 15.00
WMEL Eric Lindros 8.00 20.00
WMFP Felix Potvin 8.00 20.00
WMIK Ilya Kovalchuk 15.00 40.00
WMJA Jaromir Jagr 10.00 25.00
JSY/JSY
WMJG J-S Giguere 6.00 15.00
WMJJ Jaromir Jagr 10.00 25.00
JSY/STK
WMJR Jeremy Roenick 12.50 30.00
WMJT Joe Thornton 12.50 30.00
WMKA Paul Kariya 8.00 20.00
JSY/JSY
WMKO Olaf Kolzig 8.00 20.00
WMLE John LeClair 8.00 20.00
WMMB Martin Brodeur 20.00 50.00
WMML Mario Lemieux 30.00 80.00
WMMM Mike Modano 12.50 30.00
WMMN Markus Naslund 8.00 20.00
WMPA Zigmund Palffy 8.00 20.00
WMPB Pavel Bure 8.00 20.00
WMPF Peter Forsberg 15.00 40.00
WMPK Paul Kariya 8.00 20.00
JSY/STK
WMPR Keith Primeau 6.00 15.00
WMRB Ray Bourque 20.00 50.00
Boston
WMRO Patrick Roy 25.00 60.00
WMSG Simon Gagne 8.00 20.00
WMSS Sergei Samsonov 8.00 20.00
WMSY Steve Yzerman 20.00 50.00
WMTH Jose Theodore 10.00 25.00
WMZP Zigmund Palffy 8.00 20.00

2002-03 SPx Winning Materials Gold

This 35-card set paralleled the base insert set but each card was serial-numbered out of 15 in gold foil on the card front. All cards carried a "WM" prefix on the card backs. This set is not priced due to scarcity.
NOT PRICED DUE TO SCARCITY

2002-03 SPx Winning Materials Silver

This 35-card set paralleled the base insert set but each card was serial-numbered out of 50 in silver foil on the card front. All cards carried a "WM" prefix on the card backs.
*STARS: .75X TO 2X BASIC CARDS

2002-03 SPx Xtreme Talents

This 28-card set featured game jersey swatches. Cards were serial-numbered out of 99.

*MULT.COLOR: .75X TO 1.5X BASE HI
ALL CARDS CARRY X PREFIX

2002-03 SPx Xtreme Talents Gold

This 28-card set paralleled the base insert set but each card was serial-numbered out of 15 in gold foil on the card front. All cards carried a "X" prefix on the card backs. This set is not priced due to scarcity.
NOT PRICED DUE TO SCARCITY

2002-03 SPx Xtreme Talents Silver

This 28-card set paralleled the base insert set but each card was serial-numbered out of 50 in silver foil on the card front. All cards carried an "x" prefix on the card backs.
*STARS: .75X TO 2X BASIC CARDS

2003-04 SPx

This 240-card set consisted of several different subsets. Cards 1-100 were base veteran cards; cards 101-130 made up the Lasting Impressions subset and each card was serial-numbered out of 750; cards 131-155 made up the Xcite subset and each was serial-numbered out of 750; cards 156-175 made up the Next Generation subset and each was serial-numbered out of 999; cards 176-190 made up the Profiles subset and each was serial-numbered out of 250. Cards 191-207 and 230-240 were rookie cards that carried jersey swatches and were serial-numbered out of 999. Cards 208-229 were also rookie jersey cards but they also carried certified "cut" autographs; print runs for these can be found below. Cards 231-240 were only available in packs of UD Rookie Update.

COMP.SET w/o SP's (100) 25.00 50.00
*MULT.COLOR RC JSY: 1X TO 2.5X HI
1 J-S Giguere .20 .50
2 Stanislav Chistov .10 .25
3 Sergei Fedorov .30 .75
4 Dany Heatley .30 .75
5 Ilya Kovalchuk .30 .75
6 Joe Thornton .40 1.00
7 Sergei Samsonov .20 .50
8 Glen Murray .10 .25
9 Felix Potvin .20 .50
10 Miroslav Satan .20 .50
11 Maxim Afinogenov .20 .50
12 Chris Drury .20 .50
13 Jarome Iginla .30 .75
14 Roman Turek .20 .50
15 Steve Reinprecht .10 .25
16 Ron Francis .20 .50
17 Jeff O'Neill .10 .25
18 Alexei Zhamnov .10 .25
19 Jocelyn Thibault .20 .50
20 Kyle Calder .10 .25
21 Joe Sakic .50 1.25
22 Teemu Selanne .25 .60
23 Peter Forsberg .60 1.50
24 David Aebischer .20 .50
25 Paul Kariya .25 .60
26 Marc Denis .20 .50
27 Rick Nash .30 .75
28 Todd Marchant .10 .25
29 Bill Guerin .20 .50
30 Marty Turco .20 .50
31 Mike Modano .40 1.00
32 Henrik Zetterberg .25 .60
33 Brendan Shanahan .25 .60
34 Steve Yzerman 1.25 3.00
35 Dominik Hasek .50 1.25
36 Ryan Smyth .10 .25
37 Ales Hemsky .20 .50
38 Tommy Salo .20 .50
39 Mike Comrie .20 .50
40 Stephen Weiss .10 .25
41 Roberto Luongo .30 .75
42 Jay Bouwmeester .10 .25
43 Olli Jokinen .20 .50
44 Zigmund Palffy .20 .50
45 Alexander Frolov .10 .25
46 Roman Cechmanek .20 .50
47 Marian Gaborik .50 1.25
48 Manny Fernandez .20 .50
49 Pierre-Marc Bouchard .10 .25
50 Jose Theodore .30 .75
51 Saku Koivu .25 .60
52 Mike Komisarek .10 .25
53 Marcel Hossa .20 .50
54 Tomas Vokoun .20 .50
55 David Legwand .20 .50
56 Scott Stevens .20 .50
57 Martin Brodeur .60 1.50
58 Patrik Elias .20 .50
59 Jamie Langenbrunner .10 .25
60 Alexei Yashin .10 .25
61 Rick DiPietro .20 .50
62 Michael Peca .10 .25
63 Mike Dunham .20 .50
64 Eric Lindros .25 .60
65 Alex Kovalev .20 .50
66 Patrick Lalime .20 .50
67 Marian Hossa .25 .60
68 Daniel Alfredsson .20 .50
69 Jason Spezza .25 .60
70 John LeClair .25 .60
71 Tony Amonte .20 .50
72 Simon Gagne .25 .60
73 Jeremy Roenick .30 .75
74 Chris Gratton .10 .25
75 Sean Burke .20 .50
76 Mike Johnson .10 .25
77 Martin Straka .10 .25
78 Mario Lemieux 1.50 4.00
79 Sebastien Caron .20 .50
80 Niko Dimitrakos .10 .25
81 Evgeni Nabokov .20 .50
82 Mike Ricci .10 .25
83 Chris Osgood .20 .50
84 Al MacInnis .20 .50
85 Keith Tkachuk .25 .60
86 Chris Pronger .20 .50
87 Nikolai Khabibulin .25 .60
88 Martin St. Louis .20 .50
89 Vincent Lecavalier .25 .60
90 Owen Nolan .20 .50
91 Alexander Mogilny .20 .50
92 Ed Belfour .25 .60
93 Mats Sundin .25 .60
94 Markus Naslund .25 .60
95 Johan Hedberg .20 .50
96 Todd Bertuzzi .25 .60
97 Ed Jovanovski .20 .50
98 Jaromir Jagr .40 1.00
99 Olaf Kolzig .20 .50
100 Peter Bondra .20 .50
101 Wayne Gretzky LI 15.00 40.00
102 Gordie Howe LI 6.00 15.00
103 Bobby Orr LI 15.00 40.00
104 Bobby Clarke LI 4.00 10.00
105 Scotty Bowman LI 4.00 10.00
106 Lanny McDonald LI 4.00 10.00
107 Stan Mikita LI 4.00 10.00
108 Ted Lindsay LI 4.00 10.00
109 Marcel Dionne LI 4.00 10.00
110 Johnny Bucyk LI 4.00 10.00
111 Jean Beliveau LI 4.00 10.00
112 Mike Bossy LI 4.00 10.00
113 Guy Lafleur LI 4.00 10.00
114 Mario Lemieux LI 8.00 20.00
115 Mark Messier LI 4.00 10.00
116 Patrick Roy LI 6.00 15.00
117 Martin Brodeur LI 5.00 12.00
118 Jarome Iginla LI 4.00 10.00
119 Mike Modano LI 4.00 10.00
120 Steve Yzerman LI 6.00 15.00
121 Peter Forsberg LI 5.00 12.00
122 Marian Gaborik LI 4.00 10.00

2003-04 SPx

123 Scott Stevens LI 4.00 10.00
124 Paul Kariya LI 4.00 10.00
125 Tie Domi LI 4.00 10.00
126 Joe Sakic LI 4.00 10.00
127 Brendan Shanahan LI 4.00 10.00
128 Jeremy Roenick LI 5.00 12.00
129 Joe Thornton LI 4.00 10.00
130 Mats Sundin LI 4.00 10.00
131 J-S Giguere Xcite 4.00 10.00
132 Marian Gaborik Xcite 4.00 10.00
133 Joe Thornton Xcite 4.00 10.00
134 Saku Koivu Xcite 4.00 10.00
135 Dany Heatley Xcite 4.00 10.00
136 Vincent Lecavalier Xcite 4.00 10.00
137 Todd Bertuzzi Xcite 4.00 10.00
138 Sergei Fedorov Xcite 4.00 10.00
139 Marty Turco Xcite 4.00 10.00
140 Paul Kariya Xcite 4.00 10.00
141 Marian Hossa Xcite 4.00 10.00
142 Alexei Yashin Xcite 4.00 10.00
143 Zigmund Palffy Xcite 4.00 10.00
144 Mario Lemieux Xcite 8.00 20.00
145 Ilya Kovalchuk Xcite 4.00 10.00
146 Henrik Zetterberg Xcite 4.00 10.00
147 Mike Modano Xcite 4.00 10.00
148 Tony Amonte Xcite 4.00 10.00
149 Jason Spezza Xcite 4.00 10.00
150 Owen Nolan Xcite 4.00 10.00
151 Ales Hemsky Xcite 4.00 10.00
152 Markus Naslund Xcite 4.00 10.00
153 Teemu Selanne Xcite 4.00 10.00
154 Sergei Samsonov Xcite 4.00 10.00
155 Martin Brodeur Xcite 5.00 12.00
156 Dany Heatley NG 6.00 15.00
157 Marian Hossa NG 5.00 12.00
158 J-S Giguere NG 5.00 12.00
159 Joe Thornton NG 8.00 20.00
160 Henrik Zetterberg NG 5.00 12.00
161 Rick Nash NG 6.00 15.00
162 Jay Bouwmeester NG 5.00 12.00
163 Jason Spezza NG 6.00 15.00
164 Pavel Datsyuk NG 5.00 12.00
165 Mike Komisarek NG 5.00 12.00
166 Ales Hemsky NG 5.00 12.00
167 Marian Gaborik NG 8.00 20.00
168 Alexander Frolov NG 5.00 12.00
169 Steve Ott NG 5.00 12.00
170 Justin Williams NG 5.00 12.00
171 Pierre-Marc Bouchard NG 5.00 12.00
172 Ryan Miller NG 5.00 12.00
173 Ilya Kovalchuk NG 6.00 15.00
174 Kyle Calder NG 5.00 12.00
175 David Aebischer NG 5.00 12.00
176 Mario Lemieux PRO 20.00 50.00
177 Joe Thornton PRO 12.50 30.00
178 Martin Brodeur PRO 15.00 40.00
179 Steve Yzerman PRO 15.00 40.00
180 Joe Sakic PRO 12.50 30.00
181 Mats Sundin PRO 10.00 25.00
182 Saku Koivu PRO 10.00 25.00
183 Sergei Fedorov PRO 12.50 30.00
184 Jeremy Roenick PRO 12.50 30.00
185 Roberto Luongo PRO 12.50 30.00
186 Mike Modano PRO 12.50 30.00
187 Todd Bertuzzi PRO 12.50 30.00
188 Zigmund Palffy PRO 12.50 30.00
189 J-S Giguere PRO 10.00 25.00
190 Markus Naslund PRO 12.50 30.00
191 Dan Fritsche JSY RC 6.00 15.00
192 Tim Gleason JSY RC 6.00 15.00
193 Lasse Kukkonen JSY RC 6.00 15.00
194 John-Michael Liles JSY RC 6.00 15.00
195 Paul Martin JSY RC 6.00 15.00
196 Esa Pirnes JSY RC 6.00 15.00
197 Tom Preissing JSY RC 6.00 15.00
198 David Hale JSY RC 6.00 15.00
199 Marek Svatos JSY RC 10.00 25.00
200 Boyd Kane JSY RC 6.00 15.00
201 Matthew Lombardi JSY RC 6.00 15.00
202 Marek Zidlicky JSY RC 6.00 15.00
203 Matthew Spiller JSY RC 6.00 15.00
204 Andrew Peters JSY RC 6.00 15.00
205 Greg Campbell JSY RC 6.00 15.00
206 Sean Bergenheim JSY RC 6.00 15.00
207 Boyd Gordon JSY RC 6.00 15.00
208 P.Sejna JSY AU/925 RC 6.00 15.00
209 M.Stajan JSY AU/925 RC 15.00 40.00
210 M.Michalek JSY AU/925 RC 6.00 15.00
211 P.Vorobiev JSY AU/925 RC 8.00 20.00
212 D.Hamhuis JSY AU/925 RC 8.00 20.00
213 C.Higgins JSY AU/925 RC 15.00 40.00
214 A.Miettinen JSY AU/925 RC 6.00 15.00
215 C.Ehrhoff JSY AU/925 RC 8.00 20.00
216 A.Semin JSY AU/925 RC 20.00 50.00
217 A.Vermette JSY AU/925 RC 6.00 15.00
218 T.Moen JSY AU/925 RC 6.00 15.00
219 J.Pitkanen JSY AU/925 RC 8.00 20.00
220 P.Bergeron JSY AU/925 RC 20.00 50.00
221 J.Hudler JSY AU/925 RC 8.00 20.00
222 M.Fleury JSY AU/500 RC 50.00 125.00
223 D.Brown JSY AU/500 RC 8.00 20.00
224 J.Lupul JSY AU/925 RC 12.00 30.00
225 T.Ruutu JSY AU/500 RC 20.00 40.00
226 J.Tootoo JSY AU/500 RC 15.00 40.00
227 E.Staal JSY AU/500 RC 50.00 100.00
228 N.Horton JSY AU/500 RC 15.00 40.00
229 T.Salmalainen JSY AU/925 RC 8.00 20.00
230 John Pohl JSY RC 6.00 15.00
231 Sergei Zinovjev JSY RC 6.00 15.00
232 Ryan Kesler JSY RC 6.00 15.00
233 Dominic Moore JSY RC 8.00 20.00
234 Peter Sarno JSY RC 6.00 15.00
235 Ryan Malone JSY RC 8.00 20.00
236 Nikolai Zherdev JSY RC 12.00 30.00
237 Fredrik Sjostrom JSY RC 6.00 15.00
238 Derek Roy JSY RC 8.00 20.00
239 Mikko Luoma JSY RC 6.00 15.00
240 Trevor Daley JSY RC 6.00 15.00

2003-04 SPx Radiance

*STARS: 10X TO 25X
*LAST.IMP/XCITE: 1X TO 2.5X
*NEXT GEN.: .75X TO 2X
*PROFILES: .5X TO 1.25X
*ROOKIE JSY: .5X TO 1.25X
*ROOKIE JSY/AU: .5X TO 1.25X
STATED PRINT RUN 50 SER.#'d SETS

2003-04 SPx Spectrum

STATED PRINT RUN 10 SER.#'d SETS
NOT PRICED DUE TO SCARCITY

2003-04 SPx Big Futures

*MULT.COLOR SWATCH: .75X TO 1.5X
PRINT RUN 99 SER.#'d SETS
*LIMITED: .75X TO 2X
LIMITED PRINT RUN 25 SER.#'d SETS
BF-AA Ari Ahonen 8.00 20.00
BF-AF Alexander Frolov 8.00 20.00
BF-AH Ales Hemsky 10.00 25.00
BF-AK Ales Kotalik 8.00 20.00
BF-AS Alexander Svitov 8.00 20.00
BF-BJ Barret Jackman 8.00 20.00
BF-BO Brooks Orpik 8.00 20.00
BF-CN Sebastien Caron 8.00 20.00
BF-DB Dan Blackburn 8.00 20.00
BF-DH Dany Heatley 10.00 25.00
BF-HZ Henrik Zetterberg 12.50 30.00
BF-IK Ilya Kovalchuk 12.50 30.00
BF-IR Igor Radulov 8.00 20.00
BF-JB Jason Bacashihua 8.00 20.00
BF-JB Jay Bouwmeester 8.00 20.00
BF-JL Jordan Leopold 8.00 20.00
BF-JS Jason Spezza 12.50 30.00
BF-JT Joe Thornton 15.00 40.00
BF-MC Mike Cammalleri 8.00 20.00
BF-MD Marc Denis 8.00 20.00
BF-MG Mathieu Garon 8.00 20.00
BF-MH Marcel Hossa 8.00 20.00
BF-MP Mark Parrish 8.00 20.00
BF-MT Marty Turco 10.00 25.00
BF-OJ Olli Jokinen 8.00 20.00
BF-PD Pavel Datsyuk 10.00 25.00
BF-PL Pascal Leclaire 8.00 20.00
BF-PMB Pierre-Marc Bouchard 8.00 20.00
BF-RE Robert Esche 10.00 25.00
BF-RN Rick Nash 12.50 30.00
BF-SC Stanislav Chistov 8.00 20.00
BF-SG Simon Gagne 10.00 25.00
BF-SO Steve Ott 8.00 20.00
BF-SW Stephen Weiss 8.00 20.00

2003-04 SPx Fantasy Franchise

PRINT RUN 75 SER.#'d SETS
*LIMITED: .6X TO 1.5X
LTD PRINT RUN 25 SER.#'d SETS
FF-BLK Bure/Lindros/Kovalev 10.00 25.00
FF-DSA Drury/Satan/Afinogenov 12.00 30.00
FF-EHJ Elias/Hossa/Jagr 12.00 30.00
FF-FGC Fedorov/Giguere/Chistov 10.00 25.00
FF-GRB Giguere/Roy/Brodeur 30.00 80.00
FF-HSL Hossa/Spezza/Lalime 12.00 30.00
FF-HYS Hull/Yzerman/Shanahan 40.00 100.00
FF-HYZ Howe/Yzerman/Zettrbrg 60.00 150.00
FF-KFB Kovalchuk/Fedorov/Bure 20.00 50.00
FF-KSF Kariya/Selanne/Forsberg 25.00 60.00
FF-KTH Kariya/Thornton/Heatley 15.00 40.00
FF-LGH Lemieux/Gretzky/Howe 125.00 250.00
FF-LRA LeClair/Roenick/Amonte 15.00 40.00
FF-MGT Modano/Guerin/Turco 20.00 50.00
FF-NBM Naslund/Bertuzzi/Morrison 15.00 40.00
FF-NSM Nolan/Sundin/Mogilny 10.00 25.00
FF-NSZ Nash/Spezza/Zetterberg 40.00 100.00
FF-SBJ Stevens/Brodeur/Jovnski 20.00 50.00
FF-TMS Joe Thornton 15.00 40.00
Glen Murray
Sergei Samsonov
FF-TWM Tkachuk/Weight/MacInnis 10.00 25.00

2003-04 SPx Hall Pass

*MULT.COLOR SWATCH: .75X TO 1.5X
PRINT RUN 75 SER.#'d SETS
*LIMITED: .75X TO 2X
LIMITED PRINT RUN 25 SER.#'d SETS
HP-BH Brett Hull 15.00 40.00
HP-CC Chris Chelios 10.00 25.00
HP-DG Doug Gilmour 10.00 25.00
HP-DH Dominik Hasek 12.50 30.00
HP-MB Martin Brodeur 25.00 60.00
HP-ML Mario Lemieux 25.00 60.00
HP-MM Mark Messier 15.00 40.00
HP-PR Patrick Roy 20.00 50.00
HP-RB Ray Bourque 12.50 30.00
HP-RF Ron Francis 10.00 25.00

2003-04 SPx Origins

*MULT.COLOR SWATCH: .75X TO 1.5X
PRINT RUN 75 SER.#'d SETS
O-AY Alexei Yashin 8.00 20.00
O-BL Brian Leetch 8.00 20.00
O-BS Brendan Shanahan 8.00 20.00
O-DH Dany Heatley 15.00 40.00
O-DW Doug Weight 8.00 20.00
O-EB Ed Belfour 12.50 30.00
O-HZ Henrik Zetterberg 15.00 40.00
O-JI Jarome Iginla 12.50 30.00
O-JJ Jaromir Jagr 15.00 40.00
O-JR Jeremy Roenick 15.00 40.00
O-JS Jason Spezza 10.00 25.00
O-JSG J-S Giguere 8.00 20.00
O-JT Joe Thornton 12.50 30.00
O-MB Martin Brodeur 20.00 50.00
O-MH Marian Hossa 10.00 25.00
O-ML Mario Lemieux 25.00 60.00
O-MN Markus Naslund 10.00 25.00
O-MS Mats Sundin 12.50 30.00
O-ON Owen Nolan 8.00 20.00
O-PB Pavel Bure 8.00 20.00
O-PE Patrik Elias 8.00 20.00
O-PF Peter Forsberg 15.00 40.00
O-PR Patrick Roy 25.00 60.00
O-SF Sergei Fedorov 15.00 40.00
O-SS Sergei Samsonov 8.00 20.00
O-TS Teemu Selanne 10.00 25.00
O-ZP Zigmund Palffy 8.00 20.00

2003-04 SPx Signature Threads

This 26-card set featured over-sized jersey swatches and certified autographs. Each card was limited to 50 serial-numbered copies.
*MULT.COLOR SWATCH: .75X TO 1.5X
ST-AF Alexander Frolov 20.00 50.00
ST-AH Ales Hemsky 15.00 40.00
ST-EL Eric Lindros 30.00 80.00
ST-HZ Henrik Zetterberg 30.00 80.00
ST-IK Ilya Kovalchuk 40.00 100.00
ST-JI Jarome Iginla 25.00 60.00
ST-JL John LeClair 15.00 40.00
ST-JR Jeremy Roenick 30.00 80.00
ST-JS Jason Spezza 50.00 125.00
ST-JT Jose Theodore 25.00 60.00
ST-JT Joe Thornton 50.00 125.00
ST-JSG J-S Giguere 15.00 40.00
ST-MC Mike Comrie 15.00 40.00
ST-MG Marian Gaborik
ST-MH Marian Hossa 20.00 50.00
ST-MN Markus Naslund 20.00 50.00
ST-MT Marty Turco 15.00 40.00
ST-PB Pavel Bure 15.00 40.00
ST-RN Rick Nash 60.00 150.00
ST-SF Sergei Fedorov 25.00 60.00
ST-SK Saku Koivu 20.00 50.00
ST-SS Sergei Samsonov 15.00 40.00
ST-SY Steve Yzerman 75.00 150.00
ST-TB Todd Bertuzzi 20.00 50.00
ST-WG Wayne Gretzky 150.00 350.00
ST-ZP Zigmund Palffy 15.00 40.00

2003-04 SPx Style

This 12-card set featured triple jersey swatches from some of the league's elite players. Cards were serial-numbered out of 99. A limited parallel was also created and serial-numbered out of 25
*MULT.COLOR SWATCH: .75X TO 1.5X
*LIMITED: .5X TO 1.25X
SPX-BG Brodeur/Giguere/Luongo 25.00 60.00
SPX-BS Bertuzzi/Shanny/Tkachuk 12.50 30.00
SPX-BT Belfour/Turco/Esche 12.50 30.00
SPX-DS Domi/Stock/Shelley 12.50 30.00
SPX-GS Gretzky/Spezza/Thornton 75.00 200.00
SPX-HH Hejduk/Hossa/Jagr 20.00 50.00
SPX-HN Howe/Nash/Bertuzzi 30.00 80.00
SPX-HT Howe/Thornton/Bertuzzi 25.00 60.00
SPX-JB Jovanovski/Blake/Chara 12.50 30.00
SPX-LH Lemieux/Heatley/Fedorov 25.00 60.00
SPX-NZ Naslund/Zettrbrg/Sundin 25.00 60.00
SPX-RB Roy/Brodeur/Giguere 25.00 60.00

2003-04 SPx VIP

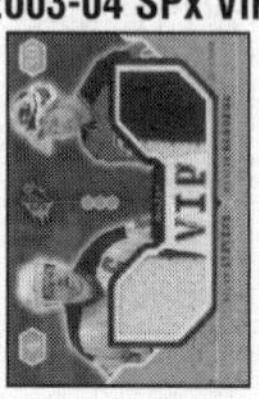

*MULT.COLOR SWATCH: .75X TO 1.5X
PRINT RUN 50 SER.#'d SETS
*LIMITED: .6X TO 1.5X
LTD PRINT RUN 25 SER.#'d SETS
VIP-DA Chris Drury 12.50 30.00
Maxim Afinogenov
VIP-FG S.Fedorov/J.Giguere 15.00 40.00
VIP-FS P.Forsberg/J.Sakic 20.00 50.00
VIP-KH S.Koivu/Marcel Hossa 12.50 30.00
VIP-LS V.Lecavalier/M.St. Louis 15.00 40.00
VIP-MG M.Modano/B.Guerin 12.50 30.00
VIP-NB M.Naslund/T.Bertuzzi 12.50 30.00
VIP-PF Z.Palffy/A.Frolov 12.50 30.00
VIP-SB S.Stevens/M.Brodeur 25.00 60.00
VIP-SK T.Selanne/P.Kariya 12.50 30.00
VIP-TM J.Thornton/G.Murray 12.50 30.00
VIP-YS S.Yzerman/B.Shanahan 25.00 60.00

2003-04 SPx Winning Materials

PRINT RUN 99 SER.#'d SETS
*LIMITED: .6X TO 1.5X
LTD PRINT RUN 25 SER.#'d SETS
WM-AD Adam Deadmarsh 6.00 15.00
WM-BE Ed Belfour 8.00 20.00
WM-BL Rob Blake 6.00 15.00
WM-BO Peter Bondra 6.00 15.00
WM-CD Chris Drury 6.00 15.00
WM-DB Dan Blackburn 6.00 15.00
WM-DH Dominik Hasek 12.50 30.00
WM-EB Ed Belfour 8.00 20.00
WM-FO Peter Forsberg 12.50 30.00
WM-GR Wayne Gretzky 40.00 100.00
WM-GY Wayne Gretzky 40.00 100.00
WM-JB Jay Bouwmeester 6.00 15.00
WM-JF Jeff Friesen 6.00 15.00
WM-JG Jaromir Jagr 12.50 30.00
WM-JI Jarome Iginla 10.00 25.00
WM-JJ Jaromir Jagr 12.50 30.00
WM-JR Jeremy Roenick 12.50 30.00
WM-JS Joe Sakic 15.00 40.00
WM-JZ Jason Spezza 12.50 30.00
WM-MD Mike Dunham 6.00 15.00
WM-MH Marian Hossa 8.00 20.00
WM-MM Mark Messier 15.00 40.00
WM-MN Markus Naslund 8.00 20.00
WM-MO Mike Modano 12.50 30.00
WM-MS Mats Sundin 8.00 20.00
WM-MT Marty Turco 6.00 15.00
WM-PB Pavel Bure 8.00 20.00
WM-PF Peter Forsberg 12.50 30.00
WM-PK Paul Kariya 8.00 20.00
WM-PR Patrick Roy 20.00 50.00
WM-RB Ray Bourque 10.00 25.00
WM-RN Rick Nash 15.00 40.00
WM-RY Patrick Roy 20.00 50.00
WM-SA Jason Spezza 12.50 30.00
WM-SB Sean Burke 6.00 15.00
WM-SF Sergei Fedorov 12.50 30.00
WM-SW Stephen Weiss 6.00 15.00
WM-TA Tony Amonte 6.00 15.00
WM-TB Todd Bertuzzi 8.00 20.00
WM-TH Jose Theodore 12.50 30.00
WM-TS Teemu Selanne 8.00 20.00
WM-WG Wayne Gretzky 40.00 100.00

2005-06 SPx

COMP.SET w/o SP's (90) 12.50 25.00
133-153 PRINT RUN 1999 SER.#'d SETS
154-188 PRINT RUN 1499 SER.#'d SETS
189-191 PRINT RUN 499 SER.#'d SETS
192-221/244-293 999 SER.#'d SETS
*MULTI.COLOR JSY: 1X TO 2.5X HI
1 J-S Giguere .20 .50
2 Sergei Fedorov .30 .75
3 Ilya Kovalchuk .30 .75
4 Kari Lehtonen .25 .60
5 Marian Hossa .25 .60
6 Patrice Bergeron .20 .50
7 Joe Thornton .40 1.00
8 Andrew Raycroft .20 .50
9 Glen Murray .15 .30
10 Maxim Afinogenov .15 .30
11 Chris Drury .20 .50
12 Jarome Iginla .30 .75
13 Miikka Kiprusoff .25 .60
14 Tony Amonte .20 .50
15 Erik Cole .15 .30
16 Eric Staal .25 .60
17 Tuomo Ruutu .15 .30
18 Nikolai Khabibulin .25 .60
19 Joe Sakic .50 1.25
20 David Aebischer .20 .50
21 Milan Hejduk .25 .60
22 Alex Tanguay .20 .50
23 Rick Nash .30 .75
24 Nikolai Zherdev .25 .60
25 Mike Modano .25 .60
26 Bill Guerin .20 .50
27 Marty Turco .20 .50
28 Steve Yzerman 1.00 2.50
29 Brendan Shanahan .25 .60
30 Henrik Zetterberg .25 .60
31 Nicklas Lidstrom .25 .60
32 Ty Conklin .20 .50
33 Chris Pronger .20 .50
34 Ryan Smyth .15 .30
35 Roberto Luongo .30 .75
36 Stephen Weiss .15 .30
37 Joe Nieuwendyk .20 .50
38 Jeremy Roenick .30 .75
39 Luc Robitaille .20 .50
40 Alexander Frolov .20 .50
41 Marian Gaborik .50 1.25
42 Manny Fernandez .20 .50
43 Saku Koivu .25 .60
44 Jose Theodore .30 .75
45 Michael Ryder .20 .50
46 Mike Ribeiro .15 .30
47 Paul Kariya .25 .60
48 Tomas Vokoun .20 .50
49 David Legwand .20 .50
50 Martin Brodeur 1.25 3.00
51 Patrik Elias .20 .50
52 Alexander Mogilny .20 .50
53 Scott Gomez .20 .50
54 Alexei Yashin .15 .30
55 Rick DiPietro .20 .50
56 Miroslav Satan .20 .50
57 Jaromir Jagr .40 1.00
58 Tom Poti .15 .30
59 Kevin Weekes .20 .50
60 Dany Heatley .30 .75
61 Daniel Alfredsson .20 .50
62 Martin Havlat .20 .50
63 Dominik Hasek .50 1.25
64 Jason Spezza .25 .60
65 Peter Forsberg .40 1.00
66 Keith Primeau .12 .30
67 Simon Gagne .25 .60
68 Robert Esche .20 .50
69 Shane Doan .15 .30
70 Brett Hull .30 .75
71 Curtis Joseph .25 .60
72 Mario Lemieux 1.50 4.00
73 Zigmund Palffy .20 .50
74 Mark Recchi .20 .50
75 Evgeni Nabokov .20 .50
76 Patrick Marleau .20 .50
77 Jonathan Cheechoo .25 .60
78 Keith Tkachuk .25 .60
79 Doug Weight .20 .50
80 Vincent Lecavalier .25 .60
81 Sean Burke .20 .50
82 Brad Richards .25 .60
83 Martin St. Louis .20 .50
84 Mats Sundin .25 .60
85 Ed Belfour .25 .60
86 Jason Allison .15 .30
87 Eric Lindros .25 .60
88 Markus Naslund .25 .60
89 Brendan Morrison .10 .30
90 Olaf Kolzig .20 .50
91 Bernie Geoffrion 75.00 175.00
92 Bobby Hull 50.00 100.00
93 Bobby Clarke 60.00 125.00
94 Borje Salming 30.00 75.00
95 Brian Leetch 125.00 250.00
96 Bryan Trottier 350.00 600.00
97 Cam Neely 75.00 200.00
98 Dominik Hasek 350.00 600.00
99 Doug Weight 200.00 400.00
100 Ed Jovanovski 25.00 60.00
101 Gerry Cheevers 75.00 150.00
102 Gilbert Perreault 250.00 400.00
103 Gordie Howe 500.00 700.00
104 Grant Fuhr 50.00 125.00
105 Guy Lafleur 75.00 150.00
106 Jari Kurri 30.00 60.00
107 Jeremy Roenick 125.00 225.00
108 Johnny Bucyk 50.00 100.00
109 Luc Robitaille 60.00 150.00
110 Marcel Dionne 30.00 80.00
111 Martin Brodeur SP 600.00 800.00
112 Mats Sundin SP 600.00 800.00
113 Mike Bossy 40.00 80.00
114 Mike Modano SP 300.00 500.00
115 Michael Peca 25.00 60.00
116 Miroslav Satan SP 250.00 500.00
117 Owen Nolan FF SSP /10 800.00 1000.00
118 Peter Stastny 50.00 100.00
119 Phil Esposito SP 150.00 300.00
120 Ray Bourque SP 500.00 1000.00
121 Roberto Luongo 60.00 150.00
122 Rogie Vachon 40.00 80.00
123 Ron Hextall 100.00 200.00
124 S Bowman FF SSP /10 800.00 1100.00
125 W Gretzky FF SSP /25 800.00 1200.00
126 Clark Gillies SP 250.00 500.00
127 Lanny McDonald 100.00 200.00
128 Tiger Williams 30.00 75.00
129 J Beliveau FF SSP /25 300.00 500.00
130 W Gretzky FF SSP 15 2000.00 3000.00
131 Butch Goring FF 25.00 60.00
132 Guy Lapointe FF 60.00 125.00
133 Duncan Keith JSY RC 4.00 10.00
134 Jaroslav Balastik JSY RC 4.00 10.00
135 Jay McClement JSY RC 4.00 10.00
136 Jeff Hoggan JSY RC 4.00 10.00
137 Andrew Alberts JSY RC 4.00 10.00
138 Kevin Dallman JSY RC 4.00 10.00
139 Maxime Talbot JSY RC 4.00 10.00
140 Raitis Ivanans JSY RC 4.00 10.00
141 Niklas Nordgren JSY RC 4.00 10.00
142 Kevin Nastiuk JSY RC 5.00 12.00
143 Jim Slater JSY RC 5.00 12.00
144 George Parros JSY RC 4.00 10.00
145 David Leneveu JSY RC 5.00 12.00
146 Andrew Wozniewski JSY RC 4.00 10.00
147 Ryan Hollweg JSY RC 4.00 10.00
148 Brett Lebda JSY RC 4.00 10.00
149 Patrick Eaves JSY RC 6.00 15.00
150 Ryane Clowe JSY RC 4.00 10.00
151 Josh Gorges JSY RC 4.00 10.00
152 Brad Winchester JSY RC 4.00 10.00
153 Matt Foy JSY RC 4.00 10.00
154 Wojtek Wolski JSY AU RC 15.00 40.00
155 Rene Bourque JSY AU RC 8.00 20.00
156 Gilbert Brule JSY AU RC 15.00 40.00
157 Jeff Woywitka JSY AU RC 8.00 20.00
158 H.Toivonen JSY AU RC 10.00 25.00
159 Al Montoya JSY AU RC 12.00 30.00
160 Yann Danis JSY AU RC 8.00 20.00
161 Alexander Perezhogin JSY AU RC 8.00 20.00
162 Cam Barker JSY AU RC 8.00 20.00
163 Zach Parise JSY AU RC 20.00 40.00
164 Dion Phaneuf JSY AU RC 40.00 80.00
165 Mike Richards JSY AU RC 12.00 30.00
166 Cam Ward JSY AU RC 20.00 50.00
167 Robert Nilsson JSY AU RC 8.00 20.00
168 Petteri Nokelainen JSY AU RC 8.00 20.00
169 A.Steen JSY AU RC 15.00 40.00
170 Ryan Getzlaf JSY AU RC 25.00 60.00
171 Corey Perry JSY AU RC 15.00 40.00
172 Rostislav Olesz JSY AU RC 10.00 25.00
173 H.Lundqvist JSY AU RC 40.00 80.00
174 Petr Prucha JSY AU RC 12.00 30.00
175 Jim Howard JSY AU RC 12.00 30.00
176 Johan Franzen JSY AU RC 12.00 30.00
177 Thomas Vanek JSY AU RC 30.00 60.00
178 Andrej Meszaros JSY AU RC 8.00 20.00
179 Brandon Bochenski JSY AU RC 8.00 20.00
180 Jussi Jokinen JSY AU RC 12.00 30.00
181 Braydon Coburn JSY AU RC 8.00 20.00
182 Ryan Suter JSY AU RC 8.00 20.00
183 Peter Budaj JSY AU RC 12.00 30.00
184 Brent Seabrook JSY AU RC 8.00 20.00
185 Keith Ballard JSY AU RC 8.00 20.00
186 Milan Jurcina JSY AU RC 8.00 20.00
187 Anthony Stewart JSY AU RC 8.00 20.00
188 Eric Nystrom JSY AU RC 8.00 20.00
189 Jeff Carter JSY AU RC 50.00 100.00
190 A.Ovechkin JSY AU RC 300.00 450.00
191 Sidney Crosby JSY AU RC 600.00 800.00
192 Lee Stempniak RC 5.00 12.00
193 Andy Roach RC 2.00 5.00
194 Colin Hemingway RC 2.00 5.00
195 Mark Streit RC 2.00 5.00
196 Wade Skolney RC 2.00 5.00
197 Chris Campoli RC 2.00 5.00
198 Paul Ranger RC 2.00 5.00
199 Kyle Brodziak RC 2.00 5.00
200 Chris Holt RC 2.00 5.00
201 Brian McGrattan RC 2.00 5.00
202 Adam Berkhoel RC 5.00 12.00
203 Nick Tarnasky RC 2.00 5.00
204 Evgeny Artyukhin RC 2.00 5.00
205 Timo Helbling RC 2.00 5.00
206 Derek Boogaard RC 2.00 5.00
207 Michael Wall RC 5.00 12.00
208 Steve Goertzen RC 2.00 5.00
209 Junior Lessard RC 2.00 5.00
210 Vojtech Polak RC 2.00 5.00
211 Andrew Penner RC 2.00 5.00
212 Jordan Sigalet RC 4.00 10.00
213 Kevin Colley RC 2.00 5.00
214 Dimitri Patzold RC 2.00 5.00
215 Christoph Schubert RC 2.00 5.00
216 Zenon Konopka RC 2.00 5.00
217 Staffan Kronwall RC 2.00 5.00
218 Erik Christensen RC 2.00 5.00
219 Brian Eklund RC 3.00 8.00
220 Rob McVicar RC 5.00 12.00
221 Tomas Fleischmann RC 3.00 8.00
222 Chris Thorburn RC 8.00 20.00
223 Daniel Paille RC 8.00 20.00
224 Andrew Ladd RC 10.00 25.00
225 Danny Richmond RC 8.00 20.00
226 Brad Richardson RC 8.00 20.00
227 Ole-Kristian Tollefsen RC 8.00 20.00
228 Alexandre Picard RC 10.00 25.00
229 Kyle Quincey RC 8.00 20.00
230 Valtteri Filppula RC 8.00 20.00
231 Jeff Tambellini RC 8.00 20.00
232 Mikko Koivu RC 10.00 25.00
233 Maxim Lapierre RC 8.00 20.00
234 Andrei Kostitsyn RC 10.00 25.00
235 Barry Tallackson RC 8.00 20.00
236 Jeremy Colliton RC 8.00 20.00
237 R.J. Umberger RC 10.00 25.00
238 Ben Eager RC 8.00 20.00
239 Ryan Whitney RC 8.00 20.00
240 Steve Bernier RC 10.00 25.00
241 Ryan Craig RC 8.00 20.00
242 Kevin Bieksa RC 8.00 20.00
243 Jakub Klepis RC 6.00 15.00
244 Dustin Penner RC 4.00 10.00
245 Ben Walter RC 2.00 5.00
246 Eric Healey RC 2.00 5.00
247 Nathan Paetsch RC 2.00 5.00
248 Jiri Novotny RC 2.00 5.00
249 Richie Regehr RC 2.00 5.00
250 Chad Larose RC 2.00 5.00
251 Martin St. Pierre RC 2.00 5.00
252 Corey Crawford RC 3.00 8.00
253 James Wisniewski RC 2.00 5.00
254 Vitaly Kolesnik RC 5.00 12.00
255 Geoff Platt RC 2.00 5.00
256 Joakim Lindstrom RC 2.00 5.00
257 Danny Syvret RC 2.00 5.00
258 Kyle Brodziak RC 2.00 5.00
259 J-F Jacques RC 2.00 5.00
260 Matt Greene RC 2.00 5.00
261 Greg Jacina RC 2.00 5.00
262 Rob Globke RC 2.00 5.00
263 Yanick Lehoux RC 2.00 5.00
264 Connor James RC 2.00 5.00
265 Richard Petiot RC 2.00 5.00
266 Petr Kanko RC 2.00 5.00
267 Matt Ryan RC 2.00 5.00
268 J-P Cote RC 2.00 5.00
269 Jonathan Ferland 2.00 5.00
270 Greg Zanon 2.00 5.00
271 Kevin Klein RC 2.00 5.00
272 Pekka Rinne RC 5.00 10.00
273 Cam Janssen RC 2.00 5.00
274 Jason Ryznar RC 2.00 5.00
275 Bruno Gervais RC 2.00 5.00
276 Stefan Ruzicka RC 2.00 5.00
277 Alexandre Picard RC 2.00 5.00
278 Matt Jones RC 2.00 5.00
279 Colby Armstrong RC 5.00 12.00
280 Doug Murray RC 2.00 5.00
281 Grant Stevenson RC 2.00 5.00
282 Dennis Wideman RC 2.00 5.00
283 Chris Beckford-Tseu RC 5.00 12.00
284 Gerald Coleman RC 2.00 5.00
285 Darren Reid RC 2.00 5.00
286 Doug O'Brien RC 2.00 5.00
287 Jay Harrison RC 2.00 5.00
288 Rick Rypien RC 2.00 5.00
289 Alexandre Burrows RC 2.00 5.00
290 Tomas Mojzis RC 2.00 5.00
291 David Steckel RC 2.00 5.00
292 Mike Green RC 2.00 5.00
293 Joey Tenute RC 2.00 5.00

2005-06 SPx Spectrum

COMMON CARD (1-90) 8.00 20.00
*STARS: 15X TO 40X BASE HI
1-90 PRINT RUN 25 SER.#'d SETS
91-132 PRINT RUN 1 SER.#'d SET
91-132 NOT PRICED DUE TO SCARCITY
*ROOKIE JSY: .75 X TO 2X
*ROOKIE JSY/AU: 1X TO 2.5X
*ROOKIE: .6X TO 1.5X
133-221 PRINT RUN 25 SER.#'d SETS
28 Steve Yzerman 25.00 60.00
50 Martin Brodeur 25.00 60.00
72 Mario Lemieux 25.00 60.00
156 Gilbert Brule 50.00 125.00
164 Dion Phaneuf 100.00 250.00
166 Cam Ward 75.00 150.00
170 Ryan Getzlaf 75.00 150.00
173 Henrik Lundqvist 100.00 250.00
189 Jeff Carter 100.00 250.00
190 Alexander Ovechkin 500.00 750.00
191 Sidney Crosby 1200.00 1800.00

2005-06 SPx Winning Combos

PRINT RUN 350 SER.#'d SETS
WC-AB David Aebischer 4.00 10.00
Rob Blake
WC-AN Sergei Fedorov 6.00 15.00
Teemu Selanne
WC-BA Martin Biron 4.00 10.00
Maxim Afinogenov
WC-BB Raymond Bourque 8.00 20.00
Rob Blake
WC-BE Martin Brodeur 10.00 25.00
Patrik Elias
WC-BF Dustin Brown 4.00 10.00
Alexander Frolov
WC-BH Jay Bouwmeester 4.00 10.00
Nathan Horton
WC-BK Mike Bossy 6.00 15.00
Jari Kurri
WC-BL Ray Bourque 8.00 20.00
Brian Leetch
WC-BM Todd Bertuzzi 4.00 10.00
Brendan Morrison
WC-BN Martin Biron 4.00 10.00
Mikka Noronen
WC-BO Glenn Murray 6.00 15.00
Joe Thornton
WC-BP Rob Blake 4.00 10.00
Chris Pronger
WC-BT Martin Brodeur 10.00 25.00
Jose Theodore
WC-CH Zdeno Chara 4.00 10.00
Martin Havlat
WC-CN Dan Cloutier 4.00 10.00
Markus Naslund
WC-CP Ty Conklin 4.00 10.00
Chris Pronger
WC-DA Bill Guerin 6.00 15.00
Mike Modano
WC-DB Chris Drury 4.00 10.00
Daniel Briere
WC-DN Marc Denis 6.00 15.00
Rick Nash
WC-DR Marcel Dionne 8.00 20.00
Luc Robitaille
WC-ED Ryan Smyth 4.00 10.00
Ales Hemsky
WC-EJ Eric Staal 4.00 10.00
Justin Williams
WC-EM Ed Belfour 8.00 20.00
Marty Turco
WC-FG Sergei Fedorov 6.00 15.00
Jean-Sebastian Giguere
WC-FL Jay Bouwmeester 6.00 15.00
Roberto Luongo
WC-FP Peter Forsberg 6.00 15.00
Keith Primeau
WC-FR Sergei Fedorov 6.00 15.00
Jeremy Roenick
WC-FS Peter Forsberg 10.00 25.00
Joe Sakic
WC-GC Wayne Gretzky 75.00 200.00
Sidney Crosby
WC-GF Marian Gaborik 6.00 15.00
Manny Fernandez
WC-GM Wayne Gretzky 20.00 50.00
Mark Messier
WC-GR Simon Gagne 4.00 10.00
Brad Richards
WC-HA Dany Heatley 8.00 20.00
Daniel Alfredsson
WC-HD Brett Hull 6.00 15.00
Shane Doan
WC-HH Marcel Hossa 6.00 15.00
Marian Hossa
WC-HJ Brett Hull 6.00 15.00
Curtis Joseph
WC-HK Marcel Hossa 6.00 15.00
Saku Koivu
WC-JM Jaromir Jagr 10.00 25.00
Mark Messier
WC-JP Joe Thornton 6.00 15.00
Patrice Bergeron
WC-JY Jaromir Jagr 6.00 15.00
Alexei Yashin
WC-KI Mikka Kiprusoff 8.00 20.00
Jarome Iginla
WC-KN Miikka Kiprusoff 6.00 15.00
Evgeni Nabokov

WC-KR Nikolai Khabibulin 4.00 10.00
Tuomo Ruutu
WC-LA Luc Robitaille 8.00 20.00
Jeremy Roenick
WC-LF Mario Lemieux 10.00 25.00
John LeClair
WC-LJ Mario Lemieux 12.00 30.00
Jaromir Jagr
WC-LK Guy Lafleur 6.00 15.00
Saku Koivu
WC-MI Marian Hossa 6.00 15.00
Ilya Kovalchuk
WC-MM Mike Modano 6.00 15.00
Brenden Morrow
WC-MN Brendan Morrison 4.00 10.00
Markus Naslund
WC-MP Mike Ribeiro 6.00 15.00
Patrice Bergeron
WC-MT Mark Messier 6.00 15.00
Bryan Trottier
WC-NA Owen Nolan 4.00 10.00
Nik Antropov
WC-ND Ladislav Nagy 4.00 10.00
Shane Doan
WC-NY Mike Bossy 6.00 15.00
Bryan Trottier
WC-NZ Rick Nash 6.00 15.00
Nikolai Zherdev
WC-OT Dany Heatley 6.00 15.00
Martin Havlat
WC-PE Keith Primeau 4.00 10.00
Robert Esche
WC-PG Keith Primeau 4.00 10.00
Simon Gagne
WC-PH Michael Peca 4.00 10.00
Ales Hemsky
WC-PR Zigmund Palffy 4.00 10.00
Mark Recchi
WC-PS Mark Parrish 4.00 10.00
Miroslav Satan
WC-RB Andrew Raycroft 6.00 15.00
Patrice Bergeron
WC-RC Wade Redden 4.00 10.00
Zdeno Chara
WC-RK Michael Ryder 4.00 10.00
Saku Koivu
WC-RL Andrew Raycroft 6.00 15.00
Kari Lehtonen
WC-RR Michael Ryder 4.00 10.00
Mike Ribeiro
WC-RT Mike Ribeiro 6.00 15.00
Jose Theodore
WC-RW Henrik Zetterberg 6.00 15.00
Niklas Lidstrom
WC-SA Jason Spezza 6.00 15.00
Daniel Alfredsson
WC-SB Jason Spezza 6.00 15.00
Patrice Bergeron
WC-SC Ryan Smyth 4.00 10.00
Ty Conklin
WC-SF Martin St. Louis 6.00 15.00
Ruslan Fedotenko
WC-SH Joe Sakic 6.00 15.00
Milan Hejduk
WC-SL Martin St.Louis 6.00 15.00
Vincent Lecavalier
WC-SN Mats Sundin 6.00 15.00
Owen Nolan
WC-SR Scott Stevens 4.00 10.00
Brian Rafalski
WC-ST Marty Turco 4.00 10.00
Brenden Morrow
WC-SW Matt Stajan 4.00 10.00
Justin Williams
WC-SY Brendan Shanahan 10.00 25.00
Steve Yzerman
WC-TB Brad Richards 6.00 15.00
Vincent Lecavalier
WC-TH Alex Tanguay 4.00 10.00
Milan Hejduk
WC-TM Marty Turco 8.00 20.00
Mike Modano
WC-TO Mats Sundin 6.00 15.00
Ed Belfour
WC-VA Ed Jovanovski 4.00 10.00
Brendan Morrison
WC-VH Tomas Vokoun 6.00 15.00
Dominik Hasek
WC-WH Stephen Weiss 4.00 10.00
Nathan Horton
WC-WL Peter Worrell 4.00 10.00
Georges Laraque
WC-WM Doug Weight 4.00 10.00
Al MacInnis
WC-WT Doug Weight 4.00 10.00
Keith Tkachuk
WC-ZD Henrik Zetterberg 4.00 10.00
Kris Draper
WC-ZL Henrik Zetterberg 6.00 15.00
Manny Legace

2005-06 SPx Winning Combos Autographs

*AUTO: 2XTO 5X BASIC WC
PRINT RUN 25 SER.#'d SETS
AWC-BT Martin Brodeur
Jose Theodore 100.00 250.00
AWC-GC W.Gretzky/S.Crosby 1500.00 2000.00
AWC-HK Marian Hossa
Ilya Kovalchuk 75.00 150.00

2005-06 SPx Winning Combos Gold

*GOLD: .6X TO 1.5X BASIC WC
PRINT RUN 99 SER.#'d SETS

2005-06 SPx Winning Combos Spectrum

PRINT RUN 10 SER.#'d SETS
NOT PRICED DUE TO SCARCITY

2005-06 SPx Winning Materials

PRINT RUN 350 SER.#'d SETS
WM-AE David Aebischer 3.00 8.00
WM-AF Alexander Frolov 3.00 8.00
WM-AH Ales Hemsky 4.00 10.00
WM-AR Andrew Raycroft 4.00 10.00
WM-AT Alex Tanguay 4.00 10.00
WM-BG Bill Guerin 4.00 10.00
WM-BH Brett Hull 5.00 12.00
WM-BL Brian Leetch 4.00 10.00
WM-BM Brendan Morrison 3.00 8.00
WM-BR Brad Richards 4.00 10.00
WM-BS Brendan Shanahan 4.00 10.00
WM-BT Bryan Trottier 4.00 10.00
WM-BY Mike Bossy 4.00 10.00
WM-CD Chris Drury 4.00 10.00
WM-CJ Curtis Joseph 4.00 10.00
WM-CP Chris Pronger 4.00 10.00
WM-DA Daniel Alfredsson 4.00 10.00
WM-DB Daniel Briere 4.00 10.00
WM-DH Dany Heatley 6.00 15.00
WM-DW Doug Weight 3.00 8.00
WM-EB Ed Belfour 4.00 10.00
WM-ED Eric Daze 3.00 8.00
WM-EJ Ed Jovanovski 3.00 8.00
WM-GL Guy Lafleur 5.00 12.00
WM-HA Dominik Hasek 10.00 25.00
WM-HO Marian Hossa 4.00 10.00
WM-HV Martin Havlat 4.00 10.00
WM-HZ Henrik Zetterberg 5.00 12.00
WM-IK Ilya Kovalchuk 6.00 15.00
WM-JG Jean-Sebastian Giguere 4.00 10.00
WM-JI Jarome Iginla 6.00 15.00
WM-JJ Jaromir Jagr 6.00 15.00
WM-JL John LeClair 4.00 10.00
WM-JO Jose Theodore 5.00 12.00
WM-JR Jeremy Roenick 5.00 12.00
WM-JS Joe Sakic 10.00 25.00
WM-JT Joe Thornton 8.00 20.00
WM-JW Justin Williams 3.00 8.00
WM-KD Kris Draper 3.00 8.00
WM-KF Miikka Kiprusoff 5.00 12.00
WM-KL Kari Lehtonen 4.00 10.00
WM-KP Keith Primeau 3.00 8.00
WM-KT Keith Tkachuk 4.00 10.00
WM-LN Ladislav Nagy 3.00 8.00
WM-LR Luc Robitaille 4.00 10.00
WM-LX Mario Lemieux 15.00 40.00
WM-MB Martin Brodeur 12.00 30.00
WM-MC Bryan McCabe 4.00 10.00
WM-MD Marcel Dionne 4.00 10.00
WM-MG Marian Gaborik 8.00 20.00
WM-MH Milan Hejduk 4.00 10.00
WM-ML Manny Legace 3.00 8.00
WM-MM Mike Modano 5.00 12.00
WM-MN Markus Naslund 4.00 10.00
WM-MP Mark Parrish 3.00 8.00
WM-MR Mike Ribeiro 3.00 8.00
WM-MS Mark Messier 5.00 12.00
WM-MW Brenden Morrow 3.00 8.00
WM-NA Nik Antropov 3.00 8.00
WM-NH Nathan Horton 3.00 8.00
WM-NK Nikolai Khabibulin 4.00 10.00
WM-NZ Nikolai Zherdev 3.00 8.00
WM-OK Olaf Kolzig 4.00 10.00
WM-ON Owen Nolan 4.00 10.00
WM-PB Patrice Bergeron 4.00 10.00
WM-PE Michael Peca 3.00 8.00
WM-PF Peter Forsberg 6.00 15.00
WM-PM Patrick Marleau 4.00 10.00
WM-RE Robert Esche 3.00 8.00
WM-RF Ruslan Fedotenko 3.00 8.00
WM-RL Roberto Luongo 6.00 15.00
WM-RN Rick Nash 5.00 12.00
WM-RS Ryan Smyth 4.00 10.00
WM-RY Michael Ryder 4.00 10.00
WM-RZ Richard Zednik 3.00 8.00
WM-SA Miroslav Satan 4.00 10.00
WM-SC Sidney Crosby 40.00 80.00
WM-SD Shane Doan 4.00 10.00
WM-SF Sergei Fedorov 5.00 12.00
WM-SG Simon Gagne 4.00 10.00
WM-SK Saku Koivu 4.00 10.00
WM-SL Martin St. Louis 4.00 10.00
WM-SP Jason Spezza 5.00 12.00
WM-ST Matt Stajan 3.00 8.00
WM-SU Mats Sundin 4.00 10.00
WM-SW Stephen Weiss 3.00 8.00
WM-SY Steve Yzerman 12.00 30.00
WM-TC Ty Conklin 3.00 8.00
WM-TR Tuomo Ruutu 4.00 10.00
WM-TS Teemu Selanne 4.00 10.00
WM-TU Marty Turco 4.00 10.00
WM-VL Vincent Lecavalier 4.00 10.00
WM-WG Wayne Gretzky 25.00 50.00
WM-ZC Zdeno Chara 4.00 10.00
WM-ZP Zigmund Palffy 4.00 10.00

2005-06 SPx Winning Materials Autographs

*AUTO: 1.5X TO 4X BASIC WM
PRINT RUN 50 SER.#'d SETS
AWM-HA Dominik Hasek 40.00 100.00
AWM-IK Ilya Kovalchuk 30.00 80.00
AWM-JI Jarome Iginla 30.00 80.00
AWM-JO Joe Thornton 30.00 80.00
AWM-KP Keith Primeau 20.00 50.00
AWM-MB Martin Brodeur 60.00 150.00
AWM-MO Mike Modano 30.00 80.00
AWM-PR Patrick Roy 100.00 200.00
AWM-RN Rick Nash 30.00 80.00
AWM-VL Vincent Lecavalier 30.00 80.00
AWM-WG Wayne Gretzky 200.00 350.00

2005-06 SPx Winning Materials Gold

*GOLD: .6X TO 1.5X BASIC WM
PRINT RUN 99 SER.#'d SETS
WM-ES Eric Staal 12.50 30.00
WM-MB Martin Brodeur 20.00 50.00
WM-PK Paul Kariya 8.00 20.00
WM-SC Sidney Crosby 100.00 250.00

2005-06 SPx Winning Materials Spectrum

PRINT RUN 10 SER.#'d SETS
NOT PRICED DUE TO SCARCITY

2005-06 SPx Xcitement Legends

PRINT RUN 499 SER.#'d SETS
XL-BB Bill Barber 2.00 5.00
XL-BC Bobby Clarke 3.00 8.00
XL-BG Bernie Geoffrion 3.00 8.00
XL-BH Bobby Hull 4.00 10.00
XL-BN Bob Nystrom 2.00 5.00
XL-BO Johnny Bower 3.00 8.00
XL-BP Brad Park 2.00 5.00
XL-BT Bryan Trottier 2.00 5.00
XL-BU Johnny Bucyk 3.00 8.00
XL-CG Clark Gillies 2.00 5.00
XL-CN Cam Neely 4.00 10.00
XL-DC Don Cherry 3.00 8.00
XL-DM Dickie Moore 3.00 8.00
XL-DS Denis Savard 2.00 5.00
XL-DT Dave Taylor 2.00 5.00
XL-FM Frank Mahovlich 3.00 8.00
XL-GA Glenn Anderson 2.00 5.00
XL-GC Gerry Cheevers 4.00 10.00
XL-GF Grant Fuhr 4.00 10.00
XL-GH Gordie Howe 6.00 15.00
XL-GL Guy Lafleur 4.00 10.00
XL-GO Butch Goring 2.00 5.00
XL-GP Gilbert Perreault 3.00 8.00
XL-HL Hakan Loob 2.00 5.00
XL-JB Jean Beliveau 4.00 10.00
XL-JK Jari Kurri 3.00 8.00
XL-KH Ken Hodge 2.00 5.00
XL-KM Ken Morrow 2.00 5.00
XL-LA Guy Lapointe 2.00 5.00
XL-LM Lanny McDonald 2.00 5.00
XL-MB Mike Bossy 3.00 8.00
XL-MD Marcel Dionne 3.00 8.00
XL-MN Mats Naslund 2.00 5.00
XL-PE Phil Esposito 4.00 10.00
XL-PR Patrick Roy 8.00 20.00
XL-PS Peter Stastny 2.00 5.00
XL-RH Ron Hextall 3.00 8.00
XL-RK Red Kelly 2.00 5.00
XL-RL Reggie Leach 2.00 5.00
XL-RM Rick Martin 2.00 5.00
XL-RR Rene Robert 2.00 5.00
XL-RV Rogie Vachon 3.00 8.00
XL-SA Derek Sanderson 3.00 8.00
XL-SB Scotty Bowman 3.00 8.00
XL-SM Stan Mikita 3.00 8.00
XL-TE Tony Esposito 4.00 10.00
XL-TO Terry O'Reilly 2.00 5.00
XL-TW Dave "Tiger" Williams 2.00 5.00
XL-WC Wayne Cashman 2.00 5.00
XL-WG Wayne Gretzky 10.00 25.00

2005-06 SPx Xcitement Legends Gold

*GOLD: .75X TO 2X
PRINT RUN 99 SER.#'d SETS

2005-06 SPx Xcitement Legends Spectrum

PRINT RUN 5 SER.#'d SETS
NOT PRICED DUE TO SCARCITY

2005-06 SPx Xcitement Rookies

PRINT RUN 999 SER.#'d SETS
XR-AA Andrew Alberts 2.00 5.00
XR-AM Andrej Meszaros 2.00 5.00
XR-AO Alexander Ovechkin 15.00 30.00
XR-AP Alexander Perezhogin 2.00 5.00
XR-AS Alexander Steen 3.00 8.00
XR-AW Andrew Wozniewski 2.00 5.00
XR-BB Brandon Bochenski 2.00 5.00
XR-BC Braydon Coburn 2.00 5.00
XR-BS Brent Seabrook 2.00 5.00
XR-CB Cam Barker 2.00 5.00
XR-CC Chris Campoli 2.00 5.00
XR-CP Corey Perry 4.00 10.00
XR-CW Cam Ward 4.00 10.00
XR-DK Duncan Keith 2.00 5.00
XR-DL David Leneveu 2.00 5.00
XR-DP Dion Phaneuf 8.00 20.00
XR-EN Eric Nystrom 2.00 5.00
XR-GB Gilbert Brule 4.00 10.00
XR-HL Henrik Lundqvist 8.00 20.00
XR-HT Hannu Toivonen 3.00 8.00
XR-JC Jeff Carter 4.00 10.00
XR-JF Johan Franzen 2.00 5.00
XR-JH Jim Howard 3.00 8.00
XR-JJ Jussi Jokinen 3.00 8.00
XR-JM Jay McClement 2.00 5.00
XR-JS Jim Slater 2.00 5.00
XR-JW Jeff Woywitka 2.00 5.00
XR-KB Keith Ballard 2.00 5.00
XR-KD Kevin Dallman 2.00 5.00
XR-KN Kevin Nastiuk 2.00 5.00
XR-MF Matt Foy 2.00 5.00
XR-MJ Milan Jurcina 2.00 5.00
XR-MO Alvaro Montoya 3.00 8.00
XR-MR Mike Richards 3.00 8.00
XR-MT Maxime Talbot 2.00 5.00
XR-PB Peter Budaj 2.00 5.00
XR-PN Petteri Nokelainen 2.00 5.00
XR-PP Petr Prucha 3.00 8.00
XR-RB Rene Bourque 2.00 5.00
XR-RC Ryane Clowe 2.00 5.00
XR-RG Ryan Getzlaf 5.00 12.00
XR-RN Robert Nilsson 2.00 5.00
XR-RO Rostislav Olesz 2.00 5.00
XR-RS Ryan Suter 2.00 5.00
XR-SC Sidney Crosby 40.00 80.00
XR-ST Anthony Stewart 2.00 5.00
XR-TV Thomas Vanek 5.00 12.00
XR-WW Wojtek Wolski 3.00 8.00
XR-YD Yann Danis 2.00 5.00
XR-ZP Zach Parise 4.00 10.00

2005-06 SPx Xcitement Rookies Gold

PRINT RUN 99 SER.#'d SETS

2005-06 SPx Xcitement Rookies Spectrum

PRINT RUN 5 SER.#'d SETS
NOT PRICED DUE TO SCARCITY

2005-06 SPx Xcitement Superstars

PRINT RUN 499 SER.#'d SETS
XS-AT Alex Tanguay 2.50 6.00
XS-BG Bill Guerin 1.50 4.00
XS-BH Brett Hull 3.00 8.00
XS-BL Brian Leetch 1.50 4.00
XS-BR Brad Richards 2.50 6.00
XS-BS Brendan Shanahan 2.50 6.00
XS-CP Chris Pronger 2.50 6.00
XS-DA Daniel Alfredsson 2.50 6.00
XS-DH Dany Heatley 4.00 10.00
XS-EB Ed Belfour 2.50 6.00
XS-ED Eric Daze 1.50 4.00
XS-EJ Ed Jovanovski 1.50 4.00
XS-EN Evgeni Nabokov 2.50 6.00
XS-HA Dominik Hasek 5.00 12.00
XS-HK Milan Hejduk 1.50 4.00
XS-HV Martin Havlat 2.50 6.00
XS-HZ Henrik Zetterberg 2.50 6.00
XS-IK Ilya Kovalchuk 4.00 10.00
XS-JI Jarome Iginla 4.00 10.00
XS-JJ Jaromir Jagr 4.00 10.00
XS-JO Joe Thornton 4.00 10.00
XS-JR Jeremy Roenick 2.50 6.00
XS-JS Joe Sakic 5.00 12.00
XS-JT Jose Theodore 3.00 8.00
XS-KD Kris Draper 1.50 4.00
XS-KP Keith Primeau 1.50 4.00
XS-KT Keith Tkachuk 1.50 4.00
XS-LR Luc Robitaille 2.50 6.00
XS-MB Martin Brodeur 6.00 15.00
XS-MG Marian Gaborik 4.00 10.00
XS-MH Marian Hossa 2.50 6.00
XS-ML Mario Lemieux 8.00 20.00
XS-MM Mark Messier 2.50 6.00
XS-MN Markus Naslund 2.50 6.00
XS-MO Mike Modano 4.00 10.00
XS-MP Mark Parrish 1.50 4.00
XS-MS Mats Sundin 2.50 6.00
XS-MT Marty Turco 2.50 6.00
XS-OK Olaf Kolzig 2.50 6.00
XS-ON Owen Nolan 1.50 4.00
XS-RB Rob Blake 1.50 4.00
XS-RL Roberto Luongo 4.00 10.00
XS-RN Rick Nash 4.00 10.00
XS-SD Shane Doan 1.50 4.00
XS-SF Sergei Fedorov 3.00 8.00
XS-SG Simon Gagne 2.50 6.00
XS-SK Saku Koivu 2.50 6.00
XS-SL Martin St. Louis 2.50 6.00
XS-SY Steve Yzerman 8.00 20.00
XS-VL Vincent Lecavalier 2.50 6.00

2005-06 SPx Xcitement Superstars Gold

*GOLD: .5X TO 1.25X
PRINT RUN 99 SER.#'d SETS

2005-06 SPx Xcitement Superstars Spectrum

PRINT RUN 5 SER.#'d SETS
NOT PRICED DUE TO SCARCITY

2006-07 SPx

1 Chris Pronger .20 .50
2 Teemu Selanne .25 .60
3 Jean-Sebastien Giguere .20 .50
4 Kari Lehtonen .25 .60
5 Marian Hossa .20 .50
6 Ilya Kovalchuk .30 .75
7 Patrice Bergeron .25 .60
8 Zdeno Chara .12 .30
9 Brad Boyes .12 .30
10 Ryan Miller .25 .60
11 Chris Drury .12 .30
12 Alex Tanguay .20 .50
13 Dion Phaneuf .30 .75
14 Jarome Iginla .30 .75
15 Miikka Kiprusoff .25 .60
16 Eric Staal .25 .60
17 Cam Ward .25 .60
18 Rod Brind'Amour .20 .50
19 Nikolai Khabibulin .25 .60
20 Martin Havlat .20 .50
21 Tuomo Ruutu .12 .30
22 Joe Sakic .50 1.25
23 Marek Svatos .12 .30
24 Jose Theodore .25 .60
25 Milan Hejduk .12 .30
26 Rick Nash .25 .60
27 Sergei Fedorov .25 .60
28 Fredrik Modin .12 .30
29 Eric Lindros .25 .60
30 Mike Modano .25 .60
31 Brenden Morrow .20 .50
32 Marty Turco .20 .50
33 Pavel Datsyuk .20 .50
34 Gordie Howe 1.25 3.00
35 Nicklas Lidstrom .25 .60
36 Henrik Zetterberg .25 .60
37 Dominik Hasek .40 1.00
38 Ryan Smyth .20 .50
39 Ales Hemsky .12 .30
40 Joffrey Lupul .12 .30
41 Wayne Gretzky 2.50 6.00
42 Olli Jokinen .12 .30
43 Todd Bertuzzi .20 .50
44 Ed Belfour .25 .60
45 Jay Bouwmeester .12 .30
46 Alexander Frolov .12 .30
47 Rob Blake .12 .30
48 Marian Gaborik .30 .75
49 Manny Fernandez .20 .50
50 Pavol Demitra .12 .30
51 Alexei Kovalev .12 .30
52 Cristobal Huet .30 .75
53 Saku Koivu .25 .60
54 Michael Ryder .20 .50
55 Mike Ribeiro .12 .30
56 Paul Kariya .25 .60
57 Tomas Vokoun .20 .50
58 Jason Arnott .12 .30
59 Martin Brodeur 1.00 2.50
60 Brian Gionta .12 .30
61 Patrik Elias .12 .30
62 Scott Gomez .12 .30
63 Rick DiPietro .20 .50
64 Miroslav Satan .12 .30
65 Alexei Yashin .12 .30
66 Brendan Shanahan .25 .60
67 Henrik Lundqvist .30 .75
68 Jaromir Jagr .40 1.00
69 Petr Prucha .12 .30
70 Daniel Alfredsson .20 .50
71 Jason Spezza .25 .60
72 Dany Heatley .30 .75
73 Martin Gerber .25 .60
74 Jeff Carter .25 .60
75 Peter Forsberg .40 1.00
76 Simon Gagne .25 .60
77 Shane Doan .12 .30
78 Jeremy Roenick .30 .75
79 Curtis Joseph .25 .60
80 Mark Recchi .12 .30
81 Sidney Crosby 2.50 6.00
82 Marc-Andre Fleury .25 .60
83 Mario Lemieux 1.50 4.00
84 Patrick Marleau .20 .50
85 Joe Thornton .40 1.00
86 Jonathan Cheechoo .25 .60
87 Keith Tkachuk .20 .50
88 Doug Weight .12 .30
89 Brad Richards .20 .50
90 Vincent Lecavalier .25 .60
91 Martin St. Louis .25 .60
92 Mats Sundin .25 .60
93 Andrew Raycroft .20 .50
94 Michael Peca .12 .30
95 Alexander Steen .20 .50
96 Roberto Luongo .30 .75
97 Markus Naslund .25 .60
98 Brendan Morrison .12 .30
99 Olaf Kolzig .25 .60
100 Alexander Ovechkin 1.50 4.00
101 Teemu Selanne JSY 10.00 25.00
102 Ilya Kovalchuk JSY 12.00 30.00
103 Jarome Iginla JSY 15.00 40.00
104 Mark Recchi JSY 8.00 20.00
105 Eric Staal JSY 10.00 25.00
106 Joe Sakic JSY 15.00 50.00
107 Sergei Fedorov JSY 10.00 25.00
108 Mike Modano JSY 10.00 25.00
109 Brendan Shanahan JSY 10.00 25.00
110 Mats Sundin JSY 8.00 20.00
111 Bill Ranford JSY 12.00 30.00
112 Roberto Luongo JSY 12.00 30.00
113 Alexei Kovalev JSY 8.00 20.00
114 Paul Kariya JSY 12.00 30.00
115 Jaromir Jagr JSY 15.00 40.00
116 Peter Forsberg JSY 15.00 40.00
117 Richard Brodeur JSY 10.00 25.00
118 Peter Stastny JSY 10.00 25.00
119 Ron Hextall JSY 15.00 40.00
120 Eric Lindros JSY 10.00 25.00
121 Dave Williams JSY 8.00 20.00
122 Cam Neely JSY AU 25.00 60.00
123 Ray Bourque JSY AU 60.00 125.00
124 Gilbert Perreault JSY AU 25.00 60.00
125 Lanny McDonald JSY AU 30.00 60.00
126 Gordie Howe JSY AU 150.00 250.00
127 Grant Fuhr JSY AU 30.00 80.00
128 Wayne Gretzky JSY AU 300.00 450.00
129 Guy Lafleur JSY AU 60.00 125.00
130 Patrick Roy JSY AU 200.00 350.00
131 Martin Brodeur JSY AU 100.00 200.00
132 Mike Bossy JSY AU 40.00 80.00
133 Dominik Hasek JSY AU 40.00 80.00
134 Sidney Crosby JSY AU 175.00 300.00
135 Mario Lemieux SP JSY AU 200.00 350.00
136 Al MacInnis JSY AU 25.00 50.00
137 Borje Salming JSY AU 20.00 50.00
138 Darryl Sittler SP JSY AU 250.00350.00
139 Steve Shutt JSY AU 20.00 50.00
140 Ed Belfour JSY AU 40.00 80.00
141 Bobby Clarke JSY AU 25.00 50.00
142 Billy Smith JSY AU 15.00 40.00
143 Dustin Byfuglien JSY RC 2.00 5.00
144 Drew Stafford JSY AU RC 20.00 50.00
145 Frank Doyle JSY RC 2.00 5.00
146 Carsen Germyn JSY RC 2.00 5.00
147 David Printz JSY RC 2.00 5.00
148 Masi Marjamaki JSY RC 2.00 5.00
149 Konstantin Pushkaryov JSY RC 2.00 5.00
150 Michel Ouellet JSY RC 6.00 15.00
151 Billy Thompson JSY RC 2.00 5.00
152 Filip Novak JSY RC 2.00 5.00
153 Miroslav Kopriva JSY RC 2.00 5.00
154 Jonas Johansson JSY RC 2.00 5.00
155 Shane O'Brien JSY RC 2.00 5.00
156 John Oduya JSY RC 2.00 5.00
157 Fredrik Norrena JSY RC 4.00 10.00
158 Niklas Backstrom JSY RC 5.00 12.00
159 D.J. King JSY RC 2.00 5.00
160 Patrick Thoresen JSY RC 4.00 10.00
161 Dustin Boyd JSY AU RC 6.00 15.00
162 Mikko Lehtonen JSY RC 2.00 5.00
163 Roman Polak JSY RC 2.00 5.00
164 Yan Stastny JSY AU RC 6.00 15.00
165 Mark Stuart JSY AU RC 6.00 15.00
166 Eric Fehr JSY AU RC 6.00 15.00
167 Ryan Potulny JSY AU RC 6.00 15.00
168 Ben Ondrus JSY AU RC 6.00 15.00
169 Brendan Bell JSY AU RC 6.00 15.00
170 Ian White JSY AU RC 6.00 15.00
171 Jeremy Williams JSY AU RC 6.00 15.00
172 Marc-Antoine Pouliot JSY AU RC 6.00 15.00
173 Noah Welch JSY AU RC 6.00 15.00
174 Shea Weber JSY AU RC 6.00 15.00
175 Jarkko Immonen JSY AU RC 6.00 15.00
176 Tomas Kopecky JSY AU RC 6.00 15.00
177 Matt Carle JSY AU RC 6.00 15.00
178 Ryan Shannon JSY AU RC 6.00 15.00
179 Anze Kopitar JSY AU RC 30.00 60.00
180 Travis Zajac JSY AU RC 8.00 20.00
181 Nigel Dawes JSY AU RC 6.00 15.00
182 Kristopher Letang JSY AU RC 6.00 15.00
183 Marc-Edouard Vlasic JSY AU RC 6.00 15.00
184 Ladislav Smid JSY AU RC 6.00 15.00
185 Loui Eriksson JSY AU RC 6.00 15.00
186 Paul Stastny JSY AU RC 30.00 60.00
187 Alexei Kaigorodov RC 2.00 5.00
188 Patrick O'Sullivan JSY AU RC 15.00 30.00
189 Phil Kessel JSY AU RC 25.00 60.00
190 Guillaume Latendresse
JSY AU RC 25.00 60.00
191 Jordan Staal JSY AU RC 75.00 175.00
192 Luc Bourdon JSY AU RC 15.00 30.00
193 Evgeni Malkin JSY AU RC 125.00 200.00
194 Keith Yandle JSY AU RC 4.00 10.00
195 Alexander Radulov
JSY AU RC 25.00 50.00
196 Rob Collins RC 2.00 5.00
197 Steve Regier RC 2.00 5.00
198 Matt Koalska RC 2.00 5.00
199 Ryan Caldwell RC 2.00 5.00
200 David Liffiton RC 2.00 5.00
201 Erik Reitz RC 2.00 5.00
202 Adam Burish RC 2.00 5.00
203 Alex Brooks RC 2.00 5.00
204 Joel Perrault RC 2.00 5.00
205 Nate Thompson RC 2.00 5.00
206 Janis Sprukts RC 2.00 5.00
207 Alexei Mikhnov RC 2.00 5.00
208 Dave Bolland RC 2.00 5.00
209 Michael Blunden RC 2.00 5.00
210 Lars Jonsson RC 2.00 5.00
211 Triston Grant RC 2.00 5.00
212 Matt Lashoff RC 2.00 5.00

2006-07 SPx Spectrum

COMMONS 4.00 10.00
*STARS: 12X TO 30X BASE HI
*FLASHBACK FABS: .75X TO 1.5X
PRINT RUN 25 #'d SETS
*BASE RCs: 1.5X TO 3X
*JSY RCs: .75X TO 2X
81 Sidney Crosby 120.00 300.00
128 Wayne Gretzky JSY AU 350.00 600.00
134 Sidney Crosby JSY AU 350.00 500.00
193 Evgeni Malkin JSY AU 350.00 500.00

2006-07 SPx SPxcitement

PRINT RUN 999 #'d SETS
X1 Chris Pronger 1.25 3.00
X2 Teemu Selanne 1.50 4.00
X3 Ilya Kovalchuk 2.00 5.00
X4 Kari Lehtonen 1.50 4.00
X5 Marian Hossa 1.25 3.00
X6 Ray Bourque 2.50 6.00
X7 Cam Neely 2.00 5.00
X8 Patrice Bergeron 1.25 3.00
X9 Brad Boyes 1.00 2.50
X10 Phil Esposito 1.50 4.00
X11 Gilbert Perreault 1.25 3.00
X12 Ryan Miller 1.50 4.00
X13 Chris Drury 1.00 2.50
X14 Lanny McDonald 1.25 3.00
X15 Jarome Iginla 2.00 5.00
X16 Miikka Kiprusoff 1.50 4.00
X17 Alex Tanguay 1.25 3.00
X18 Dion Phaneuf 2.00 5.00
X19 Nikolai Khabibulin 1.25 3.00
X20 Martin Havlat 1.25 3.00
X21 Tuomo Ruutu 1.00 2.50
X22 Joe Sakic 3.00 8.00
X23 Jose Theodore 1.50 4.00
X24 Milan Hejduk 1.00 2.50
X25 Marek Svatos 1.00 2.50
X26 Rick Nash 1.50 4.00
X27 Sergei Fedorov 1.50 4.00
X28 Gilbert Brule 1.00 2.50
X29 Mike Modano 1.50 4.00
X30 Marty Turco 1.25 3.00
X31 Eric Lindros 1.25 3.00
X32 Brenden Morrow 1.25 3.00
X33 Gordie Howe 2.00 5.00
X34 Henrik Zetterberg 1.50 4.00
X35 Pavel Datsyuk 1.25 3.00
X36 Nicklas Lidstrom 1.50 4.00
X37 Ted Lindsay 1.00 2.50
X38 Grant Fuhr 1.50 4.00
X39 Wayne Gretzky 6.00 15.00
X40 Ales Hemsky 1.00 2.50
X41 Ryan Smyth 1.25 3.00
X42 Jay Bouwmeester 1.00 2.50
X43 Nathan Horton 1.00 2.50
X44 Olli Jokinen 1.00 2.50
X45 Todd Bertuzzi 1.25 3.00
X46 Ed Belfour 1.50 4.00
X47 Alexander Frolov 1.00 2.50
X48 Rob Blake 1.25 3.00
X49 Rogie Vachon 1.25 3.00
X50 Marian Gaborik 2.00 5.00
X51 Manny Fernandez 1.25 3.00
X52 Pavol Demitra 1.00 2.50
X53 Patrick Roy 5.00 12.00
X54 Guy Lafleur 2.50 6.00
X55 Saku Koivu 1.50 4.00
X56 Cristobal Huet 2.00 5.00
X57 Michael Ryder 1.25 3.00
X58 Paul Kariya 1.50 4.00
X59 Tomas Vokoun 1.25 3.00
X60 Martin Brodeur 3.00 8.00
X61 Patrik Elias 1.00 2.50
X62 Brian Gionta 1.00 2.50
X63 Mike Bossy 1.25 3.00
X64 Miroslav Satan 1.00 2.50
X65 Alexei Yashin 1.00 2.50
X66 Jaromir Jagr 2.50 6.00
X67 Henrik Lundqvist 2.00 5.00
X68 Brendan Shanahan 1.50 4.00
X69 Dany Heatley 2.00 5.00
X70 Jason Spezza 1.50 4.00
X71 Daniel Alfredsson 1.25 3.00
X72 Martin Gerber 1.50 4.00
X73 Peter Forsberg 2.50 6.00
X74 Simon Gagne 1.25 3.00
X75 Jeff Carter 1.50 4.00
X76 Shane Doan 1.00 2.50
X77 Jeremy Roenick 1.50 4.00
X78 Owen Nolan 1.25 3.00
X79 Mario Lemieux 5.00 12.00
X80 Sidney Crosby 8.00 20.00
X81 Marc-Andre Fleury 1.50 4.00
X82 Joe Thornton 2.50 6.00
X83 Jonathan Cheechoo 1.25 3.00
X84 Patrick Marleau 1.25 3.00
X85 Doug Weight 1.00 2.50
X86 Keith Tkachuk 1.25 3.00
X87 Joe Mullen 1.00 2.50
X88 Vincent Lecavalier 1.50 4.00
X89 Martin St. Louis 1.25 3.00
X90 Brad Richards 1.25 3.00
X91 Borje Salming 1.25 3.00
X92 Darryl Sittler 1.50 4.00
X93 Mats Sundin 1.25 3.00
X94 Andrew Raycroft 1.25 3.00
X95 Alexander Steen 1.25 3.00
X96 Markus Naslund 1.25 3.00
X97 Roberto Luongo 2.00 5.00
X98 Richard Brodeur 3.00
X99 Alexander Ovechkin 3.00 8.00
X100 Olaf Kolzig 1.25 3.00

2006-07 SPx SPxcitement Spectrum

*STARS: 1.5X TO 4X BASE HI
PRINT RUN 99 #'d SETS
X39 Wayne Gretzky 25.00 60.00
X80 Sidney Crosby 40.00 100.00

2006-07 SPx SPxcitement Autographs

PRINT RUN 10 #'d SETS
NOT PRICED DUE TO SCARCITY
X1 Chris Pronger
X3 Ilya Kovalchuk
X4 Kari Lehtonen
X5 Marian Hossa
X6 Ray Bourque
X7 Cam Neely
X8 Patrice Bergeron
X11 Gilbert Perreault
X15 Jarome Iginla
X17 Alex Tanguay
X18 Dion Phaneuf
X19 Nikolai Khabibulin
X20 Martin Havlat
X23 Jose Theodore
X24 Milan Hejduk
X25 Marek Svatos
X26 Rick Nash
X30 Marty Turco
X33 Gordie Howe
X34 Henrik Zetterberg
X36 Nicklas Lidstrom
X38 Grant Fuhr
X39 Wayne Gretzky
X40 Ales Hemsky
X41 Ryan Smyth
X42 Jay Bouwmeester
X43 Nathan Horton
X47 Alexander Frolov
X48 Rob Blake
X50 Marian Gaborik
X53 Patrick Roy
X54 Guy Lafleur
X55 Saku Koivu
X56 Cristobal Huet
X57 Michael Ryder
X60 Martin Brodeur
X61 Patrik Elias
X63 Mike Bossy
X64 Miroslav Satan
X69 Dany Heatley
X76 Shane Doan
X77 Jeremy Roenick
X79 Mario Lemieux

X80 Sidney Crosby
X81 Marc-Andre Fleury
X82 Joe Thornton
X83 Jonathan Cheechoo
X85 Doug Weight
X88 Vincent Lecavalier
X91 Borje Salming
X92 Darryl Sittler
X96 Markus Naslund
X97 Roberto Luongo

2006-07 SPx Winning Materials

WMAF Alexander Frolov 2.00 5.00
WMAH Ales Hemsky 2.00 5.00
WMAM Al MacInnis 2.00 5.00
WMAN Glenn Anderson 2.00 5.00
WMAO Alexander Ovechkin 6.00 15.00
WMAS Alexander Steen 2.50 6.00
WMAT Alex Tanguay 2.50 6.00
WMAY Alexei Yashin 2.00 5.00
WMBB Brad Boyes 2.00 5.00
WMBC Bobby Clarke 3.00 8.00
WMBG Bill Guerin 2.00 5.00
WMBL Brian Leetch 3.00 8.00
WMBM Bryan McCabe 2.00 5.00
WMBO Pierre-Marc Bouchard 2.00 5.00
WMBR Brad Richards 2.50 6.00
WMBS Billy Smith 3.00 8.00
WMBT Bryan Trottier 2.50 6.00
WMCA Jeff Carter 3.00 8.00
WMCC Chris Chelios 2.50 6.00
WMCD Chris Drury 2.00 5.00
WMCH Cristobal Huet 3.00 8.00
WMCJ Curtis Joseph 3.00 8.00
WMCN Cam Neely 3.00 8.00
WMCP Chris Pronger 2.50 6.00
WMCW Cam Ward 3.00 8.00
WMDA Daniel Alfredsson 2.50 6.00
WMDH Dany Heatley 4.00 10.00
WMDP Dion Phaneuf 4.00 10.00
WMDW Doug Weight 2.00 5.00
WMEB Ed Belfour 3.00 8.00
WMES Eric Staal 3.00 8.00
WMGA Simon Gagne 3.00 8.00
WMGF Grant Fuhr 3.00 8.00
WMGI Brian Gionta 2.00 5.00
WMHA Martin Havlat 2.50 6.00
WMHE Milan Hejduk 2.00 5.00
WMHK Dominik Hasek 4.00 10.00
WMHL Henrik Lundqvist 4.00 10.00
WMHO Tomas Holmstrom 2.00 5.00
WMHZ Henrik Zetterberg 3.00 8.00
WMIK Ilya Kovalchuk 4.00 10.00
WMJB Jay Bouwmeester 2.00 5.00
WMJC Jonathan Cheechoo 3.00 8.00
WMJG Jean-Sebastien Giguere 2.50 6.00
WMJI Jarome Iginla 4.00 10.00
WMJJ Jaromir Jagr 4.00 10.00
WMJL Joffrey Lupul 2.00 5.00
WMJS Joe Sakic 5.00 12.00
WMJT Jose Theodore 3.00 8.00
WMJW Justin Williams 2.00 5.00
WMKC Kyle Calder 2.00 5.00
WMKD Kris Draper 2.00 5.00
WMKL Kari Lehtonen 3.00 8.00
WMKT Keith Tkachuk 2.50 6.00
WMLM Lanny McDonald 2.50 6.00
WMMA Maxim Afinogenov 2.00 5.00
WMMB Martin Brodeur 6.00 15.00
WMMC Mike Cammalleri 2.00 5.00
WMMF Manny Fernandez 2.50 6.00
WMMG Marian Gaborik 4.00 10.00
WMMH Marian Hossa 2.50 6.00
WMMM Mike Modano 3.00 8.00
WMMN Markus Naslund 3.00 8.00
WMMO Brendan Morrison 2.00 5.00
WMMR Michael Ryder 2.50 6.00
WMMS Miroslav Satan 2.00 5.00
WMMT Marty Turco 2.50 6.00
WMMW Brenden Morrow 2.50 6.00
WMNL Nicklas Lidstrom 3.00 8.00
WMOJ Olli Jokinen 2.00 5.00
WMOK Olaf Kolzig 3.00 8.00
WMPB Patrice Bergeron 3.00 8.00
WMPD Pavel Datsyuk 2.50 6.00
WMPE Patrik Elias 2.00 5.00
WMPF Peter Forsberg 4.00 10.00
WMPK Paul Kariya 3.00 8.00
WMPM Patrick Marleau 2.50 6.00
WMPP Petr Prucha 2.00 5.00
WMPT Pierre Turgeon 2.00 5.00
WMRD Rick DiPietro 2.50 6.00
WMRE Robert Esche 2.50 6.00
WMRE Mark Recchi 2.00 5.00
WMRL Roberto Luongo 4.00 10.00
WMRN Rick Nash 3.00 8.00
WMRO Rob Blake 2.50 6.00
WMRS Ryan Smyth 2.50 6.00
WMSA Borje Salming 2.50 6.00
WMSC Sidney Crosby 20.00 50.00
WMSD Shane Doan 2.00 5.00
WMSF Sergei Federov 3.00 8.00
WMSG Scott Gomez 2.00 5.00
WMSK Saku Koivu 3.00 8.00
WMSP Jason Spezza 3.00 8.00
WMSS Sergei Samsonov 2.50 6.00
WMST Martin St. Louis 2.50 6.00
WMTH Joe Thornton 4.00 10.00
WMTR Tuomo Ruutu 2.00 5.00
WMTS Teemu Selanne 3.00 8.00
WMTV Tomas Vokoun 2.50 6.00
WMVL Vincent Lecavalier 3.00 8.00

2006-07 SPx Winning Materials Spectrum

PRINT RUN 99 #'d SETS

2006-07 SPx Winning Materials Autographs

PRINT RUN 10 #'d SETS
NOT PRICED DUE TO SCARCITY
WMAF Alexander Frolov
WMAH Ales Hemsky
WMAM Al MacInnis
WMAN Glenn Anderson
WMAT Alex Tanguay
WMAY Alexei Yashin
WMBB Brad Boyes
WMBC Bobby Clarke
WMBM Bryan McCabe
WMBO PierreMarc Bouchard
WMBS Billy Smith
WMCA Jeff Carter
WMCD Chris Drury
WMCH Cristobal Huet
WMCN Cam Neely
WMCP Chris Pronger
WMDH Dany Heatley
WMDP Dion Phaneuf
WMDW Doug Weight
WMEB Ed Belfour
WMES Eric Staal
WMGF Grant Fuhr
WMHA Martin Havlat
WMHE Milan Hejduk
WMHK Dominik Hasek
WMHZ Henrik Zetterberg
WMIK Ilya Kovalchuk
WMJB Jay Bouwmeester
WMJC Jonathan Cheechoo
WMJI Jarome Iginla
WMJT Jose Theodore
WMKC Kyle Calder
WMKD Kris Draper
WMKL Kari Lehtonen
WMMA Maxim Afinogenov
WMMB Martin Brodeur
WMMC Mike Cammalleri
WMMG Marian Gaborik
WMMH Marian Hossa
WMMN Markus Naslund
WMMR Michael Ryder
WMMS Miroslav Satan
WMMT Marty Turco
WMNL Nicklas Lidstrom
WMPB Patrice Bergeron
WMPE Patrik Elias
WMPM Patrick Marleau
WMRE Robert Esche
WMRL Roberto Luongo
WMRN Rick Nash
WMRO Rob Blake
WMRS Ryan Smyth
WMSA Borje Salming
WMSC Sidney Crosby
WMSD Shane Doan
WMSG Scott Gomez
WMSK Saku Koivu
WMSS Sergei Samsonov
WMTH Joe Thornton
WMTR Tuomo Ruutu
WMTV Tomas Vokoun
WMVL Vincent Lecavalier

1998-99 SPx Finite

The 1998-99 SPx Finite hobby-only Series One was issued with a total of 180 cards. The three-card packs retail for $5.99 each. The 90 regular player cards (1-90) are sequentially numbered to 9,500 and feature color action player photos with a unique bronze foil emblem embedded in the center of the cards. The set contains the subsets: Global Impact (91-120) sequentially numbered to 6,950, NHL Sure Shots, (121-150) numbered to 3,900, Marquee Performers (151-170) numbered to 2,625, and Living Legends (171-180) numbered to 1,620.

COMP.BASE SET (90) 30.00 80.00
COMP.GLOB.IMPACT.SET (30) 60.00 120.00
COMP.SURE SHOTS SET (30) 30.00 60.00
COMP. MARQ.PERF.SET (20) 125.00 250.00
COMP.LIVING.LEG.SET (10) 200.00400.00
1 Teemu Selanne .60 1.50
2 Guy Hebert .50 1.25
3 Josef Marha .20 .50
4 Travis Green .20 .50
5 Sergei Samsonov .50 1.25
6 Jason Allison .20 .50
7 Byron Dafoe .50 1.25
8 Dominik Hasek 1.25 3.00
9 Michael Peca .20 .50
10 Erik Rasmussen .20 .50
11 Matthew Barnaby .20 .50
12 Theo Fleury .20 .50
13 Derek Morris .20 .50
14 Valeri Bure .20 .50
15 Trevor Kidd .50 1.25
16 Sami Kapanen .20 .50
17 Bates Battaglia .20 .50
18 Tony Amonte .50 1.25
19 Dmitri Nabokov .20 .50
20 Daniel Cleary .20 .50
21 Jeff Hackett .50 1.25
22 Joe Sakic 1.25 3.00
23 Valeri Kamensky .50 1.25
24 Patrick Roy 3.00 8.00
25 Wade Belak .20 .50
26 Joe Nieuwendyk .50 1.25
27 Mike Keane .20 .50
28 Jere Lehtinen .20 .50
29 Ed Belfour .60 1.50
30 Steve Yzerman 3.00 8.00
31 Dmitri Mironov .20 .50
32 Brendan Shanahan .60 1.50
33 Nicklas Lidstrom .60 1.50
34 Doug Weight .50 1.25
35 Janne Niinimaa .20 .50
36 Bill Guerin .50 1.25
37 Ray Whitney .20 .50
38 Robert Svehla .20 .50
39 Ed Jovanovski .20 .50
40 Vladimir Tsyplakov .20 .50
41 Jozef Stumpel .50 1.25
42 Rob Blake .50 1.25
43 Mark Recchi .50 1.25
44 Andy Moog .50 1.25
45 Matt Higgins RC .20 .50
46 Martin Brodeur 1.50 4.00
47 Doug Gilmour .50 1.25
48 Brendan Morrison .50 1.25
49 Patrik Elias .50 1.25
50 Trevor Linden .50 1.25
51 Bryan Berard .20 .50
52 Zdeno Chara .20 .50
53 Wayne Gretzky 4.00 10.00
54 Marc Savard .20 .50
55 Daniel Goneau .20 .50
56 Pat Lafontaine .60 1.50
57 Alexei Yashin .20 .50
58 Marian Hossa .60 1.50
59 Wade Redden .20 .50
60 John LeClair .60 1.50
61 Alexandre Daigle .20 .50
62 Rod Brind'Amour .50 1.25
63 Chris Therien .20 .50
64 Keith Tkachuk .60 1.50
65 Brad Isbister .20 .50
66 Nikolai Khabibulin .50 1.25
67 Robert Dome .20 .50
68 Alexei Morozov .20 .50
69 Stu Barnes .20 .50
70 Tom Barrasso .50 1.25
71 Owen Nolan .50 1.25
72 Marco Sturm .50 1.25
73 Patrick Marleau .20 .50
74 Pierre Turgeon .50 1.25
75 Chris Pronger .50 1.25
76 Pavol Demitra .50 1.25
77 Grant Fuhr .50 1.25
78 Stephane Richer .50 1.25
79 Zac Bierk RC .50 1.25
80 Alexander Selivanov .20 .50
81 Mike Johnson .50 1.25
82 Mats Sundin .60 1.50
83 Alyn McAuley .20 .50
84 Pavel Bure .60 1.50
85 Todd Bertuzzi .60 1.50
86 Garth Snow .50 1.25
87 Peter Bondra .50 1.25
88 Olaf Kolzig .50 1.25
89 Jan Bulis .20 .50
90 Sergei Gonchar .20 .50
91 Pavel Bure GI .60 1.50
92 Joe Sakic GI 2.00 5.00
93 Steve Yzerman GI 5.00 12.00
94 Jaromir Jagr GI 1.50 4.00
95 Peter Forsberg GI 2.50 6.00
96 Brendan Shanahan GI 1.00 2.50
97 Brett Hull GI 1.25 3.00
98 Alexei Yashin GI .75 2.00
99 Wayne Gretzky GI 6.00 15.00
100 Eric Lindros GI 1.00 2.50
101 Sergei Samsonov GI .75 2.00
102 John LeClair GI 1.00 2.50
103 Dominik Hasek GI 2.00 5.00
104 Teemu Selanne GI 1.00 2.50
105 Martin Brodeur GI 2.50 6.00
106 Tony Amonte GI .75 2.00
107 Theo Fleury GI .75 2.00
108 Rob Blake GI .75 2.00
109 Mike Modano GI 1.50 4.00
110 Peter Bondra GI .75 2.00
111 Brian Leetch GI 1.00 2.50
112 Nicklas Lidstrom GI 1.00 2.50
113 Doug Weight GI .75 2.00
114 Zigmund Palffy GI .75 2.00
115 Saku Koivu GI 1.00 2.50
116 Paul Kariya GI 1.00 2.50
117 Ray Bourque GI 1.50 4.00
118 Mats Sundin GI 1.00 2.50
119 Patrick Roy GI 5.00 12.00
120 Chris Chelios GI 1.00 2.50
121 Sergei Samsonov SS 1.50 4.00
122 Mike Johnson SS .60 1.50
123 Patrik Elias SS 1.50 4.00
124 Josef Marha SS .60 1.50
125 Dan Cloutier SS .60 1.50
126 Cameron Mann SS .60 1.50
127 Mattias Ohlund SS .60 1.50
128 Daniel Cleary SS .60 1.50
129 Anders Eriksson SS .60 1.50
130 Patrick Marleau SS .60 1.50
131 Jan Bulis SS .60 1.50
132 Alyn McAuley SS .60 1.50
133 Joe Thornton SS 3.00 8.00
134 Andrei Zyuzin SS .60 1.50
135 Richard Zednik SS .60 1.50
136 Derek Morris SS .60 1.50
137 Bates Battaglia SS .60 1.50
138 Mike Watt SS .60 1.50
139 Olli Jokinen SS 1.50 4.00
140 Marian Hossa SS 2.00 5.00
141 Daniel Goneau SS .60 1.50
142 Erik Rasmussen SS .60 1.50
143 Daniel Briere SS .60 1.50
144 Norm Maracle RC SS 3.00 8.00
145 Brendan Morrison SS 1.50 4.00
146 Brad Isbister SS .60 1.50
147 Robert Dome SS .60 1.50
148 Zac Bierk SS .60 1.50
149 Alexei Morozov SS .60 1.50
150 Marco Sturm SS .60 1.50
151 Wayne Gretzky MP 12.00 30.00
152 Eric Lindros MP 2.00 5.00
153 Paul Kariya MP 2.00 5.00
154 Patrick Roy MP 8.00 20.00
155 Sergei Samsonov MP 2.00 5.00
156 Steve Yzerman MP 8.00 20.00
157 Teemu Selanne MP 2.00 5.00
158 Brendan Shanahan MP 2.00 5.00
159 Dominik Hasek MP 4.00 10.00
160 Mark Messier MP 2.00 5.00
161 Martin Brodeur MP 6.00 15.00
162 Mats Sundin MP 2.00 5.00
163 Joe Sakic MP 4.00 10.00
164 John LeClair MP 2.00 5.00
165 Jaromir Jagr MP 4.00 10.00
166 Peter Forsberg MP 4.00 10.00
167 Theo Fleury MP 1.50 4.00
168 Peter Bondra MP 1.50 4.00
169 Mike Modano MP 3.00 8.00
170 Pavel Bure MP 2.00 5.00
171 Patrick Roy LL 15.00 40.00
172 Eric Lindros LL 6.00 15.00
173 Dominik Hasek LL 10.00 20.00
174 Jaromir Jagr LL 6.00 15.00
175 Steve Yzerman LL 15.00 40.00
176 Martin Brodeur LL 15.00 40.00
177 Ray Bourque LL 6.00 15.00
178 Peter Forsberg LL 10.00 25.00
179 Paul Kariya LL 6.00 15.00
180 Wayne Gretzky LL 20.00 50.00
S99 Wayne Gretzky SAMPLE.60 1.50

1998-99 SPx Finite Radiance

This 180-card silver foil parallel features the same players as in the SPx Finite base set, but with an extra added altered technology. Base radiance cards (#1-90) were serial numbered to 4750. Global impact radiance parallels (#91-120) were serial numbered to 3475, sure shots radiance parallels (#121-150) were numbered to 1300, and marquee performers radiance parallels (#151-170) were numbered to 875. Living legends radiance parallels (#171-180) were also serial numbered to 540.

*SINGLES 1-150: 1X TO 2X BASIC CARDS
*M.P.: 1.25X TO 2.5X BASIC CARDS
*LIV.LEG.: 1X TO 2X BASIC CARDS

1998-99 SPx Finite Spectrum

Sequentially numbered to 5500, this 180-card rainbow foil parallel again offers the same players as in the SPx Finite base set, but with an even further modified technology. Base spectrum parallels (#1-90) were serial numbered to 300. Global impact spectrum parallels (#91-120) were serial numbered to 225, sure shots spectrum parallels (#121-150) were numbered to 75, and marquee performers spectrum parallels (#151-170) were numbered to 25. Living legends spectrum parallels (#171-180) were also serial numbered to 1/1 and are not priced due to scarcity.

*STARS 1-90: 10X TO 25X BASIC CARDS
*GLOB.IMP.: 8X TO 20X BASIC CARDS
*S.S.: 6X TO 15X BASIC CARDS
*M.P.: 10X TO 25X BASIC CARDS

1998-99 SPx Top Prospects

The 1998-99 SPx Top Prospects set was issued in one series totaling 90 cards and features action color player photos with player information on the backs. Only 1,999 of cards 61-90 were printed. Cards 79 and 80 were only available signed.

COMPLETE SET (90) 60.00 150.00
COMP.SET w/o SP's (60) 20.00 50.00
1 Paul Kariya .60 1.50
2 Teemu Selanne .60 1.50
3 Ray Bourque 1.00 2.50
4 Sergei Samsonov .40 1.00
5 Joe Thornton 1.00 2.50
6 Dominik Hasek 1.25 3.00
7 Theo Fleury .40 1.00
8 Keith Primeau .20 .50
9 Tony Amonte .40 1.00
10 Doug Gilmour .40 1.00
11 J-P Dumont .20 .50
12 Chris Chelios .60 1.50
13 Peter Forsberg 1.50 4.00
14 Patrick Roy 3.00 8.00
15 Joe Sakic 1.25 3.00
16 Milan Hedjuk RC 3.00 8.00
17 Chris Drury .40 1.00
18 Mike Modano 1.00 2.50
19 Brett Hull .75 2.00
20 Ed Belfour .60 1.50
21 Steve Yzerman 3.00 8.00
22 Brendan Shanahan .60 1.50
23 Sergei Fedorov 1.00 2.50
24 Chris Osgood .40 1.00
25 Nicklas Lidstrom .60 1.50
26 Bill Guerin .20 .50
27 Doug Weight .40 1.00
28 Tom Poti .20 .50
29 Mark Parrish RC 1.00 2.50
30 Rob Blake .40 1.00
31 Pavel Rosa RC .40 1.00
32 Vincent Damphousse .20 .50
33 Saku Koivu .60 1.50
34 Mike Dunham .20 .50
35 Martin Brodeur 1.50 4.00
36 Zigmund Palffy .40 1.00
37 Eric Brewer .20 .50
38 Wayne Gretzky 4.00 10.00
39 Brian Leetch .60 1.50
40 Manny Malhotra .20 .50
41 Petr Nedved .20 .50
42 Alexei Yashin .20 .50
43 Eric Lindros .60 1.50
44 John LeClair .40 1.00
45 John Vanbiesbrouck .40 1.00
46 Keith Tkachuk .40 1.00
47 Jeremy Roenick .75 2.00
48 Daniel Briere .20 .50
49 Jaromir Jagr 1.00 2.50
50 Patrick Marleau .40 1.00
51 Al MacInnis .20 .50
52 Chris Pronger .40 1.00
53 Vincent Lecavalier .60 1.50
54 Curtis Joseph .60 1.50
55 Mats Sundin .60 1.50
56 Tomas Kaberle RC 1.00 2.50
57 Mark Messier .60 1.50
58 Pavel Bure .60 1.50
59 Bill Muckalt RC .40 1.00
60 Peter Bondra .40 1.00
61 Brian Finley RC 1.00 2.50
62 Roberto Luongo 2.00 5.00
63 Mike Van Ryn 1.50 4.00
64 Harold Druken 1.50 4.00
65 Daniel Tkaczuk 1.50 4.00
66 Brenden Morrow RC 5.00 12.00
67 Jani Rita RC 1.50 4.00
68 Tommi Santala RC 1.50 4.00
69 Teemu Virkkunen RC 1.50 4.00
70 Arto Laaktikainen RC 1.50 4.00
71 Ilkka Mikkola RC 1.50 4.00
72 Miko Jokela RC 1.50 4.00
73 Kirill Safronov RC 1.50 4.00
74 Denis Shvidki 1.50 4.00
75 Denis Arkhipov RC 1.50 4.00
76 Maxim Afinogenov 2.00 5.00
77 Alexander Zevakhin RC 1.50 4.00
78 Alexei Volkov RC 1.50 4.00
79 Daniel Sedin AU 6.00 15.00
80 Henrik Sedin AU 6.00 15.00
81 Jimmie Olvestad RC 1.50 4.00
82 Mattias Weinhandl RC 1.50 4.00
83 Mathias Tjarnqvist RC 1.50 4.00
84 Jakob Johansson RC 1.50 4.00
85 Barrett Heisten RC 1.50 4.00
86 Tim Connolly RC 2.00 5.00
87 Andy Hilbert RC 1.50 4.00
88 David Legwand 1.50 4.00
89 Joe Blackburn RC 1.50 4.00
90 Dave Tanabe RC 1.50 4.00

1998-99 SPx Top Prospects Radiance

Randomly inserted in Finite Radiance hot packs only, this 90-card set is parallel to the base SPx Top Prospects set and is crash numbered to 100. A crash numbered 1 of 1 Spectrum parallel was also available and found only in Finite Spectrum hot packs. Spectrum parallels not priced due to scarcity.

*STARS: 10X TO 25X BASIC CARDS
*SP's: 1.25X TO 3X BASIC CARDS
*ROOKIES:2X TO 5X BASIC CARDS

1998-99 SPx Top Prospects Highlight Heroes

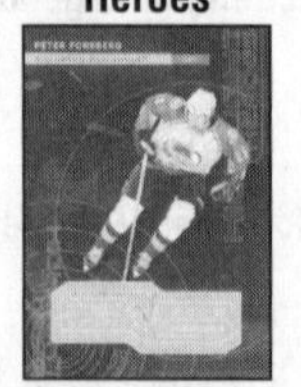

Randomly inserted in packs at the rate of 1:8, this 30-card set features action color photos of top NHL players.

COMPLETE SET (30) 75.00 150.00
H1 Paul Kariya 1.50 4.00
H2 Teemu Selanne 1.50 4.00
H3 Ray Bourque 2.50 6.00
H4 Sergei Samsonov 1.25 3.00
H5 Dominik Hasek 3.00 8.00
H6 Theo Fleury .30 .75
H7 Doug Gilmour 1.25 3.00
H8 Joe Sakic 3.00 8.00
H9 Patrick Roy 8.00 20.00
H10 Peter Forsberg 4.00 10.00
H11 Mike Modano 2.50 6.00
H12 Brett Hull 2.00 5.00
H13 Brendan Shanahan 1.50 4.00
H14 Steve Yzerman 8.00 20.00
H15 Sergei Fedorov 2.50 6.00
H16 Saku Koivu 1.50 4.00
H17 Martin Brodeur 4.00 10.00
H18 Wayne Gretzky 10.00 25.00
H19 Zigmund Palffy 1.25 3.00
H20 John Vanbiesbrouck 1.25 3.00
H21 Eric Lindros 1.50 4.00
H22 John LeClair 1.50 4.00
H23 Keith Tkachuk 1.50 4.00
H24 Jeremy Roenick 2.00 5.00
H25 Jaromir Jagr 2.50 6.00
H26 Vincent Lecavalier 1.50 4.00
H27 Mats Sundin 1.50 4.00
H28 Curtis Joseph 1.50 4.00
H29 Pavel Bure 1.50 4.00
H30 Peter Bondra 1.25 3.00

1998-99 SPx Top Prospects Lasting Impressions

COMPLETE SET (30) 40.00 80.00
STATED ODDS 1:3
L1 Vincent Lecavalier .75 2.00
L2 John Vanbiesbrouck .60 1.50
L3 Paul Kariya .75 2.00
L4 Keith Tkachuk .75 2.00
L5 Mike Modano 1.25 3.00
L6 Dominik Hasek 1.50 4.00
L7 Teemu Selanne .75 2.00
L8 Mats Sundin .75 2.00
L9 Brendan Shanahan .75 2.00
L10 Pavel Bure .75 2.00
L11 Theo Fleury .15 .40
L12 Curtis Joseph .75 2.00
L13 Joe Sakic 1.50 4.00
L14 Eric Lindros .75 2.00
L15 Peter Bondra .60 1.50
L16 Brett Hull 1.00 2.50
L17 Ray Bourque 1.25 3.00
L18 Jaromir Jagr 1.25 3.00
L19 Steve Yzerman 4.00 10.00
L20 Jeremy Roenick 1.00 2.50
L21 Martin Brodeur 2.00 5.00
L22 Saku Koivu .75 2.00
L23 Patrick Roy 4.00 10.00
L24 John LeClair .75 2.00
L25 Doug Gilmour .60 1.50
L26 Sergei Fedorov 1.25 3.00
L27 Wayne Gretzky 5.00 12.00
L28 Peter Forsberg 2.00 5.00
L29 Zigmund Palffy .60 1.50
L30 Sergei Samsonov .60 1.50

1998-99 SPx Top Prospects Premier Stars

COMPLETE SET (30) 100.00 200.00
STATED ODDS 1:17
PS1 Wayne Gretzky 15.00 40.00
PS2 Sergei Samsonov 2.00 5.00
PS3 Ray Bourque 4.00 10.00
PS4 Dominik Hasek 5.00 12.00
PS5 Martin Brodeur 6.00 15.00
PS6 Brian Leetch 2.50 6.00
PS7 Mike Richter 2.50 6.00
PS8 Eric Lindros 2.50 6.00
PS9 John LeClair 2.50 6.00
PS10 John Vanbiesbrouck 2.00 5.00
PS11 Jaromir Jagr 4.00 10.00
PS12 Vincent Lecavalier 2.50 6.00
PS13 Mats Sundin 2.50 6.00
PS14 Curtis Joseph 2.50 6.00
PS15 Peter Bondra 2.00 5.00
PS16 Wayne Gretzky 15.00 40.00
PS17 Teemu Selanne 2.50 6.00
PS18 Paul Kariya 2.50 6.00
PS19 Theo Fleury .50 1.25
PS20 Tony Amonte 2.00 5.00
PS21 Patrick Roy 12.50 30.00
PS22 Joe Sakic 5.00 12.00
PS23 Peter Forsberg 6.00 15.00
PS24 Mike Modano 4.00 10.00
PS25 Brett Hull 3.00 8.00
PS26 Steve Yzerman 12.50 30.00
PS27 Brendan Shanahan 2.50 6.00
PS28 Doug Weight 2.00 5.00
PS29 Keith Tkachuk 2.50 6.00
PS30 Mark Messier 2.50 6.00

1998-99 SPx Top Prospects Winning Materials .

Randomly inserted into packs at the rate of 1:251, this 12-card set features color player photos with pieces of the pictured player's game-used jersey and stick cut and affixed to the card.

CJ Curtis Joseph 8.00 20.00
CO Chris Osgood 8.00 20.00
EL Eric Lindros 8.00 20.00
FP Felix Potvin 8.00 20.00
JJ Jaromir Jagr 12.50 30.00
JL John LeClair 8.00 20.00
JS Joe Sakic 15.00 40.00
JV John Vanbiesbrouck 8.00 20.00
MR Mike Richter 8.00 20.00
MS Mats Sundin 8.00 20.00
PR Patrick Roy 30.00 80.00
RB Ray Bourque 15.00 40.00

1998-99 SPx Top Prospects Year of the Great One

Randomly inserted into packs at the rate of 1:17, this 30-card set features unique photos of Wayne Gretzky with notable quotes about his career from his father, various coaches, NHL greats and former teammates.

COMPLETE SET (30) 150.00 300.00
COMMON GRETZKY (WG1-WG30) 5.00 12.00

1992 Sport-Flash

This 15-card standard-size set was produced by Sport-Flash as the first series of "Hockey Stars since 1940". The accompanying certification of limited edition claims that the production run was 200,000 sets. Each set contained one autographed hockey card signed by the player. On a bright yellow card face, the fronts display close-up color photos enclosed by blue and black border stripes. The player's name appears in the bottom yellow border. The backs are bilingual and present biography, player profile, and career statistics. The cards are numbered on both sides.

COMPLETE SET (15) 4.00 10.00
1 Jacques Laperriere .24 .60
2 Larry Carriere .20 .50
3 Chuck Rayner .30 .75
4 Jean Beliveau .80 2.00
5 BoomBoom Geoffrion .60 1.50
6 Gilles Gilbert .30 .75
7 Marcel Bonin .20 .50
8 Leon Rochefort .20 .50
9 Maurice Richard 2.00 5.00
10 Rejean Houle .20 .50
11 Pierre Mondou .20 .50
12 Yvan Cournoyer .30 .75
13 Henri Richard .40 1.00
14 Checklist Card .04 .10
15 Certification of Limited Edition .04 .10

1992 Sport-Flash Autographs

Random inserts in the Sport-Flash sets. Each card is signed in blue Sharpie on the card front.

COMPLETE SET (15) 80.00 200.00
1 Jacques Laperriere 4.00 10.00
2 Larry Carriere 4.00 10.00
3 Chuck Rayner 4.00 10.00
4 Jean Beliveau 12.00 30.00
5 BoomBoom Geoffrion 12.00 30.00
6 Gilles Gilbert 4.00 10.00
7 Marcel Bonin 4.00 10.00
8 Leon Rochefort 4.00 10.00
9 Maurice Richard 20.00 50.00
10 Rejean Houle 4.00 10.00
11 Pierre Mondou 4.00 10.00
12 Yvan Cournoyer 8.00 20.00
13 Henri Richard 8.00 20.00
14 Checklist Card .20 .50
NNO Certification of Limited Edition .04 .10

1989-91 Sports Illustrated for Kids I

This multi-sport set was issued as a premium with the pages of SI for Kids magazine. Each month, a perforated sheet of nine cards was offered as an inducement to buy the issue. The cards are standard size.

COMPLETE SET (23) 24.00 60.00
1 Mario Lemieux 6.00 15.00
15 Joe Nieuwendyk .30 .75
19 Wayne Gretzky 6.00 15.00

25 Steve Yzerman 2.00 5.00
30 Sean Burke .20 .50
82 Al MacInnis .30 .75
96 Pat LaFontaine .80 2.00
100 Mark Messier 2.00 5.00
116 Brian Leetch 1.00 2.50
118 Denis Savard .30 .75
126 Dale Hawerchuk .30 .75
134 Ray Bourque 1.20 3.00
143 Grant Fuhr .50 1.25
193 Brett Hull 1.20 3.00
214 Gordie Howe 1.20 3.00
224 Ron Hextall .30 .75
228 Bernie Nicholls .20 .50
238 Chris Chelios .50 1.25
250 Mike Liut .20 .50
252 Joe Mullen .20 .50
254 Steve Larmer .20 .50
300 Paul Coffey .50 1.25
317 Bobby Orr 4.00 10.00

1992-00 Sports Illustrated for Kids II

This multi-sport set was issued as a premium with the pages of SI for Kids magazine. Each month, a perforated sheet of nine cards was offered as an inducement to buy the issue. The cards are standard size.

COMPLETE SET (61) 50.00 125.00
957 Scott Stevens .20 .50
9 Tom Barrasso .20 .50
10 Mike Eruzione .60 1.50
20 Brian Bellows .20 .50
33 Ed Belfour .25 .60
42 Mark Messier .25 .60
93 Patrick Roy 3.00 8.00
117 Jaromir Jagr .40 1.00
125 Mario Lemieux 3.00 8.00
135 Eric Lindros .25 .60
153 Wayne Gretzky 3.00 8.00
154 Alexander Mogilny .20 .50
191 Manon Rheaume 2.00 5.00
200 Teemu Selanne .60 1.50
211 Bobby Hull .80 2.00
241 Luc Robitaille .20 .50
246 Mike Gartner .20 .50
259 Sergei Fedorov .30 .75
265 Cam Neely .20 .50
284 Mike Richter .25 .60
303 Pavel Bure .25 .60
309 Doug Gilmour .20 .50
317 Phil Esposito .60 1.50
333 Jeremy Roenick .25 .60
338 John Vanbiesbrouck .20 .50
347 Mark Messier .25 .60
356 Felix Potvin .20 .50
366 Scott Stevens .20 .50
377 Paul Kariya 1.60 4.00
382 Jim Carey .20 .50
399 Eric Lindros .25 .60
413 Martin Brodeur 1.60 4.00
420 Paul Coffey .20 .50
425 Peter Forsberg 1.60 4.00
432 Karyn Bye .20 .50
435 Peter Bondra .20 .50
442 Dominik Hasek .60 1.50
453 Mario Lemieux 3.00 8.00
465 Brendan Shanahan .25 .60
474 Steve Yzerman 3.00 8.00
499 Joe Sakic .60 1.50
525 Jaromir Jagr
527 Cammi Granato .40 1.00
540 Ed Jovanovski .20 .50
546 Daren Puppa .20 .50
547 Wayne Gretzky 3.00 8.00
551 Erin Whitten .20 .50
557 Sergei Fedorov .40 .75
559 Patrick Roy 3.00 8.00
585 Chris Chelios .40 .60
595 Mats Sundin .25 .60
601 Mats Sundin .25 .60
618 Claude Lemieux .20 .50
623 Eric Lindros .25 .60
638 Brett Hull .30 .75
657 John LeClair .25 .60
666 Mark Johnson .20 .50
710 Teemu Selanne .60 1.50
715 Pavel Bure .25 .60
755 Peter Forsberg 1.50 4.00
765 Jaromir Jagr .40 1.00
767 Martin Brodeur 1.50 4.00
792 Paul Kariya 1.60 4.00
794 Eric Lindros .25 .60
805 Mike Modano .50 1.25
864 Ed Belfour
872 Wayne Gretzky 3.00 8.00
880 Paul Kariya 1.50 4.00
885 Al MacInnis .20 .50
907 Scott Gomez .20 .50
913 Roman Turek .20 .50
921 Pavle Bure .25 .60
930 Mark Recchi .20 .50
939 Ray Bourque .60 1.50
946 Theo Fleury .20 .50
NNO Bobby Orr 3x5
NNO Wayne Gretzky

2001-04 Sports Illustrated for Kids III

This multi-sport set was issued as a premium with the pages of SI for Kids magazine. Each month, a perforated sheet of nine cards was offered as an inducement to buy the issue. The cards are standard size.

9 Chris Pronger .20 .50
11 Mark Messier .25 .60
20 Tony Amonte .20 .50
31 Nadine Muzerall .20 .50
36 Zigmund Palffy .20 .50
37 Brian Leetch .20 .50
49 Joe Sakic .60 1.50
60 Sean Burke .20 .50
66 Alexei Kovalev .20 .50
76 Adam Oates .20 .50
82 Patrik Elias .20 .50
96 Nicklas Lidstrom .25 .60
106 Patrick Roy 3.00 8.00
108 Keith Tkachuk .25 .60
109 Peter Bondra
121 Curtis Joseph .30 .75
127 Maria Rooth .20 .50
135 Brendan Shanahan .25 .60
139 Jeremy Roenick .25 .60
150 Nikolai Khabibulin .20 .50
159 Jaromir Jagr .40 1.00
168 Martin Brodeur 1.50 4.00
178 Jarome Iginla .20 .50
198 Ron Francis .20 .50
204 Jose Theodore .25 .60
214 Mats Sundin .25 .60
217 Peter Forsberg 1.50 4.00
225 Evgeni Nabokov .20 .50
232 Dany Heatley .40 1.00
238 Owen Nolan .20 .50
251 Markus Naslund .25 .60
260 Joe Sakic .60 1.50
265 Jaromir Jagr .40 1.00
277 Brett Hull .30 .75
280 Todd Bertuzzi .25 .60
296 Milan Hejduk .25 .60
300 J-S Giguere .20 .50
301 Hayley Wickenheiser
307 Scott Stevens .20 .50
316 Joe Thornton .40 1.00
321 Al MacInnis .20 .50
330 Marty Turco .20 .50
340 Wayne Gretzky 4.00 10.00
343 Marian Hossa .25 .60
358 Alex Tanguay .20 .50
367 Martin Brodeur 3.00 8.00
371 Robert Lang .20 .50
384 Ilya Kovalchuk .40 1.00
395 Dwayne Roloson .20 .50
403 Martin St. Louis .20 .50
413 Evgeni Nabokov .20 .50
450 Natalie Darwitz
469 Marty Sertich
534 Rich Nash

1977-79 Sportscasters

This huge multi-sport set features color action player photos printed on cards with rounded corners and measuring approximately 4 3/4" by 6 1/4". The backs carry player information including the players' awards and records held. The cards checklisted below are the 65 hockey players only. This set was created in both Swedish and Finnish.

COMPLETE SET (65) 250.00 500.00
102 Bobby Orr 15.00 30.00
206 Gordie Howe 10.00 20.00
213 Yvan Cournoyer 2.50 5.00
Serge Savard
319 Phil Esposito 7.50 15.00
Tony Esposito
509 USA vs. Czechoslovakia 1.50 3.00
520 Bobby Hull 7.50 15.00
607 Gump Worsley 4.00 8.00
708 1976 USSR Team 2.50 5.00
717 Brad Park 2.50 5.00
1014 Jean Beliveau 5.00 10.00
10214 USSR Hockey Team 7.50 15.00
10308 Alexander Yakushev 2.50 5.00
1119 Bob Hodges 1.50 3.00
1215 USSR vs. Czechoslovakia 1.50 3.00
1322 Stan Mikita 5.00 10.00
1423 Ken Dryden 7.50 15.00
1513 Yvan Cournoyer 2.50 5.00
1709 Denis Potvin 2.50 5.00
1823 Garry Unger 1.50 3.00
1915 Canada vs. CSSR
1916 1977 Montreal Canadians 5.00 10.00
2112 Hockey Equipment .50 1.00
2724 Dennis Hull 2.00 4.00
2908 Phil Esposito 6.00 12.00
3103 Bobby Clarke 2.50 5.00
3303 Rod Gilbert 2.00 4.00
3503 The Spengler Cup .50 1.00
3807 Guy Lafleur 6.00 12.00
4024 The Stanley Cup 2.50 5.00
4304 Major and Minor Penalties
4306 Rogie Vachon 2.50 5.00
4403 Jaroslav Jirik .50 1.00
4420 Gerry Cheevers 2.50 5.00
4513 Steve Shutt 2.00 4.00
4614 In The Corners 1.00 2.00
4621 Bryan Trottier 2.50 5.00
4716 Bryan Trottier 4.00 8.00
Clark Gillies
Mike Bossy
4718 Darryl Sittler 5.00 10.00
5003 Bobby Hull 7.50 15.00
5004 Facemasks 5.00 10.00
5101 Czechoslovakia 1977 1.00 2.00
5118 Guy Lafleur 4.00 8.00
5514 Jaroslav Holik 1.00 2.00
Jiri Holik
5523 Bobby Hull WHA 10.00 20.00
5605 Montreal Forum 5.00 10.00
6012 Bobby Clarke 4.00 8.00
6103 Eddie Giacomin 2.50 5.00
6217 Lester Patrick
6309 The Howe Family 10.00 20.00
6416 Pete Stemkowski 2.50 5.00
7006 Hockey Hall of Fame 2.00 4.00
7104 Tommy Abrahamsson 2.50 5.00
Christian Abrahamsson
7112 Ulf Nilsson 2.50 5.00
Anders Hedberg
7301 Larry Robinson 4.00 8.00
(NHL vs. USSR
7311 1976 Czechoslovakia Team 2.50 5.00
7417 1978 USSR Champs 2.50 5.00
7424 Vaclav Nedomansky 2.50 5.00
7603 NCAA Hockey Champs 5.00 10.00
7710 Wayne Gretzky 150.00 300.00
7724 Expansion Whalers/Oilers 2.50 5.00
7804 Real Cloutier 1.50 3.00
8018 John Davidson 5.00 10.00
8119 Jacques Lemaire 5.00 10.00
8205 Scotty Bowman 10.00 20.00
8223 Dave Dryden 2.50 5.00

1991 Stadium Club Charter Member

These cards are part of a multi-sport set issued to collectors who joined the Topps Stadium Club.

42 Ed Belfour .30 .75
43 Ed Belfour .30 .75
44 Ray Bourque .30 .75
45 Paul Coffey .30 .75
46 Wayne Gretzky 1.60 4.00
47 Wayne Gretzky 1.60 4.00
48 Brett Hull .30 .75
49 Brett Hull .30 .75
50 Mario Lemieux 1.20 3.00

1991 Stadium Club Members Only

These cards are part of a multi-sport set issued to collectors who joined the Topps Stadium Club. They were issued in a 50-card boxed set, along with baseball, football and basketball cards.

COMPLETE SET (13) 4.80 12.00
38 Pavel Bure .80 2.00
39 Guy Carbonneau .04 .10
40 Paul Coffey .30 .75
41 Mike Gartner .10 .25
42 Mike Gartner .10 .25
43 Michel Goulet .04 .10
44 Wayne Gretzky 2.00 5.00
45 Brett Hull .40 1.00
46 Brian Leetch .20 .50
47 Mario Lemieux 1.20 3.00
48 Mario Lemieux 1.20 3.00
49 Mark Messier .30 .75
50 Patrick Roy 1.20 3.00

1991-92 Stadium Club

The 1991-92 Topps Stadium Club hockey set contains 400 standard-size cards. The fronts feature full-bleed glossy color player photos. At the bottom, the player's name appears in an aqua stripe that is bordered in gold. In the lower left or right corner the Stadium Club logo overlays the stripe. Against the background of a colorful drawing of a hockey rink, the horizontally oriented backs have a biography, The Sporting News Hockey Scouting Report (which consists of strengths and evaluative comments), statistics (last season and career totals), and a miniature photo of the player's first Topps card. There are many cards in the set that can be found with or without "The Sporting News" on the card back; these variations (no added premium) are 13, 16, 22, 46, 50, 60, 68, 149, 190, 204, 230, 249, 264, 276, 297, 298, 307, 320, 332, 339, 341, 342, 348, 351, and 362. There are no key Rookie Cards in this set.

COMPLETE SET (400) 10.00 25.00
1 Wayne Gretzky 1.00 2.50
2 Randy Moller .02 .10
3 Ray Ferraro .02 .10
4 Craig Wolanin .02 .10
5 Shayne Corson .02 .10
6 Chris Chelios .15 .40
7 Joe Mullen .08 .25
8 Ken Wregget .08 .25
9 Rob Cimetta .02 .10
10 Mike Liut .08 .25
11 Martin Gelinas .02 .10
12 Mario Marois .02 .10
13 Rick Vaive .02 .10
14 Brad McCrimmon .02 .10
15 Mark Hunter .02 .10
16 Jim Wiemer .02 .10
17 Sergio Momesso .02 .10
18 Claude Lemieux .02 .10
19 Brian Hayward .08 .25
20 Pat Flatley .02 .10
21 Mark Osborne .02 .10
22 Mike Hudson .02 .10
23 Rejean Lemelin .08 .25
24 Slava Fetisov .08 .25
25 Bobby Smith .08 .25
26 Kris King .02 .10
27 Randy Velischek .02 .10
28 Steve Bozek .02 .10
29 Mike Foligno .02 .10
30 Scott Arniel .02 .10
31 Sergei Makarov .02 .10
32 Rick Zombo .02 .10
33 Christian Ruuttu .02 .10
34 Gino Cavallini .02 .10
35 Rick Tocchet .08 .25
36 Jiri Hrdina .02 .10
37 Peter Bondra .08 .25
38 Craig Ludwig .02 .10
39 Mikael Andersson .02 .10
40 Bob Kudelski .02 .10
41 Guy Carbonneau .08 .25
42 Geoff Smith .02 .10
43 Russ Courtnall .02 .10
44 Michal Pivonka .02 .10
45 Todd Krygier .02 .10
46 Jeremy Roenick .20 .50
47 Doug Brown .02 .10
48 Paul Cavallini .02 .10
49 Ron Sutter .02 .10
50 Paul Ranheim .02 .10
51 Mike Gartner .08 .25
52 Greg Adams .02 .10
53 Dave Capuano .02 .10
54 Mike Krushelnyski .02 .10
55 Ulf Dahlen .02 .10
56 Steven Finn .02 .10
57 Ed Olczyk .02 .10
58 Steve Duchesne .02 .10
59 Bob Probert .08 .25
60 Joe Nieuwendyk .08 .25
61 Petr Klima .02 .10
62 Uwe Krupp .02 .10
63 Jay Miller .02 .10
64 Cam Neely .15 .40
65 Phil Housley .08 .25
66 Michel Goulet .08 .25
67 Brett Hull .25 .60
68 Mike Ridley .02 .10
69 Esa Tikkanen .02 .10
70 Kjell Samuelsson .02 .10
71 Corey Millen RC .02 .10
72 Doug Lidster .02 .10
73 Ron Francis .08 .25
74 Scott Young .02 .10
75 Bob Sweeney .02 .10
76 Sean Burke .08 .25
77 Pierre Turgeon .08 .25
78 David Reid .02 .10
79 Al MacInnis .08 .25
80 Mike Hough .02 .10
81 Steve Yzerman .60 1.50
82 Derek King .02 .10
83 Brad Shaw .02 .10
84 Trevor Linden .08 .25
85 Rick Meagher .02 .10
86 Stephane Richer .08 .25
87 Brian Bellows .02 .10
88 Pete Peeters .08 .25
89 Adam Creighton .02 .10
90 Brent Ashton .02 .10
91 Bryan Trottier .15 .40
92 Mike Richter .15 .40
93 Dave Andreychuk .08 .25
94 Randy Carlyle .02 .10
95 Dave Christian .02 .10
96 Doug Gilmour .08 .25
97 Tony Granato .02 .10
98 Jeff Norton .02 .10
99 Neal Broten .08 .25
100 Jody Hull .02 .10
101 Shawn Burr .02 .10
102 Pat Verbeek .02 .10
103 Ken Daneyko .02 .10
104 Peter Zezel .02 .10
105 Kirk McLean .08 .25
106 Kelly Miller .02 .10
107 Patrick Roy .75 2.00
108 Adam Oates .08 .25
109 Steve Thomas .02 .10
110 Scott Mellanby .02 .10
111 Mark Messier .15 .40
112 Larry Murphy .08 .25
113 Mark Janssens .02 .10
114 Doug Bodger .02 .10
115 Ron Tugnutt .08 .25
116 Glenn Anderson .08 .25
117 Dave Gagner .02 .10
118 Dino Ciccarelli .08 .25
119 Randy Burridge .02 .10
120 Kelly Hrudey .08 .25
121 Jimmy Carson .02 .10
122 Bruce Driver .02 .10
123 Pat LaFontaine .15 .40
124 Wendel Clark .08 .25
125 Peter Sidorkiewicz .08 .25
126 Gary Roberts .08 .25
127 Petr Svoboda .02 .10
128 Vincent Riendeau .08 .25
129 Brian Skrudland .02 .10
130 Tim Kerr .02 .10
131 Doug Wilson .08 .25
132 Pat Elynuik .02 .10
133 Craig MacTavish .02 .10
134 Troy Mallette .02 .10
135 Mike Ramsey .02 .10
136 Tony Hrkac .02 .10
137 Craig Simpson .02 .10
138 Jon Casey .08 .25
139 Steve Kasper .02 .10
140 Kevin Hatcher .08 .25
141 Dave Barr .02 .10
142 Brad Lauer .02 .10
143 Gary Suter .02 .10
144 John MacLean .08 .25
145 Dean Evason .02 .10
146 Vincent Damphousse .02 .10
147 Craig Janney .08 .25
148 Jeff Brown .02 .10
149 Geoff Courtnall .08 .25
150 Igor Larionov .02 .10
151 Jan Erixon .02 .10
152 Bob Essensa .08 .25
153 Gaetan Duchesne .02 .10
154 Jyrki Lumme .02 .10
155 Tom Barrasso .08 .25
156 Curtis Leschyshyn .02 .10
157 Benoit Hogue .02 .10
158 Gary Leeman .02 .10
159 Luc Robitaille .08 .25
160 Jamie Macoun .02 .10
161 Bob Carpenter .02 .10
162 Kevin Dineen .02 .10
163 Gary Nylund .02 .10
164 Dale Hunter .02 .10
165 Gerard Gallant .02 .10
166 Jacques Cloutier .08 .25
167 Troy Murray .02 .10
168 Phil Bourque .02 .10
169 Grant Ledyard .02 .10
170 Joel Otto .02 .10
171 Paul Ysebaert UER .02 .10
(Photo actually
Miko Sillinger)
172 Luke Richardson .02 .10
173 Ron Hextall .08 .25
174 Mario Lemieux .75 2.00
175 Garry Galley .02 .10
176 Murray Craven .02 .10
177 Walt Poddubny .02 .10
178 Scott Pearson .02 .10
179 Kevin Lowe .08 .25
180 Brent Sutter .02 .10
181 Dirk Graham .02 .10
182 Pelle Eklund .02 .10
183 Sylvain Cote .02 .10
184 Rod Brind'Amour .15 .40
185 Fredrik Olausson .02 .10
186 Kelly Kisio .02 .10
187 Mike Modano .30 .75
188 Calle Johansson .02 .10
189 John Tonelli .02 .10
190 Glen Wesley .02 .10
191 Bob Errey .02 .10
192 Rich Sutter .02 .10
193 Kirk Muller .02 .10
194 Rob Zettler .02 .10
195 Alexander Mogilny .15 .40
196 Adrien Plavsic .02 .10
197 Daniel Marois .02 .10
198 Yves Racine .02 .10
199 Brendan Shanahan .15 .40
200 Rob Brown .02 .10
201 Brian Leetch .15 .40
202 Dave McLlwain .02 .10
203 Charlie Huddy .02 .10
204 David Volek .02 .10
205 Trent Yawney .02 .10
206 Brian MacLellan .02 .10
207 Thomas Steen .02 .10
208 Sylvain Lefebvre .02 .10
209 Tomas Sandstrom .02 .10
210 Mike McPhee .02 .10
211 Andy Moog .15 .40
212 Paul Coffey .15 .40
213 Denis Savard .08 .25
214 Eric Desjardins .08 .25
215 Wayne Presley .02 .10
216 Stephane Morin UER .02 .10
(Photo actually
Jeff Jackson)
217 Ric Nattress .02 .10
218 Troy Gamble .08 .25
219 Terry Carkner .02 .10
220 Dave Hannan .02 .10
221 Randy Wood .02 .10
222 Brian Mullen .02 .10
223 Garth Butcher .02 .10
224 Tim Cheveldae .08 .25
225 Rod Langway .02 .10
226 Stephen Leach .02 .10
227 Perry Berezan .02 .10
228 Zarley Zalapski .02 .10
229 Patrick Sundstrom .02 .10
230 Steve Smith .02 .10
231 Daren Puppa .08 .25
232 Dave Taylor .08 .25
233 Ray Bourque .25 .60
234 Kevin Stevens .08 .25
235 Frank Musil .02 .10
236 Mike Keane .02 .10
237 Brian Propp .02 .10
238 Brent Fedyk .02 .10
239 Rob Ramage .02 .10
240 Robert Kron .02 .10
241 Mike McNeil .02 .10
242 Greg Gilbert .02 .10
243 Dan Quinn .02 .10
244 Chris Nilan .02 .10
245 Bernie Nicholls .08 .25
246 Don Beaupre .08 .25
247 Keith Acton .02 .10
248 Gord Murphy .02 .10
249 Bill Ranford .08 .25
250 Dave Chyzowski .02 .10
251 Clint Malarchuk .08 .25
252 Larry Robinson .08 .25
253 Dave Poulin .02 .10
254 Paul MacDermid .02 .10
255 Doug Smail .02 .10
256 Mark Recchi .15 .40
257 Brian Bradley .02 .10
258 Grant Fuhr .15 .40
259 Owen Nolan .15 .40
260 Hubie McDonough .02 .10
261 Mikko Makela .02 .10
262 Mathieu Schneider .02 .10
263 Peter Stastny .08 .25
264 Jim Hrivnak .08 .25
265 Scott Stevens .08 .25
266 Mike Tomlak .02 .10
267 Marty McSorley .08 .25
268 Johan Garpenlov .02 .10
269 Mike Vernon .08 .25
270 Steve Larmer .08 .25
271 Phil Sykes .02 .10
272 Jay Mazur .02 .10
273 John Ogrodnick .02 .10
274 Dave Ellett .02 .10
275 Randy Gilhen .02 .10
276 Tom Chorske .02 .10
277 James Patrick .02 .10
278 Darin Kimble .02 .10
279 Paul Cyr .02 .10
280 Petr Nedved .08 .25
281 Tony McKegney .02 .10
282 Alexei Kasatonov .02 .10
283 Stephen Lebeau .02 .10
284 Everett Sanipass .02 .10
285 Tony Tanti .02 .10
286 Kevin Miller .02 .10
287 Moe Mantha .02 .10
288 Alan May .02 .10
289 John Cullen .02 .10
290 Daniel Berthiaume .08 .25
291 Mark Pederson .02 .10
292 Laurie Boschman .02 .10
293 Neil Wilkinson .02 .10
294 Rick Wamsley .08 .25
295 Ken Linseman .02 .10
296 Jamie Leach .02 .10
297 Chris Terreri .08 .25
298 Cliff Ronning .02 .10
299 Bobby Holik .08 .25
300 Mats Sundin .15 .40
301 Carey Wilson .02 .10
302 Teppo Numminen .02 .10
303 Dave Lowry .02 .10
304 Joe Reekie .02 .10
305 Keith Primeau .02 .10
306 David Shaw .02 .10
307 Nick Kypreos .02 .10
308 Dave Manson .02 .10
309 Mick Vukota .02 .10
310 Todd Elik .02 .10
311 Michel Petit .02 .10
312 Dale Hawerchuk .08 .25
313 Joe Murphy .02 .10
314 Chris Dahlquist .02 .10
315 Petri Skriko .02 .10
316 Sergei Fedorov .25 .60
317 Lee Norwood .02 .10
318 Garry Valk .02 .10
319 Glen Featherstone .02 .10
320 Dave Snuggerud .02 .10
321 Doug Evans .02 .10
322 Marc Bureau .02 .10
323 John Vanbiesbrouck .08 .25
324 John McIntyre .02 .10
325 Wes Walz .02 .10
326 Daryl Reaugh .08 .25
327 Paul Fenton .02 .10
328 Ulf Samuelsson .02 .10
329 Andrew Cassels .02 .10
330 Alexei Gusarov RC .08 .25
331 John Druce .02 .10
332 Adam Graves .08 .25
333 Ed Belfour .15 .40
334 Murray Baron .02 .10
335 John Tucker .02 .10
336 Todd Gill .02 .10
337 Martin Hostak .02 .10
338 Gino Odjick .02 .10
339 Eric Weinrich .02 .10
340 Todd Ewen .02 .10
341 Mike Hartman .02 .10
342 Danton Cole .02 .10
343 Jaromir Jagr .30 .75
344 Mike Craig .02 .10
345 Mark Fitzpatrick .08 .25
346 Darren Turcotte .02 .10
347 Ron Wilson .02 .10
348 Rob Blake .08 .25
349 Dale Kushner .02 .10
350 Jeff Beukeboom .02 .10
351 Tim Bergland .02 .10
352 Peter Ing .08 .25
353 Wayne McBean .02 .10
354 Jim McKenzie .02 .10
355 Theo Fleury .02 .10
356 Jocelyn Lemieux .02 .10
357 Ken Hodge Jr. .02 .10
358 Shawn Anderson .02 .10
359 Dimitri Khristich .02 .10
360 Jon Morris .02 .10
361 Darrin Shannon .02 .10
362 Chris Joseph .02 .10
363 Normand Lacombe .02 .10
364 Frank Pietrangelo .08 .25
365 Joey Kocur .08 .25
366 Anatoli Semenov .02 .10
367 Bob Bassen .02 .10
368 Brad Jones .02 .10
369 Glenn Healy .08 .25
370 Don Sweeney .02 .10
371 Brad Dalgarno .02 .10
372 Al Iafrate .08 .25
373 Patrick Lebeau RC UER .02 .10
(Photo actually
Brent Gilchrist)
374 Terry Yake .02 .10
375 Roger Johansson .02 .10
376 Paul Broten .02 .10
377 Andre Racicot RC .08 .25
378 Scott Thornton .02 .10
379 Zdeno Ciger .02 .10
380 Paul Stanton .02 .10
381 Ray Sheppard .08 .25
382 Kevin Haller RC .02 .10
383 Vladimir Ruzicka .02 .10
384 Bryan Marchment RC .08 .25
385 Bill Berg .02 .10
386 Mike Ricci .15 .40
387 Pat Conacher .02 .10
388 Brian Glynn .02 .10
389 Joe Sakic .30 .75
390 Mikhail Tatarinov .02 .10
391 Stephane Matteau .02 .10
392 Mark Tinordi .02 .10
393 Robert Reichel .02 .10
394 Tim Sweeney .02 .10
395 Rick Tabaracci .08 .25
396 Ken Sabourin .02 .10
397 Jeff Lazaro .02 .10
398 Checklist 1-133 .02 .10
399 Checklist 134-266 .02 .10
400 Checklist 267-400 .02 .10

1992 Stadium Club Members Only

These seven cards were issued as part of a multi-sport set given to collectors who joined the Topps Stadium Club. The cards mimicked the basic SC design of that season, but featured a special Members Only seal.

44 Mike Gartner .20 .50
45 Chris Kontos .20 .50
46 Jari Kurri .20 .50
47 Eric Lindros 1.60 4.00
48 Reggie Savage .20 .50
49 Teemu Selanne .80 2.00
50 Teemu Selanne .80 2.00

1992-93 Stadium Club

This 501-card standard-size set features full-bleed color action player photos. The Stadium Club logo appears at the bottom and intersects a gold foil double stripe carrying the team name. The horizontal backs show an artist's rendering of a hockey rink as the background. A mini-reproduction of the player's first Topps card is shown as well as biography, statistics, and The Sporting News Skills Rating System. The Members Choice (241-250 and 251-260) subsets, showing full-bleed color photos, closes the first series and opens the second series. These backs have the same art work background with 1991-92 season statistics. The only notable Rookie Card is Guy Hebert.

COMPLETE SET (501) 8.00 20.00
COMPLETE SERIES 1 (250) 4.00 10.00
COMPLETE SERIES 2 (251) 4.00 10.00
1 Brett Hull .20 .50
2 Theo Fleury .07 .20
3 Joe Sakic .25 .60
4 Mike Modano .20 .50
5 Dmitri Mironov .02 .10
6 Yves Racine .02 .10
7 Igor Kravchuk .02 .10
8 Philippe Bozon .02 .10
9 Stephane Richer .07 .20
10 Dave Lowry .02 .10
11 Dean Evason .02 .10
12 Mark Fitzpatrick .07 .20
13 Dave Poulin .02 .10
14 Phil Housley .07 .20
15 Adrien Plavsic .02 .10
16 Claude Boivin .02 .10
17 Bill Guerin RC .50 1.25
18 Wayne Gretzky .75 2.00
19 Steve Yzerman .60 1.50
20 Joe Mullen .07 .20
21 Brad McCrimmon .02 .10
22 Dan Quinn .02 .10
23 Rob Blake .07 .20
24 Wayne Presley .02 .10
25 Zarley Zalapski .02 .10
26 Bryan Trottier .07 .20
27 Peter Sidorkiewicz .07 .20
28 John MacLean .07 .20
29 Brad Schlegel .02 .10
30 Marc Bureau .02 .10
31 Troy Murray .02 .10
32 Tony Amonte .07 .20
33 Rob DiMaio .02 .10
34 Joe Murphy .02 .10
35 Jim Waite .07 .20
36 Ron Sutter .02 .10
37 Joe Nieuwendyk .07 .20
38 Kevin Haller .02 .10
39 Andrew Cassels .02 .10
40 Dale Hunter .07 .20
41 Craig Janney .07 .20
42 Sergio Momesso .02 .10
43 Nicklas Lidstrom .10 .30
44 Luc Robitaille .07 .20
45 Adam Creighton .02 .10
46 Norm Maciver .02 .10
47 Mikhail Tatarinov .02 .10
48 Gary Roberts .02 .10
49 Gord Hynes .02 .10
50 Claude Lemieux .02 .10
51 Brad May .02 .10
52 Paul Stanton .02 .10
53 Rick Wamsley .07 .20
54 Steve Larmer .07 .20
55 Darrin Shannon .02 .10
56 Pat Falloon .02 .10
57 Chris Dahlquist .02 .10
58 John Vanbiesbrouck .07 .20
59 Sylvain Turgeon .02 .10
60 Jay More .02 .10
61 Randy Burridge .02 .10
62 Slava Kozlov UER .07 .20
63 Daniel Marois .02 .10
64 Curt Giles .02 .10
65 Brad Shaw .02 .10
66 Bill Ranford .07 .20
67 Frank Musil .02 .10
68 Steve Leach .02 .10
69 Michel Goulet .07 .20
70 Mathieu Schneider .02 .10
71 Steve Kasper .02 .10
72 Darryl Sydor .02 .10
73 Brian Leetch .10 .30
74 Chris Terreri .07 .20
75 Jim Johnson .02 .10
76 Rick Tocchet .07 .20
77 Teppo Numminen .02 .10
78 Owen Nolan .07 .20
79 Grant Ledyard .02 .10
80 Trevor Linden .07 .20
81 Luciano Borsato .02 .10
82 Derek King .02 .10
83 Robert Cimetta .02 .10
84 Geoff Smith .02 .10
85 Ray Sheppard .02 .10
86 Dimitri Khristich .02 .10
87 Chris Chelios .10 .30
88 Alexander Godynyuk .02 .10
89 Perry Anderson .02 .10
90 Neal Broten .07 .20
91 Brian Benning .02 .10
92 Brent Thompson .02 .10
93 Claude LaPointe .02 .10
94 Mario Lemieux .60 1.50
95 Pat LaFontaine .10 .30
96 Frank Pietrangelo .07 .20
97 Gerald Diduck .02 .10
98 Paul DiPietro .02 .10
99 Valeri Zelepukin .02 .10
100 Rick Zombo .02 .10
101 Daniel Berthiaume .07 .20
102 Tom Fitzgerald .02 .10
103 Ken Baumgartner .02 .10
104 Esa Tikkanen .02 .10
105 Steve Chiasson .02 .10

106 Bobby Holik .07 .20
107 Dominik Hasek .40 1.00
108 Jeff Hackett .07 .20
109 Paul Broten .02 .10
110 Kevin Stevens .02 .10
111 Geoff Sanderson .07 .20
112 Donald Audette .02 .10
113 Jarmo Myllys .02 .10
114 Brian Skrudland .02 .10
115 Andrei Lomakin .02 .10
116 Keith Tkachuk .10 .30
117 John McIntyre .02 .10
118 Jacques Cloutier .07 .20
119 Michel Picard .02 .10
120 Dave Babych .02 .10
121 Dave Gagner .07 .20
122 Bob Carpenter .02 .10
123 Ray Ferraro .02 .10
124 Glenn Anderson .07 .20
125 Craig MacTavish .02 .10
126 Shawn Burr .02 .10
127 Tim Bergland .02 .10
128 Al MacInnis .07 .20
129 Jeff Beukeboom .02 .10
130 Ken Wregget .07 .20
131 Arturs Irbe .10 .30
132 Dave Andreychuk .07 .20
133 Patrick Roy .60 1.50
134 Benoit Brunet .02 .10
135 Rick Tabaracci .07 .20
136 Jamie Baker .02 .10
137 Yanic Dupre .02 .10
138 Jari Kurri .10 .30
139 Adam Burt .02 .10
140 Peter Stastny .07 .20
141 Brad Jones .02 .10
142 Jeff Odgers .02 .10
143 Anatoli Semenov UER .02 .10
144 Paul Ranheim .02 .10
145 Sylvain Cote .02 .10
146 Brent Ashton .02 .10
147 Doug Bodger .02 .10
148 Bryan Marchment .02 .10
149 Bob Kudelski .02 .10
150 Adam Graves .02 .10
151 Scott Stevens .07 .20
152 Russ Courtnall .02 .10
153 Darcy Wakaluk .07 .20
154 Pelle Eklund .02 .10
155 Robert Kron .02 .10
156 Randy Ladouceur .02 .10
157 Ed Olczyk .02 .10
158 Jiri Hrdina .02 .10
159 John Tonelli .02 .10
160 John Cullen .02 .10
161 Jan Erixon .02 .10
162 David Shaw .02 .10
163 Brian Bradley .02 .10
164 Russ Romaniuk .02 .10
165 Eric Weinrich .02 .10
166 Steve Heinze .02 .10
167 Jeremy Roenick .15 .40
168 Mark Pederson .02 .10
169 Paul Coffey .10 .30
170 Bob Errey .02 .10
171 Brian Lawton .02 .10
172 Vincent Riendeau .07 .20
173 Marc Fortier .02 .10
174 Marc Bergevin .02 .10
175 Jim Sandlak .02 .10
176 Bob Bassen .02 .10
177 Uwe Krupp .02 .10
178 Paul MacDermid .02 .10
179 Bob Corkum .02 .10
180 Robert Reichel .02 .10
181 John LeClair .25 .60
182 Mike Hudson .02 .10
183 Mark Recchi .07 .20
184 Rollie Melanson .07 .20
185 Gordie Roberts .02 .10
186 Clint Malarchuk .07 .20
187 Kris King .02 .10
188 Adam Oates .07 .20
189 Jarrod Skalde .02 .10
190 Mike Lalor .02 .10
191 Vincent Damphousse .02 .10
192 Peter Ahola .02 .10
193 Kirk McLean .07 .20
194 Murray Baron .02 .10
195 Michel Petit .02 .10
196 Stephane Fiset .07 .20
197 Pat Verbeek .02 .10
198 Jon Casey .07 .20
199 Tim Cheveldae .07 .20
200 Mike Ridley .02 .10
201 Scott Lachance .02 .10
202 Rod Brind'Amour .07 .20
203 Bret Hedican UER RC .07 .20
204 Wendel Clark .07 .20
205 Shawn McEachern .02 .10
206 Randy Wood .02 .10
207 Ulf Dahlen .02 .10
208 Andy Brickley .02 .10
209 Scott Niedermayer UER .02 .10
210 Bob Essensa .07 .20
211 Patrick Poulin .02 .10
212 Johan Garpenlov .02 .10
213 Marty McInnis .02 .10
214 Josef Beranek .02 .10
215 Rod Langway .02 .10
216 Dave Christian .02 .10
217 Sergei Makarov .02 .10
218 Gerard Gallant .02 .10
219 Neil Wilkinson UER .02 .10
220 Tomas Sandstrom .07 .20
221 Shayne Corson .02 .10
222 John Ogrodnick .02 .10
223 Keith Acton .02 .10
224 Paul Fenton .02 .10
225 Rob Zettler .02 .10
226 Todd Elik .02 .10
227 Petr Svoboda .02 .10
228 Zdeno Ciger .02 .10
229 Kevin Miller .02 .10
230 Rich Pilon .02 .10
231 Pat Jablonski .07 .20
232 Greg Adams .02 .10
233 Martin Brodeur .50 1.25
234 Dave Taylor .07 .20
235 Kelly Buchberger .02 .10
236 Steve Konroyd .02 .10
237 Guy Larose .02 .10
238 Patrice Brisebois .02 .10
239 Checklist 1-125 .02 .10
240 Checklist 126-250 .02 .10
241 Mark Messier MC .10 .25
242 Mike Richter MC .06 .15
243 Ed Belfour MC .07 .20
244 Sergei Fedorov MC .12 .30
245 Adam Oates MC .07 .20
246 Pavel Bure MC .08 .20
247 Luc Robitaille MC .07 .20
248 Brian Leetch MC .07 .20
249 Ray Bourque MC .12 .30
250 Tony Amonte MC .06 .15
251 Mario Lemieux MC .30 .75
252 Patrick Roy MC .30 .75
253 Nicklas Lidstrom MC .07 .20
254 Steve Yzerman MC .30 .75
255 Jeremy Roenick MC .07 .20
256 Wayne Gretzky MC .40 1.00
257 Kevin Stevens MC .02 .10
258 Brett Hull MC .10 .30
259 Pat Falloon MC .02 .10
260 Guy Carbonneau MC .07 .20
261 Todd Gill .02 .10
262 Mike Sullivan .02 .10
263 Jeff Brown .02 .10
264 Joe Reekie .02 .10
265 Geoff Courtnall .02 .10
266 Mike Richter .10 .30
267 Ray Bourque .25 .60
268 Mike Craig .02 .10
269 Scott King .02 .10
270 Don Beaupre .07 .20
271 Ted Donato .02 .10
272 Gary Leeman .02 .10
273 Steve Weeks .07 .20
274 Keith Brown .02 .10
275 Greg Paslawski .02 .10
276 Pierre Turgeon .07 .20
277 Jimmy Carson .02 .10
278 Tom Fergus .02 .10
279 Glen Wesley .02 .10
280 Tomas Forslund .02 .10
281 Tony Granato .02 .10
282 Phil Bourque .02 .10
283 Dave Ellett .02 .10
284 David Bruce .02 .10
285 Stu Barnes .02 .10
286 Peter Bondra .07 .20
287 Garth Butcher .02 .10
288 Ron Hextall .07 .20
289 Guy Carbonneau .07 .20
290 Louie DeBrusk .02 .10
291 Dave Barr .02 .10
292 Ken Sutton .02 .10
293 Brian Bellows .02 .10
294 Mike McNeill .02 .10
295 Rob Brown .02 .10
296 Corey Millen .02 .10
297 Joe Juneau UER .07 .20
298 Jeff Chychrun UER .02 .10
299 Igor Larionov .02 .10
300 Sergei Fedorov .20 .50
301 Kevin Hatcher .02 .10
302 Al Iafrate .07 .20
303 James Black .02 .10
304 Steph Beauregard .07 .20
305 Joel Otto .02 .10
306 Nelson Emerson .02 .10
307 Gaetan Duchesne .02 .10
308 J.J. Daigneault .02 .10
309 Jamie Macoun .02 .10
310 Laurie Boschman .02 .10
311 Mike Gartner .07 .20
312 Tony Tanti .02 .10
313 Steve Duchesne .02 .10
314 Martin Gelinas .02 .10
315 Dominic Roussel .07 .20
316 Cam Neely .10 .30
317 Craig Wolanin .02 .10
318 Randy Gilhen .02 .10
319 David Volek .02 .10
320 Alexander Mogilny .07 .20
321 Jyrki Lumme .02 .10
322 Jeff Reese .02 .10
323 Greg Gilbert .02 .10
324 Jeff Norton .02 .10
325 Jim Hrivnak .07 .20
326 Eric Desjardins .07 .20
327 Curtis Joseph .10 .30
328 Ric Nattress .02 .10
329 Jamie Leach .02 .10
330 Christian Ruuttu .02 .10
331 Doug Brown .02 .10
332 Randy Carlyle .02 .10
333 Ed Belfour .10 .30
334 Doug Smail .02 .10
335 Hubie McDonough .02 .10
336 Pat MacLeod .02 .10
337 Don Sweeney .02 .10
338 Felix Potvin .10 .30
339 Kent Manderville .02 .10
340 Sergei Nemchinov .02 .10
341 Calle Johansson .02 .10
342 Dirk Graham .02 .10
343 Craig Billington .07 .20
344 Valeri Kamensky .02 .10
345 Mike Vernon .07 .20
346 Fredrik Olausson .02 .10
347 Peter Ing .07 .20
348 Mikael Andersson .02 .10
349 Mike Keane .02 .10
350 Stephane Quintal .02 .10
351 Tom Chorske .02 .10
352 Ron Francis .07 .20
353 Dana Murzyn .02 .10
354 Craig Ludwig .02 .10
355 Bob Probert .07 .20
356 Glenn Healy .07 .20
357 Troy Loney .02 .10
358 Vladimir Ruzicka .02 .10
359 Doug Gilmour .07 .20
360 Darren Turcotte .02 .10
361 Kelly Miller .02 .10
362 Dennis Vaske .02 .10
363 Stephane Matteau .02 .10
364 Brian Hayward .07 .20
365 Kevin Dineen .02 .10
366 Igor Ulanov .02 .10
367 Sylvain Lefebvre .02 .10
368 Petr Klima .02 .10
369 Steve Thomas .07 .20
370 Daren Puppa .07 .20
371 Brendan Shanahan .10 .30
372 Charlie Huddy .02 .10
373 Cliff Ronning .02 .10
374 Brian Propp .02 .10
375 Larry Murphy .07 .20
376 Bruce Driver .02 .10
377 Rob Pearson .02 .10
378 Paul Ysebaert .02 .10
379 Mark Osborne .02 .10
380 Doug Weight .10 .30
381 Kerry Huffman UER .02 .10
382 Michal Pivonka .02 .10
383 Steve Smith .02 .10
384 Steven Finn .02 .10
385 Kevin Lowe .07 .20
386 Mike Ramsey .02 .10
387 Kirk Muller .02 .10
388 John LeBlanc RC .02 .10
389 Rich Sutter .02 .10
390 Brent Fedyk .02 .10
391 Kelly Hrudey .07 .20
392 Slava Fetisov .02 .10
393 Glen Murray UER .02 .10
394 James Patrick .02 .10
395 Tom Draper .02 .10
396 Mark Hunter .02 .10
397 Wayne McBean .02 .10
398 Joe Sacco .02 .10
399 Dino Ciccarelli .07 .20
400 Brian Noonan .02 .10
401 Guy Hebert RC .40 1.00
402 Peter Douris .02 .10
403 Gilbert Dionne .02 .10
404 Doug Lidster .02 .10
405 John Druce .02 .10
406 Alexei Kasatonov .02 .10
407 Chris Lindberg .02 .10
408 Mike Ricci .07 .20
409 Tom Kurvers .02 .10
410 Pat Elynuik .02 .10
411 Mike Donnelly .02 .10
412 Grant Fuhr .10 .30
413 Curtis Leschyshyn .02 .10
414 Derian Hatcher .02 .10
415 Michel Mongeau .02 .10
416 Tom Barrasso .07 .20
417 Joey Kocur .07 .20
418 Vladimir Konstantinov .10 .30
419 Dale Hawerchuk .07 .20
420 Brian Mullen .02 .10
421 Mark Greig .02 .10
422 Claude Vilgrain .02 .10
423 Gary Suter .02 .10
424 Garry Galley .02 .10
425 Benoit Hogue .02 .10
426 Jeff Finley RC .02 .10
427 Bobby Smith .07 .20
428 Brent Sutter .02 .10
429 Ron Wilson .02 .10
430 Andy Moog .10 .30
431 Stephan Lebeau .02 .10
432 Troy Mallette .02 .10
433 Peter Zezel .02 .10
434 Mike Hough .02 .10
435 Mark Tinordi .02 .10
436 Dave Manson .02 .10
437 Jim Paek .02 .10
438 Frantisek Kucera .02 .10
439 Rob Zamuner RC .07 .20
440 Ulf Samuelsson .02 .10
441 Perry Berezan .02 .10
442 Murray Craven .02 .10
443 Mark Messier .10 .30
444 Alexander Semak .02 .10
445 Gord Murphy .02 .10
446 Jocelyn Lemieux .02 .10
447 Paul Cavallini .02 .10
448 Bernie Nicholls .07 .20
449 Brent Gilchrist .02 .10
450 Randy McKay .02 .10
451 Alexei Gusarov .02 .10
452 Mike McPhee .02 .10
453 Kimbi Daniels .02 .10
454 Kelly Kisio .02 .10
455 Bob Sweeney .02 .10
456 Luke Richardson .02 .10
457 Petr Nedved .07 .20
458 Craig Berube .02 .10
459 Kay Whitmore .07 .20
460 Randy Velischek .02 .10
461 David Williams RC .02 .10
462 Scott Mellanby .02 .10
463 Terry Carkner .02 .10
464 Dale Craigwell .02 .10
465 Kevin Todd .02 .10
466 Kjell Samuelsson .02 .10
467 Denis Savard .07 .20
468 Adam Foote .07 .20
469 Stephane Morin .02 .10
470 Doug Wilson .07 .20
471 Shawn Cronin .02 .10
472 Brian Glynn UER .02 .10
473 Craig Simpson .02 .10
474 Todd Krygier .02 .10
475 Brad Miller .02 .10
476 Yvon Corriveau .02 .10
477 Patrick Flatley .02 .10
478 Mats Sundin .10 .30
479 Joe Cirella .02 .10
480 Gino Cavallini .02 .10
481 Marty McSorley .02 .10
482 Brad Marsh .02 .10
483 Bob McGill .02 .10
484 Randy Moller .02 .10
485 Keith Primeau .02 .10
486 Darin Kimble .02 .10
487 Mike Krushelnyski .02 .10
488 Sutter Brothers .02 .10
489 Pavel Bure .10 .30
490 Ray Whitney RC .20 .50
491 Dave McLlwain .02 .10
492 Per Djoos .02 .10
493 Garry Valk .02 .10
494 Mike Bullard .02 .10
495 Greg Hawgood .02 .10
496 Terry Yake .02 .10
497 Mike Hartman .02 .10
498 Jaromir Jagr .20 .50
499 Checklist 251-384 .02 .10
500 Checklist 385-500 .02 .10
501 Eric Lindros .10 .30

1993-94 Stadium Club

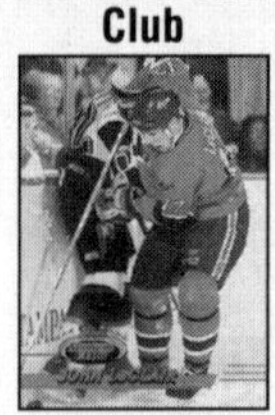

This 500-card standard-size set features borderless color player action shots on the card fronts. The set was issued in two series of 250 cards each. Cards were printed for both the Canadian and U.S. markets. The O-Pee-Chee version has a U.S.A. copyright on back for series one cards only. The player's name appears in gold foil at the bottom, atop blue and gold foil stripes. Included is a ten-card Award Winners subset (141-150) that features the 1992-93 NHL Trophy winners. Rookie Cards include Jason Arnott, Chris Osgood, Jocelyn Thibault and German Titov.

COMPLETE SET (500) 15.00 30.00
COMPLETE SERIES 1 (250) 7.50 15.00
COMPLETE SERIES 2 (250) 7.50 15.00
*SER.1 OPC CARDS: 1X TO 1.5X U.S. CARDS
1 Guy Carbonneau .01 .05
2 Joe Cirella .01 .05
3 Laurie Boschman .01 .05
4 Arturs Irbe .02 .10
5 Adam Creighton .01 .05
6 Mike McPhee .01 .05
7 Jeff Beukeboom .01 .05
8 Kevin Todd .01 .05
9 Yvon Corriveau .01 .05
10 Eric Lindros .08 .25
11 Martin Rucinsky .01 .05
12 Michel Goulet .02 .10
13 Scott Pellerin RC .01 .05
14 Mike Eagles .01 .05
15 Steve Heinze .01 .05
16 Gerard Gallant .01 .05
17 Kelly Miller .01 .05
18 Petr Nedved .02 .10
19 Joe Mullen .02 .10
20 Pat LaFontaine .08 .25
21 Garth Butcher .01 .05
22 Jeff Reese .01 .05
23 Dave Andreychuk .02 .10
24 Patrick Flatley .01 .05
25 Tomas Sandstrom .01 .05
26 Andre Racicot .02 .10
27 Patrice Brisebois .01 .05
28 Neal Broten .02 .10
29 Mark Freer .01 .05
30 Kelly Kisio .01 .05
31 Scott Mellanby .02 .10
32 Joe Sakic .20 .50
33 Kerry Huffman .01 .05
34 Evgeny Davydov .01 .05
35 Mark Messier .08 .25
36 Pat Verbeek .01 .05
37 Greg Gilbert .01 .05
38 John Tucker .01 .05
39 Claude Lemieux .01 .05
40 Shayne Corson .01 .05
41 Gordie Roberts .01 .05
42 Jiri Slegr .01 .05
43 Kevin Dineen .01 .05
44 Johan Garpenlov .01 .05
45 Sergei Fedorov .15 .40
46 Rich Sutter .01 .05
47 Dave Hannan .01 .05
48 Sylvain Lefebvre .01 .05
49 Pat Elynuik .01 .05
50 Ray Ferraro .01 .05
51 Brent Ashton .01 .05
52 Paul Stanton .01 .05
53 Kevin Haller .01 .05
54 Kelly Hrudey .02 .10
55 Russ Courtnall .01 .05
56 Alexei Zhamnov .02 .10
57 Andrei Lomakin .01 .05
58 Keith Brown .01 .05
59 Glen Murray .01 .05
60 Kay Whitmore .02 .10
61 Stephane Richer .02 .10
62 Todd Gill .01 .05
63 Bob Sweeney .01 .05
64 Mike Richter .08 .25
65 Brett Hull .10 .30
66 Sylvain Cote .01 .05
67 Kirk Muller .01 .05
68 Ronnie Stern .01 .05
69 Josef Beranek .01 .05
70 Steve Yzerman .50 1.25
71 Don Beaupre .02 .10
72 Ed Courtenay .01 .05
73 Zdeno Ciger .01 .05
74 Andrew Cassels .01 .05
75 Roman Hamrlik .02 .10
76 Benoit Hogue .01 .05
77 Andrei Kovalenko .01 .05
78 Rod Brind'Amour .02 .10
79 Tom Barrasso .02 .10
80 Al Iafrate .01 .05
81 Brett Hedican .01 .05
82 Peter Bondra .02 .10
83 Ted Donato .01 .05
84 Chris Lindberg .01 .05
85 John Vanbiesbrouck .02 .10
86 Ron Sutter .01 .05
87 Luc Robitaille .02 .10
88 Brian Leetch .08 .25
89 Randy Wood .01 .05
90 Dirk Graham .01 .05
91 Alexander Mogilny .02 .10
92 Mike Keane .01 .05
93 Adam Oates .02 .10
94 Viacheslav Butsayev .01 .05
95 John LeClair .08 .25
96 Joe Nieuwendyk .02 .10
97 Mikael Andersson .01 .05
98 Jaromir Jagr .15 .40
99 Ed Belfour .08 .25
100 David Reid .01 .05
101 Darius Kasparaitis .01 .05
102 Zarley Zalapski .01 .05
103 Christian Ruuttu .01 .05
104 Phil Housley .02 .10
105 Al MacInnis .02 .10
106 Tommy Sjodin .01 .05
107 Richard Smehlik .01 .05
108 Jyrki Lumme .01 .05
109 Dominic Roussel .02 .10
110 Mike Gartner .02 .10
111 Bernie Nicholls .01 .05
112 Mark Howe .01 .05
113 Rich Pilon .01 .05
114 Jeff Odgers .01 .05
115 Gilbert Dionne .01 .05
116 Peter Zezel .01 .05
117 Don Sweeney .01 .05
118 Jimmy Carson .01 .05
119 Igor Korolev .01 .05
120 Bob Kudelski .01 .05
121 Dave Lowry .01 .05
122 Steve Kasper .01 .05
123 Mike Ridley .01 .05
124 Dave Tippett .01 .05
125 Cliff Ronning .01 .05
126 Bruce Driver .01 .05
127 Stephane Matteau .01 .05
128 Joel Otto .01 .05
129 Alexei Kovalev .02 .10
130 Mike Modano .15 .40
131 Bill Ranford .02 .10
132 Petr Svoboda .01 .05
133 Roger Johansson .01 .05
134 Marc Bureau .01 .05
135 Keith Tkachuk .08 .25
136 Mark Recchi .02 .10
137 Bob Probert .02 .10
138 Uwe Krupp .01 .05
139 Mike Sullivan .01 .05
140 Doug Gilmour .02 .10
141 Teemu Selanne .08 .25
142 Dave Poulin .01 .05
143 Mario Lemieux TW .08 .25
144 Ed Belfour .08 .25
145 Pierre Turgeon .02 .10
146 Mario Lemieux TW .08 .25
147 Chris Chelios .08 .25
148 Mario Lemieux TW .08 .25
149 Doug Gilmour .02 .10
150 Ed Belfour .08 .25
151 Paul Ranheim .01 .05
152 Gino Cavallini .01 .05
153 Kevin Hatcher .01 .05
154 Marc Bergevin .01 .05
155 Marty McSorley .01 .05
156 Brian Bellows .01 .05
157 Patrick Poulin .01 .05
158 Kevin Stevens .01 .05
159 Bobby Holik .01 .05
160 Ray Bourque .15 .40
161 Bryan Marchment .01 .05
162 Curtis Joseph .08 .25
163 Kirk McLean .02 .10
164 Teppo Numminen .01 .05
165 Kevin Lowe .01 .05
166 Tim Cheveldae .02 .10
167 Brad Dalgarno .01 .05
168 Glenn Anderson .02 .10
169 Frank Musil .01 .05
170 Eric Desjardins .02 .10
171 Doug Zmolek .01 .05
172 Mark Lamb .01 .05
173 Craig Ludwig .01 .05
174 Rob Gaudreau RC .01 .05
175 Bob Carpenter .01 .05
176 Mike Ricci .01 .05
177 Brian Skrudland .01 .05
178 Dominik Hasek .30 .75
179 Pat Conacher .01 .05
180 Mark Janssens .01 .05
181 Brent Fedyk .01 .05
182 Rob DiMaio .01 .05
183 Dave Manson .01 .05
184 Janne Ojanen .01 .05
185 Ryan Walter .01 .05
186 Michael Nylander .01 .05
187 Steve Leach .01 .05
188 Jeff Brown .01 .05
189 Shawn McEachern .01 .05
190 Jeremy Roenick .12 .30
191 Darrin Shannon .01 .05
192 Wendel Clark .02 .10
193 Kevin Miller .01 .05
194 Paul DiPietro .01 .05
195 Steve Thomas .01 .05
196 Nicklas Lidstrom .08 .25
197 Ed Olczyk .01 .05
198 Robert Reichel .01 .05
199 Neil Brady .01 .05
200 Wayne Gretzky .60 1.50
201 Adrien Plavsic .01 .05
202 Joe Juneau .02 .10
203 Brad May .02 .10
204 Igor Kravchuk .01 .05
205 Keith Acton .01 .05
206 Ken Daneyko .01 .05
207 Sean Burke .02 .10
208 Jay More .01 .05
209 John Cullen .01 .05
210 Teemu Selanne .08 .25
211 Brent Sutter .01 .05
212 Brian Bradley .01 .05
213 Donald Audette .01 .05
214 Philippe Bozon .01 .05
215 Derek King .01 .05
216 Cam Neely .08 .25
217 Keith Primeau .01 .05
218 Steve Smith .01 .05
219 Ken Sutton .01 .05
220 Dale Hawerchuk .02 .10
221 Alexei Zhitnik .01 .05
222 Glen Wesley .01 .05
223 Nelson Emerson .01 .05
224 Pat Falloon .01 .05
225 Darryl Sydor .01 .05
226 Tony Amonte .02 .10
227 Brian Mullen .01 .05
228 Gary Suter .01 .05
229 David Shaw .01 .05
230 Troy Murray .01 .05
231 Patrick Roy .50 1.25
232 Mitchel Petit .01 .05
233 Wayne Presley .01 .05
234 Keith Jones .01 .05
235 Gary Roberts .01 .05
236 Steve Larmer .02 .10
237 Valeri Kamensky .02 .10
238 Ulf Dahlen .01 .05
239 Danton Cole .01 .05
240 Vincent Damphousse .01 .05
241 Yuri Khmylev .01 .05
242 Stephane Quintal .01 .05
243 Peter Taglianetti .01 .05
244 Gary Leeman .01 .05
245 Sergei Nemchinov .01 .05
246 Rob Blake .02 .10
247 Steve Chiasson .01 .05
248 Vladimir Malakhov .01 .05
249 Checklist 1-125 .01 .05
250 Checklist 126-250 .01 .05
251 Kjell Samuelsson .01 .05
252 Terry Carkner .01 .05
253 Bill Lindsay .01 .05
254 Bob Essensa .02 .10
255 Jocelyn Lemieux .01 .05
256 Joe Sacco .01 .05
257 Marty McInnis .01 .05
258 Warren Rychel .01 .05
259 David Maley .01 .05
260 Grant Fuhr .02 .10
261 Scott Young .01 .05
262 Ed Ronan .01 .05
263 Micah Aivazoff RC .01 .05
264 Murray Craven .01 .05
265 Slava Fetisov .01 .05
266 Chris Dahlquist .01 .05
267 Norm Maciver .01 .05
268 Alexander Godynyuk .01 .05
269 Mikael Renberg .08 .25
270 Adam Graves .01 .05
271 Randy Ladouceur .01 .05
272 Frank Pietrangelo .02 .10
273 Basil McRae .01 .05
274 Bryan Smolinski .01 .05
275 Daren Puppa .02 .10
276 Darcy Wakaluk .02 .10
277 Dimitri Khristich .01 .05
278 Vladimir Vujtek .01 .05
279 Tom Kurvers .01 .05
280 Felix Potvin .08 .25
281 Keith Brown .01 .05
282 Thomas Steen .01 .05
283 Larry Murphy .02 .10
284 Bob Corkum .01 .05
285 Tony Granato .01 .05
286 Cam Russell .01 .05
287 John MacLean .02 .10
288 Shawn Antoski .01 .05
289 Pelle Eklund .01 .05
290 Chris Pronger .10 .30
291 Alexander Karpovtsev .01 .05
292 Paul Laus RC .01 .05
293 Jaroslav Otevrel .01 .05
294 Dino Ciccarelli .02 .10
295 Guy Hebert .02 .10
296 Dave Karpa .01 .05
297 Denis Savard .02 .10
298 Jim Johnson .01 .05
299 Kirk Maltby RC .01 .05
300 Alexandre Daigle .01 .05
301 Dave Poulin .01 .05
302 James Patrick .01 .05
303 Jon Casey .02 .10
304 Yves Racine .01 .05
305 Craig Simpson .01 .05
306 Mike Krushelnyski .01 .05
307 Mark Fitzpatrick .02 .10
308 Charlie Huddy .01 .05
309 Todd Ewen .01 .05
310 Mario Lemieux .50 1.25
311 Dan Keczmer RC .01 .05
312 Sergei Zubov .01 .05
313 Shawn Burr .01 .05
314 Valeri Zelepukin .01 .05
315 Stephane Fiset .02 .10
316 C.J. Young .01 .05
317 Luciano Borsato .01 .05
318 Darcy Loewen .01 .05
319 Mike Vernon .02 .10
320 Chris Gratton .01 .05
321 Matthew Barnaby .02 .10
322 Mike Rathje .01 .05
323 Sergio Momesso .01 .05
324 David Volek .01 .05
325 Ron Tugnutt .02 .10
326 Jeff Hackett .01 .05
327 Robb Stauber .02 .10
328 Chris Terreri .02 .10
329 Rick Tocchet .02 .10
330 John Vanbiesbrouck .02 .10
331 Drake Berehowsky .01 .05
332 Alexei Kasatonov .01 .05
333 Vladimir Konstantinov .02 .10
334 John Blue .02 .10
335 Craig Janney .02 .10
336 Curtis Leschyshyn .01 .05
337 Todd Krygier .01 .05
338 Boris Mironov .01 .05
339 Joby Messier RC .01 .05
340 Tommy Soderstrom .02 .10
341 Randy Cunneyworth .01 .05
342 Mark Ferner RC .01 .05
343 Stephan Lebeau .01 .05
344 Jody Hull .01 .05
345 Jason Arnott RC .50 1.25
346 Gerard Gallant .01 .05
347 Stephane Richer .02 .10
348 Jeff Shantz RC .01 .05
349 Brian Skrudland .01 .05
350 Chris Osgood RC .75 2.00
351 Gary Shuchuk .01 .05
352 Martin Brodeur .30 .75
353 Bob Rouse .01 .05
354 Doug Bodger .01 .05
355 Mike Craig .01 .05
356 Ulf Samuelsson .01 .05
357 Trevor Linden .02 .10
358 Dennis Vaske .01 .05
359 Alexei Yashin .01 .05
360 Paul Ysebaert .01 .05
361 Shaun Van Allen .01 .05
362 Sandis Ozolinsh .01 .05
363 Todd Elik .01 .05
364 German Titov RC .01 .05
365 Alexander Semak .01 .05
366 Allen Pedersen .01 .05
367 Greg Johnson .01 .05
368 Anatoli Semenov .01 .05
369 Scott Mellanby .02 .10
370 Mats Sundin .08 .25
371 Mattias Norstrom RC .01 .05
372 Glen Featherstone .01 .05
373 Sergei Petrenko .01 .05
374 Mike Donnelly .01 .05
375 Nikolai Borschevsky .01 .05
376 Rob Zamuner .01 .05
377 Steven King .01 .05
378 Rick Tabaracci .02 .10
379 Dave Lowry .01 .05
380 Pierre Turgeon .02 .10
381 Garry Galley .01 .05
382 Doug Weight .02 .10
383 Scott Stevens .02 .10
384 Mark Tinordi .01 .05
385 Ron Francis .02 .10
386 Mark Greig .01 .05
387 Sean Hill .01 .05
388 Slava Kozlov .02 .10
389 Brendan Shanahan .08 .25
390 Theo Fleury .01 .05
391 Mathieu Schneider .01 .05
392 Tom Fitzgerald .01 .05
393 Markus Naslund .08 .25
394 Travis Green .02 .10
395 Troy Loney .01 .05
396 Gord Donnelly .01 .05
397 Owen Nolan .02 .10
398 Steve Larmer .02 .10
399 Dave Archibald .01 .05
400 Jari Kurri .08 .25
401 Jim Paek .01 .05
402 Andrei Lomakin .01 .05
403 Scott Niedermayer .01 .05
404 Bob Errey .01 .05
405 Michal Pivonka .01 .05
406 Doug Lidster .01 .05
407 Garry Valk .01 .05
408 Geoff Sanderson .02 .10
409 Stewart Malgunas RC .01 .05
410 Craig MacTavish .01 .05
411 Jaroslav Modry RC .01 .05
412 Shawn Chambers .01 .05
413 Geoff Courtnall .01 .05
414 Mark Hardy .01 .05
415 Martin Straka .01 .05
416 Randy Burridge .01 .05
417 Kent Manderville .01 .05
418 Darren Rumble .01 .05
419 Bill Houlder .01 .05
420 Chris Chelios .08 .25
421 Jim Hrivnak .02 .10
422 Benoit Brunet .01 .05
423 Aaron Ward RC .01 .05
424 Alexei Gusarov .01 .05
425 Mats Sundin .02 .10
426 Kjell Samuelsson .01 .05
427 Mikael Andersson .01 .05
428 Ulf Dahlen .01 .05
429 Nicklas Lidstrom .08 .25
430 Tommy Soderstrom .01 .05
431 Darren Madeley RC .01 .05
432 Kevin Dahl .01 .05
433 Ron Hextall .02 .10
434 Patrick Carnback RC .01 .05
435 Randy Moller .01 .05
436 Dave Gagner .02 .10
437 Corey Millen .01 .05
438 Olaf Kolzig .02 .10
439 Gord Murphy .01 .05
440 Cam Stewart RC .01 .05
441 Darren McCarty RC .20 .50
442 Frantisek Kucera .01 .05
443 Ted Drury .01 .05
444 Troy Mallette .01 .05
445 Robin Bawa RC .01 .05
446 Steven Rice .01 .05
447 Pat Elynuik .01 .05
448 Jim Cummins RC .01 .05
449 Rob Niedermayer .02 .10
450 Paul Coffey .08 .25
451 Calle Johansson .01 .05
452 Mike Needham .01 .05
453 Glenn Healy .02 .10
454 Dixon Ward .01 .05
455 Al Iafrate .01 .05
456 Jon Casey .02 .10
457 Kevin Stevens .01 .05
458 Tony Amonte .02 .10
459 Chris Chelios .08 .25
460 Pat LaFontaine .02 .10
461 Jamie Baker .01 .05
462 Andre Faust .01 .05
463 Bobby Dollas .01 .05
464 Steven Finn .01 .05
465 Scott Lachance .01 .05
466 Mike Hough .01 .05
467 Bill Guerin .01 .05
468 Dimitri Filimonov .01 .05
469 Dave Ellett .01 .05
470 Andy Moog .02 .10
471 Scott Thomas RC .01 .05
472 Trent Yawney .01 .05
473 Tim Sweeney .01 .05
474 Shjon Podein RC .01 .05
475 J.J. Daigneault .01 .05
476 Darren Turcotte .01 .05
477 Esa Tikkanen .01 .05
478 Vitali Karamnov .01 .05
479 Jocelyn Thibault RC .30 .75
480 Pavel Bure .08 .25
481 Steve Konowalchuk .01 .05
482 Sylvain Turgeon .01 .05
483 Jeff Daniels .01 .05
484 Dallas Drake RC .01 .05
485 Iain Fraser RC .01 .05
486 Joe Reekie .01 .05

487 Evgeny Davydov .01 .05
488 Jozef Stumpel .01 .05
489 Brent Thompson .01 .05
490 Terry Yake .01 .05
491 Derek Plante RC .01 .05
492 Dimitri Yushkevich .01 .05
493 Wayne McBean .01 .05
494 Derian Hatcher .01 .05
495 Jeff Norton .01 .05
496 Adam Foote .01 .05
497 Mike Peluso .01 .05
498 Rob Pearson .01 .05
499 Checklist 251-375 .01 .05
500 Checklist 376-500 .01 .05

1993-94 Stadium Club Members Only Master Set

Issued to Stadium Club members only, this set parallels the basic cards with the exception of the words "Topps' Stadium Club Members Only" printed on the card front.

COMPLETE SET (500) 320.00 800.00
*STARS: 8X TO 20X BASIC CARD

1993-94 Stadium Club First Day Issue

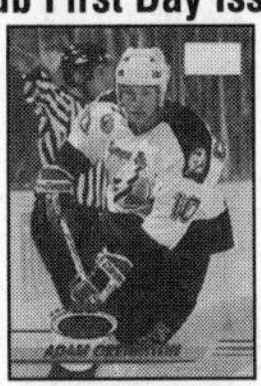

Randomly inserted at a rate of 1:24 packs, the 500-cards parallel the basic Stadium Club set. The O-Pee-Chee version has a U.S.A. copyright on back for series one cards only. The cards of Wayne Gretzky, Vincent Damphousse, Luc Robitaille and Wayne Presley can be found with the logo in either upper corner.

*STARS: 30X TO 80X BASIC CARDS
*RCs: 12.5X TO 30X BASIC CARDS
*SER.1 OPC: 1X TO 1.25X BASIC CARD

1993-94 Stadium Club All-Stars

Randomly inserted at the rate of 1:24 first-series packs, each of these 23 standard-size cards features two 1992-93 All-Stars, one from each conference. Both sides carry a posed color player photo superimposed over a stellar background. The cards are unnumbered.

1 Patrick Roy 6.00 15.00
Ed Belfour
2 Ray Bourque 2.00 5.00
Paul Coffey
3 Al Iafrate 1.50 4.00
Chris Chelios
4 Jaromir Jagr 2.00 5.00
Brett Hull
5 Pat LaFontaine 4.00 10.00
Steve Yzerman
6 Kevin Stevens 2.00 5.00
Pavel Bure
7 Craig Billington .75 2.00
Jon Casey
8 Steve Duchesne .75 2.00
Steve Chiasson
9 Scott Stevens .75 2.00
Phil Housley
10 Peter Bondra 1.50 4.00
Kelly Kisio
11 Adam Oates 1.50 4.00
Brian Bradley
12 Alexander Mogilny 1.50 4.00
Jari Kurri
13 Peter Sidorkiewicz .75 2.00
Mike Vernon
14 Zarley Zalapski .75 2.00
Dave Manson
15 Brad Marsh .75 2.00
Randy Carlyle
16 Kirk Muller .75 2.00
Gary Roberts
17 Joe Sakic 3.00 8.00
Doug Gilmour
18 Mark Recchi 1.50 4.00
Luc Robitaille
19 Kevin Lowe .75 2.00
Garth Butcher
20 Rick Tocchet 2.00 5.00
Jeremy Roenick
21 Pierre Turgeon 2.00 5.00
Mike Modano
22 Mike Gartner 2.00 5.00
Teemu Selanne
23 Mario Lemieux 10.00 25.00
Wayne Gretzky

1993-94 Stadium Club All-Stars Members Only

Issued to Stadium Club members only, this set parallels the basic cards with the exception of the words "Topp's Stadium Club Members Only" printed on the card front.

*STARS: 2.5X TO 5X ALL-STARS CARD

1993-94 Stadium Club Finest

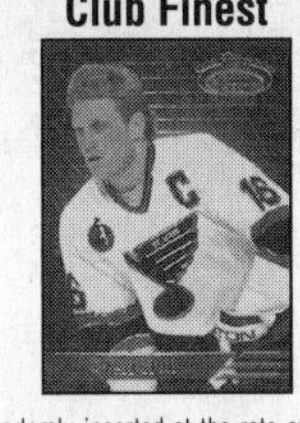

Randomly inserted at the rate of 1:24 second-series packs, these 12 standard-size cards feature color player action cutouts on their multicolored metallic fronts. The player's name in gold lettering appears on a silver bar at the lower left. The horizontal back carries a color player photo on the left. The player's name and position appear at the top, with biography, career highlights, and statistics following below on a background that resembles blue ruffled silk. The cards are numbered on the back as "X of 12."

COMPLETE SET (12) 20.00 40.00
1 Wayne Gretzky 6.00 15.00
2 Jeff Brown .20 .50
3 Brett Hull 1.25 3.00
4 Paul Coffey 1.00 2.50
5 Felix Potvin 1.00 2.50
6 Mike Gartner .40 1.00
7 Luc Robitaille .40 1.00
8 Marty McSorley .20 .50
9 Gary Roberts .20 .50
10 Mario Lemieux 5.00 12.00
11 Patrick Roy 5.00 12.00
12 Ray Bourque 1.50 4.00
NNO Redemption Single .40 1.00
NNO Redemption Set 1.50 4.00

1993-94 Stadium Club Finest Members Only

Issued to Stadium Club members only, this set parallels the basic cards with the exception of the words "Topp's Stadium Club Members Only" printed on the card front.

*STARS: 2.5X TO 5X FINEST CARD

1993-94 Stadium Club Master Photos

Inserted one per U.S. box, and issued in two 12-card series, these 24 oversized cards measure 5" by 7". The fronts feature color player action shots framed by prismatic foil lines and set on a white card face. The cards are numbered on the back for both series as "X of 12," but are listed below as 1-24 to avoid confusion. Winner cards, which could be redeemed for one 5" X 7" card of each of the three players listed on the reverse, were inserted 1:24 packs of '93-94 Stadium Club

*WINNER: 3X TO 8X BASIC CARDS
1 Pat LaFontaine .40 1.00
2 Doug Gilmour .15 .40
3 Ray Bourque .60 1.50
4 Teemu Selanne .40 1.00
5 Eric Lindros .40 1.00
6 Ray Ferraro .10 .20
7 Patrick Roy 2.00 5.00
8 Wayne Gretzky 2.50 6.00
9 Brett Hull .50 1.25
10 John Vanbiesbrouck .15 .40
11 Adam Oates .15 .40
12 Tom Barrasso .15 .40
13 Esa Tikkanen .10 .20
14 Jari Kurri .40 1.00
15 Grant Fuhr .15 .40
16 Scott Lachance .10 .20
17 Theo Fleury .10 .20
18 Adam Graves .10 .20
19 Rick Tabaracci .15 .40
20 Pierre Turgeon .15 .40
21 Steven Finn .10 .20
22 Craig Janney .15 .40
23 Mathieu Schneider .10 .20
24 Felix Potvin .40 1.00

1993-94 Stadium Club Team USA

Randomly inserted at the rate of 1:12 second-series packs, these 23 standard-size cards feature color player action shots on their borderless fronts. The player's name appears in gold-foil lettering over a blue stripe near the bottom. The gold foil USA Hockey logo appears in an upper corner. The cards are numbered on the back as "X of 23."

1 Mark Beaufait .40 1.00
2 Jim Campbell .60 1.50
3 Ted Crowley .40 1.00
4 Mike Dunham .60 1.50
5 Chris Ferraro .40 1.00
6 Peter Ferraro .40 1.00
7 Brett Hauer .40 1.00
8 Darby Hendrickson .40 1.00
9 Jon Hillebrandt .40 1.00
10 Chris Imes .40 1.00
11 Craig Johnson .40 1.00
12 Peter Laviolette .40 1.00
13 Jeff Lazaro .40 1.00
14 John Lilley .40 1.00
15 Todd Marchant .60 1.50
16 Matt Martin .40 1.00
17 Ian Moran .40 1.00
18 Travis Richards .40 1.00
19 Barry Richter .40 1.00
20 David Roberts .40 1.00
21 Brian Rolston .60 1.50
22 David Sacco .40 1.00
23 Jim Storm .40 1.00

1994 Stadium Club Members Only

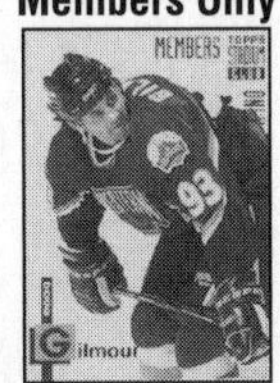

Issued to Stadium Club members, this 50-card standard-size set features 45 players who were involved with the 1994 All-Star game, Western Conference All-Stars (1-22), Eastern Conference All-Stars (23-45), and five Stadium Club Finest cards. The fronts have full-bleed color action player photos. The player's name is printed in the bottom left corner, the words "Topps Stadium Club Members Only" in gold foil appear in one of the top corners. On a black background, the horizontal backs carry a color player close-up shot, along with a player profile.

COMP.FACT SET (50) 8.00 20.00
1 Felix Potvin .30 .75
2 Chris Chelios .20 .50
3 Paul Coffey .20 .50
4 Pavel Bure .60 1.50
5 Wayne Gretzky 1.60 4.00
6 Brett Hull .30 .75
7 Al MacInnis .10 .25
8 Rob Blake .10 .25
9 Alexei Kasatonov .04 .10
10 Teemu Selanne .50 1.25
11 Sandis Ozolinsh .10 .25
12 Shayne Corson .04 .10
13 Dave Andreychuk .06 .15
14 Dave Taylor .04 .10
15 Sergei Fedorov .50 1.25
16 Brendan Shanahan .40 1.00
17 Arturs Irbe .20 .50
18 Joe Nieuwendyk .10 .25
19 Russ Courtnall .04 .10
20 Jeremy Roenick .30 .75
21 Doug Gilmour .30 .75
22 Curtis Joseph .30 .75
23 Patrick Roy 1.20 3.00
24 Brian Leetch .20 .50
25 Ray Bourque .40 1.00
26 Alexander Mogilny .20 .50
27 Mark Messier .30 .75
28 Eric Lindros .60 1.50
29 Garry Galley .04 .10
30 Scott Stevens .06 .15
31 Al Iafrate .04 .10
32 Larry Murphy .04 .10
33 Joe Mullen .04 .10
34 Mark Recchi .20 .50
35 Adam Graves .06 .15
36 Geoff Sanderson .04 .10
37 Adam Oates .20 .50
38 Pierre Turgeon .20 .50
39 Joe Sakic .50 1.25
40 John Vanbiesbrouck .20 .50
41 Brian Bradley .04 .10
42 Alexei Yashin .10 .25
43 Bob Kudelski .04 .10
44 Jaromir Jagr .80 2.00
45 Mike Richter .30 .75
46 Martin Brodeur .60 1.50
New Jers
47 Mikael Renberg .10 .25
48 Derek Plante .04 .10
49 Jason Arnott .10 .25
50 Alexandre Daigle .04 .10

1994-95 Stadium Club

This 270-card standard-size set was issued in one series. Due to the NHL lock-out, series two was replaced on the production schedule by Finest; therefore, this set does not have a comprehensive player selection. There are 12 cards per pack and 24 packs per box. The card fronts feature a full-bleed photo with the player's name and set name printed in gold foil along the bottom. The backs feature two player photos and previous year stats. Subsets include Power Players (55-60), Great Expectations (110-119), Shutouts (178-190), Rink Report (201-204), and Trophy Winners (264-270). There are no key Rookie Cards in this set.

COMPLETE SET (270) 15.00 30.00
1 Mark Messier .10 .30
2 Brad May .02 .10
3 Mike Ricci .02 .10
4 Scott Stevens .05 .15
5 Keith Tkachuk .10 .30
6 Guy Hebert .05 .15
7 Jason Arnott .02 .10
8 Cam Neely .10 .30
9 Adam Graves .02 .10
10 Pavel Bure .10 .30
11 Jeff Odgers .02 .10
12 Dimitri Khristich .02 .10
13 Patrick Poulin .02 .10
14 Mike Donnelly .02 .10
15 Felix Potvin .10 .30
16 Keith Primeau .02 .10
17 Fred Knipscheer .02 .10
18 Mike Keane .02 .10
19 Vitali Prokhorov .02 .10
20 Ray Ferraro .02 .10
21 Shane Churla .02 .10
22 Rob Niedermayer .05 .15
23 Adam Creighton .02 .10
24 Tommy Soderstrom .05 .15
25 Theo Fleury .02 .10
26 Jim Storm .02 .10
27 Bret Hedican .02 .10
28 Sean Hill .02 .10
29 Bill Ranford .05 .15
30 Derek Plante .05 .15
31 Dave McLlwain .02 .10
32 Iain Fraser .02 .10
33 Patrick Roy .60 1.50
34 Martin Straka .02 .10
35 Bruce Driver .02 .10
36 Brian Skrudland .02 .10
37 Bob Errey .02 .10
38 Randy Cunneyworth .02 .10
39 John Slaney .02 .10
40 Ray Sheppard .05 .15
41 Sergei Nemchinov .02 .10
42 Dave Ellett .02 .10
43 Vincent Riendeau .05 .15
44 Trent Yawney .02 .10
45 Dave Gagner .05 .15
46 Igor Korolev .02 .10
47 Gary Shuchuk .02 .10
48 Rob Zamuner .02 .10
49 Frantisek Kucera .02 .10
50 Joe Mullen .05 .15
51 Ron Hextall .05 .15
52 J.J. Daigneault .02 .10
53 Patrik Carnback .02 .10
54 Steven Rice .02 .10
55 Brian Leetch PP .10 .30
56 Al MacInnis PP .05 .15
57 Luc Robitaille PP .05 .15
58 Dave Andreychuk PP .05 .15
59 Jeremy Roenick PP .15 .40
60 Mario Lemieux PP .60 1.50
61 Dave Manson .02 .10
62 Pat Falloon .02 .10
63 Jesse Belanger .02 .10
64 Philippe Boucher .02 .10
65 Sergio Momesso .02 .10
66 Evgeny Davydov .02 .10
67 Alexei Gusarov .02 .10
68 Jaromir Jagr .20 .50
69 Randy Ladouceur .02 .10
70 Chris Chelios .10 .30
71 John Druce .02 .10
72 Kris Draper .02 .10
73 Joey Kocur .02 .10
74 Rich Tabaracci .02 .10
75 Mikael Andersson .02 .10
76 Mark Osborne .02 .10
77 Ray Bourque .20 .50
78 Dimitri Yushkevich .02 .10
79 Mike Vernon .05 .15
80 Steve Thomas .02 .10
81 Steve Duchesne .02 .10
82 Dean Evason .02 .10
83 Jason Smith .02 .10
84 Bryan Marchment .02 .10
85 Boris Mironov .02 .10
86 Jeff Norton .02 .10
87 Donald Audette .02 .10
88 Eric Lindros .10 .30
89 Garry Valk .02 .10
90 Mats Sundin .10 .30
91 Gerald Diduck .02 .10
92 Jeff Shantz .02 .10
93 Scott Niedermayer .02 .10
94 Troy Mallette .02 .10
95 John Vanbiesbrouck .05 .15
96 Ron Francis .05 .15
97 Slava Kozlov .05 .15
98 Ken Baumgartner .02 .10
99 Wayne Gretzky .75 2.00
100 Brett Hull .15 .40
101 Marc Bergevin .02 .10
102 Owen Nolan .05 .15
103 Bryan Smolinski .02 .10
104 Lyle Odelein .02 .10
105 Mike Ridley .02 .10
106 Trevor Kidd .05 .15
107 Derian Hatcher .02 .10
108 Derek King .02 .10
109 Rob Zettler .02 .10
110 Alexandre Daigle GE .02 .10
111 Chris Pronger GE .05 .15
112 Chris Gratton GE .02 .10
113 John Slaney GE .02 .10
114 Jocelyn Thibault GE .10 .30
115 Jason Arnott GE .02 .10
116 Alexei Yashin GE .02 .10
117 Rob Niedermayer GE .05 .15
118 Jason Allison GE .02 .10
119 Martin Brodeur GE .30 .75
120 Pat Verbeek .02 .10
121 Kelly Buchberger .02 .10
122 Doug Lidster .02 .10
123 Sergei Makarov .02 .10
124 Kris King .02 .10
125 Dominik Hasek .25 .60
126 Martin Rucinsky .02 .10
127 Kerry Huffman .02 .10
128 Gord Murphy .02 .10
129 Bobby Holik .02 .10
130 Kirk Muller .02 .10
131 Christian Ruuttu .02 .10
132 Jyrki Lumme .02 .10
133 Ken Wregget .05 .15
134 Dale Hunter .02 .10
135 Rob Blake .02 .10
136 Petr Klima .02 .10
137 Steve Heinze .02 .10
138 Chris Osgood .20 .50
139 John Lilley .02 .10
140 Dave Andreychuk .05 .15
141 Zarley Zalapski .02 .10
142 Curtis Joseph .10 .30
143 Brent Gilchrist .02 .10
144 Vladimir Malakhov .02 .10
145 Mikael Renberg .05 .15
146 Robert Kron .02 .10
147 Dean McAmmond .02 .10
148 Doug Bodger .02 .10
149 Ray Whitney .02 .10
150 Brian Leetch .10 .30
151 Martin Lapointe .02 .10
152 Teppo Numminen .02 .10
153 Scott Young .02 .10
154 Nick Kypreos .02 .10
155 Ed Belfour .10 .30
156 Greg Adams .02 .10
157 Brian Benning .02 .10
158 Bob Carpenter .02 .10
159 Vladimir Konstantinov .05 .15
160 Rick Tocchet .05 .15
161 Joe Sacco .02 .10
162 Darren Puppa .05 .15
163 Randy Burridge .02 .10
164 Darryl Sydor .02 .10
165 Jay More .02 .10
166 Joe Nieuwendyk .05 .15
167 Mike Eastwood .02 .10
168 Murray Baron .02 .10
169 Brent Fedyk .02 .10
170 Russ Courtnall .02 .10
171 Sean Burke .05 .15
172 Uwe Krupp .02 .10
173 Kevin Lowe .02 .10
174 Guy Carbonneau .02 .10
175 Alexei Yashin .05 .15
176 Thomas Steen .02 .10
177 Sandis Ozolinsh .02 .10
178 Patrick Roy SO .40 1.00
179 Dominik Hasek SO .15 .40
180 Ed Belfour SO .10 .30
181 Mike Richter SO .10 .30
182 Ron Hextall SO .05 .15
183 Daren Puppa SO .05 .15
184 Jon Casey SO .05 .15
185 Felix Potvin SO .05 .15
186 Martin Brodeur SO .30 .75
187 Darcy Wakaluk SO .05 .15
188 Kirk McLean SO .05 .15
189 Mike Vernon SO .05 .15
190 Arturs Irbe SO .05 .15
191 Dino Ciccarelli .05 .15
192 Steven Finn .02 .10
193 Pierre Sevigny .02 .10
194 Jim Dowd .02 .10
195 Chris Gratton .02 .10
196 Wayne Presley .02 .10
197 Joel Otto .02 .10
198 Fredrik Olausson .02 .10
199 Jody Hull .02 .10
200 Cliff Ronning .02 .10
201 Darren Turcotte RR .02 .10
202 Al Iafrate RR .02 .10
203 Eric Lindros RR .10 .30
204 Sandis Ozolinsh RR .02 .10
205 Petr Nedved .05 .15
206 Mark Lamb .02 .10
207 Shaun Van Allen .02 .10
208 Kelly Hrudey .05 .15
209 Nikolai Borschevsky .02 .10
210 Glen Wesley .02 .10
211 Shawn McEachern .02 .10
212 Mark Janssens .02 .10
213 Brian Mullen .02 .10
214 Craig Ludwig .02 .10
215 Mike Rathje .02 .10
216 Stephane Matteau .02 .10
217 Tim Cheveldae .05 .15
218 Brent Sutter .02 .10
219 Gord Dineen .02 .10
220 Kevin Hatcher .02 .10
221 Todd Simon RC .02 .10
222 Bill Lindsay .02 .10
223 Kirk McLean .05 .15
224 Chris Joseph .02 .10
225 Valeri Zelepukin .02 .10
226 Terry Yake .02 .10
227 Benoit Brunet .02 .10
228 Nicklas Lidstrom .10 .30
229 Zdeno Ciger .02 .10
230 Gary Roberts .02 .10
231 Andy Moog .10 .30
232 Ed Patterson .02 .10
233 Philippe Bozon .02 .10
234 Brent Hughes .02 .10
235 Chris Pronger .10 .30
236 Travis Green .05 .15
237 Pat Conacher .02 .10
238 Bob Rouse .02 .10
239 Yves Racine .02 .10
240 Nelson Emerson .02 .10
241 Oleg Petrov .02 .10
242 Steve Larmer .05 .15
243 Dan Laperriere .02 .10
244 John McIntyre .02 .10
245 Alexander Semak .02 .10
246 Stephane Fiset .05 .15
247 Peter Bondra .05 .15
248 Dale Hawerchuk .05 .15
249 Jamie Baker .02 .10
250 Sergei Fedorov .20 .50
251 Derek Mayer .02 .10
252 Ivan Droppa .02 .10
253 Kent Manderville .02 .10
254 Sergei Zholtok .02 .10
255 Murray Craven .02 .10
256 Todd Krygier .02 .10
257 Brent Grieve RC .02 .10
258 Esa Tikkanen .02 .10
259 Brad Dalgarno .02 .10
260 Russ Romaniuk .02 .10
261 Stu Barnes .02 .10
262 Dan Keczmer .02 .10
263 Eric Desjardins .05 .15
264 Martin Brodeur TW .30 .75
265 Adam Graves TW .02 .10
266 Cam Neely TW .05 .15
267 Ray Bourque TW .10 .30
268 Sergei Fedorov TW .12 .30
269 Dominik Hasek TW .15 .40
270 Wayne Gretzky TW .60 1.50

1994-95 Stadium Club Members Only Master Set

Issued to Stadium Club members only, this set parallels the basic cards with the exception of the words "Topp's Stadium Club Members Only" printed on the card front.

*STARS: 3X TO 8X BASIC CARD

1994-95 Stadium Club First Day Issue

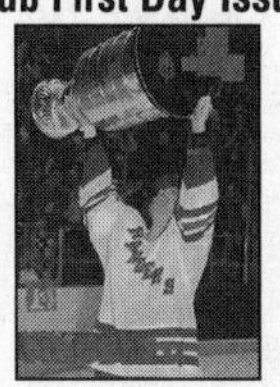

This is a parallel to the 270 card basic set, inserted at a rate of 1:24 packs. The only difference is the silver foil "First Day Issue" logo on the card front.

*STARS: 30X TO 60X BASIC CARDS
*RC's: 10X TO 25X BASIC CARDS

1994-95 Stadium Club Dynasty and Destiny

According to published odds, the five cards in this set were randomly inserted at the rate of 1:24 packs. Collector and dealer reports suggest they are available at a much easier rate than listed. Each card features two players; one veteran and an up and coming player with the same type of skills. Photos and stats for each player are on the backs. Each card is numbered out of ten, signifying that five more cards were to be included in the never-produced second series.

COMPLETE SET (5) 6.00 12.00
1 Tom Barrasso 1.25 3.00
Arturs Irbe
2 Mark Messier 1.50 4.00
Eric Lindros
3 Brett Hull 2.00 5.00
Pavel Bure
4 Luc Robitaille 1.25 3.00
Mikael Renberg
5 Chris Chelios 1.50 4.00
Chris Pronger

1994-95 Stadium Club Dynasty and Destiny Members Only

Issued to Stadium Club members only, this set parallels the basic cards with the exception of the words "Topp's Stadium Club Members Only" printed on the card front.

*STARS: .75X TO 2X BASIC CARD

1994-95 Stadium Club Finest Inserts

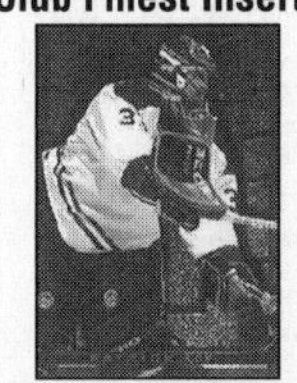

The nine cards in this set were inserted at the rate of 1:12 packs. The cards offer a completely different design from those of the basic Finest set which was released later in the season. These cards feature a cut-out player photo on a blue textured background. The player name is printed on a multi-color bar on the bottom of the card. Backs feature a small photo on the left with text information and limited stats. Cards are numbered out of nine.

COMPLETE SET (9) 20.00 40.00
1 Mario Lemieux 5.00 12.00
2 Brett Hull 1.25 3.00
3 Mark Messier 1.00 2.50
4 Wayne Gretzky 6.00 15.00
5 Pavel Bure 1.00 2.50
6 Sergei Fedorov 1.50 4.00
7 Brian Leetch 1.00 2.50
8 Ray Bourque 1.50 4.00
9 Patrick Roy 5.00 12.00

1994-95 Stadium Club Finest Inserts Members Only

Issued to Stadium Club members only, this set parallels the basic cards with the exception of the words "Topp's Stadium Club Members Only" printed on the card front.

*STARS: .75X TO 2X BASIC CARD

1994-95 Stadium Club Super Teams

The 26 cards in this set were inserted at the rate of 1:24 packs. The card fronts feature a photo of multiple players, or team action shot. The team name and set name are printed in speckled silver foil. Unlike most other inserts, these cards were part of an interactive game which allowed the holder to redeem the card for prizes if the pictured team won a division, conference or Stanley Cup championship. The backs have contest information and the teams record from the 1993-94 season. Holders of the New Jersey Devils card were able to redeem it for complete, specially stamped sets of Stadium Club and Finest. Winning division (Calgary, Detroit, Philadelphia, Quebec) and conference (Detroit, New Jersey) team cards were redeemable for packages of special stamped cards featuring members of that team.

COMPLETE SET (26) 40.00 80.00
1 Anaheim Mighty Ducks 1.00 4.00
(Bob Corkum et al.)
2 Boston Bruins 2.00 4.00
(Adam Oates/Ray Bourque)
3 Buffalo Sabres 1.50 4.00
(Dominik Hasek et al.)
4 Calgary Flames 1.00 4.00
(Andrei Trefilov/Theoren Fleury)
5 Chicago Blackhawks 2.00 4.00
(Ed Belfour et al.)
6 Dallas Stars 1.00 4.00
(Mike Modano/Trent Klatt/
Paul Broten)
7 Detroit Red Wings 2.50 6.00
(Steve Yzerman et al.)
8 Edmonton Oilers 1.00 4.00
(Bill Ranford/Bob Beers)
9 Florida Panthers 1.00 4.00
(Line change)
10 Hartford Whalers 1.00 4.00
(Sean Burke/Jim Storm/
Ted Crowley)
11 Los Angeles Kings 2.00 5.00
(Lined up for anthem)
12 Montreal Canadiens 2.00 5.00
(Patrick Roy)
13 New Jersey Devils 4.00 10.00
(Martin Brodeur)
14 New York Islanders 1.00 4.00
(Darius Kasparaitis/Yan Kaminsky)
15 New York Rangers 2.50 6.00
(Stanley Cup parade with
Mark Messier raising cup)
16 Ottawa Senators 1.00 4.00
(Practice session)
17 Philadelphia Flyers 1.50 4.00
(Eric Lindros/Mark Recchi/Jason
Bowen)
18 Pittsburgh Penguins 2.50 6.00
(Ron Francis/Joe Mullen)
19 Quebec Nordiques 2.50 6.00
(Joe Sakic et al.)
20 St. Louis Blues 2.00 5.00
(Curtis Joseph)
21 San Jose Sharks 1.00 4.00
(Tom Pederson/Sergei Makarov)
22 Tampa Bay Lightning 1.00 4.00
(Denis Savard/Petr Klima)
23 Toronto Maple Leafs 2.00 5.00
(Doug Gilmour/Dave Andreychuk)
24 Vancouver Canucks 2.50 6.00
(Pavel Bure et al.)
25 Washington Capitals 1.00 4.00
(Byron Dafoe/Dave Poulin/
Kevin Hatcher/Calle Johansson)
26 Winnipeg Jets 2.50 6.00
(Teemu Selanne/Alexei Zhamnov)

1994-95 Stadium Club Super Team Winner Cards

These cards were the prizes of the interactive game which allowed the holder to redeem the card if the pictured team won a division, conference or Stanley Cup championship. Holders of the New Jersey Devils card were able to redeem it for complete, specially stamped sets of Stadium Club and Finest. Winning division (Calgary, Detroit, Philadelphia, Quebec) and conference (Detroit, New Jersey) team cards were redeemable for packages of special stamped cards featuring members of that team.

COMPLETE SET (270) 50.00 100.00
*SUPER TEAM CARDS: 2X TO 5X BASIC CARDS

1995 Stadium Club Members Only

Topps produced a 50-card boxed set for each of the four major sports. With their club membership, members received one set of their choice and had the option of purchasing additional sets for $10.00 each. The five Finest cards (46-50) represent Topps' selection of the top 1994-95 rookies. The color action photos on the fronts have brightly-colored backgrounds and carry the distinctive Topps Stadium Club Members Only gold foil seal. The backs present a second color photo and player profile.

COMP. FACT SET (50)	10.00	25.00
1 Patrick Roy	1.00	2.50
2 Ray Bourque	.20	.50
3 Brian Leetch	.20	.50
4 Cam Neely	.16	.40
5 Jaromir Jagr	.60	1.50
6 Alexander Mogilny	.16	.40
7 John Vanbiesbrouck	.40	1.00
8 Geoff Sanderson	.06	.15
9 Mark Recchi	.10	.25
10 Scott Stevens	.04	.10
11 Roman Hamrlik	.06	.15
12 Dominik Hasek	.40	1.00
13 Joe Sakic	.40	1.00
14 Alexei Yashin	.20	.50
15 Eric Lindros	.60	1.50
16 Adam Oates	.10	.25
17 Ulf Samuelsson	.04	.10
18 Wendel Clark	.06	.15
19 Mark Messier	.30	.75
20 Pierre Turgeon	.10	.25
21 Mark Tinordi	.04	.10
22 Ron Francis	.10	.25
23 Jeff Brown	.04	.10
24 Tom Kurvers	.04	.10
25 Mike Modano	.30	.75
26 Mats Sundin	.20	.50
27 Jeremy Roenick	.20	.50
28 Kevin Hatcher	.04	.10
29 Curtis Joseph	.20	.50
30 Paul Coffey	.20	.50
31 Jason Arnott	.10	.25
32 Wayne Gretzky	1.20	3.00
33 Theo Fleury	.20	.50
34 Al MacInnis	.08	.20
35 Ed Belfour	.20	.50
36 Sergei Fedorov	.40	1.00
37 Brett Hull	.30	.75
38 Chris Chelios	.20	.50
39 Keith Tkachuk	.30	.75
40 Felix Potvin	.20	.50
41 Pavel Bure	.40	1.00
42 Ulf Dahlen	.04	.10
43 Teemu Selanne	.40	1.00
44 Doug Gilmour	.20	.50
45 Phil Housley	.06	.15
46 Paul Kariya FIN	2.40	6.00
47 Peter Forsberg FIN	2.00	5.00
48 Jim Carey FIN	.60	1.50
49 Todd Marchant FIN	.20	.50
50 Blaine Lacher FIN	.30	.75

1995-96 Stadium Club

The 1995-96 Stadium Club set was issued in one series totaling 225 cards. The 10-card packs retail for $2.50. The set features two subsets: Extreme Corps (163-189) and Extreme Rookies (190-207). One EC or ER subset card was included per hobby or retail pack (1:2 Canadian packs), making them somewhat more difficult to obtain than regular singles. Of note is the Stadium Club logo on the card fronts, which features the brand name translated into the primary language of the player featured. Rookie Cards in this set include Daniel Alfredsson.

COMPLETE SET (225)	25.00	50.00
1 Alexander Mogilny	.05	.15
2 Ray Bourque	.20	.50
3 Garry Galley	.02	.10
4 Glen Wesley	.02	.10
5 Dave Andreychuk	.05	.15
6 Daren Puppa	.05	.15
7 Shayne Corson	.02	.10
8 Kelly Hrudey	.05	.15
9 Russ Courtnall	.02	.10
10 Chris Chelios	.07	.20
11 Ulf Samuelsson	.02	.10
12 Mike Vernon	.05	.15
13 Al MacInnis	.05	.15
14 Joel Otto	.02	.10
15 Patrick Roy	.60	1.50
16 Steve Thomas	.05	.15
17 Pat Verbeek	.02	.10
18 Joe Nieuwendyk	.05	.15
19 Todd Krygier	.02	.10
20 Steve Yzerman	.60	1.50
21 Bill Ranford UER misnumbered #2	.05	.15
22 Ron Francis	.05	.15
23 Sylvain Cote	.02	.10
24 Grant Fuhr	.07	.20
25 Brendan Shanahan	.07	.20
26 John MacLean	.05	.15
27 Darren Turcotte	.02	.10
28 Bernie Nicholls	.02	.10
29 Sean Burke	.05	.15
30 Brian Leetch	.05	.15
31 Dave Gagner	.02	.10
32 Rick Tocchet	.05	.15
33 Ron Hextall	.05	.15
34 Paul Coffey	.07	.20
35 John Vanbiesbrouck	.05	.15
36 Rod Brind'Amour	.05	.15
37 Brian Savage	.02	.10
38 Nelson Emerson	.02	.10
39 Brian Bradley	.02	.10
40 Adam Oates	.05	.15
41 Kirk McLean	.05	.15
42 Kevin Hatcher	.02	.10
43 Mike Keane	.02	.10
44 Don Beaupre	.05	.15
45 Scott Stevens	.05	.15
46 Dale Hawerchuk	.07	.20
47 Scott Young	.02	.10
48 Mark Recchi	.05	.15
49 Mike Richter	.07	.20
50 Kevin Stevens	.02	.10
51 Mike Ridley	.02	.10
52 Joe Murphy	.02	.10
53 Stephane Fiset	.05	.15
54 Donald Audette	.02	.10
55 Ed Belfour	.07	.20
56 Rob Blake	.05	.15
57 Adam Graves	.02	.10
58 Arturs Irbe	.05	.15
59 Mathieu Schneider	.02	.10
60 Dominik Hasek	.25	.60
61 Andrew Cassels	.02	.10
62 Johan Garpenlov	.02	.10
63 Kyle McLaren RC	.02	.10
64 Petr Nedved	.05	.15
65 Owen Nolan	.05	.15
66 Keith Primeau	.02	.10
67 Mark Tinordi	.02	.10
68 Dimitri Khristich	.02	.10
69 Chris Pronger	.07	.20
70 Jaromir Jagr	.20	.50
71 Mike Ricci	.05	.15
72 Trevor Kidd	.05	.15
73 Stu Barnes	.02	.10
74 Doug Weight	.05	.15
75 Mats Sundin	.07	.20
76 Scott Niedermayer	.02	.10
77 John LeClair	.07	.20
78 Derian Hatcher	.02	.10
79 Brad May	.02	.10
80 Felix Potvin	.07	.20
81 Derek King	.02	.10
82 Guy Hebert	.05	.15
83 Shawn McEachern	.02	.10
84 Slava Kozlov	.05	.15
85 Martin Brodeur	.30	.75
86 Ray Whitney	.05	.15
87 Martin Straka	.02	.10
88 Keith Jones	.05	.15
89 Roman Hamrlik	.05	.15
90 Keith Tkachuk	.07	.20
91 Jim Dowd	.02	.10
92 Sergei Zubov	.02	.10
93 Bryan McCabe	.02	.10
94 Rob Niedermayer	.05	.15
95 Alexei Zhamnov	.05	.15
96 Zarley Zalapski	.02	.10
97 Alexandre Daigle	.02	.10
98 Jocelyn Thibault	.07	.20
99 Zigmund Palffy	.05	.15
100 Luc Robitaille	.05	.15
101 Radek Bonk	.02	.10
102 Todd Marchant	.02	.10
103 Todd Harvey	.05	.15
104 Blaine Lacher	.05	.15
105 Peter Forsberg	.30	.75
106 Jeff Friesen	.02	.10
107 Kenny Jonsson	.02	.10
108 Brett Lindros	.02	.10
109 David Oliver	.02	.10
110 Mikael Renberg	.05	.15
111 Alexander Selivanov	.02	.10
112 Stanislav Neckar	.02	.10
113 Oleg Tverdovsky	.02	.10
114 Shean Donovan	.02	.10
115 Jim Carey	.05	.15
116 Tony Granato	.02	.10
117 Tony Amonte	.05	.15
118 Tomas Sandstrom	.02	.10
119 Rick Tabaracci	.05	.15
120 Ray Ferraro	.02	.10
121 Brian Noonan	.02	.10
122 Miroslav Satan RC	.60	1.50
123 Sergio Momesso	.02	.10
124 Gary Suter	.02	.10
125 Eric Desjardins	.05	.15
126 Steve Duchesne	.02	.10
127 Zdeno Ciger	.02	.10
128 Cliff Ronning	.02	.10
129 Nicklas Lidstrom	.07	.20
130 Bill Guerin	.05	.15
131 Igor Korolev	.02	.10
132 Roman Oksiuta	.02	.10
133 Jesse Belanger	.02	.10
134 Chris Gratton	.02	.10
135 Chris Osgood	.05	.15
136 Pat Peake	.02	.10
137 Viktor Kozlov	.05	.15
138 Aaron Gavey	.02	.10
139 Zdenek Nedved	.02	.10
140 Rhett Warrener	.02	.10
141 Marko Kiprusoff	.02	.10
142 Dan Quinn	.02	.10
143 Alexei Zhitnik	.02	.10
144 Larry Murphy	.05	.15
145 Phil Housley	.05	.15
146 Don Sweeney	.02	.10
147 Jason Dawe	.02	.10
148 Marcus Ragnarsson RC	.05	.15
149 Andrei Nikolishin	.02	.10
150 Dino Ciccarelli	.05	.15
151 Jari Kurri	.07	.20
152 Bob Probert	.05	.15
153 Randy McKay	.02	.10
154 Michael Nylander	.02	.10
155 Wendel Clark	.05	.15
156 Antti Tormanen RC	.02	.10
157 Nikolai Khabibulin	.05	.15
158 Tom Barrasso	.05	.15
159 Vincent Damphousse	.02	.10
160 Trevor Linden	.05	.15
161 Valeri Kamensky	.05	.15
162 Mike Gartner	.05	.15
163 Cam Neely EC SP	.20	.50
164 Pat LaFontaine EC SP	.20	.50
165 Theo Fleury EC SP	.20	.50
166 Jeremy Roenick EC SP	.30	.75
167 Joe Sakic EC SP	1.00	2.50
168 Mike Modano EC SP	.60	1.50
169 Sergei Fedorov EC SP	.60	1.50
170 Scott Mellanby EC SP	.20	.50
171 Jason Arnott EC SP	.25	.60
172 Geoff Sanderson EC SP	.20	.50
173 Wayne Gretzky EC SP	4.00	8.00
174 Paul Kariya EC SP	1.25	3.00
175 Pierre Turgeon EC SP	.20	.50
176 Stephane Richer EC SP	.20	.50
177 Kirk Muller EC SP	.20	.50
178 Mark Messier EC SP	.20	.50
179 Craig Janney EC SP	.20	.50
180 Mario Lemieux EC SP	3.00	6.00
181 Eric Lindros EC SP	.20	.50
182 Alexei Yashin EC SP	.20	.50
183 Brett Hull EC SP	.50	1.25
184 Doug Gilmour EC SP	.30	.75
185 Petr Klima EC SP	.20	.50
186 Pavel Bure EC SP	.20	.50
187 Joe Juneau EC SP	.20	.50
188 Teemu Selanne EC SP	.20	.50
189 Claude Lemieux EC SP	.20	.50
190 Vitali Yachmenev ER SP	.20	.50
191 Jason Bonsignore ER SP	.20	.50
192 Jeff O'Neill ER SP	.20	.50
193 Brendan Witt ER SP	.20	.50
194 Brian Holzinger RC RC ER SP	.20	.50
195 Eric Daze ER SP	.20	.50
196 Ed Jovanovski ER SP	.20	.50
197 Deron Quint ER SP	.20	.50
198 Marty Murray ER SP	.20	.50
199 Jere Lehtinen ER SP	.20	.50
200 Radek Dvorak RC ER	.30	.75
201 Aki-Petteri Berg RC ER	.20	.50
202 Chad Kilger RC ER	.20	.50
203 Saku Koivu ER SP	.30	.75
204 Todd Bertuzzi RC ER	1.50	4.00
205 Niklas Sundstrom ER SP	.20	.50
206 Daniel Alfredsson RC ER	1.25	3.00
207 Shane Doan RC ER	1.25	3.00
208 Richard Park	.02	.10
209 Peter Bondra	.05	.15
210 Bryan Smolinski	.02	.10
211 Tommy Salo	.05	.15
212 Patrick Poulin	.02	.10
213 Mathieu Dandenault RC	.02	.10
214 Steve Rucchin	.05	.15
215 Ray Sheppard	.02	.10
216 Robert Svehla RC	.02	.10
217 Olaf Kolzig	.05	.15
218 Alexei Kovalev	.02	.10
219 Ian Moran	.02	.10
220 Valeri Bure	.02	.10
221 Dean Malkoc	.02	.10
222 Jason Doig	.02	.10
223 David Nemirovsky RC	.02	.10
224 Jamie Pushor	.02	.10
225 Ricard Persson	.02	.10

1995-96 Stadium Club Members Only Master Set

Parallel to base set that was only available to members of Topps Stadium Club. Cards are distinguishable by an embossed Members only logo.

*STARS: 10X TO 20X BASIC CARDS
*RC's:2X TO 5X BASIC CARDS

1995-96 Stadium Club Extreme North

Randomly inserted in packs at a rate of 1:48, this 9-card set focuses on some of the best players on Canadian teams. The cards are printed on diffraction foil.

COMPLETE SET (9)	20.00	40.00
EN1 Pavel Bure	2.00	5.00
EN2 Teemu Selanne	2.00	5.00
EN3 Felix Potvin	2.00	5.00
EN4 Patrick Roy	8.00	20.00
EN5 Theo Fleury	1.25	3.00
EN6 Bill Ranford	1.25	3.00
EN7 Pierre Turgeon	1.25	3.00
EN8 Doug Gilmour	1.25	3.00
EN9 Alexander Mogilny	1.25	3.00

1995-96 Stadium Club Extreme North Members Only Master Set

Issued to Stadium Club members only, this set parallels the basic cards with the exception of the words "Topp's Stadium Club Members Only" printed on the card front.

*STARS: .75X TO 2X BASIC INSERTS

1995-96 Stadium Club Fearless

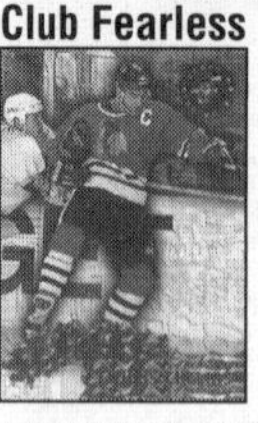

Randomly inserted at a rate of 1:24 retail, and 1:48 hobby and Canadian packs, this 9-card set features hockey's toughest players on double diffraction foil-stamped cards.

COMPLETE SET (9)	8.00	15.00
F1 Brendan Shanahan	1.50	4.00
F2 Chris Chelios	1.50	4.00
F3 Keith Primeau	.75	2.00
F4 Scott Stevens	1.25	3.00
F5 Rick Tocchet	1.25	3.00
F6 Kevin Stevens	.75	2.00
F7 Ulf Samuelsson	.75	2.00
F8 Wendel Clark	1.25	3.00
F9 Keith Tkachuk	1.50	4.00

1995-96 Stadium Club Fearless Members Only Master Set

Issued to Stadium Club members only, this set parallels the basic cards with the exception of the words "Topp's Stadium Club Members Only" printed on the card front.

*STARS: .75X TO 2X BASIC INSERTS

1995-96 Stadium Club Generation TSC

COMPLETE SET (9)	15.00	30.00
GT1 Paul Kariya	1.50	4.00
GT2 Teemu Selanne	1.50	4.00
GT3 Jaromir Jagr	2.00	5.00
GT4 Peter Forsberg	3.00	8.00
GT5 Martin Brodeur	4.00	10.00
GT6 Jim Carey	.75	2.00
GT7 Mikael Renberg	.75	2.00
GT8 Scott Niedermayer	.75	2.00
GT9 Ed Jovanovski	.75	2.00

1995-96 Stadium Club Generation TSC Members Only Master Set

Issued to Stadium Club members only, this set parallels the basic cards with the exception of the words "Topp's Stadium Club Members Only" printed on the card front.

*STARS: 2.5X TO 5X BASIC INSERTS

1995-96 Stadium Club Metalists

Randomly inserted at a rate of 1:48 hobby, 1:96 retail, and 1:192 Canadian packs, this 12-card set showcases players who have won two or more major awards during their career on the first ever laser-cut foil hockey cards.

COMPLETE SET (12)	40.00	80.00
M1 Wayne Gretzky	10.00	25.00
M2 Mario Lemieux	8.00	20.00
M3 Patrick Roy	8.00	20.00
M4 Ray Bourque	1.50	4.00
M5 Ed Belfour	1.50	4.00
M6 Tom Barrasso	1.00	2.50
M7 Joe Mullen	1.00	2.50
M8 Brian Leetch	1.00	2.50
M9 Mark Messier	1.50	4.00
M10 Dominik Hasek	3.00	8.00
M11 Paul Coffey	1.00	2.50
M12 Guy Carbonneau	1.00	2.50

1995-96 Stadium Club Metalists Members Only Master Set

Issued to Stadium Club members only, this set parallels the basic cards with the exception of the words "Topp's Stadium Club Members Only" printed on the card front.

*STARS: .75X TO 2X BASIC INSERTS

1995-96 Stadium Club Nemeses

Randomly inserted at a rate of 1:24 hobby, 1:48 retail, and 1:96 Canadian packs, this 9-card set highlights two rival players together on one card. The cards use etched foil on each side.

COMPLETE SET (9)	25.00	60.00
N1 Eric Lindros Scott Stevens	1.50	4.00
N2 W.Gretzky/M.Lemieux	10.00	25.00
N3 Claude Lemieux Cam Neely	1.50	4.00
N4 Pavel Bure Mike Richter	1.50	4.00
N5 Brian Leetch Ray Bourque	2.50	6.00
N6 Martin Brodeur Dominik Hasek	4.00	10.00
N7 Doug Gilmour Sergei Fedorov	2.50	6.00
N8 Mark Messier Joel Otto	1.50	4.00
N9 Paul Kariya Peter Forsberg	6.00	15.00

1995-96 Stadium Club Nemeses Members Only Master Set

Issued to Stadium Club members only, this set parallels the basic cards with the exception of the words "Topp's Stadium Club Members Only" printed on the card front.

*STARS: .75X TO 2X BASIC INSERTS

1995-96 Stadium Club Power Streak

Randomly inserted at a rate of 1:12 retail, and 1:24 hobby and Canadian packs, this set features 10 players who have sustained prolonged goal scoring streaks. The cards are printed using Power Matrix technology.

COMPLETE SET (10)	12.50	25.00
PS1 Pierre Turgeon	.75	2.00
PS2 Eric Lindros	2.00	5.00
PS3 Ron Francis	1.25	3.00
PS4 Paul Coffey	2.00	5.00
PS5 Mikael Renberg	1.25	3.00
PS6 John LeClair	2.00	5.00
PS7 Dino Ciccarelli	1.25	3.00
PS8 Wendel Clark	1.25	3.00
PS9 Brett Hull	2.00	5.00
PS10 Stephane Richer	.75	2.00

1995-96 Stadium Club Power Streak Members Only Master Set

Issued to Stadium Club members only, this set parallels the basic cards with the exception of the words "Topp's Stadium Club Members Only" printed on the card front.

*STARS: 2.5X TO 5X BASIC INSERTS

1995-96 Stadium Club Master Photo Test

This nine-card set measures approximately 3" by 5" and features color action player photos from the 1995-96 Stadium Club set inside a black border bearing the words Master Photo. The backs carry the TSC, NHL, and NHLPA logos. No further information on origin or distribution is available. The cards are unnumbered and checklisted below in alphabetical order. This may be an incomplete checklist; additional information would be appreciated.

COMPLETE SET (9)	25.00	60.00
1 Jason Arnott	2.00	5.00
2 Theo Fleury	4.00	10.00
3 Doug Gilmour	4.00	10.00
4 Trevor Linden	4.00	10.00
5 Kirk McLean	2.00	5.00
6 Alexander Mogilny	2.00	5.00
7 Felix Potvin	4.00	10.00
8 Mats Sundin	6.00	15.00
9 Alexei Yashin	2.00	5.00

1996 Stadium Club Members Only

This 50-card set was available through the direct marketing arm of the Topps Stadium Club. The first 45 cards feature the competitors in the 1996 NHL All-Star Game. The players are pictured in their AS sweaters over a stylized background. the back includes a portrait and player profile. The final five cards in the set picture some of the year's top rookies on Finest-style technology.

COMPLETE SET (50)	8.00	20.00
1 Wayne Gretzky	1.60	4.00
2 Paul Kariya	1.00	2.50
3 Brett Hull	.30	.75
4 Chris Chelios	.24	.60
5 Paul Coffey	.24	.60
6 Ed Belfour	.24	.60
7 Theo Fleury	.24	.60
8 Owen Nolan	.10	.25
9 Al MacInnis	.10	.25
10 Alexander Mogilny	.20	.50
11 Kevin Hatcher	.04	.10
12 Doug Weight	.16	.40
13 Felix Potvin	.20	.50
14 Teemu Selanne	.50	1.25
15 Sergei Fedorov	.50	1.25
16 Larry Murphy	.04	.10
17 Joe Sakic	.50	1.25
18 Mats Sundin	.24	.60
19 Nicklas Lidstrom	.10	.25
20 Peter Forsberg	.60	1.50
21 Chris Osgood	.24	.60
22 Mike Gartner	.06	.15
23 Denis Savard Craig MacTavish	.06	.15
24 Mario Lemieux	1.20	3.00
25 Jaromir Jagr	.80	2.00
26 Brendan Shanahan	.50	1.25
27 Scott Stevens	.06	.15
28 Ray Bourque	.30	.75
29 Martin Brodeur	.60	1.50
30 Eric Lindros	.80	2.00
31 Peter Bondra	.24	.60
32 Scott Mellanby	.04	.10
33 Brian Leetch	.24	.60
34 John Vanbiesbrouck	.24	.60
35 Pat Verbeek	.08	.20
36 Cam Neely	.20	.50
37 Roman Hamrlik	.16	.40
38 Daniel Alfredsson	.20	.50
39 Pierre Turgeon	.20	.50
40 Mark Messier	.30	.75
41 Eric Desjardins	.04	.10
42 Dominik Hasek	.50	1.25
43 John LeClair	.40	1.00
44 Mathieu Schneider	.04	.10
45 Ron Francis	.20	.50
46 Saku Koivu	1.20	3.00
47 Ed Jovanovski	.80	2.00
48 Vitali Yachmenev	.40	1.00
49 Petr Sykora	.80	2.00
50 Eric Daze	.80	2.00

1999-00 Stadium Club Promos

Sent out to dealers with the press release for Stadium Club, this 6-card set debuts the new card design for the 1999-2000 brand.

COMPLETE SET (6)	1.20	2.00
PP1 Chris Osgood	.40	.50
PP2 Steve Konowalchuk	.10	.25
PP3 Jeremy Roenick	.40	1.00
PP4 Rod Brind'Amour	.20	.50
PP5 Mattias Norstrom	.10	.25
PP6 Clarke Wilm	.10	.25

1999-00 Stadium Club

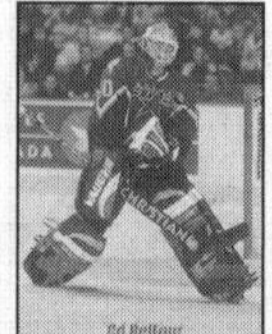

Released as a 200-card set, Stadium Club featured flawless player action shots and blue foil highlights on every base card. Stadium Club was packaged in 24-pack boxes with packs containing six cards and one checklist. Packs carried a suggested retail price of $2.00.

COMPLETE SET (200)	30.00	60.00
1 Jaromir Jagr	.30	.75
2 Mats Sundin	.20	.50
3 Mark Messier	.20	.50
4 Paul Kariya	.20	.50
5 Ray Bourque	.30	.75
6 Tony Amonte	.15	.40
7 Dominik Hasek	.40	1.00
8 Peter Forsberg	.50	1.25
9 Pavel Bure	.20	.50
10 Nicklas Lidstrom	.20	.50
11 Kenny Jonsson	.05	.15
12 Brian Leetch	.20	.50
13 Eric Lindros	.20	.50
14 Al MacInnis	.15	.40
15 Keith Tkachuk	.20	.50
16 Martin Brodeur	.50	1.25
17 Saku Koivu	.20	.50
18 Jeff Friesen	.05	.15
19 Olaf Kolzig	.15	.40
20 Mike Modano	.30	.75
21 Jarome Iginla	.25	.60
22 Alexei Kovalev	.05	.15
23 Vincent Lecavalier	.20	.50
24 Greg Johnson	.05	.15
25 Ron Francis	.15	.40
26 Steve Konowalchuk	.05	.15
27 Luc Robitaille	.15	.40
28 Alexei Yashin	.05	.15
29 Mark Parrish	.05	.15
30 Todd Warriner	.05	.15
31 Brett Hull	.25	.60
32 Steve Dubinsky	.05	.15
33 Rod Brind'Amour	.15	.40
34 Bill Muckalt	.05	.15
35 Bryan Berard	.05	.15
36 Manny Malhotra	.15	.40
37 Jozef Stumpel	.15	.40
38 Sergei Fedorov	.30	.75
39 Roman Vopat	.15	.40
40 Teemu Selanne	.20	.50
41 Teppo Numminen	.05	.15
42 Mats Lindgren	.05	.15
43 Chris Gratton	.05	.15
44 Owen Nolan	.15	.40
45 Scott Niedermayer	.05	.15
46 Sergei Krivokrasov	.05	.15
47 Joe Sakic	.40	1.00
48 Bill Guerin	.05	.15
49 Shayne Corson	.05	.15
50 Eric Daze	.15	.40
51 Clarke Wilm	.05	.15
52 Magnus Arvedson	.05	.15
53 Sergei Berezin	.05	.15
54 Derian Hatcher	.05	.15
55 Jeremy Roenick	.25	.60
56 Adam Oates	.15	.40
57 Dixon Ward	.05	.15
58 Petr Nedved	.15	.40
59 Joe Reekie	.05	.15
60 Milan Hejduk	.20	.50
61 Mike Grier	.05	.15
62 Martin Straka	.05	.15
63 Petr Sykora	.05	.15
64 Harry York	.05	.15
65 John LeClair	.20	.50
66 Patrick Roy	1.00	2.50
67 Arturs Irbe	.15	.40
68 Murray Baron	.05	.15
69 Felix Potvin	.20	.50
70 Pavol Demitra	.15	.40
71 Ray Whitney	.15	.40
72 Patrick Marleau	.20	.50
73 Tom Fitzgerald	.05	.15
74 Jamal Mayers	.05	.15
75 Joe Thornton	.30	.75
76 Craig Rivet	.05	.15
77 Ed Belfour	.20	.50
78 Stephane Fiset	.15	.40
79 Alexander Karpovtsev	.05	.15
80 Miroslav Satan	.05	.15
81 Doug Weight	.15	.40
82 Marian Hossa	.20	.50
83 Markus Naslund	.20	.50
84 Derek Morris	.05	.15
85 Mike Richter	.20	.50
86 Scott Young	.05	.15
87 Darcy Tucker	.05	.15
88 Jason Allison	.05	.15
89 Chris Osgood	.15	.40
90 Doug Gilmour	.15	.40
91 Ron Tugnutt	.15	.40
92 Adam Deadmarsh	.05	.15
93 Byron Dafoe	.15	.40
94 Rick Tocchet	.15	.40
95 Mike Johnson	.05	.15
96 Guy Hebert	.15	.40
97 Cory Stillman	.15	.40
98 Daniel Alfredsson	.15	.40
99 Tom Barrasso	.15	.40
100 Peter Bondra	.15	.40
101 Rob Blake	.15	.40
102 Gary Roberts	.05	.15
103 Cliff Ronning	.15	.40
104 Jason Woolley	.05	.15
105 Keith Primeau	.05	.15
106 Brendan Shanahan	.20	.50
107 Alexei Zhamnov	.15	.40
108 Bobby Holik	.05	.15
109 Mark Recchi	.15	.40
110 Eric Brewer	.05	.15
111 Mike Ricci	.15	.40
112 Pierre Turgeon	.15	.40
113 Martin Rucinsky	.05	.15
114 Chris McAllister RC	.05	.15
115 Patrik Elias	.15	.40
116 Alexander Selivanov	.05	.15
117 Fredrik Olausson	.05	.15
118 Curtis Joseph	.20	.50
119 Wade Redden	.05	.15
120 Nikolai Khabibulin	.15	.40
121 Chris Drury	.15	.40
122 Chris Chelios	.20	.50
123 Vincent Damphousse	.05	.15

124 Mattias Ohlund .15 .40
125 Mike Dunham .15 .40
126 John Vanbiesbrouck .15 .40
127 John MacLean .15 .40
128 Jocelyn Thibault .15 .40
129 Jan Hrdina .05 .15
130 Mariusz Czerkawski .05 .15
131 Pavel Kubina .05 .15
132 Scott Stevens .15 .40
133 Mattias Norstrom .05 .15
134 Sami Kapanen .05 .15
135 Sergei Samsonov .15 .40
136 Tom Poti .05 .15
137 Steve Shields .15 .40
138 Anson Carter .15 .40
139 Chris McAlpine .05 .15
140 Rob Niedermayer .05 .15
141 Michael Peca .05 .15
142 Valeri Bure .05 .15
143 Joe Nieuwendyk .15 .40
144 Jose Theodore .25 .60
145 Steve Yzerman 1.00 2.50
146 Chris Pronger .15 .40
147 Marty McInnis .05 .15
148 Jere Lehtinen .15 .40
149 Adam Graves .05 .15
150 Deron Quint .05 .15
151 Ray Ferraro .05 .15
152 Niklas Sundstrom .05 .15
153 Damian Rhodes .15 .40
154 Zigmund Palffy .15 .40
155 Valeri Kamensky .15 .40
156 Oleg Tverdovsky .15 .40
157 Bill Ranford .15 .40
158 Kelly Buchberger .05 .15
159 Trevor Linden .05 .15
160 Bryan McCabe .05 .15
161 Dan Cloutier .05 .15
162 Olli Jokinen .15 .40
163 Theo Fleury .05 .15
164 Dave Andreychuk .15 .40
165 Gord Murphy .05 .15
166 Steve Duchesne .15 .40
167 Marc Savard .05 .15
168 Maxim Afinogenov .05 .15
169 Mark Eaton RC .25 .60
170 Pavel Patera RC .05 .15
171 Nikolai Antropov RC .75 2.00
172 Ivan Novoseltsev RC .50 1.25
173 Jochen Hecht RC 1.00 2.50
174 Mike Ribeiro .05 .15
175 Yuri Butsayev RC .05 .15
176 Jorgen Jonsson RC .05 .15
177 Dan Hinote RC .05 .15
178 Dave Tanabe .05 .15
179 John Grahame RC .50 1.25
180 Mika Alatalo RC .15 .40
181 Patrik Stefan RC .50 1.25
182 Mike Fisher RC .40 1.00
183 Niclas Havelid RC .20 .50
184 Paul Comrie RC .05 .15
185 Michal Rozsival RC .05 .15
186 Oleg Saprykin RC .50 1.25
187 Martin Skoula RC .25 .60
188 Simon Gagne .20 .50
189 Brian Rafalski RC .50 1.25
190 J-P Dumont .15 .40
191 Martin Biron .15 .40
192 Rico Fata .05 .15
193 Jan Hlavac .05 .15
194 Alex Tanguay .15 .40
195 Brad Stuart .15 .40
196 Brian Boucher .20 .50
197 Steve Kariya RC .40 1.00
198 Scott Gomez .05 .15
199 Tim Connolly .25 .60
200 David Legwand .15 .40

1999-00 Stadium Club First Day Issue

Randomly inserted in Retail packs at the rate of one in 12, this 200-card set parallels the base Stadium Club set. Each card is enhanced with a foil "First Day Issue" stamp and is sequentially numbered to 150.
*STARS: 12.5X TO 30X BASIC CARDS
*ROOKIES: 3X TO 8X BASIC CARDS

1999-00 Stadium Club One of a Kind

Randomly inserted in Hobby packs, this 200-card set parallels the base Stadium Club set. Each card is sequentially numbered to 150.
*STARS: 12.5X TO 30X BASIC CARDS
*ROOKIES: 3X TO 8X BASIC CARDS

1999-00 Stadium Club Printing Plates Black

Randomly inserted in Hobby packs, one version of each color proof exists for the 200 different cards in the set. These are the proofs that were used in the printing process of Stadium Club.
NOT PRICED DUE TO SCARCITY

1999-00 Stadium Club Printing Plates Cyan

Randomly inserted in Hobby packs, one version of each color proof exists for the 200 different cards in the set. These are the proofs that were used in the printing process of Stadium Club.
NOT PRICED DUE TO SCARCITY

1999-00 Stadium Club Printing Plates Magenta

Randomly inserted in Hobby packs, one version of each color proof exists for the 200 different cards in the set. These are the proofs that were used in the printing process of Stadium Club.
NOT PRICED DUE TO SCARCITY

1999-00 Stadium Club Printing Plates Yellow

Randomly inserted in Hobby packs, one version of each color proof exists for the 200 different cards in the set. These are the proofs that were used in the printing process of Stadium Club.
NOT PRICED DUE TO SCARCITY

1999-00 Stadium Club Capture the Action

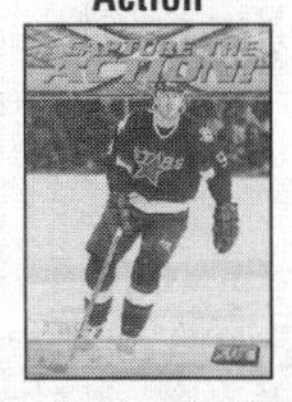

Randomly inserted in packs at the rate of 1:12, this 30-card set features blue borders on the top and bottom framing full color close up "in the game" action photographs. Game view parallels were also created and inserted at 1:118. The parallels were serial numbered to just 100.
COMPLETE SET (30) 40.00 80.00
*GAME VIEW: 6X TO 15X BASIC CARDS
CA1 Bill Muckalt .60 1.50
CA2 Chris Drury .75 2.00
CA3 Milan Hejduk 1.25 3.00
CA4 Mark Parrish .60 1.50
CA5 Marian Hossa 1.00 2.50
CA6 Manny Malhotra .75 2.00
CA7 J-P Dumont .75 2.00
CA8 Eric Brewer .60 1.50
CA9 Vincent Lecavalier 1.00 2.50
CA10 Jan Hrdina .60 1.50
CA11 Paul Kariya 1.00 2.50
CA12 Peter Forsberg 2.50 6.00
CA13 Eric Lindros 1.00 2.50
CA14 Martin Brodeur 2.50 6.00
CA15 Teemu Selanne 1.00 2.50
CA16 Keith Tkachuk 1.00 2.50
CA17 Mats Sundin 1.00 2.50
CA18 Pavel Bure 1.00 2.50
CA19 Mike Modano 1.50 4.00
CA20 Nicklas Lidstrom 1.00 2.50
CA21 Ray Bourque 1.50 4.00
CA22 Dominik Hasek 2.00 5.00
CA23 Patrick Roy 5.00 12.00
CA24 Mark Messier 1.00 2.50
CA25 Steve Yzerman 5.00 12.00
CA26 Jaromir Jagr 1.50 4.00
CA27 Paul Coffey 1.00 2.50
CA28 Brett Hull 1.25 3.00
CA29 Al MacInnis .75 2.00
CA30 Larry Murphy .75 2.00

1999-00 Stadium Club Chrome

Randomly inserted in packs at the rate of 1:4, this 50-card set utilizes the base card style, but issues this set on an all foil card stock. Chrome refractor parallels were also created and inserted at a rate of 1:8.
COMPLETE SET (50) 30.00 60.00
*REFRACTORS: .75X TO 2X BASIC CARDS
1 Jaromir Jagr 1.00 2.50
2 Mats Sundin .60 1.50
3 Mark Messier .60 1.50
4 Paul Kariya .60 1.50
5 Ray Bourque 1.00 2.50
6 Tony Amonte .50 1.25
7 Dominik Hasek 1.25 3.00
8 Peter Forsberg 1.50 4.00
9 Pavel Bure .60 1.50
10 Nicklas Lidstrom .60 1.50
11 Brian Leetch .50 1.25
12 Eric Lindros .60 1.50
13 Al MacInnis .50 1.25
14 Keith Tkachuk .60 1.50
15 Martin Brodeur 1.50 4.00
16 Saku Koivu .60 1.50
17 Jeff Friesen .50 1.25
18 Mike Modano 1.00 2.50
19 Vincent Lecavalier .60 1.50
20 Luc Robitaille .50 1.25
21 Brett Hull .75 2.00
22 Teemu Selanne .60 1.50
23 Joe Sakic 1.25 3.00
24 Jeremy Roenick .75 2.00
25 John LeClair .60 1.50
26 Patrick Roy 3.00 8.00
27 Joe Thornton 1.00 2.50
28 Ed Belfour .60 1.50
29 Doug Weight .50 1.25
30 Marian Hossa .60 1.50
31 Chris Osgood .50 1.25
32 Daniel Alfredsson .50 1.25
33 Peter Bondra .50 1.25
34 Brendan Shanahan .60 1.50
35 Curtis Joseph .60 1.50
36 Chris Drury .50 1.25
37 Sergei Samsonov .50 1.25
38 Anson Carter .50 1.25
39 Joe Nieuwendyk .50 1.25
40 Steve Yzerman 3.00 8.00
41 Zigmund Palffy .50 1.25
42 Theo Fleury .50 1.25
43 Patrik Stefan 1.00 2.50
44 Simon Gagne .60 1.50
45 J-P Dumont .50 1.25
46 Alex Tanguay .50 1.25
47 Steve Kariya .50 1.25
48 Scott Gomez .50 1.25
49 Tim Connolly .75 2.00
50 David Legwand .50 1.25

1999-00 Stadium Club Chrome Oversized

Inserted one per hobby box, this 20-card set utilizes the same design as the base set on oversized cards. Refractor parallels were also created and inserted randomly.
COMPLETE SET (20) 50.00 100.00
*REFRACTORS: .75X TO 2X BASIC CARDS
1 Jaromir Jagr 1.50 4.00
2 Mats Sundin 1.00 2.50
3 Paul Kariya 1.00 2.50
4 Ray Bourque 1.50 4.00
5 Dominik Hasek 2.00 5.00
6 Peter Forsberg 2.50 6.00
7 Pavel Bure 1.00 2.50
8 Eric Lindros 1.00 2.50
9 Martin Brodeur 2.50 6.00
10 Mike Modano 1.50 4.00
11 Teemu Selanne 1.00 2.50
12 Joe Sakic 2.00 5.00
13 Patrick Roy 5.00 12.00
14 Marian Hossa 1.00 2.50
15 Curtis Joseph 1.00 2.50
16 Steve Yzerman 5.00 12.00
17 Theo Fleury .75 2.00
18 Patrik Stefan 1.50 4.00
19 Steve Kariya .75 2.00
20 David Legwand .75 2.00

1999-00 Stadium Club Co-Signers

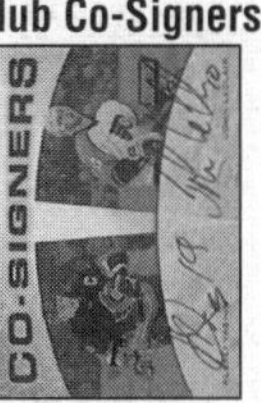

Randomly inserted in Hobby packs at the rate of 1:237, this 15-card set features two autographs on each card. Some cards were issued in exchange form.
CS1 Chris Drury / Brendan Morrison 10.00 25.00
CS2 Brendan Morrison / Marian Hossa 10.00 25.00
CS3 Marian Hossa / Chris Drury 10.00 25.00
CS4 Jaromir Jagr / Mats Sundin 30.00 80.00
CS5 Jaromir Jagr / Alexei Yashin 25.00 60.00
CS6 John LeClair / Jaromir Jagr 40.00 100.00
CS7 Alexei Yashin / Mats Sundin 10.00 25.00
CS8 Mats Sundin / John LeClair 10.00 25.00
CS9 Alexei Yashin / John LeClair 10.00 25.00
CS10 Chris Osgood / Ed Belfour 30.00 80.00
CS11 Chris Osgood / Curtis Joseph 30.00 80.00
CS12 Ed Belfour / Curtis Joseph 30.00 80.00
CS13 Ray Bourque / Al MacInnis 50.00 100.00
CS14 Al MacInnis / Wade Redden 10.00 25.00
CS15 Wade Redden / Ray Bourque 25.00 60.00

1999-00 Stadium Club Eyes of the Game

Randomly seeded in packs at the rate of 1:15, this 10-card set features colored borders on the top and bottom and close up portrait photography of each respective player. Refractor parallels were also created and inserted at a rate of 1:75.
COMPLETE SET (10) 8.00 15.00
*REFRACTORS: 1.5X TO 4X BASIC CARDS
EG1 Jaromir Jagr 1.00 2.50
EG2 Peter Forsberg 1.50 4.00
EG3 Paul Kariya .60 1.50
EG4 Teemu Selanne .60 1.50
EG5 Joe Sakic 1.25 3.00
EG6 Eric Lindros .60 1.50
EG7 Jason Allison .50 1.25
EG8 Mats Sundin .60 1.50
EG9 Pavol Demitra .50 1.25
EG10 Rod Brind'Amour .50 1.25

1999-00 Stadium Club Goalie Cam

Randomly seeded in packs at the rate of 1:24, this 7-card set puts collectors on the ice with photography taken from goalie cams.
COMPLETE SET (7) 8.00 15.00
GC1 Dominik Hasek 2.00 5.00
GC2 Martin Brodeur 2.50 6.00
GC3 Byron Dafoe .75 2.00
GC4 Olaf Kolzig .75 2.00
GC5 Mike Richter 1.00 2.50
GC6 Ron Tugnutt .75 2.00
GC7 Tom Barrasso .75 2.00

1999-00 Stadium Club Lone Star Signatures

Released as a tier insert program, cards LS1-LS3 are seeded at 1:1675, cards LS4-LS9 are seeded at 1:558, card LS10 is seeded at 1:2233, and cards LS11-13 are seeded at 1:419. Each card features an authentic player autograph. Some players were released in exchange card form.
LS1 Jaromir Jagr 40.00 100.00
LS2 Alexei Yashin 5.00 12.00
LS3 Mats Sundin 20.00 50.00
LS4 Ray Bourque 30.00 80.00
LS5 Al MacInnis 6.00 15.00
LS6 Wade Redden 5.00 12.00
LS7 Chris Osgood 6.00 15.00
LS8 Ed Belfour 8.00 20.00
LS9 Curtis Joseph 20.00 50.00
LS10 John LeClair 8.00 20.00
LS11 Chris Drury 6.00 15.00
LS12 Brendan Morrison 6.00 15.00
LS13 Marian Hossa 8.00 20.00

1999-00 Stadium Club Onyx Extreme

Randomly inserted in packs at the rate of 1:15, this 10-card set features black textured borders around full color action player photos. Each card is enhanced with silver foil highlights. A die-cut parallel was also created and inserted at a rate of 1:75.
COMPLETE SET (10) 8.00 15.00
*DIE-CUTS: 1.5X TO 4X BASIC CARDS
OE1 Jaromir Jagr 1.00 2.50
OE2 Peter Forsberg 1.50 4.00
OE3 Dominik Hasek 1.25 3.00
OE4 Eric Lindros .50 1.25
OE5 Paul Kariya .50 1.25
OE6 Joe Sakic 1.25 3.00
OE7 Nicklas Lidstrom .50 1.25
OE8 Teemu Selanne .50 1.25
OE9 John LeClair .50 1.25
OE10 Pavel Bure .50 1.25

1999-00 Stadium Club Souvenirs

Randomly inserted in Hobby packs at 1:118 for jerseys and 1:197 for stick cards, this 6-card set features swatches of game used memorabilia. Stick cards were issued in redemption form. The MacInnis card appears to be short printed.
SAM Al MacInnis S 5.00 12.00
SCO Chris Osgood J 5.00 12.00
SEB Ed Belfour S 5.00 12.00
SJL John LeClair S 10.00 25.00
SMH Marian Hossa J 5.00 12.00
SMS Mats Sundin J 5.00 12.00

2000-01 Stadium Club

Released in mid December 2000, Stadium Club consists of a 260-card base set divided up into 227 regular player cards and 33 Draft Pick cards. Base set features a full bleed color photo on the top and a name box along the bottom enhanced with silver holofoil and textured like ice. Stadium Club was packaged in 24-pack boxes with packs containing seven cards and carried a suggested retail price of $2.45.
COMPLETE SET (260) 40.00 80.00
1 Pavel Bure .20 .50
2 Brendan Shanahan .20 .50
3 Chris Pronger .15 .40
4 Doug Weight .15 .40
5 Peter Forsberg .50 1.25
6 Jaromir Jagr .30 .75
7 Ed Belfour .20 .50
8 Rod Brind'Amour .15 .40
9 Mike Richter .20 .50
10 Mike Ricci .15 .40
11 Dimitri Yushkevich .05 .15
12 Dominik Hasek .40 1.00
13 Teemu Selanne .20 .50
14 Ed Jovanovski .05 .15
15 Damian Rhodes .15 .40
16 Martin Brodeur .50 1.25
17 Keith Primeau .05 .15
18 Byron Dafoe .15 .40
19 Jeff Hackett .15 .40
20 Brad Isbister .05 .15
21 Jeremy Roenick .25 .60
22 Jocelyn Thibault .15 .40
23 Ray Bourque .40 1.00
24 Steve Yzerman 1.00 2.50
25 Mike Dunham .15 .40
26 Bill Guerin .15 .40
27 Dan Cloutier .15 .40
28 Pavol Demitra .15 .40
29 Richard Smehlik .05 .15
30 Ron Francis .15 .40
31 Zigmund Palffy .15 .40
32 David Legwand .15 .40
33 Scott Stevens .15 .40
34 Daniel Alfredsson .15 .40
35 Michal Rozsival .05 .15
36 John LeClair .20 .50
37 Vincent Lecavalier .20 .50
38 Jason Allison .05 .15
39 Kenny Jonsson .05 .15
40 Patrick Roy 1.00 2.50
41 Derian Hatcher .05 .15
42 Chris Osgood .15 .40
43 Owen Nolan .15 .40
44 Mike York .05 .15
45 Ryan Smyth .15 .40
46 Alexei Kovalev .05 .15
47 Roman Turek .15 .40
48 Mark Recchi .15 .40
49 Ray Ferraro .05 .15
50 Sergei Samsonov .15 .40
51 Paul Kariya .20 .50
52 Jarome Iginla .25 .60
53 Martin Biron .15 .40
54 Tom Poti .05 .15
55 Trevor Linden .05 .15
56 Pierre Turgeon .15 .40
57 Scott Gomez .05 .15
58 Mattias Ohlund .05 .15
59 Tony Amonte .15 .40
60 Yannick Tremblay .05 .15
61 Cliff Ronning .05 .15
62 Marc Savard .05 .15
63 Viktor Kozlov .05 .15
64 Pavel Kubina .05 .15
65 Arturs Irbe .15 .40
66 Stephane Fiset .15 .40
67 John Madden .15 .40
68 Steve Shields .15 .40
69 Theo Fleury .05 .15
70 Chris Simon .05 .15
71 Andy Delmore .05 .15
72 Radek Bonk .05 .15
73 Michal Handzus .05 .15
74 Tommy Salo .15 .40
75 Felix Potvin .20 .50
76 Teppo Numminen .05 .15
77 Bobby Holik .05 .15
78 Phil Housley .15 .40
79 Sergei Gonchar .05 .15
80 Shawn McEachern .05 .15
81 Simon Gagne .20 .50
82 Mike Sillinger .05 .15
83 Tim Connolly .05 .15
84 Eric Daze .15 .40
85 Andrew Brunette .15 .40
86 Mike Modano .30 .75
87 Chris Drury .15 .40
88 Nicklas Lidstrom .20 .50
89 Joe Thornton .30 .75
90 Michael Peca .15 .40
91 Matt Cullen .05 .15
92 Robyn Regehr .05 .15
93 Todd Marchant .05 .15
94 Brett Hull .25 .60
95 Rob Blake .15 .40
96 Sergei Zholtok .05 .15
97 Eric Lindros .20 .50
98 Jean-Sebastien Aubin .15 .40
99 Jason Arnott .05 .15
100 Keith Tkachuk .20 .50
101 Wade Redden .05 .15
102 Sean Burke .15 .40
103 Marian Hossa .20 .50
104 Robert Lang .05 .15
105 Curtis Joseph .20 .50
106 Jeff Friesen .05 .15
107 Dennis Bonvie .05 .15
108 Alexander Korolyuk .05 .15
109 Eric Lacroix .05 .15
110 Todd Bertuzzi .20 .50
111 Bates Battaglia .05 .15
112 Jozef Stumpel .05 .15
113 Alexei Zhamnov .05 .15
114 Milan Hejduk .20 .50
115 Chris Chelios .20 .50
116 Adam Graves .05 .15
117 Patrik Stefan .05 .15
118 Guy Hebert .15 .40
119 Anson Carter .15 .40
120 Fred Brathwaite .15 .40
121 Maxim Afinogenov .05 .15
122 Eric Messier .05 .15
123 Ray Whitney .15 .40
124 Bob Bassen .05 .15
125 Patrick Lalime .15 .40
126 Jonas Hoglund .05 .15
127 Mike Johnson .05 .15
128 Peter Schaefer .05 .15
129 Olaf Kolzig .15 .40
130 Jamie Langenbrunner .05 .15
131 Scott Niedermayer .05 .15
132 Mariusz Czerkawski .05 .15
133 Petr Buzek .05 .15
134 Michal Grosek .05 .15
135 Valeri Bure .05 .15
136 Igor Korolev .05 .15
137 Oleg Tverdovsky .05 .15
138 Fredrik Modin .05 .15
139 Kyle McLaren .05 .15
140 Todd Gill .05 .15
141 Miroslav Satan .15 .40
142 Jeff O'Neill .05 .15
143 Steve Sullivan .05 .15
144 Jon Klemm .05 .15
145 Joe Nieuwendyk .15 .40
146 Luc Robitaille .15 .40
147 Patrice Brisebois .05 .15
148 Travis Green .05 .15
149 Patric Kjellberg .05 .15
150 Mats Sundin .20 .50
151 Brian Rolston .05 .15
152 Patrik Elias .15 .40
153 Markus Naslund .20 .50
154 Trevor Letowski .05 .15
155 Brad Stuart .15 .40
156 Doug Gilmour .15 .40
157 Alexander Mogilny .15 .40
158 Glen Wesley .05 .15
159 Petr Nedved .15 .40
160 Peter Bondra .20 .50
161 Alex Tanguay .15 .40
162 Steve Rucchin .05 .15
163 Nikolai Antropov .05 .15
164 Anders Eriksson .05 .15
165 Martin Rucinsky .05 .15
166 Trevor Kidd .05 .15
167 Zdeno Chara .05 .15
168 Adam Oates .15 .40
169 Eric Desjardins .15 .40
170 Petr Sykora .05 .15
171 Brenden Morrow .15 .40
172 AL MacInnis .15 .40
173 Ethan Moreau .05 .15
174 Chris Tamer .05 .15
175 Jaroslav Spacek .05 .15
176 Paul Mara .05 .15
177 Bryan Smolinski .05 .15
178 Yanic Perreault .05 .15
179 Vaclav Prospal .05 .15
180 Vitali Yachmenev .05 .15
181 Pavel Trnka .05 .15
182 Joe Sakic .40 1.00
183 Vincent Damphousse .05 .15
184 Sergei Fedorov .30 .75
185 Brian Rafalski .15 .40
186 Jochen Hecht .05 .15
187 Shane Doan .15 .40
188 Saku Koivu .20 .50
189 Richard Zednik .05 .15
190 Brian Boucher .20 .50
191 Jeff Halpern .15 .40
192 Matt Cooke .05 .15
193 Darcy Tucker .05 .15
194 Brian Leetch .15 .40
195 Glen Murray .05 .15
196 Robert Svehla .05 .15
197 Kimmo Timonen .05 .15
198 Claude Lapointe .05 .15
199 Brian Savage .05 .15
200 Sami Kapanen .05 .15
201 Scott Pellerin .05 .15
202 Cam Stewart .05 .15
203 Sergei Krivokrasov .05 .15
204 Manny Fernandez .15 .40
205 Darby Hendrickson .05 .15
206 Jamie McLennan .15 .40
207 Kevyn Adams .15 .40
208 Lyle Odelein .05 .15
209 Marc Denis .15 .40
210 Ron Tugnutt .15 .40
211 Tyler Wright .40 1.00
212 Geoff Sanderson .05 .15
213 Mark Messier .20 .50
214 Mike Vernon .15 .40
215 Dave Andreychuk .15 .40
216 Chris Murray .05 .15
217 Joe Juneau .05 .15
218 Vladimir Malakhov .05 .15
219 Paul Coffey .20 .50
220 Roberto Luongo .25 .60
221 Roman Hamrlik .15 .40
222 Sandis Ozolinsh .05 .15
223 Gary Roberts .05 .15
224 Boyd Devereaux .05 .15
225 Scott Thornton .05 .15
226 Igor Larionov .05 .15
227 John Vanbiesbrouck .15 .40
228 Milan Kraft 1.00 2.50
229 Steven McCarthy .40 1.00
230 Kris Beech .05 .15
231 Henrik Sedin .40 1.00
232 Daniel Sedin .40 1.00
233 Oleg Saprykin .40 1.00
234 Maxime Ouellet .40 1.00
235 Taylor Pyatt .40 1.00
236 Brent Johnson .40 1.00
237 Shawn Heins .40 1.00
238 Mika Noronen .40 1.00
239 Samuel Pahlsson .40 1.00
240 Dimitri Kalinin .40 1.00
241 Marian Gaborik RC 2.50 6.00
242 Petr Svoboda RC .40 1.00
243 Niclas Wallin RC .40 1.00
244 Dale Purinton RC .40 1.00
245 Justin Williams RC .75 2.00
246 Roman Simicek RC .40 1.00
247 Brad Tapper RC .40 1.00
248 Rostislav Klesla RC .75 2.00
249 Martin Havlat RC 1.50 4.00
250 Scott Hartnell RC .75 2.00
251 Andrew Raycroft RC 1.50 4.00
252 Ossi Vaananen RC .40 1.00
253 Steven Reinprecht RC .40 1.00
254 Josef Vasicek RC .40 1.00
255 Petr Hubacek RC .40 1.00
256 Lubomir Sekeras RC .40 1.00
257 David Aebischer RC 1.25 3.00
258 Jani Hurme RC .75 2.00
259 Marty Turco RC 1.50 4.00
260 Jarno Kultanen RC .40 1.00

2000-01 Stadium Club Beam Team

Randomly inserted in packs at the rate of 1:53, this luminescent card features player photos on an ice rink background with laser cut accents and die cut borders. Each card is sequentially numbered to 500.
COMPLETE SET (30) 150.00 300.00
BT1 Paul Kariya 4.00 10.00
BT2 Peter Forsberg 10.00 25.00
BT3 Mike Modano 6.00 15.00
BT4 Steve Yzerman 20.00 50.00
BT5 Pavel Bure 5.00 12.00
BT6 Jaromir Jagr 6.00 15.00
BT7 Brett Hull 5.00 12.00
BT8 Joe Sakic 8.00 20.00
BT9 Scott Gomez 3.00 8.00
BT10 Teemu Selanne 4.00 10.00
BT11 Vincent Lecavalier 4.00 10.00
BT12 Patrick Roy 20.00 50.00
BT13 Martin Brodeur 10.00 25.00
BT14 Dominik Hasek 8.00 20.00
BT15 Joe Thornton 6.00 15.00
BT16 Valeri Bure 3.00 8.00
BT17 Ed Belfour 4.00 10.00
BT18 Ray Bourque 8.00 20.00
BT19 Mark Messier 5.00 12.00
BT20 Curtis Joseph 4.00 10.00
BT21 Jason Arnott 3.00 8.00
BT22 Brian Boucher 4.00 10.00
BT23 Tony Amonte 3.00 8.00
BT24 Milan Hejduk 4.00 10.00
BT25 Mark Recchi 3.00 8.00
BT26 Patrik Elias 3.00 8.00
BT27 Zigmund Palffy 3.00 8.00
BT28 Jeremy Roenick 5.00 12.00
BT29 Eric Lindros 6.00 15.00
BT30 Chris Pronger 3.00 8.00

2000-01 Stadium Club Capture the Action

Randomly inserted in packs at the rate of 1:12, this 15-card set features a base card design with borders along the top and bottom and places color action photography against a maroon and purple background. A game view parallel was also created, these

cards had a stated print run of 100 sets.
COMPLETE SET (15) 10.00 20.00
*GAME VIEW: 6X TO 15X BASIC CARDS
CA1 Jaromir Jagr 1.00 2.50
CA2 Martin Brodeur 1.50 4.00
CA3 Scott Gomez .50 1.25
CA4 Ed Belfour .60 1.50
CA5 Dominik Hasek 1.25 3.00
CA6 Olaf Kolzig .50 1.25
CA7 Pavel Bure .60 1.50
CA8 John LeClair .60 1.50
CA9 Curtis Joseph .60 1.50
CA10 Chris Pronger .50 1.25
CA11 Peter Forsberg 1.50 4.00
CA12 Teemu Selanne .60 1.50
CA13 Patrik Stefan .50 1.25
CA14 Vincent Lecavalier .60 1.50
CA15 Tim Connolly .50 1.25

2000-01 Stadium Club Co-Signers

Randomly inserted in Hobby packs at the rate of 1:644, this four card set features a split card design with two players and their authentic autographs along the bottom in a whited out box.
CO1 Pavel Bure 15.00 40.00
Pavol Demitra
CO2 Scott Gomez 60.00 150.00
Martin Brodeur
CO3 Nikolai Antropov 15.00 40.00
Daniel Alfredsson
CO4 Anson Carter 15.00 40.00
Mike York

2000-01 Stadium Club Glove Save

Randomly inserted in packs at the rate of 1:10, this 10-card set features an all die cut embossed card in the shape of a goalie glove.
COMPLETE SET (10) 20.00 40.00
GS1 Martin Brodeur 4.00 10.00
GS2 Ed Belfour 1.50 4.00
GS3 Patrick Roy 8.00 20.00
GS4 Curtis Joseph 1.50 4.00
GS5 Brian Boucher 1.25 3.00
GS6 Roman Turek 1.25 3.00
GS7 Olaf Kolzig 1.25 3.00
GS8 Dominik Hasek 3.00 8.00
GS9 Chris Osgood 1.25 3.00
GS10 Fred Brathwaite 1.25 3.00

2000-01 Stadium Club Lone Star Signatures

Randomly inserted in packs at the rate of 1:118 overall, this 10-card set features a base design with the player framed in the middle of an "ice rink" with a whited out portion centered along the bottom for an authentic player autograph.
LS1 Pavel Bure 6.00 15.00
LS2 Martin Brodeur 30.00 80.00
LS3 Scott Gomez 6.00 15.00
LS4 Daniel Alfredsson 6.00 15.00
LS5 Nikolai Antropov 6.00 15.00
LS6 Jose Theodore 15.00 40.00
LS7 Anson Carter 6.00 15.00
LS8 Pavol Demitra 6.00 15.00
LS9 Mike York 6.00 15.00
LS10 Brad Stuart 6.00 15.00

2000-01 Stadium Club Souvenirs

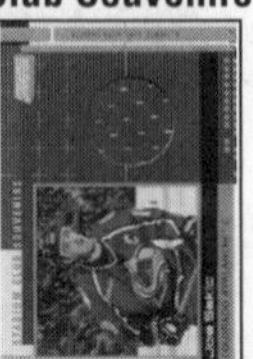

Randomly inserted in packs at the rate of 1:88 overall, this eight card set features full color player photos coupled with a circular swatch of a game worn jersey.
SCS1 Wade Redden 6.00 15.00
SCS2 Joe Sakic 12.50 30.00
SCS3 Derian Hatcher 6.00 15.00
SCS4 Jeff Hackett 6.00 15.00
SCS5 Kenny Jonsson 6.00 15.00
SCS6 Sergei Samsonov 6.00 15.00
SCS7 Darren McCarty 10.00 25.00
SCS8 Tie Domi 6.00 15.00

2000-01 Stadium Club Special Forces

Randomly inserted in packs at the rate of 1:8, this 20-card set features a base design with purple borders along the top and bottom and full color player photography set against a holofoil background in the shape of an ice rink.
COMPLETE SET (20) 15.00 30.00
SF1 Scott Stevens .40 1.00
SF2 Chris Pronger .40 1.00
SF3 Paul Kariya .50 1.25
SF4 Peter Forsberg 1.25 3.00
SF5 Mike Modano .75 2.00
SF6 Steve Yzerman 2.50 6.00
SF7 Pavel Bure .60 1.50
SF8 Jaromir Jagr .75 2.00
SF9 John LeClair .60 1.50
SF10 Mats Sundin .50 1.25
SF11 Owen Nolan .40 1.00
SF12 Brendan Shanahan .75 2.00
SF13 Pavol Demitra .40 1.00
SF14 Nicklas Lidstrom .50 1.25
SF15 Ron Francis .40 1.00
SF16 Patrick Roy 2.50 6.00
SF17 Martin Brodeur 1.25 3.00
SF18 Dominik Hasek 1.00 2.50
SF19 Keith Tkachuk .50 1.25
SF20 Curtis Joseph .50 1.25

2001-02 Stadium Club

Released in November 2001, this 140-card set carried an SRP of $3.00 for a 6-card pack. The base set consisted of 100 veteran cards, 10 transactions cards (inserted 1:4), 10 Premium Prospects cards (inserted 1:4) and 20 rookies (inserted 1:8).
COMPLETE SET (140) 60.00 120.00
1 Martin Brodeur .50 1.25
2 Peter Forsberg .50 1.25
3 Chris Pronger .15 .40
4 Paul Kariya .20 .50
5 Mike Modano .30 .75
6 Curtis Joseph .20 .50
7 Jason Allison .08 .20
8 Brendan Shanahan .20 .50
9 Peter Bondra .20 .50
10 Mark Messier .20 .50
11 Owen Nolan .15 .40
12 Saku Koivu .20 .50
13 Tony Amonte .15 .40
14 Vincent Lecavalier .20 .50
15 Marian Hossa .20 .50
16 Pavel Bure .20 .50
17 Daniel Sedin .08 .20
18 Mario Lemieux 1.25 3.00
19 Rick DiPietro .15 .40
20 Zigmund Palffy .15 .40
21 Ron Tugnutt .15 .40
22 Ron Francis .15 .40
23 Maxim Afinogenov .08 .20
24 Steve Yzerman 1.00 2.50
25 Ray Ferraro .08 .20
26 Tommy Salo .15 .40
27 Marian Gaborik .40 1.00
28 Claude Lemieux .08 .20
29 David Legwand .15 .40
30 Roman Cechmanek .15 .40
31 Jarome Iginla .25 .60
32 Sergei Fedorov .30 .75
33 Bill Guerin .15 .40
34 Brian Leetch .15 .40
35 Alexei Kovalev .15 .40
36 Pavol Demitra .15 .40
37 Olaf Kolzig .15 .40
38 Jose Theodore .25 .60
39 Johan Hedberg .15 .40
40 Teemu Selanne .15 .40
41 Adam Deadmarsh .08 .20
42 Miroslav Satan .15 .40
43 Henrik Sedin .08 .20
44 Ed Belfour .20 .50
45 Sean Burke .15 .40
46 Patrik Elias .15 .40
47 Daniel Alfredsson .15 .40
48 Evgeni Nabokov .15 .40
49 Markus Naslund .20 .50
50 Mats Sundin .20 .50
51 Milan Hejduk .20 .50
52 Eric Belanger .08 .20
53 Darren McCarty .08 .20
54 Keith Tkachuk .20 .50
55 Steve Sullivan .08 .20
56 Mark Recchi .15 .40
57 Rob Blake .15 .40
58 Manny Fernandez .15 .40
59 Patrick Lalime .15 .40
60 Adam Oates .15 .40
61 Joe Sakic .40 1.00
62 Lubomir Visnovsky .08 .20
63 Jeff Halpern .08 .20
64 Shane Willis .08 .20
65 Todd Bertuzzi .20 .50
66 Jeff Friesen .08 .20
67 Mike Dunham .15 .40
68 Alex Tanguay .15 .40
69 J-P Dumont .08 .20
70 Patrick Marleau .15 .40
71 Martin Straka .08 .20
72 Petr Sykora .08 .20
73 Arturs Irbe .15 .40
74 Patrik Stefan .08 .20
75 Brad Richards .15 .40
76 Mike Comrie .15 .40
77 Jason Arnott .08 .20
78 Tie Domi .15 .40
79 Martin Havlat .15 .40
80 Roberto Luongo .25 .60
81 Nicklas Lidstrom .20 .50
82 Simon Gagne .20 .50
83 Marc Savard .08 .20
84 John LeClair .20 .50
85 Gary Roberts .08 .20
86 Ryan Smyth .08 .20
87 Patrick Roy 1.00 2.50
88 Petr Nedved .08 .20
89 Brent Johnson .15 .40
90 Scott Gomez .08 .20
91 Joe Thornton .30 .75
92 Felix Potvin .20 .50
93 Chris Drury .15 .40
94 Keith Primeau .08 .20
95 Rod Brind'Amour .15 .40
96 Joe Nieuwendyk .15 .40
97 Espen Knutsen .08 .20
98 Adam Foote .15 .40
99 Brad Isbister .08 .20
100 Marc Denis .15 .40
101 Eric Lindros .20 .50
102 Alexei Yashin .08 .20
103 Dominik Hasek .40 1.00
104 Michael Peca .08 .20
105 Brett Hull .25 .60
106 Pierre Turgeon .15 .40
107 Doug Weight .15 .40
108 Alexander Mogilny .15 .40
109 Jaromir Jagr .30 .75
110 Jeremy Roenick .25 .60
111 Dany Heatley PP 2.00 5.00
112 Rostislav Klesla PP 1.50 4.00
113 Pavel Brendl PP 1.25 3.00
114 Barrett Heisten PP 1.25 3.00
115 Miikka Kiprusoff PP 1.25 3.00
116 Kris Beech PP 1.25 3.00
117 Pierre Dagenais PP 1.25 3.00
118 Bryan Allen PP 1.25 3.00
119 Jason Williams PP 1.25 3.00
120 Milan Kraft PP 1.25 3.00
121 Ilya Kovalchuk RC 6.00 15.00
122 Peter Smrek RC 1.25 3.00
123 Jiri Dopita RC 1.00 2.50
124 Jeff Jillson RC 1.00 2.50
125 Jukka Hentunen RC 1.00 2.50
126 Vaclav Nedorost RC 1.00 2.50
127 Timo Parssinen RC 1.25 3.00
128 Niklas Hagman RC 1.00 2.50
129 Andreas Salomonsson RC 1.00 2.50
130 Scott Nichol RC 1.25 3.00
131 Dan Blackburn RC 1.50 4.00
132 Kristian Huselius RC 1.25 3.00
133 Ivan Ciernik RC 1.25 3.00
134 Scott Clemmensen RC 1.00 2.50
135 Pascal Dupuis RC 1.00 2.50
136 Jason Chimera RC 1.00 2.50
137 Erik Cole RC 1.00 2.50
138 Brian Sutherby RC 1.00 2.50
139 Pavel Datsyuk RC 5.00 12.00
140 Niko Kapanen RC 1.25 3.00

2001-02 Stadium Club Award Winners

This 140-card set paralleled the base set but each card was serial-numbered out of 100 and carried an "Award Winner" stamp. Collectors could redeem cards from this set for special NHL Award Winners sets if the card they held was of a player who won an NHL award during the 2001/02 season.
*STARS: 8X TO 20X BASIC CARDS
*ROOKIES: .5X TO 1.25X BASIC CARDS
31 Jarome Iginla 10.00 25.00
38 Jose Theodore 40.00 100.00
81 Nicklas Lidstrom 10.00 25.00
111 Dany Heatley 20.00 50.00

2001-02 Stadium Club Master Photos

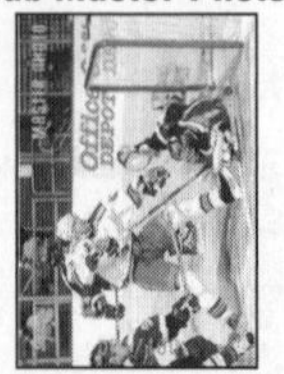

This 140-card set paralleled the base set but each card was serial-numbered out of 100 and carried a silver "Master Photo" stamp. Stated odds for this set was 1:45.
*STARS: 8X TO 20X BASIC CARDS
*ROOKIES: 1.25X TO 3X BASIC CARDS

2001-02 Stadium Club Gallery

This 40-card set was inserted at 1:5 and featured color artist renditions of some of the top players in the league. Cards were printed on glossy stock and had white borders that resembled a picture frame.
COMPLETE SET (40) 30.00 60.00
G1 Curtis Joseph .60 1.50
G2 Brendan Shanahan .60 1.50
G3 Mats Sundin .60 1.50
G4 Patrik Elias .50 1.25
G5 Martin Havlat .50 1.25
G6 Joe Sakic 1.25 3.00
G7 Mike Modano 1.00 2.50
G8 Chris Drury .50 1.25
G9 Scott Stevens .50 1.25
G10 Olaf Kolzig .50 1.25
G11 Roberto Luongo .75 2.00
G12 Roman Cechmanek .50 1.25
G13 Ed Belfour .60 1.50
G14 Teemu Selanne .60 1.50
G15 Henrik Sedin .40 1.00
G16 Jaromir Jagr 1.00 2.50
G17 Marian Gaborik 1.25 3.00
G18 John LeClair .60 1.50
G19 Keith Tkachuk .60 1.50
G20 Paul Kariya .60 1.50
G21 Mario Lemieux 4.00 10.00
G22 Sergei Fedorov 1.00 2.50
G23 Martin Brodeur 1.50 4.00
G24 Pavel Bure .60 1.50
G25 Mike Comrie .50 1.25
G26 Zigmund Palffy .50 1.25
G27 Milan Hejduk .60 1.50
G28 Nicklas Lidstrom .60 1.50
G29 Patrick Roy 3.00 8.00
G30 Bill Guerin .50 1.25
G31 Evgeni Nabokov .50 1.25
G32 Tony Amonte .50 1.25
G33 Peter Forsberg 1.50 4.00
G34 Rick DiPietro .50 1.25
G35 Saku Koivu .60 1.50
G36 Chris Pronger .50 1.25
G37 Steve Yzerman 3.00 8.00
G38 Daniel Sedin .40 1.00
G39 Vincent Lecavalier .60 1.50
G40 Mark Messier .60 1.50

2001-02 Stadium Club Gallery Gold

This set paralleled the base gallery set but was serial-numbered out of 50 and inserted at a rate of 1:319. The words "Gold Edition" were printed under the player's name on the card fronts.
*GOLD: 10X TO 25X BASIC INSERTS

2001-02 Stadium Club Heart and Soul

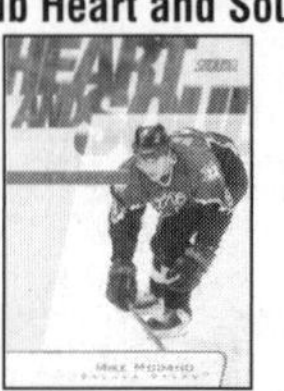

This 10-card set was inserted at a rate of 1:20 and featured full color action photos on white card fronts. The words "Heart and Soul" were printed in dark blue across the card top.
COMPLETE SET (10) 15.00 30.00
HS1 Mark Messier 1.00 2.50
HS2 Patrick Roy 4.00 10.00
HS3 Steve Yzerman 4.00 10.00
HS4 Mario Lemieux 5.00 12.00
HS5 Chris Pronger .60 1.50
HS6 Scott Stevens .60 1.50
HS7 Peter Forsberg 2.00 5.00
HS8 Curtis Joseph .60 1.50
HS9 Mike Modano 1.25 3.00
HS10 Brendan Shanahan 1.25 3.00

2001-02 Stadium Club Lone Star Signatures

Inserted at a rate of 1:120, this 7-card set featured authentic player autographs. Color player photos were printed on the top two-thirds of the card front, and a white autograph area was at the card bottom.
LS1 Milan Hejduk 8.00 20.00
LS2 Olaf Kolzig 8.00 20.00
LS3 Marian Gaborik 12.50 30.00
LS4 Martin Havlat 8.00 20.00
LS5 Patrik Elias 8.00 20.00
LS6 Adam Oates 8.00 20.00
LS7 Ilya Kovalchuk 12.50 30.00

2001-02 Stadium Club New Regime

Consisting of 11 regular insert cards and 9 autograph cards, this set featured goalie prospects from around the league. Regular cards were inserted at 1:9. Autographed cards carried a white autograph space at the bottom of each card and a Topps certified stamp on the card backs. The Turco, Hedberg and Aebischer auto cards were inserted at 1:210, all other autos were inserted at 1:140.
NR1 Marty Turco 2.00 5.00
NR2 David Aebischer 2.00 5.00
NR3 Brent Johnson 2.00 5.00
NR4 Evgeni Nabokov 2.00 5.00
NR5 Marc Denis 2.00 5.00
NR6 Roberto Luongo 2.50 6.00
NR7 Manny Fernandez 2.00 5.00
NR8 Roman Cechmanek 2.00 5.00
NR9 Jani Hurme 2.00 5.00
NR10 Johan Hedberg 2.00 5.00
NR11 Rick DiPietro 2.00 5.00
NRABJ Brent Johnson AU 8.00 20.00
NRADA David Aebischer AU 10.00 25.00
NRAEN Evgeni Nabokov AU 8.00 20.00
NRAJHE Johan Hedberg AU 8.00 20.00
NRAMD Marc Denis AU 8.00 20.00
NRAMF Manny Fernandez AU 8.00 20.00
NRAMT Marty Turco AU 10.00 25.00
NRARC Roman Cechmanek AU 8.00 20.00
NRARL Roberto Luongo AU 10.00 25.00

2001-02 Stadium Club NHL Passport

This 20-card set was inserted at 1:10 and featured international stars who also represent their homelands during world competitions. Cards carried color player photos and a small replica of the player's homeland flag.
COMPLETE SET (20) 20.00 40.00
NHLP1 Peter Forsberg 1.50 4.00
NHLP2 Nicklas Lidstrom .60 1.50
NHLP3 Mats Sundin .60 1.50
NHLP4 Pavel Bure .75 2.00
NHLP5 Sergei Fedorov 1.25 3.00
NHLP6 Alexei Kovalev .50 1.25
NHLP7 Saku Koivu .60 1.50
NHLP8 Teemu Selanne .60 1.50
NHLP9 Roman Cechmanek .50 1.25
NHLP10 Patrik Elias .50 1.25
NHLP11 Milan Hejduk .60 1.50
NHLP12 Petr Sykora .50 1.25
NHLP13 Chris Drury .50 1.25
NHLP14 Bill Guerin .50 1.25
NHLP15 John LeClair .75 2.00
NHLP16 Mike Modano 1.00 2.50
NHLP17 Paul Kariya .60 1.50
NHLP18 Mario Lemieux 4.00 10.00
NHLP19 Joe Sakic 1.25 3.00
NHLP20 Steve Yzerman 3.00 8.00

2001-02 Stadium Club Perennials

This 15-card set was inserted at 1:7 and highlighted players who make the all-star team on a consistent basis.
COMPLETE SET (15) 20.00 40.00
P1 Pavel Bure .75 2.00
P2 Joe Sakic 1.25 3.00
P3 Martin Brodeur 1.50 4.00
P4 Peter Forsberg 1.50 4.00
P5 Patrick Roy 3.00 8.00
P6 John LeClair .75 2.00
P7 Paul Kariya .60 1.50
P8 Steve Yzerman 3.00 8.00
P9 Mario Lemieux 4.00 10.00
P10 Ed Belfour .60 1.50
P11 Keith Tkachuk .60 1.50
P12 Sergei Fedorov 1.25 3.00
P13 Curtis Joseph .60 1.50
P14 Zigmund Palffy .60 1.50
P15 Tony Amonte .60 1.50

2001-02 Stadium Club Souvenirs

This 35-card hobby only set featured one, two or three swatches of game-worn jerseys from the pictured player(s). Single player cards were inserted at 1:16, dual player cards were inserted at 1:986 and serial-numbered to 25 each. Triple player cards were inserted at 1:3616 and were serial-numbered to 25.
AZ Alexei Zhamnov 4.00 10.00
CO Chris Osgood 6.00 15.00
JI Jarome Iginla 15.00 40.00
JT Joe Thornton 8.00 20.00
MB Martin Brodeur 15.00 40.00
MP Matt Pettinger 4.00 10.00
MR Mark Recchi 6.00 15.00
MT Marty Turco 6.00 15.00
PB Pavel Bure 4.00 10.00
PF Peter Forsberg 15.00 40.00
PK Paul Kariya 8.00 20.00
PM Patrick Marleau 6.00 15.00
SB Sean Burke 6.00 15.00
SF Sergei Fedorov 10.00 25.00
SK Saku Koivu 4.00 10.00
TD Tie Domi 6.00 15.00
TK Tomas Kloucek 4.00 10.00
JHA Jeff Hackett 4.00 10.00
JHL Jan Hlavac 4.00 10.00
MAS Marc Savard 4.00 10.00
MIS Miroslav Satan 6.00 15.00
EBMB Ed Belfour 60.00 120.00
Martin Brodeur
JHSK Jeff Hackett 20.00 50.00
Saku Koivu
JSCD Joe Sakic 30.00 80.00
Chris Drury
MTEB Marty Turco 30.00 80.00
Ed Belfour
PFCD Peter Forsberg 30.00 80.00
Chris Drury
PFJS Peter Forsberg 60.00 120.00
Joe Sakic
PRMB Patrick Roy 60.00 120.00
Martin Brodeur
SFPB Sergei Fedorov 30.00 80.00
Pavel Bure
SSPB Sergei Samsonov 20.00 50.00
Pavel Bure
TDDM Tie Domi 20.00 50.00
Darren McCarty
TKMM Tomas Kloucek 20.00 50.00
Mike Mottau
EBMBPR Ed Belfour 100.00 250.00
Martin Brodeur
Patrick Roy
JSCDPF Joe Sakic 150.00 300.00
Chris Drury
Peter Forsberg
JTJASS Joe Thornton 75.00 150.00
Jason Allison
Sergei Samsonov

2001-02 Stadium Club Toronto Fall Expo

This 6-card set was available only by wrapper redemption from the Topps booth at the 2001 Toronto Fall expo. The cards paralleled the base set, but carry a expo logo on the card fronts and were numbered "# of 6" on the card backs.
COMPLETE SET (6) 1.60 4.00
1 Marian Hossa .40 1.00
2 Peter Forsberg .80 2.00
3 Daniel Alfredsson .20 .50
4 Nicklas Lidstrom .20 .50
5 Brendan Shanahan .30 .75
6 Pavel Bure .40 1.00

2002-03 Stadium Club

Released in mid-November, this 140-card set featured full-color action photos on the card fronts and player stats on the card backs. SP's were inserted at a rate of 1:8.
COMPLETE SET (140) 75.00 150.00
COMP.SET w/o SP's (120) 25.00 50.00
1 Jose Theodore .25 .60
2 Jarome Iginla .25 .60
3 Nicklas Lidstrom .20 .50
4 Ron Francis .15 .40
5 Jaromir Jagr .30 .75
6 Mario Lemieux 1.25 3.00
7 Owen Nolan .15 .40
8 Martin Brodeur .50 1.25
9 Joe Sakic .40 1.00
10 Ilya Kovalchuk .25 .60
11 Mike Modano .30 .75
12 Jason Allison .08 .20
13 Sean Burke .15 .40
14 Mats Sundin .20 .50
15 Markus Naslund .20 .50
16 Jeremy Roenick .25 .60
17 Eric Lindros .20 .50
18 Brent Johnson .15 .40
19 Sergei Fedorov .30 .75
20 Sergei Samsonov .15 .40
21 Chris Drury .15 .40
22 Ryan Smyth .08 .20
23 Scott Hartnell .08 .20
24 Simon Gagne .20 .50
25 Dan Cloutier .15 .40
26 Vincent Lecavalier .20 .50
27 Martin Havlat .15 .40
28 Patrik Elias .15 .40
29 Roberto Luongo .25 .60
30 Rob Blake .15 .40
31 J-P Dumont .08 .20
32 Jeff O'Neill .08 .20
33 Pavel Datsyuk .20 .50
34 Dan Blackburn .15 .40
35 Alexei Kovalev .15 .40
36 Olaf Kolzig .15 .40
37 Milan Hejduk .20 .50
38 Steve Yzerman 1.00 2.50
39 Marc Denis .15 .40
40 Michael Peca .08 .20
41 Saku Koivu .20 .50
42 Marian Gaborik .40 1.00
43 Brad Richards .15 .40
44 Alexander Mogilny .15 .40
45 Mike Comrie .15 .40
46 Peter Forsberg .50 1.25
47 Dany Heatley .25 .60
48 Steve Sullivan .08 .20
49 Keith Tkachuk .20 .50
50 Todd Bertuzzi .20 .50
51 Evgeni Nabokov .15 .40
52 David Legwand .15 .40
53 Scott Stevens .15 .40
54 Eric Daze .08 .20
55 Martin Biron .15 .40
56 Zigmund Palffy .15 .40
57 Paul Kariya .20 .50
58 Krys Kolanos .08 .20
59 Pavel Bure .20 .50
60 Darcy Tucker .08 .20
61 Marian Hossa .20 .50
62 Roman Cechmanek .15 .40
63 Mark Parrish .08 .20
64 Arturs Irbe .15 .40
65 Brian Rolston .08 .20
66 Marty Turco .15 .40
67 Peter Bondra .20 .50
68 Johan Hedberg .15 .40
69 Chris Pronger .15 .40
70 Patrick Lalime .15 .40
71 Mike Dunham .15 .40
72 Kristian Huselius .08 .20
73 Patrick Roy 1.00 2.50
74 Joe Thornton .30 .75
75 Andrew Brunette .08 .20
76 Alexei Yashin .08 .20
77 John LeClair .20 .50
78 Miroslav Satan .15 .40
79 Doug Weight .15 .40
80 Gary Roberts .08 .20
81 Tommy Salo .15 .40
82 Daniel Alfredsson .15 .40
83 Marco Sturm .08 .20
84 Rostislav Klesla .08 .20
85 Richard Zednik .08 .20
86 Roman Turek .15 .40
87 Brian Leetch .15 .40
88 Chris Osgood .15 .40
89 Brendan Morrison .15 .40
90 Jocelyn Thibault .15 .40
91 Teemu Selanne .20 .50
92 J-S Giguere .15 .40
93 Nikolai Khabibulin .20 .50
94 Pavol Demitra .15 .40
95 Brendan Shanahan .20 .50
96 Mark Recchi .15 .40
97 Felix Potvin .20 .50
98 Shane Doan .08 .20
99 Erik Cole .08 .20
100 Brett Hull .25 .60
101 Curtis Joseph .20 .50
102 Bobby Holik .08 .20
103 Ed Belfour .20 .50
104 Bill Guerin .15 .40
105 Petr Sykora .08 .20
106 Scott Young .08 .20
107 Adam Oates .15 .40
108 Jeff Friesen .08 .20
109 Darius Kasparaitis .08 .20
110 Tony Amonte .15 .40
111 Marcel Hossa .15 .40
112 Jamie Lundmark .08 .20
113 Pavel Brendl .08 .20
114 Jaroslav Svoboda .08 .20
115 Stephen Weiss .08 .20
116 Martin Prusek RC .15 .40
117 Jani Rita .08 .20
118 Petr Cajanek .08 .20
119 Trent Hunter .08 .20
120 Jonathan Cheechoo .10 .25
121 Stanislav Chistov RC 2.50 6.00
122 Alexander Svitov RC 4.00 10.00
123 Alexander Frolov RC 4.00 10.00
124 Alexei Smirnov RC 2.00 5.00
125 Chuck Kobasew RC 2.50 6.00
126 Rick Nash RC 6.00 15.00
127 Henrik Zetterberg RC 6.00 15.00
128 Jay Bouwmeester RC 4.00 10.00
129 Ales Hemsky RC 5.00 12.00
130 Martin Gerber RC 2.00 5.00
131 Ron Hainsey RC 2.00 5.00

132 P-M Bouchard RC 4.00 10.00
133 Jason Spezza RC 6.00 15.00
134 Kurt Sauer RC 2.00 5.00
135 Lasse Pirjeta RC 2.00 5.00
136 Adam Hall RC 2.00 5.00
137 Dennis Seidenberg RC 3.00 8.00
138 Patrick Sharp RC 2.00 5.00
139 Steve Eminger RC 2.00 5.00
140 Dmitri Bykov RC 2.00 5.00

2002-03 Stadium Club Silver Decoy Cards

This 140-card set paralleled the base set but was printed on thicker card stock and carried a silver finish on the card fronts. They were inserted at one-per pack to discourage pack searching.
*DECOYS: .5X TO 1.25X BASIC CARDS

2002-03 Stadium Club Proofs

This 140-card proof set paralleled the base set but carried a "Proof" stamp and serial-numbering. Base cards were serial-numbered to 250 and rookies were serial-numbered to 100.
*STARS: 1.5X TO 4X BASIC CARDS
*ROOKIES: .75X TO 2X

2002-03 Stadium Club Beam Team

This 15-card set was inserted at a rate of 1:18.
COMPLETE SET (15) 20.00 40.00
BT1 Steve Yzerman 3.00 8.00
BT2 Mario Lemieux 4.00 10.00
BT3 Patrick Roy 3.00 8.00
BT4 Jarome Iginla .75 2.00
BT5 Jose Theodore .75 2.00
BT6 Brendan Shanahan 1.00 2.50
BT7 Chris Pronger .50 1.25
BT8 Dany Heatley .75 2.00
BT9 Joe Thornton 1.00 2.50
BT10 Peter Forsberg 1.50 4.00
BT11 Ron Francis .50 1.25
BT12 Owen Nolan .50 1.25
BT13 Todd Bertuzzi .60 1.50
BT14 Rob Blake .50 1.25
BT15 Paul Kariya .60 1.50

2002-03 Stadium Club Champions Fabric

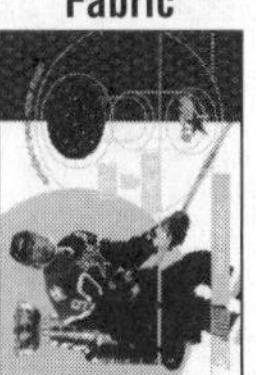

Inserted at 1:68, this 10-card set featured swatches of game jerseys.
*MULT.COLOR SWATCH: .5X TO 1.25X HI
FC1 Rob Blake 4.00 10.00
FC2 Derian Hatcher 4.00 10.00
FC3 Alex Tanguay 4.00 10.00
FC4 Martin Brodeur 10.00 25.00
FC5 Milan Hejduk 4.00 10.00
FC6 Mike Modano 6.00 15.00
FC7 Scott Niedermayer 4.00 10.00
FC8 Brian Leetch 4.00 10.00
FC9 Sergei Zubov 4.00 10.00
FC10 Chris Drury 4.00 10.00

2002-03 Stadium Club Champions Patches

A parallel to the basic Champions Fabrics jerseys, this 9-card set featured swatches of game-worn jersey patches. Each card was serial-numberde to 25 copies each. Please note that Topps did not produce a patch variation of the Chris Drury card.
*PATCHES: 2X TO 5X BASIC JERSEY

2002-03 Stadium Club Lone Star Signatures Blue

Inserted at 1:56 packs, this 14-card set featured authentic player autographs in blue

ink.
LSBG Brian Gionta 8.00 20.00
LSBR Brad Richards 8.00 20.00
LSCP Chris Pronger SP 12.50 30.00
LSDB Daniel Briere 8.00 20.00
LSEC Erik Cole 8.00 20.00
LSED Eric Daze 8.00 20.00
LSIL Ilya Kovalchuk 15.00 40.00
LSJI Jarome Iginla 15.00 40.00
LSJT Jose Theodore 15.00 40.00
LSPL Patrick Lalime 8.00 20.00
LSRK Rostislav Klesla 8.00 20.00
LSSG Simon Gagne 12.50 30.00
LSSW Stephen Weiss 8.00 20.00
LSTB Todd Bertuzzi 12.50 30.00

2002-03 Stadium Club Lone Star Signatures Red

Inserted at 1:144, this set paralleled the basic autograph set but player autographs were signed in red ink.
*RED SIGS: .5X TO 1.25X BLUE

2002-03 Stadium Club Passport

Inserted at 1:40, this 14-card set featured swatches of game-worn jerseys affixed to a passport style card front. All cards carried a NHLP prefix.
*MULT.COLOR SWATCH: .5X TO 1.25X HI
1 Saku Koivu 6.00 15.00
2 Daniel Alfredsson 4.00 10.00
3 Eric Lindros 6.00 15.00
4 Mats Sundin 6.00 15.00
5 Todd Bertuzzi 6.00 15.00
6 Simon Gagne 6.00 15.00
7 Marian Hossa 6.00 15.00
8 Paul Kariya 6.00 15.00
9 Vincent Lecavalier 6.00 15.00
10 Miroslav Satan 4.00 10.00
11 Markus Naslund 6.00 15.00
12 Zigmund Palffy 4.00 10.00
13 Tony Amonte 4.00 10.00
14 Brian Rolston 4.00 10.00
15 Maxim Afinogenov 4.00 10.00
16 Sergei Samsonov 4.00 10.00
17 Marco Sturm 4.00 10.00

2002-03 Stadium Club Puck Stops Here

COMPLETE SET (15) 10.00 20.00
STATED ODDS 1:6
PSH1 Brent Johnson .50 1.25
PSH2 Roman Cechmanek .50 1.25
PSH3 Evgeni Nabokov .50 1.25
PSH4 Jose Theodore .75 2.00
PSH5 Martin Biron .50 1.25
PSH6 Chris Osgood .50 1.25
PSH7 Marty Turco .50 1.25
PSH8 Nikolai Khabibulin .60 1.50
PSH9 Roberto Luongo .75 2.00
PSH10 Martin Brodeur 1.25 3.00
PSH11 Sean Burke .50 1.25
PSH12 Tommy Salo .50 1.25
PSH13 Mike Richter .60 1.50
PSH14 Patrick Roy 1.50 4.00
PSH15 J-S Giguere .50 1.25

2002-03 Stadium Club St. Patrick Relics

This 16-card set honored the career of Patrick Roy. Single swatch jersey only odds were 1:237 and single swatch stick only cards were inserted at 1:3160. All other print runs are listed below. Print runs of 25 or less not priced due to scarcity.
ALL CARDS CARRY SP PREFIX
*MULT.COLOR SWATCH: .75X TO 1.5X
SAS Patrick Roy 100.00 250.00
Stick Auto/50
CAJ Patrick Roy 12.50 30.00
Colorado Jersey
MCJ Patrick Roy 12.50 30.00
Montreal Jersey
CAJA Patrick Roy 60.00 150.00
Colorado Jersey Auto/250
MCJA Patrick Roy 60.00 150.00
Montreal Jersey Auto/250
SPS Patrick Roy 12.50 30.00
Stick
CAJP Patrick Roy 30.00 80.00
Colorado Patch/100
MCJP Patrick Roy 30.00 80.00
Montreal Patch/100
CAMCJ P.Roy DUAL JSY/500 30.00 80.00
CAMCJA Patrick Roy 200.00 500.00
Dual Jersey Auto/50
CAMCJS Patrick Roy 100.00 250.00
Jersey/Stick/50
CAMCJSA Patrick Roy 200.00 500.00
Jersey/Stick Auto/25
CAJPA Patrick Roy
Colorado Patch Auto/10
MCJPA Patrick Roy
Montreal Patch Auto/10
CAMCJP Patrick Roy
Dual Patch/25
CAMCJPA Patrick Roy
Dual Patch Auto/5

2002-03 Stadium Club World Stage

COMPLETE SET (20) 15.00 30.00
STATED ODDS 1:7
WS1 Sergei Fedorov 1.25 3.00
WS2 Chris Drury .50 1.25
WS3 Martin Brodeur 1.50 4.00
WS4 Joe Sakic 1.25 3.00
WS5 Mike Modano 1.00 2.50
WS6 Jeremy Roenick .75 2.00
WS7 Brett Hull .75 2.00
WS8 Ilya Kovalchuk .75 2.00
WS9 Nicklas Lidstrom .60 1.50
WS10 Jaromir Jagr 1.00 2.50
WS11 Alexei Yashin .50 1.25
WS12 Zigmund Palffy .50 1.25
WS13 Marian Gaborik .75 2.00
WS14 Teemu Selanne .60 1.50
WS15 Alexei Kovalev .50 1.25
WS16 Patrik Elias .50 1.25
WS17 Peter Bondra .50 1.25
WS18 Pavel Bure .75 2.00
WS19 Mats Sundin .60 1.50
WS20 Daniel Alfredsson .50 1.25

2002-03 Stadium Club YoungStars Relics

This 29-card set featured memorabilia worn during the NHL/Topps YoungStars game played in 2002. Single jersey swatch cards (S1-S23) were inserted at 1:28. Double swatch cards (DS1-DS6) were serial-numbered to 100. Odds for the MVP autographed puck were stated at 1:936 and there were only 200 copies available.
*MULT.COLOR SWATCH: .5X TO 1.25X HI
ALL CARDS CARRY YS PREFIX
S1 Ilya Kovalchuk 12.50 30.00
S2 Pavel Datsyuk 8.00 20.00
S3 Mike Comrie 5.00 12.00
S4 Dan Blackburn 5.00 12.00
S5 Dany Heatley 6.00 15.00
S6 Marian Gaborik 8.00 20.00
S7 Kristian Huselius 5.00 12.00
S8 David Legwand 5.00 12.00
S9 Roberto Luongo 8.00 20.00
S10 Brad Richards 5.00 12.00
S11 Justin Williams 5.00 12.00
S12 Kyle Calder 5.00 12.00
S13 Dave Tanabe 5.00 12.00
S14 Brenden Morrow 5.00 12.00
S15 Scott Hartnell 5.00 12.00
S16 Mike Fisher 5.00 12.00
S17 Tim Connolly 5.00 12.00
S18 Nick Boynton 5.00 12.00
S19 Paul Mara 5.00 12.00
S20 Mike Ribeiro 5.00 12.00
S21 Robyn Regehr 5.00 12.00
S22 Andrew Ference 5.00 12.00
S23 Karel Rachunek 5.00 12.00
DS1 Dany Heatley 25.00 60.00
Ilya Kovalchuk
DS2 David Legwand 10.00 25.00
Scott Hartnell
DS3 Kristian Huselius 20.00 50.00
Roberto Luongo
DS4 M.Gaborik/P.Datsyuk 25.00 60.00
DS5 Justin Williams 10.00 25.00
Mike Comrie
DS6 Brad Richards 10.00 25.00
Dan Blackburn
APIK Ilya Kovalchuk 25.00 60.00
Puck Auto/200

1994-95 Stars HockeyKaps

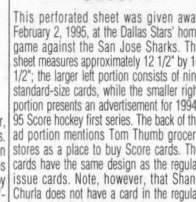

Measuring approximately 1 3/4" in diameter, this set of 25 caps features the Dallas Stars. The caps were given away at Stars games on February 6, 9, 16 and 18. Additional caps could be obtained through a mail-in offer by sending a SASE along with proof-of-purchase from one 46 oz. or one six-pack of 10 oz. Tropicana Twister. A HockeyKap collector game board was also available through a mail-in offer for two proofs-of-purchase of the above-mentioned products. The fronts feature color head shots with a white border. The player's last name is printed in the white border. The backs are blank. The caps are unnumbered and checklisted below in alphabetical order.
COMPLETE SET (25) 2.80 7.00
1 Dave Barr .10 .25
2 Brad Berry .10 .25
3 Neal Broten .20 .50
4 Paul Broten .10 .25
5 Paul Cavallini .10 .25
6 Shane Churla .20 .50
7 Russ Courtnall .16 .40
8 Mike Craig .10 .25
9 Ulf Dahlen .16 .40
10 Dean Evason .10 .25
11 Dave Gagner .16 .40
12 Bob Gainey CO .16 .40
13 Brent Gilchrist .10 .25
14 Derian Hatcher .16 .40
15 Doug Jarvis ACO .04 .10
16 Jim Johnson .10 .25
17 Trent Klatt .10 .25
18 Grant Ledyard .10 .25
19 Craig Ludwig .10 .25
20 Mike McPhee .10 .25
21 Mike Modano .60 1.50
22 Andy Moog .40 1.00
23 Mark Tinordi .10 .25
24 Darcy Wakaluk .16 .40
25 Rick Wilson ACO .04 .10

1994-95 Stars Pinnacle Sheet

Produced by Pinnacle, this promo sheet was given out at Reunion Arena for the Dallas Stars game vs. the Red Wings on April 1, 1995. The sheet measures approximately 12 1/2" by 10 1/2". The left, perforated portion displays nine standard-size player cards, while the right portion consists of an advertisement to purchase 12-packs of Coke products at participating Texaco retailers. The design is the same as the 1994-95 Pinnacle hockey series, with the same numbering. The cards are listed below, beginning at the upper left of the sheet and moving toward the lower right corner.
COMPLETE SHEET (9) 2.00 5.00
3 Mike Modano .60 1.50
55 Derian Hatcher .20 .50
133 Russ Courtnall .20 .50
157 Darcy Wakaluk .20 .50
185 Brent Gilchrist .10 .25
262 Todd Harvey .20 .50
315 Andy Moog .40 1.00
334 Dave Gagner .20 .50
433 Paul Broten .10 .25

1994-95 Stars Postcards

This 23-postcard set of the Dallas Stars was produced by the club for promotional giveaways and autograph signings. The cards feature full-bleed action photos on the fronts, while the backs contain biographical and statistical information. As the cards are unnumbered, they are listed below in alphabetical order.
COMPLETE SET (23) 6.00 15.00
1 Paul Broten .20 .50
2 Paul Cavallini .20 .50
3 Shane Churla .30 .75
4 Gord Donnelly .20 .50
5 Mike Donnelly .20 .50
6 Dean Evason .20 .50
7 Dave Gagner .30 .75
8 Brent Gilchrist .20 .50
9 Todd Harvey .30 .75
10 Derian Hatcher .30 .75
11 Kevin Hatcher .20 .50
12 Mike Kennedy .20 .50
13 Trent Klatt .20 .50
14 Mike Lalor .20 .50
15 Grant Ledyard .20 .50
16 Craig Ludwig .20 .50
17 Richard Matvichuk .30 .75
18 Corey Millen .20 .50
19 Mike Modano 1.20 3.00
20 Andy Moog .80 2.00
21 Darcy Wakaluk .30 .75
22 Peter Zezel .20 .50
23 Doug Zmolek .20 .50

1994-95 Stars Score Sheet

This perforated sheet was given away February 2, 1995, at the Dallas Stars' home game against the San Jose Sharks. The sheet measures approximately 12 1/2" by 10 1/2"; the larger left portion consists of nine standard-size cards, while the smaller right portion presents an advertisement for 1994-95 Score hockey first series. The back of the ad portion mentions Tom Thumb grocery stores as a place to buy Score cards. The cards have the same design as the regular issue cards. Note, however, that Shane Churla does not have a card in the regular series; this is his only appearance on a 1994-95 Score card. The cards are listed below beginning in the upper left and moving across and down toward the lower right.
COMPLETE SHEET (9) 2.00 5.00
17 Mike McPhee .10 .25
43 Russ Courtnall .10 .25
68 Mark Tinordi .10 .25
94 Paul Cavallini .10 .25
113 Neal Broten .20 .50
148 Derian Hatcher .20 .50
173 Andy Moog .40 1.00
188 Mike Modano .60 1.50
NNO Shane Churla .40 1.00

1995-96 Stars Score Sheet

This perforated sheet was given away at a Dallas Stars game at Reunion Arena and measures approximately 12 1/2" by 10 1/2". The left portion displays nine cards with color action player photos while the right consists of sponsor logos and an advertisement to purchase six packs of Coke products at participating Texaco retailers. The cards are listed below beginning at the upper left of the sheet and moving toward the lower right corner.
COMPLETE SHEET (1) 2.00 5.00
12 Kevin Hatcher .10 .25
38 Todd Harvey .20 .50
64 Andy Moog .40 1.00
89 Greg Adams .20 .50
120 Mike Modano .80 2.00
197 Darcy Wakaluk .20 .50
225 Derian Hatcher .20 .50
229 Joe Nieuwendyk .40 1.00
261 Brent Gilchrist .10 .25

1996-97 Stars Postcards

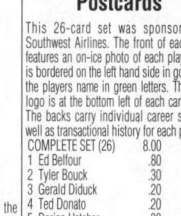

This 27-postcard set was produced by the club for promotional giveaways and autograph signings. The cards feature full color action photos on the front; the backs have biographical information and complete career stats. As the cards are unnumbered, they are listed below alphabetically.
COMPLETE SET 6.00 15.00
1 Greg Adams .20 .50
2 Bob Bassen .20 .50
3 Neal Broten .30 .75
4 Guy Carbonneau .20 .50
5 Bob Gainey .20 .50
6 Brent Gilchrist .20 .50
7 Todd Harvey .30 .75
8 Derian Hatcher .30 .75
9 Ken Hitchcock CO .20 .50
10 Benoit Hogue .20 .50
11 Bill Huard .20 .50
12 Arturs Irbe .30 .75
13 Mike Kennedy .20 .50
14 Mike Lalor .20 .50
15 Jamie Langenbrunner .30 .75
16 Grant Ledyard .20 .50
17 Jere Lehtinen .30 .75
18 Craig Ludwig .20 .50
19 Grant Marshall .20 .50
20 Richard Matvichuk .20 .50
21 Mike Modano 1.00 2.50
22 Joe Nieuwendyk .30 .75
23 Andy Moog .60 1.50
24 Dave Reid .20 .50
25 Darryl Sydor .20 .50
26 Pat Verbeek .30 .75
27 Sergei Zubov .20 .50

1996-97 Stars Score Sheet

For the third straight season, Score and the Stars teamed up to distribute a special, perforated card sheet, this time at a match

against the Edmonton Oilers on Sunday, February 23, as well as at a local card show the weekend following. The majority of the cards mirror those found in the 1996-97 Score set. Of note are the cards of Pat Verbeek and Sergei Zubov, which were updated to show them as members of the Stars; Jere Lehtinen, which features green ink on the back instead of red; and Derian Hatcher, who is not included in the regular Score set. Although it typically is sold in sheet form, it is listed below as singles because the unique cards have led to many dealers breaking it up.
COMPLETE SHEET 2.00 5.00
39 Greg Adams .20 .50
72 Mike Modano .80 2.00
86 Todd Harvey .20 .50
94 Pat Verbeek .20 .50
104 Andy Moog .40 1.00
152 Joe Nieuwendyk .30 .75
171 Sergei Zubov .20 .50
246 Jere Lehtinen .20 .50
NNO Derian Hatcher .20 .50

1999-00 Stars Postcards

This 27-card set pictures the 1999-00 Dallas Stars and was sponsored by Southwest Airlines. Each card measures 4 1/4" by 6 1/4".
COMPLETE SET (27) 8.00 20.00
1 Keith Aldridge .20 .50
2 Ed Belfour .80 2.00
3 Guy Carbonneau .30 .75
4 Shawn Chambers .20 .50
5 Manny Fernandez .30 1.00
6 Aaron Gavey .20 .50
7 Derian Hatcher .30 .75
8 Brett Hull .80 2.00
9 Mike Keane .20 .50
10 Jamie Langenbrunner .30 .75
11 Jere Lehtinen .40 1.00
12 Alan Letang .20 .50
13 Juha Lind .20 .50
14 Warren Luhning .20 .50
15 Brad Lukowich .20 .50
16 Grant Marshall .20 .50
17 Richard Matvichuk .20 .50
18 Mike Modano 1.20 3.00
19 Chris Murray .20 .50
20 Joe Nieuwendyk .40 1.00
21 Pavel Patera .20 .50
22 Derek Plante .20 .50
23 Jamie Pushor .20 .50
24 Brian Skrudland .20 .50
25 Blake Sloan .20 .50
26 Darryl Sydor .20 .50
27 Sergei Zubov .20 .50

2000-01 Stars Postcards

This 26-card set was sponsored by Southwest Airlines. The front of each card features an on-ice photo of each player and is bordered on the left hand side in gold with the players name in green letters. The team logo is at the bottom left of each card front. The backs carry individual career stats as well as transactional history for each player.
COMPLETE SET (26) 8.00 20.00
1 Ed Belfour .80 2.00
2 Tyler Bouck .30 .75
3 Gerald Diduck .20 .50
4 Ted Donato .20 .50
5 Derian Hatcher .30 .75
6 Sami Helenius .20 .50
7 Ken Hitchcock HCO .20 .50
8 Brett Hull .80 2.00
9 Richard Jackman .20 .50
10 Mike Keane .20 .50
11 Jamie Langenbrunner .20 .50
12 Jere Lehtinen .60 1.50
13 Brad Lukowich .20 .50
14 Roman Lyashenko .30 .75
15 Grant Marshall .20 .50
16 Richard Matvichuk .20 .50
17 Mike Modano .80 2.00
18 Brenden Morrow .60 1.50
19 Kirk Muller .20 .50
20 Joe Nieuwendyk .30 .75
21 Jon Sim .20 .50
22 Blake Sloan .20 .50
23 Darryl Sydor .20 .50
24 Marty Turco .80 2.00
25 Shaun Van Allen .20 .50
26 Sergei Zubov .20 .50

2001-02 Stars Postcards

This set features the Dallas Stars. Singles were often handed out at player appearances. Sets could be obtained from the club with a donation to the Stars Foundation charity. The cards measures 4 X 6. The cards are listed in alphabetical order.
COMPLETE SET (26) 8.00 20.00
COMMON CARD (1-26)
1 Ed Belfour .80 2.00
2 Benoit Brunet .20 .50
3 Rob DiMaio .20 .50
4 John Erskine .20 .50
5 Derian Hatcher .31 .78
6 Sami Helenius .31 .78
7 Ken Hitchcock CO .20 .50
8 Benoit Hogue .20 .50
9 Valeri Kamensky .20 .50
10 Niko Kapanen .40 1.00
11 Jamie Langenbrunner .40 1.00
12 Jere Lehtinen .40 1.00
13 Brad Lukowich .20 .50
14 Roman Lyashenko .20 .50
15 Dave Manson .20 .50
16 Richard Matvichuk .20 .50
17 Mike Modano 1.20 3.00
18 Brenden Morrow .40 1.00
19 Kirk Muller .20 .50
20 Joe Nieuwendyk .40 1.00
21 Martin Rucinsky .20 .50
22 Darryl Sydor .20 .50
23 Marty Turco .62 1.56
24 Pierre Turgeon .31 .78
25 Pat Verbeek .20 .50
26 Sergei Zubov .20 .50

2001-02 Stars Team Issue

Little is known about this team issued set, but the cards below are known to exist. Please forward any additional info to hockeymag@beckett.com.
1 Brenden Morrow
2 Derian Hatcher
3 John Erskine
4 Niko Kapanen

2002-03 Stars Postcards

Issued by the team, this 24-card set measured 4" X 8". Card backs carried career stats for each player.
COMPLETE SET (24) 10.00 20.00
1 Scott Pellerin .20 .50
2 Sami Helenius .20 .50
3 John Erskine .40 1.00
4 Stephane Robidas .20 .50
5 Jere Lehtinen .60 1.50
6 Sergei Zubov .20 .50
7 Kirk Muller .20 .50
8 Brenden Morrow .40 1.00
9 Mike Modano 1.25 3.00
10 Richard Matvichuk .20 .50
11 Manny Malhotra .20 .50
12 Derian Hatcher .20 .50
13 Scott Young .20 .50
14 Niko Kapanen .20 .50
15 Bill Guerin .60 1.50
16 Aaron Downey .75 2.00
17 Rob Dimaio .20 .50
18 Pierre Turgeon .30 .75
19 Marty Turco 1.25 3.00
20 Ron Tugnutt .40 1.00
21 Darryl Sydor .20 .50
22 Ulf Dahlen .20 .50
23 Philippe Boucher .20 .50
24 Jason Arnott .30 .75

2003-04 Stars Postcards

These cards were issued by the Stars for use at team events. Complete sets could also be purchased through the team. Although the majority of the cards are in colour, several late-season call-ups were issued in black and white.
COMPLETE SET (31) 10.00 20.00
1 Jason Arnott .20 .50
2 Stu Barnes .20 .50
3 Philippe Boucher .20 .50
4 Trevor Daley .20 .50
5 Rob DiMaio .20 .50
6 Aaron Downey .40 1.00
7 John Erskine .20 .50
8 Steve Gainey .20 .50
9 Bill Guerin .40 1.00
10 Niko Kapanen .30 .75
11 Jon Klemm .20 .50
12 Jere Lehtinen .40 1.00
13 Jeff MacMillan .20 .50
14 Richard Matvichuk .20 .50
15 Antti Miettinen .20 .50
16 Mike Modano .75 2.00
17 Gavin Morgan .20 .50
18 Brenden Morrow .60 1.50

19 Teppo Numminen .20 .50
20 David Oliver .20 .50
21 Steve Ott .75 2.00
22 Blake Sloan .20 .50
23 Mike Smith .40 1.00
24 Don Sweeney .20 .50
25 Mathias Tjarnqvist .20 .50
26 Ron Tugnutt .30 .75
27 Marty Turco .75 2.00
28 Pierre Turgeon .20 .50
29 Rob Valicevic .20 .50
30 Scott Young .20 .50
31 Sergei Zubov .20 .50

2006-07 Stars Team Postcards

Set includes a card of American Idol finalist Celena Rae, who sang the national anthems and was an intermission host for the Stars this season.

COMPLETE SET (28) 15.00 30.00
1 Krys Barch .75 2.00
2 Matthew Barnaby .75 2.00
3 Stu Barnes .40 1.00
4 Philippe Boucher .40 1.00
5 Trevor Daley .40 1.00
6 Loui Eriksson .75 2.00
7 Niklas Hagman .40 1.00
8 Jeff Halpern .40 1.00
9 Jussi Jokinen .40 1.00
10 Jon Klemm .40 1.00
11 Jere Lehtinen .75 2.00
12 Eric Lindros .75 2.00
13 Joel Lundqvist .75 2.00
14 Antti Miettinen .40 1.00
15 Mike Modano 1.25 3.00
16 Brenden Morrow .75 2.00
17 Steve Ott .75 2.00
18 Mike Ribeiro .40 1.00
19 Stephane Robidas .40 1.00
20 Mike Smith .75 2.00
21 Patrik Stefan .40 1.00
22 Darryl Sydor .40 1.00
23 Marty Turco .75 2.00
24 Sergei Zubov .40 1.00
25 Dave Tippett CO .10 .25
26 Celena Rae .40 1.00
27 Brett Hull 1.25 3.00
28 Craig Ludwig .40 1.00

1975-76 Stingers Kahn's

This set of 14 photos was issued on wrappers of Kahn's Wieners and Beef Franks and features players of the Cincinnati Stingers of the WHA. The wrappers are approximately 2 11/16" wide and 11 5/8" long. The wiener wrappers are predominantly yellow and carry a 2" by 1 1/4" black-and-white posed photo of the player with a facsimile autograph inscribed across the picture. The beef frank wrappers are identical in design but predominantly red in color. The wrappers are unnumbered and checklisted below in alphabetical order.

COMPLETE SET (14) 62.50 125.00
1 Serge Aubry 5.00 10.00
2 Bryan Campbell 5.00 10.00
3 Rick Dudley 7.50 15.00
4 Pierre Guite 5.00 10.00
5 John Hughes 5.00 10.00
6 Claude Larose 6.00 12.00
7 Jacques Locas UER 5.00 10.00
(Misspelled Jacque)
8 Bernie MacNeil 5.00 10.00
9 Mike Pelyk 5.00 10.00
10 Ron Plumb 5.00 10.00
11 Dave Smedsmo 5.00 10.00
12 Dennis Sobchuk 5.00 10.00
13 Gene Sobchuk 5.00 10.00
14 Gary Veneruzzo 5.00 10.00

1976-77 Stingers Kahn's

This set of six photos was issued on wrappers of Kahn's Wieners and features players of the Cincinnati Stingers of the WHA. The wrappers are approximately 2 11/16" wide and 11 5/8" long. On a predominantly yellow wrapper with red lettering, a 2" by 1 1/4" black and white player action photo appears, with a facsimile autograph inscribed across the picture. The wrappers are unnumbered and checklisted below in alphabetical order. This set is distinguished from the previous year by the fact that these card photo poses (for the players in both sets) appear to be taken in an action sequence compared to the posed photographs taken the previous year.

COMPLETE SET (6) 62.50 125.00
1 Rick Dudley 15.00 30.00
2 Dave Inkpen 12.50 25.00
3 John Hughes 10.00 20.00
4 Claude Larose 12.50 25.00
5 Jacques Locas 10.00 20.00
6 Ron Plumb 10.00 20.00
7 Dennis Sobchuk 10.00 20.00

1997-98 Studio

The 1997-98 Studio set was issued in one series totaling 110 cards and was distributed in five-card packs with an 8x10 Studio Portrait enclosed. The fronts feature color player portraits, while the backs carry an action player photos and player information.

COMPLETE SET (110) 15.00 30.00
1 Wayne Gretzky 1.00 2.50
2 Dominik Hasek .30 .75
3 Eric Lindros .15 .40
4 Paul Kariya .15 .40
5 Jaromir Jagr .25 .60
6 Brendan Shanahan .15 .40
7 Patrick Roy .75 2.00
8 Keith Tkachuk .15 .40
9 Mark Messier .15 .40
10 Steve Yzerman .75 2.00
11 Brett Hull .20 .50
12 Jarome Iginla .20 .50
13 Mike Modano .25 .60
14 Pavel Bure .15 .40
15 Peter Forsberg .40 1.00
16 Ryan Smyth .10 .30
17 John Vanbiesbrouck .10 .30
18 Teemu Selanne .15 .40
19 Saku Koivu .15 .40
20 Martin Brodeur .40 1.00
21 Sergei Fedorov .25 .60
22 John LeClair .15 .40
23 Joe Sakic .30 .75
24 Jose Theodore 2.00 .50
25 Marc Denis .10 .30
26 Dainius Zubrus .15 .40
27 Bryan Berard .10 .30
28 Ray Bourque .25 .60
29 Curtis Joseph .15 .40
30 Chris Chelios .15 .40
31 Alexei Yashin .02 .10
32 Adam Oates .10 .30
33 Anson Carter .02 .10
34 Jim Campbell .02 .10
35 Jason Arnott .02 .10
36 Derek Plante .02 .10
37 Guy Hebert .10 .30
38 Oleg Tverdovsky .02 .10
39 Ed Jovanovski .10 .30
40 Jeremy Roenick .20 .50
41 Scott Mellanby .10 .30
42 Keith Primeau .02 .10
43 Ron Hextall .02 .10
44 Daren Puppa .10 .30
45 Jim Carey .10 .30
46 Zigmund Palffy .10 .30
47 Jaroslav Svejkovsky .10 .30
48 Daymond Langkow .10 .30
49 Mikael Renberg .10 .30
50 Pat LaFontaine .15 .40
51 Mike Grier .02 .10
52 Stephane Fiset .10 .30
53 Luc Robitaille .10 .30
54 Joe Thornton .40 1.00
55 Joe Nieuwendyk .10 .30
56 Mike Dunham .10 .30
57 Mark Recchi .10 .30
58 Ed Belfour .15 .40
59 Mike Richter .15 .40
60 Peter Bondra .10 .30
61 Trevor Kidd .10 .30
62 Sean Burke .10 .30
63 Nikolai Khabibulin .10 .30
64 Pierre Turgeon .10 .30
65 Dino Ciccarelli .02 .10
66 Felix Potvin .15 .40
67 Mats Sundin .15 .40
68 Joe Juneau .10 .30
69 Mike Vernon .10 .30
70 Adam Deadmarsh .02 .10
71 Damian Rhodes .10 .30
72 Mike Peca .02 .10
73 J-S Giguere .10 .30
74 Ron Francis .10 .30
75 Roman Hamrlik .10 .30
76 Vincent Damphousse .02 .10
77 Jocelyn Thibault .10 .30
78 Claude Lemieux .02 .10
79 Steve Shields RC .25 .60
80 Dimitri Khristich .02 .10
81 Theo Fleury .02 .10
82 Sandis Ozolinsh .02 .10
83 Ethan Moreau .02 .10
84 Geoff Sanderson .10 .30
85 Paul Coffey .15 .40
86 Brian Leetch .15 .40
87 Chris Osgood .10 .30
88 Kirk McLean .10 .30
89 Mike Gartner .10 .30
90 Chris Gratton .10 .30
91 Eric Fichaud .10 .30
92 Alexandre Daigle .02 .10
93 Doug Gilmour .10 .30
94 Daniel Alfredsson .10 .30
95 Doug Weight .10 .30
96 Derian Hatcher .02 .10
97 Wade Redden .02 .10
98 Jeff Friesen .10 .30
99 Tony Amonte .10 .30
100 Janne Niinimaa .10 .30
101 Trevor Linden .10 .30
102 Grant Fuhr .10 .30
103 Chris Phillips .02 .10
104 Sergei Berezin .02 .10
105 Brendan Shanahan CL .10 .30
106 Steve Yzerman CL .15 .40
107 Teemu Selanne CL .15 .40
108 Eric Lindros CL .15 .40
109 Wayne Gretzky CL .15 .40
110 Patrick Roy CL .15 .40
P3 Eric Lindros PROMO 1.00 2.50

1997-98 Studio Press Proofs Silver

Randomly inserted in packs, this 110-card set is parallel to the base set. The difference is found in the silver holographic foil and micro-etched borders. Each card is numbered 1 of 1000.

*STARS: 15X TO 40X BASIC CARDS
*RC's: 10X TO 25X BASIC CARDS

1997-98 Studio Press Proofs Gold

Randomly inserted in packs, this 110-card set is parallel to the regular Studio set. The difference is found in the special gold holographic foil and micro-etched borders. Each card is numbered as 1 of 250.

*STARS: 30X TO 60X BASIC CARDS
*RC's: 15X TO 40X BASIC CARDS

1997-98 Studio Hard Hats

Randomly inserted in packs, this 24-card set displays color portraits of young and veteran stars printed on plastic card stock and featuring a die-cut helmet in the background. The cards are individually numbered to 3000.

COMPLETE SET (24) 75.00 150.00
1 Wayne Gretzky 15.00 40.00
2 Eric Lindros 3.00 8.00
3 Paul Kariya 3.00 8.00
4 Bryan Berard .75 2.00
5 Dainius Zubrus .75 2.00
6 Daymond Langkow .75 2.00
7 Keith Tkachuk 1.50 4.00
8 Ryan Smyth 1.50 4.00
9 Brendan Shanahan 3.00 8.00
10 Steve Yzerman 12.00 30.00
11 Teemu Selanne 3.00 8.00
12 Jarome Iginla 4.00 10.00
13 Zigmund Palffy 1.50 4.00
14 Sergei Berezin .75 2.00
15 Saku Koivu 3.00 8.00
16 Peter Forsberg 8.00 20.00
17 Joe Sakic 6.00 15.00
18 Pavel Bure 3.00 8.00
19 Jaromir Jagr 5.00 12.00
20 Brett Hull 4.00 10.00
21 Sergei Fedorov 4.00 10.00
22 Mike Grier .75 2.00
23 Ethan Moreau .75 2.00
24 Mats Sundin 3.00 8.00

1997-98 Studio Portraits

Inserted one per pack, this 36-card set is a partial parallel 8" by 10" version of the base set and features portraits of the top stars printed on large cards with a signable UV coating.

COMPLETE SET (36) 30.00 60.00
1 Wayne Gretzky 2.00 5.00
2 Dominik Hasek .60 1.50
3 Eric Lindros .30 .75
4 Paul Kariya .30 .75
5 Jaromir Jagr .50 1.25
6 Brendan Shanahan .30 .75
7 Patrick Roy 1.50 4.00
8 Keith Tkachuk .30 .75
9 Mark Messier .30 .75
10 Steve Yzerman 1.50 4.00
11 Brett Hull .40 1.00
12 Jarome Iginla .40 1.00
13 Mike Modano .50 1.25
14 Pavel Bure .30 .75
15 Peter Forsberg .75 2.00
16 Ryan Smyth .25 .60
17 John Vanbiesbrouck .25 .60
18 Teemu Selanne .30 .75
19 Saku Koivu .30 .75
20 Martin Brodeur .75 2.00
21 Sergei Fedorov .50 1.25
22 Joe Thornton .75 2.00
23 Joe Sakic .60 1.50
24 Bryan Berard .25 .60
25 John LeClair .30 .75
26 Marc Denis .25 .60
27 Dainius Zubrus .30 .75
28 Chris Chelios .30 .75
29 Jason Arnott .10 .20
30 Jeremy Roenick .40 1.00
31 Zigmund Palffy .25 .60
32 Jaroslav Svejkovsky .25 .60
33 Mike Richter .30 .75
34 Felix Potvin .30 .75
35 Brian Leetch .30 .75
36 Chris Osgood .25 .60
NNOA Martin Brodeur AU/700 40.00 100.00
NNOB Jarome Iginla AU/1000 15.00 40.00
NNOC Ryan Smyth AU/1000 6.00 15.00

1997-98 Studio Silhouettes

Randomly inserted in packs, this 24-card set features laser die-cutting of star players' facial features. The cards are sequentially numbered to 1,500. An 8"x10" parallel was also created and inserted into packs. These parallels were numbered to 3000.

COMPLETE SET (24) 150.00 300.00
*8x10's: .3X TO .5X BASIC INSERTS
1 Wayne Gretzky 25.00 60.00
2 Eric Lindros 4.00 10.00
3 Patrick Roy 20.00 50.00
4 Martin Brodeur 10.00 25.00
5 Paul Kariya 4.00 10.00
6 Mark Messier 4.00 10.00
7 Dominik Hasek 8.00 20.00
8 Brett Hull 5.00 12.00
9 Pavel Bure 4.00 10.00
10 Steve Yzerman 20.00 50.00
11 Brendan Shanahan 4.00 10.00
12 Joe Sakic 8.00 20.00
13 Peter Forsberg 10.00 25.00
14 Sergei Fedorov 6.00 15.00
15 John LeClair 4.00 10.00
16 John Vanbiesbrouck 3.00 8.00
17 Teemu Selanne 4.00 10.00
18 Keith Tkachuk 4.00 10.00
19 Mike Modano 6.00 15.00
20 Felix Potvin 4.00 10.00
21 Ryan Smyth 3.00 8.00
22 Jaromir Jagr 6.00 15.00
23 Brian Leetch 4.00 10.00
24 Jarome Iginla 5.00 12.00

1995-96 Summit

The 1995-96 Summit set was issued in one series totaling 200 cards. The 7-card packs had a suggested retail of $1.99 each. The set was highlighted by a double thick 24-point card stock. The Cool Trade redemption card was randomly inserted in 1:72 packs, and was redeemable for NHL Cool Trade Upgrade cards of Patrick Roy, Chris Chelios, Ray Bourque and Cam Neely. Rookie Cards include Daniel Alfredsson, Radek Dvorak, Chad Kilger, and Kyle McLaren.

COMPLETE SET (200) 8.00 20.00
1 Mark Messier .10 .30
2 Paul Kariya .10 .30
3 Alexei Zhamnov .05 .15
4 Adam Oates .05 .15
5 Dale Hunter .05 .15
6 Valeri Kamensky .05 .15
7 Pavel Bure .10 .30
8 Theo Fleury .02 .10
9 Mats Sundin .10 .30
10 Joe Murphy .02 .10
11 Brian Bellows .02 .10
12 Owen Nolan .05 .15
13 Brett Hull .15 .40
14 Mike Modano .20 .50
15 Ulf Dahlen .02 .10
16 Paul Coffey .10 .30
17 Jaromir Jagr .20 .50
18 Jason Arnott .02 .10
19 Eric Lindros .10 .30
20 Jesse Belanger .02 .10
21 Alexandre Daigle .02 .10
22 Darren Turcotte .02 .10
23 Brian Leetch .05 .15
24 Wayne Gretzky .75 2.00
25 Mathieu Schneider .02 .10
26 Mark Recchi .05 .15
27 Martin Brodeur .30 .75
28 Igor Korolev .02 .10
29 Jocelyn Thibault .10 .30
30 Chris Pronger .10 .30
31 Sergei Fedorov .15 .40
32 Jari Kurri .10 .30
33 Ray Bourque .20 .50
34 Pat LaFontaine .10 .30
35 Don Beaupre .05 .15
36 Dave Andreychuk .05 .15
37 Oleg Tverdovsky .02 .10
38 Geoff Sanderson .02 .10
39 Chris Chelios .10 .30
40 Phil Housley .05 .15
41 Kevin Hatcher .02 .10
42 Ron Francis .05 .15
43 Pierre Turgeon .05 .15
44 Mikael Renberg .05 .15
45 Chris Gratton .02 .10
46 Tommy Soderstrom .05 .15
47 Stu Barnes .02 .10
48 Alexander Mogilny .05 .15
49 Craig Janney .02 .10
50 Scott Niedermayer .02 .10
51 Jim Carey .05 .15
52 Stephane Richer .05 .15
53 Dave Gagner .02 .10
54 Teemu Selanne .10 .30
55 Kelly Hrudey .05 .15
56 Roman Hamrlik .05 .15
57 Scott Mellanby .02 .10
58 Guy Hebert .05 .15
59 Gary Suter .02 .10
60 Travis Green .05 .15
61 Joe Sakic .25 .60
62 Doug Gilmour .05 .15
63 Peter Bondra .05 .15
64 Vincent Damphousse .02 .10
65 Dino Ciccarelli .05 .15
66 Adam Graves .02 .10
67 Kevin Stevens .02 .10
68 Jeff Friesen .02 .10
69 Kirk McLean .05 .15
70 Brad May .02 .10
71 Bill Ranford .05 .15
72 Derian Hatcher .02 .10
73 Glen Wesley .02 .10
74 Sergei Zubov .02 .10
75 John LeClair .10 .30
76 Igor Larionov .02 .10
77 Ray Sheppard .02 .10
78 Ulf Samuelsson .02 .10
79 Rod Brind'Amour .05 .15
80 Felix Potvin .10 .30
81 Cam Neely .10 .30
82 Jeremy Roenick .15 .40
83 Slava Kozlov .05 .15
84 Arturs Irbe .05 .15
85 Daren Puppa .05 .15
86 Rob Blake .05 .15
87 Steve Heinze .02 .10
88 Tom Barrasso .05 .15
89 Luc Robitaille .05 .15
90 Al MacInnis .05 .15
91 Petr Nedved .05 .15
92 Joe Mullen .05 .15
93 Mark Tinordi .02 .10
94 Tomas Sandstrom .02 .10
95 Dale Hawerchuk .05 .15
96 Andy Moog .10 .30
97 Alexei Kovalev .02 .10
98 David Oliver .02 .10
99 Patrick Poulin .02 .10
100 Tony Granato .02 .10
101 Alexei Yashin .02 .10
102 Trevor Linden .05 .15
103 Rick Tocchet .05 .15
104 Brett Lindros .02 .10
105 Rob Niedermayer .05 .15
106 John MacLean .05 .15
107 Pat Verbeek .05 .15
108 Ray Ferraro .02 .10
109 Mike Ricci .05 .15
110 Doug Weight .05 .15
111 Bill Guerin .05 .15
112 Ken Wregget .05 .15
113 Teppo Numminen .02 .10
114 Mike Vernon .05 .15
115 Mike Richter .10 .30
116 Dan Quinn .02 .10
117 Peter Forsberg .30 .75
118 Mario Lemieux .60 1.50
119 Geoff Courtnall .02 .10
120 Ed Belfour .10 .30
121 Kirk Muller .02 .10
122 Chris Osgood .05 .15
123 Radek Bonk .02 .10
124 Brendan Shanahan .10 .30
125 Sean Burke .05 .15
126 Larry Murphy .05 .15
127 Blaine Lacher .05 .15
128 Russ Courtnall .02 .10
129 Claude Lemieux .05 .15
130 John Vanbiesbrouck .05 .15
131 Wendel Clark .05 .15
132 Nelson Emerson .02 .10
133 Ron Hextall .05 .15
134 Scott Stevens .05 .15
135 Bernie Nicholls .02 .10
136 Brian Skrudland .02 .10
137 Sandis Ozolinsh .05 .15
138 Trevor Kidd .05 .15
139 Joe Juneau .02 .10
140 Keith Primeau .02 .10
141 Petr Klima .02 .10
142 Viktor Kozlov .02 .10
143 Mike Gartner .05 .15
144 Zigmund Palffy .05 .15
145 Steve Duchesne .02 .10
146 Brian Bradley .02 .10
147 Michal Pivonka .02 .10
148 Todd Harvey .05 .15
149 Patrick Roy .60 1.50
150 Gary Roberts .02 .10
151 Shayne Corson .02 .10
152 Keith Tkachuk .10 .30
153 Dimitri Khristich .02 .10
154 Steve Yzerman .60 1.50
155 Shawn McEachern .02 .10
156 Bryan Smolinski .02 .10
157 Vladimir Malakhov .02 .10
158 Andrew Cassels .02 .10
159 Dominik Hasek .25 .60
160 Stephane Fiset .05 .15
161 Steve Thomas .05 .15
162 Joe Nieuwendyk .05 .15
163 Sergio Momesso .02 .10
164 Jyrki Lumme .02 .10
165 Tony Amonte .05 .15
166 Yanic Perreault .02 .10
167 Brian Savage .02 .10
168 Brian Holzinger RC .10 .30
169 Radek Dvorak RC .20 .50
170 Jamie Langenbrunner .02 .10
171 Ed Jovanovski .10 .30
172 Bryan McCabe .02 .10
173 Jere Lehtinen .05 .15
174 Antti Tormanen .02 .10
175 Aki-Petteri Berg RC .05 .15
176 Ryan Smyth .05 .15
177 Shean Donovan .02 .10
178 Darby Hendrickson .02 .10
179 Chad Kilger RC .02 .10
180 Vitali Yachmenev .02 .10
181 Deron Quint .02 .10
182 Daniel Alfredsson RC .25 .60
183 Jeff O'Neill .02 .10
184 Corey Hirsch .05 .15
185 Sandy Moger RC .02 .10
186 Saku Koivu .10 .30
187 Niklas Sundstrom .05 .15
188 Shane Doan RC .30 .75
189 Brendan Witt .02 .10
190 Eric Daze .05 .15
191 Marty Murray .02 .10
192 Byron Dafoe .05 .15
193 Todd Bertuzzi RC .40 1.00
194 Kyle McLaren RC .02 .10
195 Marcus Ragnarsson RC .05 .15
196 Robert Svehla RC .02 .10
197 Valeri Bure .02 .10
198 Paul Coffey .10 .30
199 Checklist (1-198) .02 .10
200 Checklist (inserts) .02 .10
NNO Cool Trade Exchange .05 .10

1995-96 Summit Artist's Proofs

This set is a parallel version of the regular Summit issue. The card fronts use a gold prismatic foil background, while the words "Artist's Proof" are stamped on the back. The cards were randomly inserted 1:36 packs.

*STARS: 20X TO 50X BASIC CARDS
*ROOKIES: 12X TO 30X BASIC CARDS

1995-96 Summit Ice

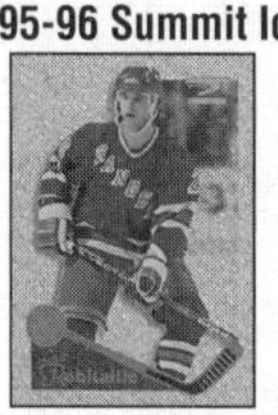

This lower end parallel set of the basic Summit issue features silver prismatic foil print technology on the front, and the words "Summit Ice" on the back. The cards were randomly inserted at a rate of 1:7 packs.

*STARS: 6X TO 12X BASIC CARDS
*RCs: 4X TO 8X BASIC CARDS

1995-96 Summit GM's Choice

Randomly inserted at a rate of 1:37 packs, this 21-card set features Pinnacle consultant Mike McPhee selecting his top choices for an all-star "dream team". The appearance of the cards is boosted by the use of a holographic gold-foil background.

COMPLETE SET (21) 25.00 50.00
1 Patrick Roy 4.00 10.00
2 Martin Brodeur 2.00 5.00
3 Chris Chelios 1.00 2.50
4 Brian Leetch .40 1.00
5 Eric Lindros 1.00 2.50
6 Keith Tkachuk 1.00 2.50
7 Pavel Bure 1.00 2.50
8 Scott Stevens 4.00 1.00
9 Paul Coffey 1.00 2.50
10 Mario Lemieux 4.00 10.00
11 Jaromir Jagr 1.50 4.00
12 Cam Neely 1.00 2.50
13 Ray Bourque 1.00 2.50
14 Al MacInnis .40 1.00
15 Sergei Fedorov 1.00 2.50
16 Mark Messier 1.00 2.50
17 Brett Hull 1.00 2.50
18 Wayne Gretzky 6.00 15.00
19 Paul Kariya 1.00 2.50
20 Brendan Shanahan 1.00 2.50
21 Mike McPhee .20 .50

1995-96 Summit In The Crease

Randomly inserted at a rate of 1:91 packs, this 15-card set showcases some of the hottest goaltenders in the league on cards utilizing Spectroetch technology.

COMPLETE SET (15) 25.00 60.00

1 Martin Brodeur 6.00 15.00
2 Dominik Hasek 4.00 10.00
3 Patrick Roy 10.00 25.00
4 Ed Belfour 2.00 5.00
5 Felix Potvin 2.00 5.00
6 Jim Carey 1.25 3.00
7 Jocelyn Thibault 1.25 3.00
8 Stephane Fiset 1.25 3.00
9 Chris Osgood 2.00 5.00
10 Ron Hextall 2.00 5.00
11 Mike Richter 2.00 5.00
12 Andy Moog 1.25 3.00
13 Sean Burke 1.25 3.00
14 Kirk McLean 1.25 3.00
15 John Vanbiesbrouck 2.00 5.00

1995-96 Summit Mad Hatters

Randomly inserted at a rate of 1:23 packs, this 15-card set pays tribute -- not surprisingly -- to some of the top hat trick artists of the 1994-95 season on Spectroetched cards.

COMPLETE SET (15) 15.00 30.00
1 Eric Lindros 1.50 4.00
Owen Nolan
Bernie Nicholls
2 Brett Hull 2.00 5.00
3 John LeClair .75 2.00
4 Cam Neely 1.50 4.00
5 Alexei Zhamnov .60 1.50
6 Jason Arnott .60 1.50
7 Pavel Bure 1.50 4.00
8 Wendel Clark .75 2.00
9 Sergei Fedorov 2.00 5.00
10 Jaromir Jagr 2.50 6.00
11 Peter Bondra .75 2.00
12 Alexei Yashin .60 1.50
13 Joe Nieuwendyk .75 2.00
14 Luc Robitaille .75 2.00
15 Todd Harvey .60 1.50

1996-97 Summit

This 200-card set was distributed in seven-card packs with a suggested retail price of $2.99. The fronts featured color action player photos while the backs carried player information. A 25-card "Rookies" subset and three checklists were included in this set. Key rookies included Kevin Hodson and Ethan Moreau.

COMPLETE SET (200) 15.00 30.00
1 Joe Sakic .30 .75
2 Dominik Hasek .30 .75
3 Paul Coffey .15 .40
4 Todd Gill .02 .10
5 Pat Verbeek .02 .10
6 John LeClair .15 .40
7 Joe Juneau .02 .10
8 Scott Mellanby .08 .25
9 Scott Stevens .08 .25
10 Ron Francis .08 .25
11 Larry Murphy .08 .25
12 Sandis Ozolinsh .02 .10
13 Luc Robitaille .08 .25
14 Grant Fuhr .08 .25
15 Adam Oates .08 .25
16 Keith Primeau .02 .10
17 Mark Recchi .08 .25
18 Brian Bradley .02 .10
19 Zdeno Ciger .02 .10
20 Zigmund Palffy .08 .25
21 Damian Rhodes .08 .25
22 Russ Courtnall .02 .10
23 Mike Modano .25 .60
24 Geoff Sanderson .08 .25
25 Michal Pivonka .02 .10
26 Randy Burridge .02 .10
27 Dimitri Khristich .02 .10
28 Mike Gartner .08 .25
29 Cam Neely .15 .40
30 Mathieu Schneider .02 .10
31 Steve Thomas .02 .10
32 Mario Lemieux .75 2.00
33 Darryl Sydor .02 .10
34 Alexei Yashin .02 .10
35 Brett Hull .20 .50
36 Trevor Kidd .08 .25
37 Alexei Zhamnov .08 .25
38 Uwe Krupp .02 .10
39 Brian Skrudland .02 .10

40 Igor Larionov .02 .10
41 Nikolai Khabibulin .08 .25
42 Pavel Bure .15 .40
43 Chris Chelios .15 .40
44 Andrew Cassels .02 .10
45 Owen Nolan .08 .25
46 Todd Harvey .02 .10
47 Jari Kurri .08 .25
48 Olaf Kolzig .08 .25
49 Greg Johnson .02 .10
50 Dominic Roussel .08 .25
51 Mats Sundin .15 .40
52 Robert Svehla .02 .10
53 Sandy Moger .02 .10
54 Darren Turcotte .02 .10
55 Teppo Numminen .02 .10
56 Benoit Hogue .02 .10
57 Scott Niedermayer .02 .10
58 Alexander Selivanov .02 .10
59 Valeri Kamensky .08 .25
60 Ken Wregget .08 .25
61 Travis Green .08 .25
62 Peter Bondra .08 .25
63 Vladimir Konstantinov .08 .25
64 Craig Janney .08 .25
65 Joe Nieuwendyk .08 .25
66 John Vanbiesbrouck .08 .25
67 Wayne Gretzky 1.00 2.50
68 Kirk McLean .08 .25
69 Alexei Zhitnik .02 .10
70 Mike Ricci .02 .10
71 Jeff Beukeboom .02 .10
72 Felix Potvin .15 .40
73 Mikael Renberg .08 .25
74 Jamie Baker .02 .10
75 Guy Hebert .08 .25
76 Steve Yzerman .75 2.00
77 Daren Puppa .08 .25
78 Scott Young .02 .10
79 Martin Gelinas .02 .10
80 Dave Gagner .08 .25
81 Tomas Sandstrom .02 .10
82 Alexei Kovalev .02 .10
83 Ray Whitney .02 .10
84 Vyacheslav Kozlov .02 .10
85 Jaromir Jagr .25 .60
86 Joe Murphy .02 .10
87 Patrick Roy .75 2.00
88 Ray Sheppard .08 .25
89 Chris Terreri .08 .25
90 Pierre Turgeon .08 .25
91 Theo Fleury .02 .10
92 Doug Weight .08 .25
93 Tom Barrasso .08 .25
94 Jim Carey .15 .40
95 Greg Adams .02 .10
96 Brian Leetch .15 .40
97 Ed Belfour .15 .40
98 Stephane Fiset .08 .25
99 Stephane Richer .08 .25
100 Ron Hextall .08 .25
101 Mike Vernon .08 .25
102 Jocelyn Thibault .15 .40
103 Jason Arnott .02 .10
104 Keith Tkachuk .15 .40
105 Sergei Fedorov .20 .50
106 Alexandre Daigle .02 .10
107 Alexander Mogilny .08 .25
108 German Titov .02 .10
109 Sean Burke .08 .25
110 Arturs Irbe .08 .25
111 Mark Messier .15 .40
112 Nicklas Lidstrom .15 .40
113 Claude Lemieux .02 .10
114 Martin Brodeur .40 1.00
115 Bernie Nicholls .02 .10
116 Paul Kariya .15 .40
117 Eric Lindros .15 .40
118 Doug Gilmour .08 .25
119 Sergei Zubov .02 .10
120 Adam Graves .02 .10
121 Phil Housley .08 .25
122 Bob Bassen .02 .10
123 Rod Brind'Amour .08 .25
124 Dave Andreychuk .08 .25
125 Corey Hirsch .08 .25
126 Kelly Hrudey .08 .25
127 Pat LaFontaine .15 .40
128 Slava Fetisov .02 .10
129 Oleg Tverdovsky .08 .25
130 Andy Moog .08 .25
131 Stu Barnes .02 .10
132 Roman Hamrlik .08 .25
133 Teemu Selanne .15 .40
134 Trevor Linden .08 .25
135 Chris Osgood .08 .25
136 Vincent Damphousse .02 .10
137 Shayne Corson .02 .10
138 Jeremy Roenick .20 .50
139 Brendan Shanahan .15 .40
140 Wendel Clark .08 .25
141 Ray Bourque .25 .60
142 Peter Forsberg .40 1.00
143 John MacLean .08 .25
144 Jeff Friesen .02 .10
145 Mike Richter .15 .40
146 Dave Reid .02 .10
147 Rob Niedermayer .08 .25
148 Petr Nedved .08 .25
149 Sylvain Lefebvre .02 .10
150 Curtis Joseph .15 .40
151 Eric Daze .08 .25
152 Saku Koivu .15 .40
153 Jere Lehtinen .02 .10
154 Todd Bertuzzi .15 .40
155 Chad Kilger .02 .10
156 Stephane Yelle .02 .10
157 Bryan McCabe .02 .10
158 Aaron Gavey .02 .10
159 Kyle McLaren .02 .10
160 Valeri Bure .02 .10
161 Antti Tormanen .02 .10
162 Brendan Witt .02 .10
163 Ed Jovanovski .08 .25
164 Aki Berg .02 .10
165 Marcus Ragnarsson .02 .10
166 Miroslav Satan .02 .10
167 Daniel Alfredsson .08 .25
168 Jeff O'Neill .02 .10
169 Radek Dvorak .02 .10
170 Petr Sykora .02 .10
171 Vitali Yachmenev .02 .10
172 Niklas Andersson .02 .10
173 Nolan Baumgartner .02 .10
174 Brandon Convery .02 .10
175 Ralph Intranuovo .02 .10
176 Niklas Sundblad .02 .10
177 Patrick Labrecque RC .08 .25
178 Eric Fichaud .08 .25
179 Martin Biron RC .75 2.00
180 Steve Sullivan RC .20 .50
181 Peter Ferraro .02 .10
182 Jose Theodore .20 .50
183 Kevin Hodson RC .15 .40
184 Ethan Moreau RC .15 .40
185 Curtis Brown .02 .10
186 Daymond Langkow .08 .25
187 Jan Caloun RC .02 .10
188 Landon Wilson .02 .10
189 Tommy Salo .08 .25
190 Anders Eriksson .02 .10
191 David Nemirovsky .02 .10
192 Jamie Langenbrunner .02 .10
193 Zdenek Nedved .02 .10
194 Todd Hlushko .02 .10
195 Alexei Yegorov RC .02 .10
196 Jamie Pushor .02 .10
197 Anders Myrvold .02 .10
198 Mark Messier CL .15 .40
199 Brett Hull CL .15 .40
200 Pavel Bure CL .15 .40

1996-97 Summit Artist's Proofs

Randomly inserted in packs at a rate of 1:35, this 200-card parallel set to the regular 1996-97 Summit set was distinguished in design by a holographic foil stamped Artist's Proof logo on the front. Values are listed below for only the most heavily traded singles. Values for all other cards can be determined by using the multipliers listed in the header below against the base set.
*STARS: 30X TO 80X BASIC CARDS
*RCs: 12.5X TO 30X BASIC CARDS

1996-97 Summit Ice

Randomly inserted in packs at the rate of 1:6, this 200-card parallel set featured prismatic foil printing which distinguished it from the regular Summit set. Values for all singles can be determined by using the multipliers below on the corresponding card from the base set.
*STARS: 6X TO 15X BASIC CARDS
*ROOKIES: 2.5X TO 6X BASIC CARDS

1996-97 Summit Metal

*METAL: 2X TO 4X BASIC CARD

1996-97 Summit Premium Stock

A parallel to the standard Summit set, Premium Stock was distributed only to hobby outlets, and featured enhanced card stock with mirrored-foil backgrounds. Many of the Premium Stock cards came damaged out of the packs as the cards were highly condition sensitive.
*STARS: 2X TO 4X BASIC CARDS
*ROOKIES: .75X TO 1.5X BASIC CARDS

1996-97 Summit High Voltage

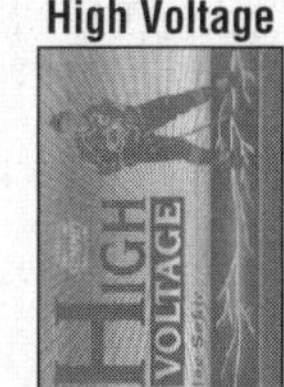

This 16-card Spectroetch insert set spotlighted the high-energy play of the NHL's superstar elite. The fronts featured a color player image on a silver and black lightning displayed background. The backs carried another player photo with player information. Just 1,500 copies of each card in this set were produced and sequentially numbered. A parallel "Mirage" version of these cards was randomly inserted into packs and sequentially numbered to 600.
COMPLETE SET (16) 60.00 150.00
*MIRAGE: .75TO 2X BASIC INSERTS

1 Mark Messier 4.00 10.00
2 Joe Sakic 8.00 20.00
3 Paul Kariya 4.00 10.00
4 Daniel Alfredsson 2.00 5.00
5 Wayne Gretzky 15.00 40.00
6 Peter Forsberg 6.00 15.00
7 Eric Daze 2.00 5.00
8 Mario Lemieux 12.00 30.00
9 Eric Lindros 4.00 10.00
10 Jeremy Roenick 4.00 10.00
11 Alexander Mogilny 2.00 5.00
12 Teemu Selanne 4.00 10.00
13 Sergei Fedorov 4.00 10.00
14 Saku Koivu 4.00 10.00
15 Jaromir Jagr 6.00 15.00
16 Brett Hull 4.00 10.00
P16 Eric Lindros PROMO 2.00 5.00

1996-97 Summit In The Crease

This 16-card insert set featured the NHL's top goalies. A gold-foil stamped print technology was utilized which gave the cards a distinctive feel and look, and created a sense of depth in the cards. 6,000 copies of each of the cards in this set were produced and sequentially numbered. A premium stock parallel was also created. The premium stock version had an enhanced foil background and was numbered with the prefix PSITC.
COMPLETE SET (16) 30.00 80.00
*PREM.STOCK: .75X TO 2X BASIC INSERTS
1 Patrick Roy 10.00 25.00
2 Mike Richter 3.00 8.00
3 Ed Belfour 3.00 8.00
4 Daren Puppa 2.00 5.00
5 Curtis Joseph 3.00 8.00
6 Jim Carey 2.00 5.00
7 Damian Rhodes 2.00 5.00
8 Martin Brodeur 6.00 15.00
9 Felix Potvin 3.00 8.00
10 John Vanbiesbrouck 2.00 5.00
11 Jocelyn Thibault 2.00 5.00
12 Nikolai Khabibulin 2.00 5.00
13 Chris Osgood 2.00 5.00
14 Dominik Hasek 4.00 10.00
15 Corey Hirsch 2.00 5.00
16 Ron Hextall 2.00 5.00

1996-97 Summit Untouchables

This 18-card insert set was an all-foil version of the regular series which honored 12 skaters who amassed 100 or more points and six goaltenders who notched 30 wins during the 1995-96 season. Although the cards were intended to mention this fact, all the goalie cards read 100 points along the bottom front, the same as the skaters. No corrected versions were produced. Just 1,000 copies of this set were produced and each card was sequentially numbered.
COMPLETE SET (18) 75.00 200.00
1 Mario Lemieux 15.00 40.00
2 Jaromir Jagr 6.00 15.00
3 Joe Sakic 8.00 20.00
4 Ron Francis 2.00 5.00
5 Peter Forsberg 6.00 15.00
6 Eric Lindros 3.00 8.00
7 Paul Kariya 3.00 8.00
8 Teemu Selanne 3.00 8.00
9 Alexander Mogilny 2.00 5.00
10 Sergei Fedorov 4.00 10.00
11 Doug Weight 2.00 5.00
12 Wayne Gretzky 20.00 50.00
13 Chris Osgood 2.00 5.00
14 Jim Carey 2.00 5.00
15 Patrick Roy 15.00 40.00
16 Martin Brodeur 10.00 25.00
17 Felix Potvin 3.00 8.00
18 Ron Hextall 3.00 8.00

2006-07 Sunkist

COMPLETE SET (10) 10.00 20.00
1 Alex Kovalev .40 1.00
2 Jason Spezza .75 2.00
3 Mats Sundin 1.25 3.00
4 Jarome Iginla 1.25 3.00
5 Ryan Smyth .75 2.00
6 Markus Naslund .75 2.00
7 Alexander Ovechkin 2.00 5.00
8 Vincent Lecavalier 1.25 3.00
9 Joe Thornton 1.50 4.00
10 Miikka Kiprusoff 1.25 3.00

1910-11 Sweet Caporal Postcards

These black-and-white photo postcards apparently were used by the artists working

on the C55 cards of the next year, 1911-12. Printed by the British American Tobacco Co. in England, these cards were distributed by Imperial Tobacco of Canada. One card was reportedly packed in each 50-cigarette tin of Sweet Caporal cigarettes. The backs show the postcard design. The cards are checklisted below according to teams as follows: Quebec Bulldogs (1-8), Ottawa Senators (10-17), Renfrew Millionaires (18-26), Montreal Wanderers (27-36), and Montreal Canadiens (37-45).
COMPLETE SET (45) 9000.00 18000.00
1 Paddy Moran 250.00 500.00
2 Joe Hall 175.00 350.00
3 Barney Holden 100.00 200.00
4 Joe Malone 500.00 1000.00
5 Ed Oatman 100.00 200.00
6 Tom Dunderdale 175.00 350.00
7 Ken Mallen 100.00 200.00
8 Jack MacDonald 100.00 200.00
9 Fred Lake 100.00 200.00
10 Albert Kerr 100.00 200.00
11 Marty Walsh 175.00 350.00
12 Hamby Shore 100.00 200.00
13 Alex Currie 100.00 200.00
14 Bruce Ridpath 100.00 200.00
15 Bruce Stuart 175.00 350.00
16 Percy Lesueur 175.00 350.00
17 Jack Darragh 175.00 350.00
18 Steve Vair 100.00 200.00
19 Don Smith 100.00 200.00
20 Cyclone Taylor 600.00 1200.00
21 Bert Lindsay 125.00 250.00
22 H.L.(Larry) Gilmour 175.00 350.00
23 Bobby Rowe 100.00 200.00
24 Sprague Cleghorn 300.00 600.00
25 Odie Cleghorn 125.00 250.00
26 Skein Ronan 100.00 200.00
27 Walter Smaill 125.00 250.00
28 Ernest(Moose) Johnson 200.00 400.00
29 Jack Marshall 175.00 350.00
30 Harry Hyland 175.00 350.00
31 Art Ross 600.00 1200.00
32 Riley Hern 175.00 350.00
33 Gordon Roberts 175.00 350.00
34 Frank Glass 100.00 200.00
35 Ernest Russell 200.00 400.00
36 James Gardner 175.00 350.00
37 Art Bernier 100.00 200.00
38 Georges Vezina 2000.00 4000.00
39 G.(Henri) Dallaire 100.00 200.00
40 R.(Rocket) Power 100.00 200.00
41 Didier(Pit) Pitre 175.00 350.00
42 Newsy Lalonde 600.00 1200.00
43 Eugene Payan 100.00 200.00
44 George Poulin 100.00 200.00
45 Jack Laviolette 200.00 400.00

1934-35 Sweet Caporal

This colorful set of 48 large (approximately 6 3/4" by 10 1/2") pictures were actually inserts in Montreal Forum programs during Canadiens and Maroons home games during the 1934-35 season. Apparently a different photo was inserted each game. Players in the checklist below are identified as part of the following teams, Montreal Canadiens (MC), Montreal Maroons (MM), Boston Bruins (BB), Chicago Blackhawks (CBH), Detroit Red Wings (DRW), New York Rangers (NYR), and Toronto Maple Leafs (TML). Card backs contain player biography and an ad for Sweet Caporal Cigarettes, both in French. The cards are unnumbered.
COMPLETE SET (48) 2500.00 5000.00
1 Gerald Carson MC 25.00 50.00
2 Nels Crutchfield MC 25.00 50.00
3 Wilfrid Cude MC 30.00 60.00
4 Roger Jenkins MC 25.00 50.00
5 Aurel Joliat MC 175.00 350.00
6 Joe Lamb MC 25.00 50.00
7 Wildor Larochelle MC 25.00 50.00
8 Pete Lepine MC 25.00 50.00
9 Georges Mantha MC 25.00 50.00
10 Sylvio Mantha MC 50.00 100.00
11 Jack McGill MC 25.00 50.00
12 Armand Mondou MC 25.00 50.00
13 Paul Marcel Raymond MC 25.00 50.00
14 Jack Riley MC 25.00 50.00
15 Russ Blinco MM 25.00 50.00
16 Herb Cain MM 40.00 80.00
17 Lionel Conacher MM 125.00 250.00
18 Alex Connell MM 62.50 125.00
19 Stewart Evans MM 25.00 50.00
20 Norman Gainor MM 25.00 50.00
21 Paul Haynes MM 25.00 50.00
22 Gus Marker MM 25.00 50.00
23 Baldy Northcott MM 30.00 60.00
24 Earl Robinson MM 25.00 50.00
25 Hooley Smith MM 50.00 100.00
26 Dave Trottier MM 25.00 50.00
27 Jimmy Ward MM 25.00 50.00
28 Cy Wentworth MM 30.00 60.00
29 Eddie Shore BB 250.00 500.00
30 Babe Siebert BB 62.50 125.00
31 Nels Stewart BB 75.00 150.00
32 Cecil(Tiny) Thompson BB 75.00 150.00
33 Lorne Chabot CBH 50.00 100.00
34 Harold March CBH 25.00 50.00
35 Howie Morenz CBH 400.00 800.00
36 Larry Aurie DRW 25.00 50.00
37 Ebbie Goodfellow DRW 50.00 100.00
38 Herbie Lewis DRW 25.00 50.00
39 Cooney Weiland DRW 50.00 100.00
40 Bill Cook NYR 50.00 100.00
41 Fred(Bun) Cook NYR 50.00 100.00
42 Ivan(Ching) Johnson NYR 67.50 135.00
43 Dave Kerr NYR 40.00 80.00
44 Frank(King) Clancy TML 200.00 400.00
45 Charlie Conacher TML 200.00 400.00
46 Red Horner TML 62.50 125.00
47 Busher Jackson TML 75.00 150.00
48 Joe Primeau TML 100.00 200.00

1981-82 TCMA

1 Norm Ullman 1.20 3.00
2 Gump Worsley 2.00 5.00
3 J.C. Tremblay .60 1.50
4 Lou Fontinato .60 1.50
5 Johnny Bucyk 1.20 3.00
6 Harry Howell .80 2.00
7 Henri Richard 2.00 5.00
8 Andy Bathgate 1.20 3.00
9 Bobby Orr 10.00 25.00
10 Frank Mahovlich 2.00 5.00
11 Jean Beliveau 4.00 10.00
12 Jacques Plante 4.00 10.00
13 Stan Mikita 2.80 7.00

1935 TCTA

Card measures approximately 3 1/2" x 5 1/2" and is in black and white.
NNO Maple Leaf Arena 25.00 50.00

1974 Team Canada L'Equipe WHA

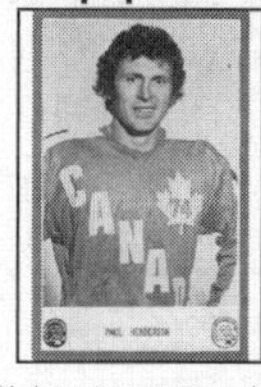

This 24-photo set measures approximately 4 1/8" by 7 1/2" and features posed, glossy, black-and-white player photos on thin stock. The pictures are attached to red poster board. The player's name and two Team Canada L'Equipe logos appear in the white margin at the bottom. The backs are blank. The cards are unnumbered and checklisted below in alphabetical order.
COMPLETE SET (24) 25.00 50.00
1 Ralph Backstrom 1.00 2.00
2 Serge Bernier .75 1.50
3 Gerry Cheevers 5.00 10.00
4 Al Hamilton 1.00 2.00
5 Billy Harris CO .50 1.00
6 Jim Harrison .75 1.50
7 Ben Hatskin OWN .75 1.50
8 Paul Henderson 2.00 4.00
9 Rejean Houle 1.00 2.00
10 Mark Howe 4.00 8.00
11 Marty Howe 1.00 2.00
12 Bill Hunter .50 1.00
13 Gordon W. Juckes .50 1.00
14 Rick Ley 1.00 2.00
15 Frank Mahovlich 4.00 8.00
16 John McKenzie 1.00 2.00
17 Don McLeod .75 1.50
18 Rick Noonan .75 1.50
19 Brad Selwood .75 1.50
20 Rick Smith .75 1.50
21 Pat Stapleton 1.00 2.00
22 Marc Tardif 1.00 2.00
23 Mike Walton 1.00 2.00
24 Tom Webster 1.00 2.00

1996-97 Team Out

The 1996-97 Team Out set was issued in one series totaling 89 cards. The cards were intended for use in a game, which is explained in the instructions included with the set. While the game itself never quite took off, the cards were quite popular with superstar and team collectors, which led to a fairly wide break of the product.
COMPLETE SET (89) 10.00 25.00
1 Paul Kariya .60 1.50
2 Luc Robitaille .10 .25
3 John LeClair .20 .50
4 Theo Fleury .20 .50
5 Scott Mellanby .10 .25
6 Adam Graves .10 .25
7 Esa Tikkanen .04 .10
8 Slava Kozlov .10 .25
9 Eric Daze .10 .25
10 Ryan Smyth .10 .25
11 Shayne Corson .10 .25
12 Kevin Stevens .10 .25
13 Murray Craven .04 .10
14 Keith Tkachuk .20 .50
15 Zigmund Palffy .20 .50
16 Eric Lindros .40 1.00
17 Mario Lemieux 1.00 2.50
18 Joe Sakic .40 1.00
19 Wayne Gretzky 1.20 3.00
20 Mark Messier .20 .50
21 Sergei Fedorov .40 1.00
22 Jason Arnott .10 .25
23 Chris Gratton .10 .25
24 Pierre Turgeon .10 .25
25 Mike Modano .20 .50
26 Saku Koivu .20 .50
27 Alexei Yashin .10 .25
28 Steve Yzerman .80 2.00
29 Peter Forsberg .40 1.00
30 Adam Oates .20 .50
31 Brett Hull .20 .50
32 Jaromir Jagr .40 1.00
33 Pavel Bure .40 1.00
34 Teemu Selanne .30 .75
35 Stephane Richer .04 .10
36 Mike Gartner .10 .25
37 Claude Lemieux .10 .25
38 Rick Tocchet .10 .25
39 Alexander Mogilny .10 .25
40 Peter Bondra .10 .25
41 Mats Sundin .10 .25
42 Daniel Alfredsson .10 .25
43 Owen Nolan .04 .10
44 Joe Juneau .10 .25
45 Mikael Renberg .10 .25
46 Chris Chelios .20 .50
47 Ray Bourque .30 .75
48 Scott Stevens .10 .25
49 Paul Coffey .20 .50
50 Glen Wesley .04 .10
51 Nicklas Lidstrom .20 .50
52 Scott Niedermayer .10 .25
53 Larry Murphy .04 .10
54 Sandis Ozolinsh .10 .25
55 Vladimir Malakhov .04 .10
56 Robert Svehla .04 .10
57 Steve Duchesne .04 .10
58 Sergei Gonchar .04 .10
59 Darius Kasparaitis .10 .25
60 Patrick Roy 1.00 2.50
61 Martin Brodeur .40 1.00
62 Mike Richter .20 .50
63 John Vanbiesbrouck .20 .50
64 Ron Hextall .10 .25
65 Nikolai Khabibulin .10 .25
66 Grant Fuhr .10 .25
67 Kirk McLean .10 .25
68 Jim Carey .20 .50
69 Dominik Hasek .30 .75
70 Ed Belfour .20 .50
71 Chris Osgood .20 .50
72 Guy Hebert .10 .25
73 Trevor Kidd .10 .25
74 Felix Potvin .20 .50
75 Roman Hamrlik .10 .25
76 Alexei Zhitnik .10 .25
77 Al MacInnis .04 .10
78 Brian Leetch .20 .50
79 Rob Blake .10 .25
80 Derian Hatcher .04 .10
81 Mathieu Schneider .04 .10
82 Gary Suter .04 .10
83 Jeff Brown .04 .10
84 Jyrki Lumme .04 .10
85 Ed Jovanovski .10 .25
86 Eric Desjardins .10 .25
87 Stephane Quintal .04 .10
88 Marcus Ragnarsson .04 .10
89 Zarley Zalapski .04 .10

2005-06 The Cup

1-100 PRINT RUN 249 SER. #'d SETS
PATCH AU PRINT RUN SER. 199 #'d SETS
AU RC PRINT RUN SER. 249 #'d SETS
1 Jean-Sebastien Giguere 4.00 10.00
2 Teemu Selanne 8.00 20.00
3 Ilya Kovalchuk 10.00 25.00
4 Marian Hossa 6.00 15.00
5 Kari Lehtonen 6.00 15.00
6 Cam Neely 8.00 20.00
7 Patrice Bergeron 6.00 15.00
8 Ray Bourque 8.00 20.00
9 Johnny Bucyk 6.00 15.00
10 Phil Esposito 5.00 12.00
11 Don Cherry 8.00 20.00
12 Brian Leetch 8.00 20.00
13 Gerry Cheevers 5.00 12.00
14 Gilbert Perreault 5.00 12.00
15 Chris Drury 4.00 10.00
16 Ryan Miller 8.00 20.00
17 Jarome Iginla 10.00 25.00
18 Lanny McDonald 4.00 10.00
19 Miikka Kiprusoff 12.00 30.00
20 Joe Mullen 4.00 10.00
21 Eric Staal 12.50 30.00
22 Doug Weight 4.00 10.00
23 Martin Gerber 4.00 10.00
24 Nikolai Khabibulin 8.00 20.00
25 Denis Savard 8.00 20.00
26 Bobby Hull 8.00 20.00
27 Tony Esposito 6.00 15.00
28 Joe Sakic 15.00 40.00
29 Alex Tanguay 6.00 15.00
30 Milan Hejduk 6.00 15.00
31 Jose Theodore 8.00 20.00
32 Marek Svatos 8.00 20.00
33 Rick Nash 12.00 30.00
34 Sergei Fedorov 8.00 20.00
35 Mike Modano 8.00 20.00
36 Marty Turco 8.00 20.00
37 Brenden Morrow 6.00 15.00
38 Steve Yzerman 20.00 50.00
39 Gordie Howe 15.00 40.00
40 Brendan Shanahan 6.00 15.00
41 Scotty Bowman 4.00 10.00
42 Pavel Datsyuk 6.00 15.00
43 Henrik Zetterberg 6.00 15.00
44 Chris Pronger 4.00 10.00
45 Wayne Gretzky 50.00 100.00
46 Grant Fuhr 8.00 20.00
47 Roberto Luongo 10.00 25.00
48 Olli Jokinen 4.00 10.00
49 Jeremy Roenick 6.00 15.00
50 Luc Robitaille 10.00 25.00
51 Rogie Vachon 4.00 10.00
52 Marian Gaborik 10.00 25.00
53 Saku Koivu 5.00 12.00
54 Jean Beliveau 10.00 25.00
55 Steve Shutt 5.00 12.00
56 Patrick Roy 20.00 50.00
57 Guy Lafleur 8.00 20.00
58 Guy Lapointe 4.00 10.00
59 Michael Ryder 8.00 20.00
60 Tomas Vokoun 10.00 25.00
61 Paul Kariya 6.00 15.00
62 Martin Brodeur 15.00 40.00
63 Patrik Elias 4.00 10.00
64 Alexei Yashin 6.00 15.00
65 Mike Bossy 5.00 12.00
66 Denis Potvin 4.00 10.00
67 Bryan Trottier 8.00 20.00
68 Clark Gillies 8.00 20.00
69 Jaromir Jagr 15.00 40.00
70 Dominik Hasek 15.00 40.00
71 Dany Heatley 12.00 30.00
72 Jason Spezza 10.00 25.00
73 Daniel Alfredsson 6.00 15.00
74 Peter Forsberg 15.00 40.00
75 Ron Hextall 4.00 10.00
76 Simon Gagne 5.00 12.00
77 Bobby Clarke 5.00 12.00
78 Keith Primeau 4.00 10.00
79 Bernie Parent 6.00 15.00
80 Shane Doan 4.00 10.00
81 Curtis Joseph 8.00 20.00
82 Mario Lemieux 20.00 50.00
83 Marc-Andre Fleury 12.00 30.00
84 Jonathan Cheechoo 10.00 25.00
85 Evgeni Nabokov 6.00 15.00
86 Joe Thornton 12.00 30.00
87 Patrick Marleau 5.00 12.00
88 Keith Tkachuk 5.00 12.00
89 Martin St. Louis 5.00 12.00
90 Vincent Lecavalier 6.00 15.00
91 Brad Richards 8.00 20.00
92 Ed Belfour 6.00 15.00
93 Darryl Sittler 6.00 15.00
94 Mats Sundin 10.00 25.00
95 Eric Lindros 8.00 20.00
96 Doug Gilmour 5.00 12.00
97 Markus Naslund 6.00 15.00
98 Todd Bertuzzi 6.00 15.00
99 Ed Jovanovski 4.00 10.00
100 Olaf Kolzig 6.00 15.00
101 Ryan Getzlaf JSY AU RC 150.00350.00
102 Ryan Whitney JSY AU RC 60.00100.00
103 R.J. Umberger JSY AU RC 40.00100.00
104 Cam Ward JSY AU RC 75.00 250.00
105 Brent Seabrook JSY AU RC 40.00 100.00
106 Eric Nystrom JSY AU RC 40.00 100.00
107 Gilbert Brule JSY AU RC 125.00350.00
108 Hannu Toivonen JSY AU RC 60.00 150.00
109 Robert Nilsson JSY AU RC 50.00 125.00
110 Rostislav Olesz JSY AU RC 75.00 200.00
111 Ryan Suter JSY AU RC 40.00 100.00
112 Jussi Jokinen JSY AU RC 100.00 200.00
113 Zach Parise JSY AU RC 150.00 350.00
114 Wojtek Wolski JSY AU RC 100.00 300.00
115 Andrej Meszaros JSY AU RC 50.00 150.00
116 Johan Franzen JSY AU RC 40.00125.00
117 Peter Budaj JSY AU RC 75.00 175.00
118 David Leneveu JSY AU RC 40.00 100.00
119 Andrew Alberts JSY AU RC 25.0060.00
120 Steve Bernier JSY AU RC 100.00250.00
121 Mikko Koivu JSY AU RC 75.00 200.00
122 Chris Campoli JSY AU RC 30.0080.00
123 Evgeny Artyukhin JSY AU RC 30.00 80.00
124 Christoph Schubert JSY AU RC 30.00 80.00
125 Tomas Fleischmann JSY AU RC 40.00 80.00
126 Maxime Talbot JSY AU RC 50.00 125.00
127 Jordan Sigalet JSY AU RC 40.00100.00
128 Danny Richmond JSY AU RC 30.00 100.00
129 Maxim Lapierre JSY AU RC 50.00 125.00
130 Dimitri Patzold JSY AU RC 40.0080.00
131 Rene Bourque JSY AU RC 40.00100.00
132 Yann Danis JSY AU RC 30.00 80.00
133 Brad Winchester JSY AU RC 40.00 100.00
134 Jim Slater JSY AU RC 40.00 100.00
135 Petr Prucha JSY AU RC 75.00 175.00
136 Jim Howard JSY AU RC 75.00 175.00
137 Patrick Eaves JSY AU RC 60.00150.00
138 Ryane Clowe JSY AU RC 50.00 100.00
139 Braydon Coburn JSY AU RC 30.00 80.00
140 Brad Richardson JSY AU RC 40.00 80.00
141 Milan Jurcina JSY AU RC 30.00 80.00
142 Jeff Woywitka JSY AU RC 25.00 60.00
143 Andrei Kostitsyn JSY AU RC 100.00 200.00
144 Derek Boogaard AU RC 12.00 30.00
145 Barry Tallackson JSY AU RC 30.00 80.00
146 Jakub Klepis JSY AU RC 30.00 80.00
147 Alvaro Montoya JSY AU RC 50.00 150.00
148 Andrew Ladd JSY AU RC 50.00 150.00
149 Brandon Bochenski JSY AU RC 40.00 100.00
150 Jeff Tambellini JSY AU RC 40.0080.00
151 Jaroslav Balastik JSY AU RC 40.00 100.00
152 Lee Stempniak JSY AU RC 50.00 125.00
153 Kevin Dallman JSY AU RC 25.0060.00
154 Niklas Nordgren JSY AU RC 25.00 60.00
155 Kevin Nastiuk JSY AU RC 30.00 80.00

156 Ryan Craig JSY AU RC 60.00 150.00
157 Erik Christensen JSY AU RC 75.00 200.00
158 Chris Thorburn JSY AU RC 25.00 60.00
159 Josh Gorges JSY AU RC 30.00 80.00
160 Matt Foy JSY AU RC 25.00 60.00
161 O.Tollefsen JSY AU RC 25.00 60.00
162 Kevin Bieksa JSY AU RC 50.00 125.00
163 Kyle Quincey JSY AU RC 40.00 100.00
164 A.Wozniewski JSY AU RC 30.00 80.00
165 Jeff Hoggan JSY AU RC 25.00 60.00
166 Jeremy Colliton JSY AU RC 25.00 60.00
167 Alexandre Picard JSY AU RC 50.00 125.00
168 Ben Eager JSY AU RC 25.00 60.00
169 Daniel Paille JSY AU RC 40.00 100.00
170 Valtteri Filppula JSY AU RC 75.00 150.00
171 A.Perezhogin JSY AU RC 60.00 100.00
172 Mike Richards JSY AU RC 60.00 150.00
173 Corey Perry JSY AU RC 125.00 350.00
174 Alexander Steen JSY AU RC 75.00 225.00
175 Thomas Vanek JSY AU RC 300.00 600.00
176 Jeff Carter JSY AU RC 75.00 250.00
177 Henrik Lundqvist JSY AU RC 200.00 500.00
178 Dion Phaneuf JSY AU/99 RC 500.00 1500.00
179 A.Ovechkin JSY AU/99 RC 1500.00 3500.00
180 Sidney Crosby JSY AU/99 RC 5000.00 10000.00
181 Brett Lebda AU RC 15.00 30.00
182 Jay McClement AU RC 15.00 40.00
183 Cam Barker JSY AU RC 50.00 100.00
184 P.Nokelainen AU RC 10.00 25.00
185 Keith Ballard AU RC 10.00 25.00
186 Duncan Keith AU RC 20.00 40.00
187 George Parros AU RC 15.00 40.00
188 Adam Berkhoel AU RC 15.00 30.00
189 Anthony Stewart AU RC 12.00 30.00
190 Ryan Hollweg AU RC 12.00 30.00
191 Ben Walter AU RC 10.00 25.00

2005-06 The Cup Gold

*1-100 GOLD: 1X TO 2.5X BASE HI
PRINT RUN 25 SER. #'d SETS
2 Teemu Selanne 20.00 50.00
3 Ilya Kovalchuk 25.00 60.00
8 Ray Bourque 25.00 50.00
10 Phil Esposito 20.00 50.00
16 Ryan Miller 20.00 50.00
17 Jarome Iginla 25.00 60.00
19 Miikka Kiprusoff 20.00 50.00
26 Bobby Hull 20.00 50.00
28 Joe Sakic 25.00 60.00
35 Mike Modano 20.00 50.00
38 Steve Yzerman 40.00 100.00
39 Gordie Howe 25.00 60.00
45 Wayne Gretzky 300.00 450.00
50 Luc Robitaille 20.00 50.00
52 Marian Gaborik 20.00 50.00
56 Patrick Roy 60.00 150.00
57 Guy Lafleur 25.00 60.00
62 Martin Brodeur 30.00 80.00
69 Jaromir Jagr 25.00 60.00
70 Dominik Hasek 25.00 60.00
71 Dany Heatley 25.00 60.00
72 Jason Spezza 20.00 50.00
74 Peter Forsberg 25.00 60.00
75 Ron Hextall 20.00 50.00
77 Bobby Clarke 20.00 50.00
82 Mario Lemieux 60.00 150.00
83 Marc-Andre Fleury 20.00 50.00
84 Jonathan Cheechoo 20.00 50.00
86 Joe Thornton 25.00 60.00
90 Vincent Lecavalier 20.00 50.00

2005-06 The Cup Autographed Rookie Patches Gold Rainbow

#'d TO PLAYER'S JERSEY NUMBER
LOW PRINT RUNS NOT PRICED DUE TO SCARCITY
UNIQUE SWATCHES MAY EARN SUBSTANTIAL PREMIUM
101 Ryan Getzlaf/51 150.00 350.00
102 Ryan Whitney/19
103 R.J. Umberger/20 75.00 150.00
104 Cam Ward/30 150.00 350.00
105 Brent Seabrook/7
106 Eric Nystrom/23 100.00 250.00
107 Gilbert Brule/17 200.00 350.00
108 Hannu Toivonen/33 100.00 250.00
109 Robert Nilsson/21 125.00 200.00
110 Rostislav Olesz/85 40.00 100.00
111 Ryan Suter/20 60.00 150.00
112 Jussi Jokinen/36 EXCH 75.00 200.00
113 Zach Parise/9
114 Wojtek Wolski/8
115 Andrej Meszaros/14
116 Johan Franzen/39 50.00 100.00
117 Peter Budaj/31 125.00 250.00
118 David Leneveu/30 60.00 150.00
119 Andrew Alberts/41 40.00 100.00
120 Steve Bernier/26 200.00 400.00
121 Mikko Koivu/21 100.00 250.00
123 Evgeny Artyukhin/76 30.00 60.00
124 Christoph Schubert/5
125 Tomas Fleischmann/43 60.00 125.00
126 Maxime Talbot/25 50.00 100.00
127 Jordan Sigalet/57 50.00 100.00
128 Danny Richmond/51 30.00 60.00
129 Maxim Lapierre/40 30.00 60.00
130 Dimitri Patzold/30 40.00 80.00
131 Rene Bourque/14
132 Yann Danis/75 40.00 100.00
133 Brad Winchester/26 40.00 100.00
134 Jim Slater/23 30.00 80.00
135 Petr Prucha/25 100.00 200.00
136 Jim Howard/35 90.00 150.00
137 Patrick Eaves/44 75.00 200.00
138 Ryane Clowe/29 75.00 150.00
139 Braydon Coburn/4
140 Brad Richardson/12
141 Milan Jurcina/68 30.00 60.00
142 Jeff Woywitka/29 30.00 60.00
143 Andrei Kostitsyn/46 75.00 200.00
145 Barry Tallackson/27 40.00 80.00
146 Jakub Klepis/38 50.00 125.00
147 Alvaro Montoya/29 100.00 200.00
148 Andrew Ladd/16
149 Brandon Bochenski/10
151 Jaroslav Balastik/40
152 Lee Stempniak/12
153 Kevin Dallman/38 30.00 60.00
154 Niklas Nordgren/44 30.00 60.00
155 Kevin Nastiuk/35 40.00 80.00
156 Ryan Craig/34 40.00 100.00
157 Erik Christensen/16
159 Josh Gorges/6
160 Matt Foy/83 30.00 60.00
161 Ole-Kristian Tollefsen/55 30.00 60.00
162 Kevin Bieksa/25 60.00 150.00
164 Andrew Wozniewski/56 30.00 60.00
165 Jeff Hoggan/22 40.00 100.00
166 Jeremy Colliton/27 40.00 80.00
167 Alexandre Picard/19 30.00 60.00
168 Ben Eager/55 30.00 60.00
169 Daniel Paille/20 75.00 150.00
171 Alexander Perezhogin/42 50.00 100.00
172 Mike Richards/18
173 Corey Perry/61 100.00 250.00
174 Alexander Steen/10
175 Thomas Vanek/26 300.00 600.00
176 Jeff Carter/17 150.00 300.00
177 Henrik Lundqvist/30 250.00 500.00
178 Dion Phaneuf/3
179 Alexander Ovechkin/8
180 Sidney Crosby/87 2500.00 4000.00
183 Cam Barker/25 60.00 150.00

2005-06 The Cup Black Rainbow

PRINT RUN 1 SER. #'d SET
NOT PRICED DUE TO SCARCITY
1 Jean-Sebastien Giguere
2 Teemu Selanne
3 Ilya Kovalchuk
4 Marian Hossa
5 Kari Lehtonen
6 Cam Neely
7 Patrice Bergeron
8 Ray Bourque
9 Johnny Bucyk
10 Phil Esposito
11 Don Cherry
12 Brian Leetch
13 Gerry Cheevers
14 Gilbert Perreault
15 Chris Drury
16 Ryan Miller
17 Jarome Iginla
18 Lanny McDonald
19 Miikka Kiprusoff
20 Joe Mullen
21 Eric Staal
22 Doug Weight
23 Martin Gerber
24 Nikolai Khabibulin
25 Denis Savard
26 Bobby Hull
27 Tony Esposito
28 Joe Sakic
29 Alex Tanguay
30 Milan Hejduk
31 Jose Theodore
32 Marek Svatos
33 Rick Nash
34 Sergei Fedorov
35 Mike Modano
36 Marty Turco
37 Brenden Morrow
38 Steve Yzerman
39 Gordie Howe
40 Brendan Shanahan
41 Scotty Bowman
42 Pavel Datsyuk
43 Henrik Zetterberg
44 Chris Pronger
45 Wayne Gretzky
46 Grant Fuhr
47 Roberto Luongo
48 Olli Jokinen
49 Jeremy Roenick
50 Luc Robitaille
51 Rogie Vachon
52 Marian Gaborik
53 Saku Koivu
54 Jean Beliveau
55 Steve Shutt
56 Patrick Roy
57 Guy Lafleur
58 Guy Lapointe
59 Michael Ryder
60 Tomas Vokoun
61 Paul Kariya
62 Martin Brodeur
63 Patrik Elias
64 Alexei Yashin
65 Mike Bossy
66 Denis Potvin
67 Bryan Trottier
68 Clark Gillies
69 Jaromir Jagr
70 Dominik Hasek
71 Dany Heatley
72 Jason Spezza
73 Daniel Alfredsson
74 Peter Forsberg
75 Ron Hextall
76 Simon Gagne
77 Bobby Clarke
78 Keith Primeau
79 Bernie Parent
80 Shane Doan
81 Curtis Joseph
82 Mario Lemieux
83 Marc-Andre Fleury
84 Jonathan Cheechoo
85 Evgeni Nabokov
86 Joe Thornton
87 Patrick Marleau
88 Keith Tkachuk
89 Martin St. Louis
90 Vincent Lecavalier
91 Brad Richards
92 Ed Belfour
93 Darryl Sittler
94 Mats Sundin
95 Eric Lindros
96 Doug Gilmour
97 Markus Naslund
98 Todd Bertuzzi
99 Ed Jovanovski
100 Olaf Kolzig

2005-06 The Cup Black Rainbow Rookies

PRINT RUN 1 SER. #'d SET
NOT PRICED DUE TO SCARCITY
101 Ryan Getzlaf
102 Ryan Whitney
103 R.J. Umberger
104 Cam Ward
105 Brent Seabrook
106 Eric Nystrom
107 Gilbert Brule
108 Hannu Toivonen
109 Robert Nilsson
110 Rostislav Olesz
111 Ryan Suter
112 Jussi Jokinen
113 Zach Parise
114 Wojtek Wolski
115 Andrej Meszaros
116 Johan Franzen
117 Peter Budaj
118 David Leneveu
119 Andrew Alberts
120 Steve Bernier
121 Mikko Koivu
122 Chris Campoli
123 Evgeny Artyukhin
124 Christoph Schubert
125 Tomas Fleischmann
126 Maxime Talbot
127 Jordan Sigalet
128 Danny Richmond
129 Maxim Lapierre
130 Dimitri Patzold
131 Rene Bourque
132 Yann Danis
133 Brad Winchester
134 Jim Slater
135 Petr Prucha
136 Jim Howard
137 Patrick Eaves
138 Ryane Clowe
139 Braydon Coburn
140 Brad Richardson
141 Milan Jurcina
142 Jeff Woywitka
143 Andrei Kostitsyn
144 Derek Boogaard
145 Barry Tallackson
146 Jakub Klepis
147 Alvaro Montoya
148 Andrew Ladd
149 Brandon Bochenski
150 Jeff Tambellini
151 Jaroslav Balastik
152 Lee Stempniak
153 Kevin Dallman
154 Niklas Nordgren
155 Kevin Nastiuk
156 Ryan Craig
157 Erik Christensen
158 Chris Thorburn
159 Josh Gorges
160 Matt Foy
161 Ole-Kristian Tollefsen
162 Kevin Bieksa
163 Kyle Quincey
164 Andrew Wozniewski
165 Jeff Hoggan
166 Jeremy Colliton
167 Alexandre Picard
168 Ben Eager
169 Daniel Paille
170 Valtteri Filppula
171 Alexander Perezhogin
172 Mike Richards
173 Corey Perry
174 Alexander Steen
175 Thomas Vanek
176 Jeff Carter
177 Henrik Lundqvist
178 Dion Phaneuf
179 Alexander Ovechkin
180 Sidney Crosby
181 Brett Lebda
182 Jay McClement
183 Cam Barker
184 Petteri Nokelainen
185 Keith Ballard
186 Duncan Keith
187 George Parros
188 Adam Berkhoel
189 Anthony Stewart
190 Ryan Hollweg
191 Ben Walter

2005-06 The Cup Dual NHL Shields

PRINT RUN 1 SER. #'d SET
NOT PRICED DUE TO SCARCITY
DSAM Alexei Yashin
Miroslav Satan
DSBE Martin Brodeur
Patrik Elias
DSBG Martin Brodeur
Scott Gomez
DSBS Patrice Bergeron
Sergei Samsonov
DSCO Sidney Crosby
Alexander Ovechkin
DSDZ Pavel Datsyuk
Henrik Zetterberg
DSFG Peter Forsberg
Simon Gagne
DSGK Marian Gaborik
Mikko Koivu
DSGL Wayne Gretzky
Mario Lemieux
DSGS Jean-Sebastien Giguere
Teemu Selanne
DSHA Martin Havlat
Daniel Alfredsson
DSHB Marian Hossa
Peter Bondra
DSHS Dany Heatley
Jason Spezza
DSIK Jarome Iginla
Miikka Kiprusoff
DSIL Jarome Iginla
Martin St. Louis
DSIN Jarome Iginla
Rick Nash
DSJC Joffrey Lupul
Corey Perry
DSJD Curtis Joseph
Shane Doan
DSJL Jaromir Jagr
Henrik Lundqvist
DSJM Jeff Carter
Mike Richards
DSKD Ilya Kovalchuk
Pavel Datsyuk
DSKG Keith Primeau
Simon Gagne
DSKJ Miikka Kiprusoff
Olli Jokinen
DSKO Ilya Kovalchuk
Alexander Ovechkin
DSKS Paul Kariya
Teemu Selanne
DSKT Saku Koivu
Jose Theodore
DSKV Paul Kariya
Tomas Vokoun
DSLB Roberto Luongo
Jay Bouwmeester
DSLC Mario Lemieux
Sidney Crosby
DSLJ Mario Lemieux
Jaromir Jagr
DSMA Mats Sundin
Alexander Steen
DSMB Glen Murray
Patrice Bergeron
DSME Mats Sundin
Eric Lindros
DSMG Mike Modano
Bill Guerin
DSMN Brendan Morrison
Markus Naslund
DSMT Mike Modano
Marty Turco
DSNB Markus Naslund
Todd Bertuzzi
DSNZ Markus Naslund
Henrik Zetterberg
DSPC Chris Pronger
Ty Conklin
DSPK Alexander Perezhogin
Saku Koivu
DSPM Peter Forsberg
Mats Sundin
DSRD Luc Robitaille
Pavol Demitra
DSRM Ryan Smyth
Michael Peca
DSRO Roberto Luongo
Olli Jokinen
DSRR Mike Ribeiro
Michael Ryder
DSRT Andrew Raycroft
Hannu Toivonen
DSSA Mats Sundin
Daniel Alfredsson
DSSB Mats Sundin
Ed Belfour
DSSF Joe Sakic
Peter Forsberg
DSST Joe Sakic
Alex Tanguay
DSWT Doug Weight
Keith Tkachuk
DSYP Alexei Yashin
Mark Parrish

2005-06 The Cup Dual NHL Shields Autographs

PRINT RUN 1 SER. #'d SET
NOT PRICED DUE TO SCARCITY
ADSAM Alexei Yashin
Miroslav Satan
ADSAR Ales Hemsky
Ryan Smyth
ADSBL Ray Bourque
Brian Leetch
ADSGK Marian Gaborik
Mikko Koivu
ADSJM Jeff Carter
Mike Richards
ADSKG Keith Primeau
Simon Gagne
ADSKH Ilya Kovalchuk
Marian Hossa
ADSKJ Miikka Kiprusoff
Olli Jokinen
ADSKO Ilya Kovalchuk
Alexander Ovechkin
ADSKT Saku Koivu
Jose Theodore
ADSLA Jeremy Roenick
Luc Robitaille
ADSLK Kari Lehtonen
Ilya Kovalchuk
ADSLL Martin St. Louis
Vincent Lecavalier
ADSLP Henrik Lundqvist
Petr Prucha
ADSMB Glen Murray
Patrice Bergeron
ADSMT Mike Modano
Marty Turco
ADSNB Markus Naslund
Todd Bertuzzi
ADSNZ Markus Naslund
Henrik Zetterberg
ADSPB Chris Pronger
Rob Blake
ADSPC Chris Pronger
Ty Conklin
ADSPK Alexander Perezhogin
Saku Koivu
ADSRB Patrick Roy
Martin Brodeur
ADSRG Rick Nash
Gilbert Brule
ADSRM Ryan Smyth
Michael Peca
ADSRT Andrew Raycroft
Hannu Toivonen
ADSSG Eric Staal
Martin Gerber
ADSTC Joe Thornton
Jonathan Cheechoo
ADSTL Jose Theodore
Roberto Luongo
ADSYP Alexei Yashin
Mark Parrish

2005-06 The Cup Emblems of Endorsement

PRINT RUN 15 SER. #'d SETS
NOT PRICED DUE TO SCARCITY
EEAF Alexander Frolov
EEAO Alexander Ovechkin
EEAR Andrew Raycroft
EEAT Alex Tanguay
EEAY Alexei Yashin
EEBH Bobby Hull
EEBL Brian Leetch
EEBO Jay Bouwmeester
EEBQ Ray Bourque
EEBS Billy Smith
EEBY Mike Bossy
EECD Chris Drury
EECN Cam Neely
EECP Chris Pronger
EEDG Doug Gilmour
EEDH Dany Heatley
EEDS Darryl Sittler
EEDW Doug Weight
EEEB Ed Belfour
EEEN Evgeni Nabokov
EEES Eric Staal
EEFM Frank Mahovlich
EEGC Gerry Cheevers
EEGE Martin Gerber
EEGF Grant Fuhr/12
EEGL Guy Lafleur
EEGM Glen Murray
EEHK Dominik Hasek
EEHO Marian Hossa
EEHV Martin Havlat
EEHZ Henrik Zetterberg
EEIK Ilya Kovalchuk
EEJB Jean Beliveau
EEJC Jonathan Cheechoo
EEJG Jean-Sebastien Giguere
EEJI Jarome Iginla
EEJM Joe Mullen
EEJO Joe Thornton
EEJP Joni Pitkanen
EEJT Jose Theodore
EEKD Kris Draper
EEKL Kari Lehtonen
EEKP Keith Primeau
EELM Larry Murphy
EELR Luc Robitaille
EELU Joffrey Lupul
EEMB Martin Brodeur
EEMC Bryan McCabe
EEMG Marian Gaborik
EEMH Milan Hejduk
EEMK Miikka Kiprusoff
EEML Manny Legace
EEMM Mike Modano
EEMN Markus Naslund
EEMS Miroslav Satan
EEMT Marty Turco
EEMU Lanny McDonald
EEMW Brenden Morrow
EEOJ Olli Jokinen
EEOK Olaf Kolzig
EEPB Patrice Bergeron
EEPH Dion Phaneuf
EEPM Patrick Marleau
EEPR Patrick Roy
EERB Rob Blake
EERH Ron Hextall
EERL Roberto Luongo/10
EERM Ryan Miller
EERN Rick Nash
EERS Ryan Smyth
EERV Rogie Vachon
EERY Michael Ryder
EESC Sidney Crosby
EESG Simon Gagne
EESK Saku Koivu
EESL Martin St. Louis
EESN Scott Niedermayer
EESS Steve Shutt
EESV Marek Svatos
EETB Todd Bertuzzi
EETE Tony Esposito
EETI Dave Williams
EETV Tomas Vokoun
EEVL Vincent Lecavalier
EEWR Wade Redden
EEZC Zdeno Chara

2005-06 The Cup Hardware Heroes

PRINT RUNS VARY
NOT PRICED DUE TO SCARCITY
HHAR Andrew Raycroft/1
HHBH Bobby Hull/3
HHBS Billy Smith/1
HHBT Bryan Trottier/1
HHCD Chris Drury/1
HHCN Cam Neely/1
HHCP Chris Pronger/1
HHDG Doug Gilmour/1
HHDH Dany Heatley/1
HHDT Dave Taylor/1
HHEN Evgeni Nabokov/1
HHFM Frank Mahovlich/1
HHGF Grant Fuhr/1
HHIK Ilya Kovalchuk/1
HHJB John Bucyk/2
HHJM Joe Mullen/2
HHJS Jean-Sebastien Giguere/1
HHJT Jose Theodore/1
HHKD Kris Draper/1
HHLU Luc Robitaille/1
HHMD Marcel Dionne/1
HHMH Milan Hejduk/1
HHMN Markus Naslund/1
HHRH Ron Hextall/1
HHRN Rick Nash/1
HHRO Rob Blake/1
HHSK Saku Koivu/1
HHSN Scott Niedermayer/1
HHBL1 Brian Leetch/1
HHBL2 Brian Leetch/2
HHBL3 Brian Leetch/1
HHBO1 Mike Bossy/1
HHBO2 Mike Bossy/3
HHBO3 Mike Bossy/1
HHBP1 Bernie Parent/2
HHBP2 Bernie Parent/2
HHDO1 Dominik Hasek/2
HHDO2 Dominik Hasek/6
HHDO3 Dominik Hasek/2
HHDP1 Denis Potvin/1
HHDP2 Denis Potvin/3
HHEB2 Ed Belfour/2
HHGH1 Gordie Howe/6
HHGH2 Gordie Howe/6
HHGL1 Guy Lafleur/3
HHGL2 Guy Lafleur/2
HHGL3 Guy Lafleur/3
HHGP1 Gilbert Perreault/1
HHGP2 Gilbert Perreault/1
HHJB1 Jean Beliveau/1
HHJB2 Jean Beliveau/1
HHJI1 Jarome Iginla/1
HHJI2 Jarome Iginla/1
HHJI3 Jarome Iginla/1
HHJI4 Jarome Iginla/2
HHLM1 Lanny McDonald/1
HHLM2 Lanny McDonald/1
HHMB1 Martin Brodeur/1
HHMB2 Martin Brodeur/2
HHMP1 Michael Peca/1
HHMP2 Michael Peca/1
HHPE1 Phil Esposito/5
HHPE2 Phil Esposito/2
HHPE3 Phil Esposito/2
HHPR1 Patrick Roy/2
HHPR2 Patrick Roy/3
HHPR3 Patrick Roy/1
HHRB1 Ray Bourque/1
HHRB2 Ray Bourque/5
HHRB3 Ray Bourque/1
HHSB1 Scotty Bowman/1
HHSB2 Scotty Bowman/1
HHSL1 Martin St. Louis/1
HHSL2 Martin St. Louis/1
HHSL3 Martin St. Louis/1
HHTE1 Tony Esposito/1
HHTE2 Tony Esposito/3
HHWG1 Wayne Gretzky/7
HHWG2 Wayne Gretzky/2
HHWG3 Wayne Gretzky/8
HHWG4 Wayne Gretzky/5
HHWG5 Wayne Gretzky/1
HHWG6 Wayne Gretzky/3
HHWG7 Wayne Gretzky/1
HHWG8 Wayne Gretzky/1

2005-06 The Cup Honorable Numbers

PRINT RUNS VARY
HNAH Ales Hemsky/83 25.00 60.00
HNAO Alexander Ovechkin/8
HNAR Andrew Raycroft/1
HNAT Alex Tanguay/18
HNAY Alexei Yashin/79 30.00 80.00
HNBH Bobby Hull/9
HNBI Martin Biron/43 25.00 50.00
HNBK Rob Blake/4
HNBL Brian Leetch/22 75.00 150.00
HNBM Bryan McCabe/24 30.00 80.00
HNBT Bryan Trottier/19 40.00 100.00
HNBY Mike Bossy/22
HNCD Chris Drury/23 40.00 100.00
HNCH Jonathan Cheechoo/14
HNCN Cam Neely/8
HNCP Chris Pronger/44 30.00 60.00
HNDA David Aebischer/1
HNDG Doug Gilmour/93 40.00 80.00
HNDH Dany Heatley/15
HNDP Dion Phaneuf/3
HNDR Dwayne Roloson/30 25.00 50.00
HNDS Darryl Sittler/27 40.00 80.00
HNDW Doug Weight/39 25.00 50.00
HNED Eric Daze/55 15.00 40.00
HNER Eric Staal/12
HNGC Gerry Cheevers/30 40.00 100.00
HNGE Martin Gerber/29 40.00 80.00
HNGF Grant Fuhr/31 60.00 100.00
HNGL Guy Lafleur/10
HNGM Glen Murray/27 40.00 80.00
HNGP Gilbert Perreault/11
HNHK Dominik Hasek/39 75.00 125.00
HNHO Marian Hossa/18
HNHV Martin Havlat/9
HNIK Ilya Kovalchuk/17 75.00 150.00
HNJB Jean Beliveau/4
HNJC Jeff Carter/17
HNJI Jarome Iginla/12
HNJO Joe Thornton/19
HNJS Jean-Sebastien Giguere/35 60.00 125.00
HNJT Jose Theodore/60 50.00 100.00
HNKL Kari Lehtonen/32 75.00 175.00
HNKP Keith Primeau/25 25.00 50.00
HNLR Luc Robitaille/20 75.00 150.00
HNLU Joffrey Lupul/15
HNMB Martin Brodeur/30 150.00 350.00
HNMC Lanny McDonald/9
HNMG Marian Gaborik/10
HNMH Milan Hejduk/23
HNMK Miikka Kiprusoff/34 60.00 125.00
HNMN Markus Naslund/19
HNMO Brendan Morrison/7
HNMP Mark Parrish/37 20.00 50.00
HNMS Marek Svatos/40 40.00 80.00
HNMT Marty Turco/35 40.00 80.00
HNMW Brenden Morrow/10
HNOK Olaf Kolzig/37 75.00 200.00
HNPB Patrice Bergeron/37 30.00 80.00
HNPE Michael Peca/37 30.00 60.00
HNPM Patrick Marleau/12
HNPO Denis Potvin/5
HNPR Patrick Roy/33 300.00 500.00
HNRB Ray Bourque/77 60.00 150.00
HNRE Robert Esche/42 25.00 50.00
HNRH Ron Hextall/27 60.00 150.00
HNRL Roberto Luongo/1
HNRN Rick Nash/61 60.00 150.00
HNSA Miroslav Satan/81 25.00 60.00
HNSC Sidney Crosby/87 500.00 900.00
HNSG Simon Gagne/12
HNSK Saku Koivu/11
HNSL Martin St. Louis/26 30.00 60.00
HNST Matt Stajan/14
HNTB Todd Bertuzzi/44 30.00 60.00
HNTE Tony Esposito/35 75.00 150.00
HNTV Tomas Vokoun/29 40.00 100.00
HNVL Vincent Lecavalier/4
HNWG Wayne Gretzky/9
HNZP Zigmund Palffy/33 40.00 80.00
HNDS2 Denis Savard/18

2005-06 The Cup Legendary Cuts

PRINT RUNS VARY
NOT PRICED DUE TO SCARCITY
LCBC Bun Cook/2
LCBH Bryan Hextall/1
LCBM Bert McInenly/1
LCCO Bill Cook/3
LCCW Bill Cowley/1
LCDC Dit Clapper/1
LCDH Doug Harvey/5
LCES Eddie Shore/1
LCFS Frank Selke/2
LCHD Hap Day/6
LCHS Harold Starr/1
LCJP Jacques Plante/3
LCKC King Clancy/5
LCMO Bill Mosienko/3
LCSA Sid Abel/2
LCSH Syd Howe/1
LCSY Syl Apps/1
LCTB Toe Blake/2

2005-06 The Cup Limited Logos

PRINT RUNS VARY
LLAO Alexander Ovechkin 200.00 500.00
LLAT Alex Tanguay 50.00 125.00
LLAY Alexei Yashin 30.00 80.00
LLBH Bobby Hull/25
LLBI Martin Biron 50.00 125.00
LLBL Rob Blake 30.00 80.00
LLBS Billy Smith 30.00 80.00
LLBY Mike Bossy 60.00 150.00
LLCD Chris Drury 40.00 100.00
LLCN Cam Neely
LLCP Chris Pronger 50.00 125.00
LLDA David Aebischer 25.00 60.00
LLDG Doug Gilmour/15 150.00 250.00
LLDH Dany Heatley/14 125.00 250.00
LLDP Denis Potvin 50.00 125.00
LLDS Darryl Sittler/5
LLDW Doug Weight/35 40.00 80.00
LLED Eric Daze 30.00 80.00
LLEN Evgeni Nabokov/20 100.00 200.00
LLES Eric Staal 50.00 125.00
LLFM Frank Mahovlich/20 75.00 150.00
LLGE Martin Gerber 50.00 100.00
LLGF Grant Fuhr/45 50.00 100.00
LLGM Glen Murray 50.00 125.00
LLGP Gilbert Perreault 60.00 150.00
LLHA Dominik Hasek 60.00 100.00
LLHJ Milan Hejduk 30.00 80.00
LLHV Martin Havlat 30.00 80.00
LLIK Ilya Kovalchuk 75.00 175.00
LLJC Jonathan Cheechoo/25 50.00 100.00
LLJI Jarome Iginla 75.00 200.00
LLJO Joe Thornton 75.00 175.00
LLJS Jean-Sebastien Giguere 30.00 80.00
LLJT Jose Theodore 40.00 100.00
LLKD Kris Draper 25.00 60.00
LLKP Keith Primeau 20.00 50.00
LLLF Guy Lafleur/10
LLLM Lanny McDonald/25 40.00 100.00
LLLU Luc Robitaille 50.00 125.00
LLMB Martin Brodeur 125.00 250.00
LLMC Bryan McCabe 25.00 60.00
LLMG Marian Gaborik 50.00 125.00
LLMH Marian Hossa 75.00 125.00
LLMK Miikka Kiprusoff 75.00 200.00
LLML Manny Legace/10
LLMM Mike Modano 60.00 150.00
LLMN Markus Naslund 50.00 125.00
LLMO Brendan Morrison 25.00 60.00
LLMP Michael Peca/30 30.00 80.00
LLMT Marty Turco 40.00 100.00
LLMW Brenden Morrow 30.00 80.00
LLOJ Olli Jokinen 25.00 60.00
LLOK Olaf Kolzig 50.00 125.00
LLPB Patrice Bergeron/25 75.00 200.00
LLPM Patrick Marleau/30 40.00 100.00
LLPR Patrick Roy/21 250.00 500.00
LLRB Ray Bourque/45 75.00 150.00
LLRE Robert Esche 20.00 50.00
LLRL Roberto Luongo/40 75.00 200.00
LLRM Ryan Miller 75.00 200.00
LLRN Rick Nash/20
LLRS Ryan Smyth 60.00 125.00
LLRV Rogie Vachon/20
LLRY Michael Ryder 50.00 100.00
LLSA Miroslav Satan 25.00 60.00
LLSC Sidney Crosby 500.00 800.00
LLSD Shane Doan 40.00 100.00
LLSG Simon Gagne 30.00 80.00
LLSK Saku Koivu 40.00 100.00
LLSL Martin St. Louis/25 60.00 150.00
LLSN Scott Niedermayer 25.00 60.00
LLSS Steve Shutt 40.00 100.00
LLSW Stephen Weiss 25.00 60.00

LLTB Todd Bertuzzi 30.00 80.00
LLTC Ty Conklin 25.00 60.00
LLTE Tony Esposito/15
LLTV Tomas Vokoun 50.00 125.00
LLVL Vincent Lecavalier 90.00 150.00
LLZP Zigmund Palffy 30.00 80.00

2005-06 The Cup Noble Numbers

PRINT RUNS VARY
UNDER 24 NOT PRICED DUE TO SCARCITY
NNBB Rob Blake
Jay Bouwmeester/4
NNBC Martin Brodeur 60.00 100.00
Gerry Cheevers/30
NNBE Ray Bourque
Phil Esposito/7
NNBL Jean Beliveau
Vincent Lecavalier/4
NNBS Mike Bossy 30.00 60.00
Steve Shutt/22
NNDZ Pavel Datsyuk
Nikolai Zherdev/13
NNFJ Grant Fuhr 40.00 100.00
Curtis Joseph/31
NNFS Peter Forsberg 50.00 125.00
Borje Salming/21
NNGM Simon Gagne
Patrick Marleau/12
NNGT Jean-Sebastien Giguere 30.00 80.00
Marty Turco/35
NNGV Martin Gerber 40.00 100.00
Tomas Vokoun/29
NNHD Milan Hejduk 25.00 60.00
Chris Drury/23
NNHM Bobby Hull
Lanny McDonald/9
NNHR Dany Heatley
Tuomo Ruutu/15
NNIG Jarome Iginla
Simon Gagne/12
NNJJ Jaromir Jagr 40.00 100.00
Milan Jurcina/68
NNJS Jason Spezza
Shane Doan/19
NNKA Saku Koivu
Daniel Alfredsson/11
NNKC Ilya Kovalchuk 60.00 125.00
Jeff Carter/17
NNKL Miikka Kiprusoff 30.00 80.00
Manny Legace/34
NNLA Roberto Luongo
David Aebischer/1
NNLM Henrik Lundqvist 75.00 125.00
Ryan Miller/30
NNLR Roberto Luongo
Andrew Raycroft/1
NNMJ Larry Murphy 25.00 50.00
Ed Jovanovski/55
NNMK Mike Modano
Paul Kariya/9
NNMM Lanny McDonald
Joe Mullen/7
NNMS Frank Mahovlich 40.00 80.00
Darryl Sittler/27
NNMT Joe Mullen
Keith Tkachuk/7
NNNP Rick Nash 30.00 80.00
Corey Perry/61
NNPB Chris Pronger 25.00 60.00
Todd Bertuzzi/44
NNPK Gilbert Perreault
Saku Koivu/11
NNPM Denis Potvin
Larry Murphy/5
NNSC Brendan Shanahan
Jonathan Cheechoo/14
NNSD Mats Sundin
Pavel Datsyuk/13
NNSE Peter Stastny 40.00 100.00
Patrik Elias/26
NNSI Eric Staal
Jarome Iginla/12
NNSL Peter Stastny 30.00 80.00
Martin St. Louis/26
NNSM Eric Staal
Patrick Marleau/12
NNSR Jason Spezza
Brad Richards/19
NNSS Mats Sundin
Teemu Selanne/13
NNST Denis Savard
Alex Tanguay/18
NNTN Joe Thornton
Markus Naslund/19
NNTS Joe Thornton
Jason Spezza/19
NNYS Steve Yzerman 125.00 250.00
Joe Sakic/19
NNYT Steve Yzerman 100.00 200.00
Joe Thornton/19
NNZS Henrik Zetterberg 50.00 100.00
Marek Svatos/40

2005-06 The Cup Noble Numbers Dual

PRINT RUN 10 SER. #'d SETS
NOT PRICED DUE TO SCARCITY
DNNBE Martin Brodeur
Patrik Elias
DNNBJ Todd Bertuzzi
Ed Jovanovski
DNNCL Sidney Crosby
Mario Lemieux
DNNCO Sidney Crosby
Alexander Ovechkin
DNNCV Gerry Cheevers
Rogie Vachon
DNNDV Marcel Dionne
Rogie Vachon
DNNDZ Pavel Datsyuk
Henrik Zetterberg
DNNEH Patrik Elias
Martin Havlat
DNNFD Sergei Fedorov
Pavel Datsyuk
DNNFG Peter Forsberg
Simon Gagne
DNNFI Saku Koivu
Teemu Selanne
DNNFN Sergei Fedorov
Rick Nash
DNNFR Grant Fuhr
Bill Ranford
DNNFS Peter Forsberg
Mats Sundin
DNNGH Marian Gaborik
Marian Hossa
DNNGL Wayne Gretzky
Mario Lemieux
DNNGS Jean-Sebastien Giguere
Teemu Selanne
DNNHI Dany Heatley
Jarome Iginla
DNNHS Bobby Hull
Denis Savard
DNNJA Joe Sakic
Alex Tanguay
DNNJH Jaromir Jagr
Dominik Hasek
DNNJJ Joe Sakic
Joe Thornton
DNNKS Paul Kariya
Teemu Selanne
DNNKT Saku Koivu
Jose Theodore
DNNKV Paul Kariya
Tomas Vokoun
DNNLB Guy Lafleur
Mike Bossy
DNNLG Martin St. Louis
Simon Gagne
DNNLJ Mario Lemieux
Jaromir Jagr
DNNLL Martin St. Louis
Vincent Lecavalier
DNNLR Vincent Lecavalier
Brad Richards
DNNMG Mike Modano
Bill Guerin
DNNMM Lanny McDonald
Joe Mullen
DNNMR Mike Modano
Jeremy Roenick
DNNMS Lanny McDonald
Darryl Sittler
DNNNK Evgeni Nabokov
Nikolai Khabibulin
DNNPJ Peter Forsberg
Joe Sakic
DNNPR Patrick Roy
Ray Bourque
DNNRB Patrick Roy
Martin Brodeur
DNNSL Mats Sundin
Eric Lindros
DNNSP Billy Smith
Denis Potvin
DNNSR Brendan Shanahan
Luc Robitaille
DNNSS Darryl Sittler
Borje Salming
DNNST Eric Staal
Joe Thornton
DNNTB Bryan Trottier
Mike Bossy
DNNTG Keith Tkachuk
Bill Guerin
DNNYL Steve Yzerman
Mario Lemieux
DNNYS Steve Yzerman
Brendan Shanahan

2005-06 The Cup Patch Variation

PRINT RUN 10 SER. #'d SETS
NOT PRICED DUE TO SCARCITY

2005-06 The Cup Patch Variation Autographs

PRINT RUN 1 SER. #'d SET
NOT PRICED DUE TO SCARCITY

2005-06 The Cup Platinum Rookies

COMMON CARD 12.00 30.00
SEMISTARS/GOALIES 15.00 40.00
PRINT RUN 25 SER. #'d SETS
101 Ryan Getzlaf 50.00 125.00
102 Ryan Whitney 20.00 50.00
103 R.J. Umberger 15.00 40.00
104 Cam Ward 60.00 125.00
105 Brent Seabrook 20.00 50.00
106 Eric Nystrom 12.00 30.00
107 Gilbert Brule 30.00 80.00
108 Hannu Toivonen 25.00 60.00
109 Robert Nilsson 15.00 40.00
110 Rostislav Olesz 20.00 50.00
111 Ryan Suter 12.00 30.00
112 Jussi Jokinen 20.00 50.00
113 Zach Parise 40.00 100.00
114 Wojtek Wolski 40.00 100.00
115 Andrej Meszaros 25.00 60.00
116 Johan Franzen 15.00 40.00
117 Peter Budaj 20.00 50.00
118 David Leneveu 15.00 40.00
119 Andrew Alberts 12.00 30.00
120 Steve Bernier 30.00 80.00
121 Mikko Koivu 30.00 80.00
122 Chris Campoli 15.00 40.00
123 Evgeny Artyukhin 12.00 30.00
124 Christoph Schubert 15.00 40.00
125 Tomas Fleischmann 15.00 40.00
126 Maxime Talbot 15.00 40.00
127 Jordan Sigalet 20.00 50.00
128 Danny Richmond 12.00 30.00
129 Maxim Lapierre 12.00 30.00
130 Dimitri Patzold 12.00 30.00
131 Rene Bourque 12.00 30.00
132 Yann Danis 20.00 50.00
133 Brad Winchester 12.00 30.00
134 Jim Slater 12.00 30.00
135 Petr Prucha 40.00 100.00
136 Jim Howard 25.00 60.00
137 Patrick Eaves 20.00 50.00
138 Ryane Clowe 20.00 50.00
139 Braydon Coburn 12.00 30.00
140 Brad Richardson 12.00 30.00
141 Milan Jurcina 12.00 30.00
142 Jeff Woywitka 12.00 30.00
143 Andrei Kostitsyn 25.00 60.00
144 Derek Boogaard 15.00 40.00
145 Barry Tallackson 12.00 30.00
146 Jakub Klepis 12.00 30.00
147 Alvaro Montoya 25.00 60.00
148 Andrew Ladd 15.00 40.00
149 Brandon Bochenski 20.00 50.00
150 Jeff Tambellini 12.00 30.00
151 Jaroslav Balastik 12.00 30.00
152 Lee Stempniak 15.00 40.00
153 Kevin Dallman 12.00 30.00
154 Niklas Nordgren 12.00 30.00
155 Kevin Nastiuk 12.00 30.00
156 Ryan Craig 15.00 40.00
157 Erik Christensen 20.00 50.00
158 Chris Thorburn 12.00 30.00
159 Josh Gorges 12.00 30.00
160 Matt Foy 15.00 40.00
161 Ole-Kristian Tollefsen 12.00 30.00
162 Kevin Bieksa 20.00 50.00
163 Kyle Quincey 15.00 40.00
164 Andrew Wozniewski 12.00 30.00
165 Jeff Hoggan 12.00 30.00
166 Jeremy Colliton 12.00 30.00
167 Alexandre Picard 20.00 50.00
168 Ben Eager 12.00 30.00
169 Daniel Paille 15.00 40.00
170 Valtteri Filppula 20.00 50.00
171 Alexander Perezhogin 25.00 60.00
172 Mike Richards 25.00 60.00
173 Corey Perry 30.00 80.00
174 Alexander Steen 25.00 60.00
175 Thomas Vanek 75.00 150.00
176 Jeff Carter 40.00 100.00
177 Henrik Lundqvist 100.00 200.00
178 Dion Phaneuf 100.00 200.00
179 Alexander Ovechkin 250.00 400.00
180 Sidney Crosby 500.00 900.00
181 Brett Lebda 12.00 30.00
182 Jay McClement 12.00 30.00
183 Cam Barker 15.00 40.00
184 Petteri Nokelainen 12.00 30.00
185 Keith Ballard 12.00 30.00
186 Duncan Keith 12.00 30.00
187 George Parros 12.00 30.00
188 Adam Berkhoel 15.00 40.00
189 Anthony Stewart 12.00 30.00
190 Ryan Hollweg 12.00 30.00
191 Ben Walter 15.00 40.00

2005-06 The Cup Property of

PRINT RUN 1 SER. #'d SET
NOT PRICED DUE TO SCARCITY
POAT Alex Tanguay
POBH Bobby Hull
POBL Rob Blake
POCP Chris Pronger
PODG Doug Gilmour
PODH Dany Heatley
PODP Denis Potvin
POES Eric Staal
POFM Frank Mahovlich
POGH Gordie Howe
POHA Dominik Hasek
POHJ Milan Hejduk
POHZ Henrik Zetterberg
POIK Ilya Kovalchuk
POJI Jarome Iginla
POJJ Jaromir Jagr
POJK Jari Kurri
POJO Joe Thornton
POJR Jeremy Roenick
POJS Joe Sakic
POJT Jose Theodore
POLR Larry Robinson
POLU Luc Robitaille
POMG Marian Gaborik
POMH Marian Hossa
POMN Markus Naslund
PONK Nikolai Khabibulin
POPD Pavel Datsyuk
POPE Patrik Elias
POPK Paul Kariya
PORB Ray Bourque
PORN Rick Nash
POSK Saku Koivu
POSL Martin St. Louis
POSP Jason Spezza
POSU Mats Sundin
POSY Steve Yzerman
POWG Wayne Gretzky

2005-06 The Cup Scripted Numbers

PRINT RUNS VARY
UNDER 24 NOT PRICED DUE TO SCARCITY
SNBC Martin Brodeur 100.00 200.00
Gerry Cheevers/30
SNBE Ray Bourque
Phil Esposito/7
SNBL Mike Bossy
Brian Leetch/22
SNBN Ed Belfour
Evgeni Nabokov/20
SNBP Patrice Bergeron 30.00 60.00
Michael Peca/37
SNBR Ed Belfour
Luc Robitaille/20
SNBS Mike Bossy
Steve Shutt/22
SNET Marty Turco 40.00 80.00
Tony Esposito/35
SNGM Simon Gagne
Patrick Marleau/12
SNGT Jean-Sebastien Giguere 30.00 60.00
Marty Turco/35
SNGV Martin Gerber 40.00 80.00
Tomas Vokoun/29
SNHD Milan Hejduk 30.00 60.00
Chris Drury/23
SNHH Bobby Hull
Gordie Howe/9
SNHM Bobby Hull
Lanny McDonald/9
SNJV Jean Beliveau
Vincent Lecavalier/4
SNKC Ilya Kovalchuk
Jeff Carter/17
SNKL Miikka Kiprusoff 40.00 100.00
Manny Legace/34
SNLA Roberto Luongo
David Aebischer/1
SNLB Vincent Lecavalier
Rob Blake/4
SNLM Henrik Lundqvist 75.00 200.00
Ryan Miller/30
SNLR Roberto Luongo
Andrew Raycroft/1
SNMH Mike Modano
Martin Havlat/9
SNMM Lanny McDonald
Joe Mullen/7
SNMN Glen Murray 25.00 60.00
Scott Niedermayer/27
SNMS Frank Mahovlich 60.00 125.00
Darryl Sittler/27
SNND Markus Naslund
Shane Doan/19
SNNO Cam Neely
Alexander Ovechkin/8
SNNP Rick Nash 40.00 100.00
Corey Perry/61
SNPB Chris Pronger 25.00 60.00
Todd Bertuzzi/44
SNPC Dion Phaneuf
Zdeno Chara/3
SNSI Eric Staal
Jarome Iginla/12
SNSM Eric Staal
Patrick Marleau/12
SNTH Alex Tanguay
Marian Hossa/18
SNTN Joe Thornton
Markus Naslund/19
SNZS Henrik Zetterberg 30.00 80.00
Marek Svatos/40

2005-06 The Cup Scripted Numbers Dual

PRINT RUN 10 SER. #'d SETS
NOT PRICED DUE TO SCARCITY
DSNBB Martin Brodeur
Ed Belfour
DSNBN Todd Bertuzzi
Markus Naslund
DSNBR Patrice Bergeron
Michael Ryder
DSNCA Lanny McDonald
Joe Mullen
DSNCO Alex Tanguay
Milan Hejduk
DSNCZ Milan Hejduk
Marek Svatos
DSNDA Mike Modano
Brenden Morrow
DSNDM Chris Drury
Ryan Miller
DSNGA Martin Gerber
David Aebischer
DSNGC Doug Gilmour
Wendel Clark
DSNGN Jean-Sebastien Giguere
Scott Niedermayer
DSNHV Dominik Hasek
Tomas Vokoun
DSNIK Jarome Iginla
Miikka Kiprusoff
DSNIN Jarome Iginla
Rick Nash
DSNKH Ilya Kovalchuk
Marian Hossa
DSNKJ Saku Koivu
Olli Jokinen
DSNKL Miikka Kiprusoff
Kari Lehtonen
DSNKO Ilya Kovalchuk
Alexander Ovechkin
DSNLS Guy Lafleur
Steve Shutt
DSNMM Mike Modano
Joe Mullen
DSNNB Cam Neely
Ray Bourque
DSNNS Rick Nash
Eric Staal
DSNPB Chris Pronger
Rob Blake
DSNPL Keith Primeau
Vincent Lecavalier
DSNRB Patrick Roy
Martin Brodeur
DSNRC Luc Robitaille
Wendel Clark
DSNRF Patrick Roy
Grant Fuhr
DSNSM Darryl Sittler
Frank Mahovlich
DSNSV Marian Hossa
Miroslav Satan
DSNSW Eric Staal
Doug Weight
DSNTH Alex Tanguay
Dany Heatley
DSNTL Jose Theodore
Roberto Luongo
DSNTM Joe Thornton
Patrick Marleau
DSNZN Henrik Zetterberg
Markus Naslund

2005-06 The Cup Scripted Swatches

PRINT RUNS VARY
UNDER 24 NOT PRICED DUE TO SCARCITY
SSAF Alexander Frolov 40.00 80.00
SSAH Ales Hemsky 50.00 125.00
SSAO Alexander Ovechkin/15
SSAR Andrew Raycroft 50.00 100.00
SSAS Alexander Steen 60.00 125.00
SSAT Alex Tanguay 60.00 150.00
SSAY Alexei Yashin 40.00 80.00
SSBH Bobby Hull/15
SSBL Rob Blake 50.00 100.00
SSBY Mike Bossy 75.00 150.00
SSCD Chris Drury 40.00 80.00
SSCH Jonathan Cheechoo/10
SSCN Cam Neely/18
SSCP Chris Pronger/10
SSDG Doug Gilmour 40.00 100.00
SSDH Dany Heatley 60.00 150.00
SSDP Dion Phaneuf 125.00 200.00
SSDT Dave Taylor 40.00 100.00
SSDW Doug Weight 30.00 80.00
SSEN Evgeni Nabokov 75.00 125.00
SSER Eric Staal 60.00 125.00
SSGC Gerry Cheevers 75.00 150.00
SSGE Martin Gerber 60.00 100.00
SSGF Grant Fuhr 50.00 125.00
SSGL Guy Lafleur/20 150.00 250.00
SSGM Glen Murray 50.00 125.00
SSGP Gilbert Perreault/9
SSHK Dominik Hasek 75.00 150.00
SSHL Henrik Lundqvist 125.00 250.00
SSHO Marian Hossa 40.00 80.00
SSHV Martin Havlat 30.00 60.00
SSIK Ilya Kovalchuk 100.00 200.00
SSJB Jean Beliveau 150.00 250.00
SSJC Jeff Carter 60.00 100.00
SSJI Jarome Iginla 100.00 175.00
SSJO Joe Thornton 100.00 200.00
SSJS Jean-Sebastien Giguere 40.00 100.00
SSJT Jose Theodore 60.00 125.00
SSKL Kari Lehtonen 75.00 150.00
SSKP Keith Primeau 60.00 100.00
SSLR Luc Robitaille 75.00 150.00
SSLU Joffrey Lupul 40.00 80.00
SSMB Martin Brodeur 200.00 300.00
SSMC Lanny McDonald/10
SSMG Marian Gaborik 90.00 150.00
SSMH Milan Hejduk 50.00 125.00
SSMK Miikka Kiprusoff 75.00 150.00
SSMM Mike Modano 75.00 150.00
SSMN Markus Naslund 60.00 100.00
SSMO Brendan Morrison 30.00 60.00
SSMP Mark Parrish 40.00 80.00
SSMT Marty Turco 60.00 100.00
SSMW Brenden Morrow 30.00 80.00
SSOJ Olli Jokinen 40.00 80.00
SSOK Olaf Kolzig 50.00 125.00
SSPB Patrice Bergeron/10
SSPE Michael Peca 40.00 80.00
SSPM Patrick Marleau/15
SSPO Denis Potvin/15
SSRE Robert Esche 40.00 80.00
SSRH Ron Hextall/4
SSRL Roberto Luongo/5
SSRM Ryan Miller 60.00 100.00
SSRY Michael Ryder 50.00 100.00
SSSA Miroslav Satan 50.00 100.00
SSSC Sidney Crosby/10 1250.00 2500.00
SSSD Shane Doan 40.00 80.00
SSSG Simon Gagne 50.00 100.00
SSSK Saku Koivu 50.00 100.00
SSSL Martin St. Louis
SSSN Scott Niedermayer/15
SSST Matt Stajan 40.00 100.00
SSTB Todd Bertuzzi 60.00 125.00
SSTE Tony Esposito 60.00 100.00
SSTV Thomas Vanek 125.00 200.00
SSVL Vincent Lecavalier 100.00 200.00
SSZP Zigmund Palffy 40.00 80.00
SSPR1 Patrick Roy 200.00 400.00
SSPR2 Patrick Roy 200.00 400.00
SSRB1 Ray Bourque 100.00 200.00
SSRB2 Ray Bourque 75.00 150.00

2005-06 The Cup Signature Patches

PRINT RUN 75 SER. #'d SETS
UNIQUE SWATCHES MAY EARN SIGNIFICANT PREMIUM
SPAF Alexander Frolov 25.00 60.00
SPAH Ales Hemsky 25.00 60.00
SPAO Alexander Ovechkin 200.00 400.00
SPAR Andrew Raycroft 25.00 60.00
SPAT Alex Tanguay 25.00 60.00
SPAY Alexei Yashin 25.00 60.00
SPBK Rob Blake 20.00 50.00
SPBL Brian Leetch 25.00 60.00
SPBS Billy Smith 30.00 80.00
SPBY Mike Bossy 40.00 100.00
SPCD Chris Drury 25.00 60.00
SPCN Cam Neely/25 60.00 100.00
SPCP Chris Pronger 25.00 60.00
SPDA David Aebischer 20.00 50.00
SPDG Doug Gilmour 25.00 60.00
SPDH Dany Heatley 40.00 100.00
SPDO Dominik Hasek 50.00 80.00
SPDP Dion Phaneuf 75.00 175.00
SPDW Doug Weight 25.00 60.00
SPES Eric Staal 30.00 80.00
SPFM Frank Mahovlich 25.00 60.00
SPGA Glenn Anderson 20.00 50.00
SPGC Gerry Cheevers/65 40.00 80.00
SPGE Martin Gerber 25.00 60.00
SPGL Guy Lafleur 40.00 100.00
SPGM Glen Murray 30.00 80.00
SPGO Scott Gomez 25.00 60.00
SPGP Gilbert Perreault/40 50.00 125.00
SPHJ Milan Hejduk 25.00 60.00
SPHL Henrik Lundqvist 60.00 150.00
SPHV Martin Havlat 25.00 60.00
SPIK Ilya Kovalchuk 40.00 100.00
SPJC Jeff Carter 40.00 80.00
SPJI Jarome Iginla 40.00 100.00
SPJM Joe Mullen 20.00 50.00
SPJO Joe Thornton 40.00 80.00
SPJP Joni Pitkanen 15.00 40.00
SPJS Jean-Sebastien Giguere 25.00 60.00
SPJT Jose Theodore 25.00 60.00
SPKD Kris Draper 15.00 40.00
SPKP Keith Primeau 15.00 40.00
SPLM Lanny McDonald 25.00 60.00
SPLR Luc Robitaille 30.00 80.00
SPLU Joffrey Lupul 25.00 60.00
SPMB Martin Brodeur 75.00 150.00
SPMG Marian Gaborik 60.00 125.00
SPMH Marian Hossa 25.00 60.00
SPMK Miikka Kiprusoff 40.00 100.00
SPMM Mike Modano 40.00 100.00
SPMN Markus Naslund 25.00 60.00
SPMP Mark Parrish 15.00 40.00
SPMR Mike Richards 25.00 60.00
SPMS Miroslav Satan 15.00 40.00
SPMT Marty Turco 25.00 60.00
SPOJ Olli Jokinen 20.00 50.00
SPOK Olaf Kolzig 30.00 80.00
SPPB Patrice Bergeron 30.00 80.00
SPPE Corey Perry/60 30.00 80.00
SPPO Denis Potvin 30.00 80.00
SPPR Patrick Roy 100.00 250.00
SPRB Ray Bourque 40.00 100.00
SPRE Robert Esche 25.00 60.00
SPRH Ron Hextall/40 50.00 100.00
SPRL Roberto Luongo 50.00 125.00
SPRM Ryan Miller 30.00 80.00
SPRN Rick Nash/40 40.00 100.00
SPRY Michael Ryder 30.00 80.00
SPSC Sidney Crosby 500.00 750.00
SPSD Shane Doan/25 25.00 60.00
SPSG Simon Gagne 25.00 60.00
SPSH Steve Shutt 25.00 60.00
SPSK Saku Koivu 30.00 80.00
SPSL Martin St. Louis/65 20.00 50.00
SPSN Scott Niedermayer 20.00 50.00
SPSV Marek Svatos 25.00 60.00
SPTB Todd Bertuzzi 20.00 50.00
SPTI Dave Williams 20.00 50.00
SPTV Thomas Vanek 100.00 200.00
SPVL Vincent Lecavalier 30.00 80.00
SPVO Tomas Vokoun 25.00 60.00
SPWG Wayne Gretzky/25 400.00 700.00
SPWR Wade Redden 20.00 50.00
SPZC Zdeno Chara 20.00 50.00

2005-06 The Cup Stanley Cup Titlists

PRINT RUNS VARY
NOT PRICED DUE TO SCARCITY
TAT Alex Tanguay/1
TBC Bobby Clarke/2
TBH Bobby Hull/1
TBL Rob Blake/1
TBS Billy Smith/4
TBY Mike Bossy/4
TCD Chris Drury/1
TCO Chris Osgood/2
TDA David Aebischer/1
TDG Doug Gilmour/1
TDH Dominik Hasek/1
TGC Gerry Cheevers/2
TGF Grant Fuhr/5
TGH Gordie Howe/4
TGL Guy Lafleur/5
THJ Milan Hejduk/1
TJA Jason Arnott/1
TJB Jean Beliveau/10
TKD Kris Draper/3
TKM Kirk Muller/1
TLE Brian Leetch/1
TLU Luc Robitaille/1
TMB Martin Brodeur/3
TMC Lanny McDonald/1
TRF Ruslan Fedotenko/1
TSB Scotty Bowman/9
TSG Scott Gomez/2
TSN Scott Niedermayer/3
TTL Ted Lindsay/4
TVL Vincent Lecavalier/1
TWC Wayne Cashman/2
TWG Wayne Gretzky/4 EXCH
TBT1 Bryan Trottier/4
TBT2 Bryan Trottier/2
TFM1 Frank Mahovlich/4
TFM2 Frank Mahovlich/2
TGA1 Glenn Anderson/5
TGA2 Glenn Anderson/1
TJM1 Joe Mullen/2
TJM2 Joe Mullen/2
TLM1 Larry Murphy/2
TLM2 Larry Murphy/2
TPR1 Patrick Roy/2
TPR2 Patrick Roy/2

2006-07 The Cup

UNIQUE SWATCHES MAY EARN SUBSTANTIAL PREMIUM
WHITE SWATCHES MAY SELL BELOW LO
1 Teemu Selanne 5.00 12.00
2 Jean-Sebastian Giguere 4.00 10.00
3 Kari Lehtonen 5.00 12.00
4 Ilya Kovalchuk 6.00 15.00
5 Phil Esposito 8.00 20.00
6 Don Cherry 6.00 15.00
7 Ray Bourque 8.00 20.00
8 Bobby Orr 12.00 30.00
9 Cam Neely 6.00 15.00
10 Patrice Bergeron 5.00 12.00
11 Johnny Bucyk 4.00 10.00
12 Ryan Miller 5.00 12.00
13 Gilbert Perreault 5.00 12.00
14 Jarome Iginla 6.00 15.00
15 Miikka Kiprusoff 6.00 15.00
16 Al MacInnis 3.00 8.00
17 Eric Staal 5.00 12.00
18 Cam Ward 5.00 12.00
19 Bobby Hull 8.00 20.00
20 Tony Esposito 5.00 12.00
21 Stan Mikita 5.00 12.00
22 Joe Sakic 10.00 25.00
23 Patrick Roy 20.00 50.00
24 Rick Nash 5.00 12.00
25 Sergei Fedorov 5.00 12.00
26 Mike Modano 5.00 12.00
27 Dominik Hasek 8.00 20.00
28 Henrik Zetterberg 5.00 12.00
29 Gordie Howe 10.00 25.00
30 Scotty Bowman 4.00 10.00
31 Ted Lindsay 3.00 8.00
32 Red Kelly 4.00 10.00
33 Ales Hemsky 3.00 8.00
34 Grant Fuhr 6.00 15.00
35 Jari Kurri 5.00 12.00
36 Ed Belfour 5.00 12.00
37 Wayne Gretzky 30.00 80.00
38 Rob Blake 4.00 10.00
39 Marcel Dionne 5.00 12.00
40 Luc Robitaille 4.00 10.00
41 Rogie Vachon 5.00 12.00
42 Dino Ciccarelli 4.00 10.00
43 Marian Gaborik 6.00 15.00
44 Saku Koivu 5.00 12.00
45 Michael Ryder 4.00 10.00
46 Guy Lafleur 8.00 20.00
47 Larry Robinson 4.00 10.00
48 Jean Beliveau 6.00 15.00
49 Jacques Lemaire 3.00 8.00
50 Paul Kariya 5.00 12.00
51 Tomas Vokoun 4.00 10.00
52 Martin Brodeur 12.00 30.00
53 Scott Stevens 3.00 8.00
54 Alexei Yashin 3.00 8.00
55 Al Arbour 4.00 10.00
56 Mike Bossy 4.00 10.00
57 Billy Smith 5.00 12.00
58 Denis Potvin 5.00 12.00
59 Jaromir Jagr 8.00 20.00
60 Brendan Shanahan 5.00 12.00
61 Henrik Lundqvist 6.00 15.00
62 Gump Worsley 6.00 15.00
63 Andy Bathgate 3.00 8.00
64 Jason Spezza 5.00 12.00
65 Dany Heatley 6.00 15.00
66 Peter Forsberg 8.00 20.00
67 Simon Gagne 5.00 12.00
68 Bernie Parent 6.00 15.00
69 Bobby Clarke 5.00 12.00
70 Ron Hextall 5.00 12.00
71 Jeremy Roenick 5.00 12.00
72 Shane Doan 3.00 8.00
73 Sidney Crosby 50.00 100.00
74 Marc-Andre Fleury 5.00 12.00
75 Mario Lemieux 20.00 50.00
76 Peter Stastny 3.00 8.00
77 Joe Thornton 8.00 20.00
78 Jonathan Cheechoo 5.00 12.00
79 Patrick Marleau 4.00 10.00
80 Bernie Federko 4.00 10.00
81 Vincent Lecavalier 5.00 12.00
82 Mats Sundin 5.00 12.00
83 Frank Mahovlich 5.00 12.00
84 Darryl Sittler 5.00 12.00
85 Johnny Bower 4.00 10.00
86 Borje Salming 4.00 10.00
87 Roberto Luongo 6.00 15.00
88 Markus Naslund 5.00 12.00
89 Alexander Ovechkin 12.00 30.00
90 Dale Hawerchuk 3.00 8.00
91 Nate Thompson AU RC 8.00 20.00
92 Mike Brown AU RC 8.00 20.00
93 Mike Card AU RC 10.00 25.00
94 Adam Dennis AU RC 10.00 25.00
95 Carsen Germyn AU RC 10.00 25.00
96 Adam Burish AU RC 10.00 25.00
97 Drew Larman AU RC 6.00 15.00
98 Jonas Johansson AU RC 8.00 20.00
99 Joel Perrault AU RC 6.00 15.00
100 Mikko Lehtonen AU RC 8.00 20.00
101 Alex Brooks AU RC 8.00 20.00
102 Frank Doyle AU RC 8.00 20.00
103 Billy Thompson AU RC 8.00 20.00
104 Kelly Guard AU RC 10.00 25.00
105 David Printz AU RC 8.00 20.00
106 D.J. King AU RC 8.00 20.00
107 Jean-Francois Racine AU RC 10.00 25.00
108 Nathan McIver AU RC 12.00 30.00
109 Shane O'Brien JSY AU/50 RC 150.00 500.00
110 Ryan Shannon JSY AU/125 RC 100.00 250.00
111 David McKee JSY AU RC 30.00 100.00
112 Mark Stuart JSY AU RC 20.00 50.00
113 Matt Lashoff JSY AU RC 25.00 60.00
114 Drew Stafford JSY AU RC 125.00 400.00
115 Clarke MacArthur JSY AU RC 25.00 60.00
116 Michael Funk JSY AU RC 20.00 50.00
117 Brandon Prust JSY AU RC 20.00 50.00
118 Dustin Boyd JSY AU RC 50.00 125.00
119 Dustin Byfuglien JSY AU RC 30.00 80.00
120 Dave Bolland JSY AU RC 30.00 100.00
121 Michael Blunden JSY AU RC 25.00 60.00
122 Filip Novak JSY AU RC 20.00 50.00
123 Fredrik Norrena JSY AU RC 30.00 80.00
124 Niklas Grossman JSY AU RC 20.00 50.00
125 Loui Eriksson JSY AU RC 25.00 60.00
126 Tomas Kopecky JSY AU RC 25.00 60.00
127 Stefan Liv JSY AU RC 25.00 60.00
128 Patrick Thoresen JSY AU RC 25.00 60.00
129 Marc-Antoine Pouliot JSY AU RC 30.00 80.00
130 Ladislav Smid JSY AU RC 30.00 80.00
131 Janis Sprukts JSY AU RC 25.00 60.00
132 Jeff Drouin-Deslauriers
JSY AU RC 25.00 60.00
133 David Booth JSY AU RC 25.00 80.00
134 Konstantin Pushkaryov
JSY AU RC 30.00 80.00
135 Patrick O'Sullivan JSY AU RC 75.00 200.00
136 Benoit Pouliot JSY AU RC 50.00 200.00
137 Niklas Backstrom JSY AU RC 75.00 200.00
138 Guillaume Latendresse
JSY AU RC 100.00 350.00
139 Shea Weber JSY AU RC 50.00 175.00
140 Johnny Oduya JSY AU RC 20.00 50.00
141 Travis Zajac JSY AU RC 40.00 125.00
142 Masi Marjamaki JSY AU RC 25.00 60.00
143 Nigel Dawes JSY AU RC 40.00 100.00
144 Jarkko Immonen JSY AU RC 25.00 60.00
145 Josh Hennessy JSY AU RC 25.00 60.00
146 Ryan Potulny JSY AU RC 30.00 80.00
147 Jussi Timonen JSY AU RC 20.00 50.00
148 Keith Yandle JSY AU RC 20.00 50.00
149 Michel Ouellet JSY AU RC 25.00 60.00
150 Noah Welch JSY AU RC 25.00 60.00
151 Kristopher Letang JSY AU RC 75.00 200.00
152 Joe Pavelski JSY AU RC 50.00 150.00
153 Matt Carle JSY AU RC 40.00 125.00
154 Marc-Edouard Vlasic JSY AU RC 40.00 125.00
155 Yan Stastny JSY AU RC 25.00 60.00
156 Marek Schwarz JSY AU RC 40.00 100.00
157 Roman Polak JSY AU RC 30.00 80.00
158 Karri Ramo JSY AU RC 30.00 80.00
159 Blair Jones JSY AU RC 20.00 50.00
160 Brendan Bell JSY AU RC 20.00 50.00
161 Ian White JSY AU RC 25.00 60.00
162 Ben Ondrus JSY AU RC 25.00 60.00

163 Jeremy Williams JSY AU RC 25.00 60.00
164 Miroslav Kopriva JSY AU RC 20.00 50.00
165 Luc Bourdon JSY AU RC 30.00 100.00
166 Jesse Schultz JSY AU RC 25.00 60.00
167 Alexander Edler JSY AU RC 25.00 60.00
168 Eric Fehr JSY AU RC 50.00 125.00
169 Jordan Staal JSY AU/99 RC 900.00 2200.00
170 Phil Kessel JSY AU/99 RC 500.00 1200.00
171 Evgeni Malkin JSY AU/99 RC 1500.00 3000.00
172 Paul Stastny JSY AU/99 RC 500.00 1200.00
173 Anze Kopitar JSY AU/99 RC 600.00 1400.00
174 Alexander Radulov
JSY AU/99 RC 1000.00 1300.00

2006-07 The Cup Autographed Cornerstones

STATED PRINT RUN 10 #'d SETS
NOT PRICED DUE TO SCARCITY
CQAH Ales Hemsky
CQAK Anze Kopitar
CQAM Al MacInnis
CQAO Adam Oates
CQAR Andrew Raycroft
CQAY Alexei Yashin
CQBB Brad Boyes
CQBL Rob Blake
CQBS Billy Smith
CQCN Cam Neely
CQCP Chris Pronger
CQCW Cam Ward
CQDG Doug Gilmour SP
CQDH Dale Hawerchuk
CQDS Denis Savard
CQEB Ed Belfour
CQEM Evgeni Malkin
CQEN Evgeni Nabokov
CQES Eric Staal
CQFM Frank Mahovlich
CQGC Gerry Cheevers
CQGF Grant Fuhr
CQGH Gordie Howe
CQGL Guy Lafleur
CQGP Gilbert Perreault
CQHA Dominik Hasek
CQHE Dany Heatley
CQHL Henrik Lundqvist
CQHM Milan Hejduk
CQHZ Henrik Zetterberg
CQIK Ilya Kovalchuk
CQJB Jean Beliveau
CQJC Jonathan Cheechoo
CQJI Jarome Iginla
CQJK Jari Kurri
CQJR Jeremy Roenick
CQJS Jordan Staal
CQJT Joe Thornton
CQKE Phil Kessel
CQKL Kari Lehtonen
CQLM Lanny McDonald
CQLR Larry Robinson
CQMA Stan Mikita
CQMB Martin Brodeur
CQMD Marcel Dionne
CQMG Marian Gaborik
CQMI Mike Bossy
CQML Mario Lemieux
CQMM Mike Modano
CQMN Markus Naslund
CQMR Michael Ryder
CQMS Martin St. Louis
CQMT Marty Turco
CQNL Nicklas Lidstrom
CQOV Alexander Ovechkin
CQPB Patrice Bergeron
CQPE Patrik Elias
CQPH Dion Phaneuf
CQPM Patrick Marleau
CQPR Patrick Roy
CQPS Peter Stastny
CQRB Ray Bourque
CQRE Ron Ellis
CQRH Ron Hextall
CQRM Ryan Miller
CQRN Rick Nash
CQRO Luc Robitaille
CQRS Ryan Smyth
CQRV Rogie Vachon
CQSA Borje Salming
CQSC Sidney Crosby
CQSG Simon Gagne
CQSK Saku Koivu
CQSM Miroslav Satan
CQSP Jason Spezza
CQSS Scott Stevens
CQST Steve Shutt
CQTE Tony Esposito
CQTH Jose Theodore
CQTV Tomas Vokoun
CQVL Vincent Lecavalier
CQWG Wayne Gretzky

2006-07 The Cup Autographed Cornerstones Patches

STATED PRINT RUN 5 #'d SETS
NOT PRICED DUE TO SCARCITY

2006-07 The Cup Autographed NHL Shields Duals

STATED PRINT RUN 1/1
NOT PRICED DUE TO SCARCITY
DASAD Dwayne Roloson
Ales Hemsky
DASAN Jean-Sebastien Giguere
Corey Perry
DASBB Ed Belfour
Todd Bertuzzi
DASBD Chris Drury
Daniel Briere
DASBH Martin Brodeur
Dominik Hasek
DASBK Rob Blake
Anze Kopitar
DASBM Ray Bourque
Al MacInnis
DASBO Glen Murray
Brad Boyes
DASBP Dustin Boyd
Brandon Prust
DASBR Mike Modano
Brenden Morrow
DASBS Ray Bourque
Scott Stevens
DASCO Milan Hejduk
Marek Svatos
DASCT Zdeno Chara
Hannu Toivonen
DASDA Adam Oates
Dale Hawerchuk
DASDJ Jason Spezza
Dany Heatley
DASDM Dany Heatley
Martin Gerber
DASDP Michael Peca
Kris Draper
DASDS Chris Drury
Drew Stafford
DASEC Eric Staal
Cam Ward
DASEO Ryan Smyth
Ales Hemsky
DASEZ Patrik Elias
Travis Zajac
DASFK Alexander Frolov
Anze Kopitar
DASGB Marian Gaborik
Pierre-Marc Bouchard
DASGC Wendel Clark
Doug Gilmour
DASGG Scott Gomez
Brian Gionta
DASGK Jari Kurri
Wayne Gretzky
DASGL Mario Lemieux
Wayne Gretzky
DASGP Simon Gagne
Joni Pitkanen
DASGS Simon Gagne
Martin St. Louis
DASHA David Aebischer
Cristobal Huet
DASHG Simon Gagne
Dany Heatley
DASHH Michal Handzus
Martin Havlat
DASHL Dominik Hasek
Nicklas Lidstrom
DASHN Dany Heatley
Rick Nash
DASHO Dominik Hasek
Chris Osgood
DASHR Wade Redden
Dany Heatley
DASHS Milan Hejduk
Marek Svatos
DASHT Milan Hejduk
Jose Theodore
DASHV Tomas Vokoun
Dominik Hasek
DASHZ Dominik Hasek
Henrik Zetterberg
DASIA Ilya Kovalchuk
Alexander Radulov
DASIK Ilya Kovalchuk
Kari Lehtonen
DASIL Vincent Lecavalier
Jarome Iginla
DASIP Jarome Iginla
Dion Phaneuf
DASIT Jarome Iginla
Alex Tanguay
DASKB Patrice Bergeron
Phil Kessel
DASKL Phil Kessel
Guillaume Latendresse
DASKO Patrick O'Sullivan
Anze Kopitar
DASKR Saku Koivu
Michael Ryder
DASLB Martin Brodeur
Roberto Luongo
DASLD Henrik Lundqvist
Nigel Dawes
DASLH Nicklas Lidstrom
Tomas Holmstrom
DASLN Markus Naslund
Roberto Luongo
DASLP Guillaume Latendresse
Benoit Pouliot
DASLR Patrick Roy
Mario Lemieux
DASLS Jarret Stoll
Joffrey Lupul
DASLT Vesa Toskala
Kari Lehtonen
DASMB Martin Biron
Ryan Miller
DASMC Chris Higgins
Guillaume Latendresse
DASMD Chris Drury
Ryan Miller
DASMI Mike Modano
Mike Ribeiro
DASMK Evgeni Malkin
Phil Kessel
DASMM Patrick Marleau
Milan Michalek
DASMN Marian Gaborik
Benoit Pouliot
DASMO Alexander Ovechkin
Evgeni Malkin
DASMR Evgeni Malkin
Alexander Radulov
DASMS Evgeni Malkin
Jordan Staal
DASMT Mike Modano
Marty Turco
DASNB Cam Neely
Ray Bourque
DASNJ Martin Brodeur
Scott Stevens
DASNM Markus Naslund
Brendan Morrison
DASNZ Rick Nash
Nikolai Zherdev
DASPC Matt Carle
Joe Pavelski
DASPG Glen Murray
Patrice Bergeron
DASRA Jason Arnott
Alexander Radulov
DASRB Patrick Roy
Martin Brodeur
DASRL Michael Ryder
Guillaume Latendresse
DASRP Michael Peca
Andrew Raycroft
DASRT Luc Robitaille
Dave Taylor
DASSC Erik Cole
Eric Staal
DASSK Phil Kessel
Jordan Staal
DASSL Vincent Lecavalier
Martin St. Louis
DASSM Drew Stafford
Clarke MacArthur
DASSS Yan Stastny
Paul Stastny
DASST Eric Staal
Jordan Staal
DASSV Marek Svatos
Paul Stastny
DASSW Justin Williams
Eric Staal
DASTB Joe Thornton
Steve Bernier
DASTC Joe Thornton
Jonathan Cheechoo
DASTM Patrick Marleau
Joe Thornton
DASVS Tomas Vokoun
Steve Sullivan
DASWW Ian White
Jeremy Williams
DASYS Miroslav Satan
Alexei Yashin
DASZN Markus Naslund
Henrik Zetterberg

2006-07 The Cup Autographed Patches

STATED PRINT RUN 1/1
NOT PRICED DUE TO SCARCITY
2 Jean-Sebastian Giguere
3 Kari Lehtonen
4 Ilya Kovalchuk
7 Ray Bourque
9 Cam Neely
10 Patrice Bergeron
12 Ryan Miller
13 Gilbert Perreault
14 Jarome Iginla
16 Al MacInnis
17 Eric Staal
18 Cam Ward
19 Bobby Hull
20 Tony Esposito
21 Stan Mikita
23 Patrick Roy
24 Rick Nash
26 Mike Modano
27 Dominik Hasek
28 Henrik Zetterberg
29 Gordie Howe
33 Ales Hemsky
34 Grant Fuhr
35 Jari Kurri
36 Ed Belfour
37 Wayne Gretzky
38 Rob Blake
39 Marcel Dionne
40 Luc Robitaille
42 Dino Ciccarelli
43 Marian Gaborik
44 Saku Koivu
45 Michael Ryder
46 Guy Lafleur
47 Larry Robinson
51 Tomas Vokoun
52 Martin Brodeur
53 Scott Stevens
54 Alexei Yashin
56 Mike Bossy
57 Billy Smith
61 Henrik Lundqvist
62 Gump Worsley
64 Jason Spezza
65 Dany Heatley
67 Simon Gagne
69 Bobby Clarke
70 Ron Hextall
71 Jeremy Roenick
73 Sidney Crosby
74 Marc-Andre Fleury
75 Mario Lemieux
76 Peter Stastny
77 Joe Thornton
78 Jonathan Cheechoo
79 Patrick Marleau
80 Bernie Federko
81 Vincent Lecavalier
84 Darryl Sittler
86 Borje Salming
87 Roberto Luongo
88 Markus Naslund
89 Alexander Ovechkin
90 Dale Hawerchuk

2006-07 The Cup Autographed Rookie Masterpiece Pressplates

STATED PRINT RUN 1/1
NOT PRICED DUE TO SCARCITY
91 Nate Thompson
92 Mike Brown
93 Mike Card
94 Adam Dennis
95 Carsen Germyn
96 Adam Burish
97 Drew Larman
98 Jonas Johansson
99 Joel Perrault
100 Mikko Lehtonen
101 Alex Brooks
102 Frank Doyle
103 Billy Thompson
104 Kelly Guard
105 David Printz
106 D.J. King
107 Jean-Francois Racine
108 Nathan McIver
109 Shane O'Brien
110 Ryan Shannon
111 David McKee
112 Mark Stuart
113 Matt Lashoff
114 Drew Stafford
115 Clarke MacArthur
116 Michael Funk
117 Brandon Prust
118 Dustin Boyd
119 Dustin Byfuglien
120 Dave Bolland
121 Michael Blunden
122 Filip Novak
123 Fredrik Norrena
124 Niklas Grossman
125 Loui Eriksson
126 Tomas Kopecky
127 Stefan Liv
128 Patrick Thoresen
129 Marc-Antoine Pouliot
130 Ladislav Smid
131 Janis Sprukts
132 Jeff Drouin-Deslauriers
133 David Booth
134 Konstantin Pushkaryov
135 Patrick O'Sullivan
136 Benoit Pouliot
137 Niklas Backstrom
138 Guillaume Latendresse
139 Shea Weber
140 Johnny Oduya
141 Travis Zajac
142 Masi Marjamaki
143 Nigel Dawes
144 Jarkko Immonen
145 Josh Hennessy
146 Ryan Potulny
147 Jussi Timonen
148 Keith Yandle
149 Michel Ouellet
150 Noah Welch
151 Kristopher Letang
152 Joe Pavelski
153 Matt Carle
154 Marc-Edouard Vlasic
155 Yan Stastny
156 Marek Schwarz
157 Roman Polak
158 Karri Ramo
159 Blair Jones
160 Brendan Bell
161 Ian White
162 Ben Ondrus
163 Jeremy Williams
164 Miroslav Kopriva
165 Luc Bourdon
166 Jesse Schultz
167 Alexander Edler
168 Eric Fehr
169 Jordan Staal
170 Phil Kessel
171 Evgeni Malkin
172 Paul Stastny
173 Anze Kopitar
174 Alexander Radulov

2006-07 The Cup Black Rainbow

STATED PRINT RUN 1/1
NOT PRICED DUE TO SCARCITY
1 Teemu Selanne
2 Jean-Sebastian Giguere
3 Kari Lehtonen
4 Ilya Kovalchuk
5 Phil Esposito
6 Don Cherry
7 Ray Bourque
8 Bobby Orr
9 Cam Neely
10 Patrice Bergeron
11 Johnny Bucyk
12 Ryan Miller
13 Gilbert Perreault
14 Jarome Iginla
15 Miikka Kiprusoff
16 Al MacInnis
17 Eric Staal
18 Cam Ward
19 Bobby Hull
20 Tony Esposito
21 Stan Mikita
22 Joe Sakic
23 Patrick Roy
24 Rick Nash
25 Sergei Fedorov
26 Mike Modano
27 Dominik Hasek
28 Henrik Zetterberg
29 Gordie Howe
30 Scotty Bowman
31 Ted Lindsay
32 Red Kelly
33 Ales Hemsky
34 Grant Fuhr
35 Jari Kurri
36 Ed Belfour
37 Wayne Gretzky
38 Rob Blake
39 Marcel Dionne
40 Luc Robitaille
41 Rogie Vachon
42 Dino Ciccarelli
43 Marian Gaborik
44 Saku Koivu
45 Michael Ryder
46 Guy Lafleur
47 Larry Robinson
48 Jean Beliveau
49 Jacques Lemaire
50 Paul Kariya
51 Tomas Vokoun
52 Martin Brodeur
53 Scott Stevens
54 Alexei Yashin
55 Al Arbour
56 Mike Bossy
57 Billy Smith
58 Denis Potvin
59 Jaromir Jagr
60 Brendan Shanahan
61 Henrik Lundqvist
62 Gump Worsley
63 Andy Bathgate
64 Jason Spezza
65 Dany Heatley
66 Peter Forsberg
67 Simon Gagne
68 Bernie Parent
69 Bobby Clarke
70 Ron Hextall
71 Jeremy Roenick
72 Shane Doan
73 Sidney Crosby
74 Marc-Andre Fleury
75 Mario Lemieux
76 Peter Stastny
77 Joe Thornton
78 Jonathan Cheechoo
79 Patrick Marleau
80 Bernie Federko
81 Vincent Lecavalier
82 Mats Sundin
83 Frank Mahovlich
84 Darryl Sittler
85 Johnny Bower
86 Borje Salming
87 Roberto Luongo
88 Markus Naslund
89 Alexander Ovechkin
90 Dale Hawerchuk

2006-07 The Cup Cornerstones

STATED PRINT RUN 25 #'d SETS
CQAH Ales Hemsky 20.00 50.00
CQAK Anze Kopitar 40.00 100.00
CQAM Al MacInnis 15.00 40.00
CQAO Adam Oates
CQAR Andrew Raycroft 15.00 40.00
CQAY Alexei Yashin 12.00 30.00
CQBB Brad Boyes 12.00 30.00
CQBL Rob Blake 20.00 50.00
CQBS Billy Smith 20.00 50.00
CQCJ Curtis Joseph 20.00 50.00
CQCN Cam Neely 25.00 60.00
CQCP Chris Pronger 25.00 60.00
CQCW Cam Ward 25.00 60.00
CQDA Daniel Alfredsson 20.00 50.00
CQDC Dino Ciccarelli 12.00 30.00
CQDG Doug Gilmour SP 20.00 50.00
CQDH Dale Hawerchuk 20.00 50.00
CQDS Denis Savard 30.00 80.00
CQEB Ed Belfour 20.00 50.00
CQEL Eric Lindros 20.00 50.00
CQEM Evgeni Malkin 75.00 200.00
CQEN Evgeni Nabokov 15.00 40.00
CQES Eric Staal
CQFM Frank Mahovlich 20.00 50.00
CQGC Gerry Cheevers 15.00 40.00
CQGF Grant Fuhr 15.00 40.00
CQGH Gordie Howe 30.00 80.00
CQGL Guy Lafleur
CQGP Gilbert Perreault 25.00 60.00
CQHA Dominik Hasek 30.00 80.00
CQHE Dany Heatley 25.00 60.00
CQHL Henrik Lundqvist 25.00 60.00
CQHM Milan Hejduk 12.00 30.00
CQHZ Henrik Zetterberg 25.00 60.00
CQIK Ilya Kovalchuk 25.00 60.00
CQJB Jean Beliveau
CQJC Jonathan Cheechoo 25.00 60.00
CQJI Jarome Iginla 25.00 60.00
CQJJ Jaromir Jagr 30.00 80.00
CQJK Jari Kurri 25.00 60.00
CQJO Joe Sakic 40.00 100.00
CQJR Jeremy Roenick 25.00 60.00
CQJS Jordan Staal 60.00 150.00
CQJT Joe Thornton 30.00 80.00
CQKE Phil Kessel 25.00 60.00
CQKL Kari Lehtonen 25.00 60.00
CQLM Lanny McDonald 25.00 60.00
CQLR Larry Robinson 25.00 60.00
CQMA Stan Mikita 25.00 60.00
CQMB Martin Brodeur 50.00 125.00
CQMD Marcel Dionne 25.00 60.00
CQMG Marian Gaborik 25.00 60.00
CQMH Marian Hossa 25.00 60.00
CQMI Mike Bossy 25.00 50.00
CQML Mario Lemieux 60.00 150.00
CQMM Mike Modano 25.00 60.00
CQMN Markus Naslund 25.00 60.00
CQMR Michael Ryder 25.00 60.00
CQMS Martin St. Louis 25.00 60.00
CQMT Marty Turco 25.00 60.00
CQNL Nicklas Lidstrom 25.00 60.00
CQOK Olaf Kolzig 25.00 60.00
CQOV Alexander Ovechkin 50.00 125.00
CQPB Patrice Bergeron 25.00 60.00
CQPD Pavel Datsyuk 25.00 60.00
CQPE Patrik Elias 12.00 30.00
CQPF Peter Forsberg 30.00 80.00
CQPH Dion Phaneuf 25.00 60.00
CQPK Paul Kariya 25.00 60.00
CQPM Patrick Marleau 25.00 60.00
CQPR Patrick Roy 60.00 150.00
CQPS Peter Stastny 15.00 40.00
CQRB Ray Bourque 30.00 80.00
CQRD Rick DiPietro 25.00 60.00
CQRE Ron Ellis
CQRH Ron Hextall 25.00 60.00
CQRL Roberto Luongo 30.00 80.00
CQRM Ryan Miller 30.00 80.00
CQRN Rick Nash 30.00 80.00
CQRO Luc Robitaille 25.00 60.00
CQRS Ryan Smyth 15.00 40.00
CQRV Rogie Vachon 25.00 60.00
CQSA Borje Salming 12.00 30.00
CQSC Sidney Crosby 100.00 250.00
CQSF Sergei Fedorov 25.00 60.00
CQSG Simon Gagne 25.00 60.00
CQSH Brendan Shanahan 25.00 60.00
CQSK Saku Koivu 25.00 60.00
CQSM Miroslav Satan 25.00 60.00
CQSP Jason Spezza 25.00 60.00
CQSS Scott Stevens 20.00 50.00
CQST Steve Shutt 12.00 30.00
CQSU Mats Sundin 25.00 60.00
CQTE Tony Esposito 25.00 60.00
CQTH Jose Theodore 25.00 60.00
CQTS Teemu Selanne 30.00 80.00
CQTV Tomas Vokoun 25.00 60.00
CQVL Vincent Lecavalier 25.00 60.00
CQWG Wayne Gretzky 75.00 200.00

2006-07 The Cup Cornerstones Patches

STATED PRINT RUN 10 #'d SETS
NOT PRICED DUE TO SCARCITY
CQAH Ales Hemsky
CQAK Anze Kopitar
CQAM Al MacInnis
CQAO Adam Oates
CQAR Andrew Raycroft
CQAY Alexei Yashin
CQBB Brad Boyes
CQBL Rob Blake
CQBS Billy Smith
CQCJ Curtis Joseph
CQCN Cam Neely
CQCP Chris Pronger
CQCW Cam Ward
CQDA Daniel Alfredsson
CQDC Dino Ciccarelli
CQDG Doug Gilmour SP
CQDH Dale Hawerchuk
CQDS Denis Savard
CQEB Ed Belfour
CQEL Eric Lindros
CQEM Evgeni Malkin
CQEN Evgeni Nabokov
CQES Eric Staal
CQGC Gerry Cheevers
CQGF Grant Fuhr
CQGH Gordie Howe
CQGL Guy Lafleur
CQGP Gilbert Perreault
CQHA Dominik Hasek
CQHE Dany Heatley
CQHL Henrik Lundqvist
CQHM Milan Hejduk
CQHZ Henrik Zetterberg
CQIK Ilya Kovalchuk
CQJC Jonathan Cheechoo
CQJI Jarome Iginla
CQJJ Jaromir Jagr
CQJK Jari Kurri
CQJO Joe Sakic
CQJR Jeremy Roenick
CQJS Jordan Staal
CQJT Joe Thornton
CQKE Phil Kessel
CQKL Kari Lehtonen
CQLR Larry Robinson
CQMA Stan Mikita
CQMB Martin Brodeur
CQMD Marcel Dionne
CQMG Marian Gaborik
CQMH Marian Hossa
CQMI Mike Bossy
CQML Mario Lemieux
CQMM Mike Modano
CQMN Markus Naslund
CQMR Michael Ryder
CQMS Martin St. Louis
CQMT Marty Turco
CQNL Nicklas Lidstrom
CQOK Olaf Kolzig
CQOV Alexander Ovechkin
CQPB Patrice Bergeron
CQPD Pavel Datsyuk
CQPE Patrik Elias
CQPF Peter Forsberg
CQPH Dion Phaneuf
CQPK Paul Kariya
CQPM Patrick Marleau
CQPR Patrick Roy
CQPS Peter Stastny
CQRB Ray Bourque
CQRD Rick DiPietro
CQRH Ron Hextall
CQRL Roberto Luongo
CQRM Ryan Miller
CQRN Rick Nash
CQRO Luc Robitaille
CQRS Ryan Smyth
CQSA Borje Salming
CQSC Sidney Crosby
CQSF Sergei Federov
CQSG Simon Gagne
CQSH Brendan Shanahan
CQSK Saku Koivu
CQSM Miroslav Satan
CQSP Jason Spezza
CQSS Scott Stevens
CQST Steve Shutt
CQSU Mats Sundin
CQTE Tony Esposito
CQTH Jose Theodore
CQTS Teemu Selanne
CQTV Tomas Vokoun
CQVL Vincent Lecavalier
CQWG Wayne Gretzky

2006-07 The Cup Enshrinements

STATED PRINT RUN 50 #'d SETS
EAK Anze Kopitar 40.00 100.00
EAR Andrew Raycroft 15.00 40.00
EBO Bobby Orr 150.00 250.00
EBP Benoit Pouliot 15.00 40.00
ECD Chris Drury 10.00 25.00
ECN Cam Neely 20.00 50.00
ECW Cam Ward 15.00 40.00
EDB Dustin Boyd 10.00 25.00
EDH Dominik Hasek 25.00 60.00
EDP Dion Phaneuf 25.00 60.00
EDS Drew Stafford 20.00 50.00
EEM Evgeni Malkin 100.00 200.00
EES Eric Staal 10.00 25.00
EFM Frank Mahovlich 15.00 40.00
EGH Gordie Howe 40.00 100.00
EGL Guillaume Latendresse 30.00 80.00
EGR Wayne Gretzky 200.00 400.00
EHE Dany Heatley
EHZ Henrik Zetterberg 25.00 60.00
EIK Ilya Kovalchuk 25.00 60.00
EJB Johnny Bucyk 10.00 25.00
EJC Jonathan Cheechoo 20.00 50.00
EJG Jean-Sebastian Giguere 20.00 50.00
EJI Jarome Iginla 25.00 60.00
EJK Jari Kurri
EJM Joe Mullen 10.00 25.00
EJS Jordan Staal 50.00 125.00
EJT Joe Thornton 25.00 60.00
EKL Kari Lehtonen 15.00 40.00
ELR Larry Robinson 10.00 25.00
EMB Martin Brodeur 40.00 100.00
EMD Marcel Dionne 15.00 40.00
EMF Marc-Andre Fleury 25.00 60.00
EMG Marian Gaborik 25.00 60.00
EML Mario Lemieux 75.00 150.00
EMR Michael Ryder 10.00 25.00
EMS Marek Svatos
EMT Marty Turco 15.00 40.00
ENL Nicklas Lidstrom 20.00 50.00
EPK Phil Kessel 25.00 60.00
EPL Pat LaFontaine 20.00 50.00
EPR Patrick Roy 75.00 150.00
EPS Paul Stastny 30.00 80.00
ERA Alexander Radulov 40.00 100.00
ERB Ray Bourque 30.00 80.00
ERH Ron Hextall 15.00 40.00
ERL Roberto Luongo
ERM Ryan Miller 25.00 60.00
ERN Rick Nash 20.00 50.00
ERS Ryan Smyth 20.00 50.00
ESC Sidney Crosby 200.00 350.00
ESS Steve Shutt 10.00 25.00
EST Scott Stevens 15.00 40.00
ETE Tony Esposito 20.00 50.00
ETV Tomas Vokoun 15.00 40.00
ETZ Travis Zajac 15.00 40.00
EVA Thomas Vanek 15.00 40.00
EVL Vincent Lecavalier 20.00 50.00
EVT Vesa Toskala 15.00 40.00
EWG Wayne Gretzky 200.00 400.00

2006-07 The Cup Gold

*GOLD: 1X TO 2.5X HI COLUMN
STATED PRINT RUN 25 #'d SETS
1 Teemu Selanne 15.00 40.00
2 Jean-Sebastian Giguere 12.00 30.00
3 Kari Lehtonen 15.00 40.00
4 Ilya Kovalchuk 20.00 50.00
5 Phil Esposito 25.00 60.00
6 Don Cherry 40.00
7 Ray Bourque 25.00 60.00
8 Bobby Orr 50.00 120.00
9 Cam Neely 20.00 50.00
10 Patrice Bergeron 15.00 40.00
11 Johnny Bucyk 25.00
12 Ryan Miller 15.00 40.00
13 Gilbert Perreault 15.00 40.00
14 Jarome Iginla 20.00 50.00
15 Miikka Kiprusoff 15.00 40.00
16 Al MacInnis 8.00 20.00
17 Eric Staal 15.00 40.00
18 Cam Ward 15.00 40.00
19 Bobby Hull 25.00 60.00
20 Tony Esposito 15.00 40.00
21 Stan Mikita 15.00 40.00
22 Joe Sakic 30.00 80.00
23 Patrick Roy 60.00 150.00
24 Rick Nash 15.00 40.00
25 Sergei Fedorov 15.00 40.00
26 Mike Modano 15.00 40.00
27 Dominik Hasek 25.00 60.00
28 Henrik Zetterberg 15.00 40.00
29 Gordie Howe 30.00 80.00
30 Scotty Bowman 25.00
31 Ted Lindsay 8.00 20.00
32 Red Kelly 8.00
33 Ales Hemsky 8.00 20.00
34 Grant Fuhr 20.00 50.00
35 Jari Kurri 15.00 40.00
36 Ed Belfour 15.00 40.00
37 Wayne Gretzky 80.00 200.00
38 Rob Blake 12.00 30.00
39 Marcel Dionne 15.00 40.00
40 Luc Robitaille 12.00 30.00
41 Rogie Vachon 15.00 40.00
42 Dino Ciccarelli 20.00
43 Marian Gaborik 20.00 50.00
44 Saku Koivu 15.00 40.00
45 Michael Ryder 12.00 30.00
46 Guy Lafleur 25.00 60.00
47 Larry Robinson 12.00 30.00
48 Jean Beliveau 20.00 50.00
49 Jacques Lemaire 20.00
50 Paul Kariya 15.00 40.00
51 Tomas Vokoun 12.00 30.00
52 Martin Brodeur 40.00 100.00
53 Scott Stevens 10.00
54 Alexei Yashin 8.00 20.00
55 Al Arbour 8.00
56 Mike Bossy 12.00 30.00
57 Billy Smith 15.00 40.00
58 Denis Potvin 12.00 30.00
59 Jaromir Jagr 25.00 60.00
60 Brendan Shanahan 15.00 40.00
61 Henrik Lundqvist 20.00 50.00
62 Gump Worsley 12.00
63 Andy Bathgate 8.00 20.00
64 Jason Spezza 15.00 40.00
65 Dany Heatley 20.00 50.00
66 Peter Forsberg 25.00 60.00
67 Simon Gagne 15.00 40.00

68 Bernie Parent 30.00
69 Bobby Clarke 15.00 40.00
70 Ron Hextall 12.00
71 Jeremy Roenick 20.00 50.00
72 Shane Doan 8.00 20.00
73 Sidney Crosby 80.00 200.00
74 Marc-Andre Fleury 15.00 40.00
75 Mario Lemieux 60.00 150.00
76 Peter Stastny 8.00 20.00
77 Joe Thornton 25.00 60.00
78 Jonathan Cheechoo 15.00 40.00
79 Patrick Marleau 12.00 30.00
80 Bernie Federko 20.00
81 Vincent Lecavalier 15.00 40.00
82 Mats Sundin 15.00 40.00
83 Frank Mahovlich 15.00 40.00
84 Darryl Sittler 15.00 40.00
85 Johnny Bower 12.00 30.00
86 Borje Salming 12.00 30.00
87 Roberto Luongo 20.00 50.00
88 Markus Naslund 15.00 40.00
89 Alexander Ovechkin 40.00 100.00
90 Dale Hawerchuk 8.00 20.00

2006-07 The Cup Gold Patches

STATED PRINT RUN 10 #'d SETS
NOT PRICED DUE TO SCARCITY
1 Teemu Selanne
2 Jean-Sebastian Giguere
3 Kari Lehtonen
4 Ilya Kovalchuk
5 Phil Esposito
7 Ray Bourque
9 Cam Neely
10 Patrice Bergeron
12 Ryan Miller
13 Gilbert Perreault
14 Jarome Iginla
15 Miikka Kiprusoff
16 Al MacInnis
17 Eric Staal
18 Cam Ward
19 Bobby Hull
20 Tony Esposito
21 Stan Mikita
22 Joe Sakic
23 Patrick Roy
24 Rick Nash
25 Sergei Fedorov
26 Mike Modano
27 Dominik Hasek
28 Henrik Zetterberg
29 Gordie Howe
33 Ales Hemsky
34 Grant Fuhr
35 Jari Kurri
36 Ed Belfour
37 Wayne Gretzky
38 Rob Blake
39 Marcel Dionne
40 Luc Robitaille
42 Dino Ciccarelli
43 Marian Gaborik
44 Saku Koivu
45 Michael Ryder
46 Guy Lafleur
47 Larry Robinson
50 Paul Kariya
51 Tomas Vokoun
52 Martin Brodeur
53 Scott Stevens
54 Alexei Yashin
56 Mike Bossy
57 Billy Smith
58 Denis Potvin
59 Jaromir Jagr
60 Brendan Shanahan
61 Henrik Lundqvist
62 Gump Worsley
64 Jason Spezza
65 Dany Heatley
66 Peter Forsberg
67 Simon Gagne
69 Bobby Clarke
70 Ron Hextall
71 Jeremy Roenick
72 Shane Doan
73 Sidney Crosby
74 Marc-Andre Fleury
75 Mario Lemieux
76 Peter Stastny
77 Joe Thornton
78 Jonathan Cheechoo
79 Patrick Marleau
80 Bernie Federko
81 Vincent Lecavalier
82 Mats Sundin
84 Darryl Sittler
85 Johnny Bower
86 Borje Salming
87 Roberto Luongo
88 Markus Naslund
89 Alexander Ovechkin
90 Dale Hawerchuk

2006-07 The Cup Gold Rainbow Autographed Rookie Patches

PRINT RUNS VARY
UNIQUE SWATCHES MAY EARN
SUBSTANTIAL PREMIUM
WHITE SWATCHES: .5X to 1X LO
109 Shane O'Brien/37 30.00 80.00
110 Ryan Shannon/38 30.00 80.00
111 David McKee/41 40.00 100.00
112 Mark Stuart/45 25.00 60.00
113 Matt Lashoff/49 30.00 80.00
114 Drew Stafford/21
115 Clarke MacArthur/41
116 Michael Funk/3
117 Brandon Prust/37
118 Dustin Boyd/41 30.00 80.00
119 Dustin Byfuglien/52 30.00 80.00
120 Dave Bolland/36 40.00 100.00
121 Michael Blunden/28 30.00 80.00
122 Filip Novak/17 25.00 60.00
123 Fredrik Norrena/30 50.00 125.00
124 Niklas Grossman/2
125 Loui Eriksson/21
126 Tomas Kopecky/32 30.00 80.00
127 Stefan Liv/32 30.00 80.00
128 Patrick Thoresen/28 30.00 80.00
129 Marc-Antoine Pouliot/36 30.00 80.00
130 Ladislav Smid/5
131 Janis Sprukts/38 40.00 100.00
132 Jeff Drouin-Deslauriers/39 25.00 60.00
133 David Booth/46 25.00 60.00
134 Konstantin Pushkaryov/5
135 Patrick O'Sullivan/12
136 Benoit Pouliot/67 40.00 100.00
137 Niklas Backstrom/32 100.00 250.00
138 Guillaume Latendresse/84 75.00 200.00
139 Shea Weber/6
140 Johnny Oduya/29 30.00 80.00
141 Travis Zajac/19
142 Masi Marjamaki/58 40.00 100.00
143 Nigel Dawes/10
144 Jarkko Immonen/38 25.00 60.00
145 Josh Hennessy/36 30.00 80.00
146 Ryan Potulny/11
147 Jussi Timonen/46
148 Keith Yandle/3
149 Michel Ouellet/7
150 Noah Welch/4
151 Kristopher Letang/58
152 Joe Pavelski/8
153 Matt Carle/18
154 Marc-Edouard Vlasic/44 40.00 100.00
155 Yan Stastny/43 25.00 60.00
156 Marek Schwarz/40
157 Roman Polak/46 25.00 60.00
158 Karri Ramo/31 30.00 80.00
159 Blair Jones/49 20.00 50.00
160 Brendan Bell/36 25.00 60.00
161 Ian White/7
162 Ben Ondrus/46 30.00 80.00
163 Jeremy Williams/48 30.00 80.00
164 Miroslav Kopriva/31 25.00 60.00
165 Luc Bourdon/4
166 Jesse Schultz/20 30.00 80.00
167 Alexander Edler/23 30.00 80.00
168 Eric Fehr/3
169 Jordan Staal/11 1500.00 5000.00
170 Phil Kessel/81 150.00 400.00
171 Evgeni Malkin/71 800.00 1200.00
172 Paul Stastny/62 500.00 1000.00
173 Anze Kopitar/11
174 Alexander Radulov/47 100.00 200.00

2006-07 The Cup Gold Rainbow Autographed Rookies

PRINT RUNS VARY
91 Nate Thompson/52 10.00 25.00
92 Mike Brown/70 10.00 25.00
93 Mike Card/33 10.00 25.00
94 Adam Dennis/35
95 Carsen Germyn/39 10.00 25.00
96 Adam Burish/37 8.00 20.00
97 Drew Larman/50 10.00 25.00
98 Jonas Johansson/45 8.00 20.00
99 Joel Perrault/26 10.00 25.00
100 Mikko Lehtonen/42 8.00 20.00
101 Alex Brooks/8
102 Frank Doyle/1
103 Billy Thompson/31
104 Kelly Guard/32 12.00 30.00
105 David Printz/28 12.00 30.00
106 D.J. King/19 15.00 40.00
107 Jean-Francois Racine/35 12.00 30.00
108 Nathan McIver/45 10.00 25.00

2006-07 The Cup Hardware Heroes

PRINT RUNS VARY
NOT PRICED DUE TO SCARCITY
HHAB Andy Bathgate/1
HHEL Elmer Lach/1
HHJL Jacques Lemaire/2
HHMS Milt Schmidt/1
HHPP Pierre Pilote/3
HHBO1 Bobby Orr/8
HHBO2 Bobby Orr/1
HHBO3 Bobby Orr/2
HHBO4 Bobby Orr/3
HHBO5 Bobby Orr/2

2006-07 The Cup Hardware Heroes Patches

PRINT RUNS VARY
NOT PRICED DUE TO SCARCITY
HHCW Cam Ward/1
HHJC Jonathan Cheechoo/1
HHJK Jari Kurri/1
HHJT Joe Thornton/1
HHLR Larry Robinson/2
HHNL Nicklas Lidstrom/4
HHSM Stan Mikita/2
HHML1 Mario Lemieux/1
HHML2 Mario Lemieux/2
HHML3 Mario Lemieux/6
HHML4 Mario Lemieux/2

2006-07 The Cup Honorable Numbers

PRINT RUNS VARY
LOWER PRINT RUNS NOT PRICED DUE TO SCARCITY
HNAH Ales Hemsky/83
HNAK Anze Kopitar/11
HNAM Al MacInnis/2
HNAO Adam Oates/12
HNAR Andrew Raycroft/1
HNBC Bobby Clarke/16
HNBL Rob Blake/4
HNBS Billy Smith/31 50.00 125.00
HNCH Jonathan Cheechoo/14
HNCN Cam Neely/8
HNCW Cam Ward/30 30.00 80.00
HNDC Dino Ciccarelli/20 30.00 80.00
HNDE Denis Savard/18 50.00 125.00
HNDH Dale Hawerchuk/10
HNDS Darryl Sittler/27 30.00 80.00
HNDW Doug Wilson/24
HNEM Evgeni Malkin/71 150.00 400.00
HNEN Evgeni Nabokov/20 40.00 100.00
HNES Eric Staal/12
HNGF Grant Fuhr/31 40.00 100.00
HNGH Gordie Howe/9
HNGL Guillaume Latendresse/84 50.00 125.00
HNGO Scott Gomez/23 50.00 100.00
HNGP Gilbert Perreault/11
HNHA Dominik Hasek/39 50.00 125.00
HNHE Dany Heatley/15
HNHL Henrik Lundqvist/30 100.00 250.00
HNHM Milan Hejduk/23 40.00 100.00
HNHZ Henrik Zetterberg/40
HNIK Ilya Kovalchuk/17
HNJC Jeff Carter/17 50.00 125.00
HNJG Jean-Sebastien Giguere/35 30.00 80.00
HNJI Jarome Iginla/12
HNJK Jari Kurri/17
HNJM Joe Mullen/7
HNJR Jordan Staal/11
HNJS Jason Spezza/19
HNJT Joe Thornton/19 75.00 150.00
HNKL Kari Lehtonen/32 40.00 100.00
HNLA Guy Lafleur/10
HNLE Loui Eriksson/21 30.00 80.00
HNLM Lanny McDonald/9
HNLR Larry Robinson/19 30.00 80.00
HNMA Stan Mikita/21 50.00 125.00
HNMB Martin Brodeur/30 100.00 250.00
HNMC Matt Carle/18 50.00 125.00
HNMD Marcel Dionne/16
HNMG Marian Gaborik/10
HNMH Martin Havlat/24 30.00 80.00
HNMI Mike Bossy/22 40.00 100.00
HNML Mario Lemieux/66 125.00 300.00
HNMM Mike Modano/9
HNMN Markus Naslund/19 60.00 150.00
HNMR Michael Ryder/73 30.00 80.00
HNMS Martin St. Louis/26 30.00 80.00
HNMT Marty Turco/35
HNMU Larry Murphy/55 15.00 40.00
HNNL Nicklas Lidstrom/5
HNNZ Nikolai Zherdev/13
HNOV Alexander Ovechkin/8
HNPA Paul Henderson/19 60.00 125.00
HNPB Patrice Bergeron/37 30.00 80.00
HNPE Patrik Elias/26 25.00 60.00
HNPH Dion Phaneuf/3
HNPK Phil Kessel/81 30.00 80.00
HNPL Pat LaFontaine/16
HNPM Patrick Marleau/12
HNPO Patrick O'Sullivan/12
HNPR Patrick Roy/33 150.00 400.00
HNPS Paul Stastny/26 100.00 250.00
HNRA Alexander Radulov/47 50.00 125.00
HNRE Ron Ellis/6
HNRH Ron Hextall/27 40.00 100.00
HNRL Roberto Luongo/1
HNRM Ryan Miller/30 60.00 150.00
HNRN Rick Nash/61 30.00 80.00
HNRO Luc Robitaille/20
HNRS Ryan Smyth/94 30.00 60.00
HNSA Borje Salming/21 30.00 80.00
HNSC Sidney Crosby/87 250.00 600.00
HNSG Simon Gagne/12
HNSH Steve Shutt/22 25.00 60.00
HNSK Saku Koivu/11
HNSM Miroslav Satan/81 25.00 60.00
HNSS Scott Stevens/4
HNST Peter Stastny/26 30.00 80.00
HNSV Marek Svatos/40 25.00 60.00
HNSW Shea Weber/6
HNTE Tony Esposito/35 50.00 125.00
HNTH Jose Theodore/60 15.00 40.00
HNTV Tomas Vokoun/29 30.00 80.00
HNTW Tiger Williams/22 30.00 80.00
HNVL Vincent Lecavalier/4
HNWG Wayne Gretzky/99 250.00 600.00
HNZC Zdeno Chara/33 25.00 60.00

2006-07 The Cup Jerseys

STATED PRINT RUN 25 #'d SETS
1 Teemu Selanne 20.00 50.00
2 Jean-Sebastian Giguere 12.00 30.00
3 Kari Lehtonen 10.00 25.00
4 Ilya Kovalchuk
7 Ray Bourque 20.00 50.00
9 Cam Neely 10.00 25.00
10 Patrice Bergeron 10.00 25.00
12 Ryan Miller 10.00 25.00
13 Gilbert Perreault
14 Jarome Iginla 10.00 25.00
15 Miikka Kiprusoff 20.00 50.00
16 Al MacInnis 10.00 25.00
17 Eric Staal 10.00 25.00
18 Cam Ward 10.00 25.00
19 Bobby Hull 12.00 30.00
20 Tony Esposito 10.00 25.00
21 Stan Mikita 10.00 25.00
22 Joe Sakic 25.00 60.00
23 Patrick Roy 50.00 125.00
24 Rick Nash 12.00 30.00
25 Sergei Fedorov 12.00 30.00
26 Mike Modano 10.00 25.00
27 Dominik Hasek 15.00 40.00
28 Henrik Zetterberg 12.00 30.00
29 Gordie Howe
33 Ales Hemsky 10.00 25.00
34 Grant Fuhr 12.00 30.00
35 Jari Kurri 20.00 50.00
36 Ed Belfour 12.00 30.00
37 Wayne Gretzky 125.00 300.00
38 Rob Blake 10.00 25.00
39 Marcel Dionne 12.00 30.00
40 Luc Robitaille 15.00 40.00
42 Dino Ciccarelli 6.00 15.00
43 Marian Gaborik 15.00 40.00
44 Saku Koivu 20.00 50.00
45 Michael Ryder 10.00 25.00
46 Guy Lafleur 20.00 50.00
47 Larry Robinson 6.00 15.00
48 Jean Beliveau
50 Paul Kariya 15.00 40.00
51 Tomas Vokoun 15.00 40.00
52 Martin Brodeur 40.00 80.00
53 Scott Stevens 10.00 25.00
54 Alexei Yashin 6.00 15.00
56 Mike Bossy
57 Billy Smith 10.00 25.00
59 Jaromir Jagr 20.00 50.00
60 Brendan Shanahan 15.00 40.00
62 Gump Worsley 12.00 30.00
64 Jason Spezza 10.00 25.00
65 Dany Heatley 12.00 30.00
66 Peter Forsberg 20.00 50.00
67 Simon Gagne 15.00 40.00
69 Bobby Clarke 12.00 30.00
70 Ron Hextall 15.00 40.00
71 Jeremy Roenick
72 Shane Doan 6.00 15.00
73 Sidney Crosby 100.00 250.00
74 Marc-Andre Fleury 15.00 40.00
75 Mario Lemieux 40.00 100.00
76 Peter Stastny 6.00 15.00
77 Joe Thornton 15.00 40.00
78 Jonathan Cheechoo 10.00 25.00
79 Patrick Marleau 15.00 40.00
80 Bernie Federko
81 Vincent Lecavalier 20.00 50.00
82 Mats Sundin 10.00 25.00
84 Darryl Sittler 10.00 25.00
86 Borje Salming 10.00 25.00
87 Roberto Luongo 20.00 50.00
88 Markus Naslund 10.00 25.00
89 Alexander Ovechkin 30.00 80.00
90 Dale Hawerchuk 10.00 25.00

2006-07 The Cup Legendary Cuts

PRINT RUNS VARY
NOT PRICED DUE TO SCARCITY
LCAB Sid Abel
LCFS Frank Selke
LCHD Hap Day/5
LCTH Tim Horton

2006-07 The Cup Limited Logos

STATED PRINT RUN 50 #'d SETS
UNIQUE SWATCHES MAY EARN
SUBSTANTIAL PREMIUM
SINGLE COLOR SWATCH: .5X TO 1X LO
LLAF Alexander Frolov 50.00 150.00
LLAH Ales Hemsky 30.00 80.00
LLAK Anze Kopitar 125.00 300.00
LLAM Al MacInnis 50.00 125.00
LLAO Adam Oates 40.00 100.00
LLAR Andrew Raycroft 30.00 80.00
LLAT Alex Tanguay 50.00 125.00
LLAY Alexei Yashin 30.00 80.00
LLBB Brad Boyes 25.00 60.00
LLBC Bobby Clarke 40.00 100.00
LLBF Bernie Federko 40.00 80.00
LLBG Brian Gionta 30.00 80.00
LLBL Bill Ranford 30.00 60.00
LLBO Mike Bossy 50.00 150.00
LLBS Billy Smith 30.00 80.00
LLCA Jeff Carter 50.00 150.00
LLCN Cam Neely 50.00 150.00
LLCW Cam Ward 30.00 80.00
LLDA David Aebischer 30.00 80.00
LLDB Daniel Briere 40.00 125.00
LLDC Dino Ciccarelli 30.00 80.00
LLDE Denis Savard 40.00 125.00
LLDG Doug Gilmour 50.00 150.00
LLDH Dale Hawerchuk 40.00 100.00
LLDO Dominik Hasek 40.00 125.00
LLDR Dwayne Roloson 30.00 80.00
LLDS Darryl Sittler 30.00 80.00
LLDW Doug Wilson 25.00 60.00
LLEM Evgeni Malkin 150.00 350.00
LLES Eric Staal 25.00 60.00
LLGA Glenn Anderson 25.00 60.00
LLGE Martin Gerber
LLGH Gordie Howe/25 700.00 1400.00
LLGL Guy Lafleur 50.00 125.00
LLGP Gilbert Perreault 40.00 100.00
LLHE Dany Heatley
LLHL Henrik Lundqvist 100.00 250.00
LLHZ Henrik Zetterberg 30.00 80.00
LLIK Ilya Kovalchuk 40.00 125.00
LLJC Jonathan Cheechoo 30.00 80.00
LLJG Jean-Sebastien Giguere 40.00 100.00
LLJI Jarome Iginla 50.00 150.00
LLJK Jari Kurri 40.00 100.00
LLJM Joe Mullen 25.00 60.00
LLJR Jeremy Roenick 40.00 100.00
LLJS Jordan Staal 100.00 300.00
LLJT Joe Thornton 50.00 150.00
LLKL Kari Lehtonen 30.00 80.00
LLLM Lanny McDonald 25.00 60.00
LLLR Larry Robinson 30.00 80.00
LLMB Martin Brodeur 125.00 250.00
LLMG Marian Gaborik 30.00 80.00
LLMH Martin Havlat 25.00 60.00
LLMI Milan Hejduk 25.00 60.00
LLML Mario Lemieux 150.00 350.00
LLMM Mike Modano 40.00 100.00
LLMR Michael Ryder 25.00 60.00
LLMS Marek Svatos 25.00 60.00
LLMT Marty Turco 30.00 80.00
LLMU Larry Murphy
LLNK Nikolai Khabibulin 30.00 80.00
LLNL Nicklas Lidstrom 40.00 100.00
LLNZ Nikolai Zherdev
LLOV Alexander Ovechkin 100.00 250.00
LLPA Paul Henderson 75.00 150.00
LLPB Patrice Bergeron 40.00 100.00
LLPE Patrik Elias 25.00 60.00
LLPH Dion Phaneuf 40.00 100.00
LLPK Phil Kessel/25 75.00 175.00
LLPL Pat LaFontaine 60.00 125.00
LLPM Patrick Marleau 30.00 80.00
LLPR Patrick Roy 250.00 500.00
LLPS Peter Stastny 30.00 80.00
LLRL Roberto Luongo 40.00 100.00
LLRM Ryan Miller 40.00 125.00
LLRN Rick Nash 50.00 150.00
LLRS Ryan Smyth 30.00 80.00
LLRV Rogie Vachon 40.00 100.00
LLSA Borje Salming 40.00 100.00
LLSC Sidney Crosby 300.00 750.00
LLSG Simon Gagne 30.00 80.00
LLSH Steve Shutt 30.00 80.00
LLSK Saku Koivu 30.00 80.00
LLSM Miroslav Satan 30.00 80.00
LLSS Scott Stevens 30.00 80.00
LLST Martin St. Louis 40.00 125.00
LLTB Todd Bertuzzi 30.00 80.00
LLTH Jose Theodore 25.00 60.00
LLTU Darcy Tucker 40.00 100.00
LLTV Tomas Vokoun 30.00 80.00
LLVL Vincent Lecavalier 40.00 125.00
LLVT Vesa Toskala 30.00 80.00
LLWC Wendel Clark 40.00 100.00
LLWG Wayne Gretzky 400.00 600.00
LLZC Zdeno Chara 25.00 60.00

2006-07 The Cup Masterpiece Pressplates

STATED PRINT RUN 1/1
FOUR COLORS FOR EACH PLATE
NOT PRICED DUE TO SCARCITY
1 Teemu Selanne
2 Jean-Sebastian Giguere
3 Kari Lehtonen
4 Ilya Kovalchuk
5 Phil Esposito
6 Don Cherry
7 Ray Bourque
8 Bobby Orr
9 Cam Neely
10 Patrice Bergeron
11 Johnny Bucyk
12 Ryan Miller
13 Gilbert Perreault
14 Jarome Iginla
15 Miikka Kiprusoff
16 Al MacInnis
17 Eric Staal
18 Cam Ward
19 Bobby Hull
20 Tony Esposito
21 Stan Mikita
22 Joe Sakic
23 Patrick Roy
24 Rick Nash
25 Sergei Fedorov
26 Mike Modano
27 Dominik Hasek
28 Henrik Zetterberg
29 Gordie Howe
30 Scotty Bowman
31 Ted Lindsay
32 Red Kelly
33 Ales Hemsky
34 Grant Fuhr
35 Jari Kurri
36 Ed Belfour
37 Wayne Gretzky
38 Rob Blake
39 Marcel Dionne
40 Luc Robitaille
41 Rogie Vachon
42 Dino Ciccarelli
43 Marian Gaborik
44 Saku Koivu
45 Michael Ryder
46 Guy Lafleur
47 Larry Robinson
48 Jean Beliveau
49 Jacques Lemaire
50 Paul Kariya
51 Tomas Vokoun
52 Martin Brodeur
53 Scott Stevens
54 Alexei Yashin
55 Al Arbour
56 Mike Bossy
57 Billy Smith
58 Denis Potvin
59 Jaromir Jagr
60 Brendan Shanahan
61 Henrik Lundqvist
62 Gump Worsley
63 Andy Bathgate
64 Jason Spezza
65 Dany Heatley
66 Peter Forsberg
67 Simon Gagne
68 Bernie Parent
69 Bobby Clarke
70 Ron Hextall
71 Jeremy Roenick
72 Shane Doan
73 Sidney Crosby
74 Marc-Andre Fleury
75 Mario Lemieux
76 Peter Stastny
77 Joe Thornton
78 Jonathan Cheechoo
79 Patrick Marleau
80 Bernie Federko
81 Vincent Lecavalier
82 Mats Sundin
83 Frank Mahovlich
84 Darryl Sittler
85 Johnny Bower
86 Borje Salming
87 Roberto Luongo
88 Markus Naslund
89 Alexander Ovechkin
90 Dale Hawerchuk

2006-07 The Cup Masterpiece Pressplates (Artifacts)

STATED PRINT RUN 1/1
FOUR COLORS OF EACH PLATE
NOT PRICED DUE TO SCARCITY
201 Dustin Byfuglien
202 Yan Stastny
203 Mark Stuart
204 Eric Fehr
205 Bill Thomas
206 Joel Perrault
207 Carsen Germyn
208 Ryan Potulny
209 David Printz
210 Rob Collins
211 Steve Regier
212 Matt Koalska
213 Masi Marjamaki
214 Konstantin Pushkaryov
215 Ben Ondrus
216 Brendan Bell
217 Ian White
218 Jeremy Williams
219 Marc-Antoine Pouliot
220 Noah Welch
221 Michel Ouellet
222 Shea Weber
223 Jarkko Immonen
224 David Liffiton
225 Tomas Kopecky
226 Billy Thompson
227 Filip Novak
228 Matt Carle
229 Erik Reitz
230 Miroslav Kopriva

2006-07 The Cup Masterpiece Pressplates (Be A Player Portraits)

STATED PRINT RUN 1/1
NOT PRICED DUE TO SCARCITY
101 Yan Stastny
102 Mark Stuart
103 Evgeni Malkin
104 Patrick Thoresen
105 Patrick O'Sullivan
106 Tomas Kopecky
107 Marc-Antoine Pouliot
108 Konstantin Pushkaryov
109 Phil Kessel
110 Luc Bourdon
111 Shea Weber
112 Guillaume Latendresse
113 Jordan Staal
114 Paul Stastny
115 Anze Kopitar
116 Jarkko Immonen
117 Travis Zajac
118 Nigel Dawes
119 Kristopher Letang
120 Ryan Potulny
121 Ryan Shannon
122 Marc-Edouard Vlasic
123 Noah Welch
124 Ladislav Smid
125 Matt Carle
126 Loui Eriksson
127 Brendan Bell
128 Ian White
129 Jeremy Williams
130 Eric Fehr

2006-07 The Cup Masterpiece Pressplates (Bee Hive)

STATED PRINT RUN 1/1
FOUR COLORS OF EACH PLATE
NOT PRICED DUE TO SCARCITY
101 David McKee
102 Ryan Shannon
103 Shane O'Brien
104 Matt Lashoff
105 Phil Kessel
106 Mark Stuart
107 Yan Stastny
108 Clarke MacArthur
109 Drew Stafford
110 Brandon Prust
111 Dustin Boyd
112 Michael Blunden
113 Dave Bolland
114 Paul Stastny
115 Fredrik Norrena
116 Loui Eriksson
117 Tomas Kopecky
118 Stefan Liv
119 Jeff Drouin-Deslauriers
120 Alexei Mikhnov
121 Ladislav Smid
122 Patrick Thoresen
123 Marc-Antoine Pouliot
124 David Booth
125 Anze Kopitar
126 Patrick O'Sullivan
127 Konstantin Pushkaryov
128 Benoit Pouliot
129 Mikhail Grabovski
130 Guillaume Latendresse
131 Alexander Radulov
132 Shea Weber
133 Travis Zajac
134 Johnny Oduya
135 Blake Comeau
136 Nigel Dawes
137 Jarkko Immonen
138 Josh Hennessy
139 Kelly Guard
140 Martin Houle
141 Ryan Potulny
142 Enver Lisin
143 Keith Yandle
144 Evgeni Malkin
145 Kristopher Letang
146 Jordan Staal
147 Michel Ouellet
148 Noah Welch
149 Joe Pavelski
150 Marc-Edouard Vlasic
151 Matt Carle
152 Marek Schwarz
153 Blair Jones
154 Ian White
155 Brendan Bell
156 Kris Newbury
157 Jesse Schultz
158 Alexander Edler
159 Luc Bourdon
160 Eric Fehr

2006-07 The Cup Masterpiece Pressplates (Black Diamond)

STATED PRINT RUN 1/1
FOUR COLORS OF EACH PLATE
NOT PRICED DUE TO SCARCITY
148 Roman Polak
149 Joel Perrault
150 Yan Stastny
151 Konstantin Pushkaryov
152 Jarkko Immonen
153 Marc-Antoine Pouliot
154 Jeremy Williams
155 Michel Ouellet
156 Tomas Kopecky
157 Keith Yandle
158 Marc-Edouard Vlasic
159 Shane O'Brien
160 Ryan Shannon
161 John Oduya
162 Fredrik Norrena
163 Kristopher Letang
164 Niklas Backstrom
165 D.J. King
166 Patrick Thoresen
167 Patrick Fischer
168 Mikko Lehtonen

2006-07 The Cup Masterpiece Pressplates (Marquee Rookies)

STATED PRINT RUN 1/1
FOUR COLORS OF EACH PLATE
NOT PRICED DUE TO SCARCITY
501 Dustin Byfuglien
502 Yan Stastny
503 Mark Stuart
504 Eric Fehr
505 Bill Thomas
506 Joel Perrault
507 Frank Doyle
508 Carsen Germyn
509 Ryan Potulny
510 David Printz
511 Rob Collins
512 Steve Regier
513 Matt Koalska
514 Ryan Caldwell
515 Masi Marjamaki
516 Cole Jarrett
517 Konstantin Pushkaryov
518 Ben Ondrus
519 Brendan Bell
520 Ian White
521 Jeremy Williams
522 Marc-Antoine Pouliot
523 Noah Welch
524 Michel Ouellet
525 Shea Weber
526 Jarkko Immonen
527 David Liffiton
528 Tomas Kopecky
529 Billy Thompson
530 Filip Novak
531 Matt Carle
532 Dan Jancevski
533 Erik Reitz
534 Miroslav Kopriva
535 Jonas Johansson
536 Shane O'Brien
537 Ryan Shannon
538 Patrick O'Sullivan
539 Anze Kopitar
540 John Oduya
541 Travis Zajac
542 Fredrik Norrena
543 Phil Kessel
544 Guillaume Latendresse
545 Nigel Dawes
546 Jordan Staal
547 Kristopher Letang
548 Paul Stastny
549 Niklas Backstrom
550 D.J. King
551 Marc-Edouard Vlasic
552 Patrick Thoresen
553 Ladislav Smid
554 Loui Eriksson
555 Patrick Fischer
556 Mikko Lehtonen
557 Roman Polak
558 Luc Bourdon
559 Keith Yandle
560 Enver Lisin
561 Adam Burish
562 Alexei Kaigorodov
563 Alex Brooks
564 Evgeni Malkin
565 Nate Thompson
566 Janis Sprukts
567 Alexander Radulov
568 Alexei Mikhnov
569 Dave Bolland
570 Michael Blunden
571 Lars Jonsson
572 Triston Grant
573 Matt Lashoff
574 Dustin Boyd
575 Brandon Prust
576 Alexander Edler
577 Jan Hejda
578 Drew Stafford
579 Kelly Guard
580 Patrick Coulombe
581 Nathan McIver
582 Mike Brown
583 Jean-Francois Racine

584 Adam Dennis
585 Drew Larman
586 Mike Card
587 Michael Funk
588 Stefan Liv
589 David Booth
590 Blair Jones
591 Jussi Timonen
592 David McKee
593 Michael Ryan
594 Peter Harrold
595 Joe Pavelski
596 Karl Goehring
597 Benoit Pouliot
598 Jesse Schultz
599 Jeff Drouin-Deslauriers
600 Martin Houle

2006-07 The Cup Masterpiece Pressplates (MVP)

STATED PRINT RUN 1/1
FOUR COLORS OF EACH PLATE
NOT PRICED DUE TO SCARCITY
298 Patrick O'Sullivan
299 Phil Kessel
300 Guillaume Latendresse
301 Jordan Staal
302 Paul Stastny
303 Evgeni Malkin
304 Luc Bourdon
305 Alexei Kaigorodov
306 Anze Kopitar
307 Travis Zajac
308 Nigel Dawes
309 Kristopher Letang
310 Marc-Edouard Vlasic
311 Patrick Thoresen
312 Ladislav Smid
313 Loui Eriksson
314 Shane O'Brien
315 Ryan Shannon
316 John Oduya
317 Fredrik Norrena
318 Niklas Backstrom
319 D.J. King
320 Patrick Fischer
321 Mikko Lehtonen
322 Roman Polak
323 Ben Ondrus
324 Bill Thomas
325 Billy Thompson
326 Brendan Bell
327 Carsen Germyn
328 Keith Yandle
329 Dan Jancevski
330 David Liffiton
331 David Printz
332 Dustin Byfuglien
333 Eric Fehr
334 Erik Reitz
335 Filip Novak
336 Frank Doyle
337 Ian White
338 Jarkko Immonen
339 Jeremy Williams
340 Joel Perrault
341 Jonas Johansson
342 Konstantin Pushkaryov
343 Marc-Antoine Pouliot
344 Mark Stuart
345 Masi Marjamaki
346 Matt Carle
347 Matt Koalska
348 Michel Ouellet
349 Miroslav Kopriva
350 Noah Welch
351 Rob Collins
352 Ryan Caldwell
353 Ryan Potulny
354 Shea Weber
355 Enver Lisin
356 Tomas Kopecky
357 Yan Stastny

2006-07 The Cup Masterpiece Pressplates (Power Play)

STATED PRINT RUN 1/1
FOUR COLORS FOR EACH PLATE
NOT PRICED DUE TO SCARCITY
101 Yan Stastny
102 Mark Stuart
103 Carsen Germyn
104 Dustin Byfuglien
105 Tomas Kopecky
106 Marc-Antoine Pouliot
107 Konstantin Pushkaryov
108 Erik Reitz
109 Miroslav Kopriva
110 Shea Weber
111 David Printz
112 Steve Regier
113 Ryan Caldwell
114 Masi Marjamaki
115 Matt Koalska
116 Jarkko Immonen
117 Cole Jarrett
118 Rob Collins
119 Filip Novak
120 Ryan Potulny
121 Bill Thomas
122 Joel Perrault
123 Noah Welch
124 Michel Ouellet
125 Matt Carle
126 Ben Ondrus
127 Brendan Bell
128 Ian White
129 Jeremy Williams
130 Eric Fehr

2006-07 The Cup Masterpiece Pressplates (SP Authentic Autographs)

STATED PRINT RUN 1/1
FOUR COLORS FOR EACH PLATE
NOT PRICED DUE TO SCARCITY
161 Ryan Shannon
162 Shane O'Brien
163 Phil Kessel
164 Mark Stuart
165 Matt Lashoff
166 Yan Stastny
167 Nate Thompson
168 Drew Stafford
169 Dustin Boyd
170 Brandon Prust
171 Dave Bolland
172 Michael Blunden
173 Dustin Byfuglien
174 Paul Stastny
175 Karri Ramo
176 Loui Eriksson
177 Tomas Kopecky
178 Ladislav Smid
179 Marc-Antoine Pouliot
181 Patrick Thoresen
182 Janis Sprukts
183 Patrick O'Sullivan
184 Anze Kopitar
185 Konstantin Pushkaryov
186 Guillaume Latendresse
187 Shea Weber
188 Alexander Radulov
189 Travis Zajac
190 Jarkko Immonen
191 Nigel Dawes
192 Kelly Guard
193 Ryan Potulny
194 Benoit Pouliot
195 Keith Yandle
196 Evgeni Malkin
197 Noah Welch
198 Jordan Staal
199 Michel Ouellet
200 Kristopher Letang
201 Matt Carle
202 Marc-Edouard Vlasic
204 Jeremy Williams
205 Ian White
206 Jesse Schultz
207 Brendan Bell
208 Luc Bourdon
210 Eric Fehr

2006-07 The Cup Masterpiece Pressplates (SP Authentic)

STATED PRINT RUN 1/1
FOUR COLORS OF EACH PLATE
NOT PRICED DUE TO SCARCITY
211 Daren Machesney
212 Nathan McIver
213 Patrick Coulombe
214 Jesse Schultz
215 Kris Newbury
216 Blair Jones
217 Marek Schwarz
218 David Backes
219 Joe Pavelski
220 Patrick Fischer
221 Bill Thomas
222 Triston Grant
223 Lars Jonsson
224 David Printz
225 Jussi Timonen
226 Martin Houle
227 Josh Hennessy
228 Blake Comeau
229 Masi Marjamaki
230 Ben Ondrus
231 Fredrik Norrena
232 Johnny Oduya
233 Enver Lisin
234 Mikhail Grabovski
235 Mikko Lehtonen
236 Niklas Backstrom
237 Miroslav Kopriva
238 Benoit Pouliot
239 Peter Harrold
240 David Booth
241 Drew Larman
242 Jan Hejda
243 Jeff Drouin-Deslauriers
244 Stefan Liv
245 Adam Burish
246 Michael Funk
247 Mike Card
248 Adam Dennis
249 Clarke MacArthur
250 David McKee

2006-07 The Cup Masterpiece Pressplates (SP Game Used)

STATED PRINT RUN 1/1
FOUR COLORS OF EACH PLATE
NOT PRICED DUE TO SCARCITY
101 Shane O'Brien
102 Ryan Shannon
103 Yan Stastny
104 Mark Stuart
105 Nate Thompson
106 Phil Kessel
107 Matt Lashoff
108 Dave Bolland
109 Michael Blunden
110 Dustin Byfuglien
111 Paul Stastny
112 Fredrik Norrena
113 Loui Eriksson
114 Tomas Kopecky
115 Alexei Mikhnov
116 Marc-Antoine Pouliot
117 Patrick Thoresen
118 Ladislav Smid
119 Janis Sprukts
120 Konstantin Pushkaryov
121 Patrick O'Sullivan
122 Anze Kopitar
123 Benoit Pouliot
124 Miroslav Kopriva
125 Niklas Backstrom
126 Guillaume Latendresse
127 Alexander Radulov
128 Shea Weber
129 Mikko Lehtonen
130 Alex Brooks
131 John Oduya
132 Travis Zajac
133 Drew Stafford
134 Masi Marjamaki
135 Jarkko Immonen
136 Nigel Dawes
137 Alexei Kaigorodov
138 Lars Jonsson
139 Ryan Potulny
140 Triston Grant
141 Enver Lisin
142 Brandon Prust
143 Keith Yandle
144 Patrick Fischer
145 Noah Welch
146 Michel Ouellet
147 Jordan Staal
148 Kristopher Letang
149 Evgeni Malkin
150 Matt Carle
151 Marc-Edouard Vlasic
152 D.J. King
153 Roman Polak
154 Ben Ondrus
155 Brendan Bell
156 Ian White
157 Dustin Boyd
158 Luc Bourdon
159 Eric Fehr
160 Jonas Johansson

2006-07 The Cup Masterpiece Pressplates (SPx Autographs)

STATED PRINT RUN 1/1
FOUR COLORS OF EACH PLATE
NOT PRICED DUE TO SCARCITY
144 Drew Stafford
161 Dustin Boyd
164 Yan Stastny
165 Mark Stuart
166 Eric Fehr
167 Ryan Potulny
168 Ben Ondrus
169 Brendan Bell
170 Ian White
171 Jeremy Williams
172 Marc-Antoine Pouliot
173 Noah Welch
174 Shea Weber
175 Jarkko Immonen
176 Tomas Kopecky
177 Matt Carle
178 Ryan Shannon
179 Anze Kopitar
180 Travis Zajac
181 Nigel Dawes
182 Kristopher Letang
183 Marc-Edouard Vlasic
184 Ladislav Smid
185 Loui Eriksson
186 Paul Stastny
188 Patrick O'Sullivan
189 Phil Kessel
190 Guillaume Latendresse
191 Jordan Staal
192 Luc Bourdon
193 Evgeni Malkin
194 Keith Yandle/1
195 Alexander Radulov/1

2006-07 The Cup Masterpiece Pressplates (SPx)

STATED PRINT RUN 1/1
FOUR COLORS OF EACH PLATE
NOT PRICED DUE TO SCARCITY
143 Dustin Byfuglien
145 Frank Doyle
146 Carsen Germyn
147 David Printz
148 Masi Marjamaki
149 Konstantin Pushkaryov
150 Michel Ouellet
151 Billy Thompson
152 Filip Novak
153 Miroslav Kopriva
154 Jonas Johansson
155 Shane O'Brien
156 John Oduya
157 Fredrik Norrena
158 Niklas Backstrom
159 D.J. King
160 Patrick Thoresen
162 Mikko Lehtonen
163 Roman Polak

2006-07 The Cup Masterpiece Pressplates (Sweet Beginnings)

STATED PRINT RUN 1/1
FOUR COLORS OF EACH PLATE
NOT PRICED DUE TO SCARCITY
101 Shane O'Brien
102 Ryan Shannon
103 David McKee
104 Phil Kessel
105 Yan Stastny
106 Mark Stuart
107 Matt Lashoff
108 Clarke MacArthur
109 Drew Stafford
110 Masi Marjamaki
111 Michael Funk
112 Brandon Prust
113 Dustin Boyd
114 Dustin Byfuglien
115 Dave Bolland
116 Michael Blunden
117 Paul Stastny
118 Fredrik Norrena
119 Niklas Grossman
120 Loui Eriksson
121 Tomas Kopecky
122 Stefan Liv
123 Patrick Thoresen
124 Marc-Antoine Pouliot
125 Ladislav Smid
126 Janis Sprukts
127 Jeff Drouin-Deslauriers
128 David Booth
129 Konstantin Pushkaryov
130 Anze Kopitar
131 Patrick O'Sullivan
132 Benoit Pouliot
133 Guillaume Latendresse
134 Mikhail Grabovski
135 Shea Weber
136 Alexander Radulov
137 Travis Zajac
138 Nigel Dawes
139 Jarkko Immonen
140 Josh Hennessy
141 Jussi Timonen
142 Ryan Potulny
143 Keith Yandle
144 Michel Ouellet
145 Jordan Staal
146 Evgeni Malkin
147 Noah Welch
148 Kristopher Letang
149 Matt Carle
150 Marc-Edouard Vlasic
151 Joe Pavelski
152 Marek Schwarz
153 Karri Ramo
154 Blair Jones
155 Ian White
156 Jeremy Williams
157 Luc Bourdon
158 Jesse Schultz
159 Alexander Edler
160 Eric Fehr

2006-07 The Cup Masterpiece Pressplates (Trilogy)

STATED PRINT RUN 1/1
FOUR COLORS OF EACH PLATE
NOT PRICED DUE TO SCARCITY
101 Shane O'Brien
102 Ryan Shannon
103 Yan Stastny
104 Mark Stuart
105 Phil Kessel
106 Carsen Germyn
107 Dustin Byfuglien
108 Paul Stastny
109 Filip Novak
110 Fredrik Norrena
111 Loui Eriksson
112 Tomas Kopecky
113 Marc-Antoine Pouliot
114 Patrick Thoresen
115 Ladislav Smid
116 Konstantin Pushkaryov
117 Patrick O'Sullivan
118 Anze Kopitar
119 Erik Reitz
120 Miroslav Kopriva
121 Niklas Backstrom
122 Dan Jancevski
123 Guillaume Latendresse
124 Shea Weber
125 Mikko Lehtonen
126 Frank Doyle
127 John Oduya
128 Travis Zajac
129 Rob Collins
130 Steve Regier
131 Matt Koalska
132 Ryan Caldwell
133 Masi Marjamaki
134 Keith Yandle
135 Enver Lisin
136 Jarkko Immonen
137 David Liffiton
138 Nigel Dawes
139 Alexei Kaigorodov
140 Ryan Potulny
141 David Printz
142 Bill Thomas
143 Joel Perrault
144 Patrick Fischer
145 Noah Welch
146 Michel Ouellet
147 Jordan Staal
148 Kristopher Letang
149 Evgeni Malkin
150 Matt Carle
151 Marc-Edouard Vlasic
152 D.J. King
153 Roman Polak
154 Ben Ondrus
155 Brendan Bell
156 Ian White
157 Jeremy Williams
158 Luc Bourdon
159 Eric Fehr
160 Jonas Johansson

2006-07 The Cup Masterpiece Pressplates (Ultimate Collection Autographs)

STATED PRINT RUN 1/1
FOUR COLORS OF EACH PLATE
NOT PRICED DUE TO SCARCITY
103 Matt Lashoff
104 Phil Kessel
105 Mark Stuart
106 Michael Blunden
107 Dave Bolland
108 Paul Stastny
109 Loui Eriksson
111 Ladislav Smid
112 Patrick Thoresen
113 Marc-Antoine Pouliot
114 Anze Kopitar
115 Patrick O'Sullivan
116 Guillaume Latendresse
117 Alexander Radulov
118 Shea Weber
119 Travis Zajac
120 Nigel Dawes
121 Dustin Boyd
122 Ryan Potulny
123 Benoit Pouliot
124 Keith Yandle
125 Evgeni Malkin
126 Kristopher Letang
127 Jordan Staal
128 Noah Welch
129 Marc-Edouard Vlasic
130 Matt Carle
131 Drew Stafford
132 Eric Fehr

2006-07 The Cup Masterpiece Pressplates (Ultimate Collection)

STATED PRINT RUN 1/1
FOUR COLORS OF EACH PLATE
NOT PRICED DUE TO SCARCITY
61 David McKee
62 Ryan Shannon
63 Clarke MacArthur
64 Andrej Sekera
65 Michael Funk
66 Adam Dennis
67 Mike Card
68 Brandon Prust
69 Troy Brouwer
70 Adam Burish
71 Fredrik Norrena
72 Stefan Liv
73 Tomas Kopecky
74 Jeff Drouin-Deslauriers
75 David Booth
76 Janis Sprukts
77 Barry Brust
78 Konstantin Pushkaryov
79 Shawn Belle
80 Niklas Backstrom
81 Mikhail Grabovski
82 Johnny Oduya
83 Blake Comeau
84 Jarkko Immonen
85 Josh Hennessy
86 Kelly Guard
87 Jussi Timonen
88 Martin Houle
89 Michel Ouellet
90 Yan Stastny
91 Roman Polak
92 Marek Schwarz
93 David Backes
94 Blair Jones
95 Karri Ramo
96 Ian White
97 Brendan Bell
98 Kris Newbury
99 Jean-Francois Racine
100 Jesse Schultz
101 Alexander Edler
102 Daren Machesney

2006-07 The Cup Masterpiece Pressplates (Victory)

STATED PRINT RUN 1/1
FOUR COLORS OF EACH PLATE
NOT PRICED DUE TO SCARCITY
201 Tomas Kopecky
202 Billy Thompson
203 Dustin Byfuglien
204 Yan Stastny
205 Eric Fehr
206 Ben Ondrus
207 Rob Collins
208 Brendan Bell
209 Frank Doyle
210 Noah Welch
211 Filip Novak
212 Ian White
213 Konstantin Pushkaryov
214 Dan Jancevski
215 Shea Weber
216 Michel Ouellet
217 Marc-Antoine Pouliot
218 Carsen Germyn
219 Matt Carle
220 Steve Regier
221 Mark Stuart
222 Bill Thomas
223 Jarkko Immonen
224 Erik Reitz
225 Joel Perrault
226 Ryan Potulny
227 Jeremy Williams
228 Masi Marjamaki
229 Miroslav Kopriva
230 Matt Koalska
281 Shane O'Brien
282 Jonas Johansson
283 Ryan Shannon
284 Patrick O'Sullivan
285 Anze Kopitar
286 John Oduya
287 Travis Zajac
288 Fredrik Norrena
289 Phil Kessel
290 Guillaume Latendresse
291 Nigel Dawes
292 Jordan Staal
293 Kristopher Letang
294 Paul Stastny
295 Niklas Backstrom
296 D.J. King
297 Marc-Edouard Vlasic
298 Patrick Thoresen
299 Ladislav Smid
300 Loui Eriksson
301 Patrick Fischer
302 Mikko Lehtonen
303 Roman Polak
304 Evgeni Malkin
305 Luc Bourdon
306 Alexei Kaigorodov
307 Alex Brooks
308 Nate Thompson
309 Janis Sprukts
310 Alexander Radulov
311 Keith Yandle
312 Enver Lisin
313 Cole Jarrett
314 Ryan Caldwell
315 David Printz
316 David Liffiton
317 Adam Burish
318 Dave Bolland
319 Michael Blunden
320 Matt Lashoff
321 Alexei Mikhnov
322 Jan Hejda
323 Lars Jonsson
324 Triston Grant
325 Alexander Edler
326 Brandon Prust
327 Dustin Boyd
328 Drew Stafford
329 Kelly Guard
330 Nathan McIver

2006-07 The Cup NHL Shields Duals

STATED PRINT RUN 1/1
NOT PRICED DUE TO SCARCITY
DSHAM Alexander Radulov
Mikko Lehtonen
DSHAS Daniel Alfredsson
Jason Spezza
DSHBE Luc Bourdon
Alexander Edler
DSHBN Joe Nieuwendyk
Jay Bouwmeester
DSHBW Noah Welch
Luc Bourdon
DSHCO Sidney Crosby
Alexander Ovechkin
DSHCV Matt Carle
Marc-Edouard Vlasic
DSHCW Shea Weber
Matt Carle
DSHDA Maxim Afinogenov
Chris Drury
DSHDB Dustin Boyd
Brandon Prust
DSHDG Pavol Demitra
Marian Gaborik
DSHDJ Curtis Joseph
Shane Doan
DSHDL Nicklas Lidstrom
Pavel Datsyuk
DSHDS Miroslav Satan
Rick DiPietro
DSHDY Alexei Yashin
Rick DiPietro
DSHEC Ed Belfour
Curtis Joseph
DSHEM Eric Lindros
Mike Ribeiro
DSHEO Ed Belfour
Olli Jokinen
DSHFC Peter Forsberg
Jeff Carter
DSHFD Pavel Datsyuk
Sergei Federov
DSHFG Peter Forsberg
Simon Gagne
DSHFL Nicklas Lidstrom
Peter Forsberg
DSHFP Eric Fehr
Ryan Potulny
DSHFZ Nikolai Zherdev
Sergei Federov
DSHGF Manny Fernandez
Marian Gaborik
DSHHD Henrik Sedin
Daniel Sedin
DSHHR Martin Havlat
Tuomo Ruutu
DSHIB Jarome Iginla
Dustin Boyd
DSHJA Jordan Staal
Anze Kopitar
DSHJB Brendan Shanahan
Jaromir Jagr
DSHJD Jason Spezza
Dany Heatley
DSHJJ Curtis Joseph
Ed Jovanovski
DSHJK Jordan Staal
Kristopher Letang
DSHJN Curtis Joseph
Ladislav Nagy
DSHJO Joe Sakic
Joe Thornton
DSHJS Jaromir Jagr
Martin Straka
DSHKC Mike Cammalleri
Anze Kopitar
DSHKH Marian Hossa
Ilya Kovalchuk
DSHKK Saku Koivu
Alexei Kovalev
DSHKO Phil Kessel
Patrick O'Sullivan
DSHKR Paul Kariya
Alexander Radulov
DSHKS Paul Kariya
Steve Sullivan
DSHKZ Olaf Kolzig
Richard Zednik
DSHLC Chris Chelios
Nicklas Lidstrom
DSHLE Martin Brodeur
Zach Parise
DSHLL Roberto Luongo
Trevor Linden
DSHLP Guillaume Latendresse
Benoit Pouliot
DSHLR Vincent Lecavalier
Brad Richards
DSHLS Manny Legace
Curtis Sanford
DSHLY Chris Drury
Drew Stafford
DSHLZ Sergei Zubov
Jere Lehtinen
DSHML Mike Modano
Eric Lindros
DSHNL Pascal LeClaire
Rick Nash
DSHNR Joe Nieuwendyk
Gary Roberts
DSHOS Shane O'Brien
Ryan Shannon
DSHOW Michel Ouellet
Noah Welch
DSHPA Phil Kessel
Anze Kopitar
DSHPH Derian Hatcher
Joni Pitkanen
DSHPJ Paul Stastny
Jordan Staal
DSHPL Ladislav Smid
Patrick Thoresen
DSHPN Chris Pronger
Scott Niedermayer
DSHPT Raffi Torres
Fernando Pisani
DSHPY Yan Stastny
Phil Kessel
DSHRE Martin Erat
Alexander Radulov
DSHRL John LeClair
Mark Recchi
DSHRP Ryan Smyth
Patrick Thoresen
DSHRW Robert Lang
Kris Draper
DSHSA Mats Sundin
Daniel Alfredsson
DSHSD Brendan Shanahan
Nigel Dawes
DSHSF Joe Sakic
Peter Forsberg
DSHSG Teemu Selanne
Jean-Sebastien Giguere
DSHSH Joe Sakic
Milan Hejduk
DSHSK Teemu Selanne
Paul Kariya
DSHSL Mark Stuart
Matt Lashoff
DSHSP Teemu Selanne
Chris Pronger
DSHSR Brian Rafalski
Scott Stevens
DSHSS Mats Sundin
Alexander Steen
DSHST Joe Sakic
Jose Theodore
DSHTO Mats Sundin
Andrew Raycroft
DSHTP Michael Peca
Darcy Tucker
DSHTS Jose Theodore
Paul Stastny
DSHTT Hannu Toivonen
Tim Thomas
DSHTW Doug Weight
Keith Tkachuk
DSHVK Paul Kariya
Tomas Vokoun
DSHWB Rod Brind'Amour
Cam Ward
DSHWG Doug Weight
Bill Guerin
DSHZD Travis Zajac
Nigel Dawes
DSHZG Sergei Zubov
Sergei Gonchar

2006-07 The Cup Property of

Confirmed sales include: Larry Robinson, $272.
STATED PRINT RUN 1/1
NOT PRICED DUE TO SCARCITY
POAK Anze Kopitar
POAM Al MacInnis
POBO Bobby Orr
POBU Peter Budaj
POCG Clark Gillies
PODC Dino Ciccarelli
PODH Dale Hawerchuk
PODT Dave Taylor
POEL Eric Lindros
POEM Evgeni Malkin
POES Eric Staal
POGH Gordie Howe
POHA Dominik Hasek
POHE Dany Heatley
POKE Phil Kessel
POKL Kari Lehtonen
POLR Larry Robinson
POMB Martin Brodeur
POMD Marcel Dionne

POML Mario Lemieux
POMM Mike Modano
POMT Marty Turco
PONL Nicklas Lidstrom
POPR Patrick Roy
POPT Pierre Turgeon
PORB Rob Blake
PORG Ryan Getzlaf
POSD Bobby Clarke
POST Jordan Staal
POTV Thomas Vanek
POWG Wayne Gretzky
POWW Wojtek Wolski

2006-07 The Cup Rookies Black

STATED PRINT RUN 1/1
NOT PRICED DUE TO SCARCITY
91 Nate Thompson
92 Mike Brown
93 Mike Card
94 Adam Dennis
95 Carsen Germyn
96 Adam Burish
97 Drew Larman
98 Jonas Johansson
99 Joel Perrault
100 Mikko Lehtonen
101 Alex Brooks
102 Frank Doyle
103 Billy Thompson
104 Kelly Guard
105 David Printz
106 D.J. King
107 Jean-Francois Racine
108 Nathan McIver
109 Shane O'Brien
110 Ryan Shannon
111 David McKee
112 Mark Stuart
113 Matt Lashoff
114 Drew Stafford
115 Clarke MacArthur
116 Michael Funk
117 Brandon Prust
118 Dustin Boyd
119 Dustin Byfuglien
120 Dave Bolland
121 Michael Blunden
122 Filip Novak
123 Fredrik Norrena
124 Niklas Grossman
125 Loui Eriksson
126 Tomas Kopecky
127 Stefan Liv
128 Patrick Thoresen
129 Marc-Antoine Pouliot
130 Ladislav Smid
131 Janis Sprukts
132 Jeff Drouin-Deslauriers
133 David Booth
134 Konstantin Pushkaryov
135 Patrick O'Sullivan
136 Benoit Pouliot
137 Niklas Backstrom
138 Guillaume Latendresse
139 Shea Weber
140 Johnny Oduya
141 Travis Zajac
142 Masi Marjamaki
143 Nigel Dawes
144 Jarkko Immonen
145 Josh Hennessy
146 Ryan Potulny
147 Jussi Timonen
148 Keith Yandle
149 Michel Ouellet
150 Noah Welch
151 Kristopher Letang
152 Joe Pavelski
153 Matt Carle
154 Marc-Edouard Vlasic
155 Yan Stastny
156 Marek Schwarz
157 Roman Polak
158 Karri Ramo
159 Blair Jones
160 Brendan Bell
161 Ian White
162 Ben Ondrus
163 Jeremy Williams
164 Miroslav Kopriva
165 Luc Bourdon
166 Jesse Schultz
167 Alexander Edler
168 Eric Fehr
169 Jordan Staal
170 Phil Kessel
171 Evgeni Malkin
172 Paul Stastny
173 Anze Kopitar
174 Alexander Radulov

2006-07 The Cup Rookies Platinum

STATED PRINT RUN 25 #'d SETS
91 Nate Thompson 8.00 20.00
92 Mike Brown 10.00 25.00
93 Mike Card 8.00 20.00
94 Adam Dennis 10.00 25.00
95 Carsen Germyn 8.00 20.00
96 Adam Burish 8.00 20.00
97 Drew Larman 8.00 20.00
98 Jonas Johansson 8.00 20.00
99 Joel Perrault 8.00 20.00
100 Mikko Lehtonen 8.00 20.00
101 Alex Brooks 8.00 20.00
102 Frank Doyle 10.00 25.00
103 Billy Thompson 10.00 25.00
104 Kelly Guard 10.00 25.00
105 David Printz 8.00 20.00
106 D.J. King 8.00 20.00
107 Jean-Francois Racine 10.00 25.00
108 Nathan McIver 8.00 20.00
109 Shane O'Brien 8.00 20.00
110 Ryan Shannon 8.00 20.00
111 David McKee 15.00 40.00
112 Mark Stuart 8.00 20.00
113 Matt Lashoff 10.00 25.00
114 Drew Stafford 40.00 100.00
115 Clarke MacArthur 8.00 20.00
116 Michael Funk 8.00 20.00
117 Brandon Prust 8.00 20.00
118 Dustin Boyd 15.00 40.00
119 Dustin Byfuglien 8.00 20.00
120 Dave Bolland 8.00 20.00
121 Michael Blunden 8.00 20.00
122 Filip Novak 8.00 20.00
123 Fredrik Norrena 15.00 40.00
124 Niklas Grossman 8.00 20.00
125 Loui Eriksson 10.00 25.00
126 Tomas Kopecky 15.00 40.00
127 Stefan Liv 15.00 40.00
128 Patrick Thoresen 15.00 40.00
129 Marc-Antoine Pouliot 15.00 40.00
130 Ladislav Smid 8.00 20.00
131 Janis Sprukts 8.00 20.00
132 Jeff Drouin-Deslauriers 10.00 25.00
133 David Booth 8.00 20.00
134 Konstantin Pushkaryov 8.00 20.00
135 Patrick O'Sullivan 15.00 40.00
136 Benoit Pouliot 15.00 40.00
137 Niklas Backstrom 25.00 60.00
138 Guillaume Latendresse 50.00 125.00
139 Shea Weber 15.00 40.00
140 Johnny Oduya 8.00 20.00
141 Travis Zajac 20.00 50.00
142 Masi Marjamaki 10.00 25.00
143 Nigel Dawes 8.00 20.00
144 Jarkko Immonen 8.00 20.00
145 Josh Hennessy 8.00 20.00
146 Ryan Potulny 15.00 40.00
147 Jussi Timonen 8.00 20.00
148 Keith Yandle 8.00 20.00
149 Michel Ouellet 15.00 40.00
150 Noah Welch 8.00 20.00
151 Kristopher Letang 15.00 40.00
152 Joe Pavelski 15.00 40.00
153 Matt Carle 15.00 40.00
154 Marc-Edouard Vlasic 15.00 40.00
155 Yan Stastny 8.00 20.00
156 Marek Schwarz 15.00 40.00
157 Roman Polak 8.00 20.00
158 Karri Ramo 10.00 25.00
159 Blair Jones 10.00 25.00
160 Brendan Bell 8.00 20.00
161 Ian White 8.00 20.00
162 Ben Ondrus 8.00 20.00
163 Jeremy Williams 8.00 20.00
164 Miroslav Kopriva 10.00 25.00
165 Luc Bourdon 15.00 40.00
166 Jesse Schultz 8.00 20.00
167 Alexander Edler 8.00 20.00
168 Eric Fehr 15.00 40.00
169 Jordan Staal 100.00 250.00
170 Phil Kessel 30.00 80.00
171 Evgeni Malkin 100.00 250.00
172 Paul Stastny 50.00 125.00
173 Anze Kopitar 75.00 200.00
174 Alexander Radulov 30.00 80.00

2006-07 The Cup Scripted Swatches

STATED PRINT RUN 25 #'d SETS
SSAO Alexander Ovechkin 60.00 150.00
SSAR Andrew Raycroft 30.00 60.00
SSAT Alex Tanguay 40.00 80.00
SSBO Mike Bossy
SSBR Bill Ranford 40.00 80.00
SSBS Borje Salming 40.00 80.00
SSCD Chris Drury 30.00 60.00
SSCN Cam Neely
SSCW Cam Ward 40.00 80.00
SSDB Daniel Briere 40.00 80.00
SSDC Dino Ciccarelli
SSDH Dale Hawerchuk 40.00 80.00
SSDS Denis Savard 30.00 80.00
SSDT Dave Taylor/10 150.00 250.00
SSDW Dave Williams
SSEM Evgeni Malkin 250.00 350.00
SSES Eric Staal
SSGA Glenn Anderson 30.00 60.00
SSGC Gerry Cheevers 40.00 80.00
SSGF Grant Fuhr 40.00 80.00
SSGL Guy Lafleur 50.00 100.00
SSGP Gilbert Perreault 40.00 80.00
SSHA Dominik Hasek
SSHE Dany Heatley
SSHL Henrik Lundqvist 150.00 250.00
SSHZ Henrik Zetterberg
SSIK Ilya Kovalchuk 60.00 125.00
SSJC Jonathan Cheechoo 40.00 80.00
SSJG Jean-Sebastien Giguere 40.00 80.00
SSJI Jarome Iginla 60.00 125.00
SSJK Jari Kurri 50.00 100.00
SSJM Joe Mullen 20.00 50.00
SSJS Jason Spezza
SSJT Joe Thornton 60.00 125.00
SSLR Larry Robinson
SSMB Martin Brodeur 200.00 300.00
SSMD Marcel Dionne 40.00 80.00
SSMG Marian Gaborik
SSMH Martin Havlat 20.00 50.00
SSMI Milan Hejduk 40.00 80.00
SSML Mario Lemieux 200.00 400.00
SSMM Mike Modano 40.00 80.00
SSMN Markus Naslund 40.00 80.00
SSMR Michael Ryder 30.00 60.00
SSMS Martin St. Louis 30.00 60.00
SSMT Marty Turco 30.00 60.00
SSNL Nicklas Lidstrom 40.00 80.00
SSPB Patrice Bergeron 60.00 125.00
SSPH Dion Phaneuf
SSPK Phil Kessel 60.00 125.00
SSPL Pat LaFontaine 40.00 80.00
SSPM Patrick Marleau 25.00 60.00
SSPR Patrick Roy 300.00 500.00
SSRA Alexander Radulov 75.00 150.00
SSRB Ray Bourque 75.00 150.00
SSRE Ron Ellis 25.00 60.00
SSRH Ron Hextall 40.00 100.00
SSRL Roberto Luongo
SSRM Ryan Miller 40.00 100.00
SSRN Rick Nash 40.00 100.00
SSRO Luc Robitaille 40.00 80.00
SSRS Ryan Smyth 30.00 80.00
SSSC Sidney Crosby 250.00 450.00
SSSG Simon Gagne 40.00 80.00
SSSH Steve Shutt 20.00 50.00
SSSK Saku Koivu 40.00 100.00
SSSS Scott Stevens 60.00 125.00
SSST Jordan Staal
SSTE Tony Esposito 50.00 100.00
SSTH Jose Theodore 30.00 60.00
SSTV Tomas Vokoun 30.00 60.00
SSVL Vincent Lecavalier 60.00 125.00

2006-07 The Cup Scripted Swatches Duals

STATED PRINT RUN 5 #'d SETS
NOT PRICED DUE TO SCARCITY
DSAR Ryan Smyth
Ales Hemsky
DSDB Darryl Sittler
Borje Salming
DSDR Luc Robitaille
Marcel Dionne
DSGC Simon Gagne
Jeff Carter
DSGH Wayne Gretzky
Gordie Howe
DSGL Mario Lemieux
Wayne Gretzky
DSHS Jason Spezza
Dany Heatley
DSKF Grant Fuhr
Jari Kurri
DSKL Ilya Kovalchuk
Kari Lehtonen
DSLM Mario Lemieux
Evgeni Malkin
DSLN Markus Naslund
Roberto Luongo
DSLR Guy Lafleur
Larry Robinson
DSLS Vincent Lecavalier
Martin St. Louis
DSMM Lanny McDonald
Al MacInnis
DSNB Cam Neely
Ray Bourque
DSOM Alexander Ovechkin
Evgeni Malkin
DSPP Peter Stastny
Paul Stastny
DSPR Patrick Roy
Ray Bourque
DSRB Patrick Roy
Martin Brodeur
DSSS Eric Staal
Jordan Staal
DSTC Joe Thornton
Jonathan Cheechoo
DSTI Jarome Iginla
Alex Tanguay
DSZL Nicklas Lidstrom
Henrik Zetterberg

2006-07 The Cup Signature Patches

STATED PRINT RUN 75 #'d SETS
UNIQUE SWATCHES MAY EARN
SUBSTANTIAL PREMIUM
WHITE SWATCHES: .5X TO 1X LO
SPAF Alexander Frolov 20.00 50.00
SPAH Ales Hemsky 20.00 50.00
SPAK Anze Kopitar 60.00 150.00
SPAM Al MacInnis 25.00 60.00
SPAO Alexander Ovechkin 100.00 250.00
SPAR Alexander Radulov 75.00 200.00
SPAT Alex Tanguay 25.00 60.00
SPBC Bobby Clarke 30.00 80.00
SPBR Martin Brodeur 75.00 150.00
SPBS Billy Smith 30.00 80.00
SPCH Cristobal Huet 25.00 60.00
SPCN Cam Neely 25.00 60.00
SPCW Cam Ward 25.00 60.00
SPDA David Aebischer 20.00 50.00
SPDB Daniel Briere 30.00 80.00
SPDC Dino Ciccarelli 25.00 60.00
SPDH Dale Hawerchuk 25.00 60.00
SPDI Dion Phaneuf 40.00 100.00
SPDS Denis Savard 25.00 60.00
SPDT Dave Taylor 30.00 80.00
SPDW Doug Wilson 15.00 40.00
SPEL Patrik Elias 15.00 40.00
SPEM Evgeni Malkin 100.00 250.00
SPES Eric Staal 20.00 50.00
SPGC Gerry Cheevers 30.00 80.00
SPGF Grant Fuhr 30.00 80.00
SPGH Gordie Howe/25 175.00 300.00
SPGL Guy Lafleur 40.00 80.00
SPGO Scott Gomez/25 20.00 50.00
SPGP Gilbert Perreault 25.00 60.00
SPHA Dominik Hasek 40.00 80.00
SPHE Dany Heatley
SPHZ Henrik Zetterberg 40.00 80.00
SPIK Ilya Kovalchuk 30.00 80.00
SPJC Jonathan Cheechoo 25.00 60.00
SPJG Jean-Sebastien Giguere 25.00 60.00
SPJI Jarome Iginla 30.00 80.00
SPJK Jari Kurri 30.00
SPJO Jordan Staal 100.00 250.00
SPJR Jeremy Roenick 25.00 60.00
SPJS Jason Spezza 30.00 80.00
SPJT Joe Thornton 40.00 80.00
SPKL Kari Lehtonen 25.00 60.00
SPLA Guillaume Latendresse 50.00 125.00
SPLB Luc Bourdon 40.00 80.00
SPLM Lanny McDonald
SPLR Larry Robinson 25.00 60.00
SPLX Mario Lemieux/25 200.00 400.00
SPMB Mike Bossy 30.00 80.00
SPMC Matt Carle 25.00 60.00
SPMD Marcel Dionne/25 60.00 150.00
SPMG Marian Gaborik 100.00
SPMI Milan Hejduk 25.00 60.00
SPMM Mike Modano 30.00 80.00
SPMR Michael Ryder 25.00 60.00
SPMS Martin St. Louis 20.00 50.00
SPMT Marty Turco 20.00 50.00
SPNL Nicklas Lidstrom 30.00 80.00
SPPA Brad Park
SPPB Patrice Bergeron 30.00 80.00
SPPH Paul Henderson 20.00 50.00
SPPK Phil Kessel 40.00 100.00
SPPM Patrick Marleau 20.00 50.00
SPPO Patrick O'Sullivan 30.00 80.00
SPPS Paul Stastny 60.00 125.00
SPRA Andrew Raycroft 20.00 50.00
SPRE Ron Ellis 15.00 40.00
SPRH Ron Hextall 25.00 60.00
SPRI Richard Brodeur 20.00 50.00
SPRL Roberto Luongo
SPRM Ryan Miller 30.00 80.00
SPRN Rick Nash 30.00 80.00
SPRO Luc Robitaille 30.00 80.00
SPRS Ryan Smyth 25.00 60.00
SPRV Rogie Vachon 30.00 80.00
SPSA Borje Salming 20.00 50.00
SPSC Sidney Crosby 300.00 600.00
SPSE Scott Stevens 20.00 50.00
SPSG Simon Gagne 20.00 50.00
SPSK Saku Koivu 20.00 50.00
SPSM Stan Mikita 25.00 60.00
SPSS Steve Shutt 20.00 50.00
SPST Peter Stastny 20.00 50.00
SPSU Brent Sutter 15.00 40.00
SPSV Marek Svatos 20.00 50.00
SPTB Todd Bertuzzi 20.00 50.00
SPTE Tony Esposito 30.00 80.00
SPTH Jose Theodore 15.00 40.00
SPTV Tomas Vokoun 25.00 60.00
SPVL Vincent Lecavalier 25.00 60.00
SPWG Wayne Gretzky/25 400.00 600.00
SPBO1 Ray Bourque 40.00 100.00
SPBO2 Ray Bourque 40.00 100.00
SPPR1 Patrick Roy 100.00 200.00
SPPR2 Patrick Roy 75.00 175.00

2006-07 The Cup Stanley Cup Signatures

STATED PRINT RUN 25 #'d SETS
CSAA Al Arbour 30.00 60.00
CSAM Al MacInnis 40.00 80.00
CSAT Alex Tanguay 30.00 60.00
CSBA Bob Baun 30.00 60.00
CSBC Bobby Clarke 30.00 60.00
CSBD Butch Bouchard 30.00 60.00
CSBH Bobby Hull 50.00 100.00
CSBI Bill Ranford 40.00 80.00
CSBO Bobby Orr 250.00 350.00
CSBP Bernie Parent 40.00 80.00
CSBR Martin Brodeur 100.00 175.00
CSBS Billy Smith 40.00 80.00
CSBU Johnny Bucyk 30.00 60.00
CSCG Clark Gillies
CSCM Craig MacTavish 25.00 50.00
CSCS Clint Smith
CSCW Cam Ward 40.00 80.00
CSDG Doug Gilmour 30.00 60.00
CSDH Dominik Hasek 50.00 100.00
CSDP Denis Potvin 25.00 50.00
CSES Eric Staal 30.00 60.00
CSFM Frank Mahovlich 40.00 80.00
CSFR Frank Mahovlich 30.00 60.00
CSGA Glenn Anderson
CSGC Gerry Cheevers 30.00 60.00
CSGF Grant Fuhr 40.00 80.00
CSGH Gordie Howe 60.00 150.00
CSGL Guy Lafleur 50.00 100.00
CSHE Milan Hejduk 25.00 50.00
CSJB Jean Beliveau
CSJK Jari Kurri 40.00 100.00
CSJL Jacques Lemaire
CSJM Joe Mullen 30.00 60.00
CSJO Johnny Bower
CSKE Red Kelly 30.00 60.00
CSLA Larry Murphy
CSLE Elmer Lach 40.00 80.00
CSLR Larry Robinson 25.00 50.00
CSMB Mike Bossy 40.00 80.00
CSML Mario Lemieux 125.00 250.00
CSMM Mike Modano 50.00 100.00
CSMS Milt Schmidt 40.00 80.00
CSMU Joe Mullen 30.00 60.00
CSNL Nicklas Lidstrom
CSPE Phil Esposito
CSPR Patrick Roy 150.00 250.00
CSRB Ray Bourque 50.00 100.00
CSRK Red Kelly 30.00 60.00
CSRL Reggie Leach
CSRO Patrick Roy 150.00 250.00
CSRV Rogie Vachon 30.00 60.00
CSSB Scotty Bowman 40.00 80.00
CSSH Steve Shutt 25.00 50.00
CSSM Stan Mikita 30.00 60.00
CSSS Scott Stevens
CSST Martin St. Louis 25.00 50.00
CSTL Ted Lindsay 30.00 60.00
CSVL Vincent Lecavalier 30.00 60.00
CSWG Wayne Gretzky 250.00 400.00

2006-07 The Cup Stanley Cup Titlists

PRINT RUNS VARY
NOT PRICED DUE TO SCARCITY
TAA Al Arbour/4
TBB Bob Baun/4
TBO Bobby Orr/2
TBU Johnny Bucyk/2
TCG Clark Gillies/4
TEL Elmer Lach/3
TJB Johnny Bower/4
TJL Jacques Lemaire/8
TMS Milt Schmidt/2
TRK Red Kelly/8

2006-07 The Cup Stanley Cup Titlists Patches

PRINT RUNS VARY
NOT PRICED DUE TO SCARCITY
TAM Al MacInnis/1
TCW Cam Ward/1
TES Eric Staal/1
TJK Jari Kurri/5
TLR Larry Robinson/6
TML Mario Lemieux/2
TRB Ray Bourque/1
TRE Ron Ellis/1
TSS Scott Stevens/3

2002-03 Thrashers Postcards

This 20-card set was issued by the team.
COMPLETE SET (20) 10.00 25.00
1 Lubos Bartecko .40 1.00
2 Yuri Butsayev .40 1.00
3 Jeff Cowan .40 1.00
4 Dany Heatley 2.00 5.00
5 Milan Hnilicka .40 1.00
6 Tony Hrkac .40 1.00
7 Frantisek Kaberle .40 1.00
8 Ilya Kovalchuk 2.00 5.00
9 Slava Kozlov .40 1.00
10 Francis Lessard .40 1.00
11 Pasi Nurminen .60 1.50
12 Jeff Odgers .60 1.50
13 Kamil Piros .40 1.00
14 Dan Snyder .75 2.00
15 Patrik Stefan .40 1.00
16 Per Svartvadet .40 1.00
16 Andy Sutton .40 1.00
17 Chris Tamer .40 1.00
18 Brad Tapper .40 1.00
20 J.P. Vigier .40 1.00

2003-04 Thrashers Postcards

Issued by the team at public events or in response to fan requests, these are standard postcard size. The checklist may not be complete.

COMPLETE SET (23) 10.00 25.00
1 Serge Aubin .40 1.00
2 Jeff Cowan .40 1.00
3 Byron Dafoe .60 1.50
4 Garnet Exelby .60 1.50
5 Bob Hartley CO .20 .50
6 Frank Kaberle .40 1.00
7 Tomas Kloucek .40 1.00
8 Slava Kozlov .40 1.00
9 Ilya Kovalchuk 2.00 5.00
10 Brad Larsen .40 1.00
11 Francis Lessard .40 1.00
12 Ivan Majesky .40 1.00
13 Shawn McEachern .40 1.00
14 Pasi Nurminen .40 1.00
15 Ronald Petrovicky .40 1.00
16 Randy Robitaille .40 1.00
17 Marc Savard .60 1.50
18 Ben Simon .40 1.00
19 Patrik Stefan .40 1.00
20 Andy Sutton .40 1.00
21 Chris Tamer .40 1.00
22 Daniel Tjarnqvist .40 1.00
23 J.P. Vigier .40 1.00

2000-01 Titanium

Released in April 2001, this 150-card set had a hobby SRP of $14.99 for a 5-card pack and a retail SRP of $3.99 for a 3-card pack. Hobby packs featured a memorabilia card in every pack. The set also boasted 50 randomly inserted Short Prints of rookies and prospects, serial numbered to just 99 in hobby packs and 199 in retail. The base cards were printed on a premium holographic foil base containing a color action player photo on a team logo background.

COMPLETE SET w/o SP's (100) 25.00 50.00
1 Paul Kariya .30 .75
2 Teemu Selanne .30 .75
3 Donald Audette .10 .25
4 Jason Allison .10 .25
5 Byron Dafoe .25 .60
6 Bill Guerin .25 .60
7 Joe Thornton .50 1.25
8 J-P Dumont .10 .25
9 Doug Gilmour .25 .60
10 Dominik Hasek .60 1.50
11 Jarome Iginla .40 1.00
12 Marc Savard .10 .25
13 Mike Vernon .25 .60
14 Ron Francis .25 .60
15 Arturs Irbe .25 .60
16 Tony Amonte .25 .60
17 Steve Sullivan .10 .25
18 Jocelyn Thibault .25 .60
19 Ray Bourque .50 1.25
20 Peter Forsberg .75 2.00
21 Milan Hejduk .30 .75
22 Patrick Roy 1.50 4.00
23 Joe Sakic .60 1.50
24 Alex Tanguay .25 .60
25 Geoff Sanderson .10 .25
26 Ron Tugnutt .25 .60
27 Ed Belfour .30 .75
28 Brett Hull .40 1.00
29 Mike Modano .50 1.25
30 Joe Nieuwendyk .25 .60
31 Sergei Fedorov .50 1.25
32 Manny Legace .25 .60
33 Nicklas Lidstrom .30 .75
34 Brendan Shanahan .30 .75
35 Steve Yzerman 1.50 4.00
36 Tommy Salo .25 .60
37 Ryan Smyth .10 .25
38 Doug Weight .25 .60
39 Pavel Bure .30 .75
40 Trevor Kidd .25 .60
41 Rob Blake .25 .60
42 Ziggy Palffy .25 .60
43 Luc Robitaille .25 .60
44 Jamie Storr .25 .60
45 Manny Fernandez .25 .60
46 Scott Pellerin .10 .25
47 Saku Koivu .30 .75
48 Trevor Linden .25 .60
49 Martin Rucinsky .10 .25
50 Jose Theodore .40 1.00
51 David Legwand .25 .60
52 Cliff Ronning .10 .25
53 Jason Arnott .10 .25
54 Martin Brodeur .75 2.00
55 Patrik Elias .25 .60
56 Alexander Mogilny .25 .60
57 Tim Connolly .10 .25
58 Mariusz Czerkawski .10 .25
59 John Vanbiesbrouck .25 .60
60 Theo Fleury .10 .25
61 Brian Leetch .25 .60
62 Mark Messier .30 .75
63 Mike Richter .30 .75
64 Radek Bonk .10 .25
65 Marian Hossa .30 .75
66 Patrick Lalime .25 .60
67 Alexei Yashin .10 .25
68 Brian Boucher .25 .60
69 Simon Gagne .30 .75
70 John LeClair .30 .75
71 Eric Lindros .30 .75
72 Sean Burke .25 .60
73 Jeremy Roenick .40 1.00
74 Keith Tkachuk .30 .75
75 Jaromir Jagr .50 1.25
76 Alexei Kovalev .25 .60
77 Mario Lemieux 2.00 5.00
78 Garth Snow .25 .60
79 Martin Straka .10 .25
80 Pavol Demitra .25 .60
81 Chris Pronger .25 .60
82 Roman Turek .25 .60
83 Pierre Turgeon .25 .60
84 Vincent Damphousse .10 .25
85 Patrick Marleau .25 .60
86 Owen Nolan .25 .60
87 Steve Shields .25 .60
88 Mike Johnson .10 .25
89 Vincent Lecavalier .30 .75
90 Sergei Berezin .10 .25
91 Curtis Joseph .30 .75
92 Gary Roberts .10 .25
93 Mats Sundin .30 .75
94 Andrew Cassels .10 .25
95 Brendan Morrison .25 .60
96 Markus Naslund .30 .75
97 Felix Potvin .30 .75
98 Peter Bondra .30 .75
99 Olaf Kolzig .25 .60
100 Adam Oates .25 .60
101 Samuel Pahlsson SP 6.00 15.00
102 Scott Fankhouser SP 6.00 15.00
103 Tomi Kallio SP 6.00 15.00
104 Brad Tapper RC 8.00 20.00
105 Andrew Raycroft RC 25.00 60.00
106 Denis Hamel SP 6.00 15.00
107 Jeff Cowan RC 15.00 40.00
108 Oleg Saprykin SP 6.00 15.00
109 Josef Vasicek RC 8.00 20.00
110 Shane Willis SP 6.00 15.00
111 David Aebischer RC 30.00 80.00
112 Serge Aubin RC 8.00 20.00
113 Marc Denis SP 6.00 15.00
114 Chris Nielsen RC 8.00 20.00
115 David Vyborny SP 6.00 15.00
116 Marty Turco RC 75.00 200.00
117 Mike Comrie RC 40.00 100.00
118 Shawn Horcoff RC 30.00 80.00
119 Dominic Pittis SP 6.00 15.00
120 Roberto Luongo SP 8.00 20.00
121 Ivan Novoseltsev SP 6.00 15.00
122 Serge Payer SP 6.00 15.00
123 Denis Shvidki SP 6.00 15.00
124 Steven Reinprecht RC 20.00 50.00
125 Lubomir Visnovsky RC 15.00 40.00
126 Marian Gaborik RC 200.00 350.00
127 Filip Kuba SP 6.00 15.00
128 Mathieu Garon SP 6.00 15.00
129 Eric Landry RC 8.00 20.00
130 Andrei Markov SP 6.00 15.00
131 Marian Cisar SP 6.00 15.00
132 Scott Hartnell RC 20.00 50.00
133 Rick DiPietro RC 75.00 200.00
134 Martin Havlat RC 60.00 150.00
135 Jani Hurme RC 15.00 40.00
136 Petr Schastlivy SP 6.00 15.00
137 Ruslan Fedotenko RC 15.00 40.00
138 Justin Williams RC 25.00 60.00
139 Robert Esche SP 6.00 15.00
140 Milan Kraft SP 6.00 15.00
141 Brent Johnson SP 6.00 15.00
142 Reed Low RC 8.00 20.00
143 Evgeni Nabokov SP 6.00 15.00
144 Alexander Kharitonov RC 8.00 20.00
145 Dieter Kochan RC 15.00 40.00
146 Brad Richards SP 15.00 40.00
147 Adam Mair SP 6.00 15.00
148 Daniel Sedin SP 6.00 15.00
149 Henrik Sedin SP 6.00 15.00
150 Trent Whitfield SP 6.00 15.00

2000-01 Titanium Blue

This 100-card set paralleled the Pacific Private Stock Titanium base set. The cards had a blue tone and were serial numbered to the depicted player's jersey number. This set is not priced due to scarcity of many of the cards.

NOT PRICED DUE TO SCARCITY

2000-01 Titanium Gold

This 100-card set paralleled the Pacific Private Stock Titanium base set. The cards had a gold tone and were serial numbered to 99. They were available in random hobby packs only.

*STARS: 5X TO 12X BASIC CARDS

2000-01 Titanium Premiere Date

Inserted at a rate of 1 per hobby box, this 100-card set paralleled the Pacific Private Stock Titanium base set. The cards were serial numbered to 185.

*STARS: 5X TO 10X BASIC CARDS

2000-01 Titanium Red

This 100-card set paralleled the Pacific Private Stock Titanium base set. The cards had a red tone and were serial numbered to 299. They were available in random retail packs only.

*STARS: 4X TO 8X BASIC CARDS

2000-01 Titanium Retail

Released through retail channels, this 150-card set is the same as the hobby set in most ways. The base cards were printed on a premium holographic foil base containing a color action player photo on a team logo background. SP's were serial numbered out of 199.

*RETAIL SINGLES SAME VALUE AS HOBBY
*RETAIL RC's: .2X TO .5X HOBBY CARDS

2000-01 Titanium All-Stars

Randomly inserted and serial-numbered to 1000, this die-cut set actually represents two different sets of all-star players. All-stars from the North American team and from the World team are featured. Card numbers do not carry a NA or W prefix, but it is added below for checklisting purposes.

COMPLETE SET (20) 50.00 100.00
1W Dominik Hasek 2.50 6.00
1NA Paul Kariya 1.25 3.00
2W Peter Forsberg 3.00 8.00
2NA Bill Guerin 1.00 2.50
3W Sergei Fedorov 2.50 6.00
3NA Ray Bourque 2.50 6.00
4W Nicklas Lidstrom 1.25 3.00
4NA Patrick Roy 6.00 15.00
5W Pavel Bure 1.50 4.00
5NA Joe Sakic 2.50 6.00
6W Ziggy Palffy 1.00 2.50
6NA Brett Hull 1.50 4.00
7W Marian Hossa 1.25 3.00
7NA Martin Brodeur 3.00 8.00
8W Evgeni Nabokov 5.00 12.00
8NA Theo Fleury 1.00 2.50
9W Mats Sundin 1.25 3.00
9NA Mario Lemieux 8.00 20.00
10A North-American Team/100 8.00 20.00
10W World Team/100 8.00 20.00

2000-01 Titanium Game Gear

Inserted at a rate of 1:1 hobby and 1:49 retail, these cards feature game-used swatches of jerseys or sticks. Cards 1-50 were stick cards and 51-150 were jersey cards. Each stick card is serial numbered and the total is listed beside the player's name below. Cards 152-155 are dual player cards and carry two swatches of jersey. Dual player cards are serial numbered out of 100.

1 Phil Housley/212 6.00 15.00
2 Martin Gelinas/255 6.00 15.00
3 Sami Kapanen/246 6.00 15.00
4 Sandis Ozolinsh/244 6.00 15.00
5 Tony Amonte/251 6.00 15.00
6 Alexei Zhamnov/206 6.00 15.00
7 Peter Forsberg/235 12.00 30.00
8 Patrick Roy/255 15.00 40.00
9 Joe Sakic/224 12.00 30.00
10 Stephane Yelle/253 6.00 15.00
11 Marc Denis/253 6.00 15.00
12 Kevin Dineen/248 2.50 6.00
13 Ron Tugnutt/253 6.00 15.00
14 Ted Donato/247 6.00 15.00
15 Brett Hull/224 10.00 25.00
16 Chris Chelios/252 8.00 20.00
17 Steve Yzerman/212 20.00 50.00
18 Olli Jokinen/249 6.00 15.00
19 Rob Blake/253 6.00 15.00
20 Rob Blake/251 6.00 15.00
21 Nelson Emerson/193 6.00 15.00
22 Ziggy Palffy/252 6.00 15.00
23 Zigmund Palffy 6.00 15.00
24 Bryan Smolinski/213 6.00 15.00
25 Jozef Stumpel/252 6.00 15.00
26 Jeff Hackett/245 6.00 15.00
27 Trevor Linden/246 8.00 20.00
28 Trevor Linden/247 6.00 15.00
29 Eric Weinrich/252 6.00 15.00
30 Alexander Mogilny/251 6.00 15.00
31 Mariusz Czerkawski/251 6.00 15.00
32 Radek Dvorak/205 6.00 15.00
33 Theo Fleury/203 6.00 15.00
34 Adam Graves/242 6.00 15.00
35 Valeri Kamensky/237 6.00 15.00
36 Brian Leetch/206 6.00 15.00
37 Sandy McCarthy/214 6.00 15.00
38 Kirk McLean/254 6.00 15.00
39 Kirk McLean/251 6.00 15.00
40 Petr Nedved/253 6.00 15.00
41 Daniel Alfredsson/251 6.00 15.00
42 John LeClair/248 8.00 20.00
43 Teppo Numminen/254 6.00 15.00
44 Mario Lemieux/254 20.00 50.00
45 Roman Turek/255 6.00 15.00
46 Yanic Perreault/245 6.00 15.00
47 Gary Roberts/211 6.00 15.00
48 Andrew Cassels/254 6.00 15.00
49 Felix Potvin/254 8.00 20.00
50 Steve Konowalchuk/243 6.00 15.00
51 Guy Hebert 2.50 6.00
52 Guy Hebert 2.50 6.00
53 Mike Leclerc 2.50 6.00
54 Teemu Selanne 8.00 20.00
55 Per Johan Axelsson 2.50 6.00
56 Byron Dafoe 2.50 6.00
57 Andre Savage 2.50 6.00
58 Stu Barnes 2.50 6.00
59 Dominik Hasek 8.00 20.00
60 Erik Rasmussen 2.50 6.00
61 Rob Ray 2.50 6.00
62 Richard Smehlik 2.50 6.00
63 Alexei Zhitnik 2.50 6.00
64 Fred Brathwaite 2.50 6.00
65 Valeri Bure 2.50 6.00
66 Rico Fata 2.50 6.00
67 Phil Housley 2.50 6.00
68 Jarome Iginla 5.00 12.00
69 Marc Savard 2.50 6.00
70 Jeff Shantz 2.50 6.00
71 Cory Stillman 2.50 6.00
72 Boris Mironov 2.50 6.00
73 Alexei Zhamnov 2.50 6.00
74 Peter Forsberg 10.00 25.00
75 Jon Klemm 2.50 6.00
76 Aaron Miller 2.50 6.00
77 Dave Reid 2.50 6.00
78 Patrick Roy 15.00 40.00
79 Joe Sakic 10.00 25.00
80 Lyle Odelein 2.50 6.00
81 Ed Belfour 4.00 10.00
82 Derian Hatcher 2.50 6.00
83 Benoit Hogue 2.50 6.00
84 Brett Hull 6.00 15.00
85 Mike Keane 2.50 6.00
86 Jamie Langenbrunner 2.50 6.00
87 Jere Lehtinen 2.50 6.00
88 Grant Marshall 2.50 6.00
89 Mike Modano 6.00 15.00
90 Joe Nieuwendyk 2.50 6.00
91 Blake Sloan 2.50 6.00
92 Darryl Sydor 2.50 6.00
93 Sergei Zubov 2.50 6.00
94 Chris Chelios 4.00 10.00
95 Mathieu Dandenault 4.00 10.00
96 Chris Osgood 2.50 6.00
97 Brendan Shanahan 4.00 10.00
98 Steve Yzerman 12.00 30.00
99 Robert Svehla 2.50 6.00
100 Benoit Brunet 2.50 6.00
101 Eric Weinrich 2.50 6.00
102 Sergei Zholtok 2.50 6.00
103 Patric Kjellberg 2.50 6.00
104 David Legwand 2.50 6.00
105 Martin Brodeur 10.00 25.00
106 Scott Niedermayer 2.50 6.00
107 Chris Terreri 2.50 6.00
108 Mariusz Czerkawski 2.50 6.00
109 Wade Flaherty 2.50 6.00
110 Kenny Jonsson 2.50 6.00
111 Theo Fleury 2.50 6.00
112 Theo Fleury 2.50 6.00
113 Adam Graves 2.50 6.00
114 Brian Leetch 2.50 6.00
115 Sylvain Lefebvre 2.50 6.00
116 Manny Malhotra 2.50 6.00
117 Petr Nedved 2.50 6.00
118 Mike Richter 4.00 10.00
119 Daniel Alfredsson 2.50 6.00
120 Alexei Yashin 2.50 6.00
121 Eric Desjardins 2.50 6.00
122 John LeClair 4.00 10.00
123 Mika Alatalo 2.50 6.00
124 Sean Burke 2.50 6.00
125 Shane Doan 2.50 6.00
126 Nikolai Khabibulin 4.00 10.00
127 Jyrki Lumme 2.50 6.00
128 Teppo Numminen 2.50 6.00
129 Jeremy Roenick 6.00 15.00
130 Jean-Sebastien Aubin 2.50 6.00
131 Rene Corbet 2.50 6.00
132 Jan Hrdina 2.50 6.00
133 Jaromir Jagr 8.00 20.00
134 Darius Kasparaitis 2.50 6.00
135 Alexei Kovalev 2.50 6.00
136 Robert Lang 2.50 6.00
137 Alexei Morozov 2.50 6.00
138 Rich Parent 2.50 6.00
139 Wayne Primeau 2.50 6.00
140 Michal Rozsival 2.50 6.00
141 Kevin Stevens 2.50 6.00
142 Martin Straka 2.50 6.00
143 Matthew Barnaby 2.50 6.00
144 Tie Domi 2.50 6.00
145 Glenn Healy 2.50 6.00
146 Curtis Joseph 4.00 10.00
147 Dimitri Yushkevich 2.50 6.00
148 Dan Cloutier 2.50 6.00
149 Felix Potvin 2.50 6.00
150 Olaf Kolzig 2.50 6.00
151 Mario Lemieux/100 60.00 150.00
152 Mario Lemieux 60.00 150.00
Jaromir Jagr/100
153 Peter Forsberg 50.00 100.00
Joe Sakic/100
154 B.Hull/M.Modano/100 50.00 100.00
155 Alexei Kovalev 15.00 40.00
Martin Straka/100

2000-01 Titanium Game Gear Patches

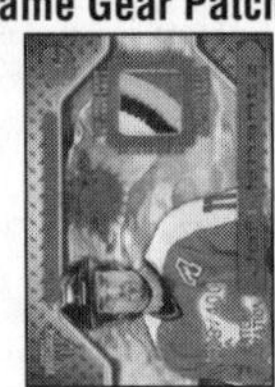

Randomly inserted in packs, these cards parallel cards 51-150 of the base game gear set. Each card features a premium swatch of jersey patch. Cards were serial numbered and the total number is listed beside the player's name below.
*PATCHES: 1.25X TO 3X JSY HI

2000-01 Titanium Three-Star Selections

Randomly inserted in packs, these cards highlight some of the top rookies, stars and goalies in the league. Cards 1-10 feature goalies and were numbered out of 1400. Cards 11-20 feature veteran stars and were numbered out of 1100. Cards 21-30 feature star rookies and are numbered to just 750.

COMPLETE SET (30) 40.00 80.00
1 Dominik Hasek 1.25 3.00
2 Patrick Roy 3.00 8.00
3 Ed Belfour .75 2.00
4 Martin Brodeur 1.50 4.00
5 Mike Richter .75 2.00
6 Brian Boucher .60 1.50
7 Roman Turek .60 1.50
8 Curtis Joseph .75 2.00
9 Felix Potvin .75 2.00
10 Olaf Kolzig .60 1.50
11 Paul Kariya .75 2.00
12 Joe Sakic 1.50 4.00
13 Mike Modano 1.25 3.00
14 Sergei Fedorov 1.25 3.00
15 Ziggy Palffy .60 1.50
16 Theo Fleury .60 1.50
17 Jaromir Jagr 1.25 3.00
18 Mario Lemieux 5.00 12.00
19 Vincent Lecavalier .75 2.00
20 Mats Sundin .75 2.00
21 Shane Willis 1.50 4.00
22 Steven Reinprecht 2.00 5.00
23 Marian Gaborik 6.00 15.00
24 Rick DiPietro 5.00 12.00
25 Martin Havlat 6.00 15.00
26 Brent Johnson 1.00 2.50
27 Evgeni Nabokov 4.00 10.00
28 Brad Richards 2.00 5.00
29 Daniel Sedin .60 1.50
30 Henrik Sedin .60 1.50

2001-02 Titanium

Released in early April 2002, this set consisted of 144 base cards and 40 rookies short printed to the particular player's jersey number. Each card featured a full color action photo on a mirrored card front with a hologram image of the player in the background. Card backs carry individual stats and a short bio. Please note that not all shortprints have been verified and cards with print runs under 25 are not priced due to scarcity.

COMP.SET w/o SP's (144) 40.00 80.00
1 Jeff Friesen .10 .25
2 J-S Giguere .25 .60
3 Paul Kariya .30 .75
4 Dany Heatley .40 1.00
5 Milan Hnilicka .25 .60
6 Patrik Stefan .10 .25
7 Byron Dafoe .25 .60
8 Bill Guerin .25 .60
9 Brian Rolston .10 .25
10 Sergei Samsonov .25 .60
11 Joe Thornton .50 1.25
12 Stu Barnes .10 .25
13 Martin Biron .25 .60
14 Tim Connolly .10 .25
15 J-P Dumont .10 .25
16 Miroslav Satan .25 .60
17 Craig Conroy .10 .25
18 Jarome Iginla .40 1.00
19 Dean McAmmond .10 .25
20 Derek Morris .10 .25
21 Marc Savard .10 .25
22 Roman Turek .25 .60
23 Tom Barrasso .25 .60
24 Ron Francis .25 .60
25 Arturs Irbe .25 .60
26 Sami Kapanen .10 .25
27 Jeff O'Neill .10 .25
28 Tony Amonte .25 .60
29 Mark Bell .10 .25
30 Kyle Calder .10 .25
31 Eric Daze .10 .25
32 Jocelyn Thibault .25 .60
33 Alexei Zhamnov .10 .25
34 Rob Blake .25 .60
35 Milan Hejduk .30 .75
36 Patrick Roy 1.50 4.00
37 Joe Sakic .60 1.50
38 Radim Vrbata .40 1.00
39 Marc Denis .25 .60
40 Rostislav Klesla .10 .25
41 Ron Tugnutt .25 .60
42 Ray Whitney .10 .25
43 Ed Belfour .30 .75
44 Jere Lehtinen .25 .60
45 Mike Modano .50 1.25
46 Joe Nieuwendyk .25 .60
47 Pierre Turgeon .25 .60
48 Sergei Fedorov .50 1.25
49 Dominik Hasek .60 1.50
50 Brett Hull .40 1.00
51 Nicklas Lidstrom .30 .75
52 Luc Robitaille .25 .60
53 Brendan Shanahan .30 .75
54 Steve Yzerman 1.50 4.00
55 Anson Carter .25 .60
56 Mike Comrie .25 .60
57 Tommy Salo .25 .60
58 Ryan Smyth .10 .25
59 Pavel Bure .30 .75
60 Viktor Kozlov .10 .25
61 Roberto Luongo .40 1.00
62 Marcus Nilsson .10 .25
63 Jason Allison .10 .25
64 Adam Deadmarsh .10 .25
65 Steve Heinze .10 .25
66 Zigmund Palffy .25 .60
67 Felix Potvin .30 .75
68 Andrew Brunette .10 .25
69 Jim Dowd .10 .25
70 Marian Gaborik .60 1.50
71 Dwayne Roloson .25 .60
72 Doug Gilmour .25 .60
73 Yanic Perreault .10 .25
74 Mike Ribeiro .10 .25
75 Brian Savage .10 .25
76 Jose Theodore .40 1.00
77 Mike Dunham .25 .60
78 Scott Hartnell .10 .25
79 David Legwand .25 .60
80 Cliff Ronning .10 .25
81 Jason Arnott .10 .25
82 Martin Brodeur .75 2.00
83 J-F Damphousse .25 .60
84 Patrik Elias .25 .60
85 Scott Stevens .25 .60
86 Mariusz Czerkawski .10 .25
87 Rick DiPietro .25 .60
88 Chris Osgood .25 .60
89 Mark Parrish .10 .25
90 Michael Peca .10 .25
91 Alexei Yashin .10 .25
92 Theo Fleury .10 .25
93 Brian Leetch .25 .60
94 Eric Lindros .30 .75
95 Mark Messier .30 .75
96 Mike Richter .30 .75
97 Mike York .10 .25
98 Daniel Alfredsson .25 .60
99 Martin Havlat .25 .60
100 Marian Hossa .30 .75
101 Patrick Lalime .25 .60
102 Todd White .10 .25
103 Roman Cechmanek .25 .60
104 Simon Gagne .30 .75
105 John LeClair .30 .75
106 Mark Recchi .25 .60
107 Jeremy Roenick .40 1.00
108 Sean Burke .25 .60
109 Daymond Langkow .25 .60
110 Claude Lemieux .10 .25
111 Johan Hedberg .25 .60
112 Alexei Kovalev .25 .60
113 Robert Lang .10 .25
114 Mario Lemieux 2.00 5.00
115 Pavol Demitra .25 .60
116 Brent Johnson .25 .60
117 Al MacInnis .25 .60
118 Chris Pronger .25 .60
119 Keith Tkachuk .30 .75
120 Doug Weight .25 .60
121 Vincent Damphousse .10 .25
122 Evgeni Nabokov .25 .60
123 Owen Nolan .25 .60
124 Teemu Selanne .30 .75
125 Nikolai Khabibulin .30 .75
126 Vincent Lecavalier .30 .75
127 Brad Richards .25 .60
128 Martin St. Louis .25 .60
129 Curtis Joseph .30 .75
130 Alexander Mogilny .25 .60
131 Gary Roberts .10 .25
132 Mats Sundin .30 .75
133 Darcy Tucker .10 .25
134 Todd Bertuzzi .30 .75
135 Dan Cloutier .25 .60
136 Brendan Morrison .25 .60
137 Markus Naslund .30 .75
138 Daniel Sedin .10 .25
139 Henrik Sedin .10 .25
140 Peter Bondra .30 .75
141 Sergei Gonchar .10 .25
142 Jaromir Jagr .50 1.25
143 Olaf Kolzig .25 .60
144 Adam Oates .25 .60
145 Ilja Bryzgalov/30 60.00 125.00
146 Timo Parssinen/29 30.00 80.00
147 Ilya Kovalchuk/17
148 Kamil Piros/25 25.00 60.00
149 Brian Pothier/3
150 Andy Hilbert/29 25.00 60.00
151 Jukka Hentunen/24
152 Erik Cole/26 75.00 200.00
153 Vaclav Nedorost/22
154 John Erskine/3
155 Niko Kapanen/39 30.00 80.00
156 Pavel Datsyuk/13
157 Jason Chimera/28 40.00 100.00
158 Ty Conklin/1
159 Jussi Markkanen/30 30.00 80.00
160 Niklas Hagman/14
161 Kristian Huselius/22
162 Jaroslav Bednar/7
163 David Cullen/24
164 Pascal Dupuis/11
165 Nick Schultz/55 25.00 60.00
166 Martin Erat/19
167 Brian Gionta/14
168 Andreas Salomonsson/15
169 Radek Martinek/24
170 Raffi Torres/16
171 Dan Blackburn/31 25.00 60.00
172 Mikael Samuelsson/37 30.00 80.00
173 Chris Neil/25 50.00 125.00
174 Jiri Dopita/20
175 Bruno St. Jacques/42
176 Krystofer Kolanos/36 25.00 60.00
177 Josef Melichar/2
178 Billy Tibbetts/12
179 Mark Rycroft/42 20.00 50.00
180 Jeff Jillson/5
181 Nikita Alexeev/15
182 Brad Leeb/38 12.50 30.00
183 Chris Corrinet/48 20.00 50.00
184 Brian Sutherby/41 30.00 80.00

2001-02 Titanium Hobby Parallel

This 144-card set directly paralleled the base hobby set with red foil highlights. Each card was also serial numbered out of 94 on the card front.
*STARS: 5X TO 12X BASIC CARD

2001-02 Titanium Premiere Date

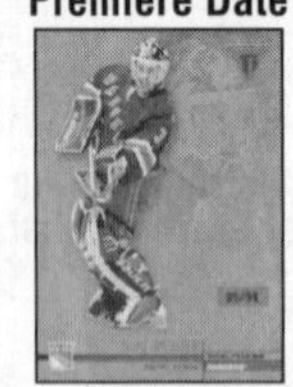

This 144-card set was a parallel to the base set but carried a premiere date stamp on the card fronts. Each card was serial numbered out of 94, and these cards were available in hobby packs only at a rate of 1:7.
*STARS: 5X TO 12X BASIC CARD

2001-02 Titanium Retail

This 184-card set resembles the hobby version, but the card stock was slightly thicker and the mirrored effect on the hobby card fronts was removed for this version. Rookies in the retail version were serial-numbered out of 534.

COMPLETE SET (184) 300.00 600.00
*STARS:SAME VALUE AS HOBBY
145 Ilja Bryzgalov RC 4.00 10.00
146 Timo Parssinen RC 3.00 8.00

147 Ilya Kovalchuk RC 20.00 50.00
148 Kamil Piros RC 3.00 8.00
149 Brian Pothier RC 3.00 8.00
150 Andy Hilbert SP 3.00 8.00
151 Jukka Hentunen RC 3.00 8.00
152 Erik Cole RC 4.00 12.00
153 Vaclav Nedorost RC 3.00 8.00
154 John Erskine RC 3.00 8.00
155 Niko Kapanen RC 3.00 8.00
156 Pavel Datsyuk RC 15.00 40.00
157 Jason Chimera RC 3.00 8.00
158 Ty Conklin RC 3.00 8.00
159 Jussi Markkanen SP 3.00 8.00
160 Niklas Hagman RC 3.00 8.00
161 Kristian Huselius RC 5.00 12.00
162 Jaroslav Bednar RC 3.00 8.00
163 David Cullen RC 3.00 8.00
164 Pascal Dupuis RC 3.00 8.00
165 Nick Schultz RC 3.00 8.00
166 Martin Erat RC 3.00 8.00
167 Brian Gionta SP 3.00 8.00
168 Andreas Salomonsson RC 3.00 8.00
169 Radek Martinek RC 3.00 8.00
170 Raffi Torres RC 4.00 10.00
171 Dan Blackburn RC 4.00 10.00
172 Mikael Samuelsson RC 3.00 8.00
173 Chris Neil RC 3.00 8.00
174 Jiri Dopita RC 3.00 8.00
175 Bruno St. Jacques RC 3.00 8.00
176 Krystofer Kolanos RC 3.00 8.00
177 Josef Melichar SP 3.00 8.00
178 Billy Tibbetts RC 3.00 8.00
179 Mark Rycroft RC 3.00 8.00
180 Jeff Jillson RC 3.00 8.00
181 Nikita Alexeev RC 3.00 8.00
182 Brad Leeb SP 3.00 8.00
183 Chris Corrinet RC 3.00 8.00
184 Brian Sutherby RC 3.00 8.00

2001-02 Titanium Retail Parallel

This 144-card set directly paralleled the base retail set with red foil highlights. Each card was also serial numbered out of 131 on the card front.
*RETAIL PARALLEL: 4X TO 10X BASIC CARD

2001-02 Titanium All-Stars

Inserted at a rate of 1:7 hobby and 1:25 retail packs, this 20 card set featured players chosen for the 2002 NHL All-Star Game. The cards carried a photo of the given player on the front alongside a bronze foil logo from the game.

COMPLETE SET (20) 20.00 40.00
1 Joe Thornton 1.00 2.50
2 Jarome Iginla .75 2.00
3 Sami Kapanen .50 1.25
4 Eric Daze .50 1.25
5 Rob Blake .50 1.25
6 Patrick Roy 3.00 8.00
7 Sergei Fedorov 1.25 3.00
8 Dominik Hasek 1.25 3.00
9 Nicklas Lidstrom .60 1.50
10 Brendan Shanahan 1.00 2.50
11 Zigmund Palffy .50 1.25
12 Jose Theodore .75 2.00
13 Patrik Elias .50 1.25
14 Alexei Yashin .50 1.25
15 Chris Pronger .50 1.25
16 Owen Nolan .50 1.25
17 Teemu Selanne .60 1.50
18 Nikolai Khabibulin .60 1.50
19 Mats Sundin .60 1.50
20 Jaromir Jagr 1.00 2.50

2001-02 Titanium Double-Sided Jerseys

Inserted at one per hobby pack and 1:25 retail, this 75-card set featured game-worn jersey swatches of two players; one on front and one on back alongside color photos of the given player.

1 Steve Rucchin 4.00 10.00
Paul Kariya
2 Jeff Friesen 2.50 6.00
Oleg Tverdovsky
3 Sergei Samsonov 4.00 10.00
Bill Guerin
4 J-P Dumont 2.50 6.00
Alexei Zhitnik
5 Marc Savard 2.50 6.00
Roman Turek
6 Roman Turek 2.50 6.00
Bob Boughner
7 Jarome Iginla 4.00 10.00
Marc Savard
8 Tony Amonte 2.50 6.00
Boris Mironov
9 Kyle Calder 2.50 6.00
Michael Nylander
10 Alexei Zhamnov 2.50 6.00
Steve Sullivan
11 Milan Hejduk 4.00 10.00
Chris Drury
12 J.Sakic/A.Tanguay 8.00 20.00
13 Patrick Roy 15.00 40.00
Rob Blake
14 Alex Tanguay 4.00 10.00
Vaclav Nedorost
15 Lyle Odelein 2.50 6.00
Jamie McLennan
16 Mike Modano 4.00 10.00
Jamie Langenbrunner
17 Felix Potvin 2.50 6.00
Zigmund Palffy
18 Adam Deadmarsh 2.50 6.00
Bryan Smolinski
19 Rob Blake 2.50 6.00
Aaron Miller
20 Jose Theodore 5.00 12.00
Felix Potvin
21 J-P Dumont 2.50 6.00
Scott Stevens
22 Cliff Ronning 2.50 6.00
Tom Fitzgerald
23 Ilya Kovalchuk 10.00 25.00
Dany Heatley
24 Eric Daze 2.50 6.00
Mark Bell
25 Eric Lindros 4.00 10.00
Theo Fleury
26 Brian Leetch 2.50 6.00
Rico Fata
27 Eric Lindros 6.00 15.00
Mark Messier
28 Mike York 2.50 6.00
Theo Fleury
29 Mike Richter 5.00 12.00
Brian Leetch
30 Daniel Alfredsson 4.00 10.00
Mats Sundin
31 Pavel Brendl 2.50 6.00
Jan Hrdina
32 Mario Lemieux 15.00 40.00
Alexei Morozov
33 Pavel Brendl 2.50 6.00
Josef Beranek
34 Martin Straka 2.50 6.00
Michal Rozsival
35 Jan Hrdina 2.50 6.00
Ian Moran
36 Alexei Kovalev 2.50 6.00
Rich Parent
37 Mike Eastwood 2.50 6.00
Fred Brathwaite
38 Scott Young 2.50 6.00
Jochen Hecht
39 Teemu Selanne 15.00 40.00
Ilya Kovalchuk/Stick
40 Vincent Lecavalier 4.00 10.00
Petr Svoboda
41 Curtis Joseph 4.00 10.00
Glenn Healy
42 Mats Sundin 8.00 20.00
Joe Sakic
43 Jaromir Jagr 6.00 15.00
Dainius Zubrus
44 Tom Barrasso 4.00 10.00
Arturs Irbe
45 Ron Francis 2.50 6.00
Jeff O'Neill
46 Rod Brind'mour 4.00 10.00
Erik Cole
47 Martin Havlat 5.00 12.00
Marian Hossa
48 Daniel Alfredsson 4.00 10.00
Patrick Lalime
49 Jiri Dopita 2.50 6.00
Roman Cechmanek
50 Jeremy Roenick 4.00 10.00
John LeClair
51 Simon Gagne 4.00 10.00
John LeClair
52 M.Modano/P.Turgeon 4.00 10.00
53 Marty Turco 5.00 12.00
Ed Belfour
54 Henrik Sedin 5.00 12.00
Daniel Sedin
55 Todd Bertuzzi 4.00 10.00
Brendan Morrison
56 Markus Naslund 4.00 10.00
Dan Cloutier
57 Brendan Morrison 4.00 10.00
Marty Turco
58 Markus Naslund 4.00 10.00
Daniel Alfredsson
59 Jeremy Roenick 4.00 10.00
Tom Barrasso
60 Martin Havlat 2.50 6.00
Roman Cechmanek
61 Ron Francis 4.00 10.00
Arturs Irbe
62 Jeff O'Neill 2.50 6.00
Erik Cole
63 Marian Hossa 2.50 6.00
Jiri Dopita
64 Patrick Lalime 4.00 10.00
Simon Gagne
65 Ed Belfour 4.00 10.00
Pierre Turgeon
66 Martin Biron 4.00 10.00
Miroslav Satan
67 M.Gaborik/M.Fernandez 6.00 15.00
68 Martin Brodeur 6.00 15.00
Jason Arnott
69 Patrik Elias 4.00 10.00
Scott Gomez
70 Jamie McLennan 2.50 6.00
Filip Kuba
71 Krystofer Kolanos 2.50 6.00
Daymond Langkow
72 Michal Handzus 2.50 6.00
Sergei Berezin
73 Steve Sullivan 2.50 6.00
Mark Bell
74 Joe Thornton 6.00 15.00
Bill Guerin
75 Jason Allison 2.50 6.00
Zigmund Palffy

2001-02 Titanium Double-Sided Patches

This 55-card set partially paralleled the jersey set but featured game-worn jersey patch swatches. Individual print runs are listed below.

1 Steve Rucchin 10.00 25.00
Paul Kariya/56
2 Jeff Friesen 10.00 25.00
Oleg Tverdovsky/213
3 Sergei Samsonov 10.00 25.00
Bill Guerin/215
4 J-P Dumont 10.00 25.00
Alexei Zhitnik/181
9 Kyle Calder 10.00 25.00
Michael Nylander/46
11 Milan Hejduk 10.00 25.00
Chris Drury/219
12 J.Sakic/A.Tanguay/259 20.00 50.00
13 Patrick Roy 30.00 80.00
Rob Blake/39
14 Alex Tanguay 10.00 25.00
Vaclav Nedorost/117
16 Mike Modano 10.00 25.00
Jamie Langenbrunner/19
17 Felix Potvin 10.00 25.00
Zigmund Palffy/174
18 Adam Deadmarsh 10.00 25.00
Bryan Smolinski/163
20 Jose Theodore 10.00 25.00
Felix Potvin/94
21 J-P Dumont 10.00 25.00
Scott Stevens/255
24 Eric Daze 10.00 25.00
Mark Bell/116
25 Eric Lindros 10.00 25.00
Theo Fleury/288
26 Brian Leetch 10.00 25.00
Rico Fata/198
27 Eric Lindros 12.50 30.00
Mark Messier/166
29 Mike Richter 12.50 30.00
Brian Leetch/104
30 Daniel Alfredsson 10.00 25.00
Mats Sundin/63
33 Pavel Brendl 10.00 25.00
Josef Beranek/39
34 Martin Straka 10.00 25.00
Michal Rozsival/302
35 Jan Hrdina 10.00 25.00
Ian Moran/88
38 Scott Young 10.00 25.00
Jochen Hecht/62
40 Vincent Lecavalier 10.00 25.00
Petr Svoboda/45
41 Curtis Joseph 10.00 25.00
Glenn Healy/140
42 Mats Sundin 20.00 50.00
JoeSakic/53
43 Jaromir Jagr 15.00 40.00
Dainius Zubrus/56
44 Tom Barrasso 10.00 25.00
Arturs Irbe/199
45 Ron Francis 10.00 25.00
Jeff O'Neill/194
46 Rod Brind'mour 10.00 25.00
Erik Cole/215
47 Martin Havlat 12.50 30.00
Marian Hossa/118
48 Daniel Alfredsson 10.00 25.00
Patrick Lalime/114
49 Jiri Dopita 10.00 25.00
Roman Cechmanek/202
50 Jeremy Roenick 10.00 25.00
John LeClair/216
51 Simon Gagne 10.00 25.00
John LeClair/169
52 M.Modano/P.Turgeon/216 15.00 40.00
53 Marty Turco 10.00 25.00
Ed Belfour/212
54 Henrik Sedin 15.00 40.00
Daniel Sedin/218
55 Todd Bertuzzi 10.00 25.00
Brendan Morrison/215
56 Markus Naslund 10.00 25.00
Dan Cloutier/164
57 Brendan Morrison 10.00 25.00
Marty Turco/119
58 Markus Naslund 10.00 25.00
Daniel Alfredsson/164
59 Jeremy Roenick 10.00 25.00
Tom Barrasso/113
60 Martin Havlat 10.00 25.00
Roman Cechmanek/109
61 Ron Francis 12.50 30.00
Arturs Irbe/154
62 Jeff O'Neill 10.00 25.00
Erik Cole/163
63 Marian Hossa 10.00 25.00
Jiri Dopita/166
64 Patrick Lalime 10.00 25.00

Simon Gagne/163
65 Ed Belfour 10.00 25.00
Pierre Turgeon/165
66 Martin Biron 10.00 25.00
Miroslav Satan/256
67 M.Gaborik/M.Fernandez/14 15.00 40.00
69 Patrik Elias 10.00 25.00
Scott Gomez/260
70 Jamie McLennan 10.00 25.00
Filip Kuba/569
71 Krystofer Kolanos 10.00 25.00
Daymond Langkow/116
72 Michal Handzus 10.00 25.00
Sergei Berezin/260
73 Steve Sullivan 10.00 25.00
Mark Bell/264
75 Jason Allison 10.00 25.00
Zigmund Palffy/106

2001-02 Titanium Rookie Team

This ten card set was inserted in hobby packs at 1:121 and each card was serial-numbered out of 70. Each card featured a player from the year's rookie class with both an action photo and a head shot.

1 Dany Heatley 10.00 25.00
2 Ilya Kovalchuk 10.00 25.00
3 Erik Cole 6.00 15.00
4 Mark Bell 4.00 10.00
5 Radim Vrbata 2.00 5.00
6 Kristian Huselius 2.00 5.00
7 Mike Ribeiro 2.00 5.00
8 Rick DiPietro 6.00 15.00
9 Raffi Torres 4.00 10.00
10 Krystofer Kolanos 2.00 5.00

2001-02 Titanium Saturday Knights

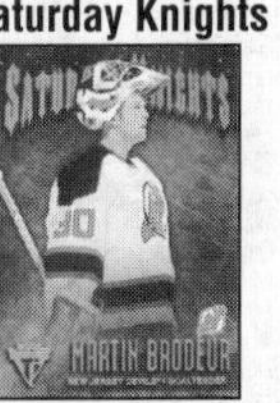

COMPLETE SET (20) 40.00 80.00
STATED ODDS 1:25 HOBBY/1:97 RETAIL
1 Paul Kariya 1.00 2.50
2 Joe Thornton 1.50 4.00
3 Jarome Iginla 1.25 3.00
4 Ed Belfour 1.00 2.50
5 Dominik Hasek 2.00 5.00
6 Brendan Shanahan 1.50 4.00
7 Steve Yzerman 5.00 12.00
8 Mike Comrie .75 2.00
9 Pavel Bure 1.25 3.00
10 Marian Gaborik 2.00 5.00
11 Jose Theodore 1.25 3.00
12 Martin Brodeur 2.50 6.00
13 Mike Peca .75 2.00
14 Eric Lindros 1.50 4.00
15 Daniel Alfredsson .75 2.00
16 Martin Havlat .75 2.00
17 Jeremy Roenick 1.25 3.00
18 Mario Lemieux 6.00 15.00
19 Curtis Joseph 1.00 2.50
20 Mats Sundin 1.00 2.50

2001-02 Titanium Three-Star Selections

This 30-card set featured top goalies, veterans and rookies with full color action photos on the card front surrounded by gold foil highlights. Cards 1-10 were seeded at 1:7 hobby packs/1:25 retail, cards 11-20 were seeded at 1:13 hobby/1:49 retail, and cards 21-30 were seeded at 1:25 hobby/1:97 retail.

COMPLETE SET (30) 50.00 100.00
1 Roman Turek .50 1.25
2 Tom Barrasso .50 1.25
3 Patrick Roy 3.00 8.00
4 Dominik Hasek 1.25 3.00
5 Martin Brodeur 1.50 4.00
6 Chris Osgood .50 1.25
7 Mike Richter .60 1.50
8 Evgeni Nabokov .50 1.25
9 Nikolai Khabibulin .60 1.50
10 Curtis Joseph .60 1.50
11 Paul Kariya .60 1.50
12 Jarome Iginla 1.00 2.50
13 Joe Sakic 1.50 4.00
14 Brendan Shanahan .60 1.50
15 Steve Yzerman 4.00 10.00
16 Eric Lindros .60 1.50
17 Mike York .50 1.25
18 Mario Lemieux 5.00 12.00
19 Mats Sundin .75 2.00
20 Jaromir Jagr 1.00 2.50
21 Dany Heatley 4.00 10.00
22 Ilya Kovalchuk 6.00 15.00
23 Erik Cole 1.50 4.00
24 Mark Bell 1.50 4.00
25 Radim Vrbata 1.50 4.00
26 Kristian Huselius 1.50 4.00
27 Mike Ribeiro 1.50 4.00
28 Rick DiPietro 1.50 4.00
29 Raffi Torres 1.50 4.00
30 Krystofer Kolanos 1.50 4.00

2002-03 Titanium

This 140-card set consisted of 100 base veteran cards and 40 rookie cards shortprinted to 99 copies each. Cards were highlighted by gold foil.

COMP.SET w/o SP's (100) 40.00 80.00
1 J-S Giguere .25 .60
2 Paul Kariya .30 .75
3 Petr Sykora .10 .25
4 Dany Heatley .40 1.00
5 Ilya Kovalchuk .40 1.00
6 Pasi Nurminen .10 .25
7 Glen Murray .10 .25
8 Brian Rolston .10 .25
9 Steve Shields .25 .60
10 Joe Thornton .50 1.25
11 Martin Biron .25 .60
12 Chris Gratton .10 .25
13 Miroslav Satan .25 .60
14 Chris Drury .30 .75
15 Jarome Iginla .40 1.00
16 Roman Turek .25 .60
17 Rod Brind'Amour .25 .60
18 Ron Francis .25 .60
19 Jeff O'Neill .10 .25
20 Kevin Weekes .25 .60
21 Tyler Arnason .25 .60
22 Theo Fleury .10 .25
23 Jocelyn Thibault .25 .60
24 Peter Forsberg .75 2.00
25 Milan Hejduk .30 .75
26 Patrick Roy 1.50 4.00
27 Joe Sakic .60 1.50
28 Andrew Cassels .10 .25
29 Marc Denis .25 .60
30 Geoff Sanderson .10 .25
31 Bill Guerin .25 .60
32 Mike Modano .50 1.25
33 Marty Turco .25 .60
34 Pierre Turgeon .25 .60
35 Sergei Fedorov .50 1.25
36 Brett Hull .40 1.00
37 Curtis Joseph .30 .75
38 Nicklas Lidstrom .30 .75
39 Brendan Shanahan .30 .75
40 Steve Yzerman 1.50 4.00
41 Anson Carter .25 .60
42 Mike Comrie .25 .60
43 Tommy Salo .25 .60
44 Ryan Smyth .10 .25
45 Kristian Huselius .10 .25
46 Olli Jokinen .25 .60
47 Roberto Luongo .40 1.00
48 Jason Allison .10 .25
49 Eric Belanger .10 .25
50 Ziggy Palffy .30 .75
51 Felix Potvin .30 .75
52 Manny Fernandez .25 .60
53 Marian Gaborik .60 1.50
54 Cliff Ronning .10 .25
55 Saku Koivu .30 .75
56 Yanic Perreault .10 .25
57 Jose Theodore .40 1.00
58 Richard Zednik .10 .25
59 Andreas Johansson .10 .25
60 David Legwand .25 .60
61 Tomas Vokoun .25 .60
62 Martin Brodeur .75 2.00
63 Scott Gomez .10 .25
64 John Madden .10 .25
65 Rick DiPietro .25 .60
66 Michael Peca .10 .25
67 Alexei Yashin .10 .25
68 Pavel Bure .30 .75
69 Eric Lindros .30 .75
70 Tom Poti .10 .25
71 Daniel Alfredsson .25 .60
72 Marian Hossa .30 .75
73 Patrick Lalime .25 .60
74 Roman Cechmanek .25 .60
75 Simon Gagne .30 .75
76 Jeremy Roenick .40 1.00
77 Tony Amonte .25 .60
78 Brian Boucher .25 .60
79 Shane Doan .10 .25
80 Johan Hedberg .25 .60
81 Alex Kovalev .25 .60
82 Mario Lemieux 2.00 5.00
83 Brent Johnson .25 .60
84 Cory Stillman .10 .25
85 Doug Weight .25 .60
86 Patrick Marleau .25 .60
87 Evgeni Nabokov .25 .60
88 Teemu Selanne .30 .75
89 Nikolai Khabibulin .30 .75
90 Vincent Lecavalier .30 .75
91 Martin St. Louis .25 .60
92 Ed Belfour .30 .75
93 Alexander Mogilny .25 .60
94 Mats Sundin .30 .75
95 Todd Bertuzzi .30 .75
96 Dan Cloutier .25 .60
97 Brendan Morrison .25 .60
98 Markus Naslund .30 .75
99 Jaromir Jagr .50 1.25
100 Michael Nylander .10 .25
101 Stanislav Chistov RC 8.00 20.00
102 Martin Gerber RC 15.00 40.00
103 Kurt Sauer RC 8.00 20.00
104 Alexei Smirnov RC 8.00 20.00
105 Shaone Morrisonn RC 8.00 20.00
106 Tim Thomas RC 12.00 30.00
107 Ryan Miller RC 60.00 125.00
108 Chuck Kobasew RC 15.00 40.00
109 Jordan Leopold RC 8.00 20.00
110 Pascal Leclaire RC 15.00 40.00
111 Rick Nash RC 100.00 225.00
112 Steve Ott RC 12.00 30.00
113 Dmitri Bykov RC 8.00 20.00
114 Henrik Zetterberg RC 75.00 150.00
115 Ales Hemsky RC 40.00 80.00
116 Jay Bouwmeester RC 15.00 40.00
117 Michael Cammalleri RC 15.00 40.00
118 Alexander Frolov RC 40.00 80.00
119 P-M Bouchard RC 15.00 40.00
120 Stephane Veilleux RC 8.00 20.00
121 Kyle Wanvig SP 8.00 20.00
122 Ron Hainsey RC 8.00 20.00
123 Vernon Fiddler RC 8.00 20.00
124 Adam Hall RC 8.00 20.00
125 Scottie Upshall RC 12.00 30.00
126 Jason Spezza RC 100.00 250.00
127 Anton Volchenkov RC 8.00 20.00
128 Dennis Seidenberg RC 8.00 20.00
129 Radovan Somik RC 8.00 20.00
130 Jeff Taffe RC 8.00 20.00
131 Sebastien Caron SP 8.00 20.00
132 Brooks Orpik RC 8.00 20.00
133 Dick Tarnstrom RC 8.00 20.00
134 Tom Koivisto RC 8.00 20.00
135 Curtis Sanford RC 8.00 20.00
136 Lynn Loyns RC 8.00 20.00
137 Alexander Svitov RC 8.00 20.00
138 Carlo Colaiacovo RC 8.00 20.00
139 Mikael Tellqvist RC 15.00 40.00
140 Steve Eminger RC 8.00 20.00

2002-03 Titanium Blue

*STARS: .5X TO 1.25X BASIC CARDS
*SP's: .05X TO .15X
STATED PRINT RUN 450 SER.#'d SETS

2002-03 Titanium Red

*STARS: 1X TO 2.5X BASE HI
*SP's: .10X TO .25X
STATED PRINT RUN 299 SER.#'d SETS

2002-03 Titanium Retail

These cards mirrored the hobby set but carried silver foil highlights.
*BASE CARDS SAME VALUE HOBBY
*SP's: .05X TO .15X HOBBY VERSION
SP PRINT RUN 1475 SER.#'d SETS

2002-03 Titanium Jerseys

Inserted one per hobby pack, this 75-card set featured swatches of game worn jerseys. Each card was individually serial-numbered. A retail variation was also created that carried silver foil in place of the gold foil on the hobby version.

*MULT.COLOR SWATCH: .5X TO 1.25X
1 Mike Leclerc/376 3.00 8.00
2 Dany Heatley/715 6.00 15.00
3 Ilya Kovalchuk/606 6.00 15.00
4 Patrik Stefan/1183 3.00 8.00
5 Joe Thornton/160 10.00 25.00
6 Martin Biron/1019 3.00 8.00
7 J-P Dumont/948 3.00 8.00
8 Rod BrindAmour/1231 3.00 8.00
9 Arturs Irbe/829 3.00 8.00
10 Jeff O'Neill/283 3.00 8.00
11 Chris Drury/514 3.00 8.00
12 Roman Turek/1160 3.00 8.00
13 Mark Bell/957 3.00 8.00
14 Sergei Berezin/304 3.00 8.00
15 Steve Sullivan/641 3.00 8.00
16 Rob Blake/1020 3.00 8.00
17 Milan Hejduk/1160 4.00 10.00
18 Patrick Roy/150 25.00 60.00
19 Rostislav Klesla/1099 3.00 8.00
20 Geoff Sanderson/1307 3.00 8.00
21 Ron Tugnutt/1338 3.00 8.00
22 Marty Turco/552 3.00 8.00
23 Sergei Fedorov/561 8.00 20.00
24 Dominik Hasek/253 8.00 20.00
25 Brett Hull/899 6.00 15.00
26 Luc Robitaille/717 3.00 8.00
27 Jason Williams/1270 3.00 8.00
28 Mike Comrie/503 3.00 8.00
29 Tommy Salo/801 3.00 8.00
30 Ryan Smyth/1052 3.00 8.00
31 Valeri Bure/1352 3.00 8.00
32 Kristian Huselius/1305 3.00 8.00
33 Roberto Luongo/1403 5.00 12.00
34 Marian Gaborik 8.00 20.00
35 Yanic Perreault/1285 3.00 8.00
36 Jose Theodore/316 5.00 12.00
37 David Legwand/857 3.00 8.00
38 Scott Walker/1307 3.00 8.00
39 Scott Gomez/872 3.00 8.00
40 Scott Stevens/1273 3.00 8.00
41 Michael Peca/553 3.00 8.00
42 Alexei Yashin/743 3.00 8.00
43 Pavel Bure/908 4.00 10.00
44 Eric Lindros/583 4.00 10.00
45 Mark Messier/809 4.00 10.00
46 Daniel Alfredsson/532 3.00 8.00
47 Martin Havlat/545 3.00 8.00
48 Patrick Lalime/826 3.00 8.00
49 Simon Gagne/1028 4.00 10.00
50 Michal Handzus/636 3.00 8.00
51 Tomi Kallio/1301 3.00 8.00
52 John LeClair/942 4.00 10.00
53 Johan Hedberg/1004 3.00 8.00
54 Mario Lemieux 15.00 40.00
55 Toby Petersen 3.00 8.00
56 Pavol Demitra/1256 3.00 8.00
57 Ray Ferraro/1288 3.00 8.00
58 Chris Pronger/1249 3.00 8.00
59 Keith Tkachuk/914 4.00 10.00
60 Sergei Varlamov/1152 3.00 8.00
61 Miikka Kiprusoff/1203 3.00 8.00
62 Patrick Marleau/730 3.00 8.00
63 Owen Nolan/439 3.00 8.00
64 Nikolai Khabibulin/1002 4.00 10.00
65 Fredrik Modin/1260 3.00 8.00
66 Alexander Mogilny/710 3.00 8.00
67 Gary Roberts/1260 3.00 8.00
68 Darcy Tucker/1260 3.00 8.00
69 Dan Cloutier/867 3.00 8.00
70 Brendan Morrison/638 3.00 8.00
71 Daniel Sedin/1105 3.00 8.00
72 Henrik Sedin/1100 3.00 8.00
73 Peter Bondra/1289 3.00 8.00
74 Jaromir Jagr/171 6.00 15.00
75 Olaf Kolzig/1303 3.00 8.00

2002-03 Titanium Jerseys Retail

*RETAIL: .6X TO 1.5X HOBBY

2002-03 Titanium Patches

This hobby-only set paralleled the basic jerseys but carried patch variations. Individual print runs are listed below. Print runs of 25 or less were not priced due to scarcity.

1 Mike Leclerc/10
2 Dany Heatley/20
3 Ilya Kovalchuk/25 20.00 50.00
4 Patrik Stefan/250 8.00 20.00
5 Joe Thornton/225 15.00 40.00
6 Martin Biron/65 8.00 20.00
8 Rod Brind'Amour/125 8.00 20.00
9 Arturs Irbe/21
10 Jeff O'neill/250 8.00 20.00
11 Chris Drury/250 8.00 20.00
13 Mark Bell/225 8.00 20.00
14 Sergei Berezin/260 8.00 20.00
15 Steve Sullivan/100 8.00 20.00
16 Rob Blake/250 8.00 20.00
17 Milan Hejduk/250 10.00 25.00
19 Rostislav Klesla/50 8.00 20.00
20 Geoff Sanderson/25
21 Ron Tugnutt/250 8.00 20.00
22 Marty Turco/195 8.00 20.00
23 Sergei Fedorov/45 20.00 50.00
24 Dominik Hasek/35 20.00 50.00
25 Brett Hull/85 15.00 40.00
27 Jason Williams/250 8.00 20.00
28 Mike Comrie/150 8.00 20.00
30 Ryan Smyth/65 8.00 20.00
31 Valeri Bure/210 8.00 20.00
32 Kristian Huselius/250 8.00 20.00
33 Roberto Luongo/250 12.50 30.00
35 Yanic Perreault/200 8.00 20.00
36 Jose Theodore/65 12.50 30.00
37 David Legwand/180 8.00 20.00
38 Scott Walker/250 8.00 20.00
39 Scott Gomez/250 8.00 20.00
40 Scott Stevens/185 8.00 20.00
42 Alexei Yashin/30 8.00 20.00
43 Pavel Bure/20
44 Mark Messier/140 10.00 25.00
45 Eric Lindros/75 10.00 25.00
46 Daniel Alfredsson/100 8.00 20.00
47 Martin Havlat/250 8.00 20.00
48 Patrick Lalime/250 8.00 20.00
49 Simon Gagne/250 10.00 25.00
50 Michal Handzus/250 8.00 20.00
53 Johan Hedberg/250 8.00 20.00
54 Mario Lemieux/60 40.00 100.00
55 Toby Petersen/250 8.00 20.00
56 Pavol Demitra/165 8.00 20.00
57 Ray Ferraro/165 8.00 20.00
58 Chris Pronger/15 8.00 20.00
59 Keith Tkachuk/145 10.00 25.00
60 Sergei Varlamov/250 8.00 20.00
61 Miikka Kiprusoff/250 8.00 20.00
62 Patrick Marleau/175 8.00 20.00
63 Owen Nolan/15
64 Nikolai Khabibulin/35 15.00 40.00
65 Fredrik Modin/250 8.00 20.00
66 Alexander Mogilny/70 8.00 20.00
67 Gary Roberts/140 8.00 20.00
69 Dan Cloutier/250 8.00 20.00
70 Brendan Morrison/40 8.00 20.00
72 Henrik Sedin/25 10.00 25.00
74 Jaromir Jagr/110 15.00 40.00
75 Olaf Kolzig/175 8.00 20.00

2002-03 Titanium Saturday Knights

COMPLETE SET (10) 15.00 30.00
STATED ODDS 1:17
1 Jarome Iginla 1.00 2.50
2 Patrick Roy 4.00 10.00
3 Joe Sakic 1.50 4.00
4 Steve Yzerman 4.00 10.00
5 Jose Theodore 1.00 2.50
6 Marian Hossa .75 2.00
7 Mario Lemieux 5.00 12.00
8 Ed Belfour .75 2.00
9 Mats Sundin .75 2.00
10 Todd Bertuzzi .75 2.00

2002-03 Titanium Masked Marauders

COMPLETE SET (8) 10.00 25.00
STATED ODDS 1:25
1 Patrick Roy 4.00 10.00
2 Marty Turco 1.25 3.00
3 Curtis Joseph 1.25 3.00
4 Jose Theodore 1.50 4.00
5 Martin Brodeur 2.50 6.00
6 Nikolai Khabibulin 1.25 3.00
7 Ed Belfour 1.25 3.00
8 Dan Cloutier 1.25 3.00

2002-03 Titanium Right on Target

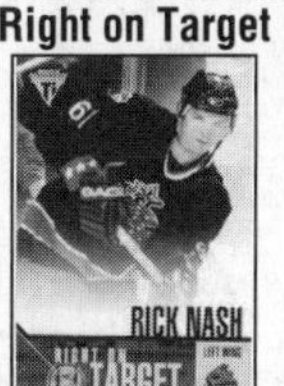

COMPLETE SET (20) 20.00 50.00
STATED ODDS 1:9
1 Stanislav Chistov 1.25 3.00
2 Ivan Huml .75 2.00
3 Chuck Kobasew 1.25 3.00
4 Jordan Leopold .75 2.00
5 Tyler Arnason .75 2.00
6 Rick Nash 3.00 8.00
7 Henrik Zetterberg 2.50 6.00
8 Ales Hemsky 2.00 5.00
9 Jay Bouwmeester 1.25 3.00
10 Stephen Weiss 1.25 3.00
11 Michael Cammalleri 1.25 3.00
12 Alexander Frolov 1.25 3.00
13 P-M Bouchard 1.25 3.00
14 Scottie Upshall 1.25 3.00
15 Rick DiPietro 1.50 4.00
16 Jamie Lundmark .75 2.00
17 Jason Spezza 2.50 6.00
18 Barret Jackman .75 2.00
19 Jonathan Cheechoo 2.00 5.00
20 Fedor Fedorov .75 2.00

2002-03 Titanium Shadows

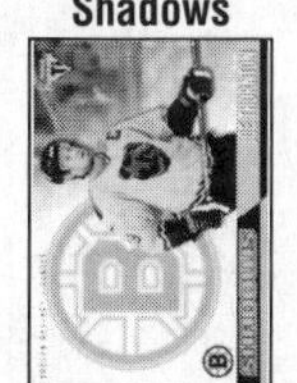

COMPLETE SET (6) 30.00 60.00
STATED ODDS 1:49
1 Ilya Kovalchuk 1.50 4.00
2 Joe Thornton 2.00 5.00
3 Patrick Roy 6.00 15.00
4 Joe Sakic 2.50 6.00
5 Steve Yzerman 6.00 15.00
6 Marian Gaborik 2.50 6.00

2003-04 Titanium

This 215-card set consisted of 100 veteran cards (1-100); 40 short-printed rookie cards (101-140) serial-numbered to 99; 50 veteran jersey cards (141-190) serial-numbered out of 875 (unless noted otherwise); 15 short-printed veteran jersey cards (191-205) serial-numbered to 99 (unless otherwise noted) and 10 short-printed rookie jersey cards (individual numbers are listed below). Titanium Hobby carried gold foil highlights

which distinguished it from the Retail brand.

COMP.SET w/o SP's (100) 15.00 30.00
PRINT RUNS UNDER 25
NOT PRICED DUE TO SCARCITY
1 Martin Gerber .25 .60
2 Steve Rucchin .10 .25
3 Petr Sykora .10 .25
4 Frantisek Kaberle .10 .25
5 Slava Kozlov .10 .25
6 Pasi Nurminen .25 .60
7 Marc Savard .10 .25
8 Mike Knuble .10 .25
9 Glen Murray .10 .25
10 Felix Potvin .25 .60
11 Andrew Raycroft .25 .60
12 Martin Biron .25 .60
13 Daniel Briere .10 .25
14 J-P Dumont .10 .25
15 Miroslav Satan .25 .60
16 Shean Donovan .10 .25
17 Miikka Kiprusoff .25 .60
18 Jordan Leopold .10 .25
19 Erik Cole .10 .25
20 Ron Francis .25 .60
21 Jeff O'Neill .10 .25
22 Josef Vasicek .10 .25
23 Kevin Weekes .25 .60
24 Mark Bell .10 .25
25 Kyle Calder .10 .25
26 Jocelyn Thibault .25 .60
27 Alexei Zhamnov .10 .25
28 Rob Blake .25 .60
29 Alex Tanguay .25 .60
30 Marc Denis .25 .60
31 Rick Nash .40 1.00
32 David Vyborny .10 .25
33 Jason Arnott .10 .25
34 Jere Lehtinen .25 .60
35 Pavel Datsyuk .30 .75
36 Dominik Hasek .60 1.50
37 Curtis Joseph .30 .75
38 Henrik Zetterberg .30 .75
39 Tommy Salo .25 .60
40 Raffi Torres .10 .25
41 Mike York .10 .25
42 Valeri Bure .10 .25
43 Viktor Kozlov .10 .25
44 Stephen Weiss .10 .25
45 Roman Cechmanek .25 .60
46 Alexander Frolov .10 .25
47 Cristobal Huet .25 .60
48 Luc Robitaille .25 .60
49 Andrew Brunette .10 .25
50 Alexandre Daigle .10 .25
51 Manny Fernandez .25 .60
52 Marian Gaborik .60 1.50
53 Dwayne Roloson .25 .60
54 Marcel Hossa .10 .25
55 Mike Ribeiro .10 .25
56 Michael Ryder .10 .25
57 Sheldon Souray .10 .25
58 David Legwand .25 .60
59 Tomas Vokoun .25 .60
60 Jeff Friesen .10 .25
61 Scott Gomez .10 .25
62 Scott Niedermayer .10 .25
63 Jason Blake .10 .25
64 Mariusz Czerkawski .10 .25
65 Trent Hunter .10 .25
66 Garth Snow .25 .60
67 Mike Dunham .25 .60
68 Brian Leetch .25 .60
69 Mark Messier .30 .75
70 Radek Bonk
71 Zdeno Chara .10 .25
72 Peter Schaefer .10 .25
73 Tony Amonte .25 .60
74 Robert Esche .25 .60
75 Michal Handzus .10 .25
76 Mark Recchi .10 .25
77 Sean Burke .25 .60
78 Shane Doan .10 .25
79 Ladislav Nagy .10 .25
80 Sebastien Caron .25 .60
81 Rico Fata .10 .25
82 Dick Tarnstrom .10 .25
83 Pavol Demitra .25 .60
84 Chris Pronger .25 .60
85 Keith Tkachuk .30 .75
86 Jonathan Cheechoo .12 .30
87 Vincent Damphousse .10 .25
88 Patrick Marleau .25 .60
89 Evgeni Nabokov .25 .60
90 Marco Sturm .10 .25
91 John Grahame .25 .60
92 Cory Stillman .10 .25
93 Joe Nieuwendyk .25 .60
94 Darcy Tucker .10 .25
95 Jason King .10 .25
96 Daniel Sedin .10 .25
97 Henrik Sedin .10 .25
98 Peter Bondra .25 .60
99 Sergei Gonchar .10 .25
100 Robert Lang .10 .25
101 Garrett Burnett RC 8.00 20.00
102 Tony Martensson RC 8.00 20.00
103 Sergei Zinovjev RC 8.00 20.00
104 Andrew Peters RC 8.00 20.00
105 Brent Krahn RC 8.00 20.00
106 Eric Staal RC 75.00 150.00
107 Travis Moen RC 8.00 20.00
108 Tuomo Ruutu RC 30.00 80.00
109 Pavel Vorobiev RC 10.00 25.00
110 Mikhail Yakubov RC 8.00 20.00
111 Cody McCormick RC 8.00 20.00
112 Dan Fritsche RC 8.00 20.00
113 Kent McDonell RC 8.00 20.00
114 Nikolai Zherdev RC 30.00 60.00
115 Trevor Daley RC 8.00 20.00
116 Antti Miettinen RC 8.00 20.00
117 Jiri Hudler RC 15.00 40.00
118 Niklas Kronwall RC 12.00 30.00
119 Nathan Robinson RC 8.00 20.00
120 Peter Sarno RC 8.00 20.00
121 Tim Gleason RC 8.00 20.00
122 Esa Pirnes RC 8.00 20.00
123 Brent Burns RC 10.00 25.00
124 Dan Hamhuis RC 10.00 25.00
125 Marek Zidlicky RC 8.00 20.00
126 David Hale RC 8.00 20.00
127 Paul Martin RC 8.00 20.00
128 Sean Bergenheim RC 8.00 20.00
129 Dominic Moore RC 8.00 20.00
130 Joni Pitkanen RC 12.00 30.00
131 Fredrik Sjostrom RC 8.00 20.00
132 Marc-Andre Fleury RC 100.00 250.00
133 Matt Murley RC 8.00 20.00
134 John Pohl RC 8.00 20.00
135 Peter Sejna RC 8.00 20.00
136 Milan Michalek RC 30.00 60.00
137 Maxim Kondratiev RC 8.00 20.00
138 Ryan Kesler RC 10.00 25.00
139 Alexander Semin RC 40.00 100.00
140 Rastislav Stana RC 8.00 20.00
141 Martin Gerber 6.00 15.00
142 Sergei Fedorov JSY 10.00 25.00
143 J-S Giguere JSY 6.00 15.00
144 Sergei Samsonov JSY 6.00 15.00
145 Ryan Miller/785 JSY 6.00 15.00
146 Jarome Iginla JSY 10.00 25.00
147 David Aebischer JSY 6.00 15.00
148 Milan Hejduk JSY 8.00 20.00
149 Joe Sakic JSY 12.50 30.00
150 Teemu Selanne JSY 8.00 20.00
151 Mike Modano JSY 10.00 25.00
152 Marty Turco JSY 6.00 15.00
153 Brendan Shanahan JSY 8.00 20.00
154 Ales Hemsky JSY 6.00 15.00
155 Ryan Smyth JSY 6.00 15.00
156 Jay Bouwmeester JSY 6.00 15.00
157 Olli Jokinen JSY 6.00 15.00
158 Roberto Luongo JSY 10.00 25.00
159 Jason Allison JSY 6.00 15.00
160 Ziggy Palffy JSY 6.00 15.00
161 Saku Koivu JSY 8.00 20.00
162 Jose Theodore JSY 10.00 25.00
163 Richard Zednik JSY 6.00 15.00
164 Martin Erat JSY 6.00 15.00
165 Scott Walker JSY 6.00 15.00
166 Patrik Elias JSY 6.00 15.00
167 Rick DiPietro JSY 6.00 15.00
168 Michael Peca JSY 6.00 15.00
169 Alexei Yashin JSY 6.00 15.00
170 Jaromir Jagr JSY 10.00 25.00
171 Eric Lindros JSY 8.00 20.00
172 Daniel Alfredsson JSY 6.00 15.00
173 Marian Hossa JSY 8.00 20.00
174 Patrick Lalime JSY 6.00 15.00
175 Jason Spezza JSY 12.50 30.00
176 Jeff Hackett JSY 6.00 15.00
177 Jeremy Roenick JSY 10.00 25.00
178 Barret Jackman JSY 6.00 15.00
179 Chris Osgood JSY 6.00 15.00
180 Doug Weight JSY 6.00 15.00
181 Nikolai Khabibulin JSY 8.00 20.00
182 Vincent Lecavalier JSY 8.00 20.00
183 Martin St. Louis/640 JSY 6.00 15.00
184 Owen Nolan JSY 6.00 15.00
185 Gary Roberts/835 JSY 6.00 15.00
186 Mats Sundin JSY 8.00 20.00
187 Dan Cloutier JSY 6.00 15.00
188 Brendan Morrison JSY 6.00 15.00
189 Markus Naslund JSY 8.00 20.00
190 Olaf Kolzig JSY 6.00 15.00
191 Ilya Kovalchuk JSY 12.50 30.00
192 Dany Heatley/39 JSY 20.00 50.00
193 Joe Thornton JSY 12.50 30.00
194 Peter Forsberg JSY 15.00 40.00
195 Paul Kariya JSY .30 .75
196 Bill Guerin JSY 8.00 20.00
197 Brett Hull JSY 12.50 30.00
198 Nicklas Lidstrom JSY 8.00 20.00
199 Steve Yzerman JSY 20.00 50.00
200 Martin Brodeur JSY 20.00 50.00
201 Pavel Bure JSY 8.00 20.00
202 John LeClair JSY 8.00 20.00
203 Mario Lemieux JSY 20.00 50.00
204 Ed Belfour JSY 8.00 20.00
205 Todd Bertuzzi JSY 8.00 20.00
206 Joffrey Lupul/15
207 Patrice Bergeron/37 125.00 200.00
208 Matthew Lombardi/18
209 Nathan Horton/16
210 Dustin Brown/23
211 Christopher Higgins/88 25.00 60.00
212 Jordin Tootoo/55 30.00 80.00
213 Antoine Vermette/20
214 Matt Stajan/14
215 Boyd Gordon/15

2003-04 Titanium Hobby Jersey Number Parallels

This 190-card partial parallel set differed from the base set in that the player's jersey number was on the card front in place of the team logo. Cards 1-100 were serial-numbered to 150 sets; cards 101-140 were numbered to 199 sets and cards 141-190 were serial-numbered to 50 sets.

*STARS: 5X TO 12X
1-100 PRINT RUN 150 SER.#'d SETS
*ROOKIES 101-140: .06X TO .15X
101-140 PRINT RUN 199 SER.#'d SETS

*JSYS: 1.25X TO 3X
JSY PRINT RUN 50 SER.#'d SETS

2003-04 Titanium Patches

*PATCH: 1 X TO 2.5X BASIC JERSEYS
PRINT RUNS OF 25 OR LESS NOT PRICED
DUE TO SCARCITY

2003-04 Titanium Retail

The Retail set carried silver foil highlights that distinguished it form the Hobby set.
*STARS: SAME VALUE AS HOBBY
*JSYS: 1X TO 2.5X
JSY PRINT RUN 170 SER.#'d SETS
RC PRINT RUN 750 SER.#'d SETS
101 Garrett Burnett RC 2.50 6.00
102 Tony Martensson RC 2.50 6.00
103 Sergei Zinovjev RC 2.50 6.00
104 Andrew Peters RC 2.50 6.00
105 Brent Krahn RC 2.50 6.00
106 Eric Staal RC 10.00 25.00
107 Travis Moen RC 2.50 6.00
108 Tuomo Ruutu RC 4.00 10.00
109 Pavel Vorobiev RC 2.50 6.00
110 Mikhail Yakubov RC 2.50 6.00
111 Cody McCormick RC 2.50 6.00
112 Dan Fritsche RC 2.50 6.00
113 Kent McDonell RC 2.50 6.00
114 Nikolai Zherdev RC 6.00 15.00
115 Trevor Daley RC 2.50 6.00
116 Antti Miettinen RC 2.50 6.00
117 Jiri Hudler RC 3.00 8.00
118 Niklas Kronwall RC 2.50 6.00
119 Nathan Robinson RC 2.50 6.00
120 Peter Sarno RC 2.50 6.00
121 Tim Gleason RC 2.50 6.00
122 Esa Pirnes RC 2.50 6.00
123 Brent Burns RC 2.50 6.00
124 Dan Hamhuis RC 2.50 6.00
125 Marek Zidlicky RC 2.50 6.00
126 David Hale RC 2.50 6.00
127 Paul Martin RC 2.50 6.00
128 Sean Bergenheim RC 2.50 6.00
129 Dominic Moore RC 2.50 6.00
130 Joni Pitkanen RC 3.00 8.00
131 Fredrik Sjostrom RC 2.50 6.00
132 Marc-Andre Fleury RC 12.00 30.00
133 Matt Murley RC 2.50 6.00
134 John Pohl RC 2.50 6.00
135 Peter Sejna RC 2.50 6.00
136 Milan Michalek RC 4.00 10.00
137 Maxim Kondratiev RC 2.50 6.00
138 Ryan Kesler RC 2.50 6.00
139 Alexander Semin RC 4.00 10.00
140 Rastislav Stana RC 2.50 6.00

2003-04 Titanium Retail Jersey Number Parallels

This 140-card partial parallel set differed from the base set in that the player's jersey number was on the card front in place of the team logo. Cards 1-100 were serial-numbered to 250 sets and cards 101-140 were serial-numbered to 225 sets.
*STARS: 4X TO 10X BASE HI
*ROOKIES 101-140: .5X TO 1.25X RETAIL HI

2003-04 Titanium Highlight Reels

COMPLETE SET (8) 12.50 25.00
STATED ODDS 1:17 HOBBY
1 Ilya Kovalchuk 1.00 2.50
2 Joe Thornton 1.25 3.00
3 Peter Forsberg 2.00 5.00
4 Joe Sakic 1.50 4.00
5 Dominik Hasek 1.50 4.00
6 Steve Yzerman 2.50 6.00
7 Martin Brodeur 2.00 5.00
8 Mario Lemieux 3.00 8.00

2003-04 Titanium Masked Marauders

COMPLETE SET (10) 10.00 20.00
STATED ODDS 1:9
1 J-S Giguere .60 1.50
2 David Aebischer .60 1.50
3 Marty Turco .60 1.50
4 Dominik Hasek 1.50 4.00
5 Jose Theodore 1.00 2.50
6 Martin Brodeur 2.00 5.00
7 Rick DiPietro .60 1.50
8 Patrick Lalime .60 1.50
9 Nikolai Khabibulin .75 2.00
10 Ed Belfour .75 2.00

2003-04 Titanium Right on Target

COMPLETE SET (16) 10.00 20.00
STATED ODDS 1:5
1 Joffrey Lupul .30 .75
2 Patrice Bergeron 1.50 4.00
3 Eric Staal .75 2.00
4 Rick Nash .50 1.25
5 Henrik Zetterberg .40 1.00
6 Ales Hemsky .30 .75
7 Jay Bouwmeester .30 .75
8 Nathan Horton .75 2.00
9 Michael Ryder .30 .75
10 Jordin Tootoo .60 1.50
11 Jason Spezza .40 1.00
12 Joni Pitkanen .30 .75
13 Marc-Andre Fleury 2.00 5.00
14 Barret Jackman .30 .75
15 Matt Stajan .75 2.00
16 Jason King .30 .75

2003-04 Titanium Stat Masters

COMPLETE SET (10) 8.00 15.00
STATED ODDS 1:9
1 Sergei Fedorov .75 2.00
2 Ilya Kovalchuk .75 2.00
3 Peter Forsberg 1.50 4.00
4 Rick Nash .75 2.00
5 Pavel Datsyuk .60 1.50
6 Brett Hull .75 2.00
7 Marian Hossa .60 1.50
8 Mario Lemieux 2.50 6.00
9 Todd Bertuzzi .60 1.50
10 Markus Naslund .60 1.50

2000-01 Titanium Draft Day Edition

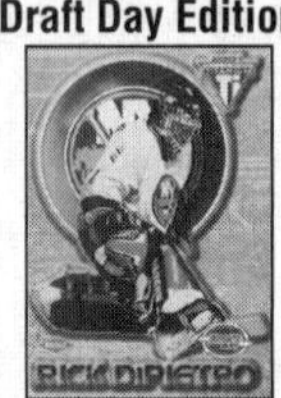

This 176-card set was released at the 2001 NHL Draft in 2-card packs containing one jersey card and one short-printed first year player per pack. Cards 1-100 were jersey cards while cards 101-176 were shortprinted prospect cards. The set introduced 25 new players not included in Titanium. The short prints were serial numbered to 1000. Jersey card print runs are listed below. Cards with print runs less than 20 are nt priced due to scarcity.
COMP.SET w/o JSYs (76) 150.00 350.00
1 J-S Giguere/1010 3.00 8.00
2 Mike Leclerc/520 3.00 8.00
3 P.J. Axelsson/520 3.00 8.00
4 Byron Dafoe/520 3.00 8.00
5 Kyle McLaren/520 3.00 8.00
6 Sergei Samsonov/520 6.00 15.00
7 Don Sweeney/535 3.00 8.00
8 Joe Thornton/535 8.00 20.00
9 Eric Weinrich/1020 3.00 8.00
10 Stu Barnes/535 3.00 8.00
11 Dominik Hasek/535 8.00 20.00
12 Erik Rasmussen/1020 3.00 8.00
13 Fred Brathwaite/1010 3.00 8.00
14 Valeri Bure/1020 3.00 8.00
15 Marc Savard/1020 3.00 8.00
16 Tony Amonte/1020 3.00 8.00
17 Eric Daze/1020 3.00 8.00
18 Boris Mironov/1020 3.00 8.00
19 Michael Nylander/1020 3.00 8.00
20 Steve Sullivan/1020 3.00 8.00
21 Jocelyn Thibault/1020 3.00 8.00
22 Alexei Zhamnov/1020 3.00 8.00
23 Chris Dingman/520 3.00 8.00
24 Peter Forsberg/520 8.00 20.00
25 Patrick Roy/68 75.00 200.00
26 Joe Sakic/535 8.00 20.00
27 Lyle Odelein/535 3.00 8.00
28 Ed Belfour/110 10.00 25.00
29 Derian Hatcher/990 3.00 8.00
30 Brett Hull/115 12.00 30.00
31 Jamie Langenbrunner/985 3.00 8.00
32 Jere Lehtinen/520 3.00 8.00
33 Mike Modano/1015 6.00 15.00
34 Joe Nieuwendyk/1015 3.00 8.00
35 Darryl Sydor/835 3.00 8.00
36 Chris Chelios/520 4.00 10.00
37 Mathieu Dandenault/520 3.00 8.00
38 Nicklas Lidstrom/110 6.00 15.00
39 Darren McCarty/520 3.00 8.00
40 Chris Osgood/1020 3.00 8.00
41 Brendan Shanahan/520 6.00 15.00
42 Steve Yzerman/105 25.00 60.00
43 Anson Carter/55 12.50 30.00
44 Ryan Smyth/1015 3.00 8.00
45 Doug Weight/520 3.00 8.00
46 Pavel Bure/55 15.00 40.00
47 Robert Svehla/1015 3.00 8.00
48 Felix Potvin/100 10.00 25.00
49 Benoit Brunet/1015 3.00 8.00
50 Jeff Hackett/520 3.00 8.00
51 Sergei Zholtok/1010 3.00 8.00
52 Mike Dunham/1020 3.00 8.00
53 Tom Fitzgerald/520 3.00 8.00
54 Patric Kjellberg/520 3.00 8.00
55 David Legwand/520 3.00 8.00
56 Cliff Ronning/520 3.00 8.00
57 Kimmo Timonen/520 3.00 8.00
58 Scott Walker/520 3.00 8.00
59 Bobby Holik/520 3.00 8.00
60 Scott Niedermayer/995 3.00 8.00
61 Mariusz Czerkawski/1020 3.00 8.00
62 Kenny Jonsson/520 3.00 8.00
63 Claude Lapointe/1015 3.00 8.00
64 Chris Terreri/1020 3.00 8.00
65 Theo Fleury/870 3.00 8.00
66 Brian Leetch/520 3.00 8.00
67 Petr Nedved/1015 3.00 8.00
68 Mike Richter/1010 4.00 10.00
69 Mike York/1015 3.00 8.00
70 Daniel Alfredsson/520 3.00 8.00
71 Alexei Yashin/285 3.00 8.00
72 Eric Desjardins/520 3.00 8.00
73 John LeClair/520 4.00 10.00
74 Mika Alatalo/535 3.00 8.00
75 Sean Burke/1010 3.00 8.00
76 Shane Doan/535 3.00 8.00
77 Jyrki Lumme/520 3.00 8.00
78 Jeremy Roenick/520 6.00 15.00
79 Radoslav Suchy/1015 3.00 8.00
80 Jean-Sebastien Aubin/1015 3.00 8.00
81 Jan Hrdina/1020 3.00 8.00
82 Jaromir Jagr/520 8.00 20.00
83 Darius Kasparaitis/1010 3.00 8.00
84 Alexei Kovalev/1015 3.00 8.00
85 Milan Kraft/1015 3.00 8.00
86 Mario Lemieux/115 25.00 60.00
87 Kevin Stevens/1020 3.00 8.00
88 Martin Straka/1010 3.00 8.00
89 Dallas Drake/535 3.00 8.00
90 Cory Stillman/1010 3.00 8.00
91 Vincent Damphousse/1015 3.00 8.00
92 Teemu Selanne/1020 4.00 10.00
93 Vincent Lecavalier/535 6.00 15.00
94 Shayne Corson/1010 3.00 8.00
95 Tie Domi/535 3.00 8.00
96 Curtis Joseph/535 6.00 15.00
97 Mats Sundin/535 6.00 15.00
98 Peter Bondra/15
99 Ulf Dahlen/535 3.00 8.00
100 Dainius Zubrus/520 3.00 8.00
101 Samuel Pahlsson 1.50 4.00
102 Scott Fankhouser 1.50 4.00
103 Tomi Kallio 1.50 4.00
104 Brad Tapper RC 2.00 5.00
105 Andrew Raycroft RC 6.00 15.00
106 Denis Hamel 1.50 4.00
107 Jeff Cowan RC 2.00 5.00
108 Oleg Saprykin 1.50 4.00
109 Josef Vasicek RC 2.00 5.00
110 Shane Willis 1.50 4.00
111 David Aebischer RC 6.00 15.00
112 Serge Aubin RC 2.00 5.00
113 Marc Denis 1.50 4.00
114 Chris Nielsen RC 2.00 5.00
115 David Vyborny 1.50 4.00
116 Marty Turco RC 8.00 20.00
117 Mike Comrie RC 3.00 8.00
118 Shawn Horcoff RC 3.00 8.00
119 Dominic Pittis 1.50 4.00
120 Roberto Luongo 2.00 5.00
121 Ivan Novoseltsev 1.50 4.00
122 Serge Payer 1.50 4.00
123 Denis Shvidki 1.50 4.00
124 Steven Reinprecht RC 3.00 8.00
125 Lubomir Visnovsky RC 2.00 5.00
126 Marian Gaborik RC 12.50 30.00
127 Filip Kuba 1.50 4.00
128 Mathieu Garon 1.50 4.00
129 Eric Landry RC 2.00 5.00
130 Andrei Markov 1.50 4.00
131 Marian Cisar 1.50 4.00
132 Scott Hartnell RC 2.50 6.00
133 Rick DiPietro RC 6.00 15.00
134 Martin Havlat RC 8.00 20.00
135 Jani Hurme RC 3.00 8.00
136 Petr Schastlivy 1.50 4.00
137 Ruslan Fedotenko RC 1.50 4.00
138 Justin Williams RC 3.00 8.00
139 Robert Esche 1.50 4.00
140 Milan Kraft 1.50 4.00
141 Brent Johnson 1.50 4.00
142 Reed Low RC 2.00 5.00
143 Evgeni Nabokov 6.00 15.00
144 Alexander Kharitonov RC 2.00 5.00
145 Dieter Kochan RC 2.00 5.00
146 Brad Richards 1.50 4.00
147 Adam Mair 1.50 4.00
148 Daniel Sedin 1.50 4.00
149 Henrik Sedin 1.50 4.00
150 Trent Whitfield 1.50 4.00
151 Marc Chouinard RC 2.00 5.00
152 Jonas Ronnqvist RC 2.00 5.00
153 Petr Tenkrat RC 2.00 5.00
154 Ronald Petrovicky RC 2.00 5.00
155 Craig Adams RC 2.00 5.00
156 Niclas Wallin RC 2.00 5.00
157 Rostislav Klesla RC 3.00 8.00
158 Petteri Nummelin RC 2.00 5.00
159 Tyler Bouck RC 2.00 5.00
160 Michel Riesen RC 2.00 5.00
161 Eric Belanger RC 2.00 5.00
162 Roman Simicek RC 2.00 5.00
163 Xavier Delisle 1.50 4.00
164 Greg Classen RC 2.00 5.00
165 Mike Commodore RC 2.00 5.00
166 Sascha Goc RC 2.00 5.00
167 Jeff Ulmer RC 2.00 5.00
168 Shane Hnidy RC 2.00 5.00
169 Roman Cechmanek RC 2.00 5.00
170 Todd Fedoruk RC 2.00 5.00
171 Ossi Vaananen RC 2.00 5.00
172 Bryce Salvador RC 2.00 5.00
173 Mark Smith RC 2.00 5.00
174 Mike Brown RC 2.00 5.00
175 Jakub Cutta RC 2.00 5.00
176 Johan Hedberg RC 3.00 8.00

2000-01 Titanium Draft Day Edition Patches

This 74-card set was the parallel set to the jersey cards in the base set (cards 1-100). Please note that the cards have different print runs which are player specific, and the set did not include patch cards for all of the players that had jersey cards. Cards with print runs less than 25 are not priced due to scarcity.
1 J-S Giguere/115 10.00 25.00
2 Mike Leclerc/114 10.00 25.00
3 P.J. Axelsson/114 10.00 25.00
4 Byron Dafoe/70 10.00 25.00
6 Sergei Samsonov/43 20.00 50.00
8 Joe Thornton/24 40.00 100.00
9 Eric Weinrich/116 10.00 25.00
10 Stu Barnes/57 10.00 25.00
12 Erik Rasmussen/113 10.00 25.00
13 Fred Brathwaite/106 10.00 25.00
14 Valeri Bure/110 10.00 25.00
15 Marc Savard/106 10.00 25.00
16 Tony Amonte/110 10.00 25.00
17 Eric Daze/114 10.00 25.00
18 Boris Mironov/116 10.00 25.00
19 Michael Nylander/113 10.00 25.00
20 Steve Sullivan/113 10.00 25.00
21 Jocelyn Thibault/113 10.00 25.00
22 Alexei Zhamnov/116 10.00 25.00
23 Chris Dingman/120 10.00 25.00
24 Peter Forsberg/112 20.00 50.00
27 Lyle Odelein/114 10.00 25.00
29 Derian Hatcher/114 10.00 25.00
31 Jamie Langenbrunner/109 10.00 25.00
33 Mike Modano/112 20.00 50.00
34 Joe Nieuwendyk/106 10.00 25.00
35 Darryl Sydor/107 10.00 25.00
36 Chris Chelios/112 20.00 50.00
37 Matthieu Dandenault/115 10.00 25.00
40 Chris Osgood/106 10.00 25.00
41 Brendan Shanahan/117 20.00 50.00
44 Ryan Smyth/24
45 Doug Weight/110 10.00 25.00
46 Pavel Bure/116 20.00 50.00
47 Robert Svehla/105 10.00 25.00
49 Benoit Brunet/111 10.00 25.00
51 Sergei Zholtok/103 10.00 25.00
52 Mike Dunham/113 10.00 25.00
54 Patric Kjellberg/118 10.00 25.00
55 David Legwand/116 10.00 25.00
56 Cliff Ronning/56 10.00 25.00
58 Scott Walker/94 10.00 25.00
59 Bobby Holik/49 10.00 25.00
60 Scott Niedermayer/102 10.00 25.00
61 Mariusz Czerkawski/79 10.00 25.00
62 Kenny Jonsson/92 10.00 25.00
63 Claude Lapointe/40 10.00 25.00
64 Chris Terreri/72 10.00 25.00
65 Theo Fleury/38 10.00 25.00
66 Brian Leetch/111 10.00 25.00
67 Petr Nedved/34 10.00 25.00
68 Mike Richter/114 25.00 60.00
69 Mike York/109 10.00 25.00
70 Daniel Alfredsson/56 10.00 25.00
71 Alexei Yashin/46 10.00 25.00
73 John LeClair/89 20.00 50.00
74 Mika Alatalo/117 10.00 25.00
75 Sean Burke/111 10.00 25.00
77 Jyrki Lumme/108 10.00 25.00
78 Jeremy Roenick/42 30.00 80.00
79 Radoslav Suchy/107 10.00 25.00
80 Jean-Sebastien Aubin/112 10.00 25.00
81 Jan Hrdina/112 10.00 25.00
83 Darius Kasparaitis/114 10.00 25.00
84 Alexei Kovalev/114 10.00 25.00
85 Milan Kraft/112 10.00 25.00
87 Kevin Stevens/115 10.00 25.00
88 Martin Straka/108 10.00 25.00
89 Dallas Drake/36 10.00 25.00
90 Cory Stillman/114 10.00 25.00
91 Vincent Damphousse/114 10.00 25.00
92 Teemu Selanne/118 15.00 40.00
94 Shayne Corson/38 10.00 25.00
95 Tie Domi/110 10.00 25.00

2000-01 Titanium Draft Day Promos

Produced as promotional give-aways, this 76-card set resembles the base set in every way except that they are numbered XXXX/1000 and have the word "sample" printed across the back. According to reports, approximately 150 sets were produced. A few of these cards have found their way to the secondary market, but not enough market information is available to price them at this time.
NOT PRICED DUE TO SCARCITY

2001-02 Titanium Draft Day Edition

Released in conjunction with the 2002 NHL Entry Draft, this 172-card set featured jersey cards and short printed prospects. Cards 1-100 carried game-worn jersey swatches of

the given player, while cards 101-172 were short printed to just 780. An autographed version of the Ilya Kovalchuk card was also randomly seeded in packs and numbered to just 500 copies.
1 Jeff Friesen 3.00 6.00
2 Paul Kariya 5.00 12.00
3 Oleg Tverdovsky 3.00 6.00
4 Dany Heatley 5.00 12.00
5 Milan Hnilicka 4.00 10.00
6 Tomi Kallio 3.00 6.00
7 Ilya Kovalchuk 6.00 15.00
8 Patrik Stefan 3.00 6.00
9 Bill Guerin 4.00 10.00
10 Kyle McLaren 3.00 6.00
11 Joe Thornton 6.00 15.00
12 Martin Biron 4.00 10.00
13 J-P Dumont 3.00 6.00
14 Erik Rasmussen 3.00 6.00
15 Jarome Iginla 6.00 15.00
16 Marc Savard 3.00 6.00
17 Roman Turek 4.00 10.00
18 Erik Cole 3.00 6.00
19 Jeff O'Neill 3.00 6.00
20 Tony Amonte 4.00 10.00
21 Kyle Calder 3.00 6.00
22 Tom Fitzgerald 3.00 6.00
23 Phil Housley 3.00 6.00
24 Steve Sullivan 3.00 6.00
25 Rob Blake 4.00 10.00
26 Vaclav Nedorost 2.00 5.00
27 Joe Sakic 8.00 20.00
28 Alex Tanguay 4.00 10.00
29 Marc Denis 4.00 10.00
30 Rostislav Klesla 3.00 6.00
31 Ron Tugnutt 4.00 10.00
32 Jason Arnott 3.00 6.00
33 Derian Hatcher 3.00 6.00
34 Mike Modano 6.00 15.00
35 Pierre Turgeon 4.00 10.00
36 Sergei Zubov 3.00 6.00
37 Dominik Hasek 8.00 20.00
38 Brett Hull 5.00 12.00
39 Mike Comrie 4.00 10.00
40 Jochen Hecht 2.00 5.00
41 Jason Allison 2.00 5.00
42 Adam Deadmarsh 2.00 5.00
43 Felix Potvin 5.00 12.00
44 Manny Fernandez 4.00 10.00
45 Marian Gaborik 6.00 15.00
46 Filip Kuba 2.00 5.00
47 Jamie McLennan 2.00 5.00
48 Sergei Berezin 2.00 5.00
49 Jeff Hackett 4.00 10.00
50 Jukka Hentunen 2.00 5.00
51 Martin Brodeur 10.00 25.00
52 Scott Gomez 2.00 5.00
53 Bobby Holik 2.00 5.00
54 Jamie Langenbrunner 2.00 5.00
55 Scott Stevens 4.00 10.00
56 Mats Lindgren 2.00 5.00
57 Kip Miller 2.00 5.00
58 Chris Osgood 4.00 10.00
59 Theo Fleury 3.00 8.00
60 Brian Leetch 4.00 10.00
61 Eric Lindros 5.00 12.00
62 Mark Messier 5.00 12.00
63 Mike Richter 5.00 12.00
64 Daniel Alfredsson 4.00 10.00
65 Martin Havlat 4.00 10.00
66 Marian Hossa 5.00 12.00
67 Patrick Lalime 4.00 10.00
68 Roman Cechmanek 3.00 8.00
69 Jiri Dopita 2.00 5.00
70 Simon Gagne 5.00 12.00
71 John LeClair 5.00 12.00
72 Jeremy Roenick 6.00 15.00
73 Michal Handzus 2.00 5.00
74 Krystofer Kolanos 2.00 5.00
75 Daymond Langkow 2.00 5.00
76 Teppo Numminen 2.00 5.00
77 Kris Beech 2.00 5.00
78 Johan Hedberg 3.00 8.00
79 Robert Lang 2.00 5.00
80 Mario Lemieux 15.00 40.00
81 Rich Parent 2.00 5.00
82 Toby Petersen 2.00 5.00
83 Mike Eastwood 2.00 5.00
84 Ray Ferraro 2.00 5.00
85 Patrick Marleau 4.00 10.00
86 Evgeni Nabokov 4.00 10.00
87 Owen Nolan 4.00 10.00
88 Vincent Lecavalier 5.00 12.00
89 Tom Barrasso 4.00 10.00
90 Mats Sundin 5.00 12.00
91 Dimitri Yushkevich 2.00 5.00
92 Todd Bertuzzi 5.00 12.00
93 Andrew Cassels 2.00 5.00
94 Dan Cloutier 4.00 10.00
95 Brendan Morrison 4.00 10.00
96 Markus Naslund 5.00 12.00
97 Daniel Sedin 2.00 5.00
98 Henrik Sedin 3.00 6.00
99 Peter Bondra 5.00 12.00
100 Jaromir Jagr 8.00 20.00
101 Ilja Bryzgalov RC 3.00 8.00
102 Andy McDonald SP 2.00 5.00
103 Timo Parssinen RC 2.00 5.00
104 Dany Heatley SP 4.00 10.00
105 Ilya Kovalchuk RC 12.00 30.00
106 Pasi Nurminen RC 2.50 6.00
107 Kamil Piros RC 2.00 5.00
108 Brian Pothier RC 2.00 5.00
109 Daniel Tjarnqvist SP 2.00 5.00
110 Andy Hilbert SP 2.00 5.00
111 Ales Kotalik RC 2.50 6.00
112 Mika Noronen SP 2.00 5.00
113 Erik Cole RC 3.00 8.00
114 Tyler Arnason RC 2.50 6.00
115 Mark Bell SP 2.00 5.00
116 Vaclav Nedorost RC 2.00 5.00
117 Radim Vrbata SP 2.00 5.00
118 Brian Willsie SP 2.00 5.00
119 Mathieu Darche RC 2.00 5.00
120 Rostislav Klesla SP 4.00 10.00
121 Jody Shelley RC 2.50 6.00
122 Martin Spanhel RC 2.00 5.00
123 John Erskine RC 2.00 5.00
124 Niko Kapanen RC 2.50 6.00
125 Sean Avery RC 2.00 5.00
126 Pavel Datsyuk RC 8.00 20.00
127 Maxim Kuznetsov SP 2.00 5.00
128 Jason Chimera RC 2.00 5.00
129 Ty Conklin RC 2.00 5.00
130 Jussi Markkanen SP 2.00 5.00
131 Niklas Hagman RC 2.00 5.00
132 Kristian Huselius RC 2.50 6.00
133 Stephen Weiss RC 4.00 10.00
134 Jaroslav Bednar RC 2.00 5.00
135 David Cullen RC 2.00 5.00
136 Pascal Dupuis RC 2.00 5.00
137 Nick Schultz RC 2.00 5.00
138 Mathieu Garon SP 2.00 5.00
139 Marcel Hossa RC 2.00 5.00
140 Mike Ribeiro SP 2.00 5.00
141 Bubba Berenzweig SP 2.00 5.00
142 Martin Erat RC 2.00 5.00
143 Jukka Hentunen RC 2.00 5.00
144 Nathan Perrott RC 2.00 5.00
145 Christian Berglund RC 2.00 5.00
146 Scott Clemmensen RC 2.00 5.00
147 J-F Damphousse SP 2.00 5.00
148 Brian Gionta SP 2.00 5.00
149 Andreas Salomonsson RC 2.00 5.00
150 Radek Martinek RC 2.00 5.00
151 Raffi Torres RC 2.50 6.00
152 Dan Blackburn RC 3.00 8.00
153 Mikael Samuelsson RC 2.00 5.00
154 Chris Neil RC 2.00 5.00
155 Pavel Brendl SP 2.00 5.00
156 Jiri Dopita RC 2.00 5.00
157 Bruno St. Jacques RC 2.00 5.00
158 Billy Tibbetts RC 2.00 5.00
159 Darcy Hordichuk SP 2.00 5.00
160 Krystofer Kolanos RC 2.00 5.00
161 Josef Melichar RC 2.00 5.00
162 Mark Rycroft RC 2.00 5.00
163 Sergei Varlamov SP 2.00 5.00
164 Matt Bradley SP 2.00 5.00
165 Jeff Jillson RC 2.00 5.00
166 Vesa Toskala SP 2.00 5.00
167 Nikita Alexeev RC 2.00 5.00
168 Alexei Ponikarovsky SP 2.00 5.00
169 Chris Corrinet RC 2.00 5.00
170 Stephen Peat SP 2.00 5.00
171 Matt Pettinger SP 2.00 5.00
172 Brian Sutherby RC 2.00 5.00
1AU Ilya Kovalchuk/500 AU 20.00 50.00

1993 Titrex Guy Lafleur Insert

This standard-size card was inserted in Canadian packages of Power Bar, made by Titrex International, a firm specializing in dietary products. Also included in the package was an order form in French for ordering the 24-card Guy Lafleur Collection set. The card features on its front and back a horizontal borderless shot of Guy Lafleur on ice wearing a Titrex jersey, with the Guy Lafleur Collection logo appearing at the bottom. The front has a glossy finish, and Lafleur's name is highlighted in gold foil. The unglossy back carries the Titrex logo at the upper left, and also has the years Lafleur played for each hockey team within a gray stripe down the left edge. The card is unnumbered.
1 Guy Lafleur 1.20 3.00
(Wearing Titrex jersey)

1994 Titrex Guy Lafleur

This 24-card standard size set presents the progression of Guy Lafleur's career. The cards were printed on heavier card stock and came with a card storage album measuring approximately 6 1/4" by 8" and a certificate of authenticity. The borderless fronts feature both horizontal and vertical black-and-white photos. The Guy Lafleur Collection emblem appears inside a red rectangle at the bottom. On a white background with a fading red stripe to the left, the backs carry horizontal and vertical black-and-white photos with the date and a brief photo description (in French and English) below. The cards are unnumbered and checklisted below in chronological order. The set could be obtained by mailing in the order form (plus 24.95 Canadian) that accompanied the 1993 Titrex Guy Lafleur Power Bar Insert in packages of Titrex's Power Bar.
COMPLETE SET (24) 12.00 30.00
COMMON LAFLEUR (1-24) .80 2.00

1954-55 Topps

Topps introduced its first hockey set in 1954-55. The issue includes 60 cards of players on the four American (Boston, Chicago, Detroit and New York) teams. Cards measure approximately 2 5/8" by 3 3/4". Color fronts feature the player on a white background with facsimile autograph and team logo. The player's name, team name and position appear in bottom borders that are in team colors. The backs, printed in red and blue, contain player biographies, 1953-54 statistics and a hockey fact section. The cards were printed in the USA. Rookie Cards include Camille Henry and Doug Mohns. An early and very popular card of Gordie Howe is the main attraction in this set.
COMPLETE SET (60) 3000.00 4500.00
1 Dick Gamble 90.00 150.00
2 Bob Chrystal 20.00 40.00
3 Harry Howell 60.00 100.00
4 Johnny Wilson 20.00 40.00
5 Red Kelly 90.00 150.00
6 Real Chevrefils 20.00 40.00
7 Bob Armstrong 20.00 40.00
8 Gordie Howe 1200.00 1800.00
9 Benny Woit 20.00 40.00
10 Gump Worsley 125.00 200.00
11 Andy Bathgate 60.00 100.00
12 Bucky Hollingworth RC 20.00 40.00
13 Ray Timgren 20.00 40.00
14 Jack Evans 20.00 40.00
15 Paul Ronty 20.00 40.00
16 Glen Skov 20.00 40.00
17 Gus Mortson 20.00 40.00
18 Doug Mohns RC 75.00 125.00
19 Leo Labine 25.00 60.00
20 Bill Gadsby 50.00 80.00
21 Jerry Toppazzini 25.00 60.00
22 Wally Hergesheimer 20.00 40.00
23 Danny Lewicki 20.00 40.00
24 Metro Prystai 20.00 40.00
25 Fern Flaman 25.00 60.00
26 Al Rollins 25.00 60.00
27 Marcel Pronovost 25.00 60.00
28 Lou Jankowski 20.00 40.00
29 Nick Mickoski 20.00 40.00
30 Frank Martin 20.00 40.00
31 Lorne Ferguson 20.00 40.00
32 Camille Henry RC 25.00 60.00
33 Pete Conacher 25.00 60.00
34 Marty Pavelich 20.00 40.00
35 Don McKenney RC 25.00 60.00
36 Fleming Mackell 25.00 60.00
37 Jim Henry 25.00 60.00
38 Hal Laycoe 20.00 40.00
39 Alex Delvecchio 90.00 150.00
40 Larry Wilson 20.00 40.00
41 Allan Stanley 60.00 100.00
42 George Sullivan 20.00 40.00
43 Jack McIntyre 20.00 40.00
44 Ivan Irwin RC 20.00 40.00
45 Tony Leswick 20.00 40.00
46 Bob Goldham 20.00 40.00
47 Cal Gardner 25.00 60.00
48 Ed Sandford 20.00 40.00
49 Bill Quackenbush 50.00 80.00
50 Warren Godfrey 20.00 40.00
51 Ted Lindsay 90.00 150.00
52 Earl Reibel 25.00 60.00
53 Don Raleigh 20.00 40.00
54 Bill Mosienko 50.00 80.00
55 Larry Popein 20.00 40.00
56 Edgar Laprade 25.00 60.00
57 Bill Dineen 25.00 60.00
58 Terry Sawchuk 400.00 700.00
59 Marcel Bonin RC 20.00 40.00
60 Milt Schmidt 150.00 250.00

1957-58 Topps

After a two year hiatus, Topps returned to producing hockey cards for 1957-58. Reportedly, Topps spent the interim evaluating the hockey card market. Cards in this 66-card set were reduced to measure the standard 2 1/2" by 3 1/2". The players in this set are from the four U.S. based teams. The cards are in team order: Boston 1-18, Chicago 19-33, Detroit 34-50 and New York 51-66. Bilingual backs feature 1956-57 statistics, a short player biography and a cartoon question and answer section. Rookie Cards in this include Johnny Bucyk, Glenn Hall, Pierre Pilote, and Norm Ullman.
COMPLETE SET (66) 1500.00 3000.00
1 Real Chevrefils 30.00 50.00
2 Jack Bionda RC 12.00 20.00

3 Bob Armstrong 12.00 20.00
4 Fern Flaman 15.00 25.00
5 Jerry Toppazzini 12.00 20.00
6 Larry Regan RC 12.00 20.00
7 Bronco Horvath RC 18.00 30.00
8 Jack Caffery 12.00 20.00
9 Leo Labine 15.00 25.00
10 Johnny Bucyk RC 150.00 250.00
11 Vic Stasiuk 12.00 20.00
12 Doug Mohns 15.00 25.00
13 Don McKenney 12.00 20.00
14 Don Simmons RC 15.00 25.00
15 Allan Stanley 18.00 30.00
16 Fleming Mackell 15.00 25.00
17 Larry Hillman RC 15.00 25.00
18 Leo Boivin 15.00 25.00
19 Bob Bailey 12.00 20.00
20 Glenn Hall RC 250.00 400.00
21 Ted Lindsay 40.00 80.00
22 Pierre Pilote RC 60.00 100.00
23 Jim Thomson 12.00 20.00
24 Eric Nesterenko 15.00 25.00
25 Gus Mortson 12.00 20.00
26 Ed Litzenberger RC 18.00 30.00
27 Elmer Vasko RC 18.00 30.00
28 Jack McIntyre 12.00 20.00
29 Ron Murphy 12.00 20.00
30 Glen Skov 12.00 20.00
31 Hec Lalande RC 12.00 20.00
32 Nick Mickoski 12.00 20.00
33 Wally Hergesheimer 12.00 20.00
34 Alex Delvecchio 30.00 50.00
35 Terry Sawchuk UER 150.00 250.00
(Misspelled Sawchuck on card front)
36 Guyle Fielder RC 15.00 25.00
37 Tom McCarthy 12.00 20.00
38 Al Arbour 25.00 40.00
39 Billy Dea 12.00 20.00
40 Lorne Ferguson 12.00 20.00
41 Warren Godfrey 12.00 20.00
42 Gordie Howe 300.00 500.00
43 Marcel Pronovost 15.00 25.00
44 Bill McNeil RC 12.00 20.00
45 Earl Reibel 12.00 20.00
46 Norm Ullman RC 150.00 250.00
47 Johnny Wilson 12.00 20.00
48 Red Kelly 30.00 50.00
49 Bill Dineen 15.00 25.00
50 Forbes Kennedy RC 15.00 25.00
51 Harry Howell 25.00 40.00
52 Jean-Guy Gendron RC 15.00 25.00
53 Gump Worsley 60.00 100.00
54 Larry Popein 12.00 20.00
55 Jack Evans 12.00 20.00
56 George Sullivan 12.00 20.00
57 Gerry Foley RC 12.00 20.00
58 Andy Hebenton RC 15.00 25.00
59 Larry Cahan 12.00 20.00
60 Andy Bathgate 25.00 40.00
61 Danny Lewicki 12.00 20.00
62 Dean Prentice 15.00 25.00
63 Camille Henry 15.00 25.00
64 Lou Fontinato RC 25.00 40.00
65 Bill Gadsby 18.00 30.00
66 Dave Creighton 30.00 50.00

1958-59 Topps

The 1958-59 Topps set contains 66 color standard-size cards of players from the four U.S. based teams. Bilingual backs feature 1957-58 statistics, player biographies and a cartoon information section on the player. The set features the Rookie Card of Bobby Hull. Due to being the last card and subject to wear as well as being chronically off-center, the Hull card is quite scarce in top grades. Other Rookie Cards include Eddie Shack and Ken Wharram.

COMPLETE SET (66) 3000.00 4500.00
1 Bob Armstrong 25.00 40.00
2 Terry Sawchuk 100.00 175.00
3 Glen Skov 10.00 20.00
4 Leo Labine 12.50 25.00
5 Dollard St.Laurent 10.00 20.00
6 Danny Lewicki 10.00 20.00
7 John Hanna RC 10.00 20.00
8 Gordie Howe UER 300.00 500.00
(Misspelled Gordy on card front)
9 Vic Stasiuk 10.00 20.00
10 Larry Regan 10.00 20.00
11 Forbes Kennedy 10.00 20.00
12 Elmer Vasko 12.50 25.00
13 Glenn Hall 90.00 150.00
14 Ken Wharram RC 12.50 25.00
15 Len Lunde RC 10.00 20.00
16 Ed Litzenberger 12.50 25.00
17 Norm Johnson RC 10.00 20.00
18 Earl Ingarfield RC 10.00 20.00
19 Les Colwill RC 10.00 20.00
20 Leo Boivin 12.50 25.00
21 Andy Bathgate 25.00 40.00
22 Johnny Wilson 10.00 20.00
23 Larry Cahan 10.00 20.00
24 Marcel Pronovost 12.50 25.00
25 Larry Hillman 12.50 25.00
26 Jim Bartlett RC 10.00 20.00
27 Nick Mickoski 10.00 20.00
28 Larry Popein 10.00 20.00
29 Fleming Mackell 12.50 25.00
30 Eddie Shack RC 150.00 250.00
31 Jack Evans 10.00 20.00
32 Dean Prentice 12.50 25.00
33 Claude Laforge RC 10.00 20.00
34 Bill Gadsby 18.00 30.00
35 Bronco Horvath 12.50 25.00
36 Pierre Pilote 30.00 50.00
37 Earl Balfour 10.00 20.00
38 Gus Mortson 10.00 20.00
39 Gump Worsley 50.00 80.00
40 Johnny Bucyk 75.00 125.00
41 Lou Fontinato 12.50 25.00
42 Tod Sloan 10.00 20.00
43 Charlie Burns RC 10.00 20.00
44 Don Simmons 12.50 25.00
45 Jerry Toppazzini 10.00 20.00
46 Andy Hebenton 10.00 20.00
47 Pete Goegan UER 10.00 20.00
(Misspelled Geogan on card front)
48 George Sullivan 10.00 20.00
49 Hank Ciesla RC 10.00 20.00
50 Doug Mohns 10.00 20.00
51 Jean-Guy Gendron 10.00 20.00
52 Alex Delvecchio 25.00 40.00
53 Eric Nesterenko 12.50 25.00
54 Camille Henry 12.50 25.00
55 Lorne Ferguson 10.00 20.00
56 Fern Flaman 12.50 25.00
57 Earl Reibel 10.00 20.00
58 Warren Godfrey 10.00 20.00
59 Ron Murphy 10.00 20.00
60 Harry Howell 18.00 30.00
61 Red Kelly 25.00 40.00
62 Don McKenney 10.00 20.00
63 Ted Lindsay 25.00 40.00
64 Al Arbour 12.50 25.00
65 Norm Ullman 60.00 100.00
66 Bobby Hull RC 2200.00 3000.00

1959-60 Topps

The 1959-60 Topps set contains 66 color standard-size cards of players from the four U.S. based teams. The fronts have the player's name and position at the bottom with team name and logo at the top. Bilingual backs feature 1958-59 statistics, a short biography and a cartoon question section.

COMPLETE SET (66) 1200.00 2000.00
1 Eric Nesterenko 30.00 50.00
2 Pierre Pilote 25.00 40.00
3 Elmer Vasko 15.00 25.00
4 Peter Goegan 10.00 20.00
5 Lou Fontinato 15.00 25.00
6 Ted Lindsay 25.00 40.00
7 Leo Labine 15.00 25.00
8 Alex Delvecchio 25.00 40.00
9 Don McKenney UER 10.00 20.00
(Misspelled McKenny on card front)
10 Earl Ingarfield 10.00 20.00
11 Don Simmons 15.00 25.00
12 Glen Skov 10.00 20.00
13 Tod Sloan 10.00 20.00
14 Vic Stasiuk 10.00 20.00
15 Gump Worsley 35.00 60.00
16 Andy Hebenton 15.00 25.00
17 Dean Prentice 15.00 25.00
18 Action picture 10.00 20.00
19 Fleming Mackell 15.00 25.00
20 Harry Howell 15.00 25.00
21 Larry Popein 10.00 20.00
22 Len Lunde 10.00 20.00
23 Johnny Bucyk 35.00 60.00
24 Jean-Guy Gendron 10.00 20.00
25 Barry Cullen 10.00 20.00
26 Leo Boivin 15.00 25.00
27 Warren Godfrey 10.00 20.00
28 Action Picture 18.00 30.00
(Glenn Hall and Camille Henry)
29 Fern Flaman 15.00 25.00
30 Jack Evans 10.00 20.00
31 John Hanna 10.00 20.00
32 Glenn Hall 60.00 100.00
33 Murray Balfour RC 15.00 25.00
34 Andy Bathgate 25.00 40.00
35 Al Arbour 15.00 25.00
36 Jim Morrison 10.00 20.00
37 Nick Mickoski 10.00 20.00
38 Jerry Toppazzini 10.00 20.00
39 Bob Armstrong 10.00 20.00
40 Charlie Burns UER 10.00 20.00
(Misspelled Charley on card front)
41 Bill McNeil 10.00 20.00
42 Terry Sawchuk 90.00 150.00
43 Dollard St.Laurent 10.00 20.00
44 Marcel Pronovost 15.00 25.00
45 Norm Ullman 35.00 60.00
46 Camille Henry 15.00 25.00
47 Bobby Hull 400.00 600.00
48 Action Picture 50.00 80.00
(Gordie Howe and Jack Evans)
49 Lou Marcon RC 10.00 20.00
50 Earl Balfour 10.00 20.00
51 Jim Bartlett 10.00 20.00
52 Forbes Kennedy 10.00 20.00
53 Action Picture 10.00 20.00
(Nick Mickoski and Johnny Hanna)
54 Action Picture 18.00 30.00
(Norm Johnson, Gump Worsley and Harry Howell)
55 Brian Cullen 10.00 20.00
56 Bronco Horvath 15.00 25.00
57 Eddie Shack 60.00 100.00
58 Doug Mohns 15.00 25.00
59 George Sullivan 10.00 20.00
60 Pierre Pilote/Flem Mackell IA 10.00 20.00
61 Ed Litzenberger 10.00 20.00
62 Bill Gadsby 18.00 30.00
63 Gordie Howe 250.00 400.00
64 Claude Laforge 10.00 20.00
65 Red Kelly 25.00 40.00
66 Ron Murphy 30.00 50.00

1960-61 Topps

The 1960-61 Topps set contains 66 color standard-size cards featuring players from Boston (1-20), Chicago (23-42) and New York (45-63). In addition to player and team names, the typical card front features color patterns according to the player's team. The backs are bilingual and have 1959-60 statistics and a cartoon trivia quiz. Cards titled "All-Time Greats" are an attractive feature to this set and include the likes of Georges Vezina and Eddie Shore. The All-Time Great players are indicated by ATG in the checklist below. Stan Mikita's Rookie Card is part of this set. The existence of an album issued by Topps to store this set has recently been confirmed. It is valued at approximately $150.

COMPLETE SET (66) 1100.00 1800.00
1 Lester Patrick ATG 45.00 80.00
2 Paddy Moran ATG 12.00 20.00
3 Joe Malone ATG 18.00 30.00
4 Ernest (Moose) Johnson ATG 9.00 15.00
5 Nels Stewart ATG 18.00 30.00
6 Bill(Red) Hay RC 9.00 15.00
7 Eddie Shack 50.00 80.00
8 Cy Denneny ATG 9.00 15.00
9 Jim Morrison 7.00 12.00
10 Bill Cook ATG 9.00 15.00
11 Johnny Bucyk 30.00 50.00
12 Murray Balfour 7.00 12.00
13 Leo Labine 7.00 12.00
14 Stan Mikita RC 300.00 400.00
15 George Hay ATG 9.00 15.00
16 Mervyn(Red) Dutton ATG 9.00 15.00
17 Dickie Boon ATG UER 7.00 12.00
(Misspelled Boone on card fr)
18 George Sullivan 7.00 12.00
19 Georges Vezina ATG 40.00 60.00
20 Eddie Shore ATG 35.00 60.00
21 Ed Litzenberger 7.00 12.00
22 Bill Gadsby 12.00 20.00
23 Elmer Vasko 7.00 12.00
24 Charlie Burns 7.00 12.00
25 Glenn Hall 50.00 80.00
26 Dit Clapper ATG 18.00 30.00
27 Art Ross ATG 30.00 50.00
28 Jerry Toppazzini 7.00 12.00
29 Frank Boucher ATG 9.00 15.00
30 Jack Evans 7.00 12.00
31 Jean-Guy Gendron 7.00 12.00
32 Chuck Gardiner ATG 15.00 25.00
33 Ab McDonald 7.00 12.00
34 Frank Fredrickson ATG 9.00 15.00
UER (Misspelled Fredrick)
35 Frank Nighbor ATG 15.00 25.00
36 Gump Worsley 30.00 50.00
37 Dean Prentice 9.00 15.00
38 Hugh Lehman ATG 9.00 15.00
39 Jack McCartan RC 15.00 25.00
40 Don McKenney UER 7.00 12.00
(Misspelled McKenny on card front)
41 Ron Murphy 7.00 12.00
42 Andy Hebenton 7.00 12.00
43 Don Simmons 9.00 15.00
44 Herb Gardiner ATG 9.00 15.00
45 Andy Bathgate 15.00 25.00
46 Cyclone Taylor ATG 18.00 30.00
47 King Clancy ATG 30.00 50.00
48 Newsy Lalonde ATG 18.00 30.00
49 Harry Howell 9.00 15.00
50 Ken Schinkel RC 7.00 12.00
51 Tod Sloan 7.00 12.00
52 Doug Mohns 9.00 15.00
53 Camille Henry 9.00 15.00
54 Bronco Horvath 7.00 12.00
55 Tiny Thompson ATG 25.00 40.00
56 Bob Armstrong 7.00 12.00
57 Fern Flaman 9.00 15.00
58 Bobby Hull 300.00 500.00
59 Howie Morenz ATG 40.00 60.00
60 Dick Irvin ATG 18.00 30.00
61 Lou Fontinato 7.00 12.00
62 Leo Boivin 9.00 15.00
63 Moose Goheen ATG 9.00 15.00
64 Al Arbour 9.00 15.00
65 Pierre Pilote 18.00 30.00
66 Vic Stasiuk 7.00 12.00

1960-61 Topps Stamps

There are 52 stamps in this scarce set. They were issued as pairs as an insert in with the 1960-61 Topps Hockey regular issue cards. The players in the set are either members of the Boston Bruins (BB), Chicago Blackhawks (CBH), New York Rangers (NYR), or All-Time Greats (ATG). The stamps are unnumbered, so they are listed below alphabetically. Stan Mikita's stamp is notable in that it appears in Stan's Rookie Card year. Dallas Smith's stamp precedes his RC by one year. Intact pairs of stamps with tabs are more difficult to find and would be valued 50 percent higher than the sum of the two players.

COMPLETE SET (52) 900.00 1500.00
1 Murray Balfour 15.00 30.00
2 Andy Bathgate 15.00 30.00
3 Leo Boivin 12.50 25.00
4 Dickie Boon 15.00 30.00
5 Frank Boucher 20.00 40.00
6 Johnny Bucyk 20.00 40.00
7 Charlie Burns 10.00 20.00
8 King Clancy 30.00 60.00
9 Dit Clapper 20.00 40.00
10 Sprague Cleghorn 20.00 40.00
11 Alex Connell 15.00 30.00
12 Bill Cook 15.00 30.00
13 Cy Denneny 15.00 30.00
14 Jack Evans 10.00 20.00
15 Frank Fredrickson 15.00 30.00
16 Chuck Gardiner 15.00 30.00
17 Herb Gardiner 15.00 30.00
18 Eddie Gerard 15.00 30.00
19 Moose Goheen 15.00 30.00
20 Glenn Hall 25.00 50.00
21 Doug Harvey 20.00 40.00
22 Bill(Red) Hay 15.00 30.00
23 George Hay 15.00 30.00
24 Andy Hebenton 10.00 20.00
25 Camille Henry 12.50 25.00
26 Bronco Horvath 10.00 20.00
27 Harry Howell 12.50 25.00
28 Bobby Hull 75.00 150.00
29 Dick Irvin 15.00 30.00
30 Ernest(Moose) Johnson 15.00 30.00
31 Newsy Lalonde 20.00 40.00
32 Albert Langlois 15.00 30.00
33 Hugh Lehman 15.00 30.00
34 Joe Malone 20.00 40.00
35 Don McKenney 10.00 20.00
36 Stan Mikita 50.00 100.00
37 Doug Mohns 10.00 20.00
38 Paddy Moran 15.00 30.00
39 Howie Morenz 30.00 60.00
40 Ron Murphy 10.00 20.00
41 Frank Nighbor 25.00 50.00
42 Murray Oliver 10.00 20.00
43 Pierre Pilote 10.00 20.00
44 Dean Prentice 10.00 20.00
45 Andre Pronovost 10.00 20.00
46 Art Ross 25.00 50.00
47 Dallas Smith 10.00 20.00
48 Nels Stewart 10.00 20.00
49 Cyclone Taylor 15.00 30.00
50 Elmer Vasko 10.00 20.00
51 Georges Vezina 40.00 80.00
52 Gump Worsley 20.00 40.00

1961-62 Topps

The 1961-62 Topps set contains 66 color standard-size cards featuring players from Boston, Chicago and New York. The card numbering in this set is basically by team order, e.g., Boston Bruins (1-22), Chicago Blackhawks (23-44), and New York Rangers (45-65). Bilingual backs contain 1960-61 statistics and brief career highlights. For the first time, Topps cards were printed in Canada. Rookie Cards include New York Ranger stars Rod Gilbert and Jean Ratelle. The set marks the debut of team and checklist cards within Topps hockey card sets.

COMPLETE SET (66) 750.00 1500.00
1 Phil Watson CO 15.00 25.00
2 Ted Green RC 25.00 40.00
3 Earl Balfour 7.00 12.00
4 Dallas Smith RC 15.00 25.00
5 Andre Pronovost UER 7.00 12.00
(Misspelled Provonost on card back)
6 Dick Meissner 7.00 12.00
7 Leo Boivin 9.00 15.00
8 Johnny Bucyk 25.00 40.00
9 Jerry Toppazzini 7.00 12.00
10 Doug Mohns 9.00 15.00
11 Charlie Burns 7.00 12.00
12 Don McKenney 7.00 12.00
13 Bob Armstrong 7.00 12.00
14 Murray Oliver 7.00 12.00
15 Orland Kurtenbach RC 15.00 25.00
16 Terry Gray 7.00 12.00
17 Don Head 9.00 15.00
18 Pat Stapleton RC 15.00 25.00
19 Cliff Pennington 7.00 12.00
20 Team Picture 25.00 40.00
21 Action Picture 8.00 14.00
(Earl Balfour and Fern Flaman)
22 Action Picture 15.00 25.00
(Andy Bathgate and Glenn Hall)
23 Rudy Pilous CO RC 9.00 15.00
24 Pierre Pilote 15.00 25.00
25 Elmer Vasko 7.00 12.00
26 Reg Fleming RC 9.00 15.00
27 Ab McDonald 7.00 12.00
28 Eric Nesterenko 9.00 15.00
29 Bobby Hull 200.00 350.00
30 Ken Wharram 9.00 15.00
31 Dollard St.Laurent 7.00 12.00
32 Glenn Hall 40.00 60.00
33 Murray Balfour 7.00 12.00
34 Ron Murphy 7.00 12.00
35 Bill(Red) Hay 7.00 12.00
36 Stan Mikita 125.00 200.00
37 Denis DeJordy RC 25.00 40.00
38 Wayne Hillman 9.00 15.00
39 Rino Robazzo 7.00 12.00
40 Bronco Horvath 7.00 12.00
41 Bob Turner 7.00 12.00
42 Blackhawks Team 25.00 40.00
43 Action Picture 8.00 14.00
(Ken Wharram)
44 Action Picture 15.00 25.00
(Dollard St.Laurent helps Glenn Hall)
45 Doug Harvey CO 25.00 40.00
46 Junior Langlois 7.00 12.00
47 Irv Spencer 7.00 12.00
48 George Sullivan 7.00 12.00
49 Earl Ingarfield 7.00 12.00
50 Gump Worsley 25.00 40.00
51 Harry Howell 9.00 15.00
52 Larry Cahan 7.00 12.00
53 Andy Bathgate 12.00 20.00
54 Dean Prentice 9.00 15.00
55 Andy Hebenton 7.00 12.00
56 Camille Henry 9.00 15.00
57 Jean-Guy Gendron 7.00 12.00
58 Pat Hannigan 7.00 12.00
59 Ted Hampson 7.00 12.00
60 Jean Ratelle RC 75.00 150.00
61 Al Lebrun 7.00 12.00
62 Rod Gilbert RC 75.00 150.00
63 Team Picture 25.00 40.00
64 Action Picture 12.00 20.00
(Dick Meissner and Gump Worsley)
65 Action Picture 12.00 20.00
(Gump Worsley)
66 Checklist Card 175.00 300.00

1962-63 Topps

The 1962-63 Topps set contains 66 color standard-size cards featuring players from Boston, Chicago, and New York. The card numbering in this set is by team order, e.g., Boston Bruins (1-22), Chicago Blackhawks (23-44), and New York Rangers (45-65). Included within the numbering sequence are team cards. Bilingual backs feature 1961-62 statistics and career highlights. The cards were printed in Canada. Rookie Cards include Vic Hadfield, Chico Maki, and Jim "The Chief" Neilson.

COMPLETE SET (66) 800.00 1300.00
1 Phil Watson CO 15.00 25.00
2 Bob Perreault 9.00 15.00
3 Bruce Gamble RC 20.00 40.00
4 Warren Godfrey 6.00 12.00
5 Leo Boivin 9.00 15.00
6 Doug Mohns 9.00 15.00
7 Ted Green 9.00 15.00
8 Pat Stapleton 9.00 15.00
9 Dallas Smith 9.00 15.00
10 Don McKenney 7.00 12.00
11 Johnny Bucyk 18.00 30.00
12 Murray Oliver 7.00 12.00
13 Jerry Toppazzini 7.00 12.00
14 Cliff Pennington 7.00 12.00
15 Charlie Burns 7.00 12.00
16 Jean-Guy Gendron 7.00 12.00
17 Irv Spencer 7.00 12.00
18 Wayne Connelly 7.00 12.00
19 Andre Pronovost 7.00 12.00
20 Terry Gray 7.00 12.00
21 Tom Williams RC 9.00 15.00
22 Bruins Team 25.00 40.00
23 Rudy Pilous CO 7.00 12.00
24 Glenn Hall 35.00 50.00
25 Denis DeJordy 9.00 15.00
26 Jack Evans 7.00 12.00
27 Elmer Vasko 7.00 12.00
28 Pierre Pilote 12.00 20.00
29 Bob Turner 7.00 12.00
30 Dollard St.Laurent 7.00 12.00
31 Wayne Hillman 9.00 15.00
32 Al McNeil 6.00 12.00
33 Bobby Hull 200.00 350.00
34 Stan Mikita 60.00 125.00
35 Bill(Red) Hay 7.00 12.00
36 Murray Balfour 7.00 12.00
37 Chico Maki RC 12.00 20.00
38 Ab McDonald 7.00 12.00
39 Ken Wharram 9.00 15.00
40 Ron Murphy 6.00 12.00
41 Eric Nesterenko 8.00 12.00
42 Reg Fleming 8.00 15.00
43 Murray Hall 7.00 12.00
44 Blackhawks Team 25.00 40.00
45 Gump Worsley 25.00 40.00
46 Harry Howell 7.00 12.00
47 Albert Langlois 7.00 12.00
48 Larry Cahan 7.00 12.00
49 Jim Neilson RC 12.00 20.00
50 Al Lebrun 7.00 12.00
51 Earl Ingarfield 7.00 12.00
52 Andy Bathgate 12.00 20.00
53 Dean Prentice 9.00 15.00
54 Andy Hebenton 7.00 12.00
55 Ted Hampson 7.00 12.00
56 Dave Balon 7.00 12.00
57 Bert Olmstead 9.00 15.00
58 Jean Ratelle 30.00 50.00
59 Rod Gilbert 30.00 50.00
60 Vic Hadfield RC 35.00 60.00
61 Frank Paice 7.00 12.00
62 Camille Henry 9.00 15.00
63 Bronco Horvath 7.00 12.00
64 Pat Hannigan 7.00 12.00
65 Rangers Team 25.00 40.00
66 Checklist Card 150.00 250.00

1962-63 Topps Hockey Bucks

These "bucks" are actually inserts printed to look like Canadian currency on thin paper stock. They were distributed as an inserted folded in one buck per wax pack. Since these bucks are unnumbered, they are ordered below in alphabetical order by player's name. The bucks are approximately 4 1/16" by 1 11/16"; there is no information on the backs, just a green-patterned design.

COMPLETE SET (24) 600.00 1000.00
1 Dave Balon 20.00 40.00
2 Andy Bathgate 20.00 40.00
3 Leo Boivin 20.00 40.00
4 Johnny Bucyk 25.00 50.00
5 Reg Fleming 20.00 40.00
6 Warren Godfrey 20.00 40.00
7 Ted Green 20.00 40.00
8 Glenn Hall 40.00 80.00
9 Bill(Red) Hay 20.00 40.00
10 Andy Hebenton 20.00 40.00
11 Harry Howell 20.00 40.00
12 Bobby Hull 100.00 200.00
13 Earl Ingarfield 20.00 40.00
14 Albert Langlois 20.00 40.00
15 Ab McDonald 20.00 40.00
16 Don McKenney 20.00 40.00
17 Stan Mikita 50.00 100.00
18 Doug Mohns 20.00 40.00
19 Murray Oliver 20.00 40.00
20 Pierre Pilote 25.00 50.00
21 Dean Prentice 20.00 40.00
22 Jerry Toppazzini 20.00 40.00
23 Elmer Vasko 20.00 40.00
24 Gump Worsley 40.00 80.00

1963-64 Topps

The 1963-64 Topps standard-size set contains 66 color cards featuring players and team cards from Boston (1-21), Chicago (22-43) and New York (44-65). Bilingual backs contain 1962-63 statistics and a short player biography. A question section, the answer for which could be obtained by rubbing the edge of a coin over a blank space under the question, also appears on the card backs. The cards were printed in Canada. The notable Rookie Cards in this set are Ed Johnston, Gilles Villemure, and Ed Westfall. Jacques Plante makes his first appearance in a Topps set.

COMPLETE SET (66) 700.00 1000.00
1 Milt Schmidt CO 15.00 25.00
2 Ed Johnston RC 25.00 50.00
3 Doug Mohns 8.00 12.00
4 Tom Johnson 8.00 12.00
5 Leo Boivin 8.00 12.00
6 Bob McCord 6.00 10.00
7 Ted Green 8.00 12.00
8 Ed Westfall RC 18.00 30.00
9 Charlie Burns 6.00 10.00
10 Murray Oliver 8.00 12.00
11 Johnny Bucyk 15.00 25.00
12 Tom Williams 8.00 12.00
13 Dean Prentice 8.00 12.00
14 Bob Leiter 6.00 10.00
15 Andy Hebenton 6.00 10.00
16 Jean-Guy Gendron 6.00 10.00
17 Wayne Rivers 6.00 10.00
18 Jerry Toppazzini 6.00 10.00
19 Forbes Kennedy 6.00 10.00
20 Orland Kurtenbach 8.00 12.00
21 Bruins Team 25.00 40.00
22 Billy Reay CO 8.00 12.00
23 Glenn Hall 25.00 40.00
24 Denis DeJordy 8.00 12.00
25 Pierre Pilote 10.00 15.00
26 Elmer Vasko 6.00 10.00
27 Wayne Hillman 8.00 12.00
28 Al McNeil 6.00 10.00
29 Howie Young 8.00 12.00
30 Ed Van Impe RC 9.00 15.00
31 Reg Fleming 10.00 15.00
Gordie Howe also shown
32 Bob Turner 6.00 10.00
33 Bobby Hull 150.00 250.00
34 Bill(Red) Hay 6.00 10.00
35 Murray Balfour 6.00 10.00
36 Stan Mikita 60.00 100.00
37 Ab McDonald 6.00 10.00
38 Ken Wharram 8.00 12.00
39 Eric Nesterenko 8.00 12.00
40 Ron Murphy 6.00 10.00
41 Chico Maki 6.00 10.00
42 John McKenzie 10.00 15.00
43 Blackhawks Team 25.00 40.00
44 George Sullivan 6.00 10.00
45 Jacques Plante 75.00 125.00
46 Gilles Villemure RC 18.00 30.00
47 Doug Harvey 18.00 30.00
48 Harry Howell 8.00 12.00
49 Albert Langlois 6.00 10.00
50 Jim Neilson 8.00 12.00
51 Larry Cahan 6.00 10.00
52 Andy Bathgate 10.00 15.00
53 Don McKenney 6.00 10.00
54 Vic Hadfield 9.00 15.00
55 Earl Ingarfield 6.00 10.00
56 Camille Henry 6.00 10.00
57 Rod Gilbert 18.00 30.00
58 Phil Goyette 10.00 15.00
(Gordie Howe also shown in background)
59 Don Marshall 8.00 12.00
60 Dick Meissner 6.00 10.00
61 Val Fonteyne 6.00 10.00
62 Ken Schinkel 6.00 10.00
63 Jean Ratelle 18.00 30.00
64 Don Johns 6.00 10.00
65 Rangers Team 25.00 40.00
66 Checklist Card 125.00 200.00

1964-65 Topps

The 1964-65 Topps hockey set features 110 color cards of players from all six NHL teams. The size of the card is larger than in previous years at 2 1/2" by 4 11/16". Colorful fronts contain a solid player background with team name at the top and player name and position at the bottom. Bilingual backs have 1963-64 statistics, a brief player bio and a cartoon section featuring a fact about the player. The cards were printed in Canada. Eleven of the numbers in the last series (56-110) appear to have been short printed. They are designated SP below. Rookie Cards include single prints of Gary Dornhoefer and Marcel Paille found in the last series. Other Rookie Cards include Roger Crozier, Jim Pappin, Pit Martin, Rod Seiling and Lou Angotti.

COMPLETE SET (110) 4000.00 6000.00
1 Pit Martin RC 60.00 125.00
2 Gilles Tremblay 12.00 20.00
3 Terry Harper 15.00 25.00
4 John Ferguson 25.00 40.00
5 Elmer Vasko 12.00 20.00
6 Terry Sawchuk UER 65.00 100.00
(Misspelled Sawchuck on card back)
7 Bill(Red) Hay 12.00 20.00
8 Gary Bergman RC 15.00 25.00
9 Doug Barkley 12.00 20.00
10 Bob McCord 12.00 20.00
11 Parker MacDonald 12.00 20.00
12 Glenn Hall 35.00 60.00
13 Albert Langlois 12.00 20.00
14 Camille Henry 12.00 20.00
15 Norm Ullman 18.00 30.00
16 Ab McDonald 12.00 20.00
17 Charlie Hodge 12.00 20.00
18 Orland Kurtenbach 12.00 20.00
19 Dean Prentice 12.00 20.00
20 Bobby Hull 200.00 350.00
21 Ed Johnston 15.00 25.00
22 Denis DeJordy 12.00 20.00
23 Claude Provost 12.00 20.00
24 Rod Gilbert 25.00 40.00
25 Doug Mohns 12.00 20.00
26 Al McNeil 12.00 20.00
27 Billy Harris 12.00 20.00
28 Ken Wharram 12.00 20.00
29 George Sullivan 12.00 20.00
30 John McKenzie 12.00 20.00
31 Stan Mikita 65.00 100.00
32 Ted Green 12.00 20.00
33 Jean Beliveau 50.00 100.00
34 Arnie Brown 12.00 20.00
35 Reg Fleming 12.00 20.00
36 Jim Mikol 12.00 20.00
37 Dave Balon 12.00 20.00
38 Billy Reay CO 12.00 20.00
39 Marcel Pronovost 15.00 25.00
40 Johnny Bower 35.00 60.00
41 Wayne Hillman 12.00 20.00
42 Floyd Smith 12.00 20.00
43 Toe Blake CO 18.00 30.00
44 Red Kelly 18.00 30.00
45 Punch Imlach CO 15.00 25.00
46 Dick Duff 15.00 25.00
47 Roger Crozier RC 35.00 60.00
48 Henri Richard 60.00 100.00
49 Larry Jeffrey 12.00 20.00
50 Leo Boivin 12.00 20.00
51 Ed Westfall 14.00 22.00
52 Jean-Guy Talbot 12.00 20.00
53 Jacques Laperriere 15.00 25.00
54 1st Series Checklist 175.00 300.00
55 2nd Series Checklist 250.00 400.00
56 Ron Murphy 25.00 50.00
57 Bob Baun 25.00 50.00
58 Tom Williams SP 75.00 150.00
59 Pierre Pilote SP 150.00 250.00
60 Bob Pulford 25.00 50.00
61 Red Berenson 25.00 50.00
62 Vic Hadfield 25.00 50.00
63 Bob Leiter 25.00 60.00
64 Jim Pappin RC 35.00 60.00
65 Earl Ingarfield 25.00 50.00
66 Lou Angotti RC 30.00 50.00
67 Rod Seiling RC 30.00 50.00
68 Jacques Plante 100.00 175.00
69 George Armstrong UER 40.00 100.00
70 Milt Schmidt CO 30.00 50.00
71 Eddie Shack 65.00 100.00
72 Gary Dornhoefer RC SP 100.00 200.00
73 Chico Maki SP 100.00 200.00
74 Gilles Villemure SP 75.00 200.00
75 Carl Brewer 25.00 50.00
76 Bruce MacGregor 25.00 60.00
77 Bob Nevin 25.00 50.00
78 Ralph Backstrom 30.00 80.00

79 Murray Oliver 25.00 60.00
80 Bobby Rousseau SP 75.00 150.00
81 Don McKenney 25.00 60.00
82 Ted Lindsay 45.00 75.00
83 Harry Howell 35.00 60.00
84 Doug Robinson 25.00 60.00
85 Frank Mahovlich 75.00 125.00
86 Andy Bathgate 35.00 60.00
87 Phil Goyette 25.00 60.00
88 J.C. Tremblay 85.00 60.00
89 Gordie Howe 300.00 500.00
90 Murray Balfour 25.00 60.00
91 Eric Nesterenko SP 75.00 150.00
92 Marcel Paille RC SP 150.00 250.00
93 Sid Abel CO 25.00 60.00
94 Dave Keon 60.00 125.00
95 Alex Delvecchio 45.00 75.00
96 Bill Gadsby 25.00 50.00
97 Don Marshall 25.00 50.00
98 Bill Hicke SP 75.00 150.00
99 Ron Stewart 25.00 60.00
100 Johnny Bucyk 45.00 75.00
101 Tom Johnson 25.00 50.00
102 Tim Horton 80.00 150.00
103 Jim Neilson 25.00 50.00
104 Allan Stanley 25.00 50.00
105 Tim Horton AS SP 175.00 300.00
106 Stan Mikita AS SP 175.00 300.00
107 Bobby Hull AS 125.00 200.00
108 Ken Wharram AS 25.00 60.00
109 Pierre Pilote AS 35.00 60.00
110 Glenn Hall AS 90.00 150.00

1965-66 Topps

The 1965-66 Topps set contains 128 standard-size cards. Bilingual backs contain 1964-65 statistics, a short biography and a scratch-off question section. The cards were printed in Canada. The cards are grouped by team: Montreal (1-10, 67-76), Toronto (11-20, 77-86), New York (21-30, 87-95), Boston (31-40, 96-105), Detroit (41-53, 106-112) and Chicago (54-65, 113-120). Cards 122-128 are quite scarce and considered single prints. The seven cards were not included on checklist card 121. Rookie Cards include Gerry Cheevers, Yvan Cournoyer, Phil Esposito, Ed Giacomin, Paul Henderson, Ken Hodge and Dennis Hull. Eleven cards in the set were double printed including Cournoyer's Rookie Card.

COMPLETE SET (128) 1700.00 2700.00
1 Toe Blake CO 35.00 60.00
2 Gump Worsley 18.00 30.00
3 Jacques Laperriere 6.00 10.00
4 Jean-Guy Talbot 5.00 8.00
5 Ted Harris 5.00 8.00
6 Jean Beliveau 35.00 60.00
7 Dick Duff 6.00 10.00
8 Claude Provost DP 4.00 6.00
9 Red Berenson 6.00 10.00
10 John Ferguson 6.00 10.00
11 Punch Imlach CO 6.00 10.00
12 Terry Sawchuk 45.00 75.00
13 Bob Baun 6.00 10.00
14 Kent Douglas 5.00 8.00
15 Red Kelly 12.00 20.00
16 Jim Pappin 6.00 10.00
17 Dave Keon 30.00 50.00
18 Bob Pulford 6.00 10.00
19 George Armstrong 9.00 15.00
20 Orland Kurtenbach 5.00 8.00
21 Ed Giacomin RC 90.00 150.00
22 Harry Howell 6.00 10.00
23 Rod Seiling 5.00 8.00
24 Mike McMahon 5.00 8.00
25 Jean Ratelle 15.00 25.00
26 Doug Robinson 5.00 8.00
27 Vic Hadfield 6.00 10.00
28 Garry Peters UER 5.00 8.00
(Misspelled Gary on card front)
29 Don Marshall 6.00 10.00
30 Bill Hicke 5.00 8.00
31 Gerry Cheevers RC 100.00 175.00
32 Leo Boivin 6.00 10.00
33 Albert Langlois 5.00 8.00
34 Murray Oliver DP 4.00 6.00
35 Tom Williams 5.00 8.00
36 Ron Schock 5.00 8.00
37 Ed Westfall 6.00 10.00
38 Gary Dornhoefer 6.00 10.00
39 Bob Dillabough 5.00 8.00
40 Paul Popiel 5.00 8.00
41 Sid Abel CO 6.00 10.00
42 Roger Crozier 6.00 10.00
43 Doug Barkley 5.00 8.00
44 Bill Gadsby 5.00 8.00
45 Bryan Watson RC 9.00 15.00
46 Bob McCord 5.00 8.00
47 Alex Delvecchio 12.00 15.00
48 Andy Bathgate 9.00 15.00
49 Norm Ullman 9.00 15.00
50 Ab McDonald 5.00 8.00
51 Paul Henderson RC 30.00 50.00
52 Pit Martin 6.00 10.00
53 Billy Harris DP 4.00 6.00
54 Billy Reay CO 6.00 10.00
55 Glenn Hall 18.00 30.00
56 Pierre Pilote 9.00 15.00
57 Al McNeil 5.00 8.00
58 Camille Henry 5.00 8.00
59 Bobby Hull 125.00 200.00
60 Stan Mikita 40.00 60.00
61 Ken Wharram 5.00 8.00
62 Bill(Red) Hay 5.00 8.00
63 Fred Stanfield RC 6.00 10.00
64 Dennis Hull DP RC 18.00 30.00
65 Ken Hodge RC 20.00 40.00
66 Checklist Card 125.00 200.00
67 Charlie Hodge 6.00 10.00
68 Terry Harper 5.00 8.00
69 J.C. Tremblay 6.00 10.00
70 Bobby Rousseau DP 4.00 6.00
71 Henri Richard 30.00 50.00
72 Dave Balon 5.00 8.00
73 Ralph Backstrom 6.00 10.00
74 Jim Roberts RC 6.00 10.00
75 Claude Larose 6.00 10.00
76 Yvan Cournoyer RC UER DP 70.00 100.00
77 Johnny Bower DP 15.00 25.00
78 Carl Brewer 6.00 10.00
79 Tim Horton 30.00 50.00
80 Marcel Pronovost 6.00 10.00
81 Frank Mahovlich 25.00 40.00
82 Ron Ellis RC 18.00 30.00
83 Larry Jeffrey 5.00 8.00
84 Pete Stemkowski RC 6.00 10.00
85 Eddie Joyal 5.00 8.00
86 Mike Walton RC 6.00 10.00
87 George Sullivan 5.00 8.00
88 Don Simmons 6.00 10.00
89 Jim Neilson 6.00 10.00
90 Arnie Brown 5.00 8.00
91 Rod Gilbert 15.00 25.00
92 Phil Goyette 5.00 8.00
93 Bob Nevin 6.00 10.00
94 John McKenzie 6.00 10.00
95 Ted Taylor 5.00 8.00
96 Milt Schmidt CO DP 6.00 10.00
97 Ed Johnston 6.00 10.00
98 Ted Green 6.00 10.00
99 Don Awrey RC 6.00 10.00
100 Bob Woytowich DP 4.00 6.00
101 Johnny Bucyk 12.00 20.00
102 Dean Prentice 6.00 10.00
103 Ron Stewart 5.00 8.00
104 Reg Fleming 5.00 8.00
105 Parker MacDonald 5.00 8.00
106 Hank Bassen 6.00 10.00
107 Gary Bergman 5.00 8.00
108 Gordie Howe DP 90.00 150.00
109 Floyd Smith 5.00 8.00
110 Bruce MacGregor 5.00 8.00
111 Ron Murphy 5.00 8.00
112 Don McKenney 5.00 8.00
113 Denis DeJordy DP 4.00 6.00
114 Elmer Vasko 5.00 8.00
115 Matt Ravlich 5.00 8.00
116 Phil Esposito RC 200.00 400.00
117 Chico Maki 5.00 8.00
118 Doug Mohns 6.00 10.00
119 Eric Nesterenko 6.00 10.00
120 Pat Stapleton 6.00 10.00
121 Checklist Card 125.00 200.00
122 Gordie Howe SP 250.00 400.00
(600 Goals)
123 Toronto Maple Leafs 50.00 80.00
Team Card SP
124 Chicago Blackhawks 50.00 80.00
Team Card SP
125 Detroit Red Wings 50.00 80.00
Team Card SP
126 Montreal Canadiens 50.00 80.00
Team Card SP
127 New York Rangers 50.00 80.00
Team Card SP
128 Boston Bruins 125.00 200.00
Team Card SP

1966-67 Topps

At 132 standard-size cards, the 1966-67 issue was the largest Topps set to date. The front features a distinctive wood grain border with a television screen look. Bilingual backs feature a short biography, 1965-66 and career statistics. The cards are grouped by team: Montreal (1-10/67-75), Toronto (11-20/76-84), New York (21-30/85-93), Boston (31-41/94-101), Detroit (42-52/102-109) and Chicago (53-64/110-117). The cards were printed in Canada. The key card in the set is Bobby Orr's Rookie Card. Other Rookie Cards include Emile Francis, Harry Sinden and Peter Mahovlich. The backs of card numbers 127-132 form a puzzle of Bobby Orr.

COMPLETE SET (132) 2600.00 4000.00
1 Toe Blake CO 30.00 80.00
2 Gump Worsley 12.00 20.00
3 Jean-Guy Talbot 6.00 10.00
4 Gilles Tremblay 6.00 10.00
5 J.C. Tremblay 7.00 12.00
6 Jim Roberts 7.00 12.00
7 Bobby Rousseau 6.00 10.00
8 Henri Richard 20.00 35.00
9 Claude Provost 6.00 10.00
10 Claude Larose 7.00 12.00
11 Punch Imlach CO 7.00 12.00
12 Johnny Bower 15.00 25.00
13 Terry Sawchuk 40.00 65.00
14 Mike Walton 7.00 12.00
15 Pete Stemkowski 6.00 10.00
16 Allan Stanley 7.00 12.00
17 Eddie Shack 18.00 30.00
18 Brit Selby RC 7.00 12.00
19 Bob Pulford 7.00 12.00
20 Marcel Pronovost 7.00 12.00
21 Emile Francis RC 12.00 20.00
22 Rod Seiling 6.00 10.00
23 Ed Giacomin 30.00 50.00
24 Don Marshall 7.00 12.00
25 Orland Kurtenbach 6.00 10.00
26 Rod Gilbert 12.00 20.00
27 Bob Nevin 7.00 12.00
28 Phil Goyette 6.00 10.00
29 Jean Ratelle 12.00 20.00
30 Earl Ingarfield 6.00 10.00
31 Harry Sinden RC 25.00 40.00
32 Ed Westfall 7.00 12.00
33 Joe Watson RC 7.00 12.00
34 Bob Woytowich 6.00 10.00
35 Bobby Orr RC 1800.00 2500.00
36 Gilles Marotte RC 7.00 12.00
37 Ted Green 7.00 12.00
38 Tom Williams 6.00 10.00
39 Johnny Bucyk 12.00 20.00
40 Wayne Connelly 6.00 10.00
41 Pit Martin 7.00 12.00
42 Sid Abel CO 6.00 10.00
43 Roger Crozier 7.00 12.00
44 Andy Bathgate 7.00 12.00
45 Dean Prentice 6.00 10.00
46 Paul Henderson 9.00 15.00
47 Gary Bergman 6.00 10.00
48 Bryan Watson 7.00 12.00
49 Bob Wall 6.00 10.00
50 Leo Boivin 7.00 12.00
51 Bert Marshall 6.00 10.00
52 Norm Ullman 9.00 15.00
53 Billy Reay CO 7.00 12.00
54 Glenn Hall 15.00 25.00
55 Wally Boyer 6.00 10.00
56 Fred Stanfield 6.00 10.00
57 Pat Stapleton 7.00 12.00
58 Matt Ravlich 6.00 10.00
59 Pierre Pilote 7.00 12.00
60 Eric Nesterenko 7.00 12.00
61 Doug Mohns 7.00 12.00
62 Stan Mikita 30.00 50.00
63 Phil Esposito 75.00 125.00
64 Leading Scorer 50.00 75.00
(Bobby Hull)
65 Vezina Trophy 15.00 25.00
(Charlie Hodge/
Gump Worsley)
66 Checklist Card 200.00 400.00
67 Jacques Laperriere 7.00 12.00
68 Terry Harper 6.00 10.00
69 Ted Harris 6.00 10.00
70 John Ferguson 7.00 12.00
71 Dick Duff 7.00 12.00
72 Yvan Cournoyer 30.00 50.00
73 Jean Beliveau 30.00 50.00
74 Dave Balon 6.00 10.00
75 Ralph Backstrom 7.00 12.00
76 Jim Pappin 6.00 10.00
77 Frank Mahovlich 18.00 30.00
78 Dave Keon 18.00 30.00
79 Red Kelly 12.00 20.00
80 Tim Horton 25.00 40.00
81 Ron Ellis 7.00 12.00
82 Kent Douglas 6.00 10.00
83 Bob Baun 6.00 10.00
84 George Armstrong 9.00 15.00
85 Bernie Geoffrion 15.00 25.00
86 Vic Hadfield 6.00 10.00
87 Wayne Hillman 6.00 10.00
88 Jim Neilson 6.00 10.00
89 Al McNeil 6.00 10.00
90 Arnie Brown 6.00 10.00
91 Harry Howell 7.00 12.00
92 Red Berenson 7.00 12.00
93 Reg Fleming 6.00 10.00
94 Ron Stewart 6.00 10.00
95 Murray Oliver 6.00 10.00
96 Ron Murphy 6.00 10.00
97 John McKenzie 7.00 12.00
98 Bob Dillabough 6.00 10.00
99 Ed Johnston 7.00 12.00
100 Ron Schock 6.00 10.00
101 Dallas Smith 6.00 10.00
102 Alex Delvecchio 12.00 20.00
103 Peter Mahovlich RC 18.00 30.00
104 Bruce MacGregor 6.00 10.00
105 Murray Hall 6.00 10.00
106 Floyd Smith 6.00 10.00
107 Hank Bassen 6.00 10.00
108 Val Fonteyne 6.00 10.00
109 Gordie Howe 125.00 200.00
110 Chico Maki 6.00 10.00
111 Doug Jarrett 6.00 10.00
112 Bobby Hull 90.00 150.00
113 Dennis Hull 7.00 12.00
114 Ken Hodge 9.00 15.00
115 Denis DeJordy 7.00 12.00
116 Lou Angotti 6.00 10.00
117 Ken Wharram 6.00 10.00
118 Montreal Canadiens 15.00 25.00
Team Card
119 Detroit Red Wings 15.00 25.00
Team Card
120 Checklist Card 200.00 400.00
121 Gordie Howe AS 60.00 100.00
122 Jacques Laperriere AS 7.00 12.00
123 Pierre Pilote AS 7.00 12.00
124 Stan Mikita AS 20.00 40.00
125 Bobby Hull AS 50.00 80.00
126 Glenn Hall AS 15.00 30.00
127 Jean Beliveau AS 15.00 30.00
128 Allan Stanley AS 7.00 12.00
129 Pat Stapleton AS 7.00 12.00
130 Gump Worsley AS 15.00 30.00
131 Frank Mahovlich AS 15.00 30.00
132 Bobby Rousseau AS 15.00 30.00

1966-67 Topps USA Test

This 66-card standard-size set was apparently a test issue with limited distribution solely in America as it is quite scarce. The cards feature the same format as the 1966-67 Topps regular hockey cards. The primary difference is that the card backs in this scarce issue are only printed in English, i.e., no French. The card numbering has some similarities to the regular issue, e.g., Bobby Orr is number 35 in both sets, however there are also many differences from the regular Topps Canadian version which was mass produced. The wood grain border on the front of the cards is slightly lighter than that of the regular issue.

COMPLETE SET (66) 8000.00 12000.00
1 Dennis Hull 50.00 80.00
2 Gump Worsley 70.00 120.00
3 Dallas Smith 30.00 50.00
4 Gilles Tremblay 30.00 50.00
5 J.C. Tremblay 30.00 50.00
6 Ralph Backstrom 30.00 50.00
7 Bobby Rousseau 30.00 50.00
8 Henri Richard 125.00 200.00
9 Claude Provost 30.00 50.00
10 Red Berenson 30.00 50.00
11 Punch Imlach CO 30.00 50.00
12 Johnny Bower 70.00 120.00
13 Yvan Cournoyer 90.00 150.00
14 Mike Walton 30.00 50.00
15 Pete Stemkowski 30.00 50.00
16 Allan Stanley 40.00 70.00
17 George Armstrong 40.00 70.00
18 Harry Howell 35.00 60.00
19 Vic Hadfield 30.00 50.00
20 Marcel Pronovost 35.00 60.00
21 Pete Mahovlich 35.00 60.00
22 Rod Seiling 30.00 50.00
23 Gordie Howe 500.00 800.00
24 Don Marshall 30.00 50.00
25 Orland Kurtenbach 30.00 50.00
26 Rod Gilbert 50.00 80.00
27 Bob Nevin 30.00 50.00
28 Phil Goyette 30.00 50.00
29 Jean Ratelle 60.00 100.00
30 Dave Keon 90.00 150.00
31 Jean Beliveau 175.00 300.00
32 Ed Westfall 30.00 50.00
33 Ron Murphy 30.00 50.00
34 Wayne Hillman 30.00 50.00
35 Bobby Orr 5000.00 8000.00
36 Boom Boom Geoffrion 90.00 150.00
37 Ted Green 30.00 50.00
38 Tom Williams 30.00 50.00
39 Johnny Bucyk 50.00 80.00
40 Bobby Hull 350.00 600.00
41 Ted Harris 30.00 50.00
42 Red Kelly 50.00 80.00
43 Roger Crozier 35.00 60.00
44 Ken Wharram 30.00 50.00
45 Dean Prentice 30.00 50.00
46 Paul Henderson 50.00 80.00
47 Gary Bergman 30.00 50.00
48 Arnie Brown 30.00 50.00
49 Jim Pappin 30.00 50.00
50 Denis DeJordy 35.00 60.00
51 Frank Mahovlich 90.00 150.00
52 Norm Ullman 50.00 80.00
53 Chico Maki 30.00 50.00
54 Reg Fleming 30.00 50.00
55 Jim Neilson 30.00 50.00
56 Bruce MacGregor 30.00 50.00
57 Pat Stapleton 30.00 50.00
58 Matt Ravlich 30.00 50.00
59 Pierre Pilote 40.00 70.00
60 Eric Nesterenko 30.00 50.00
61 Doug Mohns 30.00 50.00
62 Stan Mikita 175.00 300.00
63 Alex Delvecchio 60.00 100.00
64 Ed Johnston 35.00 60.00
65 John Ferguson 35.00 60.00
66 John McKenzie 50.00 80.00

1967-68 Topps

The 1967-68 Topps set features 132 standard-size cards. Players on the six expansion teams (Los Angeles, Minnesota, Oakland, Philadelphia, Pittsburgh, and St. Louis) were not included until 1968-69. Bilingual backs feature a short biography, 1966-67 and career records. The backs are identical in format to the 1966-67 cards. The cards are grouped by team: Montreal (1-10/67-75), Toronto (11-20/76-83), New York (21-31/84-91), Boston (32-42/92-100), Detroit (43-52/101-108) and Chicago (53-63/109-117). The cards were printed in Canada. Rookie Cards include Jacques Lemaire, Derek Sanderson, Glen Sather, and Rogatien Vachon.

COMPLETE SET (132) 2000.00 3000.00
1 Gump Worsley 25.00 40.00
2 Dick Duff 6.00 10.00
3 Jacques Lemaire RC 40.00 60.00
4 Claude Larose 6.00 10.00
5 Gilles Tremblay 5.00 8.00
6 Terry Harper 5.00 8.00
7 Jacques Laperriere 6.00 10.00
8 Garry Monahan 5.00 8.00
9 Carol Vadnais RC 6.00 10.00
10 Ted Harris 5.00 8.00
11 Dave Keon 12.00 20.00
12 Pete Stemkowski 5.00 8.00
13 Allan Stanley 6.00 10.00
14 Ron Ellis 6.00 10.00
15 Mike Walton 6.00 10.00
16 Tim Horton 20.00 35.00
17 Brian Conacher 5.00 8.00
18 Bruce Gamble 6.00 10.00
19 Bob Pulford 6.00 10.00
20 Duane Rupp 5.00 8.00
21 Larry Jeffrey 5.00 8.00
22 Wayne Hillman 5.00 8.00
23 Don Marshall 6.00 10.00
24 Red Berenson 6.00 10.00
25 Phil Goyette 5.00 8.00
26 Camille Henry 5.00 8.00
27 Rod Seiling 5.00 8.00
28 Bob Nevin 6.00 10.00
29 Bernie Geoffrion 15.00 30.00
30 Reg Fleming 5.00 8.00
31 Jean Ratelle 9.00 15.00
32 Phil Esposito 45.00 75.00
33 Derek Sanderson RC 75.00 125.00
34 Eddie Shack 15.00 25.00
35 Ross Lonsberry RC 6.00 10.00
36 Fred Stanfield 5.00 8.00
37 Don Awrey UER 5.00 8.00
(Photo actually
Skip Krake)
38 Glen Sather RC 18.00 30.00
39 John McKenzie 6.00 10.00
40 Tom Williams 5.00 8.00
41 Dallas Smith 5.00 8.00
42 Johnny Bucyk 12.00 20.00
43 Gordie Howe 90.00 150.00
44 Gary Jarrett 5.00 8.00
45 Dean Prentice 5.00 8.00
46 Bert Marshall 5.00 8.00
47 Gary Bergman 5.00 8.00
48 Roger Crozier 6.00 10.00
49 Howie Young 5.00 8.00
50 Doug Roberts 5.00 8.00
51 Alex Delvecchio 12.00 20.00
52 Floyd Smith 5.00 8.00
53 Doug Shelton 5.00 8.00
54 Gerry Goyer 5.00 8.00
55 Wayne Maki 5.00 8.00
56 Dennis Hull 6.00 10.00
57 Dave Dryden RC 9.00 15.00
58 Paul Terbenche 5.00 8.00
59 Gilles Marotte 5.00 8.00
60 Eric Nesterenko 6.00 10.00
61 Pat Stapleton 6.00 10.00
62 Pierre Pilote 6.00 10.00
63 Doug Mohns 5.00 8.00
64 Triple Winner 18.00 30.00
(Stan Mikita)
65 Vezina Trophy 12.00 20.00
(Glenn Hall/
Denis DeJordy)
66 Checklist Card 125.00 225.00
67 Ralph Backstrom 6.00 10.00
68 Bobby Rousseau 5.00 8.00
69 John Ferguson 6.00 10.00
70 Yvan Cournoyer 18.00 30.00
71 Claude Provost 5.00 8.00
72 Henri Richard 15.00 25.00
73 J.C. Tremblay 6.00 10.00
74 Jean Beliveau 25.00 40.00
75 Rogatien Vachon RC 50.00 80.00
76 Johnny Bower 12.00 20.00
77 Wayne Carleton 5.00 8.00
78 Jim Pappin 5.00 8.00
79 Frank Mahovlich 15.00 25.00
80 Larry Hillman 5.00 8.00
81 Marcel Pronovost 6.00 10.00
82 Murray Oliver 5.00 8.00
83 George Armstrong 9.00 15.00
84 Harry Howell 5.00 8.00
85 Ed Giacomin 18.00 30.00
86 Gilles Villemure 6.00 10.00
87 Orland Kurtenbach 5.00 8.00
88 Vic Hadfield 6.00 10.00
89 Arnie Brown 5.00 8.00
90 Rod Gilbert 9.00 15.00
91 Jim Neilson 5.00 8.00
92 Bobby Orr 450.00 700.00
93 Skip Krake UER RC 5.00 8.00
(Photo actually
Don Awrey)
94 Ted Green 6.00 10.00
95 Ed Westfall 6.00 10.00
96 Ed Johnston 6.00 10.00
97 Gary Doak RC 6.00 10.00
98 Ken Hodge 6.00 10.00
99 Gerry Cheevers 30.00 50.00
100 Ron Murphy 5.00 8.00
101 Norm Ullman 9.00 15.00
102 Bruce MacGregor 5.00 8.00
103 Paul Henderson 6.00 10.00
104 Jean-Guy Talbot 5.00 8.00
105 Bart Crashley 5.00 8.00
106 Roy Edwards 6.00 10.00
107 Jim Watson 5.00 8.00
108 Ted Hampson 5.00 8.00
109 Bill Orban 5.00 8.00
110 Geoffrey Powis 5.00 8.00
111 Chico Maki 5.00 8.00
112 Doug Jarrett 5.00 8.00
113 Bobby Hull 75.00 125.00
114 Stan Mikita 25.00 40.00
115 Denis DeJordy 6.00 10.00
116 Pit Martin 6.00 10.00
117 Ken Wharram 5.00 8.00
118 Calder Trophy 150.00 300.00
(Bobby Orr)
119 Norris Trophy 5.00 8.00
(Harry Howell)
120 Checklist Card 125.00 225.00
121 Harry Howell AS 5.00 8.00
122 Pierre Pilote AS 5.00 8.00
123 Ed Giacomin AS 9.00 15.00
124 Bobby Hull AS 50.00 80.00
125 Ken Wharram AS 5.00 8.00
126 Stan Mikita AS 15.00 25.00
127 Tim Horton AS 12.00 20.00
128 Bobby Orr AS 175.00 300.00
129 Glenn Hall AS 12.00 20.00
130 Don Marshall AS 5.00 8.00
131 Gordie Howe AS 60.00 100.00
132 Norm Ullman AS 12.00 20.00

1968-69 Topps

The 1968-69 Topps set consists of 132 standard-size cards featuring all 12 teams including the first cards of players from the six expansion teams. The fronts feature a horizontal format with the player in the foreground and an artistically rendered hockey scene in the background. The backs include a short biography, 1967-68 and career statistics as well as a cartoon-illustrated fact about the player. The cards are grouped by team: Boston (1-11), Chicago (12-22), Detroit (23-33), Los Angeles (34-44), Minnesota (45-55), Montreal (56-66), New York (67-77), Oakland (78-88), Philadelphia (89-99), Pittsburgh (100-110), St. Louis (111-120) and Toronto (122-132). With O-Pee-Chee printing cards for the Canadian market, text on back is English only. For the first time since 1960-61, Topps cards were printed in the U.S. The only Rookie Card of consequence is Bernie Parent.

COMPLETE SET (132) 450.00 750.00
1 Gerry Cheevers 12.00 20.00
2 Bobby Orr 150.00 250.00
3 Don Awrey UER 2.00 4.00
(Photo actually
Skip Krake)
4 Ted Green 2.50 5.00
5 Johnny Bucyk 3.50 7.00
6 Derek Sanderson 15.00 25.00
7 Phil Esposito 18.00 30.00
8 Ken Hodge 2.50 5.00
9 John McKenzie 2.50 5.00
10 Fred Stanfield 2.00 4.00
11 Tom Williams 2.00 4.00
12 Denis DeJordy 2.50 5.00
13 Doug Jarrett 2.00 4.00
14 Gilles Marotte 2.00 4.00
15 Pat Stapleton 2.50 5.00
16 Bobby Hull 35.00 50.00
17 Chico Maki 2.00 4.00
18 Pit Martin 2.50 5.00
19 Doug Mohns 2.00 4.00
20 Stan Mikita 12.00 20.00
21 Jim Pappin 2.00 4.00
22 Ken Wharram 2.00 4.00
23 Roger Crozier 2.50 5.00
24 Bob Baun 2.50 5.00
25 Gary Bergman 2.00 4.00
26 Kent Douglas 2.00 4.00
27 Ron Harris 2.00 4.00
28 Alex Delvecchio 3.50 7.00
29 Gordie Howe 45.00 70.00
30 Bruce MacGregor 2.00 4.00
31 Frank Mahovlich 7.00 12.00
32 Dean Prentice 2.00 4.00
33 Pete Stemkowski 2.00 4.00
34 Terry Sawchuk 25.00 40.00
35 Larry Cahan 2.00 4.00
36 Real Lemieux 2.00 4.00
37 Bill White RC 3.00 6.00
38 Gord Labossiere 2.00 4.00
39 Ted Irvine 2.00 4.00
40 Eddie Joyal 2.00 4.00
41 Dale Rolfe 2.00 4.00
42 Lowell MacDonald RC 3.00 6.00
43 Skip Krake UER 2.00 4.00
(Photo actually
Don Awrey)
44 Terry Gray 2.00 4.00
45 Cesare Maniago 2.50 5.00
46 Mike McMahon 2.00 4.00
47 Wayne Hillman 2.00 4.00
48 Larry Hillman 2.00 4.00
49 Bob Woytowich 2.00 4.00
50 Wayne Connelly 2.00 4.00
51 Claude Larose 2.00 4.00
52 Danny Grant RC 5.00 10.00
53 Andre Boudrias 2.00 4.00
54 Ray Cullen RC 2.00 4.00
55 Parker MacDonald 2.00 4.00
56 Gump Worsley 6.00 10.00
57 Terry Harper 2.00 4.00
58 Jacques Laperriere 2.50 5.00
59 J.C. Tremblay 2.50 5.00
60 Ralph Backstrom 2.50 5.00
61 Jean Beliveau 9.00 15.00
62 Yvan Cournoyer 7.00 12.00
63 Jacques Lemaire 9.00 15.00
64 Henri Richard 7.00 12.00
65 Bobby Rousseau 2.00 4.00
66 Gilles Tremblay 2.00 4.00
67 Ed Giacomin 7.00 12.00
68 Arnie Brown 2.00 4.00
69 Harry Howell 2.50 5.00
70 Jim Neilson 2.00 4.00
71 Rod Seiling 2.00 4.00
72 Rod Gilbert 3.50 7.00
73 Phil Goyette 2.00 4.00
74 Vic Hadfield 2.50 5.00
75 Don Marshall 2.50 5.00
76 Bob Nevin 2.50 5.00
77 Jean Ratelle 3.50 7.00
78 Charlie Hodge 2.50 5.00
79 Bert Marshall 2.00 4.00
80 Billy Harris 2.00 4.00
81 Carol Vadnais 2.50 5.00
82 Howie Young 2.00 4.00
83 John Brenneman 2.00 4.00
84 Gerry Ehman 2.00 4.00
85 Ted Hampson 2.00 4.00
86 Bill Hicke 2.00 4.00
87 Gary Jarrett 2.00 4.00
88 Doug Roberts 2.00 4.00
89 Bernie Parent RC 40.00 60.00
90 Joe Watson 2.00 4.00
91 Ed Van Impe 2.00 4.00
92 Larry Zeidel 2.00 4.00
93 John Miszuk 2.00 4.00
94 Gary Dornhoefer 2.00 4.00
95 Leon Rochefort 2.00 4.00
96 Brit Selby 2.00 4.00
97 Forbes Kennedy 2.00 4.00
98 Ed Hoekstra 2.00 4.00
99 Garry Peters 2.00 4.00
100 Les Binkley RC 5.00 10.00
101 Leo Boivin 2.50 5.00
102 Earl Ingarfield 2.00 4.00
103 Lou Angotti 2.00 4.00
104 Andy Bathgate 3.00 6.00
105 Wally Boyer 2.00 4.00
106 Ken Schinkel 2.00 4.00
107 Ab McDonald 2.00 4.00
108 Charlie Burns 2.00 4.00
109 Val Fonteyne 2.00 4.00
110 Noel Price 2.00 4.00
111 Glenn Hall 6.00 10.00
112 Bob Plager RC 6.00 12.00
113 Jim Roberts 2.50 5.00
114 Red Berenson 2.00 4.00
115 Larry Keenan 2.00 4.00
116 Camille Henry 2.00 4.00
117 Gary Sabourin 2.00 4.00
118 Ron Schock 2.00 4.00
119 Gary Veneruzzo 2.00 4.00
120 Gerry Melnyk 2.00 4.00
121 Checklist Card 60.00 100.00
122 Johnny Bower 6.00 10.00
123 Tim Horton 8.00 15.00
124 Pierre Pilote 3.00 6.00
125 Marcel Pronovost 2.50 5.00
126 Ron Ellis 2.50 5.00
127 Paul Henderson 2.50 5.00
128 Dave Keon 4.00 7.00
129 Bob Pulford 2.50 5.00
130 Floyd Smith 2.00 4.00
131 Norm Ullman 3.00 6.00
132 Mike Walton 3.00 6.00

1969-70 Topps

The 1969-70 Topps set consists of 132 standard-size cards. The backs contain 1968-69 and career statistics, a short biography and a cartoon-illustrated fact about the player. Those players in this set who were also included in the insert set of stamps have a place on the card back for placing that player's stamp. This is not recommended as it would be considered a means of defacing the card and lowering its grade. The cards are grouped by team: Montreal (1-11), St. Louis (12-21), Boston (22-32), New York (33-43), Toronto (44-54), Detroit (55-65), Chicago (66-76), Oakland (77-87), Philadelphia (88-98), Los Angeles (99-109), Pittsburgh (110-120) and Minnesota (121-131). The only notable Rookie Card in the set is Serge Savard.

COMPLETE SET (132) 350.00 500.00
1 Gump Worsley 8.00 15.00
2 Ted Harris 1.50 3.00
3 Jacques Laperriere 2.00 4.00
4 Serge Savard RC 10.00 20.00
5 J.C. Tremblay 2.00 4.00
6 Yvan Cournoyer 2.50 5.00
7 John Ferguson 2.00 4.00
8 Jacques Lemaire 2.50 5.00
9 Bobby Rousseau 1.50 3.00
10 Jean Beliveau 7.00 12.00
11 Henri Richard 5.00 8.00
12 Glenn Hall 5.00 8.00
13 Bob Plager 1.50 3.00
14 Jim Roberts 1.50 3.00
15 Jean-Guy Talbot 2.00 4.00
16 Andre Boudrias 1.50 3.00
17 Camille Henry 1.50 3.00
18 Ab McDonald 1.50 3.00
19 Gary Sabourin 1.50 3.00
20 Red Berenson 1.50 3.00
21 Phil Goyette 1.50 3.00
22 Gerry Cheevers 6.00 10.00
23 Ted Green 1.50 3.00
24 Bobby Orr 75.00 125.00
25 Dallas Smith 1.50 3.00
26 Johnny Bucyk 3.00 6.00
27 Ken Hodge 2.00 4.00
28 John McKenzie 2.00 4.00
29 Ed Westfall 2.00 4.00
30 Phil Esposito 12.00 20.00
31 Derek Sanderson 9.00 15.00
32 Fred Stanfield 1.50 3.00
33 Ed Giacomin 6.00 10.00
34 Arnie Brown 1.50 3.00
35 Jim Neilson 1.50 3.00
36 Rod Seiling 1.50 3.00
37 Rod Gilbert 2.50 5.00
38 Vic Hadfield 2.00 4.00
39 Don Marshall 1.50 3.00
40 Bob Nevin 1.50 3.00
41 Ron Stewart 1.50 3.00
42 Jean Ratelle 2.50 5.00
43 Walt Tkaczuk RC 2.50 5.00
44 Bruce Gamble 2.00 4.00
45 Tim Horton 7.00 12.00
46 Ron Ellis 2.00 4.00
47 Paul Henderson 2.00 4.00
48 Brit Selby 1.50 3.00
49 Floyd Smith 1.50 3.00
50 Mike Walton 1.50 3.00
51 Dave Keon 2.50 5.00
52 Murray Oliver 1.50 3.00
53 Bob Pulford 2.00 4.00
54 Norm Ullman 2.50 5.00
55 Roger Crozier 2.00 4.00
56 Roy Edwards 2.00 4.00
57 Bob Baun 1.50 3.00
58 Gary Bergman 1.50 3.00
59 Carl Brewer 1.50 3.00
60 Wayne Connelly 1.50 3.00
61 Gordie Howe 30.00 50.00
62 Frank Mahovlich 5.00 8.00
63 Bruce MacGregor 1.50 3.00
64 Alex Delvecchio 3.00 6.00
65 Pete Stemkowski 1.50 3.00
66 Denis DeJordy 2.00 4.00
67 Doug Jarrett 1.50 3.00
68 Gilles Marotte 1.50 3.00
69 Pat Stapleton 2.00 4.00
70 Bobby Hull 25.00 40.00
71 Dennis Hull 2.00 4.00
72 Doug Mohns 1.50 3.00
73 Jim Pappin 1.50 3.00
74 Ken Wharram 1.50 3.00

75 Pit Martin 2.00 4.00
76 Stan Mikita 7.00 12.00
77 Charlie Hodge 2.00 4.00
78 Gary Smith 2.00 4.00
79 Harry Howell 2.00 4.00
80 Bert Marshall 1.50 3.00
81 Doug Roberts 1.50 3.00
82 Carol Vadnais 2.00 4.00
83 Gerry Ehman 1.50 3.00
84 Bill Hicke 1.50 3.00
85 Gary Jarrett 1.50 3.00
86 Ted Hampson 1.50 3.00
87 Earl Ingarfield 1.50 3.00
88 Doug Favell RC 5.00 10.00
89 Bernie Parent 15.00 25.00
90 Larry Hillman 1.50 3.00
91 Wayne Hillman 1.50 3.00
92 Ed Van Impe 1.50 3.00
93 Joe Watson 1.50 3.00
94 Gary Dornhoefer 2.00 4.00
95 Reg Fleming 1.50 3.00
96 Jean-Guy Gendron 1.50 3.00
97 Jim Johnson 1.50 3.00
98 Andre Lacroix 2.00 4.00
99 Gerry Desjardins RC 5.00 8.00
100 Dale Rolfe 1.50 3.00
101 Bill White 1.50 3.00
102 Bill Flett 1.50 3.00
103 Ted Irvine 1.50 3.00
104 Ross Lonsberry 1.50 3.00
105 Leon Rochefort 1.50 3.00
106 Eddie Shack 2.50 5.00
107 Dennis Hextall RC 2.50 5.00
108 Eddie Joyal 1.50 3.00
109 Gord Labossiere 1.50 3.00
110 Les Binkley 2.00 4.00
111 Tracy Pratt 1.50 3.00
112 Bryan Watson 1.50 3.00
113 Bob Woytowich 1.50 3.00
114 Keith McCreary 1.50 3.00
115 Dean Prentice 1.50 3.00
116 Glen Sather 2.00 4.00
117 Ken Schinkel 1.50 3.00
118 Wally Boyer 1.50 3.00
119 Val Fonteyne 1.50 3.00
120 Ron Schock 1.50 3.00
121 Cesare Maniago 2.00 4.00
122 Leo Boivin 1.50 3.00
123 Bob McCord 1.50 3.00
124 John Miszuk 1.50 3.00
125 Danny Grant 2.00 4.00
126 Claude Larose 1.50 3.00
127 Jean-Paul Parise 2.00 4.00
128 Tom Williams 1.50 3.00
129 Charlie Burns 1.50 3.00
130 Ray Cullen 1.50 3.00
131 Danny O'Shea 1.50 3.00
132 Checklist Card 35.00 60.00

1970-71 Topps

The 1970-71 Topps set consists of 132 standard-size cards. Card fronts have solid player backgrounds that differ in color according to team. The player's name, team and position are at the bottom. The backs feature the player's 1969-70 and career statistics as well as a short biography. Players from the expansion Buffalo Sabres and Vancouver Canucks are included. For the most part, cards are grouped by team. However, team names on front are updated on some cards to reflect transactions that occurred late in the off-season. Rookie Cards include Wayne Cashman, Brad Park and Gilbert Perreault.

COMPLETE SET (132) 300.00 400.00
1 Gerry Cheevers 8.00 15.00
2 Johnny Bucyk 2.00 5.00
3 Bobby Orr 50.00 75.00
4 Don Awrey .75 1.50
5 Fred Stanfield .75 1.50
6 John McKenzie 1.00 2.50
7 Wayne Cashman RC 5.00 8.00
8 Ken Hodge 1.00 2.50
9 Wayne Carleton .75 1.50
10 Garnet Bailey RC 1.00 2.00
11 Phil Esposito 10.00 20.00
12 Lou Angotti .75 1.50
13 Jim Pappin .75 1.50
14 Dennis Hull 1.00 2.50
15 Bobby Hull 20.00 40.00
16 Doug Mohns .75 1.50
17 Pat Stapleton 1.00 2.50
18 Pit Martin 1.00 2.50
19 Eric Nesterenko 1.00 2.50
20 Stan Mikita 7.00 12.00
21 Roy Edwards 1.00 2.50
22 Frank Mahovlich 1.50 4.00
23 Ron Harris .75 1.50
24 Bob Baun 1.00 2.50
25 Pete Stemkowski .75 1.50
26 Garry Unger 1.00 2.50
27 Bruce MacGregor .75 1.50
28 Larry Jeffrey .75 1.50
29 Gordie Howe 35.00 50.00
30 Billy Dea .75 1.50
31 Denis DeJordy 1.00 2.50
32 Matt Ravlich .75 1.50
33 Dave Amadio .75 1.50
34 Gilles Marotte .75 1.50
35 Eddie Shack 1.50 4.00
36 Bob Pulford 1.00 2.50
37 Ross Lonsberry 1.00 2.50
38 Gord Labossiere .75 1.50
39 Eddie Joyal .75 1.50
40 Gump Worsley 1.50 4.00
41 Bob McCord .75 1.50
42 Leo Boivin 1.00 2.50
43 Tom Reid .75 1.50
44 Charlie Burns .75 1.50
45 Bob Barlow .75 1.50
46 Bill Goldsworthy 1.00 2.50
47 Danny Grant 1.00 2.50
48 Norm Beaudin .75 1.50
49 Rogatien Vachon 3.00 6.00
50 Yvan Cournoyer 1.50 4.00
51 Serge Savard 1.50 4.00
52 Jacques Laperriere 1.00 2.50
53 Terry Harper .75 1.50
54 Ralph Backstrom 1.00 2.50
55 Jean Beliveau 6.00 10.00
56 Claude Larose UER .75 1.50
(Misspelled LaRose on both sides)
57 Jacques Lemaire 1.50 4.00
58 Peter Mahovlich 1.00 2.50
59 Tim Horton 6.00 10.00
60 Bob Nevin .75 1.50
61 Dave Balon .75 1.50
62 Vic Hadfield 1.00 2.50
63 Rod Gilbert 1.50 4.00
64 Ron Stewart .75 1.50
65 Ted Irvine .75 1.50
66 Arnie Brown .75 1.50
67 Brad Park RC 18.00 25.00
68 Ed Giacomin 1.50 4.00
69 Gary Smith 1.00 2.50
70 Carol Vadnais 1.00 2.50
71 Doug Roberts .75 1.50
72 Harry Howell 1.00 2.50
73 Joe Szura .75 1.50
74 Mike Laughton .75 1.50
75 Gary Jarrett .75 1.50
76 Bill Hicke .75 1.50
77 Paul Andrea .75 1.50
78 Bernie Parent 9.00 15.00
79 Joe Watson .75 1.50
80 Ed Van Impe .75 1.50
81 Larry Hillman .75 1.50
82 George Swarbrick .75 1.50
83 Bill Sutherland .75 1.50
84 Andre Lacroix 1.00 2.50
85 Gary Dornhoefer 1.00 2.50
86 Jean-Guy Gendron .75 1.50
87 Al Smith 1.00 2.50
88 Bob Woytowich .75 1.50
89 Duane Rupp .75 1.50
90 Jim Morrison .75 1.50
91 Ron Schock .75 1.50
92 Ken Schinkel .75 1.50
93 Keith McCreary .75 1.50
94 Bryan Hextall 1.00 2.50
95 Wayne Hicks .75 1.50
96 Gary Sabourin .75 1.50
97 Ernie Wakely 1.00 2.50
98 Bob Wall .75 1.50
99 Barclay Plager 1.00 2.50
100 Jean-Guy Talbot .75 1.50
101 Gary Veneruzzo .75 1.50
102 Tim Ecclestone .75 1.50
103 Red Berenson 1.00 2.50
104 Larry Keenan .75 1.50
105 Bruce Gamble 1.00 2.50
106 Jim Dorey .75 1.50
107 Mike Pelyk .75 1.50
108 Rick Ley .75 1.50
109 Mike Walton .75 1.50
110 Norm Ullman 1.50 4.00
111 Brit Selby .75 1.50
112 Garry Monahan .75 1.50
113 George Armstrong 1.50 4.00
114 Gary Doak .75 1.50
115 Darryl Sly .75 1.50
116 Wayne Maki .75 1.50
117 Orland Kurtenbach .75 1.50
118 Murray Hall .75 1.50
119 Marc Reaume .75 1.50
120 Pat Quinn 3.00 5.00
121 Andre Boudrias .75 1.50
122 Paul Popiel .75 1.50
123 Paul Terbenche .75 1.50
124 Howie Menard .75 1.50
125 Gerry Meehan RC 1.50 4.00
126 Skip Krake .75 1.50
127 Phil Goyette .75 1.50
128 Reg Fleming .75 1.50
129 Don Marshall 1.00 2.50
130 Bill Inglis .75 1.50
131 Gilbert Perreault RC 20.00 40.00
132 Checklist Card 35.00 60.00

1970-71 Topps/OPC Sticker Stamps

This set consists of 33 unnumbered, full-color sticker stamps measuring 2 1/2" by 3 1/2". The backs are blank. The checklist below is ordered alphabetically for convenience. The sticker cards were issued as an insert in the regular issue wax packs of the 1970-71 Topps hockey as well as in first series wax packs of 1970-71 O-Pee-Chee.

COMPLETE SET (33) 250.00 400.00
1 Jean Beliveau 15.00 30.00
2 Red Berenson 6.00 12.00
3 Wayne Carleton 6.00 12.00
4 Tim Ecclestone 6.00 12.00
5 Ron Ellis 6.00 12.00
6 Phil Esposito 15.00 30.00
7 Tony Esposito 20.00 40.00
8 Bill Flett 6.00 12.00
9 Ed Giacomin 10.00 20.00
10 Rod Gilbert 10.00 20.00
11 Danny Grant 6.00 12.00
12 Bill Hicke 6.00 12.00
13 Gordie Howe 25.00 50.00
14 Bobby Hull 20.00 40.00
15 Earl Ingarfield 6.00 12.00
16 Eddie Joyal 6.00 12.00
17 Dave Keon 15.00 30.00
18 Andre Lacroix 6.00 12.00
19 Jacques Laperriere 6.00 12.00
20 Jacques Lemaire 10.00 20.00
21 Frank Mahovlich 10.00 20.00
22 Keith McCreary 6.00 12.00
23 Stan Mikita 10.00 20.00
24 Bobby Orr 50.00 100.00
25 Jean-Paul Parise 6.00 12.00
26 Jean Ratelle 7.50 20.00
27 Derek Sanderson 12.50 25.00
28 Frank St.Marseille 6.00 12.00
29 Ron Schock 6.00 12.00
30 Garry Unger 6.00 12.00
31 Carol Vadnais 6.00 12.00
32 Ed Van Impe 6.00 12.00
33 Bob Woytowich 6.00 12.00

1971-72 Topps

The 1971-72 Topps set consists of 132 standard-size cards. For the first time, Topps included the player's NHL year-by-year career record on back. A short player biography and a cartoon-illustrated fact about the player also appear on back. A League Leaders (1-6) subset is exclusive to the Topps set of this year. The only noteworthy Rookie Card is of Ken Dryden. An additional key card in the set is Gordie Howe (70). Howe does not have a basic card in the 1971-72 O-Pee-Chee set.

COMPLETE SET (132) 200.00 350.00
1 Goal Leaders 12.50 30.00
Phil Esposito
Johnny Bucyk
Bobby Hull
2 Assists Leaders 12.50 30.00
Bobby Orr
Phil Esposito
Johnny Bucyk
3 Scoring Leaders 9.00 15.00
Phil Esposito
Bobby Orr
Johnny Bucyk
4 Goalies Win Leaders 6.00 10.00
Tony Esposito
Ed Johnston
Gerry Cheevers
Ed Giacomin
5 Shutouts Leaders 3.00 6.00
Ed Giacomin
Tony Esposito
Cesare Maniago
6 Goals Against 7.00 12.00
Average Leaders
Jacques Plante
Ed Giacomin
Tony Esposito
7 Fred Stanfield .60 1.50
8 Mike Robitaille .60 1.50
9 Vic Hadfield 1.00 2.00
10 Jacques Plante 9.00 15.00
11 Bill White .60 1.50
12 Andre Boudrias .60 1.50
13 Jim Lorentz .60 1.50
14 Arnie Brown .60 1.50
15 Yvan Cournoyer 1.50 3.00
16 Bryan Hextall .60 1.50
17 Gary Croteau .60 1.50
18 Gilles Villemure 1.00 2.00
19 Serge Bernier 1.00 2.00
20 Phil Esposito 7.00 12.00
21 Charlie Burns .60 1.50
22 Doug Barrie .60 1.50
23 Eddie Joyal .60 1.50
24 Rosaire Paiement .60 1.50
25 Pat Stapleton 1.00 2.00
26 Garry Unger 1.00 2.00
27 Al Smith 1.00 2.00
28 Bob Woytowich .60 1.50
29 Marc Tardif 1.00 2.00
30 Norm Ullman 1.50 3.00
31 Tom Williams .60 1.50
32 Ted Harris .60 1.50
33 Andre Lacroix 1.00 2.00
34 Mike Byers .60 1.50
35 Johnny Bucyk 2.00 4.00
36 Roger Crozier 1.00 2.00
37 Alex Delvecchio 1.50 3.00
38 Frank St.Marseille .60 1.50
39 Pit Martin 1.00 2.00
40 Brad Park 6.00 10.00
41 Greg Polis .60 1.50
42 Orland Kurtenbach .60 1.50
43 Jim McKenny .60 1.50
44 Bob Nevin .60 1.50
45 Ken Dryden RC 75.00 125.00
46 Carol Vadnais 1.00 2.00
47 Bill Flett .60 1.50
48 Jim Johnson .60 1.50
49 Al Hamilton .60 1.50
50 Bobby Hull 25.00 50.00
51 Chris Bordeleau .60 1.50
52 Tim Ecclestone .60 1.50
53 Rod Seiling .60 1.50
54 Gerry Cheevers 3.00 6.00
55 Bill Goldsworthy 1.00 2.00
56 Ron Schock .60 1.50
57 Jim Dorey .60 1.50
58 Wayne Maki .60 1.50
59 Terry Harper .60 1.50
60 Gilbert Perreault 9.00 15.00
61 Ernie Hicke .60 1.50
62 Wayne Hillman .60 1.50
63 Denis DeJordy 1.00 2.00
64 Ken Schinkel .60 1.50
65 Derek Sanderson 3.00 6.00
66 Barclay Plager 1.00 2.00
67 Paul Henderson 1.00 2.00
68 Jude Drouin .60 1.50
69 Keith Magnuson 1.00 2.00
70 Gordie Howe 30.00 60.00
71 Jacques Lemaire 1.50 3.00
72 Doug Favell 1.00 2.00
73 Bert Marshall .60 1.50
74 Gerry Meehan 1.00 2.00
75 Walt Tkaczuk 1.00 2.00
76 Bob Berry RC 1.50 3.00
77 Syl Apps RC 1.50 3.00
78 Tom Webster 1.00 2.00
79 Danny Grant 1.00 2.00
80 Dave Keon 1.50 3.00
81 Ernie Wakely 1.50 3.00
82 John McKenzie 1.00 2.00
83 Doug Roberts .60 1.50
84 Peter Mahovlich 1.00 2.00
85 Dennis Hull 1.00 2.00
86 Juha Widing .60 1.50
87 Gary Doak .60 1.50
88 Phil Goyette .60 1.50
89 Gary Dornhoefer 1.00 2.00
90 Ed Giacomin 1.50 3.00
91 Red Berenson 1.00 2.00
92 Mike Pelyk .60 1.50
93 Gary Jarrett .60 1.50
94 Bob Pulford 1.00 2.00
95 Dale Tallon 1.00 2.00
96 Eddie Shack 1.50 3.00
97 Jean Ratelle 1.50 3.00
98 Jim Pappin .60 1.50
99 Roy Edwards 1.00 2.00
100 Bobby Orr 30.00 50.00
101 Ted Hampson .60 1.50
102 Mickey Redmond 1.50 3.00
103 Bob Plager 1.00 2.00
104 Bruce Gamble 1.00 2.00
105 Frank Mahovlich 1.50 3.00
106 Tony Featherstone .60 1.50
107 Tracy Pratt .60 1.50
108 Ralph Backstrom 1.00 2.00
109 Murray Hall .60 1.50
110 Tony Esposito 12.00 20.00
111 Checklist Card 35.00 60.00
112 Jim Neilson .60 1.50
113 Ron Ellis 1.00 2.00
114 Bobby Clarke 18.00 30.00
115 Ken Hodge 1.00 2.00
116 Jim Roberts 1.00 2.00
117 Cesare Maniago 1.00 2.00
118 Jean Pronovost 1.00 2.00
119 Gary Bergman .60 1.50
120 Henri Richard 1.50 3.00
121 Ross Lonsberry .60 1.50
122 Pat Quinn 1.00 2.00
123 Rod Gilbert 1.50 3.00
124 Gary Smith 1.00 2.00
125 Stan Mikita 6.00 10.00
126 Ed Van Impe .60 1.50
127 Wayne Connelly .60 1.50
128 Dennis Hextall 1.00 2.00
129 Wayne Cashman 1.50 3.00
130 J.C. Tremblay 1.00 2.00
131 Bernie Parent 1.50 3.00
132 Dunc McCallum RC 2.00 5.00

1972-73 Topps

The 1972-73 production marked Topps' largest set to date at 176 standard-size cards. Expansion plays a part in the increase as the Atlanta Flames and New York Islanders join the league. Tan borders include team name down the left side. A tan colored bar that crosses the bottom portion of the player photo includes the player's name and team logo. The back contains the year-by-year NHL career record of the player, a short biography and a cartoon illustrated fact about the player. The key cards in the set are the first Topps cards of Marcel Dionne and Guy Lafleur. The set was printed on two sheets of 132 cards creating 88 double-printed cards. The double prints are noted in the checklist below by DP. Topps gives collectors a look at the various NHL hardware in the Trophy subset (170-176).

COMPLETE SET (176) 200.00 400.00
1 World Champions DP 3.00 6.00
Boston Bruins Team
2 Playoff Game 1 .40 1.00
Bruins 6
Rangers 5
3 Playoff Game 2 .40 1.00
Bruins 2
Rangers 1
4 Playoff Game 3 .40 1.00
Rangers 5
Bruins 2
5 Playoff Game 4 DP .25 .50
Bruins 3
Rangers 2
6 Playoff Game 5 DP .40 1.00
Rangers 3
Bruins 2
7 Playoff Game 6 DP .25 .50
Bruins 3
Rangers 0
8 Stanley Cup Trophy 2.50 5.00
9 Ed Van Impe DP .25 .50
10 Yvan Cournoyer DP .60 1.50
11 Syl Apps DP .60 1.50
12 Bill Plager RC .60 1.50
13 Ed Johnston DP .25 .50
14 Walt Tkaczuk .50 1.25
15 Dale Tallon DP .25 .50
16 Gerry Meehan .50 1.25
17 Reggie Leach 1.50 3.00
18 Marcel Dionne DP 6.00 12.00
19 Andre Dupont RC .60 1.50
20 Tony Esposito 7.00 12.00
21 Bob Berry DP .25 .50
22 Craig Cameron .40 1.00
23 Ted Harris .40 1.00
24 Jacques Plante 7.00 12.00
25 Jacques Lemaire DP .60 1.50
26 Simon Nolet DP .25 .50
27 Keith McCreary DP .25 .50
28 Duane Rupp .40 1.00
29 Wayne Cashman .60 1.50
30 Brad Park 3.00 6.00
31 Roger Crozier .50 1.25
32 Wayne Maki .40 1.00
33 Tim Ecclestone .40 1.00
34 Rick Smith .40 1.00
35 Garry Unger DP .25 .50
36 Serge Bernier DP .25 .50
37 Brian Glennie .40 1.00
38 Gerry Desjardins DP .25 .50
39 Danny Grant .50 1.25
40 Bill White DP .25 .50
41 Gary Dornhoefer DP .25 .50
42 Peter Mahovlich .50 1.25
43 Greg Polis DP .25 .50
44 Larry Hale DP .25 .50
45 Dallas Smith .40 1.00
46 Orland Kurtenbach DP .25 .50
47 Steve Atkinson .40 1.00
48 Joey Johnston DP .25 .50
49 Gary Bergman .40 1.00
50 Jean Ratelle .60 1.50
51 Rogatien Vachon DP .60 1.50
52 Phil Roberto DP .25 .50
53 Brian Spencer DP .25 .50
54 Jim McKenny DP .25 .50
55 Gump Worsley .60 1.50
56 Stan Mikita DP 2.50 5.00
57 Guy Lapointe .50 1.25
58 Lew Morrison DP .25 .50
59 Ron Schock DP .25 .50
60 Johnny Bucyk 1.25 2.50
61 Goals Leaders 6.00 10.00
Phil Esposito
Vic Hadfield
Bobby Hull
62 Assists Leaders DP 6.00 12.00
Bobby Orr
Phil Esposito
Jean Ratelle
63 Scoring Leaders DP 6.00 12.00
Phil Esposito
Bobby Orr
Jean Ratelle
64 Goals Against 3.00 6.00
Average Leaders
Tony Esposito
Gilles Villemure
Gump Worsley
65 Penalty Minutes .40 1.00
Leaders DP
Bryan Watson
Keith Magnuson
Gary Dornhoefer
66 Jim Neilson .40 1.00
67 Nick Libett DP .25 .50
68 Jim Lorentz .40 1.00
69 Gilles Meloche RC 3.00 5.00
70 Pat Stapleton .50 1.25
71 Frank St.Marseille DP .25 .50
72 Butch Goring .50 1.25
73 Paul Henderson DP .25 .50
74 Doug Favell .50 1.25
75 Jocelyn Guevremont DP .25 .50
76 Tom Miller .40 1.00
77 Bill MacMillan .40 1.00
78 Doug Mohns .40 1.00
79 Guy Lafleur DP 10.00 20.00
80 Rod Gilbert DP .60 1.50
81 Gary Doak .40 1.00
82 Dave Burrows DP .25 .50
83 Gary Croteau .40 1.00
84 Tracy Pratt DP .25 .50
85 Carol Vadnais DP .25 .50
86 Jacques Caron DP .25 .50
87 Keith Magnuson .60 1.50
88 Dave Keon .60 1.50
89 Mike Corrigan .40 1.00
90 Bobby Clarke 8.00 15.00
91 Dunc Wilson DP .25 .50
92 Gerry Hart .40 1.00
93 Lou Nanne .50 1.25
94 Checklist 1-176 DP 15.00 25.00
95 Red Berenson DP .25 .50
96 Bob Plager .40 1.00
97 Jim Rutherford RC 3.00 6.00
98 Rick Foley DP .25 .50
99 Pit Martin DP .25 .50
100 Bobby Orr DP 25.00 50.00
101 Stan Gilbertson .40 1.00
102 Barry Wilkins .40 1.00
103 Terry Crisp DP .25 .50
104 Cesare Maniago DP .25 .50
105 Marc Tardif .40 1.00
106 Don Luce DP .25 .50
107 Mike Pelyk .40 1.00
108 Juha Widing DP .25 .50
109 Phil Myre DP RC 1.50 3.00
110 Vic Hadfield .50 1.25
111 Arnie Brown DP .25 .50
112 Ross Lonsberry DP .25 .50
113 Dick Redmond .40 1.00
114 Gary Smith .50 1.25
115 Bill Goldsworthy .50 1.25
116 Bryan Watson .40 1.00
117 Dave Balon DP .25 .50
118 Bill Mikkelson DP .25 .50
119 Terry Harper DP .25 .50
120 Gilbert Perreault DP 3.00 6.00
121 Tony Esposito AS1 3.00 6.00
122 Bobby Orr AS1 12.00 20.00
123 Brad Park AS1 1.50 3.00
124 Phil Esposito AS1 2.50 5.00
(Brother Tony pictured in background)
125 Rod Gilbert AS1 .40 1.00
126 Bobby Hull AS1 9.00 15.00
127 Ken Dryden AS2 DP 8.00 20.00
128 Bill White AS2 DP .25 .50
129 Pat Stapleton AS2 DP .25 .50
130 Jean Ratelle AS2 DP .60 1.50
131 Yvan Cournoyer AS2 DP .60 1.50
132 Vic Hadfield AS2 DP .25 .50
133 Ralph Backstrom DP .25 .50
134 Bob Baun DP .25 .50
135 Fred Stanfield DP .25 .50
136 Barclay Plager DP .25 .50
137 Gilles Villemure .50 1.25
138 Ron Harris DP .25 .50
139 Bill Flett DP .25 .50
140 Frank Mahovlich 2.00 4.00
141 Alex Delvecchio DP .60 1.50
142 Paul Popiel .40 1.00
143 Jean Pronovost DP .25 .50
144 Denis DeJordy DP .25 .50
145 Richard Martin DP 1.50 3.00
146 Ivan Boldirev RC .60 1.50
147 Jack Egers .40 1.00
148 Jim Pappin .40 1.00
149 Rod Seiling .40 1.00
150 Phil Esposito 5.00 10.00
151 Gary Edwards .50 1.25
152 Ron Ellis DP .25 .50
153 Jude Drouin .40 1.00
154 Ernie Hicke DP .25 .50
155 Mickey Redmond .60 1.50
156 Joe Watson DP .25 .50
157 Bryan Hextall .40 1.00
158 Andre Boudrias .40 1.00
159 Ed Westfall .50 1.25
160 Ken Dryden 18.00 30.00
161 Rene Robert DP RC 1.00 2.50
162 Bert Marshall DP .25 .50
163 Gary Sabourin .40 1.00
164 Dennis Hull .50 1.25
165 Ed Giacomin DP .60 1.50
166 Ken Hodge .50 1.25
167 Gilles Marotte DP .25 .50
168 Norm Ullman DP .60 1.50
169 Barry Gibbs .40 1.00
170 Art Ross Trophy .75 1.50
171 Hart Memorial Trophy .75 1.50
172 James Norris Trophy .75 1.50
173 Vezina Trophy DP .75 1.50
174 Calder Trophy DP .75 1.50
175 Lady Byng Trophy DP .75 1.50
176 Conn Smythe Trophy DP .75 1.50

1973-74 Topps

Once again increasing in size, the 1973-74 Topps set consists of 198 standard-size cards. The fronts of the cards have distinct colored borders including blue and green. This differs from O-Pee-Chee which used red borders for cards 1-198. The backs contain the player's 1972-73 season record, career numbers, a short biography and a cartoon-illustrated fact about the player. Team cards (92-107) give team and player records on the back. Since the set was printed on two 132-card sheets, there are 66 double-printed cards. These double prints are noted in the checklist below by DP. Rookie Cards include Bill Barber, Billy Smith and Dave Schultz. Ken Dryden (10) is only in the Topps set.

COMPLETE SET (198) 125.00 200.00
1 Goal Leaders 1.25 3.00
Phil Esposito
Rick MacLeish
2 Assists Leaders 1.25 3.00
Phil Esposito
Bobby Clarke
3 Scoring Leaders 1.25 3.00
Phil Esposito
Bobby Clarke
4 Goals Against 2.50 6.00
Average Leaders
Ken Dryden
Tony Esposito
5 Penalty Min. Leaders 1.25 3.00
Jim Schoenfeld
Dave Schultz
6 Power Play Goals 1.25 3.00
Leaders
Phil Esposito
Rick MacLeish
7 Paul Henderson DP .20 .40
8 Gregg Sheppard DP UER .20 .40
(Misspelled Greg on card front)
9 Rod Seiling DP .20 .40
10 Ken Dryden DP 25.00 40.00
11 Jean Pronovost DP .20 .40
12 Dick Redmond .30 .75
13 Keith McCreary DP .20 .40
14 Ted Harris DP .20 .40
15 Garry Unger .40 1.00
16 Neil Komadoski .30 .75
17 Marcel Dionne 6.00 10.00
18 Ernie Hicke DP .20 .40
19 Andre Boudrias .30 .75
20 Bill Flett .30 .75
21 Marshall Johnston .30 .75
22 Gerry Meehan .30 .75
23 Ed Johnston DP .20 .40
24 Serge Savard .50 1.25
25 Walt Tkaczuk .40 1.00
26 Johnny Bucyk .75 2.00
27 Dave Burrows .30 .75
28 Cliff Koroll .30 .75
29 Rey Comeau DP .20 .40
30 Barry Gibbs .30 .75
31 Wayne Stephenson .40 1.00
32 Dan Maloney DP .20 .40
33 Henry Boucha DP .20 .40
34 Gerry Hart .30 .75
35 Bobby Schmautz .30 .75
36 Ross Lonsberry DP .20 .40
37 Ted McAneeley .30 .75
38 Don Luce DP .20 .40
39 Jim McKenny DP .20 .40
40 Frank Mahovlich .50 1.25
41 Bill Fairbairn .30 .75
42 Dallas Smith .30 .75
43 Bryan Hextall .30 .75
44 Keith Magnuson .40 1.00
45 Dan Bouchard .40 1.00
46 Jean-Paul Parise DP .20 .40
47 Barclay Plager .40 1.00
48 Mike Corrigan .30 .75
49 Nick Libett DP .20 .40
50 Bobby Clarke 7.00 12.00
51 Bert Marshall DP .20 .40
52 Craig Patrick .40 1.00
53 Richard Lemieux .30 .75
54 Tracy Pratt DP .20 .40
55 Ron Ellis DP .20 .40
56 Jacques Lemaire .50 1.25
57 Steve Vickers DP .20 .40
58 Carol Vadnais .30 .75
59 Jim Rutherford DP .20 .40
60 Dennis Hull .40 1.00
61 Pat Quinn DP .20 .40
62 Bill Goldsworthy DP .20 .40
63 Fran Huck .30 .75
64 Rogatien Vachon DP .20 .40
65 Gary Bergman DP .20 .40
66 Bernie Parent .50 1.25
67 Ed Westfall .40 1.00
68 Ivan Boldirev .40 1.00
69 Don Tannahill DP .20 .40
70 Gilbert Perreault DP 3.00 6.00
71 Mike Pelyk DP .20 .40
72 Guy Lafleur DP 7.50 15.00
73 Jean Ratelle .50 1.25
74 Gilles Gilbert DP RC 2.00 4.00
75 Greg Polis .30 .75
76 Doug Jarrett DP .20 .40
77 Phil Myre DP .20 .40
78 Fred Harvey DP .20 .40
79 Jack Egers .30 .75
80 Terry Harper .30 .75
81 Bill Barber RC 6.00 10.00
82 Roy Edwards DP .20 .40
83 Brian Spencer .40 1.00
84 Reggie Leach DP .20 .40
85 Dave Keon .50 1.25
86 Jim Schoenfeld .75 2.00
87 Henri Richard DP .20 .40
88 Rod Gilbert DP .20 .40
89 Don Marcotte DP .20 .40
90 Tony Esposito 3.00 6.00
91 Joe Watson .30 .75
92 Flames Team .75 1.50
93 Bruins Team .75 1.50
94 Sabres Team DP .75 1.50
95 Golden Seals Team DP .75 1.50
96 Blackhawks Team .75 1.50
97 Red Wings Team DP .75 1.50
98 Kings Team DP .75 1.50
99 North Stars Team .75 1.50
100 Canadiens Team .75 1.50
101 Islanders Team .75 1.50
102 Rangers Team DP .75 1.50
103 Flyers Team DP .75 1.50
104 Penguins Team .75 1.50
105 Blues Team .75 1.50
106 Maple Leafs Team .75 1.50
107 Canucks Team .75 1.50
108 Roger Crozier DP .20 .40
109 Tom Reid .30 .75
110 Hilliard Graves .30 .75
111 Don Lever .40 1.00
112 Jim Pappin .30 .75
113 Ron Schock DP .20 .40
114 Gerry Desjardins .40 1.00
115 Yvan Cournoyer DP .20 .40
116 Checklist Card 12.00 20.00
117 Bob Leiter .30 .75
118 Ab DeMarco .30 .75
119 Doug Favell .40 1.00
120 Phil Esposito 3.00 6.00
121 Mike Robitaille .30 .75
122 Real Lemieux .30 .75
123 Jim Neilson .30 .75
124 Tim Ecclestone DP .20 .40
125 Jude Drouin .30 .75
126 Gary Smith DP .20 .40
127 Walt McKechnie .30 .75
128 Lowell MacDonald .30 .75
129 Dale Tallon DP .20 .40
130 Billy Harris .40 1.00
131 Randy Manery DP .20 .40
132 Darryl Sittler DP 3.00 6.00
133 Ken Hodge .40 1.00
134 Bob Plager .40 1.00
135 Rick MacLeish .75 2.00
136 Dennis Hextall .30 .75
137 Jacques Laperriere DP .20 .40
138 Butch Goring .40 1.00
139 Rene Robert .40 1.00
140 Ed Giacomin .50 1.25
141 Alex Delvecchio DP .20 .40
142 Jocelyn Guevremont .30 .75
143 Joey Johnston .30 .75
144 Bryan Watson DP .20 .40
145 Stan Mikita 3.00 5.00
146 Cesare Maniago .40 1.00
147 Craig Cameron .30 .75
148 Norm Ullman DP .20 .40
149 Dave Schultz RC 6.00 12.00
150 Bobby Orr 18.00 30.00
151 Phil Roberto .30 .75
152 Curt Bennett .30 .75
153 Gilles Villemure DP .20 .40
154 Chuck Lefley .30 .75
155 Richard Martin 1.00 2.50
156 Juha Widing .30 .75
157 Orland Kurtenbach .30 .75
158 Bill Collins DP .20 .40

159 Bob Stewart .30 .75
160 Syl Apps .40 1.00
161 Danny Grant .40 1.00
162 Billy Smith RC 15.00 25.00
163 Brian Glennie .30 .75
164 Pit Martin DP .20 .40
165 Brad Park 2.00 4.00
166 Wayne Cashman DP .20 .40
167 Gary Dornhoefer .30 .75
168 Steve Durbano RC .30 .75
169 Jacques Richard .30 .75
170 Guy Lapointe .40 1.00
171 Jim Lorentz .30 .75
172 Bob Berry DP .20 .40
173 Dennis Kearns .30 .75
174 Red Berenson .40 1.00
175 Gilles Meloche DP .20 .40
176 Al McDonough .30 .75
177 Dennis O'Brien .30 .75
178 Germaine Gagnon UER DP .20 .40
179 Rick Kehoe DP .20 .40
180 Bill White .30 .75
181 Vic Hadfield DP .20 .40
182 Derek Sanderson 1.50 3.00
183 Andre Dupont DP .20 .40
184 Gary Sabourin .30 .75
185 Larry Romanchych .30 .75
186 Peter Mahovlich .40 1.00
187 Dave Dryden .40 1.00
188 Gilles Marotte .30 .75
189 Bobby Lalonde .30 .75
190 Mickey Redmond .40 1.00
191 Series A .30 .75
Canadiens 4
Sabres 2
192 Series B .30 .75
Flyers 4
North Stars 2
193 Series C .30 .75
Blackhawks 4
Blues 1
194 Series D .30 .75
Rangers 4
Bruins
195 Series E .30 .75
Canadiens 4
Flyers 1
196 Series F .30 .75
Blackhawks 4
Rangers 1
197 Series G .30 .75
Canadiens 4
Blackhawks 2
198 Stanley Cup Champs 1.00 2.50

1974-75 Topps

Topps produced a set of 264 standard-size cards for 1974-75. Design of card fronts offers a hockey stick down the left side. The team name, player name and team logo appear at the bottom in a border that features one of the team colors. The backs feature the player's 1973-74 and career statistics, a short biography and a cartoon-illustrated fact about the player. Players from the 1974-75 expansion Washington Capitals and Kansas City Scouts (presently New Jersey Devils) appear in this set. The set marks the return of coach cards, including Don Cherry and Scotty Bowman.

COMPLETE SET (264) 125.00 200.00
1 Goal Leaders 1.50 3.00
Phil Esposito
Bill Goldsworthy
2 Assists Leaders 3.00 5.00
Bobby Orr
Dennis Hextall
3 Scoring Leaders 2.00 4.00
Phil Esposito
Bobby Clarke
4 Goals Against Average .60 1.50
Leaders
Doug Favell
Bernie Parent
5 Penalty Min. Leaders .25 .50
Bryan Watson
Dave Schultz
6 Power Play Goal .25 .50
Leaders
Mickey Redmond
Rick MacLeish
7 Gary Bromley .30 .75
8 Bill Barber 2.00 4.00
9 Emile Francis CO .25 .60
10 Gilles Gilbert .60 1.50
11 John Davidson RC 4.00 8.00
12 Ron Ellis .30 .75
13 Syl Apps .25 .60
14 Flames Leaders .25 .50
Jacques Richard
Tom Lysiak
Keith McCreary
15 Dan Bouchard .30 .75
16 Ivan Boldirev .30 .75
17 Gary Coalter .25 .60
18 Bob Berry .25 .60
19 Red Berenson .30 .75
20 Stan Mikita 2.00 4.00
21 Fred Shero CO RC 1.25 2.50
22 Gary Smith .30 .75
23 Bill Mikkelson .25 .60
24 Jacques Lemaire UER .60 1.50
(Shown in Sabres
sweater)
25 Gilbert Perreault 2.00 4.00
26 Cesare Maniago .30 .75
27 Bobby Schmautz .25 .60
28 Bruins Leaders 4.00 8.00
Phil Esposito
Bobby Orr
Johnny Bucyk
29 Steve Vickers .30 .75
30 Lowell MacDonald .25 .60
31 Fred Stanfield .25 .60
32 Ed Westfall .30 .75
33 Curt Bennett .25 .60
34 Bep Guidolin CO .25 .60
35 Cliff Koroll .25 .60
36 Gary Croteau .25 .60
37 Mike Corrigan .25 .60
38 Henry Boucha .25 .60
39 Ron Low .30 .75
40 Darryl Sittler 2.50 5.00
41 Tracy Pratt .25 .60
42 Sabres Leaders .25 .50
Richard Martin
Rene Robert
43 Larry Carriere .25 .60
44 Gary Dornhoefer .30 .75
45 Denis Herron RC 1.25 2.50
46 Doug Favell .30 .75
47 Dave Gardner .25 .60
48 Morris Mott .25 .60
49 Marc Boileau CO .25 .60
50 Brad Park 1.50 3.00
51 Bob Leiter .25 .60
52 Tom Reid .25 .60
53 Serge Savard .60 1.50
54 Checklist 1-132 7.00 12.00
55 Terry Harper .25 .60
56 Golden Seals .25 .50
Leaders
Joey Johnston
Walt McKechnie
57 Guy Charron .25 .60
58 Pit Martin .25 .60
59 Chris Evans .25 .60
60 Bernie Parent .60 1.50
61 Jim Lorentz .25 .60
62 Dave Kryskow .25 .60
63 Lou Angotti CO .25 .60
64 Bill Flett .25 .60
65 Vic Hadfield .30 .75
66 Wayne Merrick .25 .60
67 Andre Dupont .25 .60
68 Tom Lysiak RC .60 1.50
69 Blackhawks Leaders .25 .50
Jim Pappin
Stan Mikita
J.P. Bordeleau
70 Guy Lapointe .30 .75
71 Gerry O'Flaherty .25 .60
72 Marcel Dionne 3.00 6.00
73 Brent Hughes .25 .60
74 Butch Goring .30 .75
75 Keith Magnuson .25 .60
76 Red Kelly CO .25 .60
77 Pete Stemkowski .25 .60
78 Jim Roberts .25 .60
79 Don Luce .25 .60
80 Don Awrey .25 .60
81 Rick Kehoe .30 .75
82 Billy Smith 3.00 6.00
83 Jean-Paul Parise .25 .60
84 Red Wings Leaders .25 .50
Mickey Redmond
Marcel Dionne
Bill Hogaboam
85 Ed Van Impe .25 .60
86 Randy Manery .25 .60
87 Barclay Plager .30 .75
88 Inge Hammarstrom .25 .60
89 Ab DeMarco .25 .60
90 Bill White .25 .60
91 Al Arbour CO .60 1.50
92 Bob Stewart .25 .60
93 Jack Egers .25 .60
94 Don Lever .25 .60
95 Reggie Leach .30 .75
96 Dennis O'Brien .25 .60
97 Peter Mahovlich .30 .75
98 Kings Leaders .25 .50
Butch Goring
Frank St.Marseille
Don Kozak
99 Gerry Meehan .25 .60
100 Bobby Orr 15.00 30.00
101 Jean Potvin RC .25 .60
102 Rod Seiling .25 .60
103 Keith McCreary .25 .60
104 Phil Maloney CO .25 .60
105 Denis Dupere .25 .60
106 Steve Durbano .25 .60
107 Bob Plager UER .30 .75
(Photo actually
Barclay Plager)
108 Chris Oddleifson .25 .60
109 Jim Neilson .25 .60
110 Jean Pronovost .30 .75
111 Don Kozak .25 .60
112 North Stars .30 .75
Leaders
Bill Goldsworthy
Dennis Hextall
Danny Grant
113 Jim Pappin .25 .60
114 Richard Lemieux .25 .60
115 Dennis Hextall .25 .60
116 Bill Hogaboam .25 .60
117 Canucks Leaders .25 .50
Dennis Ververgaert
Bob Schmautz
Andre Boudrias
Don Tannahill
118 Jimmy Anderson CO .25 .60
119 Walt Tkaczuk .30 .75
120 Mickey Redmond .30 .75
121 Jim Schoenfeld .60 1.50
122 Jocelyn Guevremont .25 .60
123 Bob Nystrom .60 1.50
124 Canadiens Leaders 1.00 2.00
Yvan Cournoyer
Frank Mahovlich
Claude Larose
125 Lew Morrison .25 .60
126 Terry Murray .30 .75
127 Richard Martin AS .30 .75
128 Ken Hodge AS .25 .50
129 Phil Esposito AS 1.25 2.50
130 Bobby Orr AS 7.00 12.00
131 Brad Park AS .60 1.50
132 Gilles Gilbert AS .25 .50
133 Lowell MacDonald AS .25 .50
134 Bill Goldsworthy AS .25 .50
135 Bobby Clarke AS 2.00 4.00
136 Bill White AS .25 .50
137 Dave Burrows AS .25 .50
138 Bernie Parent AS .60 1.50
139 Jacques Richard .25 .60
140 Yvan Cournoyer .60 1.50
141 Rangers Leaders .60 1.50
Rod Gilbert
Brad Park
142 Rene Robert .30 .75
143 J. Bob Kelly .25 .60
144 Ross Lonsberry .25 .60
145 Jean Ratelle .60 1.50
146 Dallas Smith .25 .60
147 Bernie Geoffrion CO 1.25 2.50
148 Ted McAneeley .25 .60
149 Pierre Plante .25 .60
150 Dennis Hull .30 .75
151 Dave Keon .60 1.50
152 Dave Dunn .25 .60
153 Michel Belhumeur .30 .75
154 Flyers Leaders 1.00 2.00
Bobby Clarke
Dave Schultz
155 Ken Dryden 7.50 15.00
156 John Wright .25 .60
157 Larry Romanchych .25 .60
158 Ralph Stewart .25 .60
159 Mike Robitaille .25 .60
160 Ed Giacomin 1.00 2.00
161 Don Cherry CO RC 15.00 25.00
162 Checklist 133-264 7.00 12.00
163 Rick MacLeish .60 1.50
164 Greg Polis .25 .60
165 Carol Vadnais .25 .60
166 Pete Laframboise .25 .60
167 Ron Schock .25 .60
168 Lanny McDonald RC 7.00 12.00
169 Scouts Emblem .40 1.00
Draft Selections
on back
170 Tony Esposito 2.50 5.00
171 Pierre Jarry .25 .60
172 Dan Maloney .30 .75
173 Peter McDuffe .30 .75
174 Danny Grant .30 .75
175 John Stewart .25 .60
176 Floyd Smith CO .25 .60
177 Bert Marshall .25 .60
178 Chuck Lefley UER .25 .60
(Photo actually
Pierre Bouchard)
179 Gilles Villemure .30 .75
180 Borje Salming RC 7.00 12.00
181 Doug Mohns .25 .60
182 Barry Wilkins .25 .60
183 Penguins Leaders .30 .75
Lowell MacDonald
Syl Apps
184 Gregg Sheppard .25 .60
185 Joey Johnston .25 .60
186 Dick Redmond .25 .60
187 Simon Nolet .25 .60
188 Ron Stackhouse .25 .60
189 Marshall Johnston .25 .60
190 Richard Martin .60 1.50
191 Andre Boudrias .25 .60
192 Steve Atkinson .25 .60
193 Nick Libett .25 .60
194 Bob Murdoch .25 .60
Los Angeles Kings
195 Denis Potvin RC 15.00 25.00
196 Dave Schultz 1.00 2.00
197 Blues Leaders .25 .50
Garry Unger
Pierre Plante
198 Jim McKenny .25 .60
199 Gerry Hart .25 .60
200 Phil Esposito 2.00 4.00
201 Rod Gilbert .60 1.50
202 Jacques Laperriere .30 .75
203 Barry Gibbs .25 .60
204 Billy Reay CO .30 .75
205 Gilles Meloche .30 .75
206 Wayne Cashman .30 .75
207 Dennis Ververgaert .25 .60
208 Phil Roberto .25 .60
209 Quarter Finals .35 .75
Flyers sweep
Flames
210 Quarter Finals .35 .75
Rangers over
Canadiens
211 Quarter Finals .35 .75
Bruins sweep
Maple Leafs
212 Quarter Finals .35 .75
Blackhawks over
L.A. Kings
213 Stanley Cup Semifinals .35 .75
Flyers over Rangers
214 Stanley Cup Semifinals .35 .75
Bruins over
Blackhawks
215 Stanley Cup Finals .35 .75
Flyers over Bruins
216 Stanley Cup Champions .60 1.50
217 Joe Watson .25 .60
218 Wayne Stephenson .30 .75
219 Maple Leaf Leaders .60 1.50
Darryl Sittler
Norm Ullman
Paul Henderson
Denis Dupere
220 Bill Goldsworthy .30 .75
221 Don Marcotte .25 .60
222 Alex Delvecchio CO .25 .60
223 Stan Gilbertson .25 .60
224 Mike Murphy .25 .60
225 Jim Rutherford .30 .75
226 Phil Russell .25 .60
227 Lynn Powis .25 .60
228 Billy Harris .25 .60
229 Bob Pulford CO .25 .60
230 Ken Hodge .30 .75
231 Bill Fairbairn .25 .60
232 Guy Lafleur 7.00 12.00
233 Islanders Leaders 1.25 2.50
Billy Harris
Ralph Stewart
Denis Potvin
234 Fred Stanfield .25 .60
235 Rogatien Vachon .60 1.50
236 Norm Ullman .60 1.50
237 Garry Unger .30 .75
238 Jack Gordon CO .25 .60
239 Johnny Bucyk .60 1.50
240 Bob Dailey .25 .60
241 Dave Burrows .25 .60
242 Len Frig .25 .60
243 Masterson Trophy .60 1.50
Henri Richard
244 Hart Trophy 1.25 2.50
Phil Esposito
245 Byng Trophy .40 1.00
Johnny Bucyk
246 Ross Trophy 1.25 2.50
Phil Esposito
247 Prince of Wales .30 .75
Trophy
248 Norris Trophy 7.00 12.00
Bobby Orr
249 Vezina Trophy .60 1.50
Bernie Parent
250 Stanley Cup .30 .75
251 Smythe Trophy .60 1.50
Bernie Parent
252 Calder Trophy 3.00 6.00
Denis Potvin
253 Campbell Trophy .30 .75
254 Pierre Bouchard .25 .60
255 Jude Drouin .25 .60
256 Capitals Emblem .40 1.00
(Draft Selections
on back)
257 Michel Plasse .30 .75
258 Juha Widing .25 .60
259 Bryan Watson .25 .60
260 Bobby Clarke 4.00 8.00
261 Scotty Bowman CO RC 15.00 30.00
262 Craig Patrick .30 .75
263 Craig Cameron .25 .60
264 Ted Irvine .60 1.50

1975-76 Topps

At 330 standard-size cards, the 1975-76 Topps set stands as the company's largest until 1990-91. Fronts feature team name at top and player name at the bottom. The player's position appears in a puck at the bottom. The backs contain year-by-year and NHL career records, a short biography and a cartoon-illustrated hockey fact or referee's signal with interpretation. For the first time, team cards (81-98) with team checklist on back appear in a Topps set.

COMPLETE SET (330) 75.00 150.00
1 Stanley Cup Finals .60 1.50
Philadelphia 4
Buffalo 2
2 Semi-Finals .20 .50
Philadelphia 4
N.Y. Islanders 3
3 Semi-Finals .20 .50
Buffalo 4
Montreal 2
4 Quarter Finals .20 .50
N.Y. Islanders 4
Pittsburgh 2
5 Quarter Finals .20 .50
Montreal 4
Vancouver 1
6 Quarter Finals .20 .50
Buffalo 4
Chicago 1
7 Quarter Finals .20 .50
Philadelphia 4
Toronto 0
8 Curt Bennett .20 .50
9 Johnny Bucyk .50 1.25
10 Gilbert Perreault 1.25 3.00
11 Darryl Edestrand .20 .50
12 Ivan Boldirev .20 .50
13 Nick Libett .20 .50
14 Jim McElmury .20 .50
15 Frank St.Marseille .20 .50
16 Blake Dunlop .20 .50
17 Yvon Lambert .20 .50
18 Gerry Hart .20 .50
19 Steve Vickers .20 .50
20 Rick MacLeish .25 .60
21 Bob Paradise .20 .50
22 Red Berenson .25 .60
23 Lanny McDonald 1.50 4.00
24 Mike Robitaille .20 .50
25 Ron Low .25 .60
26 Bryan Hextall .20 .50
27 Carol Vadnais .20 .50
28 Jim Lorentz .20 .50
29 Gary Simmons .25 .60
30 Stan Mikita 1.25 3.00
31 Bryan Watson .20 .50
32 Guy Charron .20 .50
33 Bob Murdoch .20 .50
34 Norm Gratton .20 .50
35 Ken Dryden 9.00 15.00
36 Jean Potvin .20 .50
37 Rick Middleton 1.50 3.00
38 Ed Van Impe .20 .50
39 Rick Kehoe .25 .60
40 Garry Unger .25 .60
41 Ian Turnbull .25 .60
42 Dennis Ververgaert .20 .50
43 Mike Marson .20 .50
44 Randy Manery .20 .50
45 Gilles Gilbert .25 .60
46 Rene Robert .25 .60
47 Bob Stewart .20 .50
48 Pit Martin .20 .50
49 Danny Grant .25 .60
50 Peter Mahovlich .25 .60
51 Dennis Patterson .20 .50
52 Mike Murphy .20 .50
53 Dennis O'Brien .20 .50
54 Garry Howatt .20 .50
55 Ed Giacomin .60 1.50
56 Andre Dupont .20 .50
57 Chuck Arnason .20 .50
58 Bob Gassoff RC .20 .50
59 Ron Ellis .25 .60
60 Andre Boudrias .20 .50
61 Yvon Labre .20 .50
62 Hilliard Graves .20 .50
63 Wayne Cashman .25 .60
64 Danny Gare RC 1.00 2.00
65 Rick Hampton .20 .50
66 Darcy Rota .20 .50
67 Bill Hogaboam .20 .50
68 Denis Herron .25 .60
69 Sheldon Kannegiesser .20 .50
70 Yvan Cournoyer UER .50 1.25
(Misspelled Yvon
on card front)
71 Ernie Hicke .20 .50
72 Bert Marshall .20 .50
73 Derek Sanderson .75 2.00
74 Tom Bladon .25 .60
75 Ron Schock .20 .50
76 Larry Sacharuk .20 .50
77 George Ferguson .20 .50
78 Ab DeMarco .20 .50
79 Tom Williams .20 .50
80 Phil Roberto .20 .50
81 Bruins Team 1.00 2.50
(Checklist back)
82 Seals Team 1.00 2.50
(Checklist back)
83 Sabres Team UER 1.00 2.50
(Gary Desjardins& sic;
checklist back)
84 Blackhawks Team UER 1.00 2.50
(Germain Gagnon& sic;
checklist back)
85 Flames Team 1.00 2.50
(Checklist back)
86 Kings Team 1.00 2.50
(Checklist back)
87 Red Wings Team 1.00 2.50
(Checklist back)
88 Scouts Team UER 1.00 2.50
(Dennis Dupere& sic;
checklist back)
89 North Stars Team 1.00 2.50
(Checklist back)
90 Canadiens Team 1.00 2.50
(Checklist back)
91 Maple Leafs Team 1.00 2.50
(Checklist back)
92 Islanders Team 1.00 2.50
(Checklist back)
93 Penguins Team 1.00 2.50
(Checklist back)
94 Rangers Team 1.00 2.50
(Checklist back)
95 Flyers Team UER 1.00 2.50
(Philadelphia mis-
spelled on card back;
checklist back)
96 Blues Team 1.00 2.50
(Checklist back)
97 Canucks Team UER 1.00 2.50
(242 Robitaille should
be 24 and 42 Ververgaert
not shown;
checklist back)
98 Capitals Team 1.00 2.50
(Checklist back)
99 Checklist 1-110 6.00 10.00
100 Bobby Orr 12.00 20.00
101 Germaine Gagnon UER .20 .50
(Misspelled Germain
on both sides)
102 Phil Russell .20 .50
103 Billy Lochead .20 .50
104 Robin Burns .20 .50
105 Gary Edwards .25 .60
106 Dwight Bialowas .20 .50
107 Doug Risebrough RC UER 1.00 2.00
(Photo actually
Bob Gainey)
108 Dave Lewis .20 .50
109 Bill Fairbairn .20 .50
110 Ross Lonsberry .20 .50
111 Ron Stackhouse .20 .50
112 Claude Larose .20 .50
113 Don Luce .20 .50
114 Errol Thompson .20 .50
115 Gary Smith .25 .60
116 Jack Lynch .20 .50
117 Jacques Richard .20 .50
118 Dallas Smith .20 .50
119 Dave Gardner .20 .50
120 Mickey Redmond .25 .60
121 John Marks .20 .50
122 Dave Hudson .20 .50
123 Bob Nevin .20 .50
124 Fred Barrett .20 .50
125 Gerry Desjardins .25 .60
126 Guy Lafleur UER 4.00 10.00
(Listed as Defense
on card front)
127 Jean-Paul Parise .20 .50
128 Walt Tkaczuk .25 .60
129 Gary Dornhoefer .25 .60
130 Syl Apps .20 .50
131 Bob Plager .25 .60
132 Stan Weir .20 .50
133 Tracy Pratt .20 .50
134 Jack Egers .20 .50
135 Eric Vail .20 .50
136 Al Sims .20 .50
137 Larry Patey .20 .50
138 Jim Schoenfeld .25 .60
139 Cliff Koroll .20 .50
140 Marcel Dionne 1.50 4.00
141 Jean-Guy Lagace .20 .50
142 Juha Widing .20 .50
143 Lou Nanne .20 .50
144 Serge Savard .50 1.25
145 Glenn Resch 1.25 3.00
146 Ron Greschner RC 1.00 2.00
147 Dave Schultz .25 .60
148 Barry Wilkins .20 .50
149 Floyd Thomson .20 .50
150 Darryl Sittler .50 1.25
151 Paulin Bordeleau .20 .50
152 Ron Lalonde .20 .50
153 Larry Romanchych .20 .50
154 Larry Carriere .20 .50
155 Andre Savard .20 .50
156 Dave Hrechkosy .20 .50
157 Bill White .20 .50
158 Dave Kryskow .20 .50
159 Denis Dupere .20 .50
160 Rogatien Vachon .60 1.50
161 Doug Rombough .20 .50
162 Murray Wilson .20 .50
163 Bob Bourne RC 1.00 2.00
164 Gilles Marotte .20 .50
165 Vic Hadfield .25 .60
166 Reggie Leach .25 .60
167 Jerry Butler .20 .50
168 Inge Hammarstrom .20 .50
169 Chris Oddleifson .20 .50
170 Greg Joly .20 .50
171 Checklist 111-220 6.00 10.00
172 Pat Quinn .25 .60
173 Dave Forbes .20 .50
174 Len Frig .20 .50
175 Richard Martin .25 .60
176 Keith Magnuson .20 .50
177 Dan Maloney .20 .50
178 Craig Patrick .25 .60
179 Tom Williams .20 .50
180 Bill Goldsworthy .25 .60
181 Steve Shutt .50 1.25
182 Ralph Stewart .20 .50
183 John Davidson 1.25 3.00
184 Bob Kelly .20 .50
185 Ed Johnston .25 .60
186 Dave Burrows .20 .50
187 Dave Dunn .20 .50
188 Dennis Kearns .20 .50
189 Bill Clement 1.25 3.00
190 Gilles Meloche .25 .60
191 Bob Leiter .20 .50
192 Jerry Korab .20 .50
193 Joey Johnston .20 .50
194 Walt McKechnie .20 .50
195 Wilf Paiement .20 .50
196 Bob Berry .20 .50
197 Dean Talafous .20 .50
198 Guy Lapointe .25 .60
199 Clark Gillies RC 2.00 4.00
200 Phil Esposito 1.25 3.00
201 Greg Polis .20 .50
202 Jimmy Watson .25 .60
203 Gord McRae .25 .60
204 Lowell MacDonald .20 .50
205 Barclay Plager .25 .60
206 Don Lever .25 .60
207 Bill Mikkelson .20 .50
208 Goals Leaders 1.25 3.00
Phil Esposito
Guy Lafleur
Richard Martin
209 Assists Leaders 1.50 4.00
Bobby Clarke
Bobby Orr
Pete Mahovlich
210 Scoring Leaders 2.00 5.00
Bobby Orr
Phil Esposito
Marcel Dionne
211 Penalty Min. Leaders .20 .50
Dave Schultz
Andre Dupont
Phil Russell
212 Power Play .60 1.50
Goal Leaders
Phil Esposito
Richard Martin
Danny Grant
213 Goals Against 2.00 5.00
Average Leaders
Bernie Parent
Rogatien Vachon
Ken Dryden
214 Barry Gibbs .20 .50
215 Ken Hodge .25 .60
216 Jocelyn Guevremont .20 .50
217 Warren Williams .20 .50
218 Dick Redmond .20 .50
219 Jim Rutherford .25 .60
220 Simon Nolet .20 .50
221 Butch Goring .25 .60
222 Glen Sather .25 .60
223 Mario Tremblay RC 1.50 3.00
224 Jude Drouin .20 .50
225 Rod Gilbert .50 1.25
226 Bill Barber .50 1.25
227 Gary Inness .25 .60
228 Wayne Merrick .20 .50
229 Rod Seiling .20 .50
230 Tom Lysiak .25 .60
231 Bob Dailey .20 .50
232 Michel Belhumeur .25 .60
233 Bill Hajt .20 .50
234 Jim Pappin .20 .50
235 Gregg Sheppard .20 .50
236 Gary Bergman .20 .50
237 Randy Rota .20 .50
238 Neil Komadoski .20 .50
239 Craig Cameron .20 .50
240 Tony Esposito 1.25 3.00
241 Larry Robinson 2.50 6.00
242 Billy Harris .20 .50
243 Jean Ratelle .50 1.25
244 Ted Irvine UER .20 .50
(Photo actually
Ted Harris)
245 Bob Neely .20 .50
246 Bobby Lalonde .20 .50
247 Ron Jones .20 .50
248 Rey Comeau .20 .50
249 Michel Plasse .25 .60
250 Bobby Clarke 2.50 6.00
251 Bobby Schmautz .20 .50
252 Peter McNab RC 1.25 2.50
253 Al MacAdam .20 .50
254 Dennis Hull .25 .60
255 Terry Harper .20 .50
256 Peter McDuffe .25 .60
257 Jean Hamel .20 .50
258 Jacques Lemaire .50 1.25
259 Bob Nystrom .25 .60
260 Brad Park .75 2.00
261 Cesare Maniago .25 .60
262 Don Saleski .20 .50
263 J. Bob Kelly .20 .50
264 Bob Hess .20 .50
265 Blaine Stoughton .25 .60
266 John Gould .20 .50
267 Checklist 221-330 6.00 10.00
268 Dan Bouchard .25 .60
269 Don Marcotte .20 .50
270 Jim Neilson .20 .50
271 Craig Ramsay .20 .50
272 Grant Mulvey RC .25 .60
273 Larry Giroux .20 .50
274 Real Lemieux .20 .50
275 Denis Potvin 2.50 6.00
276 Don Kozak .20 .50
277 Tom Reid .20 .50
278 Bob Gainey 1.50 4.00
279 Nick Beverley .20 .50
280 Jean Pronovost .25 .60
281 Joe Watson .20 .50
282 Chuck Lefley .20 .50
283 Borje Salming 2.00 5.00
284 Garnet Bailey .20 .50
285 Gregg Boddy .20 .50
286 Bobby Clarke AS1 1.25 3.00
287 Denis Potvin AS1 1.25 3.00
288 Bobby Orr AS1 6.00 10.00
289 Richard Martin AS1 .20 .50
290 Guy Lafleur AS1 1.50 4.00
291 Bernie Parent AS1 .50 1.25
292 Phil Esposito AS2 .75 2.00
293 Guy Lapointe AS2 .20 .50
294 Borje Salming AS2 1.00 2.50
295 Steve Vickers AS2 .20 .50
296 Rene Robert AS2 .20 .50
297 Rogatien Vachon AS2 .50 1.25
298 Buster Harvey .20 .50
299 Gary Sabourin .20 .50
300 Bernie Parent .50 1.25
301 Terry O'Reilly .25 .60
302 Ed Westfall .25 .60
303 Pete Stemkowski .20 .50
304 Pierre Bouchard .20 .50
305 Pierre Larouche RC 2.00 4.00
306 Lee Fogolin .20 .50
307 Gerry O'Flaherty .20 .50
308 Phil Myre .25 .60
309 Pierre Plante .20 .50
310 Dennis Hextall .20 .50
311 Jim McKenny .20 .50
312 Vic Venasky .20 .50
313 Flames Leaders .20 .50
Eric Vail
Tom Lysiak
Tom Lysiak
Tom Lysiak
314 Bruins Leaders 2.00 5.00
Phil Esposito
Bobby Orr
Phil Esposito
Johnny Bucyk
315 Sabres Leaders .20 .50
Richard Martin
Rene Robert
Rene Robert
Richard Martin
316 Seals Leaders .20 .50
Dave Hrechkosy
Larry Patey
Stan Weir
Stan Weir
Larry Patey
Dave Hrechkosy
317 Blackhawks Leaders .20 .50
Stan Mikita
Jim Pappin
Stan Mikita
Stan Mikita
Stan Mikita
318 Red Wings Leaders .20 .50
Danny Grant
Marcel Dionne
Marcel Dionne
Danny Grant
319 Scouts Leaders .20 .50
Simon Nolet
Wilf Paiement
Simon Nolet
Guy Charron
Simon Nolet
320 Kings Leaders .20 .50
Bob Nevin
Bob Nevin
Bob Nevin
Bob Nevin
Juha Widing
Bob Berry
321 North Stars Leaders .20 .50
Bill Goldsworthy
Dennis Hextall
Dennis Hextall
Bill Goldsworthy
322 Canadiens Leaders .60 1.50
Guy Lafleur
Pete Mahovlich
Guy Lafleur
Guy Lafleur
323 Islanders Leaders .60 1.50
Bob Nystrom
Denis Potvin
Denis Potvin
Clark Gillies
324 Rangers Leaders .20 .50
Steve Vickers
Steve Vickers
Rod Gilbert
Rod Gilbert

Jean Ratelle
325 Flyers Leaders .20 .50
Reggie Leach
Bobby Clarke
Bobby Clarke
Reggie Leach
326 Penguins Leaders .20 .50
Jean Pronovost
Ron Schock
Ron Schock
Jean Pronovost
327 Blues Leaders .20 .50
Garry Unger
Garry Unger
Garry Unger
Garry Unger
Larry Sacharuk
328 Maple Leafs Leaders .60 1.50
Darryl Sittler
Darryl Sittler
Darryl Sittler
Darryl Sittler
329 Canucks Leaders .20 .50
Don Lever
Don Lever
Andre Boudrias
Andre Boudrias
330 Capitals Leaders .20 .50
Tommy Williams
Garnet Bailey
Tommy Williams
Garnet Bailey
Tommy Williams

1976-77 Topps

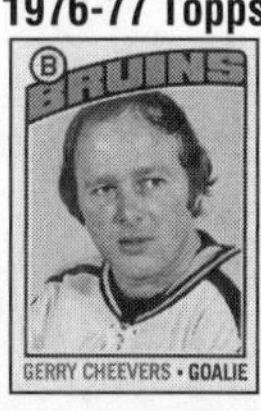

GERRY CHEEVERS • GOALIE

he 1976-77 Topps set contains 264 color tandard-size cards. The fronts contain team name and logo at the top with player name nd position at the bottom. The backs feature 975-76 and career statistics, career ighlights and a cartoon-illustrated fact. The rst cards of Colorado Rockies (formerly ansas City) players appear this year. ookie Cards in this set include Bryan rottier and Dennis Maruk.

OMPLETE SET (264) 100.00 200.00
Goals Leaders .75 2.00
Reggie Leach
Guy Lafleur
Pierre Larouche
Assists Leaders .75 2.00
Bobby Clarke
Peter Mahovlich
Guy Lafleur
Gilbert Perrault
Jean Ratelle
Scoring Leaders .75 2.00
Guy Lafleur
Bobby Clarke
Gilbert Perreault
Penalty Min. Leaders .20 .50
Steve Durbano
Bryan Watson
Dave Schultz
Power Play Goals .75 2.00
Leaders
Phil Esposito
Guy Lafleur
Richard Martin
Pierre Larouche
Denis Potvin
Goals Against 1.25 3.00
Average Leaders
Ken Dryden
Glenn Resch
Michel Larocque
Gary Doak .20 .50
Jacques Richard .20 .50
Wayne Dillon .20 .50
0 Bernie Parent .75 2.00
1 Ed Westfall .25 .60
2 Dick Redmond .20 .50
3 Bryan Hextall .20 .50
4 Jean Pronovost .25 .60
5 Peter Mahovlich .25 .60
6 Danny Grant .25 .60
7 Phil Myre .25 .60
8 Wayne Merrick .20 .50
9 Steve Durbano .20 .50
0 Derek Sanderson .60 1.50
1 Mike Murphy .20 .50
2 Borje Salming 1.00 2.50
3 Mike Walton .20 .50
4 Randy Manery .20 .50
5 Ken Hodge .25 .60
6 Mel Bridgman RC .40 1.00
7 Jerry Korab .20 .50
8 Gilles Gratton .25 .60
9 Andre St.Laurent .20 .50
0 Yvan Cournoyer .40 1.00
1 Phil Russell .20 .50
2 Dennis Hextall .20 .50
3 Lowell MacDonald .20 .50
4 Dennis O'Brien .20 .50
5 Gerry Meehan .20 .50
6 Gilles Meloche .25 .60
7 Wilf Paiement .25 .60
8 Bob MacMillan RC .40 1.00
9 Ian Turnbull .25 .60
0 Rogatien Vachon .40 1.00
1 Nick Beverley .20 .50
2 Rene Robert .25 .60
3 Andre Savard .20 .50
4 Bob Gainey 1.00 2.50
5 Joe Watson .20 .50
6 Billy Smith 1.00 2.50
7 Darcy Rota .20 .50
48 Rick Lapointe RC .20 .50
49 Pierre Jarry .20 .50
50 Syl Apps .20 .50
51 Eric Vail .20 .50
52 Greg Joly .20 .50
53 Don Lever .20 .50
54 Bob Murdoch .20 .50
Seals Right Wing
55 Denis Herron .25 .60
56 Mike Bloom .20 .50
57 Bill Fairbairn .20 .50
58 Fred Stanfield .20 .50
59 Steve Shutt .75 2.00
60 Brad Park .60 1.50
61 Gilles Villemure .25 .60
62 Bert Marshall .20 .50
63 Chuck Lefley .20 .50
64 Simon Nolet .20 .50
65 Reggie Leach RB .25 .60
Most Goals Playoffs
66 Darryl Sittler RB .40 1.00
Most Points Game
67 Bryan Trottier RB 3.00 8.00
Most Points
Season, Rookie
68 Garry Unger RB .25 .60
Most Consecutive
Games& Lifetime
69 Ron Low .25 .60
70 Bobby Clarke 1.50 4.00
71 Michel Bergeron RC .20 .50
72 Ron Stackhouse .20 .50
73 Bill Hogaboam .20 .50
74 Bob Murdoch .20 .50
Kings Defenseman
75 Steve Vickers .20 .50
76 Pit Martin .20 .50
77 Gerry Hart .20 .50
78 Craig Ramsay .20 .50
79 Michel Larocque .25 .60
80 Jean Ratelle .40 1.00
81 Don Saleski .20 .50
82 Bill Clement .40 1.00
83 Dave Burrows .20 .50
84 Wayne Thomas .25 .60
85 John Gould .20 .50
86 Dennis Maruk RC 1.00 2.00
87 Ernie Hicke .20 .50
88 Jim Rutherford .25 .60
89 Dale Tallon .20 .50
90 Rod Gilbert .40 1.00
91 Marcel Dionne 1.25 3.00
92 Chuck Arnason .20 .50
93 Jean Potvin .20 .50
94 Don Luce .20 .50
95 Johnny Bucyk .40 1.00
96 Larry Goodenough .20 .50
97 Mario Tremblay .25 .60
98 Nelson Pyatt .20 .50
99 Brian Glennie .20 .50
100 Tony Esposito .75 2.00
101 Dan Maloney .20 .50
102 Barry Wilkins .20 .50
103 Dean Talafous .20 .50
104 Ed Staniowski .20 .50
105 Dallas Smith .20 .50
106 Jude Drouin .20 .50
107 Pat Hickey .20 .50
108 Jocelyn Guevremont .20 .50
109 Doug Risebrough .40 1.00
110 Reggie Leach .25 .60
111 Dan Bouchard .25 .60
112 Chris Oddleifson .20 .50
113 Rick Hampton .20 .50
114 John Marks .20 .50
115 Bryan Trottier RC 20.00 35.00
116 Checklist 1-132 3.00 6.00
117 Greg Polis .20 .50
118 Peter McNab .40 1.00
119 Jim Roberts .20 .50
120 Gerry Cheevers .75 2.00
121 Rick MacLeish .25 .60
122 Billy Lochead .20 .50
123 Tom Reid .20 .50
124 Rick Kehoe .25 .60
125 Keith Magnuson .20 .50
126 Clark Gillies .40 1.00
127 Rick Middleton .75 2.00
128 Bill Hajt .20 .50
129 Jacques Lemaire .40 1.00
130 Terry O'Reilly .40 1.00
131 Andre Dupont .20 .50
132 Flames Team .75 2.00
(Checklist back)
133 Bruins Team .75 2.00
(Checklist back)
134 Sabres Team .75 2.00
(Checklist back)
135 Seals Team .75 2.00
(Checklist back)
136 Blackhawks Team .75 2.00
(Checklist back)
137 Red Wings Team .75 2.00
(Checklist back)
138 Scouts Team .75 2.00
(Checklist back)
139 Kings Team .75 2.00
(Checklist back)
140 North Stars Team .75 2.00
(Checklist back)
141 Canadiens Team .75 2.00
(Checklist back)
142 Islanders Team .75 2.00
(Checklist back)
143 Rangers Team .75 2.00
(Checklist back)
144 Flyers Team .75 2.00
(Checklist back)
145 Penguins Team .75 2.00
(Checklist back)
146 Blues Team .75 2.00
(Checklist back)
147 Maple Leafs Team .75 2.00
(Checklist back)
148 Canucks Team .75 2.00
(Checklist back)
149 Capitals Team .75 2.00
(Checklist back)
150 Dave Schultz .40 1.00
151 Larry Robinson 1.50 4.00
152 Al Smith .25 .60
153 Bob Nystrom .25 .60
154 Ron Greschner UER .20 .50
(Shown as Penguin on
front should be Ranger)
155 Gregg Sheppard .20 .50
156 Alain Daigle .20 .50
157 Ed Van Impe .20 .50
158 Tim Young RC .25 .60
159 Gary Bergman .20 .50
160 Ed Giacomin .60 1.50
161 Yvon Labre .20 .50
162 Jim Lorentz .20 .50
163 Guy Lafleur 2.50 6.00
164 Tom Bladon .25 .60
165 Wayne Cashman .25 .60
166 Pete Stemkowski .20 .50
167 Grant Mulvey .20 .50
168 Yves Belanger .25 .60
169 Bill Goldsworthy .25 .60
170 Denis Potvin 1.50 4.00
171 Nick Libett .20 .50
172 Michel Plasse .25 .60
173 Lou Nanne .20 .50
174 Tom Lysiak .25 .60
175 Dennis Ververgaert .20 .50
176 Gary Simmons .25 .60
177 Pierre Bouchard .20 .50
178 Bill Barber .60 1.50
179 Darryl Edestrand .20 .50
180 Gilbert Perreault .75 2.00
181 Dave Maloney RC .40 1.00
182 Jean-Paul Parise .20 .50
183 Bobby Sheehan .20 .50
184 Pete Lopresti .25 .60
185 Don Kozak .20 .50
186 Guy Charron .20 .50
187 Stan Gilbertson .20 .50
188 Bill Nyrop .20 .50
189 Bobby Schmautz .20 .50
190 Wayne Stephenson .25 .60
191 Brian Spencer .20 .50
192 Gilles Marotte .20 .50
193 Lorne Henning .20 .50
194 Bob Neely .20 .50
195 Dennis Hull .25 .60
196 Walt McKechnie .20 .50
197 Curt Ridley .20 .50
198 Dwight Bialowas .20 .50
199 Pierre Larouche .40 1.00
200 Ken Dryden 6.00 12.00
201 Ross Lonsberry .20 .50
202 Curt Bennett .20 .50
203 Hartland Monahan .20 .50
204 John Davidson .75 2.00
205 Serge Savard .40 1.00
206 Garry Howatt .20 .50
207 Darryl Sittler 1.25 3.00
208 J.P. Bordeleau .20 .50
209 Henry Boucha .20 .50
210 Richard Martin .25 .60
211 Vic Venasky .20 .50
212 Buster Harvey .20 .50
213 Bobby Orr 10.00 20.00
214 French Connection .75 2.00
Richard Martin
Gilbert Perreault
Rene Robert
215 LCB Line 1.00 2.50
Reggie Leach
Bobby Clarke
Bill Barber
216 Long Island Lightning 1.25 3.00
Clark Gillies
Bryan Trottier
Billy Harris
217 Checking Line .40 1.00
Bob Gainey
Doug Jarvis
Jim Roberts
218 Bicentennial Line .25 .60
Lowell MacDonald
Syl Apps
Jean Pronovost
219 Bob Kelly .20 .50
220 Walt Tkaczuk .25 .60
221 Dave Lewis .20 .50
222 Danny Gare .40 1.00
223 Guy Lapointe .25 .60
224 Hank Nowak .20 .50
225 Stan Mikita 1.00 2.50
226 Vic Hadfield .25 .60
227 Bernie Wolfe .25 .60
228 Bryan Watson .20 .50
229 Ralph Stewart .20 .50
230 Gerry Desjardins .25 .60
231 John Bednarski .20 .50
232 Yvon Lambert .20 .50
233 Orest Kindrachuk .20 .50
234 Don Marcotte .20 .50
235 Bill White .20 .50
236 Red Berenson .25 .60
237 Al MacAdam .20 .50
238 Rick Blight .20 .50
239 Butch Goring .25 .60
240 Cesare Maniago .25 .60
241 Jim Schoenfeld .25 .60
242 Cliff Koroll .20 .50
243 Mickey Redmond .25 .60
244 Rick Chartraw .20 .50
245 Phil Esposito 1.00 2.50
246 Dave Forbes .20 .50
247 Joe Watson .20 .50
248 Ron Schock .20 .50
249 Fred Barrett .20 .50
250 Glenn Resch .75 2.00
251 Ivan Boldirev .20 .50
252 Billy Harris .20 .50
253 Lee Fogolin .20 .50
254 Murray Wilson .20 .50
255 Gilles Gilbert .25 .60
256 Gary Dornhoefer .25 .60
257 Carol Vadnais .25 .60
258 Checklist 133-264 3.00 6.00
259 Errol Thompson .20 .50
260 Garry Unger .25 .60
261 J. Bob Kelly .20 .50
262 Terry Harper .20 .50
263 Blake Dunlop .20 .50
264 Stanley Cup Champs .60 1.50

1976-77 Topps Glossy Inserts

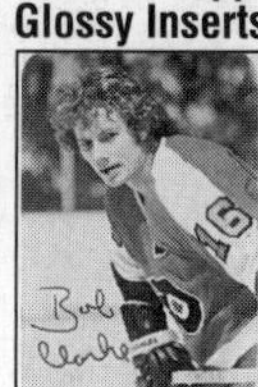

This 22-card insert set was issued with the 1976-77 Topps hockey card set but not with the O-Pee-Chee hockey cards unlike the glossy insert produced "jointly" by Topps and O-Pee-Chee the next year. This set is very similar to (but much more difficult to find than) the glossy insert set of the following year. The cards were printed in the United States. These rounded-corner cards are approximately 2 1/4" by 3 1/4".

COMPLETE SET (22) 40.00 80.00
1 Bobby Clarke 2.00 4.00
2 Brad Park 1.25 2.50
3 Tony Esposito 1.50 3.00
4 Marcel Dionne 2.00 4.00
5 Ken Dryden 7.50 15.00
6 Glenn Resch 1.00 2.00
7 Phil Esposito 2.50 5.00
8 Darryl Sittler 1.50 3.00
9 Gilbert Perreault 1.00 2.00
10 Denis Potvin 2.00 4.00
11 Guy Lafleur 4.00 8.00
12 Bill Barber 1.00 2.00
13 Syl Apps .50 1.00
14 Johnny Bucyk 1.00 2.00
15 Bryan Trottier 7.50 15.00
16 Dennis Hull .50 1.00
17 Guy Lapointe .75 1.50
18 Rod Gilbert 1.25 2.50
19 Richard Martin .75 1.50
20 Bobby Orr 12.50 25.00
21 Reggie Leach .75 1.50
22 Jean Ratelle 1.25 2.50

1977-78 Topps

The 1977-78 Topps set consists of 264 standard-size cards. Cards 203 (Stan Gilbertson) and 255 (Bill Fairbairn) differ from those of O-Pee-Chee. Card fronts have team name and logo, player name and position at the bottom. Yearly statistics including minor league numbers are featured on the back along with a short biography and a cartoon-illustrated fact about the player. After the initial print run, Topps changed the photos on card numbers 131, 138, 149 and 152. Two of the changes (138 and 149) were necessary corrections. Rookie Cards include Mike Milbury and Mike Palmateer.

COMPLETE SET (264) 45.00 90.00
1 Goals Leaders 1.00 2.50
Steve Shutt
Guy Lafleur
Marcel Dionne
2 Assists Leaders .60 1.50
Guy Lafleur
Marcel Dionne
Larry Robinson
Borje Salming
Tim Young
3 Scoring Leaders .75 2.00
Guy Lafleur
Marcel Dionne
Steve Shutt
4 Penalty Min. Leaders .15 .40
Dave(Tiger) Williams
Dennis Polonich
Bob Gassoff
5 Power Play Goals .30 .75
Leaders
Lanny McDonald
Phil Esposito
Tom Williams
6 Goals Against 1.00 2.50
Average Leaders
Michel Larocque
Ken Dryden
Glenn Resch
7 Game Winning .60 1.50
Goals Leaders
Gilbert Perreault
Steve Shutt
Guy Lafleur
Rick MacLeish
Peter McNab
8 Shutouts Leaders 1.25 3.00
Ken Dryden
Rogatien Vachon
Bernie Parent
Dunc Wilson
9 Brian Spencer .10 .25
10 Denis Potvin AS2 .30 .75
11 Nick Fotiu .30 .75
12 Bob Murray .10 .25
13 Pete Lopresti .15 .40
14 J. Bob Kelly .10 .25
15 Rick MacLeish .30 .75
16 Terry Harper .10 .25
17 Willi Plett RC .30 .75
18 Peter McNab .15 .40
19 Wayne Thomas .15 .40
20 Pierre Bouchard .10 .25
21 Dennis Maruk .30 .75
22 Mike Murphy .10 .25
23 Cesare Maniago .15 .40
24 Paul Gardner RC .10 .25
25 Rod Gilbert .30 .75
26 Orest Kindrachuk .10 .25
27 Bill Hajt .10 .25
28 John Davidson .30 .75
29 Jean-Paul Parise .10 .25
30 Larry Robinson AS1 1.25 3.00
31 Yvon Labre .10 .25
32 Walt McKechnie .10 .25
33 Rick Kehoe .15 .40
34 Randy Holt .10 .25
35 Garry Unger .15 .40
36 Lou Nanne .10 .25
37 Dan Bouchard .15 .40
38 Darryl Sittler .75 2.00
39 Bob Murdoch .10 .25
40 Jean Ratelle .30 .75
41 Dave Maloney .10 .25
42 Danny Gare .30 .75
43 Jimmy Watson .10 .25
44 Tom Williams .10 .25
45 Serge Savard .30 .75
46 Derek Sanderson .30 .75
47 John Marks .10 .25
48 Al Cameron .10 .25
49 Dean Talafous .10 .25
50 Glenn Resch .30 .75
51 Ron Schock .10 .25
52 Gary Croteau .10 .25
53 Gerry Meehan .10 .25
54 Ed Staniowski .10 .25
55 Phil Esposito .75 2.00
56 Dennis Ververgaert .10 .25
57 Rick Wilson .10 .25
58 Jim Lorentz .10 .25
59 Bobby Schmautz .10 .25
60 Guy Lapointe AS2 .15 .40
61 Ivan Boldirev .10 .25
62 Bob Nystrom .10 .25
63 Rick Hampton .10 .25
64 Jack Valiquette .10 .25
65 Bernie Parent .60 1.50
66 Dave Burrows .10 .25
67 Butch Goring .15 .40
68 Checklist 1-132 2.00 4.00
69 Murray Wilson .10 .25
70 Ed Giacomin .30 .75
71 Flames Team .50 1.25
(checklist back)
72 Bruins Team .50 1.25
(checklist back)
73 Sabres Team .50 1.25
(checklist back)
74 Blackhawks Team .50 1.25
(checklist back)
75 Barons Team .50 1.25
(checklist back)
76 Rockies Team .50 1.25
(checklist back)
77 Red Wings Team .50 1.25
(checklist back)
78 Kings Team .50 1.25
(checklist back)
79 North Stars Team .50 1.25
(checklist back)
80 Canadiens Team .50 1.25
(checklist back)
81 Islanders Team .50 1.25
(checklist back)
82 Rangers Team .50 1.25
(checklist back)
83 Flyers Team .50 1.25
(checklist back)
84 Penguins Team .50 1.25
(checklist back)
85 Blues Team .50 1.25
(checklist back)
86 Maple Leafs Team .50 1.25
(checklist back)
87 Canucks Team .50 1.25
(checklist back)
88 Capitals Team .50 1.25
(checklist back)
89 Keith Magnuson .10 .25
90 Walt Tkaczuk .15 .40
91 Bill Nyrop .10 .25
92 Michel Plasse .15 .40
93 Bob Bourne .15 .40
94 Lee Fogolin .10 .25
95 Gregg Sheppard .10 .25
96 Hartland Monahan .10 .25
97 Curt Bennett .10 .25
98 Bob Dailey .10 .25
99 Bill Goldsworthy .15 .40
100 Ken Dryden AS1 3.00 8.00
101 Grant Mulvey .10 .25
102 Pierre Larouche .30 .75
103 Nick Libett .10 .25
104 Rick Smith .10 .25
105 Bryan Trottier 4.00 10.00
106 Pierre Jarry .10 .25
107 Red Berenson .15 .40
108 Jim Schoenfeld .15 .40
109 Gilles Meloche .15 .40
110 Lanny McDonald AS2 .60 1.50
111 Don Lever .10 .25
112 Greg Polis .10 .25
113 Gary Sargent RC .10 .25
114 Earl Anderson .10 .25
115 Bobby Clarke 1.25 3.00
116 Dave Lewis .10 .25
117 Darcy Rota .10 .25
118 Andre Savard .10 .25
119 Denis Herron .15 .40
120 Steve Shutt AS1 .30 .75
121 Mel Bridgman .10 .25
122 Buster Harvey .10 .25
123 Roland Eriksson .10 .25
124 Dale Tallon .10 .25
125 Gilles Gilbert .15 .40
126 Billy Harris .10 .25
127 Tom Lysiak .15 .40
128 Jerry Korab .10 .25
129 Bob Gainey .60 1.50
130 Wilf Paiement .15 .40
131A Tom Bladon ERR 1.00 2.00
Photo actually Bob Dailey
131B Tom Bladon COR .10 .25
132 Ernie Hicke .10 .25
133 J.P. LeBlanc .10 .25
134 Mike Milbury RC 2.50 5.00
135 Pit Martin .10 .25
136 Steve Vickers .10 .25
137 Don Awrey .10 .25
138A Bernie Wolfe ERR 1.00 2.00
(Photo actually
Al MacAdam looking
straight ahead)
138B Bernie Wolfe COR .10 .25
139 Doug Jarvis .30 .75
140 Borje Salming AS1 .60 1.50
141 Bob MacMillan .10 .25
142 Wayne Stephenson .15 .40
143 Dave Forbes .10 .25
144 Jean Potvin .10 .25
145 Guy Charron .10 .25
146 Cliff Koroll .10 .25
147 Danny Grant .15 .40
148 Bill Hogaboam UER .10 .25
(Photo actually
Michel Bergeron)
149A Al MacAdam ERR 1.00 2.00
(Photo actually
Bernie Wolfe&
looking left)
149B Al MacAdam COR .10 .25
150 Gerry Desjardins .15 .40
151 Yvon Lambert .10 .25
152A Rick Lapointe ERR 1.00 2.00
Photo actually Larr Goodenough
152B Rick Lapointe COR .10 .25
153 Ed Westfall .15 .40
154 Carol Vadnais .10 .25
155 Johnny Bucyk .30 .75
156 J.P. Bordeleau .10 .25
157 Ron Stackhouse .10 .25
158 Glen Sharpley .10 .25
159 Michel Bergeron .10 .25
160 Rogatien Vachon AS2 .30 .75
161 Fred Stanfield .10 .25
162 Gerry Hart .10 .25
163 Mario Tremblay .15 .40
164 Andre Dupont .10 .25
165 Don Marcotte .10 .25
166 Wayne Dillon .10 .25
167 Claude Larose .10 .25
168 Eric Vail .10 .25
169 Tom Edur .10 .25
170 Tony Esposito .60 1.50
171 Andre St.Laurent .10 .25
172 Dan Maloney .10 .25
173 Dennis O'Brien .10 .25
174 Blair Chapman .10 .25
175 Dennis Kearns .10 .25
176 Wayne Merrick .10 .25
177 Michel Larocque .15 .40
178 Bob Kelly .10 .25
179 Dave Farrish .10 .25
180 Richard Martin AS2 .30 .75
181 Gary Doak .10 .25
182 Jude Drouin .10 .25
183 Barry Dean .10 .25
184 Gary Smith .15 .40
185 Reggie Leach .30 .75
186 Ian Turnbull .15 .40
187 Vic Venasky .10 .25
188 Wayne Bianchin .10 .25
189 Doug Risebrough .15 .40
190 Brad Park .30 .75
191 Craig Ramsay .10 .25
192 Ken Hodge .15 .40
193 Phil Myre .15 .40
194 Garry Howatt .10 .25
195 Stan Mikita .75 2.00
196 Garnet Bailey .10 .25
197 Dennis Hextall .10 .25
198 Nick Beverley .10 .25
199 Larry Patey .10 .25
200 Guy Lafleur AS1 2.00 5.00
201 Don Edwards RC 2.50 2.50
202 Gary Dornhoefer .15 .40
203 Stan Gilbertson .10 .25
204 Alex Pirus .10 .25
205 Peter Mahovlich .15 .40
206 Bert Marshall .10 .25
207 Gilles Gratton .15 .40
208 Alain Daigle .10 .25
209 Chris Oddleifson .10 .25
210 Gilbert Perreault AS2 .60 1.50
211 Mike Palmateer RC 2.50 5.00
212 Billy Lochead .10 .25
213 Dick Redmond .10 .25
214 Guy Lafleur RB .60 1.50
Most Points&
RW& Season
215 Ian Turnbull RB .10 .25
Most Goals&
Defenseman& Game
216 Guy Lafleur RB .60 1.50
Longest Point
Scoring Streak
217 Steve Shutt RB .30 .75
Most Goals&
LW& Season
218 Guy Lafleur RB .60 1.50
Most Assists&
RW& Season
219 Lorne Henning .10 .25
220 Terry O'Reilly .30 .75
221 Pat Hickey .10 .25
222 Rene Robert .15 .40
223 Tim Young .15 .40
224 Dunc Wilson .15 .40
225 Dennis Hull .15 .40
226 Rod Seiling .15 .40
227 Bill Barber .30 .75
228 Dennis Polonich .10 .25
229 Billy Smith .60 1.50
230 Yvan Cournoyer .30 .75
231 Don Luce .10 .25
232 Mike McEwen RC .15 .40
233 Don Saleski .10 .25
234 Wayne Cashman .30 .75
235 Phil Russell .10 .25
236 Mike Corrigan .10 .25
237 Guy Chouinard .15 .40
238 Steve Jensen .10 .25
239 Jim Rutherford .15 .40
240 Marcel Dionne AS1 1.25 2.50
241 Rejean Houle .10 .25
242 Jocelyn Guevremont .10 .25
243 Jim Harrison .10 .25
244 Don Murdoch .10 .25
245 Rick Green RC .30 .75
246 Rick Middleton .30 .75
247 Joe Watson .10 .25
248 Syl Apps .10 .25
249 Checklist 133-264 2.00 4.00
250 Clark Gillies .30 .75
251 Bobby Orr 9.00 15.00
252 Nelson Pyatt .10 .25
253 Gary McAdam .10 .25
254 Jacques Lemaire .30 .75
255 Bill Fairbairn .10 .25
256 Ron Greschner .15 .40
257 Ross Lonsberry .10 .25
258 Dave Gardner .10 .25
259 Rick Blight .10 .25
260 Gerry Cheevers .30 .75
261 Jean Pronovost .15 .40
262 Semi-Finals .15 .40
Canadiens Skate
Past Islanders
263 Semi-Finals .15 .40
Bruins Advance
to Finals
264 Finals .30 .75
Canadiens Win
20th Stanley Cup

1977-78 Topps/O-Pee-Chee Glossy

This set of 22 numbered cards was issued with either square or round corners as an insert with both the Topps and O-Pee-Chee hockey cards of 1977-78. Cards were numbered on the back and measure 2 1/4" by 3 1/4". They are essentially the same as the O-Pee-Chee insert issue of the same year. The O-Pee-Chee inserts have the same card numbers and pictures, same values, but different copyright lines on the reverses. The cards are priced below for the round cornered version; the square cornered cards are worth approximately 10 percent more than the prices below.

COMPLETE SET (22) 7.50 15.00
1 Wayne Cashman .20 .40
2 Gerry Cheevers .75 1.50
3 Bobby Clarke .75 1.50
4 Marcel Dionne .75 1.50
5 Ken Dryden 2.00 4.00
6 Clark Gillies .20 .40
7 Guy Lafleur 1.25 2.50
8 Reggie Leach .18 .35
9 Rick MacLeish .25 .50
10 Dave Maloney .13 .25
11 Richard Martin .20 .40
12 Don Murdoch .13 .25
13 Brad Park .38 .75
14 Gilbert Perreault .50 1.00
15 Denis Potvin .75 1.50
16 Jean Ratelle .38 .75
17 Glenn Resch .38 .75
18 Larry Robinson .75 1.50
19 Steve Shutt .38 .75
20 Darryl Sittler .63 1.25
21 Rogatien Vachon .38 .75
22 Tim Young .13 .25

1978-79 Topps

The 1978-79 Topps set consists of 264 standard-size cards. Card fronts have team name, logo and player position in the top left corner. The player's name is within the top border. A short biography, yearly statistics including minor leagues and a facsimile autograph are included on the back.

COMPLETE SET (264) 40.00 80.00
1 Mike Bossy HL 4.00 8.00
Goals by Rookie
2 Phil Esposito HL .40 1.00
29th Hat Trick
3 Guy Lafleur HL .40 1.00
Scores Against
Every Team
4 Darryl Sittler HL .25 .60
Goals In Nine
Straight Games
5 Garry Unger HL .05 .15
803 Consecutive Games
6 Gary Edwards .08 .25
7 Rick Blight .05 .15
8 Larry Patey .05 .15
9 Craig Ramsay .05 .15
10 Bryan Trottier AS1 2.00 5.00
11 Don Murdoch .05 .15
12 Phil Russell .05 .15
13 Doug Jarvis .08 .25
14 Gene Carr .05 .15
15 Bernie Parent .40 1.00

16 Perry Miller .05 .15
17 Kent-Erik Andersson .05 .15
18 Gregg Sheppard .05 .15
19 Dennis Owchar .05 .15
20 Rogatien Vachon .25 .60
21 Dan Maloney .05 .15
22 Guy Charron .05 .15
23 Dick Redmond .05 .15
24 Checklist 1-132 1.00 2.50
25 Anders Hedberg .08 .25
26 Mel Bridgman .08 .25
27 Lee Fogolin .05 .15
28 Gilles Meloche .08 .25
29 Garry Howatt .05 .15
30 Darryl Sittler AS2 .60 1.50
31 Curt Bennett .05 .15
32 Andre St.Laurent .05 .15
33 Blair Chapman .05 .15
34 Keith Magnuson .05 .15
35 Pierre Larouche .25 .60
36 Michel Plasse .08 .25
37 Gary Sargent .05 .15
38 Mike Walton .05 .15
39 Robert Picard RC .05 .15
40 Terry O'Reilly AS2 .08 .25
41 Dave Farrish .05 .15
42 Gary McAdam .05 .15
43 Joe Watson .05 .15
44 Yves Belanger .08 .25
45 Steve Jensen .05 .15
46 Bob Stewart .05 .15
47 Darcy Rota .05 .15
48 Dennis Hextall .05 .15
49 Bert Marshall .05 .15
50 Ken Dryden AS1 2.50 6.00
51 Peter Mahovlich .08 .25
52 Dennis Ververgaert .05 .15
53 Inge Hammarstrom .05 .15
54 Doug Favell .08 .25
55 Steve Vickers .05 .15
56 Syl Apps .05 .15
57 Errol Thompson .05 .15
58 Don Luce .05 .15
59 Mike Milbury .25 .60
60 Yvan Cournoyer .25 .60
61 Kirk Bowman .05 .15
62 Billy Smith .25 .60
63 Goal Leaders 1.50 4.00
Guy Lafleur
Mike Bossy
Steve Shutt
64 Assist Leaders .60 1.50
Bryan Trottier
Guy Lafleur
Darryl Sittler
65 Scoring Leaders .60 1.50
Guy Lafleur
Bryan Trottier
Darryl Sittler
66 Penalty Minutes .10 .30
Leaders
Dave Schultz
Dave(Tiger) Williams
Dennis Polonich
67 Power Play Goal 1.00 2.50
Leaders
Mike Bossy
Phil Esposito
Steve Shutt
68 Goals Against 1.00 2.50
Average Leaders
Ken Dryden
Bernie Parent
Gilles Gilbert
69 Game Winning .50 1.25
Goal Leaders
Guy Lafleur
Bill Barber
Darryl Sittler
Bob Bourne
70 Shutout Leaders 1.00 2.50
Bernie Parent
Ken Dryden
Don Edwards
Tony Esposito
Mike Palmateer
71 Bob Kelly .05 .15
72 Ron Stackhouse .05 .15
73 Wayne Dillon .05 .15
74 Jim Rutherford .08 .25
75 Stan Mikita .60 1.50
76 Bob Gainey .40 1.00
77 Gerry Hart .05 .15
78 Lanny McDonald .40 1.00
79 Brad Park .40 1.00
80 Richard Martin .25 .60
81 Bernie Wolfe .08 .25
82 Bob MacMillan .05 .15
83 Brad Maxwell .05 .15
84 Mike Fidler .05 .15
85 Carol Vadnais .05 .15
86 Don Lever .05 .15
87 Phil Myre .08 .25
88 Paul Gardner .05 .15
89 Bob Murray .05 .15
90 Guy Lafleur AS1 1.50 4.00
91 Bob Murdoch .05 .15
92 Ron Ellis .08 .25
93 Jude Drouin .05 .15
94 Jocelyn Guevremont .05 .15
95 Gilles Gilbert .08 .25
96 Bob Sirois .05 .15
97 Tom Lysiak .08 .25
98 Andre Dupont .05 .15
99 Per-Olov Brasar .05 .15
100 Phil Esposito .75 2.00
101 J.P. Bordeleau .05 .15
102 Pierre Mondou RC .25 .60
103 Wayne Bianchin .05 .15
104 Dennis O'Brien .05 .15
105 Glenn Resch .25 .60
106 Dennis Polonich .05 .15
107 Kris Manery .05 .15
108 Bill Hajt .05 .15
109 Jere Gillis .05 .15
110 Garry Unger .08 .25
111 Nick Beverley .05 .15
112 Pat Hickey .05 .15
113 Rick Middleton .25 .60
114 Orest Kindrachuk .05 .15
115 Mike Bossy RC 30.00 60.00
116 Pierre Bouchard .05 .15
117 Alain Daigle .05 .15
118 Terry Martin .05 .15
119 Tom Edur .05 .15
120 Marcel Dionne .75 2.00
121 Barry Beck RC .40 1.00
122 Billy Lochead .05 .15
123 Paul Harrison .08 .25
124 Wayne Cashman .25 .60
125 Rick MacLeish .25 .60
126 Bob Bourne .08 .25
127 Ian Turnbull .05 .15
128 Gerry Meehan .05 .15
129 Eric Vail .05 .15
130 Gilbert Perreault .25 .60
131 Bob Dailey .05 .15
132 Dale McCourt RC .25 .60
133 John Wensink RC .25 .60
134 Bill Nyrop .05 .15
135 Ivan Boldirev .05 .15
136 Lucien DeBlois RC .05 .15
137 Brian Spencer .05 .15
138 Tim Young .05 .15
139 Ron Sedlbauer .05 .15
140 Gerry Cheevers .40 1.00
141 Dennis Maruk .08 .25
142 Barry Dean .05 .15
143 Bernie Federko RC 3.00 6.00
144 Stefan Persson RC .05 .15
145 Wilf Paiement .08 .25
146 Dale Tallon .05 .15
147 Yvon Lambert .05 .15
148 Greg Joly .05 .15
149 Dean Talafous .05 .15
150 Don Edwards AS2 .05 .15
151 Butch Goring .08 .25
152 Tom Bladon .05 .15
153 Bob Nystrom .05 .15
154 Ron Greschner .08 .25
155 Jean Ratelle .25 .60
156 Russ Anderson .05 .15
157 John Marks .05 .15
158 Michel Larocque .08 .25
159 Paul Woods .05 .15
160 Mike Palmateer .08 .25
161 Jim Lorentz .05 .15
162 Dave Lewis .05 .15
163 Harvey Bennett .05 .15
164 Rick Smith .05 .15
165 Reggie Leach .25 .60
166 Wayne Thomas .08 .25
167 Dave Forbes .05 .15
168 Doug Wilson RC 3.00 6.00
169 Dan Bouchard .08 .25
170 Steve Shutt AS2 .25 .60
171 Mike Kaszycki .05 .15
172 Dennis Herron .08 .25
173 Rick Bowness .08 .25
174 Rick Hampton .05 .15
175 Glen Sharpley .05 .15
176 Bill Barber .25 .60
177 Ron Duguay RC .75 2.00
178 Jim Schoenfeld .08 .25
179 Pierre Plante .05 .15
180 Jacques Lemaire .25 .60
181 Stan Jonathan .05 .15
182 Billy Harris .05 .15
183 Chris Oddleifson .05 .15
184 Jean Pronovost .08 .25
185 Fred Barrett .05 .15
186 Ross Lonsberry .05 .15
187 Mike McEwen .05 .15
188 Rene Robert .08 .25
189 J. Bob Kelly .05 .15
190 Serge Savard AS2 .08 .25
191 Dennis Kearns .05 .15
192 Flames Team .20 .50
(checklist back)
193 Bruins Team .20 .50
(checklist back)
194 Sabres Team .20 .50
(checklist back)
195 Blackhawks Team .20 .50
(checklist back)
196 Rockies Team .20 .50
(checklist back)
197 Red Wings Team .20 .50
(checklist back)
198 Kings Team .20 .50
(checklist back)
199 North Stars Team .20 .50
(checklist back)
200 Canadiens Team .20 .50
(checklist back)
201 Islanders Team .20 .50
(checklist back)
202 Rangers Team .20 .50
(checklist back)
203 Flyers Team .20 .50
(checklist back)
204 Penguins Team .20 .50
(checklist back)
205 Blues Team .20 .50
(checklist back)
206 Maple Leafs Team .20 .50
(checklist back)
207 Canucks Team .20 .50
(checklist back)
208 Capitals Team .20 .50
(checklist back)
209 Danny Gare .08 .25
210 Larry Robinson AS1 .60 1.50
211 John Davidson .25 .60
212 Peter McNab .08 .25
213 Rick Kehoe .05 .15
214 Terry Harper .05 .15
215 Bobby Clarke .75 2.00
216 Bryan Maxwell UER .05 .15
(Photo actually
Brad Maxwell)
217 Ted Bulley .05 .15
218 Red Berenson .08 .25
219 Ron Grahame .08 .25
220 Clark Gillies AS1 .08 .25
221 Dave Maloney .05 .15
222 Derek Smith .05 .15
223 Wayne Stephenson .08 .25
224 John Van Boxmeer .05 .15
225 Dave Schultz .08 .25
226 Reed Larson RC .25 .60
227 Rejean Houle .05 .15
228 Doug Hicks .05 .15
229 Mike Murphy .05 .15
230 Pete Lopresti .08 .25
231 Jerry Korab .08 .25
232 Ed Westfall .08 .25
233 Greg Malone .05 .15
234 Paul Holmgren .25 .60
235 Walt Tkaczuk .08 .25
236 Don Marcotte .05 .15
237 Ron Low .08 .25
238 Rick Chartraw .05 .15
239 Cliff Koroll .05 .15
240 Borje Salming AS1 .40 1.00
241 Roland Eriksson .05 .15
242 Ric Seiling .05 .15
243 Jim Bedard .08 .25
244 Peter Lee .08 .25
245 Denis Potvin AS2 .60 1.50
246 Greg Polis .05 .15
247 Jimmy Watson .05 .15
248 Bobby Schmautz .05 .15
249 Doug Risebrough .08 .25
250 Tony Esposito .50 1.25
251 Nick Libett .05 .15
252 Ron Zanussi .05 .15
253 Andre Savard .05 .15
254 Dave Burrows .05 .15
255 Ulf Nilsson .25 .60
256 Richard Mulhern .05 .15
257 Don Saleski .05 .15
258 Wayne Merrick .05 .15
259 Checklist 133-264 1.00 2.50
260 Guy Lapointe .08 .25
261 Grant Mulvey .05 .15
262 Stanley Cup: Semis .10 .30
Canadiens sweep
Maple Leafs
263 Stanley Cup: Semis .10 .30
Bruins skate
past Flyers
264 Stanley Cup: Finals .40 1.00
Canadiens win 3rd
Straight Cup

1978-79 Topps Team Inserts

This set of 17 team inserts measures the standard size. Each team insert consists of two decals: a team logo and a second decal consisting of three mini-decals. The mini-decals picture hockey equipment (mask, stick(s), or puck), a hockey word (center, defense, goal!, goalie, score! or wing), and a number between zero and nine. The backs are blank. Several different combinations of the stickers are known to exist.

COMPLETE SET (17) 7.50 15.00
1 Atlanta Flames .75 1.50
2 Boston Bruins .75 1.50
3 Buffalo Sabres .50 1.00
4 Chicago Blackhawks .75 1.50
5 Colorado Rockies .75 1.50
6 Detroit Red Wings .75 1.50
7 Los Angeles Kings .50 1.00
8 Minnesota North Stars .50 1.00
9 Montreal Canadiens .75 1.50
10 New York Islanders .50 1.00
11 New York Rangers .75 1.50
12 Philadelphia Flyers .50 1.00
13 Pittsburgh Penguins .50 1.00
14 St. Louis Blues .50 1.00
15 Toronto Maple Leafs .75 1.50
16 Vancouver Canucks .50 1.00
17 Washington Capitals .50 1.00

1979-80 Topps

The 1979-80 Topps set consists of 264 standard-size cards. Card numbers 81 and 82 (Stanley Cup Playoffs), 163 (Ulf Nilsson RB) and 261 (NHL Entries) differ from those of O-Pee-Chee. Unopened packs consist of ten cards plus a piece of bubble gum. The fronts contain a blue border that is prone to chipping. The player's name, team and position are at the top with team logo at the bottom. Career and 1978-79 statistics, short biography and a cartoon-illustrated fact about the player appear on the back. Included in this set are players from the four remaining WHA franchises that were absorbed by the NHL. The franchises are the Edmonton Oilers, Hartford Whalers, Quebec Nordiques and Winnipeg Jets. The set features the Rookie Card of Wayne Gretzky and the last cards of a Hall of Fame crop including Gordie Howe, Bobby Hull, Ken Dryden and Stan Mikita.

COMPLETE SET (264) 400.00 600.00
1 Goal Leaders 1.25 3.00
Mike Bossy
Marcel Dionne
Guy Lafleur
2 Assist Leaders .60 1.50
Bryan Trottier
Guy Lafleur
Marcel Dionne
Bob MacMillan
3 Scoring Leaders .60 1.50
Bryan Trottier
Marcel Dionne
Guy Lafleur
4 Penalty Minutes .15 .40
Leaders
Dave(Tiger) Williams
Randy Holt
Dave Schultz
5 Power Play .75 2.00
Goal Leaders
Mike Bossy
Marcel Dionne
Paul Gardner
Lanny McDonald
6 Goals Against 1.00 2.50
Average Leaders
Ken Dryden
Glenn Resch
Bernie Parent
7 Game Winning 1.00 2.50
Goals Leaders
Guy Lafleur
Mike Bossy
Bryan Trottier
Jean Pronovost
Ted Bulley
8A Shutout Leaders ERR 3.00 8.00
Ken Dryden
Tony Esposito
Mario Lessard
Mike Palmateer
Bernie Parent
(Palmateer and Lessard
photos switched)
8B Shutout Leaders COR 1.25 3.00
Ken Dryden
Tony Esposito
Mario Lessard
Mike Palmateer
Bernie Parent
9 Greg Malone .15 .40
10 Rick Middleton .25 .60
11 Greg Smith .15 .40
12 Rene Robert .25 .60
13 Doug Risebrough .25 .60
14 Bob Kelly .15 .40
15 Walt Tkaczuk .25 .60
16 John Marks .15 .40
17 Willie Huber .15 .40
18 Wayne Gretzky RC UER 250.00 550.00
(Games played should
be 80 not 60)
19 Ron Sedlbauer .15 .40
20 Glenn Resch AS2 .25 .60
21 Blair Chapman .15 .40
22 Ron Zanussi .15 .40
23 Brad Park .25 .60
24 Yvon Lambert .15 .40
25 Andre Savard .15 .40
26 Jimmy Watson .15 .40
27 Hal Philipoff .15 .40
28 Dan Bouchard .25 .60
29 Bob Sirois .15 .40
30 Ulf Nilsson .25 .60
31 Mike Murphy .15 .40
32 Stefan Persson .15 .40
33 Garry Unger .25 .60
34 Rejean Houle .15 .40
35 Barry Beck .25 .60
36 Tim Young .15 .40
37 Rick Dudley .15 .40
38 Wayne Stephenson .25 .60
39 Peter McNab .25 .60
40 Borje Salming AS2 .25 .60
41 Tom Lysiak .15 .40
42 Don Maloney RC .40 1.00
43 Mike Rogers .25 .60
44 Dave Lewis .15 .40
45 Peter Lee .15 .40
46 Marty Howe .25 .60
47 Serge Bernier .15 .40
48 Paul Woods .15 .40
49 Bob Sauve .25 .60
50 Larry Robinson AS1 .60 1.50
51 Tom Gorence .15 .40
52 Gary Sargent .15 .40
53 Thomas Gradin RC .40 1.00
54 Dean Talafous .15 .40
55 Bob Murray .15 .40
56 Bob Bourne .25 .60
57 Larry Patey .15 .40
58 Ross Lonsberry .15 .40
59 Rick Smith .15 .40
60 Guy Chouinard .25 .60
61 Danny Gare .25 .60
62 Jim Bedard .25 .60
63 Dale McCourt .15 .40
64 Steve Payne RC .25 .60
65 Pat Hughes .15 .40
66 Mike McEwen .15 .40
67 Reg Kerr .15 .40
68 Walt McKechnie .15 .40
69 Michel Plasse .25 .60
70 Denis Potvin AS1 .40 1.00
71 Dave Dryden .25 .60
72 Gary McAdam .15 .40
73 Andre St.Laurent .15 .40
74 Jerry Korab .15 .40
75 Rick MacLeish .40 1.00
76 Dennis Kearns .15 .40
77 Jean Pronovost .25 .60
78 Ron Greschner .25 .60
79 Wayne Cashman .40 1.00
80 Tony Esposito .40 1.00
81 Cup Semi-Finals .15 .40
Canadiens squeak
past Bruins
82 Cup Semi-Finals .15 .40
Rangers upset
Islanders in Six
83 Stanley Cup Finals .15 .40
Canadiens Make It
Four Straight Cups
84 Brian Sutter .75 2.00
85 Gerry Cheevers .40 1.00
86 Pat Hickey .15 .40
87 Mike Kaszycki .15 .40
88 Grant Mulvey .15 .40
89 Derek Smith .15 .40
90 Steve Shutt .40 1.00
91 Robert Picard .15 .40
92 Dan Labraaten .15 .40
93 Glen Sharpley .15 .40
94 Denis Herron .25 .60
95 Reggie Leach .40 1.00
96 John Van Boxmeer .15 .40
97 Dave(Tiger) Williams .25 .60
98 Butch Goring .25 .60
99 Don Marcotte .15 .40
100 Bryan Trottier AS1 1.00 2.50
101 Serge Savard AS2 .40 1.00
102 Cliff Koroll .15 .40
103 Gary Smith .25 .60
104 Al MacAdam .15 .40
105 Don Edwards .25 .60
106 Errol Thompson .15 .40
107 Andre Lacroix .25 .60
108 Marc Tardif .25 .60
109 Rick Kehoe .25 .60
110 John Davidson .25 .60
111 Behn Wilson RC .15 .40
112 Doug Jarvis .25 .60
113 Tom Rowe .15 .40
114 Mike Milbury .25 .60
115 Billy Harris .15 .40
116 Greg Fox .15 .40
117 Curt Fraser RC .15 .40
118 Jean-Paul Parise .15 .40
119 Ric Seiling .15 .40
120 Darryl Sittler .40 1.00
121 Rick Lapointe .15 .40
122 Jim Rutherford .25 .60
123 Mario Tremblay .25 .60
124 Randy Carlyle .40 1.00
125 Bobby Clarke .60 1.50
126 Wayne Thomas .25 .60
127 Ivan Boldirev .15 .40
128 Ted Bulley .15 .40
129 Dick Redmond .15 .40
130 Clark Gillies AS1 .25 .60
131 Checklist 1-132 2.00 4.00
132 Vaclav Nedomansky .15 .40
133 Richard Mulhern .15 .40
134 Dave Schultz .25 .60
135 Guy Lapointe .25 .60
136 Gilles Meloche .25 .60
137 Randy Pierce UER .15 .40
(Photo actually
Ron Delorme)
138 Cam Connor .15 .40
139 George Ferguson .15 .40
140 Bill Barber .25 .60
141 Mike Walton .15 .40
142 Wayne Babych RC .15 .40
143 Phil Russell .15 .40
144 Bobby Schmautz .15 .40
145 Carol Vadnais .15 .40
146 John Tonelli RC 2.00 4.00
147 Peter Marsh .15 .40
148 Thommie Bergman .15 .40
149 Richard Martin .40 1.00
150 Ken Dryden AS1 2.00 5.00
151 Kris Manery .15 .40
152 Guy Charron .15 .40
153 Lanny McDonald .25 .60
154 Ron Stackhouse .15 .40
155 Stan Mikita .60 1.50
156 Paul Holmgren .25 .60
157 Perry Miller .15 .40
158 Gary Croteau .15 .40
159 Dave Maloney .15 .40
160 Marcel Dionne AS2 .75 2.00
161 Mike Bossy RB 1.00 2.50
Most Goals
RW Season
162 Don Maloney RB .15 .40
Rookie Most Points
Playoff Series
163 Ulf Nilsson RB .15 .40
Highest Scoring
Percentage Season
164 Brad Park RB .15 .40
Most Career Playoff
Goals Defenseman
165 Bryan Trottier RB .40 1.00
Most Points, Period
166 Al Hill .15 .40
167 Gary Bromley .25 .60
168 Don Murdoch .15 .40
169 Wayne Merrick .15 .40
170 Bob Gainey .40 1.00
171 Jim Schoenfeld .25 .60
172 Gregg Sheppard .15 .40
173 Dan Bolduc .15 .40
174 Blake Dunlop .15 .40
175 Gordie Howe 14.00 20.00
176 Richard Brodeur .25 .60
177 Tom Younghans .15 .40
178 Andre Dupont .15 .40
179 Ed Johnstone .15 .40
180 Gilbert Perreault .40 1.00
181 Bob Lorimer .15 .40
182 John Wensink .15 .40
183 Lee Fogolin .15 .40
184 Greg Carroll .15 .40
185 Bobby Hull 10.00 15.00
186 Harold Snepsts .15 .40
187 Peter Mahovlich .25 .60
188 Eric Vail .15 .40
189 Phil Myre .25 .60
190 Wilf Paiement .15 .40
191 Charlie Simmer RC 2.00 4.00
192 Per-Olov Brasar .15 .40
193 Lorne Henning .15 .40
194 Don Luce .15 .40
195 Steve Vickers .15 .40
196 Bob Miller .15 .40
197 Mike Palmateer .25 .60
198 Nick Libett .15 .40
199 Pat Ribble .15 .40
200 Guy Lafleur AS1 1.25 3.00
201 Mel Bridgman .25 .60
202 Morris Lukowich RC .15 .40
203 Don Lever .15 .40
204 Tom Bladon .15 .40
205 Garry Howatt .15 .40
206 Bobby Smith RC 2.00 4.00
207 Craig Ramsay .25 .60
208 Ron Duguay .25 .60
209 Gilles Gilbert .25 .60
210 Bob MacMillan .15 .40
211 Pierre Mondou .15 .40
212 J.P. Bordeleau .15 .40
213 Reed Larson .25 .60
214 Dennis Ververgaert .15 .40
215 Bernie Federko .40 1.00
216 Mark Howe .75 2.00
217 Bob Nystrom .15 .40
218 Orest Kindrachuk .15 .40
219 Mike Fidler .15 .40
220 Phil Esposito .40 1.00
221 Bill Hajt .15 .40
222 Mark Napier .25 .60
223 Dennis Maruk .25 .60
224 Dennis Polonich .15 .40
225 Jean Ratelle .25 .60
226 Bob Dailey .15 .40
227 Alain Daigle .15 .40
228 Ian Turnbull .15 .40
229 Jack Valiquette .15 .40
230 Mike Bossy AS2 5.00 10.00
231 Brad Maxwell .15 .40
232 Dave Taylor 2.00 5.00
233 Pierre Larouche .40 1.00
234 Rod Schutt .15 .40
235 Rogatien Vachon .25 .60
236 Ryan Walter RC .40 1.00
237 Checklist 133-264 2.00 4.00
238 Terry O'Reilly .25 .60
239 Real Cloutier .25 .60
240 Anders Hedberg .25 .60
241 Ken Linseman RC 1.00 2.50
242 Billy Smith .25 .60
243 Rick Chartraw .15 .40
244 Flames Team .60 1.50
(checklist back)
245 Bruins Team .60 1.50
(checklist back)
246 Sabres Team .60 1.50
(checklist back)
247 Blackhawks Team .60 1.50
(checklist back)
248 Rockies Team .60 1.50
(checklist back)
249 Red Wings Team .60 1.50
(checklist back)
250 Kings Team .60 1.50
(checklist back)
251 North Stars Team .60 1.50
(checklist back)
252 Canadiens Team .60 1.50
(checklist back)
253 Islanders Team .60 1.50
(checklist back)
254 Rangers Team .60 1.50
(checklist back)
255 Flyers Team .60 1.50
(checklist back)
256 Penguins Team .60 1.50
(checklist back)
257 Blues Team .60 1.50
(checklist back)
258 Maple Leafs Team .60 1.50
(checklist back)
259 Canucks Team .60 1.50
(checklist back)
260 Capitals Team .60 1.50
(checklist back)
261 New NHL Entries 7.00 12.00
(checklist back)
262 Jean Hamel .15 .40
263 Stan Jonathan .15 .40
264 Russ Anderson .40 1.00

1979-80 Topps Team Inserts

This set of 21 team inserts measures the standard size, 2 1/2" by 3 1/2". They were issued one per wax pack. Each team insert consists of two decals: a team logo decal, and a second decal that is subdivided into three mini-decals. The three mini-decals picture a pair of hockey sticks, a hockey word (goal, wing, score, defense), and a one-digit number. The horizontally oriented back has an offer for personalized trading cards which expired 12/31/80.

COMPLETE SET (21) 9.00 18.00
1 Atlanta Flames .75 1.50
2 Boston Bruins .75 1.50
3 Buffalo Sabres .50 1.00
4 Chicago Blackhawks .75 1.50
5 Colorado Rockies .75 1.50
6 Detroit Red Wings .75 1.50
7 Edmonton Oilers .75 1.50
8 Hartford Whalers .50 1.00
9 Los Angeles Kings .50 1.00
10 Minnesota North Stars .50 1.00
11 Montreal Canadiens .75 1.50
12 New York Islanders .50 1.00
13 New York Rangers .75 1.50
14 Philadelphia Flyers .50 1.00
15 Pittsburgh Penguins UER .75 1.50
(Triangle in Penguins
logo is upside down)
16 Quebec Nordiques .75 1.50
17 St. Louis Blues .50 1.00
18 Toronto Maple Leafs .75 1.50
19 Vancouver Canucks .50 1.00
20 Washington Capitals .50 1.00
21 Winnipeg Jets .50 1.00

1980-81 Topps

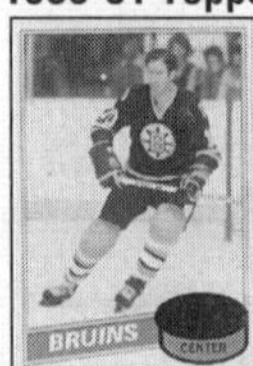

The 1980-81 Topps set features 26[4] standard-size cards. The fronts contain [a] puck (black ink) at the bottom right whic[h] can be scratched-off to reveal the player[s] name. Yearly statistics including mino[r] leagues, a short biography and a cartoo[n] illustrated hockey fact are included on th[e] back. Members of the U.S. Olympic team a[re] designated by USA.

COMPLETE SET (264) 150.00 275.0[0]
*SCRATCHED: .25X to .40X
1 Phila. Flyers RB .30 .7[5]
35 Game Streak& Long-
est in Sports History
2 Ray Bourque RB 5.00 10.0[0]
65 Pts.; Record for
Rookie Defenseman
3 Wayne Gretzky RB 10.00 20.0[0]
Youngest Ever&
50-goal Scorer
4 Charlie Simmer RB .10 .3[0]
Scores in 13th Straight
Game& NHL Record
5 Billy Smith RB .10 .3[0]
First Goalie to
Score a Goal
6 Jean Ratelle .15 .4[0]
7 Dave Maloney .07 .2[0]
8 Phil Myre .15 .4[0]
9 Ken Morrow USA RC .40 1.0[0]
10 Guy Lafleur .75 2.0[0]
11 Bill Derlago .07 .2[0]
12 Doug Wilson .30 .7[5]
13 Craig Ramsay .07 .2[0]
14 Pat Boutette .07 .2[0]
15 Eric Vail .07 .2[0]
16 Mike Foligno .10 .3[0]
Red Wings Scoring Leaders
(checklist back)
17 Bobby Smith .50 1.2[5]
18 Rick Kehoe .15 .4[0]
19 Joel Quenneville .07 .2[0]
20 Marcel Dionne .40 1.0[0]
21 Kevin McCarthy .07 .2[0]
22 Jim Craig USA RC 2.50 6.0[0]
23 Steve Vickers .07 .2[0]
24 Ken Linseman .15 .4[0]
25 Mike Bossy 1.50 4.0[0]
26 Serge Savard .30 .7[5]
27 Grant Mulvey .10 .3[0]
Blackhawks Scoring Leaders
(checklist back)
28 Pat Hickey .07 .2[0]
29 Peter Sullivan .07 .2[0]
30 Blaine Stoughton .15 .4[0]
31 Mike Liut RC 1.50 4.0[0]
32 Blair MacDonald .07 .2[0]
33 Rick Green .07 .2[0]
34 Al MacAdam .07 .2[0]
35 Robbie Ftorek .07 .2[0]
36 Dick Redmond .07 .2[0]
37 Ron Duguay .07 .2[0]
38 Danny Gare .10 .3[0]
Sabres Scoring Leaders
(checklist back)
39 Brian Propp RC 1.25 3.0[0]
40 Bryan Trottier .60 1.5[0]
41 Rich Preston .07 .2[0]
42 Pierre Mondou .07 .2[0]
43 Reed Larson .07 .2[0]
44 George Ferguson .07 .2[0]
45 Guy Chouinard .15 .4[0]
46 Billy Harris .07 .2[0]
47 Gilles Meloche .15 .4[0]
48 Blair Chapman .07 .2[0]
49 Mike Gartner 1.50 4.0[0]
Capitals Scoring Leaders
(checklist back)
50 Darryl Sittler .30 .7[5]
51 Richard Martin .15 .4[0]
52 Ivan Boldirev .07 .2[0]
53 Craig Norwich .07 .2[0]
54 Dennis Polonich .07 .2[0]
55 Bobby Clarke .40 1.0[0]
56 Terry O'Reilly .15 .4[0]
57 Carol Vadnais .07 .2[0]
58 Bob Gainey .30 .7[5]
59 Blaine Stoughton .10 .3[0]
Whalers Scoring Leaders
(checklist back)
60 Billy Smith .15 .4[0]
61 Mike O'Connell RC .15 .4[0]
62 Lanny McDonald .15 .4[0]
63 Lee Fogolin .07 .2[0]
64 Rocky Saganiuk .07 .2[0]
65 Rolf Edberg .07 .2[0]
66 Paul Shmyr .07 .2[0]
67 Michel Goulet RC 5.00 10.0[0]
68 Dan Bouchard .15 .4[0]
69 Mark Johnson USA RC .15 .4[0]
70 Reggie Leach .15 .4[0]
71 Bernie Federko .10 .3[0]
Blues Scoring Leaders
(checklist back)
72 Peter Mahovlich .15 .4[0]
73 Anders Hedberg .15 .4[0]
74 Brad Park .15 .4[0]
75 Clark Gillies .15 .4[0]
76 Doug Jarvis .07 .2[0]
77 John Garrett .15 .4[0]
78 Dave Hutchinson .07 .2[0]
79 John Anderson RC .07 .2[0]
80 Gilbert Perreault .30 .7[5]
81 Marcel Dionne AS1 .30 .7[5]
82 Guy Lafleur AS1 .40 1.0[0]
83 Charlie Simmer AS1 .10 .3[0]
84 Larry Robinson AS1 .10 .3[0]
85 Borje Salming AS1 .10 .3[0]
86 Tony Esposito AS1 .30 .7[5]
87 Wayne Gretzky AS2 12.50 25.0[0]
88 Danny Gare AS2 .10 .3[0]
89 Steve Shutt AS2 .10 .3[0]
90 Barry Beck AS2 .10 .3[0]
91 Mark Howe AS2 .10 .3[0]
92 Don Edwards AS2 .10 .3[0]
93 Tom McCarthy RC .07 .2[0]
94 Peter McNab/Rick Middleton .15 .4[0]
Bruins Scoring Leaders
(checklist back)
95 Mike Palmateer .15 .4[0]
96 Jim Schoenfeld .15 .4[0]

7 Jordy Douglas .07 .20
8 Keith Brown RC .07 .20
9 Dennis Ververgaert .07 .20
00 Phil Esposito .30 .75
01 Jack Brownschidle .07 .20
02 Bob Nystrom .07 .20
03 Steve Christoff USA RC .10 .30
04 Rob Palmer .07 .20
05 Dave(Tiger) Williams .15 .40
06 Kent Nilsson .10 .30
Flames Scoring Leaders
checklist back)
07 Morris Lukowich .15 .40
08 Jack Valiquette .07 .20
09 Richie Dunn .07 .20
10 Rogatien Vachon .15 .40
11 Mark Napier .07 .20
12 Gordie Roberts .07 .20
13 Stan Jonathan .07 .20
14 Brett Callighen .07 .20
15 Rick MacLeish .15 .40
16 Ulf Nilsson .15 .40
17 Rick Kehoe .10 .30
Penguins Scoring Leaders
(checklist back)
18 Dan Maloney .07 .20
19 Terry Ruskowski .07 .20
20 Denis Potvin .40 1.00
21 Wayne Stephenson .15 .40
22 Rich Leduc .07 .20
23 Checklist 1-132 1.75 3.50
24 Don Lever .07 .20
25 Jim Rutherford .15 .40
26 Ray Allison .07 .20
27 Mike Ramsey USA RC .75 2.00
28 Stan Smyl .10 .30
Canucks Scoring Leaders
(checklist back)
29 Al Secord RC 1.00 2.50
30 Denis Herron .15 .40
31 Bob Dailey .07 .20
32 Dean Talafous .07 .20
33 Ian Turnbull .07 .20
34 Ron Sedlbauer .07 .20
35 Tom Bladon .07 .20
36 Bernie Federko .60 1.50
37 Dave Taylor .75 2.00
38 Bob Lorimer .07 .20
39 Al MacAdam/Steve Payne .10 .30
North Stars Scoring Leaders
(checklist back)
40 Ray Bourque RC 30.00 80.00
41 Glen Hanlon .15 .40
42 Willy Lindstrom .07 .20
43 Mike Rogers .07 .20
44 Tony McKegney RC .07 .20
45 Behn Wilson .07 .20
46 Lucien DeBlois .07 .20
47 Dave Burrows .07 .20
48 Paul Woods .07 .20
49 Phil Esposito .30 .75
Rangers Scoring Leaders
(checklist back)
50 Tony Esposito .40 1.00
51 Pierre Larouche .15 .40
52 Brad Maxwell .07 .20
53 Stan Weir .07 .20
54 Ryan Walter .07 .20
55 Dale Hoganson .07 .20
56 Anders Kallur .07 .20
57 Paul Reinhart RC .30 .75
58 Greg Millen .15 .40
59 Ric Seiling .07 .20
60 Mark Howe .40 1.00
61 Goals Leaders .10 .30
Danny Gare (1)
Charlie Simmer (1)
Blaine Stoughton (1)
62 Assists Leaders 5.00 10.00
Wayne Gretzky (1)
Marcel Dionne (2)
Guy Lafleur (3)
63 Scoring Leaders 5.00 10.00
Marcel Dionne (1)
Wayne Gretzky (1)
Guy Lafleur (3)
64 Penalty Minutes .10 .30
Leaders
Jimmy Mann (1)
Dave(Tiger) Williams (2)
Paul Holmgren (3)
65 Power Play Goals .10 .30
Leaders
Charlie Simmer (1)
Marcel Dionne (2)
Danny Gare (2)
Steve Shutt (2)
Darryl Sittler (2)
66 Goals Against Average .10 .30
Leaders
Bob Sauve (1)
Denis Herron (2)
Don Edwards (3)
67 Game-Winning Goals .10 .30
Leaders
Danny Gare (1)
Peter McNab (2)
Blaine Stoughton (2)
68 Shutout Leaders .40 1.00
Tony Esposito (1)
Gerry Cheevers (2)
Bob Sauve (2)
Rogatien Vachon (2)
69 Perry Turnbull RC .07 .20
70 Barry Beck .15 .40
71 Charlie Simmer .10 .30
Kings Scoring Leaders
(checklist back)
72 Paul Holmgren .15 .40
73 Willie Huber .07 .20
74 Tim Young .07 .20
75 Gilles Gilbert .15 .40
76 Dave Christian USA RC .75 2.00
77 Lars Lindgren .07 .20
78 Real Cloutier .07 .20
79 Laurie Boschman RC .07 .20
80 Steve Shutt .07 .20
81 Bob Murray .07 .20
82 Wayne Gretzky 7.50 15.00
Oilers Scoring Leaders
(checklist back)
183 John Van Boxmeer .07 .20
184 Nick Fotiu .15 .40
185 Mike McEwen .07 .20
186 Greg Malone .07 .20
187 Mike Foligno RC 1.00 2.50
188 Dave Langevin RC .07 .20
189 Mel Bridgman .07 .20
190 John Davidson .15 .40
191 Mike Milbury .15 .40
192 Ron Zanussi .07 .20
193 Darryl Sittler .10 .30
Maple Leafs Scoring Leaders
(checklist back)
194 John Marks .07 .20
195 Mike Gartner RC 10.00 25.00
196 Dave Lewis .07 .20
197 Kent Nilsson RC 1.25 3.00
198 Rick Ley .07 .20
199 Derek Smith .07 .20
200 Bill Barber .15 .40
201 Guy Lapointe .15 .40
202 Vaclav Nedomansky .07 .20
203 Don Murdoch .07 .20
204 Mike Bossy .40 1.00
Islanders Scoring Leaders
(checklist back)
205 Pierre Hamel .30 .75
206 Mike Eaves .07 .20
207 Doug Halward .07 .20
208 Stan Smyl RC .30 .75
209 Mike Zuke .07 .20
210 Borje Salming .15 .40
211 Walt Tkaczuk .15 .40
212 Grant Mulvey .07 .20
213 Rob Ramage RC .75 2.00
214 Tom Rowe .07 .20
215 Don Edwards .07 .20
216 Guy Lafleur .30 .75
Pierre Larouche
Canadiens Scoring Leaders
(checklist back)
217 Dan Labraaten .07 .20
218 Glen Sharpley .07 .20
219 Stefan Persson .07 .20
220 Peter McNab .07 .20
221 Doug Hicks .07 .20
222 Bengt Gustafsson RC .07 .20
223 Michel Dion .15 .40
224 Jimmy Watson .07 .20
225 Wilf Paiement .07 .20
226 Phil Russell .07 .20
227 Morris Lukowich .10 .30
Jets Scoring Leaders
(checklist back)
228 Ron Stackhouse .07 .20
229 Ted Bulley .07 .20
230 Larry Robinson .30 .75
231 Don Maloney .07 .20
232 Rob McClanahan USA RC .10 .30
233 Al Sims .07 .20
234 Errol Thompson .07 .20
235 Glenn Resch .15 .40
236 Bob Miller .07 .20
237 Gary Sargent .07 .20
238 Real Cloutier .10 .30
Nordiques Scoring Leaders
(checklist back)
239 Rene Robert .15 .40
240 Charlie Simmer .50 1.25
241 Thomas Gradin .07 .20
242 Rick Vaive RC .75 2.00
243 Ron Wilson RC .07 .20
244 Brian Sutter .15 .40
245 Dale McCourt .07 .20
246 Yvon Lambert .07 .20
247 Tom Lysiak .07 .20
248 Ron Greschner .07 .20
249 Reggie Leach .10 .30
Flyers Scoring Leaders
(checklist back)
250 Wayne Gretzky UER 25.00 60.00
(1978-79 GP should
be 80& not 60)
251 Rick Middleton .15 .40
252 Al Smith .15 .40
253 Fred Barrett .07 .20
254 Butch Goring .15 .40
255 Robert Picard .07 .20
256 Marc Tardif .07 .20
257 Checklist 133-264 1.75 3.50
258 Barry Long .07 .20
259 Rene Robert .10 .30
Rockies Scoring Leaders
(checklist back)
260 Danny Gare .15 .40
261 Rejean Houle .07 .20
262 Stanley Cup Semifinals .10 .30
Islanders-Sabres
263 Stanley Cup Semifinals .10 .30
Flyers-North Stars
264 Stanley Cup Finals .40 1.00
Islanders win 1st

1980-81 Topps Team Posters

The 1980-81 Topps pin-up posters were issued as folded inserts (approximately 5" by 7" horizontal) to the 1980-81 Topps regular hockey issue. These 16 numbered posters are in full color with a white border on very thin stock. The posters feature posed shots (on ice) of the entire 1979-80 hockey team. The name of the team is indicated in large letters to the left of the hockey puck, which contains the designation 1979-80 Season. Fold lines or creases are natural and do not detract from the condition of the poster. For some reason the Edmonton Oilers, Quebec Nordiques, and Winnipeg Jets were not included in this set.

COMPLETE SET (16) 12.50 25.00
1 New York Islanders .75 1.50
2 New York Rangers 1.00 2.00
3 Philadelphia Flyers .75 1.50
4 Boston Bruins 1.25 2.50
5 Hartford Whalers 2.00 4.00
(Gordie Howe included)
6 Buffalo Sabres .75 1.50
7 Chicago Blackhawks 1.25 2.50
8 Detroit Red Wings 1.25 2.50
9 Minn. North Stars 1.00 2.00
10 Toronto Maple Leafs 1.25 2.50
11 Montreal Canadiens 1.25 2.50
12 Colorado Rockies 1.25 2.50
13 Los Angeles Kings 1.50 3.00
(Jack Carlson)
14 Vancouver Canucks .75 1.50
15 St. Louis Blues .75 1.50
16 Washington Capitals .75 1.50

1981 Topps Thirst Break

These small premiums were issued as part of a multi-sport themed gum product that was tested in limited parts of the U.S. They actually are wrappers, about the size of a Bazooka Joe comic, and feature a rendition of the player. They are extremely condition sensitive.

43 Gerry Cheevers 2.80 7.00
44 Dave Schultz 2.00 5.00
50 Bobby Hull 4.00 10.00
51 Bobby Hull 4.00 10.00
52 Bobby Hull 4.00 10.00

1981-82 Topps

Topps regionalized distribution of its 198-card standard-size set for 1981-82, and issued two types of wax boxes, commonly referred to as either "East" boxes or "West" boxes. There is no way to differentiate which type of box you have without opening the packs. While the first 66 cards of the set were distributed nationally in both pack types, cards numbered 67 East through 132 East and 67 West through 132 West were distributed regionally. The card fronts contain the Topps logo at the top, with team logo, player name and position at the bottom. The team name appears in large letters placed over the bottom portion of the photo. The backs feature player biographies and yearly statistics including minor leagues. As for the regionally distributed portions of the set, the card numbering is in order by team starting with Boston.

COMPLETE SET (198) 35.00 70.00
1 Dave Babych RC .20 .50
2 Bill Barber .08 .25
3 Barry Beck .08 .25
4 Mike Bossy .75 2.00
5 Ray Bourque 3.00 6.00
6 Guy Chouinard .02 .10
7 Dave Christian .08 .25
8 Bill Derlago .02 .10
9 Marcel Dionne .20 .50
10 Brian Engblom .02 .10
11 Tony Esposito .20 .50
12 Bernie Federko .20 .50
13 Bob Gainey .20 .50
14 Danny Gare .02 .10
15 Thomas Gradin .08 .25
16 Wayne Gretzky UER 8.00 20.00
(1978-79 GP should
be 80& not 60)
17 Rick Kehoe .02 .10
18 Jari Kurri RC 2.50 6.00
19 Guy Lafleur .40 1.00
20 Mike Liut .20 .50
21 Dale McCourt .02 .10
22 Rick Middleton .02 .10
23 Mark Napier .02 .10
24 Kent Nilsson .08 .25
25 Wilf Paiement .02 .10
26 Willi Plett .02 .10
27 Denis Potvin .20 .50
28 Paul Reinhart .02 .10
29 Jacques Richard .02 .10
30 Pat Riggin RC .08 .25
31 Larry Robinson .08 .25
32 Mike Rogers .02 .10
33 Borje Salming .08 .25
34 Steve Shutt .02 .10
35 Charlie Simmer .20 .50
36 Darryl Sittler .20 .50
37 Bobby Smith .08 .25
38 Stan Smyl .02 .10
39 Peter Stastny RC 1.50 4.00
40 Dave Taylor .20 .50
41 Bryan Trottier .20 .50
42 Ian Turnbull .02 .10
43 Eric Vail .02 .10
44 Rick Vaive .08 .25
45 Behn Wilson .02 .10
46 Rick Middleton .08 .25
Bruins Leaders
47 Danny Gare .02 .10
Sabres Leaders
48 Kent Nilsson .02 .10
Flames Leaders
49 Tom Lysiak .02 .10
Blackhawks Leaders
50 Lanny McDonald .08 .25
Rockies Leaders
51 Dale McCourt .02 .10
Red Wings Leaders
52 Wayne Gretzky 1.50 3.00
Oilers Leaders
53 Mike Rogers .02 .10
Whalers Leaders
54 Marcel Dionne .08 .25
Kings Leaders
55 Bobby Smith .08 .25
North Stars Leaders
56 Steve Shutt .08 .25
Canadiens Leaders
57 Mike Bossy .02 .10
Islanders Leaders
58 Anders Hedberg .02 .10
Rangers Leaders
59 Bill Barber .02 .10
Flyers Leaders
60 Rick Kehoe .02 .10
Penguins Leaders
61 Peter Stastny .02 .10
Nordiques Leaders
62 Bernie Federko .08 .25
Blues Leaders
63 Wilf Paiement .02 .10
Maple Leafs Leaders
64 Thomas Gradin .02 .10
Canucks Leaders
65 Dennis Maruk .02 .10
Capitals Leaders
66 Dave Christian .02 .10
Jets Leaders
E67 Dwight Foster .02 .10
E68 Steve Kasper RC .40 1.00
E69 Peter McNab .02 .10
E70 Mike O'Connell .08 .25
E71 Terry O'Reilly .08 .25
E72 Brad Park .08 .25
E73 Dick Redmond .02 .10
E74 Rogatien Vachon .08 .25
E75 Don Edwards .02 .10
E76 Tony McKegney .02 .10
E77 Bob Sauve .08 .25
E78 Andre Savard .02 .10
E79 Derek Smith .02 .10
E80 John Van Boxmeer .02 .10
E81 Pat Boutette .02 .10
E82 Mark Howe .20 .50
E83 Dave Keon .20 .50
E84 Warren Miller .02 .10
E85 Al Sims .02 .10
E86 Blaine Stoughton .08 .25
E87 Bob Bourne .02 .10
E88 Clark Gillies .08 .25
E89 Butch Goring .08 .25
E90 Anders Kallur .02 .10
E91 Ken Morrow .08 .25
E92 Stefan Persson .02 .10
E93 Billy Smith .08 .25
E94 Mike Allison .02 .10
E95 John Davidson .08 .25
E96 Ron Duguay .02 .10
E97 Ron Greschner .02 .10
E98 Anders Hedberg .08 .25
E99 Ed Johnstone .02 .10
E100 Dave Maloney .02 .10
E101 Don Maloney .02 .10
E102 Ulf Nilsson .08 .25
E103 Bobby Clarke .20 .50
E104 Bob Dailey .02 .10
E105 Paul Holmgren .02 .10
E106 Reggie Leach .08 .25
E107 Ken Linseman .08 .25
E108 Rick MacLeish .08 .25
E109 Pete Peeters .20 .50
E110 Brian Propp .20 .50
E111 Checklist 1-132 .40 1.00
E112 Randy Carlyle .08 .25
E113 Paul Gardner .02 .10
E114 Peter Lee .02 .10
E115 Greg Millen .08 .25
E116 Rod Schutt .02 .10
E117 Mike Gartner 2.50 5.00
E118 Rick Green .02 .10
E119 Bob Kelly .02 .10
E120 Dennis Maruk .08 .25
E121 Mike Palmateer .08 .25
E122 Ryan Walter .02 .10
E123 Bill Barber SA .08 .25
E124 Barry Beck SA .08 .25
E125 Mike Bossy SA .20 .50
E126 Ray Bourque SA 1.25 2.50
E127 Danny Gare SA .02 .10
E128 Rick Kehoe SA .02 .10
E129 Rick Middleton SA .08 .25
E130 Denis Potvin SA .20 .50
E131 Mike Rogers SA .02 .10
E132 Bryan Trottier SA .20 .50
W67 Keith Brown .05 .15
W68 Ted Bulley .05 .15
W69 Tim Higgins .05 .15
W70 Reg Kerr .05 .15
W71 Tom Lysiak .05 .15
W72 Grant Mulvey .05 .15
W73 Bob Murray .05 .15
W74 Terry Ruskowski .05 .15
W75 Denis Savard RC 5.00 10.00
W76 Glen Sharpley .05 .15
W77 Darryl Sutter RC .20 .50
W78 Doug Wilson .20 .50
W79 Lucien DeBlois .05 .15
W80 Paul Gagne .05 .15
W81 Merlin Malinowski .05 .15
W82 Lanny McDonald .08 .25
W83 Joel Quenneville .05 .15
W84 Rob Ramage .02 .10
W85 Glenn Resch .08 .25
W86 Steve Tambellini .05 .15
W87 Mike Foligno .20 .50
W88 Gilles Gilbert .08 .25
W89 Willie Huber .05 .15
W90 Mark Kirton .05 .15
W91 Jim Korn .05 .15
W92 Reed Larson .02 .10
W93 Gary McAdam .05 .15
W94 Vaclav Nedomansky .05 .15
W95 John Ogrodnick .20 .50
W96 Billy Harris .05 .15
W97 Jerry Korab .05 .15
W98 Mario Lessard .08 .25
W99 Don Luce .05 .15
W100 Larry Murphy RC 4.00 8.00
W101 Mike Murphy .05 .15
W102 Kent-Erik Andersson .05 .15
W103 Don Beaupre RC 1.25 3.00
W104 Steve Christoff .05 .15
W105 Dino Ciccarelli RC 5.00 10.00
W106 Craig Hartsburg .02 .10
W107 Al MacAdam .05 .15
W108 Tom McCarthy .05 .15
W109 Gilles Meloche .08 .25
W110 Steve Payne .05 .15
W111 Gordie Roberts .02 .10
W112 Greg Smith .05 .15
W113 Tim Young .05 .15
W114 Wayne Babych .05 .15
W115 Blair Chapman .05 .15
W116 Tony Currie .05 .15
W117 Blake Dunlop .05 .15
W118 Ed Kea .05 .15
W119 Rick Lapointe .05 .15
W120 Checklist 1-132 .60 1.50
W121 Jorgen Pettersson .05 .15
W122 Brian Sutter .08 .25
W123 Perry Turnbull .05 .15
W124 Mike Zuke .05 .15
W125 Marcel Dionne SA .20 .50
W126 Tony Esposito SA .20 .50
W127 Bernie Federko SA .08 .25
W128 Mike Liut SA .20 .50
W129 Dale McCourt SA .05 .15
W130 Charlie Simmer SA .08 .25
W131 Bobby Smith SA .05 .15
W132 Dave Taylor SA .20 .50

1984-85 Topps

After a two year hiatus, Topps returned to hockey with a set of 165 standard size cards. The set contains 66 single print cards which are noted in the checklist by SP. Teams from the United States have a greater player representation than the Canadian teams. Card fronts (much like 1983 Topps baseball) are color coordinated by team and feature two photos. A small photo at bottom right has player name, position and team name to the left. Card backs contain complete career statistics. Cards are in team order starting with Boston.

COMPLETE SET (165) 25.00 50.00
1 Ray Bourque .75 2.00
2 Keith Crowder SP .08 .20
3 Tom Fergus .02 .10
4 Doug Keans RC .02 .10
5 Gord Kluzak SP .08 .20
6 Mike Krushelnyski SP .08 .20
7 Nevin Markwart .02 .10
8 Rick Middleton .05 .15
9 Mike O'Connell .02 .10
10 Terry O'Reilly SP .08 .20
11 Barry Pederson .02 .10
12 Pete Peeters .05 .15
13 Dave Andreychuk RC SP 2.00 5.00
14 Tom Barrasso RC 1.25 3.00
15 Real Cloutier SP .08 .20
16 Mike Foligno .05 .15
17 Bill Hajt SP .08 .20
18 Phil Housley SP .40 1.00
19 Gilbert Perreault .05 .15
20 Larry Playfair SP .08 .20
21 Craig Ramsay SP .08 .20
22 Mike Ramsey .02 .10
23 Lindy Ruff SP .08 .20
24 Ed Beers .02 .10
25 Rejean Lemelin SP .05 .15
26 Lanny McDonald .05 .15
27 Murray Bannerman .05 .15
28 Keith Brown SP .08 .20
29 Curt Fraser .02 .10
30 Steve Larmer .50 1.50
31 Tom Lysiak .02 .10
32 Bob Murray .02 .10
33 Jack O'Callahan SP .08 .20
34 Rich Preston .02 .10
35 Denis Savard .08 .25
36 Darryl Sutter .02 .10
37 Doug Wilson .05 .15
38 Ivan Boldirev .02 .10
39 Colin Campbell SP .08 .20
40 Ron Duguay SP .08 .20
41 Dwight Foster SP .08 .20
42 Danny Gare SP .08 .20
43 Ed Johnstone .02 .10
44 Reed Larson SP .08 .20
45 Eddie Mio SP .08 .20
46 John Ogrodnick .02 .10
47 Brad Park .05 .15
48 Greg Stefan RC SP .08 .20
49 Steve Yzerman RC 20.00 50.00
50 Paul Coffey .75 2.00
51 Wayne Gretzky 4.00 8.00
52 Jari Kurri .50 1.25
53 Bob Crawford .02 .10
54 Ron Francis .60 1.50
55 Marty Howe .02 .10
56 Mark Johnson SP .08 .20
57 Greg Malone SP .08 .20
58 Greg Millen SP .08 .20
59 Ray Neufeld .02 .10
60 Joel Quenneville SP .08 .20
61 Risto Siltanen .02 .10
62 Sylvain Turgeon RC .05 .15
63 Mike Zuke SP .08 .20
64 Marcel Dionne .08 .25
65 Brian Engblom SP .08 .20
66 Jim Fox SP .08 .20
67 Bernie Nicholls .30 .75
68 Terry Ruskowski SP .08 .20
69 Charlie Simmer .05 .15
70 Don Beaupre .05 .15
71 Brian Bellows .20 .50
72 Neal Broten SP .08 .20
73 Dino Ciccarelli .08 .25
74 Paul Holmgren SP .08 .20
75 Al MacAdam SP .08 .20
76 Dennis Maruk .05 .15
77 Brad Maxwell SP .08 .20
78 Tom McCarthy SP .08 .20
79 Gilles Meloche SP .08 .20
80 Steve Payne .02 .10
81 Guy Lafleur .08 .25
82 Larry Robinson .05 .15
83 Bobby Smith .05 .15
84 Mel Bridgman .02 .10
85 Joe Cirella .02 .10
86 Don Lever .02 .10
87 Dave Lewis .02 .10
88 Jan Ludvig .02 .10
89 Glenn Resch .05 .15
90 Pat Verbeek RC 2.00 5.00
91 Mike Bossy .20 .50
92 Bob Bourne .02 .10
93 Greg Gilbert RC .02 .10
94 Clark Gillies SP .08 .20
95 Butch Goring SP .08 .20
96 Pat LaFontaine RC SP 3.00 8.00
97 Ken Morrow .02 .10
98 Bob Nystrom SP .08 .20
99 Stefan Persson SP .08 .20
100 Denis Potvin .05 .15
101 Billy Smith SP .05 .15
102 Brent Sutter SP .08 .25
103 John Tonelli .05 .15
104 Bryan Trottier .08 .25
105 Barry Beck .02 .10
106 Glen Hanlon SP .08 .20
107 Anders Hedberg SP .08 .20
108 Pierre Larouche SP .05 .15
109 Don Maloney SP .08 .20
110 Mark Osborne SP .08 .20
111 Larry Patey .02 .10
112 James Patrick RC .08 .25
113 Mark Pavelich SP .08 .20
114 Mike Rogers SP .08 .20
115 Reijo Ruotsalainen SP .08 .20
116 Peter Sundstrom RC SP .08 .20
117 Bob Froese .05 .15
118 Mark Howe .05 .15
119 Tim Kerr SP .05 .15
120 Dave Poulin RC .40 1.00
121 Darryl Sittler SP .08 .25
122 Ron Sutter RC .08 .25
123 Mike Bullard SP .08 .20
124 Ron Flockhart SP .08 .20
125 Rick Kehoe .05 .15
126 Kevin McCarthy SP .08 .20
127 Mark Taylor .02 .10
128 Dan Bouchard SP .08 .20
129 Michel Goulet .08 .25
130 Peter Stastny SP .08 .25
131 Bernie Federko .05 .15
132 Mike Liut .05 .15
133 Joe Mullen SP .40 1.00
134 Rob Ramage .02 .10
135 Brian Sutter .05 .15
136 John Anderson SP .08 .20
137 Dan Daoust .02 .10
138 Rick Vaive .02 .10
139 Darcy Rota SP .08 .20
140 Stan Smyl SP .08 .20
141 Tony Tanti .02 .10
142 Dave Christian SP .08 .20
143 Mike Gartner SP .60 1.50
144 Bengt Gustafsson SP .08 .20
145 Doug Jarvis .02 .10
146 Al Jensen .02 .10
147 Rod Langway .08 .25
148 Pat Riggin .05 .15
149 Scott Stevens SP .75 2.00
150 Dave Babych .02 .10
151 Laurie Boschman .02 .10
152 Dale Hawerchuk .40 1.00
153 Michel Goulet AS .05 .15
154 Wayne Gretzky AS 1.00 2.50
155 Mike Bossy AS .08 .25
156 Rod Langway AS .02 .10
157 Ray Bourque AS .08 .25
158 Tom Barrasso AS .20 .50
159 Mark Messier AS .08 .25
160 Bryan Trottier AS .08 .25
161 Jari Kurri AS .08 .25
162 Denis Potvin AS .05 .15
163 Paul Coffey AS .08 .25
164 Pat Riggin AS .05 .15
165 Checklist 1-165 SP .60 1.50

1985-86 Topps

This set of 165 standard-size cards is very similar to Topps' hockey set of the previous season in that there are 66 single prints. The single prints are noted in the checklist by SP. Unopened packs consist of 12 cards plus one sticker and a piece of bubble gum. The fronts have player name and position at the bottom with the team logo at the top right or left. Backs contain complete career statistics and personal notes. The key Rookie Card is Mario Lemieux.

COMPLETE SET (165) 125.00 225.00
1 Lanny McDonald .40 1.00
2 Mike O'Connell SP .20 .50
3 Curt Fraser SP .20 .50
4 Steve Penney .08 .25
5 Brian Engblom .08 .25
6 Ron Sutter .08 .25
7 Joe Mullen .40 1.00
8 Rod Langway .20 .50
9 Mario Lemieux RC ! 60.00 150.00
10 Dave Babych .08 .25
11 Bob Nystrom .08 .25
12 Andy Moog SP 1.00 2.50
13 Dino Ciccarelli .40 1.00
14 Dwight Foster SP .20 .50
15 James Patrick SP .40 1.00
16 Thomas Gradin SP .20 .50
17 Mike Foligno .20 .50
18 Mario Gosselin RC .20 .50
19 Mike Zuke SP .20 .50
20 John Anderson SP .20 .50
21 Dave Pichette .08 .25
22 Nick Fotiu SP .20 .50
23 Tom Lysiak .08 .25
24 Peter Zezel RC .40 1.00
25 Denis Potvin .20 .50
26 Bob Carpenter .08 .25
27 Murray Bannerman SP .20 .50
28 Gordie Roberts SP .20 .50
29 Steve Yzerman 8.00 20.00
30 Phil Russell .08 .25
31 Peter Stastny .40 1.00
32 Craig Ramsay SP .20 .50
33 Terry Ruskowski SP .20 .50
34 Kevin Dineen RC SP 1.25 3.00
35 Mark Howe .20 .50
36 Glenn Resch .20 .50
37 Danny Gare SP .20 .50
38 Doug Bodger RC .20 .50
39 Mike Rogers .08 .25
40 Ray Bourque 2.00 4.00
41 John Tonelli .20 .50
42 Mel Bridgman .08 .25
43 Sylvain Turgeon SP .20 .50
44 Mark Johnson .08 .25
45 Doug Wilson .20 .50
46 Mike Gartner .40 1.00
47 Brent Peterson .08 .25
48 Paul Reinhart SP .20 .50
49 Mike Krushelnyski .08 .25
50 Brian Bellows .40 1.00
51 Chris Chelios 2.00 4.00
52 Barry Pederson SP .20 .50
53 Murray Craven SP .20 .50
54 Pierre Larouche SP .20 .50
55 Reed Larson .08 .25
56 Pat Verbeek SP .08 .25
57 Randy Carlyle .08 .25
58 Ray Neufeld SP .20 .50
59 Keith Brown SP .20 .50
60 Bryan Trottier .40 1.00
61 Jim Fox SP .20 .50
62 Scott Stevens .40 1.00
63 Phil Housley .40 1.00
64 Rick Middleton .20 .50
65 Steve Payne .08 .25
66 Dave Lewis .08 .25
67 Mike Bullard .08 .25
68 Stan Smyl SP .20 .50
69 Mark Pavelich SP .20 .50
70 John Ogrodnick .08 .25
71 Bill Derlago SP .20 .50
72 Brad Marsh SP .40 1.00
73 Denis Savard .40 1.00
74 Mark Fusco .08 .25
75 Pete Peeters .20 .50
76 Doug Gilmour 3.00 6.00
77 Mike Ramsey .08 .25
78 Anton Stastny SP .20 .50
79 Steve Kasper SP .20 .50
80 Bryan Erickson SP .20 .50
81 Clark Gillies .20 .50
82 Keith Acton .08 .25
83 Pat Flatley .20 .50
84 Kirk Muller RC ! 1.00 2.50
85 Paul Coffey 1.50 3.00
86 Ed Olczyk RC .20 .50
87 Charlie Simmer SP .40 1.00
88 Mike Liut .08 .25
89 Dave Maloney .08 .25
90 Marcel Dionne .20 .50
91 Tim Kerr .20 .50
92 Ivan Boldirev SP .20 .50
93 Ken Morrow SP .20 .50
94 Don Maloney SP .20 .50
95 Rejean Lemelin .20 .50
96 Curt Giles .08 .25
97 Bob Bourne .08 .25
98 Joe Cirella .08 .25
99 Dave Christian SP .20 .50
100 Darryl Sutter .20 .50
101 Kelly Kisio .20 .50
102 Mats Naslund .20 .50
103 Joel Quenneville SP .20 .50
104 Bernie Federko .20 .50
105 Tom Barrasso .40 1.00
106 Rick Vaive .08 .25
107 Brent Sutter .08 .25
108 Wayne Babych .08 .25
109 Dale Hawerchuk .40 1.00
110 Pelle Lindbergh SP 5.00 10.00
111 Dennis Maruk SP .40 1.00
112 Reijo Ruotsalainen SP .20 .50
113 Tom Fergus SP .20 .50
114 Bob Murray SP .20 .50
115 Patrik Sundstrom .08 .25
116 Ron Duguay SP .40 1.00
117 Alan Haworth SP .20 .50
118 Greg Malone .08 .25
119 Bill Hajt .08 .25
120 Wayne Gretzky 10.00 20.00
121 Craig Redmond .08 .25
122 Kelly Hrudey RC 1.25 3.00
123 Tomas Sandstrom RC 1.25 3.00
124 Neal Broten .20 .50
125 Moe Mantha SP .20 .50
126 Greg Gilbert SP .20 .50
127 Bruce Driver RC SP .40 1.00
128 Dave Poulin .20 .50
129 Morris Lukowich SP .20 .50
130 Mike Bossy .60 1.25
131 Larry Playfair SP .20 .50
132 Steve Larmer .40 1.00
133 Doug Keans SP .20 .50
134 Bob Manno .08 .25
135 Brian Sutter .08 .25
136 Pat Riggin .20 .50
137 Pat LaFontaine 1.25 3.00
138 Barry Beck SP .20 .50
139 Rich Preston SP .20 .50
140 Ron Francis 1.00 2.50

141 Brian Propp SP .40 1.00
142 Don Beaupre .20 .50
143 Dave Andreychuk SP .40 1.00
144 Ed Beers .08 .25
145 Paul MacLean .08 .25
146 Troy Murray SP .20 .50
147 Larry Robinson .20 .50
148 Bernie Nicholls .40 1.00
149 Glen Hanlon SP .40 1.00
150 Michel Goulet .40 1.00
151 Doug Jarvis SP .20 .50
152 Warren Young .08 .25
153 Tony Tanti .08 .25
154 Tomas Jonsson SP .20 .50
155 Jari Kurri .75 2.00
156 Tony McKegney .08 .25
157 Greg Stefan SP .40 1.00
158 Brad McCrimmon SP .40 1.00
159 Keith Crowder SP .20 .50
160 Gilbert Perreault .20 .50
161 Tim Bothwell SP .20 .50
162 Bob Crawford SP .20 .50
163 Paul Gagne SP .20 .50
164 Dan Daoust SP .20 .50
165 Checklist 1-165 SP 1.00 2.50

1985-86 Topps Box Bottoms

This 16-card standard-size set was issued in sets of four on the bottom of the 1985-86 Topps wax pack boxes. Complete box bottom panels are valued at a 25 percent premium above the prices listed below. The back, written in English, includes statistical information. The cards are lettered rather than numbered. The key card in the set is Mario Lemieux, pictured in his Rookie Card year.

COMPLETE SET (16) 26.00 65.00
A Brian Bellows .24 .60
B Ray Bourque 1.00 2.50
C Bob Carpenter .16 .40
D Chris Chelios 1.60 4.00
E Marcel Dionne .50 1.25
F Ron Francis 1.00 2.50
G Wayne Gretzky 10.00 25.00
H Tim Kerr .16 .40
I Mario Lemieux 20.00 50.00
J John Ogrodnick .16 .40
K Gilbert Perreault .30 .75
L Glenn Resch .24 .60
M Reijo Ruotsalainen .16 .40
N Brian Sutter .24 .60
O John Tonelli .16 .40
P Doug Wilson .24 .60

1985-86 Topps Sticker Inserts

This set of 33 "Hockey Helmet Stickers" features stickers of 12 All-Star players (1-12) and 21 stickers of team logos, pucks, and numbers. The stickers were inserted in with the 1985-86 Topps hockey regular issue wax packs and as such are also 2 1/2" by 3 1/2". The card backs are printed in blue and red on white card stock. These inserts were also included in some O-Pee-Chee packs that year, which may explain why this particular year of stickers is relatively plentiful. The last seven team stickers can be found with the team logos on the top or bottom.

COMPLETE SET (33) 8.00 20.00
1 John Ogrodnick .10 .25
2 Wayne Gretzky 4.00 10.00
3 Jari Kurri .40 1.00
4 Paul Coffey .60 1.50
5 Ray Bourque .60 1.50
6 Pelle Lindbergh 1.60 4.00
7 John Tonelli .10 .25
8 Dale Hawerchuk .30 .75
9 Mike Bossy .40 1.00
10 Rod Langway .10 .25
11 Doug Wilson .10 .25
12 Tom Barrasso .14 .35
13 Toronto Maple Leafs .10 .25
14 Buffalo Sabres .06 .15
15 Detroit Red Wings .10 .25
16 Pittsburgh Penguins .06 .15
17 New York Rangers .10 .25
18 Calgary Flames .06 .15
19 Winnipeg Jets .06 .15
20 Quebec Nordiques .06 .15
21 Chicago Blackhawks .10 .25
22 Los Angeles Kings .06 .15
23 Montreal Canadiens .10 .25
24 Vancouver Canucks .06 .15
25 Hartford Whalers .06 .15
26 Philadelphia Flyers .06 .15
27 New Jersey Devils .06 .15
28 St. Louis Blues .06 .15
29 Minnesota North Stars .06 .15
30 Washington Capitals .06 .15
31 Boston Bruins .10 .25
32 New York Islanders .06 .15
33 Edmonton Oilers .06 .15

1986-87 Topps

This set of 198 cards measures the standard size. There are 66 double prints that are noted in the checklist by DP. Card fronts feature player name, team, team logo and position at the bottom with a team colored stripe up the right border. Card backs contain complete career statistics and career

highlights. The key Rookie Card in this set is Patrick Roy.

COMPLETE SET (198) 90.00 150.00
1 Ray Bourque 1.00 2.50
2 Pat LaFontaine DP .60 1.50
3 Wayne Gretzky 10.00 20.00
4 Lindy Ruff .05 .15
5 Brad McCrimmon .05 .15
6 Dave(Tiger) Williams .15 .40
7 Denis Savard DP .15 .40
8 Lanny McDonald .05 .15
9 John Vanbiesbrouck DP RC 6.00 12.00
10 Greg Adams RC .40 1.00
11 Steve Yzerman 8.00 15.00
12 Craig Hartsburg .05 .15
13 John Anderson DP .05 .15
14 Bob Bourne DP .05 .15
15 Kjell Dahlin .05 .15
16 Dave Andreychuk .40 1.00
17 Rob Ramage DP .05 .15
18 Ron Greschner DP .05 .15
19 Bruce Driver .05 .15
20 Peter Stastny .15 .40
21 Dave Christian .05 .15
22 Doug Keans .05 .15
23 Scott Bjugstad .05 .15
24 Doug Bodger DP .05 .15
25 Troy Murray DP .05 .15
26 Al Iafrate .40 1.00
27 Kelly Hrudey .40 1.00
28 Doug Jarvis .05 .15
29 Rich Sutter .05 .15
30 Marcel Dionne .15 .40
31 Curt Fraser .05 .15
32 Doug Lidster .05 .15
33 Brian MacLellan .05 .15
34 Barry Pederson .05 .15
35 Craig Laughlin .05 .15
36 Ilkka Sinisalo DP .05 .15
37 John MacLean RC 1.00 2.50
38 Brian Mullen .05 .15
39 Duane Sutter DP .05 .15
40 Brian Engblom .05 .15
41 Chris Cichocki .05 .15
42 Gordie Roberts .05 .15
43 Ron Francis .60 1.50
44 Joe Mullen .40 1.00
45 Moe Mantha DP .05 .15
46 Pat Verbeek .05 .15
47 Clint Malarchuk RC .40 1.00
48 Bob Brooke DP .05 .15
49 Darryl Sutter DP .05 .15
50 Stan Smyl DP .05 .15
51 Greg Stefan .15 .40
52 Bill Hajt DP .05 .15
53 Patrick Roy RC 40.00 100.00
54 Gord Kluzak .05 .15
55 Bob Froese DP .05 .15
56 Grant Fuhr 1.00 2.50
57 Mark Hunter DP .05 .15
58 Dana Murzyn RC .05 .15
59 Mike Gartner .40 1.00
60 Dennis Maruk .05 .15
61 Rich Preston .05 .15
62 Larry Robinson DP .05 .15
63 Dave Taylor DP .05 .15
64 Bob Murray DP .05 .15
65 Ken Morrow .05 .15
66 Mike Ridley RC .40 1.00
67 John Tucker RC .05 .15
68 Miroslav Frycer .05 .15
69 Danny Gare .15 .40
70 Randy Burridge RC .40 1.00
71 Dave Poulin .05 .15
72 Brian Sutter .15 .40
73 Dave Babych .05 .15
74 Dale Hawerchuk DP .40 1.00
75 Brian Bellows .05 .15
76 Dave Pasin DP .05 .15
77 Pete Peeters DP .05 .15
78 Tomas Jonsson DP .05 .15
79 Gilbert Perreault DP .05 .15
80 Glenn Anderson DP .40 1.00
81 Don Maloney .05 .15
82 Ed Olczyk DP .05 .15
83 Mike Bullard DP .05 .15
84 Tom Fergus .05 .15
85 Dave Lewis .05 .15
86 Brian Propp .15 .40
87 John Ogrodnick .05 .15
88 Kevin Dineen DP .40 1.00
89 Don Beaupre .15 .40
90 Mike Bossy DP .50 1.25
91 Tom Barrasso DP .40 1.00
92 Michel Goulet DP .05 .15
93 Doug Gilmour 1.25 3.00
94 Kirk Muller .40 1.00
95 Larry Melnyk DP .05 .15
96 Bob Gainey DP .40 1.00
97 Steve Kasper .05 .15
98 Petr Klima RC .15 .40
99 Neal Broten DP .05 .15
100 Al Secord DP .05 .15
101 Bryan Erickson DP .05 .15
102 Rejean Lemelin .05 .15
103 Sylvain Turgeon .05 .15
104 Bob Nystrom .05 .15
105 Bernie Federko .15 .40
106 Doug Wilson DP .05 .15
107 Alan Haworth .05 .15
108 Jari Kurri .60 1.50
109 Ron Sutter .05 .15
110 Reed Larson DP .05 .15
111 Terry Ruskowski DP .05 .15
112 Mark Johnson DP .05 .15
113 James Patrick .05 .15
114 Paul MacLean .05 .15
115 Mike Ramsey DP .05 .15
116 Kelly Kisio DP .05 .15
117 Brent Sutter .05 .15
118 Joel Quenneville .05 .15
119 Curt Giles DP .05 .15
120 Tony Tanti DP .05 .15
121 Doug Sulliman DP .05 .15
122 Mario Lemieux 18.00 30.00
123 Mark Howe DP .05 .15
124 Bob Sauve .15 .40
125 Anton Stastny .05 .15
126 Scott Stevens DP .40 1.00
127 Mike Foligno .05 .15
128 Reijo Ruotsalainen DP .05 .15
129 Denis Potvin .15 .40
130 Keith Crowder .05 .15
131 Bob Janecyk DP .05 .15
132 John Tonelli .05 .15
133 Mike Liut DP .05 .15
134 Tim Kerr DP .05 .15
135 Al Jensen .05 .15
136 Mel Bridgman .05 .15
137 Paul Coffey DP .60 1.50
138 Dino Ciccarelli DP .15 .40
139 Steve Larmer .40 1.00
140 Mike O'Connell .05 .15
141 Clark Gillies .15 .40
142 Phil Russell DP .05 .15
143 Dirk Graham DP RC .40 1.00
144 Randy Carlyle .05 .15
145 Charlie Simmer .05 .15
146 Ron Flockhart DP .05 .15
147 Tom Laidlaw .05 .15
148 Dave Tippett RC .05 .15
149 Wendel Clark DP RC 3.00 8.00
150 Bob Carpenter DP .05 .15
151 Bill Watson .05 .15
152 Roberto Romano DP RC .05 .15
153 Doug Shedden .05 .15
154 Phil Housley .40 1.00
155 Bryan Trottier .40 1.00
156 Patrik Sundstrom DP .05 .15
157 Rick Middleton DP .05 .15
158 Glenn Resch .15 .40
159 Bernie Nicholls DP .40 1.00
160 Ray Ferraro RC 1.00 2.50
161 Mats Naslund DP .05 .15
162 Pat Flatley DP .05 .15
163 Joe Cirella .05 .15
164 Rod Langway DP .05 .15
165 Checklist 1-99 .40 1.00
166 Carey Wilson .05 .15
167 Murray Craven .05 .15
168 Paul Gillis .05 .15
169 Borje Salming .05 .15
170 Perry Turnbull .05 .15
171 Chris Chelios 1.25 3.00
172 Keith Acton .05 .15
173 Al MacInnis 2.00 5.00
174 Russ Courtnall RC 1.00 2.50
175 Brad Marsh .05 .15
176 Guy Carbonneau .15 .40
177 Ray Neufeld .05 .15
178 Craig MacTavish RC .40 1.00
179 Rick Lanz .05 .15
180 Murray Bannerman .05 .15
181 Brent Ashton .05 .15
182 Jim Peplinski .05 .15
183 Mark Napier .05 .15
184 Laurie Boschman .05 .15
185 Larry Murphy .15 .40
186 Mark Messier .40 1.00
187 Risto Siltanen .05 .15
188 Bobby Smith .15 .40
189 Gary Suter RC .75 2.00
190 Peter Zezel .05 .15
191 Rick Vaive .05 .15
192 Dale Hunter .15 .40
193 Mike Krushelnyski .05 .15
194 Scott Arniel .05 .15
195 Larry Playfair .05 .15
196 Doug Risebrough .05 .15
197 Kevin Lowe .05 .15
198 Checklist 100-198 .40 1.00

1986-87 Topps Box Bottoms

This sixteen-card standard-size set was issued in sets of four on the bottom of the 1986-87 Topps wax pack boxes. Complete box bottom panels are valued at a 25 percent premium above the prices listed below. The front presents a color action photo with various color borders, with the team's logo in the lower right hand corner. The back includes statistical information, is written in English, and is printed on blue with black ink. The cards are lettered rather than numbered.

COMPLETE SET (16) 14.00 35.00
A Greg Adams .20 .50
B Mike Bossy .40 1.00
C Dave Christian .10 .25
D Mike Foligno .10 .25
E Michel Goulet .20 .50
F Wayne Gretzky 6.00 15.00
G Tim Kerr .10 .25
H Jari Kurri .60 1.50
I Mario Lemieux 8.00 20.00
J Lanny McDonald .20 .50
K Bernie Nicholls .20 .50
L Mike Ridley .20 .50
M Larry Robinson .20 .50
N Denis Savard .20 .50
O Brian Sutter .10 .25
P Bryan Trottier .30 .75

1986-87 Topps Sticker Inserts

This set of 33 "Hockey Helmet Stickers" features stickers of 12 All-Star players (1-12) and 21 stickers of team logos, pucks, and numbers. The stickers were inserted in with the 1986-87 Topps hockey regular issue wax packs and as such are also 2 1/2" by 3 1/2". The card backs are printed in blue and red on white card stock. The last seven team stickers can be found with the team logos on the top or bottom.

COMPLETE SET (33) 12.00 30.00
1 John Vanbiesbrouck 3.20 8.00
2 Michel Goulet .20 .50
3 Wayne Gretzky 4.00 10.00
4 Mike Bossy .40 1.00
5 Paul Coffey .60 1.50
6 Mark Howe .16 .40
7 Bob Froese .16 .40
8 Mats Naslund .16 .40
9 Mario Lemieux 4.00 10.00
10 Jari Kurri .60 1.50
11 Ray Bourque .80 2.00
12 Larry Robinson .20 .50
13 Toronto Maple Leafs .10 .25
14 Buffalo Sabres .06 .15
15 Detroit Red Wings .10 .25
16 Pittsburgh Penguins .06 .15
17 New York Rangers .10 .25
18 Calgary Flames .06 .15
19 Winnipeg Jets .06 .15
20 Quebec Nordiques .06 .15
21 Chicago Blackhawks .10 .25
22 Los Angeles Kings .06 .15
23 Montreal Canadiens .10 .25
24 Vancouver Canucks .06 .15
25 Hartford Whalers .06 .15
26 Philadelphia Flyers .06 .15
27 New Jersey Devils .06 .15
28 St. Louis Blues .06 .15
29 Minnesota North Stars .06 .15
30 Washington Capitals .06 .15
31 Boston Bruins .10 .25
32 New York Islanders .06 .15
33 Edmonton Oilers .06 .15

1987-88 Topps

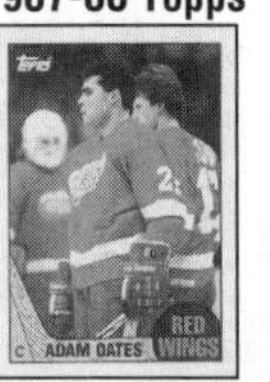

The 1987-88 Topps hockey set contains 198 standard size cards. There are 66 double printed cards which are indicated by DP below. Again, unopened packs had 12 cards plus one sticker and a piece of gum. The fronts feature a design that includes a hockey stick at the bottom with which the player's name is located. At bottom right, the team name appears in a large puck. The card backs contain career statistics, game winning goals from 1986-87 and highlights.

COMPLETE SET (198) 60.00 120.00
1 Denis Potvin DP .08 .25
2 Rick Tocchet RC 3.00 6.00
3 Dave Andreychuk .20 .50
4 Stan Smyl .08 .25
5 Dave Babych DP .01 .05
6 Pat Verbeek .02 .10
7 Esa Tikkanen RC 1.50 4.00
8 Mike Ridley .08 .25
9 Randy Carlyle .08 .25
10 Greg Paslawski RC .02 .10
11 Neal Broten .08 .25
12 Wendel Clark DP 1.00 2.50
13 Bill Ranford RC DP UER 2.00 5.00
(Date of birth is 12-12-66; should be 12-14-66)
14 Doug Wilson .08 .25
15 Mario Lemieux 10.00 20.00
16 Mats Naslund .08 .25
17 Mel Bridgman .02 .10
18 James Patrick DP .01 .05
19 Rollie Melanson .08 .25
20 Lanny McDonald .08 .25
21 Peter Stastny .08 .25
22 Murray Craven .02 .10
23 Ulf Samuelsson DP RC .60 1.50
24 Michael Thelven DP UER .01 .05
(Misspelled Thelvin on card front)
25 Scott Stevens .20 .50
26 Petr Klima .08 .25
27 Brent Sutter DP .01 .05
28 Tomas Sandstrom .20 .50
29 Tim Bothwell .02 .10
30 Bob Carpenter DP .01 .05
31 Brian MacLellan DP .01 .05
32 John Chabot .02 .10
33 Phil Housley DP .08 .25
34 Patrik Sundstrom DP .01 .05
35 Dave Ellett .08 .25
36 John Vanbiesbrouck 4.00 8.00
37 Dave Lewis .02 .10
38 Tom McCarthy DP .01 .05
39 Dave Poulin .08 .25
40 Mike Foligno .08 .25
41 Gordie Roberts .02 .10
42 Luc Robitaille RC 10.00 20.00
43 Duane Sutter .02 .10
44 Pete Peeters .08 .25
45 John Anderson .02 .10
46 Aaron Broten .02 .10
47 Keith Brown .02 .10
48 Bobby Smith .08 .25
49 Don Maloney .02 .10
50 Mark Hunter .02 .10
51 Moe Mantha .02 .10
52 Charlie Simmer .08 .25
53 Wayne Gretzky 7.50 15.00
54 Mark Howe .08 .25
55 Bob Gould .02 .10
56 Steve Yzerman DP 3.00 6.00
57 Larry Playfair .02 .10
58 Alain Chevrier .08 .25
59 Steve Larmer .20 .50
60 Bryan Trottier .20 .50
61 Stewart Gavin DP .01 .05
62 Russ Courtnall DP .20 .50
63 Mike Ramsey DP .01 .05
64 Bob Brooke .02 .10
65 Rick Wamsley DP .01 .05
66 Ken Morrow DP .01 .05
67 Gerard Gallant RC UER .02 .10
(Misspelled Gerald on card front)
68 Kevin Hatcher RC .60 1.50
69 Cam Neely .75 2.00
70 Sylvain Turgeon DP .01 .05
71 Peter Zezel .02 .10
72 Al MacInnis 1.00 2.50
73 Terry Ruskowski DP .01 .05
74 Troy Murray .02 .10
75 Jim Fox DP .01 .05
76 Kelly Kisio .02 .10
77 Michel Goulet DP .08 .25
78 Tom Barrasso DP .08 .25
79 Bruce Driver DP .01 .05
80 Craig Simpson DP RC .08 .25
81 Dino Ciccarelli .08 .25
82 Gary Nylund DP .01 .05
83 Bernie Federko .08 .25
84 John Tonelli DP .01 .05
85 Brad McCrimmon DP .01 .05
86 Dave Tippett DP .01 .05
87 Ray Bourque DP .50 1.25
88 Dave Christian .08 .25
89 Glen Hanlon .08 .25
90 Brian Curran .02 .10
91 Paul MacLean .08 .25
92 Jimmy Carson DP RC .08 .25
93 Willie Huber .02 .10
94 Brian Bellows .08 .25
95 Doug Jarvis DP .01 .05
96 Clark Gillies .08 .25
97 Tony Tanti .02 .10
98 Pelle Eklund DP RC .08 .25
99 Paul Coffey .60 1.50
100 Brent Ashton DP .01 .05
101 Mark Johnson .02 .10
102 Greg Johnston .02 .10
103 Ron Flockhart .02 .10
104 Ed Olczyk .02 .10
105 Mike Bossy .25 .60
106 Chris Chelios .60 1.50
107 Gilles Meloche .08 .25
108 Rod Langway .08 .25
109 Ray Ferraro DP .20 .50
110 Ron Duguay DP .01 .05
111 Al Secord DP .01 .05
112 Mark Messier .20 .50
113 Ron Sutter .02 .10
114 Darren Veitch .02 .10
115 Rick Middleton DP .01 .05
116 Doug Sulliman .02 .10
117 Dennis Maruk DP .01 .05
118 Dave Taylor .08 .25
119 Kelly Hrudey .20 .50
120 Tom Fergus .02 .10
121 Christian Ruuttu RC .02 .10
122 Brian Benning RC .02 .10
123 Adam Oates RC 5.00 10.00
124 Kevin Dineen .15 .40
125 Doug Bodger DP .01 .05
126 Joe Mullen .10 .30
127 Denis Savard .08 .25
128 Brad Marsh .08 .25
129 Marcel Dionne DP .08 .25
130 Bryan Erickson .02 .10
131 Reed Larson DP .01 .05
132 Don Beaupre .08 .25
133 Larry Murphy DP .08 .25
134 John Ogrodnick DP .01 .05
135 Greg Adams DP .01 .05
136 Pat Flatley .02 .10
137 Scott Arniel DP .01 .05
138 Dana Murzyn .02 .10
139 Greg C. Adams .02 .10
140 Bob Sauve .08 .25
141 Mike O'Connell .02 .10
142 Walt Poddubny DP .01 .05
143 Paul Reinhart .02 .10
144 Tim Kerr DP .08 .25
145 Brian Lawton .02 .10
146 Gino Cavallini RC .02 .10
147 Doug Keans DP .01 .05
148 Jari Kurri .20 .50
149 Dale Hawerchuk .20 .50
150 Randy Cunneyworth RC .02 .10
151 Jay Wells .02 .10
152 Mike Liut DP .08 .25
153 Steve Konroyd .02 .10
154 John Tucker .02 .10
155 Rick Vaive DP .01 .05
156 Bob Murray .02 .10
157 Kirk Muller DP .20 .50
158 Brian Propp .02 .10
159 Ron Greschner .02 .10
160 Rob Ramage .02 .10
161 Craig Laughlin .02 .10
162 Steve Kasper DP .01 .05
163 Patrick Roy 10.00 25.00
164 Shawn Burr DP RC .08 .25
165 Craig Hartsburg DP .01 .05
166 Dean Evason RC .08 .25
167 Bob Bourne .02 .10
168 Mike Gartner .20 .50
169 Ron Hextall RC 4.00 10.00
170 Joe Cirella .02 .10
171 Dan Quinn DP .01 .05
172 Tony McKegney .02 .10
173 Pat LaFontaine DP .20 .50
174 Allen Pedersen DP .01 .05
175 Doug Gilmour .08 .25
176 Gary Suter DP .01 .05
177 Barry Pederson DP .01 .05
178 Grant Fuhr DP .20 .50
179 Wayne Presley RC .08 .25
180 Wilf Paiement .08 .25
181 Doug Smail .02 .10
182 Doug Crossman DP .01 .05
183 Bernie Nicholls UER .08 .25
(Misspelled Nichols on card front)
184 Dirk Graham UER .08 .25
(Misspelled Dick on card front)
185 Anton Stastny .02 .10
186 Greg Stefan .08 .25
187 Ron Francis .20 .50
188 Steve Thomas DP .15 .40
189 Kelly Miller RC .08 .25
190 Tomas Jonsson .02 .10
191 John MacLean .20 .50
192 Larry Robinson DP .08 .25
193 Doug Wickenheiser DP .01 .05
194 Keith Crowder DP .01 .05
195 Bob Froese .08 .25
196 Jim Johnson .02 .10
197 Checklist 1-99 .30 .75
198 Checklist 100-198 .30 .75

1987-88 Topps Box Bottoms

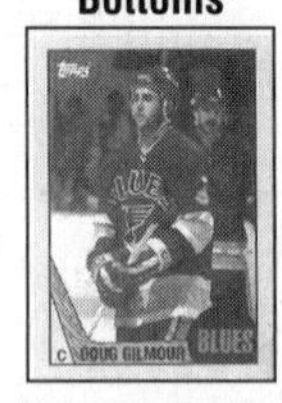

This sixteen-card standard-size set was issued in sets of four on the bottom of the 1987-88 Topps wax pack boxes. The cards feature team scoring leaders. Complete box bottom panels are valued at a 25 percent premium above the prices listed below. The cards are in the same design as the 1987-88 Topps regular issues except they are bordered in yellow. The backs are printed in red and black ink and give statistical information. The cards are lettered rather than numbered.

COMPLETE SET (16) 10.00 25.00
A Wayne Gretzky 4.00 10.00
B Tim Kerr .10 .25
C Steve Yzerman 2.00 5.00
D Luc Robitaille 1.60 4.00
E Doug Gilmour .40 1.00
F Ray Bourque .80 2.00
G Joe Mullen .20 .50
H Larry Murphy .20 .50
I Dale Hawerchuk .24 .60
J Ron Francis .40 1.00
K Walt Poddubny .06 .15
L Mats Naslund .16 .40
M Michel Goulet .20 .50
N Denis Savard .20 .50
O Bryan Trottier .24 .60
P Russ Courtnall .20 .50

1987-88 Topps Sticker Inserts

This set of 33 "Hockey Helmet Stickers" features stickers of 12 All-Star players (1-12) and 21 stickers of team logos, pucks, and numbers. The stickers were inserted in with the 1987-88 Topps hockey regular issue wax packs and as such are also 2 1/2" by 3 1/2". The card backs are printed in blue and red on white card stock. The last seven team stickers can be found with the team logos on the top or bottom.

COMPLETE SET (33) 8.00 20.00
1 Ray Bourque .80 2.00
2 Ron Hextall 1.00 2.50
3 Mark Howe .16 .40
4 Jari Kurri .30 .75
5 Wayne Gretzky 3.20 8.00
6 Michel Goulet .16 .40
7 Larry Murphy .16 .40
8 Mike Liut .16 .40
9 Al MacInnis .20 .50
10 Tim Kerr .10 .25
11 Mario Lemieux 4.00 10.00
12 Luc Robitaille 1.60 4.00
13 Toronto Maple Leafs .10 .25
14 Buffalo Sabres .06 .15
15 Detroit Red Wings .10 .25
16 Pittsburgh Penguins .06 .15
17 New York Rangers .10 .25
18 Calgary Flames .06 .15
19 Winnipeg Jets .06 .15
20 Quebec Nordiques .06 .15
21 Chicago Blackhawks .06 .15
22 Los Angeles Kings .06 .15
23 Montreal Canadiens .10 .25
24 Vancouver Canucks .06 .15
25 Hartford Whalers .06 .15
26 Philadelphia Flyers .06 .15
27 New Jersey Devils .06 .15
28 St. Louis Blues .06 .15
29 Minnesota North Stars .06 .15
30 Washington Capitals .06 .15
31 Boston Bruins .10 .25
32 New York Islanders .06 .15
33 Edmonton Oilers .06 .15

1988-89 Topps

The 1988-89 Topps hockey set contains 1 standard size cards. There are 66 doub printed cards that are indicated by DP in checklist below. The fronts feature color borders and each player's team logo. T backs contain yearly statistics, play statistics, game winning goals from 1987- and highlights. Wayne Gretzky (120) appea as a King for the first time. The pre conference photo has Gretzky holding new Kings jersey. Be careful of counter Brett Hull RCs.

COMPLETE SET (198) 30.00 60.0
1 Mario Lemieux DP 2.50 5.0
2 Bob Joyce DP .01
3 Joel Quenneville DP .01
4 Tony McKegney .02
5 Stephane Richer DP .20
6 Mark Howe DP .01
7 Brent Sutter DP .01
8 Gilles Meloche DP .01
9 Jimmy Carson DP .01
10 John MacLean .08
11 Gary Leeman .02
12 Gerard Gallant DP .01
13 Marcel Dionne .08
14 Dave Christian DP .01
15 Gary Nylund .02
16 Joe Nieuwendyk RC 1.50 4.0
17 Billy Smith DP .08
18 Christian Ruuttu .02
19 Randy Cunneyworth .02
20 Brian Lawton .02
21 Scott Mellanby DP RC .40 1.0
22 Peter Stastny DP .01
23 Gord Kluzak .02
24 Sylvain Turgeon .02
25 Clint Malarchuk .08
26 Denis Savard .08
27 Craig Simpson .02
28 Petr Klima .02
29 Pat Verbeek .02
30 Moe Mantha .02
31 Chris Nilan .02
32 Barry Pederson .02
33 Randy Burridge .02
34 Ron Hextall .40 1.0
35 Gaston Gingras .02
36 Kevin Dineen DP .01
37 Tom Laidlaw .02
38 Paul MacLean DP .01
39 John Chabot DP .01
40 Lindy Ruff .02
41 Dan Quinn DP .01
42 Don Beaupre .08
43 Gary Suter .02
44 Mikko Makela DP RC .01
45 Mark Johnson DP .01
46 Dave Taylor .08
47 Ulf Dahlen DP RC .20
48 Jeff Sharples .02
49 Chris Chelios .40 1.0
50 Mike Gartner DP .08
51 Darren Pang DP RC .20
52 Ron Francis .20
53 Ken Morrow .02
54 Michel Goulet .08
55 Ray Sheppard RC .60 1.5
56 Doug Gilmour .08
57 David Shaw DP .01
58 Cam Neely DP .08
59 Grant Fuhr DP .20
60 Scott Stevens .08
61 Bob Brooke .02
62 Dave Hunter .02
63 Alan Kerr .02
64 Brad Marsh .02
65 Dale Hawerchuk DP .08
66 Brett Hull DP RC 12.50 30.0
67 Patrik Sundstrom DP .01
68 Greg Stefan .08
69 James Patrick .02
70 Dale Hunter DP .01
71 Al Iafrate .08
72 Bob Carpenter .02
73 Ray Bourque DP .40 1.0
74 John Tucker DP .01
75 Carey Wilson .02
76 Joe Mullen .08
77 Rick Vaive .02
78 Shawn Burr DP .01
79 Murray Craven DP .01
80 Clark Gillies .08
81 Bernie Federko .08
82 Tony Tanti .02
83 Greg Gilbert .02
84 Kirk Muller .08
85 Dave Tippett .02
86 Kevin Hatcher DP .08
87 Rick Middleton DP .01
88 Bobby Smith .08
89 Doug Wilson DP .01
90 Scott Arniel .02
91 Brian Mullen .02
92 Mike O'Connell DP .01
93 Mark Messier DP .20
94 Sean Burke RC 1.25 3.0
95 Brian Bellows DP .01
96 Doug Bodger .02
97 Bryan Trottier .20
98 Anton Stastny .02
99 Checklist 1-99 .20
100 Dave Poulin DP .01
101 Bob Bourne DP .01
102 John Vanbiesbrouck .08
103 Allen Pedersen .02

104 Mike Ridley .02 .10
105 Andrew McBain .02 .10
106 Troy Murray DP .01 .05
107 Tom Barrasso .08 .25
108 Tomas Jonsson .02 .10
109 Rob Brown RC .02 .10
110 Hakan Loob DP .01 .05
111 Ilkka Sinisalo DP .01 .05
112 Dave Archibald .02 .10
113 Doug Halward .02 .10
114 Ray Ferraro .02 .10
115 Doug Brown RC .02 .10
116 Patrick Roy DP 1.50 4.00
117 Greg Millen .08 .25
118 Ken Linseman .02 .10
119 Phil Housley DP .08 .25
120 Wayne Gretzky 8.00 20.00
(Holding up Kings sweater)
121 Tomas Sandstrom .08 .25
122 Brendan Shanahan RC 6.00 15.00
123 Pat LaFontaine .20 .50
124 Luc Robitaille DP .75 2.00
125 Ed Olczyk DP .01 .05
126 Ron Sutter .02 .10
127 Mike Liut .08 .25
128 Brent Ashton DP .01 .05
129 Tony Hrkac RC .02 .10
130 Kelly Miller .02 .10
131 Alan Haworth .02 .10
132 Dave McLlwain RC .02 .10
133 Mike Ramsey .02 .10
134 Bob Sweeney RC .02 .10
135 Dirk Graham DP .01 .05
136 Ulf Samuelsson .20 .50
137 Petri Skriko .02 .10
138 Aaron Broten DP .01 .05
139 Jim Fox .02 .10
140 Randy Wood DP RC .01 .05
141 Larry Murphy .08 .25
142 Daniel Berthiaume DP .01 .05
143 Kelly Kisio .02 .10
144 Neal Broten .02 .10
145 Reed Larson .02 .10
146 Peter Zezel DP .01 .05
147 Jari Kurri .20 .50
148 Jim Johnson .02 .10
149 Gino Cavallini DP .01 .05
150 Glen Hanlon DP .08 .25
151 Bengt Gustafsson .02 .10
152 Mike Bullard DP .01 .05
153 John Ogrodnick .02 .10
154 Steve Larmer .08 .25
155 Kelly Hrudey .08 .25
156 Mats Naslund .02 .10
157 Bruce Driver .02 .10
158 Randy Hillier .02 .10
159 Craig Hartsburg .02 .10
160 Rollie Melanson .08 .25
161 Adam Oates DP .60 1.50
162 Greg Adams DP .01 .05
163 Dave Andreychuk DP .08 .25
164 Dave Babych .02 .10
165 Brian Noonan RC .02 .10
166 Glen Wesley RC .02 .10
167 Dave Ellett .02 .10
168 Brian Propp .02 .10
169 Bernie Nicholls .08 .25
170 Walt Poddubny .02 .10
171 Steve Konroyd .02 .10
172 Doug Sulliman DP .01 .05
173 Mario Gosselin .08 .25
174 Brian Benning .02 .10
175 Dino Ciccarelli .08 .25
176 Steve Kasper .02 .10
177 Rick Tocchet .40 1.00
178 Brad McCrimmon .02 .10
179 Paul Coffey .40 1.00
180 Pete Peeters .08 .25
181 Bob Probert DP RC .60 1.50
182 Steve Duchesne DP RC .40 1.00
183 Russ Courtnall .08 .25
184 Mike Foligno DP .01 .05
185 Wayne Presley DP .01 .05
186 Rejean Lemelin .08 .25
187 Mark Hunter .02 .10
188 Joe Cirella .02 .10
189 Glenn Anderson DP .08 .25
190 John Anderson .02 .10
191 Pat Flatley .02 .10
192 Rod Langway .02 .10
193 Brian MacLellan .02 .10
194 Pierre Turgeon RC 4.00 10.00
195 Brian Hayward .08 .25
196 Steve Yzerman DP 1.25 3.00
197 Doug Crossman .02 .10
198 Checklist 100-198 .20 .50

1988-89 Topps Box Bottoms

This sixteen-card standard-size set was issued in sets of four on the bottom of the 1988-89 Topps wax pack boxes. The cards feature team scoring leaders. Complete box bottom panels are valued at a 25 percent premium above the prices listed below. The cards are in the same design as the 1988-89 Topps regular issues except they are bordered only in gray. The backs are printed in purple on orange background and give statistical information. The cards are lettered rather than numbered.

COMPLETE SET (16) 5.60 14.00
A Ron Francis .30 .75
B Wayne Gretzky 2.40 6.00
C Pat LaFontaine .30 .75
D Bobby Smith .10 .25
E Bernie Federko .10 .25
F Kirk Muller .20 .50
G Ed Olczyk .06 .15
H Denis Savard .20 .50
I Ray Bourque .60 1.50
J Murray Craven and Brian Propp .06 .15
K Dale Hawerchuk .20 .50
L Steve Yzerman 1.20 3.00
M Dave Andreychuk .16 .40
N Mike Gartner .20 .50
O Hakan Loob .10 .25
P Luc Robitaille .40 1.00

1988-89 Topps Sticker Inserts

This set of 33 "Hockey Helmet Stickers" features stickers of 12 All-Star players (1-12) and 21 stickers of team logos, pucks, and numbers. The stickers were inserted in with the 1988-89 Topps hockey regular issue wax packs and as such are also 2 1/2" by 3 1/2". The card backs are printed in blue and red on white card stock. The last seven team stickers can be found with the team logos on the top or bottom.

COMPLETE SET (33) 6.00 15.00
1 Luc Robitaille .60 1.50
2 Mario Lemieux 1.60 4.00
3 Hakan Loob .10 .25
4 Scott Stevens .16 .40
5 Ray Bourque .30 .75
6 Grant Fuhr .20 .50
7 Michel Goulet .16 .40
8 Wayne Gretzky 2.00 5.00
9 Cam Neely .30 .75
10 Brad McCrimmon .10 .25
11 Gary Suter .10 .25
12 Patrick Roy 2.00 5.00
13 Toronto Maple Leafs .10 .25
14 Buffalo Sabres .06 .15
15 Detroit Red Wings .10 .25
16 Pittsburgh Penguins .06 .15
17 New York Rangers .10 .25
18 Calgary Flames .06 .15
19 Winnipeg Jets .06 .15
20 Quebec Nordiques .06 .15
21 Chicago Blackhawks .10 .25
22 Los Angeles Kings .06 .15
23 Montreal Canadiens .10 .25
24 Vancouver Canucks .06 .15
25 Hartford Whalers .06 .15
26 Philadelphia Flyers .06 .15
27 New Jersey Devils .06 .15
28 St. Louis Blues .06 .15
29 Minnesota North Stars .06 .15
30 Washington Capitals .06 .15
31 Boston Bruins .10 .25
32 New York Islanders .06 .15
33 Edmonton Oilers .06 .15

1989-90 Topps

The 1989-90 Topps set contains 198 standard-size cards. There are 66 double-printed cards which are marked as DP in the checklist below. The fronts feature blue borders on top and bottom that are prone to chipping. An ice blue border is on either side. A team logo and the player's name are at the bottom. The backs contain yearly statistics, playoff statistics, game-winning goals from 1988-89 and highlights. The key Rookie Card in this set is Joe Sakic.

COMPLETE SET (198) 15.00 30.00
1 Mario Lemieux 2.00 4.00
2 Ulf Dahlen DP .02 .10
3 Terry Carkner RC .02 .10
4 Tony McKegney .02 .10
5 Denis Savard .08 .25
6 Derek King DP RC .20 .50
7 Lanny McDonald .08 .25
8 John Tonelli .02 .10
9 Tom Kurvers DP .02 .10
10 Dave Archibald .02 .10
11 Peter Sidorkiewicz RC .08 .25
12 Esa Tikkanen .08 .25
13 Dave Barr .02 .10
14 Brent Sutter .08 .25
15 Cam Neely .20 .50
16 Calle Johansson RC .02 .10
17 Patrick Roy DP .75 2.00
18 Dale DeGray DP .02 .10
19 Phil Bourque RC .02 .10
20 Kevin Dineen .02 .10
21 Mike Bullard DP .02 .10
22 Gary Leeman .02 .10
23 Greg Stefan DP .08 .25
24 Brian Mullen .02 .10
25 Pierre Turgeon DP .30 .75
26 Bob Rouse DP .02 .10
27 Peter Zezel .02 .10
28 Jeff Brown DP .20 .50
29 Andy Brickley DP RC .02 .10
30 Mike Gartner .08 .25
31 Darren Pang .08 .25
32 Pat Verbeek .02 .10
33 Petri Skriko DP .02 .10
34 Tom Laidlaw .02 .10
35 Randy Wood .02 .10
36 Tom Barrasso DP .08 .25
37 John Tucker DP .02 .10
38 Andrew McBain .02 .10
39 David Shaw DP .02 .10
40 Rejean Lemelin .08 .25
41 Dino Ciccarelli DP .08 .25
42 Jeff Sharples .02 .10
43 Jari Kurri .20 .50
44 Murray Craven DP .02 .10
45 Cliff Ronning DP RC .50 1.25
46 Dave Babych .02 .10
47 Bernie Nicholls DP .08 .25
48 Jon Casey RC .08 .25
49 Al MacInnis .08 .25
50 Bob Errey DP RC .08 .25
51 Glen Wesley .02 .10
52 Dirk Graham .02 .10
53 Guy Carbonneau DP .08 .25
54 Tomas Sandstrom .08 .25
55 Rod Langway DP .02 .10
56 Patrik Sundstrom .02 .10
57 Michel Goulet .08 .25
58 Dave Taylor .08 .25
59 Phil Housley .08 .25
60 Pat LaFontaine DP .20 .50
61 Kirk McLean DP RC .30 .75
62 Ken Linseman .02 .10
63A Randy Cunneyworth ERR 2.50 6.00
(Pittsburgh Penguins)
63B Randy Cunneyworth COR .02 .10
64 Tony Hrkac DP .02 .10
65 Mark Messier DP .20 .50
66 Carey Wilson DP .02 .10
67 Stephen Leach RC .02 .10
68 Christian Ruuttu .02 .10
69 Dave Ellett .02 .10
70 Ray Ferraro .02 .10
71 Colin Patterson .02 .10
72 Tim Kerr .08 .25
73 Bob Joyce .02 .10
74 Doug Gilmour DP .08 .25
75 Lee Norwood DP .02 .10
76 Dale Hunter .08 .25
77 Jim Johnson DP .02 .10
78 Mike Foligno DP .02 .10
79 Al Iafrate DP .08 .25
80 Rick Tocchet DP .08 .25
81 Greg Hawgood DP RC .02 .10
82 Steve Thomas .08 .25
83 Steve Yzerman DP .75 2.00
84 Mike McPhee .02 .10
85 David Volek DP RC .02 .10
86 Brian Benning .02 .10
87 Neal Broten .08 .25
88 Luc Robitaille .08 .25
89 Trevor Linden RC .50 1.25
90 James Patrick DP .02 .10
91 Brian Lawton .02 .10
92 Sean Burke DP .08 .25
93 Scott Stevens .08 .25
94 Pat Elynuik DP RC .02 .10
95 Paul Coffey .20 .50
96 Jan Erixon DP .02 .10
97 Mike Liut .08 .25
98 Wayne Presley .02 .10
99 Craig Simpson .08 .25
100 Kjell Samuelsson RC .08 .25
101 Shawn Burr DP .02 .10
102 John MacLean .08 .25
103 Tom Fergus .02 .10
104 Mike Krushelnyski .02 .10
105 Gary Nylund .02 .10
106 Dave Andreychuk .08 .25
107 Bernie Federko .08 .25
108 Gary Suter .08 .25
109 Dave Gagner DP .08 .25
110 Ray Bourque .30 .75
111 Geoff Courtnall RC .40 1.00
112 Doug Wilson .08 .25
113 Joe Sakic RC 6.00 15.00
114 John Vanbiesbrouck .08 .25
115 Dave Poulin .02 .10
116 Rick Meagher .02 .10
117 Kirk Muller DP .08 .25
118 Mats Naslund .02 .10
119 Ray Sheppard .20 .50
120 Jeff Norton RC .02 .10
121 Randy Burridge DP .02 .10
122 Dale Hawerchuk DP .08 .25
123 Steve Duchesne .08 .25
124 John Anderson .02 .10
125 Rick Vaive DP .02 .10
126 Randy Hillier .02 .10
127 Jimmy Carson .02 .10
128 Larry Murphy .08 .25
129 Paul MacLean DP .02 .10
130 Joe Cirella .02 .10
131 Kelly Miller DP .02 .10
132 Alain Chevrier DP .08 .25
133 Ed Olczyk .02 .10
134 Dave Tippett .02 .10
135 Bob Sweeney .02 .10
136 Brian Leetch RC 3.00 6.00
137 Greg Millen .08 .25
138 Joe Nieuwendyk .20 .50
139 Brian Propp .02 .10
140 Mike Ramsey .02 .10
141 Mike Allison .02 .10
142 Shawn Chambers RC .02 .10
143 Peter Stastny DP .08 .25
144 Glen Hanlon .08 .25
145 John Cullen RC .08 .25
146 Kevin Hatcher .02 .10
147 Brendan Shanahan .20 .50
148 Paul Reinhart .02 .10
149 Bryan Trottier .20 .50
150 Dave Manson RC .20 .50
151 Marc Habscheid DP .02 .10
152 Dan Quinn .02 .10
153 Stephane Richer DP .08 .25
154 Doug Bodger DP .02 .10
155 Ron Hextall .20 .50
156 Wayne Gretzky 1.50 4.00
157 Steve Tuttle DP .02 .10
158 Charlie Huddy DP .02 .10
159 Dave Christian DP .02 .10
160 Andy Moog .08 .25
161 Tony Granato RC .20 .50
162 Sylvain Cote .02 .10
163 Mike Vernon .30 .75
164 Steve Chiasson RC .08 .25
165 Mike Ridley .02 .10
166 Kelly Hrudey .08 .25
167 Bob Carpenter DP .02 .10
168 Zarley Zalapski RC .20 .50
169 Derek Laxdal .02 .10
170 Clint Malarchuk DP .08 .25
171 Kelly Kisio .02 .10
172 Gerard Gallant .02 .10
173 Ron Sutter .02 .10
174 Chris Chelios .20 .50
175 Ron Francis .20 .50
176 Gino Cavallini .02 .10
177 Brian Bellows DP .02 .10
178 Greg C. Adams DP .02 .10
179 Steve Larmer .08 .25
180 Aaron Broten .02 .10
181 Brent Ashton DP .02 .10
182 Gerald Diduck DP .02 .10
183 Paul MacDermid .02 .10
184 Walt Poddubny DP .02 .10
185 Adam Oates .20 .50
186 Brett Hull 1.25 3.00
187 Scott Arniel .02 .10
188 Bobby Smith .08 .25
189 Guy Lafleur .08 .25
190 Craig Janney RC .30 .75
191 Mark Howe .08 .25
192 Grant Fuhr DP .20 .50
193 Rob Brown .02 .10
194 Steve Kasper DP .02 .10
195 Pete Peeters .08 .25
196 Joe Mullen .08 .25
197 Checklist 1-99 .02 .10
198 Checklist 100-198 DP .02 .10

1989-90 Topps Box Bottoms

This sixteen-card standard-size set was issued in sets of four on the bottom of the 1989-90 Topps wax pack boxes. The cards feature sixteen NHL star players who were scoring leaders on their teams. Complete box bottom panels are valued at a 25 percent premium above the prices listed below. A color action photo appears on the front and the player's name, team, and team logo at the bottom of the picture. The back is printed in red and black ink and gives the player's position and statistical information. The cards are lettered rather than numbered. The set features such NHL stars as Wayne Gretzky, Brett Hull, and Mario Lemieux.

COMPLETE SET (16) 4.00 10.00
A Mario Lemieux 1.60 4.00
B Mike Ridley .10 .25
C Tomas Sandstrom .10 .25
D Petri Skriko .10 .25
E Wayne Gretzky 1.60 4.00
F Brett Hull .80 2.00
G Tim Kerr .10 .25
H Mats Naslund .10 .25
I Jari Kurri .20 .50
J Steve Larmer .20 .50
K Cam Neely .30 .75
L Steve Yzerman .80 2.00
M Kevin Dineen .10 .25
N Dave Gagner .16 .40
O Joe Mullen .16 .40
P Pierre Turgeon .30 .75

1989-90 Topps Sticker Inserts

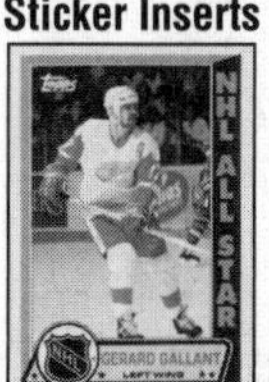

This 33-card standard-size set was issued as a one per pack insert in the 1989-90 Topps Hockey packs. This set is divided into the first 12 cards being the 1989-90 NHL all-stars and the next 21 cards being the various team logos along with some number stickers and stickers of hockey pucks. For some reason Topps apparently printed these sticker cards on sheets in such a way that there were three complete sets of 33 and then three more rows of 11 double-printed cards instead of merely printing four complete sets on the printing sheet.

COMPLETE SET (33) 4.00 10.00
1 Chris Chelios .30 .75
2 Gerard Gallant DP .06 .15
3 Mario Lemieux 2.00 5.00
4 Al MacInnis .20 .50
5 Joe Mullen DP .10 .25
6 Patrick Roy 1.60 4.00
7 Ray Bourque .30 .75
8 Rob Brown .10 .25
9 Geoff Courtnall DP .10 .25
10 Steve Duchesne DP .06 .15
11 Wayne Gretzky 2.00 5.00
12 Mike Vernon .16 .40
13 Toronto Maple Leafs .06 .15
14 Buffalo Sabres .06 .15
15 Detroit Red Wings .06 .15
16 Pittsburgh Penguins .06 .15
17 New York Rangers .06 .15
18 Calgary Flames .06 .15
19 Winnipeg Jets .06 .15
20 Quebec Nordiques .06 .15
21 Chicago Blackhawks .06 .15
22 Los Angeles Kings .06 .15
23 Montreal Canadiens .06 .15
24 Vancouver Canucks .06 .15
25 Hartford Whalers .06 .15
26 Philadelphia Flyers .06 .15
27 New Jersey Devils DP .04 .10
28 St. Louis Blues DP .04 .10
29 Minn. North Stars DP .04 .10
30 Washington Capitals DP .04 .10
31 Boston Bruins DP .04 .10
32 New York Islanders DP .04 .10
33 Edmonton Oilers DP .04 .10

1990-91 Topps

The 1990-91 Topps hockey set contains 396 standard-size cards. The fronts feature color action photos with color borders (according to team) on all four sides. A hockey stick is superimposed over the picture at the top border. The backs have yearly statistics, playoff statistics, and game winning goals from 1989-90. Included in the set is a three-card Tribute to Wayne Gretzky (1-3). Team cards have action scenes with the team's previous season standings and power play stats on back.

COMPLETE SET (396) 5.00 15.00
COMP.FACT.SET (396) 10.00 20.00
1 Gretzky Tribute .40 1.00
Indianapolis Racers
2 Gretzky Tribute .20 .50
3 Gretzky Tribute .20 .50
4 Brett Hull HL .08 .25
5 Jari Kurri HL .02 .10
6 Bryan Trottier HL .02 .10
7 Jeremy Roenick RC .40 1.00
8 Brian Propp .01 .05
9 Jim Hrivnak RC .02 .10
10 Mick Vukota .01 .05
11 Tom Kurvers .01 .05
12 Ulf Dahlen .01 .05
13 Bernie Nicholls .02 .10
14 Peter Sidorkiewicz .02 .10
15 Peter Zezel .01 .05
16 Mike Hartman .01 .05
17 Kings Team .01 .05
18 Jim Sandlak .01 .05
19 Rob Brown .01 .05
20 Paul Ranheim RC .01 .05
21 Rick Zombo .01 .05
22 Paul Gillis .01 .05
23 Brian Hayward .02 .10
24 Brent Ashton .01 .05
25 Mark Lamb .01 .05
26 Rick Tocchet .02 .10
27 Slava Fetisov RC .02 .10
28 Denis Savard .02 .10
29 Chris Chelios .08 .25
30 Janne Ojanen .01 .05
31 Don Maloney .01 .05
32 Allan Bester .02 .10
33 Geoff Smith .01 .05
34 Daniel Shank .01 .05
35 Mikael Andersson RC .01 .05
36 Gino Cavallini .01 .05
37 Rob Murphy .01 .05
38 Flames Team .01 .05
39 Laurie Boschman .01 .05
40 Craig Wolanin .01 .05
41 Phil Bourque .01 .05
42 Alexander Mogilny RC .40 1.00
43 Ray Bourque .15 .40
44 Mike Liut .02 .10
45 Ron Sutter .01 .05
46 Bob Kudelski RC .01 .05
47 Larry Murphy .02 .10
48 Darren Turcotte RC .01 .05
49 Paul Ysebaert RC .01 .05
50 Alan Kerr .01 .05
51 Randy Carlyle .01 .05
52 Iiro Jarvi .01 .05
53 Don Barber .01 .05
54 Carey Wilson .01 .05
55 Joey Kocur RC .15 .40
56 Steve Larmer .02 .10
57 Paul Cavallini .01 .05
58 Shayne Corson .01 .05
59 Canucks Team .01 .05
60 Sergei Makarov RC .01 .05
61 Kjell Samuelsson .01 .05
62 Tony Granato .01 .05
63 Tom Fergus .01 .05
64 Martin Gelinas RC .15 .40
65 Tom Barrasso .02 .10
66 Pierre Turgeon .02 .10
67 Randy Cunneyworth .01 .05
68 Michal Pivonka RC .02 .10
69 Cam Neely .08 .25
70 Brian Bellows .01 .05
71 Pat Elynuik .01 .05
72 Doug Crossman .01 .05
73 Sylvain Turgeon .01 .05
74 Shawn Burr .01 .05
75 John Vanbiesbrouck .02 .10
76 Steve Bozek .01 .05
77 Brett Hull .20 .50
78 Zarley Zalapski .01 .05
79 Wendel Clark .02 .10
80 Flyers Team .01 .05
81 Kelly Miller .01 .05
82 Mark Pederson .01 .05
83 Adam Creighton .01 .05
84 Scott Young .01 .05
85 Petr Klima .01 .05
86 Steve Duchesne .01 .05
87 Joe Nieuwendyk .02 .10
88 Andy Brickley .01 .05
89 Phil Housley .02 .10
90 Neal Broten .02 .10
91 Al Iafrate .02 .10
92 Steve Thomas .01 .05
93 Guy Carbonneau .02 .10
94 Steve Chiasson .01 .05
95 Mike Tomlak .01 .05
96 Roger Johansson .01 .05
97 Randy Wood .01 .05
98 Jim Johnson .01 .05
99 Bob Sweeney .01 .05
100 Dino Ciccarelli .02 .10
101 Rangers Team .01 .05
102 Mike Ramsey .01 .05
103 Kelly Hrudey .02 .10
104 Dave Ellett .01 .05
105 Bob Brooke .01 .05
106 Greg Adams .01 .05
107 Joe Cirella .01 .05
108 Jari Kurri .02 .10
109 Pete Peeters .02 .10
110 Paul MacLean .01 .05
111 Doug Wilson .02 .10
112 Pat Verbeek .01 .05
113 Bob Beers RC .01 .05
114 Mike O'Connell .01 .05
115 Brian Bradley .01 .05
116 Paul Coffey .08 .25
117 Doug Brown .01 .05
118 Aaron Broten .01 .05
119 Bob Essensa RC .15 .40
120 Wayne Gretzky UER .50 1.25
(1302 career assists not 13102)
121 Vincent Damphousse .01 .05
122 Nordiques Team .01 .05
123 Mike Foligno .01 .05
124 Russ Courtnall .01 .05
125 Rick Meagher .01 .05
126 Craig Fisher .01 .05
127 Al MacInnis .02 .10
128 Derek King .01 .05
129 Dale Hunter .01 .05
130 Mark Messier UER .08 .25
(Shown as LW& should be C)
131 James Patrick UER .01 .05
(Orange border& should be blue)
132 Checklist 1-132 UER .01 .05
(54 Cary Wilson should be Carey)
133 Red Wings Team .08 .25
134 Barry Pederson .01 .05
135 Gary Leeman .01 .05
136 Doug Gilmour .02 .10
137 Mike McPhee .01 .05
138 Bob Murray .01 .05
139 Bob Carpenter .01 .05
140 Sean Burke .02 .10
141 Dale Hawerchuk .02 .10
142 Guy Lafleur .08 .25
143 Lindy Ruff .01 .05
144 Whalers Team .01 .05
145 Glenn Anderson .02 .10
146 Dave Chyzowski .01 .05
147 Kevin Hatcher .01 .05
148 Rick Vaive .01 .05
149 Adam Oates .02 .10
150 Garth Butcher .01 .05
151 Basil McRae .01 .05
152 Ilkka Sinisalo .01 .05
153 Steve Kasper .01 .05
154 Greg Paslawski .01 .05
155 Brad Marsh .01 .05
156 Esa Tikkanen .01 .05
157 Tony Tanti .01 .05
158 Mario Marois .01 .05
(oi in last name line below rest of name)
159 Sylvain Lefebvre .01 .05
160 Troy Murray .01 .05
161 Gary Roberts .01 .05
162 Randy Ladouceur .01 .05
163 John Chabot .01 .05
164 Calle Johansson .01 .05
165 Bruins Team .01 .05
166 Jeff Norton .01 .05
167 Mike Krushelnyski .01 .05
168 Dave Gagner .02 .10
169 Dave Andreychuk .02 .10
170 Dave Capuano .01 .05
171 Curtis Joseph RC .50 1.25
172 Bruce Driver .01 .05
173 Scott Mellanby .02 .10
174 John Ogrodnick .01 .05
175 Mario Lemieux .60 1.25
176 Marc Fortier .01 .05
177 Vincent Riendeau RC .02 .10
178 Mark Johnson .01 .05
179 Dirk Graham .01 .05
180 Jets Team .01 .05
(Keith Acton breaking in on Daniel Berthiaume)
181 Robb Stauber RC .02 .10
182 Christian Ruuttu .01 .05
183 Dave Tippett .01 .05
184 Pat LaFontaine .08 .25
185 Mark Howe .01 .05
186 Stephane Richer .02 .10
187 Jan Erixon .01 .05
188 Neil Sheehy .01 .05
189 Craig MacTavish .01 .05
190 Randy Burridge .01 .05
191 Bernie Federko .02 .10
192 Shawn Chambers .01 .05
193 Mark Messier AS1 .08 .25
194 Luc Robitaille AS1 .02 .10
195 Brett Hull AS1 .02 .10
196 Ray Bourque AS1 .02 .10
197 Al MacInnis AS1 .02 .10
198 Patrick Roy AS1 .20 .50
199 Wayne Gretzky AS2 .25 .60
200 Brian Bellows AS2 .01 .05
201 Cam Neely AS2 .02 .10
202 Paul Coffey AS2 .01 .05
203 Doug Wilson AS2 .01 .05
204 Daren Puppa AS2 UER .02 .10
(Misspelled Darren on front and back)
205 Gary Suter .01 .05
206 Ed Olczyk .01 .05
207 Doug Lidster .01 .05
208 John Cullen .01 .05
209 Luc Robitaille .02 .10
210 Tim Kerr .01 .05
211 Scott Stevens .02 .10
212 Craig Janney .02 .10
213 Kevin Dineen .01 .05
214 Jimmy Waite RC .02 .10
215 Benoit Hogue .01 .05
216 Curtis Leschyshyn RC .01 .05
217 Brad Lauer .01 .05
218 Joe Mullen .02 .10
219 Patrick Roy .40 1.00
220 Blues Team .01 .05
221 Brian Leetch .10 .30
222 Steve Yzerman .40 1.00
223 Stephane Beauregard RC .02 .10
224 John MacLean .02 .10
225 Trevor Linden .02 .10
226 Bill Ranford .02 .10
227 Mark Osborne .01 .05
228 Curt Giles .01 .05
229 Mikko Makela .01 .05
230 Bob Errey .01 .05
231 Jimmy Carson .01 .05
232 Kay Whitmore RC .02 .10
233 Gary Nylund .01 .05
234 Jiri Hrdina .01 .05
235 Stephen Leach .01 .05
236 Greg Hawgood .01 .05
237 Jocelyn Lemieux .01 .05
238 Daren Puppa .02 .10
239 Kelly Kisio .01 .05
240 Craig Simpson .01 .05
241 Maple Leafs Team .01 .05
242 Fredrik Olausson .01 .05
243 Ron Hextall .02 .10
244 Sergio Momesso RC .01 .05
245 Kirk Muller .01 .05
246 Petr Svoboda .01 .05
247 Daniel Berthiaume .02 .10
248 Andrew McBain .01 .05
249 Jeff Jackson UER .01 .05
(Game total for '89-90 is 65 not 0)
250 Randy Gilhen .01 .05
251 Oilers Team .01 .05
252 Rick Bennett .01 .05
253 Don Beaupre .02 .10
254 Pelle Eklund .01 .05
255 Greg Gilbert .01 .05
256 Gordie Roberts .01 .05
257 Kirk McLean .02 .10
258 Brent Sutter .01 .05
259 Brendan Shanahan .08 .25
260 Todd Krygier .01 .05
261 Larry Robinson UER .02 .10
(No '80-81 stats on card& totals wrong)
262 Sabres Team .01 .05
263 Dave Christian .01 .05
264 Checklist 133-264 .01 .05
265 Jamie Macoun .01 .05
266 Glen Hanlon .02 .10
267 Daniel Marois .01 .05
268 Doug Smail .01 .05
269 Jon Casey .02 .10
270 Brian Skrudland .01 .05
271 Michel Petit .01 .05
272 Dan Quinn .01 .05
273 Geoff Courtnall .01 .05
274 Mike Bullard .01 .05
275 Randy Gregg .01 .05
276 Keith Brown .01 .05
277 Troy Mallette .01 .05
278 Steve Tuttle .01 .05
279 Brad Shaw .01 .05
280 Mark Recchi RC .50 1.25
281 John Tonelli .01 .05
282 Doug Bodger .01 .05
283 Thomas Steen .01 .05
284 Devils Team .01 .05
285 Lee Norwood .01 .05
286 Brian MacLellan .01 .05
287 Bobby Smith .02 .10
288 Rob Cimetta .01 .05
289 Rob Zettler RC .01 .05
290 David Reid .01 .05
291 Bryan Trottier .02 .10
292 Brian Mullen .01 .05
293 Paul Reinhart .01 .05
294 Andy Moog .02 .10
295 Jeff Brown .01 .05
296 Ryan Walter .01 .05
297 Trent Yawney .01 .05
298 John Druce .01 .05
299 Dave McLlwain UER .01 .05
(Card says shoots right, should be left)
300 David Volek .01 .05
301 Tomas Sandstrom .01 .05
302 Gord Murphy RC .01 .05
303 Lou Franceschetti .01 .05
304 Dana Murzyn .01 .05
305 North Stars Team .01 .05
306 Patrik Sundstrom .01 .05
307 Kevin Lowe .01 .05
308 Dave Barr .01 .05
309 Wendell Young .02 .10
310 Darrin Shannon RC .01 .05
311 Ron Francis .02 .10
312 Stephane Fiset RC .15 .40
313 Paul Fenton .01 .05
314 Dave Taylor .02 .10
315 Islanders Team .01 .05
316 Petri Skriko .01 .05
317 Rob Ramage .01 .05
318 Murray Craven .01 .05
319 Gaetan Duchesne .01 .05
320 Brad McCrimmon .01 .05
321 Grant Fuhr .02 .10

322 Gerard Gallant .01 .05
323 Tommy Albelin .01 .05
324 Scott Arniel .01 .05
325 Mike Keane RC .01 .05
326 Penguins Team .01 .05
327 Mike Ridley .01 .05
328 Dave Babych .01 .05
329 Michel Goulet .02 .10
330 Mike Richter RC .30 .75
331 Garry Galley RC .01 .05
332 Rod Brind'Amour RC .25 .60
333 Tony McKegney .01 .05
334 Peter Stastny .02 .10
335 Greg Millen .02 .10
336 Ray Ferraro .01 .05
337 Miloslav Horava .01 .05
338 Paul MacDermid .01 .05
339 Craig Coxe .01 .05
340 Dave Snuggerud .01 .05
341 Mike Lalor .01 .05
342 Marc Habscheid .01 .05
343 Rejean Lemelin .02 .10
344 Charlie Huddy .01 .05
345 Ken Linseman .01 .05
346 Canadiens Team .01 .05
347 Troy Loney .01 .05
348 Mike Modano RC .50 1.25
349 Jeff Reese RC .01 .05
350 Pat Flatley .01 .05
351 Mike Vernon .02 .10
352 Todd Elik RC .01 .05
353 Rod Langway .01 .05
354 Moe Mantha .01 .05
355 Keith Acton .01 .05
356 Scott Pearson .01 .05
357 Perry Berezan .01 .05
358 Alexei Kasatonov RC .01 .05
359 Igor Larionov RC .15 .40
360 Kevin Stevens RC .01 .05
361 Yves Racine RC .01 .05
362 Dave Poulin .01 .05
363 Blackhawks Team .01 .05
364 Yvon Corriveau .01 .05
365 Brian Benning .01 .05
366 Hubie McDonough .01 .05
367 Ron Tugnutt .02 .10
368 Steve Smith .01 .05
369 Joel Otto .01 .05
370 Dave Lowry .01 .05
371 Clint Malarchuk .02 .10
372 Mathieu Schneider RC .01 .05
373 Mike Gartner .02 .10
374 John Tucker .01 .05
375 Chris Terreri RC .02 .10
376 Dean Evason .01 .05
377 Jamie Leach .01 .05
378 Jacques Cloutier .02 .10
379 Glen Wesley .01 .05
380 Vladimir Krutov .02 .10
381 Terry Carkner .01 .05
382 John McIntyre RC .01 .05
383 Ville Siren .01 .05
384 Joe Sakic .25 .60
385 Teppo Numminen RC .01 .05
386 Theo Fleury .15 .50
387 Glen Featherstone .01 .05
388 Stephan Lebeau RC .01 .05
389 Kevin McClelland .01 .05
390 Uwe Krupp .01 .05
391 Mark Janssens .01 .05
392 Marty McSorley .01 .05
393 Vladimir Ruzicka RC .01 .05
394 Capitals Team .01 .05
395 Mark Fitzpatrick RC .02 .10
396 Checklist 265-396 .01 .05

1990-91 Topps Tiffany

Parallel to base set, Topps only produced 3000 sets. Cards can be distinguished by a glossy coating not found on regular issued cards.

COMPLETE SET (396) 60.00 150.00
*STARS: 10X TO 25X HI COLUMN
*RC's: 5X TO 10X HI

1990-91 Topps Box Bottoms

This 16-card standard-size set was issued in sets of four on the bottom of the 1990-91 Topps wax pack boxes. The cards are lettered rather than numbered. Complete box bottom panels are valued at a 25 percent premium above the prices listed below. The front design of these cards is essentially the same as the regular issue cards. The horizontally oriented backs have special statistics in blue lettering on a pale green background. The checklist does not agree with the actual grouping of the players in the four sets.

COMPLETE SET (16) 3.20 8.00
A Alexander Mogilny .50 1.25
B Jon Casey .16 .40
C Paul Coffey .24 .60
D Wayne Gretzky 1.00 2.50
E Patrick Roy .60 1.50
F Mike Modano .30 .75
G Mario Lemieux .60 1.50
H Al MacInnis .16 .40
I Ray Bourque .24 .60
J Steve Yzerman .40 1.00
K Darren Turcotte .10 .25
L Mike Vernon .16 .40
M Pierre Turgeon .20 .50
N Doug Wilson .10 .25
O Don Beaupre .16 .40
P Sergei Makarov .10 .25

1990-91 Topps Team Scoring Leaders

The 21-cards in this standard size set was included as a one per pack insert in the 1990-91 Topps hockey packs. This set has a glossy front with a full color action shot of the team's leading scorer while the back of the card has a list of the ten leading scorers for each team.

COMPLETE SET (21) 3.00 7.50
1 Steve Larmer .08 .20
2 Brett Hull .30 .75
3 Cam Neely .20 .50
4 Stephane Richer .10 .25
5 Paul Reinhart .04 .10
6 Dino Ciccarelli .10 .25
7 Kirk Muller .10 .25
8 Joe Nieuwendyk .12 .30
9 Rick Tocchet .10 .25
10 Pat LaFontaine .10 .25
11 Dale Hawerchuk .20 .50
12 Wayne Gretzky .80 2.00
13 Gary Leeman .04 .10
14 Joe Sakic .40 1.00
15 Brian Bellows .06 .15
16 Mark Messier .30 .75
17 Mario Lemieux .60 1.50
18 John Ogrodnick .04 .10
19 Steve Yzerman .40 1.00
20 Pierre Turgeon .20 .50
21 Ron Francis .20 .50

1991-92 Topps

The 1991-92 O-Pee-Chee and Topps hockey sets contain 528 standard-size cards. Both sets feature a Guy Lafleur Tribute (1-3) and a Super Rookie (4-13) subset. Topps hockey cards were sold in 15-card packs that included a bonus team scoring leader card, whereas the O-Pee-Chee cards were sold in nine-card wax packs that included a stick of gum plus one insert card from a special 66-card insert set. The fronts have glossy color action player photos, with two different color border stripes and a white card face. In the lower right corner, the team logo appears as a hockey puck superimposed on a hockey stick. They present full player information, including biography, statistics, 1990-91 game-winning goals, and NHL playoff record (the OPC cards present player information in French as well as English). The card number appears next to a hockey skate in the upper right corner of the back. Rookie Cards in this set include Tony Amonte, Valeri Kamensky and John LeClair.

COMPLETE SET (528) 5.00 12.00
COMPLETE FACT.SET (528) 5.00 12.00
*OPC: SAME VALUE
1 Lafleur Tribute .02 .10
Goodbye Guy
2 Lafleur Tribute .02 .10
Gueeey's Last Hoorah
3 Lafleur Tribute .02 .10
Guy Bids Farewell
4 Ed Belfour SR .02 .10
5 Ken Hodge Jr. SR .01 .05
6 Rob Blake SR UER .01 .05
(Center on back& should say Defense)
7 Bobby Holik SR .01 .05
8 Sergei Fedorov SR UER .07 .20
(Name misspelled on front and in stats)
9 Jaromir Jagr SR .02 .10
10 Eric Weinrich SR .01 .05
11 Mike Richter SR .02 .10
12 Mats Sundin SR .02 .10
13 Mike Ricci SR .01 .05
14 Eric Desjardins .01 .05
15 Paul Ranheim .01 .05
16 Joe Sakic .15 .40
17 Curt Giles .01 .05
18 Mike Foligno .01 .05
19 Brad Marsh .01 .05
20 Ed Belfour .07 .20
21 Steve Smith .01 .05
22 Kirk Muller .01 .05
23 Kelly Chase .01 .05
24 Jim McKenzie .01 .05
25 Mick Vukota .01 .05
26 Tony Amonte RC .50 1.25
27 Danton Cole .01 .05
28 Jay Mazur .01 .05
29 Pete Peeters .02 .10
30 Petri Skriko .01 .05
31 Steve Duchesne .01 .05
32 Sabres Team .01 .05
33 Phil Bourque UER .01 .05
(Born Chelmford& should be Chelmsford)
34 Tim Bergland .01 .05
35 Tim Cheveldae .02 .10
36 Bill Armstrong .01 .05
37 John McIntyre .01 .05
38 Dave Andreychuk .02 .10
39 Curtis Leschyshyn .01 .05
40 Jaromir Jagr .12 .30
41 Craig Janney .02 .10
42 Doug Brown .01 .05
43 Ken Sabourin .01 .05
44 North Stars Team .01 .05
45 Fredrik Olausson UER .01 .05
(Misspelled Clausson on card front)
46 Mike Gartner UER .02 .10
(No italics or diamond 81-82 GP)
47 Mark Fitzpatrick .01 .05
48 Joe Murphy .01 .05
49 Doug Wilson .02 .10
50 Brian MacLellan .01 .05
51 Bob Bassen .01 .05
52 Robert Kron .01 .05
53 Roger Johansson .01 .05
54 Guy Carbonneau UER .02 .10
(No italics or diamond 85-86 GP)
55 Rob Ramage .01 .05
56 Bobby Holik .02 .10
57 Alan May .01 .05
58 Rick Meagher .01 .05
59 Cliff Ronning .01 .05
60 Red Wings Team .01 .05
61 Bob Kudelski .01 .05
62 Wayne McBean .01 .05
63 Craig MacTavish .01 .05
64 Owen Nolan .07 .20
65 Dale Hawerchuk .02 .10
66 Ray Bourque .08 .20
67 Sean Burke .02 .10
68 Frank Musil .01 .05
69 Joe Mullen .02 .10
70 Drake Berehowsky .01 .05
71 Darren Turcotte .01 .05
72 Randy Carlyle .01 .05
73 Paul Cyr .01 .05
74 Dave Gagner .01 .05
75 Steve Larmer .02 .10
76 Petr Svoboda .01 .05
77 Keith Acton .01 .05
78 Dimitri Khristich .01 .05
79 Brad McCrimmon .01 .05
80 Pat LaFontaine UER .07 .20
(Should be lower case a in name& not d)
81 Jeff Reese .01 .05
82 Mario Marois .01 .05
83 Rob Brown .01 .05
84 Grant Fuhr .07 .20
85 Carey Wilson .01 .05
86 Garry Galley .01 .05
87 Troy Murray .01 .05
88 Tony Granato .01 .05
89 Gord Murphy UER .01 .05
(No italics or diamond 90-91 GP)
90 Brent Gilchrist .01 .05
91 Mike Richter .07 .20
92 Eric Weinrich .01 .05
93 Marc Bureau .01 .05
94 Garth Butcher .01 .05
95 Dave McLlwain .01 .05
96 Nordiques Team .01 .05
97 Clint Malarchuk UER .02 .10
(Center on front)
98 Shawn Antoski UER .01 .05
(Admirals are in IHL& not AHL)
99 Bob Sweeney .01 .05
100 Stephen Leach .01 .05
101 Gary Nylund .01 .05
102 Lucien DeBlois .01 .05
103 Oilers Team .01 .05
104 Jimmy Carson .01 .05
105 Rod Langway .01 .05
106 Jeremy Roenick .10 .25
107 Mike Vernon .02 .10
108 Brian Leetch .02 .10
109 Mark Hunter .01 .05
110 Brian Bellows .01 .05
111 Pelle Eklund .01 .05
112 Rob Blake .02 .10
113 Mike Hough .01 .05
114 Frank Pietrangelo .01 .05
115 Christian Ruuttu .01 .05
116 Bryan Marchment RC .02 .10
117 Garry Valk .01 .05
118 Ken Daneyko UER .01 .05
(No italics or diamond 81-82 GP)
119 Russ Courtnall .01 .05
120 Ron Wilson .01 .05
121 Shayne Stevenson .01 .05
122 Bill Berg .01 .05
123 Maple Leafs Team .01 .05
124 Glenn Anderson .02 .10
125 Kevin Miller .01 .05
126 Calle Johansson .01 .05
127 Jimmy Waite .02 .10
128 Allen Pedersen .01 .05
129 Brian Mullen .01 .05
130 Ron Francis .02 .10
131 Jergus Baca .01 .05
132 Checklist 1-132 .01 .05
133 Tony Tanti .01 .05
134 Wes Walz .01 .05
135 Stephan Lebeau .01 .05
136 Ken Wregget .01 .05
137 Scott Arniel UER .01 .05
(No italics or diamond 85-86 GP)
138 Dave Taylor .02 .10
139 Steven Finn .01 .05
140 Brendan Shanahan .07 .20
141 Petr Nedved .01 .05
142 Chris Dahlquist .01 .05
143 Rich Sutter .01 .05
144 Joe Reekie .01 .05
145 Peter Ing .01 .05
146 Ken Linseman .01 .05
147 Dave Barr .01 .05
148 Al Iafrate .01 .05
149 Greg Gilbert .01 .05
150 Craig Ludwig .01 .05
151 Gary Suter .01 .05
152 Jan Erixon .01 .05
153 Mario Lemieux .50 1.25
154 Mike Liut UER .02 .10
(In stats 84-85 repeats for 85-86 thru 89-90)
155 Uwe Krupp .01 .05
156 Darin Kimble .01 .05
157 Shayne Corson .01 .05
158 Jets Team .01 .05
159 Stephane Morin UER .01 .05
(Photo actually Jeff Jackson)
160 Rick Tocchet .01 .05
161 John Tonelli UER .01 .05
(No italics or diamond 81-82 GP)
162 Adrien Plavsic .01 .05
163 Jason Miller .01 .05
164 Tim Kerr .01 .05
165 Brent Sutter .01 .05
166 Michel Petit .01 .05
167 Adam Graves .01 .05
168 Jamie Macoun .01 .05
169 Terry Yake .01 .05
170 Bruins Team .01 .05
171 Alexander Mogilny .02 .10
172 Karl Dykhuis .01 .05
Top Prospect
173 Tomas Sandstrom .01 .05
174 Bernie Nicholls .01 .05
175 Slava Fetisov .01 .05
176 Andrew Cassels .01 .05
177 Ulf Dahlen .01 .05
178 Brian Hayward .02 .10
179 Doug Lidster .01 .05
180 Dave Lowry .01 .05
181 Ron Tugnutt UER .02 .10
(Birthplace and home should be Ontario& not Quebec)
182 Ed Olczyk .01 .05
183 Paul Coffey .07 .20
184 Shawn Burr UER .01 .05
(No italics or diamond 90-91 GP)
185 Whalers Team .01 .05
186 Mark Janssens .01 .05
187 Mike Craig .01 .05
188 Gary Leeman .01 .05
189 Phil Sykes .01 .05
190 Brett Hull LL .02 .10
191 Devils Team .01 .05
192 Cam Neely .07 .20
193 Petr Klima .01 .05
194 Mike Ricci .01 .05
195 Kelly Hrudey .02 .10
196 Mark Recchi .02 .10
197 Mikael Andersson .01 .05
198 Bob Probert .01 .05
199 Craig Wolanin .01 .05
200 Scott Mellanby .01 .05
201 Wayne Gretzky HL UER .25 .60
(Thomas Sandstrom mentioned on back)
202 Laurie Boschman .01 .05
203 Gino Odjick .01 .05
204 Garth Butcher .01 .05
205 Randy Wood .01 .05
206 John Druce .01 .05
207 Doug Bodger .01 .05
208 Doug Gilmour .02 .10
209 John LeClair RC .40 1.00
210 Steve Thomas .01 .05
211 Kjell Samuelsson .01 .05
212 Daniel Marois .01 .05
213 Jiri Hrdina .01 .05
214 Darrin Shannon .01 .05
215 Rangers Team .01 .05
216 Bob McGill .01 .05
217 Dirk Graham UER .01 .05
(No italics or diamond 85-86 or 90-91 GP)
218 Thomas Steen .01 .05
219 Mats Sundin .07 .20
220 Kevin Lowe UER .02 .10
(No italics or diamond 81-82 GP)
221 Kirk McLean .02 .10
222 Jeff Brown .01 .05
223 Joe Nieuwendyk .02 .10
224 Wayne Gretzky LL .25 .60
225 Marty McSorley .01 .05
226 John Cullen .01 .05
227 Brian Propp UER .01 .05
(No italics or diamond 81-82 GP)
228 Yves Racine .01 .05
229 Dale Hunter .01 .05
230 Dennis Vaske .01 .05
231 Sylvain Turgeon .01 .05
232 Ron Sutter .01 .05
233 Chris Chelios .07 .20
234 Brian Bradley .01 .05
235 Scott Young .01 .05
236 Mike Ramsey UER .01 .05
(No italics or diamond 81-82 GP)
237 Jon Casey .02 .10
238 Nevin Markwart .01 .05
239 John MacLean .02 .10
240 Brent Ashton .01 .05
241 Tony Hrkac .01 .05
242 Canucks Team .01 .05
243 Jeff Norton .01 .05
244 Martin Gelinas .01 .05
245 Mike Ridley .01 .05
246 Pat Jablonski RC .02 .10
247 Flames Team .01 .05
248 Paul Ysebaert .01 .05
249 Sylvain Cote .01 .05
250 Marc Habscheid .01 .05
251 Todd Elik .01 .05
252 Mike McPhee .01 .05
253 James Patrick .01 .05
254 Murray Craven .01 .05
255 Trent Yawney .01 .05
256 Rob Cimetta .01 .05
257 Wayne Gretzky LL .25 .60
258 Wayne Gretzky AS .25 .60
259 Brett Hull AS .02 .10
260 Luc Robitaille AS .02 .10
261 Ray Bourque AS .02 .10
262 Al MacInnis AS .02 .10
263 Ed Belfour AS .02 .10
264 Checklist 133-264 .01 .05
265 Adam Oates AS .01 .05
266 Cam Neely AS .02 .10
267 Kevin Stevens AS .01 .05
268 Chris Chelios AS .02 .10
269 Brian Leetch AS .01 .05
270 Patrick Roy AS .12 .30
271 Ed Belfour LL .02 .10
272 Rob Zettler .01 .05
273 Donald Audette .01 .05
274 Teppo Numminen .01 .05
275 Peter Stastny UER .02 .10
(No italics or diamond 81-82 GP)
276 Dave Christian .01 .05
277 Larry Murphy .02 .10
278 Johan Garpenlov .01 .05
279 Tom Fitzgerald .01 .05
280 Gerald Diduck .01 .05
281 Gino Cavallini .01 .05
282 Theo Fleury .01 .05
283 Kings Team .01 .05
284 Jeff Beukeboom .01 .05
285 Kevin Dineen .01 .05
286 Jacques Cloutier .02 .10
287 Tom Chorske .01 .05
288 Ed Belfour LL .02 .10
289 Ray Sheppard .01 .05
290 Olaf Kolzig .02 .10
291 Terry Carkner .01 .05
292 Benoit Hogue .01 .05
293 Mike Peluso .01 .05
294 Bruce Driver .01 .05
295 Jari Kurri .07 .20
296 Peter Sidorkiewicz .01 .05
297 Scott Pearson .01 .05
298 Canadiens Team .01 .05
299 Vincent Damphousse .01 .05
300 John Carter .01 .05
301 Geoff Smith .01 .05
302 Steve Kasper UER .01 .05
(No italics or diamond 85-86 GP)
303 Brett Hull .08 .25
304 Ray Ferraro .01 .05
305 Geoff Courtnall .01 .05
306 David Shaw .01 .05
307 Bob Essensa .02 .10
308 Mark Tinordi .01 .05
309 Keith Primeau .01 .05
310 Kevin Hatcher .01 .05
311 Chris Nilan .01 .05
312 Trevor Kidd .02 .10
Top Prospect
313 Daniel Berthiaume .02 .10
314 Adam Creighton .01 .05
315 Everett Sanipass .01 .05
316 Ken Baumgartner .01 .05
317 Sheldon Kennedy .01 .05
318 Dave Capuano .01 .05
319 Don Sweeney .01 .05
320 Gary Roberts .01 .05
321 Wayne Gretzky .50 1.25
322 Theo Fleury and .01 .05
Marty McSorley UER
(Name misspelled McSorely on both sides of card)
323 Ulf Samuelsson .01 .05
324 Mike Krushelnyski .01 .05
325 Dean Evason .01 .05
326 Pat Elynuik .01 .05
327 Michal Pivonka .01 .05
328 Paul Cavallini .01 .05
329 Flyers Team .01 .05
330 Denis Savard .02 .10
331 Paul Fenton .01 .05
332 Jon Morris .01 .05
333 Daren Puppa .02 .10
334 Doug Smail .01 .05
335 Kelly Kisio .01 .05
336 Michel Goulet UER .02 .10
(No italics or diamond 81-82 GP)
337 Mike Sillinger .01 .05
338 Andy Moog .02 .10
339 Paul Stanton .01 .05
340 Greg Adams .01 .05
341 Doug Crossman UER .01 .05
(No italics or diamond 85-86 GP)
342 Kelly Miller .01 .05
343 Pat Flatley .01 .05
344 Zarley Zalapski .01 .05
345 Mark Osborne UER .01 .05
(No italics or diamond 81-82 GP)
346 Mark Messier .07 .20
347 Blues Team .01 .05
348 Neil Wilkinson .01 .05
349 Brian Skrudland .01 .05
350 Lyle Odelein .01 .05
351 Luke Richardson .01 .05
352 Zdeno Ciger .01 .05
353 John Vanbiesbrouck .02 .10
354 Lou Franceschetti .01 .05
355 Alexei Gusarov RC .02 .10
356 Bill Ranford .02 .10
357 Normand Lacombe .01 .05
358 Randy Burridge .01 .05
359 Brian Benning .01 .05
360 Dave Hannan .01 .05
361 Todd Gill .01 .05
362 Peter Bondra .02 .10
363 Mike Hartman .01 .05
364 Trevor Linden .01 .05
365 John Ogrodnick .01 .05
366 Steve Konroyd .01 .05
367 Mike Modano .15 .40
368 Glenn Healy .02 .10
369 Stephane Richer .02 .10
370 Vincent Riendeau .01 .05
371 Randy Moller .01 .05
372 Penguins Team .01 .05
373 Murray Baron .01 .05
374 Troy Crowder .01 .05
375 Rick Tabaracci .02 .10
376 Brent Fedyk .01 .05
377 Randy Velischek .01 .05
378 Esa Tikkanen .01 .05
379 Rich Pilon .01 .05
380 Jeff Lazaro .01 .05
381 Dave Ellett .01 .05
382 Jeff Hackett .02 .10
383 Stephane Matteau .01 .05
384 Capitals Team .01 .05
385 Wayne Presley .01 .05
386 Grant Ledyard .01 .05
387 Kip Miller .01 .05
388 Dean Kennedy .01 .05
389 Hubie McDonough .01 .05
390 Anatoli Semenov .01 .05
391 Daryl Reaugh .02 .10
392 Mathieu Schneider .01 .05
393 Dan Quinn .01 .05
394 Claude Lemieux .01 .05
395 Phil Housley .01 .05
396 Checklist 265-396 .01 .05
397 Steve Bozek .01 .05
398 Bobby Smith .02 .10
399 Mark Pederson .01 .05
400 Kevin Todd RC .01 .05
401 Sergei Fedorov .15 .40
402 Tom Barrasso .02 .10
403 Brett Hull HL .02 .10
404 Bob Carpenter UER .01 .05
(No italics or diamond 85-86 or 90-91 GP)
405 Luc Robitaille .02 .10
406 Mark Hardy .01 .05
407 Neil Sheehy .01 .05
408 Mike McNeil .01 .05
409 Dave Manson .01 .05
410 Mike Tomlak .01 .05
411 Robert Reichel .01 .05
412 Islanders Team .01 .05
413 Patrick Roy .40 1.00
414 Shaun Van Allen RC .01 .05
415 Dale Kushner .01 .05
416 Pierre Turgeon .02 .10
417 Curtis Joseph .07 .20
418 Randy Gilhen .01 .05
419 Jyrki Lumme .01 .05
420 Neal Broten .01 .05
421 Kevin Stevens .01 .05
422 Chris Terreri .02 .10
423 David Reid .01 .05
424 Steve Yzerman .40 1.00
425 Ed Belfour LL .02 .10
426 Jim Johnson .01 .05
427 Joey Kocur .01 .05
428 Joel Otto .01 .05
429 Dino Ciccarelli .02 .10
430 Blackhawks Team .01 .05
431 Claude Lapointe RC .01 .05
432 Chris Joseph .01 .05
433 Gaetan Duchesne .01 .05
434 Mike Keane .01 .05
435 Dave Chyzowski .01 .05
436 Glen Featherstone .01 .05
437 Jim Paek RC .01 .05
438 Doug Evans .01 .05
439 Alexei Kasatonov UER .01 .05
(Misspelled Alexi on card front)
440 Ken Hodge Jr. .01 .05
441 Dave Snuggerud .01 .05
442 Brad Shaw .01 .05
443 Gerard Gallant .01 .05
444 Jiri Latal .01 .05
445 Peter Zezel .01 .05
446 Troy Gamble .02 .10
447 Craig Coxe .01 .05
448 Adam Oates .02 .10
449 Todd Krygier .01 .05
450 Andre Racicot RC .02 .10
451 Patrik Sundstrom .01 .05
452 Glen Wesley UER .01 .05
(No italics or diamond 90-91 GP)
453 Jocelyn Lemieux .01 .05
454 Rick Zombo .01 .05
455 Derek King .01 .05
456 J.J. Daigneault .01 .05
457 Rick Vaive .01 .05
458 Larry Robinson .01 .05
459 Rick Wamsley .02 .10
460 Craig Simpson .01 .05
461 Corey Millen RC .01 .05
462 Sergio Momesso .01 .05
463 Paul MacDermid .01 .05
464 Wendel Clark .02 .10
465 Mikhail Tatarinov .01 .05
466 Mark Howe .01 .05
467 Jay Miller .01 .05
468 Grant Jennings .01 .05
469 Paul Gillis .01 .05
470 Ron Hextall .02 .10
471 Alexander Godynyuk .01 .05
472 Bryan Trottier .07 .20
473 Kevin Haller RC .01 .05
474 Troy Mallette .01 .05
475 Jim Wiemer .01 .05
476 David Maley .01 .05
477 Moe Mantha UER .01 .05
(Photo actually Paul MacDermid)
478 Brad Jones .01 .05
479 Craig Muni .01 .05
480 Igor Larionov .01 .05
481 Scott Stevens .02 .10
482 Sergei Makarov .01 .05
483 Mike Lalor .01 .05
484 Tony McKegney .01 .05
485 Perry Berezan .01 .05
486 Derrick Smith .01 .05
487 Jim Hrivnak .01 .05
488 David Volek .01 .05
489 Sylvain Lefebvre .01 .05
490 Rod Brind'Amour .02 .10
491 Al MacInnis .02 .10
492 Jamie Leach .01 .05
493 Robert Dirk .01 .05
494 Gordie Roberts .01 .05
495 Mike Hudson .01 .05
496 Frank Breault .01 .05
497 Rejean Lemelin .02 .10
498 Kris King .01 .05
499 Pat Verbeek .01 .05
500 Bryan Fogarty .01 .05
501 Perry Anderson .01 .05
502 Joe Cirella .01 .05
503 Mikko Makela .01 .05
504 Paul Coffey HL UER .02 .10
(Misspelled Coffee and Dennis Potvin on card back; date 12/22/90 in English& but 12/23/90 in French)
505 Don Beaupre .02 .10
506 Brian Glynn .01 .05
507 Dave Poulin .01 .05
508 Steve Chiasson .01 .05
509 Myles O'Connor .01 .05
510 Ilkka Sinisalo .01 .05
511 Nick Kypreos .01 .05
512 Doug Houda UER .01 .05
(No position after name on back)
513 Valeri Kamensky RC .02 .10
514 Sergei Nemchinov .01 .05
515 Dimitri Mironov .02 .10
516 Brett Hull Hart .02 .10
517 Ray Bourque Norris .02 .10
518 Ed Belfour Calder .02 .10
519 Ed Belfour UER .02 .10
Vezina Trophy
(Georges misspelled as George)
520 Wayne Gretzky Byng .25 .60
521 Dirk Graham Selke .01 .05
522 Wayne Gretzky Ross .25 .60
523 Mario Lemieux Smythe .25 .60
524 Wayne Gretzky HL .25 .60
525 Sharks Logo .01 .05
526 Lightning Logo .01 .05
(Card back states team will play in Orlando for 1992-93 if arena is not complete. The Lightning played at Tampa Expo Hall.)
527 Senators Logo .01 .05
528 Checklist 397-528 .01 .05

1991-92 Topps/Bowman Preview Sheet

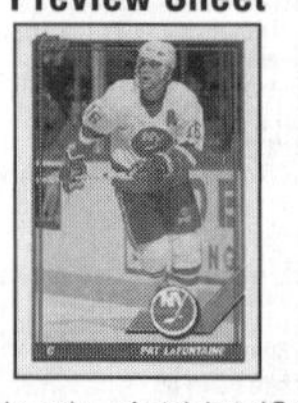

This nine-card unperforated sheet of Topps and Bowman hockey cards was sent to dealers to show them the graphic design of the coming year's hockey cards. The fronts of these preview cards are identical to the regular issue. In blue lettering, the backs have the player's name, the words "Pre-Production Sample", "1991 Topps (or as the case may be, Bowman) Card", and a tagline. The cards are unnumbered on the back and hence are listed below beginning with the upper left corner, counting across, and ending with the lower right corner. The cards are arranged so that Topps and Bowman cards alternate with one another.

COMPLETE SET (9) 4.00 10.00
1 Mario Lemieux 1.00 2.50
(Topps)
2 Wayne Gretzky 1.20 3.00
(Bowman)
3 Joe Sakic .50 1.25
(Topps)
4 Ray Bourque .30 .75
(Bowman)
5 Ed Belfour .30 .75
(Topps)
6 Mark Messier .40 1.00
(Bowman)
7 Pat LaFontaine .20 .50
(Topps)
8 Steve Yzerman .60 1.50
(Bowman)
9 Brett Hull .40 1.00
(Topps)

1991-92 Topps Team Scoring Leaders

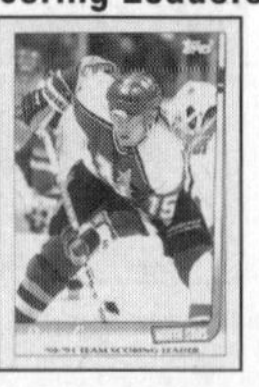

This 21-card standard-size set was inserted at a rate of one per '91-92 Topps pack and features the top scorer from every team on the front, while the back ranks the top 10 point leaders for that team.

COMPLETE SET (21) 2.40 6.00
1 Pat Verbeek .16 .40
2 Dale Hawerchuk .16 .40
3 Steve Yzerman .60 1.50
4 Brian Leetch .20 .50
5 Mark Recchi .16 .40
6 Esa Tikkanen .04 .10
7 Dave Gagner .04 .10
8 Joe Sakic .40 1.00

Vincent Damphousse .16 .40
) Wayne Gretzky 1.20 3.00
1 Phil Housley .04 .10
2 Pat LaFontaine .16 .40
3 Rick Tocchet .16 .40
4 Theo Fleury UER .16 .40
(Misspelled Fluery on card back)
5 John MacLean .04 .10
6 Kevin Hatcher .04 .10
7 Trevor Linden .16 .40
8 Russ Courtnall .04 .10
9 Ray Bourque .20 .50
0 Brett Hull .24 .60
1 Steve Larmer .04 .10

1992-93 Topps

he 1992-93 Topps set contains 529 andard-size cards. Topps switched to white ard stock this year allowing for a better oking product. Card fronts have team and ayer name at the bottom. Colorful backs clude yearly statistics, playoff statistics d game- winning goals from 1991-92. The rly print-run cards of Randy Moller (407) ffer from a print flaw which appears to be ge finger impression on the card face. The ly Rookie Card of note is Guy Hebert.

OMPLETE SET (529) 8.00 20.00
OMP.FACT.SET (549) 12.50 30.00
Wayne Gretzky .60 1.50
Brett Hull .10 .30
Felix Potvin .08 .25
Mark Tinordi .01 .05
Paul Coffey HL .05 .12
Tony Amonte .05 .12
Pat Falloon .01 .05
Pavel Bure .05 .15
Nicklas Lidstrom .02 .10
Dominic Roussel .01 .05
Nelson Emerson .01 .05
Donald Audette .01 .05
Gilbert Dionne .01 .05
Vladimir Konstantinov .08 .25
Kevin Todd .01 .05
Steve Leach .01 .05
Ed Olczyk .01 .05
Jim Hrivnak .02 .10
Gilbert Dionne .01 .05
Mike Vernon .02 .10
Dave Christian .01 .05
Ed Belfour .08 .25
Andrew Cassels .01 .05
Jaromir Jagr .12 .30
Arturs Irbe .08 .25
Petr Klima .01 .05
Randy Gilhen .01 .05
Ulf Dahlen .01 .05
Kelly Hrudey .02 .10
Dave Ellett .01 .05
Tom Fitzgerald .01 .05
Cam Neely .08 .25
Greg Paslawski .01 .05
Brad May .01 .05
Slava Kozlov .02 .10
Mark Hunter .01 .05
Steve Chiasson .01 .05
Joe Murphy .01 .05
Darryl Sydor .01 .05
Ron Hextall .02 .10
Jim Sandlak .01 .05
Dave Lowry .01 .05
Claude Lemieux .01 .05
Gerald Diduck .01 .05
Mike McPhee .01 .05
Rod Langway .01 .05
Guy Larose .01 .05
Craig Billington .02 .10
Daniel Marois .01 .05
Todd Nelson RC .01 .05
Jari Kurri .08 .25
Keith Brown .01 .05
Valeri Kamensky .01 .05
Jim Johnson .01 .05
Vincent Damphousse .01 .05
Pat Elynuik .01 .05
Jeff Beukeboom .01 .05
Paul Ysebaert .01 .05
Ken Sutton .01 .05
Dale Craigwell .01 .05
Marc Bergevin .01 .05
Stephane Beauregard .02 .10
Bob Probert .02 .10
Jergus Baca .01 .05
Brian Propp .01 .05
Jacques Cloutier .02 .10
Jim Thomson RC .01 .05
Anatoli Semenov .01 .05
Stephan Lebeau .01 .05
Rick Tocchet .02 .10
James Patrick .01 .05
Rob Brown .01 .05
Peter Ahola .01 .05
Bob Corkum .01 .05
Brent Sutter .01 .05
Neil Wilkinson .01 .05
Mark Osborne .01 .05
Ron Wilson .01 .05
Todd Richards .01 .05
Robert Kron .01 .05
Cliff Ronning .01 .05
Zarley Zalapski .01 .05
Randy Burridge .01 .05
Jarrod Skalde .01 .05
Gary Leeman .01 .05
Mike Ricci .02 .10
Dennis Vaske .01 .05
88 John LeBlanc RC .01 .05
89 Brad Shaw .01 .05
90 Rod Brind'Amour .02 .10
91 Colin Patterson .01 .05
92 Gerard Gallant .01 .05
93 Per Djoos .01 .05
94 Claude Lapointe .01 .05
95 Bob Errey .01 .05
96 Norm Maciver .01 .05
97 Todd Elik .01 .05
98 Chris Chelios .08 .25
99 Keith Primeau .01 .05
100 Jim Waite .02 .10
101 Luc Robitaille .02 .10
102 Keith Tkachuk .08 .25
103 Benoit Hogue .01 .05
104 Brian Mullen .01 .05
105 Joe Nieuwendyk .02 .10
106 Randy McKay .01 .05
107 Michal Pivonka .01 .05
108 Darcy Wakaluk .02 .10
109 Andy Brickley .01 .05
110 Patrick Roy .20 .50
Goals Against
Average Leader
111 Bob Sweeney .01 .05
112 Guy Hebert RC .20 .50
113 Joe Mullen .02 .10
114 Gord Murphy .01 .05
115 Evgeny Davydov .01 .05
116 Gary Roberts .01 .05
117 Pelle Eklund .01 .05
118 Tom Kurvers .01 .05
119 John Tonelli .01 .05
120 Fredrik Olausson .01 .05
121 Mike Donnelly .01 .05
122 Doug Gilmour .02 .10
123 Wayne Gretzky .30 .75
Assists Leader
124 Curtis Leschyshyn .01 .05
125 Guy Carbonneau .02 .10
126 Bill Ranford .02 .10
127 Ulf Samuelsson .01 .05
128 Joey Kocur .02 .10
129 Kevin Miller .01 .05
130 Kirk McLean .02 .10
131 Kevin Dineen .01 .05
132 John Cullen .01 .05
133 Al Iafrate .02 .10
134 Craig Janney .02 .10
135 Patrick Flatley .01 .05
136 Dominik Hasek .30 .75
137 Benoit Brunet .01 .05
138 Dave Babych .01 .05
139 Doug Brown .01 .05
140 Mike Lalor .01 .05
141 Thomas Steen .01 .05
142 Frank Musil .01 .05
143 Dan Quinn .01 .05
144 Dmitri Mironov .01 .05
145 Bob Kudelski .01 .05
146 Mike Bullard .01 .05
147 Randy Carlyle .01 .05
148 Kent Manderville .01 .05
149 Kevin Hatcher .01 .05
150 Steve Kasper .01 .05
151 Mikael Andersson .01 .05
152 Alexei Kasatonov .01 .05
153 Jan Erixon .01 .05
154 Craig Ludwig .01 .05
155 Dave Poulin .01 .05
156 Scott Stevens .02 .10
157 Robert Reichel .01 .05
158 Uwe Krupp .01 .05
159 Brian Noonan .01 .05
160 Stephane Richer .02 .10
161 Brent Thompson .01 .05
162 Glenn Anderson .02 .10
163 Joe Cirella .01 .05
164 Dave Andreychuk .02 .10
165 Vladimir Konstantinov .08 .25
166 Mike McNeill .01 .05
167 Darrin Shannon .01 .05
168 Rob Pearson .01 .05
169 John Vanbiesbrouck .02 .10
170 Randy Wood .01 .05
171 Marty McSorley .01 .05
172 Mike Hudson .01 .05
173 Paul Fenton .01 .05
174 Jeff Brown .01 .05
175 Mark Greig .01 .05
176 Gordie Roberts .01 .05
177 Josef Beranek .01 .05
178 Shawn Burr .01 .05
179 Marc Bureau .01 .05
180 Mikhail Tatarinov .01 .05
181 Robert Cimetta .01 .05
182 Paul Coffey UER .08 .25
(Still pictured
as a Penguin)
183 Bob Essensa .02 .10
184 Joe Reekie .01 .05
185 Jeff Hackett .02 .10
186 Tomas Forslund .01 .05
187 Claude Vilgrain .01 .05
188 John Druce .01 .05
189 Patrice Brisebois .01 .05
190 Peter Douris .01 .05
191 Brent Ashton .01 .05
192 Eric Desjardins .02 .10
193 Nick Kypreos .01 .05
194 Dana Murzyn .01 .05
195 Don Beaupre .02 .10
196 Jeff Chychrun .01 .05
197 Dave Barr .01 .05
198 Brian Glynn .01 .05
199 Keith Acton .01 .05
200 Igor Kravchuk .01 .05
201 Shayne Corson .01 .05
202 Curt Giles .01 .05
203 Darren Turcotte .01 .05
204 David Volek .01 .05
205 Ray Whitney RC .15 .40
206 Donald Audette .01 .05
207 Steve Yzerman .40 1.00
208 Craig Berube .01 .05
209 Bob McGill .01 .05
210 Stu Barnes .01 .05
211 Rob Blake .02 .10
212 Mario Lemieux .40 1.00
213 Dominic Roussel .02 .10
214 Sergio Momesso .01 .05
215 Brad Marsh .01 .05
216 Mark Fitzpatrick .02 .10
217 Ken Baumgartner .01 .05
218 Greg Gilbert .01 .05
219 Ric Nattress .01 .05
220 Theo Fleury .01 .05
221 Ray Bourque .15 .40
222 Steve Thomas .02 .10
223 Scott Niedermayer .01 .05
224 Jeff Lazaro .01 .05
225 Tim Cheveldae .01 .05
Kirk McLean
Wins Leaders
226 Marc Fortier .01 .05
227 Rob Zettler .01 .05
228 Kevin Todd .01 .05
229 Tony Amonte .02 .10
230 Mark Lamb .01 .05
231 Chris Dahlquist .01 .05
232 James Black .01 .05
233 Paul Cavallini .01 .05
234 Gino Cavallini .01 .05
235 Tony Tanti .01 .05
236 Mike Ridley .01 .05
237 Curtis Joseph .08 .25
238 Mike Craig .01 .05
239 Luciano Borsato .01 .05
240 Brian Bellows .01 .05
241 Barry Pederson .01 .05
242 Tony Granato .01 .05
243 Jim Paek .01 .05
244 Tim Bergland .01 .05
245 Jay More .01 .05
246 Lauire Boschman .01 .05
247 Doug Bodger .01 .05
248 Murray Craven .01 .05
249 Kris Draper .02 .10
250 Brian Benning .01 .05
251 Jarmo Myllys .01 .05
252 Sergei Fedorov .12 .30
253 Mathieu Schneider .01 .05
254 Dave Gagner .02 .10
255 Michel Goulet .02 .10
256 Alexander Godynyuk .01 .05
257 Ray Sheppard .01 .05
258 Mark Messier AS .08 .15
259 Kevin Stevens AS .01 .05
260 Brett Hull AS .08 .25
261 Brian Leetch AS .02 .10
262 Ray Bourque AS .08 .20
263 Patrick Roy AS .20 .50
264 Mike Gartner AS .01 .05
265 Mario Lemieux AS .20 .50
266 Luc Robitaille AS .01 .05
267 Mark Recchi AS .01 .05
268 Phil Housley AS .01 .05
269 Scott Stevens AS .01 .05
270 Kirk McLean AS .01 .05
271 Steve Duchesne .01 .05
272 Jiri Hrdina .01 .05
273 John MacLean .02 .10
274 Mark Messier .08 .25
275 Geoff Smith .01 .05
276 Russ Courtnall .01 .05
277 Yves Racine .01 .05
278 Tom Draper .01 .05
279 Charlie Huddy .01 .05
280 Trevor Kidd .02 .10
281 Garth Butcher .01 .05
282 Mike Sullivan .01 .05
283 Adam Burt .01 .05
284 Troy Murray .01 .05
285 Stephane Fiset .02 .10
286 Perry Anderson .01 .05
287 Sergei Nemchinov .01 .05
288 Rick Zombo .01 .05
289 Pierre Turgeon .02 .10
290 Kevin Lowe .02 .10
291 Brian Bradley .01 .05
292 Martin Gelinas UER .01 .05
(Transaction date should
be 8-9-88 not 8-9-89)
293 Brian Leetch .08 .25
294 Peter Bondra .02 .10
295 Brendan Shanahan .08 .25
296 Dale Hawerchuk .02 .10
297 Mike Hough .01 .05
298 Rollie Melanson .02 .10
299 Brad Jones .01 .05
300 Jocelyn Lemieux .01 .05
301 Brad McCrimmon .01 .05
302 Marty McInnis .01 .05
303 Chris Terreri .01 .05
304 Dean Evason .01 .05
305 Glenn Healy .02 .10
306 Ken Hodge Jr. .01 .05
307 Mike Liut .02 .10
308 Gary Suter .01 .05
309 Neal Broten .02 .10
310 Tim Cheveldae .02 .10
311 Tom Fergus .01 .05
312 Petr Svoboda .01 .05
313 Tom Chorske .01 .05
314 Paul Ysebaert .01 .05
Plus/Minus Leader
315 Steve Smith .01 .05
316 Stephane Morin .01 .05
317 Pat MacLeod .01 .05
318 Dino Ciccarelli .02 .10
319 Peter Zezel .01 .05
320 Chris Lindberg .01 .05
321 Grant Ledyard .01 .05
322 Ron Francis .02 .10
323 Adrien Plavsic .01 .05
324 Ray Ferraro .01 .05
325 Wendel Clark .02 .10
326 Corey Millen .01 .05
327 Mark Pederson .01 .05
328 Patrick Poulin .01 .05
329 Adam Graves .01 .05
330 Bobby Holik .02 .10
331 Kelly Kisio .01 .05
332 Peter Sidorkiewicz .02 .10
333 Vladimir Ruzicka .01 .05
334 J.J. Daigneault .01 .05
335 Troy Mallette .01 .05
336 Craig MacTavish .01 .05
337 Michel Petit .01 .05
338 Claude Loiselle .01 .05
339 Teppo Numminen .01 .05
340 Brett Hull .08 .25
Goal Scoring Leader
341 Sylvain Lefebvre .01 .05
342 Perry Berezan .01 .05
343 Kevin Stevens .01 .05
344 Randy Ladouceur .01 .05
345 Pat LaFontaine .08 .25
346 Glen Wesley .01 .05
347 Michel Goulet HL .01 .05
348 Jamie Macoun .01 .05
349 Owen Nolan .02 .10
350 Grant Fuhr .08 .25
351 Tim Kerr .01 .05
352 Kjell Samuelsson .01 .05
353 Pavel Bure .08 .25
354 Murray Baron .01 .05
355 Paul Broten .01 .05
356 Craig Simpson .01 .05
357 Ken Daneyko .01 .05
358 Greg Hawgood .01 .05
359 Johan Garpenlov .01 .05
360 Garry Galley .01 .05
361 Paul DiPietro .01 .05
362 Jamie Leach .01 .05
363 Clint Malarchuk .02 .10
364 Dan Lambert .01 .05
365 Joe Juneau UER .02 .10
(Shoots left not right)
366 Scott Lachance .01 .05
367 Mike Richter .08 .25
368 Sheldon Kennedy .01 .05
369 John McIntyre .01 .05
370 Glen Murray UER .01 .05
(Misspelled Glenn
on both sides)
371 Ron Sutter .01 .05
372 David Williams RC .01 .05
373 Bill Lindsay RC .01 .05
374 Todd Gill .01 .05
375 Sylvain Turgeon .01 .05
376 Dirk Graham .01 .05
377 Brad Schlegel .01 .05
378 Bob Carpenter .01 .05
379 Jon Casey .02 .10
380 Andrei Lomakin .01 .05
381 Kay Whitmore .02 .10
382 Alexander Mogilny .02 .10
383 Garry Valk .01 .05
384 Bruce Driver .01 .05
385 Jeff Reese .01 .05
386 Brent Gilchrist .01 .05
387 Kerry Huffman .01 .05
388 Bobby Smith .02 .10
389 Dave Manson .01 .05
390 Russ Romaniuk .01 .05
391 Paul MacDermid .01 .05
392 Louie DeBrusk .01 .05
393 Dave McLlwain .01 .05
394 Andy Moog .08 .25
395 Tie Domi .08 .25
396 Pat Jablonski .02 .10
397 Troy Loney .01 .05
398 Jimmy Carson .01 .05
399 Eric Weinrich .01 .05
400 Jeremy Roenick .12 .30
401 Brent Fedyk .01 .05
402 Geoff Sanderson .02 .10
403 Doug Lidster .01 .05
404 Mike Gartner .02 .10
405 Derian Hatcher .01 .05
406 Gaetan Duchesne .01 .05
407 Randy Moller .01 .05
408 Brian Skrudland .01 .05
409 Luke Richardson .01 .05
410 Mark Recchi .02 .10
411 Steve Konroyd .01 .05
412 Troy Gamble .02 .10
413 Greg Johnston .01 .05
414 Denis Savard .02 .10
415 Mats Sundin .08 .25
416 Bryan Trottier .02 .10
417 Don Sweeney .01 .05
418 Pat Falloon .01 .05
419 Alexander Semak .01 .05
420 David Shaw .01 .05
421 Tomas Sandstrom .01 .05
422 Petr Nedved .02 .10
423 Peter Ing .02 .10
424 Wayne Presley .01 .05
425 Rick Wamsley .02 .10
426 Rob Zamuner RC .02 .10
427 Claude Boivin .01 .05
428 Sylvain Cote .01 .05
429 Kevin Stevens HL .01 .05
430 Randy Velischek .01 .05
431 Derek King .01 .05
432 Terry Yake .01 .05
433 Philippe Bozon .01 .05
434 Rich Sutter .01 .05
435 Brian Lawton .01 .05
436 Brian Hayward .02 .10
437 Robert Dirk .01 .05
438 Bernie Nicholls .01 .05
439 Michel Picard .01 .05
440 Nicklas Lidstrom .08 .25
441 Mike Modano .15 .40
442 Phil Bourque .01 .05
443 Wayne McBean .01 .05
444 Scott Mellanby .01 .05
445 Kevin Haller .01 .05
446 Dave Taylor UER .02 .10
(Games played total
***& should be 1030)
447 Larry Murphy .02 .10
448 David Bruce .01 .05
449 Steven Finn .01 .05
450 Mike Krushelnyski .01 .05
451 Adam Creighton .01 .05
452 Al MacInnis .02 .10
453 Rick Tabaracci .02 .10
454 Bob Bassen .01 .05
455 Kelly Buchberger .01 .05
456 Phil Housley .02 .10
457 Darren Puppa .02 .10
458 Slava Fetisov .01 .05
459 Doug Smail .01 .05
460 Paul Stanton .01 .05
461 Steve Weeks .02 .10
462 Valeri Zelepukin .01 .05
463 Stephane Matteau .01 .05
464 Dale Hunter .02 .10
465 Terry Carkner .01 .05
466 Vincent Riendeau .02 .10
467 Sergei Makarov .01 .05
468 Igor Ulanov .01 .05
469 Peter Stastny .02 .10
470 Dimitri Khristich .01 .05
471 Joel Otto .01 .05
472 Geoff Courtnall .01 .05
473 Mike Ramsey .01 .05
474 Yvon Corriveau .01 .05
475 Adam Oates .02 .10
476 Esa Tikkanen .01 .05
477 Doug Weight .08 .25
478 Mike Keane .01 .05
479 Kelly Miller .01 .05
480 Nelson Emerson .01 .05
481 Shawn McEachern .01 .05
482 Doug Wilson .02 .10
483 Jeff Odgers .01 .05
484 Stephane Quintal .01 .05
485 Christian Ruuttu .01 .05
486 Paul Ranheim .01 .05
487 Craig Wolanin .01 .05
488 Rob DiMaio .01 .05
489 Shawn Cronin .01 .05
490 Kirk Muller .01 .05
491 Patrick Roy .20 .50
Save Pct. Leader
492 Rich Pilon .01 .05
493 Pat Verbeek .01 .05
494 Ken Wregget .02 .10
495 Joe Sakic .15 .40
496 Zdeno Ciger .01 .05
497 Steve Larmer .02 .10
498 Calle Johansson .01 .05
499 Trevor Linden .02 .10
500 John LeClair .15 .40
501 Bryan Marchment .01 .05
502 Todd Krygier .01 .05
503 Tom Barrasso .02 .10
504 Mario Lemieux LL .20 .50
505 Daniel Berthiaume UER .02 .10
(Headings on back are
for non-goalies)
506 Jamie Baker .01 .05
507 Greg Adams .01 .05
508 Patrick Roy .40 1.00
509 Kris King .01 .05
510 Jyrki Lumme .01 .05
511 Darin Kimble .01 .05
512 Igor Larionov .01 .05
513 Martin Brodeur .30 .75
514 Denny Felsner RC .02 .10
515 Yanic Dupre .01 .05
516 Bill Guerin RC .40 1.00
517 Bret Hedican RC UER .02 .10
(Misspelled Brett
on both sides)
518 Mike Hartman .01 .05
519 Steve Heinze UER .01 .05
(Photo actually
Gord Hynes)
520 Frantisek Kucera .01 .05
521 David Reid .01 .05
522 Frank Pietrangelo .02 .10
523 Martin Rucinsky .01 .05
524 Tony Hrkac .01 .05
525 Checklist 1-132 .01 .05
526 Checklist 133-264 .01 .05
527 Checklist 265-396 .01 .05
528 Checklist 397-528 UER .01 .05
(529 not listed)
529 Eric Lindros UER .08 .25
(Acquired 6-30-92
not 6-20-92)

1992-93 Topps Gold

Gold foil versions of all 529 cards in the 1992-93 Topps Hockey set were produced: one was inserted in each foil pack, three in each jumbo pack, and 20 were included in factory sets as a bonus. Deciding against producing Gold checklists, Topps made cards 525-528 of players not featured in the basic set. On a white card face, the fronts display color action player photos inside a two-color picture frame. The player's name and team name appear in two short colored bars toward the bottom of the picture. The backs carry biography, statistics, and player profile. The following cards were printed in a horizontal format: 90, 164, 195, 225, 272, 307, 324, 337, 350, 366, 413 and 420.

*STARS: 4X TO 10X BASIC CARDS
*RC's: 1.5X TO 4X BASIC CARDS
525G Al Conroy .20 .50
526G Jeff Norton .20 .50
527G Rob Robinson .20 .50
528G Adam Foote .40 1.00

1993-94 Topps Premier Promo Sheet

This nine-card promo sheet measures approximately 7 3/4" by 10 3/4" and features white-bordered color player photos on the front. The player's name and position appear at the bottom of each card within a team color-coded stripe, and the Premier logo is displayed in the lower left. The horizontal backs carry color player action shots on their left sides. At the top, the player's name, uniform number, team, and position appear within a team color-coded stripe. Below this, and to the right of the player photo, appear the player's biography and stats on a background that resembles white ruffled silk. The team, NHL, and NHLPA logos in the lower left round out the back.

COMPLETE SET (9) 1.60 4.00
1 Patrick Roy .60 1.50
15 Mike Vernon .16 .40
22 Jamie Baker .10 .25
100 Theo Fleury .16 .40
156 Geoff Sanderson .16 .40
244 Dave Lowry .10 .25
257 Scott Lachance .10 .25
601 Mark Messier .20 .50
602 Ray Bourque .20 .50

1993-94 Topps/OPC Premier

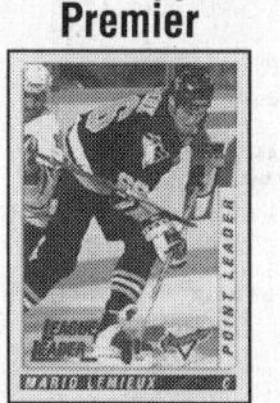

Both series of the 1993-94 Topps (and O-Pee-Chee) Premier hockey set consisted of 264 standard-size cards. The fronts feature white-bordered color player photos. The player's name and position appear at the bottom of each card within a team color-coded stripe, and the Premier logo is displayed in the lower left. The horizontal backs carry color player action shots on their left sides. Topical subsets featured are Super Rookies (121-130), and 1st Team All-Stars, 2nd Team All-Stars, and League Leaders scattered throughout the set. Except for some information in French on the backs, the O-Pee-Chee Premier set is identical to the Topps Premier set.

COMPLETE SET (528) 10.00 20.00
COMPLETE SERIES 1 (264) 5.00 10.00
COMPLETE SERIES 2 (264) 5.00 10.00
*OPC CARDS: SAME VALUE
1 Patrick Roy .40 1.00
2 Alexei Zhitnik .01 .05
3 Uwe Krupp .01 .05
4 Todd Gill .01 .05
5 Paul Stanton .01 .05
6 Petr Nedved .02 .10
7 Dale Hawerchuk .02 .10
8 Kevin Miller .01 .05
9 Nicklas Lidstrom .07 .20
10 Joe Sakic .15 .40
11 Thomas Steen .01 .05
12 Peter Bondra .02 .10
13 Brian Noonan .01 .05
14 Glen Featherstone .01 .05
15 Mike Vernon .02 .10
16 Janne Ojanen .01 .05
17 Neil Brady .01 .05
18 Dimitri Yushkevich .01 .05
19 Rob Zamuner .01 .05
20 Zarley Zalapski .01 .05
21 Mike Sullivan .01 .05
22 Jamie Baker .01 .05
23 Craig MacTavish .01 .05
24 Mark Tinordi .01 .05
25 Brian Leetch .07 .20
26 Brian Skrudland .01 .05
27 Keith Tkachuk .07 .20
28 Patrick Flatley .01 .05
29 Doug Bodger .01 .05
30 Felix Potvin .07 .20
31 Shawn Antoski .01 .05
32 Eric Desjardins .02 .10
33 Mike Donnelly .01 .05
34 Kjell Samuelsson .01 .05
35 Nelson Emerson .01 .05
36 Phil Housley .02 .10
37 Mario Lemieux LL .07 .20
38 Shayne Corson .01 .05
39 Steve Smith .01 .05
40 Bob Kudelski .01 .05
41 Joe Cirella .01 .05
42 Sergei Nemchinov .01 .05
43 Kerry Huffman .01 .05
44 Bob Beers .01 .05
45 Al Iafrate .01 .05
46 Mike Modano .12 .30
47 Pat Verbeek .01 .05
48 Joel Otto .01 .05
49 Dino Ciccarelli .02 .10
50 Adam Oates .02 .10
51 Pat Elynuik .01 .05
52 Bobby Holik .01 .05
53 Johan Garpenlov .01 .05
54 Jeff Beukeboom .01 .05
55 Tommy Soderstrom .02 .10
56 Rob Blake .02 .10
57 Marty McInnis .01 .05
58 Dixon Ward .01 .05
59 Patrice Brisebois .01 .05
60 Ed Belfour .07 .20
61 Donald Audette .01 .05
62 Mike Ricci .01 .05
63 Fredrik Olausson .01 .05
64 Norm Maciver .01 .05
65 Andrew Cassels .01 .05
66 Tim Cheveldae .02 .10
67 David Reid .01 .05
68 Philippe Bozon .01 .05
69 Drake Berehowsky .01 .05
70 Tony Amonte .02 .10
71 Dave Manson .01 .05
72 Rick Tocchet .02 .10
73 Steve Kasper .01 .05
74 Assist Leader .02 .10
Adam Oates
75 Ulf Dahlen .01 .05
76 Chris Lindberg .01 .05
77 Doug Wilson .02 .10
78 Mike Ridley .01 .05
79 Viacheslav Butsayev .01 .05
80 Scott Stevens .02 .10
81 Cliff Ronning .01 .05
82 Andrei Lomakin .01 .05
83 Shawn Burr .01 .05
84 Benoit Brunet .01 .05
85 Valeri Kamensky .02 .10
86 Randy Carlyle .01 .05
87 Chris Joseph .01 .05
88 Dirk Graham .01 .05
89 Ken Sutton .01 .05
90 Luc Robitaille AS .02 .10
91 Mario Lemieux AS .07 .20
92 Teemu Selanne AS .07 .20
93 Ray Bourque AS .07 .20
94 Chris Chelios AS .07 .20
95 Ed Belfour AS .07 .20
96 Keith Jones .01 .05
97 Sylvain Turgeon .01 .05
98 Jim Johnson .01 .05
99 Michael Nylander .01 .05
100 Theo Fleury .01 .05
101 Shawn Chambers .01 .05
102 Alexander Semak .01 .05
103 Ron Sutter .01 .05
104 Glenn Anderson .02 .10
105 Jaromir Jagr .12 .30
106 Adam Graves .01 .05
107 Nikolai Borschevsky .01 .05
108 Vladimir Konstantinov .02 .10
109 Robb Stauber .02 .10
110 Arturs Irbe .02 .10
111 Felix Potvin .02 .10
G.A.A. Leader
112 Darius Kasparaitis .01 .05
113 Kirk McLean .02 .10
114 Glen Wesley .01 .05
115 Rod Brind'Amour .02 .10
116 Mike Eagles .01 .05
117 Brian Bradley .01 .05
118 Dave Christian .01 .05
119 Randy Wood .01 .05
120 Craig Janney .02 .10
121 Eric Lindros SR .07 .20
122 Tommy Soderstrom SR .02 .10
123 Shawn McEachern SR .01 .05
124 Andrei Kovalenko SR .01 .05
125 Joe Juneau SR .02 .10
126 Felix Potvin SR .02 .10
127 Dixon Ward SR .01 .05
128 Alexei Zhamnov SR .02 .10
129 Vladimir Malakhov SR .01 .05
130 Teemu Selanne SR .07 .20
131 Neal Broten .02 .10
132 Ulf Samuelsson .01 .05
133 Mark Janssens .01 .05
134 Claude Lemieux .01 .05
135 Mike Richter .07 .20
136 Doug Weight .02 .10
137 Rob Pearson .01 .05
138 Sylvain Cote .01 .05
139 Mike Keane .01 .05
140 Benoit Hogue .01 .05
141 Michel Petit .01 .05
142 Mark Freer .01 .05
143 Doug Zmolek .01 .05
144 Tony Granato .01 .05
145 Paul Coffey .07 .20
146 Ted Donato .01 .05
147 Brent Sutter .01 .05
148 Alexander Mogilny .08 .25
Teemu Selanne
Goal Scoring Leaders
149 James Patrick .01 .05
150 Mikael Andersson .01 .05
151 Steve Duchesne .01 .05
152 Terry Carkner .01 .05
153 Russ Courtnall .01 .05
154 Brian Mullen .01 .05
155 Martin Straka .01 .05
156 Geoff Sanderson .02 .10
157 Mark Howe .01 .05
158 Stephane Richer .02 .10
159 Doug Crossman .01 .05
160 John Vanbiesbrouck .02 .10
161 Bob Essensa .02 .10
162 Wayne Presley .01 .05
163 Mathieu Schneider .01 .05
164 Jiri Slegr .01 .05
165 Stephane Fiset .02 .10
166 Wendell Young .02 .10
167 Kevin Dineen .01 .05
168 Sandis Ozolinsh .02 .10
169 Mike Krushelnyski .01 .05
170 Kevin Stevens AS .01 .05
171 Pat LaFontaine AS .02 .10
172 Alexander Mogilny AS .02 .10
173 Larry Murphy AS .01 .05
174 Al Iafrate AS .01 .05
175 Tom Barrasso AS .02 .10
176 Derek King .01 .05
177 Bob Probert .02 .10
178 Gary Suter .01 .05
179 David Shaw .01 .05
180 Luc Robitaille .02 .10
181 John LeClair .07 .20
182 Troy Murray .01 .05
183 Dave Gagner .02 .10
184 Darcy Loewen .01 .05
185 Mario Lemieux LL .07 .20
186 Pat Jablonski .02 .10
187 Alexei Kovalev .02 .10
188 Todd Krygier .01 .05
189 Larry Murphy .02 .10
190 Pierre Turgeon .02 .10
191 Craig Ludwig .01 .05
192 Brad May .02 .10
193 John MacLean .02 .10
194 Ron Wilson .01 .05
195 Eric Weinrich .01 .05

196 Steve Chiasson .01 .05
197 Dmitri Kvartalnov .01 .05
198 Andrei Kovalenko .01 .05
199 Rob Gaudreau RC .01 .05
200 Evgeny Davydov .01 .05
201 Adrien Plavsic .01 .05
202 Brian Bellows .01 .05
203 Doug Evans .01 .05
204 Tom Barrasso .02 .10
Wins Leader
205 Joe Nieuwendyk .02 .10
206 Jari Kurri .07 .20
207 Bob Rouse .01 .05
208 Yvon Corriveau .01 .05
209 John Blue .02 .10
210 Dimitri Khristich .01 .05
211 Brent Fedyk .01 .05
212 Jody Hull .01 .05
213 Chris Terreri .02 .10
214 Mike McPhee .01 .05
215 Chris Kontos .01 .05
216 Greg Gilbert .01 .05
217 Sergei Zubov .01 .05
218 Grant Fuhr .02 .10
219 Charlie Huddy .01 .05
220 Mario Lemieux .40 1.00
221 Sheldon Kennedy .01 .05
222 Curtis Joseph .07 .20
Save Pct. Leader
223 Brad Dalgarno .01 .05
224 Bret Hedican .01 .05
225 Trevor Linden .02 .10
226 Darryl Sydor .01 .05
227 Jay More .01 .05
228 Dave Poulin .01 .05
229 Frank Musil .01 .05
230 Mark Recchi .02 .10
231 Craig Simpson .01 .05
232 Gino Cavallini .01 .05
233 Vincent Damphousse .01 .05
234 Luciano Borsato .01 .05
235 Dave Andreychuk .02 .10
236 Ken Daneyko .01 .05
237 Chris Chelios .07 .20
238 Andrew McBain .01 .05
239 Rick Tabaracci .02 .10
240 Steve Larmer .02 .10
241 Sean Burke .02 .10
242 Rob DiMaio .01 .05
243 Jim Paek .01 .05
244 Dave Lowry .01 .05
245 Alexander Mogilny .02 .10
246 Darren Turcotte .01 .05
247 Brendan Shanahan .07 .20
248 Peter Taglianetti .01 .05
249 Scott Mellanby .02 .10
250 Guy Carbonneau .01 .05
251 Claude LaPointe .01 .05
252 Pat Conacher .01 .05
253 Roger Johansson .01 .05
254 Cam Neely .07 .20
255 Garry Galley .01 .05
256 Keith Primeau .01 .05
257 Scott Lachance .01 .05
258 Bill Ranford .02 .10
259 Pat Falloon .01 .05
260 Pavel Bure .07 .20
261 Darrin Shannon .01 .05
262 Mike Foligno .01 .05
263 Checklist 1-132 .01 .05
264 Checklist 133-264 .01 .05
265 Peter Douris .01 .05
266 Warren Rychel .01 .05
267 Owen Nolan .02 .10
268 Mark Osborne .01 .05
269 Teppo Numminen .01 .05
270 Rob Niedermayer .02 .10
271 Mark Lamb .01 .05
272 Curtis Joseph .07 .20
273 Joe Murphy .01 .05
274 Bernie Nicholls .01 .05
275 Gord Roberts .01 .05
276 Al MacInnis .02 .10
277 Ken Wregget .02 .10
278 Calle Johansson .01 .05
279 Tom Kurvers .01 .05
280 Steve Yzerman .40 1.00
281 Roman Hamrlik .02 .10
282 Esa Tikkanen .01 .05
283 Darrin Madeley RC .01 .05
284 Robert Dirk .01 .05
285 Derek Plante RC .01 .05
286 Ron Tugnutt .02 .10
287 Frank Pietrangelo .02 .10
288 Paul DiPietro .01 .05
289 Alexander Godynyuk .01 .05
290 Kirk Maltby RC .01 .05
291 Olaf Kolzig .02 .10
292 Vitali Karamnov .01 .05
293 Alexei Gusarov .01 .05
294 Bryan Erickson .01 .05
295 Jocelyn Lemieux .01 .05
296 Bryan Trottier .02 .10
297 Dave Ellett .01 .05
298 Tim Watters .01 .05
299 Joe Juneau .02 .10
300 Steve Thomas .01 .05
301 Mark Greig .01 .05
302 Jeff Reese .01 .05
303 Steven King .01 .05
304 Don Beaupre .02 .10
305 Denis Savard .02 .10
306 Greg Smyth .01 .05
307 Jaroslav Modry RC .01 .05
308 Petr Svoboda .01 .05
309 Mike Craig .01 .05
310 Eric Lindros .07 .20
311 Dana Murzyn .01 .05
312 Sean Hill .01 .05
313 Andre Racicot .02 .10
314 John Vanbiesbrouck .02 .10
315 Doug Lidster .01 .05
316 Garth Butcher .01 .05
317 Alexei Yashin .01 .05
318 Sergei Fedorov .12 .30
319 Louie DeBrusk .01 .05
320 Dominik Hasek .07 .20
321 Michal Pivonka .01 .05
322 Bobby Holik .01 .05
323 Roman Hamrlik .02 .10
324 Petr Svoboda .01 .05
325 Jaromir Jagr .07 .20
326 Steven Finn .01 .05
327 Stephane Richer .02 .10
328 Claude Loiselle .01 .05
329 Joe Sacco .01 .05
330 Wayne Gretzky .50 1.25
331 Sylvain Lefebvre .01 .05
332 Sergei Bautin .01 .05
333 Craig Simpson .01 .05
334 Don Sweeney .01 .05
335 Dominic Roussel .02 .10
336 Scott Thomas RC .01 .05
337 Geoff Courtnall .01 .05
338 Tom Fitzgerald .01 .05
339 Kevin Haller .01 .05
340 Troy Loney .01 .05
341 Ronnie Stern .01 .05
342 Mark Astley RC .01 .05
343 Jeff Daniels .01 .05
344 Marc Bureau .01 .05
345 Micah Aivazoff RC .01 .05
346 Matthew Barnaby .02 .10
347 C.J. Young .01 .05
348 Dale Craigwell .01 .05
349 Ray Ferraro .01 .05
350 Ray Bourque .10 .30
351 Stu Barnes .01 .05
352 Allan Conroy RC .01 .05
353 Shawn McEachern .01 .05
354 Garry Valk .01 .05
355 Christian Ruuttu .01 .05
356 Darren Rumble .01 .05
357 Stu Grimson .01 .05
358 Alexander Karpovtsev .01 .05
359 Wendel Clark .02 .10
360 Michal Pivonka .01 .05
361 Peter Popovic RC .01 .05
362 Kevin Dahl .01 .05
363 Jeff Brown .01 .05
364 Daren Puppa .02 .10
365 Dallas Drake RC .01 .05
366 Dean McAmmond .01 .05
367 Martin Rucinsky .01 .05
368 Shane Churla .01 .05
369 Todd Ewen .01 .05
370 Kevin Stevens .01 .05
371 David Volek .01 .05
372 J.J. Daigneault .01 .05
373 Marc Bergevin .01 .05
374 Craig Billington .02 .10
375 Mike Gartner .02 .10
376 Jimmy Carson .01 .05
377 Bruce Driver .01 .05
378 Steve Heinze .01 .05
379 Patrick Carnback RC .01 .05
380 Wayne Gretzky CAN .07 .20
381 Jeff Brown CAN .01 .05
382 Gary Roberts CAN .01 .05
383 Ray Bourque CAN .07 .20
384 Mike Gartner CAN .01 .05
385 Felix Potvin CAN .07 .20
386 Michel Goulet .02 .10
387 Dave Tippett .01 .05
388 Jim Waite .02 .10
389 Yuri Khmylev .01 .05
390 Doug Gilmour .02 .10
391 Brad McCrimmon .01 .05
392 Brent Severyn RC .01 .05
393 Jocelyn Thibault RC .25 .60
394 Boris Mironov .01 .05
395 Marty McSorley .01 .05
396 Shaun Van Allen .01 .05
397 Gary Leeman .01 .05
398 Ed Olczyk .01 .05
399 Darcy Wakaluk .02 .10
400 Murray Craven .01 .05
401 Martin Brodeur .20 .50
402 Paul Laus RC .01 .05
403 Bill Houlder .01 .05
404 Robert Reichel .01 .05
405 Alexandre Daigle .01 .05
406 Brent Thompson .01 .05
407 Keith Acton .01 .05
408 Dave Karpa .01 .05
409 Igor Korolev .01 .05
410 Chris Gratton .02 .10
411 Vincent Riendeau .02 .10
412 Darren McCarty RC .15 .40
413 Bob Carpenter .01 .05
414 Joe Cirella .01 .05
415 Stephane Matteau .01 .05
416 Jozef Stumpel .01 .05
417 Rich Pilon .01 .05
418 Mattias Norstrom RC .01 .05
419 Dmitri Moronov .01 .05
420 Alexei Zhamnov .02 .10
421 Bill Guerin .01 .05
422 Greg Hawgood .01 .05
423 Randy Cunneyworth .01 .05
424 Ron Francis .02 .10
425 Brett Hull .08 .25
426 Tim Sweeney .01 .05
427 Mike Rathje .01 .05
428 Dave Babych .01 .05
429 Chris Tancill .01 .05
430 Mark Messier .07 .20
431 Bob Sweeney .01 .05
432 Terry Yake .01 .05
433 Joe Reekie .01 .05
434 Tomas Sandstrom .01 .05
435 Kevin Hatcher .01 .05
436 Bill Lindsay .01 .05
437 Jon Casey .02 .10
438 Dennis Vaske .01 .05
439 Allen Pedersen .01 .05
440 Pavel Bure .07 .20
441 Sergei Fedorov .07 .20
442 Arturs Irbe .02 .10
443 Darius Kasparaitis .01 .05
444 Evgeny Davydov .01 .05
445 Vladimir Malakhov .01 .05
446 Tom Barrasso .02 .10
447 Jeff Norton .01 .05
448 David Emma .01 .05
449 Pelle Eklund .01 .05
450 Jeremy Roenick .10 .25
451 Jesse Belanger .01 .05
452 Vitali Prokhorov .01 .05
453 Arto Blomsten .01 .05
454 Peter Zezel .01 .05
455 Kelly Kisio .01 .05
456 Zdeno Ciger .01 .05
457 Greg Johnson .01 .05
458 Dave Archibald .01 .05
459 Vladimir Vujtek .01 .05
460 Mats Sundin .07 .20
461 Dan Keczmer .01 .05
462 Stephan Lebeau .01 .05
463 Dominik Hasek .20 .50
464 Kevin Lowe .01 .05
465 Gord Murphy .01 .05
466 Bryan Smolinski .01 .05
467 Josef Beranek .01 .05
468 Ron Hextall .02 .10
469 Randy Ladouceur .01 .05
470 Scott Niedermayer .01 .05
471 Kelly Hrudey .02 .10
472 Mike Needham .01 .05
473 John Tucker .01 .05
474 Kelly Miller .01 .05
475 Jyrki Lumme .01 .05
476 Andy Moog .02 .10
477 Glen Murray .01 .05
478 Mark Fermer RC .01 .05
479 John Cullen .01 .05
480 Gilbert Dionne .01 .05
481 Paul Ranheim .01 .05
482 Mike Hough .01 .05
483 Teemu Selanne .07 .20
484 Aaron Ward RC .01 .05
485 Chris Pronger .02 .10
486 Glenn Healy .02 .10
487 Curtis Leschyshyn .01 .05
488 Jim Montgomery RC .01 .05
489 Travis Green .02 .10
490 Pat LaFontaine .07 .20
491 Bobby Dollas RC .01 .05
492 Alexei Kasatonov .01 .05
493 Corey Millen .01 .05
494 Slava Kozlov .02 .10
495 Igor Kravchuk .01 .05
496 Dimitri Filimonov .01 .05
497 Jeff Odgers .01 .05
498 Joe Mullen .02 .10
499 Gary Shuchuk .01 .05
500 Jeremy Roenick USA .10 .25
501 Tom Barrasso USA .02 .10
502 Keith Tkachuk USA .07 .20
503 Phil Housley USA .02 .10
504 Tony Granato USA .01 .05
505 Brian Leetch USA .07 .20
506 Anatoli Semenov .01 .05
507 Steve Leach .01 .05
508 Brian Skrudland .01 .05
509 Kirk Muller .01 .05
510 Gary Roberts .01 .05
511 Gerard Gallant .01 .05
512 Joey Kocur .01 .05
513 Tie Domi .02 .10
514 Kay Whitmore .02 .10
515 Vladimir Malakhov .01 .05
516 Stewart Malgunas RC .01 .05
517 Jamie Macoun .01 .05
518 Alan May .01 .05
519 Guy Hebert .02 .10
520 Derian Hatcher .01 .05
521 Richard Smehlik .01 .05
522 Joby Messier RC .01 .05
523 Trent Klatt .01 .05
524 Tom Chorske .01 .05
525 Iain Fraser RC .01 .05
526 Dan Laperriere .01 .05
527 Checklist 265-396 .01 .05
528 Checklist 397-528 .01 .05

1993-94 Topps/OPC Premier Gold

Every regular Premier 12-card pack included 11 regular cards plus one Premier Gold card. Also, one in four packs contained 10 regular cards plus two Premier Gold cards; and four Gold cards were inserted in every Topps jumbo pack. Aside from the gold-foil, the Premier Gold cards are identical to their regular issue counterparts. The four regular issue Premier checklists (263, 264, 527, and 528) were replaced by Gold cards of players not included in the basic set. The cards are numbered on the back. Except for some information in French on the backs, the O-Pee-Chee Premier Gold set is identical to the Topps Premier Gold set.

*TOPPS STARS: 2X TO 5X BASIC CARDS
*TOPPS GOLD RCs: 1.25X to 3X
*OPC STARS: 2.5X TO 6X BASIC CARDS
*OPC GOLD RCs: 1.5X to 4X
263G Martin Lapointe CL REP .50 1.25
264G Kevin Miehm CL REP .50 1.25
527G Myles O'Connor CL REP .50 1.25
528G Jamie Leach CL REP .50 1.25

1993-94 Topps Premier Black Gold

Randomly inserted in Topps packs, these 24 standard-size cards feature on their white-bordered fronts color player action shots set on ghosted and darkened backgrounds. Gold foil inner borders at the top and bottom carry multiple Premier Black Gold logos. The player's name appears in white lettering within a black stripe across the lower gold-foil inner margin. The horizontal back carries a color action cutout set on a bluish background on the left. Career highlights appear within a purple area on the right. The player's name and team name appear within a black bar across the top. The cards are numbered on the back. Collectors could also find in packs a Winner Card A, redeemable for the entire 12-card first-series set; a Winner Card B, redeemable for the 12-card second series; and a Winner Card AB, redeemable for the entire 24 card set. The Winner cards expired May 31, 1994.

1 Teemu Selanne .60 1.50
2 Steve Duchesne .15 .40
3 Felix Potvin .60 1.50
4 Shawn McEachern .15 .40
5 Adam Oates .30 .75
6 Paul Coffey .60 1.50
7 Wayne Gretzky 4.00 10.00
8 Alexei Zhamnov .30 .75
9 Mario Lemieux 3.00 8.00
10 Gary Suter .15 .40
11 Tom Barrasso .30 .75
12 Joe Juneau .30 .75
13 Eric Lindros .60 1.50
14 Ed Belfour .60 1.50
15 Ray Bourque 1.00 2.50
16 Steve Yzerman 3.00 8.00
17 Andrei Kovalenko .15 .40
18 Curtis Joseph .60 1.50
19 Phil Housley .30 .75
20 Pierre Turgeon .30 .75
21 Brett Hull .75 2.00
22 Patrick Roy 3.00 8.00
23 Larry Murphy .30 .75
24 Pat LaFontaine .60 1.50
A Winner 1-12 Expired .75 2.00
B Winner 13-24 Expired .60 1.50
AB Winner 1-24 Expired .60 1.50

1993-94 Topps Premier Finest

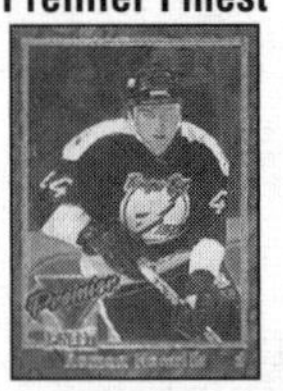

Randomly inserted in both Topps and OPC second-series packs, these 12 standard-size cards feature on their metallic fronts color player action shots framed by a gold line and bordered in blue. The player's name and position appear in gold lettering in the lower blue margin. The cards are numbered on the back as "X of 12."

1 Alexandre Daigle .20 .50
2 Roman Hamrlik .40 1.00
3 Eric Lindros .75 2.00
4 Owen Nolan .40 1.00
5 Mats Sundin .75 2.00
6 Mike Modano 1.25 3.00
7 Pierre Turgeon .40 1.00
8 Joe Murphy .20 .50
9 Wendel Clark .40 1.00
10 Mario Lemieux 4.00 10.00
11 Dale Hawerchuk .40 1.00
12 Rob Ramage .20 .50

1993-94 Topps Premier Team USA

Randomly inserted at a rate of 1:12 second-series Topps Premier packs, these 23 standard-size cards feature borderless color player photos on their fronts. The player's name and the USA Hockey logo appear at the bottom in gold foil. The red, white, and blue back carries the player's name and position at the top, followed below by biography, player photo, career highlights, and statistics. The cards are numbered on the back as "X of 23."

1 Mike Dunham .75 2.00
2 Ian Moran .40 1.00
3 Peter Laviolette .40 1.00
4 Darby Hendrickson .40 1.00
5 Brian Rolston .75 2.00
6 Mark Beaufait .40 1.00
7 Travis Richards .40 1.00
8 John Lilley .40 1.00
9 Chris Ferraro .75 2.00
10 Jon Hillebrandt .40 1.00
11 Chris Imes .40 1.00
12 Ted Crowley .40 1.00
13 David Sacco .40 1.00
14 Todd Marchant .75 2.00
15 Peter Ferraro .40 1.00
16 David Roberts .40 1.00
17 Jim Campbell .75 2.00
18 Barry Richter .40 1.00
19 Craig Johnson .40 1.00
20 Brett Hauer .40 1.00
21 Jeff Lazaro .40 1.00
22 Jim Storm .40 1.00
23 Matt Martin .40 1.00

1994-95 Topps/OPC Premier

This 550-card set was issued in two series of 275 cards each. OPC packs contained 14 cards and Topps packs contained 12 cards. Both boxes contained 36 packs. It was announced in press material that no more than 2,000 cases of each series of the OPC version were printed. Because of this shorter quantity, OPC versions earn a slight premium. Card fronts feature a full white border with a color bar enclosing the player's name near the bottom. Position runs vertically down the right side of the name, team name directly below it. All text is printed in silver foil. Backs have a black border with a cutout player photo, full stats including playoffs, and personal information. The OPC back text is in French and English. The Topps version is in English only. Since some of the cards have no written text, such as the All-Star cards, they are impossible to positively identify as being from one set or the other. Both versions have "The Topps Company, Inc." printed on the back. Several subsets appear scattered throughout the set, including All-Stars, Goaltending Duos, League Leaders, Rookie Sensations, Team of the Future, Tools of the Game, The Trade and Power.

COMPLETE SET (550) 20.00 40.00
COMPLETE SERIES 1 (275) 7.50 15.00
COMPLETE SERIES 2 (275) 12.50 25.00
1 Mark Messier .08 .25
2 Darren Turcotte .01 .05
3 Mikhail Shtalenkov RC .01 .05
4 Rob Gaudreau .01 .05
5 Tony Amonte .02 .10
6 Stephane Quintal .01 .05
7 Iain Fraser .01 .05
8 Doug Weight .02 .10
9 German Titov .01 .05
10 Larry Murphy .02 .10
11 Danton Cole .01 .05
12 Pat Peake .01 .05
13 Chris Terreri .02 .10
14 Yuri Khmylev .01 .05
15 Paul Coffey .08 .25
16 Brian Savage .01 .05
17 Rod Brind'Amour .02 .10
18 Nathan Lafayette .01 .05
19 Gord Murphy .01 .05
20 Al Iafrate .01 .05
21 Kevin Miller .01 .05
22 Peter Zezel .01 .05
23 Sylvain Turgeon .01 .05
24 Mark Tinordi .01 .05
25 Jari Kurri .02 .10
26 Benoit Hogue .01 .05
27 Jeff Reese .01 .05
28 Brian Noonan .01 .05
29 Denis Tsygurov RC .01 .05
30 James Patrick .01 .05
31 Bob Corkum .01 .05
32 Valeri Kamensky .02 .10
33 Ray Whitney .01 .05
34 Joe Murphy .01 .05
35 Dominik Hasek AS .08 .25
36 Ray Bourque AS .08 .25
37 Brian Leetch AS .08 .25
38 Dave Andreychuk AS .02 .10
39 Pavel Bure AS .08 .25
40 Sergei Fedorov AS .08 .25
41 Bob Beers .01 .05
42 Byron Dafoe RC .15 .40
43 Lyle Odelein .01 .05
44 Markus Naslund .08 .25
45 Dean Chynoweth RC .01 .05
46 Trent Klatt .01 .05
47 Murray Craven .01 .05
48 Dave Mackey .01 .05
49 Norm Maciver .01 .05
50 Alexander Mogilny .02 .10
51 David Reid .01 .05
52 Nicklas Lidstrom .08 .25
53 Tom Fitzgerald .01 .05
54 Roman Hamrlik .02 .10
55 Wendel Clark .02 .10
56 Dominic Roussel .02 .10
57 Alexei Zhitnik .01 .05
58 Valeri Zelepukin .01 .05
59 Calle Johansson .01 .05
60 Craig Janney .02 .10
61 Randy Wood .01 .05
62 Curtis Leschyshyn .01 .05
63 Stephan Lebeau .01 .05
64 Dallas Drake .01 .05
65 Vincent Damphousse .01 .05
66 Scott Lachance .01 .05
67 Dirk Graham .01 .05
68 Kevin Smyth .01 .05
69 Denis Savard .02 .10
70 Mike Richter .08 .25
71 Ronnie Stern .01 .05
72 Kirk Maltby .01 .05
73 Kjell Samuelsson .01 .05
74 Neal Broten .02 .10
75 Trevor Linden .02 .10
76 Todd Elik .01 .05
77 Andrew McBain .01 .05
78 Alexei Kudashov .01 .05
79 Ken Daneyko .01 .05
80 Dominik Hasek .08 .25
Grant Fuhr DUO
81 Andy Moog .08 .25
Darcy Wakaluk DUO
82 John Vanbiesbrouck .02 .10
Mark Fitzpatrick DUO
83 Martin Brodeur .08 .25
Chris Terreri DUO
84 Tom Barrasso .02 .10
Ken Wregget DUO
85 Kirk McLean .02 .10
Kay Whitmore DUO
86 Darryl Sydor .01 .05
87 Chris Osgood .15 .40
88 Ted Donato .01 .05
89 Dave Lowry .01 .05
90 Mark Recchi .02 .10
91 Jim Montgomery .01 .05
92 Bill Houlder .01 .05
93 Richard Smehlik .01 .05
94 Benoit Brunet .01 .05
95 Teemu Selanne .08 .25
96 Paul Ranheim .01 .05
97 Andrei Kovalenko .01 .05
98 Grant Ledyard .01 .05
99 Brent Grieve RC .01 .05
100 Joe Juneau .02 .10
101 Martin Gelinas .01 .05
102 Jamie Macoun .01 .05
103 Craig MacTavish .01 .05
104 Micah Aivazoff .01 .05
105 Stephane Richer .02 .10
106 Eric Weinrich .01 .05
107 Pat Elynuik .01 .05
108 Tomas Sandstrom .01 .05
109 Darrin Madeley .01 .05
110 Al MacInnis .02 .10
111 Cam Stewart .01 .05
112 Dixon Ward .01 .05
113 Vlastimil Kroupa .01 .05
114 Rob DiMaio .01 .05
115 Pierre Turgeon .02 .10
116 Mike Hough .01 .05
117 John LeClair .08 .25
118 Dave Hannan .01 .05
119 Todd Ewen .01 .05
120 Stanley Cup Card .02 .10
121 Dave Manson .01 .05
122 Jocelyn Lemieux .01 .05
123 Jocelyn Thibault .08 .25
124 Scott Pearson .01 .05
125 Patrick Roy AS .20 .50
126 Scott Stevens AS .02 .10
127 Al MacInnis AS .02 .10
128 Adam Graves AS .01 .05
129 Cam Neely AS .02 .10
130 Wayne Gretzky AS .30 .75
131 Tom Chorske .01 .05
132 John Tucker .01 .05
133 Steve Smith .01 .05
134 Kay Whitmore .02 .10
135 Adam Oates .02 .10
136 Bill Berg .01 .05
137 Wes Walz .01 .05
138 Jeff Beukeboom .01 .05
139 Ron Francis .02 .10
140 Alexandre Daigle .01 .05
141 Josef Beranek .01 .05
142 Tom Pederson .01 .05
143 Jamie McLennan .02 .10
144 Scott Mellanby .02 .10
145 Slava Kozlov .02 .10
146 Marty McSorley .01 .05
147 Tim Sweeney .01 .05
148 Luciano Borsato .01 .05
149 Jason Dawe .01 .05
150 Wayne Gretzky LL .30 .75
151 Pavel Bure LL .08 .25
152 Dominik Hasek LL .08 .25
153 Scott Stevens LL .02 .10
154 Wayne Gretzky LL .30 .75
155 Mike Richter LL .08 .25
156 Dominik Hasek LL .08 .25
157 Ted Drury .01 .05
158 Peter Popovic .01 .05
159 Alexei Kasatonov .01 .05
160 Mats Sundin .08 .25
161 Brad Shaw .01 .05
162 Bret Hedican .01 .05
163 Mike McPhee .01 .05
164 Martin Straka .01 .05
165 Dimitri Mironov .01 .05
166 Andrei Trefilov .01 .05
167 Joe Reekie .01 .05
168 Gary Suter .01 .05
169 Greg Gilbert .01 .05
170 Igor Larionov .01 .05
171 Mike Sillinger .01 .05
172 Igor Kravchuk .01 .05
173 Glen Murray .01 .05
174 Shawn Chambers .01 .05
175 John MacLean .02 .10
176 Yves Racine .01 .05
177 Andrei Lomakin .01 .05
178 Patrick Flatley .01 .05
179 Igor Ulanov .01 .05
180 Pat LaFontaine .08 .25
181 Mathieu Schneider .01 .05
182 Peter Stastny .02 .10
183 Tony Granato .01 .05
184 Peter Douris .01 .05
185 Alexei Kovalev .01 .05
186 Geoff Courtnall .01 .05
187 Richard Matvichuk .01 .05
188 Troy Murray .01 .05
189 Todd Gill .01 .05
190 Martin Brodeur RS .08 .25
191 Mikael Renberg RS .02 .10
192 Alexei Yashin RS .01 .05
193 Jason Arnott RS .01 .05
194 Derek Plante RS .01 .05
195 Alexandre Daigle RS .01 .05
196 Bryan Smolinski RS .01 .05
197 Jesse Belanger RS .01 .05
198 Chris Pronger RS .02 .10
199 Chris Osgood RS .02 .10
200 Jeremy Roenick .12 .30
201 Johan Garpenlov .01 .05
202 Dave Karpa .01 .05
203 Darren McCarty .01 .05
204 Claude Lemieux .01 .05
205 Geoff Sanderson .02 .10
206 Tom Barrasso .02 .10
207 Kevin Dineen .01 .05
208 Sylvain Cote .01 .05
209 Brent Gretzky .01 .05
210 Shayne Corson .01 .05
211 Darius Kasparaitis .01 .05
212 Peter Andersson .01 .05
213 Robert Reichel .01 .05
214 Jozef Stumpel .01 .05
215 Brendan Shanahan .08 .25
216 Craig Muni .01 .05
217 Alexei Zhamnov .02 .10
218 Robert Lang .01 .05
219 Brian Bellows .01 .05
220 Steven King .01 .05
221 Sergei Zubov .01 .05
222 Kelly Miller .01 .05
223 Ilya Byakin .01 .05
224 Chris Tamer RC .01 .05
225 Doug Gilmour .02 .10
226 Shawn Antoski .01 .05
227 Andrew Cassels .01 .05
228 Craig Wolanin .01 .05
229 Jon Casey .02 .10
230 Mike Modano .15 .40
231 Bill Guerin .02 .10
232 Gaetan Duchesne .01 .05
233 Steve Dubinsky .01 .05
234 Jason Bowen .01 .05
235 Steve Yzerman .50 1.25
236 Dave Poulin .01 .05
237 Michael Nylander .01 .05
238 Felix Potvin FUT .02 .10
239 Sandis Ozolinsh FUT .01 .05
240 Scott Niedermayer FUT .01 .05
241 Eric Lindros FUT .08 .25
242 Keith Tkachuk FUT .08 .25
243 Teemu Selanne FUT .08 .25
244 Marty McInnis .01 .05
245 Bob Kudelski .01 .05
246 Paul Cavallini .01 .05
247 Brian Bradley .01 .05
248 Robb Stauber .02 .10
249 Jay Wells .01 .05
250 Mario Lemieux .50 1.25
251 Tommy Albelin .01 .05
252 Paul DiPietro .01 .05
253 Mike Gartner .02 .10
254 Darrin Shannon .01 .05
255 Alexander Karpovtsev .01 .05
256 Dave Babych .01 .05
257 Greg Johnson .01 .05
258 Frank Musil .01 .05
259 Michal Pivonka .01 .05
260 Arturs Irbe .02 .10
261 Paul Broten .01 .05
262 Don Sweeney .01 .05
263 Doug Brown .01 .05
264 Bobby Dollas .01 .05
265 Brian Skrudland .01 .05
266 Dan Plante RC .01 .05
267 Chad Penney .01 .05
268 Steve Leach .01 .05
269 Damian Rhodes .02 .10
270 Glenn Anderson .02 .10
271 Randy McKay .01 .05
272 Jeff Brown .01 .05
273 Steve Konowalchuk .01 .05
274 Checklist 1-136 .01 .05
275 Checklist 137-275 .01 .05
276 Sergei Fedorov .08 .25
277 Adam Oates .02 .10
278 Mark Messier .08 .25
279 Doug Gilmour .02 .10
280 Wayne Gretzky .30 .75
281 Rick Tocchet .02 .10
282 Guy Carbonneau .01 .05
283 Peter Bondra .02 .10
284 Valeri Karpov RC .01 .05
285 Ed Belfour .08 .25
286 Petr Nedved .02 .10
287 Mikael Andersson .01 .05
288 Boris Mironov .01 .05
289 Donald Audette .01 .05
290 Kevin Stevens .01 .05
291 Cliff Ronning .01 .05
292 Bruce Driver .01 .05
293 Mariusz Czerkawski RC .10 .30
294 Mikael Renberg .02 .10
295 Theo Fleury .01 .05
296 Robert Kron .01 .05
297 Wendel Clark .02 .10
298 Dave Gagner .02 .10
299 Ulf Dahlen .01 .05
300 Keith Tkachuk .08 .25
301 Mike Ridley .01 .05
302 Mike Vernon .02 .10
303 Troy Mallette .01 .05
304 Derek King .01 .05
305 Kirk Muller .01 .05
306 Rob Niedermayer .02 .10
307 Ian Laperriere RC .01 .05
308 Mike Donnelly .01 .05
309 Joe Sacco .01 .05
310 Patrick Roy .20 .50
311 Tom Barrasso .02 .10
312 Dominik Hasek .08 .25
313 Felix Potvin .08 .25
314 Mike Richter .08 .25
315 Bobby Holik .01 .05
316 Patrick Poulin .01 .05
317 Stephane Matteau .01 .05
318 Petr Klima .01 .05
319 Fredrik Olausson .01 .05
320 Dale Hawerchuk .02 .10
321 Jim Dowd .01 .05
322 Chris Therien .01 .05
323 Ravil Gusmanov RC .01 .05
324 Vincent Riendeau .02 .10
325 Pavel Bure .08 .25
326 Jimmy Carson .01 .05
327 Steve Chiasson .01 .05
328 Ken Wregget .02 .10
329 Kenny Jonsson .01 .05
330 Keith Primeau .01 .05
331 Bob Errey .01 .05
332 Derian Hatcher .01 .05
333 Stephane Fiset .02 .10
334 Brent Severyn .01 .05

5 Ray Ferraro .01 .05
6 Pavol Demitra .02 .10
7 Valeri Bure .01 .05
8 Guy Hebert .02 .10
9 Matt Johnson RC .01 .05
0 Curtis Joseph .08 .25
1 Rob Pearson .01 .05
2 Jeff Shantz .01 .05
3 Eric Charron RC .01 .05
4 Jason Smith .01 .05
5 Mats Sundin .02 .10
Wendel Clark
6 Rick Tocchet .02 .10
Luc Robitaille
7 Al MacInnis .02 .10
Phil Housley
8 Mike Vernon .02 .10
Steve Chiasson
9 Craig Simpson .01 .05
0 Adam Graves .01 .05
1 Kevin Haller .01 .05
2 Nelson Emerson .01 .05
3 Phil Housley .02 .10
4 Shawn McEachern .01 .05
5 Felix Potvin .08 .25
6 Sergio Momesso .01 .05
7 Glen Wesley .01 .05
8 David Shaw .01 .05
9 Terry Carkner .01 .05
0 John Vanbiesbrouck .02 .10
1 Dean Evason .01 .05
2 Michal Sykora .01 .05
3 Troy Loney .01 .05
4 Sylvain Lefebvre .01 .05
5 Alexei Yashin .01 .05
6 Gilbert Dionne .01 .05
7 Rick Tabaracci .02 .10
8 Paul Ysebaert .01 .05
9 Craig Johnson .01 .05
0 Scott Stevens .02 .10
1 Philippe Boucher .01 .05
2 Garry Valk .01 .05
3 Jason Muzzatti .02 .10
4 Chris Joseph .01 .05
5 Wayne Gretzky .60 1.50
6 Teppo Numminen .01 .05
7 Oleg Petrov .01 .05
8 Patrik Juhlin RC .01 .05
9 Zarley Zalapski .01 .05
0 Martin Brodeur TOTF .08 .25
1 Chris Pronger .02 .10
2 Sergei Zubov .01 .05
3 Mikael Renberg .02 .10
4 Brett Lindros .01 .05
5 Peter Forsberg .15 .40
6 Brandon Convery .01 .05
7 Steve Heinze .01 .05
8 Glenn Healy .02 .10
9 Brian Benning .01 .05
0 Pat Verbeek .01 .05
1 Ulf Samuelsson .01 .05
2 Turner Stevenson .01 .05
3 Bob Rouse .01 .05
4 Steve Konroyd .01 .05
5 Russ Courtnall .01 .05
6 Sergei Makarov .01 .05
7 Kirk McLean .02 .10
8 Steven Finn .01 .05
9 Yan Kaminsky .01 .05
0 Eric Lindros .08 .25
1 Steve Duchesne .01 .05
2 John Slaney .01 .05
3 Bernie Nicholls .02 .10
4 Kelly Buchberger .01 .05
5 Paul Kariya .08 .25
6 Michel Petit .01 .05
7 Cale Hulse RC .01 .05
8 Sheldon Kennedy .01 .05
9 Brad May .01 .05
0 Daren Puppa .02 .10
1 Janne Laukkanen .01 .05
2 Mats Sundin .08 .25
3 Trevor Kidd .02 .10
4 Greg Adams .01 .05
5 Pavel Bure .08 .25
6 Teemu Selanne .08 .25
7 Brett Hull .08 .25
8 Steve Larmer .02 .10
9 Cam Neely .02 .10
0 Ray Bourque .15 .40
1 Andrei Nikolishin .01 .05
2 Jim Paek .01 .05
3 John Cullen .01 .05
4 Darcy Wakaluk .02 .10
5 Peter Forsberg .30 .75
6 Yves Racine .01 .05
7 Jody Hull .01 .05
8 Ron Sutter .01 .05
9 Ray Sheppard .02 .10
0 Sandis Ozolinsh .01 .05
1 Brent Grieve .01 .05
2 Shaun Van Allen .01 .05
3 Craig Berube .01 .05
4 Vladislav Boulin RC .01 .05
5 Bill Ranford .02 .10
6 Denny Felsner .01 .05
7 Jamie Storr .02 .10
8 Brian Rolston .01 .05
9 Chris Gratton .01 .05
0 Dominik Hasek .20 .50
1 Garth Butcher .01 .05
2 Jyrki Lumme .01 .05
3 Sergei Nemchinov .01 .05
4 Tie Domi .02 .10
5 Gary Roberts .01 .05
6 Dave McLlwain .01 .05
7 John Gruden RC .01 .05
8 Vladimir Konstantinov .02 .10
9 Adam Deadmarsh .01 .05
0 Brian Leetch .08 .25
1 Scott Stevens .02 .10
2 Mark Tinordi .01 .05
3 Al Iafrate .01 .05
4 Ray Bourque .08 .25
5 Patrick Roy .40 1.00
6 Viktor Gordiouk .01 .05
7 Owen Nolan .02 .10
8 Stu Barnes .01 .05
9 Zigmund Palffy .02 .10
0 Jaromir Jagr .15 .40
1 Andrei Nazarov .01 .05
462 Kelly Hrudey .02 .10
463 Jason Wiemer RC .01 .05
464 Oleg Tverdovsky .02 .10
465 Brett Hull .12 .30
466 Luke Richardson .01 .05
467 Jason Allison .01 .05
468 Dimitri Yushkevich .01 .05
469 Todd Simon RC .01 .05
470 Martin Brodeur .30 .60
471 Thomas Steen .01 .05
472 Vesa Viitakoski .01 .05
473 Todd Harvey .01 .05
474 Kent Manderville .01 .05
475 Chris Chelios .08 .25
476 Joby Messier .01 .05
477 Jassen Cullimore .01 .05
478 Jamie Pushor .01 .05
479 Bryan Smolinski .01 .05
480 Joe Sakic .20 .50
481 David Wilkie .01 .05
482 Craig Billington .02 .10
483 Pat Neaton .01 .05
484 Chris Pronger .08 .25
485 Brian Leetch .08 .25
486 Chris Chelios .08 .25
487 Jeff Brown .01 .05
488 Al MacInnis .02 .10
489 Paul Coffey .08 .25
490 Ray Bourque .08 .25
491 Phil Housley .02 .10
492 Larry Murphy .02 .10
493 Sergei Zubov .01 .05
494 Scott Stevens .02 .10
495 Steve Thomas .01 .05
496 Jim Waite .02 .10
497 Mike Keane .01 .05
498 Rob Blake .02 .10
499 John Lilley .01 .05
500 Brian Leetch .08 .25
501 Derek Plante .01 .05
502 Tim Cheveldae .02 .10
503 Vladimir Vujtek .01 .05
504 Esa Tikkanen .01 .05
505 Cam Neely .08 .25
506 Dale Hunter .01 .05
507 Marc Bergevin .01 .05
508 Joel Otto .01 .05
509 Brent Fedyk .01 .05
510 Dave Andreychuk .02 .10
511 Andy Moog .08 .25
512 Jaroslav Modry .01 .05
513 Sergei Krivokrasov .01 .05
514 Brett Lindros .01 .05
515 Cory Stillman RC .01 .05
516 Jon Rohloff RC .01 .05
517 Joe Mullen .02 .10
518 Evgeny Davydov .01 .05
519 Scott Young .01 .05
520 Sergei Fedorov .12 .30
521 Pat Falloon .01 .05
522 Bill Lindsay .01 .05
523 Ron Tugnutt .02 .10
524 Anatoli Semenov .01 .05
525 Geoff Courtnall .01 .05
526 Luc Robitaille .02 .10
527 Geoff Sanderson .02 .10
528 Esa Tikkanen .01 .05
529 Brendan Shanahan .08 .25
530 Jason Arnott .01 .05
531 Michal Grosek RC .01 .05
532 Steve Larmer .02 .10
533 Eric Fichaud RC .02 .10
534 Dimitri Khristich .01 .05
535 Garry Galley .01 .05
536 Aaron Gavey .01 .05
537 Joe Nieuwendyk .02 .10
538 Mike Craig .01 .05
539 Scott Niedermayer .01 .05
540 Luc Robitaille .02 .10
541 Dino Ciccarelli .02 .10
542 Sean Burke .02 .10
543 Jiri Slegr .01 .05
544 Jesse Belanger .01 .05
545 Sean Hill .01 .05
546 Vladimir Malakhov .01 .05
547 Jeff Friesen .01 .05
548 Mike Ricci .01 .05
549 Checklist 276-414 .01 .05
550 Checklist 415-550 .01 .05

1994-95 Topps/OPC Premier Special Effects

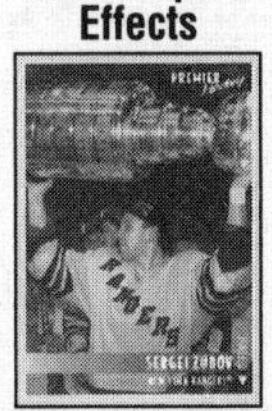

One card from this parallel set was issued in every other pack of OPC and Topps Premier. The cards can be differentiated from the basic set by the reflective rainbow foil which appears in the card background when held at an angle to a light source. Card backs are the same. The OPC versions are slightly more desirable because they were printed in smaller quantities than the Topps cards. Cards 274, 275, 549 and 550 replaced the checklists with players not featured in the basic set.
*SER.1 STARS: 4X TO 10X BASIC CARDS
*SER.1 ROOKIES: 1.5X TO 4X BASIC CARDS
*SER.2 STARS: 6X TO 15X BASIC CARDS
*SER.2 FX ROOKIES: 3X TO 8X BASIC CARDS
*OPC VERSIONS: .75X TO 1.5X TOPPS

1994-95 Topps Finest Inserts

The 23 cards in this set were randomly inserted at a rate of 1:36 Topps Premier

series one packs. The set includes all players who scored at least 40 goals in 1993-94. Cards feature an isolated player photo over a textured rainbow background. A reflective rainbow border is broken up by the player name and his goal scoring mark. Premier Finest is written across the top of the card. Backs have a small player photo with brief personal information, and scoring breakdown by division. Cards are numbered "X" of 23.
COMPLETE SET (23) 20.00 50.00
1 Pavel Bure 1.50 4.00
2 Brett Hull 2.00 5.00
3 Sergei Fedorov 2.00 5.00
4 Dave Andreychuk .75 2.00
5 Brendan Shanahan 2.00 5.00
6 Ray Sheppard .75 2.00
7 Adam Graves .40 1.00
8 Cam Neely 2.00 5.00
9 Mike Modano 2.00 5.00
10 Wendel Clark .75 2.00
11 Jeremy Roenick 2.00 5.00
12 Eric Lindros 2.00 5.00
13 Luc Robitaille .75 2.00
14 Steve Thomas .40 1.00
15 Geoff Sanderson .75 2.00
16 Gary Roberts .40 1.00
17 Kevin Stevens .40 1.00
18 Keith Tkachuk .75 2.00
19 Theo Fleury .40 1.00
20 Robert Reichel .40 1.00
21 Mark Recchi .75 2.00
22 Vincent Damphousse .40 1.00
23 Bob Kudelski .40 1.00

1994-95 Topps/OPC Premier The Go To Guy

This 15-card set was issued in both Topps and OPC Premier series two product at the rate of 1:36 packs. There is no difference between the cards inserted in each product.
COMPLETE SET (15) 15.00 30.00
1 Wayne Gretzky 5.00 12.00
2 Joe Sakic 1.50 4.00
3 Brett Hull 1.00 2.50
4 Mike Modano 1.25 3.00
5 Pavel Bure .75 2.00
6 Pat LaFontaine .75 2.00
7 Theo Fleury .15 .40
8 Jeremy Roenick 1.00 2.50
9 Sergei Fedorov 1.00 2.50
10 Eric Lindros .75 2.00
11 Kirk Muller .15 .40
12 Steve Yzerman 4.00 10.00
13 Alexander Mogilny .30 .75
14 Doug Gilmour .30 .75
15 Mark Messier .75 2.00

1994-96 Topps Finest Bronze

This trio of sets were made available to collectors exclusively through Topps Stadium Club program. The sets cost approximately $95 each, including shipping, from the club. Each bronze card features embossed color action player images on a metallic background of the team logo in a marbleized black border and thin gold frame. The gold backs carry player information and career statistics. Cards 1-6 were issued as a first series in 1994.
1 Jaromir Jagr 12.00 30.00
2 Eric Lindros 12.00 30.00
3 Patrick Roy 20.00 50.00
4 Pavel Bure 10.00 25.00
5 Teemu Selanne 10.00 25.00
6 Doug Gilmour 8.00 20.00
7 Sergei Fedorov 10.00 25.00
8 Brett Hull 10.00 25.00
9 Paul Kariya 16.00 40.00
10 Cam Neely 8.00 20.00
11 Mats Sundin 8.00 20.00
12 Martin Brodeur 10.00 25.00
13 Jeremy Roenick 8.00 20.00
14 Brian Leetch 6.00 15.00
15 Mark Messier 8.00 20.00
16 Mario Lemieux 20.00 50.00
17 Peter Forsberg 12.00 30.00
18 Felix Potvin 8.00 20.00
19 Alexander Mogilny 4.00 10.00
20 Ray Bourque 12.00 30.00
21 Ed Jovanovski 6.00 15.00
22 Mikael Renberg 4.00 10.00

1995-96 Topps

The 385-card set was issued in two series of 220 and 165 cards, respectively. The 13-card packs had an SRP of $1.29.
COMPLETE SET (385) 12.50 25.00

COMPLETE SERIES 1 (220) 7.50 15.00
COMPLETE SERIES 2 (165) 5.00 10.00
1 Eric Lindros MM .07 .20
2 Dominik Hasek MM .07 .20
3 Jeremy Roenick MM .10 .25
4 Paul Coffey MM .07 .20
5 Mark Messier MM .07 .20
6 Peter Bondra MM .02 .10
7 Paul Kariya MM .07 .20
8 Chris Chelios .07 .20
9 Martin Brodeur MM .07 .20
10 Brett Hull MM .07 .20
11 Mike Vernon MM .02 .10
12 Trevor Linden MM .02 .10
13 Pat LaFontaine MM .02 .10
14 Geoff Sanderson MM .02 .10
15 Cam Neely MM .02 .10
16 Brendan Shanahan MM .07 .20
17 Jason Arnott MM .01 .05
18 Mikael Renberg MM .02 .10
19 Mats Sundin MM .07 .20
20 Pavel Bure MM .07 .20
21 Pierre Turgeon MM .02 .10
22 Alexei Zhamnov MM .01 .05
23 Blaine Lacher .02 .10
24 Brian Holzinger RC .07 .20
25 Theo Fleury .01 .05
26 Eric Daze .02 .10
27 Mike Kennedy RC .01 .05
28 Darren McCarty .01 .05
29 Todd Marchant .01 .05
30 Andrew Cassels .01 .05
31 Rob Niedermayer .02 .10
32 Eric Lacroix RC .01 .05
33 Steve Rucchin RC .01 .05
34 Turner Stevenson .01 .05
35 Sergei Brylin .01 .05
36 Mathieu Schneider .01 .05
37 Pat Verbeek .01 .05
38 Steve Larouche RC .01 .05
39 Rod Brind'Amour .02 .10
40 Luc Robitaille .02 .10
41 Brett Lindros .01 .05
42 Shean Donovan RC .01 .05
43 David Roberts .01 .05
44 Cory Cross .01 .05
45 Todd Warriner .01 .05
46 Yevgeny Namestnikov .01 .05
47 Sergei Gonchar .01 .05
48 Nikolai Khabibulin .02 .10
49 Alexei Zhitnik .01 .05
50 Ray Bourque .12 .30
51 Paul Kruse .01 .05
52 Murray Craven .01 .05
53 Andy Moog .07 .20
54 Keith Primeau .01 .05
55 Shayne Corson .01 .05
56 Johan Garpenlov .01 .05
57 Marek Malik .01 .05
58 Tony Granato .01 .05
59 Bob Corkum .01 .05
60 Patrick Roy .40 1.00
61 Chris McAlpine RC .01 .05
62 Chris Marinucci RC .01 .05
63 Jeff Beukeboom .01 .05
64 Radek Bonk .01 .05
65 John LeClair .07 .20
66 Len Barrie .01 .05
67 Teppo Numminen .01 .05
68 Ray Whitney .02 .10
69 Jeff Norton .01 .05
70 Chris Gratton .01 .05
71 Benoit Hogue .01 .05
72 Bret Hedican .01 .05
73 Keith Jones .02 .10
74 John Cullen .01 .05
75 Brian Leetch .02 .10
76 Dave Reid .01 .05
77 Dino Ciccarelli .02 .10
78 Gary Roberts .01 .05
79 Tony Amonte .02 .10
80 Mike Modano .12 .30
81 Doug Brown .01 .05
82 Scott Thornton .01 .05
83 Bill Lindsay .01 .05
84 Frantisek Kucera .01 .05
85 Wayne Gretzky .50 1.25
86 Joe Sacco .01 .05
87 Benoit Brunet .01 .05
88 Bill Guerin .02 .10
89 Travis Green .02 .10
90 Alexei Kovalev .01 .05
91 Stanislav Neckar .01 .05
92 Rob Dimaio .01 .05
93 Chris Joseph .01 .05
94 Craig Martin RC .01 .05
95 Craig Janney .01 .05
96 Greg Gilbert .01 .05
97 Alexander Semak .01 .05
98 Mike Gartner .02 .10
99 Cliff Ronning .01 .05
100 Mario Lemieux .40 1.00
101 Jassen Cullimore .01 .05
102 Steve Duchesne .01 .05
103 Derek Plante .01 .05
104 John Gruden .01 .05
105 Michal Sykora .01 .05
106 Trent Klatt .01 .05
107 Nicklas Lidstrom .07 .20
108 Luke Richardson .01 .05
109 Steven Rice .01 .05
110 Stu Barnes .01 .05
111 John Druce .01 .05
112 Guy Hebert .02 .10
113 Vladimir Malakhov .01 .05
114 Claude Lemieux .01 .05
115 Kirk Muller .01 .05
116 Darren Langdon RC .01 .05
117 Rob Gaudreau .01 .05
118 Karl Dykhuis .01 .05
119 Richard Park .01 .05
120 Dave Manson .01 .05
121 Andrei Nazarov .01 .05
122 Bernie Nicholls .01 .05
123 Mikael Andersson .01 .05
124 Todd Gill .01 .05
125 Trevor Linden .02 .10
126 Kelly Miller .01 .05
127 Don Sweeney .01 .05
128 Jason Dawe .01 .05
129 Steve Chiasson .01 .05
130 Ed Belfour .07 .20
131 Kerry Huffman .01 .05
132 Tim Taylor .01 .05
133 Kirk Maltby .02 .10
134 Jody Hull .01 .05
135 Sean Burke .02 .10
136 Philippe Boucher .01 .05
137 Valeri Karpov .01 .05
138 Yves Racine .01 .05
139 Patrick Flatley .01 .05
140 John MacLean .02 .10
141 Sergei Nemchinov .01 .05
142 Don Beaupre .02 .10
143 Kevin Dineen .01 .05
144 Ulf Samuelsson .01 .05
145 Al MacInnis .02 .10
146 Igor Korolev .01 .05
147 Pat Falloon .01 .05
148 Brian Bradley .01 .05
149 Josef Beranek .01 .05
150 Mats Sundin .07 .20
152 Keith Tkachuk .07 .20
153 Mariusz Czerkawski .01 .05
154 Trevor Kidd .02 .10
155 Garry Galley .01 .05
156 Gary Suter .01 .05
157 Grant Ledyard .01 .05
158 Doug Weight .02 .10
159 Jesse Belanger .01 .05
160 Mike Vernon .02 .10
161 Robert Kron .01 .05
162 Marty McSorley .01 .05
163 Todd Krygier .01 .05
164 Scott Niedermayer .01 .05
165 Mark Recchi .02 .10
166 Phil Housley .02 .10
167 Ron Hextall .02 .10
168 Richard Smehlik .01 .05
169 Chris Tamer .01 .05
170 Alexei Yashin .01 .05
171 Sergei Makarov .01 .05
172 Patrice Tardif .01 .05
173 Milos Holan .01 .05
174 J.C. Bergeron .01 .05
175 Dave Andreychuk .02 .10
176 Martin Gelinas .01 .05
177 Dale Hunter .02 .10
178 Kevin Haller .01 .05
179 Jeff Shantz .01 .05
180 Adam Oates .02 .10
181 Ronnie Stern .01 .05
182 Jamie Langenbrunner .02 .10
183 Mark Fitzpatrick .02 .10
184 Adam Burt .01 .05
185 Sergei Fedorov .12 .30
186 Robert Lang .01 .05
187 Craig Conroy RC .01 .05
188 Ken Daneyko .01 .05
189 Marko Tuomainen .01 .05
190 Ken Wregget .02 .10
191 Mike Rathje .01 .05
192 Dimitri Yushkevich .01 .05
193 Roman Hamrlik .02 .10
194 Russ Courtnall .01 .05
195 Teemu Selanne .07 .20
196 Jon Rohloff .01 .05
197 Derian Hatcher .01 .05
198 Mark Tinordi .01 .05
199 Patrice Brisebois .01 .05
200 Jaromir Jagr .12 .30
201 Randy McKay .01 .05
202 Derek King .01 .05
203 Tony Twist .02 .10
204 Jyrki Lumme .01 .05
205 Steve Smith .01 .05
206 Bob Rouse .01 .05
207 Dave Ellett .01 .05
208 Kevin Dean .01 .05
209 Rusty Fitzgerald RC .01 .05
210 Jim Carey .02 .10
211 Kenny Jonsson .01 .05
212 Mike Richter .07 .20
213 Glen Wesley .01 .05
214 Donald Audette .01 .05
215 Curtis Joseph .07 .20
216 Joe Juneau .01 .05
217 Paul Kariya .07 .20
218 1995 Stanley Cup Champions .02 .10
219 Checklist 1-110 .01 .05
220 Checklist 111-220 .01 .05
221 Cam Neely .07 .20
222 Wayne Primeau RC .01 .05
223 Yanic Perreault .01 .05
224 Pierre Turgeon .02 .10
225 Alexander Mogilny .02 .10
226 Daren Puppa .02 .10
227 Ulf Dahlen .01 .05
228 Tomas Sandstrom .01 .05
229 Shayne Corson .01 .05
230 Chris Chelios .07 .20
231 Stephane Richer .02 .10
232 Paul Ranheim .01 .05
233 Joe Nieuwendyk .02 .10
234 Doug Gilmour .02 .10
235 Jeremy Roenick .10 .25
236 Joel Otto .01 .05
237 Steve Yzerman .40 1.00
238 Petr Klima .01 .05
239 Jari Kurri .07 .20
240 Mark Messier .07 .20
241 Bill Ranford .02 .10
242 Grant Fuhr .07 .20
243 Brent Severyn .01 .05
244 Ron Francis .02 .10
245 Ray Ferraro .01 .05
246 Martin Straka .01 .05
247 Gerald Diduck .01 .05
248 Dimitri Khristich .01 .05
249 Wade Flaherty RC .02 .10
250 Pat LaFontaine .07 .20
251 Darren Turcotte .01 .05
252 John Vanbiesbrouck .02 .10
253 Brian Bellows .01 .05
254 Dave Gagner .01 .05
255 Larry Murphy .02 .10
256 Steve Thomas .02 .10
257 Robert Svehla RC .01 .05
258 Deron Quint .01 .05
259 Kjell Samuelsson .01 .05
260 Scott Mellanby .01 .05
261 Dan Quinn .01 .05
262 Tom Barrasso .02 .10
263 Zarley Zalapski .01 .05
264 Rick Tocchet .02 .10
265 Paul Coffey .07 .20
266 Joe Sakic .15 .40
267 Aki-Petteri Berg RC .02 .10
268 Jeff Brown .01 .05
269 Wendel Clark .02 .10
270 Vincent Damphousse .01 .05
271 Dale Hawerchuk .07 .20
272 Rhett Warrener RC .01 .05
273 Kevin Hatcher .01 .05
274 Calle Johansson .01 .05
275 Scott Stevens .02 .10
276 Geoff Courtnall .01 .05
277 Kirk McLean .02 .10
278 Steve Heinze .01 .05
279 Sylvain Lefebvre .01 .05
280 Joe Murphy .01 .05
281 Mike Keane .01 .05
282 Kevin Stevens .01 .05
283 Miroslav Satan RC .25 .60
284 Stephane Fiset .02 .10
285 Jeff O'Neill .01 .05
286 Denny Lambert .01 .05
287 Marcus Ragnarsson RC .02 .10
288 Adam Deadmarsh .01 .05
289 Eric Weinrich .01 .05
290 Eric Desjardins .02 .10
291 Tim Cheveldae .02 .10
292 Glenn Healy .02 .10
293 Byron Dafoe .02 .10
294 Tom Fitzgerald .01 .05
295 Adam Graves .01 .05
296 Arturs Irbe UER .02 .10
front reads "Aturs"
297 Shaun Van Allen .01 .05
298 Kelly Buchberger .01 .05
299 Bob Probert .02 .10
300 Pavel Bure .07 .20
301 Chad Kilger RC .01 .05
302 Dominik Hasek .15 .40
303 Bobby Holik .01 .05
304 Petr Nedved .02 .10
305 Owen Nolan .02 .10
306 Saku Koivu .07 .20
307 Rob Blake .02 .10
308 Chris Pronger .07 .20
309 Kyle McLaren RC .01 .05
310 Peter Bondra .02 .10
311 Nelson Emerson .01 .05
312 Bryan McCabe .01 .05
313 Darcy Wakaluk .02 .10
314 Shane Doan RC .20 .50
315 Felix Potvin .07 .20
316 Jim Dowd .01 .05
317 Roman Oksiuta .01 .05
318 Geoff Sanderson .01 .05
319 Radek Dvorak RC .15 .40
320 Paul Ysebaert .01 .05
321 Shawn McEachern .01 .05
322 Vyacheslav Kozlov .02 .10
323 Marty McInnis .01 .05
324 Ted Donato .01 .05
325 Martin Brodeur .20 .50
326 Patrick Poulin .01 .05
327 Eric Lindros .07 .20
328 Dallas Drake .01 .05
329 Sean Hill .01 .05
330 Michal Pivonka .01 .05
331 Alexei Zhamnov .02 .10
332 Cory Stillman .01 .05
333 Sergei Zubov .01 .05
334 Tommy Soderstrom .02 .10
335 Patrik Carnback .01 .05
336 Joe Dziedzic .01 .05
337 Steve Duchesne .01 .05
338 Marty Murray .01 .05
339 Todd Bertuzzi RC .50 1.25
340 Jason Arnott .01 .05
341 Niklas Sundstrom .02 .10
342 Alexandre Daigle .01 .05
343 Jocelyn Thibault .07 .20
344 Mikhail Shtalenkov .01 .05
345 Chris Osgood .02 .10
346 Brendan Witt .01 .05
347 Ian Laperriere .01 .05
348 Zigmund Palffy .02 .10
349 Brian Savage .01 .05
350 Mike Peca .02 .10
351 Vitali Yachmenev .01 .05
352 Luc Robitaille .02 .10
353 Mikael Renberg .02 .10
354 Ed Jovanovski .07 .20
355 Jason Doig .01 .05
356 Todd Harvey .02 .10
357 Viktor Kozlov .02 .10
358 Valeri Bure .01 .05
359 Peter Forsberg .20 .50
360 Jeff Friesen .01 .05
361 Andrei Nikolishin .01 .05
362 Brian Rolston .01 .05
363 Jamie Storr .02 .10
364 Chris Therien .01 .05
365 Oleg Tverdovsky .01 .05
366 David Oliver .01 .05
367 Alexander Selivanov .01 .05
368 Alex Stojanov .01 .05
369 Daniel Alfredsson RC .25 .60
370 Brendan Shanahan .07 .20
371 Yuri Khmylev .01 .05
372 Brett Hull .10 .25
373 Sergei Fedorov MM .07 .20
374 Jaromir Jagr MM .07 .20
375 Wayne Gretzky MM .40 1.00
376 Alexander Mogilny MM .02 .10
377 Patrick Roy MM .30 .75
378 Ed Belfour MM .07 .20
379 Luc Robitaille MM .02 .10
380 Peter Forsberg MM .07 .20
381 Adam Oates MM .02 .10
382 Theo Fleury MM .01 .05
383 Jim Carey MM .01 .05
384 Checklist 221-304 .01 .05
385 Checklist 305-385 .01 .05

1995-96 Topps OPC Inserts

The 1995-96 OPC Insert set is a parallel to the 1995-96 Topps set. The set is identical save for the silver foil OPC logo in place of the gold foil Topps. The cards were inserted one per second series Canadian foil pack; cards from both series were included in this manner and were not available in separate packs as in the past. Several of the cards on the D printing sheet were short printed according to Topps Canada.
*STARS: 6X TO 15X BASIC CARDS
*ROOKIES: 2.5X TO 6X BASIC CARDS
*SP's: 10X TO 25X

1995-96 Topps Canadian Gold

These ten cards featured some of the top players to don their whites in Canadian rinks; they were randomly inserted at a rate of 1:36 series 1 Canadian retail packs. These packs, unlike the American ones, contained just five cards each.
COMPLETE SET (10) 30.00 60.00
1CG Patrick Roy 12.50 30.00
2CG Alexei Yashin 2.00 5.00
3CG Jason Arnott 2.00 5.00
4CG Trevor Kidd 2.00 5.00
5CG Pavel Bure 2.50 6.00
6CG Theo Fleury 2.00 5.00
7CG Pierre Turgeon 2.00 5.00
8CG Felix Potvin 2.50 6.00
9CG Teemu Selanne 2.50 6.00
10CG Mats Sundin 2.50 6.00

1995-96 Topps Canadian World Juniors

The cards in this set, featuring the member of the World Champion Canadian junior team, could be found randomly inserted at a rate of 1:18 series one Canadian Topps packs.
COMPLETE SET (22) 10.00 20.00
1CJ Wade Redden .60 1.50
2CJ Jamie Storr .40 1.00
3CJ Larry Courville .40 1.00
4CJ Jason Allison .60 1.50
5CJ Alexandre Daigle .40 1.00
6CJ Marty Murray .40 1.00
7CJ Bryan McCabe .60 1.50
8CJ Ryan Smyth .75 2.00
9CJ Lee Sorochan .40 1.00
10CJ Todd Harvey .40 1.00
11CJ Nolan Baumgartner .40 1.00
12CJ Denis Pederson .40 1.00
13CJ Shean Donovan .40 1.00
14CJ Jason Botterill .40 1.00
15CJ Jeff Friesen .40 1.00
16CJ Darcy Tucker .60 1.50
17CJ Chad Allan .40 1.00
18CJ Dan Cloutier .60 1.50
19CJ Eric Daze .40 1.00
20CJ Jeff O'Neill .40 1.00
21CJ Jamie Rivers .40 1.00
22CJ Ed Jovanovski .60 1.50

1995-96 Topps Hidden Gems

The cards in this chase set focus on star players who were mined in the sixth round or later of the NHL entry draft. The cards were randomly inserted in series 1 packs at a rate of 1:24.
COMPLETE SET (15) 8.00 20.00
1HG Theo Fleury .75 2.00
2HG Luc Robitaille .75 2.00
3HG Doug Gilmour .75 2.00
4HG Dominik Hasek 2.00 5.00

5HG Pavel Bure 1.25 3.00
6HG Peter Bondra .75 2.00
7HG Steve Larmer .40 1.00
8HG David Oliver .40 1.00
9HG Gary Suter .40 1.00
10HG Brett Hull 1.25 3.00
11HG Kevin Stevens .40 1.00
12HG Ron Hextall .75 2.00
13HG Kirk McLean .40 1.00
14HG Andy Moog .75 2.00
15HG Rick Tocchet .40 1.00

1995-96 Topps Home Grown Canada

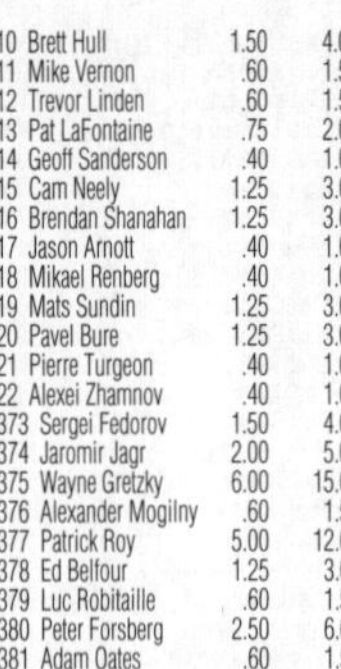

These cards, randomly inserted in Canadian series two retail packs only (HGC1-HGC15) at a rate of 1:36 and randomly inserted in Canadian series 2 hobby packs only (HGC16-HGC30) at a rate of 1:36, feature players born in the Great White North. The hobby-only cards are somewhat harder to find, as Topps announced that an indeterminate number of the 1-15 cards were inserted in their place, resulting in fewer of the 16-30 cards being released.

COMPLETE SET (30) 40.00 80.00
HGC1 Patrick Roy 6.00 15.00
HGC2 Wendel Clark .60 1.50
HGC3 Pierre Turgeon .60 1.50
HGC4 Doug Gilmour .60 1.50
HGC5 Theo Fleury .30 .75
HGC6 Eric Lindros 1.25 3.00
HGC7 Paul Kariya 1.25 3.00
HGC8 Bill Ranford .60 1.50
HGC9 Ray Bourque 2.00 5.00
HGC10 Brendan Shanahan 1.25 3.00
HGC11 Paul Coffey 1.25 3.00
HGC12 Trevor Linden .60 1.50
HGC13 Trevor Kidd .60 1.50
HGC14 Alexandre Daigle .30 .75
HGC15 Chris Pronger 1.25 3.00
HGC16 Steve Yzerman 6.00 15.00
HGC17 Todd Harvey .60 1.50
HGC18 Felix Potvin 1.25 3.00
HGC19 Luc Robitaille .60 1.50
HGC20 Wayne Gretzky 8.00 20.00
HGC21 Keith Primeau .30 .75
HGC22 Al MacInnis .60 1.50
HGC23 Cam Neely 1.25 3.00
HGC24 Ed Belfour 1.25 3.00
HGC25 Joe Juneau .30 .75
HGC26 Adam Graves .30 .75
HGC27 Mark Recchi .60 1.50
HGC28 Stephane Richer .60 1.50
HGC29 Mark Messier 1.25 3.00
HGC30 Mario Lemieux 6.00 15.00

1995-96 Topps Home Grown USA

This 10-card set features some of the top US-born players in the NHL. The cards were randomly inserted at a rate of 1:36 series two US packs.

COMPLETE SET (10) 10.00 20.00
HGA1 Brian Leetch .60 1.50
HGA2 Jeremy Roenick 1.50 4.00
HGA3 Mike Modano 2.00 5.00
HGA4 Pat LaFontaine 1.25 3.00
HGA5 Keith Tkachuk 1.25 3.00
HGA6 Chris Chelios 1.25 3.00
HGA7 Darren Turcotte .30 .75
HGA8 John Vanbiesbrouck .60 1.50
HGA9 John LeClair 1.25 3.00
HGA10 Mike Richter 1.25 3.00

1995-96 Topps Marquee Men Power Boosters

This 33-card set is a parallel to the Marquee Men cards found in the base Topps issue, with numbering on the back matching those cards as well. Cards 1-22 were randomly inserted in series 1 packs at a rate of 1:36; cards 373-383 used the same odds in series 2 packs. Because there were more cards distributed throughout the series 1 production run (22 to 11) the series one cards are somewhat more difficult to acquire. These cards can be differentiated from the base issues by the use of much thicker 28-point card stock and the prismatic foil front.

COMPLETE SET (33) 30.00 80.00
1 Eric Lindros 1.25 3.00
2 Dominik Hasek 2.50 6.00
3 Jeremy Roenick 1.50 4.00
4 Paul Coffey .75 2.00
5 Mark Messier 1.25 3.00
6 Peter Bondra .60 1.50
7 Paul Kariya 1.25 3.00
8 Chris Chelios 1.25 3.00
9 Martin Brodeur 3.00 8.00
10 Brett Hull 1.50 4.00
11 Mike Vernon .60 1.50
12 Trevor Linden .60 1.50
13 Pat LaFontaine .75 2.00
14 Geoff Sanderson .40 1.00
15 Cam Neely 1.25 3.00
16 Brendan Shanahan 1.25 3.00
17 Jason Arnott .40 1.00
18 Mikael Renberg .40 1.00
19 Mats Sundin 1.25 3.00
20 Pavel Bure 1.25 3.00
21 Pierre Turgeon .40 1.00
22 Alexei Zhamnov .40 1.00
373 Sergei Fedorov 1.50 4.00
374 Jaromir Jagr 2.00 5.00
375 Wayne Gretzky 6.00 15.00
376 Alexander Mogilny .60 1.50
377 Patrick Roy 5.00 12.00
378 Ed Belfour 1.25 3.00
379 Luc Robitaille .60 1.50
380 Peter Forsberg 2.50 6.00
381 Adam Oates .60 1.50
382 Theo Fleury .40 1.00
383 Jim Carey .40 1.00

1995-96 Topps Mystery Finest

These unique chase cards featured three top positional stars on the back and an opaque protective foil covering on the front. When removed, it would reveal a full frontal shot of one of the three players on the back, hence the mystery. The cards, which utilized the Finest technology, were randomly inserted 1:36 series 2 packs. A parallel refractor version of the set also existed. These cards were much more difficult to pull, coming out of 1:216 packs. Multipliers for these cards are included in the headers below.

COMPLETE SET (22) 50.00 100.00
*REFRACTORS: 1.5X TO 4X BASIC INSERTS
M1 Wayne Gretzky 10.00 25.00
M2 Mario Lemieux 8.00 20.00
M3 Mark Messier 1.50 4.00
M4 Eric Lindros 1.50 4.00
M5 Sergei Fedorov 2.50 6.00
M6 Joe Sakic 3.00 8.00
M7 Brett Hull 2.00 5.00
M8 Jaromir Jagr 2.50 6.00
M9 Teemu Selanne 1.50 4.00
M10 Brendan Shanahan 1.50 4.00
M11 Cam Neely 1.50 4.00
M12 Mikael Renberg .75 2.00
M13 Paul Kariya 1.50 4.00
M14 Keith Tkachuk 1.50 4.00
M15 Pavel Bure 1.50 4.00
M16 Brian Leetch .75 2.00
M17 Scott Stevens .75 2.00
M18 Chris Chelios 1.50 4.00
M19 Dominik Hasek 3.00 8.00
M20 Patrick Roy 8.00 20.00
M21 Martin Brodeur 4.00 10.00
M22 Felix Potvin 1.50 4.00

1995-96 Topps New To The Game

This 22-card set featured some of the top players just beginning to make their marks in the NHL. The cards were inserted one per US series 1 retail packs.

COMPLETE SET (22) 4.00 8.00
1NG Jim Carey .20 .50
2NG Sergei Brylin .10 .25
3NG Todd Marchant .10 .25
4NG Oleg Tverdovsky .10 .25
5NG Paul Kariya .40 1.00
6NG Adam Deadmarsh .10 .25
7NG Mike Kennedy .10 .25
8NG Roman Oksiuta .10 .25
9NG Kenny Jonsson .10 .25
10NG Peter Forsberg 1.00 2.50
11NG Alexander Selivanov .10 .25
12NG Chris Therien .10 .25
13NG Brian Rolston .10 .25
14NG David Oliver .10 .25
15NG Blaine Lacher .20 .50
16NG Sergei Krivokrasov .10 .25
17NG Todd Harvey .20 .50
18NG Jeff Friesen .10 .25
19NG Mariusz Czerkawski .10 .25
20NG Ian Laperriere .10 .25
21NG Brian Savage .10 .25
22NG Andrei Nikolishin .10 .25

1995-96 Topps Power Lines

These ten three player-cards feature the top lines of the 1994-95 NHL season. The cards were randomly inserted in 1:12 series 1 packs.

COMPLETE SET (10) 4.00 8.00

1PL Eric Lindros .20 .50
John LeClair
Mikael Renberg
2PL Keith Tkachuk .20 .50
Teemu Selanne
Alexei Zhamnov
3PL Adam Graves .20 .50
Mark Messier
Pat Verbeek
4PL Pat Poulin .20 .50
Jeremy Roenick
Tony Amonte
5PL Kevin Stevens .75 2.00
Jaromir Jagr
Ron Francis
6PL Jason Dawe .20 .50
Pat Lafontaine
Alexander Mogilny
7PL Adam Oates .20 .50
Cam Neely
Mariusz Czerkawski
8PL Slava Kozlov 1.00 2.50
Sergei Fedorov
Doug Brown
9PL Vin Damphousse .20 .50
Pierre Turgeon
Mark Recchi
10PL Mike Peluso .20 .50
Bobby Holik
Randy McKay

1995-96 Topps Profiles

Mark Messier knows a bit about hockey, as he demonstrates here with his choices of and commentary on some of the game's finest. The cards were inserted in both series 1 (1-10) and series 2 (11-20) packs at a rate of 1:12.

COMPLETE SET (20) 12.00 30.00
PF1 Wayne Gretzky 4.00 10.00
PF2 Brian Leetch .30 .75
PF3 Patrick Roy 2.50 6.00
PF4 Jaromir Jagr 1.00 2.50
PF5 Sergei Fedorov 1.00 2.50
PF6 Martin Brodeur 1.50 4.00
PF7 Eric Lindros .60 1.50
PF8 Jeremy Roenick .75 2.00
PF9 John Vanbiesbrouck .30 .75
PF10 Cam Neely .60 1.50
PF11 Pavel Bure .60 1.50
PF12 Paul Coffey .60 1.50
PF13 Scott Stevens .30 .75
PF14 Dominik Hasek 1.25 3.00
PF15 Mario Lemieux 2.50 6.00
PF16 Ed Belfour .60 1.50
PF17 Doug Gilmour .30 .75
PF18 Teemu Selanne .60 1.50
PF19 Brett Hull .75 2.00
PF20 Joe Sakic 1.25 3.00

1995-96 Topps Rink Leaders

Topps selected players who are top guys both on the ice and in the dressing room for this ten-card tribute. The cards were randomly inserted in series 1 hobby packs at a rate of 1:36.

COMPLETE SET (10) 30.00 60.00
1RL Mark Messier 2.00 5.00
2RL Mario Lemieux 10.00 25.00
3RL Ray Bourque 3.00 8.00
4RL Brett Hull 2.50 6.00
5RL Pat LaFontaine 2.00 5.00
6RL Scott Stevens 1.00 2.50
7RL Keith Tkachuk 2.00 5.00
8RL Doug Gilmour 1.00 2.50
9RL Chris Chelios 2.00 5.00
10RL Wayne Gretzky 12.50 30.00

1995-96 Topps Young Stars

Topps honors fifteen of the brightest young stars in the game with this set which utilizes the Power Matrix printing technology. The cards were randomly inserted at 1:24 series 2 packs.

COMPLETE SET (15) 12.00 25.00
YS1 Paul Kariya 1.00 2.50

YS2 Martin Brodeur 2.50 6.00
YS3 Mikael Renberg .50 1.25
YS4 Peter Forsberg 2.50 6.00
YS5 Alexei Yashin UER .25 .60
front reads "Alexi"
YS6 Jeff Friesen .25 .60
YS7 Oleg Tverdovsky .25 .60
YS8 Jim Carey .50 1.25
YS9 Alexei Kovalev .25 .60
YS10 Jason Arnott .25 .60
YS11 Teemu Selanne 1.00 2.50
YS12 Chris Osgood .50 1.25
YS13 Roman Hamrlik .50 1.25
YS14 Scott Niedermayer .25 .60
YS15 Jaromir Jagr 1.50 4.00

1998-99 Topps

The 1998-99 Topps set was issued in one series totaling 242 cards. The 11-card packs retail for $1.29 each. The fronts featured color action photos and the backs carried player information and statistics.

COMPLETE SET (242) 12.50 25.00
1 Peter Forsberg .30 .75
2 Petr Sykora .02 .10
3 Byron Dafoe .08 .25
4 Ron Francis .08 .25
5 Alexei Yashin .02 .10
6 Dave Ellett .02 .10
7 Jamie Langenbrunner .02 .10
8 Doug Weight .08 .25
9 Jason Woolley .02 .10
10 Paul Coffey .10 .30
11 Uwe Krupp .02 .10
12 Tomas Sandstrom .02 .10
13 Scott Mellanby .02 .10
14 Vladimir Tsyplakov .02 .10
15 Martin Rucinsky .02 .10
16 Mikael Renberg .08 .25
17 Marco Sturm .02 .10
18 Eric Lindros .10 .30
19 Sean Burke .02 .10
20 Martin Brodeur .30 .75
21 Boyd Devereaux .02 .10
22 Kelly Buchberger .02 .10
23 Scott Stevens .08 .25
24 Jamie Storr .08 .25
25 Anders Eriksson .02 .10
26 Gary Suter .02 .10
27 Theo Fleury .02 .10
28 Steve Leach .02 .10
29 Felix Potvin .10 .30
30 Brett Hull .15 .40
31 Mike Grier .02 .10
32 Cale Hulse .02 .10
33 Larry Murphy .08 .25
34 Rick Tocchet .08 .25
35 Eric Desjardins .08 .25
36 Igor Kravchuk .02 .10
37 Rob Niedermayer .02 .10
38 Bryan Smolinski .02 .10
39 Valeri Kamensky .02 .10
40 Ryan Smyth .08 .25
41 Bruce Driver .02 .10
42 Mike Johnson .02 .10
43 Rob Zamuner .02 .10
44 Steve Duchesne .02 .10
45 Martin Straka .02 .10
46 Bill Houlder .02 .10
47 Craig Conroy .02 .10
48 Guy Hebert .08 .25
49 Colin Forbes .02 .10
50 Mike Modano .20 .50
51 Jamie Pushor .02 .10
52 Jarome Iginla .15 .40
53 Paul Kariya .10 .30
54 Mattias Ohlund .08 .25
55 Sergei Berezin .08 .25
56 Peter Zezel .02 .10
57 Teppo Numminen .02 .10
58 Dale Hunter .02 .10
59 Sandy Moger .02 .10
60 John LeClair .10 .30
61 Wade Redden .02 .10
62 Patrik Elias .08 .25
63 Rob Blake .08 .25
64 Todd Marchant .02 .10
65 Claude Lemieux .02 .10
66 Trevor Kidd .08 .25
67 Sergei Fedorov .20 .50
68 Joe Sakic .25 .60
69 Derek Morris .02 .10
70 Alexei Morozov .02 .10
71 Mats Sundin .10 .30
72 Daymond Langkow .08 .25
73 Kevin Hatcher .02 .10
74 Damian Rhodes .08 .25
75 Brian Leetch .10 .30
76 Saku Koivu .10 .30
77 Rick Tabaracci .02 .10
78 Bernie Nicholls .02 .10
79 Alyn McCauley .02 .10
80 Patrice Brisebois .02 .10
81 Bret Hedican .02 .10
82 Sandy McCarthy .02 .10
83 Viktor Kozlov .02 .10
84 Derek King .02 .10
85 Alexander Selivanov .02 .10
86 Mike Vernon .08 .25
87 Jeff Beukeboom .02 .10
88 Tommy Salo .08 .25
89 Adam Graves .02 .10
90 Randy McKay .02 .10
91 Rich Pilon .02 .10
92 Richard Zednik .02 .10
93 Jeff Hackett .08 .25
94 Michael Peca .02 .10
95 Brent Gilchrist .02 .10
96 Stu Grimson .02 .10
97 Bob Probert .02 .10
98 Stu Barnes .02 .10
99 Ruslan Salei .02 .10
100 Al MacInnis .08 .25
101 Ken Daneyko .02 .10
102 Paul Ranheim .02 .10
103 Marty McInnis .02 .10
104 Marian Hossa .10 .30
105 Darren McCarty .02 .10
106 Guy Carbonneau .02 .10
107 Dallas Drake .02 .10
108 Sergei Samsonov .08 .25
109 Teemu Selanne .10 .30
110 Checklist .02 .10
111 Jaromir Jagr .20 .50
112 Joe Thornton .20 .50
113 Jon Klemm .02 .10
114 Grant Fuhr .08 .25
115 Nikolai Khabibulin .08 .25
116 Rod Brind'Amour .08 .25
117 Trevor Linden .08 .25
118 Vincent Damphousse .02 .10
119 Dino Ciccarelli .08 .25
120 Pat Verbeek .02 .10
121 Sandis Ozolinsh .02 .10
122 Garth Snow .08 .25
123 Ed Belfour .10 .30
124 Keith Primeau .02 .10
125 Jason Allison .02 .10
126 Peter Bondra .08 .25
127 Ulf Samuelsson .02 .10
128 Jeff Friesen .02 .10
129 Jason Bonsignore .02 .10
130 Daniel Alfredsson .08 .25
131 Bobby Holik .02 .10
132 Jozef Stumpel .02 .10
133 Brian Bellows .02 .10
134 Chris Osgood .08 .25
135 Alexei Zhamnov .02 .10
136 Mattias Norstrom .02 .10
137 Drake Berehowsky .02 .10
138 Mark Messier .10 .30
139 Geoff Courtnall .02 .10
140 Marc Bureau .02 .10
141 Don Sweeney .02 .10
142 Wendel Clark .08 .25
143 Scott Niedermayer .02 .10
144 Chris Therien .02 .10
145 Kirk Muller .02 .10
146 Wayne Primeau .02 .10
147 Tony Granato .02 .10
148 Derian Hatcher .02 .10
149 Daniel Briere .02 .10
150 Fredrik Olausson .02 .10
151 Joe Juneau .08 .25
152 Michal Grosek .02 .10
153 Janne Laukkanen .02 .10
154 Keith Tkachuk .10 .30
155 Marty McSorley .02 .10
156 Owen Nolan .08 .25
157 Mark Tinordi .02 .10
158 Steve Washburn .02 .10
159 Luke Richardson .02 .10
160 Kris King .02 .10
161 Joe Nieuwendyk .08 .25
162 Travis Green .02 .10
163 Dominik Hasek .25 .60
164 Dimitri Khristich .02 .10
165 Dave Manson .02 .10
166 Chris Chelios .10 .30
167 Claude LaPointe .02 .10
168 Kris Draper .02 .10
169 Brad Isbister .02 .10
170 Patrick Marleau .02 .10
171 Jeremy Roenick .15 .40
172 Darren Langdon .02 .10
173 Kevin Dineen .02 .10
174 Luc Robitaille .08 .25
175 Steve Yzerman .60 1.50
176 Sergei Zubov .02 .10
177 Ed Jovanovski .02 .10
178 Sami Kapanen .02 .10
179 Adam Oates .08 .25
180 Pavel Bure .10 .30
181 Chris Pronger .08 .25
182 Pat Falloon .02 .10
183 Darcy Tucker .02 .10
184 Zigmund Palffy .08 .25
185 Curtis Brown .02 .10
186 Curtis Joseph .10 .30
187 Valeri Zelepukin .02 .10
188 Russ Courtnall .02 .10
189 Adam Foote .02 .10
190 Patrick Roy .60 1.50
191 Cory Stillman .02 .10
192 Alexei Zhitnik .02 .10
193 Olaf Kolzig .08 .25
194 Mark Fitzpatrick .02 .10
195 Eric Daze .08 .25
196 Zarley Zalapski .02 .10
197 Niklas Sundstrom .02 .10
198 Bryan Berard .08 .25
199 Jason Arnott .02 .10
200 Mike Richter .10 .30
201 Ken Baumgartner .02 .10
202 Jason Dawe .02 .10
203 Nicklas Lidstrom .10 .30
204 Tony Amonte .08 .25
205 Kjell Samuelsson .02 .10
206 Ray Bourque .20 .50
207 Alexander Mogilny .08 .25
208 Pierre Turgeon .08 .25
209 Tom Barrasso .08 .25
210 Richard Matvichuk .02 .10
211 Sergei Krivokrasov .02 .10
212 Ted Drury .02 .10
213 Matthew Barnaby .02 .10
214 Denis Pederson .02 .10
215 John Vanbiesbrouck .08 .25
216 Brendan Shanahan .10 .30
217 Jocelyn Thibault .08 .25
218 Nelson Emerson .02 .10
219 Wayne Gretzky .75 2.00
220 Checklist .02 .10
221 Ramzi Abid RC .30 .75
222 Mark Bell RC .30 .75
223 Michael Henrich RC .30 .75
224 Vincent Lecavalier .40 1.00
225 Rico Fata .02 .10
226 Bryan Allen .02 .10
227 Daniel Tkaczuk .08 .25
228 Brad Stuart RC .30 .75
229 Derrick Walser RC .08 .25
230 Jonathan Cheechoo RC 3.00 8.00
231 Sergei Varlamov .02 .10
232 Scott Gomez RC 2.00 5.00
233 Jeff Heerema RC .30 .75
234 David Legwand .25 .60
235 Manny Malhotra .02 .10
236 Michael Rupp RC .30 .75
237 Alex Tanguay .30 .75
238 Mathieu Biron RC .02 .10
239 Bujar Amidovski RC .02 .10
240 Brian Finley RC .30 .75
241 Philippe Sauve RC .75 2.00
242 Jiri Fischer RC .30 .75

1998-99 Topps O-Pee-Chee

This 242-card parallel set, offered only in Canadian hobby packs, offers the same players as the Topps base set, but was emblazoned with the O-Pee-Chee foil stamp logo.

*STARS: 5X TO 12X BASIC CARD
*ROOKIES: 1.5X TO 4X BASIC CARD

1998-99 Topps Autographs

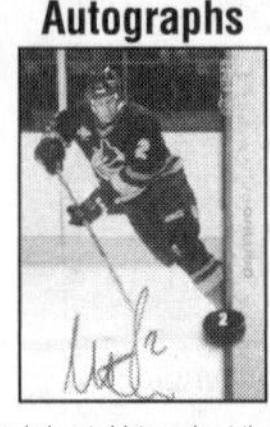

Randomly inserted into packs at the rate of 1:209, this nine-card set features autographed color action player photos with player information on the backs.

A1 Jason Allison 4.00 10.00
A2 Sergei Samsonov 6.00 15.00
A3 John LeClair 8.00 20.00
A4 Mattias Ohlund 4.00 10.00
A5 Jaromir Jagr 20.00 50.00
A6 Keith Tkachuk 6.00 15.00
A7 Patrik Elias 4.00 10.00
A8 Dominik Hasek 25.00 60.00
A9 Brian Leetch 8.00 20.00

1998-99 Topps Blast From The Past

Randomly inserted in packs at a rate of 1:23, this 10-card insert set features early reprint cards of true heroes of the game including Gordie Howe, Phil Esposito and Stan Mikita. These cards resemble the originals in every way except a small note on the back that states "Reprint X of 10".

COMPLETE SET (10) 25.00 50.00
1 Wayne Gretzky 5.00 12.00
2 Mark Messier 2.00 5.00
3 Ray Bourque 3.00 8.00
4 Patrick Roy 4.00 10.00
5 Grant Fuhr 2.00 5.00
6 Brett Hull 2.00 5.00
7 Gordie Howe 5.00 12.00
8 Stan Mikita 2.50 6.00
9 Bobby Hull 3.00 8.00
10 Phil Esposito 2.50 6.00

1998-99 Topps Blast From The Past Autographs

Randomly inserted into packs at the rate of 1:1,878, this 4-card set mirrored the basic inserts but included autographs of the retired players. The Mikita card had insertion odds of 1:3,756.

7 Gordie Howe 60.00 150.00
8 Stan Mikita 30.00 80.00
9 Bobby Hull 40.00 100.00
10 Phil Esposito 30.00 80.00

1998-99 Topps Board Members

Randomly inserted in packs at a rate of 1:36, this 15-card insert features color action photography of superstar defensemen on vibrant foilboard.

COMPLETE SET (15) 15.00 40.00
B1 Chris Pronger 1.25 3.00

B2 Chris Chelios 2.50 6.0
B3 Brian Leetch 2.50 6.0
B4 Ray Bourque 4.00 10.0
B5 Mattias Ohlund .75 2.0
B6 Nicklas Lidstrom 2.50 6.0
B7 Sergei Zubov .75 2.0
B8 Scott Niedermayer .75 2.0
B9 Larry Murphy .75 2.0
B10 Sandis Ozolinsh .75 2.0
B11 Rob Blake 1.25 3.0
B12 Scott Stevens .75 2.0
B13 Derian Hatcher .75 2.0
B14 Kevin Hatcher .75 2.0
B15 Wade Redden .75 2.0

1998-99 Topps Ice Age 2000

Randomly inserted in packs at a rate of 1:
this 15-card insert was printed with d
matrix technology.

COMPLETE SET (15) 8.00 15.0
I1 Paul Kariya .60 1.5
I2 Marco Sturm .20 .5
I3 Jarome Iginla .75 2.0
I4 Denis Pederson .20 .5
I5 Wade Redden .20 .5
I6 Jason Allison .20 .5
I7 Chris Pronger .50 1.2
I8 Peter Forsberg 1.50 4.0
I9 Saku Koivu .60 1.5
I10 Eric Lindros .60 1.5
I11 Sergei Samsonov .50 1.2
I12 Mattias Ohlund .50 1.2
I13 Joe Thornton 1.00 2.5
I14 Mike Johnson .20 .5
I15 Nikolai Khabibulin .50 1.2

1998-99 Topps Loca Legends

Randomly inserted in packs at a rate of 1:
this worldly 15-card insert honors playe
on foilboard cards that actually depict t
player's country of origin.

COMPLETE SET (15) 30.00 60.0
L1 Peter Forsberg 2.50 6.0
L2 Mats Sundin 1.00 2.5
L3 Zigmund Palffy .75 2.0
L4 Jaromir Jagr 1.50 4.0
L5 Dominik Hasek 2.00 5.0
L6 Martin Brodeur 2.50 6.0
L7 Wayne Gretzky 6.00 15.0
L8 Patrick Roy 5.00 12.0
L9 Eric Lindros 1.00 2.5
L10 Joe Sakic 2.00 5.0
L11 Mark Messier 1.00 2.5
L12 Mike Modano 1.50 4.0
L13 Sergei Fedorov 1.50 4.0
L14 Pavel Bure 1.00 2.5
L15 Teemu Selanne 1.00 2.5

1998-99 Topps Mystery Finest Bronze

Sequentially numbered and arranged jersey (home, away and All-Star), this 2 card insert honors the 20 best players in NHL today. The set was also grouped a randomly inserted in Bronze 1:36; Silv 1:72; and Gold 1:108 variations. Refrac parallels for each color were also crea and inserted at the following rates: bronze 1:108, silver at 1:216, and gold at 1:324.

COMPLETE SET (20) 40.00 80.0
*REFRACTORS: .75X TO 2X BASIC INSER
*SILVERS: .75X TO 1.5X BASIC INSERTS
*SILVER REF.: 1.25X TO 3X BASIC INSER

*GOLDS: 1X TO 2X BASIC INSERTS
*GOLD.REF.: 4X TO 10X BASIC INSERTS
M1 Teemu Selanne 1.50 4.00
M2 Olaf Kolzig 1.25 3.00
M3 Pavel Bure 1.50 4.00
M4 Wayne Gretzky 10.00 25.00
M5 Mike Modano 2.50 6.00
M6 Jaromir Jagr 2.50 6.00
M7 Dominik Hasek 3.00 8.00
M8 Peter Forsberg 4.00 10.00
M9 Eric Lindros 1.50 4.00
M10 John LeClair 1.50 4.00
M11 Zigmund Palffy 1.25 3.00
M12 Martin Brodeur 4.00 10.00
M13 Keith Tkachuk 1.50 4.00
M14 Peter Bondra 1.25 3.00
M15 Nicklas Lidstrom 1.50 4.00
M16 Patrick Roy 8.00 20.00
M17 Chris Chelios 1.25 3.00
M18 Saku Koivu 1.50 4.00
M19 Mark Messier 1.50 4.00
M20 Joe Sakic 3.00 8.00

1998-99 Topps Season's Best

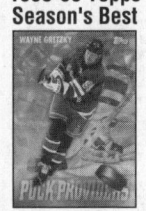

Randomly inserted in packs at a rate of 1:8, this 30-card insert features color action photography in five distinct categories: NetMinders salutes the league's top goalies, Sharpshooters features the top scoring leaders, Puck Providers showcases assist leaders, Performers Plus features those that lead ice time by plus/minus ratio, and Ice Hot introduces the powerful rookies.

COMPLETE SET (30) 25.00 50.00
SB1 Dominik Hasek 1.50 4.00
SB2 Martin Brodeur 2.00 5.00
SB3 Ed Belfour .75 2.00
SB4 Curtis Joseph .75 2.00
SB5 Jeff Hackett .60 1.50
SB6 Tom Barrasso .60 1.50
SB7 Mike Johnson .60 1.50
SB8 Sergei Samsonov .60 1.50
SB9 Patrik Elias .60 1.50
SB10 Patrick Marleau .75 2.00
SB11 Mattias Ohlund .60 1.50
SB12 Marco Sturm .60 1.50
SB13 Teemu Selanne .75 2.00
SB14 Peter Bondra .60 1.50
SB15 Pavel Bure 1.00 2.50
SB16 John LeClair 1.00 2.50
SB17 Zigmund Palffy .60 1.50
SB18 Keith Tkachuk .75 2.00
SB19 Jaromir Jagr 1.25 3.00
SB20 Wayne Gretzky 5.00 12.00
SB21 Peter Forsberg 2.00 5.00
SB22 Ron Francis .60 1.50
SB23 Adam Oates .60 1.50
SB24 Jozef Stumpel .60 1.50
SB25 Chris Pronger .60 1.50
SB26 Larry Murphy .60 1.50
SB27 Jason Allison .30 .75
SB28 John LeClair 1.00 2.50
SB29 Randy McKay .30 .75
SB30 Dainius Zubrus .60 1.50

1999-00 Topps Arena Giveaways

These promo cards were issued in various NHL cities as part of a stadium giveaway program that included six cards per team. Manufacturers Topps, Upper Deck, and Pacific were all represented with two cards per team set.

COMPLETE SET 15.00 30.00
ANA-LK Ladislav Kohn
ANA-OT Oleg Tverdovsky
ATL-MJ Matt Johnson .50
ATL-PS Patrik Stefan 1.00
BOS-JG Jonathan Girard
BOS-JT Joe Thornton
BUF-MA Maxim Afinogenov
BUF-MB Martin Biron
CAL-DG Denis Gauthier
CAL-RR Robyn Regehr
CAR-BB Bates Battaglia
CAR-DT David Tanabe
CHI-ED Eric Daze
CHI-JD J-P Dumont
COL-AT Alex Tanguay
COL-MD Marc Denis
DAL-BM Brenden Morrow .80 2.00
DAL-JS Jon Sim
DET-JF Jiri Fischer
DET-MD Mathieu Dandenault
EDM-GL Georges Laraque
EDM-PC Paul Comrie
FLO-IN Ivan Novoseltsev
FLO-OK Oleg Kvasha
LA-FK Frantisek Kaberle .20 .50
LA-JS Jamie Storr .40 1.00
NAS-DL David Legwand
NAS-TV Tomas Vokoun
NJ-PE Patrik Elias
NJ-SG Scott Gomez
NYI-OJ Olli Jokinen
NYI-RL Roberto Luongo
NYR-KJ Kim Johnsson
NYR-MY Mike York
OTT-MF Mike Fisher
OTT-MH Marian Hossa
PHO-RS Radoslav Suchy
PHO-TL Trevor Letowski
PIT-AF Andrew Ference
PIT-JH Jan Hrdina
SJ-BS Brad Stuart
SJ-MS Marco Sturm
STL-JH Jochen Hecht
STL-TN Tyson Nash
TB-PM Paul Mara
TB-VL Vincent Lecavalier
TOR-NA Nikolai Antropov
TOR-TK Tomas Kaberle
VAN-EJ Ed Jovanovski
VAN-SK Steve Kariya
WAS-JH Jeff Halpern
WAS-RZ Richard Zednik

1999-00 Topps/OPC

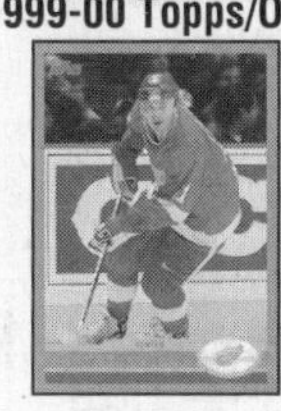

Released as a 286-card set, there are actually a total of 330-cards in this release. Five versions of cards 276-286 were released. The complete set prices below reflect sets with one version of cards 276-286. Base cards feature full color action shots with blue borders and gold foil highlights. The O-Pee-Chee version of this set exactly parallels the base set, but book at a slight premium.

COMPLETE SET (275) 25.00 50.00
COMPLETE SET (330) 60.00 120.00
FIVE VERSIONS OF MM 276-286 EXIST
EACH VERSION SAME VALUE
*OPC: 1X TO 1.5X TOPPS
1 Joe Sakic .25 .60
2 Alexei Yashin .02 .10
3 Paul Kariya .10 .30
4 Keith Tkachuk .10 .30
5 Jaromir Jagr .20 .50
6 Mike Modano .20 .50
7 Eric Lindros .10 .30
8 Zigmund Palffy .08 .25
9 Dominik Hasek .25 .60
10 Pavel Bure .10 .30
11 Ray Bourque .20 .50
12 Peter Forsberg .30 .75
13 Al MacInnis .08 .25
14 Steve Yzerman .60 1.50
15 Mats Sundin .10 .30
16 Patrick Roy .60 1.50
17 Teemu Selanne .10 .30
18 Keith Primeau .02 .10
19 John LeClair .10 .30
20 Martin Brodeur .30 .75
21 Joe Thornton .20 .50
22 Rob Blake .08 .25
23 Ron Francis .08 .25
24 Grant Fuhr .08 .25
25 Nicklas Lidstrom .10 .30
26 Vladimir Orszagh RC .02 .10
27 Glen Wesley .02 .10
28 Adam Deadmarsh .02 .10
29 Zdeno Chara .02 .10
30 Brian Leetch .10 .30
31 Valeri Bure .02 .10
32 Ryan Smyth .02 .10
33 Jean-Sebastien Aubin .08 .25
34 Dave Reid .02 .10
35 Ed Jovanovski .02 .10
36 Anders Eriksson .02 .10
37 Mike Ricci .02 .10
38 Todd Bertuzzi .10 .30
39 Shawn Bates .02 .10
40 Kip Miller .02 .10
41 Jozef Stumpel .08 .25
42 Jeremy Roenick .15 .40
43 Todd Marchant .02 .10
44 Josh Holden .02 .10
45 Rob Niedermayer .02 .10
46 Cory Sarich .02 .10
47 Nikolai Khabibulin .08 .25
48 Marty McInnis .02 .10
49 Marty Reasoner .08 .25
50 Gary Roberts .02 .10
51 Manny Malhotra .08 .25
52 Adam Foote .02 .10
53 Luc Robitaille .08 .25
54 Bryan Marchment .02 .10
55 Mark Janssens .02 .10
56 Steve Heinze .02 .10
57 Cory Stillman .02 .10
58 Guy Hebert .08 .25
59 Mike Richter .10 .30
60 Jamie Langenbrunner .02 .10
61 Wade Redden .02 .10
62 Steve Smith .02 .10
63 Daniil Markov .02 .10
64 Erik Rasmussen .02 .10
65 Glen Murray .02 .10
66 Alexei Kovalev .02 .10
67 Peter Bondra .08 .25
68 Dimitri Khristich .02 .10
69 Sami Kapanen .02 .10
70 Tom Poti .02 .10
71 Trevor Linden .02 .10
72 Tomas Vokoun .08 .25
73 Steve Webb .02 .10
74 Jarome Iginla .15 .40
75 Scott Mellanby .02 .10
76 Mattias Ohlund .02 .10
77 Steve Konowalchuk .02 .10
78 Bryan Berard .08 .25
79 Chris Pronger .08 .25
80 Teppo Numminen .02 .10
81 John MacLean .02 .10
82 Jeff Hackett .08 .25
83 Ray Whitney .02 .10
84 Chris Osgood .08 .25
85 Doug Zmolek .02 .10
86 Curtis Brown .02 .10
87 Reid Simpson .02 .10
88 Milan Hejduk .10 .30
89 Donald Audette .02 .10
90 Saku Koivu .10 .30
91 Martin Straka .02 .10
92 Mark Messier .10 .30
93 Richard Zednik .02 .10
94 Curtis Joseph .10 .30
95 Colin Forbes .02 .10
96 Jeff Friesen .02 .10
97 Eric Brewer .02 .10
98 Darius Kasparaitis .02 .10
99 Marian Hossa .10 .30
100 Petr Sykora .02 .10
101 Vladimir Malakhov .02 .10
102 Jamie Storr .08 .25
103 Doug Gilmour .08 .25
104 Doug Weight .08 .25
105 Derian Hatcher .02 .10
106 Chris Drury .08 .25
107 Arturs Irbe .08 .25
108 Fred Brathwaite .08 .25
109 Jason Allison .02 .10
110 Roman Hamrlik .02 .10
111 Rico Fata .02 .10
112 Janne Niinimaa .02 .10
113 Kenny Jonsson .02 .10
114 Marco Sturm .02 .10
115 Steve Thomas .02 .10
116 Garth Snow .08 .25
117 Rick Tocchet .08 .25
118 Jean-Marc Pelletier .08 .25
119 Bobby Holik .02 .10
120 Sergei Fedorov .20 .50
121 J-P Dumont .08 .25
122 Jason Woolley .02 .10
123 James Patrick .02 .10
124 Blake Sloan .10 .30
125 Marcus Nilsson .02 .10
126 Shayne Corson .02 .10
127 Tom Fitzgerald .02 .10
128 Brian Rolston .02 .10
129 Ron Tugnutt .08 .25
130 Mark Recchi .08 .25
131 Matthew Barnaby .02 .10
132 Olaf Kolzig .08 .25
133 Paul Mara .02 .10
134 Patrick Marleau .10 .30
135 Magnus Arvedson .02 .10
136 Felix Potvin .10 .30
137 Bill Guerin .08 .25
138 Brett Hull .15 .40
139 Vitali Yachmenev .02 .10
140 Ruslan Salei .02 .10
141 Mark Parrish .02 .10
142 Randy Cunneyworth .02 .10
143 Damian Rhodes .08 .25
144 Daniel Briere .02 .10
145 Craig Conroy .02 .10
146 Sergei Gonchar .02 .10
147 Vincent Lecavalier .10 .30
148 Adam Graves .02 .10
149 Doug Bodger .02 .10
150 Jeff O'Neill .02 .10
151 Darby Hendrickson .02 .10
152 Sergei Samsonov .08 .25
153 Ed Belfour .10 .30
154 Robert Svehla .02 .10
155 Cliff Ronning .02 .10
156 Brendan Morrison .08 .25
157 Daniel Alfredsson .08 .25
158 Eric Desjardins .08 .25
159 Mike Vernon .08 .25
160 Vadim Sharifijanov .02 .10
161 Jaroslav Svejkovsky .02 .10
162 Michael Peca .08 .25
163 Shane Willis .02 .10
164 Sandis Ozolinsh .02 .10
165 Mathieu Dandenault .02 .10
166 Martin Rucinsky .02 .10
167 Scott Stevens .02 .10
168 Sami Salo .02 .10
169 Tom Barrasso .08 .25
170 Chris Gratton .02 .10
171 Markus Naslund .10 .30
172 Mike Johnson .02 .10
173 Bob Boughner .02 .10
174 Todd Simpson .02 .10
175 Fredrik Olausson .02 .10
176 Jocelyn Thibault .08 .25
177 Juha Ylonen .02 .10
178 Brad Bombardir .02 .10
179 Jan Hrdina .02 .10
180 Adrian Aucoin .02 .10
181 Mike Eagles .02 .10
182 Petr Nedved .08 .25
183 Rem Murray .02 .10
184 Mikael Renberg .08 .25
185 Mike Eastwood .02 .10
186 Byron Dafoe .08 .25
187 Tony Amonte .08 .25
188 Darren McCarty .02 .10
189 Sergei Krivokrasov .02 .10
190 Dave Lowry .02 .10
191 Michal Handzus .08 .25
192 Tie Domi .08 .25
193 Brian Holzinger .02 .10
194 Jason Arnott .02 .10
195 Jose Theodore .15 .40
196 Brendan Shanahan .10 .30
197 Derek Morris .02 .10
198 Steve Rucchin .02 .10
199 Kevin Hodson .08 .25
200 Oleg Kvasha .02 .10
201 John Vanbiesbrouck .08 .25
202 Adam Oates .08 .25
203 Anson Carter .08 .25
204 Sebastien Bordeleau .02 .10
205 Pavol Demitra .08 .25
206 Owen Nolan .08 .25
207 Pavel Rosa .02 .10
208 Petr Svoboda .02 .10
209 Tomas Kaberle .02 .10
210 Claude Lapointe .02 .10
211 Todd Harvey .02 .10
212 Trent McCleary .02 .10
213 Vyacheslav Kozlov .02 .10
214 Marc Denis .08 .25
215 Joe Nieuwendyk .08 .25
216 Kelly Buchberger .02 .10
217 Tommy Albelin .02 .10
218 Kyle McLaren .02 .10
219 Chris Chelios .10 .30
220 Joel Bouchard .02 .10
221 Mats Lindgren .02 .10
222 Jyrki Lumme .02 .10
223 Pierre Turgeon .08 .25
224 Bill Muckalt .02 .10
225 Antti Aalto .02 .10
226 Jere Lehtinen .08 .25
227 Theo Fleury .02 .10
228 Dmitri Mironov .02 .10
229 Scott Niedermayer .02 .10
230 Sean Burke .08 .25
231 Eric Daze .08 .25
232 Alexei Zhitnik .02 .10
233 Christian Matte .02 .10
234 Patrik Elias .08 .25
235 Alexandre Korolyuk .02 .10
236 Sergei Berezin .02 .10
237 Ray Ferraro .02 .10
238 Rod Brind'Amour .08 .25
239 Darcy Tucker .02 .10
240 Darryl Sydor .02 .10
241 Mike Dunham .08 .25
242 Marc Bergevin .02 .10
243 Ray Sheppard .02 .10
244 Miroslav Satan .08 .25
245 Andreas Dackell .02 .10
246 Mike Grier .02 .10
247 Alexei Zhamnov .02 .10
248 David Legwand .08 .25
249 Daniel Tkaczuk .02 .10
250 Roberto Luongo .15 .40
251 Simon Gagne .10 .30
252 Jamie Lundmark .08 .25
253 Alexandre Giroux RC .02 .10
254 Dusty Jamieson RC .08 .25
255 Jamie Chamberlain RC .08 .25
256 Radim Vrbata RC 2.50 6.00
257 Scott Cameron RC .08 .25
258 Simon Lajeunesse RC .40 1.00
259 Tim Connolly .02 .10
260 Kris Beech .02 .10
261 Brian Finley .08 .25
262 Alex Auld RC .40 1.00
263 Martin Grenier RC .08 .25
264 Sheldon Keefe RC .40 1.00
265 Justin Mapletoft RC .08 .25
266 Edward Hill RC .08 .25
267 Nolan Yonkman RC .15 .40
268 Oleg Saprykin RC .40 1.00
269 Branislav Mezei RC .10 .30
270 Chris Kelly RC .08 .25
271 Pavel Brendl RC 1.50 4.00
272 Brett Lysak RC .10 .30
273 Matt Carkner RC .08 .25
274 Luke Sellars RC .15 .40
275 Brad Ralph RC .08 .25
276A Ray Bourque MM .40 1.00
277A Peter Forsberg MM .60 1.50
278A Joe Nieuwendyk MM .10 .30
279A Dominik Hasek MM .50 1.25
280A Jaromir Jagr MM .40 1.00
281A Paul Kariya MM .10 .30
282A Eric Lindros MM .10 .25
283A Mark Messier MM .10 .30
284A Patrick Roy MM 1.25 3.00
285A Joe Sakic MM .50 1.25
286A Steve Yzerman MM 1.25 3.00

1999-00 Topps/OPC All-Topps

Randomly inserted in Topps and OPC packs at the rate of 1:18, this 15-card set features top players on a card with full color action shots and holographic foil highlights. Card backs carry an "AT" prefix.

COMPLETE SET (15) 20.00 40.00
AT1 Dominik Hasek 1.50 4.00
AT2 Martin Brodeur 2.00 5.00
AT3 Ray Bourque 1.25 3.00
AT4 Al MacInnis .60 1.50
AT5 Nicklas Lidstrom .75 2.00
AT6 Brian Leetch .75 2.00
AT7 John LeClair 1.00 2.50
AT8 Paul Kariya .75 2.00
AT9 Keith Tkachuk .75 2.00
AT10 Eric Lindros 1.25 3.00
AT11 Peter Forsberg 2.00 5.00
AT12 Steve Yzerman 4.00 10.00
AT13 Jaromir Jagr 1.25 3.00
AT14 Teemu Selanne .75 2.00
AT15 Pavel Bure 1.00 2.50

1999-00 Topps/OPC Autographs

Randomly inserted in Topps and OPC packs at the rate of 1:517, this 10-card set features authentic player autographs.

TA1 Joe Sakic 12.50 30.00
TA2 Dominik Hasek 15.00 40.00
TA3 Curtis Joseph 10.00 25.00
TA4 Alexei Yashin 8.00 20.00
TA5 Mats Sundin 12.50 30.00
TA6 Chris Drury 8.00 20.00
TA7 Milan Hejduk 10.00 25.00
TA8 Marian Hossa 10.00 25.00
TA9 Vincent Lecavalier 10.00 25.00
TA10 Joe Thornton 12.50 30.00

1999-00 Topps/OPC A-Men

COMPLETE SET (6) 6.00 12.00
STATED ODDS 1:10 TOPPS/1:8 OPC
AM1 Jaromir Jagr .75 2.00
AM2 Peter Forsberg 1.25 3.00
AM3 Paul Kariya 1.25 3.00
AM4 Teemu Selanne 1.25 3.00
AM5 Joe Sakic 1.00 2.50
AM6 Eric Lindros .75 2.00

1999-00 Topps/OPC Fantastic Finishers

COMPLETE SET (6) 4.00 8.00
STATED ODDS 1:10 TOPPS/1:8 OPC
FF1 Teemu Selanne .50 1.25
FF2 Jaromir Jagr .75 2.00
FF3 Tony Amonte .40 1.00
FF4 Alexei Yashin .40 1.00
FF5 John LeClair .60 1.50
FF6 Joe Sakic 1.00 2.50

1999-00 Topps/OPC Ice Futures

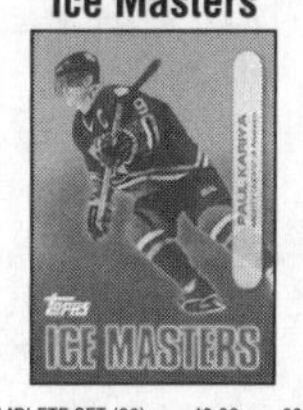

COMPLETE SET (6) 1.50 3.00
STATED ODDS 1:10 TOPPS/1:8 OPC
IF1 Mark Parrish .15 .40
IF2 Chris Drury .50 1.25
IF3 Bill Muckalt .15 .40
IF4 Marian Hossa .15 .40
IF5 Milan Hejduk .50 1.25
IF6 Brendan Morrison .50 1.25

1999-00 Topps/OPC Ice Masters

COMPLETE SET (20) 40.00 80.00
STATED ODDS 1:30
IM1 Joe Sakic 2.00 5.00
IM2 Dominik Hasek 2.00 5.00
IM3 Eric Lindros 1.50 4.00
IM4 Jaromir Jagr 1.50 4.00
IM5 John LeClair 1.25 3.00
IM6 Mats Sundin 1.25 3.00
IM7 Ray Bourque 1.50 4.00
IM8 Mike Modano 1.50 4.00
IM9 Peter Forsberg 2.50 6.00
IM10 Brian Leetch 1.25 3.00
IM11 Martin Brodeur 2.50 6.00
IM12 Al MacInnis 1.00 2.50
IM13 Paul Kariya 1.25 3.00
IM14 Alexei Yashin 1.00 2.50
IM15 Steve Yzerman 5.00 12.00
IM16 Ed Belfour 1.25 3.00
IM17 Keith Tkachuk 1.25 3.00
IM18 Patrick Roy 5.00 12.00
IM19 Nicklas Lidstrom 1.25 3.00
IM20 Teemu Selanne 1.25 3.00

1999-00 Topps/OPC Now Starring

COMPLETE SET (15) 10.00 20.00
STATED ODDS 1:18
NS1 Anson Carter .75 2.00
NS2 Marian Hossa .75 2.00
NS3 Michael Peca .75 2.00
NS4 Kenny Jonsson .60 1.50
NS5 Petr Sykora .60 1.50
NS6 Chris Drury .75 2.00
NS7 Byron Dafoe .75 2.00
NS8 Wade Redden .60 1.50

NS9 Jeff Friesen .60 1.50
NS10 Jamie Langenbrunner .60 1.50
NS11 Mike Johnson .60 1.50
NS12 Keith Primeau .60 1.50
NS13 Vincent Lecavalier .75 2.00
NS14 Mattias Ohlund .75 2.00
NS15 Pavol Demitra .75 2.00

1999-00 Topps/OPC Positive Performers

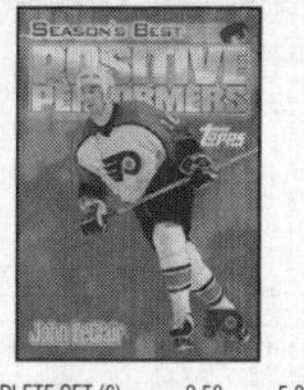

COMPLETE SET (6) 2.50 5.00
STATED ODDS 1:10 TOPPS/1:8 OPC
PP1 Alexander Karpovtsev .15 .40
PP2 John LeClair .60 1.50
PP3 Eric Lindros .75 2.00
PP4 Magnus Arvedson .15 .40
PP5 Al MacInnis .40 1.00
PP6 Jere Lehtinen .40 1.00

1999-00 Topps/OPC Postmasters

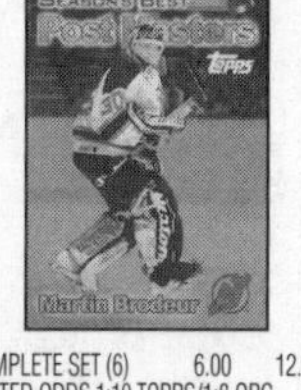

COMPLETE SET (6) 6.00 12.00
STATED ODDS 1:10 TOPPS/1:8 OPC
PM1 Dominik Hasek 1.00 2.50
PM2 Byron Dafoe .40 1.00
PM3 Nikolai Khabibulin .40 1.00
PM4 Ed Belfour .50 1.25
PM5 Patrick Roy 2.50 6.00
PM6 Martin Brodeur 1.25 3.00

1999-00 Topps Stanley Cup Heroes

Randomly inserted in Topps and OPC packs at the rate of 1:23, this 20-card die cut set features full color player shots in the foreground and the Stanley cup in the background. A refractor parallel was also created and inserted at a rate of 1:120.

COMPLETE SET (20) 50.00 100.00
*REFRACTORS: 2X TO 4X BASIC INSERTS
SC1 Mario Lemieux 6.00 15.00
SC2 Mike Bossy 2.00 5.00
SC3 Guy Lafleur 2.00 5.00
SC4 Rocket Richard 8.00 20.00
SC5 Lanny McDonald 3.00 8.00
SC6 Frank Mahovlich 1.00 2.50
SC7 Steve Yzerman 6.00 15.00
SC8 Mark Messier 1.50 4.00
SC9 Patrick Roy 6.00 15.00
SC10 Joe Sakic 2.50 6.00
SC11 Jaromir Jagr 3.00 8.00
SC12 Peter Forsberg 3.00 8.00
SC13 Claude Lemieux 1.00 2.50
SC14 Martin Brodeur 3.00 8.00
SC15 Brian Leetch 1.50 4.00
SC16 Mike Richter 1.50 4.00
SC17 Theo Fleury 1.00 2.50
SC18 Chris Osgood 1.25 3.00
SC19 Ed Belfour 1.50 4.00
SC20 Joe Nieuwendyk 1.25 3.00

1999-00 Topps Stanley Cup Heroes Autographs

Randomly inserted in Topps and OPC packs at the rate of 1:697, this 6-card set features a die cut card and authentic player autographs.

COMPLETE SET (6) 200.00 400.00
SCA1 Mario Lemieux 150.00 250.00
SCA2 Mike Bossy 30.00 80.00
SCA3 Guy Lafleur 40.00 100.00
SCA4 Rocket Richard 200.00 300.00
SCA5 Lanny McDonald 25.00 60.00
SCA6 Frank Mahovlich 20.00 50.00

1999-00 Topps/OPC Top of the World

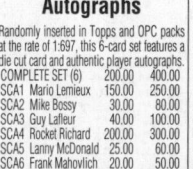

COMPLETE SET (20) 30.00 60.00
STATED ODDS 1:30
TW1 Teemu Selanne 1.00 2.50
TW2 Saku Koivu 1.00 2.50
TW3 Jere Lehtinen .75 2.00
TW4 Peter Forsberg 2.50 6.00
TW5 Mats Sundin 1.00 2.50
TW6 Nicklas Lidstrom 1.00 2.50
TW7 Alexei Yashin 1.00 2.50
TW8 Nikolai Khabibulin .75 2.00
TW9 Pavel Bure 1.25 3.00
TW10 John LeClair 1.25 3.00
TW11 Keith Tkachuk 1.00 2.50
TW12 Mike Modano 1.50 4.00
TW13 Paul Kariya 1.00 2.50
TW14 Joe Sakic 2.00 5.00
TW15 Martin Brodeur 2.50 6.00
TW16 Dominik Hasek 2.00 5.00
TW17 Jaromir Jagr 1.50 4.00
TW18 Peter Bondra .75 2.00
TW19 Olaf Kolzig .75 2.00
TW20 Marco Sturm .75 2.00

2000 Topps AS Sittler

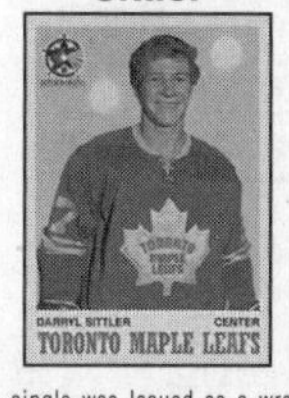

This single was Issued as a wrapper redemption at the 2000 NHL All-Star Game by Topps.

1 Darryl Sittler 1.20 3.00

2000-01 Topps/OPC

Released as a 330-card set, Topps/OPC features action player photography set on a card with silver borders and gold foil highlights. Topps/OPC was packaged in 36-pack boxes with packs containing 10 cards and carried a suggested retail price of $1.29. Card numbers 251-270 were exclusive to Topps or OPC. "A" version cards are found in Topps, "B" version cards are found in OPC.

COMPLETE SET (330) 15.00 30.00
1 Jaromir Jagr .20 .50
2 Patrick Roy .60 1.50
3 Paul Kariya .10 .30
4 Mats Sundin .10 .30
5 Ron Francis .08 .25
6 Pavel Bure .10 .30
7 John LeClair .10 .30
8 Olaf Kolzig .08 .25
9 Chris Pronger .08 .25
10 Jeremy Roenick .15 .40
11 Owen Nolan .08 .25
12 Theo Fleury .02 .10
13 Zigmund Palffy .08 .25
14 Patrik Stefan .02 .10
15 Jarome Iginla .15 .40
16 Joe Thornton .20 .50
17 Tony Amonte .08 .25
18 Mike Modano .20 .50
19 Alexander Mogilny .08 .25
20 Mark Messier .10 .30
21 Dominik Hasek .25 .60
22 Steve Yzerman .60 1.50
23 Marian Hossa .10 .30
24 David Legwand .08 .25
25 Jose Theodore .15 .40
26 Vincent Lecavalier .10 .30
27 Mike Ricci .02 .10
28 Scott Stevens .08 .25
29 Kevin Weekes .08 .25
30 Sean Burke .08 .25
31 Alexei Kovalev .02 .10
32 Trevor Linden .02 .10
33 Joe Juneau .02 .10
34 Niklas Sundstrom .02 .10
35 Dan Cloutier .08 .25
36 Drake Berehowsky .02 .10
37 Jonas Hoglund .02 .10
38 Sami Kapanen .02 .10
39 Matthew Barnaby .02 .10
40 Anson Carter .08 .25
41 Miroslav Satan .08 .25
42 Mark Recchi .08 .25
43 Pavol Demitra .08 .25
44 Peter Bondra .08 .25
45 Mike Richter .10 .30
46 Guy Hebert .08 .25

47 Robert Svehla .02 .10
48 Martin Skoula .02 .10
49 Ed Belfour .10 .30
50 Alexei Zhamnov .02 .10
51 Fred Brathwaite .08 .25
52 Andrew Brunette .02 .10
53 Byron Dafoe .08 .25
54 Claude Lemieux .02 .10
55 Sergei Berezin .02 .10
56 Felix Potvin .10 .30
57 Rod Brind'Amour .08 .25
58 Doug Gilmour .10 .30
59 Brett Hull .15 .40
60 Nicklas Lidstrom .10 .30
61 Mike York .02 .10
62 Al MacInnis .08 .25
63 Brian Boucher .10 .30
64 Teemu Selanne .10 .30
65 Mike Vernon .08 .25
66 Bill Guerin .08 .25
67 Ray Bourque .25 .60
68 Bryan McCabe .02 .10
69 Ray Ferraro .02 .10
70 Stephane Fiset .02 .10
71 Sergei Gonchar .02 .10
72 Mattias Ohlund .02 .10
73 Todd Marchant .02 .10
74 Derek Morris .02 .10
75 Brian Rolston .02 .10
76 Damian Rhodes .08 .25
77 Chris Drury .08 .25
78 Curtis Joseph .10 .30
79 Teppo Numminen .02 .10
80 Petr Nedved .02 .10
81 Doug Weight .08 .25
82 Arturs Irbe .08 .25
83 Chris Osgood .08 .25
84 Chris Gratton .02 .10
85 Jocelyn Thibault .08 .25
86 Oleg Tverdovsky .02 .10
87 Derian Hatcher .02 .10
88 Ray Whitney .02 .10
89 Saku Koivu .10 .30
90 Cliff Ronning .02 .10
91 Claude Lapointe .02 .10
92 Fredrik Modin .02 .10
93 Chris Simon .02 .10
94 Todd Harvey .02 .10
95 Martin Rucinsky .02 .10
96 Valeri Bure .02 .10
97 Brad Isbister .02 .10
98 Daymond Langkow .08 .25
99 Todd Bertuzzi .10 .30
100 Roman Turek .08 .25
101 Kenny Jonsson .02 .10
102 Mike Dunham .08 .25
103 Rob Blake .08 .25
104 Darius Kasparaitis .02 .10
105 Daniel Alfredsson .08 .25
106 Bobby Holik .02 .10
107 Tommy Salo .08 .25
108 Sergei Samsonov .08 .25
109 Joe Sakic .25 .60
110 Bryan Smolinski .02 .10
111 Luc Robitaille .08 .25
112 Ryan Smyth .02 .10
113 Eric Daze .08 .25
114 Mariusz Czerkawski .02 .10
115 Brendan Shanahan .10 .30
116 Brian Rafalski .02 .10
117 Mark Parrish .02 .10
118 Jamie Langenbrunner .02 .10
119 Peter Forsberg .30 .75
120 Phil Housley .02 .10
121 Jeff O'Neill .02 .10
122 Stu Barnes .02 .10
123 Glen Murray .02 .10
124 Jeff Hackett .08 .25
125 Sergei Fedorov .20 .50
126 Kyle McLaren .02 .10
127 Michael Nylander .02 .10
128 Sergei Zubov .02 .10
129 Steve Rucchin .02 .10
130 Nelson Emerson .02 .10
131 Martin Brodeur .30 .75
132 Mike Grier .02 .10
133 Paul Coffey .10 .30
134 Radek Bonk .02 .10
135 Marc Savard .02 .10
136 Milan Hejduk .10 .30
137 Curtis Brown .02 .10
138 Viktor Kozlov .02 .10
139 Jason Woolley .02 .10
140 Adam Foote .02 .10
141 Radek Dvorak .02 .10
142 Jason Arnott .02 .10
143 German Titov .02 .10
144 Scott Thornton .02 .10
145 Brendan Morrison .08 .25
146 Keith Tkachuk .10 .30
147 Patrik Elias .08 .25
148 Donald Audette .02 .10
149 Jochen Hecht .02 .10
150 Dave Scatchard .02 .10
151 Tom Barrasso .08 .25
152 Adam Deadmarsh .02 .10
153 Brian Leetch .08 .25
154 Sergei Krivokrasov .02 .10
155 Randy Robitaille .02 .10
156 Petr Sykora .02 .10
157 Dave Andreychuk .02 .10
158 Mathieu Biron .08 .25
159 Sergei Zholtok .02 .10
160 Shawn McEachern .02 .10
161 Steve Shields .08 .25
162 Petr Svoboda .02 .10
163 Nikolai Antropov .02 .10
164 Michal Handzus .02 .10
165 Martin Straka .02 .10
166 Shane Doan .02 .10
167 Eric Desjardins .02 .10
168 Peter Schaefer .02 .10
169 Adam Oates .08 .25
170 Scott Niedermayer .02 .10
171 Dallas Drake .02 .10
172 Josh Green .02 .10
173 Mike Sillinger .02 .10
174 Adam Graves .02 .10
175 Lubos Bartecko .02 .10
176 Steve Konowalchuk .02 .10
177 Jozef Stumpel .02 .10
178 Vincent Damphousse .02 .10
179 Tomas Kaberle .02 .10
180 Maxim Afinogenov .02 .10
181 Marty McInnis .02 .10
182 Chris Chelios .10 .30
183 Joe Nieuwendyk .08 .25
184 Petr Buzek .02 .10
185 Calle Johansson .02 .10
186 Jeff Friesen .02 .10
187 Paul Mara .02 .10
188 Markus Naslund .10 .30
189 Scott Young .02 .10
190 Trevor Letowski .02 .10
191 Steve Thomas .02 .10
192 Martin Biron .08 .25
193 Jason Allison .02 .10
194 Bob Probert .02 .10
195 Jere Lehtinen .08 .25
196 Tom Poti .02 .10
197 Eric Lindros .10 .30
198 Rob Niedermayer .02 .10
199 Gary Roberts .02 .10
200 Richard Zednik .02 .10
201 Dainius Zubrus .02 .10
202 Tom Fitzgerald .02 .10
203 Scott Gomez .02 .10
204 Travis Green .02 .10
205 Pierre Turgeon .08 .25
206 Ed Jovanovski .02 .10
207 Trevor Kidd .08 .25
208 Jan Hrdina .02 .10
209 Valeri Zelepukin .02 .10
210 Vaclav Prospal .02 .10
211 Matt Cullen .02 .10
212 Karlis Skrastins .02 .10
213 Robyn Regehr .02 .10
214 Darren McCarty .02 .10
215 John Madden .02 .10
216 Scott Mellanby .02 .10
217 Tim Connolly .02 .10
218 Pat Verbeek .02 .10
219 Richard Matvichuk .02 .10
220 Rick Tocchet .02 .10
221 Jan Hlavac .02 .10
222 Jeff Halpern .02 .10
223 Patrick Marleau .08 .25
224 Robert Lang .02 .10
225 Wade Redden .02 .10
226 Stephane Richer .02 .10
227 Kim Johnsson .02 .10
228 Greg Adams .02 .10
229 Alex Tanguay .08 .25
230 Andre Savage .02 .10
231 Slava Kozlov .02 .10
232 Steve Sullivan .02 .10
233 Alexander Selivanov .02 .10
234 Tommy Westlund .02 .10
235 Darcy Tucker .02 .10
236 Simon Gagne .10 .30
237 Brad Stuart .02 .10
238 Jean-Sebastien Aubin .08 .25
239 Mike Johnson .02 .10
240 Shayne Corson .02 .10
241 Michael Peca .02 .10
242 Keith Primeau .02 .10
243 Martin Lapointe .02 .10
244 Tie Domi .08 .25
245 Janne Niinimaa .02 .10
246 Brenden Morrow .08 .25
247 Sandis Ozolinsh .02 .10
248 Ron Tugnutt .08 .25
249 Andrei Nazarov .02 .10
250 Bates Battaglia .02 .10
251A Dean Sylvester .02 .10
251B Yannick Tremblay .02 .10
252A Hal Gill .02 .10
252B Grant Fuhr .08 .25
253A Vladimir Tsyplakov .02 .10
253B Cory Stillman .02 .10
254A Sean Hill .02 .10
254B Jason Wiemer .02 .10
255A Michal Grosek .02 .10
255B Martin Gelinas .02 .10
256A Darryl Sydor .02 .10
256B Mike Keane .02 .10
257A Igor Larionov .02 .10
257B Ethan Moreau .02 .10
258A Jaroslav Spacek .02 .10
258B Jason Smith .02 .10
259A Mattias Norstrom .02 .10
259B Kelly Buchberger .02 .10
260A Ladislav Kohn .02 .10
260B Benoit Brunet .02 .10
261A Patric Kjellberg .02 .10
261B Brian Savage .02 .10
262A Marty Reasoner .02 .10
262B Sheldon Souray .02 .10
263A Zdeno Chara .02 .10
263B Greg Johnson .02 .10
264A Mathieu Schneider .02 .10
264B Magnus Arvedson .02 .10
265A John Vanbiesbrouck .08 .25
265B Patrick Lalime .08 .25
266A Jyrki Lumme .02 .10
266B Wayne Primeau .02 .10
267A Janne Laukkanen .02 .10
267B Igor Korolev .02 .10
268A Alexander Korolyuk .02 .10
268B Yanic Perreault .02 .10
269A Pavel Kubina .02 .10
269B Adrian Aucoin .02 .10
270A Ulf Dahlen .02 .10
270B Andrew Cassels .02 .10
271 Roberto Luongo .15 .40
272 Harold Druken .02 .10
273 Marc Denis .08 .25
274 Oleg Saprykin .02 .10
275 Glen Metropolit .02 .10
276 Mark Eaton .02 .10
277 Dmitri Yakushin .02 .10
278 Scott Hannan .02 .10
279 Dave Tanabe .02 .10
280 Jiri Fischer .02 .10
281 Dmitri Nabokov .02 .10
282 Ivan Novoseltsev .02 .10
283 Manny Fernandez .08 .25
284 Maxim Balmochnyk .02 .10
285 Brian Campbell .02 .10
286 Sergei Varlamov .02 .10
287 Ville Nieminen RC .02 .10
288 Colin White RC .15 .40
289 Mike Fisher .02 .10
290 Matt Elich RC .08 .25
291 Zenith Komarniski .02 .10
292 Eric Nickulas RC .08 .25
293 Steven McCarthy .02 .10
294 Jason Krog .02 .10
295 Robert Esche .02 .10
296 Adam Mair .02 .10
297 Ladislav Nagy .02 .10
298 Sergei Vyshedkevich .10 .30
299 Steve Begin .02 .10
300 Brad Ference .02 .10
301 Andy Delmore .02 .10
302 Brent Sopel RC .10 .30
303 Evgeni Nabokov .08 .25
304 David Gosselin RC .10 .30
305 Travis Hansen .02 .10
306 Ray Giroux .02 .10
307 Serge Aubin RC .10 .30
308 Shane Willis .02 .10
309 Vitali Vishnevski .02 .10
310 Richard Jackman .02 .10
311 Petr Schastlivy .02 .10
312 Ryan Bonni .02 .10
313 Alexei Tezikov .02 .10
314 Zac Bierk .08 .25
315 Mike Ribeiro .02 .10
316 Darryl Laplante .02 .10
317 Kyle Calder .02 .10
318 Dimitri Kalinin .02 .10
319 J-S Giguere .08 .25
320 Willie Mitchell RC .08 .25
321 Stephen Valiquette RC .10 .30
322 Brian Willsie .02 .10
323 Jarkko Ruutu .02 .10
324 Jon Sim .02 .10
325 Jonathan Girard .02 .10
326 Martin Brodeur HL .50 1.25
327 Ray Bourque HL .40 1.00
328 The Bure Brothers HL .10 .30
329 Steve Yzerman HL 1.00 2.50
330 Brett Hull HL .25 .60

2000-01 Topps/OPC Parallel

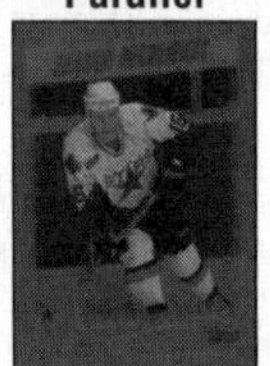

Randomly inserted in Topps packs at the rate of 1:39 and OPC packs at the rate of 1:31, this 330-card set parallels the base Topps/OPC set on cards enhanced with an all foil card stock. Each card is sequentially numbered to 100. Topps Parallels are found in O-Pee-Chee packs and O-Pee-Chee Parallels are found in Topps packs. Card numbers 251-270 were exclusive to Topps or OPC. "A" version cards are found in Topps, "B" version cards are found in OPC.
*STARS: 25X TO 60X BASIC CARDS
*ROOKIES: 10X TO 25X BASIC CARDS

2000-01 Topps/OPC Autographs

Randomly inserted in packs at the rate of 1:502, this 11-card set features authentic player autographs on a card front that has action photography set against a whiteout background..
ACP Chris Pronger 6.00 15.00
AFB Fred Brathwaite 6.00 15.00
AJL John LeClair 10.00 25.00
AJT Jose Theodore 12.50 30.00
AMM Mike Modano 15.00 40.00
AMR Mark Recchi 6.00 15.00
ARB Ray Bourque 30.00 80.00
ART Roman Turek 6.00 15.00
ASG Scott Gomez 6.00 15.00
ATA Tony Amonte EXCH 6.00 15.00
AVB Valeri Bure 6.00 15.00

2000-01 Topps/OPC Combos

Randomly inserted in Topps packs at the rate of 1:12 and OPC packs at the rate of 1:24, this 10-card set features original artist rendered pictures that pair up some of the NHL's finest.
COMPLETE SET (10) 30.00 60.00
*JUMBOS: .5X TO 1.25X
JUMBOS: ONE PER BOX
TC1 Pavel Bure 2.50 6.00
Valeri Bure
TC2 Teemu Selanne 2.50 6.00
Paul Kariya
TC3 John LeClair 2.50 6.00
Tony Amonte
TC4 Curtis Joseph 3.00 8.00
Dominik Hasek
TC5 M.Modano/P.Forsberg 4.00 10.00
TC6 Raymond Bourque 4.00 10.00
Chris Pronger
TC7 Vincent Lecavalier 2.50 6.00
Joe Thornton
TC8 Patrick Roy 5.00 12.00
Martin Brodeur
TC9 S.Yzerman/B.Hull 5.00 12.00
TC10 Jaromir Jagr 4.00 10.00
Mario Lemieux

2000-01 Topps/OPC Game-Worn Sweaters

Randomly inserted in packs at the rate of 1:460, this six card set features swatches of authentic game worn jerseys.
GWAG Adam Graves 8.00 20.00
GWBH Bobby Holik 30.00 80.00
GWDL David Legwand 8.00 20.00
GWDM Darren McCarty 8.00 20.00
GWJJ Jaromir Jagr 12.50 30.00
GWTD Tie Domi 8.00 20.00

2000-01 Topps/OPC Hobby Masters

This 10-card set was inserted in Topps Hobby packs at the rate of 1:18 and OPC packs at the rate of 1:20.
COMPLETE SET (10) 20.00 40.00
HM1 Martin Brodeur 2.50 6.00
HM2 Pavel Bure 1.25 3.00
HM3 Peter Forsberg 2.50 6.00
HM4 Dominik Hasek 2.00 5.00
HM5 Jaromir Jagr 1.50 4.00
HM6 Curtis Joseph 1.00 2.50
HM7 Paul Kariya 1.00 2.50
HM8 Mike Modano 1.25 3.00
HM9 Patrick Roy 5.00 12.00
HM10 Steve Yzerman 5.00 12.00

2000-01 Topps/OPC Lemieux Reprints

Randomly inserted in packs at the rate of 1:12, this 23-card set pays tribute to Mario Lemieux by reprinting both his base Topps and O-Pee-Chee cards.
COMPLETE SET (23) 50.00 100.00
COMMON CARD (1-23) 3.00 8.00

2000-01 Topps/OPC Lemieux Reprints Autographs

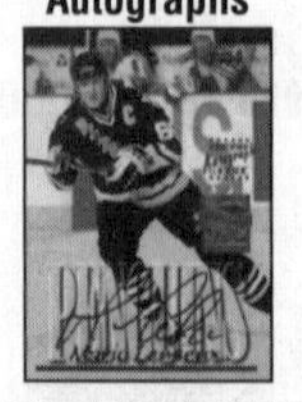

Randomly seeded in packs at the rate of 1:5456, this 23-card set parallels the base Lemieux Reprints set on cards enhanced with a Mario Lemieux autograph.
COMMON CARD (1-23) 60.00 150.00

2000-01 Topps/OPC NHL Draft

Randomly inserted in packs at the rate of 1:31, this 14-card set features seven number one draft selections and seven of the NHL's standout players.
COMPLETE SET (14) 20.00 40.00

D1 Vincent Lecavalier 1.25 3.00
D2 Eric Lindros 2.00 5.00
D3 Mike Modano 2.00 5.00
D4 Owen Nolan 1.00 2.50
D5 Patrik Stefan 1.00 2.50
D6 Mats Sundin 1.25 3.00
D7 Joe Thornton 2.00 5.00
D8 Pavel Bure 1.50 4.00
D9 Anson Carter 1.00 2.50
D10 Pavol Demitra 1.00 2.50
D11 Doug Gilmour 1.25 3.00
D12 Dominik Hasek 2.50 6.00
D13 Brett Hull 1.50 4.00
D14 Luc Robitaille 1.00 2.50

2000-01 Topps/OPC Own the Game

Randomly inserted in packs at the rate of 1:7, this 30-card set spotlights NHL leaders in each of these three categories: Points (OTG1-OTG10), Wins (OTG11-OTG20), and Rookie Points (OTG21-OTG30).
COMPLETE SET (30) 30.00 60.00
OTG1 Jaromir Jagr 1.50 4.00
OTG2 Pavel Bure 1.25 3.00
OTG3 Mark Recchi .75 2.00
OTG4 Paul Kariya 1.00 2.50
OTG5 Teemu Selanne 1.00 2.50
OTG6 Owen Nolan .75 2.00
OTG7 Tony Amonte .75 2.00
OTG8 Mike Modano 1.50 4.00
OTG9 Joe Sakic 2.00 5.00
OTG10 Steve Yzerman 5.00 12.00
OTG11 Martin Brodeur 2.50 6.00
OTG12 Roman Turek .75 2.00
OTG13 Olaf Kolzig .75 2.00
OTG14 Curtis Joseph 1.00 2.50
OTG15 Arturs Irbe .75 2.00
OTG16 Patrick Roy 5.00 12.00
OTG17 Ed Belfour 1.00 2.50
OTG18 Chris Osgood .75 2.00
OTG19 Guy Hebert .75 2.00
OTG20 Steve Shields .75 2.00
OTG21 Scott Gomez .75 2.00
OTG22 Alex Tanguay .75 2.00
OTG23 Mike York .75 2.00
OTG24 Simon Gagne .75 2.00
OTG25 Jan Hlavac .60 1.50
OTG26 Trevor Letowski .60 1.50
OTG27 Brad Stuart .60 1.50
OTG28 Maxim Afinogenov .75 2.00
OTG29 Tim Connolly .75 2.00
OTG30 Jochen Hecht .75 2.00

2000-01 Topps Stanley Cup Heroes

Randomly inserted in packs at the rate of 1:55, this five card set features top NHL stars of the past on an all foil die cut card in the shape of the Stanley Cup.
COMPLETE SET (5) 20.00 40.00
SHBG Bob Gainey 4.00 10.00
SHBP Bernie Parent 5.00 12.00
SHBT Bryan Trottier 5.00 12.00
SHLR Larry Robinson 5.00 12.00
SHTL Ted Lindsay 4.00 10.00

2000-01 Topps Stanley Cup Heroes Autographs

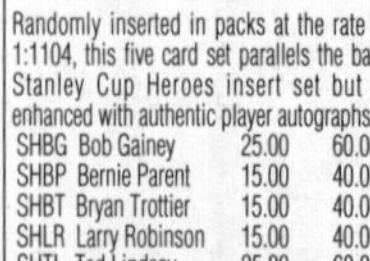

Randomly inserted in packs at the rate of 1:1104, this five card set parallels the base Stanley Cup Heroes insert set but is enhanced with authentic player autographs.
SHBG Bob Gainey 25.00 60.00
SHBP Bernie Parent 15.00 40.00
SHBT Bryan Trottier 15.00 40.00
SHLR Larry Robinson 15.00 40.00
SHTL Ted Lindsay 25.00 60.00

2000-01 Topps/OPC 1000 Point Club

Randomly inserted in packs at the rate of 1:27, this 16-card set spotlights players that have accumulated more than 1000 points on an all foil insert card.
COMPLETE SET (16) 25.00 50.00

PC1 Mark Messier 1.50 4.00
PC2 Steve Yzerman 6.00 15.00
PC3 Ron Francis 1.00 2.50
PC4 Paul Coffey 1.25 3.00
PC5 Ray Bourque 2.50 6.00
PC6 Doug Gilmour 1.25 3.00
PC7 Adam Oates 1.00 2.50
PC8 Larry Murphy 1.00 2.50
PC9 Dave Andreychuk 1.00 2.50
PC10 Luc Robitaille 1.00 2.50
PC11 Phil Housley 1.00 2.50
PC12 Brett Hull 1.50 4.00
PC13 Al MacInnis 1.00 2.50
PC14 Pierre Turgeon 1.00 2.50
PC15 Joe Sakic 2.50 6.00
PC16 Pat Verbeek 1.00 2.50

2001-02 Topps

2001 Topps was released in August as a 360-card set with cards #330-360 in packs as redemption cards for to be determined rookies. The list of rookies redeemable for these cards was not made public until November. Pack SRP was $1.49 for a 10-card pack and there were 36 packs per box. Cards carrying a "U" prefix were available in packs of Topps Chrome at 1:4. These cards were inserted as updates for players who had changed teams since the release of the base set. The "U" was added for checklisting purposes only, it was not printed on the cards.
COMPLETE SET (360) 125.00 250.00
COMP.SET w/o ROOK.RED. (330) 25.00 50.00
1 Mario Lemieux .75 2.00
2 Steve Yzerman .60 1.50
3 Martin Brodeur .30 .75
4 Brian Leetch .10 .25
5 Tony Amonte .10 .25
6 Bill Guerin .10 .25
7 Olaf Kolzig .10 .25
8 Pavel Bure .12 .30
9 Patrick Marleau .10 .25
10 Mariusz Czerkawski .02 .10
11 Teemu Selanne .12 .30
12 Alex Tanguay .10 .25
13 Keith Primeau .02 .10
14 Alexei Yashin .02 .10
14U Alexei Yashin .02 .10
15 Markus Naslund .12 .30
16 Chris Pronger .10 .25
17 Sergei Zubov .02 .10
18 Marian Gaborik .25 .60
19 Mats Sundin .12 .30
20 Kevin Weekes .02 .10
21 J.P. Dumont .02 .10
22 Nicklas Lidstrom .12 .30
23 Ron Francis .10 .25
24 Doug Weight .10 .25
24U Doug Weight .12 .30
25 Zigmund Palffy .10 .25
26 Jason Allison .02 .10
27 Joe Sakic .25 .60
28 Paul Kariya .12 .30
29 Marian Hossa .12 .30
30 Owen Nolan .10 .25
31 Jason Arnott .02 .10
32 Jaromir Jagr .20 .50
32U Jaromir Jagr .25 .60
33 Justin Williams .02 .10
34 Peter Bondra .12 .30
35 Chris Drury .10 .25
36 Radek Bonk .02 .10
37 Theo Fleury .02 .10
38 Keith Tkachuk .12 .30
39 Rick DiPietro .10 .25
40 Ed Jovanovski .10 .25
41 Scott Stevens .10 .25
42 John LeClair .12 .30
43 Jochen Hecht .02 .10
44 Vincent Lecavalier .12 .30
45 Henrik Sedin .02 .10
46 David Aebischer .10 .25
47 Patrick Roy .60 1.50
48 Valeri Bure .02 .10
49 Dominik Hasek .25 .60
49U Dominik Hasek .30 .75
50 Ray Ferraro .02 .10
51 Milan Hejduk .12 .30
52 Mike Modano .20 .50
53 Sergei Fedorov .20 .50
54 Luc Robitaille .10 .25
55 Mark Messier .12 .30
56 Sean Burke .10 .25
57 Jeff Friesen .02 .10
58 Alexander Mogilny .10 .25
58U Alexander Mogilny .10 .25
59 Roman Cechmanek .10 .25
60 Martin Straka .02 .10
61 Pavol Demitra .10 .25
62 Curtis Joseph .12 .30
63 Daniel Sedin .02 .10
64 Brad Richards .10 .25
65 Simon Gagne .12 .30
66 Saku Koivu .12 .30
67 Jamie McLennan .02 .10
68 Roberto Luongo .15 .40
69 Brendan Shanahan .12 .30
70 Espen Knutsen .02 .10
71 Rob Blake .10 .25
72 Steve Sullivan .02 .10
73 Arturs Irbe .10 .25
74 Maxim Afinogenov .02 .10
75 Patrik Stefan .02 .10
76 Scott Gomez .02 .10
77 Brad Isbister .02 .10
78 Robert Lang .02 .10
79 Pierre Turgeon .12 .30
79U Pierre Turgeon .10 .25
80 Gary Roberts .02 .10
81 Adam Oates .10 .25
82 Evgeni Nabokov .10 .25
83 Petr Nedved .02 .10
84 Mike Dunham .10 .25
85 Chris Osgood .10 .25
85U Chris Osgood .10 .25
86 Brett Hull .15 .40
86U Brett Hull .15 .40
87 Peter Forsberg .30 .75
88 Joe Thornton .20 .50
89 Ray Bourque .25 .60
90 Ed Belfour .12 .30
91 Patrik Elias .10 .25
92 Michael York .02 .10
93 Martin Havlat .10 .25
94 Jeremy Roenick .15 .40
94U Jeremy Roenick .15 .40
95 Alexei Kovalev .10 .25
96 Al MacInnis .10 .25
97 Marco Sturm .02 .10
98 Jose Theodore .15 .40
99 Joe Nieuwendyk .10 .25
100 Darren McCarty .02 .10
101 Mark Recchi .10 .25
102 Daniel Alfredsson .10 .25
103 Miroslav Satan .10 .25
104 Sergei Samsonov .10 .25
105 Roman Turek .10 .25
105U Roman Turek .10 .25
106 Jarome Iginla .15 .40
107 Jeff O'Neill .02 .10
108 Tommy Salo .10 .25
109 Petr Sykora .02 .10
110 Adam Deadmarsh .02 .10
111 Oleg Tverdovsky .02 .10
112 Damian Rhodes .10 .25
113 Bob Probert .02 .10
114 Jere Lehtinen .10 .25
115 Cale Hulse .02 .10
116 Andy Sutton .02 .10
117 Wade Redden .02 .10
118 Brad Stuart .10 .25
119 Tomas Kaberle .02 .10
120 Sergei Gonchar .02 .10
121 Jean-Sebastien Aubin .10 .25
122 Adam Graves .02 .10
123 Teppo Numminen .02 .10
124 Martin Rucinsky .02 .10
125 Scott Young .02 .10
126 Pat Verbeek .02 .10
127 Michael Nylander .02 .10
128 Marc Savard .02 .10
129 Brian Rolston .02 .10
130 Sandis Ozolinsh .02 .10
131 Mike Grier .02 .10
132 Eric Belanger .02 .10
133 Patrick Lalime .10 .25
134 Steve Thomas .02 .10
135 Viktor Kozlov .02 .10
136 Manny Legace .10 .25
137 Oleg Saprykin .02 .10
138 Sami Kapanen .02 .10
139 Janne Niinimaa .02 .10
140 Scott Hartnell .02 .10
141 Tim Connolly .02 .10
142 Travis Green .02 .10
143 Matthew Barnaby .02 .10
144 Brendan Morrison .10 .25
145 Darcy Tucker .02 .10
146 Gary Suter .02 .10
147 Mattias Ohlund .02 .10
148 Patric Kjellberg .02 .10
149 Lubomir Visnovsky .02 .10
150 Claude Lapointe .10 .25
151 Martin Skoula .02 .10
152 Mike Vernon .10 .25
153 Stu Barnes .02 .10
154 Brenden Morrow .10 .25
155 Jim Dowd .02 .10
156 Shane Doan .02 .10
157 Peter Schaefer .02 .10
158 Jeff Halpern .02 .10
159 Sergei Berezin .02 .10
160 Mike Ricci .02 .10
161 Radek Dvorak .02 .10
162 Brian Savage .02 .10
163 Bryan Smolinski .02 .10
164 Derian Hatcher .02 .10
165 Shane Willis .02 .10
166 Ron Tugnutt .10 .25
167 Peter Worrell .02 .10
168 Richard Zednik .02 .10
169 Todd Marchant .02 .10
170 Andrew Brunette .02 .10
171 Derek Morris .02 .10
172 Kyle Calder .02 .10
173 Felix Potvin .12 .30
174 Bobby Holik .02 .10
175 Manny Fernandez .10 .25
176 Rick Tocchet .02 .10
177 Jonas Hoglund .02 .10
178 Todd Bertuzzi .12 .30
179 Garth Snow .10 .25
180 Cliff Ronning .02 .10
181 Martin Lapointe .02 .10
182 Jason Smith .02 .10
183 Byron Dafoe .10 .25
184 Rob Niedermayer .02 .10
185 Steve Rucchin .02 .10
186 Alexei Zhamnov .02 .10
187 Mike Richter .12 .30
188 Michal Handzus .02 .10
189 Pavel Kubina .02 .10
190 Donald Brashear .02 .10
191 Trevor Letowski .02 .10
192 Randy McKay .02 .10

193 Trevor Linden .02 .10
194 Mike Sillinger .02 .10
195 David Vyborny .02 .10
196 Dave Tanabe .02 .10
197 Scott Niedermayer .02 .10
198 Anson Carter .10 .25
199 Mike Leclerc .02 .10
200 Dave Scatchard .02 .10
201 Jan Hrdina .02 .10
202 Brian Holzinger .02 .10
203 Steve Konowalchuk .02 .10
204 Tie Domi .10 .25
205 Brent Johnson .10 .25
206 Shawn McEachern .02 .10
207 Jozef Stumpel .02 .10
208 Jamie Langenbrunner .02 .10
209 Jocelyn Thibault .10 .25
210 Donald Audette .02 .10
211 Serge Aubin .02 .10
212 Andrew Cassels .02 .10
213 Tyson Nash .02 .10
214 Colin White .02 .10
215 Tom Poti .02 .10
216 Rod Brind'Amour .10 .25
217 Fred Brathwaite .10 .25
218 Marc Denis .10 .25
219 Roman Simicek .02 .10
220 Jan Hlavac .02 .10
221 Darius Kasparaitis .02 .10
222 Vincent Damphousse .02 .10
223 Bob Boughner .02 .10
224 Yanic Perreault .02 .10
225 Chris Simon .02 .10
226 Chris Gratton .02 .10
227 Josef Vasicek .02 .10
228 Slava Kozlov .02 .10
229 Kelly Buchberger .02 .10
230 Jeff Hackett .02 .10
231 Taylor Pyatt .02 .10
232 Niklas Sundstrom .02 .10
233 Dan Cloutier .10 .25
234 Eric Daze .10 .25
235 Ryan Smyth .02 .10
236 Marty McInnis .02 .10
237 John Madden .02 .10
238 Claude Lemieux .02 .10
239 Steve Heinze .02 .10
240 Nikolai Antropov .02 .10
241 Cory Stillman .02 .10
242 Geoff Sanderson .02 .10
243 Trevor Kidd .10 .25
244 David Legwand .10 .25
245 Eric Desjardins .02 .10
246 Fredrik Modin .02 .10
247 Brett Clark .02 .10
248 Bryan Muir .02 .10
249 Ron Sutter .02 .10
250 Ken Klee .02 .10
251 Steve Halko .02 .10
252 Steve McKenna .02 .10
253 Marc Bergevin .02 .10
254 Scott Lachance .02 .10
255 Jamie Rivers .02 .10
256 Dixon Ward .02 .10
257 Gord Murphy .02 .10
258 Bret Hedican .02 .10
259 Bob Corkum .02 .10
260 Brent Sopel .02 .10
261 Todd Simpson .02 .10
262 Reid Simpson .02 .10
263 Chris McAlpine .02 .10
264 Deron Quint .02 .10
265 Josh Holden .02 .10
266 Mike Mottau .02 .10
267 Jakub Cutta .02 .10
268 Maxime Ouellet .10 .25
269 Peter Smrek RC .60 1.50
270 Daniel Corso .02 .10
271 Rostislav Klesla .10 .25
272 Mika Noronen .10 .25
273 Kris Beech .02 .10
274 Sheldon Keefe .02 .10
275 Miikka Kiprusoff .10 .25
276 Mathieu Garon .10 .25
277 Jason Chimera RC .60 1.50
278 Mark Bell .02 .10
279 Chris Nielsen .02 .10
280 Eric Chouinard .02 .10
281 Pierre Dagenais .02 .10
282 Branislav Mezei .02 .10
283 Milan Kraft .02 .10
284 Tomas Kloucek .02 .10
285 Petr Schastlivy .02 .10
286 Lee Goren .02 .10
287 Daniel Tkaczuk .02 .10
288 Andreas Lilja .02 .10
289 Tomas Divisek RC .60 1.50
290 Alexei Ponikarovsky .02 .10
291 Mikael Samuelsson RC .60 1.50
292 Petr Svoboda .02 .10
293 Mike Comrie .10 .25
294 Johan Hedberg .10 .25
295 Tyler Moss .02 .10
296 Martin Spanhel RC .60 1.50
297 Mike Brown .02 .10
298 Derek Gustafson .10 .25
299 Matt Pettinger .02 .10
300 Mike Commodore .02 .10
301 Antti-Jussi Niemi .02 .10
302 Brad Tapper .02 .10
303 Rick Berry .02 .10
304 Andrew Raycroft .02 .10
305 Bryan Allen .02 .10
306 Ivan Novoseltsev .02 .10
307 Jason Williams .02 .10
308 Gregg Naumenko .02 .10
309 Jiri Bicek .02 .10
310 Mathieu Darche RC .60 1.50
311 Brian Campbell .02 .10
312 Jeff Farkas .02 .10
313 Rico Fata .02 .10
314 Kristian Kudroc .02 .10
315 Roman Cechmanek AS .10 .25
316 Nicklas Lidstrom AS .12 .30
317 Ray Bourque AS .25 .60
318 Joe Sakic AS .25 .60
319 Patrik Elias AS .10 .25
320 Jaromir Jagr AS .20 .50
321 John Madden/Randy McKay .02 .10
322 Mark Recchi .10 .25
323 Vincent Damphousse .02 .10
324 Patrick Roy .60 1.50
325 Jaromir Jagr .20 .50
326 Mario Lemieux 2.00 5.00
327 Mario Lemieux 2.00 5.00
328 Mario Lemieux 2.00 5.00
329 Mario Lemieux 2.00 5.00
330 Mario Lemieux 2.00 5.00
331 Ilya Kovalchuk RC 6.00 15.00
332 Dan Blackburn RC 1.00 2.50
333 Vaclav Nedorost RC 1.00 2.50
334 Krys Kolanos RC 1.00 2.50
335 Kristian Huselius RC 2.00 5.00
336 Martin Erat RC 1.00 2.50
337 Timo Parssinen RC 1.00 2.50
338 Scott Nichol RC 1.00 2.50
339 Nick Schultz RC 1.00 2.50
340 Jukka Hentunen RC 1.00 2.50
341 Pascal Dupuis RC 1.00 2.50
342 Radek Martinek RC 1.00 2.50
343 Scott Clemmensen RC 1.00 2.50
344 Jeff Jillson RC 1.00 2.50
345 Brian Sutherby RC 1.00 2.50
346 Nikita Alexeev RC 1.00 2.50
347 Niklas Hagman RC 1.00 2.50
348 Erik Cole RC 2.00 5.00
349 Pavel Datsyuk RC 3.00 8.00
350 Ilja Bryzgalov RC 2.00 5.00
351 Chris Neil RC 2.00 5.00
352 Mark Rycroft RC 1.00 2.50
353 Kamil Piros RC 1.00 2.50
354 Niko Kapanen RC 1.00 2.50
355 Jiri Dopita RC 1.00 2.50
356 Andreas Salomonsson RC 1.00 2.50
357 Ivan Ciernik RC 1.00 2.50
358 Jaroslav Bednar RC 1.00 2.50
359 Ty Conklin RC 1.00 2.50
360 Raffi Torres RC 2.00 5.00

2001-02 Topps Heritage Parallel

Inserted at a rate of 1:1, this 110-card set parallels the first 110 cards of the Topps base set. The card fronts carry the same photo as the base cards, but use the 1971-72 Topps design. Card backs are the same as the base set. A limited parallel to these inserts was also created, these parallels look the same but carry different colored foil and serial numbering out of 50.
*STARS: 1.25X TO 2.5X BASIC CARDS
*LIMITED: 40X TO 80X BASIC CARDS

2001-02 Topps OPC Parallel

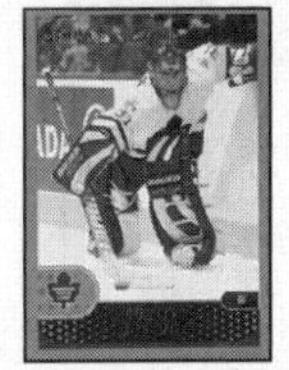

Inserted at a rate of 1:4, this 330-card set parallel the base set except that card fronts carried the O-Pee-Chee stamp in silver. Card backs were the same as the base cards.
*STARS: 1.5X TO 4X BASIC CARDS

2001-02 Topps Autographs

This 10-card set was inserted into hobby packs at a rate of 1:507 and retail packs at 1:390. Card fronts were a blue and white ice design with the white portion being where the players signed. Card backs carried a Topps certified sticker.
ACD Chris Drury 10.00 25.00
AEN Evgeni Nabokov 10.00 25.00
AGR Gary Roberts 8.00 20.00
AJA Jason Arnott 8.00 20.00
AMY Mike York 8.00 20.00
ARF Ron Francis 8.00 20.00
ASG Simon Gagne 12.00 30.00
AVL Vincent Lecavalier 20.00 50.00
AMHA Martin Havlat 8.00 20.00
AMHE Milan Hejduk 12.00 30.00

2001-02 Topps Captain's Cloth

Available only in hobby packs, this 3-card set featured four swatches of game-used jerseys from four different players who were the captains of their respective teams. Each swatch was affixed in the shape of a "C" on the card front. Card backs carried photos and bios of each player along with the Topps

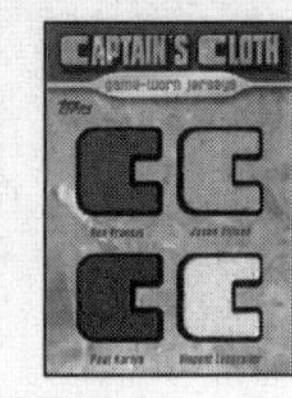

certified sticker.
CC1 Jaromir Jagr 150.00 300.00
Joe Sakic
Paul Kariya
Vincent Lecavalier
CC2 Chris Pronger 100.00 200.00
Saku Koivu
Tony Amonte
Jaromir Jagr
CC3 Ron Francis 100.00 200.00
Jason Allison
Paul Kariya
Vincent Lecavalier

2001-02 Topps Game-Worn Jersey

Inserted at 1:253 hobby and 1:195 retail, this 10-card set featured game-worn jersey swatches of the featured players. Card backs carried a Topps certified sticker.
*MULT.COLORS: 1X TO 1.5X BASIC CARDS
JBB Brian Boucher 6.00 15.00
JBH Brett Hull 10.00 25.00
JCD Chris Drury 8.00 20.00
JEB Ed Belfour 8.00 20.00
JJA Jason Arnott 6.00 15.00
JMY Mike York 6.00 15.00
JPK Paul Kariya 8.00 20.00
JRF Ron Francis 6.00 15.00
JSG Simon Gagne 8.00 20.00
JVL Vincent Lecavalier 6.00 15.00

2001-02 Topps Jumbo Jersey Autographs

Inserted at stated odds of 1:16,895 hobby and 1:12,996 retail, this 6-card set featured larger than normal swatches of game-worn jerseys. The jersey swatches were also signed by the featured player. Due to scarcity, we are unable to price or verify all of these cards at this time.
JJA-CD Chris Drury
JJA-JA Jason Arnott
JJA-MY Mike York
JJA-RF Ron Francis
JJA-SG Simon Gagne
JJA-VL Vincent Lecavalier

2001-02 Topps Mario Lemieux Reprints

Inserted at 1:12 hobby and 1:10 retail, this 10-card set featured reprints of past Topps cards of Mario Lemieux.
COMPLETE SET (10) 20.00 50.00
COMMON CARD (1-10) 2.50 6.00

2001-02 Topps Mario Returns Autographs

Numbered to just 66 sets, this 5-card set parallels the Mario Returns base cards, but also feature a certified autograph on the card front. These cards were inserted at 1:7679 hobby and 1:5907 retail.
COMMON CARD (1-5) 100.00 250.00

2001-02 Topps Own The Game

This 30-card set was inserted at 1:6 hobby and 1:5 retail. Cards were produced on foil stock and featured league leaders in points, wins and rookie points.
COMPLETE SET (30) 15.00 30.00
OTG1 Jaromir Jagr .60 1.50
OTG2 Joe Sakic .75 2.00
OTG3 Patrik Elias .30 .75
OTG4 Jason Allison .12 .30
OTG5 Alexei Kovalev .30 .75
OTG6 Martin Straka .12 .30
OTG7 Pavel Bure .50 1.25
OTG8 Doug Weight .30 .75
OTG9 Peter Forsberg .75 2.00
OTG10 Zigmund Palffy .30 .75
OTG11 Brad Richards .30 .75
OTG12 Shane Willis .12 .30
OTG13 Martin Havlat .30 .75
OTG14 Lubomir Visnovsky .12 .30
OTG15 Marian Gaborik .75 2.00
OTG16 Ruslan Fedotenko .30 .75
OTG17 Steven Reinprecht .12 .30
OTG18 Daniel Sedin .12 .30
OTG19 Karel Rachunek .12 .30
OTG20 David Vyborny .12 .30
OTG21 Martin Brodeur 1.00 2.50
OTG22 Patrick Roy 2.00 5.00
OTG23 Dominik Hasek .75 2.00
OTG24 Olaf Kolzig .30 .75
OTG25 Arturs Irbe .30 .75
OTG26 Patrick Lalime .30 .75
OTG27 Tommy Salo .30 .75
OTG28 Roman Cechmanek .30 .75
OTG29 Ed Belfour .40 1.00
OTG30 Curtis Joseph .40 1.00

2001-02 Topps Rookie Reprints

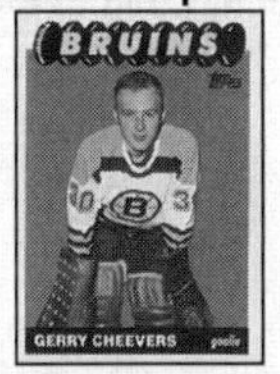

This 4-card set was inserted in 1:22 hobby and 1:17 retail packs and featured reprints of rookie cards of four NHL Hall-of-Famers.
COMPLETE SET (4) 10.00 20.00
1 Denis Potvin 2.00 5.00
2 Yvan Cournoyer 2.00 5.00
3 Phil Esposito 2.00 5.00
4 Gerry Cheevers 2.00 5.00

2001-02 Topps Rookie Reprint Autographs

This 4-card set paralleled the regular rookie reprint set but included authentic autographs from the featured players. A Topps certified sticker was placed on the card backs of this set.
1 Denis Potvin 15.00 40.00
2 Yvan Cournoyer 15.00 40.00
3 Phil Esposito 15.00 40.00
4 Gerry Cheevers 15.00 40.00

2001-02 Topps Shot Masters

COMPLETE SET (18) 15.00 30.00
STATED ODDS 1:13 HOBBY/1:10 RETAIL
SM1 Mario Lemieux 2.50 6.00
SM2 Pavel Bure .50 1.25
SM3 Brett Hull .50 1.25
SM4 Joe Sakic .75 2.00
SM5 Jaromir Jagr .60 1.50
SM6 Steve Yzerman 2.00 5.00
SM7 Milan Hejduk .40 1.00
SM8 Tony Amonte .30 .75
SM9 Zigmund Palffy .30 .75
SM10 Paul Kariya .40 1.00
SM11 Bill Guerin .30 .75
SM12 Peter Bondra .40 1.00
SM13 Patrik Elias .30 .75
SM14 Alexei Kovalev .30 .75
SM15 John LeClair .50 1.25
SM16 Alexei Yashin 1.00 2.50
SM17 Teemu Selanne .40 1.00
SM18 Alexander Mogilny .30 .75

2001-02 Topps Stanley Cup Heroes

Inserted at 1:66 hobby and 1:51 retail, this 4-card set features vintage players on a chrome die-cut design.
COMPLETE SET (4) 15.00 30.00
SCHDP Denis Potvin 4.00 10.00
SCHGC Gerry Cheevers 5.00 12.00
SCHPE Phil Esposito 4.00 10.00
SCHYC Yvan Cournoyer 5.00 12.00

2001-02 Topps Stanley Cup Heroes Autographs

This set paralleled the base heroes set but included player autographs and a Topps certified sticker on the card backs. Odds for this set were 1:1584 hobby and 1:1218 retail.
SCHADP Denis Potvin 15.00 40.00
SCHAGC Gerry Cheevers 15.00 40.00
SCHAPE Phil Esposito 20.00 50.00
SCHAYC Yvan Cournoyer 15.00 40.00

2001-02 Topps Stars of the Game

Inserted at 1:12 hobby and 1:10 retail, this 10-card set highlighted players who were recognized most often as one of the "Three Stars of the Game" media voting during the 2000/01 season.
COMPLETE SET (10) 8.00 15.00
SG1 Mario Lemieux 2.50 6.00
SG2 Sean Burke .30 .75
SG3 Pavel Bure .50 1.25
SG4 Joe Sakic .75 2.00
SG5 Patrik Elias .30 .75
SG6 Mike Modano .60 1.50
SG7 Curtis Joseph .40 1.00
SG8 Alexei Kovalev .30 .75
SG9 Sergei Fedorov .75 2.00
SG10 Tommy Salo .30 .75

2002-03 Topps

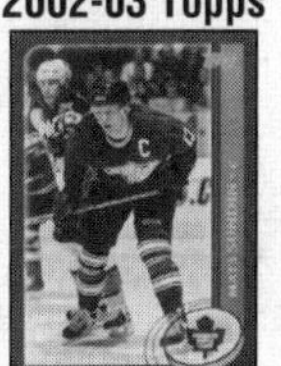

This 340-card set was released as a 330 card set and an available 10-card rookie update set. The rookie update set was available by mail by sending in special redemption cards found in packs. Cards with a "U" prefix were update cards found in packs of Topps Chrome. The "U" prefix is for checklisting purposes only.
COMPLETE SET (340) 25.00 50.00
COMP.SET w/o ROOK.RED. (330) 20.00 40.00
1 Patrick Roy .60 1.50
2 Mario Lemieux .75 2.00
3 Martin Brodeur .30 .75
4 Steve Yzerman .60 1.50
5 Jaromir Jagr .20 .50
6 Chris Pronger .10 .25
7 John LeClair .12 .30
8 Paul Kariya .12 .30
9 Tony Amonte .10 .25
9U Tony Amonte .10 .25
10 Joe Thornton .20 .50
11 Ilya Kovalchuk .15 .40
12 Jarome Iginla .15 .40
13 Mike Modano .20 .50
14 Vincent Lecavalier .12 .30
15 Michael Peca .02 .10
16 Pavel Bure .12 .30
17 Eric Lindros .12 .30
18 Felix Potvin .12 .30
19 Ron Francis .10 .25
20 Miroslav Satan .10 .25
21 Rostislav Klesla .02 .10
22 Mike Comrie .10 .25
23 Daniel Alfredsson .10 .25
24 Sean Burke .10 .25
25 David Legwand .10 .25
26 Marian Gaborik .25 .60
27 Saku Koivu .12 .30
28 Owen Nolan .10 .25
29 Mats Sundin .12 .30
30 J-P Dumont .02 .10
31 Chris Drury .10 .25
31U Chris Drury .10 .25
32 Markus Naslund .12 .30
33 Anson Carter .10 .25
34 Dwayne Roloson .02 .10
35 Brad Isbister .02 .10
36 Daniel Briere .02 .10
37 Martin St. Louis .10 .25
38 Shayne Corson .02 .10
39 Keith Tkachuk .12 .30
40 Mark Recchi .10 .25
41 Patrice Brisebois .02 .10
42 Niklas Hagman .02 .10
43 Marc Denis .10 .25
44 Robyn Regehr .02 .10
45 Byron Dafoe .10 .25
46 Sergei Fedorov .20 .50
47 Andrew Brunette .02 .10
48 Denis Arkhipov .02 .10
49 Martin Havlat .10 .25
50 Mike Rathje .02 .10
51 Mattias Ohlund .02 .10
52 Ulf Dahlen .02 .10
53 Tim Connolly .02 .10
54 Valeri Bure .02 .10
55 Brian Boucher .10 .25
56 Pascal Dupuis .02 .10
57 Brian Leetch .10 .25
58 Daniel Sedin .02 .10
59 Kenny Jonsson .02 .10
60 Erik Cole .02 .10
61 Patrick Lalime .10 .25
62 Mike Leclerc .02 .10
63 Patrick Marleau .10 .25
64 Tom Poti .02 .10
65 Lubos Bartecko .02 .10
66 Tom Barrasso .10 .25
67 Ryan Smyth .02 .10
68 Sami Kapanen .02 .10
69 Michal Handzus .02 .10
70 Martin Straka .02 .10
71 Peter Forsberg .30 .75
72 Marc Savard .02 .10
73 Jeff Friesen .02 .10
73U Jeff Friesen .02 .10
74 Manny Fernandez .10 .25
75 Jason Smith .02 .10
76 Mike Ribeiro .02 .10
77 Steve Heinze .02 .10
78 Adam Foote .02 .10
79 Sandy McCarthy .02 .10
80 Toni Lydman .02 .10
81 Tie Domi .10 .25
82 Scott Stevens .10 .25
83 Radim Vrbata .02 .10
84 Oleg Petrov .02 .10
85 Marty Turco .10 .25
86 Kristian Huselius .02 .10
87 Jeremy Roenick .15 .40
88 Gary Roberts .02 .10
89 Dean McAmmond .02 .10
90 Chris Chelios .12 .30
91 Andy McDonald .02 .10
92 Brett Hull .15 .40
93 Danny Markov .02 .10
94 Eric Daze .10 .25
95 Alex Tanguay .10 .25
96 Petr Nedved .02 .10
97 Simon Gagne .12 .30
98 Roman Turek .10 .25
99 Milan Hejduk .12 .30
100 Mariusz Czerkawski .02 .10
100U Mariusz Czerkawski .02 .10
101 Jaroslav Modry .02 .10
102 Dan Cloutier .10 .25
103 Mark Bell .02 .10
104 Brendan Witt .02 .10
105 Teemu Selanne .12 .30
106 Johan Hedberg .10 .25
107 Mike Ricci .02 .10
108 Roberto Luongo .15 .40
109 Vaclav Prospal .02 .10
110 Zigmund Palffy .10 .25
111 Ed Jovanovski .02 .10
112 Scott Gomez .02 .10
113 Pierre Turgeon .10 .25
114 Niklas Sundstrom .02 .10
115 Martin Biron .10 .25
116 Keith Primeau .02 .10
117 J-S Giguere .10 .25
118 Filip Kuba .02 .10
119 Dave Tanabe .02 .10
120 Brian Savage .02 .10
121 Alexei Zhamnov .02 .10
122 Brent Johnson .10 .25
123 Dan Blackburn .10 .25
124 Eric Belanger .02 .10
125 Janne Niinimaa .02 .10
126 Jonas Hoglund .02 .10
127 Marian Hossa .12 .30
128 Mike Richter .12 .30
129 Peter Bondra .12 .30
130 Rod Brind'Amour .10 .25
131 Shane Doan .02 .10
132 Viktor Kozlov .02 .10
133 Yanic Perreault .02 .10
134 Sergei Samsonov .10 .25
135 Nikolai Khabibulin .12 .30
136 Rob Ray .02 .10
137 Roman Cechmanek .10 .25
138 Patrik Stefan .02 .10
139 Matt Cullen .02 .10
140 Kim Johnsson .02 .10
141 Jim Dowd .02 .10
142 Glen Murray .02 .10
143 Dominik Hasek .25 .60
144 Brad Richards .10 .25
145 Cory Stillman .02 .10
146 Josef Vasicek .02 .10
147 Alexei Kovalev .10 .25
148 Adam Deadmarsh .02 .10
149 Brendan Morrison .10 .25
150 Eric Brewer .02 .10
151 Jason Arnott .02 .10
152 Brenden Morrow .02 .10
153 Manny Legace .02 .10
154 Michael Nylander .02 .10
155 Pavol Demitra .02 .10
156 Olaf Kolzig .10 .25
157 Sergei Berezin .02 .10
158 Teppo Numminen .02 .10
159 Vladimir Orszagh .02 .10
160 Brian Rafalski .02 .10
161 Doug Gilmour .10 .25
162 Jere Lehtinen .10 .25
163 Mark Parrish .02 .10
164 Petr Sykora .02 .10
164U Petr Sykora .02 .10
165 Sergei Zholtok .02 .10
166 Wade Redden .02 .10
167 Scott Niedermayer .02 .10
168 Olli Jokinen .10 .25
169 Kyle Calder .02 .10
170 Jamie Langenbrunner .02 .10
171 Darcy Tucker .02 .10
172 Alexei Morozov .02 .10
173 Adam Oates .10 .25
173U Adam Oates .10 .25
174 Chris Osgood .10 .25
175 Espen Knutsen .02 .10
176 Jochen Hecht .02 .10
177 Maxim Afinogenov .02 .10
178 Radek Dvorak .02 .10
179 Steve Sullivan .02 .10
180 Trevor Linden .02 .10
181 Tomi Kallio .02 .10
182 Robert Lang .02 .10
182U Robert Lang .02 .10
183 Milan Hnilicka .10 .25
184 Justin Williams .02 .10
185 Greg Johnson .02 .10
186 Craig Conroy .02 .10
187 Alexander Mogilny .10 .25
188 Adrian Aucoin .02 .10
189 Fredrik Modin .02 .10
190 Jose Theodore .15 .40
191 Ray Whitney .02 .10
192 Mikael Renberg .02 .10
193 Mike Sillinger .02 .10
194 Richard Zednik .02 .10
195 Mike Dunham .10 .25
196 Joe Sakic .25 .60
197 Fred Brathwaite .10 .25
198 Chris Simon .02 .10
199 Al MacInnis .10 .25
200 Georges Laraque .02 .10
201 Jozef Stumpel .02 .10
202 Theo Fleury .02 .10
203 Rob Blake .10 .25
204 Todd White .02 .10
205 Dany Heatley .15 .40
206 Scott Hartnell .02 .10
207 Oleg Tverdovsky .02 .10
208 Krys Kolanos .02 .10
209 Ian Laperriere .02 .10
210 Vincent Damphousse .02 .10
211 Nick Boynton .02 .10
212 Curtis Joseph .12 .30
212U Curtis Joseph .12 .30
213 Henrik Sedin .02 .10
214 Kris Beech .02 .10
215 Sandis Ozolinsh .02 .10
216 Ron Tugnutt .10 .25
217 Todd Bertuzzi .12 .30
218 Tommy Salo .10 .25
219 Martin Lapointe .02 .10
220 Derian Hatcher .02 .10
221 David Vyborny .02 .10
222 Jocelyn Thibault .10 .25
223 Nicklas Lidstrom .12 .30
224 Marcus Nilsson .02 .10
225 Sergei Zubov .02 .10
226 Bryan McCabe .02 .10
227 Claude Lemieux .02 .10
228 Jean-Luc Grand-Pierre .02 .10
229 Bill Guerin .10 .25
229U Bill Guerin .10 .25
230 Sergei Brylin .02 .10
231 Bryan Smolinski .02 .10
232 Luc Robitaille .10 .25
233 Alexei Yashin .02 .10
234 Evgeni Nabokov .10 .25
235 Pavel Datsyuk .12 .30
236 Martin Erat .02 .10
237 Stu Barnes .02 .10
238 Derek Morris .02 .10
239 Bates Battaglia .02 .10
240 Jason Allison .02 .10
241 Peter Worrell .02 .10
242 Mark Messier .12 .30
243 Shawn Bates .02 .10
244 Daymond Langkow .02 .10
245 Ed Belfour .12 .30
245U Ed Belfour .12 .30
246 Jan Hrdina .02 .10
247 Pavel Kubina .02 .10
248 Scott Young .02 .10
249 Curtis Brown .02 .10
250 Brian Rolston .02 .10
251 Jiri Dopita .02 .10
252 Kimmo Timonen .02 .10
253 Marco Sturm .02 .10
254 Arturs Irbe .10 .25
255 Joe Nieuwendyk .10 .25
256 Sergei Gonchar .02 .10
257 Doug Weight .10 .25
258 Jeff O'Neill .02 .10
259 Mike York .02 .10
260 Radek Bonk .02 .10
261 Patrik Elias .10 .25
262 Phil Housley .02 .10
263 Brendan Shanahan .12 .30
264 Sheldon Keefe .02 .10
265 Rick DiPietro .10 .25
266 J-F Fortin .02 .10
267 Jason Chimera .02 .10
268 Andy Hilbert .02 .10
269 Brian Gionta .02 .10
270 Sergei Varlamov .02 .10
271 Alex Auld .02 .10
272 Pavel Brendl .02 .10
273 Branko Radivojevic .02 .10
274 Kamil Piros .02 .10
275 Steve Gainey .02 .10
276 Mike Mottau .02 .10
277 Jimmie Olvestad .02 .10
278 Jeff Jillson .02 .10
279 Ilja Bryzgalov .10 .25
280 Taylor Pyatt .02 .10
281 Andrew Raycroft .10 .25
282 Christian Berglund .02 .10
283 Patrick DesRochers .02 .10
284 Lukas Krajicek .02 .10
285 Riku Hahl .02 .10
286 Ivan Huml .02 .10
287 Jani Rita .02 .10
288 Kristian Kudroc .02 .10
289 Juraj Kolnik .02 .10
290 John Erskine .02 .10
291 Brian Sutherby .02 .10
292 Bruno St-Jacques .02 .10
293 Nick Schultz .02 .10
294 Pasi Nurminen .02 .10
295 Norm Milley .02 .10
296 Marcel Hossa .02 .10
297 Ales Kotalik .02 .10
298 Bryan Allen .02 .10
299 Mika Noronen .10 .25
300 Tyler Arnason .10 .25
301 Petr Schastlivy .02 .10
302 Mike Van Ryn .02 .10
303 Steve Montador .02 .10
304 Denis Shvidki .02 .10
305 Stephen Weiss .02 .10
306 Nikita Alexeev .02 .10

307 Vaclav Nedorost .02 .10
308 Raffi Torres .02 .10
309 Guillaume Lefebvre .02 .10
310 Sean Avery .02 .10
311 Shane Endicott .02 .10
312 Ty Conklin .10 .25
313 J-F Damphousse .10 .25
314 Jeremy Roenick .15 .40
315 Ron Francis .10 .25
316 Brendan Shanahan .20 .50
317 Patrick Roy .60 1.50
318 Luc Robitaille .10 .25
319 Jose Theodore .15 .40
320 Patrick Roy .60 1.50
321 Sergei Gonchar .02 .10
322 Bryan McCabe .02 .10
323 Chris Chelios .12 .30
324 Nicklas Lidstrom .12 .30
325 Simon Gagne .12 .30
326 Brendan Shanahan .20 .50
327 Jaromir Jagr .20 .50
328 Jarome Iginla .15 .40
329 Mats Sundin .12 .30
330 Joe Sakic .25 .60
331 Henrik Zetterberg RC 3.00 8.00
332 P-M Bouchard RC 1.25 3.00
333 Alexander Frolov RC 1.25 3.00
334 Alexander Svitov RC 1.00 2.50
335 Jason Spezza RC 2.00 5.00
336 Jay Bouwmeester RC 1.25 3.00
337 Ales Hemsky RC 2.00 5.00
338 Rick Nash RC 2.50 6.00
339 Chuck Kobasew RC 1.00 2.50
340 Stanislav Chistov RC 1.25 3.00

2002-03 Topps OPC Blue Parallel

Inserted at 1:6 for the regular cards and 1:1,813 for the rookie redemption card, this 331-card set paralleled the base Topps set but carried blue borders and blue foil highlights. The O-Pee-Chee logo was printed on the card fronts in place of the Topps logo and each card was serial-numbered out of 500.
*STARS: 3X TO 8X BASIC CARDS
*ROOKIES: 1.25X TO 3X

2002-03 Topps OPC Red Parallel

Inserted at 1:25 for the regular cards and 1:9,869 for the rookie redemption card, this 331-card set paralleled the base Topps set but carried red borders and red foil highlights. The O-Pee-Chee logo was printed on the card fronts in place of the Topps logo and each card was serial-numbered out of 100.
*STARS: 8X TO 20X BASIC CARDS
*ROOKIES: 4X TO 10X

2002-03 Topps Captain's Cloth

This 17-card set fetured swatches of game jersey from team captains around the league. Single swatch cards were serial-numbered to 100 and inserted at 1:939. Multi-swatch cards were serial-numbered to 50 and inserted at 1:2691.
CC1 Lemieux/Sakic/Francis 75.00 200.00
CC2 Keith Primeau 60.00 150.00
John LeClair
Mark Recchi
CC3 Hatcher/Zubov/Modano 75.00 150.00
CC4 Chris Pronger 60.00 125.00
Paul Kariya
Ron Francis
CC5 Saku Koivu 40.00 100.00
Markus Naslund
Mats Sundin
CC6 Lemieux/Sundin/Primeau 75.00 200.00
CC7 Paul Kariya 60.00 150.00
Saku Koivu
Joe Sakic
CC8 Mario Lemieux 20.00 50.00
CC9 Keith Primeau 12.50 30.00
CC10 Markus Naslund 10.00 25.00
CC11 Mats Sundin 10.00 25.00
CC12 Paul Kariya 10.00 25.00
CC13 Joe Sakic 15.00 40.00
CC14 Saku Koivu 12.50 30.00
CC15 Ron Francis 12.50 30.00
CC16 Derian Hatcher 12.50 30.00
CC17 Chris Pronger 12.50 30.00

2002-03 Topps Coast to Coast

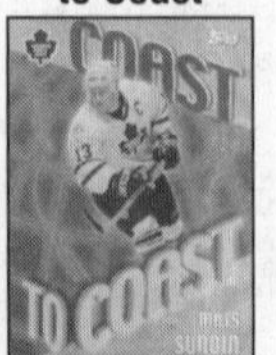

COMPLETE SET (10) 10.00 20.00
STATED ODDS 1:12
CC1 Mario Lemieux 4.00 10.00
CC2 Pavel Bure .75 2.00
CC3 Jarome Iginla .75 2.00
CC4 Mats Sundin .60 1.50
CC5 Peter Bondra .60 1.50
CC6 Ilya Kovalchuk .75 2.00
CC7 Joe Thornton 1.00 2.50
CC8 Paul Kariya .60 1.50
CC9 Joe Sakic 1.25 3.00
CC10 Patrik Elias .75 2.00

2002-03 Topps First Round Fabric

STATED ODDS 1:216
ALL CARDS CARRY FRF PREFIX
DB Dan Blackburn 6.00 15.00
EL Eric Lindros 8.00 20.00
KP Keith Primeau 6.00 15.00
MB Martin Biron 6.00 15.00
MM Mike Modano 10.00 25.00
MN Markus Naslund 10.00 25.00
MS Mats Sundin 10.00 25.00
PM Patrick Marleau 6.00 15.00
RD Radek Dvorak 6.00 15.00
SN Scott Niedermayer 6.00 15.00
JPD J-P Dumont 6.00 15.00

2002-03 Topps First Round Fabric Autographs

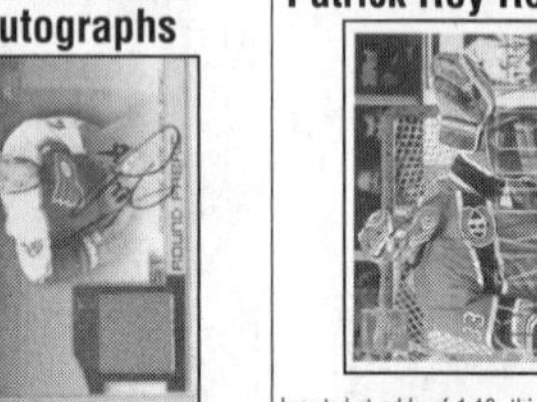

This autographed parallel was inserted at 1:1191 packs.
ALL CARDS CARRY FRF PREFIX
KP Keith Primeau 12.50 30.00
MB Martin Biron 12.50 30.00
MM Mike Modano 20.00 50.00
MS Mats Sundin 20.00 50.00
RD Radek Dvorak 12.50 30.00
SN Scott Niedermayer 15.00 40.00

2002-03 Topps/OPC Hometown Heroes

This 40-card set was split into two subsets: Canadian and USA heroes. Cards HHC1-HHC20 were available only in OPC packs and cards HHU1-HHU20 were inserted into Topps packs. Odds were 1:12.
COMP.CANADA SET (20) 10.00 20.00
COMP.USA SET (20) 15.00 30.00
HHC1 Jarome Iginla .60 1.50
HHC2 Ed Jovanovski .40 1.00
HHC3 Ryan Smyth .40 1.00
HHC4 Mike York .40 1.00
HHC5 Mats Sundin .50 1.25
HHC6 Todd Bertuzzi .50 1.25
HHC7 Markus Naslund .50 1.25
HHC8 Saku Koivu .50 1.25
HHC9 Jose Theodore .60 1.50
HHC10 Daniel Alfredsson .40 1.00
HHC11 Patrick Lalime .40 1.00
HHC12 Roman Turek .40 1.00
HHC13 Mike Comrie .40 1.00
HHC14 Tommy Salo .40 1.00
HHC15 Anson Carter .40 1.00
HHC16 Doug Gilmour .40 1.00
HHC17 Yanic Perreault .40 1.00
HHC18 Radek Bonk .40 1.00
HHC19 Darcy Tucker .40 1.00
HHC20 Curtis Joseph .50 1.25
HHU1 Martin Brodeur 1.25 3.00
HHU2 Joe Sakic .75 2.50
HHU3 Mario Lemieux 3.00 8.00
HHU4 Steve Yzerman 2.50 6.00
HHU5 Paul Kariya .50 1.25
HHU6 Mike Modano .75 2.00
HHU7 Brett Hull .60 1.50
HHU8 Bill Guerin .40 1.00
HHU9 Tony Amonte .40 1.00
HHU10 Jeremy Roenick .60 1.50
HHU11 John LeClair .50 1.25
HHU12 Brendan Shanahan .75 2.00
HHU13 Owen Nolan .40 1.00
HHU14 Al MacInnis .40 1.00
HHU15 Chris Pronger .40 1.00
HHU16 Doug Weight .40 1.00
HHU17 Ilya Kovalchuk .60 1.50
HHU18 Joe Thornton .75 2.00
HHU19 Patrick Roy 2.50 6.00
HHU20 Ron Francis .40 1.00

2002-03 Topps Own The Game

COMPLETE SET (20) 5.00 10.00
STATED ODDS 1:6
OTG1 Jarome Iginla .25 .60
OTG2 Markus Naslund .20 .50
OTG3 Todd Bertuzzi .20 .50
OTG4 Mats Sundin .20 .50
OTG5 Jaromir Jagr .30 .75
OTG6 Jarome Iginla .25 .60
OTG7 Mats Sundin .20 .50
OTG8 Bill Guerin .15 .40
OTG9 Glen Murray .15 .40
OTG10 Markus Naslund .20 .50
OTG11 Dany Heatley .25 .60
OTG12 Ilya Kovalchuk .25 .60
OTG13 Kristian Huselius .15 .40
OTG14 Erik Cole .15 .40
OTG15 Pavel Datsyuk .20 .50
OTG16 Dominik Hasek .40 1.00
OTG17 Martin Brodeur .50 1.25
OTG18 Evgeni Nabokov .15 .40
OTG19 Byron Dafoe .15 .40
OTG20 Brent Johnson .15 .40

2002-03 Topps Patrick Roy Reprints

Inserted at odds of 1:18, this 14-card set featured reprints of goalie great Patrick Roy. Each card carried a gold foil Topps logo on the card front.
COMMON CARD (1-14) 2.50 6.00

2002-03 Topps Patrick Roy Reprints Autographs

This 14-card set paralleled the regular reprint set but included a certified autograph on each card. This set was serial-numbered to just 33.
COMMON CARD (1-14) 60.00 150.00

2002-03 Topps Rookie Reprints

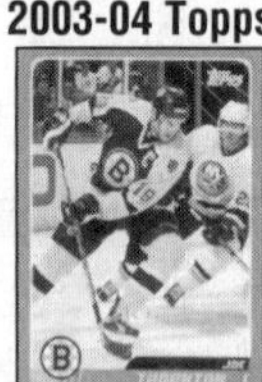

STATED ODDS 1:18
1 Pat LaFontaine 2.00 5.00
2 Mike Gartner 2.00 5.00
3 Pete Mahovlich 3.00 8.00
4 Andy Bathgate 3.00 8.00
5 Gump Worsley 3.00 8.00
6 Danny Gare 2.00 5.00
7 Harry Howell 2.00 5.00
8 Andy Moog 2.00 5.00
9 Keith Magnuson 2.00 5.00
10 Milt Schmidt 3.00 8.00
11 Glen Sather 2.00 5.00
12 Dick Duff 2.00 5.00
13 Garry Unger 2.00 5.00
14 Darren Pang 2.00 5.00
15 Chico Resch 3.00 8.00

2002-03 Topps Rookie Reprint Autographs

This autographed parallel was inserted at 1:1191 packs.
1 Pat LaFontaine 15.00 40.00
2 Mike Gartner 15.00 40.00
3 Pete Mahovlich 30.00 60.00
4 Andy Bathgate 25.00 60.00
5 Gump Worsley 25.00 60.00
6 Danny Gare 15.00 40.00
7 Harry Howell 15.00 40.00
8 Andy Moog 20.00 50.00
9 Keith Magnuson 40.00 100.00
10 Milt Schmidt 30.00 80.00
11 Glen Sather 30.00 80.00
12 Dick Duff 20.00 50.00
13 Garry Unger 30.00 80.00
14 Darren Pang 15.00 40.00
15 Chico Resch 25.00 60.00

2002-03 Topps Signs of the Future

Inserted at 1:1191, this 6-card set featured certified player autographs. All cards carried a "SF" prefix on the card back.
DL David Legwand 12.50 30.00
IK Ilya Kovalchuk 15.00 40.00
KK Krys Kolanos 12.50 30.00
MC Mike Comrie 12.50 30.00
MH Martin Havlat 12.50 30.00
RV Radim Vrbata 12.50 30.00

2002-03 Topps Stanley Cup Heroes

COMPLETE SET (5) 25.00 40.00
STATED ODDS 1:36
ALL CARDS CARRY SCH PREFIX
DS Derek Sanderson 4.00 10.00
JF John Ferguson 4.00 10.00
RL Reggie Leach 4.00 10.00
RM Rick MacLeish 4.00 10.00
SS Steve Shutt 4.00 10.00

2002-03 Topps Stanley Cup Heroes Autographs

This autographed parallel was inserted at 1:375 hobby packs.
ALL CARDS CARRY SCHA PREFIX
DS Derek Sanderson 15.00 40.00
JF John Ferguson 12.50 30.00
RL Reggie Leach 12.50 30.00
RM Rick MacLeish 12.50 30.00
SS Steve Shutt 12.50 30.00

2002-03 Topps Promos

This set was released in late-Spring of 2002 to generate early buzz around the release of the 2002-03 Topps set.
COMPLETE SET (6) 1.60 4.00
PP1 Simon Gagne 1.00
PP2 Jason Allison .40 1.00
PP3 Sergei Gonchar .20 .50
PP4 Wade Redden .20 .50
PP5 Byron Dafoe .40 1.00
PP6 Patrik Elias .40 1.00

2003-04 Topps

Released in late-August, this 330-card set featured full-color action photos with blue-green borders on the card fronts. A rookie redemption card redeemable for cards 331-340 was also randomly inserted at 1:36. Cards PP1-PP6 were promos sent out to announce the products release.
COMPLETE SET (340) 40.00 80.00
1 Joe Thornton .20 .50
2 Chris Osgood .10 .25
3 Brian Rafalski .02 .10
4 Chris Chelios .12 .30
5 Marian Gaborik .25 .60
6 Pavel Bure .12 .30
7 Ladislav Nagy .02 .10
8 Stephen Weiss .02 .10
9 Mike Modano .20 .50
10 Paul Kariya .12 .30
11 Daymond Langkow .02 .10
12 Patrick Lalime .10 .25
13 Alyn McCauley .02 .10
14 Steve Rucchin .02 .10
15 Mike Johnson .02 .10
16 Georges Laraque .02 .10
17 Brian Sutherby .02 .10
18 Petr Sykora .02 .10
19 Joe Sakic .25 .60
20 Henrik Sedin .02 .10
21 Nikolai Khabibulin .12 .30
22 Kevin Weekes .10 .25
23 Jan Bulis .02 .10
24 Ales Kotalik .02 .10
25 Niko Kapanen .02 .10
26 Jaroslav Modry .02 .10
27 Dan Cloutier .10 .25
28 Olli Jokinen .10 .25
29 Todd Marchant .02 .10
30 Jaromir Jagr .20 .50
31 Rick Nash .15 .40
32 Sami Kapanen .02 .10
33 Brian Boucher .10 .25
34 P.J. Stock .02 .10
35 Teemu Selanne .12 .30
36 Ossi Vaananen .02 .10
37 Jan Hlavac .02 .10
38 Ville Nieminen .02 .10
39 Jere Lehtinen .10 .25
40 Markus Naslund .12 .30
41 Anson Carter .10 .25
42 Steve Sullivan .02 .10
43 Dwayne Roloson .10 .25
44 Frantisek Kaberle .02 .10
45 Cory Stillman .02 .10
46 Shawn Horcoff .02 .10
47 Robert Lang .02 .10
48 Barret Jackman .10 .25
49 Joe Nieuwendyk .10 .25
50 Alexei Kovalev .10 .25
51 Niclas Wallin .02 .10
52 Cory Sarich .02 .10
53 Brendan Witt .02 .10
54 Mike Fisher .02 .10
55 Ed Belfour .12 .30
56 Sergei Zubov .02 .10
57 Ryan Miller .10 .25
58 Tyler Arnason .10 .25
59 Matt Cooke .02 .10
60 Brian Leetch .10 .25
61 Pavel Datsyuk .12 .30
62 Miikka Kiprusoff .10 .25
63 Michal Handzus .02 .10
64 Steve Shields .10 .25
65 Jason Arnott .02 .10
66 Miroslav Satan .10 .25
67 Nick Schultz .02 .10
68 Daniel Briere .02 .10
69 Alexei Yashin .02 .10
70 Martin Straka .02 .10
71 Martin Biron .10 .25
72 Michael Peca .02 .10
73 Simon Gagne .12 .30
74 Alexei Morozov .02 .10
75 Owen Nolan .10 .25
76 Niklas Hagman .02 .10
77 Kim Johnsson .02 .10
78 David Legwand .10 .25
79 Mark Parrish .02 .10
80 Marcel Hossa .02 .10
81 Mike Rathje .02 .10
82 Ruslan Fedotenko .02 .10
83 Bryan Berard .02 .10
84 Richard Zednik .02 .10
85 Viktor Kozlov .02 .10
86 John Madden .02 .10
87 Roman Hamrlik .02 .10
88 Eric Lindros .12 .30
89 Patrik Elias .10 .25
90 Sergei Fedorov .15 .40
91 Pavel Kubina .02 .10
92 Chris Phillips .02 .10
93 Marc Savard .02 .10
94 Janne Niinimaa .02 .10
95 Michael Nylander .02 .10
96 Radek Bonk .02 .10
97 Dmitri Bykov .02 .10
98 Dave Scatchard .02 .10
99 Marian Hossa .12 .30
100 Mario Lemieux .75 2.00
101 Mark Messier .12 .30
102 Tim Connolly .02 .10
103 Henrik Zetterberg .12 .30
104 Brendan Morrison .10 .25
105 Craig Conroy .02 .10
106 Darcy Tucker .02 .10
107 Steve Konowalchuk .02 .10
108 Valeri Bure .02 .10
109 Rod Brind'Amour .10 .25
110 Jeremy Roenick .15 .40
111 Zdeno Chara .02 .10
112 Mathieu Schneider .02 .10
113 Scott Hartnell .02 .10
114 Vincent Damphousse .02 .10
115 Brian Gionta .02 .10
116 Jeff O'Neill .02 .10
117 Pascal Dupuis .02 .10
118 Patrik Stefan .02 .10
119 Eric Daze .10 .25
120 Jose Theodore .15 .40
121 Yanic Perreault .02 .10
122 Shawn McEachern .02 .10
123 Daniel Alfredsson .10 .25
124 Peter Bondra .10 .25
125 Doug Weight .10 .25
126 Chris Drury .10 .25
127 Ed Jovanovski .10 .25
128 Scott Stevens .10 .25
129 Adam Foote .02 .10
130 Curtis Joseph .12 .30
131 Phil Housley .02 .10
132 Philippe Boucher .02 .10
133 Patrice Brisebois .02 .10
134 Josef Vasicek .02 .10
135 Peter Worrell .02 .10
136 Mike Knuble .02 .10
137 Jocelyn Thibault .10 .25
138 Keith Primeau .10 .25
139 Marc Chouinard .02 .10
140 Mats Sundin .12 .30
141 Martin Skoula .02 .10
142 Sergei Gonchar .02 .10
143 Pavol Demitra .10 .25
144 Tie Domi .10 .25
145 Denis Arkhipov .02 .10
146 Oleg Saprykin .02 .10
147 Tommy Salo .10 .25
148 Andrei Markov .02 .10
149 Brent Johnson .10 .25
150 Jarome Iginla .15 .40
151 Darryl Sydor .02 .10
152 Bryan Smolinski .02 .10
153 Roberto Luongo .15 .40
154 Sandis Ozolinsh .02 .10
155 Alexander Svitov .02 .10
156 J.P. Dumont .02 .10
157 Mike York .02 .10
158 Martin Brodeur .30 .75
159 Scott Gomez .02 .10
160 Peter Forsberg .30 .75
161 Kimmo Timonen .02 .10
162 Derek Morris .02 .10
163 Justin Williams .02 .10
164 Mike Comrie .10 .25
165 Mattias Weinhandl .02 .10
166 Dimitri Kalinin .02 .10
167 John LeClair .12 .30
168 Evgeni Nabokov .10 .25
169 Alexander Mogilny .10 .25
170 Derian Hatcher .02 .10
171 Adam Deadmarsh .02 .10
172 Alexei Smirnov .02 .10
173 Nikolai Antropov .02 .10
174 Radoslav Suchy .02 .10
175 Nick Boynton .02 .10
176 Marc Denis .10 .25
177 Ivan Huml .02 .10
178 Dan Blackburn .10 .25
179 Roman Cechmanek .10 .25
180 Tony Amonte .10 .25
181 Jason Blake .02 .10
182 Erik Cole .02 .10
183 P-M Bouchard .02 .10
184 Reed Low .02 .10
185 Geoff Sanderson .02 .10
186 Andrei Zyuzin .02 .10
187 J-S Giguere .10 .25
188 Patrick Marleau .10 .25
189 Nicklas Lidstrom .12 .30
190 Ilya Kovalchuk .15 .40
191 Petr Nedved .02 .10
192 Vincent Lecavalier .12 .30
193 Andreas Johansson .02 .10
194 Dennis Seidenberg .02 .10
195 Alex Tanguay .10 .25
196 Slava Kozlov .02 .10
197 Eric Brewer .02 .10
198 Adam Hall .02 .10
199 Steve Reinprecht .02 .10
200 Todd Bertuzzi .12 .30
201 Rob Blake .10 .25
202 Olaf Kolzig .10 .25
203 Roman Turek .10 .25
204 Brian Rolston .02 .10
205 Bill Guerin .10 .25
206 Johan Hedberg .10 .25
207 Vladimir Orszagh .02 .10
208 Jordan Leopold .02 .10
209 Donald Brashear .02 .10
210 Saku Koivu .12 .30
211 Dave Andreychuk .02 .10
212 Luc Robitaille .10 .25
213 Shaun Van Allen .02 .10
214 Trevor Linden .02 .10
215 Jason Allison .02 .10
216 Marty Turco .10 .25
217 Kyle McLaren .02 .10
218 Daniel Sedin .02 .10
219 Eric Belanger .02 .10
220 Mattias Ohlund .02 .10
221 Brad Richards .10 .25
222 Kyle Calder .02 .10
223 Alexander Frolov .02 .10
224 Tomas Kaberle .02 .10
225 Martin Havlat .10 .25
226 Patrick Roy .60 1.50
227 Jamie Lundmark .02 .10
228 Wade Redden .02 .10
229 Mark Recchi .10 .25
230 Tomas Vokoun .10 .25
231 Scott Niedermayer .02 .10
232 Bob Boughner .02 .10
233 Rick Dipietro .10 .25
234 Chris Gratton .02 .10
235 Keith Tkachuk .12 .30
236 Rostislav Klesla .02 .10
237 Ruslan Salei .02 .10
238 Jeff Friesen .02 .10
239 Felix Potvin .12 .30
240 Dany Heatley .15 .40
241 Brad Stuart .02 .10
242 Andrew Cassels .02 .10
243 Ray Whitney .02 .10
244 Chris Pronger .02 .10
245 Garth Snow .10 .25
246 Sean Hill .02 .10
247 Kristian Huselius .02 .10
248 Jamie Langenbrunner .02 .10
249 Martin St. Louis .10 .25
250 Ron Francis .10 .25
251 Tyler Wright .02 .10
252 Doug Gilmour .10 .25
253 Mike Dunham .10 .25
254 Jozef Stumpel .02 .10
255 Andrew Brunette .02 .10
256 Bobby Holik .02 .10
257 Brendan Shanahan .12 .30
258 Martin Gelinas .02 .10
259 Sergei Berezin .02 .10
260 Zigmund Palffy .10 .25
261 Yannick Tremblay .02 .10
262 Pasi Nurminen .10 .25
263 Robyn Regehr .02 .10
264 Espen Knutsen .02 .10
265 Al MacInnis .10 .25
266 Adam Oates .10 .25
267 Ryan Smyth .02 .10
268 Marco Sturm .02 .10
269 Tom Poti .02 .10
270 Brett Hull .15 .40
271 David Aebischer .10 .25
272 Milan Hejduk .12 .30
273 Steve McKenna .02 .10
274 Dick Tarnstrom .02 .10
275 Kenny Jonsson .02 .10
276 Glen Murray .02 .10
277 Stu Barnes .02 .10
278 Jay Bouwmeester .02 .10
279 Darius Kasparaitis BM .02 .10
280 Scott Stevens BM .10 .25
281 Zdeno Chara BM .02 .10
282 Donald Brashear BM .02 .10
283 Reed Low BM .02 .10
284 Jody Shelley BM .02 .10
285 Eric Cairns BM .02 .10
286 Brendan Witt BM .02 .10
287 Rob Ray BM .02 .10
288 Georges Laraque BM .02 .10
289 Brett Hull SH .15 .40
290 Martin Brodeur SH .30 .75
291 J-S Giguere SH .10 .25
292 Paul Kariya SH .12 .30
293 New Jersey Devils .12 .30
Stanley Cup Champions
294 Marty Turco AS .10 .25
295 Patrick Lalime AS .10 .25
296 Paul Kariya AS .12 .30
297 Nicklas Lidstrom AS .12 .30
298 Al MacInnis AS .10 .25
299 Scott Stevens AS .10 .25
300 Marian Gaborik AS .25 .60
301 Dany Heatley AS .15 .40
302 Jaromir Jagr AS .20 .50
303 Olli Jokinen AS .10 .25
304 Bill Guerin AS .10 .25
305 Todd Bertuzzi AS .12 .30
306 Bruno St. Jacques .02 .10
307 Mathieu Darche .02 .10
308 Mathias Johansson .02 .10
309 Joe DiPenta RC .12 .30
310 Milan Bartovic RC .12 .30
311 Rick Mrozik RC .02 .10
312 Kent McDonell RC .12 .30
313 Fernando Pisani .02 .10
314 Kip Brennan .02 .10
315 Miroslav Zalesak .02 .10
316 Peter Sejna RC .75 2.00
317 Matt Stajan RC 1.50 4.00
318 Ivan Ciernik .02 .10
319 Shaone Morrisonn .02 .10
320 Garnet Exelby .02 .10
321 Ari Ahonen .02 .10
322 Mike Rupp .02 .10
323 Kris Vernarsky .02 .10
324 Tomas Kurka .02 .10
325 Brandon Reid .02 .10
326 Jim Vandermeer .02 .10
327 Jared Aulin .02 .10
328 Cristobal Huet .10 .25
329 Alexei Ponikarovsky .02 .10
330 Alexei Semenov .02 .10
331 Patrice Bergeron RC 2.50 6.00
332 Jiri Hudler RC 1.50 4.00
333 Antti Miettinen RC .75 2.00
334 Eric Staal RC 2.50 6.00
335 Nathan Horton RC 2.00 5.00
336 Joffrey Lupul RC .75 2.00
337 Tuomo Ruutu RC 2.00 5.00
338 Jordin Tootoo RC 2.00 5.00
339 Dustin Brown RC .75 2.00
340 Marc-Andre Fleury RC 3.00 8.00
PP1 Marian Hossa .12 .30
PP2 Jaromir Jagr .25 .60
PP3 Curtis Joseph .20 .50
PP4 Mike Modano .25 .60
PP5 Markus Naslund .12 .30
PP6 Alexei Yashin .02 .10
NNO Rookie Redemption .20 .50

2003-04 Topps Blue

This 330-card set paralleled the base set but carried blue glitter borders and the O-Pee-Chee logo. These parallels were inserted at 1:4 and each card was serial numbered out of 500. The Rookie Redemption parallel card was inserted at 1:1298.
*STARS: 4X TO 10X BASIC CARDS
*ROOKIES: .75X TO 2X

2003-04 Topps Gold

This 330-card set paralleled the base set but carried gold glitter borders and the O-Pee-Chee logo. These parallels were inserted at 1:28 and each card was serial numbered out of 50. The Rookie Redemption parallel card was inserted at 1:9028. A "Golden Ticket" card redeemable for the entire gold parallel set was also randomly inserted at a rate of 1:97,056, due to scarcity, that card was not priced.
*STARS: 10X TO 25X BASIC CARDS
*ROOKIES: 2.5X TO 6X

2003-04 Topps Red

This 330-card set paralleled the base set but carried red glitter borders and the O-Pee-Chee logo. These parallels were inserted at 1:21and each card was serial numbered out of 100. The Rookie Redemption parallel card was inserted at 1:5468.
*STARS: 8X TO 20X BASIC CARDS
*ROOKIES: 2X TO 4X

2003-04 Topps First Overall Fabrics

SINGLE JSY.ODDS 1:4734
SINGLE PRINT RUN 50 SER.#'D SETS
DUAL JSY.ODDS 1:3769
DUAL PRINT RUN 25 SER.#'d SETS
ALL CARDS CARRY "FO" PREFIX
EL Eric Lindros 20.00 50.00
IL Ilya Kovalchuk 25.00 60.00
JT Joe Thornton 30.00 80.00
ML Mario Lemieux 50.00 125.00
MM Mike Modano 20.00 50.00
MS Mats Sundin 15.00 40.00
RN Rick Nash 20.00 50.00
VL Vincent Lecavalier 20.00 50.00

TIK J.Thornton/I.Kovalchuk 50.00 125.00
TVL J.Thornton/V.Lecavalier 50.00125.00
LMM M.Lemieux/M.Modano 75.00 200.00
LRN M.Lemieux/R.Nash 75.00 200.00
MMS M.Modano/M.Sundin 75.00200.00
SEL M.Sundin/E.Lindros 50.00 125.00
NIK R.Nash/I.Kovalchuk 60.00 150.00
LEL V.Lecavalier/E.Lindros 30.00 80.00

2003-04 Topps First Round Fabrics

INGLE JSY.ODDS 1:238
UAL JSY.ODDS 1:9706
LL CARDS CARRY A "FR" PREFIX
Y Alexei Yashin 6.00 15.00
G Bill Guerin 6.00 15.00
B Jay Bouwmeester 6.00 15.00
I Jarome Iginla 12.50 30.00
J Jaromir Jagr 10.00 25.00
L Jamie Lundmark 6.00 15.00
P Jason Spezza 10.00 25.00
B Todd Bertuzzi 6.00 15.00
GJI B.Guerin/J.Iginla 30.00 80.00
JJL J.Jagr/J.Lundmark
SJB J.Spezza/J.Bouwmeester 30.0080.00
BAY T.Bertuzzi/A.Yashin 50.00 125.00

2003-04 Topps/OPC Idols

serted at 1:12, this 60-card insert set onsisted of 3 subsets: Canadian Idols; USA dols and International Idols. USA and ternational Idols were found in Topps acks while Canadian Idols were found in anadian packs.
I1 Dany Heatley .30 .75
I2 Martin Brodeur .60 1.50
I3 Todd Bertuzzi .25 .60
I4 Mario Lemieux 1.50 4.00
I5 Joe Thornton .40 1.00
I6 Ed Belfour .25 .60
I7 Michael Peca .08 .20
I8 Jarome Iginla .30 .75
I9 Marty Turco .20 .50
I10 Steve Yzerman 1.25 3.00
I11 Patrick Lalime .20 .50
I12 Jose Theodore .30 .75
I13 Rick Nash .30 .75
I14 Joe Sakic .50 1.25
I15 Vincent Lecavalier .25 .60
I16 Mark Messier .25 .60
I17 Brendan Shanahan .25 .60
I18 Patrick Roy 1.25 3.00
I19 Paul Kariya .25 .60
I20 Jocelyn Thibault .20 .50
1 Marian Gaborik .50 1.25
2 Alex Kovalev .20 .50
3 Patrik Elias .20 .50
4 Daniel Alfredsson .20 .50
5 Alexei Yashin .08 .20
6 Peter Bondra .20 .50
7 Milan Hejduk .25 .60
8 Sergei Fedorov .30 .75
9 Alexander Mogilny .20 .50
10 Olli Jokinen .20 .50
11 Pavel Bure .25 .60
12 Jaromir Jagr .40 1.00
13 Nicklas Lidstrom .25 .60
14 Ilya Kovalchuk .30 .75
15 Teemu Selanne .25 .60
16 Marian Hossa .25 .60
17 Markus Naslund .25 .60
18 Peter Forsberg .60 1.50
19 Saku Koivu .25 .60
20 Mats Sundin .25 .60
JI1 Bill Guerin .20 .50
JI2 Jeremy Roenick .30 .75
JI3 Doug Weight .20 .50
JI4 Chris Drury .20 .50
JI5 Mike Modano .40 1.00
JI6 Chris Chelios .25 .60
JI7 Scott Gomez .08 .20
JI8 Brian Rolston .08 .20
JI9 Keith Tkachuk .25 .60
JI10 Mark Parrish .08 .20
JI11 John LeClair .25 .60
JI12 Mike Dunham .20 .50
JI13 Tyler Arnason .20 .50
JI14 Tony Amonte .20 .50
JI15 Mike York .08 .20
JI16 David Legwand .20 .50
JI17 Brian Leetch .20 .50
JI18 Brent Johnson .20 .50
JI19 Erik Cole .08 .20
JI20 Jamie Langenbrunner .08 .20

2003-04 Topps Lost Rookies

his 11-card set features "rookie" cards of uperstars who didn't have a card issued uring their rookie season. Cards from this et were inserted at 1:12.

BH Brett Hull .60 1.50
BS Brendan Shanahan .50 1.25
CJ Curtis Joseph .50 1.25
EB Ed Belfour .50 1.25
JR Jeremy Roenick .60 1.50
JS Joe Sakic 1.00 2.50
ML Mario Lemieux 3.00 8.00
MM Mike Modano .75 2.00
PR Patrick Roy 3.00 8.00
RF Ron Francis .50 1.25
SY Steve Yzerman 2.50 6.00

2003-04 Topps Own the Game

COMPLETE SET (20) 6.00 12.00
STATED ODDS 1:6
OTG1 Peter Forsberg .60 1.50
OTG2 Markus Naslund .20 .50
OTG3 Joe Thornton .30 .75
OTG4 Milan Hejduk .20 .50
OTG5 Todd Bertuzzi .20 .50
OTG6 Henrik Zetterberg .20 .50
OTG7 Tyler Arnason .15 .40
OTG8 Rick Nash .25 .60
OTG9 Ales Kotalik .15 .40
OTG10 Niko Kapanen .15 .40
OTG11 Martin Brodeur .60 1.50
OTG12 Patrick Lalime .15 .40
OTG13 Ed Belfour .20 .50
OTG14 Patrick Roy 1.00 2.50
OTG15 J-S Giguere .15 .40
OTG16 Jody Shelley .15 .40
OTG17 Reed Low .15 .40
OTG18 Matt Johnson .15 .40
OTG19 Wade Belak .15 .40
OTG20 Peter Worrell .15 .40

2003-04 Topps Signs of Toughness

STATED ODDS 1:1277
GL Georges Laraque 15.00 40.00
KS Kevin Sawyer 15.00 40.00
PW Peter Worrell 15.00 40.00
RR Rob Ray 20.00 50.00
SM Sandy McCarthy 15.00 40.00
SP Scott Parker 15.00 40.00
PJS P.J. Stock 15.00 40.00

2003-04 Topps Signs of Youth

STATED ODDS 1:635
BG Brian Gionta 5.00 12.00
BR Brad Richards 12.50 30.00
IK Ilya Kovalchuk 15.00 40.00
KH Kristian Huselius 10.00 25.00
RN Rick Nash 20.00 50.00
SW Stephen Weiss 10.00 25.00

2003-04 Topps Stanley Cup Heroes

STATED ODDS 1:36
BC Bobby Clarke 4.00 10.00
BN Bobby Nystrom 4.00 10.00
BS Billy Smith 4.00 10.00
DS Dave Schultz 4.00 10.00
GF Grant Fuhr 5.00 12.00
JL Jacques Lemaire 4.00 10.00
SS Serge Savard 4.00 10.00

2003-04 Topps Stanley Cup Heroes Autographs

STATED ODDS 1:250
BC Bobby Clarke 15.00 40.00
BN Bobby Nystrom 12.50 30.00
BS Billy Smith 12.50 30.00
DS Dave Schultz 12.50 30.00
GF Grant Fuhr 15.00 40.00
JL Jacques Lemaire 12.50 30.00
SS Serge Savard

2003-04 Topps Tough Materials

SINGLE JSY.ODDS 1:191
DUAL JSY.ODDS 1:1505
DL Darren Langdon 6.00 15.00
EC Eric Cairns 6.00 15.00
GL Georges Laraque 8.00 20.00
KS Kevin Sawyer 6.00 15.00
PW Peter Worrell 8.00 20.00
RL Reed Low 6.00 15.00
RR Rob Ray 8.00 20.00
SM Sandy McCarthy 6.00 15.00
SP Scott Parker 6.00 15.00
PJS P.J. Stock 8.00 20.00
GLSP G.Laraque/S.Parker 20.00 50.00
KSRL K.Sawyer/R.Low 12.50 30.00
PSRR P.Stock/R.Ray 20.00 50.00
PWDL P.Worrell/D.Langdon 20.00 50.00
SMEC S.McCarthy/E.Cairns 15.00 40.00

2003-04 Topps Tough Materials Signed

STATED ODDS 1:1277
GL Georges Laraque 15.00 40.00
KS Kevin Sawyer 15.00 40.00
PW Peter Worrell 15.00 40.00
RR Rob Ray 15.00 40.00
SM Sandy McCarthy 15.00 40.00
SP Scott Parker 15.00 40.00
PJS P.J. Stock 15.00 40.00

2003 Topps All-Star Block Party

Given away exclusively at the Topps booth during the 2003 NHL All-Star block party, this 6-card set resembles the base Topps set but carried different numbering and an All-Star log on the card fronts. Each card was numbered "X of 6".
COMPLETE SET (6) 12.00
1 Patrick Roy 2.00 5.00
2 Jaromir Jagr .80 2.00
3 Jarome Iginla .40 1.00
4 Henrik Zetterberg 1.60 3.00
5 Rick Nash 1.60 4.00
6 Jay Bouwmeester 1.20 2.00

2004 Topps NHL All-Star FANtasy

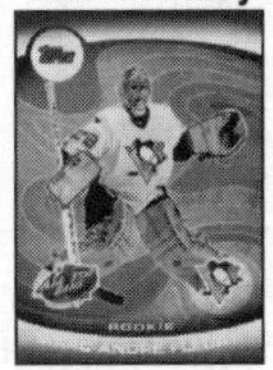

This 6-card set was given away via a wrapper redemption at the Topps booth during the 2004 NHL All-Star weekend. Cards are numbered "X of 6" on the card backs.
COMPLETE SET (6) 6.00 15.00
1 Marian Gaborik .60 1.50
2 Dwayne Roloson .60 1.50
3 Patrice Bergeron 1.50 5.00
4 Marc-Andre Fleury 2.00 5.00
5 Eric Staal 1.00 2.00
6 Tuomo Ruutu 1.25 3.00

2001-02 Topps Archives

Released in mid-February 2002, this 81-card set had an SRP of $4.00 for a 8-card pack and featured reprints of past Topps/OPC rookie cards. Each card was embossed with a gold Topps Archives stamp in the top right corner and printed on 24-point white card stock.
COMPLETE SET (81) 30.00 60.00
1 Andy Bathgate .50 1.25
2 Bill Gadsby .50 1.25
3 Tony Esposito .75 2.00
4 Harry Howell .40 1.00
5 Larry Robinson .40 1.00
6 Jacques Plante .75 2.00
7 Pierre Pilote .50 1.25
8 Glenn Hall .50 1.25
9 Dale Hunter .25 .60
10 Guy Lapointe .25 .60
11 Norm Ullman .40 1.00
12 Bryan Trottier .60 1.50
13 Alex Delvecchio .50 1.25
14 Stan Mikita .60 1.50
15 Neal Broten .25 .60
16 Bernie Parent .50 1.25
17 Johnny Bucyk .50 1.25
18 Rick Middleton .40 1.00
19 Bobby Clarke .50 1.25
20 Billy Smith .50 1.25
21 Peter Stastny .40 1.00
22 Tim Kerr .25 .60
23 Gerry Cheevers .60 1.50
24 Andy Moog .40 1.00
25 Dennis Hull .40 1.00
26 Nick Fotiu .25 .60
27 Marcel Dionne .40 1.00
28 Guy Lafleur .60 1.50
29 Yvan Cournoyer .50 1.25
30 Brian Mullen .25 .60
31 Wayne Cashman .25 .60
32 Steve Shutt .40 1.00
33 Grant Fuhr .40 1.00
34 Ed Johnston .40 1.00
35 Clark Gillies .25 .60
36 Rick MacLeish .25 .60
37 Denis Potvin .40 1.00
38 Bill Clement .25 .60
39 Darryl Sittler .50 1.25
40 Pierre Larouche .25 .60
41 Vic Hadfield .25 .60
42 Derek Sanderson .40 1.00
43 Reggie Leach .25 .60
44 Brian Propp .25 .60
45 Barry Melrose .40 1.00
46 Danny Gare .25 .60
47 Darren Pang .40 1.00
48 Dick Duff .25 .60
49 Joel Quenneville .25 .60
50 John Ferguson .40 1.00
51 Ed Westfall .25 .60
52 Johnny Bower .50 1.25
53 Serge Savard .50 1.25
54 Keith Magnuson .25 .60
55 Ken Hodge .25 .60
56 Garry Unger .25 .60
57 Lindy Ruff .25 .60
58 Glenn Resch .40 1.00
59 Gump Worsley .50 1.25
60 Bernie Federko .25 .60
61 Mike Foligno .25 .60
62 Milt Schmidt .40 1.00
63 Mike Bossy .40 1.00
64 Ron Low .40 1.00
65 Jacques Lemaire .50 1.25
66 Dave Schultz .40 1.00
67 Glen Sather .40 1.00
68 Doug Wilson .25 .60
69 Terry Sawchuk 1.00 2.50
70 Mike Milbury .25 .60
71 Terry O'Reilly .40 1.00
72 Red Kelly .50 1.25
73 Peter McNab .25 .60
74 Paul Holmgren .25 .60
75 Ken Linseman .25 .60
76 Tim Horton .50 1.25
77 Bobby Smith .25 .60
78 Bobby Hull .75 2.00
79 Pat LaFontaine .40 1.00
80 Pete Mahovlich .25 .60
81 Mike Gartner .40 1.00

2001-02 Topps Archives Arena Seats

This 28-card set was inserted at a rate of 1:10 and featured a piece of an arena seat from either Boston Gardens, Maple Leaf Gardens or the Montreal Forum. Each card carried a reprinted card photo alongside the seat piece.
ASAD Alex Delvecchio 5.00 12.00
ASBF Bernie Federko 5.00 12.00
ASBS Bobby Smith 5.00 12.00
ASBT Bryan Trottier 5.00 12.00
ASDH Dennis Hull 5.00 12.00
ASDS Derek Sanderson 5.00 12.00
ASDSI Darryl Sittler 5.00 12.00
ASDWI Doug Wilson 5.00 12.00
ASGC Gerry Cheevers 6.00 15.00
ASGHA Glenn Hall 6.00 15.00
ASGL Guy Lapointe 5.00 12.00
ASGLA Guy Lafleur 5.00 12.00
ASJB John Bucyk 5.00 12.00
ASJL Jacques Lemaire 5.00 12.00
ASKH Ken Hodge 5.00 12.00
ASLR Larry Robinson 5.00 12.00
ASMD Marcel Dionne 5.00 12.00
ASNB Neal Broten 5.00 12.00
ASNU Norm Ullman 5.00 12.00
ASPL Pierre Larouche 5.00 12.00
ASPP Pierre Pilote 5.00 12.00
ASSM Stan Mikita 6.00 15.00
ASSSA Serge Savard 5.00 12.00
ASSSH Steve Shutt 5.00 12.00
ASTE Tony Esposito 6.00 15.00
ASTO Terry O'Reilly 5.00 12.00
ASWC Wayne Cashman 5.00 12.00
ASYC Yvan Cournoyer 5.00 12.00

2001-02 Topps Archives Autographs

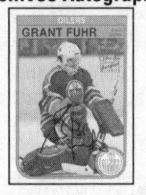

Inserted at an overall rate of 1:17 hobby or retail packs, these cards were reprints of rookie cards of past players adorned with authentic autographs. The set was skip-numbered and a true checklist was never released, therefore the cards are listed in the original checklist order.
1 Gerry Cheevers 10.00 25.00
2 Yvan Cournoyer 10.00 25.00
3 Denis Potvin 10.00 25.00
4 John Bucyk 10.00 25.00
5 Glenn Hall 10.00 25.00
6 Pierre Pilote 10.00 25.00
7 Norm Ullman 10.00 25.00
8 Jacques Lemaire 10.00 25.00
9 Grant Fuhr 15.00 40.00
10 Stan Mikita 20.00 50.00
11 Guy Lafleur 20.00 50.00
12 Tony Esposito 25.00 60.00
13 Alex Delvecchio 10.00 25.00
14 Dennis Hull 10.00 25.00
15 Marcel Dionne 10.00 25.00
16 Bobby Clarke 20.00 50.00
17 Darryl Sittler 10.00 25.00
18 Dave Schultz SP 30.00 80.00
19 Bryan Trottier 10.00 25.00
20 Billy Smith SP 30.00 80.00
21 Terry O'Reilly 25.00 60.00
22 Serge Savard SP 15.00 40.00
23 Vic Hadfield SP 60.00 150.00
24 Rick Middleton 10.00 25.00
25 Peter McNab 10.00 25.00
26 Peter Stastny SP 40.00 100.00
27 Ken Linseman 10.00 25.00
28 Ed Westfall SP 60.00 150.00
29 Clark Gillies 25.00 60.00
30 Bobby Hull SP 75.00 200.00

2001-02 Topps Archives Autoproofs

Inserted at a rate of 1:1696 hobby or retail packs, these cards were actual vintage cards that were bought back by Topps, autographed by the player and then randomly inserted into packs. Each card was serial-numbered out of 50. The three cards listed below are the only cards known to exist. Due to scarcity and volatility, these cards are not priced.
1 Marcel Dionne
2 Bobby Clarke
3 Denis Potvin
4 Guy Lafleur
Assists Leaders

2001-02 Topps Archives Relics

This 15-card set featured smaller rookie reprint photos alongside swatches of game-used jerseys and sticks. Jersey cards were inserted at 1:8 and stick cards were inserted at 1:264. Jersey swatches were affixed using a rubber seal around the swatch.
*MULT.COLOR SWATCH : .75X TO 1.5X HI
JAD Alex Delvecchio J 5.00 12.00
JAM Andy Moog J 5.00 12.00
JBC Bobby Clarke J 15.00 40.00
JBM Brian Mullen J 5.00 12.00
JEW Ed Westfall J 5.00 12.00
JGF Grant Fuhr J 8.00 20.00
JLR Larry Robinson J 6.00 15.00
JMG Mike Gartner J 6.00 15.00
JPM Pete Mahovlich J 5.00 12.00
JSM Stan Mikita J 6.00 15.00
JBIS Billy Smith J 6.00 15.00
JBOS Bobby Smith J 5.00 12.00
SBC Bobby Clarke S 15.00 40.00
SDH Dale Hawerchuk S 8.00 20.00
STE Tony Esposito S 15.00 40.00

2003-04 Topps C55

This 165-card set was released in late December and pays homage to the original 1911-12 C55 set. Ten different players have two different cards each depicting them in either a cropped head and shoulders shot or a full length body shot, the cards are noted below with a "B" suffix (for checklisting purposes only). The set is considered incomplete without these 10 variation cards.

A complete original C55 set was also inserted into packs at a rate of 1:6390. Since the buyback cards were not altered, prices can be found under the original set listing.
COMPLETE SET (165) 30.00 60.00
COMP.SET w/o SP's
1 Peter Forsberg .50 1.25
1B Peter Forsberg Full Length .50 1.25
2 Brian Leetch .15 .40
3 Jarome Iginla .25 .60
4 Scott Stevens .15 .40
5 Nicklas Lidstrom .20 .50
6 Patrick Lalime .15 .40
7 Henrik Zetterberg .20 .50
7B Henrik Zetterberg Full Length .20 .50
8 Patrick Marleau .15 .40
9 Mike Modano .30 .75
10 Marian Hossa .20 .50
11 Owen Nolan .15 .40
12 John Madden .10 .25
13 Mats Sundin .20 .50
14 Adam Hall .10 .25
15 Ron Francis .15 .40
16 Peter Bondra .15 .40
17 Ilya Kovalchuk .25 .60
17B Ilya Kovalchuk Full Length .25 .60
18 Miroslav Satan .15 .40
19 Joe Sakic .40 1.00
20 Vincent Lecavalier .20 .50
21 Rick Nash .25 .60
21B Rick Nash Full Length .25 .60
22 Anson Carter .15 .40
23 Doug Weight .15 .40
24 Rick DiPietro .15 .40
25 Tyler Arnason .15 .40
26 Mike Johnson .10 .25
27 Jeremy Roenick .25 .60
28 Teemu Selanne .20 .50
29 Roberto Luongo .25 .60
30 Martin Brodeur .50 1.25
30B Martin Brodeur Full Length .50 1.25
31 Bill Guerin .15 .40
32 Tim Connolly .10 .25
33 Roman Turek .15 .40
34 Olli Jokinen .15 .40
35 Radek Bonk .10 .25
36 Steve Rucchin .10 .25
37 Barret Jackman .15 .40
38 Dominik Hasek .40 1.00
39 Petr Nedved .10 .25
40 Marian Gaborik .40 1.00
40B Marian Gaborik Full Length .40 1.00
41 Josef Vasicek .10 .25
42 Ladislav Nagy .10 .25
43 Felix Potvin .15 .40
44 Jay Bouwmeester .15 .40
45 Sergei Gonchar .10 .25
46 Niklas Hagman .10 .25
47 Glen Murray .10 .25
48 Kyle Calder .10 .25
49 Ed Belfour .20 .50
50 Milan Hejduk .20 .50
51 Alex Kovalev .15 .40
52 Petr Sykora .10 .25
53 Scott Hartnell .10 .25
54 Tony Amonte .15 .40
55 Ed Jovanovski .15 .40
56 Sergei Zubov .10 .25
57 Mark Recchi .15 .40
58 Markus Naslund .20 .50
59 Zigmund Palffy .15 .40
60 Marty Turco .15 .40
61 Jocelyn Thibault .15 .40
62 Martin Biron .15 .40
63 Roman Hamrlik .10 .25
64 Stanislav Chistov .10 .25
65 Tomas Kaberle .10 .25
66 Mario Lemieux 1.25 3.00
66B Mario Lemieux Full Length 1.25 3.00
67 Rob Blake .15 .40
68 Jaromir Jagr .30 .75
69 Nikolai Khabibulin .20 .50
70 Brett Hull .25 .60
71 Slava Kozlov .10 .25
72 Michael Peca .10 .25
73 Jeff O'Neill .10 .25
74 Joe Nieuwendyk .15 .40
75 Yanic Perreault .10 .25
76 Derian Hatcher .10 .25
77 Chris Gratton .10 .25
78 Olaf Kolzig .15 .40
79 Alexei Yashin .10 .25
80 Martin St. Louis .15 .40
81 Chris Pronger .15 .40
82 Dick Tarnstrom .10 .25
83 Nick Schultz .10 .25
84 Ossi Vaananen .10 .25
85 Tie Domi .15 .40
86 Patrik Elias .15 .40
87 Jim Vandermeer .10 .25
88 Alexei Morozov .10 .25
89 Alexander Mogilny .15 .40
90 Dany Heatley .25 .60
91 Marcel Hossa .10 .25
92 Mike Comrie .15 .40
92B Mike Comrie Full Length .15 .40
93 Niko Kapanen .10 .25
94 David Legwand .15 .40
95 Alex Tanguay .15 .40
96 Alyn McCauley .10 .25
97 Brendan Morrison .15 .40
98 Chris Drury .15 .40
99 Paul Kariya .20 .50
100 Joe Thornton .30 .75
100B Joe Thornton Full Length .30 .75
101 Tomas Vokoun .15 .40
102 Tommy Salo .15 .40
103 Brad Richards .15 .40
104 Geoff Sanderson .10 .25
105 Daniel Briere .10 .25
106 Mike Dunham .15 .40
107 Kyle McLaren .10 .25
108 Zdeno Chara .10 .25
109 Curtis Joseph .20 .50
110 Todd Bertuzzi .20 .50
111 Saku Koivu .20 .50
112 Martin Havlat .15 .40
113 Dave Andreychuk .10 .25
114 Dan Cloutier .15 .40
115 Pavol Demitra .15 .40
116 Dave Scatchard .10 .25
117 Ryan Smyth .10 .25
118 Craig Conroy .10 .25
119 Eric Brewer .10 .25
120 J-S Giguere .15 .40
120B J-S Giguere Full Length .15 .40
121 Alexander Frolov .10 .25
122 Al MacInnis .15 .40
123 Martin Straka .10 .25
124 Brian Rolston .10 .25
125 Jamie Langenbrunner .10 .25
126 Pierre-Marc Bouchard .10 .25
127 Jan Bulis .10 .25
128 Rostislav Klesla .10 .25
129 Pasi Nurminen .15 .40
130 Jose Theodore .25 .60
131 Tuomo Ruutu RC 2.00 5.00
132 Andrew Peters RC 1.00 2.50
133 Jordin Tootoo RC 1.50 4.00
134 Joe DiPenta RC 1.00 2.50
135 Milan Bartovic RC 1.00 2.50
136 Rick Mrozik RC 1.00 2.50
137 Kent McDonell RC 1.00 2.50
138 Antti Miettinen RC 1.00 2.50
139 Alexander Semin RC 1.50 4.00
140 Dustin Brown RC 1.00 2.50
141 Peter Sejna RC 1.00 2.50
142 Matt Stajan RC 1.50 4.00
143 Brent Burns RC 1.00 2.50
144 Paul Martin RC 1.00 2.50
145 Antoine Vermette RC 1.00 2.50
146 Sean Bergenheim RC 1.00 2.50
147 Joni Pitkanen RC 1.00 2.50
148 Patrice Bergeron RC 2.50 6.00
149 Eric Staal RC 3.00 8.00
150 Dan Hamhuis RC 1.00 2.50
151 Marc-Andre Fleury RC 4.00 10.00
152 Jiri Hudler RC 1.25 3.00
153 David Hale RC 1.00 2.50
154 Milan Michalek RC 1.50 4.00
155 John-Michael Liles RC 1.00 2.50

2003-04 Topps C55 Minis

These mini-cards were inserted one per pack and parallel the base set. There were several different parallels of the mini set that carried differing card backs, those sets proceed this set listing.
*STARS: .5X TO 1.25X BASE HI
*ROOKIES: .5X TO 1.25X

2003-04 Topps C55 Minis American Back

*BLACK STARS: .75X TO 2X BASE HI
*BLACK ROOKIES: .6X TO 1.5X
BLACK ODDS 1:9
*RED STARS: 2X TO 5X
*RED ROOKIES: .75X TO 2X
RED ODDS 1:33

2003-04 Topps C55 Minis Bazooka Back

This 165-card parallel set was the toughest pull of the variations. It is believed that only 5 copies of each card exist.
STATED ODDS 1:687
NOT PRICED DUE TO SCARCITY

2003-04 Topps C55 Minis Brooklyn Back

*STARS: .75X TO 2X BASE HI
*ROOKIES: .6X TO 1.5X
STATED ODDS 1:9

2003-04 Topps C55 Minis Hat Trick Back

*STARS: 2X TO 5X BASE HI
*ROOKIES: .75X TO 2X
STATED ODDS 1:38

2003-04 Topps C55 Minis O Canada Back

*BLACK STARS: .75X TO 2X BASE HI
*BLACK ROOKIES: .6X TO 1.5X
BLACK ODDS 1:9
*RED STARS: 2X TO 5X
*RED ROOKIES: .75X TO 2X
RED ODDS 1:33

2003-04 Topps C55 Minis Stanley Cup Back

*STARS: .6X TO 1.5X
*ROOKIES: .6X TO 1.5X
STATED ODDS 1:4

2003-04 Topps C55 Autographs

This 12-card set featured certified autographs on mini-cards. Each card was held in a grey "C55" holder and shrink wrapped in clear plastic.
GROUP A ODDS 1:81
GROUP B ODDS 1:417

GROUP C ODDS 1:71
TA-CD Chris Drury C 6.00 15.00
TA-EC Erik Cole A 6.00 15.00
TA-HZ Henrik ZetterbergÂ A 10.00 25.00
TA-IK Ilya KovalchukÂ B 12.50 30.00
TA-JG J-S Giguere AÂ 8.00 20.00
TA-KH Kristian Huselius A 6.00 15.00
TA-MH Marian Hossa A 8.00 20.00
TA-PE Patrik EliasÂ C 6.00 15.00
TA-RN Rick NashÂ AÂ Â 10.00 25.00
TA-RV Radim Vrbata C 6.00 15.00
TA-SW Steve WeissÂ A 6.00 15.00
TA-TB Todd BertuzziÂ C 8.00 20.00

2003-04 Topps C55 Award Winners

These decoy cards represented trophy winners from the previous campaign. Cards from this set and the Stanley Cup Winners set were inserted one per non-memorabilia pack.

1 Mighty Ducks of Anaheim .20 .50
2 New Jersey Devils .20 .50
3 Ottawa Senators .20 .50
4 Barret Jackman .20 .50
5 Brendan Shanahan .25 .60
6 Peter Forsberg .40 1.00
7 Martin Brodeur .40 1.00
8 Alexander Mogilny .20 .50
9 Steve Yzerman .75 2.00
10 Nicklas Lidstrom .25 .60
11 Markus Naslund .25 .60
12 Milan Hejduk .25 .60
13 Peter Forsberg .40 1.00
14 Jere Lehtinen .20 .50
15 J-S Giguere .20 .50
16 Martin Brodeur .40 1.00

2003-04 Topps C55 Relics

This 45-card set featured jersey swatches on mini-cards. Each card was held in a grey "C55" holder and shrink wrapped in clear plastic.

GROUP A ODDS 1:15788
GROUP B ODDS 1:948
GROUP C ODDS 1:268
GROUP D ODDS 1:56
GROUP E ODDS 1:15
TRAH Adam Hall E 3.00 8.00
TRAS Alexander Svitov E 3.00 8.00
TRAY Alexei Yashin E 3.00 8.00
TRBG Bill Guerin E 3.00 8.00
TRBH Brett Hull D 8.00 20.00
TRBM Brendan Morrison D 3.00 8.00
TRBRA Branko Radivojevic E 3.00 8.00
TRBR Brad Richards D 4.00 10.00
TRDA Daniel Alfredsson D 4.00 10.00
TRDH Dany Heatley C 6.00 15.00
TRDL David Legwand C 4.00 10.00
TREB Ed Belfour D 6.00 15.00
TRGL Georges Laraque E 3.00 8.00
TRIK Ilya Kovalchuk D 8.00 20.00
TRJB Jay Bouwmeester E 3.00 8.00
TRJI Jarome Iginla E 6.00 15.00
TRJJ Jaromir Jagr E 8.00 20.00
TRJL Jordan Leopold E 3.00 8.00
TRJS Jason Spezza E 6.00 15.00
TRJT Jose Theodore E 6.00 15.00
TRJTH Joe Thornton E 8.00 20.00
TRMC Mike Comrie B 8.00 20.00
TRMG Marian Gaborik E 8.00 20.00
TRMHE Milan Hejduk D 5.00 12.00
TRMH Marian Hossa E 5.00 12.00
TRML Mario Lemieux A 250.00 400.00
TRMM Mike Modano B 50.00 125.00
TRMN Markus Naslund D 5.00 12.00
TRMS Mats Sundin D 5.00 12.00
TRMTÂ Marty Turco E 4.00 10.00
TRNK Nikolai Khabibulin E 5.00 12.00
TRNS Nick Schultz E 3.00 8.00
TRPB Pavel Bure E 5.00 12.00
TRPK Paul Kariya B 30.00 80.00
TRPL Patrick Lalime D 4.00 10.00
TRRB Rob Blake E 4.00 10.00
TRRL Roberto Luongo C 6.00 15.00
TRRM Ryan Miller E 5.00 12.00
TRRN Rick Nash E 6.00 15.00
TRSK Saku Koivu E 5.00 12.00
TRSN Scott Niedermayer B 30.00 80.00
TRSP Scott Parker E 3.00 8.00
TRTB Todd Bertuzzi E 5.00 12.00
TRTC Tim Connolly B 20.00 50.00
TRVL Vincent Lecavalier B 50.00 125.00

2003-04 Topps C55 Stanley Cup Winners

These decoy cards represented Cup winners from previous years. Cards from this set and the Award Winners set were inserted one per non-memorabilia pack.

1 Ottawa Senators .30 .75
2 New York Rangers .30 .75
3 Boston Bruins .30 .75
4 Montreal Canadiens .30 .75
5 Montreal Canadiens .30 .75
6 Toronto Maple Leafs .30 .75
7 New York Rangers .30 .75
8 Chicago Blackhawks .30 .75
9 Montreal Maroons .30 .75
10 Detroit Red Wings .30 .75
11 Detroit Red Wings .30 .75
12 Chicago Blackhawks .30 .75
13 Boston Bruins .30 .75
14 New York Rangers .30 .75
15 Boston Bruins .30 .75
16 Toronto Maple Leafs .30 .75
17 Detroit Red Wings .30 .75
18 Montreal Canadiens .30 .75
19 Toronto Maple Leafs .30 .75
20 Montreal Canadiens .30 .75
21 Toronto Maple Leafs .30 .75
22 Toronto Maple Leafs .30 .75
23 Toronto Maple Leafs .30 .75
24 Detroit Red Wings .30 .75
25 Toronto Maple Leafs .30 .75
26 Detroit Red Wings .30 .75
27 Montreal Canadiens .30 .75
28 Detroit Red Wings .30 .75
29 Detroit Red Wings .30 .75
30 Montreal Canadiens .30 .75
31 Montreal Canadiens .30 .75
32 Montreal Canadiens .30 .75
33 Montreal Canadiens .30 .75
34 Montreal Canadiens .30 .75
35 Chicago Blackhawks .30 .75
36 Toronto Maple Leafs .30 .75
37 Toronto Maple Leafs .30 .75
38 Toronto Maple Leafs .30 .75
39 Montreal Canadiens .30 .75
40 Montreal Canadiens .30 .75
41 Toronto Maple Leafs .30 .75
42 Montreal Canadiens .30 .75
43 Montreal Canadiens .30 .75
44 Boston Bruins .30 .75
45 Montreal Canadiens .30 .75
46 Boston Bruins .30 .75
47 Montreal Canadiens .30 .75
48 Philadelphia Flyers .30 .75
49 Philadelphia Flyers .30 .75
50 Montreal Canadiens .30 .75
51 Montreal Canadiens .30 .75
52 Montreal Canadiens .30 .75
53 Montreal Canadiens .30 .75
54 New York Islanders .30 .75
55 New York Islanders .30 .75
56 New York Islanders .30 .75
57 New York Islanders .30 .75
58 Edmonton Oilers .30 .75
59 Edmonton Oilers .30 .75
60 Montreal Canadiens .30 .75
61 Edmonton Oilers .30 .75
62 Edmonton Oilers .30 .75
63 Calgary Flames .30 .75
64 Edmonton Oilers .30 .75
65 Pittsburgh Penguins .30 .75
66 Pittsburgh Penguins .30 .75
67 Montreal Canadiens .30 .75
68 New York Rangers .30 .75
69 New Jersey Devils .30 .75
70 Colorado Avalanche .30 .75
71 Detroit Red Wings .30 .75
72 Detroit Red Wings .30 .75
73 Dallas Stars .30 .75
74 New Jersey Devils .30 .75
75 Colorado Avalanche .30 .75
76 Detroit Red Wings .30 .75
77 New Jersey Devils .30 .75

2002-03 Topps Factory Set

Available only in gift box factory sets, this 340-card set paralleled the regular Topps and OPC sets but featured gold foil highlights instead of the silver highlights found on cards distributed in packs. Each gift box contained 330 veteran cards, a redemption card for a 10-card rookie subset, a 20-card Hometown Heroes set, and a Patrick Roy Reprint card.

COMPLETE FACTORY SET (340) 25.00 50.00
COMP.BASE SET (330) 20.00 40.00
*STARS: .5X TO 1.25X REG.TOPPS
*ROOKIES: .6X TO 1.5X REG.TOPPS

2002-03 Topps Factory Set Hometown Heroes

This 20-card set was inserted into every gift box of Topps and OPC Complete factory set. The cards paralleled the regular Hometown Heroes cards found in packs but did not carry the same glossy finish. Cards HHU1-

HHU20 were available in Topps and HHC1-HHC20 were available in OPC.
*SAME VALUE AS REGULAR HOME.HERO

2002-03 Topps Factory Set Patrick Roy Reprints

Available in gift boxes of Topps and OPC Complete factory set, this 14-card set paralleled the reprints available in packs, but carried a silver foil logo.

COMPLETE SET (14) 30.00 60.00
COMMON ROY (1-14) 2.50 6.00

1999-00 Topps/OPC Chrome

The 1999-00 Topps/OPC Chrome set released as a 297-card set printed on 16-point foil stock and consisted of 247 regular player cards and 39 subset cards, (24) 1999 NHL Draft Picks, 4-CHL Stars, and 11-Magic Moments which is comprised of five different versions of each card highlighting five significant moments in each player's career. Packaged in 24-pack boxes and 4-card packs, Topps/OPC Chrome packs carried a suggested retail price of $3.00.

COMPLETE SET (297) 150.00 300.00
COMP.SET w/MMs (341) 200.00 400.00
FIVE VERSIONS OF MM 276-286 EXIST
ALL VERSIONS SAME VALUE
*OPC CHROME: 1X TO 1.5X TOPPS CHROME
1 Joe Sakic 1.00 2.50
2 Alexei Yashin .25 .60
3 Paul Kariya .50 1.25
4 Keith Tkachuk .50 1.25
5 Jaromir Jagr .75 2.00
6 Mike Modano .75 2.00
7 Eric Lindros .50 1.25
8 Zigmund Palffy .40 1.00
9 Dominik Hasek 1.00 2.50
10 Pavel Bure .50 1.25
11 Ray Bourque .75 2.00
12 Peter Forsberg 1.25 3.00
13 Al MacInnis .40 1.00
14 Steve Yzerman 2.50 6.00
15 Mats Sundin .50 1.25
16 Patrick Roy 2.50 6.00
17 Teemu Selanne .50 1.25
18 Keith Primeau .25 .60
19 John LeClair .50 1.25
20 Martin Brodeur 1.25 3.00
21 Joe Thornton .75 2.00
22 Rob Blake .40 1.00
23 Ron Francis .40 1.00
24 Grant Fuhr .40 1.00
25 Nicklas Lidstrom .50 1.25
26 Vladimir Orszagh RC .25 .60
27 Glen Wesley .25 .60
28 Adam Deadmarsh .25 .60
29 Zdeno Chara .25 .60
30 Brian Leetch .50 1.25
31 Valeri Bure .25 .60
32 Ryan Smyth .25 .60
33 Jean-Sebastien Aubin .40 1.00
34 Dave Reid .25 .60
35 Ed Jovanovski .25 .60
36 Anders Eriksson .25 .60
37 Mike Ricci .25 .60
38 Todd Bertuzzi .50 1.25
39 Shawn Bates .25 .60
40 Kip Miller .25 .60
41 Jozef Stumpel .40 1.00
42 Jeremy Roenick .60 1.50
43 Todd Marchant .25 .60
44 Josh Holden .25 .60
45 Rob Niedermayer .25 .60
46 Cory Sarich .25 .60
47 Nikolai Khabibulin .40 1.00
48 Marty McInnis .25 .60
49 Marty Reasoner .40 1.00
50 Gary Roberts .25 .60
51 Manny Malhotra .40 1.00
52 Adam Foote .25 .60
53 Luc Robitaille .40 1.00
54 Bryan Marchment .25 .60
55 Mark Janssens .25 .60
56 Steve Heinze .25 .60
57 Cory Stillman .25 .60
58 Guy Hebert .40 1.00
59 Mike Richter .50 1.25
60 Jamie Langenbrunner .25 .60
61 Wade Redden .25 .60
62 Steve Smith .25 .60
63 Daniil Markov .25 .60
64 Erik Rasmussen .25 .60
65 Glen Murray .25 .60
66 Alexei Kovalev .25 .60
67 Peter Bondra .40 1.00
68 Dimitri Khristich .25 .60
69 Sami Kapanen .25 .60
70 Tom Poti .25 .60
71 Trevor Linden .25 .60
72 Tomas Vokoun .40 1.00
73 Steve Webb .25 .60
74 Jarome Iginla .60 1.50
75 Scott Mellanby .25 .60
76 Mattias Ohlund .25 .60
77 Steve Konowalchuk .25 .60
78 Bryan Berard .40 1.00
79 Chris Pronger .40 1.00
80 Teppo Numminen .25 .60
81 John MacLean .25 .60
82 Jeff Hackett .40 1.00
83 Ray Whitney .25 .60
84 Chris Osgood .40 1.00
85 Doug Zmolek .25 .60
86 Curtis Brown .25 .60
87 Reid Simpson .25 .60
88 Milan Hejduk .50 1.25
89 Donald Audette .25 .60
90 Saku Koivu .50 1.25
91 Martin Straka .25 .60
92 Mark Messier .50 1.25
93 Richard Zednik .25 .60
94 Curtis Joseph .50 1.25
95 Colin Forbes .25 .60
96 Jeff Friesen .25 .60
97 Eric Brewer .25 .60
98 Darius Kasparaitis .25 .60
99 Marian Hossa .50 1.25
100 Petr Sykora .25 .60
101 Vladimir Malakhov .25 .60
102 Jamie Storr .40 1.00
103 Doug Gilmour .40 1.00
104 Doug Weight .40 1.00
105 Derian Hatcher .25 .60
106 Chris Drury .40 1.00
107 Arturs Irbe .40 1.00
108 Fred Brathwaite .40 1.00
109 Jason Allison .25 .60
110 Roman Hamrlik .25 .60
111 Rico Fata .25 .60
112 Janne Niinimaa .25 .60
113 Kenny Jonsson .25 .60
114 Marco Sturm .25 .60
115 Steve Thomas .25 .60
116 Garth Snow .40 1.00
117 Rick Tocchet .40 1.00
118 Jean-Marc Pelletier .40 1.00
119 Bobby Holik .25 .60
120 Sergei Fedorov .75 2.00
121 J-P Dumont .40 1.00
122 Jason Woolley .25 .60
123 James Patrick .25 .60
124 Blake Sloan .50 1.25
125 Marcus Nilsson .25 .60
126 Shayne Corson .25 .60
127 Tom Fitzgerald .25 .60
128 Brian Rolston .25 .60
129 Ron Tugnutt .40 1.00
130 Mark Recchi .40 1.00
131 Matthew Barnaby .25 .60
132 Olaf Kolzig .40 1.00
133 Paul Mara .25 .60
134 Patrick Marleau .50 1.25
135 Magnus Arvedson .25 .60
136 Felix Potvin .50 1.25
137 Bill Guerin .40 1.00
138 Brett Hull .60 1.50
139 Vitali Yachmenev .25 .60
140 Ruslan Salei .25 .60
141 Mark Parrish .25 .60
142 Randy Cunneyworth .25 .60
143 Damian Rhodes .40 1.00
144 Daniel Briere .25 .60
145 Craig Conroy .25 .60
146 Sergei Gonchar .25 .60
147 Vincent Lecavalier .50 1.25
148 Adam Graves .25 .60
149 Doug Bodger .25 .60
150 Jeff O'Neill .25 .60
151 Darby Hendrickson .25 .60
152 Sergei Samsonov .40 1.00
153 Ed Belfour .50 1.25
154 Robert Svehla .25 .60
155 Cliff Ronning .25 .60
156 Brendan Morrison .40 1.00
157 Daniel Alfredsson .40 1.00
158 Eric Desjardins .40 1.00
159 Mike Vernon .40 1.00
160 Vadim Sharifijanov .25 .60
161 Jaroslav Svejkovsky .25 .60
162 Michael Peca .40 1.00
163 Shane Willis .25 .60
164 Sandis Ozolinsh .25 .60
165 Mathieu Dandenault .25 .60
166 Martin Rucinsky .25 .60
167 Scott Stevens .25 .60
168 Sami Salo .25 .60
169 Tom Barrasso .40 1.00
170 Chris Gratton .25 .60
171 Markus Naslund .50 1.25
172 Mike Johnson .25 .60
173 Bob Boughner .25 .60
174 Todd Simpson .25 .60
175 Fredrik Olausson .25 .60
176 Jocelyn Thibault .40 1.00
177 Juha Ylonen .25 .60
178 Brad Bombardir .25 .60
179 Jan Hrdina .25 .60
180 Adrian Aucoin .25 .60
181 Mike Eagles .25 .60
182 Petr Nedved .40 1.00
183 Rem Murray .25 .60
184 Mikael Renberg .40 1.00
185 Mike Eastwood .25 .60
186 Byron Dafoe .40 1.00
187 Tony Amonte .40 1.00
188 Darren McCarty .25 .60
189 Sergei Krivokrasov .25 .60
190 Dave Lowry .25 .60
191 Michal Handzus .40 1.00
192 Tie Domi .40 1.00
193 Brian Holzinger .25 .60
194 Jason Arnott .25 .60
195 Jose Theodore .60 1.50
196 Brendan Shanahan .50 1.25
197 Derek Morris .25 .60
198 Steve Rucchin .25 .60
199 Kevin Hodson .40 1.00
200 Oleg Kvasha .25 .60
201 John Vanbiesbrouck .40 1.00
202 Adam Oates .40 1.00
203 Anson Carter .40 1.00
204 Sebastien Bordeleau .25 .60
205 Pavol Demitra .40 1.00
206 Owen Nolan .40 1.00
207 Pavel Rosa .25 .60
208 Petr Svoboda .25 .60
209 Tomas Kaberle .25 .60
210 Claude Lapointe .25 .60
211 Todd Harvey .25 .60
212 Trent McCleary .25 .60
213 Vyacheslav Kozlov .25 .60
214 Marc Denis .40 1.00
215 Joe Nieuwendyk .40 1.00
216 Kelly Buchberger .25 .60
217 Tommy Albelin .25 .60
218 Kyle McLaren .25 .60
219 Chris Chelios .50 1.25
220 Joel Bouchard .25 .60
221 Mats Lindgren .25 .60
222 Jyrki Lumme .25 .60
223 Pierre Turgeon .40 1.00
224 Bill Muckalt .25 .60
225 Antti Aalto .25 .60
226 Jere Lehtinen .40 1.00
227 Theo Fleury .25 .60
228 Dmitri Mironov .25 .60
229 Scott Niedermayer .25 .60
230 Sean Burke .40 1.00
231 Eric Daze .40 1.00
232 Alexei Zhitnik .25 .60
233 Christian Matte .25 .60
234 Patrik Elias .40 1.00
235 Alexandre Korolyuk .25 .60
236 Sergei Berezin .25 .60
237 Ray Ferraro .25 .60
238 Rod Brind'Amour .40 1.00
239 Darcy Tucker .25 .60
240 Darryl Sydor .25 .60
241 Mike Dunham .40 1.00
242 Marc Bergevin .25 .60
243 Ray Sheppard .25 .60
244 Miroslav Satan .40 1.00
245 Andreas Dackell .25 .60
246 Mike Grier .25 .60
247 Alexei Zhamnov .25 .60
248 David Legwand .40 1.00
249 Daniel Tkaczuk .25 .60
250 Roberto Luongo .60 1.50
251 Simon Gagne .50 1.25
252 Jamie Lundmark .40 1.00
253 Alexandre Giroux RC .40 1.00
254 Dusty Jamieson RC .40 1.00
255 Jamie Chamberlain RC .40 1.00
256 Radim Vrbata RC 2.00 5.00
257 Scott Cameron RC .40 1.00
258 Simon Lajeunesse RC .60 1.50
259 Tim Connolly .25 .60
260 Kris Beech .25 .60
261 Brian Finley .40 1.00
262 Alex Auld RC .60 1.50
263 Martin Grenier RC .40 1.00
264 Sheldon Keefe RC 1.25 3.00
265 Justin Mapletoft RC .40 1.00
266 Edward Hill RC .40 1.00
267 Nolan Yonkman RC .50 1.25
268 Oleg Saprykin RC 1.00 2.50
269 Branislav Mezei RC 1.25 3.00
270 Chris Kelly RC .40 1.00
271 Pavel Brendl RC 2.00 5.00
272 Brett Lysak RC .50 1.25
273 Matt Carkner RC .40 1.00
274 Luke Sellars RC .50 1.25
275 Brad Ralph RC .40 1.00
276A Ray Bourque MM 1.25 3.00
277A Peter Forsberg MM 2.00 5.00
278A Joe Nieuwendyk MM .40 1.00
279A Dominik Hasek MM 1.50 4.00
280A Jaromir Jagr MM 1.25 3.00
281A Paul Kariya MM .50 1.25
282A Eric Lindros MM
283A Mark Messier MM .50 1.25
284A Patrick Roy MM 4.00 10.00
285A Joe Sakic MM 1.50 4.00
286A Steve Yzerman MM 5.00 12.00
287 Alex Tanguay .40 1.00
288 Brad Stuart .40 1.00
289 Brian Boucher .50 1.25
290 Steve Kariya RC .60 1.50
291 Scott Gomez .25 .60
292 Mikko Eloranta RC .60 1.50
293 Patrik Stefan RC 1.00 2.50
294 John Madden RC 1.00 2.50
295 Per Svartvadet RC .60 1.50
296 Jiri Fischer .25 .60
297 Nikolai Antropov RC 1.25 3.00

1999-00 Topps/OPC Chrome Refractors

Randomly inserted in Topps and OPC packs at 1:12, this 297-card set parallels the base set and is enhanced by the rainbow holo-foil refractor effect. Above the card number on the back, the word "REFRACTOR" appears.

*STARS: 5X TO 10X BASIC CARD
*ROOKIES: 1.25X TO 3X BASIC CARDS
*MM STARS: 2X TO 5X BASIC CARDS

1999-00 Topps/OPC Chrome All-Topps

Randomly seeded in Topps and OPC packs at 1:24, this 15-card set features brilliant action photography of the best active players at a particular position, while the card backs contain comparisons with all-time greats at

that same position. Refractor parallels of this set were also randomly inserted at 1:120.

COMPLETE SET (15) 20.00 40.00
*REFRACTORS: 1.5X TO 3X BASIC INSERTS
AT1 Dominik Hasek 2.00 5.00
AT2 Martin Brodeur 2.50 6.00
AT3 Ray Bourque 1.50 4.00
AT4 Al MacInnis .75 2.00
AT5 Nicklas Lidstrom 1.00 2.50
AT6 Brian Leetch 1.00 2.50
AT7 John LeClair 1.00 2.50
AT8 Paul Kariya 1.00 2.50
AT9 Keith Tkachuk 1.00 2.50
AT10 Eric Lindros 1.00 2.50
AT11 Peter Forsberg 2.50 6.00
AT12 Steve Yzerman 5.00 12.00
AT13 Jaromir Jagr 1.50 4.00
AT14 Teemu Selanne 1.00 2.50
AT15 Pavel Bure 1.00 2.50

1999-00 Topps/OPC Chrome A-Men

Randomly inserted in Topps and OPC packs at 1:24, this 6-card set focuses on the NHL's leading assist men. Action photos are set against a silver foil background. Refractor parallels of this set were also randomly inserted at 1:120.

COMPLETE SET (6) 10.00 20.00
*REFRACTORS: 1.5X TO 3X BASIC INSERTS
AM1 Jaromir Jagr 1.50 4.00
AM2 Peter Forsberg 2.50 6.00
AM3 Paul Kariya 1.50 4.00
AM4 Teemu Selanne 1.50 4.00
AM5 Joe Sakic 2.00 5.00
AM6 Eric Lindros 1.50 4.00

1999-00 Topps/OPC Chrome Fantastic Finishers

Randomly inserted in Topps and OPC packs at 1:24, this 6-card set features the NHL's top goal scorers. Action player photos are set against a foil true-life background. Refractor parallels of this set were also randomly inserted at 1:120.

COMPLETE SET (6) 6.00 12.00
*REFRACTORS: 1.5X TO 3X BASIC INSERTS
FF1 Teemu Selanne 1.00 2.50
FF2 Jaromir Jagr 1.50 4.00
FF3 Tony Amonte .75 2.00
FF4 Alexei Yashin .75 2.00
FF5 John LeClair 1.00 2.50
FF6 Joe Sakic 2.00 5.00

1999-00 Topps/OPC Chrome Ice Futures

Randomly inserted in Topps and OPC packs at 1:24, this 6-card set focuses on the NHL's hottest prospects. Action photos are set against a blue foil checkerboard background. Refractor parallels of this set were also randomly inserted at 1:120.

COMPLETE SET (6) 6.00 12.00
*REFRACTORS: 1.5X TO 3X BASIC INSERTS
IF1 Mark Parrish 1.00 2.50
IF2 Chris Drury 1.00 2.50
IF3 Bill Muckalt 1.00 2.50
IF4 Marian Hossa 1.25 3.00
IF5 Milan Hejduk 1.00 2.50
IF6 Brendan Morrison 1.00 2.50

1999-00 Topps/OPC Chrome Ice Masters

Randomly inserted in Topps and OPC packs at 1:18, this 20-card set showcases some of hockey's elite players on a blue and silver foil card that is textured like ice. Refractor parallels of this set were also randomly inserted at 1:90.

COMPLETE SET (20) 25.00 50.00
*REFRACTORS: 1.5X TO 3X BASIC INSERTS
IM1 Joe Sakic 1.50 4.00
IM2 Dominik Hasek 1.50 4.00
IM3 Eric Lindros .75 2.00
IM4 Jaromir Jagr 1.25 3.00
IM5 John LeClair .75 2.00
IM6 Mats Sundin .75 2.00
IM7 Ray Bourque 1.25 3.00
IM8 Mike Modano 1.25 3.00
IM9 Peter Forsberg 2.00 5.00
IM10 Brian Leetch .75 2.00
IM11 Martin Brodeur 2.00 5.00
IM12 Al MacInnis .60 1.50
IM13 Paul Kariya .75 2.00
IM14 Alexei Yashin .60 1.50
IM15 Steve Yzerman 4.00 10.00
IM16 Ed Belfour .75 2.00
IM17 Keith Tkachuk .75 2.0
IM18 Patrick Roy 4.00 10.0
IM19 Nicklas Lidstrom .75 2.0
IM20 Teemu Selanne .75 2.0

1999-00 Topps/OPC Chrome Positive Performers

Randomly inserted in Topps and OPC pack at 1:24, this 6-card set features players wi the best plus/minus rating in th game.Refractor parallels of this set were als randomly inserted at 1:120.

COMPLETE SET (6) 4.00 8.0
*REFRACTORS: 1.5X TO 3X BASIC INSERT
PP1 Alexander Karpovtsev .60 1.5
PP2 John LeClair 1.00 2.5
PP3 Eric Lindros 1.00 2.5
PP4 Magnus Arvedson .60 1.5
PP5 Al MacInnis .75 2.0
PP6 Jere Lehtinen .75 2.0

1999-00 Topps/OPC Chrome Postmasters

Randomly inserted in Topps and OPC pack at 1:24, this 6-card set focuses on the NHL toughest goaltenders. Refractor parallels this set were also randomly inserted a 1:120.

COMPLETE SET (6) 10.00 20.0
*REFRACTORS: 1.5X TO 3X BASIC INSERT
PM1 Dominik Hasek 2.00 5.0
PM2 Byron Dafoe .75 2.0
PM3 Nikolai Khabibulin .75 2.0
PM4 Ed Belfour 1.00 2.5
PM5 Patrick Roy 5.00 12.0
PM6 Martin Brodeur 2.50 6.0

2000-01 Topps Chrome

Released in late January 2001, this 251-ca set is comprised of 160 veteran cards, Season Highlight cards, 55 NHL Prospect and 30 Chrome Expansion cards. Carc #241-251 were sequentially numbered 1250. Base cards have silver borders and a printed on an all chrome card stock. Tw parallel versions were issued for th Expansion cards, numbers 240-251, ar these cards are also sequentially numbere to 1250. Topps Chrome was packaged 24-pack boxes with packs containing fo cards and carried a suggested retail price $3.00.

COMPLETE SET (250) 100.00 200.0
COMP.SET w/o SP's (240) 30.00 60.0
1 Jaromir Jagr .75 2.0
2 Patrick Roy 2.50 6.0
3 Paul Kariya .50 1.2
4 Mats Sundin .50 1.2
5 Ron Francis .40 1.0
6 Pavel Bure .50 1.2
7 John LeClair .50 1.2
8 Olaf Kolzig .40 1.0
9 Chris Pronger .40 1.0
10 Jeremy Roenick .60 1.5
11 Owen Nolan .40 1.0
12 Theo Fleury .20 .5
13 Zigmund Palffy .40 1.0
14 Patrik Stefan .20 .5
15 Jarome Iginla .60 1.5
16 Joe Thornton .75 2.0
17 Tony Amonte .40 1.0
18 Mike Modano .75 2.0
19 Mark Messier .50 1.2
20 Dominik Hasek 1.00 2.5
21 Steve Yzerman 2.50 6.0
22 Marian Hossa .50 1.2
23 David Legwand .40 1.0
24 Jose Theodore .60 1.5
25 Vincent Lecavalier .50 1.2
26 Scott Stevens .40 1.0
27 Mark Parrish .20 .5
28 Sean Burke .40 1.0
29 Alexei Kovalev .20 .5
30 Dan Cloutier .20 .5
31 Sami Kapanen .20 .5
32 Anson Carter .40 1.0
33 Miroslav Satan .40 1.0
34 Mark Recchi .40 1.0
35 Pavol Demitra .40 1.0
36 Peter Bondra .50 1.2
37 Mike Richter .50 1.2
38 Guy Hebert .40 1.0
39 Martin Skoula .20 .5
40 Ed Belfour .50 1.2
41 Fred Brathwaite .40 1.0
42 Andrew Brunette .20 .5
43 Byron Dafoe .40 1.0
44 Felix Potvin .50 1.2
45 Rod Brind'Amour .40 1.0

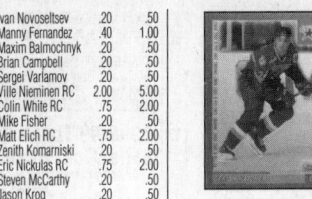

46 Doug Gilmour .40 1.00
47 Brett Hull .60 1.50
48 Nicklas Lidstrom .50 1.25
49 Mike York .20 .50
50 Al MacInnis .40 1.00
51 Brian Boucher .50 1.25
52 Teemu Selanne .50 1.25
53 Bill Guerin .40 1.00
54 Ray Bourque .75 2.00
55 Ray Ferraro .20 .50
56 Sergei Gonchar .20 .50
57 Mattias Ohlund .20 .50
58 Todd Marchant .20 .50
59 Damian Rhodes .20 .50
60 Chris Drury .40 1.00
61 Curtis Joseph .50 1.25
62 Teppo Numminen .20 .50
63 Petr Nedved .20 .50
64 Doug Weight .40 1.00
65 Arturs Irbe .40 1.00
66 Chris Osgood .40 1.00
67 Jocelyn Thibault .40 1.00
68 Oleg Tverdovsky .20 .50
69 Derian Hatcher .20 .50
70 Ray Whitney .20 .50
71 Saku Koivu .50 1.25
72 Cliff Ronning .20 .50
73 Claude Lapointe .20 .50
74 Chris Simon .20 .50
75 Martin Rucinsky .20 .50
76 Valeri Bure .20 .50
77 Brad Isbister .20 .50
78 Roman Turek .40 1.00
79 Kenny Jonsson .20 .50
80 Mike Dunham .40 1.00
81 Rob Blake .40 1.00
82 Daniel Alfredsson .40 1.00
83 Tommy Salo .40 1.00
84 Sergei Samsonov .40 1.00
85 Joe Sakic 1.00 2.50
86 Bryan Smolinski .20 .50
87 Luc Robitaille .40 1.00
88 Mariusz Czerkawski .20 .50
89 Brendan Shanahan .50 1.25
90 Brian Rafalski .20 .50
91 Jamie Langenbrunner .20 .50
92 Peter Forsberg 1.25 3.00
93 Phil Housley .20 .50
94 Glen Murray .20 .50
95 Jeff Hackett .40 1.00
96 Sergei Fedorov .75 2.00
97 Sergei Zubov .20 .50
98 Martin Brodeur 1.25 3.00
99 Mike Grier .20 .50
100 Paul Coffey .50 1.25
101 Radek Bonk .20 .50
102 Milan Hejduk .50 1.25
103 Viktor Kozlov .40 1.00
104 Jason Arnott .20 .50
105 Brendan Morrison .40 1.00
106 Keith Tkachuk .50 1.25
107 Patrik Elias .40 1.00
108 Jochen Hecht .20 .50
109 Brian Leetch .40 1.00
110 Petr Sykora .20 .50
111 Dave Andreychuk .40 1.00
112 Steve Shields .40 1.00
113 Nikolai Antropov .20 .50
114 Martin Straka .20 .50
115 Eric Desjardins .40 1.00
116 Adam Oates .40 1.00
117 Adam Graves .20 .50
118 Jozef Stumpel .20 .50
119 Vincent Damphousse .20 .50
120 Maxim Afinogenov .20 .50
121 Chris Chelios .50 1.25
122 Joe Nieuwendyk .40 1.00
123 Petr Buzek .20 .50
124 Jeff Friesen .20 .50
125 Markus Naslund .50 1.25
126 Trevor Letowski .20 .50
127 Steve Thomas .20 .50
128 Jason Allison .20 .50
129 Jere Lehtinen .40 1.00
130 Tom Poti .20 .50
131 Eric Lindros .50 1.25
132 Rob Niedermayer .40 1.00
133 Gary Roberts .20 .50
134 Scott Gomez .20 .50
135 Pierre Turgeon .40 1.00
136 Trevor Kidd .40 1.00
137 Jan Hrdina .20 .50
138 John Madden .20 .50
139 Tim Connolly .20 .50
140 Pat Verbeek .20 .50
141 Jeff Halpern .20 .50
142 Patrick Marleau .40 1.00
143 Wade Redden .20 .50
144 Alex Tanguay .40 1.00
145 Darcy Tucker .20 .50
146 Simon Gagne .50 1.25
147 Brad Stuart .40 1.00
148 Jean-Sebastien Aubin .40 1.00
149 Mike Johnson .20 .50
150 Shayne Corson .20 .50
151 Michael Peca .20 .50
152 Keith Primeau .20 .50
153 Tie Domi .40 1.00
154 Brenden Morrow .40 1.00
155 Sandis Ozolinsh .20 .50
156 Mike Keane .20 .50
157 Patric Kjellberg .20 .50
158 Patrick Lalime .40 1.00
159 John Vanbiesbrouck .40 1.00
160 Andrew Cassels .20 .50
161 Scott Stephens HL .20 .50
162 Ed Belfour HL .50 1.25
163 Martin Brodeur HL .60 1.50
164 Mike Modano HL .40 1.00
165 Jason Arnott HL .20 .50
166 Roberto Luongo .60 1.50
167 Harold Druken .20 .50
168 Marc Denis .40 1.00
169 Oleg Saprykin .20 .50
170 Glen Metropolit .20 .50
171 Daniel Sedin .20 .50
172 Dmitri Yakushin .20 .50
173 Scott Hannan .20 .50
174 Dave Tanabe .20 .50
175 Jiri Fischer .20 .50
176 Dmitri Nabokov .20 .50
177 Ivan Novoseltsev .20 .50
178 Manny Fernandez .40 1.00
179 Maxim Balmochnykh .20 .50
180 Brian Campbell .20 .50
181 Sergei Varlamov .20 .50
182 Ville Nieminen RC 2.00 5.00
183 Colin White RC .75 2.00
184 Mike Fisher .20 .50
185 Matt Elich RC .75 2.00
186 Zenith Komarniski .20 .50
187 Eric Nickulas RC .75 2.00
188 Steven McCarthy .20 .50
189 Jason Krog .20 .50
190 Robert Esche .20 .50
191 Adam Mair .20 .50
192 Ladislav Nagy .20 .50
193 Sergei Vyshedkevich RC .75 2.00
194 Steve Begin .20 .50
195 Brad Ference .20 .50
196 Andy Delmore .20 .50
197 Brent Sopel RC .75 2.00
198 Evgeni Nabokov .40 1.00
199 David Gosselin RC .75 2.00
200 Tavis Hansen .20 .50
201 Ray Giroux .20 .50
202 Serge Aubin RC .75 2.00
203 Shane Willis .20 .50
204 Vitali Vishnevsky .20 .50
205 Richard Jackman .20 .50
206 Petr Schastlivy .20 .50
207 Ryan Bonni .20 .50
208 Alexei Tezikov .20 .50
209 Henrik Sedin .20 .50
210 Mike Ribeiro .20 .50
211 Darryl Laplante .20 .50
212 Kyle Calder .20 .50
213 Dimitri Kalinin .20 .50
214 J-S Giguere .20 .50
215 Willie Mitchell RC .75 2.00
216 Steve Valiquette RC .75 2.00
217 Brian Willsie .20 .50
218 Jarkko Ruutu .20 .50
219 Jon Sim .20 .50
220 Jonathan Girard .20 .50
221 Ron Tugnutt .40 1.00
222 Lyle Odelein .20 .50
223 Jean-Luc Grand-Pierre .20 .50
224 Geoff Sanderson .20 .50
225 Robert Kron .20 .50
226 Kevin Dineen .20 .50
227 Kevyn Adams .20 .50
228 Tyler Wright .20 .50
229 Jamie Pushor .20 .50
230 David Vyborny .20 .50
231 Jamie McLennan .20 .50
232 Jeff Nielsen .20 .50
233 Scott Pellerin .20 .50
234 Darby Hendrickson .20 .50
235 Jim Dowd .20 .50
236 Filip Kuba .20 .50
237 Stacy Roest .20 .50
238 Sean O'Donnell .20 .50
239 Aaron Gavey .20 .50
240 Sergei Krivokrasov .20 .50
241 Justin Williams RC 2.00 5.00
242 Marian Gaborik RC 8.00 20.00
243 Marty Turco RC 4.00 10.00
244 David Aebischer RC 3.00 8.00
245 Rostislav Klesla RC 2.50 6.00
246 Petr Hubacek RC 2.00 5.00
247 Scott Hartnell RC 2.00 5.00
248 Martin Havlat RC 4.00 10.00
249 Steven Reinprecht RC 2.00 5.00
250 Andrew Raycroft RC 3.00 8.00
251 Rick DiPietro RC 2.00 5.00

2000-01 Topps Chrome Blue

Randomly inserted in packs, this 11-card set parallels the base rookie cards from the Topps Chrome set, card numbers 241-251. Each card is enhanced with a blue border and is sequentially numbered to 1250.
*BLUE: SAME VALUE AS BASIC CARDS

2000-01 Topps Chrome Red

Randomly inserted in packs, this 11-card set parallels the base rookie cards from the Topps Chrome set, card numbers 241-251. Each card is enhanced with a red border and is sequentially numbered to 1250.
*REDS SAME VALUE AS BASIC CARDS

2000-01 Topps Chrome OPC Refractors

Randomly inserted in packs at the rate of 1:9 for card numbers 1-220, and 1:383 for card numbers 241-251, this 251-card set parallels the base Topps Chrome set

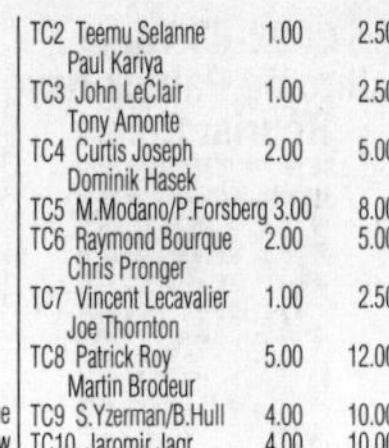

enhanced with the O-Pee-Chee logo in the lower right hand corner and the rainbow holofoil refractor effect. Card numbers 241-251 are all sequentially numbered to 35.
*STARS: 1.5X TO 4X BASIC CARDS
*EXPANSION REF.: 1.5X TO 4X BASIC CARDS
*ROOKIE REF: 2X TO 4X BASIC CARDS

2000-01 Topps Chrome OPC Refractors Blue

Randomly inserted in packs at the rate of 1:383, this 11-card set parallels the last 11 cards in the base Topps Chrome set, card numbers 241-251. Each card is enhanced with a blue border, the rainbow holofoil refractor effect, and is sequentially numbered to 35.
*BLUE.OPC.REF.: 2X TO 4X BASIC CARDS

2000-01 Topps Chrome OPC Refractors Red

Randomly inserted in packs at the rate of 1:383, this 11-card set parallels the last 11 cards in the base Topps Chrome set, card numbers 241-251. Each card is enhanced with a red border, the rainbow holofoil refractor effect, and is sequentially numbered to 35.
*RED.OPC.REF.: 2X TO 4X BASIC CARDS

2000-01 Topps Chrome Refractors

Randomly inserted in packs at the rate of 1:9 for card numbers 1-220, and randomly inserted for card numbers 241-250, this 250-card set parallels the base Topps Chrome set enhanced with the Topps Chrome logo in one of the front lower corners and the rainbow holofoil refractor effect. Card numbers 241-251 are all sequentially numbered to 25.
*STARS: 2X TO 5X BASIC CARDS
*EXPANSION REF.: 1.5X TO 4X BASIC CARDS
*ROOKIE REF.: 3X TO 5X BASIC CARDS

2000-01 Topps Chrome Refractors Blue

Randomly inserted in packs, this 11-card set parallels the last 11 cards in the base Topps Chrome set, card numbers 241-251. Each card is enhanced with a blue border, the rainbow holofoil refractor effect, and is sequentially numbered to 25.
*BLUE.REF.: 3X TO 5X BASIC CARDS

2000-01 Topps Chrome Refractors Red

Randomly inserted in packs, this 11-card set parallels the last 11 cards in the base Topps Chrome set, card numbers 241-251. Each card is enhanced with a red border, the rainbow holofoil refractor effect, and is sequentially numbered to 25.
*RED.REF.: 3X TO 5X BASIC CARDS

2000-01 Topps Chrome Combos

Randomly inserted in packs at the rate of one in 20, this 10-card set features original artwork of two top NHL players. The bottom of the card has their names and a brief explanation why they are paired in a green box. Cards are printed on all chrome card stock. Refractor parallels of this set were also randomly inserted at 1:200.
COMPLETE SET (10) 15.00 40.00
TC1 Pavel Bure 1.00 2.50
Valeri Bure
TC2 Teemu Selanne 1.00 2.50
Paul Kariya
TC3 John LeClair 1.00 2.50
Tony Amonte
TC4 Curtis Joseph 2.00 5.00
Dominik Hasek
TC5 M.Modano/P.Forsberg 3.00 8.00
TC6 Raymond Bourque 2.00 5.00
Chris Pronger
TC7 Vincent Lecavalier 1.00 2.50
Joe Thornton
TC8 Patrick Roy 5.00 12.00
Martin Brodeur
TC9 S.Yzerman/B.Hull 4.00 10.00
TC10 Jaromir Jagr 4.00 10.00
Mario Lemieux

2000-01 Topps Chrome Hobby Masters Refractors

Randomly inserted in Hobby packs at the rate of 1:400, this 10-card set features a player photo with a diagonal line above the lower right hand corner with the player's name and the words "Hobby Master" in yellow. Backgrounds are enhanced with the rainbow holofoil refractor effect.
COMPLETE SET (10) 75.00 150.00
HM1 Martin Brodeur 10.00 25.00
HM2 Pavel Bure 6.00 15.00
HM3 Peter Forsberg 10.00 25.00
HM4 Dominik Hasek 8.00 20.00
HM5 Jaromir Jagr 6.00 15.00
HM6 Curtis Joseph 5.00 12.00
HM7 Paul Kariya 5.00 12.00
HM8 Mike Modano 5.00 12.00
HM9 Patrick Roy 20.00 50.00
HM10 Steve Yzerman 20.00 50.00

2000-01 Topps Chrome Mario Lemieux Reprints

Randomly inserted in packs at the rate of 1:18, this 23-card set features reprinted versions of Mario Lemieux's cards dating back to 85-86 Topps and OPC. Cards are printed on an all chrome card stock. Refractor parallels of this set were also randomly inserted at 1:180.
COMPLETE SET (23) 75.00 150.00
COMMON LEMIEUX (1-23) 4.00 10.00
COMMON LEM.REF. (1-23) 12.50 30.00

2000-01 Topps Chrome Rocket's Flare

Randomly inserted in packs at the rate of 1:14, this 10-card set features top players on a die cut card stock. The bottom of the card is red and the player's name appears in a black name box. A silver die cut "diamond shape" appears behind a full color player action photo. Refractor parallels of this set were also randomly inserted at 1:140.
COMPLETE SET (10) 10.00 20.00
*REFRACTORS: .8X TO 2X BASIC INSERTS
RF1 Pavel Bure 1.00 2.50
RF2 Paul Kariya 1.00 2.50
RF3 John LeClair 1.00 2.50
RF4 Jaromir Jagr 1.50 4.00
RF5 Luc Robitaille .75 2.00
RF6 Milan Hejduk 1.00 2.50
RF7 Tony Amonte .75 2.00
RF8 Patrik Elias .75 2.00
RF9 Miroslav Satan .75 2.00
RF10 Teemu Selanne 1.00 2.50

2000-01 Topps Chrome 1000 Point Club Refractors

Randomly inserted in Retail packs at the rate of 1:250, this 16-card set features 1000 point club members on an all holofoil refractor card. Player photos are in full color, and the words, "1000 Point Club" appear on the top of the card. Card numbers carry a "1000PC" prefix.
1 Mark Messier 5.00 12.00
2 Steve Yzerman 20.00 50.00
3 Ron Francis 3.00 8.00
4 Paul Coffey 4.00 10.00
5 Ray Bourque 8.00 20.00
6 Doug Gilmour 3.00 8.00
7 Adam Oates 3.00 8.00
8 Larry Murphy 3.00 8.00
9 Dave Andreychuk 3.00 8.00
10 Luc Robitaille 3.00 8.00
11 Phil Housley 3.00 8.00
12 Brett Hull 5.00 12.00
13 Al MacInnis 3.00 8.00
14 Pierre Turgeon 3.00 8.00
15 Joe Sakic 10.00 25.00
16 Pat Verbeek 3.00 8.00

2001-02 Topps Chrome

Released in late February 2002, this 182-card set carried an SRP of $3.00 for a 4-card pack. Cards were printed on a chromium card stock. Short printed rookie cards were inserted at 1:3. Update cards for 2001-02 Topps were also randomly seeded in packs at 1:3. Update cards are listed with the base Topps set.
COMPLETE SET (182) 200.00 400.00
1 Mario Lemieux 2.50 6.00
2 Steve Yzerman 2.00 5.00
3 Martin Brodeur 1.25 3.00
4 Brian Leetch .40 1.00
5 Tony Amonte .40 1.00
6 Bill Guerin .40 1.00
7 Olaf Kolzig .40 1.00
8 Pavel Bure .50 1.25
9 Patrick Marleau .40 1.00
10 Mariusz Czerkawski .20 .50
11 Teemu Selanne .50 1.25
12 Alex Tanguay .40 1.00
13 Keith Primeau .20 .50
14 Alexei Yashin .20 .50
15 Markus Naslund .50 1.25
16 Chris Pronger .40 1.00
17 Sergei Zubov .20 .50
18 Marian Gaborik 1.00 2.50
19 Mats Sundin .50 1.25
20 David Legwand .40 1.00
21 J-P Dumont .20 .50
22 Nicklas Lidstrom .50 1.25
23 Ron Francis .40 1.00
24 Doug Weight .40 1.00
25 Zigmund Palffy .40 1.00
26 Jason Allison .20 .50
27 Joe Sakic 1.00 2.50
28 Paul Kariya .50 1.25
29 Marian Hossa .50 1.25
30 Owen Nolan .40 1.00
31 Jason Arnott .20 .50
32 Jaromir Jagr .75 2.00
33 Claude Lemieux .20 .50
34 Peter Bondra .40 1.00
35 Chris Drury .40 1.00
36 Radek Bonk .20 .50
37 Theo Fleury .20 .50
38 Keith Tkachuk .50 1.25
39 Rick DiPietro .40 1.00
40 Ed Jovanovski .40 1.00
41 Scott Stevens .40 1.00
42 John LeClair .50 1.25
43 Ryan Smyth .20 .50
44 Vincent Lecavalier .50 1.25
45 Henrik Sedin .20 .50
46 David Aebischer .40 1.00
47 Patrick Roy 2.50 6.00
48 Valeri Bure .20 .50
49 Dominik Hasek 1.00 2.50
50 Ray Ferraro .20 .50
51 Milan Hejduk .50 1.25
52 Mike Modano .75 2.00
53 Sergei Fedorov .75 2.00
54 Luc Robitaille .40 1.00
55 Mark Messier .50 1.25
56 Sean Burke .40 1.00
57 Jeff Friesen .20 .50
58 Alexander Mogilny .40 1.00
59 Roman Cechmanek .40 1.00
60 Martin Straka .20 .50
61 Pavol Demitra .40 1.00
62 Curtis Joseph .50 1.25
63 Daniel Sedin .20 .50
64 Brad Richards .40 1.00
65 Simon Gagne .50 1.25
66 Saku Koivu .50 1.25
67 Eric Daze .40 1.00
68 Roberto Luongo .60 1.50
69 Brendan Shanahan .50 1.25
70 Espen Knutsen .20 .50
71 Rob Blake .40 1.00
72 Steve Sullivan .20 .50
73 Arturs Irbe .40 1.00
74 Maxim Afinogenov .20 .50
75 Dan Cloutier .40 1.00
76 Josef Vasicek .20 .50
77 Vincent Damphousse .20 .50
78 Robert Lang .20 .50
79 Pierre Turgeon .40 1.00
80 Gary Roberts .20 .50
81 Adam Oates .40 1.00
82 Evgeni Nabokov .40 1.00
83 Petr Nedved .20 .50
84 Mike Dunham .40 1.00
85 Chris Osgood .40 1.00
86 Brett Hull .60 1.50
87 Peter Forsberg 1.25 3.00
88 Joe Thornton .75 2.00
89 Marc Denis .40 1.00
90 Ed Belfour .50 1.25
91 Patrik Elias .40 1.00
92 Michael York .20 .50
93 Martin Havlat .40 1.00
94 Jeremy Roenick .60 1.50
95 Alexei Kovalev .40 1.00
96 Al MacInnis .40 1.00
97 Marco Sturm .20 .50
98 Jose Theodore .60 1.50
99 Joe Nieuwendyk .40 1.00
100 Darren McCarty .20 .50
101 Mark Recchi .40 1.00
102 Daniel Alfredsson .40 1.00
103 Miroslav Satan .40 1.00
104 Sergei Samsonov .40 1.00
105 Roman Turek .40 1.00
106 Jarome Iginla .60 1.50
107 Jeff O'Neill .20 .50
108 Tommy Salo .40 1.00
109 Petr Sykora .20 .50
110 Adam Deadmarsh .20 .50
111 Oleg Tverdovsky .20 .50
112 Sami Kapanen .20 .50
113 Scott Hartnell .20 .50
114 Jere Lehtinen .40 1.00
115 Darcy Tucker .20 .50
116 Stu Barnes .20 .50
117 Jim Dowd .20 .50
118 Derek Morris .20 .50
119 Felix Potvin .50 1.25
120 Manny Fernandez .40 1.00
121 Jason Smith .20 .50
122 Byron Dafoe .20 .50
123 Teppo Numminen .20 .50
124 Mike Richter .50 1.25
125 Anson Carter .40 1.00
126 Jocelyn Thibault .40 1.00
127 Dany Heatley .60 1.50
128 Marc Savard .20 .50
129 Brian Rolston .20 .50
130 Martin Biron .40 1.00
131 Mark Parrish .20 .50
132 Mike Peca .20 .50
133 Patrick Lalime .40 1.00
134 Eric Lindros .50 1.25
135 Brian Boucher .50 1.25
136 Nikolai Khabibulin .50 1.25
137 John Madden .20 .50
138 Rostislav Klesla .20 .50
139 Mika Noronen .40 1.00
140 Kris Beech .20 .50
141 Miikka Kiprusoff .40 1.00
142 Mathieu Garon .40 1.00
143 Mark Bell .20 .50
144 Jussi Markkanen .40 1.00
145 Mike Comrie .40 1.00
146 Johan Hedberg .40 1.00
147 Andrew Raycroft .40 1.00
148 Daniel Corso .20 .50
149 Ilya Kovalchuk RC 6.00 15.00
150 Dan Blackburn RC 1.50 4.00
151 Vaclav Nedorost RC 1.50 4.00
152 Krys Kolanos RC 1.50 4.00
153 Kristian Huselius RC 1.50 4.00
154 Martin Erat RC 1.50 4.00
155 Timo Parssinen RC 1.50 4.00
156 Scott Nichol RC 1.50 4.00
157 Nick Schultz RC 1.50 4.00
158 Jukka Hentunen RC 1.50 4.00
159 Pascal Dupuis RC 1.50 4.00
160 Radek Martinek RC 1.50 4.00
161 Scott Clemmensen RC 1.50 4.00
162 Jeff Jillson RC 1.50 4.00
163 Brian Sutherby RC 1.50 4.00
164 Nikita Alexeev RC 1.50 4.00
165 Niklas Hagman RC 1.50 4.00
166 Erik Cole RC 1.50 4.00
167 Pavel Datsyuk RC 3.00 8.00
168 Ilja Bryzgalov RC 2.00 5.00
169 Chris Neil RC 1.50 4.00
170 Mark Rycroft RC 1.50 4.00
171 Kamil Piros RC 1.50 4.00
172 Niko Kapanen RC 1.50 4.00
173 Jiri Dopita RC 1.50 4.00
174 Andreas Salomonsson RC 1.50 4.00
175 Ivan Ciernik RC 1.50 4.00
176 Jaroslav Bednar RC 1.50 4.00
177 Ty Conklin RC 1.50 4.00
178 Richard Scott RC 1.50 4.00
179 Raffi Torres RC 2.00 5.00
180 Vaclav Pletka RC 1.50 4.00
181 Mikael Samuelsson RC 1.50 4.00
182 Mike Farrell RC 1.50 4.00

2001-02 Topps Chrome Refractors

This 182-cards set paralleled the base set with the rainbow holofoil refractor effect. Refractors were inserted at a rate of 1:6 packs.
*STARS: 1.5X TO 4X BASIC CARDS
*SP's: .75X TO 2X BASIC CARDS

2001-02 Topps Chrome Black Border Refractors

Serial-numbered to just 50 copies each, this 182-card set paralleled the base set with a rainbow holofoil refractor effect and black borders.
*STARS: 5X TO 12X BASIC CARD
*SP's: 1.5X TO 4X BASIC CARDS

2001-02 Topps Chrome Mario Lemieux Reprints

Inserted at 1:12, 10-card set featured reprints of past Topps cards of Mario Lemieux on chrome stock. Refractor parallels of this set were also created and inserted at 1:120.
COMPLETE SET (10) 30.00 60.00
COMMON LEMIEUX 3.00 8.00
*REFRACTORS: 1.25X TO 3X BASIC CARD

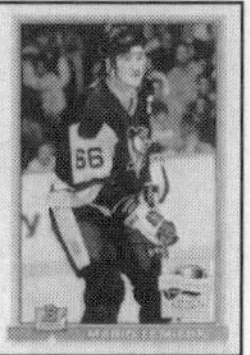

2001-02 Topps Chrome Mario Returns

This 5-card set highlighted the return of Mario Lemieux to the NHL. Cards from this set were inserted at odds of 1:24. Refractor parallels of this set were also created and inserted at 1:240.
COMPLETE SET (5) 25.00 50.00
COMMON LEMIEUX (MR1-MR5) 4.00 10.00
REFRACTORS: 1.25X TO 3X BASIC CARD

2001-02 Topps Chrome Reprints

This 10-card set featured rookie card reprints of past greats on chrome stock. Cards from this set were inserted at 1:12 packs. A refractor parallel was also created and inserted at 1:120
COMPLETE SET (10) 15.00 40.00
*REFRACTORS: 1.25X TO 3X BASIC CARD
1 Billy Smith 2.00 5.00
2 Wayne Cashman 2.00 5.00
3 Barry Melrose 2.00 5.00
4 Bernie Federko 2.00 5.00
5 Neal Broten 2.00 5.00
6 Bill Clement 2.00 5.00
7 Guy Lapointe 2.00 5.00
8 Bernie Parent 2.00 5.00
9 Larry Robinson 2.00 5.00
10 Ken Hodge 2.00 5.00

2001-02 Topps Chrome Reprint Autographs

Inserted at 1:247, this 10-card set paralleled the reprints set but was enhanced with authentic autographs of the featured players. Card backs carried a Topps authentic sticker.
1 Billy Smith 12.50 30.00
2 Wayne Cashman 12.50 30.00
3 Barry Melrose 15.00 40.00
4 Bernie Federko 12.50 30.00
5 Neal Broten 12.50 30.00
6 Bill Clement 12.50 30.00
7 Guy Lapointe 12.50 30.00
8 Bernie Parent 20.00 50.00
9 Larry Robinson 15.00 40.00
10 Ken Hodge 12.50 30.00

2002 Topps Chrome All-Star Fantasy

Available as wrapper redemptions from the Topps booth at the NHL All-Star Fantasy in Los Angeles, this 6-card set featured players involved in All-Star events. Each card was numbered "x of 6" on the card back. The card front carried the All-Star logo.
COMPLETE SET (6) 6.00 15.00
1 Paul Kariya 1.20 3.00
2 Zigmund Palffy .40 1.00
3 Joe Sakic 1.20 3.00
4 Jaromir Jagr 1.20 3.00
5 Dominik Hasek .80 2.00
6 Ilya Kovalchuk 2.00 5.00

2002-03 Topps Chrome

Released in February, this 181-card set consisted of 148 base veteran cards and 33 shortprinted rookie cards. Rookies were inserted at 1:3.

COMPLETE SET (182) 150.00 300.00
COMMON RC (149-182) 2.00 5.00
1 Patrick Roy 2.50 6.00
2 Mario Lemieux 3.00 8.00
3 Martin Brodeur 1.25 3.00
4 Steve Yzerman 2.50 6.00
5 Jaromir Jagr .75 2.00
6 Chris Pronger .40 1.00
7 John LeClair .50 1.25
8 Paul Kariya .50 1.25
9 Tony Amonte .40 1.00
10 Joe Thornton .75 2.00
11 Ilya Kovalchuk .60 1.50
12 Jarome Iginla .60 1.50
13 Mike Modano .75 2.00
14 Vincent Lecavalier .50 1.25
15 Michael Peca .20 .50
16 Pavel Bure .50 1.25
17 Eric Lindros .50 1.25
18 Felix Potvin .50 1.25
19 Ron Francis .40 1.00
20 Miroslav Satan .40 1.00
21 Rostislav Klesla .20 .50
22 Mike Comrie .40 1.00
23 Daniel Alfredsson .40 1.00
24 Sean Burke .40 1.00
25 David Legwand .40 1.00
26 Marian Gaborik 1.00 2.50
27 Saku Koivu .50 1.25
28 Owen Nolan .40 1.00
29 Mats Sundin .50 1.25
30 J-P Dumont .20 .50
31 Chris Drury .40 1.00
32 Markus Naslund .50 1.25
33 Anson Carter .40 1.00
34 Daniel Briere .20 .50
35 Keith Tkachuk .50 1.25
36 Mark Recchi .40 1.00
37 Marc Denis .40 1.00
38 Sergei Fedorov .75 2.00
39 Andrew Brunette .20 .50
40 Martin Havlat .40 1.00
41 Brian Leetch .40 1.00
42 Erik Cole .20 .50
43 Patrick Lalime .40 1.00
44 Patrick Marleau .40 1.00
45 Ryan Smyth .20 .50
46 Sami Kapanen .20 .50
47 Martin Straka .20 .50
48 Peter Forsberg 1.25 3.00
49 Jeff Friesen .20 .50
50 Manny Fernandez .40 1.00
51 Scott Stevens .40 1.00
52 Radim Vrbata .20 .50
53 Marty Turco .40 1.00
54 Kristian Huselius .20 .50
55 Jeremy Roenick .60 1.50
56 Gary Roberts .20 .50
57 Chris Chelios .50 1.25
58 Brett Hull .60 1.50
59 Eric Daze .40 1.00
60 Alex Tanguay .40 1.00
61 Simon Gagne .50 1.25
62 Roman Turek .40 1.00
63 Milan Hejduk .50 1.25
64 Mariusz Czerkawski .20 .50
65 Dan Cloutier .40 1.00
66 Teemu Selanne .50 1.25
67 Johan Hedberg .40 1.00
68 Mike Ricci .20 .50
69 Roberto Luongo .60 1.50
70 Zigmund Palffy .40 1.00
71 Ed Jovanovski .40 1.00
72 Scott Gomez .20 .50
73 Pierre Turgeon .40 1.00
74 Martin Biron .40 1.00
75 Keith Primeau .20 .50
76 J-S Giguere .40 1.00
77 Alexei Zhamnov .20 .50
78 Brent Johnson .40 1.00
79 Dan Blackburn .40 1.00
80 Mike Richter .50 1.25
81 Peter Bondra .40 1.00
82 Rod Brind'Amour .40 1.00
83 Shane Doan .20 .50
84 Sergei Samsonov .40 1.00
85 Nikolai Khabibulin .50 1.25
86 Roman Cechmanek .40 1.00
87 Glen Murray .20 .50
88 Brad Richards .40 1.00
89 Alexei Kovalev .40 1.00
90 Adam Deadmarsh .20 .50
91 Brendan Morrison .40 1.00
92 Jason Arnott .20 .50
93 Brenden Morrow .40 1.00
94 Pavol Demitra .40 1.00
95 Olaf Kolzig .40 1.00
96 Doug Gilmour .40 1.00
97 Jere Lehtinen .40 1.00
98 Petr Sykora .20 .50
99 Wade Redden .20 .50
100 Adam Oates .40 1.00
101 Chris Osgood .40 1.00
102 Espen Knutsen .20 .50
103 Maxim Afinogenov .20 .50
104 Steve Sullivan .20 .50
105 Robert Lang .20 .50
106 Milan Hnilicka .40 1.00
107 Craig Conroy .20 .50
108 Alexander Mogilny .40 1.00
109 Jose Theodore .60 1.50
110 Mike Dunham .40 1.00
111 Joe Sakic 1.00 2.50
112 Al MacInnis .40 1.00
113 Marian Hossa .50 1.25
114 Rob Blake .40 1.00
115 Dany Heatley .60 1.50
116 Scott Hartnell .20 .50
117 Krys Kolanos .20 .50
118 Vincent Damphousse .20 .50
119 Curtis Joseph .50 1.25
120 Todd Bertuzzi .50 1.25
121 Tommy Salo .40 1.00
122 Jocelyn Thibault .40 1.00
123 Nicklas Lidstrom .50 1.25
124 Bryan McCabe .20 .50
125 Bill Guerin .40 1.00
126 Luc Robitaille .40 1.00
127 Alexei Yashin .20 .50
128 Evgeni Nabokov .40 1.00
129 Pavel Datsyuk .50 1.25
130 Stu Barnes .20 .50
131 Derek Morris .20 .50
132 Jason Allison .20 .50
133 Mark Messier .50 1.25
134 Ed Belfour .50 1.25
135 Scott Young .20 .50
136 Marco Sturm .20 .50
137 Arturs Irbe .40 1.00
138 Joe Nieuwendyk .40 1.00
139 Sergei Gonchar .20 .50
140 Doug Weight .40 1.00
141 Jeff O'Neill .20 .50
142 Mike York .20 .50
143 Patrik Elias .40 1.00
144 Brendan Shanahan .50 1.25
145 Rick DiPietro .40 1.00
146 Jani Rita .20 .50
147 Stephen Weiss .20 .50
148 Nikita Alexeev .20 .50
149 Micki DuPont RC 2.00 5.00
150 Ivan Majesky RC 2.00 5.00
151 Jason Spezza RC 6.00 15.00
152 Eric Godard RC 2.00 5.00
153 Shawn Thornton RC 2.00 5.00
154 Jeff Paul RC 2.00 5.00
155 Lasse Pirjeta RC 2.00 5.00
156 Adam Hall RC 2.00 5.00
157 Mikael Tellqvist RC 2.00 5.00
158 Tomi Pettinen RC 2.00 5.00
159 Radovan Somik RC 2.00 5.00
160 Jordan Leopold RC 2.00 5.00
161 Dmitri Bykov RC 2.00 5.00
162 Tim Thomas RC 2.00 5.00
163 Martin Gerber RC 3.00 8.00
164 Tom Koivisto RC 2.00 5.00
165 Patrick Sharp RC 2.00 5.00
166 Steve Eminger RC 2.00 5.00
167 Anton Volchenkov RC 2.00 5.00
168 Scottie Upshall RC 2.00 5.00
169 Ron Hainsey RC 2.00 5.00
170 Kurt Sauer RC 2.00 5.00
171 Jeff Taffe RC 2.00 5.00
172 Dennis Seidenberg RC 2.00 5.00
173 Stanislav Chistov RC 2.00 5.00
174 Chuck Kobasew RC 2.00 5.00
175 Rick Nash RC 6.00 15.00
176 Ales Hemsky RC 4.00 10.00
177 Jay Bouwmeester RC 3.00 8.00
178 Alexei Smirnov RC 2.00 5.00
179 Alexander Svitov RC 2.00 5.00
180 P-M Bouchard RC 3.00 8.00
181 Alexander Frolov RC 4.00 10.00
182 Henrik Zetterberg RC 5.00 12.00

2002-03 Topps Chrome Black Border Refractors

Inserted at 1:20, these refractor parallels mirrored the base set but carried black borders. Cards were serial-numbered to 100 copies each.

*STARS: 2.5X TO 6X BASIC CARD
*SP's: 1.25X TO 3X

2002-03 Topps Chrome Refractors

*STARS: 1.25X TO 3X BASIC CARDS
*SP's: .75X TO 2X

2002-03 Topps Chrome e-Topps Decoy Cards

This 6-card set was inserted into packs of Topps Chrome as decoy cards to discourage pack searching. The cards advertised the upcoming release of 2003 e-Topps and pictured different player's e-Topps cards.

1 Jarome Iginla .30 .75
2 Pavel Bure .30 .75
3 Patrick Roy .30 .75
4 Mats Sundin .30 .75
5 Jaromir Jagr .30 .75
6 Martin Brodeur .30 .75

2002-03 Topps Chrome Chromographs

Inserted at 1:134, this 6-card set carried authentic player autographs.

CGBG Brian Gionta 4.00 10.00
CGBR Brad Richards 6.00 15.00
CGCJ Curtis Joseph 15.00 40.00
CGEC Erik Cole 4.00 10.00
CGRV Radim Vrbata 4.00 10.00
CGSW Stephen Weiss 4.00 10.00

2002-03 Topps Chrome Chromograph Refractors

*REFRACTORS: 1X TO 2.5X BASIC AUTO
STATED ODDS 1:1205

2002-03 Topps Chrome First Round Fabric Patches

This 9-card set featured swatches of game jersey patches. Cards were serial-numbered to 50 copies each.

ALL CARDS CARRY FRFP PREFIX
DB Dan Blackburn 12.50 30.00
EL Eric Lindros 15.00 40.00
JP J-P Dumont 12.50 30.00
KP Keith Primeau 12.50 30.00
MB Martin Biron 12.50 30.00
MM Mike Modano 30.00 80.00
MN Markus Naslund 15.00 40.00
MS Mats Sundin 15.00 40.00
PM Patrick Marleau 12.50 30.00
RD Radek Dvorak 12.50 30.00
SN Scott Niedermayer 12.50 30.00

2002-03 Topps Chrome Patrick Roy Reprints

COMPLETE SET (25) 25.00 50.00
STATED ODDS 1:6
1 1986-87 Topps 1.00 2.50
2 1987-88 Topps 1.00 2.50
3 1988-89 Topps 1.00 2.50
4 1989-90 Topps 1.00 2.50
5 1990-91 Topps 1.00 2.50
6 1991-92 Topps 1.00 2.50
7 1992-93 Topps 1.00 2.50
8 1993-94 Premier 1.00 2.50
9 1994-95 Premier 1.00 2.50
10 1995-96 Topps 1.00 2.50
11 1998-99 Topps 1.00 2.50
12 1999-00 Topps 1.00 2.50
13 2000-01 Topps 1.00 2.50
14 2001-02 Topps 1.00 2.50
15 1986-87 OPC 1.00 2.50
16 1987-88 OPC 1.00 2.50
17 1988-89 OPC 1.00 2.50
18 1989-90 OPC 1.00 2.50
19 1990-91 OPC 1.00 2.50
20 1991-92 OPC 1.00 2.50
21 1992-93 OPC 1.00 2.50
22 1998-99 OPC 1.00 2.50
23 1999-00 OPC 1.00 2.50
24 2000-01 OPC 1.00 2.50
25 2001-02 OPC 1.00 2.50

2002-03 Topps Chrome Patrick Roy Reprints Refractors

*REFRACTOR: 2X TO 5X BASIC CARD

2002-03 Topps Chrome Patrick Roy Reprint Autographs

Inserted at 1:904 and serial-numbered to 400 copies each, this 2-card set carried certified autographs of Patrick Roy on reprints of his rookie cards.

COMMON CARD 40.00 80.00
COA Patrick Roy OPC 30.00 80.00
CTA Patrick Roy TOPPS 30.00 80.00

2002-03 Topps Chrome Patrick Roy Reprint Autograph Refractors

Inserted at 1:11,452, this 2-card set paralleled the basic autograph set on refractor card fronts. Each card was serial-numbered out of 33.

*REFRACTOR: 1.5X TO 4X BASIC AUTOGRAPH
COA Patrick Roy OPC 125.00 300.00
CTA Patrick Roy Topps 125.00 300.00

2002-03 Topps Chrome Patrick Roy Reprint Relics

This 4-card set featured jersey or patch swatches affixed to reprints of Roy's rookie cards. Jersey swatches were inserted at 1:1446 and patch swatches were inserted at 1:19,376. Jersey cards were serial-numbered to 250 and patches to 10. Patch cards are not priced due to scarcity.

PRJO1 Patrick Roy 25.00 60.00
OPC Jersey
PRJT1 Patrick Roy 25.00 60.00
Topps Jersey
PRP1 Patrick Roy
OPC Patch
PRPT1 Patrick Roy
Topps Patch

2002-03 Topps Chrome Patrick Roy Reprint Relics Refractors

Inserted at a rate of 1:5812, this 2-card set paralleled the base jersey cards on a refractor card front. Cards were serial-numbered to just 33 copies each.

PRJO1 Patrick Roy 75.00 200.00
OPC Jersey
PRJT1 Patrick Roy 75.00 200.00
Topps Jersey

1998-99 Topps Gold Label Class 1

This 100-card set features color player photos printed on 35-point spectral-reflective rainbow polycarbonate stock with gold stamping. Each card showcases an NHL player on three different versions of his base card. Displayed in the foreground of the Class 1 set is a photo of the player with an action shot appearing in the background featuring players skating and goalies standing upright. Three parallel versions of this set were also produced: The Black Label Parallel with the Black Topps Gold Label logo inserted at 1:18, the Red Label Parallel identified by the Red Topps Gold Label logo and sequentially numbered to 100 (inserted 1:73), and the One to One Parallel printed on special silver foil backs and numbered 1 of 1.

COMPLETE SET (100) 40.00 80.00
*BLACK STARS: 2.5X TO 5X BASIC CARDS
*BLACK ROOKIES: 1.25X TO 3X
*RED STARS: 10X TO 25X BASIC CARDS
*RED ROOKIES: 8X TO 20X
NINE DIFFERENT 1 OF 1 PARALLELS EXIST
1 Brendan Shanahan .50 1.25
2 Mike Modano .75 2.00
3 Chris Chelios .50 1.25
4 Wayne Gretzky 3.00 8.00
5 Jaromir Jagr .75 2.00
6 Mark Messier .50 1.25
7 Teemu Selanne .50 1.25
8 Theo Fleury .10 .30
9 Ray Bourque .75 2.00
10 Martin Brodeur 1.25 3.00
11 Alexei Yashin .10 .30
12 Keith Tkachuk .50 1.25
13 Eric Lindros .50 1.25
14 Owen Nolan .40 1.00
15 Al MacInnis .40 1.00
16 Peter Bondra .40 1.00
17 Saku Koivu .50 1.25
18 Doug Weight .40 1.00
19 Robert Reichel .10 .30
20 Sergei Fedorov .75 2.00
21 Peter Forsberg 1.25 3.00
22 Ron Francis .40 1.00
23 Dimitri Khristich .10 .30
24 Ed Belfour .50 1.25
25 Oleg Kvasha RC .50 1.25
26 Ray Whitney .10 .30
27 Kenny Jonsson .10 .30
28 Randy McKay .10 .30
29 Pavol Demitra .40 1.00
30 Pierre Turgeon .40 1.00
31 Steve Yzerman 2.50 6.00
32 Ryan Smyth .40 1.00
33 Tony Amonte .40 1.00
34 Dominik Hasek 1.00 2.50
35 Jarome Iginla .60 1.50
36 Jari Kapanen .10 .30
37 Patrik Elias .40 1.00
38 Daniel Cleary .10 .30
39 Curtis Joseph .50 1.25
40 Joe Juneau .10 .30
41 Adam Graves .10 .30
42 Trevor Linden .40 1.00
43 Olli Jokinen .40 1.00
44 Joe Nieuwendyk .40 1.00
45 Sergei Samsonov .40 1.00
46 Rico Fata .10 .30
47 Mark Recchi .40 1.00
48 Rick Tocchet .40 1.00
49 Chris Pronger .40 1.00
50 Jason Allison .10 .30
51 Paul Kariya .50 1.25
52 Stu Barnes .10 .30
53 Mats Sundin .50 1.25
54 Mike Richter .50 1.25
55 Cliff Ronning .10 .30
56 Keith Primeau .10 .30
57 Guy Hebert .40 1.00
58 Nicklas Lidstrom .50 1.25
59 John Vanbiesbrouck .40 1.00
60 Jeff Friesen .10 .30
61 Vincent Lecavalier 1.00 2.50
62 Alexander Mogilny .40 1.00
63 Olaf Kolzig .40 1.00
64 Doug Gilmour .40 1.00
65 Joe Sakic 1.00 2.50
66 Mike Johnson .10 .30
67 Vincent Damphousse .10 .30
68 Eric Brewer .10 .30
69 Daniel Alfredsson .40 1.00
70 Nikolai Khabibulin .40 1.00
71 Marco Sturm .10 .30
72 Marty Reasoner .40 1.00
73 Bill Muckalt RC .10 .30
74 Pavel Bure .50 1.25
75 Bill Guerin .10 .30
76 Chris Osgood .40 1.00
77 Patrick Roy 2.50 6.00
78 Tom Barrasso .40 1.00
79 Alyn McCauley .10 .30
80 Adam Oates .40 1.00
81 Joe Thornton .75 2.00
82 Brendan Morrison .40 1.00
83 Mike Dunham .40 1.00
84 Jeremy Roenick .60 1.50
85 Brian Leetch .50 1.25
86 John LeClair .50 1.25
87 Mattias Ohlund .40 1.00
88 Wade Redden .10 .30
89 Mark Parrish RC 1.25 3.00
90 Milan Hejduk RC 1.25 3.00
91 Michael Peca .40 1.00
92 Brett Hull .60 1.50
93 Manny Malhotra .10 .30
94 Patrick Marleau .40 1.00
95 Grant Fuhr .40 1.00
96 Rob Blake .40 1.00
97 Damian Rhodes .40 1.00
98 Eric Daze .40 1.00
99 Rod Brind'Amour .40 1.00
100 Scott Stevens .40 1.00

1998-99 Topps Gold Label Class 2

Randomly inserted into packs at the rate of one in six, this 100-card set features color player photos printed on 35-point spectral-reflective rainbow polycarbonate stock with gold stamping. Each card showcases an NHL player on three different version of his base card. Displayed in the foreground of the Class 2 set is a photo of the player with an action shot appearing in the background featuring players shooting and goalies sprawling. Three parallel versions of this set were also produced: The Black Label Parallel with the Black Topps Gold Label logo inserted at a rate 1:36, the Red Label Parallel identified by the Red Topps Gold Label logo and sequentially numbered to 50 (inserted at 1:146), and the One to One Parallel printed on special silver foil backs and numbered 1 of 1.

COMPLETE SET (100) 100.00 200.00
*STARS: 1X TO 2.5X CLASS 1 BASIC CARDS
*BLACK: 2X TO 4X CL.1 BASIC CARDS
*RED: 20X TO 40X CL.1 BASIC CARDS

1998-99 Topps Gold Label Class 3

Randomly inserted into packs at the rate of 1:12, this 100-card set features color player photos printed on 35-point spectral-reflective rainbow polycarbonate stock with gold stamping. Each card showcases an NHL player on three different version of his base card. Displayed in the foreground of the Class 3 set is a photo of the player with an action shot appearing in the background featuring players with their masks off. Three parallel versions of this set were also produced: The Black Label Parallel with the Black Topps Gold Label logo, the Red Label Parallel identified by the Red Topps Gold Label logo and sequentially numbered to 25 (inserted at 1:293) and the One to One Parallel printed on special silver foil backs and numbered 1 of 1.

COMPLETE SET (100) 150.00 300.00
*STARS: 1.5X TO 4X CLASS 1 BASIC CARDS
*BLACK: 6X TO 12X CL.1 BASIC CARDS
*RED: 60X TO 150X CL.1 BASIC CARDS

1998-99 Topps Gold Label Goal Race '99

Randomly inserted in packs at the rate of 1:18, this 10-card set features color action photos of the top players who strike fear in the hearts of goalies night after night. Three parallel versions of this set were also produced: Black Label Parallel with the Black Topps Gold Label logo and insertion rate of 1:54; Red Label Parallel with the Red Topps Gold Label logo, insertion rate of 1:795, and sequentially numbered to 92; and One of One parallel version printed on special silver foil backs and sequentially numbered 1 of 1.

*BLACK: 1.25X TO 2.5X BASIC INSERTS
*RED: 3X TO 8X BASIC INSERTS
GR1 Eric Lindros 2.50 6.00
GR2 John LeClair 2.50 6.00
GR3 Teemu Selanne 2.50 6.00
GR4 Paul Kariya 2.50 6.00
GR5 Jaromir Jagr 4.00 10.00
GR6 Keith Tkachuk 2.50 6.00
GR7 Theo Fleury 2.50 6.00
GR8 Brendan Shanahan 2.50 6.00
GR9 Tony Amonte 2.00 5.00
GR10 Joe Sakic 5.00 12.00

1999-00 Topps Gold Label Class 1

This 100-card set features color player photos printed on 35-point spectral-reflective rainbow polycarbonate stock with gold stamping. Each card showcases an NHL player on three different versions of his base card. Displayed in the foreground of the Class 1 set is a photo of the player with an action shot appearing in the background featuring players skating and goalies standing upright. Three parallel versions of this set were also produced: The Black Label Parallel with the Black Topps Gold Label logo (inserted 1:18), the Red Label Parallel identified by the Red Topps Gold Label logo and sequentially numbered to 100 (inserted 1:32), and the One to One Parallel numbered 1 of 1.

COMPLETE SET (100) 30.00 60.00
*CLASS 1 BLACK: 3X TO 6X BASIC CARDS
*CLASS 1 BLACK RC's: 1.5X TO 3X
CLASS 1 BLACK STATED ODDS 1:18
*CLASS 1 RED: 20X TO 40X BASIC CARDS
*CLASS 1 RED RC's: 10X TO 20X
CLASS 1 RED PRINT RUN 100 SERIAL #'d SETS
NINE DIFFERENT 1 OF 1 PARALLELS EXIST
1 Dominik Hasek .75 2.00
2 Al MacInnis .30 .75
3 Luc Robitaille .30 .75
4 Steve Yzerman 2.00 5.00
5 Michael Peca .30 .75
6 Keith Tkachuk .40 1.00
7 Saku Koivu .40 1.00
8 Tony Amonte .30 .75
9 Peter Bondra .30 .75
10 Pavel Bure .40 1.00
11 Ron Francis .30 .75
12 Eric Lindros .40 1.00
13 Paul Kariya .40 1.00
14 Theo Fleury .08 .25
15 Jaromir Jagr .60 1.50
16 Patrick Roy 2.00 5.00
17 Zigmund Palffy .30 .75
18 Ed Belfour .40 1.00
19 Sergei Samsonov .30 .75
20 Nicklas Lidstrom .40 1.00
21 Pavol Demitra .30 .75
22 Sergei Fedorov .60 1.50
23 Teemu Selanne .40 1.00
24 Martin Brodeur 1.00 2.50
25 John LeClair .40 1.00
26 Ray Bourque .60 1.50
27 Peter Forsberg 1.00 2.50
28 Doug Weight .30 .75
29 Brian Leetch .40 1.00
30 Mark Recchi .30 .75
31 Jason Allison .08 .25
32 Rob Blake .30 .75
33 Scott Niedermayer .08 .25
34 Chris Pronger .30 .75
35 Joe Sakic .75 2.00
36 Mark Messier .40 1.00
37 Daniel Alfredsson .30 .75
38 Guy Hebert .30 .75
39 Bobby Holik .08 .25
40 Joe Thornton .60 1.50
41 Ron Tugnutt .30 .75
42 Jeff Friesen .08 .25
43 Jeremy Roenick .50 1.25
44 Wade Redden .08 .25
45 Chris Osgood .30 .75
46 Arturs Irbe .30 .75
47 Valeri Bure .08 .25
48 Chris Drury .30 .75
49 Owen Nolan .30 .75
50 Kenny Jonsson .08 .25
51 Petr Sykora .08 .25
52 Byron Dafoe .30 .75
53 Brett Hull .50 1.25
54 Mike Richter .40 1.00
55 Brendan Shanahan .40 1.00
56 Mats Sundin .40 1.00
57 Miroslav Satan .30 .75
58 Markus Naslund .40 1.00
59 Rod Brind'Amour .30 .75
60 Joe Nieuwendyk .30 .75
61 Petr Nedved .30 .75
62 Sergei Berezin .30 .75
63 Trevor Linden .30 .75
64 Marian Hossa .40 1.00
65 Pierre Turgeon .30 .75
66 Vincent Lecavalier .40 1.00
67 Sami Kapanen .08 .25
68 Andrew Brunette .08 .25
69 Brian Savage .08 .25
70 Derian Hatcher .08 .25
71 Curtis Joseph .40 1.00
72 Scott Stevens .30 .75
73 Radek Bonk .08 .25
74 Jarome Iginla .50 1.25
75 Adam Graves .08 .25
76 Alexander Selivanov .08 .25
77 Alexander Mogilny .30 .75
78 Cliff Ronning .30 .75
79 Vincent Damphousse .08 .25
80 Alexei Kovalev .08 .25
81 Yanic Perreault .08 .25
82 Alexander Korolyuk .08 .25
83 Jozef Stumpel .30 .75
84 Viktor Kozlov .08 .25
85 Mike Modano .60 1.50
86 David Legwand .08 .25
87 Scott Gomez .08 .25
88 Tim Connolly .08 .25
89 Brad Stuart .30 .75
90 Peter Schaefer .08 .25
91 Alex Tanguay .30 .75
92 Simon Gagne .40 1.00
93 Dave Tanabe .08 .25
94 Roberto Luongo .50 1.25
95 Martin Biron .30 .75
96 Mike Fisher RC .50 1.25
97 Patrik Stefan RC 1.25 3.00
98 Nikolai Antropov RC .75 2.00
99 Jochen Hecht RC 1.00 2.50
100 Steve Kariya RC .50 1.25

1999-00 Topps Gold Label Class 2

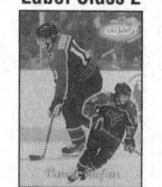

Randomly inserted into packs, this 100-card set features color player photos printed on 35-point spectral-reflective rainbow polycarbonate stock with gold stamping. Each card showcases an NHL player on three different version of his base card. Displayed in the foreground of the Class 2 set is a photo of the player with an action shot appearing in the background featuring players shooting and goalies sprawling. Three parallel versions of this set were also produced: The Black Label Parallel with the Black Topps Gold Label logo, the Red Label Parallel identified by the Red Topps Gold Label logo and sequentially numbered to 50, and the One to One Parallel numbered 1 of 1.

COMPLETE SET (100) 75.00 150.00
*CLASS 2: 1X TO 2.5X CLASS 1 BASIC CARDS
*BLACK STARS: 6X TO 12X CLASS 1 BASIC CARDS
*BLACK ROOKIE: 4X TO 8X CLASS 1 BASIC CARDS
*RED STARS: 35X TO 75X CLASS 1 BASIC CARDS
*RED ROOKIE: 20X TO 40X CLASS 1 BASIC CARDS

1999-00 Topps Gold Label Class 3

Randomly inserted into packs this 100-card set features color player photos printed on 35-point spectral-reflective rainbow polycarbonate stock with gold stamping. Each card showcases an NHL player on three different version of his base card. Displayed in the foreground of the Class 3 set is a photo of the player with an action shot appearing in the background featuring

players celebrating and goalies with their masks off. Three parallel versions of this set were also produced: The Black Label Parallel with the Black Topps Gold Label logo (inserted 1:72), the Red Label Parallel identified by the Red Topps Gold Label logo and sequentially numbered to 25 (inserted 1:129) and the One to One Parallel numbered 1 of 1.
COMPLETE SET (100) 150.00 300.00
*CLASS 3 : 1.5X TO 4X CLASS 1 BASIC CARDS
*BLACK STARS: 24X TO 50X CLASS 1 BASIC CARDS
*BLACK ROOKIE: 6X TO 12X CLASS 1 BASIC CARDS
*RED STARS: 60X TO 120X CLASS 1 BASIC CARDS
*RED ROOKIE: 20X TO 40X CLASS 1 BASIC CARDS

1999-00 Topps Gold Label Fresh Gold

Randomly inserted in packs at one in 30, this 20-card set focuses on young stars looking to make their mark on the game. Each card features an action foreground shot and a silhouette background shot. Black and Red Label parallels of this set were also randomly inserted in packs. Black parallels were inserted at 1:150 and were red parallels were inserted at 1:644 and serial numbered to 25. Card backs carry an "FG" prefix.
COMPLETE SET (20) 15.00 30.00
*BLACK: 2X TO 4X BASIC CARDS
*RED: 12.5X TO 25X BASIC CARDS
1/1 GOLD, BLACK, RED EXIST
1/1's NOT PRICED DUE TO SCARCITY
FG1 Sergei Samsonov .75 2.00
FG2 Joe Thornton 2.00 5.00
FG3 Wade Redden .75 2.00
FG4 Chris Drury .75 2.00
FG5 Petr Sykora .75 2.00
FG6 Patrik Stefan 2.00 5.00
FG7 Anson Carter .75 2.00
FG8 Martin Biron .75 2.00
FG9 Alex Tanguay .75 2.00
FG10 Milan Hejduk 1.25 3.00
FG11 Mark Parrish .75 2.00
FG12 David Legwand .75 2.00
FG13 Brendan Morrison .75 2.00
FG14 Scott Gomez .75 2.00
FG15 Tim Connolly 1.25 3.00
FG16 Marian Hossa 1.25 3.00
FG17 Jan Hrdina .75 2.00
FG18 Steve Kariya .75 2.00
FG19 Jochen Hecht 1.50 4.00
FG20 Vincent Lecavalier 1.25 3.00

1999-00 Topps Gold Label Prime Gold

Randomly inserted in packs at one in 20, this 15-card set showcases 15 veterans who have set their own standards, and have influenced how future players will be evaluated. The foreground features a full color action shot that is set against a silhouette background shot. Black and Red label parallels were also released of this set. Black parallels were inserted at 1:100 and were red parallels were inserted at 1:859 and serial numbered to 25. Card backs carry a "PG" prefix.
COMPLETE SET (15) 30.00 60.00
*BLACK: 2X TO 4X BASIC CARDS
*RED: 12.5X TO 25X BASIC CARDS
1/1 GOLD, BLACK, RED EXIST
1/1's NOT PRICED DUE TO SCARCITY
PG1 Dominik Hasek 3.00 8.00
PG2 Paul Kariya 1.50 4.00
PG3 Theo Fleury 1.25 3.00
PG4 Jaromir Jagr 2.50 6.00
PG5 Zigmund Palffy 1.25 3.00
PG6 Nicklas Lidstrom 1.50 4.00
PG7 Teemu Selanne 1.50 4.00
PG8 John LeClair 1.50 4.00
PG9 Ray Bourque 2.50 6.00
PG10 Peter Forsberg 4.00 10.00
PG11 Joe Sakic 3.00 8.00
PG12 Jeremy Roenick 2.00 5.00
PG13 Mike Modano 2.50 6.00
PG14 Pavel Bure 1.50 4.00
PG15 Curtis Joseph 1.50 4.00

1999-00 Topps Gold Label Quest for the Cup

Randomly seeded in packs at 1:12, this 10-card set celebrates the 10 teams most likely to contend for the 2000 Stanley Cup. Card fronts feature the player that best represents

his respective team set against the teams full color logo and the Stanley cup itself. Card backs carry a "QC" prefix. Black, red and gold parallels were also created and seeded randomly. Black parallels were inserted at 1:60. Red parallels were inserted at 1:1289 and were serial numbered to 25. Gold, black and red 1/1's also exist, but are not priced due to scarcity.
COMPLETE SET (10) 15.00 30.00
*BLACK: 2X TO 4X BASIC CARDS
*RED: 25X TO 50X BASIC CARDS
QC1 Steve Yzerman 4.00 10.00
QC2 Keith Tkachuk .75 2.00
QC3 Eric Lindros .75 2.00
QC4 Patrick Roy 4.00 10.00
QC5 Martin Brodeur 2.00 5.00
QC6 Chris Pronger .60 1.50
QC7 Daniel Alfredsson .60 1.50
QC8 Owen Nolan .60 1.50
QC9 Brett Hull 1.00 2.50
QC10 Mats Sundin .75 2.00

2000-01 Topps Gold Label Class 1

This 115-card set features color player photos printed on 35-point spectral-reflective rainbow styrene stock with gold stamping. Each card showcases an NHL player on three different versions of his base card. Displayed in the foreground of the Class 1 set is a photo of the player with an action shot appearing in the background featuring players skating and goalies standing upright. The last 15 cards in the set were sequentially numbered to 999. A gold parallel version of this set was also available in random packs where the same photos were used on gold tinted stock. In that version, cards 1-100 were sequentially numbered to 399 and cards 101-115 were numbered to 99. Topps Gold Label was packaged in 24-pack boxes with packs containing five cards and carried a suggested retail price of $5.00.
COMPLETE SET (115) 75.00 150.00
*GOLD STARS: 1.5X TO 3X BASIC CARDS
*GOLD ROOKIES: 1X TO 1.5X BASIC CARDS
1 Ray Bourque .75 2.00
2 Brendan Shanahan .40 1.00
3 Mark Recchi .30 .75
4 Olaf Kolzig .30 .75
5 Brett Hull .50 1.25
6 Valeri Bure .08 .25
7 Joe Thornton .60 1.50
8 Pavel Bure .40 1.00
9 Jeff Hackett .30 .75
10 Patrik Elias .30 .75
11 Marian Hossa .40 1.00
12 Patrick Marleau .30 .75
13 Markus Naslund .40 1.00
14 Jaromir Jagr .60 1.50
15 Tim Connolly .08 .25
16 Zigmund Palffy .30 .75
17 Peter Forsberg 1.00 2.50
18 Byron Dafoe .30 .75
19 Patrik Stefan .08 .25
20 Arturs Irbe .30 .75
21 Jocelyn Thibault .30 .75
22 Bill Guerin .30 .75
23 Keith Primeau .08 .25
24 Mats Sundin .40 1.00
25 Adam Oates .30 .75
26 Owen Nolan .30 .75
27 Mike Richter .40 1.00
28 Luc Robitaille .30 .75
29 Chris Drury .30 .75
30 Maxim Afinogenov .08 .25
31 Jarome Iginla .50 1.25
32 Joe Nieuwendyk .30 .75
33 Maxim Sushinski .08 .25
34 Daniel Alfredsson .30 .75
35 Pierre Turgeon .30 .75
36 Jason Allison .08 .25
37 Mario Lemieux 2.50 6.00
38 Sergei Fedorov .60 1.50
39 Paul Kariya .40 1.00
40 Scott Stevens .30 .75
41 Keith Tkachuk .40 1.00
42 Curtis Joseph .40 1.00
43 Peter Bondra .40 1.00
44 Roman Turek .30 .75
45 Alexei Kovalev .30 .75
46 Brian Boucher .40 1.00
47 Mark Messier .40 1.00
48 Saku Koivu .40 1.00
49 Tommy Salo .30 .75
50 Ron Tugnutt .30 .75
51 Patrick Roy 2.00 5.00
52 Fred Brathwaite .30 .75
53 Donald Audette .08 .25
54 Doug Gilmour .30 .75
55 Alexander Mogilny .30 .75
56 John LeClair .40 1.00
57 Scott Young .08 .25
58 Jeff Friesen .08 .25
59 Simon Gagne .40 1.00
60 Theo Fleury .08 .25
61 Scott Gomez .08 .25
62 Guy Hebert .30 .75
63 Roberto Luongo .50 1.25
64 Mike Modano .60 1.50
65 Joe Sakic .75 2.00
66 Dominik Hasek .75 2.00
67 Pavol Demitra .30 .75
68 Daniel Sedin .08 .25
69 Vincent Lecavalier .40 1.00
70 Jeremy Roenick .50 1.25
71 Martin Brodeur 1.00 2.50
72 Rob Blake .30 .75
73 Ed Belfour .40 1.00
74 Tony Amonte .30 .75
75 Miroslav Satan .30 .75
76 Alexei Yashin .08 .25
77 Henrik Sedin .08 .25
78 David Legwand .30 .75
79 Steve Yzerman 2.00 5.00
80 Ron Francis .30 .75
81 Milan Hejduk .40 1.00
82 Teemu Selanne .40 1.00
83 Brad Isbister .30 .75
84 Jean-Sebastien Aubin .30 .75
85 Chris Pronger .30 .75
86 Nicklas Lidstrom .40 1.00
87 Brad Richards .08 .25
88 Brent Johnson .08 .25
89 Oleg Saprykin .08 .25
90 Anson Carter .30 .75
91 Brian Leetch .30 .75
92 Evgeni Nabokov .30 .75
93 Ian Laperriere .08 .25
94 Peter White .08 .25
95 Wes Walz .08 .25
96 Jason Arnott .08 .25
97 Tommy Albelin .08 .25
98 Jeff Toms .08 .25
99 Brad Brown .08 .25
100 Garry Valk .08 .25
101 Andrew Raycroft RC 4.00 10.00
102 Marian Gaborik RC 12.50 30.00
103 David Aebischer RC 5.00 12.00
104 Scott Hartnell RC 2.50 6.00
105 Marty Turco RC 8.00 20.00
106 Justin Williams RC 3.00 8.00
107 Steven Reinprecht RC 1.25 3.00
108 Josef Vasicek RC 1.25 3.00
109 Martin Havlat RC 8.00 20.00
110 Rostislav Klesla RC 3.00 8.00
111 Jani Hurme RC 2.50 6.00
112 Rick DiPietro RC 5.00 12.00
113 Alexander Kharitonov RC 1.25 3.00
114 Matt Pettinger RC 1.25 3.00
115 Roman Cechmanek RC 1.50 4.00

2000-01 Topps Gold Label Class 2

Randomly inserted into packs, this 115-card set features color player photos printed on 35-point spectral-reflective rainbow styrene stock with gold stamping. Each card showcases an NHL player on three different versions of his base card. Displayed in the foreground of the Class 2 set is a photo of the player with an action shot appearing in the background featuring players shooting and goalies defending the net. The last 15 cards in the set were sequentially numbered to 666. A gold parallel version of this set was also available in random packs where the same photos were used on gold tinted stock. In that version, cards 1-100 were sequentially numbered to 299 and cards 101-115 were numbered to 66.
*STARS: 1.5X TO 3X CLASS 1 BASIC CARDS
*ROOKIES: 1X TO 1.5X CLASS 1 BASIC CARDS
*GOLD STARS: 3X TO 5X CLASS 1 BASIC CARDS
*GOLD ROOKIE: 1X TO 2X CLASS 1 BASIC CARDS

2000-01 Topps Gold Label Class 3

Randomly inserted into packs, this 115-card set features color player photos printed on 35-point spectral-reflective rainbow styrene stock with gold stamping. Each card showcases an NHL player on three different version of his base card. Displayed in the foreground of the Class 3 set is a photo of the player with an action shot appearing in the background featuring players defending and goalies playing the puck. The last 15 cards in the set were sequentially numbered to 333. A gold parallel version of this set was also available in random packs where the same photos were used on gold tinted stock. In that version, cards 1-100 were sequentially numbered to 199 and cards 101-115 were numbered to 33.
*STARS: 3X TO 5X CLASS 1 BASIC CARDS
*ROOKIES: X TO 1.5X CLASS 1 BASIC CARDS
*GOLD STARS: 4X TO 8X CLASS 1 BASIC CARDS
*GOLD ROOKIE: 2X TO 4X CLASS 1 BASIC CARDS

2000-01 Topps Gold Label Autographs

This 10-card set features authentic autographs of each player accompanied by an action photo and a large team logo on a reflective silver background. Each card also carries the Topps Certified Autograph stamp on front and a Topps Genuine Issue sticker on card back. These cards were available in random packs at stated odds of 1:57. The Gomez card was originally issued as an exchange card.

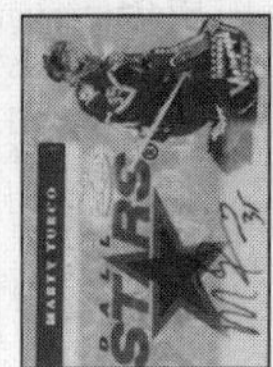

GLA-BB Brian Boucher 4.00 10.00
GLA-BR Brad Richards 6.00 15.00
GLA-JW Justin Williams 4.00 10.00
GLA-MG Marian Gaborik 12.50 30.00
GLA-MK Milan Kraft 4.00 10.00
GLA-MT Marty Turco 10.00 25.00
GLA-MY Mike York 4.00 10.00
GLA-RB Ray Bourque 20.00 50.00
GLA-SG Scott Gomez 4.00 10.00
GLA-SH Scott Hartnell 4.00 10.00

2000-01 Topps Gold Label Behind the Mask

This 10-card set was available in random packs at a stated odd of 1:7. The card fronts featured a color action shot of the player in the foreground over a larger player photo in the background. The players name is stamped in gold on the front along with a color team logo. A sparkle-texture treated parallel numbered 1 of 1 was also randomly available.
COMPLETE SET (10) 10.00 20.00
BTM1 Curtis Joseph
BTM2 Ed Belfour .75 2.00
BTM3 Dominik Hasek 1.50 4.00
BTM4 Martin Brodeur 2.00 5.00
BTM5 Brian Boucher .75 2.00
BTM6 Roman Turek .75 2.00
BTM7 Olaf Kolzig .75 2.00
BTM8 Patrick Roy 4.00 10.00
BTM9 Arturs Irbe .75 2.00
BTM10 Mike Richter .75 2.00

2000-01 Topps Gold Label Bullion

This 10-card set features photos of three teammates on a gold team logo background. These cards were available in random packs at stated odds of 1:21. A sparkle-texture treated parallel numbered 1 of 1 was also randomly available.
COMPLETE SET (10) 30.00 60.00
B1 M.Brodeur/S.Gomez/J.Arnott 4.00 10.00
B2 E.Belfour/M.Modano/B.Hull 3.00 8.00
B3 Steve Yzerman 6.00 12.00
Brendan Shanahan
Sergei Fedorov
B4 Patrick Roy 6.00 15.00
Ray Bourque
Peter Forsberg
B5 RomanTurek 2.00 5.00
Chris Pronger
Pavol Demitra
B6 Mats Sundin 4.00 10.00
Curtis Joseph
Tie Domi
B7 Jeremy Roenick 3.00 8.00
Keith Tkachuk
Teppo Numminen
B8 Jeff Friesen 3.00 8.00
Patrick Marleau
Owen Nolan
B9 Mark Messier 2.00 5.00
Brian Leetch
Mike Richter
B10 Daniel Sedin 2.00 5.00
Markus Naslund
Henrik Sedin

2000-01 Topps Gold Label Game-Worn Jerseys

This 6-card set was randomly available in packs at stated odds of 1:37. The card fronts featured a swatch of game-used jersey from the player featured along with an action photo of the player on a sparkle-texture treated foil. The card backs also contained a Topps Genuine Issue sticker.
GLJ-JL John LeClair 5.00 12.00
GLJ-KT Keith Tkachuk 5.00 12.00
GLJ-MB Martin Brodeur 10.00 25.00
GLJ-PF Peter Forsberg 10.00 25.00
GLJ-PM Patrick Marleau 5.00 12.00
GLJ-SF Sergei Fedorov 6.00 15.00

2000-01 Topps Gold Label Golden Greats

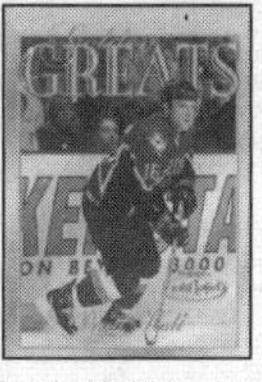

This 15-card set highlights players who scored 50-plus goals in a single season. The card fronts carry a gold-bordered action photo of the player. These cards were available in random packs at stated odds of 1:5. A sparkle-texture treated parallel numbered 1 of 1 was also randomly available.
GG1 Pavel Bure 1.25 3.00
GG2 Paul Kariya 1.00 2.50
GG3 Jaromir Jagr 1.50 4.00
GG4 John LeClair 1.25 3.00
GG5 Steve Yzerman 5.00 12.00
GG6 Brett Hull 1.25 3.00
GG7 Alexander Mogilny .75 2.00
GG8 Joe Sakic 2.00 5.00
GG9 Keith Tkachuk 1.00 2.50
GG10 Teemu Selanne 1.00 2.50
GG11 Sergei Fedorov 2.00 5.00
GG12 Luc Robitaille .75 2.00
GG13 Mike Modano 1.50 4.00
GG14 Brendan Shanahan 1.50 4.00
GG15 Jeremy Roenick 1.25 3.00

2000-01 Topps Gold Label New Generation

This 15-card set featured a color action photo of each player in the foreground and a larger photo of the players face in the background all set on a blue-bordered card front which also displayed the players name, position, and team logo. These cards were available in random packs at stated odds of 1:14. A sparkle-texture treated parallel numbered 1 of 1 was also randomly available.
NG1 Scott Gomez .75 2.00
NG2 Vincent Lecavalier 1.50 4.00
NG3 Joe Thornton 2.50 6.00
NG4 Alex Tanguay 1.25 3.00
NG5 Marian Hossa 1.50 4.00
NG6 Brad Stuart .75 2.00
NG7 Henrik Sedin .75 2.00
NG8 Marian Gaborik 4.00 10.00
NG9 Roberto Luongo 2.00 5.00
NG10 David Legwand .75 2.00
NG11 Daniel Sedin .75 2.00
NG12 Patrik Stefan .75 2.00
NG13 Brian Boucher 1.25 3.00
NG14 Chris Drury 1.25 3.00
NG15 Tim Connolly .75 2.00

2000-01 Topps Heritage

Topps Heritage was released in 2000-01 as a 247-card set. The cards had the same design as that of the 1954-55 Topps set. The rookies from the set were short-printed and serial numbered to 1955. They were available in packs at a rate of 1:12.
COMP.SET w/o SP's 25.00 50.00
1 Ray Bourque .75 2.00
2 Martin Brodeur 1.00 2.50
3 Jaromir Jagr .60 1.50
4 Vincent Lecavalier .40 1.00
5 Olaf Kolzig .30 .75
6 Alexei Yashin .10 .30
7 Mark Messier .40 1.00
8 Paul Kariya .40 1.00
9 Pavel Bure .40 1.00
10 Steve Yzerman 2.00 5.00
11 Patrik Stefan .10 .30
12 Joe Thornton .60 1.50
13 Mats Sundin .40 1.00
14 Brett Hull .50 1.25
15 Zigmund Palffy .30 .75
16 Peter Bondra .40 1.00
17 Owen Nolan .30 .75
18 Tony Amonte .30 .75
19 Henrik Sedin .10 .30
20 Keith Tkachuk .40 1.00
21 Tim Connolly .10 .30
22 Doug Weight .30 .75
23 Ed Belfour .40 1.00
24 Patrick Roy 2.00 5.00
25 Brad Richards .10 .30
26 Dominik Hasek .75 2.00
27 Brendan Shanahan .40 1.00
28 Teemu Selanne .40 1.00
29 Scott Gomez .10 .30
30 John LeClair .40 1.00
31 Chris Pronger .30 .75
32 Ron Francis .30 .75
33 Daniel Sedin .10 .30
34 Curtis Joseph .40 1.00
35 Roman Turek .30 .75
36 Jeremy Roenick .50 1.25
37 Mark Recchi .30 .75
38 Patrik Elias .30 .75
39 Saku Koivu .40 1.00
40 Luc Robitaille .30 .75
41 Sergei Fedorov .60 1.50
42 Peter Forsberg 1.00 2.50
43 Milan Kraft .30 .75
44 Jason Allison .10 .30
45 Mike Modano .60 1.50
46 Roberto Luongo .50 1.25
47 David Legwand .30 .75
48 Pierre Turgeon .30 .75
49 Maxime Ouellet .30 .75
50 Oleg Saprykin .10 .30
51 Pavol Demitra .30 .75
52 Adam Oates .30 .75
53 Doug Gilmour .30 .75
54 Joe Sakic .75 2.00
55 Daniel Alfredsson .30 .75
56 Brian Leetch .30 .75
57 Bill Guerin .30 .75
58 Brent Johnson .10 .30
59 Scott Stevens .30 .75
60 Rob Blake .30 .75
61 Nicklas Lidstrom .40 1.00
62 Milan Hejduk .40 1.00
63 Arturs Irbe .30 .75
64 Maxim Afinogenov .10 .30
65 Taylor Pyatt .10 .30
66 Tommy Salo .30 .75
67 Theo Fleury .10 .30
68 Marian Hossa .40 1.00
69 Simon Gagne .40 1.00
70 Jarome Iginla .50 1.25
71 Alexander Mogilny .30 .75
72 Chris Drury .30 .75
73 Mario Lemieux 2.50 6.00
74 Petr Hubacek RC 3.00 10.00
75 Marty Turco RC 10.00 25.00
76 Rostislav Klesla RC 6.00 15.00
77 Martin Havlat RC 10.00 25.00
78 David Aebischer RC 8.00 20.00
79 Reto Von Arx RC 3.00 10.00
80 Mike Comrie RC 6.00 15.00
81 Tomas Kloucek RC 3.00 10.00
82 Steven Reinprecht RC 3.00 10.00
83 Brad Tapper RC 3.00 10.00
84 Petr Svoboda RC 3.00 10.00
85 Marian Gaborik RC 10.00 25.00
86 Josef Vasicek RC 3.00 10.00
87 Lubomir Visnovsky RC 3.00 10.00
88 Roman Cechmanek RC 3.00 8.00
89 Reed Low RC 3.00 10.00
90 Jani Hurme RC 3.00 8.00
91 Petteri Nummelin RC 3.00 10.00
92 Colin White RC 3.00 10.00
93 Andrew Raycroft RC 6.00 15.00
94 Greg Classen RC 3.00 10.00
95 Alexander Kharitonov RC 3.00 10.00
96 Rick DiPietro RC 8.00 20.00
97 Justin Williams RC 6.00 15.00
98 Eric Belanger RC 3.00 10.00
99 Scott Hartnell RC 3.00 10.00
100 Michel Riesen RC 3.00 10.00
101 Brian Boucher .30 .75
102 Mike Richter .40 1.00
103 John Vanbiesbrouck .30 .75
104 Jamie McLennan .10 .30
105 Andrei Markov .10 .30
106 Ron Tugnutt .30 .75
107 Jean-Sebastien Aubin .30 .75
108 Brad Stuart .10 .30
109 Gary Roberts .10 .30
110 Rod Brind'Amour .30 .75
111 Keith Primeau .10 .30
112 Jeff Halpern .10 .30
113 Jochen Hecht .10 .30
114 Valeri Bure .10 .30
115 Donald Audette .10 .30
116 Brenden Morrow .30 .75
117 Mike Mottau .10 .30
118 Kevin Weekes .10 .30
119 Jamie Storr .30 .75
120 Shane Willis .10 .30
121 Matt Cooke .10 .30
122 Martin Lapointe .10 .30
123 Alexei Kovalev .30 .75
124 Felix Potvin .40 1.00
125 Sean Burke .30 .75
126 Jeff Hackett .30 .75
127 Brad Isbister .10 .30
128 Derian Hatcher .10 .30
129 Marc Savard .10 .30
130 Sergei Samsonov .30 .75
131 Maxim Sushinski .10 .30
132 Radek Bonk .10 .30
133 Mika Noronen .10 .30
134 Adam Graves .10 .30
135 Sheldon Keefe .10 .30
136 Markus Naslund .40 1.00
137 Trevor Letowski .10 .30
138 Jeff Friesen .10 .30
139 Alex Tanguay .30 .75
140 Byron Dafoe .30 .75
141 Chris Osgood .30 .75
142 Mike York .10 .30
143 Scott Young .10 .30
144 Sami Kapanen .10 .30
145 Evgeni Nabokov .30 .75
146 Brendan Morrison .30 .75
147 Joe Nieuwendyk .30 .75
148 Tomi Kallio .10 .30
149 Guy Hebert .30 .75
150 Randy McKay .10 .30
151 Mike Johnson .10 .30
152 Miroslav Satan .30 .75
153 Patrick Marleau .30 .75
154 Jocelyn Thibault .30 .75
155 Martin Straka .10 .30
156 Fred Brathwaite .30 .75
157 Cliff Ronning .10 .30
158 Denis Shvidki .10 .30
159 Espen Knutsen .10 .30
160 Alexei Zhamnov .10 .30
161 Georges Laraque .10 .30
162 Jose Theodore .50 1.25
163 Rick Tocchet .10 .30
164 Donald Brashear .10 .30
165 Darren Langdon .10 .30
166 Rob Ray .10 .30
167 Matthew Barnaby .10 .30
168 Chris Simon .10 .30
169 Ken Belanger .10 .30
170 Tie Domi .30 .75
171 Roman Hamrlik .10 .30
172 Olli Jokinen .30 .75
173 Steve Rucchin .10 .30
174 Jim Cummins .10 .30
175 Tyson Nash .10 .30
176 Scott Parker .10 .30
177 Matt Johnson .10 .30
178 Sandy McCarthy .10 .30
179 Daniel Cleary .10 .30
180 Michal Handzus .10 .30
181 Nikolai Antropov .10 .30
182 Scott Thornton .10 .30
183 Shane Doan .10 .30
184 Wade Redden .10 .30
185 Ray Whitney .10 .30
186 Teppo Numminen .10 .30
187 Pat Verbeek .10 .30
188 Bobby Holik .10 .30
189 Mike Dunham .30 .75
190 Rob Niedermayer .10 .30
191 Ray Ferraro .10 .30
192 Steve Sullivan .10 .30
193 Sergei Zubov .10 .30
194 Scott Walker .10 .30
195 Geoff Sanderson .10 .30
196 Bob Probert .10 .30
197 Andrew Brunette .10 .30
198 Marty Murray .10 .30
199 Steve Staios .10 .30
200 Kay Whitmore .10 .30
201 Jonas Hoglund .10 .30
202 Niklas Andersson .10 .30
203 Joaquin Gage .10 .30
204 Mike Ricci .10 .30
205 Bryan Helmer .10 .30
206 Patrick Traverse .10 .30
207 Mike Rucinski .10 .30
208 Brantt Myhres .10 .30
209 Claude Lapointe .10 .30
210 Frank Musil .10 .30
211 Sandis Ozolinsh .10 .30
212 Tomas Vokoun .30 .75
213 Jarrod Skalde .10 .30
214 Sergei Gonchar .10 .30
215 Anson Carter .30 .75
216 Steve Yzerman AS 1.00 2.50
217 Mike Modano AS .30 .75
218 Paul Kariya AS .20 .50
219 Brendan Shanahan AS .30 .75
220 Pavel Bure AS .30 .75
221 Jaromir Jagr AS .30 .75
222 Chris Pronger AS .30 .75
223 Nicklas Lidstrom AS .20 .50
224 Rob Blake AS .10 .30
225 Eric Desjardins AS .10 .30
226 Olaf Kolzig AS .10 .30
227 Roman Turek AS .10 .30
228 S.Stevens/C.Pronger LL .10 .30
229 S.Gomez/A.Tanguay LL .20 .50
230 P.Bure/O.Nolan LL .30 .75
231 M.Brodeur/R.Turek LL .40 1.00
232 M.Czerkawski/O.Nolan LL .10 .30
233 J.Theodore/E.Belfour LL .20 .50
234 J.Madden/T.Amonte LL .20 .50
235 J.Jagr/P.Kariya LL .20 .50
236 E.Desjardins/N.Lidstrom LL .20 .50
237 B.Boucher/R.Turek LL .10 .30
238 Steve Yzerman AW 1.00 2.50
239 Scott Stevens AW .10 .30
240 Scott Gomez AW .15 .40
241 Roman Turek AW .10 .30
242 Pavol Demitra AW .10 .30
243 Pavel Bure AW .40 1.00
244 Olaf Kolzig AW .10 .30
245 Jaromir Jagr AW .30 .75
246 Chris Pronger AW .10 .30
247 New Jersey Devils SC .10 .30

2000-01 Topps Heritage Chrome Parallel

Randomly inserted in packs of Topps Heritage, the 100-card parallel set featured the chrome version of the base set. The cards were serial numbered to 555.
*STARS: 3X TO 6X BASIC CARDS
*ROOKIES: .25X TO .6X

2000-01 Topps Heritage Arena Relics

Randomly inserted in packs of 2000-01 Topps Heritage at a rate of 1:128, this 15-card set featured original pieces from the old arenas. The 2 autographed cards were available in packs at a rate of 1:12345. The multi-piece arena relic was available in packs at a rate of 1:11536.

OSA-JT Joe Thornton 10.00 25.00
OSA-MM Mark Messier 10.00 25.00
OSA-MS Mats Sundin 10.00 25.00
OSA-SK Saku Koivu 10.00 25.00
OSA-SY Steve Yzerman 12.50 30.00
OSA-TA Tony Amonte 10.00 25.00
OSA-BG Bill Gadsby 10.00 25.00
OSA-GH Gordie Howe 12.50 30.00
OSA-LW Gump Worsley 10.00 25.00
OSA-MR Maurice Richard 20.00 50.00
OSA-MS Milt Schmidt 10.00 25.00
OSA-TK Ted Kennedy 10.00 25.00
OSA Multi Arena Relic/55 200.00 500.00
HAA-GH Gordie Howe AU/25 250.00 500.00
HAA-LW Gump Worsley AU/25 75.00 200.00

2000-01 Topps Heritage Autographs

This 12-card set was randomly inserted in packs at a rate of 1:184 for the current players and 1:97 for the reprints of former NHL players. Please note that at the time of its release Topps included Joe Thornton and Tony Amonte as exchange/redemption cards. Tony Amonte did not sign his cards, the exchange card was redeemable for a similar card from other Topps issues.

HA-AG Adam Graves 10.00 25.00
HA-CJ Curtis Joseph 10.00 25.00
HA-JH Jeff Hackett 5.00 12.00
HA-JT Joe Thornton 15.00 40.00
HA-SF Sergei Fedorov 15.00 40.00
HA-TA Exchange Card
HA-AB Andy Bathgate 10.00 25.00
HA-AD Alex Delvecchio 10.00 25.00
HA-GH Gordie Howe 60.00 150.00
HA-LW Gump Worsley 15.00 40.00
HA-RK Red Kelly 10.00 25.00
HA-TL Ted Lindsay 10.00 25.00

2000-01 Topps Heritage Autoproofs

Randomly inserted in 2000-01 Topps Heritage packs, this 6-card set was created by using original 1954-55 Topps Hockey cards and having the featured player autograph the card. The cards were then serial numbered to 10 for each player. Please note that the Gordie Howe and Andy Bathgate cards were issued as exchange/redemption cards. These cards are not priced due to scarcity.

5 Red Kelly
8 Gordie Howe
10 Gump Worsley
11 Andy Bathgate
39 Alex Delvecchio
51 Ted Lindsay

2000-01 Topps Heritage Heroes

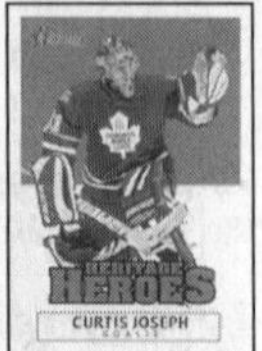

COMPLETE SET (20) 25.00 50.00
STATED ODDS: 1:14
HH1 Ray Bourque 1.50 4.00
HH2 Jaromir Jagr 1.25 3.00
HH3 Steve Yzerman 4.00 10.00
HH4 Mike Modano 1.25 3.00
HH5 Patrick Roy 4.00 10.00
HH6 Martin Brodeur 2.00 5.00
HH7 Mark Messier 1.00 2.50
HH8 Peter Forsberg 2.00 5.00
HH9 Scott Stevens .60 1.50
HH10 Teemu Selanne .75 2.00
HH11 Pavel Bure 1.00 2.50
HH12 Curtis Joseph .75 2.00
HH13 John LeClair 1.00 2.50
HH14 Brett Hull 1.00 2.50
HH15 Keith Tkachuk .75 2.00
HH16 Tony Amonte .60 1.50
HH17 Ed Belfour .75 2.00
HH18 Brendan Shanahan 1.25 3.00
HH19 Dominik Hasek 1.50 4.00
HH20 Paul Kariya .75 2.00

2000-01 Topps Heritage New Tradition

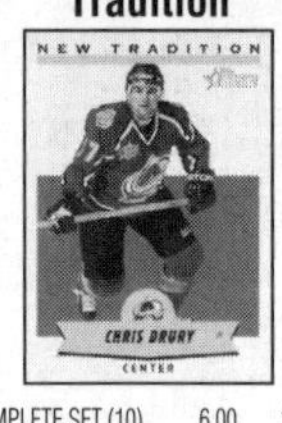

COMPLETE SET (10) 6.00 12.00
STATED ODDS: 1:8
NT1 Marian Hossa .50 1.25
NT2 Daniel Sedin .40 1.00
NT3 Milan Hejduk .50 1.25
NT4 Vincent Lecavalier .50 1.25
NT5 Joe Thornton .75 2.00
NT6 Scott Gomez .40 1.00
NT7 Chris Drury .40 1.00
NT8 Brian Boucher .40 1.00
NT9 Henrik Sedin .40 1.00
NT10 Marian Gaborik 2.00 5.00

2000-01 Topps Heritage Original Six Relics

Randomly inserted in packs at a rate of 1:409, this 16-card set featured original pieces from game-used hockey sticks or jerseys. The 2 autographed jersey cards that were available in packs at a rate of 1:8240. The multi-piece relics were available in packs at a rate of 1:11,536. The jersey cards were available in packs at a rate of 1:51. Tony Amonte did not sign his autograph cards, the exchange card was redeemed for similar cards from other Topps issues.

*MULT.COLOR STICK/SWATCH: 1X TO 2X
OSJ-AZ Alexei Zhamnov J 5.00 12.00
OSJ-CO Chris Osgood J 5.00 12.00
OSJ-JT Joe Thornton J 8.00 20.00
OSJ-SK Saku Koivu J 5.00 12.00
OSJ-TD Tie Domi J 5.00 12.00
OSJ-TF Theo Fleury J 5.00 12.00
OSS-BP Bob Probert S 5.00 12.00
OSS-JA Jason Allison S 10.00 25.00
OSS-JH Jeff Hackett S 10.00 25.00
OSS-MM Mark Messier S 10.00 25.00
OSS-MS Mats Sundin S 10.00 25.00
OSS-SY Steve Yzerman S 15.00 40.00
OSJ Alexei Zhamnov 125.00 250.00
Theo Fleury
Chris Osgood
Joe Thornton
Saku Koivu
Tie Domi/55
OSJA-JH Jeff Hackett 40.00 80.00
JSY AU/25
OSJA-JT Joe Thornton 75.00 200.00
JSY AU/25

2001-02 Topps Heritage

Released in early December 2001, this 187-card set borrowed from the 1957-58 Topps design. This set carried an SRP of $3.00 for an 8-card pack, and each pack included a stick of gum. Rookies were seeded at 1:3.

COMPLETE SET (187) 100.00 200.00
1 Mario Lemieux 2.50 6.00
2 Evgeni Nabokov .30 .75
3 Nicklas Lidstrom .40 1.00
4 Patrik Elias .30 .75
5 Olaf Kolzig .30 .75
6 Mats Sundin .40 1.00
7 Jason Allison .10 .30
8 Mike Modano .60 1.50
9 Keith Tkachuk .40 1.00
10 John LeClair .40 1.00
11 Pavel Bure .40 1.00
12 Tony Amonte .30 .75
13 Zigmund Palffy .30 .75
14 Mark Messier .40 1.00
15 Sean Burke .30 .75
16 Markus Naslund .40 1.00
17 Milan Hejduk .40 1.00
18 Teemu Selanne .40 1.00
19 Espen Knutsen .10 .30
20 David Legwand .30 .75
21 Saku Koivu .40 1.00
22 Ron Francis .30 .75
23 Ray Ferraro .10 .30
24 Brendan Shanahan .40 1.00
25 Rick DiPietro .30 .75
26 Brad Richards .30 .75
27 Henrik Sedin .10 .30
28 Marian Hossa .40 1.00
29 Marian Gaborik .75 2.00
30 Ed Belfour .40 1.00
31 Miroslav Satan .30 .75
32 Roberto Luongo .50 1.25
33 Brian Leetch .30 .75
34 Chris Pronger .30 .75
35 Peter Bondra .40 1.00
36 Keith Primeau .10 .30
37 Johan Hedberg .30 .75
38 Steve Yzerman 2.00 5.00
39 Peter Forsberg 1.00 2.50
40 Jarome Iginla .50 1.25
41 Jose Theodore .50 1.25
42 Curtis Joseph .40 1.00
43 Martin Havlat .30 .75
44 Sergei Fedorov .60 1.50
45 Arturs Irbe .30 .75
46 Martin Brodeur 1.00 2.50
47 Owen Nolan .30 .75
48 Daniel Sedin .10 .30
49 Mark Recchi .30 .75
50 Adam Deadmarsh .10 .30
51 Tommy Salo .30 .75
52 Alexei Kovalev .30 .75
53 Steve Sullivan .10 .30
54 Paul Kariya .40 1.00
55 Vincent Lecavalier .40 1.00
56 Alex Tanguay .30 .75
57 Joe Thornton .60 1.50
58 Brent Johnson .30 .75
59 Roman Cechmanek .30 .75
60 Petr Sykora .10 .30
61 J-P Dumont .10 .30
62 Mike Comrie .30 .75
63 Daniel Alfredsson .30 .75
64 Eric Daze .30 .75
65 Felix Potvin .40 1.00
66 Chris Drury .30 .75
67 Manny Fernandez .30 .75
68 Claude Lemieux .10 .30
69 Rob Blake .30 .75
70 Bill Guerin .30 .75
71 Mike Dunham .30 .75
72 Simon Gagne .40 1.00
73 Jeff Friesen .10 .30
74 Joe Sakic .75 2.00
75 Jason Arnott .10 .30
76 Patrick Roy 2.00 5.00
77 Josef Vasicek .30 .75
78 Marty Turco .30 .75
79 Al MacInnis .30 .75
80 Anson Carter .30 .75
81 Tomi Kallio .10 .30
82 Eric Belanger .10 .30
83 Patrick Lalime .30 .75
84 Scott Young .10 .30
85 Scott Gomez .10 .30
86 Marc Denis .30 .75
87 Jeff O'Neill .10 .30
88 Sergei Samsonov .30 .75
89 Robert Lang .10 .30
90 Byron Dafoe .30 .75
91 Scott Stevens .30 .75
92 Adam Oates .30 .75
93 Patrick Marleau .30 .75
94 Petr Nedved .10 .30
95 Ryan Smyth .10 .30
96 Adam Foote .10 .30
97 Marc Savard .10 .30
98 Brad Isbister .10 .30
99 Martin Straka .10 .30
100 Joe Nieuwendyk .30 .75
101 Shane Willis .10 .30
102 Pavol Demitra .30 .75
103 Jeff Halpern .10 .30
104 Sergei Zubov .10 .30
105 David Vyborny .10 .30
106 Gary Roberts .10 .30
107 Martin Biron .30 .75
108 Lubomir Visnovsky .10 .30
109 Fredrik Modin .10 .30
110 Brenden Morrow .30 .75
111 Stanley Cup .40 1.00
112 Nicklas Lidstrom AS .20 .50
113 Jaromir Jagr AS .30 .75
114 Patrik Elias AS .20 .50
115 Joe Sakic AS .40 1.00
116 Dominik Hasek AS .40 1.00
117 Rob Blake AS .15 .40
118 Scott Stevens AS .15 .40
119 Roman Cechmanek AS .15 .40
120 Mario Lemieux AS 1.25 3.00
121 Pavel Bure AS .30 .75
122 Luc Robitaille AS .20 .50
123 Jaromir Jagr .30 .75
Joe Sakic LL
124 Pavel Bure .30 .75
Joe Sakic LL
125 Patrik Elias .40 1.00
Joe Sakic LL
126 Brian Leetch .20 .50
Nicklas Lidstrom LL
127 Arturs Irbe .15 .40
Tommy Salo LL
128 M.Brodeur/P.Roy LL 1.00 2.50
129 Marty Turco .15 .40
Roman Cechmanek LL
130 Joe Sakic AW .40 1.00
131 Patrick Roy AW 1.00 2.50
132 Pavel Bure AW .30 .75
133 Evgeni Nabokov AW .15 .40
134 Nicklas Lidstrom AW .20 .50
135 Dominik Hasek AW .40 1.00
136 John Madden AW .05 .15
137 Jaromir Jagr AW .30 .75
138 Ilya Kovalchuk RC 6.00 15.00
139 Niko Kapanen RC 2.00 5.00
140 Brian Sutherby RC 2.00 5.00
141 Jeff Jillson RC 2.00 5.00
142 Jiri Dopita RC 2.00 5.00
143 Andreas Salomonsson RC 2.00 5.00
144 Timo Parssinen RC 2.00 5.00
145 Vaclav Nedorost RC 2.00 5.00
146 Kristian Huselius RC 2.00 5.00
147 Dan Blackburn RC 1.50 4.00
148 Nikita Alexeev RC 2.00 5.00
149 Peter Smrek RC 2.00 5.00
150 Krys Kolanos RC 2.00 5.00
151 Pavel Datsyuk RC 5.00 12.00
152 Jaroslav Bednar RC 2.00 5.00
153 Chris Neil RC 2.00 5.00
154 Erik Cole RC 2.50 6.00
155 Niklas Hagman RC 2.00 5.00
156 Jason Chimera RC 2.00 5.00
157 Scott Clemmensen RC 2.00 5.00
158 Andrew Brunette .30 .75
159 Dominik Hasek 2.50 6.00
160 Jaromir Jagr .60 1.50
161 Doug Weight 1.00 2.50
162 Brett Hull 1.50 4.00
163 Pierre Turgeon 1.00 2.50
164 Jeremy Roenick 1.50 4.00
165 Alexander Mogilny 1.00 2.50
166 Luc Robitaille 1.00 2.50
167 Michael Peca .30 .75
168 Roman Turek 1.00 2.50
169 Martin Lapointe .30 .75
170 Alexei Yashin .30 .75
171 Adam Graves .30 .75
172 Valeri Bure .30 .75
173 Tim Connolly .30 .75
174 Kris Beech .30 .75
175 Donald Audette .30 .75
176 Jochen Hecht .30 .75
177 Fred Brathwaite 1.00 2.50
178 Rob Niedermayer .30 .75
179 Eric Lindros .40 1.00
180 Bill Muckalt .30 .75
181 Eric Weinrich .30 .75
182 Taylor Pyatt .30 .75
183 Pavel Brendl 1.00 2.50
184 Craig Berube .30 .75
185 Dany Heatley .50 1.25
186 Ken Sutton .30 .75
187 Slava Kozlov .30 .75

2001-02 Topps Heritage Refractors

Printed on chrome reflective stock, this 110-card set paralleled the base set and was serial numbered to just 558 sets.

*REFRACTORS: 3X TO 6X BASIC CARD

2001-02 Topps Heritage Arena Relics

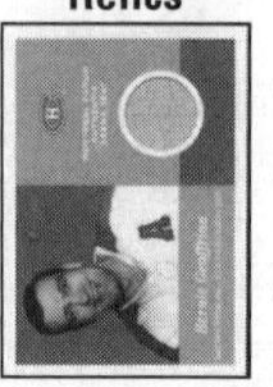

This 13-card hobby only set featured pieces of arena seats from the Montreal Forum and Boston Gardens. Cards featuring single players were inserted at 1:149. Dual player cards were serial-numbered to 100 and inserted at 1:994 Dual payer cards included two pieces of arena seats. Autographed versions of this set were inserted at 1:1491 for single player and 1:3976 for dual player. Autographed cards with dual players were serial-numbered out of 25 and are not priced due to scarcity.

RBG Bernie Geoffrion 6.00 15.00
RHR Henri Richard 6.00 15.00
RJBE Jean Beliveau 10.00 25.00
RJBU John Bucyk 6.00 15.00
RJB/BG J.Bucyk/B.Geoffrion 20.00 50.00
RJB/HR John Bucyk 20.00 50.00
Henri Richard
RJB/JB John Bucyk 30.00 80.00
Jean Beliveau
ARBG Bernie Geoffrion AU 30.00 80.00
ARHR Henri Richard AU 40.00 100.00
ARJBE Jean Beliveau AU 30.00 80.00
ARJBU John Bucyk AU 60.00 150.00
ARJB/BG John Bucyk AU
Bernie Geoffrion AU
ARJB/HR John Bucyk AU
Henri Richard AU
ARJB/JB John Bucyk AU
Jean Beliveau AU

2001-02 Topps Heritage Autographs

This 16-card set featured authentic autographs of current and former players on the classic 1957-58 design. Current player cards were inserted at 1:156, reprints were inserted at 1:91 and cards #ABG, AHR and AJBE were inserted at 1:182. Overall odds of autograph cards were 1:44.

AAA Al Arbour 10.00 25.00
ABG Bernie Geoffrion 10.00 25.00
AGH Glenn Hall 10.00 25.00
AHH Harry Howell 10.00 25.00
AHR Henri Richard 10.00 25.00
AIK Ilya Kovalchuk 20.00 50.00
AJH Johan Hedberg 10.00 25.00
AJW Justin Williams 10.00 25.00
AMG Marian Gaborik 15.00 40.00
AMS Miroslav Satan 10.00 25.00
ANU Norm Ullman 10.00 25.00
AOK Olaf Kolzig 10.00 25.00
APP Pierre Pilote 10.00 25.00
AVL Vincent Lecavalier 10.00 25.00
AJBE Jean Beliveau 15.00 40.00
AJBU John Bucyk 15.00 40.00

2001-02 Topps Heritage Captain's Cloth

This 6-card set featured game-worn jersey swatches from team captains from around the league. Cards from this set were randomly inserted at 1:76 hobby packs.

*MULT.COLOR SWATCH: .75X TO 1.5X
CCAO Adam Oates 6.00 15.00
CCDH Derian Hatcher 6.00 15.00
CCED Eric Desjardins 8.00 20.00
CCPK Paul Kariya 8.00 20.00
CCSK Saku Koivu 8.00 20.00
CCVL Vincent Lecavalier 6.00 15.00

2001-02 Topps Heritage Jerseys

This 10-card hobby only set was inserted at overall odds of 1:17 packs. Cards from this set featured swatches of game-worn jerseys from the featured players.

JBL Brian Leetch 6.00 15.00
JJI Jarome Iginla 8.00 20.00
JJL John LeClair 6.00 15.00
JJT Joe Thornton 8.00 20.00
JMB Martin Brodeur 12.50 30.00
JMS Martin Straka 6.00 15.00
JPF Peter Forsberg 10.00 25.00
JPM Patrick Marleau 6.00 15.00
JRL Robert Lang 6.00 15.00
JSF Sergei Fedorov 8.00 20.00

2001-02 Topps Heritage Salute

This 9-card set featured 6 reprints from the 1957-58 Topps set and 3 "cards that never were" (S7-S9). Cards from this set were inserted at 1:16.

COMPLETE SET (9) 1.00 30.00
S1 John Bucyk 2.50 6.00
S2 Al Arbour 2.00 5.00
S3 Glenn Hall 2.50 6.00
S4 Harry Howell 2.00 5.00
S5 Pierre Pilote 2.00 5.00
S6 Norm Ullman 2.00 5.00
S7 Jean Beliveau 2.50 6.00
S8 Henri Richard 2.00 5.00
S9 Bernie Geoffrion 2.50 6.00

2001 Topps Heritage Avalanche NHL All-Star Game

This six card set was produced by Topps as a wrapper redemption for the 2001 All-Star Fan Fest. Base cards feature full color player action photos set against a white background with the Avalanche logo in the upper left hand corner and a blue and red border along the card bottom. Overlaying the pictures is a facsimile of the featured player's autograph.

COMPLETE SET (6) 12.00 30.00
1 Ray Bourque 3.20 8.00

2 Patrick Roy 4.00 10.00
3 Peter Forsberg 3.20 8.00
4 Joe Sakic 2.40 6.00
5 Milan Hejduk 1.60 4.00
6 Chris Drury 1.60 4.00

2002-03 Topps Heritage

Released in December 2002, this 180-card set borrowed from the classic "woodgrain" design of 1966-67 Topps. Cards 131-180 were inserted at a rate of 1:4. Original 1966-67 cards were also repurchased and randomly inserted into packs at 1:1687.

COMPLETE SET (180) 125.00 250.00
COMP.SET w/o SP's (130) 40.00 80.00
1 Nicklas Lidstrom .40 1.00
2 Jarome Iginla .50 1.25
3 Jose Theodore .50 1.25
4 Ron Francis .30 .75
5 Joe Thornton .60 1.50
6 Jaromir Jagr .60 1.50
7 Mario Lemieux 2.50 6.00
8 Roberto Luongo .50 1.25
9 Dany Heatley .50 1.25
10 Pavel Bure .40 1.00
11 Brett Hull .50 1.25
12 Keith Tkachuk .40 1.00
13 Mats Sundin .40 1.00
14 Pavel Datsyuk .40 1.00
15 Daniel Alfredsson .30 .75
16 Marian Gaborik .75 2.00
17 Peter Forsberg 1.00 2.50
18 Miroslav Satan .30 .75
19 Martin Brodeur 1.00 2.50
20 Jeremy Roenick .50 1.25
21 Teemu Selanne .40 1.00
22 Todd Bertuzzi .40 1.00
23 Erik Cole .10 .30
24 Jason Allison .10 .30
25 Sean Burke .30 .75
26 Eric Daze .30 .75
27 Patrick Roy 2.00 5.00
28 Simon Gagne .40 1.00
29 Nikolai Khabibulin .40 1.00
30 Alexei Yashin .10 .30
31 Denis Arkhipov .10 .30
32 Steve Yzerman 2.00 5.00
33 Mike Modano .60 1.50
34 Joe Sakic .75 2.00
35 Sergei Samsonov .30 .75
36 Saku Koivu .40 1.00
37 Paul Kariya .40 1.00
38 Doug Weight .30 .75
39 Tie Domi .30 .75
40 Kevin Weekes .30 .75
41 Rostislav Klesla .10 .30
42 Zigmund Palffy .30 .75
43 Chris Osgood .30 .75
44 Owen Nolan .30 .75
45 Markus Naslund .40 1.00
46 Martin Biron .30 .75
47 Ryan Smyth .10 .30
48 Mike Dunham .30 .75
49 Martin Havlat .30 .75
50 Patrik Elias .30 .75
51 Peter Bondra .40 1.00
52 Craig Conroy .10 .30
53 Rob Blake .30 .75
54 Mike Richter .40 1.00
55 Stephen Weiss .10 .30
56 Johan Hedberg .30 .75
57 Brendan Morrison .30 .75
58 Chris Pronger .30 .75
59 Patrick Lalime .30 .75
60 David Legwand .30 .75
61 Jocelyn Thibault .30 .75
62 Mike Comrie .30 .75
63 Sergei Fedorov .60 1.50
64 Michael Peca .10 .30
65 Tommy Salo .30 .75
66 Scott Stevens .30 .75
67 Mark Recchi .30 .75
68 Vincent Damphousse .10 .30
69 Vincent Lecavalier .40 1.00
70 Olaf Kolzig .30 .75
71 Shane Doan .10 .30
72 Marty Turco .30 .75
73 Marian Hossa .40 1.00
74 Eric Lindros .40 1.00
75 Brent Johnson .30 .75
76 John LeClair .40 1.00
77 Dan Cloutier .30 .75
78 Radim Vrbata .10 .30
79 Ilya Kovalchuk .50 1.25
80 Brendan Shanahan .40 1.00
81 Stu Barnes .10 .30
82 Alexander Mogilny .30 .75
83 Felix Potvin .40 1.00
84 Jeff O'Neill .10 .30
85 Glen Murray .30 .75
86 Marc Denis .30 .75
87 Brad Richards .30 .75
88 Roman Cechmanek .30 .75
89 Brian Leetch .30 .75
90 Roman Turek .30 .75
91 Andrew Brunette .10 .30
92 Krys Kolanos .10 .30
93 Alyn McCauley .10 .30
94 J-S Giguere .30 .75
95 Alexei Kovalev .30 .75
96 Peter Worrell .10 .30
97 Alexei Zhamnov .10 .30
98 Evgeni Nabokov .30 .75
99 Pavol Demitra .30 .75
100 Chris Drury .30 .75
101 Jarome Iginla .50 1.25
102 Patrick Roy 1.00 2.50
103 Dany Heatley .20 .50
104 Nicklas Lidstrom .20 .50
105 Jose Theodore .25 .60
106 Michael Peca .05 .15
107 Ron Francis .15 .40
108 J.Iginla/M.Sundin .30 .75
109 J.Iginla/M.Sundin .30 .75
110 J.Allison/A.Oates .30 .75
111 P.Datsyuk/D.Heatley .30 .75
112 C.Chelios/J.Roenick .30 .75
113 N.Lidstrom/S.Gonchar .30 .75
114 K.Sawyer/P.Worrell .30 .75
115 R.Turek/M.Brodeur .30 .75
116 P.Roy/J.Theodore .50 1.25
117 P.Roy/R.Cechmanek .40 1.00
118 Joe Sakic .40 1.00
119 Jarome Iginla .50 1.25
120 Markus Naslund .40 1.00
121 Nicklas Lidstrom .40 1.00
122 Chris Chelios .40 1.00
123 Patrick Roy 1.00 2.50
124 Mats Sundin .40 1.00
125 Bill Guerin .30 .75
126 Brendan Shanahan .30 .75
127 Rob Blake .30 .75
128 Sergei Gonchar .10 .30
129 Jose Theodore .50 1.25
130 Stanley Cup Champions UER .40 1.00
Card reads 2002-03 Champions
131 Henrik Zetterberg RC 6.00 15.00
132 Martin Gerber RC 3.00 8.00
133 Alexander Frolov RC 4.00 10.00
134 Alexei Smirnov RC 2.00 5.00
135 Stanislav Chistov RC 2.00 5.00
136 Alexander Svitov RC 2.00 5.00
137 Adam Hall RC 2.00 5.00
138 Jay Bouwmeester RC 3.00 8.00
139 Ales Hemsky RC 5.00 12.00
140 Rick Nash RC 8.00 20.00
141 Chuck Kobasew RC 2.50 6.00
142 Shawn Thornton RC 2.00 5.00
143 Dennis Seidenberg RC 2.00 5.00
144 Ron Hainsey RC 2.00 5.00
145 Kurt Sauer RC 2.00 5.00
146 Lasse Pirjeta RC 2.00 5.00
147 Jason Spezza RC 8.00 20.00
148 Tom Koivisto RC 2.00 5.00
149 P-M Bouchard RC 4.00 10.00
150 Patrick Sharp RC 2.00 5.00
151 Scottie Upshall RC 2.00 5.00
152 Steve Eminger RC 2.00 5.00
153 Radovan Somik RC 2.00 5.00
154 Anton Volchenkov RC 2.00 5.00
155 Dmitri Bykov RC 2.00 5.00
156 Bobby Holik SP .40 1.00
157 Curtis Joseph SP .40 1.00
158 Jeff Friesen SP .40 1.00
159 Petr Sykora SP .40 1.00
160 Ed Belfour SP 1.00 2.50
161 Darius Kasparaitis SP .40 1.00
162 Scott Young SP .40 1.00
163 Bill Guerin SP .75 2.00
164 Adam Oates SP .75 2.00
165 Tony Amonte SP .75 2.00
166 Jochen Hecht SP .40 1.00
167 Randy McKay SP .40 1.00
168 Jamie Lundmark SP .40 1.00
169 Mariusz Czerkawski SP .40 1.00
170 Bryan Berard SP .40 1.00
171 Shawn McEachern SP .40 1.00
172 Brian Boucher SP .75 2.00
173 Jiri Dopita SP .40 1.00
174 Erik Rasmussen SP .40 1.00
175 Robert Lang SP .40 1.00
176 Steve Shields SP .75 2.00
177 Kelly Buchberger SP .40 1.00
178 Andrew Cassels SP .40 1.00
179 Oleg Tverdovsky SP .40 1.00
180 Ron Tugnutt SP .75 2.00
NNO Checklist 1 of 6 .10 .30
NNO Checklist 4 of 6 .10 .30
NNO Checklist 3 of 6 .10 .30
NNO Checklist 2 of 6 .10 .30
NNO Checklist 6 of 6 .10 .30
NNO Checklist 5 of 6 .10 .30

2002-03 Topps Heritage Chrome Parallel

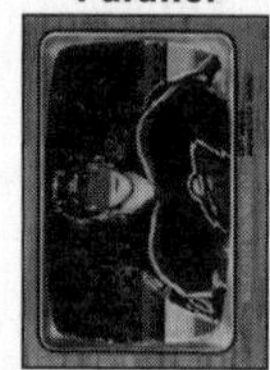

This 100-card set paralleled the base set on chrome card stock. Each card was serial-numbered out of 667 on the cardbacks.

*STARS: 2X TO 5X BASIC CARD

2002-03 Topps Heritage Autographs

Inserted at 1:55, this 9-card set featured certified player autographs in blue ink.

AM Al MacInnis 6.00 15.00
BM Bryan McCabe 6.00 15.00
CD Chris Drury 6.00 15.00

EC Erik Cole	6.00	15.00
KK Krys Kolanos	6.00	15.00
MP Mike Peca	6.00	15.00
PE Patrik Elias	6.00	15.00
SW Stephen Weiss	6.00	15.00
TB Todd Bertuzzi	8.00	20.00

2002-03 Topps Heritage Autographs Black

Inserted at 1:155, this parallel set carried player autographs in black ink.
*BLACK: .75X TO 2X BASIC AUTO

2002-03 Topps Heritage Autographs Red

Inserted at 1:495, this parallel set carried player autographs in red ink.
*RED: 1.5X TO 4X BASIC AUTO

2002-03 Topps Heritage Calder Cloth

This 8-card set featured swatches of game jerseys from past Calder trophy winners. Cards in group "A" were inserted at 1:1160 and cards in group "B" were inserted at 1:217.

ALL CARD CARRY CC PREFIX

BL Brian Leetch B	6.00	15.00
CD Chris Drury A	15.00	40.00
DA Daniel Alfredsson B	6.00	15.00
DH Dany Heatley B	15.00	40.00
MB Martin Brodeur A	20.00	50.00
PF Peter Forsberg A	15.00	40.00
SG Scott Gomez B	6.00	15.00
SS Sergei Samsonov A	10.00	25.00

2002-03 Topps Heritage Calder Cloth Patches

*PATCHES: 1.25X TO 3X BASIC JERSEYS
PATCH ODDS 1:2774

2002-03 Topps Heritage Crease Piece

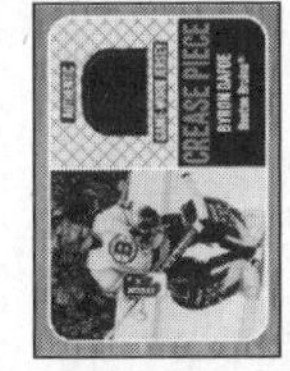

Inserted at 1:39, this 9-card set carried swatches of goalie game jerseys.

ALL CARDS CARRY CP PREFIX

BB Brian Boucher	4.00	10.00
BD Byron Dafoe	4.00	10.00
DB Dan Blackburn	4.00	10.00
DC Dan Cloutier	4.00	10.00
FP Felix Potvin	6.00	15.00
ML Manny Legace	4.00	10.00
MT Marty Turco	6.00	15.00
PL Patrick Lalime	4.00	10.00
SB Sean Burke	4.00	10.00

2002-03 Topps Heritage Crease Piece Patches

*PATCH: 1X TO 2.5X BASE HI
STATED ODDS 1:775

2002-03 Topps Heritage Great Skates

This 10-card memorabilia set was inserted at 1:50.

ALL CARDS CARRY GS PREFIX

AK Alexei Kovalev	5.00	12.00
AT Alex Tanguay	5.00	12.00
BL Brian Leetch	5.00	12.00
BM Brendan Morrison	5.00	12.00
MH Milan Hejduk	6.00	15.00
MR Mark Recchi	5.00	12.00
MS Marco Sturm	5.00	12.00

SG Simon Gagne	6.00	15.00
TA Tony Amonte	5.00	12.00
MHO Marian Hossa	6.00	15.00

2002-03 Topps Heritage Great Skates Patches

*PATCH: 1.25X TO 3X BASE HI
STATED ODDS 1:1550

2002-03 Topps Heritage Reprint Autographs

Inserted at 1:139, this 5-card set partially paralleled the base reprint set but included certified autographs on the cardfronts. Cards carried a TMLA prefix on the cardbacks.

ES Eddie Shack	15.00	40.00
JB Johnny Bower	15.00	40.00
JP Jim Pappin	10.00	25.00
RK Red Kelly	10.00	25.00
RP Bob Pulford	15.00	40.00

2002-03 Topps Heritage Reprint Relics

Inserted at 1:127, this 7-card set paralleled the base reprint set but also featured a piece of stadium seat from Maple Leaf Gardens. Cards carried a TMLS prefix on the cardbacks.

ES Eddie Shack	10.00	25.00
JB Johnny Bower	10.00	25.00
JP Jim Pappin	8.00	20.00
RK Red Kelly	8.00	20.00
RP Robert Pulford	8.00	20.00
TH Tim Horton	12.50	30.00
TS Terry Sawchuk	25.00	60.00

2002-03 Topps Heritage Reprints

Inserted at 1:8, this 7-card set featured reprinted versions of original 1966-67 cards of members of the Toronto Maple Leafs. Cards carried a TML prefix on the cardbacks.

ES Eddie Shack	1.00	2.50
JB Johnny Bower	1.25	3.00
JP Jim Pappin	1.00	2.50
RK Red Kelly	1.25	3.00
RP Robert Pulford	1.00	2.50
TH Tim Horton	1.25	3.00
TS Terry Sawchuk	1.50	4.00

2002-03 Topps Heritage USA Test Parallel

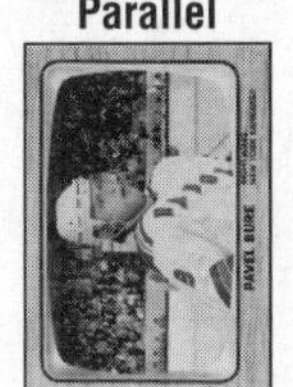

In keeping with the tradition of the 1966-67 Topps set, this 10-card parallel set featured a sampling of players with a much lighter woodgrain borders. This set was inserted at 1:20.

2 Jarome Iginla	1.50	4.00
3 Jose Theodore	1.50	4.00
6 Jaromir Jagr	2.00	5.00
7 Mario Lemieux	8.00	20.00
10 Pavel Bure	1.25	3.00
13 Mats Sundin	1.25	3.00
17 Peter Forsberg	3.00	8.00
27 Patrick Roy	6.00	15.00
32 Steve Yzerman	6.00	15.00
79 Ilya Kovalchuk	1.50	4.00

1999 Topps Pearson Award

This card was available only by mail for those who voted online for Jaromir Jagr for the 1999 Lester B.Pearson award.

1 Jaromir Jagr	6.00	15.00

1996-97 Topps Picks

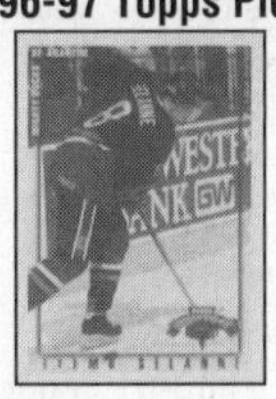

This limited production 90-card set was distributed in seven-card packs (five-cards in Canadian packs) with a suggested retail price of $.99. Topps and Fleer card companies joined together to each select a team of 90 hockey players. The cards in Topps set all have odd numbers because Topps had the first pick of players. Each card features color player photos with player career statistics, biographical information, and a "Topps Prediction" section which gave the upcoming season's goals, assists, wins and shutouts totals for each player as predicted by the Topps Sports Department. Each pack contained an official NHL/NHLPA Draft Game registration form which allowed the collectors the chance to draft their own players and create teams in order to win prizes in a fantasy league.

COMPLETE SET (90)	5.00	15.00
1 Jaromir Jagr	.20	.50
3 Mario Lemieux	.60	1.50
5 Peter Forsberg	.30	.75
7 Teemu Selanne	.10	.30
9 Alexander Mogilny	.05	.15
11 Patrick Roy	.60	1.50
13 Jim Carey	.10	.30
15 Pavel Bure	.10	.30
17 Sergei Fedorov	.15	.40
19 Chris Chelios	.10	.30
21 Sandis Ozolinsh	.01	.05
23 Doug Weight	.05	.15
25 Mark Messier	.10	.30
27 Martin Brodeur	.30	.75
29 Brett Hull	.15	.40
31 Steve Yzerman	.60	1.50
33 Kevin Hatcher	.01	.05
35 Roman Hamrlik	.05	.15
37 Petr Nedved	.05	.15
39 Valeri Kamensky	.05	.15
41 Gary Suter	.01	.05
43 Mats Sundin	.10	.30
45 Trevor Linden	.05	.15
47 Jeremy Roenick	.15	.40
49 Al MacInnis	.05	.15
51 Mike Modano	.20	.50
53 Mathieu Schneider	.01	.05
55 Michal Pivonka	.01	.05
57 Owen Nolan	.05	.15
59 Martin Rucinsky	.01	.05
61 Joe Nieuwendyk	.05	.15
63 Mark Recchi	.05	.15
65 Geoff Sanderson	.05	.15
67 Vyacheslav Kozlov	.01	.05
69 Pat Verbeek	.01	.05
71 Brian Bradley	.01	.05
73 Steve Duchesne	.01	.05
75 Steve Thomas	.01	.05
77 Eric Daze	.05	.15
79 Alexei Kovalev	.01	.05
81 Kevin Stevens	.01	.05
83 Curtis Joseph	.10	.30
85 Bill Ranford	.05	.15
87 Luc Robitaille	.05	.15
89 Claude Lemieux	.01	.05
91 Sergei Gonchar	.01	.05
93 Eric Desjardins	.05	.15
95 Garry Galley	.01	.05
97 Oleg Tverdovsky	.05	.15
99 Rob Niedermayer	.05	.15
101 Scott Mellanby	.05	.15
103 Adam Deadmarsh	.01	.05
105 Cliff Ronning	.01	.05
107 Russ Courtnall	.01	.05
109 Keith Primeau	.01	.05
111 Rick Tocchet	.05	.15
113 Scott Young	.01	.05
115 Scott Stevens	.05	.15
117 Al Iafrate	.01	.05
119 Ray Ferraro	.01	.05
121 Todd Bertuzzi	.10	.30
123 Alexander Selivanov	.01	.05
125 Steve Chiasson	.01	.05
127 Dave Andreychuk	.05	.15
129 Ray Sheppard	.05	.15
131 Bernie Nicholls	.01	.05
133 Tony Amonte	.05	.15
135 Nelson Emerson	.01	.05
137 Cam Neely	.10	.30
139 Shayne Corson	.01	.05
141 Bill Guerin	.01	.05
143 Joe Murphy	.01	.05
145 Cory Stillman	.01	.05
147 Radek Bonk	.01	.05
149 Geoff Courtnall	.01	.05
151 Chad Kilger	.01	.05
153 Sylvain Cote	.01	.05
155 Glen Wesley	.01	.05
157 Jeff Norton	.01	.05
159 Rob Blake	.05	.15
161 Calle Johansson	.01	.05
163 Uwe Krupp	.01	.05
165 James Patrick	.01	.05
167 Dmitri Mironov	.01	.05
169 Vladimir Konstantinov	.05	.15
171 Mattias Norstrom	.01	.05
173 David Wilkie	.01	.05
175 Bryan McCabe	.01	.05
177 Barry Richter	.01	.05
179 Ed Belfour	.10	.30

1996-97 Topps Picks 500 Club

Randomly inserted at the rate of 1:36 packs, this eight-card insert set featured the eight active players who had scored their 500th career goal by the end of the 1995-96 season. The set featured color player photos and player information printed on rainbow diffraction foilboard.

COMPLETE SET (8)	12.00	30.00
FC1 Wayne Gretzky	6.00	15.00
FC2 Mike Gartner	.75	2.00
FC3 Jari Kurri	.75	2.00
FC4 Dino Ciccarelli	.75	2.00
FC5 Mario Lemieux	4.00	10.00
FC6 Mark Messier	1.25	3.00
FC7 Steve Yzerman	3.00	8.00
FC8 Dale Hawerchuk	.75	2.00

1996-97 Topps Picks Fantasy Team

Randomly inserted at the rate of 1:24 packs, this 22 card set featured a dream team made up of the elite hockey stars which any NHL general manager would want playing for him. Printed with Power Matrix technology, the fronts displayed color player photos while the backs carried player information.

COMPLETE SET (7)	20.00	50.00
FT1 Patrick Roy	3.00	8.00
FT2 Chris Osgood	.40	1.00
FT3 Martin Brodeur	2.00	5.00
FT4 Ray Bourque	1.25	3.00
FT5 Brian Leetch	.75	2.00
FT6 Chris Chelios	.75	2.00
FT7 Paul Coffey	.75	2.00
FT8 Ed Jovanovski	.40	1.00
FT9 Roman Hamrlik	.40	1.00
FT10 Wayne Gretzky	4.00	10.00
FT11 Paul Kariya	1.25	3.00
FT12 Brett Hull	1.25	3.00
FT13 Pavel Bure	1.25	3.00
FT14 Jaromir Jagr	1.50	4.00
FT15 Mario Lemieux	3.00	8.00
FT16 Peter Forsberg	1.50	4.00
FT17 Sergei Fedorov	1.25	3.00
FT18 Jeremy Roenick	1.25	3.00
FT19 Alexander Mogilny	.75	2.00
FT20 Joe Sakic	2.00	5.00
FT21 Teemu Selanne	1.25	3.00
FT22 Eric Lindros	1.25	3.00

1996-97 Topps Picks Ice D

Randomly inserted at the rate of 1:24 packs, this 15-card set featured five of the best defensemen and ten top goalies. Color player photos were printed on rainbow prismatic foil with player information on the backs.

COMPLETE SET (15)	20.00	40.00
ID1 Brian Leetch	1.25	3.00
ID2 Ray Bourque	2.00	5.00
ID3 Chris Chelios	1.25	3.00
ID4 Scott Stevens	1.00	2.50
ID5 Ed Jovanovski	1.00	2.50
ID6 Martin Brodeur	3.00	8.00
ID7 Patrick Roy	4.00	10.00
ID8 Chris Osgood	1.00	2.50
ID9 Jim Carey	1.25	3.00
ID10 Dominik Hasek	2.50	6.00
ID11 Ron Hextall	1.00	2.50
ID12 John Vanbiesbrouck	1.00	2.50
ID13 Mike Richter	1.25	3.00
ID14 Felix Potvin	1.25	3.00
ID15 Grant Fuhr	1.00	2.50

1996-97 Topps Picks OPC Inserts

Randomly inserted in Canadian packs only at the rate of 1:4, this 90-card set was parallel to the regular 1996-97 Topps NHL Picks set. These inserts are differentiated in that OPC cards have foil backgrounds and feature the OPC logo on the front. Values for

the cards can be determined by using the multipliers below on the base cards.
*OPC STARS: 5X TO 10X BASIC CARDS

1996-97 Topps Picks Rookie Stars

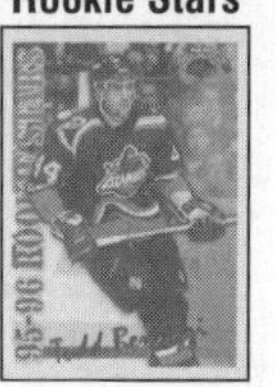

Inserted at the rate of one per pack, this 18-card set showcased hockey's best and brightest young stars. The fronts displayed color player photos while the back carried player information. OPC parallels were also created and inserted in random Canadian packs.

COMPLETE SET (18)	5.00	10.00
RS1 Daniel Alfredsson	.20	.50
RS2 Jere Lehtinen	.60	1.50
RS3 Vitali Yachmenev	.20	.50
RS4 Eric Daze	.20	.50
RS5 Saku Koivu	.60	1.50
RS6 Petr Sykora	.20	.50
RS7 Marcus Ragnarsson	.20	.50
RS8 Valeri Bure	.20	.50
RS9 Cory Stillman	.20	.50
RS10 Todd Bertuzzi	.60	1.50
RS11 Ed Jovanovski	.40	1.00
RS12 Miroslav Satan	.40	1.00
RS13 Kyle McLaren	.20	.50
RS14 Byron Dafoe	.40	1.00
RS15 Eric Fichaud	.20	.50
RS16 Corey Hirsch	.20	.50
RS17 Jeff O'Neill	.20	.50
RS18 Niklas Sundstrom	.20	.50

1996-97 Topps Picks Top Shelf

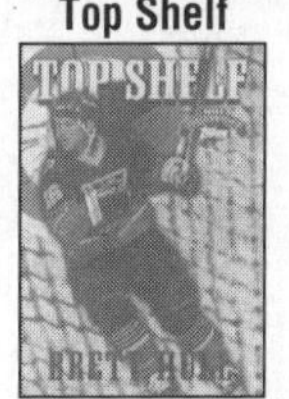

Randomly inserted at the rate of 1:12 packs, this 15-card set featured red foil-stamped cards of the league's top scorers and award winners of the 1995-96 season. The fronts displayed color player photos while the backs carried player information.

COMPLETE SET (15)	15.00	40.00
TS1 John LeClair	.60	1.50
TS2 Wayne Gretzky	4.00	10.00
TS3 Eric Lindros	1.00	2.50
TS4 Paul Kariya	1.00	2.50
TS5 Mark Messier	1.00	2.50
TS6 Jaromir Jagr	1.50	4.00
TS7 Peter Forsberg	1.50	4.00
TS8 Teemu Selanne	1.00	2.50
TS9 Alexander Mogilny	.60	1.50
TS10 Brett Hull	1.25	3.00
TS11 Sergei Fedorov	1.25	3.00
TS12 Joe Sakic	2.00	5.00
TS13 Mats Sundin	1.00	2.50
TS14 Theo Fleury	.60	1.50
TS15 Steve Yzerman	2.50	6.00

1999-00 Topps Premier Plus

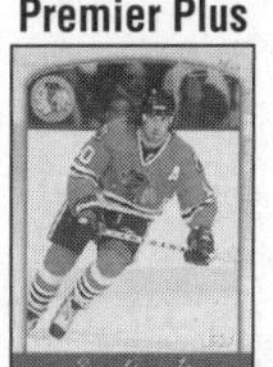
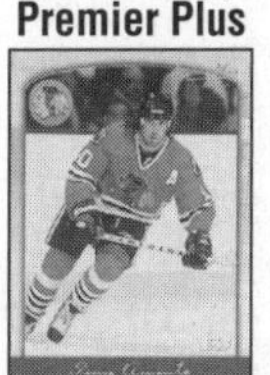

Topps Premier Plus was released as a 140-card set comprised of 81 veteran cards and 59 prospect cards. Printed on a canvas card-stock, this set features crystal clear player action shots with a blue name box across the bottom for veterans and a red name box across the bottom for the prospects. Packaged at 24-packs per box and eight cards per pack, packs carried a suggested retail price of $2.50.

COMPLETE SET (140)	40.00	80.00
1 Curtis Joseph	.20	.50
2 Peter Bondra	.15	.40
3 Theo Fleury	.05	.15
4 Steve Yzerman	1.00	2.50
5 Peter Forsberg	.50	1.25
6 Ray Bourque	.30	.75
7 Dominik Hasek	.40	1.00
8 Chris Drury	.15	.40
9 Brett Hull	.25	.60
10 Chris Osgood	.15	.40
11 Luc Robitaille	.15	.40
12 Bobby Holik	.15	.40
13 John LeClair	.20	.50
14 Jeremy Roenick	.25	.60
15 Owen Nolan	.15	.40
16 Wade Redden	.05	.15
17 Teemu Selanne	.20	.50
18 Doug Weight	.15	.40
19 Vincent Lecavalier	.20	.50
20 Pierre Turgeon	.15	.40
21 Ron Francis	.15	.40
22 Sergei Samsonov	.15	.40
23 Patrick Roy	1.00	2.50
24 Mark Messier	.20	.50
25 Al MacInnis	.15	.40
26 Mark Parrish	.05	.15
27 Ron Tugnutt	.15	.40
28 Joe Nieuwendyk	.15	.40
29 Valeri Bure	.05	.15
30 Jason Allison	.05	.15
31 Tony Amonte	.15	.40
32 Scott Niedermayer	.05	.15
33 Kenny Jonsson	.05	.15
34 Jaromir Jagr	.30	.75
35 Sergei Berezin	.15	.40
36 Olaf Kolzig	.15	.40
37 Byron Dafoe	.15	.40
38 Adam Deadmarsh	.05	.15
39 Alexei Zhitnik	.05	.15
40 Paul Kariya	.20	.50
41 Chris Pronger	.15	.40
42 Markus Naslund	.20	.50
43 Damian Rhodes	.15	.40
44 Marian Hossa	.20	.50
45 Adam Graves	.05	.15
46 Scott Stevens	.15	.40
47 Nicklas Lidstrom	.20	.50
48 Ed Belfour	.20	.50
49 Miroslav Satan	.15	.40
50 Rob Blake	.15	.40
51 Petr Nedved	.15	.40
52 Mark Recchi	.15	.40
53 Jeff Friesen	.05	.15
54 Mats Sundin	.20	.50
55 Arturs Irbe	.15	.40
56 Derian Hatcher	.05	.15
57 Mike Modano	.30	.75
58 Brendan Shanahan	.20	.50
59 Zigmund Palffy	.15	.40
60 Saku Koivu	.20	.50
61 Brian Leetch	.20	.50
62 Rod Brind'Amour	.15	.40
63 Keith Tkachuk	.20	.50
64 Pavol Demitra	.15	.40
65 Magnus Arvedson	.05	.15
66 Martin Brodeur	.50	1.25
67 Chris Chelios	.20	.50
68 Joe Sakic	.40	1.00
69 Anson Carter	.15	.40
70 Sergei Fedorov	.30	.75
71 Pavel Bure	.20	.50
72 Petr Sykora	.05	.15
73 Daniel Alfredsson	.15	.40
74 Guy Hebert	.15	.40
75 Jere Lehtinen	.15	.40
76 Mike Richter	.20	.50
77 Michael Peca	.15	.40
78 Sandis Ozolinsh	.05	.15
79 Joe Thornton	.30	.75
80 Eric Lindros	.20	.50
81 Milan Hejduk	.20	.50
82 Ladislav Nagy RC	1.00	2.50
83 Francis Bouillon RC	.15	.40
84 Mark Eaton RC	.30	.75
85 Robert Valicevic RC	.15	.40
86 Sami Helenius RC	.15	.40
87 Travis Brigley RC	.15	.40
88 Glen Metropolit RC	.60	1.50
89 Alan Letang RC	.15	.40
90 Brad Chartrand RC	.15	.40
91 Marc Rodgers RC	.15	.40
92 Hans Jonsson RC	.15	.40
93 Kim Johnsson RC	.15	.40
94 Richard Lintner RC	.15	.40
95 Andrew Ference	.15	.40
96 Jeff Halpern RC	.75	2.00
97 Brad Lukowich RC	.15	.40
98 Tyson Nash RC	.20	.50
99 Oleg Saprykin RC	.75	2.00
100 John Grahame RC	.75	2.00
101 Patrik Stefan RC	.75	2.00
102 Jason Blake RC	.15	.40
103 Kyle Calder RC	.20	.50
104 John Madden RC	.75	2.00
105 Dan Hinote RC	.60	1.25
106 Pavel Patera RC	.15	.40
107 Yuri Butsayev RC	.15	.40
108 Paul Comrie RC	.15	.40
109 Ivan Novoseltsev RC	.60	1.50
110 Niclas Havelid RC	.20	.50
111 Brian Rafalski RC	.60	1.50
112 Jorgen Jonsson RC	.15	.40
113 Mike Fisher RC	.50	1.25
114 Mika Alatalo RC	.15	.40
115 Michal Rozsival RC	.15	.40
116 Jochen Hecht RC	1.00	2.50
117 Nikolai Antropov RC	1.00	2.50
118 Steve Kariya RC	.60	1.50
119 Brian Campbell RC	.15	.40
120 Maxim Afinogenov	.05	.15
121 Roberto Luongo	.25	.60
122 Petr Buzek	.05	.15
123 Per Svartvadet RC	.15	.40
124 Dave Tanabe	.05	.15
125 Brad Stuart	.15	.40
126 Michael York	.05	.15
127 Jiri Fischer	.05	.15
128 Peter Schaefer	.15	.40
129 Martin Biron	.15	.40
130 Rico Fata	.05	.15
131 J-P Dumont	.15	.40
132 Martin Skoula RC	.60	1.50
133 Alex Tanguay	.15	.40
134 Mike Ribeiro	.15	.40
135 David Legwand	.15	.40
136 Scott Gomez	.05	.15
137 Tim Connolly	.05	.15
138 Jan Hlavac	.05	.15
139 Simon Gagne	.20	.50
140 Brian Boucher	.20	.50
CTW1 Chris Drury AU	10.00	20.00

1999-00 Topps Premier Plus Parallel

Randomly inserted in packs at 1:16, this die-cut foil parallel is labeled on the back "Limited Edition of 250." Cards are randomly inserted into packs.
*STARS: 12.5X TO 30X BASIC CARDS
*ROOKIES: 3X TO 8X

1999-00 Topps Premier Plus Calling All Calders

Randomly inserted in packs at 1:16, this 10-card set features Calder Trophy winners spanning from the late 1980's to 1999. This foil insert places player action shots against a background that shows The Calder Trophy.

COMPLETE SET (10)	12.00	25.00
CAC1 Chris Drury	.75	2.00
CAC2 Sergei Samsonov	1.00	2.50
CAC3 Daniel Alfredsson	.75	2.00
CAC4 Peter Forsberg	2.50	6.00
CAC5 Martin Brodeur	2.50	6.00
CAC6 Teemu Selanne	.75	2.00
CAC7 Pavel Bure	1.25	3.00
CAC8 Ed Belfour	1.00	2.50
CAC9 Joe Nieuwendyk	.75	2.00
CAC10 Brian Leetch	1.00	2.50

1999-00 Topps Premier Plus Club Signings

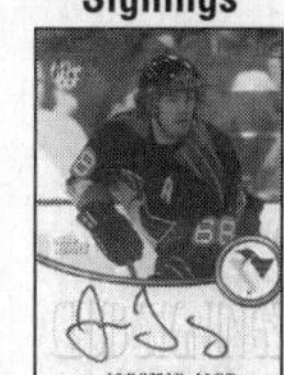

Randomly inserted in packs, this 9-card set featured authentic player autographs. Single autographs were inserted at 1:476 and dual autos were inserted at 1:1905.

CS1 Ray Bourque	30.00	80.00
CS2 Cam Neely	20.00	50.00
CS3 Curtis Joseph	12.50	30.00
CS4 Johnny Bower	10.00	25.00
CS5 Jaromir Jagr	25.00	60.00
CS6 Mario Lemieux	40.00	100.00
CSC1 Ray Bourque / Cam Neely	60.00	150.00
CSC2 Curtis Joseph / Johnny Bower	40.00	100.00
CSC3 Jaromir Jagr / Mario Lemieux	150.00	300.00

1999-00 Topps Premier Plus Code Red

COMPLETE SET (8)	20.00	40.00
STATED ODDS 1:40		
CR1 Keith Tkachuk	1.50	4.00
CR2 Teemu Selanne	1.50	4.00
CR3 Zigmund Palffy	1.50	4.00
CR4 Steve Yzerman	8.00	20.00
CR5 Theo Fleury	1.50	4.00
CR6 Jaromir Jagr	2.50	6.00
CR7 Peter Bondra	1.25	3.00
CR8 Pavel Bure	2.00	5.00

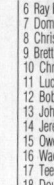

1999-00 Topps Premier Plus Feature Presentations

COMPLETE SET (8) 8.00 15.00
STATED ODDS 1:10
FP1 Joe Sakic 1.25 3.00
FP2 Mark Messier .75 2.00
FP3 Steve Yzerman 3.00 8.00
FP4 Mike Modano 1.00 2.50
FP5 Paul Kariya .75 2.00
FP6 Pavel Bure .75 2.00
FP7 Jaromir Jagr 1.00 2.50
FP8 Ray Bourque 1.00 2.50

1999-00 Topps Premier Plus Game Pieces

Randomly inserted in packs, this 5-card set consists of a card front displaying a piece of game-used stick (inserted at 1:960) or game-used sweater (inserted at 1:190) from the league's top veterans and prospects.
GPCD Chris Drury S 40.00 100.00
GPDL David Legwand S 8.00 15.00
GPDW Doug Weight J 8.00 15.00
GPMR Mike Richter S 15.00 40.00
GPNL Nicklas Lidstrom J 8.00 15.00
GPSG Scott Gomez J 8.00 15.00

1999-00 Topps Premier Plus Imperial Guard

COMPLETE SET(8) 20.00 40.00
STATED ODDS 1:40
IG1 Ed Belfour 1.50 4.00
IG2 Patrick Roy 8.00 20.00
IG3 Martin Brodeur 4.00 10.00
IG4 Dominik Hasek 3.00 8.00
IG5 Curtis Joseph 1.50 4.00
IG6 John Vanbiesbrouck 1.25 3.00
IG7 Mike Richter 1.50 4.00
IG8 Byron Dafoe 1.25 3.00

1999-00 Topps Premier Plus Premier Rookies

Randomly inserted in packs at 1:12, this 10-card set features some of the NHL's eligible Calder Trophy winners. A parallel variation numbered to just 250 was also created and inserted at 1:229.
COMPLETE SET (10) 10.00 20.00
*PARALLEL: 1.5X TO 4X BASIC CARDS
PR1 Alex Tanguay 1.50 4.00
PR2 Brad Stuart 1.25 3.00
PR3 Peter Schaefer .75 2.00
PR4 Scott Gomez .75 2.00
PR5 Patrik Stefan .75 2.00
PR6 Jochen Hecht 1.25 3.00
PR7 David Legwand 1.50 4.00
PR8 Steve Kariya 1.50 4.00
PR9 J-P Dumont 1.00 2.50
PR10 Simon Gagne 1.50 4.00

1999-00 Topps Premier Plus Premier Team

Seeded in packs at 1:12, this 10-card set pictures NHL superstars who have separated themselves from the rest of the league. Card

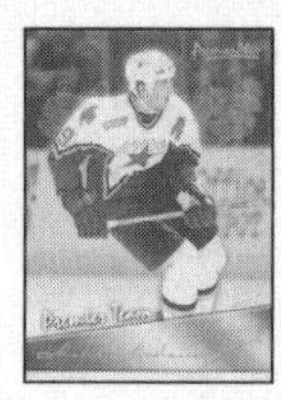

backs carry a "PT" prefix. A parallel variation numbered to just 250 was also created and inserted at 1:299.
COMPLETE SET (10) 15.00 30.00
*PARALLEL: 4X TO 10X BASIC CARDS
PT1 Paul Kariya .75 2.00
PT2 Jaromir Jagr 1.25 3.00
PT3 Eric Lindros .75 2.00
PT4 Mike Modano 1.25 3.00
PT5 Mats Sundin .75 2.00
PT6 Peter Forsberg 2.00 5.00
PT7 Steve Yzerman 4.00 10.00
PT8 Patrick Roy 4.00 10.00
PT9 Martin Brodeur 2.00 5.00
PT10 Dominik Hasek 1.50 4.00

1999-00 Topps Premier Plus Signing Bonus

Randomly inserted in packs at 1:229, this 5-card set features five of the NHL's top prospects. Each card is autographed and contains the "Topps Certified Autograph" stamp and 3M authentication sticker. Card backs carry an "SB" prefix.
SB1 David Legwand 5.00 12.00
SB2 Scott Gomez 5.00 12.00
SB3 Peter Schaefer 5.00 12.00
SB4 Patrik Stefan 5.00 12.00
SB5 Alex Tanguay 10.00 25.00

1999-00 Topps Premier Plus The Next Ones

COMPLETE SET (8) 6.00 12.00
STATED ODDS 1:10
TNO1 Vincent Lecavalier 1.00 2.50
TNO2 Marian Hossa 1.00 2.50
TNO3 Chris Drury .75 2.00
TNO4 Joe Thornton 1.50 4.00
TNO5 Steve Kariya .30 .75
TNO6 David Legwand .75 2.00
TNO7 Patrik Stefan .30 .75
TNO8 Milan Hejduk 1.00 2.50

1999-00 Topps Premiere Plus Promos

This set of six promo cards was widely distributed prior to the release of the Premier Plus set. The cards feature the same photos as the base cards, but different numbers, including a PP-prefix.
COMPLETE SET (6) 3.00 5.00
PP1 Curtis Joseph 1.00 1.50
PP2 J.P. Dumont .40 .50
PP3 Marian Hossa .50 1.50
PP4 Saku Koivu .75 .75
PP5 Chris Drury .50 1.00
PP6 Ron Francis .40 .50

2000-01 Topps Premier Plus

Topps Premier Plus was issued as a 140-card set with an additional NNO card of Scott Gomez with the checklist on the back. The card design had an embossed front and looked like the base Topps 2000-01. The card backs had a small photo of the featured player and some of his statistics from his NHL career.
COMPLETE SET (140) 30.00 60.00
1 Scott Gomez .05 .15
2 Brian Boucher .20 .50
3 Patrik Stefan .05 .15
4 David Legwand .15 .40
5 Tim Connolly .05 .15
6 Jaromir Jagr .30 .75
7 Owen Nolan .15 .40
8 Patrick Roy 1.00 2.50
9 Joe Thornton .30 .75
10 Paul Kariya .20 .50
11 Mark Messier .20 .50
12 Jeremy Roenick .25 .60
13 Jeff Friesen .05 .15
14 Al MacInnis .15 .40
15 Curtis Joseph .20 .50
16 Olaf Kolzig .15 .40
17 Dominik Hasek .40 1.00
18 Arturs Irbe .15 .40
19 Joe Sakic .40 1.00
20 Sergei Fedorov .30 .75
21 Zigmund Palffy .15 .40
22 Jason Arnott .05 .15
23 Marian Hossa .20 .50
24 Pierre Turgeon .15 .40
25 Ron Tugnutt .15 .40
26 Valeri Bure .05 .15
27 Tony Amonte .15 .40
28 Jeff Hackett .15 .40
29 Mariusz Czerkawski .05 .15
30 Wade Redden .05 .15
31 Mark Recchi .15 .40
32 Jean-Sebastien Aubin .15 .40
33 Jason Allison .05 .15
34 Michael Peca .15 .40
35 Teemu Selanne .20 .50
36 Martin Brodeur .50 1.25
37 Simon Gagne .20 .50
38 Chris Simon .05 .15
39 Doug Weight .15 .40
40 Jocelyn Thibault .15 .40
41 Ed Belfour .20 .50
42 Ray Bourque .40 1.00
43 Mike Richter .20 .50
44 Curtis Leschyshyn .05 .15
45 Pavol Demitra .15 .40
46 Alexei Kovalev .15 .40
47 Brad Stuart .15 .40
48 Jarome Iginla .25 .60
49 Ron Francis .15 .40
50 Brendan Shanahan .20 .50
51 Rob Blake .15 .40
52 Miroslav Satan .15 .40
53 Theo Fleury .05 .15
54 John LeClair .20 .50
55 Roman Turek .15 .40
56 Brett Hull .25 .60
57 Peter Forsberg .50 1.25
58 Steve Yzerman 1.00 2.50
59 Derian Hatcher .05 .15
60 Pavel Bure .20 .50
61 Patrik Elias .15 .40
62 Daniel Alfredsson .15 .40
63 Adam Oates .15 .40
64 Andrew Brunette .05 .15
65 Chris Pronger .15 .40
66 Mario Lemieux 1.25 3.00
67 Keith Tkachuk .20 .50
68 Markus Naslund .20 .50
69 Mike Modano .30 .75
70 Nicklas Lidstrom .20 .50
71 Scott Stevens .15 .40
72 Vincent Lecavalier .20 .50
73 Luc Robitaille .15 .40
74 Mats Sundin .20 .50
75 Milan Hejduk .20 .50
76 Rod Brind'amour .15 .40
77 Tommy Salo .15 .40
78 Byron Dafoe .15 .40
79 Doug Gilmour .15 .40
80 Guy Hebert .15 .40
81 Keith Primeau .05 .15
82 Chris Drury .15 .40
83 Saku Koivu .20 .50
84 Alexei Yashin .05 .15
85 Martin St. Louis .15 .40
86 Steve McCarthy .05 .15
87 Henrik Sedin .05 .15
88 Kris Beech .05 .15
89 Dimitri Kalinin .05 .15
90 Maxime Ouellet .15 .40
91 Shawn Heins .05 .15
92 Mika Noronen .05 .15
93 Taylor Pyatt .05 .15
94 Brent Johnson .15 .40
95 Oleg Saprykin .05 .15
96 Daniel Tkaczuk .05 .15
97 Daniel Sedin .05 .15
98 Milan Kraft .05 .15
99 Jeff Farkas .05 .15
100 Denis Shvidki .05 .15
101 Mathieu Garon .15 .40
102 Mike Mottau .05 .15
103 Andrei Markov .05 .15
104 Brad Richards .15 .40
105 Brian Swanson RC .20 .50
106 Josef Vasicek RC .20 .50
107 Reto Von Arx RC .20 .50
108 Lubomir Sekeras RC .20 .50
109 Ruslan Fedotenko RC .20 .50
110 Roman Simicek RC .20 .50
111 Michel Riesen RC .05 .15
112 Petteri Nummelin RC .20 .50
113 Brad Tapper RC .20 .50
114 Alexander Kharitonov RC .20 .50
115 Andrew Raycroft RC 1.25 3.00
116 Ossi Vaananen RC .20 .50
117 Tyler Bouck RC .20 .50
118 Steven Reinprecht RC .20 .50
119 Rostislav Klesla RC .75 2.00
120 Martin Havlat RC 1.50 4.00
121 Scott Hartnell RC .50 1.25
122 David Aebischer RC 1.25 3.00
123 Bryce Salvador RC .20 .50
124 Jani Hurme RC .60 1.50
125 Eric Belanger RC .20 .50
126 Marty Turco RC 1.50 4.00
127 Rick DiPietro RC 1.25 3.00
128 Justin Williams RC .75 2.00
129 Dale Purinton RC .20 .50
130 Marian Gaborik RC 2.00 5.00
131 Petr Svoboda RC .20 .50
132 Niclas Wallin RC .20 .50
133 Petr Hubacek RC .20 .50
134 Colin White RC .20 .50
135 Greg Classen RC .20 .50
136 Roman Cechmanek RC .25 .60
137 Eric Boulton RC .20 .50
138 Sascha Goc RC .20 .50
139 Lubomir Visnovsky RC .05 .15
140 Ronald Petrovicky .20 .50
NNO Scott Gomez .05 .15
Oversized CL

2000-01 Topps Premier Plus Blue Ice

Randomly inserted in packs of 2000-01 Topps Premier Plus at a rate of 1:15, this 140-card set is parallel to the base set. The cards were serial numbered to 250.The card design was the same as the base set with the exceptions of a red border instead of blue and the ice in the photo was blue, the cards were die-cut on all 4 sides and the card front used an embossed foilboard design.
*STARS: 4X TO 10X BASIC CARDS
*BLUE RC'S: 1.5X TO 3X BASIC CARDS

2000-01 Topps Premier Plus Aspirations

COMPLETE SET (10) 10.00 20.00
STATED ODDS 1:16
PA1 Scott Gomez .75 2.00
PA2 Vincent Lecavalier 1.25 3.00
PA3 Maxim Afinogenov .75 2.00
PA4 Milan Hejduk 1.25 3.00
PA5 Joe Thornton 2.00 5.00
PA6 Marian Hossa 1.25 3.00
PA7 Oleg Saprykin .75 2.00
PA8 Shane Willis .75 2.00
PA9 David Legwand 1.00 2.50
PA10 Tim Connolly .75 2.00

2000-01 Topps Premier Plus Club Signings

The Signings were randomly inserted in packs of 2000-01 Topps Premier Plus at a rate of 1:219 for the single signed cards and a rate of 1:1751 for the dual signed cards.
CS-1 Billy Smith 8.00 20.00
CS-2 John Vanbiesbrouck 8.00 20.00
CS-3 John LeClair 8.00 20.00
CS-4 Bobby Clarke 12.50 30.00
CS-5 Luc Robitaille 8.00 20.00
CS-6 Marcel Dionne 8.00 20.00
CSC-1 J.V'brouck/B.Smith 40.00 100.00
CSC-2 John LeClair 30.00 80.00
Bobby Clarke
CSC-3 Luc Robitaille 30.00 60.00
Marcel Dionne

2000-01 Topps Premier Plus Game-Used Memorabilia

Randomly inserted in packs of 2000-01 Topps Premier Plus at a rate of 1:66 for the jersey cards, 1:658 for the stick cards, and 1:1752 for the combo relic cards. The 18-card set featured pieces of game-used memorabilia from the NHL.
*MULT.COLOR SWATCH: 1X TO 2X
GPAO Adam Oates S 8.00 20.00
GPEB Ed Belfour S 20.00 50.00
GPJI Jarome Iginla J 12.00 30.00
GPJV John Vanbiesbrouck S 12.00 30.00
GPKB Kris Beech J 4.00 10.00
GPMB Max Balmochnyk J 4.00 10.00
GPMT Marty Turco J 8.00 20.00
GPOS Oleg Saprykin J 4.00 10.00
GPRF Rico Fata J 4.00 10.00
GPTP Taylor Pyatt J 4.00 10.00
GPTS Teemu Selanne S 12.00 30.00
GPVB Valeri Bure J 4.00 10.00
GPAOKB Kris Beech 8.00 20.00
Adam Oates
GPEBMT Marty Turco 30.00 80.00
Ed Belfour
GPJIRF Rico Fata 20.00 50.00
Jarome Iginla
GPJVTP Taylor Pyatt 20.00 50.00
John Vanbiesbrouck
GPTSMB Max Balmochnyk 12.00 30.00
Teemu Selanne
GPVBOS Oleg Saprykin 8.00 20.00
Valeri Bure

2000-01 Topps Premier Plus Masters of the Break

COMPLETE SET (20) 30.00 60.00
STATED ODDS 1:24
MB1 Jaromir Jagr 1.50 4.00
MB2 Teemu Selanne 1.00 2.50
MB3 Pavel Bure 1.25 3.00
MB4 Tony Amonte .75 2.00
MB5 Milan Hejduk 1.00 2.50
MB6 Patrik Elias .75 2.00
MB7 Paul Kariya 1.00 2.50
MB8 Peter Forsberg 2.50 6.00
MB9 Sergei Fedorov 2.00 5.00
MB10 Mike Modano 1.50 4.00
MB11 Martin Brodeur 2.50 6.00
MB12 Patrick Roy 5.00 12.00
MB13 Ed Belfour 1.00 2.50
MB14 Curtis Joseph 1.00 2.50
MB15 Dominik Hasek 2.00 5.00
MB16 Olaf Kolzig .60 1.50
MB17 Roman Turek .60 1.50
MB18 Brian Boucher 1.00 2.50
MB19 Mike Richter 1.00 2.50
MB20 Tommy Salo .60 1.50

2000-01 Topps Premier Plus Private Signings

Randomly inserted in packs of Topps Premier Plus at a rate of 1:175 for the rookies and 1:350 for the veterans and 1:526 for the Gomez. This 13-card set featured autographs from some of the top players in the NHL. The cards carried a 'PS' prefix except for the Gomez which carried a 'CT' prefix for the card number. Exchange expiration was 03/01/02.
CTW1 Scott Gomez Calder 8.00 20.00
PSBR Brad Richards 8.00 20.00
PSBS Brad Stuart 8.00 20.00
PSCP Chris Pronger 8.00 20.00
PSDS Daniel Sedin 8.00 20.00
PSEN Evgeni Nabokov 12.50 30.00
PSHS Henrik Sedin 8.00 20.00
PSJW Justin Williams 8.00 20.00
PSMB Martin Brodeur 30.00 80.00
PSMG Marian Gaborik 20.00 50.00
PSMK Milan Kraft 8.00 20.00
PSMT Marty Turco 15.00 40.00
PSSH Scott Hartnell 8.00 20.00

2000-01 Topps Premier Plus Rookies

Randomly inserted in packs of 2000-01 Topps Premier Plus at a rate of 1:12, the 10-card set highlighted the top newcomers to the NHL. A blue ice parallel variation numbered to just 250 was also created and inserted at 1:213.
COMPLETE SET (10) 10.00 20.00
*BLUE ICE: 1.5X TO 3X BASIC CARDS
PR1 Marian Gaborik 3.00 8.00
PR2 Henrik Sedin .40 1.00
PR3 Rostislav Klesla 1.00 2.50
PR4 Brad Richards 1.50 4.00
PR5 Justin Williams 1.00 2.50
PR6 Josef Vasicek .40 1.00
PR7 Daniel Sedin .40 1.00
PR8 Maxime Ouellet 1.25 3.00
PR9 Andrei Markov .40 1.00
PR10 Oleg Saprykin .75 2.00

2000-01 Topps Premier Plus Team

Randomly inserted in packs of 2000-01 Topps Premier Plus at a rate of 1:12, the 10-card set highlighted the top players from the NHL. A blue ice parallel variation numbered to just 250 was also created and inserted at 1:213.
COMPLETE SET (10) 8.00 15.00
*BLUE ICE: 1X TO 1.5X BASIC CARDS
PT1 Paul Kariya .50 1.25
PT2 Peter Forsberg 1.50 4.00
PT3 John LeClair .50 1.25
PT4 Mike Modano 1.00 2.50
PT5 Martin Brodeur 1.50 4.00
PT6 Pavel Bure .50 1.25
PT7 Curtis Joseph .50 1.25
PT8 Jaromir Jagr 1.00 2.50
PT9 Chris Pronger .50 1.25
PT10 Teemu Selanne .50 1.25

2000-01 Topps Premier Plus Trophy Tribute

COMPLETE SET (15) 15.00 30.00
STATED ODDS 1:16
TT1 Dominik Hasek 1.25 3.00
TT2 Jaromir Jagr 1.00 2.50
TT3 Patrick Roy 3.00 8.00
TT4 Chris Pronger .50 1.25
TT5 Paul Kariya .60 1.50
TT6 Ed Belfour .60 1.50
TT7 Mark Messier .75 2.00
TT8 Ray Bourque 1.25 3.00
TT9 Steve Yzerman 3.00 8.00
TT10 Sergei Fedorov 1.25 3.00
TT11 Brett Hull .75 2.00
TT12 Ron Francis .50 1.25
TT13 Pavel Bure .75 2.00
TT14 Teemu Selanne .60 1.50
TT15 Brian Leetch .50 1.25

2000-01 Topps Premier Plus World Premier

COMPLETE SET (20) 30.00 60.00
STATED ODDS 1:24
WP1 Patrick Roy 5.00 12.00
WP2 Martin Brodeur 2.50 6.00
WP3 Chris Pronger .75 2.00
WP4 Sergei Zubov .60 1.50
WP5 Scott Stevens .75 2.00
WP6 Ray Bourque 2.00 5.00
WP7 Nicklas Lidstrom 1.00 2.50
WP8 Rob Blake .75 2.00
WP9 Paul Kariya 1.00 2.50
WP10 John LeClair 1.25 3.00
WP11 Keith Tkackuk 1.00 2.50
WP12 Brendan Shanahan 1.50 4.00
WP13 Vincent Lecavalier 1.00 2.50
WP14 Steve Yzerman 5.00 12.00
WP15 Mike Modano 1.50 4.00
WP16 Peter Forsberg 2.50 6.00
WP17 Pavel Bure 1.25 3.00
WP18 Teemu Selanne 1.00 2.50
WP19 Brett Hull 1.25 3.00
WP20 Jaromir Jagr 1.50 4.00

2003-04 Topps Pristine

This 190-card set was released in January and was packaged 5 packs per box with 8 cards per pack. Each pack contained two additional packs with a memorabilia card and a "uncirculated" card in each pack. Uncircualted cards were incased in clear plastic slabs. Rookies in the set each had three different variations; common, uncommon and rare. Unpriced 1/1 Press

Plates in 4 different colors also exist for each card below.
COMMON RC PRINT RUN 1199 SER.#'d SETS
UNCOMMON PRINT RUN 699 SER.#'d SETS
RARE PRINT RUN 199 SER.#'d SETS
1 J-S Giguere .75 2.00
2 Slava Kozlov .40 1.00
3 Steve Shields .75 2.00
4 Martin Biron .75 2.00
5 Roman Turek .75 2.00
6 Kevin Weekes .75 2.00
7 Kyle Calder .40 1.00
8 Patrik Elias .75 2.00
9 Rob Blake .75 2.00
10 Marty Turco .75 2.00
11 Bill Guerin .75 2.00
12 Nicklas Lidstrom 1.00 2.50
13 Mike Comrie .75 2.00
14 Roberto Luongo 1.25 3.00
15 Ziggy Palffy .75 2.00
16 Paul Kariya 1.00 2.50
17 Stanislav Chistov .40 1.00
18 Andrew Brunette .40 1.00
19 Richard Zednik .40 1.00
20 Martin Brodeur 2.50 6.00
21 Alexei Yashin .40 1.00
22 Brian Leetch .75 2.00
23 Patrick Lalime .75 2.00
24 Simon Gagne 1.00 2.50
25 Mike Johnson .40 1.00
26 Mario Lemieux 4.00 10.00
27 Alyn McCauley .40 1.00
28 Kyle McLaren .40 1.00
29 Brent Johnson .75 2.00
30 Vincent Lecavalier 1.00 2.50
31 Ed Belfour 1.00 2.50
32 Todd Bertuzzi 1.00 2.50
33 Brendan Morrison .75 2.00
34 Olaf Kolzig .75 2.00
35 Ilya Kovalchuk 1.25 3.00
36 Johan Hedberg .75 2.00
37 Mike Knuble .40 1.00
38 Ales Kotalik .40 1.00
39 Chris Drury .75 2.00
40 Joe Thornton 1.50 4.00
41 Dominik Hasek 2.00 5.00
42 Daniel Alfredsson .75 2.00
43 Marc Denis .75 2.00
44 Mike Modano 1.50 4.00
45 Sergei Fedorov 1.25 3.00
46 Henrik Zetterberg 1.00 2.50
47 Tommy Salo .75 2.00
48 Olli Jokinen .75 2.00
49 Felix Potvin 1.00 2.50
50 Dany Heatley 1.25 3.00
51 Marian Gaborik 2.00 5.00
52 Saku Koivu 1.00 2.50
53 Tomas Vokoun .75 2.00
54 Eric Brewer .40 1.00
55 Rick DiPietro .75 2.00
56 Mike Dunham .75 2.00
57 Marian Hossa 1.00 2.50
58 Jeremy Roenick 1.25 3.00
59 Brian Boucher .75 2.00
60 Milan Hejduk 1.00 2.50
61 Patrick Marleau .75 2.00
62 Pavol Demitra .75 2.00
63 Al MacInnis .75 2.00
64 Nikolai Khabibulin 1.00 2.50
65 Mats Sundin 1.00 2.50
66 Miroslav Satan .75 2.00
67 Sergei Gonchar .40 1.00
68 Pasi Nurminen .75 2.00
69 Glen Murray .40 1.00
70 Brett Hull 1.25 3.00
71 Jarome Iginla 1.25 3.00
72 Ron Francis .75 2.00
73 Tyler Arnason .40 1.00
74 Joe Sakic 2.00 5.00
75 David Aebischer .75 2.00
76 Geoff Sanderson .40 1.00
77 Derian Hatcher .40 1.00
78 Jocelyn Thibault .75 2.00
79 Curtis Joseph 1.00 2.50
80 Markus Naslund 1.00 2.50
81 Kristian Huselius .40 1.00
82 Alexander Frolov .40 1.00
83 Petr Sykora .40 1.00
84 Dwayne Roloson .75 2.00
85 Jose Theodore 1.25 3.00
86 David Legwand .75 2.00
87 Scott Stevens .75 2.00
88 Michael Peca .40 1.00
89 Alex Kovalev .75 2.00
90 Jaromir Jagr 1.50 4.00
91 Tony Amonte .75 2.00
92 Daymond Langkow .40 1.00
93 Martin Straka .40 1.00
94 Evgeni Nabokov .75 2.00
95 Chris Pronger .75 2.00
96 Martin St. Louis .75 2.00
97 Alexander Mogilny .75 2.00
98 Owen Nolan .75 2.00
99 Dan Cloutier .75 2.00
100 Peter Forsberg 2.50 6.00
101 Tuomo Ruutu C RC 4.00 10.00
102 Tuomo Ruutu U 4.00 10.00
103 Tuomo Ruutu R 12.00 30.00
104 Marc-Andre Fleury C RC 10.00 25.00
105 Marc-Andre Fleury U 6.00 15.00
106 Marc-Andre Fleury R 25.00 60.00
107 Patrice Bergeron C RC 8.00 20.00
108 Patrice Bergeron U 6.00 15.00
109 Patrice Bergeron R 25.00 60.00
110 Milan Michalek C RC 3.00 8.00
111 Milan Michalek U 2.00 5.00
112 Milan Michalek R 12.50 30.00
113 Dominic Moore C RC 2.50 6.00

114 Dominic Moore U 2.00 5.00
115 Dominic Moore R 10.00 25.00
116 Dustin Brown C RC 2.50 6.00
117 Dustin Brown U 2.00 5.00
118 Dustin Brown R 10.00 25.00
119 Nathan Horton C RC 4.00 10.00
120 Nathan Horton U 3.00 8.00
121 Nathan Horton R 12.50 30.00
122 Chris Higgins C RC 4.00 10.00
123 Chris Higgins U 3.00 8.00
124 Chris Higgins R 12.50 30.00
125 Antti Miettinen C RC 2.50 6.00
126 Antti Miettinen U 2.00 5.00
127 Antti Miettinen R 10.00 25.00
128 Tom Preissing C RC 2.50 6.00
129 Tom Preissing U 2.00 5.00
130 Tom Preissing R 10.00 25.00
131 Marek Svatos C RC 4.00 10.00
132 Marek Svatos U 3.00 8.00
133 Marek Svatos R 10.00 25.00
134 Peter Sejna C RC 2.50 6.00
135 Peter Sejna U 2.00 5.00
136 Peter Sejna R 10.00 25.00
137 Matt Stajan C RC 4.00 10.00
138 Matt Stajan U 4.00 10.00
139 Matt Stajan R 12.50 30.00
140 Jiri Hudler C RC 3.00 8.00
141 Jiri Hudler U 2.50 6.00
142 Jiri Hudler R 10.00 25.00
143 Joni Pitkanen C RC 3.00 8.00
144 Joni Pitkanen U 2.00 5.00
145 Joni Pitkanen R 10.00 25.00
146 Garnet Exelby C 2.50 6.00
147 Garnet Exelby U 2.00 5.00
148 Garnet Exelby R 10.00 25.00
149 Eric Staal C RC 10.00 25.00
150 Eric Staal U 6.00 15.00
151 Eric Staal R 25.00 60.00
152 Sean Bergenheim C RC 2.50 6.00
153 Sean Bergenheim U 2.00 5.00
154 Sean Bergenheim R 10.00 25.00
155 Gregory Campbell C RC 2.50 6.00
156 Gregory Campbell U 2.00 5.00
157 Gregory Campbell R 10.00 25.00
158 Dan Hamhuis C RC 2.50 6.00
159 Dan Hamhuis U 2.00 5.00
160 Dan Hamhuis R 10.00 25.00
161 Maxim Kondratiev C RC 2.50 6.00
162 Maxim Kondratiev U 2.00 5.00
163 Maxim Kondratiev R 10.00 25.00
164 Matthew Lombardi C RC 2.50 6.00
165 Matthew Lombardi U 2.00 5.00
166 Matthew Lombardi R 10.00 25.00
167 Alexander Semin C RC 6.00 15.00
168 Alexander Semin U 5.00 12.00
169 Alexander Semin R 12.00 30.00
170 John-Michael Liles C RC 2.50 6.00
171 John-Michael Liles U 2.00 5.00
172 John-Michael Liles R 8.00 20.00
173 Andrew Peters C RC 2.50 6.00
174 Andrew Peters U 2.00 5.00
175 Andrew Peters R 10.00 25.00
176 Dan Fritsche C RC 2.50 6.00
177 Dan Fritsche U 2.00 5.00
178 Dan Fritsche R 8.00 20.00
179 Antoine Vermette C RC 2.50 6.00
180 Antoine Vermette U 2.00 5.00
181 Antoine Vermette R 10.00 25.00
182 David Hale C RC 2.50 6.00
183 David Hale U 2.00 5.00
184 David Hale R 10.00 25.00
185 Joffrey Lupul C RC 3.00 8.00
186 Joffrey Lupul U 2.50 6.00
187 Joffrey Lupul R 10.00 25.00
188 Jordin Tootoo C RC 4.00 10.00
189 Jordin Tootoo U 3.00 8.00
190 Jordin Tootoo R 10.00 25.00

2003-04 Topps Pristine Gold Refractor Die Cuts

One per box in boxtopper packs.
*STARS: 3X TO 8X
*COMMON ROOKIE: 2X TO 5X
*UNCOMMON ROOKIE: 3X TO 8X
*RARE ROOKIE: 1X TO 2.5X
PRINT RUN 33 SER.#'d SETS
149 Eric Staal C 40.00 100.00
150 Eric Staal U 50.00 120.00

2003-04 Topps Pristine Refractors

*STARS: 2.5X TO 6X
1-100 PRINT RUN 59 SER.#'d SETS
*COMMON ROOKIE: .6X TO 1.5X
COMMON PRINT RUN 499 SER.#'d SETS
*UNCOMMON ROOKIE: .75X TO 2X
UNCOMMON PRINT RUN 199 SER.#'d SETS
*RARE ROOKIE: 1X TO 2.5X
RARE PRINT RUN 59 SER.#'d SETS

2003-04 Topps Pristine Autographs

This 7-card set featured certified autographs on silver metallic cards. A Gold metallic parallel was also created.
GROUP A ODDS 1:11
GROUP B ODDS 1:26
GROUP C ODDS 1:8
PE-MN Markus Naslund B 8.00 20.00
PE-JG J-S Giguere A 5.00 12.00
PE-MH Milan Hejduk A 5.00 12.00
PE-RN Rick Nash A 12.50 30.00
PE-MT Marty Turco C 6.00 15.00
PE-MS Martin St. Louis C 8.00 20.00
PE-SC Stanislav Chistov C 5.00 12.00

2003-04 Topps Pristine Autographs Gold

*GOLD: 1.5X TO 4X BASIC INSERTS
STATED PRINT RUN 25 SER.#'d SETS

2003-04 Topps Pristine Jersey Portions

GROUP A ODDS 4:5
GROUP B ODDS 1:27
PPJ-BMN Brendan Morrison A 2.50 6.00
PPJ-PL Patrick Lalime B 2.50 6.00
PPJ-KP Keith Primeau A 2.50 6.00
PPJ-DC Dan Cloutier A 2.50 6.00
PPJ-RF Ron Francis A 2.50 6.00
PPJ-ML Manny Legace A 4.00 10.00
PPJ-BRI Brad Richards A 5.00 12.00
PPJ-MHE Milan Hejduk A 3.00 8.00
PPJ-JW Justin Williams A 2.50 6.00
PPJ-MHO Marian Hossa A 3.00 8.00
PPJ-MA Maxim Afinogenov A 2.50 6.00
PPJ-MG Marian Gaborik B 6.00 15.00
PPJ-IK Ilya Kovalchuk A 5.00 12.00
PPJ-RB Rob Blake A 2.50 6.00
PPJ-DA Daniel Alfredsson A 2.50 6.00
PPJ-MB Martin Biron A 2.50 6.00
PPJ-MSU Mats Sundin A 3.00 8.00
PPJ-TV Tomas Vokoun A 2.50 6.00
PPJ-DBL Dan Blackburn A 2.50 6.00
PPJ-JD J-P Dumont A 2.50 6.00
PPJ-BRO Brian Rolston A 2.50 6.00
PPJ-RL Roberto Luongo A 3.00 8.00
PPJ-ED Eric Desjardins A 2.50 6.00
PPJ-DH Dany Heatley A 5.00 12.00
PPJ-PR Patrick Roy B 12.50 30.00
PPJ-ZP Zigmund Palffy A 2.50 6.00
PPJ-MSA Miroslav Satan A 2.50 6.00
PPJ-DL David Legwand B 2.50 6.00
PPJ-MT Marty Turco B 2.50 6.00
PPJ-TB Todd Bertuzzi B 3.00 8.00
PPJ-EL Eric Lindros A 3.00 8.00
PPJ-SK Saku Koivu A 3.00 8.00
PPJ-FP Felix Potvin A 3.00 8.00
PPJ-PM Patrick Marleau A 2.50 6.00
PPJ-BMW Brenden Morrow A 2.50 6.00

2003-04 Topps Pristine Jersey Portion Refractors

*STARS: 2X TO 5X
PRINT RUN 25 SER.#'d SETS

2003-04 Topps Pristine Mini

Inserted at just one per box on average, these smaller cards were inserted into a fourth pack.
MINI AUTO ODDS 1:318
PM-OK Olaf Kolzig 2.00 5.00
PM-JTH Jose Theodore 3.00 8.00
PM-PL Patrick Lalime 2.00 5.00
PM-PS Peter Sejna 2.00 5.00
PM-RT Roman Turek 2.00 5.00
PM-JL Joffrey Lupul 3.00 8.00
PM-TV Tomas Vokoun 2.00 5.00
PM-ES Eric Staal 8.00 20.00
PM-DH Dominik Hasek 3.00 8.00
PM-SC Sebastien Caron 2.00 5.00
PM-RL Roberto Luongo 3.00 8.00
PM-MD Mike Dunham 2.00 5.00
PM-RE Robert Esche 2.00 5.00
PM-NH Nathan Horton 4.00 10.00
PM-FP Felix Potvin 2.50 6.00
PM-MSO Matt Stajan 3.00 8.00
PM-CO Chris Osgood 2.00 5.00
PM-KW Kevin Weekes 2.00 5.00
PM-JT Jocelyn Thibault 2.00 5.00
PM-RD Rick DiPietro 2.00 5.00
PM-EB Ed Belfour 2.50 6.00
PM-MB Martin Brodeur 4.00 10.00
PM-DB Dustin Brown 2.00 5.00
PM-MDE Marc Denis 2.00 5.00
PM-EN Evgeni Nabokov 2.00 5.00
PM-DC Dan Cloutier 2.00 5.00
PM-TS Tommy Salo 2.00 5.00
PM-NK Nikolai Khabibulin 2.50 6.00
PM-JSG J-S Giguere 2.00 5.00
PM-MAF Marc-Andre Fleury 8.00 20.00
PM-SB Sean Burke 2.00 5.00
PM-RC Roman Cechmanek 2.00 5.00
PM-JTO Jordin Tootoo 5.00 12.00
PM-MBI Martin Biron 2.00 5.00
PM-JHU Jiri Hudler 3.00 8.00
PM-DR Dwayne Roloson 2.00 5.00
PM-PN Pasi Nurminen 2.00 5.00
PM-DA David Aebischer 2.00 5.00
PM-MT Marty Turco 2.00 5.00
PM-AM Antti Miettinen 2.00 5.00
PMA-JG J-S Giguere AU 15.00 40.00

2003-04 Topps Pristine Patches

*MULT.COLOR SWATCH: .75X TO 2X
STATED ODDS 1:16
STATED PRINT RUN 50 SER.#'d SETS
REFRACTOR PRINT RUN 10 SER.#'d SETS
REF.NOT PRICED DUE TO SCARCITY
PP-JI Jarome Iginla 20.00 50.00
PP-PL Patrick Lalime 8.00 20.00
PP-DB Dan Blackburn 8.00 20.00
PP-IK Ilya Kovalchuk 15.00 40.00
PP-MB Martin Biron 12.00 30.00
PP-JL John LeClair 8.00 20.00
PP-AT Alex Tanguay 12.00 30.00
PP-KH Kristian Huselius 8.00 20.00
PP-BRO Brian Rolston 8.00 20.00
PP-MM Mike Modano 15.00 40.00
PP-MN Markus Naslund 12.00 30.00
PP-SG Simon Gagne 12.00 30.00
PP-MT Marty Turco 12.00 30.00
PP-PF Peter Forsberg 15.00 40.00
PP-JW Justin Williams 8.00 20.00
PP-MG Marian Gaborik 20.00 50.00
PP-MHO Marian Hossa 12.00 30.00
PP-BM Brendan Morrison 8.00 20.00
PP-VL Vincent Lecavalier 15.00 40.00
PP-RB Rob Blake 8.00 20.00
PP-FP Felix Potvin 12.00 30.00
PP-PR Patrick Roy 30.00 80.00
PP-MST Marco Sturm 8.00 20.00
PP-JS Joe Sakic 15.00 40.00
PP-ML Manny Legace 12.00 30.00
PP-RL Roberto Luongo 15.00 40.00
PP-MC Mike Comrie 8.00 20.00
PP-SK Saku Koivu 12.00 30.00
PP-DH Dany Heatley 15.00 40.00
PP-MSA Miroslav Satan 12.00 30.00
PP-MHE Milan Hejduk 8.00 20.00
PP-DL David Legwand 8.00 20.00
PP-PD Pavel Datsyuk 12.00 30.00
PP-DA Daniel Alfredsson 12.00 30.00
PP-KP Keith Primeau 8.00 20.00
PP-MA Maxim Afinogenov 12.00 30.00
PP-ZP Zigmund Palffy 12.00 30.00
PP-EL Eric Lindros 15.00 40.00
PP-JD J-P Dumont 8.00 20.00
PP-MSU Mats Sundin 12.00 30.00
PP-TB Todd Bertuzzi 12.00 30.00

2003-04 Topps Pristine Popular Demand Relics

GROUP A ODDS 1:127
GROUP B ODDS 1:12
GROUP C ODDS 1:5
PD-TC Tim Connolly A 4.00 10.00
PD-SN Scott Niedermayer B 4.00 10.00
PD-TD Tie Domi B 4.00 10.00
PD-PD Pavel Datsyuk C 6.00 15.00
PD-PB Pavel Bure C 5.00 12.00
PD-JL John LeClair B 5.00 12.00
PD-MN Markus Naslund A 6.00 15.00
PD-JB Jay Bouwmeester C 4.00 10.00
PD-JI Jarome Iginla B 5.00 12.00
PD-SG Simon Gagne A 12.50 30.00
PD-JTH Jose Theodore C 6.00 15.00
PD-MR Mark Recchi B 4.00 10.00
PD-MM Mike Modano B 6.00 15.00
PD-JSP Jason Spezza B 6.00 15.00
PD-JJ Jaromir Jagr C 8.00 20.00
PD-NK Nikolai Khabibulin C 4.00 10.00
PD-AY Alexei Yashin C 4.00 10.00
PD-MST Marco Sturm B 4.00 10.00
PD-ML Mario Lemieux A 20.00 50.00
PD-BG Bill Guerin C 4.00 10.00
PD-AZ Alexei Zhamnov B 4.00 10.00
PD-PK Paul Kariya A 8.00 20.00
PD-KH Kristian Huselius C 4.00 10.00
PD-MSK Martin Straka C 4.00 10.00
PD-JT Joe Thornton C 8.00 20.00

2003-04 Topps Pristine Popular Demand Relic Refractors

GRP.A PRINT RUN 10 SER.#'d SETS
GRP.A NOT PRICED DUE TO SCARCITY
*GRP.B/C REFRACTOR: 1.5X TO 4X
GRP.B/C PRINT RUN 25 SER.#'d SETS

2003-04 Topps Pristine Stick Portions

STATED ODDS 1:27
REFRACTOR PRINT RUN 10 SER.#'d SETS
REF.NOT PRICED DUE TO SCARCITY
PPS-VB Valeri Bure 4.00 10.00
PPS-MM Mark Messier 8.00 20.00
PPS-DW Doug Weight 5.00 12.00
PPS-JI Jarome Iginla 6.00 15.00
PPS-ED Eric Desjardins 4.00 10.00
PPS-DA Daniel Alfredsson 5.00 12.00
PPS-AO Adam Oates 5.00 12.00
PPS-SY Steve Yzerman 20.00 50.00
PPS-PS Patrik Stefan 4.00 10.00
PPS-CJ Curtis Joseph 5.00 12.00
PPS-MS Mats Sundin 5.00 12.00
PPS-JL John LeClair 5.00 12.00

2001-02 Topps Reserve

Released in late January 2002, this 121-card hobby only set featured color player photos on gold sparkle card stock. Each 10-pack box contained an autographed team logo puck, a PSA graded serial-numbered rookie card, a non-graded serial-numbered rookie cards and two jersey cards. Rookie cards were serial-numbered to 1599, 1099, or 699. Approximately half of each rookie print run was graded.
COMP.SET w/o SP's (100) 40.00 80.00
1 Joe Sakic 1.00 2.50
2 Patrik Elias .40 1.00
3 Mario Lemieux 3.00 8.00
4 Chris Pronger .40 1.00
5 Simon Gagne .50 1.25
6 Steve Yzerman 2.50 6.00
7 Bill Guerin .40 1.00
8 Pavel Bure .50 1.25
9 Mark Messier .50 1.25
10 Evgeni Nabokov .40 1.00
11 Peter Bondra .50 1.25
12 Martin Havlat .40 1.00
13 Mike Dunham .40 1.00
14 Mike Comrie .40 1.00
15 Ed Belfour .50 1.25
16 Tony Amonte .40 1.00
17 Patrik Stefan .15 .40
18 Paul Kariya .50 1.25
19 Patrick Roy 2.50 6.00
20 Sean Burke .40 1.00
21 Vincent Lecavalier .50 1.25
22 Henrik Sedin .15 .40
23 Petr Sykora .15 .40
24 Marian Gaborik 1.00 2.50
25 Rod Brind'Amour .40 1.00
26 Miroslav Satan .40 1.00
27 Zigmund Palffy .40 1.00
28 Sergei Fedorov .75 2.00
29 Ron Tugnutt .40 1.00
30 Jason Allison .15 .40
31 Marian Hossa .50 1.25
32 John LeClair .50 1.25
33 Keith Tkachuk .50 1.25
34 Adam Oates .50 1.25
35 Johan Hedberg .40 1.00
36 Saku Koivu .50 1.25
37 Peter Forsberg 1.00 2.50
38 Jarome Iginla .60 1.50
39 Nicklas Lidstrom .50 1.25
40 Martin Brodeur 1.25 3.00
41 Daniel Alfredsson .40 1.00
42 Alexei Kovalev .40 1.00
43 Mats Sundin .50 1.25
44 Brian Leetch .40 1.00
45 Owen Nolan .40 1.00
46 Cliff Ronning .15 .40
47 Mike Modano .75 2.00
48 Milan Hejduk .40 1.00
49 Joe Thornton .75 2.00
50 Ray Ferraro .15 .40
51 Geoff Sanderson .15 .40
52 Roberto Luongo .60 1.50
53 Manny Fernandez .40 1.00
54 Mark Recchi .40 1.00
55 Curtis Joseph .50 1.25
56 Philippe Boucher .15 .40
57 Patrick Lalime .40 1.00
58 Rick DiPietro .40 1.00
59 Adam Deadmarsh .15 .40
60 Pierre Turgeon .40 1.00
61 Roman Turek .40 1.00
62 Jeff Friesen .15 .40
63 Eric Lindros .50 1.25
64 Martin Straka .15 .40
65 Markus Naslund .50 1.25
66 J-P Dumont .15 .40
67 Daniel Sedin .15 .40
68 Alexei Yashin .15 .40
69 Felix Potvin .50 1.25
70 Chris Drury .40 1.00
71 Martin Biron .40 1.00
72 Tommy Salo .40 1.00
73 Stanislav Neckar .15 .40
74 Jaromir Jagr .60 1.50
75 Brendan Shanahan .50 1.25
76 Jose Theodore .60 1.50
77 Teemu Selanne .50 1.25
78 Alexander Mogilny .40 1.00
79 Niclas Havelid .15 .40
80 Colin Forbes .15 .40
81 Michael Peca .15 .40
82 Jason Arnott .15 .40
83 Arturs Irbe .40 1.00
84 Garry Valk .15 .40
85 Roman Cechmanek .40 1.00
86 Scott Gomez .15 .40
87 Chris McAllister .15 .40
88 Shane Doan .15 .40
89 David Harlock .15 .40
90 Jeff O'Neill .15 .40
91 Rob Blake .40 1.00
92 Dominik Hasek 1.00 2.50
93 Olaf Kolzig .40 1.00
94 Brent Johnson .40 1.00
95 Jeremy Roenick .60 1.50
96 Brad Richards .40 1.00
97 Steve Sullivan .15 .40
98 Alex Tanguay .40 1.00
99 Brett Hull .60 1.50
100 Doug Weight .40 1.00
101 Niklas Hagman/1099 RC 3.00 8.00
102 Scott Clemmensen/1099 RC 3.00 8.00
103 Brian Sutherby/1099 RC 3.00 8.00
104 Erik Cole/1599 RC 3.00 8.00
105 Vaclav Nedorost/1599 RC 3.00 8.00
106 Jaroslav Bednar/1099 RC 3.00 8.00
107 Nick Schultz/699 RC 3.00 8.00
108 Jiri Dopita/699 RC 3.00 8.00
109 Krys Kolanos/1599 RC 3.00 8.00
110 Jukka Hentunen/1099 RC 3.00 8.00
111 Niko Kapanen/699 RC 4.00 10.00
112 Timo Parssinen/1099 RC 3.00 8.00
113 Kristian Huselius/1599 RC 3.00 8.00
114 A.Salomonsson RC/699 3.00 8.00
115 Ilya Kovalchuk/1599 RC 8.00 20.00
116 Dan Blackburn/1599 RC 3.00 8.00
117 Pavel Datsyuk/699 RC 12.50 30.00
118 Peter Smrek/699 RC 3.00 8.00
119 Jeff Jillson/1099 RC 3.00 8.00
120 Nikita Alexeev/1599 RC 3.00 8.00
121 Scott Nichol/699 RC 3.00 8.00

2001-02 Topps Reserve Emblems

This 56-card set paralleled the base jersey set but each card carried a piece of the team logo from the player's jersey. Each card was inserted at 1:32. Each card carried a "TRL" prefix.
*EMBLEMS: 1X TO 2.5X JERSEYS

2001-02 Topps Reserve Jerseys

Inserted at 1:4 packs, this 56-card set featured swatches of game-worn jerseys alongside color player photos on team colored card fronts. All cards carried a "TR" prefix that has been left off of the listing below for checklisting purposes.
*MULT.COLOR SWATCH: 1X TO 1.5X
AK Alexei Kovalev 3.00 8.00
AO Adam Oates 3.00 8.00
AZ Alexei Zhamnov 3.00 8.00
BB Brian Boucher 3.00 8.00
BL Brian Leetch 5.00 12.00
CD Chris Drury 4.00 10.00
DH Derian Hatcher 3.00 8.00
DM Darren McCarty 4.00 10.00
DY Dimitri Yushkevich 3.00 8.00
EB Ed Belfour 5.00 12.00
ED Eric Desjardins 3.00 8.00
JH Jeff Hackett 3.00 8.00
JI Jarome Iginla 6.00 15.00
JL John LeClair 4.00 10.00
JS Joe Sakic 6.00 15.00
JT Joe Thornton 8.00 20.00
KJ Kenny Jonsson 3.00 8.00
KO Krzysztof Oliwa 3.00 8.00
MB Martin Brodeur 8.00 20.00
MC Mariusz Czerkawski 3.00 8.00
ML Mario Lemieux 12.50 30.00
MM Mike Mottau 3.00 8.00
MP Matt Pettinger 3.00 8.00
MR Mark Recchi 4.00 10.00
MT Marty Turco 5.00 12.00
MY Mike York 3.00 8.00
OS Oleg Saprykin 3.00 8.00
PB Pavel Bure 5.00 12.00
PF Peter Forsberg 6.00 15.00
PK Paul Kariya 5.00 12.00
PM Patrick Marleau 4.00 10.00
PR Patrick Roy 10.00 25.00
RL Robert Lang 3.00 8.00
SB Sean Burke 3.00 8.00
SF Sergei Fedorov 6.00 15.00
SG Simon Gagne 5.00 12.00
SK Saku Koivu 5.00 12.00
SM Shawn McEachern 3.00 8.00
SS Sergei Samsonov 5.00 12.00
SZ Sergei Zubov 3.00 8.00
TA Tony Amonte 4.00 10.00
TD Tie Domi 4.00 10.00
TF Theo Fleury 3.00 8.00
TK Tomas Kloucek 3.00 8.00
TL Trevor Letowski 3.00 8.00
TV Tomas Vokoun 5.00 12.00
VL Vincent Lecavalier 5.00 12.00
WR Wade Redden 3.00 8.00
DAB Daniel Briere 4.00 10.00
DOB Donald Brashear 4.00 10.00
JAI Jason Allison 4.00 10.00
JAR Jason Arnott 4.00 10.00
MIS Miroslav Satan 4.00 10.00
MSA Marc Savard 4.00 10.00
MST Martin Straka 4.00 10.00
ROF Ron Francis 4.00 10.00

2001-02 Topps Reserve Name Plates

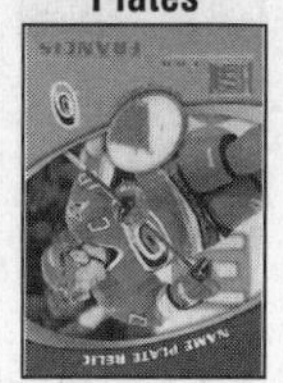

This 56-card set paralleled the base jersey set but each card carried a piece of the name plate from the player's jersey. These cards were inserted at 1:32. Each card carried a "TRN" prefix.
*NAME PLATES: 1X TO 2.5X JERSEYS

2001-02 Topps Reserve Numbers

This 56-card set paralleled the base jersey set but each card carried a piece of the jersey number from the player's jersey. These cards were inserted at 1:29 packs. Each card carried a "TR#" prefix. Please note that card #JAH did not have a parent card in the base jersey set, thus it is priced seperately below.
*NUMBERS: 1X TO 2.5X JERSEYS
JAH Jan Hlavac 12.50 30.00

2001-02 Topps Reserve Patches

This 56-card set paralleled the base jersey set but each card carried jersey patch from the player's jersey. These cards were inserted at 1:257. Each card carried a "TRP" prefix.
*PATCHES: 1.25X TO 3X JERSEYS

2000-01 Topps Stars

Released in late January 2001 as a 150-card set, Topps Stars features 97 veteran players, 3 retired stars on a gold background, 35 prospects on a silver background(card numbers 101-125 and 141-150) and 15 veteran spotlight cards, numbers 126-140. Base card stock has a blue background with silver glitter and silver foil highlights around full color player action photography. Topps Stars was packaged in 24 pack boxes with packs containing six cards and carried a suggested retail price of $3.00.
COMPLETE SET (150) 30.00 60.00
1 Vincent Lecavalier .20 .50
2 Patrick Roy 1.00 2.50
3 Scott Gomez .05 .15
4 Steve Yzerman 1.00 2.50
5 Paul Kariya .20 .50
6 Dominik Hasek .40 1.00
7 Mike Modano .30 .75
8 Zigmund Palffy .15 .40
9 John LeClair .20 .50
10 Mats Sundin .20 .50
11 Owen Nolan .15 .40
12 Tony Amonte .15 .40
13 Patrik Stefan .05 .15
14 Brett Hull .25 .60
15 Chris Pronger .15 .40
16 Jeremy Roenick .25 .60
17 Martin Brodeur .50 1.25
18 Doug Weight .15 .40
19 Ray Bourque .40 1.00
20 Olaf Kolzig .15 .40
21 Jaromir Jagr .30 .75
22 Daniel Alfredsson .15 .40
23 Jeff Hackett .05 .15
24 Jason Allison .05 .15
25 Joe Sakic .40 1.00
26 Brendan Shanahan .20 .50
27 David Legwand .05 .15
28 Tim Connolly .05 .15
29 Mark Recchi .15 .40
30 Brad Stuart .15 .40
31 Pierre Turgeon .15 .40
32 Ed Belfour .20 .50
33 Valeri Bure .05 .15
34 Pavel Bure .20 .50
35 Teemu Selanne .20 .50
36 Patrik Elias .15 .40
37 Mattias Ohlund .05 .15
38 Rod Brind'Amour .15 .40
39 Derian Hatcher .05 .15
40 Peter Forsberg .50 1.25
41 Eric Lindros .20 .50
42 Curtis Joseph .20 .50
43 Keith Tkachuk .20 .50
44 Mike Ricci .05 .15
45 Al MacInnis .15 .40
46 Nicklas Lidstrom .20 .50
47 Rob Blake .15 .40
48 Scott Stevens .15 .40
49 Milan Hejduk .20 .50
50 Theo Fleury .05 .15
51 Joe Thornton .30 .75
52 Tommy Salo .15 .40
53 Eric Desjardins .15 .40
54 Pavol Demitra .15 .40
55 Adam Oates .15 .40
56 Jeff Friesen .05 .15
57 Mariusz Czerkawski .05 .15
58 Luc Robitaille .15 .40
59 Jeff O'Neill .05 .15
60 Andrew Brunette .05 .15
61 Fred Brathwaite .15 .40
62 Robert Svehla .05 .15
63 Kimmo Timonen .05 .15
64 Teppo Numminen .05 .15
65 Nikolai Antropov .05 .15
66 Marian Hossa .20 .50
67 Joe Nieuwendyk .15 .40
68 Michael Peca .05 .15
69 Saku Koivu .20 .50
70 Alexei Kovalev .15 .40
71 Sergei Gonchar .05 .15
72 Brian Leetch .15 .40
73 Ryan Smyth .05 .15
74 Jarome Iginla .25 .60
75 Byron Dafoe .05 .15
76 Ray Whitney .05 .15
77 Wade Redden .05 .15
78 Pavel Kubina .05 .15
79 Markus Naslund .20 .50
80 Brian Boucher .20 .50
81 Martin Rucinsky .05 .15
82 Roman Turek .15 .40
83 Jocelyn Thibault .15 .40
84 Miroslav Satan .15 .40
85 Cliff Ronning .05 .15
86 Mike Richter .20 .50
87 Chris Chelios .20 .50
88 Arturs Irbe .15 .40
89 Steve Thomas .05 .15
90 Felix Potvin .20 .50
91 Jason Arnott .05 .15
92 Mark Messier .20 .50
93 Scott Pellerin .05 .15
94 John Vanbiesbrouck .15 .40
95 Dave Andreychuk .15 .40
96 Paul Coffey .20 .50
97 Ron Tugnutt .15 .40
98 Larry Robinson .15 .40
99 Billy Smith .15 .40
100 Mario Lemieux 2.00 5.00
101 Martin Havlat RC 2.00 5.00
102 Petr Hubacek RC .40 1.00
103 Niclas Wallin RC .40 1.00
104 Alexander Khavanov RC .40 1.00
105 Roman Cechmanek RC .50 1.25
106 Bryce Salvador RC .40 1.00
107 Jonas Ronnqvist RC .40 1.00
108 Rostislav Klesla RC 1.00 2.50
109 Justin Williams RC .40 1.00
110 Sascha Goc RC .40 1.00
111 Andrew Raycroft RC 1.50 4.00
112 Marty Turco RC 2.00 5.00
113 Marian Gaborik RC 2.00 5.00
114 Josef Vasicek RC .40 1.00
115 Steven Reinprecht RC .40 1.00
116 Jani Hurme RC .40 1.00
117 David Aebischer RC 1.50 4.00
118 Dale Purinton RC .40 1.00
119 Jarno Kultanen RC .40 1.00
120 Petr Svoboda RC .40 1.00
121 Eric Belanger RC .40 1.00
122 Petteri Nummelin RC .40 1.00
123 Michel Riesen RC .40 1.00
124 Jason Labarbera RC .40 1.00
125 Tyler Bouck RC .40 1.00
126 Martin Brodeur SL .25 .60
127 Pavel Bure SL .10 .30
128 Peter Forsberg SL .25 .60
129 Scott Gomez SL .10 .25
130 Dominik Hasek SL .20 .50
131 Brett Hull SL .12 .30
132 Jaromir Jagr SL .15 .40
133 Curtis Joseph SL .12 .30
134 Paul Kariya SL .20 .50
135 Chris Pronger SL .10 .25
136 Patrick Roy SL .50 1.25
137 Joe Sakic SL .20 .50
138 Teemu Selanne SL .10 .25
139 Steve Yzerman SL .50 1.25
140 Vincent Lecavalier SL .10 .25
141 Samuel Pahlsson SL .10 .25
142 Maxime Ouellet SL .10 .25
143 Kris Beech SL .10 .25
144 Henrik Sedin SL .10 .25
145 Daniel Sedin SL .10 .25
146 Milan Kraft SL .10 .25
147 Marty Turco SL .10 .25
148 Oleg Saprykin SL .10 .25
149 Brent Johnson SL .10 .25
150 Marian Gaborik SL .10 .25

2000-01 Topps Stars Blue

Randomly inserted in packs at the rate of 1:8, this 150-card set parallels the base set enhanced with blue foil. Card numbers 126-140 are sequentially numbered to 99, and the rest are sequentially numbered to 299.
*BLUE STARS: 4X TO 10X BASIC CARDS

*BLUE YNG.STARS: 3X TO 8X BASIC CARDS
*BLUE RC's:1.5X TO 3X BASIC CARDS

2000-01 Topps Stars All-Star Authority

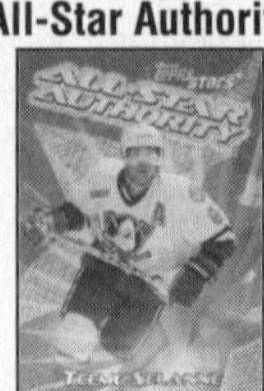

COMPLETE SET (11) 8.00 15.00
STATED ODDS 1:9
ASA1 Ray Bourque .60 1.50
ASA2 Brett Hull .40 1.00
ASA3 Mark Messier .40 1.00
ASA4 Patrick Roy 2.00 5.00
ASA5 Jaromir Jagr .60 1.50
ASA6 Dominik Hasek .60 1.50
ASA7 Teemu Selanne .40 1.00
ASA8 Steve Yzerman 2.00 5.00
ASA9 Joe Sakic .60 1.50
ASA10 Paul Bure .50 1.25
ASA11 John LeClair .40 1.00

2000-01 Topps Stars Autographs

Randomly inserted in packs at the rate of 1:15 (combined odds between Game Gear and Autographs), this 10-card set features a framed player photo on the left side of the card front with a whiteout area extending from the left card border down along the bottom border of the card where the player autograph appears. Each card is enhanced with gold foil highlights.
ABB Brian Boucher 6.00 15.00
ACP Chris Pronger 10.00 25.00
ALR Larry Robinson 10.00 25.00
AML Mario Lemieux 75.00 200.00
AMM Mike Modano 15.00 40.00
AMY Mike York 6.00 15.00
AVL Vincent Lecavalier 12.50 30.00
ABSM Billy Smith 12.50 30.00
ABST Brad Stuart 6.00 15.00

2000-01 Topps Stars Game Gear

Randomly inserted in packs at the rate of 1:15 (combined odds between Game Gear and Autographs), this 18-card set featured either a swatch of game worn jersey or game used stick. Two different game gear autograph cards were also available, and randomly inserted in packs at the rate of 1:5568 for the jersey cards and 1:12528 for the stick cards. The Don Cherry suit cards were randomly inserted at 1:49 Canadian packs or 1:392 Canadian packs for the autographed version.
*MULT.COLOR SWATCH: .75X TO 1.5X
GGAG Adam Graves J 3.00 8.00
GGCP Chris Pronger J 4.00 10.00
GGDC Don Cherry Suit 10.00 25.00
GGDCA D.Cherry Suit/AU 40.00 100.00
GGDL David Legwand J 3.00 8.00
GGDM Darren McCarty J 3.00 8.00
GGJA Jason Allison J 3.00 8.00
GGKT Keith Tkachuk S 10.00 25.00
GGMC Mariusz Czerkawski J 3.00 8.00
GGML Martin Lapointe J 3.00 8.00
GGMM Mike Modano S 10.00 25.00
GGMR Mike Richter J 4.00 10.00
GGPH Phil Housley J 3.00 8.00
GGPR Patrick Roy J 20.00 50.00
GGRT Ron Tugnutt S 10.00 25.00
GGSZ Sergei Zubov J 3.00 8.00
GGTA Tony Amonte J 3.00 8.00
GGTS Teemu Selanne J 4.00 10.00
GGZP Zigmund Palffy S 10.00 25.00
GGMR Mark Recchi S 10.00 25.00
GGCP Chris Pronger J/AU 100.00 200.00
GGMM Mike Modano S/AU 150.00 300.00

2000-01 Topps Stars Progression

Randomly inserted in packs at the rate of 1:11, this nine-card set features three players of the same position on an all foil card stock. Three portrait style photos are set against a blue background with yellow foil highlights. From left to right, the photos feature an established veteran star, an established star, and a young star.

COMPLETE SET (9) 15.00 40.00
P1 Mario Lemieux 3.00 8.00
Mike Modano
Vincent Lecavalier
P2 Mario Lemieux 3.00 8.00
Peter Forsberg
Patrik Stefan
P3 Mario Lemieux 3.00 8.00
Steve Yzerman
Scott Gomez
P4 Billy Smith 3.00 8.00
Patrick Roy
Roberto Luongo
P5 Billy Smith 2.00 5.00
Martin Brodeur
Marty Turco
P6 Billy Smith 1.25 3.00
Ed Belfour
Brian Boucher
P7 Larry Robinson .75 2.00
Scott Stevens
Rostislav Klesla
P8 Larry Robinson 2.00 5.00
Ray Bourque
Brad Stuart
P9 Larry Robinson .75 2.00
Chris Pronger
Martin Skoula

2000-01 Topps Stars Walk of Fame

COMPLETE SET (10) 10.00 20.00
STATED ODDS 1:10
WF1 Pavel Bure .60 1.50
WF2 Paul Kariya .60 1.50
WF3 Jaromir Jagr .75 2.00
WF4 Peter Forsberg 1.25 3.00
WF5 Mike Modano .60 1.50
WF6 Patrick Roy 2.50 6.00
WF7 Steve Yzerman 2.50 6.00
WF8 Dominik Hasek 1.00 2.50
WF9 John LeClair .60 1.50
WF10 Martin Brodeur 1.25 3.00

1995-96 Topps SuperSkills

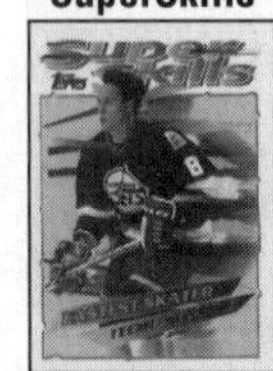

The 1995-96 Topps SuperSkills set was issued in one series totaling 90 cards. The 11-card packs originally retailed for $3.99. The set was a special one-off project designed to capitalize on Topps sponsorship of the SuperSkills program held in conjunction with the 1996 All-Star Game in Boston. The set features the players who were expected to compete in the following categories: Puck Control (1-18), Fastest Skater (19-36), Hardest Shot (37-54), Accuracy Shooting (55-72) and Rapid Fire/Breakaway Relay (73-90). The packs clearly identified which conference and event the cards inside would picture. A one-card-per-pack parallel set, "Platinum", is identical to the basic set save for a platinum trim along the edges of the cards. Multipliers can be found in the header below to determine values for these.
COMPLETE SET (90) 8.00 20.00
COMPLETE PLATINUM SET (90) 18.00 45.00
*PLATINUM: .75X to 1.5X BASIC CARDS
1 Mario Lemieux .80 2.00
2 Adam Oates .15 .40
3 Donald Audette .01 .05
4 Andrew Cassels .01 .05
5 Pat LaFontaine .15 .40
6 Mathieu Schneider .01 .05
7 Scott Stevens .01 .05
8 Mikael Renberg .15 .40
9 Pierre Turgeon .15 .40
10 Steve Yzerman .80 2.00
11 Russ Courtnall .01 .05
12 Oleg Tverdovsky .15 .40
13 Craig Janney .01 .05
14 Doug Gilmour .20 .50
15 Wayne Gretzky 1.20 3.00
16 Paul Kariya .60 1.50
17 Joe Sakic .40 1.00
18 Peter Forsberg .40 1.00
19 Brian Leetch .20 .50
20 Jaromir Jagr .40 1.00
21 Geoff Sanderson .01 .05
22 Rob Niedermayer .15 .40
23 Ray Ferraro .01 .05
24 Alexandre Daigle .01 .05
25 Joe Juneau .15 .40
26 Don Sweeney .01 .05
27 Scott Niedermayer .01 .05
28 Mike Gartner .01 .05
29 Paul Coffey .15 .40
30 Pavel Bure .40 1.00
31 Teemu Selanne .30 .75
32 Mats Sundin .20 .50
33 Trevor Linden .15 .40
34 Sergei Fedorov .30 .75
35 Theo Fleury .20 .50
36 Alexander Mogilny .15 .40
37 Garry Galley .01 .05
38 Stu Barnes .01 .05
39 Glen Wesley .01 .05
40 Eric Lindros .40 1.00
41 Stephane Richer .01 .05
42 John LeClair .20 .50
43 Pat Verbeek .15 .40
44 Bill Guerin .01 .05
45 Wendel Clark .15 .40
46 Mike Modano .20 .50
47 Keith Primeau .15 .40
48 Brett Hull .24 .60
49 Al MacInnis .15 .40
50 Chris Chelios .20 .50
51 Keith Tkachuk .20 .50
52 Dave Andreychuk .01 .05
53 Kevin Hatcher .01 .05
54 Chris Pronger .01 .05
55 Brendan Shanahan .20 .50
56 Luc Robitaille .15 .40
57 Ray Bourque .15 .75
58 Mark Recchi .15 .40
59 Brian Bradley .01 .05
60 Mark Messier .24 .60
61 Kevin Stevens .01 .05
62 John MacLean .01 .05
63 Cam Neely .20 .50
64 Rick Tocchet .01 .05
65 Jeremy Roenick .20 .50
66 Phil Housley .01 .05
67 Jason Arnott .15 .40
68 Todd Harvey .01 .05
69 Jeff Friesen .15 .40
70 Alexei Zhamnov .15 .40
71 David Oliver .01 .05
72 Bernie Nicholls .01 .05
73 Jim Carey .15 .40
74 Mike Richter .15 .40
75 Dominik Hasek .30 .75
76 Sean Burke .01 .05
77 Ron Hextall .15 .40
78 John Vanbiesbrouck .20 .50
79 Tom Barrasso .15 .40
80 Martin Brodeur .40 1.00
81 Patrick Roy .80 2.00
82 Trevor Kidd .15 .40
83 Andy Moog .15 .40
84 Mike Vernon .01 .05
85 Felix Potvin .20 .50
86 Bill Ranford .15 .40
87 Kelly Hrudey .15 .40
88 Grant Fuhr .15 .40
89 Kirk McLean .15 .40
90 Ed Belfour .20 .50

1995-96 Topps SuperSkills Super Rookies

Inserted one per Topps SuperSkills pack, this 15-card set features the cream of the 1995-96 rookie crop on 20 point all-foil board stock with gild-edge technology.
COMPLETE SET (15) 4.80 12.00
SR1 Ed Jovanovski .30 .75
SR2 Jason Bonsignore .10 .25
SR3 Jeff O'Neill .40 1.00
SR4 Cory Stillman .10 .25
SR5 Chad Kilger .20 .50
SR6 Aki Berg .20 .50
SR7 Todd Bertuzzi 1.20 3.00
SR8 Shane Doan .40 1.00
SR9 Kyle McLaren .20 .50
SR10 Radek Dvorak .20 .50
SR11 Saku Koivu 1.20 3.00
SR12 Daniel Alfredsson .40 1.00
SR13 Antti Tormanen .10 .25
SR14 Niklas Sundstrom .20 .50
SR15 Vitali Yachmenev .10 .25

2002-03 Topps Total

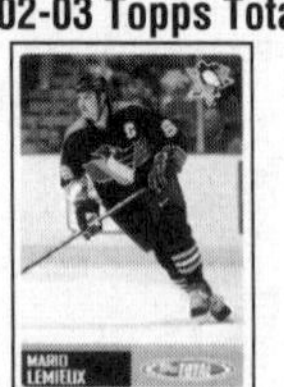

Released in late February, this 440-card set was one of the largest base sets of the year.
COMPLETE SET (440) 15.00 40.00
1 Nicklas Lidstrom .15 .40
2 Mikko Eloranta .05 .15
3 Richard Park .05 .15
4 Eric Lindros .15 .40
5 Vincent Lecavalier .15 .40
6 Dany Heatley .20 .50
7 Roman Turek .12 .30
8 Rostislav Klesla .05 .15
9 Paul Kariya .15 .40
10 Marian Hossa .15 .40
11 Patrick Roy .75 2.00
12 Henrik Sedin .05 .15
13 Adam Graves .05 .15
14 Ian Laperriere .05 .15
15 Jiri Fischer .05 .15
16 Nick Schultz .05 .15
17 Steve Sullivan .05 .15
18 Sandis Ozolinsh .05 .15
19 Evgeni Nabokov .12 .30
20 Dimitri Khristich .05 .15
21 Danny Markov .05 .15
22 Adam Foote .05 .15
23 David Vyborny .05 .15
24 Jocelyn Thibault .12 .30
25 Mike Leclerc .05 .15
26 Pavol Demitra .12 .30
27 Scott Mellanby .05 .15
28 Brent Sopel .05 .15
29 Brad Isbister .05 .15
30 Sami Salo .05 .15
31 Jose Theodore .20 .50
32 Simon Gagne .15 .40
33 Rem Murray .05 .15
34 Mike Ricci .05 .15
35 Kim Johnsson .05 .15
36 Adam Oates .12 .30
37 Taylor Pyatt .05 .15
38 Rod Brind'Amour .12 .30
39 Mike Modano .25 .60
40 Jason Woolley .05 .15
41 Dimitri Yushkevich .05 .15
42 Craig Johnson .05 .15
43 Tony Hrkac .05 .15
44 Scott Young .05 .15
45 Marian Gaborik .30 1.00
46 Patrik Stefan .05 .15
47 Jon Klemm .05 .15
48 Andy McDonald .05 .15
49 Chris Pronger .12 .30
50 Frantisek Kaberle .05 .15
51 J-S Giguere .12 .30
52 Luc Robitaille .05 .15
53 Scott Stevens .12 .30
54 Roberto Luongo .20 .50
55 Teppo Numminen .05 .15
56 Alyn McCauley .05 .15
57 John Grahame .12 .30
58 David Legwand .12 .30
59 Hal Gill .05 .15
60 Mattias Ohlund .05 .15
61 Radim Vrbata .05 .15
62 Doug Gilmour .12 .30
63 Vaclav Prospal .05 .15
64 Brian Leetch .12 .30
65 Sheldon Keefe .05 .15
66 Randy McKay .05 .15
67 Mikael Samuelsson .05 .15
68 Pavel Bure .15 .40
69 Zdeno Chara .05 .15
70 P.J. Stock .05 .15
71 Shawn McEachern .05 .15
72 Radek Martinek .05 .15
73 Mike Rathje .05 .15
74 Kenny Jonsson .05 .15
75 Jamie Langenbrunner .05 .15
76 Chris Phillips .05 .15
77 Zigmund Palffy .12 .30
78 Stu Barnes .05 .15
79 Robert Reichel .05 .15
80 Jason Allison .05 .15
81 Dimitri Kalinin .05 .15
82 Chris Simon .05 .15
83 Arturs Irbe .12 .30
84 Tony Amonte .12 .30
85 Ruslan Salei .05 .15
86 Pascal Rheaume .05 .15
87 Marc Denis .12 .30
88 Marc Chouinard .05 .15
89 Jim Dowd .05 .15
90 Claude Lemieux .05 .15
91 Alexei Zhamnov .05 .15
92 Al MacInnis .12 .30
93 Cory Stillman .05 .15
94 Bob Boughner .05 .15
95 Kris Draper .05 .15
96 Mario Lemieux 1.00 2.50
97 Sean Burke .12 .30
98 Wes Walz .05 .15
99 Brenden Morrow .12 .30
100 Dave Andreychuk .05 .15
101 Jaromir Jagr .25 .60
102 Markus Naslund .15 .40
103 Nick Boynton .05 .15
104 Sean Hill .05 .15
105 Trevor Linden .05 .15
106 Bryan Berard .05 .15
107 Chris Neilson .05 .15
108 Marco Sturm .05 .15
109 Oleg Petrov .05 .15
110 Scott Gomez .05 .15
111 Luke Richardson .05 .15
112 Manny Malhotra .05 .15
113 Valeri Bure .05 .15
114 Marcel Hossa .05 .15
115 Todd Marchant .05 .15
116 Radek Bonk .05 .15
117 Matt Bradley .05 .15
118 Jochen Hecht .05 .15
119 Dan McGillis .05 .15
120 Adrian Aucoin .05 .15
121 Eric Belanger .05 .15
122 Peter Forsberg .40 1.00
123 Alexei Morozov .05 .15
124 Jimmie Olvestad .05 .15
125 Ed Jovanovski .12 .30
126 Chris Drury .12 .30
127 Alexander Mogilny .12 .30
128 Stephen Weiss .05 .15
129 Manny Legace .12 .30
130 Jarome Iginla .20 .50
131 Doug Weight .12 .30
132 Martin St. Louis .12 .30
133 Alexander Khavanov .05 .15
134 Chris Chelios .15 .40
135 Viktor Kozlov .05 .15
136 Bret Hedican .05 .15
137 Denis Arkhipov .05 .15
138 Jere Lehtinen .12 .30
139 Mathieu Schneider .05 .15
140 Tomas Kaberle .05 .15
141 Brian Gionta .05 .15
142 Janne Niinimaa .05 .15
143 Mark Parrish .05 .15
144 Todd White .05 .15
145 Geoff Sanderson .05 .15
146 Yanic Perreault .05 .15
147 Roman Hamrlik .05 .15
148 Mike Fisher .05 .15
149 Jiri Dopita .05 .15
150 Claude Lapointe .05 .15
151 Vaclav Nedorost .05 .15
152 Mikael Renberg .05 .15
153 Jozef Stumpel .05 .15
154 Felix Potvin .15 .40
155 Chris Gratton .05 .15
156 Adam Deadmarsh .05 .15
157 Sergei Fedorov .25 .60
158 Mike Sillinger .05 .15
159 Kris Beech .05 .15
160 Grant Marshall .05 .15
161 Brent Johnson .12 .30
162 Alexei Kovalev .12 .30
163 Darren McCarty .05 .15
164 Marc Savard .05 .15
165 Janne Laukkanen .05 .15
166 Phil Housley .05 .15
167 Tomas Holmstrom .05 .15
168 Bill Guerin .12 .30
169 Darius Kasparaitis .05 .15
170 Jaroslav Modry .05 .15
171 Martin Gelinas .05 .15
172 Peter Bondra .12 .30
173 Steven Reinprecht .05 .15
174 Anson Carter .12 .30
175 Eric Brewer .05 .15
176 Magnus Arvedson .05 .15
177 Patrice Brisebois .05 .15
178 Sergei Brylin .05 .15
179 Vitali Vishnevski .05 .15
180 Marcus Nilsson .05 .15
181 Niklas Sundstrom .05 .15
182 Daymond Langkow .12 .30
183 Craig Conroy .05 .15
184 Gary Roberts .05 .15
185 Justin Williams .05 .15
186 Matt Cooke .05 .15
187 Pierre Turgeon .12 .30
188 Steve Konowalchuk .05 .15
189 Yannick Tremblay .05 .15
190 Tom Poti .05 .15
191 Sergei Zholtok .05 .15
192 Robyn Regehr .05 .15
193 Mike Richter .15 .40
194 Shawn Bates .05 .15
195 Pavel Trnka .05 .15
196 Martin Straka .05 .15
197 Jonas Hoglund .05 .15
198 Filip Kuba .05 .15
199 Chris Osgood .12 .30
200 Brad May .05 .15
201 David Aebischer .12 .30
202 Fred Brathwaite .12 .30
203 Lubos Bartecko .05 .15
204 Marty Turco .12 .30
205 Petr Nedved .05 .15
206 Shayne Corson .05 .15
207 Sergei Samsonov .12 .30
208 Patrik Elias .12 .30
209 Martin Erat .05 .15
210 Krystofer Kolanos .05 .15
211 Joe Thornton .25 .60
212 Ivan Novoseltsev .05 .15
213 Eric Messier .05 .15
214 Daniel Cleary .05 .15
215 Alex Tanguay .12 .30
216 Robert Lang .05 .15
217 Wade Redden .05 .15
218 Scott Walker .05 .15
219 Milan Hejduk .15 .40
220 Ken Daneyko .05 .15
221 J-P Dumont .05 .15
222 Ian Moran .05 .15
223 Christian Berglund .05 .15
224 Alexei Yashin .05 .15
225 Brad Stuart .05 .15
226 Donald Brashear .05 .15
227 Curtis Brown .12 .30
228 John LeClair .15 .40
229 Manny Fernandez .12 .30
230 Maxim Afinogenov .05 .15
231 Roman Cechmanek .12 .30
232 Tyler Wright .05 .15
233 Slava Kozlov .05 .15
234 Tyler Arnason .12 .30
235 Sandy McCarthy .05 .15
236 Pascal Dupuis .05 .15
237 Olaf Kolzig .12 .30
238 Kyle Calder .05 .15
239 Jeremy Roenick .20 .50
240 Mathieu Dandenault .05 .15
241 Jeff O'Neill .05 .15
242 Dave Tanabe .05 .15
243 Calle Johansson .05 .15
244 Greg deVries .05 .15
245 Andrew Brunette .05 .15
246 Dan Hinote .05 .15
247 Jason Smith .05 .15
248 Mark Bell .05 .15
249 Pavel Kubina .05 .15
250 Teemu Selanne .15 .40
251 Vladimir Orszagh .05 .15
252 Brad Ference .05 .15
253 Darryl Sydor .05 .15
254 Vitali Yachmenev .05 .15
255 Scott Hartnell .05 .15
256 Fredrik Modin .05 .15
257 Alexei Zhitnik .05 .15
258 Brett Hull .20 .50
259 Glen Murray .05 .15
260 Michael Peca .05 .15
261 Owen Nolan .12 .30
262 Tie Domi .12 .30
263 Ville Nieminen .05 .15
264 Rob Blake .12 .30
265 Greg Johnson .05 .15
266 Andrei Markov .05 .15
267 Josef Vasicek .05 .15
268 Ryan Smyth .05 .15
269 Vincent Damphousse .05 .15
270 Mark Recchi .12 .30
271 Rob Niedermayer .05 .15
272 Mariusz Czerkawski .05 .15
273 Glen Wesley .05 .15
274 Brian Boucher .12 .30
275 Bryan McCabe .05 .15
276 Ron Tugnutt .12 .30
277 Daniel Briere .05 .15
278 Igor Larionov .05 .15
279 Keith Tkachuk .15 .40
280 Mats Sundin .15 .40
281 Dwayne Roloson .12 .30
282 Andrew Cassels .05 .15
283 Brendan Morrison .12 .30
284 Bryan Smolinski .05 .15
285 Jan Hlavac .05 .15
286 Jamal Mayers .05 .15
287 Kevin Weekes .12 .30
288 Tim Connolly .05 .15
289 Steve Yzerman .75 2.00
290 Derek Morris .05 .15
291 Derian Hatcher .05 .15
292 Steve Shields .12 .30
293 Martin Brodeur .40 1.00
294 Marcus Ragnarsson .05 .15
295 Scott Thornton .05 .15
296 Oleg Kvasha .05 .15
297 Mike York .05 .15
298 Tomi Kallio .05 .15
299 Martin Skoula .05 .15
300 Jeff Halpern .05 .15
301 Ed Belfour .15 .40
302 Andrew Ference .05 .15
303 Nikolai Khabibulin .15 .40
304 Bryce Salvador .05 .15
305 Lubomir Visnovsky .05 .15
306 Dan Cloutier .12 .30
307 Andy Delmore .05 .15
308 Martin Lapointe .05 .15
309 Daniel Sedin .05 .15
310 Kelly Buchberger .05 .15
311 Darcy Tucker .05 .15
312 Sergei Berezin .05 .15
313 Ruslan Fedotenko .05 .15
314 Mark Messier .15 .40
315 Mike Comrie .12 .30
316 Bobby Holik .05 .15
317 Shane Doan .05 .15
318 Michal Handzus .05 .15
319 Joe Sakic .30 .75
320 Kristian Huselius .05 .15
321 Ben Clymer .05 .15
322 Mattias Norstrom .05 .15
323 Pavel Datsyuk .15 .40
324 Richard Matvichuk .05 .15
325 Dainius Zubrus .05 .15
326 Craig Rivet .05 .15
327 Eric Desjardins .05 .15
328 Patrick Marleau .12 .30
329 Mike Grier .05 .15
330 Steve Rucchin .05 .15
331 Kimmo Timonen .05 .15
332 Brendan Witt .05 .15
333 Sami Kapanen .05 .15
334 Todd Bertuzzi .15 .40
335 Ilya Kovalchuk .20 .50
336 Donald Audette .05 .15
337 Georges Laraque .05 .15
338 Jason Arnott .05 .15
339 John Madden .05 .15
340 Petr Sykora .05 .15
341 Tommy Salo .12 .30
342 Daniel Alfredsson .12 .30
343 Eric Weinrich .05 .15
344 Radek Dvorak .05 .15
345 Stephane Yelle .05 .15
346 Sergei Zubov .05 .15
347 Milan Hnilicka .12 .30
348 Lubomir Sekeras .05 .15
349 Espen Knutsen .05 .15
350 Travis Green .05 .15
351 Jan Hrdina .05 .15
352 Paul Laus .05 .15
353 Bates Battaglia .05 .15
354 Miroslav Satan .12 .30
355 Craig Berube .05 .15
356 Sean O'Donnell .05 .15
357 Joe Nieuwendyk .12 .30
358 Patrick Lalime .12 .30
359 Brian Rafalski .05 .15
360 Michael Nylander .05 .15
361 Jean-Luc Grand Pierre .05 .15
362 Ron Francis .12 .30
363 Andrei Nikolishin .05 .15
364 Dallas Drake .05 .15
365 Eric Daze .05 .15
366 Andreas Dackell .05 .15
367 Scott Niedermayer .05 .15
368 Chris Clark .05 .15
369 Brendan Shanahan .15 .40
370 Tomas Vokoun .12 .30
371 Johan Hedberg .12 .30
372 Nikita Alexeev .05 .15
373 Dave Scatchard .05 .15
374 Matt Cullen .05 .15
375 Steve Thomas .05 .15
376 Brian Rolston .05 .15
377 Richard Zednik .05 .15
378 Sergei Gonchar .05 .15
379 Keith Primeau .05 .15
380 Jeff Friesen .05 .15
381 Keith Carney .05 .15
382 Kirk Maltby .05 .15
383 Erik Cole .05 .15
384 Martin Biron .12 .30
385 Jody Shelley .05 .15
386 Brad Richards .12 .30
387 Michal Rozsival .05 .15
388 Martin Havlat .12 .30
389 Igor Korolev .05 .15
390 Ladislav Nagy .05 .15
391 Curtis Joseph .15 .40
392 Toni Lydman .05 .15
393 Antti Laaksonen .05 .15
394 Jeff Jillson .05 .15
395 Saku Koivu .15 .40
396 Trevor Letowski .05 .15
397 Ray Whitney .05 .15
398 Olli Jokinen .12 .30
399 Colin White .05 .15
400 Mike Dunham .12 .30
401 Dan Blackburn .12 .30
402 Ron Hainsey RC .60 1.50
403 Scottie Upshall RC .60 1.50
404 Anton Volchenkov RC .60 1.50
405 Dmitri Bykov RC .60 1.50
406 Steve Eminger RC .60 1.50
407 Lasse Pirjeta RC .60 1.50
408 Tomi Pettinen RC .60 1.50
409 Ales Hemsky RC 2.00 3.00
410 Chuck Kobasew RC 1.00 2.50
411 Jason Spezza RC 2.50 5.00
412 Jeff Paul RC .60 1.50
413 Adam Hall RC .60 1.50
414 Rick Nash RC 2.50 5.00
415 Kurt Sauer RC .60 1.50
416 Alexander Frolov RC 1.25 3.00
417 Patrick Sharp RC .60 1.50
418 Alexei Smirnov RC .60 1.50
419 Tom Koivisto RC .60 1.50
420 Jay Bouwmeester RC 1.25 2.50
421 Mikael Tellqvist RC .60 1.50
422 P-M Bouchard RC 1.25 2.50
423 Radovan Somik RC .60 1.50
424 Ivan Majesky RC .60 1.50
425 Jamie Lundmark .05 .15
426 Henrik Zetterberg RC 2.50 4.00
427 Dennis Seidenberg RC .60 1.50
428 Jeff Taffe RC .60 1.50
429 Martin Gerber RC 1.00 2.50
430 Lynn Loyns RC .60 1.50
431 Micki DuPont RC .60 1.50
432 Jonathan Cheechoo .08 .20
433 Eric Godard RC .60 1.50
434 Stanislav Chistov RC .05 .15
435 Alexander Svitov RC .60 1.50
436 Fedor Fedorov .05 .15
437 Stephane Veilleux RC .60 1.50
438 Curtis Sanford RC .05 .15
439 Jordan Leopold RC .60 1.50
440 Carlo Colaiacovo RC .60 1.50

2002-03 Topps Total Award Winners

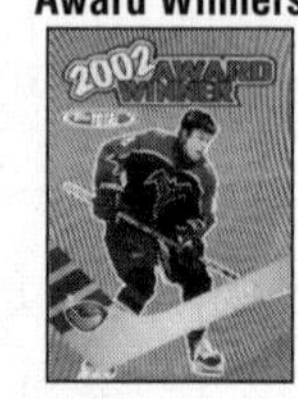

COMPLETE SET (10) 8.00 15.00
STATED ODDS 1:36
AW1 Jarome Iginla .75 2.00
AW2 Patrick Roy 2.50 6.00
AW3 Nicklas Lidstrom .60 1.50
AW4 Jose Theodore .75 2.00
AW5 Dany Heatley .75 2.00
AW6 Ron Francis .50 1.25
AW7 Eric Daze .50 1.25
AW8 Chris Chelios .60 1.50
AW9 Saku Koivu .60 1.50
AW10 Michael Peca .50 1.25

2002-03 Topps Total Production

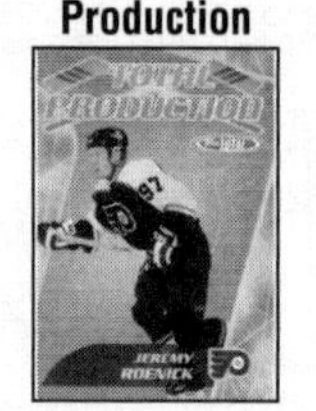

COMPLETE SET (15) 6.00 12.00
STATED ODDS 1:12
TP1 Jarome Iginla .40 1.00
TP2 Joe Sakic .60 1.50
TP3 Mats Sundin .30 .75
TP4 Peter Forsberg .75 2.00
TP5 Bill Guerin .25 .60
TP6 Brendan Shanahan .50 1.25
TP7 Sergei Fedorov .60 1.50
TP8 Pavel Bure .40 1.00
TP9 Jeremy Roenick .40 1.00
TP10 Tony Amonte .25 .60
TP11 Teemu Selanne .30 .75
TP12 Alexander Mogilny .25 .60
TP13 Markus Naslund .30 .75
TP14 Todd Bertuzzi .30 .75
TP15 Jaromir Jagr .50 1.25

2002-03 Topps Total Signatures

Inserted at a rate of 1:926, this 6-card set looked like the base set but carried certified autographs on the card fronts. As of press time, not all cards have been verified.
BG Brian Gionta 6.00 15.00
EC Erik Cole 6.00 15.00
KK Krystofer Kolanos EXISTS?
RK Rostislav Klesla 12.50 30.00
RV Radim Vrbata 6.00 15.00
SW Stephen Weiss EXISTS?

2002-03 Topps Total Team Checklists

COMPLETE SET (30) 6.00 15.00
TTC1 Ilya Kovalchuk .40 1.00
TTC2 Joe Thornton .40 1.00
TTC3 Miroslav Satan .10 .25
TTC4 Jarome Iginla .40 1.00
TTC5 Ron Francis .10 .25
TTC6 Jocelyn Thibault .10 .25
TTC7 Patrick Roy 1.25 3.00

TTC8 Rick Nash .40 1.00
TTC9 Mike Modano .40 1.00
TTC10 Steve Yzerman .75 2.00
TTC11 Tommy Salo .10 .25
TTC12 Roberto Luongo .40 1.00
TTC13 Jason Allison .10 .25
TTC14 Paul Kariya .30 .75
TTC15 Marian Gaborik .40 1.00
TTC16 Jose Theodore .40 1.00
TTC17 Mike Dunham .20 .50
TTC18 Martin Brodeur .75 2.00
TTC19 Michael Peca .10 .25
TTC20 Pavel Bure .30 .75
TTC21 Daniel Alfredsson .20 .50
TTC22 John LeClair .10 .25
TTC23 Tony Amonte .10 .25
TTC24 Mario Lemieux 1.25 3.00
TTC25 Owen Nolan .20 .50
TTC26 Keith Tkachuk .20 .50
TTC27 Nikolai Khabibulin .30 .75
TTC28 Mats Sundin .30 .75
TTC29 Todd Bertuzzi .10 .25
TTC30 Jaromir Jagr .60 1.50

2002-03 Topps Total Topps

COMPLETE SET (20) 8.00 15.00
STATED ODDS 1:6
TT1 Jarome Iginla .25 .60
TT2 Patrick Roy 1.00 2.50
TT3 Nicklas Lidstrom .20 .50
TT4 Jose Theodore .25 .60
TT5 Joe Sakic .40 1.00
TT6 Mats Sundin .25 .60
TT7 Ilya Kovalchuk .25 .60
TT8 Joe Thornton .30 .75
TT9 Mike Modano .30 .75
TT10 Brett Hull .25 .60
TT11 Steve Yzerman 1.00 2.50
TT12 Curtis Joseph .20 .50
TT13 Paul Kariya .20 .50
TT14 Patrik Elias .12 .30
TT15 Martin Brodeur .50 1.25
TT16 Eric Lindros .20 .50
TT17 Daniel Alfredsson .12 .30
TT18 Mario Lemieux 1.25 3.00
TT19 Owen Nolan .12 .30
TT20 Jaromir Jagr .30 .75

2003-04 Topps Traded

Released in late-April, this 165-card set consisted of 84 veterans who were traded earlier in the season and rookies who made their debut late in the season.

COMPLETE SET (165) 25.00 50.00
TT1 Felix Potvin .10 .25
TT2 Chris Drury .10 .25
TT3 Karel Rachunek .02 .10
TT4 Miikka Kiprusoff .10 .25
TT5 Justin Williams .02 .10
TT6 Bryan Berard .02 .10
TT7 Jim Vandermeer .02 .10
TT8 Shayne Corson .02 .10
TT9 Teemu Selanne .12 .30
TT10 Peter Worrell .02 .10
TT11 Darryl Sydor .02 .10
TT12 Todd Marchant .02 .10
TT13 Ray Whitney .02 .10
TT14 Robert Lang .02 .10
TT15 Adam Oates .10 .25
TT16 Jozef Stumpel .02 .10
TT17 Luc Robitaille .10 .25
TT18 Roman Cechmanek .10 .25
TT19 Martin Straka .02 .10
TT20 Sergei Fedorov .15 .40
TT21 Michael Nylander .02 .10
TT22 Steve Sullivan .02 .10
TT23 Steve Konowalchuk .02 .10
TT24 Valeri Bure .02 .10
TT25 Jaromir Jagr .20 .50
TT26 Peter Bondra .10 .25
TT27 Mike Grier .02 .10
TT28 Cory Stillman .02 .10
TT29 Joe Nieuwendyk .10 .25
TT30 Brian Leetch .10 .25
TT31 Johan Hedberg .10 .25
TT32 Andrew Raycroft .10 .25
TT33 Chuck Kobasew .02 .10
TT34 Brett McLean .02 .10
TT35 Craig Andersson .02 .10
TT36 Michael Leighton .10 .25
TT37 Matthew Barnaby .02 .10
TT38 Philippe Sauve .10 .25
TT39 Chris Gratton .02 .10
TT40 Radek Dvorak .02 .10
TT41 Raffi Torres .02 .10
TT42 Ossi Vaananen .02 .10
TT43 Trent Klatt .02 .10
TT44 Alexander Daigle .02 .10
TT45 Sergei Gonchar .02 .10
TT46 Niklas Sundstrom .02 .10
TT47 Michael Ryder .02 .10
TT48 Igor Larionov .02 .10
TT49 Jan Hrdina .02 .10
TT50 Cliff Ronning .02 .10
TT51 Trent Hunter .02 .10
TT52 Alexei Zhamnov .02 .10
TT53 Tommy Salo .10 .25
TT54 Danny Markov .02 .10
TT55 Sean Burke .10 .25
TT56 Shane Doan .02 .10
TT57 Konstantin Koltsov .02 .10
TT58 Mike Danton .02 .10
TT59 John Grahame .10 .25
TT60 Dimitry Afanasenkov .02 .10
TT61 Bryan Marchment .02 .10
TT62 Mikael Tellqvist .10 .25
TT63 Jason King .02 .10
TT64 Anson Carter .10 .25
TT65 Steve Shields .10 .25
TT66 Ron Francis .10 .25
TT67 Petr Nedved .02 .10
TT68 Alexander Svitov .02 .10
TT69 Ville Nieminen .02 .10
TT70 Martin Skoula .02 .10
TT71 Steve Yzerman .60 1.50
TT72 Jason Spezza .12 .30
TT73 Stanislav Chistov .02 .10
TT74 Pascal Leclaire .10 .25
TT75 Mike Comrie .10 .25
TT76 Brent Johnson .10 .25
TT77 Mike Rupp .02 .10
TT78 Derek Morris .02 .10
TT79 Geoff Sanderson .02 .10
TT80 Martin Rucinsky .02 .10
TT81 Shaone Morrisonn .02 .10
TT82 Paul Kariya .12 .30
TT83 Alex Kovalev .10 .25
TT84 Jeff Jillson .02 .10
TT85 Kari Lehtonen RC 3.00 8.00
TT86 Karl Stewart RC .75 2.00
TT87 Sergei Zinovjev RC .75 2.00
TT88 Carl Corazzini RC .75 2.00
TT89 Andrew Peters RC .75 2.00
TT90 Derek Roy RC .75 2.00
TT91 Matthew Lombardi RC .75 2.00
TT92 Alan Rourke RC .75 2.00
TT93 Pavel Vorobiev RC .75 2.00
TT94 Lasse Kukkonen RC .75 2.00
TT95 Travis Moen RC .75 2.00
TT96 Matt Keith RC .75 2.00
TT97 Marek Svatos RC 2.00 5.00
TT98 Cody McCormick RC .75 2.00
TT99 Mike Green RC .75 2.00
TT100 Mikhail Kuleshov RC .75 2.00
TT101 Dan Fritsche RC .75 2.00
TT102 Nikolai Zherdev RC 2.00 5.00
TT103 Aaron Johnson RC .75 2.00
TT104 Tim Jackman RC .75 2.00
TT105 Trevor Daley RC .75 2.00
TT106 Nathan Robinson RC .75 2.00
TT107 Niklas Kronwall RC .75 2.00
TT108 Darryl Bootland RC .75 2.00
TT109 Tony Salmelainen RC .75 2.00
TT110 Mike Bishai RC .75 2.00
TT111 Gregory Campbell RC .75 2.00
TT112 Tim Gleason RC .75 2.00
TT113 Dustin Brown .75 2.00
TT114 Noah Clarke RC .75 2.00
TT115 Chris Kunitz RC .75 2.00
TT116 Tony Martensson RC .75 2.00
TT117 Brent Burns RC .75 2.00
TT118 Chris Higgins RC 1.25 3.00
TT119 Dan Hamhuis RC .75 2.00
TT120 Marek Zidlicky RC .75 2.00
TT121 Andrew Hutchinson RC .75 2.00
TT122 Paul Martin RC .75 2.00
TT123 Aleksandr Suglobov RC .75 2.00
TT124 David Hale RC .75 2.00
TT125 Sean Bergenheim RC .75 2.00
TT126 Jed Ortmeyer RC .75 2.00
TT127 Lawrence Nycholat RC .75 2.00
TT128 Dominic Moore RC .75 2.00
TT129 Fedor Tyutin RC .75 2.00
TT130 Garth Murray RC .75 2.00
TT131 Antoine Vermette RC .75 2.00
TT132 Joni Pitkanen RC .75 2.00
TT133 Antero Niittymaki RC 2.00 5.00
TT134 Matthew Spiller RC .75 2.00
TT135 Fredrik Sjostrom RC .75 2.00
TT136 Ryan Malone RC .75 2.00
TT137 Matt Murley RC .75 2.00
TT138 Andy Chiodo RC .75 2.00
TT139 Tom Preissing RC .75 2.00
TT140 Wade Brookbank RC .75 2.00
TT141 Ryan Kesler RC .75 2.00
TT142 Nathan Smith RC .75 2.00
TT143 Boyd Gordon RC .75 2.00
TT144 Alexander Semin RC .75 2.00
TT145 Rastislav Stana RC .75 2.00
TT146 Cory Larose RC .75 2.00
TT147 Rob Scuderi RC .75 2.00
TT148 Ryan Barnes RC .75 2.00
TT149 Matt Ellison RC .75 2.00
TT150 Milan Michalek RC .75 2.00
TT151 Kyle Wellwood RC .75 2.00
TT152 Jame Pollock RC .75 2.00
TT153 Dwayne Zinger RC .75 2.00
TT154 Dan Ellis RC .75 2.00
TT155 Patrick Leahy RC .75 2.00
TT156 Jozef Balej RC .75 2.00
TT157 Colton Orr RC .75 2.00
TT158 Julien Vauclair RC .75 2.00
TT159 Darcy Verot RC .75 2.00
TT160 Christian Ehrhoff RC .75 2.00
TT161 Boyd Kane RC .75 2.00
TT162 Tuomas Pihlman RC .75 2.00
TT163 John-Michael Liles RC .75 2.00
TT164 Anton Babchuk RC .75 2.00
TT165 Owen Fussey RC .75 2.00

2003-04 Topps Traded Blue

*STARS: 5X TO 12X BASE HI
*ROOKIES: .75X TO 2X
PRINT RUN 500 SER.#'d SETS

2003-04 Topps Traded Gold

*STARS: 10X TO 25X BASE HI
*ROOKIES: 1.5X TO 4X
PRINT RUN 50 SER.#'d SETS

2003-04 Topps Traded Red

*STARS: 8X TO 20X BASE HI
*ROOKIES: 1.25X TO 3X
PRINT RUN 100 SER.#'d SETS

2003-04 Topps Traded Franchise Fabrics

Memorabilia in Topps Traded was inserted at an overall rate of 3:24. No further insertion info was made available.

*MULT.COLOR SWATCH: .5X TO 1.25X
FF-VL Vincent Lecavalier 5.00 12.00
FF-JTH Jose Theodore 5.00 12.00
FF-RN Rick Nash 5.00 12.00
FF-JSG J-S Giguere 3.00 8.00
FF-DA Daniel Alfredsson 3.00 8.00
FF-MB Martin Brodeur 15.00 40.00
FF-PM Patrick Marleau 4.00 10.00
FF-MS Mats Sundin 4.00 10.00
FF-MR Mark Recchi 3.00 8.00
FF-KP Keith Primeau 3.00 8.00
FF-AY Alexei Yashin 3.00 8.00
FF-IK Ilya Kovalchuk
FF-ZP Zigmund Palffy 3.00 8.00
FF-RL Roberto Luongo 5.00 12.00
FF-TB Todd Bertuzzi
FF-JS Joe Sakic 5.00 12.00
FF-ML Mario Lemieux 20.00 50.00
FF-MG Marian Gaborik 5.00 12.00
FF-MT Marty Turco 3.00 8.00
FF-JT Joe Thornton 5.00 12.00
FF-TV Tomas Vokoun 3.00 8.00
FF-JI Jarome Iginla 5.00 12.00
FF-BG Bill Guerin 3.00 8.00

2003-04 Topps Traded Future Phenoms

Memorabilia in Topps Traded was inserted at an overall rate of 3:24. No further insertion info was made available.

*MULT.COLOR SWATCH: .5X TO 1.25X
FP-NH Nathan Horton 4.00 10.00
FP-DH Dan Hamhuis 2.00 5.00
FP-SB Sean Bergenheim 2.00 5.00
FP-RR Robyn Regehr 2.00 5.00
FP-AH Adam Hall 2.00 5.00
FP-NB Nick Boynton 2.00 5.00
FP-MW Mattias Weinhandl 2.00 5.00
FP-JB Jay Bouwmeester 4.00 10.00
FP-SC Stanislav Chistov 2.00 5.00
FP-MS Matthew Stajan 4.00 10.00
FP-DA David Aebischer 4.00 10.00
FP-AM Antti Miettinen 2.00 5.00
FP-SW Stephen Weiss 2.00 5.00
FP-JOL Joffrey Lupul 4.00 10.00
FP-JL Jordan Leopold 2.00 5.00
FP-JLU Jamie Lundmark 2.00 5.00
FP-MR Mike Ribeiro 2.00 5.00
FP-AV Antoine Vermette 2.00 5.00
FP-BR Brad Richards 5.00 12.00
FP-AF Alexander Frolov 4.00 10.00
FP-BJ Barret Jackman 2.00 5.00
FP-PD Pavel Datsyuk 4.00 10.00
FP-PS Peter Sejna 2.00 5.00
FP-JP Joni Pitkanen 2.00 5.00
FP-RM Ryan Miller 5.00 12.00
FP-AT Alex Tanguay 4.00 10.00

1963-64 Toronto Star

This set of 42 photos was distributed one per week with the Toronto Star and was also available as a complete set directly. The photos measure approximately 4 3/4" by 6 3/4" and are entitled, "Hockey Stars in Action." There is a short write-up on the back of each photo. The player's team is identified in the checklist below, Boston Bruins (BB), Chicago Blackhawks (CBH), Detroit Red Wings (DRW), Montreal Canadiens (MC), New York Rangers (NYR), and Toronto Maple Leafs (TML). Since the photos are unnumbered, they are listed below in alphabetical order.

COMPLETE SET (42) 150.00 300.00
1 George Armstrong TML 4.00 8.00
2 Andy Bathgate NYR 4.00 8.00
3 Bob Baun TML 2.50 5.00
4 Jean Beliveau MC 7.50 15.00
5 Leo Boivin BB 2.50 5.00
6 Johnny Bower TML 5.00 10.00
7 Carl Brewer TML 2.50 5.00
8 Johnny Bucyk BB 4.00 8.00
9 Alex Delvecchio DRW 5.00 10.00
10 Kent Douglas TML 2.00 4.00
11 Dick Duff TML 2.50 5.00
12 Bill Gadsby DRW 3.00 6.00
13 Jean-Guy Gendron BB 2.00 4.00
14 BoomBoom Geoffrion MC 7.50 15.00
15 Glenn Hall CBH 6.00 12.00
16 Doug Harvey NYR 5.00 10.00
17 Bill(Red) Hay CBH 2.50 5.00
18 Camille Henry NYR 2.50 5.00
19 Tim Horton TML 7.50 15.00
20 Gordie Howe DRW 25.00 50.00
21 Bobby Hull CBH 15.00 30.00
22 Red Kelly TML 5.00 10.00
23 Dave Keon TML 7.50 15.00
24 Parker MacDonald DRW 2.00 4.00
25 Frank Mahovlich TML 7.50 15.00
26 Stan Mikita CBH 7.50 15.00
27 Dickie Moore MC 5.00 10.00
28 Eric Nesterenko CBH 2.50 5.00
29 Marcel Pronovost DRW 2.50 5.00
30 Claude Provost MC 2.50 5.00
31 Bob Pulford TML 3.00 6.00
32 Henri Richard MC 7.50 15.00
33 Terry Sawchuk DRW 10.00 20.00
34 Eddie Shack TML 5.00 10.00
35 Allan Stanley TML 3.00 6.00
36 Ron Stewart TML 2.00 4.00
37 Jean-Guy Talbot MC 2.50 5.00
38 Gilles Tremblay MC 2.00 4.00
39 J.C. Tremblay MC 2.50 5.00
40 Norm Ullman DRW 4.00 8.00
41 Elmer(Moose) Vasko CBH 2.00 4.00
42 Ken Wharram CBH 2.50 5.00

1964-65 Toronto Star

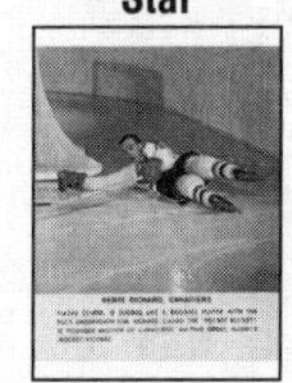

This set of 48 photos was distributed one per week with the Toronto Star and was also available as a complete set directly. The direct complete sets also included a booklet and glossy photo of Dave Keon in the mail-away package. These blank-backed photos measure approximately 4 1/8" by 5 1/8". The player's team is identified in the checklist below, Boston Bruins (BB), Chicago Blackhawks (CBH), Detroit Red Wings (DRW), Montreal Canadiens (MC), New York Rangers (NYR), and Toronto Maple Leafs (TML). Since the photos are unnumbered, they are listed below in alphabetical order. There was an album (actually a folder) available for each team to slot in cards. However when the cards were placed in the album it rendered the card's caption unreadable as only the action photo was visible.

COMPLETE SET (48) 150.00 300.00
1 Dave Balon MC 2.00 4.00
2 Andy Bathgate TML 4.00 8.00
3 Bob Baun TML 3.00 6.00
4 Jean Beliveau MC 7.50 15.00
5 Red Berenson MC 2.50 5.00
6 Leo Boivin BB 3.00 6.00
7 Carl Brewer TML 2.50 5.00
8 Alex Delvecchio DRW 4.00 8.00
9 Rod Gilbert NYR 4.00 8.00
10 Ted Green BB 2.50 5.00
11 Glenn Hall CBH 5.00 10.00
12 Billy Harris TML 2.00 4.00
13 Bill(Red) Hay CBH 2.00 4.00
14 Paul Henderson DRW 3.00 6.00
15 Wayne Hillman CBH 2.00 4.00
16 Charlie Hodge MC 3.00 6.00
17 Tim Horton TML 7.50 15.00
18 Gordie Howe DRW 20.00 40.00
19 Harry Howell NYR 3.00 6.00
20 Bobby Hull CBH 12.50 25.00
21 Larry Jeffrey DRW 2.00 4.00
22 Tom Johnson BB 3.00 6.00
23 Forbes Kennedy BB 2.00 4.00
24 Dave Keon TML 6.00 12.00
25 Orland Kurtenbach BB 2.50 5.00
26 Jacques Laperriere MC 2.50 5.00
27 Parker MacDonald DRW 2.00 4.00
28 Al MacNeil CBH 2.00 4.00
29 Frank Mahovlich TML 6.00 12.00
30 Chico Maki CBH 2.00 4.00
31 Don McKenney TML 2.00 4.00
32 John McKenzie CBH 2.50 5.00
33 Stan Mikita CBH 6.00 12.00
34 Jim Neilson NYR 2.00 4.00
35 Jim Pappin TML 2.00 4.00
36 Pierre Pilote CBH 3.00 6.00
37 Jacques Plante NYR 10.00 20.00
38 Marcel Pronovost DRW 3.00 6.00
39 Claude Provost MC 2.00 4.00
40 Bob Pulford TML 3.00 6.00
41 Henri Richard MC 6.00 12.00
42 Wayne Rivers BB 2.00 4.00
43 Floyd Smith DRW 2.00 4.00
44 Allan Stanley TML 4.00 8.00
45 Ron Stewart TML 2.00 4.00
46 J.C. Tremblay MC 2.50 5.00
47 Norm Ullman DRW 4.00 8.00
48 Elmer Vasko CBH 2.00 4.00
xx Album/Folder 12.50 25.00

1971-72 Toronto Sun

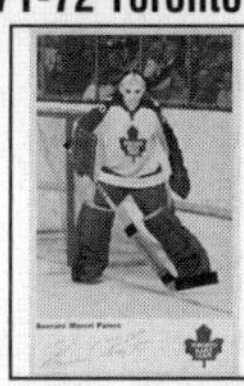

This set of 294 photo cards with two punch holes has never been very popular with collectors. The photos are quite fragile, printed on thin paper, and measure approximately 5" by 7". The checklist below is in team order as follows: Boston Bruins (1-21), Buffalo Sabres (22-41), California Golden Seals (42-61), Chicago Blackhawks (62-82), Detroit Red Wings (83-103), Los Angeles Kings (104-124), Minnesota North Stars (125-145), Montreal Canadiens (146-166), New York Rangers (167-186), Philadelphia Flyers (187-208), Pittsburgh Penguins (209-230), St. Louis Blues (231-252), Toronto Maple Leafs (253-274), and Vancouver Canucks (275-294). The cards were intended to fit in a two-ring binder specially made to hold the cards. Also included was and introduction photo, with text by Scott Young.

COMPLETE SET (294) 300.00 600.00
1 Boston Bruins Team Crest 1.50 3.00
2 Don Awrey .50 1.00
3 Garnet Bailey .50 1.00
4 Ivan Boldirev .50 1.00
5 Johnny Bucyk 3.00 6.00
6 Wayne Cashman .75 1.50
7 Gerry Cheevers 4.00 8.00
8 Phil Esposito 10.00 20.00
9 Ted Green .75 1.50
10 Ken Hodge .75 1.50
11 Ed Johnston 1.50 3.00
12 Reggie Leach 1.50 3.00
13 Don Marcotte .50 1.00
14 John McKenzie .50 1.00
15 Bobby Orr 30.00 60.00
16 Derek Sanderson 4.00 8.00
17 Dallas Smith .50 1.00
18 Richard Allan Smith .50 1.00
19 Fred Stanfield .50 1.00
20 Mike Walton .75 1.50
21 Ed Westfall .75 1.50
22 Buffalo Sabres Team Crest 1.00 2.00
23 Doug Barrie .50 1.00
24 Roger Crozier 2.00 4.00
25 Dave Dryden 1.00 2.00
26 Dick Duff .75 1.50
27 Phil Goyette .50 1.00
28 Al Hamilton .50 1.00
29 Larry Keenan .50 1.00
30 Danny Lawson .50 1.00
31 Don Luce .50 1.00
32 Richard Martin 1.00 2.00
33 Ray McKay .50 1.00
34 Gerry Meehan .75 1.50
35 Kevin O'Shea .50 1.00
36 Gilbert Perreault 4.00 8.00
37 Tracy Pratt .50 1.00
38 Mike Robitaille .50 1.00
39 Eddie Shack 2.00 4.00
40 Jim Watson .50 1.00
41 Rod Zaine .50 1.00
42 California Seals Team Crest 1.50 3.00
43 Wayne Carleton .50 1.00
44 Lyle Carter .50 1.00
45 Gary Croteau .50 1.00
46 Norm Ferguson .50 1.00
47 Stan Gilbertson .50 1.00
48 Ernie Hicke .50 1.00
49 Gary Jarrett .50 1.00
50 Joey Johnston .50 1.00
51 Marshall Johnston .50 1.00
52 Bert Marshall .50 1.00
53 Walt McKechnie .50 1.00
54 Don O'Donoghue .50 1.00
55 Gerry Pinder .75 1.50
56 Dick Redmond .50 1.00
57 Robert Sheehan .50 1.00
58 Paul Shmyr .50 1.00
59 Ron Stackhouse SP 6.00 12.00
60 Carol Vadnais .50 1.00
61 Tom Williams .50 1.00
62 Chicago Blackhawks Team Crest 1.50 3.00
63 Lou Angotti .50 1.00
64 Bryan Campbell .50 1.00
65 Tony Esposito 10.00 20.00
66 Bobby Hull 15.00 30.00
67 Dennis Hull 1.00 2.00
68 Doug Jarrett .50 1.00
69 Jerry Korab .50 1.00
70 Cliff Koroll .50 1.00
71 Darryl Maggs .50 1.00
72 Keith Magnuson .75 1.50
73 Chico Maki .75 1.50
74 Dan Maloney .50 1.00
75 Pit Martin .75 1.50
76 Stan Mikita 6.00 12.00
77 Eric Nesterenko .50 1.00
78 Danny O'Shea .50 1.00
79 Jim Pappin .50 1.00
80 Gary Smith 1.00 2.00
81 Pat Stapleton .50 1.00
82 Bill White .50 1.00
83 Detroit Red Wings Team Crest 1.50 3.00
84 Red Berenson .75 1.50
85 Gary Bergman .75 1.50
86 Arnie Brown .50 1.00
87 Guy Charron .50 1.00
88 Bill Collins .50 1.00
89 Brian Conacher .50 1.00
90 Joe Daley 1.50 3.00
91 Alex Delvecchio 3.00 6.00
92 Marcel Dionne 7.50 15.00
93 Tim Ecclestone .50 1.00
94 Ron Harris .50 1.00
95 Gerry Hart .50 1.00
96 Gordie Howe 25.00 50.00
97 Al Karlander .50 1.00
98 Nick Libett .75 1.50
99 Ab McDonald .50 1.00
100 James Niekamp .50 1.00
101 Mickey Redmond 2.00 4.00
102 Leon Rochefort .50 1.00
103 Al Smith .75 1.50
104 Los Angeles Kings Team Crest 1.00 2.00
105 Ralph Backstrom .75 1.50
106 Bob Berry .75 1.50
107 Mike Byers .50 1.00
108 Larry Cahan .50 1.00
109 Paul Curtis .50 1.00
110 Denis DeJordy 1.50 3.00
111 Gary Edwards 1.00 2.00
112 Bill Flett .50 1.00
113 Butch Goring .75 1.50
114 Lucien Grenier .50 1.00
115 Larry Hillman .50 1.00
116 Dale Hoganson .50 1.00
117 Harry Howell 1.50 3.00
118 Eddie Joyal .50 1.00
119 Real Lemieux .50 1.00
120 Ross Lonsberry .50 1.00
121 Al McDonough .50 1.00
122 Jean Potvin .50 1.00
123 Bob Pulford 1.50 3.00
124 Juha Widing .75 1.50
125 Minnesota North Stars Team Crest 1.00 2.00
126 Fred Barrett .50 1.00
127 Charlie Burns .50 1.00
128 Jude Drouin .50 1.00
129 Barry Gibbs .50 1.00
130 Gilles Gilbert 2.00 4.00
131 Bill Goldsworthy 1.00 2.00
132 Danny Grant .75 1.50
133 Ted Hampson .50 1.00
134 Ted Harris .50 1.00
135 Fred Harvey .50 1.00
136 Cesare Maniago 2.00 4.00
137 Doug Mohns .75 1.50
138 Lou Nanne .75 1.50
139 Bob Nevin .75 1.50
140 Dennis O'Brien .50 1.00
141 Murray Oliver .50 1.00
142 Jean-Paul Parise .75 1.50
143 Dean Prentice .75 1.50
144 Tom Reid .50 1.00
145 Gump Worsley 3.00 6.00
146 Montreal Canadiens Team Crest 1.50 3.00
147 Pierre Bouchard .50 1.00
148 Yvan Cournoyer 3.00 6.00
149 Ken Dryden 25.00 50.00
150 Terry Harper .75 1.50
151 Rejean Houle .75 1.50
152 Guy Lafleur 15.00 30.00
153 Jacques Laperriere 1.00 2.00
154 Guy Lapointe 1.50 3.00
155 Claude Larose .50 1.00
156 Jacques Lemaire 2.00 4.00
157 Frank Mahovlich 6.00 12.00
158 Pete Mahovlich .75 1.50
159 Phil Myre 1.50 3.00
160 Larry Pleau .75 1.50
161 Henri Richard 6.00 12.00
162 Phil Roberto .50 1.00
163 Serge Savard 1.50 3.00
164 Marc Tardif .75 1.50
165 J.C. Tremblay .75 1.50
166 Rogatien Vachon 3.00 6.00
167 New York Rangers Team Crest 1.50 3.00
168 Dave Balon .50 1.00
169 Ab DeMarco .50 1.00
170 Jack Egers .50 1.00
171 Bill Fairbairn .50 1.00
172 Ed Giacomin 4.00 8.00
173 Rod Gilbert 2.00 4.00
174 Vic Hadfield .75 1.50
175 Ted Irvine .50 1.00
176 Bruce MacGregor .50 1.00
177 Jim Neilson .50 1.00
178 Brad Park 3.00 6.00
179 Jean Ratelle 2.00 4.00
180 Dale Rolfe .50 1.00
181 Bobby Rousseau .75 1.50
182 Glen Sather 1.50 3.00
183 Rod Seiling .50 1.00
184 Pete Stemkowski .75 1.50
185 Walt Tkaczuk .75 1.50
186 Gilles Villemure 1.50 3.00
187 Philadelphia Flyers Team Crest 1.50 3.00
188 Barry Ashbee 1.00 2.00
189 Serge Bernier .50 1.00
190 Larry Brown .50 1.00
191 Bobby Clarke 10.00 20.00
192 Gary Dornhoefer .75 1.50
193 Doug Favell 1.50 3.00
194 Bruce Gamble 2.00 4.00
195 Jean-Guy Gendron .50 1.00
196 Larry Hale .50 1.00
197 Wayne Hillman .50 1.00
198 Brent Hughes .50 1.00
199 Jim Johnson .50 1.00
200 Bob Kelly .50 1.00
201 Andre Lacroix .75 1.50
202 Bill Lesuk .50 1.00
203 Rick MacLeish 1.00 2.00
204 Larry Mickey .50 1.00
205 Simon Nolet .50 1.00
206 Pierre Plante .50 1.00
207 Ed Van Impe .50 1.00
208 Joe Watson .50 1.00
209 Pittsburgh Penguins Team Crest 1.00 2.00
210 Syl Apps .75 1.50
211 Les Binkley 1.50 3.00
212 Wally Boyer .50 1.00
213 Darryl Edestrand .50 1.00
214 Roy Edwards 1.50 3.00
215 Nick Harbaruk .50 1.00
216 Bryan Hextall .75 1.50
217 Bill Hicke .50 1.00
218 Tim Horton 5.00 10.00
219 Sheldon Kannegiesser .50 1.00
220 Bob Leiter .50 1.00
221 Keith McCreary .50 1.00
222 Joe Noris .50 1.00
223 Greg Polis .50 1.00
224 Jean Pronovost .75 1.50
225 Rene Robert .75 1.50
226 Duane Rupp .50 1.00
227 Ken Schinkel .50 1.00
228 Ron Schock .50 1.00
229 Bryan Watson .75 1.50
230 Bob Woytowich .50 1.00
231 St. Louis Blues Team Crest 1.00 2.00
232 Al Arbour 1.50 3.00
233 John Arbour .50 1.00
234 Chris Bordeleau .50 1.00
235 Carl Brewer .75 1.50
236 Gene Carr .50 1.00
237 Wayne Connelly .50 1.00
238 Terry Crisp .75 1.50
239 Jim Lorentz .50 1.00
240 Peter McDuffe 1.00 2.00
241 George Morrison .50 1.00
242 Michel Parizeau .50 1.00
243 Noel Picard .50 1.00
244 Barclay Plager .75 1.50
245 Bob Plager .75 1.50
246 Jim Roberts .50 1.00
247 Gary Sabourin .50 1.00
248 Jim Shires .50 1.00
249 Frank St.Marseille .50 1.00
250 Bill Sutherland .50 1.00
251 Garry Unger 1.00 2.00
252 Ernie Wakely 1.50 3.00
253 Toronto Maple Leafs Team Crest 1.50 3.00
254 Bob Baun .75 1.50
255 Jim Dorey .50 1.00
256 Denis Dupere .50 1.00
257 Ron Ellis .75 1.50
258 Brian Glennie .50 1.00
259 Jim Harrison .50 1.00
260 Paul Henderson 1.00 2.00
261 Dave Keon 3.00 6.00
262 Rick Ley .50 1.00
263 Billy MacMillan .50 1.00
264 Don Marshall .50 1.00
265 Jim McKenny .50 1.00
266 Garry Monahan .50 1.00
267 Bernie Parent 6.00 12.00
268 Mike Pelyk .50 1.00
269 Jacques Plante 10.00 20.00
270 Brad Selwood .50 1.00
271 Darryl Sittler 6.00 12.00
272 Brian Spencer 1.00 2.00
273 Guy Trottier .50 1.00
274 Norm Ullman 2.50 5.00
275 Vancouver Canucks Team Crest 1.00 2.00
276 Andre Boudrias .50 1.00
277 George Gardiner .50 1.00
278 Jocelyn Guevremont .75 1.50
279 Murray Hall .50 1.00
280 Danny Johnson .50 1.00
281 Dennis Kearns .50 1.00
282 Orland Kurtenbach .75 1.50
283 Bobby Lalonde .50 1.00
284 Wayne Maki .50 1.00
285 Rosaire Paiement .75 1.50
286 Paul Popiel .50 1.00
287 Pat Quinn 1.00 2.00
288 John Schella .50 1.00
289 Bobby Schmautz .75 1.50
290 Fred Speck .50 1.00
291 Dale Tallon .75 1.50
292 Ron Ward .50 1.00
293 Barry Wilkins .50 1.00
294 Dunc Wilson 1.50 3.00
xx Binder 12.50 25.00
NNO Introduction Card 2.00 4.00
(Written by Scott Young)

1972 Tower Hockey Instructions Booklets

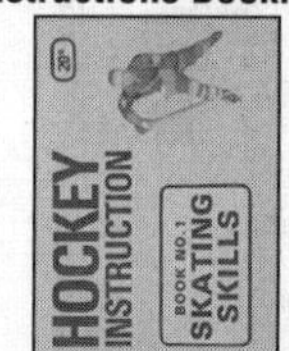

Sponsored by Towers and Donimart stores, we have very little information about these oddball hockey instruction booklets.

1 Skating Skills 10.00 20.00

1936 Triumph Postcards

This eleven-card set was issued as a supplement to The Triumph (a newspaper). The cards measure approximately 3 1/2" by 5 1/2" and are in the postcard format. The borderless fronts feature full-length black and white posed action shots. The player's name and team name appear in the lower left corner. The back carries the typical postcard design with each player's name and biographical information in the upper corner. Different dates appear on the back of the cards, which represent the date each card was distributed. The cards were issued three the first week with The Triumph, then one per week thereafter. The cards are unnumbered and checklisted below in alphabetical order. The date mentioned below is the issue date as noted on the card back in Canadian style, day/month/year.

COMPLETE SET (11) 650.00 1300.00
1 Lionel Conacher 125.00 250.00
22/2/36
2 Harvey(Busher) Jackson 125.00 250.00
18/1/36
3 Ivan(Ching) Johnson 62.50 125.00
8/2/36
4 Herbie Lewis 40.00 80.00
7/3/36
5 Sylvio Mantha 62.50 125.00
18/1/36
6 Nick Metz 40.00 80.00
15/2/36
7 Baldy Northcott 45.00 90.00
Montreal Maroons
1/2/36
8 Eddie Shore 250.00 500.00
25/1/36
9 Paul Thompson 40.00 80.00
29/2/36
10 Roy Worters 62.50 125.00
New York Americans
18/1/36
11 Charley Conacher 40.00 80.00

2004-05 UD All-World

Released in June, this 120-card set featured NHL players who spent the lockout season playing in Europe as well as European legends. Two subsets, "Up Close & Personal" and "Euro-Legends" were inserted at 1:8 odds. Please note that cards #'s 108 and 119 do not exist and that card #110 is used on three different cards. Those cards are noted below with "A,B and C" suffixes.

COMPLETE SET (120)
1 Roman Turek .25 .60
2 Jiri Fischer .20 .50
3 Martin Rucinsky .20 .50
4 Ales Hemsky .25 .60
5 Milan Hejduk .30 .75
6 Zigmund Palffy .25 .60
7 Peter Stastny .20 .50
8 Petr Nedved .20 .50
9 Radek Bonk .20 .50
10 Roman Hamrlik .20 .50
11 Martin Havlat .25 .60
12 Jarkko Ruutu .20 .50
13 Matti Hagman .20 .50
14 Tomas Vokoun .25 .60
15 Mika Noronen .25 .60
16 Jari Kurri .40 1.00
17 Teemu Selanne .30 .75
18 Dwayne Roloson .25 .60
19 Saku Koivu .30 .75
20 Erik Cole .20 .50
21 Marco Sturm .20 .50
22 Mike York .20 .50
23 Ryan Malone .20 .50
24 Alex Kovalev .25 .60
25 Brad Richards .25 .60
26 Ilya Kovalchuk .40 1.00
27 Nikolai Khabibulin .30 .75
28 Vincent Lecavalier .30 .75
29 Jaromir Jagr .50 1.25
30 Alexander Frolov .25 .60
31 Nikolai Zherdev .25 .60
32 Maxim Afinogenov .20 .50
33 Pavel Datsyuk .30 .75
34 Nikolai Antropov .20 .50
35 Evgeni Nabokov .25 .60
36 Patrik Elias .25 .60
37 Petr Sykora .20 .50
38 Sergei Gonchar .20 .50
39 Michael Nylander .20 .50
40 Fedor Fedorov .20 .50
41 Alexei Zhamnov .20 .50
42 Pavol Demitra .25 .60
43 Miroslav Satan .25 .60
44 Borje Salming .40 1.00
45 Ulf Nilsson .20 .50
46 Tyler Arnason .20 .50
47 Mats Naslund .40 1.00
48 Jose Theodore .40 1.00
49 Marty Turco .25 .60
50 Kent Nilsson .20 .50
51 Marian Gaborik .60 1.50
52 Mike Comrie .25 .60
53 Sheldon Souray .20 .50
54 Zdeno Chara .20 .50
55 Hakan Loob .20 .50
56 Thomas Steen .20 .50
57 Daniel Alfredsson .25 .60
58 Jonathan Cheechoo .25 .60
59 Michael Ryder .20 .50
60 Brendan Morrison .25 .60
61 Justin Williams .20 .50
62 Tomas Holmstrom .20 .50
63 Adrian Aucoin .20 .50
64 Daniel Sedin .20 .50
65 Henrik Sedin .20 .50
66 Markus Naslund .30 .75
67 Peter Forsberg .75 2.00
68 Anders Hedberg .20 .50
69 Ladislav Nagy .20 .50
70 Marcel Hossa .20 .50
71 Marian Hossa .30 .75
72 Trent Hunter .20 .50
73 Dick Tarnstrom .20 .50
74 Olli Jokinen .25 .60
75 Fredrik Modin .20 .50
76 Henrik Zetterberg .30 .75
77 Miikka Kiprusoff .25 .60
78 Joe Thornton .50 1.25
79 Rick Nash .40 1.00
80 Martin St. Louis .25 .60
81 Alex Tanguay .25 .60
82 David Aebischer .25 .60
83 Martin Gelinas .20 .50
84 Daniel Briere .20 .50
85 Dany Heatley .40 1.00
86 Niko Kapanen .20 .50
87 Igor Larionov .20 .50
88 Richard Zednik .20 .50
89 Jochen Hecht .20 .50
90 Vladislav Tretiak .25 .60
91 Wayne Gretzky UCP 4.00 10.00
92 Gordie Howe UCP 3.00 8.00
93 Patrick Roy UCP 4.00 10.00
94 Joe Thornton UCP 2.50 6.00
95 Rick Nash UCP 2.50 6.00
96 Martin Brodeur UCP 4.00 10.00
97 Marty Turco UCP 2.00 5.00
98 Jarome Iginla UCP 2.50 6.00
99 Joe Sakic UCP 3.00 8.00
100 Peter Forsberg UCP 3.00 8.00
101 Mario Lemieux UCP 4.00 10.00
102 Markus Naslund UCP 2.00 5.00
103 Martin St. Louis UCP 2.00 5.00
104 Mike Bossy UCP 2.00 5.00
105 Jose Theodore UCP 2.50 6.00
106 Matti Hagman EL 2.00 5.00
107 Teemu Selanne EL 2.00 5.00
109 Borje Salming EL 2.50 6.00
110A Ulf Nilsson EL 3.00 8.00
110B Jari Kurri EL 2.50 6.00
110C Igor Larionov EL 3.00 8.00
111 Anders Hedberg EL 2.00 5.00
112 Vladislav Tretiak EL 4.00 10.00
113 Mats Naslund EL 3.00 8.00
114 Peter Stastny EL 2.00 5.00
115 Thomas Steen EL 2.00 5.00
116 Hakan Loob EL 2.50 6.00
117 Kent Nilsson EL 2.00 5.00
118 Saku Koivu EL 2.00 5.00
120 Jaromir Jagr EL 3.00 8.00

2004-05 UD All-World Gold

*GOLD: 8X TO 20X BASE CARD
PRINT RUN 50 SER.#'d SETS

2004-05 UD All-World Autographs

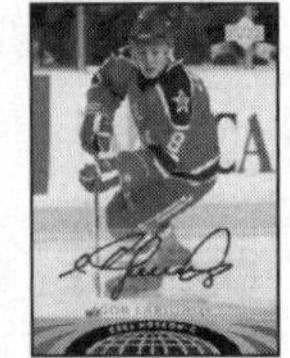

1-90 STATED ODDS 1:24
91-119 PRINT RUN 10 SER.#'d SETS
91-119 NOT PRICED DUE TO SCARCITY
SKIP NUMBERED SET
1 Roman Turek 6.00 10.00
4 Ales Hemsky 8.00 20.00
5 Milan Hejduk 8.00 20.00
6 Zigmund Palffy SP
7 Peter Stastny 8.00 20.00
11 Martin Havlat 10.00 25.00
12 Jarkko Ruutu 4.00 10.00
13 Matti Hagman 6.00 10.00
15 Mika Noronen 6.00 10.00
16 Jari Kurri 8.00 20.00
18 Dwayne Roloson 12.00 30.00
20 Erik Cole 8.00 15.00
26 Ilya Kovalchuk SP
27 Nikolai Khabibulin SP 40.00 80.00
28 Vincent Lecavalier SP
30 Alexander Frolov 6.00 15.00
31 Nikolai Zherdev 8.00 15.00
32 Maxim Afinogenov 6.00 15.00
44 Borje Salming 12.00 30.00
45 Ulf Nilsson 10.00 25.00
46 Tyler Arnason 6.00 15.00
47 Mats Naslund 15.00 40.00
48 Jose Theodore SP
50 Kent Nilsson 6.00 15.00
51 Marian Gaborik 20.00 50.00
52 Mike Comrie 6.00 15.00
53 Sheldon Souray 6.00 15.00
54 Zdeno Chara 6.00 15.00
55 Hakan Loob 12.00 30.00
56 Thomas Steen 6.00 15.00
57 Daniel Alfredsson SP
58 Jonathan Cheechoo 10.00 25.00
59 Michael Ryder SP
60 Brendan Morrison 6.00 15.00
61 Justin Williams 8.00 15.00
66 Markus Naslund SP
68 Anders Hedberg 6.00 15.00
69 Ladislav Nagy 6.00 10.00
70 Marcel Hossa 6.00 10.00
71 Marian Hossa SP
72 Trent Hunter 6.00 15.00
76 Henrik Zetterberg SP 25.00 60.00
78 Joe Thornton 15.00 40.00
79 Rick Nash SP 60.00 150.00
80 Martin St. Louis SP
81 Alex Tanguay SP
82 David Aebischer SP 15.00 40.00
84 Daniel Briere 12.00 30.00
85 Dany Heatley SP
87 Igor Larionov 10.00 25.00
88 Richard Zednik 6.00 15.00
90 Vladislav Tretiak 20.00 50.00
91 Wayne Gretzky
92 Gordie Howe
94 Joe Thornton
95 Rick Nash
97 Marty Turco
102 Markus Naslund
103 Martin St. Louis
104 Mike Bossy
106 Matti Hagman
108 Jari Kurri 10.00 25.00
109 Borje Salming 10.00 25.00
110 Ulf Nilsson
111 Anders Hedberg
112 Vladislav Tretiak 12.00 30.00
113 Mats Naslund
114 Peter Stastny
115 Thomas Steen
116 Hakan Loob
117 Kent Nilsson 6.00 10.00
119 Igor Larionov 6.00 15.00

2004-05 UD All-World Dual Autographs

PRINT RUN 25 SER.#'d SETS
AD-PS Ziggy Palffy/Peter Stastny 25.00 60.00
AD-HH Milan Hejduk/Ales Hemsky 30.00 80.00
AD-HN Matti Hagman/Mika Noronen 25.00 60.00
AD-AF Maxim Afinogenov
Alexander Frolov 20.00 50.00
AD-FZ Alexander Frolov
Nikolai Zherdev 30.00 80.00
AD-JA Joe Thornton/Alex Tanguay 75.00 200.00
AD-KK Jari Kurri/Saku Koivu 75.00 200.00
AD-KL Jari Kurri/Hakan Loob 30.00 80.00
AD-LK V.Lecavalier/N.Khabibulin 60.00 150.00
AD-LS Hakan Loob/Thomas Steen 30.00 80.00
AD-MM Marian Hossa/Marcel Hossa
AD-NN Mats Naslund/Markus Naslund
AD-NT R.Nash/J.Thornton 100.00 250.00
AD-SC Sheldon Souray/Zdeno Chara 25.00 60.00
AD-SN Borje Salming/Kent Nilsson 30.00 80.00

2004-05 UD All-World Triple Autographs

PRINT RUN 20 SER.#'d SETS
NOT PRICED DUE TO SCARCITY
AT-CWR Cheechoo/J.Williams/J.Ruutu
AT-KHK Jari Kurri/Matti Hagman/Saku Koivu
AT-KSN Jari Kurri/Peter Stastny/Mats Naslund
AT-LTZ Igor Larionov/Vladislav Tretiak/Nikolai Zherdev
AT-NLN Mats Naslund/Hakan Loob/Kent Nilsson
AT-RCM M.Ryder/Cheechoo/B.Morrison
AT-SHH Peter Stastny/Milan Hejduk/Ales Hemsky
AT-SLN Thomas Steen/Hakan Loob/Ulf Nilsson
AT-TAR Jose Theodore/David Aebischer/Dwayne Roloson
AT-ZFA Nikolai Zherdev/Alexander Frolov/Maxim Afinogenov

2004-05 UD All-World Quad Autographs

PRINT RUN 15 SER.#'d SETS
NOT PRICED DUE TO SCARCITY
AQ-SWE Thomas Steen/Kent Nilsson/Michael Ryder/Justin Williams
AQ-YFW Jonathan Cheechoo
Justin Williams
Alexander Frolov
Trent Hunter
AQ-NAM Mats Naslund/Markus Naslund/Marian Hossa/Marcel Hossa
AQ-ALS Jari Kurri/Kent Nilsson/Hakan Loob/Matti Hagman
AQ-RUS Ilya Kovalchuk/Maxim Afinogenov/Vladislav Tretiak/Igor Larionov
AQ-GOL Jose Theodore/David Aebischer/Evgeni Nabokov/Dwayne Roloson
AQ-GSC Joe Thornton
Rick Nash
Dany Heatley
Daniel Briere
AQ-OAS Peter Stastny/Mats Naslund/Ulf Nilsson/Hakan Loob

2004-05 UD All-World Five Autographs

PRINT RUN 10 SER.#'d SETS
NOT PRICED DUE TO SCARCITY
AF-GOL Vladislav Tretiak/Nikolai Khabibulin/Evgeni Nabokov/David Aebischer/Marty Turco
AF-YAO Peter Stastny/Ziggy Palffy/Ales Hemsky/Thomas Steen/Martin Havlat
AF-YGN Vincent Lecavalier/Ilya Kovalchuk/Alexander Frolov/Nikolai Zherdev/Nikolai Khabibulin
AF-AST Jari Kurri/Peter Stastny/Igor Larionov/Borje Salming/Vladislav Tretiak

2004-05 UD All-World Six Autographs

PRINT RUN 5 SER.#'d SETS
NOT PRICED DUE TO SCARCITY
AS-RUS Ilya Kovalchuk/Brad Richards/Vincent Lecavalier/Alexander Frolov/Nikolai Zherdev/Maxim Afinogenov
AS-SWT Joe Thornton
Rick Nash
Martin St. Louis
Dany Heatley
Daniel Briere
Alex Tanguay
AS-SWD Markus Naslund
Marian Gaborik
Michael Ryder
Henrik Zetterberg
Justin Williams
Jonathan Cheechoo

2005-06 UD Artifacts

COMP.SET w/o SP'S (100) 15.00 30.00
AL/AS PRINT RUN 899 SER.#'d SETS
RC PRINT RUN 750 SER.#'d SETS
GOLD & AUTO 1/1's EXIST
1 J-S Giguere .12 .30
2 Sergei Fedorov .20 .50
3 Jeffrey Lupul .08 .20
4 Dany Heatley .20 .50
5 Ilya Kovalchuk .20 .50
6 Kari Lehtonen .12 .30
7 Andrew Raycroft .12 .30
8 Joe Thornton .25 .60
9 Glen Murray .08 .20
10 Sergei Samsonov .12 .30
11 Patrice Bergeron .08 .20
12 Martin Biron .12 .30
13 Maxim Afinogenov .08 .20
14 Chris Drury .12 .30
15 Jarome Iginla .20 .50
16 Miikka Kiprusoff .12 .30
17 Jordan Leopold .08 .20
18 Eric Staal .08 .20
19 Justin Williams .08 .20
20 Erik Cole .08 .20
21 Tuomo Ruutu .08 .20
22 Eric Daze .12 .30
23 Tyler Arnason .08 .20
24 Joe Sakic .30 .75
25 Rob Blake .12 .30
26 David Aebischer .12 .30
27 Milan Hejduk .15 .40
28 Alex Tanguay .12 .30
29 Geoff Sanderson .08 .20
30 Rick Nash .20 .50
31 Nikolai Zherdev .12 .30
32 Mike Modano .25 .60
33 Bill Guerin .12 .30
34 Brenden Morrow .12 .30
35 Marty Turco .12 .30
36 Manny Legace .12 .30
37 Pavel Datsyuk .15 .40
38 Brendan Shanahan .15 .40
39 Steve Yzerman .60 1.50
40 Henrik Zetterberg .15 .40
41 Ty Conklin .12 .30
42 Ryan Smyth .08 .20
43 Stephen Weiss .08 .20
44 Roberto Luongo .20 .50
45 Olli Jokinen .12 .30
46 Alexander Frolov .08 .20
47 Dustin Brown .08 .20
48 Luc Robitaille .12 .30
49 Dwayne Roloson .12 .30
50 Marian Gaborik .25 .60
51 Mike Ribeiro .08 .20
52 Michael Ryder .08 .20
53 Jose Theodore .15 .40
54 Saku Koivu .15 .40
55 Steve Sullivan .08 .20
56 Jordin Tootoo .08 .20
57 Tomas Vokoun .12 .30
58 Martin Brodeur .60 1.50
59 Scott Gomez .08 .20
60 Jeff Friesen .08 .20
61 Patrik Elias .12 .30
62 Tom Poti .08 .20
63 Mark Messier .15 .40
64 Jaromir Jagr .25 .60
65 Mark Parrish .08 .20
66 Rick DiPietro .12 .30
67 Alexei Yashin .08 .20
68 Daniel Alfredsson .12 .30
69 Dominik Hasek .30 .75
70 Marian Hossa .15 .40
71 Jason Spezza .15 .40
72 Martin Havlat .12 .30
73 Robert Esche .12 .30
74 Keith Primeau .12 .30
75 Simon Gagne .12 .30
76 Michal Handzus .08 .20
77 Brett Hull .20 .50
78 Mike Comrie .12 .30
79 Shane Doan .08 .20
80 Marc-Andre Fleury .12 .30
81 Mario Lemieux .75 2.00
82 Mark Recchi .12 .30
83 Evgeni Nabokov .12 .30
84 Patrick Marleau .12 .30
85 Jonathan Cheechoo .12 .30
86 Mike Sillinger .08 .20
87 Doug Weight .12 .30
88 Keith Tkachuk .15 .40
89 Brad Richards .12 .30
90 Fredrik Modin .08 .20
91 Martin St. Louis .12 .30
92 Vincent Lecavalier .15 .40
93 Ed Belfour .15 .40
94 Owen Nolan .12 .30
95 Mats Sundin .15 .40
96 Nik Antropov .08 .20
97 Ed Jovanovski .12 .30
98 Markus Naslund .15 .40
99 Trevor Linden .08 .20
100 Olaf Kolzig .12 .30
101 Glenn Anderson AL 1.50 4.00
102 Bill Barber AL 1.50 4.00
103 Jean Beliveau AL 2.00 5.00
104 Mike Bossy AL 2.00 5.00
105 Johnny Bower AL 2.00 5.00
106 Scotty Bowman AL 1.50 4.00
107 Johnny Bucyk AL 2.00 5.00
108 Wayne Cashman AL 1.50 4.00
109 Gerry Cheevers AL 1.50 4.00
110 Don Cherry AL 1.50 4.00
111 Bobby Clarke AL 2.00 5.00
112 Gordie Howe AL 2.50 6.00
113 Wayne Gretzky AL 4.00 10.00
114 Marcel Dionne AL 1.50 4.00
115 Phil Esposito AL 1.50 4.00
116 Tony Esposito AL 2.00 5.00
117 Grant Fuhr AL 2.00 5.00
118 Bernie Geoffrion AL 2.00 5.00
119 Clark Gillies AL 1.50 4.00
120 Butch Goring AL 1.50 4.00
121 Glenn Hall AL 2.00 5.00
122 Paul Henderson AL 1.50 4.00
123 Ron Hextall AL 1.50 4.00
124 Al Iafrate AL 1.50 4.00
125 Red Kelly AL 2.00 5.00
126 Jari Kurri AL 2.00 5.00
127 Guy LaFleur AL 2.00 5.00
128 Igor Larionov AL 1.50 4.00
129 Reggie Leach AL 1.50 4.00
130 Hakan Loob AL 1.50 4.00
131 Frank Mahovlich AL 1.50 4.00
132 Rick Martin AL 1.50 4.00
133 Lanny McDonald AL 1.50 4.00
134 Stan Mikita AL 2.00 5.00
135 Dickie Moore AL 2.00 5.00
136 Ken Morrow AL 1.50 4.00
137 Larry Murphy AL 1.50 4.00
138 Cam Neely AL 2.00 5.00
139 Mats Naslund AL 1.50 4.00
140 Bob Nystrom AL 1.50 4.00
141 Terry O'Reilly AL 2.00 5.00
142 Brad Park AL 1.50 4.00
143 Gilbert Perreault AL 2.00 5.00
144 Rene Robert AL 1.50 4.00
145 Derek Sanderson AL 1.50 4.00
146 Denis Savard AL 1.50 4.00
147 Peter Stastny AL 1.50 4.00
148 Thomas Steen AL 1.50 4.00
149 Dave Taylor AL 1.50 4.00
150 Bryan Trottier AL 1.50 4.00
151 Sergei Fedorov AS 2.00 5.00
152 Ilya Kovalchuk AS 2.00 5.00
153 Dany Heatley AS 2.00 5.00
154 Joe Thornton AS 2.00 5.00
155 Glen Murray AS 1.50 4.00
156 Jarome Iginla AS 2.00 5.00
157 Eric Daze AS 1.50 4.00
158 Joe Sakic AS 2.00 5.00
159 Rob Blake AS 1.50 4.00
160 Milan Hejduk AS 1.50 4.00
161 Alex Tanguay AS 1.50 4.00
162 Rick Nash AS 2.00 5.00
163 Mike Modano AS 2.00 5.00
164 Bill Guerin AS 1.50 4.00
165 Marty Turco AS 1.50 4.00
166 Brendan Shanahan AS 1.50 4.00
167 Steve Yzerman AS 3.00 8.00
168 Pavel Datsyuk AS 1.50 4.00
169 Roberto Luongo AS 2.00 5.00
170 Luc Robitaille AS 1.50 4.00
171 Marian Gaborik AS 2.00 5.00
172 Jose Theodore AS 1.50 4.00
173 Saku Koivu AS 1.50 4.00
174 Tomas Vokoun AS 1.50 4.00
175 Martin Brodeur AS 2.00 5.00
176 Scott Gomez AS 1.50 4.00
177 Patrik Elias AS 1.50 4.00
178 Mark Messier AS 2.00 5.00
179 Jaromir Jagr AS 2.00 5.00
180 Alexei Yashin AS 1.50 4.00
181 Mark Parrish AS 1.50 4.00
182 Dominik Hasek AS 2.00 5.00
183 Marian Hossa AS 1.50 4.00
184 Daniel Alfredsson AS 1.50 4.00
185 Keith Primeau AS 1.50 4.00
186 Simon Gagne AS 1.50 4.00
187 Brett Hull AS 1.50 4.00
188 Shane Doan AS 1.50 4.00
189 Mario Lemieux AS 3.00 8.00
190 Mark Recchi AS 1.50 4.00
191 Evgeni Nabokov AS 1.50 4.00
192 Keith Tkachuk AS 1.50 4.00
193 Martin St. Louis AS 1.50 4.00
194 Vincent Lecavalier AS 1.50 4.00
195 Ed Belfour AS 1.50 4.00
196 Mats Sundin AS 1.50 4.00
197 Owen Nolan AS 1.50 4.00
198 Markus Naslund AS 1.50 4.00
199 Ed Jovanovski AS 1.50 4.00
200 Olaf Kolzig AS 1.50 4.00
201 Corey Perry RC 6.00 15.00
202 Braydon Coburn RC 3.00 8.00
203 Hannu Toivonen RC 5.00 12.00
204 Thomas Vanek RC 10.00 25.00
205 Dion Phaneuf RC 15.00 40.00
206 Cam Ward RC 8.00 20.00
207 Brent Seabrook RC 3.00 8.00
208 Wojtek Wolski RC 6.00 15.00
209 Gilbert Brule RC 5.00 12.00
210 Jussi Jokinen RC 5.00 12.00
211 Jim Howard RC 5.00 12.00
212 Brad Winchester RC 3.00 8.00
213 Rostislav Olesz RC 3.00 8.00
214 George Parros RC 3.00 8.00
215 Matt Foy RC 3.00 8.00
216 Alexander Perezhogin RC 3.00 8.00
217 Ryan Suter RC 3.00 8.00
218 Zach Parise RC 6.00 15.00
219 Henrik Lundqvist RC 12.00 30.00
220 Robert Nilsson RC 3.00 8.00
221 Andrej Meszaros RC 3.00 8.00
222 Jeff Carter RC 8.00 20.00
223 David Leneveu RC 3.00 8.00
224 Sidney Crosby RC 175.00 300.00
225 Ryane Clowe RC 3.00 8.00
226 Jeff Woywitka RC 3.00 8.00
227 Evgeny Artyukhin RC 3.00 8.00
228 Alexander Steen RC 5.00 12.00
229 Rob McVicar RC 3.00 8.00
230 Alexander Ovechkin RC 50.00 100.00
231 Peter Budaj RC 4.00 10.00
232 Rene Bourque RC 3.00 8.00
233 Yann Danis RC 3.00 8.00
234 Eric Nystrom RC 2.00 5.00
235 Mike Richards RC 6.00 15.00
236 Kevin Nastiuk RC 2.00 5.00
237 Petteri Nokelainen RC 2.00 5.00
238 Ryan Getzlaf RC 8.00 20.00
239 Johan Franzen RC 2.00 5.00
240 Brandon Bochenski RC 2.00 5.00
241 Patrick Eaves RC 3.00 8.00
242 Jim Slater RC 2.00 5.00
243 Dustin Penner RC 3.00 8.00
244 Zenon Konopka RC 2.00 5.00
245 Michael Wall RC 2.00 5.00
246 Adam Berkhoel RC 2.00 5.00
247 Andrew Alberts RC 2.00 5.00
248 Milan Jurcina RC 2.00 5.00
249 Ben Walter RC 2.00 5.00
250 Jordan Sigalet RC 3.00 8.00
251 Nathan Paetsch RC 2.00 5.00
252 Chris Thorburn RC 2.00 5.00
253 Daniel Paille RC 2.00 5.00
254 Mark Giordano RC 2.00 5.00
255 Niklas Nordgren RC 2.00 5.00
256 Andrew Ladd RC 3.00 8.00
257 Chad Larose RC 2.00 5.00
258 Danny Richmond RC 2.00 5.00
259 Duncan Keith RC 2.00 5.00
260 Cam Barker RC 2.00 5.00
261 Martin St. Pierre RC 2.00 5.00
262 Corey Crawford RC 2.00 5.00
263 James Wisniewski RC 2.00 5.00
264 Brad Richardson RC 2.00 5.00
265 Vitaly Kolesnik RC 2.00 5.00
266 Alexandre Picard RC 2.00 5.00
267 Ole-Kristian Tollefsen RC 2.00 5.00
268 Steven Goertzen RC 2.00 5.00
269 Geoff Platt RC 2.00 5.00
270 Joakim Lindstrom RC 2.00 5.00
271 Junior Lessard RC 2.00 5.00
272 Vojtech Polak RC 2.00 5.00
273 Brett Lebda RC 2.00 5.00
274 Kyle Quincey RC 2.00 5.00
275 Valtteri Filppula RC 2.00 5.00
276 Danny Syvret RC 2.00 5.00
277 Kyle Brodziak RC 2.00 5.00
278 J-F Jacques RC 2.00 5.00
279 Matt Greene RC 2.00 5.00
280 Anthony Stewart RC 2.00 5.00
281 Greg Jacina RC 2.00 5.00
282 Petr Taticek RC 2.00 5.00
283 Yanick Lehoux RC 2.00 5.00
284 Jeff Tambellini RC 2.00 5.00
285 Petr Kanko RC 2.00 5.00
286 Richard Petiot RC 2.00 5.00
287 Mikko Koivu RC 4.00 10.00
288 Derek Boogaard RC 2.00 5.00
289 Jonathan Ferland RC 2.00 5.00
290 Maxim Lapierre RC 2.00 5.00
291 Jean-Philippe Cote RC 2.00 5.00
292 Andrei Kostitsyn RC 3.00 8.00
293 Greg Zanon RC 2.00 5.00
294 Kevin Klein RC 2.00 5.00
295 Pekka Rinne RC 2.00 5.00
296 Barry Tallackson RC 2.00 5.00
297 Cam Janssen RC 2.00 5.00
298 Jason Ryznar RC 2.00 5.00
299 Jeremy Colliton RC 2.00 5.00
300 Chris Campoli RC 2.00 5.00
301 Bruno Gervais RC 2.00 5.00
302 Petr Prucha RC 4.00 10.00
303 Ryan Hollweg RC 2.00 5.00
304 Al Montoya RC 3.00 8.00
305 Brian McGrattan RC 2.00 5.00
306 Christoph Schubert RC 2.00 5.00
307 R.J. Umberger RC 3.00 8.00
308 Stefan Ruzicka RC 2.00 5.00
309 Ben Eager RC 2.00 5.00
310 Alexandre Picard RC 2.00 5.00
311 Keith Ballard RC 2.00 5.00
312 Matt Jones RC 2.00 5.00
313 Maxime Talbot RC 2.00 5.00
314 Erik Christensen RC 2.00 5.00
315 Ryan Whitney RC 2.00 5.00
316 Colby Armstrong RC 3.00 8.00
317 Josh Gorges RC 2.00 5.00
318 Dimitri Patzold RC 2.00 5.00
319 Steve Bernier RC 5.00 10.00
320 Grant Stevenson RC 2.00 5.00
321 Doug Murrray RC 2.00 5.00
322 Jay McClement RC 2.00 5.00
323 Jeff Hoggan RC 2.00 5.00
324 Colin Hemingway RC 2.00 5.00
325 Dennis Wideman RC 2.00 5.00
326 Lee Stempniak RC 3.00 8.00
327 Chris Beckford-Tseu RC 2.00 5.00
328 Gerald Coleman RC 2.00 5.00
329 Nick Tarnasky RC 2.00 5.00
330 Paul Ranger RC 2.00 5.00
331 Darren Reid RC 2.00 5.00
332 Ryan Craig RC 2.00 5.00
333 Andrew Wozniewski RC 2.00 5.00
334 Staffan Kronwall RC 2.00 5.00
335 Jay Harrison RC 2.00 5.00
336 Kevin Bieksa RC 2.00 5.00
337 Rick Rypien RC 2.00 5.00
338 Rob McVicar 2.00 5.00
339 Tomas Mojzis RC 2.00 5.00
340 Tomas Fleischmann RC 2.00 5.00
341 Jakub Klepis RC 2.00 5.00
342 Mike Green RC 2.00 5.00

2005-06 UD Artifacts Blue

*1-100: 4X TO 10X BASE HI
*101-200: .5X TO 1.25X
PRINT RUN 75 SER.#'d SETS

2005-06 UD Artifacts Green

*1-100: 10X TO 25X BASE HI
*101-200: .75X TO 2X
PRINT RUN 25 SER.#'d SETS

2005-06 UD Artifacts Pewter

*1-100: 4X TO 10X BASE HI
*101-200: .5X TO 1.25X
PRINT RUN 100 SER.#'d SETS

2005-06 UD Artifacts Red

*1-100: 5X TO 12X BASE HI
*101-200: .6X TO 1.5X
PRINT RUN 50 SER.#'d SETS

2005-06 UD Artifacts Auto Facts

UNLISTED STARS 8.00 20.00
PRINT RUN 100 SER.#'d SETS
PEWTER PRINT RUN 10 SETS
BLUE PRINT RUN 1 SET
PEWTER/BLUE NOT PRICED
DUE TO SCARCITY
AF-ML Manny Legace 6.00 15.00
AF-RZ Richard Zednik 4.00 10.00
AF-TS Tony Salmelainen 4.00 10.00
AF-AF Alexander Frolov 6.00 15.00
AF-AH Ales Hemsky 6.00 15.00
AF-HZ Henrik Zetterberg 8.00 20.00
AF-NO Mika Noronen 4.00 10.00
AF-HO Marcel Hossa 4.00 10.00
AF-IK Ilya Kovalchuk 15.00 40.00
AF-GF Grant Fuhr 10.00 25.00
AF-GL Georges Laraque 4.00 10.00
AF-TR Tuomo Ruutu 6.00 15.00
AF-JG J-S Giguere 6.00 15.00
AF-ZC Zdeno Chara 4.00 10.00
AF-JT Joe Thornton 15.00 40.00
AF-SK Saku Koivu 8.00 20.00
AF-DL David Legwand 4.00 10.00
AF-NY Bob Nystrom 4.00 10.00
AF-BB Brad Boyes 4.00 10.00
AF-ES Eric Staal 10.00 25.00
AF-DM Darren McCarty 8.00 20.00
AF-MH Martin Havlat 8.00 20.00
AF-VL Vincent Lecavalier 10.00 25.00
AF-RS Ryan Smyth 6.00 15.00
AF-RB Rob Blake 4.00 10.00
AF-AT Alex Tanguay 6.00 15.00
AF-DS Denis Savard 6.00 15.00
AF-SW Stephen Weiss 4.00 10.00
AF-CN Cam Neely 12.00 30.00
AF-DU Dustin Brown 4.00 10.00
AF-DC Don Cherry 12.00 30.00
AF-HS Marian Hossa 8.00 20.00
AF-CP Chris Pronger 6.00 15.00
AF-BO Mike Bossy 10.00 25.00
AF-MP Mark Popovic 4.00 10.00
AF-PB Patrice Bergeron 10.00 25.00
AF-BC Bobby Clarke 8.00 20.00
AF-MO Brendan Morrison 4.00 10.00
AF-SL Martin St. Louis 6.00 15.00
AF-MC Mike Cammalleri 6.00 15.00
AF-RL Roberto Luongo 12.00 30.00
AF-MN Markus Naslund 8.00 20.00
AF-BR Brad Richards 6.00 15.00
AF-MG Marian Gaborik 15.00 40.00
AF-CD Chris Drury 6.00 15.00
AF-ST Matt Stajan 6.00 15.00
AF-KH Ken Hodge 4.00 10.00
AF-MA Maxim Afinogenov 6.00 15.00
AF-SC Dave Schultz 6.00 15.00
AF-CE Christian Ehrhoff 4.00 10.00
AF-CO Bob Cole 4.00 10.00
AF-RN Rick Nash 10.00 25.00
AF-SU Mats Sundin 10.00 25.00
AF-KL Kari Lehtonen 10.00 25.00
AF-MM Mike Modano 10.00 25.00
AF-BM Bryan McCabe 4.00 10.00
AF-RK Ryan Kesler 4.00 10.00
AF-BI Martin Biron 6.00 15.00
AF-RF Ruslan Fedotenko 4.00 10.00
AF-MF Marc-Andre Fleury 15.00 40.00
AF-LN Ladislav Nagy 4.00 10.00
AF-SG Simon Gagne 8.00 20.00
AF-JB Jay Bouwmeester 4.00 10.00
AF-NZ Nikolai Zherdev 4.00 10.00
AF-AM Antti Miettinen 4.00 10.00
AF-RH Ron Hextall 20.00 40.00
AF-JR Jeremy Roenick 10.00 25.00
AF-JL Jeffrey Lupul 6.00 15.00
AF-GW Gump Worsley 8.00 20.00
AF-OK Dave Taylor 4.00 10.00
AF-RE Robert Esche 8.00 20.00
AF-KD Kris Draper 6.00 15.00
AF-JS Jason Spezza 8.00 20.00
AF-JW Justin Williams 6.00 15.00
AF-JK Jari Kurri 8.00 20.00
AF-WC Wayne Cashman 4.00 10.00
AF-PW Peter Worrell 4.00 10.00
AF-AR Andrew Raycroft 6.00 15.00
AF-RY Michael Ryder 8.00 20.00
AF-TC Ty Conklin 4.00 10.00
AF-HE Milan Hejduk 8.00 20.00
AF-NA Nikolai Antropov 4.00 10.00
AF-TH Trent Hunter 4.00 10.00
AF-EC Erik Cole 4.00 10.00
AF-MT Marty Turco 6.00 15.00
AF-BL Brian Leetch 8.00 20.00
AF-DA David Aebischer 6.00 15.00
AF-NH Nathan Horton 4.00 10.00
AF-JC Jonathan Cheechoo 10.00 25.00
AF-LR Luc Robitaille 6.00 15.00
AF-SS Steve Sullivan 4.00 10.00
AF-JI Jarome Iginla 15.00 40.00
AF-RM Ryan Miller 6.00 15.00
AF-MR Mike Ribeiro 4.00 10.00

AF-TL Trevor Linden 12.00 30.00
AF-PS Philippe Sauve 4.00 10.00

2005-06 UD Artifacts Auto Facts Copper

*COPPER: .75 TO 1.25 VALUE BASE
PRINT RUN 75 SER.#'d SETS
AF-DH Dominik Hasek 20.00 50.00
AF-WG Wayne Gretzky 100.00 200.00
AF-MB Martin Brodeur 40.00 100.00
AF-GH Gordie Howe 50.00 125.00

2005-06 UD Artifacts Auto Facts Silver

*SILVER: .5X TO 1.25X BASIC AUTO
PRINT RUN 50 SER.#'d SETS
AF-GH Gordie Howe 60.00 150.00
AF-DH Dominik Hasek 25.00 60.00
AF-WG Wayne Gretzky 150.00 250.00
AF-MB Martin Brodeur 50.00 125.00

2005-06 UD Artifacts Frozen Artifacts

COMMON CARD 2.00 5.00
UNLISTED STARS 3.00 8.00
PRINT RUN 275 SER.#'d SETS
*COPPER/SILVER: .5X TO 1.25X HI
COPPER PRINT RUN 125 SER.#'d SETS
SILVER PRINT RUN 50 SER.#'d SETS
*MAROON: .75X TO 2X
MAROON PRINT RUN 25 SER.#'d SETS
PEWTER PRINT RUN 10 SER.#'d SETS
GOLD & AUTO 1/1'S EXIST
UNDER 25 NOT PRICED DUE TO SCARCITY
FA-AM Al MacInnis 2.00 5.00
FA-KD Kris Draper 3.00 8.00
FA-MT Marty Turco 2.00 5.00
FA-JB Jean Beliveau 4.00 10.00
FA-SA Denis Savard 2.00 5.00
FA-BO Jay Bouwmeester 2.00 5.00
FA-MO Alexander Mogilny 2.00 5.00
FA-RE Mark Recchi 2.00 5.00
FA-BM Brendan Morrison 2.00 5.00
FA-EB Ed Belfour 3.00 8.00
FA-JT Jocelyn Thibault 2.00 5.00
FA-ML Mario Lemieux 10.00 25.00
FA-EL Eric Lindros 3.00 8.00
FA-DW Doug Weight 2.00 5.00
FA-MH Martin Havlat 2.00 5.00
FA-BG Bernie Geoffrion 3.00 8.00
FA-DH Dominik Hasek 5.00 12.00
FA-DS Darryl Sittler 3.00 8.00
FA-JW Justin Williams 2.00 5.00
FA-RA Bill Ranford 2.00 5.00
FA-JO Jose Theodore 4.00 10.00
FA-JK Jari Kurri 3.00 8.00
FA-SL Martin St. Louis 2.00 5.00
FA-DC Dan Cloutier 2.00 5.00
FA-JL Joffrey Lupul 2.00 5.00
FA-BH Brett Hull 3.00 8.00
FA-GR Gary Roberts 2.00 5.00
FA-NH Nathan Horton 2.00 5.00
FA-BR Brad Richards 2.00 5.00
FA-HO Marcel Hossa 2.00 5.00
FA-BT Bryan Trottier 2.00 5.00
FA-RB Ray Bourque 5.00 12.00
FA-HZ Henrik Zetterberg 3.00 8.00
FA-RH Ron Hextall 6.00 15.00
FA-TE Tony Esposito 3.00 8.00
FA-PK Paul Kariya 3.00 8.00
FA-RL Roberto Luongo 4.00 10.00
FA-BS Borje Salming 3.00 8.00
FA-AF Alexander Frolov 2.00 5.00
FA-RD Rick DiPietro 2.00 5.00
FA-WG Wayne Gretzky 15.00 40.00
FA-DR Derek Roy 2.00 5.00
FA-CO Chris Osgood 2.00 5.00
FA-ON Owen Nolan 2.00 5.00
FA-MG Marian Gaborik 4.00 10.00
FA-GU Bill Guerin 2.00 5.00
FA-BC Bobby Clarke 2.00 5.00
FA-DU Dustin Brown 2.00 5.00
FA-MR Mike Ribeiro 2.00 5.00

2005-06 UD Artifacts Frozen Artifacts Dual

*DUAL: 1X TO 2.5X FA BASE
DUAL PRINT RUN 65 SER.#'d SETS
*DUAL COPPER: 1X TO 2.5X FA BASE
COPPER PRINT RUN 50 SER.#'d SETS
*DUAL SILVER: 1.25X TO 3X FA BASE
SILVER PRINT RUN 25 SER.#'d SETS
MAROON PRINT RUN 15 SER.#'d SETS
PEWTER PRINT RUN 10 SER.#'d SETS
GOLD & AUTO 1/1'S EXIST
UNDER 25 NOT PRICED DUE TO SCARCITY

2005-06 UD Artifacts Frozen Artifacts Patches

*PATCHES: 2X TO 5X FA BASE
PATCH PRINT RUN 50 SER.#'d SETS
SILVER PATCH PRINT RUN 5 SETS
DUAL PATCH PRINT RUN 15 SETS
PEWTER & AUTO 1/1'S EXIST
UNDER 25 NOT PRICED DUE TO SCARCITY
FP-WG Wayne Gretzky 60.00 150.00
FP-MG Marian Gaborik 15.00 40.00
FP-ML Mario Lemieux 25.00 60.00
FP-RB Ray Bourque 20.00 50.00
FP-DH Dominik Hasek 15.00 40.00

2005-06 UD Artifacts Goalie Gear

PRINT RUN 50 SER.#'d SETS
SILVER PATCH PRINT RUN 5 SETS
DUAL PATCH PRINT RUN 15 SETS
PEWTER, AUTO & DUAL AUTO 1/1's EXIST
UNDER 25 NOT PRICED DUE TO SCARCITY
FG-EB Ed Belfour 12.00 30.00
FG-DH Dominik Hasek 25.00 60.00
FG-JO Jose Theodore 15.00 40.00
FG-RD Rick DiPietro 8.00 20.00
FG-JT Jocelyn Thibault 8.00 20.00
FG-TE Tony Esposito 8.00 20.00
FG-CO Chris Osgood 8.00 20.00
FG-GC Gerry Cheevers 8.00 20.00
FG-RA Bill Ranford 12.00 30.00
FG-MT Marty Turco 8.00 20.00
FG-RL Roberto Luongo 10.00 25.00

2005-06 UD Artifacts Remarkable Artifacts

PRINT RUN 1 SET
DUAL PRINT RUN 1 SET
NOT PRICED DUE TO SCARCITY

2005-06 UD Artifacts Treasured Patches

*PATCHES: 2X TO 5X TS BASE
PATCH PRINT RUN 50 SER.#'d SETS
SILVER PATCH PRINT RUN 5 SETS
DUAL PATCH PRINT RUN 15 SETS
PEWTER, AUTO & DUAL AUTO 1/1's EXIST
UNDER 25 NOT PRICED DUE TO SCARCITY
TP-SY Steve Yzerman 30.00 80.00
TP-HA Dominik Hasek 25.00 60.00
TP-MB Martin Brodeur 30.00 80.00
TP-MM Mike Modano 20.00 50.00
TP-PF Peter Forsberg 20.00 50.00
TP-ML Mario Lemieux 25.00 60.00
TP-JS Joe Sakic 15.00 40.00
TP-MG Marian Gaborik 20.00 50.00
TP-JJ Jaromir Jagr 25.00 60.00
TP-WG Wayne Gretzky 100.00 250.00

2005-06 UD Artifacts Treasured Swatches

PRINT RUN 275 SER.#'d SETS
*COPPER/SILVER: .5X TO 1.25X HI
COPPER PRINT RUN 125 SER.#'d SETS
SILVER PRINT RUN 50 SER.#'d SETS
*MAROON: .75X TO 2X HI
MAROON PRINT RUN 25 SER.#'d SETS
PEWTER PRINT RUN 10 SER.#'d SETS
BLUE & AUTO 1/1'S EXIST
UNDER 25 NOT PRICED DUE TO SCARCITY
TS-TB Todd Bertuzzi 3.00 8.00
TS-JT Joe Thornton 4.00 10.00
TS-BL Brian Leetch 3.00 8.00
TS-PD Pavel Datsyuk 3.00 8.00
TS-MP Michael Peca 2.00 5.00
TS-EB Ed Belfour 3.00 8.00
TS-ST Matt Stajan 2.00 5.00
TS-ZP Zigmund Palffy 2.00 5.00
TS-TR Tuomo Ruutu 2.00 5.00
TS-PE Patrik Elias 2.00 5.00
TS-JS Joe Sakic 5.00 12.00
TS-JR Jeremy Roenick 3.00 8.00
TS-JI Jarome Iginla 3.00 8.00
TS-ML Mario Lemieux 10.00 25.00
TS-SK Saku Koivu 3.00 8.00
TS-VL Vincent Lecavalier 3.00 8.00
TS-DA Daniel Alfredsson 2.00 5.00
TS-MH Milan Hejduk 3.00 8.00
TS-RN Rick Nash 4.00 10.00
TS-JJ Jaromir Jagr 5.00 12.00
TS-MD Marc Denis 2.00 5.00
TS-JO Jose Theodore 3.00 8.00
TS-CP Chris Pronger 2.00 5.00
TS-JG J-S Giguere 2.00 5.00
TS-SP Jason Spezza 3.00 8.00
TS-NK Nikolai Khabibulin 3.00 8.00
TS-SS Scott Stevens 2.00 5.00
TS-KP Keith Primeau 2.00 5.00
TS-SU Mats Sundin 3.00 8.00
TS-MB Martin Brodeur 10.00 25.00
TS-TS Teemu Selanne 3.00 8.00
TS-MG Marian Gaborik 4.00 10.00
TS-SL Martin St. Louis 2.00 5.00
TS-MM Mike Modano 4.00 10.00
TS-PF Peter Forsberg 4.00 10.00
TS-CJ Curtis Joseph 3.00 8.00
TS-SY Steve Yzerman 8.00 20.00
TS-SF Sergei Fedorov 3.00 8.00
TS-BS Brendan Shanahan 3.00 8.00
TS-HO Marian Hossa 3.00 8.00
TS-HA Dominik Hasek 5.00 12.00
TS-RS Ryan Smyth 2.00 5.00
TS-AT Alex Tanguay 2.00 5.00
TS-MS Mark Messier 3.00 8.00
TS-DH Dany Heatley 3.00 8.00
TS-MN Markus Naslund 3.00 8.00
TS-SD Shane Doan 2.00 5.00
TS-IK Ilya Kovalchuk 4.00 10.00
TS-WG Wayne Gretzky 15.00 40.00

2005-06 UD Artifacts Treasured Swatches Dual

*DUAL: 1X TO 2.5X TS BASE
DUAL PRINT RUN 65 SER.#'d SETS
*DUAL COPPER: 1X TO 2.5X TS BASE
COPPER PRINT RUN 50 SER.#'d SETS
*DUAL SILVER: 1.25X TO 3X TS BASE
SILVER PRINT RUN 25 SER.#'d SETS
MAROON PRINT RUN 15 SER.#'d SETS
PEWTER PRINT RUN 10 SER.#'d SETS
BLUE & AUTO 1/1'S EXIST
UNDER 25 NOT PRICED DUE TO SCARCITY
SCARCITY

2006-07 UD Artifacts

AS/LEGEND PRINT RUN 999 #'d SETS
RC PRINT RUN 999 #'d SETS
1 Alexander Ovechkin 1.25 3.00
2 Olaf Kolzig .25 .60
3 Roberto Luongo .30 .75
4 Markus Naslund .25 .60
5 Brendan Morrison .12 .30
6 Mats Sundin .25 .60
7 Darcy Tucker .12 .30
8 Alexander Steen .20 .50
9 Andrew Raycroft .20 .50
10 Michael Peca .12 .30
11 Brad Richards .20 .50
12 Vincent Lecavalier .25 .60
13 Martin St. Louis .20 .50
14 Keith Tkachuk .25 .60
15 Doug Weight .12 .30
16 Patrick Marleau .20 .50
17 Joe Thornton .40 1.00
18 Jonathan Cheechoo .25 .60
19 Vesa Toskala .20 .50
20 Mark Recchi .12 .30
21 Sidney Crosby 1.50 4.00
22 Marc-Andre Fleury .20 .50
23 Colby Armstrong .12 .30
24 Shane Doan .12 .30
25 Curtis Joseph .25 .60
26 Jeremy Roenick .30 .75
27 Mike Richards .20 .50
28 Peter Forsberg .60 1.50
29 Simon Gagne .25 .60
30 Jeff Carter .20 .50
31 Jason Spezza .25 .60
32 Dany Heatley .30 .75
33 Daniel Alfredsson .20 .50
34 Martin Gerber .20 .50
35 Brendan Shanahan .25 .60
36 Jaromir Jagr .40 1.00
37 Henrik Lundqvist .30 .75
38 Petr Prucha .12 .30
39 Miroslav Satan .12 .30
40 Rick DiPietro .20 .50
41 Alexei Yashin .12 .30
42 Patrik Elias .12 .30
43 Martin Brodeur .75 2.00
44 Brian Gionta .12 .30
45 Paul Kariya .25 .60
46 Tomas Vokoun .20 .50
47 Saku Koivu .25 .60
48 Cristobal Huet .20 .50
49 Michael Ryder .20 .50
50 Alex Kovalev .12 .30
51 Pavol Demitra .12 .30
52 Marian Gaborik .50 1.25
53 Manny Fernandez .20 .50
54 Alexander Frolov .12 .30
55 Rob Blake .20 .50
56 Nathan Horton .12 .30
57 Olli Jokinen .12 .30
58 Todd Bertuzzi .20 .50
59 Ed Belfour .25 .60
60 Ales Hemsky .12 .30
61 Joffrey Lupul .12 .30
62 Ryan Smyth .20 .50
63 Henrik Zetterberg .25 .60
64 Pavel Datsyuk .25 .60
65 Nicklas Lidstrom .25 .60
66 Dominik Hasek .50 1.25
67 Mike Modano .30 .75
68 Marty Turco .20 .50
69 Brenden Morrow .20 .50
70 Eric Lindros .25 .60
71 Fredrik Modin .12 .30
72 Rick Nash .30 .75
73 Sergei Fedorov .25 .60
74 Joe Sakic .50 1.25
75 Milan Hejduk .20 .50
76 Jose Theodore .25 .60
77 Marek Svatos .12 .30
78 Martin Havlat .20 .50
79 Nikolai Khabibulin .25 .60
80 Tuomo Ruutu .20 .50
81 Eric Staal .25 .60
82 Cam Ward .25 .60
83 Rod Brind'Amour .25 .60
84 Jarome Iginla .30 .75
85 Miikka Kiprusoff .25 .60
86 Dion Phaneuf .30 .75
87 Alex Tanguay .20 .50
88 Ryan Miller .25 .60
89 Chris Drury .12 .30
90 Daniel Briere .12 .30
91 Brad Boyes .12 .30
92 Patrice Bergeron .25 .60
93 Zdeno Chara .12 .30
94 Marc Savard .12 .30
95 Ilya Kovalchuk .30 .75
96 Marian Hossa .20 .50
97 Kari Lehtonen .25 .60
98 Teemu Selanne .25 .60
99 Jean-Sebastien Giguere .20 .50
100 Chris Pronger .20 .50
101 Glenn Anderson 1.50 4.00
102 Jean Beliveau 2.50 6.00
103 Bob Bourne 1.50 4.00
104 Mike Bossy 2.00 5.00
105 Richard Brodeur 2.00 5.00
106 Johnny Bucyk 2.00 5.00
107 Gerry Cheevers 2.00 5.00
108 Don Cherry 2.50 6.00
109 Wendel Clark 2.00 5.00
110 Bobby Clarke 2.00 5.00
111 Phil Esposito 2.50 6.00
112 Tony Esposito 2.00 5.00
113 Grant Fuhr 2.00 5.00
114 Doug Gilmour 2.00 5.00
115 Peter Stastny 1.50 4.00
116 Glenn Hall 2.00 5.00
117 Ron Hextall 2.00 5.00
118 Guy Lafleur 2.50 6.00
119 Guy Lapointe 1.50 4.00
120 Reggie Leach 1.50 4.00
121 Ted Lindsay 1.50 4.00
122 Lanny McDonald 2.00 5.00
123 Joe Mullen 1.50 4.00
124 Kirk Muller 1.50 4.00
125 Cam Neely 2.00 5.00
126 Bob Nystrom 1.50 4.00
127 Terry O'Reilly 1.50 4.00
128 Bernie Parent 2.00 5.00
129 Gilbert Perreault 2.00 5.00
130 Denis Potvin 1.50 4.00
131 Bill Ranford 1.50 4.00
132 Derek Sanderson 2.00 5.00
133 Denis Savard 2.00 5.00
134 Steve Shutt 1.50 4.00
135 Darryl Sittler 2.00 5.00
136 Billy Smith 2.00 5.00
137 Thomas Steen 1.50 4.00
138 Rick Vaive 1.50 4.00
139 Ron Ellis 1.50 4.00
140 Doug Wilson 1.50 4.00
141 Wayne Gretzky 6.00 15.00
142 Patrick Roy 4.00 10.00
143 Gordie Howe 3.00 8.00
144 Ray Bourque 2.00 5.00
145 Al MacInnis 1.50 4.00
146 Mike Krushelnyski 1.50 4.00
147 Mario Lemieux 4.00 10.00
148 Bob Probert 2.00 5.00
149 Dave Williams 2.00 5.00
150 Clark Gillies 1.50 4.00
151 Teemu Selanne 2.00 5.00
152 Ilya Kovalchuk 2.50 6.00
153 Marian Hossa 1.50 4.00
154 Patrice Bergeron 2.00 5.00
155 Cristobal Huet 1.50 4.00
156 Ryan Miller 2.00 5.00
157 Miikka Kiprusoff 2.00 5.00
158 Jarome Iginla 2.50 6.00
159 Eric Staal 2.00 5.00
160 Nikolai Khabibulin 2.00 5.00
161 Joe Sakic 2.50 6.00
162 Alex Tanguay 1.50 4.00
163 Rick Nash 2.50 6.00
164 Mike Modano 2.50 6.00
165 Marty Turco 1.50 4.00
166 Henrik Zetterberg 2.00 5.00
167 Pavel Datsyuk 2.00 5.00
168 Brendan Shanahan 2.00 5.00
169 Ales Hemsky 1.50 4.00
170 Chris Pronger 1.50 4.00
171 Roberto Luongo 2.50 6.00
172 Olli Jokinen 1.50 4.00
173 Alexander Frolov 1.50 4.00
174 Marian Gaborik 2.50 6.00
175 Saku Koivu 2.00 5.00
176 Michael Ryder 1.50 4.00
177 Paul Kariya 2.00 5.00
178 Tomas Vokoun 1.50 4.00
179 Martin Brodeur 3.00 8.00
180 Patrik Elias 1.50 4.00
181 Brian Gionta 1.50 4.00
182 Miroslav Satan 1.50 4.00
183 Jaromir Jagr 3.00 8.00
184 Henrik Lundqvist 2.50 6.00
185 Dany Heatley 2.50 6.00
186 Ed Belfour 2.00 5.00
187 Jason Spezza 2.00 5.00
188 Peter Forsberg 2.50 6.00
189 Simon Gagne 2.00 5.00
190 Shane Doan 1.50 4.00
191 Sidney Crosby 8.00 20.00
192 Marc-Andre Fleury 1.50 4.00
193 Joe Thornton 3.00 8.00
194 Patrick Marleau 1.50 4.00
195 Jonathan Cheechoo 2.00 5.00
196 Martin St. Louis 1.50 4.00
197 Vincent Lecavalier 2.00 5.00
198 Brad Richards 1.50 4.00
199 Mats Sundin 2.00 5.00
200 Markus Naslund 2.00 5.00
201 Dustin Byfuglien RC 1.50 4.00
202 Yan Stastny RC 1.50 4.00
203 Mark Stuart RC 1.50 4.00
204 Eric Fehr RC 1.50 4.00
205 Bill Thomas RC 2.00 5.00
206 Joel Perrault RC 1.50 4.00
207 Carsen Germyn RC 1.50 4.00
208 Ryan Potulny RC 2.00 5.00
209 David Printz RC 1.50 4.00
210 Rob Collins RC 1.50 4.00
211 Steve Regier RC 1.50 4.00
212 Matt Koalska RC 1.50 4.00
213 Masi Marjamaki RC 1.50 4.00
214 Konstantin Pushkarev RC 1.50 4.00
215 Ben Ondrus RC 1.50 4.00
216 Brendan Bell RC 1.50 4.00
217 Ian White RC 1.50 4.00
218 Jeremy Williams RC 1.50 4.00
219 Marc-Antoine Pouliot RC 2.00 5.00
220 Noah Welch RC 2.00 5.00
221 Michel Ouellet RC 2.00 5.00
222 Shea Weber RC 1.50 4.00
223 Jarkko Immonen RC 1.50 4.00
224 David Liffiton RC 1.50 4.00
225 Tomas Kopecky RC 1.50 4.00
226 Billy Thompson RC 2.00 5.00
227 Filip Novak RC 1.50 4.00
228 Matt Carle RC 2.50 6.00
229 Erik Reitz RC 1.50 4.00
230 Miroslav Kopriva RC 1.50 4.00
231 Ryan Shannon 2.50 6.00
232 Benoit Pouliot 2.50 6.00
233 Phil Kessel 6.00 15.00
234 Drew Stafford 5.00 12.00
235 Dustin Boyd 2.50 6.00
236 Josh Hennessey 2.50 6.00
237 Dave Bolland 2.50 6.00
238 Paul Stastny 8.00 20.00
239 Fredrik Norrena 3.00 8.00
240 Loui Eriksson 2.50 6.00
241 Derek Meech 2.50 6.00
242 Ladislav Smid 2.50 6.00
243 Janis Sprukts 2.50 6.00
244 Anze Kopitar 10.00 25.00
245 Niklas Backstrom 3.00 8.00
246 Guillaume Latendresse 6.00 15.00
247 Alexander Radulov 6.00 15.00
248 Travis Zajac 3.00 8.00
249 Blake Comeau 2.50 6.00
250 Nigel Dawes 2.50 6.00
251 Alexei Kaigorodov 2.50 6.00
252 Martin Houle 2.50 6.00
253 Enver Lisin 2.50 6.00
254 Evgeni Malkin 30.00 60.00
255 Marc-Edouard Vlasic 2.50 6.00
256 Marek Schwarz 3.00 8.00
257 Karri Ramo 2.50 6.00
258 Kris Newbury 2.50 6.00
259 Luc Bourdon 3.00 8.00
260 Darren Machesney 2.50 6.00
261 Jordan Staal 20.00 50.00
262 Patrick O'Sullivan 3.00 8.00
263 Patrik Thoresen 2.50 6.00
265 Mikhail Grabovski 2.50 6.00
265 Jesse Schultz 2.50 6.00
266 Michael Blunden 2.50 6.00
267 David Booth 2.50 6.00
268 Brandon Prust 2.50 6.00
269 Matt Lashoff 2.50 6.00
270 Niklas Grossman 2.50 6.00
271 Joe Pavelski 3.00 8.00
272 Clarke MacArthur 2.50 6.00

2006-07 UD Artifacts Gold

*1-100 5X TO 12X HI
*101-230 .75X TO 2X HI
PRINT RUN 25 SER. #'d SETS

2006-07 UD Artifacts Radiance

COMPLETE SET (230)
PRINT RUN 1/1
NOT PRICED DUE TO SCARCITY

2006-07 UD Artifacts Autographed Radiance Parallel

COMPLETE SET (111)
STATED PRINT RUN 1/1
NOT PRICED DUE TO SCARCITY

2006-07 UD Artifacts Red

*RED 1-100 2X TO 5X HI
*RED 101-230 SAME AS BASE
PRINT RUN 100 SER. #'d SETS

2006-07 UD Artifacts Auto-Facts

The Billy Smith card mistakenly pictures Chico Resch.
STATED ODDS 1:10
GOLD 1/1s EXIST
GOLDS NOT PRICED DUE TO SCARCITY
AFAA Adrian Aucoin 3.00 8.00
AFAH Ales Hemsky 5.00 12.00
AFAK Andrei Kostitsyn 8.00 20.00
AFAO Alexander Ovechkin SP 100.00 175.00
AFAP Alexandre Picard 3.00 8.00
AFBB Bob Bourne 3.00 8.00
AFBC Bobby Clarke 8.00 20.00
AFBE Jean Beliveau SP 50.00 125.00
AFBI Martin Biron 3.00 8.00
AFBL Brett Lebda 3.00 8.00
AFBN Bob Nystrom 3.00 8.00
AFBO Jay Bouwmeester 10.00 25.00
AFBP Bob Probert 8.00 20.00
AFBR Brad Boyes 3.00 8.00
AFBS Billy Smith UER 8.00 20.00
AFBU Johnny Bucyk SP 6.00 15.00
AFBW Ben Walter 3.00 8.00
AFBY Mike Bossy 6.00 15.00
AFCA Jeff Carter 6.00 15.00
AFCD Chris Drury 5.00 12.00
AFCG Clark Gillies 5.00 12.00
AFCK Chuck Kobasew 3.00 8.00
AFCN Cam Neely 10.00 25.00
AFCP Corey Perry 5.00 12.00
AFDA David Aebischer 6.00 15.00
AFDB Doug Bodger 3.00 8.00
AFDE Derek Boogaard 5.00 12.00
AFDP Dion Phaneuf 15.00 40.00
AFDR Dwayne Roloson 5.00 12.00
AFDS Denis Savard 5.00 12.00
AFDW Doug Wilson 3.00 8.00
AFFP Fernando Pisani 3.00 8.00
AFGA Glenn Anderson SP 6.00 15.00
AFGF Grant Fuhr SP 15.00 40.00
AFGL Guy Lafleur SP 20.00 50.00
AFHO Gordie Howe 30.00 60.00
AFHR Ryan Hollweg 3.00 8.00
AFHZ Henrik Zetterberg SP 20.00 50.00
AFIK Ilya Kovalchuk SP 20.00 50.00
AFJB Jaroslav Balastik 3.00 8.00
AFJC Jonathan Cheechoo 8.00 20.00
AFJH Jeff Halpern 3.00 8.00
AFJI Jarome Iginla SP 20.00 50.00
AFJL Joffrey Lupul SP 8.00 20.00
AFJM Joe Mullen 5.00 12.00
AFJT Jose Theodore SP 12.00 30.00
AFKD Kris Draper 3.00 8.00
AFKM Kirk Muller 3.00 8.00
AFLE Reggie Leach 8.00 20.00
AFLN Ladislav Nagy 3.00 8.00
AFLS Lee Stempniak 3.00 8.00
AFMA Marian Gaborik SP 20.00 50.00
AFMB Martin Brodeur SP 75.00 175.00
AFMC Mike Cammalleri 3.00 8.00
AFMG Martin Gerber 5.00 12.00
AFMI Mike Richards 5.00 12.00
AFMK Miikka Kiprusoff SP 15.00 40.00
AFML Mario Lemieux SP 200.00 350.00
AFMR Michael Ryder 5.00 12.00
AFMS Marek Svatos 5.00 12.00
AFMT Mikael Tellqvist 5.00 12.00
AFNH Nathan Horton 5.00 12.00
AFOJ Olli Jokinen 3.00 8.00
AFPB Pierre-Marc Bouchard SP 30.00 60.00
AFPE Phil Esposito SP 100.00 200.00
AFPM Patrick Marleau 8.00 20.00
AFRA Ray Bourque SP 25.00 60.00
AFRB Rob Blake SP 25.00 50.00
AFRE Ron Ellis 5.00 12.00
AFRF Ruslan Fedotenko 3.00 8.00
AFRG Ryan Getzlaf 6.00 15.00
AFRH Ron Hextall SP 20.00 50.00
AFRI Richard Brodeur 5.00 12.00
AFRK Rostislav Klesla 3.00 8.00
AFRL Rod Langway 3.00 8.00
AFRM Ryan Malone SP 12.00 30.00
AFRO Mike Ribeiro 3.00 8.00
AFRS Ryan Smyth 12.00 30.00
AFRY Ryan Miller 15.00 30.00
AFSC Sidney Crosby 125.00 225.00
AFSG Scott Gomez 3.00 8.00
AFSH Scott Hartnell 3.00 8.00
AFSS Steve Shutt 3.00 8.00
AFSW Stephen Weiss 3.00 8.00
AFTE Tony Esposito SP 20.00 50.00
AFTH Joe Thornton SP 25.00 50.00
AFTL Ted Lindsay 6.00 15.00
AFTS Tomas Steen 3.00 8.00
AFTV Thomas Vanek 10.00 25.00
AFVO Tomas Vokoun 5.00 12.00
AFWC Wendel Clark 20.00 50.00
AFWG Wayne Gretzky SP 125.00 250.00
AFWI Dave Williams 5.00 12.00
AFWR Wade Redden SP 15.00 40.00
AFZC Zdeno Chara 5.00 12.00

2006-07 UD Artifacts Auto-Facts Gold

COMPLETE SET (95)
PRINT RUN 1/1
NOT PRICED DUE TO SCARCITY
AFAA Adrian Aucoin
AFAH Ales Hemsky
AFAK Andrei Kostitsyn
AFAO Alexander Ovechkin
AFAP Alexandre Picard
AFBB Bob Bourne
AFBC Bobby Clarke
AFBE Jean Beliveau
AFBI Martin Biron
AFBL Brett Lebda
AFBN Bob Nystrom
AFBO Jay Bouwmeester
AFBP Bob Probert
AFBR Brad Boyes
AFBS Billy Smith
AFBU Johnny Bucyk
AFBW Ben Walter
AFBY Mike Bossy
AFCA Jeff Carter
AFCD Chris Drury
AFCG Clark Gillies
AFCK Chuck Kobasew
AFCN Cam Neely
AFCP Corey Perry
AFDA David Aebischer
AFDB Doug Bodger
AFDE Derek Boogaard
AFDP Dion Phaneuf
AFDR Dwayne Roloson
AFDS Denis Savard
AFDW Doug Wilson
AFFP Fernando Pisani
AFGA Glenn Anderson
AFGF Grant Fuhr
AFGL Guy Lafleur
AFHO Gordie Howe
AFHR Ryan Hollweg
AFHZ Henrik Zetterberg
AFIK Ilya Kovalchuk
AFJB Jaroslav Balastik
AFJC Jonathan Cheechoo
AFJH Jeff Halpern
AFJI Jarome Iginla
AFJL Joffrey Lupul
AFJM Joe Mullen
AFJT Jose Theodore
AFKD Kris Draper
AFKM Kirk Muller
AFLE Reggie Leach
AFLN Ladislav Nagy
AFLS Lee Stempniak
AFMA Marian Gaborik
AFMB Martin Brodeur
AFMC Mike Cammalleri
AFMG Martin Gerber
AFMI Mike Richards
AFMK Miikka Kiprusoff
AFML Mario Lemieux
AFMR Michael Ryder
AFMS Marek Svatos
AFMT Mikael Tellqvist
AFNH Nathan Horton
AFOJ Olli Jokinen
AFPB Pierre-Marc Bouchard
AFPE Phil Esposito
AFPM Patrick Marleau
AFRA Ray Bourque
AFRB Rob Blake
AFRE Ron Ellis
AFRF Ruslan Fedotenko
AFRG Ryan Getzlaf
AFRH Ron Hextall
AFRI Richard Brodeur
AFRK Rostislav Klesla
AFRL Rod Langway
AFRM Ryan Malone
AFRO Mike Ribeiro
AFRS Ryan Smyth
AFRY Ryan Miller
AFSC Sidney Crosby
AFSG Scott Gomez
AFSH Scott Hartnell
AFSS Steve Shutt
AFSW Stephen Weiss
AFTE Tony Esposito
AFTH Joe Thornton
AFTL Ted Lindsay
AFTS Tomas Steen
AFTV Thomas Vanek
AFVO Tomas Vokoun
AFWC Wendel Clark
AFWG Wayne Gretzky
AFWI Dave Williams
AFWR Wade Redden
AFZC Zdeno Chara

2006-07 UD Artifacts Frozen Artifacts

PRINT RUN 250 SER. #'d SETS
FAAO Adam Oates 2.00 5.00
FAAT Alex Tanguay 2.50 6.00
FABG Brian Gionta 2.50 6.00
FABM Brenden Morrow 2.50 6.00
FABP Brad Park 2.50 6.00
FABR Bill Ranford 2.50 6.00
FABS Brad Stuart 2.00 5.00
FACC Chris Chelios 2.50 6.00
FACD Chris Drury 2.50 6.00
FACK Chuck Kobasew 2.00 5.00
FACP Chris Pronger 2.50 6.00
FACW Cam Ward 3.00 8.00
FADA Daniel Alfredsson 2.50 6.00
FADS Darryl Sittler 2.50 6.00
FAES Eric Staal 3.00 8.00
FAGA Glenn Anderson 2.50 6.00
FAHZ Henrik Zetterberg 4.00 10.00
FAJB Jay Bouwmeester 2.50 6.00
FAJC Jeff Carter 2.50 6.00
FAJI Jarome Iginla 5.00 12.00
FAJL Joffrey Lupul 2.50 6.00
FAJO Jonathan Cheechoo 2.50 6.00
FAJS Joe Sakic 5.00 12.00
FALM Lanny McDonald 2.50 6.00
FAMC Bryan McCabe 2.00 5.00
FAMH Milan Hejduk 2.50 6.00
FAMK Miikka Kiprusoff 3.00 8.00
FAMM Mike Modano 4.00 10.00
FAMO Brendan Morrison 2.50 6.00
FAMR Mark Recchi 2.00 5.00
FANL Nicklas Lidstrom 2.50 6.00
FAPB Patrice Bergeron 3.00 8.00
FAPD Pavol Demitra 2.00 5.00
FAPE Patrik Elias 2.00 5.00
FAPM Patrick Marleau 2.50 6.00
FAPR Patrick Roy 10.00 25.00
FAPS Peter Stastny 2.00 5.00
FARB Rod Brind'Amour 2.50 6.00
FARL Roberto Luongo 4.00 10.00
FARM Ryan Miller 3.00 8.00
FARS Ryan Smyth 3.00 8.00
FASG Simon Gagne 3.00 8.00
FASK Saku Koivu 3.00 8.00
FASP Jason Spezza 3.00 8.00
FASS Steve Shutt 2.50 6.00
FASU Steve Sullivan 2.00 5.00
FASW Stephen Weiss 2.00 5.00
FATS Teemu Selanne 3.00 8.00
FATV Tomas Vokoun 3.00 8.00
FAWC Wendel Clark 3.00 8.00

2006-07 UD Artifacts Frozen Artifacts Black

FAAO Adam Oates
FAAT Alex Tanguay
FABG Brian Gionta
FABM Brenden Morrow
FABP Brad Park
FABR Bill Ranford
FABS Brad Stuart
FACC Chris Chelios
FACD Chris Drury
FACK Chuck Kobasew
FACP Chris Pronger
FACW Cam Ward
FADA Daniel Alfredsson
FADS Darryl Sittler
FAES Eric Staal
FAGA Glenn Anderson
FAHZ Henrik Zetterberg
FAJB Jay Bouwmeester
FAJC Jeff Carter
FAJI Jarome Iginla
FAJL Joffrey Lupul
FAJO Jonathan Cheechoo
FAJS Joe Sakic
FALM Lanny McDonald
FAMC Bryan McCabe
FAMH Milan Hejduk
FAMK Miikka Kiprusoff
FAMM Mike Modano
FAMO Brendan Morrison
FAMR Mark Recchi
FANL Nicklas Lidstrom
FAPB Patrice Bergeron
FAPD Pavol Demitra
FAPE Patrik Elias
FAPM Patrick Marleau
FAPR Patrick Roy
FAPS Peter Stastny
FARB Rod Brind'Amour
FARL Roberto Luongo
FARM Ryan Miller
FARS Ryan Smyth
FASG Simon Gagne
FASK Saku Koivu
FASP Jason Spezza
FASS Steve Shutt
FASU Steve Sullivan
FASW Stephen Weiss
FATS Teemu Selanne
FATV Tomas Vokoun
FAWC Wendel Clark

2006-07 UD Artifacts Frozen Artifacts Blue

*BLUE .75X TO 1.5X HI
PRINT RUN 50 SER. #'d SETS

2006-07 UD Artifacts Frozen Artifacts Platinum

PRINT RUN 10 SER. #'d SETS
NOT PRICED DUE TO SCARCITY

2006-07 UD Artifacts Frozen Artifacts Red

*RED .5X TO 1.25X HI
PRINT RUN 100 SER. #'d SETS

2006-07 UD Artifacts Frozen Artifacts Autographed Black

PRINT RUN 1/1
NOT PRICED DUE TO SCARCITY
FABR Bill Ranford
FACD Chris Drury
FACK Chuck Kobasew
FACP Chris Pronger
FADS Darryl Sittler
FAGA Glenn Anderson
FAHZ Henrik Zetterberg
FAJB Jay Bouwmeester
FAJC Jeff Carter
FAJI Jarome Iginla
FAJL Joffrey Lupul
FAJO Jonathan Cheechoo
FAMH Milan Hejduk
FAMK Miikka Kiprusoff
FAPM Patrick Marleau
FAPR Patrick Roy
FAPS Peter Stastny
FARL Roberto Luongo
FARM Ryan Miller
FARS Ryan Smyth
FASK Saku Koivu
FASS Steve Shutt
FASW Stephen Weiss
FATV Tomas Vokoun
FAWC Wendel Clark

2006-07 UD Artifacts Frozen Artifacts Patches Blue

PRINT RUN 25 SER. #'d SETS
BLUE SAME PRICE AS RED

2006-07 UD Artifacts Frozen Artifacts Patches Gold

PRINT RUN 10 SER. #'d SETS
NOT PRICED DUE TO SCARCITY

2006-07 UD Artifacts Frozen Artifacts Patches Platinum

PRINT RUN 5 SER. #'d SETS
NOT PRICED DUE TO SCARCITY

2006-07 UD Artifacts Frozen Artifacts Patches Red

PRINT RUN 35 SER. #'d SETS
FAAO Adam Oates 12.00 25.00
FAAT Alex Tanguay 15.00 40.00
FABG Brian Gionta 10.00 25.00
FABM Brenden Morrow 15.00 40.00
FABP Brad Park 10.00 25.00
FABR Bill Ranford 15.00 40.00
FABS Brad Stuart 10.00 25.00
FACC Chris Chelios 15.00 40.00
FACD Chris Drury 15.00 40.00
FACK Chuck Kobasew 10.00 25.00
FACP Chris Pronger 15.00 40.00
FACW Cam Ward 15.00 40.00
FADA Daniel Alfredsson 15.00 40.00
FADS Darryl Sittler 15.00 40.00
FAES Eric Staal 15.00 40.00
FAGA Glenn Anderson 15.00 40.00
FAHZ Henrik Zetterberg 15.00 40.00
FAJB Jay Bouwmeester 10.00 25.00
FAJC Jeff Carter 15.00 40.00
FAJI Jarome Iginla 20.00 50.00
FAJL Joffrey Lupul 10.00 25.00
FAJO Jonathan Cheechoo 10.00 25.00
FAJS Joe Sakic 30.00 60.00
FALM Lanny McDonald 15.00 40.00
FAMC Bryan McCabe 10.00 25.00
FAMH Milan Hejduk 15.00 40.00
FAMK Miikka Kiprusoff 20.00 50.00
FAMM Mike Modano 20.00 50.00
FAMO Brendan Morrison 10.00 25.00
FAMR Mark Recchi 10.00 25.00
FANL Nicklas Lidstrom 15.00 40.00
FAPB Patrice Bergeron 15.00 40.00
FAPD Pavol Demitra 10.00 25.00
FAPE Patrik Elias 10.00 25.00
FAPM Patrick Marleau 15.00 40.00
FAPR Patrick Roy 50.00 100.00
FAPS Peter Stastny 10.00 25.00
FARB Rod Brind'Amour 15.00 40.00
FARL Roberto Luongo 20.00 50.00
FARM Ryan Miller 15.00 40.00
FARS Ryan Smyth 15.00 40.00
FASG Simon Gagne 15.00 40.00
FASK Saku Koivu 15.00 40.00
FASP Jason Spezza 15.00 40.00
FASS Steve Shutt 15.00 40.00
FASU Steve Sullivan 10.00 25.00
FASW Stephen Weiss 10.00 25.00
FATS Teemu Selanne 15.00 40.00
FATV Tomas Vokoun 15.00 40.00
FAWC Wendel Clark 15.00 40.00

2006-07 UD Artifacts Frozen Artifacts Patches Autographed Black Tag Parallel

COMPLETE SET (24)
PRINT RUN 1/1
NOT PRICED DUE TO SCARCITY
FACD Chris Drury
FACK Chuck Kobasew
FACP Chris Pronger
FADS Darryl Sittler
FAGA Glenn Anderson
FAHZ Henrik Zetterberg
FAJB Jay Bouwmeester
FAJC Jeff Carter
FAJI Jarome Iginla
FAJL Joffrey Lupul
FAJO Jonathan Cheechoo
FAMH Milan Hejduk
FAMK Miikka Kiprusoff
FAPM Patrick Marleau
FAPR Patrick Roy
FAPS Peter Stastny
FARL Roberto Luongo
FARM Ryan Miller
FARS Ryan Smyth
FASK Saku Koivu
FASS Steve Shutt
FASW Stephen Weiss
FATV Tomas Vokoun
FAWC Wendel Clark

2006-07 UD Artifacts Rookie Redemptions

STATED ODDS 1:10 PACKS
RED1 Anaheim Ducks 3.00 8.00
RED2 Atlanta Thrashers 3.00 8.00
RED3 Boston Bruins 12.00 30.00
RED4 Buffalo Sabres 10.00 25.00
RED5 Calgary Flames 8.00 20.00
RED6 Carolina Hurricanes 3.00 8.00
RED7 Chicago Blackhawks 3.00 8.00
RED8 Colorado Avalanche 12.00 30.00
RED9 Columbus Blue Jackets 3.00 8.00
RED10 Dallas Stars 3.00 8.00
RED11 Detroit Red Wings 5.00 12.00
RED12 Edmonton Oilers 8.00 20.00
RED13 Florida Panthers 3.00 8.00
RED14 Los Angeles Kings 15.00 40.00
RED15 Minnesota Wild 6.00 15.00
RED16 Montreal Canadiens 12.00 30.00
RED17 Nashville Predators 12.00 30.00
RED18 New Jersey Devils 6.00 15.00
RED19 New York Islanders 3.00 8.00
RED20 New York Rangers 3.00 8.00
RED21 Ottawa Senators 3.00 8.00
RED22 Philadelphia Flyers 3.00 8.00
RED23 Phoenix Coyotes 3.00 8.00
RED24 Pittsburgh Penguins 75.00 150.00
RED25 San Jose Sharks 6.00 15.00
RED26 St. Louis Blues 3.00 8.00
RED27 Tampa Bay Lightning 3.00 8.00
RED28 Toronto Maple Leafs 6.00 15.00
RED29 Vancouver Canucks 6.00 15.00
RED30 Washington Capitals 3.00 8.00
RED31 Wild Card 25.00 60.00
RED32 Wild Card 10.00 25.00
RED33 Wild Card 3.00 8.00
RED34 Wild Card 10.00 25.00
RED35 Wild Card 5.00 15.00
RED36 Wild Card 5.00 15.00
RED37 Wild Card 5.00 15.00
RED38 Wild Card 5.00 15.00
RED39 Wild Card 6.00 15.00
RED40 Wild Card 5.00 15.00
RED41 Wild Card 5.00 15.00
RED42 Wild Card 5.00 15.00

2006-07 UD Artifacts Treasured Patches Black

TSAF Alexander Frolov
TSAH Ales Hemsky
TSAK Alex Kovalev
TSAM Al MacInnis
TSAO Alexander Ovechkin
TSAR Jason Arnott
TSBB Bob Bourne
TSBC Bobby Clarke
TSBG Bill Guerin
TSBL Rob Blake
TSBP Bob Probert
TSBS Borje Salming
TSCJ Curtis Joseph
TSCN Cam Neely
TSDG Doug Gilmour
TSDW Dave Williams
TSEB Ed Belfour
TSEL Eric Lindros
TSGF Grant Fuhr
TSIK Ilya Kovalchuk
TSJA Jason Allison
TSJG Jean-Sebastien Giguere
TSJJ Jaromir Jagr
TSJN Joe Nieuwendyk
TSJT Joe Thornton
TSKP Keith Primeau
TSKT Keith Tkachuk
TSMB Martin Brodeur
TSMF Manny Fernandez
TSMH Marian Hossa
TSML Mario Lemieux
TSMM Mike Modano
TSMN Markus Naslund
TSMR Mark Recchi
TSMT Marty Turco
TSNK Nikolai Khabibulin
TSOK Olaf Kolzig
TSPF Peter Forsberg
TSPK Paul Kariya
TSRB Ray Bourque
TSRN Rick Nash
TSRV Rick Vaive
TSRY Michael Ryder
TSSC Sidney Crosby
TSSF Sergei Fedorov
TSSG Scott Gomez
TSSK Saku Koivu
TSSN Scott Niedermayer
TSWE Doug Weight

2006-07 UD Artifacts Treasured Patches Blue

*BLUE SAME PRICE AS RED
PRINT RUN 25 SER. #'d SETS

2006-07 UD Artifacts Treasured Patches Platinum

COMPLETE SET (50)
PRINT RUN 5 SER. #'d SETS
NOT PRICED DUE TO SCARCITY

2006-07 UD Artifacts Treasured Patches Red

PRINT RUN 35 SER. #'d SETS
TSAF Alexander Frolov 10.00 25.00
TSAH Ales Hemsky 10.00 25.00
TSAK Alex Kovalev 8.00 20.00
TSAM Al MacInnis 8.00 20.00
TSAO Alexander Ovechkin
TSAR Jason Arnott 8.00 20.00
TSBB Bob Bourne 8.00 20.00
TSBC Bobby Clarke 15.00 40.00
TSBG Bill Guerin 8.00 20.00
TSBL Rob Blake 10.00 25.00
TSBN Bob Nystrom 8.00 20.00
TSBP Bob Probert 15.00 40.00
TSBS Borje Salming 15.00 40.00
TSCJ Curtis Joseph 15.00 40.00
TSCN Cam Neely 15.00 40.00
TSDG Doug Gilmour 15.00 40.00
TSDW Dave Williams 15.00 40.00
TSEB Ed Belfour 15.00 40.00
TSEL Eric Lindros 15.00 40.00
TSGF Grant Fuhr 15.00 40.00
TSIK Ilya Kovalchuk 20.00 50.00
TSJA Jason Allison 8.00 20.00
TSJG Jean-Sebastien Giguere 10.00 25.00
TSJJ Jaromir Jagr 20.00 50.00
TSJN Joe Nieuwendyk 10.00 25.00
TSJT Joe Thornton 20.00 50.00
TSKP Keith Primeau 8.00 20.00
TSKT Keith Tkachuk 10.00 25.00
TSMB Martin Brodeur 25.00 60.00
TSMF Manny Fernandez 10.00 25.00
TSMH Marian Hossa 15.00 40.00
TSML Mario Lemieux 30.00 80.00
TSMM Mike Modano 20.00 50.00
TSMN Markus Naslund 15.00 40.00
TSMR Mark Recchi 8.00 20.00
TSMT Marty Turco 15.00 40.00
TSNK Nikolai Khabibulin 15.00 40.00
TSOK Olaf Kolzig 20.00 50.00
TSPF Peter Forsberg 20.00 50.00
TSPK Paul Kariya 15.00 40.00
TSRB Ray Bourque 15.00 40.00
TSRN Rick Nash 20.00 50.00
TSRV Rick Vaive 8.00 20.00
TSRY Michael Ryder 15.00 40.00
TSSC Sidney Crosby 100.00 175.00
TSSF Sergei Fedorov 15.00 40.00
TSSG Scott Gomez 8.00 20.00
TSSK Saku Koivu 15.00 40.00
TSSN Scott Niedermayer 10.00 25.00
TSWE Doug Weight 10.00 25.00

2006-07 UD Artifacts Treasured Patches Autographed Black Tag Parallel

COMPLETE SET (24)
PRINT RUN 1/1
NOT PRICED DUE TO SCARCITY
TSAF Alexander Frolov
TSAH Ales Hemsky
TSAO Alexander Ovechkin
TSBB Bob Bourne
TSBL Rob Blake
TSBP Bob Probert
TSBS Borje Salming
TSCN Cam Neely
TSDW Dave Williams
TSGF Grant Fuhr
TSIK Ilya Kovalchuk
TSJT Joe Thornton
TSMB Martin Brodeur
TSMH Marian Hossa
TSML Mario Lemieux
TSMN Markus Naslund
TSMT Marty Turco
TSRB Ray Bourque
TSRN Rick Nash
TSRY Michael Ryder
TSSC Sidney Crosby
TSSG Scott Gomez
TSSK Saku Koivu
TSWE Doug Weight

2006-07 UD Artifacts Treasured Swatches

PRINT RUN 250 SER. #'d SETS
TSAF Alexander Frolov 2.00 5.00
TSAH Ales Hemsky 2.50 6.00
TSAK Alex Kovalev 2.00 5.00
TSAM Al MacInnis 2.00 5.00
TSAO Alexander Ovechkin 10.00 25.00
TSAR Jason Arnott 2.00 5.00
TSBB Bob Bourne 2.00 5.00
TSBC Bobby Clarke 3.00 8.00
TSBG Bill Guerin 2.00 5.00
TSBL Rob Blake 2.50 6.00
TSBN Bob Nystrom 2.00 5.00
TSBP Bob Probert 4.00 10.00
TSBS Borje Salming 2.50 6.00
TSCJ Curtis Joseph 3.00 8.00
TSCN Cam Neely 3.00 8.00
TSDG Doug Gilmour 3.00 8.00
TSDW Dave Williams 2.50 6.00
TSEB Ed Belfour 3.00 8.00
TSEL Eric Lindros 3.00 8.00
TSGF Grant Fuhr 3.00 8.00
TSIK Ilya Kovalchuk 5.00 12.00
TSJA Jason Allison 2.00 5.00
TSJG Jean-Sebastien Giguere 2.50 6.00
TSJJ Jaromir Jagr 5.00 12.00
TSJN Joe Nieuwendyk 2.00 5.00
TSJT Joe Thornton 5.00 12.00
TSKP Keith Primeau 2.00 5.00
TSKT Keith Tkachuk 3.00 8.00
TSMB Martin Brodeur 8.00 20.00
TSMF Manny Fernandez 2.50 6.00
TSMH Marian Hossa 3.00 8.00
TSML Mario Lemieux 12.00 30.00
TSMM Mike Modano 5.00 12.00
TSMN Markus Naslund 3.00 8.00
TSMR Mark Recchi 2.00 5.00
TSMT Marty Turco 3.00 8.00
TSNK Nikolai Khabibulin 3.00 8.00
TSOK Olaf Kolzig 3.00 8.00
TSPF Peter Forsberg 5.00 12.00
TSPK Paul Kariya 3.00 8.00
TSRB Ray Bourque 5.00 12.00
TSRN Rick Nash 4.00 10.00
TSRV Rick Vaive 2.00 5.00
TSRY Michael Ryder 2.50 6.00
TSSC Sidney Crosby 15.00 40.00
TSSF Sergei Fedorov 3.00 8.00
TSSG Scott Gomez 2.00 5.00
TSSK Saku Koivu 3.00 8.00
TSSN Scott Niedermayer 2.00 5.00
TSWE Doug Weight 2.00 5.00

2006-07 UD Artifacts Treasured Swatches Black

COMPLETE SET (50)
PRINT RUN 1/1
NOT PRICED DUE TO SCARCITY
TSAF Alexander Frolov
TSAH Ales Hemsky
TSAK Alex Kovalev
TSAM Al MacInnis
TSAO Alexander Ovechkin
TSAR Jason Arnott
TSBB Bob Bourne
TSBC Bobby Clarke
TSBG Bill Guerin
TSBL Rob Blake
TSBN Bob Nystrom
TSBP Bob Probert
TSBS Borje Salming
TSCJ Curtis Joseph
TSCN Cam Neely
TSDG Doug Gilmour
TSDW Dave Williams
TSEB Ed Belfour
TSEL Eric Lindros
TSGF Grant Fuhr
TSIK Ilya Kovalchuk
TSJA Jason Allison
TSJG Jean-Sebastien Giguere
TSJJ Jaromir Jagr
TSJN Joe Nieuwendyk
TSJT Joe Thornton
TSKP Keith Primeau
TSKT Keith Tkachuk
TSMB Martin Brodeur
TSMF Manny Fernandez
TSMH Marian Hossa
TSML Mario Lemieux
TSMM Mike Modano
TSMN Markus Naslund
TSMR Mark Recchi
TSMT Marty Turco
TSNK Nikolai Khabibulin
TSOK Olaf Kolzig
TSPF Peter Forsberg
TSPK Paul Kariya
TSRB Ray Bourque
TSRN Rick Nash
TSRV Rick Vaive
TSRY Michael Ryder
TSSC Sidney Crosby
TSSF Sergei Fedorov
TSSG Scott Gomez
TSSK Saku Koivu
TSSN Scott Niedermayer
TSWE Doug Weight

2006-07 UD Artifacts Treasured Swatches Blue

*BLUE: .75X TO 1.5X HI
PRINT RUN 50 SER. #'d SETS

2006-07 UD Artifacts Treasured Swatches Platinum

PRINT RUN 10 SER. #'d SETS
NOT PRICED DUE TO SCARCITY

2006-07 UD Artifacts Treasured Swatches Red

*RED: .50X TO 1.25X HI
PRINT RUN 100 SER. #'d SETS

2006-07 UD Artifacts Treasured Swatches Autographed Black

COMPLETE SET (26)
PRINT RUN 1/1
NOT PRICED DUE TO SCARCITY
TSAF Alexander Frolov
TSAH Ales Hemsky
TSAO Alexander Ovechkin
TSBB Bob Bourne
TSBL Rob Blake
TSBN Bob Nystrom
TSBP Bob Probert
TSBS Borje Salming
TSCN Cam Neely
TSDW Dave Williams
TSGF Grant Fuhr
TSIK Ilya Kovalchuk
TSJT Joe Thornton
TSMB Martin Brodeur
TSMH Marian Hossa
TSML Mario Lemieux
TSMN Markus Naslund
TSMT Marty Turco
TSRB Ray Bourque
TSRN Rick Nash
TSRV Rick Vaive
TSRY Michael Ryder
TSSC Sidney Crosby
TSSG Scott Gomez
TSSK Saku Koivu
TSWE Doug Weight

2006-07 UD Artifacts Tundra Tandems

PRINT RUN 125 SER. #'d SETS
TTAB Andrew Raycroft 5.00 12.00
Bryan McCabe
TTAD Maxim Afinogenov 4.00 10.00
Chris Drury
TTAG Glenn Anderson 30.00 80.00
Wayne Gretzky/50
TTAK Glenn Anderson 4.00 10.00
Mike Krushelnyski
TTAM Matt Stajan 5.00 12.00
Alexander Steen
TTAS Sergei Samsonov 4.00 10.00
Alex Kovalev
TTBB Brad Boyes 6.00 15.00
Patrice Bergeron
TTBE Martin Brodeur 8.00 20.00
Patrik Elias
TTBJ Brendan Shanahan 8.00 20.00
Jaromir Jagr
TTBN Bob Nystrom 4.00 10.00
Bob Bourne
TTBO Johnny Bucyk 8.00 20.00
Ray Bourque
TTBR Brian Rolston 4.00 10.00
Pierre-Marc Bouchard
TTCA Cam Neely 8.00 20.00
Adam Oates
TTCE Curtis Joseph 5.00 12.00
Ed Jovanovski
TTCG Wendel Clark 10.00 25.00
Doug Gilmour
TTCL Dino Ciccarelli 4.00 10.00
Rod Langway
TTCN Mike Comrie 4.00 10.00
Ladislav Nagy
TTCR Cam Neely 8.00 20.00
Ray Bourque
TTDB Darryl Sittler 8.00 20.00
Borje Salming
TTDD Daniel Alfredsson 6.00 15.00
Dany Heatley
TTDH Tomas Holmstrom 5.00 12.00
Pavel Datsyuk
TTDO Trevor Daley 4.00 10.00
Steve Ott
TTDR Richard Brodeur 5.00 12.00
Dave Williams
TTDW Kris Draper 4.00 10.00
Jason Williams
TTEJ Ed Belfour 5.00 12.00
Jay Bouwmeester
TTFB Rob Blake 4.00 10.00
Alexander Frolov
TTFG Peter Forsberg 6.00 15.00
Simon Gagne
TTFP Manny Fernandez 4.00 10.00
Mark Parrish
TTFR Grant Fuhr 8.00 20.00
Bill Ranford
TTGC Simon Gagne 5.00 12.00
Jeff Carter
TTGD Marian Gaborik 5.00 12.00
Pavol Demitra
TTGG Scott Gomez 4.00 10.00
Brian Gionta
TTGP Guy Lafleur 8.00 20.00
Peter Stastny
TTHD Henrik Sedin 5.00 12.00
Daniel Sedin
TTHK Marian Hossa 8.00 20.00
Ilya Kovalchuk
TTHO Dominik Hasek 8.00 20.00
Chris Osgood
TTHP Marcel Hossa 4.00 10.00
Petr Prucha
TTHS Milan Hejduk 4.00 10.00
Marek Svatos
TTHU Scott Hartnell 4.00 10.00
Scottie Upshall
TTIT Jarome Iginla 6.00 15.00
Alex Tanguay
TTJA Joe Mullen 4.00 10.00
Al MacInnis
TTJH Jason Spezza 6.00 15.00
Dany Heatley
TTJJ Joffrey Lupul 4.00 10.00
Jarret Stoll
TTKA Paul Kariya 4.00 10.00
Jason Arnott
TTKH Nikolai Khabibulin 4.00 10.00
Martin Havlat
TTKK Saku Koivu 5.00 12.00
Alex Kovalev
TTKL Ilya Kovalchuk 6.00 15.00
Kari Lehtonen
TTKO Olaf Kolzig 12.00 30.00
Alexander Ovechkin
TTKP Miikka Kiprusoff 8.00 20.00
Dion Phaneuf
TTLB Guy Lafleur 15.00 40.00
Jean Beliveau
TTLC Mario Lemieux 40.00 80.00
Sidney Crosby
TTLM John LeClair 4.00 10.00
Mark Recchi
TTLN Markus Naslund 6.00 15.00
Roberto Luongo
TTLR Vincent Lecavalier 6.00 15.00
Brad Richards
TTLS Guy Lafleur 6.00 15.00
Steve Shutt
TTLZ Luc Robitaille 4.00 10.00
Zigmund Palffy
TTMB Ryan Miller 6.00 15.00
Martin Biron
TTMC Larry Murphy 4.00 10.00
Chris Chelios
TTME Lanny McDonald 6.00 15.00
Ron Ellis
TTML Mike Modano 6.00 15.00
Eric Lindros
TTMM Lanny McDonald 4.00 10.00
Al MacInnis
TTMR Miroslav Satan 4.00 10.00
Rick DiPietro
TTMS Glen Murray 4.00 10.00
Marc Savard
TTMT Bryan McCabe 6.00 15.00
Darcy Tucker
TTNF Rick Nash 6.00 15.00
Sergei Fedorov
TTNG Scott Niedermayer 4.00 10.00
Jean-Sebastien Giguere
TTNH Nicklas Lidstrom 6.00 15.00
Henrik Zetterberg
TTNO Markus Naslund 4.00 10.00
Mattias Ohlund
TTNP Chris Pronger 5.00 12.00
Scott Niedermayer
TTNR Joe Nieuwendyk 4.00 10.00
Gary Roberts
TTNY Mike York 4.00 10.00
Trent Hunter
TTOT Olli Jokinen 4.00 10.00
Todd Bertuzzi
TTPJ Patrick Roy 15.00 40.00
Joe Sakic
TTPK Patrick Roy 10.00 25.00
Kirk Muller
TTPM Patrick Marleau 4.00 10.00
Mark Bell
TTPT Pascal Leclaire 4.00 10.00
Ty Conklin
TTRB Patrick Roy 15.00 40.00
Ray Bourque
TTRD Shane Doan 4.00 10.00
Jeremy Roenick
TTRK Tuomo Ruutu 4.00 10.00
Nikolai Khabibulin
TTRM Mark Recchi 4.00 10.00
Ryan Malone
TTRR Mike Ribeiro 4.00 10.00
Michael Ryder
TTRS Ryan Smyth 4.00 10.00
Shawn Horcoff
TTSF Martin St. Louis 4.00 10.00
Ruslan Fedotenko
TTSJ Sami Kapanen 4.00 10.00
Joni Pitkanen
TTSM Marc Denis 4.00 10.00
Sean Burke
TTSP Teemu Selanne 6.00 15.00
Corey Perry
TTST Joe Sakic 8.00 20.00
Jose Theodore
TTSV Darryl Sittler 8.00 20.00
Rick Vaive
TTSW Eric Staal 6.00 15.00
Cam Ward
TTTC Joe Thornton 8.00 20.00
Jonathan Cheechoo
TTTG Keith Tkachuk 4.00 10.00
Bill Guerin
TTTM Marty Turco 4.00 10.00
Brenden Morrow
TTTO Mats Sundin 5.00 12.00
Michael Peca
TTTW Doug Weight 4.00 10.00
Keith Tkachuk
TTVE Tomas Vokoun 4.00 10.00
Martin Erat
TTWA Wade Redden 4.00 10.00
Andrej Meszaros
TTWB Justin Williams 4.00 10.00
Rod Brind'Amour
TTWG Doug Weight 4.00 10.00
Bill Guerin
TTWS Denis Savard 4.00 10.00
Doug Wilson
TTZM Zdeno Chara 4.00 10.00
Milan Jurcina

2006-07 UD Artifacts Tundra Tandems Black

COMPLETE SET (100)
PRINT RUN 1/1
NOT PRICED DUE TO SCARCITY

2006-07 UD Artifacts Tundra Tandems Blue

*BLUE: .75X TO 1.5X HI
PRINT RUN 25 SER. #'d SETS
TTAG Glenn Anderson 75.00 125.00
Wayne Gretzky
TTKO Olaf Kolzig 30.00 75.00
Alexander Ovechkin
TTLC Mario Lemieux 60.00 100.00
Sidney Crosby
TTPJ Patrick Roy 25.00 60.00
Joe Sakic
TTRB Patrick Roy 25.00 60.00
Ray Bourque

2006-07 UD Artifacts Tundra Tandems Gold

PRINT RUN 10 SER. #'d SETS
NOT PRICED DUE TO SCARCITY

2006-07 UD Artifacts Tundra Tandems Red

* RED: .50X TO 1.25X HI
PRINT RUN 50 SER. #'d SETS

2006-07 UD Artifacts Tundra Tandems Dual Patches Red

PRINT RUN 25 SER. #'d SETS
NOT PRICED DUE TO SCARCITY
TTLC Mario Lemieux 100.00 175.00
Sidney Crosby

2002-03 UD Artistic Impressions

Released in mid-April 2003, this 135-card set featured artist renderings of the featured player's on the card fronts. Rookies in this set were inserted at 1:4.

COMPLETE SET (135) 60.00 125.00
COMP.SET w/o SP's (90) 20.00 40.00
1 J-S Giguere .20 .50
2 Paul Kariya .25 .60
3 Dany Heatley .40 1.00
4 Ilya Kovalchuk .40 1.00
5 Ray Bourque .60 1.50
6 Joe Thornton .50 1.25
7 Bobby Orr 2.00 5.00
8 Sergei Samsonov .20 .50
9 Maxim Afinogenov .10 .25
10 Martin Biron .20 .50
11 Miroslav Satan .20 .50
12 Roman Turek .20 .50
13 Jarome Iginla .30 .75
14 Arturs Irbe .20 .50
15 Ron Francis .20 .50
16 Jeff O'Neill .10 .25
17 Alexei Zhamnov .10 .25
18 Eric Daze .20 .50
19 Jocelyn Thibault .20 .50
20 Rob Blake .20 .50
21 Patrick Roy 1.50 4.00
22 Joe Sakic .60 1.50
23 Peter Forsberg .75 2.00
24 Ray Bourque .60 1.50
25 Marc Denis .20 .50
26 Espen Knutsen .10 .25
27 Rostislav Klesla .10 .25
28 Marty Turco .20 .50
29 Bill Guerin .20 .50
30 Mike Modano .50 1.25
31 Steve Yzerman 1.50 4.00
32 Nicklas Lidstrom .25 .60
33 Sergei Fedorov .50 1.25
34 Curtis Joseph .25 .60
35 Brendan Shanahan .25 .60
36 Gordie Howe 1.50 4.00
37 Mike Comrie .20 .50
38 Tommy Salo .20 .50
39 Wayne Gretzky 2.00 5.00
40 Roberto Luongo .30 .75
41 Kristian Huselius .10 .25
42 Zigmund Palffy .20 .50
43 Felix Potvin .25 .60
44 Jason Allison .10 .25
45 Manny Fernandez .20 .50
46 Marian Gaborik .60 1.50
47 Saku Koivu .25 .60
48 Doug Gilmour .20 .50
49 Jose Theodore .30 .75
50 David Legwand .20 .50
51 Tomas Vokoun .20 .50
52 Martin Brodeur .75 2.00
53 Patrik Elias .20 .50
54 Joe Nieuwendyk .20 .50
55 Alexei Yashin .10 .25
56 Michael Peca .10 .25
57 Chris Osgood .20 .50
58 Eric Lindros .25 .60
59 Pavel Bure .25 .60
60 Brian Leetch .20 .50
61 Martin Havlat .20 .50
62 Marian Hossa .25 .60
63 Daniel Alfredsson .20 .50
64 John LeClair .25 .60
65 Jeremy Roenick .30 .75
66 Simon Gagne .25 .60
67 Tony Amonte .20 .50
68 Sean Burke .20 .50
69 Daniel Briere .10 .25
70 Alex Kovalev .20 .50
71 Johan Hedberg .20 .50
72 Mario Lemieux 2.00 5.00
73 Teemu Selanne .25 .60
74 Evgeni Nabokov .20 .50
75 Owen Nolan .20 .50
76 Chris Pronger .20 .50
77 Doug Weight .20 .50
78 Keith Tkachuk .25 .60
79 Brad Richards .20 .50
80 Nikolai Khabibulin .25 .60
81 Vincent Lecavalier .25 .60
82 Mats Sundin .25 .60
83 Ed Belfour .25 .60
84 Alexander Mogilny .20 .50
85 Todd Bertuzzi .25 .60
86 Dan Cloutier .20 .50
87 Markus Naslund .25 .60
88 Jaromir Jagr .50 1.25
89 Peter Bondra .20 .50
90 Olaf Kolzig .20 .50
91 Jonathan Hedstrom RC .75 2.00
92 Henrik Zetterberg RC 3.00 8.00
93 Steve Ott RC 1.25 3.00
94 Jay Bouwmeester RC 1.50 4.00
95 Rick Nash RC 4.00 10.00
96 Pascal LeClaire RC 1.25 3.00
97 Jason Spezza RC 3.00 8.00
98 Dick Tarnstrom RC .75 2.00
99 Alexei Smirnov RC 1.00 2.50

100 Ron Hainsey RC .75 2.00
101 Michael Leighton RC 1.00 2.50
102 Ian MacNeil RC .75 2.00
103 Anton Volchenkov RC .75 2.00
104 Ales Hemsky RC 1.50 4.00
105 Steve Eminger RC .75 2.00
106 Shaone Morrisonn RC .75 2.00
107 Levente Szuper RC .75 2.00
108 Brooks Orpik RC .75 2.00
109 Curtis Sanford RC 1.00 2.50
110 Jared Aulin RC .75 2.00
111 Eric Godard RC .75 2.00
112 Jim Fahey RC .75 2.00
113 Rickard Wallin RC .75 2.00
114 Mike Cammalleri RC 1.00 2.50
115 Mikael Tellqvist RC .75 2.00
116 Chuck Kobasew RC 1.00 2.50
117 Scottie Upshall RC 1.25 3.00
118 Jerred Smithson RC .75 2.00
119 Jeff Taffe RC .75 2.00
120 Cody Rudkowsky RC .75 2.00
121 Alexander Frolov RC 1.50 4.00
122 Alexander Svitov RC 1.00 2.50
123 Stanislav Chistov RC 1.00 2.50
124 P-M Bouchard RC 1.50 4.00
125 Patrick Sharp RC .75 2.00
126 Ryan Miller RC 2.50 6.00
127 Tomas Malec RC .75 2.00
128 Curtis Murphy RC .75 2.00
129 Jordan Leopold RC .75 2.00
130 Carlo Colaiacovo RC 1.00 2.50
131 Alexei Semenov RC .75 2.00
132 Craig Andersson RC .75 2.00
133 Jim Vandermeer RC .75 2.00
134 Ray Emery RC 2.00 5.00
135 Paul Manning RC .75 2.00

2002-03 UD Artistic Impressions Gold

*STARS: 1.5X TO 4X
STATED PRINT RUN 199 SER.#'d SETS
*SP's: .75X TO 2X
SP STATED PRINT RUN 75 SER.#'d SETS

2002-03 UD Artistic Impressions Artist's Touch

Singles in this 25-card memorabilia set were serial-numbered to 499 copies each.
*MULT.COLOR SWATCH: .5X TO 1.25X HI
ATBS Brendan Shanahan 3.00 8.00
ATCJ Curtis Joseph 3.00 8.00
ATDH Dany Heatley 4.00 10.00
ATFP Felix Potvin 3.00 8.00
ATIK Ilya Kovalchuk 5.00 12.00
ATJI Jarome Iginla 4.00 10.00
ATJJ Jaromir Jagr 4.00 10.00
ATJR Jeremy Roenick 4.00 10.00
ATJS Joe Sakic 5.00 12.00
ATJT Joe Thornton 5.00 12.00
ATMB Martin Brodeur 8.00 20.00
ATMD Mike Dunham 3.00 8.00
ATML Mario Lemieux 10.00 25.00
ATMM Mike Modano 5.00 12.00
ATMS Mats Sundin 3.00 8.00
ATOK Olaf Kolzig 3.00 8.00
ATPF Peter Forsberg 5.00 12.00
ATPK Paul Kariya 3.00 8.00
ATPR Patrick Roy 10.00 25.00
ATRB Ray Bourque 5.00 12.00
ATSB Sean Burke 3.00 8.00
ATSF Sergei Fedorov 4.00 10.00
ATSG Simon Gagne 3.00 8.00
ATTH Jose Theodore 4.00 10.00
ATZP Zigmund Palffy 3.00 8.00

2002-03 UD Artistic Impressions Artist's Touch Gold

*STARS: .5X TO 1.25X BASIC INSERTS
STATED PRINT RUN 199 SER.#'d SETS

2002-03 UD Artistic Impressions Artwork Originals

Randomly inserted, these one of one framed prints were the original art used for the set. Several of the pieces were signed by the player though we are unable to verify which ones exactly as only a few have been verified. These pieces are not priced due to scarcity.
AI1 Ray Bourque AU
AI2 Martin Brodeur AU
AI3 Simon Gagne
AI4 Mike Comrie
AI5 Dany Heatley
AI6 Gordie Howe
AI7 Jarome Iginla
AI8 Curtis Joseph
AI9 Ilya Kovalchuk
AI10 John LeClair
AI11 Markus Naslund
AI12 Nikolai Khabibulin
AI13 Patrick Roy
AI14 Sergei Samsonov AU
AI15 Jose Theodore
AI16 Joe Thornton AU
AI17 Steve Yzerman AU
AI18 Martin Havlat
AI19 Marty Turco
AI20 Brad Richards

2002-03 UD Artistic Impressions Artwork Signed

Inserted at one per case, these framed prints of the artwork used for the set carried certified player autographs under the print in the frame.
AI1 Ray Bourque 60.00 150.00
AI2 Martin Brodeur 100.00 200.00
AI3 Pavel Bure 30.00 80.00
AI4 Mike Comrie 25.00 60.00
AI5 Dany Heatley 40.00 100.00
AI6 Gordie Howe 200.00 400.00
AI7 Jarome Iginla 30.00 80.00
AI8 Curtis Joseph 50.00 125.00
AI9 Ilya Kovalchuk 60.00 150.00
AI10 John LeClair 25.00 60.00
AI11 Markus Naslund 25.00 60.00
AI12 Bobby Orr 300.00 600.00
AI13 Patrick Roy 100.00 250.00
AI14 Sergei Samsonov 25.00 60.00
AI15 Jose Theodore 50.00 125.00
AI16 Joe Thornton 60.00 150.00
AI17 Steve Yzerman 75.00 200.00

2002-03 UD Artistic Impressions Beckett Promos

Inserted into copies of the June 2003 issue of Beckett Hockey Collector, this 90-card set parallels the base set but carried a silver foil "UD Promo" stamp across the card fronts. Due to the type of distribution and the wide range of prices realized by these cards in the secondary market, they are not priced.
NOT PRICED DUE TO SCARCITY

2002-03 UD Artistic Impressions Common Ground

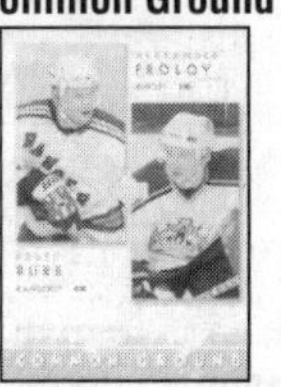

COMPLETE SET (22) 20.00 40.00
STATED ODDS 1:8
CG1 Patrick Roy 2.00 5.00
Pascal Leclaire
CG2 Ales Hemsky 1.25 3.00
Jaromir Jagr
CG3 Wayne Gretzky 2.50 6.00
Jason Spezza
CG4 Jay Bouwmeester 1.25 3.00
Nicklas Lidstrom
CG5 Roman Cechmanek 1.25 3.00
Levente Szuper
CG6 R.Nash/M.Lemieux 2.00 5.00
CG7 Ray Bourque 1.50 4.00
Jay Bouwmeester
CG8 Pierre-Marc Bouchard 1.25 3.00
Saku Koivu
CG9 G.Howe/R.Nash 1.50 4.00
CG10 Alexander Frolov 1.25 3.00
Pavel Bure
CG11 Rob Blake 1.25 3.00
Brooks Orpik
CG12 Henrik Zetterberg 1.25 3.00
Mats Sundin
CG13 Sergei Samsonov 1.25 3.00
Stanislav Chistov
CG14 Jordan Leopold 1.25 3.00
Ray Bourque
CG15 Bill Guerin 1.25 3.00
Chuck Kobasew
CG16 Alexander Svitov 1.25 3.00
Sergei Federov
CG17 Jeremy Roenick 1.50 4.00
Scottie Upshall
CG18 Carlo Colaiacovo 1.25 3.00
Nicklas Lidstrom
CG19 Steve Yzerman 1.25 3.00
Steve Ott
CG20 J.Taffe/M.Modano 1.25 3.00
CG21 Peter Forsberg 2.00 5.00
Henrik Zetterberg
CG22 P.LeClaire/M.Brodeur 1.50 4.00

2002-03 UD Artistic Impressions Common Ground Gold

*STARS: 1.5X TO 4X BASIC INSERTS
STATED PRINT RUN 150 SER.#'d SETS

2002-03 UD Artistic Impressions Flashbacks

STATED ODDS 1:20
UD1 Joe Sakic 2.00 5.00
UD2 Mike Modano 1.50 4.00
UD3 Mario Lemieux 3.00 8.00
UD4 Brian Leetch .75 2.00
UD5 Ron Francis .75 2.00
UD6 Pavel Bure .75 2.00
UD7 Ray Bourque 2.00 5.00
UD8 Sergei Fedorov 1.50 4.00
UD9 Jaromir Jagr 1.50 4.00
UD10 Jeremy Roenick 1.00 2.50
UD11 Gordie Howe 2.50 6.00

2002-03 UD Artistic Impressions Flashbacks Gold

*STARS: .75X TO 2X BASIC INSERTS
STATED PRINT RUN 75 SER.#'d SETS

2002-03 UD Artistic Impressions Great Depictions

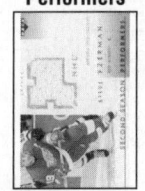

COMPLETE SET (12) 20.00 40.00
STATED ODDS 1:20
GD1 Wayne Gretzky 3.00 8.00
GD2 Patrick Roy 2.50 6.00
GD3 Martin Brodeur 2.50 6.00
GD4 Bobby Orr 3.00 8.00
GD5 Ilya Kovalchuk 1.00 2.50
GD6 Mario Lemieux 3.00 8.00
GD7 Ray Bourque 2.00 5.00
GD8 Steve Yzerman 2.50 6.00
GD9 Gordie Howe 2.00 5.00
GD10 Pavel Bure .75 2.00
GD11 Marian Gaborik 1.50 4.00
GD12 Joe Thornton 1.25 3.00

2002-03 UD Artistic Impressions Great Depictions Gold

*STARS: .75X TO 2X BASIC INSERTS
STATED PRINT RUN 75 SER.#'d SETS

2002-03 UD Artistic Impressions Performers

Singles in this 6-card memorabilia set were serial-numbered to 199.
*MULT.COLOR SWATCH: .5X TO 1.25X HI
SSJJ Jaromir Jagr 4.00 10.00
SSJL John LeClair 3.00 8.00
SSMB Martin Brodeur 12.50 30.00
SSMM Mark Messier 3.00 8.00
SSPR Patrick Roy 15.00 40.00
SSSY Steve Yzerman 12.50 30.00

2002-03 UD Artistic Impressions Performers Gold

*STARS: .5X TO 1.25X BASIC INSERTS
STATED PRINT RUN 75 SER.#'d SETS

2002-03 UD Artistic Impressions Retrospectives

This 100-card set was inserted one per pack. These cards were smaller versions of the base card with colorful borders.
COMPLETE SET (100) 30.00 60.00
STATED ODDS 1:1
R1 J-S Giguere .25 .60
R2 Paul Kariya .30 .75
R3 Dany Heatley .40 1.00
R4 Ilya Kovalchuk .40 1.00
R5 Ray Bourque .60 1.50
R6 Joe Thornton .50 1.25
R7 Bobby Orr 2.00 5.00
R8 Sergei Samsonov .25 .60
R9 Maxim Afinogenov .25 .60
R10 Martin Biron .25 .60
R11 Miroslav Satan .25 .60
R12 Roman Turek .25 .60
R13 Jarome Iginla .40 1.00
R14 Arturs Irbe .25 .60
R15 Ron Francis .25 .60
R16 Jeff O'Neill .25 .60
R17 Alexei Zhamnov .25 .60
R18 Eric Daze .25 .60
R19 Jocelyn Thibault .25 .60
R20 Rob Blake .25 .60
R21 Patrick Roy 2.00 5.00
R22 Joe Sakic .60 1.50
R23 Peter Forsberg .75 2.00
R24 Ray Bourque .60 1.50
R25 Marc Denis .25 .60
R26 Espen Knutsen .25 .60
R27 Rostislav Klesla .25 .60
R28 Marty Turco .25 .60
R29 Bill Guerin .25 .60
R30 Mike Modano .50 1.25
R31 Steve Yzerman 1.50 4.00
R32 Nicklas Lidstrom .30 .75
R33 Sergei Fedorov .50 1.25
R34 Curtis Joseph .30 .75
R35 Brendan Shanahan .30 .75
R36 Gordie Howe 1.50 4.00
R37 Mike Comrie .25 .60
R38 Tommy Salo .25 .60
R39 Wayne Gretzky 2.00 5.00
R40 Roberto Luongo .40 1.00
R41 Kristian Huselius .25 .60
R42 Zigmund Palffy .25 .60
R43 Felix Potvin .30 .75
R44 Jason Allison .25 .60
R45 Manny Fernandez .25 .60
R46 Marian Gaborik .60 1.50
R47 Saku Koivu .30 .75
R48 Doug Gilmour .25 .60
R49 Jose Theodore .40 1.00
R50 David Legwand .25 .60
R51 Tomas Vokoun .25 .60
R52 Martin Brodeur 1.50 4.00
R53 Patrik Elias .25 .60
R54 Joe Nieuwendyk .25 .60
R55 Alexei Yashin .25 .60
R56 Michael Peca .25 .60
R57 Chris Osgood .25 .60
R58 Eric Lindros .30 .75
R59 Pavel Bure .30 .75
R60 Brian Leetch .25 .60
R61 Martin Havlat .25 .60
R62 Marian Hossa .30 .75
R63 Daniel Alfredsson .25 .60
R64 John LeClair .30 .75
R65 Jeremy Roenick .40 1.00
R66 Simon Gagne .30 .75
R67 Tony Amonte .25 .60
R68 Sean Burke .25 .60
R69 Daniel Briere .25 .60
R70 Alexei Kovalev .25 .60
R71 Johan Hedberg .25 .60
R72 Mario Lemieux 2.00 5.00
R73 Teemu Selanne .30 .75
R74 Evgeni Nabokov .25 .60
R75 Owen Nolan .25 .60
R76 Chris Pronger .25 .60
R77 Doug Weight .25 .60
R78 Keith Tkachuk .30 .75
R79 Brad Richards .25 .60
R80 Nikolai Khabibulin .30 .75
R81 Vincent Lecavalier .30 .75
R82 Mats Sundin .30 .75
R83 Ed Belfour .30 .75
R84 Alexander Mogilny .25 .60
R85 Todd Bertuzzi .30 .75
R86 Dan Cloutier .25 .60
R87 Markus Naslund .30 .75
R88 Jaromir Jagr .50 1.25
R89 Peter Bondra .25 .60
R90 Olaf Kolzig .25 .60
R91 Jason Spezza 2.50 6.00
R92 Rick Nash 3.00 8.00
R93 Jay Bouwmeester 2.00 5.00
R94 Stanislav Chistov 2.00 5.00
R95 P-M Bouchard 2.00 5.00
R96 Pascal LeClaire 2.00 5.00
R97 Brooks Orpik .75 2.00
R98 Steve Ott 1.25 3.00
R99 Alexander Frolov 1.50 4.00
R100 Alexander Svitov 1.00 2.50

2002-03 UD Artistic Impressions Retrospectives Gold

*STARS: 6X TO 15X BASIC INSERTS
STATED PRINT RUN 25 SER.#'d SETS
SKIP NUMBERED SET

2002-03 UD Artistic Impressions Retrospectives Signed

This autographed partial parallel set was serial-numbered to just 25 copies each. Cards are not priced due to scarcity.
STATED PRINT RUN 25 SER.#'d SETS
NOT PRICED DUE TO SCARCITY
SKIP NUMBERED SET

2002-03 UD Artistic Impressions Retrospectives Silver

*STARS: 1.5X TO 4X BASIC CARDS
STATED PRINT RUN 99 SER.#'d SETS

2002-03 UD Artistic Impressions Right Track

Singles in this 11-card memorabilia set were serial-numbered to 299.
*MULT.COLOR SWATCH: .5X TO 1.25X HI
RTAF Alexander Frolov 3.00 8.00
RTDB Daniel Briere 3.00 8.00
RTDH Dany Heatley 5.00 12.00
RTJA Jared Aulin 6.00 15.00
RTJL Jamie Lundmark 4.00 10.00

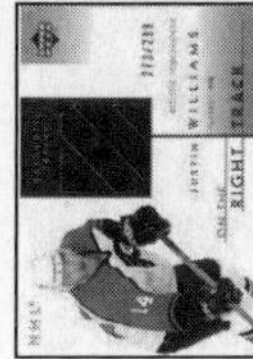

RTJW Justin Williams 3.00 8.00
RTKC Kyle Calder 3.00 8.00
RTMA Maxim Afinogenov 3.00 8.00
RTME Martin Erat 3.00 8.00
RTSC Stanislav Chistov 5.00 12.00
RTSR Steve Reinprecht 3.00 8.00

2002-03 UD Artistic Impressions Right Track Gold

*STARS: .5X TO 1.25X BASIC INSERTS
STATED PRINT RUN 175 SER.#'d SETS

2006-07 UD Biography of a Season

COMPLETE SET (15) 4.00 10.00
BOS1 Eric Staal .40 1.00
BOS2 Brendan Shanahan .40 1.00
BOS3 Mats Sundin .40 1.00
BOS4 Evgeni Malkin .75 2.00
BOS5 Evgeni Malkin .75 2.00
BOS6 Ryan Miller .75 2.00
BOS7 Patrick Roy .75 2.00
BOS8 Chris Pronger .40 1.00
BOS9 Sidney Crosby 1.25 3.00
BOS10 Alexander Ovechkin .75 2.00
BOS11 Daniel Briere .40 1.00
BOS12 Zach Parise .40 1.00
BOS13 Mark Recchi .40 1.00
BOS14 Joe Sakic .75 2.00
BOS15 Sidney Crosby 1.25 3.00

2001-02 UD Challenge for the Cup

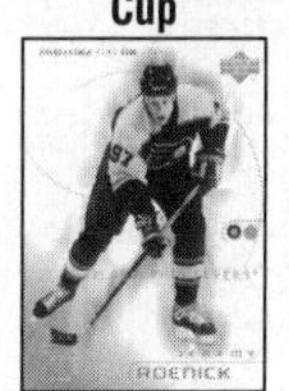

Released in mid-March 2002, this 135-card set carried an SRP of $4.99 per 5-card pack. Cards 91-135 were short printed to 1000 copies each of which 320 copies of each card were graded by Beckett Grading Services.
COMP.SET w/o SP's (90) 20.00 40.00
1 Paul Kariya .40 1.00
2 Jeff Friesen .10 .30
3 Dany Heatley .50 1.25
4 Milan Hnilicka .30 .75
5 Joe Thornton .60 1.50
6 Bill Guerin .30 .75
7 Miroslav Satan .30 .75
8 Martin Biron .30 .75
9 Jarome Iginla .50 1.25
10 Roman Turek .30 .75
11 Craig Conroy .10 .30
12 Jeff O'Neill .10 .30
13 Arturs Irbe .30 .75
14 Tony Amonte .30 .75
15 Steve Sullivan .10 .30
16 Rob Blake .30 .75
17 Joe Sakic .75 2.00
18 Milan Hejduk .40 1.00
19 Chris Drury .30 .75
20 Patrick Roy 2.00 5.00
21 Espen Knutsen .10 .30
22 Ray Whitney .10 .30
23 Pierre Turgeon .30 .75
24 Ed Belfour .40 1.00
25 Mike Modano .60 1.50
26 Sergei Zubov .10 .30
27 Dominik Hasek .75 2.00
28 Steve Yzerman 2.00 5.00
29 Brendan Shanahan .40 1.00
30 Nicklas Lidstrom .40 1.00
31 Luc Robitaille .30 .75
32 Mike Comrie .30 .75
33 Ryan Smyth .30 .75
34 Tommy Salo .30 .75
35 Roberto Luongo .50 1.25
36 Valeri Bure .10 .30
37 Pavel Bure .40 1.00
38 Felix Potvin .40 1.00
39 Jason Allison .10 .30
40 Zigmund Palffy .30 .75
41 Manny Fernandez .30 .75
42 Marian Gaborik .75 2.00
43 Andrew Brunette .10 .30
44 Brian Savage .10 .30
45 Jeff Hackett .10 .30
46 Oleg Petrov .10 .30
47 Cliff Ronning .10 .30
48 Mike Dunham .30 .75
49 Scott Walker .10 .30
50 Martin Brodeur 1.00 2.50
51 Scott Niedermayer .10 .30
52 Scott Gomez .10 .30
53 Patrik Elias .30 .75
54 Alexei Yashin .10 .30
55 Chris Osgood .30 .75
56 Mike Peca .10 .30
57 Mark Messier .40 1.00
58 Theo Fleury .10 .30
59 Eric Lindros .40 1.00
60 Brian Boucher .30 .75
61 John LeClair .40 1.00
62 Jeremy Roenick .50 1.25
63 Keith Primeau .10 .30
64 Michal Handzus .10 .30
65 Claude Lemieux .10 .30
66 Sean Burke .30 .75
67 Alexei Kovalev .30 .75
68 Mario Lemieux 2.50 6.00
69 Johan Hedberg .30 .75
70 Martin Straka .10 .30
71 Owen Nolan .30 .75
72 Evgeni Nabokov .30 .75
73 Teemu Selanne .40 1.00
74 Doug Weight .30 .75
75 Brent Johnson .30 .75
76 Pavol Demitra .30 .75
77 Chris Pronger .30 .75
78 Keith Tkachuk .40 1.00
79 Vincent Lecavalier .40 1.00
80 Brad Richards .30 .75
81 Nikolai Khabibulin .40 1.00
82 Curtis Joseph .40 1.00
83 Alexander Mogilny .30 .75
84 Mats Sundin .40 1.00
85 Trevor Linden .10 .30
86 Markus Naslund .40 1.00
87 Brendan Morrison .30 .75
88 Jaromir Jagr .60 1.50
89 Olaf Kolzig .30 .75
90 Peter Bondra .40 1.00
91 Ilja Bryzgalov RC 2.00 6.00
92 Timo Parssinen RC 1.25 3.00
93 Kevin Sawyer RC 1.25 3.00
94 Brian Pothier RC 1.25 3.00
95 Ilya Kovalchuk RC 10.00 25.00
96 Kamil Piros RC 1.25 3.00
97 Ivan Huml RC 1.25 3.00
98 Jukka Hentunen RC 1.25 3.00
99 Scott Nichol RC 1.25 3.00
100 Erik Cole RC 2.00 5.00
101 Jaroslav Obsut RC 1.25 3.00
102 Vaclav Nedorost RC 1.25 3.00
103 Martin Spanhel RC 1.25 3.00
104 Niko Kapanen RC 1.25 3.00
105 Pavel Datsyuk RC 6.00 15.00
106 Ty Conklin RC 1.25 3.00
107 Niklas Hagman RC 1.25 3.00
108 Kristian Huselius RC 1.25 3.00
109 Jaroslav Bednar RC 1.25 3.00
110 Pascal Dupuis RC 1.25 3.00
111 Mike Matteucci RC 1.25 3.00
112 Nick Schultz RC 1.25 3.00
113 Travis Roche RC 1.25 3.00
114 Martti Jarventie SP 1.25 3.00
115 Martin Erat RC 1.25 3.00
116 Pavel Skrbek RC 1.25 3.00
117 Josef Boumedienne RC 1.25 3.00
118 Andreas Salomonsson RC 1.25 3.00
119 Scott Clemmensen RC 1.25 3.00
120 Mikael Samuelsson RC 1.25 3.00
121 Dan Blackburn RC 1.25 3.00
122 Richard Scott RC 1.25 3.00
123 Radek Martinek RC 1.25 3.00
124 Raffi Torres RC 2.50 6.00
125 Ivan Ciernik RC 1.25 3.00
126 Jiri Dopita RC 1.25 3.00
127 Vaclav Pletka RC 1.25 3.00
128 Krys Kolanos RC 1.25 3.00
129 David Cullen RC 1.25 3.00
130 Jeff Jillson RC 1.25 3.00
131 Mark Rycroft RC 1.25 3.00
132 Ryan Tobler RC 1.25 3.00
133 Nikita Alexeev RC 1.25 3.00
134 Brian Sutherby RC 1.25 3.00
135 Chris Corrinet RC 1.25 3.00

2001-02 UD Challenge for the Cup 500 Game Winner

This 2-card set highlighted the career wins of Patrick Roy. Each card carried a swatch of game-worn jersey. One card also carried an authentic autograph and was serial-numbered to 25. The jersey only card was serial-numbered out of 300. Please note that both cards are numbered 500PR, the "A" on the autograph card is for checklisting only.
500PR Patrick Roy/300 60.00 150.00
500PRA Patrick Roy AU/25 400.00 800.00

2001-02 UD Challenge for the Cup All-Time Lineup

Serial-numbered out of 6, this 6-card set was not priced due to scarcity.
AT1 Bobby Hull
AT2 Wayne Gretzky
AT3 Gordie Howe
AT4 Bobby Orr
AT5 Ray Bourque
AT6 Patrick Roy

2001-02 UD Challenge for the Cup Backstops

Cards from this 10-card goalie set were serial-numbered out of 35 each.
BB1 Roman Turek 12.00 30.00

BB2 Arturs Irbe 12.00 30.00
BB3 Patrick Roy 40.00 100.00
BB4 Dominik Hasek 25.00 60.00
BB5 Tommy Salo 12.00 30.00
BB6 Martin Brodeur 30.00 80.00
BB7 Roman Cechmanek 12.00 30.00
BB8 Evgeni Nabokov 12.00 30.00
BB9 Curtis Joseph 15.00 40.00
BB10 Olaf Kolzig 15.00 40.00

2001-02 UD Challenge for the Cup Century Men

Cards from this 10-card set were serial-numbered to just 100 copies each.
COMPLETE SET (10) 125.00 250.00
CM1 Jeremy Roenick 8.00 20.00
CM2 Joe Sakic 10.00 25.00
CM3 Steve Yzerman 12.50 30.00
CM4 Sergei Fedorov 8.00 20.00
CM5 Luc Robitaille 6.00 15.00
CM6 Mark Messier 6.00 15.00
CM7 Jaromir Jagr 10.00 25.00
CM8 Mario Lemieux 15.00 40.00
CM9 Brett Hull 8.00 20.00
CM10 Pavel Bure 6.00 15.00

2001-02 UD Challenge for the Cup Cornerstones

Cards from this 10-card set were serial-numbered to just 250.
COMPLETE SET (10) 75.00 150.00
CR1 Paul Kariya 1.50 4.00
CR2 Ilya Kovalchuk 8.00 20.00
CR3 Joe Sakic 3.00 8.00
CR4 Mike Modano 2.50 6.00
CR5 Steve Yzerman 6.00 15.00
CR6 Pavel Bure 2.00 5.00
CR7 Mario Lemieux 10.00 25.00
CR8 Chris Pronger 1.25 3.00
CR9 Mats Sundin 1.50 4.00
CR10 Jaromir Jagr 2.50 6.00

2001-02 UD Challenge for the Cup Future Famers

Cards in this 6-card set were serial-numbered to just 25. This set was not priced due to scarcity.
FF1 Joe Sakic
FF2 Patrick Roy
FF3 Brett Hull
FF4 Luc Robitaille
FF5 Steve Yzerman
FF6 Mark Messier

2001-02 UD Challenge for the Cup Jerseys

Inserted at odds of 1:36, this 23-card set consisted of 4 different subsets: Terrific 200, Franchise Players, Then & Now, and Unstoppable Combos. The Then & Now and the Unstoppable Combos subsets featured two swatches of game used jerseys while the other subsets featured one swatch.
TCJ Curtis Joseph 4.00 10.00
TCO Chris Osgood 4.00 10.00
TDH Dominik Hasek 8.00 20.00
TEB Ed Belfour 6.00 15.00
TFP Felix Potvin 4.00 10.00
TMB Martin Brodeur 12.00 30.00

TMR Mike Richter 4.00 10.00
TPR Patrick Roy SP 20.00 50.00
TSB Sean Burke 4.00 10.00
TTB Tom Barrasso 4.00 10.00
FPDW Doug Weight 4.00 10.00
FPEL Eric Lindros SP 5.00 12.00
FPJA Jason Allison 5.00 12.00
FPJL John LeClair 5.00 12.00
FPML Mario Lemieux 10.00 25.00
FPNL Nicklas Lidstrom 5.00 12.00
FPPF Peter Forsberg 8.00 20.00
FPRB Ray Bourque 8.00 20.00
FPSY Steve Yzerman 10.00 25.00
FPTA Tony Amonte 4.00 10.00
TNAM Al MacInnis Dual 8.00 20.00
TNBS Brendan Shanahan Dual 8.00 20.00
TNCJ Curtis Joseph Dual 8.00 20.00
TNJS Joe Sakic Dual 10.00 25.00
TNKP Keith Primeau Dual 8.00 20.00
TNPR Patrick Roy Dual 15.00 40.00
TNRB Ray Bourque Dual 10.00 25.00
UCLB John LeClair 4.00 10.00
Brian Boucher
UCLL Eric Lindros 4.00 10.00
Brian Leetch
UCMB Mike Modano 4.00 10.00
Ed Belfour
UCPD Zigmund Palffy 4.00 10.00
Adam Deadmarsh
UCSH Joe Sakic 15.00 40.00
Milan Hejduk
UCSJ Mats Sundin 5.00 12.00
Curtis Joseph
UCSY Brendan Shanahan 12.00 30.00
Steve Yzerman

2001-02 UD Challenge for the Cup Jersey Autographs

This 15-card set partially paralleled the base jersey set but also included authentic autographs from the featured players. Single jersey cards were serial-numbered to 75 while dual jersey cards were serial-numbered to 25.

TBE Ed Belfour 20.00 50.00
TBR Martin Brodeur 40.00 100.00
TJO Curtis Joseph 15.00 40.00
TPO Felix Potvin 15.00 40.00
TPR Patrick Roy 60.00 150.00
TRI Mike Richter 15.00 40.00
FPAL Jason Allison 15.00 40.00
FPBO Ray Bourque 25.00 60.00
FPJI Jarome Iginla 25.00 60.00
FPPB Pavel Bure 50.00 125.00
FPWE Doug Weight 15.00 40.00
FPYZ Steve Yzerman 30.00 80.00
TNBO Ray Bourque Dual 40.00 100.00
TNEB Ed Belfour Dual 40.00 100.00
TNJO Curtis Joseph Dual 30.00 80.00
TNKP Keith Primeau Dual 30.00 80.00
TNMA Al MacInnis Dual 30.00 80.00
UCAP Jason Allison 50.00 125.00
Zigmund Palffy
UCBB Ray Bourque 100.00 250.00
Rob Blake
UCLG John LeClair 40.00 100.00
Simon Gagne
UCST Sergei Samsonov 40.00 100.00
Joe Thornton

2002 UD Chicago National Spokesmen

Given away exclusively at the Upper Deck booth during the 2002 Chicago National Convention, this set highlighted player spokesmen from the four major sports. Please note that only the hockey players are listed below.

COMPLETE HOCKEY SET (3) 40.00
N8 Wayne Gretzky 4.80 20.00
N9 Bobby Orr 4.80 20.00
N10 Gordie Howe 4.80 10.00

1998-99 UD Choice

The 1998-99 Upper Deck UD Choice set was issued with a total of 220 cards. The 12-card packs retail for $1.29 each. The set contains the subsets: GM's Choice (221-242), Crease Lightning (244-252), and Jr. Showcase (253-307). The fronts feature color action photos surrounded by a white border.

COMPLETE SET (310) 15.00 30.00
1 Guy Hebert .08 .25
2 Mikhail Shtalenkov .03 .10
3 Josef Marha .03 .10
4 Paul Kariya .10 .30
5 Travis Green .03 .10
6 Steve Rucchin .03 .10
7 Matt Cullen .03 .10
8 Teemu Selanne .10 .30
9 Antti Aalto .03 .10
10 Byron Dafoe .08 .25
11 Ted Donato .03 .10
12 Dimitri Khristich .03 .10
13 Sergei Samsonov .08 .25
14 Jason Allison .03 .10
15 Ray Bourque .20 .50
16 Kyle McLaren .03 .10
17 Cameron Mann .03 .10
18 Shawn Bates .03 .10
19 Joe Thornton .20 .50
20 Vaclav Varada .03 .10
21 Brian Holzinger .03 .10
22 Miroslav Satan .08 .25
23 Dominik Hasek .25 .60
24 Michael Peca .03 .10
25 Erik Rasmussen .03 .10
26 Alexei Zhitnik .03 .10
27 Geoff Sanderson .08 .25
28 Donald Audette .03 .10
29 Derek Morris .03 .10
30 German Titov .03 .10
31 Valeri Bure .03 .10
32 Michael Nylander .03 .10
33 Cory Stillman .03 .10
34 Theo Fleury .03 .10
35 Jarome Iginla .15 .40
36 Gary Roberts .03 .10
37 Jeff O'Neill .03 .10
38 Bates Battaglia .08 .25
39 Keith Primeau .03 .10
40 Sami Kapanen .03 .10
41 Glen Wesley .03 .10
42 Trevor Kidd .08 .25
43 Nelson Emerson .03 .10
44 Daniel Cleary .03 .10
45 Eric Daze .08 .25
46 Chris Chelios .10 .30
47 Gary Suter .03 .10
48 Alexei Zhamnov .03 .10
49 Jeff Hackett .08 .25
50 Dmitri Nabokov .03 .10
51 Tony Amonte .08 .25
52 Jean-Yves Leroux .03 .10
53 Eric Messier .03 .10
54 Patrick Roy .60 1.50
55 Claude Lemieux .03 .10
56 Peter Forsberg .30 .75
57 Adam Deadmarsh .03 .10
58 Valeri Kamensky .03 .10
59 Joe Sakic .25 .60
60 Sandis Ozolinsh .03 .10
61 Jamie Langenbrunner .03 .10
62 Joe Nieuwendyk .08 .25
63 Ed Belfour .10 .30
64 Juha Lind .03 .10
65 Derian Hatcher .03 .10
66 Sergei Zubov .03 .10
67 Darryl Sydor .03 .10
68 Jere Lehtinen .03 .10
69 Mike Modano .20 .50
70 Larry Murphy .08 .25
71 Igor Larionov .03 .10
72 Darren McCarty .03 .10
73 Steve Yzerman .60 1.50
74 Chris Osgood .08 .25
75 Sergei Fedorov .20 .50
76 Brendan Shanahan .10 .30
77 Nicklas Lidstrom .10 .30
78 Vyacheslav Kozlov .03 .10
79 Dean McAmmond .03 .10
80 Roman Hamrlik .03 .10
81 Curtis Joseph .10 .30
82 Ryan Smyth .08 .25
83 Boris Mironov .03 .10
84 Bill Guerin .08 .25
85 Doug Weight .08 .25
86 Janne Niinimaa .03 .10
87 Ray Whitney .03 .10
88 Robert Svehla .03 .10
89 John Vanbiesbrouck .08 .25
90 Scott Mellanby .03 .10
91 Ed Jovanovski .03 .10
92 Dave Gagner .03 .10
93 Dino Ciccarelli .08 .25
94 Rob Niedermayer .03 .10
95 Rob Blake .08 .25
96 Yanic Perreault .03 .10
97 Stephane Fiset .08 .25
98 Luc Robitaille .08 .25
99 Glen Murray .03 .10
100 Jozef Stumpel .08 .25
101 Vladimir Tsyplakov .03 .10
102 Donald MacLean .03 .10
103 Shayne Corson .03 .10
104 Vladimir Malakhov .03 .10
105 Saku Koivu .10 .30
106 Andy Moog .08 .25
107 Matt Higgins RC .08 .25
108 Dave Manson .03 .10
109 Mark Recchi .08 .25
110 Vincent Damphousse .03 .10
111 Brian Savage .03 .10
112 Petr Sykora .03 .10
113 Scott Stevens .08 .25
114 Patrik Elias .08 .25
115 Bobby Holik .03 .10
116 Martin Brodeur .30 .75
117 Doug Gilmour .08 .25
118 Jason Arnott .03 .10
119 Scott Niedermayer .03 .10
120 Brendan Morrison .08 .25
121 Zigmund Palffy .08 .25
122 Trevor Linden .08 .25
123 Bryan Berard .08 .25
124 Zdeno Chara .03 .10
125 Kenny Jonsson .03 .10
126 Robert Reichel .03 .10
127 Bryan Smolinski .03 .10
128 Wayne Gretzky .75 2.00
129 Brian Leetch .10 .30
130 Pat Lafontaine .10 .30
131 Dan Cloutier .03 .10
132 Niklas Sundstrom .03 .10
133 Marc Savard .08 .25
134 Adam Graves .03 .10
135 Mike Richter .10 .30
136 Jeff Beukeboom .03 .10
137 Daniel Goneau .03 .10
138 Shawn McEachern .03 .10
139 Damian Rhodes .08 .25
140 Wade Redden .03 .10
141 Alexei Yashin .03 .10
142 Marian Hossa .10 .30
143 Chris Phillips .03 .10
144 Daniel Alfredsson .08 .25
145 Vaclav Prospal .03 .10
146 Andreas Dackell .03 .10
147 Sean Burke .03 .10
148 Alexandre Daigle .03 .10
149 Rod Brind'Amour .08 .25
150 Chris Gratton .08 .25
151 Paul Coffey .10 .30
152 Eric Lindros .10 .30
153 John LeClair .10 .30
154 Chris Therien .03 .10
155 Keith Carney .03 .10
156 Craig Janney .03 .10
157 Teppo Numminen .03 .10
158 Jeremy Roenick .15 .40
159 Oleg Tverdovsky .03 .10
160 Keith Tkachuk .10 .30
161 Brad Isbister .03 .10
162 Nikolai Khabibulin .08 .25
163 Daniel Briere .03 .10
164 Juha Ylonen .03 .10
165 Tom Barrasso .08 .25
166 Alexei Morozov .03 .10
167 Stu Barnes .03 .10
168 Jaromir Jagr .20 .50
169 Ron Francis .08 .25
170 Peter Skudra .03 .10
171 Robert Dome .03 .10
172 Kevin Hatcher .03 .10
173 Patrick Marleau .03 .10
174 Jeff Friesen .03 .10
175 Owen Nolan .08 .25
176 John MacLean .03 .10
177 Mike Vernon .08 .25
178 Marcus Ragnarsson .03 .10
179 Andrei Zyuzin .03 .10
180 Mike Ricci .08 .25
181 Marco Sturm .03 .10
182 Steve Duchesne .03 .10
183 Brett Hull .15 .40
184 Pierre Turgeon .08 .25
185 Chris Pronger .08 .25
186 Pavol Demitra .08 .25
187 Jamie McLennan .08 .25
188 Al MacInnis .08 .25
189 Jim Campbell .03 .10
190 Geoff Courtnall .03 .10
191 Daren Puppa .08 .25
192 Daymond Langkow .08 .25
193 Stephane Richer .08 .25
194 Paul Ysebaert .03 .10
195 Alexander Selivanov .03 .10
196 Rob Zamuner .03 .10
197 Mikael Renberg .08 .25
198 Mathieu Schneider .03 .10
199 Mike Johnson .03 .10
200 Alyn McCauley .03 .10
201 Sergei Berezin .08 .25
202 Wendel Clark .08 .25
203 Mats Sundin .10 .30
204 Tie Domi .08 .25
205 Jyrki Lumme .03 .10
206 Mattias Ohlund .08 .25
207 Garth Snow .08 .25
208 Pavel Bure .10 .30
209 Dave Scatchard .03 .10
210 Alexander Mogilny .08 .25
211 Mark Messier .10 .30
212 Todd Bertuzzi .10 .30
213 Peter Bondra .08 .25
214 Joe Juneau .08 .25
215 Olaf Kolzig .08 .25
216 Jan Bulis .03 .10
217 Adam Oates .08 .25
218 Richard Zednik .03 .10
219 Calle Johansson .03 .10
220 Phil Housley .03 .10
221 Dominik Hasek GM .10 .30
222 Ray Bourque GM .10 .30
223 Chris Chelios GM .08 .25
224 Paul Kariya GM .10 .30
225 Wayne Gretzky GM .40 1.00
226 Jaromir Jagr GM .10 .30
227 Rob Blake GM .03 .10
228 Adam Foote GM .03 .10
229 Peter Forsberg GM .10 .30
230 Joe Sakic GM .10 .30
231 Mark Recchi GM .03 .10
232 Patrick Roy GM .10 .30
233 Nicklas Lidstrom GM .08 .25
234 Rob Blake GM .03 .10
235 John LeClair GM .10 .30
236 Wayne Gretzky GM .40 1.00
237 Eric Lindros GM .10 .30
238 Brian Leetch GM .03 .10
239 Scott Stevens GM .08 .25
240 Paul Kariya GM .10 .30
241 Peter Forsberg GM .10 .30
242 Teemu Selanne GM .10 .30
243 Patrick Roy CRL .10 .30
244 Dominik Hasek CRL .10 .30
245 Martin Brodeur CRL .10 .30
246 Mike Richter CRL .08 .25
247 John Vanbiesbrouck CRL .08 .25
248 Chris Osgood CRL .08 .25
249 Ed Belfour CRL .10 .30
250 Tom Barrasso CRL .03 .10
251 Curtis Joseph CRL .10 .30
252 Sean Burke CRL .03 .10
253 Josh Holden .08 .10
254 Daniel Tkaczuk .03 .10
255 Manny Malhotra .03 .10
256 Eric Brewer .03 .10
257 Alex Tanguay .08 .25
258 Roberto Luongo .15 .40
259 Vincent Lecavalier .15 .40
260 Mathieu Garon .08 .25
261 Brad Ference .10 .30
262 Jesse Wallin .03 .10
263 Zenith Komarniski .03 .10
264 Sean Blanchard RC .08 .25
265 Cory Sarich .03 .10
266 Mike Van Ryn .03 .10
267 Steve Begin .03 .10
268 Matt Cooke RC .08 .25
269 Daniel Corso .03 .10
270 Brett McLean .03 .10
271 J-P Dumont .08 .10
272 Jason Ward .03 .10
273 Brian Willsie RC .08 .25
274 Matt Bradley RC .03 .10
275 Olli Jokinen .08 .25
276 Teemu Elomo .03 .10
277 Timo Vertala .03 .10
278 Mika Noronen .10 .25
279 Pasi Petrilainen .03 .10
280 Timo Ahmaoja .03 .10
281 Eero Somervuori .03 .10
282 Maxim Afinogenov .30 .75
283 Maxim Balmochnykh .03 .10
284 Artem Chubarov .03 .10
285 Vitali Vishnevsky .03 .10
286 Denis Shvidki .03 .10
287 Dmitri Vlasenkov .03 .10
288 Magnus Nilsson RC .08 .25
289 Mikael Holmqvist RC .08 .25
290 Mattias Karlin RC .03 .10
291 Pierre Hedin .03 .10
292 Henrik Petre .03 .10
293 Johan Forsander .03 .10
294 Daniel Sedin .03 .10
295 Henrik Sedin .03 .10
296 Marcus Nilsson .03 .10
297 Paul Mara .03 .10
298 Brian Gionta RC 1.25 3.00
299 Chris Hajt RC .08 .25
300 Mike Mottau RC .20 .50
301 Jean-Marc Pelletier RC .20 .50
302 David Legwand .20 .50
303 Ty Jones .03 .10
304 Nikos Tselios .03 .10
305 Jesse Boulerice .03 .10
306 Jeff Farkas .02 *.10
307 Toby Petersen .03 .10
308 Wayne Gretzky CL .10 .30
309 Patrick Roy CL .08 .25
310 Steve Yzerman CL .08 .25

1998-99 UD Choice Blow-Ups

Inserted as box-toppers in UD choice, these oversized cards resembled the base set but were approximately 5" x 7". Cards were numbered "X of 5".

COMPLETE SET (5) 20.00
1 Patrick Roy 2.00 5.00
2 Steve Yzerman 2.00 5.00
3 John LeClair .80 2.00
4 Martin Brodeur 1.20 3.00
5 Peter Forsberg 4.00

1998-99 UD Choice Draw Your Own Trading Card

Inserted one in every pack, this insert asks collectors to submit an 8.5" x 11" piece of paper, their rendering of a trading card of their favorite NHL star. The selected winners' works were featured in the next season's UD Choice Hockey product.

NNO Wayne Gretzky .20 .50

1998-99 UD Choice Hometeam Heroes

This set of 20-cards features members of the Detroit Red Wings. The cards were inserted one-per-pack of UD Choice throughout Michigan at retail outlets.

COMPLETE SET(20) 6.00 12.00
RW1 Steve Yzerman 2.00 5.00
RW2 Sergei Fedorov 1.25 3.00
RW3 Nicklas Lidstrom .40 1.00
RW4 Vyacheslav Kozlov .40 1.00
RW5 Chris Osgood .75 2.00
RW6 Darren McCarty .40 1.00
RW7 Brendan Shanahan 1.25 3.00
RW8 Igor Larionov .20 .50
RW9 Martin Lapointe .20 .50
RW10 Doug Brown .20 .50
RW11 Kirk Maltby .20 .50
RW12 Kris Draper .20 .50
RW13 Tomas Holmstrom .20 .50
RW14 Larry Murphy .20 .50
RW15 Slave Fetisov .20 .50
RW16 Anders Eriksson .20 .50
RW17 Brent Gilchrist .20 .50
RW18 Joey Kocur .20 .50
RW19 Mike Knuble .20 .50
RW20 Kevin Hodson .20 .50

1998-99 UD Choice Mini Bobbing Head

Randomly inserted in packs at a rate of 1:4, this 30-card insert features specially enhanced miniatures that fold into a stand-up figure with a removable bobbing head.

BH1 Wayne Gretzky 2.00 5.00
BH2 Keith Tkachuk .30 .75
BH3 Ray Bourque .50 1.25
BH4 Brett Hull .40 1.00
BH5 Jaromir Jagr .50 1.25
BH6 John LeClair .30 .75
BH7 Martin Brodeur .75 2.00
BH8 Eric Lindros .30 .75
BH9 Mark Messier .30 .75
BH10 John Vanbiesbrouck .25 .60
BH11 Paul Kariya .30 .75
BH12 Luc Robitaille .25 .60
BH13 Zigmund Palffy .25 .60
BH14 Peter Forsberg .75 2.00
BH15 Teemu Selanne .30 .75
BH16 Mike Modano .50 1.25
BH17 Mats Sundin .30 .75
BH18 Dominik Hasek .60 1.50
BH19 Joe Sakic .60 1.50
BH20 Rob Blake .25 .60
BH21 Patrick Roy 1.50 4.00
BH22 Sergei Samsonov .25 .60
BH23 Chris Chelios .30 .75
BH24 Brendan Shanahan .30 .75
BH25 Theo Fleury .10 .25
BH26 Ed Belfour .30 .75
BH27 Steve Yzerman 1.50 4.00
BH28 Saku Koivu .30 .75
BH29 Brian Leetch .30 .75
BH30 Pavel Bure .30 .75

1998-99 UD Choice Preview

The 1998-99 UD Choice Preview set was issued in one series totaling 60 cards. The 6-card packs retail for $.79 each. Set is skip numbered.

COMPLETE SET (110) 7.50 15.00
219 Calle Johansson .08 .20
1 Guy Hebert .20 .50
3 Josef Marha .08 .20
5 Travis Green .08 .20
7 Matt Cullen .08 .20
9 Antti Aalto .08 .20
11 Ted Donato .08 .20
13 Sergei Samsonov .20 .50
15 Ray Bourque .40 1.00
17 Cameron Mann .08 .20
19 Joe Thornton .40 1.00
21 Brian Holzinger .08 .20
23 Dominik Hasek .50 1.25
25 Erik Rasmussen .08 .20
27 Geoff Sanderson .08 .20
29 Derek Morris .08 .20
31 Valeri Bure .08 .20
33 Cory Stillman .08 .20
35 Jarome Iginla .30 .75
37 Jeff O'Neill .08 .20
39 Keith Primeau .08 .20
41 Glen Wesley .08 .20
43 Nelson Emerson .08 .20
45 Eric Daze .20 .50
47 Gary Suter .08 .20
49 Jeff Hackett .20 .50
51 Tony Amonte .20 .50
53 Eric Messier .08 .20
55 Claude Lemieux .08 .20
57 Adam Deadmarsh .08 .20
59 Joe Sakic .50 1.25
61 Jamie Langenbrunner .08 .20
63 Ed Belfour .25 .60
65 Derian Hatcher .08 .20
67 Daryl Sydor .20 .50
69 Mike Modano .40 1.00
71 Igor Larionov .08 .20
73 Steve Yzerman 1.25 3.00
75 Sergei Fedorov .40 1.00
77 Nicklas Lidstrom .25 .60
78 Slava Kozlov .20 .50
79 Dean McAmmond .08 .20
81 Curtis Joseph .25 .60
83 Boris Mironov .08 .20
85 Doug Weight .20 .50
87 Ray Whitney .08 .20
89 John Vanbiesbrouck .20 .50
90 Scott Mellanby .08 .20
91 Ed Jovanovksi .08 .20
93 Dino Ciccarelli .20 .50
95 Rob Blake .20 .50
97 Stephane Fiset .20 .50
99 Glen Murray .08 .20
101 Vladimir Tsyplakov .08 .20
103 Shayne Corson .08 .20
105 Saku Koivu .25 .60
107 Matt Higgins .08 .20
109 Mark Recchi .20 .50
111 Brian Savage .08 .20
113 Scott Stevens .20 .50
115 Bobby Holik .08 .20
117 Doug Gilmour .20 .50
119 Scott Niedermayer .08 .20
121 Zigmund Palffy .20 .50
123 Bryan Berard .08 .20
125 Kenny Jonsson .08 .20
127 Bryan Smolinski .20 .50
129 Brian Leetch .25 .60
131 Dan Cloutier .20 .50
133 Marc Savard .08 .20
135 Mike Richter .25 .60
137 Daniel Goneau .08 .20
139 Damian Rhodes .20 .50
141 Alexei Yashin .08 .20
143 Chris Phillips .08 .20
147 Sean Burke .20 .50
149 Rod Brind'Amour .20 .50
151 Paul Coffey .25 .60
153 John LeClair .25 .60
157 Teppo Numminen .08 .20
159 Oleg Tverdovsky .08 .20
161 Brad Isbister .08 .20
163 Daniel Briere .08 .20
165 Tom Barrasso .20 .50
167 Stu Barnes .08 .20
169 Ron Francis .08 .20
171 Robert Dome .08 .20
173 Patrick Marleau .25 .60
175 Owen Nolan .20 .50
177 Mike Vernon .20 .50
179 Andrei Zyuzin .08 .20
181 Marco Sturm .20 .50
183 Brett Hull .30 .75
185 Chris Pronger .20 .50
187 Jamie McLennan .20 .50
189 Jim Campbell .20 .50
190 Geoff Courtnall .08 .20
191 Daren Puppa .20 .50
193 Stephane Richer .20 .50
195 Alexander Selivanov .08 .20
197 Mikael Renberg .20 .50
199 Mike Johnson .08 .20
201 Sergei Berezin .20 .50
203 Mats Sundin .25 .60
205 Jyrki Lumme .08 .20
207 Garth Snow .20 .50
209 Dave Scatchard .08 .20
211 Mark Messier .25 .60
213 Peter Bondra .20 .50
215 Olaf Kolzig .08 .20
217 Adam Oates .20 .50

1998-99 UD Choice Prime Choice Reserve

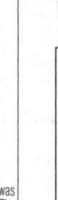

This hobby-only parallel showcases the same players found in the UD Choice base set, except each card is foil-stamped with the words "Prime Choice Reserve". The set is sequentially numbered to 100.

*STARS: 25X TO 60X BASIC CARDS
*RC's: 20X TO 50X BASIC CARDS

1998-99 UD Choice Reserve

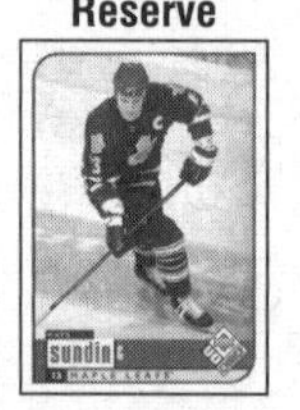

Randomly inserted in packs at a rate of 1:6, this 310-card parallel showcases the same players found in the UD Choice base set, except each card sports a distinctive foil treatment.

*STARS: 3X TO 6X BASIC CARDS
*RC's: 2X TO 4X BASIC CARDS
STATED ODDS 1:6

1998-99 UD Choice StarQuest Blue

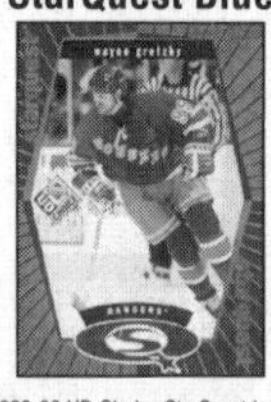

The 1998-99 UD Choice StarQuest insert set salutes 30 of the NHL's top players with each of four 30-card tiers representing a different insert ratio. The cards feature color action player photos in different colored borders and with a different number of stars in the left bottom corner according to which tier the card is from. StarQuest Blue has one star and is inserted two per pack; StarQuest Green has two stars with an insertion rate of 1:7; StarQuest Red features three stars and an insertion rate of 1:23; StarQuest Gold is a limited-edition set and displays four stars. Only 100 sequentially numbered Gold sets were made.

COMPLETE SET (30) 8.00 15.00
*GREEN: 1.5X TO 3X BASIC INSERTS
*RED: 4X TO 8X BASIC INSERTS
*GOLD: 25X TO 50X BASIC INSERTS
SQ1 Wayne Gretzky 1.25 3.00
SQ2 Pavel Bure .20 .50
SQ3 Patrick Roy 1.00 2.50
SQ4 Dominik Hasek .40 1.00
SQ5 Teemu Selanne .20 .50
SQ6 Sergei Samsonov .15 .40
SQ7 Brian Leetch .20 .50
SQ8 Saku Koivu .20 .50
SQ9 Brendan Shanahan .20 .50
SQ10 Alexei Yashin .15 .40
SQ11 Joe Sakic .40 1.00
SQ12 Patrik Elias .15 .40
SQ13 Theo Fleury .15 .40
SQ14 Peter Bondra .15 .40
SQ15 John LeClair .20 .50
SQ16 Jaromir Jagr .30 .75
SQ17 Ed Belfour .20 .50
SQ18 Steve Yzerman 1.00 2.50
SQ19 Mats Sundin .20 .50
SQ20 Peter Forsberg .50 1.25
SQ21 Ray Bourque .30 .75
SQ22 Brett Hull .25 .60
SQ23 Martin Brodeur .50 1.25
SQ24 Mike Modano .30 .75
SQ25 Paul Kariya .20 .50
SQ26 Tony Amonte .15 .40
SQ27 Mike Johnson .15 .40
SQ28 Eric Lindros .20 .50
SQ29 Mark Messier .20 .50
SQ30 Keith Tkachuk .20 .50

2002 Upper Deck Collectors Club

COMPLETE SET (20) 16.00 40.00
NHL1 Wayne Gretzky 2.00 5.00
NHL2 Gordie Howe 1.20 2.00
NHL3 Bobby Orr 2.00 5.00
NHL4 Ray Bourque .80 2.00
NHL5 Mario Lemieux 1.60 4.00
NHL6 Patrick Roy 1.60 4.00
NHL7 Steve Yzerman 1.60 4.00
NHL8 Jaromir Jagr .80 1.50
NHL9 Dominik Hasek .40 1.00
NHL10 Martin Brodeur .80 2.00
NHL11 Joe Sakic .80 2.00
NHL12 Paul Kariya .80 1.50
NHL13 Teemu Selanne .40 1.00
NHL14 Chris Pronger .20 .50
NHL15 Pavel Bure .40 1.00
NHL16 Peter Forsberg .80 1.50
NHL17 Nicklas Lidstrom .40 1.00
NHL18 Ilya Kovalchuk 2.00 3.00
NHL19 Kristian Huselius .40 .50
NHL20 Dan Blackburn .80 1.00

2002 Upper Deck Collectors Club Jerseys

One memorabilia card was included in each UD Collector's Club boxed set. The Yzerman features a swatch from a game jersey and appears to be slightly more scarce than the Bourque, which features a practice jersey swatch.

COMPLETE SET (2) 40.00 100.00
RB-J Ray Bourque 16.00 40.00
SY-J Steve Yzerman 30.00 75.00

2002-03 UD Foundations

Released in November 2002, this 167-card set consited of 100 veteran base cards (#1-100), 20 "Speceial Efforts" subset cards (101-121), and 46 "New Foundations" prospect cards (#122-167). All subset cards were serial-numbered out of 1250. Cards 164-167 were available only in packs of UD Rookie Update.

COMP.SET w/o SP's (100) 20.00 40.00
1 Andy Moog .20 .50
2 Bill Ranford .20 .50
3 Cam Neely .25 .60
4 Bobby Orr 1.50 4.00
5 Terry O'Reilly .12 .30
6 Ray Bourque .50 1.25
7 Phil Esposito .60 1.50
8 Clark Gillies .12 .30
9 Grant Fuhr .20 .50
10 Dale Hawerchuk .12 .30
11 Kent Nilsson .12 .30
12 Willi Plett .12 .30
13 Al Secord .12 .30
14 Denis Savard .20 .50
15 Bob Probert .12 .30
16 Steve Larmer .12 .30
17 Patrick Roy 1.25 3.00
18 Ray Bourque .50 1.25
19 Andy Moog .20 .50
20 Alex Delvecchio .25 .60
21 Borje Salming .20 .50
22 Dino Ciccarelli .12 .30
23 Gordie Howe 1.25 3.00
24 John Ogrodnick .12 .30

25 Marcel Dionne .25 .60
26 Mark Howe .12 .30
27 Ron Duguay .12 .30
28 Steve Yzerman 1.25 3.00
29 Andy Moog .20 .50
30 Bill Ranford .20 .50
31 Grant Fuhr .20 .50
32 Mark Messier .30 .75
33 Marty McSorley .12 .30
34 Wayne Gretzky 1.50 4.00
35 Glenn Anderson .12 .30
36 Gordie Howe 1.25 3.00
37 Mark Howe .12 .30
38 Gordie Howe 1.25 3.00
39 Butch Goring .20 .50
40 Charlie Simmer .12 .30
41 Ron Duguay .12 .30
42 Marcel Dionne .25 .60
43 Marty McSorley .12 .30
44 Wayne Gretzky 1.50 4.00
45 Wayne Gretzky 1.50 4.00
46 Brian Bellows .12 .30
47 Dino Ciccarelli .12 .30
48 Mike Modano .40 1.00
49 Brian Bellows .12 .30
50 Denis Savard .20 .50
51 Guy Lafleur .30 .75
52 Mats Naslund .12 .30
53 Doug Gilmour .20 .50
54 Patrick Roy 1.25 3.00
55 Rod Langway .12 .30
56 Ryan Walter .12 .30
57 Yvan Cournoyer .25 .60
58 Martin Brodeur .75 2.00
59 Bob Nystrom .12 .30
60 Butch Goring .20 .50
61 Clark Gillies .12 .30
62 Mike Bossy .25 .60
63 Glenn Anderson .12 .30
64 Guy Lafleur .30 .75
65 Mark Messier .25 .60
66 Marcel Dionne .25 .60
67 Phil Esposito .40 1.00
68 Ron Duguay .12 .30
69 Steve Larmer .12 .30
70 Wayne Gretzky 1.50 4.00
71 Brian Propp .12 .30
72 Jeremy Roenick .30 .75
73 Mark Howe .12 .30
74 Ron Hextall .20 .50
75 Tim Kerr .12 .30
76 Anton Stastny .12 .30
77 Dale Hunter .12 .30
78 Guy Lafleur .30 .75
79 Ron Hextall .20 .50
80 Wendel Clark .20 .50
81 Wilf Paiement .12 .30
82 Brett Hull .30 .75
83 Bernie Federko .12 .30
84 Dale Hawerchuk .12 .30
85 Grant Fuhr .20 .50
86 Tony Twist .12 .30
87 Wayne Gretzky 1.50 4.00
88 Borje Salming .20 .50
89 Mats Sundin .25 .60
90 Glenn Anderson .12 .30
91 Grant Fuhr .20 .50
92 Wendel Clark .20 .50
93 Wilf Paiement .12 .30
94 Harold Snepsts .12 .30
95 Pavel Bure .25 .60
96 Tony Tanti .12 .30
97 Dale Hunter .12 .30
98 Dino Ciccarelli .12 .30
99 Rod Langway .12 .30
100 Dale Hawerchuk .12 .30
101 Wayne Gretzky SE 3.00 8.00
102 Gordie Howe SE 2.50 6.00
103 Bobby Orr SE 3.00 8.00
104 Gordie Howe SE 2.50 6.00
105 Wayne Gretzky SE 3.00 8.00
106 Wayne Gretzky SE 3.00 8.00
107 Cam Neely SE .50 1.25
108 Ray Bourque SE 1.00 2.50
109 Phil Esposito SE 1.00 2.50
110 Grant Fuhr SE .50 1.25
111 Denis Savard SE .50 1.25
112 Patrick Roy SE 2.50 6.00
113 Steve Yzerman SE 2.50 6.00
114 Marcel Dionne SE .60 1.50
115 Guy Lafleur SE .75 2.00
116 Bernie Federko SE .30 .75
117 Wayne Gretzky SE 3.00 8.00
118 Ray Bourque SE 1.00 2.50
118 Phil Esposito SE 1.00 2.50
119 Mike Bossy SE .60 1.50
120 Patrick Roy SE 2.50 6.00
121 Bob Nystrom SE .30 .75
122 Pasi Nurminen NF .75 2.00
123 Mark Hartigan NF .75 2.00
124 Henrik Tallinder NF .75 2.00
125 Micki Dupont NF RC 1.50 4.00
126 Riku Hahl NF .75 2.00
127 Andrej Nedorost NF .75 2.00
128 Ales Pisa NF .75 2.00
129 Jani Rita NF .75 2.00
130 Stephen Weiss NF 2.00 5.00
131 Lukas Krajicek NF .75 2.00
132 Sylvain Blouin NF RC 1.50 4.00
133 Marcel Hossa NF .75 2.00
134 Adam Hall NF RC 1.50 4.00
135 Jan Lasak NF .75 2.00
136 Ray Schultz NF RC 1.50 4.00
137 Trent Hunter NF .75 2.00
138 Martin Prusek NF .75 2.00
139 Branko Radivojevic NF .75 2.00
140 Sebastien Centomo NF .75 2.00
141 Karel Pilar NF .75 2.00
142 Sebastien Charpentier NF .75 2.00
143 Stanislav Chistov NF RC 2.00 5.00
144 Alexei Smirnov NF RC 1.50 4.00
145 Joe Thornton SE 1.00 2.50
146 Chuck Kobasew NF RC 1.50 4.00
147 Patrick Roy SE 5.00 12.00
148 Mike Modano SE 2.00 5.00
149 Rick Nash NF RC 6.00 15.00
150 Mike Comrie SE 1.00 2.50
151 Henrik Zetterberg NF RC 6.00 15.00
152 Ales Hemsky NF RC 2.50 6.00
153 Jay Bouwmeester NF RC 2.00 5.00
154 Pavel Bure SE 1.25 3.00
155 Alexander Frolov NF RC 2.50 6.00
156 P-M Bouchard NF RC 2.00 5.00
157 Ron Hainsey NF RC 1.50 4.00
158 Sean Burke SE 1.00 2.50
159 Mario Lemieux SE 3.00 8.00
160 Anton Volchenkov NF RC 1.50 4.00
161 Mats Sundin SE 1.25 3.00
162 Alexander Svitov NF RC 1.50 4.00
163 Steve Eminger NF RC 1.50 4.00
164 Jason Spezza NF RC 6.00 15.00
165 Pascal LeClaire NF RC 2.50 6.00
166 Ari Ahonen NF RC 1.50 4.00
167 Steve Ott NF RC 1.50 4.00

2002-03 UD Foundations 1000 Point Club

This 39-card memorabilia set featured swatches of game jerseys or sticks. Jersey cards were serial-numbered to 110 and stick cards were serial-numbered to 150. Gold jersey parallels numbered to 15 and silver jersey parallels numbered to 85 were also created. Silver prices can be found by using the multipliers below; gold cards are not priced due to scarcity.

*MULT.COLOR SWATCH: .5X TO 1.25X HI
*SILVER JSY: .5X TO 1.25X BASE HI
BT Bryan Trottier JSY 5.00 12.00
DC Dino Ciccarelli JSY 4.00 10.00
DE Denis Savard JSY 4.00 10.00
DP Denis Potvin JSY 4.00 10.00
GL Guy Lafleur JSY 4.00 10.00
JB Johnny Bucyk JSY 5.00 12.00
LA Guy Lafleur JSY 4.00 10.00
MB Mike Bossy JSY 6.00 15.00
MG Michel Goulet JSY 4.00 10.00
SY Steve Yzerman JSY 12.50 30.00
WG Wayne Gretzky JSY 25.00 60.00
YZ Steve Yzerman STK 12.50 30.00
AN Glenn Anderson STK 4.00 10.00
AN2 Glenn Anderson STK 4.00 10.00
BE Jean Beliveau STK 8.00 20.00
BO Mike Bossy STK 6.00 15.00
BO1 Ray Bourque STK 8.00 20.00
BO2 Ray Bourque STK 8.00 20.00
BU Johnny Bucyk STK 5.00 12.00
CI Dino Ciccarelli STK 4.00 10.00
DI Marcel Dionne STK 4.00 10.00
DI2 Marcel Dionne STK 4.00 10.00
ES Phil Esposito STK 4.00 10.00
ES2 Phil Esposito STK 4.00 10.00
GA Mike Gartner STK 4.00 10.00
GR Wayne Gretzky STK 20.00 50.00
HA Dale Hawerchuk STK 8.00 20.00
HA2 Dale Hawerchuk STK 8.00 20.00
HO Gordie Howe STK 25.00 60.00
KU Jari Kurri STK 6.00 15.00
KU2 Jari Kurri STK 6.00 15.00
LA1 Guy Lafleur STK 4.00 10.00
LA2 Guy Lafleur STK 4.00 10.00
LA3 Guy Lafleur STK 4.00 10.00
MC Lanny McDonald STK 4.00 10.00
MI Stan Mikita STK 4.00 10.00
PO Denis Potvin STK 4.00 10.00
SA Denis Savard STK 4.00 10.00
TR Bryan Trottier STK 5.00 12.00

2002-03 UD Foundations Calder Winners

Gold parallels of this memorabilia set numbered to 15 and silver parallels numbered to 85 were also created. Silver prices can be found by using the multipliers below; gold cards are not priced due to scarcity.

PRINT RUN 110 SER.#'d SETS
*SILVER: .5X TO 1.25X BASIC JERSEY
TBT Bryan Trottier 6.00 15.00
TMB Mike Bossy 8.00 20.00
TPB Pavel Bure 5.00 12.00
TRB Ray Bourque 8.00 20.00
TWP Willi Plett 5.00 12.00

2002-03 UD Foundations Canadian Heroes

Singles in this 22-card set were serial-numbered to 150. Gold parallels numbered to 50 and silver parallels numbered to 95 were also created. Prices for those parallels can be found by using the multipliers below.

*MULT.COLOR SWATCH: .5X TO 1.25X HI
*SILVER: .5X TO 1.25X BASIC INSERTS
*GOLD: .75X TO 2X
CBO Ray Bourque 8.00 20.00
CBT Bryan Trottier 5.00 12.00
CCN Cam Neely 5.00 12.00
CDC Dino Ciccarelli 5.00 12.00
CGF Grant Fuhr 10.00 25.00
CGL Guy Lafleur 5.00 12.00
CHS Harold Snepsts 5.00 12.00
CJB Johnny Bucyk 5.00 12.00
CMB Mike Bossy 5.00 12.00
CMG Michel Goulet 5.00 12.00
CMH Mark Howe 5.00 12.00
CMM Marty McSorley 5.00 12.00
CPR Patrick Roy 12.50 30.00
CRD Ron Duguay 5.00 12.00
CRO Patrick Roy 12.50 30.00
CRV Rick Vaive 5.00 12.00
CSA Denis Savard 5.00 12.00
CSY Steve Yzerman 12.50 30.00
CTT Tony Twist 5.00 12.00
CWC Wendel Clark 5.00 12.00
CWG Wayne Gretzky 25.00 60.00
CWP Willi Plett 5.00 12.00

2002-03 UD Foundations Classic Greats

Singles in this 17-card memorabilia set were serial-numbered to 150. Gold parallels numbered to 50 and silver parallels numbered to 95 were also created. Prices for those parallels can be found by using the multipliers below.

*SILVER: .5X TO 1.25X BASIC INSERTS
*GOLD: .75X TO 2X
GBN Bob Nystrom 5.00 12.00
GBO Ray Bourque 8.00 20.00
GBR Bill Ranford 5.00 12.00
GBS Borje Salming 5.00 12.00
GCN Cam Neely 5.00 12.00
GDC Dino Ciccarelli 5.00 12.00
GDP Denis Potvin 5.00 12.00
GDS Denis Savard 5.00 12.00
GGF Grant Fuhr 10.00 25.00
GGL Guy Lafleur 5.00 12.00
GMB Mike Bossy 5.00 12.00
GMG Michel Goulet 5.00 12.00
GMH Mark Howe 5.00 12.00
GRB Ray Bourque 8.00 20.00
GRD Ron Duguay 5.00 12.00
GWC Wendel Clark 6.00 15.00
GWG Wayne Gretzky 25.00 60.00

2002-03 UD Foundations Defense First

Singles in this 8-card memorabilia set were serial-numbered to 1000. Gold parallels numbered to 15 and silver parallels numbered to 85 were also created. Silver prices can be found by using the multipliers below; gold cards are not priced due to scarcity.

*SILVER: .5X TO 1.25X BASE JSY
DBO Ray Bourque 8.00 20.00
DBS Borje Salming 5.00 12.00
DDP Denis Potvin 5.00 12.00
DGF Grant Fuhr 10.00 25.00
DHS Harold Snepsts 5.00 12.00
DMH Mark Howe 5.00 12.00
DMM Marty McSorley 5.00 12.00
DRB Ray Bourque 8.00 20.00

2002-03 UD Foundations Lasting Impressions Sticks

STAT.PRINT RUN 150 SER.#'d SETS
L-BN Bob Nystrom 6.00 15.00
L-BO Bobby Orr 50.00 125.00
L-BR Bill Ranford 6.00 15.00
L-CN Cam Neely 6.00 15.00
L-JP Jacques Plante 12.50 30.00
L-MN Mats Naslund 8.00 20.00
L-WC Wendel Clark 6.00 15.00
L-YC Yvan Cournoyer 6.00 15.00

2002-03 UD Foundations Milestones

Gold parallels of this memorabilia set numbered to 50 and silver parallels numbered to 95 were also created. Prices for those parallels can be found by using the multipliers below.

PRINT RUN 150 SER.#'d SETS
*SILVER: .5X TO 1.25X BASE JSY
*GOLD: .75X TO 2X
NBO Ray Bourque 8.00 20.00
NBT Bryan Trottier 5.00 12.00
NCN Cam Neely 10.00 25.00
NDP Denis Potvin 5.00 12.00
NGF Grant Fuhr 10.00 25.00
NMB Mike Bossy 5.00 12.00
NPR Patrick Roy 12.50 30.00
NSY Steve Yzerman 12.50 30.00
NWG Wayne Gretzky 25.00 60.00

2002-03 UD Foundations Playoff Performers

Gold parallels of this memorabilia set numbered to 50 and silver parallels numbered to 95 were also created. Prices for those parallels can be found by using the multipliers below.

PRINT RUN 150 SER.#'d SETS
*SILVER: .5X TO 1.25X BASE JSY
*GOLD: .75X TO 2X
PBN Bob Nystrom 5.00 12.00
PBS Borje Salming 5.00 12.00
PBT Bryan Trottier 5.00 12.00
PCN Cam Neely 5.00 12.00
PDC Dino Ciccarelli 5.00 12.00
PGF Grant Fuhr 8.00 20.00
PJB Johnny Bucyk 5.00 12.00
PMB Mike Bossy 5.00 12.00
PMG Michel Goulet 5.00 12.00
PMM Marty McSorley 5.00 12.00
PPB Pavel Bure 5.00 12.00
PPR Patrick Roy 12.50 30.00
PRB Ray Bourque 8.00 20.00
PRO Patrick Roy 12.50 30.00
PSY Steve Yzerman 12.50 30.00
PWG Wayne Gretzky 25.00 60.00

2002-03 UD Foundations Power Stations

Singles in this 11-card set were serial-numbered to 110. Gold parallels onumbered to 15 and silver parallels numbered to 85 were also created. Silver prices can be found by using the multipliers below; gold cards are not priced due to scarcity.

*SILVER: .5X TO 1.25X BASE JSY
SBN Bob Nystrom 5.00 12.00
SCN Cam Neely 5.00 12.00
SDC Dino Ciccarelli 5.00 12.00
SHS Harold Snepsts 5.00 12.00
SMB Mike Bossy 5.00 12.00
SMH Mark Howe 5.00 12.00
SMM Marty McSorley 5.00 12.00
SRV Rick Vaive 5.00 12.00
STT Tony Twist 5.00 12.00
SWC Wendel Clark 5.00 12.00
SWP Willi Plett 5.00 12.00

2002-03 UD Foundations Signs of Greatness

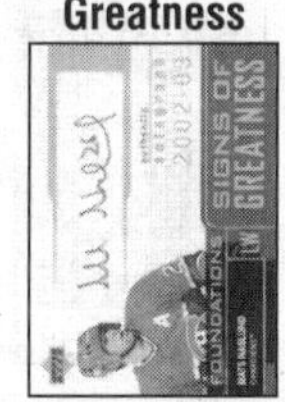

Inserted at 1:53, this 36-card set featured certified player autogrpahs. Known shortprints are listed below.

SGAS Al Secord/26 30.00 80.00
SGBB Brian Bellows/26 25.00 60.00
SGBC Bobby Clarke SP 10.00 25.00
SGBO Bobby Orr/48 200.00 400.00
SGBP Brian Propp/87 12.00 30.00
SGBS Billy Smith 10.00 25.00
SGCG Clark Gillies/26 20.00 50.00
SGCN Cam Neely SP 15.00 40.00
SGCS Charlie Simmer/26 30.00 80.00
SGDC Dino Ciccarelli SP 10.00 25.00
SGDH Dale Hawerchuk 10.00 25.00
SGDP Denis Potvin 10.00 25.00
SGDS Denis Savard SP 10.00 25.00
SGFM Frank Mahovlich SP 10.00 25.00
SGGA Glenn Anderson 10.00 25.00
SGGF Grant Fuhr SP 15.00 40.00
SGGH Gordie Howe/43 75.00 200.00
SGGL Guy Lafleur SP 20.00 50.00
SGGP Gilbert Perreault SP 10.00 25.00
SGJB Jean Beliveau SP 15.00 40.00
SGJBU Johnny Bucyk 10.00 25.00
SGJK Jari Kurri 12.50 30.00
SGLM Lanny McDonald 10.00 25.00
SGMB Mike Bossy 10.00 25.00
SGMD Marcel Dionne SP 10.00 25.00
SGMG Mike Gartner 12.50 30.00
SGMGU Michel Goulet SP 10.00 25.00
SGMN Mats Naslund/87 15.00 40.00
SGPS Peter Stastny 10.00 25.00
SGRA Ray Bourque/23 25.00 60.00
SGRB Ray Bourque/23 25.00 60.00
SGRH Ron Hextall/51 30.00 80.00
SGSL Steve Larmer/26 12.50 30.00
SGSM Stan Mikita SP 10.00 25.00
SGTL Ted Lindsay SP 10.00 25.00
SGWG Wayne Gretzky/46 150.00 400.00

2000-01 UD Heroes

The 2000-01 UD Heroes set consisted of 180 cards. There were 30 rookies and 2 checklist cards. The set design for the card fronts had a photo of the featured player in action and a gold-foil UD Heroes stamp on the bottom of the card by the player name. The card backs used a small photo cut from the card front photo and included the player's vitals and his stats.

COMPLETE SET (180) 30.00 60.00
1 Steve Rucchin .05 .15
2 Marty McInnis .05 .15
3 Oleg Tverdovsky .05 .15
4 Guy Hebert .15 .40
5 Patrik Stefan .05 .15
6 Donald Audette .05 .15
7 Andrew Brunette .05 .15
8 Jason Allison .05 .15
9 Sergei Samsonov .15 .40
10 Joe Thornton .30 .75
11 Byron Dafoe .15 .40
12 Dominik Hasek .40 1.00
13 Miroslav Satan .15 .40
14 Doug Gilmour .15 .40
15 J-P Dumont .05 .15
16 Fred Brathwaite .15 .40
17 Valeri Bure .05 .15
18 Marc Savard .05 .15
19 Cory Stillman .05 .15
20 Ron Francis .15 .40
21 Arturs Irbe .15 .40
22 Jeff O'Neill .05 .15
23 Sandis Ozolinsh .05 .15
24 Tony Amonte .15 .40
25 Jocelyn Thibault .15 .40
26 Alexei Zhamnov .05 .15
27 Steve Sullivan .05 .15
28 Chris Drury .15 .40
29 Milan Hejduk .20 .50
30 Alex Tanguay .15 .40
31 Peter Forsberg .50 1.25
32 Adam Deadmarsh .05 .15
33 Marc Denis .15 .40
34 Ron Tugnutt .15 .40
35 Tyler Wright .05 .15
36 David Vyborny .05 .15
37 Brett Hull .25 .60
38 Ed Belfour .20 .50
39 Joe Nieuwendyk .15 .40
40 Sergei Zubov .05 .15
41 Jere Lehtinen .15 .40
42 Sergei Fedorov .30 .75
43 Martin Lapointe .05 .15
44 Chris Osgood .15 .40
45 Pat Verbeek .05 .15
46 Nicklas Lidstrom .20 .50
47 Doug Weight .15 .40
48 Tommy Salo .15 .40
49 Ryan Smyth .05 .15
50 Sean Brown .05 .15
51 Ray Whitney .05 .15
52 Trevor Kidd .15 .40
53 Viktor Kozlov .15 .40
54 Denis Shvidki .05 .15
55 Rob Blake .15 .40
56 Zigmund Palffy .15 .40
57 Luc Robitaille .15 .40
58 Glen Murray .05 .15
59 Manny Fernandez .15 .40
60 Scott Pellerin .05 .15
61 Maxim Sushinski .05 .15
62 Saku Koivu .20 .50
63 Jose Theodore .25 .60
64 Martin Rucinsky .05 .15
65 Darryl Shannon .05 .15
66 Cliff Ronning .05 .15
67 Randy Robitaille .05 .15
68 David Legwand .15 .40
69 Mike Dunham .05 .15
70 Alexander Mogilny .15 .40
71 Patrik Elias .15 .40
72 Bobby Holik .05 .15
73 Scott Stevens .15 .40
74 Mariusz Czerkawski .05 .15
75 Tim Connolly .05 .15
76 Aris Brimanis .05 .15
77 John Vanbiesbrouck .15 .40
78 Brian Leetch .15 .40
79 Mike York .05 .15
80 Theo Fleury .05 .15
81 Mike Richter .20 .50
82 Alexei Yashin .05 .15
83 Ricard Persson .05 .15
84 Radek Bonk .05 .15
85 Patrick Lalime .15 .40
86 Simon Gagne .20 .50
87 Brian Boucher .10 .25
88 Keith Primeau .05 .15
89 Mark Greig .05 .15
90 Teppo Numminen .05 .15
91 Shane Doan .05 .15
92 Keith Tkachuk .10 .25
93 Sean Burke .15 .40
94 Milan Kraft .15 .40
95 Alexei Kovalev .15 .40
96 Jean-Sebastien Aubin .15 .40
97 Martin Straka .05 .15
98 Vincent Damphousse .05 .15
99 Steve Shields .15 .40
100 Brad Stuart .15 .40
101 Owen Nolan .15 .40
102 Chris Pronger .15 .40
103 Pavol Demitra .15 .40
104 Roman Turek .15 .40
105 Pierre Turgeon .15 .40
106 Dan Cloutier .05 .15
107 Brad Richards .15 .40
108 Paul Mara .05 .15
109 Gary Roberts .05 .15
110 Sergei Berezin .05 .15
111 Mats Sundin .20 .50
112 Bryan McCabe .05 .15
113 Henrik Sedin .05 .15
114 Daniel Sedin .05 .15
115 Greg Hawgood .05 .15
116 Adam Oates .05 .15
117 Olaf Kolzig .15 .40
118 Sergei Gonchar .05 .15
119 Bobby Orr 1.25 3.00
120 Cam Neely .20 .50
121 Gilbert Perreault .20 .50
122 Bobby Hull .40 1.00
123 Stan Mikita .30 .75
124 Tony Esposito .30 .75
125 Gordie Howe .40 1.00
126 Wayne Gretzky 1.25 3.00
127 Marcel Dionne .20 .50
128 Maurice Richard .75 2.00
129 Guy Lafleur .30 .75
130 Jean Beliveau .20 .50
131 Bryan Trottier .20 .50
132 Denis Potvin .50
133 Mike Bossy .20 .50
134 Bobby Clarke .30 .75
135 Bernie Parent .20 .50
136 Mario Lemieux 1.25 3.00
137 Michel Goulet .20 .50
138 Frank Mahovlich .20 .50
139 Paul Kariya .20 .50
140 Teemu Selanne .20 .50
141 Patrick Roy 1.00 2.50
142 Joe Sakic .40 1.00
143 Peter Forsberg .50 1.25
144 Ray Bourque .40 1.00
145 Mike Modano .30 .75
146 Steve Yzerman 1.00 2.50
147 Brendan Shanahan .20 .50
148 Pavel Bure .20 .50
149 Martin Brodeur .50 1.25
150 Scott Gomez .05 .15
151 Mark Messier .20 .50
152 Marian Hossa .20 .50
153 John LeClair .10 .25
154 Jeremy Roenick .25 .60
155 Jaromir Jagr .30 .75
156 Jeff Friesen .05 .15
157 Vincent Lecavalier .20 .50
158 Curtis Joseph .20 .50
159 Jonas Ronnqvist RC .20 .50
160 Jeff Cowan RC .20 .50
161 David Aebischer RC 1.25 3.00
162 Rostislav Klesla RC .50 1.25
163 Tyler Bouck RC .20 .50
164 Michel Riesen RC .20 .50
165 Steven Reinprecht RC .20 .50
166 Marian Gaborik RC 2.50 6.00
167 David Gosselin RC .20 .50
168 Scott Hartnell RC .50 1.25
169 Colin White RC .20 .50
170 Rick DiPietro RC 1.25 3.00
171 Johan Holmqvist RC .20 .50
172 Jani Hurme RC .50 1.25
173 Martin Havlat RC 1.50 4.00
174 Justin Williams RC .50 1.25
175 Roman Cechmanek RC .25 .60
176 Roman Simicek RC .20 .50
177 Zdenek Blatny RC .20 .50
178 Jordan Krestanovich RC .20 .50
179 Mark Messier CL .10 .30
180 Wayne Gretzky CL .60 1.50

2000-01 UD Heroes Game-Used Twigs

In 2000-01 UD Heroes inserted the Game-Used Twigs cards in packs at a rate of 1:83. The 20-card set featured a piece of a game-used hockey stick on the card. The card numbering had a 'T' prefix.

*MULT.COLOR STICK: 1X TO 2X
T-BH Bobby Hull 12.00 30.00
T-BO Bobby Orr 60.00 150.00
T-BO Mike Bossy 5.00 12.00
T-CJ Curtis Joseph 5.00 12.00
T-DH Dominik Hasek 6.00 15.00
T-GH Gordie Howe 15.00 40.00
T-GP Gilbert Perreault 5.00 12.00
T-JJ Jaromir Jagr 6.00 15.00
T-JL John LeClair 5.00 12.00
T-MB Martin Brodeur 10.00 25.00
T-ML Mario Lemieux 15.00 40.00
T-MM Mark Messier 5.00 12.00
T-MS Mats Sundin 5.00 12.00
T-PK Paul Kariya 5.00 12.00
T-PR Patrick Roy 15.00 40.00
T-RB Ray Bourque 6.00 15.00
T-SY Steve Yzerman 15.00 40.00
T-TF Theo Fleury 5.00 12.00
T-TS Teemu Selanne 5.00 12.00
T-WG Wayne Gretzky 40.00 100.00

2000-01 UD Heroes Game-Used Twigs Gold

In 2000-01 UD Heroes inserted the Game-Used Twigs Gold cards in packs. The 10-card combo set featured a piece of a game-used hockey stick from both players on the card. The card numbering had a 'C' prefix. The cards were serial numbered to 50.

C-BO Ray Bourque / Bobby Orr 150.00 400.00
C-FL Theo Fleury / John LeClair 30.00 75.00
C-GM Wayne Gretzky / Mark Messier 125.00 300.00
C-HB Bobby Hull / Mike Bossy 60.00 150.00
C-HP Dominik Hasek / Gilbert Perreault 30.00 75.00
C-HY Gordie Howe / Steve Yzerman 150.00 400.00
C-JS Curtis Joseph / Mats Sundin 30.00 75.00
C-KS Paul Kariya / Teemu Selanne 30.00 75.00
C-LJ M.Lemieux/J.Jagr 75.00 200.00
C-RB Patrick Roy / Martin Brodeur 60.00 150.00

2000-01 UD Heroes NHL Leaders

COMPLETE SET (10) 10.00 20.00
STATED ODDS 1:13
L1 Paul Kariya .50 1.25
L2 Ray Bourque 1.25 3.00
L3 Joe Sakic 1.25 3.00
L4 Steve Yzerman 3.00 8.00
L5 Mark Messier .75 2.00
L6 Alexei Yashin .50 1.25
L7 John LeClair .75 2.00
L8 Keith Tkachuk .60 1.50
L9 Jaromir Jagr 1.00 2.50
L10 Al MacInnis .50 1.25

2000-01 UD Heroes Player Idols

Inserted into packs at a rate of 1:23, This 6-card set featured young stars and their idols.

COMPLETE SET (6) 12.00 25.00
PI1 Brendan Shanahan / Mark Messier 1.00 2.50
PI2 M.Brodeur/P.Roy 3.00 8.00
PI3 Maxim Afinogenov / Pavel Bure 1.00 2.50
PI4 Paul Kariya / Wayne Gretzky 3.00 8.00
PI5 Vincent Lecavalier / Mario Lemieux 4.00 10.00
PI6 Roman Turek / Dominik Hasek 1.50 4.00

2000-01 UD Heroes Second Season Heroes

COMPLETE SET (10) 20.00 40.00
STATED ODDS 1:13
SS1 Patrick Roy 4.00 10.00
SS2 Peter Forsberg 2.00 5.00
SS3 Mike Modano 1.00 2.50
SS4 Ed Belfour 1.00 2.50
SS5 Steve Yzerman 4.00 10.00
SS6 Wayne Gretzky 5.00 12.00
SS7 Martin Brodeur 2.00 5.00
SS8 Mark Messier 1.00 2.50

SS9 John LeClair 1.00 2.50
SS10 Jaromir Jagr 1.25 3.00

2000-01 UD Heroes Signs of Greatness

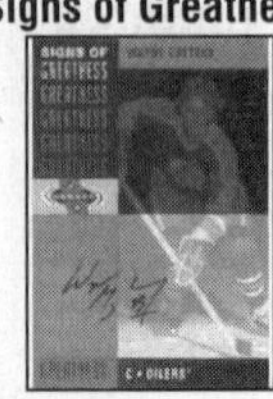

Randomly inserted in 2000-01 UD Heroes packs at a rate of 1:71, this 33-card set featured autograph cards from the top current and former player from the NHL. Please note that at time of release the Orr and Yzerman cards were inserted into packs as redemption cards, also note there are some short prints specified below.

BC Bobby Clarke 10.00 25.00
BH Bobby Hull SP 20.00 50.00
BO Bobby Orr SP 75.00 200.00
BP Bernie Parent 10.00 25.00
BT Bryan Trottier 10.00 25.00
CN Cam Neely 10.00 25.00
DP Denis Potvin 8.00 20.00
FM Frank Mahovlich 10.00 25.00
FP Felix Potvin 12.50 30.00
GH Gordie Howe SP 50.00 100.00
GL Guy Lafleur 15.00 40.00
GP Gilbert Perreault 10.00 25.00
JB Jean Beliveau 10.00 25.00
JL John LeClair 6.00 15.00
JR Jeremy Roenick SP 20.00 50.00
KJ Kenny Jonsson 4.00 10.00
MA Marc Denis 4.00 10.00
MD Marcel Dionne 10.00 25.00
MG Michel Goulet 10.00 25.00
ML Mario Lemieux SP 75.00 150.00
MM Mark Messier SP 50.00 100.00
MS Miroslav Satan 4.00 10.00
MY Mike York 4.00 10.00
PA Pavel Brendl 4.00 10.00
PB Pavel Bure SP 6.00 15.00
PB Peter Bondra 4.00 10.00
RL Roberto Luongo 8.00 20.00
RT Roman Turek 4.00 10.00
SG Scott Gomez 6.00 15.00
SM Stan Mikita 10.00 25.00
SY Steve Yzerman 30.00 80.00
TS Tommy Salo 4.00 10.00
WG Wayne Gretzky SP 100.00 200.00

2000-01 UD Heroes Timeless Moments

COMPLETE SET (10) 10.00 20.00
STATED ODDS 1:13
TM1 Teemu Selanne .60 1.50
TM2 Dominik Hasek 1.25 3.00
TM3 Patrick Roy 3.00 8.00
TM4 Brett Hull .75 2.00
TM5 Pavel Bure .75 2.00
TM6 Martin Brodeur 1.50 4.00
TM7 Mike York .50 1.25
TM8 Brian Boucher .60 1.50
TM9 Jaromir Jagr 1.00 2.50
TM10 Curtis Joseph .60 1.50

2000-01 UD Heroes Today's Snipers

COMPLETE SET (6) 5.00 10.00
STATED ODDS 1:23
TS1 Paul Kariya .60 1.50
TS2 Brendan Shanahan .75 2.00
TS3 Pavel Bure .75 2.00
TS4 John LeClair .75 2.00
TS5 Jaromir Jagr 1.00 2.50
TS6 Mats Sundin .60 1.50

2001-02 UD Honor Roll

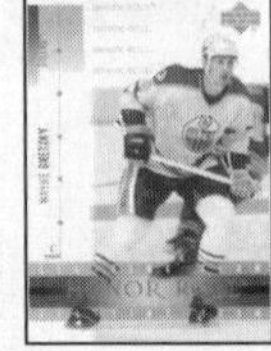

Released in mid-March 2002, this 100-card set carried an SRP of $2.99 fro a 5-card pack. The set consisted of 60 regular cards, 30 shortprinted rookies serial-numbered to 1499 and 10 dual jersey cards serial-numbered to 1000. Dual jersey cards featured one rookie and one veteran player.

COMP.SET w/o SP's (60) 20.00 40.00
1 Bobby Hull .40 1.00
2 Wayne Gretzky .75 2.00
3 Gordie Howe .60 1.50
4 Bobby Orr .60 1.50
5 Ray Bourque .25 .60
6 Patrick Roy .60 1.50
7 Luc Robitaille .10 .25
8 Mario Lemieux .75 2.00
9 Jaromir Jagr .20 .50
10 Chris Pronger .10 .25
11 Rob Blake .10 .25
12 Martin Brodeur .30 .75
13 Paul Kariya .12 .30
14 Joe Sakic .25 .60
15 Pavel Bure .12 .30
16 Nicklas Lidstrom .12 .30
17 Brian Leetch .10 .25
18 Dominik Hasek .25 .60
19 Brendan Shanahan .12 .30
20 Steve Yzerman .60 1.50
21 Teemu Selanne .12 .30
22 Al MacInnis .10 .25
23 Scott Stevens .10 .25
24 Curtis Joseph .12 .30
25 Dany Heatley .15 .40
26 Joe Thornton .20 .50
27 Mark Parrish .10 .25
28 Rostislav Klesla .10 .25
29 Brad Stuart .10 .25
30 Rick DiPietro .10 .25
31 Bobby Hull .40 1.00
32 Wayne Gretzky .75 2.00
33 Gordie Howe .60 1.50
34 Bobby Orr .60 1.50
35 Ray Bourque .25 .60
36 Patrick Roy .60 1.50
37 Luc Robitaille .10 .25
38 Mario Lemieux .75 2.00
39 Jaromir Jagr .20 .50
40 Chris Pronger .10 .25
41 Rob Blake .10 .25
42 Martin Brodeur .30 .75
43 Paul Kariya .12 .30
44 Joe Sakic .25 .60
45 Pavel Bure .15 .40
46 Nicklas Lidstrom .12 .30
47 Brian Leetch .10 .25
48 Dominik Hasek .25 .60
49 Brendan Shanahan .20 .50
50 Steve Yzerman .60 1.50
51 Teemu Selanne .12 .30
52 Al MacInnis .10 .25
53 Scott Stevens .10 .25
54 Curtis Joseph .12 .30
55 Dany Heatley .15 .40
56 Joe Thornton .20 .50
57 Mark Parrish .10 .25
58 Rostislav Klesla .10 .25
59 Brad Stuart .10 .25
60 Rick DiPietro .10 .25
61 Ilja Bryzgalov RC 3.00 8.00
62 Mike Weaver RC 2.00 5.00
63 Kamil Piros RC 2.00 5.00
64 Ben Simon RC 2.00 5.00
65 Ivan Huml RC 2.00 5.00
66 Ales Kotalik RC 2.00 5.00
67 Scottie Nichol RC 2.00 5.00
68 Kelly Fairchild RC 2.00 5.00
69 Vaclav Nedorost RC 2.00 5.00
70 Niko Kapanen RC 2.50 6.00
71 Pavel Datsyuk RC 8.00 20.00
72 Sean Avery RC 2.00 5.00
73 Kristian Huselius RC 2.50 6.00
74 Nick Smith RC 2.00 5.00
75 Nick Schultz RC 2.00 5.00
76 Marcel Hossa RC 2.00 5.00
77 Olivier Michaud RC 2.00 5.00
78 Martin Erat RC 2.00 5.00
79 Christian Berglund RC 2.00 5.00
80 Andreas Salomonsson RC 2.00 5.00
81 Radek Martinek RC 2.00 5.00
82 Richard Scott RC 2.00 5.00
83 Ivan Ciernik RC 2.00 5.00
84 Bruno St. Jacques RC 2.00 5.00
85 Dan Focht RC 2.00 5.00
86 Jeff Jillson RC 2.00 5.00
87 Mark Rycroft RC 2.00 5.00
88 Nikita Alexeev RC 2.00 5.00
89 Justin Kurtz RC 2.00 5.00
90 Chris Corrinet RC 2.00 5.00
91 Martin Spanhel 6.00 15.00
Tony Amonte JSY
92 Matt Davidson 8.00 20.00
Chris Drury JSY
93 Jaroslav Bednar 6.00 15.00
Zigmund Palffy JSY
94 Raffi Torres 8.00 20.00
Brendan Shanahan JSY
95 Mikael Samuelsson 6.00 15.00
Sergei Fedorov JSY
96 Dan Blackburn 6.00 15.00
Mike Richter JSY
97 Tomas Divisek 6.00 15.00
John LeClair JSY
98 Jiri Dopita 6.00 15.00
Pavol Demitra JSY
99 Krys Kolanos 6.00 15.00
Mike Modano JSY
100 Ilya Kovalchuk 12.50 30.00
Jaromir Jagr JSY

2001-02 UD Honor Roll Defense First

Inserted at 1:40, this 6-card set highlights the league's most defensive minded forwards.

COMPLETE SET (6) 10.00 20.00
DF1 Mike Modano 1.25 3.00
DF2 Jere Lehtinen .75 2.00
DF3 Steve Yzerman 4.00 10.00
DF4 Sergei Fedorov 1.25 3.00

DF5 John Madden .75 2.00
DF6 Michael Peca .75 2.00

2001-02 UD Honor Roll Honor Society

Serial-numbered to just 100 copies each, this 4-card set featured dual game-worn jersey swatches of the featured players. A gold parallel of this set was also created and serial-numbered to just 25 copies each. As of press time, not all cards have been verified.

*MULT.COLOR SWATCH: 1X TO 1.5X HI
*GOLD: 2X TO 5X BASIC CARD
HS-BB Pavel Bure 20.00 50.00
Valeri Bure
HS-CH Roman Cechmanek 20.00 50.00
Dominik Hasek
HS-HK Milan Hejduk 20.00 50.00
Paul Kariya
HS-RB Patrick Roy 30.00 80.00
Martin Brodeur

HS-LH M.Lemieux/D.Hasek 25.00 60.00
HS-RB Patrick Roy 30.00 80.00
Martin Brodeur
HS-SR Joe Sakic 20.00 50.00
Luc Robitaille
HS-SS Mats Sundin 12.50 30.00
Scott Stevens
HS-TM Alex Tanguay 12.50 30.00
Al MacInnis

2001-02 UD Honor Roll Jerseys

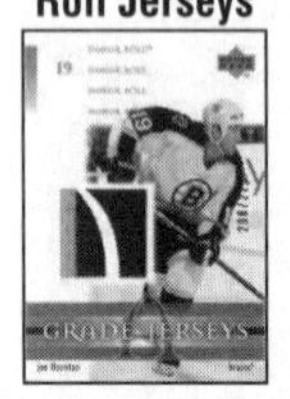

Serial-numbered to 225 copies each, this 31-card set featured game-worn jersey swatches of the featured players. A gold parallel was also created and serial-numbered to just 50 copies each.

*MULT.COLOR SWATCH: 1X TO 1.5X
*GOLD: 1.25X TO 3X BASIC CARD
J-BB Brian Boucher 4.00 10.00
J-BH Brett Hull 6.00 15.00
J-BL Brian Leetch 5.00 12.00
J-BS Brendan Shanahan 5.00 12.00
J-CD Chris Drury 4.00 10.00
J-DL David Legwand 4.00 10.00
J-DW Doug Weight 4.00 10.00
J-EB Ed Belfour 5.00 12.00
J-EL Eric Lindros 5.00 12.00
J-JH Jochen Hecht 4.00 10.00
J-JL John LeClair 4.00 10.00
J-JN Joe Nieuwendyk 4.00 10.00
J-JS Joe Sakic 8.00 20.00
J-JT Joe Thornton 6.00 15.00
J-LI Eric Lindros 5.00 12.00
J-LR Luc Robitaille 5.00 12.00
J-MB Martin Brodeur 8.00 20.00
J-ML Mario Lemieux 12.50 30.00
J-MM Mike Modano 6.00 15.00
J-MN Markus Naslund 4.00 10.00
J-MO Maxime Ouellet 4.00 10.00
J-MS Miroslav Satan 4.00 10.00
J-NL Nicklas Lidstrom 4.00 10.00
J-PB Peter Bondra 4.00 10.00
J-PD Pavol Demitra 4.00 10.00
J-PK Paul Kariya 5.00 12.00
J-RB Ray Bourque 8.00 20.00
J-RL Roberto Luongo 6.00 15.00
J-SF Sergei Fedorov 6.00 15.00
J-SS Sergei Samsonov 5.00 12.00
J-SU Mats Sundin 5.00 12.00
J-TC Tim Connolly 4.00 10.00

2001-02 UD Honor Roll Original Six

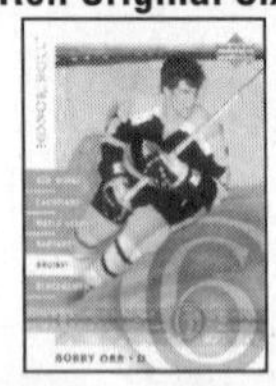

This 6-card set was inserted at 1:40 packs.

COMPLETE SET (6) 20.00 40.00
OS1 Bobby Orr 4.00 10.00
OS2 Bobby Hull 2.50 6.00
OS3 Gordie Howe 4.00 10.00
OS4 Patrick Roy 4.00 10.00
OS5 Wayne Gretzky 5.00 12.00
OS6 Curtis Joseph .75 2.00

2001-02 UD Honor Roll Playoff Matchups

Serial-numbered to 200 copies each, this 6-card set featured dual game-worn jersey swatches of the featured players. A gold parallel was also created and serial-numbered to 25.

*GOLD: 1.5X TO 4X BASIC CARD
HS-HT Brett Hull 12.50 30.00
Keith Tkachuk

2001-02 UD Honor Roll Pucks

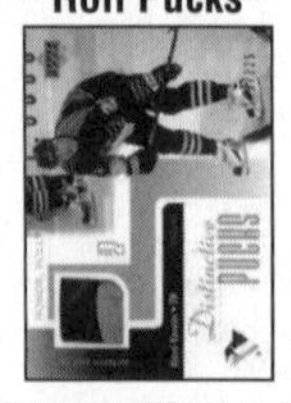

Serial-numbered to 225 copies each, this 12-card set featured a piece of game-used puck on each card. A gold parallel was also created and serial-numbered to 100 each.

GOLD: 1X TO 2.5X BASIC CARD
P-AK Alexei Kovalev 8.00 20.00
P-BL Brian Leetch 8.00 20.00
P-JI Jarome Iginla 15.00 40.00
P-MH Marian Hossa 10.00 25.00
P-MM Mark Messier 10.00 25.00
P-MS Mats Sundin 10.00 25.00
P-PB Pavel Bure 10.00 25.00
P-PE Patrik Elias 8.00 20.00
P-PO Peter Bondra 10.00 25.00
P-SK Saku Koivu 10.00 25.00
P-SS Scott Stevens 8.00 20.00
P-VL Vincent Lecavalier 10.00 25.00

2001-02 UD Honor Roll Sharp Skaters

This 6-card set was inserted at 1:40 packs.

COMPLETE SET (6) 10.00 20.00
SS1 Paul Kariya .75 2.00
SS2 Mike Modano 1.25 3.00
SS3 Sergei Fedorov 1.50 4.00
SS4 Pavel Bure 1.00 2.50
SS5 Marian Hossa .75 2.00
SS6 Simon Gagne .75 2.00

2001-02 UD Honor Roll Student of the Game

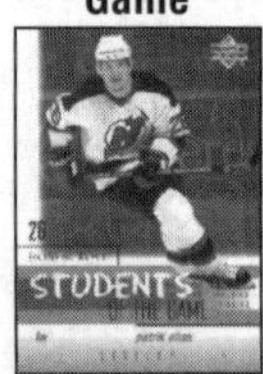

This 6-card set was inserted at 1:40 packs.

COMPLETE SET (6) 10.00 20.00
SG1 Paul Kariya .75 2.00
SG2 Joe Sakic 1.50 4.00
SG3 Mike Modano 1.25 3.00
SG4 Steve Yzerman 4.00 10.00
SG5 Patrik Elias .75 2.00
SG6 Mats Sundin .75 2.00

2001-02 UD Honor Roll Tough Customers

This 6-card set was inserted at 1:40 packs.

COMPLETE SET (6) 4.00 8.00
TC1 Martin Lapointe .60 1.50
TC2 Rob Blake .60 1.50
TC3 Scott Stevens .60 1.50
TC4 Jeremy Roenick .75 2.00
TC5 Owen Nolan .60 1.50
TC6 Chris Pronger .60 1.50

2001-02 UD Honor Roll Tribute to 500

This 2-card set featured swatches of game-used jerseys from Patrick Roy. Each card was serial-numbered to 500 copies each.

1 Patrick Roy 40.00 100.00
Montreal
2 Patrick Roy 40.00 100.00
Colorado

2002-03 UD Honor Roll

This 166-card set consisted of 100 veteran cards, 45 shortprinted rookie cards and 21 Dean's List jersey card rookies. Rookies #101-145 were serial-numbered to 1499 each and the jersey cards #146-166 were inserted at 1:48.

COMP.SET w/o SP's (100) 12.50 25.00
*MULT.COLOR JSY: .75X TO 1.5X
1 Paul Kariya .12 .30
2 J-S Giguere .10 .25
3 Ilya Kovalchuk .15 .40
4 Dany Heatley .15 .40
5 Joe Thornton .20 .50
6 Sergei Samsonov .10 .25
7 Miroslav Satan .10 .25
8 Martin Biron .10 .25
9 Chris Drury .10 .25
10 Jarome Iginla .15 .40
11 Ron Francis .10 .25
12 Arturs Irbe .10 .25
13 Tyler Arnason .10 .25
14 Jocelyn Thibault .10 .25
15 Patrick Roy .60 1.50
16 Joe Sakic .25 .60
17 Peter Forsberg .30 .75
18 Rob Blake .10 .25
19 Ray Whitney .08 .20
20 Marc Denis .10 .25
21 Mike Modano .20 .50
22 Marty Turco .10 .25
23 Bill Guerin .10 .25
24 Steve Yzerman .60 1.50
25 Sergei Fedorov .20 .50
26 Nicklas Lidstrom .12 .30
27 Brett Hull .15 .40
28 Curtis Joseph .12 .30
29 Brendan Shanahan .12 .30
30 Mike Comrie .12 .30
31 Tommy Salo .10 .25
32 Roberto Luongo .15 .40
33 Kristian Huselius .08 .20
34 Felix Potvin .12 .30
35 Zigmund Palffy .12 .30
36 Marian Gaborik .25 .60
37 Manny Fernandez .12 .30
38 Jose Theodore .15 .40
39 Saku Koivu .12 .30
40 Patrik Elias .12 .30
41 Martin Brodeur .30 .75
42 David Legwand .10 .25
43 Tomas Vokoun .10 .25
44 Alexei Yashin .08 .20
45 Chris Osgood .10 .25
46 Michael Peca .08 .20
47 Eric Lindros .12 .30
48 Mike Richter .12 .30
49 Pavel Bure .12 .30
50 Marian Hossa .12 .30
51 Daniel Alfredsson .12 .30
52 Jeremy Roenick .15 .40
53 John LeClair .12 .30
54 Roman Cechmanek .10 .25
55 Sean Burke .10 .25
56 Tony Amonte .10 .25
57 Alex Kovalev .10 .25
58 Mario Lemieux .75 2.00
59 Owen Nolan .10 .25
60 Evgeni Nabokov .10 .25
61 Keith Tkachuk .12 .30
62 Brent Johnson .10 .25
63 Nikolai Khabibulin .12 .30
64 Vincent Lecavalier .12 .30
65 Mats Sundin .12 .30
66 Ed Belfour .12 .30
67 Todd Bertuzzi .12 .30
68 Markus Naslund .12 .30
69 Olaf Kolzig .10 .25
70 Jaromir Jagr .20 .50
71 Paul Kariya .12 .30
72 Shawn McEachern .08 .20
73 Joe Thornton .20 .50
74 Stu Barnes .08 .20
75 Craig Conroy .08 .20
76 Ron Francis .10 .25
77 Alexei Zhamnov .08 .20
78 Joe Sakic .25 .60
79 Ray Whitney .08 .20
80 Derian Hatcher .08 .20
81 Steve Yzerman .60 1.50
82 Jason Smith .08 .20
83 Valeri Bure .08 .20
84 Mattias Norstrom .08 .20
85 Andrew Brunette .08 .20
86 Saku Koivu .12 .30
87 Greg Johnson .08 .20
88 Scott Stevens .10 .25
89 Michael Peca .08 .20
90 Brian Leetch .10 .25
91 Daniel Alfredsson .10 .25
92 Keith Primeau .08 .20
93 Teppo Numminen .08 .20
94 Mario Lemieux .75 2.00
95 Owen Nolan .10 .25
96 Chris Pronger .10 .25
97 Vincent Lecavalier .12 .30
98 Mats Sundin .12 .30
99 Markus Naslund .12 .30
100 Steve Konowalchuk .08 .20
101 Alexei Smirnov RC 3.00 8.00
102 Martin Gerber RC 5.00 12.00
103 Kurt Sauer RC 3.00 8.00
104 Tim Thomas RC 5.00 12.00
105 Jordan Leopold RC 3.00 8.00
106 Dany Sabourin RC 3.00 8.00
107 Levente Szuper RC 3.00 8.00
108 Shawn Thornton RC 3.00 8.00
109 Matt Henderson RC 3.00 8.00
110 Lasse Pirjeta RC 3.00 8.00
111 Pascal LeClaire RC 5.00 12.00
112 Dmitri Bykov RC 3.00 8.00
113 Kari Haakana RC 3.00 8.00
114 Craig Andersson RC 3.00 8.00
115 Mike Cammalleri RC 3.00 8.00
116 Stephane Veilleux RC 3.00 8.00
117 Adam Hall RC 3.00 8.00
118 Greg Koehler RC 3.00 8.00
119 Vernon Fiddler RC 3.00 8.00
120 Ray Emery RC 5.00 12.00
121 Eric Godard RC 3.00 8.00
122 Dennis Seidenberg RC 3.00 8.00
123 Jeff Taffe RC 3.00 8.00
124 Dick Tarnstrom RC 3.00 8.00
125 Tom Koivisto RC 3.00 8.00
126 Curtis Sanford RC 3.00 8.00
127 Cody Rudkowsky RC 3.00 8.00
128 Carlo Colaiacovo RC 3.00 8.00
129 Paul Manning RC 3.00 8.00
130 Shaone Morrisonn RC 3.00 8.00
131 Ryan Miller RC 8.00 20.00
132 Jerred Smithson RC 3.00 8.00
133 Alexei Semenov RC 3.00 8.00
134 Michael Leighton RC 3.00 8.00
135 Ian MacNeil RC 3.00 8.00
136 Jared Aulin RC 3.00 8.00
137 Curtis Murphy RC 3.00 8.00
138 Jim Vandermeer RC 3.00 8.00
139 Steve Ott RC 3.00 8.00
140 Brooks Orpik RC 3.00 8.00
141 Jim Fahey RC 3.00 8.00
142 Matt Walker RC 3.00 8.00
143 Rickard Wallin RC 3.00 8.00
144 Tomas Malec RC 3.00 8.00
145 Jonathan Hedstrom RC 3.00 8.00
146 Stanislav Chistov JSY RC 5.00 12.00
147 Chuck Kobasew JSY RC 5.00 12.00
148 Micki Dupont JSY RC 5.00 12.00
149 Jeff Paul JSY RC 5.00 12.00
150 Rick Nash JSY RC 20.00 50.00
151 Henrik Zetterberg JSY RC 15.00 40.00
152 Ales Hemsky JSY RC 10.00 25.00
153 Jay Bouwmeester JSY RC 6.00 15.00
154 Alexander Frolov JSY RC 10.00 25.00
155 P-M Bouchard JSY RC 6.00 15.00
156 Sylvain Blouin JSY RC 5.00 12.00
157 Ron Hainsey JSY RC 5.00 12.00
158 Scottie Upshall JSY RC 5.00 12.00
159 Tomi Pettinen JSY RC 5.00 12.00
160 Jason Spezza JSY RC 15.00 40.00
161 Anton Volchenkov JSY RC 5.00 12.00
162 Radovan Somik JSY RC 5.00 12.00
163 Lynn Loyns JSY RC 5.00 12.00
164 Alexander Svitov JSY RC 5.00 12.00
165 Mikael Tellqvist JSY RC 5.00 12.00
166 Steve Eminger JSY RC 5.00 12.00

2002-03 UD Honor Roll Grade A Jerseys

*MULT.COLOR SWATCH: .5X TO 1.25X
SINGLE JSY.ODDS 1:26
TRIPLE JSY.ODDS 1:480
GAED Eric Daze 3.00 8.00
GAJJ Jaromir Jagr 5.00 12.00
GAMB Martin Brodeur 8.00 20.00
GAMD Mike Dunham 3.00 8.00
GAMM Mike Modano 4.00 10.00
GAMS Mats Sundin 3.00 8.00
GAOK Olaf Kolzig 3.00 8.00
GAPF Peter Forsberg 5.00 12.00
GAPK Paul Kariya 3.00 8.00
GAPR Patrick Roy 10.00 25.00
GARB Ray Bourque 5.00 12.00
GASA Miroslav Satan 3.00 8.00
GASG Simon Gagne 3.00 8.00
GASK Saku Koivu 3.00 8.00
TJKB Jaromir Jagr 15.00 40.00
Olaf Kolzig
Peter Bondra
TPRG Keith Primeau 25.00 60.00
Jeremy Roenick
Simon Gagne
TRFS Patrick Roy 50.00 125.00
Peter Forsberg
Joe Sakic
TSTM Sergei Samsonov 15.00 40.00
Joe Thornton
Glen Murray
TYFS Yzerman/Fedorov/Shanny 30.00 80.00

2002-03 UD Honor Roll Signature Class

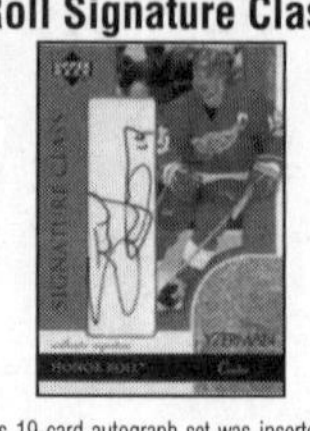

This 19-card autograph set was inserted at 1:480. The Orr and Howe cards were not priced due to scarcity. Printed print runs were provided by Upper Deck.

AS Alexander Svitov 10.00 25.00
BO Bobby Orr/10
BR Pavel Brendl 6.00 15.00
DH Dany Heatley 10.00 25.00
GH Gordie Howe/9
HZ Henrik Zetterberg 75.00 150.00
JB Jay Bouwmeester 12.00 30.00
JL John LeClair 8.00 20.00
JS Jason Spezza 200.00 400.00
MA Maxim Afinogenov 6.00 15.00
MB Martin Brodeur SP 150.00 300.00
MF Manny Fernandez 6.00 15.00
NK Nikolai Khabibulin SP
PB Pavel Bure 6.00 15.00
PR Patrick Roy 75.00 200.00
SC Stanislav Chistov 12.50 30.00
SY Steve Yzerman 40.00 100.00
TS Teemu Selanne SP
WGO Wayne Gretzky/9

2002-03 UD Honor Roll Students of the Game

COMPLETE SET (30) 20.00 40.00
STATED ODDS 1:6
SG1 Paul Kariya .30 .75
SG2 Dany Heatley .30 .75
SG3 Joe Thornton .40 1.00
SG4 Jarome Iginla .40 1.00
SG5 Chris Drury .25 .60
SG6 Joe Sakic .60 1.50
SG7 Patrick Roy 1.50 4.00
SG8 Peter Forsberg .75 2.00
SG9 Rick Nash 1.25 3.00
SG10 Mike Modano .50 1.25
SG11 Bill Guerin .25 .60
SG12 Curtis Joseph .30 .75
SG13 Steve Yzerman 1.50 4.00
SG14 Sergei Fedorov .60 1.50
SG15 Mike Comrie .25 .60
SG16 Marian Gaborik .30 .75
SG17 Saku Koivu .30 .75
SG18 Martin Brodeur .75 2.00
SG19 Alexei Yashin .25 .60
SG20 Pavel Bure .50 1.25
SG21 Eric Lindros .50 1.25
SG22 Jason Spezza 1.00 2.50
SG23 Jeremy Roenick .40 1.00
SG24 Tony Amonte .30 .75
SG25 Mario Lemieux 2.00 5.00
SG26 Teemu Selanne .30 .75
SG27 Keith Tkachuk .30 .75
SG28 Vincent Lecavalier .30 .75
SG29 Mats Sundin .30 .75
SG30 Jaromir Jagr .75 2.00

2002-03 UD Honor Roll Team Warriors

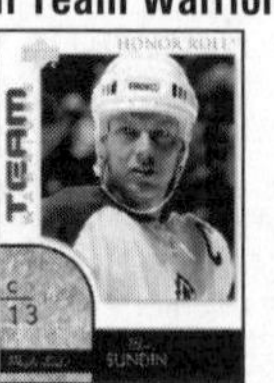

COMPLETE SET (15) 10.00 20.00
STATED ODDS 1:12
TW1 Joe Thornton .60 1.50
TW2 Jarome Iginla .50 1.25
TW3 Jeff O'Neill .30 .75
TW4 Peter Forsberg 1.00 2.50
TW5 Mike Modano .60 1.50
TW6 Brendan Shanahan .60 1.50
TW7 Adam Deadmarsh .30 .75
TW8 Saku Koivu .40 1.00
TW9 Michael Peca .30 .75
TW10 Eric Lindros .40 1.00
TW11 John LeClair .40 1.00
TW12 Mario Lemieux 2.50 6.00
TW13 Owen Nolan .30 .75
TW14 Mats Sundin .40 1.00
TW15 Todd Bertuzzi .40 1.00

2003-04 UD Honor Roll

This 191-card set consisted of several subsets: cards 1-90 were base veteran cards; cards 91-110 made up the "Students of the Game" subset and were serial-numbered out of 999; cards 111-125 made up the "Class Reunion" subset and were serial-numbered out of 500; cards 126-132 made up the "Head of the Class" subset and were serial-numbered to 250; cards 133-167 were rookie cards serial-numbered to 800 and cards 133-167 were rookie jersey cards that made up the "Dean's List" subset . The "Dean's List" jerseys were inserted at 1:24. Please note that there is no card #63 and there are two cards numbered #48.

COMPLETE SET (191)
COMP. SET w/o SP's (90) 8.00 15.00
1 J-S Giguere .10 .25
2 Sergei Fedorov .15 .40
3 Dany Heatley .15 .40
4 Ilya Kovalchuk .15 .40
5 Felix Potvin .12 .30
6 Joe Thornton .20 .50
7 Sergei Samsonov .10 .25
8 Chris Drury .10 .25
9 Daniel Briere .05 .15
10 Jarome Iginla .15 .40
11 Roman Turek .10 .25
12 Jamie Storr .10 .25
13 Ron Francis .10 .25
14 Kyle Calder .05 .15
15 Jocelyn Thibault .10 .25
16 Tyler Arnason .10 .25
17 David Aebischer .10 .25
18 Joe Sakic .25 .60
19 Paul Kariya .12 .30
20 Peter Forsberg .30 .75
21 Marc Denis .10 .25
22 Rick Nash .15 .40
23 Todd Marchant .05 .15
24 Bill Guerin .10 .25
25 Marty Turco .10 .25
26 Mike Modano .20 .50
27 Dominik Hasek .25 .60
28 Henrik Zetterberg .12 .30
29 Steve Yzerman .60 1.50
30 Ales Hemsky .10 .25
31 Mike Comrie .10 .25
32 Tommy Salo .10 .25
33 Jay Bouwmeester .05 .15
34 Olli Jokinen .10 .25
35 Roberto Luongo .15 .40
36 Alexander Frolov .05 .15
37 Jason Allison .05 .15
38 Roman Cechmanek .10 .25
39 Zigmund Palffy .10 .25
40 Manny Fernandez .10 .25
41 Marian Gaborik .25 .60
42 Pierre-Marc Bouchard .05 .15
43 Jose Theodore .15 .40
44 Marcel Hossa .05 .15
45 Saku Koivu .12 .30
46 David Legwand .10 .25
47 Tomas Vokoun .10 .25
48 Martin Brodeur .30 .75
48 Jeff Hackett .10 .25
49 Scott Gomez .05 .15
50 Scott Stevens .10 .25
51 Alexei Yashin .05 .15
52 Michael Peca .05 .15
53 Rick DiPietro .10 .25
54 Alex Kovalev .10 .25
55 Eric Lindros .12 .30
56 Mark Messier .12 .30
57 Mike Dunham .10 .25
58 Daniel Alfredsson .10 .25
59 Jason Spezza .12 .30
60 Marian Hossa .12 .30
61 Patrick Lalime .10 .25
62 John LeClair .12 .30
64 Jeremy Roenick .15 .40
65 Simon Gagne .12 .30
66 Mike Johnson .05 .15
67 Sean Burke .10 .25
68 Mario Lemieux .75 2.00
69 Martin Straka .05 .15
70 Evgeni Nabokov .10 .25
71 Patrick Marleau .10 .25
72 Vincent Damphousse .05 .15
73 Chris Pronger .10 .25
74 Chris Osgood .10 .25
75 Doug Weight .10 .25
76 Keith Tkachuk .12 .30
77 Pavol Demitra .10 .25
78 Nikolai Khabibulin .12 .30
79 Vincent Lecavalier .12 .30
80 Alexander Mogilny .10 .25
81 Ed Belfour .12 .30
82 Mats Sundin .12 .30
83 Owen Nolan .10 .25
84 Ed Jovanovski .10 .25
85 Johan Hedberg .10 .25
86 Markus Naslund .12 .30
87 Todd Bertuzzi .12 .30
88 Jaromir Jagr .20 .50
89 Olaf Kolzig .10 .25
90 Peter Bondra .10 .25
91 Marian Gaborik SOG 1.50 4.00
92 Joe Thornton SOG 1.50 4.00
93 J-S Giguere SOG .75 2.00
94 Ilya Kovalchuk SOG 1.25 3.00
95 Ales Hemsky SOG .75 2.00
96 Mike Komisarek SOG .75 2.00
97 Rick Nash SOG 1.00 2.50
98 Marty Turco SOG .75 2.00
99 Alexander Frolov SOG .75 2.00
100 Jay Bouwmeester SOG .75 2.00
101 Henrik Zetterberg SOG 1.00 2.50
102 Marian Hossa SOG 1.00 2.50
103 Ales Kotalik SOG .75 2.00
104 Vincent Lecavalier SOG .75 2.00
105 Pavel Datsyuk SOG 1.00 2.50
106 Andrew Raycroft SOG .75 2.00
107 Philippe Sauve SOG .75 2.00
108 Marcel Hossa SOG .75 2.00
109 Rick DiPietro SOG .75 2.00
110 Jason Spezza SOG 1.00 2.50
111 Brendan Shanahan CR 1.25 3.00
112 Joe Sakic CR 2.50 6.00
113 Mike Modano CR 2.00 5.00
114 Jeremy Roenick CR 1.50 4.00
115 Teemu Selanne CR 1.25 3.00
116 Mats Sundin CR 1.25 3.00
117 Sergei Fedorov CR 1.50 4.00
118 Owen Nolan CR 1.00 2.50
119 Jaromir Jagr CR 2.00 5.00
120 Peter Forsberg CR 3.00 8.00
121 Markus Naslund CR 1.25 3.00
122 Alexei Yashin CR .50 1.50
123 Manny Fernandez CR 1.00 2.50
124 Paul Kariya CR 1.25 3.00
125 Saku Koivu CR 1.25 3.00
126 Peter Forsberg HOC 4.00 10.00
127 Steve Yzerman HOC 8.00 20.00
128 Joe Thornton HOC 2.50 6.00
129 Martin Brodeur HOC 6.00 15.00
130 Mario Lemieux HOC 10.00 25.00
131 Ed Belfour HOC 1.50 4.00
132 Mike Modano HOC 2.50 6.00
133 Darryl Bootland RC 2.50 6.00
134 Trevor Daley RC 2.50 6.00
135 John-Michael Liles RC 2.50 6.00
136 Paul Martin RC 2.50 6.00
137 Esa Pirnes RC 2.50 6.00
138 Seamus Kotyk RC 2.50 6.00
139 Pat Rissmiller RC 2.50 6.00
140 Marek Svatos RC 4.00 10.00
141 Maxim Kondratiev RC 2.50 6.00
142 Marek Zidlicky RC 2.50 6.00
143 Matthew Spiller RC 2.50 6.00
144 Nathan Smith RC 2.50 6.00
145 Brent Burns RC 2.50 6.00
146 Boyd Gordon RC 2.50 6.00
147 Andrew Hutchinson RC 2.50 6.00
148 Peter Sarno RC 2.50 6.00
149 Jed Ortmeyer RC 2.50 6.00
150 Cody McCormick RC 2.50 6.00
151 Christoph Brandner RC 2.50 6.00
152 Grant McNeill RC 2.50 6.00
153 Greg Campbell RC 2.50 6.00
154 Tony Salmelainen RC 2.50 6.00
155 Kent McDonell RC 2.50 6.00
156 Martin Strbak RC 2.50 6.00
157 Matt Murley RC 2.50 6.00
158 Rastislav Stana RC 2.50 6.00
159 Karl Stewart RC 2.50 6.00
160 Ryan Malone RC 4.00 10.00
161 Wade Brookbank RC 2.50 6.00
162 Mike Stuart RC 2.50 6.00
163 Sergei Zinovjev RC 2.50 6.00
164 Julien Vauclair RC 2.50 6.00
165 Alan Rourke RC 2.50 6.00
166 John Pohl RC 2.50 6.00
167 Dominic Moore RC 2.50 6.00
168 Peter Sejna JSY RC 3.00 8.00
169 Matt Stajan JSY RC 6.00 15.00
170 Milan Michalek JSY RC 5.00 12.00
171 Pavel Vorobiev JSY RC 4.00 10.00
172 Dan Hamhuis JSY RC 3.00 8.00
173 Chris Higgins JSY RC 8.00 20.00
174 Antti Miettinen JSY RC 3.00 8.00
175 Christian Ehrhoff JSY RC 3.00 8.00
176 Alexander Semin JSY RC 6.00 15.00
177 Antoine Vermette JSY RC 3.00 8.00
178 Travis Moen JSY RC 3.00 8.00
179 Joni Pitkanen JSY RC 3.00 8.00
180 Patrice Bergeron JSY RC 10.00 25.00
181 Jiri Hudler JSY RC 4.00 10.00
182 Marc-Andre Fleury JSY RC 15.00 40.00
183 Dustin Brown JSY RC 3.00 8.00
184 Joffrey Lupul JSY RC 5.00 12.00
185 Tuomo Ruutu JSY RC 6.00 15.00
186 Jordin Tootoo JSY RC 6.00 15.00
187 Eric Staal JSY RC 12.00 30.00
188 Nathan Horton JSY RC 6.00 15.00
189 Tim Gleason JSY RC 3.00 8.00
190 Sean Bergenheim JSY RC 3.00 8.00
191 Matthew Lombardi JSY RC 3.00 8.00

2003-04 UD Honor Roll Grade A Jerseys

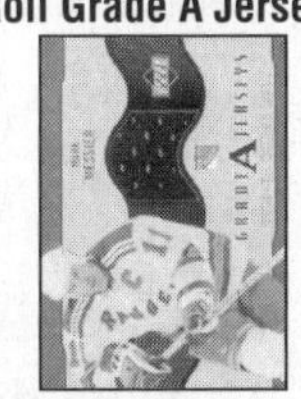

STATED ODDS 1:24
TRIPLE JSY ODDS 1:480
GAAY Alexei Yashin 3.00 8.00
GAJI Jarome Iginla 5.00 12.00
GAJT Joe Thornton 5.00 12.00
GAMB Martin Brodeur 8.00 20.00
GAML Mario Lemieux 12.50 30.00
GAMM Mark Messier 8.00 20.00
GAMS Miroslav Satan 4.00 10.00
GASG Simon Gagne 4.00 10.00
GATM Marty Turco 4.00 10.00
GAVL Vincent Lecavalier 4.00 10.00
TBOS Joe Thornton 15.00 40.00
Sergei Samsonov
Glen Murray
TCOL Paul Kariya 25.00 60.00
Joe Sakic
Peter Forsberg
TDET Dominik Hasek 30.00 80.00
Steve Yzerman
Henrik Zetterberg
TNYR Eric Lindros 20.00 50.00
Pavel Bure
Alex Kovalev
TTOR Mats Sundin 15.00 40.00
Owen Nolan
Ed Belfour
TVAN Markus Naslund 20.00 50.00
Todd Bertuzzi
Trevor Linden

2003-04 UD Honor Roll Signature Class

STATED ODDS 1:480
PRINT RUNS UNDER 25 NOT PRICED DUE TO SCARCITY
SC1 David Aebischer/10
SC2 Todd Bertuzzi/24
SC3 Martin Brodeur/10
SC4 Pavel Bure/24
SC5 Sergei Fedorov/10
SC6 Marian Gaborik/24
SC7 J-S Giguere/24
SC8 Wayne Gretzky/10
SC9 Scott Hartnell/24
SC10 Martin Havlat/24
SC11 Marian Hossa/24
SC12 Gordie Howe/10
SC13 Jarome Iginla/24
SC14 Curtis Joseph/49 20.00 50.00
SC15 Saku Koivu/10
SC16 Ilya Kovalchuk/10
SC17 John LeClair/49 12.50 30.00
SC18 Eric Lindros/24
SC19 Joe Nieuwendyk/24
SC20 Bobby Orr/10
SC21 Ziggy Palffy/24
SC22 Jeremy Roenick/24
SC23 Patrick Roy/10
SC24 Sergei Samsonov/49 12.50 30.00
SC25 Jose Theodore/49 20.00 50.00
SC26 Joe Thornton/24
SC27 Marty Turco/24
SC28 Adam Hall/24
SC29 Chuck Kobasew/24
SC30 Jason Spezza/10
SC31 Jason Blake/10
SC32 Mark Parrish/24

2004-05 UD Legendary Signatures

Released in late-summer 2004, this 100-card set featured some of the more colorful greats of the past.

COMPLETE SET (100) 40.00 80.00
1 Al Iafrate .30 .75
2 Butch Goring .30 .75
3 Bernie Federko .30 .75
4 Bernie Geoffrion .50 1.25
5 Bill Barber .30 .75
6 Bill White .30 .75
7 Bob Nystrom .30 .75
8 Bobby Clarke .50 1.25
9 Bobby Hull 1.00 2.50
10 Borje Salming .40 1.00
11 Brad Marsh .30 .75
12 Brad Park .40 1.00
13 Brian Bellows .30 .75
14 Brian Sutter .30 .75
15 Bryan Trottier .40 1.00
16 Cam Neely .60 1.50
17 Charlie Simmer .30 .75
18 Clark Gillies .30 .75
19 Craig Hartsburg .30 .75
20 Darryl Sittler .50 1.25
21 Billy Smith .40 1.00
22 Dave Schultz .40 1.00
23 Dave Taylor .30 .75
24 Tiger Williams .40 1.00
25 Denis Potvin .40 1.00
26 Dennis Hull .40 1.00
27 Denis Savard .50 1.25
28 Dino Ciccarelli .40 1.00
29 Don Cherry 1.00 2.50
30 Don Marcotte .30 .75
31 Doug Gilmour .50 1.25
32 Doug Wilson .30 .75
33 Tony Twist .30 .75
34 Errol Thompson .30 .75
35 Frank Mahovlich .50 1.25
36 Gerry Cheevers .75 2.00
37 Gilbert Perreault .50 1.25
38 Glenn Anderson .30 .75
39 Glenn Hall .50 1.25
40 Gordie Howe 1.00 2.50
41 Grant Fuhr .40 1.00
42 Guy Lafleur 1.00 2.50
43 Guy Lapointe .30 .75
44 Henri Richard .50 1.25
45 Ian Turnbull .30 .75
46 Jari Kurri .50 1.25
47 Jean Beliveau .60 1.50
48 Brian Propp .50 1.25
49 Johnny Bower .50 1.25
50 Johnny Bucyk .50 1.25
51 Ken Hodge .30 .75
52 Ken Morrow .30 .75
53 Lanny McDonald .40 1.00
54 Gump Worsley .50 1.25
55 Marcel Dionne .50 1.25
56 Mark Howe .30 .75
57 Mike Bossy .50 1.25
58 Mike Ramsey .30 .75
59 Neal Broten .30 .75
60 Pat Stapleton .30 .75
61 Richard Brodeur .40 1.00
62 Paul Coffey .50 1.25
63 Paul Henderson .40 1.00
64 Peter Mahovlich .30 .75
65 Phil Esposito .75 2.00
66 Randy Gregg .30 .75
67 Red Berenson .30 .75
68 Reggie Leach .30 .75
69 Rene Robert .30 .75
70 Rick Martin .30 .75
71 Wayne Babych .30 .75
72 Willi Plett .30 .75
73 Rod Seiling .30 .75
74 Ron Ellis .30 .75
75 Ron Duguay .30 .75
76 Rogie Vachon .50 1.25
77 Stan Jonathan .40 1.00
78 Stan Mikita .50 1.25
79 Steve Larmer .30 .75
80 Steve Shutt .40 1.00
81 Stu Grimson .30 .75
82 Ted Lindsay .50 1.25
83 Terry O'Reilly .40 1.00
84 Tony Esposito .50 1.25
85 Tony Tanti .30 .75
86 Vic Hadfield .30 .75
87 Wayne Cashman .30 .75
88 Wayne Gretzky 1.25 3.00
89 Rob McClanahan .30 .75
90 Yvan Cournoyer .50 1.25
91 Chris Nilan .40 1.00
92 Dave Christian .30 .75
93 Don Awrey .30 .75
94 J.P. Parise .30 .75
95 Jim Craig .40 1.00
96 Keith Brown .30 .75
97 Ken Linseman .30 .75
98 Mark Tinordi .30 .75
99 Harold Snepsts .30 .75
100 Michel Goulet .30 .75

2004-05 UD Legendary Signatures AKA Autographs

This 24-card set featured signatures of past greats along with their nicknames. Each card was serial-numbered out of 100.

AKA-GH Gordie Howe/Mr.Hockey 50.00 125.00
AKA-GE B.Geoffrion Boom Boom 40.00 80.00
AKA-DG Doug Gilmour/Killer 25.00 60.00
AKA-TO Terry O'Reilly/Taz 20.00 50.00
AKA-HA Glenn Hall/Mr.Goalie 20.00 50.00
AKA-JB John Bucyk/Chief 20.00 50.00
AKA-HS Dave Schultz/The Hammer 25.00 60.00
AKA-CN C.Nilan Knuckles 20.00 50.00
AKA-JE Jean Beliveau/LeGros Bill 40.00 100.00
AKA-GL G.Lafleur The Flower 40.00 80.00
AKA-RD Richard Brodeur/King 20.00 50.00
AKA-MJ Mark Johnson/Capt.America 40.00 80.00
AKA-TW Tony Twist/Twister 20.00 50.00
AKA-BH Bobby Hull/Golden Jet 40.00 100.00
AKA-SG Stu Grimson/Grim Reaper 20.00 50.00
AKA-BO Johnny Bower/China Wall 30.00 80.00
AKA-GC Gerry Cheevers/Cheesy 25.00 60.00
AKA-AI Al Iafrate/Wild Thing 20.00 50.00
AKA-TE Tony Esposito/Tony O 30.00 80.00
AKA-BN Bob Nystrom/Thor 20.00 50.00
AKA-FM Frank Mahovlich/Big M 25.00 60.00
AKA-DC Don Cherry/Grapes 40.00 80.00
AKA-YC Yvan Cournoyer/Roadrunner 40.00 100.00
AKA-LW Lorne Worsley/Gump 20.00 50.00

2004-05 UD Legendary Signatures Autographs

This 100-card autograph set paralleled the base set with certified player signatures and were inserted one per pack. Known short-print numbers are listed below.

AI Al Iafrate 5.00 12.00
BB Bill Barber 5.00 12.00
BC Bobby Clarke/34 50.00 125.00
BE Brian Bellows 5.00 12.00
BF Bernie Federko 6.00 15.00
BG Butch Goring 6.00 15.00
BH Bobby Hull/81 50.00 125.00
BI Billy Smith 10.00 25.00
BM Brad Marsh 5.00 12.00
BN Bob Nystrom 5.00 12.00
BO Johnny Bower 6.00 15.00
BP Brian Propp 6.00 15.00
BR Brian Sutter 5.00 12.00
BS Borje Salming 15.00 40.00
BT Bryan Trottier 6.00 15.00
BW Bill White 5.00 12.00
CA Cam Neely 15.00 40.00
CG Clark Gillies 5.00 12.00
CH Craig Hartsburg 5.00 12.00
CI Dino Ciccarelli 10.00 25.00
CN Chris Nilan 6.00 15.00
CS Charlie Simmer 5.00 12.00
DC Don Cherry 12.00 30.00
DE Denis Savard 6.00 15.00
DG Doug Gilmour/84 25.00 60.00
DH Dennis Hull 6.00 15.00
DM Don Marcotte 5.00 12.00
DP Denis Potvin 6.00 15.00
DS Darryl Sittler/91 20.00 50.00
DT Dave Taylor 5.00 12.00
DU Ron Duguay 5.00 12.00
DV Dave Christian 5.00 12.00
DW Doug Wilson 5.00 12.00
ET Errol Thompson 5.00 12.00
FM Frank Mahovlich/41 150.00 350.00
GA Glenn Anderson 5.00 12.00
GC Gerry Cheevers 15.00 40.00
GE Bernie Geoffrion 12.00 30.00
GF Grant Fuhr 10.00 25.00
GH Gordie Howe 40.00 100.00
GL Guy Lafleur/25 200.00 400.00
GP Gilbert Perreault/34 100.00 200.00
HA Glenn Hall 12.50 30.00
HR Henri Richard 8.00 20.00
HS Dave Schultz 6.00 15.00
IT Ian Turnbull 5.00 12.00
JB Johnny Bucyk 6.00 15.00
JC Jim Craig 15.00 40.00
JE Jean Beliveau/98 60.00 150.00
JK Jari Kurri 10.00 25.00
JP J.P. Parise 5.00 12.00
KB Keith Brown 5.00 12.00
KH Ken Hodge 5.00 12.00
KL Ken Linseman 5.00 12.00
KM Ken Morrow 5.00 12.00
LA Guy Lapointe 5.00 12.00
LM Lanny McDonald 6.00 15.00
LW Gump Worsley 20.00 50.00
LY Rod Langway 10.00 25.00
MB Mike Bossy 8.00 15.00
MD Marcel Dionne 10.00 25.00
MG Michel Goulet 5.00 12.00
MH Mark Howe 5.00 12.00
MT Mark Tinordi 5.00 12.00
NB Neal Broten 6.00 15.00
PC Paul Coffey 12.50 30.00
PE Phil Esposito/37 100.00 250.00
PH Paul Henderson 10.00 25.00
PM Peter Mahovlich 6.00 15.00
PS Pat Stapleton 5.00 12.00
RA Mike Ramsey 5.00 12.00
RB Red Berenson 5.00 12.00
RD Richard Brodeur 6.00 15.00
RE Ron Ellis 5.00 12.00
RG Randy Gregg 5.00 12.00
RL Reggie Leach 5.00 12.00
RM Rick Martin 5.00 12.00
RR Rene Robert 5.00 12.00
RS Rod Seiling 5.00 12.00
RV Rogie Vachon 10.00 25.00
SC Steve Shutt 6.00 15.00
SG Stu Grimson 5.00 12.00
SJ Stan Jonathan 6.00 15.00
SL Steve Larmer 5.00 12.00
SM Stan Mikita/91 30.00 80.00
SN Harold Snepsts 5.00 12.00
SS Stan Smyl 5.00 12.00
TE Tony Esposito/62 40.00 100.00
TI Tiger Williams 6.00 15.00
TL Ted Lindsay 10.00 25.00
TO Terry O'Reilly/96 25.00 60.00
TT Tony Tanti 5.00 12.00
TW Tony Twist 5.00 12.00
VH Vic Hadfield 5.00 12.00
VP Brad Park 6.00 15.00
WB Wayne Babych 5.00 12.00
WC Wayne Cashman 6.00 15.00
WG Wayne Gretzky 75.00 150.00
WP Willi Plett 5.00 12.00
YC Yvan Cournoyer 6.00 15.00

2004-05 UD Legendary Signatures Buybacks

This 195-card set featured past Upper Deck cards that were "bought back" by UD and autographed by the given player. The original set and print runs are listed below.

PRINT RUNS UNDER 25 NOT PRICED DUE TO SCARCITY
1 Bernie Federko UD Legends/2
2 Bernie Federko UD Legends/2
3 Bernie Geoffrion UD Retro/2
4 Bernie Geoffrion UD Legends/1
5 Bill Barber UD Legends Jerseys/10
6 Bill Barber UD Legends Milestones/17
7 Billy Smith UD Legends Sticks/8
8 Billy Smith UD Vintage Jerseys/38
9 Billy Smith UD Vintage Jerseys/15
10 Bobby Clarke UD Century Legends/2
11 Bobby Clarke UD Retro/4
12 Bobby Clarke UD Retro Generation/1
13 Bobby Clarke UD Heroes/2
14 Bobby Clarke UD Legends/2
15 Bobby Clarke UD Legends/Enshrined Stars 1
16 Bobby Clarke UD Legends/4
17 Bobby Clarke UD Legends Milestones/18
18 Bobby Clarke UD LegendsSticks/5
19 Bobby Clarke UD Vintage Jerseys/9
20 Bobby Hull UD Century Legends/1
21 Bobby Hull UD Retro/7
22 Bobby Hull UD Heroes/2
23 Bobby Hull UD Legends/1
24 Bobby Hull UD Legends Playoff Heroes/1
25 Bobby Hull UD Legends/2
26 Bobby Hull UD Legends/3
27 Bryan Trottier Upper Deck Locker All-Stars/1
28 Bryan Trottier Upper Deck/1
29 Bryan Trottier UD Century Legends/2
30 Bryan Trottier UD Heroes/3
31 Bryan Trottier UD Legends/2
32 Bryan Trottier UD Legends/4
33 Bryan Trottier UD Legends Milestones/13
34 Bryan Trottier UD Legends Sticks/6
35 Bryan Trottier UD Vintage Jerseys/19
36 Cam Neely Upper Deck/1
37 Cam Neely Upper Deck/1
38 Cam Neely Upper Deck SP/1
39 Cam Neely SP/1
40 Cam Neely UD Heroes/1
41 Cam Neely UD Legends/1
42 Cam Neely UD Legends Jerseys/11
43 Cam Neely UD Legends Milestones/10
44 Clark Gillies Upper Deck/1
45 Clark Gillies UD Legends/1
46 Clark Gillies UD Legends/5
47 Clark Gillies UD Legends Jerseys/13
48 Darryl Sittler Upper Deck AS Sittler/2
49 Darryl Sittler UD Legends/3
50 Darryl Sittler UD Legends Sticks/11
51 Denis Potvin UD Legends Jerseys/8
52 Denis Potvin UD Legends Milestones/22
53 Denis Potvin UD Legends Sticks/8
54 Doug Gilmour Upper Deck/1
55 Doug Gilmour UD Retro/4
56 Doug Gilmour Upper Deck/1
57 Doug Gilmour Upper Deck/1
58 Doug Gilmour Upper Deck/1
59 Doug Gilmour Upper Deck SP/1
60 Doug Gilmour SP Holoview Collection/1
61 Doug Gilmour SPx/1
62 Doug Gilmour SPx Finite/1
63 Doug Gilmour UD Retro/3
64 Doug Gilmour UD Heroes/1
65 Doug Gilmour UD Legends/1
66 Frank Mahovlich Upper Deck/1
67 Frank Mahovlich UD Heroes/2
68 Frank Mahovlich UD Legends/3
69 Frank Mahovlich UD Legends Sticks/1
70 Gerry Cheevers UD Retro/4
71 Gerry Cheevers UD Legends/3
72 Gerry Cheevers UD Legend/3
73 Gerry Cheevers UD Legends Jerseys/9
74 Gerry Cheevers UD Legends Sticks/11
75 Gerry Cheevers UD Vintage Jerseys/27
76 Gilbert Perreault UD Heroes/2
77 Gilbert Perreault UD Heroes Game-Used Twigs/15
78 Gilbert Perreault UD Legends/1
79 Gilbert Perreault UD Legends/4
80 Gilbert Perreault UD Legends Jerseys/10
81 Gilbert Perreault UD Legends Milestones/21
82 Gilbert Perreault UD Vintage Jerseys/17
83 Glenn Anderson Upper Deck/1
84 Glenn Anderson UD Legends/4
85 Glenn Hall UD Century Legends/1
86 Glenn Hall UD Retro/3
87 Gordie Howe UD All-Star/5
88 Gordie Howe UD Heroes/1
89 Gordie Howe UD Legends/2
90 Gordie Howe UD Legends Enshrined Stars/1
91 Gordie Howe SP Authentic/1
92 Gordie Howe UD Legends/3
93 Gordie Howe UD Legends/3
94 Gordie Howe UD Legends/3
95 Gordie Howe UD Legends Fiorentino Collection/1
96 Gordie Howe UD Legends Jerseys/10
97 Gordie Howe UD Stanley Cup Champs/1
98 Gordie Howe UD Vintage Jerseys/1
99 Gordie Howe SPx/1
100 Gordie Howe UD Piece of History/1
101 Guy Lafleur Upper Deck/1
102 Guy Lafleur UD Heroes/2
103 Guy Lafleur UD Legends/1
104 Guy Lafleur UD Legends/2
105 Guy Lafleur UD Legends/3
106 Guy Lafleur UD Legends Jerseys/13
107 Guy Lafleur UD Legends Jerseys/11
108 Guy Lafleur UD Legends Jerseys/13
109 Guy Lafleur UD Legends Jerseys/10
110 Guy Lafleur UD Legends Sticks/13
111 Henri Richard Upper Deck Locker All-Stars/1
112 Henri Richard UD Century Legends/1
113 Henri Richard UD Retro/3
114 Henri Richard UD Legends/1
115 Jari Kurri Upper Deck/1
116 Jari Kurri Upper Deck/1
117 Jari Kurri Upper Deck/1
118 Jari Kurri Upper Deck Junior Grade/1
119 Jari Kurri UD Century Legends/2
120 Jari Kurri UD Retro/4
121 Jari Kurri UD Legends/2
122 Jari Kurri UD Legends/2
123 Jari Kurri UD Legends/1
124 Jari Kurri UD Legends Sticks/5
125 Johnny Bucyk UD Century Legends/1
126 Johnny Bucyk UD Retro/5
127 Johnny Bucyk UD Legends/1
128 Johnny Bucyk UD Legends/2
129 Lanny McDonald Upper Deck Locker All-Stars/1
130 Lanny McDonald UD Retro/4
131 Lanny McDonald UD Legends/1
132 Lanny McDonald UD Legends/4
133 Lanny McDonald UD Legends Milestones/18
134 Marcel Dionne Upper Deck/2
135 Marcel Dionne UD Century Legends/2
136 Marcel Dionne UD Retro/3
137 Marcel Dionne UD Heroes/2
138 Marcel Dionne UD Legends/1
139 Marcel Dionne UD Legends/4
140 Marcel Dionne UD Legends/4
141 Marcel Dionne UD Legends Sticks/14
142 Michel Goulet Upper Deck/1
143 Michel Goulet Upper Deck/1
144 Michel Goulet

UD Heroes/3
145 Michel Goulet
UD Legends/2
146 Michel Goulet
UD Legends/4
147 Mike Bossy
UD Century Legends/1
148 Mike Bossy
UD Retro/3
149 Mike Bossy
UD Heroes/2
150 Mike Bossy
UD Heroes Game-Used/Twigs 3
151 Mike Bossy
UD Legends/2
152 Mike Bossy
UD Legends Legendary Game Jerseys/1
153 Mike Bossy
UD Legends Supreme Milestones/1
154 Mike Bossy
UD Legends/3
155 Mike Bossy
UD Legends/2
156 Mike Bossy
UD Legends Milestones/1
157 Mike Bossy
UD Legends Sticks/18
158 Mike Bossy
UD Foundations/1
159 Neal Broten 30.00 60.00
UD Legends Milestones/37
160 Paul Coffey
Upper Deck Locker All-Stars/1
161 Paul Coffey
Upper Deck/1
162 Paul Coffey
Upper Deck/2
163 Paul Coffey
Upper Deck/1
164 Paul Coffey
Upper Deck/1
165 Paul Coffey
Upper Deck Gretzky's Great Ones/1
166 Paul Coffey
Upper Deck SP/1
167 Paul Coffey
SP/2
168 Paul Coffey
SP Stars/Etoiles/1
169 Paul Coffey
SP Clearcut Winner/1
170 Paul Coffey
UD Century Legends/2
171 Paul Coffey
UD Legends/2
172 Phil Esposito
UD Retro/3
173 Phil Esposito
UD Legends/1
174 Phil Esposito
UD Legends/2
175 Phil Esposito
UD Legends Fiorentino Collection/1
176 Phil Esposito
UD Legends Jerseys/11
177 Phil Esposito
UD Legends Sticks/6
178 Phil Esposito
UD Vintage Jerseys/35
179 Rogie Vachon 40.00 80.00
UD Vintage Jerseys/30
180 Steve Shutt
UD Legends Milestones/20
181 Steve Shutt
UD Vintage Sweaters of Honor/35
182 Stan Mikita
Upper Deck Locker All-Stars/1
183 Stan Mikita
UD Retro/5
184 Stan Mikita
UD Retro Generation/2
185 Stan Mikita
UD Heroes/1
186 Ted Lindsay
UD Retro/3
187 Ted Lindsay
UD Legends/2
188 Ted Lindsay
UD Legends/4
189 Tony Esposito
UD Retro/4
190 Tony Esposito
UD Heroes/1
191 Tony Esposito
UD Legends/2
192 Tony Esposito
UD Legends Enshrined Stars/1
193 Tony Esposito
UD Legends/2
194 Tony Esposito
UD Legends/2
195 Tony Esposito
UD Legends Sticks/8

2004-05 UD Legendary Signatures HOF Inks

This 14-card set celebrated past great who have been inducted into the Hall of Fame. Each card was serial-numbered to the year in which the star was inducted and those print runs are listed below.

HOF-HR Henri Richard/79 20.00 50.00
HOF-BC Bobby Clarke/87 20.00 50.00
HOF-BO Johnny Bower/76 20.00 50.00
HOF-TE Tony Esposito/88 20.00 50.00
HOF-DS Darryl Sittler/89 20.00 50.00
HOF-GH Gordie Howe/72 75.00 200.00
HOF-CG Clarke Gillies/102 15.00 40.00
HOF-JB Johnny Bucyk/81 15.00 40.00
HOF-GF Grant Fuhr/103 25.00 60.00
HOF-GP Gilbert Perreault/90 15.00 40.00
HOF-BI Billy Smith/93 15.00 40.00
HOF-MD Marcel Dionne/92 20.00 50.00
HOF-HA Glenn Hall/75 25.00 60.00
HOF-MB Mike Bossy/91 15.00 40.00

2004-05 UD Legendary Signatures Linemates

This 13-card set featured triple autographs of great lines from the past. Each card was serial-numbered to just 50 copioes.

BBBCRL Bill Barber/Bobby Clarke
Reggie Leach 100.00 200.00
BENBCI Bellows/Broten/
Ciccarelli 40.00 100.00
BRBFWB Sutter/Federko/Babych 40.00 100.00
CGBTMB Gillies/Trottier/Bossy 75.00 200.00
CSMDDT Charlie Simmer/Marcel
Dionne/Dave Taylor 100.00 200.00
ETDSLM Thompson
Sittler/McDonald 60.00 150.00
GAWGJK Glenn Anderson/Wayne
Gretzky/Jari Kurri 300.00 500.00
RMGPRR Ric Martin/Gilbert Perreault/
Rene Robert 75.00 200.00
SCPMGL Shutt/P.Mahovlich/Lafleur 40.00 100.00
SJDMTO Jonathan/Marcotte/O'Reilly 40.00 100.00
SLDEMG Larmer/Savard/Goulet 40.00 100.00
TISSTT Williams/Smyl/Tanti 40.00 100.00
WCPEKH Wayne Cashman/Phil
Esposito/Ken Hodge 75.00 200.00

2004-05 UD Legendary Signatures Miracle Men

This 18-card set highlighted the 1980 USA Olympic hockey team. Cards were inserted one per US pack.

COMPLETE SET (18) 10.00 20.00
STATED ODDS 1:1 US
USA1 Mike Eruzione 1.50 4.00
USA2 Jim Craig 1.25 3.00
USA3 Rob McClanahan .50 1.25
USA4 Buzz Schneider .50 1.25
USA5 Mark Johnson .60 1.50
USA6 Neal Broten .60 1.50
USA7 Mark Pavelich .50 1.25
USA8 Dave Christian .60 1.50
USA9 Mike Ramsey .50 1.25
USA10 Ken Morrow .50 1.25
USA11 Steve Christoff .50 1.25
USA12 Bill Baker .50 1.25
USA13 Marc Wells .50 1.25
USA14 John Harrington .50 1.25
USA15 Dave Silk .50 1.25
USA16 Steve Janasak .50 1.25
USA17 Eric Strobel .50 1.25
USA18 Bob Suter .50 1.25

2004-05 UD Legendary Signatures Miracle Men Autographs

Inserted at 1:5 packs, this 18-card set featured certified autographs from the 1980 USA Olympic Hockey team. Please note that the Mark Johnson card was issued as a redemption and has yet to be fulfilled though UD states Johnson is committed to signing.

KNOWN PRINT RUNS LISTED BELOW
USA-JA Steve Janasak 20.00 50.00
USA-ES Eric Strobel 10.00 25.00
USA-DV Dave Christian 40.00 100.00
USA-BI Bill Baker 10.00 25.00
USA-KM Ken Morrow 25.00 60.00
USA-RO Rob McClanahan 10.00 25.00
USA-ME Mike Eruzione 30.00 60.00
USA-OB Bob Suter 10.00 25.00
USA-ST Steve Christoff 10.00 25.00
USA-SI Dave Silk 10.00 25.00
USA-JC Jim Craig/73 200.00 450.00
USA-MW Marc Wells 10.00 25.00
USA-MP Mark Pavelich 10.00 25.00
USA-BZ Buzz Schneider 10.00 25.00
USA-NB Neal Broten/73 400.00 700.00
USA-RA Mike Ramsey/97 200.00 300.00
USA-JH John Harrington 10.00 25.00
USA-MJ Mark Johnson 25.00 60.00

2004-05 UD Legendary Signatures Rearguard Retrospectives

This 6-card se featured great defensive combinations from the past. Each card carried dual autographs and was limited to 100 copies each.

BMMH Brad Marsh/Mark Howe 12.50 30.00
BSIT Borje Salming/Ian Turnbull 25.00 60.00
CHMT Craig Hartsburg/Mark Tinordi 12.50 30.00
DPKM D.Potvin/K.Morrow 25.00 60.00
DWKB Doug Wilson/Keith Brown 12.50 30.00
PCRG Paul Coffey/Randy Gregg 20.00 50.00

2004-05 UD Legendary Signatures Summit Stars

This 20-card set highlighted the 1972 Canada Cup Canadian team.

COMPLETE SET (20) 10.00 20.00
STATED ODDS 1:1 CANADIAN
CDN1 Phil Esposito 1.00 2.50
CDN2 Paul Henderson .75 2.00
CDN3 Bobby Clarke .60 1.50
CDN4 Yvan Cournoyer .60 1.50
CDN5 Brad Park .50 1.25
CDN6 Dennis Hull .50 1.25
CDN7 J.P. Parise .50 1.25
CDN8 Ron Ellis .50 1.25
CDN9 Gilbert Perreault .60 1.50
CDN10 Frank Mahovlich .60 1.50
CDN11 Peter Mahovlich .50 1.25
CDN12 Bill White .50 1.25
CDN13 Wayne Cashman .50 1.25
CDN14 Stan Mikita .60 1.50
CDN15 Red Berenson .50 1.25
CDN16 Don Awrey .50 1.25
CDN17 Vic Hadfield .50 1.25
CDN18 Rod Seiling .50 1.25
CDN19 Pat Stapleton .50 1.25
CDN20 Tony Esposito .60 1.50

2004-05 UD Legendary Signatures Summit Stars Autographs

This 20-card set paralleled the basic insert set but carried certified player autographs. Known short-print numbers are listed below.

STATED ODDS 1:5 CANADIAN
KNOWN PRINT RUNS LISTED BELOW
CDN-YC Yvan Cournoyer 12.50 30.00
CDN-PM Pete Mahovlich 6.00 15.00
CDN-BW Bill White 6.00 15.00
CDN-PS Pat Stapleton 6.00 15.00
CDN-FM Frank Mahovlich/48 100.00 200.00
CDN-PH Paul Henderson 12.50 30.00
CDN-BP Brad Park 12.50 30.00
CDN-BC Bobby Clarke/73 75.00 150.00
CDN-WC Wayne Cashman 6.00 15.00
CDN-VH Vic Hadfield 6.00 15.00
CDN-PE Phil Esposito/48 100.00 250.00
CDN-RS Rod Seiling 6.00 15.00
CDN-JP J.P. Parise 6.00 15.00
CDN-DH Dennis Hull 6.00 15.00
CDN-RE Ron Ellis 6.00 15.00
CDN-SM Stan Mikita/97 50.00 125.00
CDN-GP Gilbert Perreault/48 60.00 150.00
CDN-RB Red Berenson 6.00 15.00
CDN-TE Tony Esposito/24 250.00 500.00
CDN-DA Don Awrey 6.00 15.00

2004-05 UD Legends Classics

Released in late-2004, this 100-card set featured past greats of the NHL.

COMPLETE SET (100) 20.00 40.00
1 Al Iafrate .20 .50
2 Andy Bathgate .30 .75
3 Bernie Geoffrion .30 .75
4 Bill Barber .25 .60
5 Bob Cole .20 .50
6 Bob Nystrom .20 .50
7 Bobby Clarke .40 1.00
8 Bobby Hull .60 1.50
9 Brad Park .25 .60
10 Bryan Trottier .25 .60
11 Butch Goring .20 .50
12 Cam Neely .40 1.00
13 Clark Gillies .20 .50
14 Tiger Williams .25 .60
15 Dave Schultz .25 .60
16 Dave Taylor .20 .50
17 Derek Sanderson .20 .50
18 Dickie Moore .25 .60
19 Don Cherry .60 1.50
20 Doug Wilson .20 .50
21 Frank Mahovlich .30 .75
22 Fred Cusick .20 .50
23 Gerry Cheevers .25 .60
24 Gilbert Perreault .30 .75
25 Glenn Anderson .20 .50
26 Glenn Hall .30 .75
27 Gordie Howe .60 1.50
28 Grant Fuhr .40 1.00
29 Guy Lafleur .50 1.25
30 Jari Kurri .30 .75
31 Jean Beliveau .50 1.25
32 Johnny Bower .30 .75
33 Johnny Bucyk .30 .75
34 Ken Hodge .20 .50
35 Ken Morrow .20 .50
36 Lanny McDonald .25 .60
37 Larry Murphy .20 .50
38 Gump Worsley .30 .75
39 Marcel Dionne .30 .75
40 Mike Bossy .30 .75
41 Patrick Roy .75 2.00
42 Paul Coffey .30 .75
43 Paul Henderson .25 .60
44 Phil Esposito .50 1.25
45 Phil Esposito .50 1.25
46 Red Kelly .30 .75
47 Reggie Leach .20 .50
48 Rene Robert .20 .50
49 Rick Martin .20 .50
50 Stan Mikita .30 .75
51 Ted Lindsay .30 .75
52 Tony Esposito .30 .75
53 Wayne Cashman .20 .50
54 Wayne Gretzky 1.00 2.50
55 Darryl Sittler .30 .75
56 Gordie Howe .60 1.50
57 Gordie Howe .60 1.50
58 Paul Henderson .25 .60
59 Darryl Sittler .30 .75
60 Mike Bossy .30 .75
61 Tiger Williams .25 .60
62 Patrick Roy .75 2.00
63 Paul Coffey .30 .75
64 Marcel Dionne .30 .75
65 Mike Bossy .30 .75
66 Bobby Hull .60 1.50
67 Jari Kurri .30 .75
68 Bryan Trottier .25 .60
69 Phil Esposito .50 1.25
70 Bobby Clarke .40 1.00
71 Jean Beliveau .50 1.25
72 Stan Mikita .30 .75
73 Gilbert Perreault .30 .75
74 Glenn Hall .30 .75
75 Guy Lafleur .50 1.25
76 Ken Morrow .20 .50
77 Tony Esposito .30 .75
78 Johnny Bower .30 .75
79 Wayne Gretzky 1.00 2.50
80 Wayne Gretzky 1.00 2.50
81 Gordie Howe .60 1.50
82 Wayne Gretzky 1.00 2.50
83 Bobby Hull .60 1.50
84 Bobby Clarke .40 1.00
85 Gilbert Perreault .30 .75
86 Darryl Sittler .30 .75
87 Guy Lafleur .50 1.25
88 Glenn Hall .30 .75
89 Andy Bathgate .30 .75
90 Red Kelly .30 .75
91 Tony Esposito .30 .75
92 Jean Beliveau .50 1.25
93 Grant Fuhr .40 1.00
94 Frank Mahovlich .30 .75
95 Gerry Cheevers .25 .60
96 Phil Esposito .50 1.25
97 Bryan Trottier .25 .60
98 Dickie Moore .20 .50
99 Stan Mikita .30 .75
100 Marcel Dionne .30 .75

2004-05 UD Legends Classics Gold

COMMON GRETZKY 40.00 100.00
*GOLD: 10X TO 25X BASE HI
GOLD PRINT RUN 25 SER.'d SETS

2004-05 UD Legends Classics Platinum

PLATINUM PRINT RUN 10 SER.#'d SETS
NOT PRICED DUE TO SCARCITY

2004-05 UD Legends Classics Silver

COMMON GRETZKY 20.00 50.00
*SILVER: 5X TO 12X BASE HI
SILVER PRINT RUN 75 SER.#'d SETS

2004-05 UD Legends Classics Jacket Redemptions

Cards from this set were redeemable for Mitchell & Ness throwback jackets of the teams represented on the card.

STATED ODDS 1:384
JK1 Boston Bruins
JK2 Chicago Blackhawks 150.00 300.00
JK3 Detroit Red Wings
JK4 Montreal Canadiens 125.00 250.00
JK5 Toronto Maple Leafs 150.00 300.00

2004-05 UD Legends Classics Jersey Redemptions

Cards from this set were redeemable for Mitchell & Ness throwback jerseys of the players represented on the card. Please note, some cards have yet to be verified.

STATED ODDS 1:384
JY1 Henri Richard 60.00 150.00
JY2 Jean Beliveau 150.00 300.00
JY3 Maurice Richard 150.00 300.00
JY4 Dickie Moore
JY5 Doug Harvey 60.00 150.00
JY6 Jacques Plante 125.00 250.00
JY7 Bernie Geoffrion 60.00 150.00
JY8 Frank Mahovlich
JY9 T.Sawchuk TOR 175.00 350.00
JY10 Tim Horton 150.00 300.00
JY11 Johnny Bower 60.00 150.00
JY12 Red Kelly 75.00 150.00
JY13 Eddie Shack 60.00 150.00
JY14 Dave Keon 60.00 150.00
JY15 Marcel Pronovost 60.00 150.00
JY16 W.Gretzky EDM 300.00 700.00
JY17 Stan Mikita
JY18 Bobby Orr 250.00 500.00
JY19 Gordie Howe 250.00 500.00
JY20 T.Sawchuk DET 150.00 300.00
JY21 Bobby Clarke 125.00 250.00
JY22 Tony Esposito
JY23 P.Esposito BOS
JY24 P.Esposito NYR
JY25 Guy Lafleur 60.00 150.00
JY26 W.Gretzky AS 350.00 700.00
JY27 Bill Barber
JY28 Dave Williams
JY29 Dave Schultz 60.00 150.00
JY30 Grant Fuhr 60.00 150.00
JY31 Reggie Leach

2004-05 UD Legends Classics Pennants

Inserted one per box, these team pennants were produced by Mitchell & Ness for UD. Numbers P1-P12 were limited to 158 copies and numbers P13-P19 were limited to 88 copies.

P1 The Dynamite Line 20.00 50.00
P2 The Kid Line 12.50 30.00
P3 The Punch Line 10.00 25.00
P4 The Pony Line 12.50 30.00
P5 The Kraut Line 10.00 25.00
P6 The Production Line 20.00 50.00
P7 The Uke Line 15.00 40.00
P8 The LCB Line 10.00 25.00
P9 The Big Three 10.00 25.00
P10 The GAG Line 12.50 30.00
P11 The Triple Crown Line
P12 The French Connection 12.50 30.00
P13 Kansas City Scouts 30.00 80.00
P14 California Golden Seals 20.00 50.00
P15 Colorado Rockies 12.50 30.00
P16 Atlanta Flames 6.00 15.00
P17 Hartford Whalers 15.00 40.00
P18 Quebec Nordiques 10.00 25.00
P19 Winnipeg Jets 15.00 40.00
P20 Boston Bruins 10.00 25.00
P21 NY Rangers 6.00 15.00
P22 Chicago Blackhawks 6.00 15.00
P23 Detroit Red Wings 10.00 25.00
P24 Toronto Maple Leafs 8.00 20.00
P25 Montreal Canadiens 6.00 15.00
P26 Philadelphia Flyers 6.00 15.00
P27 LA Kings 6.00 15.00
P28 St.Louis Blues 8.00 20.00
P29 Minnesota North Stars 10.00 25.00
P30 Pittsburgh Penguins 6.00 15.00
P31 Oakland Seals 6.00 15.00
P32 Detroit Cougars 6.00 15.00
P33 Toronto St.Pats 6.00 15.00

2004-05 UD Legends Classics Signature Moments

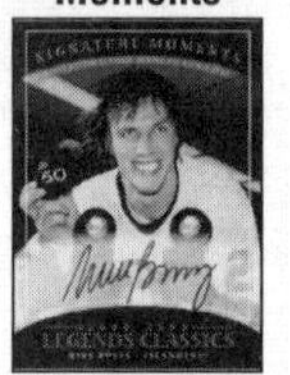

PRINT RUN 125 SER.#'d SETS
M1 Wayne Gretzky 100.00 250.00
M2 Gordie Howe 50.00 125.00
M3 Don Cherry 20.00 50.00
M4 Red Kelly 10.00 25.00
M5 Dickie Moore 8.00 20.00
M6 Andy Bathgate 10.00 25.00
M7 Terry O'Reilly 12.50 30.00
M8 Wayne Cashman 8.00 20.00
M9 Tony Esposito 15.00 40.00
M10 Ted Lindsay 15.00 40.00
M11 Stan Mikita 10.00 25.00
M12 Reggie Leach 8.00 20.00
M13 Rene Robert 8.00 20.00
M14 Rick Martin 8.00 20.00
M15 Phil Esposito 20.00 50.00
M16 Paul Henderson 8.00 20.00
M17 Paul Coffey 12.50 30.00
M18 Mike Bossy 10.00 25.00
M19 Lanny McDonald 12.50 30.00
M20 Gump Worsley 10.00 25.00
M21 Marcel Dionne 10.00 25.00
M22 Ken Morrow 8.00 20.00
M23 Ken Hodge 8.00 20.00
M24 Johnny Bucyk 10.00 25.00
M25 Johnny Bower 12.50 30.00
M26 Jari Kurri 12.50 30.00
M27 Cam Neely 15.00 40.00
M28 Jean Beliveau 20.00 50.00
M29 Guy Lafleur 20.00 50.00
M30 Gerry Cheevers 12.50 30.00
M31 Gilbert Perreault 12.50 30.00
M32 Glenn Anderson 8.00 20.00
M33 Glenn Hall 10.00 25.00
M34 Dave Taylor 8.00 20.00
M35 Grant Fuhr 20.00 50.00
M36 Frank Mahovlich 12.50 30.00
M37 Don Cherry 20.00 50.00
M38 Doug Wilson 8.00 20.00
M39 Dave Schultz 8.00 20.00
M40 Tiger Williams 10.00 25.00
M41 Dave Taylor 8.00 20.00
M42 Clark Gillies 10.00 25.00
M43 Bryan Trottier 12.50 30.00
M44 Butch Goring 8.00 20.00
M45 Bernie Geoffrion 12.50 30.00
M46 Al Iafrate 8.00 20.00
M47 Bill Barber 8.00 20.00
M48 Bob Nystrom 8.00 20.00
M49 Bobby Clarke 12.50 30.00
M50 Bobby Hull 25.00 60.00
M51 Brad Park 8.00 20.00
M52 Patrick Roy 60.00 150.00
M53 Ray Bourque 25.00 60.00
M54 Derek Sanderson 15.00 40.00
M55 Reggie Leach 8.00 20.00
M56 Jari Kurri 12.50 30.00
M57 Marcel Dionne 10.00 25.00
M58 Ken Hodge 8.00 20.00
M59 Dave Schultz 8.00 20.00
M60 Brad Park 8.00 20.00
M61 Gilbert Perreault 12.50 30.00
M62 Ken Morrow 8.00 20.00
M63 Gerry Cheevers 15.00 40.00
M64 Ted Lindsay 10.00 25.00
M65 Dave Taylor 8.00 20.00
M66 Cam Neely 20.00 50.00
M67 Johnny Bucyk 10.00 25.00
M68 Larry Murphy 8.00 20.00
M69 Fred Cusick 8.00 20.00
M70 Bob Cole 8.00 20.00

2004-05 UD Legends Classics Signatures

This 98-card set featured 4 different levels including single, dual, triple and quadruple autographs. Overall odds were 1:12 packs. An explanation of noted short-prints is below.

SP PRINT RUN 200 OR FEWER
SSP PRINT RUN 100 OR FEWER
XSP PRINT RUN 55 OR FEWER
DUAL PRINT RUN 75 SER.#'d SETS
TRIPLE PRINT RUN 25 SER.#'d SETS
QUAD PRINT RUN 10 SER.#'d SETS
QUADS NOT PRICED DUE TO SCARCITY
CS1 Wayne Gretzky XSP 200.00 400.00
CS2 Gordie Howe SSP 50.00 125.00
CS3 Don Cherry 15.00 40.00
CS4 Red Kelly 10.00 25.00
CS5 Dickie Moore 8.00 20.00
CS6 Andy Bathgate 10.00 25.00
CS7 Terry O'Reilly 12.50 30.00
CS8 Wayne Cashman 6.00 15.00
CS9 Tony Esposito XSP 40.00 100.00
CS10 Ted Lindsay XSP 20.00 50.00
CS11 Stan Mikita XSP 25.00 60.00
CS12 Reggie Leach 6.00 15.00
CS13 Rene Robert 8.00 20.00
CS14 Rick Martin 8.00 20.00
CS15 Phil Esposito XSP 75.00 150.00
CS16 Paul Henderson 8.00 20.00
CS17 Paul Coffey SSP 20.00 50.00
CS18 Mike Bossy 10.00 25.00
CS19 Lanny McDonald SP 12.50 30.00
CS20 Gump Worsley 20.00 50.00
CS21 Marcel Dionne SSP 25.00 60.00
CS22 Ken Morrow 6.00 15.00
CS23 Ken Hodge 6.00 15.00
CS24 Johnny Bucyk SP 10.00 25.00
CS25 Johnny Bower 10.00 25.00
CS26 Jari Kurri 10.00 25.00
CS27 Cam Neely SP 20.00 50.00
CS28 Jean Beliveau SSP 40.00 100.00
CS29 Guy Lafleur XSP 75.00 150.00
CS30 Gerry Cheevers 12.50 30.00
CS31 Gilbert Perreault XSP 30.00 80.00
CS32 Glenn Anderson 6.00 15.00
CS33 Glenn Hall 10.00 25.00
CS34 Grant Fuhr XSP 30.00 80.00
CS35 Frank Mahovlich XSP 30.00 80.00
CS36 Doug Wilson 6.00 15.00
CS37 Dave Schultz 8.00 20.00
CS38 Tiger Williams 8.00 20.00
CS39 Dave Taylor 6.00 15.00
CS40 Clark Gillies 6.00 15.00
CS41 Bryan Trottier/56 15.00 40.00
CS42 Butch Goring 6.00 15.00
CS43 Bernie Geoffrion SP 25.00 60.00
CS44 Al Iafrate 6.00 15.00
CS45 Bill Barber 6.00 15.00
CS46 Bob Nystrom 6.00 15.00
CS47 Bobby Clarke SP 20.00 50.00
CS48 Bobby Hull XSP 75.00 150.00
CS49 Brad Park 10.00 25.00
CS50 Patrick Roy SSP 60.00 150.00
CS51 Ray Bourque/25 150.00 400.00
CS52 Derek Sanderson 10.00 25.00
CS53 Fred Cusick 8.00 20.00
CS54 Bob Cole 6.00 15.00
CS55 Larry Murphy 8.00 20.00
DC1 T.Esposito/P.Esposito 50.00 100.00
DC2 Jean Beliveau 60.00 125.00
Guy Lafleur
DC3 Stan Mikita 30.00 80.00
Bobby Hull
DC4 Ray Bourque 40.00 100.00
Cam Neely
DC5 Mike Bossy 30.00 80.00
Bryan Trottier
DC6 Derek Sanderson 25.00 60.00
Johnny Bucyk
DC7 Rene Robert 25.00 60.00
Gilbert Perreault
DC8 C.Neely/J.Bucyk 25.00 60.00
DC9 J.Beliveau/D.Moore 30.00 80.00
DC10 B.Park/R.Bourque 40.00 100.00
DC11 Derek Sanderson 25.00 60.00
Phil Esposito
DC12 Tony Esposito 40.00 100.00
Glenn Hall
DC13 Marcel Dionne 30.00 80.00
Guy Lafleur
DC14 Gordie Howe 100.00 250.00
Bobby Hull
DC15 D.Schultz/D.Williams 25.00 60.00
DC16 Larry Murphy 25.00 60.00
Dave Taylor
DC17 Marcel Dionne 25.00 60.00
Dave Taylor
DC18 Bobby Clarke 40.00 100.00
Gilbert Perreault
DC19 Fred Cusick 25.00 60.00
Bob Cole
DC20 Bobby Clarke 30.00 80.00
Bill Barber
DC21 Andy Bathgate 40.00 100.00
Johnny Bower
DC22 Stan Mikita 25.00 60.00
Doug Wilson
TC1 Tony Esposito 200.00 400.00
Gump Worsley
Patrick Roy
TC2 Big M/Henderson/Bower 100.00 250.00
TC3 Gerry Cheevers 75.00 200.00
Phil Esposito
Derek Sanderson
TC4 Glenn Hall 125.00 250.00
Tony Esposito
Gerry Cheevers
TC5 Clark Gillies 60.00 150.00
Bryan Trottier
Mike Bossy
TC6 Barber/Clarke/Leach 75.00 200.00
TC7 Geoffrion/Howe/Beliveau 250.00500.00
TC8 Ken Hodge
Brad Park
Phil Esposito
TC9 Paul Coffey 60.00 150.00
Larry Murphy
Ray Bourque
TC10 Rick Martin 60.00 150.00
Gilbert Perreault
Rene Robert
TC11 Glenn Anderson
Wayne Gretzky
Jari Kurri
TC12 Gump Worsley 60.00 150.00
Jean Beliveau
Dickie Moore
TC13 Gordie Howe 200.00 400.00
Red Kelly
Ted Lindsay
TC14 Wayne Gretzky 300.00 600.00
Marcel Dionne
Guy Lafleur
TC15 Tony Esposito 75.00 200.00
Stan Mikita
Doug Wilson
QC1 Patrick Roy
Tony Esposito
Glenn Hall
Gerry Cheevers
QC2 Gordie Howe
Guy Lafleur
Mike Bossy
Jari Kurri
QC3 Bobby Hull
Frank Mahovlich
Ted Lindsay
Johnny Bucyk
QC4 Wayne Gretzky
Bryan Trottier
Gilbert Perreault
Marcel Dionne
QC5 Phil Esposito
Terry O'Reilly
Cam Neely
Wayne Cashman
QC6 Gordie Howe
Bobby Clarke
Cam Neely
Clark Gillies

2001-02 UD Mask Collection

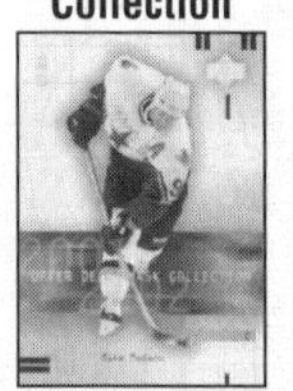

Released in June, this 190-card had a SRP of $3.99. The set featured 100 regular base cards, 40 Precious Gems rookie cards, 30 Manning the Nets subset cards and 20 Unmasked Warriors subset cards. The Precious Gems cards were serial-numbered out of 1500, the Unmasked Warriors cards were serial-numbered out of 1250, and the Manning the Nets cards were inserted at a rate of 1:3.

COMP.SET w/o SP's (100) 25.00 50.00
1 Paul Kariya .30 .75
2 Jeff Friesen .10 .25
3 Matt Cullen .10 .25
4 Dany Heatley .40 1.00
5 Lubos Bartecko .10 .25
6 Tony Hrkac .10 .25
7 Sergei Samsonov .25 .60
8 Joe Thornton .50 1.25
9 Bill Guerin .25 .60
10 P.J. Stock .10 .25
11 Stu Barnes .10 .25
12 Tim Connolly .10 .25
13 Jarome Iginla .40 1.00
14 Craig Conroy .10 .25
15 Sami Kapanen .10 .25
16 Ron Francis .25 .60
17 Tony Amonte .25 .60

18 Mark Bell .10 .25
19 Steve Sullivan .10 .25
20 Chris Drury .25 .60
21 Milan Hejduk .30 .75
22 Joe Sakic .60 1.50
23 Rob Blake .25 .60
24 Alex Tanguay .25 .60
25 Mike Sillinger .10 .25
26 Ray Whitney .10 .25
27 Rostislav Klesla .10 .25
28 Pierre Turgeon .25 .60
29 Jere Lehtinen .25 .60
30 Mike Modano .50 1.25
31 Sergei Zubov .10 .25
32 Brendan Shanahan .30 .75
33 Steve Yzerman 1.50 4.00
34 Brett Hull .40 1.00
35 Sergei Fedorov .50 1.25
36 Mike Comrie .25 .60
37 Ryan Smyth .10 .25
38 Anson Carter .25 .60
39 Viktor Kozlov .10 .25
40 Marcus Nilsson .10 .25
41 Sandis Ozolinsh .10 .25
42 Adam Deadmarsh .10 .25
43 Jason Allison .10 .25
44 Zigmund Palffy .25 .60
45 Andrew Brunette .10 .25
46 Marian Gaborik .60 1.50
47 Jim Dowd .10 .25
48 Yanic Perreault .10 .25
49 Sergei Berezin .10 .25
50 Donald Audette .10 .25
51 Francois Bouillon .10 .25
52 Karlis Skrastins .10 .25
53 David Legwand .25 .60
54 Scott Hartnell .10 .25
55 Bobby Holik .10 .25
56 Joe Nieuwendyk .25 .60
57 Patrik Elias .25 .60
58 Brian Rafalski .10 .25
59 Mark Parrish .10 .25
60 Michael Peca .10 .25
61 Alexei Yashin .10 .25
62 Petr Nedved .10 .25
63 Theo Fleury .10 .25
64 Pavel Bure .30 .75
65 Eric Lindros .30 .75
66 Martin Havlat .25 .60
67 Daniel Alfredsson .25 .60
68 Marian Hossa .30 .75
69 Radek Bonk .10 .25
70 Simon Gagne .30 .75
71 John LeClair .30 .75
72 Jeremy Roenick .40 1.00
73 Mark Recchi .25 .60
74 Michal Handzus .10 .25
75 Claude Lemieux .10 .25
76 Shane Doan .10 .25
77 Jamie Pushor .10 .25
78 Alexei Kovalev .25 .60
79 Mario Lemieux 2.00 5.00
80 Vincent Damphousse .10 .25
81 Owen Nolan .25 .60
82 Teemu Selanne .30 .75
83 Keith Tkachuk .30 .75
84 Chris Pronger .25 .60
85 Doug Weight .25 .60
86 Pavol Demitra .25 .60
87 Fredrik Modin .10 .25
88 Brad Richards .25 .60
89 Vincent Lecavalier .30 .75
90 Darcy Tucker .10 .25
91 Alexander Mogilny .10 .25
92 Mats Sundin .30 .75
93 Brendan Morrison .25 .60
94 Todd Bertuzzi .30 .75
95 Markus Naslund .30 .75
96 Ed Jovanovski .10 .25
97 Drake Berehowsky .10 .25
98 Ulf Dahlen .10 .25
99 Peter Bondra .30 .75
100 Jaromir Jagr .50 1.25
101 J-S Giguere MTN 1.25 3.00
102 Milan Hnilicka MTN 1.25 3.00
103 Byron Dafoe MTN 1.25 3.00
104 Martin Biron MTN 1.25 3.00
105 Roman Turek MTN 1.25 3.00
106 Arturs Irbe MTN 1.25 3.00
107 Jocelyn Thibault MTN 1.25 3.00
108 Patrick Roy MTN 3.00 8.00
109 Ron Tugnutt MTN 1.25 3.00
110 Ed Belfour MTN 1.50 4.00
111 Dominik Hasek MTN 2.50 6.00
112 Tommy Salo MTN 1.25 3.00
113 Roberto Luongo MTN 2.00 5.00
114 Felix Potvin MTN 1.50 4.00
115 Manny Fernandez MTN 1.25 3.00
116 Jose Theodore MTN 2.00 5.00
117 Mike Dunham MTN 1.25 3.00
118 Martin Brodeur MTN 2.50 6.00
119 Chris Osgood MTN 1.25 3.00
120 Mike Richter MTN 1.50 4.00
121 Patrick Lalime MTN 1.25 3.00
122 Roman Cechmanek MTN 1.25 3.00
123 Sean Burke MTN 1.25 3.00
124 Johan Hedberg MTN 1.25 3.00
125 Evgeni Nabokov MTN 1.25 3.00
126 Brent Johnson MTN 1.25 3.00
127 Nikolai Khabibulin MTN 1.50 4.00
128 Curtis Joseph MTN 1.50 4.00
129 Dan Cloutier MTN 1.25 3.00
130 Olaf Kolzig MTN 1.25 3.00
131 Frederic Cassivi RC 2.00 5.00
132 Ilya Kovalchuk RC 10.00 25.00
133 Pasi Nurminen RC 2.00 5.00
134 Mark Hartigan RC 2.00 5.00
135 Francis Lessard RC 2.00 5.00
136 Ivan Huml RC 2.00 5.00
137 Chris Kelleher RC 2.00 5.00
138 Erik Cole RC 2.50 5.00
139 Mike Peluso RC 2.00 5.00
140 Vaclav Nedorost RC 2.00 5.00
141 Jeff Daw RC 2.00 5.00
142 Andrej Nedorost RC 2.00 5.00
143 Sean Avery RC 2.00 5.00
144 Pavel Datsyuk RC 8.00 20.00
145 Stephen Weiss RC 6.00 10.00
146 Niklas Hagman RC 2.00 5.00
147 Kristian Huselius RC 2.50 6.00
148 Lukas Krajicek RC 2.00 5.00
149 Tony Virta RC 2.00 5.00
150 Olivier Michaud RC 2.00 10.00
151 Marcel Hossa RC 2.00 5.00
152 Martin Erat RC 2.00 5.00
153 Christian Berglund RC 2.00 5.00
154 Raffi Torres RC 2.50 6.00
155 Dan Blackburn RC 2.50 8.00
156 Martin Prusek RC 2.00 5.00
157 Chris Bala RC 2.00 5.00
158 Josh Langfeld RC 2.00 5.00
159 Jiri Dopita RC 2.00 5.00
160 Neil Little RC 2.00 5.00
161 Guillaume Lefebvre RC 2.00 5.00
162 Krys Kolanos RC 2.00 5.00
163 Branko Radivojevic RC 2.00 5.00
164 Shane Endicott RC 2.00 5.00
165 Hannes Hyvonen RC 2.00 5.00
166 Jeff Jillson RC 2.00 5.00
167 Nikita Alexeev RC 2.00 5.00
168 Gaetan Royer RC 2.00 5.00
169 Karel Pilar RC 2.00 5.00
170 Brian Sutherby RC 2.00 5.00
171 Byron Dafoe UW 2.00 5.00
172 Martin Biron UW 2.00 5.00
173 Roman Turek UW 2.00 5.00
174 Arturs Irbe UW 2.00 5.00
175 Patrick Roy UW 6.00 15.00
176 Ed Belfour UW 2.50 6.00
177 Dominik Hasek UW 5.00 12.00
178 Tommy Salo UW 2.00 5.00
179 Felix Potvin UW 2.50 6.00
180 Mike Dunham UW 2.00 5.00
181 Martin Brodeur UW 5.00 12.00
182 Chris Osgood UW 2.00 5.00
183 Mike Richter UW 2.50 6.00
184 Roman Cechmanek UW 2.00 5.00
185 Sean Burke UW 2.00 5.00
186 Johan Hedberg UW 2.00 5.00
187 Evgeni Nabokov UW 2.00 5.00
188 Nikolai Khabibulin UW 2.50 6.00
189 Curtis Joseph UW 2.50 6.00
190 Olaf Kolzig UW 2.00 5.00

2001-02 UD Mask Collection Gold

This 190-card set paralleled the base set. Each card was serial-numbered to just 50 copies each.

GOLD: 5X TO 12X BASIC CARD
GOLD MTN: 4X TO 10X BASIC CARD
GOLD PG: 2X TO 4X BASIC CARD
GOLD UW: 2X TO 5X BASIC CARD

2001-02 UD Mask Collection Double Patches

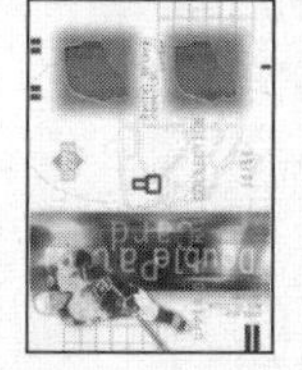

This 60-card set paralleled the jersey card set, but carried two swatches of jersey patches. Cards were serial-numbered out of 100. Swatches were affixed beside a full-color action photo on the card front. Card backs carried a congratulatory message.

*DBL.PATCH: 2X TO 5X JERSEY CARD

2001-02 UD Mask Collection Dual Jerseys

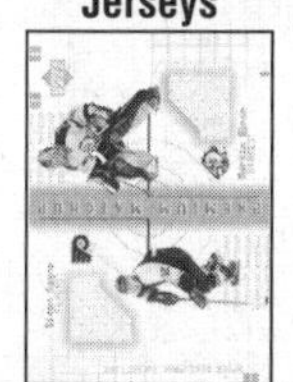

Inserted at a rate of 1:288, this 14-card set featured two game-worn swatches of the players featured. There was two subsets, Premier Matchups and Behind the Mask. Card prefixes denote subset. Swatches were affixed beside a full-color action photo on the card front. Card backs carried a congratulatory message.

*MULT.COLOR SWATCH: .5X TO 1.5X HI
MBBC Brian Boucher 10.00 25.00
Roman Cechmanek
MBBT Martin Brodeur 15.00 40.00
Jose Theodore
MBCJ Curtis Joseph 10.00 25.00
Curtis Joseph
MBFP Felix Potvin 10.00 25.00
Double Jersey
MBPR Patrick Roy 40.00 100.00
Double Jersey
MBRD Mike Richter 10.00 25.00
Mike Dunham
MBTB Jocelyn Thibault 10.00 25.00
Ed Belfour
PMAD Tony Amonte 10.00 25.00
Mike Dunham
PMAJ Jason Arnott 10.00 25.00
Curtis Joseph
PMFT Sergei Fedorov 10.00 25.00
Jocelyn Thibault
PMGB Simon Gagne 10.00 25.00
Martin Biron
PMMJ Mike Modano 10.00 25.00
Brent Johnson
PMSB Joe Sakic 12.50 30.00
Martin Brodeur
PMYR Steve Yzerman 30.00 80.00
Patrick Roy

2001-02 UD Mask Collection Gloves

Inserted at a rate of 1:144, this 13-card set featured game-used glove swatches of the featured player. Swatches were affixed beside a full-color action photo on the card front. Card backs carried a congratulatory message.

*MULT.COLOR SWATCH: .75X TO 2X HI
GGAM Alexander Mogilny 8.00 20.00
GGBD Byron Dafoe 8.00 20.00
GGBH Brett Hull 12.50 30.00
GGBS Brendan Shanahan 10.00 25.00
GGCD Chris Drury 8.00 20.00
GGEB Ed Belfour 10.00 25.00
GGJR Jeremy Roenick 12.50 30.00
GGMM Mark Messier 10.00 25.00
GGRB Ray Bourque 15.00 40.00
GGRD Rick DiPietro 10.00 25.00
GGSF Sergei Fedorov 12.50 30.00
GGSK Sami Kapanen 8.00 20.00
GGTK Keith Tkachuk 10.00 25.00

2001-02 UD Mask Collection Goalie Jerseys

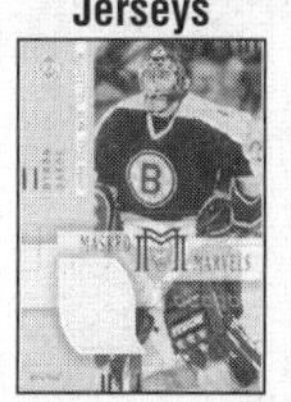

This 39-card set featured game-worn jersey swatches of NHL goalies. There were five different subsets: Masked Marvels (inserted at 1:96), Super Stoppers and Styling Tenders (inserted at 1:168), View from the Cage (inserted at 1:144), and Caged Greats (inserted at 1:288). Card prefixes denote subset. Swatches were affixed beside a full-color action photo on the card front. Card backs carried a congratulatory message.

*MULT.COLOR SWATCH: .75X TO 1.5X HI
MMBB Brian Boucher 4.00 10.00
MMBD Byron Dafoe 4.00 10.00
MMDA David Aebischer 6.00 15.00
MMJT Jocelyn Thibault 4.00 10.00
MMMD Mike Dunham 4.00 10.00
MMMT Marty Turco 6.00 15.00
MMRT Ron Tugnutt 4.00 10.00
MMSB Sean Burke 4.00 10.00
SSBD Byron Dafoe 6.00 15.00
SSBJ Brent Johnson 6.00 15.00
SSFP Felix Potvin 8.00 20.00
SSJT Jocelyn Thibault 6.00 15.00
SSMB Martin Biron 6.00 15.00
SSRL Roberto Luongo 10.00 25.00
SSRT Ron Tugnutt 6.00 15.00
SSTH Jose Theodore 10.00 25.00
SYBB Brian Boucher 6.00 15.00
SYDA David Aebischer 6.00 15.00
SYEB Ed Belfour 8.00 20.00
SYJG Jean-Sebastien Giguere 6.00 15.00
SYMD Mike Dunham 6.00 15.00
SYMN Mika Noronen 6.00 15.00
SYPR Patrick Roy 15.00 40.00
SYRC Roman Cechmanek 6.00 15.00
VCEB Ed Belfour 8.00 20.00
VCFP Felix Potvin 8.00 20.00
VCMB Martin Brodeur 12.50 30.00
VCMD Mike Dunham 6.00 15.00
VCMT Marty Turco 8.00 20.00
VCPR Patrick Roy 15.00 40.00
VCRC Roman Cechmanek 6.00 15.00
VCSB Sean Burke 6.00 15.00
CGCJ Curtis Joseph 8.00 20.00
CGCO Chris Osgood 8.00 20.00
CGDH Dominik Hasek 12.50 30.00
CGMB Martin Brodeur 15.00 40.00
CGMR Mike Richter 8.00 20.00
CGPR Patrick Roy 25.00 60.00
CGSB Sean Burke 8.00 20.00

2001-02 UD Mask Collection Goalie Pads

Inserted at a rate of 1:66, this 8-card set featured game-worn goalie pad swatches of the featured goalie. Swatches were affixed beside a full-color action photo on the card front. Card backs carried a congratulatory message.

*MULT.COLOR SWATCH: .75X TO 1.5X HI
GPBD Byron Dafoe 5.00 12.00
GPDH Dominik Hasek 8.00 20.00
GPJH Johan Hedberg 5.00 12.00
GPJT Jose Theodore 6.00 15.00
GPMB Martin Biron 5.00 12.00
GPMD Marc Denis 5.00 12.00
GPOK Olaf Kolzig 5.00 12.00
GPPR Patrick Roy 12.50 30.00

2001-02 UD Mask Collection Jerseys

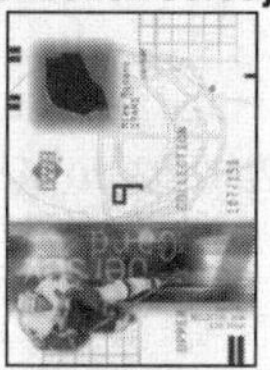

This 60-card set featured a game-worn jersey swatch of the featured player. Swatches were affixed beside a full-color action photo on the card front. Card backs carry a congratulatory message.

*MULT.COLOR SWATCH: .75X TO 1.5X HI
J-AD Adam Deadmarsh 4.00 10.00
J-AT Alex Tanguay 4.00 10.00
J-BB Brian Boucher 4.00 10.00
J-BE Mark Bell 4.00 10.00
J-BJ Brent Johnson 4.00 10.00
J-BL Rob Blake 4.00 10.00
J-BS Brendan Shanahan 6.00 15.00
J-CD Chris Drury 4.00 10.00
J-DA David Aebischer 6.00 15.00
J-DB Daniel Briere 4.00 10.00
J-EB Ed Belfour 6.00 15.00
J-EK Espen Knutsen 4.00 10.00
J-FP Felix Potvin 6.00 15.00
J-GS Geoff Sanderson 4.00 10.00
J-JA Jason Allison 4.00 10.00
J-JD J-P Dumont 4.00 10.00
J-JF Jeff Friesen 4.00 10.00
J-JG J-S Giguere 4.00 10.00
J-JI Jarome Iginla 8.00 20.00
J-JJ Jaromir Jagr 8.00 20.00
J-JN Joe Nieuwendyk 4.00 10.00
J-JT Jocelyn Thibault 4.00 10.00
J-JW Justin Williams 4.00 10.00
J-KO Slava Kozlov 4.00 10.00
J-KP Keith Primeau 4.00 10.00
J-MA Maxim Afinogenov 4.00 10.00
J-MB Martin Biron 4.00 10.00
J-MD Marc Denis 4.00 10.00
J-MH Milan Hejduk 6.00 15.00
J-ML Mario Lemieux 20.00 50.00
J-MM Mike Modano 8.00 20.00
J-MR Mike Richter 6.00 15.00
J-MS Miroslav Satan 4.00 10.00
J-MS Mats Sundin 6.00 15.00
J-MT Marty Turco 4.00 10.00
J-MY Mike York 4.00 10.00
J-NL Nicklas Lidstrom 6.00 15.00
J-PD Pavol Demitra 4.00 10.00
J-PF Peter Forsberg 10.00 25.00
J-PK Paul Kariya 6.00 15.00
J-PR Patrick Roy 12.50 30.00
J-RB Ray Bourque 10.00 25.00
J-RF Ruslan Fedotenko 4.00 10.00
J-RK Rostislav Klesla 4.00 10.00
J-RT Ron Tugnutt 4.00 10.00
J-RW Ray Whitney 4.00 10.00
J-SA Marc Savard 4.00 10.00
J-SD Shane Doan 4.00 10.00
J-SF Sergei Fedorov 8.00 20.00
J-SG Simon Gagne 6.00 15.00
J-SK Saku Koivu 6.00 15.00
J-SS Steve Sullivan 4.00 10.00
J-SY Steve Yzerman 15.00 40.00
J-TA Tony Amonte 4.00 10.00
J-TC Tim Connolly 4.00 10.00
J-TH Jose Theodore 8.00 20.00
J-TL Trevor Linden 4.00 10.00
J-TS Teemu Selanne 6.00 15.00
J-VN Ville Nieminen 4.00 10.00
J-ZP Zigmund Palffy 4.00 10.00

2001-02 UD Mask Collection Jersey and Patch

This 60-card set paralleled the jersey card set, but carried a swatch of jersey patch as well as the jersey swatch. Cards were serial-numbered out of 100. Swatches were affixed beside a full-color action photo on the card front. Card backs carried a congratulatory message.

*JSY/PATCH: 1.25X TO 3X JERSEY CARD

2001-02 UD Mask Collection Mini Masks

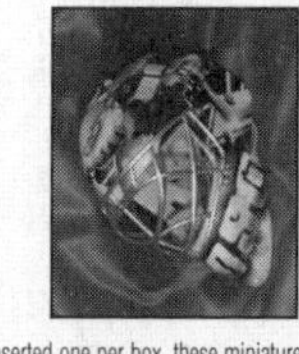

Inserted one per box, these miniature masks feature the artwork sported by some of the league's top goalies. A chrome cage parallel was also created and values can be found by using the mutlipliers below.

*CHROME MASK: .6X TO 1.5X

CJ Curtis Joseph 12.50 30.00
EN Evgeni Nabokov 15.00 40.00
JH Johan Hedberg 12.50 30.00
JT Jose Theodore 15.00 40.00
MB Martin Brodeur 15.00 40.00
PRA Patrick Roy Col. 20.00 50.00
PRC Patrick Roy Mon. 40.00 100.00
EBGD Ed Belfour Gold 25.00 60.00
EBGN Ed Belfour Green 12.50 30.00

2001-02 UD Mask Collection Signed Patches

This 8-card set featured game-worn jersey swatches that were signed by the featured player. Cards were serial-numbered out of 25. Swatches were affixed below a full-color action photo on the card front.

SPBI Martin Biron 75.00 200.00
SPCJ Curtis Joseph 125.00 300.00
SPEB Ed Belfour 150.00 300.00
SPFP Felix Potvin 125.00 300.00
SPJT Jose Theodore 200.00 500.00
SPMB Martin Brodeur 300.00 500.00
SPMR Mike Richter 200.00 300.00
SPPR Patrick Roy 300.00 600.00

2001-02 UD Mask Collection Signs of History

Little is currently known about this set other than that cards were serial-numbered out of 33 and carried an authentic autograph of Patrick Roy.

PR1 Patrick Roy 125.00 300.00
PR2 Patrick Roy 125.00 300.00
PR3 Patrick Roy 125.00 300.00
PR4 Patrick Roy 125.00 300.00

2001-02 UD Mask Collection Sticks

Inserted at a rate of 1:288, this 7-card set featured game-used stick swatches of some of the premier goalies in the league. Swatches were affixed beside a full-color action photo on the card front.

SSBB Brian Boucher 8.00 20.00
SSDH Dominik Hasek 15.00 40.00
SSFP Felix Potvin 12.50 30.00
SSJT Jose Theodore 15.00 40.00
SSMB Martin Brodeur 15.00 40.00
SSOK Olaf Kolzig 8.00 20.00
SSTS Tommy Salo 8.00 20.00

2002-03 UD Mask Collection

Released in May 2003, this 180-card set featured 90 base cards and two subsets. Cards 1-90 carried a color player photo on the card front with a smaller black and white photo of a teammate in the background. Card backs carried stats of both players. Cards 91-115 were a "Team Saviours" subset and each card was serial-numbered to the featured goalies 2001-02 saves total. Cards 116-180 made up a "Potential Gems" subset. Cards 116-157 were serial-numbered to 1750 and cards 158-180 were serial-numbered to 1250.

COMPLETE SET (180)
COMP.SET w/o SP's (90) 8.00 20.00
1 J-S Giguere .20 .50
Martin Gerber
2 Paul Kariya .25 .60
J-S Giguere
3 Byron Dafoe .20 .50
Milan Hnilicka
4 Milan Hnilicka .20 .50
Byron Dafoe
5 D.Heatley/B.Dafoe .30 .75
6 I.Kovalchuk/B.Dafoe .30 .75
7 Pasi Nurminen .20 .50
Byron Dafoe
8 Jeff Hackett .20 .50
Steve Shields
9 Steve Shields .20 .50
Jeff Hackett
10 J.Thornton/J.Hackett .40 1.00
11 Martin Biron .20 .50
Mika Noronen
12 Mika Noronen .20 .50
Martin Biron
13 Roman Turek .20 .50
Jamie McLennan
14 Jamie McLennan .20 .50
Roman Turek
15 Chris Drury .20 .50
Roman Turek
16 Jarome Iginla .25 .60
Roman Turek
17 Kevin Weekes .20 .50
Arturs Irbe
18 Arturs Irbe .20 .50
Kevin Weekes
19 Jocelyn Thibault .20 .50
Steve Passmore
20 Steve Passmore .20 .50
Jocelyn Thibault
21 P.Roy/D.Aebischer 1.25 3.00
22 David Aebischer .20 .50
Patrick Roy
23 J.Sakic/P.Roy .50 1.25
24 Marc Denis .20 .50
Jean-Francois Labbe
25 Jean-Francois Labbe .20 .50
Marc Denis
26 Marty Turco .20 .50
Ron Tugnutt
27 Ron Tugnutt .20 .50
Marty Turco
28 M.Modano/M.Turco .40 1.00
29 Bill Guerin .20 .50
Marty Turco
30 Curtis Joseph .20 .50
Manny Legace
31 Manny Legace .20 .50
Curtis Joseph
32 S.Yzerman/C.Joseph 1.25 3.00
33 Brendan Shanahan .25 .60
Curtis Joseph
34 Tommy Salo .20 .50
Jussi Markkanen
35 Jussi Markkanen .20 .50
Tommy Salo
36 Mike Comrie .20 .50
Tommy Salo
37 Roberto Luongo .20 .50
Jani Hurme
38 Jani Hurme .20 .50
Roberto Luongo
39 Felix Potvin .25 .60
Jamie Storr
40 Jamie Storr .20 .50
Felix Potvin
41 Zigmund Palffy .20 .50
Felix Potvin
42 Manny Fernandez .20 .50
Dwayne Roloson
43 Dwayne Roloson .20 .50
Manny Fernandez
44 M.Gaborik/M.Fernandez .25 .60
45 Jose Theodore .25 .60
Mathieu Garon
46 Mathieu Garon .20 .50
Jose Theodore
47 Saku Koivu .25 .60
Jose Theodore
48 Jan Lasak .20 .50
Tomas Vokoun
49 Tomas Vokoun .20 .50
Jan Lasak
50 M.Brodeur/C.Schwab .60 1.50
51 Corey Schwab .20 .50
Martin Brodeur
52 Garth Snow .20 .50
Chris Osgood
53 Chris Osgood .20 .50
Garth Snow
54 Mike Dunham .20 .50
Dan Blackburn
55 Dan Blackburn .20 .50
Mike Dunham
56 Jason Labarbera .20 .50
Dan Blackburn
57 Pavel Bure .25 .60
Mike Dunham
58 Patrick Lalime .20 .50
Martin Prusek
59 Martin Prusek .20 .50
Patrick Lalime
60 Roman Cechmanek .20 .50
Robert Esche
61 Robert Esche .20 .50
Roman Cechmanek
62 J.Roenick/R.Cechmanek .25 .60
63 John LeClair .25 .60
Roman Cechmanek
64 Brian Boucher .20 .50
Sean Burke
65 Sean Burke .20 .50
Brian Boucher
66 Jean-Marc Pelletier .20 .50
Brian Boucher
67 Tony Amonte .20 .50
Sean Burke
68 Johan Hedberg .20 .50
Jean-Sebastien Aubin
69 Jean-Sebastien Aubin .20 .50
Johan Hedberg
70 M.Lemieux/J.Hedberg 1.50 4.00
71 Sebastien Caron .20 .50
Johan Hedberg
72 Evgeni Nabokov .20 .50
Miikka Kiprusoff
73 Vesa Toskala .20 .50
Evgeni Nabokov
74 Miikka Kiprusoff .20 .50
Evgeni Nabokov
75 Brent Johnson .20 .50
Fred Brathwaite
76 Tom Barrasso .20 .50
Brent Johnson
77 Fred Brathwaite .20 .50
Brent Johnson
78 Reinhard Divis .20 .50
Brent Johnson
79 Nikolai Khabibulin .25 .60
Kevin Hodson
80 Kevin Hodson .25 .60
Nikolai Khabibulin
81 Evgeny Konstantinov .25 .60
Nikolai Khabibulin
82 Ed Belfour .25 .60
Trevor Kidd
83 Trevor Kidd .20 .50
Ed Belfour
84 M.Sundin/E.Belfour .25 .60
85 Dan Cloutier .20 .50
Peter Skudra
86 Peter Skudra .20 .50
Dan Cloutier
87 J.Jagr/O.Kolzig .40 1.00
88 Olaf Kolzig .20 .50
Craig Billington
89 Craig Billington .20 .50
Olaf Kolzig
90 Sebastien Charpentier .20 .50
Olaf Kolzig
91 Martin Brodeur/1499 3.00 8.00
92 Patrick Roy/1475 4.00 10.00
93 Curtis Joseph/1096 3.00 8.00
94 Roman Cechmanek/1042 3.00 8.00
95 Marty Turco/590 3.00 8.00
96 Jocelyn Thibault/1439 3.00 8.00
97 Jose Theodore/1836 4.00 10.00
98 J-S Giguere/1260 3.00 8.00
99 Ed Belfour/1305 3.00 8.00
100 Steve Shields/771 3.00 8.00
101 Johan Hedberg/1673 3.00 8.00
102 Martin Biron/1630 3.00 8.00
103 Dan Cloutier/1298 3.00 8.00
104 Evgeni Nabakov/1669 3.00 8.00
105 Sean Burke/1574 3.00 8.00
106 Nikolai Khabibulin/1733 3.00 8.00
107 Olaf Kolzig/1785 3.00 8.00
108 Byron Dafoe/1379 3.00 8.00
109 David Aebischer/501 3.00 8.00
110 Manny Fernandez/1032 3.00 8.00
111 Dan Blackburn/840 3.00 8.00
112 Felix Potvin/1529 3.00 8.00
113 Patrick Lalime/1373 3.00 8.00
114 Brent Johnson/1166 3.00 8.00
115 Marc Denis/1046 3.00 8.00
116 Micki Dupont RC 1.50 4.00
117 Cody Rudkowsky RC 1.50 4.00
118 Shawn Thornton RC 1.50 4.00
119 Lasse Pirjeta RC 1.50 4.00
120 Radovan Somik RC 1.50 4.00
121 Tomi Pettinen RC 1.50 4.00
122 Jonathan Hedstrom RC 1.50 4.00
123 Sylvain Blouin RC 1.50 4.00
124 Stephane Veilleux RC 1.50 4.00
125 Curtis Sanford RC 1.50 4.00
126 Kurt Sauer RC 1.50 4.00
127 Vernon Fiddler RC 1.50 4.00
128 Patrick Sharp RC 1.50 4.00
129 Greg Koehler RC 1.50 4.00
130 Dany Sabourin RC 1.50 4.00
131 Dmitri Bykov RC 1.50 4.00
132 Ivan Majesky RC 1.50 4.00
133 Ray Schultz RC 1.50 4.00
134 Matt Henderson RC 1.50 4.00
135 Tom Koivisto RC 1.50 4.00
136 Ian MacNeil RC 1.50 4.00
137 Eric Godard RC 1.50 4.00
138 Dick Tarnstrom RC 1.50 4.00
139 Jeff Paul RC 1.50 4.00
140 Darren Haydar RC 1.50 4.00
141 Levente Szuper RC 1.50 4.00
142 Dennis Seidenberg RC 2.00 5.00
143 Tim Thomas RC 2.50 6.00
144 Fernando Pisani RC 2.00 5.00
145 Alex Henry RC 1.50 4.00
146 Craig Andersson RC 1.50 4.00
147 Kari Haakana RC 1.50 4.00
148 Jared Aulin RC 1.50 4.00
149 Adam Hall RC 1.50 4.00
150 Carlo Colaiacovo RC 1.50 4.00
151 Martin Gerber RC 3.00 8.00
152 Jamie Hodson RC 1.50 4.00
153 Ray Emery RC 3.00 8.00
154 Ari Ahonen RC 1.50 4.00
155 Michael Leighton RC 1.50 4.00
156 Kris Vernarsky RC 1.50 4.00
157 Jim Vandermeer RC 1.50 4.00
158 Chuck Kobasew RC 2.00 5.00
159 Ron Hainsey RC 2.00 5.00
160 P-M Bouchard RC 3.00 8.00
161 Alexander Frolov RC 4.00 10.00
162 Henrik Zetterberg RC 6.00 15.00
163 Alexander Svitov RC 1.50 4.00
164 Mike Cammalleri RC 1.50 4.00
165 Ryan Miller RC 5.00 12.00
166 Anton Volchenkov RC 2.00 5.00
167 Brooks Orpik RC 2.00 5.00
168 Ales Hemsky RC 4.00 10.00
169 Stanislav Chistov RC 2.00 5.00
170 Shaone Morrisonn RC 2.00 5.00
171 Jason Spezza RC 6.00 15.00
172 Jay Bouwmeester RC 2.00 5.00
173 Jordan Leopold RC 2.00 5.00
174 Jeff Taffe RC 2.00 5.00
175 Pascal LeClaire RC 2.50 6.00
176 Scottie Upshall RC 2.00 5.00
177 Alexei Smirnov RC 2.00 5.00
178 Rick Nash RC 8.00 20.00
179 Mikael Tellqvist RC 2.00 5.00
180 Steve Eminger RC 2.00 5.00

2002-03 UD Mask Collection Beckett Promos

Inserted into copies of the May 2003 issue of Beckett Hockey Collector, this 90-card set parallels the base set but carried a silver foil "UD Promo" stamp across the card fronts. Due to the type of distribution and the wide range of prices realized by these cards in the secondary market, they are not priced.

NOT PRICED DUE TO SCARCITY

2002-03 UD Mask Collection Behind the Mask

Inserted at a rate of 1:60 hobby packs, this 18-card set featured swatches of game-worn jerseys.

*MULT.COLOR SWATCH: .75X TO 1.5X
BMAM Andy Moog SP 10.00 25.00
BMBI Martin Biron 6.00 15.00
BMBJ Brent Johnson 6.00 15.00
BMCJ Curtis Joseph 6.00 15.00
BMDU Mike Dunham 6.00 15.00
BMEB Ed Belfour 8.00 20.00
BMFP Felix Potvin 6.00 15.00
BMJG J-S Giguere 8.00 20.00
BMJH Johan Hedberg 6.00 15.00
BMJT Jose Theodore 6.00 15.00
BMMB Martin Brodeur 8.00 20.00
BMMD Marc Denis 6.00 15.00
BMMN Mika Noronen 6.00 15.00
BMMT Marty Turco 6.00 15.00
BMOK Olaf Kolzig 6.00 15.00
BMPR Patrick Roy 12.50 30.00
BMRC Roman Cechmanek 6.00 15.00
BMRD Rick DiPietro 6.00 15.00

2002-03 UD Mask Collection Career Wins

This 17-card set featured swatches of game-worn jerseys. Each card was serial-numbered to the given goalies career wins total as of press time.

*MULT.COLOR SWATCH: .75X TO 1.5X
CWAM Andy Moog/372 10.00 25.00
CWBD Byron Dafoe/162 10.00 25.00
CWCJ Curtis Joseph/346 10.00 25.00
CWCO Chris Osgood/253 10.00 25.00
CWEB Ed Belfour/364 12.50 30.00
CWFP Felix Potvin/237 10.00 25.00
CWJT Jocelyn Thibault/196 10.00 25.00
CWMB Martin Brodeur/324 12.50 30.00
CWMD Mike Dunham/92 10.00 25.00
CWMR Mike Richter/296 12.50 30.00
CWOK Olaf Kolzig/182 10.00 25.00
CWPR Patrick Roy/289 15.00 40.00
CWRT Ron Tugnutt/168 10.00 25.00
CWRY Patrick Roy/227 15.00 40.00
CWSB Sean Burke/281 10.00 25.00
CWTS Tommy Salo/168 10.00 25.00
CWTU Roman Turek/126 10.00 25.00

2002-03 UD Mask Collection Great Gloves

Inserted at a rate of 1:60 hobby packs, this 18-card set featured swatches of game-worn jerseys.

*MULT.COLOR SWATCH: .75X TO 1.5X
GGBB Brian Boucher 6.00 15.00
GGBR Martin Brodeur 8.00 20.00
GGCJ Curtis Joseph 6.00 15.00
GGDB Dan Blackburn 6.00 15.00
GGDU Mike Dunham 6.00 15.00
GGEB Ed Belfour 8.00 20.00
GGFP Felix Potvin 6.00 15.00
GGJG J-S Giguere 12.50 30.00
GGJT Jose Theodore 8.00 20.00
GGMB Martin Biron 6.00 15.00
GGMD Marc Denis 6.00 15.00
GGMR Mike Richter 6.00 15.00
GGMT Marty Turco 8.00 20.00
GGOK Olaf Kolzig SP 10.00 25.00
GGPR Patrick Roy 12.50 30.00
GGRC Roman Cechmanek 6.00 15.00
GGRL Roberto Luongo 8.00 20.00
GGRT Roman Turek 6.00 15.00

2002-03 UD Mask Collection Instant Offense

Serial-numbered out of 250, this 25-card set featured swatches of game-worn jerseys.

*MULT.COLOR SWATCH: .75X TO 1.5X
IOAY Alexei Yashin 4.00 10.00
IOBS Brendan Shanahan 5.00 12.00

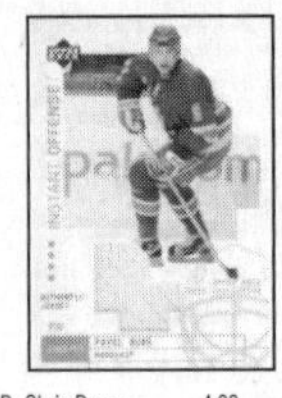

IOCD Chris Drury 4.00 10.00
IOED Eric Daze 4.00 10.00
IOEL Eric Lindros 5.00 12.00
IOJA Jason Allison 4.00 10.00
IOJI Jarome Iginla 6.00 15.00
IOJJ Jaromir Jagr 10.00 25.00
IOJR Jeremy Roenick 6.00 15.00
IOJS Joe Sakic 10.00 25.00
IOJT Joe Thornton 8.00 20.00
IOML Mario Lemieux 12.50 30.00
IOMM Mike Modano 8.00 20.00
IOMN Markus Naslund 5.00 12.00
IOMS Miroslav Satan 4.00 10.00
IOPB Pavel Bure 5.00 12.00
IOPE Patrik Elias 4.00 10.00
IOPF Peter Forsberg 12.50 30.00
IOPK Paul Kariya 5.00 12.00
IOSG Simon Gagne 5.00 12.00
IOSK Saku Koivu 5.00 12.00
IOSS Sergei Samsonov 4.00 10.00
IOSU Mats Sundin 5.00 12.00
IOSY Steve Yzerman 12.50 30.00
IOZP Zigmund Palffy 4.00 10.00

2002-03 UD Mask Collection Masked Marvels

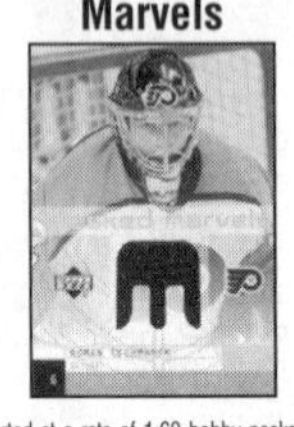

Inserted at a rate of 1:60 hobby packs, this 17-card set featured swatches of game-worn jerseys.

*MULT.COLOR SWATCH: .75X TO 1.5X
MMBI Martin Biron 4.00 10.00
MMCO Chris Osgood 4.00 10.00
MMFP Felix Potvin 5.00 12.00
MMJG J-S Giguere 8.00 20.00
MMJH Johan Hedberg 4.00 10.00
MMJT Jocelyn Thibault 4.00 10.00
MMMB Martin Brodeur 8.00 20.00
MMMD Mike Dunham 4.00 10.00
MMMR Mike Richter 6.00 15.00
MMMT Marty Turco 6.00 15.00
MMOK Olaf Kolzig SP 4.00 10.00
MMPR Patrick Roy 12.50 30.00
MMRC Roman Cechmanek 4.00 10.00
MMRL Roberto Luongo 6.00 15.00
MMRM Ryan Miller 8.00 20.00
MMRT Roman Turek 6.00 15.00
MMTH Jose Theodore SP 6.00 15.00

2002-03 UD Mask Collection Mini Masks

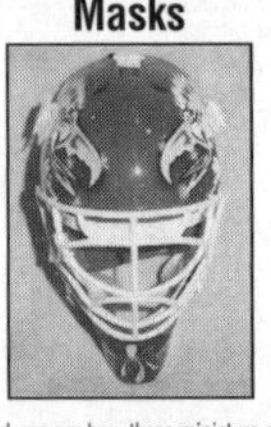

Inserted one per box, these miniature masks feature the artwork sported by some of the league's top goalies. A glitter effect parallel was also created and values can be found by using the multiplier below. Glitter parallels were limited to 25 copies each.

*GLITTER: 1.25X TO 3X
AM Andy Moog 20.00 50.00
CJ Curtis Joseph 15.00 40.00
CR Glenn Resch 12.50 30.00
EB Ed Belfour 20.00 50.00
EN Evgeni Nabokov 12.50 30.00
FP Felix Potvin 15.00 40.00
GC Gerry Cheevers 12.50 30.00
GF1 Grant Fuhr Sabres 12.50 30.00
GF2 Grant Fuhr Blues SP 20.00 50.00
JH Johan Hedberg 12.50 30.00
JP1 Jacque Plante Pretzel 15.00 40.00
JP2 Jacque Plante Alien SP 30.00 80.00
JT Jose Theodore 15.00 40.00
MB Martin Brodeur 20.00 50.00
NK Nikolai Khabibulin 20.00 50.00
PR Patrick Roy 15.00 40.00
TE Tony Esposito 20.00 50.00
TS Terry Sawchuk 15.00 40.00

2002-03 UD Mask Collection Mini Masks Autographs

STAT.PRINT RUN 25 SETS
CJ Curtis Joseph 50.00 125.00
EB Ed Belfour 125.00 250.00
EN Evgeni Nabokov 40.00 100.00
GC Gerry Cheevers 30.00 80.00
GF1 Grant Fuhr Sabres 30.00 80.00

GF2 Grant Fuhr Blues SP 50.00 125.00
JT Jose Theodore 60.00 150.00
MB Martin Brodeur 100.00 250.00
NK Nikolai Khabibulin 50.00 125.00
PR Patrick Roy 100.00 250.00
TE Tony Esposito 60.00 150.00

2002-03 UD Mask Collection Nation's Best

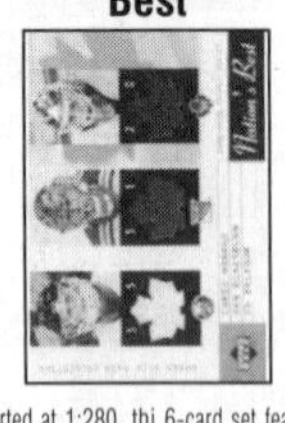

Inserted at 1:280, thi 6-card set featured jersey swatches from each of the goalies featured on the card fronts.

NDBJ Brian Boucher 12.50 30.00
Brent Johnson
Rick DiPietro
NJBT Marty Turco 12.50 30.00
Sean Burke
Curtis Joseph
NLBT Jose Theodore 30.00 80.00
Roberto Luongo
Martin Biron
NOBB Chris Osgood 12.50 30.00
Dan Blackburn
Ed Belfour
NRBP Martin Brodeur 30.00 80.00
Patrick Roy
Felix Potvin
NRDM Mike Richter 12.50 30.00
Mike Dunham
Ryan Miller

2002-03 UD Mask Collection Patches

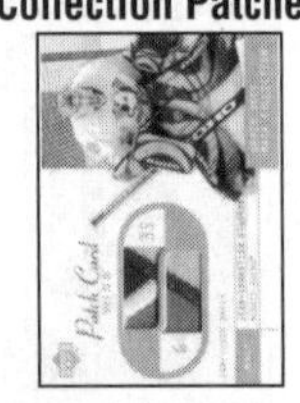

Serial-numbered to the total of goals for forwards and wins for goalies, this 42-card set featured swatches of game-worn jersey patches. Print runs under 25 are not priced due to scarcity.

*SINGLE COLOR PATCH: .25X TO .75X HI
PGBS Brendan Shanahan/37 40.00 100.00
PGDB Daniel Briere/32 25.00 60.00
PGED Eric Daze/37 25.00 60.00
PGEL Eric Lindros/37 30.00 80.00
PGGM Glen Murray/41 25.00 60.00
PGIK Ilya Kovalchuk/29 40.00 100.00
PGJA Jason Allison/19
PGJI Jarome Iginla/52 40.00 100.00
PGJJ Jaromir Jagr/31 40.00 100.00
PGJS Joe Sakic/26 40.00 100.00
PGMM Mike Modano/34 40.00 100.00
PGMN Markus Naslund/40 25.00 60.00
PGMS Mats Sundin/41 25.00 60.00
PGPB Peter Bondra/39 30.00 80.00
PGPE Patrik Elias/29 25.00 60.00
PGPK Paul Kariya/32 50.00 125.00
PGSF Sergei Fedorov/30 30.00 80.00
PGSG Simon Gagne/33 25.00 60.00
PGSY Steve Yzerman/13
PGZP Zigmund Palffy/31 25.00 60.00
PWBJ Brent Johnson/34 30.00 80.00
PWBR Martin Brodeur/38 50.00 125.00
PWCJ Curtis Joseph/29 40.00 100.00
PWCO Chris Osgood/31 25.00 60.00
PWDB Dan Blackburn/12
PWEB Ed Belfour/21
PWFP Felix Potvin/31 25.00 60.00
PWJG J-S Giguere/20
PWJH Johan Hedberg/25 25.00 60.00
PWJT Jocelyn Thibault/32 30.00 80.00
PWMB Martin Biron/31 25.00 60.00
PWMD Mike Dunham/23
PWMR Mike Richter/24 40.00 100.00
PWMT Marty Turco/15
PWOK Olaf Kolzig/31 25.00 60.00
PWPR Patrick Roy/32 200.00 400.00
PWRC Roman Cechmanek/24
PWRL Roberto Luongo/16
PWRT Roman Turek/30 25.00 60.00
PWSB Sean Burke/33 25.00 60.00
PWTH Jose Theodore/31 60.00 150.00
PWTS Tommy Salo/30 25.00 60.00

2002-03 UD Mask Collection Super Stoppers

Inserted at a rate of 1:60 hobby packs, this 8-card set featured swatches of game-worn jerseys.

*MULT.COLOR SWATCH: .75X TO 1.5X
SSCJ Curtis Joseph 5.00 12.00
SSCO Chris Osgood 4.00 10.00

SSJT Jose Theodore 6.00 15.00
SSMB Martin Brodeur 8.00 20.00
SSOK Olaf Kolzig 4.00 10.00
SSPR Patrick Roy 12.50 30.00
SSRC Roman Cechmanek 4.00 10.00
SSRT Roman Turek 4.00 10.00

2002-03 UD Mask Collection View from the Cage

Inserted at a rate of 1:140 hobby packs, this 17-card set featured swatches of game-worn jerseys.

*MULT.COLOR SWATCH: .75X TO 1.5X
VBI Martin Biron 6.00 15.00
VCJ Curtis Joseph 6.00 15.00
VEB Ed Belfour 10.00 25.00
VJG J-S Giguere 6.00 15.00
VJH Johan Hedberg 6.00 15.00
VJT Jocelyn Thibault 6.00 15.00
VMB Martin Brodeur 15.00 40.00
VMR Mike Richter 6.00 15.00
VMT Marty Turco 6.00 15.00
VOK Olaf Kolzig 6.00 15.00
VPR Patrick Roy 12.50 30.00
VRC Roman Cechmanek 6.00 15.00
VRL Roberto Luongo 8.00 20.00
VRT Roman Turek 6.00 15.00
VSB Sean Burke 6.00 15.00
VTH Jose Theodore 8.00 20.00
VTS Tommy Salo 6.00 15.00

2006-07 UD Mini Jersey Collection

COMPLETE SET (130) 75.00 125.00
1 Teemu Selanne .25 .60
2 Jean-Sebastien Giguere .20 .50
3 Chris Pronger .20 .50
4 Ilya Kovalchuk .30 .75
5 Kari Lehtonen .25 .60
6 Marian Hossa .20 .50
7 Patrice Bergeron .25 .60
8 Brad Boyes .12 .30
9 Zdeno Chara .12 .30
10 Thomas Vanek .12 .30
11 Ryan Miller .25 .60
12 Chris Drury .12 .30
13 Alex Tanguay .20 .50
14 Miikka Kiprusoff .25 .60
15 Dion Phaneuf .30 .75
16 Jarome Iginla .30 .75
17 Eric Staal .25 .60
18 Cam Ward .25 .60
19 Erik Cole .12 .30
20 Rod Brind`Amour .20 .50
21 Martin Havlat .20 .50
22 Nikolai Khabibulin .25 .60
23 Tuomo Ruutu .12 .30
24 Joe Sakic .50 1.25
25 Marek Svatos .12 .30
26 Milan Hejduk .12 .30
27 Jose Theodore .25 .60
28 Fredrik Modin .12 .30
29 Rick Nash .25 .60
30 Sergei Fedorov .25 .60
31 Nikolai Zherdev .12 .30
32 Eric Lindros .25 .60
33 Mike Modano .20 .50
34 Marty Turco .20 .50
35 Brenden Morrow .20 .50
36 Henrik Zetterberg .25 .60
37 Nicklas Lidstrom .25 .60
38 Dominik Hasek .40 1.00
39 Gordie Howe .75 2.00
40 Pavel Datsyuk .20 .50
41 Joffrey Lupul .12 .30
42 Fernando Pisani .12 .30
43 Ales Hemsky .12 .30
44 Ryan Smyth .20 .50
45 Dwayne Roloson .25 .60
46 Todd Bertuzzi .20 .50
47 Olli Jokinen .20 .50
48 Ed Belfour .25 .60
49 Rob Blake .20 .50
50 Alexander Frolov .12 .30
51 Marian Gaborik .30 .75
52 Manny Fernandez .20 .50
53 Pavol Demitra .12 .30
54 Saku Koivu .25 .60
55 Michael Ryder .20 .50
56 Patrick Roy 1.25 3.00
57 Sergei Samsonov .20 .50
58 Paul Kariya .25 .60
59 Tomas Vokoun .20 .50
60 Martin Brodeur 1.00 2.50
61 Patrik Elias .12 .30
62 Alexei Yashin .12 .30
63 Miroslav Satan .12 .30
64 Rick DiPietro .20 .50
65 Jaromir Jagr .40 1.00
66 Henrik Lundqvist .30 .75
67 Brendan Shanahan .25 .60
68 Martin Gerber .25 .60
69 Jason Spezza .25 .60
70 Dany Heatley .30 .75
71 Daniel Alfredsson .20 .50
72 Mike Richards .20 .50
73 Peter Forsberg .40 1.00
74 Simon Gagne .25 .60
75 Antero Niittymaki .20 .50
76 Jeff Carter .25 .60
77 Shane Doan .12 .30
78 Jeremy Roenick .30 .75
79 Curtis Joseph .25 .60
80 Sidney Crosby 2.00 5.00
81 Marc-Andre Fleury .25 .60
82 Jonathan Cheechoo .25 .60
83 Vesa Toskala .20 .50
84 Patrick Marleau .20 .50
85 Joe Thornton .40 1.00
86 Keith Tkachuk .20 .50
87 Vincent Lecavalier .25 .60
88 Martin St. Louis .20 .50
89 Brad Richards .20 .50
90 Mats Sundin .25 .60
91 Alexander Steen .20 .50
92 Bryan McCabe .12 .30
93 Andrew Raycroft .20 .50
94 Darcy Tucker .12 .30
95 Markus Naslund .25 .60
96 Roberto Luongo .30 .75
97 Henrik Sedin .12 .30
98 Brendan Morrison .12 .30
99 Olaf Kolzig .25 .60
100 Alexander Ovechkin 1.00 2.50
101 Yan Stastny RC 1.00 2.50
102 Mark Stuart RC 1.00 2.50
103 Phil Kessel RC 3.00 8.00
104 Ryan Shannon RC 1.00 2.50
105 Tomas Kopecky RC 1.50 4.00
106 Marc-Antoine Pouliot RC 1.50 4.00
107 Konstantin Pushkaryov RC 1.00 2.50
108 Patrick O'Sullivan RC 1.25 3.00
109 Anze Kopitar RC 3.00 8.00
110 Shea Weber RC 1.50 4.00
111 Travis Zajac RC 2.00 5.00
112 Guillaume Latendresse RC 3.00 8.00
113 Marc-Edouard Vlasic RC 1.00 2.50
114 Ladislav Smid RC 1.00 2.50
115 Loui Eriksson RC 8.00 20.00
116 Kristopher Letang RC 1.50 4.00
117 Jarkko Immonen RC 1.00 2.50
118 Nigel Dawes RC 1.00 2.50
119 Luc Bourdon RC 1.50 4.00
120 Ryan Potulny RC 1.50 4.00
121 Keith Yandle RC 1.00 2.50
122 Patrick Thoresen RC 1.50 4.00
123 Noah Welch RC 1.00 2.50
124 Jordan Staal RC 6.00 15.00
125 Matt Carle RC 1.50 4.00
126 Evgeni Malkin RC 6.00 15.00
127 Brendan Bell RC 1.00 2.50
128 Ian White RC 1.00 2.50
129 Jeremy Williams RC 1.00 2.50
130 Eric Fehr RC 15.00 40.00

2006-07 UD Mini Jersey Collection Jerseys

COMPLETE SET (21) 125.00 200.00
ONE PER PACK
AF Alexander Frolov 2.00 5.00
AO Alexander Ovechkin 4.00 10.00
DH Dany Heatley 2.00 5.00
DP Dion Phaneuf 2.00 5.00
EM Evgeni Malkin 6.00 15.00
ES Eric Staal 2.00 5.00
GH Gordie Howe SP 60.00 125.00
HL Henrik Lundqvist 2.00 5.00
IK Ilya Kovalchuk 2.00 5.00
JS Joe Sakic 3.00 8.00
JT Joe Thornton 2.00 5.00
MN Markus Naslund 2.00 5.00
MR Michael Ryder 2.00 5.00
MS Mats Sundin 2.00 5.00
MT Marty Turco 2.00 5.00
PB Patrice Bergeron 2.00 5.00
PF Peter Forsberg 2.00 5.00
PR Patrick Roy 5.00 12.00
RN Rick Nash 1.50 4.00
SC Sidney Crosby 8.00 20.00
TV Thomas Vanek 2.00 5.00

2006-07 UD Mini Jersey Collection Jersey Variations

* VARIATIONS: 1.25X TO 3X HI
AF Alexander Frolov 8.00 20.00
AO Alexander Ovechkin 12.00 30.00
DH Dany Heatley 6.00 15.00
DP Dion Phaneuf 6.00 15.00
EM Evgeni Malkin 30.00 80.00
ES Eric Staal 6.00 15.00
GH Gordie Howe 200.00 350.00
HL Henrik Lundqvist 6.00 15.00
IK Ilya Kovalchuk 6.00 15.00
JS Joe Sakic 8.00 20.00
JT Joe Thornton 8.00 20.00
MN Markus Naslund 6.00 15.00
MR Michael Ryder 6.00 15.00
MS Mats Sundin 6.00 15.00
PB Patrice Bergeron 6.00 15.00
PF Peter Forsberg 6.00 15.00
PR Patrick Roy 12.00 30.00
RN Rick Nash 6.00 15.00
SC Sidney Crosby 30.00 80.00
TV Thomas Vanek 8.00 20.00

2006-07 UD Mini Jersey Collection Jersey Autographs

STATED ODDS 1 PER CASE
AF Alexander Frolov 25.00 60.00
AO Alexander Ovechkin SP
DH Dany Heatley SP
DP Dion Phaneuf 50.00 125.00
ES Eric Staal 40.00 80.00
GH Gordie Howe SP 250.00 400.00
IK Ilya Kovalchuk SP 75.00 150.00
JT Joe Thornton SP 75.00 150.00
MN Markus Naslund 40.00 80.00
MR Michael Ryder 25.00 60.00
MT Marty Turco 40.00 80.00
PB Patrice Bergeron SP 60.00 125.00
SC Sidney Crosby SP 300.00 500.00
TV Thomas Vanek 30.00 80.00

2005-06 UD Phenomenal Beginnings

COMPLETE SET (20) 15.00 30.00
COMMON CARD (1-20) .60 1.50
NNO Sidney Crosby AU

2002-03 UD Piece of History

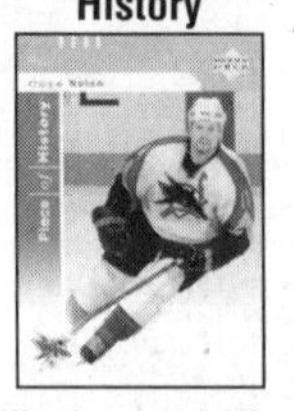

This 150-card set consisted of 90 regular base cards, 18 "Season to Remember subset cards, 12 "Tribute to Greatness" subset cards and 30 shortprinted "History in the Making" rookie cards. Subset cards were serial-numbered to 2999 and rookie cards were serial-numbered to 1500.

COMP.SET w/o SP's (90) 15.00 30.00
1 Paul Kariya .20 .50
2 J-S Giguere .15 .40
3 Ilya Kovalchuk .25 .60
4 Dany Heatley .25 .60
5 Joe Thornton .30 .75
6 Sergei Samsonov .15 .40
7 Glen Murray .08 .20
8 Miroslav Satan .15 .40
9 Tim Connolly .08 .20
10 Martin Biron .15 .40
11 Jeff O'Neill .08 .20
12 Erik Cole .08 .20
13 Ron Francis .15 .40
14 Arturs Irbe .15 .40
15 Roman Turek .15 .40
16 Marc Savard .15 .40
17 Jarome Iginla .25 .60
18 Eric Daze .15 .40
19 Steve Sullivan .08 .20
20 Jocelyn Thibault .15 .40
21 Espen Knutsen .08 .20
22 Rostislav Klesla .08 .20
23 Marc Denis .15 .40
24 Patrick Roy 1.00 2.50
25 Chris Drury .15 .40
26 Joe Sakic .40 1.00
27 Peter Forsberg .50 1.25
28 Alex Tanguay .15 .40
29 Mike Modano .30 .75
30 Marty Turco .15 .40
31 Jason Arnott .08 .20
32 Steve Yzerman 1.00 2.50
33 Sergei Fedorov .30 .75
34 Nicklas Lidstrom .20 .50
35 Brett Hull .25 .60
36 Curtis Joseph .20 .50
37 Brendan Shanahan .20 .50
38 Mike Comrie .15 .40
39 Tommy Salo .15 .40
40 Ryan Smyth .08 .20
41 Roberto Luongo .25 .60
42 Kristian Huselius .08 .20
43 Jason Allison .08 .20
44 Felix Potvin .20 .50
45 Zigmund Palffy .15 .40
46 Marian Gaborik .40 1.00
47 Manny Fernandez .15 .40
48 Jose Theodore .25 .60
49 Saku Koivu .20 .50
50 Patrik Elias .15 .40
51 Martin Brodeur .50 1.25
52 Joe Nieuwendyk .15 .40
53 Scott Hartnell .08 .20
54 Mike Dunham .15 .40
55 Alexei Yashin .08 .20
56 Chris Osgood .15 .40
57 Michael Peca .08 .20
58 Eric Lindros .20 .50
59 Mike Richter .15 .40
60 Pavel Bure .20 .50
61 Brian Leetch .15 .40
62 Patrick Lalime .15 .40
63 Marian Hossa .20 .50
64 Daniel Alfredsson .15 .40
65 Jeremy Roenick .25 .60
66 Simon Gagne .20 .50
67 Roman Cechmanek .15 .40
68 Sean Burke .15 .40
69 Daniel Briere .08 .20
70 Tony Amonte .15 .40
71 Alexei Kovalev .15 .40
72 Mario Lemieux 1.25 3.00
73 Johan Hedberg .20 .50
74 Patrick Marleau .15 .40
75 Owen Nolan .15 .40
76 Evgeni Nabokov .15 .40
77 Keith Tkachuk .20 .50
78 Chris Pronger .15 .40
79 Brent Johnson .15 .40
80 Nikolai Khabibulin .20 .50
81 Vincent Lecavalier .20 .50
82 Alexander Mogilny .15 .40
83 Mats Sundin .20 .50
84 Ed Belfour .20 .50
85 Todd Bertuzzi .20 .50
86 Dan Cloutier .15 .40
87 Markus Naslund .20 .50
88 Olaf Kolzig .15 .40
89 Peter Bondra .15 .40
90 Jaromir Jagr .30 .75
91 Wayne Gretzky SR 2.50 6.00
92 Wayne Gretzky SR 5.00 12.00
93 Mario Lemieux SR 5.00 12.00
94 Patrick Roy SR 4.00 10.00
95 Steve Yzerman SR 4.00 10.00
96 Gordie Howe SR 2.00 5.00
97 Bobby Orr SR 5.00 12.00
98 Ray Bourque SR .75 2.00
99 Brett Hull SR .75 2.00
100 Teemu Selanne SR .20 .50
101 Martin Brodeur SR 2.00 5.00
102 Jaromir Jagr SR 1.25 3.00
103 Eric Lindros SR 1.25 3.00
104 Joe Sakic SR 1.50 4.00
105 Mike Richter SR .60 1.50
106 Sergei Fedorov SR 1.50 4.00
107 Peter Forsberg SR 2.00 5.00
108 Mark Messier SR .20 .50
109 Wayne Gretzky TG 2.50 6.00
110 Wayne Gretzky TG 5.00 12.00
111 Wayne Gretzky TG 5.00 12.00
112 Gordie Howe TG 2.00 5.00
113 Gordie Howe TG 4.00 10.00
114 Gordie Howe TG 4.00 10.00
115 Bobby Orr TG 5.00 12.00
116 Bobby Orr TG 5.00 12.00
117 Bobby Orr TG 5.00 12.00
118 Ray Bourque TG .75 2.00
119 Ray Bourque TG 1.50 4.00
120 Ray Bourque TG 1.50 4.00
121 Stanislav Chistov HM RC 2.00 5.00
122 Alexei Smirnov HM RC 2.00 5.00
123 Henrik Tallinder HM 1.50 4.00
124 Micki Dupont HM RC 1.50 4.00
125 Chuck Kobasew HM RC 2.00 5.00
126 Andrej Nedorost HM 1.50 4.00
127 Rick Nash HM RC 8.00 20.00
128 Henrik Zetterberg HM RC 6.00 15.00
129 Ales Hemsky HM RC 4.00 10.00
130 Jani Rita HM 1.50 4.00
131 Stephen Weiss HM .08 .20
132 Jay Bouwmeester HM RC 3.00 8.00
133 Alexander Frolov HM RC 3.00 8.00
134 P-M Bouchard HM RC 3.00 8.00
135 Sylvain Blouin HM RC 1.50 4.00
136 Ron Hainsey HM RC 1.50 4.00
137 Adam Hall HM RC 1.50 4.00
138 Jan Lasak HM 1.50 4.00
139 Ray Schultz HM RC 1.50 4.00
140 Trent Hunter HM 1.50 4.00
141 Martin Prusek HM 1.50 4.00
142 Anton Volchenkov HM RC 1.50 4.00
143 Patrick Sharp HM RC 1.50 4.00
144 Dennis Seidenberg HM RC 2.00 5.00
145 Branko Radivojevic HM 1.50 4.00
146 Shane Endicott HM 1.50 4.00
147 Alexander Svitov HM RC 2.00 5.00
148 Sebastien Centomo HM 1.50 4.00
149 Karel Pilar HM 1.50 4.00
150 Steve Eminger HM RC 1.50 4.00

2002-03 UD Piece of History Awards Collection

COMPLETE SET (28) 25.00 50.00
STAT.ODDS 1:5 HBBY/1:6 RETAIL
AC1 Paul Kariya .50 1.25
AC2 Ray Bourque 1.00 2.50
AC3 Sergei Samsonov .40 1.00
AC4 Jarome Iginla .60 1.50
AC5 Chris Drury .40 1.00
AC6 Joe Sakic 1.00 2.50
AC7 Rob Blake .40 1.00
AC8 Peter Forsberg 1.25 3.00
AC9 Patrick Roy 2.50 6.00
AC10 Luc Robitaille .40 1.00
AC11 Brett Hull .60 1.50
AC12 Steve Yzerman 2.50 6.00
AC13 Dominik Hasek 1.00 2.50
AC14 Nicklas Lidstrom .50 1.25
AC15 Sergei Fedorov 1.00 2.50
AC16 Wayne Gretzky 3.00 8.00
AC17 Joe Nieuwendyk .40 1.00
AC18 Martin Brodeur 1.25 3.00
AC19 Brian Leetch .40 1.00
AC20 Pavel Bure .60 1.50
AC21 Claude Lemieux .40 1.00
AC22 Mario Lemieux 3.00 8.00
AC23 Evgeni Nabokov .40 1.00
AC24 Teemu Selanne .50 1.25
AC25 Chris Pronger .40 1.00
AC26 Al MacInnis .40 1.00
AC27 Jaromir Jagr .75 2.00
AC28 Olaf Kolzig .40 1.00

2002-03 UD Piece of History Exquisite Combos

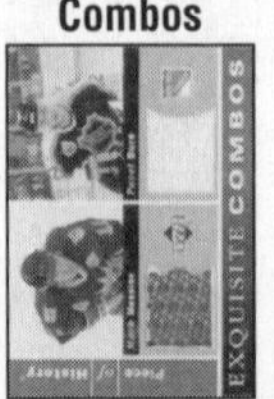

ODDS 1:168 HOBBY ONLY
ECBM Pavel Bure 12.50 30.00

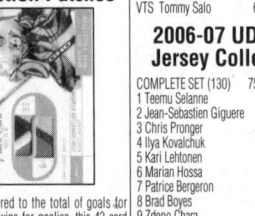

Mark Messier
ECBR Rob Blake 15.00 40.00
Patrick Roy
ECLK M.Lemieux/A.Kovalev 20.00 50.00
ECLM Eric Lindros 12.50 30.00
Mark Messier
ECNB Cam Neely 12.50 30.00
Ray Bourque

2002-03 UD Piece of History Heroes Jerseys

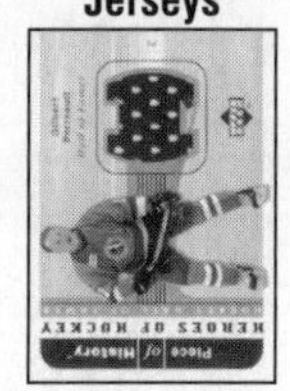

*MULT.COLOR SWATCH: .5X TO 1.25X HI
STATED ODDS 1:48
HHBS Borje Salming 4.00 10.00
HHGP Gilbert Perreault 3.00 8.00
HHJK Jari Kurri 5.00 12.00
HHMG Mike Gartner 3.00 8.00
HHPS Peter Stastny 3.00 8.00

2002-03 UD Piece of History Historical Swatches

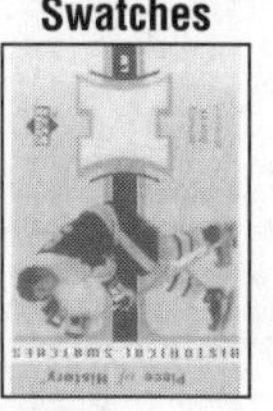

*MULT.COLOR SWATCH: .5X TO 1.25X HI
STATED ODDS 1:96
HSBS Borje Salming 6.00 15.00
HSBT Bryan Trottier 5.00 12.00
HSCN Cam Neely 15.00 40.00
HSGL Guy Lafleur 5.00 12.00
HSJB Johnny Bucyk 5.00 12.00
HSMB Mike Bossy 5.00 12.00
HSMG Michel Goulet 5.00 12.00
HSMG Mike Gartner 5.00 12.00
HSRB Ray Bourque 15.00 40.00
HSWG Wayne Gretzky 30.00 80.00

2002-03 UD Piece of History Hockey Beginnings

COMPLETE SET (8) 20.00 40.00
STATED ODDS 1:20
HB1 Bobby Orr 2.50 6.00
HB2 Ray Bourque .75 2.00
HB3 Steve Yzerman 2.00 5.00
HB4 Gordie Howe 2.00 5.00
HB5 Wayne Gretzky 2.50 6.00
HB6 Patrick Roy 2.00 5.00
HB7 Mike Bossy .60 1.50
HB8 Wayne Gretzky 2.50 6.00

2002-03 UD Piece of History Marks of Distinction

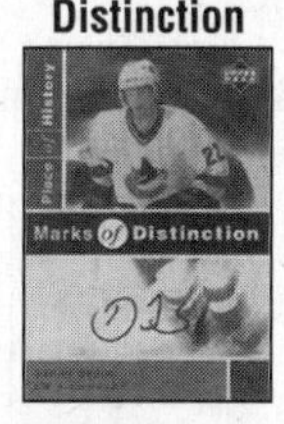

This 31-card autograph set was inserted at a rate of 1:168 hobby packs. Print runs listed below were provided by Upper Deck. Print runs of 25 or less not priced due to scarcity.

BO Bobby Orr/24
BR Rod Brind'Amour 6.00 15.00
BT Bryan Trottier/25
CN Cam Neely/25
DH Dany Heatley 12.50 30.00
DS Daniel Sedin 6.00 15.00
GA Mike Gartner/25
GH Gordie Howe/24
GL Guy Lafleur/25 75.00 100.00
GP Gilbert Perreault/25
HS Henrik Sedin 6.00 15.00
JB Johnny Bucyk/25
JI Jarome Iginla SP 12.50 30.00
JK Jari Kurri/25
JT Joe Thornton/24
MB Mike Bossy/25
MC Mike Comrie SP 15.00 40.00
MG Michel Goulet/25
MN Markus Naslund 8.00 20.00
MR Mike Richter 6.00 15.00
PA Pavel Brendl 6.00 15.00
PB Pavel Bure/24
PR Patrick Roy/24
PS Peter Stastny/25
RA Ray Bourque/24
SG Simon Gagne SP 8.00 20.00
SS Sergei Samsonov SP 12.50 30.00
SY Steve Yzerman 40.00 100.00
TS Teemu Selanne 8.00 20.00
VN Vaclav Nedorost 6.00 15.00
WG Wayne Gretzky/24

2002-03 UD Piece of History Patches

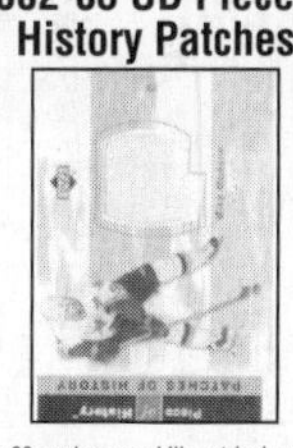

This 28-card memorabilia set had a stated print run of 25 serial-numbered sets.

PHBA Rob Blake 20.00 50.00
PHBL Brian Leetch 20.00 50.00
PHBS Brendan Shanahan 20.00 50.00
PHEL Eric Lindros 20.00 50.00
PHFP Felix Potvin 20.00 50.00
PHJS Joe Sakic 50.00 125.00
PHJT Jose Theodore 25.00 60.00
PHKP Keith Primeau 20.00 50.00
PHMA Maxim Afinogenov 20.00 50.00
PHMD Mike Dunham 20.00 50.00
PHMM Mike Modano 30.00 80.00
PHMN Markus Naslund 20.00 50.00
PHMS Mats Sundin 20.00 50.00
PHMT Marty Turco 20.00 50.00
PHPK Paul Kariya 20.00 50.00
PHPR Patrick Roy 75.00 200.00
PHRB Ray Bourque 50.00 125.00
PHRT Ron Tugnutt 20.00 50.00
PHSA Sergei Samsonov 20.00 50.00
PHSB Sean Burke 20.00 50.00
PHSF Sergei Fedorov 30.00 80.00
PHSG Simon Gagne 20.00 50.00
PHSS Steve Sullivan 20.00 50.00
PHSY Steve Yzerman 75.00 200.00
PHTH Joe Thornton 40.00 100.00
PHTS Teemu Selanne 20.00 50.00
PHWG Wayne Gretzky 125.00 300.00
PHZP Zigmund Palffy 20.00 50.00

2002-03 UD Piece of History Simply the Best

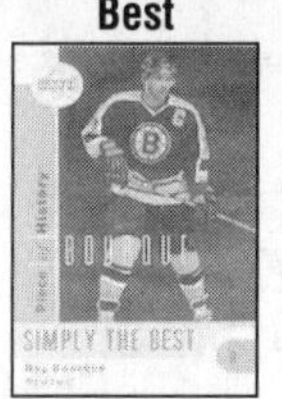

COMPLETE SET (6) 20.00 40.00
STATED ODDS 1:24
SB1 Ray Bourque 1.25 3.00
SB2 Bobby Orr 4.00 10.00
SB3 Patrick Roy 3.00 8.00
SB4 Steve Yzerman 3.00 8.00
SB5 Gordie Howe 3.00 8.00
SB6 Wayne Gretzky 4.00 10.00

2002-03 UD Piece of History Stellar Stitches

*MULT.COLOR SWATCH: .5X TO 1.25X HI
STATED ODDS 1:168 HOBBY PACKS
SSJS Joe Sakic 8.00 20.00
SSJT Joe Thornton 8.00 20.00
SSMM Mike Modano 6.00 15.00
SSMS Mats Sundin 5.00 12.00
SSPK Paul Kariya 5.00 12.00
SSSY Steve Yzerman 12.50 30.00

2002-03 UD Piece of History Threads

*MULT.COLOR SWATCH: .5X TO 1.25X HI
STATED ODDS 1:96 RETAIL PACKS
TTCD Chris Drury 5.00 12.00
TTCL Claude Lemieux 5.00 12.00
TTJT Jose Theodore 6.00 15.00
TTSF Sergei Fedorov 6.00 15.00
TTSG Simon Gagne 5.00 12.00
TTSH Scott Hartnell 5.00 12.00

2001-02 UD Playmakers

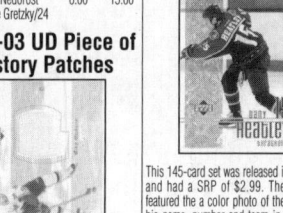

This 145-card set was released in early April and had a SRP of $2.99. The card front featured the a color photo of the player with his name, number and team in team colors in the lower right corner. The left side of the card fronts also were colored the featured team's color. Rookies in this set were short printed out of 1250.

COMP.SET w/o SP's (100) 10.00 20.00
1 Steve Shields .05 .15
2 Jeff Friesen .05 .15
3 Paul Kariya .12 .30
4 Ray Ferraro .05 .15
5 Milan Hnilicka .10 .25
6 Dany Heatley .15 .40
7 Sergei Samsonov .10 .25
8 Joe Thornton .20 .50
9 Byron Dafoe .10 .25
10 Hal Gill .05 .15
11 Miroslav Satan .10 .25
12 Stu Barnes .05 .15
13 Martin Biron .10 .25
14 Marc Savard .05 .15
15 Roman Turek .10 .25
16 Jarome Iginla .15 .40
17 Jeff O'Neill .05 .15
18 Sami Kapanen .05 .15
19 Arturs Irbe .10 .25
20 Steve Sullivan .05 .15
21 Jocelyn Thibault .10 .25
22 Tony Amonte .10 .25
23 Joe Sakic .25 .60
24 Milan Hejduk .12 .30
25 Chris Drury .10 .25
26 Patrick Roy .60 1.50
27 Rob Blake .10 .25
28 Marc Denis .10 .25
29 Ray Whitney .05 .15
30 Rostislav Klesla .05 .15
31 Ed Belfour .12 .30
32 Pierre Turgeon .10 .25
33 Mike Modano .20 .50
34 Brett Hull .15 .40
35 Dominik Hasek .25 .60
36 Brendan Shanahan .12 .30
37 Luc Robitaille .10 .25
38 Steve Yzerman .60 1.50
39 Mike Comrie .10 .25
40 Tommy Salo .10 .25
41 Ryan Smyth .05 .15
42 Anson Carter .05 .15
43 Valeri Bure .05 .15
44 Roberto Luongo .15 .40
45 Pavel Bure .12 .30
46 Felix Potvin .12 .30
47 Jason Allison .05 .15
48 Zigmund Palffy .10 .25
49 Manny Fernandez .10 .25
50 Marian Gaborik .25 .60
51 Andrew Brunette .05 .15
52 Yanic Perreault .05 .15
53 Jose Theodore .15 .40
54 Brian Savage .05 .15
55 David Legwand .10 .25
56 Mike Dunham .10 .25
57 Cliff Ronning .05 .15
58 Martin Brodeur .30 .75
59 Patrik Elias .10 .25
60 Jason Arnott .05 .15
61 Alexei Yashin .05 .15
62 Chris Osgood .10 .25
63 Mark Parrish .05 .15
64 Theo Fleury .05 .15
65 Brian Leetch .10 .25
66 Mark Messier .12 .30
67 Eric Lindros .12 .30
68 Radek Bonk .05 .15
69 Marian Hossa .12 .30
70 Martin Havlat .10 .25
71 John LeClair .12 .30
72 Mark Recchi .10 .25
73 Roman Cechmanek .10 .25
74 Jeremy Roenick .15 .40
75 Michal Handzus .05 .15
76 Shane Doan .05 .15
77 Sean Burke .10 .25
78 Alexei Kovalev .10 .25
79 Mario Lemieux .75 2.00
80 Johan Hedberg .10 .25
81 Owen Nolan .10 .25
82 Teemu Selanne .12 .30
83 Evgeni Nabokov .10 .25
84 Chris Pronger .10 .25
85 Pavol Demitra .10 .25
86 Keith Tkachuk .12 .30
87 Doug Weight .10 .25
88 Vincent Lecavalier .12 .30
89 Brad Richards .10 .25
90 Nikolai Khabibulin .12 .30
91 Wade Belak .05 .15
92 Alexander Mogilny .10 .25
93 Mats Sundin .12 .30
94 Curtis Joseph .12 .30
95 Brendan Morrison .10 .25
96 Trevor Linden .05 .15
97 Markus Naslund .12 .30
98 Peter Bondra .12 .30
99 Olaf Kolzig .10 .25
100 Jaromir Jagr .20 .50
101 Timo Parssinen RC 1.50 4.00
102 Ilja Bryzgalov RC 1.50 4.00
103 Mike Weaver RC 1.50 4.00
104 Ilya Kovalchuk RC 5.00 12.00
105 Ivan Huml RC 1.50 4.00
106 Tony Tuzzolino RC 1.50 4.00
107 Jukka Hentunen RC 1.50 4.00
108 Scott Nichol RC 1.50 4.00
109 Erik Cole RC 1.50 4.00
110 Mike Peluso RC 1.50 4.00
111 Riku Hahl RC 1.50 4.00
112 Vaclav Nedorost RC 1.50 4.00
113 Blake Bellefeuille RC 1.50 4.00
114 Niko Kapanen RC 2.00 5.00
115 John Erskine RC 1.50 4.00
116 Pavel Datsyuk RC 4.00 10.00
117 Ty Conklin RC 1.50 4.00
118 Jason Chimera RC 1.50 4.00
119 Niklas Hagman RC 1.50 4.00
120 Kristian Huselius RC 2.00 5.00
121 Kip Brennan RC 1.50 4.00
122 Pascal Dupuis RC 1.50 4.00
123 Marcel Hossa RC 1.50 4.00
124 Olivier Michaud RC 1.50 4.00
125 Martin Erat RC 1.50 4.00
126 Christian Berglund RC 1.50 4.00
127 Andreas Salomonsson RC 1.50 4.00
128 Raffi Torres RC 2.00 5.00
129 Radek Martinek RC 1.50 4.00
130 Mikael Samuelsson RC 1.50 4.00
131 Dan Blackburn RC 2.00 5.00
132 Toni Dahlman RC 1.50 4.00
133 Bruno St. Jacques RC 1.50 4.00
134 Tomas Divisek RC 1.50 4.00
135 Jiri Dopita RC 1.50 4.00
136 Krys Kolanos RC 1.50 4.00
137 Eric Meloche RC 1.50 4.00
138 Tom Kostopoulos RC 1.50 4.00
139 Jeff Jillson RC 1.50 4.00
140 Mark Rycroft RC 1.50 4.00
141 Josef Boumedienne RC 1.50 4.00
142 Nikita Alexeev RC 1.50 4.00
143 Mike Farrell RC 1.50 4.00
144 Todd Rohloff RC 1.50 4.00
145 Brian Sutherby RC 1.50 4.00

2001-02 UD Playmakers Bobble Heads

Inserted at one per hobby box, this 24-figure set featured 12 players in both home and away jerseys.

CJ-A Curtis Joseph 5.00 12.00
CJ-H Curtis Joseph 5.00 12.00
DH-A Dominik Hasek 5.00 12.00
DH-H Dominik Hasek 5.00 12.00
DW-A Doug Weight 5.00 12.00
DW-H Doug Weight 5.00 12.00
EL-A Eric Lindros 5.00 12.00
EL-H Eric Lindros 5.00 12.00
IK-A Ilya Kovalchuk 5.00 12.00
IK-H Ilya Kovalchuk 10.00 25.00
JJ-A Jaromir Jagr 5.00 12.00
JJ-H Jaromir Jagr 5.00 12.00
JS-A Joe Sakic 5.00 12.00
JS-H Joe Sakic 5.00 12.00
MB-A Martin Brodeur 5.00 12.00
MB-H Martin Brodeur 5.00 12.00
MM-A Mike Modano 5.00 12.00
MM-H Mike Modano 5.00 12.00
PB-A Pavel Bure 5.00 12.00
PB-H Pavel Bure 5.00 12.00
PR-A Patrick Roy 10.00 25.00
PR-H Patrick Roy 10.00 25.00
SY-A Steve Yzerman 10.00 25.00
SY-H Steve Yzerman 10.00 25.00

2001-02 UD Playmakers Bobble Heads Autographed

Inserted at one per case, these bobble head figures parallel the regular set but also include authentic player autographs on the base.

CJ-A Curtis Joseph 30.00 80.00
CJ-H Curtis Joseph 40.00 100.00
DW-A Doug Weight 12.50 30.00
DW-H Doug Weight 12.50 30.00
IK-A Ilya Kovalchuk 30.00 80.00
IK-H Ilya Kovalchuk 30.00 80.00
MB-A Martin Brodeur 40.00 100.00
MB-H Martin Brodeur 40.00 100.00
PB-A Pavel Bure 25.00 60.00
PB-H Pavel Bure 25.00 60.00
SY-A Steve Yzerman 50.00 125.00
SY-H Steve Yzerman 40.00 100.00

2001-02 UD Playmakers Combo Jerseys

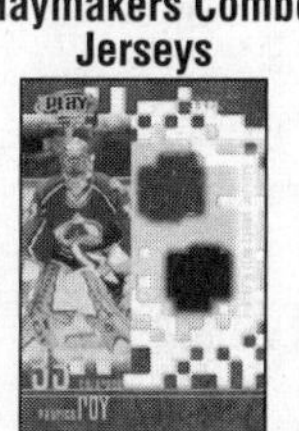

Serial-numbered to 100 copies each, this 10-card set featured dual game-worn jersey swatches of the given player. A gold parallel was also created and serial-numbered to 50.

*MULT.COLOR SWATCH: 1X TO 1.5X HI
*GOLD: 1X TO 2X BASIC INSERT
CJJI Jarome Iginla 12.50 30.00
CJJL John LeClair 10.00 25.00
CJMA Maxim Afinogenov 10.00 25.00
CJMD Mike Dunham 10.00 25.00
CJMH Milan Hejduk 10.00 25.00
CJMR Mark Recchi 10.00 25.00
CJPK Paul Kariya 10.00 25.00
CJPR Patrick Roy 25.00 60.00
CJRB Rob Blake 10.00 25.00
CJSG Simon Gagne 12.50 30.00

2001-02 UD Playmakers Jerseys

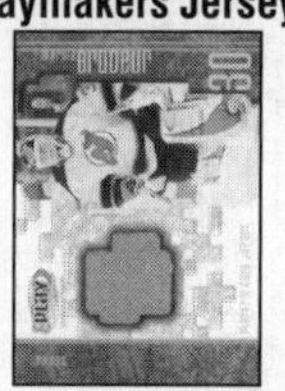

Inserted at 1:72, this 10-card set featured swatches of game-used jerseys of the featured players. A gold parallel was also created and serial-numbered out of 100.

*GOLD: 1X TO 2X BASIC INSERT
J-JI Jarome Iginla 8.00 20.00
J-MA Maxim Afinogenov 6.00 15.00
J-MB Martin Brodeur 10.00 25.00
J-ML Mario Lemieux 15.00 40.00
J-MR Mark Recchi 6.00 15.00
J-PF Peter Forsberg 8.00 20.00
J-RT Ron Tugnutt 6.00 15.00
J-SG Simon Gagne 6.00 15.00
J-TS Teemu Selanne 6.00 15.00
J-ZP Zigmund Palffy 6.00 15.00

2001-02 UD Playmakers Practice Jerseys

Inserted at 1:48, this 10-card set featured swatches of practice jerseys from the given player. A gold parallel was also created and serial-numbered to 200 copies each.

*GOLD: .75X TO 1.5X BASIC INSERT
PJEB Ed Belfour 6.00 15.00
PJJI Jarome Iginla 8.00 20.00
PJJL John LeClair 6.00 15.00
PJMH Milan Hejduk 6.00 15.00
PJMO Maxime Ouellet 5.00 12.00
PJMS Miroslav Satan 5.00 12.00
PJRB Rod Brind'Amour 5.00 12.00
PJRF Rico Fata 5.00 12.00
PJSG Simon Gagne 6.00 15.00
PJTB Tyler Bouck 5.00 12.00

2005-06 UD PowerPlay

COMPLETE SET (1-132) 50.00 100.00
COMP.SET w/o SP's (90) 8.00 15.00
IP AND IA ODDS 1:12
GR AND CC ODDS 1:24
1 J-S Giguere .15 .40
2 Joffrey Lupul .10 .25
3 Sergei Fedorov .20 .50
4 Dany Heatley .25 .60
5 Ilya Kovalchuk .25 .60
6 Kari Lehtonen .20 .50
7 Sergei Samsonov .10 .25
8 Joe Thornton .30 .75
9 Andrew Raycroft .15 .40
10 Glen Murray .10 .25
11 Ryan Miller .15 .40
12 Daniel Briere .10 .25
13 Miroslav Satan .10 .25
14 Jarome Iginla .25 .60
15 Jordan Leopold .10 .25
16 Miikka Kiprusoff .20 .50
17 Eric Staal .15 .40
18 Josef Vasicek .10 .25
19 Eric Daze .15 .40
20 Tuomo Ruutu .10 .25
21 Jocelyn Thibault .15 .40
22 Joe Sakic .40 1.00
23 Alex Tanguay .15 .40
24 Milan Hejduk .20 .50
25 Peter Forsberg .30 .75
26 Rick Nash .25 .60
27 Nikolai Zherdev .15 .40
28 Marc Denis .15 .40
29 Mike Modano .20 .50
30 Bill Guerin .10 .25
31 Marty Turco .15 .40
32 Pavel Datsyuk .20 .50
33 Brendan Shanahan .20 .50
34 Steve Yzerman .75 2.00
35 Nicklas Lidstrom .20 .50
36 Ales Hemsky .10 .25
37 Ryan Smyth .15 .40
38 Patrice Bergeron .20 .50
39 Roberto Luongo .25 .60
40 Olli Jokinen .15 .40
41 Luc Robitaille .15 .40
42 Zigmund Palffy .15 .40
43 Lubomir Visnovsky .10 .25
44 Marian Gaborik .40 1.00
45 Dwayne Roloson .15 .40
46 Michael Ryder .15 .40
47 Jose Theodore .25 .60
48 Mike Ribeiro .10 .25
49 Steve Sullivan .10 .25
50 Nathan Horton .10 .25
51 Tomas Vokoun .15 .40
52 Martin Brodeur 1.00 2.50
53 Patrik Elias .15 .40
54 Scott Niedermayer .10 .25
55 Michael Peca .10 .25
56 Mark Messier .20 .50
57 Jaromir Jagr .30 .75
58 Mark Parrish .10 .25
59 Rick DiPietro .15 .40
60 Daniel Alfredsson .15 .40
61 Marian Hossa .15 .40
62 Jason Spezza .20 .50
63 Dominik Hasek .40 1.00
64 Jeremy Roenick .25 .60
65 Keith Primeau .10 .25
66 John LeClair .20 .50
67 Brett Hull .25 .60
68 Ladislav Nagy .10 .25
69 Shane Doan .10 .25
70 Marc-Andre Fleury .15 .40
71 Mario Lemieux 1.25 3.00
72 Mark Recchi .15 .40
73 Jonathan Cheechoo .20 .50
74 Evgeni Nabokov .15 .40
75 Patrick Marleau .15 .40
76 Chris Pronger .15 .40
77 Doug Weight .15 .40
78 Keith Tkachuk .20 .50
79 Brad Richards .15 .40
80 Nikolai Khabibulin .20 .50
81 Martin St. Louis .15 .40
82 Dave Andreychuk .10 .25
83 Joe Nieuwendyk .15 .40
84 Ed Belfour .20 .50
85 Mats Sundin .20 .50
86 Brian Leetch .20 .50
87 Brendan Morrison .10 .25
88 Markus Naslund .20 .50
89 Todd Bertuzzi .20 .50
90 Olaf Kolzig .15 .40
91 Sergei Fedorov IP .40 1.00
92 Dany Heatley IP .50 1.25
93 Joe Thornton IP .60 1.50
94 Daniel Briere IP .20 .50
95 Jarome Iginla IP .50 1.25
96 Joe Sakic IP .75 2.00
97 Steve Yzerman IP 1.50 4.00
98 Martin Havlat IP .30 .75
99 Jeremy Roenick IP .50 1.25
100 Mario Lemieux IP 2.50 6.00
101 Chris Pronger IP .30 .75
102 Dave Andreychuk IP .20 .50
103 Martin St. Louis IP .30 .75
104 Mats Sundin IP .40 1.00
105 Ilya Kovalchuk IA .50 1.25
106 Andrew Raycroft IA .30 .75
107 Peter Forsberg IA .60 1.50
108 Rick Nash IA .60 1.50
109 Jose Theodore IA .50 1.25
110 Tomas Vokoun IA .30 .75
111 Jaromir Jagr IA .60 1.50
112 Mark Messier IA .40 1.00
113 Jason Spezza IA .40 1.00
114 Marc-Andre Fleury IA .30 .75
115 Jonathan Cheechoo IA .40 1.00
116 Patrick Marleau IA .30 .75
117 Nikolai Khabibulin IA .40 1.00
118 Markus Naslund IA .40 1.00
119 Dave Andreychuk CC .25 .60
120 Martin Brodeur CC 2.00 5.00
121 Joe Sakic CC 1.00 2.50
122 Patrick Roy CC 2.50 6.00
123 Wayne Gretzky CC 3.00 8.00
124 Mark Messier CC .50 1.25
125 Steve Yzerman CC 2.00 5.00
126 Andrew Raycroft GR .40 1.00
127 Martin Brodeur GR 2.50 6.00
128 Patrick Roy GR 2.50 6.00
129 Jose Theodore GR .60 1.50
130 Marc-Andre Fleury GR .40 1.00
131 Marty Turco GR .40 1.00
132 Nikolai Khabibulin GR .50 1.25
133 Sidney Crosby RC 20.00 40.00
134 Wojtek Wolski RC 2.50 6.00
135 Hannu Toivonen RC 2.00 5.00
136 Alexander Steen RC 2.00 5.00
137 Jeff Woywitka RC 1.25 3.00
138 Jussi Jokinen RC 2.00 5.00
139 Kevin Nastiuk RC 1.50 4.00
140 Brent Seabrook RC 1.50 4.00
141 Brad Winchester RC 1.50 4.00
142 Brandon Bochenski RC 1.50 4.00
143 Alexander Ovechkin RC 10.00 25.00
144 Thomas Vanek RC 3.00 8.00
145 Yann Danis RC 1.50 4.00
146 Ryan Getzlaf RC 3.00 8.00
147 Ryan Suter RC 1.50 4.00
148 Henrik Lundqvist RC 4.00 10.00
149 Johan Franzen RC 1.50 4.00
150 Rene Bourque RC 1.50 4.00
151 Eric Nystrom RC 1.50 4.00
152 Patrick Eaves RC 1.50 4.00
153 Corey Perry RC 2.50 6.00
154 Alexander Perezhogin RC 2.00 5.00
155 Zach Parise RC 2.50 6.00
156 Mike Richards RC 2.00 5.00
157 Braydon Coburn RC 1.50 4.00
158 Cam Ward RC 2.00 5.00
159 David Leneveu RC 1.50 4.00
160 Andrew Alberts RC 1.50 4.00
161 Petteri Nokelainen RC 1.50 4.00
162 Lee Stempniak RC 1.50 4.00
163 Jeff Carter RC 2.50 6.00
164 Gilbert Brule RC 2.00 5.00
165 Dion Phaneuf RC 4.00 10.00
166 Jim Howard RC 2.50 6.00
167 Rostislav Olesz RC 1.50 4.00
168 Robert Nilsson RC 1.50 4.00
169 Peter Budaj RC 1.50 4.00
170 Andrej Meszaros RC 1.50 4.00
171 Petr Prucha RC 2.00 5.00
172 Matt Foy RC 1.25 3.00
A Rookie Redemption A 10.00 25.00
B Rookie Redemption B 4.00 10.00
C Rookie Redemption C 4.00 10.00
D Rookie Redemption D 4.00 10.00

2005-06 UD PowerPlay Rainbow

PRINT RUNS EQUAL JSY #'s
NOT PRICED DUE TO SCARCITY
1 J-S Giguere
2 Joffrey Lupul
3 Sergei Fedorov
4 Dany Heatley
5 Ilya Kovalchuk
6 Kari Lehtonen
7 Sergei Samsonov
8 Joe Thornton
9 Andrew Raycroft
10 Glen Murray
11 Ryan Miller
12 Daniel Briere
13 Miroslav Satan
14 Jarome Iginla
15 Jordan Leopold
16 Miikka Kiprusoff
17 Eric Staal
18 Josef Vasicek
19 Eric Daze
20 Tuomo Ruutu
21 Jocelyn Thibault
22 Joe Sakic
23 Alex Tanguay
24 Milan Hejduk
25 Peter Forsberg
26 Rick Nash
27 Nikolai Zherdev
28 Marc Denis
29 Mike Modano
30 Bill Guerin
31 Marty Turco
32 Pavel Datsyuk
33 Brendan Shanahan
34 Steve Yzerman
35 Nicklas Lidstrom
36 Ales Hemsky
37 Ryan Smyth
38 Patrice Bergeron
39 Roberto Luongo
40 Olli Jokinen
41 Luc Robitaille
42 Zigmund Palffy
43 Lubomir Visnovsky
44 Marian Gaborik
45 Dwayne Roloson
46 Michael Ryder
47 Jose Theodore
48 Mike Ribeiro
49 Steve Sullivan
50 Nathan Horton
51 Tomas Vokoun
52 Martin Brodeur
53 Patrik Elias
54 Scott Niedermayer
55 Michael Peca
56 Mark Messier
57 Jaromir Jagr
58 Mark Parrish
59 Rick DiPietro
60 Daniel Alfredsson
61 Marian Hossa
62 Jason Spezza
63 Dominik Hasek
64 Jeremy Roenick
65 Keith Primeau
66 John LeClair
67 Brett Hull
68 Ladislav Nagy
69 Shane Doan
70 Marc-Andre Fleury
71 Mario Lemieux
72 Mark Recchi
73 Jonathan Cheechoo
74 Evgeni Nabokov
75 Patrick Marleau
76 Chris Pronger
77 Doug Weight
78 Keith Tkachuk
79 Brad Richards
80 Nikolai Khabibulin
81 Martin St. Louis
82 Dave Andreychuk
83 Joe Nieuwendyk
84 Ed Belfour
85 Mats Sundin
86 Brian Leetch
87 Brendan Morrison
88 Markus Naslund
89 Todd Bertuzzi
90 Olaf Kolzig

2005-06 UD Powerplay Power Marks

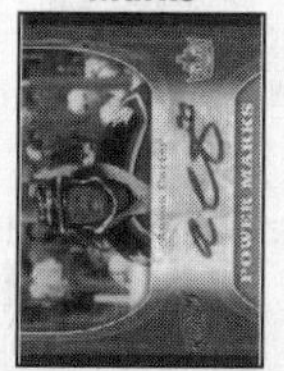

STATED ODDS 1:200
PMAC Anson Carter 10.00 25.00
PMBB Brad Boyes 10.00 25.00
PMCK Chuck Kobasew 8.00 20.00
PMDA Daniel Alfredsson SP 20.00 50.00
PMDB Dustin Brown 4.00 10.00
PMEJ Ed Jovanovski 8.00 20.00
PMEN Evgeni Nabokov SP 12.00 30.00
PMFS Fredrik Sjostrom 4.00 10.00
PMGH Gordie Howe SP 125.00 250.00

PMHA Martin Havlat 10.00 25.00
PMHE Milan Hejduk 12.00 30.00
PMHZ Henrik Zetterberg SP 20.00 50.00
PMIK Ilya Kovalchuk SP 50.00 100.00
PMJC Jonathan Cheechoo 15.00 40.00
PMJI Jarome Iginla SP 40.00 80.00
PMJP Joni Pitkanen 4.00 10.00
PMJT Joe Thornton 25.00 60.00
PMJW Justin Williams 10.00 25.00
PMKD Kris Draper 8.00 20.00
PMKP Keith Primeau 4.00 10.00
PMLR Luc Robitaille 30.00 80.00
PMMB Milan Bartovic 4.00 10.00
PMMC Mike Comrie SP 40.00 100.00
PMMG Marian Gaborik SP 20.00 50.00
PMMH Marian Hossa 20.00 50.00
PMMN Markus Naslund 15.00 40.00
PMMP Mark Popovic 4.00 10.00
PMMR Mike Ribeiro 8.00 20.00
PMMS Martin St. Louis SP 25.00 60.00
PMNK Nikolai Khabibulin SP 40.00 80.00
PMNO Mika Noronen 4.00 10.00
PMNS Nathan Smith 4.00 10.00
PMPS Peter Sejna 4.00 10.00
PMRK Ryan Kesler 4.00 10.00
PMRN Rick Nash 25.00 60.00
PMRY Michael Ryder 20.00 50.00
PMSS Sheldon Souray SP 15.00 40.00
PMWG Wayne Gretzky SP 350.00 500.00
PMZP Zigmund Palffy 12.00 30.00
PMZP Roman Turek 8.00 20.00

2005-06 UD Powerplay Specialists

*MULT.COLOR: 1.25X TO 3X HI
STATED ODDS 1:12
TSAB David Aebischer 3.00 8.00
TSAH Ales Hemsky 3.00 8.00
TSAKO Alex Kovalev 4.00 10.00
TSAS Alexei Semenov 3.00 8.00
TSAY Alexei Yashin 3.00 8.00
TSBH Brett Hull 5.00 12.00
TSBK Radek Bonk 3.00 8.00
TSBO Peter Bondra 3.00 8.00
TSBS Brendan Shanahan 4.00 10.00
TSCC Chris Chelios 4.00 10.00
TSCD Chris Drury 3.00 8.00
TSCE Christian Ehrhoff 3.00 8.00
TSDA Daniel Alfredsson 3.00 8.00
TSDH Dany Heatley 5.00 12.00
TSDO Dominik Hasek 6.00 15.00
TSDW Doug Weight 3.00 8.00
TSEB Eric Brewer 3.00 8.00
TSEJ Ed Jovanovski 3.00 8.00
TSGM Glen Murray 3.00 8.00
TSHA Derian Hatcher 3.00 8.00
TSJD J-P Dumont 3.00 8.00
TSJI Jarome Iginla 5.00 12.00
TSJJ Jaromir Jagr 8.00 20.00
TSJL John LeClair 3.00 8.00
TSJL Joffrey Lupul 3.00 8.00
TSJN Joe Nieuwendyk 3.00 8.00
TSJS J-S Giguere 3.00 8.00
TSJT Joe Thornton 6.00 15.00
TSKP Keith Primeau 3.00 8.00
TSLC Pascal Leclaire 3.00 8.00
TSLE Jordan Leopold 3.00 8.00
TSMB Martin Brodeur 10.00 25.00
TSMC Mike Comrie 3.00 8.00
TSMH Milan Hejduk 4.00 10.00
TSML Mario Lemieux 12.00 30.00
TSMM Mike Modano 6.00 15.00
TSMR Mark Recchi 3.00 8.00
TSMT Marty Turco SP 6.00 15.00
TSNA Nikolai Antropov 3.00 8.00
TSOJ Olli Jokinen 3.00 8.00
TSOK Olaf Kolzig 3.00 8.00
TSPB P-M Bouchard 3.00 8.00
TSPB Pavel Bure 4.00 10.00
TSPD Pavol Demitra 3.00 8.00
TSPK Paul Kariya SP 60.00 100.00
TSPL Patrick Lalime 3.00 8.00
TSRB Rob Blake 3.00 8.00
TSRE Robert Esche 3.00 8.00
TSRL Robert Lang 3.00 8.00
TSRT Roman Turek 3.00 8.00
TSSB Sean Burke 3.00 8.00
TSSG Scott Gomez 3.00 8.00
TSSP Jason Spezza 4.00 10.00
TSTA Tony Amonte SP 3.00 8.00
TSTH Jocelyn Thibault 3.00 8.00
TSTL Trevor Linden 8.00 20.00
TSTS Teemu Selanne 4.00 10.00
TSVL Vincent Lecavalier SP 40.00 80.00
TSVN Ville Nieminen 3.00 8.00
TSWG Wayne Gretzky SP 125.00 250.00

2005-06 UD Powerplay Specialists Patches

PRINT RUN 5 SER.#'d SETS
NOT PRICED DUE TO SCARCITY

2006-07 UD Powerplay

COMPLETE SET (130) 40.00 80.00
1 Jean-Sebastien Giguere .15 .40
2 Teemu Selanne .20 .50
3 Chris Pronger .15 .40
4 Ilya Kovalchuk .25 .60
5 Marian Hossa .15 .40
6 Kari Lehtonen .20 .50
7 Patrice Bergeron .20 .50
8 Brad Boyes .10 .25
9 Hannu Toivonen .20 .50
10 Zdeno Chara .10 .25
11 Chris Drury .10 .25
12 Ryan Miller .20 .50
13 Maxim Afinogenov .10 .25
14 Miikka Kiprusoff .20 .50
15 Jarome Iginla .25 .60
16 Dion Phaneuf .25 .60
17 Alex Tanguay .15 .40
18 Eric Staal .20 .50
19 Cam Ward .20 .50
20 Rod Brind'Amour .15 .40
21 Erik Cole .10 .25
22 Tuomo Ruutu .10 .25
23 Nikolai Khabibulin .20 .50
24 Michal Handzus .10 .25
25 Martin Havlat .15 .40
26 Marek Svatos .10 .25
27 Milan Hejduk .15 .40
28 Joe Sakic .40 1.00
29 Rick Nash .20 .50
30 Sergei Fedorov .20 .50
31 Pascal Leclaire .15 .40
32 Mike Modano .20 .50
33 Brenden Morrow .15 .40
34 Marty Turco .15 .40
35 Eric Lindros .20 .50
36 Henrik Zetterberg .20 .50
37 Nicklas Lidstrom .20 .50
38 Pavel Datsyuk .15 .40
39 Dominik Hasek .30 .75
40 Joffrey Lupul .10 .25
41 Ales Hemsky .10 .25
42 Ryan Smyth .15 .40
43 Olli Jokinen .10 .25
44 Todd Bertuzzi .15 .40
45 Jay Bouwmeester .10 .25
46 Alexander Frolov .10 .25
47 Rob Blake .15 .40
48 Mike Cammalleri .10 .25
49 Marian Gaborik .25 .60
50 Manny Fernandez .15 .40
51 Pavol Demitra .10 .25
52 Saku Koivu .20 .50
53 Cristobal Huet .25 .60
54 Alex Kovalev .10 .25
55 Michael Ryder .15 .40
56 Steve Sullivan .10 .25
57 Paul Kariya .20 .50
58 Tomas Vokoun .15 .40
59 Martin Brodeur .75 2.00
60 Patrik Elias .10 .25
61 Brian Gionta .10 .25
62 Miroslav Satan .10 .25
63 Alexei Yashin .10 .25
64 Rick DiPietro .15 .40
65 Jaromir Jagr .30 .75
66 Henrik Lundqvist .25 .60
67 Brendan Shanahan .20 .50
68 Martin Gerber .15 .40
69 Jason Spezza .20 .50
70 Dany Heatley .25 .60
71 Daniel Alfredsson .15 .40
72 Peter Forsberg .40 1.00
73 Simon Gagne .20 .50
74 Robert Esche .15 .40
75 Jeff Carter .15 .40
76 Shane Doan .10 .25
77 Curtis Joseph .20 .50
78 Jeremy Roenick .25 .60
79 Sergei Gonchar .10 .25
80 Sidney Crosby 1.25 3.00
81 Marc-Andre Fleury .15 .40
82 Joe Thornton .30 .75
83 Jonathan Cheechoo .20 .50
84 Patrick Marleau .15 .40
85 Doug Weight .10 .25
86 Keith Tkachuk .20 .50
87 Manny Legace .15 .40
88 Brad Richards .15 .40
89 Martin St. Louis .15 .40
90 Vincent Lecavalier .20 .50
91 Mats Sundin .20 .50
92 Alexander Steen .15 .40
93 Bryan McCabe .10 .25
94 Andrew Raycroft .15 .40
95 Markus Naslund .20 .50
96 Roberto Luongo .25 .60
97 Brendan Morrison .10 .25
98 Henrik Sedin .10 .25
99 Alexander Ovechkin 1.00 2.50
100 Olaf Kolzig .20 .50
101 Yan Stastny RC .60 1.50
102 Mark Stuart RC .60 1.50
103 Carsen Germyn RC .60 1.50
104 Dustin Byfuglien RC .60 1.50
105 Tomas Kopecky RC .75 2.00
106 Marc-Antoine Pouliot RC .75 2.00
107 Konstantin Pushkarev RC .60 1.50
108 Erik Reitz RC .60 1.50
109 Miroslav Kopriva RC .60 1.50
110 Shea Weber RC .75 2.00
111 David Printz RC .60 1.50
112 Steve Regier RC .60 1.50
113 Ryan Caldwell RC .60 1.50
114 Masi Marjamaki RC .60 1.50
115 Matt Koalska RC .60 1.50
116 Jarkko Immonen RC .60 1.50
117 Cole Jarrett RC .60 1.50
118 Rob Collins RC .60 1.50
119 Filip Novak RC .60 1.50
120 Ryan Potulny RC 1.00 2.50
121 Bill Thomas RC .60 1.50
122 Joel Perrault RC .60 1.50
123 Noah Welch RC .60 1.50
124 Michel Ouellet RC 1.00 2.50
125 Matt Carle RC .75 2.00
126 Ben Ondrus RC .60 1.50
127 Brendan Bell RC .60 1.50
128 Ian White RC .60 1.50
129 Jeremy Williams RC .60 1.50
130 Eric Fehr RC .75 2.00

2006-07 UD Powerplay Impact Rainbow

*STARS: 15X TO 40X BASE HI
*PROSPECTS 2X TO 5X BASE HI
PRINT RUN 25 SER. #'d SETS
80 Sidney Crosby 80.00 200.00
99 Alexander Ovechkin 30.00 80.00

2006-07 UD Powerplay Cup Celebrations

COMPLETE SET (7) 10.00 25.00
STATED ODDS 1:24
CC1 Eric Staal 1.00 2.50
CC2 Cam Ward 1.00 2.50
CC3 Dominik Hasek 1.50 4.00
CC4 Mike Modano 1.25 3.00
CC5 Martin St. Louis 1.00 2.50
CC6 Mario Lemieux 4.00 10.00
CC7 Patrick Roy 3.00 8.00

2006-07 UD Powerplay Goal Robbers

COMPLETE SET (14) 12.00 30.00
STATED ODDS 1:12
GR1 Jean-Sebastien Giguere 1.00 2.50
GR2 Kari Lehtonen 1.25 3.00
GR3 Ryan Miller 1.25 3.00
GR4 Miikka Kiprusoff 1.25 3.00
GR5 Cam Ward 1.25 3.00
GR6 Jose Theodore 1.25 3.00
GR7 Marty Turco 1.00 2.50
GR8 Marc-Andre Fleury 1.25 3.00
GR9 Roberto Luongo 1.50 4.00
GR10 Manny Fernandez 1.00 2.50
GR11 Tomas Vokoun 1.00 2.50
GR12 Martin Brodeur 2.50 6.00
GR13 Henrik Lundqvist 1.50 4.00
GR14 Cristobal Huet 1.50 4.00

2006-07 UD Powerplay In Action

COMPLETE SET (14) 10.00 25.00
STATED ODDS 1:12
IA1 Jarome Iginla .60 1.50
IA2 Joe Sakic 1.00 2.50
IA3 Rick Nash .50 1.25
IA4 Henrik Zetterberg .50 1.25
IA5 Saku Koivu .50 1.25
IA6 Martin Brodeur 2.00 5.00
IA7 Jaromir Jagr .75 2.00
IA8 Dany Heatley .60 1.50
IA9 Peter Forsberg 1.00 2.50
IA10 Sidney Crosby 3.00 8.00
IA11 Joe Thornton .75 2.00
IA12 Mats Sundin .50 1.25
IA13 Markus Naslund .50 1.25
IA14 Alexander Ovechkin 2.50 6.00

2006-07 UD Powerplay Last Man Standing

COMPLETE SET (7) 6.00 15.00
STATED ODDS 1:24
LM1 Jody Shelley 1.25 3.00
LM2 Derek Boogaard 1.25 3.00
LM3 George Parros 1.25 3.00
LM4 Donald Brashear 1.25 3.00
LM5 Georges Laraque 1.25 3.00
LM6 Chris Simon 1.25 3.00
LM7 Todd Fedoruk 1.25 3.00

2006-07 UD Powerplay Power Marks

STATED ODDS 1:400
PMAA Andrew Alberts 8.00 20.00
PMAM Andrej Meszaros 12.00 30.00
PMAO Alexander Ovechkin
PMAS Anthony Stewart 8.00 20.00
PMAY Alexei Yashin 10.00 25.00
PMBB Brad Boyes 8.00 20.00
PMBE Ben Eager 8.00 20.00
PMCD Chris Drury 10.00 25.00
PMCK Chris Kunitz 10.00 25.00
PMCP Corey Perry
PMDW Doug Weight 8.00 20.00
PMFP Fernando Pisani
PMHZ Henrik Zetterberg 20.00 40.00
PMJH Jeff Hoggan 8.00 20.00
PMJI Jarome Iginla 40.00 80.00
PMJT Joe Thornton
PMMH Marian Hossa
PMMT Maxime Talbot 12.00 30.00
PMMV Mike Van Ryn 8.00 20.00
PMPM Patrick Marleau
PMPR Paul Ranger 8.00 20.00
PMRN Rick Nash
PMRS Ryan Smyth 15.00 40.00
PMSC Sidney Crosby 100.00 200.00
PMSG Scott Gomez 8.00 20.00
PMSH Scott Hartnell 8.00 20.00
PMSK Saku Koivu
PMTH Jose Theodore 30.00 60.00
PMWG Wayne Gretzky
PMZP Zach Parise 10.00 25.00

2006-07 UD Powerplay Specialists

STATED ODDS 1:24
SAF Alexander Frolov 3.00 8.00
SAH Ales Hemsky 3.00 8.00
SAK Alex Kovalev 3.00 8.00
SAL Jason Allison 3.00 8.00
SAO Alexander Ovechkin 20.00 50.00
SAT Alex Tanguay 4.00 10.00
SBG Bill Guerin 3.00 8.00
SBL Brian Leetch 5.00 12.00
SBM Bryan McCabe 3.00 8.00
SBR Brian Rolston 3.00 8.00
SBS Brendan Shanahan 5.00 12.00
SCP Chris Pronger 4.00 10.00
SDB Donald Brashear 3.00 8.00
SDH Dominik Hasek 8.00 20.00
SDP Dion Phaneuf 8.00 20.00
SDW Doug Weight 3.00 8.00
SEB Ed Belfour 5.00 12.00
SEJ Ed Jovanovski 3.00 8.00
SES Eric Staal 5.00 12.00
SGA Simon Gagne 5.00 12.00
SGM Glen Murray 3.00 8.00
SIK Ilya Kovalchuk 8.00 20.00
SJA Jason Arnott 3.00 8.00
SJG Jean-Sebastien Giguere 4.00 10.00
SJI Jarome Iginla 8.00 20.00
SJJ Jaromir Jagr 8.00 20.00
SJL Jere Lehtinen 3.00 8.00
SJS Joe Sakic SP 15.00 40.00
SJT Joe Thornton 8.00 20.00
SKL Kari Lehtonen 5.00 12.00
SKP Keith Primeau 3.00 8.00
SMB Martin Brodeur 12.00 30.00
SMF Manny Fernandez 4.00 10.00
SMG Marian Gaborik 8.00 20.00
SMH Marian Hossa 4.00 10.00
SMK Miikka Kiprusoff 5.00 12.00
SMM Mike Modano 8.00 20.00
SMN Markus Naslund 5.00 12.00
SMO Brendan Morrison 3.00 8.00
SMP Michael Peca 3.00 8.00
SMS Marc Savard 3.00 8.00
SMT Marty Turco 4.00 10.00
SOK Olaf Kolzig 5.00 12.00
SPB Patrice Bergeron 5.00 12.00
SPD Pavel Datsyuk 4.00 10.00
SPF Peter Forsberg 8.00 20.00
SPK Paul Kariya 5.00 12.00
SPM Patrick Marleau 4.00 10.00
SRB Rob Blake 4.00 10.00
SRE Robert Esche 4.00 10.00
SRI Brad Richards 4.00 10.00
SRM Ryan Miller 5.00 12.00
SSC Sidney Crosby SP 30.00 80.00
SSF Sergei Fedorov 5.00 12.00
SSG Scott Gomez 3.00 8.00
SSN Scott Niedermayer 3.00 8.00
SSP Jason Spezza 5.00 12.00
STR Tuomo Ruutu 3.00 8.00
STS Teemu Selanne 5.00 12.00
SZC Zdeno Chara 3.00 8.00

2006-07 UD Powerplay Specialists Patches

PRINT RUN 5 SER. #'d SETS
NOT PRICED DUE TO SCARCITY

2001-02 UD Premier Collection

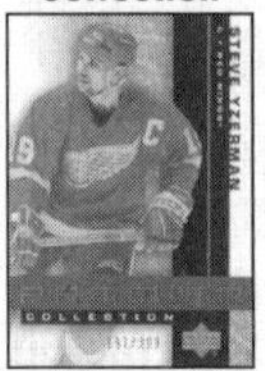

Released in early June, Premier Collection carried a SRP of $100 per pack. Each pack contained a memorabilia card, an autographed card, a serial-numbered rookie card as well as serial-numbered base cards. The base set was made up of 114 cards total, cards 1-87 were serial-numbered to 399, cards 88-108 were serial-numbered to 250 and cards 109-114 were serial-numbered to 199.

1 Paul Kariya 1.00 2.50
2 Dany Heatley 1.25 3.00
3 Joe Thornton 1.50 4.00
4 Ray Bourque 2.00 5.00
5 Bobby Orr 10.00 25.00
6 Sergei Samsonov .75 2.00
7 Tim Connolly .75 2.00
8 Jarome Iginla 1.25 3.00
9 Arturs Irbe .75 2.00
10 Jocelyn Thibault .75 2.00
11 Joe Sakic 2.00 5.00
12 Patrick Roy 5.00 12.00
13 Peter Forsberg 2.00 5.00
14 Chris Drury .75 2.00
15 Milan Hejduk 1.00 2.50
16 Rostislav Klesla .75 2.00
17 Mike Modano 1.50 4.00
18 Ed Belfour 1.00 2.50
19 Gordie Howe 3.00 8.00
20 Brendan Shanahan 1.00 2.50
21 Steve Yzerman 5.00 12.00
22 Brett Hull 1.25 3.00
23 Dominik Hasek 2.00 5.00
24 Sergei Fedorov 1.50 4.00
25 Wayne Gretzky 6.00 15.00
26 Tommy Salo .75 2.00
27 Roberto Luongo 1.25 3.00
28 Felix Potvin 1.00 2.50
29 Marian Gaborik 2.00 5.00
30 Jose Theodore 1.25 3.00
31 Mike Dunham .75 2.00
32 Martin Brodeur 2.50 6.00
33 Alexei Yashin .75 2.00
34 Eric Lindros 1.00 2.50
35 Pavel Bure 1.00 2.50
36 Marian Hossa 1.00 2.50
37 Jeremy Roenick 1.25 3.00
38 John LeClair 1.00 2.50
39 Simon Gagne 1.00 2.50
40 Sean Burke .75 2.00
41 Mario Lemieux 6.00 15.00
42 Evgeni Nabokov .75 2.00
43 Teemu Selanne 1.00 2.50
44 Keith Tkachuk 1.00 2.50
45 Chris Pronger .75 2.00
46 Brad Richards .75 2.00
47 Curtis Joseph 1.00 2.50
48 Mats Sundin 1.00 2.50
49 Markus Naslund 1.00 2.50
50 Jaromir Jagr 1.50 4.00
51 Timo Parssinen RC 3.00 8.00
52 Ben Simon RC 4.00 8.00
53 Frederic Cassivi RC 4.00 8.00
54 Ales Kotalik RC 8.00 20.00
55 Mike Peluso RC 3.00 8.00
56 Steve Moore RC 3.00 8.00
57 Martin Spanhel RC 3.00 8.00
58 Matt Davidson RC 3.00 8.00
59 Mathieu Darche RC 3.00 8.00
60 Duvie Westcott RC 3.00 8.00
61 Blake Bellefeuille RC 3.00 8.00
62 Ty Conklin RC 6.00 15.00
63 Stephen Weiss RC 10.00 25.00
64 Jaroslav Bednar RC 3.00 8.00
65 Pascal Dupuis RC 3.00 8.00
66 Nick Schultz RC 3.00 8.00
67 Travis Roche RC 3.00 8.00
68 Nathan Perrott RC 3.00 8.00
69 Scott Clemmensen RC 3.00 8.00
70 Andreas Salomonsson RC 3.00 8.00
71 Stanislav Gron RC 3.00 8.00
72 Radek Martinek RC 3.00 8.00
73 Mikael Samuelsson RC 6.00 15.00
74 Toni Dahlman RC 3.00 8.00
75 Bruno St. Jacques RC 3.00 8.00
76 Tomas Divisek RC 3.00 8.00
77 Vaclav Pletka RC 3.00 8.00
78 Eric Meloche RC 3.00 8.00
79 Tom Kostopoulos RC 3.00 8.00
80 Mark Rycroft RC 3.00 8.00
81 Martin Cibak RC 3.00 8.00
82 Josef Boumedienne RC 3.00 8.00
83 Karel Pilar RC 3.00 8.00
84 Sebastien Centomo RC 3.00 8.00
85 Justin Kurtz RC 3.00 8.00
86 Ivan Ciernik RC 3.00 8.00
87 Chris Corrinet RC 3.00 8.00
88 Ilja Bryzgalov RC 12.00 30.00
89 Pasi Nurminen RC 4.00 10.00
90 Ivan Huml RC 4.00 10.00
91 Erik Cole RC 15.00 40.00
92 Tyler Arnason RC 4.00 10.00
93 Riku Hahl RC 4.00 10.00
94 Niko Kapanen RC 4.00 10.00
95 Pavel Datsyuk RC 75.00 200.00
96 Sean Avery RC 10.00 25.00
97 Niklas Hagman RC 4.00 10.00
98 Olivier Michaud RC 4.00 10.00
99 Marcel Hossa RC 10.00 25.00
100 Martin Erat RC 8.00 20.00
101 Christian Berglund RC 4.00 10.00
102 Lukas Krajicek RC 4.00 10.00
103 Jiri Dopita RC 4.00 10.00
104 Branko Radivojevic RC 4.00 10.00
105 Shane Endicott RC 4.00 10.00
106 Jeff Jillson RC 4.00 10.00
107 Nikita Alexeev RC 4.00 10.00
108 Brian Sutherby RC 8.00 20.00
109 Ilya Kovalchuk AU RC 350.00 700.00
110 Vaclav Nedorost AU RC 10.00 25.00
111 Kristian Huselius AU RC 20.00 50.00
112 Raffi Torres AU RC 25.00 60.00
113 Dan Blackburn AU RC 12.00 30.00
114 Krys Kolanos AU RC 10.00 25.00

2001-02 UD Premier Collection Dual Jerseys

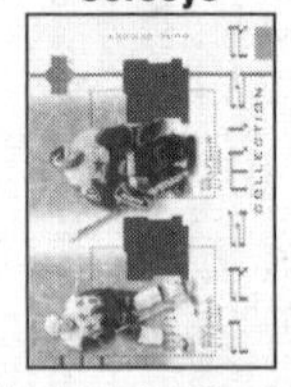

Serial-numbered to just 100 copies each, this 35-card set featured dual-swatches of game-worn jerseys from the pictured players. A black parallel to this set was also created and serial-numbered to 50 copies each. Black parallels could be identified by both numbering and a small black square in the lower right hand side of each card front.

*MULT.COLOR SWATCH: .75X TO 1.5X HI
*BLACK: .5X TO 1.25X BASE HI
DAT Tony Amonte 8.00 20.00
Jocelyn Thibault
DBA Pavel Bure 8.00 20.00
Maxim Afinogenov
DBB R.Bourque/R.Blake 15.00 40.00
DBP Rob Blake 8.00 20.00
Chris Pronger
DCB Roman Cechmanek 8.00 20.00
Brian Boucher
DDM Chris Drury 12.00 30.00
Mike Modano
DDP Adam Deadmarsh 8.00 20.00
Felix Potvin
DFB Sergei Fedorov 12.00 30.00
Pavel Bure
DFD Peter Forsberg 15.00 40.00
Chris Drury
DGH Wayne Gretzky 30.00 80.00
Brett Hull
DGK W.Gretzky/P.Kariya 25.00 60.00
DGL W.Gretzky/M.Lemieux 50.00 125.00
DGM Wayne Gretzky 50.00 125.00
Mark Messier
DHC Dominik Hasek 12.00 30.00
Roman Cechmanek
DHG Gordie Howe 50.00 125.00
Wayne Gretzky
DHJ Milan Hejduk 12.00 30.00
Jaromir Jagr
DJB Jaromir Jagr 12.00 30.00
Peter Bondra
DJP Curtis Joseph 8.00 20.00
Felix Potvin
DKI Paul Kariya 12.00 30.00
Jarome Iginla
DKS Paul Kariya 15.00 40.00
Joe Sakic
DLH Nicklas Lidstrom 12.00 30.00
Dominik Hasek
DLK M.Lemieux/P.Kariya 20.00 50.00
DLR Brian Leetch 8.00 20.00
Mike Richter
DMB Mike Modano 15.00 40.00
Ed Belfour
DRB P.Roy/M.Brodeur 30.00 80.00
DRJ Mike Richter 8.00 20.00
Curtis Joseph
DSN Teemu Selanne 8.00 20.00
Ville Nieminen
DSP Teemu Selanne 8.00 20.00
Zigmund Palffy
DSR Joe Sakic 20.00 50.00
Patrick Roy
DST Sergei Samsonov 12.00 30.00
Joe Thornton
DSY Brendan Shanahan 20.00 50.00
Steve Yzerman
DTB Jocelyn Thibault 8.00 20.00
Sean Burke
DTN Joe Thornton 12.00 30.00
Joe Nieuwendyk
DBTE Martin Brodeur 15.00 40.00
Jose Theodore
DBTO Ray Bourque 15.00 40.00
Joe Thornton

2001-02 UD Premier Collection Jerseys

This 44-card set featured game-worn jersey swatches of the pictured players. Bronze cards carried a bronze logo and were serial-numbered to 300 copies each. Silver cards carried a silver logo and were serial-numbered to 150 copies each. Gold cards carried a gold logo and were serial-numbered to 50 each.

BBS Brendan Shanahan B 5.00 12.00
BBU Pavel Bure B 5.00 12.00
BCD Chris Drury B 5.00 12.00
BEB Ed Belfour B 5.00 12.00
BEL Eric Lindros B 5.00 12.00
BIK Ilya Kovalchuk B 8.00 20.00
BJA Jaromir Jagr B 8.00 20.00
BJI Jarome Iginla B 6.00 15.00
BJJ Jaromir Jagr B 8.00 20.00
BJL John LeClair B 5.00 12.00
BJS Joe Sakic B 8.00 20.00
BJT Jose Theodore B 6.00 15.00
BMH Milan Hejduk B 5.00 12.00
BMR Mike Richter B 5.00 12.00
BMS Mats Sundin B 5.00 12.00
BOK Olaf Kolzig B 5.00 12.00
BPB Peter Bondra B 5.00 12.00
BPF Peter Forsberg B 8.00 20.00
BPK Paul Kariya B 5.00 12.00
BPR Patrick Roy B 15.00 40.00
BRB Ray Bourque B 10.00 25.00
BSF Sergei Fedorov B 6.00 15.00
BSG Simon Gagne B 5.00 12.00
BSK Saku Koivu B 5.00 12.00
BSS Sergei Samsonov B 5.00 12.00
BTA Tony Amonte B 5.00 12.00
BTF Theo Fleury B 5.00 12.00
BTS Teemu Selanne B 5.00 12.00
BWG Wayne Gretzky B 30.00 80.00
BZP Zigmund Palffy B 5.00 12.00
SCJ Curtis Joseph S 10.00 25.00
SDH Dominik Hasek S 12.00 30.00
SJS Joe Sakic S 15.00 40.00
SJT Joe Thornton S 12.50 30.00
SMB Martin Brodeur S 15.00 40.00
SMM Mike Modano S 12.50 30.00
SPK Paul Kariya S 12.00 30.00
GBH Bobby Hull G 15.00 40.00
GGH Gordie Howe G 30.00 80.00
GML Mario Lemieux G 30.00 80.00
GPR Patrick Roy G 30.00 80.00
GRB Ray Bourque G 25.00 60.00
GSY Steve Yzerman G 30.00 80.00
GWG Wayne Gretzky G 50.00 125.00

2001-02 UD Premier Collection Jerseys Black

This 44-card set paralleled the base jersey set but a black square appeared in the bottom right corner of the card front. Bronze/black cards were serial-numbered to 150, silver/black cards were serial-numbered to 75 and gold/black cards were serial-numbered to 5. Gold/black cards were not priced due to scarcity.

*BRONZE/BLACK: .5X TO 1.25X BASIC INSERTS
*SILVER/BLACK: .5X TO 1.25X BASIC INSERTS

2001-02 UD Premier Collection Signatures

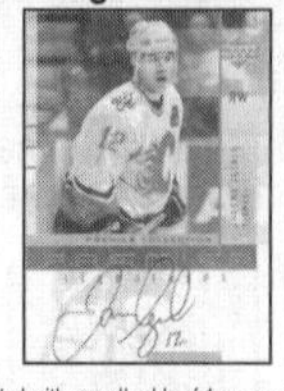

Inserted with overall odds of 1 per pack, this 40 card set featured authentic player autographs under full color action photos. Bronze, silver and gold subsets could be identified by the color of the foil in the Upper Deck logo and a small rectangle at the bottom of each card front. Though not explicitly stated, the silver and gold versions are thought to be more scarce than the bronze.

AI Arturs Irbe B 4.00 10.00
AK Alexei Kovalev B 4.00 10.00
BI Martin Biron B 4.00 10.00
HO Marian Hossa B 6.00 15.00
JH Johan Hedberg B 4.00 10.00
JT Jose Theodore B 10.00 25.00
MC Mike Comrie B 5.00 12.00
MG Marian Gaborik B 10.00 25.00
MH Martin Havlat B 4.00 10.00
MN Markus Naslund B 6.00 15.00
RK Rostislav Klesla B 4.00 10.00
RT Raffi Torres B 5.00 12.00
SA Tommy Salo B 4.00 10.00
TA Tony Amonte B 4.00 10.00
BL Rob Blake S 6.00 15.00
CN Cam Neely S 20.00 50.00
DH Dany Heatley S 10.00 25.00
DW Doug Weight S 8.00 20.00
FP Felix Potvin S 8.00 20.00
HE Milan Hejduk S 8.00 20.00
JI Jarome Iginla S 10.00 25.00
JL John LeClair S 8.00 20.00
MB Mike Bossy S 10.00 25.00
OK Olaf Kolzig S 6.00 15.00
PB Peter Bondra S 8.00 20.00
SG Simon Gagne S 8.00 20.00
ZP Zigmund Palffy S 6.00 15.00
BH Bobby Hull G 20.00 50.00
BO Bobby Orr G 150.00 300.00
BR Dan Blackburn 10.00 25.00
Mike Richter G
CJ Curtis Joseph G 8.00 20.00
GH Gordie Howe G 50.00 125.00
GR Wayne Gretzky G 125.00 250.00
IK Ilya Kovalchuk G 25.00 60.00
JS Joe Thornton 20.00 50.00
Sergei Samsonov G
PR Patrick Roy G 75.00 150.00
RB Ray Bourque G 20.00 50.00
SY Steve Yzerman G 30.00 80.00
TS Teemu Selanne G 10.00 25.00
WG Wayne Gretzky G 100.00 250.00

2001-02 UD Premier Collection Signatures Black

This 38-card set paralleled the base autograph set with the addition of black borders and serial numbering. Bronze cards were serial numbered to 100, silver cards were serial numbered to 25, and gold cards were serial numbered to 5. Gold cards are not priced due to scarcity. Black parallels could be identified by both numbering and a small black rectangle under the autograph on each card.

*BRONZE/BLACK: .6X TO 1.5X BASIC AUTO
*SILVER/BLACK: 1X TO 2.5X BASIC AUTO

2001-02 UD Premier Collection Tribute to 500

Limited to just 50 copies, this single-card set highlighted the career wins of Patrick Roy. Each card carried a swatch of game jersey from both Montreal and Colorado.

1 Patrick Roy Col./Mon. 75.00 200.00

2002-03 UD Premier Collection

Released in April, this 103-card set featured serial-numbered base cards and three different levels of rookie cards. Due to printing errors, several card numbers were duplicated or excluded. Duplicate card numbers are denoted below with a an "A" or "B" suffix, though those letters did not appear on the cards. Cards #1-72 and 88-98 were serial-numbered to 399 sets. Cards #73-77 and 99-103 carried certified player autographs and were serial-numbered to 199. Cards #78-84 carried certified autographs and swatches of jersey patches. Patch/auto cards were serial-numbered to 99 copies each.

*SINGLE COLOR PATCH: .5X TO .75X

CARDS 85,86,87 DO NOT EXIST
1 Paul Kariya 1.25 3.00
2 Ilya Kovalchuk 1.50 4.00
3 Dany Heatley 1.50 4.00
4 Byron Dafoe .75 2.00
5 Joe Thornton 1.50 4.00
6 Jeff Hackett .75 2.00
7 Sergei Samsonov .75 2.00
8 Miroslav Satan .75 2.00
9 Jarome Iginla 1.50 4.00
10 Ron Francis .75 2.00
11 Tyler Arnason .75 2.00
12 Jocelyn Thibault .75 2.00
13 Peter Forsberg 1.50 4.00
14 Joe Sakic 2.00 5.00
15 Patrick Roy 5.00 12.00
16 Milan Hejduk 1.25 3.00
17 Marc Denis .75 2.00
18 Mike Modano 1.50 4.00
19 Bill Guerin .75 2.00
20 Marty Turco .75 2.00
21 Steve Yzerman 5.00 12.00
22 Curtis Joseph 1.25 3.00
23 Brendan Shanahan 1.25 3.00
24 Nicklas Lidstrom 1.25 3.00
25 Mike Comrie .75 2.00
26 Stephen Weiss .75 2.00
27 Roberto Luongo 1.50 4.00
28 Zigmund Palffy .75 2.00
29 Marian Gaborik 1.50 4.00
30 Saku Koivu 1.25 3.00
31 Jose Theodore 1.50 4.00
32 David Legwand .75 2.00
33 Martin Brodeur 2.50 6.00
34 Michael Peca .75 2.00
35 Alexei Kovalev .75 2.00
36 Eric Lindros 1.25 3.00
37 Pavel Bure 1.25 3.00
38 Mike Dunham .75 2.00
39 Marian Hossa 1.25 3.00
40 Jeremy Roenick 1.50 4.00
41 John LeClair 1.25 3.00
42 Tony Amonte .75 2.00
43 Mario Lemieux 6.00 15.00
44A Sebastien Caron .75 2.00
44B Martin Gerber RC 10.00 25.00
45A Evgeni Nabokov .75 2.00
45B Tim Thomas RC 8.00 20.00
46A Kyle McLaren .75 2.00
46B Ryan Miller RC 50.00 100.00
47A Keith Tkachuk 1.25 3.00
47B Jordan Leopold RC 4.00 10.00
48A Vincent Lecavalier .75 2.00
48B Shaone Morrisonn RC 4.00 10.00
49A Nikolai Khabibulin 1.25 3.00
49B Levente Szuper RC 4.00 10.00
50 Mats Sundin 1.25 3.00
51A Ed Belfour 1.25 3.00
51B Jim Fahey RC 4.00 10.00
52A Todd Bertuzzi 1.25 3.00
52B Dmitri Bykov RC 4.00 10.00
53 Markus Naslund 1.25 3.00
54 Jaromir Jagr 1.50 4.00
55 Olaf Kolzig .75 2.00
56A Wayne Gretzky/299 8.00 20.00
56B Mike Cammalleri RC 12.00 30.00
57A Bobby Orr/299 10.00 25.00
57B Stephane Veilleux RC 4.00 10.00
58A Gordie Howe/299 3.00 8.00
58B Rickard Wallin RC 4.00 10.00
59A Ray Bourque/299 2.00 5.00
59B Vernon Fiddler RC 4.00 10.00
60A Alexei Semenov RC 4.00 10.00
60B Darren Haydar RC 4.00 10.00
61 Anton Volchenkov RC 4.00 10.00
62 Patrick Sharp RC 5.00 12.00
63 Dennis Seidenberg RC 4.00 10.00
64 Tomas Malec RC 4.00 10.00
65 Craig Andersson RC 6.00 15.00
66 Cody Rudkowsky RC 4.00 10.00
67A Ari Ahonen RC 4.00 10.00
67B Curtis Sanford RC 6.00 15.00
68 Adam Hall RC 4.00 10.00
69 Carlo Colaiacovo RC 8.00 20.00
70A Dick Tarnstrom RC 4.00 10.00
70B Steve Eminger RC 4.00 10.00
71A Jamie Hodson RC 4.00 10.00
71B Alexei Smirnov AU RC 10.00 25.00
72A Jarret Stoll RC 8.00 20.00
72B P-M Bouchard AU RC 20.00 50.00
73 Ron Hainsey AU RC 10.00 25.00
74 Pascal Leclaire AU RC 15.00 40.00
75 Scottie Upshall AU RC 15.00 40.00
76 Jeff Taffe AU RC 10.00 25.00
77 Mikael Tellqvist AU RC 15.00 40.00
78 S.Chistov PATCH AU RC 50.00 125.00
79 C.Kobasew PATCH AU RC 60.00 150.00
80 R.Nash PATCH AU RC 500.00 1000.00
81 H.Zetterberg PATCH AU RC 350.00 600.00
82 J.Bouwmeester PATCH AU RC 100.00 350.00
83 Jason Spezza PATCH AU RC 750.00 1300.00
84 Alexander Svitov PATCH AU RC 60.00 150.00
88 Jerred Smithson RC 4.00 10.00
89 Jim Vandermeer RC 4.00 10.00
90 Michael Leighton RC 6.00 15.00
91 Ray Emery RC 15.00 40.00
92 Tomas Zizka RC 4.00 10.00
93 Bobby Allen RC 4.00 10.00
94 Kris Vernarsky RC 4.00 10.00
95 Cristobal Huet RC 20.00 50.00
96 Fernando Pisani RC 8.00 20.00
97 Jonathan Hedstrom RC 4.00 10.00
98 Konstantin Koltsov RC 4.00 10.00
99 Ales Hemsky AU RC 75.00 150.00
100 Steve Ott AU RC 10.00 25.00
101 Alexander Frolov AU RC 50.00 125.00
102 Brooks Orpik AU RC 12.00 30.00
103 Jared Aulin AU RC 10.00 25.00

2002-03 UD Premier Collection Gold

This 58-card skip-numbered set paralleled the rookie checklist of the base set but carried gold highlights and different serial-numbering. Cards #44-70, 71A, 72A and 88-98 were serial-numbered to 199. Cards #71B, 72B, 73-77 and 99-103 were serial-numbered to 25. Cards 78-84 were serial-numbered to just 15 copies each and are not priced due to scarcity.
*GOLD: .3X TO .75X BASIC CARDS

2002-03 UD Premier Collection Jerseys Bronze

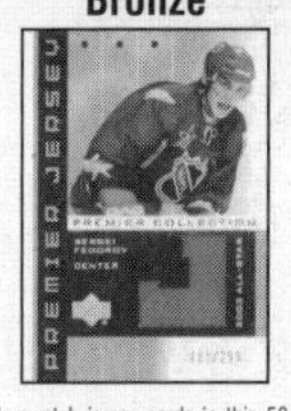

Single swatch jersey cards in this 58-card set were serial-numbered to 299. Dual jersey cards were serial-numbered to 99.
*MULT.COLOR SWATCH: .75X TO 1.5X
AA Ari Ahonen 2.00 5.00
AK Alexei Kovalev 4.00 10.00
AS Alexander Svitov 2.00 5.00
AV Anton Volchenkov 2.00 5.00
AX Alexei Semenov 2.00 5.00
BO Brooks Orpik 2.00 5.00
BS Brendan Shanahan 4.00 10.00
CD Chris Drury 4.00 10.00
CJ Curtis Joseph 4.00 10.00
EL Eric Lindros 4.00 10.00
GM Glen Murray 4.00 10.00
IK Ilya Kovalchuk 6.00 15.00
JG Jaromir Jagr 8.00 20.00
JI Jarome Iginla 6.00 15.00
JJ Jaromir Jagr 8.00 20.00
JK Jeremy Roenick 6.00 15.00
JR Jeremy Roenick 6.00 15.00
JS Joe Sakic 8.00 20.00
JT Jose Theodore 6.00 15.00
MB Martin Brodeur 12.50 30.00
MC Mike Comrie 2.00 5.00
MH Milan Hejduk 4.00 10.00
ML Mario Lemieux 15.00 40.00
MM Mike Modano 6.00 15.00
MO Mike Modano 6.00 15.00
MS Mats Sundin 4.00 10.00
OK Olaf Kolzig 4.00 10.00
PB Pavel Bure 4.00 10.00
PF Peter Forsberg 8.00 20.00
PG Peter Forsberg 8.00 20.00
PK Paul Kariya 4.00 10.00
PL Pascal Leclaire 8.00 20.00
PR Patrick Roy 15.00 40.00
RB Ray Bourque 6.00 15.00
SF Sergei Fedorov 6.00 15.00
SG Simon Gagne 4.00 10.00
SK Saku Koivu 4.00 10.00
SO Steve Ott 2.00 5.00
SS Sergei Samsonov 2.00 5.00
SV Sergei Fedorov 6.00 15.00
SY Steve Yzerman 12.50 30.00
TF Theo Fleury 4.00 10.00
TH Joe Thornton 8.00 20.00
WG Wayne Gretzky 25.00 60.00
BL Pavel Bure / Eric Lindros 10.00 25.00
BR Rob Blake / Patrick Roy 12.50 30.00
FH Peter Forsberg / Milan Hejduk 12.00 30.00
FJ Sergei Fedorov / Curtis Joseph 10.00 25.00
GL W.Gretzky/M.Lemieux 50.00 125.00
JK Jaromir Jagr / Olaf Kolzig 10.00 25.00
JR J.Spezza/R.Nash 25.00 60.00
KG Paul Kariya / Jean-Sebastien Giguere 10.00 25.00
PA Pascal Leclaire / Ari Ahonen 8.00 20.00
RG Jeremy Roenick / Simon Gagne 10.00 25.00
SR Joe Sakic / Steven Reinprecht 12.50 30.00
ST Sergei Samsonov / Joe Thornton 10.00 25.00
SY Brendan Shanahan / Steve Yzerman 15.00 40.00
TK Jose Theodore / Saku Koivu 10.00 25.00

2002-03 UD Premier Collection Jerseys Gold

*SNGL.JSY: .6X TO 1.5X BRONZE
SNGL.JSY PRINT RUN 50 SER.#'d SETS
*DUAL JSY: .6X TO 1.5X BRONZE
DUAL JSY PRINT RUN 25 SER.#'d SETS

2002-03 UD Premier Collection Jerseys Silver

*SNGL.JSY: .5X TO 1.25X BRONZE
SNGL.JSY PRINT RUN 99 SER.#'d SETS
*DUAL JSY: .5X TO 1.25X BRONZE
DUAL JSY PRINT RUN 50 SER.#'d SETS

2002-03 UD Premier Collection NHL Patches

This 10-card set featured the NHL patch from game-worn jerseys on the card fronts. Each card was serial-numberd 1 of 1.
NOT PRICED DUE TO SCARCITY
JJ1 Jaromir Jagr
JS1 Joe Sakic
MB1 Martin Brodeur
ML1 Mario Lemieux
MM1 Mike Modano
MS1 Mats Sundin
PK1 Paul Kariya
PR1 Patrick Roy
SY1 Steve Yzerman
WG1 Wayne Gretzky

2002-03 UD Premier Collection Patches

This 32-card memorabilia set was limited to 25 serial-numbered sets.
PBO Ray Bourque 75.00 200.00
PBS Brendan Shanahan 50.00 120.00
PCD Chris Drury 50.00 120.00
PCJ Curtis Joseph 50.00 120.00
PEL Eric Lindros 50.00 120.00
PGR Wayne Gretzky 200.00 350.00
PIK Ilya Kovalchuk 60.00 150.00
PJI Jarome Iginla 60.00 150.00
PJJ Jaromir Jagr 75.00 200.00
PJR Jeremy Roenick 100.00 250.00
PJS Joe Sakic 75.00 200.00
PJT Jose Theodore 60.00 150.00
PMB Martin Brodeur 125.00 300.00
PMC Mike Comrie 50.00 120.00
PMH Milan Hejduk 50.00 120.00
PML Mario Lemieux 150.00 400.00
PMM Mike Modano 60.00 150.00
PMS Mats Sundin 50.00 120.00
POK Olaf Kolzig 50.00 120.00
PPB Pavel Bure 50.00 120.00
PPF Peter Forsberg 75.00 200.00
PPK Paul Kariya 50.00 120.00
PPR Patrick Roy 150.00 400.00
PRB Ray Bourque 75.00 200.00
PSF Sergei Fedorov 60.00 150.00
PSG Simon Gagne 50.00 120.00
PSK Saku Koivu 50.00 120.00
PSS Sergei Samsonov 50.00 120.00
PSY Steve Yzerman 125.00 300.00
PTH Joe Thornton 75.00 200.00
PTS Teemu Selanne 40.00 100.00
PWG Wayne Gretzky 200.00 350.00

2002-03 UD Premier Collection Signatures Bronze

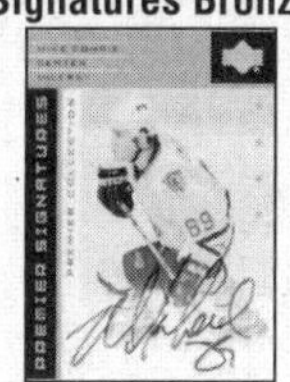

This 48-card autograph set was inserted at a rate of 1:2 packs.
SAH Adam Hall SP 5.00 12.00
SAS Alexei Smirnov 5.00 12.00
SBO Bobby Orr 75.00 150.00
SBR Pavel Brendl 5.00 12.00
SBW Jay Bouwmeester 10.00 25.00
SCK Chuck Kobasew 5.00 12.00
SDH Dany Heatley 8.00 20.00
SEB Ed Belfour 12.50 30.00
SEC Erik Cole 5.00 12.00
SGH Gordie Howe 50.00 125.00
SHZ Henrik Zetterberg 10.00 25.00
SIK Ilya Kovalchuk 12.50 30.00
SJB Jay Bouwmeester 10.00 25.00
SJI Jarome Iginla 8.00 20.00
SJL John LeClair 6.00 15.00
SJT Joe Thornton 15.00 40.00
SJW Justin Williams 5.00 12.00
SMA Maxim Afinogenov 5.00 12.00
SMB Martin Brodeur SP 30.00 80.00
SMC Mike Comrie 5.00 12.00
SMF Manny Fernandez 5.00 12.00
SMH Martin Havlat 5.00 12.00
SMN Markus Naslund 6.00 15.00
SMT Mikael Tellqvist SP 10.00 25.00
SNA Rick Nash 20.00 50.00
SNK Nikolai Khabibulin 6.00 15.00
SPB Pavel Bure SP 6.00 15.00
SPM P-M Bouchard 8.00 20.00
SPR Patrick Roy 40.00 100.00
SRA Ray Bourque 20.00 50.00
SRB Ray Bourque 20.00 50.00
SRH Ron Hainsey SP 5.00 12.00
SRN Rick Nash 12.50 30.00
SSC Stanislav Chistov 5.00 12.00
SSG Simon Gagne 6.00 15.00
SSH Scott Hartnell 5.00 12.00
SSP Jason Spezza 12.50 30.00
SSS Sergei Samsonov 5.00 12.00
SSU Scottie Upshall SP 10.00 25.00
SSV Alexander Svitov 5.00 12.00
SSY Steve Yzerman 25.00 60.00
STA Jeff Taffe SP 5.00 12.00
SWG Wayne Gretzky SP 100.00 200.00
AS-JT Joe Thornton 12.50 30.00
ASDH Dany Heatley 10.00 25.00
ASJI Jarome Iginla 8.00 20.00
ASMB Martin Brodeur 30.00 80.00
ASPR Patrick Roy SP 40.00 100.00

2002-03 UD Premier Collection Signatures Gold

*GOLD: .6X TO 1.5X BRONZE
GOLD PRINT RUN 50 SER.#'d SETS

2002-03 UD Premier Collection Signatures Silver

*SILVER: .5X TO 1.25X BRONZE
SILVER PRINT RUN 125 SER.#'d SETS

2003-04 UD Premier Collection

This 121-card set featured 59 veteran base cards; 48 short-printed rookie cards (#60-104 and #118-121) serial-numbered out of 399 each and 13 rookie autograph patch cards (#105-117). Cards 105-111 were serial-numbered to 199 and cards 112-117 were serial-numbered to 99 copies each.
COMPLETE SET (121)
COMP.SET w/o SP's (59) 50.00 100.00
*SINGLE COLOR PATCH: .4X TO .75X HI
1 J-S Giguere 1.00 2.50
2 Sergei Fedorov 1.50 4.00
3 Dany Heatley 1.50 4.00
4 Ilya Kovalchuk 1.50 4.00
5 Sergei Samsonov 1.00 2.50
6 Joe Thornton 1.50 4.00
7 Andrew Raycroft 1.00 2.50
8 Chris Drury 1.00 2.50
9 Jarome Iginla 1.50 4.00
10 Justin Williams .60 1.50
11 Jocelyn Thibault 1.00 2.50
12 Bryan Berard .60 1.50
13 David Aebischer 1.00 2.50
14 Joe Sakic 2.50 6.00
15 Paul Kariya 1.25 3.00
16 Peter Forsberg 3.00 8.00
17 Rick Nash 1.50 4.00
18 Marty Turco 1.00 2.50
19 Mike Modano 2.00 5.00
20 Brett Hull 1.50 4.00
21 Pavel Datsyuk 1.25 3.00
22 Steve Yzerman 4.00 10.00
23 Raffi Torres .60 1.50
24 Ales Hemsky .60 1.50
25 Roberto Luongo 1.50 4.00
26 Zigmund Palffy 1.00 2.50
27 Marian Gaborik 2.50 6.00
28 Jose Theodore 1.50 4.00
29 Saku Koivu 1.25 3.00
30 Tomas Vokoun 1.00 2.50
31 Scott Stevens 1.00 2.50
32 Martin Brodeur 3.00 8.00
33 Alexei Yashin .60 1.50
34 Rick DiPietro 1.00 2.50
35 Jaromir Jagr 2.00 5.00
36 Mark Messier 1.25 3.00
37 Eric Lindros 1.25 3.00
38 Jason Spezza 1.25 3.00
39 Marian Hossa 1.25 3.00
40 Patrick Lalime 1.00 2.50
41 Jeremy Roenick 1.50 4.00
42 Tony Amonte 1.00 2.50
43 Mike Comrie 1.00 2.50
44 Brian Boucher 1.00 2.50
45 Mario Lemieux 5.00 12.00
46 Evgeni Nabokov 1.00 2.50
47 Chris Osgood 1.00 2.50
48 Doug Weight 1.00 2.50
49 Keith Tkachuk 1.25 3.00
50 Nikolai Khabibulin 1.25 3.00
51 Mats Sundin 1.25 3.00
52 Owen Nolan 1.00 2.50
53 Ed Belfour 1.25 3.00
54 Ron Francis 1.00 2.50
55 Ed Jovanovski 1.00 2.50
56 Markus Naslund 1.25 3.00
57 Todd Bertuzzi 1.25 3.00
58 Brendan Morrison 1.00 2.50
59 Olaf Kolzig 1.00 2.50
60 Niklas Kronwall RC 10.00 25.00
61 Derek Roy RC 12.00 25.00
62 Tim Jackman RC 4.00 10.00
63 Timofei Shishkanov RC 4.00 10.00
64 Tomas Plekanec RC 4.00 10.00
65 Aleksander Suglobov RC 5.00 12.00
66 Kyle Wellwood RC 12.00 25.00
67 Mike Smith RC 8.00 20.00
68 Anton Babchuk RC 4.00 10.00
69 Ryan Barnes RC 4.00 10.00
70 Jason Pominville RC 12.00 30.00
71 Pavel Vorobiev RC 5.00 12.00
72 Dustin Brown RC 5.00 12.00
73 Chris Higgins RC 15.00 40.00
74 Dan Hamhuis RC 5.00 12.00
75 Marek Zidlicky RC 5.00 12.00
76 Sean Bergenheim RC 4.00 10.00
77 Antoine Vermette RC 6.00 15.00
78 Milan Michalek RC 10.00 25.00
79 Brad Boyes RC 10.00 25.00
80 Alexander Semin RC 30.00 60.00
81 Carl Corazzini RC 4.00 10.00
82 Sergei Zinovjev RC 4.00 10.00
83 Julien Vauclair RC 4.00 10.00
84 John Pohl RC 4.00 10.00
85 Benoit Dusablon RC 4.00 10.00
86 Tony Salmelainen RC 4.00 10.00
87 Bryce Lampman RC 4.00 10.00
88 Trevor Daley RC 4.00 10.00
89 Dan Ellis RC 5.00 12.00
90 Zbynek Michalek RC 4.00 10.00
91 Goran Bezina RC 4.00 10.00
92 Erik Westrum RC 5.00 12.00
93 Ryan Kesler RC 5.00 12.00
94 Owen Fussey RC 4.00 10.00
95 Josh Olson RC 4.00 10.00
96 Dan Fritsche RC 4.00 10.00
97 Michal Barinka RC 4.00 10.00
98 Kari Lehtonen RC 30.00 60.00
99 Mike Stutzel RC 4.00 10.00
100 Matt Hussey RC 4.00 10.00
101 Roman Tvrdon RC 4.00 10.00
102 Matthew Yeats RC 4.00 10.00
103 Brett Lysak 4.00 10.00
104 Thomas Pock RC 4.00 10.00
105 F.Sjostrom PATCH AU RC 40.00 100.00
106 P.Sejna PATCH AU RC 40.00 100.00
107 M.Stajan PATCH AU RC 75.00 200.00
108 N.Zherdev PATCH AU RC 100.00 250.00
109 P.Bergeron PATCH AU RC 150.00 300.00
110 J.Pitkanen PATCH AU RC 50.00 125.00
111 J.Lupul PATCH AU RC 75.00 175.00
112 J.Tootoo PATCH AU RC 150.00 350.00
113 N.Horton PATCH AU RC 250.00 400.00
114 E.Staal PATCH AU RC 400.00 600.00
115 J.Hudler PATCH AU RC 150.00 350.00
116 T.Ruutu PATCH AU RC 150.00 350.00
117 M.Fleury PATCH AU RC 550.00 1000.00
118 Fedor Tyutin RC 4.00 10.00
119 Denis Grebeshkov RC 4.00 10.00
120 Cory Larose RC 4.00 10.00
121 Andy Chiodo RC 4.00 10.00

2003-04 UD Premier Collection Legends

This 6-card set featured oversized swatches of jersey from past greats. Each card was serial-numbered out of 25.
PL-GL Guy Lafleur 20.00 50.00
PL-MB Mike Bossy 15.00 40.00
PL-MH Gordie Howe 40.00 100.00
PL-PR Patrick Roy 50.00 125.00
PL-SB Scotty Bowman 25.00 60.00
PL-WG Wayne Gretzky 150.00 250.00

2003-04 UD Premier Collection Legends Patches

This set paralleled the basic insert set with authentic patches. This set was serial-numbered out of 10.
NOT PRICED DUE TO SCARCITY

2003-04 UD Premier Collection Matchups

This 6-card set featured dual jersey swatches of two current players. Each card was serial-numbered out of 25.
PM-BT Ed Belfour / Jose Theodore 30.00 80.00
PM-GB Marian Gaborik / Todd Bertuzzi 20.00 50.00
PM-HM Ales Hemsky / Mike Modano 20.00 50.00
PM-HR Marian Hossa / Jeremy Roenick 20.00 50.00
PM-RH Patrick Roy / Dominik Hasek 25.00 60.00
PM-TB Joe Thornton / Martin Brodeur 25.00 60.00

2003-04 UD Premier Collection Matchups Patches

This set paralleled the basic insert set with authentic patches. This set was serial-numbered out of 3.
NOT PRICED DUE TO SCARCITY

2003-04 UD Premier Collection NHL Shields

This 35-card set of 1/1's featured the NHL shield patch from the given player's jersey along with a certified autograph.
NOT PRICED DUE TO SCARCITY
SH-AC Todd Bertuzzi
SH-AH Ales Hemsky
SH-CJ Curtis Joseph
SH-DA David Aebischer
SH-EL Eric Lindros
SH-ES Eric Staal
SH-GL Martin Brodeur
SH-G1 Wayne Gretzky
SH-IK Ilya Kovalchuk
SH-JH Jiri Hudler
SH-JI Jarome Iginla
SH-JL Joffrey Lupul
SH-JR Jeremy Roenick
SH-JS Jason Spezza
SH-JT Joe Thornton
SH-JR2 Jeremy Roenick
SH-JSG J-S Giguere
SH-MB Martin Brodeur
SH-MG Marian Gaborik
SH-MH Marian Hossa
SH-MN Markus Naslund
SH-MT Marty Turco
SH-MAF Marc-Andre Fleury
SH-NH Nathan Horton
SH-ON Owen Nolan
SH-PB Patrice Bergeron
SH-PR Patrick Roy
SH-RL Roberto Luongo
SH-RN Rick Nash
SH-ROY Patrick Roy
SH-SK Saku Koivu
SH-TB Todd Bertuzzi
SH-TH Jose Theodore
SH-TR Tuomo Ruutu
SH-WG Wayne Gretzky

2003-04 UD Premier Collection Signatures

This 41-card set featured player autographs in silver paint pen on black puck-like backgrounds below a full-color player photo. Cards were inserted one per pack.
PS-AC Anson Carter 6.00 15.00
PS-AH Ales Hemsky 6.00 15.00
PS-BO Pavel Bure SP 10.00 25.00
PS-BY Mike Bossy 10.00 25.00
PS-CJ Curtis Joseph 8.00 20.00
PS-DA David Aebischer 6.00 15.00
PS-DC Don Cherry 12.00 30.00
PS-EL Eric Lindros 8.00 20.00
PS-ES Eric Staal 12.00 30.00
PS-GL Guy Lafleur SP 25.00 60.00
PS-G1 Wayne Gretzky 75.00 150.00
PS-HZ Henrik Zetterberg 10.00 25.00
PS-IK Ilya Kovalchuk 12.50 30.00
PS-JH Jiri Hudler 6.00 15.00
PS-JI Jarome Iginla 10.00 25.00
PS-JR Jeremy Roenick 8.00 20.00
PS-JS Jason Spezza 10.00 25.00
PS-JT Joe Thornton 15.00 40.00
PS-JSG J-S Giguere 6.00 15.00
PS-JTH Jose Theodore 10.00 25.00
PS-MB Martin Brodeur 50.00 125.00
PS-MG Marian Gaborik 10.00 25.00
PS-MH Gordie Howe 30.00 80.00
PS-MT Marty Turco 6.00 15.00
PS-MAF Marc-Andre Fleury 15.00 40.00
PS-MAH Marian Hossa 6.00 15.00
PS-MCH Marcel Hossa 6.00 15.00
PS-MNH Markus Naslund 6.00 15.00
PS-NH Nathan Horton 6.00 15.00
PS-ON Owen Nolan 6.00 15.00
PS-PB Patrice Bergeron SP 15.00 40.00
PS-PR Patrick Roy 60.00 150.00
PS-RL Roberto Luongo 8.00 20.00
PS-RN Rick Nash 12.00 30.00
PS-ROY Patrick Roy SP 100.00 250.00
PS-SK Saku Koivu 10.00 25.00
PS-TB Todd Bertuzzi 6.00 15.00
PS-TR Tuomo Ruutu 8.00 20.00
PS-TOO Jordin Tootoo 10.00 25.00
PS-WG Wayne Gretzky 60.00 150.00
PS-ZP Zigmund Palffy 6.00 15.00

2003-04 UD Premier Collection Signatures Gold

This 38-card set paralleled the basic insert set but utilized gold paint pens. Known print runs are listed below.
NOT PRICED DUE TO SCARCITY
PS-AC Anson Carter/2
PS-AH Ales Hemsky/1
PS-BO Pavel Bure/2
PS-BY Mike Bossy/10
PS-CJ Curtis Joseph/9
PS-DA David Aebischer/10
PS-DC Don Cherry/10
PS-EL Eric Lindros/10
PS-ES Eric Staal/1
PS-GL Guy Lafleur/10
PS-G1 Wayne Gretzky EDM/10
PS-HZ Henrik Zetterberg/10
PS-IK Ilya Kovalchuk/10
PS-JH Jiri Hudler/8
PS-JI Jarome Iginla/6
PS-JR Jeremy Roenick/4
PS-JS Jason Spezza/10
PS-JT Joe Thornton/10
PS-JSG J-S Giguere/10
PS-JTH Jose Theodore/1
PS-MB Martin Brodeur/10
PS-MG Marian Gaborik/3
PS-MH Gordie Howe/7
PS-MT Marty Turco/9
PS-MAF Marc-Andre Fleury/10
PS-MAH Marian Hossa/4
PS-NH Nathan Horton/10
PS-ON Owen Nolan/8
PS-PB Patrice Bergeron/10
PS-PR Patrick Roy/10
PS-RL Roberto Luongo/10
PS-RN Rick Nash/10
PS-ROY Patrick Roy/10
PS-SK Saku Koivu/3
PS-TB Todd Bertuzzi/10
PS-TR Tuomo Ruutu/5
PS-WG Wayne Gretzky LA/8
PS-ZP Zigmund Palffy/8

2003-04 UD Premier Collection Skills

This 6-card set featured dual jersey swatches from two current players. Each card was serial-numbered out of 50.
SK-BF Martin Brodeur / Marc-Andre Fleury 25.00 60.00
SK-BT Todd Bertuzzi / Keith Tkachuk 12.50 30.00
SK-FT Peter Forsberg / Joe Thornton 12.50 30.00
SK-LT M.Lemieux/J.Thornton 25.00 60.00
SK-RR Jeremy Roenick / Tuomo Ruttu 15.00 40.00
SK-SY J.Sakic/S.Yzerman 25.00 60.00

2003-04 UD Premier Collection Skills Patches

This set paralleled the basic insert set with authentic patches. This set was serial-numbered out of 10.
NOT PRICED DUE TO SCARCITY

2003-04 UD Premier Collection Stars

This 35-card set featured jersey swatches inset in the die-cut letter "e" of the word Premier across the card front. Each card was serial-numbered out of 250.
ST-AM Alexander Mogilny 4.00 10.00
ST-BH Brett Hull 5.00 12.00
ST-DH Dan Hamhuis 4.00 10.00
ST-DW Doug Weight 4.00 10.00
ST-ES Eric Staal 10.00 25.00
ST-GM Glenn Murray 4.00 10.00
ST-IK Ilya Kovalchuk 5.00 12.00
ST-JH Jiri Hudler 4.00 10.00
ST-JI Jarome Iginla 5.00 12.00
ST-JL Joffrey Lupul 4.00 10.00
ST-JS Joe Sakic 6.00 15.00
ST-JT Jordin Tootoo 5.00 12.00
ST-JSG J-S Giguere 4.00 10.00
ST-LR Luc Robitaille 4.00 10.00
ST-MD Marc Denis 4.00 10.00
ST-MF Manny Fernandez 4.00 10.00
ST-MH Milan Hejduk 4.00 10.00
ST-MN Markus Naslund 4.00 10.00
ST-MR Mark Recchi 4.00 10.00
ST-MR Mike Ribeiro 4.00 10.00
ST-MS Martin Straka 4.00 10.00
ST-MAF Marc-Andre Fleury 10.00 25.00
ST-NH Nathan Horton 4.00 10.00
ST-NZ Nikolai Zherdev 4.00 10.00
ST-PB Patrice Bergeron 5.00 12.00
ST-PD Pavol Demitra 4.00 10.00
ST-PK Paul Kariya 4.00 10.00
ST-RC Roman Cechmanek 4.00 10.00
ST-RL Roberto Luongo 5.00 12.00
ST-SF Sergei Fedorov 5.00 12.00
ST-SS Sergei Samsonov 4.00 10.00
ST-SY Steve Yzerman 8.00 20.00
ST-TB Todd Bertuzzi 4.00 10.00
ST-TR Tuomo Ruutu 5.00 12.00
ST-VL Vincent Lecavalier 4.00 10.00

2003-04 UD Premier Collection Stars Patches

This set paralleled the basic insert set with authentic patches. This set was serial-numbered out of 100.
*PATCHES: 1.25X TO 3X JSY HI

2003-04 UD Premier Collection Super Stars

This 6-card set featured jersey swatches of current super stars serial-numbered to 100.
SS-JS Jason Spezza 12.50 30.00
SS-JT Joe Thornton 12.50 30.00
SS-MB Martin Brodeur 25.00 60.00
SS-MG Marian Gaborik 12.50 30.00
SS-ML Mario Lemieux 20.00 50.00
SS-PF Peter Forsberg 12.50 30.00

2003-04 UD Premier Collection Super Stars Patches

This set paralleled the basic insert set with authentic patches. This set was serial-numbered out of 25.

SS-JS Jason Spezza 40.00 100.00
SS-JT Joe Thornton 60.00 150.00
SS-MB Martin Brodeur 75.00 200.00
SS-MG Marian Gaborik 60.00 150.00
SS-ML Mario Lemieux 75.00 200.00
SS-PF Peter Forsberg 60.00 150.00

2003-04 UD Premier Collection Teammates

Serial-numbered out of 100, this 30-card set featured prominent players on the 30 NHL franchises and swatches of their jerseys.

PT-AM J-S Giguere 8.00 20.00
Sergei Fedorov
PT-BB1 Joe Thornton 10.00 25.00
Sergei Samsonov
PT-BB2 Joe Thornton 10.00 25.00
Patrice Bergeron
PT-CB Jocelyn Thibault 8.00 20.00
Tuomo Ruutu
PT-CH Ron Francis 15.00 40.00
Eric Staal
PT-CA1 Peter Forsberg 12.50 30.00
Joe Sakic
PT-CA2 Teemu Selanne 8.00 20.00
Paul Kariya
PT-CB1 R.Nash/M.Denis 8.00 20.00
PT-CB2 R.Nash/N.Zherdev 8.00 20.00
PT-DR1 Steve Yzerman 15.00 40.00
Dominik Hasek
PT-DR2 Steve Yzerman 15.00 40.00
Brett Hull
PT-DS1 M.Modano/M.Turco 10.00 25.00
PT-DS2 Bill Guerin 8.00 20.00
Mike Modano
PT-EO1 Wayne Gretzky 60.00 150.00
Mark Messier
PT-EO2 Raffi Torres 8.00 20.00
Ales Hemsky
PT-FP Roberto Luongo 10.00 25.00
Olli Jokinen
PT-LK Zigmund Palffy 8.00 20.00
Roman Cechmanek
PT-MC Jose Theodore 10.00 25.00
Saku Koivu
PT-MW Marian Gaborik 8.00 20.00
Manny Fernandez
PT-ND M.Brodeur/S.Stevens 12.50 30.00
PT-NR Eric Lindros 10.00 25.00
Mark Messier
PT-OS Jason Spezza 10.00 25.00
Marian Hossa
PT-PP M.Lemieux/M.Fleury 25.00 60.00
PT-PF1 Jeremy Roenick 8.00 20.00
Tony Amonte
PT-PF2 Jeremy Roenick 8.00 20.00
Joni Pitkanen
PT-SB Keith Tkachuk 8.00 20.00
Doug Weight
PT-TL Vincent Lecavalier 10.00 25.00
Nikolai Khabibulin
PT-TM1 M.Sundin/O.Nolan 8.00 20.00
PT-TM2 Ed Belfour 8.00 20.00
Mats Sundin
PT-VC Todd Bertuzzi 10.00 25.00
Markus Naslund

2003-04 UD Premier Collection Teammates Patches

This set paralleled the basic insert set with authentic patches. This set was serial-numbered out of 25.
*PATCHES: 1.5X TO 4X JSY HI
PRINT RUN 25 SERIAL #'d SETS

2000-01 UD Pros and Prospects

Upper Deck Pros and Prospects were released as a 132-card set with 42 short-printed rookie cards. The set design featured a white bordered card with copper-foil lettering, highlights, and logo. The card backs are white and blue with a small photo of the player on the top right corner. SP's are numbered to 1000 sets.

COMPLETE SET (132) 125.00 250.00
COMP.SET w/o SP's 15.00 30.00
1 Paul Kariya .30 .75
2 Teemu Selanne .30 .75
3 Guy Hebert .25 .60
4 Donald Audette .10 .25
5 Adam Burt .10 .25
6 Patrik Stefan .10 .25
7 Joe Thornton .50 1.25
8 Jason Allison .10 .25
9 Sergei Samsonov .25 .60
10 Dominik Hasek .60 1.50
11 Doug Gilmour .25 .60
12 Maxim Afinogenov .10 .25
13 Oleg Saprykin .10 .25
14 Valeri Bure .10 .25
15 Mike Vernon .25 .60
16 Ron Francis .25 .60
17 Jeff O'Neill .10 .25
18 Arturs Irbe .25 .60
19 Steve Sullivan .25 .60
20 Alexei Zhamnov .10 .25
21 Tony Amonte .25 .60
22 Ray Bourque .60 1.50
23 Patrick Roy 1.50 4.00
24 Peter Forsberg .75 2.00
25 Marc Denis .25 .60
26 Tyler Wright .10 .25
27 Mike Modano .50 1.25
28 Brett Hull .40 1.00
29 Ed Belfour .30 .75
30 Brendan Shanahan .30 .75
31 Sergei Fedorov .50 1.25
32 Steve Yzerman 1.50 4.00
33 Ryan Smyth .10 .25
34 Tommy Salo .25 .60
35 Doug Weight .25 .60
36 Pavel Bure .30 .75
37 Ray Whitney .10 .25
38 Viktor Kozlov .10 .25
39 Luc Robitaille .25 .60
40 Rob Blake .25 .60
41 Zigmund Palffy .25 .60
42 Manny Fernandez .25 .60
43 Scott Pellerin .10 .25
44 Jose Theodore .40 1.00
45 Brian Savage .10 .25
46 Martin Rucinsky .10 .25
47 David Legwand .25 .60
48 Mike Dunham .25 .60
49 Cliff Ronning .10 .25
50 Scott Gomez .10 .25
51 Scott Stevens .25 .60
52 Martin Brodeur .75 2.00
53 Tim Connolly .10 .25
54 Brad Isbister .25 .60
55 Roman Hamrlik .10 .25
56 Theo Fleury .10 .25
57 Mike Richter .30 .75
58 Mark Messier .30 .75
59 Marian Hossa .30 .75
60 Alexei Yashin .10 .25
61 Radek Bonk .10 .25
62 John LeClair .30 .75
63 Mark Recchi .25 .60
64 Simon Gagne .30 .75
65 Jeremy Roenick .40 1.00
66 Shane Doan .10 .25
67 Keith Tkachuk .30 .75
68 Jaromir Jagr .50 1.25
69 Mario Lemieux 2.50 6.00
70 Alexei Kovalev .25 .60
71 Owen Nolan .25 .60
72 Jeff Friesen .10 .25
73 Patrick Marleau .25 .60
74 Chris Pronger .25 .60
75 Roman Turek .25 .60
76 Pierre Turgeon .25 .60
77 Kevin Weekes .10 .25
78 Fredrik Modin .10 .25
79 Vincent Lecavalier .30 .75
80 Curtis Joseph .30 .75
81 Mats Sundin .30 .75
82 Gary Roberts .10 .25
83 Markus Naslund .30 .75
84 Daniel Sedin .10 .25
85 Henrik Sedin .10 .25
86 Adam Oates .25 .60
87 Peter Bondra .30 .75
88 Olaf Kolzig .25 .60
89 Mark Messier .30 .75
90 Steve Yzerman 1.50 4.00
91 Jonas Ronnqvist RC 2.00 5.00
92 Andy McDonald RC 2.00 5.00
93 Eric Nickulas RC 2.00 5.00
94 Andrew Raycroft RC 4.00 10.00
95 Jarno Kultanen RC 2.00 5.00
96 Jeff Cowan RC 2.00 5.00
97 Josef Vasicek RC 2.00 5.00
98 Reto Von Arx RC 2.00 5.00
99 David Aebischer RC 5.00 12.00
100 Serge Aubin RC 2.00 5.00
101 Rostislav Klesla RC 3.00 8.00
102 Marty Turco RC 8.00 20.00
103 Tyler Bouck RC 2.00 5.00
104 Brian Swanson RC 2.00 5.00
105 Michel Riesen RC 2.00 5.00
106 Eric Belanger RC 2.00 5.00
107 Steven Reinprecht RC 2.00 5.00
108 Marian Gaborik RC 12.50 30.00
109 Scott Hartnell RC 2.50 6.00
110 Greg Classen RC 2.00 5.00
111 Willie Mitchell RC 2.00 5.00
112 Colin White RC 2.00 5.00
113 Petr Mika RC 2.00 5.00
114 Rick DiPietro RC 5.00 12.00
115 Jason Labarbera RC 3.00 8.00
116 Martin Havlat RC 6.00 15.00
117 Jani Hurme RC 3.00 8.00
118 Petr Hubacek RC 2.00 5.00
119 Justin Williams RC 3.00 8.00
120 Roman Cechmanek RC 2.50 6.00
121 Roman Simicek RC 2.00 5.00
122 Mark Smith RC 2.00 5.00
123 Alexander Kharitonov RC 2.00 5.00
124 Matt Elich RC 2.00 5.00
125 Jakub Cutta RC 2.00 5.00
126 Fedor Fedorov RC 2.00 5.00
127 Marc-Andre Thinel RC 2.00 5.00
128 Zdenek Blatny RC 2.00 5.00
129 Jeff Bateman RC 2.00 5.00
130 Jason Jaspers RC 2.00 5.00
131 Jordan Krestanovich RC 2.00 5.00
132 Damian Surma RC 2.00 5.00

2000-01 UD Pros and Prospects Championship Rings

COMPLETE SET (8) 12.00 25.00
STATED ODDS 1:12
CR1 Patrick Roy 3.00 8.00
CR2 Brendan Shanahan 1.00 2.50
CR3 Steve Yzerman 3.00 8.00
CR4 Wayne Gretzky 4.00 10.00
CR5 Scott Stevens .60 1.50
CR6 Martin Brodeur 1.50 4.00
CR7 Mark Messier .75 2.00
CR8 Jaromir Jagr 1.00 2.50

2000-01 UD Pros and Prospects Game Jerseys

Randomly inserted in Upper Deck Pros and Prospects packs at a rate of 1:30, this 10-card set featured a swatch of game jersey. An exclusives parallel serial-numbered to 50 was also created.
*MULT.COLOR SWATCHES: 1X TO 2X
*EXCLUSIVES: 1X TO 2X BASIC INSERTS

BS Brendan Shanahan 3.00 8.00
CP Chris Pronger 3.00 8.00
JJ Jaromir Jagr 5.00 12.00
MM Mike Modano 4.00 10.00
PF Peter Forsberg 6.00 15.00
PK Paul Kariya 3.00 8.00
PR Patrick Roy 8.00 20.00
RB Ray Bourque 8.00 20.00
SF Sergei Fedorov 4.00 10.00
TS Teemu Selanne 3.00 8.00

2000-01 UD Pros and Prospects Game Jersey Autographs

Randomly inserted in Upper Deck Pros and Prospects packs at a rate of 1:96, this 10-card set featured a swatch of game jersey, and an autograph. An exclusives parallel was also created and serial-numbered to 50. Please note at the time of release the Scott Gomez and Wayne Gretzky cards were issued as exchange/redemption cards.
*MULT.COLOR SWATCHES: 1X TO 2X
*EXCLUSIVES: 1X TO 2X BASIC INSERTS

S-JL John LeClair 12.50 30.00
S-JR Jeremy Roenick 25.00 60.00
S-KT Keith Tkachuk 12.50 30.00
S-LB Lubos Bartecko 10.00 25.00
S-MM Mark Messier 250.00 400.00
S-PB Pavel Bure 12.50 30.00
S-SG Scott Gomez 10.00 25.00
S-SS Sergei Samsonov 12.50 30.00
S-SY Steve Yzerman 50.00 125.00
S-WG Wayne Gretzky 200.00 300.00

2000-01 UD Pros and Prospects Great Skates

COMPLETE SET (8) 10.00 20.00
STATED ODDS 1:12
GS1 Paul Kariya .60 1.50
GS2 Mario Lemieux 4.00 10.00
GS3 Patrick Roy 3.00 8.00
GS4 Brendan Shanahan 1.00 2.50
GS5 Pavel Bure .75 2.00
GS6 Alexei Yashin .60 1.50
GS7 John LeClair .75 2.00
GS8 Jaromir Jagr 1.00 2.50

2000-01 UD Pros and Prospects NHL Passion

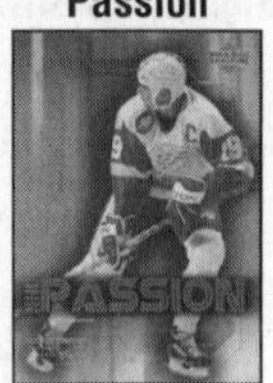

COMPLETE SET (9) 10.00 20.00
STATED ODDS 1:10
NP1 Ray Bourque 1.00 3.00
NP2 Brett Hull .75 2.00
NP3 Steve Yzerman 3.00 8.00
NP4 Mark Messier .75 2.00
NP5 John LeClair .75 2.00
NP6 Jeremy Roenick .75 2.00
NP7 Jaromir Jagr 1.00 2.50
NP8 Mario Lemieux 4.00 10.00
NP9 Curtis Joseph .60 1.50

2000-01 UD Pros and Prospects Now Appearing

COMPLETE SET (8) 10.00 20.00
STATED ODDS 1:12
NA1 Maxim Afinogenov .60 1.50
NA2 Marian Gaborik 3.00 8.00
NA3 Scott Hartnell .75 2.00
NA4 Scott Gomez .60 1.50
NA5 Rick DiPietro 3.00 8.00
NA6 Justin Williams 1.25 3.00
NA7 Daniel Sedin .60 1.50
NA8 Henrik Sedin .60 1.50

2000-01 UD Pros and Prospects ProMotion

COMPLETE SET (9) 10.00 20.00
STATED ODDS 1:10
PM1 Teemu Selanne .75 2.00
PM2 Dominik Hasek 1.50 4.00
PM3 Peter Forsberg 1.50 4.00
PM4 Sergei Fedorov 1.00 3.00
PM5 Mike Modano 1.00 2.50
PM6 Pavel Bure 1.00 2.50
PM7 Martin Brodeur 1.50 4.00
PM8 John LeClair .75 2.00
PM9 Jaromir Jagr 1.00 2.50

2000-01 UD Reserve

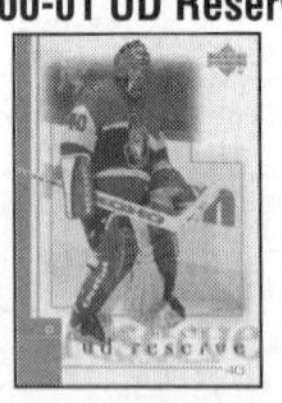

The 2000-01 UD Reserve complete set consisted of 120 cards,30 of which were rookies and 2 were checklists. The base set design used silver-foil for the Upper Deck logo and for highlights on the cards, and they had a light-blue border on the left side of the card front. The card backs had a small photo of the player on the top half and statistics below for the past couple seasons and also contained a career statistics line. The card backs also had the UD hologram on the bottom right corner.

COMPLETE SET (120) 40.00 80.00
1 Paul Kariya .25 .60
2 Steve Rucchin .08 .20
3 Teemu Selanne .25 .60
4 Damian Rhodes .08 .20
5 Patrik Stefan .08 .20
6 Byron Dafoe .20 .50
7 Jason Allison .08 .20
8 Joe Thornton .40 1.00
9 Doug Gilmour .20 .50
10 Dominik Hasek .50 1.25
11 Miroslav Satan .20 .50
12 Jarome Iginla .30 .75
13 Oleg Saprykin .08 .20
14 Valeri Bure .08 .20
15 Sandis Ozolinsh .08 .20
16 Ron Francis .20 .50
17 Sami Kapanen .08 .20
18 Steve Sullivan .20 .50
19 Alexei Zhamnov .08 .20
20 Tony Amonte .20 .50
21 Ray Bourque .50 1.25
22 Patrick Roy 1.25 3.00
23 Peter Forsberg .60 1.50
24 Joe Sakic .50 1.25
25 Ron Tugnutt .20 .50
26 Steve Heinze .08 .20
27 Mike Modano .40 1.00
28 Brett Hull .30 .75
29 Ed Belfour .25 .60
30 Brendan Shanahan .25 .60
31 Sergei Fedorov .40 1.00
32 Steve Yzerman 1.25 3.00
33 Ryan Smyth .08 .20
34 Tommy Salo .20 .50
35 Doug Weight .20 .50
36 Pavel Bure .25 .60
37 Ray Whitney .08 .20
38 Roberto Luongo .30 .75
39 Luc Robitaille .20 .50
40 Zigmund Palffy .20 .50
41 Jamie Storr .20 .50
42 Jamie McLennan .08 .20
43 Jim Dowd .08 .20
44 Brian Savage .08 .20
45 Jose Theodore .30 .75
46 Saku Koivu .25 .60
47 David Legwand .20 .50
48 Cliff Ronning .08 .20
49 Tomas Vokoun .20 .50
50 Scott Gomez .08 .20
51 Patrik Elias .20 .50
52 Martin Brodeur .60 1.50
53 Tim Connolly .08 .20
54 Roman Hamrlik .08 .20
55 John Vanbiesbrouck .20 .50
56 Theo Fleury .08 .20
57 Mark Messier .25 .60
58 Brian Leetch .25 .60
59 Marian Hossa .25 .60
60 Patrick Lalime .20 .50
61 Alexei Yashin .08 .20
62 John LeClair .25 .60
63 Mark Recchi .20 .50
64 Keith Primeau .08 .20
65 Jeremy Roenick .30 .75
66 Sean Burke .20 .50
67 Keith Tkachuk .25 .60
68 Jaromir Jagr .40 1.00
69 Milan Kraft .20 .50
70 Mario Lemieux 1.50 4.00
71 Owen Nolan .20 .50
72 Jeff Friesen .08 .20
73 Evgeni Nabokov .20 .50
74 Chris Pronger .20 .50
75 Scott Young .08 .20
76 Roman Turek .20 .50
77 Vincent Lecavalier .25 .60
78 Brad Richards .20 .50
79 Mike Johnson .08 .20
80 Curtis Joseph .25 .60
81 Mats Sundin .25 .60
82 Sergei Berezin .08 .20
83 Markus Naslund .25 .60
84 Daniel Sedin .08 .20
85 Henrik Sedin .08 .20
86 Chris Simon .08 .20
87 Peter Bondra .25 .60
88 Olaf Kolzig .20 .50
89 Andrew Raycroft RC 1.50 4.00
90 Josef Vasicek RC .40 1.00
91 David Aebischer RC 1.50 4.00
92 Rostislav Klesla RC 1.00 2.50
93 Marty Turco RC 2.00 5.00
94 Tyler Bouck RC .60 1.50
95 Shawn Horcoff RC .75 2.00
96 Eric Belanger RC .40 1.00
97 Steven Reinprecht RC .40 1.00
98 Marian Gaborik RC 2.50 6.00
99 Peter Bartos RC .40 1.00
100 Scott Hartnell RC .40 1.00
101 Greg Classen RC .40 1.00
102 Chris Mason RC .40 1.00
103 Willie Mitchell RC .40 1.00
104 Rick DiPietro RC 1.50 4.00
105 Jason Labarbera RC .50 1.25
106 Jani Hurme RC .75 2.00
107 Martin Havlat RC 2.00 5.00
108 Ruslan Fedotenko RC .40 1.00
109 Justin Williams RC 1.00 2.50
110 Petr Hubacek RC .40 1.00
111 Roman Cechmanek RC .50 1.25
112 Mark Smith RC .40 1.00
113 Alexander Khavanov RC .40 1.00
114 Alexander Kharitonov RC .40 1.00
115 Marc-Andre Thinel RC .40 1.00
116 Zdenek Blatny RC .40 1.00
117 Jordan Krestanovich RC .40 1.00
118 Jeff Bateman RC .40 1.00
119 Mark Messier CL .25 .60
120 Curtis Joseph CL .25 .60

2000-01 UD Reserve Buyback Autographs

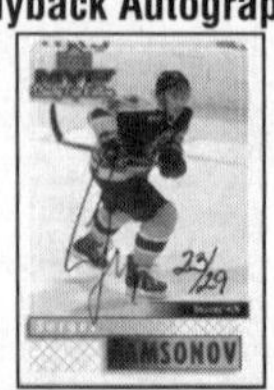

Randomly inserted in packs at a rate of 1:239, this set features 137 different original Upper Deck cards that Upper Deck bought back and had autographed. Please note these cards have print runs that vary. Cards with print runs of less than 25 are not priced due to scarcity. The Scott Gomez cards were only found in packs as exchange cards and the actual autographed buybacks have yet to be verified. For that reason only the exchange card is priced.
PRINT RUNS OF LESS THAN 20 NOT PRICED DUE TO SCARCITY

1 Wayne Gretzky 90UD/1
2 Wayne Gretzky 91UD621/1
3 Wayne Gretzky 92UD25/1
4 Wayne Gretzky 92UD33/1
5 Wayne Gretzky 96UD/1
6 Wayne Gretzky 97UD/1
7 Wayne Gretzky 98UD135/1
8 Wayne Gretzky 98UD390/1
9 Wayne Gretzky 99UD9/1
10 Wayne Gretzky 99UD10/1
11 S.Yzerman 90UD303/1
12 S.Yzerman 90UD56/1
13 S.Yzerman 91UD/1
14 S.Yzerman 92UD/1
15 S.Yzerman 93UD/1
16 S.Yzerman 94UD/1
17 S.Yzerman 95UD/1
18 S.Yzerman 96UD/1
19 S.Yzerman 97UD/1
20 S.Yzerman 98UD/1
21 S.Yzerman 99UD304/4
22 S.Yzerman 99UD49/1
23 Sergei Samsonov 99MVPSC/29
25 Scott Gomez 99MVPSCSS/27 12.50 25.00
26 Scott Gomez 99UD/9
27 Ray Bourque 90UD204/2
28 Ray Bourque 90UD320/1
29 Ray Bourque 90UD64/1
30 Ray Bourque 91UD/2
31 Ray Bourque 92UD265/2
32 Ray Bourque 92UD626/1
33 Ray Bourque 95UD/3
34 Ray Bourque 96UD/1
35 Ray Bourque 97UD/1
36 Ray Bourque 98UD/1
37 Pavel Brendl 99MVPSC/301 15.0030.00
38 Pavel Brendl 99UD/9
39 Mike Richter 90UD/6
40 Mike Richter 91UD175/1
41 Mike Richter 91UD34/1
42 Mike Richter 92UD/1
43 Mike Richter 94UD/1
44 Mike Richter 95UD/2
45 Mike Richter 96UD/1
46 Mike Richter 97UD/1
47 Mike Richter 98UD/1
48 Mike Richter 99UD/1
49 Mike Ribiero 97UD/52
50 Mike Ribiero 99OVA/1
51 Mike Ribiero 99UD/25 25.00 60.00
52 M.Modano 90UD346/13
53 M.Modano 90UD46/56 25.00 60.00
54 M.Modano 91UD160/12
55 M.Modano 91UD32/5
56 M.Modano 92UD305/69 25.00 60.00
57 M.Modano 92UD9/10
58 M.Modano 93UD294/2
59 M.Modano 93UD397/5
60 M.Modano 94UD/8
61 M.Modano 95UD/7
62 M.Modano 96UD363/3
63 M.Modano 96UD43/39 40.00 100.00
64 M.Modano 98UD256/8
65 M.Modano 98UD30/1
66 M.Modano 99UD/9
67 M.Brodeur 92UD/2
68 M.Brodeur 94UD/1
69 M.Brodeur 96UD/1
70 M.Brodeur 97UD/7
71 M.Brodeur 99UD/3
72 Mark Messier 90UD321/1
73 Mark Messier 90UD44/1
74 Mark Messier 91UD/1
75 Mark Messier 92UD242/1
76 Mark Messier 92UD34/1
77 Mark Messier 94UD/1
78 Mark Messier 99UD/4
79 Luc Robitaille 90UD/10
80 Luc Robitaille 91UD145/12
81 Luc Robitaille 91UD507/5
82 Luc Robitaille 91UD623/2
83 Luc Robitaille 91UD8/6
84 Luc Robitaille 92UD/13
85 Luc Robitaille 93UD231/12
86 Luc Robitaille 93UD293/5
87 Luc Robitaille 93UD414/13
88 Luc Robitaille 98MVP/2
89 Luc Robitaille 98UD/6
90 Luc Robitaille 99OVA/7
91 Luc Robitaille 99RETRO/3
92 Luc Robitaille 99UD/3
93 Luc Robitaille 99UV/1
94 Keith Tkachuk 92UD364/2
95 Keith Tkachuk 92UD398/2
96 Keith Tkachuk 92UD419/2
97 Keith Tkachuk 94UD/1
98 Keith Tkachuk 95UD/1
99 Keith Tkachuk 97UD/1
100 Keith Tkachuk 99UD/100 75.00200.00
101 Jose Theodore 95UD/4
102 Jose Theodore 97UD/4
103 Jose Theodore 99MVPSC/356 6.00 15.00
104 John LeClair 91UD/4
105 John LeClair 92UD/2
106 John LeClair 95UD247/1
107 John LeClair 95UD7/2
108 John LeClair 96UD118/3
109 John LeClair 96UD368/2
110 John LeClair 97UD123/7
111 John LeClair 98UD/3
112 John LeClair 99UD/2
113 Henrik Sedin 99UDGR166/3
114 Henrik Sedin 99UDGR308/1
115 Henrik Sedin EXCH 20.00 40.00
116 Henrik Sedin 99UD166/3
117 Henrik Sedin 99UD308/13
118 Gordie Howe 92UDGH19/1
119 Gordie Howe 92UDGH20/1
120 Gordie Howe 92UDGH21/1
121 Gordie Howe 92UDGH22/1
122 Gordie Howe 92UDGH23/1
123 Gordie Howe 92UDGH24/1
124 Gordie Howe 92UDGH25/1
125 Gordie Howe 92UDGH26/1
126 Gordie Howe 92UDGH27/1
127 Gordie Howe 99OVACS/1
128 Daniel Sedin 99UDGR/2
129 Daniel Sedin 99MVPSC/329 12.50 25.00
130 Daniel Sedin 99UD165/2
131 Daniel Sedin 99UD307/10
132 Curtis Joseph 90UD/10
133 Curtis Joseph 92UD/1
134 Curtis Joseph 94UD/1
135 Curtis Joseph 95UD/1
136 Curtis Joseph 97UD/1
137 Curtis Joseph 98UD/1

2000-01 UD Reserve Gold Strike

COMPLETE SET (10) 12.00 25.00
STATED ODDS 1:14
GS1 Teemu Selanne .75 2.00
GS2 Joe Sakic 1.50 4.00
GS3 Mike Modano 1.25 3.00
GS4 Sergei Fedorov 1.50 4.00
GS5 Pavel Bure 1.00 2.50
GS6 Scott Gomez .60 1.50
GS7 Theo Fleury .60 1.50
GS8 Mario Lemieux 5.00 12.00
GS9 Mats Sundin .75 2.00
GS10 Olaf Kolzig .60 1.50

2000-01 UD Reserve Golden Goalies

COMPLETE SET (10) 10.00 20.00
STATED ODDS 1:14
GG1 Guy Hebert .60 1.50
GG2 Dominik Hasek 1.50 4.00
GG3 Patrick Roy 4.00 10.00
GG4 Tommy Salo .60 1.50
GG5 Jose Theodore .75 2.00
GG6 Mike Dunham .60 1.50
GG7 Martin Brodeur 2.00 5.00
GG8 John Vanbiesbrouck .75 2.00
GG9 Roman Turek .60 1.50
GG10 Curtis Joseph 1.00 2.50

2000-01 UD Reserve On-Ice Success

COMPLETE SET (6) 6.00 12.00
STATED ODDS 1:23
OS1 Paul Kariya .75 2.00
OS2 Tony Amonte .75 2.00
OS3 Joe Sakic 1.50 4.00
OS4 Pavel Bure 1.00 2.50
OS5 Luc Robitaille .75 2.00
OS6 Mark Messier 1.00 2.50

2000-01 UD Reserve Power Portfolios

COMPLETE SET (6) 10.00 20.00
STATED ODDS 1:23
PP1 Patrick Roy 4.00 10.00
PP2 Brett Hull 1.00 2.50
PP3 Steve Yzerman 4.00 10.00
PP4 Martin Brodeur 2.00 5.00
PP5 Mark Messier 1.00 2.50
PP6 Jaromir Jagr 1.25 3.00

2000-01 UD Reserve Practice Session Jerseys

Randomly inserted in packs at a rate of 1:239, this 10-card set featured a swatch of a practice session jersey. The set used player initials for the card numbering. Autographed variations were also created and inserted at 1:479.
*AUTOS: 1.25X TO 3X BASIC INSERTS

CO Chris Osgood 4.00 10.00
JJ Jaromir Jagr 6.00 15.00
JL John LeClair 4.00 10.00

JT Joe Thornton 6.00 15.00
MA Mark Messier 10.00 25.00
MM Mike Modano 6.00 15.00
MR Mark Recchi 4.00 10.00
PF Peter Forsberg 6.00 15.00
TF Theo Fleury 4.00 10.00
TS Teemu Selanne 5.00 12.00

2000-01 UD Reserve The Big Ticket

COMPLETE SET (10) 15.00 30.00
STATED ODDS 1:14
BT1 Paul Kariya .75 2.00
BT2 Dominik Hasek 1.50 4.00
BT3 Ray Bourque 1.50 4.00
BT4 Steve Yzerman 4.00 10.00
BT5 Pavel Bure 1.00 2.50
BT6 Marian Gaborik 3.00 8.00
BT7 Martin Brodeur 2.00 5.00
BT8 John LeClair 1.00 2.50
BT9 Jaromir Jagr 1.25 3.00
BT10 Vincent Lecavalier .75 2.00

2005-06 UD Rookie Class

COMPLETE SET (50) 12.50 30.00
1 Sidney Crosby 2.50 6.00
2 Alexander Ovechkin 1.00 2.50
3 Henrik Lundqvist .30 .75
4 Marek Svatos .10 .20
5 Thomas Vanek .20 .50
6 Brad Boyes .10 .20
7 Petr Prucha .20 .50
8 Jussi Jokinen .10 .30
9 Dion Phaneuf .30 .75
10 Alexander Steen .15 .40
11 Alvaro Montoya .25 .60
12 Keith Ballard .10 .20
13 Jeff Carter .25 .60
14 Michel Ouellet .15 .40
15 Andrej Meszaros .10 .25
16 Pavel Vorobiev .10 .20
17 Mike Richards .20 .50
18 Milan Michalek .10 .20
19 Antti Miettinen .10 .20
20 Rene Bourque .10 .20
21 Chris Campoli .10 .20
22 Gilbert Brule .30 .75
23 Andrew Ladd .10 .25
24 R.J. Umberger .10 .30
25 Hannu Toivonen .15 .40
26 Ryan Miller .10 .30
27 Kyle Wellwood .10 .20
28 Fedor Tjutin .10 .20
29 Brent Seabrook .10 .20
30 Jim Howard .15 .40
31 Ryan Whitney .10 .20
32 Corey Perry .20 .50
33 Alexander Perezhogin .15 .40
34 Zach Parise .15 .40
35 Peter Budaj .10 .20
36 Mikko Koivu .20 .50
37 Rostislav Olesz .10 .30
38 Ryan Getzlaf .20 .50
39 Yann Danis .10 .20
40 Wojtek Wolski .25 .60
41 Ryan Suter .15 .40
42 Patrick Eaves .10 .20
43 Anthony Stewart .10 .20
44 Brandon Bochenski .10 .20
45 Eric Nystrom .10 .20
46 Antero Niittymaki .15 .40
47 Johan Franzen .10 .20
48 Andrei Kostitsyn .10 .30
49 Carlo Colaiacovo .10 .25
50 Cam Ward .30 .75

2005-06 UD Rookie Class Commemorative Boxtoppers

CC-1 Sidney Crosby 6.00 15.00
CC-2 Alexander Ovechkin 5.00 12.00
CC-3 Henrik Lundqvist 1.50 4.00
CC-4 Thomas Vanek 1.00 2.50
CC-5 Dion Phaneuf 1.50 4.00
CC-6 Alexander Steen 1.00 2.50
CC-7 Jeff Carter 1.00 2.50

2001-02 UD Stanley Cup Champs

This 86-card set was available in 3-card packs that were inserted one pack per box of various Upper Deck products. The cards featured action photos of past Stanley Cup winners.

1 Phil Esposito 2.00 5.00
2 Bobby Orr 8.00 20.00
3 Glenn Hall 1.00 2.50
4 Bobby Hull 1.50 4.00
5 Ray Bourque 1.50 4.00
6 Gordie Howe 4.00 10.00
7 Ted Lindsay .40 1.00
8 Terry Sawchuk 2.00 5.00
9 Grant Fuhr .60 1.50
10 Wayne Gretzky 5.00 12.00
11 Jari Kurri .75 2.00
12 Bill Ranford .40 1.00
13 Jean Beliveau 1.00 2.50
14 Yvan Cournoyer .75 2.00
15 Guy Lafleur 1.50 4.00
16 Jacques Plante 1.25 3.00
17 Maurice Richard 1.50 4.00
18 Henri Richard .40 1.00
19 Mike Bossy 1.25 3.00
20 Bob Nystrom .40 1.00
21 Ken Morrow .40 1.00
22 Bryan Trottier .40 1.00
23 Bobby Clarke 1.25 3.00
24 Bernie Parent .60 1.50
25 Tim Horton .40 1.00
26 Frank Mahovlich .75 2.00
27 Mike Vernon .60 1.50
28 Theo Fleury .40 1.00
29 Al MacInnis .60 1.50
30 Peter Forsberg 2.00 5.00
31 Dan Hinote .40 1.00
32 Milan Hejduk .75 2.00
33 Alex Tanguay .60 1.50
34 David Aebischer .60 1.50
35 Chris Drury .60 1.50
36 Rob Blake .60 1.50
37 Joe Sakic 1.50 4.00
38 Patrick Roy 4.00 10.00
39 Ville Nieminen .40 1.00
40 Steven Reinprecht .40 1.00
41 Adam Foote .40 1.00
42 Adam Deadmarsh .40 1.00
43 Jon Klemm .40 1.00
44 Sandis Ozolinsh .40 1.00
45 Mike Keane .40 1.00
46 Mike Modano 1.25 3.00
47 Brett Hull 1.00 2.50
48 Joe Nieuwendyk .60 1.50
49 Sergei Zubov .40 1.00
50 Ed Belfour .75 2.00
51 Derian Hatcher .40 1.00
52 Jamie Langenbrunner .40 1.00
53 Grant Marshall .40 1.00
54 Jere Lehtinen .60 1.50
55 Darryl Sydor .40 1.00
56 Sergei Fedorov 1.25 3.00
57 Steve Yzerman 4.00 10.00
58 Nicklas Lidstrom .75 2.00
59 Mathieu Dandenault .40 1.00
60 Slava Kozlov .40 1.00
61 Chris Osgood .60 1.50
62 Darren McCarty .40 1.00
63 Kirk Maltby .40 1.00
64 Brendan Shanahan .75 2.00
65 Tomas Holmstrom .40 1.00
66 John LeClair .75 2.00
67 Patrick Roy 4.00 10.00
68 Eric Desjardins .40 1.00
69 Scott Stevens .60 1.50
70 Patrik Elias .60 1.50
71 Randy McKay .40 1.00
72 Jason Arnott .40 1.00
73 Alexander Mogilny .60 1.50
74 Petr Sykora .40 1.00
75 Scott Gomez .40 1.00
76 Sergei Brylin .40 1.00
77 Bobby Holik .40 1.00
78 Martin Brodeur 2.00 5.00
79 John Madden .40 1.00
80 Scott Niedermayer .40 1.00
81 Claude Lemieux .40 1.00
82 Brian Leetch .60 1.50
83 Mike Richter .75 2.00
84 Mark Messier .75 2.00
85 Jaromir Jagr 1.25 3.00
86 Mario Lemieux 5.00 12.00

2001-02 UD Stanley Cup Champs Champion Signatures

Randomly inserted in box-topper packs, these cards were numbered 1 of 1 and contain a cut signature of the given player. As of press time neither card had been verified, and these cards are not priced due to scarcity.

JP Jacques Plante/1
TS Terry Sawchuk/1

2001-02 UD Stanley Cup Champs Jerseys

Randomly inserted in box topper packs, this 20-card set featured a game-worn jersey swatch of the featured player on the card front and a congratulatory message on the card back. Each card was numbered out of 200.

*MULT.COLOR SWATCH: .5X TO 1.5X HI
T-BH Brett Hull 12.50 30.00
T-BL Brian Leetch 12.50 30.00
T-BS Brendan Shanahan 15.00 40.00
T-BT Bryan Trottier 12.50 30.00
T-EB Ed Belfour 12.50 30.00
T-GL Guy Lafleur 15.00 40.00
T-JJ Jaromir Jagr 20.00 50.00
T-JS Joe Sakic 20.00 50.00
T-KM Ken Morrow 12.50 30.00
T-MB Mike Bossy 12.50 30.00
T-ME Mark Messier 12.50 30.00
T-ML Mario Lemieux 30.00 80.00
T-MM Mike Modano 12.50 30.00
T-PF Peter Forsberg 25.00 60.00
T-PR Patrick Roy 30.00 80.00
T-RB Ray Bourque 25.00 60.00
T-RO Patrick Roy 30.00 80.00
T-SF Sergei Fedorov 20.00 50.00
T-SY Steve Yzerman 30.00 80.00
T-TF Theo Fleury 12.50 30.00

2001-02 UD Stanley Cup Champs Pieces of Glory

Randomly inserted in box topper packs, this 30-card set featured pieces of a game-used jersey and stick from the featured player. Each card was serial numbered out of just 50.

G-BG Bill Guerin 15.00 40.00
G-BH Brett Hull 30.00 80.00
G-BL Brian Leetch 15.00 40.00
G-BO Mike Bossy 20.00 50.00
G-BR Bill Ranford 15.00 40.00
G-BS Brendan Shanahan 15.00 40.00
G-BT Bryan Trottier 40.00 100.00
G-CL Claude Lemieux 15.00 40.00
G-CO Chris Osgood 15.00 40.00
G-EB Ed Belfour 15.00 40.00
G-GL Guy Lafleur 50.00 125.00
G-JJ Jaromir Jagr 20.00 50.00
G-JN Joe Nieuwendyk 15.00 40.00
G-JS Joe Sakic 40.00 100.00
G-LM Lanny McDonald 15.00 40.00
G-MA Mark Messier 15.00 40.00
G-MB Martin Brodeur 50.00 125.00
G-ML Mario Lemieux 60.00 150.00
G-MM Mike Modano 20.00 50.00
G-MR Mike Richter 15.00 40.00
G-NL Nicklas Lidstrom 15.00 40.00
G-PF Peter Forsberg 40.00 100.00
G-PR Patrick Roy 60.00 150.00
G-RB Ray Bourque 25.00 60.00
G-RO Patrick Roy 60.00 150.00
G-SF Sergei Fedorov 20.00 50.00
G-SY Steve Yzerman 60.00 150.00
G-TF Theo Fleury 15.00 40.00
G-WG Wayne Gretzky 150.00 300.00

2001-02 UD Stanley Cup Champs Sticks

Randomly inserted into box topper packs, this 29-card set featured pieces of a game-used stick of the featured player on the card front and a congratulatory message on the card back. Each card was numbered out of 150.

S-AM Al MacInnis 12.50 30.00
S-AT Alex Tanguay 12.50 30.00
S-BG Bill Guerin 12.50 30.00
S-BH Brett Hull 15.00 40.00
S-BK Rob Blake 12.50 30.00
S-BL Brian Leetch 12.50 30.00
S-BO Mike Bossy 20.00 50.00
S-BS Brendan Shanahan 12.50 30.00
S-BT Bryan Trottier 15.00 40.00
S-CL Claude Lemieux 12.50 30.00
S-EB Ed Belfour 12.50 30.00
S-GH Gordie Howe 50.00 125.00
S-GL Guy Lafleur 20.00 50.00
S-JJ Jaromir Jagr 15.00 40.00
S-JN Joe Nieuwendyk 12.50 30.00
S-JS Joe Sakic 15.00 40.00
S-MB Martin Brodeur 20.00 50.00
S-ML Mario Lemieux 40.00 100.00
S-MM Mike Modano 15.00 40.00
S-MO Alexander Mogilny 12.50 30.00
S-MR Mike Richter 12.50 30.00
S-PF Peter Forsberg 15.00 40.00
S-PR Patrick Roy 25.00 60.00
S-RB Ray Bourque 15.00 40.00
S-RO Patrick Roy 25.00 60.00
S-SF Sergei Fedorov 15.00 40.00
S-SY Steve Yzerman 25.00 60.00
S-TF Theo Fleury 12.50 30.00
S-WG Wayne Gretzky 60.00 150.00

2001-02 UD Top Shelf

Released in mid-October 2001, this 156-card set carried an SRP of $9.99. The original 97-card base set consisted of 45 veteran cards (1-45), 42 rookie cards (46-66) and 10-exchange rookie cards (67-76). Cards 46-66 were issued in two versions, both versions were serial-numbered to 800 each the only difference between the two versions was that the images on front and back were reversed. Cards 67-76 were redeemable for rookie players who made their debut during the season, and they were serial-numbered to 500 each. Cards 77-135 were available in random packs of UD Rookie Update and cards 122-135 were serial-numbered to 900 each. Cards 136-141 were available by redeeming cards TR1-TR6 of the Rookie Redemption set; they were serial-numbered to just 100 copies each.

COMP.SET w/o SP's (90) 30.00 60.00
1 Paul Kariya .60 1.50
2 Patrik Stefan .20 .50
3 Joe Thornton 1.00 2.50
4 Miroslav Satan .50 1.25
5 Jarome Iginla .75 2.00
6 Jeff O'Neill .20 .50
7 Tony Amonte .50 1.25
8 Joe Sakic 1.25 3.00
9 Peter Forsberg 1.50 4.00
10 Ray Bourque 1.25 3.00
11 Milan Hejduk .60 1.50
12 Patrick Roy 3.00 8.00
13 Rostislav Klesla .20 .50
14 Mike Modano 1.00 2.50
15 Steve Yzerman 3.00 8.00
16 Luc Robitaille .50 1.25
17 Dominik Hasek 1.25 3.00
18 Tommy Salo .50 1.25
19 Pavel Bure .60 1.50
20 Zigmund Palffy .50 1.25
21 Brett Hull .75 2.00
22 Marian Gaborik 1.25 3.00
23 Saku Koivu .60 1.50
24 David Legwand .50 1.25
25 Martin Brodeur 1.50 4.00
26 Patrik Elias .50 1.25
27 Rick DiPietro .50 1.25
28 Eric Lindros .60 1.50
29 Marian Hossa .60 1.50
30 Jeremy Roenick .75 2.00
31 Roman Cechmanek .50 1.25
32 Sean Burke .50 1.25
33 Alexei Kovalev .50 1.25
34 Mario Lemieux 4.00 10.00
35 Johan Hedberg .50 1.25
36 Evgeni Nabokov .50 1.25
37 Teemu Selanne .60 1.50
38 Chris Pronger .50 1.25
39 Keith Tkachuk .60 1.50
40 Vincent Lecavalier .60 1.50
41 Curtis Joseph .60 1.50
42 Mats Sundin .60 1.50
43 Markus Naslund .60 1.50
44 Daniel Sedin .20 .50
45 Jaromir Jagr 1.00 2.50
46 Mikael Samuelsson RC 2.50 6.00
46B Mikael Samuelsson RC 2.50 6.00
47 Dan Snyder RC 4.00 10.00
47B Dan Snyder RC 4.00 10.00
48 Zdenek Kutlak RC 2.50 6.00
48B Zdenek Kutlak RC 2.50 6.00
49 Michel Larocque RC 2.50 6.00
49B Michel Larocque RC 2.50 6.00
50 Casey Hankinson RC 2.50 6.00
50B Casey Hankinson RC 2.50 6.00
51 Bill Bowler RC 2.50 6.00
51B Bill Bowler RC 2.50 6.00
52 Martin Spanhel RC 2.50 6.00
52B Martin Spanhel RC 2.50 6.00
53 Mathieu Darche RC 2.50 6.00
53B Mathieu Darche RC 2.50 6.00
54 Jason Chimera RC 2.50 6.00
54B Jason Chimera RC 2.50 6.00
55 Andrej Podkonicky RC 2.50 6.00
55B Andrej Podkonicky RC 2.50 6.00
56 Pascal Dupuis RC 2.50 6.00
56B Pascal Dupuis RC 2.50 6.00
57 Francis Belanger RC 2.50 6.00
57B Francis Belanger RC 2.50 6.00
58 Mike Jefferson RC 2.50 6.00
58B Mike Jefferson RC 2.50 6.00
59 Stanislav Gron RC 2.50 6.00
59B Stanislav Gron RC 2.50 6.00
60 Joel Kwiatkowski RC 2.50 6.00
60B Joel Kwiatkowski RC 2.50 6.00
61 Kirby Law RC 2.50 6.00
61B Kirby Law RC 2.50 6.00
62 Tomas Divisek RC 2.50 6.00
62B Tomas Divisek RC 2.50 6.00
63 Billy Tibbetts RC 2.50 6.00
63B Billy Tibbetts RC 2.50 6.00
64 Thomas Ziegler RC 2.50 6.00
64B Thomas Ziegler RC 2.50 6.00
65 Mike Brown 2.50 6.00
65B Mike Brown 2.50 6.00
66 Pat Kavanagh RC 2.50 6.00
66B Pat Kavanagh RC 2.50 6.00
67 Ilja Bryzgalov RC 6.00 15.00
68 Ilya Kovalchuk RC 25.00 60.00
69 Vaclav Nedorost RC 4.00 10.00
70 Niko Kapanen RC 4.00 10.00
71 Kristian Huselius RC 4.00 10.00
72 Dan Blackburn RC 4.00 10.00
73 Krystofer Kolanos RC 2.50 6.00
74 Jiri Dopita RC 4.00 10.00
75 Nikita Alexeev RC 4.00 10.00
76 Brian Sutherby RC 4.00 10.00
77 Dany Heatley .75 2.00
78 Sergei Samsonov .50 1.25
79 Bill Guerin .50 1.25
80 Byron Dafoe .50 1.25
81 Martin Biron .50 1.25
82 Roman Turek .50 1.25
83 Arturs Irbe .50 1.25
84 Steve Sullivan .20 .50
85 Mark Bell .20 .50
86 Rob Blake .50 1.25
87 Alex Tanguay .50 1.25
88 Chris Drury .50 1.25
89 Espen Knutsen .20 .50
90 Ed Belfour .60 1.50
91 Brendan Shanahan .60 1.50
92 Nicklas Lidstrom .60 1.50
93 Sergei Fedorov 1.00 2.50
94 Mike Comrie .50 1.25
95 Roberto Luongo .75 2.00
96 Felix Potvin .60 1.50
97 Jason Allison .20 .50
98 Joe Thornton .75 2.00
99 Joe Nieuwendyk .50 1.25
100 Brian Gionta .20 .50
101 Alexei Yashin .20 .50
102 Michael Peca .50 1.25
103 Chris Osgood .50 1.25
104 Mark Parrish .20 .50
105 Juraj Kolnik .20 .50
106 Theo Fleury .20 .50
107 Mike Richter .60 1.50
108 Brian Leetch .50 1.25
109 Pavel Bure .60 1.50
110 Martin Havlat .50 1.25
111 Adam Oates .50 1.25
112 John LeClair .60 1.50
113 Keith Primeau .20 .50
114 Owen Nolan .50 1.25
115 Pavol Demitra .50 1.25
116 Brent Johnson .50 1.25
117 Doug Weight .50 1.25
118 Nikolai Khabibulin .60 1.50
119 Brad Richards .50 1.25
120 Peter Bondra .60 1.50
121 Olaf Kolzig .50 1.25
122 Pasi Nurminen RC 4.00 10.00
123 Ivan Huml RC 3.00 8.00
124 Erik Cole RC 2.50 6.00
125 Mike Peluso RC 3.00 8.00
126 Riku Hahl RC 3.00 8.00
127 Pavel Datsyuk RC 12.00 30.00
128 Niklas Hagman RC 3.00 8.00
129 Olivier Michaud RC 4.00 10.00
130 Marcel Hossa RC 3.00 8.00
131 Martin Erat RC 3.00 8.00
132 Christian Berglund RC 3.00 8.00
133 Raffi Torres RC 6.00 15.00
134 Branko Radivojevic RC 3.00 8.00
135 Jeff Jillson RC 3.00 8.00
136 Mark Hartigan RC 15.00 40.00
137 Stephen Weiss RC 20.00 50.00
138 Jan Lasak RC 15.00 40.00
139 Trent Hunter RC 20.00 50.00
140 Evgeny Konstantinov RC 15.00 40.00
141 Sebastien Charpentier RC 15.00 40.00

2001-02 UD Top Shelf All-Star Nets

Inserted at 1:287, this 6-card set featured a piece of All-Star game-used netting. Card fronts were team colored and the netting was affixed in an "X" design. Card backs carried a congratulatory message.

NDH Dominik Hasek 25.00 60.00
NEN Evgeni Nabokov 15.00 40.00
NMB Martin Brodeur 25.00 60.00
NPR Patrick Roy 30.00 80.00
NRC Roman Cechmanek 15.00 40.00
NSB Sean Burke 15.00 40.00

2001-02 UD Top Shelf Goalie Gear

This 14-card set featured game-used equipment from some of the top goalies of the NHL, past and present. Cards from this set were inserted at a rate of 1:12. Equipment used on each card is listed below beside the player's name. Card backs carried a congratulatory message.

BJH Johan Hedberg Blocker 5.00 12.00
SCO Chris Osgood Skate 5.00 12.00
GGJH Johan Hedberg Glove 5.00 12.00
LPBB Brian Boucher Pad 5.00 12.00
LPBD Byron Dafoe Pad 5.00 12.00
LPDH Dominik Hasek Pad 10.00 25.00
LPGC Gerry Cheevers Pad 5.00 12.00
LPJH Johan Hedberg Pad 5.00 12.00
LPJT Jose Theodore Pad 6.00 15.00
LPJV John Vanbiesbrouck Pad 5.00 12.00
LPMB Martin Biron Pad 5.00 12.00
LPRC Roman Cechmanek Pad 5.00 12.00
LPRL Roberto Luongo Pad 6.00 15.00
LPSS Steve Shields Pad 5.00 12.00

2001-02 UD Top Shelf Jerseys

This 30-card set featured swatches of game-worn jersey and color player photos on a mostly silver card front. Two subsets made up this set; Stanley Cup Champions jerseys and regular jerseys. Stanley Cup jerseys were inserted at 1:30 and are denoted below with an "SC" beside the player's name. Regular jerseys were inserted at 1:20. Card backs carried a congratulatory message. Cards found in UD Update packs carry a "TJ" prefix.

*MULT.COLOR SWATCH: 1X TO 2X HI
AY Alexei Yashin 4.00 10.00
BH Brett Hull SC 5.00 12.00
BS Brendan Shanahan SC 4.00 10.00
DS Daniel Sedin 4.00 10.00
DW Doug Weight 4.00 10.00
EB Ed Belfour SC 4.00 10.00
HS Henrik Sedin 4.00 10.00
JA Jason Allison 4.00 10.00
JI Jarome Iginla 5.00 12.00
JJ Jaromir Jagr SC 6.00 15.00
JL John LeClair SC 4.00 10.00
JO Jose Theodore 5.00 12.00
JS Joe Sakic SC 8.00 20.00
JT Joe Thornton 5.00 12.00
MH Marian Hossa 4.00 10.00
ML Mario Lemieux SC 20.00 50.00
MM Mike Modano SC 6.00 15.00
MR Mike Richter SC 4.00 10.00
MT Marty Turco 4.00 10.00
PB Peter Bondra 4.00 10.00
PF Peter Forsberg SC 10.00 25.00
PK Paul Kariya 4.00 10.00
PR Patrick Roy SC 12.50 30.00
PS Patrik Stefan 4.00 10.00
RB Ray Bourque SC 10.00 25.00
SF Sergei Fedorov SC 6.00 15.00
SY Steve Yzerman SC 12.50 30.00
TS Teemu Selanne 4.00 10.00
VB Valeri Bure 4.00 10.00
VL Vincent Lecavalier 4.00 10.00
TJBS Brendan Shanahan Upd 4.00 10.00
TJCD Chris Drury Upd 4.00 10.00
TJJI Jarome Iginla Upd 4.00 10.00
TJJW Justin Williams Upd 4.00 10.00
TJMH Milan Hejduk Upd 4.00 10.00
TJMN Markus Naslund Upd 4.00 10.00
TJMS Miroslav Satan Upd 4.00 10.00
TJPD Pavol Demitra Upd 4.00 10.00
TJPK Paul Kariya Upd 8.00 20.00
TJZP Zigmund Palffy Upd 4.00 10.00

2001-02 UD Top Shelf Jersey Autographs

This 18-card set paralleled the basic jersey set, but also incorporates an autograph of the featured player along with the jersey swatch. Each card was serial-numbered out of 100 copies. Card backs carried a congratulatory message.

DS Daniel Sedin 15.00 40.00
DW Doug Weight 15.00 40.00
EB Ed Belfour SC 15.00 40.00
HS Henrik Sedin 15.00 40.00
JA Jason Allison 15.00 40.00
JI Jarome Iginla 20.00 50.00
JL John LeClair SC 15.00 40.00
JO Jose Theodore 20.00 50.00
JT Joe Thornton 20.00 50.00
MH Marian Hossa 15.00 40.00
MM Mike Modano SC 25.00 60.00
MT Marty Turco 15.00 40.00
PS Patrik Stefan 15.00 40.00
RB Ray Bourque SC 40.00 100.00
SY Steve Yzerman SC 50.00 120.00
TS Teemu Selanne 15.00 40.00
VL Vincent Lecavalier 15.00 40.00

2001-02 UD Top Shelf Patches

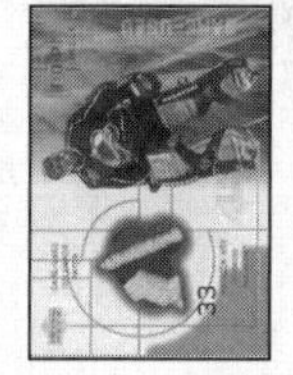

Inserted at 1:287, this 6-card set partially parallels the base jersey set but each card carried a patch swatch on the card front. Please note that the Brodeur card does not have a parent card in the base jersey set. Card backs carried a congratulatory message.

PJJ Jaromir Jagr 15.00 40.00
PMB Martin Brodeur 30.00 80.00
PMM Mike Modano 15.00 40.00
PPF Peter Forsberg 25.00 60.00
PPR Patrick Roy 30.00 80.00
PSY Steve Yzerman 30.00 80.00

2001-02 UD Top Shelf Rookie Redemption

Available in random packs of UD Rookie Update, this 10-card set of exchange cards were redeemable for a rookie who made his debut late in the 2001/02 season or in the 2002/03 season. Each card was serial-numbered to 100. Shortly after the products release, Upper Deck announced the first six players in the set. Those first six cards can be found at the end of the base set as they were numbered #136-141. The remaining 4 players were not announced until March of 2003 and carry a "TS" prefix.

TS1 Stanislav Chistov 10.00 25.00
TS2 Rick Nash 50.00 100.00
TS3 Henrik Zetterberg 40.00 80.00
TS4 Jason Spezza 50.00 125.00

2001-02 UD Top Shelf Sticks

Inserted at overall odds of 1:12, this 29-card set featured dime-sized pieces of game-used sticks from the featured player(s). Card fronts were silver-toned and carried a color picture of the featured player. Card backs carried a congratulatory message.

*SINGLE COLOR SWATCH: .25X TO .75X HI
SBH Brett Hull 8.00 20.00
SBS Brendan Shanahan 6.00 15.00
SCP Chris Pronger 6.00 15.00
SDH Dominik Hasek 8.00 20.00
SJL John LeClair 6.00 15.00
SJR Jeremy Roenick 8.00 20.00
SJS Joe Sakic 10.00 25.00
SKT Keith Tkachuk 6.00 15.00
SMB Martin Brodeur 20.00 50.00
SML Mario Lemieux 20.00 50.00
SMM Mark Messier 6.00 15.00
SNL Nicklas Lidstrom 6.00 15.00
SPB Peter Bondra 6.00 15.00
SPF Peter Forsberg 10.00 25.00
SPK Paul Kariya 6.00 15.00
SPR Patrick Roy 15.00 40.00
SRB Ray Bourque 10.00 25.00
SSF Sergei Fedorov 8.00 20.00
SSO Sandis Ozolinsh 6.00 15.00
SSY Steve Yzerman 12.50 30.00
STF Theo Fleury 6.00 15.00
SWG Wayne Gretzky 40.00 100.00
SZP Zigmund Palffy 6.00 15.00
SPBU Pavel Bure 6.00 15.00
BFJ Bure/Forsberg/Jagr 50.00 125.00
BPR Bourque/Pronger/Roy 60.00 150.00
KSF Kariya/Sakic/Fleury 40.00 100.00
LOH Lidstrom/Ozolinsh/Hasek 30.00 80.00
RSF Roy/Sakic/Forsberg 50.00 125.00

2002-03 UD Top Shelf

Released in August 2002 at an SRP of $4.99, this 165-card set featured 90 regular base cards and 45 rookie redemptions cards. Rookie redemption cards were redeemable for rookies who made their debut in the 2002-03 season. Cards 91-120 were serial-numbered to 1125 and cards 121-135 were serial-numbered to 500.

COMP.SET w/o SP's (90) 60.00 125.00
1 J-S Giguere .50 1.25
2 Jeff Friesen .20 .50
3 Paul Kariya .60 1.50
4 Ilya Kovalchuk .75 2.00
5 Dany Heatley .75 2.00
6 Joe Thornton 1.00 2.50
7 Sergei Samsonov .50 1.25
8 Bill Guerin .50 1.25
9 Martin Biron .50 1.25
10 Miroslav Satan .50 1.25
11 Maxim Afinogenov .20 .50
12 Jarome Iginla .75 2.00
13 Roman Turek .50 1.25
14 Craig Conroy .20 .50
15 Jeff O'Neill .20 .50
16 Arturs Irbe .50 1.25
17 Sami Kapanen .20 .50
18 Jocelyn Thibault .50 1.25
19 Eric Daze .50 1.25
20 Alexei Zhamnov .20 .50
21 Patrick Roy 3.00 8.00
22 Joe Sakic 1.25 3.00
23 Peter Forsberg 1.50 4.00
24 Marc Denis .50 1.25
25 Espen Knutsen .20 .50
26 Mike Modano 1.00 2.50
27 Jason Arnott .20 .50
28 Marty Turco .50 1.25
29 Steve Yzerman 3.00 8.00
30 Sergei Fedorov 1.00 2.50
31 Dominik Hasek 1.25 3.00
32 Brendan Shanahan .60 1.50
33 Ryan Smyth .20 .50
34 Tommy Salo .50 1.25
35 Mike Comrie .50 1.25
36 Roberto Luongo .75 2.00
37 Kristian Huselius .20 .50
38 Sandis Ozolinsh .20 .50
39 Zigmund Palffy .50 1.25
40 Jason Allison .20 .50
41 Felix Potvin .60 1.50
42 Manny Fernandez .50 1.25
43 Marian Gaborik 1.25 3.00
44 Andrew Brunette .20 .50
45 Jose Theodore .75 2.00
46 Saku Koivu .60 1.50

47 Richard Zednik .20 .50
48 Mike Dunham .50 1.25
49 David Legwand .50 1.25
50 Patrik Elias .50 1.25
51 Joe Nieuwendyk .50 1.25
52 Martin Brodeur 1.50 4.00
53 Scott Niedermayer .20 .50
54 Alexei Yashin .20 .50
55 Michael Peca .20 .50
56 Chris Osgood .50 1.25
57 Mike Richter .60 1.50
58 Pavel Bure .60 1.50
59 Eric Lindros .60 1.50
60 Martin Havlat .50 1.25
61 Patrick Lalime .50 1.25
62 Marian Hossa .60 1.50
63 Jeremy Roenick .75 2.00
64 Roman Cechmanek .50 1.25
65 John LeClair .60 1.50
66 Simon Gagne .60 1.50
67 Ladislav Nagy .20 .50
68 Sean Burke .50 1.25
69 Daniel Briere .20 .50
70 Johan Hedberg .50 1.25
71 Mario Lemieux 4.00 10.00
72 Alexei Kovalev .50 1.25
73 Evgeni Nabokov .50 1.25
74 Owen Nolan .50 1.25
75 Teemu Selanne .60 1.50
76 Brent Johnson .50 1.25
77 Keith Tkachuk .60 1.50
78 Chris Pronger .50 1.25
79 Brad Richards .50 1.25
80 Vincent Lecavalier .60 1.50
81 Nikolai Khabibulin .60 1.50
82 Alexander Mogilny .50 1.25
83 Mats Sundin .60 1.50
84 Curtis Joseph .60 1.50
85 Todd Bertuzzi .60 1.50
86 Brendan Morrison .50 1.25
87 Markus Naslund .60 1.50
88 Jaromir Jagr 1.00 2.50
89 Peter Bondra .60 1.50
90 Olaf Kolzig .50 1.25
91 Tim Thomas RC 6.00 15.00
92 Ivan Majesky RC 2.00 5.00
93 Jay Bouwmeester RC 6.00 15.00
94 Ron Hainsey RC 2.00 5.00
95 Ray Schultz RC 2.00 5.00
96 Tomi Pettinen RC 2.00 5.00
97 Eric Godard RC 2.00 5.00
98 Anton Volchenkov RC 2.00 5.00
99 Dennis Seidenberg RC 2.00 5.00
100 Radovan Somik RC 2.00 5.00
101 Patrick Sharp RC 2.00 5.00
102 Carlo Colaiacovo RC 2.00 5.00
103 Mikael Tellqvist RC 3.00 8.00
104 Steve Eminger RC 2.00 5.00
105 Alex Henry RC 2.00 5.00
106 Kurt Sauer RC 2.00 5.00
107 Micki Dupont RC 2.00 5.00
108 Shawn Thornton RC 2.00 5.00
109 Matt Henderson RC 2.00 5.00
110 Jeff Paul RC 2.00 5.00
111 Lasse Pirjeta RC 2.00 5.00
112 Dmitri Bykov RC 2.00 5.00
113 Kari Haakana RC 2.00 5.00
114 Sylvain Blouin RC 2.00 5.00
115 Stephane Veilleux RC 2.00 5.00
116 Greg Koehler RC 2.00 5.00
117 Lynn Loyns RC 2.00 5.00
118 Tom Koivisto RC 2.00 5.00
119 Curtis Sanford RC 3.00 8.00
120 Cody Rudkowsky RC 2.00 5.00
121 Martin Gerber RC 8.00 20.00
122 Alexei Smirnov RC 4.00 10.00
123 Stanislav Chistov RC 6.00 15.00
124 Jordan Leopold RC 6.00 15.00
125 Chuck Kobasew RC 6.00 15.00
126 Rick Nash RC 30.00 60.00
127 Henrik Zetterberg RC 12.00 30.00
128 Ales Hemsky RC 10.00 25.00
129 Alexander Frolov RC 10.00 25.00
130 P-M Bouchard RC 8.00 20.00
131 Adam Hall RC 6.00 15.00
132 Scottie Upshall RC 6.00 15.00
133 Jason Spezza RC 20.00 50.00
134 Jeff Taffe RC 6.00 15.00
135 Alexander Svitov RC 4.00 10.00

2002-03 UD Top Shelf All-Stars

*MULT.COLOR SWATCH: .75X TO 1.5X HI
PRINT RUN 50 SER.#'d SETS
ASGR Wayne Gretzky 75.00 200.00
ASJJ Jaromir Jagr 15.00 40.00
ASJS Joe Sakic 15.00 40.00
ASKT Keith Tkachuk 10.00 25.00
ASMS Mats Sundin 10.00 25.00
ASPK Paul Kariya 10.00 25.00
ASSF Sergei Fedorov 12.50 30.00
ASSS Scott Stevens 8.00 20.00
ASTA Tony Amonte 8.00 20.00
ASTF Theo Fleury 8.00 20.00
ASTS Teemu Selanne 10.00 25.00
ASWG Wayne Gretzky 75.00 200.00

2002-03 UD Top Shelf Clutch Performers

*MULT.COLOR SWATCH: .75X TO 1.5X HI
PRINT RUN 75 SER.#'d SETS
CPAD Adam Deadmarsh 6.00 15.00
CPAM Al MacInnis 6.00 15.00
CPBG Bill Guerin 6.00 15.00
CPBL Brian Leetch 6.00 15.00
CPBO Peter Bondra 8.00 20.00
CPBS Brendan Shanahan 8.00 20.00
CPCD Chris Drury 6.00 15.00
CPCJ Curtis Joseph 8.00 20.00
CPCL Claude Lemieux 6.00 15.00
CPDW Doug Weight 6.00 15.00
CPEB Ed Belfour 8.00 20.00
CPEL Eric Lindros 8.00 20.00
CPIK Ilya Kovalchuk 15.00 40.00
CPJI Jarome Iginla 10.00 25.00
CPJJ Jaromir Jagr 12.50 30.00
CPJN Joe Nieuwendyk 6.00 15.00
CPJR Jeremy Roenick 10.00 25.00
CPJS Joe Sakic 20.00 50.00
CPJT Joe Thornton 12.50 30.00
CPKT Keith Tkachuk 8.00 20.00
CPLR Luc Robitaille 6.00 15.00
CPMB Martin Brodeur 20.00 50.00
CPMH Milan Hejduk 8.00 20.00
CPML Mario Lemieux 25.00 60.00
CPMM Mike Modano 12.50 30.00
CPMR Mike Richter 8.00 20.00
CPMS Mats Sundin 8.00 20.00
CPNL Nicklas Lidstrom 8.00 20.00
CPPB Pavel Bure 8.00 20.00
CPPK Paul Kariya 8.00 20.00
CPPR Patrick Roy 25.00 60.00
CPRB Ray Bourque 20.00 50.00
CPSB Sean Burke 6.00 15.00
CPSF Sergei Fedorov 12.50 30.00
CPSGA Simon Gagne 8.00 20.00
CPSGO Sergei Gonchar 6.00 15.00
CPSSA Sergei Samsonov 6.00 15.00
CPSSU Steve Sullivan 6.00 15.00
CPSY Steve Yzerman 25.00 60.00
CPTS Teemu Selanne 8.00 20.00
CPWG Wayne Gretzky 50.00 125.00
CPZP Zigmund Palffy 6.00 15.00

2002-03 UD Top Shelf Dual Player Jerseys

Singles in this 42-card memorabilia set were serial-numbered out of 99.
RBD Marc Denis 12.50 30.00
Ed Belfour
RBK Pavel Bure 30.00 80.00
Ilya Kovalchuk
RBP Rob Blake 12.50 30.00
Chris Pronger
RBS Sergei Samsonov 12.50 30.00
Pavel Bure
RBZ Peter Bondra 12.50 30.00
Zigmund Palffy
RFA Sergei Fedorov 12.50 30.00
Maxim Afinogenov
RIW Jarome Iginla 20.00 50.00
Justin Williams
RKG Simon Gagne 12.50 30.00
Paul Kariya
RLK Rostislav Klesla 20.00 50.00
Nickalas Lidstrom
RMC Tim Connolly 12.50 30.00
Mike Modano
RNL David Legwand 12.50 30.00
Joe Nieuwendyk
RPB Felix Potvin 12.50 30.00
Martin Biron
RPT Joe Thornton 12.50 30.00
Keith Primeau
RRT Patrick Roy 40.00 100.00
Jose Theodore
RSF Ruslan Fedotenko 12.50 30.00
Miroslav Satan
RSH Scott Hartnell 12.50 30.00
Brendan Shanahan
RSR Steven Reinprecht 12.50 30.00
Steve Sullivan
RYK K.Kolanos/S.Yzerman 30.00 80.00
STAB Eric Belanger 12.50 30.00
Jason Allison
STBB Ray Bourque 30.00 80.00
Rob Blake
STBD Daniel Briere 12.50 30.00
Shane Doan
STBE Brian Leetch 12.50 30.00
Pavel Bure
STBJ Jaromir Jagr 15.00 40.00
Peter Bondra
STBL Roberto Luongo 12.50 30.00
Valeri Bure
STBN Martin Biron 12.50 30.00
Mika Noronen
STBS M.Brodeur/S.Stevens 20.00 50.00
STBT Joe Thornton 30.00 80.00
Ray Bourque
STDE Martin Erat 12.50 30.00
Mike Dunham
STDT Eric Daze 12.50 30.00
Jocelyn Thibault
STFL Nicklas Lidstrom 12.50 30.00
Sergei Fedorov
STFP Keith Primeau 12.50 30.00
Ruslan Fedotenko
STFR Mike Richter 25.00 60.00
Theo Fleury
STGB Brian Boucher 12.50 30.00
Simon Gagne
STGD Bill Guerin 12.50 30.00
Byron Dafoe
STGK Olaf Kolzig 12.50 30.00
Sergei Gonchar
STGM Mark Messier 75.00 200.00
Wayne Gretzky
STGR Mark Recchi 12.50 30.00
Simon Gagne
STGS J-S Giguere 12.50 30.00
Steve Shields
STHL David Legwand 12.50 30.00
Scott Hartnell
STHR Milan Hejduk 12.50 30.00
Steven Reinprecht
STIS Jarome Iginla 12.50 30.00
Marc Savard
STJK Jaromir Jagr 12.50 30.00
Olaf Kolzig
STKB Krys Kolanos 12.50 30.00
Sean Burke
STKF Jeff Friesen 15.00 40.00
Paul Kariya
STKT Jose Theodore 15.00 40.00
Saku Koivu
STKW Ray Whitney 12.50 30.00
Rostislav Klesla
STLD Claude Lemieux 12.50 30.00
Shane Doan
STMA Jason Arnott 12.50 30.00
Mike Modano
STMM Brenden Morrow 15.00 40.00
Mike Modano
STNL Markus Naslund 12.50 30.00
Trevor Linden
STPD Adam Deadmarsh 12.50 30.00
Zigmund Palffy
STSA Maxim Afinogenov 12.50 30.00
Miroslav Satan
STSH Dan Hinote 15.00 40.00
Joe Sakic
STSM Steve Sullivan 12.50 30.00
Tony Amonte
STSN Owen Nolan 15.00 40.00
Teemu Selanne
STST Joe Thornton 15.00 40.00
Sergei Samsonov
STTD Marc Denis 20.00 50.00
Ron Tugnutt
STTG Bill Guerin 12.50 30.00
Joe Thornton
STYH Jochen Hecht 12.50 30.00
Mike York
STYS Brendan Shanahan 20.00 50.00
Steve Yzerman

2002-03 UD Top Shelf Goal Oriented

*MULT.COLOR SWATCH: .75X TO 1.5X HI
PRINT RUN 75 SER.#'d SETS
GOAD Adam Deadmarsh 10.00 25.00
GOAT Alex Tanguay 10.00 25.00
GOBG Bill Guerin 10.00 25.00
GOBO Peter Bondra 10.00 25.00
GODA Denis Arkhipov 10.00 25.00
GODB Daniel Briere 10.00 25.00
GOED Eric Daze 10.00 25.00
GOGM Glen Murray 10.00 25.00
GOIK Ilya Kovalchuk 15.00 40.00
GOJJ Jaromir Jagr 12.50 30.00
GOJS Joe Sakic 15.00 40.00
GOJT Joe Thornton 12.50 30.00
GOMA Mats Sundin 10.00 25.00
GOMH Milan Hejduk 10.00 25.00
GOMM Mike Modano 12.50 30.00
GOMS Miroslav Satan 10.00 25.00
GOMY Mike York 10.00 25.00
GOPB Pavel Bure 10.00 25.00
GOPK Paul Kariya 10.00 25.00
GORD Radek Dvorak 10.00 25.00
GORL Robert Lang 10.00 25.00
GOSF Sergei Fedorov 15.00 40.00
GOSG Simon Gagne 10.00 25.00
GOSR Steven Reinprecht 10.00 25.00
GOSS Sergei Samsonov 10.00 25.00
GOSU Steve Sullivan 10.00 25.00
GOSY Steve Yzerman 20.00 50.00
GOTA Tony Amonte 10.00 25.00
GOTS Teemu Selanne 10.00 25.00
GOZP Zigmund Palffy 10.00 25.00

2002-03 UD Top Shelf Hardware Heroes

This 10-card memorabilia set featured quad jersey swatches. Each card was limited to 10 copies each. This set is not priced due to scarcity.
HBRBD Ed Belfour
Patrick Roy
Martin Brodeur
Mike Dunham
HFYGC Fedrv/Yze./Glmr/Clrke
HGKSD Wayne Gretzky
Paul Kariya
Joe Sakic
Pavol Demitra
HGSLJ Grtzky/Sak/Lem./Jagr
HHBRK Dominik Hasek
Ed Belfour
Patrick Roy
Olaf Kolzig
HHGLJ Howe/Grtzky/Lem./Jagr
HPMBL Chris Pronger
Al MacInnis
Rob Blake
Nicklas Lidstrom
HSRBF Joe Sakic
Patrick Roy
Rob Blake
Peter Forsberg
HSSBR Sergei Samsonov
Teemu Selanne
Pavel Bure
Luc Robitaille
HYNLR Yze./Nie-dyk/Ltch/Roy

2002-03 UD Top Shelf Milestones Jerseys

This 10-card memorabilia set featured quad jersey swatches. Each card was serial-numbered out of 25.
MBBRR Jeremy Roenick 50.00 125.00
Mark Recchi
Pavel Bure
Peter Bondra
MBMBS Ray Bourque 100.00 250.00
Pavel Bure
Teemu Selanne
Mike Modano
MGBYM Grtz./Brqe/Mess./Yze. 300.00 800.00
MGHLY Grtz./Lem./Hwe/Yze. 500.00 1000.00
MHPBJ Sean Burke 50.00 125.00
Felix Potvin
Tom Barrasso
Dominik Hasek
MLNLA Tony Amonte 50.00 125.00
John LeClair
Eric Lindros
Owen Nolan
MMHYR Mess./Hull/Robit./Yze. 300.00 600.00
MRBRJ Roy/Brodr./Cujo/Richtr 200.00 400.00
MSFRM Theo Fleury 50.00 125.00
Brendan Shanahan
Jeremy Roenick
Mark Messier
MSYVR Shan./Yze./Vbeek/Robit. 150.00 300.00

2002-03 UD Top Shelf Shooting Stars

*MULT.COLOR SWATCH: .75X TO 1.5X
SHAR Jason Arnott 8.00 20.00
SHAT Alex Tanguay 8.00 20.00
SHBG Bill Guerin 8.00 20.00
SHBH Brett Hull 12.50 30.00
SHBL Brian Leetch 8.00 20.00
SHBM Brenden Morrow 8.00 20.00
SHBO Peter Bondra 10.00 25.00
SHBS Brendan Shanahan 10.00 25.00
SHDB Daniel Briere 8.00 20.00
SHEK Espen Knutsen 8.00 20.00
SHGM Glen Murray 8.00 20.00
SHJA Jason Allison 8.00 20.00
SHJJ Jaromir Jagr 12.50 30.00
SHJN Joe Nieuwendyk 8.00 20.00
SHKK Krys Kolanos 8.00 20.00
SHLE Rob Blake 8.00 20.00
SHMA Maxim Afinogenov 8.00 20.00
SHMH Milan Hejduk 10.00 25.00
SHML Mario Lemieux 30.00 80.00
SHMM Mike Modano 12.50 30.00
SHMSA Miroslav Satan 8.00 20.00
SHMSU Mats Sundin 10.00 25.00
SHMY Mike York 8.00 20.00
SHNA Nikolai Antropov 8.00 20.00
SHNL Nicklas Lidstrom 10.00 25.00
SHPB Pavel Bure 10.00 25.00
SHPF Peter Forsberg 15.00 40.00
SHPK Paul Kariya 10.00 25.00
SHRB Ray Bourque 15.00 40.00
SHRL Robert Lang 8.00 20.00
SHSD Shane Doan 8.00 20.00
SHSF Sergei Fedorov 12.50 30.00
SHSG Simon Gagne 10.00 25.00
SHSH Scott Hartnell 8.00 20.00
SHSK Saku Koivu 10.00 25.00
SHSR Steven Reinprecht 8.00 20.00
SHSS Steve Sullivan 8.00 20.00
SHSY Steve Yzerman 25.00 60.00
SHTA Tony Amonte 8.00 20.00
SHTF Theo Fleury 8.00 20.00
SHTS Teemu Selanne 10.00 25.00
SHZP Zigmund Palffy 8.00 20.00

2002-03 UD Top Shelf Signatures

Inserted at one per box, this 36-card set featured authentic autographs of the featured players. The Yzerman card was a redemption in pack.
AK Alexei Kovalev 6.00 15.00
BB Brian Boucher SP 8.00 20.00
BG Bill Guerin 6.00 15.00
BL Rob Blake 6.00 15.00
BO Bobby Orr/96 150.00 250.00
DH Dany Heatley 12.50 30.00
DS Daniel Sedin 6.00 15.00
DW Doug Weight/92 12.50 30.00
GH Gordie Howe/27 150.00 400.00
HA Martin Havlat 8.00 20.00
HS Henrik Sedin 6.00 15.00
JA Jason Allison SP 6.00 15.00
JH Johan Hedberg SP 6.00 15.00
JI Jarome Iginla 10.00 25.00
JL John LeClair 8.00 20.00
MB Martin Biron SP 6.00 15.00
MC Mike Comrie 6.00 15.00
MH Milan Hejduk 8.00 20.00
MN Markus Naslund 8.00 20.00
MO Maxime Ouellet 6.00 15.00
PA Pavel Brendl 6.00 15.00
PB Pavel Bure 8.00 20.00
PE Peter Bondra 6.00 15.00
PR Patrick Roy SP 50.00 125.00
RB Ray Bourque SP 25.00 60.00
RD Rick DiPietro 6.00 15.00
RK Rostislav Klesla SP 8.00 20.00
RT Raffi Torres 6.00 15.00
SG Simon Gagne 8.00 20.00
SH Scott Hartnell 6.00 15.00
SS Sergei Samsonov 6.00 15.00
TH Jose Theodore 10.00 25.00
TS Tommy Salo 6.00 15.00
WG Wayne Gretzky/95 150.00 300.00
ZP Zigmund Palffy 6.00 15.00

2002-03 UD Top Shelf Stopper Jerseys

Singles in this 54-card memorabilia set were serial-numbered out of 99.
*MULT.COLOR SWATCH: .75X TO 1.5X
SSBB Brian Boucher 10.00 25.00
SSBD Byron Dafoe 10.00 25.00
SSBI Martin Biron 10.00 25.00
SSBJ Brent Johnson 10.00 25.00
SSCJ Curtis Joseph 10.00 25.00
SSDA David Aebischer 10.00 25.00
SSDB Dan Blackburn 10.00 25.00
SSDH Dominik Hasek 15.00 40.00
SSDU Mike Dunham 10.00 25.00
SSEB Ed Belfour 12.50 30.00
SSFP Felix Potvin 12.50 30.00
SSJGO J-S Giguere 10.00 25.00
SSJTO Jocelyn Thibault 10.00 25.00
SSMB Martin Brodeur 20.00 50.00
SSMD Marc Denis 10.00 25.00
SSMN Mika Noronen 10.00 25.00
SSMR Mike Richter 12.50 30.00
SSOK Olaf Kolzig 10.00 25.00
SSPR Patrick Roy 20.00 50.00
SSRC Roman Cechmanek 10.00 25.00
SSRT Ron Tugnutt 10.00 25.00
SSSB Sean Burke 10.00 25.00
SSSS Steve Shields 10.00 25.00
SSTH Jose Theodore 12.50 30.00

2002-03 UD Top Shelf Sweet Sweaters

*MULT.COLOR SWATCH: .75X TO 1.5X HI
PRINT RUN 50 SER.#'d SETS
SWAD Adam Deadmarsh 10.00 25.00
SWAT Alex Tanguay 10.00 25.00
SWBE Mark Bell 10.00 25.00
SWBG Bill Guerin 10.00 25.00
SWBH Brett Hull 20.00 50.00
SWCD Chris Drury 10.00 25.00
SWCJ Curtis Joseph 10.00 25.00
SWCL Claude Lemieux 10.00 25.00
SWDB Daniel Briere 10.00 25.00
SWDE Marc Denis 10.00 25.00
SWDG Doug Gilmour 10.00 25.00
SWFP Felix Potvin 10.00 25.00
SWJA Jason Allison 10.00 25.00
SWJF Jeff Friesen 10.00 25.00
SWJJ Jaromir Jagr 12.50 30.00
SWJO Joe Thornton 15.00 40.00
SWJS Joe Sakic 25.00 60.00
SWJT Jocelyn Thibault 10.00 25.00
SWKP Keith Primeau 10.00 25.00
SWKT Keith Tkachuk 10.00 25.00
SWMA Maxim Afinogenov 10.00 25.00
SWMB Martin Biron 10.00 25.00
SWMD Mike Dunham 10.00 25.00
SWMM Mike Modano 15.00 40.00
SWMS Mats Sundin 10.00 25.00
SWOK Olaf Kolzig 10.00 25.00
SWPB Pavel Bure 10.00 25.00
SWPK Paul Kariya 10.00 25.00
SWRB Ray Bourque 30.00 80.00
SWRK Rostislav Klesla 10.00 25.00
SWSA Miroslav Satan 10.00 25.00
SWSF Sergei Fedorov 15.00 40.00
SWSK Saku Koivu 10.00 25.00
SWSR Steven Reinprecht 10.00 25.00
SWSS Sergei Samsonov 10.00 25.00
SWSU Steve Sullivan 10.00 25.00
SWSY Steve Yzerman 30.00 80.00
SWTH Jose Theodore 12.50 30.00
SWTS Teemu Selanne 10.00 25.00
SWVN Ville Nieminen 10.00 25.00
SWWG Wayne Gretzky 75.00 200.00
SWZP Zigmund Palffy 10.00 25.00

2002-03 UD Top Shelf Triple Jerseys

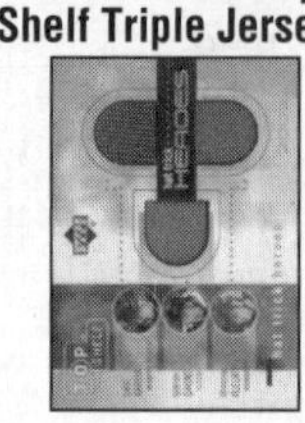

These triple jersey memorabilia cards were randomly inserted into packs. The " Hat Trick" subset cards were serial-numbered out of 25 and the "Three Stars" subset was serial-numbered to just 10 sets and was not priced due to scarcity.
HTAPS Tony Amonte 40.00 100.00
Zigmund Palffy
Teemu Selanne
HTBSB Peter Bondra 40.00 100.00
Pavel Bure
Miroslav Satan
HTGHB Bill Guerin 40.00 100.00
Peter Bondra
Marian Hossa
HTGLB Wayne Gretzky 300.00 600.00
Mario Lemieux
Pavel Bure
HTJHS Milan Hejduk 40.00 100.00
Jaromir Jagr
Teemu Selanne
HTKGF Simon Gagne 40.00 100.00
Paul Kariya
Theo Fleury
HTKYI Iginla/Kariya/Yzerman 150.00300.00
HTLJT Joe Thornton 125.00 250.00
Jaromir Jagr
Mario Lemieux
HTLRR Jeremy Roenick 125.00 250.00
John LeClair
Mark Recchi
HTNTH Milan Hejduk 40.00 100.00
Joe Thornton
Markus Naslund
HTSHR Brendan Shanahan 100.00 200.00
Brett Hull
Luc Robitaille
HTSIG Joe Sakic 60.00 150.00
Jarome Iginla
Simon Gagne
TSAPP Felix Potvin
Jason Allison
Zigmund Palffy
TSASB Martin Biron
Maxim Afinogenov
Miroslav Satan
TSDPJ Brent Johnson
Chris Pronger
Pavol Demitra
TSGTD Bill Guerin
Byron Dafoe
Joe Thornton
TSJBK Jaromir Jagr
Olaf Kolzig
Peter Bondra
TSLGC John LeClair
Roman Cechmanek
Simon Gagne
TSMMB Brenden Morrow
Ed Belfour
Mike Modano
TSSAT Jocelyn Thibault
Steve Sullivan
Tony Amonte
TSSYH Brendan Shanahan
Dominik Hasek
Steve Yzerman
TSTSR Alex Tanguay
Joe Sakic
Patrick Roy

2003 UD Toronto Fall Expo Priority Signings

This 11-card set was part of a wrapper redemption at the Upper Deck booth during the 2003 Fall Expo. Each card was hand serial-numbered and individual print runs were listed below.
CJ Curtis Joseph/41 20.00 50.00
DH Dany Heatley/25 30.00 80.00
GH Gordie Howe/40 60.00 150.00
IK Ilya Kovalchuk/78 20.00 50.00
JI Jarome Iginla/57 20.00 50.00
JS Jason Spezza/110 15.00 40.00
JT Joe Thornton/107 15.00 40.00
MB Martin Brodeur/70 50.00 125.00
PB Pavel Bure/29 25.00 60.00
PR Patrick Roy/44 75.00 200.00
RB Ray Bourque/75 25.00 60.00

2004 UD Toronto Fall Expo Pride of Canada

This 26-card set was available only at the Upper Deck booth during the 2004 Toronto Fall Expo. Each card was serial-numbered out of 75.
COMPLETE SET (26) 125.00 250.00
1 Martin Brodeur 15.00 40.00
2 Roberto Luongo 6.00 15.00
3 Jose Theodore 8.00 20.00
4 Jay Bouwmeester 4.00 10.00
5 Eric Brewer 4.00 10.00
6 Adam Foote 4.00 10.00
7 Scott Hannan 4.00 10.00
8 Ed Jovanovski 4.00 10.00
9 Scott Niedermayer 4.00 10.00
10 Wade Redden 4.00 10.00
11 Robyn Regehr 4.00 10.00
12 Shane Doan 4.00 10.00
13 Kris Draper 4.00 10.00
14 Simon Gagne 5.00 12.00
15 Dany Heatley 6.00 15.00
16 Jarome Iginla 8.00 20.00
17 Vincent Lecavalier 8.00 20.00
18 Mario Lemieux 15.00 40.00
19 Kirk Maltby 4.00 10.00
20 Patrick Marleau 4.00 10.00
21 Brenden Morrow 4.00 10.00
22 Brad Richards 4.00 10.00
23 Joe Sakic 10.00 25.00
24 Martin St. Louis 4.00 10.00
25 Ryan Smyth 4.00 10.00
26 Joe Thornton 6.00 15.00

2004 UD Toronto Fall Expo Priority Signings

Available only via wrapper redemption during the 2004 Toronto Fall Expo, this 28-card set featured authentic player autographs. Print runs are listed below. Please note, due to a production error, the Tootoo card was pulled from the redemption program though a few copies are known to have been released.
PRINT RUNS UNDER 25
NOT PRICED DUE TO SCARCITY
AH Ales Hemsky/50 10.00 25.00
AY Alexei Yashin/50 10.00 25.00
BU Pavel Bure/10
CK Chuck Kobasew/49 10.00 25.00
GR Wayne Gretzky/25 200.00 300.00
HO Marian Hossa/52 12.50 30.00
JI Jarome Iginla/7
JL John LeClair/50 10.00 25.00
JR Jeremy Roenick/31 40.00 80.00
JS Jason Spezza/39 25.00 60.00
JT Jordin Tootoo ERR
MB Martin Brodeur/14
MG Marian Gaborik/26
MH Martin Havlat/50 12.50 30.00
MN Markus Naslund/50 12.50 30.00
MP Mark Parrish/50 8.00 20.00
MT Marty Turco/35 20.00 50.00
PB Pavel Bure/60 12.50 30.00
PE Mike Peca/27 20.00 50.00
PR Patrick Roy/33 75.00 150.00
RD Rick DiPietro/20
RL Roberto Luongo/50 12.50 30.00
RN Rick Nash/61 30.00 80.00
RO Patrick Roy/10
SF Sergei Fedorov/3
SH Scott Hartnell/78 8.00 20.00
TB Todd Bertuzzi/44 20.00 50.00
WG Wayne Gretzky/9

2005 UD Toronto Fall Expo Priority Signings

PRINT RUNS UNDER 25 NOT PRICED DUE TO SCARCITY
PS-DH Dominik Hasek/5
PS-BO Brooks Orpik/40 6.00 15.00
PS-AH Ales Hemsky/22
PS-ST Matt Stajan/70 10.00 25.00
PS-AF Alexander Frolov/40 20.00 50.00

PS-PS Philippe Sauve/63 6.00 15.00
PS-DA David Aebischer/2
PS-JT Joe Thornton/5
PS-HO Marian Hossa/9
PS-RM Ryan Malone/62 10.00 25.00
PS-TB Todd Bertuzzi/10
PS-JL John LeClair/20
PS-BE Patrice Bergeron/62 12.00 30.00
PS-AY Alexei Yashin/20
PS-RO Patrick Roy/10
PS-MH Martin Havlat/24
PS-TE Tony Esposito/5
PS-TR Tuomo Ruutu/62 10.00 25.00
PS-JI Jarome Iginla/10
PS-JS Jason Spezza/10
PS-SM Stan Mikita/1
PS-MP Mark Parrish/20
PS-TH Trent Hunter/61 10.00 25.00
PS-BU Pavel Bure/10
PS-RY Michael Ryder/60 20.00 50.00
PS-LU Joffrey Lupul/64 10.00 25.00
PS-PB P-M Bouchard/61 8.00 20.00
PS-MB Martin Brodeur/5
PS-JC Jonathan Cheechoo/61 12.00 30.00
PS-ML Matthew Lombardi/61 6.00 15.00
PS-RL Roberto Luongo/20
PS-JG J-S Giguere/5
PS-GR Wayne Gretzky/25 250.00 400.00
PS-MG Marian Gaborik/10
PS-MT Marty Turco/20
PS-SL Martin St. Louis/10
PS-AR Andrew Raycroft/63 10.00 25.00
PS-SY Steve Yzerman/2
PS-RN Rick Nash/20
PS-HS Marcel Hossa/16
PS-PE Michael Peca/20
PS-RT Raffi Torres/60 10.00 25.00
PS-ES Eric Staal/62 25.00 60.00
PS-WG Wayne Gretzky/5
PS-MM Mike Modano/10
PS-MN Markus Naslund/10
PS-GH Gordie Howe/15
PS-NZ Nikolai Zherdev/61 10.00 25.00
PS-PR Patrick Roy/3

2006 UD Toronto Fall Expo Priority Signings

AVAIL. AS REDEMPTION ONLY AT EXPO
PRINT RUNS UNDER 25 NOT PRICED DUE TO SCARCITY
PSAA Aaron Asham/75 4.00 10.00
PSAK Andrei Kostitsyn/10
PSAL Andrew Ladd/10
PSAP Alexandre Picard/10
PSAS Alexander Steen/50 12.00 30.00
PSBB Brad Boyes/50 10.00 25.00
PSBO Jay Bouwmeester/26 12.00 30.00
PSBR Brad Richardson/41 8.00 20.00
PSBS Brent Seabrook/53
PSCH Chris Higgins/82 12.00 30.00
PSDP Dion Phaneuf/15 50.00 80.00
PSFS Fredrik Sjostrom/94 4.00 10.00
PSGB Gilbert Brule/21 25.00 60.00
PSGH Gordie Howe/11
PSHL Henrik Lundqvist/26 30.00 60.00
PSJB Jason Blake/75 6.00 15.00
PSJC Jeff Carter/3
PSJS Jason Spezza/11
PSJT Jeff Tambellini/52 4.00 10.00
PSMB Martin Brodeur/11
PSMG Marian Gaborik/10
PSMP Michael Peca/20
PSMR Mike Richards/4
PSPB Pierre-Marc Bouchard/6
PSRN Robert Nilsson/58 4.00 10.00
PSRU R.J. Umberger/10
PSRW Ryan Whitney/65 8.00 20.00
PSSB Steve Bernier/12
PSSC Sidney Crosby/35 175.00 250.00
PSTV Thomas Vanek/42 20.00 40.00
PSWC Wendel Clark/6
PSWG1 Wayne Gretzky/9
PSWG2 Wayne Gretzky/4
PSZP Zach Parise/12

1998-99 UD3

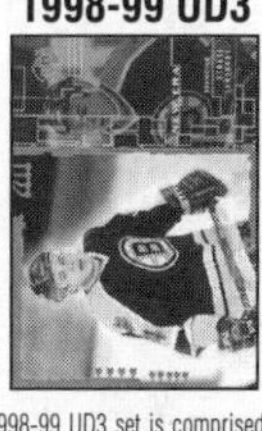

The 1998-99 UD3 set is comprised of six 60-card subsets each printed with three different technologies and features color action player photos. The Embossed technology subsets include New Era (1-30) inserted 1:1 and Three Star Spotlight (151-180) inserted 1:23. The Light F/X technology subsets include new Era (61-90) inserted 1:1 and Three Star Spotlight (91-120). The Rainbow Foil technology subsets include New Era (121-150) inserted 1:5 and Three Star Spotlight (31-60) inserted 1:1.

COMPLETE SET (180) 300.00 500.00
1 Sergei Samsonov NE .40 1.00
2 Ryan Johnson NE RC .30 .75
3 Josef Marha NE .30 .75
4 Patrick Marleau NE .30 .75
5 Derek Morris NE .30 .75
6 Jamie Storr NE .40 1.00
7 Richard Zednik NE .30 .75
8 Alyn McCauley NE .30 .75
9 Robert Dome NE .30 .75
10 Patrik Elias NE .40 1.00
11 Olli Jokinen NE .40 1.00
12 Warren Luhning NE .30 .75
13 Chris Phillips NE .30 .75
14 Mattias Ohlund NE .40 1.00
15 Joe Thornton NE .75 2.00
16 Matt Cullen NE .30 .75
17 Bates Battaglia NE .30 .75
18 Andrei Zyuzin NE .30 .75
19 Cameron Mann NE .30 .75
20 Zdeno Chara NE .30 .75
21 Marc Savard NE .30 .75
22 Alexei Morozov NE .30 .75
23 Mike Johnson NE .40 1.00
24 Vaclav Varada NE .30 .75
25 Dan Cloutier NE .30 .75
26 Brad Isbister NE .30 .75
27 Marco Sturm NE .30 .75
28 Anders Eriksson NE .30 .75
29 Jan Bulis NE .30 .75
30 Brendan Morrison NE .40 1.00
31 Wayne Gretzky TR 2.50 6.00
32 Jaromir Jagr TR .60 1.50
33 Peter Forsberg TR 1.00 2.50
34 Paul Kariya TR .40 1.00
35 Brett Hull TR .50 1.25
36 Martin Brodeur TR 1.00 2.50
37 Eric Lindros TR .50 1.25
38 Peter Bondra TR .40 1.00
39 Mike Modano TR .60 1.50
40 Theo Fleury TR .40 1.00
41 Curtis Joseph TR .40 1.00
42 Sergei Fedorov TR .60 1.50
43 Saku Koivu TR .40 1.00
44 Zigmund Palffy TR .40 1.00
45 Ed Belfour TR .40 1.00
46 Patrick Roy TR 2.00 5.00
47 Brendan Shanahan TR .40 1.00
48 Mats Sundin TR .40 1.00
49 Alexei Yashin TR .40 1.00
50 Doug Gilmour TR .40 1.00
51 Chris Osgood TR .40 1.00
52 Keith Tkachuk TR .40 1.00
53 Mark Messier TR .50 1.25
54 John Vanbiesbrouck TR .40 1.00
55 Ray Bourque TR .60 1.50
56 John LeClair TR .50 1.25
57 Dominik Hasek TR .75 2.00
58 Teemu Selanne TR .40 1.00
59 Joe Sakic TR .75 2.00
60 Steve Yzerman TR 2.00 5.00
61 Sergei Samsonov NF .40 1.00
62 Ryan Johnson NF .30 .75
63 Josef Marha NF .30 .75
64 Patrick Marleau NF .30 .75
65 Derek Morris NF .30 .75
66 Jamie Storr NF .40 1.00
67 Richard Zednik NF .30 .75
68 Alyn McCauley NF .30 .75
69 Robert Dome NF .30 .75
70 Patrik Elias NF .40 1.00
71 Olli Jokinen NF .40 1.00
72 Warren Luhning NF .30 .75
73 Chris Phillips NF .30 .75
74 Mattias Ohlund NF .40 1.00
75 Joe Thornton NF .75 2.00
76 Matt Cullen NF .30 .75
77 Bates Battaglia NF .30 .75
78 Andrei Zyuzin NF .30 .75
79 Cameron Mann NF .40 1.00
80 Zdeno Chara NF .30 .75
81 Marc Savard NF .30 .75
82 Alexei Morozov NF .40 1.00
83 Mike Johnson NF .40 1.00
84 Vaclav Varada NF .30 .75
85 Dan Cloutier NF .30 .75
86 Brad Isbister NF .30 .75
87 Marco Sturm NF .40 1.00
88 Anders Eriksson NF .30 .75
89 Jan Bulis NF .30 .75
90 Brendan Morrison NF .40 1.00
91 Wayne Gretzky TF 4.00 10.00
92 Jaromir Jagr TF 1.00 2.50
93 Peter Forsberg TF 1.50 4.00
94 Paul Kariya TF .75 2.00
95 Brett Hull TF .75 2.00
96 Martin Brodeur TF 1.50 4.00
97 Eric Lindros TF .75 2.00
98 Peter Bondra TF .75 2.00
99 Mike Modano TF 1.00 2.50
100 Theo Fleury TF .60 1.50
101 Curtis Joseph TF .75 2.00
102 Sergei Fedorov TF 1.00 2.50
103 Saku Koivu TF .75 2.00
104 Zigmund Palffy TF .75 2.00
105 Ed Belfour TF .75 2.00
106 Patrick Roy TF 3.00 8.00
107 Brendan Shanahan TF .75 2.00
108 Mats Sundin TF .75 2.00
109 Alexei Yashin TF .60 1.50
110 Doug Gilmour TF .75 2.00
111 Chris Osgood TF .75 2.00
112 Keith Tkachuk TF .75 2.00
113 Mark Messier TF .50 1.25
114 John Vanbiesbrouck TF .60 1.50
115 Ray Bourque TF 1.00 2.50
116 John LeClair TF .50 1.25
117 Dominik Hasek TF 1.25 3.00
118 Teemu Selanne TF .75 2.00
119 Joe Sakic TF 1.25 3.00
120 Steve Yzerman TF 3.00 8.00
121 Sergei Samsonov NR 1.25 3.00
122 Ryan Johnson NR 1.00 2.50
123 Josef Marha NR 1.00 2.50
124 Patrick Marleau NR 1.00 2.50
125 Derek Morris NR 1.00 2.50
126 Jamie Storr NR 1.25 3.00
127 Richard Zednik NR 1.00 2.50
128 Alyn McCauley NR 1.00 2.50
129 Robert Dome NR 1.00 2.50
130 Patrik Elias NR 1.25 3.00
131 Olli Jokinen NR 1.25 3.00
132 Warren Luhning NR 1.00 2.50
133 Chris Phillips NR 1.00 2.50
134 Mattias Ohlund NR 1.25 3.00
135 Joe Thornton NR 2.50 6.00
136 Matt Cullen NR 1.00 2.50
137 Bates Battglia NR 1.00 2.50
138 Andrei Zyuzin NR 1.00 2.50
139 Cameron Mann NR 1.00 2.50
140 Zdeno Chara NR 1.00 2.50
141 Marc Savard NR 1.00 2.50
142 Alexei Morozov NR 1.25 3.00
143 Mike Johnson NR 1.25 3.00
144 Vaclav Varada NR 1.00 2.50
145 Dan Cloutier NR 1.00 2.50
146 Brad Isbister NR 1.00 2.50
147 Marco Sturm NR 1.25 3.00
148 Anders Eriksson NR 1.00 2.50
149 Jan Bulis NR 1.00 2.50
150 Brendan Morrison NR 2.00 5.00
151 Wayne Gretzky TE 25.00 60.00
152 Jaromir Jagr TE 6.00 15.00
153 Peter Forsberg TE 10.00 25.00
154 Paul Kariya TE 4.00 10.00
155 Brett Hull TE 5.00 12.00
156 Martin Brodeur TE 10.00 25.00
157 Eric Lindros TE 4.00 10.00
158 Peter Bondra TE 4.00 10.00
159 Mike Modano TE 6.00 15.00
160 Theo Fleury TE 1.00 2.50
161 Curtis Joseph TE 1.50 4.00
162 Sergei Fedorov TE 6.00 15.00
163 Saku Koivu TE 4.00 10.00
164 Zigmund Palffy TE 4.00 10.00
165 Ed Belfour TE 4.00 10.00
166 Patrick Roy TE 20.00 50.00
167 Brendan Shanahan TE 4.00 10.00
168 Mats Sundin TE 4.00 10.00
169 Alexei Yashin TE 4.00 10.00
170 Doug Gilmour TE 4.00 10.00
171 Chris Osgood TE 4.00 10.00
172 Keith Tkachuk TE 4.00 10.00
173 Mark Messier TE .50 1.25
174 John Vanbiesbrouck TE 4.00 10.00
175 Ray Bourque TE 6.00 15.00
176 John LeClair TE 4.00 10.00
177 Dominik Hasek TE 8.00 20.00
178 Teemu Selanne TE 4.00 10.00
179 Joe Sakic TE 8.00 20.00
180 Steve Yzerman TE 20.00 50.00

1998-99 UD3 Die-Cuts

This 180-card set is a limited edition die-cut parallel version of the base set. The New Era and Three Star Spotlight SE Light F/X cards versions (61-120) are sequentially numbered to 1,000. The New Era Embossed cards (1-30) are sequentially numbered to 200 with the Three Star Spotlight Embossed ones (151-180) sequentially numbered to 100. The New Era Rainbow cards (121-150) are sequentially numbered to 50. The Three Star Spotlight Rainbow ones (31-60) are numbered 1 of 1. Cards 31-60 are not priced due to scarcity.

*DIECUTS 1-30: 6X TO 15X BASIC INSERTS
*DIECUTS 61-90: 2X TO 5X
*DIECUTS 91-120: 2X TO 5X
*DIECUTS 121-150: 10X to 25X
*DIECUTS 151-180: 2.5X TO 6X

2004-05 Ultimate Collection

Released in early-summer 2005, this 84-card set is was packaged in 4-card packs that contained 1 serial-numbered base card, 1 autograph card, 1 memorabilia card and 1 serial-numbered subset card or extra base card. Cards 1-48 were serial-numbered to 350 and the World Cup subset cards (#59-84) were serial-numbered to 299.

1 J-S Giguere 1.50 4.00
2 Dany Heatley 2.50 6.00
3 Ilya Kovalchuk 2.50 6.00
4 Joe Thornton 2.50 6.00
5 Chris Drury 1.50 4.00
6 Jarome Iginla 2.50 6.00
7 Miikka Kiprusoff 1.50 4.00
8 Eric Staal 1.50 4.00
9 Jocelyn Thibault 1.50 4.00
10 Peter Forsberg 2.50 6.00
11 Joe Sakic 3.00 8.00
12 Rick Nash 2.00 5.00
13 Mike Modano 2.00 5.00
14 Pavel Datsyuk 1.50 4.00
15 Gordie Howe 3.00 8.00
16 Steve Yzerman 5.00 12.00
17 Wayne Gretzky 8.00 20.00
18 Ryan Smyth 1.50 4.00
19 Roberto Luongo 2.50 6.00
20 Luc Robitaille 1.50 4.00
21 Marian Gaborik 2.50 6.00
22 Patrick Roy 6.00 15.00
23 Jose Theodore 2.00 5.00
24 Tomas Vokoun 1.50 4.00
25 Martin Brodeur 6.00 15.00
26 Jaromir Jagr 3.00 8.00
27 Mark Messier 2.00 5.00
28 Michael Peca 1.50 4.00
29 Dominik Hasek 3.00 8.00
30 Jason Spezza 2.00 5.00
31 Jeremy Roenick 2.00 5.00
32 Simon Gagne 2.00 5.00
33 Brett Hull 2.00 5.00
34 Mario Lemieux 6.00 15.00
35 Evgeni Nabokov 1.50 4.00
36 Keith Tkachuk 2.00 5.00
37 Vincent Lecavalier 2.00 5.00
38 Martin St. Louis 1.50 4.00
39 Mats Sundin 2.00 5.00
40 Ed Belfour 2.00 5.00
41 Markus Naslund 2.00 5.00
42 Olaf Kolzig 1.50 4.00
43 Brad Fast RC 1.50 4.00
44 Brennan Evans RC 1.50 4.00
45 Layne Ulmer RC 1.50 4.00
46 Mel Angelstad RC 1.50 4.00
47 Garret Stroshein RC 1.50 4.00
48 Marcel Goc RC 2.50 6.00
49 Alexander Ragulin RC 1.50 4.00
50 Herb Brooks 1.50 4.00
51 Cammie Granato RC 1.50 4.00
52 Foster Hewitt 1.50 4.00
53 Mike Keenan 2.00 5.00
54 Bob Cole 1.50 4.00
55 Lord Stanley 2.00 5.00
56 James Norris 2.00 5.00
57 Ken Hitchcock 1.50 4.00
58 Dave Reece 2.00 5.00
59 Mario Lemieux WC 6.00 15.00
60 Joe Thornton WC 3.00 8.00
61 Dany Heatley WC 2.50 6.00
62 Jarome Iginla WC 2.50 6.00
63 Joe Sakic WC 4.00 10.00
64 Vincent Lecavalier WC 2.00 5.00
65 Martin Brodeur WC 6.00 15.00
66 Jaromir Jagr WC 4.00 10.00
67 Milan Hejduk WC 1.50 4.00
68 Miikka Kiprusoff WC 2.00 5.00
69 Tuomo Ruutu WC 1.50 4.00
70 Teemu Selanne WC 2.00 5.00
71 Marco Sturm WC 1.50 4.00
72 Olaf Kolzig WC 1.50 4.00
73 Ilya Kovalchuk WC 2.50 6.00
74 Sergei Samsonov WC 1.50 4.00
75 Marian Hossa WC 1.50 4.00
76 Marian Gaborik WC 3.00 8.00
77 Nicklas Lidstrom WC 1.50 4.00
78 Mats Sundin WC 1.50 4.00
79 Peter Forsberg WC 2.50 6.00
80 Robert Esche WC 1.50 4.00
81 Mike Modano WC 2.00 5.00
82 Bill Guerin WC 1.50 4.00
83 Tony Amonte WC 1.50 4.00
84 Keith Tkachuk WC 1.50 4.00

2004-05 Ultimate Collection Buybacks

This 96-cards set featured cards that were "bought back" by UD, signed by the players, serial-numbered and then re-inserted into this product. Each card carried a UD hologram and a "Buyback" certificate card.

LOWER PRINT RUNS NOT PRICED DUE TO SCARCITY
1 Alex Tanguay 15.00 40.00
2002-2003 Upper Deck MVP MVP Souvenirs/28
2 Bobby Clarke
2003-2004 Trilogy Crest of Honor/12
3 Brad Richards
2001-02 Premier Base Card/1
4 Chris Drury 12.50 30.00
2002-2003 Upper Deck MVP Skate Around Jersey/32
5 Dominik Hasek
2000-01 Upper Deck Game Jersey Patches/1
6 Dominik Hasek
2001-2002 UD Mask Collection Goalie Pads/3
7 Dominik Hasek
2001-2002 UD Top Shelf Goalie Gear/7
8 Dominik Hasek
2000-2001 MVP Super Game-Used Souvenirs/5
9 Dominik Hasek
2002-03 SPx Winning Materials/1
10 Eric Staal
2003-2004 Honor Roll Dean's List/12
11 Gordie Howe
2003-2004 UD Trilogy Base Card/1
12 Gordie Howe
2003-2004 UD Trilogy Crest of Honor/12
13 Gordie Howe
2001-2002 Legends Sticks/9
14 Guy Lafleur
2003-2004 UD Trilogy Base Card/1
15 Guy Lafleur
2002-2003 UD Trilogy Crest of Honor/15
16 Ilya Kovalchuk
2003-04 UD Premier Base Card/2
17 Ilya Kovalchuk
2002-2003 Upper Deck Difference Makers/6
18 Ilya Kovalchuk
2003-04 Upper Deck Ice Ice Breakers/1
19 Ilya Kovalchuk
2001-2002 SPx Rookie Treasures/1
20 Jari Kurri
2002-2003 UD Trilogy Crest of Honor/14
21 Jarome Iginla
2001-2002 Upper Deck Next Generation Jerseys/11
22 Jarome Iginla
2002-2003 SP Game-Used Piece of History Gold/5
23 Jarome Iginla
2002-03 UD Premier Jerseys Silver/1
24 Jarome Iginla
2003-04 UD Premier Stars/1
25 Jarome Iginla
2001-2002 UD Top Shelf Jerseys/3
26 Jason Spezza 25.00 60.00
2000-2001 Upper Deck Prospects Game Jerseys/51
27 Jay Bouwmeester
2003-04 UD Trilogy Base Card/1
28 Jay Bouwmeester 15.00 40.00
2000-2001 Upper Deck Prospects Game Jerseys/56
29 Jeremy Roenick
2003-04 UD Premier Base Card/1
30 Jeremy Roenick
2001-2002 UD Mask Collection Great Gloves/8
31 Jeremy Roenick
2000-2001 UD SP Game-Used Tools of the Game/3
32 Jeremy Roenick
2000-2001 SPx Winning Materials Update/9
33 Joe Thornton
2003-04 UD Premier Base Card/1
34 Joe Thornton
2001-2002 UD SP Game-Used Authentic Fabrics/2
35 Joe Thornton
2002-2003 SP Game-Used Authentic Fabrics Gold/3
36 Joe Thornton
2002-2003 Upper Deck Difference Makers/8
37 Joe Thornton 25.00 60.00
2000-2001 UD Ice Game Jerseys Update/22
38 Joe Thornton
2002-2003 SP Game-Used Patches/2
39 Joe Thornton
2002-2003 SP Game-Used Piece of History/2
40 Joe Thornton 25.00 60.00
2002-2003 Upper Deck MVP Skate Around Jersey/24
41 Joe Thornton
2002-2003 SP Game-Used Tools of the Game/1
42 Joe Thornton
2000-2001 SPx Winning Materials Update/6
43 Jose Theodore
2001-2002 Mask Collection Stellar Stickhandlers/3
44 Jose Theodore
2001-2002 Upper Deck MVP Authentic Goalies/8
45 Jose Theodore 40.00 100.00
2001-2002 UD Mask Collection Goalie Pads/23
46 Jose Theodore 40.00 100.00
2001-2002 UD Top Shelf Goalie Gear/18
47 Jose Theodore
2002-2003 SP Game Used Piece of History /3
48 Jose Theodore
2001-2002 UD Mask Collection Super Stoppers/6
49 Jose Theodore
2002-2003 SP Game Used Patches/6
50 Marc-Andre Fleury
2003-2004 UD Honor Roll Dean's List/15
51 Markus Naslund
2001-02 UD Premier Base Card/1
52 Markus Naslund
2003-04 UD Premier Base Card/1
53 Markus Naslund
2003-04 UD Trilogy Base Card/1
54 Markus Naslund
2003-04 Uper Deck Big Playmakers/1
55 Markus Naslund
2002-2003 SP Game Used Patches/3
56 Markus Naslund
2002-2003 SP Game Used Piece of History Gold/2
57 Markus Naslund 15.00 40.00
2001-2002 UD Top Shelf Jerseys/17
58 Martin St. Louis
2003-04 UD Trilogy Base Card/1
59 Martin St. Louis
2003-04 Black Diamond Base Card/1
60 Marty Turco
2003-04 Upper Deck Big Playmakers/1
61 Marty Turco 20.00 50.00
2002-2003 Upper Deck MVP MVP Souvenirs/26
62 Marty Turco
2003-04 UD Rookie Update Superstars Jersey/1
63 Mika Noronen
2001-2002 SP Game Used Authentic Fabrics/21
64 Mika Noronen 12.50 30.00
2001-2002 UD Mask Collection Goalie Jerseys/22
65 Milan Hejduk
2001-2002 Upper Deck Stanley Cup Finals Single Jersey/9
66 Milan Hejduk 12.50 30.00
2001-2002 Upper Deck MVP Morning Skate Jerseys/20
67 Milan Hejduk
2002-03 SP Game Used Pieces of History/1
68 Milan Hejduk
2001-2002 UD Playmakers Player's Club Practice Jersey/8
69 Milan Hejduk 15.00 40.00
2001-2002 UD Top Shelf Jerseys/22
70 Nathan Horton
2003-2004 Honor Roll Dean's List/11
71 Patrick Roy
2000-2001 UD Ice Game Jerseys Update/12
71R Patrick Roy EXCH
72 Patrick Roy
2001-2002 Upper Deck Patch Names/1
73 Patrick Roy
2001-2002 Upper Deck Patch Numbers/2
74 Ray Bourque
2001-2002 UD Challenge for the Cup Franchise Players/7
75 Ray Bourque
2000-2001 Upper Deck MVP Super Game-Used Souvenirs/5
76 Ray Bourque
2000-2001 SPx Winning Materials Update/2
77 R.Nash Trilogy/3
78 Roberto Luongo
2003-04 Upper Deck Big Playmakers/1
79 Roberto Luongo
2002-03 SP Game Used Tools of the Game/2
80 Roberto Luongo
2001-2002 UD Top Shelf Goalie Gear/10
81 Roberto Luongo
2002-03 SP Game Used First Rounder Patches/1
82 Roberto Luongo
2000-2001 MVP Super Game-Used Souvenirs/5
83 Roberto Luongo
2001-2002 UD Mask Collection Super Stoppers/7
84 Roberto Luongo
2000-2001 SPx Winning Materials Update/10
85 Saku Koivu
2003-04 UD Premier Base Card/1
86 Saku Koivu
2001-2002 Upper Deck Pride of a Nation/7
87 Zigmund Palffy
2001-2002 SP Game Used Authentic Fabrics/23
87R Zigmund Palffy EXCH 15.00 40.00
88 Zigmund Palffy
2001-2002 Upper Deck MVP Combo MVP Souvenirs/7
89 Zigmund Palffy
2002-2003 Upper Deck Difference Makers/9
90 Zigmund Palffy
2001-2002 UD Playmakers Player's Club Jersey/7
91 Zigmund Palffy
2001-2002 UD Mask Collection Jerseys/5
92 Zigmund Palffy 15.00 40.00
2001-2002 Upper Deck Phenomenal Finishers/19
93 Zigmund Palffy
2000-2001 Upper Deck MVP Super Game-Used Souvenirs/5
94 Zigmund Palffy 12.50 30.00
2001-2002 Upper Deck MVP MVP Souvenirs/26
95 Zigmund Palffy
2001-2002 UD Top Shelf Sticks/6
96 Zigmund Palffy 12.50 30.00
2001-2002 UD Top Shelf Jerseys/23

2004-05 Ultimate Collection Dual Logos

This 41-card patch set featured the NHL shields from game-used jerseys of two players. Each card was serial-numbered 1/1.

NOT PRICED DUE TO SCARCITY
UL2-AF David Aebischer/Peter Forsberg
UL2-BB Ray Bourque/Ray Bourque
UL2-BE Martin Brodeur/Patrik Elias
UL2-BF Rob Blake/Adam Foote
UL2-BG Martin Brodeur/Jean Sebastian Giguere
UL2-BS Eddie Belfour/Mats Sundin
UL2-FG Sergei Fedorov/Jean-Sebastien Giguere
UL2-FS Peter Forsberg/Joe Sakic
UL2-GL W.Gretzky/M.Lemieux
UL2-GM Wayne Gretzky/Mark Messier
UL2-HA Dominik Hasek/Daniel Alfredsson
UL2-HF Milan Hejduk/Peter Forsberg
UL2-HJ Dominik Hasek/Curtis Joseph
UL2-IK Jarome Iginla/Miikka Kiprusoff
UL2-IL Jarome Iginla/Vincent LeCavalier
UL2-IS Jarome Iginla/Ryan Smith
UL2-KL Nikolai Khabibulin/Vincent Lecavalier
UL2-KS Paul Kariya/Teemu Selanne
UL2-KT Saku Koivu/Jose Theodore
UL2-LB Roberto Luongo
Martin Brodeur
UL2-LL Martin St. Louis/Vincent Lecavalier
UL2-LP John LeClair/Keith Primeau
UL2-MD Michael Peca/Rick DiPietro
UL2-MP Al MacInnis/Chris Pronger
UL2-MT M.Modano/M.Turco
UL2-NM Markus Naslund/Brendan Morrison
UL2-NR Nicklas Lidstrom/Rob Blake
UL2-NT Cam Neely/Joe Thornton
UL2-NZ R.Nash/N.Zherdev
UL2-RB P.Roy/M.Brodeur
UL2-RG Jeremy Roenick/Simon Gagne
UL2-RL P.Roy/M.Lemieux
UL2-SH Jason Spezza/Marian Hossa
UL2-SL Brendan Shanahan/Nicklas Lidstrom
UL2-SR Mats Sundin/Gary Roberts
UL2-ST Joe Sakic/Joe Thornton
UL2-SY J.Sakic/S.Yzerman
UL2-TL J.Thornton/M.Lemieux
UL2-TR Jose Theodore/Patrick Roy
UL2-VT Tomas Vokoun/Jordin Tootoo
UL2-WT Doug Weight/Keith Tkachuk

2004-05 Ultimate Collection Jerseys

PRINT RUN 250 SER.#'d SETS
UGJ-AT Alex Tanguay 4.00 10.00
UGJ-BC Bobby Clarke 5.00 12.00
UGJ-BH Bobby Hull 8.00 20.00
UGJ-BO Mike Bossy 4.00 10.00
UGJ-BT Bryan Trottier 4.00 10.00
UGJ-CJ Curtis Joseph 4.00 10.00
UGJ-DH Dany Heatley 6.00 15.00
UGJ-DO Dominik Hasek 8.00 20.00
UGJ-GH Gordie Howe 15.00 40.00
UGJ-GL Guy Lafleur 8.00 20.00
UGJ-HE Milan Hejduk 4.00 10.00
UGJ-JB Johnny Bucyk 4.00 10.00
UGJ-JI Jarome Iginla 6.00 15.00
UGJ-JJ Jaromir Jagr 10.00 25.00
UGJ-JK Jari Kurri 5.00 12.00
UGJ-JO Jose Theodore 5.00 12.00
UGJ-JR Jeremy Roenick 5.00 12.00
UGJ-JS Joe Sakic 10.00 25.00
UGJ-JT Joe Thornton 8.00 20.00
UGJ-MB Martin Brodeur 10.00 25.00
UGJ-MH Marian Hossa 4.00 10.00
UGJ-ML Mario Lemieux 15.00 40.00
UGJ-MM Mark Messier 8.00 20.00
UGJ-MN Markus Naslund 4.00 10.00
UGJ-MO Mike Modano 5.00 12.00
UGJ-MS Martin St.Louis 4.00 10.00
UGJ-NK Nikolai Khabibulin 4.00 10.00
UGJ-NZ Nikolai Zherdev 4.00 10.00
UGJ-PF Peter Forsberg 6.00 15.00
UGJ-PK Paul Kariya 4.00 10.00
UGJ-RB Ray Bourque 5.00 12.00
UGJ-RN Rick Nash 5.00 12.00
UGJ-SK Saku Koivu 4.00 10.00
UGJ-SP Jason Spezza 5.00 12.00
UGJ-SU Mats Sundin 4.00 10.00
UGJ-SY Steve Yzerman 10.00 25.00
UGJ-VL Vincent Lecavalier 4.00 10.00
UGJ-PR1 Patrick Roy 15.00 40.00
UGJ-PR2 Patrick Roy 15.00 40.00
UGJ-WG1 Wayne Gretzky AS 30.00 80.00
UGJ-WG2 Wayne Gretzky EDM 30.00 80.00

2004-05 Ultimate Collection Jerseys Gold

*GOLD: .75X TO 2X JSY HI
PRINT RUN 75 SER.#'d SETS

2004-05 Ultimate Collection Jersey Autographs

PRINT RUN 5 SER.#'d SETS
NOT PRICED DUE TO SCARCITY
UGJA-MB Martin Brodeur
UGJA-NZ Nikolai Zherdev
UGJA-JT Joe Thornton
UGJA-MN Markus Naslund
UGJA-AT Alex Tanguay
UGJA-JK Jari Kurri
UGJA-GL Guy Lafleur
UGJA-NK Nikolai Khabibulin
UGJA-BT Bryan Trottier
UGJA-BC Bobby Clarke
UGJA-MS Martin St.Louis
UGJA-VL Vincent Lecavalier
UGJA-RB Ray Bourque
UGJA-SP Jason Spezza
UGJA-BH Bobby Hull
UGJA-JO Jose Theodore
UGJA-JR Jeremy Roenick
UGJA-JB Johnny Bucyk
UGJA-JI Jarome Iginla
UGJA-DH Dany Heatley
UGJA-RN Rick Nash
UGJA-HE Milan Hejduk
UGJA-BO Mike Bossy
UGJA-GH Gordie Howe
UGJA-DO Dominik Hasek
UGJA-SK Saku Koivu
UGJA-PR1 Patrick Roy COL
UGJA-WG1 Wayne Gretzky AS
UGJA-PR2 Patrick Roy MTL
UGJA-WG2 Wayne Gretzky EDM

2004-05 Ultimate Collection Patches

*SINGLE COLOR SWATCH: .25X TO .5X HI
*4+ COLOR SWATCH: .75X TO 2X
UNIQUENESS OF PATCH MAY EARN UP TO 50% PREMIUM
PRINT RUN 35 SER.#'d SETS
UP-BL Brian Leetch 60.00 150.00
UP-NZ Nikolai Zherdev 30.00 80.00
UP-HE Milan Hejduk 30.00 80.00
UP-JJ Jaromir Jagr 60.00 150.00
UP-SF Sergei Fedorov 30.00 80.00

UP-JG J-S Giguere 40.00 100.00
UP-MB Martin Brodeur 75.00 200.00
UP-NK Nikolai Khabibulin 30.00 80.00
UP-ML Mario Lemieux 200.00 400.00
UP-VL Vincent Lecavalier 40.00 100.00
UP-JO Jose Theodore 40.00 100.00
UP-TK Keith Tkachuk 30.00 80.00
UP-PF Peter Forsberg 50.00 125.00
UP-JS Joe Sakic 75.00 200.00
UP-HA Dominik Hasek 40.00 100.00
UP-SK Saku Koivu 40.00 100.00
UP-SP Jason Spezza 40.00 100.00
UP-JR Jeremy Roenick 30.00 80.00
UP-IK Ilya Kovalchuk 50.00 125.00
UP-SY Steve Yzerman 125.00 250.00
UP-MO Mike Modano 40.00 100.00
UP-JT Joe Thornton 75.00 150.00
UP-BT Bryan Trottier 30.00 80.00
UP-BS Brendan Shanahan 40.00 100.00
UP-RN Rick Nash 50.00 125.00
UP-MM Mark Messier 75.00 200.00
UP-CJ Curtis Joseph 50.00 125.00
UP-EB Ed Belfour 50.00 125.00
UP-BH Brett Hull 40.00 100.00
UP-MH Marian Hossa 40.00 100.00
UP-SU Mats Sundin 30.00 80.00
UP-PK Paul Kariya/9
UP-MS Martin St.Louis 30.00 80.00
UP-RB1 Ray Bourque BOS 75.00 200.00
UP-WG1 Wayne Gretzky LA/25 275.00 600.00
UP-PR1 Patrick Roy COL 150.00 350.00
UP-RB2 Ray Bourque COL 75.00 200.00
UP-PR2 Patrick Roy MTL 150.00 400.00
UP-WG2 Wayne Gretzky AS/25 250.00 500.00
UP-DHA Dany Heatley JSY 30.00 80.00
UP-DHB Dany Heatley PATCH 50.00125.00
UP-MNA Markus Naslund JSY 25.0060.00
UP-MNB Markus Naslund PATCH 30.00 80.00

2004-05 Ultimate Collection Patch Autographs

*SINGLE COLOR SWATCH: .25X TO .5X HI
UNIQUENESS OF PATCH MAY EARN
UP TO 50% PREMIUM
SNGL.PRINT RUN 50 SER.#'d SETS
DUAL PRINT RUN 10 SER.#'d SETS
DUAL NOT PRICED DUE TO SCARCITY
UPA-AT Alex Tanguay 40.00 100.00
UPA-BR Brad Richards EXCH 30.00 80.00
UPA-CD Chris Drury 30.00 80.00
UPA-DH Dany Heatley 60.00 150.00
UPA-DO Dominik Hasek 75.00 200.00
UPA-EJ Ed Jovanovski 40.00 100.00
UPA-JB Jay Bouwmeester 30.00 80.00
UPA-JI Jarome Iginla 50.00 125.00
UPA-JK Jari Kurri 50.00 125.00
UPA-JO Jose Theodore 50.00 125.00
UPA-JR Jeremy Roenick 40.00 100.00
UPA-JT Joe Thornton 60.00 150.00
UPA-MB Martin Brodeur 200.00 400.00
UPA-MD Marcel Dionne 40.00 100.00
UPA-MH Milan Hejduk 30.00 80.00
UPA-MN Markus Naslund 30.00 80.00
UPA-MS Martin St.Louis 40.00 100.00
UPA-MT Marty Turco 40.00 100.00
UPA-NK Nikolai Khabibulin 50.00 125.00
UPA-NZ Nikolai Zherdev 30.00 60.00
UPA-PR Patrick Roy 200.00 400.00
UPA-RB Ray Bourque 60.00 150.00
UPA-RL Roberto Luongo 60.00 150.00
UPA-RN Rick Nash 125.00 250.00
UPA-SK Saku Koivu 40.00 100.00
UPA-SP Jason Spezza 75.00 150.00
UPA-VL Vincent Lecavalier 50.00 125.00
UPA-WG1 Wayne Gretzky AS 250.00 500.00
UPA-WG2 Wayne Gretzky LA 250.00500.00
UPA-ARJT Andrew Raycroft/Joe Thornton
UPA-ATMH Alex Tanguay/Milan Hejduk
UPA-BRMS Brad Richards/Martin St. Louis
UPA-CNRB Cam Neely/Ray Bourque
UPA-GHCN Gordie Howe/Cam Neely
UPA-IKRN I.Kovalchuk/R.Nash
UPA-JIVL Jarome Iginla/Vincent LeCavalier
UPA-PRJO Patrick Roy/Jose Theodor
UPA-PRMB P.Roy/M.Brodeur
UPA-RBJB Ray Bourque/Jay Bouwmeester
UPA-WGGH Gordie Howe/Wayne Gretzky
UPA-WGJK Wayne Gretzky/Jari Kurri

2004-05 Ultimate Collection Signatures

This 42-card set was seeded at one per pack. Known shortprints are listed below.
US-BL Brian Leetch 6.00 15.00
US-SP Jason Spezza 12.50 30.00
US-JI Jarome Iginla 12.50 30.00
US-ES Eric Staal 12.00 30.00
US-MB Martin Brodeur SP 60.00 150.00
US-BH Bobby Hull SP 50.00 125.00
US-SK Saku Koivu SP 12.50 30.00
US-NH Nathan Horton 4.00 10.00
US-VL Vincent Lecavalier SP 25.00 60.00
US-JB Jay Bouwmeester 6.00 15.00
US-ZP Zigmund Palffy 4.00 10.00
US-GH Gordie Howe 40.00 80.00
US-DH Dany Heatley 10.00 25.00
US-BB Brad Boyes 4.00 10.00
US-MS Martin St. Louis 6.00 15.00
US-MH Milan Hejduk 4.00 10.00
US-HA Dominik Hasek SP 30.00 80.00
US-CD Chris Drury 4.00 10.00
US-BT Bryan Trottier SP 12.50 30.00
US-KD Kris Draper 4.00 10.00
US-JK Jari Kurri 10.00 25.00
US-RL Roberto Luongo SP 15.00 40.00
US-KL Kari Lehtonen 8.00 20.00
US-NK Nikolai Khabibulin 8.00 20.00
US-MR Michael Ryder 8.00 20.00
US-BR Brad Richards 6.00 15.00
US-MN Markus Naslund 6.00 15.00
US-RN Rick Nash SP 25.00 60.00
US-EJ Ed Jovanovski 4.00 10.00
US-MA Marc-Andre Fleury 12.50 30.00
US-JT Joe Thornton 12.50 30.00
US-BC Bobby Clarke 10.00 25.00
US-NZ Nikolai Zherdev 6.00 15.00
US-MT Marty Turco 4.00 10.00
US-AR Andrew Raycroft 6.00 15.00
US-IK Ilya Kovalchuk 15.00 40.00
US-JO Jose Theodore SP 50.00 100.00
US-HZ Henrik Zetterberg 8.00 20.00
US-AT Alex Tanguay 4.00 10.00
US-PR1 Patrick Roy SP 250.00 400.00
US-RB1 Ray Bourque SP 25.00 60.00
US-WG1 Wayne Gretzky 100.00 250.00

2004-05 Ultimate Collection Signature Logos

This 40-card set featured certified autographs and the NHL shield patch from game-used player jerseys. Each card was serial-numbered 1/1.
PRINT RUN 1 SER.#'d SET
NOT PRICED DUE TO SCARCITY
ULA-JK Jari Kurri
ULA-BT Bryan Trottier
ULA-DH Dany Heatley
ULA-NK Nikolai Khabibulin
ULA-SG Simon Gagne
ULA-CD Chris Drury
ULA-JI Jarome Iginla
ULA-NZ Nikolai Zherdev
ULA-ES Eric Staal
ULA-BL Brian Leetch
ULA-MB Martin Brodeur
ULA-KD Kris Draper
ULA-JT Joe Thornton
ULA-BR Brad Richards
ULA-ZP Zigmund Palffy
ULA-MR Michael Ryder
ULA-MS Martin St. Louis
ULA-NH Nathan Horton
ULA-MT Marty Turco
ULA-HA Dominik Hasek
ULA-EJ Ed Jovanovski
ULA-MH Milan Hejduk
ULA-SK Saku Koivu
ULA-RL Roberto Luongo
ULA-JO Jose Theodore
ULA-AT Alex Tanguay
ULA-VL Vincent Lecavalier
ULA-AR Andrew Raycroft
ULA-RN Rick Nash
ULA-MN Markus Naslund
ULA-KP Keith Primeau
ULA-JR Jeremy Roenick
ULA-SP Jason Spezza
ULA-RB1 Ray Bourque
ULA-PR1 Patrick Roy
ULA-WG1 Wayne Gretzky NYR
ULA-PR2 Patrick Roy
ULA-WG2 Wayne Gretzky LA
ULA-RB2 Ray Bourque
ULA-WG3 Wayne Gretzky AS

2004-05 Ultimate Collection Signature Patches

This 41-card set featured certified autographs directly on game-used jersey patches. Cards were serial-numbered out of 10.
NOT PRICED DUE TO SCARCITY
SP-MS Martin St. Louis
SP-RN Rick Nash
SP-KD Kris Draper
SP-VL Vincent Lecavalier
SP-JR Jeremy Roenick
SP-ZP Ziggy Palffy
SP-KP Keith Primeau
SP-MB Martin Brodeur
SP-PR Patrick Roy
SP-NH Nathan Horton
SP-SP Jason Spezza
SP-RB Ray Bourque
SP-ES Eric Staal
SP-SK Saku Koivu
SP-NK Nikolai Khabibulin
SP-EJ Ed Jovanovski
SP-MT Marty Turco
SP-KL Kari Lehtonen
SP-CD Chris Drury
SP-MR Michael Ryder
SP-NZ Nikolai Zherdev
SP-HZ Henrik Zetterberg
SP-BU Johnny Bucyk
SP-HA Dominik Hasek
SP-JI Jarome Iginla
SP-AR Andrew Raycroft
SP-MH Milan Hejduk
SP-JB Jay Bouwmeester
SP-RL Roberto Luongo
SP-AT Alex Tanguay
SP-BL Brian Leetch
SP-MN Markus Naslund
SP-BR Brad Richards
SP-JK Jari Kurri
SP-BT Bryan Trottier
SP-JT Joe Thornton
SP-JO Jose Theodore
SP-DH Dany Heatley
SP-WG1 Wayne Gretzky EDM/5
SP-WG2 Wayne Gretzky LA
SP-WG3 Wayne Gretzky NYR

2004-05 Ultimate Collection Ultimate Cuts

This 9-card set featured "cut" signatures of past greats.
PRINT RUN 1 SER.#'d SET
NOT PRICED DUE TO SCARCITY
UC-PI Punch Imlach
UC-TB Toe Blake
UC-BM Bill Mosienko
UC-BP Babe Pratt
UC-KC King Clancy
UC-DH Doug Harvey
UC-HD Hap Day
UC-BH Bryan Hextall Sr.
UC-BD Bob Davidson

2005-06 Ultimate Collection

1 Teemu Selanne 2.00 5.00
2 Jean-Sebastien Giguere 1.50 4.00
3 Joffrey Lupul 1.25 3.00
4 Ilya Kovalchuk 3.00 8.00
5 Marian Hossa 2.00 5.00
6 Kari Lehtonen 1.50 4.00
7 Andrew Raycroft 1.50 4.00
8 Brad Boyes 1.25 3.00
9 Patrice Bergeron 2.00 5.00
10 Brian Leetch 2.00 5.00
11 Glen Murray 1.25 3.00
12 Chris Drury 1.25 3.00
13 Martin Biron 1.50 4.00
14 Daniel Briere 1.25 3.00
15 Jarome Iginla 2.50 6.00
16 Miikka Kiprusoff 1.50 4.00
17 Doug Weight 1.25 3.00
18 Eric Staal 1.50 4.00
19 Nikolai Khabibulin 2.00 5.00
20 Tuomo Ruutu 1.25 3.00
21 Marek Svatos 1.25 3.00
22 Joe Sakic 4.00 10.00
23 Jose Theodore 2.00 5.00
24 Rob Blake 1.25 3.00
25 Alex Tanguay 1.50 4.00
26 Milan Hejduk 1.50 4.00
27 Rick Nash 3.00 8.00
28 Sergei Fedorov 2.00 5.00
29 Mike Modano 2.50 6.00
30 Bill Guerin 1.25 3.00
31 Marty Turco 2.00 5.00
32 Steve Yzerman 6.00 15.00
33 Nicklas Lidstrom 2.00 5.00
34 Gordie Howe 4.00 10.00
35 Brendan Shanahan 2.00 5.00
36 Pavel Datsyuk 2.00 5.00
37 Henrik Zetterberg 2.00 5.00
38 Ryan Smyth 1.50 4.00
39 Chris Pronger 1.50 4.00
40 Ales Hemsky 1.25 3.00
41 Wayne Gretzky 10.00 25.00
42 Roberto Luongo 2.50 6.00
43 Olli Jokinen 1.25 3.00
44 Jeremy Roenick 2.50 6.00
45 Pavol Demitra 1.25 3.00
46 Luc Robitaille 1.50 4.00
47 Marian Gaborik 2.50 6.00
48 David Aebischer 1.50 4.00
49 Michael Ryder 1.25 3.00
50 Saku Koivu 2.00 5.00
51 Mike Ribeiro 1.25 3.00
52 Tomas Vokoun 1.50 4.00
53 Paul Kariya 2.00 5.00
54 Martin Brodeur 5.00 12.00
55 Patrik Elias 1.25 3.00
56 Rick DiPietro 1.50 4.00
57 Alexei Yashin 1.25 3.00
58 Miroslav Satan 1.25 3.00
59 Jaromir Jagr 3.00 8.00
60 Dominik Hasek 2.50 6.00
61 Dany Heatley 2.50 6.00
62 Jason Spezza 1.50 4.00
63 Martin Havlat 1.25 3.00
64 Daniel Alfredsson 1.50 4.00
65 Peter Forsberg 2.50 6.00
66 Simon Gagne 1.50 4.00
67 Robert Esche 1.50 4.00
68 Keith Primeau 1.25 3.00
69 Curtis Joseph 1.50 4.00
70 Shane Doan 1.25 3.00
71 Mario Lemieux 6.00 15.00
72 Ryan Malone 1.25 3.00
73 Marc-Andre Fleury 1.50 4.00
74 Joe Thornton 3.00 8.00
75 Evgeni Nabokov 1.50 4.00
76 Jonathan Cheechoo 1.50 4.00
77 Patrick Marleau 1.50 4.00
78 Keith Tkachuk 1.50 4.00
79 Brad Richards 1.50 4.00
80 Martin St. Louis 1.50 4.00
81 Vincent Lecavalier 2.00 5.00
82 Bryan McCabe 1.25 3.00
83 Eric Lindros 2.00 5.00
84 Ed Belfour 2.00 5.00
85 Mats Sundin 2.00 5.00
86 Markus Naslund 2.00 5.00
87 Brendan Morrison 1.25 3.00
88 Todd Bertuzzi 2.00 5.00
89 Ed Jovanovski 1.25 3.00
90 Olaf Kolzig 1.25 3.00
91 Sidney Crosby AU RC 900.00 1200.00
92 Alexander Ovechkin AU RC 200.00 350.00
93 Gilbert Brule AU RC 20.00 50.00
94 Corey Perry AU RC 25.00 50.00
95 Jeff Carter AU RC 30.00 60.00
96 Alexander Steen AU RC 25.00 60.00
97 Henrik Lundqvist AU RC 50.00 100.00
98 Hannu Toivonen AU RC 20.00 40.00
99 Alexander Perezhogin AU RC 20.0040.00
100 Thomas Vanek AU RC 50.00 100.00
101 Ryan Getzlaf AU RC 30.00 80.00
102 Braydon Coburn AU RC 8.00 20.00
103 Milan Jurcina AU RC 8.00 20.00
104 Andrew Alberts AU RC 8.00 20.00
105 Dion Phaneuf AU RC 40.00 80.00
106 Eric Nystrom AU RC 8.00 20.00
107 Cam Ward AU RC 25.00 50.00
108 Cam Barker AU RC 8.00 20.00
109 Brent Seabrook AU RC 8.00 20.00
110 Rene Bourque AU RC 8.00 20.00
111 Peter Budaj AU RC 12.00 30.00
112 Wojtek Wolski AU RC 20.00 50.00
113 Jussi Jokinen AU RC 15.00 40.00
114 Jim Howard AU RC 15.00 40.00
115 Johan Franzen AU RC 8.00 20.00
116 Brad Winchester AU RC 8.00 20.00
117 Rostislav Olesz AU RC 12.00 30.00
118 Anthony Stewart AU RC 10.00 25.00
119 Matt Foy AU RC 6.00 15.00
120 Yann Danis AU RC 8.00 20.00
121 Ryan Suter AU RC 10.00 25.00
122 Zach Parise AU RC 20.00 50.00
123 Robert Nilsson AU RC 8.00 20.00
124 Alvaro Montoya AU RC 15.00 40.00
125 Petr Prucha AU RC 15.00 40.00
126 Brandon Bochenski AU RC 8.00 20.00
127 Andrej Meszaros AU RC 10.00 25.00
128 Patrick Eaves AU RC 12.00 30.00
129 Mike Richards AU RC 15.00 40.00
130 Keith Ballard AU RC 8.00 20.00
131 Ryane Clowe AU RC 10.00 25.00
132 Jeff Woywitka AU RC 6.00 15.00
133 Michael Wall RC 4.00 10.00
134 Zenon Konopka RC 3.00 8.00
135 Jim Slater RC 4.00 10.00
136 Adam Berkhoel RC 4.00 10.00
137 Daniel Paille RC 3.00 8.00
138 Jordan Sigalet RC 4.00 10.00
139 Niklas Nordgren RC 3.00 8.00
140 Kevin Nastiuk RC 4.00 10.00
141 Duncan Keith RC 3.00 8.00
142 Jaroslav Balastik RC 3.00 8.00
143 Steven Goertzen RC 3.00 8.00
144 Alexandre Picard RC 5.00 12.00
145 Junior Lessard RC 3.00 8.00
146 Vojtech Polak RC 3.00 8.00
147 Brett Lebda RC 3.00 8.00
148 Valtteri Filppula RC 3.00 8.00
149 Kyle Brodziak RC 3.00 8.00
150 Matt Greene RC 3.00 8.00
151 Derek Boogaard RC 3.00 8.00
152 Brad Richardson RC 3.00 8.00
153 Mark Streit RC 3.00 8.00
154 Chris Campoli RC 3.00 8.00
155 Petteri Nokelainen RC 3.00 8.00
156 Kevin Colley RC 3.00 8.00
157 Ryan Hollweg RC 3.00 8.00
158 Jeremy Colliton RC 3.00 8.00
159 Brian McGrattan RC 3.00 8.00
160 Christoph Schubert RC 3.00 8.00
161 R.J. Umberger RC 5.00 12.00
162 Ben Eager RC 3.00 8.00
163 David Leneveu RC 4.00 10.00
164 Maxime Talbot RC 3.00 8.00
165 Josh Gorges RC 3.00 8.00
166 Dimitri Patzold RC 4.00 10.00
167 Jay McClement RC 3.00 8.00
168 Jeff Hoggan RC 3.00 8.00
169 Lee Stempniak RC 4.00 10.00
170 Andrei Kostitsyn RC 4.00 10.00
171 Timo Helbling RC 3.00 8.00
172 Paul Ranger RC 3.00 8.00
173 Ryan Craig RC 4.00 10.00
174 Evgeny Artyukhin RC 3.00 8.00
175 Andrew Wozniewski RC 3.00 8.00
176 Staffan Kronwall RC 3.00 8.00
177 Yanick Lehoux RC 3.00 8.00
178 Ryan Whitney RC 4.00 10.00
179 Erik Christensen RC 4.00 10.00
180 Andrew Ladd RC 3.00 8.00
181 Rob McVicar RC 3.00 8.00
182 Tomas Fleischmann RC 3.00 8.00
183 Jakub Klepis RC 3.00 8.00
184 Mike Green RC 3.00 8.00
185 Corey Crawford RC 3.00 8.00
186 Mikko Koivu RC 5.00 12.00
187 Steve Bernier RC 8.00 20.00
188 Cam Janssen RC 3.00 8.00
189 Barry Tallackson RC 3.00 8.00
190 Jeff Tambellini RC 3.00 8.00
191 Maxim Lapierre RC 3.00 8.00
192 Danny Richmond RC 3.00 8.00
193 Dustin Penner RC 5.00 12.00
194 Ben Walter RC 3.00 8.00
195 Chris Thorburn RC 3.00 8.00
196 Jiri Novotny RC 3.00 8.00
197 Richie Regehr RC 3.00 8.00
198 Chad Larose RC 3.00 8.00
199 James Wisniewski RC 3.00 8.00
200 Vitaly Kolesnik RC 4.00 10.00
201 Joakim Lindstrom RC 3.00 8.00
202 Ole-Kristian Tollefsen RC 3.00 8.00
203 Kyle Quincey RC 3.00 8.00
204 Danny Syvret RC 3.00 8.00
205 Jean-Francois Jacques RC 3.00 8.00
206 Greg Jacina RC 3.00 8.00
207 Petr Taticek RC 3.00 8.00
208 Rob Globke RC 3.00 8.00
209 George Parros RC 3.00 8.00
210 Petr Kanko RC 3.00 8.00
211 Richard Petiot RC 3.00 8.00
212 Jean-Philippe Cote RC 3.00 8.00
213 Kevin Klein RC 3.00 8.00
214 Pekka Rinne RC 4.00 10.00
215 Jason Ryznar RC 3.00 8.00
216 Bruno Gervais RC 3.00 8.00
217 Alexandre Picard RC 3.00 8.00
218 Stefan Ruzicka RC 3.00 8.00
219 Matt Jones RC 3.00 8.00
220 Colby Armstrong RC 8.00 20.00
221 Doug Murray RC 3.00 8.00
222 Grant Stevenson RC 3.00 8.00
223 Colin Hemingway RC 3.00 8.00
224 Kevin Dallman RC 3.00 8.00
225 Dennis Wideman RC 3.00 8.00
226 Darren Reid RC 3.00 8.00
227 Doug O'Brien RC 3.00 8.00
228 Gerald Coleman RC 3.00 8.00
229 Nick Tarnasky RC 3.00 8.00
230 Jay Harrison RC 3.00 8.00
231 Kevin Bieksa RC 3.00 8.00
232 Tomas Mojzis RC 3.00 8.00

2005-06 Ultimate Collection Gold

*STARS: 1.5X TO 3X
*ROOKIES: NOT PRICED DUE TO EARLY VOLATILITY
PRINT RUN 25 #'d SETS
32 Steve Yzerman 20.00 50.00
41 Wayne Gretzky 40.00 100.00
71 Mario Lemieux 25.00 60.00

2005-06 Ultimate Collection Autographed Patches

PRINT RUN 25 SER. #'d SETS
UNIQUE PATCHES MAY EARN
SUBSTANTIAL PREMIUMS
91 Sidney Crosby 800.00 1200.00
93 Gilbert Brule 150.00 300.00
94 Corey Perry 75.00 150.00
95 Jeff Carter 75.00 150.00
96 Alexander Steen 75.00 150.00
97 Henrik Lundqvist 125.00 250.00
98 Hannu Toivonen 40.00 100.00
99 Alexander Perezhogin
100 Thomas Vanek 100.00 200.00
101 Ryan Getzlaf
102 Braydon Coburn
103 Milan Jurcina 20.00 50.00
104 Andrew Alberts 20.00 50.00
105 Dion Phaneuf 150.00 250.00
106 Eric Nystrom
107 Cam Ward 150.00 250.00
108 Cam Barker 20.00 50.00
109 Brent Seabrook 20.00 50.00
110 Rene Bourque 25.00 60.00
111 Peter Budaj 30.00 80.00
112 Wojtek Wolski
113 Jussi Jokinen 30.00 75.00
114 Jim Howard 60.00 100.00
115 Johan Franzen 25.00 60.00
116 Brad Winchester 25.00 60.00
117 Rostislav Olesz 25.00 60.00
119 Matt Foy 20.00 50.00
120 Yann Danis
121 Ryan Suter 25.00 60.00
122 Zach Parise
123 Robert Nilsson 25.00 60.00
124 Alvaro Montoya 40.00 100.00
126 Brandon Bochenski 25.00 60.00
127 Andrej Meszaros 40.00 75.00
129 Mike Richards 50.00 100.00
130 Keith Ballard 20.00 50.00
131 Ryane Clowe 20.00 50.00
132 Jeff Woywitka 20.00 50.00

2005-06 Ultimate Collection Autographed Shields

PRINT RUN 1/1
NOT PRICED DUE TO SCARCITY
91 Sidney Crosby
92 Alexander Ovechkin
93 Gilbert Brule
94 Corey Perry
95 Jeff Carter
96 Alexander Steen
97 Henrik Lundqvist
98 Hannu Toivonen
99 Alexander Perezhogin
100 Thomas Vanek
101 Ryan Getzlaf
102 Braydon Coburn
103 Milan Jurcina
104 Andrew Alberts
105 Dion Phaneuf
107 Cam Ward
108 Cam Barker
109 Brent Seabrook
110 Rene Bourque
111 Peter Budaj
112 Worjtek Wolski
113 Jussi Jokinen
115 Johan Franzen
116 Brad Winchester
117 Rostislav Olesz
119 Matt Foy
120 Yann Danis
121 Ryan Suter
122 Zach Parise
123 Robert Nilsson
124 Alvaro Montoya
127 Andrej Meszaros
128 Patrick Eaves
129 Mike Richards
130 Keith Ballard
131 Ryane Clowe
132 Jeff Woywitka

2005-06 Ultimate Collection Endorsed Emblems

PRINT RUN 35 #'d SETS
EEAT Alex Tanguay
EEAY Alexei Yashin 15.00 30.00
EEBC Bobby Clarke 30.00 80.00
EEBI Martin Biron
EEBK Rob Blake 25.00 60.00
EEBL Brian Leetch 25.00 60.00
EEBM Brendan Morrison 15.00 30.00
EEBU Johnny Bucyk 25.00 60.00
EEBY Mike Bossy 50.00 100.00
EECD Chris Drury 25.00 60.00
EECN Cam Neely 60.00 125.00
EEDA David Aebischer 30.00 80.00
EEDB Dustin Brown 15.00 30.00
EEDG Doug Gilmour EXCH 75.00 125.00
EEDH Dany Heatley 40.00 100.00
EEDL David Legwand 25.00 60.00
EEDP Denis Potvin 50.00 100.00
EEDR Dwayne Roloson 25.00 60.00
EEDS Darryl Sittler 25.00 60.00
EEDW Doug Weight 15.00 30.00
EEEB Ed Belfour 75.00 150.00
EEES Eric Staal EXCH 60.00 100.00
EEGE Martin Gerber 25.00 60.00
EEGF Grant Fuhr 40.00 100.00
EEGL Eric Staal EXCH 75.00 150.00
EEGM Glen Murray 15.00 30.00
EEHJ Milan Hejduk 25.00 60.00
EEHK Dominik Hasek 75.00 150.00
EEHO Marian Hossa EXCH 40.00 100.00
EEHV Martin Havlat 30.00 80.00
EEHZ Henrik Zetterberg 50.00 125.00
EEIK Ilya Kovalchuk 90.00 150.00
EEJC Jonathan Cheechoo 30.00 80.00
EEJI Jarome Iginla 50.00 100.00
EEJO Joe Thornton 75.00 125.00
EEJP Joni Pitkanen 25.00 60.00
EEJR Jeremy Roenick 25.00 60.00
EEJS Jean-Sebastien Giguere 25.00 60.00
EEJT Jose Theodore 50.00 100.00
EEKL Kari Lehtonen 25.00 60.00
EEKP Keith Primeau 15.00 40.00
EELM Lanny McDonald 75.00 125.00
EELR Luc Robitaille 50.00 100.00
EELU Joffrey Lupul 25.00 60.00
EEMB Martin Brodeur 150.00 300.00
EEMC Bryan McCabe EXCH 15.00 40.00
EEML Manny Legace 15.00 40.00
EEMM Mike Modano 50.00 100.00
EEMN Markus Naslund 30.00 80.00
EEMS Matt Stajan 15.00 30.00
EEMU Larry Murphy 15.00 30.00
EEMW Brenden Morrow 25.00 60.00
EENZ Nikolai Zherdev
EEOK Olaf Kolzig 30.00 80.00
EEPA Mark Parrish 15.00 30.00
EEPB Patrice Bergeron 30.00 80.00
EEPM Patrick Marleau 25.00 60.00
EEPR Patrick Roy 125.00 250.00
EERB Ray Bourque 75.00 150.00
EERE Robert Esche 15.00 30.00
EERL Roberto Luongo 50.00 100.00
EERM Ryan Miller 60.00 125.00
EERN Rick Nash 75.00 150.00
EERS Ryan Smyth 25.00 60.00
EERY Michael Ryder 50.00 100.00
EERZ Richard Zednik 15.00 30.00
EESG Simon Gagne 30.00 80.00
EESK Saku Koivu 30.00 80.00
EESL Martin St. Louis 25.00 60.00
EESP Jason Spezza 50.00 100.00
EESV Denis Savard 30.00 80.00
EETC Ty Conklin EXCH 15.00 30.00
EEWG Wayne Gretzky 300.00 400.00

2005-06 Ultimate Collection Jerseys

PRINT RUN 250 #'d COPIES, UNLESS NOTED
JAO Alexander Ovechkin 15.00 40.00
JAS Alexander Steen 4.00 10.00
JAY Alexei Yashin 3.00 8.00
JBT Bryan Trottier 4.00 10.00
JCO Corey Perry 4.00 10.00
JCP Chris Pronger 3.00 8.00
JDH Dominik Hasek 6.00 15.00
JDP Dion Phaneuf 10.00 25.00
JDW Doug Weight 3.00 8.00
JEL Eric Lindros 3.00 8.00
JES Eric Staal 4.00 10.00
JGB Gilbert Brule 4.00 10.00
JGH Gordie Howe 15.00 40.00
JHE Dany Heatley 5.00 12.00
JHL Henrik Lundqvist 10.00 25.00
JHT Hannu Toivonen 4.00 10.00
JIK Ilya Kovalchuk 6.00 15.00
JJB Jean Beliveau 8.00 20.00
JJC Jeff Carter 4.00 10.00
JJI Jarome Iginla 5.00 12.00
JJJ Jaromir Jagr/200 6.00 15.00
JJO Joe Thornton 6.00 15.00
JJS Joe Sakic 6.00 15.00
JJT Jose Theodore 5.00 12.00
JKL Kari Lehtonen 3.00 8.00
JLR Luc Robitaille 3.00 8.00
JMA Martin St. Louis 3.00 8.00
JMB Martin Brodeur 8.00 20.00
JMG Marian Gaborik 5.00 12.00
JMH Milan Hejduk 3.00 8.00
JML Mario Lemieux 15.00 40.00
JMM Mike Modano 5.00 12.00
JMN Markus Naslund 3.00 8.00
JMS Mats Sundin 3.00 8.00
JMT Marty Turco 3.00 8.00
JPB Patrice Bergeron 3.00 8.00
JPD Pavel Datsyuk 3.00 8.00
JPE Phil Esposito 5.00 12.00
JPF Peter Forsberg 5.00 12.00
JPK Paul Kariya 3.00 8.00
JPM Patrick Marleau 3.00 8.00
JPR Patrick Roy 12.00 30.00
JRB Ray Bourque 5.00 12.00
JRG Ryan Getzlaf 5.00 12.00
JRL Roberto Luongo 5.00 12.00
JSC Sidney Crosby 30.00 60.00
JSG Simon Gagne 3.00 8.00
JSK Saku Koivu/125 8.00 20.00
JSP Jason Spezza 4.00 10.00
JSY Steve Yzerman 10.00 25.00
JTB Todd Bertuzzi 3.00 8.00
JTS Teemu Selanne 3.00 8.00
JTV Tomas Vokoun 3.00 8.00
JVA Thomas Vanek 6.00 15.00
JVL Vincent Lecavalier 3.00 8.00
JWG Wayne Gretzky 30.00 60.00

2005-06 Ultimate Collection Jerseys Dual

PRINT RUN 75 #'d COPIES
DJAL Jason Allison 5.00 12.00
Eric Lindros
DJBR Patrice Bergeron 8.00 20.00
Andrew Raycroft
DJCR Jeff Carter 10.00 25.00
Mike Richards
DJFP Peter Forsberg 10.00 25.00
Keith Primeau
DJFZ Johan Franzen 10.00 25.00
Henrik Zetterberg
DJGC Wayne Gretzky 100.00 200.00
Sidney Crosby
DJHC Dominik Hasek 10.00 25.00
Zdeno Chara
DJHY Gordie Howe 50.00 100.00
Steve Yzerman
DJJD Jason Spezza 12.00 30.00
Dany Heatley
DJJL Curtis Joseph 5.00 12.00
David Leneveu
DJKH Ilya Kovalchuk 10.00 25.00
Marian Hossa
DJKP Saku Koivu 8.00 20.00
Alexander Perezhogin
DJKV Paul Kariya 8.00 20.00
Tomas Vokoun
DJLC Mario Lemieux 90.00 150.00
Sidney Crosby
DJLS Joffrey Lupul 8.00 20.00
Teemu Selanne
DJML Alvaro Montoya 20.00 50.00
Henrik Lundqvist
DJNB Rick Nash 20.00 50.00
Gilbert Brule/30
DJOC Alexander Ovechkin 100.00 175.00
Sidney Crosby
DJPG Corey Perry 10.00 25.00
Ryan Getzlaf
DJPI Dion Phaneuf 20.00 50.00
Jarome Iginla
DJRT Patrick Roy 20.00 50.00
Jose Theodore
DJSB Brent Seabrook 6.00 15.00
Cam Barker
DJSH Joe Sakic 10.00 25.00
Milan Hejduk
DJSL Martin St. Louis 10.00 25.00
Vincent Lecavalier
DJTD Jose Theodore 8.00 20.00
Yann Danis
DJTL Hannu Toivonen 8.00 20.00
Kari Lehtonen
DJWN Cam Ward 12.00 30.00
Kevin Nastiuk

2005-06 Ultimate Collection Jerseys Triple

PRINT RUN 25 SER #'d SETS
TJFGC Peter Forsberg 30.00 60.00
Simon Gagne
Jeff Carter
TJGLC Wayne Gretzky 250.00 450.00
Mario Lemieux
Sidney Crosby
TJHSH Dany Heatley 50.00 100.00
Jason Spezza
Dominik Hasek
TJKTP Saku Koivu 30.00 60.00
Jose Theodore
Alexander Perezhogin
TJLVR Martin St. Louis 30.00 60.00
Vincent Lecavalier
Brad Richards
TJNOC Rick Nash 200.00 400.00
Alexander Ovechkin
Sidney Crosby
TJPGL Corey Perry 20.00 50.00
Ryan Getzlaf
Joffrey Lupul
TJRTB Patrick Roy
Jose Theodore
Martin Brodeur
TJSLA Mats Sundin 40.00 80.00
Eric Lindros
Jason Allison

2005-06 Ultimate Collection Marquee Attractions

PRINT RUN 250 #'d SETS
MA1 Corey Perry 3.00 8.00
MA2 Ryan Getzlaf 4.00 10.00
MA3 Jean-Sebastien Giguere 2.50 6.00
MA4 Ilya Kovalchuk 4.00 10.00
MA5 Marian Hossa 2.50 6.00
MA6 Hannu Toivonen 3.00 8.00
MA7 Patrice Bergeron 3.00 8.00
MA8 Andrew Raycroft 1.50 4.00
MA9 Thomas Vanek 4.00 10.00
MA10 Dion Phaneuf 8.00 20.00
MA11 Jarome Iginla 4.00 10.00
MA12 Eric Staal 3.00 8.00
MA13 Nikolai Khabibulin 2.50 6.00
MA14 Alex Tanguay 1.50 4.00
MA15 Milan Hejduk 2.50 6.00
MA16 Rick Nash 4.00 10.00
MA17 Mike Modano 4.00 10.00

MA18 Brenden Morrow 2.50 6.00
MA19 Marty Turco 2.50 6.00
MA20 Johan Franzen 1.50 4.00
MA21 Henrik Zetterberg 2.50 6.00
MA22 Chris Pronger 1.50 4.00
MA23 Roberto Luongo 4.00 10.00
MA24 Jeremy Roenick 3.00 8.00
MA25 Mikko Koivu 2.50 6.00
MA26 Alexander Perezhogin 1.50 4.00
MA27 Saku Koivu 3.00 8.00
MA28 Jose Theodore 4.00 10.00
MA29 Martin Brodeur 6.00 15.00
MA30 Miroslav Satan 2.50 6.00
MA31 Henrik Lundqvist 8.00 20.00
MA32 Dominik Hasek 4.00 10.00
MA33 Dany Heatley 4.00 10.00
MA34 Jason Spezza 3.00 8.00
MA35 Jeff Carter 4.00 10.00
MA36 Mike Richards 3.00 8.00
MA37 Keith Primeau 1.50 4.00
MA38 Shane Doan 1.50 4.00
MA39 Sidney Crosby 30.00 80.00
MA40 Mark Recchi 1.50 4.00
MA41 Joe Thornton 5.00 12.00
MA42 Martin St. Louis 1.50 4.00
MA43 Vincent Lecavalier 3.00 8.00
MA44 Alexander Steen 3.00 8.00
MA45 Mats Sundin 2.50 6.00
MA46 Ed Belfour 2.50 6.00
MA47 Markus Naslund 2.50 6.00
MA48 Alexander Ovechkin 12.00 30.00
MA49 Gilbert Brule 3.00 8.00
MA50 Olaf Kolzig 3.00 8.00

2005-06 Ultimate Collection Marquee Attractions Signatures

PRINT RUN 10 #'d SETS
NOT PRICED DUE TO SCARCITY

2005-06 Ultimate Collection National Heroes Jerseys

PRINT RUN 225 #'d COPIES UNLESS NOTED
NHJAF Alexander Frolov 2.50 6.00
NHJAK Alexei Kovalev 2.50 6.00
NHJAL Daniel Alfredsson 3.00 8.00
NHJAO Alexander Ovechkin 20.00 50.00
NHJAY Alexei Yashin 2.50 6.00
NHJBG Bill Guerin 2.50 6.00
NHJBR Brian Rolston 2.50 6.00
NHJCC Chris Chelios 3.00 8.00
NHJCD Chris Drury 2.50 6.00
NHJCP Chris Pronger/200 3.00 8.00
NHJDA David Aebischer 3.00 8.00
NHJDW Doug Weight 2.50 6.00
NHJFO Adam Foote 2.50 6.00
NHJFT Fedor Tyutin 2.50 6.00
NHJGA Marian Gaborik 6.00 15.00
NHJHA Michal Handzus 2.50 6.00
NHJHJ Milan Hejduk 3.00 8.00
NHJHK Dominik Hasek/200 8.00 20.00
NHJHO Marian Hossa 3.00 8.00
NHJHS Marcel Hossa 2.50 6.00
NHJHZ Henrik Zetterberg 3.00 8.00
NHJIK Ilya Kovalchuk 6.00 15.00
NHJJB Jay Bouwmeester 2.50 6.00
NHJJI Jarome Iginla 6.00 15.00
NHJJJ Jaromir Jagr 6.00 15.00
NHJJL Jere Lehtinen 2.50 6.00
NHJJO Joe Thornton 6.00 15.00
NHJJP Joni Pitkanen/200 3.00 8.00
NHJJS Joe Sakic 6.00 15.00
NHJKD Kris Draper 2.50 6.00
NHJKT Keith Tkachuk 3.00 8.00
NHJLE Jordan Leopold 2.50 5.00
NHJMB Martin Brodeur 8.00 20.00
NHJMC Bryan McCabe 2.50 6.00
NHJMG Martin Gerber/200 5.00 12.00
NHJMM Mike Modano 6.00 15.00
NHJMO Mattias Ohlund 2.50 6.00
NHJMP Mark Parrish 2.50 6.00
NHJMS Martin Straka/200 2.50 6.00
NHJMT Marty Turco 3.00 8.00
NHJNA Nik Antropov 2.50 6.00
NHJNL Nicklas Lidstrom 3.00 8.00
NHJOJ Olli Jokinen/200 3.00 8.00
NHJOK Olaf Kolzig 3.00 8.00
NHJPA Pavol Demitra 3.00 8.00
NHJPB Peter Bondra 3.00 8.00
NHJPD Pavel Datsyuk 3.00 8.00
NHJPE Patrik Elias 3.00 8.00
NHJPF Peter Forsberg 6.00 15.00
NHJRA Brian Rafalski/200 2.50 6.00
NHJRB Rob Blake 3.00 8.00
NHJRD Rick DiPietro 5.00 12.00
NHJRE Robert Esche 3.00 8.00
NHJRI Brad Richards 3.00 8.00
NHJRL Roberto Luongo 6.00 15.00
NHJRS Ryan Smyth/200 3.00 8.00
NHJSA Miroslav Satan 2.50 6.00
NHJSG Simon Gagne 3.00 8.00
NHJSO Sandis Ozolinsh 2.50 6.00
NHJSU Mats Sundin 3.00 8.00
NHJSV Marek Svatos/200 2.50 6.00
NHJTB Todd Bertuzzi/200 5.00 12.00
NHJTS Teemu Selanne 3.00 8.00
NHJTV Tomas Vokoun 3.00 8.00
NHJVK Viktor Kozlov 2.50 6.00
NHJVL Vincent Lecavalier 3.00 8.00
NHJWR Wade Redden 2.50 6.00
NHJZC Zdeno Chara 3.00 8.00

2005-06 Ultimate Collection National Heroes Patches

PRINT RUN VARIES 10-25 COPIES
NOT PRICED DUE TO SCARCITY
NHPAF Alexander Frolov/25
NHPAK Alexei Kovalev/25
NHPAL Daniel Alfredsson/25
NHPAO Alexander Ovechkin/10
NHPAY Alexei Yashin/25
NHPBG Bill Guerin/25
NHPBR Brian Rolston/25
NHPCC Chris Chelios/10
NHPCD Chris Drury/25
NHPCP Chris Pronger/10
NHPDA David Aebischer/25
NHPDH Dany Heatley/10
NHPDW Doug Weight/10
NHPFO Adam Foote/25
NHPFT Fedor Tyutin/25
NHPGA Marian Gaborik/25
NHPHA Michal Handzus/25
NHPHJ Milan Hejduk/10
NHPHK Dominik Hasek/10
NHPHO Marian Hossa/10
NHPHS Marcel Hossa/25
NHPHZ Henrik Zetterberg/10
NHPIK Ilya Kovalchuk/10
NHPJB Jay Bouwmeester/10
NHPJI Jarome Iginla/10
NHPJJ Jaromir Jagr/10
NHPJL Jere Lehtinen/25
NHPJO Joe Thornton/10
NHPJP Joni Pitkanen/25
NHPJS Joe Sakic/10
NHPKD Kris Draper/25
NHPKT Keith Tkachuk/25
NHPLE Jordan Leopold/25
NHPMB Martin Brodeur/10
NHPMC Bryan McCabe/25
NHPMG Marian Gerber/25
NHPMM Mike Modano/10
NHPMO Mattias Ohlund/25
NHPMP Mark Parrish/25
NHPMS Martin Straka/25
NHPMT Marty Turco/25
NHPNA Nik Antropov/25
NHPNL Nicklas Lidstrom/25
NHPOJ Olli Jokinen/25
NHPOK Olaf Kolzig/25
NHPPA Pavol Demitra/25
NHPPB Peter Bondra/25
NHPPD Pavel Datsyuk/25
NHPPE Patrik Elias/25
NHPPF Peter Forsberg/10
NHPRA Brian Rafalski/25
NHPRB Rob Blake/25
NHPRD Rick DiPietro/25
NHPRE Robert Esche/25
NHPRI Brad Richards/10
NHPRL Roberto Luongo/25
NHPRN Rick Nash/10
NHPRS Ryan Smyth/25
NHPSA Miroslav Satan/25
NHPSG Simon Gagne/25
NHPSK Saku Koivu/10
NHPSL Martin St. Louis/10
NHPSO Sandis Ozolinsh/25
NHPSU Mats Sundin/10
NHPSV Marek Svatos/25
NHPTB Todd Bertuzzi/25
NHPTS Teemu Selanne/25
NHPTV Tomas Vokoun/25
NHPVK Viktor Kozlov/25
NHPVL Vincent Lecavalier/10
NHPWR Wade Redden/25
NHPZC Zdeno Chara/25

2005-06 Ultimate Collection Premium Patches

PRINT RUN 35 SER. #'d SETS
UNIQUE SWATCHES MAY EARN PREMIUM
PPAO Alexander Ovechkin 75.00 150.00
PPAP Alexander Perezhogin 15.00 40.00
PPAS Alexander Steen 25.00 60.00
PPAY Alexei Yashin 25.00 60.00
PPBS Brendan Shanahan 20.00 50.00
PPCP Chris Pronger 20.00 50.00
PPCW Cam Ward 25.00 60.00
PPDH Dany Heatley/30 25.00 60.00
PPDP Dion Phaneuf 50.00 100.00
PPDW Doug Weight 15.00 40.00
PPEL Eric Lindros
PPES Eric Staal 25.00 60.00
PPGB Gilbert Brule 25.00 60.00
PPHK Dominik Hasek 25.00 60.00
PPHL Henrik Lundqvist 40.00 100.00
PPHT Hannu Toivonen 25.00 60.00
PPIK Ilya Kovalchuk 30.00 80.00
PPJC Jeff Carter 25.00 60.00
PPJF Johan Franzen 20.00 50.00
PPJI Jarome Iginla 30.00 80.00
PPJJ Jaromir Jagr 50.00 125.00
PPJO Joe Thornton 40.00 80.00
PPJR Jeremy Roenick 25.00 60.00
PPJS Joe Sakic 40.00 100.00
PPJT Jose Theodore 25.00 60.00
PPKL Kari Lehtonen 30.00 80.00
PPLR Luc Robitaille 20.00 50.00
PPMB Martin Brodeur 75.00 150.00
PPMG Marian Gaborik 30.00 80.00
PPMH Milan Hejduk 25.00 60.00
PPML Mario Lemieux 100.00 200.00
PPMM Mike Modano 30.00 80.00
PPMN Markus Naslund 20.00 50.00
PPMR Mike Richards 30.00 80.00
PPMS Mats Sundin 40.00 100.00
PPMT Marty Turco
PPPB Patrice Bergeron 20.00 50.00
PPPD Pavel Datsyuk 20.00 50.00
PPPE Corey Perry 20.00 50.00
PPPF Peter Forsberg 30.00 80.00
PPPK Paul Kariya 25.00 60.00
PPPM Patrick Marleau 20.00 50.00
PPPR Patrick Roy 100.00 200.00
PPPS Jason Spezza 25.00 60.00
PPRB Ray Bourque 30.00 80.00
PPRG Ryan Getzlaf 30.00 80.00
PPRL Roberto Luongo 30.00 80.00
PPRN Rick Nash/15
PPSC Sidney Crosby 150.00 300.00
PPSF Sergei Fedorov 20.00 50.00
PPSG Simon Gagne 20.00 50.00
PPSY Steve Yzerman 75.00 150.00
PPTB Todd Bertuzzi 20.00 50.00
PPTS Teemu Selanne 25.00 60.00
PPTV Thomas Vanek 40.00 100.00
PPVL Vincent Lecavalier 30.00 80.00
PPVO Tomas Vokoun 40.00 100.00
PPWG Wayne Gretzky 100.00 250.00

2005-06 Ultimate Collection Premium Swatches

75 SER. #'d COPIES UNLESS NOTED
PSAO Alexander Ovechkin 30.00 80.00
PSAP Alexander Perezhogin 4.00 10.00
PSAS Alexander Steen 8.00 20.00
PSAY Alexei Yashin 3.00 8.00
PSBS Brendan Shanahan 6.00 15.00
PSCP Chris Pronger 3.00 8.00
PSCW Cam Ward 8.00 20.00
PSDH Dany Heatley/35 12.00 30.00
PSDP Dion Phaneuf 10.00 25.00
PSDW Doug Weight 3.00 8.00
PSEL Eric Lindros 5.00 12.00
PSES Eric Staal 6.00 15.00
PSGB Gilbert Brule 6.00 15.00
PSHL Henrik Lundqvist 10.00 25.00
PSHT Hannu Toivonen 5.00 12.00
PSIK Ilya Kovalchuk 8.00 20.00
PSJC Jeff Carter 6.00 15.00
PSJF Johan Franzen 3.00 8.00
PSJI Jarome Iginla 6.00 15.00
PSJJ Jaromir Jagr/50 15.00 30.00
PSJO Joe Thornton 8.00 20.00
PSJR Jeremy Roenick 4.00 10.00
PSJS Joe Sakic 8.00 20.00
PSJT Jose Theodore 6.00 15.00
PSKL Kari Lehtonen 4.00 10.00
PSLR Luc Robitaille 4.00 10.00
PSMB Martin Brodeur/50 15.00 40.00
PSMG Marian Gaborik 6.00 15.00
PSMH Milan Hejduk 4.00 10.00
PSML Mario Lemieux 20.00 50.00
PSMM Mike Modano 4.00 10.00
PSMN Markus Naslund 4.00 10.00
PSMR Mike Richards 4.00 10.00
PSMS Mats Sundin 4.00 10.00
PSMT Marty Turco 4.00 10.00
PSPB Patrice Bergeron 4.00 10.00
PSPD Pavel Datsyuk 3.00 8.00
PSPE Corey Perry 4.00 10.00
PSPF Peter Forsberg 8.00 20.00
PSPM Patrick Marleau 3.00 8.00
PSPR Patrick Roy 20.00 50.00
PSPS Jason Spezza 5.00 12.00
PSRB Ray Bourque 5.00 12.00
PSRG Ryan Getzlaf 4.00 10.00
PSRL Roberto Luongo 6.00 15.00
PSSC Sidney Crosby 60.00 125.00
PSSK Saku Koivu 4.00 10.00
PSSL Martin St. Louis 4.00 10.00
PSSY Steve Yzerman 15.00 40.00
PSTB Todd Bertuzzi 4.00 10.00
PSTS Teemu Selanne 6.00 15.00
PSTV Thomas Vanek 4.00 10.00
PSVL Vincent Lecavalier 4.00 10.00
PSVO Tomas Vokoun 4.00 10.00
PSWG Wayne Gretzky 75.00 150.00

2005-06 Ultimate Collection Ultimate Achievements

PRINT RUNS VARY
UNDER 20 NOT PRICED DUE TO SCARCITY
UAAR Andrew Raycroft/29 15.00 30.00
UAAT Alex Tanguay/12
UAAY Alexei Yashin/6
UABC Bobby Clarke/3
UABH Bobby Hull/9
UABP Bernie Parent/2
UACN Cam Neely/5
UADH Dany Heatley/26 25.00 60.00
UADW Doug Weight/8
UAEN Evgeni Nabokov/10
UAES Eric Staal/2
UAGH Gordie Howe/6
UAGP Gilbert Perreault/6
UAHK Dominik Hasek/6
UAHO Marian Hossa/12
UAHV Martin Havlat/11
UAHZ Henrik Zetterberg/22 25.00 50.00
UAIK Ilya Kovalchuk/41 20.00 50.00
UAJB Jean Beliveau/2
UAJC Jonathan Cheechoo/28 25.00 50.00
UAJG Jean-Sebastien Giguere/15
UAJI Jarome Iginla/41 20.00 50.00
UAJO Joe Thornton/5
UAJR Jeremy Roenick/9
UAJT Jose Theodore/23
UALA Guy Lafleur/3
UALU Luc Robitaille/8
UAMB Martin Brodeur/4
UAMH Milan Hejduk/4
UAML Manny Legace/10
UAMM Mike Modano/6
UAMN Markus Naslund/5
UAMT Marty Turco/9
UANK Nikolai Khabibulin/16
UAON Jeff O'Neill/5
UAPB Patrice Bergeron/16
UAPE Phil Esposito/5
UAPR Patrick Roy/3
UARB Ray Bourque/5
UARL Roberto Luongo/23 40.00 75.00
UARN Rick Nash/41 15.00 40.00
UARS Ryan Smyth/6
UASG Simon Gagne/17
UASK Saku Koivu/2
UASL Martin St. Louis/24 12.50 30.00
UASN Scott Niedermayer/18
UATB Todd Bertuzzi/4
UATE Tony Esposito/3
UAVL Vincent Lecavalier/9
UAWG Wayne Gretzky/9

2005-06 Ultimate Collection Ultimate Debut Threads Jerseys

PRINT RUN 250 #'d SETS
DTJAA Andrew Alberts 3.00 8.00
DTJAK Andrei Kostsitsyn 4.00 10.00
DTJAL Andrew Ladd 4.00 10.00
DTJAM Andrej Meszaros 3.00 8.00
DTJAO Alexander Ovechkin 15.00 40.00
DTJAP Alexander Perezhogin 4.00 10.00
DTJAS Alexander Steen 4.00 10.00
DTJBB Brandon Bochenski 3.00 8.00
DTJBC Braydon Coburn 3.00 8.00
DTJBS Brent Seabrook 3.00 8.00
DTJBT Barry Tallackson 3.00 8.00
DTJBW Brad Winchester 3.00 8.00
DTJCB Cam Barker 3.00 8.00
DTJCC Chris Campoli 3.00 8.00
DTJCP Corey Perry 4.00 10.00
DTJCS Christoph Schubert 3.00 8.00
DTJCW Cam Ward 6.00 15.00
DTJDB Derek Boogaard 3.00 8.00
DTJDL David Leneveu 3.00 8.00
DTJDP Dion Phaneuf 10.00 25.00
DTJEA Evgeny Artyukhin 3.00 8.00
DTJEN Eric Nystrom 3.00 8.00
DTJGB Gilbert Brule 5.00 12.00
DTJHL Henrik Lundqvist 10.00 25.00
DTJHT Hannu Toivonen 4.00 10.00
DTJJC Jeff Carter 5.00 12.00
DTJJF Johan Franzen 3.00 8.00
DTJJH Jim Howard 4.00 10.00
DTJJJ Jussi Jokinen 4.00 10.00
DTJJK Jakub Klepis 3.00 8.00
DTJJM Jay McClement 3.00 8.00
DTJJS Jim Slater 3.00 8.00
DTJJT Jeff Tambellini 3.00 8.00
DTJJW Jeff Woywitka 3.00 8.00
DTJKB Keith Ballard 3.00 8.00
DTJMJ Milan Jurcina 3.00 8.00
DTJMK Mikko Koivu 4.00 10.00
DTJML Maxim Lapierre 3.00 8.00
DTJMO Alvaro Montoya 4.00 10.00
DTJMR Mike Richards 4.00 10.00
DTJMT Maxime Talbot 3.00 8.00
DTJPP Petr Prucha 4.00 10.00
DTJRB Rene Bourque 3.00 8.00
DTJRC Ryane Clowe 3.00 8.00
DTJRG Ryan Getzlaf 5.00 12.00
DTJRJ R.J. Umberger 3.00 8.00
DTJRN Robert Nilsson 3.00 8.00
DTJRO Rostislav Olesz 4.00 10.00
DTJRS Ryan Suter 3.00 8.00
DTJRW Ryan Whitney 3.00 8.00
DTJSB Steve Bernier 4.00 10.00
DTJSC Sidney Crosby 40.00 80.00
DTJSI Jordan Sigalet 4.00 10.00
DTJTF Tomas Fleischmann 3.00 8.00
DTJTV Thomas Vanek 8.00 20.00
DTJWW Wojtek Wolski 4.00 10.00
DTJYD Yann Danis 3.00 8.00
DTJZP Zach Parise 4.00 10.00

2005-06 Ultimate Collection Ultimate Debut Threads Jerseys Autographs

PRINT RUN 25 COPIES
NOT PRICED DUE TO SCARCITY
DAJSC Sidney Crosby 450.00 750.00

2005-06 Ultimate Collection Ultimate Debut Threads Patches

PRINT RUN 60 #'d COPIES UNLESS NOTED
UNIQUE SWATCHES MAY EARN SUBSTANTIAL PREMIUM
DTPAA Andrew Alberts 10.00 25.00
DTPAL Andrew Ladd 20.00 50.00
DTPAO Alexander Ovechkin 75.00 150.00
DTPAP Alexander Perezhogin 20.00 50.00
DTPAS Alexander Steen 20.00 50.00
DTPBB Brandon Bochenski 15.00 40.00
DTPBC Braydon Coburn 15.00 40.00
DTPBS Brent Seabrook 25.00 60.00
DTPBT Barry Tallackson 10.00 25.00
DTPBW Brad Winchester 10.00 25.00
DTPCB Cam Barker 15.00 40.00
DTPCC Chris Campoli/40 15.00 40.00
DTPCP Corey Perry 30.00 80.00
DTPCW Cam Ward 40.00 100.00
DTPDB Derek Boogaard 15.00 40.00
DTPDL David Leneveu 15.00 40.00
DTPDP Dion Phaneuf 50.00 125.00
DTPEA Evgeny Artyukhin/25 30.00 80.00
DTPEN Eric Nystrom 20.00 50.00
DTPGB Gilbert Brule/50 40.00 100.00
DTPHL Henrik Lundqvist 50.00 125.00
DTPHT Hannu Toivonen 25.00 60.00
DTPJC Jeff Carter 30.00 80.00
DTPJF Johan Franzen 10.00 25.00
DTPJH Jim Howard 20.00 50.00
DTPJJ Jussi Jokinen 20.00 50.00
DTPJK Jakub Klepis 10.00 25.00
DTPJM Jay McClement/15
DTPJS Jim Slater 20.00 50.00
DTPJT Jeff Tambellini/30 15.00 40.00
DTPJW Jeff Woywitka 15.00 40.00
DTPKB Keith Ballard 10.00 25.00
DTPMJ Milan Jurcina/30 20.00 50.00
DTPMK Mikko Koivu 20.00 50.00
DTPMO Alvaro Montoya 20.00 50.00
DTPMR Mike Richards 20.00 50.00
DTPMT Maxime Talbot 10.00 25.00
DTPPB Peter Budaj 25.00 60.00
DTPPP Petr Prucha/30 40.00 60.00
DTPRB Rene Bourque 20.00 50.00
DTPRC Ryane Clowe/10
DTPRG Ryan Getzlaf 30.00 80.00
DTPRJ R.J. Umberger/35 15.00 40.00
DTPRN Robert Nilsson 15.00 40.00
DTPRO Rostislav Olesz 15.00 40.00
DTPRS Ryan Suter 15.00 40.00
DTPRW Ryan Whitney 15.00 40.00
DTPSB Steve Bernier/25 40.00 80.00
DTPSC Sidney Crosby/1
DTPSI Jordan Sigalet/35 25.00 50.00
DTPTF Tomas Fleischmann 10.00 25.00
DTPTV Thomas Vanek 50.00 125.00
DTPWW Wojtek Wolski 20.00 50.00
DTPYD Yann Danis 20.00 50.00
DTPZP Zach Parise 30.00 80.00

2005-06 Ultimate Collection Ultimate Debut Threads Patches Autographs

PRINT RUN 10 #'d SETS
NOT PRICED DUE TO SCARCITY

2005-06 Ultimate Collection Ultimate Patches

PRINT RUN 75 SER #'d COPIES
UNIQUE PATCHES MAY EARN SUBSTANTIAL PREMIUM
PAO Alexander Ovechkin 75.00 125.00
PAS Alexander Steen 12.00 30.00
PAY Alexei Yashin 10.00 25.00
PBS Brendan Shanahan 12.00 30.00
PBT Bryan Trottier 15.00 40.00
PCO Corey Perry 10.00 25.00
PCP Chris Pronger 10.00 25.00
PDH Dominik Hasek 15.00 40.00
PDP Dion Phaneuf 20.00 50.00
PDW Doug Weight 8.00 20.00
PEL Eric Lindros 10.00 25.00
PES Eric Staal 15.00 40.00
PGB Gilbert Brule 15.00 40.00
PGH Gordie Howe/10
PHE Dany Heatley 15.00 40.00
PHL Henrik Lundqvist 20.00 50.00
PHT Hannu Toivonen 10.00 25.00
PIK Ilya Kovalchuk 15.00 40.00
PJC Jeff Carter 12.00 30.00
PJI Jarome Iginla 15.00 40.00
PJJ Jaromir Jagr 20.00 50.00
PJO Joe Thornton 20.00 50.00
PJR Jeremy Roenick 15.00 40.00
PJS Joe Sakic 20.00 50.00
PJT Jose Theodore 12.00 30.00
PKL Kari Lehtonen 10.00 25.00
PLR Luc Robitaille 10.00 25.00
PMA Martin St. Louis 8.00 20.00
PMB Martin Brodeur 25.00 60.00
PMG Marian Gaborik 20.00 50.00
PMH Milan Hejduk 10.00 25.00
PML Mario Lemieux 30.00 80.00
PMM Mike Modano 15.00 40.00
PMN Markus Naslund 12.00 30.00
PMS Mats Sundin 12.00 30.00
PMT Marty Turco 10.00 25.00
PPB Patrice Bergeron 15.00 40.00
PPD Pavel Datsyuk 10.00 25.00
PPE Phil Esposito 12.00 30.00
PPF Peter Forsberg/35 20.00 50.00
PPK Paul Kariya 10.00 25.00
PPM Patrick Marleau 8.00 20.00
PPR Patrick Roy 30.00 80.00
PRB Ray Bourque 15.00 40.00
PRG Ryan Getzlaf 15.00 40.00
PRL Roberto Luongo 15.00 40.00
PSC Sidney Crosby 125.00 250.00
PSF Sergei Fedorov 10.00 25.00
PSG Simon Gagne 8.00 20.00
PSK Saku Koivu 10.00 25.00
PSP Jason Spezza 10.00 25.00
PSY Steve Yzerman 25.00 60.00
PTB Todd Bertuzzi 10.00 25.00
PTS Teemu Selanne 10.00 25.00
PTV Tomas Vokoun 12.00 30.00
PVA Thomas Vanek 15.00 40.00
PVL Vincent Lecavalier 12.00 30.00

2005-06 Ultimate Collection Ultimate Patches Dual

PRINT RUN 25 SER #'d SETS
UNIQUE PATCHES MAY EARN SUBSTANTIAL PREMIUMS
DPAL Jason Allison 20.00 50.00
Eric Lindros
DPBR Patrice Bergeron 25.00 60.00
Andrew Raycroft
DPCR Jeff Carter
Mike Richards
DPFP Peter Forsberg
Keith Primeau
DPFZ Johan Franzen 25.00 60.00
Henrik Zetterberg
DPHC Dominik Hasek 30.00 80.00
Zdeno Chara
DPHY Gordie Howe 150.00 300.00
Steve Yzerman
DPJD Jason Spezza 40.00 100.00
Dany Heatley
DPJL Curtis Joseph 15.00 40.00
David Leneveu
DPKH Ilya Kovalchuk 30.00 80.00
Marian Hossa
DPKP Saku Koivu 15.00 40.00
Alexander Perezhogin
DPKV Paul Kariya/Tomas Vokoun 20.00 50.00
DPLC Mario Lemieux 250.00 500.00
Sidney Crosby
DPLS Joffrey Lupul 25.00 60.00
Teemu Selanne
DPML Alvaro Montoya 30.00 80.00
Henrik Lundqvist
DPNB Rick Nash
Gilbert Brule
DPOC Alexander Ovechkin 350.00 600.00
Sidney Crosby
DPPG Corey Perry
Ryan Getzlaf
DPPI Dion Phaneuf 75.00 150.00
Jarome Iginla
DPRT Patrick Roy 150.00 250.00
Jose Theodore
DPSB Brent Seabrook 15.00 40.00
Cam Barker
DPSH Joe Sakic 25.00 60.00
Milan Hejduk
DPSL Martin St. Louis 20.00 50.00
Vincent Lecavalier
DPSY Brendan Shanahan 40.00 80.00
Steve Yzerman
DPTD Jose Theodore 15.00 40.00
Yann Danis
DPTL Hannu Toivonen 40.00 100.00
Kari Lehtonen
DPWN Cam Ward 25.00 50.00
Kevin Nastiuk

2005-06 Ultimate Collection Ultimate Patches Triple

PRINT RUN 5 SER #'d SETS
NOT PRICED DUE TO SCARCITY

2005-06 Ultimate Collection Ultimate Signatures

USAO Alexander Ovechkin 60.00 100.00
USAP Alexander Perezhogin 4.00 10.00
USAR Andrew Raycroft 4.00 10.00
USAT Alex Tanguay SP 15.00 40.00
USAY Alexei Yashin 4.00 10.00
USBC Bobby Clarke 10.00 25.00
USBL Brian Leetch 6.00 15.00
USBM Brenden Morrow 4.00 10.00
USBP Bernie Parent 10.00 25.00
USBR Brad Richards 8.00 20.00
USCH Jonathan Cheechoo 6.00 15.00
USCN Cam Neely 12.00 30.00
USCW Cam Ward 8.00 20.00
USDH Dany Heatley SP 20.00 50.00
USDW Doug Weight 4.00 10.00
USEB Ed Belfour 10.00 25.00
USEC Erik Cole 4.00 10.00
USEN Eric Nystrom 4.00 10.00
USES Eric Staal EXCH 10.00 25.00
USGB Gilbert Brule 8.00 20.00
USGH Gordie Howe 40.00 80.00
USGP Gilbert Perreault 8.00 20.00
USHK Dominik Hasek 15.00 40.00
USHL Henrik Lundqvist 12.00 30.00
USHO Marian Hossa 4.00 10.00
USHT Hannu Toivonen 4.00 10.00
USHV Martin Havlat 4.00 10.00
USHZ Henrik Zetterberg 10.00 25.00
USIK Ilya Kovalchuk 15.00 40.00
USJB Jean Beliveau 12.00 30.00
USJC Jeff Carter 8.00 20.00
USJG Jean-Sebastien Giguere 4.00 10.00
USJH Jim Howard 6.00 15.00
USJI Jarome Iginla 8.00 20.00
USJO Joe Thornton 12.00 30.00
USJT Jose Theodore 6.00 15.00
USKL Kari Lehtonen 6.00 15.00
USLR Luc Robitaille 8.00 20.00
USMB Martin Brodeur 40.00 80.00
USMF Marc-Andre Fleury 12.00 30.00
USMH Milan Hejduk 4.00 10.00
USML Manny Legace 4.00 10.00
USMM Mike Modano 10.00 25.00
USMN Markus Naslund 5.00 12.00
USMS Miroslav Satan 6.00 15.00
USMT Marty Turco 4.00 10.00
USNA Evgeni Nabokov 4.00 10.00
USNK Nikolai Khabibulin 6.00 15.00
USNZ Nikolai Zherdev 4.00 10.00
USON Jeff O'Neill 4.00 10.00
USPB Patrice Bergeron 8.00 20.00
USPE Phil Esposito SP 20.00 50.00
USPR Patrick Roy SP 125.00 250.00
USPY Corey Perry 5.00 12.00
USRB Ray Bourque SP 40.00 80.00
USRG Ryan Getzlaf 8.00 20.00
USRL Roberto Luongo 10.00 25.00
USRN Rick Nash 12.00 30.00
USRO Rostislav Olesz 3.00 10.00
USRS Ryan Suter 4.00 10.00
USRW Ryan Whitney 4.00 10.00
USRY Michael Ryder 4.00 10.00
USSC Sidney Crosby 200.00 350.00
USSG Simon Gagne 4.00 10.00
USSK Saku Koivu 8.00 20.00
USSL Martin St. Louis SP 15.00 40.00
USSM Ryan Smyth 8.00 20.00
USSN Scott Niedermayer 10.00 25.00
USST Alexander Steen 6.00 15.00
USSV Marek Svatos 5.00 12.00
USTB Todd Bertuzzi 4.00 10.00
USTE Tony Esposito 20.00 40.00
USTR Tuomo Ruutu 4.00 10.00
USTV Thomas Vanek 10.00 25.00
USVL Vincent Lecavalier 8.00 20.00
USWG Wayne Gretzky SP 200.00 350.00
USWW Wojtek Wolski 6.00 15.00
USYD Yann Danis 6.00 15.00

2005-06 Ultimate Collection Ultimate Signatures Foursomes

PRINT RUN 5 SER #'d SETS
NOT PRICED DUE TO SCARCITY

2005-06 Ultimate Collection Ultimate Signatures Logos

PRINT RUN 1/1
NOT PRICED DUE TO SCARCITY

2005-06 Ultimate Collection Ultimate Signatures Pairings

PRINT RUN 25 SER. #'d SETS
NOT PRICED DUE TO SCARCITY

2005-06 Ultimate Collection Ultimate Signatures Trios

PRINT RUN 10 SER. #'d SETS
NOT PRICED DUE TO SCARCITY

2006-07 Ultimate Collection

1 Teemu Selanne 1.50 4.00
2 Ilya Kovalchuk 2.00 5.00
3 Kari Lehtonen 1.50 4.00
4 Patrice Bergeron 1.50 4.00
5 Bobby Orr 5.00 12.00
6 Ray Bourque 2.00 5.00
7 Phil Esposito 1.50 4.00
8 Ryan Miller 1.50 4.00
9 Gilbert Perreault 1.50 4.00
10 Miikka Kiprusoff 1.50 4.00
11 Jarome Iginla 2.00 5.00
12 Dion Phaneuf 1.50 4.00
13 Eric Staal 1.50 4.00
14 Cam Ward 1.50 4.00
15 Martin Havlat 1.50 4.00
16 Bobby Hull 1.50 4.00
17 Joe Sakic 2.50 6.00
18 Jose Theodore 1.50 4.00
19 Rick Nash 1.50 4.00
20 Mike Modano 1.50 4.00
21 Marty Turco 1.50 4.00
22 Henrik Zetterberg 1.50 4.00
23 Dominik Hasek 2.00 5.00
24 Nicklas Lidstrom 1.50 4.00
25 Gordie Howe 2.50 6.00
26 Ales Hemsky 1.00 2.50
27 Wayne Gretzky 8.00 20.00
28 Jari Kurri 1.00 2.50
29 Ed Belfour 1.50 4.00
30 Rob Blake 1.50 4.00
31 Marian Gaborik 2.00 5.00
32 Saku Koivu 1.50 4.00
33 Michael Ryder 1.50 4.00
34 Patrick Roy 5.00 12.00
35 Tomas Vokoun 1.50 4.00
36 Paul Kariya 1.50 4.00
37 Martin Brodeur 4.00 10.00
38 Alexei Yashin 1.00 2.50
39 Mike Bossy 1.50 4.00
40 Jaromir Jagr 2.00 5.00
41 Brendan Shanahan 1.50 4.00
42 Henrik Lundqvist 1.50 4.00
43 Dany Heatley 1.50 4.00
44 Jason Spezza 1.50 4.00
45 Peter Forsberg 2.00 5.00
46 Shane Doan 1.00 2.50
47 Sidney Crosby 10.00 25.00
48 Marc-Andre Fleury 1.50 4.00
49 Mario Lemieux 5.00 12.00
50 Joe Thornton 2.00 5.00
51 Jonathan Cheechoo 1.50 4.00
52 Patrick Marleau 1.50 4.00
53 Brad Richards 1.50 4.00
54 Vincent Lecavalier 1.50 4.00
55 Martin St. Louis 1.50 4.00
56 Mats Sundin 1.50 4.00
57 Andrew Raycroft 1.50 4.00
58 Markus Naslund 1.50 4.00
59 Roberto Luongo 2.00 5.00
60 Alexander Ovechkin 4.00 10.00
61 David McKee RC 3.00 8.00
62 Ryan Shannon RC 2.00 5.00
63 Clarke MacArthur RC 2.00 5.00
64 Andrej Sekera RC 2.00 5.00
65 Michael Funk RC 2.00 5.00
66 Adam Dennis RC 2.00 5.00
67 Mike Card RC 2.00 5.00
68 Brandon Prust RC 2.00 5.00
69 Troy Brouwer RC 3.00 8.00
70 Adam Burish RC 2.00 5.00
71 Fredrik Norrena RC 3.00 8.00
72 Stefan Liv RC 2.00 5.00
73 Tomas Kopecky RC 3.00 8.00
74 Jeff Drouin-Deslauriers RC 2.00 5.00
75 David Booth RC 2.00 5.00
76 Janis Sprukts RC 2.00 5.00
77 Barry Brust RC 2.00 5.00
78 Konstantin Pushkaryov RC 2.00 5.00
79 Shawn Belle RC 2.00 5.00
80 Niklas Backstrom RC 4.00 10.00
81 Mikhail Grabovski RC 2.00 5.00
82 Johnny Oduya RC 2.00 5.00
83 Blake Comeau RC 2.00 5.00
84 Jarkko Immonen RC 2.00 5.00
85 Josh Hennessy RC 2.00 5.00
86 Kelly Guard RC 2.00 5.00
87 Jussi Timonen RC 2.00 5.00
88 Martin Houle RC 2.00 5.00
89 Michel Ouellet RC 4.00 10.00
90 Yan Stastny RC 2.00 5.00
91 Roman Polak RC 2.00 5.00
92 Marek Schwarz RC 3.00 8.00
93 David Backes RC 3.00 8.00
94 Blair Jones RC 2.00 5.00
95 Karri Ramo RC 2.00 5.00
96 Ian White RC 2.00 5.00
97 Brendan Bell RC 2.00 5.00
98 Kris Newbury RC 2.00 5.00
99 Jean-Francois Racine RC 2.00 5.00
100 Jesse Schultz RC 2.00 5.00
101 Alexander Edler RC 2.00 5.00
102 Daren Machesney RC 2.00 5.00
103 Matt Lashoff AU RC 6.00 15.00
104 Phil Kessel AU/99 RC 125.00 250.00
105 Mark Stuart AU RC 6.00 15.00
106 Michael Blunden AU RC 6.00 15.00
107 Dave Bolland AU RC 6.00 15.00
108 Paul Stastny AU RC 25.00 60.00
109 Loui Eriksson AU RC 6.00 15.00
110 Niklas Grossman AU RC 6.00 15.00
111 Ladislav Smid AU RC 6.00 15.00
112 Patrick Thoresen AU RC 10.00 25.00

113 Marc-Antoine Pouliot AU RC 10.00 25.00
114 Anze Kopitar AU RC 25.00 60.00
115 Patrick O'Sullivan AU RC 10.00 25.00
116 Guillaume Latendresse AU RC 25.00 60.00
117 Alexander Radulov AU RC 25.00 60.00
118 Shea Weber AU RC 10.00 25.00
119 Travis Zajac AU RC 12.00 30.00
120 Nigel Dawes AU RC 6.00 15.00
121 Dustin Boyd AU RC 10.00 25.00
122 Ryan Potulny AU RC 10.00 25.00
123 Benoit Pouliot AU RC 10.00 25.00
124 Keith Yandle AU RC 6.00 15.00
125 Evgeni Malkin AU/99 RC 350.00 600.00
126 Kristopher Letang AU RC 10.00 25.00
127 Jordan Staal AU/99 RC 350.00 600.00
128 Noah Welch AU RC 6.00 15.00
129 Marc-Edouard Vlasic AU RC 6.00 15.00
130 Matt Carle AU RC 10.00 25.00
131 Drew Stafford AU RC 20.00 50.00
132 Eric Fehr AU RC 10.00 25.00

2006-07 Ultimate Collection Autographed Jerseys

STATED PRINT RUN 50 #'d SETS
AJ-AF Alexander Frolov 6.00 15.00
AJ-AH Ales Hemsky 6.00 15.00
AJ-AR Andrew Raycroft 10.00 25.00
AJ-BB Brad Boyes 6.00 15.00
AJ-BH Bobby Hull 20.00 50.00
AJ-BM Brenden Morrow 10.00 25.00
AJ-BO Mike Bossy 10.00 25.00
AJ-BP Brad Park 10.00 25.00
AJ-BS Billy Smith 12.00 30.00
AJ-CN Cam Neely 15.00 40.00
AJ-CW Cam Ward 12.00 30.00
AJ-DH Dany Heatley 15.00 40.00
AJ-DP Denis Potvin 10.00 25.00
AJ-DT Dave Taylor 12.00 30.00
AJ-EL Patrik Elias 6.00 15.00
AJ-EM Evgeni Malkin 60.00 150.00
AJ-ES Eric Staal 12.00 30.00
AJ-GC Gerry Cheevers 10.00 25.00
AJ-GF Grant Fuhr 15.00 40.00
AJ-GL Guy Lafleur 20.00 50.00
AJ-GP Gilbert Perreault 12.00 30.00
AJ-HA Dominik Hasek 20.00 50.00
AJ-IK Ilya Kovalchuk 15.00 40.00
AJ-JB Jean Beliveau 15.00 40.00
AJ-JG Jean-Sebastien Giguere 10.00 25.00
AJ-JI Jarome Iginla 15.00 40.00
AJ-JK Jari Kurri 12.00 30.00
AJ-JR Jeremy Roenick 15.00 40.00
AJ-JS Jordan Staal 50.00 125.00
AJ-JT Joe Thornton 20.00 50.00
AJ-KL Kari Lehtonen 12.00 30.00
AJ-LM Lanny McDonald 10.00 25.00
AJ-LR Larry Robinson 10.00 25.00
AJ-MB Martin Brodeur 50.00 125.00
AJ-MG Marian Gaborik 15.00 40.00
AJ-MK Miikka Kiprusoff 12.00 30.00
AJ-ML Mario Lemieux 60.00 150.00
AJ-MM Mike Modano 15.00 40.00
AJ-MT Marty Turco 10.00 25.00
AJ-NL Nicklas Lidstrom 12.00 30.00
AJ-PE Phil Esposito 20.00 50.00
AJ-PH Dion Phaneuf 15.00 40.00
AJ-PK Phil Kessel 20.00 50.00
AJ-PM Patrick Marleau 10.00 25.00
AJ-PR Patrick Roy 60.00 150.00
AJ-RB Ray Bourque 20.00 50.00
AJ-RM Ryan Miller 12.00 30.00
AJ-RN Rick Nash 12.00 30.00
AJ-RV Rogie Vachon 12.00 30.00
AJ-RY Michael Ryder 10.00 25.00
AJ-SA Borje Salming 10.00 25.00
AJ-SC Sidney Crosby 150.00 250.00
AJ-SG Simon Gagne 12.00 30.00
AJ-TE Tony Esposito 12.00 30.00
AJ-TH Jose Theodore 12.00 30.00
AJ-TV Tomas Vokoun 10.00 25.00
AJ-VL Vincent Lecavalier 12.00 30.00
AJ-WG Wayne Gretzky 150.00 250.00

2006-07 Ultimate Collection Autographed Patches

STATED PRINT RUN 15 #'d SETS
NOT PRICED DUE TO SCARCITY
AJ-AF Alexander Frolov
AJ-AH Ales Hemsky
AJ-AR Andrew Raycroft
AJ-BB Brad Boyes
AJ-BM Brenden Morrow
AJ-BO Mike Bossy
AJ-BP Brad Park
AJ-BS Billy Smith
AJ-CN Cam Neely
AJ-CW Cam Ward
AJ-DH Dany Heatley
AJ-DP Denis Potvin
AJ-DT Dave Taylor
AJ-EL Patrik Elias
AJ-EM Evgeni Malkin
AJ-ES Eric Staal
AJ-GC Gerry Cheevers
AJ-GF Grant Fuhr
AJ-GL Guy Lafleur
AJ-GP Gilbert Perreault
AJ-HA Dominik Hasek
AJ-IK Ilya Kovalchuk
AJ-JB Jean Beliveau
AJ-JG Jean-Sebastien Giguere
AJ-JI Jarome Iginla
AJ-JK Jari Kurri
AJ-JR Jeremy Roenick
AJ-JS Jordan Staal
AJ-JT Joe Thornton
AJ-KL Kari Lehtonen
AJ-LM Lanny McDonald
AJ-LR Larry Robinson
AJ-MB Martin Brodeur
AJ-MG Marian Gaborik
AJ-MK Miikka Kiprusoff
AJ-ML Mario Lemieux
AJ-MM Mike Modano
AJ-MT Marty Turco
AJ-NL Nicklas Lidstrom
AJ-PE Phil Esposito
AJ-PH Dion Phaneuf
AJ-PK Phil Kessel
AJ-PM Patrick Marleau
AJ-PR Patrick Roy
AJ-RB Ray Bourque
AJ-RM Ryan Miller
AJ-RN Rick Nash
AJ-RV Rogie Vachon
AJ-RY Michael Ryder
AJ-SA Borje Salming
AJ-SC Sidney Crosby
AJ-SG Simon Gagne
AJ-TH Jose Theodore
AJ-TV Tomas Vokoun
AJ-VL Vincent Lecavalier
AJ-WG Wayne Gretzky

2006-07 Ultimate Collection Jerseys

STATED PRINT RUN 200 #'d SETS
UJ-AO Alexander Ovechkin 12.00 30.00
UJ-BC Bobby Clarke 5.00 12.00
UJ-BI Billy Smith 5.00 12.00
UJ-BR Martin Brodeur 12.00 30.00
UJ-BS Brendan Shanahan 5.00 12.00
UJ-CN Cam Neely 6.00 15.00
UJ-CW Cam Ward 5.00 12.00
UJ-DA Daniel Alfredsson 4.00 10.00
UJ-DH Dominik Hasek 8.00 20.00
UJ-DP Dion Phaneuf 8.00 20.00
UJ-DT Dave Taylor 4.00 10.00
UJ-EL Eric Lindros 5.00 12.00
UJ-EM Evgeni Malkin 15.00 40.00
UJ-ES Eric Staal 5.00 12.00
UJ-GC Gerry Cheevers 6.00 15.00
UJ-GF Grant Fuhr 6.00 15.00
UJ-GL Guy Lafleur 8.00 20.00
UJ-GP Gilbert Perreault 5.00 12.00
UJ-GW Gump Worsley 4.00 10.00
UJ-HE Dany Heatley 6.00 15.00
UJ-HL Henrik Lundqvist 8.00 20.00
UJ-HZ Henrik Zetterberg 5.00 12.00
UJ-IK Ilya Kovalchuk 6.00 15.00
UJ-JB Jean Beliveau 6.00 15.00
UJ-JI Jarome Iginla 6.00 15.00
UJ-JJ Jaromir Jagr 8.00 20.00
UJ-JK Jari Kurri 5.00 12.00
UJ-JS Joe Sakic 10.00 25.00
UJ-JT Joe Thornton 8.00 20.00
UJ-KL Kari Lehtonen 5.00 12.00
UJ-LM Lanny McDonald 4.00 10.00
UJ-LR Larry Robinson 4.00 10.00
UJ-MB Mike Bossy 4.00 10.00
UJ-MD Marcel Dionne 5.00 12.00
UJ-MG Marian Gaborik 8.00 20.00
UJ-MH Milan Hejduk 3.00 8.00
UJ-ML Mario Lemieux 15.00 40.00
UJ-MM Mike Modano 5.00 12.00
UJ-MN Markus Naslund 5.00 12.00
UJ-MR Michael Ryder 4.00 10.00
UJ-MS Mats Sundin 5.00 12.00
UJ-NL Nicklas Lidstrom 5.00 12.00
UJ-PB Patrice Bergeron 5.00 12.00
UJ-PF Peter Forsberg 8.00 20.00
UJ-PK Paul Kariya 5.00 12.00
UJ-PO Denis Potvin 4.00 10.00
UJ-PR Patrick Roy 15.00 40.00
UJ-PS Peter Stastny 3.00 8.00
UJ-RB Ray Bourque 10.00 25.00
UJ-RL Roberto Luongo 8.00 20.00
UJ-RN Rick Nash 5.00 12.00
UJ-SA Borje Salming 4.00 10.00
UJ-SC Sidney Crosby 25.00 60.00
UJ-SM Stan Mikita 5.00 12.00
UJ-SP Jason Spezza 5.00 12.00
UJ-SS Scott Stevens 3.00 8.00
UJ-ST Martin St. Louis 4.00 10.00
UJ-TS Teemu Selanne 5.00 12.00
UJ-TV Tomas Vokoun 4.00 10.00
UJ-VL Vincent Lecavalier 5.00 12.00

2006-07 Ultimate Collection Jerseys Dual

STATED PRINT RUN 50 #'d SETS
UJ2-CM Sidney Crosby 40.00 100.00
Evgeni Malkin
UJ2-CP Bobby Clarke 15.00 40.00
Gilbert Perreault
UJ2-DB Darryl Sittler 8.00 20.00
Borje Salming
UJ2-DV Marcel Dionne 8.00 20.00
Rogie Vachon
UJ2-EE Phil Esposito 12.00 30.00
Tony Esposito
UJ2-FG Peter Forsberg 12.00 30.00
Simon Gagne
UJ2-GL Mario Lemieux 50.00 125.00
Wayne Gretzky
UJ2-HL Dominik Hasek 10.00 25.00
Nicklas Lidstrom
UJ2-HS Ryan Smyth 8.00 20.00
Ales Hemsky
UJ2-JL Jaromir Jagr 20.00 50.00
Henrik Lundqvist
UJ2-KA Paul Kariya 10.00 25.00
Jason Arnott
UJ2-KI Jarome Iginla 15.00 40.00
Miikka Kiprusoff
UJ2-KS Teemu Selanne 8.00 20.00
Jari Kurri
UJ2-LN Markus Naslund 10.00 25.00
Roberto Luongo
UJ2-LS Vincent Lecavalier 10.00 25.00
Martin St. Louis
UJ2-ME Lanny McDonald 6.00 15.00
Ron Ellis
UJ2-ML Mike Modano 10.00 25.00
Eric Lindros
UJ2-MM Joe Mullen 6.00 15.00
Al MacInnis
UJ2-NB Cam Neely 15.00 40.00
Patrice Bergeron
UJ2-NL Pascal LeClaire 8.00 20.00
Rick Nash
UJ2-RB Patrick Roy 15.00 40.00
Ray Bourque
UJ2-RD Jeremy Roenick 6.00 15.00
Shane Doan
UJ2-RP Denis Potvin 10.00 25.00
Larry Robinson
UJ2-SH Jason Spezza 10.00 25.00
Dany Heatley
UJ2-SS Joe Sakic 15.00 40.00
Peter Stastny
UJ2-SW Eric Staal 8.00 20.00
Cam Ward
UJ2-TC Joe Thornton 12.00 30.00
Jonathan Cheechoo
UJ2-TH Milan Hejduk 6.00 15.00
Jose Theodore
UJ2-ZD Pavel Datsyuk 10.00 25.00
Henrik Zetterberg

2006-07 Ultimate Collection Jerseys Triple

STATED PRINT RUN 25 #'d SETS
UJ3-CMS Sidney Crosby 150.00 300.00
Evgeni Malkin
Jordan Staal
UJ3-ENK Phil Esposito 40.00 100.00
Cam Neely
Phil Kessel
UJ3-GHL Mario Lemieux 200.00 350.00
Wayne Gretzky
Gordie Howe
UJ3-LRS Guy Lafleur 25.00 60.00
Steve Shutt
Larry Robinson
UJ3-OMK Ilya Kovalchuk 75.00 150.00
Alexander Ovechkin
Evgeni Malkin
UJ3-RBL Patrick Roy 75.00 150.00
Martin Brodeur
Roberto Luongo
UJ3-SBG Mike Bossy 30.00 80.00
Denis Potvin
Billy Smith
UJ3-SFL Nicklas Lidstrom 40.00 100.00
Peter Forsberg
Mats Sundin
UJ3-SSH Darryl Sittler 25.00 60.00
Borje Salming
Paul Henderson
UJ3-STS Joe Sakic 40.00 100.00
Joe Thornton
Eric Staal

2006-07 Ultimate Collection Patches

STATED PRINT RUN 75 #'d SETS
UNIQUE SWATCHES MAY EARN SUBSTANTIAL PREMIUM
UJ-AO Alexander Ovechkin 25.00 60.00
UJ-BC Bobby Clarke 15.00 40.00
UJ-BI Billy Smith 15.00 40.00
UJ-BR Martin Brodeur 25.00 60.00
UJ-BS Brendan Shanahan 15.00 40.00
UJ-CN Cam Neely 15.00 40.00
UJ-CW Cam Ward 15.00 40.00
UJ-DA Daniel Alfredsson 10.00 25.00
UJ-DH Dominik Hasek 20.00 50.00
UJ-DP Dion Phaneuf 15.00 40.00
UJ-DT Dave Taylor 10.00 25.00
UJ-EL Eric Lindros 15.00 40.00
UJ-EM Evgeni Malkin 40.00 100.00
UJ-ES Eric Staal 15.00 40.00
UJ-GC Gerry Cheevers 10.00 25.00
UJ-GF Grant Fuhr 15.00 40.00
UJ-GL Guy Lafleur 15.00 40.00
UJ-GP Gilbert Perreault 15.00 40.00
UJ-GW Gump Worsley 15.00 40.00
UJ-HE Dany Heatley 20.00 50.00
UJ-HL Henrik Lundqvist 20.00 50.00
UJ-HZ Henrik Zetterberg 15.00 40.00
UJ-IK Ilya Kovalchuk 20.00 50.00
UJ-JI Jarome Iginla 20.00 50.00
UJ-JJ Jaromir Jagr 20.00 50.00
UJ-JK Jari Kurri 20.00 50.00
UJ-JS Joe Sakic 25.00 60.00
UJ-JT Joe Thornton 20.00 50.00
UJ-KL Kari Lehtonen 15.00 40.00
UJ-LM Lanny McDonald 10.00 25.00
UJ-LR Larry Robinson 10.00 25.00
UJ-MB Mike Bossy 10.00 25.00
UJ-MD Marcel Dionne 10.00 25.00
UJ-MG Marian Gaborik 20.00 50.00
UJ-MH Milan Hejduk 8.00 20.00
UJ-ML Mario Lemieux 30.00 80.00
UJ-MM Mike Modano 15.00 40.00
UJ-MN Markus Naslund 15.00 40.00
UJ-MR Michael Ryder 10.00 25.00
UJ-MS Mats Sundin 15.00 40.00
UJ-NL Nicklas Lidstrom 15.00 40.00
UJ-PB Patrice Bergeron 15.00 40.00
UJ-PF Peter Forsberg 20.00 50.00
UJ-PK Paul Kariya 15.00 40.00
UJ-PR Patrick Roy 30.00 80.00
UJ-PS Peter Stastny 8.00 20.00
UJ-RB Ray Bourque 20.00 50.00
UJ-RL Roberto Luongo 20.00 50.00
UJ-RN Rick Nash 15.00 40.00
UJ-SA Borje Salming 10.00 25.00
UJ-SC Sidney Crosby 50.00 125.00
UJ-SM Stan Mikita 15.00 40.00
UJ-SP Jason Spezza 15.00 40.00
UJ-SS Scott Stevens 10.00 25.00
UJ-ST Martin St. Louis 10.00 25.00
UJ-TS Teemu Selanne 15.00 40.00
UJ-TV Tomas Vokoun 10.00 25.00
UJ-VL Vincent Lecavalier 15.00 40.00

2006-07 Ultimate Collection Patches Dual

STATED PRINT RUN 25 #'d SETS
NOT YET PRICED DUE TO LACK OF MARKET DATA
UJ2-CM Sidney Crosby 300.00 400.00
Evgeni Malkin
UJ2-CP Bobby Clarke 25.00 60.00
Gilbert Perreault
UJ2-DB Darryl Sittler 20.00 50.00
Borje Salming
UJ2-DV Marcel Dionne 40.00 100.00
Rogie Vachon/15
UJ2-EE Phil Esposito 30.00 80.00
Tony Esposito
UJ2-FG Peter Forsberg 20.00 50.00
Simon Gagne
UJ2-GL Mario Lemieux 250.00 350.00
Wayne Gretzky
UJ2-HL Dominik Hasek 25.00 60.00
Nicklas Lidstrom
UJ2-HS Ryan Smyth 15.00 40.00
Ales Hemsky
UJ2-JL Jaromir Jagr 30.00 80.00
Henrik Lundqvist
UJ2-KA Paul Kariya 20.00 50.00
Jason Arnott
UJ2-KI Jarome Iginla 25.00 60.00
Miikka Kiprusoff
UJ2-KS Teemu Selanne 60.00 150.00
Jari Kurri
UJ2-LN Markus Naslund 25.00 60.00
Roberto Luongo
UJ2-LS Vincent Lecavalier 30.00 80.00
Martin St. Louis
UJ2-ME Lanny McDonald 12.00 30.00
Ron Ellis
UJ2-ML Mike Modano 25.00 60.00
Eric Lindros
UJ2-MM Joe Mullen 30.00 80.00
Al MacInnis
UJ2-NB Cam Neely 30.00 80.00
Patrice Bergeron
UJ2-NL Pascal LeClaire 30.00 80.00
Rick Nash
UJ2-RB Patrick Roy 75.00 175.00
Ray Bourque
UJ2-RD Jeremy Roenick 25.00 60.00
Shane Doan
UJ2-SH Jason Spezza 30.00 80.00
Dany Heatley
UJ2-SS Joe Sakic 30.00 80.00
Peter Stastny
UJ2-SW Eric Staal 15.00 40.00
Cam Ward
UJ2-TC Joe Thornton
Jonathan Cheechoo
UJ2-TH Milan Hejduk 20.00 50.00
Jose Theodore
UJ2-ZD Pavel Datsyuk 40.00 100.00
Henrik Zetterberg

2006-07 Ultimate Collection Patches Triple

STATED PRINT RUN 5 #'d SETS
NOT PRICED DUE TO SCARCITY

2006-07 Ultimate Collection Premium Patches

STATED PRINT RUN 25 #'d SETS
UNIQUE SWATCHES MAY EARN PREMIUM
PS-AF Alexander Frolov 25.00 60.00
PS-AH Ales Hemsky 25.00 60.00
PS-AK Alexei Kovalev 20.00 40.00
PS-AM Al MacInnis 20.00 40.00
PS-AR Andrew Raycroft 30.00 60.00
PS-AS Alexander Steen 30.00 60.00
PS-AT Alex Tanguay 30.00 60.00
PS-AY Alexei Yashin 20.00 40.00
PS-BL Rob Blake 30.00 60.00
PS-BO Mike Bossy 30.00 60.00
PS-BS Borje Salming 30.00 60.00
PS-CD Chris Drury 20.00 40.00
PS-CJ Curtis Joseph 40.00 80.00
PS-CN Cam Neely 40.00 80.00
PS-CW Cam Ward 40.00 80.00
PS-DB Daniel Briere 30.00 60.00
PS-DH Dominik Hasek 50.00 100.00
PS-EL Eric Lindros 40.00 80.00
PS-ES Eric Staal 30.00 60.00
PS-GW Gump Worsley 50.00 100.00
PS-HA Martin Havlat 30.00 60.00
PS-HE Milan Hejduk 25.00 60.00
PS-HT Hannu Toivonen 30.00 60.00
PS-IK Ilya Kovalchuk 25.00 80.00
PS-JB Jay Bouwmeester 20.00 40.00
PS-JG Jean-Sebastien Giguere 30.00 60.00
PS-JJ Jaromir Jagr 50.00 100.00
PS-JL Jere Lehtinen 30.00 80.00
PS-JM Joe Mullen 20.00 40.00
PS-JP Joni Pitkanen 20.00 40.00
PS-JR Jeremy Roenick 40.00 80.00
PS-JT Joe Thornton 50.00 100.00
PS-KL Kari Lehtonen 30.00 60.00
PS-LM Lanny McDonald 30.00 60.00
PS-MA Maxim Afinogenov 20.00 40.00
PS-MB Martin Brodeur 60.00 150.00
PS-MG Marian Gaborik 40.00 80.00
PS-MH Marian Hossa 30.00 60.00
PS-MK Miikka Kiprusoff 40.00 100.00
PS-MM Mike Modano 40.00 80.00
PS-MN Markus Naslund 40.00 80.00
PS-MP Michael Peca 20.00 40.00
PS-MR Mark Recchi 20.00 40.00
PS-MS Miroslav Satan 25.00 60.00
PS-MT Marty Turco 30.00 60.00
PS-OK Olaf Kolzig 40.00 80.00
PS-PD Pavel Datsyuk 30.00 60.00
PS-PE Patrik Elias 30.00 60.00
PS-PL Pascal LeClaire 30.00 60.00
PS-PM Patrick Marleau 30.00 60.00
PS-RB Ray Bourque 50.00 100.00
PS-RE Ron Ellis/20 40.00 80.00
PS-RM Ryan Miller 40.00 80.00
PS-RS Ryan Smyth 30.00 60.00
PS-SF Sergei Fedorov 40.00 80.00
PS-SZ Sergei Zubov 20.00 40.00
PS-ZC Zdeno Chara 20.00 40.00

2006-07 Ultimate Collection Premium Swatches

STATED PRINT RUN 50 #'d SETS
PS-AF Alexander Frolov 5.00 12.00
PS-AH Ales Hemsky 5.00 12.00
PS-AK Alexei Kovalev 5.00 12.00
PS-AM Al MacInnis 5.00 12.00
PS-AR Andrew Raycroft 8.00 20.00
PS-AS Alexander Steen 8.00 20.00
PS-AT Alex Tanguay 8.00 20.00
PS-AY Alexei Yashin 5.00 12.00
PS-BL Rob Blake 8.00 20.00
PS-BO Mike Bossy 8.00 20.00
PS-BS Borje Salming 8.00 20.00
PS-CD Chris Drury 5.00 12.00
PS-CJ Curtis Joseph 8.00 20.00
PS-CN Cam Neely 10.00 25.00
PS-CW Cam Ward 8.00 20.00
PS-DB Daniel Briere 8.00 20.00
PS-DG Doug Gilmour 10.00 25.00
PS-DH Dominik Hasek 12.00 30.00
PS-EL Eric Lindros 8.00 20.00
PS-ES Eric Staal 8.00 20.00
PS-GW Gump Worsley 8.00 20.00
PS-HA Martin Havlat 8.00 20.00
PS-HE Milan Hejduk 5.00 12.00
PS-HT Hannu Toivonen 8.00 20.00
PS-IK Ilya Kovalchuk 12.00 30.00
PS-JB Jay Bouwmeester 5.00 12.00
PS-JG Jean-Sebastien Giguere 8.00 20.00
PS-JJ Jaromir Jagr 12.00 30.00
PS-JL Jere Lehtinen 5.00 12.00
PS-JM Joe Mullen 5.00 12.00
PS-JP Joni Pitkanen 5.00 12.00
PS-JR Jeremy Roenick 10.00 25.00
PS-JT Joe Thornton 12.00 30.00
PS-KL Kari Lehtonen 10.00 25.00
PS-LM Lanny McDonald 8.00 20.00
PS-MA Maxim Afinogenov 5.00 12.00
PS-MB Martin Brodeur 20.00 50.00
PS-MG Marian Gaborik 12.00 30.00
PS-MH Marian Hossa 8.00 20.00
PS-MK Miikka Kiprusoff 10.00 25.00
PS-MM Mike Modano 10.00 25.00
PS-MN Markus Naslund 10.00 25.00
PS-MP Michael Peca 5.00 12.00
PS-MR Mark Recchi 5.00 12.00
PS-MS Miroslav Satan 5.00 12.00
PS-MT Marty Turco 8.00 20.00
PS-MU Larry Murphy 5.00 12.00
PS-OK Olaf Kolzig 8.00 20.00
PS-PD Pavel Datsyuk 8.00 20.00
PS-PE Patrik Elias 5.00 12.00
PS-PL Pascal LeClaire 8.00 20.00
PS-PM Patrick Marleau 8.00 20.00
PS-RB Ray Bourque 10.00 25.00
PS-RE Ron Ellis 8.00 20.00
PS-RM Ryan Miller 10.00 25.00
PS-RS Ryan Smyth 8.00 20.00
PS-SF Sergei Fedorov 10.00 25.00
PS-SS Scott Stevens 5.00 12.00
PS-SZ Sergei Zubov 5.00 12.00
PS-ZC Zdeno Chara 5.00 12.00

2006-07 Ultimate Collection Rookies Autographed NHL Shields

STATED PRINT RUN 1/1
NOT PRICED DUE TO SCARCITY

2006-07 Ultimate Collection Rookies Autographed Patches

STATED PRINT RUN 25 #'d SETS
UNIQUE SWATCHES MAY EARN SUBSTANTIAL PREMIUM
103 Matt Lashoff 20.00 50.00
104 Phil Kessel 60.00 150.00
105 Mark Stuart 20.00 50.00
106 Michael Blunden 20.00 50.00
107 Dave Bolland 20.00 50.00
108 Paul Stastny 75.00 200.00
109 Loui Eriksson 20.00 50.00
110 Niklas Grossman 20.00 50.00
111 Ladislav Smid 20.00 50.00
112 Patrick Thoresen 25.00 60.00
113 Marc-Antoine Pouliot 25.00 60.00
114 Anze Kopitar 75.00 200.00
115 Patrick O'Sullivan 30.00 80.00
116 Guillaume Latendresse 75.00 200.00
117 Alexander Radulov 60.00 150.00
118 Shea Weber 25.00 60.00
119 Travis Zajac 30.00 80.00
120 Nigel Dawes 20.00 50.00
121 Dustin Boyd 30.00 80.00
122 Ryan Potulny 25.00 60.00
123 Benoit Pouliot 30.00 80.00
124 Keith Yandle 20.00 50.00
125 Evgeni Malkin 250.00 400.00
126 Kristopher Letang 30.00 80.00
127 Jordan Staal 200.00 350.00
128 Noah Welch 20.00 50.00
129 Marc-Edouard Vlasic 20.00 50.00
130 Matt Carle 30.00 80.00
131 Drew Stafford 60.00 150.00
132 Eric Fehr 25.00 60.00

2006-07 Ultimate Collection Signatures

US-AH Ales Hemsky 3.00 8.00
US-AK Anze Kopitar 15.00 40.00
US-AM Al MacInnis 3.00 8.00
US-AR Andrew Raycroft 5.00 12.00
US-AT Alex Tanguay 5.00 12.00
US-BB Brad Boyes 3.00 8.00
US-BC Bobby Clarke 6.00 15.00
US-BF Bernie Federko 3.00 8.00
US-BH Bobby Hull SP 20.00 50.00
US-BM Mike Bossy SP 20.00 50.00
US-BO Pierre-Marc Bouchard 3.00 8.00
US-BP Bernie Parent 5.00 12.00
US-BR Richard Brodeur 5.00 12.00
US-BU Johnny Bucyk 3.00 8.00
US-CA Colby Armstrong 3.00 8.00
US-CH Jonathan Cheechoo 6.00 15.00
US-CI Dino Ciccarelli 3.00 8.00
US-CN Cam Neely 8.00 20.00
US-CW Cam Ward 8.00 20.00
US-DC Don Cherry 15.00 40.00
US-DH Dominik Hasek SP 20.00 50.00
US-DR Dwayne Roloson 6.00 15.00
US-DS Denis Savard 5.00 12.00
US-EM Evgeni Malkin 30.00 80.00
US-ES Eric Staal 6.00 15.00
US-GB Gilbert Brule 6.00 15.00
US-GC Gerry Cheevers 12.00 30.00
US-GF Grant Fuhr SP 12.00 30.00
US-GH Gordie Howe 25.00 50.00
US-GL Guillaume Latendresse 12.00 30.00
US-GP Gilbert Perreault 6.00 15.00
US-HA Dale Hawerchuk 3.00 8.00
US-HE Dany Heatley SP 20.00 40.00
US-HL Henrik Lundqvist 8.00 20.00
US-IK Ilya Kovalchuk 8.00 20.00
US-JA Jason Arnott 3.00 8.00
US-JB Jean Beliveau SP 50.00 100.00
US-JG Jean-Sebastien Giguere 5.00 12.00
US-JI Jarome Iginla SP 10.00 25.00
US-JK Jari Kurri 6.00 15.00
US-JM Joe Mullen 3.00 8.00
US-JO Johnny Bower 5.00 12.00
US-KL Kari Lehtonen 6.00 15.00
US-LR Larry Robinson 5.00 12.00
US-MB Martin Brodeur SP 60.00 150.00
US-MC Matt Carle 5.00 12.00
US-MD Marcel Dionne 6.00 15.00
US-MF Marc-Andre Fleury 6.00 15.00
US-MG Marian Gaborik 8.00 20.00
US-MH Martin Havlat 5.00 12.00
US-MI Milan Hejduk 3.00 8.00
US-ML Mario Lemieux SP 100.00 200.00
US-MM Mike Modano 8.00 20.00
US-MR Michael Ryder 5.00 12.00
US-MS Marek Svatos 3.00 8.00
US-MT Marty Turco 5.00 12.00
US-NL Nicklas Lidstrom 6.00 15.00
US-OR Bobby Orr 100.00 175.00
US-PB Patrice Bergeron 6.00 15.00
US-PE Patrik Elias 3.00 8.00
US-PH Phil Esposito SP 10.00 25.00
US-PK Phil Kessel 10.00 25.00
US-PM Patrick Marleau SP 8.00 20.00
US-PO Denis Potvin 5.00 12.00
US-PR Patrick Roy SP 100.00 200.00
US-PS Paul Stastny 20.00 40.00
US-RA Alexander Radulov 10.00 25.00
US-RB Ray Bourque SP 40.00 100.00
US-RH Ron Hextall 6.00 15.00
US-RM Ryan Miller 8.00 20.00
US-RN Rick Nash 6.00 15.00
US-RS Ryan Smyth 5.00 12.00
US-SB Steve Bernier 3.00 8.00
US-SC Sidney Crosby 100.00 200.00
US-SG Simon Gagne 6.00 15.00
US-SK Saku Koivu SP 50.00 80.00
US-SP Peter Stastny 3.00 8.00
US-SS Scott Stevens 3.00 8.00
US-ST Jordan Staal 30.00 60.00
US-TE Tony Esposito SP 12.00 30.00
US-TH Joe Thornton SP 30.00 60.00
US-TL Ted Lindsay 3.00 8.00
US-TO Terry O'Reilly 5.00 12.00
US-TV Tomas Vokoun 5.00 12.00
US-VL Vincent Lecavalier SP 20.00 50.00
US-VT Vesa Toskala 5.00 12.00
US-WG Wayne Gretzky 100.00 200.00

2006-07 Ultimate Collection Ultimate Achievements

PRINT RUNS VARY
UNDER 10 NOT PRICED DUE TO SCARCITY
UA-BC Bobby Clarke/89 10.00 25.00
UA-BH Bobby Hull/58 15.00 40.00
UA-BO Bobby Orr/6 1000.00 1500.00
UA-BP Bernie Parent/47 15.00 40.00
UA-CN Cam Neely/9
UA-CW Cam Ward/15 50.00 100.00
UA-DH Dany Heatley/50 15.00 40.00
UA-EM Evgeni Malkin/6
UA-ES Eric Staal/28 15.00 40.00
UA-GF Grant Fuhr/23 30.00 60.00
UA-GH Gordie Howe/26 60.00 125.00
UA-GL Guy Lafleur/60 20.00 50.00
UA-GP Gilbert Perreault/72 10.00 25.00
UA-HA Dominik Hasek/41 20.00 50.00
UA-IK Ilya Kovalchuk/52 12.00 30.00
UA-JB Jean Beliveau/10 75.00 150.00
UA-JC Jonathan Cheechoo/56 10.00 25.00
UA-JI Jarome Iginla/52 15.00 40.00
UA-JK Jari Kurri/68 10.00 25.00
UA-JT Joe Thornton/96 12.00 30.00
UA-LR Luc Robitaille/63 25.00 60.00
UA-MB Martin Brodeur/43 40.00 100.00
UA-MD Marcel Dionne/53 15.00 40.00
UA-MF Marc-Andre Fleury/40 20.00 40.00
UA-MG Marian Gaborik/38 30.00 60.00
UA-MH Milan Hejduk/50 6.00 15.00
UA-MI Mike Bossy/9 125.00 200.00
UA-MK Miikka Kiprusoff/42 20.00 50.00
UA-ML Mario Lemieux/8
UA-MM Mike Modano/23 30.00 60.00
UA-NL Nicklas Lidstrom/80 12.00 30.00
UA-PE Phil Esposito/76 15.00 40.00
UA-PR Patrick Roy/23 200.00 300.00
UA-PS Peter Stastny/70 8.00 20.00
UA-RN Rick Nash/41 15.00 40.00
UA-SC Sidney Crosby/39 150.00 300.00
UA-SK Saku Koivu/71 12.00 30.00
UA-TV Tomas Vokoun/36 12.00 30.00
UA-VL Vincent Lecavalier/78 12.00 30.00
UA-WG Wayne Gretzky/10 750.00 1000.00

2006-07 Ultimate Collection Ultimate Debut Threads Jerseys

STATED PRINT RUN 150 #'d SETS
DJ-AK Anze Kopitar 8.00 20.00
DJ-AR Alexander Radulov 8.00 20.00
DJ-BB Brendan Bell 3.00 8.00
DJ-BO Dave Bolland 3.00 8.00
DJ-BP Benoit Pouliot 4.00 10.00
DJ-BT Billy Thompson 4.00 10.00
DJ-CG Carsen Germyn 3.00 8.00
DJ-DB Dustin Byfuglien 3.00 8.00
DJ-DK D.J. King 3.00 8.00
DJ-DP David Printz 3.00 8.00
DJ-DS Drew Stafford 6.00 15.00
DJ-DU Dustin Boyd 4.00 10.00
DJ-EF Eric Fehr 4.00 10.00
DJ-EM Evgeni Malkin 15.00 40.00
DJ-FD Frank Doyle 4.00 10.00
DJ-FN Filip Novak 3.00 8.00
DJ-GL Guillaume Latendresse 8.00 20.00
DJ-IW Ian White 3.00 8.00
DJ-JI Jarkko Immonen 3.00 8.00
DJ-JJ Jonas Johansson 3.00 8.00
DJ-JO John Oduya 3.00 8.00
DJ-JW Jeremy Williams 3.00 8.00
DJ-KL Kristopher Letang 5.00 12.00
DJ-KP Konstantin Pushkaryov 3.00 8.00
DJ-KY Keith Yandle 3.00 8.00
DJ-LB Luc Bourdon 5.00 12.00
DJ-LE Loui Eriksson 5.00 12.00
DJ-LS Ladislav Smid 3.00 8.00
DJ-MB Michael Blunden 3.00 8.00
DJ-MC Matt Carle 4.00 10.00
DJ-MI Mikko Lehtonen 3.00 8.00
DJ-MK Miroslav Kopriva 4.00 10.00
DJ-ML Matt Lashoff 3.00 8.00
DJ-MM Masi Marjamaki 3.00 8.00
DJ-MO Michel Ouellet 4.00 10.00
DJ-MP Marc-Antoine Pouliot 4.00 10.00
DJ-MS Mark Stuart 3.00 8.00
DJ-MV Marc-Edouard Vlasic 3.00 8.00
DJ-NB Niklas Backstrom 4.00 10.00
DJ-ND Nigel Dawes 5.00 12.00
DJ-NO Fredrik Norrena 4.00 10.00
DJ-NW Noah Welch 3.00 8.00
DJ-ON Ben Ondrus 3.00 8.00
DJ-PK Phil Kessel 8.00 20.00
DJ-PO Patrick O'Sullivan 4.00 10.00
DJ-PR Brandon Prust 3.00 8.00
DJ-PS Paul Stastny 12.00 30.00
DJ-PT Patrick Thoresen 4.00 10.00
DJ-RO Roman Polak 3.00 8.00
DJ-RP Ryan Potulny 4.00 10.00
DJ-RS Ryan Shannon 3.00 8.00
DJ-SO Shane O'Brien 3.00 8.00
DJ-ST Jordan Staal 15.00 40.00
DJ-SW Shea Weber 5.00 12.00
DJ-TK Tomas Kopecky 4.00 10.00
DJ-TZ Travis Zajac 4.00 10.00
DJ-YS Yan Stastny 3.00 8.00

2006-07 Ultimate Collection Ultimate Debut Threads Jerseys Autographs

STATED PRINT RUN 35 #'d SETS
DJ-AK Anze Kopitar 25.00 60.00
DJ-AR Alexander Radulov 20.00 50.00
DJ-BB Brendan Bell 8.00 20.00
DJ-BO Dave Bolland 8.00 20.00
DJ-BP Benoit Pouliot 12.00 30.00
DJ-BT Billy Thompson 8.00 20.00
DJ-CG Carsen Germyn 8.00 20.00
DJ-DB Dustin Byfuglien 8.00 20.00
DJ-DK D.J. King 8.00 20.00
DJ-DP David Printz 8.00 20.00
DJ-DS Drew Stafford 20.00 50.00
DJ-DU Dustin Boyd 12.00 30.00
DJ-EF Eric Fehr 12.00 30.00
DJ-EM Evgeni Malkin 60.00 150.00
DJ-FD Frank Doyle 12.00 30.00
DJ-FN Filip Novak 8.00 20.00
DJ-GL Guillaume Latendresse 25.00 60.00
DJ-IW Ian White 8.00 20.00
DJ-JI Jarkko Immonen 8.00 20.00
DJ-JJ Jonas Johansson 8.00 20.00
DJ-JO John Oduya 8.00 20.00
DJ-JW Jeremy Williams 8.00 20.00
DJ-KL Kristopher Letang 12.00 30.00
DJ-KP Konstantin Pushkaryov 8.00 20.00
DJ-KY Keith Yandle 8.00 20.00
DJ-LB Luc Bourdon 12.00 30.00
DJ-LE Loui Eriksson 8.00 20.00
DJ-LS Ladislav Smid 8.00 20.00
DJ-MB Michael Blunden 8.00 20.00
DJ-MC Matt Carle 12.00 30.00
DJ-MI Mikko Lehtonen 8.00 20.00
DJ-MK Miroslav Kopriva 8.00 20.00
DJ-ML Matt Lashoff 8.00 20.00
DJ-MM Masi Marjamaki 8.00 20.00
DJ-MO Michel Ouellet 15.00 40.00
DJ-MP Marc-Antoine Pouliot 12.00 30.00
DJ-MS Mark Stuart 8.00 20.00
DJ-MV Marc-Edouard Vlasic 8.00 20.00
DJ-NB Niklas Backstrom 15.00 40.00
DJ-ND Nigel Dawes 8.00 20.00
DJ-NO Fredrik Norrena 12.00 30.00
DJ-NW Noah Welch 8.00 20.00
DJ-ON Ben Ondrus 8.00 20.00
DJ-PK Phil Kessel 20.00 50.00
DJ-PO Patrick O'Sullivan 12.00 30.00
DJ-PR Brandon Prust 8.00 20.00
DJ-PS Paul Stastny 30.00 80.00
DJ-PT Patrick Thoresen 12.00 30.00
DJ-RO Roman Polak 8.00 20.00
DJ-RP Ryan Potulny 12.00 30.00
DJ-RS Ryan Shannon 8.00 20.00
DJ-SO Shane O'Brien 8.00 20.00
DJ-ST Jordan Staal 50.00 125.00
DJ-SW Shea Weber 12.00 30.00
DJ-TK Tomas Kopecky 12.00 30.00
DJ-TZ Travis Zajac 15.00 40.00
DJ-YS Yan Stastny 8.00 20.00

2006-07 Ultimate Collection Ultimate Debut Threads Patches

STATED PRINT RUN 25 #'d SETS
DJ-AK Anze Kopitar 50.00 125.00
DJ-AR Alexander Radulov 40.00 100.00
DJ-BB Brendan Bell 15.00 40.00
DJ-BO Dave Bolland 15.00 40.00
DJ-BP Benoit Pouliot 20.00 50.00
DJ-BT Billy Thompson 15.00 40.00
DJ-CG Carsen Germyn 15.00 40.00
DJ-DB Dustin Byfuglien 15.00 40.00
DJ-DK D.J. King 15.00 40.00
DJ-DP David Printz 12.00 30.00
DJ-DS Drew Stafford 40.00 100.00
DJ-DU Dustin Boyd 20.00 50.00
DJ-EF Eric Fehr 20.00 50.00
DJ-EM Evgeni Malkin 100.00 250.00
DJ-FD Frank Doyle 20.00 50.00
DJ-FN Filip Novak 12.00 30.00
DJ-GL Guillaume Latendresse 50.00 125.00
DJ-IW Ian White 12.00 30.00
DJ-JI Jarkko Immonen 15.00 40.00
DJ-JJ Jonas Johansson 12.00 30.00
DJ-JO John Oduya 12.00 30.00
DJ-JW Jeremy Williams 12.00 30.00
DJ-KL Kristopher Letang 20.00 50.00
DJ-KP Konstantin Pushkaryov 12.00 30.00
DJ-KY Keith Yandle 12.00 30.00
DJ-LB Luc Bourdon 20.00 50.00
DJ-LE Loui Eriksson 20.00 50.00
DJ-LS Ladislav Smid 12.00 30.00
DJ-MB Michael Blunden 12.00 30.00
DJ-MC Matt Carle 20.00 50.00
DJ-MI Mikko Lehtonen 12.00 30.00
DJ-MK Miroslav Kopriva 12.00 30.00
DJ-ML Matt Lashoff 12.00 30.00
DJ-MM Masi Marjamaki 12.00 30.00
DJ-MO Michel Ouellet 25.00 60.00
DJ-MP Marc-Antoine Pouliot 20.00 50.00
DJ-MS Mark Stuart 12.00 30.00
DJ-MV Marc-Edouard Vlasic 12.00 30.00
DJ-NB Niklas Backstrom 25.00 60.00
DJ-ND Nigel Dawes 12.00 30.00
DJ-NO Fredrik Norrena 20.00 50.00
DJ-NW Noah Welch 12.00 30.00
DJ-ON Ben Ondrus 12.00 30.00
DJ-PK Phil Kessel 40.00 100.00
DJ-PO Patrick O'Sullivan 20.00 50.00
DJ-PR Brandon Prust 12.00 30.00
DJ-PS Paul Stastny 60.00 150.00
DJ-PT Patrick Thoresen 20.00 50.00
DJ-RO Roman Polak 12.00 30.00
DJ-RP Ryan Potulny 20.00 50.00
DJ-RS Ryan Shannon 12.00 30.00
DJ-SO Shane O'Brien 12.00 30.00
DJ-ST Jordan Staal 100.00 250.00
DJ-SW Shea Weber 20.00 50.00
DJ-TK Tomas Kopecky 20.00 50.00
DJ-TZ Travis Zajac 25.00 60.00
DJ-YS Yan Stastny 12.00 30.00

2006-07 Ultimate Collection Ultimate Debut Threads Patches Autographs

STATED PRINT RUN 10 #'d SETS
NOT PRICED DUE TO SCARCITY

2006-07 Ultimate Collection Ultimate Signatures Logos

STATED PRINT RUN 1/1
NOT PRICED DUE TO SCARCITY

1991-92 Ultimate Original Six

Produced by the Ultimate Trading Card Company, this 100-card standard-size set celebrates the 75th anniversary of the NHL by featuring players from the original six teams in the NHL. The cards were available only in foil packs, with a production run reportedly of 25,000 foil cases. Each foil pack included a sweepstake card; prizes offered included 250 autographed Bobby Hull holograms and 500 sets autographed by those players living at the time. The fronts feature color action photos with white borders, with the player's name in a silver bar at the top and the lower left corner of the picture rolled back to allow space for the producer's logo. The backs have a career summary presented in the format of a newspaper article (with different headlines), with biography and career statistics appearing in a silver box toward the bottom of the card. The cards are numbered on the back and checklisted below as follows: Team Checklists (1-6), Montreal Canadiens (7-17), New York Rangers (18-29), Toronto Maple Leafs (30-46), Boston Bruins (47-56), Chicago Blackhawks (57-65), Detroit Red Wings (66-72), Ultimate Hall of Fame (73-78), All Ultimate Team (79-84), Referees (85-87), Bobby Hull (88-92), and Great Moments (93-97). The cards were produced in both English and French versions. Either version is valued the same.

COMPLETE SET (100) 2.40 6.00
1 Montreal Canadiens .04 .10
Checklist
2 New York Rangers .02 .05
Checklist
3 Toronto Maple Leafs .02 .05
Checklist
4 Boston Bruins .02 .05
Checklist
5 Chicago Blackhawks .02 .05
Checklist
6 Detroit Red Wings .02 .05
Checklist
7 Ralph Backstrom .02 .05
8 Emile(Butch) Bouchard .06 .15
9 John Ferguson .04 .10
10 BoomBoom Geoffrion .24 .60
11 Phil Goyette .02 .05
12 Doug Harvey .16 .40
13 Don Marshall .04 .10
14 Henri Richard .20 .50
15 Dollard St.Laurent .02 .05
16 Jean-Guy Talbot .04 .10
17 Gump Worsley .16 .40
18 Andy Bathgate .08 .20
19 Lou Fontinato .02 .05
20 Ed Giacomin .08 .20
21 Vic Hadfield .04 .10
22 Camille Henry .02 .05
23 Harry Howell .06 .15
24 Orland Kurtenbach .04 .10
25 Jim Neilson .02 .05
26 Bob Nevin .02 .05
27 Dean Prentice .04 .10
28 Leo Reise Jr. .02 .05
29 George Sullivan .02 .05
30 Bob Baun .04 .10
31 Gus Bodnar .02 .05
32 Johnny Bower .08 .20
33 Bob Davidson .02 .05
34 Ron Ellis .04 .10
35 Billy Harris .02 .05
36 Larry Hillman .02 .05
37 Tim Horton .30 .75
38 Red Kelly .12 .30
39 Dave Keon .08 .20
40 Frank Mahovlich .20 .50
41 Eddie Shack .08 .20
42 Tod Sloan .02 .05
43 Sid Smith .04 .10
44 Allan Stanley .08 .20
45 Gaye Stewart .02 .05
46 Harry Watson .06 .15
47 Wayne Carleton .02 .05
48 Fern Flaman .04 .10
49 Ken Hodge UER .04 .10
(Photo actually
Ed Westfall)
50 Leo Labine .02 .05
51 Harry Lumley .08 .20
52 John McKenzie .04 .10
53 Doug Mohns .04 .10
54 Fred Stanfield .02 .05
55 Jerry Toppazzini .02 .05
56 Ed Westfall .04 .10
57 Bobby Hull .40 1.00
58 Ed Litzenberger .02 .05
59 Gilles Marotte .02 .05
60 Ab McDonald .02 .05
61 Bill Mosienko .06 .15
62 Jim Pappin .02 .05
63 Pierre Pilote .06 .15
64 Elmer Vasko .02 .05
65 Johnny Wilson .02 .05
66 Sid Abel .08 .20
67 Gary Bergman .02 .05
68 Alex Delvecchio .12 .30
69 Bill Gadsby .08 .20
70 Ted Lindsay .16 .40
71 Marcel Pronovost .06 .15
72 Norm Ullman .08 .20
73 BoomBoom Geoffrion .24 .60
74 Andy Bathgate .08 .20
75 Allan Stanley .08 .20
76 Fern Flaman .06 .15
77 Bobby Hull .40 1.00
78 Norm Ullman .08 .20
79 Red Kelly .12 .30
80 Johnny Bower .12 .30
81 Henri Richard .20 .50
82 Bobby Hull .40 1.00
83 BoomBoom Geoffrion .24 .60
84 Tim Horton .30 .75
85 Bill Friday REF .02 .05
86 Bruce Hood REF .02 .05
87 Ron Wicks REF .02 .05
88 Bobby Hull .20 .50
Electric Slap Shot
89 Bobby Hull .20 .50
The Point Race
90 Bobby Hull .20 .50
1960-61 Stanley Cup
91 Bobby Hull .20 .50
The Curse of Muldoon
is lifted
92 Bobby Hull .20 .50
Million Dollar Man
93 Bobby Baun .02 .05
Baun's Heroics
94 Ted Lindsay .06 .15
Lindsay's comeback
95 Henri Richard .06 .15
Richard's 99-year record
96 Bobby Hull .20 .50
Hull breaks 50 goal
barrier
97 Tim Horton .10 .25
A Tribute to Horton
98 Keith McCreary .02 .05
99 Checklist 1 .02 .05
100 Checklist 2 .02 .05
NNO Bobby Hull Hologram 10.00 25.00

1991-92 Ultimate Original Six Box Bottoms

This four-card standard-size set was issued on the bottom of foil boxes. The cards feature on the fronts four-color or black and white action photos, with the lower left corner turned upward to allow space for the Ultimate logo. The player's name appears in black in a silver border at the top and the NHL logo is placed toward the end of the silver bar. Bobby Hull's card features red to black screened bars on two sides enclosing an artwork collage. The cards are unnumbered and checklisted below in alphabetical order.

COMPLETE SET (4) .60 1.50
1 Ed Giacomin .20 .50
2 Bobby Hull .40 1.00
The Golden Jet
3 Marcel Pronovost .10 .25
4 Eddie Shack .10 .25

1999-00 Ultimate Victory

The 1999-00 Upper Deck Ultimate Victory set was released as a 120-card set, which features 90 veteran cards, 20 short-printed prospects, and 10 Ultimate Hockey Legacy Wayne Gretzky cards on a front foil card-stock. This product was released in 5-card packs and 24-pack boxes.

COMPLETE SET (120) 60.00 125.00
COMP.SET w/o SP's (90) 10.00 20.00
1 Paul Kariya .25 .60
2 Teemu Selanne .25 .60
3 Jason Marshall .08 .25
4 David Harlock .08 .25
5 Ray Ferraro .08 .25
6 Kelly Buchberger .08 .25
7 Sergei Samsonov .20 .50
8 Ray Bourque .40 1.00
9 Darren Van Impe .08 .25
10 Dominik Hasek .50 1.25
11 Miroslav Satan .20 .50
12 Geoff Sanderson .20 .50
13 Valeri Bure .08 .25
14 Cale Hulse .08 .25
15 Cory Stillman .08 .25
16 Ron Francis .20 .50
17 Andrei Kovalenko .08 .25
18 Sami Kapanen .08 .25
19 Tony Amonte .20 .50
20 Steve Sullivan .08 .25
21 Doug Gilmour .20 .50
22 Milan Hejduk .25 .60
23 Joe Sakic .50 1.25
24 Patrick Roy 1.25 3.00
25 Chris Drury .20 .50
26 Peter Forsberg .60 1.50
27 Mike Modano .40 1.00
28 Brett Hull .30 .75
29 Ed Belfour .25 .60
30 Blake Sloan .08 .25
31 Steve Yzerman 1.25 3.00
32 Chris Osgood .20 .50
33 Brendan Shanahan .25 .60
34 Larry Murphy .20 .50
35 Doug Weight .20 .50
36 Christian Laflamme .08 .25
37 Alexander Selivanov .08 .25
38 Pavel Bure .25 .60
39 Jaroslav Spacek .08 .25
40 Viktor Kozlov .20 .50
41 Luc Robitaille .20 .50
42 Zigmund Palffy .20 .50
43 Rob Blake .20 .50
44 Saku Koivu .25 .60
45 Patrick Poulin .08 .25
46 Brian Savage .08 .25
47 David Legwand .20 .50
48 Sergei Krivokrasov .08 .25
49 Robert Valicevic RC .08 .25
50 Martin Brodeur .60 1.50
51 Scott Stevens .20 .50
52 Krzysztof Oliwa .08 .25
53 Jamie Heward .08 .25
54 Mariusz Czerkawski .08 .25
55 Kenny Jonsson .08 .25
56 Mike Richter .25 .60
57 Theo Fleury .08 .25
58 Tim Taylor .08 .25
59 Brian Leetch .25 .60
60 Andreas Dackell .08 .25
61 Marian Hossa .25 .60
62 Ron Tugnutt .20 .50
63 Craig Berube .08 .25
64 Eric Lindros .25 .60
65 John LeClair .25 .60
66 Dallas Drake .08 .25
67 Keith Tkachuk .25 .60
68 Jeremy Roenick .30 .75
69 Jaromir Jagr .40 1.00
70 Martin Straka .08 .25
71 Rob Brown .08 .25
72 Marcus Ragnarsson .08 .25
73 Steve Shields .20 .50
74 Owen Nolan .20 .50
75 Jeff Friesen .08 .25
76 Pavol Demitra .20 .50
77 Roman Turek .20 .50
78 Mike Eastwood .08 .25
79 Vincent Lecavalier .25 .60
80 Dan Cloutier .20 .50
81 Stan Drulia .08 .25
82 Mats Sundin .25 .60
83 Igor Korolev .08 .25
84 Curtis Joseph .25 .60
85 Mark Messier .25 .60
86 Harry York .20 .50
87 Peter Schaefer .08 .25
88 Olaf Kolzig .20 .50
89 Steve Konowalchuk .08 .25
90 Peter Bondra .25 .60
91 Patrik Stefan SP RC 1.25 3.00
92 Brian Campbell SP RC 1.25 3.00
93 Mikko Eloranta SP RC 1.25 3.00
94 Oleg Saprykin SP RC 1.25 3.00
95 Kyle Calder SP RC 1.50 4.00
96 Jonathan Sim SP RC 1.25 3.00
97 Marc Rodgers SP RC 1.25 3.00
98 Paul Comrie SP RC 1.25 3.00
99 Ivan Novoseltsev SP RC 1.25 3.00
100 Jason Blake SP RC 1.25 3.00
101 Brian Rafalski SP RC 2.00 5.00
102 Jorgen Jonsson SP RC 1.25 3.00
103 Nikolai Antropov SP RC 2.00 5.00
104 Steve Kariya SP RC 1.50 4.00
105 Glen Metropolit RC 1.25 3.00
106 Jochen Hecht SP RC 2.00 5.00
107 Sheldon Keefe SP RC 1.25 3.00
108 Branislav Mezei SP RC 1.25 3.00
109 Pavel Brendl SP RC 1.25 3.00
110 Milan Kraft SP RC 1.25 3.00
111 Wayne Gretzky 1.50 4.00
112 Wayne Gretzky 1.50 4.00
113 Wayne Gretzky 1.50 4.00
114 Wayne Gretzky 1.50 4.00
115 Wayne Gretzky 1.50 4.00
116 Wayne Gretzky 1.50 4.00
117 Wayne Gretzky 1.50 4.00
118 Wayne Gretzky 1.50 4.00
119 Wayne Gretzky 1.50 4.00
120 Wayne Gretzky 1.50 4.00

1999-00 Ultimate Victory 1/1

Randomly inserted in packs, this 120-card set features the base card in a one of one parallel.
NOT PRICED DUE TO SCARCITY

1999-00 Ultimate Victory Parallel

Randomly inserted in packs, this 120-card parallel set features the base card etched with a vertical rainbow effect.
*STARS: 1.25X TO 3X BASIC CARDS
*SP's: .6X TO 1.5X BASIC CARDS

1999-00 Ultimate Victory Parallel 100

Randomly inserted in packs, this 120-card parallel set is printed on a bronze version of the base card and serial numbered to 100.
*STARS: 5X TO 12X BASIC CARDS
*SP's: 2X TO 5X BASIC CARDS

1999-00 Ultimate Victory Frozen Fury

COMPLETE SET (10) 12.00 25.00
STATED ODDS 1:23
FF1 Eric Lindros 1.25 3.00
FF2 Paul Kariya .75 2.00
FF3 Pavel Bure 1.00 2.50
FF4 Steve Kariya .30 .75
FF5 Mike Modano 1.25 3.00
FF6 Patrik Stefan .30 .75
FF7 Martin Brodeur 2.00 5.00
FF8 Jaromir Jagr 1.25 3.00
FF9 Joe Sakic 1.50 4.00
FF10 Steve Yzerman 4.00 10.00

1999-00 Ultimate Victory Legendary Fabrics

Randomly inserted in packs, this five-card set featured single and dual game-worn jersey swatches with the addition of certified autographs on two cards in the set. Lower print runs are not priced due to scarcity.

BOS Bobby Orr/4 AU
LFBO Bobby Orr/99 100.00 250.00
LFWG Wayne Gretzky/99 100.00 250.00
UFS Wayne Gretzky
Bobby Orr/10 AU
UF Wayne Gretzky 300.00 600.00
Bobby Orr/99

1999-00 Ultimate Victory Net Work

COMPLETE SET (10) 12.00 25.00
STATED ODDS 1:11
NW1 Dominik Hasek 1.50 4.00
NW2 Patrick Roy 5.00 12.00
NW3 Chris Osgood .75 2.00
NW4 Ed Belfour 1.00 2.50
NW5 Mike Richter 1.00 2.50
NW6 Roman Turek .75 2.00
NW7 Steve Shields .75 2.00
NW8 Curtis Joseph .75 2.00
NW9 Guy Hebert .75 2.00
NW10 Martin Brodeur 2.00 5.00

1999-00 Ultimate Victory Smokin Guns

COMPLETE SET (12) 8.00 15.00
STATED ODDS 1:11
SG1 Jaromir Jagr .75 2.00
SG2 Paul Kariya .50 1.25
SG3 Sergei Fedorov 1.00 2.50
SG4 Steve Kariya .20 .50
SG5 Peter Forsberg 1.25 3.00
SG6 Marian Hossa .50 1.25
SG7 Theo Fleury .50 1.25
SG8 Patrik Stefan .75 2.00
SG9 Pavel Bure .60 1.50
SG10 Eric Lindros .75 2.00
SG11 Brett Hull .60 1.50
SG12 Teemu Selanne .50 1.25

1999-00 Ultimate Victory Stature

COMPLETE SET (12) 6.00 12.00
STATED ODDS 1:6
S1 Paul Kariya .30 .75
S2 Joe Sakic .60 1.50
S3 Peter Forsberg .75 2.00
S4 Mike Modano .50 1.25
S5 Brendan Shanahan .50 1.25
S6 Pavel Bure .40 1.00
S7 Martin Brodeur .75 2.00
S8 Theo Fleury .25 .60
S9 Eric Lindros .50 1.25
S10 Keith Tkachuk .30 .75
S11 Jaromir Jagr .50 1.25
S12 Ray Bourque .50 1.25

1999-00 Ultimate Victory The Victors

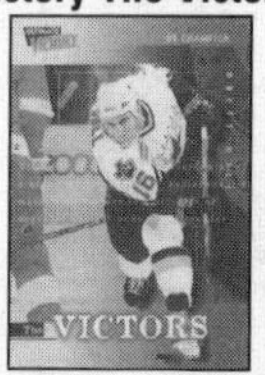

COMPLETE SET (8) 10.00 20.00
STATED ODDS 1:23
V1 Mark Messier .75 2.00
V2 Brett Hull .75 2.00
V3 Steve Yzerman 3.00 8.00
V4 Jaromir Jagr 1.00 2.50
V5 Patrick Roy 3.00 8.00
V6 Martin Brodeur 1.50 4.00
V7 Peter Forsberg 1.50 4.00
V8 Theo Fleury .60 1.50

1999-00 Ultimate Victory UV Extra

COMPLETE SET (8) 12.00 25.00
STATED ODDS 1:23
UV1 Jaromir Jagr 1.00 2.50
UV2 Patrick Roy 3.00 8.00
UV3 Pavel Bure .60 1.50
UV4 Bobby Orr 4.00 10.00
UV5 Paul Kariya 1.25 3.00
UV6 Peter Forsberg 1.50 4.00
UV7 Steve Yzerman 3.00 8.00
UV8 Eric Lindros 1.00 2.50

1992-93 Ultra

The 1992-93 Ultra hockey set consists of 450 standard-size cards. The fronts have glossy color action player photos that are full-bleed except at the bottom where a diagonal gold-foil stripe edges a "blue ice" border. The player's name and team appear on two team color-coded bars that overlay the bottom border. The horizontally oriented backs display action and close-up cut-out player photos against a hockey rink background. The Roenick Harding promo was issued in advance of the series and pictures the two men (the latter, the president of Fleer) in front of the Chicago skyline.

COMPLETE SET (450) 15.00 30.00
COMPLETE SERIES 1 (250) 10.00 20.00
COMPLETE SERIES 2 (200) 5.00 10.00
1 Brent Ashton .02 .10
2 Ray Bourque .25 .60
3 Steve Heinze .02 .10
4 Joe Juneau UER .07 .20
(Shoots left not right)
5 Stephen Leach .02 .10
6 Andy Moog .10 .30
7 Cam Neely .10 .30
8 Adam Oates .07 .20
9 Dave Poulin .02 .10
10 Vladimir Ruzicka .02 .10
11 Glen Wesley .02 .10
12 Dave Andreychuk .07 .20
13 Keith Carney RC .08 .25
14 Tom Draper .02 .10
15 Dale Hawerchuk .07 .20
16 Pat LaFontaine .10 .30
17 Brad May .07 .20
18 Alexander Mogilny .07 .20
19 Mike Ramsey .02 .10
20 Ken Sutton .02 .10
21 Theo Fleury .02 .10
22 Gary Leeman .02 .10
23 Al MacInnis .07 .20
24 Sergei Makarov .02 .10
25 Joe Nieuwendyk .07 .20
26 Joel Otto .02 .10
27 Paul Ranheim .02 .10
28 Robert Reichel .02 .10
29 Gary Roberts .02 .10
30 Gary Suter .02 .10
31 Mike Vernon .07 .20
32 Ed Belfour .10 .30
33 Rob Brown .02 .10
34 Chris Chelios .10 .30
35 Michel Goulet .07 .20
36 Dirk Graham .02 .10
37 Mike Hudson .02 .10
38 Igor Kravchuk .02 .10
39 Steve Larmer .07 .20
40 Dean McAmmond RC .02 .10
41 Jeremy Roenick .15 .40
42 Steve Smith .02 .10
43 Brent Sutter .02 .10
44 Shawn Burr .02 .10
45 Jimmy Carson .02 .10
46 Tim Cheveldae .07 .20
47 Dino Ciccarelli .07 .20
48 Sergei Fedorov .20 .50
49 Vladimir Konstantinov .10 .30
50 Slava Kozlov .07 .20
51 Nicklas Lidstrom .10 .30
52 Brad McCrimmon .02 .10
53 Bob Probert .07 .20
54 Paul Ysebaert .02 .10
55 Steve Yzerman .40 1.00
56 Josef Beranek .02 .10
57 Shayne Corson .02 .10
58 Brian Glynn .02 .10
59 Petr Klima .02 .10
60 Kevin Lowe .07 .20
61 Norm Maciver .02 .10
62 Dave Manson .02 .10
63 Joe Murphy .02 .10
64 Bernie Nicholls .07 .20
65 Bill Ranford .07 .20
66 Craig Simpson .02 .10
67 Esa Tikkanen .02 .10
68 Sean Burke .07 .20
69 Adam Burt .02 .10
70 Andrew Cassels .02 .10
71 Murray Craven .02 .10
72 John Cullen .02 .10
73 Randy Cunneyworth .02 .10
74 Tim Kerr .02 .10
75 Geoff Sanderson .07 .20
76 Eric Weinrich .02 .10
77 Zarley Zalapski .02 .10
78 Peter Ahola .02 .10
79 Rob Blake .07 .20
80 Paul Coffey .10 .30
81 Mike Donnelly .02 .10
82 Tony Granato .02 .10
83 Wayne Gretzky .60 1.50
84 Kelly Hrudey .07 .20
85 Jari Kurri .10 .30
86 Corey Millen .02 .10
87 Luc Robitaille .07 .20
88 Tomas Sandstrom .07 .20
89 Neal Broten .07 .20
90 Jon Casey .07 .20
91 Russ Courtnall .02 .10
92 Ulf Dahlen .02 .10
93 Todd Elik .02 .10
94 Dave Gagner .07 .20
95 Jim Johnson .02 .10
96 Mike Modano UER .20 .50
(Born in Livonia,
Michigan not Minnesota)
97 Bobby Smith .07 .20
98 Mark Tinordi .02 .10
99 Darcy Wakaluk .07 .20
100 Brian Bellows .02 .10
101 Benoit Brunet .02 .10
102 Guy Carbonneau .07 .20
103 Vincent Damphousse .02 .10
104 Eric Desjardins .07 .20
105 Gilbert Dionne .02 .10
106 Mike Keane .02 .10
107 Kirk Muller .02 .10
108 Patrick Roy .40 1.00
109 Denis Savard .07 .20
110 Mathieu Schneider .02 .10
111 Brian Skrudland .02 .10
112 Tom Chorske .02 .10
113 Zdeno Ciger .02 .10
114 Claude Lemieux .07 .20
115 John MacLean .07 .20
116 Scott Niedermayer .02 .10
117 Stephane Richer .07 .20
118 Peter Stastny .07 .20
119 Scott Stevens .07 .20
120 Chris Terreri .07 .20
121 Kevin Todd .02 .10
122 Valeri Zelepukin .02 .10
123 Ray Ferraro .02 .10
124 Mark Fitzpatrick .07 .20
125 Patrick Flatley .02 .10
126 Glenn Healy .07 .20
127 Benoit Hogue .02 .10
128 Derek King .02 .10
129 Uwe Krupp .02 .10
130 Scott Lachance .02 .10
131 Steve Thomas .02 .10
132 Pierre Turgeon .07 .20
133 Tony Amonte .07 .20
134 Paul Broten .02 .10
135 Mike Gartner .07 .20
136 Adam Graves .07 .20
137 Alexei Kovalev .07 .20
138 Brian Leetch .10 .30
139 Mark Messier .10 .30
140 Sergei Nemchinov .02 .10
141 James Patrick .02 .10
142 Mike Richter .10 .30
143 Darren Turcotte .02 .10
144 John Vanbiesbrouck .07 .20
145 Dominic Lavoie .02 .10
146 Lonnie Loach RC .02 .10
147 Andrew McBain .02 .10
148 Darren Rumble .02 .10
149 Sylvain Turgeon .02 .10
150 Peter Sidorkiewicz .07 .20
151 Brian Benning .02 .10
152 Rod Brind'Amour .07 .20
153 Viacheslav Butsayev RC .02 .10
154 Kevin Dineen .02 .10
155 Pelle Eklund .02 .10
156 Garry Galley .02 .10
157 Eric Lindros .10 .30
158 Mark Recchi .07 .20
159 Dominic Roussel .07 .20
160 Tommy Soderstrom RC .07 .20
161 Dimitri Yushkevich RC .07 .20
162 Tom Barrasso .07 .20
163 Ron Francis .07 .20
164 Jaromir Jagr .20 .50
165 Mario Lemieux .40 1.00
166 Joe Mullen .07 .20
167 Larry Murphy .07 .20
168 Jim Paek .02 .10
169 Kjell Samuelsson .02 .10
170 Ulf Samuelsson .02 .10
171 Kevin Stevens .02 .10
172 Rick Tocchet .07 .20
173 Alexei Gusarov .02 .10
174 Ron Hextall .07 .20
175 Mike Hough .02 .10
176 Claude Lapointe .02 .10
177 Owen Nolan .07 .20
178 Mike Ricci .07 .20
179 Joe Sakic .25 .60
180 Mats Sundin .10 .30
181 Mikhail Tatarinov .02 .10
182 Bob Bassen .02 .10
183 Jeff Brown .02 .10
184 Garth Butcher .02 .10
185 Paul Cavallini .02 .10
186 Brett Hull .20 .50
187 Craig Janney .07 .20
188 Curtis Joseph .10 .30
189 Brendan Shanahan .10 .30
190 Ron Sutter .02 .10
191 David Bruce .02 .10
192 Dale Craigwell .02 .10
193 Dean Evason .02 .10

194 Pat Falloon .02 .10
195 Jeff Hackett .07 .20
196 Kelly Kisio .02 .10
197 Brian Lawton .02 .10
198 Neil Wilkinson .02 .10
199 Doug Wilson .07 .20
200 Marc Bergevin .02 .10
201 Roman Hamrlik RC .08 .25
202 Pat Jablonski .07 .20
203 Michel Mongeau .02 .10
204 Peter Taglianetti .02 .10
205 Steve Tuttle .02 .10
206 Wendell Young .07 .20
207 Glenn Anderson .07 .20
208 Wendel Clark .07 .20
209 Dave Ellett .02 .10
210 Grant Fuhr .10 .30
211 Doug Gilmour .07 .20
212 Jamie Macoun .02 .10
213 Felix Potvin .10 .30
214 Bob Rouse .02 .10
215 Joe Sacco .02 .10
216 Peter Zezel .02 .10
217 Greg Adams .02 .10
218 Dave Babych .02 .10
219 Pavel Bure .10 .30
220 Geoff Courtnall .02 .10
221 Doug Lidster .02 .10
222 Trevor Linden .07 .20
223 Jyrki Lumme .02 .10
224 Kirk McLean .07 .20
225 Sergio Momesso .02 .10
226 Petr Nedved .07 .20
227 Cliff Ronning .02 .10
228 Jim Sandlak .02 .10
229 Don Beaupre .07 .20
230 Peter Bondra .07 .20
231 Kevin Hatcher .02 .10
232 Dale Hunter .07 .20
233 Al Iafrate .07 .20
234 Calle Johansson .02 .10
235 Dimitri Khristich .02 .10
236 Kelly Miller .02 .10
237 Michal Pivonka .02 .10
238 Mike Ridley .02 .10
239 Luciano Borsato .02 .10
240 Bob Essensa .07 .20
241 Phil Housley .07 .20
242 Troy Murray .02 .10
243 Teppo Numminen .02 .10
244 Fredrik Olausson .02 .10
245 Ed Olczyk .02 .10
246 Darrin Shannon .02 .10
247 Thomas Steen .02 .10
248 Checklist 1 .02 .10
249 Checklist 2 .02 .10
250 Checklist 3 .02 .10
251 Ted Donato .02 .10
252 Dmitri Kvartalnov RC .02 .10
253 Gord Murphy .02 .10
254 Gregori Panteleyev RC .02 .10
255 Gordie Roberts .02 .10
256 David Shaw .02 .10
257 Don Sweeney .02 .10
258 Doug Bodger .02 .10
259 Gord Donnelly .02 .10
260 Yuri Khmylev RC .02 .10
261 Daren Puppa .07 .20
262 Richard Smehlik RC .02 .10
263 Petr Svoboda .02 .10
264 Bob Sweeney .02 .10
265 Randy Wood .02 .10
266 Kevin Dahl RC .02 .10
267 Chris Dahlquist .02 .10
268 Roger Johansson .02 .10
269 Chris Lindberg .02 .10
270 Frank Musil .02 .10
271 Ronnie Stern .02 .10
272 Carey Wilson .02 .10
273 Dave Christian .02 .10
274 Karl Dykhuis .02 .10
275 Greg Gilbert .02 .10
276 Sergei Krivokrasov .02 .10
277 Frantisek Kucera .02 .10
278 Bryan Marchment .02 .10
279 Stephane Matteau .02 .10
280 Brian Noonan .02 .10
281 Christian Ruuttu .02 .10
282 Steve Chiasson .02 .10
283 Dino Ciccarelli .07 .20
284 Gerard Gallant .02 .10
285 Mark Howe .02 .10
286 Keith Primeau .02 .10
287 Yves Racine .02 .10
288 Vincent Riendeau .07 .20
289 Ray Sheppard .02 .10
290 Mike Sillinger .02 .10
291 Kelly Buchberger .02 .10
292 Shayne Corson .02 .10
293 Brent Gilchrist .02 .10
294 Craig MacTavish .02 .10
295 Scott Mellanby .02 .10
296 Craig Muni .02 .10
297 Luke Richardson .02 .10
298 Ron Tugnutt .07 .20
299 Shaun Van Allen .02 .10
300 Steve Konroyd .02 .10
301 Nick Kypreos .02 .10
302 Robert Petrovicky RC .02 .10
303 Frank Pietrangelo .07 .20
304 Patrick Poulin .02 .10
305 Pat Verbeek .02 .10
306 Eric Weinrich .02 .10
307 Jim Hiller RC .02 .10
308 Charlie Huddy .02 .10
309 Lonnie Loach .02 .10
310 Marty McSorley .02 .10
311 Robb Stauber .07 .20
312 Darryl Sydor .02 .10
313 Dave Taylor .07 .20
314 Alexei Zhitnik .02 .10
315 Shane Churla .02 .10
316 Russ Courtnall .02 .10
317 Mike Craig .02 .10
318 Gaetan Duchesne .02 .10
319 Derian Hatcher .02 .10
320 Craig Ludwig .02 .10
321 Richard Matvichuk RC .07 .20
322 Mike McPhee .02 .10
323 Tommy Sjodin RC .02 .10
324 Brian Bellows .02 .10
325 Patrice Brisebois .02 .10
326 J.J.Daigneault .02 .10
327 Kevin Haller .02 .10
328 Sean Hill RC .02 .10
329 Stephan Lebeau .02 .10
330 John LeClair .20 .50
331 Lyle Odelein .02 .10
332 Andre Racicot .07 .20
333 Ed Ronan RC .02 .10
334 Craig Billington .07 .20
335 Ken Daneyko .02 .10
336 Bruce Driver .02 .10
337 Slava Fetisov .02 .10
338 Bill Guerin RC .60 1.50
339 Bobby Holik .07 .20
340 Alexei Kasatonov .02 .10
341 Alexander Semak .02 .10
342 Tom Fitzgerald .02 .10
343 Travis Green RC .08 .25
344 Darius Kasparaitis .02 .10
345 Danny Lorenz RC .02 .10
346 Vladimir Malakhov .02 .10
347 Marty McInnis .02 .10
348 Brian Mullen .02 .10
349 Jeff Norton .02 .10
350 David Volek .02 .10
351 Jeff Beukeboom .02 .10
352 Phil Bourque .02 .10
353 Paul Broten .02 .10
354 Mark Hardy .02 .10
355 Steven King RC .02 .10
356 Kevin Lowe .07 .20
357 Ed Olczyk .02 .10
358 Doug Weight .10 .30
359 Sergei Zubov RC .20 .50
360 Jamie Baker .02 .10
361 Daniel Berthiaume .07 .20
362 Chris Luongo RC .07 .20
363 Norm Maciver .02 .10
364 Brad Marsh .02 .10
365 Mike Peluso .02 .10
366 Brad Shaw .02 .10
367 Peter Sidorkiewicz .07 .20
368 Keith Acton .02 .10
369 Stephane Beauregard .07 .20
370 Terry Carkner .02 .10
371 Brent Fedyk .02 .10
372 Andrei Lomakin .02 .10
373 Ryan McGill RC .02 .10
374 Ric Nattress .02 .10
375 Greg Paslawski .02 .10
376 Peter Ahola .02 .10
377 Jeff Daniels .02 .10
378 Troy Loney .02 .10
379 Shawn McEachern .02 .10
380 Mike Needham RC .02 .10
381 Paul Stanton .02 .10
382 Martin Straka RC .20 .50
383 Ken Wregget .07 .20
384 Steve Duchesne .02 .10
385 Ron Hextall .07 .20
386 Kerry Huffman .02 .10
387 Andrei Kovalenko RC .07 .20
388 Bill Lindsay RC .02 .10
389 Mike Ricci .07 .20
390 Martin Rucinsky .02 .10
391 Scott Young .02 .10
392 Philippe Bozon .02 .10
393 Nelson Emerson .02 .10
394 Guy Hebert RC .20 .50
395 Igor Korolev RC .07 .20
396 Kevin Miller .02 .10
397 Vitali Prokhorov RC .02 .10
398 Rich Sutter .02 .10
399 John Carter .02 .10
400 Johan Garpenlov .02 .10
401 Arturs Irbe .08 .25
402 Sandis Ozolinsh .02 .10
403 Tom Pederson RC .02 .10
404 Michel Picard .02 .10
405 Doug Zmolek RC .02 .10
406 Mikael Andersson .02 .10
407 Bob Beers .02 .10
408 Brian Bradley .02 .10
409 Adam Creighton .02 .10
410 Doug Crossman .02 .10
411 Ken Hodge Jr. .02 .10
412 Chris Kontos RC .02 .10
413 Rob Ramage .02 .10
414 John Tucker .02 .10
415 Rob Zamuner RC .07 .20
416 Ken Baumgartner .02 .10
417 Drake Berehowsky .02 .10
418 Nikolai Borschevsky RC .02 .10
419 John Cullen .02 .10
420 Mike Foligno .02 .10
421 Mike Krushelnyski .02 .10
422 Dmitri Mironov .02 .10
423 Rob Pearson .02 .10
424 Gerald Diduck .02 .10
425 Robert Dirk .02 .10
426 Tom Fergus .02 .10
427 Gino Odjick .02 .10
428 Adrien Plavsic .02 .10
429 Anatoli Semenov .02 .10
430 Jiri Slegr .02 .10
431 Dixon Ward RC .07 .20
432 Paul Cavallini .02 .10
433 Sylvain Cote .02 .10
434 Pat Elynuik .02 .10
435 Jim Hrivnak .02 .10
436 Keith Jones RC .08 .25
437 Steve Konowalchuk RC .07 .20
438 Todd Krygier .02 .10
439 Paul MacDermid .02 .10
440 Sergei Bautin RC .02 .10
441 Evgeny Davydov .02 .10
442 John Druce .02 .10
443 Troy Murray .02 .10
444 Teemu Selanne .40 1.00
445 Rick Tabaracci .07 .20
446 Keith Tkachuk .10 .30
447 Alexei Zhamnov .07 .20
448 Checklist 4 .02 .10
449 Checklist 5 .02 .10
450 Checklist 6 .02 .10
NNO Jeremy Roenick/Harding Promo

1992-93 Ultra All-Stars

This 12-card standard-size set was randomly inserted in 1992-93 Ultra first series foil packs. The cards depict First Team All-Stars by conference. The glossy color action player photos on the fronts are full-bleed except at the bottom where a diagonal gold-foil stripe edges a beige marbleized border. A gold-foil insignia with a star is superimposed on the beige border.

COMPLETE SET (12) 8.00 20.00
1 Paul Coffey UER .50 1.25
(Photo on back actually Kevin Stevens)
2 Ray Bourque .75 2.00
3 Patrick Roy 1.50 4.00
4 Mario Lemieux 1.50 4.00
5 Kevin Stevens UER .15 .40
(Photo on back actually Paul Coffey)
6 Jaromir Jagr .75 2.00
7 Chris Chelios .50 1.25
8 Al MacInnis .30 .75
9 Ed Belfour .50 1.25
10 Wayne Gretzky 2.00 5.00
11 Luc Robitaille .30 .75
12 Brett Hull .75 2.00

1992-93 Ultra Award Winners

This ten-card standard-size set was randomly inserted in 1992-93 Ultra first series foil packs. The cards feature 1991-92 award winners. The glossy color action player photos on the fronts are full-bleed except at the bottom where a gold-foil stripe edges into a marbleized border.

COMPLETE SET (10) 6.00 15.00
1 Mark Messier .60 1.50
2 Brian Leetch .50 1.25
3 Guy Carbonneau .30 .75
4 Patrick Roy 1.50 4.00
5 Mario Lemieux 1.50 4.00
6 Wayne Gretzky 2.00 5.00
7 Mark Fitzpatrick .30 .75
8 Ray Bourque .75 2.00
9 Pavel Bure .50 1.25
10 Mark Messier .50 1.25

1992-93 Ultra Imports

Randomly inserted in second series 1992-93 Ultra foil packs, this 25-card set measures the standard size. The cards depict foreign players in the National Hockey League. Fronts feature color action cut-out player photos against a purple surreal background showing the player on ice with a globe design in the distance. The player's name is silver foil stamped at the bottom. The horizontal backs carry a close-up of the player, the player's name, and player information. The background is similar to the front.

COMPLETE SET (25) 8.00 20.00
1 Nikolai Borschevsky .20 .50
2 Pavel Bure .75 2.00
3 Sergei Fedorov 1.00 2.50
4 Roman Hamrlik .20 .50
5 Arturs Irbe .40 1.00
6 Jaromir Jagr 1.25 3.00
7 Dimitri Khristich .20 .50
8 Petr Klima .20 .50
9 Andrei Kovalenko .20 .50
10 Alexei Kovalev .40 1.00
11 Jari Kurri .75 2.00
12 Dmitri Kvartalnov .20 .50
13 Nicklas Lidstrom .75 2.00
14 Vladimir Malakhov .20 .50
15 Dmitri Mironov .20 .50
16 Alexander Mogilny .40 1.00
17 Petr Nedved .20 .50
18 Fredrik Olausson .20 .50
19 Sandis Ozolinsh .20 .50
20 Ulf Samuelsson .20 .50
21 Teemu Selanne 2.00 5.00
22 Richard Smehlik .20 .50
23 Tommy Soderstrom .20 .50
24 Peter Stastny .40 1.00
25 Mats Sundin .75 2.00

1992-93 Ultra Jeremy Roenick

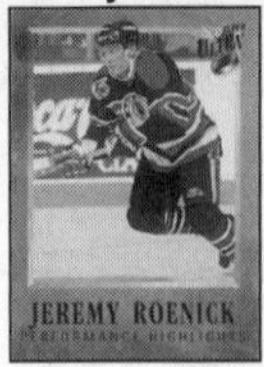

Randomly inserted in first series 1992-93 Ultra foil packs, this 12-card set measures the standard size. Two of the cards (11, 12) were available through a mail-in offer which was not available in Canada. The set, which features color action photos on front and career highlights on back, spotlights the career of Chicago Blackhawks' Jeremy Roenick. Roenick personally autographed more than 2,000 of his cards. Stated odds suggest the likelihood of pulling an autographed card at 1:8,000 packs.

COMPLETE SET (10) 10.00 20.00
COMMON ROENICK (1-10) .75 2.00
11 Jeremy Roenick 1.25 3.00
Impressive Impressions
12 Jeremy Roenick 1.25 3.00
Roenick on Roenick
AU Jeremy Roenick AU 60.00 150.00

1992-93 Ultra Rookies

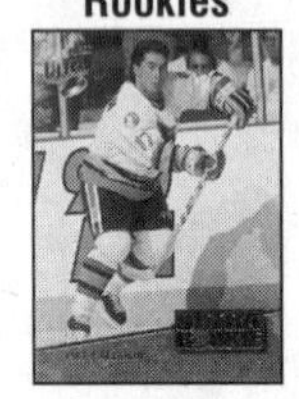

This eight-card standard-size set was randomly inserted in 1992-93 Ultra series one foil packs. The card fronts feature color, action player photos. A brown marbleized border runs diagonally across the bottom. This border is separated from the photo by a thin gold foil stripe. The player's name and the words "Ultra Rookie" are printed in gold foil on the marbleized border. The backs show a close-up picture with a player profile against a gray marbleized background.

1 Tony Amonte .20 .50
2 Donald Audette .20 .50
3 Pavel Bure .75 2.00
4 Gilbert Dionne .20 .50
5 Nelson Emerson .20 .50
6 Pat Falloon .20 .50
7 Nicklas Lidstrom .75 2.00
8 Kevin Todd .20 .50

1993-94 Ultra

The 1993-94 Ultra hockey set consists of 500 standard-size cards. Both the first and second series contained 250 cards. The color action player photos on the fronts are full-bleed except at the bottom where a diagonal gold foil stripe separates the picture from a gray ice border. The player's name, team name, and position are gold foil-stamped on team color-coded bars.

COMPLETE SET (500) 20.00 40.00
COMPLETE SERIES 1 (250) 10.00 20.00
COMPLETE SERIES 2 (250) 10.00 20.00
1 Ray Bourque .20 .50
2 Andy Moog .05 .15
3 Brian Benning .02 .10
4 Brian Bellows .02 .10
5 Claude Lemieux .02 .10
6 Jamie Baker .02 .10
7 Steve Duchesne .02 .10
8 Ed Courtenay .02 .10
9 Glenn Anderson .05 .15
10 Sergei Bautin .02 .10
11 Al Iafrate .02 .10
12 Gary Shuchuk .02 .10
13 Matthew Barnaby .05 .15
14 Tim Cheveldae .05 .15
15 Sean Burke .05 .15
16 Ray Ferraro .02 .10
17 Josef Beranek .02 .10
18 Bob Beers .02 .10
19 Greg Adams .02 .10
20 John Cullen .02 .10
21 Kirk Muller .02 .10
22 Ed Belfour .10 .30
23 Kevin Dahl .02 .10
24 Rob Blake .05 .15
25 Mike Gartner .05 .15
26 Tom Barrasso .05 .15
27 Garth Butcher .02 .10
28 Don Beaupre .05 .15
29 Kirk McLean .05 .15
30 Felix Potvin .10 .30
31 Doug Bodger .02 .10
32 Dino Ciccarelli .05 .15
33 Andrew Cassels .02 .10
34 Patrick Flatley .02 .10
35 Jason Bowen RC .02 .10
36 Brian Bradley .02 .10
37 Pavel Bure .10 .30
38 Dave Ellett .02 .10
39 Patrick Roy .60 1.50
40 Chris Chelios .10 .30
41 Theo Fleury .02 .10
42 Jimmy Carson .02 .10
43 Adam Graves .02 .10
44 Ron Francis .05 .15
45 Nelson Emerson .02 .10
46 Peter Bondra .05 .15
47 Sergio Momesso .02 .10
48 Teemu Selanne .10 .30
49 Joe Juneau .05 .15
50 Russ Courtnall .02 .10
51 Shayne Corson .02 .10
52 Patrice Brisebois .02 .10
53 John MacLean .05 .15
54 Daniel Berthiaume .05 .15
55 Stephane Fiset .05 .15
56 Pat Falloon .02 .10
57 Dave Andreychuk .05 .15
58 Evgeny Davydov .02 .10
59 Dimitri Khristich .02 .10
60 Darryl Sydor .02 .10
61 Dirk Graham .02 .10
62 Chris Lindberg .02 .10
63 Tony Granato .02 .10
64 Corey Hirsch .05 .15
65 Jaromir Jagr .20 .50
66 Bret Hedican .02 .10
67 Pat Elynuik .02 .10
68 Petr Nedved .05 .15
69 Thomas Steen .02 .10
70 Philippe Boucher .02 .10
71 Paul Coffey .10 .30
72 Mike Lenarduzzi RC .02 .10
73 Iain Fraser RC .02 .10
74 Rod Brind'Amour .05 .15
75 Shawn Chambers .02 .10
76 Geoff Courtnall .02 .10
77 Todd Gill .02 .10
78 Mathieu Schneider .02 .10
79 Vincent Damphousse .02 .10
80 Igor Kravchuk .02 .10
81 Ulf Dahlen .02 .10
82 Dmitri Kvartalnov .02 .10
83 Johan Garpenlov .02 .10
84 Valeri Kamensky .05 .15
85 Bob Kudelski .02 .10
86 Bernie Nicholls .02 .10
87 Alexei Zhitnik .02 .10
88 Kelly Miller .02 .10
89 Bob Essensa .05 .15
90 Drake Berehowsky .02 .10
91 Jon Casey .05 .15
92 Dave Gagner .05 .15
93 Dave Manson .02 .10
94 Eric Desjardins .05 .15
95 Scott Niedermayer .02 .10
96 Chris Luongo .02 .10
97 Dave Karpa .02 .10
98 Rob Gaudreau RC .02 .10
99 Nikolai Borschevsky .02 .10
100 Phil Housley .05 .15
101 Michal Pivonka .02 .10
102 Dixon Ward .02 .10
103 Grant Fuhr .05 .15
104 Dallas Drake RC .02 .10
105 Michael Nylander .02 .10
106 Glenn Healy .05 .15
107 Kevin Dineen .05 .15
108 Roman Hamrlik .05 .15
109 Trevor Linden .05 .15
110 Doug Gilmour .05 .15
111 Keith Tkachuk .10 .30
112 Sergei Krivokrasov .02 .10
113 Al MacInnis .05 .15
114 Wayne Gretzky .75 2.00
115 Alexei Kovalev .05 .15
116 Mario Lemieux .60 1.50
117 Brett Hull .15 .40
118 Kevin Hatcher .02 .10
119 Cliff Ronning .02 .10
120 Viktor Gordiouk .02 .10
121 Sergei Fedorov .20 .50
122 Patrick Poulin .02 .10
123 Benoit Hogue .02 .10
124 Garry Galley .02 .10
125 Pat Jablonski .02 .10
126 Jyrki Lumme .02 .10
127 Dimitri Mironov .02 .10
128 Alexei Zhamnov .05 .15
129 Steve Larmer .05 .15
130 Joe Nieuwendyk .05 .15
131 Kelly Hrudey .05 .15
132 Brian Leetch .10 .30
133 Shawn McEachern .02 .10
134 Craig Janney .05 .15
135 Dale Hunter .02 .10
136 Jiri Slegr .02 .10
137 Mats Sundin .10 .30
138 Cam Neely .10 .30
139 Derian Hatcher .02 .10
140 Shjon Podein RC .05 .15
141 Gilbert Dionne .02 .10
142 Scott Pellerin RC .02 .10
143 Norm Maciver .02 .10
144 Andrei Kovalenko .02 .10
145 Arturs Irbe .05 .15
146 Wendel Clark .05 .15
147 Fredrik Olausson .02 .10
148 Mike Ridley .02 .10
149 Dale Hawerchuk .05 .15
150 Vladimir Konstantinov .05 .15
151 Geoff Sanderson .05 .15
152 Stephane Richer .05 .15
153 Darren Rumble .02 .10
154 Owen Nolan .05 .15
155 Kelly Kisio .02 .10
156 Adam Oates .05 .15
157 Trent Klatt .02 .10
158 Bill Ranford .05 .15
159 Paul DiPietro .02 .10
160 Darius Kasparaitis .02 .10
161 Eric Lindros .10 .30
162 Chris Kontos .02 .10
163 Joe Murphy .02 .10
164 Robert Reichel .02 .10
165 Jari Kurri .10 .30
166 Alexander Semak .02 .10
167 Brad Shaw .02 .10
168 Mike Ricci .02 .10
169 Sandis Ozolinsh .02 .10
170 Joby Messier RC .02 .10
171 Joe Mullen .05 .15
172 Curtis Joseph .10 .30
173 Yuri Khmylev .02 .10
174 Slava Kozlov .05 .15
175 Pat Verbeek .02 .10
176 Derek King .02 .10
177 Ryan McGill .02 .10
178 Chris LiPuma RC .02 .10
179 Grigori Pantaleyev .02 .10
180 Richard Matvichuk .02 .10
181 Steven Rice .02 .10
182 Sean Hill .02 .10
183 Mark Messier .10 .30
184 Larry Murphy .05 .15
185 Igor Korolev .02 .10
186 Jeremy Roenick .15 .40
187 Gary Roberts .02 .10
188 Robert Lang .02 .10
189 Scott Stevens .05 .15
190 Sylvain Turgeon .02 .10
191 Martin Rucinsky .02 .10
192 J.F. Quintin .02 .10
193 Dave Poulin .02 .10
194 Mike Modano .20 .50
195 Doug Weight .05 .15
196 Mike Keane .02 .10
197 Pierre Turgeon .05 .15
198 Dimitri Yushkevich .02 .10
199 Rob Zamuner .02 .10
200 Richard Smehlik .02 .10
201 Steve Yzerman .60 1.50
202 Tony Amonte .05 .15
203 Sergei Nemchinov .02 .10
204 Ulf Samuelsson .02 .10
205 Kevin Miehm .02 .10
206 Brent Sutter .02 .10
207 Mike Vernon .05 .15
208 Luc Robitaille .05 .15
209 Chris Terreri .05 .15
210 Philippe Bozon .02 .10
211 John Tucker .02 .10
212 Jozef Stumpel .02 .10
213 Mark Tinordi .02 .10
214 Bruce Driver .02 .10
215 John LeClair .10 .30
216 Steve Thomas .02 .10
217 Tommy Soderstrom .05 .15
218 Kevin Miller .02 .10
219 Pat LaFontaine .10 .30
220 Nicklas Lidstrom .10 .30
221 Terry Yake .02 .10
222 Valeri Zelepukin .02 .10
223 Jeff Brown .02 .10
224 Chris Simon RC .30 .75
225 Rick Tocchet .05 .15
226 Gary Suter .02 .10
227 Marty McSorley .02 .10
228 Mike Richter .10 .30
229 Kevin Stevens .02 .10
230 Doug Wilson .05 .15
231 Steve Smith .02 .10
232 Bryan Smolinski .02 .10
233 Tommy Sjodin .02 .10
234 Zarley Zalapski .02 .10
235 Vladimir Malakhov .02 .10
236 Mark Recchi .05 .15
237 David Littman RC .02 .10
238 Alexander Mogilny .05 .15
239 Keith Primeau .02 .10
240 Tyler Wright .02 .10
241 Stephan Lebeau .02 .10
242 Joe Sakic .25 .60
243 Sergei Zubov .02 .10
244 Martin Straka .02 .10
245 Brendan Shanahan .10 .30
246 Tomas Sandstrom .02 .10
247 Milan Tichy RC .02 .10
248 C.J. Young .02 .10
249 Checklist .10 .30
Eric Lindros
250 Checklist .10 .30
Teemu Selanne
251 Patrick Carnback RC .02 .10
252 Todd Ewen .02 .10
253 Stu Grimson .02 .10
254 Guy Hebert .05 .15
255 Sean Hill .02 .10
256 Bill Houlder .02 .10
257 Alexei Kasatonov .02 .10
258 Steven King .02 .10
259 Troy Loney .02 .10
260 Joe Sacco .02 .10
261 Anatoli Semenov .02 .10
262 Tim Sweeney .02 .10
263 Ron Tugnutt .05 .15
264 Shaun Van Allen .02 .10
265 Terry Yake .02 .10
266 Jon Casey .05 .15
267 Ted Donato .02 .10
268 Steve Leach .02 .10
269 David Reid .02 .10
270 Cam Stewart RC .02 .10
271 Don Sweeney .02 .10
272 Glen Wesley .02 .10
273 Donald Audette .02 .10
274 Dominik Hasek .40 1.00
275 Sergei Petrenko .02 .10
276 Derek Plante RC .02 .10
277 Craig Simpson .02 .10
278 Bob Sweeney .02 .10
279 Randy Wood .02 .10
280 Ted Drury .02 .10
281 Trevor Kidd .05 .15
282 Kelly Kisio .02 .10
283 Frank Musil .02 .10
284 Jason Muzzatti RC .05 .15
285 Joel Otto .02 .10
286 Paul Ranheim .02 .10
287 Wes Walz .02 .10
288 Ivan Droppa RC .02 .10
289 Michel Goulet .05 .15
290 Stephane Matteau .02 .10
291 Brian Noonan .02 .10
292 Patrick Poulin .02 .10
293 Rich Sutter .02 .10
294 Kevin Todd .02 .10
295 Eric Weinrich .02 .10
296 Neal Broten .05 .15
297 Mike Craig .02 .10
298 Dean Evason .02 .10
299 Grant Ledyard .02 .10
300 Mike McPhee .02 .10
301 Andy Moog .05 .15
302 Jarkko Varvio .02 .10
303 Micah Aivazoff RC .02 .10
304 Terry Carkner .02 .10
305 Steve Chiasson .02 .10
306 Greg Johnson .02 .10
307 Darren McCarty RC .30 .75
308 Chris Osgood RC 1.00 2.50
309 Bob Probert .05 .15
310 Ray Sheppard .05 .15
311 Mike Sillinger .02 .10
312 Jason Arnott RC .60 1.50
313 Fred Brathwaite RC .25 .60
314 Kelly Buchberger .02 .10
315 Zdeno Ciger .02 .10
316 Craig MacTavish .02 .10
317 Dean McAmmond .02 .10
318 Luke Richardson .02 .10
319 Vladimir Vujtek .02 .10
320 Jesse Belanger .02 .10
321 Brian Benning .02 .10
322 Keith Brown .02 .10
323 Evgeny Davydov .02 .10
324 Tom Fitzgerald .02 .10
325 Alexander Godynyuk .02 .10
326 Scott Levins RC .02 .10
327 Andrei Lomakin .02 .10
328 Scott Mellanby .05 .15
329 Gord Murphy .02 .10
330 Rob Niedermayer .05 .15
331 Brent Severyn RC .02 .10
332 Brian Skrudland .02 .10
333 John Vanbiesbrouck .05 .15
334 Mark Greig .02 .10
335 Bryan Marchment .02 .10
336 James Patrick .02 .10
337 Robert Petrovicky .02 .10
338 Frank Pietrangelo .02 .10
339 Chris Pronger .05 .15
340 Brian Propp .02 .10
341 Darren Turcotte .02 .10
342 Pat Conacher .02 .10
343 Mark Hardy .02 .10
344 Charlie Huddy .02 .10
345 Shawn McEachern .02 .10
346 Warren Rychel .02 .10
347 Robb Stauber .05 .15
348 Dave Taylor .05 .15
349 Benoit Brunet .02 .10
350 Guy Carbonneau .02 .10
351 J.J. Daigneault .02 .10
352 Kevin Haller .02 .10
353 Gary Leeman .02 .10
354 Lyle Odelein .02 .10
355 Andre Racicot .05 .15
356 Ron Wilson .02 .10
357 Martin Brodeur .40 1.00
358 Ken Daneyko .02 .10
359 Bill Guerin .02 .10
360 Bobby Holik .02 .10
361 Corey Millen .02 .10
362 Jaroslav Modry RC .02 .10
363 Jason Smith RC .02 .10
364 Brad Dalgarno .02 .10
365 Travis Green .05 .15
366 Ron Hextall .05 .15
367 Steve Junker .02 .10
368 Tom Kurvers .02 .10
369 Scott Lachance .02 .10
370 Marty McInnis .02 .10
371 Glenn Healy .05 .15
372 Alexander Karpovtsev .02 .10
373 Steve Larmer .05 .15
374 Doug Lidster .02 .10
375 Kevin Lowe .02 .10
376 Mattias Norstrom RC .02 .10
377 Esa Tikkanen .02 .10
378 Craig Billington .05 .15
379 Robert Burakovsky RC .02 .10
380 Alexandre Daigle .02 .10
381 Dmitri Filimonov .02 .10
382 Darrin Madeley RC .02 .10
383 Vladimir Ruzicka .02 .10
384 Alexei Yashin .02 .10
385 Vyacheslav Butsayev .02 .10
386 Pelle Eklund .02 .10
387 Brent Fedyk .02 .10
388 Greg Hawgood .02 .10
389 Milos Holan RC .02 .10
390 Stewart Malgunas RC .02 .10
391 Mikael Renberg .10 .30
392 Dominic Roussel .05 .15
393 Doug Brown .02 .10
394 Marty McSorley .02 .10
395 Markus Naslund .10 .30
396 Mike Ramsey .02 .10
397 Peter Taglianetti .02 .10
398 Bryan Trottier .05 .15
399 Ken Wregget .05 .15
400 Iain Fraser .02 .10
401 Martin Gelinas .02 .10
402 Kerry Huffman .02 .10
403 Claude Lapointe .02 .10
404 Curtis Leschyshyn .02 .10
405 Chris Lindberg .02 .10
406 Jocelyn Thibault RC .40 1.00
407 Murray Baron .02 .10
408 Bob Bassen .02 .10
409 Phil Housley .05 .15
410 Jim Hrivnak .02 .10
411 Tony Hrkac .02 .10
412 Vitali Karamnov .05 .15
413 Jim Montgomery RC .02 .10
414 Vitali Kroupa RC .02 .10
415 Igor Larionov .05 .15
416 Sergei Makarov .02 .10
417 Jeff Norton .02 .10
418 Mike Rathje .02 .10
419 Jim Waite .05 .15
420 Ray Whitney .02 .10
421 Mikael Andersson .02 .10
422 Donald Dufresne .02 .10
423 Chris Gratton .05 .15
424 Brent Gretzky RC .02 .10

425 Petr Klima .02 .10
426 Bill McDougall RC .02 .10
427 Daren Puppa .05 .15
428 Denis Savard .05 .15
429 Ken Baumgartner .02 .10
430 Sylvain Lefebvre .02 .10
431 Jamie Macoun .02 .10
432 Matt Martin RC .02 .10
433 Mark Osborne .02 .10
434 Rob Pearson .02 .10
435 Damian Rhodes RC .05 .15
436 Peter Zezel .02 .10
437 Shawn Antoski .02 .10
438 Jose Charbonneau .02 .10
439 Murray Craven .02 .10
440 Gerald Diduck .02 .10
441 Dana Murzyn .02 .10
442 Gino Odjick .02 .10
443 Kay Whitmore .05 .15
444 Randy Burridge .02 .10
445 Sylvain Cote .02 .10
446 Keith Jones .02 .10
447 Olaf Kolzig .05 .15
448 Todd Krygier .02 .10
449 Pat Peake .02 .10
450 Dave Poulin .02 .10
451 Stephane Beauregard .05 .15
452 Luciano Borsato .02 .10
453 Nelson Emerson .02 .10
454 Boris Mironov .02 .10
455 Teppo Numminen .02 .10
456 Stephane Quintal .02 .10
457 Paul Ysebaert .02 .10
458 Adrian Aucoin RC .10 .30
459 Todd Brost RC .02 .10
460 Martin Gendron RC .02 .10
461 David Harlock .02 .10
462 Corey Hirsch .05 .15
463 Todd Hlushko RC .02 .10
464 Fabian Joseph RC .02 .10
465 Paul Kariya 2.00 5.00
466 Brett Lindros RC .02 .10
467 Ken Lovsin RC .02 .10
468 Jason Marshall .02 .10
469 Derek Mayer RC .02 .10
470 Dwayne Norris RC .02 .10
471 Russ Romaniuk .02 .10
472 Brian Savage RC .10 .30
473 Trevor Sim RC .02 .10
474 Chris Therien RC .02 .10
475 Brad Turner RC .02 .10
476 Todd Warriner RC .02 .10
477 Craig Woodcroft RC .02 .10
478 Mark Beaufait RC .02 .10
479 Jim Campbell .02 .10
480 Ted Crowley RC .02 .10
481 Mike Dunham .05 .15
482 Chris Ferraro RC .02 .10
483 Peter Ferraro .02 .10
484 Brett Hauer RC .02 .10
485 Darby Hendrickson RC .02 .10
486 Chris Imes RC .02 .10
487 Craig Johnson RC .02 .10
488 Peter Laviolette RC .02 .10
489 Jeff Lazaro .02 .10
490 John Lilley RC .02 .10
491 Todd Marchant .02 .10
492 Ian Moran RC .02 .10
493 Travis Richards RC .05 .15
494 Barry Richter RC .02 .10
495 David Roberts RC .02 .10
496 Brian Rolston .02 .10
497 David Sacco RC .02 .10
498 Checklist Card .02 .10
499 Checklist Card .02 .10
500 Checklist Card .02 .10

1993-94 Ultra Adam Oates

As part of Ultra's Signature series, this 12-card standard-size set presents career highlights of Adam Oates. These cards were randomly inserted throughout all packs, and Oates autographed more than 2,000 of his cards. Stated odds suggest the likelihood of pulling an autographed card at 1:10,000 packs. Two additional cards (11, 12) were available only by mail for ten Ultra wrappers plus 1.00.

COMPLETE SET (10) 2.00 4.00
COMMON OATES (1-10) .20 .50
COMMON MAIL-IN (11-12) .75 2.00
NNO Adam Oates/AU 20.00 50.00

1993-94 Ultra All-Rookies

Randomly inserted at a rate of 1:20 19-card first-series jumbo packs, this 10-card standard-size set features on its borderless fronts color player action cutouts "breaking out" of their simulated ice backgrounds. The player's name appears in gold-foil lettering at a lower corner. The blue back carries the player's name at the top in gold-foil lettering, followed below by career highlights and a color player action cutout. The cards are numbered on the back as "X of 10."

COMPLETE SET (10) 5.00 12.00
1 Philippe Boucher .75 2.00
2 Viktor Gordiouk .40 1.00
3 Corey Hirsch .75 2.00
4 Chris LiPuma .40 1.00
5 David Littman .40 1.00
6 Joby Messier .40 1.00
7 Chris Simon .75 2.00
8 Bryan Smolinski .75 2.00
9 Jozef Stumpel .75 2.00
10 Milan Tichy .40 1.00

1993-94 Ultra All-Stars

Randomly inserted into all first series packs, this 18-card standard-size set focuses on 18 of the NHL's best players. The set numbering is by conference All-Stars, Wales (1-9) and Campbell (10-18).

COMPLETE SET (18) 12.50 25.00
1 Patrick Roy 2.50 6.00
2 Ray Bourque .75 2.00
3 Pierre Turgeon .25 .60
4 Pat LaFontaine .50 1.25
5 Alexander Mogilny .25 .60
6 Kevin Stevens .15 .40
7 Adam Oates .25 .60
8 Al Iafrate .15 .40
9 Kirk Muller .15 .40
10 Ed Belfour .50 1.25
11 Teemu Selanne .50 1.25
12 Steve Yzerman 2.50 6.00
13 Luc Robitaille .25 .60
14 Chris Chelios .50 1.25
15 Wayne Gretzky 3.00 8.00
16 Doug Gilmour .25 .60
17 Pavel Bure .50 1.25
18 Phil Housley .25 .60

1993-94 Ultra Award Winners

Randomly inserted into all first series packs, this six-card standard-size set honors NHL award winners of the previous season. Each borderless front features the player with his award. The back has an action photo and career highlights. The cards are numbered "X of 6".

COMPLETE SET (6) 3.00 8.00
1 Ed Belfour .60 1.50
Jennings/Vezina Trophies
2 Chris Chelios .60 1.50
Norris Trophy
3 Doug Gilmour .30 .75
Selke Trophy
4 Mario Lemieux 2.00 5.00
5 Dave Poulin .20 .50
King Clancy Trophy
6 Teemu Selanne .60 1.50
Calder Trophy

1993-94 Ultra Premier Pivots

Randomly inserted in all series II packs, these ten standard-size cards feature some of the NHL's greatest centers. The borderless fronts have color player action shots on motion-streaked backgrounds. The player's name appears in silver foil at the upper right. The cards are numbered on the back as "X of 10."

COMPLETE SET (10) 10.00 20.00
1 Doug Gilmour .20 .50
2 Wayne Gretzky 2.50 6.00
3 Pat LaFontaine .40 1.00
4 Mario Lemieux 2.00 5.00
5 Eric Lindros .40 1.00
6 Mark Messier .40 1.00
7 Adam Oates .20 .50
8 Jeremy Roenick .50 1.25
9 Pierre Turgeon .20 .50
10 Steve Yzerman 2.00 5.00

1993-94 Ultra Promo Sheet

This (approximately) 11" by 8 1/2" sheet features some of the cards of the 1993-94 Ultra set. It is arranged in three rows with three cards each, the middle card in the middle row is not a player's card but a title card. The backs are also identical to the cards' backs.

NNO Joe Juneau 2.00 5.00
Sergei Fedorov, Mats Sundin, Mark Recchi, Jeremy Roenick, Alexei Kovalev

1993-94 Ultra Prospects

Randomly inserted into first series foil packs, the Ultra Prospects set consists of ten standard-size cards. Borderless fronts feature the player emerging from a solid background. The backs contain a photo and career highlights. The cards are numbered as "X of 10".

COMPLETE SET (10) 4.00 8.00
1 Iain Fraser .40 1.00
2 Rob Gaudreau .40 1.00
3 Dave Karpa .40 1.00
4 Trent Klatt .40 1.00
5 Mike Lenarduzzi .40 1.00
6 Kevin Miehm .40 1.00
7 Michael Nylander .40 1.00
8 J.F. Quintin .40 1.00
9 Gary Shuchuk .40 1.00
10 Tyler Wright .40 1.00

1993-94 Ultra Red Light Specials

Randomly inserted in series 2 packs, this ten-card standard-size set highlights some of the NHL's best goal scorers. The borderless fronts feature two color player action shots, one superimposed upon the other. The player's name appears in red foil at the bottom. The horizontal back carries an on-ice close-up of the player set off to the right. The player's name appears in red foil at the upper left, followed below by the player's goal-scoring highlights, all on the red-screened background from the player close-up. The cards are numbered on the back as "X of 10."

COMPLETE SET (10) 6.00 15.00
1 Dave Andreychuk .40 1.00
2 Pavel Bure .75 2.00
3 Mike Gartner .40 1.00
4 Brett Hull 1.00 2.50
5 Jaromir Jagr 1.25 3.00
6 Mario Lemieux 2.00 5.00
7 Alexander Mogilny .40 1.00
8 Mark Recchi .40 1.00
9 Luc Robitaille .40 1.00
10 Teemu Selanne .75 2.00

1993-94 Ultra Scoring Kings

Randomly inserted into all first series packs, this six-card standard-size set showcases six of the NHL's top scorers. Borderless fronts have action player photos. Backs feature a player photo and career highlights. The player's name appears in gold at the top. The card are numbered "X of 6".

COMPLETE SET (6) 12.50 25.00
1 Pat LaFontaine .60 1.50
2 Wayne Gretzky 4.00 10.00
3 Brett Hull .75 2.00
4 Mario Lemieux 3.00 8.00
5 Pierre Turgeon .30 .75
6 Steve Yzerman 3.00 8.00

1993-94 Ultra Speed Merchants

Randomly inserted in second series jumbo packs, this 10-card standard-size set sports fronts of motion-streaked color player action cutouts set on borderless indigo backgrounds highlighted by ice spray. The cards are numbered on the back as "X of 10."

COMPLETE SET (10) 40.00 80.00
1 Pavel Bure 3.00 8.00
2 Russ Courtnall 1.00 2.50
3 Sergei Fedorov 5.00 12.00
4 Mike Gartner 1.50 4.00
5 Al Iafrate 1.00 2.50
6 Pat LaFontaine 3.00 8.00
7 Alexander Mogilny 1.50 4.00
8 Rob Niedermayer 1.50 4.00
9 Geoff Sanderson 1.00 2.50
10 Teemu Selanne 3.00 8.00

1993-94 Ultra Wave of the Future

Randomly inserted in series II packs, these 20 standard-size cards highlight players in their first or second NHL season. The borderless fronts feature color player action shots with "rippled" on-ice backgrounds. The player's name appears in gold foil at a lower corner.The cards are numbered on the back as "X of 20."

COMPLETE SET (20) 6.00 15.00
1 Jason Arnott .40 1.00
2 Martin Brodeur 2.00 5.00
3 Alexandre Daigle .20 .50
4 Ted Drury .20 .50
5 Chris Gratton .20 .50
6 Milos Holan .20 .50
7 Greg Johnson .20 .50
8 Boris Mironov .20 .50
9 Jaroslav Modry .20 .50
10 Markus Naslund .60 1.50
11 Rob Niedermayer .40 1.00
12 Chris Osgood .75 2.00
13 Derek Plante .20 .50
14 Chris Pronger .60 1.50
15 Mike Rathje .20 .50
16 Mikael Renberg .40 1.00
17 Jason Smith .20 .50
18 Jocelyn Thibault .60 1.50
19 Jarkko Varvio .20 .50
20 Alexei Yashin .20 .50

1994-95 Ultra

The 1994-95 Ultra hockey set consists of two series of 200 and 150 cards, for a total of 350 standard-size cards. The suggested retail price for 12-card packs was $1.99, and $2.69 for 15-card packs. Every pack included one insert card, and one "Hot Pack" consisting exclusively of insert cards was seeded once every two boxes (or 1:72 packs). Full-bleed card fronts have the player's name, team and Ultra logo in gold foil at the bottom. The backs also have a full-bleed photo with two smaller inset photos. Stats are at the bottom. Each series is arranged alphabetically by team and the player's within each team alphabetized. Rookie Cards include Mariusz Czerkawski and Eric Fichaud.

COMPLETE SET (400) 17.50 35.00
COMPLETE SERIES 1 (250) 10.00 20.00
COMPLETE SERIES 2 (150) 7.50 15.00
1 Bob Corkum .02 .10
2 Todd Ewen .02 .10
3 Guy Hebert .05 .15
4 Bill Houlder .02 .10
5 Stephan Lebeau .02 .10
6 Joe Sacco .02 .10
7 Anatoli Semenov .02 .10
8 Tim Sweeney .02 .10
9 Terry Yake .02 .10
10 Ray Bourque .20 .50
11 Mariusz Czerkawski RC .15 .40
12 Ted Donato .02 .10
13 Cam Neely .10 .30
14 Adam Oates .05 .15
15 Vincent Riendeau .05 .15
16 Bryan Smolinski .02 .10
17 Don Sweeney .02 .10
18 Glen Wesley .02 .10
19 Donald Audette .02 .10
20 Doug Bodger .02 .10
21 Jason Dawe .02 .10
22 Dominik Hasek .25 .60
23 Dale Hawerchuk .05 .15
24 Pat LaFontaine .10 .30
25 Brad May .02 .10
26 Alexander Mogilny .05 .15
27 Derek Plante .02 .10
28 Richard Smehlik .02 .10
29 Theo Fleury .05 .15
30 Trevor Kidd .05 .15
31 Frank Musil .02 .10
32 Michael Nylander .02 .10
33 James Patrick .02 .10
34 Robert Reichel .05 .15
35 Gary Roberts .02 .10
36 German Titov .02 .10
37 Wes Walz .02 .10
38 Zarley Zalapski .02 .10
39 Ed Belfour .10 .30
40 Chris Chelios .10 .30
41 Dirk Graham .02 .10
42 Bernie Nicholls .05 .15
43 Patrick Poulin .02 .10
44 Jeremy Roenick .12 .30
45 Steve Smith .02 .10
46 Gary Suter .02 .10
47 Brent Sutter .02 .10
48 Neal Broten .05 .15
49 Paul Cavallini .02 .10
50 Dean Evason .02 .10
51 Dave Gagner .05 .15
52 Derian Hatcher .02 .10
53 Trent Klatt .02 .10
54 Grant Ledyard .02 .10
55 Mike Modano .20 .50
56 Andy Moog .10 .30
57 Mark Tinordi .02 .10
58 Dino Ciccarelli .05 .15
59 Paul Coffey .10 .30
60 Sergei Fedorov .20 .50
61 Vladimir Konstantinov .05 .15
62 Nicklas Lidstrom .10 .30
63 Darren McCarty .02 .10
64 Chris Osgood .20 .50
65 Keith Primeau .02 .10
66 Ray Sheppard .05 .15
67 Steve Yzerman .60 1.50
68 Jason Arnott .02 .10
69 Bob Beers .02 .10
70 Ilya Byakin .02 .10
71 Zdeno Ciger .02 .10
72 Igor Kravchuk .02 .10
73 Boris Mironov .02 .10
74 Fredrik Olausson .02 .10
75 Scott Pearson .02 .10
76 Bill Ranford .05 .15
77 Doug Weight .05 .15
78 Stu Barnes .02 .10
79 Jesse Belanger .02 .10
80 Bob Kudelski .02 .10
81 Andrei Lomakin .02 .10
82 Dave Lowry .02 .10
83 Gord Murphy .02 .10
84 Rob Niedermayer .05 .15
85 Brian Skrudland .02 .10
86 John Vanbiesbrouck .05 .15
87 Sean Burke .05 .15
88 Ted Drury .02 .10
89 Alexander Godynyuk .02 .10
90 Robert Kron .02 .10
91 Chris Pronger .10 .30
92 Brian Propp .02 .10
93 Geoff Sanderson .05 .15
94 Darren Turcotte .02 .10
95 Pat Verbeek .02 .10
96 Rob Blake .05 .15
97 Mike Donnelly .02 .10
98 John Druce .02 .10
99 Kelly Hrudey .05 .15
100 Jari Kurri .05 .15
101 Robert Lang .02 .10
102 Marty McSorley .02 .10
103 Luc Robitaille .05 .15
104 Alexei Zhitnik .02 .10
105 Brian Bellows .02 .10
106 Patrice Brisebois .02 .10
107 Vincent Damphousse .02 .10
108 Eric Desjardins .05 .15
109 Gilbert Dionne .02 .10
110 Mike Keane .02 .10
111 John LeClair .10 .30
112 Lyle Odelein .02 .10
113 Patrick Roy .60 1.50
114 Mathieu Schneider .02 .10
115 Martin Brodeur .30 .75
116 Jim Dowd .02 .10
117 Bill Guerin .05 .15
118 Claude Lemieux .02 .10
119 John MacLean .05 .15
120 Corey Millen .02 .10
121 Scott Niedermayer .02 .10
122 Stephane Richer .05 .15
123 Scott Stevens .05 .15
124 Valeri Zelepukin .02 .10
125 Patrick Flatley .02 .10
126 Travis Green .05 .15
127 Ron Hextall .05 .15
128 Benoit Hogue .02 .10
129 Darius Kasparaitis .02 .10
130 Vladimir Malakhov .02 .10
131 Marty McInnis .02 .10
132 Steve Thomas .02 .10
133 Pierre Turgeon .05 .15
134 Dennis Vaske .02 .10
135 Glenn Anderson .05 .15
136 Jeff Beukeboom .02 .10
137 Adam Graves .02 .10
138 Steve Larmer .05 .15
139 Brian Leetch .10 .30
140 Mark Messier .10 .30
141 Petr Nedved .05 .15
142 Sergei Nemchinov .02 .10
143 Mike Richter .10 .30
144 Sergei Zubov .02 .10
145 Craig Billington .05 .15
146 Alexandre Daigle .02 .10
147 Evgeny Davydov .02 .10
148 Scott Levins .02 .10
149 Norm Maciver .02 .10
150 Troy Mallette .02 .10
151 Brad Shaw .02 .10
152 Alexei Yashin .02 .10
153 Josef Beranek .02 .10
154 Jason Bowen .02 .10
155 Rod Brind'Amour .05 .15
156 Kevin Dineen .02 .10
157 Garry Galley .02 .10
158 Mark Recchi .05 .15
159 Mikael Renberg .05 .15
160 Tommy Soderstrom .05 .15
161 Dimitri Yushkevich .02 .10
162 Tom Barrasso .05 .15
163 Ron Francis .05 .15
164 Jaromir Jagr .20 .50
165 Mario Lemieux .60 1.50
166 Shawn McEachern .02 .10
167 Joe Mullen .05 .15
168 Larry Murphy .05 .15
169 Ulf Samuelsson .02 .10
170 Kevin Stevens .02 .10
171 Martin Straka .02 .10
172 Wendel Clark .05 .15
173 Stephane Fiset .05 .15
174 Iain Fraser .02 .10
175 Andrei Kovalenko .02 .10
176 Sylvain Lefebvre .02 .10
177 Owen Nolan .05 .15
178 Mike Ricci .02 .10
179 Martin Rucinsky .02 .10
180 Joe Sakic .25 .60
181 Scott Young .02 .10
182 Steve Duchesne .02 .10
183 Brett Hull .15 .40
184 Curtis Joseph .10 .30
185 Al MacInnis .05 .15
186 Kevin Miller .02 .10
187 Jim Montgomery .02 .10
188 Vitali Prokhorov .02 .10
189 Brendan Shanahan .10 .30
190 Peter Stastny .05 .15
191 Esa Tikkanen .02 .10
192 Ulf Dahlen .02 .10
193 Todd Elik .02 .10
194 Johan Garpenlov .02 .10
195 Arturs Irbe .05 .15
196 Vlastimil Kroupa .02 .10
197 Igor Larionov .02 .10
198 Sergei Makarov .02 .10
199 Jeff Norton .02 .10
200 Sandis Ozolinsh .02 .10
201 Mike Rathje .02 .10
202 Brian Bradley .02 .10
203 Shawn Chambers .02 .10
204 Danton Cole .02 .10
205 Chris Gratton .02 .10
206 Roman Hamrlik .05 .15
207 Chris Joseph .02 .10
208 Petr Klima .02 .10
209 Daren Puppa .05 .15
210 John Tucker .02 .10
211 Dave Andreychuk .05 .15
212 Ken Baumgartner .02 .10
213 Dave Ellett .02 .10
214 Mike Gartner .05 .15
215 Todd Gill .02 .10
216 Doug Gilmour .05 .15
217 Jamie Macoun .02 .10
218 Dmitri Mironov .02 .10
219 Felix Potvin .10 .30
220 Mats Sundin .10 .30
221 Jeff Brown .02 .10
222 Pavel Bure .10 .30
223 Murray Craven .02 .10
224 Bret Hedican .02 .10
225 Nathan Lafayette .02 .10
226 Trevor Linden .05 .15
227 Jyrki Lumme .02 .10
228 Kirk McLean .05 .15
229 Gino Odjick .02 .10
230 Cliff Ronning .02 .10
231 Peter Bondra .05 .15
232 Sylvain Cote .02 .10
233 Kevin Hatcher .02 .10
234 Dale Hunter .02 .10
235 Calle Johansson .02 .10
236 Dimitri Khristich .02 .10
237 Pat Peake .02 .10
238 Michal Pivonka .02 .10
239 Rick Tabaracci .05 .15
240 Tim Cheveldae .05 .15
241 Dallas Drake .02 .10
242 Nelson Emerson .02 .10
243 Dave Manson .02 .10
244 Teppo Numminen .02 .10
245 Stephane Quintal .02 .10
246 Teemu Selanne .10 .30
247 Keith Tkachuk .10 .30
248 Checklist .02 .10
249 Checklist .02 .10
250 Checklist .02 .10
251 John Lilley .02 .10
252 Mikhail Shtalenkov .02 .10
253 Garry Valk .02 .10
254 John Gruden RC .02 .10
255 Brent Hughes .02 .10
256 Al Iafrate .02 .10
257 Alexei Kasatonov .02 .10
258 Mikko Makela .02 .10
259 Marc Potvin .02 .10
260 Jon Rohloff RC .02 .10
261 Jozef Stumpel .02 .10
262 Grant Fuhr .05 .15
263 Viktor Gordiouk .02 .10
264 Yuri Khmylev .02 .10
265 Craig Muni .02 .10
266 Craig Simpson .02 .10
267 Denis Tsygurov RC .02 .10
268 Steve Chiasson .02 .10
269 Phil Housley .05 .15
270 Joel Otto .02 .10
271 Andrei Trefilov .02 .10
272 Vesa Viitakoski .02 .10
273 Tony Amonte .05 .15
274 Brent Grieve .02 .10
275 Bernie Nicholls .05 .15
276 Christian Soucy RC .05 .15
277 Paul Ysebaert .02 .10
278 Shane Churla .02 .10
279 Russ Courtnall .02 .10
280 Craig Ludwig .02 .10
281 Jarkko Varvio .02 .10
282 Darcy Wakaluk .05 .15
283 Greg Johnson .02 .10
284 Slava Kozlov .05 .15
285 Martin Lapointe .02 .10
286 Tim Taylor RC .02 .10
287 Mike Vernon .05 .15
288 Jason York RC .02 .10
289 Fred Brathwaite .05 .15
290 Kelly Buchberger .02 .10
291 Shayne Corson .02 .10
292 Dean McAmmond .02 .10
293 Vladimir Vujtek .02 .10
294 Doug Barrault .02 .10
295 Keith Brown .02 .10
296 Mark Fitzpatrick .05 .15
297 Mike Hough .02 .10
298 Scott Mellanby .05 .15
299 Jimmy Carson .02 .10
300 Andrew Cassels .02 .10
301 Andrei Nikolishin .02 .10
302 Steven Rice .02 .10
303 Glen Wesley .02 .10
304 Rob Brown .02 .10
305 Tony Granato .02 .10
306 Wayne Gretzky .75 2.00
307 Dan Quinn .02 .10
308 Darryl Sydor .02 .10
309 Rick Tocchet .05 .15
310 Donald Brashear RC .02 .10
311 Valeri Bure .02 .10
312 Jim Montgomery .02 .10
313 Kirk Muller .02 .10
314 Oleg Petrov .02 .10
315 Peter Popovic .02 .10
316 Yves Racine .02 .10
317 Turner Stevenson .02 .10
318 Ken Daneyko .02 .10
319 David Emma .02 .10
320 Brian Rolston .02 .10
321 Alexander Semak .02 .10
322 Jason Smith .02 .10
323 Chris Terreri .05 .15
324 Ray Ferraro .02 .10
325 Derek King .02 .10
326 Scott Lachance .02 .10
327 Brett Lindros .02 .10
328 Jamie McLennan .05 .15
329 Zigmund Palffy .05 .15
330 Corey Hirsch .05 .15
331 Alexei Kovalev .02 .10
332 Stephane Matteau .02 .10
333 Petr Nedved .05 .15
334 Mattias Norstrom .02 .10
335 Mark Osborne .02 .10
336 Randy Cunneyworth .02 .10
337 Pavol Demitra .05 .15
338 Pat Elynuik .02 .10
339 Sean Hill .02 .10
340 Darrin Madeley .02 .10
341 Sylvain Turgeon .02 .10
342 Vladislav Boulin RC .02 .10
343 Ron Hextall .05 .15
344 Patrik Juhlin RC .02 .10
345 Eric Lindros .10 .30
346 Shjon Podein .02 .10
347 Chris Therien .02 .10
348 John Cullen .02 .10
349 Markus Naslund .10 .30
350 Luc Robitaille .05 .15
351 Kjell Samuelsson .02 .10
352 Tomas Sandstrom .02 .10
353 Ken Wregget .05 .15
354 Wendel Clark .05 .15
355 Adam Deadmarsh .02 .10
356 Peter Forsberg .50 1.25
357 Valeri Kamensky .05 .15
358 Uwe Krupp .02 .10
359 Janne Laukkanen .02 .10
360 Sylvain Lefebvre .02 .10
361 Jocelyn Thibault .10 .30
362 Bill Houlder .02 .10
363 Craig Janney .05 .15
364 Pat Falloon .02 .10
365 Jeff Friesen .02 .10
366 Viktor Kozlov .02 .10
367 Andrei Nazarov .02 .10
368 Jeff Odgers .02 .10
369 Michal Sykora .02 .10
370 Mikael Andersson .02 .10
371 Eric Charron RC .02 .10
372 Chris LiPuma .02 .10
373 Denis Savard .05 .15
374 Jason Wiemer RC .02 .10
375 Nikolai Borschevsky .02 .10
376 Eric Fichaud RC .05 .15
377 Kenny Jonsson .02 .10
378 Mike Ridley .02 .10
379 Mats Sundin .10 .30
380 Greg Adams .02 .10
381 Shawn Antoski .02 .10
382 Geoff Courtnall .02 .10
383 Martin Gelinas .02 .10
384 Sergio Momesso .02 .10
385 Jiri Slegr .02 .10
386 Jason Allison .02 .10
387 Don Beaupre .05 .15
388 Joe Juneau .05 .15
389 Steve Konowalchuk .02 .10
390 Kelly Miller .02 .10
391 Dave Poulin .02 .10
392 Tie Domi .05 .15
393 Michal Grosek RC .02 .10
394 Russ Romaniuk .02 .10
395 Darrin Shannon .02 .10
396 Thomas Steen .02 .10
397 Igor Ulanov .02 .10
398 Alexei Zhamnov .05 .15
399 Checklist .02 .10
400 Checklist .02 .10

1994-95 Ultra All-Rookies

Randomly inserted in first series jumbo packs, this 10-card standard-size set reflects top rookies from the 1993-94 campaign. On acetate stock, the player is on the right superimposed over an ice-like surface. The left side is clear with the set title. The left portion of the back has a brief write-up and

photo. Two distinct versions of each card in this set exist; one version carries the words "All-Rookie 1994-95" in a dark, greyish silver tint; the other in a bright, sparkling silver tint.
COMPLETE SET (10) 6.00 15.00
1 Jason Arnott .75 2.00
2 Martin Brodeur 8.00 10.00
3 Alexandre Daigle .75 2.00
4 Chris Gratton .40 1.00
5 Boris Mironov .40 1.00
6 Derek Plante .40 1.00
7 Chris Pronger .75 2.00
8 Mikael Renberg .40 1.00
9 Bryan Smolinski .40 1.00
10 Alexei Yashin .75 2.00

1994-95 Ultra All-Stars

Randomly inserted into first series foil packs at a rate of 1:2, this standard-size set focuses on 12 players who participated in the 1994 NHL All-Star Game in New York. The set is arranged according to Eastern (1-6) and Western Conferences (7-12). Horizontally designed, the front features the player in his All-Star jersey. The background is colorful and flashy. The All-Star logo also appears on front. The backs are much the same with an up-close player photo.
COMPLETE SET (12) 3.00 6.00
1 Ray Bourque .25 .60
2 Brian Leetch .15 .40
3 Eric Lindros .15 .40
4 Mark Messier .15 .40
5 Alexander Mogilny .10 .20
6 Patrick Roy .75 2.00
7 Pavel Bure .15 .40
8 Chris Chelios .15 .40
9 Paul Coffey .15 .40
10 Wayne Gretzky 1.00 2.50
11 Brett Hull .20 .50
12 Felix Potvin .15 .40

1994-95 Ultra Award Winners

Randomly inserted into first series foil packs, this 8-card standard-size set honors NHL award winners of the previous season. Horizontally designed, the fronts have an action photo and, to the left, the player in his tux at the awards ceremony. The backs have a write-up and a player photo.
COMPLETE SET (8) 6.00 12.00
1 Ray Bourque .60 1.50
2 Martin Brodeur 1.00 2.50
3 Sergei Fedorov .60 1.50
4 Adam Graves .15 .30
5 Wayne Gretzky 2.50 6.00
6 Dominik Hasek .75 2.00
7 Brian Leetch .40 1.00
8 Cam Neely .40 1.00

1994-95 Ultra Global Greats

Randomly inserted in second series 15-card jumbo packs at a rate of 1:12, this 10-card standard-size set features superstars who hail from outside North America. On the front, a player photo is superimposed over a background of colorful globes. The back features a write-up and a photo over the same background.
COMPLETE SET (10) 8.00 15.00
1 Sergei Fedorov 1.50 4.00
2 Dominik Hasek 2.00 5.00
3 Arturs Irbe .50 1.25
4 Jaromir Jagr 1.50 4.00
5 Jari Kurri .50 1.25
6 Alexander Mogilny .50 1.25
7 Petr Nedved .50 1.25
8 Mikael Renberg .50 1.25
9 Teemu Selanne 1.00 2.50
10 Alexei Yashin .30 .75

1994-95 Ultra Power

Randomly inserted in first series foil packs and distributed one set per hobby case, this 10-card standard-size set focuses on high scoring forwards. The card fronts contain a player photo superimposed over a glossy and circular background. The backs are horizontal with a player photo, highlights and a similar background.
COMPLETE SET (10) 4.00 8.00
1 Dave Andreychuk .30 .75
2 Jason Arnott .20 .50
3 Chris Gratton .20 .50
4 Adam Graves .20 .50
5 Eric Lindros .60 1.50
6 Cam Neely .60 1.50
7 Mikael Renberg .30 .75
8 Jeremy Roenick .60 1.50
9 Brendan Shanahan .60 1.50
10 Keith Tkachuk .60 1.50

1994-95 Ultra Premier Pad Men

Randomly inserted in first series foil packs at a rate of 1:37, this 6-card standard-size set spotlights leading goaltenders. On front, a gold embossed design serves as background to the player photo. The backs have a solid color background that coordinates with the player's team. A player photo and write-up are in the foreground.
COMPLETE SET (6) 10.00 20.00
1 Dominik Hasek 2.00 5.00
2 Arturs Irbe .50 1.25
3 Curtis Joseph 1.00 2.50
4 Felix Potvin 1.00 2.50
5 Mike Richter 1.00 2.50
6 Patrick Roy 8.00 20.00

1994-95 Ultra Premier Pivots

Randomly inserted in second series foil packs at a rate of 1:4, this 10-card standard-size set spotlights leading NHL centers. The fronts contain a player photo superimposed over a brown checkered background. The backs are similar except for the addition of some player highlights.
COMPLETE SET (10) 6.00 12.00
1 Jason Arnott .15 .30
2 Sergei Fedorov .60 1.50
3 Doug Gilmour .20 .50
4 Wayne Gretzky 2.50 6.00
5 Pat LaFontaine .40 1.00
6 Eric Lindros .40 1.00
7 Mark Messier .40 1.00
8 Mike Modano .60 1.50
9 Adam Oates .20 .50
10 Steve Yzerman 2.00 5.00

1994-95 Ultra Prospects

Randomly inserted in second series 12-card foil packs at a rate of 1:12, this 10-card standard-size set focuses on some of the rookie crop from the 1994-95 season. The fronts have an embossed player photo superimposed over a background containing the set name. The backs have a photo and write-up.
COMPLETE SET (10) 15.00 30.00
1 Peter Forsberg 5.00 12.00
2 Todd Harvey .75 2.00
3 Paul Kariya 2.00 5.00
4 Viktor Kozlov .75 2.00
5 Brett Lindros .75 2.00
6 Mike Peca .75 2.00
7 Brian Rolston .75 2.00
8 Jamie Storr 1.50 4.00
9 Oleg Tverdovsky .75 2.00
10 Jason Wiemer .75 2.00

1994-95 Ultra Red Light Specials

Randomly inserted in second series foil packs at a rate of 1:12, this 10-card standard-size set presents top goal scorers. The fronts are horizontally designed with a player photo superimposed over three action strips of the player. The set logo is in red foil at bottom left. The backs offer a photo and highlights.
COMPLETE SET (10) 2.00 4.00
1 Dave Andreychuk .10 .30
2 Pavel Bure .25 .60
3 Mike Gartner .10 .30
4 Adam Graves .10 .20
5 Brett Hull .30 .75
6 Cam Neely .25 .60
7 Gary Roberts .10 .20
8 Teemu Selanne .25 .60
9 Brendan Shanahan .25 .60
10 Kevin Stevens .10 .20

1994-95 Ultra Scoring Kings

Randomly inserted in first series foil packs, this 7-card standard-size set showcases seven of the NHL's top scorers. The fronts provide three player photos with a gold foil set logo at bottom left. The backs have a player photo and write-up.
COMPLETE SET (7) 5.00 10.00
1 Pavel Bure .25 .60
2 Sergei Fedorov .40 1.00
3 Doug Gilmour .10 .30
4 Wayne Gretzky 1.50 4.00
5 Mario Lemieux 1.25 3.00
6 Eric Lindros .25 .60
7 Steve Yzerman 1.25 3.00

1994-95 Ultra Sergei Fedorov

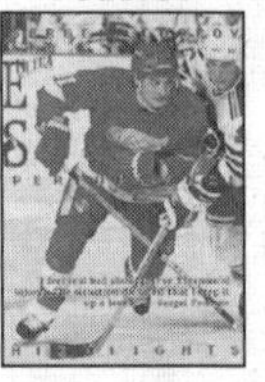

Measuring the standard-size, the first ten cards were randomly inserted in first series foil packs. Card Nos. 11 and 12 were available through a mail-in offer. The set chronicles various stages of Fedorov's career and his abilities. The front offers a photo with a quote from an opposing player, teammate or executive. In addition to providing career information, horizontal backs contain a player photo. An indeterminate number of cards were autographed by Fedorov, and randomly inserted in series one packs.
COMPLETE SET (10) 5.00 10.00
COMMON FEDOROV (1-10) .60 1.50
COMMON MAIL-IN (11-12) .75 2.00

1994-95 Ultra Speed Merchants

Randomly inserted in second series foil packs at the rate of 1:2, this 10-card standard-size set salutes the league's fastest and hardest-to-defend skaters. A player photo is superimposed over an action-oriented background with the player's name and set title in gold foil at the bottom. The backs contain a checkered flag background with a photo and highlights.
COMPLETE SET (10) 1.25 2.50
1 Pavel Bure .20 .50
2 Russ Courtnall .05 .15
3 Sergei Fedorov .30 .75
4 Al Iafrate .05 .15
5 Pat LaFontaine .20 .50
6 Brian Leetch .20 .50
7 Mike Modano .30 .75
8 Alexander Mogilny .10 .25
9 Jeremy Roenick .20 .50
10 Geoff Sanderson .10 .25

1995-96 Ultra

These 400 standard-size cards represent the two series release of the 1995-96 Ultra issue. Issued in 12-card packs, the suggested retail price per pack was $2.49. Each series one pack contains two insert cards. One was a Gold Medallion parallel insert while the other was from one of the five series one Ultra insert sets. Second series packs did not guarantee an insert per pack. The cards are printed on 20-point stock. Key RCs in the set include Daniel Alfredsson, Todd Bertuzzi, Chad Kilger and Kyle McLaren. The Cool Trade Exchange card was randomly inserted 1:360 series two packs, making it the hardest to pull of the five available. The card could be redeemed, until the expiration date of 3/1/97, for special Emotion cards of Jeremy Roenick, Paul Kariya, Saku Koivu and Martin Brodeur.
COMPLETE SET (400) 20.00 50.00
COMPLETE SERIES 1 (200) 10.00 25.00
COMPLETE SERIES 2 (200) 10.00 25.00
1 Guy Hebert .05 .15
2 Milos Holan .02 .10
3 Paul Kariya .10 .30
4 Denny Lambert .02 .10
5 Stephan Lebeau .02 .10
6 Oleg Tverdovsky .02 .10
7 Shaun Van Allen .02 .10
8 Ray Bourque .20 .50
9 Mariusz Czerkawski .02 .10
10 Blaine Lacher .05 .15
11 Sandy Moger RC .02 .10
12 Cam Neely .10 .30
13 Adam Oates .05 .15
14 Bryan Smolinski .02 .10
15 Donald Audette .02 .10
16 Jason Dawe .02 .10
17 Garry Galley .02 .10
18 Dominik Hasek .25 .60
19 Brian Holzinger RC .05 .15
20 Pat LaFontaine .10 .30
21 Alexander Mogilny .05 .15
22 Alexei Zhitnik .02 .10
23 Steve Chiasson .02 .10
24 Theo Fleury .02 .10
25 Phil Housley .05 .15
26 Trevor Kidd .05 .15
27 Joel Otto .02 .10
28 Gary Roberts .02 .10
29 Zarley Zalapski .02 .10
30 Ed Belfour .10 .30
31 Chris Chelios .10 .30
32 Eric Daze .05 .15
33 Sergei Krivokrasov .02 .10
34 Bernie Nicholls .02 .10
35 Jeremy Roenick .15 .40
36 Gary Suter .02 .10
37 Todd Harvey .05 .15
38 Derian Hatcher .02 .10
39 Mike Kennedy RC .02 .10
40 Grant Ledyard .02 .10
41 Mike Modano .20 .50
42 Andy Moog .10 .30
43 Mike Torchia RC .05 .15
44 Paul Coffey .10 .30
45 Sergei Fedorov .20 .50
46 Vladimir Konstantinov .05 .15
47 Slava Kozlov .05 .15
48 Keith Primeau .02 .10
49 Ray Sheppard .02 .10
50 Mike Vernon .05 .15
51 Steve Yzerman .60 1.50
52 Jason Arnott .02 .10
53 Shayne Corson .02 .10
54 Igor Kravchuk .02 .10
55 Todd Marchant .02 .10
56 David Oliver .02 .10
57 Bill Ranford .05 .15
58 Doug Weight .05 .15
59 Stu Barnes .02 .10
60 Jesse Belanger .02 .10
61 Gord Murphy .02 .10
62 Rob Niedermayer .05 .15
63 Brian Skrudland .02 .10
64 John Vanbiesbrouck .05 .15
65 Sean Burke .05 .15
66 Andrew Cassels .02 .10
67 Frantisek Kucera .02 .10
68 Andrei Nikolishin .02 .10
69 Chris Pronger .10 .30
70 Geoff Sanderson .02 .10
71 Kevin Smyth .02 .10
72 Darren Turcotte .02 .10
73 Rob Blake .05 .15
74 Wayne Gretzky .75 2.00
75 Kelly Hrudey .05 .15
76 Marty McSorley .02 .10
77 Jamie Storr .05 .15
78 Darryl Sydor .05 .15
79 Rick Tocchet .05 .15
80 Vincent Damphousse .02 .10
81 Vladimir Malakhov .02 .10
82 Mark Recchi .05 .15
83 Patrick Roy .60 1.50
84 Brian Savage .02 .10
85 Pierre Turgeon .05 .15
86 Martin Brodeur .30 .75
87 Neal Broten .05 .15
88 Sergei Brylin .02 .10
89 John MacLean .05 .15
90 Scott Niedermayer .02 .10
91 Stephane Richer .05 .15
92 Scott Stevens .05 .15
93 Ray Ferraro .02 .10
94 Scott Lachance .02 .10
95 Brett Lindros .02 .10
96 Kirk Muller .02 .10
97 Zigmund Palffy .05 .15
98 Tommy Salo RC .50 1.25
99 Mathieu Schneider .02 .10
100 Tommy Soderstrom .05 .15
101 Glenn Healy .05 .15
102 Darren Langdon RC .02 .10
103 Steve Larmer .05 .15
104 Brian Leetch .05 .15
105 Mark Messier .10 .30
106 Mattias Norstrom .02 .10
107 Pat Verbeek .02 .10
108 Sergei Zubov .02 .10
109 Don Beaupre .05 .15
110 Radek Bonk .02 .10
111 Alexandre Daigle .02 .10
112 Steve Larouche RC .02 .10
113 Stanislav Neckar .02 .10
114 Alexei Yashin .02 .10
115 Rod Brind'Amour .05 .15
116 Eric Desjardins .05 .15
117 Ron Hextall .05 .15
118 John LeClair .10 .30
119 Eric Lindros .10 .30
120 Mikael Renberg .05 .15
121 Chris Therien .02 .10
122 Ron Francis .05 .15
123 Jaromir Jagr .20 .50
124 Joe Mullen .05 .15
125 Larry Murphy .05 .15
126 Ulf Samuelsson .02 .10
127 Kevin Stevens .02 .10
128 Ken Wregget .05 .15
129 Wendel Clark .05 .15
130 Adam Deadmarsh .02 .10
131 Stephane Fiset .05 .15
132 Peter Forsberg .30 .75
133 Curtis Leschyshyn .02 .10
134 Owen Nolan .05 .15
135 Mike Ricci .05 .15
136 Joe Sakic .25 .60
137 Denis Chasse .02 .10
138 Steve Duchesne .02 .10
139 Brett Hull .15 .40
140 Curtis Joseph .10 .30
141 Ian Laperriere .02 .10
142 Brendan Shanahan .10 .30
143 Esa Tikkanen .02 .10
144 Ulf Dahlen .02 .10
145 Jeff Friesen .02 .10
146 Arturs Irbe .05 .15
147 Craig Janney .02 .10
148 Sergei Makarov .02 .10
149 Sandis Ozolinsh .02 .10
150 Ray Whitney .05 .15
151 Chris Gratton .02 .10
152 Roman Hamrlik .05 .15
153 Petr Klima .02 .10
154 Brantt Myhres RC .02 .10
155 Daren Puppa .05 .15
156 Jason Wiemer .02 .10
157 Paul Ysebaert .02 .10
158 Dave Andreychuk .05 .15
159 Tie Domi .05 .15
160 Doug Gilmour .05 .15
161 Kenny Jonsson .02 .10
162 Felix Potvin .10 .30
163 Mike Ridley .02 .10
164 Mats Sundin .10 .30
165 Jeff Brown .02 .10
166 Pavel Bure .10 .30
167 Geoff Courtnall .02 .10
168 Russ Courtnall .02 .10
169 Trevor Linden .05 .15
170 Kirk McLean .05 .15
171 Roman Oksiuta .02 .10
172 Peter Bondra .05 .15
173 Jim Carey .05 .15
174 Martin Gendron .02 .10
175 Dale Hunter .05 .15
176 Calle Johansson .02 .10
177 Michal Pivonka .02 .10
178 Mark Tinordi .02 .10
179 Nelson Emerson .02 .10
180 Nikolai Khabibulin .05 .15
181 Dave Manson .02 .10
182 Teppo Numminen .02 .10
183 Teemu Selanne .10 .30
184 Keith Tkachuk .10 .30
185 Alexei Zhamnov .05 .15
186 Martin Brodeur SC .30 .75
187 Neal Broten .05 .15
188 Bob Carpenter .02 .10
189 Ken Daneyko .02 .10
190 Bruce Driver .02 .10
191 Bill Guerin .05 .15
192 Claude Lemieux .02 .10
193 John MacLean .05 .15
194 Scott Niedermayer .02 .10
195 Stephane Richer .05 .15
196 Scott Stevens .05 .15
197 Presentation Card .05 .15
Stanley Cup Champions
198 Checklist (1-83) .02 .10
199 Checklist (84-169) .02 .10
200 Checklist (170-200) .02 .10
201 Todd Krygier .02 .10
202 Steve Rucchin .05 .15
203 Mike Sillinger .02 .10
204 Ted Donato .02 .10
205 Shawn McEachern .02 .10
206 Joe Mullen .05 .15
207 Kevin Stevens .02 .10
208 Don Sweeney .02 .10
209 Mark Astley .02 .10
210 Randy Burridge .02 .10
211 Jason Dawe .02 .10
212 Mike Peca .05 .15
213 Michael Nylander .02 .10
214 Cory Stillman .02 .10
215 Pavel Torgajev RC .02 .10
216 Tony Amonte .05 .15
217 Joe Murphy .02 .10
218 Bob Probert .05 .15
219 Denis Savard .05 .15
220 Stephane Fiset .05 .15
221 Valeri Kamensky .05 .15
222 Sylvain Lefebvre .02 .10
223 Claude Lemieux .02 .10
224 Sandis Ozolinsh .02 .10
225 Patrick Roy .60 1.50
226 Scott Young .02 .10
227 Greg Adams .02 .10
228 Guy Carbonneau .10 .30
229 Dave Gagner .02 .10
230 Kevin Hatcher .02 .10
231 Darcy Wakaluk .05 .15
232 Dino Ciccarelli .05 .15
233 Greg Johnson .02 .10
234 Igor Larionov .02 .10
235 Darren McCarty .02 .10
236 Chris Osgood .05 .15
237 Zdeno Ciger .02 .10
238 Bryan Marchment .02 .10
239 Boris Mironov .02 .10
240 Peter White .02 .10
241 Jody Hull .02 .10
242 Scott Mellanby .02 .10
243 Gord Murphy .02 .10
244 Jason Woolley .02 .10
245 Gerald Diduck .02 .10
246 Nelson Emerson .02 .10
247 Brendan Shanahan .10 .30
248 Glen Wesley .02 .10
249 Tony Granato .02 .10
250 Dimitri Khristich .02 .10
251 Jari Kurri .10 .30
252 Eric Lacroix .02 .10
253 Yanic Perreault .02 .10
254 Patrice Brisebois .02 .10
255 Benoit Brunet .02 .10
256 Valeri Bure .02 .10
257 Stephane Quintal .02 .10
258 Jocelyn Thibault .10 .30
259 Shawn Chambers .02 .10
260 Jim Dowd .02 .10
261 Bill Guerin .05 .15
262 Bobby Holik .02 .10
263 Steve Thomas .05 .15
264 Esa Tikkanen .02 .10
265 Wendel Clark .05 .15
266 Travis Green .05 .15
267 Brett Lindros .02 .10
268 Kirk Muller .02 .10
269 Zigmund Palffy .05 .15
270 Mathieu Schneider .02 .10
271 Alexander Semak .02 .10
272 Dennis Vaske .02 .10
273 Ray Ferraro .02 .10
274 Adam Graves .02 .10
275 Alexei Kovalev .02 .10
276 Mike Richter .10 .30
277 Luc Robitaille .05 .15
278 Ulf Samuelsson .02 .10
279 Steve Duchesne .02 .10
280 Trent McCleary RC .02 .10
281 Dan Quinn .02 .10
282 Martin Straka .02 .10
283 Karl Dykhuis .02 .10
284 Pat Falloon .02 .10
285 Joel Otto .02 .10
286 Kjell Samuelsson .02 .10
287 Garth Snow .05 .15
288 Mario Lemieux .60 1.50
289 Norm Maciver .02 .10
290 Dmitri Mironov .02 .10
291 Markus Naslund .10 .30
292 Petr Nedved .05 .15
293 Tomas Sandstrom .02 .10
294 Bryan Smolinski .02 .10
295 Sergei Zubov .02 .10
296 Shayne Corson .02 .10
297 Geoff Courtnall .02 .10
298 Grant Fuhr .10 .30
299 Dale Hawerchuk .10 .30
300 Al MacInnis .05 .15
301 Brian Noonan .02 .10
302 Chris Pronger .10 .30
303 Andrei Nazarov .02 .10
304 Owen Nolan .05 .15
305 Ray Sheppard .02 .10
306 Chris Terreri .05 .15
307 Brian Bellows .02 .10
308 Brian Bradley .02 .10
309 John Cullen .02 .10
310 Alexander Selivanov .02 .10
311 Mike Gartner .05 .15
312 Benoit Hogue .02 .10
313 Sergio Momesso .02 .10
314 Larry Murphy .05 .15
315 Dave Babych .02 .10
316 Bret Hedican .02 .10
317 Alexander Mogilny .05 .15
318 Mike Ridley .02 .10
319 Peter Bondra .05 .15
320 Jim Carey .05 .15
321 Sylvain Cote .02 .10
322 Sergei Gonchar .02 .10
323 Joe Juneau .02 .10
324 Steve Konowalchuk .02 .10
325 Pat Peake .02 .10
326 Dallas Drake .02 .10
327 Igor Korolev .02 .10
328 Darren Turcotte .02 .10
329 Daniel Alfredsson RC .50 1.25
330 Aki-Petteri Berg RC .05 .15
331 Todd Bertuzzi RC .75 2.00
332 Jason Bonsignore .02 .10
333 Curtis Brown RC .10 .30
334 Byron Dafoe .05 .15
335 Eric Daze .05 .15
336 Shane Doan RC .30 .75
337 Jason Doig .02 .10
338 Radek Dvorak RC .20 .50
339 Joe Dziedzic .02 .10
340 Darby Hendrickson .02 .10
341 Brian Holzinger RC .10 .30
342 Ed Jovanovski .05 .15
343 Chad Kilger RC .02 .10
344 Saku Koivu .10 .30
345 Darren Langdon .02 .10
346 Jamie Langenbrunner .02 .10
347 Jere Lehtinen .05 .15
348 Bryan McCabe .02 .10
349 Kyle McLaren RC .02 .10
350 Marty Murray .02 .10
351 Jeff O'Neill .02 .10
352 Deron Quint .02 .10
353 Marcus Ragnarsson RC .05 .15
354 Tommy Salo .20 .50
355 Miroslav Satan RC .50 1.25
356 Jamie Storr .05 .15
357 Niklas Sundstrom .05 .15
358 Robert Svehla RC .02 .10
359 Denis Pederson .02 .10
360 Antti Tormanen .02 .10
361 Brendan Witt .02 .10
362 Vitali Yachmenev .02 .10
363 Stephane Yelle .02 .10
364 Tom Barrasso NE .05 .15
365 Ed Belfour NE .10 .30
366 Martin Brodeur NE .30 .75
367 Sean Burke NE .05 .15
368 Jim Carey NE .02 .10
369 Stephane Fiset NE .05 .15
370 Dominik Hasek NE .25 .60
371 Ron Hextall NE .05 .15
372 Nikolai Khabibulin NE .05 .15
373 Kirk McLean NE .05 .15
374 Chris Osgood NE .05 .15
375 Felix Potvin NE .05 .15
376 Daren Puppa NE .05 .15
377 Patrick Roy NE .60 1.50
378 John Vanbiesbrouck NE .05 .15
379 Pavel Bure UC .10 .30
380 Chris Chelios UC .10 .30
381 Sergei Fedorov UC .20 .50
382 Theo Fleury UC .02 .10
383 Peter Forsberg UC .30 .75
384 Ron Francis UC .05 .15
385 Wayne Gretzky UC .75 2.00
386 Brett Hull UC .15 .40
387 Jaromir Jagr UC .20 .50
388 Paul Kariya UC .10 .30
389 Pat LaFontaine UC .05 .15
390 Brian Leetch UC .05 .15
391 Mario Lemieux UC .60 1.50
392 Eric Lindros UC .20 .50
393 Mark Messier UC .10 .30
394 Mike Modano UC .10 .30
395 Adam Oates UC .05 .15
396 Jeremy Roenick UC .15 .40
397 Joe Sakic UC .25 .60
398 Alexei Zhamnov UC .05 .15
399 Checklist .02 .10
400 Checklist .02 .10
NNO Cool Trade Exchange .75 2.00

1995-96 Ultra Gold Medallion

This 200-card standard-size set is a parallel to the basic Ultra series one issue. These cards were issued one per series one pack. No Gold Medallion version exists for series two cards. The fronts have the same photo as the regular cards except the entire background is gold. The Ultra Gold Medallion logo is in the middle of the card and is embossed for effect. The words "Gold Medallion Edition" are located under the player's name. The backs are identical to the regular cards. Gold Medallion version also could be found for series one insert cards. Values for those are included under the appropriate insert header.
*STARS: 3X TO 6X BASIC CARDS
*ROOKIES: 1.5X TO 3X BASIC CARDS

1995-96 Ultra All-Rookies

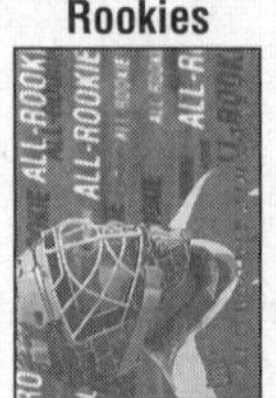

These ten cards, which were randomly inserted at a rate of 1:4 series one retail packs, focus on the top rookies from the 1994-95 campaign. Gold Medallion parallel versions of these cards also were available at indeterminate odds.
COMPLETE SET (10) 6.00 15.00
*GOLD MED: .75X TO 2X BASIC INSERTS
1 Jim Carey .40 1.00
2 Mariusz Czerkawski .40 1.00
3 Peter Forsberg 2.00 5.00
4 Jeff Friesen .40 1.00
5 Paul Kariya 1.50 4.00
6 Blaine Lacher .40 1.00
7 Ian Laperriere .40 1.00
8 Todd Marchant .40 1.00
9 Roman Oksiuta .40 1.00
10 David Oliver .40 1.00

1995-96 Ultra Crease Crashers

These twenty cards capture a goalie's worst nightmare -- a soft-handed forward with a propensity for invading a netminder's home turf. The cards were randomly inserted in series two retail packs only at a rate of 1:18.

COMPLETE SET (20)	20.00	40.00
1 Jason Arnott	1.00	2.00
2 Rod Brind'Amour	1.00	2.50
3 Theo Fleury	1.00	2.50
4 Todd Harvey	1.00	2.50
5 John LeClair	1.50	4.00
6 Claude Lemieux	1.00	2.50
7 Trevor Linden	1.00	2.50
8 Eric Lindros	1.50	4.00
9 Darren McCarty	1.00	2.50
10 Scott Mellanby	1.00	2.50
11 Mark Messier	1.50	4.00
12 Cam Neely	1.50	4.00
13 Owen Nolan	1.00	2.50
14 Keith Primeau	1.00	2.50
15 Jeremy Roenick	2.00	5.00
16 Tomas Sandstrom	1.00	2.50
17 Brendan Shanahan	1.50	4.00
18 Kevin Stevens	1.00	2.50
19 Rick Tocchet	1.00	2.50
20 Keith Tkachuk	1.50	4.00

1995-96 Ultra Extra Attackers

When pulling the goalie and down late in the game, these are the guys you'd love to tap on the shoulder. The cards were randomly inserted in series two hobby packs only at a rate of 1:18.

COMPLETE SET (20)	40.00	80.00
1 Peter Bondra	.60	1.50
2 Eric Daze	.60	1.50
3 Radek Dvorak	.60	1.50
4 Sergei Fedorov	2.00	5.00
5 Peter Forsberg	3.00	8.00
6 Ron Francis	.60	1.50
7 Wayne Gretzky	8.00	20.00
8 Brett Hull	1.50	4.00
9 Jaromir Jagr	2.00	5.00
10 Ed Jovanovski	.60	1.50
11 Paul Kariya	1.25	3.00
12 Saku Koivu	1.25	3.00
13 Mario Lemieux	6.00	15.00
14 Mike Modano	2.00	5.00
15 Alexander Mogilny	.60	1.50
16 Adam Oates	.60	1.50
17 Joe Sakic	2.50	6.00
18 Niklas Sundstrom	.60	1.50
19 Mats Sundin	1.25	3.00
20 Steve Yzerman	6.00	15.00

1995-96 Ultra High Speed

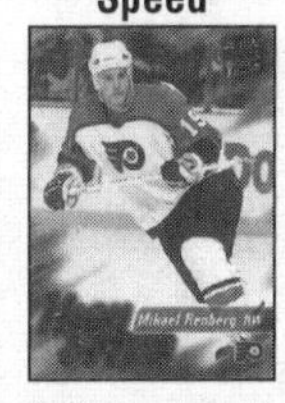

Young stars in a hurry to reach the upper echelon of the NHL pay scale, and some already there trying to prove they're worth it, are featured in this 20-card set. Collectors could find these cards randomly inserted at a rate of 1:5 series two packs.

COMPLETE SET (20)	10.00	20.00
1 Daniel Alfredsson	.75	2.00
2 Jason Arnott	.20	.50
3 Todd Bertuzzi	.75	2.00
4 Radek Bonk	.20	.50
5 Martin Brodeur	2.00	5.00
6 Alexandre Daigle	.20	.50
7 Shane Doan	.40	1.00
8 Peter Forsberg	1.50	4.00
9 Roman Hamrlik	.20	.50
10 Todd Harvey	.20	.50
11 Paul Kariya	.75	2.00
12 Travis Green	.20	.50
13 Chris Osgood	.40	1.00
14 Zigmund Palffy	.40	1.00
15 Marcus Ragnarsson	.20	.50
16 Mikael Renberg	.20	.50
17 Brian Savage	.20	.50
18 Robert Svehla	.20	.50
19 Jocelyn Thibault	.40	1.00
20 Brendan Witt	.20	.50

1995-96 Ultra Premier Pad Men

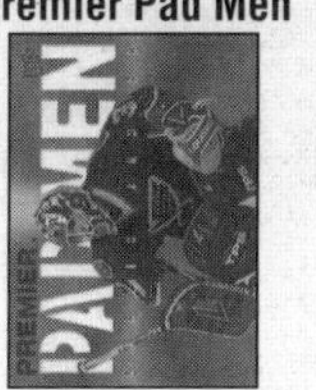

Cards from this 12-card standard-size set was inserted 1:36 series one packs. This set features leading NHL goaltenders on a special gold foil embossed design. There is also a Gold Medallion parallel version of each card that were inserted at 1:360. Multipliers can be found in the header to determine values for these.

COMPLETE SET (12)	20.00	40.00
*GOLD MED: 1.25X TO 2X BASIC INSERTS		
1 Ed Belfour	1.00	2.50
2 Martin Brodeur	8.00	20.00
3 Sean Burke	.50	1.25
4 Jim Carey	.50	1.25
5 Dominik Hasek	2.00	5.00
6 Curtis Joseph	1.00	2.50
7 Blaine Lacher	.50	1.25
8 Andy Moog	1.00	2.50
9 Felix Potvin	1.00	2.50
10 Patrick Roy	8.00	20.00
11 John Vanbiesbrouck	.50	1.25
12 Mike Vernon	.50	1.25

1995-96 Ultra Premier Pivots

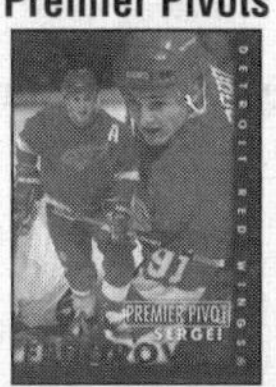

These 10 standard-size cards were inserted into first series packs at a rate of 1:4. Leading NHL centers are showcased on these cards. There also are Gold Medallion versions of each of these cards which were inserted at 1:40. Multipliers can be found in the header to determine values for these.

COMPLETE SET (10)	6.00	12.00
*GOLD MED: .75X TO 2X BASIC INSERTS		
1 Sergei Fedorov	.60	1.50
2 Ron Francis	.20	.50
3 Wayne Gretzky	2.50	6.00
4 Eric Lindros	.40	1.00
5 Mark Messier	.40	1.00
6 Adam Oates	.20	.50
7 Jeremy Roenick	.50	1.25
8 Joe Sakic	.75	2.00
9 Mats Sundin	.40	1.00
10 Alexei Zhamnov	.20	.50

1995-96 Ultra Red Light Specials

These 10 standard-size cards were inserted into series one packs at a rate of 1:3. These cards feature players who lit the lamp on a regular basis during the '94-95 season. There is also a Gold Medallion parallel version of each card inserted at 1:30. Multipliers can be found in the header to determine values for these.

COMPLETE SET (10)	1.50	3.00
*GOLD MED: .75X TO 2X BASIC INSERTS		
1 Peter Bondra	.10	.30
2 Theo Fleury	.10	.20
3 Brett Hull	.30	.75
4 Jaromir Jagr	.40	1.00
5 John LeClair	.25	.60
6 Eric Lindros	.25	.60
7 Cam Neely	.25	.60
8 Owen Nolan	.10	.30
9 Ray Sheppard	.10	.20
10 Alexei Zhamnov	.10	.30

1995-96 Ultra Rising Stars

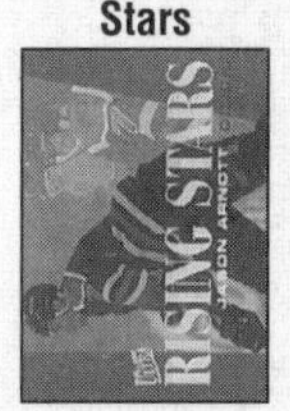

These 10 standard-size cards were randomly inserted 1:4 series one packs. There are also Gold Medallion parallel versions of these cards which were randomly inserted at 1:40. Multipliers can be found in the header below to determine values for these.

COMPLETE SET (10)	1.00	2.00
*GOLD MED: .75X TO 2X BASIC INSERTS		
1 Jason Arnott	.10	.20
2 Alexandre Daigle	.10	.20
3 Roman Hamrlik	.10	.30
4 Trevor Kidd	.10	.30
5 Scott Niedermayer	.10	.20
6 Keith Primeau	.10	.20
7 Mikael Renberg	.10	.30
8 Jocelyn Thibault	.25	.60
9 Alexei Yashin	.10	.20
10 Alexei Zhitnik	.10	.20

1995-96 Ultra Ultraview

This 10-card set features the NHL's best on clear acrylic. The cards were randomly inserted at a rate of 1:55 series two packs. A parallel version of these cards could be found in complete set form in randomly inserted Ultraview Hot Packs. These sets, which bore the Hot Pack logo, were found in 1:360 packs. Because they were found in complete set form, dealers tended to discount them slightly at time of sale. Multipliers can be found in the header to determine value for these.

COMPLETE SET (10)	20.00	40.00
1 Sergei Fedorov	1.25	3.00
2 Wayne Gretzky	6.00	15.00
3 Dominik Hasek	2.00	5.00
4 Jaromir Jagr	1.50	4.00
5 Brian Leetch	.75	2.00
6 Mario Lemieux	5.00	12.00
7 Eric Lindros	1.00	2.50
8 Jeremy Roenick	1.25	3.00
9 Joe Sakic	2.00	5.00
10 Alexei Zhamnov	.75	2.00

1995-96 Ultra Ultraview Hot Pack

These parallels to the Ultraview singles were found in "Hot Packs" (packs which contained only inserts). In this case, a 10-card pack would contain a complete set of Ultraviews, each with a special Hot Pack notation on the front. Although these packs were extremely rare, the distribution method actually hurt the value. Because they were found in set form, they tend to be worth slightly less than the regular Ultraview cards, which were found 1:55.

*HOT PACK: .25X TO .5X BASIC INSERTS

1996-97 Ultra

The 1996-97 Ultra set was issued in one series totaling 180 cards. Ten-card packs retailed for $2.49. Key rookies include Dainius Zubrus, Patrick Lalime, and Sergei Berezin. Card fronts feature a color action photo with player information on the back.

COMPLETE SET (180)	15.00	30.00
1 Guy Hebert	.05	.15
2 Paul Kariya	.10	.30
3 Jari Kurri	.05	.15
4 Roman Oksiuta	.02	.10
5 Ruslan Salei RC	.02	.10
6 Teemu Selanne	.10	.30
7 Darren Van Impe	.02	.10
8 Ray Bourque	.20	.50
9 Kyle McLaren	.02	.10
10 Adam Oates	.05	.15
11 Bill Ranford	.05	.15
12 Rick Tocchet	.05	.15
13 Donald Audette	.02	.10
14 Curtis Brown	.02	.10
15 Jason Dawe	.02	.10
16 Dominik Hasek	.25	.60
17 Pat LaFontaine	.10	.30
18 Jay McKee RC	.02	.10
19 Derek Plante	.02	.10
20 Wayne Primeau	.02	.10
21 Theo Fleury	.02	.10
22 Dave Gagner	.05	.15
23 Jonas Hoglund	.02	.10
24 Jarome Iginla	.12	.40
25 Trevor Kidd	.05	.15
26 Robert Reichel	.02	.10
27 German Titov	.02	.10
28 Tony Amonte	.05	.15
29 Ed Belfour	.10	.30
30 Chris Chelios	.10	.30
31 Eric Daze	.05	.15
32 Ethan Moreau RC	.10	.30
33 Gary Suter	.02	.10
34 Adam Deadmarsh	.02	.10
35 Peter Forsberg	.30	.75
36 Valeri Kamensky	.05	.15
37 Claude Lemieux	.02	.10
38 Sandis Ozolinsh	.02	.10
39 Patrick Roy	.60	1.50
40 Joe Sakic	.25	.60
41 Landon Wilson	.02	.10
42 Derian Hatcher	.02	.10
43 Jamie Langenbrunner	.02	.10
44 Mike Modano	.20	.50
45 Andy Moog	.05	.15
46 Joe Nieuwendyk	.05	.15
47 Pat Verbeek	.02	.10
48 Sergei Zubov	.02	.10
49 Anders Eriksson	.02	.10
50 Sergei Fedorov	.20	.50
51 Vladimir Konstantinov	.05	.15
52 Slava Kozlov	.05	.15
53 Nicklas Lidstrom	.10	.30
54 Chris Osgood	.05	.15
55 Brendan Shanahan	.10	.30
56 Steve Yzerman	.60	1.50
57 Jason Arnott	.02	.10
58 Mike Grier RC	.30	.75
59 Curtis Joseph	.10	.30
60 Rem Murray RC	.02	.10
61 Jeff Norton	.02	.10
62 Miroslav Satan	.02	.10
63 Doug Weight	.05	.15
64 Radek Dvorak	.02	.10
65 Ed Jovanovski	.05	.15
66 Scott Mellanby	.05	.15
67 Rob Niedermayer	.05	.15
68 Ray Sheppard	.05	.15
69 Robert Svehla	.02	.10
70 John Vanbiesbrouck	.05	.15
71 Steve Washburn RC	.02	.10
72 Jeff Brown	.02	.10
73 Sean Burke	.05	.15
74 Hnat Domenichelli	.02	.10
75 Keith Primeau	.02	.10
76 Geoff Sanderson	.05	.15
77 Rob Blake	.05	.15
78 Stephane Fiset	.05	.15
79 Dimitri Khristich	.02	.10
80 Mattias Norstrom	.02	.10
81 Ed Olczyk	.02	.10
82 Jamie Storr	.05	.15
83 Jan Vopat	.02	.10
84 Vitali Yachmenev	.02	.10
85 Shayne Corson	.02	.10
86 Vincent Damphousse	.02	.10
87 Saku Koivu	.10	.30
88 Mark Recchi	.05	.15
89 Stephane Richer	.05	.15
90 Jocelyn Thibault	.10	.30
91 David Wilkie	.02	.10
92 Dave Andreychuk	.05	.15
93 Martin Brodeur	.30	.75
94 Scott Niedermayer	.02	.10
95 Scott Stevens	.05	.15
96 Petr Sykora	.02	.10
97 Steve Thomas	.02	.10
98 Bryan Berard	.10	.30
99 Todd Bertuzzi	.10	.30
100 Eric Fichaud	.05	.15
101 Travis Green	.05	.15
102 Kenny Jonsson	.02	.10
103 Zigmund Palffy	.05	.15
104 Christian Dube	.02	.10
105 Daniel Goneau RC	.02	.10
106 Wayne Gretzky	.75	2.00
107 Alexei Kovalev	.02	.10
108 Brian Leetch	.10	.30
109 Mark Messier	.10	.30
110 Mike Richter	.10	.30
111 Luc Robitaille	.05	.15
112 Niklas Sundstrom	.02	.10
113 Daniel Alfredsson	.05	.15
114 Radek Bonk	.02	.10
115 Andreas Dackell RC	.02	.10
116 Alexandre Daigle	.02	.10
117 Steve Duchesne	.02	.10
118 Wade Redden	.02	.10
119 Damian Rhodes	.05	.15
120 Alexei Yashin	.02	.10
121 Rod Brind'Amour	.05	.15
122 Paul Coffey	.10	.30
123 Eric Desjardins	.05	.15
124 Ron Hextall	.05	.15
125 John LeClair	.10	.30
126 Eric Lindros	.10	.30
127 Janne Niinimaa	.10	.30
128 Mikael Renberg	.05	.15
129 Dainius Zubrus RC	.30	.75
130 Mike Gartner	.05	.15
131 Craig Janney	.05	.15
132 Nikolai Khabibulin	.05	.15
133 Dave Manson	.02	.10
134 Teppo Numminen	.02	.10
135 Jeremy Roenick	.15	.40
136 Keith Tkachuk	.10	.30
137 Oleg Tverdovsky	.05	.15
138 Tom Barrasso	.05	.15
139 Ron Francis	.05	.15
140 Kevin Hatcher	.02	.10
141 Jaromir Jagr	.20	.50
142 Patrick Lalime RC	.75	2.00
143 Mario Lemieux	.60	1.50
144 Jim Campbell	.02	.10
145 Grant Fuhr	.05	.15
146 Brett Hull	.15	.40
147 Al MacInnis	.05	.15
148 Pierre Turgeon	.05	.15
149 Harry York RC	.10	.30
150 Kelly Hrudey	.05	.15
151 Al Iafrate	.02	.10
152 Bernie Nicholls	.02	.10
153 Owen Nolan	.05	.15
154 Darren Turcotte	.02	.10
155 Brian Bradley	.02	.10
156 Dino Ciccarelli	.05	.15
157 Roman Hamrlik	.05	.15
158 Daymond Langkow	.05	.15
159 Daren Puppa	.05	.15
160 Alexander Selivanov	.02	.10
161 Sergei Berezin RC	.40	1.00
162 Wendel Clark	.05	.15
163 Doug Gilmour	.05	.15
164 Larry Murphy	.05	.15
165 Felix Potvin	.10	.30
166 Mats Sundin	.10	.30
167 Pavel Bure	.10	.30
168 Trevor Linden	.05	.15
169 Kirk McLean	.05	.15
170 Alexander Mogilny	.05	.15
171 Esa Tikkanen	.02	.10
172 Peter Bondra	.05	.15
173 Andrew Brunette RC	.25	.60
174 Jim Carey	.10	.30
175 Sergei Gonchar	.02	.10
176 Phil Housley	.05	.15
177 Joe Juneau	.02	.10
178 Michal Pivonka	.02	.10
179 Checklist (1-143)	.02	.10
180 Checklist (143-180/inserts)	.02	.10
S125 John LeClair promo	.20	.50

1996-97 Ultra Gold Medallion

A one-per-pack parallel, these cards differ from the base cards by the use of gold foil to highlight the player's name on the card front. The words "Gold Medallion" are also included. Values for the cards can be determined by using the multipliers below on the corresponding base card.

*STARS: 3X TO 6X BASIC CARDS
*ROOKIES: 1.25X TO 3X BASIC CARDS

1996-97 Ultra Clear the Ice

Ten players recognized as some of the elite at their position are the subject of this set, which was randomly inserted in packs at the stingy rate of 1:350.

COMPLETE SET (10)	50.00	100.00
1 Jim Carey	4.00	10.00
2 Peter Forsberg	10.00	25.00
3 Dominik Hasek	8.00	20.00
4 Jaromir Jagr	6.00	15.00
5 John LeClair	4.00	10.00
6 Eric Lindros	4.00	10.00
7 Mark Messier	4.00	10.00
8 Patrick Roy	20.00	50.00
9 Brendan Shanahan	4.00	10.00
10 Keith Tkachuk	4.00	10.00

1996-97 Ultra Mr. Momentum

Randomly inserted in retail packs only at a rate of 1:36, these ten cards offer simple fronts and three-photo, text-laden backs.

COMPLETE SET (10)	20.00	40.00
1 Peter Bondra	1.00	2.50
2 Pavel Bure	2.00	5.00
3 Ron Francis	1.00	2.50
4 Brett Hull	2.50	6.00
5 Jaromir Jagr	3.00	8.00
6 Pat LaFontaine	2.00	5.00
7 Eric Lindros	2.00	5.00
8 Mark Messier	2.00	5.00
9 Mats Sundin	2.00	5.00
10 Steve Yzerman	6.00	15.00

1996-97 Ultra Power

The 16 cards in this set were randomly inserted in packs at a rate of 1:16. The cards feature fiery lettering and a glitter-enhanced design. Card fronts also feature a color action photo, with biographical info on the back. The checklist was mirrored in the Red Line and Blue Line sets, although photo choice and card numbering varied slightly.

COMPLETE SET (16)	30.00	60.00
1 Ray Bourque	2.00	5.00
2 Chris Chelios	1.25	3.00
3 Paul Coffey	1.25	3.00
4 Sergei Fedorov	2.00	5.00
5 Wayne Gretzky	8.00	20.00
6 Roman Hamrlik	.60	1.50
7 Ed Jovanovski	.60	1.50
8 Paul Kariya	1.25	3.00
9 Vladimir Konstantinov	.60	1.50
10 Brian Leetch	1.25	3.00
11 Mario Lemieux	6.00	15.00
12 Nicklas Lidstrom	1.25	3.00
13 Alexander Mogilny	.60	1.50
14 Adam Oates	.60	1.50
15 Joe Sakic	2.50	6.00
16 Teemu Selanne	1.25	3.00

1996-97 Ultra Power Blue Line

Randomly inserted in hobby packs only at a rate of 1:90, this tough insert features eight top defensive players. The cards are sequentially numbered on the back out of 1,082.

COMPLETE SET (8)	12.00	25.00
1 Ray Bourque	4.00	10.00
2 Chris Chelios	2.50	6.00
3 Paul Coffey	2.50	6.00
4 Roman Hamrlik	1.25	3.00
5 Ed Jovanovski	1.25	3.00
6 Vladimir Konstantinov	1.25	3.00
7 Brian Leetch	2.50	6.00
8 Nicklas Lidstrom	2.50	6.00

1996-97 Ultra Power Red Line

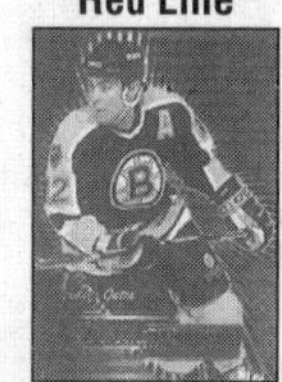

Eight of the absolute best offensive weapons grace this tough insert set, randomly seeded only in hobby packs at a rate of 1:90. The cards are sequentially numbered on the back out of 1,082.

COMPLETE SET (8)	40.00	80.00
1 Sergei Fedorov	4.00	10.00
2 Wayne Gretzky	15.00	40.00
3 Paul Kariya	2.50	6.00
4 Mario Lemieux	12.50	30.00
5 Alexander Mogilny	1.25	3.00
6 Adam Oates	1.25	3.00
7 Joe Sakic	5.00	12.00
8 Teemu Selanne	2.50	6.00

1996-97 Ultra Rookies

Randomly inserted in packs at a rate of 1:9, these cards offer a single player photo with the player's name with "Rookie" written on the left-hand side. Flip sides give a smaller photo with several pieces of information about each athlete.

COMPLETE SET (20)	8.00	20.00
1 Bryan Berard	.40	1.00
2 Sergei Berezin	.40	1.00
3 Curtis Brown	.40	1.00
4 Jim Campbell	.40	1.00
5 Christian Dube	.40	1.00
6 Anders Eriksson	.40	1.00
7 Eric Fichaud	.75	2.00
8 Daniel Goneau	.40	1.00
9 Mike Grier	.75	2.00
10 Jarome Iginla	3.00	8.00
11 Jamie Langenbrunner	.40	1.00
12 Jay McKee	.40	1.00
13 Ethan Moreau	.40	1.00
14 Rem Murray	.40	1.00
15 Janne Niinimaa	.40	1.00
16 Wayne Primeau	.40	1.00
17 Wade Redden	.75	2.00
18 Jamie Storr	.75	2.00
19 David Wilkie	.40	1.00
20 Landon Wilson	.40	1.00

2005-06 Ultra

COMP.SET w/o SP's (250)	25.00	60.00
251-271 STATED ODDS 1:24		
1 J-S Giguere	.10	.30
2 Teemu Selanne	.15	.40
3 Petr Sykora	.10	.20
4 Rob Niedermayer	.10	.20
5 Scott Niedermayer	.10	.20
6 Sandis Ozolinsh	.10	.20
7 Joffrey Lupul	.10	.20
8 Kari Lehtonen	.15	.40
9 Ilya Kovalchuk	.20	.50
10 Peter Bondra	.10	.30
11 Marian Hossa	.15	.40
12 Patrik Stefan	.10	.20
13 Bobby Holik	.10	.20
14 Marc Savard	.10	.20
15 Andrew Raycroft	.10	.30
16 Patrice Bergeron	.10	.30
17 Joe Thornton	.25	.60
18 Glen Murray	.10	.20
19 Brian Leetch	.15	.40
20 Nick Boynton	.10	.20
21 Sergei Samsonov	.10	.30
22 Shawn McEachern	.10	.20
23 Martin Biron	.10	.30
24 Chris Drury	.10	.30
25 Daniel Briere	.10	.20
26 Derek Roy	.10	.20
27 Maxim Afinogenov	.10	.20
28 J.P. Dumont	.10	.20
29 Mika Noronen	.10	.30
30 Miikka Kipruosoff	.20	.50
31 Jarome Iginla	.20	.50
32 Tony Amonte	.10	.30
33 Matthew Lombardi	.10	.20
34 Robyn Regehr	.10	.20
35 Jordan Leopold	.10	.20
36 Chuck Kobasew	.10	.20
37 Phillippe Sauve	.10	.30
38 Darren McCarty	.10	.20
39 Martin Gerber	.10	.30
40 Eric Staal	.10	.30
41 Erik Cole	.10	.20
42 Justin Williams	.10	.30
43 Glen Wesley	.10	.20
44 Oleg Tverdovsky	.10	.20
45 Cory Stillman	.10	.20
46 Rod Brind'Amour	.10	.30
47 Nikolai Khabibulin	.15	.40
48 Tuomo Ruutu	.10	.20
49 Eric Daze	.10	.30
50 Tyler Arnason	.10	.30
51 Adrian Aucoin	.10	.20
52 Kyle Calder	.10	.20
53 Mark Bell	.10	.20
54 David Aebischer	.10	.30
55 Joe Sakic	.30	.75
56 Milan Hejduk	.15	.40
57 Alex Tanguay	.10	.30
58 Rob Blake	.10	.30
59 John-Michael Liles	.10	.20
60 Pierre Turgeon	.10	.20
61 Marc Denis	.10	.30
62 Rick Nash	.20	.50
63 Nikolai Zherdev	.10	.30
64 Rostislav Klesla	.10	.20
65 Bryan Berard	.10	.20
66 Sergei Fedorov	.20	.50
67 Marty Turco	.10	.30
68 Mike Modano	.15	.40
69 Brenden Morrow	.10	.30
70 Bill Guerin	.10	.30
71 Sergei Zubov	.10	.20
72 Jere Lehtinen	.10	.30
73 Manny Legace	.20	.50
74 Steve Yzerman	.60	1.50
75 Brendan Shanahan	.15	.40
76 Pavel Datsyuk	.15	.40
77 Nicklas Lidstrom	.15	.40
78 Chris Chelios	.15	.40
79 Henrik Zetterberg	.15	.40
80 Ty Conklin	.10	.30
81 Michael Peca	.10	.20
82 Ryan Smyth	.10	.20
83 Raffi Torres	.10	.20
84 Chris Pronger	.10	.30
85 Ales Hemsky	.10	.20
86 Roberto Luongo	.20	.50
87 Joe Nieuwendyk	.10	.30
88 Stephen Weiss	.10	.20
89 Olli Jokinen	.10	.30
90 Jay Bouwmeester	.10	.20
91 Nathan Horton	.10	.20
92 Mathieu Garon	.10	.30
93 Jeremy Roenick	.20	.50
94 Luc Robitaille	.10	.30
95 Pavol Demitra	.10	.30
96 Dustin Brown	.10	.20
97 Alexander Frolov	.10	.30
98 Dwayne Roloson	.10	.30
99 Marian Gaborik	.30	.75
100 Alexandre Daigle	.10	.20
101 Pierre-Marc Bouchard	.10	.20
102 Filip Kuba	.10	.20
103 Manny Fernandez	.10	.30
104 Saku Koivu	.15	.40
105 Jose Theodore	.20	.50
106 Mike Ribeiro	.10	.20
107 Michael Ryder	.10	.30
108 Sheldon Souray	.10	.20
109 Richard Zednik	.10	.20
110 Tomas Vokoun	.10	.30
111 Paul Kariya	.15	.40
112 Steve Sullivan	.10	.20
113 David Legwand	.10	.30
114 Kimmo Timonen	.10	.20
115 Scott Walker	.10	.20
116 Martin Brodeur	.75	2.00
117 Scott Gomez	.15	.40
118 Patrik Elias	.10	.30
119 Alexander Mogilny	.10	.30
120 Brian Rafalski	.10	.20
121 John Madden	.10	.20
122 Rick DiPietro	.10	.30
123 Alexei Yashin	.10	.20
124 Miroslav Satan	.10	.30
125 Trent Hunter	.10	.20
126 Brent Sopel	.10	.20
127 Mark Parrish	.10	.20
128 Kevin Weekes	.10	.30
129 Jaromir Jagr	.25	.60

130 Marcel Hossa .10 .20
131 Steve Rucchin .10 .20
132 Tom Poti .10 .20
133 Dominik Hasek .30 .75
134 Jason Spezza .15 .40
135 Dany Heatley .20 .50
136 Martin Havlat .10 .30
137 Wade Redden .10 .20
138 Zdeno Chara .15 .40
139 Daniel Alfredsson .10 .30
140 Robert Esche .10 .30
141 Peter Forsberg .30 .75
142 Simon Gagne .15 .40
143 Keith Primeau .10 .25
144 Joni Pitkanen .10 .20
145 Kim Johnsson .10 .20
146 Sami Kapanen .10 .20
147 Curtis Joseph .15 .40
148 Shane Doan .10 .20
149 Jamie Lundmark .10 .20
150 Ladislav Nagy .10 .20
151 Mike Ricci .10 .20
152 Petr Nedved .10 .20
153 Jocelyn Thibault .10 .30
154 Mario Lemieux 1.00 2.50
155 Mark Recchi .10 .30
156 Zigmund Palffy .10 .30
157 John LeClair .15 .40
158 Ryan Malone .10 .20
159 Marc-Andre Fleury .10 .30
160 Evgeni Nabokov .10 .30
161 Patrick Marleau .10 .30
162 Jonathan Cheechoo .20 .50
163 Marco Sturm .10 .20
164 Brad Stuart .10 .20
165 Patrick Lalime .10 .30
166 Doug Weight .10 .30
167 Keith Tkachuk .15 .40
168 Mark Rycroft .10 .20
169 Barret Jackman .10 .25
170 Dallas Drake .10 .20
171 Sean Burke .10 .30
172 Martin St. Louis .10 .30
173 Vincent Lecavalier .15 .40
174 Brad Richards .10 .30
175 Ruslan Fedotenko .10 .20
176 Fredrik Modin .10 .20
177 Dave Andreychuk .10 .30
178 Pavel Kubina .10 .20
179 Ed Belfour .15 .40
180 Mats Sundin .15 .40
181 Eric Lindros .15 .40
182 Jeff O'Neill .10 .20
183 Bryan McCabe .10 .20
184 Tie Domi .10 .30
185 Matt Stajan .10 .20
186 Nik Antropov .10 .20
187 Jason Allison .10 .20
188 Dan Cloutier .10 .30
189 Markus Naslund .15 .40
190 Brendan Morrison .10 .25
191 Todd Bertuzzi .15 .40
192 Ed Jovanovski .10 .30
193 Mattias Ohlund .10 .20
194 Trevor Linden .10 .30
195 Anson Carter .10 .30
196 Ryan Kesler .10 .20
197 Olaf Kolzig .10 .30
198 Jeff Friesen .10 .20
199 Brian Willsie .10 .20
200 Brendan Witt .97 .20
201 Braydon Coburn RC 1.50 4.00
202 Jim Slater RC 1.50 4.00
203 Adam Berkhoel RC 1.50 4.00
204 Andrew Alberts RC 1.50 4.00
205 Kevin Dallman RC 1.50 4.00
206 Milan Jurcina RC 1.50 4.00
207 Niklas Nordgren RC 1.50 4.00
208 Kevin Nastiuk RC 1.50 4.00
209 Brent Seabrook RC 2.00 5.00
210 Rene Bourque RC 1.50 4.00
211 Duncan Keith RC 1.50 4.00
212 Cam Barker RC 2.00 5.00
213 Peter Budaj RC 2.00 5.00
214 Jaroslav Balastik RC 1.50 4.00
215 Jussi Jokinen RC 2.00 5.00
216 Brett Lebda RC 1.50 4.00
217 Johan Franzen RC 2.00 5.00
218 Brad Winchester RC 1.50 4.00
219 Kyle Brodziak RC 1.50 4.00
220 George Parros RC 1.50 4.00
221 Derek Boogaard RC 1.50 4.00
222 Matthew Foy RC 1.50 4.00
223 Yann Danis RC 2.00 5.00
224 Mark Streit RC 1.50 4.00
225 Raitis Ivanans RC 1.50 4.00
226 Ryan Suter RC 2.00 5.00
227 Petteri Nokelainen RC 1.50 4.00
228 Chris Campoli RC 1.50 4.00
229 Ryan Hollweg RC 1.50 4.00
230 Petr Prucha RC 2.00 5.00
231 Al Montoya RC 2.00 5.00
232 Chris Holt RC 1.50 4.00
233 Brandon Bochenski RC 1.50 4.00
234 Andrej Meszaros RC 1.50 4.00
235 Brian McGrattan RC 1.50 4.00
236 Patrick Eaves RC 2.00 6.00
237 Wade Skolney RC 1.50 4.00
238 Keith Ballard RC 1.50 4.00
239 David Leneveu RC 1.50 4.00
240 Maxime Talbot RC 1.50 4.00
241 Ryane Clowe RC 1.50 4.00
242 Josh Gorges RC 1.50 4.00
243 Jay McClement RC 1.50 4.00
244 Jeff Hoggan RC 1.50 4.00
245 Lee Stempniak RC 2.00 5.00
246 Andy Roach RC 1.50 4.00
247 Timo Helbling RC 1.50 4.00
248 Paul Ranger RC 1.50 4.00
249 Andrew Wozniewski RC 1.50 4.00
250 Anthony Stewart RC 2.00 5.00
251 Sidney Crosby RC 90.00 150.00
252 Alexander Ovechkin RC 25.00 60.00
253 Corey Perry RC 4.00 10.00
254 Jeff Carter RC 5.00 12.00
255 Gilbert Brule RC 4.00 10.00
256 Wojtek Wolski RC 4.00 10.00
257 Jeff Woywitka RC 1.50 4.00
258 Hannu Toivonen RC 3.00 8.00
259 Alexander Perezhogin RC 2.00 5.00
260 Zach Parise RC 5.00 12.00
261 Dion Phaneuf RC 10.00 25.00
262 Mike Richards RC 3.00 8.00
263 Cam Ward RC 5.00 12.00
264 Robert Nilsson RC 2.00 5.00
265 Eric Nystrom RC 2.00 5.00
266 Alexander Steen RC 3.00 8.00
267 Ryan Getzlaf RC 6.00 15.00
268 Rostislav Olesz RC 2.00 5.00
269 Henrik Lundqvist RC 10.00 25.00
270 Jim Howard RC 2.00 5.00
271 Thomas Vanek RC 6.00 15.00

2005-06 Ultra Gold

*STARS: 2X TO 5X BASE HI
*ROOKIES: X TO X
*ROOKIES 251-271: .75X TO 2X
ONE PER NON-INSERT PACK
251 Sidney Crosby 150.00 250.00
252 Alexander Ovechkin 75.00 150.00
261 Dion Phaneuf 30.00 75.00
263 Cam Ward 15.00 40.00

2005-06 Ultra Difference Makers

COMPLETE SET (12) 20.00 40.00
STATED ODDS 1:32
DM1 Rick Nash .50 1.25
DM2 Pavel Datsyuk .40 1.00
DM3 Steve Yzerman 1.50 4.00
DM4 Todd Bertuzzi .40 1.00
DM5 Jeff Carter .50 1.25
DM6 Sidney Crosby 6.00 15.00
DM7 Tuomo Ruutu .40 1.00
DM8 Patrice Bergeron .40 1.00
DM9 Alexander Ovechkin 3.00 8.00
DM10 Martin St. Louis .40 1.00
DM11 Jarome Iginla .50 1.25
DM12 Andrew Raycroft .40 1.00

2005-06 Ultra Difference Makers Jerseys

STATED ODDS 1:164
DMJ-AO Alexander Ovechkin 12.00 30.00
DMJ-AR Andrew Raycroft 4.00 10.00
DMJ-JC Jeff Carter 5.00 12.00
DMJ-JI Jarome Iginla 5.00 12.00
DMJ-PB Patrice Bergeron 4.00 10.00
DMJ-PD Pavel Datsyuk 4.00 10.00
DMJ-RN Rick Nash 8.00 20.00
DMJ-SC Sidney Crosby 30.00 80.00
DMJ-SL Martin St. Louis 4.00 10.00
DMJ-SY Steve Yzerman 10.00 25.00
DMJ-TB Todd Bertuzzi 4.00 10.00
DMJ-TR Tuomo Ruutu 4.00 10.00

2005-06 Ultra Difference Makers Jersey Autographs

PRINT RUN 10 SER.#'d SETS
NOT PRICED DUE TO SCARCITY
DAJ-AO Alexander Ovechkin
DAJ-AR Andrew Raycroft
DAJ-JC Jeff Carter
DAJ-JI Jarome Iginla
DAJ-PB Patrice Bergeron
DAJ-RN Rick Nash
DAJ-SC Sidney Crosby
DAJ-SL Martin St. Louis
DAJ-TR Tuomo Ruutu

2005-06 Ultra Difference Makers Patches

*PATCHES: 1.5X TO 4X BASE JSY
PRINT RUN 25 SER.#'d SETS

2005-06 Ultra Difference Makers Patch Autographs

PRINT RUN 5 SER.#'d SETS
NOT PRICED DUE TO SCARCITY
DAP-AO Alexander Ovechkin
DAP-AR Andrew Raycroft
DAP-JC Jeff Carter
DAP-JI Jarome Iginla
DAP-PB Patrice Bergeron
DAP-RN Rick Nash
DAP-SC Sidney Crosby
DAP-SL Martin St. Louis
DAP-TR Tuomo Ruutu

2005-06 Ultra Fresh Ink

STATED ODDS 1:360
FI-AM Al Montoya 10.00 25.00
FI-AO Alexander Ovechkin 75.00 150.00
FI-AP Alexander Perezhogin 8.00 20.00
FI-AR Andrew Raycroft SP
FI-AS Alexander Steen 12.00 30.00
FI-AT Alex Tanguay SP 12.50 30.00
FI-AW Andrew Wozniewski 4.00 10.00
FI-AY Alexei Yashin 8.00 20.00
FI-BG Boyd Gordon 4.00 10.00
FI-BL Brett Lebda 4.00 10.00
FI-BM Brenden Morrow 4.00 10.00
FI-BO Derek Boogaard 8.00 20.00
FI-CA Mike Cammalleri 4.00 10.00
FI-CB Cam Barker 8.00 20.00
FI-CD Chris Drury 4.00 10.00
FI-CE Christian Ehrhoff 4.00 10.00
FI-CK Chris Kunitz 4.00 10.00
FI-CP Corey Perry SP 12.00 30.00
FI-CW Cam Ward 12.00 30.00
FI-DB Dustin Brown 4.00 10.00
FI-DL David Leneveu 8.00 20.00
FI-DP Dion Phaneuf 30.00 60.00
FI-DR Dwayne Roloson 4.00 10.00
FI-DW Doug Weight 4.00 10.00
FI-EJ Ed Jovanovski 8.00 20.00
FI-EN Eric Nystrom 4.00 10.00
FI-ES Eric Staal SP 25.00 60.00
FI-GB Gilbert Brule 12.00 30.00
FI-GM Glen Murray 6.00 15.00
FI-GP George Parros 4.00 10.00
FI-HO Jeff Hoggan 4.00 10.00
FI-HT Hannu Toivonen 10.00 25.00
FI-HV Martin Havlat SP
FI-HZ Henrik Zetterberg 10.00 25.00
FI-IK Ilya Kovalchuk SP 25.00 60.00
FI-IL Ian Laperriere 4.00 10.00
FI-JA Jaroslav Balastik 4.00 10.00
FI-JB Jay Bouwmeester SP 8.00 20.00
FI-JC Jeff Carter 15.00 40.00
FI-JG Josh Gorges 4.00 10.00
FI-JH Jochen Hecht 4.00 10.00
FI-JI Jarome Iginla 30.00 75.00
FI-JI Jim Howard 10.00 25.00
FI-JL Joffrey Lupul 4.00 10.00
FI-JM Jay McClement 4.00 10.00
FI-JN Jocelyn Thibault 4.00 10.00
FI-JO Jeff O'Neill
FI-JR Jeremy Roenick SP 30.00 80.00
FI-JS Jason Spezza SP 20.00 50.00
FI-JT Joe Thornton SP 25.00 60.00
FI-JW Jeff Woywitka 4.00 10.00
FI-KD Kevin Dallman 4.00 10.00
FI-KP Keith Primeau 4.00 10.00
FI-KW Kevin Weekes 6.00 15.00
FI-LN Ladislav Nagy SP
FI-MB Martin Brodeur SP 75.00 125.00
FI-MC Bryan McCabe 6.00 15.00
FI-MO Brendan Morrison 4.00 10.00
FI-MP Michael Peca 4.00 10.00
FI-MR Mike Richards 12.00 30.00
FI-MS Matt Stajan 10.00 25.00
FI-MT Marty Turco SP 12.00 30.00
FI-NI Rob Niedermayer 6.00 15.00
FI-NN Niklas Nordgren 4.00 10.00
FI-NS Robert Nilsson 4.00 10.00
FI-NZ Nikolai Zherdev 8.00 20.00
FI-ON Owen Nolan 6.00 15.00
FI-PB Patrice Bergeron SP
FI-PE Mark Popovic SP 4.00 10.00
FI-RE Robert Esche 4.00 10.00
FI-RF Ruslan Fedotenko 4.00 10.00
FI-RG Ryan Getzlaf SP 25.00 60.00
FI-RH Ryan Hollweg 4.00 10.00
FI-RI Raitis Ivanans 4.00 10.00
FI-RK Ryan Kesler 4.00 10.00
FI-RL Roberto Luongo 10.00 25.00
FI-RN Rick Nash SP
FI-RO Rostislav Olesz 8.00 20.00
FI-RS Ryan Smyth 6.00 15.00
FI-RZ Richard Zednik 4.00 10.00
FI-SA Miroslav Satan 4.00 10.00
FI-SB Sean Burke 4.00 10.00
FI-SC Sidney Crosby SP 150.00 250.00
FI-SD Shane Doan 4.00 10.00
FI-SG Simon Gagne 15.00 40.00
FI-SK Saku Koivu SP 25.00 60.00
FI-SN Scott Niedermayer 6.00 15.00
FI-SS Sheldon Souray 4.00 10.00
FI-ST Anthony Stewart 6.00 15.00
FI-SU Ryan Suter 8.00 20.00
FI-TH Jose Theodore Sp 20.00 50.00
FI-TI Timo Helbling 4.00 10.00
FI-TL Trevor Linden 12.00 30.00
FI-TR Tuomo Ruutu 6.00 15.00
FI-TS Timofei Shishkanov 4.00 10.00
FI-TV Thomas Vanek 15.00 40.00
FI-VL Vincent Lecavalier 20.00 50.00
FI-WW Wojtek Wolski 12.00 30.00
FI-YD Yann Danis
FI-ZC Zdeno Chara 8.00 20.00
FI-ZP Zach Parise 20.00 50.00

2005-06 Ultra Ice

COMMON CARD (1-200) 2.00 5.00
*STARS: 5X TO 12X
*ROOKIES 201-250: 1X TO 2.5X
*ROOKIES 251-271: 1.25X TO 3X
PRINT RUN 25 SER.#'d SETS
251 Sidney Crosby 300.00 550.00
252 Alexander Ovechkin 150.00 300.00

2005-06 Ultra Rookie Uniformity Jerseys

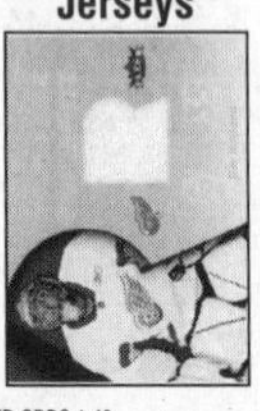

STATED ODDS 1:48
RU-AA Andrew Alberts 3.00 8.00
RU-AM Andrej Meszaros 3.00 8.00
RU-AO Alexander Ovechkin 12.00 30.00
RU-AP Alexander Perezhogin 4.00 10.00
RU-AS Alexander Steen 4.00 10.00
RU-AW Andrew Wozniewski 3.00 8.00
RU-BB Brandon Bochenski 3.00 8.00
RU-BC Braydon Coburn 4.00 10.00
RU-BL Brett Lebda 3.00 8.00
RU-BS Brent Seabrook 3.00 8.00
RU-BW Brad Winchester 3.00 8.00
RU-CB Cam Barker 3.00 8.00
RU-CP Corey Perry 5.00 12.00
RU-CW Cam Ward 6.00 15.00
RU-DK Duncan Keith 3.00 8.00
RU-DL David Leneveu 3.00 8.00
RU-DP Dion Phaneuf 8.00 20.00
RU-EN Eric Nystrom 3.00 8.00
RU-GB Gilbert Brule 6.00 15.00
RU-GP George Parros 3.00 8.00
RU-HL Henrik Lundqvist 8.00 20.00
RU-HO Jeff Hoggan 3.00 8.00
RU-HT Hannu Toivonen 4.00 10.00
RU-JB Jaroslav Balastik 3.00 8.00
RU-JC Jeff Carter 5.00 12.00
RU-JF Johan Franzen 3.00 8.00
RU-JG Josh Gorges 3.00 8.00
RU-JH Jim Howard 4.00 10.00
RU-JJ Jussi Jokinen 4.00 10.00
RU-JM Jay McClement 3.00 8.00
RU-JS Jim Slater 3.00 8.00
RU-JW Jeff Woywitka 3.00 8.00
RU-KB Keith Ballard 3.00 8.00
RU-KD Kevin Dallman 3.00 8.00
RU-KN Kevin Nastiuk 3.00 8.00
RU-MF Matthew Foy 3.00 8.00
RU-MJ Milan Jurcina 3.00 8.00
RU-MO Al Montoya 4.00 10.00
RU-MR Mike Richards 4.00 10.00
RU-MT Maxime Talbot 3.00 8.00
RU-NN Niklas Nordgren 3.00 8.00
RU-PB Peter Budaj 3.00 8.00
RU-PE Patrick Eaves 3.00 8.00
RU-PN Petteri Nokelainen 3.00 8.00
RU-PP Petr Prucha 4.00 10.00
RU-RB Rene Bourque 3.00 8.00
RU-RC Ryane Clowe 3.00 8.00
RU-RG Ryan Getzlaf 5.00 12.00
RU-RH Ryan Hollweg 3.00 8.00
RU-RI Raitis Ivanans 3.00 8.00
RU-RN Robert Nilsson 3.00 8.00
RU-RO Rostislav Olesz 4.00 10.00
RU-RS Ryan Suter 4.00 10.00
RU-SC Sidney Crosby 30.00 80.00
RU-ST Anthony Stewart 3.00 8.00
RU-TH Timo Helbling 3.00 8.00
RU-TV Thomas Vanek 6.00 15.00
RU-WW Wojtek Wolski 5.00 12.00
RU-YD Yann Danis 3.00 8.00
RU-ZP Zach Parise 4.00 10.00

2005-06 Ultra Rookie Uniformity Jersey Autographs

*AUTOS: 2X TO 5X BASE JSY
PRINT RUN 25 SER.#'d SETS
ARU-AO Alexander Ovechkin 250.00 400.00
ARU-DP Dion Phaneuf 75.00 150.00
ARU-HL Henrik Lundqvist 75.00 150.00
ARU-SC Sidney Crosby 400.00 700.00
ARU-TV Thomas Vanek 50.00 125.00

2005-06 Ultra Rookie Uniformity Patches

*PATCHES: 2X TO 4X BASE JSY
PATCH PRINT RUN 35 SER.#'d SETS

2005-06 Ultra Scoring Kings

COMPLETE SET (40) 25.00 50.00
STATED ODDS 1:12
SK1 Mario Lemieux 2.00 5.00
SK2 Martin St. Louis .25 .60
SK3 Joe Thornton .50 1.25
SK4 Mats Sundin .30 .75
SK5 Jarome Iginla .40 1.00
SK6 Mike Modano .50 1.25
SK7 Steve Yzerman 1.25 3.00
SK8 Joe Sakic .60 1.50
SK9 Alex Tanguay .25 .60
SK10 Dany Heatley .40 1.00
SK11 Sidney Crosby 4.00 10.00
SK12 Jeremy Roenick .40 1.00
SK13 Jason Spezza .30 .75
SK14 Patrik Elias .25 .60
SK15 Jaromir Jagr .50 1.25
SK16 Brad Richards .25 .60
SK17 Markus Naslund .30 .75
SK18 Alexander Ovechkin 2.00 5.00
SK19 Doug Weight .25 .60
SK20 Ilya Kovalchuk .40 1.00
SK21 Peter Forsberg .50 1.25
SK22 Sergei Fedorov .40 1.00
SK23 Marian Hossa .30 .75
SK24 Milan Hejduk .30 .75
SK25 Bill Guerin .25 .60
SK26 Shane Doan .25 .60
SK27 Mike Ribeiro .25 .60
SK28 Martin Havlat .25 .60
SK29 Corey Perry .40 1.00
SK30 Mike Richards .40 1.00
SK31 Ryan Getzlaf .40 1.00
SK32 Keith Tkachuk .30 .75
SK33 Glen Murray .25 .60
SK34 Brendan Shanahan .30 .75
SK35 Paul Kariya .30 .75
SK36 Marian Gaborik .50 1.25
SK37 Luc Robitaille .25 .60
SK38 Daniel Alfredsson .25 .60
SK39 Vincent Lecavalier .30 .75
SK40 Eric Daze .25 .60

2005-06 Ultra Scoring Kings Jerseys

STATED ODDS 1:72
SKJ-AO Alexander Ovechkin 12.00 30.00
SKJ-AT Alex Tanguay 3.00 8.00
SKJ-BG Bill Guerin 3.00 8.00
SKJ-BR Brad Richards 3.00 8.00
SKJ-BS Brendan Shanahan 3.00 8.00
SKJ-CP Corey Perry 3.00 8.00
SKJ-DA Daniel Alfredsson 3.00 8.00
SKJ-DH Dany Heatley 4.00 10.00
SKJ-DW Doug Weight 3.00 8.00
SKJ-ED Eric Daze 3.00 8.00
SKJ-GM Glen Murray 3.00 8.00
SKJ-HO Marian Hossa 3.00 8.00
SKJ-HV Martin Havlat 3.00 8.00
SKJ-IK Ilya Kovalchuk 4.00 10.00
SKJ-JI Jarome Iginla 5.00 12.00
SKJ-JJ Jaromir Jagr 5.00 12.00
SKJ-JR Jeremy Roenick 4.00 10.00
SKJ-JS Jason Spezza 4.00 10.00
SKJ-JS Joe Sakic 6.00 15.00
SKJ-JT Joe Thornton 5.00 12.00
SKJ-KT Keith Tkachuk 3.00 8.00
SKJ-LR Luc Robitaille 3.00 8.00
SKJ-MG Marian Gaborik 5.00 12.00
SKJ-MH Milan Hejduk 3.00 8.00
SKJ-ML Mario Lemieux 12.00 30.00
SKJ-MM Mike Modano 5.00 12.00
SKJ-MN Markus Naslund 3.00 8.00
SKJ-MR Mike Ribeiro 3.00 8.00
SKJ-MS Mats Sundin 3.00 8.00
SKJ-PE Patrik Elias 3.00 8.00
SKJ-PF Peter Forsberg 6.00 15.00
SKJ-PK Paul Kariya 3.00 8.00
SKJ-RG Ryan Getzlaf 3.00 8.00
SKJ-RI Mike Richards 3.00 8.00
SKJ-SC Sidney Crosby 30.00 80.00
SKJ-SD Shane Doan 3.00 8.00
SKJ-SF Sergei Fedorov 4.00 10.00
SKJ-SL Martin St. Louis 3.00 8.00
SKJ-SY Steve Yzerman 6.00 15.00
SKJ-VL Vincent Lecavalier 3.00 8.00

2005-06 Ultra Scoring Kings Jersey Autographs

PRINT RUN 20 SER.#'d SETS
NOT PRICED DUE TO SCARCITY
KAJ-AO Alexander Ovechkin
KAJ-AT Alex Tanguay
KAJ-BR Brad Richards
KAJ-CP Corey Perry
KAJ-DA Daniel Alfredsson
KAJ-DH Dany Heatley
KAJ-DW Doug Weight
KAJ-ED Eric Daze
KAJ-GM Glen Murray
KAJ-HO Marian Hossa
KAJ-HV Martin Havlat
KAJ-IK Ilya Kovalchuk
KAJ-JI Jarome Iginla
KAJ-JR Jeremy Roenick
KAJ-JS Jason Spezza
KAJ-JT Joe Thornton
KAJ-MH Milan Hejduk
KAJ-MM Mike Modano
KAJ-MN Markus Naslund
KAJ-MR Mike Ribiero
KAJ-MS Mats Sundin
KAJ-RG Ryan Getzlaf
KAJ-RI Mike Richards
KAJ-SC Sidney Crosby
KAJ-SD Shane Doan
KAJ-SL Martin St. Louis
KAJ-VL Vincent Lecavalier

2005-06 Ultra Scoring Kings Patches

*PATCHES: 1.25X TO 3X BASE JSY
PRINT RUN 50 SER.#'d SETS
SKP-AO Alexander Ovechkin 75.00 200.00
SKP-CP Corey Perry 20.00 50.00
SKP-RG Ryan Getzlaf 20.00 50.00
SKP-SC Sidney Crosby 100.00 250.00

2005-06 Ultra Scoring Kings Patch Autographs

PRINT RUN 10 SER.#'d SETS
NOT PRICED DUE TO SCARCITY
KAP-AO Alexander Ovechkin
KAP-AT Alex Tanguay
KAP-BR Brad Richards
KAP-CP Corey Perry
KAP-DA Daniel Alfredsson
KAP-DH Dany Heatley
KAP-DW Doug Weight
KAP-ED Eric Daze
KAP-GM Glen Murray
KAP-HO Marian Hossa
KAP-HV Martin Havlat
KAP-IK Ilya Kovalchuk
KAP-JI Jarome Iginla
KAP-JR Jeremy Roenick
KAP-JS Jason Spezza
KAP-JT Joe Thornton
KAP-MH Milan Hejduk
KAP-MM Mike Modano
KAP-MN Markus Naslund
KAP-MR Mike Ribeiro
KAP-RG Ryan Getzlaf
KAP-RI Mike Richards
KAP-SC Sidney Crosby
KAP-SD Shane Doan
KAP-SL Martin St. Louis
KAP-VL Vincent Lecavalier

2005-06 Ultra Super Six

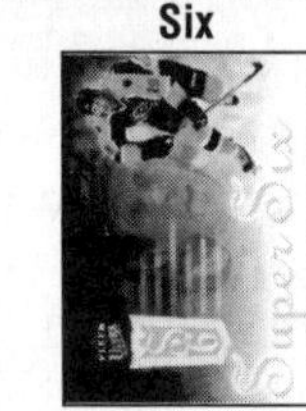

COMPLETE SET (8) 10.00 25.00
COMMON CARD (1-8)
SS1 Mario Lemieux 2.50 6.00
SS2 Joe Thornton .60 1.50
SS3 Martin Brodeur 2.00 5.00
SS4 Ray Bourque .75 2.00
SS5 Joe Sakic .75 2.00
SS6 Patrick Roy 2.00 5.00
SS7 Ray Bourque .75 2.00
SS8 Patrick Roy 2.00 5.00

2005-06 Ultra Super Six Jerseys

STATED ODDS 1:288
SSJ-JS Joe Sakic 8.00 20.00
SSJ-JT Joe Thornton 6.00 15.00
SSJ-MB Martin Brodeur 8.00 20.00
SSJ-ML Mario Lemieux 15.00 30.00
SSJ-PR1 Patrick Roy 15.00 30.00
SSJ-PR2 Patrick Roy 15.00 30.00
SSJ-RB1 Ray Bourque 6.00 15.00
SSJ-RB2 Ray Bourque 6.00 15.00

2005-06 Ultra Super Six Jersey Autographs

PRINT RUN 3 SER.#'d SETS
NOT PRICED DUE TO SCARCITY
SAJ-JT Joe Thornton
SAJ-MB Martin Brodeur
SAJ-PR1 Patrick Roy
SAJ-PR2 Patrick Roy
SAJ-RB1 Ray Bourque
SAJ-RB2 Ray Bourque

2005-06 Ultra Super Six Patches

PATCH PRINT RUN 6 SER.#'d SETS
NOT PRICED DUE TO SCARCITY
UNPRICED PATCH AU 1/1's EXIST

2006-07 Ultra

COMPLETE SET (251) 100.00 250.00
1 Jean-Sebastien Giguere .15 .40
2 Chris Pronger .15 .40
3 Andy McDonald .10 .25
4 Corey Perry .15 .40
5 Teemu Selanne .20 .50
6 Ryan Getzlaf .15 .40
7 Scott Niedermayer .10 .25
8 Kari Lehtonen .20 .50
9 Steve Rucchin .10 .25
10 Marian Hossa .15 .40
11 Ilya Kovalchuk .25 .60
12 Slava Kozlov .10 .25
13 Bobby Holik .10 .25
14 Patrice Bergeron .20 .50
15 Brad Boyes .10 .25
16 Marc Savard .10 .25
17 Brad Stuart .10 .25
18 Marco Sturm .10 .25
19 Glen Murray .10 .25
20 Zdeno Chara .10 .25
21 Thomas Vanek .15 .40
22 Ryan Miller .15 .40
23 Maxim Afinogenov .10 .25
24 Ales Kotalik .10 .25
25 Chris Drury .10 .25
26 Martin Biron .15 .40
27 Daniel Briere .15 .40
28 Miikka Kiprusoff .20 .50
29 Jarome Iginla .25 .60
30 Chuck Kobasew .10 .25
31 Kristian Huselius .10 .25
32 Daymond Langkow .10 .25
33 Dion Phaneuf .25 .60
34 Alex Tanguay .15 .40
35 Cam Ward .20 .50
36 Andrew Ladd .10 .25
37 Eric Staal .15 .40
38 Justin Williams .10 .25
39 Erik Cole .10 .25
40 Mike Commodore .10 .25
41 Rod Brind'Amour .15 .40
42 Nikolai Khabibulin .20 .50
43 Tuomo Ruutu .10 .25
44 Kyle Calder .10 .25
45 Martin Havlat .15 .40
46 Rene Bourque .10 .25
47 Duncan Keith .10 .25
48 Jose Theodore .20 .50
49 Joe Sakic .40 1.00
50 Milan Hejduk .15 .40
51 Andrew Brunette .10 .25
52 Marek Svatos .10 .25
53 Pierre Turgeon .10 .25
54 Peter Budaj .15 .40
55 Fredrik Modin .10 .25
56 Nikolai Zherdev .10 .25
57 Rick Nash .25 .60
58 Sergei Fedorov .20 .50
59 Rostislav Klesla .10 .25
60 Bryan Berard .10 .25
61 David Vyborny .10 .25
62 Marty Turco .15 .40
63 Mike Modano .30 .75
64 Sergei Zubov .10 .25
65 Brenden Morrow .10 .25
66 Jussi Jokinen .10 .25
67 Eric Lindros .20 .50
68 Jere Lehtinen .10 .25
69 Tomas Holmstrom .10 .25
70 Henrik Zetterberg .20 .50
71 Nicklas Lidstrom .20 .50
72 Pavel Datsyuk .15 .40
73 Chris Osgood .15 .40
74 Kris Draper .10 .25
75 Steve Yzerman .75 2.00
76 Ales Hemsky .10 .25
77 Jarret Stoll .10 .25
78 Joffrey Lupul .10 .25
79 Dwayne Roloson .15 .40
80 Ryan Smyth .15 .40
81 Shawn Horcoff .10 .25
82 Fernando Pisani .10 .25
83 Todd Bertuzzi .15 .40
84 Nathan Horton .15 .40
85 Alex Auld .15 .40
86 Olli Jokinen .10 .25
87 Jay Bouwmeester .10 .25
88 Rostislav Olesz .10 .25
89 Joe Nieuwendyk .15 .40
90 Alexander Frolov .10 .25
91 Mathieu Garon .15 .40
92 Mike Cammalleri .15 .40
93 Rob Blake .15 .40
94 Lubomir Visnovsky .10 .25
95 Dustin Brown .10 .25
96 Marian Gaborik .40 1.00
97 Manny Fernandez .15 .40
98 Mark Parrish .10 .25
99 Pierre-Marc Bouchard .10 .25
100 Brian Rolston .10 .25
101 Pavol Demitra .10 .25
102 Saku Koivu .20 .50
103 Cristobal Huet .15 .40
104 Alex Kovalev .10 .25
105 Michael Ryder .15 .40
106 David Aebischer .15 .40
107 Mike Ribeiro .10 .25
108 Chris Higgins .15 .40
109 Tomas Vokoun .15 .40
110 Steve Sullivan .10 .25
111 David Legwand .10 .25
112 Paul Kariya .20 .50
113 Jason Arnott .10 .25
114 Kimmo Timonen .10 .25
115 Martin Brodeur 1.00 2.50
116 Brian Rafalski .10 .25
117 Patrik Elias .10 .25
118 Brian Gionta .10 .25
119 Scott Gomez .10 .25
120 Zach Parise .10 .25
121 Alexei Yashin .10 .25
122 Rick DiPietro .15 .40
123 Miroslav Satan .10 .25
124 Trent Hunter .10 .25
125 Jason Blake .10 .25
126 Mike Sillinger .10 .25
127 Henrik Lundqvist .25 .60
128 Martin Straka .10 .25
129 Jaromir Jagr .30 .75
130 Petr Prucha .10 .25
131 Brendan Shanahan .20 .50
132 Matt Cullen .10 .25
133 Martin Gerber .15 .40
134 Jason Spezza .20 .50
135 Wade Redden .10 .25
136 Dany Heatley .25 .60
137 Daniel Alfredsson .15 .40
138 Patrick Eaves .10 .25
139 Ray Emery .15 .40
140 Peter Forsberg .50 1.25
141 Antero Niittymaki .15 .40
142 Joni Pitkanen .10 .25
143 Simon Gagne .20 .50
144 Keith Primeau .10 .25
145 Jeff Carter .15 .40
146 Robert Esche .15 .40
147 Mike Richards .15 .40
148 Ladislav Nagy .10 .25
149 Curtis Joseph .20 .50
150 Mike Comrie .10 .25
151 Shane Doan .10 .25
152 Ed Jovanovski .10 .25
153 Jeremy Roenick .20 .50
154 Sidney Crosby 1.25 3.00
155 Marc-Andre Fleury .15 .40
156 Ryan Malone .10 .25
157 Colby Armstrong .10 .25
158 Ryan Whitney .10 .25
159 John LeClair .15 .40
160 Evgeni Nabokov .15 .40
161 Joe Thornton .30 .75
162 Patrick Marleau .15 .40
163 Vesa Toskala .15 .40
164 Jonathan Cheechoo .20 .50
165 Steve Bernier .10 .25
166 Mark Bell .10 .25
167 Keith Tkachuk .20 .50
168 Curtis Sanford .15 .40
169 Doug Weight .10 .25
170 Bill Guerin .10 .25
171 Lee Stempniak .10 .25
172 Petr Cajanek .10 .25
173 Evgeni Artyukhin .10 .25
174 Brad Richards .15 .40
175 Martin St. Louis .15 .40
176 Vincent Lecavalier .20 .50
177 Vaclav Prospal .10 .25
178 Marc Denis .15 .40
179 Ruslan Fedotenko .10 .25
180 Andrew Raycroft .15 .40
181 Mats Sundin .20 .50

182 Bryan McCabe .10 .25
183 Alexander Steen .15 .40
184 Kyle Wellwood .10 .25
185 Darcy Tucker .10 .25
186 Tomas Kaberle .10 .25
187 Michael Peca .10 .25
188 Markus Naslund .20 .50
189 Roberto Luongo .25 .60
190 Henrik Sedin .10 .25
191 Mattias Ohlund .10 .25
192 Brendan Morrison .10 .25
193 Ryan Kesler .10 .25
194 Daniel Sedin .10 .25
195 Olaf Kolzig .20 .50
196 Alexander Ovechkin 1.00 2.50
197 Brian Pothier .10 .25
198 Dainius Zubrus .10 .25
199 Chris Clark .10 .25
200 Matt Pettinger .10 .25
201 Yan Stastny RC 1.50 4.00
202 Mark Stuart RC 1.25 3.00
203 Carsen Germyn RC 1.25 3.00
204 Dustin Byfuglien RC 1.25 3.00
205 Dan Jancevski RC 1.25 3.00
206 Tomas Kopecky RC 1.50 4.00
207 Marc-Antoine Pouliot RC 1.50 4.00
208 Konstantin Pushkaryov RC 1.25 3.00
209 Erik Reitz RC 1.25 3.00
210 Miroslav Kopriva RC 1.25 3.00
211 Shea Weber RC 1.50 4.00
212 Frank Doyle RC 1.25 3.00
213 Rob Collins RC 1.25 3.00
214 Steve Regier RC 1.25 3.00
215 Ryan Caldwell RC 1.25 3.00
216 Masi Marjamaki RC 1.25 3.00
217 Jarkko Immonen RC 1.25 3.00
218 Billy Thompson RC 1.25 3.00
219 Filip Novak RC 1.25 3.00
220 Ryan Potulny RC 1.50 4.00
221 Bill Thomas RC 1.25 3.00
222 Joel Perrault RC 1.25 3.00
223 Noah Welch RC 1.50 4.00
224 Michel Ouellet RC 1.50 4.00
225 Matt Carle RC 1.50 4.00
226 Ben Ondrus RC 1.25 3.00
227 Brendan Bell RC 1.25 3.00
228 Ian White RC 1.25 3.00
229 Jeremy Williams RC 1.25 3.00
230 Eric Fehr RC 1.50 4.00
231 Patrick Thoreson RR 2.00 5.00
232 Ryan Shannon RR 2.00 5.00
233 Anze Kopitar RR 10.00 25.00
234 Travis Zajac RR 3.00 8.00
235 Nigel Dawes RR 2.00 5.00
236 Kris Letang RR 3.00 8.00
237 Marc Edouard Vlasic RR 2.00 5.00
238 Keith Yandle RR 2.00 5.00
239 Alexei Mikhnov RR 2.00 5.00
240 Ladislav Smid RR 2.00 5.00
241 Loui Eriksson RR 2.00 5.00
242 Luc Bourdon RR 2.00 5.00
243 Alexander Radulov RR 6.00 15.00
244 Alexei Kaigorodov RR 2.00 5.00
245 Enver Lisin RR 2.00 5.00
246 Patrick O'Sullivan RR 3.00 8.00
247 Jordan Staal RR 20.00 50.00
248 Paul Stastny RR 8.00 20.00
249 Guillaume Latendresse RR 8.00 20.00
250 Phil Kessel RR 6.00 15.00
251 Evgeni Malkin RR 30.00 60.00

2006-07 Ultra Gold Medallion

STARS 2X to 5X BASE HI
ROOKIES .75X to 2X BASE HI
ONE PER PACK
ROOKIE REDEMPTIONS: 1X to 1.5X HI
231 Patrick Thoreson 12.00 30.00
233 Anze Kopitar 25.00 60.00
234 Travis Zajac 12.00 30.00
242 Luc Bourdon 12.00 30.00
243 Alexander Radulov 20.00 50.00
246 Patrick O'Sullivan 12.00 30.00
247 Jordan Staal 30.00 80.00
248 Paul Stastny 20.00 50.00
249 Guillaume Latendresse 25.00 60.00
250 Phil Kessel 20.00 50.00
251 Evgeni Malkin 60.00 125.00

2006-07 Ultra Ice Medallion

STARS: 6X to 15X BASE HI
ROOKIES: 1.5X to 3X BASE HI
STATED PRINT RUN 100 #'d SETS
ROOKIE REDEMPTIONS 1.5X to 3X HI
ROOKIE RED. PRINT RUN 25 #'d SETS
154 Sidney Crosby 30.00 80.00
196 Alexander Ovechkin 20.00 50.00
233 Anze Kopitar 40.00 80.00
247 Jordan Staal 50.00 125.00
249 Guillaume Latendresse 30.00 80.00
251 Evgeni Malkin 150.00 250.00

2006-07 Ultra Action

STATED ODDS 1:12
UA1 Kari Lehtonen .75 2.00
UA2 Jarome Iginla 1.25 3.00
UA3 Dion Phaneuf .75 2.00
UA4 Eric Staal .75 2.00
UA5 Joe Sakic 1.25 3.00
UA6 Marek Svatos .40 1.00
UA7 Rick Nash 1.25 3.00
UA8 Mike Modano 1.25 3.00
UA9 Henrik Zetterberg .75 2.00
UA10 Brendan Shanahan .75 2.00
UA11 Chris Pronger .75 2.00
UA12 Roberto Luongo .75 2.00
UA13 Marian Gaborik 1.25 3.00
UA14 Saku Koivu .75 2.00
UA15 Paul Kariya .75 2.00
UA16 Martin Brodeur 2.50 6.00
UA17 Alexei Yashin .40 1.00
UA18 Jaromir Jagr 1.25 3.00
UA19 Dominik Hasek 1.25 3.00
UA20 Dany Heatley 1.25 3.00
UA21 Peter Forsberg 1.25 3.00
UA22 Shane Doan .40 1.00
UA23 Sidney Crosby 4.00 10.00
UA24 Joe Thornton 1.25 3.00
UA25 Evgeni Nabokov .75 2.00
UA26 Martin St. Louis .75 2.00
UA27 Vincent Lecavalier .75 2.00
UA28 Alexander Ovechkin 3.00 8.00
UA29 Mats Sundin .75 2.00
UA30 Markus Naslund .75 2.00

2006-07 Ultra Difference Makers

STATED ODDS 1:12
DM1 Ilya Bryzgalov .75 2.00
DM2 Ilya Kovalchuk 1.25 3.00
DM3 Patrice Bergeron .75 2.00
DM4 Ryan Miller .75 2.00
DM5 Jarome Iginla 1.25 3.00
DM6 Miikka Kiprusoff .75 2.00
DM7 Eric Staal .75 2.00
DM8 Markus Naslund .75 2.00
DM9 Alex Tanguay .75 2.00
DM10 Jose Theodore 1.25 3.00
DM11 Rick Nash 1.25 3.00
DM12 Marty Turco .75 2.00
DM13 Pavel Datsyuk .75 2.00
DM14 Henrik Zetterberg .75 2.00
DM15 Chris Pronger .75 2.00
DM16 Roberto Luongo 1.25 3.00
DM17 Michael Ryder .75 2.00
DM18 Saku Koivu .75 2.00
DM19 Mats Sundin .75 2.00
DM20 Martin Brodeur 2.50 6.00
DM21 Jaromir Jagr 1.25 3.00
DM22 Henrik Lundqvist 1.25 3.00
DM23 Daniel Alfredsson .75 2.00
DM24 Dany Heatley 1.25 3.00
DM25 Jason Spezza .75 2.00
DM26 Peter Forsberg 1.25 3.00
DM27 Alexander Ovechkin 3.00 8.00
DM28 Sidney Crosby 4.00 10.00
DM29 Joe Thornton 1.25 3.00
DM30 Vincent Lecavalier .75 2.00

2006-07 Ultra Fresh Ink

STATED ODDS 1:200
IAL Andrew Ladd SP
IAM Al Montoya 8.00 20.00
IAO Alexander Ovechkin SP 60.00 100.00
IBB Brad Boyes SP 8.00 20.00
IBL Brian Leetch SP 15.00 40.00
IBM Brenden Morrow SP
IBR Martin Brodeur SP
ICD Chris Drury SP 10.00 25.00
ICK Chuck Kobasew 4.00 10.00
ICO Chris Osgood SP 10.00 25.00
IDB Daniel Briere SP 10.00 25.00
IDC Dan Cloutier SP 12.00 40.00
IDL David Leneveu 8.00 20.00
IDR Dwayne Roloson 8.00 20.00
IEN Evgeni Nabokov 6.00 15.00
IGM Glen Murray SP 15.00 40.00
IHE Milan Hejduk SP
IJB Jay Bouwmeester SP 12.00 30.00
IJH Jeff Halpern 6.00 15.00
IJI Jarome Iginla SP 25.00 60.00
IJL Jason Labarbera 6.00 15.00
IJO Jeff O'Neill SP 8.00 20.00
IJT Jose Theodore SP 15.00 40.00
IJV Josef Vasicek 8.00 20.00
IMB Martin Biron 6.00 15.00
IMC Mike Cammalleri SP 8.00 20.00
IMG Marian Gaborik SP 15.00 40.00
IMH Michal Handzus 6.00 15.00
IMN Mika Noronen 5.00 12.00
IMR Michael Ryder SP 10.00 25.00
IMS Marc Savard 6.00 15.00
IMT Mikael Tellqvist 10.00 25.00
IMZ Marek Zidlicky SP 8.00 20.00
INA Nikolai Antropov SP 8.00 20.00
IOK Olaf Kolzig SP 12.00 25.00
IPS Philippe Sauve 4.00 10.00
IRF Ruslan Fedotenko SP 8.00 20.00
IRM Ryan Malone SP 10.00 25.00
IRS Ryan Smyth SP 12.00 30.00
ISC Sidney Crosby SP 150.00 250.00
ISG Scott Gomez SP 10.00 25.00
ISH Scott Hartnell SP 8.00 20.00
ISK Saku Koivu SP 10.00 25.00
ISS Sergei Samsonov SP 6.00 15.00
ISU Ryan Suter 8.00 20.00
ITB Todd Bertuzzi SP 15.00 40.00
ITC Ty Conklin SP 8.00 20.00
ITG Tim Gleason 5.00 12.00

2006-07 Ultra Scoring Kings

STATED ODDS 1:12
SK1 Alex Tanguay .75 2.00
SK2 Alexander Ovechkin 3.00 8.00
SK3 Brad Richards .75 2.00
SK4 Brendan Shanahan .75 2.00
SK5 Daniel Alfredsson .75 2.00
SK6 Dany Heatley 1.25 3.00
SK7 Eric Staal .75 2.00
SK8 Henrik Zetterberg .75 2.00
SK9 Ilya Kovalchuk 1.25 3.00
SK10 Jarome Iginla 1.25 3.00
SK11 Jaromir Jagr 1.25 3.00
SK12 Jason Spezza .75 2.00
SK13 Joe Sakic 1.25 3.00
SK14 Joe Thornton 1.25 3.00
SK15 Jonathan Cheechoo .75 2.00
SK16 Ryan Smyth .40 1.00
SK17 Marian Gaborik 1.25 3.00
SK18 Markus Naslund .75 2.00
SK19 Mats Sundin .75 2.00
SK20 Michael Ryder .40 1.00
SK21 Mike Modano 1.25 3.00
SK22 Patrice Bergeron .75 2.00
SK23 Paul Kariya .75 2.00
SK24 Pavel Datsyuk .75 2.00
SK25 Peter Forsberg 1.25 3.00
SK26 Rick Nash 1.25 3.00
SK27 Saku Koivu .75 2.00
SK28 Sidney Crosby 4.00 10.00
SK29 Simon Gagne .75 2.00
SK30 Vincent Lecavalier .75 2.00

2006-07 Ultra Uniformity

STATED ODDS 1:12
UAH Ales Hemsky 3.00 8.00
UAO Alexander Ovechkin 10.00 25.00
UBL Rob Blake 3.00 8.00
UBM Brendan Morrison 3.00 8.00
UBR Martin Brodeur 8.00 20.00
UBS Brad Stuart 3.00 8.00
UCC Carlo Colaiacovo 3.00 8.00
UCD Chris Drury 3.00 8.00
UCP Chris Pronger 4.00 10.00
UDE Pavol Demitra 3.00 8.00
UDH Dan Hamhuis 3.00 8.00
UDL David Legwand 3.00 8.00
UDM Darren McCarty 3.00 8.00
UEB Ed Belfour 4.00 10.00
UED Eric Daze 3.00 8.00
UEJ Ed Jovanovski 3.00 8.00
UEL Eric Lindros 4.00 10.00
UEN Evgeni Nabokov 4.00 10.00
UES Eric Staal 4.00 10.00
UFP Fernando Pisani 3.00 8.00
UGE Martin Gerber 3.00 8.00
UHA Dominik Hasek SP 8.00 20.00
UJA Jason Arnott 3.00 8.00
UJG Jean-Sebastien Giguere 3.00 8.00
UJK Jason King 3.00 8.00
UJL Jere Lehtinen 3.00 8.00
UJS Joe Sakic 8.00 20.00
UJT Joe Thornton 6.00 15.00
UJW Justin Williams 3.00 8.00
UKO Mikko Koivu 3.00 8.00
UKT Keith Tkachuk 3.00 8.00
ULN Ladislav Nagy 3.00 8.00
ULR Luc Robitaille 4.00 10.00
UMB Martin Biron 3.00 8.00
UMC Bryan McCabe 3.00 8.00
UMD Marc Denis 3.00 8.00
UMG Marian Gaborik 6.00 15.00
UMK Miikka Kiprusoff 5.00 12.00
UMM Mike Modano 5.00 12.00
UMN Markus Naslund 4.00 10.00
UMP Mark Parrish 3.00 8.00
UMR Michael Ryder 4.00 10.00
UMS Marek Svatos 3.00 8.00
UNA Nikolai Antropov 3.00 8.00
UPB Pierre-Marc Bouchard 3.00 8.00
UPD Pavel Datsyuk 4.00 10.00
UPE Michael Peca 3.00 8.00
UPF Peter Forsberg 6.00 15.00
UPL Patrick Lalime 3.00 8.00
UPP Petr Prucha 3.00 8.00
URB Radek Bonk 3.00 8.00
URE Robert Esche 3.00 8.00
URR Robyn Regehr 3.00 8.00
URZ Richard Zednik 3.00 8.00
USG Simon Gagne 4.00 10.00
USK Saku Koivu 4.00 10.00
UST Martin Straka 3.00 8.00
USU Mats Sundin 4.00 10.00
USW Stephen Weiss 3.00 8.00
UTS Teemu Selanne 4.00 10.00

2006-07 Ultra Uniformity Patches

NOT PRICED DUE TO SCARCITY
PRINT RUN 25 SER. #'d SETS
UPAH Ales Hemsky
UPAO Alexander Ovechkin 40.00 100.00
UPBM Rob Blake 20.00 50.00
UPBO_ Radek Bonk
UPBO Brendan Morrison
UPBR Martin Brodeur
UPBS Brad Stuart
UPCC Carlo Colaiacovo
UPCD Chris Drury 12.00 30.00
UPCP Chris Pronger 20.00 50.00
UPDE Pavol Demitra 12.00 30.00
UPDH Dan Hamhuis
UPDL David Legwand
UPDM Darren McCarty
UPEB Ed Belfour 25.00 60.00
UPED Eric Daze
UPEJ Ed Jovanovski
UPEL Eric Lindros 25.00 60.00
UPEN Evgeni Nabokov
UPES Eric Staal
UPFP Fernando Pisani
UPGA Martin Gerber
UPHA Dominik Hasek
UPJA Jason Arnott
UPJG Jean-Sebastien Giguere 20.00 50.00
UPJK Jason King
UPJL Jere Lehtinen
UPJS Joe Sakic 40.00 100.00
UPJT Joe Thornton 30.00 80.00
UPJW Justin Williams
UPKO Mikko Koivu
UPKT Keith Tkachuk
UPLN Ladislav Nagy
UPLR Luc Robitaille
UPMB Martin Biron 20.00 50.00
UPMD Bryan McCabe
UPMG Marc Denis
UPMK Marian Gaborik
UPMM Miikka Kiprusoff 25.00 60.00
UPMN Mike Modano
UPMO Markus Naslund 25.00 60.00
UPMP Mark Parrish
UPMR Michael Ryder 20.00 50.00
UPMS Marek Svatos 12.00 30.00
UPNA Nikolai Antropov
UPPA Pierre-Marc Bouchard 12.00 30.00
UPPB_ Peter Forsberg
UPPB Pavel Datsyuk 20.00 50.00
UPPD_ Michael Peca 12.00 30.00
UPPL Patrick Lalime
UPPP Petr Prucha
UPRE Robert Esche
UPRR Robyn Regehr
UPRZ Richard Zednik
UPSG Simon Gagne 25.00 60.00
UPSK Saku Koivu 25.00 60.00
UPST Martin Straka
UPSU Mats Sundin 25.00 60.00
UPSW Stephen Weiss
UPTS Teemu Selanne 25.00 60.00

2006-07 Ultra Uniformity Autographed Jerseys

AUTOS: 2X to 5X BASE JERSEY
PRINT RUN 35 SER. #'d SETS

1961-62 Union Oil WHL

This 12-drawing set features players from the Los Angeles Blades (1-8) and the San Francisco Seals (9-12) of the Western Hockey League. The black-and-white drawings by artist Sam Patrick measure approximately 6" by 8" and are printed on textured white paper. The back of each drawing carries the player's career highlights and biographical information. The Union Oil name and logo at the bottom round out the backs. The cards are unnumbered and listed below alphabetically within teams. Reportedly only eight cards were issued to the public, making four of the cards extremely scarce.

COMPLETE SET (12) 50.00 100.00
1 Jack Bownass 3.00 6.00
2 Ed Diachuk 3.00 6.00
3 Leo LaBine 5.00 10.00
4 Willie O'Ree 20.00 40.00
5 Bruce Carmichael 3.00 6.00
6 Gordon Haworth 4.00 8.00
7 Fleming Mackell 5.00 10.00
8 Robert Solinger 3.00 6.00
9 Gary Edmundson 3.00 6.00
10 Al Nicholson 3.00 6.00
11 Orland Kurtenbach 7.50 15.00
12 Tom Thurlby 3.00 6.00

1990-91 Upper Deck

The 1990-91 Upper Deck Hockey set contains 550 standard-size cards. The set was released in two series of 400 and 150 cards, respectively. The card fronts feature color action photos, bordered on the right and bottom in the team's colors with the team logo in the lower right hand corner. The player's name and position in black lettering appear in a pale blue bar at the top of the card front. Two-thirds of back shows another color action photo, while the remaining third presents biographical information and career statistics in pale blue box running the length of the card. The second (or extended) series contains 150 cards and includes newest rookies, traded players, All Stars, Heroes of the NHL, and members of the Canadian National Junior Team. It should also be noted that the Canada's Captains card (473) shows Eric Lindros along with Kris Draper and Steven Rice. The French version of 1990-91 Upper Deck was produced in smaller quantities compared to the English version; multipliers can be found in the header below to determine values for these.

COMPLETE SET (550) 25.00 60.00
COMPLETE LO SERIES (400) 12.50 30.00
COMPLETE HI SERIES (150) 12.50 30.00
COMP.HI FACT.SERIES (150) 15.00 30.00
*FRENCH: 1X TO 1.5X HI COLUMN
1 David Volek .02 .10
2 Brian Propp .02 .10
3 Wendel Clark .07 .20
4 Adam Creighton .02 .10
5 Mark Osborne .02 .10
6 Murray Craven .02 .10
7 Doug Crossman .02 .10
8 Mario Marois .02 .10
9 Curt Giles .02 .10
10 Rick Wamsley .07 .20
11 Troy Mallette .02 .10
12 John Cullen .02 .10
13 Miloslav Horava .02 .10
14 Kevin Stevens RC .02 .10
15 David Shaw .02 .10
16 Randy Wood .02 .10
17 Peter Zezel .02 .10
18 Glenn Healy RC .07 .20
19 Sergio Momesso RC .02 .10
20 Don Maloney .02 .10
21 Craig Muni .02 .10
22 Phil Housley .07 .20
23 Martin Gelinas RC .25 .60
24 Alexander Mogilny RC .60 1.50
25 John Byce .02 .10
26 Joe Nieuwendyk .07 .20
27 Ron Tugnutt .07 .20
28 Don Barber .02 .10
29 Gary Roberts .02 .10
30 Basil McRae .02 .10
31 Phil Bourque .02 .10
32 Mike Richter RC .40 1.00
33 Zarley Zalapski .02 .10
34 Bernie Nicholls .07 .20
35 Bob Corkum RC .02 .10
36 Rod Brind'Amour RC .60 1.50
37 Mark Fitzpatrick RC UER .07 .20
(Back says catches right& not left)
38 Gino Cavallini .02 .10
39 Mick Vukota .02 .10
40 Mike Lalor .02 .10
41 Dave Andreychuk .07 .20
42 Bill Ranford .07 .20
43 Pierre Turgeon .07 .20
44 Mark Messier .15 .40
45 Rob Blake RC .40 1.00
46 Mike Modano RC 1.00 2.50
47 Theo Fleury .25 .60
48 Neal Broten .07 .20
49 Paul Gillis .02 .10
50 Doug Bodger .02 .10
51 Stephan Lebeau RC .02 .10
52 Larry Robinson .07 .20
53 Dale Hawerchuk .07 .20
54 Wayne Gretzky .75 2.00
55 Ed Belfour RC UER 1.00 2.50
(Turned pro with Gears should be Generals)
56 Steve Yzerman .60 1.50
57 Rod Langway .02 .10
58 Bernie Federko .07 .20
59 Mario Lemieux Streak .40 1.00
60 Doug Lidster .02 .10
61 Dave Christian .02 .10
62 Rob Ramage .02 .10
63 Jeremy Roenick RC .60 1.50
64 Ray Bourque .25 .60
65 Jon Morris .02 .10
66 Sergei Svoboda .07 .20
67 Ron Francis .07 .20
68 Ron Sutter .02 .10
69 Peter Sidorkiewicz .07 .20
70 Sylvain Turgeon .02 .10
71 Dave Ellett .02 .10
72 Bobby Smith .07 .20
73 Luc Robitaille .07 .20
74 Pat Elynuik .02 .10
75 Jason Soules .02 .10
76 Dino Ciccarelli .07 .20
77 Vladimir Krutov .07 .20
78 Lee Norwood .02 .10
79 Brian Bradley .07 .20
80 Michal Pivonka RC .07 .20
81 Mark LaForest .02 .10
82 Trent Yawney .02 .10
83 Tom Fergus .02 .10
84 Andy Brickley .02 .10
85 Dave Manson .02 .10
86 Gord Murphy RC .02 .10
87 Scott Young .02 .10
88 Tommy Albelin .02 .10
89 Ken Wregget .07 .20
90 Brad Shaw .02 .10
91 Mario Gosselin .07 .20
92 Paul Fenton .02 .10
93 Brian Skrudland .02 .10
94 Thomas Steen .02 .10
95 John Tonelli .02 .10
96 Steve Chiasson UER .02 .10
(Back photo actually Yves Racine)
97 Mike Ridley .02 .10
98 Garth Butcher .02 .10
99 Daniel Shank .02 .10
100 Checklist 1-100 .02 .10
101 Jamie Macoun .02 .10
102 Wendell Young .07 .20
103 Laurie Boschman .02 .10
104 Paul Ranheim RC .02 .10
105 Doug Smail .02 .10
106 Shawn Chambers .02 .10
107 Steve Weeks .07 .20
108 Gaetan Duchesne .02 .10
109 Kevin Hatcher .02 .10
110 Paul Reinhart .02 .10
111 Shawn Burr .02 .10
112 Troy Murray .02 .10
113 John Chabot .02 .10
114 Jacques Cloutier .07 .20
115 Rick Zombo .02 .10
116 Kjell Samuelsson .02 .10
117 Tim Watters .02 .10
118 Pat Flatley .02 .10
119 Tom Laidlaw .02 .10
120 Ilkka Sinisalo .02 .10
121 Tom Barrasso .07 .20
122 Bob Essensa RC .25 .60
123 Sergei Makarov RC .07 .20
124 Paul Coffey .15 .40
125 Bob Beers RC .02 .10
126 Brian Bellows .07 .20
127 Mike Liut .07 .20
128 Igor Larionov RC .40 1.00
129 Craig Simpson .02 .10
130 Kelly Miller .02 .10
131 Dirk Graham .02 .10
132 Jimmy Carson .02 .10
133 Michel Goulet .07 .20
134 Gerard Gallant .02 .10
135 Bruce Hoffort .02 .10
136 Steve Duchesne .02 .10
137 Bryan Trottier .07 .20
138 Pelle Eklund .02 .10
139 Gary Nylund .02 .10
140 Steve Kasper .02 .10
141 Joel Otto .02 .10
142 Rob Brown .02 .10
143 Al MacInnis .07 .20
144 Mario Lemieux 1.00 2.00
145 Peter Eriksson .02 .10
146 Jari Kurri .07 .20
147 Petri Skriko .02 .10
148 Steve Smith .02 .10
149 Calle Johansson .02 .10
150 Stewart Gavin .02 .10
151 Randy Ladouceur .02 .10
152 Vincent Riendeau RC .07 .20
153 Patrick Roy UER .60 1.50
(Feet and inches reversed in stat table)
154 Brett Hull .30 .75
155 Craig Fisher .02 .10
156 Cam Neely .15 .40
157 Al Iafrate .07 .20
158 Bob Carpenter .02 .10
159 Doug Brown .02 .10
160 Tom Kurvers .02 .10
161 John MacLean .07 .20
162 Guy Lafleur .15 .40
163 Peter Stastny .07 .20
164 Joe Sakic .40 1.00
165 Robb Stauber RC .07 .20
166 Daren Puppa .07 .20
167 Esa Tikkanen .02 .10
168 Mike Ramsey .02 .10
169 Craig MacTavish .02 .10
170 Christian Ruuttu .02 .10
171 Brian Hayward .07 .20
172 Pat Verbeek .02 .10
173 Adam Oates .07 .20
174 Chris Chelios .15 .40
175 Curtis Joseph RC .75 2.00
176 Slava Fetisov RC .15 .40
177 Dave Poulin .02 .10
178 Mark Recchi RC .60 1.50
179 Daniel Marois .02 .10
180 Mark Johnson .02 .10
181 Michel Petit .02 .10
182 Brian Mullen .02 .10
183 Chris Terreri RC .07 .20
184 Tony Hrkac .02 .10
185 James Patrick .02 .10
186 Craig Ludwig .02 .10
187 Uwe Krupp .02 .10
188 Guy Carbonneau .07 .20
189 Dave Snuggerud .02 .10
190 Joe Murphy RC .02 .10
191 Jeff Brown .02 .10
192 Dean Evason .02 .10
193 Petr Svoboda .02 .10
194 Dave Babych .02 .10
195 Steve Tuttle .02 .10
196 Randy Burridge .02 .10
197 Tony Tanti .02 .10
198 Bob Sweeney .02 .10
199 Brad Marsh .02 .10
200 Checklist 101-200 .02 .10
201 Conn Smythe Trophy .07 .20
202 Calder Trophy .02 .10
Sergei Makarov
203 Lady Byng Trophy .15 .40
Brett Hull
204 Norris Trophy .07 .20
Ray Bourque
205 Art Ross Trophy .40 1.00
Wayne Gretzky
206 Hart Trophy .07 .20
Mark Messier
207 Vezina Trophy .30 .75
Patrick Roy
208 Frank Selke Trophy .02 .10
209 William Jennings .02 .10
Trophy
Andy Moog and
Reggie Lemelin
210 Aaron Broten .02 .10
211 John Carter .02 .10
212 Marty McSorley .02 .10
213 Greg Millen .07 .20
214 Dave Taylor .07 .20
215 Rejean Lemelin .07 .20
216 Dave McLlwain .02 .10
217 Don Beaupre .07 .20
218 Paul MacDermid .02 .10
219 Dale Hunter .02 .10
220 Brent Ashton .02 .10
221 Steve Thomas .02 .10
222 Ed Olczyk .02 .10
223 Doug Wilson .07 .20
224 Vincent Damphousse .02 .10
225 Rob DiMaio .02 .10
226 Hubie McDonough .02 .10
227 Ron Hextall .07 .20
228 Dave Chyzowski .02 .10
229 Larry Murphy .07 .20
230 Mike Bullard .02 .10
231 Kelly Hrudey .07 .20
232 Andy Moog .07 .20
233 Todd Elik RC .02 .10
234 Craig Janney .07 .20
235 Peter Lappin .02 .10
236 Scott Stevens .07 .20
237 Fredrik Olausson .02 .10
238 Geoff Courtnall .02 .10
239 Greg Paslawski .02 .10
240 Alan May .02 .10
241 Allan Bester .07 .20
242 Steve Larmer .07 .20
243 Gary Leeman .02 .10
244 Denis Savard .07 .20
245 Eric Weinrich RC .02 .10
246 Pat LaFontaine .15 .40
247 Tim Kerr .02 .10
248 Dave Gagner .02 .10
249 Brent Sutter .02 .10
250 Claude Vilgrain RC .02 .10
251 Tomas Sandstrom .02 .10
252 Joe Mullen .07 .20
253 Brian Leetch .20 .50
254 Mike Vernon .07 .20
255 Daniel Dore .02 .10
256 Trevor Linden .07 .20
257 Dave Barr .02 .10
258 John Ogrodnick .02 .10
259 Russ Courtnall .02 .10
260 Dan Quinn .02 .10
261 Mark Howe .02 .10
262 Kevin Lowe .02 .10
263 Rick Tocchet .07 .20
264 Grant Fuhr .07 .20
265 Andrew Cassels RC .07 .20
266 Kevin Dineen .02 .10
267 Kirk Muller .02 .10
268 Randy Cunneyworth .02 .10
269 Brendan Shanahan .15 .40
270 Dave Tippett .02 .10
271 Doug Gilmour .07 .20
272 Tony Granato .02 .10
273 Gary Suter .02 .10
274 Darren Turcotte RC .02 .10
275 Murray Baron .02 .10
276 Stephane Richer .07 .20
277 Mike Gartner .07 .20
278 Kirk McLean .07 .20
279 John Vanbiesbrouck .07 .20
280 Shayne Corson .02 .10
281 Paul Cavallini .02 .10
282 Petr Klima .02 .10
283 Ulf Dahlen .02 .10
284 Glenn Anderson .07 .20
285 Rick Meagher .02 .10
286 Alexei Kasatonov RC .02 .10
287 Ulf Samuelsson .02 .10
288 Patrik Sundstrom .02 .10
289 Ray Ferraro .02 .10
290 Janne Ojanen .02 .10
291 Jeff Jackson .02 .10
292 Jiri Hrdina .02 .10
293 Joe Cirella .02 .10
294 Brad McCrimmon .02 .10
295 Curtis Leschyshyn RC .02 .10
296 Kelly Kisio .02 .10
297 Jyrki Lumme RC .02 .10
298 Mark Janssens .02 .10
299 Stan Smyl .02 .10
300 Checklist 201-300 .02 .10
301 Joe Sakic .15 .40
(Quebec Nordiques TC)
302 Petri Skriko .02 .10
303 Steve Yzerman .15 .40
(Detroit Red Wings TC)
304 Tim Kerr .02 .10
305 Mario Lemieux TC .30 .75
306 Pat LaFontaine .07 .20
(New York Islanders TC)
307 Wayne Gretzky .40 1.00
(Los Angeles Kings TC)
308 Brian Bellows TC .02 .10
309 Rod Langway TC .02 .10
310 Gary Leeman TC .02 .10
311 Kirk Muller TC .02 .10
312 Brett Hull .07 .20
(St. Louis Blues TC)
313 Thomas Steen TC .02 .10
314 Ron Francis TC .07 .20
315 Brian Leetch .07 .20
(New York Rangers TC)
316 Jeremy Roenick .15 .40
(Chicago Blackhawks TC)
317 Patrick Roy .30 .75
(Montreal Canadiens TC)
318 Pierre Turgeon .07 .20
(Buffalo Sabres TC)
319 Al MacInnis TC .07 .20
320 Ray Bourque TC .07 .20
321 Mark Messier .07 .20
(Edmonton Oilers TC)
322 Jody Hull RC .02 .10
323 Chris Joseph .02 .10
324 Adam Burt RC .02 .10
325 Jason Herter RC .02 .10
326 Geoff Smith ART .02 .10
327 Brad Shaw ART .02 .10
328 Rich Sutter .02 .10
329 Barry Pederson .02 .10
330 Paul MacLean .02 .10
331 Randy Carlyle .02 .10
332 Donald Dufresne .02 .10
333 Brent Hughes RC .02 .10
334 Mathieu Schneider RC .02 .10
335 Jason Miller .02 .10
336 Sergei Makarov ART .02 .10
337 Bob Essensa ART .07 .20
338 Claude Loiselle .02 .10
339 Wayne Presley .02 .10
340 Tony McKegney .02 .10
341 Charlie Huddy .02 .10
342 Greg Adams UER .02 .10
(Front photo actually Igor Larionov)
343 Mike Tomlak .02 .10
344 Adam Graves RC .30 .75
345 Michel Mongeau RC .02 .10
346 Mike Modano UER ART .07 .20
('89 Entry Draft should say '88)
347 Rod Brind'Amour ART .07 .20
348 Dana Murzyn .02 .10
349 Dave Lowry RC .02 .10
350 Star Rookie CL .02 .10
351 First Four Picks .20 .50
Owen Nolan
Keith Primeau
Petr Nedved
Mike Ricci
Top Ten Draft Pick CL
352 Owen Nolan FDP RC .40 1.00
353 Petr Nedved RC .20 .50
354 Keith Primeau RC .40 1.00
355 Mike Ricci RC UER .25 .60
(Born October& not November 27)
356 Jaromir Jagr RC 1.25 3.00
357 Scott Scissons RC .02 .10
358 Darryl Sydor RC .20 .50
359 Derian Hatcher RC .02 .10
360 John Slaney RC .02 .10
361 Drake Berehowsky RC .02 .10
362 Luke Richardson .02 .10
363 Lucien DeBlois .02 .10
364 Dave Reid RC .02 .10
365 Mats Sundin RC .75 2.00
366 Jan Erixon .02 .10
367 Troy Loney .02 .10
368 Chris Nilan .02 .10
369 Gord Dineen .02 .10
370 Jeff Bloemberg .02 .10
371 John Druce .02 .10
372 Brian MacLellan .02 .10
373 Bruce Driver .02 .10
374 Marc Habscheid .02 .10
375 Paul Ysebaert RC .02 .10
376 Rick Vaive .02 .10
377 Glen Wesley .02 .10
378 Mike Foligno .02 .10
379 Garry Galley RC .02 .10
380 Dean Kennedy .02 .10
381 Daniel Berthiaume .07 .20
382 Mike Keane RC .02 .10
383 Frank Musil .02 .10
384 Mike McPhee .02 .10
385 Jon Casey .07 .20
386 Jeff Norton .02 .10
387 John Tucker .02 .10
388 Alan Kerr .02 .10

389 Bob Rouse .02 .10
390 Gerald Diduck .02 .10
391 Greg Hawgood .02 .10
392 Randy Velischek .02 .10
393 Tim Cheveldae RC .07 .20
394 Mike Krushelnyski .02 .10
395 Glen Hanlon .07 .20
396 Lou Franceschetti .02 .10
397 Scott Arniel .02 .10
398 Terry Carkner .02 .10
399 Clint Malarchuk .07 .20
400 Checklist 301-400 .02 .10
401 Mikhail Tatarinov RC .02 .10
402 Benoit Hogue .02 .10
403 Frank Pietrangelo .07 .20
404 Paul Stanton .02 .10
405 Anatoli Semenov RC .02 .10
406 Bobby Smith .07 .20
407 Derek King .02 .10
408 J.C. Bergeron RC .02 .10
409 Brian Propp .02 .10
410 Jiri Latal .02 .10
411 Joey Kocur RC .25 .60
412 Daniel Berthiaume .07 .20
413 Dave Ellett .02 .10
414 Jay Miller RC .02 .10
415 Stephane Beauregard RC .07 .20
416 Mark Hardy .02 .10
417 Todd Krygier .02 .10
418 Randy Moller .02 .10
419 Doug Crossman .02 .10
420 Ray Sheppard .07 .20
421 Sylvain Lefebvre .02 .10
422 Chris Chelios .15 .40
423 Joe Mullen .07 .20
424 Pete Peeters .07 .20
425 Bryan Trottier .07 .20
426 Denis Savard .07 .20
427 Ken Daneyko .02 .10
428 Eric Desjardins RC .20 .50
429 Zdeno Ciger RC .02 .10
430 Brad McCrimmon .02 .10
431 Ed Olczyk .02 .10
432 Peter Ing .07 .20
433 Bob Kudelski RC .02 .10
434 Troy Gamble RC .07 .20
435 Phil Housley .07 .20
436 Scott Stevens .07 .20
437 Normand Rochefort .02 .10
438 Geoff Courtnall .02 .10
439 Ken Baumgartner .02 .10
440 Kris King RC .02 .10
441 Troy Crowder RC .02 .10
442 Chris Nilan .02 .10
443 Dale Hawerchuk .07 .20
444 Kevin Miller RC .02 .10
445 Keith Acton .02 .10
446 Jeff Chychrun .02 .10
447 Claude Lemieux .02 .10
448 Bob Probert .07 .20
449 Brian Hayward .07 .20
450 Craig Berube .02 .10
451 Team Canada .15 .40
452 Mike Sillinger RC .02 .10
453 Jason Marshall RC .02 .10
454 Patrice Brisebois RC .02 .10
455 Brad May RC .07 .20
456 Pierre Sevigny RC .02 .10
457 John Slaney .02 .10
458 Felix Potvin RC .75 2.00
459 Scott Thornton RC .08 .25
460 Greg Johnson RC .02 .10
461 Scott Niedermayer RC .40 1.00
462 Steven Rice RC .02 .10
463 Trevor Kidd RC .40 1.00
464 Dale Craigwell RC .02 .10
465 Kent Manderville RC .02 .10
466 Kris Draper RC .40 1.00
467 Martin Lapointe RC .40 1.00
468 Chris Snell RC .02 .10
469 Pat Falloon RC .02 .10
470 David Harlock RC .02 .10
471 Karl Dykhuis RC .02 .10
472 Mike Craig RC .02 .10
473 Canada's Captains .75 2.00
Kris Draper
Steven Rice
Eric Lindros
474 Brett Hull AS .15 .40
475 Darren Turcotte AS .02 .10
476 Wayne Gretzky AS .40 1.00
477 Steve Yzerman AS .30 .75
478 Theo Fleury AS .02 .10
479 Pat LaFontaine AS .07 .20
480 Trevor Linden AS .07 .20
481 Jeremy Roenick AS .15 .40
482 Scott Stevens AS .07 .20
483 Adam Oates AS .07 .20
484 Vincent Damphousse AS .02 .10
485 Brian Leetch AS .15 .40
486 Kevin Hatcher AS .02 .10
487 Mark Recchi AS .07 .20
488 Rick Tocchet AS .07 .20
489 Ray Bourque AS .07 .20
490 Joe Sakic AS .20 .50
491 Chris Chelios AS .07 .20
492 John Cullen AS .02 .10
493 Cam Neely AS .07 .20
494 Mark Messier AS .15 .40
495 Mike Vernon AS .07 .20
496 Patrick Roy AS .30 .75
497 Al MacInnis AS .07 .20
498 Paul Coffey AS .07 .20
499 Steve Larmer AS .07 .20
500 Checklist 401-500 .02 .10
501 Heroes Checklist .02 .10
502 Red Kelly HERO .02 .10
503 Eric Nesterenko HERO .02 .10
504 Darryl Sittler HERO .02 .10
505 Jim Schoenfeld HERO .02 .10
506 Serge Savard HERO .02 .10
507 Glenn Resch HERO .07 .20
508 Lanny McDonald HERO .02 .10
509 Bobby Clarke HERO .07 .20
510 Phil Esposito HERO .07 .20
511 Harry Howell HERO .02 .10
512 Rod Gilbert HERO .02 .10
513 Pit Martin HERO .02 .10
514 Jimmy Watson HERO .02 .10
515 Denis Potvin HERO .02 .10
516 Robert Ray RC .20 .50
517 Danton Cole RC .02 .10
518 Gino Odjick RC .02 .10
519 Donald Audette RC .20 .50
520 Rick Tabaracci RC .07 .20
521 Sergei Fedorov .30 .75
Johan Garpenlov
(Young Guns Checklist)
522 Kip Miller YG RC .02 .10
523 Johan Garpenlov YG RC .02 .10
524 Stephane Morin YG RC .02 .10
525 Sergei Fedorov YG RC UER 1.25 3.00
(Birthplace listed
as Pskow should be
Appatity)
526 Pavel Bure YG RC 1.50 4.00
527 Wes Walz YG RC .02 .10
528 Robert Kron YG RC .02 .10
529 Ken Hodge Jr. YG RC .02 .10
530 Garry Valk YG RC .02 .10
531 Tim Sweeney YG RC .02 .10
532 Mark Pederson YG .02 .10
533 Robert Reichel YG RC .15 .40
534 Bobby Holik YG RC .20 .50
535 Stephane Matteau YG RC .02 .10
536 Peter Bondra YG RC .60 1.50
537 Dimitri Khristich RC .02 .10
538 Vladimir Ruzicka RC .02 .10
539 Al Iafrate .07 .20
540 Rick Bennett .02 .10
541 Daryl Reaugh RC .02 .10
542 Martin Hostak .02 .10
543 Kari Takko .07 .20
544 Jocelyn Lemieux .02 .10
545 Gretzky's 2000th Point .40 1.00
546 Hull's 50 Goals .15 .40
547 Neil Wilkinson RC .02 .10
548 Bryan Fogarty .02 .10
549 Zamboni Machine .07 .20
550 Checklist 501-550 .02 .10

1990-91 Upper Deck Holograms

The nine standard-size cards in this set were randomly inserted in 1990-91 Upper Deck foil packs (low and high series). The cards are best described as stereograms because the players show movement when the cards are slowly rotated. On the fronts, the stereograms are enclosed by a frame with rounded corners. The Upper Deck logo and title line "Hockey Superstars" appear in a bar at the top. The backs are blank and can be peeled off to stick the stereogram on a surface. The cards are unnumbered and checklisted below in alphabetical order.

COMPLETE SET (9) 4.00 10.00
1 Wayne Gretzky .80 2.00
Stopping
2 Wayne Gretzky .80 2.00
Shooting
3 Wayne Gretzky .80 2.00
Standing
4 Brett Hull .30 .75
5 Mark Messier .30 .75
6 Mark Messier and .30 .75
Brett Hull
7 Mark Messier and .40 1.00
Steve Yzerman
8 Steve Yzerman .40 1.00
9 Steve Yzerman .40 1.00

1990-91 Upper Deck Promos

The 1990-91 Upper Deck Promo set is a two-card set featuring Wayne Gretzky and Patrick Roy both numbered as card number 241. The cards were first handed out as samples at the 1990 National Sports Collectors Convention in Arlington. The Arlington National promos were issued as a set in a special screw-down holder commemorating the National; these sets are much more limited and are rarely offered for sale. The photos on the front and back of both of the cards were changed in the regular set, as were the card numbers.

COMPLETE SET (2) 20.00 50.00
241A Wayne Gretzky UER 8.00 20.00
(Wrong height, feet
and inches reversed)
241B Patrick Roy UER 6.00 15.00
(Wrong height, feet
and inches reversed)

1990-91 Upper Deck Sheets

As an advertising promotion, Upper Deck produced hockey commemorative sheets that were given away during the 1990-91 season at selected games in large arenas. Each sheet measures 8 1/2" by 11" and is printed on card stock. The fronts of the team commemorative sheets feature the team logo and a series of Upper Deck cards of star players on that team. Some of these sheets have a brief history of the team, which is tied in with an Upper Deck advertisement. The All-Star game sheet is distinguished by a hockey stick facsimile autographed by those All-Star players whose cards are displayed. All the sheets have an Upper Deck stamp indicating the production quota; in addition, some of the sheets have the serial number. The backs are blank. The sheets are listed below in chronological order.

COMPLETE SET (11) 64.00 160.00
1 Toronto Maple Leafs 10.00 25.00
vs. Detroit Red Wings
Nov. 17, 1990 (20,000)
Al Iafrate
Ed Olczyk
Vincent Damphousse
Wendel Clark
Gary Leeman
Drake Berehowsky
2 Detroit Red Wings I 6.00 15.00
vs. Boston Bruins
Dec. 4, 1990 (22,000)
Keith Primeau
Shawn Burr
Steve Yzerman
Jimmy Carson
Tim Cheveldae
Steve Chiasson
3 Los Angeles Kings 6.00 15.00
vs. Calgary Flames
Dec. 13, 1990 (19,500)
Steve Duchesne
Luc Robitaille
Rob Blake
Wayne Gretzky
Tony Granato
Tomas Sandstrom
4 New York Rangers I 4.00 10.00
vs. Hartford Whalers
Jan. 13, 1991 (25,700)
Mike Richter
Ray Sheppard
Troy Mallette
Normand Rochefort
Mark Janssens
Dennis Vial
John Ogrodnick
Lindy Ruff
Brian Leetch
5 New York Rangers II 4.80 12.00
vs. Chicago Blackhawks
Jan. 17, 1991 (25,700)
David Shaw
Miloslav Horava
Darren Turcotte
Jan Erixon
Kelly Kisio
Brian Mullen
Bernie Nicholls
John Vanbiesbrouck
James Patrick
6 Campbell All-Stars 12.00 30.00
Chicago Stadium
Jan. 19, 1991 (15,100)
Wayne Gretzky
Chris Chelios
Luc Robitaille
Brett Hull
Al MacInnis
Mike Vernon
7 Wales All-Stars 10.00 25.00
Chicago Stadium
Jan. 19, 1991 (15,100)
Ray Bourque
Rick Tocchet
Joe Sakic
Paul Coffey
Cam Neely
Patrick Roy
8 St. Louis Blues 4.00 10.00
vs. Buffalo Sabres
Jan. 29, 1991 (21,000)
Jeff Brown
Vincent Riendeau
Brent Hull
Paul Cavallini
Curtis Joseph
Gino Cavallini
Adam Oates
Scott Stevens
Rod Brind'Amour
9 Detroit Red Wings II 4.80 12.00
vs. Minnesota North Stars
Feb. 16, 1991 (23,000)
Joey Kocur
Rick Zombo
Sergei Fedorov
Gerard Gallant
Johan Garpenlov
Glen Hanlon
Dave Barr
John Chabot
Bob Probert
10 New York Rangers III 4.00 10.00
vs. New York Islanders
Feb. 18, 1991 (25,700)
Tie Domi
Randy Moller
Mike Gartner
Kevin Miller
Mark Hardy
Jody Hull
Kris King
Bob Froese
Paul Broten
11 All-Rookie Team 8.00 20.00
June 21, 1991 (16,000)
Eric Weinrich
Jaromir Jagr
Ed Belfour
Sergei Fedorov
Rob Blake
Ken Hodge

1991-92 Upper Deck

The 1991-92 UD set was released in two series of 500 and 200 cards, respectively. The front design features action photos with white borders. The player's name and position appear in the top white border, while the team name is given in the bottom white border. Biographical information, statistics, or player profile are displayed on the back alongside a second color photo. The All-Rookie Team and the Star Rookies are marked by the abbreviations ART and SR respectively in the list below. A randomly inserted Glasnost card (SP1) featuring Wayne Gretzky, Brett Hull and Valeri Kamensky and ballots by which fans could vote for their favorite NHL All-Stars were included in foil packs. Special subsets include members of the teams that participated in the IIHF World Junior Championships (650--699).

COMPLETE SET (700) 20.00 40.00
COMPLETE LO SET (500) 15.00 25.00
COMPLETE HI SET (200) 5.00 10.00
COMP.HI FACT.SET (200) 6.00 12.00
*FRENCH: SAME VALUE
1 Vladimir Malakhov SS RC .08 .25
2 Alexei Zhamnov SS RC .20 .50
3 Dimitri Filiminov SS RC .01 .05
4 Alexander Semak SS RC .01 .05
5 Slava Kozlov SS RC .20 .50
6 Sergei Fedorov SS .08 .25
7 Canada Cup Checklist .30 .75
Eric Lindros and
Brett Hull
8 Al MacInnis CC .01 .05
9 Eric Lindros CC .08 .25
10 Bill Ranford CC .04 .10
11 Paul Coffey CC .05 .15
12 Dale Hawerchuk CC .01 .05
13 Wayne Gretzky CC .40 1.00
14 Mark Messier CC .08 .25
15 Steve Larmer CC .01 .05
16 Zigmund Palffy CC RC .75 2.00
17 Josef Beranek CC RC .01 .05
18 Jiri Slegr CC RC .05 .15
19 Martin Rucinsky CC RC .10 .30
20 Jaromir Jagr CC .08 .25
21 Teemu Selanne CC RC 1.25 3.00
22 Janne Laukkanen CC RC .01 .05
23 Markus Ketterer CC RC .01 .05
24 Jari Kurri CC .05 .15
25 Janne Ojanen CC .01 .05
26 Nicklas Lidstrom CC RC 1.00 2.50
27 Tomas Forslund CC RC .01 .05
28 Johan Garpenlov CC .01 .05
29 Niclas Andersson CC RC .01 .05
30 Tomas Sandstrom CC .01 .05
31 Mats Sundin CC .08 .25
32 Mike Modano CC .08 .25
33 Brett Hull CC .08 .25
34 Mike Richter CC .05 .15
35 Brian Leetch CC .05 .15
36 Jeremy Roenick CC .10 .30
37 Chris Chelios CC .05 .15
38 Wayne Gretzky 99 .40 1.00
39 Ed Belfour ART .08 .25
40 Sergei Fedorov ART .08 .25
41 Ken Hodge Jr. ART .01 .05
42 Jaromir Jagr ART .08 .25
43 Rob Blake ART .01 .05
44 Eric Weinrich ART .01 .05
45 The 50/50 Club .40 1.00
Mario Lemieux
Wayne Gretzky
Brett Hull
46 Russ Romaniuk RC .01 .05
47 Mario Lemieux/Geo.Bush .40 1.00
48 Michel Picard RC .01 .05
49 Dennis Vaske .01 .05
50 Eric Murano .01 .05
51 Enrico Ciccone .01 .05
52 Shaun Van Allen RC .01 .05
53 Stu Barnes .01 .05
54 Pavel Bure .08 .25
55 Neil Wilkinson .01 .05
56 Tony Hrkac .01 .05
57 Brian Mullen .01 .05
58 Jeff Hackett .05 .15
59 Brian Hayward .05 .15
60 Craig Coxe .01 .05
61 Rob Zettler .01 .05
62 Bob McGill .01 .05
63 Draft Picks Checklist .05 .15
(Martin Lapointe
and Jamie Pushor)
64 Peter Forsberg RC 2.00 5.00
65 Patrick Poulin RC .01 .05
66 Martin Lapointe .05 .15
67 Tyler Wright RC .01 .05
68 Philippe Boucher RC .01 .05
69 Glen Murray RC .40 1.00
70 Martin Rucinsky RC .10 .30
71 Zigmund Palffy RC .75 2.00
72 Jassen Cullimore RC .01 .05
73 Jamie Pushor RC .01 .05
74 Andrew Verner RC .01 .05
75 Jason Dawe RC .01 .05
76 Jamie Matthews RC .01 .05
77 Sandy McCarthy RC .10 .30
78 Cam Neely .05 .15
(Boston Bruins TC)
79 Dale Hawerchuk .01 .05
(Buffalo Sabres TC)
80 Theoren Fleury .01 .05
(Calgary Flames TC)
81 Ed Belfour .08 .25
(Chicago Blackhawks TC)
82 Sergei Fedorov .08 .25
(Detroit Red Wings TC)
83 Esa Tikkanen .01 .05
(Edmonton Oilers TC)
84 John Cullen .01 .05
(Hartford Whalers TC)
85 Tomas Sandstrom .01 .05
(Los Angeles Kings TC)
86 Dave Gagner .01 .05
(Minnesota North Stars TC)
87 Russ Courtnall .01 .05
(Montreal Canadiens TC)
88 John MacLean .01 .05
(New Jersey Devils TC)
89 David Volek .01 .05
(New York Islanders TC)
90 Darren Turcotte .01 .05
(New York Rangers TC)
91 Rick Tocchet .01 .05
(Philadelphia Flyers TC)
92 Mark Recchi .05 .15
(Pittsburgh Penguins TC)
93 Mats Sundin .08 .25
(Quebec Nordiques TC)
94 Adam Oates .01 .05
(St. Louis Blues TC)
95 Neil Wilkinson .01 .05
(San Jose Sharks TC)
96 Dave Ellett .01 .05
(Toronto Maple Leafs TC)
97 Trevor Linden .01 .05
(Vancouver Canucks TC)
98 Kevin Hatcher .01 .05
(Washington Capitals TC)
99 Ed Olczyk .01 .05
(Winnipeg Jets TC)
100 Checklist 1-100 .01 .05
101 Bob Essensa .05 .15
102 Uwe Krupp .01 .05
103 Pelle Eklund .01 .05
104 Christian Ruuttu .01 .05
105 Kevin Dineen .01 .05
106 Phil Housley .05 .15
107 Pat Jablonski RC .05 .15
108 Jarmo Kekalainen .01 .05
109 Pat Elynuik .01 .05
110 Corey Millen RC .01 .05
111 Petr Klima .01 .05
112 Mike Ridley .01 .05
113 Peter Stastny .05 .15
114 Jyrki Lumme .01 .05
115 Chris Terreri .05 .15
116 Tom Barrasso .05 .15
117 Bill Ranford .05 .15
118 Peter Ing .05 .15
119 John Tanner .01 .05
120 Troy Gamble .05 .15
121 Stephane Matteau .01 .05
122 Rick Tocchet .05 .15
123 Wes Walz .01 .05
124 Dave Andreychuk .05 .15
125 Mike Craig .01 .05
126 Dale Hawerchuk .05 .15
127 Dean Evason .01 .05
128 Craig Janney .05 .15
129 Tim Cheveldae .05 .15
130 Rick Wamsley .05 .15
131 Peter Bondra .05 .15
132 Scott Stevens .05 .15
133 Kelly Miller .01 .05
134 Mats Sundin .08 .25
135 Mick Vukota .01 .05
136 Vincent Damphousse .01 .05
137 Patrick Roy .50 1.25
138 Hubie McDonough .01 .05
139 Curtis Joseph .08 .25
140 Brent Sutter .01 .05
141 Tomas Sandstrom .01 .05
142 Kevin Miller .01 .05
143 Mike Ricci .08 .25
144 Sergei Fedorov .20 .50
145 Luc Robitaille .05 .15
146 Steve Yzerman .50 1.25
147 Andy Moog .08 .25
148 Rob Blake .05 .15
149 Kirk Muller .01 .05
150 Daniel Berthiaume .05 .15
151 John Druce .01 .05
152 Garry Valk .01 .05
153 Brian Leetch .08 .25
154 Kevin Stevens .01 .05
155 Darren Turcotte .01 .05
156 Mario Lemieux .50 1.25
157 Dimitri Khristich .01 .05
158 Brian Glynn .01 .05
159 Benoit Hogue UER .01 .05
(Back photo act-
ually Dean Kennedy)
160 Mike Modano .25 .60
161 Jimmy Carson .01 .05
162 Steve Thomas .01 .05
163 Mike Vernon .05 .15
164 Ed Belfour .25 .60
165 Joel Otto .01 .05
166 Jeremy Roenick .10 .30
167 Johan Garpenlov .01 .05
168 Russ Courtnall .01 .05
169 John MacLean .05 .15
170 J.J. Daigneault .01 .05
171 Sylvain Lefebvre .01 .05
172 Tony Granato .01 .05
173 David Volek .01 .05
174 Trevor Linden .05 .15
175 Mike Richter .08 .25
176 Pierre Turgeon .05 .15
177 Paul Coffey .08 .25
178 Jan Erixon .01 .05
179 Rick Vaive .01 .05
180 Dave Gagner .01 .05
181 Thomas Steen .01 .05
182 Esa Tikkanen .01 .05
183 Sean Burke .05 .15
184 Paul Cavallini .01 .05
185 Alexei Kasatonov .01 .05
186 Kevin Lowe .05 .15
187 Gino Cavallini .01 .05
188 Doug Gilmour .05 .15
189 Rod Brind'Amour .08 .25
190 Gary Roberts .05 .15
191 Kirk McLean .05 .15
192 Kevin Haller RC .01 .05
193 Pat Verbeek .01 .05
194 Dave Snuggerud .01 .05
195 Gino Odjick .01 .05
196 Dave Ellett .01 .05
197 Don Beaupre .05 .15
198 Rob Brown .01 .05
199 Marty McSorley .01 .05
200 Checklist 101-200 .01 .05
201 Joe Mullen .05 .15
202 Dave Capuano .01 .05
203 Paul Stanton .01 .05
204 Terry Carkner .01 .05
205 Jon Casey .05 .15
206 Ken Wregget .05 .15
207 Gaetan Duchesne .01 .05
208 Cliff Ronning .01 .05
209 Dale Hunter .01 .05
210 Danton Cole .01 .05
211 Jeff Brown .01 .05
212 Mike Foligno .01 .05
213 Michel Mongeau .01 .05
214 Doug Brown .01 .05
215 Todd Krygier .01 .05
216 Jon Morris .01 .05
217 David Reid .01 .05
218 John McIntyre .01 .05
219 Guy Lafleur's Farewell .08 .25
220 Vincent Riendeau .05 .15
221 Tim Hunter .01 .05
222 Dave McLlwain .01 .05
223 Robert Reichel .01 .05
224 Glenn Healy .05 .15
225 Robert Kron .01 .05
226 Pat Flatley .01 .05
227 Petr Nedved .05 .15
228 Mark Janssens .01 .05
229 Michal Pivonka .01 .05
230 Ulf Samuelsson .01 .05
231 Zarley Zalapski .01 .05
232 Neal Broten .01 .05
233 Bobby Holik .05 .15
234 Cam Neely .08 .25
235 John Cullen .01 .05
236 Brian Bellows .01 .05
237 Chris Nilan .01 .05
238 Mikael Andersson .01 .05
239 Bob Probert .05 .15
240 Teppo Numminen .01 .05
241 Peter Zezel .01 .05
242 Denis Savard .05 .15
243 Al MacInnis .05 .15
244 Stephane Richer .01 .05
245 Theo Fleury .01 .05
246 Mark Messier .08 .25
247 Mike Gartner .05 .15
248 Daren Puppa .05 .15
249 Louie DeBrusk RC .01 .05
250 Glenn Anderson .05 .15
251 Ken Hodge Jr. .01 .05
252 Adam Oates .05 .15
253 Pat LaFontaine .08 .25
254 Adam Creighton .01 .05
255 Ray Bourque .20 .50
256 Jaromir Jagr .20 .50
257 Steve Larmer .05 .15
258 Keith Primeau .01 .05
259 Mike Liut .05 .15
260 Brian Propp .01 .05
261 Stephan Lebeau .01 .05
262 Kelly Hrudey .05 .15
263 Joe Nieuwendyk .05 .15
264 Grant Fuhr .08 .25
265 Guy Carbonneau .05 .15
266 Martin Gelinas .01 .05
267 Alexander Mogilny .08 .25
268 Adam Graves .05 .15
269 Anatoli Semenov .01 .05
270 Dave Taylor .05 .15
271 Dirk Graham .01 .05
272 Gary Leeman .01 .05
273 Valeri Kamensky RC .05 .15
274 Marc Bureau .01 .05
275 James Patrick .01 .05
276 Dino Ciccarelli .05 .15
277 Ron Tugnutt .05 .15
278 Paul Ysebaert .01 .05
279 Laurie Boschman .01 .05
280 Dave Manson .01 .05
281 Dave Chyzowski .01 .05
282 Shayne Corson .01 .05
283 Steve Chiasson .01 .05
284 Craig MacTavish .01 .05
285 Petr Svoboda .01 .05
286 Craig Simpson .01 .05
287 Ron Hoover .01 .05
288 Vladimir Ruzicka .01 .05
289 Randy Wood .01 .05
290 Doug Lidster .01 .05
291 Kay Whitmore .05 .15
292 Bruce Driver .01 .05
293 Bobby Smith .05 .15
294 Claude Lemieux .01 .05
295 Mark Tinordi .01 .05
296 Mark Osborne .01 .05
297 Brad Shaw .01 .05
298 Igor Larionov .01 .05
299 Ron Francis .05 .15
300 Checklist 201-300 .01 .05
301 Bob Kudelski .01 .05
302 Larry Murphy .05 .15
303 Brent Ashton .01 .05
304 Brad Jones .01 .05
305 Gord Donnelly .01 .05
306 Murray Craven .01 .05
307 Chris Dahlquist .01 .05
308 Jim Paek RC .01 .05
309 Ron Sutter .01 .05
310 Mike Tomlak .01 .05
311 Ray Ferraro .01 .05
312 Dave Hannan .01 .05
313 Randy McKay .01 .05
314 Rod Langway .01 .05
315 Shawn Burr .01 .05
316 Calle Johansson .01 .05
317 Rich Sutter .01 .05
318 Al Iafrate .05 .15
319 Bob Bassen .01 .05
320 Mike Krushelnyski .01 .05
321 Sergei Makarov .01 .05
322 Darrin Shannon .01 .05
323 Terry Yake .01 .05
324 John Vanbiesbrouck .05 .15
325 Peter Sidorkiewicz .05 .15
326 Troy Mallette .01 .05
327 Ron Hextall .05 .15
328 Mathieu Schneider .01 .05
329 Bryan Trottier .08 .25
330 Kris King .01 .05
331 Daniel Marois .01 .05
332 Shayne Stevenson .01 .05
333 Joe Sakic .25 .60
334 Petri Skriko .01 .05
335 Dominik Hasek RC 1.25 3.00
336 Scott Pearson .01 .05
337 Bryan Fogarty .01 .05
338 Don Sweeney .01 .05
339 Rick Tabaracci .05 .15
340 Steven Finn .01 .05
341 Gary Suter .01 .05
342 Troy Crowder .01 .05
343 Jim Hrivnak .05 .15
344 Eric Weinrich .01 .05
345 John LeClair RC .40 1.00
346 Mark Recchi .08 .25
347 Dan Currie RC .01 .05
348 Ulf Dahlen .01 .05
349 Robert Ray .01 .05
350 Steve Smith .01 .05
351 Shawn Antoski .01 .05
352 Cam Russell .01 .05
353 Scott Thornton .01 .05
354 Chris Chelios .08 .25
355 Sergei Nemchinov .01 .05
356 Bernie Nicholls .05 .15
357 Jeff Norton .01 .05
358 Dan Quinn .01 .05
359 Michel Petit .01 .05
360 Eric Desjardins .05 .15
361 Kevin Hatcher .01 .05
362 Jiri Sejba .01 .05
363 Mark Pederson .01 .05
364 Jeff Lazaro .01 .05
365 Alexei Gusarov RC .05 .15
366 Jari Kurri .08 .25
367 Owen Nolan .08 .25
368 Clint Malarchuk .05 .15
369 Patrik Sundstrom .01 .05
370 Glen Wesley .01 .05
371 Wayne Presley .01 .05
372 Craig Muni .01 .05
373 Brent Fedyk .01 .05
374 Michel Goulet .05 .15
375 Tim Sweeney .01 .05
376 Gary Shuchuk .01 .05
377 Andre Racicot RC .05 .15
378 Jay Mazur .01 .05
379 Andrew Cassels .01 .05
380 Brian Noonan .01 .05
381 Sergei Kharin .01 .05
382 Derek King .01 .05
383 Fredrik Olausson .01 .05
384 Tom Fergus .01 .05
385 Zdeno Ciger .01 .05
386 Wendel Clark .05 .15
387 Ed Olczyk .01 .05
388 Basil McRae .01 .05
389 Tom Fitzgerald .01 .05
390 Ray Sheppard .05 .15
391 Bob Sweeney .01 .05
392 Gord Murphy .01 .05
393 John Chabot .01 .05
394 Jeff Beukeboom .01 .05
395 Rick Zombo .01 .05
396 Kjell Samuelsson .01 .05
397 Garth Butcher .01 .05
398 Phil Bourque .01 .05
399 Lou Franceschetti .01 .05
400 Checklist 301-400 .01 .05
401 Kevin Todd RC .05 .15
402 Ken Baumgartner .01 .05
403 Peter Douris .01 .05
404 Jiri Latal .01 .05
405 Marc Potvin RC .01 .05
406 Gary Nylund .01 .05
407 Yvon Corriveau .01 .05
408 Sheldon Kennedy .01 .05
409 David Shaw .01 .05
410 Slava Fetisov .01 .05
411 Mario Doyon .01 .05
412 Jamie Macoun .01 .05
413 Curtis Leschyshyn .01 .05
414 Mike Peluso RC .01 .05
415 Brian Benning .01 .05
416 Stu Grimson RC .05 .15
417 Ken Sabourin .01 .05
418 Luke Richardson .01 .05
419 Ken Quinney .01 .05
420 Mike Donnelly RC .01 .05
421 Darcy Loewen .01 .05
422 Brian Skrudland .01 .05
423 Joel Savage .01 .05
424 Adrien Plavsic .01 .05
425 Jergus Baca .01 .05
426 Greg Adams .01 .05
427 Tom Chorske .01 .05
428 Scott Scissons .01 .05
429 Dale Kushner .01 .05
430 Todd Richards .01 .05
431 Kip Miller .01 .05
432 Jason Prosofsky .01 .05
433 Stephane Morin .01 .05

4 Brian McReynolds .01 .05
5 Ken Daneyko .01 .05
6 Chris Joseph .01 .05
7 Wayne Gretzky .60 1.50
8 Jocelyn Lemieux .01 .05
9 Garry Galley .01 .05
0 Super Rookie Checklist .30 .75
Tony Amonte&
Doug Weight&
and Steven Rice
1 Steven Rice SR .01 .05
2 Patrice Brisebois SR .01 .05
3 Jimmy Waite SR .05 .15
4 Doug Weight SR RC .40 1.00
5 Nelson Emerson SR .01 .05
6 Jarrod Skalde SR RC .01 .05
7 Jamie Leach SR .01 .05
8 Gilbert Dionne SR RC .05 .15
9 Trevor Kidd SR .05 .15
0 Tony Amonte SR RC .40 1.00
1 Pat Murray SR .01 .05
2 Stephane Fiset SR .05 .15
3 Patrick Lebeau SR RC .01 .05
4 Chris Taylor SR RC .01 .05
5 Chris Tancill SR RC .01 .05
6 Mark Greig SR .01 .05
7 Mike Sillinger SR .01 .05
8 Ken Sutton SR RC .01 .05
9 Len Barrie SR RC .01 .05
0 Felix Potvin SR .40 1.00
1 Brian Sakic SR RC .01 .05
2 Slava Kozlov SR RC .20 .50
3 Matt DelGuidice .01 .05
4 Brett Hull .20 .50
5 Norm Foster .01 .05
6 Alexander Godynyuk .01 .05
7 Geoff Courtnall .05 .15
8 Frantisek Kucera .01 .05
9 Benoit Brunet RC .01 .05
0 Mark Vermette .01 .05
1 Tim Watters .01 .05
2 Paul Ranheim .01 .05
3 Martin Hostak .01 .05
4 Joe Murphy .01 .05
5 Claude Boivin RC .01 .05
6 John Ogrodnick .01 .05
7 Doug Bodger .01 .05
8 Shawn Cronin .01 .05
9 Mark Hunter .01 .05
0 Dave Tippett .01 .05
1 Rob DiMaio .01 .05
2 Lyle Odelein .01 .05
3 Joe Reekie .01 .05
4 Randy Velischek .01 .05
5 Myles O'Connor .01 .05
6 Craig Wolanin .01 .05
7 Mike McPhee .01 .05
8 Claude Lapointe RC .01 .05
9 Troy Loney .01 .05
0 Bob Beers .01 .05
1 Sylvain Couturier .01 .05
2 Kimbi Daniels .01 .05
3 Darryl Shannon .01 .05
4 Jim McKenzie .01 .05
5 Don Gibson .01 .05
6 Ralph Barahona .01 .05
7 Murray Baron .01 .05
8 Yves Racine .01 .05
9 Larry Robinson .05 .15
0 Checklist 401-500 .01 .05
1 Canada Cup Checklist .40 1.00
Paul Coffey and
Wayne Gretzky
2 Dirk Graham CC .01 .05
3 Rick Tocchet CC .01 .05
4 Eric Desjardins CC .01 .05
5 Shayne Corson CC .01 .05
6 Theo Fleury CC .01 .05
7 Luc Robitaille CC .05 .15
8 Tony Granato CC .01 .05
9 Eric Weinrich CC .01 .05
0 Gary Suter CC .01 .05
1 Kevin Hatcher CC .01 .05
2 Craig Janney CC .01 .05
3 Darren Turcotte CC .01 .05
4 Chris Winnes RC .01 .05
5 Kelly Kisio .01 .05
6 Joe Day RC .01 .05
7 Ed Courtenay RC .01 .05
8 Andrei Lomakin .01 .05
9 Kirk Muller .01 .05
0 Rick Lessard .01 .05
1 Scott Thornton .01 .05
2 Luke Richardson .01 .05
3 Mike Eagles .01 .05
4 Mike McNeill .01 .05
5 Ken Priestlay .01 .05
6 Louie DeBrusk .01 .05
7 Dave McLlwain .01 .05
8 Gary Leeman .01 .05
9 Adam Foote RC .15 .40
0 Kevin Dineen .01 .05
1 David Reid .01 .05
2 Arturs Irbe .08 .25
3 Mark Osiecki RC .01 .05
4 Steve Thomas .01 .05
5 Vincent Damphousse .01 .05
6 Stephane Richer .05 .15
7 Jarmo Myllys .01 .05
8 Carey Wilson .01 .05
9 Scott Stevens .05 .15
0 Uwe Krupp .01 .05
1 Dave Christian .01 .05
2 Scott Mellanby .01 .05
3 Peter Ahola RC .01 .05
4 Todd Elik .01 .05
5 Mark Messier .15 .40
6 Derian Hatcher .05 .15
7 Rod Brind'Amour .08 .25
8 Dave Manson .01 .05
9 Darryl Sydor .05 .15
0 Paul Broten .01 .05
1 Andrew Cassels .01 .05
2 Tom Draper RC .05 .15
3 Grant Fuhr .08 .25
4 Pierre Turgeon .05 .15
5 Pavel Bure .08 .25
6 Pat LaFontaine .08 .25
7 Dave Thomlinson .01 .05
8 Doug Gilmour .05 .15
9 Craig Billington RC .05 .15

560 Dean Evason .01 .05
561 Brendan Shanahan .08 .25
562 Mike Hough .01 .05
563 Dan Quinn .01 .05
564 Jeff Daniels .01 .05
565 Troy Murray .01 .05
566 Bernie Nicholls .05 .15
567 Randy Burridge .01 .05
568 Todd Hartje RC .01 .05
569 Charlie Huddy .01 .05
570 Steve Duchesne .01 .05
571 Sergio Momesso .01 .05
572 Brian Lawton .01 .05
573 Ray Sheppard .01 .05
574 Adam Graves .05 .15
575 Rollie Melanson .05 .15
576 Steve Kasper .01 .05
577 Jim Sandlak .01 .05
578 Pat MacLeod RC .01 .05
579 Sylvain Turgeon .01 .05
580 James Black RC .01 .05
581 Darrin Shannon .01 .05
582 Todd Krygier .01 .05
583 Dominic Roussel RC .05 .15
584 Young Guns Checklist .20 .50
Nicklas Lidstrom
585 Donald Audette YG .01 .05
586 Tomas Forslund YG .01 .05
587 Nicklas Lidstrom YG .40 1.00
588 Geoff Sanderson YG RC .10 .25
589 Valeri Zelepukin YG RC .01 .05
590 Igor Ulanov YG RC .05 .15
591 Corey Foster YG RC .01 .05
592 Dan Lambert YG RC .01 .05
593 Pat Falloon YG .01 .05
594 Vladimir Konstantinov YG RC .40
1.00
595 Josef Beranek YG .01 .05
596 Brad May YG .01 .05
597 Jeff Odgers YG RC .01 .05
598 Rob Pearson YG RC .01 .05
599 Luciano Borsato YG RC .01 .05
600 Checklist 501-600 .01 .05
601 Peter Douris .01 .05
602 Mark Fitzpatrick .05 .15
603 Randy Gilhen .01 .05
604 Corey Millen .01 .05
605 Jason Cirone RC .01 .05
606 Kyosti Karjalainen RC .01 .05
607 Garry Galley .01 .05
608 Brent Thompson RC .01 .05
609 Alexander Godynyuk .01 .05
610 All-Star Checklist .08 .25
Mark Messier
Mike Richter
Brian Leetch
611 Mario Lemieux AS .40 .75
612 Brian Leetch AS .05 .15
613 Kevin Stevens AS .01 .05
614 Patrick Roy AS .30 .75
615 Paul Coffey AS .05 .15
616 Joe Sakic AS .08 .25
617 Jaromir Jagr AS .08 .25
618 Alexander Mogilny AS .05 .15
619 Owen Nolan AS .05 .15
620 Mark Messier AS .08 .25
621 Wayne Gretzky AS .40 1.00
622 Brett Hull AS .08 .25
623 Luc Robitaille AS .05 .15
624 Phil Housley AS .01 .05
625 Ed Belfour AS .08 .25
626 Steve Yzerman AS .25 .60
627 Adam Oates AS .01 .05
628 Trevor Linden AS .01 .05
629 Jeremy Roenick AS .10 .30
630 Theo Fleury AS .01 .05
631 Sergei Fedorov AS .08 .25
632 Al MacInnis AS .01 .05
633 Ray Bourque AS .08 .25
634 Mike Richter AS .05 .15
635 Al Secord HERO .05 .15
636 Marcel Dionne HERO .08 .25
637 Ken Morrow HERO .05 .15
638 Guy Lafleur HERO .08 .25
639 Ed Mio HERO .05 .15
640 Clark Gillies HERO .05 .15
641 Bob Nystrom HERO .05 .15
642 Pete Peeters HERO .05 .15
643 Ulf Nilsson HERO .05 .15
644 Stephan Lebeau and .01 .05
Patrick Lebeau
645 The Sutter Brothers .01 .05
Brian Sutter
Duane Sutter
Darryl Sutter
Brent Sutter
Rich Sutter
Ron Sutter
646 Gino Cavallini and .01 .05
Paul Cavallini
647 Valeri Bure .08 .25
and Pavel Bure
648 Chris Ferraro and .05 .15
Peter Ferraro
649 World Jr. Checklist .08 .25
CCCP Team Photo
650 Darius Kasparaitis RC .20 .50
651 Alexei Yashin RC .30 .75
652 Nikolai Khabibulin RC .75 2.00
653 Denis Metlyuk RC .01 .05
654 Konstantin Korotkov RC .01 .05
655 Alexei Kovalev RC .60 1.50
656 Alexander Kuzminsky RC .01 .05
657 Alexander Cherbayev RC .01 .05
658 Sergei Krivokrasov RC .05 .15
659 Sergei Zholtok RC .05 .15
660 Alexei Zhitnik RC .08 .25
661 Sandis Ozolinch RC .20 .50
662 Boris Mironov RC .08 .25
663 Pauli Jaks RC .05 .15
664 Gaetan Voisard RC .01 .05
665 Nicola Celio RC .01 .05
666 Marc Weber RC .01 .05
667 Bernhard Schumperli RC .01 .05
668 Laurent Bucher RC .01 .05
669 Michael Blaha RC .01 .05
670 Tiziano Gianini RC .01 .05
671 Marko Kiprusoff RC .05 .15
672 Janne Gronvall RC .01 .05
673 Juha Ylonen RC .08 .25
674 Sami Kapanen RC .40 1.00

675 Marko Tuomainen RC .01 .05
676 Jarkko Varvio RC .01 .05
677 Tuomas Gronman RC .01 .05
678 Andreas Naumann RC .01 .05
679 Steffen Ziesche RC .01 .05
680 Jens Schwabe RC .01 .05
681 Thomas Schubert RC .01 .05
682 Hans-Jorg Mayer RC .01 .05
683 Marc Seliger RC .08 .25
684 Trevor Kidd RC .05 .15
685 Martin Lapointe RC .08 .25
686 Tyler Wright RC .05 .15
687 Kimbi Daniels RC .01 .05
688 Karl Dykhuis RC .01 .05
689 Jeff Nelson RC .01 .05
690 Jassen Cullimore RC .01 .05
691 Turner Stevenson RC .01 .05
692 Scott Lachance RC .05 .15
693 Mike Dunham RC .40 1.00
694 Brent Bilodeau RC .01 .05
695 Ryan Sittler RC .01 .05
696 Peter Ferraro RC .08 .25
697 Pat Peake RC .01 .05
698 Keith Tkachuk RC .75 2.00
699 Brian Rolston RC .40 1.00
700 Checklist 601-700 .01 .05
SP1 Glasnost On Ice 1.50 4.00
Wayne Gretzky
Valeri Kamensky
Brett Hull

1991-92 Upper Deck Award Winner Holograms

This nine-card standard-size hologram set features award-winning hockey players with their respective trophies for most outstanding performance. The name of the award appears in the left border stripe, while the player's name and position are printed in the bottom border stripe. The backs have a color photo of the player with the trophy as well as biographical information. The holograms were randomly inserted into foil packs and subdivided into three groups: AW1-AW3 (low series); AW5-AW7 (late winter, low series); and AW4, AW8, and AW9 (high series). The holograms are numbered on the back with an "AW" prefix.

COMPLETE SET (9) 3.00 8.00
AW1 Wayne Gretzky 1.00 2.50
Art Ross Trophy
AW2 Ed Belfour .40 1.00
William M. Jennings
Trophy
AW3 Brett Hull .30 .75
Hart Trophy
AW4 Ed Belfour .40 1.00
Calder Trophy
AW5A Ray Bourque ERR .30 .75
Norris Trophy
(No best defenseman
notation on back)
AW5B Ray Bourque COR .30 .75
Norris Trophy
(Best defenseman
notation on back)
AW6 Wayne Gretzky 1.00 2.50
Lady Byng Trophy
AW7 Ed Belfour .40 1.00
Vezina Trophy
AW8 Dirk Graham .05 .10
Frank J. Selke Trophy
AW9 Mario Lemieux .75 2.00

1991-92 Upper Deck Box Bottoms

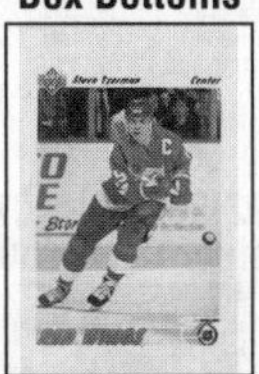

These five box bottoms are printed on glossy cover stock and measure approximately 5 1/2" by 9". Though they were issued with both French and English hockey sets, the New York Rangers' Mark Messier box bottom was available only with the high series. Each bottom features a four-color action photo enclosed by white borders. The Upper Deck logo, player's name, and position appear above the photo while the team name and the 75th NHL Anniversary logo appear beneath the picture superimposed on small black lines. The box bottoms are unnumbered and checklisted below alphabetically.

COMPLETE SET (5) 2.00 5.00
1 Wayne Gretzky .80 2.00
2 Brett Hull .24 .60
3 Mark Messier .24 .60
4 Mark Messier .40 1.00
5 Steve Yzerman .60 1.50

1991-92 Upper Deck Brett Hull Heroes

This ten-card standard-size set was inserted in 1991-92 Upper Deck low series foil packs (French as well as English editions). On a light gray textured background, the fronts have color player photos cut out and superimposed on an emblem. The textured background is enclosed by thin tan border stripes. On the same textured background, the backs summarize various moments in Hull's career. Brett Hull personally signed and numbered 2,500 of the checklist card number 9; these autographed cards were randomly inserted in packs. The signed cards are numbered by hand on the front.

COMMON HULL HEROES (1-9) .40 1.00
AU1 Brett Hull 25.00 60.00
(Certified autograph)
NNO Hull Header SP 2.00 5.00

1991-92 Upper Deck Euro-Stars

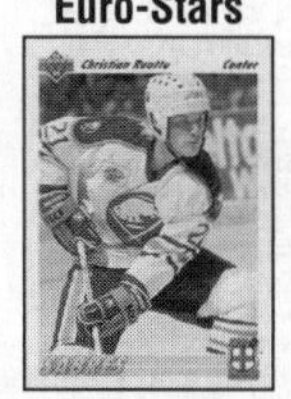

This 18-card standard-size set spotlights NHL players from Finland, the former Soviet Union, Czechoslovakia, and Sweden. One Euro-Star card was inserted in each 1991-92 Upper Deck Hockey jumbo pack in both English and French editions. The front design of the cards is the same as the regular issue except that a Euro-Stars emblem featuring a segment of the player's homeland flag, appears in the lower right corner. On a textured background, the backs present career summary.

*FRENCH VERSION: SAME VALUE
1 Jarmo Kekalainen .08 .25
2 Alexander Mogilny .30 .75
3 Bobby Holik .20 .50
4 Anatoli Semenov .08 .25
5 Petr Nedved .20 .50
6 Jaromir Jagr .60 1.50
7 Tomas Sandstrom .20 .50
8 Robert Kron .08 .25
9 Sergei Fedorov .60 1.50
10 Esa Tikkanen .20 .50
11 Christian Ruuttu .08 .25
12 Peter Bondra .30 .75
13 Mats Sundin .50 1.25
14 Dominik Hasek 1.25 3.00
15 Johan Garpenlov .08 .25
16 Alexander Godynyuk .08 .25
17 Ulf Samuelsson .08 .25
18 Igor Larionov .20 .50

1991-92 Upper Deck Sheets

For the second straight year, Upper Deck produced hockey commemorative sheets that were given away during the 1991-92 season at selected games in large arenas. Each sheet measures approximately 8 1/2" by 11" and is printed on card stock. The fronts of the team commemorative sheets feature the team logo and a series of Upper Deck cards of star players on that team. The Alumni sheet features player portraits by sports artist Alan Studt. All the sheets have an Upper Deck stamp indicating the production quota and the serial number. The backs are blank. The sheets are listed below in chronological order.

COMPLETE SET (19) 90.00 225.00
1 Los Angeles Kings 25th 6.00 15.00
vs. Edmonton Oilers
Oct. 8, 1991 (20,000)
Rob Blake
Jari Kurri
Tomas Sandstrom
Wayne Gretzky
Marty McSorley
Kelly Hrudey
2 New York Rangers I 4.00 10.00
vs. Calgary Flames
Nov. 4, 1991 (21,500)
Randy Moller
Paul Broten
Jody Hull
Jan Erixon
Mark Janssens
Brian Leetch
Mike Gartner
Joey Kocur
Mark Hardy
3 St. Louis Blues 4.00 10.00
vs. Philadelpha Flyers
Nov. 5, 1991 (21,500)
Adam Oates
Nelson Emerson
Paul Cavallini
Curtis Joseph
Brett Hull
Jeff Brown
4 New Jersey Devils 10th 4.00 10.00
vs. Chicago Blackhawks
Dec. 21, 1991 (24,000)
(New Jersey Devils
Tenth Anniversary)
Walt Poddubny
John MacLean
Scott Stevens
Peter Stastny
Claude Lemieux
Stephane Richer
5 Calgary Flames I 4.80 12.00
Tenth Annual Clinic
Dec. 27, 1991 (26,000)
Robert Reichel
Doug Gilmour
Theoren Fleury
Al MacInnis
Joel Otto
Gary Roberts
6 New York Rangers II 4.00 10.00
vs. St. Louis Blues
Jan. 8, 1992 (23,000)
Mike Richter
Kris King
Tie Domi
Tony Amonte
Mark Messier
Joe Cirella
James Patrick
Sergei Nemchinov
7 Philadelphia Flyers I 4.00 10.00
Alumni vs. NHL Heroes
Jan. 17, 1992 (21,000)
Bill Barber
Bill Clement
Keith Allen
Joe Watson
Bobby Clarke
Bernie Parent
8 Campbell All-Stars 10.00 25.00
Philadelphia Spectrum
Jan. 18, 1992 (13,500)
Brett Hull
Al MacInnis
Luc Robitaille
Chris Chelios
Wayne Gretzky
Ed Belfour
9 Wales All-Stars 10.00 25.00
Philadelphia Spectrum
Jan. 18, 1992 (13,500)
Mario Lemieux
Patrick Roy
Kevin Stevens
Paul Coffey
Jaromir Jagr
Ray Bourque
10 Detroit Red Wings I 4.80 12.00
vs. Toronto Maple Leafs
Feb. 7, 1992 (25,000)
Niklas Lidstrom
Steve Yzerman
Tim Cheveldae
Bob Probert
Steve Chiasson
Sergei Fedorov
11 Washington Capitals 4.00 10.00
vs. New York Rangers
Feb. 7, 1992 (20,500)
Kevin Hatcher
Dimitri Khristich
Calle Johansson
Michal Pivonka
Al Iafrate
Dino Ciccarelli
12 Minnesota North Stars 8.00 20.00
Dream Team
Feb.15, 1992 (19,000)
Brian Bellows
Neal Broten
Bill Goldsworthy
Curt Giles
Jon Casey
Craig Hartsburg
13 Pittsburgh Penguins 8.00 20.00
vs. Toronto Maple Leafs
Feb. 18, 1992 (21,000)
Kevin Stevens
Jaromir Jagr
Ulf Samuelsson
Tom Barrasso
Mark Recchi
Joe Mullen
14 New York Rangers III 4.00 10.00
vs. Philadelphia Flyers
Feb. 23, 1992 (23,000)
John Vanbiesbrouck
Kris King
Normand Rochefort
John Ogrodnick
Mark Messier
Jeff Beukeboom
Adam Graves
Darren Turcotte
15 Edmonton Oilers 4.80 12.00
vs. Philadelphia Flyers
Feb. 28, 1992 (22,000)
Kevin Lowe
Craig MacTavish
Esa Tikkanen
Bill Ranford
Craig Simpson
Vincent Damphousse
16 Minnesota North Stars 8.00 20.00
vs. Detroit Red Wings
March 14, 1992 (19,000)
Bobby Smith
Dave Gagner
Mike Modano
Ulf Dahlen
Mark Tinordi
Basil McRae
17 Calgary Flames II 4.80 12.00
vs. Minnesota North Stars
Eighth Fan
Appreciation Night
March 28, 1992 (24,000)
Mike Vernon
Joe Nieuwendyk
Gary Suter
Paul Ranheim
Sergei Makarov
Carey Wilson
18 Detroit Red Wings II 4.00 10.00
vs. Chicago Blackhawks
March 31, 1992 (25,000)
Paul Ysebaert
Yves Racine
Vladimir Konstantinov
Ray Sheppard
Kevin Miller
Jimmy Carson
19 Philadelphia Flyers II 4.00 10.00
April 5, 1992 (21,000)
Mike Ricci
Kevin Dineen
Garry Galley
Steve Duchesne
Rod Brind'Amour
Claude Boivin

1992-93 Upper Deck

The 1992-93 Upper Deck hockey set contains 640 standard-size cards. The set was released in two series of 440 and 200 cards, respectively. Action photos on the fronts are bordered by the player's name and team logo at the bottom. Special subsets featured include Team Checklists (1-24), Bloodlines (35-39), '92 World Juniors (222-236), Russian Stars from Moscow Dynamo (333-353), Rookie Report (354-368), '92 World Championships (369-386), Team USA (392-397), Star Rookies (398-422), and Award Winners (431-440). Pavel Bure is showcased on a special card (SP2) that was randomly inserted in first series foil and jumbo packs. Another special card (SP3) titled "World Champions", honors Canada's 1993 IIHF World Junior Champions team. High series subsets featured are Lethal Lines (453-456), Young Guns (554-583), and World Junior Champions (584-619). The World Junior Champions subset is grouped according to national teams as follows: Canada (585-594), Sweden (595-599), Czechoslovakia (600-604), USA (605-609), Russia (610-614), and Finland (615-619). An Upper Deck Profiles (620-640) subset closes out the set. Card No. 88, Eric Lindros, was short-printed (SP) as it was not included in second series packaging. This was brought about because of a controversy over Lindros' head being superimposed on a teammate's body.

COMPLETE SET (640) 25.00 50.00
COMPLETE LO SET (440) 10.00 20.00
COMPLETE HI SET (200) 15.00 30.00
1 Andy Moog TC .02 .10
2 Donald Audette TC .01 .05
3 Tomas Forslund TC .01 .05
4 Steve Larmer TC .01 .05
5 Tim Cheveldae TC .01 .05
6 Vincent Damphousse TC .01 .05
7 Pat Verbeek TC .01 .05
8 Luc Robitaille TC .02 .10
9 Mike Modano TC .08 .20
10 Denis Savard TC .01 .05
11 Kevin Todd TC .01 .05
12 Ray Ferraro TC .01 .05
13 Tony Amonte TC .05 .12
14 Peter Sidorkiewicz TC .01 .05
15 Rod Brind'Amour TC .01 .05
16 Jaromir Jagr TC .08 .25
17 Owen Nolan TC .01 .05
18 Nelson Emerson TC .01 .05
19 Pat Falloon TC .01 .05
20 Anatoli Semenov TC .01 .05
21 Doug Gilmour TC .02 .10
22 Kirk McLean TC .01 .05
23 Don Beaupre TC .02 .10
24 Phil Housley TC .01 .05
25 Wayne Gretzky .60 1.50
26 Mario Lemieux .40 1.00
27 Valeri Kamensky .01 .05
28 Jaromir Jagr .15 .40
29 Brett Hull .15 .40
30 Neil Wilkinson .01 .05
31 Dominic Roussel .02 .10
32 Kent Manderville .01 .05
33 Gretzky 1500 .40 1.00
34 Presidents' Cup .08 .25
35 Kip Miller BL .01 .05
Kevin Miller
Kelly Miller
36 Brian Sakic BL .08 .25
Joe Sakic
37 Wayne Gretzky BL .30 .75
Keith Gretzky
Brent Gretzky
38 Jamie Linden BL .02 .10
Trevor Linden
39 Geoff Courtnall BL .01 .05
Russ Courtnall
40 Dale Craigwell .01 .05
41 Peter Ahola .01 .05
42 Robert Reichel .01 .05
43 Chris Terreri .02 .10
44 John Vanbiesbrouck .02 .10
45 Alexander Semak .01 .05
46 Mike Sullivan .01 .05
47 Bob Sweeney .01 .05
48 Corey Millen .01 .05
49 Murray Craven .01 .05
50 Dennis Vaske .01 .05
51 David Williams RC .01 .05
52 Tom Fitzgerald .01 .05
53 Corey Foster .01 .05
54 Al Iafrate .02 .10
55 John LeClair .20 .50
56 Stephane Richer .02 .10
57 Claude Boivin .01 .05
58 Rick Tabaracci .02 .10
59 Johan Garpenlov .01 .05
60 Checklist 1-110 .01 .05
61 Steve Leach .01 .05
62 Trent Klatt RC .02 .10
63 Darryl Sydor .01 .05
64 Brian Glynn .01 .05
65 Mike Craig .01 .05
66 Gary Leeman .01 .05
67 Jim Waite .02 .10
68 Jason Marshall .01 .05
69 Robert Kron .01 .05
70 Yanic Perreault RC .20 .50
71 Daniel Marois .01 .05
72 Mark Osborne .01 .05
73 Mark Tinordi .01 .05
74 Brad May .01 .05
75 Kimbi Daniels .01 .05
76 Kay Whitmore .02 .10
77 Luciano Borsato .01 .05
78 Kris King .01 .05
79 Felix Potvin .08 .25
80 Benoit Brunet .01 .05
81 Shawn Antoski .01 .05
82 Randy Gilhen .01 .05
83 Dimitri Mironov .01 .05
84 Dave Manson .01 .05
85 Sergio Momesso .01 .05
86 Cam Neely .08 .25
87 Mike Krushelnyski .01 .05
88 Eric Lindros UER SP .08 .25
(8 games with Canadian
Olympic Team not 7)
89 Wendel Clark .02 .10
90 Enrico Ciccone .01 .05
91 Jarrod Skalde .01 .05
92 Dominik Hasek .30 .75
93 Dave McLlwain .01 .05
94 Russ Courtnall .01 .05
95 Tim Sweeney .01 .05
96 Alexei Kasatonov .01 .05
97 Chris Lindberg .01 .05
98 Steven Rice .01 .05
99 Tie Domi .08 .25
100 Paul Stanton .01 .05
101 Brad Schlegel .01 .05
102 David Bruce .01 .05
103 Mikael Andersson .01 .05
104 Shawn Chambers .01 .05
105 Rob Ramage .01 .05
106 Joe Reekie .01 .05
107 Sylvain Turgeon .01 .05
108 Rob Murphy .01 .05
109 Brad Shaw .01 .05
110 Darren Rumble RC .01 .05
111 Kyosti Karjalainen .01 .05
112 Mike Vernon .02 .10
113 Michel Goulet .02 .10
114 Garry Valk .01 .05
115 Peter Bondra .02 .10
116 Paul Coffey .08 .25
117 Brian Noonan .01 .05
118 John McIntyre .01 .05
119 Scott Mellanby .01 .05
120 Jim Sandlak .01 .05
121 Mats Sundin .08 .25
122 Brendan Shanahan .08 .25
123 Kelly Buchberger .01 .05
124 Doug Smail .01 .05
125 Craig Janney .02 .10
126 Mike Gartner .02 .10
127 Alexei Gusarov .01 .05
128 Joe Nieuwendyk .02 .10
129 Troy Murray .01 .05
130 Jamie Baker .01 .05
131 Dale Hunter .02 .10
132 Darrin Shannon .01 .05
133 Adam Oates .02 .10
134 Trevor Kidd .02 .10
135 Steve Larmer .02 .10
136 Fredrik Olausson .01 .05
137 Jyrki Lumme .01 .05
138 Tony Amonte .02 .10
139 Calle Johansson .01 .05
140 Rob Blake .02 .10
141 Phil Bourque .01 .05
142 Yves Racine .01 .05
143 Rich Sutter .01 .05
144 Joe Mullen .02 .10
145 Mike Richter .08 .25
146 Pat MacLeod .01 .05
147 Claude Lapointe .01 .05
148 Paul Broten .01 .05
149 Patrick Roy .40 1.00
150 Doug Wilson .02 .10
151 Jim Hrivnak .02 .10
152 Joe Murphy .01 .05
153 Randy Burridge .01 .05
154 Thomas Steen .01 .05
155 Steve Yzerman .40 1.00
156 Pavel Bure .08 .25
157 Sergei Fedorov .15 .40
158 Trevor Linden .02 .10
159 Chris Chelios .08 .25
160 Cliff Ronning .01 .05
161 Jeff Beukeboom .01 .05
162 Denis Savard .02 .10
163 Claude Lemieux .01 .05
164 Mike Keane .01 .05
165 Pat LaFontaine .08 .25
166 Nelson Emerson .01 .05
167 Alexander Mogilny .02 .10

168 Jamie Leach .01 .05
169 Darren Turcotte .01 .05
170 Checklist 111-220 .01 .05
171 Steve Thomas .02 .10
172 Brian Bellows .01 .05
173 Mike Ridley .01 .05
174 Dave Gagner .02 .10
175 Pierre Turgeon .02 .10
176 Paul Ysebaert .01 .05
177 Brian Propp .01 .05
178 Nicklas Lidstrom .08 .25
179 Kelly Miller .01 .05
180 Kirk Muller .01 .05
181 Bob Bassen .01 .05
182 Tony Tanti .01 .05
183 Mikhail Tatarinov .01 .05
184 Ron Sutter .01 .05
185 Tony Granato .01 .05
186 Curtis Joseph .08 .25
187 Uwe Krupp .01 .05
188 Esa Tikkanen .01 .05
189 Ulf Samuelsson .01 .05
190 Jon Casey .02 .10
191 Derek King .01 .05
192 Greg Adams .01 .05
193 Ray Ferraro .01 .05
194 Dave Christian .01 .05
195 Eric Weinrich .01 .05
196 Josef Beranek .01 .05
197 Tim Cheveldae .02 .10
198 Kevin Hatcher .01 .05
199 Brent Sutter .01 .05
200 Bruce Driver .01 .05
201 Tom Draper .01 .05
202 Ted Donato .01 .05
203 Ed Belfour .08 .25
204 Pat Verbeek .01 .05
205 John Druce .01 .05
206 Neal Broten .02 .10
207 Doug Bodger .01 .05
208 Troy Loney .01 .05
209 Mark Pederson .01 .05
210 Todd Elik .01 .05
211 Ed Olczyk .01 .05
212 Paul Cavallini .01 .05
213 Stephan Lebeau .01 .05
214 Dave Ellett .01 .05
215 Doug Gilmour .02 .10
216 Luc Robitaille .02 .10
217 Bob Essensa .02 .10
218 Jari Kurri .08 .25
219 Dimitri Khristich .01 .05
220 Joel Otto .01 .05
221 Checklist 221-280 .01 .05
222 Jonas Hoglund RC .08 .25
223 Rolf Wanhainen RC .01 .05
224 Stefan Klockare RC .01 .05
225 Johan Norgren RC .01 .05
226 Roger Kyro RC .01 .05
227 Niklas Sundblad RC .01 .05
228 Calle Carlsson RC .01 .05
229 Jakob Karlsson RC .01 .05
230 Fredrik Jax RC .01 .05
231 Bjorn Nord RC .01 .05
232 Kristian Gahn RC .01 .05
233 Mikael Renberg RC .20 .50
234 Markus Naslund RC 1.00 2.50
235 Peter Forsberg .40 1.00
236 Michael Nylander RC .08 .25
237 Stanley Cup Centennial .01 .05
238 Rick Tocchet .02 .10
239 Igor Kravchuk .01 .05
240 Geoff Courtnall .01 .05
241 Larry Murphy .02 .10
242 Mark Messier .08 .25
243 Tom Barrasso .02 .10
244 Glen Wesley .01 .05
245 Randy Wood .01 .05
246 Gerard Gallant .01 .05
247 Kip Miller .01 .05
248 Bob Probert .02 .10
249 Gary Suter .01 .05
250 Ulf Dahlen .01 .05
251 Dan Lambert .01 .05
252 Bobby Holik .02 .10
253 Jimmy Carson .01 .05
254 Ken Hodge Jr. .01 .05
255 Joe Sakic .20 .50
256 Kevin Dineen .01 .05
257 Al MacInnis .02 .10
258 Vladimir Ruzicka .01 .05
259 Ken Daneyko .01 .05
260 Guy Carbonneau .02 .10
261 Michal Pivonka .01 .05
262 Bill Ranford .02 .10
263 Petr Nedved .02 .10
264 Rod Brind'Amour .02 .10
265 Ray Bourque .20 .50
266 Joe Sacco .01 .05
267 Vladimir Konstantinov .08 .25
268 Eric Desjardins .02 .10
269 Dave Andreychuk .02 .10
270 Kelly Hrudey .02 .10
271 Grant Fuhr .08 .25
272 Dirk Graham .01 .05
273 Frank Pietrangelo .02 .10
274 Jeremy Roenick .12 .30
275 Kevin Stevens .01 .05
276 Phil Housley .02 .10
277 Patrice Brisebois .01 .05
278 Slava Fetisov .01 .05
279 Doug Weight .08 .25
280 Checklist 281-330 .01 .05
281 Dean Evason .01 .05
282 Martin Gelinas .01 .05
283 Philippe Bozon .01 .05
284 Brian Leetch .08 .25
285 Theo Fleury .01 .05
286 Pat Falloon .01 .05
287 Derian Hatcher .01 .05
288 Andrew Cassels .01 .05
289 Gary Roberts .01 .05
290 Bernie Nicholls .02 .10
291 Ron Francis .02 .10
292 Tom Kurvers .01 .05
293 Geoff Sanderson .02 .10
294 Slava Kozlov .02 .10
295 Valeri Zelepukin .01 .05
296 Ray Sheppard .01 .05
297 Scott Stevens .02 .10
298 Sergei Nemchinov .01 .05
299 Kirk McLean .02 .10
300 Igor Ulanov .01 .05
301 Brian Benning .01 .05
302 Dale Hawerchuk .02 .10
303 Kevin Todd .01 .05
304 John Cullen .01 .05
305 Mike Modano .15 .40
306 Donald Audette .01 .05
307 Vincent Damphousse .01 .05
308 Jeff Hackett .02 .10
309 Craig Simpson .01 .05
310 Don Beaupre .02 .10
311 Adam Creighton .01 .05
312 Pat Elynuik .01 .05
313 David Volek .01 .05
314 Sergei Makarov .01 .05
315 Craig Billington .02 .10
316 Zarley Zalapski .01 .05
317 Brian Mullen .01 .05
318 Rob Pearson .01 .05
319 Garry Galley .01 .05
320 James Patrick .01 .05
321 Owen Nolan .02 .10
322 Marty McSorley .01 .05
323 James Black .01 .05
324 Jacques Cloutier .02 .10
325 Benoit Hogue .01 .05
326 Teppo Numminen .01 .05
327 Mark Recchi .02 .10
328 Paul Ranheim .01 .05
329 Andy Moog .08 .25
330 Shayne Corson .01 .05
331 J.J. Daigneault .01 .05
332 Mark Fitzpatrick .02 .10
333 Russian Stars CL .01 .05
Alexander Yudin
Dmitri Yushkevich
Yan Kaminsky
Alexander Andriyevski
334 Alexei Yashin RS .01 .05
335 Darius Kasparaitis RS .01 .05
336 Alexander Yudin RS RC .01 .05
337 Sergei Bautin RS RC .01 .05
338 Igor Korolev RS RC .02 .10
339 Sergei Klimovich RS RC .02 .10
340 Andrei Nikolishin RS RC .01 .05
341 Vitali Karamnov RS RC .01 .05
342 Alex. Andriyevski RS RC .01 .05
343 Sergei Sorokin RS RC .01 .05
344 Yan Kaminsky RS RC .01 .05
345 Andrei Trefilov RS RC .01 .05
346 Sergei Petrenko RS RC .01 .05
347 Ravil Khaidarov RS RC .01 .05
348 Dmitri Frolov RS .01 .05
349 Ravil Yakubov RS RC .01 .05
350 Dmitri Yushkevich RS RC .02 .10
351 Alex Karpovtsev RS RC .02 .10
352 Igor Dorofeyev RS RC .01 .05
353 Alexander Galchenyuk RS RC .01 .05
354 Joe Juneau RR .01 .05
355 Pat Falloon RR .01 .05
356 Gilbert Dionne RR .01 .05
357 Vladimir Konstantinov .08 .25
358 Rick Tabaracci RR .01 .05
359 Tony Amonte RR .05 .12
360 Scott Lachance RR .01 .05
361 Tom Draper RR .01 .05
362 Pavel Bure RR .08 .20
363 Nicklas Lidstrom RR .02 .10
364 Keith Tkachuk RR .08 .25
365 Kevin Todd RR .01 .05
366 Dominik Hasek RR .08 .25
367 Igor Kravchuk RR .01 .05
368 Shawn McEachern RR .01 .05
369 '92 World Champion-ships Checklist .20 .50
Arto Blomsten
Peter Forsberg
370 Dieter Hegen RC .01 .05
371 Stefan Ustorf RC .01 .05
372 Ernst Kopf RC .01 .05
373 Raimond Hilger RC .01 .05
374 Mats Sundin .08 .25
375 Peter Forsberg .40 1.00
376 Arto Blomsten RC .01 .05
377 Tommy Soderstom RC .02 .10
378 Michael Nylander RC .02 .10
379 David Jensen RC .01 .05
380 Chris Winnes .01 .05
381 Ray LeBlanc .02 .10
382 Joe Sacco .01 .05
383 Dennis Vaske .01 .05
384 Jorg Eberle RC .01 .05
385 Trevor Kidd .02 .10
386 Pat Falloon .01 .05
387 Rob Brown .01 .05
388 Adam Graves .01 .05
389 Peter Zezel .01 .05
390 Checklist 391-440 .01 .05
391 Don Sweeney .01 .05
392 Sean Hill RC .01 .05
393 Ted Donato .01 .05
394 Marty McInnis .01 .05
395 C.J. Young RC .01 .05
396 Ted Drury RC .01 .05
397 Scott Young .01 .05
398 Star Rookie CL .02 .10
Scott Lachance
Keith Tkachuk
399 Joe Juneau SR UER .01 .05
(Olympic stats should read 8 games, 9 assists 15 points, and 4 PIM)
400 Steve Heinze SR .01 .05
401 Glen Murray SR .01 .05
402 Keith Carney SR RC .08 .25
403 Dean McAmmond SR RC .01 .05
404 Karl Dykhuis SR .01 .05
405 Martin Lapointe SR .02 .10
406 Scott Niedermayer SR .01 .05
407 Ray Whitney SR RC .15 .40
408 Martin Brodeur SR .40 1.00
409 Scott Lachance SR .01 .05
410 Marty McInnis SR .01 .05
411 Bill Guerin SR RC .60 1.50
412 Shawn McEachern SR .01 .05
413 Denny Felsner SR RC .02 .10
414 Bret Hedican SR RC .02 .10
415 Drake Berehowsky SR .01 .05
416 Patrick Poulin SR .01 .05
417 Vladimir Vujtek SR RC .01 .05
418 Steve Konowalchuk SR RC .02 .10
419 Keith Tkachuk SR .08 .25
420 Evgeny Davydov SR .01 .05
421 Yanick Dupre SR .01 .05
422 Jason Woolley SR RC .01 .05
423 Back-to-Back .30 .75
Brett Hull
Wayne Gretzky
424 Tomas Sandstrom .02 .10
425 Craig MacTavish .01 .05
426 Stu Barnes .01 .05
427 Gilbert Dionne .01 .05
428 Andrei Lomakin .01 .05
429 Tomas Forslund .01 .05
430 Andre Racicot .02 .10
431 Pavel Bure AW .08 .20
Calder Memorial
432 Mark Messier AW .08 .20
Lester B. Pearson
433 Mario Lemieux Ross .25 .60
434 Brian Leetch AW .02 .10
Norris
435 Wayne Gretzky AW .30 .75
Lady Byng
436 Mario Lemieux Smythe .25 .60
437 Mark Messier AW .08 .20
Hart
438 Patrick Roy AW .25 .60
Vezina
439 Guy Carbonneau AW .02 .10
Frank J. Selke
440 Patrick Roy AW .25 .60
William M. Jennings
441 Russ Courtnall .01 .05
442 Jeff Reese .01 .05
443 Brent Fedyk .01 .05
444 Kerry Huffman .01 .05
445 Mark Freer .01 .05
446 Christian Ruuttu .01 .05
447 Nick Kypreos .01 .05
448 Mike Hurlbut RC .01 .05
449 Bob Sweeney .01 .05
450 Checklist 491-540 .01 .05
451 Perry Berezan .01 .05
452 Phil Bourque .01 .05
453 New York Rangers LL .08 .25
Mark Messier
Tony Amonte
Adam Graves
454 Pittsburgh Penguins LL .15 .40
Mario Lemieux
Kevin Stevens
Rick Tocchet
455 Boston Bruins LL .02 .10
Adam Oates
Joe Juneau
Dmitri Kvartalnov
456 Buffalo Sabres LL .02 .10
Pat LaFontaine
Dave Andreychuk
Alexander Mogilny
457 Zdeno Ciger .01 .05
458 Pat Jablonski .02 .10
459 Brent Gilchrist .01 .05
460 Yvon Corriveau .01 .05
461 Dino Ciccarelli .02 .10
462 David Emma .01 .05
463 Corey Hirsch RC .08 .25
464 Jamie Baker .01 .05
465 John Cullen .01 .05
466 Lonnie Loach RC .01 .05
467 Louie DeBrusk .01 .05
468 Brian Mullen .01 .05
469 Gaeten Duchesne .01 .05
470 Eric Lindros .08 .25
471 Brian Bellows .01 .05
472 Bill Lindsay RC .01 .05
473 Dave Archibald .01 .05
474 Reggie Savage .01 .05
475 Tommy Soderstrom .02 .10
476 Vincent Damphousse .01 .05
477 Mike Ricci .02 .10
478 Bob Carpenter .01 .05
479 Kevin Haller .01 .05
480 Peter Sidorkiewicz .02 .10
481 Peter Andersson RC .01 .05
482 Kevin Miller .01 .05
483 Jean-Francois Quintin RC .01 .05
484 Philippe Boucher .01 .05
485 Jozef Stumpel .01 .05
486 Vitali Prokhorov RC .01 .05
487 Stan Drulia RC .01 .05
488 Jay More .01 .05
489 Mike Needham RC .01 .05
490 Glenn Mulvenna RC .01 .05
491 Ed Ronan RC .01 .05
492 Grigori Panteleyev RC .01 .05
493 Kevin Dahl RC .01 .05
494 Ryan McGill RC .01 .05
495 Robb Stauber .02 .10
496 Vladimir Vujtek RC .01 .05
497 Tomas Jelinek RC .01 .05
498 Patrik Kjellberg RC .08 .25
499 Sergei Bautin .01 .05
500 Bobby Holik .02 .10
501 Guy Hebert RC .30 .75
502 Chris Kontos RC .01 .05
503 Vyatcheslav Butsayev RC .01 .05
504 Yuri Khymlev RC .01 .05
505 Richard Matvichuk RC .02 .10
506 Dominik Hasek .20 .50
507 Ed Courtenay .01 .05
508 Jeff Daniels .01 .05
509 Doug Zmolek RC .01 .05
510 Vitali Karamnov .01 .05
511 Norm Maciver .01 .05
512 Terry Yake .01 .05
513 Steve Duchesne .01 .05
514 Andrei Trefilov .01 .05
515 Jiri Slegr .01 .05
516 Sergei Zubov RC .25 .60
517 Dave Karpa RC .01 .05
518 Sean Burke .02 .10
519 Adrien Plavsic .01 .05
520 Michael Nylander .01 .05
521 John MacLean .02 .10
522 Jason Ruff RC .01 .05
523 Sean Hill .01 .05
524 Mike Sillinger .01 .05
525 Dan Laperriere RC .01 .05
526 Peter Ahola .01 .05
527 Guy Larose .01 .05
528 Tommy Sjodin RC .01 .05
529 Rob DiMaio .01 .05
530 Mark Howe .01 .05
531 Greg Paslawski .01 .05
532 Ron Hextall .02 .10
533 Keith Jones RC .08 .25
534 Chris Luongo RC .01 .05
535 Anatoli Semenov .01 .05
536 Stephane Beauregard .02 .10
537 Pat Elynuik .01 .05
538 Mike McPhee .01 .05
539 Jody Hull .01 .05
540 Stephane Matteau .01 .05
541 Shayne Corson .01 .05
542 Mikhail Kravets RC .01 .05
543 Kevin Miehm RC .01 .05
544 Brian Bradley .01 .05
545 Mathieu Schneider .01 .05
546 Steve Chiasson .01 .05
547 Warren Rychel RC .01 .05
548 John Tucker .01 .05
549 Todd Ewen .01 .05
550 Checklist 591-640 .01 .05
551 Petr Klima .01 .05
552 Robert Lang RC .01 .05
553 Eric Weinrich .01 .05
554 Young Guns Checklist .01 .05
555 Roman Hamrlik YG RC .20 .50
556 Martin Rucinsky YG .01 .05
557 Patrick Poulin YG .01 .05
558 Tyler Wright YG .01 .05
559 Martin Straka YG RC .30 .75
560 Jim Hiller YG RC .01 .05
561 Dmitri Kvartalnov YG RC .01 .05
562 Scott Niedermayer YG .01 .05
563 Darius Kasparaitis YG .01 .05
564 Richard Smehlik YG RC .01 .05
565 Shawn McEachern YG .01 .05
566 Alexei Zhitnik YG .01 .05
567 Andrei Kovalenko YG RC .02 .10
568 Sandis Ozolinsh YG .01 .05
569 Robert Petrovicky YG RC .01 .05
570 Dimitri Yushkevich YG .02 .10
571 Scott Lachance YG .01 .05
572 Nikolai Borschevsky YG .01 .05
573 Alexei Kovalev YG .02 .10
574 Teemu Selanne YG .40 1.00
575 Steven King YG RC .01 .05
576 Guy Leveque YG RC .01 .05
577 Vladimir Malakhov YG .01 .05
578 Alexei Zhamnov YG .02 .10
579 Viktor Gordiouk YG RC .01 .05
580 Dixon Ward YG RC .02 .10
581 Igor Korolev YG .01 .05
582 Sergei Krivokrasov YG .01 .05
583 Rob Zamuner YG RC .02 .10
584 World Jr. .01 .05
Championship Checklist
585 Manny Legace RC .75 2.00
586 Paul Kariya RC 3.00 8.00
587 Alexandre Daigle RC .20 .50
588 Nathan Lafayette RC .02 .10
589 Mike Rathje RC .01 .05
590 Chris Gratton RC .20 .50
591 Chris Pronger RC 1.25 3.00
592 Brent Tully RC .01 .05
593 Rob Niedermayer RC UER .30 .75
(Hometown is Cassiar not Kassier)
594 Darcy Werenka RC .01 .05
595 Peter Forsberg .40 1.00
596 Kenny Jonsson RC .08 .25
597 Niklas Sundstrom RC .20 .50
598 Reine Rauhala RC .01 .05
599 Daniel Johansson RC .01 .05
600 David Vyborny RC .20 .50
601 Jan Vopat RC .02 .10
602 Pavol Demitra RC .60 1.50
603 Michal Cerny RC .01 .05
604 Ondrej Steiner RC .01 .05
605 Jim Campbell RC .02 .10
606 Todd Marchant RC .02 .10
607 Mike Pomichter RC .02 .10
608 John Emmons RC .01 .05
609 Adam Deadmarsh RC .20 .50
610 Nikolai Semin RC .01 .05
611 Igor Alexandrov RC .01 .05
612 Vadim Sharifjanov RC .08 .25
613 Viktor Kozlov RC .30 .75
614 Nikolai Tsulygin RC .01 .05
615 Jere Lehtinen RC .60 1.50
616 Ville Peltonen RC .02 .10
617 Saku Koivu RC 1.25 3.00
618 Kimmo Rintanen RC .01 .05
619 Jonni Vauhkonen RC .01 .05
620 Brett Hull .08 .25
621 Wayne Gretzky .30 .75
622 Jaromir Jagr .08 .25
623 Darius Kasparaitis .01 .05
624 Bernie Nicholls .01 .05
625 Gilbert Dionne .01 .05
626 Ray Bourque .08 .25
627 Mike Ricci .02 .10
628 Phil Housley .02 .10
629 Chris Chelios .08 .25
630 Kevin Stevens .01 .05
631 Roman Hamrlik .02 .10
632 Sergei Fedorov .08 .25
633 Alexei Kovalev .02 .10
634 Shawn McEachern .01 .05
635 Tony Amonte .05 .12
636 Brian Bellows .01 .05
637 Adam Oates .02 .10
638 Denis Savard .02 .10
639 Doug Gilmour .02 .10
640 Brian Leetch .02 .10
SP2 Pavel Bure .08 .25
All-Rookie Team
SP3 World Jr. Champs 1.00 2.50
Gold medal winner
Canada

1992-93 Upper Deck All-Rookie Team

This seven-card set was inserted only in low series U.S. foil packs and features six of the NHL's brightest rookies from the 1991-92 season. The fronts show a triple-pose player photo and have a diagonal silver foil stripe in the lower right corner with the words "All-Rookie Team". The backs provide biographical information and a color photo of the player in civilian dress. The checklist card has a group photo of all six players. The cards are numbered on the back with an "AR" prefix.

COMPLETE SET (7) 6.00 15.00
AR1 Tony Amonte .40 1.00
AR2 Gilbert Dionne .40 1.00
AR3 Kevin Todd .40 1.00
AR4 Nicklas Lidstrom 2.00 5.00
AR5 Vladimir Konstantinov 2.00 5.00
AR6 Dominik Hasek 2.00 5.00
AR7 Checklist Card .75 2.00
Tony Amonte
Gilbert Dionne
Kevin Todd
Nicklas Lidstrom
Vladimir Konstantinov
Dominik Hasek

1992-93 Upper Deck All-World Team

This six-card set was randomly inserted only in Canadian low series foil packs. These standard size cards are full bleed with a gold "All-World Team" logo at the bottom of the card. The cards are numbered on the back with a "W" prefix.

W1 Wayne Gretzky 4.00 10.00
W2 Brett Hull 1.00 2.50
W3 Jaromir Jagr 1.00 2.50
W4 Nicklas Lidstrom .60 1.50
W5 Vladimir Konstantinov .60 1.50
W6 Patrick Roy 3.00 8.00

1992-93 Upper Deck Ameri/Can Holograms

Randomly inserted in high series foil packs, this six-card hologram standard-size set spotlights the top rookies of either U.S. or Canadian heritage at each position. The cards have the photo superimposed over the hologram.

1 Joe Juneau .10 .25
2 Keith Tkachuk .50 1.25
3 Steve Heinze .10 .25
4 Scott Lachance .10 .25
5 Scott Niedermayer .10 .25
6 Dominic Roussel .20 .50

1992-93 Upper Deck Calder Candidates

Randomly inserted into 1992-93 Upper Deck U.S. high series retail foil packs only, this 20-card standard-size set spotlights top rookies eligible to win the Calder Memorial Trophy for the 1992-93 season. The full-bleed photos on the front are bordered on the top by a gold foil stripe. The team name and player's name appears in bar that shades from black to white. On a background consisting of a stone slab carved with an image of the Calder trophy, the backs present a career summary. The card number appears in a white stripe that cuts across the top of the card. The cards are numbered with a "CC" prefix.

COMPLETE SET (20) 10.00 25.00
CC1 Dixon Ward .40 1.00
CC2 Igor Korolev .40 1.00
CC3 Felix Potvin 1.50 4.00
CC4 Rob Zamuner .40 1.00
CC5 Scott Niedermayer .75 2.00
CC6 Eric Lindros 2.00 5.00
CC7 Alexei Zhitnik .40 1.00
CC8 Roman Hamrlik .40 1.00
CC9 Joe Juneau 1.00 2.50
CC10 Teemu Selanne 2.00 5.00
CC11 Alexei Kovalev .75 2.00
CC12 Vladimir Malakhov .40 1.00
CC13 Darius Kasparaitis .40 1.00
CC14 Shawn McEachern .40 1.00
CC15 Keith Tkachuk 1.50 4.00
CC16 Scott Lachance .40 1.00
CC17 Andrei Kovalenko .40 1.00
CC18 Patrick Poulin .40 1.00
CC19 Evgeny Davydov .40 1.00
CC20 Dimitri Yushkevich .40 1.00

1992-93 Upper Deck Euro-Rookie Team

This six-card standard-size set was randomly inserted in 1992-93 Upper Deck low series packs. The cards feature cut-out color player photos superimposed on a hologram that shows the player in action. The horizontal fronts are bordered on the left and top by gray wood-textured panels. The team logo appears at the top left on a tan wood-textured panel. The horizontal backs feature a player profile on a tan background bordered by gray wood-textured panels. The cards are numbered on the back with an "ERT" prefix.

COMPLETE SET (6) 3.00 8.00
ERT1 Pavel Bure .75 2.00
ERT2 Nicklas Lidstrom .75 2.00
ERT3 Dominik Hasek 2.00 5.00
ERT4 Peter Ahola .20 .50
ERT5 Alexander Semak .20 .50
ERT6 Tomas Forslund .20 .50

1992-93 Upper Deck Euro-Rookies

One per high series jumbo pack, this 20-card standard-size set spotlights European born rookies. The color action player photos on the fronts are full-bleed except on the right side, where a black stripe carries the player's name in bronze foil lettering. At the upper right corner appears a bronze foil "Euro-Rookies" seal, with the flag of the player's country immediately to the right. The cards are numbered on the back with an "ER" prefix.

COMPLETE SET (20) 4.00 10.00
ER1 Richard Smehlik .20 .50
ER2 Michael Nylander .30 .75
ER3 Igor Korolev .20 .50
ER4 Robert Lang .20 .50
ER5 Sergei Krivokrasov .20 .50
ER6 Teemu Selanne .75 2.00
ER7 Darius Kasparaitis .20 .50
ER8 Alexei Zhamnov .30 .75
ER9 Jiri Slegr .20 .50
ER10 Alexei Kovalev .60 1.50
ER11 Roman Hamrlik .40 1.00
ER12 Dimitri Yushkevich .20 .50
ER13 Alexei Zhitnik .20 .50
ER14 Andrei Kovalenko .20 .50
ER15 Vladimir Malakhov .20 .50
ER16 Sandis Ozolinsh .40 1.00
ER17 Evgeny Davydov .20 .50
ER18 Viktor Gordiouk .20 .50
ER19 Martin Straka .30 .75
ER20 Robert Petrovicky .20 .50

1992-93 Upper Deck Euro-Stars

This 20-card standard-size set, issued one per low series jumbo pack, features action color player photos with a silver foil border. The borders are prone to chipping. The pictures are silver-foil stamped with the player's name and with the "Euro Sta emblem which hangs down from a whi red, and blue ribbon at the upper rig corner. The backs display player prof information against a light gray panel wit black, silver, and gold frame design. T cards are numbered on the back with an prefix.

COMPLETE SET (20) 4.00 10.0
E1 Sergei Fedorov .75 2.0
E2 Pavel Bure .60 1.5
E3 Dominik Hasek 1.00 2.5
E4 Vladimir Ruzicka .15 .3
E5 Peter Ahola .15 .3
E6 Kyosti Karjalainen .15 .3
E7 Igor Kravchuk .15 .3
E8 Evgeny Davydov .15 .3
E9 Nicklas Lidstrom .60 1.5
E10 Vlad. Konstantinov .60 1.5
E11 Josef Beranek .15 .3
E12 Valeri Zelepukin .15 .3
E13 Sergei Nemchinov .15 .3
E14 Jaromir Jagr 1.00 2.5
E15 Igor Ulanov .15 .3
E16 Sergei Makarov .15 .3
E17 Andrei Lomakin .15 .3
E18 Mats Sundin .60 1.5
E19 Jarmo Myllys .15 .3
E20 Valeri Kamensky .15 .3

1992-93 Upper Dec Gordie Howe Heroe

Randomly inserted in high series foil pac this 10-card "Hockey Heroes" standard-s set showcases Gordie Howe, the NH former all-time leader in goals, assists, a points. The backs capture highlights Howe's career. The cards are numbered the back and continue from where Gretzky Heroes left off.

COMPLETE SET (10) 8.00 15.
COMMON HOWE (19-27) .75 2.
NNO G.Howe Header SP 1.50 4.

1992-93 Upper Dec Gordie Howe Select

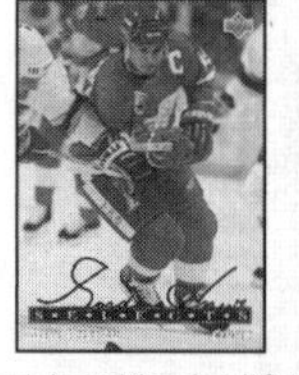

Randomly inserted throughout U.S. hi series hobby packs only, this 20-card standard-size features Gordie How selections of ten current NHL superstars a ten rookies who he believes are the NH best. The fronts carry full-bleed color pla photos. Howe's signature in gold foil sits top of a black bar (carrying the wo "Selects") toward the bottom of the pictu with the player's name and posit immediately below. The backs have a co head shot in an oval and a quote of How evaluation of the player's strengths. A sm color player cut-out of Howe and the playe statistics complete the back. The cards numbered on the back with a "G" prefix.

COMPLETE SET (20) 15.00 40.
G1 Brian Bellows .15
G2 Luc Robitaille .30
G3 Pat LaFontaine .60 1.
G4 Kevin Stevens .15
G5 Wayne Gretzky 4.00 10.0
G6 Steve Larmer .30
G7 Brett Hull 1.25 3.0
G8 Jeremy Roenick 1.00 2.5
G9 Mario Lemieux 3.00 8.0
G10 Steve Yzerman 3.00 8.0
G11 Joe Juneau .15
G12 Vladimir Malakhov .15
G13 Alexei Kovalev .30
G14 Eric Lindros .75 2.0
G15 Teemu Selanne 1.50 4.0
G16 Patrick Poulin .15
G17 Shawn McEachern .15
G18 Keith Tkachuk .75 2.0
G19 Andrei Kovalenko .15
G20 Ted Donato .15

1992-93 Upper Dec Sheets

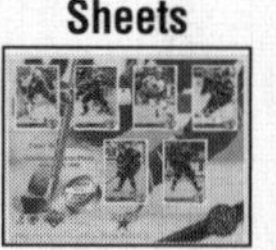

For the third straight year, Upper De produced hockey commemorative she that were given away during the 1992- season at selected games in large aren Each sheet measures 8 1/2" by 11" and printed on card stock. The fronts of the te commemorative sheets feature a series Upper Deck cards of star players of particular team and the team logo. The 19 ll-Star Game sheets feature a series of pper Deck cards of players that participated the 16-All-Star Game. All the sheets have an pper Deck stamp indicating the production uota and the serial number. Sheets without production quantity number are listed as NO. The backs of the sheets are blank. The layers are listed as they appear from left to ght.

COMPLETE SET (17) 60.00 150.00
'91-92 All-Rookie Team 4.00 10.00
June 1992 (17,000)
Gilbert Dionne
Kevin Todd
Vladimir Konstantinov
Tony Amonte
Nicklas Lidstrom
Dominik Hasek
New York Rangers 4.00 10.00
Defending Season Champs
Undated (18,000)
Peter Andersson
Phil Bourque
Joe Kocur
Doug Weight
Randy Gilhen
John Vanbiesbrouck
Adam Graves
Mark Messier
Gordie Howe Birthday 4.00 10.00
Undated (NNO)
65th Birthday
Celebration Tour
(Nine Howe Hockey Heroes
Cards Pictured)
Gordie Howe Birthday 4.00 10.00
Undated (NNO)
Hamilton McDonald's
Wayne Gretzky Heroes 6.00 15.00
Mail-In (NNO)
New York Rangers 2.00 5.00
vs. Quebec Nordiques
Oct. 29, 1992 (18,000)
Paul Broten
Mike Richter
Sergei Nemchinov
Tie Domi
Kris King
Jeff Beukeboom
Brian Leetch Norris
Tony Amonte
Los Angeles Kings 4.00 10.00
vs. Vancouver Canucks
Nov. 12, 1992 (18,000)
Luc Robitaille
Paul Coffey
Tony Granato
Rob Blake
Tomas Sandstrom
Kelly Hrudey
Minnesota North Stars 6.00 15.00
vs. San Jose Sharks
Nov. 28, 1992 (16,500)
Edmonton Oilers 2.00 5.00
vs. Calgary Flames
Dec. 8, 1992 (18,500)
Brian Glynn
Scott Mellanby
Dave Manson
Craig MacTavish
Bernie Nicholls
Bill Ranford
) Philadelphia Flyers 2.00 5.00
vs. Pittsburgh Penguins
Dec. 17, 1992 (19,000)
Kevin Dineen
Mark Recchi
Garry Galley
Dominic Roussel
Brian Benning
Rod Brind'Amour
1 Minnesota North Stars 6.00 15.00
vs. Tampa Bay Lightning
Jan. 30, 1993 (16,500)
Dave Gagner
Neal Broten
Ulf Dahlen
Todd Elik
Tommy Sjodin
Gaetan Duchesne
2 Campbell All-Stars 4.00 10.00
Montreal Forum
Feb. 6, 1993 (NNO)
Ed Belfour
Paul Coffey
Chris Chelios
Steve Yzerman
Brett Hull
Pavel Bure
3 Wales All-Stars 4.00 10.00
Montreal Forum
Feb. 6, 1993 (NNO)
Patrick Roy
Brian Leetch
Ray Bourque
Kevin Stevens
Mario Lemieux
Jaromir Jagr
4 Washington Capitals 4.00 10.00
vs. St. Louis Blues
Feb. 21, 1993 (17,000)
Jim Hrivnak
Mike Ridley
Peter Bondra
Dale Hunter
Kelly Miller
Don Beaupre
5 Los Angeles Kings 4.00 10.00
vs. Ottawa Senators
Mar.4, 1993 (18,000)
Jari Kurri
Corey Millen
Marty McSorley
Darryl Sydor
Wayne Gretzky
Robb Stauber
6 Quebec Nordiques 6.00 15.00
vs. Hartford Whalers
Mar. 8, 1993 (15,000)
7 St.Louis Blues 2.00 5.00
vs. Vancouver Canucks
Mar. 30, 1993 (17,500)

1992-93 Upper Deck Wayne Gretzky Heroes

Randomly inserted in low series foil packs, this ten-card "Hockey Heroes" standard-size set pays tribute to Wayne Gretzky by chronicling his career. Inside white borders on a gray ice background, the fronts display color photos that are cut out to fit a emblem design. On a gray ice background accented by black, the backs (which continue the numbering from where the Hull Heroes left off) capture highlights in Gretzky's career.

COMPLETE SET (10) 20.00 40.00
COMMON GRETZKY (10-18) 2.00 5.00
NNO W.Gretzky Header SP 5.00 10.00

1992-93 Upper Deck World Junior Grads

Randomly inserted in Canadian high series foil packs, this 20-card standard-size set features top players in the world who have participated in the IIHF Junior Championships. Beneath a black stripe carrying the player's name, the fronts display full-bleed color action player photos. The top portion of a globe and the words "World Junior Grads" are silver foil-stamped at the bottom of the picture. On the backs, a full-size globe serves as a panel for displaying a career summary and a color action player cut-out. The back also includes the year the player participated in the IIHF World Junior Championships. The cards are numbered on the back with a "WG" prefix.

WG1 Scott Niedermayer .40 1.00
WG2 Slava Kozlov .40 1.00
WG3 Chris Chelios .75 2.00
WG4 Jari Kurri .75 2.00
WG5 Pavel Bure 1.50 4.00
WG6 Jaromir Jagr 2.00 5.00
WG7 Steve Yzerman 6.00 15.00
WG8 Joe Sakic 2.00 5.00
WG9 Alexei Kovalev .40 1.00
WG10 Wayne Gretzky 8.00 20.00
WG11 Mario Lemieux 6.00 15.00
WG12 Eric Lindros 1.50 4.00
WG13 Pat Falloon .40 1.00
WG14 Trevor Linden .40 1.00
WG15 Brian Leetch .75 2.00
WG16 Sergei Fedorov 3.00 8.00
WG17 Mats Sundin .75 2.00
WG18 Alexander Mogilny .40 1.00
WG19 Jeremy Roenick 1.50 4.00
WG20 Luc Robitaille .75 2.00

1993-94 Upper Deck

The 1993-94 Upper Deck hockey set contains 575 standard-size cards. The set was released in two series of 310 and 265 cards, respectively. The fronts feature a photo with team color-coded inner borders. The player's name, position and team name are at the bottom. The backs have a photo in the upper half with yearly statistics in the bottom portion. The following subsets are included: 100-Point Club (220-235), NHL Star Rookies (236-249), World Jr. Championships - which include Canada (250-260/531-550), Czechoslovakia (261-267/573), Finland (268-271), Russia (272-279/571/574) and USA (551-568) - All-Rookie Team (280-285) and Team Point Leaders (286-309). The set closes with an All-World Junior Team subset (569-574). A special card (SP4) was randomly inserted in Upper Deck series one packs commemorating Teemu Selanne's record-breaking 76 goal rookie season. A Wayne Gretzky card commemorating his 802nd NHL goal was randomly inserted at a rate of 1:36 Parkhurst series two packs. This card is identical to his regular Upper Deck card for '93-94, with the exception of a gold foil stamp that indicates his 802nd goal. The silver version of this card was handed out to Canadian dealers as a promotion for Parkhurst series two, and also given to each of the 16,005 fans attending the next game at the Great Western Forum following the event.

COMPLETE SET (575) 15.00 30.00
COMPLETE SERIES 1 (310) 7.50 15.00
COMPLETE SERIES 2 (265) 7.50 15.00
1 Guy Hebert .02 .10
2 Bob Bassen .01 .05
3 Theo Fleury .01 .05
4 Ray Whitney .01 .05
5 Donald Audette .01 .05
6 Martin Rucinsky .01 .05
7 Lyle Odelein .01 .05
8 John Vanbiesbrouck .02 .10
9 Tim Cheveldae .02 .10
10 Jock Callander .01 .05
11 Nick Kypreos .01 .05
12 Jarrod Skalde .01 .05
13 Gary Shuchuk .01 .05
14 Kris King .01 .05
15 Josef Beranek .01 .05
16 Sean Hill .01 .05
17 Bob Kudelski .01 .05
18 Jiri Slegr .01 .05
19 Dmitri Kvartalnov .01 .05
20 Drake Berehowsky .01 .05
21 Jean-Francois Quintin .01 .05
22 Randy Wood .01 .05
23 Jim McKenzie .01 .05
24 Steven King .01 .05
25 Scott Niedermayer .01 .05
26 Alexander Andrijevski .01 .05
27 Alexei Kovalev .02 .10
28 Steve Konowalchuk .01 .05
29 Vladimir Malakhov .01 .05
30 Eric Lindros .08 .25
31 Mathieu Schneider .01 .05
32 Russ Courtnall .01 .05
33 Ron Sutter .01 .05
34 Radek Hamr RC .01 .05
35 Pavel Bure .08 .25
36 Joe Sacco .01 .05
37 Robert Petrovicky .01 .05
38 Anatoli Fedotov RC .01 .05
39 Pat Falloon .01 .05
40 Martin Straka .01 .05
41 Brad Werenka .01 .05
42 Mike Richter .08 .25
43 Mike McPhee .01 .05
44 Sylvain Turgeon .01 .05
45 Tom Barrasso .02 .10
46 Anatoli Semenov .01 .05
47 Joe Murphy .01 .05
48 Rob Pearson .01 .05
49 Patrick Roy .50 1.25
50 Dallas Drake RC .01 .05
51 Mark Messier .08 .25
52 Scott Pellerin RC .01 .05
53 Teppo Numminen .01 .05
54 Chris Kontos .01 .05
55 Richard Matvichuk .01 .05
56 Dale Craigwell .01 .05
57 Mike Eastwood .01 .05
58 Bernie Nicholls .01 .05
59 Travis Green .02 .10
60 Shjon Podein RC .01 .05
61 Darrin Madeley RC .01 .05
62 Dixon Ward .01 .05
63 Andre Faust .01 .05
64 Tony Amonte .02 .10
65 Joe Cirella .01 .05
66 Michel Petit .01 .05
67 David Lowry .01 .05
68 Shawn Chambers .01 .05
69 Joe Sakic .20 .50
70 Michael Nylander .01 .05
71 Peter Andersson .01 .05
72 Sandis Ozolinsh UER .01 .05
(Petri Skriko on back)
73 Joby Messier RC .01 .05
74 John Blue .02 .10
75 Pat Elynuik .01 .05
76 Keith Osborne RC .01 .05
77 Greg Adams .01 .05
78 Chris Gratton .02 .10
79 Louie DeBrusk .01 .05
80 Todd Harkins RC .01 .05
81 Neil Brady .01 .05
82 Philippe Boucher .01 .05
83 Darryl Sydor .01 .05
84 Oleg Petrov .01 .05
85 Andrei Kovalenko .01 .05
86 Dave Andreychuk .02 .10
87 Jeff Daniels .01 .05
88 Kevin Todd .01 .05
89 Mark Tinordi .01 .05
90 Garry Galley .01 .05
91 Shawn Burr .01 .05
92 Tom Pederson .01 .05
93 Warren Rychel .01 .05
94 Stu Barnes .01 .05
95 Peter Bondra .02 .10
96 Brian Skrudland .01 .05
97 Doug MacDonald RC .01 .05
98 Rob Niedermayer .02 .10
99 Wayne Gretzky .60 1.50
100 Peter Taglianetti .01 .05
101 Don Sweeney .01 .05
102 Andrei Lomakin .01 .05
103 Checklist 1-103 .01 .05
104 Sergio Momesso .01 .05
105 Dave Archibald .01 .05
106 Karl Dykhuis .01 .05
107 Scott Mellanby .02 .10
108 Paul DiPietro .01 .05
109 Neal Broten .02 .10
110 Chris Terreri .02 .10
111 Craig MacTavish .01 .05
112 Jody Hull .01 .05
113 Philippe Bozon .01 .05
114 Geoff Courtnall .01 .05
115 Ed Olczyk .01 .05
116 Ray Bourque .15 .40
117 Gilbert Dionne .01 .05
118 Valeri Kamensky .02 .10
119 Scott Stevens .02 .10
120 Pelle Eklund .01 .05
121 Brian Bradley .01 .05
122 Steve Thomas .01 .05
123 Don Beaupre .02 .10
124 Joel Otto .01 .05
125 Arturs Irbe .02 .10
126 Kevin Stevens .01 .05
127 Dimitri Yushkevich .01 .05
128 Adam Graves .01 .05
129 Chris Chelios .08 .25
130 Jeff Brown .01 .05
131 Paul Ranheim .01 .05
132 Shayne Corson .01 .05
133 Curtis Leschyshyn .01 .05
134 John MacLean .02 .10
135 Dimitri Khristich .01 .05
136 Dino Ciccarelli .02 .10
137 Pat LaFontaine .08 .25
138 Patrick Poulin .01 .05
139 Jaromir Jagr .15 .40
140 Kevin Hatcher .01 .05
141 Christian Ruuttu .01 .05
142 Ulf Samuelsson .01 .05
143 Ted Donato .01 .05
144 Bob Essensa .02 .10
145 Dave Gagner .02 .10
146 Tony Granato .01 .05
147 Ed Belfour .08 .25
148 Kirk Muller .01 .05
149 Rob Gaudreau RC .01 .05
150 Nicklas Lidstrom .08 .25
151 Gary Roberts .01 .05
152 Trent Klatt .01 .05
153 Ray Ferraro .01 .05
154 Michal Pivonka .01 .05
155 Mike Foligno .01 .05
156 Kirk McLean .02 .10
157 Curtis Joseph .08 .25
158 Roman Hamrlik .01 .05
159 Felix Potvin .08 .25
160 Brett Hull .10 .30
161 Alexei Zhitnik UER .01 .05
(Listed as being drafted in 1990; should be 1991)
162 Alexei Zhamnov .02 .10
163 Grant Fuhr .02 .10
164 Nikolai Borschevsky .01 .05
165 Tomas Jelinek .01 .05
166 Thomas Steen .01 .05
167 John LeClair .08 .25
168 Vladimir Vujtek .01 .05
169 Richard Smehlik .01 .05
170 Alexandre Daigle .01 .05
171 Sergei Fedorov .15 .40
172 Steve Larmer .02 .10
173 Darius Kasparaitis .01 .05
174 Igor Kravchuk .01 .05
175 Owen Nolan .02 .10
176 Rob DiMaio .01 .05
177 Mike Vernon .02 .10
178 Alexander Semak .01 .05
179 Rick Tocchet .02 .10
180 Bill Ranford .02 .10
181 Sergei Zubov .01 .05
182 Tommy Soderstrom .02 .10
183 Al Iafrate .01 .05
184 Eric Desjardins .02 .10
185 Bret Hedican .01 .05
186 Joe Mullen .02 .10
187 Doug Bodger .01 .05
188 Tomas Sandstrom .01 .05
189 Glen Murray .01 .05
190 Chris Pronger .02 .10
191 Mike Craig .01 .05
192 Jim Paek .01 .05
193 Doug Zmolek .01 .05
194 Yves Racine .01 .05
195 Keith Tkachuk .08 .25
196 Chris Lindberg .01 .05
197 Kelly Buchberger .01 .05
198 Mark Janssens .01 .05
199 Peter Zezel .01 .05
200 Bob Probert .02 .10
201 Brad May .02 .10
202 Rob Zamuner .02 .10
203 Stephane Fiset .02 .10
204 Derian Hatcher .02 .10
205 Mike Gartner .02 .10
206 Checklist 104-206 .01 .05
207 Todd Krygier .01 .05
208 Glen Wesley .01 .05
209 Fredrik Olausson .01 .05
210 Patrick Flatley .01 .05
211 Cliff Ronning .01 .05
212 Kevin Dineen .01 .05
213 Zarley Zalapski .01 .05
214 Stephane Matteau .01 .05
215 Dave Ellett .01 .05
216 Kelly Hrudey .02 .10
217 Steve Duchesne .01 .05
218 Bobby Holik .01 .05
219 Brad Dalgarno .01 .05
220 Mats Sundin 100 CL .02 .10
221 Pat LaFontaine 100 .02 .10
222 Mark Recchi 100 .02 .10
223 Joe Sakic 100 .08 .25
224 Pierre Turgeon 100 .02 .10
225 Craig Janney 100 .02 .10
226 Adam Oates 100 .02 .10
227 Steve Yzerman 100 .25 .60
228 Mats Sundin 100 .02 .10
229 Theo Fleury 100 .02 .10
230 Kevin Stevens 100 .01 .05
231 Luc Robitaille 100 .02 .10
232 Brett Hull 100 .02 .10
233 Rick Tocchet 100 .02 .10
234 Alexander Mogilny 100 .02 .10
235 Jeremy Roenick 100 .05 .15
236 Guy Leveque .01 .05
Turner Stevenson
SR CL
237 Adam Bennett SR RC .01 .05
238 Dody Wood SR RC .01 .05
239 Niclas Andersson SR .01 .05
240 Jason Bowen SR RC .01 .05
241 Steve Junker SR RC .01 .05
242 Bryan Smolinski SR .01 .05
243 Chris Simon SR RC .30 .75
244 Sergei Zholtok SR .01 .05
245 Dan Ratushny SR RC .01 .05
246 Guy Leveque SR .01 .05
247 Scott Thomas SR RC .01 .05
248 Turner Stevenson SR .01 .05
249 Dan Keczmer SR .01 .05
250 Alexandre Daigle WJC CL .01 .05
251 Adrian Aucoin WJC RC .08 .25
252 Jason Smith WJC .01 .05
253 Ralph Intranuovo WJC RC .01 .05
254 Jason Dawe WJC .01 .05
255 Jeff Bes WJC RC .01 .05
256 Tyler Wright WJC .01 .05
257 Martin Lapointe WJC .01 .05
258 Jeff Shantz WJC RC .01 .05
259 Martin Gendron WJC RC .01 .05
260 Philippe DeRouville WJC RC .01 .05
261 Frantisek Kaberle WJC RC .02 .10
262 Radim Bicanek WJC RC .02 .10
263 Tomas Klimt WJC RC .02 .10
264 Tomas Nemcicky WJC RC .02 .10
265 Richard Kapus WJC RC .02 .10
266 Patrik Krisak WJC RC .02 .10
267 Roman Kadera WJC RC .02 .10
268 Kimmo Timonen WJC RC .30 .75
269 Jukka Ollila WJC RC .02 .10
270 Tuomas Gronman WJC .01 .05
271 Mikko Luovi WJC RC .02 .10
272 Sergei Gonchar WJC RC .30 .75
273 Maxim Golanov WJC RC .02 .10
274 Oleg Belov WJC RC .02 .10
275 Sergei Klimovich WJC RC .02 .10
276 Sergei Brylin WJC RC .01 .05
277 Alexei Yashin WJC .01 .05
278 Vitali Tomilin WJC RC .02 .10
279 Alexander Cherbaev .01 .05
WJC
280 Eric Lindros ART .08 .25
281 Teemu Selanne ART .08 .25
282 Joe Juneau ART .02 .10
283 Vladimir Malakhov ART .01 .05
284 Scott Niedermayer ART .01 .05
285 Felix Potvin ART .02 .10
286 Adam Oates TL .02 .10
287 Pat LaFontaine TL .02 .10
288 Theo Fleury TL .02 .10
289 Jeremy Roenick TL .05 .15
290 Steve Yzerman TL .25 .60
291 Petr Klima TL .01 .05
Doug Weight TL
292 Geoff Sanderson TL .02 .10
293 Luc Robitaille TL .02 .10
294 Mike Modano TL .02 .10
295 Vincent Damphousse TL .01 .05
296 Claude Lemieux TL .01 .05
297 Pierre Turgeon TL .02 .10
298 Mark Messier TL .02 .10
299 Norm Maciver TL .01 .05
300 Mark Recchi TL .02 .10
301 Mario Lemieux TL .25 .60
302 Mats Sundin TL .02 .10
303 Craig Janney TL .02 .10
304 Kelly Kisio TL .01 .05
305 Brian Bradley TL .01 .05
306 Doug Gilmour TL .02 .10
307 Pavel Bure TL .02 .10
308 Peter Bondra TL .02 .10
309 Teemu Selanne TL .08 .25
310 Checklist 207-310 .01 .05
311 Terry Yake .01 .05
312 Bob Sweeney .01 .05
313 Robert Reichel .01 .05
314 Jeremy Roenick .10 .30
315 Paul Coffey .08 .25
316 Geoff Sanderson .02 .10
317 Rob Blake .02 .10
318 Patrice Brisebois .01 .05
319 Jaroslav Modry RC .01 .05
320 Scott Lachance .01 .05
321 Glenn Healy .02 .10
322 Martin Gelinas .01 .05
323 Craig Janney .02 .10
324 Bill McDougall RC .01 .05
325 Shawn Antoski .01 .05
326 Olaf Kolzig .02 .10
327 Adam Oates .02 .10
328 Dirk Graham .01 .05
329 Brent Gilchrist .01 .05
330 Zdeno Ciger .01 .05
331 Pat Verbeek .01 .05
332 Jari Kurri .08 .25
333 Kevin Haller .01 .05
334 Martin Brodeur .30 .75
335 Norm Maciver .01 .05
336 Dominic Roussel .02 .10
337 Iain Fraser RC .01 .05
338 Vitali Karamnov .01 .05
339 Rene Corbet RC .01 .05
340 Wendel Clark .02 .10
341 Mike Ridley .01 .05
342 Nelson Emerson .01 .05
343 Joe Juneau .02 .10
344 Vesa Viitakoski RC .01 .05
345 Steve Chiasson .01 .05
346 Andrew Cassels .01 .05
347 Pierre Turgeon .02 .10
348 Brian Leetch .08 .25
349 Alexei Yashin .01 .05
350 Mark Recchi .02 .10
351 Ron Francis .02 .10
352 Mike Ricci .01 .05
353 Igor Korolev .01 .05
354 Brent Gretzky RC .01 .05
355 Dave Poulin .01 .05
356 Cam Neely .08 .25
357 Gary Suter .01 .05
358 Dave Manson .01 .05
359 Robert Kron .01 .05
360 Ulf Dahlen .01 .05
361 Rod Brind'Amour .02 .10
362 Alexei Gusarov .01 .05
363 Vitali Prokhorov .01 .05
364 Dimitri Rhodes RC .02 .10
365 Paul Ysebaert .01 .05
366 Vladimir Konstantinov .02 .10
367 Steven Rice .01 .05
368 Brian Propp .01 .05
369 Valeri Zelepukin .01 .05
370 David Volek .01 .05
371 Sergei Nemchinov .01 .05
372 Pavol Demitra .08 .25
373 Brent Fedyk .01 .05
374 Larry Murphy .02 .10
375 Dave Karpa .01 .05
376 Dave Babych .01 .05
377 Keith Jones .01 .05
378 Neil Wilkinson .01 .05
379 Jozef Stumpel .01 .05
380 Vincent Damphousse .01 .05
381 Tom Kurvers .01 .05
382 Doug Gilmour .02 .10
383 Trevor Linden .02 .10
384 Kelly Miller .01 .05
385 Tim Sweeney .01 .05
386 Mikhail Tatarinov .01 .05
387 Dominic Hasek .30 .75
388 Steve Yzerman .50 1.25
389 Scott Pearson .01 .05
390 Brian Bellows .01 .05
391 Claude Lemieux .01 .05
392 Marty McInnis .01 .05
393 Jim Sandlak .01 .05
394 Jocelyn Thibault RC .40 1.00
395 John Cullen .01 .05
396 Joe Nieuwendyk .02 .10
397 Mike Modano .15 .40
398 Ray Sheppard .02 .10
399 Trevor Kidd .02 .10
400 Checklist .01 .05
401 Frank Pietrangelo .02 .10
402 Stephan Lebeau .01 .05
403 Stephane Richer .02 .10
404 Greg Gilbert .01 .05
405 Dmitri Filimonov .01 .05
406 Vyacheslav Butsayev .01 .05
407 Mario Lemieux .50 1.25
408 Kevin Miller .01 .05
409 John Tucker .01 .05
410 Murray Craven .01 .05
411 Dale Hawerchuk .02 .10
412 Al MacInnis .02 .10
413 Keith Primeau .01 .05
414 Luc Robitaille .02 .10
415 Benoit Brunet .01 .05
416 Tom Chorske .01 .05
417 Derek King .01 .05
418 Troy Mallette .01 .05
419 Mats Sundin .08 .25
420 Kent Manderville .01 .05
421 Kip Miller .01 .05
422 Jarkko Varvio .01 .05
423 Jason Arnott RC .40 1.00
424 Craig Billington .02 .10
425 Stewart Malgunas RC .01 .05
426 Ron Tugnutt .02 .10
427 Alexei Kudashov RC .01 .05
428 Harijs Vitolinsh .01 .05
429 Bill Houlder .01 .05
430 Craig Simpson .01 .05
431 Wes Walz .01 .05
432 Micah Aivazoff RC .01 .05
433 Scott Levins RC .01 .05
434 Ron Hextall .02 .10
435 Fred Brathwaite RC .30 .75
436 Chad Penney RC .01 .05
437 Vlastimil Kroupa RC .01 .05
438 Troy Loney .01 .05
439 Matthew Barnaby .02 .10
440 Kevin Todd .01 .05
441 Paul Cavallini .01 .05
442 Doug Weight .02 .10
443 Egeny Davydov .01 .05
444 Dominic Lavoie .01 .05
445 Peter Popovic RC .01 .05
446 Sergei Makarov .01 .05
447 Matt Martin RC .01 .05
448 Teemu Selanne .08 .25
449 Todd Ewen .01 .05
450 Sergei Petrenko .01 .05
451 Jeff Shantz .01 .05
452 Greg Johnson .01 .05
453 Brent Severyn RC .01 .05
454 Shawn McEachern .01 .05
455 Pierre Sevigny .01 .05
456 Benoit Hogue .01 .05
457 Esa Tikkanen .01 .05
458 Brian Glynn .01 .05
459 Doug Brown .01 .05
460 Mike Rathje .01 .05
461 Rudy Poeschek .01 .05
462 Jason Woolley .01 .05
463 Patrick Carnback RC .01 .05
464 Cam Stewart RC .01 .05
465 Petr Svoboda .01 .05
466 Ted Drury .01 .05
467 Ladislav Karabin RC .01 .05
468 Paul Broten .01 .05
469 Alexander Godynyuk .01 .05
470 Bob Jay RC .01 .05
471 Steve Larmer .02 .10
472 Jim Montgomery RC .01 .05
473 Darren Puppa .01 .05
474 Alexei Kasatonov .01 .05
475 Derek Plante RC .01 .05
476 German Titov RC .01 .05
477 Steve Dubinsky RC .01 .05
478 Andy Moog .02 .10
479 Aaron Ward RC .01 .05
480 Dean McAmmond .01 .05
481 Randy Gilhen .01 .05
482 Jason Muzzatti RC .02 .10
483 Corey Millen .01 .05
484 Alexander Karpovtsev .01 .05
485 Bill Huard RC .01 .05
486 Mikael Renberg .08 .25
487 Marty McSorley .01 .05
488 Alexander Mogilny .02 .10
489 Michal Sykora RC .01 .05
490 Checklist .01 .05
491 Tom Tilley .01 .05
492 Boris Mironov .01 .05
493 Sandy McCarthy .01 .05
494 Mark Astley RC .01 .05
495 Slava Kozlov .02 .10
496 Brian Benning .01 .05
497 Eric Weinrich .01 .05
498 Robert Burakovsky RC .01 .05
499 Patrick Lebeau .01 .05
500 Markus Naslund .08 .25
501 Jimmy Waite .02 .10
502 Denis Savard .02 .10
503 Jose Charbonneau .01 .05
504 Randy Burridge .01 .05
505 Arto Blomsten .01 .05
506 Shaun Van Allen .01 .05
507 Jon Casey .02 .10
508 Darren McCarty RC .30 .75
509 Roman Oksiuta RC .01 .05
510 Jody Hull .01 .05
511 Scott Scissons .01 .05
512 Jeff Norton .01 .05
513 Dmitri Mironov .01 .05
514 Sergei Bautin .01 .05
515 Garry Valk .01 .05
516 Keith Carney .01 .05
517 James Black .01 .05
518 Pat Peake .01 .05
519 Chris Osgood RC .60 1.00
520 Kirk Maltby RC .01 .05
521 Gord Murphy .01 .05
522 Mattias Norstrom RC .01 .05
523 Milos Holan RC .01 .05
524 Dave McLwain .01 .05
525 Phil Housley .02 .10
526 Petr Klima .01 .05
527 John McIntyre .01 .05
528 Enrico Ciccone .01 .05
529 Stephane Quintal .01 .05
530 World Junior .02 .10
Checklist
531 Anson Carter WJC RC .30 .75
532 Jeff Friesen WJC RC .30 .75
533 Yanick Dube WJC RC .01 .05
534 Jason Botterill WJC RC .08 .25
535 Todd Harvey WJC RC .01 .05
536 Manny Fernandez WJC RC .30 .75
537 Jason Allison WJC RC .30 .75
538 Jamie Storr WJC RC .30 .75
539 Rick Girrard WJC RC .01 .05
540 Martin Gendron WJC .01 .05
541 Joel Bouchard WJC RC .01 .05
542 Mike Peca WJC RC .30 .75
543 Nick Stajduhar WJC RC .01 .05
544 Brendan Witt WJC RC .01 .05
545 Aaron Gavey WJC RC .01 .05
546 Chris Armstrong WJC RC .01 .05
547 Curtis Bowen WJC RC .01 .05
548 Brandon Convery WJC RC .01 .05
549 Bryan McCabe WJC RC .08 .25
550 Marty Murray WJC RC .01 .05
551 Ryan Sittler WJC .01 .05
552 Jason McBain WJC RC .01 .05
553 Richard Park WJC RC .01 .05
554 Aaron Ellis WJC RC .02 .10
555 Toby Kvalevog WJC RC .02 .10
556 Jay Pandolfo WJC RC .01 .05
557 John Emmons WJC .01 .05
558 David Wilkie WJC RC .01 .05
559 John Varga WJC RC .01 .05
560 Jason Bonsignore WJC RC .01 .05
561 Deron Quint WJC RC .01 .05
562 Adam Deadmarsh WJC .01 .05
563 Jon Coleman WJC RC .01 .05
564 Bob Lachance WJC RC .01 .05
565 Chris O'Sullivan WJC RC .01 .05
566 J.Langenbrunner WJC RC .30 .75
567 Kevin Hilton WJC RC .01 .05
568 Kevyn Adams WJC RC .01 .05
569 Saku Koivu WJC .08 .25
570 Mats Lindgren WJC RC .01 .05
571 Valeri Bure WJC RC .30 .75
572 Edvin Frylen WJC RC .01 .05
573 Jaroslav Miklenda WJC RC .02 .10
574 Vadim Sharifjanov WJC .02 .10
575 Checklist Card .01 .05
99B1 W.Gretzky 802 Silver 6.00 15.00
99B2 W.Gretzky 802 Gold 4.00 10.00
SP4 Teemu Selanne Hologram .08 .25

1993-94 Upper Deck Award Winners

Randomly inserted at a rate of 1:30 Canadian first-series foil packs, this eight-card set measures the standard size. The fronts feature a black-and-white photo of the player and his trophy. The player's name appears at the bottom and in silver-foil letters on the left side.

COMPLETE SET (8) 6.00 12.00
AW1 Mario Lemieux 1.50 4.00
AW2 Teemu Selanne .30 .75
Calder Trophy
AW3 Ed Belfour .30 .75
Jennings Trophy
Vezina Trophy
AW4 Patrick Roy 1.50 4.00
Conn Smythe Trophy
AW5 Chris Chelios .30 .75
Jack Norris Trophy
AW6 Doug Gilmour .15 .30
Frank J. Selke Trophy
AW7 Pierre Turgeon .15 .30
Lady Byng Trophy
AW8 Dave Poulin .05 .15
King Clancy

1993-94 Upper Deck Future Heroes

Randomly inserted at a rate of 1:30 first-series U.S. hobby packs, this 10-card set measures the standard size. The tan-bordered fronts feature sepia-toned action player photos with the player's name in white lettering within a black bar above the photo. The set's title appears below the photo, with the word "Heroes" printed in copper foil. On a gray background, the back carries a player profile. The cards are numbered on the back and continue where the Howe Heroes left off.

COMPLETE SET (10) 6.00 12.00
28 Felix Potvin .30 .75
29 Pat Falloon .05 .15
30 Pavel Bure .30 .75
31 Eric Lindros .30 .75
32 Teemu Selanne .30 .75
33 Jaromir Jagr .50 1.25
34 Alexander Mogilny .15 .30
35 Joe Juneau .15 .30
36 Checklist 2.00 5.00
NNO Header Card .75 2.00

1993-94 Upper Deck Gretzky's Great Ones

Randomly inserted in series one packs and one per series one jumbo, this 10-card set measures the standard size. The fronts feature color player photos with blue and gray bars above, below, and to the left. The player's name and the words "Gretzky's Great Ones" in copper-foil letters appear below and above the photo, respectively.The cards are numbered on the back with a "GG" prefix.

COMPLETE SET (10) 2.50 5.00
GG1 Denis Savard .10 .20
GG2 Chris Chelios .20 .50
GG3 Brett Hull .25 .60
GG4 Mario Lemieux 1.00 2.50
GG5 Mark Messier .20 .50
GG6 Paul Coffey .20 .50
GG7 Theo Fleury .05 .10
GG8 Luc Robitaille .10 .20
GG9 Marty McSorley .05 .10
GG10 Grant Fuhr .10 .20

1993-94 Upper Deck Gretzky Box Bottom

Issued on the bottom of Upper Deck boxes, this card measures approximately 5" by 7" and features Wayne Gretzky on the front. The design is the same as his regular issue card. The back is blank. The card is unnumbered.

1 Wayne Gretzky .40 1.00

1993-94 Upper Deck Gretzky Sheet

This sheet was mailed to collectors who ordered Wayne Gretzky's 24-Karat Gold Card commemorating his NHL record breaking 802nd goal after Upper Deck had unexpected production difficulties. It could also be ordered through the Upper Deck Authenticated catalog. It measures 8 1/2" by 11". The front features a white border and three color action photos of Wayne Gretzky set against a background with the number "802". A seal on the front carries the serial number and the production figure (30,000). The back is blank.

1 Wayne Gretzky 8.00 20.00

1993-94 Upper Deck Hat Tricks

Inserted one per series one jumbo pack, this 20-card set measures the standard size. The fronts feature color player photos that are borderless, except on the right, where a strip that fades from brown to black carries the player's name. The cards are numbered on the back with an "HT" prefix.

COMPLETE SET (20) 3.00 6.00
HT1 Adam Graves .05 .10
HT2 Geoff Sanderson .10 .20
HT3 Gary Roberts .05 .10
HT4 Robert Reichel .05 .10
HT5 Adam Oates .10 .20
HT6 Steve Yzerman 1.00 2.50
HT7 Alexei Kovalev .10 .20
HT8 Vincent Damphousse .05 .10
HT9 Rob Gaudreau .05 .10
HT10 Pat LaFontaine .20 .50
HT11 Pierre Turgeon .10 .20
HT12 Rick Tocchet .10 .20
HT13 Michael Nylander .05 .10
HT14 Steve Larmer .10 .20
HT15 Alexander Mogilny .10 .20
HT16 Owen Nolan .10 .20
HT17 Luc Robitaille .10 .20
HT18 Jeremy Roenick .25 .60
HT19 Kevin Stevens .05 .10
HT20 Mats Sundin .20 .50

1993-94 Upper Deck Next In Line

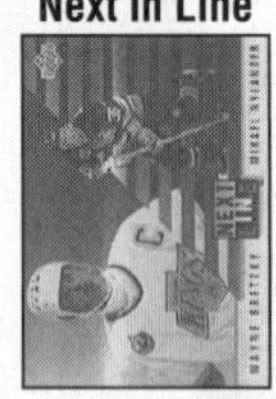

Randomly inserted in all first-series packs, this six-card set measures the standard-size. The horizontal metallic and prismatic fronts feature photos of two NHL players, diagonally divided in the middle. The players' names appear under the photos. The cards are numbered on the back with an "NL" prefix.

COMPLETE SET (6) 7.50 15.00
NL1 Wayne Gretzky 2.50 6.00
Michael Nylander
NL2 Brett Hull .75 2.00
Patrick Poulin
NL3 Steve Yzerman 2.50 6.00
Joe Sakic
NL4 Ray Bourque 2.00 5.00
Brian Leetch
NL5 Doug Gilmour 1.00 2.50
Keith Tkachuk
NL6 Patrick Roy 1.25 3.00
Felix Potvin

1993-94 Upper Deck NHL's Best

Randomly inserted at a rate of 1:30 first-series U.S. retail packs, this 10-card set measures the standard size. The fronts feature color action player photos that are borderless, except at the bottom, where a black bar carries the player's name. The cards are numbered on the back with an "HB" prefix.

COMPLETE SET (10) 5.00 10.00
HB1 Alexander Mogilny .15 .30
HB2 Rob Gaudreau .05 .15
HB3 Brett Hull .40 1.00
HB4 Dallas Drake .05 .15
HB5 Pavel Bure .30 .75
HB6 Alexei Kovalev .15 .30
HB7 Mario Lemieux 1.50 4.00
HB8 Eric Lindros .30 .75
HB9 Wayne Gretzky 2.00 5.00
HB10 Joe Juneau .15 .30

1993-94 Upper Deck NHLPA/Roots

Teamed with the NHL Players Association, Upper Deck issued these clothing tags as a promotion for a new line of clothing produced by the clothing manufacturer, Roots Canada. Called "Hang Out," each article of clothing came with one of ten "hang tag" cards featuring on their fronts a full-bleed photo of the NHL player wearing the clothing. The clothing tags measure the standard size and are punch holed in the upper left corner. Versions of these cards without the punch hole also exist. With a faded and enlarged Upper Deck logo, the backs carry the player's name and an advertisement for the NHLPA apparel. The cards are numbered on the back. The entire set could also be purchased by mail. The first series came out in 1993, while the second series came out in 1994. Reportedly 5,000 sets of the third series were produced. The backs of cards 21-30 also have a NHLPA apparel advertisement but sport a different design than cards 1-20.

COMPLETE SET (30) 16.00 40.00
COMPLETE SERIES 1 (10) 6.00 15.00
COMPLETE SERIES 2 (10) 6.00 15.00
COMPLETE SERIES 3 (10) 6.00 15.00
1 Trevor Linden .50 1.25
2 Patrick Roy 4.00 10.00
3 Felix Potvin .60 1.50
4 Steve Yzerman 4.00 10.00
5 Doug Gilmour .60 1.50
6 Wendel Clark .50 1.25
7 Kirk McLean .50 1.25
8 Larry Murphy .16 .40
9 Guy Carbonneau .16 .40
10 Mike Ricci .50 1.25
11 Doug Gilmour .60 1.50
12 Sergei Fedorov 1.20 3.00
13 Shayne Corson .16 .40
14 Alexei Yashin .50 1.25
15 Pavel Bure 1.60 4.00
16 Joe Sakic 1.60 4.00
17 Teemu Selanne 1.20 3.00
18 Dave Andreychuk .50 1.25
19 Al MacInnis .50 1.25
20 Rob Blake .50 1.25
21 Doug Gilmour .60 1.50
22 Steve Larmer .16 .40
23 Eric Lindros 1.60 4.00
24 Mike Modano .80 2.00
25 Vincent Damphousse .50 1.25
26 Mike Gartner .50 1.25
27 John Vanbiesbrouck .60 1.50
28 Theo Fleury .60 1.50
29 Ken Baumgartner .16 .40
30 Jeremy Roenick .60 1.50

1993-94 Upper Deck Program of Excellence

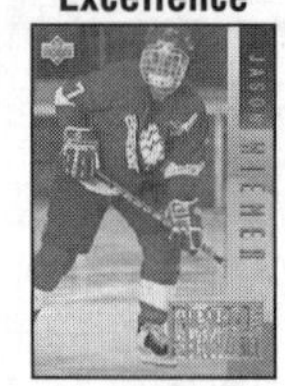

Randomly inserted at a rate of 1:30 Canadian second series packs, this 15-card set measures the standard size. The fronts feature color action player photos that are borderless, except at the right, where the margin carries the player's name in silver-foil letters. The silver-foil "Program of Excellence" logo rests at the lower right. The cards are numbered on the back with an "E" prefix.

COMPLETE SET (15) 10.00 20.00
E1 Adam Smith .05 .15
E2 Jason Podollan .05 .15
E3 Jason Wiemer .05 .15
E4 Jeff O'Neill .15 .30
E5 Daniel Goneau .05 .15
E6 Christian Laflamme .05 .15
E7 Daymond Langkow .05 .15
E8 Jeff Friesen 1.00 2.50
E9 Wayne Primeau .05 .15
E10 Paul Kariya 5.00 12.00
E11 Rob Niedermayer .15 .30
E12 Eric Lindros .30 .75
E13 Mario Lemieux 1.50 4.00
E14 Steve Yzerman 1.50 4.00
E15 Alexandre Daigle .05 .15

1993-94 Upper Deck Silver Skates

The first ten standard-size die-cut cards (H1-H10) listed below were randomly inserted in U.S. second-series hobby packs, while the second ten (R1-R10) were inserted in U.S. retail packs. The fronts feature color player action cutouts set on red and black backgrounds. The trade cards were randomly inserted in both hobby and jumbo packs and could be redeemed for a silver or gold retail set. These cards picture Gretzky, and because the majority were redeemed, they have become highly sought after in their own right.

*RETAIL GOLD EXCH: .75X TO 1.5X BASIC INSERTS
H1 Mario Lemieux 1.50 4.00
H2 Pavel Bure .30 .75
H3 Eric Lindros .30 .75
H4 Rob Niedermayer .15 .30
H5 Chris Pronger .15 .30
H6 Adam Oates .15 .30
H7 Pierre Turgeon .15 .30
H8 Alexei Yashin .05 .15
H9 Joe Sakic .60 1.50
H10 Alexander Mogilny .15 .30
R1 Wayne Gretzky 2.00 5.00
R2 Teemu Selanne .30 .75
R3 Alexandre Daigle .05 .15
R4 Chris Gratton .15 .30
R5 Brett Hull .40 1.00
R6 Steve Yzerman 1.50 4.00
R7 Doug Gilmour .15 .30
R8 Jaromir Jagr .50 1.25
R9 Jason Arnott .60 1.50
R10 Jeremy Roenick .40 1.00
NNO W.Gretzky Gold Trade 20.00 50.00
NNO W.Gretzky Silver Trade 15.00 40.00

1993-94 Upper Deck SP

Inserted one per second-series pack and two per second-series jumbo, these 180 standard-size cards feature color player action shots on their fronts. The photos are borderless, except at the bottom, where a team color-coded margin carries the player's name and position in white lettering. The player's team name appears in a silver-foil arc above him.

1 Sean Hill .15 .40
2 Troy Loney .15 .40
3 Joe Sacco .15 .40
4 Anatoli Semenov .15 .40
5 Ron Tugnutt .30 .75
6 Terry Yake .15 .40
7 Ray Bourque 1.25 3.00
8 Jon Casey .30 .75
9 Joe Juneau .30 .75
10 Cam Neely .75 2.00
11 Adam Oates .30 .75
12 Bryan Smolinski .15 .40
13 Matthew Barnaby .30 .75
14 Philippe Boucher .15 .40
15 Grant Fuhr .30 .75
16 Dale Hawerchuk .30 .75
17 Pat LaFontaine .75 2.00
18 Alexander Mogilny .30 .75
19 Craig Simpson .15 .40
20 Ted Drury .15 .40
21 Theo Fleury .15 .40
22 Al MacInnis .30 .75
23 Joe Nieuwendyk .30 .75
24 Joel Otto .15 .40
25 Gary Roberts .15 .40
26 Vesa Viitakoski .05 .10
27 Ed Belfour .75 2.00
28 Chris Chelios .75 2.00
29 Joe Murphy .15 .40
30 Patrick Poulin .15 .40
31 Jeremy Roenick 1.00 2.50
32 Jeff Shantz .15 .40
33 Kevin Todd .15 .40
34 Neal Broten .30 .75
35 Paul Cavallini .15 .40
36 Russ Courtnall .15 .40
37 Derian Hatcher .15 .40
38 Mike Modano 1.00 2.50
39 Andy Moog .30 .75
40 Jarkko Varvio .15 .40
41 Dino Ciccarelli .30 .75
42 Paul Coffey .75 2.00
43 Dallas Drake .05 .10
44 Sergei Fedorov 1.00 2.50
45 Keith Primeau .15 .40
46 Bob Probert .30 .75
47 Steve Yzerman 2.00 5.00
48 Jason Arnott .40 1.00
49 Shayne Corson .15 .40
50 Dave Manson .15 .40
51 Dean McAmmond .15 .40
52 Bill Ranford .30 .75
53 Doug Weight .30 .75
54 Brad Werenka .15 .40
55 Evgeny Davydov .15 .40
56 Scott Levins .05 .10
57 Scott Mellanby .30 .75
58 Rob Niedermayer .30 .75
59 Brian Skrudland .15 .40
60 John Vanbiesbrouck .30 .75
61 Robert Kron .15 .40
62 Michael Nylander .15 .40
63 Robert Petrovicky .15 .40
64 Chris Pronger .30 .75
65 Geoff Sanderson .30 .75
66 Darren Turcotte .15 .40
67 Pat Verbeek .15 .40
68 Rob Blake .30 .75
69 Tony Granato .15 .40
70 Wayne Gretzky 4.00 10.00
71 Kelly Hrudey .30 .75
72 Shawn McEachern .15 .40
73 Luc Robitaille .30 .75
74 Darryl Sydor .15 .40
75 Alexei Zhitnik .15 .40
76 Brian Bellows .15 .40
77 Vincent Damphousse .15 .40
78 Stephan Lebeau .15 .40
79 John LeClair .75 2.00
80 Kirk Muller .15 .40
81 Patrick Roy 2.50 6.00
82 Pierre Sevigny .15 .40
83 Claude Lemieux .15 .40
84 Corey Millen .15 .40
85 Bernie Nicholls .15 .40
86 Scott Niedermayer .15 .40
87 Stephane Richer .30 .75
88 Alexander Semak .15 .40
89 Scott Stevens .30 .75
90 Ray Ferraro .15 .40
91 Darius Kasparaitis .15 .40
92 Scott Lachance .15 .40
93 Vladimir Malakhov .15 .40
94 Marty McInnis .15 .40
95 Steve Thomas .15 .40
96 Pierre Turgeon .30 .75
97 Tony Amonte .30 .75
98 Mike Gartner .30 .75
99 Adam Graves .15 .40
100 Alexander Karpovtsev .15 .40
101 Alexei Kovalev .30 .75
102 Brian Leetch .75 2.00
103 Mark Messier .75 2.00
104 Esa Tikkanen .15 .40
105 Craig Billington .30 .75
106 Robert Burakovsky .05 .10
107 Alexandre Daigle .15 .40
108 Pavol Demitra .40 1.00
109 Dmitri Filimonov .15 .40
110 Bob Kudelski .15 .40
111 Norm Maciver .15 .40
112 Alexei Yashin .15 .40
113 Josef Beranek .15 .40
114 Rod Brind'Amour .30 .75
115 Milos Holan .05 .10
116 Eric Lindros .75 2.00
117 Mark Recchi .30 .75
118 Mikael Renberg .40 1.00
119 Dimitri Yushkevich .15 .40
120 Tom Barrasso .30 .75
121 Jaromir Jagr 1.25 3.00
122 Mario Lemieux 2.50 6.00
123 Markus Naslund .75 2.00
124 Kevin Stevens .15 .40
125 Martin Straka .15 .40
126 Rick Tocchet .30 .75
127 Martin Gelinas .15 .40
128 Owen Nolan .30 .75
129 Mike Ricci .15 .40
130 Joe Sakic 1.25 3.00
131 Chris Simon .60 1.50
132 Mats Sundin .75 2.00
133 Jocelyn Thibault .75 2.00
134 Philippe Bozon .15 .40
135 Jeff Brown .15 .40
136 Phil Housley .30 .75
137 Brett Hull 1.00 2.50
138 Craig Janney .30 .75
139 Curtis Joseph .75 2.00
140 Brendan Shanahan .75 2.00
141 Pat Falloon .15 .40
142 Johan Garpenlov .15 .40
143 Rob Gaudreau .15 .40
144 Vlastimil Kroupa .05 .10
145 Sergei Makarov .15 .40
146 Sandis Ozolinsh .15 .40
147 Mike Rathje .15 .40
148 Brian Bradley .15 .40
149 Chris Gratton .30 .75
150 Brent Gretzky .05 .10
151 Roman Hamrlik .15 .40
152 Petr Klima .15 .40
153 Denis Savard .30 .75
154 Rob Zamuner .15 .40
155 Dave Andreychuk .30 .75
156 Nikolai Borschevsky .15 .40
157 Dave Ellett .15 .40
158 Doug Gilmour .30 .75
159 Alexei Kudashov .05 .10
160 Felix Potvin .75 2.00
161 Greg Adams .15 .40
162 Pavel Bure .75 2.00
163 Geoff Courtnall .15 .40
164 Trevor Linden .30 .75
165 Kirk McLean .30 .75
166 Jiri Slegr .15 .40
167 Dixon Ward .15 .40
168 Peter Bondra .30 .75
169 Kevin Hatcher .15 .40
170 Al Iafrate .15 .40
171 Dimitri Khristich .15 .40
172 Pat Peake .15 .40
173 Mike Ridley .15 .40
174 Arto Blomsten .15 .40
175 Nelson Emerson .15 .40
176 Boris Mironov .15 .40
177 Teemu Selanne .75 2.00
178 Keith Tkachuk .75 2.00
179 Paul Ysebaert .15 .40
180 Alexei Zhamnov .30 .75

1994-95 Upper Deck

The 1994-95 Upper Deck set was issued in two series of 270 and 300 cards for a total of 570 standard-size cards. The product was available in three packaging versions per series: US Hobby, US Retail and Canadian. The fronts have a team color coded bar on the left border. The team name, position and player name are within the bar in gold foil. Due to a printing error, card numbers 22, 65, 85 and 200 each appear with two different numbers. Each variation was printed in the same quantity, so neither version carries a premium. Subsets include Shooter's Edge (227-234), Super Rookies (235-270), World Junior Championship teams including Canada (496-505), Czech Republic (506-509), Finland (510-512), Russia (513-517), Sweden (518-521) and USA (522-525), as well as Calder Candidates (526-540), and 1994 World Tour (541-570).

COMPLETE SET (570) 20.00 50.00
COMPLETE SERIES 1 (270) 10.00 25.00
COMPLETE SERIES 2 (300) 10.00 25.00
1 Wayne Gretzky .75 2.00
2 German Titov .02 .10
3 Guy Hebert .05 .15
4 Tony Amonte .05 .15
5 Dino Ciccarelli .05 .15
6 Geoff Sanderson .05 .15
7 Alexei Zhamnov .05 .15
8 John MacLean .05 .15
9 Brent Fedyk .02 .10
10 Adam Graves .02 .10
11 Adam Oates .05 .15
12 Ron Francis .05 .15
13 Bobby Dollas .02 .10
14 Ray Ferraro .02 .10
15 Paul Broten .02 .10
16 Ulf Dahlen .02 .10
17 Pat LaFontaine .10 .30
18 Craig Janney .05 .15
19 Garry Galley .02 .10
20 Gary Roberts .02 .10
21 Bill Ranford .05 .15
22 Mario Lemieux 200B .60 1.50
23 Glen Murray .02 .10
24 Paul Coffey .10 .30
25 Corey Millen .02 .10
26 Chris Chelios .10 .30
27 Ronnie Stern .02 .10
28 Zdeno Ciger .02 .10
29 Tony Granato .02 .10
30 Donald Audette .02 .10
31 Russ Courtnall .02 .10
32 Mike Gartner .05 .15
33 Marty McSorley .02 .10
34 Jeff Brown .02 .10
35 Mark Janssens .02 .10
36 Patrick Poulin .02 .10
37 Sergei Fedorov .20 .50
38 Tim Sweeney .02 .10
39 John Slaney .02 .10
40 Steve Larmer .05 .15
41 Dave Karpa .02 .10
42 Esa Tikkanen .02 .10
43 Joel Otto .02 .10
44 Doug Weight .05 .15
45 Murray Craven .02 .10
46 John Vanbiesbrouck .05 .15
47 Nelson Emerson .02 .10
48 Dean Evason .02 .10
49 Evgeny Davydov .02 .10
50 Craig Simpson .02 .10
51 Mats Sundin .10 .30
52 Chris Pronger .10 .30
53 Stephan Lebeau .02 .10
54 Martin Gelinas .02 .10
55 Bob Rouse .02 .10
56 Christian Ruuttu .02 .10
57 Gilbert Dionne .02 .10
58 Mike Modano .20 .50
59 Derek King .02 .10
60 Peter Stastny .05 .15
61 Ted Donato .02 .10
62 Mark Messier .10 .30
63 Dave Manson .02 .10
64 Johan Garpenlov .02 .10
65 Igor Larionov .02 .10
66 Kirk Muller .02 .10
67 Dave Ellett .02 .10
68 Dale Hunter .02 .10
69 Brent Gretzky .02 .10
70 Tom Barrasso .05 .15
71 Philippe Boucher .02 .10
72 Jesse Belanger .02 .10
73 Scott Stevens .05 .15
74 Gary Suter .02 .10
75 Tim Cheveldae .05 .15
76 Dimitri Khristich .02 .10
77 Pierre Turgeon .05 .15
78 Mike Richter .10 .30
79 Michael Nylander .02 .10
80 Sergei Krivokrasov .02 .10
81 Andy Moog UER .10 .30
(Darcy Wakaluk on back)
82 Al Iafrate .02 .10
83 Bernie Nicholls .05 .15
84 Darren Turcotte .02 .10
85 Sergio Momesso .02 .10
86 Petr Klima .02 .10
87 Alexandre Daigle .02 .10
88 Joe Juneau .05 .15
89 Glen Wesley .02 .10
90 Teemu Selanne .10 .30
91 Curtis Joseph .10 .30
92 Scott Mellanby .05 .15
93 Jaromir Jagr .20 .50
94 Mark Recchi .05 .15
95 Jiri Slegr .02 .10
96 Martin Brodeur .30 .75
97 Scott Pearson .02 .10
98 Eric Lindros .10 .30
99 Larry Murphy .05 .15
100 Sergei Zubov .02 .10
101 Mathieu Schneider .02 .10
102 Dale Hawerchuk .05 .15
103 Owen Nolan .05 .15
104 Darryl Sydor .02 .10
105 Anatoli Semenov .02 .10
106 Marty McInnis .02 .10
107 Derek Mayer .02 .10
108 Steve Duchesne .02 .10
109 Geoff Smith .02 .10
110 Zarley Zalapski .02 .10
111 Rod Brind'Amour .05 .15
112 Nicklas Lidstrom .10 .30
113 Teppo Numminen .02 .10
114 Denny Felsner .02 .10
115 Wendel Clark .05 .15
116 Arturs Irbe .05 .15
117 Josef Beranek .02 .10
118 Brian Bradley .02 .10
119 Eric Weinrich .02 .10
120 Kevin Todd .02 .10
121 Patrick Roy .60 1.50
122 Guy Carbonneau .02 .10
123 Tom Kurvers .02 .10
124 Sergei Makarov .02 .10
125 Pat Peake .02 .10
126 Danton Cole .02 .10
127 Derian Hatcher .02 .10
128 Kjell Samuelsson .02 .10
129 Alexei Yashin .02 .10
130 Chris Osgood .05 .15
131 Kent Manderville .02 .10
132 Jim Montgomery .02 .10
133 Kirk McLean .05 .15
134 Kelly Buchberger .02 .10
135 Peter Bondra .05 .15
136 Stephane Matteau .02 .10
137 Oleg Petrov .02 .10
138 Doug Gilmour .05 .15
139 Vladimir Malakhov .02 .10
140 Peter Zezel .02 .10
141 Mike Vernon .05 .15
142 Derek Plante .02 .10
143 Valeri Zelepukin .02 .10
144 Kevin Haller .02 .10
145 Keith Tkachuk .10 .30
146 Claude Boivin .02 .10
147 Jocelyn Thibault .10 .30
148 Jyrki Lumme .02 .10
149 Ray Whitney .02 .10
150 Al MacInnis .05 .15
151 Kelly Miller .02 .10
152 Ray Sheppard .05 .15
153 Aaron Ward .02 .10
154 Damian Rhodes .05 .15
155 Jozef Stumpel .02 .10
156 Sergei Nemchinov .02 .10
157 Richard Matvichuk .02 .10
158 Sean Burke .05 .15
159 Todd Marchant .02 .10
160 Ryan McGill .02 .10
161 Sean Hill .02 .10
162 Iain Fraser .02 .10
163 Shawn McEachern .02 .10
164 Petr Nedved .05 .15
165 John Lilley .02 .10
166 Joe Sacco .02 .10
167 Jason Dawe .02 .10
168 Mike Rathje .02 .10
169 Phil Housley .05 .15
170 Ron Hextall .05 .15
171 Yves Racine .02 .10
172 Boris Mironov .02 .10
173 Vitali Prokhorov .02 .10
174 Roman Hamrlik .05 .15
175 Robert Lang .02 .10
176 Jody Hull .02 .10
177 Mike Ridley .02 .10
178 Dmitri Filimonov .02 .10
179 Rene Corbet .02 .10
180 Rob Pearson .02 .10
181 Richard Smehlik .02 .10
182 Rob Gaudreau .02 .10
183 Bill Houlder .02 .10
184 Igor Korolev .02 .10
185 Chris Joseph .02 .10
186 Shane Churla .02 .10
187 Rick Tabaracci .05 .15
188 Alexander Godynyuk .02 .10
189 Vladimir Konstantinov .05 .15
190 Markus Naslund .10 .30
191 Tom Chorske .02 .10
192 Thomas Steen .02 .10
193 Patrice Brisebois .02 .10
194 Luc Robitaille .05 .15
195 Michal Sykora .02 .10
196 Troy Mallette .02 .10
197 Steve Chiasson .02 .10
198 Jimmy Carson .02 .10
199 Mike Donnelly .02 .10
200 Mike Sillinger .02 .10
201 Martin Rucinsky .02 .10
202 Adam Bennett .02 .10
203 Matt Johnson RC .02 .10
204 Daren Puppa .05 .15
205 Ted Drury .02 .10
206 Jon Casey .05 .15
207 Alexei Kovalev .02 .10
208 Alexei Kasatonov .02 .10
209 Ulf Samuelsson .02 .10
210 Justin Hocking RC .02 .10
211 Greg Adams .02 .10
212 Greg Johnson .02 .10
213 Mike Craig .02 .10
214 Steve Konowalchuk .02 .10
215 Luke Richardson .02 .10
216 Pavol Demitra .05 .15
217 Brian Benning .02 .10
218 Corey Hirsch .05 .15
219 Alexander Semak .02 .10
220 Travis Green .05 .15
221 Turner Stevenson .02 .10
222 Dimitri Mironov .02 .10
223 Christian Soucy RC .05 .15
224 Rick Tocchet .05 .15
225 Craig MacTavish .02 .10
226 Wayne Gretzky 802 .75 2.00
Record Breaker
227 Pavel Bure .10 .30
228 Wayne Gretzky .10 .30
229 Brett Hull .10 .30
230 Mike Gartner .05 .15
231 Brian Leetch .10 .30
232 Al MacInnis .05 .15
233 Dominik Hasek .10 .30
234 Mark Messier .10 .30
235 Paul Kariya .10 .30
236 Jamie Storr .05 .15
237 Jeff Friesen .02 .10
238 Kenny Jonsson .02 .10
239 Mariusz Czerkawski RC .15 .40
240 Brett Lindros .02 .10
241 Andrei Nikolishin .02 .10
242 Jason Allison .02 .10
243 Oleg Tverdovsky .05 .15
244 Brian Savage .02 .10
245 Peter Forsberg .50 1.25
246 Patrik Juhlin RC .02 .10
247 Jassen Cullimore .02 .10
248 Chris Therien .02 .10
249 Kevin Brown RC .02 .10
250 Jeff Nelson .02 .10
251 Janne Laukkanen .02 .10
252 Jamie McLennan .05 .15
253 Craig Johnson .02 .10
254 Ravil Gusmanov RC .02 .10
255 Valeri Bure .02 .10
256 Valeri Karpov RC .02 .10
257 Mike Peca .02 .10
258 Brian Rolston .02 .10
259 Brandon Convery .02 .10
260 Mark Lawrence RC .02 .10
261 Adam Deadmarsh .02 .10
262 Jason Wiemer RC .02 .10
263 Alexander Cherbayev .02 .10
264 Sergei Gonchar .02 .10
265 Viktor Kozlov .02 .10
266 Vladislav Boulin RC .02 .10

267 Todd Harvey	.02	.10
268 Cory Stillman RC	.02	.10
269 David Oliver RC	.02	.10
270 Andrei Nazarov	.02	.10
271 Mikael Renberg	.05	.15
272 Andrei Kovalenko	.02	.10
273 Neal Broten	.05	.15
274 Ed Olczyk	.02	.10
275 Steve Thomas	.02	.10
276 Joe Nieuwendyk	.05	.15
277 Rob Gaudreau	.02	.10
278 Pat Verbeek	.02	.10
279 Eric Desjardins	.05	.15
280 Vincent Damphousse	.02	.10
281 John Cullen	.02	.10
282 Garry Valk	.02	.10
283 Daniel Lacroix	.02	.10
284 Mike Ricci	.02	.10
285 Dominik Hasek	.25	.60
286 Geoff Courtnall	.02	.10
287 Rob Niedermayer	.05	.15
288 Alexander Karpovtsev	.02	.10
289 Martin Straka	.02	.10
290 Ed Belfour	.10	.30
291 Dave Lowry	.02	.10
292 Brendan Shanahan	.10	.30
293 Jari Kurri	.05	.15
294 Steven Rice	.02	.10
295 Scott Levins	.02	.10
296 Ray Bourque	.20	.50
297 Mikael Andersson	.02	.10
298 Darius Kasparaitis	.02	.10
299 Chris Simon	.02	.10
300 Steve Yzerman	.60	1.50
301 Don McSween	.02	.10
302 Brian Noonan	.02	.10
303 Claude Lemieux	.02	.10
304 Radek Bonk RC	.25	.60
305 Jason Arnott	.02	.10
306 Ian Laperriere RC	.02	.10
307 Pat Falloon	.02	.10
308 Kris King	.02	.10
309 Brian Bellows	.02	.10
310 Uwe Krupp	.02	.10
311 Paul Cavallini	.02	.10
312 Shaun Van Allen	.02	.10
313 Dave Andreychuk	.05	.15
314 Bobby Holik	.02	.10
315 Theo Fleury	.02	.10
316 Mark Osborne	.02	.10
317 Andrew Cassels	.02	.10
318 Chris Tamer	.02	.10
319 Trevor Linden	.05	.15
320 Tom Fitzgerald	.02	.10
321 Ron Tugnutt	.05	.15
322 Jeremy Roenick	.15	.40
323 Todd Marchant	.02	.10
324 Scott Niedermayer	.02	.10
325 Tim Taylor RC	.02	.10
326 Mike Kennedy RC	.02	.10
327 Steve Heinze	.02	.10
328 David Sacco	.02	.10
329 Sergei Brylin	.02	.10
330 John LeClair	.10	.30
331 Brian Skrudland	.02	.10
332 Kevin Hatcher	.02	.10
333 Brett Hull	.15	.40
334 Alexander Mogilny	.05	.15
335 Sylvain Lefebvre	.02	.10
336 Sylvain Turgeon	.02	.10
337 Keith Primeau	.02	.10
338 Eric Fichaud RC	.05	.15
339 Jeff Beukeboom	.02	.10
340 Cory Cross RC	.02	.10
341 J.J. Daigneault	.02	.10
342 Stephen Leach	.02	.10
343 Zigmund Palffy	.05	.15
344 Igor Korolev	.02	.10
345 Chris Gratton	.02	.10
346 Joe Mullen	.05	.15
347 Brent Gilchrist	.02	.10
348 Adam Creighton	.02	.10
349 Dimitri Yushkevich	.02	.10
350 Wes Walz	.02	.10
351 Shayne Corson	.02	.10
352 Eric Lacroix	.02	.10
353 Maxim Bets	.02	.10
354 Sylvain Cote	.02	.10
355 Valeri Kamensky	.05	.15
356 Shjon Podein	.02	.10
357 Robert Reichel	.02	.10
358 Cliff Ronning	.02	.10
359 Bill Guerin	.05	.15
360 Dallas Drake	.02	.10
361 Robert Petrovicky	.02	.10
362 Ken Wregget	.05	.15
363 Todd Elik	.02	.10
364 Cam Neely	.10	.30
365 Darren McCarty	.02	.10
366 Shean Donovan RC	.02	.10
367 Felix Potvin	.10	.30
368 Yuri Khmylev	.02	.10
369 Mark Tinordi	.02	.10
370 Craig Billington	.05	.15
371 Patrick Flatley	.02	.10
372 Jocelyn Lemieux	.02	.10
373 Slava Kozlov	.05	.15
374 Trent Klatt	.02	.10
375 Geoff Sarjeant RC	.02	.10
376 Bob Kudelski	.02	.10
377 Stanislav Neckar RC	.02	.10
378 Jon Rohloff RC	.02	.10
379 Jeff Shantz	.02	.10
380 Dale Craigwell	.02	.10
381 Adrien Plavsic	.02	.10
382 Dave Gagner	.05	.15
383 Dave Archibald	.02	.10
384 Gilbert Dionne	.02	.10
385 Troy Loney	.02	.10
386 Dean McAmmond	.02	.10
387 Pauli Jaks	.05	.15
388 Stephane Richer	.05	.15
389 Don Beaupre	.05	.15
390 Kevin Stevens	.02	.10
391 Brad May	.02	.10
392 Neil Wilkinson	.02	.10
393 Kevin Lowe	.02	.10
394 Fredrik Olausson	.02	.10
395 Trevor Kidd	.05	.15
396 Brent Grieve	.02	.10
397 Dominic Roussel	.05	.15
398 Bret Hedican	.02	.10
399 Bryan Smolinski	.02	.10
400 Doug Lidster	.02	.10
401 Bob Errey	.02	.10
402 Pierre Sevigny	.02	.10
403 Rob Brown	.02	.10
404 Joe Sakic	.25	.60
405 Nikolai Borschevsky	.02	.10
406 Martin Lapointe	.02	.10
407 Jean-Yves Roy RC	.02	.10
408 Robert Kron	.02	.10
409 Tie Domi	.05	.15
410 Jim Dowd	.02	.10
411 Keith Jones	.02	.10
412 Scott Lachance	.02	.10
413 Bob Corkum	.02	.10
414 Denis Chasse RC	.02	.10
415 Denis Savard	.05	.15
416 Joe Murphy	.02	.10
417 Vyacheslav Butsayev	.02	.10
418 Mattias Norstrom	.02	.10
419 Sergei Zholtok	.02	.10
420 Nikolai Khabibulin	.05	.15
421 Pat Elynuik	.02	.10
422 Doug Brown	.02	.10
423 Dave McLlwain	.02	.10
424 James Patrick	.02	.10
425 Alexander Selivanov RC	.20	.50
426 Scott Thornton	.02	.10
427 Todd Ewen	.02	.10
428 Peter Popovic	.02	.10
429 Jarkko Varvio	.02	.10
430 Paul Ranheim	.02	.10
431 Kevin Dineen	.02	.10
432 Kelly Hrudey	.05	.15
433 Michal Grosek	.02	.10
434 Slava Fetisov	.02	.10
435 Ivan Droppa	.02	.10
436 Benoit Hogue	.02	.10
437 Sheldon Kennedy	.02	.10
438 Gord Murphy	.02	.10
439 Jamie Baker	.02	.10
440 Todd Gill	.02	.10
441 Mark Recchi	.05	.15
442 Ted Crowley	.02	.10
443 Ryan Smyth RC	.75	2.00
444 Brian Leetch	.10	.30
445 Bob Sweeney	.02	.10
446 Don Sweeney	.02	.10
447 Byron Dafoe RC	.40	1.00
448 Nathan Lafayette	.02	.10
449 Keith Carney	.02	.10
450 Stephane Fiset	.05	.15
451 Kevin Miller	.02	.10
452 Craig Darby RC	.02	.10
453 Vlastimil Kroupa	.02	.10
454 Rob Zettler	.02	.10
455 Glenn Healy	.05	.15
456 Todd Simon	.02	.10
457 Mark Fitzpatrick	.05	.15
458 Drake Berehowsky	.02	.10
459 Darcy Wakaluk	.05	.15
460 Enrico Ciccone	.02	.10
461 Tomas Sandstrom	.02	.10
462 Mikhail Shtalenkov	.02	.10
463 Igor Kravchuk	.02	.10
464 Jamie Allison	.02	.10
465 Gino Odjick	.02	.10
466 Norm Maciver	.02	.10
467 Terry Carkner	.02	.10
468 Rob Zamuner	.02	.10
469 Pavel Bure	.10	.30
470 Patrice Tardif RC	.02	.10
471 Andrei Lomakin	.02	.10
472 Kirk Maltby	.02	.10
473 Jaroslav Modry	.02	.10
474 Tommy Soderstrom	.05	.15
475 Patrik Carnback	.02	.10
476 Jeff Reese	.02	.10
477 Todd Krygier	.02	.10
478 John McIntyre	.02	.10
479 Joey Kocur	.02	.10
480 Steve Rucchin RC	.20	.50
481 Bob Bassen	.02	.10
482 Marek Malik RC	.02	.10
483 Darrin Shannon	.02	.10
484 Shawn Burr	.02	.10
485 Louie DeBrusk	.02	.10
486 Olaf Kolzig	.05	.15
487 Cam Stewart	.02	.10
488 Rob Blake	.05	.15
489 Eric Charron	.02	.10
490 Sandis Ozolinsh	.02	.10
491 Paul Ysebaert	.02	.10
492 Kris Draper	.02	.10
493 Stu Barnes	.02	.10
494 Doug Bodger	.02	.10
495 Blaine Lacher RC	.05	.15
496 Ed Jovanovski RC	.20	.50
497 Eric Daze RC	.40	1.00
498 Dan Cloutier RC	.40	1.00
499 Chad Allen RC	.02	.10
500 Todd Harvey	.02	.10
501 Jamie Rivers RC	.02	.10
502 Bryan McCabe	.02	.10
503 Darcy Tucker RC	.60	1.50
504 Wade Redden RC	.25	.60
505 Nolan Baumgartner RC	.02	.10
506 Marek Malik RC	.02	.10
507 Petr Cajanek RC	.40	1.00
508 Jan Hlavac RC	.40	1.00
509 Ladislav Kohn RC	.02	.10
510 Kimmo Timonen	.05	.15
511 Antti Aalto RC	.05	.15
512 Tommi Rajamaki RC	.05	.15
513 Vitali Yachmenev RC	.02	.10
514 Vadim Epantchinsev RC	.05	.15
515 Dmitri Klevakin RC	.05	.15
516 Nikolai Zavarukhin RC	.02	.10
517 Alexander Korolyuk RC	.25	.60
518 Anders Eriksson	.05	.15
519 Jesper Mattsson RC	.05	.15
520 Mattias Ohlund RC	.40	1.00
521 Anders Soderberg RC	.05	.15
522 Bryan Berard RC	.25	.60
523 Jason Bonsignore	.02	.10
524 Deron Quint	.02	.10
525 Richard Park	.02	.10
526 Jeff Friesen	.02	.10
527 Paul Kariya	.10	.30
528 Peter Forsberg	.30	.75
529 Zigmund Palffy CC	.05	.15
530 Kenny Jonsson	.02	.10
531 Jamie Storr	.05	.15
532 Alexander Selivanov	.05	.15
533 Mike Peca CC	.02	.10
534 Mariusz Czerkawski	.02	.10
535 Jason Allison	.02	.10
536 Todd Harvey	.02	.10
537 Brett Lindros	.02	.10
538 Radek Bonk	.02	.10
539 Blaine Lacher	.05	.15
540 Oleg Tverdovsky	.05	.15
541 Wayne Gretzky	.10	.30
542 Radek Bonk	.02	.10
543 Mariusz Czerkawski	.02	.10
544 Jaromir Jagr	.10	.30
545 Dominik Hasek	.10	.30
546 Todd Harvey	.02	.10
547 Mike Peca WT	.02	.10
548 Mats Sundin	.05	.15
549 Doug Weight WT	.05	.15
550 Steve Yzerman	.10	.30
551 Brett Lindros	.02	.10
552 Alexander Mogilny	.05	.15
553 Patrik Juhlin WT	.02	.10
554 Alexei Yashin	.02	.10
555 Peter Forsberg	.10	.30
556 Michael Nylander WT	.02	.10
557 Teemu Selanne	.10	.30
558 Marek Malik	.02	.10
559 Jari Kurri WT	.05	.15
560 Kenny Jonsson	.02	.10
561 Mikael Renberg	.05	.15
562 Adam Deadmarsh WT	.02	.10
563 Mark Messier	.10	.30
564 Rob Blake WT	.02	.10
565 Janne Laukkanen WT	.02	.10
566 Theo Fleury WT	.02	.10
567 Alexei Kovalev	.02	.10
568 Jamie Storr	.05	.15
569 Brett Hull	.10	.30
570 Valeri Karpov	.02	.10

1994-95 Upper Deck Electric Ice

This is a parallel set to the regular Upper Deck issue and is inserted in packs at the rate of 1:35. The backs are identical to the regular set. The only difference on the front is that the words "Electric Ice" are at the bottom which, along with the player's name and bar enclosing his position, are all in electric foil.

*STARS: 8X TO 20X BASIC CARDS
*ROOKIES: 4X TO 10X BASIC CARDS

1994-95 Upper Deck Ice Gallery

This 15-card set features some of the NHL's top players, along with a few journeymen. The cards were inserted 1:25 packs in Upper Deck series one. The cards feature a close-up headshot with a wide black and gray border. An action photo and text appear on the back. The cards are numbered with an "IG" prefix.

IG1 Steve Yzerman	5.00	12.00
IG2 Jason Arnott	.30	.75
IG3 Jeremy Roenick	1.25	3.00
IG4 Brendan Shanahan	1.00	2.50
IG5 Scott Stevens	.50	1.25
IG6 Scott Niedermayer	.30	.75
IG7 Adam Graves	.30	.75
IG8 Mike Modano	1.50	4.00
IG9 Kirk Muller	.30	.75
IG10 Alexandre Daigle	.30	.75
IG11 Martin Brodeur	2.50	6.00
IG12 Garry Valk	.30	.75
IG13 Teemu Selanne	1.00	2.50
IG14 Pat LaFontaine	1.00	2.50
IG15 Wayne Gretzky	6.00	15.00

1994-95 Upper Deck Predictor Canadian

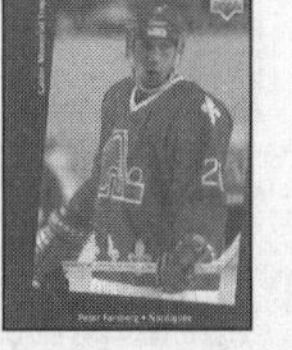

The Calder Predictors (C1-C15) were inserted at a rate of 1:20 first series Canadian packs, while the Pearson/Norris cards (C16-C35) were inserted at a rate of 1:20 series two Canadian packs. C1 (Peter Forsberg) was the winning card that could be redeemed for a gold foil Calder set, while C15 (Long Shot) could be redeemed for a silver version. Either C23 (Eric Lindros) or C31 (Paul Coffey) could be redeemed for a 20-card gold foil Pearson/Norris set, while C24 (Jaromir Jagr) netted the collector a silver version of cards C16-C25, and C29 (Chris Chelios) could be redeemed for a silver version of cards C26-C35.

*EXCH.CARDS: .2X TO .5X BASIC INSERTS
*GOLD/SILVER CALDER EXCH: EQUAL VALUE

C1 Peter Forsberg	5.00	12.00
C2 Paul Kariya	1.25	3.00
C3 Viktor Kozlov	.40	1.00
C4 Jason Allison	.40	1.00
C5 Mariusz Czerkawski	1.50	4.00
C6 Valeri Karpov	.40	1.00
C7 Brett Lindros	.40	1.00
C8 Valeri Bure	.40	1.00
C9 Andrei Nikolishin	.40	1.00
C10 Mike Peca	.40	1.00
C11 Kenny Jonsson	.40	1.00
C12 Alexander Cherbayev	.40	1.00
C13 Brian Rolston	.40	1.00
C14 Oleg Tverdovsky	.60	1.50
C15 Calder Long Shot	.40	1.00
C16 Wayne Gretzky	8.00	20.00
C17 Brett Hull	1.50	4.00
C18 Doug Gilmour	.60	1.50
C19 Jeremy Roenick	1.50	4.00
C20 John Vanbiesbrouck	.60	1.50
C21 Sergei Fedorov	2.00	5.00
C22 Mark Messier	1.25	3.00
C23 Eric Lindros	1.25	3.00
C24 Jaromir Jagr	2.00	5.00
C25 Pearson Long Shot	.40	1.00
C26 Ray Bourque	2.00	5.00
C27 Sandis Ozolinsh	.40	1.00
C28 Brian Leetch	1.25	3.00
C29 Chris Chelios	1.25	3.00
C30 Scott Stevens	.60	1.50
C31 Paul Coffey	1.25	3.00
C32 Rob Blake	.60	1.50
C33 Al MacInnis	.60	1.50
C34 Scott Niedermayer	.40	1.00
C35 Norris Long Shot	.40	1.00

1994-95 Upper Deck Predictor Hobby

The Hart Predictors (H1-H15) were inserted at a rate of 1:20 first series U.S. hobby packs, while the Art Ross/Vezina cards (H16-H35) were inserted at a rate of 1:20 second series U.S. hobby packs. H8 (Eric Lindros) was redeemable for a gold foil version of the Hart set, while card H15 (Long Shot) was redeemable for a silver version. Either H24 (Jaromir Jagr) or H31 (Dominik Hasek) could be redeemed for a 20-card gold foil version of the Art Ross/Vezina set, while H23 (Eric Lindros) and H27 (Ed Belfour) won gold foil versions of cards H16-H25, and H26-H35, respectively.

*EXCH.CARDS: 2X TO 5X BASIC CARDS

H1 Wayne Gretzky	8.00	20.00
H2 Pavel Bure	1.25	3.00
H3 Doug Gilmour	.60	1.50
H4 Mark Messier	1.25	3.00
H5 Patrick Roy	6.00	15.00
H6 Sergei Fedorov	2.00	5.00
H7 Chris Chelios	1.25	3.00
H8 Eric Lindros	1.25	3.00
H9 Alexander Mogilny	.60	1.50
H10 Peter Forsberg	5.00	12.00
H11 Brian Leetch	1.25	3.00
H12 Martin Brodeur	3.00	8.00
H13 Jeremy Roenick	1.50	4.00
H14 Paul Kariya	1.25	3.00
H15 Hart Long Shot	.40	1.00
H16 Wayne Gretzky	8.00	20.00
H17 Joe Sakic	2.50	6.00
H18 Sergei Fedorov	2.00	5.00
H19 Pavel Bure	1.25	3.00
H20 Adam Oates	.60	1.50
H21 Doug Gilmour	.60	1.50
H22 Steve Yzerman	6.00	15.00
H23 Eric Lindros	1.25	3.00
H24 Jaromir Jagr	2.00	5.00
H25 Art Ross Long Shot	.40	1.00
H26 Patrick Roy	6.00	15.00
H27 Ed Belfour	1.25	3.00
H28 Felix Potvin	1.25	3.00
H29 Martin Brodeur	3.00	8.00
H30 Mike Richter	1.25	3.00
H31 Dominik Hasek	2.50	6.00
H32 John Vanbiesbrouck	.60	1.50
H33 Curtis Joseph	1.25	3.00
H34 Kirk McLean	.60	1.50
H35 Vezina Long Shot	.40	1.00

1994-95 Upper Deck Predictor Retail

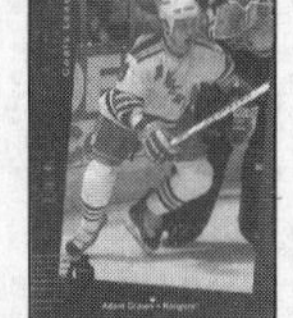

The Scoring Predictors (R1-R30) were inserted at a rate of 1:20 series one U.S. retail packs, while the Playoff Scoring cards (R31-R60) were inserted at a rate of 1:20 series two U.S. retail packs. Cards R10 (Goals Long Shot), R20 (Assists Long Shot), R28 (Eric Lindros), R29 (Jaromir Jagr), and R30 (Points Long shot) were all redeemable for a 30 card gold foil version of Scoring Predictors. Cards R40 (Goals Long Shot), R50 (Assists Long Shot), and R52 (Sergei Fedorov) were all redeemable for a 30 card gold foil version of the Playoff Scoring Predictors. Cards R39 (Jaromir Jagr), and R60 (Points Long Shot) won gold foil versions of cards R31-40, and R51-60, respectively.

*EXCH.CARDS: .2X TO .5X BASIC INSERTS
ONE EXCH.SET VIA MAIL PER PRED.WINNER

R1 Pavel Bure	1.25	3.00
R2 Brett Hull	1.50	4.00
R3 Teemu Selanne	1.25	3.00
R4 Sergei Fedorov	2.00	5.00
R5 Adam Graves	.40	1.00
R6 Dave Andreychuk	.60	1.50
R7 Brendan Shanahan	1.25	3.00
R8 Jeremy Roenick	1.50	4.00
R9 Eric Lindros	1.25	3.00
R10 Goals Long Shot	.40	1.00
R11 Doug Gilmour	.60	1.50
R12 Adam Oates	.60	1.50
R13 Brian Leetch	1.25	3.00
R14 Ray Bourque	2.00	5.00
R15 Joe Juneau	.60	1.50
R16 Craig Janney	.60	1.50
R17 Pat LaFontaine	1.25	3.00
R18 Jaromir Jagr	2.00	5.00
R19 Wayne Gretzky	8.00	20.00
R20 Assists Long Shot	.40	1.00
R21 Wayne Gretzky	8.00	20.00
R22 Pat LaFontaine	1.25	3.00
R23 Sergei Fedorov	2.00	5.00
R24 Steve Yzerman	6.00	15.00
R25 Pavel Bure	1.25	3.00
R26 Adam Oates	.60	1.50
R27 Doug Gilmour	.60	1.50
R28 Eric Lindros	1.25	3.00
R29 Jaromir Jagr	2.00	5.00
R30 Points Long Shot	.40	1.00
R31 Pavel Bure	1.25	3.00
R32 Brett Hull	1.50	4.00
R33 Cam Neely	1.25	3.00
R34 Mark Messier	1.25	3.00
R35 Dave Andreychuk	.60	1.50
R36 Sergei Fedorov	2.00	5.00
R37 Mike Modano	2.00	5.00
R38 Adam Graves	.40	1.00
R39 Jaromir Jagr	2.00	5.00
R40 Playoff Goals Long Shot	.40	1.00
R41 Theo Fleury	.40	1.00
R42 Wayne Gretzky	8.00	20.00
R43 Steve Yzerman	6.00	15.00
R44 Adam Oates	.60	1.50
R45 Brian Leetch	1.25	3.00
R46 Al MacInnis	.60	1.50
R47 Pat LaFontaine	1.25	3.00
R48 Scott Stevens	.60	1.50
R49 Doug Gilmour	.60	1.50
R50 Playoff Assists Long Shot	.40	1.00
R51 Brian Leetch	1.25	3.00
R52 Sergei Fedorov	2.00	5.00
R53 Pavel Bure	1.25	3.00
R54 Mark Messier	1.25	3.00
R55 Pat LaFontaine	1.25	3.00
R56 Doug Gilmour	.60	1.50
R57 Brett Hull	1.50	4.00
R58 Theo Fleury	.40	1.00
R59 Wayne Gretzky	8.00	20.00
R60 Playoff Points Long Shot	.40	1.00

1994-95 Upper Deck SP Inserts

The 1994-95 Upper Deck SP Insert set was released in two series of 90 cards for a total of 180. One SP Insert was found in each Upper Deck hobby pack, with two per retail pack.

COMPLETE SET (180)	50.00	100.00
*DIE CUTS: 1.2X TO 3X BASIC INSERTS		
SP1 Maxim Bets	.15	.40
SP2 Stephan Lebeau	.15	.40
SP3 Garry Valk	.15	.40
SP4 Ray Bourque	.75	2.00
SP5 Mariusz Czerkawski	.30	.75
SP6 Cam Neely	.50	1.25
SP7 Adam Oates	.25	.60
SP8 Dominik Hasek	1.00	2.50
SP9 Dale Hawerchuk	.25	.60
SP10 Alexander Mogilny	.25	.60
SP11 Theo Fleury	.15	.40
SP12 Trevor Kidd	.25	.60
SP13 Joe Nieuwendyk	.25	.60
SP14 Gary Roberts	.15	.40
SP15 Ed Belfour	.50	1.25
SP16 Chris Chelios	.50	1.25
SP17 Jeremy Roenick	.60	1.50
SP18 Neal Broten	.25	.60
SP19 Russ Courtnall	.15	.40
SP20 Derian Hatcher	.15	.40
SP21 Mike Modano	.75	2.00
SP22 Paul Coffey	.50	1.25
SP23 Slava Kozlov	.25	.60
SP24 Keith Primeau	.15	.40
SP25 Steve Yzerman	2.50	6.00
SP26 Jason Arnott	.15	.40
SP27 Bill Ranford	.25	.60
SP28 Doug Weight	.25	.60
SP29 Bob Kudelski	.15	.40
SP30 Rob Niedermayer	.25	.60
SP31 John Vanbiesbrouck	.25	.60
SP32 Andrew Cassels	.15	.40
SP33 Chris Pronger	.50	1.25
SP34 Geoff Sanderson	.25	.60
SP35 Rob Blake	.25	.60
SP36 Wayne Gretzky	3.00	8.00
SP37 Jari Kurri	.25	.60
SP38 Alexei Zhitnik	.15	.40
SP39 Vincent Damphousse	.15	.40
SP40 Kirk Muller	.15	.40
SP41 Oleg Petrov	.15	.40
SP42 Patrick Roy	2.50	6.00
SP43 Martin Brodeur	1.25	3.00
SP44 Stephane Richer	.25	.60
SP45 Scott Stevens	.25	.60
SP46 Darius Kasparaitis	.15	.40
SP47 Vladimir Malakhov	.15	.40
SP48 Pierre Turgeon	.25	.60
SP49 Alexei Kovalev	.15	.40
SP50 Brian Leetch	.50	1.25
SP51 Mark Messier	.50	1.25
SP52 Mike Richter	.50	1.25
SP53 Craig Billington	.25	.60
SP54 Alexandre Daigle	.15	.40
SP55 Alexei Yashin	.15	.40
SP56 Josef Beranek	.15	.40
SP57 Rod Brind'Amour	.25	.60
SP58 Mark Recchi	.25	.60
SP59 Mikael Renberg	.25	.60
SP60 Jaromir Jagr	.75	2.00
SP61 Mario Lemieux	2.50	6.00
SP62 Kevin Stevens	.15	.40
SP63 Owen Nolan	.25	.60
SP64 Mike Ricci	.15	.40
SP65 Joe Sakic	1.00	2.50
SP66 Brett Hull	.60	1.50
SP67 Craig Janney	.25	.60
SP68 Curtis Joseph	.50	1.25
SP69 Brendan Shanahan	.50	1.25
SP70 Ulf Dahlen	.15	.40
SP71 Arturs Irbe	.25	.60
SP72 Sergei Makarov	.15	.40
SP73 Sandis Ozolinsh	.15	.40
SP74 Brian Bradley	.15	.40
SP75 Chris Gratton	.15	.40
SP76 Denis Savard	.25	.60
SP77 Dave Andreychuk	.25	.60
SP78 Mike Gartner	.25	.60
SP79 Dimitri Mironov	.15	.40
SP80 Felix Potvin	.50	1.25
SP81 Jeff Brown	.15	.40
SP82 Geoff Courtnall	.15	.40
SP83 Trevor Linden	.25	.60
SP84 Kirk McLean	.25	.60
SP85 Peter Bondra	.25	.60
SP86 Kevin Hatcher	.15	.40
SP87 Dimitri Khristich	.15	.40
SP88 Teemu Selanne	.50	1.25
SP89 Keith Tkachuk	.50	1.25
SP90 Alexei Zhamnov	.25	.60
SP91 Paul Kariya	.50	1.25
SP92 Valeri Karpov	.15	.40
SP93 Oleg Tverdovsky	.25	.60
SP94 Al Iafrate	.15	.40
SP95 Blaine Lacher	.15	.40
SP96 Bryan Smolinski	.15	.40
SP97 Donald Audette	.15	.40
SP98 Yuri Khymlev	.15	.40
SP99 Pat LaFontaine	.50	1.25
SP100 Derek Plante	.15	.40
SP101 Steve Chiasson	.15	.40
SP102 Phil Housley	.25	.60
SP103 Michael Nylander	.15	.40
SP104 Robert Reichel	.15	.40
SP105 Tony Amonte	.25	.60
SP106 Bernie Nicholls	.25	.60
SP107 Gary Suter	.15	.40
SP108 Paul Cavallini	.15	.40
SP109 Todd Harvey	.15	.40
SP110 Kevin Hatcher	.15	.40
SP111 Andy Moog	.50	1.25
SP112 Dino Ciccarelli	.25	.60
SP113 Sergei Fedorov	.75	2.00
SP114 Nicklas Lidstrom	.50	1.25
SP115 Mike Vernon	.25	.60
SP116 Shayne Corson	.15	.40
SP117 David Oliver	.15	.40
SP118 Ryan Smyth	1.50	4.00
SP119 Jesse Belanger	.15	.40
SP120 Mark Fitzpatrick	.25	.60
SP121 Scott Mellanby	.25	.60
SP122 Andrei Nikolishin	.15	.40
SP123 Darren Turcotte	.15	.40
SP124 Pat Verbeek	.15	.40
SP125 Glen Wesley	.15	.40
SP126 Tony Granato	.15	.40
SP127 Marty McSorley	.15	.40
SP128 Jamie Storr	.25	.60
SP129 Rick Tocchet	.25	.60
SP130 Brian Bellows	.15	.40
SP131 Valeri Bure	.15	.40
SP132 Turner Stevenson	.15	.40
SP133 John MacLean	.25	.60
SP134 Scott Niedermayer	.15	.40
SP135 Brian Rolston	.15	.40
SP136 Brett Lindros	.15	.40
SP137 Jamie McLennan	.25	.60
SP138 Zigmund Palffy	.25	.60
SP139 Steve Thomas	.15	.40
SP140 Adam Graves	.15	.40
SP141 Petr Nedved	.25	.60
SP142 Sergei Zubov	.15	.40
SP143 Don Beaupre	.25	.60
SP144 Radek Bonk	.50	1.25
SP145 Pavol Demitra	.25	.60
SP146 Sylvain Turgeon	.15	.40
SP147 Ron Hextall	.25	.60
SP148 Patrik Juhlin	.15	.40
SP149 Eric Lindros	.50	1.25
SP150 Ron Francis	.25	.60
SP151 Markus Naslund	.50	1.25
SP152 Luc Robitaille	.25	.60
SP153 Martin Straka	.15	.40
SP154 Wendel Clark	.25	.60
SP155 Adam Deadmarsh	.15	.40
SP156 Peter Forsberg	2.00	5.00
SP157 Janne Laukkanen	.15	.40
SP158 Steve Duchesne	.15	.40
SP159 Al MacInnis	.25	.60
SP160 Esa Tikkanen	.15	.40
SP161 Jeff Friesen	.15	.40
SP162 Viktor Kozlov	.15	.40
SP163 Ray Whitney	.15	.40
SP164 Roman Hamrlik	.25	.60
SP165 Alexander Selivanov	.40	1.00
SP166 Jason Wiemer	.15	.40
SP167 Doug Gilmour	.25	.60
SP168 Kenny Jonsson	.15	.40
SP169 Mike Ridley	.15	.40
SP170 Mats Sundin	.50	1.25
SP171 Pavel Bure	.50	1.25
SP172 Martin Gelinas	.15	.40
SP173 Mike Peca	.15	.40
SP174 Jason Allison	.15	.40
SP175 Joe Juneau	.25	.60
SP176 Pat Peake	.15	.40
SP177 Mark Tinordi	.15	.40
SP178 Tim Cheveldae	.25	.60
SP179 Nelson Emerson	.15	.40
SP180 Dave Manson	.15	.40

1995-96 Upper Deck

The 1995-96 Upper Deck set was issued in two series totaling 570 cards. The set is distinguished primarily through the inclusion of a number of noteworthy rookie cards in the Star Rookie (496-507) and Program of Excellence (508-525) subsets. The Cool Trade Exchange card was randomly inserted in 1:82 series 2 packs. The card could be redeemed for special die-cut cards of Wayne Gretzky, Sergei Fedorov, Peter Forsberg and Doug Gilmour.

COMPLETE SET (570)	50.00	100.00
COMPLETE SERIES 1 (270)	10.00	20.00
COMPLETE SERIES 2 (300)	20.00	40.00
1 Cam Neely	.10	.30
2 Donald Audette	.02	.10
3 Derian Hatcher	.02	.10
4 Mike Vernon	.05	.15
5 Darryl Sydor	.05	.15
6 Patrice Brisebois	.02	.10
7 John LeClair	.10	.30
8 Luc Robitaille	.05	.15
9 Todd Krygier	.02	.10
10 Steve Chiasson	.02	.10
11 Sergei Krivokrasov	.02	.10
12 Marko Tuomainen	.02	.10
13 Paul Ranheim	.02	.10
14 Brian Rolston	.02	.10
15 Alexei Yashin	.02	.10
16 Joe Mullen	.05	.15
17 Dallas Drake	.02	.10
18 Tony Amonte	.05	.15
19 Gary Roberts	.02	.10
20 Geoff Sanderson	.02	.10
21 Gord Murphy	.02	.10
22 Dean Evason	.02	.10
23 Brantt Myhres RC	.02	.10
24 Sergei Makarov	.02	.10
25 Joe Juneau	.02	.10
26 Greg Adams	.02	.10
27 Yuri Khmylev	.02	.10
28 Yanic Perreault	.02	.10
29 Jason Arnott	.02	.10
30 Glenn Healy	.05	.15
31 Sergei Brylin	.02	.10
32 Ian Laperriere	.02	.10
33 Trevor Linden	.05	.15
34 Nicklas Lidstrom	.10	.30
35 Don Sweeney	.02	.10
36 Brian Savage	.02	.10
37 Richard Matvichuk	.05	.15
38 Dale Hawerchuk	.10	.30
39 Patrick Roy	.60	1.50
40 Alexander Semak	.02	.10
41 Kirk Maltby	.05	.15
42 Jiri Slegr	.02	.10
43 Joe Sacco	.02	.10
44 Claude Lemieux	.02	.10
45 Eric Weinrich	.02	.10
46 Ron Francis	.05	.15
47 Jamie Storr	.05	.15
48 Felix Potvin	.10	.30
49 Steve Duchesne	.02	.10
50 Jody Hull	.02	.10
51 Dave Manson	.02	.10
52 Marty McInnis	.02	.10
53 James Patrick	.02	.10
54 Joe Sakic	.25	.60
55 Andrei Nikolishin	.02	.10
56 Adrian Aucoin	.02	.10
57 Wade Flaherty RC	.05	.15
58 Marek Malik	.02	.10
59 Jason Allison	.02	.10
60 Stephane Matteau	.02	.10
61 Jason Dawe	.02	.10
62 Ray Whitney	.05	.15
63 Bill Lindsay	.02	.10
64 Alexei Zhamnov	.05	.15
65 Adam Deadmarsh	.02	.10
66 Vincent Damphousse	.02	.10
67 Josef Beranek	.02	.10
68 Stanislav Neckar	.02	.10
69 Alexei Kasatonov	.02	.10
70 Jon Casey	.05	.15
71 Todd Marchant	.02	.10
72 Mike Sillinger	.02	.10
73 Markus Naslund	.10	.30
74 John MacLean	.05	.15
75 Mike Ridley	.02	.10
76 Petr Svoboda	.02	.10
77 Milos Holan	.02	.10
78 John Tucker	.02	.10
79 Doug Brown	.02	.10

80 Ted Donato .02 .10
81 Dimitri Yushkevich .02 .10
82 Brett Lindros .02 .10
83 Brian Bradley .02 .10
84 Mario Lemieux .60 1.50
85 Nikolai Khabibulin .05 .15
86 Larry Murphy .05 .15
87 Mike Donnelly .02 .10
88 Brian Holzinger RC .10 .30
89 Steve Larouche .02 .10
90 Ray Ferraro .02 .10
91 Mikhail Shtalenkov .02 .10
92 Viktor Kozlov .05 .15
93 Jon Klemm .02 .10
94 Mark Tinordi .02 .10
95 Bret Hedican .02 .10
96 Kevin Stevens .02 .10
97 Bernie Nicholls .02 .10
98 Pat Verbeek .02 .10
99 Wayne Gretzky .75 2.00
100 Rene Corbet .02 .10
101 Shayne Corson .02 .10
102 Cliff Ronning .02 .10
103 Olaf Kolzig .05 .15
104 Dominik Hasek .25 .60
105 Corey Millen .02 .10
106 Patrick Flatley .02 .10
107 Chris Therien .02 .10
108 Ken Wregget .05 .15
109 Paul Ysebaert .02 .10
110 Mike Gartner .05 .15
111 Michal Grosek .02 .10
112 Craig Billington .05 .15
113 Steve Yzerman .60 1.50
114 Neal Broten .05 .15
115 Tom Barrasso .05 .15
116 Brent Fedyk .02 .10
117 Todd Gill .02 .10
118 Petr Klima .02 .10
119 Dave Karpa .02 .10
120 Geoff Courtnall .02 .10
121 Kelly Buchberger .02 .10
122 Eric LaCroix .02 .10
123 Janne Laukkanen .02 .10
124 Radek Bonk .02 .10
125 Sergio Momesso .02 .10
126 Esa Tikkanen .02 .10
127 Jon Rohloff .02 .10
128 Ken Klee RC .02 .10
129 Johan Garpenlov .02 .10
130 Sean Burke .05 .15
131 Shean Donovan .02 .10
132 Alexei Kovalev .02 .10
133 Sylvain Cote .02 .10
134 Jeff Friesen .02 .10
135 Scott Pearson .02 .10
136 Kirk McLean .05 .15
137 Glen Wesley .02 .10
138 Bob Kudelski .02 .10
139 Craig Johnson .02 .10
140 Zigmund Palffy .05 .15
141 Kris King .02 .10
142 Rusty Fitzgerald RC .02 .10
143 Trevor Kidd .05 .15
144 Dave Ellett .02 .10
145 Kelly Hrudey .05 .15
146 Igor Kravchuk .02 .10
147 Mats Sundin .10 .30
148 Shawn Chambers .02 .10
149 Bob Corkum .02 .10
150 Shjon Podein .02 .10
151 Murray Craven .02 .10
152 Roman Hamrlik .05 .15
153 Lyle Odelein .02 .10
154 Vyacheslav Kozlov .05 .15
155 David Emma .02 .10
156 Benoit Brunet .02 .10
157 Jozef Stumpel .02 .10
158 Darrin Madeley .05 .15
159 Keith Primeau .02 .10
160 Jeff Norton .02 .10
161 Mathieu Schneider .02 .10
162 Trent Klatt .02 .10
163 Pat Peake .02 .10
164 Rob Gaudreau .02 .10
165 Doug Bodger .02 .10
166 Sergei Nemchinov .02 .10
167 David Oliver .02 .10
168 Sandis Ozolinsh .02 .10
169 Mark Messier .10 .30
170 Chris Chelios .10 .30
171 Teemu Selanne .10 .30
172 Robert Svehla RC .02 .10
173 Nikolai Borschevsky .02 .10
174 Chris Pronger .10 .30
175 Dave Lowry .02 .10
176 Owen Nolan .05 .15
177 Sylvain Turgeon .02 .10
178 Nelson Emerson .02 .10
179 Theo Fleury .02 .10
180 Patrik Carnback .02 .10
181 Kevin Smyth .02 .10
182 Jeff Shantz .02 .10
183 Bob Carpenter .02 .10
184 Brendan Shanahan .10 .30
185 Tomas Sandstrom .02 .10
186 Eric Desjardins .05 .15
187 Alexei Zhitnik .02 .10
188 Alexander Mogilny .05 .15
189 Mariusz Czerkawski .02 .10
190 Vladimir Konstantinov .05 .15
191 Andy Moog .10 .30
192 Peter Popovic .02 .10
193 Marty McSorley .02 .10
194 Mikael Renberg .05 .15
195 Alek Stojanov RC .02 .10
196 Rick Tabaracci .05 .15
197 Adam Oates .05 .15
198 Garry Galley .02 .10
199 Todd Harvey .05 .15
200 Martin Lapointe .02 .10
201 Tony Granato .02 .10
202 Turner Stevenson .02 .10
203 Jeff Beukeboom .02 .10
204 Adam Foote .05 .15
205 Daren Puppa .05 .15
206 Paul Kariya .10 .30
207 German Titov .02 .10
208 Patrick Poulin .02 .10
209 Jesse Belanger .02 .10
210 Steven Rice .02 .10
211 Martin Brodeur .30 .75
212 Rob Pearson .02 .10
213 Igor Larionov .02 .10
214 Pavel Bure .10 .30
215 Sergei Fedorov .10 .30
216 Ed Belfour .10 .30
217 Mark Messier .10 .30
218 Steve Yzerman .30 .75
219 Mats Sundin .10 .30
220 Mike Modano .20 .50
221 Alexander Mogilny .05 .15
222 Wayne Gretzky .40 1.00
223 Keith Primeau .02 .10
224 Adam Graves .02 .10
225 Owen Nolan .05 .15
226 Paul Coffey .10 .30
227 Jeremy Roenick .15 .40
228 Felix Potvin .10 .30
229 Trevor Kidd .05 .15
230 Ray Bourque .10 .30
231 Mario Lemieux 5 .30 .75
232 Peter Bondra .05 .15
233 Brett Hull .10 .30
234 Alexei Zhamnov .05 .15
235 Theo Fleury .02 .10
236 Brian Leetch .05 .15
237 Cam Neely .05 .15
238 Chris Chelios .10 .30
239 Adam Graves .02 .10
240 Doug Gilmour .05 .15
241 Jeremy Roenick .15 .40
242 Joe Sakic .10 .30
243 Keith Tkachuk .10 .30
244 Luc Robitaille .05 .15
245 Paul Kariya .10 .30
246 Owen Nolan .05 .15
247 John LeClair .10 .30
248 Paul Coffey .10 .30
249 Peter Bondra .05 .15
250 Ray Bourque .10 .30
251 Brett Hull .10 .30
252 Wayne Gretzky .40 1.00
253 Teemu Selanne .10 .30
254 Ray Sheppard .02 .10
255 Ron Francis .05 .15
256 Kevin Hatcher .02 .10
257 Brett Lindros .02 .10
258 Claude Lemieux .02 .10
259 Saku Koivu .10 .30
260 Radek Dvorak RC .20 .50
261 Niklas Sundstrom .05 .15
262 Chad Kilger RC .25 .60
263 Vitali Yachmenev .02 .10
264 Jeff O'Neill .02 .10
265 Brendan Witt .02 .10
266 Jason Bonsignore .02 .10
267 Aki-Petteri Berg RC .05 .15
268 Eric Daze .05 .15
269 Shane Doan RC .40 1.00
270 Daymond Langkow RC .20 .50
271 Alexandre Daigle .02 .10
272 Brian Noonan .02 .10
273 Guy Carbonneau .10 .30
274 Rick Tocchet .05 .15
275 Teppo Numminen .02 .10
276 Brian Skrudland .02 .10
277 Andrei Trefilov .02 .10
278 Joe Murphy .02 .10
279 Sergei Fedorov .20 .50
280 Doug Weight .05 .15
281 Robert Lang .02 .10
282 Darryl Shannon .02 .10
283 Cory Stillman .02 .10
284 Gary Suter .02 .10
285 Joe Nieuwendyk .05 .15
286 Terry Carkner .02 .10
287 Dimitri Khristich .02 .10
288 Alexander Karpovtsev .02 .10
289 Garth Snow .05 .15
290 Al MacInnis .05 .15
291 Doug Gilmour .05 .15
292 Mike Eastwood .02 .10
293 Steve Heinze .02 .10
294 Phil Housley .05 .15
295 Tim Taylor .02 .10
296 Curtis Joseph .10 .30
297 Patrick Roy .60 1.50
298 Ted Drury .02 .10
299 Igor Korolev .02 .10
300 Ray Bourque .20 .50
301 Darren McCarty .02 .10
302 Miroslav Satan RC .40 1.00
303 Adam Burt .02 .10
304 Valeri Bure .02 .10
305 Sergei Gonchar .02 .10
306 Jason York .02 .10
307 Brent Grieve .02 .10
308 Greg Johnson .02 .10
309 Kevin Hatcher .02 .10
310 Rob Niedermayer .05 .15
311 Nelson Emerson .02 .10
312 Mark Janssens .02 .10
313 Tommy Soderstrom .05 .15
314 Joey Kocur .02 .10
315 Craig Janney .02 .10
316 Alexander Selivanov .02 .10
317 Russ Courtnall .02 .10
318 Petr Sykora RC .50 1.25
319 Rick Zombo .02 .10
320 Randy Burridge .02 .10
321 John Vanbiesbrouck .05 .15
322 Dmitri Mironov .02 .10
323 Sean Hill .02 .10
324 Rod Brind'Amour .05 .15
325 Wendel Clark .05 .15
326 Brent Gilchrist .02 .10
327 Tyler Wright .02 .10
328 Scott Daniels .02 .10
329 Adam Graves .02 .10
330 Dean Malkoc .02 .10
331 Jamie Macoun .02 .10
332 Sandy Moger RC .02 .10
333 Mike Peca .05 .15
334 Greg Johnson .02 .10
335 Jason Woolley .02 .10
336 Rob Dimaio .02 .10
337 Damian Rhodes .05 .15
338 Gino Odjick .02 .10
339 Peter Bondra .05 .15
340 Todd Ewen .02 .10
341 Matthew Barnaby .10 .30
342 Sylvain Lefebvre .02 .10
343 Oleg Petrov .02 .10
344 Jim Carey .05 .15
345 Stu Barnes .02 .10
346 Kelly Miller .02 .10
347 Antti Tormanen RC .02 .10
348 Ray Sheppard .02 .10
349 Igor Larionov .02 .10
350 Kjell Samuelsson .02 .10
351 Benoit Hogue .02 .10
352 Jeff Brown .02 .10
353 Nolan Baumgartner .02 .10
354 Denis Pederson .02 .10
355 Shawn Burr .02 .10
356 Jyrki Lumme .02 .10
357 Kevin Haller .02 .10
358 John Cullen .02 .10
359 Martin Gelinas .02 .10
360 Shawn McEachern .02 .10
361 Sandy McCarthy .02 .10
362 Grant Marshall .02 .10
363 Dean McAmmond .02 .10
364 Kevin Todd .02 .10
365 Bobby Holik .02 .10
366 Joel Otto .02 .10
367 Dave Andreychuk .05 .15
368 Ronnie Stern .02 .10
369 Jocelyn Thibault .10 .30
370 Dave Gagner .02 .10
371 Bryan Marchment .02 .10
372 Jari Kurri .10 .30
373 Bill Guerin .05 .15
374 Eric Lindros .10 .30
375 Adam Creighton .02 .10
376 Dimitri Yushkevich .02 .10
377 Peter Zezel .02 .10
378 Valeri Karpov .02 .10
379 Patrick Labrecque .02 .10
380 Mick Vukota .02 .10
381 Ulf Dahlen .02 .10
382 Enrico Ciccone .02 .10
383 Scott Niedermayer .02 .10
384 Ville Peltonen .02 .10
385 Blaine Lacher .05 .15
386 Pat LaFontaine .10 .30
387 Jeff Hackett .05 .15
388 Mike Keane .02 .10
389 Pierre Turgeon .05 .15
390 Scott Lachance .02 .10
391 Jason Wiemer .02 .10
392 Michal Pivonka .02 .10
393 Denis Bonvie RC .02 .10
394 Glen Murray .02 .10
395 Bobby Dollas .02 .10
396 Paul Coffey .10 .30
397 Stephane Fiset .05 .15
398 Jere Lehtinen .05 .15
399 Scott Mellanby .05 .15
400 Robert Kron .02 .10
401 Doug Lidster .02 .10
402 Don Beaupre .05 .15
403 Arturs Irbe .05 .15
404 Brian Bellows .02 .10
405 Corey Hirsch .05 .15
406 Pavel Bure .10 .30
407 Chris Gratton .02 .10
408 Oleg Tverdovsky .02 .10
409 Derek Plante .02 .10
410 Dan Keczmer .02 .10
411 Donald Brashear .05 .15
412 Andrei Vasilyev RC .02 .10
413 Tommy Salo RC .40 1.00
414 Kevin Lowe .05 .15
415 Dody Wood .02 .10
416 Denis Chasse .02 .10
417 Aaron Gavey .02 .10
418 Scott Walker .02 .10
419 Richard Park .02 .10
420 Mike Modano .10 .30
421 Kyle McLaren RC .02 .10
422 Jeremy Roenick .15 .40
423 Mark Fitzpatrick .05 .15
424 Landon Wilson RC .02 .10
425 Steve Rucchin .05 .15
426 Stephane Richer .05 .15
427 Martin Straka .05 .15
428 Ron Hextall .05 .15
429 Joe Dziedzic .02 .10
430 Peter Forsberg .30 .75
431 Dino Ciccarelli .05 .15
432 Robert Dirk .02 .10
433 Wayne Primeau RC .02 .10
434 Denis Savard .05 .15
435 Keith Carney .02 .10
436 Tom Fitzgerald .02 .10
437 Cale Hulse .02 .10
438 Mike Richter .10 .30
439 Marcus Ragnarsson RC .05 .15
440 Roman Vopat .02 .10
441 Zdenek Nedved .02 .10
442 Dale Hunter .05 .15
443 Bob Sweeney .02 .10
444 Randy McKay .02 .10
445 Chris Osgood .05 .15
446 Andrei Kovalenko .02 .10
447 Darius Kasparaitis .02 .10
448 Ulf Samuelsson .02 .10
449 Chris Joseph .02 .10
450 Chris Terreri .05 .15
451 Keith Jones .05 .15
452 Tim Cheveldae .05 .15
453 Stephen Leach .02 .10
454 Michael Nylander .02 .10
455 Ed Belfour .10 .30
456 Claude Lemieux .02 .10
457 Mike Ricci .02 .10
458 Shane Churla .02 .10
459 Kris Draper .02 .10
460 Byron Dafoe .05 .15
461 Troy Mallette .02 .10
462 Petr Nedved .05 .15
463 Kenny Jonsson .02 .10
464 Keith Tkachuk .10 .30
465 Jaromir Jagr .20 .50
466 Vladimir Malakhov .02 .10
467 Guy Hebert .05 .15
468 Brad May .02 .10
469 Bob Probert .05 .15
470 Sandis Ozolinsh .02 .10
471 Oleg Mikulchik .02 .10
472 Steve Thomas .05 .15
473 Travis Green .05 .15
474 Sergei Zubov .02 .10
475 Bill Houlder .02 .10
476 Roman Oksiuta .02 .10
477 Jamie Rivers .02 .10
478 Rob Blake .05 .15
479 Todd Elik .02 .10
480 Zarley Zalapski .02 .10
481 Darren Turcotte .02 .10
482 Scott Stevens .05 .15
483 Pat Falloon .02 .10
484 Grant Fuhr .10 .30
485 Martin Rucinsky .02 .10
486 Brett Hull .15 .40
487 Brian Leetch .05 .15
488 Shaun Van Allen .02 .10
489 Valeri Kamensky .05 .15
490 Mark Recchi .05 .15
491 Jason Muzzatti .05 .15
492 Andrew Cassels .02 .10
493 Nick Kypreos .02 .10
494 Bryan Smolinski .02 .10
495 Owen Nolan .05 .15
496 Bryan McCabe .02 .10
497 Mathieu Dandenault RC .25 .60
498 Deron Quint .02 .10
499 Jason Doig .02 .10
500 Marty Murray .02 .10
501 Ed Jovanovski .10 .30
502 Stefan Ustorf .02 .10
503 Jamie Langenbrunner .02 .10
504 Daniel Alfredsson RC .50 1.25
505 Darby Hendrickson .02 .10
506 Brett McLean RC .05 .15
507 Daniel Cleary RC .05 .15
508 Todd Robinson .02 .10
509 Arron Asham RC .05 .15
510 Daniel Corso RC .40 1.00
511 Darren Van Oene RC .02 .10
512 Trevor Wasyluk RC .10 .30
513 Josh Holden RC .02 .10
514 Etienne Drapeau RC .05 .15
515 Matt Osborne .02 .10
516 Zenith Komarniski RC .05 .15
517 Chris Phillips RC .20 .50
518 Chris Fleury RC .02 .10
519 Coy Sarich RC .05 .15
520 Glenn Crawford RC .02 .10
521 Francois Methot .02 .10
522 Geoff Peters .02 .10
523 Joey Tetarenko .05 .15
524 Randy Petruk RC .05 .15
525 Mathieu Garon RC 1.00 2.50
526 Daymond Langkow .10 .30
527 Craig Mills RC .02 .10
528 Rhett Warrener .02 .10
529 Marc Denis RC 1.00 2.50
530 Jose Theodore RC 2.50 6.00
531 Curtis Brown RC .10 .30
532 Chad Allen .02 .10
533 Denis Gauthier RC .02 .10
534 Brad Larsen .02 .10
535 Jamie Wright RC .05 .15
536 Mike Watt RC .05 .15
537 Jason Holland RC .05 .15
538 Robb Gordon RC .02 .10
539 Hnat Domenichelli RC .05 .15
540 Ondrej Kratena .05 .15
541 Michal Bros .05 .15
542 Marek Posmyk .05 .15
543 Marek Melanovsky RC .05 .15
544 Jan Tomajko .05 .15
545 Ales Pisa RC .05 .15
546 Miika Elomo RC .05 .15
547 Timo Salonen RC .05 .15
548 Teemu Riihijarvi RC .05 .15
549 Antti-Jussi Niemi .05 .15
550 Pasi Petrilainen RC .05 .15
551 Toni Lydman RC .05 .15
552 Dmitri Nabokov .05 .15
553 Alexei Morozov .10 .30
554 Sergei Samsonov .05 .15
555 Alexei Vasilyev .05 .15
556 Andrei Petrunin .02 .10
557 Dimitri Rjabykin .05 .15
558 Sergei Zimakov RC .05 .15
559 Peter Nylander .02 .10
560 Marcus Nilsson UER RC .30 .75
561 Niklas Anger RC .05 .15
562 Per Anton Lundstrom RC .05 .15
563 Patrik Wallenberg RC .05 .15
564 Per Ragnar Bergkvist RC .05 .15
565 Mike Sylvia .02 .10
566 Marty Reasoner .05 .15
567 Reg Berg .02 .10
568 Tom Poti RC .20 .50
569 Chris Drury RC 2.50 6.00
570 Michael McBain .02 .10
NNO Cool Trade Exchange .10 .25

1995-96 Upper Deck Electric Ice

The Electric Ice cards were inserted one per retail pack, or two per jumbo. These cards featured the Electric Ice logo on a silver foil background.

*STARS: 5X TO 10X BASIC CARDS
*ROOKIES: 1X TO 2.5X BASIC CARDS
529 Marc Denis 5.00 12.00
530 Jose Theodore 8.00 20.00

1995-96 Upper Deck Electric Ice Gold

These cards were inserted at the rate of 1:35 retail packs only, and could be differentiated from basic UD cards by the inclusion of the words Electric Ice embossed in gold down the side of the card front. The card J-171 is a recently confirmed jumbo version of the Electric Ice Gold Selanne card. The J prefix was added for checklisting purposes. It is not known whether other jumbo versions exist for Electric Ice Gold cards.

*STARS: 40X TO 100X BASIC CARDS
*ROOKIES: 8X TO 20X BASIC CARDS
530 Jose Theodore 30.00 80.00
569 Chris Drury 30.00 60.00

1995-96 Upper Deck All-Star Game Predictors

The thirty cards in this set were handed out one per person at the Upper Deck booth at the All-Star FanFest in Boston. The winning card, no. 21 Ray Bourque, was redeemable for a full thirty card set of All-Star Game Predictors that contained different photos than the original give-aways. Prices below are for the cards handed out at the All-Star game. Separate multipliers to determine values for the redeemed versions can be found in the header below. The redeemed Bourque card is actually worth about 33 percent of the game card; this is due to the mass redemption of the Bourque game card, making it extremely difficult to locate in the secondary market.

*REDEEMED CARDS: 2X TO 3X BASIC PREDICTORS
1 Wayne Gretzky 80.00 200.00
2 Sergei Fedorov 20.00 50.00
3 Brett Hull 16.00 40.00
4 Alexander Mogilny 6.00 15.00
5 Joe Sakic 20.00 50.00
6 Paul Kariya 30.00 75.00
7 Teemu Selanne 20.00 50.00
8 Paul Coffey 10.00 25.00
9 Chris Chelios 16.00 40.00
10 Doug Gilmour 10.00 25.00
11 Peter Forsberg 24.00 60.00
12 Jeremy Roenick 16.00 40.00
13 Theo Fleury 10.00 25.00
14 Mike Modano 16.00 40.00
15 Steve Yzerman 50.00 125.00
16 Mario Lemieux 60.00 150.00
17 Jaromir Jagr 24.00 60.00
18 Eric Lindros 20.00 50.00
19 Mark Messier 16.00 40.00
20 Brendan Shanahan 16.00 40.00
21 Ray Bourque 80.00 200.00
22 Cam Neely 16.00 40.00
23 Ron Francis 6.00 15.00
24 John LeClair 16.00 40.00
25 Brian Leetch 10.00 25.00
26 Peter Bondra 10.00 25.00
27 Scott Stevens 6.00 15.00
28 Adam Oates 6.00 15.00
29 Martin Brodeur 24.00 60.00
30 Longshot 2.00 5.00

1995-96 Upper Deck Freeze Frame

Twenty top stars are featured in this multiple photo insert set which utilizes Upper Deck's Light FX foil printing technology. The cards were randomly inserted at a rate of 1:34 series one packs. Jumbo versions of these cards, measuring 3 1/2" by 6", were inserted one per series one box. Multipliers can be found in the header below to determine values for these.

COMPLETE SET (20) 25.00 60.00
*JUMBOS: .5X TO 1X BASIC CARDS
F1 Peter Forsberg 2.50 6.00
F2 Wayne Gretzky 6.00 15.00
F3 Eric Lindros 1.25 3.00
F4 Jaromir Jagr 2.00 5.00
F5 Cam Neely 1.25 3.00
F6 Jeremy Roenick 1.25 3.00
F7 Mark Messier 1.25 3.00
F8 Sergei Fedorov 1.25 3.00
F9 Paul Kariya 1.25 3.00
F10 Pavel Bure 1.25 3.00
F11 Dominik Hasek 2.50 5.00
F12 Theo Fleury .40 1.00
F13 Alexei Zhamnov .40 1.00
F14 Martin Brodeur 3.00 8.00
F15 Brett Hull 1.25 3.00
F16 Mario Lemieux 4.00 10.00
F17 Paul Coffey .60 1.50
F18 Brian Leetch .60 1.50
F19 Ray Bourque 1.25 3.00
F20 Jim Carey .40 1.00

1995-96 Upper Deck Gretzky Collection

This 24 card set, which focuses on the many remarkable achievements in the career of Wayne Gretzky, was released through four separate products. Cards G1-G9, along with an NNO header card, could be found in 1995-96 Collector's Choice retail and hobby packs at a rate of 1:11. Cards G10-G13 and an NNO header card were randomly inserted in packs of Upper Deck series 1 at a rate of 1:29. Cards G14-17 along with an NNO header card were randomly inserted in packs of Upper Deck series 2 at a rate of 1:29. Finally, cards G18-G20, along with an NNO header card, were randomly inserted at a rate of 1:45 packs of SP. The cards share a similar design element, but with added foil enhancements for each step up the premium ladder. A jumbo version of cards G1-G10 were produced and inserted into some Collector's Choice boxes. Multipliers can be found in the header below to determine value for these.

COMPLETE SET (24) 75.00 150.00
COMMON CC (G1-G9/HDR) 2.00 5.00
COMMON UD (G10-G17/HDR'S) 4.00 10.00
COMMON SP (G18-G20/HDR) 12.50 30.00
*G1-G10 JUMBOS: .75X TO 1.5X BASIC CARDS

1995-96 Upper Deck NHL All-Stars

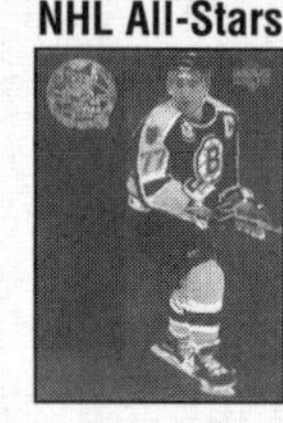

Randomly inserted in packs at a rate of 1:34 series 2 packs, these twenty two-sided cards highlight the participants in the 1995-96 All-Star Game. The cards utilize the UD Light FX technology. Players from the Western Conference have a teal left border, while players from the Eastern Conference have purple left border. There also were jumbo version of these cards inserted one per series 2 box. Multipliers can be found in the header below to determine value for these.

*JUMBOS: .5X TO 1X BASIC INSERTS
AS1 Ray Bourque / Paul Coffey 1.00 2.50
AS2 Scott Stevens / Chris Chelios .75 2.00
AS3 Jaromir Jagr / Brett Hull 1.25 3.00
AS4 Brendan Shanahan / Pavel Bure .75 2.00
AS5 M.Lemieux/W.Gretzky 8.00 20.00
AS6 Martin Brodeur / Ed Belfour 2.00 5.00
AS7 Brian Leetch / Nicklas Lidstrom .75 2.00
AS8 Roman Hamrlik / Gary Suter .75 2.00
AS9 Eric Desjardins / Al MacInnis .75 2.00
AS10 Cam Neely / Alexander Mogilny .75 2.00
AS11 Peter Bondra / Theo Fleury .75 2.00
AS12 Daniel Alfredsson / Teemu Selanne .75 2.00
AS13 Pat Verbeek / Owen Nolan .75 2.00
AS14 John LeClair / Paul Kariya 2.00 5.00
AS15 Pierre Turgeon / Sergei Fedorov 1.00 2.50
AS16 Mark Messier / Doug Weight .75 2.00
AS17 Eric Lindros / Peter Forsberg 2.50 6.00
AS18 Ron Francis / Mats Sundin .75 2.00
AS19 John Vanbiesbrouck / Chris Osgood .75 2.00
AS20 Dominik Hasek / Felix Potvin 2.00 5.00

1995-96 Upper Deck Predictor Hobby

The 40 cards in this set were randomly inserted in series 1 hobby packs (H1-H20) at the rate of 1:30, and series 2 hobby packs (H21-H40) at the rate of 1:23. Each card was a potential winner in an interactive game based on season-end award recipients: if the player pictured on your card came in first or second in the voting for that award, you could redeem your card for a complete set of Predictors from that distribution category. Cards H1-H10 were contestants for the Hart Trophy, cards H11-H20 were goalies competing for the Vezina Trophy, cards H21-H30 were contestants for the Calder Trophy, and cards H31-H40 were vying for the James Norris Trophy. The cards of Mario Lemieux, Mark Messier, Jim Carey, Vezina Long Shot, Daniel Alfredsson, Eric Daze, Chris Chelios and Ray Bourque may be somewhat harder to locate now, because, as winners, many of them were redeemed and destroyed.

*EXCH CARDS: .2X TO .5X BASIC INSERTS
H1 Eric Lindros 1.00 2.50
H2 Jaromir Jagr 1.50 4.00
H3 Paul Coffey 1.00 2.50
H4 Mario Lemieux 4.00 10.00
H5 Martin Brodeur 2.50 6.00
H6 Sergei Fedorov 1.00 2.50
H7 Wayne Gretzky 6.00 15.00
H8 Peter Forsberg 1.50 4.00
H9 Mark Messier 1.25 3.00
H10 Hart Long Shot .40 1.00
H11 Martin Brodeur 2.50 6.00
H12 Mike Richter 1.00 2.50
H13 Dominik Hasek 2.00 5.00
H14 Patrick Roy 4.00 10.00
H15 Blaine Lacher .40 1.00
H16 Jim Carey .40 1.00
H17 Felix Potvin 1.25 3.00
H18 Ed Belfour 1.25 3.00
H19 John Vanbiesbrouck .75 2.00
H20 Vezina Long Shot .40 1.00
H21 Vitali Yachmenev .40 1.00
H22 Saku Koivu 1.00 2.50
H23 Daniel Alfredsson 2.00 5.00
H24 Ed Jovanovski .40 1.00
H25 Aki Berg .40 1.00
H26 Radek Dvorak .40 1.00
H27 Shane Doan .75 2.00
H28 Nicklas Sundstrom .40 1.00
H29 Eric Daze .40 1.00
H30 Calder Long Shot .40 1.00
H31 Paul Coffey .75 2.00
H32 Ray Bourque 1.25 3.00
H33 Brian Leetch .75 2.00
H34 Chris Chelios 1.25 3.00
H35 Scott Stevens .40 1.00
H36 Nicklas Lidstrom 1.00 2.50
H37 Sergei Zubov .40 1.00
H38 Larry Murphy .40 1.00
H39 Roman Hamrlik .40 1.00
H40 Norris Long Shot .40 1.00

1995-96 Upper Deck Predictor Retail

The 60 cards in this interactive set were randomly inserted in retail packs from both series. R1-R30 were inserted at a rate of 1:30 series 1 retail packs, and 1:17 Value Added retail packs, while cards R31-R60 were inserted at a rate of 1:23 retail series 2 packs. A card could be redeemed if the player pictured finished first or second in the race for the scoring category featured. Cards R1-R10 battled for the assists crown, R11-R20 aimed to be the most prolific snipers, R21-R30 aimed to reach the top of the point scoring heap, R31-R40 were shooting for Art Ross, R41-R50 were in search of Lester B. Pearson, and R51-R60 were players looking to be awarded the Conn Smythe. However, a printing error at the printing plant reversed the intended categories on cards R1-R10 and R11-R20. In light of this, Upper Deck decided to honour a card as a winner if the player pictured won in either category. The cards of Mario Lemieux (R32, R42), Jaromir Jagr, Patrick Roy, Ron Francis and the Long Shots in the Assists, Goals, Points, and Smythe categories may be somewhat harder to find, as many were redeemed as winners.

*EXCH CARDS: .2X TO .5X BASIC INSERTS
R1 Cam Neely 1.25 3.00
R2 Eric Lindros 1.25 3.00
R3 Jaromir Jagr 2.00 5.00
R4 Brendan Shanahan 1.25 3.00
R5 Brett Hull 1.50 4.00
R6 Alexander Mogilny .60 1.50
R7 Owen Nolan .60 1.50
R8 Theo Fleury .40 1.00
R9 Pavel Bure 1.25 3.00
R10 Assists Long Shot .40 1.00
R11 Ron Francis .60 1.50
R12 Paul Coffey 1.25 3.00
R13 Wayne Gretzky 6.00 15.00
R14 Joe Sakic 2.50 6.00
R15 Steve Yzerman 4.00 10.00
R16 Adam Oates .60 1.50
R17 Joe Juneau .40 1.00
R18 Brian Leetch .60 1.50
R19 Pat LaFontaine 1.25 3.00
R20 Goals Long Shot .40 1.00
R21 Eric Lindros 1.25 3.00
R22 Jaromir Jagr 2.00 5.00
R23 Wayne Gretzky 6.00 15.00
R24 Sergei Fedorov 1.50 4.00
R25 Peter Forsberg 2.00 5.00
R26 Pavel Bure 1.25 3.00
R27 Joe Sakic 2.50 6.00
R28 Alexei Zhamnov .40 1.00
R29 Pat LaFontaine 1.25 3.00
R30 Points Long Shot .40 1.00
R31 Wayne Gretzky 6.00 15.00
R32 Mario Lemieux 4.00 10.00
R33 Eric Lindros 1.25 3.00
R34 Sergei Fedorov 1.50 4.00
R35 Alexander Mogilny .60 1.50
R36 Joe Sakic 2.50 6.00
R37 Peter Forsberg 2.00 5.00
R38 Jaromir Jagr 2.00 5.00
R39 Mark Messier 1.25 3.00
R40 Ross Long Shot .40 1.00
R41 Wayne Gretzky 6.00 15.00
R42 Mario Lemieux 4.00 10.00
R43 Paul Kariya 1.25 3.00
R44 Sergei Fedorov 1.50 4.00
R45 Joe Sakic 2.50 6.00
R46 Jaromir Jagr 2.00 5.00
R47 Jeremy Roenick 1.50 4.00
R48 Ray Bourque 1.25 3.00
R49 Teemu Selanne 1.25 3.00
R50 Pearson Long Shot .40 1.00
R51 Wayne Gretzky 6.00 15.00
R52 Eric Lindros 1.25 3.00
R53 Mario Lemieux 4.00 10.00
R54 Peter Forsberg 2.00 5.00

R55 Patrick Roy 5.00 12.00
R56 Mark Messier 1.25 3.00
R57 Martin Brodeur 2.50 6.00
R58 Steve Yzerman 4.00 10.00
R59 Mike Modano 1.50 4.00
R60 Smythe Long Shot .40 1.00

1995-96 Upper Deck Special Edition

This 180-card set was inserted one per hobby pack over both series of 1995-96 Upper Deck cards. Cards 1-90 were found in series 1 packs, while 91-180 were in series 2.

COMPLETE SET (180) 30.00 60.00
*GOLDS: 8X TO 20X BASIC INSERTS
SE1 Paul Kariya .25 .60
SE2 Oleg Tverdovsky .10 .20
SE3 Guy Hebert .10 .30
SE4 Ray Bourque .25 .60
SE5 Adam Oates .10 .30
SE6 Mariusz Czerkawski .10 .20
SE7 Blaine Lacher .10 .30
SE8 Garry Galley .10 .20
SE9 Donald Audette .10 .20
SE10 Pat LaFontaine .25 .60
SE11 Alexei Zhitnik .10 .20
SE12 Joe Nieuwendyk .10 .30
SE13 Phil Housley .10 .30
SE14 German Titov .10 .20
SE15 Trevor Kidd .10 .30
SE16 Bernie Nicholls .10 .20
SE17 Chris Chelios .25 .60
SE18 Tony Amonte .10 .30
SE19 Ed Belfour .25 .60
SE20 Jon Klemm .10 .20
SE21 Peter Forsberg .60 1.50
SE22 Adam Deadmarsh .10 .30
SE23 Stephane Fiset .10 .30
SE24 Dave Gagner .10 .20
SE25 Kevin Hatcher .10 .20
SE26 Mike Modano .40 1.00
SE27 Keith Primeau .10 .20
SE28 Dino Ciccarelli .10 .30
SE29 Nicklas Lidstrom .25 .60
SE30 Steve Yzerman 1.25 3.00
SE31 Doug Weight .10 .30
SE32 Bill Ranford .10 .30
SE33 Stu Barnes .10 .20
SE34 Scott Mellanby .10 .30
SE35 Rob Niedermayer .10 .30
SE36 Andrew Cassels .10 .20
SE37 Darren Turcotte .10 .20
SE38 Andrei Nikolishin .10 .20
SE39 Sean Burke .10 .30
SE40 Rick Tocchet .10 .30
SE41 Jari Kurri .25 .60
SE42 Rob Blake .10 .30
SE43 Mark Recchi .10 .30
SE44 Pierre Turgeon .10 .30
SE45 Vladimir Malakhov .10 .20
SE46 Valeri Bure .10 .20
SE47 Stephane Richer .10 .30
SE48 Bill Guerin .10 .30
SE49 Scott Stevens .10 .30
SE50 Claude Lemieux .10 .20
SE51 Zigmund Palffy .10 .30
SE52 Kirk Muller .10 .20
SE53 Todd Bertuzzi .10 .30
SE54 Brett Lindros .10 .20
SE55 Brian Leetch .10 .30
SE56 Alexei Kovalev .10 .20
SE57 Adam Graves .10 .20
SE58 Mike Richter .25 .60
SE59 Alexei Yashin .10 .20
SE60 Alexandre Daigle .10 .20
SE61 Don Beaupre .10 .30
SE62 Radek Bonk .10 .20
SE63 John LeClair .25 .60
SE64 Rod Brind'Amour .10 .30
SE65 Ron Hextall .10 .30
SE66 Ron Francis .10 .30
SE67 Markus Naslund .25 .60
SE68 Tom Barrasso .10 .30
SE69 Ian Laperriere .10 .20
SE70 Esa Tikkanen .10 .20
SE71 Al MacInnis .10 .30
SE72 Ulf Dahlen .10 .20
SE73 Craig Janney .10 .20
SE74 Jeff Friesen .10 .20
SE75 Chris Gratton .10 .30
SE76 Roman Hamrlik .10 .30
SE77 Alexander Selivanov .10 .20
SE78 Daren Puppa .10 .30
SE79 Dave Andreychuk .10 .30
SE80 Doug Gilmour .10 .30
SE81 Kenny Jonsson .10 .20
SE82 Trevor Linden .10 .30
SE83 Kirk McLean .10 .30
SE84 Jeff Brown .10 .20
SE85 Keith Jones .10 .20
SE86 Joe Juneau .10 .20
SE87 Jim Carey .10 .30
SE88 Keith Tkachuk .25 .60
SE89 Teemu Selanne .25 .60
SE90 Igor Korolev .10 .20
SE91 Mike Sillinger .10 .20
SE92 Steve Rucchin .10 .20
SE93 Valeri Karpov .10 .20
SE94 Cam Neely .25 .60
SE95 Shawn McEachern .10 .20
SE96 Kevin Stevens .10 .20
SE97 Ted Donato .10 .20
SE98 Dominik Hasek .50 1.25
SE99 Randy Burridge .10 .20
SE100 Jason Dawe .10 .20
SE101 Theo Fleury .10 .20
SE102 Michael Nylander .10 .20
SE103 Rick Tabaracci .10 .30
SE104 Jeremy Roenick .30 .75
SE105 Bob Probert .10 .30
SE106 Patrick Poulin .10 .20
SE107 Gary Suter .10 .20
SE108 Claude Lemieux .10 .20
SE109 Sandis Ozolinsh .10 .20
SE110 Patrick Roy 1.25 3.00
SE111 Joe Sakic .50 1.25
SE112 Derian Hatcher .10 .20
SE113 Greg Adams .10 .20
SE114 Todd Harvey .10 .30
SE115 Sergei Fedorov .40 1.00
SE116 Chris Osgood .10 .30
SE117 Vyacheslav Kozlov .10 .30
SE118 Paul Coffey .25 .60
SE119 Jason Arnott .10 .20
SE120 David Oliver .10 .20
SE121 Todd Marchant .10 .20
SE122 John Vanbiesbrouck .10 .30
SE123 Jody Hull .10 .20
SE124 Jason Woolley .10 .20
SE125 Brendan Shanahan .25 .60
SE126 Nelson Emerson .10 .20
SE127 Geoff Sanderson .10 .30
SE128 Wayne Gretzky 1.50 4.00
SE129 Marty McSorley .10 .20
SE130 Yanic Perreault .10 .20
SE131 Jocelyn Thibault .25 .60
SE132 Brian Savage .10 .20
SE133 Vincent Damphousse .10 .20
SE134 John MacLean .10 .30
SE135 Martin Brodeur .60 1.50
SE136 Steve Thomas .10 .30
SE137 Scott Niedermayer .10 .30
SE138 Travis Green .10 .30
SE139 Wendel Clark .10 .30
SE140 Tommy Soderstrom .10 .30
SE141 Mark Messier .25 .60
SE142 Ulf Samuelsson .10 .20
SE143 Ray Ferraro .10 .20
SE144 Luc Robitaille .10 .30
SE145 Daniel Alfredsson 1.00 2.50
SE146 Martin Straka .10 .20
SE147 Steve Duchesne .10 .20
SE148 Eric Lindros .25 .60
SE149 Mikael Renberg .10 .30
SE150 Eric Desjardins .10 .30
SE151 Joel Otto .10 .20
SE152 Mario Lemieux 1.25 3.00
SE153 Jaromir Jagr .40 1.00
SE154 Petr Nedved .10 .30
SE155 Sergei Zubov .10 .20
SE156 Tomas Sandstrom .10 .20
SE157 Brett Hull .30 .75
SE158 Grant Fuhr .25 .60
SE159 Shayne Corson .10 .20
SE160 Chris Pronger .25 .60
SE161 Ray Sheppard .10 .30
SE162 Arturs Irbe .10 .30
SE163 Owen Nolan .10 .30
SE164 Andrei Nazarov .10 .20
SE165 Paul Ysebaert .10 .20
SE166 Brian Bradley .10 .20
SE167 Petr Klima .10 .20
SE168 Felix Potvin .25 .60
SE169 Mats Sundin .25 .60
SE170 Larry Murphy .10 .30
SE171 Benoit Hogue .10 .20
SE172 Pavel Bure .25 .60
SE173 Alexander Mogilny .10 .30
SE174 Cliff Ronning .10 .20
SE175 Pat Peake .10 .20
SE176 Sylvain Cote .10 .20
SE177 Peter Bondra .10 .30
SE178 Dallas Drake .10 .30
SE179 Tim Cheveldae .10 .30
SE180 Darren Turcotte .10 .20

1996-97 Upper Deck

This two-series, 390-card set was distributed in 12-card packs with the suggested retail price of $2.49. The set was highlighted by the use of actual game dating for much of the photography, the selection of which included some of the most memorable moments of the '96 season. The set is noteworthy for including Wayne Gretzky in his new uniform as a New York Ranger both in the set and on all packaging. The set also contained a 15-card Star Rookie subset (#181-195), a 13-card Through the Glass subset (#196-208), a 10-card On-Ice Insight subset (359-368) and four checklist cards. Several key rookies appeared in this set, including Joe Thornton, Patrick Marleau, Daniel Tkaczuk, and Dainius Zubrus. The "Meet the Stars" promotion was continued in this set, which gave the collector an opportunity to win a chance to meet "The Great One" himself. Trivia cards were inserted one in every four packs and Instant Win cards one in every 56 packs. These cards are not widely traded, but are now worth about ten cents each.

COMPLETE SET (390) 40.00 80.00
COMPLETE SERIES 1 (210) 15.00 30.00
COMPLETE SERIES 2 (180) 25.00 50.00
1 Paul Kariya .15 .40
2 Guy Hebert .08 .25
3 J.F. Jomphe RC .02 .10
4 Joe Sacco .02 .10
5 Jason York .02 .10
6 Alex Hicks .02 .10
7 Mikhail Shtalenkov .02 .10
8 Bill Ranford .08 .25
9 Kyle McLaren .02 .10
10 Rick Tocchet .08 .25
11 Jon Rohloff .02 .10
12 Jozef Stumpel .02 .10
13 Cam Neely .15 .40
14 Ray Bourque .25 .60
15 Pat LaFontaine .15 .40
16 Brian Holzinger .08 .25
17 Alexei Zhitnik .02 .10
18 Donald Audette .02 .10
19 Jason Dawe .02 .10
20 Wayne Primeau .02 .10
21 Mike Peca .02 .10
22 Theo Fleury .02 .10
23 Sandy McCarthy .02 .10
24 Zarley Zalapski .02 .10
25 Trevor Kidd .08 .25
26 Steve Chiasson .02 .10
27 Michael Nylander .02 .10
28 Ronnie Stern .02 .10
29 Eric Daze .08 .25
30 Jeff Hackett .08 .25
31 Chris Chelios .15 .40
32 Tony Amonte .08 .25
33 Bob Probert .08 .25
34 Eric Weinrich .02 .10
35 Jeremy Roenick .20 .50
36 Mike Ricci .02 .10
37 Sandis Ozolinsh .02 .10
38 Patrick Roy .75 2.00
39 Uwe Krupp .02 .10
40 Stephane Yelle .02 .10
41 Adam Deadmarsh .02 .10
42 Scott Young .02 .10
43 Mike Modano .25 .60
44 Derian Hatcher .02 .10
45 Todd Harvey .02 .10
46 Brent Fedyk .02 .10
47 Grant Marshall .02 .10
48 Jamie Langenbrunner .02 .10
49 Jere Lehtinen .02 .10
50 Steve Yzerman .75 2.00
51 Igor Larionov .02 .10
52 Vladimir Konstantinov .08 .25
53 Chris Osgood .08 .25
54 Jamie Pushor .02 .10
55 Darren McCarty .02 .10
56 Nicklas Lidstrom .15 .40
57 Jason Arnott .02 .10
58 Doug Weight .08 .25
59 Todd Marchant .02 .10
60 David Oliver .02 .10
61 Luke Richardson .02 .10
62 Jason Bonsignore .02 .10
63 John Vanbiesbrouck .08 .25
64 Stu Barnes .02 .10
65 Martin Straka .02 .10
66 Ed Jovanovski .08 .25
67 Robert Svehla .02 .10
68 Gord Murphy .02 .10
69 Tom Fitzgerald .02 .10
70 Jeff O'Neill .02 .10
71 Jason Muzzatti .02 .10
72 Sean Burke .08 .25
73 Jeff Brown .02 .10
74 Andrew Cassels .02 .10
75 Geoff Sanderson .02 .10
76 Dimitri Khristich .02 .10
77 Vitali Yachmenev .02 .10
78 Kevin Stevens .02 .10
79 Yanic Perreault .02 .10
80 Craig Johnson .02 .10
81 John Slaney .02 .10
82 Saku Koivu .15 .40
83 Jocelyn Thibault .15 .40
84 Vladimir Malakhov .02 .10
85 Turner Stevenson .02 .10
86 Vincent Damphousse .02 .10
87 Mark Recchi .08 .25
88 Patrice Brisebois .02 .10
89 Dave Andreychuk .08 .25
90 Bill Guerin .02 .10
91 Martin Brodeur .40 1.00
92 Scott Niedermayer .02 .10
93 Petr Sykora .02 .10
94 Stephane Richer .08 .25
95 John MacLean .02 .10
96 Eric Fichaud .08 .25
97 Zigmund Palffy .08 .25
98 Alexander Semak .02 .10
99 Bryan McCabe .02 .10
100 Darby Hendrickson .02 .10
101 Kenny Jonsson .02 .10
102 Marty McInnis .02 .10
103 Alexei Kovalev .02 .10
104 Ulf Samuelsson .02 .10
105 Jeff Beukeboom .02 .10
106 Marty McSorley .02 .10
107 Niklas Sundstrom .02 .10
108 Wayne Gretzky 1.00 2.50
with Mark Messier
109 Mike Richter .15 .40
110 Alexei Yashin .02 .10
111 Randy Cunneyworth .02 .10
112 Damian Rhodes .08 .25
113 Daniel Alfredsson .08 .25
114 Antti Tormanen .02 .10
115 Ted Drury .02 .10
116 Janne Laukkanen .02 .10
117 Sean Hill .02 .10
118 John LeClair .15 .40
119 Ron Hextall .08 .25
120 Dale Hawerchuk .08 .25
121 Rod Brind'Amour .08 .25
122 Pat Falloon .02 .10
123 Eric Desjardins .08 .25
124 Joel Otto .02 .10
125 Alexei Zhamnov .08 .25
126 Nikolai Khabibulin .08 .25
127 Craig Janney .08 .25
128 Deron Quint .02 .10
129 Oleg Tverdovsky .08 .25
130 Chad Kilger .02 .10
131 Teppo Numminen .02 .10
132 Tom Barrasso .08 .25
133 Ron Francis .08 .25
134 Petr Nedved .08 .25
135 Ken Wregget .08 .25
136 Joe Dziedzic .02 .10
137 Tomas Sandstrom .02 .10
138 Dmitri Mironov .02 .10
139 Shayne Corson .02 .10
140 Grant Fuhr .08 .25
141 Al MacInnis .08 .25
142 Stephen Leach .02 .10
143 Murray Baron .02 .10
144 Chris Pronger .08 .25
145 Jamie Rivers .02 .10
146 Owen Nolan .08 .25
147 Chris Terreri .08 .25
148 Marcus Ragnarsson .02 .10
149 Shean Donovan .02 .10
150 Ray Whitney .02 .10
151 Michal Sykora .02 .10
152 Viktor Kozlov .02 .10
153 Roman Hamrlik .08 .25
154 Bill Houlder .02 .10
155 Mikael Andersson .02 .10
156 Petr Klima .02 .10
157 Jason Wiemer .02 .10
158 Rob Zamuner .02 .10
159 Paul Ysebaert .02 .10
160 Mats Sundin .15 .40
161 Larry Murphy UER .08 .25
(bio info that of Mats Sundin)
162 Doug Gilmour .08 .25
163 Todd Warriner .02 .10
164 Dimitri Yushkevich .02 .10
165 Kirk Muller .02 .10
166 Jamie Macoun .02 .10
167 Alexander Mogilny .08 .25
168 Corey Hirsch .02 .10
169 Trevor Linden .08 .25
170 Markus Naslund .15 .40
171 Martin Gelinas .02 .10
172 Jyrki Lumme .02 .10
173 Bret Hedican .02 .10
174 Jim Carey .15 .40
175 Sergei Gonchar .02 .10
176 Joe Juneau .02 .10
177 Brendan Witt .02 .10
178 Dale Hunter .02 .10
179 Steve Konowalchuk .02 .10
180 Peter Bondra .08 .25
181 Jarome Iginla .20 .50
182 Ralph Intranuovo .02 .10
183 Anders Eriksson .02 .10
184 Andrew Brunette RC .25 .60
185 Steve Sullivan RC .25 .60
186 Brandon Convery .02 .10
187 Ethan Moreau RC .15 .40
188 Marko Kiprusoff .02 .10
189 Jason McBain .02 .10
190 Mark Kolesar RC .02 .10
191 Greg DeVries RC .02 .10
192 Alexei Yegorov RC .02 .10
193 Sebastien Bordeleau RC .02 .10
194 Nick Stajduhar .02 .10
195 Jan Caloun RC .02 .10
196 Dino Ciccarelli TTG .08 .25
197 Ron Hextall TTG .08 .25
198 Murray Baron TTG .02 .10
199 Patrick Roy TTG .15 .40
200 Scott Mellanby TTG .08 .25
201 Tie Domi TTG .08 .25
202 Glenn Healy TTG .08 .25
203 Keith Primeau TTG .02 .10
204 Joe Sakic TTG .15 .40
205 Jeremy Roenick TTG .02 .10
206 Sergei Fedorov TTG .15 .40
207 Claude Lemieux TTG .02 .10
208 Theo Fleury TTG .02 .10
209 Checklist (1-104) .02 .10
210 Checklist (105-210) .02 .10
211 Teemu Selanne .15 .40
212 Jari Kurri .08 .25
213 Darren Van Impe .02 .10
214 Steve Rucchin .02 .10
215 Ruslan Salei RC .02 .10
216 Adam Oates .08 .25
217 Don Sweeney .02 .10
218 Steve Staios RC .02 .10
219 Barry Richter .02 .10
220 Mattias Timander RC .02 .10
221 Ted Donato .02 .10
222 Dominik Hasek .30 .75
223 Derek Plante .02 .10
224 Vaclav Varada RC .02 .10
225 Andrei Trefilov .02 .10
226 Curtis Brown .02 .10
227 German Titov .02 .10
228 Robert Reichel .02 .10
229 Cory Stillman .02 .10
230 Chris O'Sullivan .02 .10
231 Corey Millen .02 .10
232 Jonas Hoglund .02 .10
233 Alexei Zhamnov .08 .25
234 Ed Belfour .15 .40
235 Gary Suter .02 .10
236 Kevin Miller .02 .10
237 Tuomas Gronman .02 .10
238 Enrico Ciccone .02 .10
239 Peter Forsberg .40 1.00
240 Joe Sakic .30 .75
241 Valeri Kamensky .08 .25
242 Landon Wilson .02 .10
243 Claude Lemieux .02 .10
244 Eric Lacroix .02 .10
245 Joe Nieuwendyk UER .08 .25
(front Joe Nieuwendky)
246 Sergei Zubov .02 .10
247 Benoit Hogue .02 .10
248 Arturs Irbe .08 .25
249 Pat Verbeek .02 .10
250 Sergei Fedorov .20 .50
251 Vyacheslav Kozlov .02 .10
252 Brendan Shanahan .15 .40
253 Kevin Hodson RC .15 .40
254 Greg Johnson .02 .10
255 Tomas Holmstrom RC .60 1.50
256 Curtis Joseph .15 .40
257 Dean McAmmond .02 .10
258 Ryan Smyth .15 .40
259 Mike Grier RC .30 .75
260 Miroslav Satan .02 .10
261 Rem Murray RC .02 .10
262 Rob Niedermayer .08 .25
263 Ray Sheppard .08 .25
264 Dave Lowry .02 .10
265 Scott Mellanby .08 .25
266 Rhett Warrener .02 .10
267 Per Gustafsson RC .02 .10
268 Paul Coffey .15 .40
269 Nelson Emerson .02 .10
270 Kevin Dineen .02 .10
271 Keith Primeau .02 .10
272 Hnat Domenichelli .02 .10
273 Ray Ferraro .02 .10
274 Stephane Fiset .08 .25
275 Kai Nurminen RC .02 .10
276 Dan Bylsma RC .02 .10
277 Mattias Norstrom .02 .10
278 Rob Blake .08 .25
279 Jose Theodore .20 .50
280 Martin Rucinsky .02 .10
281 Darcy Tucker .02 .10
282 David Wilkie .02 .10
283 Valeri Bure .02 .10
284 Steve Thomas .02 .10
285 Brian Rolston .02 .10
286 Scott Stevens .08 .25
287 Shawn Chambers .02 .10
288 Denis Pederson .02 .10
289 Lyle Odelein .02 .10
290 Travis Green .02 .10
291 Todd Bertuzzi .15 .40
292 Niclas Andersson .02 .10
293 Darius Kasparaitis .02 .10
294 Bryan Berard .15 .40
295 Daniel Goneau RC .02 .10
296 Christian Dube .02 .10
297 Adam Graves .02 .10
298 Sergei Nemchinov .02 .10
299 Mark Messier .15 .40
300 Brian Leetch .15 .40
301 Radek Bonk .02 .10
302 Alexandre Daigle .02 .10
303 Andreas Dackell RC .02 .10
304 Steve Duchesne .02 .10
305 Wade Redden .02 .10
306 Eric Lindros .15 .40
307 Mikael Renberg .08 .25
308 Shjon Podein .02 .10
309 Dainius Zubrus RC .30 .75
310 Janne Niinimaa .15 .40
311 Karl Dykhuis .02 .10
312 Jeremy Roenick .20 .50
313 Keith Tkachuk .15 .40
314 Shane Doan .02 .10
315 Cliff Ronning .02 .10
316 Mike Gartner .08 .25
317 Dave Manson .02 .10
318 Shawn Antoski .02 .10
319 Kevin Hatcher .02 .10
320 Jaromir Jagr .25 .60
321 Mario Lemieux .75 2.00
322 Bryan Smolinski .02 .10
323 Stefan Bergkvist RC .02 .10
324 Brett Hull .20 .50
325 Joe Murphy .02 .10
326 Stephane Matteau .02 .10
327 Geoff Courtnall .02 .10
328 Jim Campbell .02 .10
329 Harry York RC .15 .40
330 Kelly Hrudey .08 .25
331 Al Iafrate .02 .10
332 Jeff Friesen .02 .10
333 Darren Turcotte .02 .10
334 Bernie Nicholls .02 .10
335 Ville Peltonen .02 .10
336 Dino Ciccarelli .08 .25
337 Chris Gratton .08 .25
338 Daren Puppa .08 .25
339 Alexander Selivanov .02 .10
340 Daymond Langkow .08 .25
341 Felix Potvin .15 .40
342 Wendel Clark .08 .25
343 Mathieu Schneider .02 .10
344 Dave Ellet .02 .10
345 Fredrik Modin RC .40 1.00
346 Sergei Berezin RC .40 1.00
347 Pavel Bure .15 .40
348 Kirk McLean .08 .25
349 Mike Sillinger .02 .10
350 Russ Courtnall .02 .10
351 Scott Walker .02 .10
352 Esa Tikkanen .02 .10
353 Pat Peake .02 .10
354 Olaf Kolzig .08 .25
355 Michal Pivonka .02 .10
356 Richard Zednik RC .20 .50
357 Phil Housley .08 .25
358 Anson Carter .08 .25
359 Eric Daze OII .08 .25
360 Felix Potvin OII .15 .40
361 Wayne Gretzky OII .15 .40
362 Ed Jovanovski OII .08 .25
363 Mike Modano OII .08 .25
364 Peter Bondra OII .08 .25
365 Patrick Roy OII .15 .40
366 Ray Bourque OII .15 .40
367 Roman Hamrlik OII .08 .25
368 John LeClair OII .15 .40
369 Adam Colagiacomo RC .40 1.00
370 Joe Thornton RC 6.00 15.00
371 Patrick DesRochers RC .40 1.00
372 Pierre-Luc Therrien RC .40 1.00
373 Nick Boynton RC .40 1.00
374 Andrew Ference RC .40 1.00
375 Jean-Francois Fortin RC .40 1.00
376 Daniel Tetrault RC .40 1.00
377 Luc Theoret RC .40 1.00
378 Mike Van Ryn RC .40 1.00
379 Scott Barney RC .40 1.00
380 Harold Druken RC .40 1.00
381 Dylan Gyori RC .40 1.00
382 Chris Heron RC .40 1.00
383 Chad Hinz RC .40 1.00
384 Patrick Marleau RC 1.50 4.00
385 Serge Payer RC .40 1.00
386 Jeremy Reich RC .40 1.00
387 Daniel Tkaczuk RC .40 1.00
388 Jason Ward RC .40 1.00
389 Checklist (211-298) .02 .10
390 Checklist (299-390) .02 .10

1996-97 Upper Deck Game Jerseys

Inserted 1:2500 packs, these highly popular inserts featured swatches of actual game-worn jerseys as part of the card stock. Five cards were inserted in series one packs, while the remaining eight cards were distributed with series two.

*MULT.COLOR SWATCH: .75X TO 1.5X HI
GJ1 Steve Yzerman 75.00 200.00
GJ2 Brett Hull 40.00 100.00
GJ3 Doug Gilmour 30.00 80.00
GJ4 Jaromir Jagr 60.00 150.00
GJ5 Ray Bourque 40.00 100.00
GJ6 Mario Lemieux 75.00 200.00
GJ7 John Vanbiesbrouck 30.00 80.00
GJ8 Eric Lindros 30.00 80.00
GJ9 Mike Modano 40.00 100.00
GJ10 Pavel Bure 30.00 80.00
GJ11 Mark Messier 60.00 150.00
GJ12 Theo Fleury 30.00 80.00
GJ13 Mats Sundin UER 30.00 80.00

1996-97 Upper Deck Generation Next

Randomly inserted in packs at a rate of 1:4, this double-fronted, series two insert paired up two top players on each card. Both sides were enhanced with silver and gold foil.

COMPLETE SET (40) 50.00 100.00
X1 Paul Kariya 5.00 12.00
Wayne Gretzky
X2 Trevor Linden 2.00 5.00
Peter Forsberg
X3 Joe Sakic 1.50 4.00
Rob Niedermayer
X4 Chris O'Sullivan .40 1.00
Eric Weinrich
X5 Jocelyn Thibault 4.00 10.00
Patrick Roy
X6 Brett Hull 1.25 3.00
Daniel Alfredsson
X7 Chris Osgood .75 2.00
John Vanbiesbrouck
X8 Ray Bourque 1.50 4.00
Roman Hamrlik
X9 Paul Coffey 1.25 3.00
Sandis Ozolinsh
X10 Doug Gilmour 1.25 3.00
Sergei Fedorov
X11 Chris Chelios 1.25 3.00
Ed Jovanovski
X12 Jason Arnott 1.25 3.00
Jeremy Roenick
X13 Doug Weight 3.00 8.00
Steve Yzerman
X14 Brendan Shanahan 1.25 3.00
Todd Bertuzzi
X15 Wendel Clark 1.25 3.00
Keith Tkachuk
X16 Saku Koivu 1.25 3.00
Teemu Selanne
X17 Jaromir Jagr 1.25 3.00
Zigmund Palffy
X18 Ed Belfour 1.50 4.00
Martin Brodeur
X19 Eric Daze .75 2.00
Owen Nolan
X20 Valeri Kamensky .40 1.00
Vitali Yachmenev
X21 Jarome Iginla 2.50 6.00
Mike Modano
X22 Anders Eriksson 1.25 3.00
Niklas Lidstrom
X23 Brian Leetch 1.25 3.00
Bryan Berard
X24 Jari Kurri .40 1.00
Niklas Sundstrom
X25 Adam Deadmarsh .40 1.00
Scott Mellanby
X26 Peter Bondra .40 1.00
Petr Sykora
X27 Curtis Joseph 1.25 3.00
Eric Fichaud
X28 Dominik Hasek 2.50 6.00
Roman Turek
X29 Alexander Mogilny .40 1.00
Valeri Bure
X30 Daymond Langkow .40 1.00
Theo Fleury
X31 Bernie Nicholls .75 2.00
Sergei Berezin
X32 Chris Gratton .75 2.00
Rick Tocchet
X33 Felix Potvin 1.25 3.00
Grant Fuhr
X34 Keith Primeau .40 1.00
Kevin Stevens
X35 Rob Blake .40 1.00
Wade Redden
X36 Chris Pronger .75 2.00
Scott Stevens
X37 Gary Suter .40 1.00
Kyle McLaren
X38 Jonas Hoglund .75 2.00
Mats Sundin
X39 Larry Murphy .40 1.00
Sergei Zubov
X40 Adam Oates .75 2.00
Joe Juneau

1996-97 Upper Deck Hart Hopefuls Bronze

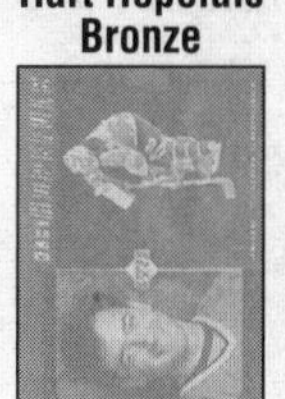

Randomly inserted in packs at a rate of 1:30, this series two-only insert consisted of twenty players vying for the title of league MVP and the chance to take home the Hart Trophy. Cards were numbered "One of 5000" on the back. Silver and gold parallels were also created. Silver were inserted at 1:150 and only 1000 were printed. Gold were inserted at 1:1500 and only 100 were produced.

*SILVERS: 1.5X TO 3X BASIC INSERTS
*GOLD: 4X TO 8X BASIC INSERTS
HH1 Wayne Gretzky 8.00 20.00
HH2 Mark Messier 1.00 2.50
HH3 Eric Lindros 1.00 2.50
HH4 Sergei Fedorov 1.25 3.00
HH5 Saku Koivu 1.00 2.50
HH6 John Vanbiesbrouck .75 2.00
HH7 Peter Forsberg 2.50 6.00
HH8 Keith Tkachuk 1.00 2.50
HH9 Paul Kariya 1.00 2.50
HH10 Martin Brodeur 2.50 6.00
HH11 Patrick Roy 6.00 15.00
HH12 Alexander Mogilny .75 2.00
HH13 Brett Hull 1.25 3.00
HH14 Pavel Bure 1.00 2.50
HH15 Teemu Selanne 1.00 2.50
HH16 Mario Lemieux 6.00 15.00
HH17 Jeremy Roenick 1.25 3.00
HH18 Jaromir Jagr 1.50 4.00
HH19 Steve Yzerman 5.00 12.00
HH20 Joe Sakic 2.00 5.00

1996-97 Upper Deck Lord Stanley's Heroes Quarterfinals

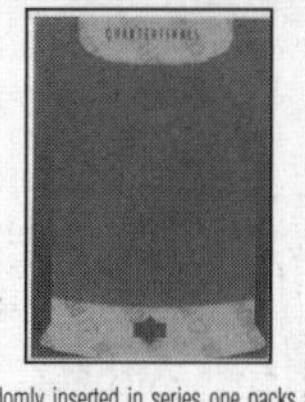

Randomly inserted in series one packs at a rate of 1:37, this 20-card set featured numbered inserts (one of 5,000) on cel chrome technology. A player's head photo was displayed on acetate in the middle of the trophy. Semifinals and finals parallel variations were also produced and inserted randomly. Semifinals parallels were inserted at 1:185 and only 1000 sets were produced. Finals parallels were inserted at 1:1850 and only 100 sets were produced.

*FINALS:10X TO 20X BASIC INSERTS
*SEMI-FINALS: 1.5X TO 3X BASIC INSERTS
LS1 Wayne Gretzky 8.00 20.00
LS2 Mark Messier 1.50 4.00
LS3 Mario Lemieux 8.00 20.00
LS4 Jaromir Jagr 3.00 8.00
LS5 Martin Brodeur 5.00 12.00
LS6 Patrick Roy 6.00 15.00
LS7 Joe Sakic 4.00 10.00
LS8 Peter Forsberg 5.00 12.00
LS9 Theo Fleury 1.50 4.00
LS10 Paul Coffey 1.50 4.00
LS11 Doug Gilmour 1.50 4.00
LS12 Paul Kariya 1.50 4.00
LS13 Eric Lindros 1.50 4.00
LS14 Sergei Fedorov 2.50 6.00
LS15 Eric Daze 1.50 4.00
LS16 Teemu Selanne 1.50 4.00
LS17 Keith Tkachuk 1.50 4.00
LS18 Pavel Bure 1.50 4.00
LS19 Mats Sundin 1.50 4.00
LS20 Saku Koivu 1.50 4.00

1996-97 Upper Deck Power Performers

Randomly inserted in series two packs at a rate of 1:13, these cards featured a layered design on gold foil. Thirty of the league's toughest physical competitors were highlighted in the set.

COMPLETE SET (30) 15.00 40.00
P1 Brendan Shanahan 1.50 4.00
P2 Mikael Renberg .40 1.00
P3 John LeClair .75 2.00
P4 Keith Primeau .40 1.00
P5 Adam Graves .40 1.00
P6 Jason Arnott .40 1.00
P7 Todd Bertuzzi .75 2.00
P8 Ed Jovanovski .40 1.00
P9 Scott Stevens .40 1.00
P10 Chris Gratton .40 1.00
P11 Bill Guerin .40 1.00
P12 Vladimir Konstantinov .75 2.00
P13 Mike Grier .40 1.00
P14 Theo Fleury .75 2.00
P15 Chris Chelios .75 2.00
P16 Trevor Linden .75 2.00
P17 Claude Lemieux .40 1.00
P18 Owen Nolan .75 2.00
P19 Jarome Iginla 3.00 8.00
P20 Joe Nieuwendyk .75 2.00
P21 Kevin Hatcher .40 1.00
P22 Dino Ciccarelli .40 1.00
P23 Adam Deadmarsh .40 1.00
P24 Chris Pronger .75 2.00
P25 Mike Ricci .40 1.00
P26 Rod Brind'Amour .75 2.00
P27 Derian Hatcher .40 1.00
P28 Mats Sundin 1.50 4.00
P29 Doug Gilmour .75 2.00
P30 Todd Harvey .40 1.00

1996-97 Upper Deck Superstar Showdown

Randomly inserted in first series packs at a rate of 1:4, this 60-card set featured 30 different one-on-one match-ups of the NHL's top stars. Each of the card fronts displayed a single player photo with a die-cut design that enabled the cards to be matched together in pairs.

COMPLETE SET (60) 40.00 80.00
SS1A Pavel Bure .60 1.50
SS1B Paul Kariya .60 1.50
SS2A Patrick Roy 3.00 8.00
SS2B John Vanbiesbrouck .40 1.00
SS3A Eric Lindros .60 1.50
SS3B Ed Jovanovski .40 1.00
SS4A Theo Fleury .15 .40
SS4B Doug Gilmour .40 1.00
SS5A Wayne Gretzky 4.00 10.00
SS5B Mario Lemieux 3.00 8.00
SS6A Keith Tkachuk .60 1.50
SS6B Brendan Shanahan .60 1.50
SS7A Ray Bourque 1.00 2.50
SS7B Brian Leetch .60 1.50
SS8A Peter Forsberg 1.50 4.00
SS8B Sergei Fedorov .75 2.00
SS9A Mark Messier .60 1.50
SS9B Scott Stevens .40 1.00
SS10A Teemu Selanne .60 1.50
SS10B Alexander Mogilny .40 1.00
SS11A Felix Potvin .60 1.50
SS11B Jocelyn Thibault .60 1.50
SS12A Martin Brodeur 1.50 4.00
SS12B Eric Fichaud .40 1.00
SS13A Roman Hamrlik .40 1.00
SS13B Jaromir Jagr 1.00 2.50
SS14A Jim Carey .60 1.50
SS14B Saku Koivu .60 1.50
SS15A Jeremy Roenick .75 2.00
SS15B Brett Hull .75 2.00
SS16A Joe Sakic 1.25 3.00
SS16B Steve Yzerman 3.00 8.00
SS17A Doug Weight .40 1.00
SS17B Pat LaFontaine .60 1.50
SS18A Daniel Alfredsson .40 1.00
SS18B Eric Daze .40 1.00
SS19A Mike Modano 1.00 2.50
SS19B Jason Arnott .15 .40
SS20A Paul Coffey .60 1.50
SS20B Sandis Ozolinsh .15 .40
SS21A Zigmund Palffy .40 1.00
SS21B Petr Sykora .15 .40
SS22A Ed Belfour .60 1.50
SS22B Ron Hextall .40 1.00
SS23A Mats Sundin .60 1.50
SS23B Mikael Renberg .40 1.00
SS24A Vitali Yachmenev .15 .40
SS24B Alexei Zhamnov .40 1.00
SS25A Oleg Tverdovsky .40 1.00
SS25B Kyle McLaren .15 .40
SS26A Dominik Hasek 1.25 3.00
SS26B Petr Nedved .40 1.00
SS27A Chris Chelios .60 1.50
SS27B Chris Pronger .40 1.00
SS28A Rob Niedermayer .40 1.00
SS28B Scott Niedermayer .15 .40
SS29A Keith Primeau .15 .40
SS29B Bob Probert .40 1.00
SS30A Bill Ranford .40 1.00
SS30B Chris Osgood .40 1.00

1997-98 Upper Deck

The 1997-98 Upper Deck set was issued in two series totaling 420 cards and was distributed in 12-card packs with a suggested retail price of $2.49. The fronts feature color player photos, while the backs carry player information and career statistics. Series 1 contains the following subsets: Star Rookie (181-195), Fan Favorites (196-208) and two checklists (209-210). Series 2 contains the following subsets: Physical Force (389-398), Program of Excellence (399-418) and two checklists (419-420).

COMPLETE SET (420) 25.00 60.00
COMP.SER. 1 (210) 10.00 20.00
COMP.SER. 2 (210) 15.00 40.00
1 Teemu Selanne .15 .40
2 Steve Rucchin .02 .10
3 Kevin Todd .02 .10
4 Darren Van Impe .02 .10
5 Mark Janssens .02 .10
6 Guy Hebert .08 .25
7 Sean Pronger .02 .10
8 Jason Allison .02 .10
9 Ray Bourque .25 .60
10 Landon Wilson .02 .10
11 Anson Carter .08 .25
12 Jean-Yves Roy .02 .10
13 Kyle McLaren .02 .10
14 Don Sweeney .02 .10
15 Brian Holzinger .02 .10
16 Matthew Barnaby .02 .10
17 Wayne Primeau .02 .10
18 Steve Shields RC .40 1.00
19 Jason Dawe .02 .10
20 Donald Audette .02 .10
21 Dixon Ward .02 .10
22 Hnat Domenichelli .02 .10
23 Trevor Kidd .08 .25
24 Jarome Iginla .20 .50
25 Sandy McCarthy .02 .10
26 Marty McInnis .02 .10
27 Jonas Hoglund .02 .10
28 Aaron Gavey .02 .10
29 Keith Primeau .02 .10
30 Geoff Sanderson .08 .25
31 Sean Burke .08 .25
32 Steven Rice .02 .10
33 Stu Grimson .02 .10
34 Jeff O'Neill .02 .10
35 Curtis Leschyshyn .02 .10
36 Chris Chelios .15 .40
37 Sergei Krivokrasov .02 .10
38 Jeff Hackett .08 .25
39 Bob Probert .02 .10
40 Chris Terreri .08 .25
41 Eric Daze .08 .25
42 Alexei Zhamnov .02 .10
43 Patrick Roy .75 2.00
44 Sandis Ozolinsh .02 .10
45 Eric Messier RC .08 .25
46 Adam Deadmarsh .02 .10
47 Claude Lemieux .02 .10
48 Mike Ricci .02 .10
49 Stephane Yelle .02 .10
50 Joe Nieuwendyk .08 .25
51 Derian Hatcher .02 .10
52 Jere Lehtinen .02 .10
53 Roman Turek .08 .25
54 Darryl Sydor .02 .10
55 Todd Harvey .02 .10
56 Mike Modano .25 .60
57 Steve Yzerman .75 2.00
58 Martin Lapointe .02 .10
59 Darren McCarty .02 .10
60 Mike Vernon .08 .25
61 Kirk Maltby .02 .10
62 Kris Draper .02 .10
63 Vladimir Konstantinov .08 .25
64 Todd Marchant .02 .10
65 Doug Weight .08 .25
66 Jason Arnott .02 .10
67 Mike Grier .02 .10
68 Mats Lindgren .02 .10
69 Bryan Marchment .02 .10
70 Rem Murray .02 .10
71 Radek Dvorak .02 .10
72 John Vanbiesbrouck .08 .25
73 Robert Svehla .02 .10
74 Bill Lindsay .02 .10
75 Paul Laus .02 .10
76 Kirk Muller .02 .10
77 Dave Nemirovsky .02 .10
78 Roman Vopat .02 .10
79 Jan Vopat .02 .10
80 Dimitri Khristich .02 .10
81 Glen Murray .02 .10
82 Mattias Norstrom .02 .10
83 Ian Laperriere .02 .10
84 Mark Recchi .08 .25
85 Jose Theodore .20 .50
86 Vincent Damphousse .02 .10
87 Sebastien Bordeleau .02 .10
88 Darcy Tucker .02 .10
89 Martin Rucinsky .02 .10
90 Jocelyn Thibault .08 .25
91 Doug Gilmour .08 .25
92 Brian Rolston .02 .10
93 Jay Pandolfo .02 .10
94 John MacLean .02 .10
95 Scott Stevens .08 .25
96 Dave Andreychuk .02 .10
97 Denis Pederson .02 .10
98 Bryan Berard .08 .25
99 Zigmund Palffy .08 .25
100 Bryan McCabe .02 .10
101 Rich Pilon .02 .10
102 Eric Fichaud .08 .25
103 Todd Bertuzzi .15 .40
104 Robert Reichel .02 .10
105 Christian Dube .02 .10
106 Niklas Sundstrom .02 .10
107 Mike Richter .15 .40
108 Adam Graves .02 .10
109 Wayne Gretzky 1.00 2.50
110 Bruce Driver .02 .10
111 Esa Tikkanen .02 .10
112 Daniel Alfredsson .08 .25
113 Ron Tugnutt .08 .25
114 Steve Duchesne .02 .10
115 Bruce Gardiner RC .02 .10
116 Sergei Zholtok .02 .10
117 Alexandre Daigle .02 .10
118 Wade Redden .02 .10
119 Mikael Renberg .08 .25
120 Trent Klatt .02 .10
121 Rod Brind'Amour .08 .25
122 Dainius Zubrus .15 .40
123 John LeClair .15 .40
124 Janne Niinimaa .08 .25
125 Vaclav Prospal RC .15 .40
126 Keith Tkachuk .15 .40
127 Jeremy Roenick .20 .50
128 Mike Gartner .08 .25
129 Nikolai Khabibulin .08 .25
130 Chad Kilger .02 .10
131 Shane Doan .02 .10
132 Cliff Ronning .02 .10
133 Patrick Lalime .08 .25
134 Greg Johnson .02 .10
135 Ron Francis .08 .25
136 Darius Kasparaitis .02 .10
137 Petr Nedved .08 .25
138 Jason Woolley .02 .10
139 Fredrik Olausson .02 .10
140 Harry York .02 .10
141 Brett Hull .20 .50
142 Chris Pronger .08 .25
143 Jim Campbell .02 .10
144 Libor Zabransky RC .02 .10
145 Grant Fuhr .08 .25
146 Pavol Demitra .08 .25
147 Owen Nolan .08 .25
148 Stephen Guolla RC .02 .10
149 Marcus Ragnarsson .02 .10
150 Bernie Nicholls .02 .10
151 Todd Gill .02 .10
152 Shean Donovan .02 .10
153 Corey Schwab .08 .25
154 Dino Ciccarelli .08 .25
155 Chris Gratton .08 .25
156 Alexander Selivanov .02 .10
157 Roman Hamrlik .08 .25
158 Daymond Langkow .08 .25
159 Paul Ysebaert .02 .10
160 Steve Sullivan .02 .10
161 Sergei Berezin .02 .10
162 Fredrik Modin .02 .10
163 Todd Warriner .02 .10
164 Wendel Clark .08 .25
165 Jason Podollan .02 .10
166 Darby Hendrickson .02 .10
167 Martin Gelinas .02 .10
168 Pavel Bure .15 .40
169 Trevor Linden .08 .25
170 Mike Sillinger .02 .10
171 Corey Hirsch .08 .25
172 Lonny Bohonos .02 .10
173 Markus Naslund .15 .40
174 Steve Konowalchuk .02 .10
175 Dale Hunter .02 .10
176 Joe Juneau .08 .25
177 Adam Oates .08 .25
178 Bill Ranford .08 .25
179 Pat Peake .02 .10
180 Sergei Gonchar .02 .10
181 Mike LeClerc RC .40 1.00
182 Randy Robitaille RC .20 .50
183 Paxton Schafer RC .02 .10
184 Rumun Ndur RC .02 .10
185 Christian Laflamme RC .02 .10
186 Wade Belak RC .08 .25
187 Mike Knuble RC .02 .10
188 Steve Kelly .02 .10
189 Patrik Elias RC 1.00 2.50
190 Ken Belanger RC .02 .10
191 Colin Forbes RC .02 .10
192 Juha Ylonen .02 .10
193 David Cooper RC .02 .10
194 D.J. Smith RC .02 .10
195 Jaroslav Svejkovsky .08 .25
196 Tie Domi .08 .25
197 Bob Probert .02 .10
198 Doug Gilmour .08 .25
199 Dino Ciccarelli .02 .10
200 Martin Gelinas .02 .10
201 Tony Twist .02 .10
202 Claude Lemieux .02 .10
203 Vladimir Konstantinov .08 .25
204 Ulf Samuelsson .02 .10
205 Chris Simon .02 .10
206 Gino Odjick .02 .10
207 Mike Grier .02 .10
208 Tony Amonte .08 .25
209 Wayne Gretzky CL .15 .40
210 Patrick Roy CL .15 .40
211 Paul Kariya .15 .40
212 J.J. Daigneault .02 .10
213 Dmitri Mironov .02 .10
214 Joe Sacco .02 .10
215 Richard Park .02 .10
216 Espen Knutsen RC .50 1.25
217 Dave Karpa .02 .10
218 Joe Thornton .40 1.00
219 Sergei Samsonov .08 .25
220 P.J. Axelsson .02 .10
221 Ted Donato .02 .10
222 Dean Chynoweth .02 .10
223 Rob Tallas RC .02 .10
224 Mattias Timander .02 .10
225 Dominik Hasek .30 .75
226 Erik Rasmussen .02 .10
227 Mike Peca .02 .10
228 Rob Ray .02 .10
229 Vaclav Varada .02 .10
230 Curtis Brown .02 .10
231 Jay McKee .02 .10
232 Theo Fleury .02 .10
233 Derek Morris RC .20 .50
234 Chris Dingman RC .02 .10
235 Chris O'Sullivan .02 .10
236 Rick Tabaracci .08 .25
237 Tommy Albelin .02 .10
238 Todd Simpson .02 .10
239 Sami Kapanen .02 .10
UER numbered 229
240 Gary Roberts .02 .10
241 Kevin Dineen .02 .10
242 Kevin Haller .02 .10
243 Nelson Emerson .02 .10
244 Glen Wesley .02 .10
245 Tony Amonte .08 .25
246 Eric Weinrich .02 .10
247 Daniel Cleary .08 .25
248 Jeff Shantz .02 .10
249 Jean-Yves Leroux RC .02 .10
250 Ethan Moreau .02 .10
251 Craig Mills .02 .10
252 Peter Forsberg .40 1.00
253 Joe Sakic .30 .75
254 Valeri Kamensky .08 .25
255 Adam Foote .02 .10
256 Josef Marha .02 .10
257 Christian Matte RC .02 .10
258 Aaron Miller .02 .10
259 Ed Belfour .15 .40
260 Jamie Langenbrunner .02 .10
261 Juha Lind RC .02 .10
262 Pat Verbeek .02 .10
263 Sergei Zubov .02 .10
264 Dave Reid .02 .10
265 Greg Adams .02 .10
266 Sergei Fedorov .25 .60
267 Nicklas Lidstrom .15 .40
268 Brendan Shanahan .15 .40
269 Chris Osgood .08 .25
270 Aaron Ward .02 .10
271 Vyacheslav Kozlov .02 .10
272 Kevin Hodson .08 .25
273 Curtis Joseph .15 .40
274 Ryan Smyth .08 .25
275 Dean McAmmond .02 .10
276 Boris Mironov .02 .10
277 Dennis Bonvie .02 .10
278 Kelly Buchberger .02 .10
279 Kevin Lowe .02 .10
280 Ray Sheppard .02 .10
281 Rob Niedermayer .02 .10
282 Scott Mellanby .02 .10
283 Terry Carkner .02 .10
284 Ed Jovanovski .08 .25
285 Gord Murphy .02 .10
286 Tom Fitzgerald .02 .10
287 Jamie Storr .08 .25
288 Olli Jokinen RC 1.00 2.50
289 Vladimir Tsyplakov .02 .10
290 Luc Robitaille .08 .25
291 Vitali Yachmenev .02 .10
292 Donald MacLean .02 .10
293 Saku Koivu .15 .40
294 Andy Moog .08 .25
295 Patrice Brisebois .02 .10
296 Brad Brown RC .02 .10
297 Turner Stevenson .02 .10
298 Shayne Corson .02 .10
299 Brian Savage .02 .10
300 Martin Brodeur .40 1.00
301 Scott Niedermayer .02 .10
302 Krzysztof Oliwa RC .02 .10
303 Valeri Zelepukin .02 .10
304 Bobby Holik .02 .10
305 Ken Daneyko .02 .10
306 Lyle Odelein .02 .10
307 Travis Green .02 .10
308 Steve Webb RC .02 .10
309 Dan Plante .02 .10
310 Bryan Smolinski .02 .10
311 Claude Lapointe .02 .10
312 Kenny Jonsson .02 .10
313 Ulf Samuelsson .02 .10
314 Jeff Beukeboom .02 .10
315 Mike Keane .02 .10
316 Brian Leetch .15 .40
317 Shane Chrula .02 .10
318 Pat LaFontaine .15 .40
319 Alexei Kovalev .02 .10
320 Radek Bonk .02 .10
321 Alexei Yashin .02 .10
322 Damian Rhodes .08 .25
323 Andreas Dackell .02 .10
324 Magnus Arvedson .02 .10
325 Chris Phillips .02 .10
326 Marian Hossa RC 2.50 6.00
327 Chris Gratton .08 .25
328 Shjon Podein .02 .10
329 Paul Coffey .15 .40
330 Luke Richardson .02 .10
331 Eric Lindros .15 .40
332 Eric Desjardins .08 .25
333 Joel Otto .02 .10
334 Craig Janney .02 .10
335 Oleg Tverdovsky .02 .10
336 Teppo Numminen .02 .10
337 Jim McKenzie .02 .10
338 Dallas Drake .02 .10
339 Rick Tocchet .08 .25
340 Brad Isbister .02 .10
341 Alexei Morozov .08 .25
342 Jaromir Jagr .25 .60
343 Kevin Hatcher .02 .10
344 Ken Wregget .08 .25
345 Chris Tamer .02 .10
346 Robert Dome .02 .10
347 Neil Wilkinson .02 .10
348 Chris McAlpine .02 .10
349 Joe Murphy .02 .10
350 Robert Petrovicky .02 .10
351 Marc Bergevin .02 .10
352 Al MacInnis .08 .25
353 Pierre Turgeon .08 .25
354 Patrick Marleau .25 .60
355 Marco Sturm RC .40 1.00
356 Mike Vernon .08 .25
357 Al Iafrate .02 .10
358 Jeff Friesen .02 .10
359 Viktor Kozlov .02 .10
360 Tony Granato .02 .10
361 Mikael Renberg .08 .25
362 Daren Puppa .08 .25
363 Roman Hamrlik .02 .10
364 Rob Zamuner .02 .10
365 Cory Cross .02 .10
366 Patrick Poulin .02 .10
367 Felix Potvin .15 .40
368 Tie Domi .08 .25
369 Mats Sundin .15 .40
370 Jeff Ware .02 .10
371 Alyn McCauley .08 .25
372 Mathieu Schneider .02 .10
373 Craig Wolanin .02 .10
374 Mark Messier .15 .40
375 Kirk McLean .08 .25
376 Donald Brashear .02 .10
377 Arturs Irbe .08 .25
378 Jyrki Lumme .02 .10
379 Gino Odjick .02 .10
380 Mattias Ohlund .08 .25
381 Jan Bulis RC .08 .25
382 Andrew Brunette .08 .25
383 Calle Johansson .02 .10
384 Brendan Witt .02 .10
385 Mark Tinordi .02 .10
386 Ken Klee .02 .10
387 Chris Simon .02 .10
388 Richard Zednik .02 .10
389 Ed Jovanovski .08 .25
390 Darren McCarty .02 .10
391 Darius Kasparaitis .02 .10
392 Bryan Marchment .02 .10
393 Matthew Barnaby .02 .10
394 Chris Chelios .15 .40
395 Ulf Samuelsson .02 .10
396 Scott Stevens .08 .25
397 Derian Hatcher .02 .10
398 Chris Pronger .08 .25
399 Mathieu Chouinard RC .60 1.50
400 Jake McCracken RC .40 1.00
401 Bryan Allen RC .30 .75
402 Christian Chartier RC .30 .75
403 Jonathan Girard RC .40 1.00
404 Abe Herbst RC .08 .25
405 Stephen Peat RC .08 .25
406 Robyn Regehr RC .30 .75
407 Blair Betts RC .08 .25
408 Eric Chouinard RC .50 1.25
409 Brett DeCecco RC .08 .25
410 Rico Fata RC .40 1.00
411 Simon Gagne RC 2.50 6.00
412 Vincent Lecavalier RC 3.00 8.00
413 Manny Malhotra RC .30 .75
414 Norm Milley RC .40 1.00
415 Justin Papineau RC .40 1.00
416 Garrett Prosofsky RC .02 .10
417 Mike Ribeiro RC .60 1.50
418 Brad Richards RC 2.50 6.00
419 Wayne Gretzky CL .15 .40
420 Patrick Roy CL .15 .40

1997-98 Upper Deck Blow-Ups 3 x 5

Inserted as box-toppers or in special retail packs, these oversized cards resembled the base set but were approximately 3 1/2" x 5". Cards were numbered X of 10. The prefixes below are for checklisting only and designate whether the cards were available in series 1 or series 2 packs.

COMPLETE SET (20)
1-1 Wayne Gretzky 4.00 10.00
1-2 Steve Yzerman
1-3 Bryan Berard .60 1.50
1-4 Owen Nolan .60 1.50
1-5 Pavel Bure 1.60 4.00
1-6 Patrick Roy
1-7 Teemu Selanne 1.20 3.00
1-8 Brett Hull .80 2.00
1-9 Keith Tkachuk
1-10 John Vanbiesbrouck .60 1.50
2-1 Paul Kariya
2-2 Joe Thornton
2-3 Joe Sakic
2-4 Martin Brodeur
2-5 Slava Kozlov
2-6 Mark Messier
2-7 Jaromir Jagr
2-8 Eric Lindros
2-9 Peter Forsberg
2-10 Sergei Samsonov

1997-98 Upper Deck Blow-Ups 5 x 7

Inserted as box-toppers in various distribution forms of Upper Deck, these oversized cards resembled the base set but were approximately 5" x 7". Cards were numbered "X of 5" (the suffixes below are for checklisting only). The checklist below is not complete, please forward any further information to hockeymag@beckett.com.

COMPLETE SET (14)
1A Mark Messier
1B Patrick Roy 3.20 8.00
1C Paul Kariya
2A Jaromir Jagr 1.60 4.00
2B Teemu Selanne 1.20 3.00
3A Joe Sakic 1.20 3.00
3B Eric Lindros 1.00 2.50
4A Peter Forsberg 1.60 4.00
4B Martin Brodeur 1.60 4.00
4C Keith Tkachuk .80 2.00
5A Sergei Samsonov .60 1.50
5B Pavel Bure 1.20 3.00
5C Slava Kozlov .60 1.50
5D John Vanbiesbrouck .60 1.50

1997-98 Upper Deck Game Dated Moments

Randomly inserted in packs at the rate of 1:1500, this 60-card set features color player photos of their top moments of last year and printed on 24 pt. embossed Light F/X cards. The set is skip numbered. It is important to note that these cards are printed on card stock that is approximately 3X thicker than the base set and carry silver foil highlights that distinguish them from the base set cards that also carry the Game Dated stamp.

1 Teemu Selanne 25.00 60.00
9 Ray Bourque 40.00 100.00
30 Geoff Sanderson 10.00 25.00
43 Patrick Roy 100.00 250.00
47 Claude Lemieux 6.00 15.00
57 Steve Yzerman 100.00 250.00
59 Darren McCarty 10.00 25.00
60 Mike Vernon 12.00 30.00
63 Vladimir Konstantinov 15.00 40.00
64 Todd Marchant 6.00 15.00
72 John Vanbiesbrouck 15.00 40.00
84 Mark Recchi 15.00 40.00
85 Jose Theodore 30.00 80.00
91 Doug Gilmour 15.00 40.00
98 Bryan Berard 10.00 25.00
105 Christian Dube 6.00 15.00
107 Mike Richter 20.00 50.00
109 Wayne Gretzky 150.00 400.00
112 Daniel Alfredsson 20.00 50.00
118 Wade Redden 6.00 15.00
121 Rod Brind'Amour 15.00 40.00
124 Janne Niinimaa 6.00 15.00
126 Keith Tkachuk 15.00 40.00
133 Patrick Lalime 15.00 40.00
135 Ron Francis 15.00 40.00
141 Brett Hull 30.00 80.00
143 Jim Campbell 6.00 15.00
147 Owen Nolan 15.00 40.00
154 Dino Ciccarelli 6.00 15.00
168 Pavel Bure 30.00 80.00
211 Paul Kariya 30.00 60.00
218 Joe Thornton 40.00 100.00
219 Sergei Samsonov 12.00 30.00
225 Dominik Hasek 50.00 120.00
227 Mike Peca 6.00 15.00
232 Theo Fleury 10.00 25.00
240 Gary Roberts 6.00 15.00
245 Tony Amonte 12.00 30.00
252 Peter Forsberg 50.00 120.00
253 Joe Sakic 50.00 120.00
266 Sergei Fedorov 30.00 80.00
267 Nicklas Lidstrom 25.00 60.00
268 Brendan Shanahan 25.00 60.00
271 Slava Kozlov 6.00 15.00
273 Curtis Joseph 25.00 60.00
274 Ryan Smyth 20.00 50.00
282 Scott Mellanby 6.00 15.00
290 Luc Robitaille 20.00 50.00
300 Martin Brodeur 60.00 150.00
316 Brian Leetch 15.00 40.00
325 Chris Phillips 6.00 15.00
329 Paul Coffey 15.00 40.00
331 Eric Lindros 30.00 80.00
335 Oleg Tverdovsky 6.00 15.00
342 Jaromir Jagr 40.00 100.00
353 Pierre Turgeon 15.00 40.00
354 Patrick Marleau 30.00 80.00
360 Tony Granato 6.00 15.00
369 Mats Sundin 25.00 60.00
374 Mark Messier 30.00 80.00

1997-98 Upper Deck Game Jerseys

Randomly inserted in packs at the rate of 1:2,500, this 15-card set features color player photos with an actual piece of the player's game-worn jersey embedded in the card. Patrick Roy autographed 33 cards inserted in Series 1 packs, and Wayne Gretzky signed 99 cards containing remnants of his 1997 All-Star Game jersey inserted in Series 2 packs.

GJ1 Patrick Roy HOME 100.00 250.00
GJ2 Patrick Roy AWAY 125.00 300.00
GJ3 Dominik Hasek 50.00 125.00
GJ4 Jarome Iginla 40.00 100.00
GJ5 Sergei Fedorov 40.00 100.00
GJ6 Tony Amonte 20.00 50.00
GJ7 Joe Sakic 60.00 150.00
GJ8 Wayne Gretzky 200.00 500.00
GJ9 Saku Koivu 20.00 50.00
GJ11 Mike Richter 20.00 50.00
GJ12 Doug Weight 20.00 50.00
GJ13 Brendan Shanahan 20.00 50.00
GJ14 Brian Leetch 20.00 50.00
GJ1S Patrick Roy AU/33 400.00 800.00
GJ8S Wayne Gretzky AU/99 400.00 1000.00

1997-98 Upper Deck Sixth Sense Masters

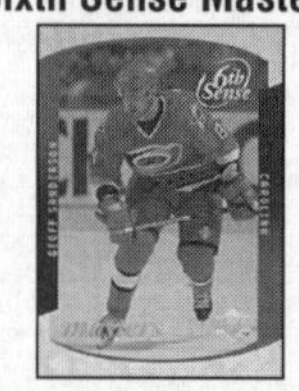

Randomly inserted in Series 2 packs, this 30-card set features color photos of the NHL's brightest stars. Only 2,000 of each card were produced and are sequentially numbered. A holographic die-cut parallel version labeled "Wizards" was also produced and limited to 100 copies each.

COMPLETE SET (30) 125.00 250.00
*WIZARDS: 2.5X TO 6X BASIC INSERTS
SS1 Wayne Gretzky 20.00 50.00
SS2 Jaromir Jagr 5.00 12.00
SS3 Sergei Fedorov 4.00 10.00
SS4 Brett Hull 4.00 10.00
SS5 Brian Leetch 2.00 5.00
SS6 Joe Thornton 6.00 15.00
SS7 Ray Bourque 4.00 10.00
SS8 Teemu Selanne 3.00 8.00
SS9 Paul Kariya 3.00 8.00
SS10 Doug Weight 2.00 5.00
SS11 Mark Messier 3.00 8.00
SS12 Adam Oates 2.00 5.00
SS13 Mats Sundin 3.00 8.00
SS14 Brendan Shanahan 3.00 8.00
SS15 Saku Koivu 3.00 8.00
SS16 Doug Gilmour 2.00 5.00
SS17 Eric Lindros 3.00 8.00
SS18 Tony Amonte 2.00 5.00
SS19 Joe Sakic 6.00 15.00
SS20 Steve Yzerman 15.00 40.00
SS21 Peter Forsberg 8.00 20.00
SS22 Geoff Sanderson 2.00 5.00
SS23 Keith Tkachuk 2.00 5.00
SS24 Pavel Bure 4.00 10.00
SS25 Ron Francis 2.00 5.00
SS26 Zigmund Palffy 2.00 5.00
SS27 Daniel Alfredsson 2.00 5.00
SS28 Bryan Berard 2.00 5.00
SS29 Mike Modano 5.00 12.00
SS30 Patrick Roy 15.00 40.00

1997-98 Upper Deck Smooth Grooves

COMPLETE SET (60) 40.00 80.00
STATED ODDS 1:4
SG1 Wayne Gretzky 5.00 12.00
SG2 Patrick Roy 4.00 10.00
SG3 Patrick Marleau 1.25 3.00
SG4 Martin Brodeur 2.00 5.00
SG5 Zigmund Palffy .50 1.25
SG6 Joe Thornton 2.00 5.00
SG7 Chris Chelios .75 2.00
SG8 Teemu Selanne .75 2.00
SG9 Paul Kariya .75 2.00
SG10 Tony Amonte .50 1.25
SG11 Mark Messier .75 2.00
SG12 Jarome Iginla 1.00 2.50
SG13 Mats Sundin .75 2.00
SG14 Brendan Shanahan .75 2.00
SG15 Ed Jovanovski .50 1.25
SG16 Brett Hull 1.00 2.50
SG17 Brian Rolston .20 .50
SG18 Saku Koivu .75 2.00
SG19 Steve Yzerman 4.00 10.00
SG20 Doug Weight .50 1.25
SG21 Peter Forsberg 2.00 5.00
SG22 Brian Leetch .75 2.00
SG23 Alexei Yashin .20 .50
SG24 Owen Nolan .50 1.25
SG25 Mike Grier .20 .50
SG26 Jere Lehtinen .20 .50
SG27 Vaclav Prospal .75 2.00
SG28 Sandis Ozolinsh .20 .50
SG29 Mike Modano 1.25 3.00
SG30 Sergei Samsonov .50 1.25
SG31 Curtis Joseph .75 2.00
SG32 Daymond Langkow .50 1.25
SG33 Doug Gilmour .50 1.25
SG34 Bryan Berard .50 1.25
SG35 Joe Sakic 1.50 4.00
SG36 Wade Redden .20 .50
SG37 Keith Tkachuk .75 2.00
SG38 Jaromir Jagr 1.25 3.00
SG39 Dominik Hasek 1.50 4.00
SG40 Patrick Lalime .50 1.25
SG41 Janne Niinima .20 .50
SG42 Oleg Tverdovsky .20 .50
SG43 Vitali Yachmenev .20 .50
SG44 Rob Niedermayer .20 .50
SG45 Nicklas Lidstrom .75 2.00
SG46 Jim Campbell .20 .50
SG47 Roman Hamrlik .50 1.25
SG48 Eric Lindros .75 2.00
SG49 Brian Holzinger .20 .50
SG50 John LeClair .75 2.00
SG51 Sergei Berezin .20 .50
SG52 Jaroslav Svejkovsky .50 1.25
SG53 Mike Richter .75 2.00
SG54 John Vanbiesbrouck .50 1.25
SG55 Keith Primeau .20 .50
SG56 Adam Oates .50 1.25
SG57 Jeremy Roenick 1.00 2.50
SG58 Pavel Bure .75 2.00
SG59 Dainius Zubrus .75 2.00
SG60 Jose Theodore 1.00 2.50

1997-98 Upper Deck The Specialists

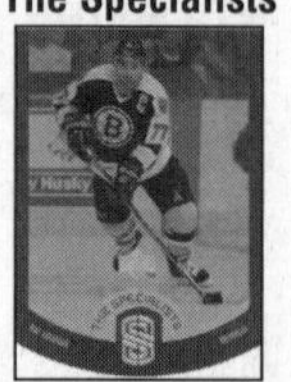

Randomly inserted in Series 1 packs, this 30-card set features black-and-white action photos of the NHL brightest stars. Only 4,000 of each card were produced and numbered.

COMPLETE SET (30) 50.00 100.00
1 Wayne Gretzky 5.00 12.00
2 Patrick Roy 4.00 10.00
3 Jaromir Jagr 2.00 5.00

4 Joe Sakic 2.50 6.00
5 Mark Messier 1.25 3.00
6 Eric Lindros 1.25 3.00
7 John Vanbiesbrouck 1.00 2.50
8 Teemu Selanne 1.25 3.00
9 Paul Kariya 1.25 3.00
10 Pavel Bure 1.25 3.00
11 Sergei Fedorov 2.00 5.00
12 Peter Bondra 1.00 2.50
13 Mats Sundin 1.25 3.00
14 Brendan Shanahan 1.25 3.00
15 Keith Tkachuk 1.25 3.00
16 Brett Hull 1.50 4.00
17 Jeremy Roenick 1.50 4.00
18 Dominik Hasek 2.50 6.00
19 Steve Yzerman 4.00 10.00
20 John LeClair 1.25 3.00
21 Peter Forsberg 3.00 8.00
22 Zigmund Palffy 1.00 2.50
23 Tony Amonte 1.00 2.50
24 Jarome Iginla 1.25 3.00
25 Curtis Joseph 1.25 3.00
26 Mike Modano 2.00 5.00
27 Ray Bourque 2.00 5.00
28 Brian Leetch 1.25 3.00
29 Bryan Berard 1.00 2.50
30 Martin Brodeur 3.00 8.00

1997-98 Upper Deck The Specialists Level 2 Die Cuts

Randomly inserted in Series 1 packs, this 30-card set is a crash numbered, laser die-cut parallel version of The Specialists Level 1 set. Only 100 of each card was produced and serially numbered.
*STARS: 2.5X TO 6X BASIC CARDS

1997-98 Upper Deck Three Star Selects

Randomly inserted in Series 1 packs at the rate of 1:4, this 60-card set features color photos on die-cut cards of three top players that fit together to form 20 different sets.
COMPLETE SET (60) 40.00 80.00
1A Eric Lindros .75 2.00
1B Wayne Gretzky 5.00 12.00
1C Peter Forsberg 2.00 5.00
2A Dominik Hasek 1.50 4.00
2B Patrick Roy 4.00 10.00
2C John Vanbiesbrouck .75 2.00
3A Joe Sakic 1.50 4.00
3B Steve Yzerman 4.00 10.00
3C Paul Kariya .75 2.00
4A Bryan Berard .20 .50
4B Brian Leetch .40 1.00
4C Chris Chelios .40 1.00
5A Teemu Selanne .75 2.00
5B Jaromir Jagr 1.25 3.00
5C Pavel Bure .75 2.00
6A Owen Nolan .40 1.00
6B Brendan Shanahan .75 2.00
6C Keith Tkachuk .40 1.00
7A Sergei Fedorov 1.00 2.50
7B Niklas Sundstrom .20 .50
7C Mike Peca .20 .50
8A Janne Niinimaa .20 .50
8B Saku Koivu .75 2.00
8C Jere Lehtinen .20 .50
9A Tony Amonte .40 1.00
9B John LeClair .40 1.00
9C Brett Hull 1.00 2.50
10A Martin Brodeur 2.00 5.00
10B Curtis Joseph .75 2.00
10C Mike Richter .75 2.00
11A Ray Bourque 1.00 2.50
11B Mark Messier .75 2.00
11C Scott Stevens .20 .50
12A Patrick Lalime .40 1.00
12B Marc Denis .40 1.00
12C Jose Theodore 1.00 2.50
13A Adam Deadmarsh .20 .50
13B Doug Weight .40 1.00
13C Bill Guerin .20 .50
14A Daniel Alfredsson .40 1.00
14B Mats Sundin .75 2.00
14C Nicklas Lidstrom .75 2.00
15A Jim Campbell .20 .50
15B Dainius Zubrus .40 1.00
15C Daymond Langkow .20 .50
16A Mike Grier .20 .50
16B Mike Modano 1.25 3.00
16C Jeremy Roenick 1.00 2.50
17A Jason Arnott .20 .50
17B Trevor Linden .40 1.00
17C Rod Brind'Amour .40 1.00
18A Adam Oates .40 1.00
18B Doug Gilmour .40 1.00
18C Joe Juneau .20 .50
19A Sergei Berezin .20 .50
19B Alexander Mogilny .40 1.00
19C Alexei Zhamnov .20 .50
20A Derian Hatcher .20 .50
20B Wade Redden .20 .50
20C Sandis Ozolinsh .20 .50

1997 Upper Deck Crash the All-Star Game

Distributed one per attendee of the 1997 NHL All-Star Game in San Jose, these one-off Crash the Game cards were redeemable for a special set if the player pictured scored a goal in the contest. The Western Conference cards (1-11) were rumored to be the only ones distributed, although a few copies of each of the Eastern Conference cards have surfaced as well. The complete set price below includes both conferences. The winners are numbered AR1 thru AR20, and feature gold foil and a record of the player's performance in the game.
1 Tony Amonte 8.00 20.00
2 Paul Kariya 50.00 125.00
3 Brett Hull 16.00 40.00
4 Teemu Selanne 24.00 60.00
5 Steve Yzerman 40.00 100.00
6 Owen Nolan 8.00 20.00
7 Mats Sundin 12.00 30.00
8 Pavel Bure 32.00 80.00
9 Brendan Shanahan 24.00 60.00
10 Sandis Ozolinsh 8.00 20.00
11 Keith Tkachuk 12.00 30.00
12 Ray Bourque 16.00 40.00
13 Eric Lindros 32.00 80.00
14 Mark Messier 16.00 40.00
15 John LeClair 20.00 50.00
16 Jaromir Jagr 40.00 100.00
17 Dino Ciccarelli 8.00 20.00
18 Peter Bondra 12.00 30.00
19 Brian Leetch 16.00 40.00
20 Wayne Gretzky 80.00 200.00
AR1 Tony Amonte 4.00 10.00
AR2 Paul Kariya 20.00 50.00
AR3 Brett Hull 6.00 15.00
AR4 Teemu Selanne 10.00 25.00
AR5 Steve Yzerman 16.00 40.00
AR6 Owen Nolan 6.00 15.00
AR7 Mats Sundin 8.00 20.00
AR8 Pavel Bure 10.00 25.00
AR9 Brendan Shanahan 10.00 25.00
AR10 Sandis Ozolinsh 4.00 10.00
AR11 Keith Tkachuk 6.00 15.00
AR12 Ray Bourque 4.00 10.00
AR13 Eric Lindros 20.00 50.00
AR14 Mark Messier 6.00 15.00
AR15 John LeClair 8.00 20.00
AR16 Jaromir Jagr 16.00 40.00
AR17 Dino Ciccarelli 4.00 10.00
AR18 Peter Bondra 5.00 12.50
AR19 Brian Leetch 5.00 12.50
AR20 Wayne Gretzky 32.00 80.00

1998-99 Upper Deck

The 1998-99 Upper Deck set was issued in two series of 210 cards each for a total of 420 cards and was distributed in 10-card packs with a suggested retail price of $2.49. The fronts feature a color action player photo with player information on the backs. Series 1 contains the following subsets: Star Rookies, Rookie Rewind, and three Checklist cards. Series 2 contains the subset Program of Excellence which consists of the top Canadian prospects, eight Calder Candidates, and three Checklist cards.
COMPLETE SET (420) 75.00 150.00
1 Antti Aalto SR .40 1.00
2 Cameron Mann SR .40 1.00
3 Norm Maracle SR RC .60 1.50
4 Daniel Cleary SR .40 1.00
5 Brendan Morrison SR .60 1.50
6 Marian Hossa SR .60 1.50
7 Daniel Briere SR .60 1.50
8 Mike Crowley RC .40 1.00
9 Darryl Laplante RC .40 1.00
10 Sven Butenschon SR .40 1.00
11 Yan Golubovsky RC .40 1.00
12 Olli Jokinen SR .40 1.00
13 J-S Giguere .60 1.50
14 Mike Watt SR .40 1.00
15 Ryan Johnson SR RC .40 1.00
16 Teemu Selanne RR .60 1.50
17 Paul Kariya RR .60 1.50
18 Pavel Bure RR .60 1.50
19 Joe Thornton RR 1.50 4.00
20 Dominik Hasek RR 1.50 4.00
21 Bryan Berard RR .40 1.00
22 Chris Phillips RR .40 1.00
23 Sergei Fedorov RR 1.25 3.00
24 Sergei Samsonov RR .60 1.50
25 Marc Denis RR .60 1.50
26 Patrick Marleau RR .60 1.50
27 Jaromir Jagr RR 1.25 3.00
28 Saku Koivu RR .60 1.50
29 Peter Forsberg RR 2.00 5.00
30 Mike Modano RR 1.25 3.00
31 Paul Kariya .15 .40
32 Matt Cullen .02 .10
33 Josef Marha .02 .10
34 Teemu Selanne .15 .40
35 Pavel Trnka .02 .10
36 Tom Askey RC .02 .10
37 Tim Taylor .02 .10
38 Ray Bourque .25 .60
39 Sergei Samsonov .08 .25
40 Don Sweeney .02 .10
41 Jason Allison .02 .10
42 Steve Heinze .02 .10
43 Erik Rasmussen .02 .10
44 Dominik Hasek .30 .75
45 Geoff Sanderson .02 .10
46 Michael Peca .02 .10
47 Brian Holzinger .02 .10
48 Vaclav Varada .02 .10
49 Steve Begin .02 .10
50 Denis Gauthier .02 .10
51 Derek Morris .02 .10
52 Valeri Bure .02 .10
53 Hnat Domenichelli .02 .10
54 Cory Stillman .02 .10
55 Jarome Iginla .20 .50
56 Tyler Moss .02 .10
57 Sami Kapanen .02 .10
58 Trevor Kidd .08 .25
59 Glen Wesley .02 .10
60 Nelson Emerson .02 .10
61 Jeff O'Neill .02 .10
62 Bates Battaglia .02 .10
63 Doug Gilmour .08 .25
64 Christian LaFlamme .02 .10
65 Chris Chelios .15 .40
66 Paul Coffey .15 .40
67 Eric Weinrich .02 .10
68 Eric Daze .08 .25
69 Peter Forsberg .40 1.00
70 Eric Messier .02 .10
71 Eric Lacroix .02 .10
72 Adam Deadmarsh .02 .10
73 Claude Lemieux .02 .10
74 Patrick Roy .75 2.00
75 Marc Denis .08 .25
76 Brett Hull .20 .50
77 Mike Keane .02 .10
78 Joe Nieuwendyk .08 .25
79 Darryl Sydor .02 .10
80 Ed Belfour .15 .40
81 Jamie Langenbrunner .02 .10
82 Petr Buzek .02 .10
83 Nicklas Lidstrom .15 .40
84 Mathieu Dandenault .02 .10
85 Steve Yzerman .75 2.00
86 Martin Lapointe .02 .10
87 Brendan Shanahan .15 .40
88 Anders Eriksson .02 .10
89 Tomas Holmstrom .02 .10
90 Doug Weight .08 .25
91 Janne Niinimaa .02 .10
92 Bill Guerin .08 .25
93 Kelly Buchberger .02 .10
94 Mike Grier .02 .10
95 Craig Millar .02 .10
96 Roman Hamrlik .02 .10
97 Ray Whitney .02 .10
98 Viktor Kozlov .02 .10
99 Peter Worrell RC .20 .50
100 Kevin Weekes .08 .25
101 Ed Jovanovski .08 .25
102 Bill Lindsay .02 .10
103 Jozef Stumpel .08 .25
104 Luc Robitaille .08 .25
105 Yanic Perreault .02 .10
106 Donald MacLean .02 .10
107 Jamie Storr .08 .25
108 Ian Laperriere .02 .10
109 Jason Morgan RC .02 .10
110 Vincent Damphousse .02 .10
111 Mark Recchi .08 .25
112 Vladimir Malakhov .02 .10
113 Dave Manson .02 .10
114 Jose Theodore .20 .50
115 Brian Savage .02 .10
116 Jonas Hoglund .02 .10
117 Krzysztof Oliwa .02 .10
118 Martin Brodeur .40 1.00
119 Patrik Elias .08 .25
120 Jason Arnott .02 .10
121 Scott Stevens .08 .25
122 Sheldon Souray RC .40 1.00
123 Brian Rolston .02 .10
124 Trevor Linden .08 .25
125 Warren Luhning .02 .10
126 Zdeno Chara .02 .10
127 Bryan Berard .08 .25
128 Bryan Smolinski .02 .10
129 Jason Dawe .02 .10
130 Kevin Stevens .02 .10
131 P.J. Stock RC .40 1.00
132 Marc Savard .08 .25
133 Pat LaFontaine .15 .40
134 Dan Cloutier .08 .25
135 Wayne Gretzky 1.00 2.50
136 Niklas Sundstrom .02 .10
137 Damian Rhodes .08 .25
138 Magnus Arvedson .02 .10
139 Alexei Yashin .02 .10
140 Chris Phillips .02 .10
141 Janne Laukkanen .02 .10
142 Shawn McEachern .02 .10
143 John LeClair .15 .40
144 Alexandre Daigle .02 .10
145 Dainius Zubrus .02 .10
146 Joel Otto .02 .10
147 Mike Sillinger .02 .10
148 John Vanbiesbrouck .08 .25
149 Chris Gratton .08 .25
150 Eric Desjardins .08 .25
151 Juha Ylonen .02 .10
152 Brad Isbister .02 .10
153 Oleg Tverdovsky .02 .10
154 Keith Tkachuk .15 .40
155 Teppo Numminen .02 .10
156 Cliff Ronning .02 .10
157 Nikolai Khabibulin .08 .25
158 Alexei Morozov .02 .10
159 Kevin Hatcher .02 .10
160 Darius Kasparaitis .02 .10
161 Jaromir Jagr .25 .60
162 Tom Barrasso .08 .25
163 Tomas Gronman .02 .10
164 Robert Dome .02 .10
165 Peter Skudra .02 .10
166 Marcus Ragnarsson .02 .10
167 Mike Vernon .08 .25
168 Andrei Zyuzin .02 .10
169 Marco Sturm .02 .10
170 Mike Ricci .02 .10
171 Patrick Marleau .02 .10
172 Pierre Turgeon .02 .10
173 Pavol Demitra .08 .25
174 Chris Pronger .08 .25
175 Pascal Rheaume .02 .10
176 Al MacInnis .08 .25
177 Tony Twist .02 .10
178 Jim Campbell .02 .10
179 Mikael Renberg .08 .25
180 Jason Bonsignore .02 .10
181 Zac Bierk RC .40 1.00
182 Alexander Selivanov .02 .10
183 Stephane Richer .02 .10
184 Sandy McCarthy .02 .10
185 Alyn McCauley .02 .10
186 Sergei Berezin .08 .25
187 Mike Johnson .02 .10
188 Wendel Clark .08 .25
189 Tie Domi .08 .25
190 Yannick Tremblay .02 .10
191 Curtis Joseph .15 .40
192 Fredrik Modin .02 .10
193 Pavel Bure .15 .40
194 Todd Bertuzzi .15 .40
195 Mark Messier .15 .40
196 Bret Hedican .02 .10
197 Mattias Ohlund .02 .10
198 Garth Snow .08 .25
199 Adam Oates .08 .25
200 Peter Bondra .08 .25
201 Sergei Gonchar .02 .10
202 Jan Bulis .02 .10
203 Joe Juneau .08 .25
204 Brian Bellows .02 .10
205 Olaf Kolzig .08 .25
206 Richard Zednik .02 .10
207 Wayne Gretzky CL .40 1.00
208 Patrick Roy CL .40 1.00
209 Steve Yzerman CL .40 1.00
210 Mike Dunham .08 .25
211 Johan Davidsson .02 .10
212 Guy Hebert .08 .25
213 Mike Leclerc .02 .10
214 Steve Rucchin .02 .10
215 Travis Green .02 .10
216 Josef Marha .02 .10
217 Ted Donato .02 .10
218 Joe Thornton .25 .60
219 Kyle McLaren .02 .10
220 Peter Nordstrom RC .02 .10
221 Byron Dafoe .08 .25
222 Jonathon Girard .02 .10
223 Antti Laaksonen RC .40 1.00
224 Jason Holland .02 .10
225 Miroslav Satan .08 .25
226 Alexei Zhitnik .02 .10
227 Donald Audette .02 .10
228 Matthew Barnaby .02 .10
229 Rumun Ndur .02 .10
230 Ken Wregget .08 .25
231 Andrew Cassels .02 .10
232 Theo Fleury .08 .25
233 Phil Housley .08 .25
234 Martin St. Louis RC 2.00 5.00
235 Mike Rucinski RC .02 .10
236 Gary Roberts .02 .10
237 Keith Primeau .02 .10
238 Martin Gelinas .02 .10
239 Nolan Pratt RC .08 .25
240 Ray Sheppard .02 .10
241 Ron Francis .08 .25
242 Ty Jones .02 .10
243 Tony Amonte .08 .25
244 Chad Kilger .02 .10
245 Alexei Zhamnov .08 .25
246 Remi Royer RC .02 .10
247 Milan Hejduk RC 1.00 2.50
248 Joe Sakic .30 .75
249 Valeri Kamensky .08 .25
250 Sandis Ozolinsh .02 .10
251 Shean Donovan .02 .10
252 Wade Belak .02 .10
253 Jamie Wright .02 .10
254 Sergei Zubov .02 .10
255 Richard Matvichuk .02 .10
256 Mike Modano .25 .60
257 Pat Verbeek .02 .10
258 Jere Lehtinen .08 .25
259 Derian Hatcher .02 .10
260 Jason Botterill .02 .10
261 Igor Larionov .02 .10
262 Sergei Fedorov .25 .60
263 Chris Osgood .08 .25
264 Vyacheslav Kozlov .08 .25
265 Larry Murphy .02 .10
266 Darren McCarty .02 .10
267 Doug Brown .02 .10
268 Kris Draper .02 .10
269 Uwe Krupp .02 .10
270 Fredrik Lindquist RC .02 .10
271 Dean McAmmond .02 .10
272 Ryan Smyth .08 .25
273 Boris Mironov .02 .10
274 Tom Poti .02 .10
275 Todd Marchant .02 .10
276 Sean Brown .02 .10
277 Rob Niedermayer .02 .10
278 Robert Svehla .02 .10
279 Scott Mellanby .02 .10
280 Radek Dvorak .02 .10
281 Jaroslav Spacek RC .02 .10
282 Mark Parrish RC .40 1.00
283 Ryan Johnson .02 .10
284 Glen Murray .02 .10
285 Rob Blake .08 .25
286 Steve Duchesne .08 .25
287 Vladimir Tsyplakov .02 .10
288 Stephane Fiset .08 .25
289 Mattias Norstrom .02 .10
290 Saku Koivu .15 .40
291 Shayne Corson .08 .25
292 Brad Brown .02 .10
293 Patrice Brisebois .02 .10
294 Terry Ryan .02 .10
295 Jocelyn Thibault .08 .25
296 Miroslav Guren .02 .10
297 Darren Turcotte .08 .25
298 Sebastien Bordeleau .02 .10
299 Jan Vopat .02 .10
300 Blair Atcheynum .02 .10
301 Andrew Brunette .08 .25
302 Sergei Krivokrasov .02 .10
303 Marian Cisar .02 .10
304 Patrick Cote .02 .10
305 J.J. Daigneault .02 .10
306 Greg Johnson .02 .10
307 Chris Terreri .08 .25
308 Scott Niedermayer .02 .10
309 Vadim Sharifijanov .02 .10
310 Petr Sykora .02 .10
311 Sergei Brylin .02 .10
312 Denis Pederson .02 .10
313 Bobby Holik .02 .10
314 Bryan Muir RC .02 .10
315 Zigmund Palffy .08 .25
316 Mike Watt .02 .10
317 Tommy Salo .08 .25
318 Kenny Jonsson .02 .10
319 Dmitri Nabokov .02 .10
320 John MacLean .02 .10
321 Zarley Zalapski .02 .10
322 Brian Leetch .15 .40
323 Todd Harvey .02 .10
324 Mike Richter .15 .40
325 Mike Knuble .02 .10
326 Jeff Beukeboom .02 .10
327 Daniel Alfredsson .08 .25
328 Vaclav Prospal .02 .10
329 Wade Redden .02 .10
330 Igor Kravchuk .02 .10
331 Andreas Dackell .02 .10
332 Mike Maneluk RC .02 .10
333 Eric Lindros .15 .40
334 Rod Brind'Amour .08 .25
335 Colin Forbes .02 .10
336 Dimitri Tertyshny RC .02 .10
337 Shjon Podein .02 .10
338 Chris Therien .02 .10
339 Jeremy Roenick .20 .50
340 Jyrki Lumme .02 .10
341 Rick Tocchet .08 .25
342 Dallas Drake .02 .10
343 Keith Carney .02 .10
344 Greg Adams .02 .10
345 Jan Hrdina RC .40 1.00
346 German Titov .02 .10
347 Stu Barnes .02 .10
348 Kevin Hatcher .02 .10
349 Martin Straka .02 .10
350 Jean-Sebastien Aubin RC .40 1.00
351 Jeff Friesen .02 .10
352 Tony Granato .02 .10
353 Scott Hannan RC .02 .10
354 Owen Nolan .08 .25
355 Stephane Matteau .02 .10
356 Bryan Marchment .02 .10
357 Geoff Courtnall .08 .25
358 Brent Johnson RC .75 2.00
359 Jamie Rivers .02 .10
360 Terry Yake .02 .10
361 Jamie McLennan .08 .25
362 Grant Fuhr .08 .25
363 Michal Handzus RC .40 1.00
364 Bill Ranford .08 .25
365 John Cullen .02 .10
366 Craig Janney .02 .10
367 Daren Puppa .08 .25
368 Pavel Kubina RC .20 .50
369 Wendel Clark .08 .25
370 Mats Sundin .15 .40
371 Felix Potvin .15 .40
372 Daniil Markov RC .02 .10
373 Derek King .02 .10
374 Steve Thomas .02 .10
375 Tomas Kaberle RC .40 1.00
376 Alexander Mogilny .08 .25
377 Bill Muckalt RC .02 .10
378 Brian Noonan .02 .10
379 Markus Naslund .15 .40
380 Brad May .02 .10
381 Matt Cooke RC .02 .10
382 Calle Johansson .02 .10
383 Dale Hunter .02 .10
384 Jaroslav Svejkovsky .02 .10
385 Dmitri Mironov .02 .10
386 Matt Herr RC .02 .10
387 Nolan Baumgartner .02 .10
388 Wayne Gretzky CL .15 .40
389 Steve Yzerman CL .08 .25
390 Wayne Gretzky .15 .40
Steve Yzerman CL
391 Brian Finley PE RC .60 1.50
392 Maxime Ouellet PE RC .75 2.00
393 Kurtis Foster PE RC .60 1.50
394 Barret Jackman PE RC .75 2.00
395 Ross Lupaschuk PE RC .60 1.50
396 Steven McCarthy PE RC .60 1.50
397 Peter Reynolds PE RC .60 1.50
398 Bart Rushmer PE RC .60 1.50
399 Jonathan Zion PE RC .60 1.50
400 Kris Beech PE RC .60 1.50
401 Brandin Cote PE RC .60 1.50
402 Scott Kelman PE RC .60 1.50
403 Jamie Lundmark PE RC .75 2.00
404 Derek MacKenzie PE RC .60 1.50
405 Rory McDade PE RC .60 1.50
406 David Morisset PE RC .60 1.50
407 Mirko Murovic PE RC .60 1.50
408 Taylor Pyatt PE RC .75 2.00
409 Charlie Stephens PE .60 1.50
410 Kyle Wanvig PE RC .60 1.50
411 Krzystof Wieckowski PE RC .60 1.50
412 Michael Zigomanis PE RC .60 1.50
413 Rico Fata CC .60 1.50
414 Vincent Lecavalier CC 1.00 2.50
415 Chris Drury CC .60 1.50
416 Oleg Kvasha CC RC .60 1.50
417 Eric Brewer CC .60 1.50
418 Josh Green CC RC .60 1.50
419 Marty Reasoner CC .60 1.50
420 Manny Malhotra CC .60 1.50

1998-99 Upper Deck Exclusives

Randomly inserted into hobby packs only, this 420-card set is parallel to the base set. Cards are serial numbered to only 100 copies. An exclusive 1 of 1 parallel also exists and randomly inserted into packs.
*STARS: 75X TO 150X BASIC CARDS
*ROOKIES: 25X TO 60X BASIC CARDS
*SR, RR STARS: 5X TO 12X BASIC CARDS
*SR,RR,PE,CC RC's: 4X TO 10X BASIC CARDS

1998-99 Upper Deck Blow-Ups 5 x 7

Inserted as box-toppers in various distribution forms of Upper Deck, these oversized cards resembled differentr insert sets but were approximately 5" x 7". Cards were numbered the same as the basic insert card.
85 Steve Yzerman
Upper Deck
P3 Steve Yzerman
Profiles
FF20 Steve Yzerman 3.20 8.00
Fantastic Finishers
FT1 Steve Yzerman 3.20 8.00
Frozen in Time
LS14 Steve Yzerman 3.20 8.00
Lord Stanley's Heroes

1998-99 Upper Deck Fantastic Finishers

Randomly inserted into Series 1 packs at a rate of 1:12, this 30-card set features color action photos of players considered to be the more prolific and gifted finishers in the NHL. Three Tier Quantum parallel versions of this insert set were also produced and inserted into Series 1 packs. Tier 1 cards were sequentially numbered to 1,500; Tier 2 cards were sequentially numbered to 50; and Tier 3 cards were sequentially numbered to 1.
*QUANTUM 1: 1X TO 2X BASIC INSERTS
*QUANTUM 2: 20X TO 40X BASIC INSERTS
FF1 Wayne Gretzky 6.00 15.00
FF2 Peter Bondra .75 2.00
FF3 Sergei Samsonov .75 2.00
FF4 Jaromir Jagr 1.50 4.00
FF5 Brendan Shanahan 1.00 2.50
FF6 Joe Sakic 2.00 5.00
FF7 Brett Hull 1.50 4.00
FF8 Paul Kariya 1.00 2.50
FF9 Keith Tkachuk 1.00 2.50
FF10 Zigmund Palffy .75 2.00
FF11 Eric Lindros 1.00 2.50
FF12 Mike Modano 1.50 4.00
FF13 Pavel Bure 1.00 2.50
FF14 Mats Sundin .75 2.00
FF15 Patrik Elias .75 2.00
FF16 Tony Amonte .75 2.00
FF17 Peter Forsberg 2.50 6.00
FF18 Alexei Yashin .75 2.00
FF19 Mark Recchi .75 2.00
FF20 Steve Yzerman 4.00 10.00
FF21 Doug Weight .75 2.00
FF22 Jeremy Roenick 1.25 3.00
FF23 Teemu Selanne 1.00 2.50
FF24 Owen Nolan .75 2.00
FF25 John LeClair 1.00 2.50
FF26 Jason Allison .75 2.00
FF27 Mike Johnson .75 2.00
FF28 Theo Fleury .75 2.00
FF29 Nicklas Lidstrom 1.00 2.50
FF30 Joe Nieuwendyk .75 2.00

1998-99 Upper Deck Frozen In Time

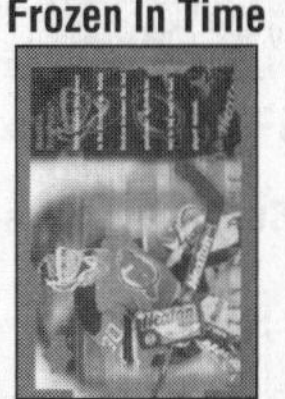

Randomly inserted in Series 1 packs at a rate of 1:23, this 30-card set features color action photos of some of the key moments throughout the careers of the highlighted players. Three Tier Quantum parallel versions of this insert set were also produced and inserted into Series 1 packs. Tier 1 cards were sequentially numbered to 1,000; Tier 2 cards were sequentially numbered to 25; and Tier 3 cards were numbered to 1.
COMPLETE SET (30) 50.00 100.00
*QUANTUM 1: 1X TO 2X BASIC INSERTS
*QUANTUM 2: 25X TO 50X BASIC INSERTS
FT1 Steve Yzerman 4.00 10.00
FT2 Peter Forsberg 2.50 6.00
FT3 Sergei Samsonov 1.25 3.00
FT4 Martin Brodeur 2.50 6.00
FT5 Theo Fleury .75 2.00
FT6 Paul Kariya 1.50 4.00
FT7 Rob Blake 1.25 3.00
FT8 Jari Kurri .75 2.00
FT9 Eric Lindros 1.50 4.00
FT10 Dominik Hasek 2.00 5.00
FT11 Patrick Roy 4.00 10.00
FT12 Saku Koivu 1.50 4.00
FT13 Mike Modano 1.50 4.00
FT14 Alexei Morozov .75 2.00
FT15 Chris Osgood 1.25 3.00
FT16 Doug Gilmour 1.25 3.00
FT17 Owen Nolan 1.25 3.00
FT18 Mike Johnson 1.25 3.00
FT19 Keith Tkachuk 1.50 4.00
FT20 Adam Oates 1.25 3.00
FT21 Chris Chelios 1.50 4.00
FT22 Brendan Shanahan 1.50 4.00
FT23 Joe Sakic 2.00 5.00
FT24 Pavel Bure 1.50 4.00
FT25 Ray Bourque 2.00 5.00
FT26 Ed Belfour 1.50 4.00
FT27 John LeClair 1.50 4.00
FT28 Teemu Selanne 1.50 4.00
FT29 Jaromir Jagr 1.50 4.00
FT30 Wayne Gretzky 6.00 15.00

1998-99 Upper Deck Game Jerseys

Randomly inserted into Series 1 and Series 2 packs at the rate of one in 2,500 retail and 1:288 hobby, this 24-card set features color action player photos with a piece from an actual game-worn jersey embedded in the cards. Four of the player's autographed some of their cards. The number of cards each player autographed follow the player's name in the checklist below.
*MULT.COLORS: 1X TO 1.5X BASIC INS.
GJ1 Wayne Gretzky 75.00 200.00
GJ2 Vincent Lecavalier 25.00 60.00
GJ3 Bobby Hull 25.00 60.00
GJ4 Curtis Joseph 10.00 25.00
GJ5 Roberto Luongo 15.00 40.00
GJ6 Martin Brodeur 25.00 60.00
GJ8 Ed Belfour 10.00 25.00
GJ9 Al MacInnis 6.00 15.00
GJ10 Derian Hatcher 6.00 15.00
GJ11 Daniel Tkaczuk 6.00 15.00
GJ12 Manny Malhotra 6.00 15.00
GJ13 Eric Brewer 6.00 15.00
GJ14 Alex Tanguay 8.00 20.00
GJ15 Brendan Shanahan 10.00 25.00
GJ16 Chris Osgood 8.00 20.00
GJ16 Jaromir Jagr 25.00 60.00
GJ17 Dominik Hasek 25.00 60.00
GJ18 Doug Gilmour 8.00 20.00
GJ19 Mats Sundin 10.00 25.00
GJ20 Darryl Sydor 6.00 15.00
GJ21 Chris Therien 6.00 15.00
GJ22 Darius Kasparaitis 6.00 15.00
GJ23 Alexei Zhamnov 6.00 15.00
GJ24 Joe Nieuwendyk 8.00 20.00
GJA1 Bobby Hull AU/9 900.00 1500.00
GJA2 W.Gretzky AU/99 300.00 600.00
GJA3 V.Lecavalier AU/100 125.00 300.00
GJA4 Gretzky 2Swatch AU/99 400.00 750.00

1998-99 Upper Deck Generation Next

Randomly inserted in Series 2 packs at the rate of 1:23, this 30-card set features color action photos of ten of the top players in the NHL on one side with one of three heir apparent pictured on the other. Quantum parallels of this set were also produced and inserted into Series 2 packs. Three different Quantum parallel sets exist, and each Quantum set was broken into three levels or "tiers". Quantum 1 had tiers that featured ten cards sequentially numbered to 1,000; ten numbered to 500; and ten cards sequentially numbered to 250. Quantum 2 had tiers that contained ten cards sequentially numbered to 75; ten numbered to 25; and ten cards sequentially numbered to 10. Quantum 3 had tiers with ten cards sequentially numbered to 3; ten sequentially numbered to 2; and ten cards numbered to 1. The card numbers in each tier were the same for each set, the card numbers are listed below. Tiers were grouped by serial numbers in descending order. Quantum 2, Tier 3 and Quantum 3 cards are not priced due to their scarcity.

COMPLETE SET (30) 30.00 60.00
*GN Q1/TIER 1: .75X TO 1.5X BASIC INSERTS
*GN Q1/TIER 2: 1.5X TO 3X BASIC INSERTS
*GN Q1/TIER 3: 2.5X TO 5X BASIC INSERTS
*GN Q2/TIER 1: 10X TO 20X BASIC INSERTS
*GN Q2/TIER 2: 25X TO 50X BASIC INSERTS
TIER 1 CARDS: 1,4,7,10,13,16,19,22,25,28
TIER 2 CARDS: 2,5,8,11,14,17,20,23,26,29
TIER 3 CARDS: 3,6,9,12,15,18,21,24,27,30
GN1 Wayne Gretzky / Sergei Samsonov 2.00 5.00
GN2 Wayne Gretzky / Marian Hossa 2.00 5.00
GN3 Wayne Gretzky / Vincent Lecavalier 2.00 5.00
GN4 Steve Yzerman / Brendan Morrison 1.50 4.00
GN5 Steve Yzerman / Marty Reasoner 1.50 4.00
GN6 Steve Yzerman / Manny Malhotra 1.50 4.00
GN7 Patrick Roy / J-S Giguere 1.50 4.00
GN8 Patrick Roy / Jose Theodore 2.00 5.00
GN9 Patrick Roy / Marc Denis 1.50 4.00
GN10 Eric Lindros / Patrick Marleau .60 1.50
GN11 Eric Lindros / Brad Isbister .60 1.50
GN12 Eric Lindros / Joe Thornton .60 1.50
GN13 Brendan Shanahan / Josh Green .60 1.50
GN14 Brendan Shanahan / Ty Jones .60 1.50
GN15 Brendan Shanahan / Mike Watt .60 1.50
GN16 Ray Bourque / Mattias Ohlund .60 1.50
GN17 Ray Bourque / Tom Poti .60 1.50
GN18 Ray Bourque / Eric Brewer .75 2.00
GN19 Paul Kariya / Daniel Briere .60 1.50
GN20 Paul Kariya / Rico Fata .60 1.50
GN21 Paul Kariya / Chris Drury .60 1.50
GN22 Jaromir Jagr / Robert Dome .60 1.50
GN23 Jaromir Jagr / Richard Zednik .60 1.50
GN24 Jaromir Jagr / Oleg Kvasha .60 1.50
GN25 Peter Forsberg / Olli Jokinen 1.25 3.00
GN26 Peter Forsberg / Niklas Sundstrom 1.00 2.50
GN27 Peter Forsberg / Brendan Morrison 1.00 2.50
GN28 Pavel Bure / Vadim Sharifijanov .60 1.50
GN29 Pavel Bure / Dmitri Nabokov .60 1.50
GN30 Pavel Bure / Sergei Samsonov .60 1.50

1998-99 Upper Deck Lord Stanley's Heroes

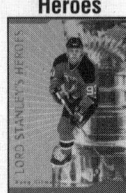

Randomly inserted into Series 1 packs at a rate of one in six, this 30-card set features color action photos of players vying for their chance at claiming the Stanley Cup. Three Tier Quantum parallel versions of this insert set were also produced and inserted into Series 1 packs. Tier 1 cards were sequentially numbered to 2,000; Tier 2 cards were sequentially numbered to 100; and Tier 3 cards were numbered to 1.

COMPLETE SET (30) 30.00 60.00
*QUANTUM 1: .6X TO 1.5X BASIC INSERTS
*QUANTUM 2: 8X TO 20X BASIC INSERTS
LS1 Wayne Gretzky 4.00 10.00
LS2 Joe Sakic 1.25 3.00
LS3 Jaromir Jagr 1.00 2.50
LS4 Brendan Shanahan .60 1.50
LS5 Martin Brodeur 1.50 4.00
LS6 Theo Fleury .15 .40
LS7 Doug Gilmour .40 1.00
LS8 Ron Francis .40 1.00
LS9 Sergei Fedorov 1.00 2.50
LS10 Patrick Roy 3.00 8.00
LS11 Mark Messier .60 1.50
LS12 Peter Forsberg 1.50 4.00
LS13 Brian Leetch .60 1.50
LS14 Steve Yzerman 3.00 8.00
LS15 Sergei Samsonov .40 1.00
LS16 Eric Lindros .60 1.50
LS17 Paul Kariya .60 1.50
LS18 Saku Koivu .60 1.50
LS19 Bryan Berard .40 1.00
LS20 Chris Pronger .40 1.00
LS21 Keith Tkachuk .60 1.50
LS22 Doug Weight .40 1.00
LS23 Ed Belfour .60 1.50
LS24 Mats Sundin .60 1.50
LS25 John LeClair .60 1.50
LS26 Pavel Bure .60 1.50
LS27 Dominik Hasek 1.25 3.00
LS28 Mike Modano 1.00 2.50
LS29 Curtis Joseph .60 1.50
LS30 Teemu Selanne .60 1.50

1998-99 Upper Deck Profiles

Randomly inserted into Series 2 packs at the rate of one in 12, this 30-card set features color action photos of some of the greatest current players in the NHL. Three Tier Quantum parallel versions of this insert set were also produced and inserted into Series 2 packs. Tier 1 cards were sequentially numbered to 1,500; Tier 2 cards were sequentially numbered to 50; and Tier 3 cards were numbered to 1.

COMPLETE SET (30) 30.00 60.00
*QUANTUM 1: .75X TO 1.5X BASIC INSERTS
*QUANTUM 2: 10X TO 25X BASIC INSERTS
P1 Marty Reasoner .50 1.25
P2 Brett Hull 1.00 2.50
P3 Steve Yzerman 4.00 10.00
P4 Eric Lindros .75 2.00
P5 Eric Brewer .60 1.50
P6 Martin Brodeur 2.00 5.00
P7 John Vanbiesbrouck .50 1.25
P8 Teemu Selanne .75 2.00
P9 Wayne Gretzky 5.00 12.00
P10 Jaromir Jagr 1.25 3.00
P11 Peter Forsberg 2.00 5.00
P12 Manny Malhotra .50 1.25
P13 Sergei Samsonov .50 1.25
P14 Brendan Shanahan .75 2.00
P15 Doug Gilmour .60 1.50
P16 Vincent Lecavalier .75 2.00
P17 Dominik Hasek 1.50 4.00
P18 Mike Modano 1.25 3.00
P19 Saku Koivu .75 2.00
P20 Curtis Joseph .75 2.00
P21 Paul Kariya .75 2.00
P22 Doug Weight .60 1.50
P23 Ray Bourque 1.50 4.00
P24 Patrick Roy 4.00 10.00
P25 John LeClair .75 2.00
P26 Chris Drury .50 1.25
P27 Theo Fleury .60 1.50
P28 Mats Sundin .60 1.50
P29 Sergei Fedorov 1.00 2.50
P30 Rico Fata .60 1.50

1998-99 Upper Deck Wayne Gretzky Game Jersey Autographs

These cards could be found in packs of Black Diamond, Upper Deck MVP, SP Authentic, and SPx Top Prospects. Each product had one version of the card numbered to 40 sets. The cards contain an actual piece of a game worn Wayne Gretzky jersey embedded in the cards and an authentic autograph.

COMMON CARD 200.00 500.00

1998-99 Upper Deck Year of the Great One

Randomly inserted into Series 2 packs at the rate of 1:6, this 30-card set features color photos of Hockey great, Wayne Gretzky. Three Tier Quantum parallel versions of this insert set were also produced and inserted into Series 2 packs. Tier 1 cards were sequentially numbered to 1,999; Tier 2 cards were sequentially numbered to 99; and Tier 3 cards were numbered to 1.

COMPLETE SET (30) 40.00 80.00
COMMON CARD (GO1-GO30) 1.50 4.00
COMMON QUANTUM 1 (1-30) 6.00 15.00
COMMON QUANTUM 2 (1-30) 25.00 60.00

1998 Upper Deck Willie O'Ree Commemorative Card

This card was issued by Upper Deck of the 1998 NHL All-Stars game in Vancouver. It was available at All-Star activities throughout the weekend.

22 Willie O'Ree 5.00 10.00

1999-00 Upper Deck

Upper Deck was released as a 335-card two series set with 270 regular issue cards and 65 short prints. Series one is comprised of 135 regular cards and 35 short prints for a total of 170 cards, and series two was comprised of 135 regular cards and 30 short prints for a total of 165 cards. Base cards have a blue and black border along the bottom edge of the card with enhanced bronze foil stamping. Upper Deck was released in 24-pack boxes with packs containing 10 cards and carried a suggested retail price of $2.99.

COMPLETE SET (335) 40.00 100.00
SP STATED ODDS 1:4
1 Wayne Gretzky .60 1.50
2 Wayne Gretzky .60 1.50
3 Wayne Gretzky .60 1.50
4 Wayne Gretzky .60 1.50
5 Wayne Gretzky .60 1.50
6 Wayne Gretzky .60 1.50
7 Wayne Gretzky .60 1.50
8 Wayne Gretzky .60 1.50
9 Wayne Gretzky .60 1.50
10 Wayne Gretzky .60 1.50
11 Paul Kariya .20 .50
12 Matt Cullen .02 .10
13 Steve Rucchin .15 .40
14 Fredrik Olausson .02 .10
15 Damian Rhodes .15 .40
16 Jody Hull .02 .10
17 Ray Bourque .30 .75
18 Joe Thornton .30 .75
19 Jonathan Girard .02 .10
20 Shawn Bates .02 .10
21 Byron Dafoe .15 .40
22 Dominik Hasek .40 1.00
23 Michael Peca .15 .40
24 Miroslav Satan .15 .40
25 Dixon Ward .02 .10
26 Valeri Bure .02 .10
27 Derek Morris .02 .10
28 Jarome Iginla .25 .60
29 Rico Fata .02 .10
30 J-S Giguere .15 .40
31 Arturs Irbe .15 .40
32 Sami Kapanen .02 .10
33 Gary Roberts .02 .10
34 Bates Battaglia .02 .10
35 J-P Dumont .15 .40
36 Ty Jones .02 .10
37 Tony Amonte .15 .40
38 Anders Eriksson .02 .10
39 Peter Forsberg .50 1.25
40 Adam Foote .02 .10
41 Chris Drury .15 .40
42 Milan Hejduk .20 .50
43 Brett Hull .25 .60
44 Ed Belfour .20 .50
45 Jamie Langenbrunner .02 .10
46 Derian Hatcher .02 .10
47 Jon Sim RC .15 .40
48 Joe Nieuwendyk .15 .40
49 Steve Yzerman 1.00 2.50
50 Brendan Shanahan .20 .50
51 Nicklas Lidstrom .20 .50
52 Igor Larionov .02 .10
53 Vyacheslav Kozlov .02 .10
54 Bill Guerin .02 .10
55 Mike Grier .02 .10
56 Tommy Salo .15 .40
57 Tom Poti .02 .10
58 Mark Parrish .02 .10
59 Pavel Bure .20 .50
60 Scott Mellanby .02 .10
61 Chris Allen RC .02 .10
62 Rob Blake .15 .40
63 Pavel Rosa .02 .10
64 Donald Audette .02 .10
65 Vladimir Tsyplakov .02 .10
66 Manny Legace .15 .40
67 Saku Koivu .20 .50
68 Eric Weinrich .02 .10
69 Jeff Hackett .15 .40
70 Arron Asham .02 .10
71 Trevor Linden .15 .40
72 Cliff Ronning .15 .40
73 David Legwand .15 .40
74 Kimmo Timonen .02 .10
75 Sergei Krivokrasov .02 .10
76 Mike Dunham .15 .40
77 Martin Brodeur .50 1.25
78 Patrik Elias .15 .40
79 Petr Sykora .02 .10
80 Vadim Sharifijanov .02 .10
81 John Madden RC .20 .50
82 Eric Brewer .02 .10
83 Dmitri Nabokov .02 .10
84 Kenny Jonsson .02 .10
85 Zdeno Chara .02 .10
86 Wayne Gretzky 1.25 3.00
87 Mike Richter .20 .50
88 Adam Graves .02 .10
89 Manny Malhotra .15 .40
90 Alexei Yashin .02 .10
91 Sami Salo .15 .40
92 Marian Hossa .02 .10
93 Shawn McEachern .20 .50
94 Eric Lindros .20 .50
95 Jean-Marc Pelletier .02 .10
96 Rod Brind'Amour .15 .40
97 Mark Recchi .15 .40
98 Eric Desjardins .15 .40
99 Robert Reichel .02 .10
100 Keith Tkachuk .20 .50
101 Robert Esche RC .60 1.50
102 Oleg Tverdovsky .02 .10
103 Trevor Letowski .02 .10
104 Jaromir Jagr .30 .75
105 Tom Barrasso .15 .40
106 Jan Hrdina .02 .10
107 Matthew Barnaby .15 .40
108 Vincent Damphousse .02 .10
109 Jeff Friesen .02 .10
110 Patrick Marleau .20 .50
111 Mike Ricci .15 .40
112 Scott Hannan .02 .10
113 Pavol Demitra .15 .40
114 Al MacInnis .15 .40
115 Lubos Bartecko .02 .10
116 Jochen Hecht RC .20 .50
117 Vincent Lecavalier .20 .50
118 Paul Mara .02 .10
119 Kevin Hodson .15 .40
120 Dan Cloutier .15 .40
121 Mats Sundin .20 .50
122 Daniil Markov .02 .10
123 Sergei Berezin .02 .10
124 Steve Thomas .02 .10
125 Tomas Kaberle .02 .10
126 Mark Messier .20 .50
127 Bill Muckalt .15 .40
128 Kevin Weekes .02 .10
129 Josh Holden .15 .40
130 Jaroslav Svejkovsky .02 .10
131 Adam Oates .15 .40
132 Peter Bondra .15 .40
133 Jan Bulis .02 .10
134 Wayne Gretzky CL .60 1.50
135 Wayne Gretzky CL .60 1.50
136 Wayne Gretzky SP 1.50 4.00
137 Eric Lindros SP .25 .60
138 Jaromir Jagr SP .40 1.00
139 Paul Kariya SP .25 .60
140 Steve Yzerman SP 1.25 3.00
141 Patrick Roy SP 1.25 3.00
142 Chris Drury SP .20 .50
143 Sergei Samsonov SP .20 .50
144 Brett Hull SP .30 .75
145 Dominik Hasek SP .50 1.25
146 Keith Tkachuk SP .25 .60
147 Alexei Yashin SP .20 .50
148 Martin Brodeur SP .60 1.50
149 Pavel Bure SP .25 .60
150 Paul Mara SP .20 .50
151 Peter Bondra SP .20 .50
152 Mike Modano SP .40 1.00
153 Teemu Selanne SP .20 .50
154 Peter Forsberg SP .60 1.50
155 Brendan Shanahan SP .20 .50
156 Ray Bourque SP .40 1.00
157 Saku Koivu SP .25 .60
158 John LeClair SP .25 .60
159 Joe Sakic SP .50 1.25
160 David Legwand SP .20 .50
161 Patrik Stefan YG RC .40 1.00
162 Nick Boynton YG SP RC .40 1.00
163 Roberto Luongo YG SP .50 1.25
164 Rico Fata SP .20 .50
165 Daniel Sedin YG SP .20 .50
166 Henrik Sedin YG SP .20 .50
167 Brad Stuart YG SP .20 .50
168 Tony Amonte SP .20 .50
169 Oleg Saprykin YG RC .50 1.25
170 Denis Shvidki YG SP .20 .50
171 Guy Hebert .15 .40
172 Niclas Havelid RC .20 .50
173 Oleg Tverdovsky .02 .10
174 Teemu Selanne .20 .50
175 Damian Rhodes .15 .40
176 Nelson Emerson .02 .10
177 Per Svartvadet RC .02 .10
178 Ray Ferraro .02 .10
179 Kelly Buchberger .02 .10
180 Norm Maracle .15 .40
181 Patrik Stefan .02 .10
182 Dave Andreychuk .15 .40
183 Sergei Samsonov .15 .40
184 John Grahame RC .20 .50
185 Jason Allison .02 .10
186 Kyle McLaren .02 .10
187 Anson Carter .15 .40
188 Martin Biron .15 .40
189 Brian Campbell RC .20 .50
190 Curtis Brown .02 .10
191 Alexei Zhitnik .02 .10
192 David Moravec RC .02 .10
193 Oleg Saprykin .02 .10
194 Grant Fuhr .15 .40
195 Phil Housley .15 .40
196 Marc Savard .02 .10
197 Robyn Regehr .02 .10
198 Martin Gelinas .02 .10
199 Ron Francis .15 .40
200 Jeff O'Neil .02 .10
201 Keith Primeau .02 .10
202 Paul Ranheim .02 .10
203 Kyle Calder RC .20 .50
204 Jocelyn Thibault .15 .40
205 Wendel Clark .15 .40
206 Doug Gilmour .15 .40
207 Josef Marha .02 .10
208 Alexei Zhamnov .02 .10
209 Dan Hinote RC .20 .50
210 Patrick Roy 1.00 2.50
211 Joe Sakic .40 1.00
212 Alex Tanguay .15 .40
213 Sandis Ozolinsh .02 .10
214 Adam Deadmarsh .02 .10
215 Jere Lehtinen .15 .40
216 Mike Modano .30 .75
217 Darryl Sydor .15 .40
218 Sergei Zubov .02 .10
219 Pavel Patera RC .02 .10
220 Jamie Pushor .02 .10
221 Chris Osgood .15 .40
222 Tomas Holmstrom .02 .10
223 Chris Chelios .20 .50
224 Sergei Fedorov .30 .75
225 Jiri Fischer .02 .10
226 Paul Comrie RC .02 .10
227 Frantisek Musil .02 .10
228 Janne Niinimaa .02 .10
229 Doug Weight .15 .40
230 Trevor Kidd .15 .40
231 Oleg Kvasha .15 .40
232 Viktor Kozlov .02 .10
233 Rob Niedermayer .02 .10
234 Luc Robitaille .15 .40
235 Aki Berg .02 .10
236 Bryan Smolinski .15 .40
237 Jozef Stumpel .15 .40
238 Zigmund Palffy .15 .40
239 Stephane Fiset .15 .40
240 Jason Blake RC .15 .40
241 Scott Lachance .02 .10
242 Vladimir Malakhov .02 .10
243 Mike Ribeiro .02 .10
244 Brian Savage .02 .10
245 Tomas Vokoun .02 .10
246 Randy Robitaille .02 .10
247 Sergei Nemchinov .02 .10
248 Brendan Morrison .15 .40
249 Scott Niedermayer .02 .10
250 Scott Stevens .15 .40
251 Scott Gomez .02 .10
252 Mark Lawrence .02 .10
253 Felix Potvin .20 .50
254 Olli Jokinen .15 .40
255 Tim Connolly .02 .10
256 Mariusz Czerkaswki .02 .10
257 Valeri Kamensky .02 .10
258 Brian Leetch .20 .50
259 Petr Nedved .15 .40
260 Theo Fleury .02 .10
261 Kevin Hatcher .02 .10
262 Mike York .02 .10
263 Ron Tugnutt .15 .40
264 Chris Phillips .02 .10
265 Daniel Alfredsson .15 .40
266 Radek Bonk .02 .10
267 Wade Redden .02 .10
268 John Vanbiesbrouck .15 .40
269 John LeClair .20 .50
270 Simon Gagne .20 .50
271 Nikolai Khabibulin .15 .40
272 Daniel Briere .02 .10
273 Jeremy Roenick .25 .60
274 Andrew Ference .02 .10
275 Alexei Kovalev .02 .10
276 Martin Straka .02 .10
277 Alexei Morozov .15 .40
278 Steve Shields .15 .40
279 Marco Sturm .15 .40
280 Niklas Sundstrom .02 .10
281 Brad Stuart .15 .40
282 Owen Nolan .15 .40
283 Roman Turek .15 .40
284 Chris Pronger .15 .40
285 Jim Campbell .02 .10
286 Michal Handzus .15 .40
287 Pierre Turgeon .15 .40
288 Darcy Tucker .02 .10
289 Andrei Zyuzin .02 .10
290 Stephen Guolla .02 .10
291 Curtis Joseph .20 .50
292 Jonas Hoglund .02 .10
293 Bryan Berard .02 .10
294 Mike Johnson .15 .40
295 Garth Snow .15 .40
296 Jason Strudwick .02 .10
297 Steve Kariya RC .20 .50
298 Markus Naslund .20 .50
299 Mattias Ohlund .15 .40
300 Alexander Mogilny .15 .40
301 Olaf Kolzig .15 .40
302 Alexei Tezikov RC .20 .50
303 Alexander Volchkov RC .15 .40
304 Steve Yzerman CL .20 .50
305 Curtis Joseph CL .15 .40
306 Pavel Brendl YG SP RC .40 1.00
307 Daniel Sedin YG SP .20 .50
308 Henrik Sedin YG SP .20 .50
309 Sheldon Keefe YG SP RC .40 1.00
310 Ryan Jardine YG SP RC .40 1.00
311 Maxime Ouellet YG SP .20 .50
312 Barret Jackman YG SP .20 .50
313 Kristian Kudroc YG SP RC .40 1.00
314 Branislav Mezei YG SP RC .40 1.00
315 Denis Shvidki YG SP .20 .50
316 Brian Finley YG SP .20 .50
317 Jonathan Cheechoo YG SP 2.50 6.00
318 Mark Bell YG SP .20 .50
319 Taylor Pyatt YG SP .20 .50
320 Norm Milley YG SP .20 .50
321 Jamie Lundmark YG SP .20 .50
322 Alexander Buturlin RC .40 1.00
323 Jaroslav Kristek YG SP RC .40 1.00
324 Kris Beech YG SP .20 .50
325 Scott Kelman YG SP .20 .50
326 Milan Kraft RC .40 1.00
327 Mattias Weinhandl YG SP .20 .50
328 Alexei Volkov YG SP .20 .50
329 Andrei Shefer RC .40 1.00
330 Mathieu Chouinard YG SP .20 .50
331 Justin Papineau YG SP .20 .50
332 Mike Van Horn SP .20 .50
333 Jeff Heerema YG SP .20 .50
334 Michael Zigomanis YG SP .20 .50
335 Bryan Kazarian YG SP RC .40 1.00

1999-00 Upper Deck Exclusives

Randomly inserted in packs, this 335-card set parallels the base Upper Deck set with gold foil highlights. Each card is sequentially numbered to 100. Unpriced 1/1 exclusive parallels also exist.

COMMON GRETZKY (1-10) 20.00 50.00
*STARS: 40X TO 100X BASIC CARDS
*ROOKIES: 12.5X TO 30X BASIC CARDS
*EXCL.STARS SP's: 10X TO 25X BASIC CARDS
*YG SP's: 1.25X TO 4X BASIC CARDS
*YG SP ROOKIES: 2X TO 5X BASIC CARDS

1999-00 Upper Deck 500 Goal Club

Randomly inserted in various Upper Deck products, these cards feature players who attained the 500-goal mark during their career. The front pictures the player and includes a swatch of game-worn jersey or game-used stick. An autographed version of each card, serial-numbered to 25, was also available. Michel Goulet and Stan Mikita were randomly available in Black Diamond with stated odds of 1:1788. Bobby Hull and Brett Hull were randomly available in SP Authentic with stated odds of 1:1339. Gordie Howe was randomly available in Upper Deck Series II packs with stated odds of 1:2989. Bryan Trottier and Mike Bossy were randomly available in Upper Deck MVP SC Edition with stated odds of 1:3995. Luc Robitaille and Marcel Dionne were randomly available in Upper Deck Ovation with stated odds of 1:947. Dino Ciccarelli and Steve Yzerman were randomly available in Upper Deck PowerDeck with stated odds of 1:330. Gilbert Perreault and Maurice Richard were randomly available in Upper Deck Ultimate Victory with stated odds of 1:1113. Guy Lafleur and Jean Beliveau were randomly available in Wayne Gretzky Hockey with stated odds of 1:1259.

500BH Bobby Hull AU/25 250.00 500.00
500BH Bobby Hull 50.00 125.00
500BT Bryan Trottier AU/25 200.00 400.00
500BT Bryan Trottier 15.00 40.00
500DC Dino Ciccarelli 30.00 80.00
500DC Dino Ciccarelli AU/25 150.00 300.00
500GH Gordie Howe 60.00 150.00
500GH Gordie Howe AU/25 500.00 800.00
500GL Guy Lafleur AU/25 150.00 350.00
500GL Guy Lafleur 125.00 300.00
500GP Gilbert Perreault 15.00 40.00
500GP G.Perreault AU/25 400.00 600.00
500JB Jean Beliveau AU/25 300.00 500.00
500JB Jean Beliveau 100.00 250.00
500LR Luc Robitaille AU/25 350.00 500.00
500LR Luc Robitaille 20.00 50.00
500MB Mike Bossy AU/25 400.00 500.00
500MB Mike Bossy 20.00 50.00
500MD Marcel Dionne AU/25 125.00 250.00
500MD Marcel Dionne 20.00 50.00
500MG Michel Goulet AU/25 150.00 300.00
500MG Michel Goulet 15.00 40.00
500MR Maurice Richard 75.00 200.00
500MR M.Richard AU/25 300.00 700.00
500SM Stan Mikita AU/25 200.00 400.00
500SM Stan Mikita 50.00 125.00
500SY Steve Yzerman AU/25 400.00 800.00
500SY Steve Yzerman 60.00 150.00
500BHU Brett Hull AU/25 250.00 500.00
500BHU Brett Hull 40.00 80.00

1999-00 Upper Deck All-Star Class

Randomly inserted in Series Two packs at the rate of 1:23, this 20-card set features an all blue foil card stock with full color action player photos. Silver and gold parallels were also created and inserted randomly. Silver parallels were limited to 100 serial numbered sets. Gold parallels were numbered 1/1 and are not priced due to scarcity.

COMPLETE SET (20) 30.00 60.00
*SILVER STARS: 10X TO 25X BASIC CARDS
AS1 Dominik Hasek 2.00 5.00
AS2 Patrick Roy 5.00 12.00
AS3 Jaromir Jagr 1.50 4.00
AS4 Paul Kariya 1.00 2.50
AS5 Teemu Selanne 1.00 2.50
AS6 Keith Tkachuk 1.00 2.50
AS7 Pavel Bure 1.00 2.50
AS8 John LeClair 1.00 2.50
AS9 Mats Sundin 1.00 2.50
AS10 Steve Yzerman 5.00 12.00
AS11 Peter Forsberg 2.50 6.00
AS12 Eric Lindros 1.00 2.50
AS13 Steve Kariya 1.25 3.00
AS14 Ed Belfour 1.00 2.50
AS15 Nicklas Lidstrom .75 2.00
AS16 Ray Bourque 1.50 4.00
AS17 Sandis Ozolinsh .75 2.00
AS18 Al MacInnis .75 2.00
AS19 Martin Brodeur 2.50 6.00
AS20 Patrik Stefan 1.50 4.00

1999-00 Upper Deck Crunch Time

Randomly inserted in Series One packs at the rate of 1:4, this 30-card set features an all foil card stock with concentric laser rays coming out from behind an action player shot. Background foil color matches the respective player's team colors. Silver and gold parallels were also created and inserted randomly. Silver parallels were limited to 100 serial numbered sets. Unpriced gold parallels were numbered 1/1.

COMPLETE SET (30) 15.00 30.00
*SILVER STARS: 25X TO 60X BASIC CARDS
CT1 Vincent Lecavalier .40 1.00
CT2 Steve Yzerman 2.00 5.00
CT3 Peter Bondra .30 .75
CT4 Jean-Marc Pelletier .30 .75
CT5 Brendan Shanahan .40 1.00
CT6 Joe Sakic .75 2.00
CT7 J-S Giguere .30 .75
CT8 Brett Hull .50 1.25
CT9 Jaromir Jagr .60 1.50
CT10 Eric Brewer .30 .75
CT11 Sergei Samsonov .30 .75
CT12 Alexei Yashin .20 .50
CT13 Mats Sundin .40 1.00
CT14 Mike Modano .60 1.50
CT15 Al MacInnis .30 .75
CT16 Paul Mara .20 .50
CT17 David Legwand .30 .75
CT18 Eric Lindros .40 1.00
CT19 Peter Forsberg 1.00 2.50
CT20 Ray Bourque .60 1.50
CT21 Teemu Selanne .40 1.00
CT22 John LeClair .40 1.00
CT23 Dominik Hasek .75 2.00
CT24 Martin Brodeur 1.00 2.50
CT25 Tony Amonte .30 .75
CT26 Keith Tkachuk .40 1.00
CT27 Patrick Roy 2.00 5.00
CT28 Pavel Bure .40 1.00
CT29 Paul Kariya .40 1.00
CT30 Curtis Joseph .40 1.00

1999-00 Upper Deck Fantastic Finishers

Randomly inserted in Series One packs at the rate of 1:11, this 15-card set features a gray and white border and blue foil stamping. Silver and gold parallels were also created and inserted randomly. Silver parallels were limited to 100 serial numbered sets. Gold parallels were numbered 1/1 and are unpriced due to scarcity.

COMPLETE SET (15) 12.00 25.00
*SILVER STARS: 20X TO 50X BASIC CARDS
FF1 Brett Hull .60 1.50
FF2 John LeClair .50 1.25
FF3 Eric Lindros .50 1.25
FF4 Jaromir Jagr .75 2.00
FF5 Sergei Samsonov .40 1.00
FF6 Teemu Selanne .50 1.25
FF7 Alexei Yashin .40 1.00
FF8 Keith Tkachuk .50 1.25
FF9 Pavel Bure .50 1.25
FF10 Peter Forsberg 1.25 3.00
FF11 Brendan Shanahan .50 1.25
FF12 Tony Amonte .40 1.00
FF13 Paul Kariya .50 1.25
FF14 Steve Yzerman 2.50 6.00
FF15 Joe Sakic 1.00 2.50

1999-00 Upper Deck Game Jerseys

Randomly inserted in Series One packs at the rate of 1:287, this 18-card set features player action shots with a swatch of a game worn jersey in the shape of the NHL logo. A special Wayne Gretzky jersey card was released that features a swatch of an NHL jersey and a CHL jersey which are sequentially numbered to 99, and a special Nagano Olympic Gretzky jersey was issued as well. Several players have signed versions that are sequentially numbered to 25.

BH Brett Hull 10.00 25.00
DH Dominik Hasek 12.50 30.00
EL Eric Lindros 8.00 25.00
JJ Jaromir Jagr 12.50 30.00
JL John LeClair 8.00 25.00
JS Joe Sakic 15.00 40.00
MB Martin Brodeur 20.00 50.00
MM Mike Modano 10.00 25.00
PF Peter Forsberg 20.00 50.00
PR Patrick Roy 20.00 50.00
RB Ray Bourque 20.00 50.00
SF Sergei Fedorov 10.00 25.00
SS Sergei Samsonov 8.00 25.00
SY Steve Yzerman 20.00 50.00
TS Teemu Selanne 8.00 25.00
WG1 Wayne Gretzky 30.00 80.00
WG2 W.Gretzky Dual/99 300.00 600.00
WG3 Wayne Gretzky Nagano 125.00 300.00
BHS B.Hull AU/25 150.00 300.00

RBS R.Bourque AU/25 150.00 300.00
SYS S.Yzerman AU/25 250.00 500.00
WGS1 W.Gretzky AU/25 400.00 800.00

1999-00 Upper Deck Game Jerseys Series II

Randomly inserted in Series Two packs at the rate of 1:287, this 16-card set features player action photography coupled with a swatch of a game worn jersey. A special Canadian jersey card was issued for Steve Yzerman, and several players have autographed versions that are sequentially numbered to 25.

AM Al MacInnis 8.00 20.00
CJ Curtis Joseph 8.00 20.00
DH Dominik Hasek 15.00 40.00
EB Ed Belfour 8.00 20.00
JJ Jaromir Jagr 12.50 30.00
JL John LeClair 20.00 50.00
JR Jeremy Roenick 12.50 30.00
JT Joe Thornton 10.00 25.00
MB Martin Brodeur 20.00 50.00
PF Peter Forsberg 20.00 50.00
PK Paul Kariya 15.00 40.00
PR Patrick Roy 20.00 50.00
SF Sergei Fedorov 10.00 25.00
SY Steve Yzerman 20.00 50.00
TS Temmu Selanne 15.00 40.00
WG Wayne Gretzky 30.00 80.00
CJS C.Joseph AU/25 100.00 250.00
EBS E.Belfour AU/25 100.00 250.00
SYC Steve Yzerman CAN 20.00 50.00
SYS S.Yzerman AU/25 250.00 500.00
WGS W.Gretzky AU/25 400.00 800.00

1999-00 Upper Deck Game Jersey Patch

Randomly inserted in Series One packs, this 17-card set features premium swatches of game jersey patches. Unpriced 1/1 parallels also exist.

WG1P Wayne Gretzky 400.00 800.00
WG2P Wayne Gretzky 400.00 800.00
BHP Brett Hull 125.00 300.00
DHP Dominik Hasek 125.00 300.00
ELP Eric Lindros 75.00 200.00
JJP Jaromir Jagr 125.00 300.00
JLP John LeClair 75.00 200.00
JSP Joe Sakic 125.00 300.00
MBP Martin Brodeur 150.00 400.00
MMP Mike Modano 100.00 250.00
PFP Peter Forsberg 125.00 300.00
PRP Patrick Roy 150.00 400.00
RBP Ray Bourque 125.00 300.00
SFP Sergei Fedorov 125.00 300.00
SSP Sergei Samsonov 75.00 200.00
SYP Steve Yzerman 150.00 400.00
TSP Teemu Selanne 75.00 200.00

1999-00 Upper Deck Game Jersey Patch Series II

Randomly inserted in Series Two packs at a rate of 1:7500, this 14-card set features premium swatches of game used jersey patches. Unpriced 1/1 parallels also exist.

CJP Curtis Joseph 125.00 300.00
DHP Dominik Hasek 125.00 300.00
EBP Ed Belfour 125.00 300.00
JJP Jaromir Jagr 125.00 300.00
JLP John LeClair 60.00 150.00
JTP Joe Thornton 100.00 250.00
KTP Keith Tkachuk 60.00 150.00
MBP Martin Brodeur 150.00 400.00
PFP Peter Forsberg 125.00 300.00
PKP Paul Kariya 75.00 200.00
PRP Patrick Roy 150.00 400.00
SFP Sergei Fedorov 100.00 250.00
SYP Steve Yzerman 150.00 400.00
WGP Wayne Gretzky 400.00 800.00

1999-00 Upper Deck Game Pads

Randomly inserted in Series Two packs at the rate of 1:5000, this single card issue features a swatch of Curtis Joseph game used goalie pads.

CJGP Curtis Joseph 20.00 50.00

1999-00 Upper Deck Gretzky Profiles

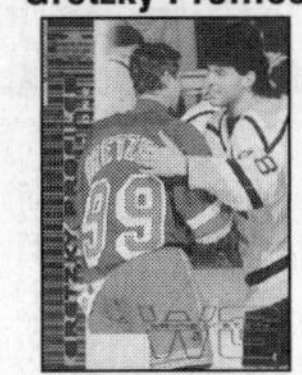

Randomly inserted in Series One Hobby packs at the rate of 1:23, this 10-card set pays tribute to the career of Wayne Gretzky. Both silver and gold parallels were also created. Silver parallels were serial numbered to 100, and gold to 1/1. Gold parallels not priced due to scarcity.

COMPLETE SET (10) 40.00 80.00
COMMON CARD (GP1-GP10) 4.00 10.00
COMMON SILVER (1-10) 30.00 80.00

1999-00 Upper Deck Headed for the Hall

Randomly seeded in Series Two pack, this 15-card set features top NHL players on an all silver foil card stock with foil stamp highlights. Silver and gold parallels were also created. Silver parallels were limited to 100 serial numbered sets. Unpriced gold parallels were numbered 1/1.

COMPLETE SET (15) 20.00 40.00
*SILVER STARS: 8X TO 20X BASIC CARDS

HOF1 Wayne Gretzky 5.00 12.00
HOF2 Dominik Hasek 1.50 4.00
HOF3 Ray Bourque 1.25 3.00
HOF4 Steve Yzerman 4.00 10.00
HOF5 Jaromir Jagr 1.25 3.00
HOF6 Brett Hull 1.00 2.50
HOF7 Eric Lindros .75 2.00
HOF8 Adam Oates .60 1.50
HOF9 Brian Leetch .75 2.00
HOF10 Patrick Roy 4.00 10.00
HOF11 Mark Messier .75 2.00
HOF12 Luc Robitaille .60 1.50
HOF13 Joe Sakic 1.50 4.00
HOF14 Chris Chelios .75 2.00
HOF15 Curtis Joseph .75 2.00

1999-00 Upper Deck Ice Gallery

Randomly inserted in Series Two packs at the rate of 1:72, this 10-card set features silver foil borders along the top and the two sided of the card with blue foil highlights. Silver and gold parallels were also created and inserted randomly. Silver parallels were limited to 100 serial numbered sets. Unpriced gold parallels were numbered 1/1.

COMPLETE SET (10) 40.00 80.00
*SILVER STARS: 4X TO 10X BASIC CARDS
IG1 Jaromir Jagr 4.00 10.00
IG2 Paul Kariya 3.00 8.00
IG3 Peter Forsberg 6.00 15.00
IG4 Dominik Hasek 5.00 12.00
IG5 Patrick Roy 12.50 30.00
IG6 Teemu Selanne 3.00 8.00
IG7 Eric Lindros 3.00 8.00
IG8 Patrik Stefan 4.00 10.00
IG9 Steve Kariya 3.00 8.00
IG10 Pavel Bure 3.00 8.00

1999-00 Upper Deck Marquee Attractions

Randomly seeded in Series One packs, this 15-card set features an all silver foil card stock with color player photography and blue foil highlights. Silver and gold parallels were also created. Silver parallels were limited to 100 serial numbered sets. Gold parallels were numbered 1/1 and are not priced.

COMPLETE SET (15) 12.00 25.00
*SILVER STARS: 20X TO 50X BASIC CARDS
MA1 Ray Bourque .75 2.00
MA2 Paul Kariya .50 1.25
MA3 Eric Lindros .50 1.25
MA4 Jaromir Jagr .75 2.00
MA5 Dominik Hasek 1.00 2.50
MA6 Patrick Roy 2.50 6.00
MA7 Alexei Yashin .40 1.00
MA8 Mats Sundin .50 1.25
MA9 Steve Yzerman 2.50 6.00
MA10 Pavel Bure .50 1.25
MA11 Vincent Lecavalier .50 1.25
MA12 Teemu Selanne .50 1.25
MA13 Mike Modano .75 2.00
MA14 Keith Tkachuk .50 1.25
MA15 Peter Forsberg 1.25 3.00

1999-00 Upper Deck New Ice Age

Randomly seeded in Series One packs, this 20-card set features foil card stock with color player photography and highlights several players ready to take the NHL in the 21st Century. Silver and gold parallels were also created. Silver parallels were limited to 100 serial numbered sets. Unpriced gold parallels were numbered 1/1.

COMPLETE SET (20) 20.00 40.00
*SILVER STARS: 10X TO 25X BASIC CARDS
N1 Jaromir Jagr 1.50 4.00
N2 Paul Kariya 1.00 2.50
N3 Sergei Samsonov .75 2.00
N4 Vadim Sharifijanov .40 1.00
N5 Ty Jones .40 1.00
N6 Teemu Selanne 1.00 2.50
N7 Martin Brodeur 2.50 6.00
N8 David Legwand .75 2.00
N9 Vincent Lecavalier 1.00 2.50
N10 Paul Mara .75 2.00
N11 Jean-Marc Pelletier .40 1.00
N12 J-S Giguere .75 2.00
N13 Marian Hossa 1.00 2.50
N14 Milan Hejduk 1.00 2.50
N15 Chris Drury .75 2.00
N16 Rico Fata .40 1.00
N17 Patrik Elias .75 2.00
N18 Eric Brewer .75 2.00
N19 Joe Thornton 1.50 4.00
N20 J-P Dumont .75 2.00

1999-00 Upper Deck NHL Scrapbook

Randomly seeded in Series Two packs, this 15-card set features a shadowed background with a full color player photograph and gold foil highlights. Silver and gold parallels were also created. Silver parallels were limited to 100 serial numbered sets. Gold parallels were numbered 1/1 and are not priced due to scarcity.

COMPLETE SET (15) 12.00 25.00
*SILVER: 20X TO 50X BASIC CARDS
SB1 Patrick Roy 2.50 6.00
SB2 Ray Bourque .75 2.00
SB3 Steve Yzerman 2.50 6.00
SB4 Jaromir Jagr .75 2.00
SB5 Paul Kariya .60 1.50
SB6 Peter Forsberg 1.25 3.00
SB7 Pavel Bure .60 1.50
SB8 Curtis Joseph .60 1.50
SB9 Brett Hull .60 1.50
SB10 Eric Lindros .60 1.50
SB11 Teemu Selanne .60 1.50
SB12 Brendan Shanahan .60 1.50
SB13 John LeClair .60 1.50
SB14 Steve Kariya .60 1.50
SB15 Patrik Stefan .75 2.00

1999-00 Upper Deck PowerDeck Inserts

Randomly inserted in Series 1 Hobby packs at the rate of 1:23 for base cards and one in 288 for Gretzky SP cards, this 9-card set is an actual CD-ROM that contains footage, interviews, and a photo gallery that can be viewed with a PC.

COMPLETE SET (9) 75.00 150.00
PD1 Dominik Hasek 3.00 8.00
PD2 Paul Kariya 2.00 5.00
PD3 Jaromir Jagr 2.50 6.00
PD4 Steve Yzerman 8.00 20.00
PD5 Patrick Roy 8.00 20.00
PD6 Brett Hull 2.00 5.00
PD7 Wayne Gretzky 12.50 25.00
PD8 Wayne Gretzky SP 30.00 80.00
PD9 Wayne Gretzky SP 30.00 80.00

1999-00 Upper Deck Sixth Sense

Randomly inserted in Series Two packs, this 20-card set highlights top players on a "framed" card stock with foil stamp highlights. Silver and gold parallels were also created. Silver parallels were limited to 100 serial numbered sets. Gold parallels were numbered 1/1 and are not priced due to scarcity.

COMPLETE SET (20) 12.00 25.00
*SILVER STARS: 25X TO 60X BASIC CARDS
SS1 Paul Kariya .40 1.00
SS2 Patrick Roy 2.00 5.00
SS3 Brett Hull .50 1.25
SS4 Eric Lindros .40 1.00
SS5 Sergei Samsonov .40 1.00
SS6 Peter Forsberg 1.00 2.50
SS7 Patrik Stefan .60 1.50
SS8 Steve Yzerman 2.00 5.00
SS9 Jaromir Jagr .60 1.50
SS10 David Legwand .40 1.00
SS11 Steve Kariya .50 1.25
SS12 Tim Connolly .40 1.00
SS13 Pavel Bure .40 1.00
SS14 Brendan Shanahan .40 1.00
SS15 Martin Brodeur 1.00 2.50
SS16 Dominik Hasek .75 2.00
SS17 Mats Sundin .40 1.00
SS18 Vincent Lecavalier .40 1.00
SS19 Keith Tkachuk .40 1.00
SS20 Mike Modano .60 1.50

1999-00 Upper Deck Ultimate Defense

Randomly inserted in Series Two packs, this 10-card set features top goalies on an all foil card with color borders to match each respective goalie's team colors and blue foil highlights. Silver and gold parallels were also created. Silver parallels were limited to 100 serial numbered sets. Gold parallels were numbered 1/1 and are not priced due to scarcity.

COMPLETE SET (10) 10.00 20.00
*SILVER STARS: 12.5X TO 30X BASIC CARDS
UD1 Byron Dafoe .60 1.50
UD2 Dominik Hasek 1.50 4.00
UD3 Patrick Roy 4.00 10.00
UD4 Chris Osgood .60 1.50
UD5 Ed Belfour .75 2.00
UD6 Roman Turek .60 1.50
UD7 Mike Richter .75 2.00
UD8 Nikolai Khabibulin .60 1.50
UD9 Martin Brodeur 2.00 5.00
UD10 Curtis Joseph .60 1.50

1999-00 Upper Deck Arena Giveaways

These promo cards were issued in various NHL cities and included 6 cards per team. Manufacturers Topps, Upper Deck, and Pacific were all represented with two cards per team set. The cards have the word's Tomorrow's Stars across the top, and are numbered with a team-coded prefix. They are extremely difficult to find in the secondary market, and command strong prices. Only the Upper Deck cards are listed below as the other cards can be found with the manufacturer's listings.

COMPLETE SET (56) 15.00 40.00
AM1 Ladislav Kohn .20 .50
AM2 Mike Leclerc .20 .50
AT1 Patrik Stefan .40 1.00
AT2 Shean Donovan .20 .50
BB1 Jonathan Girard .40 1.00
BB2 Sergei Samsonov 1.25 3.00
BS1 Maxim Afinogenov .75 2.00
BS2 Cory Sarich .20 .50
CA1 Alex Tanguay 1.25 3.00
CA2 Chris Drury 1.25 3.00
CB1 J-P Dumont .40 1.00
CB2 Bryan McCabe .20 .50
CF1 Robyn Regehr .20 .50
CF2 Derek Morris .40 1.00
CH1 Dave Tanabe .20 .50
CH2 Jeff O'Neill .40 1.00
DR1 Jiri Fischer .40 1.00
DR2 Darryl Laplante .20 .50
DS1 Brenden Morrow .75 2.00
DS2 Jamie Langenbrunner .40 1.00
EO1 Paul Comrie .20 .50
EO2 Boyd Devereaux .20 .50
FP1 Ivan Novoseltsev .40 1.00
FP2 Mark Parrish .40 1.00
LK1 Frantisek Kaberle .20 .50
LK2 Aki Berg .20 .50
MC1 Mike Ribeiro .20 .50
MC2 Arron Asham .20 .50
ND1 Scott Gomez .75 2.00
ND2 Sheldon Souray .20 .50
NI1 Roberto Luongo 2.50 6.00
NI2 Tim Connolly .75 2.00
NP1 David Legwand .40 1.00
NP2 Randy Robitaille .20 .50
NR1 Michael York .40 1.00
NR2 Manny Malhotra .20 .50
OS1 Mike Fisher .40 1.00
OS2 Chris Phillips .20 .50
PC1 Trevor Letowski .75 2.00
PC2 Shane Doan .75 2.00
PF1 Simon Gagne 1.25 3.00
PF2 Daymond Langkow .40 1.00
PP1 Andrew Ference .20 .50
PP2 Michal Rozsival .20 .50
SB1 Jochen Hecht .40 1.00
SB2 Michal Handzus .75 2.00
SS1 Brad Stuart .40 1.00
SS2 Jeff Friesen .40 1.00
TL1 Paul Mara .20 .50
TL2 Andrei Zyuzin .20 .50
TM1 Nikolai Antropov .75 2.00
TM2 Danny Markov .20 .50
VC1 Steve Kariya .75 2.00
VC2 Peter Schaefer .20 .50
WC1 Jeff Halpern .40 1.00
WC2 Alexei Tezikov .20 .50

2006-07 Upper Deck Arena Giveaways

ANA1 Corey Perry 1.25 3.00
ANA2 Teemu Selanne 1.50 4.00
ANA3 Andy McDonald .75 2.00
ANA4 Scott Niedermayer .75 2.00
ANA5 Jean-Sebastien Giguere 1.25 3.00
ANA6 Chris Pronger 1.25 3.00
ATL1 Marian Hossa 1.25 3.00
ATL2 Slava Kozlov .75 2.00
ATL3 Bobby Holik .75 2.00
ATL4 Ilya Kovalchuk 2.00 5.00
ATL5 Steve Rucchin .75 2.00
ATL6 Kari Lehtonen 1.50 4.00
BOS1 Brad Boyes .75 2.00
BOS2 Hannu Toivonen 1.25 3.00
BOS3 Patrice Bergeron 1.50 4.00
BOS4 Zdeno Chara .75 2.00
BOS5 Marc Savard .75 2.00
BOS6 Glen Murray .75 2.00
BUF1 Ryan Miller 1.50 4.00
BUF2 Thomas Vanek 1.25 3.00
BUF3 Daniel Briere 1.25 3.00
BUF4 Jason Pominville .75 2.00
BUF5 Maxim Afinogenov .75 2.00
BUF6 Chris Drury .75 2.00
CAR1 Eric Staal 1.50 4.00
CAR2 Cam Ward 1.50 4.00
CAR3 Justin Williams .75 2.00
CAR4 Erik Cole .75 2.00
CAR5 Andrew Ladd .75 2.00
CAR6 Rod Brind`Amour 1.25 3.00
CGY1 Jarome Iginla 2.00 5.00
CGY2 Dion Phaneuf 2.00 5.00
CGY3 Chuck Kobasew .75 2.00
CGY4 Alex Tanguay 1.25 3.00
CGY5 Daymond Langkow .75 2.00
CGY6 Miikka Kiprusoff 1.50 4.00
CHI1 Tuomo Ruutu .75 2.00
CHI2 Martin Havlat 1.25 3.00
CHI3 Brent Seabrook .75 2.00
CHI4 Adrian Aucoin .75 2.00
CHI5 Bryan Smolinski .75 2.00
CHI6 Nikolai Khabibulin 1.50 4.00
CLB1 Rick Nash 1.50 4.00
CLB2 Pascal LeClaire 1.25 3.00
CLB3 Adam Foote .75 2.00
CLB4 Fredrik Modin .75 2.00
CLB5 Gilbert Brule 1.50 4.00
CLB6 Sergei Fedorov 1.50 4.00
COL1 Jose Theodore 1.50 4.00
COL2 Wojtek Wolski .75 2.00
COL3 John-Michael Liles .75 2.00
COL4 Joe Sakic 3.00 8.00
COL5 Marek Svatos .75 2.00
COL6 Milan Hejduk .75 2.00
DAL1 Brenden Morrow 1.25 3.00
DAL1 Brenden Morrow 1.25 3.00
DAL2 Jussi Jokinen .75 2.00
DAL2 Jussi Jokinen .75 2.00
DAL3 Sergei Zubov .75 2.00
DAL3 Sergei Zubov .75 2.00
DAL4 Mike Modano 1.50 4.00
DAL4 Mike Modano 1.50 4.00
DAL5 Eric Lindros 1.50 4.00
DAL5 Eric Lindros 1.50 4.00
DAL6 Marty Turco 1.25 3.00
DET1 Kris Draper .75 2.00
DET2 Dominik Hasek 2.50 6.00
DET3 Chris Chelios 1.25 3.00
DET4 Henrik Zetterberg 1.50 4.00
DET5 Nicklas Lidstrom 1.50 4.00
DET6 Pavel Datsyuk 1.25 3.00
EDM1 Ales Hemsky .75 2.00
EDM2 Fernando Pisani .75 2.00
EDM3 Jarret Stoll .75 2.00
EDM4 Ryan Smyth 1.25 3.00
EDM5 Joffrey Lupul .75 2.00
EDM6 Dwayne Roloson 1.50 4.00
FLA1 Jay Bouwmeester .75 2.00
FLA2 Nathan Horton .75 2.00
FLA3 Stephen Weiss .75 2.00
FLA4 Olli Jokinen .75 2.00
FLA5 Ed Belfour 1.50 4.00
FLA6 Todd Bertuzzi 1.25 3.00
LAK1 Alexander Frolov .75 2.00
LAK2 Lubomir Visnovsky .75 2.00
LAK3 Dustin Brown .75 2.00
LAK4 Rob Blake 1.25 3.00
LAK5 Craig Conroy .75 2.00
LAK6 Mike Cammalleri .75 2.00
MIN1 Marian Gaborik 2.00 5.00
MIN2 Pierre-Marc Bouchard .75 2.00
MIN3 Brian Rolston .75 2.00
MIN4 Pavol Demitra .75 2.00
MIN5 Mark Parrish .75 2.00
MIN6 Manny Fernandez 1.25 3.00
NJD1 Martin Brodeur 5.00 12.00
NJD2 Brian Gionta .75 2.00
NJD3 Zach Parise 1.25 3.00
NJD4 Brian Rafalski .75 2.00
NJD5 Scott Gomez .75 2.00
NJD6 Patrik Elias .75 2.00
NSH1 Tomas Vokoun 1.25 3.00
NSH2 David Legwand .75 2.00
NSH3 Kimmo Timonen .75 2.00
NSH4 Paul Kariya 1.50 4.00
NSH5 Jason Arnott .75 2.00
NSH6 Steve Sullivan .75 2.00
NYI1 Rick DiPietro 1.25 3.00
NYI2 Jeff Tambellini .75 2.00
NYI3 Jason Blake .75 2.00
NYI4 Trent Hunter .75 2.00
NYI5 Alexei Yashin .75 2.00
NYI6 Miroslav Satan .75 2.00
NYR1 Jaromir Jagr 2.50 6.00
NYR2 Petr Prucha .75 2.00
NYR3 Martin Straka .75 2.00
NYR4 Henrik Lundqvist 2.00 5.00
NYR5 Michael Nylander .75 2.00
NYR6 Brendan Shanahan 1.50 4.00
OTT1 Jason Spezza 1.50 4.00
OTT2 Chris Phillips .75 2.00
OTT3 Dany Heatley 2.00 5.00
OTT4 Wade Redden .75 2.00
OTT5 Martin Gerber 1.50 4.00
OTT6 Daniel Alfredsson 1.25 3.00
PHI1 Peter Forsberg 2.50 6.00
PHI2 Robert Esche 1.25 3.00
PHI3 Joni Pitkanen .75 2.00
PHI4 Simon Gagne 1.50 4.00
PHI5 Antero Niittymaki 1.25 3.00
PHI6 Jeff Carter 1.50 4.00
PHX1 Shane Doan .75 2.00
PHX2 Ladislav Nagy .75 2.00
PHX3 Ed Jovanovski .75 2.00
PHX4 Jeremy Roenick 2.00 5.00
PHX5 Owen Nolan 1.25 3.00
PHX6 Curtis Joseph 1.50 4.00
PIT1 Sidney Crosby 12.00 30.00
PIT2 Colby Armstrong .75 2.00
PIT3 Sergei Gonchar .75 2.00
PIT4 Ryan Malone .75 2.00
PIT5 Mark Recchi .75 2.00
PIT6 Marc-Andre Fleury 1.50 4.00
SJS1 Joe Thornton 2.50 6.00
SJS2 Vesa Toskala 1.25 3.00
SJS3 Steve Bernier .75 2.00
SJS4 Patrick Marleau 1.25 3.00
SJS5 Evgeni Nabokov 1.25 3.00
SJS6 Jonathan Cheechoo 1.50 4.00
STL1 Keith Tkachuk 1.25 3.00
STL2 Barret Jackman .75 2.00
STL3 Lee Stempniak .75 2.00
STL4 Manny Legace 1.25 3.00
STL5 Bill Guerin .75 2.00
STL6 Doug Weight .75 2.00
TBL1 Martin St. Louis 1.25 3.00
TBL2 Vaclav Prospal .75 2.00
TBL3 Ruslan Fedotenko .75 2.00
TBL4 Vincent Lecavalier 1.50 4.00
TBL5 Marc Denis 1.25 3.00
TBL6 Brad Richards 1.25 3.00
TOR1 Mats Sundin 1.50 4.00
TOR2 Darcy Tucker .75 2.00
TOR3 Alexander Steen 1.25 3.00
TOR4 Andrew Raycroft 1.25 3.00
TOR5 Michael Peca .75 2.00
TOR6 Bryan McCabe .75 2.00
VAN1 Markus Naslund 1.50 4.00
VAN2 Henrik Sedin .75 2.00
VAN3 Roberto Luongo 2.00 5.00
VAN4 Brendan Morrison .75 2.00
VAN5 Trevor Linden .75 2.00
VAN6 Daniel Sedin .75 2.00
WSH1 Shaone Morrisonn .75 2.00
WSH2 Alexander Semin 1.25 3.00
WSH3 Alexander Ovechkin 5.00 12.00
WSH4 Richard Zednik .75 2.00
WSH5 Dainius Zubrus .75 2.00
WSH6 Olaf Kolzig 1.50 4.00

1999-00 Upper Deck Sobey's Memorial Cup

Released by Upper Deck in conjunction with Sobey's grocery stores and Kraft, this 16-card set features players and designs from the 1999-2000 Upper Deck NHL Prospects set and pays tribute the 2000 Memorial Cup tournament. The cards were available in 4-card cello packs over a four-week period at Sobey's stores in the Halifax area. The cards mirror the UD CHL series issued earlier that year, but feature several small design changes, including the addition of a Sobey's logo.

COMPLETE SET (16) 10.00 25.00
1 Alexei Volkov .80 2.00
2 Justin Papineau .80 2.00
3 Michael Henrich .40 1.00
4 Kris Beech .40 1.00
5 Mark Bell 1.20 4.00
6 Andrei Shefer .40 1.00
7 Pavel Brendl .40 1.00
8 Blake Robson .40 1.00
9 Ben Knopp .40 1.00
10 Maxime Ouellet .80 2.00
11 Thatcher Bell .40 1.00
12 Brian Finley .80 2.00
13 Jared Aulin 2.00 4.00
14 Jared Newman .40 1.00
15 Brad Boyes 4.00 10.00
16 Miguel Delisle .40 1.00

2000-01 Upper Deck

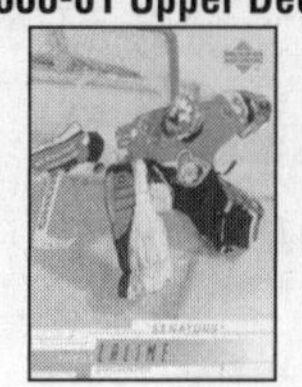

Released as a 440-card set, Upper Deck is comprised of 180 veteran cards and 50 short printed prospect cards (181-230) in series one, and 180 veteran cards and 30 short printed prospect cards (411-440) in series two. Base cards have full color action photography and foil highlights. Upper Deck was packaged in 24-pack boxes with packs containing 10 cards and carried a suggested retail price of $2.99.

COMPLETE SET (230) 200.00 400.00
COMP.SER.1 (230) 125.00 250.00
COMP.SER.1 w/o SP's (180) 15.00 30.00
COMP.SER.2 (210) 100.00 200.00
COMP.SER.2 w/o SP's (180) 10.00 25.00
1 Paul Kariya .20 .50
2 Steve Rucchin .02 .10
3 Oleg Tverdovsky .02 .10
4 Mike Leclerc .02 .10
5 Ladislav Kohn .02 .10
6 Guy Hebert .15 .40
7 Dean Sylvester .02 .10
8 Andrew Brunette .15 .40
9 Ray Ferraro .02 .10
10 Donald Audette .02 .10
11 Damian Rhodes .02 .10
12 Patrik Stefan .02 .10
13 Joe Thornton .30 .75
14 Brian Rolston .02 .10
15 John Grahame .15 .40
16 Jason Allison .02 .10
17 Kyle McLaren .02 .10
18 Andre Savage .02 .10
19 Martin Biron .15 .40
20 Doug Gilmour .15 .40
21 Chris Gratton .02 .10
22 Miroslav Satan .15 .40
23 Maxim Afinogenov .02 .10
24 Dimitri Kalinin .02 .10
25 Oleg Saprykin .02 .10
26 Valeri Bure .02 .10
27 Derek Morris .02 .10
28 Marc Savard .02 .10
29 Clarke Wilm .02 .10
30 Fred Brathwaite .15 .40
31 Ron Francis .15 .40
32 Sami Kapanen .02 .10
33 Bates Battaglia .02 .10
34 Arturs Irbe .15 .40
35 Dave Tanabe .02 .10
36 Rod Brind'Amour .15 .40
37 Michal Grosek .02 .10
38 Steve Sullivan .02 .10
39 Eric Daze .15 .40
40 Bryan McCabe .02 .10
41 Michael Nylander .02 .10
42 Alexei Zhamnov .02 .10
43 Milan Hejduk .20 .50
44 Ray Bourque .40 1.00
45 Patrick Roy 1.00 2.50
46 Peter Forsberg .50 1.25
47 Martin Skoula .02 .10
48 Shjon Podein .02 .10
49 Aaron Miller .02 .10
50 Espen Knutsen .02 .10
51 Jamie Pushor .02 .10
52 Kevyn Adams .02 .10
53 Marc Denis .15 .40
54 Ron Tugnutt .15 .40
55 Mike Modano .30 .75
56 Joe Nieuwendyk .15 .40
57 Mike Keane .02 .10
58 Darryl Sydor .02 .10
59 Brenden Morrow .15 .40
60 Jere Lehtinen .15 .40
61 Derian Hatcher .02 .10
62 Brendan Shanahan .20 .50
63 Sergei Fedorov .30 .75
64 Darren McCarty .02 .10
65 Tomas Holmstrom .02 .10
66 Chris Osgood .15 .40
67 Nicklas Lidstrom .20 .50
68 Ryan Smyth .15 .40
69 Igor Ulanov .02 .10
70 Tommy Salo .15 .40
71 Ethan Moreau .02 .10
72 Daniel Cleary .02 .10
73 Bill Guerin .15 .40
74 Pavel Bure .20 .50
75 Ray Whitney .15 .40
76 Lance Pitlick .02 .10
77 Trevor Kidd .15 .40
78 Mike Wilson .02 .10
79 Ivan Novoseltsev .15 .40
80 Luc Robitaille .15 .40
81 Stephane Fiset .15 .40
82 Rob Blake .15 .40
83 Jozef Stumpel .02 .10
84 Craig Johnson .02 .10
85 Glen Murray .02 .10
86 Kelly Buchberger .02 .10
87 Manny Fernandez .15 .40
88 Stacy Roest .02 .10
89 Andy Sutton .02 .10
90 Scott Pellerin .02 .10
91 Jim Dowd .02 .10
92 Dainius Zubrus .02 .10
93 Brian Savage .02 .10
94 Martin Rucinsky .02 .10
95 Craig Darby .02 .10
96 Jose Theodore .25 .60
97 David Legwand .15 .40
98 Rob Valicevic .02 .10
99 Randy Robitaille .02 .10
100 Mike Dunham .15 .40
101 Kimmo Timonen .02 .10

102 Scott Gomez .02 .10
103 Petr Sykora .02 .10
104 Alexander Mogilny .15 .40
105 John Madden .02 .10
106 Jason Arnott .02 .10
107 Sergei Brylin .02 .10
108 Scott Stevens .15 .40
109 Tim Connolly .02 .10
110 Mariusz Czerkawski .02 .10
111 Zdeno Chara .02 .10
112 Kenny Jonsson .02 .10
113 Claude Lapointe .02 .10
114 Theo Fleury .02 .10
115 Mike Richter .20 .50
116 Mike York .02 .10
117 Jan Hlavac .15 .40
118 Adam Graves .02 .10
119 Mark Messier .20 .50
120 Marian Hossa .20 .50
121 Daniel Alfredsson .15 .40
122 Mike Fisher .15 .40
123 Patrick Lalime .15 .40
124 Wade Redden .02 .10
125 Shawn McEachern .02 .10
126 John LeClair .20 .50
127 Mark Recchi .15 .40
128 Brian Boucher .20 .50
129 Simon Gagne .20 .50
130 Eric Desjardins .15 .40
131 Rick Tocchet .15 .40
132 Jeremy Roenick .25 .60
133 Travis Green .02 .10
134 Trevor Letowski .02 .10
135 Teppo Numminen .02 .10
136 Shane Doan .02 .10
137 Mike Sullivan .02 .10
138 Jaromir Jagr .30 .75
139 Robert Lang .02 .10
140 Jan Hrdina .02 .10
141 Matthew Barnaby .02 .10
142 Jean-Sebastien Aubin .15 .40
143 Jiri Slegr .02 .10
144 Owen Nolan .15 .40
145 Jeff Friesen .02 .10
146 Patrick Marleau .15 .40
147 Brad Stuart .15 .40
148 Steve Shields .15 .40
149 Todd Harvey .02 .10
150 Pavol Demitra .15 .40
151 Chris Pronger .15 .40
152 Scott Young .02 .10
153 Todd Reirden .02 .10
154 Roman Turek .15 .40
155 Marty Reasoner .15 .40
156 Mike Johnson .02 .10
157 Todd Warriner .02 .10
158 Paul Mara .02 .10
159 Dan Cloutier .15 .40
160 Fredrik Modin .02 .10
161 Curtis Joseph .20 .50
162 Steve Thomas .02 .10
163 Darcy Tucker .02 .10
164 Yanic Perreault .02 .10
165 Sergei Berezin .02 .10
166 Dimitri Yushkevich .02 .10
167 Markus Naslund .20 .50
168 Andrew Cassels .02 .10
169 Todd Bertuzzi .20 .50
170 Felix Potvin .20 .50
171 Ed Jovanovski .15 .40
172 Trent Klatt .02 .10
173 Adam Oates .15 .40
174 Chris Simon .02 .10
175 Richard Zednik .02 .10
176 Calle Johansson .02 .10
177 Andrei Nikolishin .02 .10
178 Jeff Halpern .02 .10
179 Steve Yzerman CL .20 .50
180 Curtis Joseph CL .15 .40
181 Eric Nickulas RC 2.00 5.00
182 Serge Aubin RC 2.00 5.00
183 Keith Aldridge RC 2.00 5.00
184 Mike Minard RC 2.00 5.00
185 Steven Reinprecht RC 2.00 5.00
186 David Gosselin RC 2.00 5.00
187 Andrew Berenzweig 2.00 5.00
188 Willie Mitchell RC 2.00 5.00
189 Colin White RC 2.00 5.00
190 Petr Mika RC 2.00 5.00
191 Steve Valiquette RC 2.00 5.00
192 Kyle Freadrich RC 2.00 5.00
193 Rich Parent RC 2.00 5.00
194 Greg Andrusak RC 2.00 5.00
195 Brent Sopel RC 2.00 5.00
196 Matt Pettinger RC 2.00 5.00
197 Chris Nielsen RC 2.00 5.00
198 Dany Heatley RC 25.00 60.00
199 Matt Zultek RC 2.00 5.00
200 Dmitri Afanasenkov RC 2.00 5.00
201 Tyler Bouck RC 1.25 3.00
202 Jonas Andersson RC 2.00 5.00
203 Marc-Andre Thinel RC 2.00 5.00
204 Jaroslav Svoboda RC 2.00 5.00
205 Josef Vasicek RC 2.00 5.00
206 Andrew Raycroft RC 5.00 12.00
207 Juraj Kolnik RC 2.00 5.00
208 Zdenek Blatny RC 2.00 5.00
209 Sebastien Caron RC 1.50 4.00
210 Michael Ryder RC 10.00 25.00
211 Jason Jaspers RC 2.00 5.00
212 Pavel Brendl 2.00 5.00
213 Milan Kraft 2.00 5.00
214 Justin Williams RC 3.00 8.00
215 Andreas Karlsson 2.00 5.00
216 Herbert Vasilijevs RC 2.00 5.00
217 Sergei Vyshedkevich RC 2.00 5.00
218 Johnathan Aitken RC 2.00 5.00
219 Brandon Smith RC 2.00 5.00
220 Jeff Cowan RC 2.00 5.00
221 Steve Brule RC 2.00 5.00
222 Johan Witehall RC 2.00 5.00
223 Jani Hurme RC 3.00 8.00
224 Jean-Guy Trudel RC 2.00 5.00
225 Kaspars Astashenko RC 2.00 5.00
226 Scott Hartnell RC 3.00 8.00
227 Dieter Kochan RC 2.00 5.00
228 Rostislav Klesla RC 3.00 8.00
229 Marian Gaborik RC 30.00 60.00
230 Alfie Michaud 2.00 5.00
231 Teemu Selanne .20 .50
232 Matt Cullen .02 .10
233 German Titov .02 .10
234 Vitali Vishnevski .02 .10
235 Pavel Trnka .02 .10
236 Marty McInnis .02 .10
237 Hnat Domenichelli .02 .10
238 Per Svartvadet .02 .10
239 Steve Guolla .02 .10
240 Frantisek Kaberle .02 .10
241 Steve Staios .02 .10
242 Byron Dafoe .15 .40
243 Peter Popovic .02 .10
244 Paul Coffey .20 .50
245 Sergei Samsonov .15 .40
246 Andrei Kovalenko .02 .10
247 Shawn Bates .02 .10
248 Dominik Hasek .40 1.00
249 Stu Barnes .02 .10
250 Curtis Brown .02 .10
251 Alexei Zhitnik .02 .10
252 Jay McKee .02 .10
253 Vaclav Varada .02 .10
254 Jarome Iginla .25 .60
255 Phil Housley .02 .10
256 Cory Stillman .02 .10
257 Mike Vernon .02 .10
258 Jeff Shantz .02 .10
259 Brad Werenka .02 .10
260 Jeff O'Neill .02 .10
261 Martin Gelinas .02 .10
262 Tommy Westlund .02 .10
263 Steve Halko .02 .10
264 Sandis Ozolinsh .02 .10
265 Rob DiMaio .02 .10
266 Tony Amonte .15 .40
267 Jocelyn Thibault .15 .40
268 Boris Mironov .02 .10
269 Dean McAmmond .02 .10
270 Jean-Yves Leroux .02 .10
271 Valeri Zelepukin .02 .10
272 Nolan Pratt .02 .10
273 Joe Sakic .40 1.00
274 Chris Drury .15 .40
275 Alex Tanguay .15 .40
276 Adam Deadmarsh .02 .10
277 Stephane Yelle .02 .10
278 Ron Tugnutt .15 .40
279 Geoff Sanderson .02 .10
280 Steve Heinze .02 .10
281 Jean-Luc Grand-Pierre .02 .10
282 Robert Kron .02 .10
283 Kevin Dineen .02 .10
284 Brett Hull .25 .60
285 Sergei Zubov .02 .10
286 Jamie Langenbrunner .02 .10
287 Ed Belfour .20 .50
288 Roman Lyashenko .02 .10
289 Ted Donato .02 .10
290 Martin LaPointe .02 .10
291 Chris Chelios .20 .50
292 Slava Kozlov .02 .10
293 Steve Yzerman 1.00 2.50
294 Larry Murphy .02 .10
295 Brent Gilchrist .02 .10
296 Doug Weight .15 .40
297 Eric Brewer .02 .10
298 Todd Marchant .02 .10
299 Tom Poti .15 .40
300 Mike Grier .02 .10
301 Georges Laraque .02 .10
302 Igor Larionov .02 .10
303 Roberto Luongo .25 .60
304 Olli Jokinen .15 .40
305 Viktor Kozlov .15 .40
306 Robert Svehla .02 .10
307 Mike Sillinger .02 .10
308 Jere Karalahti .02 .10
309 Zigmund Palffy .15 .40
310 Mattias Norstrom .02 .10
311 Bryan Smolinski .02 .10
312 Jamie Storr .15 .40
313 Ian Laperriere .02 .10
314 Manny Fernandez .15 .40
315 Sergei Krivokrasov .02 .10
316 Darryl Laplante .02 .10
317 Sean O'Donnell .02 .10
318 Scott Pellerin .02 .10
319 Saku Koivu .20 .50
320 Sergei Zholtok .02 .10
321 Jeff Hackett .15 .40
322 Eric Weinrich .02 .10
323 Karl Dykhuis .02 .10
324 Benoit Brunet .02 .10
325 Cliff Ronning .02 .10
326 Patric Kjellberg .02 .10
327 Drake Berehowsky .02 .10
328 Vitali Yachmenev .02 .10
329 Tomas Vokoun .15 .40
330 Greg Johnson .02 .10
331 Patrik Elias .15 .40
332 Bobby Holik .02 .10
333 Randy McKay .02 .10
334 Brian Rafalski .02 .10
335 Martin Brodeur .50 1.25
336 Sergei Brylin .02 .10
337 Brad Isbister .15 .40
338 Roman Hamrlik .02 .10
339 John Vanbiesbrouck .15 .40
340 Dave Scatchard .02 .10
341 Oleg Kvasha .02 .10
342 Mark Parrish .02 .10
343 Petr Nedved .02 .10
344 Brian Leetch .15 .40
345 Radek Dvorak .02 .10
346 Vladimir Malakhov .02 .10
347 Valeri Kamensky .02 .10
348 Rich Pilon .02 .10
349 Radek Bonk .02 .10
350 Vaclav Prospal .02 .10
351 Jason York .02 .10
352 Andreas Dackell .02 .10
353 Magnus Arvedson .02 .10
354 Rob Zamuner .02 .10
355 Daymond Langkow .15 .40
356 Keith Primeau .02 .10
357 Dan McGillis .02 .10
358 Andy Delmore .02 .10
359 Jody Hull .02 .10
360 Luke Richardson .02 .10
361 Joe Juneau .02 .10
362 Mika Alatalo .02 .10
363 Keith Tkachuk .20 .50
364 Radoslav Suchy .02 .10
365 Louie DeBrusk .02 .10
366 Sean Burke .15 .40
367 Martin Straka .02 .10
368 Alexei Kovalev .15 .40
369 Alexei Morozov .02 .10
370 Josef Beranek .02 .10
371 Milan Kraft .02 .10
372 Darius Kasparaitis .02 .10
373 Vincent Damphousse .02 .10
374 Mike Ricci .02 .10
375 Scott Thornton .02 .10
376 Niklas Sundstrom .02 .10
377 Marco Sturm .15 .40
378 Jeff Norton .02 .10
379 Pierre Turgeon .15 .40
380 Al MacInnis .15 .40
381 Jochen Hecht .02 .10
382 Sean Hill .02 .10
383 Pavol Demitra .15 .40
384 Michal Handzus .02 .10
385 Mike Eastwood .02 .10
386 Vincent Lecavalier .20 .50
387 Brian Holzinger .02 .10
388 Pavel Kubina .02 .10
389 Andrei Zyuzin .02 .10
390 Wayne Primeau .02 .10
391 Mats Sundin .20 .50
392 Gary Roberts .02 .10
393 Igor Korolev .02 .10
394 Shayne Corson .02 .10
395 Tomas Kaberle .02 .10
396 Cory Cross .02 .10
397 Peter Schaefer .02 .10
398 Adrian Aucoin .02 .10
399 Brendan Morrison .15 .40
400 Daniel Sedin .02 .10
401 Donald Brashear .02 .10
402 Henrik Sedin .02 .10
403 Joe Murphy .02 .10
404 Steve Konowalchuk .02 .10
405 Joe Reekie .02 .10
406 Sergei Gonchar .02 .10
407 Peter Bondra .20 .50
408 Olaf Kolzig .15 .40
409 Steve Yzerman CL 1.00 2.50
410 Mark Messier CL .20 .50
411 Rick DiPietro RC 8.00 20.00
412 Michel Riesen RC 2.00 5.00
413 Reto Von Arx RC 2.00 5.00
414 Martin Havlat RC 8.00 20.00
415 Matt Elich RC 2.00 5.00
416 Jonas Ronnqvist RC 2.00 5.00
417 Jason Labarbera RC 3.00 8.00
418 Marc Moro RC 2.00 5.00
419 Mark Smith RC 2.00 5.00
420 Petr Hubacek RC 2.00 5.00
421 Niclas Wallin RC 2.00 5.00
422 Brian Swanson RC 2.00 5.00
423 Petteri Nummelin RC 2.50 6.00
424 Alexandre Boikov RC 2.00 5.00
425 Ossi Vaananen RC 2.00 5.00
426 Roman Simicek RC 2.00 5.00
427 Greg Classen RC 2.00 5.00
428 Marty Turco RC 6.00 15.00
429 Shane Hnidy RC 2.00 5.00
430 Lubomir Visnovsky RC 3.00 8.00
431 Bryce Salvador RC 2.00 5.00
432 Lubomir Sekeras RC 2.00 5.00
433 David Aebischer RC 6.00 15.00
434 Peter Ratchuk RC 2.00 5.00
435 Roman Cechmanek RC 2.00 5.00
436 Eric Belanger RC 2.00 5.00
437 Alexander Kharitonov RC 2.00 5.00
438 Jeff Bateman RC 2.00 5.00
439 Damian Surma RC 2.00 5.00
440 Jordan Krestanovich RC 2.00 5.00

2000-01 Upper Deck Exclusives Tier 1

Randomly inserted in Hobby packs, this 440-card set parallels the base set enhanced with silver foil. Each card is sequentially numbered to 100.
*EXC.TIER 1 STARS: 12X TO 30X BASIC CARDS
*EXC.TIER 1 SP's: 1.25X TO 2.5X BASIC CARDS
*EXC.TIER 1 SP RC's: 1X TO 2.5X

2000-01 Upper Deck Exclusives Tier 2

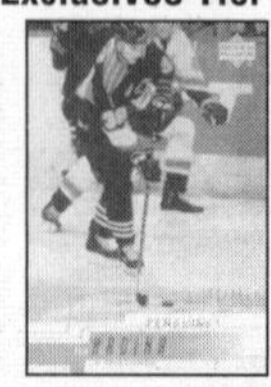

Randomly inserted in Hobby packs, this 440-card set parallels the base set enhanced with gold foil. Each card is sequentially numbered to 25.
*EXC.TIER 2 STARS: 60X TO 150X BASIC CARDS
*EXC.TIER 2 SP's: 2X TO 5X BASIC CARDS
*EXC.TIER 2 SP RC's: 1.5X TO 4X

2000-01 Upper Deck 500 Goal Club

Randomly inserted in various Upper Deck product packs, this set pays tribute to the members of the esteemed 500-goal club. Each card contains a swatch of a game worn jersey or stick in the shape of the NHL logo. Card numbers on the back carry a "500" prefix. Dale Hawerchuk and Mike Gartner were randomly found in Black Diamond and only 650 unsigned versions were produced. Pat Verbeek and Mario Lemieux were randomly available in SPx with a total of 800 unsigned cards produced of each and 25 serial-numbered autographed versions. Phil Esposito was randomly available in Upper Deck Ice with 450 unsigned cards and 25 serial-numbered signed cards produced. Dave Andreychuk and John Bucyk were randomly available in Upper Deck Legends with a total of 900 unsigned cards produced between the two players and 25 serial-numbered autographed versions of each. Frank Mahovlich and Lanny McDonald were randomly available in Upper Deck MVP with 600 unsigned cards produced and 25 serial-numbered autographed versions. Mark Messier was available in Upper Deck Vintage, 300 total cards were issued for the unsigned version, and 25 autographed copies were issued. Jari Kurri, Joe Mullen, Mark Messier, and Wayne Gretzky were all randomly available in Upper Deck Series I packs. A serial-numbered autographed version of each was also produced. Mark Messier was the only player inserted in series 2 packs.

500DA Dave Andreychuk J 12.50 30.00
500DA Dave Andreychuk AU/25 150.00 300.00
500DH Dale Hawerchuk J 20.00 50.00
500DH Dale Hawerchuk AU/25 150.00 300.00
500FM Frank Mahovlich S 50.00 100.00
500FM Frank Mahovlich AU/25 200.00 400.00
500JK Jari Kurri J 40.00 100.00
500JK Jarri Kurri AU/25 400.00 600.00
500JM Joe Mullen J 40.00 100.00
500JM Joe Mullen AU/25 100.00 250.00
500LM Lanny McDonald S 20.00 50.00
500LM Lanny McDonald AU/25 300.00 450.00
500MG Michel Goulet S 12.50 30.00
500MG Michel Goulet AU/25 100.00 250.00
500ML Mario Lemieux J 125.00 300.00
500ML M.Lemieux AU/25 800.00 1000.00
500MM Mark Messier J 30.00 80.00
500MM Mark Messier AU/25 250.00600.00
500MM Mark Messier AU/25 500.00800.00
500PE Phil Esposito/450 S 15.00 40.00
500PE Phil Esposito AU/25 200.00 400.00
500PV Pat Verbeek J 12.50 30.00
500PV Pat Verbeek AU/25 125.00 250.00
500WG Wayne Gretzky J 60.00 150.00
500WG Wayne Gretzky AU/25 1000.00 2000.00
500JBU John Bucyk S 12.50 30.00
500JBU John Bucyk AU/25 150.00 300.00
500MGA Mike Gartner J 12.50 30.00
500MGA Mike Gartner AU/25 300.00 500.00

2000-01 Upper Deck All-Star Class

COMPLETE SET (10) 8.00 15.00
STATED ODDS 1:23 SERIES 2
A1 Teemu Selanne .60 1.50
A2 Valeri Bure .60 1.50
A3 Milan Hejduk .60 1.50
A4 Mike Modano 1.00 2.50
A5 Pavel Bure 1.00 2.50
A6 Marian Hossa .60 1.50
A7 Brian Boucher .60 1.50
A8 Keith Tkachuk .60 1.50
A9 Jaromir Jagr 1.25 3.00
A10 Curtis Joseph .60 1.50

2000-01 Upper Deck Dignitaries

COMPLETE SET (10) 20.00 40.00
STATED ODDS 1:23 SERIES 1
D1 Paul Kariya .75 2.00
D2 Ray Bourque 1.50 4.00
D3 Patrick Roy 4.00 10.00

D4 Brett Hull 1.00 2.50
D5 Steve Yzerman 4.00 10.00
D6 Pavel Bure 1.00 2.50
D7 Luc Robitaille .75 2.00
D8 Brian Leetch .75 2.00
D9 Jaromir Jagr 1.25 3.00
D10 Mark Messier 1.00 2.50

2000-01 Upper Deck e-Cards

Randomly inserted in packs at the rate of 1:12, this twelve card set features an interactive number that can be entered at the Upper Deck website to see if it evolves. Cards can evolve into Game Jersey Cards sequentially numbered to 300, Autographed Cards sequentially numbered to 200, or Autographed Game Jersey Cards sequentially numbered to 50.

EC1 Sergei Samsonov .20 .50
EC2 Brett Hull .30 .75
EC3 Steve Yzerman 1.25 3.00
EC4 Pavel Bure .40 1.00
EC5 John LeClair .30 .75
EC6 Curtis Joseph .25 .60
EC7 Martin Brodeur .60 1.50
EC8 Mark Messier .30 .75
EC9 Chris Osgood .20 .50
EC10 Mike Richter .25 .60
EC11 Ray Bourque .50 1.25
EC12 Jeremy Roenick .30 .75

2000-01 Upper Deck e-Card Prizes

Winning e-Cards may be redeemed for Game Jersey Cards sequentially numbered to 300, Autographed Cards sequentially numbered to 200, or Autographed Game Jersey Cards sequentially numbered to 50. The original checklist contained a Mark Messier jersey card which was later found to be non-existent.

ABH Brett Hull AU 25.00 60.00
ACJ Curtis Joseph AU 25.00 60.00
ACO Chris Osgood AU 12.50 30.00
AJL John LeClair AU 10.00 25.00
AJR Jeremy Roenick AU 15.00 40.00
AMB Martin Brodeur AU 40.00 100.00
AMM Mark Messier AU 75.00 200.00
AMR Mike Richter AU 12.50 30.00
APB Pavel Bure AU 12.50 30.00
ARB Ray Bourque AU 30.00 80.00
ASS Sergei Samsonov AU 12.50 30.00
ASY Steve Yzerman AU 30.00 80.00
EBH Brett Hull Jersey 12.50 30.00
ECJ Curtis Joseph JSY 10.00 25.00
ECO Chris Osgood JSY 10.00 25.00
EJL John LeClair JSY 10.00 25.00
EJR Jeremy Roenick JSY 12.50 30.00
EMB Martin Brodeur JSY 25.00 60.00
EMR Mike Richter JSY 10.00 25.00
EPB Pavel Bure JSY 10.00 25.00
ERB Ray Bourque JSY 20.00 50.00
ESS Sergei Samsonov JSY 10.00 25.00
ESY Steve Yzerman JSY 15.00 40.00
SRB Ray Bourque GJ/AU 75.00 200.00
SEBH B.Hull GJ/AU 60.00 150.00
SECJ C.Joseph GJ/AU 20.00 50.00
SECO Chris Osgood GJ/AU 20.00 50.00
SEJL John LeClair GJ/AU 20.00 50.00
SEJR Jeremy Roenick GJ/AU 20.00 50.00
SEMB Martin Brodeur GJ/AU 100.00 200.00
SEMM Mark Messier GJ/AU 25.00 60.00
SEMR Mike Richter GJ/AU 20.00 50.00
SEPB P.Bure GJ/AU 20.00 50.00
SESS S.Samsonov GJ/AU 20.00 50.00
SESY S.Yzerman GJ/AU 75.00 200.00

2000-01 Upper Deck Fantastic Finishers

COMPLETE SET (11) 15.00 30.00
STATED ODDS 1:23 SERIES 1
FF1 Paul Kariya .75 2.00
FF2 Teemu Selanne .75 2.00
FF3 Peter Forsberg 2.00 5.00
FF4 Brett Hull 1.00 2.50
FF5 Steve Yzerman 4.00 10.00
FF6 Pavel Bure 1.00 2.50
FF7 John LeClair 1.00 2.50
FF8 Keith Tkachuk .75 2.00
FF9 Jaromir Jagr 1.25 3.00
FF10 Owen Nolan .60 1.50
FF11 Mats Sundin .75 2.00

2000-01 Upper Deck Frozen in Time

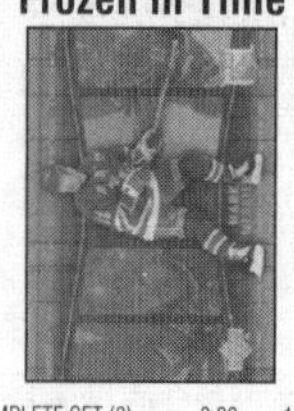

COMPLETE SET (8) 8.00 15.00
STATED ODDS 1:12 SERIES 2
FT1 Doug Gilmour .60 1.50
FT2 Ray Bourque 1.25 3.00
FT3 Brett Hull .75 2.00
FT4 Steve Yzerman 3.00 8.00
FT5 Mark Messier .75 2.00
FT6 Jeremy Roenick .75 2.00
FT7 Jaromir Jagr 1.00 2.50
FT8 Curtis Joseph .60 1.50

2000-01 Upper Deck Fun-Damentals

COMPLETE SET (9) 10.00 20.00
STATED ODDS 1:10 SERIES 2
F1 Paul Kariya .60 1.50
F2 Dominik Hasek 1.25 3.00
F3 Peter Forsberg 1.50 4.00
F4 Mike Modano 1.00 2.50
F5 Sergei Fedorov 1.25 3.00
F6 Pavel Bure .75 2.00
F7 Marian Hossa .60 1.50
F8 Jaromir Jagr 1.00 2.50
F9 Curtis Joseph .60 1.50

2000-01 Upper Deck Game Jerseys

Randomly inserted in packs at the rate of 1:287, this 25-card set features full color player photography and a swatch of a game worn jersey.

BS Brendan Shanahan Ser.1 8.00 20.00
BS Brendan Shanahan Ser.2 8.00 20.00
CP Chris Pronger Ser.1 8.00 20.00
JJ Jaromir Jagr Ser.2 12.50 30.00
JJ Jaromir Jagr Ser.1 12.50 30.00
JL John LeClair Ser.1 8.00 20.00
JN Joe Nieuwendyk Ser.1 8.00 20.00
JS Joe Sakic Ser.2 12.50 30.00
JS Joe Sakic Ser.1 12.50 30.00
JT Joe Thornton Ser.1 10.00 25.00
KT Keith Tkachuk Ser.1 8.00 20.00
MB Martin Brodeur Ser.1 25.00 60.00
MS Mats Sundin Ser.2 8.00 20.00
MS Mats Sundin Ser.1 8.00 20.00
PB Pavel Bure Ser.2 8.00 20.00
PE Peter Bondra Ser.1 8.00 20.00
PF Peter Forsberg Ser.2 15.00 40.00
PK Paul Kariya Ser.1 8.00 20.00
PK Paul Kariya Ser.2 8.00 20.00
SF Sergei Fedorov Ser.2 10.00 25.00
SF Sergei Fedorov Ser.1 10.00 25.00
TS Teemu Selanne Ser.2 8.00 20.00
TS Teemu Selanne Ser.1 8.00 20.00
WG Wayne Gretzky Ser.1 30.00 80.00
WG Wayne Gretzky AS Ser.2 30.00 80.00

2000-01 Upper Deck Game Jersey Autographs

Randomly inserted in Hobby packs at the rate of 1:287, this 18-card set features color action photography coupled with both and authentic player signature and a swatch of a game worn jersey.

HBH Brett Hull Ser.1 40.00 100.00
HCO Chris Osgood Ser.2 10.00 25.00
HJH Jochen Hecht Ser.1 10.00 25.00
HJL John LeClair Ser.2 15.00 40.00
HJR Jeremy Roenick Ser.2 25.00 60.00
HJT Joe Thornton Ser.2 25.00 60.00
HKT Keith Tkachuk Ser.2 15.00 40.00
HMA Martin Biron Ser.1 10.00 25.00
HMR Mike Richter Ser.2 15.00 40.00
HMY Mike York Ser.1 10.00 25.00
HNL Nicklas Lidstrom Ser.1 15.00 40.00
HPB Pavel Bure Ser.1 15.00 40.00
HSG Scott Gomez Ser.1 10.00 25.00
HSS Sergei Samsonov Ser.2 10.00 25.00
HSS Sergei Samsonov Ser.1 10.00 25.00
HSY Steve Yzerman Ser.2 60.00 150.00
HSY Steve Yzerman Ser.1 60.00 150.00
HTC Tim Connolly Ser.1 10.00 25.00

2000-01 Upper Deck Game Jersey Autographs Canadian

Randomly inserted in Canadian Hobby packs at the rate of 1:287, this set features four of Canada's own bright stars. Each card contains both an authentic player signature and a swatch of a game worn jersey.

CCJ Curtis Joseph Ser.1 15.00 40.00
CJT Jose Theodore Ser.2 25.00 60.00
CMM Mark Messier Ser.2 100.00 250.00
CRL Roberto Luongo Ser.1 15.00 40.00

2000-01 Upper Deck Game Jersey Autographs Exclusives

Randomly inserted in packs, this 36-card set partially paralleled the basic jersey set in an autographed version that was hand numbered to 25. The Gretzky, Hecht, and Richter cards were issued as exchanges.

NOT PRICED DUE TO SCARCITY
EBH Brett Hull Ser.1
EBS Brendan Shanahan Ser.1
ECP Chris Pronger Ser.1
EJH Jochen Hecht Ser.1
EJJ Jaromir Jagr Ser.1
EJL John LeClair Ser.1
EJN Joe Nieuwendyk Ser.1
EJS Joe Sakic Ser.1
EJT Joe Thornton Ser.1
EKT Keith Tkachuk Ser.1
EMB Martin Brodeur Ser.1
EMB Martin Biron Ser.1
EMS Mats Sundin Ser.1
EMY Mike York Ser.1
ENL Nicklas Lidstrom Ser.1
EPB Pavel Bure Ser.1
EPE Peter Bondra Ser.1
EPK Paul Kariya Ser.1
ESF Sergei Fedorov Ser.1
ESG Scott Gomez Ser.1
ESY Steve Yzerman Ser.1
ETC Tim Connolly Ser.1
ETS Teemu Selanne Ser.1
EWG Wayne Gretzky Ser.1
ESCO Chris Osgood Ser.2
ESJL John LeClair Ser.2
ESJN Joe Nieuwendyk Ser.2
ESJR Jeremy Roenick Ser.2
ESJT Joe Thornton Ser.2
ESKT Keith Tkachuk Ser.2
ESMR Mike Richter Ser.2
ESPB Pavel Bure Ser.2
ESSF Sergei Fedorov Ser.2
ESSS Sergei Samsonov Ser.2
ESSY Steve Yzerman Ser.2
ESWG Wayne Gretzky AS Ser.2

2000-01 Upper Deck Game Jersey Combos

Randomly inserted in series one packs, this 15-card set features a dual player card design with two swatches of game worn jerseys. Each card is sequentially numbered to 50.

DBF Raymond Bourque 100.00 250.00
Peter Forsberg
DBH Ed Belfour 60.00 150.00
Dominik Hasek
DCL Tim Connolly 20.00 50.00
Roberto Luongo
DFB Sergei Fedorov 30.00 80.00
Pavel Bure
DGB Scott Gomez 75.00 200.00
Martin Brodeur
DGH Wayne Gretzky 175.00 450.00
Brett Hull
DGL W.Gretzky/M.Lemieux 200.00 500.00
DGM Wayne Gretzky 125.00 300.00
Mark Messier
DJL Jaromir Jagr 100.00 250.00
Mario Lemieux
DLC John LeClair 20.00 50.00
Bobby Clarke
DSJ Mats Sundin 20.00 50.00
Curtis Joseph
DSK Teemu Selanne 20.00 50.00
Payl Kariya
DTS Joe Thornton 20.00 50.00
Sergei Samsonov

DYL Mike York 20.00 50.00
Brian Leetch
DYS S.Yzrmn/B.Shnahan 150.00 400.00

2000-01 Upper Deck Game Jersey Doubles

Randomly inserted in series two packs, this 10-card set features top NHL players in action coupled with two swatches of game worn jerseys. Each jersey swatch represents either more than one team played on, or a team and an all-star jersey. Each card is sequentially numbered to 100.

DBH Brett Hull 20.00 50.00
DBS Brendan Shanahan 12.50 30.00
DDH Dominik Hasek 25.00 60.00
DFP Felix Potvin 12.50 30.00
DJJ Jaromir Jagr 30.00 80.00
DJN Joe Nieuwendyk 12.50 30.00
DJS Joe Sakic 30.00 80.00
DPB Pavel Bure 12.50 30.00
DTS Teemu Selanne 12.50 30.00
DWG Wayne Gretzky AS 125.00 300.00

2000-01 Upper Deck Game Jersey Patches

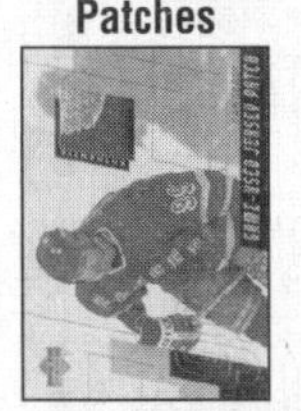

Randomly inserted in series one packs at the rate of 1:2500 and series two packs at the rate of one in 5000, this 36-card set features premium swatches of game worn jersey emblems and patches.

BHP Brett Hull Ser.1 50.00 125.00
BSP Brendan Shanahan Ser.1 40.00 100.00
CJP Curtis Joseph Ser.1 40.00 100.00
DHP Dominik Hasek Ser.1 50.00 125.00
ELP Eric Lindros Ser.1 40.00 100.00
JHP Jochen Hecht Ser.1 30.00 80.00
JJP Jaromir Jagr Ser.1 60.00 150.00
JLP John LeClair Ser.1 40.00 100.00
JSP Joe Sakic Ser.1 75.00 200.00
JTP Joe Thornton Ser.1 75.00 200.00
KTP Keith Tkachuk Ser.1 40.00 100.00
MBP Martin Brodeur Ser.1 125.00 300.00
MMP Mark Messier Ser.1 40.00 100.00
MYP Mike York Ser.1 30.00 80.00
PBP Pavel Bure Ser.1 40.00 100.00
PBS Brendan Shanahan Ser.2 40.00 100.00
PCO Chris Osgood Ser.2 30.00 80.00
PFP Peter Forsberg Ser.1 60.00 150.00
PJJ Jaromir Jagr Ser.2 60.00 150.00
PJL John LeClair Ser.2 40.00 100.00
PKP Paul Kariya Ser.1 40.00 100.00
PKT Keith Tkachuk Ser.2 40.00 100.00
PPF Peter Forsberg Ser.2 75.00 200.00
PPK Paul Kariya Ser.2 40.00 100.00
PRP Patrick Roy Ser.1 125.00 300.00
PSF Sergei Fedorov Ser.2 60.00 150.00
PSY Steve Yzerman Ser.2 75.00 200.00
PTS Teemu Selanne Ser.2 40.00 100.00
PWG W.Gretzky AS Ser.2 250.00 500.00
SFP Sergei Fedorov Ser.1 50.00 125.00
SGP Scott Gomez Ser.1 30.00 80.00
SSP Sergei Samsonov Ser.1 30.00 80.00
SYP Steve Yzerman Ser.1 75.00 200.00
TCP Tim Connolly Ser.1 30.00 80.00
TSP Teemu Selanne Ser.1 40.00 100.00
WGP Wayne Gretzky Ser.1 200.00 500.00

2000-01 Upper Deck Game Jersey Patch Autographs Exclusives

Randomly inserted in packs, this 28-card set parallels the base Game Jersey Patches set enhanced with player autographs. Series 1 cards are numbered one of one, series 2 cards are numbered to the featured player's jersey number. Cards with print runs under 25 are not priced due to scarcity.

BHP Brett Hull Ser.1
BSP Brendan Shanahan Ser.1
CJP Curtis Joseph Ser.1
DHP Dominik Hasek Ser.1
ELP Eric Lindros Ser.1
JHP Jochen Hecht Ser.1
JJP Jaromir Jagr Ser.1
JLP John LeClair Ser.1
JSP Joe Sakic Ser.1
JTP Joe Thornton Ser.1
KTP Keith Tkachuk Ser.1
MBP Martin Brodeur Ser.1
MMP Mark Messier Ser.1
MYP Mike York Ser.1
PBP Pavel Bure Ser.1
PFP Peter Forsberg Ser.1
PKP Paul Kariya Ser.1
PRP Patrick Roy Ser.1
SFP Sergei Fedorov Ser.1
SGP Scott Gomez Ser.1
SSP Sergei Samsonov Ser.1
SYP Steve Yzerman Ser.1
TCP Tim Connolly Ser.1
TSP Teemu Selanne Ser.1
WGP Wayne Gretzky Ser.1
PSJL John LeClair/10
PSSY Steve Yzerman/19
PSWG W.Gretzky AS/99 500.00 1200.00

2000-01 Upper Deck Game Jersey Patch Exclusives Series II

Randomly inserted in series two packs, this 13-card set features premium swatches of game worn player jerseys. Each card is sequentially numbered to 25. These cards are not priced due to scarcity.

EBS Brendan Shanahan
ECO Chris Osgood
EJJ Jaromir Jagr
EJL John LeClair
EKT Keith Tkachuk
EPF Peter Forsberg
EPK Paul Kariya
ESF Sergei Fedorov
ESY Steve Yzerman
ETS Teemu Selanne
EWG Wayne Gretzky AS

2000-01 Upper Deck Gate Attractions

COMPLETE SET (11) 15.00 30.00
STATED ODDS 1:11 SERIES 1
GA1 Paul Kariya .75 2.00
GA2 Dominik Hasek 1.25 3.00
GA3 Ray Bourque 1.25 3.00
GA4 Patrick Roy 3.00 8.00
GA5 Mike Modano .75 2.00
GA6 Steve Yzerman 3.00 8.00
GA7 Pavel Bure .75 2.00
GA8 Martin Brodeur 1.50 4.00
GA9 John LeClair .75 2.00
GA10 Jaromir Jagr 1.00 2.50
GA11 Curtis Joseph .75 2.00

2000-01 Upper Deck Lord Stanley's Heroes

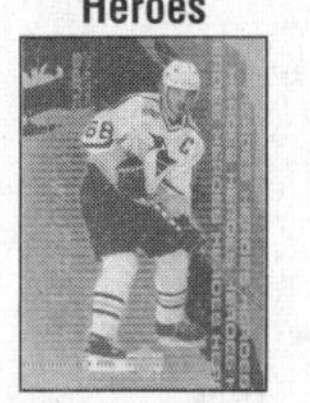

COMPLETE SET (9) 10.00 20.00
STATED ODDS 1:10 SERIES 2
L1 Patrick Roy 3.00 8.00
L2 Joe Sakic 1.25 3.00
L3 Brett Hull .75 2.00
L4 Steve Yzerman 2.50 6.00
L5 Brendan Shanahan 1.00 2.50
L6 Martin Brodeur 1.25 3.00
L7 Scott Gomez .75 2.00
L8 Mark Messier .75 2.00
L9 Jaromir Jagr 1.00 2.50

2000-01 Upper Deck Number Crunchers

COMPLETE SET (10) 10.00 20.00
STATED ODDS 1:9 SERIES 1
NC1 Peter Forsberg 1.50 4.00
NC2 Brendan Shanahan 1.00 2.50
NC3 John LeClair .75 2.00
NC4 Eric Lindros 1.00 2.50
NC5 Keith Tkachuk .60 1.50
NC6 Jeremy Roenick .75 2.00
NC7 Jaromir Jagr 1.00 2.50
NC8 Owen Nolan .60 1.50
NC9 Chris Pronger .60 1.50
NC10 Mark Messier .75 2.00

2000-01 Upper Deck Profiles

COMPLETE SET (10) 12.00 25.00
STATED ODDS 1:23 SERIES 2
P1 Dominik Hasek 1.50 4.00
P2 Joe Sakic 1.50 4.00
P3 Mike Modano 1.25 3.00
P4 Brendan Shanahan 1.25 3.00
P5 Pavel Bure 1.00 2.50
P6 Martin Brodeur 2.00 5.00
P7 John LeClair 1.00 2.50
P8 Jaromir Jagr 1.25 3.00
P9 Mats Sundin .75 2.00
P10 Olaf Kolzig .60 1.50

2000-01 Upper Deck Prospects In Depth

COMPLETE SET (10) 10.00 20.00
STATED ODDS 1:11 SERIES 1
P1 Patrik Stefan 1.00 2.50
P2 Maxim Afinogenov 1.00 2.50
P3 Alex Tanguay 1.00 2.50
P4 Brenden Morrow 1.00 2.50
P5 Scott Gomez 1.00 2.50
P6 Tim Connolly 1.00 2.50
P7 Mike York 1.00 2.50
P8 Simon Gagne 1.25 3.00
P9 Brian Boucher 1.25 3.00
P10 Jochen Hecht 1.00 2.50

2000-01 Upper Deck Rise to Prominence

COMPLETE SET (8) 5.00 12.00
STATED ODDS 1:12 SERIES 2
RP1 Paul Kariya .60 1.50
RP2 Pavel Bure .75 2.00
RP3 Jose Theodore .75 2.00
RP4 Scott Gomez .50 1.25
RP5 Marian Hossa .60 1.50
RP6 Brian Boucher .50 1.25
RP7 Roman Turek .50 1.25
RP8 Vincent Lecavalier .60 1.50

2000-01 Upper Deck Signs of Greatness

Randomly inserted in series two packs, this nine card set features an all white borderless card stock. The player'n name appears along the top of the card in gray tone, and full color action photography is centered on the card. Each card is autographed and numbered out of 250. The Amonte card has yet to be confirmed and it is believed that he never signed.

SBO Bobby Orr 100.00 250.00
SCJ Curtis Joseph 20.00 40.00
SKT Keith Tkachuk 20.00 40.00
SMB Martin Brodeur 30.00 80.00
SMY Mike York 12.50 30.00
SPB Pavel Brendl 12.50 30.00
SSS Sergei Samsonov 20.00 40.00
SWG Wayne Gretzky 100.00 250.00

2000-01 Upper Deck Skilled Stars

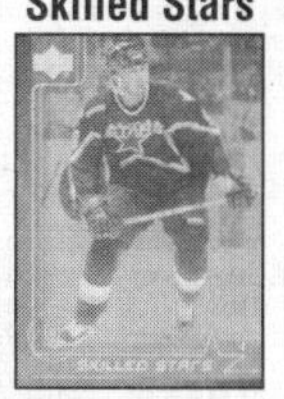

COMPLETE SET (20) 15.00 30.00
STATED ODDS 1:5 SERIES 1
SS1 Paul Kariya .50 1.25
SS2 Teemu Selanne .50 1.25
SS3 Dominik Hasek 1.00 2.50
SS4 Valeri Bure .40 1.00
SS5 Patrick Roy 2.50 6.00
SS6 Peter Forsberg 1.25 3.00
SS7 Ed Belfour .50 1.25
SS8 Mike Modano .75 2.00
SS9 Sergei Fedorov 1.00 2.50
SS10 Brendan Shanahan .75 2.00
SS11 Pavel Bure .60 1.50
SS12 Zigmund Palffy .40 1.00
SS13 Martin Brodeur 1.25 3.00
SS14 Tim Connolly .40 1.00
SS15 John LeClair .40 1.00
SS16 Jeremy Roenick .60 1.50
SS17 Jaromir Jagr .75 2.00
SS18 Vincent Lecavalier .50 1.25
SS19 Mats Sundin .50 1.25
SS20 Olaf Kolzig .40 1.00

2000-01 Upper Deck Triple Threat

Randomly inserted in series two pack at the rate of 1:72, this 10-card set pairs three players of the same position that dominate year after year. Base cards feature a doctored action shot where three players are present doing what they do best. Cards are all silver foil and are enhanced with light blue foil highlights.

COMPLETE SET (10) 30.00 80.00
TT1 Paul Kariya 4.00 10.00
Scott Gomez
Milan Hejduk
TT2 Roy/Brodeur/Belfour 10.00 25.00
TT3 Peter Forsberg 6.00 15.00
Mats Sundin
Henrik Sedin
TT4 Brett Hull 4.00 10.00
Jeremy Roenick
John LeClair
TT5 Yzerman/Sakic/Modano 8.00 20.00
TT6 Brendan Shanahan 4.00 10.00
Keith Tkachuk
Mark Messier
TT7 Pavel Bure 3.00 8.00
Sergei Samsonov
Sergei Fedorov
TT8 Raymond Bourque 4.00 10.00
Chris Pronger
Rob Blake
TT9 Jaromir Jagr 4.00 10.00
Teemu Selanne
Milan Kraft
TT10 Roman Turek 4.00 10.00
Dominik Hasek
Olaf Kolzig

2000-01 Upper Deck UD Flashback

Randomly inserted in series two packs at the rate of 1:12, this eight card set features players in action on a holofoil version of the 1990-91 Upper Deck card design.

COMPLETE SET (8) 3.00 8.00
UD1 Teemu Selanne .60 1.50
UD2 Tony Amonte .40 1.00
UD3 Milan Hejduk .60 1.50
UD4 Scott Gomez .40 1.00
UD5 Tim Connolly .40 1.00
UD6 John LeClair .75 2.00
UD7 Keith Tkachuk .60 1.50
UD8 Olaf Kolzig .40 1.00

2001-02 Upper Deck

This 441-card set was released in two different series of 231 cards and 210 cards. Series I was released in late October 2001 and Series II was released in early February 2002. Both series carried an SRP of $2.99 for an 8-card pack. Series I consisted of 180 regular base cards and 51 Young Guns subset shortprints. Series II consisted of 180 regular base cards and 30 Young Guns shortprints. Series II Young Guns had two different versions of each card which were the same value. Shortprints for both series were inserted at 1:4. The Jared Aulin card (#220B) was printed in error and is known to have been inserted into some packs, though only a handful have been verified therefore it is not priced. The "B" suffix on the Aulin card is for checklisting purposes only.

COMPLETE SET (441) 300.00 600.00
COMP.SERIES 1 (231) 150.00 300.00
COMP.SER. 1 w/o SP's (180) 15.00 30.00
COMP.SERIES 2 (210) 150.00 300.00
COMP.SER. 2 w/o SP's (180) 15.00 30.00
1 Paul Kariya .20 .50
2 Jeff Friesen .02 .10
3 Mike Leclerc .02 .10
4 Andy McDonald .02 .10
5 J-S Giguere .15 .40
6 Steve Rucchin .02 .10
7 Ray Ferraro .02 .10
8 Milan Hnilicka .15 .40
9 Patrik Stefan .02 .10
10 Jiri Slegr .02 .10
11 Jeff Odgers .02 .10
12 Steve Guolla .02 .10
13 Joe Thornton .30 .75
14 Sergei Samsonov .15 .40
15 Kyle McLaren .02 .10
16 Jonathan Girard .02 .10
17 Brian Rolston .02 .10
18 Byron Dafoe .15 .40
19 Miroslav Satan .15 .40
20 Curtis Brown .02 .10
21 Stu Barnes .02 .10
22 Maxim Afinogenov .02 .10
23 Vaclav Varada .02 .10
24 Chris Gratton .02 .10
25 Jarome Iginla .25 .60
26 Dave Lowry .02 .10
27 Derek Morris .02 .10
28 Marc Savard .02 .10
29 Oleg Saprykin .02 .10
30 Craig Conroy .02 .10
31 Jeff O'Neill .02 .10
32 Arturs Irbe .15 .40
33 Shane Willis .02 .10
34 Dave Tanabe .02 .10
35 Josef Vasicek .02 .10
36 Sami Kapanen .02 .10
37 Steve Sullivan .02 .10
38 Tony Amonte .15 .40
39 Michael Nylander .02 .10
40 Eric Daze .15 .40
41 Jocelyn Thibault .15 .40
42 Boris Mironov .02 .10
43 Ville Nieminen .02 .10
44 Alex Tanguay .15 .40
45 Milan Hejduk .20 .50
46 Chris Drury .15 .40
47 Peter Forsberg .50 1.25
48 Steven Reinprecht .02 .10
49 Ron Tugnutt .15 .40
50 Ray Whitney .02 .10
51 Geoff Sanderson .02 .10
52 Serge Aubin .02 .10
53 Espen Knutsen .02 .10
54 Rostislav Klesla .02 .10
55 Mike Modano .30 .75
56 Ed Belfour .20 .50
57 Pierre Turgeon .15 .40
58 Jamie Langenbrunner .02 .10
59 Brenden Morrow .15 .40
60 Donald Audette .02 .10
61 Steve Yzerman 1.00 2.50
62 Brett Hull .25 .60
63 Nicklas Lidstrom .20 .50
64 Darren McCarty .02 .10
65 Luc Robitaille .15 .40
66 Dominik Hasek .40 1.00
67 Mike Comrie .15 .40
68 Tommy Salo .15 .40
69 Todd Marchant .02 .10
70 Mike Grier .02 .10
71 Ryan Smyth .02 .10
72 Tom Poti .02 .10
73 Pavel Bure .20 .50
74 Marcus Nilsson .02 .10
75 Roberto Luongo .25 .60
76 Kevyn Adams .02 .10
77 Dan Boyle .02 .10
78 Robert Svehla .02 .10
79 Zigmund Palffy .15 .40
80 Eric Belanger .02 .10
81 Ian Laperriere .02 .10
82 Bryan Smolinski .02 .10
83 Jozef Stumpel .02 .10
84 Adam Deadmarsh .02 .10
85 Marian Gaborik .40 1.00
86 Lubomir Sekeras .02 .10
87 Manny Fernandez .15 .40
88 Darby Hendrickson .02 .10
89 Roman Simicek .02 .10
90 Saku Koivu .20 .50
91 Richard Zednik .02 .10
92 Oleg Petrov .02 .10
93 Patrice Brisebois .02 .10
94 Brian Savage .02 .10
95 Jan Bulis .02 .10
96 David Legwand .15 .40
97 Cliff Ronning .02 .10
98 Mike Dunham .15 .40
99 Greg Johnson .02 .10
100 Kimmo Timonen .02 .10
101 Denis Arkhipov .02 .10
102 Patrik Elias .15 .40
103 Jason Arnott .02 .10
104 Scott Niedermayer .02 .10
105 Scott Gomez .02 .10
106 Scott Stevens .15 .40
107 John Madden .02 .10
108 Rick DiPietro .15 .40
109 Mark Parrish .02 .10
110 Brad Isbister .15 .40
111 Michael Peca .02 .10
112 Kenny Jonsson .02 .10
113 Mariusz Czerkawski .02 .10
114 Mark Messier .20 .50
115 Theo Fleury .02 .10
116 Radek Dvorak .02 .10
117 Brian Leetch .15 .40
118 Eric Lindros .20 .50
119 Mike Mottau .02 .10
120 Radek Bonk .02 .10
121 Daniel Alfredsson .15 .40
122 Marian Hossa .20 .50
123 Magnus Arvedson .02 .10
124 Patrick Lalime .15 .40
125 Martin Havlat .15 .40
126 Eric Desjardins .15 .40
127 Keith Primeau .02 .10
128 Mark Recchi .15 .40
129 Justin Williams .02 .10
130 Roman Cechmanek .15 .40
131 Jeremy Roenick .25 .60
132 Sean Burke .15 .40
133 Shane Doan .02 .10
134 Paul Mara .02 .10
135 Michal Handzus .02 .10
136 Ladislav Nagy .02 .10
137 Mike Johnson .02 .10
138 Mario Lemieux 1.25 3.00
139 Alexei Kovalev .15 .40
140 Robert Lang .02 .10
141 Kevin Stevens .02 .10
142 Andrew Ference .02 .10
143 Johan Hedberg .15 .40
144 Owen Nolan .15 .40
145 Teemu Selanne .20 .50
146 Scott Thornton .02 .10
147 Patrick Marleau .15 .40
148 Alexander Korolyuk .02 .10
149 Todd Harvey .02 .10
150 Keith Tkachuk .20 .50
151 Pavol Demitra .15 .40
152 Al MacInnis .15 .40
153 Scott Young .02 .10
154 Cory Stillman .02 .10
155 Doug Weight .15 .40
156 Brad Richards .15 .40
157 Nikolai Khabibulin .20 .50
158 Martin St. Louis .15 .40
159 Fredrik Modin .02 .10
160 Matthew Barnaby .02 .10
161 Gary Roberts .02 .10
162 Jonas Hoglund .02 .10
163 Curtis Joseph .20 .50
164 Mats Sundin .20 .50
165 Darcy Tucker .02 .10
166 Shayne Corson .02 .10
167 Markus Naslund .20 .50
168 Daniel Sedin .02 .10
169 Henrik Sedin .02 .10
170 Brendan Morrison .15 .40
171 Peter Schaefer .02 .10
172 Harold Druken .02 .10
173 Peter Bondra .20 .50
174 Olaf Kolzig .15 .40
175 Sergei Gonchar .02 .10
176 Jeff Halpern .02 .10
177 Andrei Nikolishin .02 .10
178 Jaromir Jagr .30 .75
179 Steve Yzerman CL .20 .50
180 Pavel Bure CL .20 .50
181 Dan Snyder RC 2.00 5.00
182 Zdenek Kutlak RC 2.00 5.00
183 Michel Larocque RC 2.00 5.00
184 Casey Hankinson RC 2.00 5.00
185 Jody Shelley RC 2.00 5.00
186 Martin Spanhel RC 2.00 5.00
187 Mathieu Darche RC 2.00 5.00
188 Matt Davidson RC 2.00 5.00
189 Sean Selmser RC 2.00 5.00
190 Jason Chimera RC 2.00 5.00
191 Andrej Podkonicky RC 2.00 5.00
192 Mike Matteucci RC 2.00 5.00
193 Pascal Dupuis RC 2.00 5.00
194 Francis Belanger RC 2.00 5.00
195 Bill Bowler RC 2.00 5.00
196 Mike Jefferson RC 2.00 5.00
197 Stanislav Gron RC 2.00 5.00
198 Mikael Samuelsson RC 2.00 5.00
199 Peter Smrek RC 2.00 5.00
200 Joel Kwiatkowski RC 2.00 5.00
201 Tomas Divisek RC 2.00 5.00
202 Kirby Law RC 2.00 5.00
203 David Cullen RC 2.00 5.00
204 Greg Crozier RC 2.00 5.00
205 Billy Tibbetts RC 2.00 5.00
206 Dale Clarke RC 2.00 5.00
207 Jaroslav Obsut RC 2.00 5.00
208 Thomas Ziegler RC 2.00 5.00
209 Pat Kavanagh RC 2.00 5.00
210 Mike Brown 2.00 5.00
211 Ilya Kovalchuk RC 40.00 80.00
212 Ray Bourque 1.50 4.00
213 Brett Hull 1.00 2.50
214 Dominik Hasek 1.50 4.00
215 Vaclav Nedorost RC 2.00 5.00
216 Steve Yzerman 4.00 10.00
217 Mark Messier .20 .50
218 Mike Modano 1.25 3.00
219 Patrick Roy 4.00 10.00
220 John LeClair .75 2.00
220B Jared Aulin
221 Martin Brodeur 2.00 5.00
222 Tony Amonte .60 1.50
223 Zigmund Palffy .60 1.50
224 Roman Cechmanek .60 1.50
225 Jeff Jillson RC 2.00 5.00
226 Jaromir Jagr 1.25 3.00
227 Nikita Alexeev RC 2.00 5.00
228 Krystofer Kolanos RC 2.00 5.00
229 Peter Forsberg 2.00 5.00
230 Pavel Bure .20 .50
231 Brian Sutherby RC 2.00 5.00
232 Oleg Tverdovsky .02 .10
233 Steve Shields .15 .40
234 Matt Cullen .02 .10
235 Jason York .02 .10
236 Vitali Vishnevsky .02 .10
237 Marty McInnis .02 .10
238 Yannick Tremblay .02 .10
239 Dany Heatley .25 .60
240 Lubos Bartecko .02 .10
241 Damian Rhodes .15 .40
242 Ilya Kovalchuk 6.00 15.00
243 Hnat Domenichelli .02 .10
244 Bill Guerin .15 .40
245 Martin Lapointe .02 .10
246 Scott Pellerin .02 .10
247 Rob Zamuner .02 .10
248 Jozef Stumpel .02 .10
249 Glen Murray .02 .10
250 Martin Biron .15 .40
251 Tim Connolly .02 .10
252 Slava Kozlov .02 .10
253 Jay McKee .02 .10
254 J-P Dumont .02 .10
255 Alexei Zhitnik .02 .10
256 Roman Turek .15 .40
257 Igor Kravchuk .02 .10
258 Clarke Wilm .02 .10
259 Robyn Regehr .02 .10
260 Rob Niedermayer .02 .10
261 Dean McAmmond .02 .10
262 Ron Francis .15 .40
263 Martin Gelinas .02 .10
264 Rod Brind'Amour .15 .40
265 Sandis Ozolinsh .02 .10
266 Bates Battaglia .02 .10
267 Chris Dingman .02 .10
268 Igor Korolev .02 .10
269 Jaroslav Spacek .02 .10
270 Alexei Zhamnov .02 .10
271 Steve Thomas .02 .10
272 Jon Klemm .02 .10
273 Adam Foote .02 .10
274 Joe Sakic .40 1.00
275 Rob Blake .15 .40
276 Patrick Roy 1.00 2.50
277 Greg deVries .02 .10
278 Dan Hinote .02 .10
279 Marc Denis .15 .40
280 David Vyborny .02 .10
281 Tyler Wright .02 .10
282 Mike Sillinger .02 .10
283 Bruce Gardiner .02 .10
284 Sergei Zubov .02 .10
285 Jere Lehtinen .15 .40
286 Joe Nieuwendyk .15 .40
287 Darryl Sydor .02 .10
288 Rob DiMaio .02 .10
289 Valeri Kamensky .02 .10
290 Brendan Shanahan .20 .50
291 Igor Larionov .02 .10
292 Tomas Holmstrom .02 .10
293 Mathieu Dandenault .02 .10
294 Sergei Fedorov .30 .75
295 Fredrik Olausson .02 .10
296 Anson Carter .15 .40
297 Jochen Hecht .02 .10
298 Daniel Cleary .02 .10
299 Janne Niinimaa .02 .10
300 Rem Murray .02 .10
301 Eric Brewer .02 .10
302 Valeri Bure .02 .10
303 Viktor Kozlov .02 .10
304 Denis Shvidki .02 .10
305 Olli Jokinen .15 .40
306 Jason Wiemer .02 .10
307 Ryan Johnson .02 .10
308 Felix Potvin .20 .50
309 Jason Allison .02 .10
310 Mathieu Schneider .02 .10
311 Lubomir Visnovsky .02 .10
312 Mattias Norstrom .02 .10
313 Steve Heinze .02 .10
314 Jim Dowd .02 .10
315 Wes Walz .02 .10
316 Filip Kuba .02 .10
317 Andrew Brunette .02 .10
318 Sergei Zholtok .02 .10
319 Stacy Roest .02 .10
320 Jose Theodore .25 .60
321 Yanic Perreault .02 .10
322 Doug Gilmour .02 .10
323 Andreas Dackell .02 .10
324 Martin Rucinsky .02 .10
325 Chad Kilger .02 .10
326 Scott Walker .02 .10
327 Andy Delmore .02 .10
328 Patric Kjellberg .02 .10
329 Tomas Vokoun .15 .40
330 Vitali Yachmenev .02 .10
331 Bill Houlder .02 .10
332 Martin Brodeur .50 1.25
333 Bobby Holik .02 .10
334 Petr Sykora .02 .10
335 Brian Rafalski .02 .10
336 Sergei Brylin .02 .10
337 Randy McKay .02 .10
338 Alexei Yashin .02 .10
339 Roman Hamrlik .02 .10
340 Michael Peca .02 .10
341 Dave Scatchard .02 .10
342 Claude Lapointe .02 .10
343 Chris Osgood .15 .40
344 Mike Richter .20 .50
345 Mike York .02 .10
346 Eric Lindros .20 .50
347 Petr Nedved .02 .10
348 Barrett Heisten .02 .10
349 Zdeno Ciger .02 .10
350 Shawn McEachern .02 .10
351 Wade Redden .02 .10
352 Bill Muckalt .02 .10
353 Andre Roy .02 .10
354 Sami Salo .02 .10
355 Todd White .02 .10
356 John LeClair .20 .50
357 Brian Boucher .15 .40
358 Pavel Brendl .02 .10
359 Jan Hlavac .02 .10
360 Dan McGillis .02 .10
361 Simon Gagne .20 .50
362 Daymond Langkow .15 .40
363 Sergei Berezin .02 .10
364 Danny Markov .02 .10
365 Tyler Bouck .02 .10
366 Teppo Numminen .02 .10
367 Trevor Letowski .02 .10
368 Martin Straka .02 .10
369 Jan Hrdina .02 .10
370 Alexei Morozov .02 .10
371 Darius Kasparaitis .02 .10
372 Toby Petersen .02 .10
373 Kris Beech .02 .10
374 Evgeni Nabokov .15 .40
375 Mike Ricci .02 .10
376 Brad Stuart .02 .10
377 Adam Graves .02 .10
378 Vincent Damphousse .02 .10
379 Stephane Matteau .02 .10
380 Chris Pronger .15 .40
381 Brent Johnson .15 .40
382 Fred Brathwaite .15 .40
383 Dallas Drake .02 .10
384 Mike Eastwood .02 .10
385 Daniel Corso .02 .10
386 Brian Holzinger .02 .10
387 Vincent Lecavalier .20 .50
388 Jassen Cullimore .02 .10
389 Vaclav Prospal .02 .10
390 Dave Andreychuk .15 .40
391 Jimmie Olvestad .02 .10
392 Alexander Mogilny .15 .40
393 Tomas Kaberle .02 .10
394 Mikael Renberg .02 .10
395 Travis Green .02 .10
396 Robert Reichel .02 .10
397 Nikolai Antropov .02 .10
398 Andrew Cassels .02 .10
399 Dan Cloutier .15 .40

400 Ed Jovanovski .15 .40
401 Todd Bertuzzi .20 .50
402 Trent Klatt .02 .10
403 Donald Brashear .02 .10
404 Jaromir Jagr .30 .75
405 Joe Sacco .02 .10
406 Steve Konowalchuk .02 .10
407 Adam Oates .20 .50
408 Dimitri Khristich .02 .10
409 Dainius Zubrus .02 .10
410 John LeClair .20 .50
411 Martin Brodeur .50 1.25
412 Timo Parssinen RC 2.00 5.00
413 Ilja Bryzgalov RC 3.00 8.00
414 Kevin Sawyer RC 2.00 5.00
415 Kamil Piros RC 2.50 5.00
416 Ivan Huml RC 2.00 5.00
417 Scott Nichol RC 2.00 5.00
418 Jukka Hentunen RC 2.00 5.00
419 Erik Cole RC 4.00 10.00
420 Ben Simon RC 2.00 5.00
421 Niko Kapanen RC 2.00 5.00
422 Pavel Datsyuk RC 15.00 40.00
423 Ty Conklin RC 2.00 5.00
424 Wayne Gretzky SP 8.00 20.00
425 Niklas Hagman RC 2.00 5.00
426 Kristian Huselius RC 2.00 5.00
427 Jaroslav Bednar RC 2.00 5.00
428 Nick Schultz RC 2.00 5.00
429 Travis Roche RC 2.00 5.00
430 Martin Erat RC 2.00 5.00
431 Andreas Salomonsson RC 2.00 5.00
432 Josef Boumedienne RC 2.00 5.00
433 Scott Clemmensen RC 2.00 5.00
434 Dan Blackburn RC 3.00 8.00
435 Radek Martinek RC 2.00 5.00
436 Raffi Torres RC 3.00 8.00
437 Ivan Ciernik RC 2.00 5.00
438 Jiri Dopita RC 2.00 5.00
439 Mark Rycroft RC 2.00 5.00
440 Ryan Tobler RC 2.00 5.00
441 Chris Corrinet RC 2.00 5.00

2001-02 Upper Deck Exclusives

This 441-card set paralleled the base set with serial-numbering added. Regular base cards were serial-numbered to 100 copies each and Young Guns subset cards were serial-numbered to 50 copies each.
*EXCL.: 12X TO 30X BASE CARD
*EXCL.SP's: 4X TO 10X BASE CARD

2001-02 Upper Deck Crunch Timers

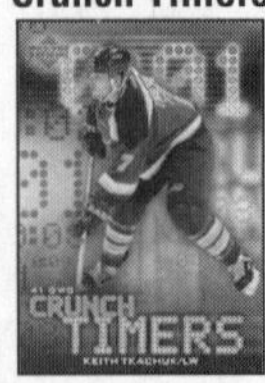

COMPLETE SET (15) 15.00 30.00
STATED ODDS 1:24 SERIES 2
CT1 Joe Sakic 1.25 3.00
CT2 Milan Hejduk .60 1.50
CT3 Chris Drury .50 1.25
CT4 Mike Modano 1.00 2.50
CT5 Brett Hull .75 2.00
CT6 Steve Yzerman 3.00 8.00
CT7 Zigmund Palffy .50 1.25
CT8 Alexei Yashin .50 1.25
CT9 Jeremy Roenick .75 2.00
CT10 Mark Recchi .50 1.25
CT11 Teemu Selanne .60 1.50
CT12 Keith Tkachuk .60 1.50
CT13 Markus Naslund .60 1.50
CT14 Jaromir Jagr 1.00 2.50
CT15 Peter Bondra .60 1.50

2001-02 Upper Deck Fantastic Finishers

COMPLETE SET (10) 10.00 20.00
STATED ODDS 1:36 SERIES 1
FF1 Pavel Bure .75 2.00
FF2 Pavol Demitra .50 1.25
FF3 Markus Naslund .60 1.50
FF4 Mario Lemieux 4.00 10.00
FF5 John LeClair .75 2.00
FF6 Keith Tkachuk .60 1.50
FF7 Marian Hossa .60 1.50
FF8 Teemu Selanne .60 1.50
FF9 Joe Sakic 1.25 3.00
FF10 Zigmund Palffy .50 1.25

2001-02 Upper Deck Franchise Cornerstones

COMPLETE SET (15) 25.00 50.00
STATED ODDS 1:24 SERIES 1
FC1 Paul Kariya .60 1.50
FC2 Pavel Bure .75 2.00
FC3 Mario Lemieux 4.00 10.00
FC4 Peter Forsberg 1.50 4.00
FC5 Vincent Lecavalier .50 1.25
FC6 Joe Sakic 1.25 3.00
FC7 Zigmund Palffy .50 1.25
FC8 Martin Brodeur 1.50 4.00
FC9 Patrick Roy 3.00 8.00
FC10 Steve Yzerman 3.00 8.00
FC11 Mike Modano 1.00 2.50
FC12 Tony Amonte .50 1.25
FC13 Teemu Selanne .60 1.50
FC14 John LeClair .75 2.00
FC15 Mats Sundin .60 1.50

2001-02 Upper Deck Game Jerseys

Inserted into random packs of Series I, this 38-card set featured swatches of game-worn jerseys and consisted of 4 subsets: All-Stars, Goalies, Next Generation, and Combos. All-Stars jerseys were denoted with an "A" prefix and inserted at 1:144. Goalie jerseys were denoted with a "GJ" prefix and inserted at 1:288. Next Generation jerseys were denoted with a "NG" prefix and inserted at 1:144. Combo jerseys were denoted with a "C" prefix fro dual jerseys or numbered using the first letter of the players' last names for triple jerseys. Combo jerseys were inserted at 1:144.
*MULT.COLOR SWATCH: 1X TO 1.5X HI
AAM Al MacInnis AS 4.00 10.00
ACC Chris Chelios AS 5.00 12.00
AGL Guy Lafleur AS 4.00 10.00
AJJ Jaromir Jagr AS 8.00 20.00
AJO Joe Sakic AS 10.00 25.00
AMM Mike Modano AS 10.00 20.00
AMS Mats Sundin AS 5.00 12.00
ATF Theo Fleury AS 4.00 10.00
ATS Teemu Selanne AS 5.00 12.00
GJBB Brian Boucher G 10.00 25.00
GJCJ Curtis Joseph G 10.00 25.00
GJDH Dominik Hasek G 12.50 30.00
GJEB Ed Belfour G 10.00 25.00
GJJH Jani Hurme G 10.00 25.00
GJJT Jocelyn Thibault G 10.00 25.00
GJMO Maxime Ouellet G 10.00 25.00
GJMR Mike Richter G 10.00 25.00
GJMT Marty Turco G 10.00 25.00
GJOK Olaf Kolzig G 10.00 25.00
GJPR Patrick Roy G 15.00 40.00
GJRC Roman Cechmanek G 10.00 25.00
GJSB Sean Burke G 10.00 25.00
GJVY Vitali Yeremeyev G 10.00 25.00
NGCB Curtis Brown NG 4.00 10.00
NGDS Daniel Sedin NG 4.00 10.00
NGED Eric Daze NG 4.00 10.00
NGHS Henrik Sedin NG 4.00 10.00
NGJH Jani Hurme NG 4.00 10.00
NGJI Jarome Iginla NG 10.00 25.00
NGJW Justin Williams NG 4.00 10.00
NGMH Marian Hossa NG 5.00 12.00
NGMM Manny Malhotra NG 4.00 10.00
NGMT Marty Turco NG 4.00 10.00
NGMY Mike York NG 4.00 10.00
NGPS Patrik Stefan NG 4.00 10.00
NGRF Ruslan Fedotenko NG 4.00 10.00
NGSD Shane Doan NG 4.00 10.00
NGVL Vincent Lecavalier NG 5.00 12.00
CFR Peter Forsberg 20.00 50.00
Patrick Roy
CHH Marian Hossa 12.50 30.00
Jani Hurme
CKS Paul Kariya 12.50 30.00
Teemu Selanne
CLJ Mario Lemieux 15.00 40.00
Jaromir Jagr
CMN Mike Modano 15.00 40.00
Joe Nieuwendyk
CPC Keith Primeau 12.50 30.00
Roman Cechmanek
CSS Henrik Sedin 12.50 30.00
Daniel Sedin
FSR Peter Forsberg 25.00 60.00
Joe Sakic
Patrick Roy
MNB Mike Modano 20.00 50.00
Joe Nieuwendyk
Ed Belfour
YSF Steve Yzerman 25.00 60.00
Brendan Shanahan
Sergei Fedorov

2001-02 Upper Deck Game Jerseys Series II

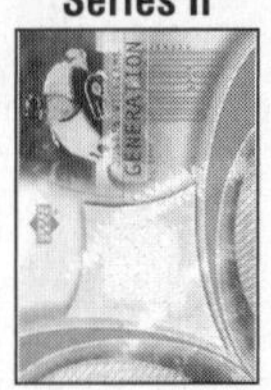

Randomly inserted into Series II packs, this 58-card set featured swatches of game-worn jersey swatches and consisted of 6 subsets: Finals Jerseys, Generation Next, Phenomenal Finishers, Superstar Sweaters, Dual Jerseys and Triple Jerseys. Single swatch jerseys were inserted at 1:144 odds, dual jerseys were inserted at 1:288. Triple swatch jerseys were serial-numbered to just 25 and were not priced due to scarcity.
*MULT.COLOR SWATCH: 1X TO 1.5X HI
FJBS Brendan Shanahan 6.00 15.00
FJCD Chris Drury 4.00 10.00
FJCL Claude Lemieux 4.00 10.00
FJCO Chris Osgood 6.00 15.00
FJEB Ed Belfour 6.00 15.00
FJJL John LeClair 4.00 10.00
FJJN Joe Nieuwendyk 4.00 10.00
FJJS Joe Sakic 10.00 25.00
FJMB Martin Brodeur 12.50 30.00
FJMH Milan Hejduk 6.00 15.00
FJMM Mike Modano 8.00 20.00
FJMS Miroslav Satan 4.00 10.00
FJPF Peter Forsberg 10.00 25.00
FJPR Patrick Roy 12.50 30.00
FJSF Sergei Fedorov 8.00 20.00
FJSS Scott Stevens 4.00 10.00
FJSY Steve Yzerman 12.50 30.00
GNJW Justin Williams 4.00 10.00
GNMB Martin Biron 4.00 10.00
GNMM Manny Malhotra 4.00 10.00
GNMO Maxime Ouellet 4.00 10.00
GNMY Mike York 4.00 10.00
GNPM Patrick Marleau 6.00 15.00
GNRB Radek Bonk 4.00 10.00
GNRF Rico Fata 4.00 10.00
GNSA Serge Aubin 4.00 10.00
GNSG Simon Gagne 6.00 15.00
PFAK Alexei Kovalev 4.00 10.00
PFBS Brendan Shanahan 6.00 15.00
PFJJ Jaromir Jagr 8.00 20.00
PFJL John LeClair 6.00 15.00
PFJS Joe Sakic 10.00 25.00
PFKP Keith Primeau 4.00 10.00
PFML Mario Lemieux 15.00 40.00
PFMN Markus Naslund 4.00 10.00
PFPK Paul Kariya 6.00 15.00
PFZP Zigmund Palffy 4.00 10.00
SSAM Al MacInnis 4.00 10.00
SSCD Chris Drury 6.00 15.00
SSMB Martin Brodeur 12.50 30.00
SSMM Mike Modano 8.00 20.00
SSPF Peter Forsberg 10.00 25.00
SSPK Paul Kariya 6.00 15.00
SSPR Patrick Roy 12.50 30.00
SSRB Ray Bourque 8.00 20.00
SSSY Steve Yzerman 12.50 30.00
SSWG Wayne Gretzky 30.00 80.00
DJBR Ray Bourque 20.00 50.00
Patrick Roy
DJFS Sergei Fedorov 10.00 25.00
Brendan Shanahan
DJMN Mike Modano 10.00 25.00
Joe Nieuwendyk
DJSB Scott Stevens 20.00 50.00
Martin Brodeur
DJSF Joe Sakic 25.00 60.00
Peter Forsberg
DJSH Miroslav Satan 10.00 25.00
Dominik Hasek
DJTD Alex Tanguay 10.00 25.00
Chris Drury
DJYL Steve Yzerman 15.00 40.00
Nicklas Lidstrom
TJNMB Joe Nieuwendyk 15.00 40.00
Mike Modano
Ed Belfour
TJRBH Patrick Roy 60.00 150.00
Joe Sakic
Milan Hejduk
TJYFS Steve Yzerman 25.00 60.00
Sergei Fedorov
Brendan Shanahan

2001-02 Upper Deck Game Jersey Autographs

Inserted randomly into both Series I and Series II, this 16-card set featured game-worn jersey swatches and authentic player autographs. Series I cards were inserted randomly at 1:288 packs. Series II cards were serial-numbered to 150 copies each.
SDS Daniel Sedin Ser.1 10.00 25.00
SDW Doug Weight Ser.1 15.00 40.00
SHS Henrik Sedin Ser.1 10.00 25.00
SJL John LeClair Ser.1 10.00 25.00
SMM Mike Modano Ser.1 25.00 60.00
SRB Ray Bourque Ser.1 30.00 80.00
SSY Steve Yzerman Ser.1 75.00 200.00
SJBO Ray Bourque Ser.2 30.00 80.00
SJCJ Curtis Joseph Ser.2 15.00 40.00
SJEB Ed Belfour Ser.2 20.00 50.00
SJJL John LeClair Ser.2 10.00 25.00
SJMB Martin Brodeur Ser.2 60.00 150.00
SJMO Maxime Ouellet Ser.2 10.00 25.00
SJRB Ray Bourque Ser.2 30.00 80.00
SJSG Simon Gagne Ser.2 10.00 25.00
SJSY Steve Yzerman Ser.2 75.00 200.00

2001-02 Upper Deck Gate Attractions

COMPLETE SET (15) 20.00 40.00
STATED ODDS 1:24 SERIES 1
GA1 Mark Messier .75 2.00
GA2 Theo Fleury .50 1.25
GA3 Keith Tkachuk .60 1.50
GA4 John LeClair .75 2.00
GA5 Mario Lemieux 4.00 10.00
GA6 Alexei Kovalev .50 1.25
GA7 Chris Drury .50 1.25
GA8 Joe Sakic 1.25 3.00
GA9 Peter Forsberg 1.50 4.00
GA10 Paul Kariya .60 1.50
GA11 Teemu Selanne .60 1.50
GA12 Steve Yzerman 3.00 8.00
GA13 Brendan Shanahan 1.00 2.50
GA14 Mike Modano 1.00 2.50
GA15 Chris Pronger .50 1.25

2001-02 Upper Deck Goalies in Action

COMPLETE SET (10) 12.50 25.00
STATED ODDS 1:36 SERIES 1
GL1 Curtis Joseph .75 2.00
GL2 Ed Belfour .75 2.00
GL3 Martin Brodeur 2.00 5.00
GL4 Evgeni Nabokov .60 1.50
GL5 Johan Hedberg .75 2.00
GL6 Patrick Roy 4.00 10.00
GL7 Tommy Salo .60 1.50
GL8 Patrick Lalime .60 1.50
GL9 Olaf Kolzig .60 1.50
GL10 Roberto Luongo 1.00 2.50

2001-02 Upper Deck Goaltender Threads

Randomly inserted at 1:240 Series II packs, this 10-card set featured swatches game-worn goalie jerseys.
*MULT.COLOR SWATCH: 1X TO 1.5X
TTBB Brian Boucher 8.00 20.00
TTCJ Curtis Joseph 8.00 20.00
TTCO Chris Osgood 8.00 20.00
TTJO Jose Theodore 10.00 25.00
TTJT Jocelyn Thibault 8.00 20.00
TTMB Martin Brodeur 15.00 40.00
TTMD Mike Dunham 8.00 20.00
TTMR Mike Richter 8.00 20.00
TTPR Patrick Roy 15.00 40.00
TTRC Roman Cechmanek 8.00 20.00

2001-02 Upper Deck Last Line of Defense

COMPLETE SET (10) 12.50 25.00
STATED ODDS 1:36 SERIES 2
LL1 Patrick Roy 4.00 10.00
LL2 Ed Belfour .75 2.00
LL3 Dominik Hasek 1.50 4.00
LL4 Felix Potvin .75 2.00
LL5 Martin Brodeur 2.00 5.00
LL6 Roman Cechmanek .60 1.50
LL7 Johan Hedberg .75 2.00
LL8 Evgeni Nabokov .60 1.50
LL9 Curtis Joseph .75 2.00
LL10 Olaf Kolzig .60 1.50

2001-02 Upper Deck Leaders of the Pack

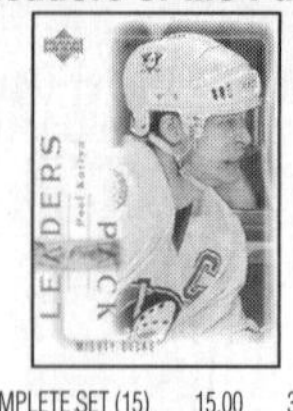

COMPLETE SET (15) 15.00 30.00
STATED ODDS 1:24 SERIES 2
LP1 Paul Kariya .60 1.50
LP2 Tony Amonte .50 1.25
LP3 Joe Sakic 1.25 3.00
LP4 Mike Modano 1.00 2.50
LP5 Steve Yzerman 3.00 8.00
LP6 Pavel Bure .75 2.00
LP7 Scott Stevens .50 1.25
LP8 Mark Messier .75 2.00
LP9 Michael Peca .50 1.25
LP10 Daniel Alfredsson .50 1.25
LP11 Mario Lemieux 4.00 10.00
LP12 Owen Nolan .50 1.25
LP13 Doug Weight .50 1.25
LP14 Chris Pronger .50 1.25
LP15 Mats Sundin .60 1.50

2001-02 Upper Deck Legendary Cut Signatures

Randomly inserted into Series I and Series II packs, this 5-card set featured "cut" signatures from some of the most recognized names in the history of the NHL. Each card was individually serial-numbered and the totals are listed below. These cards were not priced due to scarcity.
LCCC Clarence Campbell/5
Series 2
LCDH Doug Harvey/5
Series 2
LCES Eddie Shore/5
Series1 EXCH
LCJP Jacques Plante/5
Series 1
LCKC King Clancy/5
Series 2
LCLS Lord Stanley/1
Series 2
LCSA Sid Abel/5
Series 2
LCTS Terry Sawchuk/5
Series 1

2001-02 Upper Deck Patches

Inserted at 1:2500 Series I packs, this 19-card set featured swatches of game-used jersey patches.
PBS Brendan Shanahan 25.00 60.00
PDW Doug Weight 25.00 60.00
PEB Ed Belfour 30.00 80.00
PJJ Jaromir Jagr 30.00 80.00
PJL John LeClair 25.00 60.00
PJS Joe Sakic 30.00 80.00
PMH Marian Hossa 15.00 40.00
PML Mario Lemieux 60.00 150.00
PMM Mike Modano 25.00 60.00
PMO Mike Modano 25.00 60.00
PMS Mats Sundin 15.00 40.00
PPF Peter Forsberg 40.00 100.00
PPK Paul Kariya 25.00 60.00
PPR Patrick Roy 50.00 120.00
PRB Ray Bourque 40.00 100.00
PSA Joe Sakic 30.00 80.00
PSF Sergei Fedorov 30.00 80.00
PSY Steve Yzerman 50.00 125.00
PTS Teemu Selanne 15.00 40.00

2001-02 Upper Deck Patches Series II

Randomly inserted into Series II packs, this 24-card set partially paralleled Series II jersey set but featured swatches of jersey logos, name plates or numbers. Number patches were denoted with a "PN" prefix and inserted at 1:2500. Logo patches were denoted with a "PL" prefix and inserted at 1:2500. Name Plate patches were denoted with a "NA" prefix and inserted at 1:7500. Please note that the Modano Name Plate card had a "PL" prefix according to Upper Deck.
PLJJ Jaromir Jagr 30.00 80.00
PLMB Martin Brodeur 40.00 100.00
PLML Mario Lemieux 40.00 100.00
PLPF Peter Forsberg 40.00 100.00
PLPK Paul Kariya 20.00 50.00
PLPR Patrick Roy 40.00 100.00
PLSF Sergei Fedorov 30.00 80.00
PLSY Steve Yzerman 40.00 100.00
PNBS Brendan Shanahan 20.00 50.00
PNJL John LeClair 20.00 50.00
PNJS Joe Sakic 30.00 80.00
PNML Mario Lemieux 40.00 100.00
PNMM Mike Modano 25.00 60.00
PNPK Paul Kariya 20.00 50.00
PNPR Patrick Roy 40.00 100.00
PNSY Steve Yzerman 40.00 100.00
NABS Brendan Shanahan 50.00 120.00
NAJL John LeClair 40.00 100.00
NAJS Joe Sakic 75.00 200.00
NAML Mario Lemieux 100.00 250.00
NAPF Peter Forsberg 75.00 200.00
NAPR Patrick Roy 100.00 250.00
NASY Steve Yzerman 100.00 250.00
PLMM Mike Modano 60.00 150.00

2001-02 Upper Deck Pride of a Nation

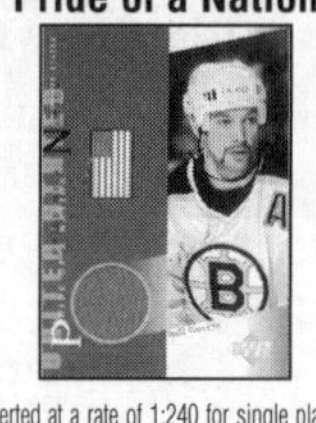

Inserted at a rate of 1:240 for single players and 1:576 for double players, this 30-card set highlighted the homelands of players of the NHL. Each card carried game-worn jersey piece(s) of the player(s) featured. Triple player cards were serial-numbered to just twenty and are not priced due to scarcity.
PNBG Bill Guerin 6.00 15.00
PNDH Dominik Hasek 8.00 20.00
PNDW Doug Weight 6.00 15.00
PNJJ Jaromir Jagr 8.00 20.00
PNJS Joe Sakic 10.00 25.00
PNMB Martin Brodeur 15.00 40.00
PNML Mario Lemieux 15.00 40.00
PNPF Peter Forsberg 8.00 20.00
PNPR Patrick Roy 15.00 40.00
PNSF Sergei Fedorov 8.00 20.00
PNSK Saku Koivu 6.00 15.00
PNSY Steve Yzerman 15.00 40.00
PNTA Tony Amonte 6.00 15.00
PNTS Teemu Selanne 6.00 15.00
PNVK Viktor Kozlov 6.00 15.00
DPAG Tony Amonte 12.50 30.00
Bill Guerin
DPFK Sergei Fedorov 12.50 30.00
Viktor Kozlov
DPFS Peter Forsberg 15.00 40.00
Mats Sundin
DPHJ Dominik Hasek 15.00 40.00
Jaromir Jagr
DPLK M.Lemieux/P.Kariya 15.00 40.00
DPLM J.LeClair/M.Modano 12.50 30.00
DPRS Patrick Roy 30.00 80.00
Joe Sakic
DPSB Scott Stevens 12.50 30.00
Martin Brodeur
DPSK Teemu Selanne 12.50 30.00
Saku Koivu
DPYS Steve Yzerman 25.00 60.00
Brendan Shanahan
TPAWL Tony Amonte
Doug Weight
Brian Leetch
TPFKK Sergei Fedorov
Alexei Kovalev
Viktor Kozlov
TPFSL Peter Forsberg
Mats Sundin
Nicklas Lidstrom
TPHJL Dominik Hasek
Jaromir Jagr
Robert Lang
TPYRL Steve Yzerman
Patrick Roy
Mario Lemieux

2001-02 Upper Deck Pride of the Leafs

Serial-numbered to just 75 sets, this 9 card set featured past and present Toronto Maple Leafs with full color action photos alongside a swatch of game-worn jersey on the card fronts.
MLBJ Borje Salming 50.00 125.00
MLCJ Curtis Joseph 30.00 80.00
MLDG Doug Gilmour 30.00 80.00
MLFP Felix Potvin 50.00 125.00
MLMS Mats Sundin 30.00 80.00
MLNA Nikolai Antropov 30.00 80.00
MLSB Sergei Berezin 30.00 80.00
MLTD Tie Domi 30.00 80.00
MLWC Wendel Clark 50.00 125.00

2001-02 Upper Deck Shooting Stars

COMPLETE SET (20) 15.00 30.00
STATED ODDS 1:9 SERIES 2
SS1 Paul Kariya .40 1.00
SS2 Bill Guerin .30 .75
SS3 Joe Sakic .75 2.00
SS4 Milan Hejduk .40 1.00
SS5 Brett Hull .50 1.25
SS6 Brendan Shanahan .60 1.50
SS7 Luc Robitaille .30 .75
SS8 Pavel Bure .60 1.50
SS9 Zigmund Palffy .30 .75
SS10 Patrik Elias .30 .75
SS11 Alexei Yashin .30 .75
SS12 John LeClair .50 1.25
SS13 Alexei Kovalev .30 .75
SS14 Mario Lemieux 2.50 6.00
SS15 Owen Nolan .30 .75
SS16 Teemu Selanne .40 1.00
SS17 Alexander Mogilny .30 .75
SS18 Markus Naslund .40 1.00
SS19 Jaromir Jagr .60 1.50
SS20 Peter Bondra .30 .75

2001-02 Upper Deck Skilled Stars

COMPLETE SET (20) 15.00 30.00
STATED ODDS 1:9 SERIES 1
SS1 Paul Kariya .40 1.00
SS2 Mario Lemieux 2.50 6.00
SS3 Chris Pronger .30 .75
SS4 Teemu Selanne .40 1.00
SS5 Owen Nolan .30 .75
SS6 Pavel Bure .50 1.25
SS7 Keith Tkachuk .40 1.00
SS8 Mike Modano .60 1.50
SS9 Peter Forsberg 1.00 2.50
SS10 Zigmund Palffy .30 .75
SS11 Martin Brodeur 1.00 2.50
SS12 Patrick Roy 2.00 5.00
SS13 Joe Sakic .75 2.00
SS14 Ray Bourque .75 2.00
SS15 Steve Yzerman 2.00 5.00
SS16 Roman Cechmanek .30 .75
SS17 Mark Messier .50 1.25
SS18 Vincent Lecavalier .40 1.00
SS19 John LeClair .50 1.25
SS20 Tony Amonte .30 .75

2001-02 Upper Deck Tandems

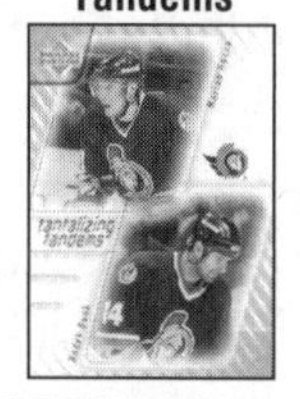

COMPLETE SET (10) 20.00 40.00
STATED ODDS 1:36 SERIES 2
T1 Sergei Samsonov 2.00 5.00
Joe Thornton
T2 Joe Sakic 4.00 10.00
Milan Hejduk
T3 Brendan Shanahan 5.00 12.00
Steve Yzerman
T4 Valeri Bure 1.25 3.00
Pavel Bure
T5 Patrik Elias 1.25 3.00
Jason Arnott
T6 Marian Hossa 1.25 3.00
Radek Bonk
T7 John LeClair 1.25 3.00
Jeremy Roenick
T8 Teemu Selanne 1.25 3.00
Owen Nolan
T9 Keith Tkachuk 1.25 3.00
Pavol Demitra
T10 Brad Richards 1.25 3.00
Vincent Lecavalier

2002-03 Upper Deck

This 456-card set was issued in two different series. Series I consisted of 180 base cards; 15 Memorable Season subset cards (181-195) inserted at 1:6; 30 Young Guns subset cards (196-225) inserted at 1:4; 9 more Memorable Seasons subset cards and 12 more Young Guns subset cards (226-246) inserted one per box. Series 2 consisted of 180 base cards and 30 Young Guns subset cards (427-456) inserted at 1:4.
COMP.SER.1 SET (246) 300.00 600.00
COMP.SER.1 SET w/o SP's (225) 60.00 125.00
COMP.SER.2 SET (210) 150.00 300.00
COMP.SER.2 SET w/o SP's (180) 15.00 30.00
1 Vitali Vishnevsky .02 .10
2 J-S Giguere .15 .40
3 Steve Rucchin .02 .10
4 Paul Kariya .20 .50
5 Andy McDonald .02 .10
6 Lubos Bartecko .02 .10
7 Ilya Kovalchuk .25 .60
8 Tomi Kallio .02 .10
9 Milan Hnilicka .15 .40
10 Patrik Stefan .02 .10
11 Joe Thornton .30 .75
12 Brian Rolston .02 .10
13 Martin Lapointe .02 .10

14 Nick Boynton .02 .10
15 Andy Hilbert .02 .10
16 Glen Murray .02 .10
17 J-P Dumont .02 .10
18 Tim Connolly .02 .10
19 Miroslav Satan .15 .40
20 Maxim Afinogenov .02 .10
21 Taylor Pyatt .02 .10
22 Jay McKee .02 .10
23 Marc Savard .02 .10
24 Roman Turek .15 .40
25 Dean McAmmond .02 .10
26 Craig Conroy .02 .10
27 Derek Morris .02 .10
28 Rod Brind'Amour .15 .40
29 Josef Vasicek .02 .10
30 Niclas Wallin .02 .10
31 Jaroslav Svoboda .02 .10
32 Sami Kapanen .02 .10
33 Erik Cole .02 .10
34 Jeff O'Neill .02 .10
35 Michael Nylander .02 .10
36 Alexei Zhamnov .02 .10
37 Jon Klemm .02 .10
38 Kyle Calder .02 .10
39 Eric Daze .02 .10
40 Steve Sullivan .02 .10
41 Stephane Yelle .02 .10
42 Rob Blake .15 .40
43 Patrick Roy 1.00 2.50
44 Radim Vrbata .02 .10
45 Chris Drury .15 .40
46 Milan Hejduk .20 .50
47 Joe Sakic .40 1.00
48 Peter Forsberg .50 1.25
49 Rostislav Klesla .02 .10
50 Marc Denis .15 .40
51 Grant Marshall .02 .10
52 Ray Whitney .02 .10
53 Espen Knutsen .02 .10
54 Mike Sillinger .02 .10
55 Bill Guerin .15 .40
56 Mike Modano .30 .75
57 Sergei Zubov .02 .10
58 Marty Turco .15 .40
59 Jason Arnott .02 .10
60 Jere Lehtinen .15 .40
61 Steve Yzerman 1.00 2.50
62 Sergei Fedorov .30 .75
63 Nicklas Lidstrom .20 .50
64 Curtis Joseph .20 .50
65 Igor Larionov .02 .10
66 Luc Robitaille .15 .40
67 Tomas Holmstrom .02 .10
68 Brett Hull .25 .60
69 Mike Comrie .15 .40
70 Marty Reasoner .02 .10
71 Tommy Salo .15 .40
72 Ryan Smyth .02 .10
73 Anson Carter .15 .40
74 Janne Niinimaa .02 .10
75 Sandis Ozolinsh .02 .10
76 Roberto Luongo .25 .60
77 Kristian Huselius .02 .10
78 Valeri Bure .02 .10
79 Brad Ference .02 .10
80 Ian Laperriere .02 .10
81 Mattias Norstrom .02 .10
82 Adam Deadmarsh .02 .10
83 Jason Allison .02 .10
84 Eric Belanger .02 .10
85 Felix Potvin .20 .50
86 Wes Walz .02 .10
87 Darby Hendrickson .02 .10
88 Dwayne Roloson .02 .10
89 Marian Gaborik .40 1.00
90 Filip Kuba .02 .10
91 Andrei Markov .02 .10
92 Jose Theodore .25 .60
93 Mike Ribeiro .02 .10
94 Richard Zednik .02 .10
95 Gino Odjick .02 .10
96 Saku Koivu .20 .50
97 Andy Delmore .02 .10
98 Tomas Vokoun .15 .40
99 Martin Erat .02 .10
100 Denis Arkhipov .02 .10
101 Scott Hartnell .02 .10
102 Scott Stevens .15 .40
103 Patrik Elias .15 .40
104 Jamie Langenbrunner .02 .10
105 Brian Gionta .02 .10
106 Joe Nieuwendyk .15 .40
107 Martin Brodeur .50 1.25
108 Roman Hamrlik .02 .10
109 Shawn Bates .02 .10
110 Steve Webb .02 .10
111 Alexei Yashin .02 .10
112 Chris Osgood .15 .40
113 Mark Parrish .02 .10
114 Petr Nedved .02 .10
115 Eric Lindros .20 .50
116 Dan Blackburn .15 .40
117 Radek Dvorak .02 .10
118 Tom Poti .02 .10
119 Pavel Bure .20 .50
120 Todd White .02 .10
121 Patrick Lalime .15 .40
122 Marian Hossa .20 .50
123 Daniel Alfredsson .15 .40
124 Wade Redden .02 .10
125 Mike Fisher .02 .10
126 Keith Primeau .02 .10
127 Jeremy Roenick .25 .60
128 Eric Weinrich .02 .10
129 Roman Cechmanek .15 .40
130 Mark Recchi .15 .40
131 Justin Williams .02 .10
132 Brad May .02 .10
133 Sean Burke .15 .40
134 Paul Mara .02 .10
135 Shane Doan .02 .10
136 Tony Amonte .15 .40
137 Daniel Briere .02 .10
138 Kris Beech .02 .10
139 Martin Straka .02 .10
140 Alexei Kovalev .15 .40
141 Mario Lemieux 1.25 3.00
142 Andrew Ference .02 .10
143 Johan Hedberg .15 .40
144 Patrick Marleau .15 .40
145 Owen Nolan .15 .40
146 Mike Rathje .02 .10
147 Evgeni Nabokov .15 .40
148 Marco Sturm .02 .10
149 Todd Harvey .02 .10
150 Pavol Demitra .15 .40
151 Doug Weight .15 .40
152 Al MacInnis .15 .40
153 Brent Johnson .15 .40
154 Keith Tkachuk .20 .50
155 Cory Stillman .02 .10
156 Brad Richards .15 .40
157 Pavel Kubina .02 .10
158 Nikolai Khabibulin .20 .50
159 Martin St. Louis .15 .40
160 Vincent Lecavalier .20 .50
161 Bryan McCabe .02 .10
162 Gary Roberts .02 .10
163 Ed Belfour .20 .50
164 Mats Sundin .20 .50
165 Tie Domi .15 .40
166 Alexander Mogilny .15 .40
167 Daniel Sedin .02 .10
168 Todd Bertuzzi .20 .50
169 Mattias Ohlund .02 .10
170 Dan Cloutier .15 .40
171 Markus Naslund .20 .50
172 Jan Hlavac .02 .10
173 Olaf Kolzig .15 .40
174 Peter Bondra .20 .50
175 Sergei Gonchar .02 .10
176 Steve Konowalchuk .02 .10
177 Chris Simon .02 .10
178 Dainius Zubrus .02 .10
179 Patrick Roy CL .75 2.00
180 Steve Yzerman CL .75 2.00
181 Paul Kariya MS .50 1.25
182 Bobby Orr MS 3.00 8.00
183 Jarome Iginla MS .60 1.50
184 Joe Sakic MS 1.00 2.50
185 Patrick Roy MS 2.50 6.00
186 Steve Yzerman MS 2.50 6.00
187 Gordie Howe MS 2.00 5.00
188 Wayne Gretzky MS 4.00 10.00
189 Wayne Gretzky MS 4.00 10.00
190 Martin Brodeur MS 1.25 3.00
191 Mario Lemieux MS 3.00 8.00
192 Brett Hull MS .60 1.50
193 Jaromir Jagr MS .75 2.00
194 Pavel Bure MS .60 1.50
195 Teemu Selanne MS .60 1.50
196 Mark Hartigan YG 1.25 3.00
197 Pasi Nurminen YG 1.25 3.00
198 Henrik Tallinder YG 1.25 3.00
199 Micki Dupont YG RC 1.25 3.00
200 Tyler Arnason YG 2.50 6.00
201 Jordan Krestanovich YG 1.25 3.00
202 Kelly Fairchild YG 1.25 3.00
203 Andrej Nedorost YG 1.25 3.00
204 Sean Avery YG 1.25 3.00
205 Stephen Weiss YG 2.00 5.00
206 Lukas Krajicek YG 1.50 4.00
207 Kyle Rossiter YG 1.25 3.00
208 Eric Beaudoin YG 1.25 3.00
209 Sylvain Blouin YG RC 1.25 3.00
210 Marcel Hossa YG 1.25 3.00
211 Adam Hall YG RC 1.25 3.00
212 Greg Koehler YG RC 1.25 3.00
213 Trent Hunter YG 1.25 3.00
214 Ray Schultz YG RC 1.25 3.00
215 Martin Prusek YG 1.25 3.00
216 Chris Bala YG 1.25 3.00
217 Josh Langfeld YG 1.25 3.00
218 Bruno St. Jacques YG 1.25 3.00
219 Branko Radivojevic YG 1.25 3.00
220 Martin Cibak YG 1.25 3.00
221 Evgeni Konstantinov YG 1.25 3.00
222 Karel Pilar YG 1.25 3.00
223 Sebastien Centomo YG 1.25 3.00
224 Sebastien Charpentier YG 1.25 3.00
225 J-F Fortin YG 1.25 3.00
226 Stanislav Chistov YG RC 6.00 15.00
227 Alexei Smirnov YG RC 5.00 12.00
228 Chuck Kobasew YG RC 6.00 15.00
229 Tony Amonte MS 20.00 50.00
230 Peter Forsberg MS 30.00 80.00
231 Chris Drury MS 25.00 60.00
232 Rick Nash YG RC 40.00 100.00
233 Brendan Shanahan MS 25.00 60.00
234 Henrik Zetterberg YG RC 50.00 125.00
235 Ales Hemsky YG RC 25.00 60.00
236 Jay Bouwmeester YG RC 20.00 50.00
237 Alexei Yashin MS 25.00 60.00
238 Alexander Frolov YG RC 20.00 50.00
239 P-M Bouchard YG RC 12.50 30.00
240 Ron Hainsey YG RC 6.00 15.00
241 Sean Burke MS 20.00 50.00
242 Owen Nolan MS 25.00 60.00
243 Chris Pronger MS 20.00 50.00
244 Mats Sundin MS 25.00 60.00
245 Alexander Svitov YG RC 6.00 15.00
246 Steve Eminger YG RC 6.00 15.00
247 Adam Oates .15 .40
248 Petr Sykora .02 .10
249 Fredrik Olausson .02 .10
250 Matt Cullen .02 .10
251 Ruslan Salei .02 .10
252 Slava Kozlov .02 .10
253 Dany Heatley .25 .60
254 Frantisek Kaberle .02 .10
255 Pasi Nurminen .02 .10
256 Shawn McEachern .02 .10
257 Sergei Samsonov .15 .40
258 Steve Shields .15 .40
259 Jonathan Girard .02 .10
260 Jozef Stumpel .02 .10
261 Bryan Berard .02 .10
262 Marty McInnis .02 .10
263 Stu Barnes .02 .10
264 Curtis Brown .02 .10
265 Chris Gratton .02 .10
266 Rhett Warrener .02 .10
267 Jochen Hecht .02 .10
268 James Patrick .02 .10
269 Jarome Iginla .25 .60
270 Martin Gelinas .02 .10
271 Chris Drury .15 .40
272 Stephane Yelle .02 .10
273 Jamie Wright .02 .10
274 Kevin Weekes .15 .40
275 Bret Hedican .02 .10
276 Ron Francis .15 .40
277 Kevyn Adams .02 .10
278 Marek Malik .02 .10
279 Bates Battaglia .02 .10
280 Theo Fleury .02 .10
281 Sergei Berezin .02 .10
282 Mark Bell .02 .10
283 Alexander Karpovtsev .02 .10
284 Steve Passmore .02 .10
285 Bob Probert .02 .10
286 Alex Tanguay .15 .40
287 Steven Reinprecht .02 .10
288 Adam Foote .02 .10
289 David Aebischer .15 .40
290 Greg deVries .02 .10
291 Dan Hinote .02 .10
292 Derek Morris .02 .10
293 Scott Parker .02 .10
294 Geoff Sanderson .02 .10
295 Andrew Cassels .02 .10
296 Jean-Luc Grand-Pierre .02 .10
297 Luke Richardson .02 .10
298 Tyler Wright .02 .10
299 Jody Shelley .02 .10
300 Ron Tugnutt .15 .40
301 Scott Young .02 .10
302 Pierre Turgeon .15 .40
303 Derian Hatcher .02 .10
304 Richard Matvichuk .02 .10
305 Kirk Muller .02 .10
306 Brendan Shanahan .20 .50
307 Chris Chelios .20 .50
308 Mathieu Dandenault .02 .10
309 Pavel Datsyuk .20 .50
310 Kris Draper .02 .10
311 Boyd Devereaux .02 .10
312 Kirk Maltby .02 .10
313 Manny Legace .15 .40
314 Jani Rita .02 .10
315 Todd Marchant .02 .10
316 Daniel Cleary .02 .10
317 Georges Laraque .02 .10
318 Mike York .02 .10
319 Jason Smith .02 .10
320 Viktor Kozlov .02 .10
321 Dimitri Yushkevich .02 .10
322 Olli Jokinen .15 .40
323 Marcus Nilsson .02 .10
324 Ivan Novoseltsev .02 .10
325 Aaron Miller .02 .10
326 Zigmund Palffy .15 .40
327 Jamie Storr .15 .40
328 Bryan Smolinski .02 .10
329 Mathieu Schneider .02 .10
330 Erik Rasmussen .02 .10
331 Andrew Brunette .02 .10
332 Richard Park .02 .10
333 Manny Fernandez .15 .40
334 Matt Johnson .02 .10
335 Ladislav Benysek .02 .10
336 Mariusz Czerkawski .02 .10
337 Sheldon Souray .02 .10
338 Chad Kilger .02 .10
339 Yanic Perreault .02 .10
340 Mathieu Garon .15 .40
341 Craig Rivet .02 .10
342 Mike Dunham .15 .40
343 David Legwand .15 .40
344 Vladimir Orszagh .02 .10
345 Kimmo Timonen .02 .10
346 Cale Hulse .02 .10
347 Oleg Tverdovsky .02 .10
348 Jeff Friesen .02 .10
349 Brian Rafalski .02 .10
350 Sergei Brylin .02 .10
351 John Madden .02 .10
352 Colin White .02 .10
353 Michael Peca .02 .10
354 Eric Cairns .02 .10
355 Dave Scatchard .02 .10
356 Brad Isbister .02 .10
357 Oleg Kvasha .02 .10
358 Mattias Timander .02 .10
359 Matthew Barnaby .02 .10
360 Bobby Holik .02 .10
361 Darius Kasparaitis .02 .10
362 Vladimir Malakhov .02 .10
363 Brian Leetch .15 .40
364 Mark Messier .20 .50
365 Mike Richter .20 .50
366 Martin Havlat .15 .40
367 Radek Bonk .02 .10
368 Petr Schastlivy .02 .10
369 Zdeno Chara .02 .10
370 Chris Neil .02 .10
371 Magnus Arvedson .02 .10
372 Pavel Brendl .02 .10
373 Donald Brashear .02 .10
374 Michal Handzus .02 .10
375 Kim Johnsson .02 .10
376 John LeClair .20 .50
377 Simon Gagne .20 .50
378 Claude Lemieux .02 .10
379 Brian Boucher .15 .40
380 Teppo Numminen .02 .10
381 Daymond Langkow .15 .40
382 Ladislav Nagy .02 .10
383 Brian Savage .02 .10
384 Ville Nieminen .02 .10
385 Randy Robitaille .02 .10
386 Alexei Morozov .02 .10
387 Jan Hrdina .02 .10
388 Michal Rozsival .02 .10
389 Alexandre Daigle .02 .10
390 Mike Ricci .02 .10
391 Vincent Damphousse .02 .10
392 Teemu Selanne .20 .50
393 Adam Graves .02 .10
394 Scott Thornton .02 .10
395 Scott Hannan .02 .10
396 Fred Brathwaite .15 .40
397 Jamal Mayers .02 .10
398 Reed Low .02 .10
399 Chris Pronger .15 .40
400 Scott Mellanby .02 .10
401 Alexander Khavanov .02 .10
402 Ruslan Fedotenko .02 .10
403 Fredrik Modin .02 .10
404 Nikita Alexeev .02 .10
405 Shane Willis .02 .10
406 Dave Andreychuk .02 .10
407 Trevor Kidd .15 .40
408 Robert Reichel .02 .10
409 Robert Svehla .02 .10
410 Alyn McCauley .02 .10
411 Tomas Kaberle .02 .10
412 Travis Green .02 .10
413 Henrik Sedin .02 .10
414 Brendan Morrison .15 .40
415 Matt Cooke .02 .10
416 Ed Jovanovski .15 .40
417 Mattias Ohlund .02 .10
418 Trevor Linden .02 .10
419 Jaromir Jagr .30 .75
420 Robert Lang .02 .10
421 Matt Pettinger .02 .10
422 Ken Klee .02 .10
423 Stephen Peat .02 .10
424 Brian Sutherby .02 .10
425 Joe Thornton .30 .75
426 Wayne Gretzky 1.25 3.00
427 Martin Gerber YG RC 6.00 15.00
428 Kurt Sauer YG RC 3.00 8.00
429 Tim Thomas YG RC 6.00 15.00
430 Jordan Leopold YG RC 3.00 8.00
431 Levente Szuper YG RC 3.00 8.00
432 Shawn Thornton YG RC 3.00 8.00
433 Jeff Paul YG RC 3.00 8.00
434 Lasse Pirjeta YG RC 3.00 8.00
435 Dmitri Bykov YG RC 3.00 8.00
436 Ryan Miller YG RC 20.00 50.00
437 Kari Haakana YG RC 3.00 8.00
438 Ivan Majesky YG RC 3.00 8.00
439 Stephane Veilleux YG RC 3.00 8.00
440 Scottie Upshall YG RC 5.00 12.00
441 Shaone Morrisonn YG RC 3.00 8.00
442 Eric Godard YG RC 3.00 8.00
443 Jason Spezza YG RC 25.00 60.00
444 Anton Volchenkov YG RC 3.00 8.00
445 Dennis Seidenberg YG RC 5.00 12.00
446 Radovan Somik YG RC 3.00 8.00
447 Patrick Sharp YG RC 3.00 8.00
448 Jeff Taffe YG RC 3.00 8.00
449 Lynn Loyns YG RC 3.00 8.00
450 Mike Cammalleri YG RC 6.00 15.00
451 Tom Koivisto YG RC 3.00 8.00
452 Curtis Sanford YG RC 4.00 10.00
453 Cody Rudkowsky YG RC 3.00 8.00
454 Carlo Colaiacovo YG RC 3.00 8.00
455 Mikael Tellqvist YG RC 6.00 15.00
456 Vernon Fiddler YG RC 3.00 8.00

2002-03 Upper Deck Exclusives

Available only in Canadian hobby packs, this 456-card set paralleled the base set but was enhanced with gold foil maple leafs across the card front and serial-numbered to 75 copies each. Cards 1-180 were available in Series I and cards 181-456 were available in Series II.
*STARS: 3X TO 8X BASE HI
*SER.1 SP's (181-225): 2X TO 5X
*SER.1 SP's (226-
*YG SP's 226-245: .75X TO 2X BASE HI

2002-03 Upper Deck All-Star Jerseys

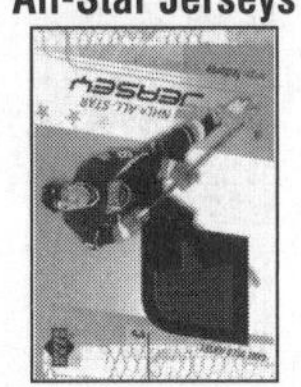

*MULT.COLOR SWATCH: .75X TO 1.5X
STATED ODDS 1:96 SERIES 1 HOBBY
ASCC Chris Chelios 3.00 8.00
ASEJ Ed Jovanovski 3.00 8.00
ASJS Joe Sakic 6.00 15.00
ASJT Jose Theodore 4.00 10.00
ASMN Markus Naslund 3.00 8.00
ASPK Paul Kariya 3.00 8.00
ASRB Rob Blake 3.00 8.00
ASSB Sean Burke 3.00 8.00
ASSF Sergei Fedorov 5.00 12.00
ASSK Sami Kapanen 3.00 8.00
ASSO Sandis Ozolinsh 3.00 8.00
ASTS Teemu Selanne 3.00 8.00
ASVD Vincent Damphousse 3.00 8.00
ASWG Wayne Gretzky 30.00 80.00

2002-03 Upper Deck All-Star Performers

*MULT.COLOR SWATCH: .75X TO 1.5X
STATED ODDS 1:96 SERIES 2
ASEJ Ed Jovanovski 4.00 10.00
ASJT Jose Theodore 5.00 12.00
ASMM Mike Modano 8.00 20.00
ASMN Markus Naslund 3.00 8.00
ASPK Paul Kariya 3.00 8.00
ASPR Patrick Roy 15.00 40.00
ASRB Rob Blake 4.00 10.00
ASSB Sean Burke 4.00 10.00
ASSK Sami Kapanen 4.00 10.00
ASSO Sandis Ozolinsh 4.00 10.00
ASTS Teemu Selanne 3.00 8.00
ASVD Vincent Damphousse 4.00 10.00
ASWG Wayne Gretzky 30.00 80.00

2002-03 Upper Deck Blow-Ups

Found in Canadian retail boxes only, this 42-card set was larger sized parallels of the base set. Cards were serial-numbered out of 299.

COMPLETE SET (42) 150.00
C1 Paul Kariya 6.00 10.00
C2 Ilya Kovalchuk 2.50 6.00
C3 Joe Thornton 2.50 6.00
C4 Roman Turek 1.50 2.00
C5 Jeff O'Neill 1.50 2.00
C6 Rob Blake 1.50 2.00
C7 Patrick Roy 8.00 15.00
C8 Joe Sakic 4.00 10.00
C9 Peter Forsberg 5.00 10.00
C10 Marc Denis 1.50 3.00
C11 Mike Modano 3.00 6.00
C12 Marty Turco 1.50 4.00
C13 Steve Yzerman 8.00 15.00
C14 Curtis Joseph 2.50 6.00
C15 Nicklas Lidstrom 2.00 4.00
C16 Mike Comrie 1.50 4.00
C17 Tommy Salo 1.50 3.00
C18 Roberto Luongo 1.50 3.00
C19 Felix Potvin 2.00 4.00
C20 Marian Gaborik 2.00 6.00
C21 Jose Theodore 2.00 4.00
C22 Saku Koivu 2.00 4.00
C23 Scott Hartnell 3.00
C24 Scott Stevens 1.50 2.00
C25 Martin Brodeur 5.00 10.00
C26 Eric Lindros 2.00 4.00
C27 Pavel Bure 2.50 6.00
C28 Marian Hossa 2.00 4.00
C29 Daniel Alfredsson 1.50 3.00
C30 Keith Primeau 1.50 2.00
C31 Sean Burke 1.50 3.00
C32 Tony Amonte 2.00 4.00
C33 Mario Lemieux 10.00 20.00
C34 Owen Nolan 1.50 3.00
C35 Al MacInnis 1.50 3.00
C36 Brad Richards 1.50 3.00
C37 Vincent Lecavalier 1.50 3.00
C38 Mats Sundin 2.00 4.00
C39 Ed Belfour 2.00 4.00
C40 Todd Bertuzzi 1.50 3.00
C41 Markus Naslund 1.50 3.00
C42 Olaf Kolzig 1.50 3.00

2002-03 Upper Deck Bright Futures

*MULT.COLOR SWATCH: .75X TO 1.5X
STATED ODDS 1:72 SERIES 2
ALL CARDS CARRY BF PREFIX
AM Alexei Morozov 4.00 10.00
BB Brian Boucher 4.00 10.00
DA Denis Arkhipov 4.00 10.00
DL David Legwand 4.00 10.00
IB Ilja Bryzgalov 4.00 10.00
JB Jaroslav Bednar 4.00 10.00
JG J-S Giguere 4.00 10.00
JL Jamie Lundmark 4.00 10.00
ME Martin Erat 4.00 10.00
MM Manny Malhotra 4.00 10.00
MP Matt Pettinger 4.00 10.00
MR Mike Ribeiro 4.00 10.00
MY Mike York 4.00 10.00
PA Timo Parssinen 4.00 10.00
PB Pavel Brendl 4.00 10.00
PS Patrik Stefan 4.00 10.00
RK Rostislav Klesla 4.00 10.00
SG Simon Gagne 4.00 10.00
TC Tim Connolly 4.00 10.00
TP Taylor Pyatt 4.00 10.00
VN Ville Nieminen 4.00 10.00

2002-03 Upper Deck CHL Graduates

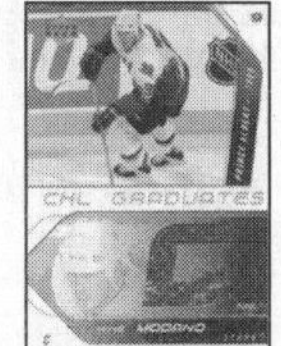

*MULT.COLOR SWATCH: .75X TO 1.5X
STATED ODDS 1:96 SERIES 1 HOBBY
CGAT Alex Tanguay 4.00 10.00
CGBL Dan Blackburn 4.00 10.00
CGDB Daniel Briere 4.00 10.00
CGDL David Legwand 4.00 10.00
CGED Eric Daze 4.00 10.00
CGEL Eric Lindros 8.00 20.00
CGGM Glen Murray 4.00 10.00
CGJA Jason Arnott 4.00 10.00
CGJF Jeff Friesen 4.00 10.00
CGJS Joe Sakic 6.00 15.00
CGJT Joe Thornton 8.00 20.00
CGKP Keith Primeau 4.00 10.00
CGMD Marc Denis 4.00 10.00
CGML Mario Lemieux 20.00 50.00
CGMM Mike Modano 8.00 20.00
CGMR Mark Recchi 4.00 10.00
CGRT Ron Tugnutt 4.00 10.00
CGSS Steve Sullivan 4.00 10.00
CGSY Steve Yzerman 12.50 30.00
CGTL Trevor Linden 4.00 10.00

2002-03 Upper Deck CHL Graduates Gold

*GOLD: 2X TO 5X BASIC JERSEY
STATED PRINT RUN 25 SER.#'d SETS

2002-03 Upper Deck Difference Makers

*MULT.COLOR SWATCH: .75X TO 1.5X
STATED ODDS 1:72 SERIES 2
BL Brian Leetch 3.00 8.00
BS Brendan Shanahan 3.00 8.00
ED Eric Daze 3.00 8.00
IK Ilya Kovalchuk 5.00 12.00
JA Jason Allison 3.00 8.00
JI Jarome Iginla 4.00 10.00
JJ Jaromir Jagr 6.00 15.00
JT Jose Theodore 4.00 10.00
JT Joe Thornton 8.00 20.00
MD Mike Dunham 3.00 8.00
ML Mario Lemieux 15.00 40.00
MM Mike Modano 8.00 20.00
MS Mats Sundin 3.00 8.00
PK Paul Kariya 3.00 8.00
PR Patrick Roy 15.00 40.00
RB Rob Blake 3.00 8.00
RT Roman Turek 3.00 8.00
SA Miroslav Satan 3.00 8.00
SS Sergei Samsonov 3.00 8.00
SY Steve Yzerman 10.00 25.00
ZP Zigmund Palffy 3.00 8.00

2002-03 Upper Deck Fan Favorites

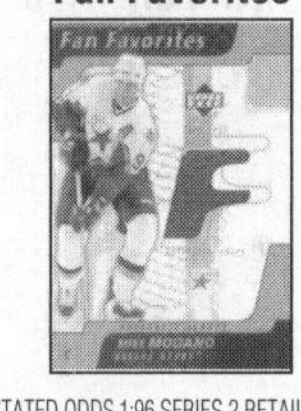

STATED ODDS 1:96 SERIES 2 RETAIL
ALL CARDS CARRY FF PREFIX
AD Adam Deadmarsh 3.00 8.00
BL Brian Leetch 3.00 8.00
JI Jarome Iginla 4.00 10.00
JJ Jaromir Jagr 6.00 15.00
KP Keith Primeau 3.00 8.00
MB Martin Brodeur 10.00 25.00
MM Mike Modano 8.00 20.00
MN Markus Naslund 3.00 8.00
NL Nicklas Lidstrom 3.00 8.00
PF Peter Forsberg 10.00 25.00
PK Paul Kariya 3.00 8.00
SD Shane Doan 3.00 8.00
SK Saku Koivu 3.00 8.00
SS Sergei Samsonov 3.00 8.00

2002-03 Upper Deck First Class

*MULT.COLOR SWATCH: .75X TO 1.5X
STATED ODDS 1:288 SERIES 1
UDJJ Jaromir Jagr 8.00 20.00
UDJS Joe Sakic 12.50 30.00
UDJT Jose Theodore 8.00 20.00
UDML Mario Lemieux 15.00 40.00
UDPK Paul Kariya 8.00 20.00
UDPR Patrick Roy 15.00 40.00
UDSY Steve Yzerman 12.50 30.00

2002-03 Upper Deck First Class Gold

This 7-card set paralleled the regular First Class jersey set but was enhanced by gold foil and serial-numbering out of 75.
*GOLD: .75X TO 2X BASIC JERSEY

2002-03 Upper Deck Game Jersey Autographs

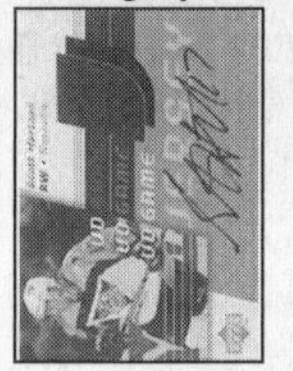

*AUTO: 2.5X TO 6X BASIC JERSEY
RANDOM INSERTS IN SERIES 2 PACKS
PRINT RUN 50 SERIAL #'d SETS
ALL CARDS CARRY SGJ PREFIX
PR Patrick Roy 100.00 250.00
SY Steve Yzerman 60.00 150.00
WG Wayne Gretzky 150.00 400.00

2002-03 Upper Deck Game Jersey Series II

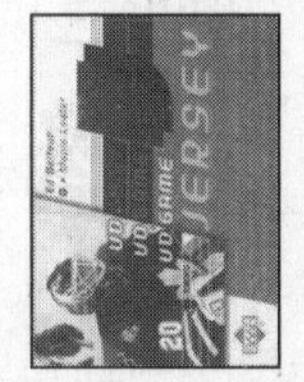

*MULT.COLOR SWATCH: .75X TO 1.5X
STATED ODDS 1:96 SERIES 2
GJEB Ed Belfour 4.00 10.00
GJHZ Henrik Zetterberg 12.00 30.00
GJIK Ilya Kovalchuk 5.00 12.00
GJJL John LeClair 3.00 8.00
GJJS Joe Sakic 6.00 15.00
GJJT Joe Thornton 6.00 15.00
GJMB Martin Brodeur 12.50 30.00
GJPB Pavel Bure 3.00 8.00
GJPR Patrick Roy 15.00 40.00
GJSG Simon Gagne 3.00 8.00
GJSH Scott Hartnell 3.00 8.00
GJSS Sergei Samsonov 3.00 8.00
GJSY Steve Yzerman 10.00 25.00
GJWG Wayne Gretzky 30.00 80.00

2002-03 Upper Deck Gifted Greats

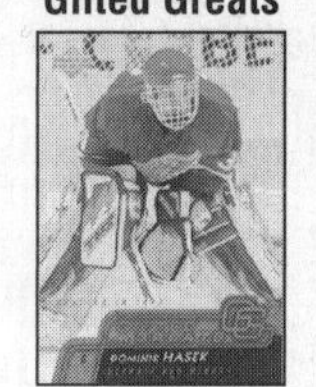

COMPLETE SET (14) 15.00 30.00
STATED ODDS 1:12 SERIES 1
GG1 Paul Kariya .40 1.00
GG2 Bobby Orr 2.50 6.00
GG3 Joe Sakic .75 2.00
GG4 Patrick Roy 2.00 5.00
GG5 Peter Forsberg 1.00 2.50
GG6 Mike Modano .60 1.50
GG7 Dominik Hasek .75 2.00
GG8 Steve Yzerman 2.00 5.00
GG9 Gordie Howe 2.00 5.00
GG10 Martin Brodeur 1.00 2.50
GG11 Wayne Gretzky 3.00 8.00
GG12 Pavel Bure .40 1.00
GG13 Mario Lemieux 2.50 6.00
GG14 Jaromir Jagr .60 1.50

2002-03 Upper Deck Goaltender Threads

*MULT.COLOR SWATCH: .75X TO 1.5X
STATED ODDS 1:96 SERIES 2
ALL CARDS CARRY GT PREFIX
*GOLD: 2X TO 5X BASE HI
GOLD PRINT RUN 25 SER.#'d SETS
FP Felix Potvin 3.00 8.00
IB Ilja Bryzgalov 3.00 8.00
JG J-S Giguere 3.00 8.00
JT Jose Theodore 4.00 10.00
MB Martin Biron 3.00 8.00
MD Mike Dunham 3.00 8.00
MN Mika Noronen 3.00 8.00
MT Marty Turco 8.00 20.00
OK Olaf Kolzig 3.00 8.00

RC Roman Cechmanek 3.00 8.00
RL Roberto Luongo 4.00 10.00
RT Roman Turek 3.00 8.00
SS Steve Shields 3.00 8.00
TH Jocelyn Thibault 3.00 8.00

2002-03 Upper Deck Good Old Days

This 14-card memorabilia set was inserted at a rate of 1:96 Series 1 packs.

*MULT.COLOR SWATCH: .75X TO 1.5X
GOAM Al MacInnis 3.00 8.00
GOBG Bill Guerin 3.00 8.00
GOBH Brett Hull 6.00 15.00
GOBS Brendan Shanahan 4.00 10.00
GOCJ Curtis Joseph 4.00 10.00
GODM Dominik Hasek 8.00 20.00
GOJN Joe Nieuwendyk 3.00 8.00
GOJS Joe Sakic 8.00 20.00
GOKP Keith Primeau 4.00 10.00
GOKT Keith Tkachuk 4.00 10.00
GOMS Mats Sundin 4.00 10.00
GOPB Pavel Bure 4.00 10.00
GOTF Theo Fleury 4.00 10.00
GOTS Teemu Selanne 4.00 10.00

2002-03 Upper Deck Hot Spots

*MULT.COLOR SWATCH: .75X TO 1.5X
STATED ODDS 1:96 SERIES 1 HOBBY
HSCL Claude Lemieux 3.00 8.00
HSDA Denis Arkhipov 3.00 8.00
HSDB Daniel Briere 3.00 8.00
HSDL David Legwand 4.00 10.00
HSDU Mike Dunham 4.00 10.00
HSIK Ilya Kovalchuk 5.00 12.00
HSMD Marc Denis 4.00 10.00
HSME Martin Erat 3.00 8.00
HSRK Rostislav Klesla 3.00 8.00
HSRW Ray Whitney 3.00 8.00
HSSD Shane Doan 3.00 8.00
HSSH Scott Hartnell 3.00 8.00

2002-03 Upper Deck Last Line of Defense

COMPLETE SET (14) 10.00 20.00
STATED ODDS 1:12 SERIES 2
LL1 J-S Giguere .40 1.00
LL2 Martin Biron .40 1.00
LL3 Patrick Roy 2.00 5.00
LL4 Curtis Joseph .50 1.25
LL5 Tommy Salo .40 1.00
LL6 Roberto Luongo .60 1.50
LL7 Jose Theodore .60 1.50
LL8 Martin Brodeur 1.25 3.00
LL9 Chris Osgood .40 1.00
LL10 Sean Burke .40 1.00
LL11 Evgeni Nabokov .40 1.00
LL12 Nikolai Khabibulin .50 1.25
LL13 Ed Belfour .50 1.25
LL14 Olaf Kolzig .40 1.00

2002-03 Upper Deck Letters of Note

*MULT.COLOR SWATCH: .75X TO 1.5X
STATED ODDS 1:144 SERIES 1
*GOLD: .75X TO 2X BASIC JERSEY
GOLD PRINT RUN 50 SER.#'d SETS
LNCD Chris Drury
LNCP Chris Pronger 6.00 15.00
LNJI Jarome Iginla 8.00 20.00
LNJS Joe Sakic 12.50 30.00
LNML Mario Lemieux 20.00 50.00
LNMM Mike Modano 10.00 25.00
LNMN Markus Naslund 6.00 15.00
LNMS Mats Sundin 6.00 15.00
LNON Owen Nolan 6.00 15.00
LNPB Peter Bondra 6.00 15.00
LNPK Paul Kariya 6.00 15.00
LNSK Saku Koivu 6.00 15.00
LNSS Scott Stevens 8.00 20.00
LNSY Steve Yzerman 15.00 40.00

2002-03 Upper Deck Number Crunchers

COMPLETE SET (14) 10.00 20.00
STATED ODDS 1:12 SERIES 2
NC1 Joe Thornton .75 2.00
NC2 Theo Fleury .30 .75
NC3 Brenden Morrow .40 1.00
NC4 Gordie Howe 2.00 5.00
NC5 Brendan Shanahan .50 1.25
NC6 Georges Laraque .30 .75
NC7 Scott Hartnell .30 .75
NC8 Eric Lindros .50 1.25
NC9 Donald Brashear .30 .75
NC10 Keith Primeau .30 .75
NC11 Jeremy Roenick .60 1.50
NC12 Keith Tkachuk .50 1.25
NC13 Ed Jovanovski .40 1.00
NC14 Todd Bertuzzi .50 1.25

2002-03 Upper Deck On the Rise

*MULT.COLOR SWATCH: .75X TO 1.5X
STATED ODDS 1:96 SERIES 1 HOBBY
ORBM Brenden Morrow 4.00 10.00
ORDB Dan Blackburn 4.00 10.00
ORIK Ilya Kovalchuk 5.00 12.00
ORKK Krystofer Kolanos 3.00 8.00
ORMB Mark Bell 3.00 8.00
ORRK Rostislav Klesla 3.00 8.00
ORSR Steven Reinprecht 3.00 8.00

2002-03 Upper Deck Patch Card Logo

STATED ODDS 1:7500 SERIES 2
NOT PRICED DUE TO SCARCITY
BS Brendan Shanahan
IK Ilya Kovalchuk
JJ Jaromir Jagr
MH Marian Hossa
ML Mario Lemieux
MN Markus Naslund
MS Mats Sundin
PR Patrick Roy
SG Simon Gagne
SK Saku Koivu
WG Wayne Gretzky

2002-03 Upper Deck Patch Card Name Plate

STATED ODDS 1:7500 SERIES 2
NOT PRICED DUE TO SCARCITY
JJ Jaromir Jagr
JR Jeremy Roenick
MB Martin Brodeur
ML Mario Lemieux
PF Peter Forsberg
PK Paul Kariya
SF Sergei Fedorov
SS Sergei Samsonov
VL Vincent Lecavalier
WG Wayne Gretzky

2002-03 Upper Deck Patch Card Numbers

STATED ODDS 1:7500 SERIES 2
NOT PRICED DUE TO SCARCITY
JS Joe Sakic
JT Joe Thornton
JT Jose Theodore
MB Martin Brodeur
ML Mario Lemieux
MM Mike Modano
OK Olaf Kolzig
PK Paul Kariya
SY Steve Yzerman
WG Wayne Gretzky

2002-03 Upper Deck Patchwork

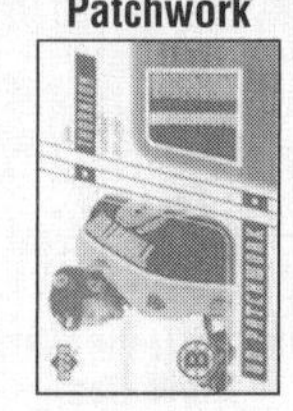

Inserted at a rate of 1:2500 Series 1 packs, this 30-card set featured swatches of game jersey patches. As of press time, not all cards have been verified.

PWAK Alexei Kovalev 40.00 100.00
PWBG Bill Guerin 40.00 100.00
PWBS Brendan Shanahan 40.00 100.00
PWCD Chris Drury 40.00 100.00
PWJJ Jaromir Jagr 60.00 150.00
PWJL John LeClair 40.00 100.00
PWJS Joe Sakic 100.00 200.00
PWJT Joe Thornton 60.00 150.00
PWKP Keith Primeau 40.00 100.00
PWMB Martin Brodeur 75.00 200.00
PWMD Mike Dunham 40.00 100.00
PWMH Milan Hejduk 60.00 150.00
PWML Mario Lemieux 200.00 400.00
PWMM Mike Modano 60.00 150.00
PWMN Markus Naslund 40.00 100.00
PWMS Mats Sundin 40.00 100.00
PWMT Marty Turco 60.00 150.00
PWNL Nicklas Lidstrom 40.00 100.00
PWPF Peter Forsberg 75.00 200.00
PWPK Paul Kariya 75.00 200.00
PWPR Patrick Roy 100.00 250.00
PWSB Sean Burke 40.00 100.00
PWSF Sergei Fedorov 60.00 150.00
PWSG Simon Gagne 40.00 100.00
PWSK Saku Koivu 40.00 100.00
PWSS Sergei Samsonov 40.00 100.00
PWSY Steve Yzerman 100.00 250.00
PWTA Tony Amonte 40.00 100.00
PWTH Jose Theodore 60.00 150.00
PWZP Zigmund Palffy 40.00 100.00

2002-03 Upper Deck Pinpoint Accuracy

*MULT.COLOR SWATCH: .75X TO 1.5X
STATED ODDS 1:96 SERIES 2
PAAT Alex Tanguay 3.00 8.00
PABS Brendan Shanahan 3.00 8.00
PACD Chris Drury 3.00 8.00
PAED Eric Daze 3.00 8.00
PAGS Geoff Sanderson 3.00 8.00
PAJI Jarome Iginla 4.00 10.00
PAJT Joe Thornton 6.00 15.00
PAMH Milan Hejduk 3.00 8.00
PAML Mario Lemieux 12.50 30.00
PAMM Mike Modano 8.00 20.00
PAMR Mark Recchi 3.00 8.00
PAPB Pavel Bure 3.00 8.00
PAPK Paul Kariya 3.00 8.00
PASF Sergei Fedorov 5.00 12.00

2002-03 Upper Deck Playbooks

Extremely limited, this 14-card set featured a "book" style folding card that opened to reveal jersey swatches. Individual print runs are listed below. This set is not priced due to scarcity. Please note that card #PL12 does not exist.

PL1 Paul Kariya/15
PL2 Ray Bourque/10
PL3 Joe Sakic/15
PL4 Patrick Roy/10
PL5 Brendan Shanahan/15
PL6 Sergei Fedorov/15
PL7 Dominik Hasek/10
PL8 Wayne Gretzky/5
PL9 Wayne Gretzky/20
PL10 Jose Theodore/15
PL11 Teemu Selanne/20
PL13 Curtis Joseph/15
PL14 Mats Sundin/15
PL15 Markus Naslund/20

2002-03 Upper Deck Playbooks Series II

Extremely limited, this 14-card set featured a folding "book" card that opened to reveal dual jersey swatches. Known print runs are listed below. This set is not priced due to scarcity.

FS Peter Forsberg
Joe Sakic
HD Milan Hejduk
Chris Drury
JK Jaromir Jagr
Olaf Kolzig/14
KG Paul Kariya
J-S Giguere/14
KT Saku Koivu
Jose Theodore
LK M.Lemieux/A.Kovalev
LL Brian Leetch
Eric Lindros
LW John LeClair
Justin Williams
MT M.Modano/M.Turco/17
RP Jeremy Roenick
Keith Primeau
RT Patrick Roy
Alex Tanguay
SL Brendan Shanahan
Nicklas Lidstrom
ST Sergei Samsonov
Joe Thornton
YF S.Yzerman/S.Fedorov

2002-03 Upper Deck Reaching Fifty

*MULT.COLOR SWATCH: .75X TO 1.5X
STATED ODDS 1:96 SERIES 2
50BH Brett Hull 4.00 10.00
50BO Peter Bondra 3.00 8.00
50JI Jarome Iginla 4.00 10.00
50JJ Jaromir Jagr 6.00 15.00
50JL John LeClair 3.00 8.00
50JS Joe Sakic 6.00 15.00
50KT Keith Tkachuk 3.00 8.00
50ML Mario Lemieux 15.00 40.00
50MM Mike Modano 8.00 20.00
50PB Pavel Bure 3.00 8.00
50PK Paul Kariya 3.00 8.00
50SF Sergei Fedorov 5.00 12.00
50SY Steve Yzerman 10.00 25.00
50WG Wayne Gretzky 30.00 80.00

2002-03 Upper Deck Reaching Fifty Gold

*STARS: 2X TO 5X BASIC JERSEY
PRINT RUN 50 SERIAL #'d SETS

2002-03 Upper Deck Saviors Jerseys

Known print runs and short prints are listed below.

*MULT.COLOR SWATCH: .75X TO 1.5X
STATED ODDS 1:96 SERIES 1
SVBB Brian Boucher 3.00 8.00
SVBD Byron Dafoe 3.00 8.00
SVBJ Brent Johnson 3.00 8.00
SVJG J-S Giguere 3.00 8.00
SVJT Jose Theodore SP 5.00 12.00
SVMB Martin Biron 3.00 8.00
SVMD Mike Dunham 3.00 8.00
SVMT Marty Turco 3.00 8.00
SVOK Olaf Kolzig 3.00 8.00
SVPR Patrick Roy SP 25.00 60.00
SVRT Roman Turek 3.00 8.00
SVTH Jocelyn Thibault/100 12.50 30.00
SVTU Ron Tugnutt/100 8.00 20.00

2002-03 Upper Deck Shooting Stars

COMPLETE SET (14) 15.00 30.00
STATED ODDS 1:12 SERIES 2
SS1 Paul Kariya .40 1.00
SS2 Jarome Iginla .50 1.25
SS3 Joe Thornton .60 1.50
SS4 Joe Sakic .75 2.00
SS5 Mike Modano .60 1.50
SS6 Gordie Howe 2.00 5.00
SS7 Steve Yzerman 2.00 5.00
SS8 Mike Comrie .30 .75
SS9 Wayne Gretzky 3.00 8.00
SS10 Pavel Bure .40 1.00
SS11 Simon Gagne .40 1.00
SS12 Mario Lemieux 2.50 6.00
SS13 Teemu Selanne .40 1.00
SS14 Jaromir Jagr .60 1.50

2002-03 Upper Deck Sizzling Scorers

COMPLETE SET (14) 8.00 15.00
STATED ODDS 1:12 SERIES 1
SS1 Ilya Kovalchuk .50 1.25
SS2 Joe Thornton .60 1.50
SS3 Jarome Iginla .50 1.25
SS4 Ron Francis .40 1.00
SS5 Joe Sakic .75 2.00
SS6 Mike Modano .60 1.50
SS7 Brendan Shanahan .40 1.00
SS8 Mike Comrie .40 1.00
SS9 Marian Gaborik .75 2.00
SS10 Patrik Elias .40 1.00
SS11 Pavel Bure .40 1.00
SS12 Jeremy Roenick .50 1.25
SS13 Mats Sundin .40 1.00
SS14 Todd Bertuzzi .40 1.00

2002-03 Upper Deck Specialists

*MULT.COLOR SWATCH: .75X TO 1.5X
STATED ODDS 1:96 SERIES 1 HOBBY
SAZ Alexei Zhamnov 3.00 8.00
SBL Brian Leetch 4.00 10.00
SCD Chris Drury 4.00 10.00
SEB Eric Belanger 3.00 8.00
SJL Jere Lehtinen 4.00 10.00
SMM Mike Modano 8.00 20.00
SMR Mark Recchi 4.00 10.00
SMS Miroslav Satan 4.00 10.00
SPB Peter Bondra 4.00 10.00
SRB Jarome Iginla 4.00 10.00
SRL Robert Lang 3.00 8.00
SSF Sergei Fedorov 5.00 12.00
SSS Sergei Samsonov 4.00 10.00
STM Todd Marchant 3.00 8.00

2002-03 Upper Deck Speed Demons

*MULT.COLOR SWATCH: .75X TO 1.5X
STATED ODDS 1:96 SERIES 1 RETAIL
SDDB Daniel Briere 3.00 8.00
SDPB Pavel Bure 3.00 8.00
SDSF Sergei Fedorov 5.00 12.00
SDSG Simon Gagne 3.00 8.00
SDSS Steve Sullivan 3.00 8.00
SDTM Todd Marchant 3.00 8.00
SDZP Zigmund Palffy 4.00 10.00

2002-03 Upper Deck Super Saviors

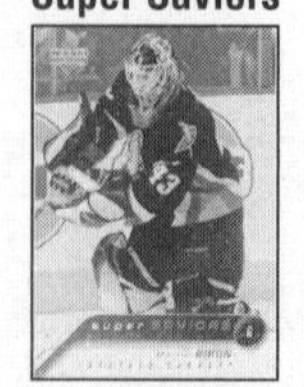

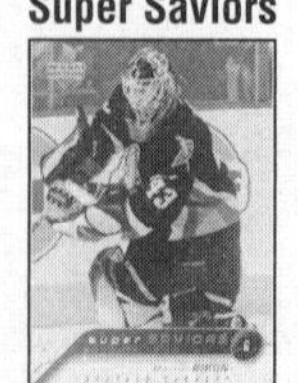

COMPLETE SET (14) 12.50 25.00
STATED ODDS 1:12 SERIES 1
SA1 Martin Biron .60 1.50
SA2 Roman Turek .60 1.50
SA3 Arturs Irbe .60 1.50
SA4 Patrick Roy 2.50 6.00
SA5 Marty Turco .60 1.50
SA6 Dominik Hasek 1.00 2.50
SA7 Jose Theodore 1.00 2.50
SA8 Martin Brodeur 1.25 3.00
SA9 Chris Osgood .60 1.50
SA10 Patrick Lalime .60 1.50
SA11 Sean Burke .60 1.50
SA12 Evgeni Nabokov .60 1.50
SA13 Brent Johnson .60 1.50
SA14 Olaf Kolzig .60 1.50

2003-04 Upper Deck

This 475-card set was issued in two different sets of 245 cards and 230 cards. The "Young Guns" rookie subset cards were inserted at odds of 1:4.

COMPLETE SERIES 1 (245) 200.00 400.00
COMP.SERIES 1 w/o SP's 20.00 40.00
COMPLETE SERIES 2 (230) 125.00 250.00
COMP.SERIES 2 w/o SP's 20.00 40.00
1 Petr Sykora .02 .10
2 Steve Rucchin .02 .10
3 Sandis Ozolinsh .02 .10
4 Jason Krog .02 .10
5 Sergei Fedorov .25 .60
6 Rob Niedermayer .02 .10
7 J-S Giguere .15 .40
8 Dany Heatley .25 .60
9 Slava Kozlov .02 .10
10 Patrik Stefan .02 .10
11 Yannick Tremblay .02 .10
12 Shawn McEachern .02 .10
13 Byron Dafoe .15 .40
14 Joe Thornton .30 .75
15 Bryan Berard .02 .10
16 P-J Axelsson .02 .10
17 Hal Gill .02 .10
18 P.J. Stock .02 .10
19 Mike Knuble .02 .10
20 Steve Shields .15 .40
21 Daniel Briere .02 .10
22 Ales Kotalik .02 .10
23 Curtis Brown .02 .10
24 JP Dumont .02 .10
25 Alexei Zhitnik .02 .10
26 Maxim Afinogenov .02 .10
27 Martin Biron .15 .40
28 Dean McAmmond .02 .10
29 Jarome Iginla .25 .60
30 Martin Gelinas .02 .10
31 Jordan Leopold .02 .10
32 Chuck Kobasew .02 .10
33 Roman Turek .15 .40
34 Jeff O'Neill .02 .10
35 Ron Francis .15 .40
36 Sean Hill .02 .10
37 Erik Cole .02 .10
38 Pavel Brendl .02 .10
39 Kevin Weekes .15 .40
40 Alexei Zhamnov .02 .10
41 Kyle Calder .02 .10
42 Tyler Arnason .15 .40
43 Igor Radulov .02 .10
44 Jocelyn Thibault .15 .40
45 Peter Forsberg .50 1.25
46 Alex Tanguay .15 .40
47 Derek Morris .02 .10
48 Rob Blake .15 .40
49 Paul Kariya .20 .50
50 Teemu Selanne .20 .50
51 David Aebischer .15 .40
52 Patrick Roy 1.00 2.50
53 Pascal Leclaire .15 .40
54 Geoff Sanderson .02 .10
55 Rick Nash .25 .60
56 Rostislav Klesla .02 .10
57 Jody Shelley .02 .10
58 Marc Denis .15 .40
59 Mike Modano .30 .75
60 Sergei Zubov .02 .10
61 Jere Lehtinen .15 .40
62 Steve Ott .02 .10
63 Niko Kapanen .02 .10
64 Jason Bacashihua .15 .40
65 Marty Turco .15 .40
66 Brett Hull .25 .60
67 Nicklas Lidstrom .20 .50
68 Mathieu Schneider .02 .10
69 Henrik Zetterberg .20 .50
70 Pavel Datsyuk .20 .50
71 Derian Hatcher .02 .10
72 Steve Yzerman 1.00 2.50
73 Manny Legace .15 .40
74 Ryan Smyth .02 .10
75 Mike York .02 .10
76 Ales Hemsky .15 .40
77 Eric Brewer .02 .10
78 Fernando Pisani .02 .10
79 Georges Laraque .02 .10
80 Tommy Salo .15 .40
81 Viktor Kozlov .02 .10
82 Kristian Huselius .02 .10
83 Stephen Weiss .02 .10
84 Jay Bouwmeester .02 .10
85 Roberto Luongo .25 .60
86 Zigmund Palffy .15 .40
87 Alexander Frolov .02 .10
88 Luc Robitaille .15 .40
89 Ian Laperriere .02 .10
90 Jared Aulin .02 .10
91 Roman Cechmanek .15 .40
92 Marian Gaborik .40 1.00
93 Pascal Dupuis .02 .10
94 Andrew Brunette .02 .10
95 Wes Walz .02 .10
96 Pierre-Marc Bouchard .02 .10
97 Willie Mitchell .02 .10
98 Manny Fernandez .15 .40
99 Saku Koivu .20 .50
100 Jan Bulis .02 .10
101 Marcel Hossa .02 .10
102 Michael Komisarek .02 .10
103 Richard Zednik .02 .10
104 Mathieu Garon .02 .10
105 Ron Hainsey .02 .10
106 David Legwand .15 .40
107 Greg Johnson .02 .10
108 Scott Hartnell .02 .10
109 Scottie Upshall .02 .10
110 Tomas Vokoun .15 .40
111 Patrik Elias .15 .40
112 Jeff Friesen .02 .10
113 Joe Nieuwendyk .15 .40
114 Scott Niedermayer .02 .10
115 Grant Marshall .02 .10
116 Scott Stevens .15 .40
117 Martin Brodeur .50 1.25
118 Jason Blake .02 .10
119 Mark Parrish .02 .10
120 Michael Peca .02 .10
121 Adrian Aucoin .02 .10
122 Rick DiPietro .15 .40
123 Eric Godard .02 .10
124 Alex Kovalev .15 .40
125 Anson Carter .15 .40
126 Mark Messier .20 .50
127 Petr Nedved .02 .10
128 Tom Poti .02 .10
129 Jamie Lundmark .02 .10
130 Mike Dunham .15 .40
131 Marian Hossa .20 .50
132 Martin Havlat .15 .40
133 Zdeno Chara .02 .10
134 Peter Schaefer .02 .10
135 Ray Emery .15 .40
136 Jason Spezza .20 .50
137 Patrick Lalime .15 .40
138 Mark Recchi .15 .40
139 Tony Amonte .15 .40
140 Keith Primeau .02 .10
141 Simon Gagne .20 .50
142 Eric Weinrich .02 .10
143 Jim Vandermeer .02 .10
144 Robert Esche .15 .40
145 Shane Doan .02 .10
146 Chris Gratton .02 .10
147 Jan Hrdina .02 .10
148 Daymond Langkow .02 .10
149 Tyson Nash .02 .10
150 Brian Boucher .15 .40
151 Mario Lemieux 1.25 3.00
152 Aleksey Morozov .02 .10
153 Ramzi Abid .02 .10
154 Dick Tarnstrom .02 .10
155 Rico Fata .02 .10
156 Brooks Orpik .02 .10
157 Vincent Damphousse .02 .10
158 Marco Sturm .02 .10
159 Mike Ricci .02 .10
160 Jim Fahey .02 .10
161 Niko Dimitrakos .02 .10
162 Kyle McLaren .02 .10
163 Evgeni Nabokov .15 .40
164 Al MacInnis .15 .40
165 Scott Mellanby .02 .10
166 Keith Tkachuk .20 .50
167 Barret Jackman .15 .40
168 Reed Low .02 .10
169 Chris Pronger .15 .40
170 Chris Osgood .15 .40
171 Vincent Lecavalier .20 .50
172 Dave Andreychuk .15 .40
173 Brad Richards .15 .40
174 Pavel Kubina .02 .10
175 Alexander Svitov .02 .10
176 John Grahame .15 .40
177 Alexander Mogilny .15 .40
178 Owen Nolan .15 .40
179 Darcy Tucker .02 .10
180 Doug Gilmour .15 .40
181 Tie Domi .15 .40
182 Phil Housley .02 .10
183 Gary Roberts .02 .10
184 Ed Belfour .20 .50
185 Markus Naslund .20 .50
186 Brendan Morrison .15 .40
187 Ed Jovanovski .15 .40
188 Matt Cooke .02 .10
189 Henrik Sedin .02 .10
190 Brandon Reid .02 .10
191 Marek Malik .02 .10
192 Alexander Auld .02 .10
193 Robert Lang .02 .10
194 Sergei Gonchar .02 .10
195 Michael Nylander .02 .10
196 Mike Grier .02 .10
197 Steve Konowalchuk .02 .10
198 Olaf Kolzig .15 .40
199 Joe Thornton CL .25 .60
200 Martin Brodeur CL .40 1.00
201 Garrett Burnett YG RC 2.00 5.00
202 Joffrey Lupul YG RC 4.00 10.00
203 Jiri Hudler YG RC 4.00 10.00
204 Patrice Bergeron YG RC 10.00 25.00
205 Matthew Lombardi YG RC 2.00 5.00
206 Eric Staal YG RC 20.00 40.00
207 Lasse Kukkonen YG RC 2.00 5.00
208 Pavel Vorobiev YG RC 2.00 5.00
209 Travis Moen YG RC 2.00 5.00
210 Tuomo Ruutu YG RC 8.00 20.00
211 Cody McCormick YG RC 2.00 5.00
212 John-Michael Liles YG RC 2.00 5.00
213 Marek Svatos YG RC 6.00 15.00
214 Dan Fritsche YG RC 2.00 5.00
215 Antti Miettinen YG RC 2.00 5.00
216 Nathan Horton YG RC 6.00 15.00
217 Dustin Brown YG RC 3.00 8.00
218 Esa Pirnes YG RC 2.00 5.00
219 Alexander Semin YG RC 10.00 25.00
220 Tim Gleason YG RC 2.00 5.00
221 Brent Burns YG RC 2.00 5.00
222 Christoph Brandner YG RC 2.00 5.00
223 Chris Higgins YG RC 10.00 25.00
224 Dan Hamhuis YG RC 2.00 5.00
225 Jordin Tootoo YG RC 6.00 15.00
226 Marek Zidlicky YG RC 2.00 5.00
227 Wade Brookbank YG RC 2.00 5.00
228 David Hale YG RC 2.00 5.00
229 Paul Martin YG RC 2.00 5.00
230 Sean Bergenheim YG RC 2.00 5.00
231 Antoine Vermette YG RC 2.00 5.00
232 Joni Pitkanen YG RC 4.00 10.00
233 Matthew Spiller YG RC 2.00 5.00
234 Marc-Andre Fleury YG RC 30.00 60.00
235 Matt Murley YG RC 2.00 5.00
236 Ryan Malone YG RC 4.00 10.00
237 Christian Ehrhoff YG RC 2.00 5.00
238 Milan Michalek YG RC 8.00 20.00
239 Andrew Peters YG RC 2.00 5.00

240 Tom Preissing YG RC 2.00 5.00
241 Peter Sejna YG RC 2.00 5.00
242 Matt Stajan YG RC 6.00 15.00
243 Maxim Kondratiev YG RC 2.00 5.00
244 Boyd Gordon YG RC 2.00 5.00
245 Marc-Andre Fleury 2.00 5.00
Eric Staal
Nathan Horton CL
246 Vaclav Prospal .02 .10
247 Stanislav Chistov .02 .10
248 Mike Leclerc .02 .10
249 Keith Carney .02 .10
250 Martin Gerber .15 .40
251 Sammy Pahlsson .02 .10
252 Ruslan Salei .02 .10
253 Marc Savard .02 .10
254 Ilya Kovalchuk .25 .60
255 Kamil Piros .02 .10
256 Frantisek Kaberle .02 .10
257 Pasi Nurminen .15 .40
258 Sergei Samsonov .15 .40
259 Brian Rolston .02 .10
260 Travis Green .02 .10
261 Glen Murray .02 .10
262 Nick Boynton .02 .10
263 Jeff Jillson .02 .10
264 Felix Potvin .20 .50
265 Andrew Raycroft .15 .40
266 Jochen Hecht .02 .10
267 Chris Drury .15 .40
268 Miroslav Satan .15 .40
269 Andy Delmore .02 .10
270 Ryan Miller .15 .40
271 Tim Connolly .15 .40
272 Oleg Saprykin .02 .10
273 Craig Conroy .02 .10
274 Steve Reinprecht .02 .10
275 Toni Lydman .02 .10
276 Robyn Regehr .02 .10
277 Jamie McLennan .02 .10
278 Jaroslav Svoboda .02 .10
279 Rod Brind'Amour .15 .40
280 Radim Vrbata .02 .10
281 Bret Hedican .02 .10
282 Danny Markov .02 .10
283 Jamie Storr .15 .40
284 Eric Daze .15 .40
285 Steve Sullivan .02 .10
286 Jon Klemm .02 .10
287 Alexander Karpovtsev .02 .10
288 Michael Leighton .15 .40
289 Joe Sakic .40 1.00
290 Steve Konowalchuk .02 .10
291 Milan Hejduk .20 .50
292 Adam Foote .02 .10
293 Dan Hinote .02 .10
294 Philippe Sauve .15 .40
295 Trevor Letowski .02 .10
296 Andrew Cassels .02 .10
297 Todd Marchant .02 .10
298 David Vyborny .02 .10
299 Darryl Sydor .02 .10
300 Jaroslav Spacek .02 .10
301 Espen Knutsen .02 .10
302 Brenden Morrow .15 .40
303 Jason Arnott .02 .10
304 Pierre Turgeon .15 .40
305 Bill Guerin .15 .40
306 Teppo Numminen .02 .10
307 Ron Tugnutt .15 .40
308 Stu Barnes .02 .10
309 Brendan Shanahan .20 .50
310 Ray Whitney .02 .10
311 Tomas Holmstrom .02 .10
312 Chris Chelios .20 .50
313 Jiri Fischer .02 .10
314 Dominik Hasek .40 1.00
315 Darren McCarty .02 .10
316 Brad Isbister .02 .10
317 Ethan Moreau .02 .10
318 Raffi Torres .02 .10
319 Mike Comrie .15 .40
320 Radek Dvorak .02 .10
321 Jason Smith .02 .10
322 Ty Conklin .15 .40
323 Adam Oates .20 .50
324 Marcus Nilsson .02 .10
325 Olli Jokinen .15 .40
326 Valeri Bure .02 .10
327 Eric Messier .02 .10
328 Branislav Mezei .02 .10
329 Steve Shields .15 .40
330 Matt Cullen .02 .10
331 Adam Deadmarsh .02 .10
332 Jason Allison .02 .10
333 Jozef Stumpel .02 .10
334 Eric Belanger .02 .10
335 Mattias Norstrom .02 .10
336 Cristobal Huet .15 .40
337 Martin Straka .02 .10
338 Antti Laaksonen .02 .10
339 Sergei Zholtok .02 .10
340 Alexandre Daigle .02 .10
341 Filip Kuba .02 .10
342 Dwayne Roloson .15 .40
343 Mike Ribeiro .02 .10
344 Donald Audette .02 .10
345 Michael Ryder .02 .10
346 Andrei Markov .02 .10
347 Jose Theodore .25 .60
348 Yanic Perreault .02 .10
349 Andreas Johansson .02 .10
350 Denis Arkhipov .02 .10
351 Rem Murray .02 .10
352 Scott Walker .02 .10
353 Adam Hall .02 .10
354 Kimmo Timonen .02 .10
355 Jason York .02 .10
356 Sergei Brylin .02 .10
357 John Madden .02 .10
358 Scott Gomez .02 .10
359 Jamie Langenbrunner .02 .10
360 Brian Gionta .02 .10
361 Brian Rafalski .02 .10
362 Corey Schwab .15 .40
363 Igor Larionov .02 .10
364 Oleg Kvasha .02 .10
365 Alexei Yashin .02 .10
366 Mariusz Czerkawski .02 .10
367 Roman Hamrlik .02 .10
368 Janne Niinimaa .02 .10
369 Arron Asham .02 .10
370 Garth Snow .02 .10
371 Jan Hlavac .02 .10
372 Matthew Barnaby .02 .10
373 Eric Lindros .20 .50
374 Brian Leetch .15 .40
375 Jussi Markkanen .15 .40
376 Mike Fisher .02 .10
377 Radek Bonk .15 .40
378 Bryan Smolinski .02 .10
379 Daniel Alfredsson .15 .40
380 Wade Redden .02 .10
381 Chris Phillips .02 .10
382 Todd White .02 .10
383 Jeremy Roenick .25 .60
384 Michal Handzus .02 .10
385 Donald Brashear .02 .10
386 John LeClair .20 .50
387 Justin Williams .02 .10
388 Kim Johnsson .02 .10
389 Eric Desjardins .02 .10
390 Jeff Hackett .15 .40
391 Ladislav Nagy .02 .10
392 Brian Savage .02 .10
393 Mike Johnson .02 .10
394 Branko Radivojevic .02 .10
395 Paul Mara .02 .10
396 David Tanabe .02 .10
397 Sean Burke .15 .40
398 Mike Sillinger .02 .10
399 Drake Berehowsky .02 .10
400 Steve McKenna .02 .10
401 Konstantin Koltsov .02 .10
402 Michal Rozsival .02 .10
403 Sebastien Caron .15 .40
404 Patrick Marleau .15 .40
405 Wayne Primeau .02 .10
406 Alexander Korolyuk .02 .10
407 Jonathan Cheechoo .05 .12
408 Mike Rathje .02 .10
409 Brad Stuart .02 .10
410 Scott Thornton .02 .10
411 Pavol Demitra .15 .40
412 Doug Weight .15 .40
413 Eric Boguniecki .02 .10
414 Petr Cajanek .02 .10
415 Brent Johnson .15 .40
416 Dallas Drake .02 .10
417 Cory Stillman .02 .10
418 Fredrik Modin .02 .10
419 Martin St. Louis .15 .40
420 Ruslan Fedotenko .02 .10
421 Dan Boyle .02 .10
422 Nikolai Khabibulin .20 .50
423 Mats Sundin .20 .50
424 Joe Nieuwendyk .15 .40
425 Nik Antropov .02 .10
426 Tomas Kaberle .02 .10
427 Bryan McCabe .02 .10
428 Mikael Tellqvist .15 .40
429 Ken Klee .02 .10
430 Daniel Sedin .02 .10
431 Magnus Arvedson .02 .10
432 Trevor Linden .02 .10
433 Todd Bertuzzi .20 .50
434 Mattias Ohlund .02 .10
435 Dan Cloutier .15 .40
436 Johan Hedberg .15 .40
437 Jason King .02 .10
438 Peter Bondra .15 .40
439 Jeff Halpern .02 .10
440 Jaromir Jagr .30 .75
441 Steve Eminger .02 .10
442 Sebastien Charpentier .15 .40
443 Dainius Zubrus .02 .10
444 Mario Lemieux 1.25 3.00
445 Jason Spezza .20 .50
446 Brent Krahn YG RC 2.00 5.00
447 Boyd Kane YG RC 2.00 5.00
448 Greg Campbell YG RC 2.00 5.00
449 Andrew Hutchinson YG RC 2.00 5.00
450 Mike Stuart YG RC 2.00 5.00
451 Nikolai Zherdev YG RC 4.00 10.00
452 Sergei Zinovjev YG RC 2.00 5.00
453 Julien Vauclair YG RC 2.00 5.00
454 Ryan Kesler YG RC 2.00 5.00
455 Fredrik Sjostrom YG RC 2.00 5.00
456 Mikhail Yakubov YG RC 2.00 5.00
457 Nathan Smith YG RC 2.00 5.00
458 Grant McNeill YG RC 2.00 5.00
459 Seamus Kotyk YG RC 2.00 5.00
460 Alan Rourke YG RC 2.00 5.00
461 John Pohl YG RC 2.00 5.00
462 Dominic Moore YG RC 2.00 5.00
463 Tony Salmelainen YG RC 2.00 5.00
464 Rastislav Stana YG RC 2.00 5.00
465 Karl Stewart YG RC 2.00 5.00
466 Darryl Bootland YG RC 2.00 5.00
467 Trevor Daley YG RC 2.00 5.00
468 Peter Sarno YG RC 2.00 5.00
469 Jed Ortmeyer YG RC 2.00 5.00
470 Nathan Robinson YG RC 2.00 5.00
471 Pat Rissmiller YG RC 2.00 5.00
472 Gretzky/Lafleur/Messier CL 6.00 15.00
473 Jose Theodore HC 3.00 8.00
474 Don Cherry HC 4.00 10.00
475 Salmlinn/Moore/Zinvjev CL 1.00 2.50

2003-04 Upper Deck 500 Goal Club

This 8-card set featured the newest members to the exclusive 500 Goal Club. Cards were inserted at 1:237 for the non-autographed cards and the autographed versions were serial-numbered to 25.
500-BS Brendan Shanahan 12.50 30.00
500-JJ Jaromir Jagr 15.00 40.00
500-JN Joe Nieuwendyk 12.50 30.00
500-JS Joe Sakic 20.00 50.00
500-RF Ron Francis 12.50 30.00
500-JJA Jaromir Jagr AU 250.00 400.00
500-JNA Joe Nieuwendyk AU 150.00 300.00
500-RFA Ron Francis AU 150.00 300.00

2003-04 Upper Deck All-Star Class

COMPLETE SET (30) 10.00 20.00
STATED ODDS 1:1 RETAIL
AS-1 J-S Giguere .25 .60
AS-2 Ilya Kovalchuk .40 1.00
AS-3 Joe Thornton .40 1.00
AS-4 Paul Kariya .30 .75
AS-5 Peter Forsberg .75 2.00
AS-6 Teemu Selanne .30 .75
AS-7 Marty Turco .25 .60
AS-8 Mike Modano .50 1.25
AS-9 Steve Yzerman 1.25 3.00
AS-10 Dominik Hasek .60 1.50
AS-11 Nicklas Lidstrom .30 .75
AS-12 Jay Bouwmeester .25 .60
AS-13 Zigmund Palffy .25 .60
AS-14 Marian Gaborik .60 1.50
AS-15 Saku Koivu .30 .75
AS-16 Martin Brodeur .75 2.00
AS-17 Alexei Yashin .25 .60
AS-18 Tom Poti .25 .60
AS-19 Jason Spezza .30 .75
AS-20 Marian Hossa .30 .75
AS-21 Jeremy Roenick .40 1.00
AS-22 Sean Burke .25 .60
AS-23 Mario Lemieux 1.50 4.00
AS-24 Patrick Marleau .25 .60
AS-25 Chris Pronger .25 .60
AS-26 Vincent Lecavalier .25 .60
AS-27 Mats Sundin .30 .75
AS-28 Ed Belfour .30 .75
AS-29 Todd Bertuzzi .30 .75
AS-30 Jaromir Jagr .50 1.25

2003-04 Upper Deck All-Star Lineup

COMPLETE SET (10) 40.00 80.00
STATED ODDS 1:40
AS1 Marian Gaborik 3.00 8.00
AS2 Dany Heatley 3.00 8.00
AS3 Joe Thornton 3.00 8.00
AS4 Mario Lemieux 6.00 15.00
AS5 Martin Brodeur 5.00 12.00
AS6 Jason Spezza 2.50 6.00
AS7 Rick Nash 3.00 8.00
AS8 Henrik Zetterberg 2.50 6.00
AS9 Ales Hemsky 2.50 6.00
AS10 Ryan Miller 2.50 6.00

2003-04 Upper Deck Big Playmakers

*MULT.COLOR SWATCH: .5X TO 1.25X
STATED ODDS 1:905
PRINT RUN 50 SERIAL #'d SETS
BP-DH Dany Heatley 20.00 50.00
BP-IK Ilya Kovalchuk 25.00 60.00
BP-JB Jason Blake 10.00 25.00
BP-JJ Jaromir Jagr 20.00 50.00
BP-JL Jamie Langenbrunner 10.00 25.00
BP-JR Jeremy Roenick 20.00 50.00
BP-JS J-S Giguere 12.50 30.00
BP-JT Joe Thornton 25.00 60.00
BP-MB Martin Brodeur 40.00 100.00
BP-MG Marian Gaborik 25.00 60.00
BP-MH Marian Hossa 15.00 40.00
BP-ML Mario Lemieux 40.00 100.00
BP-MM Mike Modano 20.00 50.00
BP-MN Markus Naslund 15.00 40.00
BP-MS Mats Sundin 15.00 40.00
BP-MT Marty Turco 12.50 30.00
BP-ON Owen Nolan 12.50 30.00
BP-PB Pavel Bure 15.00 40.00
BP-PF Peter Forsberg 25.00 60.00
BP-PL Pavel Brendl 10.00 25.00
BP-PR Patrick Roy 40.00 100.00
BP-RL Roberto Luongo 20.00 50.00
BP-RN Rick Nash 20.00 50.00
BP-SF Sergei Fedorov 20.00 50.00
BP-SK Saku Koivu 15.00 40.00
BP-TB Todd Bertuzzi 15.00 40.00
BP-TH Jocelyn Thibault 12.50 30.00
BP-TS Teemu Selanne 15.00 40.00
BP-WG Wayne Gretzky 100.00 250.00
BP-ZP Zigmund Palffy 12.50 30.00

2003-04 Upper Deck BuyBacks

This 182-card set featured cards that were "bought back" by UD and then autographed by the player. Print runs and original set ids are listed below.
1 Joe Thornton 96UD/7
2 Joe Thornton 97UD/5
3 Joe Thornton 98UD/9
4 Joe Thornton 99UD/9
5 Joe Thornton 00UD/9
6 Joe Thornton 01UD/2
7 Joe Thornton 02UD/22
8 Markus Naslund 92UD/38 20.00 50.00
9 Markus Naslund 93UD/10
10 Markus Naslund 94 UD/9
11 Markus Naslund 95 UD/10
12 Markus Naslund 96UD/4
13 Markus Naslund 97UD/5
14 Markus Naslund 98UD/10
15 Markus Naslund 99UD/10
16 Markus Naslund 00UD/10
17 Markus Naslund 01UD/9
18 Markus Naslund 02UD/21
19 Todd Bertuzzi 96UD/10
20 Todd Bertuzzi 97UD/10
21 Todd Bertuzzi 98UD/10
22 Todd Bertuzzi 00UD/10
23 Todd Bertuzzi 01 UD/9
24 Todd Bertuzzi 02UD/48 25.00 60.00
25 J-S Giguere 02UD/48 15.00 40.00
26 Bobby Orr 99UD Leg/5
27 Bobby Orr 00 UD Leg/5
28 Bobby Orr 01UD Leg/4
29 Bobby Orr 01UD Leg/5
30 Bobby Orr 02 UD/8
31 Gordie Howe 99UD Leg/9
32 Gordie Howe 00UD Leg/2
33 Gordie Howe 01UD Leg/5
34 Gordie Howe 01UD Leg/7
35 Gordie Howe 01UD Leg/4
36 Gordie Howe 02UD/23
37 Zigmund Palffy 91UD/28 20.00 50.00
38 Zigmund Palffy 94UD/4
39 Zigmund Palffy 95UD/9
40 Zigmund Palffy 96UD/10
41 Zigmund Palffy 97UD/11
42 Zigmund Palffy 98UD/14
43 Zigmund Palffy 99UD/6
44 Zigmund Palffy 00UD/10
45 Zigmund Palffy 01UD/10
46 Zigmund Palffy 01UD/1
47 Zigmund Palffy 02UD/23
48 Jason Spezza 02UD/29 100.00 200.00
49 Jason Spezza 03AS Promo/4
50 Rick Nash 00 UD CHL/2
51 Rick Nash 03 AS Promo/4
52 John LeClair 00UD/5
53 John LeClair 01UD/5
54 John LeClair 02UD/23
55 Pavel Bure 90UD/14
56 Pavel Bure 91UD/5
57 Pavel Bure 91UD/5
58 Pavel Bure 92UD/5
59 Pavel Bure 93UD/5
60 Pavel Bure 95UD/5
61 Pavel Bure 95UD/5
62 Pavel Bure 96UD/5
63 Pavel Bure 97UD/5
64 Pavel Bure 98UD/5
65 Pavel Bure 99UD/5
66 Pavel Bure 00UD/5
67 Pavel Bure 01UD/5
68 Pavel Bure 02UD/48 15.00 40.00
69 Pavel Bure MS 02UD/24
70 Mike Comrie 01UD/13
71 Mike Comrie 02UD/30 12.50 30.00
72 Sergei Fedorov 90UD/11
73 Sergei Fedorov ART 91UD/7
74 Sergei Fedorov 91UD/5
75 Sergei Fedorov 92UD/5
76 Sergei Fedorov 93UD/5
77 Sergei Fedorov 94UD/3
78 Sergei Fedorov 95UD/5
79 Sergei Fedorov 96UD/5
80 Sergei Fedorov 97UD/4
81 Sergei Fedorov 98UD/5
82 Sergei Fedorov 99UD/4
83 Sergei Fedorov 00UD/5
84 Sergei Fedorov 01UD/5
85 Sergei Fedorov 02UD/39 30.00 80.00
86 Ron Francis 90-91 UD
87 Ron Francis 91UD/5
88 Ron Francis 92UD/5
89 Ron Francis 93UD/5
90 Ron Francis 94UD/5
91 Ron Francis 95UD/5
92 Ron Francis 96UD/5
93 Ron Francis 97UD/5
94 Ron Francis 99UD/5
95 Ron Francis 00UD/5
96 Ron Francis 01UD/5
97 Ron Francis 02UD/47 20.00 50.00
98 Marian Gaborik 01UD/9
99 Marian Gaborik 02UD/48 20.00 50.00
100 Marian Hossa 97UD/17
101 Marian Hossa 98UD/1
102 Marian Hossa 99UD/10
103 Marian Hossa 00UD/10
104 Marian Hossa 01UD/10
105 Marian Hossa 02UD/48 15.00 40.00
106 Curtis Joseph 90UD/15
107 Curtis Joseph 91UD/5
108 Curtis Joseph 00UD/5
109 Curtis Joseph 01UD/5
109 Curtis Joseph 02UD/48 15.00 40.00
110 Jarome Iginla 97UD/5
111 Jarome Iginla MS 02UD/47 15.00 40.00
112 Jarome Iginla 02UD/48 15.00 40.00
113 Saku Koivu 92UD/14
114 Saku Koivu 93UD/5
115 Saku Koivu 95 UD/5
116 Saku Koivu 96UD/3
117 Saku Koivu 97UD/5
118 Saku Koivu 98UD/5
119 Saku Koivu 99UD/5
120 Saku Koivu 00UD/5
121 Saku Koivu 01UD/5
122 Saku Koivu 02UD/48 20.00 50.00
123 Ilya Kovalchuk 01 UD/1
124 Ilya Kovalchuk 01 UD/9
125 Ilya Kovalchuk 02UD/48 25.00 60.00
126 Joe Nieuwendyk 90UD/5
127 Joe Nieuwendyk 91UD/5
128 Joe Nieuwendyk 92UD/5
129 Joe Nieuwendyk 93UD/5
130 Joe Nieuwendyk 94UD/5
131 Joe Nieuwendyk 95UD/5
132 Joe Nieuwendyk 96UD/5
133 Joe Nieuwendyk 97 UD/2
134 Joe Nieuwendyk 98UD/5
135 Joe Nieuwendyk 99UD/5
136 Joe Nieuwendyk 00UD/5
137 Joe Nieuwendyk 01UD/5
138 Joe Nieuwendyk 02UD/48 12.50 30.00
139 Jeremy Roenick 90UD/14
140 Jeremy Roenick 91UD/5
141 Jeremy Roenick 92UD/5
142 Jeremy Roenick 93UD/5
143 Jeremy Roenick 94 UD/5
144 Jeremy Roenick 95UD/5
145 Jeremy Roenick 96UD/5
146 Jeremy Roenick 97UD/5
147 Jeremy Roenick 98UD/5
148 Jeremy Roenick 99UD/5
149 Jeremy Roenick 00UD/5
150 Jeremy Roenick 01UD/5
151 Jeremy Roenick 02UD/48 15.00 40.00
152 Patrick Roy 90UD/5
153 Patrick Roy 91UD/5
154 Patrick Roy 92UD/5
155 Patrick Roy 93UD/5
156 Patrick Roy 94UD/5
157 Patrick Roy 95UD/5
158 Patrick Roy 96UD/5
159 Patrick Roy 97UD/5
160 Patrick Roy 98UD/5
161 Patrick Roy 99UD/5
162 Patrick Roy 00UD/5
163 Patrick Roy 01UD/2
164 Patrick Roy 01UD/5
165 Patrick Roy 02UD/48 50.00 125.00
166 Patrick Roy MS 02UD/48 50.00 125.00
167 Sergei Samsonov 95UD/5
168 Sergei Samsonov 97UD/5
169 Sergei Samsonov 98UD/5
170 Sergei Samsonov 99UD/5
171 Sergei Samsonov 00UD/5
172 Sergei Samsonov 01UD/5
173 Sergei Samsonov 02UD/48 20.00 50.00
174 Jose Theodore 95UD/3
175 Jose Theodore 98 UD/5
176 Jose Theodore 00UD/5
177 Jose Theodore 01UD/5
178 Jose Theodore 02UD/48 15.00 40.00
179 Alexander Frolov 02UD/10
180 Alexander Frolov 03AS Promo/4
181 Stanislav Chistov 02UD/29 25.00 60.00
182 Stanislav Chistov 03AS Promo/5

2003-04 Upper Deck Canadian Exclusives

Inserted exclusively in Canadian hobby boxes, this 475 card parallel set carried distinctive red foil serial-numbering and a red foil maple leaf on the card fronts. Cards 1-445 were numbered out of 50 while cards 446-475 were numbered to 25.
*CARDS 1-200: 6X TO 15X BASE HI
*CARDS 201-245: 1X TO 2.5X
*CARDS 446-475: 1.5X TO 4X

2003-04 Upper Deck Fan Favorites

COMPLETE SET (10) 12.50 25.00
STATED ODDS 1:21
FF1 Jeremy Roenick 1.25 3.00
FF2 Todd Bertuzzi 1.00 2.50
FF3 Roberto Luongo 1.25 3.00
FF4 Georges Laraque .75 2.00
FF5 Tie Domi .75 2.00
FF6 Steve Yzerman 3.00 8.00
FF7 Mike Modano 1.50 4.00
FF8 P.J. Stock .75 2.00
FF9 Mario Lemieux 4.00 10.00
FF10 J-S Giguere .75 2.00

2003-04 Upper Deck Franchise Fabrics

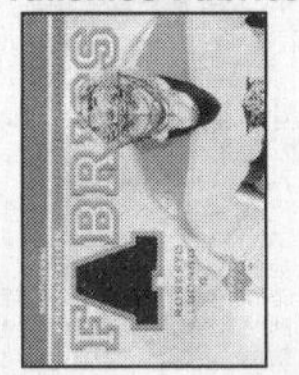

*MULT.COLOR SWATCH: .5X TO 1.25X
STATED ODDS 1:24
FF-AY Alexei Yashin 4.00 10.00
FF-BL Brian Leetch 4.00 10.00
FF-CD Chris Drury 4.00 10.00
FF-DH Dany Heatley 5.00 12.00
FF-HZ Henrik Zetterberg 4.00 10.00
FF-JI Jarome Iginla 6.00 15.00
FF-JJ Jaromir Jagr 8.00 20.00
FF-JT Joe Thornton 8.00 20.00
FF-JT Jose Theodore 6.00 15.00
FF-MB Martin Brodeur 10.00 25.00
FF-MG Marian Gaborik 8.00 20.00
FF-MH Marian Hossa 4.00 10.00
FF-ML Mario Lemieux 10.00 25.00
FF-MN Markus Naslund 4.00 10.00
FF-MS Mats Sundin 4.00 10.00
FF-MT Marty Turco 4.00 10.00
FF-NL Nicklas Lidstrom 4.00 10.00
FF-PF Peter Forsberg 6.00 15.00
FF-PK Paul Kariya 4.00 10.00
FF-RL Roberto Luongo 6.00 15.00
FF-RS Ryan Smyth 4.00 10.00
FF-SF Sergei Fedorov 6.00 15.00
FF-TB Todd Bertuzzi 4.00 10.00
FF-VL Vincent Lecavalier 4.00 10.00
FF-ZP Zigmund Palffy 4.00 10.00

2003-04 Upper Deck Gifted Greats

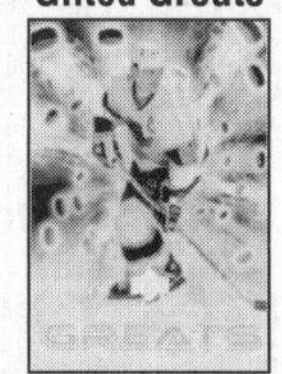

COMPLETE SET (10) 25.00 60.00
STATED ODDS 1:40
GG1 Wayne Gretzky 6.00 15.00
GG2 J-S Giguere 2.00 5.00
GG3 Joe Thornton 3.00 8.00
GG4 Mario Lemieux 6.00 15.00
GG5 Eric Lindros 2.00 5.00
GG6 Todd Bertuzzi 2.00 5.00
GG7 Marian Gaborik 4.00 10.00
GG8 Dany Heatley 3.00 8.00
GG9 Marian Hossa 2.00 5.00
GG10 Martin Brodeur 5.00 12.00

2003-04 Upper Deck HG

This 475-card parallel set featured a "high-gloss" finish and the letters "HG" embossed on the card fronts. Cards 1-200 and 246-445 were serial-numbered out of 25. Cards 201-245 and 446-475 were serial-numbered out of 10.
*STARS: 10X TO 25X BASE HI
YNG.GUNS NOT PRICED DUE TO SCARCITY

2003-04 Upper Deck Highlight Heroes

COMPLETE SET (10) 15.00 30.00
STATED ODDS 1:40
HH-AM Alexander Mogilny 2.00 5.00
HH-JJ Jaromir Jagr 3.00 8.00
HH-JS Jason Spezza 2.00 5.00
HH-JT Jocelyn Thibault 2.00 5.00
HH-MG Marian Gaborik 4.00 10.00
HH-PB Pavel Bure 2.00 5.00
HH-RN Rick Nash 2.50 6.00
HH-SS Sergei Samsonov 2.00 5.00
HH-TA Tony Amonte 2.00 5.00
HH-TS Teemu Selanne 2.00 5.00

2003-04 Upper Deck Highlight Heroes Jerseys

*MULT.COLOR SWATCH: .5X TO 1.25X
STATED ODDS 1:96
HH-AM Alexander Mogilny 5.00 12.00
HH-JJ Jaromir Jagr 8.00 20.00
HH-JS Jason Spezza 6.00 15.00
HH-JT Jocelyn Thibault 5.00 12.00
HH-MG Marian Gaborik 10.00 25.00
HH-PB Pavel Bure 6.00 15.00
HH-RN Rick Nash 8.00 20.00
HH-SS Sergei Samsonov 5.00 12.00
HH-TA Tony Amonte 5.00 12.00
HH-TS Teemu Selanne 6.00 15.00

2003-04 Upper Deck Jerseys

This 27-card memorabilia set was inserted at a rate of 1:96 for Series I and 1:72 for Series 2. Notations are made below distinguishing which cards were available in which series.
*MULT.COLOR SWATCH: .5X TO 1.25X
GJ-AK Alex Kovalev Ser. 1 6.00 15.00
GJ-BG Bill Guerin Ser. 1 6.00 15.00
GJ-EL Eric Lindros Ser. 1 6.00 15.00
GJ-IK Ilya Kovalchuk Ser. 1 8.00 20.00
GJ-JB Owen Nolan Ser. 1 6.00 15.00
GJ-JG J-S Giguere Ser. 1 6.00 15.00
GJ-JI Jarome Iginla Ser. 1 8.00 20.00
GJ-MA Maxim Afinogenov Ser. 1 6.00 15.00
GJ-MB Martin Brodeur Ser. 1 15.00 40.00
GJ-MC Mike Comrie Ser. 1 6.00 15.00
GJ-ML Mario Lemieux Ser. 1 15.00 40.00
GJ-MR Mark Recchi Ser. 1 6.00 15.00
GJ-MS Martin St. Louis Ser. 1 8.00 20.00
GJ-SK Saku Koivu Ser. 1 6.00 15.00
GJ-TB Todd Bertuzzi Ser. 1 6.00 15.00
UD-AF Alexander Frolov Ser. 2 6.00 15.00
UD-AH Ales Hemsky Ser. 2 6.00 15.00
UD-BH Brett Hull Ser. 2 8.00 20.00
UD-EJ Ed Jovanovski Ser. 2 6.00 15.00
UD-IK Ilya Kovalchuk Ser. 2 8.00 20.00
UD-JSG J-S Giguere Ser. 2 6.00 15.00
UD-MC Mike Comrie Ser. 2 6.00 15.00
UD-MH Marian Hossa Ser. 2 6.00 15.00
UD-MK Mike Komisarek Ser. 2 6.00 15.00
UD-MS Martin St. Louis Ser. 2 6.00 15.00
UD-ON Owen Nolan Ser. 2 6.00 15.00
UD-RB Rob Blake Ser. 2 6.00 15.00

2003-04 Upper Deck Jersey Autographs

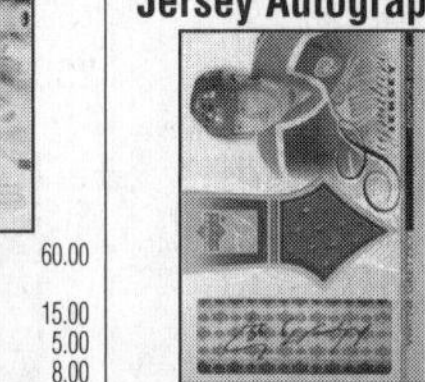

STATED ODDS 1:480 SERIES II
SJ-AH Ales Hemsky 12.00 30.00
SJ-CJ Curtis Joseph 15.00 40.00
SJ-DA David Aebischer 20.00 50.00
SJ-EL Eric Lindros 15.00 40.00
SJ-JA Jared Aulin 10.00 25.00
SJ-JI Jarome Iginla 30.00 80.00
SJ-JR Jeremy Roenick 25.00 60.00
SJ-JS Jason Spezza 60.00 125.00
SJ-JT Joe Thornton 20.00 50.00
SJ-JSG J-S Giguere 12.00 30.00
SJ-MH Marian Hossa 20.00 50.00
SJ-PR Patrick Roy 75.00 200.00
SJ-RN Rick Nash 40.00 100.00
SJ-SF Sergei Fedorov 20.00 50.00
SJ-SH Scott Hartnell 10.00 25.00
SJ-SK Saku Koivu 15.00 40.00
SJ-SS Sergei Samsonov 12.00 30.00
SJ-TB Todd Bertuzzi 12.00 30.00
SJ-WG Wayne Gretzky 225.00 350.00
SJ-ZP Zigmund Palffy 12.00 30.00

2003-04 Upper Deck Magic Moments

COMPLETE SET (15) 30.00 60.00
STATED ODDS 1:14
MM-1 J-S Giguere 1.00 2.50
MM-2 Scott Stevens 1.00 2.50
MM-3 Jason Spezza 1.00 2.50
MM-4 Steve Yzerman 3.00 8.00
MM-5 Paul Kariya 1.00 2.50
MM-6 Patrick Roy 3.00 8.00
MM-7 Joe Thornton 1.25 3.00
MM-8 Wayne Gretzky 4.00 10.00
MM-9 Marc-Andre Fleury 3.00 8.00
MM-10 Milan Hejduk 1.00 2.50
MM-11 Dominik Hasek 1.50 4.00
MM-12 Martin Brodeur 3.00 8.00
MM-13 Peter Forsberg 2.00 5.00
MM-14 Sergei Fedorov 1.25 3.00
MM-15 Jordin Tootoo 2.00 5.00

2003-04 Upper Deck Memorable Matchups

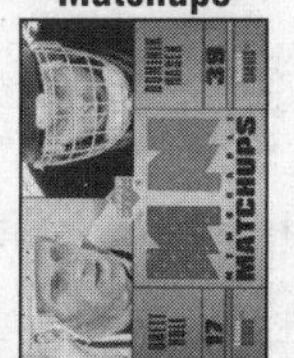

*MULT.COLOR SWATCH: .5X TO 1.25X
STATED ODDS 1:144
MM-BG T.Bertuzzi/M.Gaborik 6.00 15.00
MM-FK Sergei Fedorov 8.00 20.00
Paul Kariya
MM-GB J-S Giguere 12.50 30.00
Martin Brodeur
MM-HH Brett Hull 12.50 30.00
Dominik Hasek

MM-LS Eric Lindros 6.00 15.00
Scott Stevens
MM-NN Rob Niedermayer 5.00 12.00
Scott Niedermayer
MM-RR Jeremy Roenick 20.00 50.00
Patrick Roy
MM-TH Jose Theodore 5.00 12.00
Ales Hemsky
MM-TT Joe Thornton 8.00 20.00
Jose Theodore

2003-04 Upper Deck Mr. Hockey

COMPLETE SET (30) 40.00 80.00
COMMON CARD (GH1-GH30) 2.00 5.00

2003-04 Upper Deck NHL Best

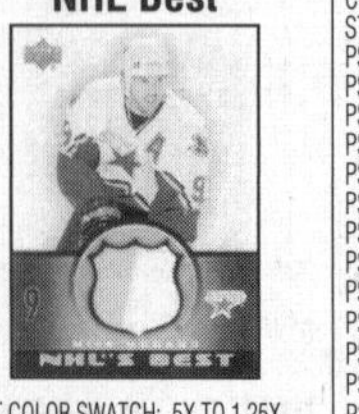

MULT.COLOR SWATCH: .5X TO 1.25X
STATED ODDS 1:48
NB-DH Dany Heatley 6.00 15.00
NB-GM Glen Murray 5.00 12.00
NB-IK Ilya Kovalchuk 6.00 15.00
NB-JG J-S Giguere 5.00 12.00
NB-JI Jarome Iginla 6.00 15.00
NB-JR Jeremy Roenick 6.00 15.00
NB-KT Keith Tkachuk 5.00 12.00
NB-MB Martin Brodeur 15.00 40.00
NB-ML Mario Lemieux 15.00 40.00
NB-MM Mike Modano 8.00 20.00
NB-NL Nicklas Lidstrom 5.00 12.00
NB-PR Patrick Roy 15.00 40.00
NB-PS Sergei Fedorov 6.00 15.00
NB-VL Vincent Lecavalier 5.00 12.00
NB-ZP Zigmund Palffy 5.00 12.00

2003-04 Upper Deck Patches

This 60-card memorabilia set was inserted at the rate of 1:7500 Series I and Series II packs. Notations are made below distinguishing cards available in each series. As of press time, not all cards have been verified.

LD1 Steve Yzerman Ser.2
LD2 Mike Modano Ser.2
LD3 Mario Lemieux Ser.2 100.00 250.00
LD4 Mats Sundin Ser.2 60.00 150.00
LD5 Joe Thornton Ser.2 75.00 200.00
LD6 Ron Francis Ser.2 60.00 125.00
LD7 Markus Naslund Ser.2 40.00 100.00
LD8 Brian Leetch Ser.2
LD9 Jeremy Roenick Ser.2 60.00 150.00
LD10 Jaromir Jagr Ser.2
SP1 Paul Kariya Ser.
SP2 Marian Gaborik Ser.2
SP3 Jeremy Roenick Ser.2 60.00 150.00
SP4 Brett Hull Ser.2 75.00 200.00
SP5 Dany Heatley Ser.2 75.00 200.00
SP6 Jarome Iginla Ser.2
SP7 Chris Drury Ser.2
SP8 Vincent Lecavalier Ser.2 50.00 125.00
SP9 Bill Guerin Ser.2 30.00 80.00
SP10 Glen Murray Ser.2 50.00 125.00
SV1 Martin Brodeur Ser.2 100.00 200.00
SV2 Roberto Luongo Ser.2 75.00 200.00
SV3 Roman Cechmanek Ser.2 40.00 100.00
SV4 Marty Turco Ser.2
SV5 Tommy Salo Ser.2 40.00 100.00
SV6 Jocelyn Thibault Ser.2
SV7 David Aebischer Ser.2 40.00 100.00
SV8 Patrick Lalime Ser.2 40.00 100.00
SV9 Dominik Hasek Ser.2 50.00 125.00
SV10 Ed Belfour Ser.2 50.00 125.00
PLG-JG J-S Giguere Ser.1 40.00 100.00
PLG-JS Jason Spezza Ser.1 75.00 200.00
PLG-JT Joe Thornton Ser.1 60.00 150.00
PLG-MB Martin Brodeur Ser.1 100.00 200.00
PLG-MG Marian Gaborik Ser.1
PLG-MH Marian Hossa Ser.1 40.00 100.00
PLG-ML Mario Lemieux Ser.1 75.00 200.00
PLG-MN Markus Naslund Ser.1 50.00 125.00
PLG-PR Patrick Roy Ser.1 150.00 300.00
PLG-RN Rick Nash Ser.1 75.00 200.00
PNM-JG J-S Giguere Ser.1 40.00 100.00
PNM-JS Jason Spezza Ser.1 75.00 200.00
PNM-JT Joe Thornton Ser.1 75.00 200.00
PNM-MB Martin Brodeur Ser.1 100.00 200.00
PNM-MG Marian Gaborik Ser.1
PNM-MH Marian Hossa Ser.1 40.00 100.00
PNM-ML Mario Lemieux Ser.1 75.00 200.00
PNM-MN Markus Naslund Ser.1 50.00 125.00
PNM-PR Patrick Roy Ser.1 150.00 300.00
PNM-RN Rick Nash Ser.1 75.00 150.00
PNR-JG J-S Giguere Ser.1 40.00 100.00
PNR-JS Jason Spezza Ser.1 75.00 200.00
PNR-JT Joe Thornton Ser.1 75.00 200.00
PNR-MB Martin Brodeur Ser.1 100.00 200.00
PNR-MG Marian Gaborik Ser.1
PNR-MH Marian Hossa Ser.1 40.00 100.00
PNR-ML Mario Lemieux Ser.1 100.00 250.00
PNR-MN Markus Naslund Ser.1 50.00 125.00
PNR-PR Patrick Roy Ser.1 150.00 300.00
PNR-RN Rick Nash Ser.1 75.00 150.00

2003-04 Upper Deck Performers

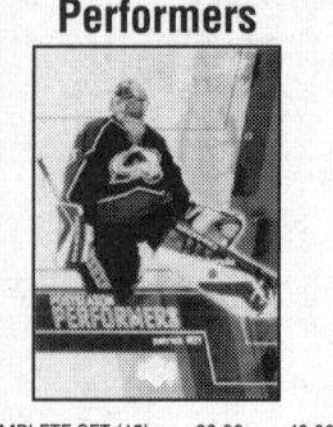

COMPLETE SET (15) 20.00 40.00
STATED ODDS 1:14
PS1 J-S Giguere .60 1.50
PS2 Scott Stevens .60 1.50
PS3 Steve Yzerman 2.50 6.00
PS4 Jeremy Roenick .75 2.00
PS5 Peter Forsberg 1.25 3.00
PS6 Jose Theodore .75 2.00
PS7 Marian Gaborik 1.00 2.50
PS8 Martin Brodeur 1.50 4.00
PS9 Ed Belfour .60 1.50
PS10 Mike Modano .75 2.00
PS11 Joe Sakic 1.00 2.50
PS12 Bobby Orr 4.00 10.00
PS13 Mario Lemieux 3.00 8.00
PS14 Wayne Gretzky 4.00 10.00
PS15 Patrick Roy 2.50 6.00

2003-04 Upper Deck Power Zone

COMPLETE SET (10) 10.00 25.00
STATED ODDS 1:21
PZ-1 Joe Thornton .75 2.00
PZ-2 Keith Tkachuk 1.00 2.50
PZ-3 Jeremy Roenick 1.25 3.00
PZ-4 Brendan Shanahan 1.00 2.50
PZ-5 Todd Bertuzzi 1.00 2.50
PZ-6 Rick Nash 1.25 3.00
PZ-7 Peter Forsberg 1.50 4.00
PZ-8 Owen Nolan 1.00 2.50
PZ-9 Mario Lemieux 4.00 10.00
PZ-10 Eric Lindros 1.00 2.50

2003-04 Upper Deck Rookie Threads

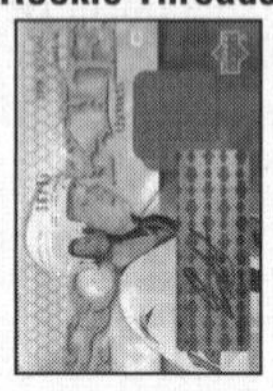

*MULT.COLOR SWATCH: .5X TO 1.25X
PRINT RUN 75 SER.#'d SETS
RT-1 Joffrey Lupul 15.00 40.00
RT-2 Dustin Brown 15.00 40.00
RT-3 Marc-Andre Fleury 40.00 100.00
RT-4 Joni Pitkanen 15.00 40.00
RT-5 Peter Sejna 12.50 30.00
RT-6 Eric Staal 30.00 80.00
RT-7 Tuomo Ruutu 30.00 80.00
RT-8 Dan Hamhuis 12.50 30.00
RT-9 Nathan Horton 25.00 60.00
RT-10 Jordin Tootoo 25.00 60.00

2003-04 Upper Deck Shooting Stars

MULT.COLOR SWATCH: .5X TO 1.25X
STATED ODDS 1:48
ST-AH Ales Hemsky 5.00 12.00
ST-AS Alexander Svitov 5.00 12.00
ST-AV Anton Volchenkov 5.00 12.00
ST-JA Jared Aulin 5.00 12.00
ST-JB Jay Bouwmeester 5.00 12.00
ST-JL Jordan Leopold 5.00 12.00
ST-JS Jason Spezza 8.00 20.00
ST-JW Justin Williams 5.00 12.00
ST-MH Marcel Hossa 5.00 12.00
ST-PM Pierre-Marc Bouchard 5.00 12.00
ST-RD Rick DiPietro 5.00 12.00
ST-RM Ryan Miller 5.00 12.00
ST-RN Rick Nash 20.00 40.00
ST-SO Steve Ott 5.00 12.00
ST-SV Alexei Smirnov 5.00 12.00

2003-04 Upper Deck Super Saviors

MULT.COLOR SWATCH: .5X TO 1.25X
STATED ODDS 1:144
SS-JG J-S Giguere 8.00 20.00
SS-MB Martin Brodeur 15.00 40.00
SS-MT Marty Turco 8.00 20.00
SS-PL Patrick Lalime 8.00 20.00
SS-PR Patrick Roy 15.00 40.00
SS-RC Roman Cechmanek 8.00 20.00

2003-04 Upper Deck Superstar Spotlight

This 15-card set featured a holographic mirrored action image on the majority of the card front with a smaller color photo of the featured player along side. This set was inserted at odds of 1:144.

SS1 J-S Giguere 4.00 10.00
SS2 Joe Thornton 6.00 15.00
SS3 Marian Gaborik 6.00 15.00
SS4 Rick Nash 5.00 12.00
SS5 Steve Yzerman 12.50 30.00
SS6 Martin Brodeur 12.50 30.00
SS7 Jason Spezza 5.00 12.00
SS8 Mike Modano 6.00 15.00
SS9 Mario Lemieux 15.00 40.00
SS10 Jaromir Jagr 6.00 15.00
SS11 Todd Bertuzzi 4.00 10.00
SS12 Dany Heatley 5.00 12.00
SS13 Patrick Roy 15.00 40.00
SS14 Bobby Orr 20.00 50.00
SS15 Gordie Howe 12.50 30.00

2003-04 Upper Deck Team Essentials

TL/TP STATED ODDS 1:96
TS STATED ODDS 1:288
*MULT.COLOR SWATCH: .5X TO 1.25X
TL-JS Joe Sakic 10.00 25.00
TL-JT Joe Thornton 8.00 20.00
TL-ML Mario Lemieux 15.00 40.00
TL-MN Markus Naslund 6.00 15.00
TL-MP Michael Peca 6.00 15.00
TL-MS Mats Sundin 6.00 15.00
TL-SS Scott Stevens 6.00 15.00
TL-SY Steve Yzerman 12.50 30.00
TP-AM Al MacInnis 6.00 15.00
TP-DA Daniel Alfredsson 6.00 15.00
TP-DH Dany Heatley 8.00 20.00
TP-JT Joe Thornton 8.00 20.00
TP-ML Mario Lemieux 12.50 30.00
TP-MM Mike Modano 8.00 20.00
TP-MS Miroslav Satan 6.00 15.00
TP-PF Peter Forsberg 10.00 25.00
TP-PK Paul Kariya 6.00 15.00
TP-VL Vincent Lecavalier 6.00 15.00
TS-DH Dany Heatley 10.00 25.00
TS-JJ Jaromir Jagr 12.50 30.00
TS-MH Milan Hejduk 8.00 20.00
TS-MH Marian Hossa 8.00 20.00
TS-PB Pavel Bure 8.00 20.00
TS-TB Todd Bertuzzi 8.00 20.00

2003-04 Upper Deck Three Stars

COMPLETE SET (15) 20.00 40.00
STATED ODDS 1:14
TS1 Paul Kariya .60 1.50
TS2 Marian Hossa .60 1.50
TS3 Dany Heatley .75 2.00
TS4 Alexei Yashin .60 1.50
TS5 Jaromir Jagr .75 2.00
TS6 Martin Brodeur 1.50 4.00
TS7 Marian Gaborik 1.00 2.50
TS8 Ziggy Palffy .60 1.50
TS9 Marty Turco .60 1.50
TS10 Mats Sundin .60 1.50
TS11 J-S Giguere .60 1.50
TS12 Mario Lemieux 3.00 8.00
TS13 Jarome Iginla .75 2.00
TS14 Markus Naslund .60 1.50
TS15 Joe Thornton .75 2.00

2003-04 Upper Deck Tough Customers

COMPLETE SET (15) 12.00 25.00
STATED ODDS 1:14
TC-1 Jody Shelley .75 2.00
TC-2 Andrei Nazarov .75 2.00
TC-3 Reed Low .75 2.00
TC-4 Andrew Peters .75 2.00
TC-5 Wade Belak .75 2.00
TC-6 Darren McCarty 1.00 2.50
TC-7 Krzysztof Oliwa .75 2.00
TC-8 P.J. Stock .75 2.00
TC-9 Matt Johnson .75 2.00
TC-10 Chris Neil .75 2.00
TC-11 Garrett Burnett .75 2.00
TC-12 Georges Laraque 1.00 2.50
TC-13 Tie Domi 1.00 2.50
TC-14 Jason Strudwick .75 2.00
TC-15 Donald Brashear .75 2.00

2003-04 Upper Deck UD Exclusives

This 230-card set paralleled cards 246-475 of the base set. Cards 246-445 were serial-numbered out of 50 and cards 446-475 were serila-numbered out of 10. Each card carried an "Exclusive" foil stamp.

*STARS: 6X TO 15X BASIC CARDS
446-475 NOT PRICED DUE TO SCARCITY

2004-05 Upper Deck

This 210-card set was released in just one series for the 2004-05 season that was ultimately canceled due to the labor dispute. The set consisted of 180 veteran cards and 30 Young Gun subset cards inserted at 1:4. Due to a lack of a true rookie class, many of the Young Gun cards were "flashbacks" of veteran players in their rookie season.

COMPLETE SET (210) 125.00 250.00
COMP.SET w/o SP's (180) 15.00 30.00
COMMON CARD (1-210) .02 .10
1 Petr Sykora .02 .10
2 Andy McDonald .02 .10
3 Sandis Ozolinsh .02 .10
4 Sergei Fedorov .25 .60
5 Joffrey Lupul .02 .10
6 J-S Giguere .15 .40
7 Dany Heatley .25 .60
8 Ilya Kovalchuk .25 .60
9 Patrik Stefan .02 .10
10 Jaroslav Modry .02 .10
11 Serge Aubin .02 .10
12 Kari Lehtonen .40 1.00
13 Joe Thornton .30 .75
14 Sergei Gonchar .02 .10
15 Patrice Bergeron .15 .40
16 Nick Boynton .02 .10
17 Sergei Samsonov .15 .40
18 Andrew Raycroft .15 .40
19 Daniel Briere .02 .10
20 Miroslav Satan .15 .40
21 Mika Noronen .15 .40
22 JP Dumont .02 .10
23 Maxim Afinogenov .02 .10
24 Martin Biron .15 .40
25 Chris Simon .02 .10
26 Jarome Iginla .25 .60
27 Robyn Regehr .02 .10
28 Jordan Leopold .02 .10
29 Chuck Kobasew .02 .10
30 Miikka Kiprusoff .15 .40
31 Jeff O'Neill .02 .10
32 Ron Francis .15 .40
33 Aaron Ward .02 .10
34 Erik Cole .02 .10
35 Eric Staal .02 .10
36 Martin Gerber .15 .40
37 Matthew Barnaby .02 .10
38 Kyle Calder .02 .10
39 Tyler Arnason .02 .10
40 Eric Daze .15 .40
41 Jocelyn Thibault .15 .40
42 Peter Forsberg .50 1.25
43 Alex Tanguay .15 .40
44 Milan Hejduk .20 .50
45 Rob Blake .15 .40
46 Paul Kariya .20 .50
47 Teemu Selanne .20 .50
48 David Aebischer .15 .40
49 Luke Richardson .02 .10
50 Rick Nash .25 .60
51 Rostislav Klesla .02 .10
52 Nikolai Zherdev .20 .50
53 Marc Denis .15 .40
54 Mike Modano .20 .50
55 Sergei Zubov .02 .10
56 Bill Guerin .15 .40
57 Jason Arnott .02 .10
58 Niko Kapanen .02 .10
59 Marty Turco .15 .40
60 Kirk Maltby .02 .10
61 Nicklas Lidstrom .20 .50
62 Kris Draper .02 .10
63 Brendan Shanahan .20 .50
64 Pavel Datsyuk .20 .50
65 Robert Lang .02 .10
66 Steve Yzerman 1.00 2.50
67 Curtis Joseph .15 .40
68 Ryan Smyth .02 .10
69 Jason Smith .02 .10
70 Ales Hemsky .15 .40
71 Eric Brewer .02 .10
72 Raffi Torres .02 .10
73 Ty Conklin .15 .40
74 Mike Van Ryn .02 .10
75 Kristian Huselius .02 .10
76 Stephen Weiss .02 .10
77 Jay Bouwmeester .02 .10
78 Roberto Luongo .25 .60
79 Craig Conroy .02 .10
80 Aaron Miller .02 .10
81 Luc Robitaille .15 .40
82 Martin Straka .02 .10
83 Mattias Norstrom .02 .10
84 Roman Cechmanek .15 .40
85 Marian Gaborik .30 .75
86 Pascal Dupuis .02 .10
87 Alexander Daigle .02 .10
88 Pierre-Marc Bouchard .02 .10
89 Filip Kuba .02 .10
90 Manny Fernandez .15 .40
91 Saku Koivu .20 .50
92 Michael Ryder .02 .10
93 Marcel Hossa .02 .10
94 Mike Ribeiro .02 .10
95 Jose Theodore .20 .50
96 Sheldon Souray .02 .10
97 David Legwand .15 .40
98 Steve Sullivan .02 .10
99 Marek Zidlicky .02 .10
100 Martin Erat .02 .10
101 Tomas Vokoun .15 .40
102 Patrik Elias .15 .40
103 Jeff Friesen .02 .10
104 Brian Rafalski .02 .10
105 Scott Niedermayer .02 .10
106 Scott Stevens .15 .40
107 Martin Brodeur 1.00 2.50
108 Oleg Kvasha .02 .10
109 Mark Parrish .02 .10
110 Michael Peca .02 .10
111 Adrian Aucoin .02 .10
112 Rick DiPietro .15 .40
113 Trent Hunter .02 .10
114 Eric Lindros .20 .50
115 Tom Poti .02 .10
116 Mark Messier .20 .50
117 Jaromir Jagr .30 .75
118 Bobby Holik .02 .10
119 Mike Dunham .15 .40
120 Marian Hossa .20 .50
121 Martin Havlat .15 .40
122 Zdeno Chara .02 .10
123 Daniel Alfredsson .15 .40
124 Jason Spezza .20 .50
125 Dominik Hasek .40 1.00
126 Jeremy Roenick .25 .60
127 Tony Amonte .02 .10
128 Keith Primeau .15 .40
129 Simon Gagne .20 .50
130 Danny Markov .02 .10
131 Robert Esche .15 .40
132 Shane Doan .02 .10
133 Mike Comrie .02 .10
134 Ladislav Nagy .02 .10
135 Brett Hull .25 .60
136 Derek Morris .02 .10
137 Brian Boucher .15 .40
138 Mario Lemieux 1.25 3.00
139 Mark Recchi .02 .10
140 Ryan Malone .02 .10
141 Dick Tarnstrom .02 .10
142 Rico Fata .02 .10
143 Marc-Andre Fleury .50 1.25
144 Alyn McCauley .02 .10
145 Marco Sturm .02 .10
146 Patrick Marleau .15 .40
147 Scott Hannan .02 .10
148 Kyle McLaren .02 .10
149 Evgeni Nabokov .15 .40
150 Al MacInnis .15 .40
151 Petr Cajanek .02 .10
152 Keith Tkachuk .20 .50
153 Barret Jackman .02 .10
154 Chris Pronger .15 .40
155 Patrick Lalime .15 .40
156 Vincent Lecavalier .20 .50
157 Dave Andreychuk .02 .10
158 Brad Richards .15 .40
159 Pavel Kubina .02 .10
160 Ruslan Fedotenko .02 .10
161 Nikolai Khabibulin .20 .50
162 Alexander Mogilny .15 .40
163 Owen Nolan .15 .40
164 Gary Roberts .02 .10
165 Brian McCabe .02 .10
166 Ed Belfour .20 .50
167 Joe Nieuwendyk .15 .40
168 Markus Naslund .20 .50
169 Brendan Morrison .15 .40
170 Todd Bertuzzi .20 .50
171 Ed Jovanovski .15 .40
172 Trevor Linden .02 .10
173 Dan Cloutier .15 .40
174 Jeff Halpern .02 .10
175 Dainius Zubrus .02 .10
176 Jason Doig .02 .10
177 Brendan Witt .02 .10
178 Olaf Kolzig .15 .40
179 Wayne Gretzky CL 1.50 4.00
180 Gordie Howe CL 1.00 2.50
181 Brad Fast YG RC 2.00 5.00
182 Brennan Evans YG RC 2.00 5.00
183 Wayne Gretzky YG 15.00 40.00
184 Mark Messier YG 6.00 15.00
185 Peter Forsberg YG 6.00 15.00
186 Steve Yzerman YG 8.00 20.00
187 Ron Francis YG 4.00 10.00
188 Patrick Roy YG 10.00 25.00
189 Mario Lemieux YG 10.00 25.00
190 Dave Andreychuk YG 4.00 10.00
191 Luc Robitaille YG 4.00 10.00
192 Gordie Howe YG 8.00 20.00
193 Don Cherry YG 8.00 20.00
194 Hobey Baker YG RC 2.00 5.00
195 Mike Modano YG 4.00 10.00
196 Denis Brodeur YG 2.00 5.00
197 Keith Tkachuk YG 2.00 5.00
198 Bob Goodenow YG 2.00 5.00
199 Cammi Granato YG RC 4.00 10.00
200 Foster Hewitt YG 2.00 5.00
201 Mike Keenan YG 2.00 5.00
202 Dick Irvin Jr. YG 2.00 5.00
203 Jeremy Roenick YG 4.00 10.00
204 James Norris YG 2.00 5.00
205 Alexander Ragulin YG RC 2.00 5.00
206 Brendan Shanahan YG 4.00 10.00
207 Lord Stanley YG 2.00 5.00
208 Gary Thorne YG 2.00 5.00
209 Scott Stevens YG 4.00 10.00
210 Joe Sakic YG 6.00 15.00

2004-05 Upper Deck 1997 Game Jerseys

This insert set recaptured the design of Upper Deck's first jersey cards from the 1997-98 season. Cards were inserted at a rate of 1:288 and carried a "97" prefix.

KNOWN PRINT RUNS LISTED BELOW
LOWER PRINT RUNS NOT PRICED DUE TO SCARCITY
BB Joe Thornton 15.00 40.00
BS Brendan Shanahan/100 25.00 60.00
GH Gordie Howe/15
JI Jarome Iginla 15.00 40.00
JS Jason Spezza 10.00 25.00
MB Martin Brodeur 25.00 60.00
MM Mike Modano 12.50 30.00
MS Martin St. Louis 10.00 25.00
PF Peter Forsberg/50 25.00 60.00
PR Patrick Roy/50 30.00 80.00
SF Sergei Fedorov 15.00 40.00
SK Saku Koivu 10.00 25.00
SU Mats Sundin 10.00 25.00
WG2 Wayne Gretzky/25

2004-05 Upper Deck Big Playmakers

STATED PRINT RUN 50 SER.#'d SETS
BP-AT Alex Tanguay 10.00 25.00
BP-BH Brett Hull 12.00 30.00
BP-EF Sergei Fedorov 12.00 30.00
BP-GH Gordie Howe 150.00 250.00
BP-HE Milan Hejduk 12.50 25.00
BP-HO Marian Hossa 12.50 25.00
BP-IK Ilya Kovalchuk 15.00 40.00
BP-JI Jarome Iginla 20.00 50.00
BP-JJ Jaromir Jagr 20.00 50.00
BP-JR Jeremy Roenick 15.00 40.00
BP-JS Joe Sakic 20.00 50.00
BP-KP Keith Primeau 10.00 25.00
BP-KT Keith Tkachuk 12.00 30.00
BP-ML Mario Lemieux 40.00 100.00
BP-MM Mike Modano 15.00 40.00
BP-MN Markus Naslund 12.00 30.00
BP-MS Martin St. Louis 10.00 25.00
BP-PB Pavel Bure 12.00 30.00
BP-PD Pavel Datsyuk 12.00 30.00
BP-SU Mats Sundin 12.00 30.00
BP-TH Joe Thornton 20.00 50.00
BP-WG Wayne Gretzky 100.00 200.00

2004-05 Upper Deck Canadian Exclusives

*1-180 EXCL.: 10X TO 25X
1-180 PRINT RUN 50 SER.#'d SETS
*181-210 YG EXCL.: 2X TO 5X
181-210 PRINT RUN 25 SER.#'d SETS

2004-05 Upper Deck Clutch Performers

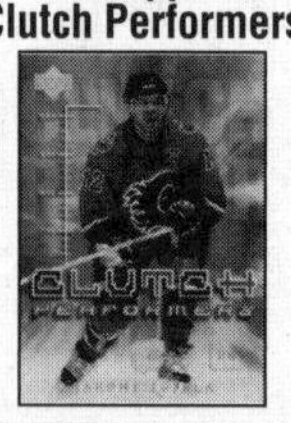

COMPLETE SET (7) 12.50 25.00
STATED ODDS 1:24
CP1 Jarome Iginla 1.50 4.00
CP2 Brad Richards .75 2.00
CP3 Joe Sakic 2.00 5.00
CP4 Joe Thornton 1.50 4.00
CP5 Keith Primeau .75 2.00
CP6 Nikolai Khabibulin 1.25 3.00
CP7 Mario Lemieux 4.00 10.00

2004-05 Upper Deck Hardware Heroes

COMPLETE SET (14) 15.00 30.00
STATED ODDS 1:12
AW1 Scott Niedermeyer .75 2.00
Norris
AW2 Martin St. Louis .75 2.00
Art Ross
AW3 Brad Richards .75 2.00
Conn Smythe
AW4 Andrew Raycroft .75 2.00
Calder
AW5 Martin Brodeur 2.50 6.00
Vezina
AW6 Iginla/Nash/Kovalchuk/Richard 2.00 5.00
AW7 Martin St. Louis .75 2.00
Hart
AW8 Brad Richards .75 2.00
Lady Byng
AW9 Kris Draper .75 2.00
Selke
AW10 Bryan Berard .75 2.00
Masterton
AW11 Jarome Iginla 1.00 2.50
Clancy
AW12 Martin Brodeur 2.50 6.00
Jennings
AW13 Detroit Red Wings 2.00 5.00
President's Trophy
AW14 Tampa Bay Lightning 2.50 6.00
Stanley Cup

2004-05 Upper Deck Heritage Classic

Inserted at 1:288, this 15-card set featured jersey swatches of players who played in the 2003-04 Heritage Classic.

KNOWN PRINT RUNS LISTED BELOW
CC-AH Ales Hemsky 15.00 40.00
CC-EB Eric Brewer 12.00 30.00
CC-GF Grant Fuhr 40.00 80.00
CC-JK Jari Kurri 30.00 80.00
CC-JT Jose Theodore/75 30.00 80.00
CC-LU Guy Lafleur/82 50.00 125.00
CC-MM Mark Messier/25 250.00 400.00
CC-MR Mike Ribeiro 12.00 30.00
CC-PC Paul Coffey/75 40.00 100.00
CC-RS Ryan Smyth 20.00 50.00
CC-RT Raffi Torres 12.00 30.00
CC-RY Michael Ryder 20.00 50.00
CC-SK Saku Koivu 20.00 50.00
CC-SS Steve Shutt 12.00 30.00
CC-TC Ty Conklin 12.00 30.00

2004-05 Upper Deck HG Glossy Gold

STATED PRINT RUN 5 SER.#'d SETS
NOT PRICED DUE TO SCARCITY

2004-05 Upper Deck HG Glossy Silver

STATED PRINT RUN 10 SER.#'d SETS
NOT PRICED DUE TO SCARCITY

2004-05 Upper Deck Jersey Autographs

STATED ODDS 1:288
SINGLE PRINT RUN 25 SER.#'d SETS
DUAL JSY PRINT RUN 10 SER.#'d SETS
DUAL NOT PRICED DUE TO SCARCITY
GJA-AA Arron Asham 12.00 40.00
GJA-AF Alexander Frolov 25.00 60.00
GJA-AH Adam Hall 15.00 30.00
GJA-AL Ales Hemsky 25.00 60.00
GJA-AS Alexander Svitov 15.00 40.00
GJA-AY Alexei Yashin 15.00 40.00
GJA-BO Brooks Orpik 15.00 40.00
GJA-BU Pavel Bure 30.00 80.00
GJA-CK Chuck Kobasew 15.00 40.00
GJA-DA David Aebischer 20.00 50.00
GJA-GH Gordie Howe 125.00 250.00
GJA-HO Marcel Hossa 15.00 30.00
GJA-HS Marian Hossa 25.00 60.00
GJA-IK Ilya Kovalchuk 60.00 150.00
GJA-JG J-S Giguere 15.00 40.00
GJA-JI Jarome Iginla 60.00 150.00
GJA-JL John LeClair 15.00 40.00
GJA-JR Jeremy Roenick 40.00 100.00
GJA-JS Jason Spezza 60.00 150.00
GJA-MC Mike Comrie
GJA-MG Marian Gaborik 60.00 150.00
GJA-MH Martin Havlat 25.00 60.00
GJA-MK Markus Naslund 30.00 80.00
GJA-MN Markus Naslund 30.00 80.00
GJA-MP Mark Parrish 12.00 40.00
GJA-MT Marty Turco 30.00 80.00
GJA-PB Pavel Bure 40.00 100.00
GJA-PE Michael Peca 15.00 30.00
GJA-PH Phil Esposito 30.00 80.00
GJA-PR Patrick Roy 125.00 300.00
GJA-RD Rick DiPietro 25.00 60.00
GJA-RF Ron Francis 25.00 60.00
GJA-RL Roberto Luongo 40.00 100.00
GJA-RN Rick Nash 50.00 125.00
GJA-SF Sergei Fedorov 30.00 80.00
GJA-TB Todd Bertuzzi 25.00 60.00
GJA-TH Joe Thornton 50.00 125.00
GJA-WG Wayne Gretzky 225.00 500.00
GJA-PA/MP Mark Parrish/Michael Peca
GJA-PB/MN Pavel Bure/Markus Naslund
GJA-PR/RL Patrick Roy/Roberto Luongo
GJA-HO/HS Marcel Hossa/Marian Hossa
GJA-WG/RN Wayne Gretzky/Rick Nash
GJA-MT/JG Marty Turco/JS Giguere

GJA-TB/MN Todd Bertuzzi/Markus Naslund
GJA-IL/PB Ilya Kovalchuk/Pavel Bure
GJA-PR/DA Patrick Roy/David Aebischer
GJA-JR/JL Jeremy Roenick/John LeClair
GJA-WG/GH Wayne Gretzky/Gordie Howe
GJA-MB/PR M.Brodeur/P.Roy
GJA-JS/AY Jason Spezza/Alexei Yashin

2004-05 Upper Deck NHL's Best

STATED ODDS 1:96
KNOWN PRINT RUNS LISTED BELOW
NB-BL Brian Leetch 6.00 15.00
NB-EB Ed Belfour 6.00 15.00
NB-GH Gordie Howe/15
NB-JT Jose Theodore 8.00 20.00
NB-MB Martin Brodeur 10.00 25.00
NB-ML Mario Lemieux/50 30.00 80.00
NB-NL Nicklas Lidstrom 6.00 15.00
NB-PF Peter Forsberg/75 15.00 40.00
NB-PR Patrick Roy/50 40.00 100.00
NB-RB Rob Blake 6.00 15.00
NB-RN Rick Nash 8.00 20.00
NB-SG Sergei Gonchar 6.00 15.00
NB-SN Scott Niedermayer 6.00 15.00
NB-TB Todd Bertuzzi 8.00 15.00
NB-WG Wayne Gretzky/25 150.00 300.00

2004-05 Upper Deck Patches

NMBR.PATCH ODDS 1:2500
LOGO PATCH ODDS 1:5000
NAME PATCH ODDS 1:7500
NOT PRICED DUE TO SCARCITY
GJPA-BB Joe Thornton/11
GJPA-JJ Jaromir Jagr/7
GJPA-JR Jeremy Roenick/8
GJPA-JS Joe Sakic/5
GJPA-MB Martin Brodeur/5
GJPA-ML Mario Lemieux/5
GJPA-MM Mark Messier/5
GJPA-MO Mike Modano/10
GJPA-MS Martin St. Louis/8
GJPA-PF Peter Forsberg/5
GJPA-PK Paul Kariya
GJPA-SY Steve Yzerman/5
GJPA-TB Todd Bertuzzi/8
GJPA-WG Wayne Gretzky/5
GJPL-BB Joe Thornton/10
GJPL-JJ Jaromir Jagr/15
GJPL-JR Jeremy Roenick/13
GJPL-JS Joe Sakic/8
GJPL-MB Martin Brodeur/8
GJPL-ML Mario Lemieux/5
GJPL-MM Mark Messier/8
GJPL-MO Mike Modano/15
GJPL-MS Martin St. Louis/13
GJPL-PF Peter Forsberg/8
GJPL-PK Paul Kariya/3
GJPL-SY Steve Yzerman/8
GJPL-TB Todd Bertuzzi/12
GJPL-WG Wayne Gretzky/5
GJPN-BB Joe Thornton/23
GJPN-JJ Jaromir Jagr/23
GJPN-JR Jeremy Roenick/20
GJPN-JS Joe Sakic/20
GJPN-MB Martin Brodeur/23
GJPN-ML Mario Lemieux/15
GJPN-MM Mark Messier/17
GJPN-MO Mike Modano/23
GJPN-MS Martin St. Louis/23
GJPN-PF Peter Forsberg/20
GJPN-PK Paul Kariya/2
GJPN-SY Steve Yzerman/20
GJPN-TB Todd Bertuzzi/23
GJPN-WG Wayne Gretzky/5

2004-05 Upper Deck School of Hard Knocks

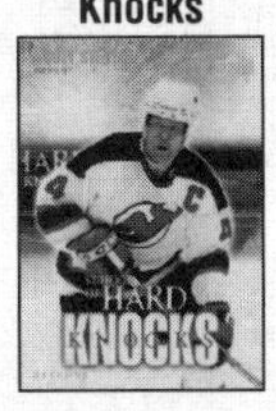

COMPLETE SET (7) 8.00 15.00
STATED ODDS 1:24
SHK1 Brendan Shanahan 1.00 2.50
SHK2 Scott Stevens 1.00 2.50
SHK3 Gary Roberts 1.00 2.50
SHK4 Jeremy Roenick 1.50 4.00
SHK5 Zdeno Chara 1.00 2.50
SHK6 Ed Jovanovski 1.00 2.50
SHK7 Todd Bertuzzi 1.00 2.50

2004-05 Upper Deck Swatch of Six

STATED ODDS 1:96
KNOWN PRINT RUNS LISTED BELOW
SS-AR Andrew Raycroft 8.00 20.00
SS-BS Brendan Shanahan 8.00 20.00
SS-EB Ed Belfour 8.00 20.00
SS-GH Gordie Howe/15
SS-GR Gary Roberts 6.00 15.00
SS-JJ Jaromir Jagr/50 15.00 40.00
SS-JO Jocelyn Thibault 6.00 15.00
SS-JT Jose Theodore 10.00 25.00
SS-MM Mark Messier/25 100.00 200.00
SS-PD Pavel Datsyuk 8.00 20.00
SS-SK Saku Koivu 8.00 20.00
SS-SY Steve Yzerman 15.00 40.00
SS-TH Joe Thornton 12.50 30.00
SS-TR Tuomo Ruutu 8.00 20.00
SS-WG Wayne Gretzky/25 150.00 300.00

2004-05 Upper Deck Three Stars

COMPLETE SET (14) 15.00 30.00
STATED ODDS 1:12
AS1 Steve Yzerman 1.50 4.00
AS2 Joe Sakic 1.25 3.00
AS3 Mats Sundin .60 1.50
AS4 Mike Modano .75 2.00
AS5 Jarome Iginla .75 2.00
AS6 Jeremy Roenick .75 2.00
AS7 Martin Brodeur 1.50 4.00
AS8 Vincent Lecavalier .60 1.50
AS9 Markus Naslund .60 1.50
AS10 Jaromir Jagr .75 2.00
AS11 Mario Lemieux 3.00 8.00
AS12 Patrick Roy 1.50 4.00
AS13 Wayne Gretzky 3.00 8.00
AS14 Gordie Howe 1.50 4.00

2004-05 Upper Deck World's Best

This 30-card retail only set featured players who have represented their countries in international competition.

COMPLETE SET (30) 12.50 30.00
WB1 Joe Sakic .60 1.50
WB2 Jarome Iginla .40 1.00
WB3 Martin St. Louis .25 .60
WB4 Martin Broduer 1.25 3.00
WB5 Mario Lemieux 1.50 4.00
WB6 Joe Thornton .50 1.25
WB7 Dany Heatley .40 1.00
WB8 Milan Hejduk .30 .75
WB9 Jaromir Jagr .50 1.25
WB10 Tomas Kaberle .25 .60
WB11 Tomas Vokoun .25 .60
WB12 Saku Koivu .30 .75
WB13 Kari Lehtonen .40 1.00
WB14 Teemu Selanne .30 .75
WB15 Olaf Kolzig .25 .60
WB16 Jochen Hecht .25 .60
WB17 Sergei Gonchar .25 .60
WB18 Ilya Kovalchuk .40 1.00
WB19 Pavel Datsyuk .30 .75
WB20 Zdeno Chara .25 .60
WB21 Pavel Demitra .25 .60
WB22 Marian Hossa .30 .75
WB23 Marian Gaborik .60 1.50
WB24 Mats Sundin .30 .75
WB25 Peter Forsberg .75 2.00
WB26 Nicklas Lidstrom .30 .75
WB27 Robert Esche .25 .60
WB28 Chris Chelios .30 .75
WB29 Mike Modano .50 1.25
WB30 Keith Tkachuk .30 .75

2004-05 Upper Deck World Cup Tribute

SINGLE ODDS 1:48
DUAL JSY ODDS 1:72
TRIPLE JSY ODDS 1:700
TRIPLE JSY PRINT RUN 25 SER.#'d SETS
AK Alex Kovalev 5.00 10.00
BB Joe Thornton 10.00 25.00
BG Bill Guerin 3.00 8.00
BH Brett Hull SP 12.00 30.00
BL Brian Leetch 4.00 10.00
BR Brad Richards 3.00 8.00
CC Chris Chelios 4.00 10.00
CD Chris Drury 3.00 8.00
DH Dany Heatley SP 12.00 30.00
HE Milan Hejduk 4.00 10.00
IK Ilya Kovalchuk SP 15.00 40.00
JB Jay Bouwmeester 3.00 8.00
JH Jochen Hecht 3.00 8.00
JI Jarome Iginla 5.00 12.00
JJ Jaromir Jagr 12.00 30.00
JS Joe Sakic 15.00 40.00
MB Martin Brodeur 25.00 60.00
MH Marian Hossa 4.00 10.00
MK Miikkaa Kiprusoff 10.00 25.00
ML Martin St. Louis 5.00 10.00
MM Mike Modano 8.00 20.00
MS Mats Sundin 4.00 10.00
NL Nicklas Lidstrom 4.00 10.00
OK Olaf Kolzig 3.00 8.00
PD Pavel Datsyuk 5.00 10.00
PE Patrik Elias 3.00 8.00
PF Peter Forsberg SP 15.00 40.00
RD Rick DiPietro 3.00 8.00
RE Robert Esche 3.00 8.00
RL Roberto Luongo 8.00 20.00
SK Saku Koivu SP 10.00 25.00
VL Vincent Lecavalier 5.00 12.00
ZC Zdeno Chara 3.00 8.00
BLBR Brian Leetch/Brian Rafalski 8.00 20.00
CCTA Chris Chelios/Tony Amonte 8.00 20.00
IKAK Ilya Kovalchuk/Alexei Kovalev 15.00 40.00
JBAF Jay Bouwmeester/Adam Foote 8.00 20.00
JHOK Jochen Hecht/Olaf Kolzig 8.0020.00
KLMK Kari Lehtonen
Miikkaa Kiprusoff 12.00 30.00
MBRL M.Brodeur/R.Luongo SP 20.0050.00
NLMO Nicklas Lidstrom
Mattias Ohlund 8.00 20.00
RCTV Roman Cechmanek
Tomas Vokoun 8.00 20.00
SNEJ Scott Niedermeyer
Ed Jovanovski 8.00 20.00
WREB Wade Redden/Eric Brewer 8.00 20.00
ZCMG Z.Chara/M.Gaborik 8.00 20.00
AKAYSS Alexei Kovalev/Alexei Yashin/Sergei Samsonov 20.00 50.00
CCRELDH Chris Chelios/Robert Esche/Brian Leetch 30.00 80.00
DHPMSD Dany Heatley/Patrick Marleau/Shane Doan 30.00 80.00
DWMOCD Doug Weight/Mike Modano/Chris Drury 40.00 100.00
EBEJWR Eric Brewer/Ed Jovanoski/Wade Redden 20.00 50.00
HZTSNL Henrik Zetterberg/Tommy Salo/Nicklas Lidstrom
JSMLJI Sakic/Lemieux/Iginla 125.00300.00
KLJPTR Kari Lehtonen/Joni Pitkanen/Tuomo Ruutu 30.00 80.00
KTDWBH Keith Tkachuk/Doug Weight/Brett Hull 50.00 125.00
MBRLJT Martin Brodeur/Roberto Luongo/Jose Theodore 125.00 300.00
MGHOMI Gaborik/Hossa/Satan 50.00 125.00
MHSKTV Martin Havlat/Martin Straka/Tomas Vokoun 20.00 50.00
MSVLBR Martin St. Louis/Vincent Lecavalier/Brad Richards 75.00 200.00
OJSKTS Olli Jokinen/Saku Koivu/Teemu Selanne 50.00 125.00
PBPDZC Peter Bondra/Pavol Demitra/Zdeno Chara 25.00 60.00
PDMAIK Pavel Datsyuk/Maxim Afinogenov/Ilya Kovalchuk 50.00 100.00
PEJJHE Elias/Jagr/Hejduk 75.00 200.00
PFSUDA Peter Forsberg/Mats Sundin/Daniel Alfredsson 60.00 150.00
SGTHRS Simon Gagne/Joe Thornton/Ryan Smyth 75.00 150.00
TASGBG Tony Amonte/Scott Gomez/Bill Guerin 40.00 100.00
TCRDRE Ty Conklin/Rick DiPietro/Robert Esche 25.00 60.00

2004-05 Upper Deck YoungStars

STATED ODDS 1:72
YS-AR Andrew Raycroft 8.00 20.00
YS-ES Eric Staal 8.00 20.00
YS-JC Jonathan Cheechoo 15.00 40.00
YS-JL Joffrey Lupul 4.00 10.00
YS-MR Michael Ryder 6.00 15.00
YS-MS Matt Stajan 5.00 12.00
YS-NZ Nikolai Zherdev 6.00 15.00
YS-PB Patrice Bergeron 12.50 30.00
YS-PS Philippe Sauve 4.00 10.00
YS-RT Raffi Torres 4.00 10.00
YS-TH Trent Hunter 4.00 10.00
YS-TR Tuomo Ruutu 8.00 20.00

2005-06 Upper Deck

COMPLETE SET (487) 400.00 800.00
COMP.SER 1 w/o SP's (200) 12.00 25.00
COMPLETE SERIES 1 (242) 300.00 600.00
COMP.SER 2 w/o SP's (200) 12.00 25.00
COMPLETE SERIES 2 (245) 250.00 500.00
YG STATED ODDS 1:4
1 Sergei Fedorov .25 .60
2 Sandis Ozolinsh .05 .15
3 Rob Niedermayer .05 .15
4 Andy McDonald .05 .15
5 Joffrey Lupul .05 .15
6 J-S Giguere .15 .40
7 Ilya Kovalchuk .25 .60
8 Patrik Stefan .05 .15
9 Kari Lehtonen .15 .40
10 Marc Savard .05 .15
11 Andy Sutton .05 .15
12 Niclas Havelid .05 .15
13 Nick Boynton .05 .15
14 Joe Thornton .30 .75
15 Andrew Raycroft .15 .40
16 P.J. Axelsson .05 .15
17 Patrice Bergeron .15 .40
18 Sergei Samsonov .15 .40
19 Chris Drury .15 .40
20 Derek Roy .05 .15
21 Maxim Afinogenov .05 .15
22 Daniel Briere .05 .15
23 Mika Noronen .15 .40
24 Jean-Pierre Dumont .05 .15
25 Jarome Iginla .25 .60
26 Jordan Leopold .05 .15
27 Robyn Regehr .05 .15
28 Marcus Nilson .05 .15
29 Shean Donovan .05 .15
30 Miikka Kiprusoff .15 .40
31 Erik Cole .05 .15
32 Bret Hedican .05 .15
33 Josef Vasicek .05 .15
34 Radim Vrbata .05 .15
35 Niclas Wallin .05 .15
36 Justin Williams .05 .15
37 Mark Bell .05 .15
38 Tuomo Ruutu .05 .15
39 Eric Daze .15 .40
40 Kyle Calder .05 .15
41 Matthew Barnaby .05 .15
42 Tyler Arnason .05 .15
43 Joe Sakic .75 2.00
44 Rob Blake .15 .40
45 Alex Tanguay .15 .40
46 Dan Hinote .05 .15
47 J-M Liles .05 .15
48 Steve Konowalchuk .05 .15
49 David Aebischer .15 .40
50 Riku Hahl .05 .15
51 Rick Nash .25 .60
52 Marc Denis .15 .40
53 Jody Shelley .05 .15
54 David Vyborny .05 .15
55 Manny Malhotra .05 .15
56 Todd Marchant .05 .15
57 Geoff Sanderson .05 .15
58 Bill Guerin .15 .40
59 Brenden Morrow .15 .40
60 Sergei Zubov .05 .15
61 Jaroslav Svoboda .05 .15
62 Steve Ott .05 .15
63 Jason Arnott .05 .15
64 Niko Kapanen .05 .15
65 Stu Barnes .05 .15
66 Steve Yzerman 1.00 2.50
67 Nicklas Lidstrom .20 .50
68 Robert Lang .05 .15
69 Manny Legace .15 .40
70 Tomas Holmstrom .05 .15
71 Kris Draper .05 .15
72 Jiri Fischer .05 .15
73 Henrik Zetterberg .20 .50
74 Ty Conklin .15 .40
75 Raffi Torres .05 .15
76 Jason Smith .05 .15
77 Radek Dvorak .05 .15
78 Ales Hemsky .15 .40
79 Shawn Horcoff .05 .15
80 Roberto Luongo .25 .60
81 Mike Van Ryn .05 .15
82 Olli Jokinen .15 .40
83 Jay Bouwmeester .05 .15
84 Nathan Horton .05 .15
85 Niklas Hagman .05 .15
86 Luc Robitaille .15 .40
87 Mathieu Garon .05 .15
88 Lubomir Visnovsky .05 .15
89 Trent Klatt .05 .15
90 Mattias Norstrom .05 .15
91 Dustin Brown .05 .15
92 Dwayne Roloson .15 .40
93 Marian Gaborik .40 1.00
94 Pascal Dupuis .05 .15
95 Filip Kuba .05 .15
96 Pierre-Marc Bouchard .05 .15
97 Alexandre Daigle .05 .15
98 Saku Koivu .20 .50
99 Richard Zednik .05 .15
100 Michael Ryder .05 .15
101 Sheldon Souray .05 .15
102 Craig Rivet .05 .15
103 Jan Bulis .05 .15
104 Pierre Dagenais .05 .15
105 Tomas Vokoun .15 .40
106 David Legwand .15 .40
107 Steve Sullivan .05 .15
108 Adam Hall .05 .15
109 Jordin Tootoo .05 .15
110 Denis Arkhipov .05 .15
111 Scott Gomez .05 .15
112 Patrik Elias .15 .40
113 Scott Stevens .15 .40
114 Sergei Brylin .05 .15
115 John Madden .05 .15
116 Jeff Friesen .05 .15
117 Paul Martin .05 .15
118 Alexei Yashin .05 .15
119 Trent Hunter .05 .15
120 Mark Parrish .05 .15
121 Garth Snow .15 .40
122 Jason Blake .05 .15
123 Janne Niinimaa .05 .15
124 Jamie Lundmark .05 .15
125 Tom Poti .05 .15
126 Jaromir Jagr .30 .75
127 Darius Kasparaitis .05 .15
128 Michael Nylander .05 .15
129 Kevin Weekes .15 .40
130 Daniel Alfredsson .15 .40
131 Dominik Hasek .40 1.00
132 Wade Redden .05 .15
133 Jason Spezza .20 .50
134 Chris Phillips .05 .15
135 Vaclav Varada .05 .15
136 Zdeno Chara .05 .15
137 Simon Gagne .20 .50
138 Joni Pitkanen .05 .15
139 Keith Primeau .05 .15
140 Michal Handzus .05 .15
141 Kim Johnsson .05 .15
142 Sami Kapanen .05 .15
143 Donald Brashear .05 .15
144 Brett Hull .25 .60
145 Tyson Nash .05 .15
146 Shane Doan .05 .15
147 Derek Morris .05 .15
148 Mike Johnson .05 .15
149 Paul Mara .05 .15
150 Mario Lemieux 1.25 3.00
151 Mark Recchi .05 .15
152 Ryan Malone .05 .15
153 Rico Fata .05 .15
154 Lasse Pirjeta .05 .15
155 Dick Tarnstrom .05 .15
156 Jonathan Cheechoo .08 .20
157 Marco Sturm .05 .15
158 Evgeni Nabokov .15 .40
159 Alyn McCauley .05 .15
160 Kyle McLaren .05 .15
161 Brad Stuart .05 .15
162 Wayne Primeau .05 .15
163 Christian Ehrhoff .05 .15
164 Keith Tkachuk .20 .50
165 Barret Jackman .05 .15
166 Patrick Lalime .15 .40
167 Dallas Drake .05 .15
168 Mark Rycroft .05 .15
169 Christian Backman .05 .15
170 Brad Richards .15 .40
171 Fredrik Modin .05 .15
172 Martin St. Louis .15 .40
173 Ruslan Fedotenko .05 .15
174 Darryl Sydor .05 .15
175 Pavel Kubina .05 .15
176 Tim Taylor .05 .15
177 Mats Sundin .20 .50
178 Matt Stajan .05 .15
179 Bryan McCabe .05 .15
180 Darcy Tucker .05 .15
181 Tomas Kaberle .05 .15
182 Owen Nolan .15 .40
183 Nikolai Antropov .05 .15
184 Ken Klee .05 .15
185 Ed Jovanovski .15 .40
186 Dan Cloutier .15 .40
187 Trevor Linden .05 .15
188 Matt Cooke .05 .15
189 Todd Bertuzzi .20 .50
190 Alex Auld .05 .15
191 Sami Salo .05 .15
192 Mattias Ohlund .05 .15
193 Olaf Kolzig .15 .40
194 Brendan Witt .05 .15
195 Jeff Halpern .05 .15
196 Dainius Zubrus .05 .15
197 Alexander Semin .05 .15
198 Boyd Gordon .05 .15
199 Joe Thornton CL .30 .75
200 Jarome Iginla CL .25 .60
201 Sidney Crosby YG RC 200.00 350.00
202 Mike Richards YG RC 5.00 10.00
203 Dion Phaneuf YG RC 12.00 30.00
204 Corey Perry YG RC 5.00 12.00
205 Alexander Steen YG RC 4.00 10.00
206 Zach Parise YG RC 6.00 15.00
207 Rostislav Olesz YG RC 3.00 8.00
208 Matt Foy YG RC 3.00 8.00
209 Brent Seabrook YG RC 4.00 8.00
210 Jeff Hoggan YG RC 3.00 8.00
211 Petteri Nokelainen YG RC 3.00 8.00
212 Andrew Wozniewski YG RC 3.00 8.00
213 Peter Budaj YG RC 3.00 8.00
214 Chris Campoli YG RC 3.00 8.00
215 Jim Howard YG RC 4.00 10.00
216 Henrik Lundqvist YG RC 12.00 30.00
217 David Leneveu YG RC 3.00 8.00
218 George Parros YG RC 3.00 8.00
219 Kevin Dallman YG RC 3.00 8.00
220 Jeff Woywitka YG RC 3.00 8.00
221 Rene Bourque YG RC 3.00 8.00
222 Jim Slater YG RC 3.00 8.00
223 Niklas Nordgren YG RC 3.00 8.00
224 Jay McClement YG RC 3.00 8.00
225 Andrew Alberts YG RC 3.00 8.00
226 Alexander Perezhogin YG RC 4.00 10.00
227 Yann Danis YG RC 4.00 10.00
228 Andrej Meszaros YG RC 3.00 8.00
229 Cam Ward YG RC 5.00 12.00
230 Duncan Keith YG RC 3.00 8.00
231 Timo Helbling YG RC 3.00 8.00
232 Keith Ballard YG RC 3.00 8.00
233 Braydon Coburn YG RC 3.00 8.00
234 Ryane Clowe YG RC 3.00 8.00
235 Ryan Hollweg YG RC 3.00 8.00
236 Maxime Talbot YG RC 3.00 8.00
237 Brett Lebda YG RC 3.00 8.00
238 Brandon Bochenski YG RC 3.00 8.00
239 Jaroslav Balastik YG RC 3.00 8.00
240 Wojtek Wolski YG RC 5.00 12.00
241 Hannu Toivonen YG RC 4.00 10.00
242 S.Crosby/C.Perry YG CL 4.00 10.00
243 Teemu Selanne .20 .50
244 Scott Niedermayer .10 .25
245 Ilya Bryzgalov .15 .40
246 Todd Fedoruk .10 .25
247 Chris Kunitz .10 .25
248 Petr Sykora .10 .25
249 Keith Carney .10 .25
250 Marian Hossa .20 .50
251 Peter Bondra .15 .40
252 Bobby Holik .10 .25
253 Mike Dunham .15 .40
254 Vyacheslav Kozlov .10 .25
255 Steve Shields .15 .40
256 Glen Murray .10 .25
257 Brian Leetch .20 .50
258 Brad Boyes .10 .25
259 Jiri Slegr .10 .25
260 Travis Green .10 .25
261 Hal Gill .10 .25
262 Marco Sturm .10 .25
263 Brad Stuart .10 .25
264 Ryan Miller .15 .40
265 Teppo Numminen .10 .25
266 Jochen Hecht .10 .25
267 Martin Biron .15 .40
268 Paul Gaustad .10 .25
269 Ales Kotalik .10 .25
270 Tim Connolly .10 .25
271 Mike Grier .10 .25
272 Tony Amonte .15 .40
273 Philippe Sauve .15 .40
274 Daymond Langkow .10 .25
275 Chuck Kobasew .10 .25
276 Chris Simon .10 .25
277 Matthew Lombardi .10 .25
278 Roman Hamrlik .10 .25
279 Stephane Yelle .10 .25
280 Eric Staal .15 .40
281 Rod Brind'Amour .15 .40
282 Cory Stillman .10 .25
283 Martin Gerber .15 .40
284 Glen Wesley .10 .25
285 Oleg Tverdovsky .10 .25
286 Nikolai Khabibulin .20 .50
287 Pavel Vorobiev .10 .25
288 Martin Lapointe .10 .25
289 Adrian Aucoin .10 .25
290 Matt Ellison .10 .25
291 Jaroslav Spacek .10 .25
292 Milan Hejduk .20 .50
293 Pierre Turgeon .10 .25
294 Ian Laperriere .10 .25
295 Marek Svatos .10 .25
296 Patrice Brisebois .10 .25
297 Antti Laaksonen .10 .25
298 Nikolai Zherdev .15 .40
299 Bryan Berard .10 .25
300 Pascal Leclaire .15 .40
301 Adam Foote .10 .25
302 Sergei Fedorov .25 .60
303 Trevor Letowski .10 .25
304 Dan Fritsche .10 .25
305 Mike Modano .20 .50
306 Marty Turco .15 .40
307 Jere Lehtinen .15 .40
308 Johan Hedberg .15 .40
309 Philippe Boucher .10 .25
310 Antti Miettinen .10 .25
311 Trevor Daley .10 .25
312 Brendan Shanahan .20 .50
313 Chris Osgood .15 .40
314 Pavel Datsyuk .20 .50
315 Chris Chelios .20 .50
316 Jason Williams .10 .25
317 Mikael Samuelsson .10 .25
318 Mathieu Schneider .10 .25
319 Ryan Smyth .10 .25
320 Chris Pronger .15 .40
321 Jussi Markkanen .10 .25
322 Georges Laraque .10 .25
323 Michael Peca .10 .25
324 Marc-Andre Bergeron .10 .25
325 Jarret Stoll .10 .25
326 Jani Rita .10 .25
327 Stephen Weiss .10 .25
328 Joe Nieuwendyk .15 .40
329 Gary Roberts .10 .25
330 Martin Gelinas .10 .25
331 Chris Gratton .10 .25
332 Juraj Kolnik .10 .25
333 Lukas Krajicek .10 .25
334 Jeremy Roenick .25 .60
335 Alexander Frolov .15 .40
336 Pavol Demitra .15 .40
337 Craig Conroy .10 .25
338 Jason LaBarbera .15 .40
339 Mike Cammalleri .10 .25
340 Tim Gleason .10 .25
341 Manny Fernandez .15 .40
342 Marc Chouinard .10 .25
343 Brian Rolston .10 .25
344 Todd White .10 .25
345 Nick Schultz .10 .25
346 Brent Burns .10 .25
347 Jose Theodore .25 .60
348 Mike Ribeiro .10 .25
349 Steve Begin .10 .25
350 Alex Kovalev .15 .40
351 Tomas Plekanec .10 .25
352 Andrei Markov .10 .25
353 Radek Bonk .10 .25
354 Chris Higgins .10 .25
355 Paul Kariya .20 .50
356 Yanic Perreault .10 .25
357 Scott Hartnell .10 .25
358 Kimmo Timonen .10 .25
359 Scott Walker .10 .25
360 Dan Hamhuis .10 .25
361 Martin Erat .10 .25
362 Martin Brodeur 1.00 2.50
363 David Hale .10 .25
364 Brian Gionta .10 .25
365 Viktor Kozlov .10 .25
366 Scott Clemmensen .15 .40
367 Jamie Langenbrunner .10 .25
368 Brian Rafalski .10 .25
369 Miroslav Satan .15 .40
370 Rick DiPietro .15 .40
371 Alexei Zhitnik .10 .25
372 Mike York .10 .25
373 Brent Sopel .10 .25
374 Martin Rucinsky .10 .25
375 Martin Straka .10 .25
376 Steve Rucchin .10 .25
377 Marcel Hossa .10 .25
378 Fedor Tjutin .10 .25
379 Dominic Moore .10 .25
380 Dany Heatley .25 .60
381 Martin Havlat .15 .40
382 Peter Schaefer .10 .25
383 Bryan Smolinski .10 .25
384 Antoine Vermette .10 .25
385 Anton Volchenkov .10 .25
386 Peter Forsberg .30 .75
387 Robert Esche .15 .40
388 Mike Rathje .10 .25
389 Eric Desjardins .10 .25
390 Patrick Sharp .10 .25
391 Mike Knuble .10 .25
392 Curtis Joseph .20 .50
393 Ladislav Nagy .10 .25
394 Geoff Sanderson .10 .25
395 Mike Comrie .15 .40
396 Oleg Saprykin .10 .25
397 Petr Nedved .10 .25
398 Zigmund Palffy .15 .40
399 John LeClair .20 .50
400 Marc-Andre Fleury .15 .40
401 Sergei Gonchar .10 .25
402 Jocelyn Thibault .15 .40
403 Sebastien Caron .10 .25
404 Patrick Marleau .15 .40
405 Vesa Toskala .15 .40
406 Marcel Goc .10 .25
407 Joe Thornton .30 .75
408 Milan Michalek .10 .25
409 Niko Dimitrakos .10 .25
410 Doug Weight .15 .40
411 Petr Cajanek .10 .25
412 Reinhard Divis .10 .25
413 Jamal Mayers .10 .25
414 Scott Young .10 .25
415 Eric Brewer .10 .25
416 Vincent Lecavalier .20 .50
417 Sean Burke .15 .40
418 Vaclav Prospal .10 .25
419 Dave Andreychuk .10 .25
420 Cory Sarich .10 .25
421 John Grahame .15 .40
422 Ed Belfour .20 .50
423 Jason Allison .10 .25
424 Jeff O'Neill .10 .25
425 Eric Lindros .20 .50
426 Tie Domi .15 .40
427 Kyle Wellwood .10 .25
428 Mikael Tellqvist .15 .40
429 Markus Naslund .20 .50
430 Henrik Sedin .10 .25
431 Daniel Sedin .10 .25
432 Ryan Kesler .10 .25
433 Brendan Morrison .10 .25
434 Anson Carter .15 .40
435 Jeff Friesen .10 .25
436 Steve Eminger .10 .25
437 Jamie Heward .10 .25
438 Mike Green RC .10 .25
439 Andrew Cassels .10 .25
440 Shaone Morrisonn .10 .25
441 Peter Forsberg CL .30 .75
442 Dany Heatley CL .25 .60
443 Alexander Ovechkin RC 40.00 80.00
444 Jeff Carter RC 5.00 12.00
445 Cam Barker RC 3.00 8.00
446 Gilbert Brule RC 5.00 12.00
447 Brad Winchester RC 3.00 8.00
448 Eric Nystrom RC 3.00 8.00
449 R.J. Umberger RC 4.00 10.00
450 Mikko Koivu RC 4.00 10.00
451 Robert Nilsson RC 3.00 8.00
452 Ryan Getzlaf RC 6.00 15.00
453 Anthony Stewart RC 3.00 8.00
454 Ryan Suter RC 4.00 10.00
455 Al Montoya RC 4.00 10.00
456 Johan Franzen RC 3.00 8.00
457 Thomas Vanek RC 8.00 20.00
458 Patrick Eaves RC 4.00 10.00
459 Jussi Jokinen RC 3.00 8.00
460 Christoph Schubert RC 3.00 8.00
461 Ryan Whitney RC 4.00 10.00
462 Evgeny Artyukhin RC 3.00 8.00
463 Jordan Sigalet RC 3.00 8.00
464 Milan Jurcina RC 3.00 8.00
465 Dimitri Patzold RC 3.00 8.00
466 Staffan Kronwall RC 3.00 8.00
467 Erik Christensen RC 3.00 8.00
468 Kyle Brodziak RC 3.00 8.00
469 Ryan Craig RC 3.00 8.00
470 Steve Bernier RC 4.00 10.00
471 Matt Greene RC 3.00 8.00
472 Barry Tallackson RC 3.00 8.00
473 Jakub Klepis RC 3.00 8.00
474 Maxim Lapierre RC 3.00 8.00
475 Danny Richmond RC 3.00 8.00
476 Tomas Fleischmann RC 3.00 8.00
477 Adam Berkhoel RC 3.00 8.00
478 Kevin Bieksa RC 3.00 8.00
479 Greg Jacina RC 3.00 8.00
480 Gerald Coleman RC 3.00 8.00
481 Jeremy Colliton RC 3.00 8.00
482 Andrei Kostitsyn RC 3.00 8.00
483 Valtteri Filppula RC 3.00 8.00
484 Dennis Wideman RC 3.00 8.00
485 Brad Richardson RC 3.00 8.00
486 Jeff Tambellini RC 3.00 8.00
487 Alexander Ovechkin
Jeff Carter CL 4.00 10.00

2005-06 Upper Deck All-Time Greatest

COMPLETE SET (90) 20.00 50.00
1 J-S Giguere .40 1.00
2 Paul Kariya .50 1.25
3 Ilya Kovalchuk .60 1.50
4 Dany Heatley .60 1.50
5 Joe Thornton .75 2.00
6 Cam Neely .50 1.25
7 Dominik Hasek .75 2.00
8 Gilbert Perreault .50 1.25
9 Jarome Iginla .60 1.50
10 Lanny McDonald .40 1.00
11 Rod Brind'Amour .40 1.00
12 Gary Roberts .25 .60
13 Tony Esposito .50 1.25
14 Stan Mikita .50 1.25
15 Joe Sakic 1.00 2.50
16 Patrick Roy 2.00 5.00
17 Rick Nash .60 1.50
18 Marc Denis .40 1.00
19 Mike Modano .60 1.50
20 Ed Belfour .50 1.25
21 Gordie Howe 1.25 3.00
22 Steve Yzerman 1.50 4.00
23 Wayne Gretzky 3.00 8.00
24 Jari Kurri .50 1.25
25 Roberto Luongo .60 1.50
26 Olli Jokinen .40 1.00
27 Wayne Gretzky 3.00 8.00
28 Luc Robitaille .25 .60
29 Marian Gaborik .75 2.00
30 Dwayne Roloson .40 1.00
31 Patrick Roy 2.00 5.00
32 Jose Theodore .60 1.50
33 Steve Sullivan .25 .60
34 Tomas Vokoun .40 1.00
35 Martin Brodeur 1.50 4.00
36 Patrik Elias .40 1.00
37 Mike Bossy .50 1.25
38 Alexei Yashin .25 .60
39 Jaromir Jagr .75 2.00
40 Brian Leetch .50 1.25
41 Daniel Alfredsson .40 1.00
42 Jason Spezza .50 1.25
43 Keith Tkachuk .50 1.25
44 Shane Doan .25 .60
45 Bobby Clarke .50 1.25
46 Ron Hextall .25 .60
47 Mario Lemieux 2.00 5.00
48 Jaromir Jagr .75 2.00
49 Doug Weight .40 1.00
50 Chris Pronger .40 1.00
51 Patrick Marleau .40 1.00
52 Evgeni Nabokov .40 1.00

53 Martin St. Louis .40 1.00
54 Vincent Lecavalier .50 1.25
55 Mats Sundin .50 1.25
56 Darryl Sittler .50 1.25
57 Markus Naslund .50 1.25
58 Trevor Linden .25 .60
59 Olaf Kolzig .40 1.00
60 Peter Bondra .40 1.00
61 Dany Heatley .60 1.50
62 Ray Bourque .60 1.50
63 Andrew Raycroft .40 1.00
64 Gilbert Perreault .50 1.25
65 Jarome Iginla .60 1.50
66 Tony Esposito .50 1.25
67 Ed Belfour .50 1.25
68 Rick Nash .60 1.50
69 Paul Kariya .50 1.25
70 Gordie Howe 1.25 3.00
71 Steve Yzerman 1.50 4.00
72 Sergei Fedorov .50 1.25
73 Wayne Gretzky 3.00 8.00
74 Luc Robitaille .40 1.00
75 Mike Modano .75 2.00
76 Guy Lafleur .60 1.50
77 Patrick Roy 2.00 5.00
78 Martin Brodeur 1.50 4.00
79 Mike Bossy .50 1.25
80 Brian Leetch .50 1.25
81 Daniel Alfredsson .40 1.00
82 Ron Hextall .40 1.00
83 Eric Lindros .50 1.25
84 Sidney Crosby 4.00 10.00
85 Mario Lemieux 2.00 5.00
86 Joe Sakic 1.00 2.50
87 Peter Forsberg .75 2.00
88 Peter Stastny .25 .60
89 Evgeni Nabokov .40 1.00
90 Teemu Selanne .50 1.25

2005-06 Upper Deck Big Playmakers

PRINT RUN 50 SER.#'d SETS
B-DHA Dominik Hasek 25.00 60.00
B-DAR Denis Arkhipov 10.00 25.00
B-MST Martin St. Louis 15.00 40.00
B-SST Scott Stevens 10.00 25.00
B-MDE Marc Denis 10.00 25.00
B-SSA Sergei Samsonov 15.00 40.00
B-MPA Michael Peca 10.00 25.00
B-ROB Rob Blake 15.00 40.00
B-BMC Brendan Morrison 10.00 25.00
B-MSU Mats Sundin 15.00 40.00
B-MME Mark Messier 25.00 60.00
B-DHE Dany Heatley 15.00 40.00
B-JBL Jay Bouwmeester 10.00 25.00
B-MHA Martin Havlat 12.00 30.00
B-MRI Mike Ribeiro 10.00 25.00
B-MHO Marian Hossa 15.00 40.00
B-JLU Jere Lehtinen 10.00 25.00
B-JOL Jordan Leopold 10.00 25.00
B-MDU Mike Dunham 10.00 25.00
B-BMO Bryan McCabe 10.00 25.00
B-DAE David Aebischer 15.00 40.00
B-MRY Michael Ryder
B-JEL Jamie Lundmark 10.00 25.00
B-RNI Rob Niedermayer 10.00 25.00
B-MBI Mike Bossy
B-MPE Mark Parrish 10.00 25.00
B-MRE Mark Recchi 10.00 25.00
B-MAH Marcel Hossa 10.00 25.00
B-JBO Jason Blake 10.00 25.00
B-MBO Martin Biron 10.00 25.00
B-PBO Peter Bondra 10.00 25.00
B-AC Anson Carter 10.00 25.00
B-AF Alexander Frolov 10.00 25.00
B-AH Adam Hall 10.00 25.00
B-AM Al MacInnis 12.00 30.00
B-AT Alex Tanguay 15.00 40.00
B-AT Alexander Mogilny 12.00 30.00
B-AY Alexei Yashin 12.00 30.00
B-BC Bobby Clarke 20.00 50.00
B-BG Bill Guerin 12.00 30.00
B-BH Brett Hull 15.00 40.00
B-BJ Barret Jackman 10.00 25.00
B-BS Brendan Shanahan 15.00 40.00
B-CC Chris Chelios 12.00 30.00
B-CD Chris Drury 12.00 30.00
B-CJ Curtis Joseph 15.00 40.00
B-CN Cam Neely 20.00 50.00
B-CP Chris Pronger 15.00 40.00
B-CS Chris Simon 10.00 25.00
B-DB Daniel Briere 15.00 40.00
B-DC Dan Cloutier 10.00 25.00
B-DL David Legwand 10.00 25.00
B-DW Doug Weight 12.00 30.00
B-EB Ed Belfour 15.00 40.00
B-ED Eric Daze 15.00 40.00
B-EJ Ed Jovanovski 10.00 25.00
B-EL Eric Lindros 15.00 40.00
B-ES Eric Staal 20.00 50.00
B-GM Glen Murray 12.00 30.00
B-GO Scott Gomez 10.00 25.00
B-GS Geoff Sanderson 10.00 25.00
B-HJ Milan Hejduk 15.00 40.00
B-IK Ilya Kovalchuk 25.00 60.00
B-JA Jason Allison 10.00 25.00
B-JC Jonathan Cheechoo 15.00 40.00
B-JG J-S Giguere 12.00 30.00
B-JI Jarome Iginla 25.00 60.00
B-JJ Jaromir Jagr 25.00 60.00
B-JK Jari Kurri 15.00 40.00
B-JL John LeClair 12.00 30.00
B-JN Joe Nieuwendyk
B-JO Jose Theodore 20.00 50.00
B-JP Joni Pitkanen 10.00 25.00
B-JR Jeremy Roenick 15.00 40.00
B-JS Jason Smith 10.00 25.00
B-JT Joe Thornton 25.00 60.00
B-JW Justin Williams 12.00 30.00
B-KP Keith Primeau 12.00 30.00
B-KT Keith Tkachuk 12.00 30.00
B-LR Luc Robitaille 12.00 30.00
B-MA Maxim Afinogenov 12.00 30.00
B-MB Martin Brodeur 30.00 80.00
B-MF Manny Fernandez 15.00 40.00
B-MG Marian Gaborik 25.00 60.00
B-ML Mario Lemieux 50.00 125.00
B-MM Mike Modano 20.00 50.00
B-MN Markus Naslund 15.00 40.00
B-MO Mattias Ohlund 10.00 25.00
B-MS Martin Straka 10.00 25.00
B-MT Marty Turco 15.00 40.00
B-NA Nik Antropov 10.00 25.00
B-NK Nikolai Khabibulin 15.00 40.00
B-NL Nicklas Lidstrom 15.00 40.00
B-OJ Olli Jokinen 10.00 25.00
B-OK Olaf Kolzig 15.00 40.00
B-ON Owen Nolan 12.00 30.00
B-PB Patrice Bergeron 15.00 40.00
B-PD Pavel Datsyuk 15.00 40.00
B-PE Patrik Elias 12.00 30.00
B-PF Peter Forsberg 25.00 60.00
B-PK Paul Kariya 15.00 40.00
B-PL Patrick Lalime 10.00 25.00
B-PM Patrick Marleau
B-PR Patrick Roy 40.00 100.00
B-RB Ray Bourque 20.00 50.00
B-RF Ruslan Fedotenko 10.00 25.00
B-RH Ron Hextall 20.00 50.00
B-RK Rostislav Klesla 10.00 25.00
B-RL Roberto Luongo 25.00 60.00
B-RN Rick Nash 20.00 40.00
B-RS Ryan Smyth 15.00 40.00
B-SB Sean Burke 10.00 25.00
B-SD Shane Doan 10.00 25.00
B-SF Sergei Fedorov 15.00 40.00
B-SG Simon Gagne 15.00 40.00
B-SH Scott Hartnell 10.00 25.00
B-SK Saku Koivu 15.00 40.00
B-SO Sandis Ozolinsh 10.00 25.00
B-SP Jason Spezza 15.00 40.00
B-SY Steve Yzerman 30.00 80.00
B-SZ Sergei Zubov 10.00 25.00
B-TA Tony Amonte 15.00 40.00
B-TB Todd Bertuzzi 15.00 40.00
B-TC Ty Conklin 10.00 25.00
B-TH Trent Hunter 10.00 25.00
B-TP Tom Poti 10.00 25.00
B-TR Tuomo Ruutu 15.00 40.00
B-TV Tomas Vokoun 15.00 40.00
B-VD Vincent Damphousse 10.00 25.00
B-VL Vincent Lecavalier 15.00 40.00
B-VN Ville Nieminen 10.00 25.00
B-WG Wayne Gretzky 100.00 250.00
B-ZC Zdeno Chara 10.00 25.00

2005-06 Upper Deck Destined for the Hall

COMPLETE SET (7) 12.00 25.00
ODDS 1:24
DH1 Steve Yzerman 4.00 10.00
DH2 Martin Brodeur 4.00 10.00
DH3 Joe Sakic 2.00 5.00
DH4 Dominik Hasek 2.00 5.00
DH5 Jaromir Jagr 1.50 4.00
DH6 Mario Lemieux 6.00 15.00
DH7 Brendan Shanahan 1.00 2.50

2005-06 Upper Deck Diary of a Phenom

COMPLETE SET (30) 20.00 40.00
COMMON CARD (DP1-DP30) .50 1.25
ONE PER RETAIL PACK

2005-06 Upper Deck Goal Celebrations

COMPLETE SETS (7) 8.00 15.00
ODDS 1:12
GC1 Ilya Kovalchuk 1.25 3.00
GC2 Dany Heatley 1.25 3.00
GC3 Jaromir Jagr 1.50 4.00
GC4 Jarome Iginla 1.25 3.00
GC5 Martin St. Louis .75 2.00
GC6 Rick Nash 1.25 3.00
GC7 Mats Sundin 1.00 2.50

2005-06 Upper Deck Goal Rush

COMPLETE SET (14) 10.00 20.00
STATED ODDS 1:12
GR1 Rick Nash .75 2.00
GR2 Martin St. Louis .60 1.50
GR3 Milan Hejduk .60 1.50
GR4 Steve Yzerman 1.50 4.00
GR5 Joe Sakic 1.25 3.00
GR6 Wayne Gretzky 3.00 8.00
GR7 Mario Lemieux 3.00 8.00
GR8 Ilya Kovalchuk .75 2.00
GR9 Patrice Bergeron .60 1.50
GR10 Markus Naslund .60 1.50
GR11 Marian Hossa .60 1.50
GR12 Mike Modano 1.00 2.50
GR13 Jarome Iginla .75 2.00
GR14 Dany Heatley .75 2.00

2005-06 Upper Deck HG Glossy

PRINT RUN 10 SER.#'d SETS
NOT PRICED DUE TO SCARCITY

2005-06 Upper Deck Hometown Heroes

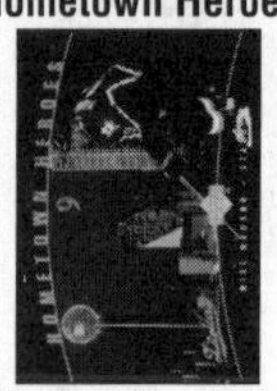

COMPLETE SET (28) 20.00 40.00
STATED ODDS 1:12
HH1 Joe Sakic 1.25 3.00
HH2 Martin Brodeur 1.50 4.00
HH3 Joe Thornton 1.00 2.50
HH4 Jarome Iginla .75 2.00
HH5 Mats Sundin .60 1.50
HH6 Steve Yzerman 1.50 4.00
HH7 Saku Koivu .60 1.50
HH8 Jaromir Jagr .75 2.00
HH9 Ilya Kovalchuk .75 2.00
HH10 Mike Modano .50 1.25
HH11 Martin St. Louis .50 1.25
HH12 Mark Messier .60 1.50
HH13 Mario Lemieux 3.00 8.00
HH14 Keith Tkachuk .60 1.50
HH15 Daniel Alfredsson .40 1.00
HH16 Evgeni Nabokov .40 1.00
HH17 Jaromir Jagr .75 2.00
HH18 Rick Nash .60 1.50
HH19 Peter Forsberg .75 2.00
HH20 Paul Kariya .50 1.25
HH21 J-S Giguere .40 1.00
HH22 Nikolai Khabibulin .50 1.25
HH23 Alexei Yashin .40 .60
HH24 Shane Doan .40 1.00
HH25 Markus Naslund .50 1.25
HH26 Dany Heatley .60 1.50
HH27 Eric Lindros .50 1.25
HH28 Olaf Kolzig .40 1.00

2005-06 Upper Deck Jerseys

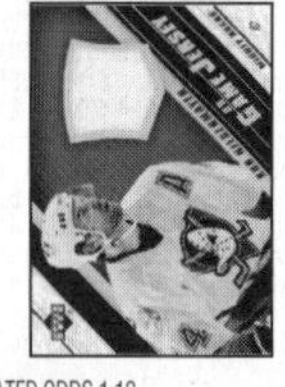

STATED ODDS 1:12
J-TRU Tuomo Ruutu 4.00 10.00
J-SST Scott Stevens 4.00 10.00
J-SKO Steve Konowalchuk 4.00 10.00
J-JOL Joffrey Lupul 4.00 10.00
J-TDO Tie Domi 4.00 10.00
J-MCO Mike Comrie 4.00 10.00
J-MHE Milan Hejduk 5.00 12.00
J-MGA Mathieu Garon 4.00 10.00
J-BGE Bernie Geoffrion SP 75.00 150.00
J-NIB Nick Boynton 4.00 10.00
J-SOT Steve Ott 4.00 10.00
J-MAH Marcel Hossa 4.00 10.00
J-MNI Marcus Nilson 4.00 10.00
J-BHU Brett Hull 6.00 15.00
J-PAS Patrik Stefan 4.00 10.00
J-PDE Pavol Demitra 4.00 10.00
J-MRY Michael Ryder 4.00 10.00
J-HSE Henrik Sedin 4.00 10.00
J-RHX Ron Hextall SP 15.00 40.00
J-PSY Petr Sykora 4.00 10.00
J-JLE Jere Lehtinen 4.00 10.00
J-DAE David Aebischer 4.00 10.00
J-DBR Donald Brashear 2.50 6.00
J-MST Matt Stajan 4.00 10.00
J-BHO Bobby Holik 4.00 10.00
J-STR Steven Reinprecht 2.50 6.00
J-SGA Simon Gagne 6.00 15.00
J-BMC Bryan McCabe 4.00 10.00
J-DAR Denis Arkhipov 2.50 6.00
J-MPA Mark Parrish 4.00 10.00
J-SOZ Sandis Ozolinsh 4.00 10.00
J-JAR Jason Arnott 4.00 10.00
J-RLU Roberto Luongo 8.00 20.00
J-JAB Jay Bouwmeester 4.00 10.00
J-RIH Riku Hahl 4.00 10.00
J-RBK Radek Bonk 4.00 10.00
J-GUL Georges Laraque 4.00 10.00
J-DSA Denis Savard SP 15.00 40.00
J-MAD Marc Denis 4.00 10.00
J-MCA Mike Cammalleri 4.00 10.00
J-MPE Michael Peca 4.00 10.00
J-SSA Sergei Samsonov 4.00 10.00
J-MGR Mike Grier 4.00 10.00
J-DSE Daniel Sedin 4.00 10.00
J-SGO Scott Gomez 4.00 10.00
J-AHE Ales Hemsky 4.00 10.00
J-MLO Matthew Lombardi 4.00 10.00
J-MBI Martin Biron 4.00 10.00
J-TSE Teemu Selanne 6.00 15.00
J-SKA Sami Kapanen 4.00 10.00
J-AA Adrian Aucoin 2.50 6.00
J-AF Adam Foote 2.50 6.00
J-AK Alexei Kovalev 2.50 6.00
J-AM Alexander Mogilny 4.00 10.00
J-AY Alexei Yashin 4.00 10.00
J-BC Bobby Clarke SP 60.00 125.00
J-BG Bill Guerin SP 2.50 6.00
J-BL Rob Blake 4.00 10.00
J-BM Brendan Morrison 2.50 6.00
J-BR Dustin Brown 2.50 6.00
J-BT Bryan Trottier 6.00 15.00
J-BW Brendan Witt 2.50 6.00
J-CC Chris Chelios SP 15.00 40.00
J-CD Chris Drury 4.00 10.00
J-CJ Curtis Joseph 6.00 15.00
J-CK Chuck Kobasew 2.50 6.00
J-CO Chris Osgood 4.00 10.00
J-CP Chris Pronger 6.00 15.00
J-DB Daniel Briere 4.00 10.00
J-DH Dany Heatley 8.00 20.00
J-DL David Legwand 4.00 10.00
J-DO Dominik Hasek 8.00 20.00
J-DW Doug Weight 4.00 10.00
J-EB Ed Belfour 6.00 15.00
J-EJ Ed Jovanovski 4.00 10.00
J-EL Eric Lindros 6.00 15.00
J-GF Grant Fuhr SP 20.00 50.00
J-GL Guy Lafleur SP 25.00 60.00
J-GM Glen Murray 4.00 10.00
J-GR Gary Roberts 4.00 10.00
J-HA Dan Hamhuis 4.00 10.00
J-JF Jeff Friesen 2.50 6.00
J-JG J-S Giguere 4.00 10.00
J-JH Jani Hurme 4.00 10.00
J-JI Jarome Iginla 8.00 20.00
J-JO Jose Theodore 6.00 15.00
J-JP Joni Pitkanen SP 4.00 10.00
J-JR Jeremy Roenick 6.00 15.00
J-JS Jason Smith 4.00 10.00
J-JS Joe Sakic SP 12.50 30.00
J-JT Joe Thornton 8.00 20.00
J-JW Justin Williams 4.00 10.00
J-KD Kris Draper 4.00 10.00
J-KL Kari Lehtonen SP 25.00 60.00
J-KP Keith Primeau 2.50 6.00
J-KT Keith Tkachuk 6.00 15.00
J-LR Luc Robitaille 6.00 15.00
J-MA Maxim Afinogenov 4.00 10.00
J-MB Martin Brodeur 12.50 30.00
J-MD Mike Dunham 4.00 10.00
J-MK Miikka Kiprusoff 8.00 20.00
J-ML Mario Lemieux SP 25.00 60.00
J-MM Mike Modano 6.00 15.00
J-MO Mattias Ohlund 4.00 10.00
J-MR Mark Recchi 4.00 10.00
J-MS Mats Sundin 6.00 15.00
J-NA Nik Antropov 4.00 10.00
J-NH Nathan Horton 4.00 10.00
J-NK Nikolai Khabibulin 6.00 15.00
J-NS Nathan Smith 4.00 10.00
J-OJ Olli Jokinen 4.00 10.00
J-OK Olaf Kolzig 4.00 10.00
J-ON Owen Nolan 4.00 10.00
J-PD Pavel Datsyuk 6.00 15.00
J-PF Peter Forsberg 8.00 20.00
J-PK Paul Kariya SP 8.00 20.00
J-PR Patrick Roy 15.00 40.00
J-PT Pierre Turgeon 4.00 10.00
J-RB Ray Bourque SP 15.00 40.00
J-RE Robert Esche 4.00 10.00
J-RM Ryan Miller 4.00 10.00
J-RN Rob Niedermayer 4.00 10.00
J-RT Raffi Torres 4.00 10.00
J-SC Stanislav Chistov 4.00 10.00
J-SF Sergei Fedorov 6.00 15.00
J-SH Scott Hartnell 4.00 10.00
J-SK Saku Koivu 6.00 15.00
J-SM Scott Mellanby 4.00 10.00
J-SP Jason Spezza 6.00 15.00
J-SU Scottie Upshall 4.00 10.00
J-SY Steve Yzerman 12.50 30.00
J-SZ Sergei Zubov 4.00 10.00
J-TA Tony Amonte 4.00 10.00
J-TC Ty Conklin 4.00 10.00
J-TO Jordin Tootoo 4.00 10.00
J-TP Tom Poti 4.00 10.00
J-VB Valeri Bure 4.00 10.00
J-VK Viktor Kozlov 4.00 10.00
J-VL Vincent Lecavalier 6.00 15.00
J-VN Ville Nieminen 4.00 10.00
J-WG Wayne Gretzky SP 40.00 100.00

2005-06 Upper Deck Jerseys Series II

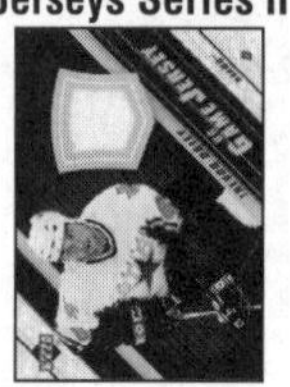

ODDS 1:12
J2AA Alex Auld 2.50 6.00
J2AC Anson Carter 2.50 6.00
J2AF Alexander Frolov 4.00 10.00
J2AK Alex Kovalev 4.00 10.00
J2AR Andrew Raycroft 4.00 10.00
J2AT Alex Tanguay 4.00 10.00
J2BG Bill Guerin 4.00 10.00
J2BI Martin Biron 4.00 10.00
J2BJ Barret Jackman 4.00 10.00
J2BL Brian Leetch 6.00 15.00
J2BM Brendan Morrison 4.00 10.00
J2BR Brad Richards 4.00 10.00
J2BS Brendan Shanahan 6.00 15.00
J2CK Matt Cooke 2.50 6.00
J2CM Mike Comrie 2.50 6.00
J2CO Chris Osgood 4.00 10.00
J2CP Chris Pronger 4.00 10.00
J2CS Cory Stillman 4.00 10.00
J2CY Tim Connolly 4.00 10.00
J2DA Daniel Alfredsson 4.00 10.00
J2DC Dan Cloutier 4.00 10.00
J2DM Dominic Moore 4.00 10.00
J2DW Doug Weight 4.00 10.00
J2DY Trevor Daley 2.50 6.00
J2EB Ed Belfour 6.00 15.00
J2EJ Ed Jovanovski 4.00 10.00
J2EL Eric Lindros 6.00 15.00
J2ES Eric Staal 8.00 20.00
J2FT Fedor Tjutin 2.50 6.00
J2GA Simon Gagne 6.00 15.00
J2GE Martin Gerber 4.00 10.00
J2GI Brian Gionta 4.00 10.00
J2GM Glen Murray 4.00 10.00
J2GO Scott Gomez 4.00 10.00
J2HJ Milan Hejduk 6.00 15.00
J2HO Marcel Hossa 2.50 6.00
J2HZ Michal Handzus 2.50 6.00
J2HZ Henrik Zetterberg 6.00 15.00
J2IK Ilya Kovalchuk 8.00 20.00
J2JA Jason Allison 4.00 10.00
J2JB Jay Bouwmeester 4.00 10.00
J2JC Jonathan Cheechoo 8.00 20.00
J2JE Jere Lehtinen 4.00 10.00
J2JG J-S Giguere 4.00 10.00
J2JH Jeff Halpern 2.50 6.00
J2JI Jarome Iginla 8.00 20.00
J2JJ Jaromir Jagr 20.00 50.00
J2JO Jose Theodore 8.00 20.00
J2JP Joni Pitkanen 2.50 6.00
J2JR Jeremy Roenick 8.00 20.00
J2JS Joe Sakic 12.00 30.00
J2JU Justin Williams 4.00 10.00
J2JW Jason Williams 4.00 10.00
J2KC Kyle Calder 4.00 10.00
J2KD Kris Draper 4.00 10.00
J2KL Kari Lehtonen 6.00 15.00
J2KP Keith Primeau 2.50 6.00
J2LE Jordan Leopold 4.00 10.00
J2LO Matthew Lombardi 4.00 10.00
J2LR Luc Robitaille 4.00 10.00
J2LU Joffrey Lupul 4.00 10.00
J2LX Mario Lemieux SP 100.00 200.00
J2MA Maxim Afinogenov 4.00 10.00
J2MB Martin Brodeur 12.00 30.00
J2MC Bryan McCabe 4.00 10.00
J2MG Marian Gaborik 12.00 30.00
J2MH Martin Havlat 4.00 10.00
J2MK Miikka Kiprusoff 6.00 15.00
J2ML Manny Legace 6.00 15.00
J2MM Mike Modano 8.00 20.00
J2MN Markus Naslund 6.00 15.00
J2MO Mattias Ohlund 4.00 10.00
J2MP Michael Peca 4.00 10.00
J2MR Mike Ribeiro 4.00 10.00
J2MS Miroslav Satan 4.00 10.00
J2MT Marty Turco 4.00 10.00
J2MW Brenden Morrow 4.00 10.00
J2NA Nik Antropov 2.50 6.00
J2NB Nick Boynton 2.50 6.00
J2NI Rob Niedermayer 2.50 6.00
J2NK Nikolai Khabibulin SP 75.00 125.00
J2NL Nicklas Lidstrom 6.00 15.00
J2NO Mika Noronen 4.00 10.00
J2NZ Nikolai Zherdev 4.00 10.00
J2OK Olaf Kolzig 4.00 10.00
J2ON Jeff O'Neill 4.00 10.00
J2PA Mark Parrish 2.50 6.00
J2PB Peter Bondra 4.00 10.00
J2PE Patrik Elias 4.00 10.00
J2PF Peter Forsberg 10.00 25.00
J2PK Paul Kariya 6.00 15.00
J2PS Patrick Sharp 4.00 10.00
J2PT Pierre Turgeon 2.50 6.00
J2RD Rick DiPietro 4.00 10.00
J2RE Robert Esche 4.00 10.00
J2RF Ruslan Fedotenko 4.00 10.00
J2RK Brian Rafalski 2.50 6.00
J2RL Roberto Luongo 8.00 20.00
J2RN Rick Nash 8.00 20.00
J2RO Brian Rolston 4.00 10.00
J2RS Ryan Smyth 4.00 10.00
J2RT Raffi Torres 2.50 6.00
J2RY Ryan Miller 4.00 10.00
J2SA Philippe Sauve 2.50 6.00
J2SB Sean Burke 4.00 10.00
J2SD Shane Doan 4.00 10.00
J2SH Shawn Horcoff 4.00 10.00
J2SK Sami Kapanen 4.00 10.00
J2SL Martin St. Louis 4.00 10.00
J2SN Scott Niedermayer 4.00 10.00
J2SO Sandis Ozolinsh 4.00 10.00
J2SP Jason Spezza 6.00 15.00
J2SR Marc Savard 4.00 10.00
J2SS Steve Sullivan 4.00 10.00
J2SU Mats Sundin 6.00 15.00
J2SV Sergei Samsonov 4.00 10.00
J2SW Stephen Weiss 4.00 10.00
J2SY Steve Yzerman SP 50.00 125.00
J2TB Todd Bertuzzi 6.00 15.00
J2TC Ty Conklin 4.00 10.00
J2TD Tie Domi 4.00 10.00
J2TH Trent Hunter 2.50 6.00
J2TL Trevor Linden 4.00 10.00
J2TO Tony Amonte 4.00 10.00
J2TP Tom Poti 4.00 10.00
J2TS Teemu Selanne 6.00 15.00
J2TV Tomas Vokoun 4.00 10.00
J2VK Viktor Kozlov 4.00 10.00
J2VL Vincent Lecavalier 6.00 15.00
J2VP Vaclav Prospal 2.50 6.00
J2WR Wade Redden 4.00 10.00
J2ZC Zdeno Chara 4.00 10.00
J2ZP Zigmund Palffy 4.00 10.00

2005-06 Upper Deck Majestic Materials

PRINT RUN 50 SER.#'d SETS
MMAF Alexander Frolov 8.00 20.00
MMAO Alexander Ovechkin 75.00 175.00
MMAP Alexander Perezhogin 12.00 30.00
MMAR Andrew Raycroft 15.00 40.00
MMAS Alexander Steen 20.00 50.00
MMAT Alex Tanguay 12.00 30.00
MMAY Alexei Yashin 15.00 40.00
MMBG Bill Guerin 8.00 20.00
MMBR Brad Richards 20.00 50.00
MMBS Brendan Shanahan 15.00 40.00
MMCH Jonathan Cheechoo 20.00 50.00
MMCP Chris Pronger 12.00 30.00
MMDA Daniel Alfredsson 15.00 40.00
MMDP Dion Phaneuf 40.00 80.00
MMDW Doug Weight 8.00 20.00
MMEB Ed Belfour 15.00 40.00
MMEJ Ed Jovanovski 8.00 20.00
MMEL Eric Lindros 15.00 40.00
MMES Eric Staal 15.00 40.00
MMGB Gilbert Brule 15.00 40.00
MMGI Brian Gionta 15.00 40.00
MMHE Milan Hejduk 8.00 20.00
MMHK Dominik Hasek 20.00 50.00
MMHL Henrik Lundqvist 30.00 80.00
MMHT Hannu Toivonen 15.00 40.00
MMHV Martin Havlat 8.00 20.00
MMHZ Henrik Zetterberg 15.00 40.00
MMIK Ilya Kovalchuk 20.00 50.00
MMJA Jason Allison 12.00 30.00
MMJB Jay Bouwmeester 15.00 40.00
MMJC Jeff Carter 20.00 50.00
MMJG J-S Giguere 8.00 20.00
MMJI Jarome Iginla 30.00 60.00
MMJJ Jaromir Jagr 25.00 60.00
MMJL Joffrey Lupul 8.00 20.00
MMJO Jose Theodore 15.00 40.00
MMJR Jeremy Roenick 15.00 40.00
MMJS Joe Sakic/40 30.00 60.00
MMJT Joe Thornton 25.00 60.00
MMKL Kari Lehtonen
MMKP Keith Primeau 8.00 20.00
MMKT Keith Tkachuk 8.00 20.00
MMLE Manny Legace
MMLR Luc Robitaille 15.00 40.00
MMMB Martin Brodeur 30.00 80.00
MMMG Marian Gaborik 25.00 60.00
MMML Mario Lemieux 50.00 125.00
MMMM Mike Modano 30.00 60.00
MMMN Markus Naslund 8.00 20.00
MMMP Michael Peca 8.00 20.00
MMMR Michael Ryder 8.00 20.00
MMMS Martin St.Louis 12.00 30.00
MMMT Marty Turco 20.00 50.00
MMMW Brenden Morrow 8.00 20.00
MMNL Nicklas Lidstrom 8.00 20.00
MMNZ Nikolai Zherdev 15.00 40.00
MMOK Olaf Kolzig 15.00 40.00
MMPB Patrice Bergeron 15.00 40.00
MMPD Pavel Datsyuk 12.50 30.00
MMPE Patrik Elias 8.00 20.00
MMPF Peter Forsberg 25.00 60.00
MMPK Paul Kariya 20.00 50.00
MMRB Rob Blake 8.00 20.00
MMRD Rick DiPietro 20.00 50.00
MMRE Mark Recchi 8.00 20.00
MMRI Mike Richards 12.00 30.00
MMRL Roberto Luongo 12.00 30.00
MMRM Ryan Miller 12.00 30.00
MMRN Rick Nash 25.00 60.00
MMRO Mike Ribeiro 8.00 20.00
MMRS Ryan Smyth 15.00 40.00
MMSA Miroslav Satan 12.00 30.00
MMSC Sidney Crosby 125.00 250.00
MMSD Shane Doan 15.00 40.00
MMSG Simon Gagne 15.00 40.00
MMSH Shawn Horcoff 8.00 20.00
MMSK Saku Koivu 15.00 40.00
MMSN Scott Niedermayer 15.00 40.00
MMSP Jason Spezza 25.00 60.00
MMSS Steve Sullivan 8.00 20.00
MMST Matt Stajan 20.00 50.00
MMSU Mats Sundin
MMSW Stephen Weiss 12.00 30.00
MMSY Steve Yzerman 30.00 80.00
MMTB Todd Bertuzzi 15.00 40.00
MMTC Ty Conklin 8.00 20.00
MMTS Teemu Selanne 12.00 30.00
MMTV Tomas Vokoun 15.00 40.00
MMVA Thomas Vanek 20.00 50.00
MMVL Vincent Lecavalier 12.00 30.00
MMZC Zdeno Chara 8.00 20.00
MMZP Zigmund Palffy 15.00 40.00

2005-06 Upper Deck NHL Generations

DUAL ODDS 1:144
TRIPLE ODDS 1:288
DAR J. Arnott/M.Ryder 5.00 12.00
DBB R.Bourque/J.Bouwmeester 8.00 20.00
DBT M.Brodeur/J.Theodore 20.00 50.00
DFD S.Fedorov/P.Datsyuk 8.00 20.00
DGB B.Guerin/D.Brown 5.00 12.00
DGL W.Gretzky/M.Lemieux 125.00 250.00
DGR S.Gagne/M.Ribeiro 5.00 12.00
DHV D.Hasek/T.Vokoun 10.00 25.00
DIN J.Iginla/R.Nash 12.00 30.00
DJH J.Jagr/M.Havlat 10.00 25.00
DKS J.Kurri/T.Selanne 15.00 40.00
DKZ I.Kovalchuk/N.Zherdev
DLH J.Lehtinen/R.Hahl 5.00 12.00
DML M.Messier/V.Lecavalier 10.00 25.00
DNZ M.Naslund/H.Zetterberg 8.00 20.00
DRB W.Redden/N.Boynton 5.00 12.00
DSC S.Stevens/Z.Chara 5.00 12.00
DST B.Shanahan/J.Thornton 12.50 30.00
DTC M.Turco/T.Conklin 8.00 20.00
DYS S.Yzerman/J.Spezza 25.00 60.00
TBLL Brodeur/Luongo/Lehtonen 30.00 60.00
TBTN Bossy/Thornton/Nash
TCGP Clarke/Gagne/Primeau 15.00 40.00
TFKA Fedorov/Kovalchuk/Afinogenov 20.00 50.00
TGYS Gretzky/Yzerman/Sakic 250.00 400.00
TLKR LaFleur/Koivu/Ribeiro 15.00 40.00
TMST Messier/Shanahan/Thornton 20.00 50.00
TNSN Neely/Shanahan/Nash 20.00 50.00
TRBL Roy/Brodeur/Luongo 75.00 150.00
TSFZ Sundin/Forsberg/Zetterberg 15.00 40.00
TSHT Sakic/Hejduk/Tanguay 20.00 50.00
TSIR Sakic/Iginla/Ribeiro 20.00 50.00
TSKJ Selanne/Koivu/Jokinen 15.00 40.00
TSTP Sakic/Thornton/Spezza 25.00 60.00

2005-06 Upper Deck Notable Numbers

STATED ODDS 1:288
PRINT RUNS VARY
UNDER 23 NOT PRICED DUE TO SCARCITY
N-SGO Sergei Gonchar/55
N-CRC Craig Conroy/22
N-RON Rob Niedermayer/44 15.00 40.00
N-RBO Ray Bourque/77 50.00 100.00
N-MAS Marco Sturm/19 20.00 50.00
N-JAL Jason Allison/41
N-PHS Philippe Sauve/30 15.00 40.00
N-SGZ Scott Gomez/23
N-MHA Michal Handzus/26
N-MDI Marcel Dionne/16
N-PSY Petr Sykora/39
N-PLE Pascal Leclaire/31 20.00 50.00
N-JAL Jamie Lundmark/21
N-MRI Mike Ricci/40
N-MPH Mark Parrish/37 25.00 60.00
N-CCH Chris Chelios/24
N-MGA Mathieu Garon/30
N-MDE Marc Denis/30
N-MNY Michael Nylander/92 8.00 20.00
N-JAR Jason Arnott/44 15.00 40.00
N-DLW Daymond Langkow/11
N-TSA Tony Salmelainen/42 15.00 40.00
N-MCO Matt Cooke/24
N-DUB Dustin Brown/23 20.00 50.00
N-PMB P-M Bouchard/96 10.00 25.00
N-MGE Martin Gerber/29 30.00 80.00
N-JLI John-Michael Liles/26 20.00 50.00
N-MSA Miroslav Satan/81 10.00 25.00
N-JEO Jeff O'Neill/92 10.00 25.00
N-JAR Jani Rita/22
N-MBY Mike Bossy/22
N-CCO Carlo Colaiacovo/45 15.00 40.00
N-MBR Martin Brodeur/30 100.00 200.00
N-RBL Rob Blake/4
N-MBA Matthew Barnaby/38 12.00 30.00
N-BRA Brian Rafalski/28 15.00 40.00
N-JTH Jocelyn Thibault/41 20.00 50.00
N-NIK Niko Kapanen/39
N-AA Adrian Aucoin/33
N-AC Anson Carter/11
N-AE David Aebischer/1
N-AF Marc-Andre Fleury/29 75.00 150.00
N-AH Ales Hemsky/83 12.00 30.00
N-AL Daniel Alfredsson/11
N-AN Nikolai Antropov/80 15.00 40.00
N-AR Andrew Raycroft/1
N-AT Alex Tanguay/18 50.00 100.00
N-AY Alexei Yashin/79 10.00 25.00
N-BA Milan Bartovic/15
N-BB Brad Boyes/26 20.00 50.00
N-BC Bobby Clarke/16
N-BI Martin Biron/43 15.00 40.00
N-BL Brian Leetch/2
N-BR Brad Richards/19
N-BS Borje Salming/21
N-BY Bryan McCabe/24 30.00 80.00
N-CA Mike Cammalleri/13
N-CB Christian Backman/55 6.00 15.00
N-CD Chris Drury/23
N-CE Christian Ehrhoff/44 12.00 30.00
N-CK Chuck Kobasew/7
N-CO Chris Osgood/30 20.00 50.00
N-CP Chris Pronger/44 25.00 60.00
N-CS Cory Stillman/61 10.00 25.00
N-DA Dave Andreychuk/25
N-DB Daniel Briere/48 20.00 50.00
N-DC Dan Cloutier/39 20.00 50.00
N-DF Dan Fritsche/49 10.00 25.00
N-DH Dominik Hasek/39 40.00 100.00
N-DL David Legwand/11
N-DM Darren McCarty/25
N-DR Dwayne Roloson/30 20.00 50.00
N-DS Darryl Sittler/27
N-DW Doug Weight/39 20.00 50.00
N-EB Ed Belfour/20
N-EC Erik Cole/26 25.00 60.00
N-ED Eric Daze/55 12.00 30.00
N-EJ Ed Jovanovski/55 15.00 40.00
N-EN Evgeni Nabokov/20
N-ES Eric Staal/12
N-FP Fernando Pisani/34
N-FR Alexander Frolov/24 25.00 60.00
N-FT Fedor Tjutin/51 10.00 25.00
N-GC Gerry Cheevers/30 30.00 80.00
N-GF Grant Fuhr/31 30.00 80.00
N-GH Gordie Howe/9
N-GI J-S Giguere/35 15.00 40.00
N-GL Georges Laraque/27 25.00 60.00
N-GM Glen Murray/27 20.00 40.00
N-HE Dany Heatley/15 25.00
N-HJ Milan Hejduk/23 20.00 40.00
N-HO Marcel Hossa/81 10.00 25.00
N-HV Martin Havlat/9
N-HZ Henrik Zetterberg/40 25.00 60.00
N-IK Ilya Kovalchuk/17
N-IL Ian Laperriere/22
N-JB Jay Bouwmeester/4
N-JC Jonathan Cheechoo/14
N-JH Jochen Hecht/55 6.00 15.00
N-JI Jarome Iginla/12
N-JK Jari Kurri/17
N-JL Joffrey Lupul/15
N-JO Jose Theodore/60 20.00 50.00
N-JP Joni Pitkanen/44 20.00 50.00
N-JS Jason Spezza/19 125.00 200.00
N-JT Joe Thornton/19
N-JV Josef Vasicek/63 8.00 20.00
N-JW Justin Williams/11
N-KD Kris Draper/33 15.00 40.00
N-KH Kristian Huselius/22
N-KL Kari Lehtonen/32 25.00 60.00
N-KP Keith Primeau/25 20.00 50.00
N-KT Kimmo Timonen/44 8.00 20.00
N-KW Kevin Weekes/80 8.00 20.00
N-LM Larry Murphy/55 12.00 30.00
N-LN Ladislav Nagy/17
N-LO Stephen Weiss/9
N-LR Luc Robitaille/20
N-MA Maxim Afinogenov/61 15.00 40.00
N-MB Brendan Morrison/7
N-MC Mike Comrie/89 8.00 20.00
N-MG Marian Gaborik/10
N-MH Marian Hossa/18
N-MJ Matt Stajan/14
N-ML Manny Legace/34 20.00 50.00
N-MM Mike Modano/9
N-MN Markus Naslund/19
N-MO Olaf Kolzig/37 50.00 100.00
N-MP Michael Peca/27 25.00 60.00
N-MR Mike Ribeiro/71 12.00 30.00
N-MS Martin St. Louis/26 20.00 50.00
N-MT Marty Turco/35 25.00 60.00
N-NA Owen Nolan/11
N-NB Nick Boynton/44
N-ND Niko Dimitrakos/23
N-NH Nathan Horton/16
N-NK Nikolai Khabibulin/53 20.00 50.00
N-NO Mika Noronen/35 20.00 50.00
N-NZ Nikolai Zherdev/13
N-PB Patrice Bergeron/37 25.00 60.00

N-PD Pavol Demitra/38
N-PE Phil Esposito/7
N-PM Patrick Marleau/12
N-PO Mark Popovic/33 10.00 25.00
N-PW Peter Worrell/28 15.00 40.00
N-RE Robert Esche/42 20.00 50.00
N-RF Ruslan Fedotenko/17
N-RH Riku Hahl/32
N-RL Roberto Luongo/1
N-RM Ryan Miller/30 15.00 60.00
N-RN Rick Nash/61 30.00 80.00
N-RO Jeremy Roenick/97 20.00 50.00
N-RS Ryan Smyth/94 20.00 50.00
N-RT Roman Turek/1
N-RV Rogie Vachon/30 30.00 60.00
N-RY Michael Ryder/73 15.00 40.00
N-RZ Richard Zednik/20
N-SB Sean Burke/41 10.00 25.00
N-SD Shane Doan/19 20.00 50.00
N-SG Simon Gagne/12
N-SK Saku Koivu/11
N-SN Scott Niedermayer/27 20.00 50.00
N-SS Sheldon Souray/44 10.00 25.00
N-SU Mats Sundin/13
N-SZ Sergei Zubov/56 6.00 15.00
N-TA Tyler Arnason/39 15.00 40.00
N-TB Todd Bertuzzi/44 25.00 60.00
N-TC Ty Conklin/1
N-TE Tony Esposito/35 25.00 60.00
N-TG Tim Gleason/42 12.00 30.00
N-TL Trevor Linden/16
N-TN Tyson Nash/18
N-TO Terry O'Reilly/24 30.00 60.00
N-TR Tuomo Ruutu/15
N-TV Steve Sullivan/26 10.00 25.00
N-VL Vincent Lecavalier/4
N-VP Vaclav Prospal/20 20.00 40.00
N-VR Mike Van Ryn/26 10.00 25.00
N-WG Wayne Gretzky/99 150.00 300.00
N-ZC Zdeno Chara/3

2005-06 Upper Deck Patches

PRINT RUN 15 SER.#'d SETS
NOT PRICED DUE TO SCARCITY

2005-06 Upper Deck Patches Series II

PRINT RUN 15 SER.#'d SETS
NOT PRICED DUE TO SCARCITY

2005-06 Upper Deck Playoff Performers

COMPLETE SET (7) 12.00 25.00
STATED ODDS 1:24
PP1 Jarome Iginla 1.00 2.50
PP2 Martin St. Louis .75 2.00
PP3 Peter Forsberg 2.00 5.00
PP4 Wayne Gretzky 4.00 10.00
PP5 Jarome Iginla 1.00 2.50
PP6 Joe Sakic 1.50 4.00
PP7 Mario Lemieux 4.00 10.00

2005-06 Upper Deck Rookie Ink

RIAA Andrew Alberts /41 12.00 30.00
RIAM Andrej Meszaros /14 60.00 100.00
RIAO Alexander Ovechkin /8
RIAP Alexander Perezhogin /42 25.00 60.00
RIAS Anthony Stewart /57 15.00 40.00
RIAW Andrew Wozniewski /55 15.00 40.00
RIBB Brandon Bochenski /10
RIBC Braydon Coburn /4
RIBS Brent Seabrook /7
RIBW Brad Winchester /26 20.00 50.00
RICB Cam Barker /25
RICC Chris Campoli /14
RICP Corey Perry /61 25.00 50.00
RICW Cam Ward /30 60.00 125.00
RIDL David Leneveu /30 20.00 50.00
RIDP Dion Phaneuf /3
RIEN Eric Nystrom /23 25.00 60.00
RIGB Gilbert Brule /17
RIGP George Parros /57 12.00 30.00
RIHL Henrik Lundqvist /30 75.00 150.00
RIHO Jeff Hoggan /22 15.00 40.00
RIHT Hannu Toivonen /33 30.00 80.00
RIJB Jaroslav Balastik /29 20.00 50.00
RIJC Jeff Carter /17 50.00 100.00
RIJF Johan Franzen /39 25.00 60.00
RIJG Josh Gorges /6
RIJH Jim Howard /35 40.00 80.00
RIJJ Jussi Jokinen /36 30.00 60.00
RIJM Jay McClement /9
RIJS Jim Slater /23 20.00 50.00
RIJW Jeff Woywitka /29 20.00 50.00
RIKB Keith Ballard /2
RIKD Kevin Dallman /58 10.00 25.00
RIKN Kevin Nastiuk /35 20.00 50.00
RIMF Matt Foy /83 10.00 25.00
RIMJ Milan Jurcina /68 12.00 30.00
RIMK Mikko Koivu /21
RIMO Alvaro Montoya /29 30.00 80.00
RIMR Mike Richards /18 40.00 100.00
RIMT Maxime Talbot /25 40.00 80.00
RIPB Peter Budaj /31 50.00 100.00
RIPE Patrick Eaves /7
RIPN Petteri Nokelainen /29 25.00 60.00
RIPP Petr Prucha /25 40.00 100.00
RIRB Rene Bourque /14
RIRC Ryane Clowe /29 25.00 60.00
RIRG Ryan Getzlaf /51 40.00 80.00
RIRH Ryan Hollweg /44 15.00 40.00
RIRI Raitis Ivanans /3
RIRN Robert Nilsson /21
RIRO Rostislav Olesz /85 12.00 30.00
RIRS Ryan Suter /20 40.00 80.00
RIRU R.J. Umberger /20 30.00 80.00
RIRW Ryan Whitney /19
RISC Sidney Crosby /87 300.00 500.00
RIST Alexander Steen /10
RITV Thomas Vanek /26 75.00 125.00
RIWW Wojtek Wolski /8
RIYD Yann Danis /75 15.00 40.00
RIZP Zach Parise /9

2005-06 Upper Deck Rookie Showcase

Available only via the Upper Deck website and one per customer, this 36-card set featured rookies making their debut in the 2005-06 season. Print run was limited to 1000 copies each.

COMMON CARD (RS1-RS36) 3.00 8.00
STATED PRINT RUN 1000 COPIES
RS1 Corey Perry 6.00 15.00
RS2 Braydon Coburn 3.00 8.00
RS3 Hannu Toivonen 5.00 12.00
RS4 Thomas Vanek 6.00 15.00
RS5 Dion Phaneuf 10.00 25.00
RS6 Cam Ward 6.00 15.00
RS7 Brent Seabrook 3.00 8.00
RS8 Wojtek Wolski 5.00 12.00
RS9 Gilbert Brule 6.00 15.00
RS10 Jussi Jokinen 5.00 12.00
RS11 Jim Howard 5.00 12.00
RS12 Brad Winchester 3.00 8.00
RS13 Rostislav Olesz 5.00 12.00
RS14 George Parros 3.00 8.00
RS15 Matt Foy 3.00 8.00
RS16 Alexander Perezhogin 5.00 12.00
RS17 Ryan Suter 5.00 12.00
RS18 Zach Parise 5.00 12.00
RS19 Robert Nilsson 5.00 12.00
RS20 Henrik Lundqvist 10.00 25.00
RS21 Andrej Meszaros 3.00 8.00
RS22 Jeff Carter 6.00 15.00
RS23 David Leneveu 5.00 12.00
RS24 Sidney Crosby 30.00 80.00
RS25 Ryane Clowe 3.00 8.00
RS26 Jeff Woywitka 3.00 8.00
RS27 Evgeni Artyukhin 3.00 8.00
RS28 Alexander Steen 5.00 12.00
RS29 Rob McVicar 3.00 8.00
RS30 Alexander Ovechkin 20.00 50.00
RS31 Yann Danis 5.00 12.00
RS32 Eric Nystrom 5.00 12.00
RS33 Mike Richards 5.00 12.00
RS34 Ryan Getzlaf 6.00 15.00
RS35 Johan Franzen 3.00 8.00
RS36 Brandon Bochenski 3.00 8.00

2005-06 Upper Deck Rookie Showcase Beckett Promos

This 36-card set was available only in copies of Beckett Hockey #180. The cards paralleled the regular Rookie Showcase cards but with a subtle color shift from gold backgrounds and details to pewter. Exact print runs were not made available.

RS1 Corey Perry 4.00 10.00
RS2 Braydon Coburn 3.00 8.00
RS3 Hannu Toivonen 3.00 8.00
RS4 Thomas Vanek 4.00 10.00
RS5 Dion Phaneuf 6.00 15.00
RS6 Cam Ward 4.00 10.00
RS7 Brent Seabrook 3.00 8.00
RS8 Wojtek Wolski 4.00 10.00
RS9 Gilbert Brule 4.00 10.00
RS10 Jussi Jokinen 3.00 8.00
RS11 Jim Howard 3.00 8.00
RS12 Brad Winchester 3.00 8.00
RS13 Rostislav Olesz 3.00 8.00
RS14 George Parros 3.00 8.00
RS15 Matt Foy 3.00 8.00
RS16 Alexander Perezhogin 3.00 8.00
RS17 Ryan Suter 3.00 8.00
RS18 Zach Parise 3.00 8.00
RS19 Robert Nilsson 3.00 8.00
RS20 Henrik Lundqvist 6.00 15.00
RS21 Andrej Meszaros 1.50 4.00
RS22 Jeff Carter 4.00 10.00
RS23 David Leneveu 3.00 8.00
RS24 Sidney Crosby 20.00 50.00
RS25 Ryane Clowe 3.00 8.00
RS26 Jeff Woywitka 3.00 8.00
RS27 Evgeny Artyukhin 3.00 8.00
RS28 Alexander Steen 3.00 8.00
RS29 Rob McVicar 3.00 8.00
RS30 Alexander Ovechkin 15.00 40.00
RS31 Yann Danis 3.00 8.00
RS32 Eric Nystrom 3.00 8.00
RS33 Mike Richards 3.00 8.00
RS34 Ryan Getzlaf 4.00 10.00
RS35 Johan Franzen 3.00 8.00
RS36 Brandon Bochenski 3.00 8.00

2005-06 Upper Deck Rookie Threads

ODDS 1:24
RTAA Andrew Alberts 3.00 8.00
RTAM Andrej Meszaros 3.00 8.00
RTAO Alexander Ovechkin 20.00 50.00
RTAP Alexander Perezhogin 6.00 15.00
RTAS Anthony Stewart 3.00 8.00
RTAW Andrew Wozniewski 3.00 8.00
RTBB Brandon Bochenski 3.00 8.00
RTBC Braydon Coburn 5.00 12.00
RTBL Brett Lebda 3.00 8.00
RTBS Brent Seabrook 3.00 8.00
RTBW Brad Winchester 3.00 8.00
RTCB Cam Barker 5.00 12.00
RTCP Corey Perry 6.00 15.00
RTCW Cam Ward 8.00 20.00
RTDK Duncan Keith 5.00 12.00
RTDL David Leneveu 3.00 8.00
RTDP Dion Phaneuf 12.00 30.00
RTEN Eric Nystrom 3.00 8.00
RTGB Gilbert Brule 6.00 15.00
RTGP George Parros 3.00 8.00
RTHL Henrik Lundqvist 12.00 30.00
RTHO Jim Howard 6.00 15.00
RTHT Hannu Toivonen 6.00 15.00
RTJB Jaroslav Balastik 3.00 8.00
RTJC Jeff Carter 6.00 15.00
RTJF Johan Franzen 3.00 8.00
RTJG Josh Gorges 3.00 8.00
RTJH Jeff Hoggan 3.00 8.00
RTJJ Jussi Jokinen 5.00 12.00
RTJM Jay McClement 3.00 8.00
RTJS Jim Slater 3.00 8.00
RTJW Jeff Woywitka 3.00 8.00
RTKB Keith Ballard 3.00 8.00
RTKD Kevin Dallman 3.00 8.00
RTKN Kevin Nastiuk 3.00 8.00
RTMF Matt Foy 5.00 12.00
RTMJ Milan Jurcina 3.00 8.00
RTMO Alvaro Montoya 8.00 20.00
RTMR Mike Richards 5.00 12.00
RTMT Maxime Talbot 3.00 8.00
RTNN Niklas Nordgren 3.00 8.00
RTPB Peter Budaj 3.00 8.00
RTPE Patrick Eaves 3.00 8.00
RTPN Petteri Nokelainen 3.00 8.00
RTPP Petr Prucha 5.00 12.00
RTRB Rene Bourque 3.00 8.00
RTRC Ryane Clowe 3.00 8.00
RTRG Ryan Getzlaf 6.00 15.00
RTRH Ryan Hollweg 3.00 8.00
RTRI Raitis Ivanans 3.00 8.00
RTRN Robert Nilsson 6.00 15.00
RTRO Rostislav Olesz 5.00 12.00
RTRS Ryan Suter 5.00 12.00
RTSC Sidney Crosby 50.00 100.00
RTST Alexander Steen 6.00 15.00
RTTH Timo Helbling 3.00 8.00
RTTV Thomas Vanek 8.00 20.00
RTWW Wojtek Wolski 8.00 20.00
RTYD Yann Danis 3.00 8.00
RTZP Zach Parise 6.00 15.00

2005-06 Upper Deck Rookie Threads Autographs

*AUTO: 1.5X TO 4X JSY HI
PRINT RUN 75 SER.#'d SETS
UNLESS NOTED BELOW
ARTAO Alexander Ovechkin
ARTAP Alexander Perezhogin
ARTCP Corey Perry
ARTHL Henrik Lundqvist
ARTJC Jeff Carter
ARTMR Mike Richards
ARTRG Ryan Getzlaf
ARTSC Sidney Crosby
ARTST Alexander Steen
ARTTV Thomas Vanek

2005-06 Upper Deck School of Hard Knocks

COMPLETE SET (7) 5.00 10.00
STATED ODDS 1:24
HK1 Scott Stevens .75 2.00
HK2 Chris Pronger .75 2.00
HK3 Chris Simon .75 2.00
HK4 Jeremy Roenick 1.00 2.50
HK5 Tie Domi .75 2.00
HK6 Ed Jovanovski .75 2.00
HK7 Brendan Shanahan .75 2.00

2005-06 Upper Deck Scrapbooks

COMPLETE SET (30) 10.00 25.00
COMMON CARD .15 .40
RANDOM INSERT IN RETAIL PACKS
HS1 Ilya Kovalchuk .25 .60
HS2 Wayne Gretzky 1.25 3.00
HS3 Joe Thornton .30 .75
HS4 Kari Lehtonen .20 .50
HS5 Dominik Hasek .40 1.00
HS6 Mario Lemieux 1.25 3.00
HS7 Jose Theodore .25 .60
HS8 Paul Kariya .25 .60
HS9 Mike Modano .30 .75
HS10 Rick Nash .25 .60
HS11 Mark Messier .20 .50
HS12 Jarome Iginla .25 .60
HS13 Peter Forsberg .50 1.25
HS14 Nikolai Khabibulin .20 .50
HS15 Dany Heatley .25 .60
HS16 Brett Hull .25 .60
HS17 Marian Gaborik .40 1.00
HS18 Mats Sundin .40 1.00
HS19 Steve Yzerman 1.00 2.50
HS20 Joe Sakic .40 1.00
HS21 Marian Hossa .20 .50
HS22 Markus Naslund .20 .50
HS23 Jaromir Jagr .40 1.00
HS24 Andrew Raycroft .15 .40
HS25 Ed Belfour .20 .50
HS26 Martin St. Louis .15 .40
HS27 Jeremy Roenick .25 .60
HS28 Brendan Shanahan .20 .50
HS29 Sergei Fedorov .25 .60
HS30 Martin Brodeur 1.00 2.50

2005-06 Upper Deck Shooting Stars

STATED ODDS 1:32
S-MMO Mike Modano 6.00 15.00
S-MRI Mike Ribeiro 3.00 8.00
S-MHO Marian Hossa 4.00 10.00
S-MHA Martin Havlat 4.00 10.00
S-MRY Michael Ryder 4.00 10.00
S-MME Mark Messier 10.00 25.00
S-AM Alexander Mogilny 3.00 8.00
S-BG Bill Guerin 3.00 8.00
S-BH Brett Hull 5.00 12.00
S-BR Brad Richards 4.00 10.00
S-BS Brendan Shanahan 4.00 10.00
S-CD Chris Drury 3.00 8.00
S-DA Daniel Alfredsson 4.00 10.00
S-DH Dany Heatley 6.00 15.00
S-EL Eric Lindros 4.00 10.00
S-GM Glen Murray 3.00 8.00
S-HZ Henrik Zetterberg 4.00 10.00
S-IK Ilya Kovalchuk 6.00 15.00
S-JI Jarome Iginla 6.00 15.00
S-JJ Jaromir Jagr SP 40.00 100.00
S-JL John LeClair 3.00 8.00
S-JR Jeremy Roenick 4.00 10.00
S-JS Joe Sakic 8.00 20.00
S-JT Joe Thornton 6.00 15.00
S-KP Keith Primeau 3.00 8.00
S-KT Keith Tkachuk 3.00 8.00
S-LR Luc Robitaille 4.00 10.00
S-MG Marian Gaborik 6.00 15.00
S-MH Milan Hejduk 3.00 8.00
S-ML Mario Lemieux SP 30.00 80.00
S-MN Markus Naslund 4.00 10.00
S-MP Mark Parrish 3.00 8.00
S-MP Michael Peca 3.00 8.00
S-MS Martin St. Louis 4.00 10.00
S-MS Mats Sundin 4.00 10.00
S-PB Peter Bondra 3.00 8.00
S-PE Patrik Elias 4.00 10.00
S-PK Paul Kariya 4.00 10.00
S-RB Rob Blake 3.00 8.00
S-RE Mark Recchi 4.00 10.00
S-RN Rick Nash
S-RS Ryan Smyth 3.00 8.00
S-SF Sergei Fedorov 4.00 10.00
S-SG Simon Gagne 4.00 10.00
S-SS Sergei Samsonov 3.00 8.00
S-SY Steve Yzerman 12.00 30.00
S-TA Tony Amonte 3.00 8.00
S-VL Vincent Lecavalier 5.00 12.00
S-ZP Zigmund Palffy 4.00 10.00

2005-06 Upper Deck Sportsfest

COMPLETE SET (3) 30.00
NHL1 Sidney Crosby 10.00 25.00
NHL2 Alexander Ovechkin 15.00
NHL3 Wayne Gretzky 10.00
NHLAU Sidney Crosby AU 1/1

2005-06 Upper Deck Stars in the Making

COMPLETE SET (14) 25.00 50.00
SM1 Sidney Crosby 8.00 20.00
SM2 Alexander Ovechkin 6.00 15.00
SM3 Jeff Carter 2.00 5.00
SM4 Corey Perry 2.00 5.00
SM5 Thomas Vanek 2.50 6.00
SM6 Henrik Lundqvist 4.00 10.00
SM7 Alexander Perezhogin 1.50 4.00
SM8 Dion Phaneuf 4.00 10.00
SM9 Hannu Toivonen 2.00 5.00
SM10 Alexander Steen 2.00 5.00
SM11 Gilbert Brule 2.50 6.00
SM12 Mike Richards 1.50 4.00
SM13 Zach Parise 2.00 5.00
SM14 Wojtek Wolski 2.50 6.00

2006-07 Upper Deck

COMPLETE SET (495) 400.00 700.00
COMP. SER. 1 w/o SPs 10.00 25.00
COMP. SER. 2 w/o SPs 10.00 25.00
YG ODDS 1:4
1 Corey Perry .12 .30
2 Ilya Bryzgalov .12 .30
3 Teemu Selanne .15 .40
4 Andy McDonald .07 .20
5 Ryan Getzlaf .12 .30
6 Francois Beauchemin .10 .25
7 Scott Niedermayer .10 .25
8 Kari Lehtonen .20 .50
9 Marian Hossa .15 .40
10 Slava Kozlov .07 .20
11 Jim Slater .07 .20
12 Garnet Exelby .10 .25
13 Bobby Holik .07 .20
14 Niclas Havelid .07 .20
15 Brad Boyes .10 .25
16 Brad Stuart .07 .20
17 Tim Thomas .12 .30
18 Marco Sturm .07 .20
19 Hannu Toivonen .15 .40
20 Glen Murray .07 .20
21 Ryan Miller .15 .40
22 Thomas Vanek .12 .30
23 Chris Drury .10 .25
24 Henrik Tallinder .07 .20
25 Jochen Hecht .10 .25
26 Brian Campbell .07 .20
27 Derek Roy .10 .25
28 Jarome Iginla .25 .60
29 Dion Phaneuf .25 .60
30 Robyn Regehr .07 .20
31 Jamie Lundmark .07 .20
32 Darren McCarty .10 .25
33 Kristian Huselius .07 .20
34 Chuck Kobasew .07 .20
35 Eric Staal .15 .40
36 Cam Ward .15 .40
37 Justin Williams .07 .20
38 Glen Wesley .07 .20
39 Mike Commodore .07 .20
40 Cory Stillman .07 .20
41 Ray Whitney .07 .20
42 Tuomo Ruutu .07 .20
43 Radim Vrbata .07 .20
44 Duncan Keith .07 .20
45 Nikolai Khabibulin .15 .40
46 Rene Bourque .07 .20
47 Patrick Sharp .07 .20
48 Jose Theodore .20 .50
49 Milan Hejduk .15 .40
50 Pierre Turgeon .10 .25
51 Andrew Brunette .07 .20
52 Wojtek Wolski .07 .20
53 John-Michael Liles .07 .20
54 Joe Sakic .40 1.00
55 Rick Nash .20 .50
56 Pascal Leclaire .12 .30
57 Adam Foote .07 .20
58 Alexandre Picard .07 .20
59 Bryan Berard .07 .20
60 Sergei Fedorov .20 .50
61 Marty Turco .15 .40
62 Brenden Morrow .15 .40
63 Jussi Jokinen .07 .20
64 Sergei Zubov .07 .20
65 Jere Lehtinen .07 .20
66 Steve Ott .10 .25
67 Philippe Boucher .07 .20
68 Pavel Datsyuk .15 .40
69 Mikael Samuelsson .07 .20
70 Tomas Holmstrom .10 .25
71 Kris Draper .07 .20
72 Jason Williams .10 .25
73 Chris Osgood .12 .30
74 Robert Lang .07 .20
75 Ales Hemsky .07 .20
76 Fernando Pisani .10 .25
77 Jarret Stoll .07 .20
78 Marc-Andre Bergeron .07 .20
79 Dwayne Roloson .15 .40
80 Ethan Moreau .07 .20
81 Raffi Torres .07 .20
82 Joe Nieuwendyk .12 .30
83 Jay Bouwmeester .07 .20
84 Nathan Horton .07 .20
85 Rostislav Olesz .07 .20
86 Martin Gelinas .10 .25
87 Stephen Weiss .07 .20
88 Mathieu Garon .12 .30
89 Mike Cammalleri .07 .20
90 Alexander Frolov .07 .20
91 Lubomir Visnovsky .07 .20
92 George Parros .07 .20
93 Dustin Brown .07 .20
94 Marian Gaborik .25 .60
95 Wes Walz .07 .20
96 Pierre-Marc Bouchard .07 .20
97 Nick Schultz .07 .20
98 Derek Boogaard .07 .20
99 Todd White .07 .20
100 Saku Koivu .20 .50
101 Cristobal Huet .25 .60
102 Alex Kovalev .07 .20
103 Chris Higgins .07 .20
104 Andrei Markov .07 .20
105 Alexander Perezhogin .07 .20
106 Mathieu Dandenault .07 .20
107 Steve Sullivan .07 .20
108 Tomas Vokoun .15 .40
109 David Legwand .07 .20
110 Marek Zidlicky .10 .25
111 Kimmo Timonen .07 .20
112 Ryan Suter .07 .20
113 Jordin Tootoo .15 .40
114 Martin Brodeur .75 2.00
115 Brian Gionta .07 .20
116 Zach Parise .12 .30
117 Brian Rafalski .07 .20
118 Jamie Langenbrunner .07 .20
119 John Madden .10 .25
120 Jay Pandolfo .07 .20
121 Miroslav Satan .07 .20
122 Rick DiPietro .15 .40
123 Alexei Zhitnik .07 .20
124 Jeff Tambellini .07 .20
125 Chris Campoli .07 .20
126 Jason Blake .07 .20
127 Trent Hunter .07 .20
128 Jaromir Jagr .30 .75
129 Petr Prucha .07 .20
130 Kevin Weekes .15 .40
131 Sandis Ozolinsh .10 .25
132 Ryan Hollweg .07 .20
133 Darius Kasparaitis .07 .20
134 Martin Straka .07 .20
135 Jason Spezza .20 .50
136 Ray Emery .12 .30
137 Andrej Meszaros .07 .20
138 Patrick Eaves .07 .20
139 Daniel Alfredsson .15 .40
140 Antoine Vermette .07 .20
141 Chris Phillips .07 .20
142 Peter Forsberg .30 .75
143 Robert Esche .12 .30
144 Mike Knuble .10 .25
145 Joni Pitkanen .07 .20
146 Mike Richards .15 .40
147 R.J. Umberger .07 .20
148 Sami Kapanen .07 .20
149 Shane Doan .07 .20
150 Keith Ballard .07 .20
151 Ladislav Nagy .07 .20
152 Mike Ricci .10 .25
153 Oleg Saprykin .07 .20
154 David Leneveu .15 .40
155 Sidney Crosby 1.25 3.00
156 Colby Armstrong .07 .20
157 John LeClair .12 .30
158 Sergei Gonchar .07 .20
159 Ryan Whitney .07 .20
160 Ryan Malone .07 .20
161 Joe Thornton .30 .75
162 Vesa Toskala .15 .40
163 Milan Michalek .07 .20
164 Marcel Goc .10 .25
165 Steve Bernier .07 .20
166 Jonathan Cheechoo .20 .50
167 Christian Ehrhoff .07 .20
168 Keith Tkachuk .12 .30
169 Barret Jackman .07 .20
170 Curtis Sanford .12 .30
171 Lee Stempniak .07 .20
172 Petr Cajanek .07 .20
173 Dallas Drake .07 .20
174 Martin St. Louis .15 .40
175 Vaclav Prospal .07 .20
176 Dan Boyle .07 .20
177 Ryan Craig .07 .20
178 Ruslan Fedotenko .07 .20
179 Paul Ranger .10 .25
180 Sean Burke .12 .30
181 Mats Sundin .20 .50
182 Darcy Tucker .07 .20
183 Alexander Steen .15 .40
184 Mikael Tellqvist .15 .40
185 Tomas Kaberle .07 .20
186 Nikolai Antropov .07 .20
187 Bryan McCabe .07 .20
188 Markus Naslund .20 .50
189 Henrik Sedin .07 .20
190 Mattias Ohlund .07 .20
191 Daniel Sedin .07 .20
192 Matt Cooke .07 .20
193 Sami Salo .10 .25
194 Ryan Kesler .07 .20
195 Brooks Laich .07 .20
196 Shaone Morrisonn .10 .25
197 Chris Clark .07 .20
198 Alexander Semin .15 .40
199 Sidney Crosby 1.50 4.00
200 Jaromir Jagr .30 .75
201 Shane O'Brien RC 2.00 5.00
202 Ryan Shannon RC 2.00 5.00
203 Yan Stastny RC 2.00 5.00
204 Phil Kessel RC 10.00 25.00
205 Carsen Germyn RC 2.00 5.00
206 Dustin Byfuglien RC 2.00 5.00
207 Paul Stastny RC 12.00 30.00
208 Fredrik Norrena RC 3.00 8.00
209 Filip Novak RC 2.00 5.00
210 Loui Eriksson RC 3.00 8.00
211 Tomas Kopecky RC 3.00 8.00
212 Marc-Antoine Pouliot RC 3.00 8.00
213 Ladislav Smid RC 2.00 5.00
214 Patrick Thoresen RC 3.00 8.00
215 Patrick O'Sullivan RC 4.00 10.00
216 Anze Kopitar RC 12.00 30.00
217 Konstantin Pushkarev RC 2.00 5.00
218 Erik Reitz RC 2.00 5.00
219 Miroslav Kopriva RC 2.00 5.00
220 Niklas Backstrom RC 3.00 8.00
221 Guillaume Latendresse RC 10.0025.00
222 Shea Weber RC 3.00 8.00
223 Mikko Lehtonen RC 2.00 5.00
224 Frank Doyle RC 2.00 5.00
225 Travis Zajac RC 3.00 8.00
226 John Oduya RC 2.00 5.00
227 Ryan Caldwell RC 2.00 5.00
228 Masi Marjamaki RC 2.00 5.00
229 Matt Koalska RC 2.00 5.00
230 Jarkko Immonen RC 2.00 5.00
231 Nigel Dawes RC 2.00 5.00
232 Ryan Potulny RC 2.00 5.00
233 David Printz RC 2.00 5.00
234 Bill Thomas RC 2.00 5.00
235 Joel Perrault RC 2.00 5.00
236 Patrick Fischer RC 2.00 5.00
237 Noah Welch RC 2.00 5.00
238 Michel Ouellet RC 3.00 8.00
239 Jordan Staal RC 30.00 60.00
240 Kristopher Letang RC 3.00 8.00
241 Matt Carle RC 3.00 8.00
242 Marc-Edouard Vlasic RC 3.00 8.00
243 D.J. King RC 2.00 5.00
244 Ben Ondrus RC 2.00 5.00
245 Brendan Bell RC 2.00 5.00
246 Ian White RC 2.00 5.00
247 Jeremy Williams RC 2.00 5.00
248 Luc Bourdon RC 3.00 8.00
249 Eric Fehr RC 3.00 8.00
250 Phil Kessel CL 3.00 8.00
251 Chris Pronger .12 .30
252 Todd Fedoruk .07 .20
253 Chris Kunitz .07 .20
254 Jean-Sebastien Giguere .12 .30
255 Rob Niedermayer .07 .20
256 Todd Marchant .07 .20
257 Samuel Pahlsson .07 .20
258 Ilya Kovalchuk .20 .50
259 Steve Rucchin .07 .20
260 Niko Kapanen .07 .20
261 Greg de Vries .07 .20
262 Johan Hedberg .12 .30
263 Andy Sutton .07 .20
264 Scott Mellanby .07 .20
265 Patrice Bergeron .15 .40
266 Zdeno Chara .07 .20
267 Andrew Alberts .07 .20
268 P.J. Axelsson .07 .20
269 Marc Savard .07 .20
270 Paul Mara .07 .20
271 Wayne Primeau .07 .20
272 Daniel Briere .12 .30
273 Ales Kotalik .07 .20
274 Jiri Novotny .07 .20
275 Martin Biron .12 .30
276 Jason Pominville .07 .20
277 Maxim Afinogenov .07 .20
278 Jaroslav Spacek .07 .20
279 Alex Tanguay .12 .30
280 Daymond Langkow .07 .20
281 Roman Hamrlik .07 .20
282 Miikka Kiprusoff .15 .40
283 Jeff Friesen .07 .20
284 Andrew Ference .07 .20
285 Stephane Yelle .07 .20
286 Rod Brind`Amour .12 .30
287 Erik Cole .07 .20
288 Andrew Ladd .07 .20
289 John Grahame .12 .30
290 Tim Gleason .07 .20
291 Kevyn Adams .07 .20
292 Martin Havlat .12 .30
293 Brent Seabrook .07 .20
294 Adrian Aucoin .07 .20
295 Brian Boucher .12 .30
296 Bryan Smolinski .07 .20
297 Martin Lapointe .07 .20
298 Michal Handzus .07 .20
299 Marek Svatos .07 .20
300 Mark Rycroft .07 .20
301 Tyler Arnason .07 .20
302 Peter Budaj .12 .30
303 Patrice Brisebois .07 .20
304 Antti Laaksonen .07 .20
305 Ian Laperriere .07 .20
306 Fredrik Modin .07 .20
307 Rostislav Klesla .07 .20
308 Nikolai Zherdev .07 .20
309 Gilbert Brule .15 .40
310 David Vyborny .07 .20
311 Manny Malhotra .07 .20
312 Jody Shelley .07 .20
313 Mike Modano .15 .40
314 Antti Miettinen .07 .20
315 Jeff Halpern .07 .20
316 Patrik Stefan .07 .20
317 Mike Ribeiro .07 .20
318 Eric Lindros .15 .40
319 Dominik Hasek .25 .60
320 Chris Chelios .12 .30
321 Johan Franzen .07 .20
322 Mathieu Schneider .07 .20
323 Henrik Zetterberg .15 .40
324 Nicklas Lidstrom .15 .40
325 Ryan Smyth .12 .30
326 Steve Staios .07 .20
327 Jussi Markkanen .12 .30
328 Joffrey Lupul .07 .20
329 Jason Smith .07 .20
330 Shawn Horcoff .07 .20
331 Petr Sykora .07 .20
332 Olli Jokinen .07 .20
333 Ed Belfour .15 .40
334 Mike Van Ryn .07 .20
335 Jozef Stumpel .07 .20
336 Alexander Auld .12 .30
337 Todd Bertuzzi .12 .30
338 Gary Roberts .07 .20
339 Rob Blake .12 .30
340 Craig Conroy .07 .20
341 Dan Cloutier .12 .30
342 Mattias Norstrom .07 .20
343 Sean Avery .07 .20
344 Oleg Tverdovsky .07 .20
345 Manny Fernandez .12 .30
346 Brian Rolston .07 .20
347 Mikko Koivu .07 .20
348 Kim Johnsson .07 .20
349 Pavol Demitra .07 .20
350 Mark Parrish .07 .20
351 Kurtis Foster .07 .20
352 Michael Ryder .12 .30
353 David Aebischer .12 .30
354 Sergei Samsonov .12 .30
355 Sheldon Souray .07 .20
356 Mike Johnson .07 .20
357 Craig Rivet .07 .20
358 Radek Bonk .07 .20
359 Paul Kariya .15 .40
360 Scott Hartnell .07 .20
361 Martin Erat .07 .20
362 Jason Arnott .07 .20
363 Chris Mason .12 .30
364 J.P. Dumont .07 .20
365 Patrik Elias .07 .20
366 Scott Gomez .07 .20
367 Colin White .07 .20
368 Sergei Brylin .07 .20
369 Paul Martin .07 .20
370 Cam Janssen .07 .20
371 Alexei Yashin .07 .20
372 Mike Sillinger .07 .20
373 Arron Asham .07 .20
374 Mike York .07 .20
375 Mike Dunham .12 .30
376 Brendan Witt .07 .20
377 Henrik Lundqvist .20 .50
378 Adam Hall .07 .20
379 Wayne Gretzky 1.00 2.50
380 Matt Cullen .07 .20
381 Michal Rozsival .07 .20
382 Michael Nylander .07 .20
383 Brendan Shanahan .15 .40
384 Dany Heatley .20 .50
385 Joe Corvo .07 .20
386 Peter Schaefer .07 .20
387 Chris Neil .07 .20
388 Wade Redden .07 .20
389 Martin Gerber .15 .40
390 Mike Fisher .07 .20
391 Simon Gagne .15 .40
392 Jeff Carter .15 .40
393 Antero Niittymaki .12 .30
394 Geoff Sanderson .07 .20
395 Fredrick Meyer .07 .20
396 Kyle Calder .07 .20
397 Curtis Joseph .15 .40
398 Ed Jovanovski .07 .20
399 Mike Comrie .07 .20
400 Nick Boynton .07 .20
401 Jeremy Roenick .20 .50
402 Georges Laraque .07 .20
403 Owen Nolan .12 .30
404 Marc-Andre Fleury .15 .40
405 Nils Ekman .07 .20
406 Jarkko Ruutu .07 .20
407 Mark Eaton .07 .20
408 Dominic Moore .07 .20
409 Mark Recchi .07 .20
410 Patrick Marleau .12 .30
411 Scott Hannan .07 .20
412 Josh Gorges .07 .20
413 Mike Grier .07 .20
414 Mark Bell .07 .20
415 Evgeni Nabokov .12 .30

416 Doug Weight .07 .20
417 Dennis Wideman .07 .20
418 Jay McClement .07 .20
419 Manny Legace .12 .30
420 Bill Guerin .07 .20
421 Jay McKee .07 .20
422 Vincent Lecavalier .15 .40
423 Marc Denis .12 .30
424 Filip Kuba .07 .20
425 Tim Taylor .07 .20
426 Brad Richards .12 .30
427 Dimitry Afanasenkov .07 .20
428 Andrew Raycroft .12 .30
429 Kyle Wellwood .07 .20
430 Michael Peca .07 .20
431 Alexei Ponikarovsky .07 .20
432 Jeff O'Neill .07 .20
433 Jean-Sebastien Aubin .12 .30
434 Matt Stajan .07 .20
435 Dany Sabourin .12 .30
436 Roberto Luongo .20 .50
437 Willie Mitchell .07 .20
438 Jan Bulis .07 .20
439 Brendan Morrison .07 .20
440 Trevor Linden .07 .20
441 Lukas Krajicek .07 .20
442 Alexander Ovechkin .75 2.00
443 Olaf Kolzig .15 .40
444 Richard Zednik .07 .20
445 Brian Pothier .07 .20
446 Donald Brashear .07 .20
447 Dainius Zubrus .07 .20
448 Ben Clymer .07 .20
449 Miikka Kiprusoff .15 .40
450 Wayne Gretzky 1.00 2.50
451 David McKee RC 2.00 5.00
452 Mark Stuart RC 2.00 5.00
453 Matt Lashoff RC 2.00 5.00
454 Mike Brown RC 2.00 5.00
455 Nate Thompson RC 2.00 5.00
456 Drew Stafford RC 6.00 15.00
457 Adam Dennis RC 2.00 5.00
458 Mike Card RC 2.00 5.00
459 Michael Funk RC 2.00 5.00
460 Michael Ryan RC 2.00 5.00
461 Dustin Boyd RC 3.00 8.00
462 Brandon Prust RC 2.00 5.00
463 Dave Bolland RC 2.00 5.00
464 Michael Blunden RC 2.00 5.00
465 Adam Burish RC 2.00 5.00
466 Stefan Liv RC 2.00 5.00
467 Alexei Mikhnov RC 2.00 5.00
468 Jeff Deslauriers RC 2.00 5.00
469 Jan Hejda RC 2.00 5.00
470 David Booth RC 2.00 5.00
471 Drew Larman RC 2.00 5.00
472 Peter Harrold RC 2.00 5.00
473 Barry Brust RC 2.00 5.00
474 Karri Ramo RC 2.00 5.00
475 Benoit Pouliot RC 3.00 8.00
476 Alex Radulov RC 10.00 25.00
477 Alex Brooks RC 2.00 5.00
478 Alexei Kaigorodov RC 2.00 5.00
479 Kelly Guard RC 2.00 5.00
480 Jussi Timonen RC 2.00 5.00
481 Martin Houle RC 2.00 5.00
482 Lars Jonsson RC 2.00 5.00
483 Triston Grant RC 2.00 5.00
484 Enver Lisin RC 2.00 5.00
485 Keith Yandle RC 2.00 5.00
486 Evgeni Malkin RC 40.00 100.00
487 Joe Pavelski RC 3.00 8.00
488 Roman Polak RC 2.00 5.00
489 Blair Jones RC 2.00 5.00
490 J-F Racine RC 2.00 5.00
491 Alexander Edler RC 2.00 5.00
492 Jesse Schultz RC 2.00 5.00
493 Nathan McIver RC 2.00 5.00
494 Patrick Coulombe RC 2.00 5.00
495 Evgeni Malkin 4.00 10.00

2006-07 Upper Deck Exclusives Parallel

VALUE: 10X TO 25X BASE HI
PRINT RUN 100 #'d SETS
YOUNG GUNS: 1.2X TO 3 X HI
204 Phil Kessel 20.00 50.00
207 Paul Stastny 25.00 60.00
215 Patrick O'Sullivan 15.00 40.00
216 Anze Kopitar 25.00 60.00
220 Niklas Backstrom 15.00 40.00
221 Guillaume Latendresse 25.00 60.00
225 Travis Zajac 15.00 40.00
239 Jordan Staal 40.00 100.00
241 Matt Carle 15.00 40.00
486 Evgeni Malkin 60.00 150.00

2006-07 Upper Deck High Gloss Parallel

PRINT RUN 10 SER. #'d SETS
NOT PRICED DUE TO SCARCITY

2006-07 Upper Deck All-Time Greatest

COMPLETE SET (28) 15.00 40.00
STATED ODDS 1:12 SER. 2 PACKS
ATG1 Teemu Selanne .50 1.25
ATG2 Ilya Kovalchuk .60 1.50
ATG3 Bobby Orr 2.50 6.00
ATG4 Gilbert Perreault .50 1.25
ATG5 Joe Sakic 1.00 2.50
ATG6 Rick Nash .50 1.25
ATG7 Mike Modano .50 1.25
ATG8 Ted Lindsay .25 .60
ATG9 Wayne Gretzky 2.50 6.00
ATG10 Marcel Dionne .50 1.25
ATG11 Marian Gaborik .60 1.50
ATG12 Tomas Vokoun .40 1.00
ATG13 Martin Brodeur 1.25 3.00
ATG14 Andy Bathgate .25 .60
ATG15 Daniel Alfredsson .40 1.00
ATG16 Bobby Clarke .50 1.25
ATG17 Shane Doan .25 .60
ATG18 Mario Lemieux 2.00 5.00
ATG19 Evgeni Nabokov .40 1.00
ATG20 Martin St. Louis .40 1.00
ATG21 Darryl Sittler .50 1.25
ATG22 Alexander Ovechkin 2.50 6.00
ATG23 Tony Esposito .50 1.25
ATG24 Mario Lemieux 2.00 5.00
ATG25 Guy Lafleur .75 2.00
ATG26 Gilbert Perreault .50 1.25
ATG27 Wayne Gretzky 2.50 6.00
ATG28 Johnny Bower .40 1.00

2006-07 Upper Deck All World

COMPLETE SET (30) 200.00 350.00
STATED ODDS 1:24 SER. 2 PACKS
AW1 Mike Modano 2.00 5.00
AW2 Nicklas Lidstrom 2.00 5.00
AW3 Joe Thornton 3.00 8.00
AW4 Teemu Selanne 2.00 5.00
AW5 Kari Lehtonen 2.00 5.00
AW6 Zdeno Chara 1.00 2.50
AW7 Jarome Iginla 2.50 6.00
AW8 Eric Staal 2.00 5.00
AW9 Martin Havlat 1.50 4.00
AW10 Milan Hejduk 1.00 2.50
AW11 Sergei Fedorov 2.00 5.00
AW12 Rick Nash 2.00 5.00
AW13 Henrik Zetterberg 2.00 5.00
AW14 Olli Jokinen 1.00 2.50
AW15 Marian Gaborik 2.50 6.00
AW16 Saku Koivu 2.00 5.00
AW17 Tomas Vokoun 1.50 4.00
AW18 Paul Kariya 2.00 5.00
AW19 Martin Gerber 2.00 5.00
AW20 Markus Naslund 2.00 5.00
AW21 Ilya Kovalchuk 15.00 30.00
AW22 Miikka Kiprusoff 20.00 50.00
AW23 Joe Sakic 30.00 80.00
AW24 Dominik Hasek 20.00 40.00
AW25 Martin Brodeur 20.00 50.00
AW26 Jaromir Jagr 20.00 40.00
AW27 Peter Forsberg 10.00 25.00
AW28 Sidney Crosby 30.00 80.00
AW29 Mats Sundin 15.00 30.00
AW30 Alexander Ovechkin 15.00 40.00

2006-07 Upper Deck Award Winners

COMPLETE SET (7) 8.00 20.00
STATED ODDS 1:24 .75 2.00
AW1 Joe Thornton 1.50 4.00
AW2 Miikka Kiprusoff 1.25 3.00
AW3 Nicklas Lidstrom .75 2.00
AW4 Alexander Ovechkin 2.50 6.00
AW5 Jaromir Jagr 1.50 4.00
AW6 Rod Brind'Amour .75 2.00
AW7 Cam Ward .75 2.00

2006-07 Upper Deck Century Marks

COMPLETE SET (7) 10.00 25.00
STATED ODDS 1:24 SER. 2 PACKS
CM1 Joe Thornton 1.25 3.00
CM2 Alexander Ovechkin 2.50 6.00
CM3 Dany Heatley 1.00 2.50
CM4 Jaromir Jagr 1.25 3.00
CM5 Sidney Crosby 5.00 12.00
CM6 Eric Staal .75 2.00
CM7 Daniel Alfredsson .60 1.50

2006-07 Upper Deck Diary of a Phenom

COMPLETE SET (25) 20.00 50.00
COMMON MALKIN 1.25 3.00
ONE PER SER. 2 FAT PACK
DP1 Evgeni Malkin 1.25 3.00
DP2 Evgeni Malkin 1.25 3.00
DP3 Evgeni Malkin 1.25 3.00
DP4 Evgeni Malkin 1.25 3.00
DP5 Evgeni Malkin 1.25 3.00
DP6 Evgeni Malkin 1.25 3.00
DP7 Evgeni Malkin 1.25 3.00
DP8 Evgeni Malkin 1.25 3.00
DP9 Evgeni Malkin 1.25 3.00
DP10 Evgeni Malkin 1.25 3.00
DP11 Evgeni Malkin 1.25 3.00
DP12 Evgeni Malkin 1.25 3.00
DP13 Evgeni Malkin 1.25 3.00
DP14 Evgeni Malkin 1.25 3.00
DP15 Evgeni Malkin 1.25 3.00
DP16 Evgeni Malkin 1.25 3.00
DP17 Evgeni Malkin 1.25 3.00
DP18 Evgeni Malkin 1.25 3.00
DP19 Evgeni Malkin 1.25 3.00
DP20 Evgeni Malkin 1.25 3.00
DP21 Evgeni Malkin 1.25 3.00
DP22 Evgeni Malkin 1.25 3.00
DP23 Evgeni Malkin 1.25 3.00
DP24 Evgeni Malkin 1.25 3.00
DP25 Evgeni Malkin 1.25 3.00

2006-07 Upper Deck Game Dated Moments

STATED ODDS 1:288
GD1 Sidney Crosby 40.00 80.00
GD2 Alexander Ovechkin 20.00 50.00
GD3 Luc Robitaille 10.00 25.00
GD4 Dion Phaneuf 15.00 40.00
GD5 Miikka Kiprusoff 12.00 30.00
GD6 Jaromir Jagr 15.00 40.00
GD7 Jonathan Cheechoo 10.00 25.00
GD8 Martin Brodeur 20.00 50.00
GD9 Ilya Bryzgalov 8.00 20.00
GD10 Joffrey Lupul 8.00 20.00
GD11 Ryan Miller 12.00 30.00
GD12 Cam Ward 10.00 25.00
GD13 Teemu Selanne 12.00 30.00
GD14 Pierre Turgeon 8.00 20.00
GD15 Joe Thornton 15.00 40.00
GD16 Brian Leetch 12.00 30.00
GD17 Henrik Lundqvist 15.00 40.00
GD18 Alexander Ovechkin 20.00 50.00
GD19 Sidney Crosby 40.00 80.00
GD20 Ilya Kovalchuk 15.00 40.00
GD21 Sidney Crosby 40.00 80.00
GD22 Alexander Ovechkin 20.00 50.00
GD23 Joe Thornton 15.00 40.00
GD24 Fernando Pisani 8.00 20.00
GD25 Ryan Smyth 10.00 25.00
GD26 Rod Brind'Amour 12.00 30.00
GD27 Shawn Horcoff 8.00 20.00
GD28 Jose Theodore 12.00 30.00
GD29 Patrick Marleau 10.00 25.00
GD30 Daniel Briere 10.00 25.00
GD31 Chris Drury 10.00 25.00
GD32 Cam Ward 10.00 25.00
GD33 Martin Havlat 8.00 20.00
GD34 Michael Ryder 10.00 25.00
GD35 Martin Brodeur 20.00 50.00
GD36 R.J. Umberger 10.00 25.00
GD37 Jarome Iginla 15.00 40.00
GD38 Marian Gaborik 15.00 40.00
GD39 Marek Svatos 8.00 20.00
GD40 Joe Sakic 15.00 40.00
GD41 Cristobal Huet 15.00 40.00
GD42 Patrice Bergeron 10.00 25.00

2006-07 Upper Deck Game Jerseys

COMMON CARD 4.00 10.00
STATED ODDS 1:12
JAA Arron Asham 4.00 10.00
JAF Alexander Frolov 4.00 10.00
JAH Ales Hemsky 4.00 10.00
JAK Alex Kovalev 4.00 10.00
JAL Jason Allison 4.00 10.00
JAM Andrej Meszaros 4.00 10.00
JAO Alexander Ovechkin SP 25.00 60.00
JAT Alex Tanguay 6.00 15.00
JAY Alexei Yashin 4.00 10.00
JBA Barret Jackman 4.00 10.00
JBB Brad Boyes 4.00 10.00
JBE Patrice Bergeron 6.00 15.00
JBG Bill Guerin 4.00 10.00
JBI Martin Biron 5.00 12.00
JBL Rob Blake 5.00 12.00
JBM Mark Bell 4.00 10.00
JBR Brian Rolston 4.00 10.00
JBS Brad Stuart 4.00 10.00
JBT Barry Tallackson 4.00 10.00
JBU Peter Budaj 5.00 12.00
JCC Chris Chelios 5.00 12.00
JCD Chris Drury 4.00 10.00
JCJ Curtis Joseph 6,00 15.00
JCO Chris Osgood 5.00 12.00
JCP Corey Perry 5.00 12.00
JCS Curtis Sanford 5.00 12.00
JDA Daniel Alfredsson 5.00 12.00
JDE Pavol Demitra 4.00 10.00
JDK Duncan Keith 4.00 10.00
JDP Daniel Paille 4.00 10.00
JDW Doug Weight 4.00 10.00
JEB Ed Belfour 6.00 15.00
JEJ Ed Jovanovski 4.00 10.00
JEL Eric Lindros 6.00 15.00
JGA Simon Gagne 5.00 12.00
JGL Georges Laraque 4.00 10.00
JHA Martin Havlat 5.00 12.00
JHE Milan Hejduk 5.00 12.00
JHO Marcel Hossa 4.00 10.00
JIK Ilya Kovalchuk SP 20.00 50.00
JJA Jason Arnott 4.00 10.00
JJB Jay Bouwmeester 4.00 10.00
JJC Jonathan Cheechoo 5.00 12.00
JJF Jeff Friesen 4.00 10.00
JJG Jean-Sebastien Giguere 5.00 12.00
JJI Jarome Iginla 8.00 20.00
JJJ Jaromir Jagr 8.00 20.00
JJL Joffrey Lupul 4.00 10.00
JJN Joe Nieuwendyk 5.00 12.00
JJO Jordan Leopold 4.00 10.00
JJS Jason Spezza 6.00 15.00
JJT Joe Thornton 8.00 20.00
JJW Jason Williams 4.00 10.00
JKD Kris Draper 4.00 10.00
JKP Keith Primeau 4.00 10.00
JKS Andrei Kostitsyn 4.00 10.00
JKT Keith Tkachuk 5.00 12.00
JLA Andrew Ladd 4.00 10.00
JLE Jere Lehtinen 4.00 10.00
JLU Jamie Lundmark 4.00 10.00
JLX Mario Lemieux SP 20.00 50.00
JMB Martin Brodeur 10.00 25.00
JMC Mike Comrie 4.00 10.00
JME Martin Erat 4.00 10.00
JMG Marian Gaborik 8.00 20.00
JMH Marian Hossa 6.00 15.00
JMI Mike Komisarek 4.00 10.00
JMK Miikka Kiprusoff 8.00 20.00
JML Manny Legace 4.00 10.00
JMM Mike Modano 8.00 20.00
JMN Markus Naslund 6.00 15.00
JMO Brendan Morrison 4.00 10.00
JMP Michael Peca 4.00 10.00
JMR Mark Recchi 4.00 10.00
JMS Marc Savard 4.00 10.00
JNK Nikolai Khabibulin 5.00 12.00
JPB Peter Bondra 5.00 12.00
JPD Pavel Datsyuk 5.00 12.00
JPF Peter Forsberg 8.00 20.00
JPP Petr Prucha 4.00 10.00
JRB Rod Brind'Amour 5.00 12.00
JRF Ruslan Fedotenko 4.00 10.00
JRH Ryan Hollweg 4.00 10.00
JRI Brad Richards 6.00 15.00
JRM Ryan Miller 6.00 15.00
JRU R.J. Umberger 4.00 10.00
JSC Sidney Crosby SP 75.00 200.00
JSG Scott Gomez 4.00 10.00
JSH Brendan Shanahan 6.00 15.00
JSM Matt Stajan 4.00 10.00
JSN Scott Niedermayer 4.00 10.00
JSS Sergei Samsonov 5.00 12.00
JST Steve Sullivan 4.00 10.00
JSU Scottie Upshall 4.00 10.00
JSW Stephen Weiss 4.00 10.00
JTC Ty Conklin 5.00 12.00
JTL Trevor Linden 6.00 15.00
JTP Tom Poti 4.00 10.00
JVL Vincent Lecavalier SP 20.00 50.00
JWR Wade Redden 4.00 10.00
J2AP Alexander Perezhogin 4.00 10.00
J2AR Andrew Raycroft 6.00 15.00
J2AS Alexander Steen 4.00 10.00
J2BB Brandon Bochenski 4.00 10.00
J2BC Bobby Clarke 5.00 12.00
J2BG Brian Gionta 4.00 10.00
J2BM Brenden Morrow 4.00 10.00
J2BP Brad Park 4.00 10.00
J2BR Bryan McCabe 4.00 10.00
J2BW Brendan Witt 4.00 10.00
J2CA Mike Cammalleri 4.00 10.00
J2CH Cristobal Huet 5.00 12.00
J2CK Chuck Kobasew 4.00 10.00
J2CN Cam Neely 6.00 15.00
J2CP Chris Pronger 4.00 10.00
J2CW Cam Ward 4.00 10.00
J2DB Daniel Briere 4.00 10.00
J2DC Dan Cloutier 4.00 10.00
J2DH Dominik Hasek 8.00 20.00
J2DP Dion Phaneuf 6.00 15.00
J2DR Dwayne Roloson 5.00 12.00
J2DS Daniel Sedin 4.00 10.00
J2DT Darcy Tucker 4.00 10.00
J2DU Ron Duguay 4.00 10.00
J2DW Dave Williams 6.00 15.00
J2EC Erik Cole 4.00 10.00
J2ES Eric Staal 6.00 15.00
J2GM Glen Murray 4.00 10.00
J2GR Gary Roberts 4.00 10.00
J2HE Dany Heatley 5.00 12.00
J2HL Henrik Lundqvist 5.00 12.00
J2HS Henrik Sedin 4.00 10.00
J2HZ Henrik Zetterberg 6.00 15.00
J2JB Jason Bacashihua 4.00 10.00
J2JC Jeff Carter 6.00 15.00
J2JJ Jussi Jokinen 4.00 10.00
J2JK Jakub Klepis 4.00 10.00
J2JP Joni Pitkanen 4.00 10.00
J2JR Jeremy Roenick 5.00 12.00
J2JS Joe Sakic 10.00 25.00
J2JT Jose Theodore 6.00 15.00
J2JW Justin Williams 4.00 10.00
J2KB Kevin Bieksa 4.00 10.00
J2KC Kyle Calder 4.00 10.00
J2KL Kari Lehtonen 6.00 15.00
J2KM Kirk Muller 4.00 10.00
J2KO Saku Koivu 6.00 15.00
J2LA Lanny McDonald 5.00 12.00
J2LM Larry Murphy 4.00 10.00
J2LX Mario Lemieux 15.00 40.00
J2MA Martin St. Louis 5.00 12.00
J2MC Mike Commodore 4.00 10.00
J2MF Manny Fernandez 5.00 12.00
J2MG Mike Grier 4.00 10.00
J2MH Michal Handzus 4.00 10.00
J2MJ Milan Jurcina 4.00 10.00
J2MP Mark Parrish 4.00 10.00
J2MR Michael Ryder 5.00 12.00
J2MS Marek Svatos 4.00 10.00
J2MT Marty Turco 5.00 12.00
J2MY Mike York 4.00 10.00
J2NH Nathan Horton 4.00 10.00
J2NL Nicklas Lidstrom 5.00 12.00
J2OJ Olli Jokinen 4.00 10.00
J2OK Olaf Kolzig 5.00 12.00
J2PE Patrik Elias/15 8.00 20.00
J2PK Paul Kariya 5.00 12.00
J2PM Patrick Marleau 5.00 12.00
J2PR Bob Probert 5.00 12.00
J2PS Peter Stastny 4.00 10.00
J2RB Ray Bourque 6.00 15.00
J2RD Rick DiPietro 5.00 12.00
J2RE Ron Ellis 4.00 10.00
J2RI Mike Ribeiro 4.00 10.00
J2RK Ryan Kesler 4.00 10.00
J2RL Roberto Luongo 15.00
J2RN Rick Nash/15 8.00 20.00
J2RO Patrick Roy 15.00 40.00
J2RS Ryan Smyth 5.00 12.00
J2SA Miroslav Satan 4.00 10.00
J2SB Steve Bernier 4.00 10.00
J2SC Stanislav Chistov 4.00 10.00
J2SD Shane Doan 4.00 10.00
J2SF Sergei Federov 5.00 12.00
J2SH Jody Shelley 4.00 10.00
J2SK Steve Konowalchuk 4.00 10.00
J2SO Sandis Ozolinsh 4.00 10.00
J2SS Sergei Samsonov 4.00 10.00
J2ST Jarret Stoll 4.00 10.00
J2SU Mats Sundin 5.00 12.00
J2SZ Sergei Zubov 4.00 10.00
J2TF Tomas Fleischmann 4.00 10.00
J2TH Tomas Holmstrom 4.00 10.00
J2TS Teemu Selanne 6.00 15.00
J2TT Tim Thomas 5.00 12.00
J2TV Tomas Vokoun 12.00
J2WG Wayne Gretzky SP 50.00 125.00
J2ZC Zdeno Chara 4.00 10.00

2006-07 Upper Deck Game Patches

STATED PRINT RUN 15 SER. #'d SETS
NOT PRICED DUE TO SCARCITY
PAA Arron Asham
PAH Ales Hemsky
PAK Alex Kovalev
PAL Jason Allison
PAM Andrej Meszaros
PAO Alexander Ovechkin
PAT Alex Tanguay
PAY Alexei Yashin
PBA Barret Jackman
PBB Brad Boyes
PBE Patrice Bergeron
PBG Bill Guerin
PBI Martin Biron
PBL Rob Blake
PBM Mark Bell
PBR Brian Rolston
PBS Brad Stuart
PBT Barry Tallackson
PBU Peter Budaj
PCC Chris Chelios
PCD Chris Drury
PCJ Curtis Joseph
PCO Chris Osgood
PCP Corey Perry
PCS Curtis Sanford
PDA Daniel Alfredsson
PDE Pavol Demitra
PDK Duncan Keith
PDP Daniel Paille
PDW Doug Weight
PEB Ed Belfour
PEJ Ed Jovanovski
PEL Eric Lindros
PGA Simon Gagne
PGL Georges Laraque
PHA Martin Havlat
PHE Milan Hejduk
PHO Marcel Hossa
PIK Ilya Kovalchuk
PJA Jason Arnott
PJB Jay Bouwmeester
PJC Jonathan Cheechoo
PJF Jeff Friesen
PJG Jean-Sebastien Giguere
PJI Jarome Iginla
PJJ Jaromir Jagr
PJL Joffrey Lupul
PJN Joe Nieuwendyk
PJO Jordan Leopold
PJS Jason Spezza
PJT Joe Thornton
PJW Jason Williams
PKD Kris Draper
PKP Keith Primeau
PKS Andrei Kostitsyn
PKT Keith Tkachuk
PLA Andrew Ladd
PLE Jere Lehtinen
PLU Jamie Lundmark
PLX Mario Lemieux
PMB Martin Brodeur
PMC Mike Comrie
PME Martin Erat
PMG Marian Gaborik
PMH Marian Hossa
PMI Mike Komisarek
PMK Miikka Kiprusoff
PML Manny Legace
PMM Mike Modano
PMN Markus Naslund
PMO Brendan Morrison
PMP Michael Peca
PMR Mark Recchi
PMS Marc Savard
PNK Nikolai Khabibulin
PPB Peter Bondra
PPD Pavel Datsyuk
PPF Peter Forsberg
PPP Petr Prucha
PRB Rod Brind'Amour
PRF Ruslan Fedotenko
PRH Ryan Hollweg
PRI Brad Richards
PRM Ryan Miller
PRU R.J. Umberger
PSC Sidney Crosby
PSG Scott Gomez
PSH Brendan Shanahan
PSN Scott Niedermayer
PSS Sergei Samsonov
PST Matt Stajan
PSU Steve Sullivan
PSW Stephen Weiss
PTC Ty Conklin
PTL Trevor Linden
PTP Tom Poti
PUP Scottie Upshall
PVL Vincent Lecavalier
PWR Wade Redden

2006-07 Upper Deck Generations Duals

PRINT RUN 100 SER. #'d SETS
G2BL Martin Brodeur 30.00 80.00
Roberto Luongo
G2BP Rob Blake 12.00 30.00
Dion Phaneuf
G2BW Ed Belfour 10.00 25.00
Cam Ward
G2DH Shane Doan 8.00 20.00
Nathan Horton
G2EG Patrik Elias 10.00 25.00
Marian Gaborik
G2FD Pavel Datsyuk 12.00 30.00
Sergei Fedorov
G2FK Alexander Frolov 8.00 20.00
Alex Kovalev
G2FS Peter Forsberg 15.00 40.00
Alexander Steen
G2GB Bill Guerin 8.00 20.00
Dustin Brown
G2GC Wayne Gretzky 75.00 200.00
Sidney Crosby
G2HH Marian Hossa 8.00 20.00
Ales Hemsky
G2HS Milan Hejduk 8.00 20.00
Marek Svatos
G2IL Jarome Iginla 12.00 30.00
Joffrey Lupul
G2JK Olli Jokinen 8.00 20.00
Mikko Koivu
G2JO Jaromir Jagr 30.00 80.00
Alexander Ovechkin
G2KD Saku Koivu 12.00 30.00
Pavel Datsyuk
G2KL Miikka Kiprusoff 15.00 40.00
Kari Lehtonen
G2LP Nicklas Lidstrom 12.00 30.00
Joni Pitkanen
G2NB Scott Niedermayer 8.00 20.00
Jay Bouwmeester
G2NZ Markus Naslund 10.00 25.00
Henrik Zetterberg
G2PG Keith Primeau 10.00 25.00
Ryan Getzlaf
G2RM Wade Redden 8.00 20.00
Andrej Meszaros
G2SN Brendan Shanahan 12.00 30.00
Rick Nash
G2SS Joe Sakic 20.00 50.00
Jason Spezza
G2TS Joe Thornton 15.00 40.00
Eric Staal
G2VH Tomas Vokoun 12.00 30.00
Dominik Hasek
G2PJD Joe Sakic 20.00 50.00
Dany Heatley
G2PSH Miroslav Satan 8.00 20.00
Martin Havlat

2006-07 Upper Deck Generations Triples

PRINT RUN 25 SER. #'d SETS
NOT PRICED DUE TO SCARCITY
G3BPB Rob Blake
Dion Phaneuf
Ray Bourque
G3BTW Ed Belfour
Marty Turco
Cam Ward
G3GCL Wayne Gretzky
Sidney Crosby
Mario Lemieux
G3HSS Milan Hejduk
Miroslav Satan
Marek Svatos
G3IML Jarome Iginla
Brenden Morrow
Joffrey Lupul
G3KJK Saku Koivu
Olli Jokinen
Mikko Koivu
G3KTL Miikka Kiprusoff
Kari Lehtonen
Hannu Toivonen
G3LTS Vincent Lecavalier
Joe Thornton
Eric Staal
G3NZS Markus Naslund
Henrik Zetterberg
Alexander Steen
G3SKO Teemu Selanne
Ilya Kovalchuk
Alexander Ovechkin
G3SSC Joe Sakic
Jason Spezza
Jeff Carter

2006-07 Upper Deck Generations Patches Dual

PRINT RUN 10 SER. #'d SETS
NOT PRICED DUE TO SCARCITY
G2PBL Martin Brodeur
Roberto Luongo
G2PBP Rob Blake
Dion Phaneuf
G2PBW Ed Belfour
Cam Ward
G2PDH Shane Doan
Nathan Horton
G2PEG Patrik Elias
Marian Gaborik
G2PFD Pavel Datsyuk
Sergei Fedorov
G2PFS Peter Forsberg
Alexander Steen
G2PGB Bill Guerin
Dustin Brown
G2PGC Sidney Crosby
Wayne Gretzky
G2PHH Marian Hossa
Ales Hemsky
G2PHS Milan Hejduk
Marek Svatos
G2PIL Jarome Iginla
Joffrey Lupul
G2PJD Joe Sakic
Dany Heatley
G2PJK Olli Jokinen
Mikko Koivu
G2PJO Jaromir Jagr
Alexander Ovechkin
G2PKD Saku Koivu
Pavel Datsyuk
G2PKL Miikka Kiprusoff
Kari Lehtonen
G2PLP Nicklas Lidstrom
Joni Pitkanen
G2PNB Scott Niedermayer
Jay Bouwmeester
G2PNZ Markus Naslund
Henrik Zetterberg
G2PPG Keith Primeau
Ryan Getzlaf
G2PRM Wade Redden
Andrej Meszaros
G2PSH Miroslav Satan
Martin Havlat
G2PSN Brendan Shanahan
Rick Nash
G2PSS Joe Sakic
Jason Spezza
G2PTS Joe Thornton
Eric Staal
G2PVH Tomas Vokoun
Dominik Hasek

2006-07 Upper Deck Generations Patches Triple

PRINT RUN 5 SER. #'d SETS
NOT PRICED DUE TO SCARCITY
G3PBPB Rob Blake
Dion Phaneuf
Ray Bourque
G3PBTW Ed Belfour
Marty Turco
Cam Ward
G3PGCL Mario Lemieux
Sidney Crosby
Wayne Gretzky
G3PHSS Milan Hejduk
Miroslav Satan
Marek Svatos
G3PIML Jarome Iginla
Brenden Morrow
Joffrey Lupul
G3PKJK Saku Koivu
Olli Jokinen
Mikko Koivu
G3PKTL Miikka Kiprusoff
Kari Lehtonen
Hannu Toivonen
G3PLTS Vincent Lecavalier
Joe Thornton
Eric Staal
G3PNZS Markus Naslund
Henrik Zetterberg
Alexander Steen
G3PSKO Teemu Selanne
Ilya Kovalchuk
Alexander Ovechkin
G3PSSC Joe Sakic
Jason Spezza
Jeff Carter

2006-07 Upper Deck Goal Rush

COMPLETE SET (14) 10.00 25.00
ODDS 1:24 SER. 2 PACKS
GR1 Jonathan Cheechoo .60 1.50
GR2 Jaromir Jagr 1.00 2.50
GR3 Dany Heatley .75 2.00
GR4 Ilya Kovalchuk .75 2.00
GR5 Rick Nash .60 1.50
GR6 Marian Gaborik .75 2.00
GR7 Markus Naslund .60 1.50
GR8 Jarome Iginla .75 2.00
GR9 Alexander Ovechkin 1.50 4.00
GR10 Simon Gagne .60 1.50
GR11 Eric Staal .60 1.50
GR12 Teemu Selanne .60 1.50
GR13 Brendan Shanahan .60 1.50
GR14 Sidney Crosby 2.50 6.00

2006-07 Upper Deck Hometown Heroes

COMPLETE SET (28) 20.00 50.00
STATED ODDS 1:12
HH29 Teemu Selanne .60 1.50
HH30 Patrice Bergeron .60 1.50
HH31 Ryan Miller .60 1.50
HH32 Miikka Kiprusoff .60 1.50
HH33 Eric Staal .60 1.50
HH34 Henrik Zetterberg .60 1.50
HH35 Michael Ryder .50 1.25
HH36 Henrik Lundqvist .75 2.00
HH37 Jason Spezza .60 1.50
HH38 Simon Gagne .60 1.50
HH39 Sidney Crosby 4.00 10.00
HH40 Jonathan Cheechoo .60 1.50
HH41 Darcy Tucker .30 .75
HH42 Alexander Ovechkin 2.00 5.00
HH43 Milan Hejduk .30 .75
HH44 Patrick Marleau .50 1.25
HH45 Cristobal Huet .75 2.00
HH46 Cam Ward .60 1.50
HH47 Vincent Lecavalier .60 1.50
HH48 Kari Lehtonen .60 1.50
HH49 Nicklas Lidstrom .60 1.50
HH50 Roberto Luongo .75 2.00
HH51 Rob Blake .50 1.25
HH52 Marian Gaborik .75 2.00
HH53 Alexander Steen .50 1.25
HH54 Doug Weight .30 .75
HH55 Marc-Andre Fleury .60 1.50
HH56 Dion Phaneuf .75 2.00

2006-07 Upper Deck Oversized Wal-Mart Exclusives

251 Chris Pronger 1.00 2.50
254 Jean-Sebastien Giguere 1.00 2.50
258 Ilya Kovalchuk 1.50 4.00
265 Patrice Bergeron 1.25 3.00
279 Alex Tanguay 1.00 2.50
282 Miikka Kiprusoff 1.25 3.00
286 Rod Brind`Amour 1.00 2.50
292 Martin Havlat 1.00 2.50
299 Marek Svatos .60 1.50
309 Gilbert Brule 1.25 3.00
313 Mike Modano 1.25 3.00
318 Eric Lindros 1.25 3.00
319 Dominik Hasek 2.00 5.00
323 Henrik Zetterberg 1.25 3.00
324 Nicklas Lidstrom 1.25 3.00
325 Ryan Smyth
333 Ed Belfour 1.25 3.00
337 Todd Bertuzzi 1.00 2.50
339 Rob Blake 1.00 2.50
345 Manny Fernandez
352 Michael Ryder
359 Paul Kariya
365 Patrik Elias .60 1.50
377 Henrik Lundqvist 1.50 4.00
379 Wayne Gretzky 4.00 10.00
383 Brendan Shanahan 1.25 3.00
384 Dany Heatley 1.50 4.00
391 Simon Gagne 1.25 3.00
392 Jeff Carter 1.25 3.00
401 Jeremy Roenick 1.50 4.00
403 Owen Nolan 1.00 2.50
404 Marc-Andre Fleury 1.25 3.00
409 Mark Recchi .75 2.00
410 Patrick Marleau 1.00 2.50
415 Evgeni Nabokov 1.00 2.50
417 Doug Weight .60 1.50
422 Vincent Lecavalier 1.25 3.00
426 Brad Richards 1.00 2.50
428 Andrew Raycroft 1.00 2.50
430 Michael Peca .60 1.50
436 Roberto Luongo 1.50 4.00
442 Alexander Ovechkin 2.00 5.00

2006-07 Upper Deck Rookie Game Dated Moments

ODDS 1:288
RGD1 Ryan Shannon 6.00 15.00
RGD2 Phil Kessel 12.00 30.00
RGD3 Mark Stuart 6.00 15.00
RGD4 Yan Stastny 6.00 15.00
RGD5 Paul Stastny 15.00 40.00
RGD6 Loui Eriksson 6.00 15.00
RGD7 Tomas Kopecky 8.00 20.00
RGD8 Patrick Thoresen 8.00 20.00
RGD9 Ladislav Smid 6.00 15.00
RGD10 Marc-Antoine Pouliot 8.00 20.00
RGD11 Patrick O'Sullivan 8.00 20.00
RGD12 Anze Kopitar 20.00 50.00

RGD13 Guillaume Latendresse 20.00 50.00
RGD14 Shea Weber 8.00 20.00
RGD15 Mikko Lehtonen 6.00 15.00
RGD16 Travis Zajac 8.00 20.00
RGD17 Nigel Dawes 6.00 15.00
RGD18 Alexei Kaigorodov 6.00 15.00
RGD19 Ryan Potulny 6.00 15.00
RGD20 Joel Perrault 6.00 15.00
RGD21 Evgeni Malkin 30.00 80.00
RGD22 Jordan Staal 25.00 60.00
RGD23 Kristopher Letang 6.00 15.00
RGD24 Noah Welch 6.00 15.00
RGD25 Marc-Edouard Vlasic 6.00 15.00
RGD26 Matt Carle 8.00 20.00
RGD27 Ian White 6.00 15.00
RGD28 Ben Ondrus 6.00 15.00
RGD29 Luc Bourdon 8.00 20.00
RGD30 Eric Fehr 6.00 15.00

2006-07 Upper Deck Rookie Headliners

COMPLETE SET (30) 100.00 175.00
ONE PER SER. 2 FAT PACK
RH1 Patrick O'Sullivan 1.50 4.00
RH2 Loui Eriksson 1.25 3.00
RH3 Enver Lisin 1.25 3.00
RH4 Luc Bourdon 1.25 3.00
RH5 Noah Welch 1.25 3.00
RH6 Travis Zajac 1.50 4.00
RH7 Ladislav Smid 1.25 3.00
RH8 Ryan Potulny 1.25 3.00
RH9 Marc-Antoine Pouliot 1.25 3.00
RH10 Dave Bolland 1.25 3.00
RH11 Nigel Dawes 1.25 3.00
RH12 Marc-Edouard Vlasic 1.25 3.00
RH13 Patrick Thoresen 1.25 3.00
RH14 Matt Lashoff 1.25 3.00
RH15 Ian White 1.25 3.00
RH16 Alexei Mikhnov 1.25 3.00
RH17 Tomas Kopecky 1.25 3.00
RH18 Kristopher Letang 1.25 3.00
RH19 Michael Blunden 1.25 3.00
RH20 Brandon Prust 1.25 3.00
RH21 Evgeni Malkin SP 12.00 30.00
RH22 Phil Kessel SP 10.00 25.00
RH23 Jordan Staal SP 10.00 25.00
RH24 Guillaume Latendresse SP 12.00 30.00
RH25 Anze Kopitar SP 10.00 25.00
RH26 Matt Carle SP 2.50 6.00
RH27 Paul Stastny SP 6.00 15.00
RH28 Alexander Radulov SP 12.00 30.00
RH29 Dustin Boyd SP 6.00 15.00
RH30 Drew Stafford SP 5.00 12.00

2006-07 Upper Deck Rookie Materials

STATED ODDS 1:24
RMBB Brendan Bell 2.00 5.00
RMBO Ben Ondrus 2.00 5.00
RMBT Billy Thompson 2.00 5.00
RMCG Carsen Germyn 2.00 5.00
RMDB Dustin Byfuglien 2.00 5.00
RMDK D.J. King 2.00 5.00
RMEF Eric Fehr 3.00 8.00
RMEM Evgeni Malkin 12.00 30.00
RMFN Filip Novak 2.00 5.00
RMGL Guillaume Latendresse 5.00 12.00
RMIW Ian White 2.00 5.00
RMJI Jarkko Immonen 2.00 5.00
RMJS Jordan Staal 12.00 30.00
RMJW Jeremy Williams 2.00 5.00
RMKL Kristopher Letang 3.00 8.00
RMKO Anze Kopitar 5.00 12.00
RMKP Konstantin Pushkaryov 2.00 5.00
RMKY Keith Yandle 2.00 5.00
RMLB Luc Bourdon 3.00 8.00
RMLE Loui Eriksson 2.00 5.00
RMLS Ladislav Smid 2.00 5.00
RMMC Matt Carle 2.50 6.00
RMMP MarcAntoine Pouliot 2.50 6.00
RMMS Mark Stuart 2.00 5.00
RMMV MarcEdouard Vlasic 2.00 5.00
RMNB Niklas Backstrom 3.00 8.00
RMND Nigel Dawes 2.00 5.00
RMNO Fredrik Norrena 3.00 8.00
RMNW Noah Welch 2.00 5.00
RMPK Phil Kessel 4.00 10.00
RMPO Patrick O'Sullivan 2.00 5.00
RMPS Paul Stastny 5.00 12.00
RMPT Patrick Thoresen 3.00 8.00
RMRO Roman Polak 2.00 5.00
RMRP Ryan Potulny 3.00 8.00
RMRS Ryan Shannon 2.00 5.00
RMSO Shane O'Brien 2.00 5.00
RMSW Shea Weber 2.50 6.00
RMTK Tomas Kopecky 2.50 6.00
RMTZ Travis Zajac 3.00 8.00
RMYS Yan Stastny 2.00 5.00

2006-07 Upper Deck Rookie Materials Patches

PRINT RUN 15 #'d SETS
NOT PRICED DUE TO SCARCITY
RMBB Brendan Bell
RMBO Ben Ondrus
RMBT Billy Thompson
RMCG Carsen Germyn
RMDB Dustin Byfuglien
RMDK D.J. King
RMEF Eric Fehr
RMEM Evgeni Malkin
RMFN Filip Novak
RMGL Guillaume Latendresse
RMIW Ian White
RMJI Jarkko Immonen
RMJS Jordan Staal
RMJW Jeremy Williams
RMKL Kristopher Letang
RMKO Anze Kopitar
RMKP Konstantin Pushkaryov
RMKY Keith Yandle
RMLB Luc Bourdon
RMLE Loui Eriksson
RMLS Ladislav Smid
RMMC Matt Carle
RMMP MarcAntoine Pouliot
RMMS Mark Stuart
RMMV MarcEdouard Vlasic
RMNB Niklas Backstrom
RMND Nigel Dawes
RMNO Fredrik Norrena
RMNW Noah Welch
RMPK Phil Kessel
RMPO Patrick O'Sullivan
RMPS Paul Stastny
RMPT Patrick Thoresen
RMRO Roman Polak
RMRP Ryan Potulny
RMRS Ryan Shannon
RMSO Shane O'Brien
RMSW Shea Weber
RMTK Tomas Kopecky
RMTZ Travis Zajac
RMYS Yan Stastny

2006-07 Upper Deck Shootout Artists

COMPLETE SET (14) 10.00 25.00
STATED ODDS 1:12
SA1 Jussi Jokinen .60 1.50
SA2 Miroslav Satan .60 1.50
SA3 Brad Richards .75 2.00
SA4 Alexander Ovechkin 3.00 8.00
SA5 Paul Kariya 1.00 2.50
SA6 Ales Hemsky .75 2.00
SA7 Mikko Koivu .75 2.00
SA8 Alexander Frolov .60 1.50
SA9 Jason Williams .60 1.50
SA10 Slava Kozlov .60 1.50
SA11 Brian Gionta .60 1.50
SA12 Vincent Lecavalier 1.00 2.50
SA13 Jaroslav Balastik .30 .75
SA14 Sergei Zubov .60 1.50

2006-07 Upper Deck Signatures

PRINT RUN 25 COPIES EXCEPT FOR SPs
RANDOM INSERTS IN SER. 2 PACKS
SAO Alexander Ovechkin SP
SAP Alexander Perezhogin 10.00 25.00
SAR Andrew Raycroft 15.00 40.00
SAT Alex Tanguay 20.00 50.00
SBB Brad Boyes 10.00 25.00
SBC Braydon Coburn 8.00 20.00
SBL Brett Lebda 10.00 25.00
SBO Jay Bouwmeester
SCP Corey Perry SP
SCS Cory Stillman 8.00 20.00
SCT Chris Thorburn 8.00 20.00
SDC Dan Cloutier 10.00 25.00
SDH Dany Heatley SP 75.00 125.00
SDL David Legwand SP
SDP Daniel Paille 10.00 25.00
SDW Doug Weight SP
SEC Erik Cole 10.00 25.00
SEL Enver Lisin 8.00 20.00
SEM Evgeni Malkin 125.00 200.00
SEN Eric Nystrom 8.00 20.00
SES Eric Staal SP
SFP Fernando Pisani 8.00 20.00
SGB Gilbert Brule 20.00 40.00
SGH Gordie Howe SP 75.00 125.00
SGL Guillaume Latendresse
SGM Glen Murray 10.00 25.00
SHL Henrik Lundqvist 30.00 80.00
SHZ Henrik Zetterberg 50.00 100.00
SJI Jarome Iginla SP
SJR Jeremy Roenick 25.00 50.00
SJS Jordan Staal 60.00 125.00
SJT Jeff Tambellini SP
SJW Justin Williams 8.00 20.00
SMB Martin Brodeur SP 125.00 200.00
SMG Marian Gaborik SP 75.00 125.00
SMM Mike Modano SP 25.00 60.00
SMN Markus Naslund 20.00 50.00
SMP Michael Peca 10.00 25.00
SMR Mike Ribeiro 8.00 20.00
SMS Martin St. Louis 15.00 40.00
SNK Nikolai Khabibulin 12.00 30.00
SPB Patrice Bergeron 15.00 40.00
SPH Dion Phaneuf 20.00 50.00
SPK Phil Kessel 25.00 60.00
SRH Ryan Hollweg 8.00 20.00
SRK Ryan Kesler 10.00 25.00
SRL Roberto Luongo 50.00 125.00
SSB Steve Bernier 12.00 30.00
SSC Sidney Crosby 200.00 300.00
SSG Simon Gagne 25.00 60.00
SSS Sergei Samsonov 10.00 25.00
SST Matt Stajan 15.00 40.00
STA Tyler Arnason 8.00 20.00
STV Thomas Vanek 25.00 60.00
SVL Vincent Lecavalier SP 200.00 300.00
SWG Wayne Gretzky SP
SYD Yann Danis 8.00 20.00
SZP Zach Parise 25.00 60.00

2006-07 Upper Deck Signature Sensations

STATED ODDS 1:288
SSAA Aaron Asham 4.00 10.00
SSAF Alexander Frolov 8.00 20.00
SSAH Adam Hall 4.00 10.00
SSAR Andrew Raycroft 8.00 20.00
SSAS Alexander Steen 10.00 25.00
SSAT Alex Tanguay 12.00 30.00
SSBB Brad Boyes 6.00 15.00
SSBL Brian Leetch 25.00 50.00
SSBO Jay Bouwmeester 8.00 20.00
SSBR Brian Rafalski 6.00 15.00
SSBW Brad Winchester
SSCH Chris Higgins 12.00 30.00
SSCK Chris Kunitz 10.00 25.00
SSCP Chris Phillips 4.00 10.00
SSDW Doug Weight 8.00 20.00
SSEJ Ed Jovanovski 6.00 15.00
SSEN Evgeni Nabokov 12.00 30.00
SSFL Marc-Andre Fleury 25.00 60.00
SSFS Fredrik Sjostrom 4.00 10.00
SSGM Glen Murray 6.00 15.00
SSHA Michal Handzus
SSHE Milan Hejduk
SSHT Hannu Toivonen 10.00 25.00
SSJB Jason Blake 4.00 10.00
SSJP Joni Pitkanen 5.00 12.00
SSJR Jeremy Roenick 12.00 30.00
SSJT Jose Theodore 10.00 25.00
SSKB Keith Ballard 4.00 10.00
SSKL Kari Lehtonen 12.00 30.00
SSKP Keith Primeau 4.00 10.00
SSKT Kimmo Timonen
SSMC Mike Comrie 5.00 12.00
SSMG Marian Gaborik 20.00 50.00
SSMH Martin Havlat 10.00 25.00
SSMK Miikka Kiprusoff 25.00 50.00
SSML Mario Lemieux 100.00 150.00
SSMP Mark Parrish 4.00 10.00
SSMS Miroslav Satan 5.00 12.00
SSNK Nikolai Khabibulin 15.00 40.00
SSPB Pierre-Marc Bouchard 6.00 15.00
SSPM Patrick Marleau
SSPR Chris Pronger 8.00 20.00
SSRB Rene Bourque 4.00 10.00
SSRF Ruslan Fedotenko 4.00 10.00
SSRN Rick Nash 20.00 50.00
SSRS Ryan Smyth 10.00 25.00
SSRU R.J. Umberger 6.00 15.00
SSRW Ryan Whitney 8.00 20.00
SSSC Sidney Crosby 150.00 250.00
SSSD Shane Doan 6.00 15.00
SSSG Scott Gomez 10.00 25.00
SSSH Shawn Horcoff
SSSS Steve Sullivan 4.00 10.00
SSTA Tyler Arnason 5.00 12.00
SSTL Trevor Linden 15.00 40.00
SSVT Vesa Toskala 12.00 30.00
SSWG Wayne Gretzky SP
SSWR Wade Redden 5.00 12.00
SSWW Wojtek Wolski 6.00 15.00

2006-07 Upper Deck Statistical Leaders

COMPLETE SET (7) 10.00 25.00
STATED ODDS 1:24
SL1 Joe Thornton 2.00 5.00
SL2 Jonathan Cheechoo .75 2.00
SL3 Alexander Ovechkin 4.00 10.00
SL4 Wade Redden .75 2.00
SL5 Martin Brodeur 3.00 8.00
SL6 Miikka Kiprusoff 2.00 5.00
SL7 Sean Avery .40 1.00

2006-07 Upper Deck Zero Men

COMPLETE SET (7) 8.00 20.00
ODDS 1:24 SER. 2 PACKS
ZM1 Martin Brodeur 3.00 8.00
ZM2 Dominik Hasek 2.00 5.00
ZM3 Roberto Luongo 1.25 3.00
ZM4 Miikka Kiprusoff 1.25 3.00
ZM5 Marty Turco 1.00 2.50
ZM6 Cam Ward 1.00 2.50
ZM7 Ed Belfour 1.00 2.50

2007 Upper Deck BAP Draft Redemption Premium

TY-SC Sidney Crosby 6.00

2006 Upper Deck Rookie Showdown

RS-SCAO Sidney Crosby 4.00 10.00
Alexander Ovechkin

2003 Upper Deck All-Star Promos

Handed out in packs at the Upper Deck booth during the 2003 NHL All-Star Block Party, this 21-card set resembled the base UD set but card fronts carried a special All-Star logo and each card (except the checklists) was serial-numbered out of 500. Each pack contained 5-cards including the checklist card. Cards S1-S6 were randomly inserted into packs and carried authentic player autographs and were rumored to be limited to just 30 copies each.
COMP.SET w/o AUTOS (15) 16.00 40.00
S1 Rick Nash 80.00 200.00
S2 Stanislav Chistov 16.00 40.00
S3 Jason Spezza 20.00 70.00
S4 Alexander Frolov 12.00 20.00
S5 Jay Bouwmeester 16.00 40.00
S6 Jordan Leopold 10.00 20.00
AS1 Joe Thornton CL .40 2.00
AS2 Rick Nash 4.00 10.00
AS3 Stanislav Chistov 2.40 5.00
AS4 Chuck Kobasew 1.60 3.00
AS5 Stephen Weiss .60 2.00
AS6 Martin Brodeur CL .80 2.00
AS7 Jason Spezza 3.20 8.00
AS8 Alexander Frolov 2.00 3.00
AS9 Carlo Colaiacovo 1.20 2.00
AS10 Alexander Svitov 1.20 2.00
AS11 Nikolai Khabibulin CL .40 1.00
AS12 Henrik Zetterberg 4.00 10.00
AS13 Jordan Leopold .80 2.00
AS14 Jay Bouwmeester 2.40 5.00
AS15 P-M Bouchard 2.40 5.00

2004 Upper Deck All-Star Promos

Available only via wrapper redemption at the Upper Deck booth during the 2004 NHL All-Star Fanfest, this 15-card set featured perennial all-stars as well as popular prospects. Each card was serial-numbered out of 750.
COMPLETE SET (15)
BB Brent Burns 4.00 15.00
CB Christoph Brandner 4.00 10.00
ES Eric Staal 6.00 15.00
FS Fredrik Sjostrom 4.00 10.00
GH Gordie Howe 5.00 15.00
JP Joni Pitkanen 4.00 10.00
JS Jason Spezza 5.00 15.00
JT Joe Thornton 6.00 15.00
MF Marc-Andre Fleury 12.50 30.00
MG Marian Gaborik 6.00 15.00
NH Nathan Horton 6.00 12.00
NZ Nikolai Zherdev 8.00 20.00
PB Patrice Bergeron 10.00 30.00
PR Patrick Roy 8.00 30.00
TO Jordin Tootoo 6.00 15.00

2007 Upper Deck All-Star Game Redemptions

Single cards were available as wrapper redemptions over the course of the three-day card show held in conjunction with the 2007 NHL All-Star Game in Dallas.
AS1 Martin Brodeur 4.00 10.00
AS2 Phil Kessel 2.00 5.00
AS3 Eric Lindros 1.50 4.00
AS4 Joe Sakic 3.00 8.00
AS5 Jordan Staal 4.00 10.00
AS6 Marty Turco 1.25 3.00
AS7 Sidney Crosby 8.00 20.00
AS8 Alexander Radulov 2.00 5.00
AS9 Brenden Morrow 1.25 3.00
AS10 Alexander Ovechkin 4.00 10.00
AS11 Evgeni Malkin 6.00 15.00
AS12 Mike Modano 2.00 5.00

2000 Upper Deck AS Sittler

This card was given away at the 2000 All-Star Fan Fest. The card features Darryl Sittler.
1 Darryl Sittler 1.20 3.00

2001 Upper Deck Avalanche NHL All-Star Game

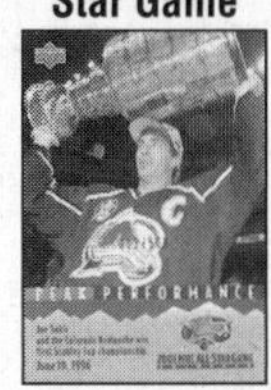

This 15-card set was produced by Upper Deck as a wrapper redemption for the 2001 All-Star Fan Fest and feature members of the host Avalanche. The cards were distributed in three-card packs, with each card serial numbered out of 500. A Wayne Gretzky e-card was given away also, these cards carried an interactive number that could be entered at the Upper Deck website to see if it "evolved" into a memorabilia winner. The e-card is listed, but not considered part of the complete set.
COMPLETE SET (15) 50.00 125.00
CA1 Ray Bourque 6.00 15.00
CA2 Adam Foote .80 2.00
CA3 Adam Deadmarsh .80 2.00
CA4 Alex Tanguay 4.00 10.00
CA5 Aaron Miller .40 1.00
CA6 Stephane Yelle .40 1.00
HH1 David Aebischer 8.00 20.00
Patrick Roy
HH2 Milan Hejduk 6.00 15.00
Peter Forsberg
HH3 Joe Sakic 6.00 15.00
Raymond Bourque
PP1 Patrick Roy 8.00 20.00
PP2 Joe Sakic 4.80 12.00
PP3 Peter Forsberg 6.00 15.00
PP4 Chris Drury 4.00 10.00
PP5 Milan Hejduk 4.00 10.00
PP6 David Aebischer 4.00 10.00
WG Wayne Gretzky e-Card 2.00 5.00

1999-00 Upper Deck Century Legends

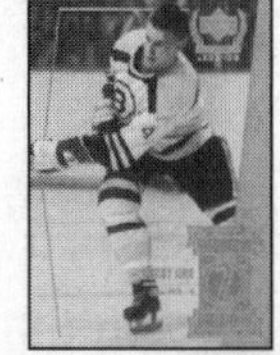

Released as an 89-card base set, Upper Deck Century Legends commemorates the NHL's timeless players spanning to the beginning of the century. Base cards feature action photography, a right side silver foil border and gold foil highlights. Card number 23 was not released. Century Legends was packaged in 24-pack boxes with 12 cards per pack and carried a suggested retail price of $4.99.
COMPLETE SET (89) 30.00 60.00
1 Wayne Gretzky 1.25 3.00
2 Bobby Orr 1.00 2.50
3 Gordie Howe .75 2.00
4 Mario Lemieux 1.00 2.50
5 Maurice Richard .50 1.25
6 Jean Beliveau .30 .75
7 Doug Harvey .20 .50
8 Bobby Hull .40 1.00
9 Jacques Plante .40 1.00
10 Eddie Shore .20 .50
11 Guy Lafleur .30 .75
12 Mark Messier .20 .50
13 Terry Sawchuk .40 1.00
14 Howie Morenz .15 .40
15 Denis Potvin .15 .40
16 Ray Bourque .30 .75
17 Glenn Hall .25 .60
18 Stan Mikita .30 .75
19 Phil Esposito .40 1.00
20 Mike Bossy .25 .60
21 Ted Lindsay .20 .50
22 Red Kelly .15 .40
23 Does not exist
24 Bobby Clarke .25 .60
25 Larry Robinson .20 .50
26 Milt Schmidt .15 .40
27 Frank Mahovlich .20 .50
28 Henri Richard .15 .40
29 Paul Coffey .20 .50
30 Bryan Trottier .15 .40
31 Dickie Moore .15 .40
32 Newsy Lalonde .15 .40
33 Syl Apps .15 .40
34 Bill Durnan .15 .40
35 Patrick Roy 1.00 2.50
36 Peter Stastny .20 .50
37 Jaromir Jagr .30 .75
38 Charlie Conacher .15 .40
39 Marcel Dionne .20 .50
40 Tim Horton .20 .50
41 Joe Malone .15 .40
42 Chris Chelios .20 .50
43 Bernie Geoffrion .30 .75
44 Dit Clapper .15 .40
45 Bill Cook .15 .40
46 Johnny Bucyk .15 .40
47 Serge Savard .20 .50
48 Jari Kurri .20 .50
49 Max Bentley .15 .40
50 Gilbert Perreault .15 .40
51 Dominik Hasek .40 1.00
52 Jaromir Jagr .30 .75
53 Peter Forsberg .50 1.25
54 Paul Kariya .20 .50
55 Patrick Roy 1.00 2.50
56 Steve Yzerman 1.00 2.50
57 Ray Bourque .30 .75
58 Pavel Bure .20 .50
59 Teemu Selanne .20 .50
60 Mike Modano .30 .75
61 Eric Lindros .20 .50
62 Brett Hull .25 .60
63 Martin Brodeur .50 1.25
64 Keith Tkachuk .20 .50
65 Joe Sakic .40 1.00
66 Mats Sundin .20 .50
67 John LeClair .20 .50
68 Alexei Yashin .02 .10
69 Peter Bondra .15 .40
70 Brendan Shanahan .20 .50
71 Sergei Samsonov .15 .40
72 Vincent Lecavalier .20 .50
73 Marian Hossa .20 .50
74 Chris Drury .15 .40
75 Milan Hejduk .20 .50
76 Paul Mara .02 .10
77 David Legwand .15 .40
78 Joe Thornton .30 .75
79 Pavel Rosa .02 .10
80 Patrik Elias .15 .40
81 Wayne Gretzky .75 2.00
82 Wayne Gretzky .75 2.00
83 Wayne Gretzky .75 2.00
84 Wayne Gretzky .75 2.00
85 Wayne Gretzky .75 2.00
86 Wayne Gretzky .75 2.00
87 Wayne Gretzky .75 2.00
88 Wayne Gretzky .75 2.00
89 Wayne Gretzky .75 2.00
90 Wayne Gretzky .75 2.00

1999-00 Upper Deck Century Legends Century Collection

Randomly inserted in packs, this 90-card die cut and holographic foil enhanced set parallels the base Century Legends set. Each card is sequentially numbered to 100.
*STARS: 25X TO 50X BASIC CARDS

1999-00 Upper Deck Century Legends All Century Team

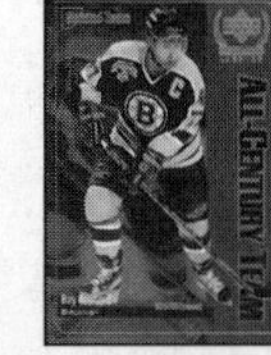

Randomly inserted in packs at the rate of 1:11, this 12-card set picks an All-Century first and second team.
COMPLETE SET (12) 40.00 80.00
AC1 Wayne Gretzky 6.00 15.00
AC2 Gordie Howe 4.00 10.00
AC3 Bobby Hull 2.50 6.00
AC4 Bobby Orr 5.00 12.00
AC5 Doug Harvey 2.00 5.00
AC6 Jacques Plante 2.00 5.00
AC7 Mario Lemieux 5.00 12.00
AC8 Maurice Richard 3.00 8.00
AC9 Ted Lindsay 2.00 5.00
AC10 Eddie Shore 2.00 5.00
AC11 Ray Bourque 4.00 10.00
AC12 Terry Sawchuk 2.50 6.00

1999-00 Upper Deck Century Legends Century Artifacts

Randomly inserted in packs, these 10 cards were issued as redemptions. Each card was redeemable for a one of one card that featured either a game used stick, jersey, autograph, cut autograph, or a Wayne Gretzky lithograph. The 1/1 cards and the lithograph are not priced due to scarcity.
C1 W.Gretzky Stick/1
C2 W.Gretzky Oilers Jersey/1
C3 W.Gretzky Rngrs Jersey/1
C4 Auto'd Card Collection/1
C5 Auto'd Puck Collection/1
C6 B.Orr Bruins Jersey/1
C7 G.Howe Wings Jersey/1
C8 W.Gretzky Litho/1
C9 J.Plante Cut Piece/1
C10 T.Sawchuk Cut Piece/1

1999-00 Upper Deck Century Legends Epic Signatures

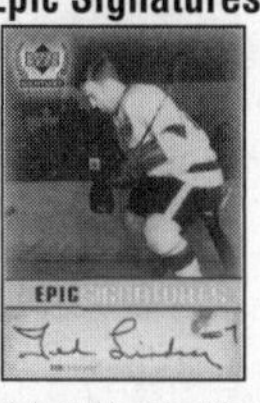

Randomly inserted in packs at the rate of 1:23, this 23-card set features authentic autographs of hockey's all time greats. The Gretzky card originally checklisted was never issued.
BC Bobby Clarke 12.50 30.00
BH Bobby Hull 20.00 50.00
BO Bobby Orr 150.00 300.00
BP Brad Park 6.00 15.00
FM Frank Mahovlich 6.00 15.00
GC Gerry Cheevers 10.00 25.00
GH Gordie Howe 75.00 150.00
JB John Bucyk 6.00 15.00
LR Larry Robinson 25.00 60.00
MB Mike Bossy 10.00 30.00
MD Marcel Dionne 8.00 20.00
ML Mario Lemieux 75.00 200.00
MR Maurice Richard 75.00 175.00
PB Pavel Bure 8.00 20.00
PE Phil Esposito 25.00 60.00
RB Ray Bourque 40.00 80.00
SM Stan Mikita 10.00 25.00
SS Sergei Samsonov 8.00 20.00
TE Tony Esposito 8.00 20.00
TL Ted Lindsay 6.00 15.00
BRH Brett Hull 15.00 40.00
JEB Jean Beliveau 12.00 30.00

1999-00 Upper Deck Century Legends Epic Signatures 100

Randomly seeded in packs, this 23-card set parallels the regular Epic Signature set. Each card is sequentially numbered out of 100.
*STARS: 1.25X TO 2.5X HI COLUMN
BO Bobby Orr 150.00 400.00
GH Gordie Howe 125.00 250.00
ML Mario Lemieux 150.00 300.00
WG Wayne Gretzky 250.00 600.00

1999-00 Upper Deck Century Legends Essence of the Game

Randomly inserted in packs at the rate of 1:11, this 8-card set couples a player of the past with a present player. The "past" side of the card is in black and white, and the "present" side of the card is in color.
COMPLETE SET (8) 25.00 50.00
E1 Wayne Gretzky 5.00 12.00
Paul Kariya
E2 Bobby Orr 5.00 12.00
Ray Bourque
E3 Mario Lemieux 4.00 10.00
Jaromir Jagr
E4 Gordie Howe 2.50 6.00
Eric Lindros
E5 Jacques Plante 5.00 12.00
Patrick Roy
E6 Maurice Richard 2.50 6.00
Pavel Bure
E7 Bobby Hull 3.00 8.00
Brett Hull
E8 Ted Lindsay 2.50 6.00
Keith Tkachuk

1999-00 Upper Deck Century Legends Greatest Moments

Randomly inserted in packs at the rate of 1:23, this 10-card set pays tribute to the career of Wayne Gretzky.
COMPLETE SET (10) 60.00 125.00
COMMON GRETZKY (GM1-GM10) 6.00 15.00

1999-00 Upper Deck Century Legends Jerseys of the Century

Randomly inserted in packs at the rate of 1:475, this 6-card set features swatches of game used jersey coupled with a player photo. Bobby Clark and Mario Lemieux cards are signed and numbered out of 25. Note: set price does not include JCA1 and JCA2.
JC1 Bobby Clarke 30.00 80.00
JC2 Mike Bossy 30.00 80.00
JC3 Larry Robinson 30.00 80.00
JC4 Ray Bourque 30.00 80.00
JC5 Mario Lemieux 75.00 200.00
JC6 Wayne Gretzky 125.00 300.00
JCA1 Bobby Clarke AU/25 150.00 400.00
JCA2 Mario Lemieux AU/25 500.00 1000.00

2002-03 Upper Deck Classic Portraits

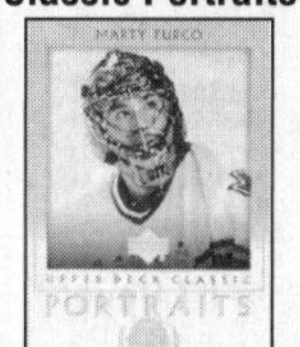

Released in February, this 138-card set consisted of 100 veteran base cards (#1-100), and 38 shortprinted rookie cards (#101-138). Cards 131-138 were only available in UD Rookie Update packs. Rookies were serial-numbered to 1500 copies each.
COMPLETE SET (138) 125.00 250.00
COMP.SET w/o SP's (100) 25.00 50.00
1 J-S Giguere .30 .75
2 Paul Kariya .40 1.00
3 Mike LeClerc .10 .30
4 Dany Heatley .50 1.25
5 Ilya Kovalchuk .50 1.25
6 Milan Hnilicka .30 .75
7 Joe Thornton .60 1.50
8 Brian Rolston .10 .30
9 Sergei Samsonov .30 .75
10 Miroslav Satan .30 .75
11 Martin Biron .30 .75
12 Tim Connolly .30 .75
13 Roman Turek .30 .75
14 Jarome Iginla .50 1.25
15 Craig Conroy .10 .30
16 Arturs Irbe .30 .75
17 Ron Francis .30 .75
18 Rod Brind'Amour .30 .75
19 Jeff O'Neill .10 .30
20 Alexei Zhamnov .10 .30
21 Eric Daze .30 .75
22 Jocelyn Thibault .30 .75
23 Rob Blake .30 .75
24 Patrick Roy 2.00 5.00
25 Joe Sakic .75 2.00
26 Peter Forsberg 1.00 2.50
27 Chris Drury .30 .75
28 Marc Denis .30 .75
29 Espen Knutsen .10 .30
30 Rostislav Klesla .10 .30
31 Marty Turco .30 .75
32 Brenden Morrow .30 .75
33 Mike Modano .60 1.50
34 Steve Yzerman 2.00 5.00
35 Nicklas Lidstrom .40 1.00
36 Sergei Fedorov .60 1.50

37 Brendan Shanahan .40 1.00
38 Curtis Joseph .40 1.00
39 Mike Comrie .30 .75
40 Tommy Salo .30 .75
41 Ryan Smyth .10 .30
42 Roberto Luongo .50 1.25
43 Viktor Kozlov .10 .30
44 Kristian Huselius .10 .30
45 Zigmund Palffy .30 .75
46 Felix Potvin .40 1.00
47 Jason Allison .10 .30
48 Manny Fernandez .30 .75
49 Andrew Brunette .10 .30
50 Marian Gaborik .75 2.00
51 Saku Koivu .40 1.00
52 Yanic Perreault .10 .30
53 Jose Theodore .50 1.25
54 Denis Arkhipov .10 .30
55 Scott Hartnell .10 .30
56 Mike Dunham .30 .75
57 Martin Brodeur 1.00 2.50
58 Patrik Elias .30 .75
59 Joe Nieuwendyk .30 .75
60 Scott Niedermayer .10 .30
61 Alexei Yashin .10 .30
62 Michael Peca .10 .30
63 Chris Osgood .30 .75
64 Eric Lindros .40 1.00
65 Pavel Bure .40 1.00
66 Brian Leetch .30 .75
67 Dan Blackburn .30 .75
68 Martin Havlat .30 .75
69 Marian Hossa .40 1.00
70 Daniel Alfredsson .30 .75
71 John LeClair .40 1.00
72 Jeremy Roenick .40 1.00
73 Keith Primeau .10 .30
74 Simon Gagne .40 1.00
75 Tony Amonte .30 .75
76 Sean Burke .30 .75
77 Daniel Briere .10 .30
78 Alexei Kovalev .30 .75
79 Johan Hedberg .30 .75
80 Mario Lemieux 2.50 6.00
81 Patrick Marleau .30 .75
82 Teemu Selanne .40 1.00
83 Evgeni Nabokov .30 .75
84 Owen Nolan .30 .75
85 Chris Pronger .30 .75
86 Doug Weight .30 .75
87 Keith Tkachuk .40 1.00
88 Brad Richards .30 .75
89 Nikolai Khabibulin .40 1.00
90 Vincent Lecavalier .40 1.00
91 Mats Sundin .40 1.00
92 Gary Roberts .10 .30
93 Ed Belfour .40 1.00
94 Alexander Mogilny .30 .75
95 Todd Bertuzzi .40 1.00
96 Brendan Morrison .30 .75
97 Markus Naslund .40 1.00
98 Jaromir Jagr .60 1.50
99 Peter Bondra .30 .75
100 Olaf Kolzig .30 .75
101 Alexei Smirnov RC 2.00 5.00
102 Stanislav Chistov RC 2.00 5.00
103 Martin Gerber RC 3.00 8.00
104 Kurt Sauer RC 2.00 5.00
105 Chuck Kobasew RC 2.00 5.00
106 Micki Dupont RC 2.00 5.00
107 Shawn Thornton RC 2.00 5.00
108 Jeff Paul RC 2.00 5.00
109 Rick Nash RC 6.00 15.00
110 Lasse Pirjeta RC 2.00 5.00
111 Henrik Zetterberg RC 6.00 15.00
112 Dmitri Bykov RC 2.00 5.00
113 Ales Hemsky RC 4.00 10.00
114 Mike Cammalleri RC 2.00 5.00
115 Ivan Majesky RC 2.00 5.00
116 Jay Bouwmeester RC 3.00 8.00
117 Alexander Frolov RC 4.00 10.00
118 P-M Bouchard RC 4.00 10.00
119 Ron Hainsey RC 2.00 5.00
120 Adam Hall RC 2.00 5.00
121 Scottie Upshall RC 2.00 5.00
122 Anton Volchenkov RC 2.00 5.00
123 Dennis Seidenberg RC 2.00 5.00
124 Patrick Sharp RC 2.00 5.00
125 Jeff Taffe RC 2.00 5.00
126 Jason Spezza RC 6.00 15.00
127 Tom Koivisto RC 2.00 5.00
128 Alexander Svitov RC 2.00 5.00
129 Carlo Colaiacovo RC 2.00 5.00
130 Steve Eminger RC 2.00 5.00
131 Jared Aulin RC 2.00 5.00
132 Pascal LeClaire RC 3.00 8.00
133 Steve Ott RC 2.00 5.00
134 Brooks Orpik RC 2.00 5.00
135 Ari Ahonen RC 2.00 5.00
136 Mike Komisarek RC 2.00 5.00
137 Ryan Miller RC 3.00 8.00
138 Ray Emery RC 2.00 5.00

2002-03 Upper Deck Classic Portraits Etched in Time

COMPLETE SET (15) 15.00 30.00
STATED ODDS 1:12
ET1 Paul Kariya .50 1.25
ET2 Joe Sakic 1.00 2.50
ET3 Patrick Roy 2.50 6.00
ET4 Mike Modano .75 2.00
ET5 Steve Yzerman 2.50 6.00
ET6 Brendan Shanahan .75 2.00
ET7 Brett Hull .60 1.50
ET8 Mike Comrie .40 1.00
ET9 Jose Theodore .50 1.25
ET10 Martin Brodeur 1.25 3.00
ET11 Pavel Bure .60 1.50
ET12 Simon Gagne .50 1.25
ET13 Mario Lemieux 3.00 8.00
ET14 Teemu Selanne .50 1.25
ET15 Mats Sundin .50 1.25

2002-03 Upper Deck Classic Portraits Genuine Greatness

COMPLETE SET (7) 20.00 40.00
STATED ODDS 1:24
GG1 Paul Kariya
GG2 Peter Forsberg 1.50 4.00
GG3 Patrick Roy 3.00 8.00
GG4 Steve Yzerman 3.00 8.00
GG5 Wayne Gretzky 4.00 10.00
GG6 Pavel Bure 1.00 2.50
GG7 Jaromir Jagr 1.00 2.50

2002-03 Upper Deck Classic Portraits Headliners

This 12-card set featured dual jersey swatches. Cards were inserted at a rate of 1:48. A limited parallel was also created and serial-numbered out of 25.

*MULT.COLOR SWATCH: .75X TO 1.5X
*LTD: 1X TO 2.5X BASE HI
DZ Eric Daze 4.00 10.00
Alexei Zhamnov
FS Peter Forsberg 15.00 40.00
Joe Sakic
JB Jaromir Jagr 4.00 10.00
Peter Bondra
KF Paul Kariya 4.00 10.00
Jeff Friesen
LF Nicklas Lidstrom 10.00 25.00
Sergei Fedorov
LK Claude Lemieux 4.00 10.00
Krys Kolanos
LM M.Lemieux/A.Morozov 12.50 30.00
RA Patrick Roy 15.00 40.00
David Aebischer
RG Jeremy Roenick 5.00 12.00
Simon Gagne
ST Sergei Samsonov 6.00 15.00
Joe Thornton
TK Jose Theodore 12.50 30.00
Saku Koivu
YH Steve Yzerman 12.50 30.00
Dominik Hasek

2002-03 Upper Deck Classic Portraits Hockey Royalty

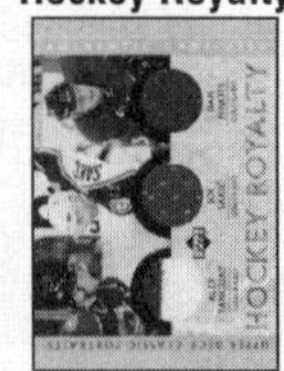

This 30-card set featured three jersey swatches per card. Each card was serial-numbered to just 90 copies. A limited parallel was also created and serial-numbered out of 25. As of press time, not all cards have been verified.

*MULT.COLOR SWATCH: .75X TO 1.5X
*LTD: 1.25X TO 3X BASE HI
BLB Sean Burke 12.50 30.00
Claude Lemieux
Daniel Briere
BPT Martin Brodeur 25.00 60.00
Felix Potvin
Jocelyn Thibault
DLH Mike Dunham 12.50 30.00
David Legwand
Scott Hartnell
DPP Adam Deadmarsh 12.50 30.00
Felix Potvin
Zigmund Palffy
DZT Eric Daze 12.50 30.00
Alexei Zhamnov
Jocelyn Thibault
GLS Gretzky/M.Lemieux/Sakic 60.00 150.00
GTD Simon Gagne 12.50 30.00
Alex Tanguay
Eric Daze
GTM Bill Guerin 20.00 50.00
Joe Thornton
Glen Murray
GWA Doug Weight 12.50 30.00
Tony Amonte
Bill Guerin
HBK Jeff Halpern 12.50 30.00
Peter Bondra
Olaf Kolzig
JHL Jaromir Jagr 12.50 30.00
Milan Hejduk
Robert Lang
KFB Sergei Fedorov 20.00 50.00
Pavel Bure
Ilya Kovalchuk
KFG Paul Kariya
Jeff Friesen
J-S Giguere EXISTS?
KGJ Steve Konowalchuk 12.50 30.00
Sergei Gonchar
Jaromir Jagr
KSI Paul Kariya 30.00 80.00
Joe Sakic
Jarome Iginla
KTK Espen Knutsen 12.50 30.00
Ron Tugnutt
Rostislav Klesla
LBL Eric Lindros 12.50 30.00
Pavel Bure
Brian Leetch
LLN M.Lemieux/Lang/Nieminen 25.00 60.00
LLT M.Lemieux/Lindros/Thornton 30.00 80.00
LRR John LeClair 20.00 50.00
Jeremy Roenick
Mark Recchi
MML Mike Modano 20.00 50.00
Brenden Morrow
Jere Lehtinen
PGF Keith Primeau 12.50 30.00
Simon Gagne
Ruslan Fedotenko
RBT Martin Brodeur 40.00 100.00
Patrick Roy
Jose Theodore
RDF Steven Reinprecht 15.00 40.00
Chris Drury
Peter Forsberg
SCA Miroslav Satan 12.50 30.00
Tim Connolly
Maxim Afinogenov
SIT Marc Savard 12.50 30.00
Jarome Iginla
Roman Turek
SLN Teemu Selanne 12.50 30.00
Jere Lehtinen
Ville Nieminen
SNL Markus Naslund 15.00 40.00
Nicklas Lidstrom
Mats Sundin
SYL Brendan Shanahan 30.00 80.00
Steve Yzerman
Nicklas Lidstrom
TSH Alex Tanguay 12.50 30.00
Joe Sakic
Dan Hinote

2002-03 Upper Deck Classic Portraits Mini-Busts

Inserted one per box, these mini-busts stood approximately 12 in. high and carried a player likeness on top of a column base. Each player had several variations including; home, away, glass and marble. Several players also had autographed versions and alternate jersey versions. Individual print runs for autographs are listed below, print runs of less than 25 are not priced due to scarcity.

1 Brendan Shanahan A 8.00 20.00
2 Brendan Shanahan G 8.00 20.00
3 Brendan Shanahan H 6.00 15.00
4 Brendan Shanahan M 6.00 15.00
5 Curtis Joseph A 8.00 20.00
6 Curtis Joseph A AU/31 40.00 100.00
7 Curtis Joseph G 8.00 20.00
8 Curtis Joseph G AU/10
9 Curtis Joseph H 6.00 15.00
10 Curtis Joseph H AU 30.00 80.00
11 Curtis Joseph M 6.00 15.00
12 Curtis Joseph M AU/25 40.00 100.00
13 Dany Heatley A 8.00 20.00
14 Dany Heatley A AU/15
15 Dany Heatley G 8.00 20.00
16 Dany Heatley G AU/10
17 Dany Heatley H 6.00 15.00
18 Dany Heatley H AU 20.00 50.00
19 Dany Heatley M 6.00 15.00
20 Dany Heatley M AU/25 30.00 80.00
21 Dominik Hasek A 8.00 20.00
22 Dominik Hasek G 8.00 20.00
23 Dominik Hasek H 6.00 15.00
24 Dominik Hasek M 6.00 15.00
25 Dominik Hasek Third 6.00 15.00
26 Gordie Howe A 20.00 50.00
27 Gordie Howe A AU/9
28 Gordie Howe G 20.00 50.00
29 Gordie Howe G AU/10
30 Gordie Howe H 15.00 40.00
31 Gordie Howe H AU SP 50.00 125.00
32 Gordie Howe M 15.00 40.00
33 Gordie Howe M AU/25 100.00 250.00
34 Gordie Howe Third 15.00 40.00
35 Gordie Howe Third AU/50 60.00 150.00
36 Ilya Kovalchuk A 8.00 20.00
37 Ilya Kovalchuk A AU/17
38 Ilya Kovalchuk G 8.00 20.00
39 Ilya Kovalchuk G AU/10
40 Ilya Kovalchuk H 6.00 15.00
41 Ilya Kovalchuk H AU 20.00 50.00
42 Ilya Kovalchuk M 6.00 15.00
43 Ilya Kovalchuk M AU/25 30.00 80.00
44 Jarome Iginla A 8.00 20.00
45 Jarome Iginla A AU/12
46 Jarome Iginla G 8.00 20.00
47 Jarome Iginla G AU/10
48 Jarome Iginla H 6.00 15.00
49 Jarome Iginla H AU 12.50 30.00
50 Jarome Iginla M 6.00 15.00
51 Jarome Iginla M AU/25 20.00 50.00
52 Jaromir Jagr A 8.00 20.00
53 Jaromir Jagr G 8.00 20.00
54 Jaromir Jagr H 6.00 15.00
55 Jaromir Jagr M 12.50 30.00
56 Jason Spezza A 8.00 20.00
57 Jason Spezza A AU/39 50.00 125.00
58 Jason Spezza G 8.00 20.00
59 Jason Spezza G AU/10
60 Jason Spezza H 6.00 15.00
61 Jason Spezza H AU 25.00 60.00
62 Jason Spezza M 10.00 25.00
63 Jason Spezza M AU/25 40.00 100.00
64 Jason Spezza Third 6.00 15.00
65 Jason Spezza Third AU/50 30.00 80.00
66 Joe Sakic A 20.00 50.00
67 Joe Sakic G 20.00 50.00
68 Joe Sakic H 12.50 30.00
69 Joe Sakic M 15.00 40.00
70 Joe Sakic Third 15.00 40.00
71 Joe Thornton A 8.00 20.00
72 Joe Thornton A AU/19
73 Joe Thornton G 8.00 20.00
74 Joe Thornton G AU/10
75 Joe Thornton H 6.00 15.00
76 Joe Thornton H AU 30.00 80.00
77 Joe Thornton M 6.00 15.00
78 Joe Thornton M AU/25 50.00 125.00
79 Joe Thornton Third 6.00 15.00
80 Joe Thornton Third AU/50 40.00 100.00
81 Mario Lemieux H 50.00 125.00
82 Mario Lemieux G 60.00 150.00
83 Martin Brodeur A 25.00 60.00
84 Martin Brodeur A AU/30 50.00 125.00
85 Martin Brodeur G 25.00 60.00
86 Martin Brodeur G AU/10
87 Martin Brodeur H 12.50 30.00
88 Martin Brodeur H AU 50.00 125.00
89 Martin Brodeur M 15.00 40.00
90 Martin Brodeur M AU/25 75.00 200.00
91 Patrick Roy A 30.00 80.00
92 Patrick Roy A AU/33 125.00 300.00
93 Patrick Roy G 30.00 80.00
94 Patrick Roy G AU/10
95 Patrick Roy H 20.00 50.00
96 Patrick Roy H AU SP 75.00 200.00
97 Patrick Roy M 25.00 60.00
98 Patrick Roy M AU/25 125.00 300.00
99 Patrick Roy Third 25.00 60.00
100 Patrick Roy Third AU/50 100.00 250.00
101 Paul Kariya A 8.00 20.00
102 Paul Kariya G 8.00 20.00
103 Paul Kariya H 6.00 15.00
104 Paul Kariya M 6.00 15.00
105 Pavel Bure A 8.00 20.00
106 Pavel Bure A AU/9
107 Pavel Bure G 8.00 20.00
108 Pavel Bure G AU/10
109 Pavel Bure H 6.00 15.00
110 Pavel Bure H AU SP 30.00 80.00
111 Pavel Bure M 6.00 15.00
112 Pavel Bure M AU/25 60.00 150.00
113 Pavel Bure Third 6.00 15.00
114 Pavel Bure Third AU/50 40.00 100.00
115 Ray Bourque Bos.A 20.00 50.00
116 Ray Bourque Bos.A AU/77 50.00 125.00
117 Ray Bourque G 20.00 50.00
118 Ray Bourque G AU/10
119 Ray Bourque Bos.H 12.50 30.00
120 Ray Bourque Bos.H AU SP 40.00 100.00
121 Ray Bourque M 15.00 40.00
122 Ray Bourque M AU/25 60.00 150.00
123 Ray Bourque Col.Third 15.00 40.00
124 Ray Bourque Col.Third AU/50 50.00 125.00

2002-03 Upper Deck Classic Portraits Pillars of Strength

COMPLETE SET (10) 10.00 20.00
STATED ODDS 1:18
PS1 Ilya Kovalchuk .60 1.50
PS2 Jarome Iginla .50 1.25
PS3 Joe Sakic 1.00 2.50
PS4 Mike Modano .75 2.00
PS5 Brendan Shanahan .75 2.00
PS6 Martin Brodeur 1.25 3.00
PS7 Eric Lindros .40 1.00
PS8 Mario Lemieux 3.00 8.00
PS9 Teemu Selanne .40 1.00
PS10 Olaf Kolzig .40 1.00

2002-03 Upper Deck Classic Portraits Portrait of a Legend

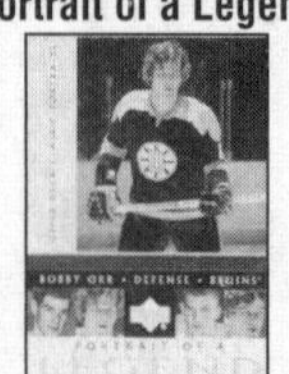

This 10-card set was dedicated to the career of Bobby Orr. Cards were inserted at 1:18.

COMPLETE SET (10) 20.00 40.00
COMMON ORR (PL1-PL10) 2.00 5.00

2002-03 Upper Deck Classic Portraits Starring Cast

This 15-card memorabilia set was inserted at 1:48. A limited parallel was also created and serial-numbered out of 50.

*MULT.COLOR SWATCH: .75X TO 1.5X
*LTD: .6X TO 1.5X BASE HI
CAT Alex Tanguay 4.00 10.00
CBG Bill Guerin 4.00 10.00
CBS Brendan Shanahan 5.00 12.00
CFP Felix Potvin 5.00 12.00
CJR Jeremy Roenick 5.00 12.00
CKT Keith Tkachuk 5.00 12.00
CMM Mike Modano 6.00 15.00
CMN Markus Naslund 5.00 12.00
CMS Mats Sundin 5.00 12.00
CPK Paul Kariya 5.00 12.00
CSA Miroslav Satan 4.00 10.00
CSB Sean Burke 4.00 10.00
CSG Simon Gagne 5.00 12.00
CSY Steve Yzerman 12.50 30.00
CZP Zigmund Palffy 4.00 10.00

2002-03 Upper Deck Classic Portraits Stitches

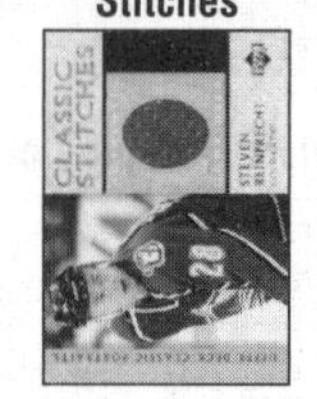

This 15-card memorabilia set was inserted at 1:24. A limited parallel was also created and serial-numbered out of 75.

*MULT.COLOR SWATCH: .75X TO 1.5X
*LTD: .5X TO 1.25X BASE HI
CAD Adam Deadmarsh 3.00 8.00
CBO Peter Bondra 3.00 8.00
CCD Chris Drury 3.00 8.00
CJF Jeff Friesen 3.00 8.00
CJI Jarome Iginla 5.00 12.00
CJT Joe Thornton 8.00 20.00
CKK Krys Kolanos 3.00 8.00
CMD Mike Dunham 3.00 8.00
CPB Pavel Bure 4.00 10.00
CRS Rostislav Klesla 3.00 8.00
CSF Sergei Fedorov 6.00 15.00
CSG Simon Gagne 4.00 10.00
CSR Steven Reinprecht 3.00 8.00
CSS Sergei Samsonov 3.00 8.00
CTH Jose Theodore 5.00 12.00

2003-04 Upper Deck Classic Portraits

Released in late-October, this 188-card set consisted of 100 veteran cards, 15 "Etched in Time" subset cards (101-115) serial-numbered to 1100, 18 Patrick Roy "Portrait of a Legend" cards (116-135) serial-numbered to 800, 25 "Pillars of Strength" subset cards (136-160) serial-numbered to 650, 6 pack issued rookies (161-166); 20 shortprinted rookies available via exchange cards (167-188) and 8 shortprinted rookies (189-196) available in packs of UD Rookie Update. Cards 161-196 were serial-numbered out of 1150.

COMP.SET w/o SP's (100) 15.00 30.00
1 Sergei Fedorov .40 1.00
2 Stanislav Chistov .10 .25
3 J-S Giguere .25 .60
4 Dany Heatley .40 1.00
5 Ilya Kovalchuk .40 1.00
6 Joe Thornton .50 1.25
7 Glen Murray .10 .25
8 Sergei Samsonov .25 .60
9 Miroslav Satan .25 .60
10 Maxim Afinogenov .25 .60
11 Chris Drury .25 .60
12 Jarome Iginla .40 1.00
13 Steve Reinprecht .10 .25
14 Roman Turek .25 .60
15 Ron Francis .25 .60
16 Jeff O'Neill .25 .60
17 Alexei Zhamnov .10 .25
18 Kyle Calder .10 .25
19 Jocelyn Thibault .25 .60
20 Teemu Selanne .30 .75
21 Peter Forsberg .75 2.00
22 Paul Kariya .30 .75
23 Joe Sakic .60 1.50
24 David Aebischer .25 .60
25 Rick Nash .40 1.00
26 Marc Denis .25 .60
27 Todd Marchant .10 .25
28 Mike Modano .50 1.25
29 Bill Guerin .25 .60
30 Marty Turco .25 .60
31 Brendan Shanahan .30 .75
32 Henrik Zetterberg .30 .75
33 Steve Yzerman 1.50 4.00
34 Dominik Hasek .50 1.25
35 Ryan Smyth .10 .25
36 Mike Comrie .25 .60
37 Ales Hemsky .25 .60
38 Tommy Salo .25 .60
39 Olli Jokinen .25 .60
40 Stephen Weiss .10 .25
41 Jay Bouwmeester .10 .25
42 Roberto Luongo .40 1.00
43 Zigmund Palffy .25 .60
44 Alexander Frolov .10 .25
45 Roman Cechmanek .25 .60
46 Marian Gaborik .60 1.50
47 P-M Bouchard .10 .25
48 Manny Fernandez .25 .60
49 Dwayne Roloson .25 .60
50 Saku Koivu .30 .75
51 Marcel Hossa .10 .25
52 Jose Theodore .40 1.00
53 Michael Komisarek .10 .25
54 David Legwand .25 .60
55 Tomas Vokoun .25 .60
56 Patrik Elias .25 .60
57 Jamie Langenbrunner .10 .25
58 Scott Stevens .25 .60
59 Martin Brodeur .75 2.00
60 Alexei Yashin .10 .25
61 Rick DiPietro .25 .60
62 Alex Kovalev .25 .60
63 Eric Lindros .30 .75
64 Pavel Bure .30 .75
65 Mike Dunham .25 .60
66 Marian Hossa .30 .75
67 Daniel Alfredsson .25 .60
68 Jason Spezza .30 .75
69 Patrick Lalime .25 .60
70 Jeremy Roenick .40 1.00
71 Tony Amonte .25 .60
72 John LeClair .30 .75
73 Simon Gagne .30 .75
74 Mike Johnson .10 .25
75 Chris Gratton .10 .25
76 Sean Burke .25 .60
77 Mario Lemieux 2.00 5.00
78 Martin Straka .10 .25
79 Sebastien Caron .25 .60
80 Mike Ricci .10 .25
81 Nicholas Dimitrakos .10 .25
82 Evgeni Nabokov .25 .60
83 Al MacInnis .25 .60
84 Keith Tkachuk .25 .60
85 Chris Pronger .25 .60
86 Chris Osgood .25 .60
87 Vincent Lecavalier .30 .75
88 Martin St. Louis .25 .60
89 Nikolai Khabibulin .30 .75
90 Alexander Mogilny .25 .60
91 Mats Sundin .30 .75
92 Owen Nolan .25 .60
93 Ed Belfour .30 .75
94 Alexander Auld .10 .25
95 Markus Naslund .30 .75
96 Todd Bertuzzi .30 .75
97 Ed Jovanovski .25 .60
98 Jaromir Jagr .50 1.25
99 Peter Bondra .25 .60
100 Olaf Kolzig .25 .60
101 J-S Giguere ET .50 1.25
102 Joe Thornton ET 1.00 2.50
103 Mario Lemieux ET 4.00 10.00
104 Peter Forsberg ET 1.50 4.00
105 Steve Yzerman ET 3.00 8.00
106 Eric Lindros ET .60 1.50
107 Marian Gaborik ET 1.25 3.00
108 Paul Kariya ET .60 1.50
109 Joe Sakic ET 1.25 3.00
110 Martin Brodeur ET 1.50 4.00
111 Ed Belfour ET .60 1.50
112 Marian Hossa ET .60 1.50
113 Gordie Howe ET 5.00 12.00
114 Wayne Gretzky ET 5.00 12.00
115 Bobby Orr ET 6.00 15.00
116 Patrick Roy PL 8.00 20.00
117 Patrick Roy PL 8.00 20.00
118 Patrick Roy PL 8.00 20.00
119 Patrick Roy PL 8.00 20.00
120 Patrick Roy PL 8.00 20.00
121 Patrick Roy PL 8.00 20.00
122 Patrick Roy PL 8.00 20.00
123 Patrick Roy PL 8.00 20.00
124 Patrick Roy PL 8.00 20.00
125 Patrick Roy PL 8.00 20.00
126 Patrick Roy PL 8.00 20.00
127 Patrick Roy PL 8.00 20.00
128 Patrick Roy PL 8.00 20.00
129 Patrick Roy PL 8.00 20.00
130 Patrick Roy PL 8.00 20.00
131 Patrick Roy PL 8.00 20.00
132 Patrick Roy PL 8.00 20.00
133 Patrick Roy PL 8.00 20.00
J-S Giguere
134 Patrick Roy 8.00 20.00
Martin Brodeur PL
135 J-S Giguere PS 8.00 20.00
136 Mario Lemieux PS 6.00 15.00
137 Gordie Howe PS 6.00 15.00
138 Keith Tkachuk PS .75 2.00
139 Peter Forsberg PS 2.50 6.00
140 Jeremy Roenick PS 1.25 3.00
141 Eric Lindros PS 1.00 2.50
142 Jaromir Jagr PS 1.50 4.00
143 Zdeno Chara PS .30 .75
144 Owen Nolan PS .75 2.00
145 Martin Brodeur PS 2.50 6.00
146 Ed Belfour PS 1.00 2.50
147 Marian Hossa PS 1.00 2.50
148 Jarome Iginla PS 1.00 2.50
149 Jocelyn Thibault PS .75 2.00
150 Marian Gaborik PS 2.00 5.00
151 Vincent Lecavalier PS .75 2.00
152 Joe Thornton PS 1.50 4.00
153 Rick Nash PS .75 2.00
154 Joe Sakic PS 2.00 5.00
155 Mike Modano PS 1.50 4.00
156 J-S Giguere PS .75 2.00
157 Olli Jokinen PS .75 2.00
158 Steve Yzerman PS 5.00 12.00
159 Jason Spezza PS .75 2.00
160 Chris Pronger PS .75 2.00
161 Joe DiPenta RC 2.50 6.00
162 Milan Bartovic RC 2.50 6.00
163 Rick Mrozik RC 2.50 6.00
164 Kent McDonell RC 2.50 6.00
165 Peter Sejna RC 2.50 6.00
166 Matt Stajan RC 3.00 8.00
167 Marc-Andre Fleury RC 8.00 20.00
168 Nathan Horton RC 4.00 10.00
169 Eric Staal RC 8.00 20.00
170 Joffrey Lupul RC 3.00 8.00
171 Dustin Brown RC 2.50 6.00
172 Jordin Tootoo RC 4.00 10.00
173 Joni Pitkanen RC 3.00 8.00
174 Milan Michalek RC 4.00 10.00
175 Pavel Vorobiev RC 2.50 6.00
176 Tuomo Ruutu RC 4.00 10.00
177 Patrice Bergeron RC 5.00 12.00
178 Antoine Vermette RC 20.00 50.00
179 Antti Miettinen RC 2.50 6.00
180 Dan Hamhuis RC 2.50 6.00
181 Sean Bergenheim RC 2.50 6.00
182 Maxim Kondratiev RC 2.50 6.00
183 Chris Higgins RC 5.00 12.00
184 John-Michael Liles RC 2.50 6.00
185 Brent Burns RC 2.50 6.00
186 Marek Svatos RC 3.00 8.00
187 Boyd Gordon RC 2.50 6.00
188 Cody McCormick RC 2.50 6.00
189 Alexander Semin RC 5.00 12.00
190 Timofei Shishkanov RC 2.50 6.00
191 Mikhail Yakubov RC 2.50 6.00
192 Ryan Kesler RC 2.50 6.00
193 Fredrik Sjostrom RC 2.50 6.00
194 Nikolai Zherdev RC 2.50 6.00
195 Derek Roy RC 3.00 8.00
196 Tomas Plekanec RC 2.50 6.00

2003-04 Upper Deck Classic Portraits Classic Colors

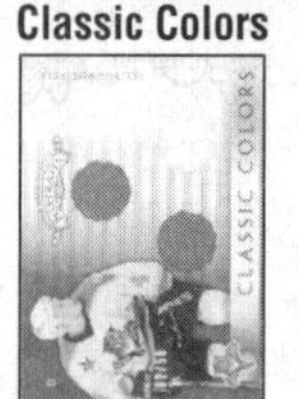

PRINT RUN 50 SERIAL #'d SETS
CC-AM Al MacInnis 8.00 20.00
CC-BH Brett Hull 20.00 50.00
CC-BS Brendan Shanahan 12.50 30.00
CC-CD Chris Drury 8.00 20.00
CC-CJ Curtis Joseph 12.50 30.00
CC-CO Chris Osgood 8.00 20.00
CC-DW Doug Weight 8.00 20.00
CC-EL Eric Lindros 12.50 30.00
CC-JA Jason Allison 8.00 20.00
CC-JB Jay Bouwmeester 8.00 20.00
CC-JJ Jaromir Jagr 20.00 50.00
CC-JS Jason Spezza 20.00 50.00
CC-JS Joe Sakic 30.00 80.00
CC-MD Mike Modano 12.50 30.00
CC-ON Ed Belfour 12.50 30.00
CC-PK Paul Kariya 12.50 30.00
CC-RN Rick Nash 25.00 60.00
CC-TA Tony Amonte 8.00 20.00
CC-TS Teemu Selanne 12.50 30.00
CC-WG Wayne Gretzky 75.00 200.00

2003-04 Upper Deck Classic Portraits Classic Stitches

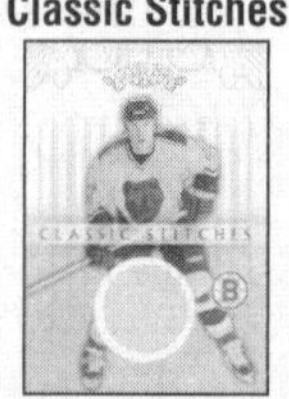

*MULT.COLOR SWATCH: .75X TO 1.5X
STATED ODDS 1:18
CS-AD Adam Deadmarsh 3.00 8.00
CS-BB Brian Boucher 3.00 8.00
CS-CP Chris Pronger 3.00 8.00
CS-EB Ed Belfour 5.00 12.00
CS-GM Glen Murray 3.00 8.00
CS-JT Joe Thornton 8.00 20.00
CS-MA Maxim Afinogenov 3.00 8.00
CS-SK Saku Koivu 5.00 12.00
CS-SY Steve Yzerman 12.50 30.00
CS-TH Jocelyn Thibault 3.00 8.00

2003-04 Upper Deck Classic Portraits Genuine Greatness

*MULT.COLOR SWATCH: .75X TO 1.5X
PRINT RUN 75 SERIAL #'d SETS
GG-DH Dany Heatley 10.00 25.00
GG-GR Wayne Gretzky 50.00 125.00
GG-JR Jeremy Roenick 10.00 25.00
GG-JS Jason Spezza 12.50 30.00
GG-JT Joe Thornton 12.50 30.00
GG-MB Martin Brodeur 15.00 40.00
GG-ML Mario Lemieux 20.00 50.00
GG-PR Patrick Roy 20.00 50.00
GG-RN Rick Nash 12.50 30.00
GG-SY Steve Yzerman 15.00 40.00
GG-WG Wayne Gretzky 50.00 125.00

2003-04 Upper Deck Classic Portraits Headliners

*MULT.COLOR SWATCH: .75X TO 1.5X
STATED ODDS 1:36
HH-EL Eric Lindros 8.00 20.00
HH-HA Marcel Hossa 5.00 12.00
HH-JJ Jaromir Jagr 10.00 25.00
HH-JT Joe Thornton 8.00 20.00
HH-MG Marian Gaborik 8.00 20.00
HH-ML Mario Lemieux 12.50 30.00
HH-MN Markus Naslund 6.00 15.00
HH-PK Paul Kariya 6.00 15.00
HH-VB Valeri Bure 5.00 12.00

2003-04 Upper Deck Classic Portraits Hockey Royalty

PRINT RUN 99 SERIAL #'d SETS
BLC Bure/Lindros/Kovalev 12.50 30.00
BNM Bertuzzi/Naslund/Morrison 12.50 30.00
BSM Belfour/Sundin/Mogilny 15.00 40.00
DSB Domi/Stock/Brashear 15.00 40.00
FSK Forsberg/Sakic/Kariya 25.00 60.00
KTH Koivu/Theodore/Hossa 25.00 60.00
LYG Lemieux/Yzerman/Gilmour 30.00 80.00
PLB Pronger/Lidstrom/Bowmster 12.50 30.00
RLA Roenick/LeClair/Amonte 20.00 50.00
YHS Yzerman/Hull/Shanahan 30.00 80.00

2003-04 Upper Deck Classic Portraits Mini-Busts

Inserted one per box, these ceramic busts carried two themes; Stanley Cup Winners and 500 Goal scorers. A bronze version was also created and limited to 25 copies each.
*BRONZE: 1X TO 2.5X
1 Patrick Roy COL 15.00 40.00
2 Patrick Roy MON/50 25.00 60.00
3 Gordie Howe SC 15.00 40.00
4 Martin Brodeur SC 15.00 40.00
5 Mike Modano SC 15.00 40.00
6 Joe Sakic SC 15.00 40.00
7 Peter Forsberg SC 15.00 40.00
8 Brett Hull DET 15.00 40.00
9 Brett Hull DAL/50 20.00 50.00
10 Ray Bourque SC 15.00 40.00
11 Jaromir Jagr PITT 15.00 40.00
12 Mario Lemieux SC 25.00 60.00
13 Steve Yzerman SC 20.00 50.00
14 Mark Messier NYR SC 15.00 40.00
15 Mark Messier EDM SC/50 20.00 50.00
16 Phil Esposito SC 15.00 40.00
17 Terry Sawchuk DET 15.00 40.00
18 Terry Sawchuk TOR/50 20.00 50.00
19 Bryan Trottier NYI SC 15.00 40.00
20 Bryan Trottier PITT SC/50 15.00 40.00
21 Bobby Clarke SC 15.00 40.00
22 Guy Lafleur SC 15.00 40.00
23 Scotty Bowman DET 20.00 50.00
24 Scotty Bowman MON/50 20.00 50.00
25 Scotty Bowman PITT/50 20.00 50.00
26 Phil Esposito 500 15.00 40.00
27 Steve Yzerman 500 20.00 50.00
28 Guy Lafleur 500 25.00 60.00
29 Mario Lemieux 500 25.00 60.00
30 Brett Hull 500 15.00 40.00
31 Jaromir Jagr 500 15.00 40.00
32 Gordie Howe 500 15.00 40.00
33 Mark Messier 500 15.00 40.00
34 Bryan Trottier 500 15.00 40.00
35 Joe Sakic 500 15.00 40.00

2003-04 Upper Deck Classic Portraits Mini-Busts Signed

This 21-card set partially parallels the regular bust but carried authentic player autographs. The busts in the 500 Goal Scorers subset were limited to 50 copies each and the Sawchuk busts were 1 of 1's. A bronze version was also created and limited to 10 copies or less each. Those busts are not priced due to scarcity.
BRONZE PRINT RUN 10 OR LESS
1 Patrick Roy COL 100.00 250.00
2 Patrick Roy MON/25 250.00 500.00
3 Gordie Howe SC 60.00 150.00
4 Martin Brodeur SC 60.00 150.00
10 Ray Bourque SC 40.00 100.00
11 Jaromir Jagr PITT 40.00 100.00
16 Phil Esposito SC 40.00 100.00
17 Terry Sawchuk DET/1
18 Terry Sawchuk TOR/1
19 Bryan Trottier NYI SC 40.00 100.00
20 Bryan Trottier PITT SC/25 100.00200.00
21 Bobby Clarke SC 25.00 60.00
22 Guy Lafleur SC 50.00 125.00
23 Scotty Bowman DET 40.00 100.00
24 Scotty Bowman MON
25 Scotty Bowman PITT/25 50.00 125.00
26 Phil Esposito 500 30.00 80.00
28 Guy Lafleur 500 50.00 125.00
31 Jaromir Jagr 500 75.00 200.00
32 Gordie Howe 500 150.00 300.00
34 Bryan Trottier 500 75.00 200.00

2003-04 Upper Deck Classic Portraits Premium Portraits

*MULT.COLOR SWATCH: .75X TO 1.5X
PRINT RUN 25 SERIAL #'d SETS
PP-JT Joe Thornton 25.00 60.00
PP-MB Martin Brodeur 30.00 80.00
PP-MH Gordie Howe 40.00 100.00
PP-ML Mario Lemieux 40.00 100.00
PP-PF Peter Forsberg 25.00 60.00
PP-PR Patrick Roy 40.00 100.00
PP-SY Steve Yzerman 40.00 100.00
PP-WG Wayne Gretzky 60.00 150.00

2003-04 Upper Deck Classic Portraits Starring Cast

*MULT.COLOR SWATCH: .75X TO 1.5X
STATED ODDS 1:36
SC-CD Chris Drury 4.00 10.00
SC-JG J-S Giguere 4.00 10.00
SC-JH Johan Hedberg 4.00 10.00
SC-MB Martin Brodeur 12.50 30.00
SC-MM Mike Modano 8.00 20.00
SC-PR Patrick Roy 12.50 30.00
SC-RN Rick Nash 8.00 20.00
SC-TA Tony Amonte 4.00 10.00
SC-TB Todd Bertuzzi 4.00 10.00

1991-92 Upper Deck Czech World Juniors

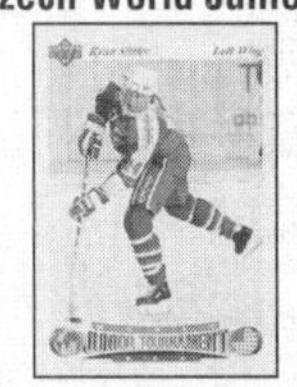

This 100 card standard-size set featured players from the 1991 World Junior Championships. Two Wayne Gretzky Holograms were inserted into the set. They are priced at the end of the listings but are not included in the set price. Inside white borders, the fronts display glossy color action photos of the players in their national team uniforms. The player's name and position appear on the top, while the World Junior Tournament logo and an emblem of their national flag overlay the bottom. The backs have a second color player photo; alongside in a gray box, the player's position and a brief profile are printed in English and Czech. The cards are sequenced in this way: C.I.S. (1-23), Switzerland (24-31), Finland (32-40), Germany (41-46), Canada (47-65), U.S.A. (66-86), Czechoslovakia (87-99). These cards were designed for distribution in Eastern Europe. An album (valued at about $5) was also made to house the set.
COMPLETE SET (100) 12.00 30.00
1 Description Card .02 .10
2 Vladislav Boulin .02 .10
3 Ravil Gusmanov .02 .10
4 Denis Vinokurov .02 .10
5 Mikhail Volkov .02 .10
6 Alexei Troschinsky .02 .10
7 Andrei Nikolishin .20 .50
8 Alexander Sverztov .02 .10
9 Artem Kopot .02 .10
10 Ildar Mukhometov .02 .10
11 Darius Kasparaitis .20 .50
12 Alexei Yashin .20 .50
13 Nikolai Khabibulin .50 1.25
14 Denis Metlyuk .02 .10
15 Konstantin Korotkov .02 .10
16 Alexei Kovalev .60 1.50
17 Alexander Kuzminsky .02 .10
18 Alexander Cherbayev .02 .10
19 Sergei Krivokrasov .20 .50
20 Sergei Zholtok .20 .50
21 Alexei Zhitnik .40 1.00
22 Sandis Ozolinsh .40 1.00
23 Boris Mironov .40 1.00
24 Pauli Jaks .02 .10
25 Gaetan Voisard .02 .10
26 Nicola Celio .02 .10
27 Marc Weber .02 .10
28 Bernhard Schumperli .02 .10
29 Laurent Bucher .02 .10
30 Michael Blaha .02 .10
31 Tiziano Gianini .02 .10
32 Tero Lehtera .02 .10
33 Mikko Luovi .02 .10
34 Marko Kiprusoff .02 .10
35 Janne Gronvall .02 .10
36 Juha Ylonen .20 .50
37 Sami Kapanen .20 .50
38 Marko Tuomainen .02 .10
39 Jarkko Varvio .02 .10
40 Tuomas Gronman .02 .10
41 Andreas Naumann .02 .10
42 Steffen Ziesche .02 .10
43 Jens Schwabe .02 .10
44 Thomas Schubert .02 .10
45 Hans-Jorg Mayer .02 .10
46 Marc Seliger .20 .50
47 Ryan Hughes .02 .10
48 Richard Matvichuk .20 .50
49 David St. Pierre .02 .10
50 Paul Kariya 2.50 6.00
51 Patrick Poulin .20 .50
52 Mike Fountain .20 .50
53 Scott Niedermayer .20 .50
54 John Slaney .02 .10
55 Brad Bombardir .02 .10
56 Andy Schneider .02 .10
57 Steve Junker .02 .10
58 Trevor Kidd .40 1.00
59 Martin Lapointe .40 1.00
60 Tyler Wright .20 .50
61 Kimbi Daniels .02 .10
62 Karl Dykhuis .20 .50
63 Jeff Nelson .02 .10
64 Jassen Cullimore .02 .10
65 Turner Stevenson .20 .50
66 Brian Mueller .02 .10
67 Chris Tucker .02 .10
68 Marty Schriner .02 .10
69 Mike Prendergast .02 .10
70 John Lilley .02 .10
71 Jim Campbell .20 .50
72 Brian Holzinger .20 .50
73 Steve Konowalchuk .20 .50
74 Chris Ferraro .02 .10
75 Chris Imes .02 .10
76 Rich Brennan .02 .10
77 Todd Hall .02 .10
78 Brian Rafalski .20 .50
79 Scott Lachance .20 .50
80 Mike Dunham .40 1.00
81 Brent Bilodeau .02 .10
82 Ryan Sittler .02 .10
83 Peter Ferraro .02 .10
84 Pat Peake .02 .10
85 Keith Tkachuk 1.50 4.00
86 Brian Rolston .40 1.00
87 Milan Hnilicka .20 .50
88 Roman Hamrlik .20 .50
89 Milan Nedoma .02 .10
90 Patrik Luza .02 .10
91 Jan Caloun .20 .50
92 Viktor Ujcik .02 .10
93 Robert Petrovicky .20 .50
94 Roman Meluzin .02 .10
95 Jan Vopat .02 .10
96 Martin Prochazka .20 .50
97 Zigmund Palffy 1.00 2.50
98 Ivan Droppa .02 .10
99 Martin Straka .20 .50
100 Checklist 1-100 .02 .10
NNO W.Gretzky Hologram 1.50 4.00
NNO W.Gretzky Hologram 1.50 4.00

1997-98 Upper Deck Diamond Vision

This 25-card set was distributed in one-card packs with a suggested retail price of $7.99. The cards feature actual NHL game footage of the named player on each card combined with the latest technology to create fluid action sequences. Inserted one in every 500 packs is a Wayne Gretzky REEL Time card which displays his greatest moments in frame-by-frame action imagery.
COMPLETE SET (25) 50.00 125.00
1 Wayne Gretzky 10.00 25.00
2 Patrick Roy 8.00 20.00
3 Jaromir Jagr 3.00 8.00
4 Steve Yzerman 6.00 15.00
5 Martin Brodeur 5.00 12.00
6 Paul Kariya 2.00 5.00
7 John Vanbiesbrouck 1.25 3.00
8 Ray Bourque 2.00 5.00
9 Theo Fleury 1.25 3.00
10 Pavel Bure 1.50 4.00
11 Brendan Shanahan 2.00 5.00
12 Brian Leetch 1.25 3.00
13 Owen Nolan 1.25 3.00
14 Peter Forsberg 3.00 8.00
15 Doug Weight 1.25 3.00
16 Teemu Selanne 2.00 5.00
17 Mats Sundin 2.00 5.00
18 Keith Tkachuk 1.25 3.00
19 Tony Amonte 1.25 3.00
20 Joe Sakic 4.00 10.00
21 Zigmund Palffy 1.25 3.00
22 Eric Lindros 1.50 4.00
23 Sergei Fedorov 2.00 5.00
24 Dominik Hasek 4.00 10.00
25 Brett Hull 2.00 5.00
RT1 Wayne Gretzky 100.00 250.00
REEL TIME

1997-98 Upper Deck Diamond Vision Signature Moves

Randomly inserted in packs at the rate of 1:5, this 25-card set is parallel to the regular Diamond Vision set only with a facsimile signature of the player pictured on the card.
COMPLETE SET (25) 200.00 500.00
*SIGNATURE MOVES: 1X TO 2X BASIC CARDS

1997-98 Upper Deck Diamond Vision Defining Moments

Randomly inserted in packs at the rate of 1:40, this six-card set features incredible action technology to show the memorable highlights of the pictured player's career.
DM1 Wayne Gretzky 50.00 120.00
DM2 Patrick Roy 40.00 100.00
DM3 Steve Yzerman 40.00 100.00
DM4 Jaromir Jagr 12.50 30.00
DM5 Joe Sakic 15.00 40.00
DM6 Brendan Shanahan 8.00 20.00

2006 Upper Deck Entry Draft

Set was issued as a wrapper redemption exclusively at the 2006 NHL Entry Draft in Vancouver.
COMPLETE SET (6) 15.00 30.00
DR6 Joe Thornton 1.50 4.00
DR5 Ilya Kovalchuk 1.50 4.00
DR4 Rick Nash 1.50 4.00
DR3 Marc-Andre Fleury 1.25 3.00
DR2 Alexander Ovechkin 4.00 10.00
DR1 Sidney Crosby 6.00 15.00

1999-00 Upper Deck Gold Reserve

1999-00 Upper Deck Gold Reserve was packaged as a two-series release. Series one contained 170 cards and series two contained 180 cards. Base cards use the same design as the 2000 Upper Deck release but are enhanced with an all-foil card stock and gold foil highlights. Prospect cards in both series were short printed and numbered out of 2500. This release was packaged in 24-pack boxes where packs contained 10 cards and carried a suggested retail price of $2.99.
COMPLETE SET (350) 200.00 400.00
COMP.SER.1 (170) 75.00 150.00
COMP.SER.1. w/o SP's (135) 20.00 40.00
COMP.SER.2 (180) 100.00 250.00
COMP.SER.2. w/o SP's (150) 15.00 30.00
1 Wayne Gretzky 1.25 3.00
2 Wayne Gretzky 1.25 3.00
3 Wayne Gretzky 1.25 3.00
4 Wayne Gretzky 1.25 3.00
5 Wayne Gretzky 1.25 3.00
6 Wayne Gretzky 1.25 3.00
7 Wayne Gretzky 1.25 3.00
8 Wayne Gretzky 1.25 3.00
9 Wayne Gretzky 1.25 3.00
10 Wayne Gretzky 1.25 3.00
11 Paul Kariya .40 1.00
12 Matt Cullen .08 .20
13 Steve Rucchin .30 .75
14 Fredrik Olausson .08 .20
15 Damian Rhodes .30 .75
16 Jody Hull .08 .20
17 Ray Bourque .60 1.50
18 Joe Thornton .60 1.50
19 Jonathan Girard .08 .20
20 Shawn Bates .08 .20
21 Byron Dafoe .30 .75
22 Dominik Hasek .75 2.00
23 Michael Peca .30 .75
24 Miroslav Satan .30 .75
25 Dixon Ward .08 .20
26 Valeri Bure .08 .20
27 Derek Morris .08 .20
28 Jarome Iginla .50 1.25
29 Rico Fata .08 .20
30 J-S Giguere .30 .75
31 Arturs Irbe .08 .20
32 Sami Kapanen .08 .20
33 Gary Roberts .08 .20
34 Bates Battaglia .08 .20
35 J-P Dumont .30 .75
36 Ty Jones .08 .20
37 Tony Amonte .30 .75
38 Anders Eriksson .08 .20
39 Peter Forsberg 1.00 2.50
40 Adam Foote .08 .20
41 Chris Drury .50 1.25
42 Milan Hejduk .40 1.00
43 Brett Hull .50 1.25
44 Ed Belfour .40 1.00
45 Jamie Langenbrunner .08 .20
46 Derian Hatcher .08 .20
47 Jon Sim RC .30 .75
48 Joe Nieuwendyk .30 .75
49 Steve Yzerman 2.00 5.00
50 Brendan Shanahan .60 1.50
51 Nicklas Lidstrom .40 1.00
52 Igor Larionov .08 .20
53 Vyacheslav Kozlov .08 .20
54 Bill Guerin .08 .20
55 Mike Grier .08 .20
56 Tommy Salo .30 .75
57 Tom Poti .08 .20
58 Mark Parrish .08 .20
59 Pavel Bure .50 1.25
60 Scott Mellanby .08 .20
61 Chris Allen RC .08 .20
62 Rob Blake .30 .75
63 Pavel Rosa .08 .20
64 Donald Audette .08 .20
65 Vladimir Tsyplakov .08 .20
66 Manny Legace .30 .75
67 Saku Koivu .40 1.00
68 Eric Weinrich .08 .20
69 Jeff Hackett .30 .75
70 Arron Asham .08 .20
71 Trevor Linden .30 .75
72 Cliff Ronning .30 .75
73 David Legwand .30 .75
74 Kimmo Timonen .08 .20
75 Sergei Krivokrasov .08 .20
76 Mike Dunham .30 .75
77 Martin Brodeur 1.00 2.50
78 Patrik Elias .30 .75
79 Petr Sykora .08 .20
80 Vadim Sharifijanov .08 .20
81 John Madden RC .75 2.00
82 Eric Brewer .08 .20
83 Dmitri Nabokov .08 .20
84 Kenny Jonsson .08 .20
85 Zdeno Chara .08 .20
86 Wayne Gretzky 2.50 6.00
87 Mike Richter .40 1.00
88 Adam Graves .08 .20
89 Manny Malhotra .30 .75
90 Alexei Yashin .08 .20
91 Sami Salo .08 .20
92 Marian Hossa .40 1.00
93 Shawn McEachern .08 .20
94 Eric Lindros .60 1.50
95 Jean-Marc Pelletier .08 .20
96 Rod Brind'Amour .30 .75
97 Mark Recchi .30 .75
98 Eric Desjardins .30 .75
99 Robert Reichel .08 .20
100 Keith Tkachuk .40 1.00
101 Robert Esche RC 2.50 6.00
102 Oleg Tverdovsky .08 .20
103 Trevor Letowski .08 .20
104 Jaromir Jagr .60 1.50
105 Tom Barrasso .30 .75
106 Jan Hrdina .08 .20
107 Matthew Barnaby .30 .75
108 Vincent Damphousse .08 .20
109 Jeff Friesen .08 .20
110 Patrick Marleau .40 1.00
111 Mike Ricci .30 .75
112 Scott Hannan .08 .20
113 Pavol Demitra .30 .75
114 Al MacInnis .30 .75
115 Lubos Bartecko .08 .20
116 Jochen Hecht RC .75 2.00
117 Vincent Lecavalier .40 1.00
118 Paul Mara .08 .20
119 Kevin Hodson .30 .75
120 Dan Cloutier .30 .75
121 Mats Sundin .40 1.00
122 Daniil Markov .08 .20
123 Sergei Berezin .08 .20
124 Steve Thomas .08 .20
125 Tomas Kaberle .08 .20
126 Mark Messier .50 1.25
127 Bill Muckalt .08 .20
128 Kevin Weekes .08 .20
129 Josh Holden .30 .75
130 Jaroslav Svejkovsky .08 .20
131 Adam Oates .30 .75
132 Peter Bondra .30 .75
133 Jan Bulis .08 .20
134 Wayne Gretzky CL 1.25 3.00
135 Wayne Gretzky CL 1.25 3.00
136 Wayne Gretzky SP 3.00 8.00
137 Eric Lindros SP .75 2.00
138 Jaromir Jagr SP .75 2.00
139 Paul Kariya SP .75 2.00
140 Steve Yzerman SP 2.50 6.00
141 Patrick Roy SP 2.50 6.00
142 Chris Drury SP .60 1.50
143 Sergei Samsonov SP .75 2.00
144 Brett Hull SP .60 1.50
145 Dominik Hasek SP 1.00 2.50
146 Keith Tkachuk SP 1.50 4.00
147 Alexei Yashin SP .75 2.00
148 Martin Brodeur SP 1.25 3.00
149 Pavel Bure SP .60 1.50
150 Paul Mara SP .75 2.00
151 Peter Bondra SP .75 2.00
152 Mike Modano SP .75 2.00
153 Teemu Selanne SP .75 2.00
154 Peter Forsberg SP 1.25 3.00
155 Brendan Shanahan SP .75 2.00
156 Ray Bourque SP .75 2.00
157 Saku Koivu SP 1.50 4.00
158 John LeClair SP .50 1.50
159 Joe Sakic SP 1.00 2.50
160 David Legwand SP .75 2.00
161 Patrik Stefan YG RC 1.00 2.50
162 Nick Boynton YG .75 2.00
163 Roberto Luongo YG 1.00 2.50
164 Rico Fata SP .75 2.00
165 Daniel Sedin YG .75 2.00
166 Henrik Sedin YG .75 2.00
167 Brad Stuart YG .75 2.00
168 Tony Amonte SP .75 2.00
169 Oleg Saprykin YG RC 1.00 2.50
170 Denis Shvidki YG .75 2.00
171 Guy Hebert .30 .75
172 Niclas Havelid RC .40 1.00
173 Oleg Tverdovsky .08 .20
174 Teemu Selanne .40 1.00
175 Damian Rhodes .30 .75
176 Nelson Emerson .08 .20
177 Per Svartvadet RC .08 .20
178 Ray Ferraro .08 .20
179 Kelly Buchberger .08 .20
180 Norm Maracle .30 .75
181 Patrik Stefan .08 .20
182 Dave Andreychuk .08 .20
183 Sergei Samsonov .30 .75
184 John Grahame RC .60 1.50
185 Jason Allison .08 .20
186 Kyle McLaren .08 .20
187 Anson Carter .30 .75
188 Martin Biron .30 .75
189 Brian Campbell RC .08 .20
190 Curtis Brown .08 .20
191 Alexei Zhitnik .08 .20
192 David Moravec RC .08 .20
193 Oleg Saprykin .30 .75
194 Grant Fuhr .30 .75
195 Phil Housley .08 .20
196 Marc Savard .08 .20
197 Robyn Regehr .08 .20
198 Martin Gelinas .08 .20
199 Ron Francis .30 .75
200 Jeff O'Neill .08 .20
201 Keith Primeau .08 .20
202 Paul Ranheim .08 .20
203 Kyle Calder RC .60 1.50
204 Jocelyn Thibault .30 .75
205 Wendel Clark .30 .75
206 Doug Gilmour .30 .75
207 Josef Marha .08 .20
208 Alexei Zhamnov .08 .20
209 Dan Hinote RC .75 2.00
210 Patrick Roy 2.00 5.00
211 Joe Sakic .75 2.00
212 Alex Tanguay .30 .75
213 Sandis Ozolinsh .08 .20
214 Adam Deadmarsh .08 .20
215 Jere Lehtinen .30 .75
216 Mike Modano .60 1.50
217 Darryl Sydor .30 .75
218 Sergei Zubov .08 .20
219 Pavel Patera RC .08 .20
220 Jamie Pushor .08 .20
221 Chris Osgood .30 .75
222 Tomas Holmstrom .08 .20
223 Chris Chelios .40 1.00
224 Sergei Fedorov .75 2.00
225 Jiri Fischer .08 .20
226 Paul Comrie RC .08 .20
227 Frantisek Musil .08 .20
228 Janne Niinimaa .08 .20
229 Doug Weight .30 .75
230 Trevor Kidd .30 .75
231 Oleg Kvasha .30 .75
232 Viktor Kozlov .08 .20
233 Rob Niedermayer .08 .20
234 Luc Robitaille .30 .75
235 Aki Berg .08 .20
236 Bryan Smolinski .08 .20
237 Jozef Stumpel .08 .20
238 Zigmund Palffy .30 .75
239 Stephane Fiset .30 .75
240 Jason Blake RC .08 .20
241 Scott Lachance .08 .20
242 Vladimir Malakhov .08 .20
243 Mike Ribeiro .08 .20
244 Brian Savage .08 .20
245 Tomas Vokoun .08 .20
246 Randy Robitaille .08 .20
247 Sergei Nemchinov .08 .20
248 Brendan Morrison .30 .75
249 Scott Niedermayer .08 .20
250 Scott Stevens .30 .75
251 Scott Gomez .08 .20
252 Mark Lawrence .08 .20
253 Felix Potvin .40 1.00
254 Olli Jokinen .30 .75
255 Tim Connolly .08 .20
256 Mariusz Czerkawski .08 .20
257 Valeri Kamensky .08 .20
258 Brian Leetch .40 1.00
259 Petr Nedved .30 .75
260 Theo Fleury .08 .20
261 Kevin Hatcher .08 .20
262 Mike York .08 .20
263 Ron Tugnutt .30 .75
264 Chris Phillips .08 .20
265 Daniel Alfredsson .30 .75
266 Radek Bonk .08 .20
267 Wade Redden .08 .20
268 John Vanbiesbrouck .30 .75
269 John LeClair .50 1.25
270 Simon Gagne .40 1.00
271 Nikolai Khabibulin .30 .75
272 Daniel Briere .08 .20
273 Jeremy Roenick .50 1.25
274 Andrew Ference .08 .20
275 Alexei Kovalev .08 .20
276 Martin Straka .08 .20
277 Alexei Morozov .30 .75
278 Steve Shields .30 .75
279 Marco Sturm .30 .75
280 Niklas Sundstrom .08 .20
281 Brad Stuart .08 .20
282 Owen Nolan .30 .75
283 Roman Turek .30 .75
284 Chris Pronger .30 .75
285 Jim Campbell .08 .20
286 Michal Handzus .30 .75
287 Pierre Turgeon .30 .75
288 Darcy Tucker .08 .20
289 Andrei Zyuzin .08 .20
290 Stephen Guolla .08 .20
291 Curtis Joseph .40 1.00
292 Jonas Hoglund .08 .20
293 Bryan Berard .08 .20
294 Mike Johnson .30 .75
295 Garth Snow .30 .75
296 Jason Strudwick .08 .20
297 Steve Kariya RC 1.00 2.50
298 Markus Naslund .40 1.00
299 Mattias Ohlund .30 .75
300 Alexander Mogilny .30 .75
301 Olaf Kolzig .30 .75
302 Alexei Tezikov RC .40 1.00
303 Alexandre Volchkov RC .30 .75
304 Steve Yzerman CL .40 1.00
305 Curtis Joseph CL .08 .20
306 Pavel Brendl RC 2.50 6.00
307 Daniel Sedin SP 3.00 8.00
308 Henrik Sedin SP 3.00 8.00
309 Sheldon Keefe RC 2.50 6.00
310 Ryan Jardine RC 2.50 6.00
311 Maxime Ouellet SP 1.25 3.00
312 Barret Jackman SP 1.25 3.00
313 Kristian Kudroc RC 2.50 6.00
314 Branislav Mezei RC 2.50 6.00
315 Denis Shvidki SP 1.25 3.00
316 Brian Finley SP 1.25 3.00
317 Jonathan Cheechoo SP 6.00 15.00
318 Mark Bell SP 1.25 3.00
319 Taylor Pyatt SP 1.25 3.00
320 Norm Milley SP 1.25 3.00
321 Jamie Lundmark SP 1.25 3.00
322 Alexander Buturlin RC 2.50 6.00
323 Jaroslav Kristek RC 2.50 6.00
324 Kris Beech SP 1.25 3.00
325 Scott Kelman SP 1.25 3.00
326 Milan Kraft RC 2.50 6.00
327 Mattias Weinhandl SP 1.25 3.00
328 Alexei Volkov SP 1.25 3.00
329 Andrei Shefer RC 2.50 6.00
330 Mathieu Chouinard SP 1.25 3.00
331 Justin Papineau SP 1.25 3.00
332 Mike Van Ryn SP 1.25 3.00
333 Jeff Heerema SP 1.25 3.00
334 Michael Zigomanis SP 1.25 3.00
335 Bryan Kazarian RC 2.50 6.00
336 Antti Aalto .30 .75
337 Andreas Karlsson RC .30 .75
338 Joel Prpic RC .30 .75
339 Travis Brigley RC .30 .75
340 Steve Passmore RC .30 .75
341 Georges Laraque RC .60 1.50
342 Brad Chartrand RC .30 .75
343 Francis Bouillon RC .30 .75
344 Karlis Skrastins RC .30 .75
345 Karel Rachunek .30 .75
346 Andy Delmore RC .30 .75
347 Martin Sonnenberg RC .30 .75
348 Ben Clymer RC .30 .75
349 Chris McAllister RC .30 .75
350 Harold Druken .30 .75

1999-00 Upper Deck Gold Reserve Game-Used Souvenirs

Randomly inserted in Gold Reserve Update packs at the rate of 1:480, this 7-card set features NHL players coupled with a swatch of a game-used puck.
GRBH Brett Hull 20.00 50.00
GREL Eric Lindros 15.00 40.00
GRPB Pavel Bure 15.00 40.00
GRPK Paul Kariya 15.00 40.00
GRPR Patrick Roy 30.00 80.00
GRSY Steve Yzerman 25.00 60.00
GRWG Wayne Gretzky 40.00 100.00

1999-00 Upper Deck Gold Reserve UD Authentics

Randomly seeded in packs at the rate of 1:480, this 6-card set features authentic player autographs on the card front. Cards that carry the "UPD" suffix are found in Gold

Reserve Update packs.
BH Brett Hull 25.00 50.00
BL Brian Leetch UPD 10.00 20.00
BM Bill Muckalt 6.00 15.00
CD Chris Drury 10.00 20.00
CJ Curtis Joseph 8.00 20.00
DL David Legwand 10.00 20.00
PB Pavel Bure 8.00 20.00
PS Patrik Stefan UPD 6.00 15.00
SS Sergei Samsonov UPD 10.00 20.00
SY Steve Yzerman UPD 30.00 80.00

1998-99 Upper Deck Gold Reserve

Distributed as a predominately retail product, this brand mirrored the regular Upper Deck brand in look and checklist, the only difference being that this set carried gold foil where Upper Deck was silver.

COMPLETE SET (420) 100.00 200.00
COMP.SER.1 SET (210) 60.00 120.00
COMP.SER.2 SET (210) 40.00 80.00
1 Antti Aalto SR 1.00 2.50
2 Cameron Mann SR 1.00 2.50
3 Norm Maracle SR RC 1.00 2.50
4 Daniel Cleary SR 1.00 2.50
5 Brendan Morrison SR 1.00 2.50
6 Marian Hossa SR 1.00 2.50
7 Daniel Briere SR 1.00 2.50
8 Mike Crowley SR RC 1.00 2.50
9 Darryl Laplante SR RC 1.00 2.50
10 Suem Butenschen SR 1.00 2.50
11 Yan Golubovsky SR RC 1.00 2.50
12 Olli Jokinen SR 1.00 2.50
13 J-S Giguere 1.00 2.50
14 Mike Watt SR 1.00 2.50
15 Ryan Johnson SR RC 1.00 2.50
16 Teemu Selanne RR 1.00 2.50
17 Paul Kariya RR 1.00 2.50
18 Pavel Bure RR 1.00 2.50
19 Joe Thornton RR 2.50 6.00
20 Dominik Hasek RR 2.50 6.00
21 Bryan Berard RR 1.00 2.50
22 Chris Phillips RR 1.00 2.50
23 Sergei Fedorov RR 2.00 5.00
24 Sergei Samsonov RR 1.00 2.50
25 Marc Denis RR 1.00 2.50
26 Patrick Marleau RR 1.00 2.50
27 Jaromir Jagr RR 2.00 5.00
28 Saku Koivu RR 1.00 2.50
29 Peter Forsberg RR 3.00 8.00
30 Mike Modano RR 2.00 5.00
31 Paul Kariya .50 1.25
32 Matt Cullen .15 .30
33 Josef Marha .15 .30
34 Teemu Selanne .50 1.25
35 Pavel Trnka .15 .30
36 Tom Askey RC .15 .30
37 Tim Taylor .15 .30
38 Ray Bourque .75 2.00
39 Sergei Samsonov .30 .75
40 Don Sweeney .15 .30
41 Jason Allison .15 .30
42 Steve Heinze .15 .30
43 Erik Rasmussen .15 .30
44 Dominik Hasek 1.00 2.50
45 Geoff Sanderson .15 .30
46 Michael Peca .15 .30
47 Brian Holzinger .15 .30
48 Vaclav Varada .15 .30
49 Steve Begin .15 .30
50 Denis Gauthier .15 .30
51 Derek Morris .15 .30
52 Valeri Bure .15 .30
53 Hnat Domenichelli .15 .30
54 Corey Stillman .15 .30
55 Jarome Iginla .60 1.50
56 Tyler Moss .15 .30
57 Sami Kapanen .15 .30
58 Trevor Kidd .30 .75
59 Glen Wesley .15 .30
60 Nelson Emerson .15 .30
61 Jeff O'Neill .15 .30
62 Bates Battaglia .15 .30
63 Doug Gilmour .30 .75
64 Christian LaFlamme .15 .30
65 Chris Chelios .50 1.25
66 Paul Coffey .50 1.25
67 Eric Weinrich .15 .30
68 Eric Daze .30 .75
69 Peter Forsberg 1.25 3.00
70 Eric Messier .15 .30
71 Eric Lacroix .15 .30
72 Adam Deadmarsh .15 .30
73 Claude Lemieux .15 .30
74 Patrick Roy 2.50 6.00
75 Marc Denis .30 .75
76 Brett Hull .60 1.50
77 Mike Keane .15 .30
78 Joe Nieuwendyk .30 .75
79 Darryl Sydor .15 .30
80 Ed Belfour .50 1.25
81 Jamie Langenbrunner .15 .30
82 Petr Buzek .15 .30
83 Nicklas Lidstrom .50 1.25
84 Mathieu Dandenault .15 .30
85 Steve Yzerman 2.50 6.00
86 Martin Lapointe .15 .30
87 Brendan Shanahan .50 1.25
88 Anders Eriksson .15 .30
89 Tomas Holmstrom .15 .30
90 Doug Weight .30 .75
91 Janne Ninnimaa .30 .75
92 Bill Guerin .30 .75
93 Kelly Buchberger .15 .30
94 Mike Grier .15 .30
95 Craig Millar .15 .30
96 Roman Hamrlik .15 .30
97 Ray Whitney .15 .30
98 Viktor Kozlov .15 .30
99 Peter Worrell RC .60 1.50
100 Kevin Weekes .30 .75
101 Ed Jovanovski .30 .75
102 Bill Lindsay .15 .30
103 Jozef Stumpel .30 .75
104 Luc Robitaille .30 .75
105 Yanic Perreault .15 .30
106 Donald MacLean .15 .30
107 Jamie Storr .30 .75
108 Ian Laperriere .15 .30
109 Jason Morgan RC .15 .30
110 Vincent Damphousse .15 .30
111 Mark Recchi .30 .75
112 Vladimir Malakhov .15 .30
113 Dave Manson .15 .30
114 Jose Theodore .60 1.50
115 Brian Savage .15 .30
116 Jonas Hoglund .15 .30
117 Krzysztof Oliwa .15 .30
118 Martin Brodeur 1.25 3.00
119 Patrik Elias .30 .75
120 Jason Arnott .30 .75
121 Scott Stevens .30 .75
122 Sheldon Souray RC 1.25 3.00
123 Brian Rolston .15 .30
124 Trevor Linden .30 .75
125 Warren Luhning .15 .30
126 Zdeno Chara .15 .30
127 Bryan Berard .30 .75
128 Bryan Smolinski .15 .30
129 Jason Dawe .15 .30
130 Kevin Stevens .15 .30
131 P.J. Stock RC 2.00 5.00
132 Marc Savard .30 .75
133 Pat LaFontaine .50 1.25
134 Dan Cloutier .30 .75
135 Wayne Gretzky 3.00 8.00
136 Niklas Sundstrom .15 .30
137 Damian Rhodes .30 .75
138 Magnus Arvedson .15 .30
139 Alexei Yashin .15 .30
140 Chris Phillips .15 .30
141 Janne Laukkanen .15 .30
142 Shawn McEachern .15 .30
143 John LeClair .50 1.25
144 Alexandre Daigle .15 .30
145 Dainius Zubrus .15 .30
146 Joel Otto .15 .30
147 Mike Sillinger .15 .30
148 John Vanbiesbrouck .30 .75
149 Chris Gratton .30 .75
150 Eric Desjardins .30 .75
151 Juha Ylonen .15 .30
152 Brad Isbister .15 .30
153 Oleg Tverdovsky .15 .30
154 Keith Tkachuk .50 1.25
155 Teppo Numminen .15 .30
156 Cliff Ronning .15 .30
157 Nikolai Khabibulin .30 .75
158 Alexei Morozov .15 .30
159 Kevin Hatcher .15 .30
160 Darius Kasparaitis .15 .30
161 Jaromir Jagr .75 2.00
162 Tom Barrasso .30 .75
163 Tuomas Gronman .15 .30
164 Robert Dome .15 .30
165 Peter Skudra .15 .30
166 Marcus Ragnarsson .15 .30
167 Mike Vernon .30 .75
168 Andrei Zyuzin .15 .30
169 Marco Sturm .15 .30
170 Mike Ricci .15 .30
171 Patrick Marleau .30 .75
172 Pierre Turgeon .15 .30
173 Pavol Demitra .30 .75
174 Chris Pronger .30 .75
175 Pascal Rheaume .15 .30
176 Al MacInnis .30 .75
177 Tony Twist .15 .30
178 Jim Campbell .15 .30
179 Mikael Renberg .30 .75
180 Jason Bonsignore .15 .30
181 Zac Bierk RC 3.00 8.00
182 Alexander Selivanov .15 .30
183 Stephane Richer .15 .30
184 Sandy McCarthy .15 .30
185 Alyn McCauley .15 .30
186 Sergei Berezin .30 .75
187 Mike Johnson .15 .30
188 Wendel Clark .30 .75
189 Tie Domi .15 .30
190 Yannick Trembley .15 .30
191 Curtis Joseph .50 1.25
192 Fredrik Modin .15 .30
193 Pavel Bure .50 1.25
194 Todd Bertuzzi .50 1.25
195 Mark Messier .50 1.25
196 Bret Hedican .15 .30
197 Mattias Ohlund .15 .30
198 Garth Snow .30 .75
199 Adam Oates .30 .75
200 Peter Bondra .30 .75
201 Sergei Gonchar .15 .30
202 Jan Bulis .15 .30
203 Joe Juneau .30 .75
204 Brian Bellows .15 .30
205 Olaf Kolzig .30 .75
206 Richard Zednik .15 .30
207 Wayne Gretzky CL 1.50 4.00
208 Patrick Roy CL 1.25 3.00
209 Steve Yzerman CL 1.25 3.00
210 Mike Dunham .30 .75
211 Johan Davidsson .15 .30
212 Guy Hebert .30 .75
213 Mike LeClerc .15 .30
214 Steve Rucchin .15 .30
215 Travis Green .15 .30
216 Josef Marha .15 .30
217 Ted Donato .15 .30
218 Joe Thornton .75 2.00
219 Kyle McLaren .15 .30
220 Peter Nordstrom RC .15 .30
221 Byron Dafoe .30 .75
222 Jonathan Girard .15 .30
223 Antti Laaksonen RC 3.00 8.00
224 Jason Holland .15 .30
225 Miroslav Satan .30 .75
226 Alexei Zhitnik .15 .30
227 Donald Audette .15 .30
228 Matthew Barnaby .15 .30
229 Rumun Ndur .15 .30
230 Ken Wregget .30 .75
231 Andrew Cassels .15 .30
232 Theo Fleury .15 .30
233 Phil Housley .30 .75
234 Martin St. Louis RC 6.00 15.00
235 Mike Rucinski RC .15 .30
236 Gary Roberts .15 .30
237 Keith Primeau .15 .30
238 Martin Gelinas .15 .30
239 Nolan Pratt RC .15 .30
240 Ray Sheppard .15 .30
241 Ron Francis .30 .75
242 Ty Jones .15 .30
243 Tony Amonte .30 .75
244 Chad Kilger .15 .30
245 Alexei Zhamnov .30 .75
246 Remi Royer RC .15 .30
247 Milan Hejduk RC 3.00 8.00
248 Joe Sakic 1.00 2.50
249 Valeri Kamensky .30 .75
250 Sandis Ozolinsh .15 .30
251 Shean Donovan .15 .30
252 Wade Belak .15 .30
253 Jamie Wright .15 .30
254 Sergei Zubov .15 .30
255 Richard Matvichuk .15 .30
256 Mike Modano .75 2.00
257 Pat Verbeek .15 .30
258 Jere Lehtinen .30 .75
259 Derian Hatcher .15 .30
260 Jason Botterill .15 .30
261 Igor Larionov .15 .30
262 Sergei Fedorov .75 2.00
263 Chris Osgood .30 .75
264 Vyacheslav Kozlov .30 .75
265 Larry Murphy .30 .75
266 Darren McCarty .15 .30
267 Doug Brown .15 .30
268 Kris Draper .15 .30
269 Uwe Krupp .15 .30
270 Fredrik Lindquist RC .15 .30
271 Dean McAmmond .15 .30
272 Ryan Smyth .30 .75
273 Boris Mironov .15 .30
274 Tom Poti .15 .30
275 Todd Marchant .15 .30
276 Sean Brown .15 .30
277 Rob Niedermayer .15 .30
278 Robert Svehla .15 .30
279 Scott Mellanby .15 .30
280 Radek Dvorak .15 .30
281 Jaroslav Spacek RC .15 .30
282 Mark Parrish RC 1.25 3.00
283 Ryan Johnson .15 .30
284 Glen Murray .15 .30
285 Rob Blake .30 .75
286 Steve Duchesne .30 .75
287 Vladimir Tsyplakov .15 .30
288 Stephane Fiset .30 .75
289 Mattias Norstrom .15 .30
290 Saku Koivu .50 1.25
291 Shayne Corson .15 .30
292 Brad Brown .15 .30
293 Patrice Brisebois .15 .30
294 Terry Ryan .15 .30
295 Jocelyn Thibault .30 .75
296 Miroslav Guren .15 .30
297 Darren Turcotte .30 .75
298 Sebastien Bordeleau .15 .30
299 Jan Vopat .15 .30
300 Blair Atcheynum .15 .30
301 Andrew Brunette .30 .75
302 Sergei Krivokrasov .15 .30
303 Marian Cisar .15 .30
304 Patrick Cote .15 .30
305 J.J. Daigneault .15 .30
306 Greg Johnson .15 .30
307 Chris Terreri .30 .75
308 Scott Niedermayer .15 .30
309 Vadim Sharifijanov .15 .30
310 Petr Sykora .15 .30
311 Sergei Brylin .15 .30
312 Denis Pederson .15 .30
313 Bobby Holik .15 .30
314 Bryan Muir RC .15 .30
315 Zigmund Palffy .30 .75
316 Mike Watt .15 .30
317 Tommy Salo .30 .75
318 Kenny Jonsson .15 .30
319 Dmitri Nabokov .15 .30
320 John Maclean .15 .30
321 Zarley Zalapski .15 .30
322 Brian Leetch .50 1.25
323 Todd Harvey .15 .30
324 Mike Richter .50 1.25
325 Mike Knuble .15 .30
326 Jeff Beukeboom .15 .30
327 Daniel Alfredsson .30 .75
328 Vaclav Prospal .15 .30
329 Wade Redden .15 .30
330 Igor Kravchuk .15 .30
331 Andreas Dackell .15 .30
332 Mike Maneluk RC .15 .30
333 Eric Lindros .50 1.25
334 Rod Brind'Amour .30 .75
335 Colin Forbes .15 .30
336 Dimitri Tertyshny RC .15 .30
337 Shjon Podein .15 .30
338 Chris Therien .15 .30
339 Jeremy Roenick .60 1.50
340 Jyrki Lumme .15 .30
341 Rick Tocchet .30 .75
342 Dallas Drake .15 .30
343 Keith Carney .15 .30
344 Greg Adams .15 .30
345 Jan Hrdina RC 1.50 4.00
346 German Titov .15 .30
347 Stu Barnes .15 .30
348 Kevin Hatcher .15 .30
349 Martin Straka .15 .30
350 Jean-Sebastien Aubin RC 1.50 4.00
351 Jeff Friesen .15 .30
352 Tony Granato .15 .30
353 Scott Hannan RC .15 .30
354 Owen Nolan .30 .75
355 Stephane Matteau .15 .30
356 Bryan Marchment .15 .30
357 Geoff Courtnall .30 .75
358 Brent Johnson RC 6.00 15.00
359 Jamie Rivers .15 .30
360 Terry Yake .15 .30
361 Jamie McLennan .30 .75
362 Grant Fuhr .30 .75
363 Michal Handzus RC 1.25 3.00
364 Bill Ranford .30 .75
365 John Cullen .15 .30
366 Craig Janney .15 .30
367 Daren Puppa .30 .75
368 Pavel Kubina RC .60 1.50
369 Wendel Clark .30 .75
370 Mats Sundin .50 1.25
371 Felix Potvin .50 1.25
372 Daniil Markov RC .15 .30
373 Derek King .15 .30
374 Steve Thomas .15 .30
375 Tomas Kaberle RC 1.25 3.00
376 Alexander Mogilny .30 .75
377 Bill Muckalt RC .15 .30
378 Brian Noonan .15 .30
379 Markus Naslund .50 1.25
380 Brad May .15 .30
381 Matt Cooke RC .15 .30
382 Calle Johansson .15 .30
383 Dale Hunter .15 .30
384 Jaroslav Svejkovsky .15 .30
385 Dmitri Mironov .15 .30
386 Matt Herr RC .15 .30
387 Nolan Baumgartner .15 .30
388 Wayne Gretzky CL .50 1.25
389 Steve Yzerman CL .30 .75
390 W.Gretzky/S.Yzerman CL .50 1.25
391 Brian Finley PE RC 1.25 3.00
392 Maxime Ouellet PE RC 3.00 8.00
393 Kurtis Foster PE RC 1.00 2.50
394 Barret Jackman PE RC 3.00 8.00
395 Ross Lupaschuk PE RC 1.00 2.50
396 Steven McCarthy PE RC 1.00 2.50
397 Peter Reynolds PE RC 1.00 2.50
398 Bart Rushmer PE RC 1.00 2.50
399 Jonathan Zion PE RC 1.00 2.50
400 Kris Beech PE RC 1.00 2.50
401 Brandin Cote PE RC 1.00 2.50
402 Scott Kelman PE RC 1.00 2.50
403 Jamie Lundmark PE RC 3.00 8.00
404 Derek Mackenzie PE RC 1.00 2.50
405 Rory McDade PE RC 1.00 2.50
406 David Morisset PE RC 1.00 2.50
407 Mirko Murovic PE RC 1.00 2.50
408 Taylor Pyatt PE RC 3.00 8.00
409 Charlie Stephens PE 1.00 2.50
410 Kyle Wanvig PE RC 1.00 2.50
411 Krzystof Wieckowk PE RC 1.00 2.50
412 Michael Zigomanis PE RC 1.00 2.50
413 Rico Fata CC 1.00 2.50
414 Vincent Lecavalier CC 1.50 4.00
415 Chris Drury CC RC 1.00 2.50
416 Oleg Kvasha CC RC 1.00 2.50
417 Eric Brewer CC 1.00 2.50
418 Josh Green CC RC 1.00 2.50
419 Marty Reasoner CC 1.00 2.50
420 Manny Malhotra CC 1.00 2.50
SY S.Yzerman Stick/200 75.00 200.00
SY S.Yzerman Stick AU/19
WG W.Gretzky Stick/200 75.00 200.00
WG W.Gretzky Stick AU/99 250.00 600.00
NNO1 W.Gretzky AU/200 200.00 500.00
NNO2 S.Yzerman AU/200 60.00 150.00

1999-00 Upper Deck Gretzky Exclusives

Inserted one pack per box of Upper Deck, these cards featured special tributes to Wayne Gretzky's career. Gold and platinum parallels to the set were also created and inserted randomly. Gold parallels were numbered to just 99. Platinum parallels were numbered 1/1 and are not priced due to scarcity.

COMPLETE SET (99) 125.00 250.00
COMMON GRETZKY (1-99) 1.25 3.00
COMMON GOLD GRETZKY (1-99) 20.00 50.00
NNO Gretzky Blues AU/99 150.00 400.00
NNO Gretzky Kings AU/99 150.00 400.00
NNO Gretzky Oilers AU/50 300.00 800.00
NNO Gretzky Rangers AU/25 400.00 1000.00

1999-00 Upper Deck Gretzky Game Jersey Autographs

These cards were randomly inserted in packs of Upper Deck Century Legend, Upper Deck Retro, and Upper Deck MVP. Each product had one version of the card numbered to 40 sets. The cards contain an actual piece of a game worn Wayne Gretzy jersey embedded in the cards and an authentic autograph.

COMMON CARD 300.00 800.00

1994 Upper Deck Gretzky 24K Gold

Issued in a heavy Plexiglas holder, this card measures the standard size and commemorates Wayne Gretzky's record-breaking 802nd goal. On a black background, the horizontal front features a 24-karat gold photo and a facsimile autograph of Gretzky, along with "802" printed in large silver numbers on the left. On the same black background, the horizontal back carries Gretzky's biography and stats in gold print. The card's serial number and the production run figure (3,500) round out the back.

1 Wayne Gretzky 40.00 100.00

2002 Upper Deck Gretzky All-Star Game

This three-card set was available via wrapper redemption from the Upper Deck booth at the NHL All-Star Fantasy in Los Angeles. The cards were individually serial numbered out of 2002 and featured highlights of Wayne Gretzky's career.

COMPLETE SET (3) 10.00 25.00
AS1 Wayne Gretzky 4.00 10.00
All-Time Leading Scorer
AS2 Wayne Gretzky 4.00 10.00
All-Time Leading Goal Scorer
AS3 Wayne Gretzky 4.00 10.00
All-Star Game Goals in a Single Period Record

2001-02 Upper Deck Gretzky Expo e-Card

Available at the Upper Deck booth during the Toronto Fall Expo, these cards featured Wayne Gretzky on the card front and a scratch-off code that could be entered into the Upper Deck web site to win prizes. A Gretzky jersey card serial-numbered out of 200 was one of the prizes and was created especially for this promotion.

WG Wayne Gretzky Jsy/200 60.00 150.00
NNO Wayne Gretzky

2005 Upper Deck Hawaii Trade Conference Signature Supremacy *

SSP12 Wayne Gretzky H
SSP13 Wayne Gretzky A

2005-06 Upper Deck Hockey Showcase

Cards were issued via a special online redemption offer through Upper Deck over an eight-week period. The stated print run was 1,000 copies of each card.

HS1 Peter Forsberg 4.00 10.00
HS2 Chris Pronger 2.00 5.00
HS3 Adam Foote 1.25 3.00
HS4 Gary Roberts 1.25 3.00
HS5 Sergei Gonchar 1.25 3.00
HS6 Brian Leetch 2.50 6.00
HS7 Darren McCarty 1.25 3.00
HS8 Michael Peca 1.25 3.00
HS9 Bobby Holik 1.25 3.00
HS10 Eric Brewer 1.25 3.00
HS11 Paul Kariya 2.50 6.00
HS12 Jason Allison 1.25 3.00
HS13 Derian Hatcher 1.25 3.00
HS14 Sean Burke 2.00 5.00
HS15 Adrian Aucoin 1.25 3.00
HS16 Jeremy Roenick 3.00 8.00
HS17 Jocelyn Thibault 2.00 5.00
HS18 Alexander Mogilny 2.00 5.00
HS19 Pierre Turgeon 1.25 3.00
HS20 Anson Carter 2.00 5.00
HS21 Tony Amonte 2.00 5.00
HS22 Curtis Joseph 2.50 6.00
HS23 Miroslav Satan 1.25 3.00
HS24 Teemu Selanne 2.50 6.00
HS25 Mike York 1.25 3.00
HS26 Dany Heatley 3.00 8.00
HS27 Zigmund Palffy 2.00 5.00
HS28 Scott Niedermayer 1.25 3.00
HS29 Jeff O'Neill 1.25 3.00
HS30 Joe Nieuwendyk 2.00 5.00
HS31 Marian Hossa 2.00 5.00
HS32 Eric Lindros 2.50 6.00
HS33 Nikolai Khabibulin 2.50 6.00
HS34 Martin Straka 1.25 3.00
HS35 Chris Osgood 2.00 5.00
HS36 Pavol Demitra 2.00 5.00
HS37 Peter Bondra 2.00 5.00
HS38 John LeClair 2.50 6.00
HS39 Cory Stillman 1.25 3.00
HS40 Alexei Zhamnov 1.25 3.00

2005-06 Upper Deck Hockey Showcase Beckett Promos

Issued as a premium in an issue of Beckett Hockey, these cards featured a background that was more bronze than the one seen on the online offer cards. Although no print run was announced, there are significantly fewer copies of this version of the card.

HS1 Peter Forsberg 4.00 10.00
HS2 Chris Pronger 2.00 5.00
HS3 Adam Foote 1.25 3.00
HS4 Gary Roberts 1.25 3.00
HS5 Sergei Gonchar 1.25 3.00
HS6 Brian Leetch 2.50 6.00
HS7 Darren McCarty 1.25 3.00
HS8 Michael Peca 1.25 3.00
HS9 Bobby Holik 1.25 3.00
HS10 Eric Brewer 1.25 3.00
HS11 Paul Kariya 2.50 6.00
HS12 Jason Allison 1.25 3.00
HS13 Derian Hatcher 1.25 3.00
HS14 Sean Burke 2.00 5.00
HS15 Adrian Aucoin 1.25 3.00
HS16 Jeremy Roenick 3.00 8.00
HS17 Jocelyn Thibault 2.00 5.00
HS18 Alexander Mogilny 2.00 5.00
HS19 Pierre Turgeon 1.25 3.00
HS20 Anson Carter 2.00 5.00
HS21 Tony Amonte 2.00 5.00
HS22 Curtis Joseph 2.50 6.00
HS23 Miroslav Satan 1.25 3.00
HS24 Teemu Selanne 2.50 6.00
HS25 Mike York 1.25 3.00
HS26 Dany Heatley 3.00 8.00
HS27 Zigmund Palffy 2.00 5.00
HS28 Scott Niedermayer 1.25 3.00
HS29 Jeff O'Neill 1.25 3.00
HS30 Joe Nieuwendyk 2.00 5.00
HS31 Marian Hossa 2.00 5.00
HS32 Eric Lindros 2.50 6.00
HS33 Nikolai Khabibulin 2.50 6.00
HS34 Martin Straka 1.25 3.00
HS35 Chris Osgood 2.00 5.00
HS36 Pavol Demitra 2.00 5.00
HS37 Peter Bondra 2.00 5.00
HS38 John LeClair 2.50 6.00
HS39 Cory Stillman 1.25 3.00
HS40 Alexei Zhamnov 1.25 3.00

1999-00 Upper Deck HoloGrFx

The 1999-00 Upper Deck HoloGrFx set was released as a 60-card one series set. The cards themselves feature NHL players on a silver rainbow foil holographic card with background color to match each player's team colors. This set was packaged as a 36-pack box with packs containing three cards at a suggested retail price of $1.99.

COMPLETE SET (60) 15.00 30.00
1 Teemu Selanne .25 .60
2 Paul Kariya .25 .60
3 Patrik Stefan RC 1.50 4.00
4 Sergei Samsonov .20 .50
5 Ray Bourque .40 1.00
6 Dominik Hasek .50 1.25
7 Brian Campbell RC .07 .20
8 Marc Savard .07 .20
9 Oleg Saprykin RC 1.50 4.00
10 Sami Kapanen .07 .20
11 Keith Primeau .07 .20
12 Tony Amonte .20 .50
13 J-P Dumont .20 .50
14 Peter Forsberg .60 1.50
15 Joe Sakic .50 1.25
16 Chris Drury .20 .50
17 Patrick Roy 1.25 3.00
18 Brett Hull .30 .75
19 Mike Modano .40 1.00
20 Ed Belfour .25 .60
21 Steve Yzerman 1.25 3.00
22 Brendan Shanahan .25 .60
23 Sergei Fedorov .40 1.00
24 Doug Weight .20 .50
25 Bill Guerin .07 .20
26 Pavel Bure .25 .60
27 Mark Parrish .07 .20
28 Luc Robitaille .20 .50
29 Zigmund Palffy .20 .50
30 Mike Ribeiro .20 .50
31 David Legwand .20 .50
32 Scott Gomez .07 .20
33 Martin Brodeur .60 1.50
34 Vadim Sharifijanov .07 .20
35 Jorgen Jonsson RC .07 .20
36 Eric Brewer .20 .50
37 Tim Connolly .07 .20
38 Theo Fleury .07 .20
39 Brian Leetch .25 .60
40 Mike Richter .25 .60
41 Marian Hossa .25 .60
42 Simon Gagne .25 .60
43 Eric Lindros .25 .60
44 John LeClair .25 .60
45 Keith Tkachuk .25 .60
46 Jeremy Roenick .30 .75
47 Jaromir Jagr .40 1.00
48 Niklas Sundstrom .07 .20
49 Jeff Friesen .07 .20
50 Brad Stuart .20 .50
51 Pavol Demitra .20 .50
52 Al MacInnis .20 .50
53 Paul Mara .20 .50
54 Vincent Lecavalier .25 .60
55 Mats Sundin .25 .60
56 Sergei Berezin .20 .50
57 Curtis Joseph .25 .60
58 Steve Kariya RC 1.00 2.50
59 Peter Bondra .20 .50
60 Olaf Kolzig .20 .50

1999-00 Upper Deck HoloGrFx Ausome

Randomly inserted in packs at 1:17, this gold parallel set features the base card enhanced with a gold foil background. Card backs carry an "AU" prefix.

*STARS: 5X TO 12X BASIC CARDS
*YNG.STARS: 4X TO 10X BASIC CARDS

1999-00 Upper Deck HoloGrFx Gretzky GrFx

Randomly inserted in packs at 1:3, this 15-card set pays tribute to The Great One by following his career from Edmonton to New York on the base HoloGrFx card stock. An AU-SOME parallel was also released for this set that featured a gold foil background. Parallels were inserted randomly at 1:105.

COMPLETE SET (15) 15.00 30.00
COMMON GRETZKY (GG1-GG15) 1.25 3.00
COMMON AUSOME (1-15) 10.00 25.00

1999-00 Upper Deck HoloGrFx Impact Zone

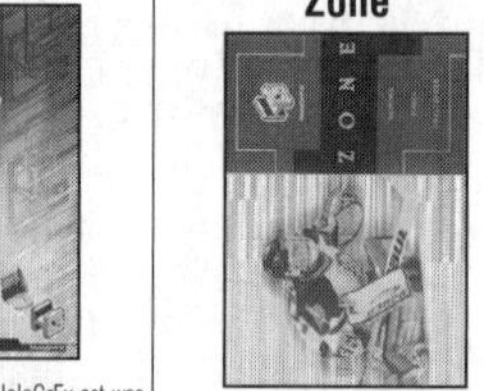

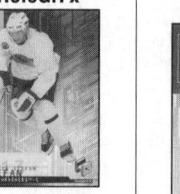

Randomly inserted in packs at 1:34, this 6-card set showcases some of the NHL's top players. The right 1/3 of the card front is black with the HoloGrFx logo and the players name, and the rest of the card features the player set against a silver rainbow foil background that has a laser etching effect. Card backs carry an "IZ" prefix. An AU-SOME gold foil parallel of this set was also released and inserted at 1:431.

COMPLETE SET (6) 15.00 30.00
*AUSOME: 2.5X TO 6X BASIC INSERTS
IZ1 Dominik Hasek 2.50 6.00
IZ2 Jaromir Jagr 2.00 5.00
IZ3 Eric Lindros 2.50 6.00
IZ4 Patrick Roy 6.00 15.00
IZ5 Paul Kariya 2.50 6.00
IZ6 Peter Forsberg 3.00 8.00

1999-00 Upper Deck HoloGrFx Pure Skill

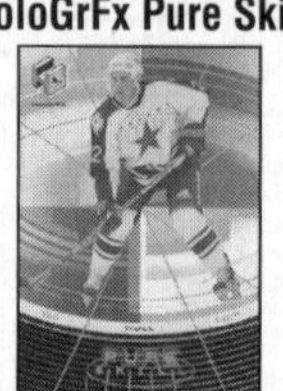

Randomly inserted in packs at 1:17, this 9-card set pictures some of the NHL's most dominating offensive threats and goalies on a silver holographic foil card. Card backs carry a "PS" prefix. A gold foil AU-SOME parallel of this set was also seeded in packs at 1:210.

COMPLETE SET (9) 12.00 25.00
*AUSOME: 2.5X TO 6X BASIC INSERTS
PS1 Paul Kariya .75 2.00
PS2 Peter Forsberg 2.00 5.00
PS3 Dominik Hasek 1.50 4.00
PS4 Sergei Samsonov .75 2.00
PS5 Teemu Selanne .75 2.00
PS6 Patrick Roy 4.00 10.00
PS7 Brett Hull 1.00 2.50
PS8 Eric Lindros .75 2.00
PS9 Jaromir Jagr 1.25 3.00

1999-00 Upper Deck HoloGrFx UD Authentics

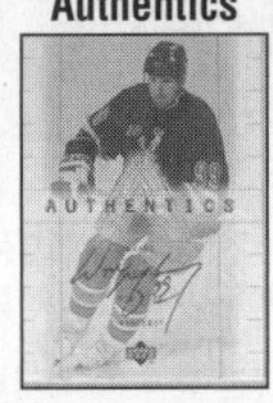

Randomly inserted in packs, this set features autographed cards of some of the NHL's top veterans and up and coming youngsters.

BH Brett Hull 15.00 40.00
BM Bill Muckalt 6.00 15.00
CD Chris Drury 10.00 25.00
DL David Legwand 6.00 15.00
PB Pavel Bure 6.00 15.00
PS Patrik Stefan 6.00 15.00
RB Ray Bourque 40.00 80.00
WG Wayne Gretzky 150.00 300.00
WG2 Wayne Gretzky Kings 150.00 300.00

1996-97 Upper Deck Ice

This retail-only set was issued in one series totaling 150 cards. Each pack contained three see-through cel cards and carried a suggested retail price of $3.99. The set is broken down into four subsets: Ice Performers (1-75), Ice Phenoms (76-105), Ice Legends (106-115), and World Juniors (116-150).

COMPLETE SET (150) 40.00 100.00
1 Kevin Todd .20 .50
2 Adam Oates .40 1.00
3 Bill Ranford .20 .50
4 Rick Tocchet .40 1.00
5 Dominik Hasek 1.00 2.50
6 Richard Smehlik .20 .50
7 Derek Plante .20 .50
8 Joel Bouchard .20 .50
9 Theo Fleury .20 .50
10 Chris Chelios .40 1.00
11 Ed Belfour .60 1.50
12 Eric Weinrich .20 .50
13 Tony Amonte .40 1.00
14 Greg Adams .20 .50
15 Jamie Langenbrunner .20 .50
16 Sergei Zubov .20 .50
17 Pat Verbeek .20 .50
18 Chris Osgood .40 1.00
19 Rem Murray RC .40 1.00
20 Jason Arnott .20 .50
21 Curtis Joseph .60 1.50
22 Bill Lindsay .20 .50
23 Ray Sheppard .20 .50
24 Martin Straka .20 .50
25 J-S Giguere RC 8.00 20.00
26 Sean Burke .40 1.00
27 Keith Primeau .20 .50
28 Geoff Sanderson .20 .50
29 Rob Blake .40 1.00
30 Ian Laperriere .20 .50
31 Byron Dafoe .40 1.00
32 Vincent Damphousse .20 .50
33 Darcy Tucker .20 .50
34 Brian Savage .20 .50
35 Bill Guerin .20 .50
36 Scott Niedermayer .20 .50
37 Steve Thomas .20 .50
38 Valeri Zelepukin .20 .50
39 Bryan Smolinski .20 .50
40 Derek King .20 .50
41 Mike Richter .60 1.50
42 Daniel Goneau RC .20 .50
43 Brian Leetch .40 1.00
44 Adam Graves .20 .50
45 Damian Rhodes .40 1.00
46 Mikael Renberg .20 .50
47 Eric Desjardins .20 .50
48 Rod Brind'Amour .40 1.00
49 Janne Niinimaa .60 1.50
50 Dale Hawerchuk .40 1.00
51 Jeremy Roenick .75 2.00
52 Mike Gartner .40 1.00
53 Cliff Ronning .20 .50
54 Patrick Lalime RC 1.00 2.50
55 Ron Francis .40 1.00
56 Petr Nedved .40 1.00
57 Bernie Nicholls .20 .50
58 Jeff Friesen .20 .50
59 Owen Nolan .40 1.00
60 Marty McSorley .20 .50
61 Pierre Turgeon .40 1.00
62 Grant Fuhr .40 1.00
63 Chris Pronger .40 1.00
64 Jim Campbell .20 .50
65 Chris Gratton .20 .50
66 Dino Ciccarelli .40 1.00
67 Felix Potvin .20 .50
68 Tie Domi .40 1.00
69 Doug Gilmour .40 1.00
70 Trevor Linden .40 1.00
71 Corey Hirsch .20 .50
72 Jim Carey .20 .50
73 Chris Simon .20 .50
74 Mark Tinordi .20 .50
75 Sergei Gonchar .20 .50
76 Paul Kariya .60 1.50
77 Teemu Selanne .60 1.50
78 Jarome Iginla .75 2.00
79 Eric Daze .20 .50
80 Sandis Ozolinsh .20 .50
81 Peter Forsberg .75 2.00
82 Mike Modano .60 1.50
83 Anders Eriksson .20 .50
84 Sergei Fedorov .60 1.50
85 Brendan Shanahan .60 1.50
86 Mike Grier RC .60 1.50
87 Doug Weight .40 1.00
88 Ed Jovanovski .20 .50
89 Saku Koivu .60 1.50
90 Jose Theodore .75 2.00
91 Jocelyn Thibault .40 1.00
92 Martin Brodeur 1.25 3.00
93 Bryan Berard .20 .50
94 Zigmund Palffy .40 1.00
95 Daniel Alfredsson .40 1.00
96 Alexei Yashin .20 .50
97 Wade Redden .20 .50
98 John LeClair .40 1.00
99 Oleg Tverdovsky .20 .50
100 Keith Tkachuk .40 1.00
101 Jaromir Jagr .75 2.00
102 Roman Hamrlik .20 .50
103 Sergei Berezin RC .40 1.00
104 Alexander Mogilny .40 1.00
105 Pavel Bure .60 1.50
106 Ray Bourque .75 2.00
107 Patrick Roy 1.50 4.00
108 Joe Sakic 1.00 2.50
109 Steve Yzerman 1.25 3.00
110 John Vanbiesbrouck .40 1.00
111 Mark Messier .60 1.50
112 Wayne Gretzky 2.00 5.00
113 Eric Lindros .60 1.50
114 Mario Lemieux 3.00 8.00
115 Brett Hull .60 1.50
116 Joe Thornton RC 12.00 30.00
117 Marc Denis .20 .50
118 Martin Biron RC 2.00 5.00
119 Jason Doig .20 .50
120 Daniel Briere RC 8.00 20.00
121 Trevor Letowski RC .40 1.00
122 Boyd Devereaux RC .40 1.00
123 Dwayne Hay RC .40 1.00
124 Hugh Hamilton RC .40 1.00
125 Brad Isbister RC .60 1.50
126 Shane Willis RC .40 1.00
127 Trent Whitfield RC .40 1.00
128 Jesse Wallin RC .40 1.00
129 Alyn McCauley .20 .50
130 Cameron Mann RC .40 1.00
131 Jeff Ware .20 .50
132 Corey Sarich .20 .50
133 Richard Jackman RC .20 .50
134 Brad Larsen .20 .50
135 Peter Schaefer RC .75 2.00
136 Christian Dube .20 .50
137 Chris Phillips .20 .50
138 Sergei Samsonov .40 1.00
139 Alexei Morozov .20 .50
140 Sergei Fedotov RC .40 1.00
141 Denis Khlopotnov RC .40 1.00
142 Andrei Markov RC .75 2.00
143 Andrei Petrunin .20 .50
144 Roman Liachenko RC .40 1.00
145 Joe Corvo RC .40 1.00
146 Erik Rasmussen .20 .50
147 Mike York RC .75 2.00
148 Brian Boucher .40 1.00
149 Paul Mara RC .40 1.00
150 Marty Reasoner .20 .50

1996-97 Upper Deck Ice Parallel

This 115-card set is a partial parallel version of the regular Upper Deck Ice set and features a special Light F/X acetate card design. The set contains three subsets: Ice Performers (1-75) inserted at the rate of 1:9 with a bronze design, Ice Phenoms (76-105) inserted at the rate of 1:47 with a silver design, and Ice Legends (106-115) inserted at the rate of 1:325 with a gold design. The World Juniors subset, present in the regular issue, is not included in the parallel version, leaving the set complete at 115 cards.

*PERF.STARS: 3X TO 8X BASIC CARDS
*PERF.ROOKIE: 1.5X TO 4X BASIC CARDS
*PHENOMS: 6X TO 15X BASIC CARDS
*PHEN.ROOKIE: 3X TO 6X BASIC CARDS
*LEGENDS: 20X TO 40X BASIC CARDS

1996-97 Upper Deck Ice Stanley Cup Foundation

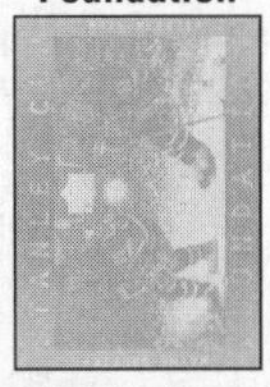

Randomly inserted in packs at a rate of 1:96, this 10-card set features color player photos of winning teammate pairs in colored borders on an acetate card. Dynasty parallels were also inserted randomly at 1:960.

*DYNASTY: 2X TO 4X BASIC INSERTS
S1 Wayne Gretzky 20.00 50.00
Mark Messier
S2 Brendan Shanahan 15.00 40.00
Steve Yzerman
S3 John Vanbiesbrouck 6.00 15.00
Ed Jovanovski
S4 Jocelyn Thibault 15.00 40.00
Saku Koivu
S5 Joe Sakic 20.00 50.00
Patrick Roy
S6 Paul Kariya 6.00 15.00
Teemu Selanne
S7 Mario Lemieux 20.00 50.00
Jaromir Jagr
S8 Jeremy Roenick 12.50 30.00
Keith Tkachuk
S9 Doug Weight 6.00 15.00
Jason Arnott
S10 John LeClair 15.00 40.00
Eric Lindros

1997-98 Upper Deck Ice

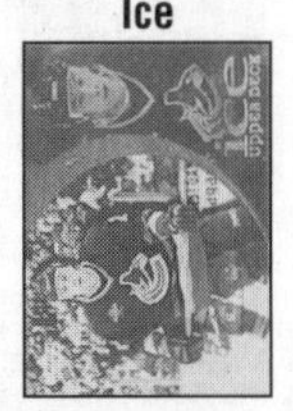

The 1997-98 Upper Deck Ice set was issued in one series totaling 90 cards and was distributed in three-card packs with a suggested retail price of $4.99. The fronts feature color action player photos printed on acetate card stock. The backs carry player information.

COMPLETE SET (90) 40.00 80.00
1 Nelson Emerson .15 .40
2 Derian Hatcher .15 .40
3 Mike Richter .50 1.25
4 Sergei Berezin .15 .40
5 Nicklas Lidstrom .50 1.25
6 Ryan Smyth .40 1.00
7 Martin Brodeur 1.25 3.00
8 Geoff Sanderson .40 1.00
9 Doug Weight .40 1.00
10 Owen Nolan .40 1.00
11 Daniel Alfredsson .40 1.00
12 Peter Bondra .40 1.00
13 Jim Campbell .15 .40
14 Rob Niedermayer .15 .40
15 Daymond Langkow .40 1.00
16 Zigmund Palffy .40 1.00
17 Adam Oates .40 1.00
18 Adam Deadmarsh .15 .40
19 Brian Holzinger .15 .40
20 Jarome Iginla .50 1.25
21 Janne Niinimaa .40 1.00
22 Dino Ciccarelli .15 .40
23 Mark Recchi .40 1.00
24 Sandis Ozolinsh .15 .40
25 Keith Primeau .15 .40
26 Ed Jovanovski .40 1.00
27 Jeremy Roenick .60 1.50
28 Alexei Yashin .15 .40
29 Felix Potvin .50 1.25
30 Chris Osgood .40 1.00
31 Marc Denis .15 .40
32 Tyler Moss RC .15 .40
33 Kevin Hodson .40 1.00
34 Jamie Storr .40 1.00
35 Roman Turek .40 1.00
36 Jose Theodore .50 1.25
37 Magnus Arvedson .15 .40
38 Daniel Cleary .15 .40
39 Mike Knuble .15 .40
40 Jaroslav Svejkovsky .40 1.00
41 Patrick Marleau .75 2.00
42 Mattias Ohlund .40 1.00
43 Sergei Samsonov .40 1.00
44 Espen Knutsen RC .75 2.00
45 Vaclav Prospal RC .50 1.25
46 Joe Thornton 1.25 3.00
47 Chris Phillips .15 .40
48 Mike Johnson RC .50 1.25
49 Dainius Zubrus .50 1.25
50 Wade Redden .15 .40
51 Derek Morris RC .60 1.50
52 Marco Sturm RC .75 2.00
53 Don MacLean .15 .40
54 Bryan Berard .15 .40
55 Richard Zednik .15 .40
56 Alexei Morozov .40 1.00
57 Erik Rasmussen .15 .40
58 Olli Jokinen RC 1.00 2.50
59 Jan Bulis RC .15 .40
60 Patrik Elias RC 2.00 5.00
61 Peter Forsberg 1.25 3.00
62 Mike Modano .50 1.25
63 Tony Amonte .40 1.00
64 Theo Fleury .15 .40
65 Ron Francis .40 1.00
66 Brett Hull .60 1.50
67 Chris Chelios .50 1.25
68 Jaromir Jagr .75 2.00
69 Sergei Fedorov .75 2.00
70 Keith Tkachuk .50 1.25
71 Mark Messier .50 1.25
72 Pat LaFontaine .50 1.25
73 Mats Sundin .50 1.25
74 John Vanbiesbrouck .40 1.00
75 John LeClair .50 1.25
76 Brian Leetch .50 1.25
77 Ray Bourque .75 2.00
78 Saku Koivu .50 1.25
79 Joe Sakic 1.00 2.50
80 Teemu Selanne .50 1.25
81 Curtis Joseph .50 1.25
82 Doug Gilmour .40 1.00
83 Patrick Roy 2.50 6.00
84 Brendan Shanahan .50 1.25
85 Paul Kariya .50 1.25
86 Pavel Bure .50 1.25
87 Dominik Hasek 1.00 2.50
88 Eric Lindros .50 1.25
89 Steve Yzerman 2.50 6.00
90 Wayne Gretzky 3.00 8.00

1997-98 Upper Deck Ice Parallel

This 90-card set is a parallel version of the base set and is divided into three partial parallel sets. Ice Performers consists of cards 1-30 with an insertion rate of 1:2; Ice Phenoms consists of cards 31-60 with an insertion rate of 1:5; Ice Legends consists of the top 30 NHL players whose cards are 61-90 and have an insertion rate of 1:11.

*PERF.STARS: .75X TO 1.5X BASIC CARDS
*PHEN.STARS: 1X TO 2X BASIC CARDS
*LEGENDS STARS: 2X TO 5X BASIC CARDS

1997-98 Upper Deck Ice Champions

Randomly inserted in packs at the rate of 1:47 and numbered out of 100, this 20-card set features color player head photos and action images printed with a Light FX/litho/acetate combination. An Ice Champions 2 Die Cuts parallel was also produced and limited to 100 copies each.

COMPLETE SET (20) 150.00 300.00
*DIE CUTS: 4X TO 8X BASIC CARDS
IC1 Wayne Gretzky 30.00 80.00
IC2 Patrick Roy 25.00 60.00
IC3 Eric Lindros 5.00 12.00
IC4 Saku Koivu 5.00 12.00
IC5 Dominik Hasek 10.00 25.00
IC6 Joe Thornton 8.00 20.00
IC7 Martin Brodeur 12.50 30.00
IC8 Teemu Selanne 5.00 12.00
IC9 Paul Kariya 5.00 12.00
IC10 Joe Sakic 10.00 25.00
IC11 Mark Messier 5.00 12.00
IC12 Peter Forsberg 12.50 30.00
IC13 Mats Sundin 5.00 12.00
IC14 Brendan Shanahan 5.00 12.00
IC15 Keith Tkachuk 5.00 12.00
IC16 Brett Hull 6.00 15.00
IC17 John Vanbiesbrouck 5.00 12.00
IC18 Jaromir Jagr 8.00 20.00
IC19 Steve Yzerman 15.00 40.00
IC20 Sergei Samsonov 5.00 12.00

1997-98 Upper Deck Ice Lethal Lines

Randomly inserted in packs at the rate of 1:11, this 30-card set features ten sets of three cards each displaying an action player photo which create an interlocking complete die-cut "lethal line" card when placed side-by-side in the correct order. A lethal line 2 parallel was also created and inserted at 1:120.

COMPLETE SET (30) 60.00 150.00
*LETH.LINE 2: 1.25X TO 3X BASIC CARDS
L1A Paul Kariya 2.00 5.00
L1B Wayne Gretzky 10.00 25.00
L1C Joe Thornton 4.00 10.00
L2A Brendan Shanahan 2.00 5.00
L2B Eric Lindros 2.00 5.00
L2C Jaromir Jagr 3.00 8.00
L3A Keith Tkachuk 1.25 3.00
L3B Mark Messier 2.00 5.00
L3C Owen Nolan 1.25 3.00
L4A Daniel Alfredsson 1.25 3.00
L4B Peter Forsberg 5.00 12.00
L4C Mats Sundin 2.00 5.00
L5A Ryan Smyth 1.25 3.00
L5B Steve Yzerman 8.00 20.00
L5C Jarome Iginla 2.50 6.00
L6A Sergei Samsonov 1.25 3.00
L6B Igor Larionov 1.25 3.00
L6C Sergei Fedorov 2.50 6.00
L7A Patrik Elias .40 1.00
L7B Alexei Morozov .40 1.00
L7C Vaclav Prospal .40 1.00
L8A John LeClair 1.25 3.00
L8B Mike Modano 2.50 6.00
L8C Brett Hull 2.50 6.00
L9A Olli Jokinen 1.25 3.00
L9B Saku Koivu 2.50 6.00
L9C Teemu Selanne 2.50 6.00
L10A Brian Leetch 1.25 3.00
L10B Patrick Roy 8.00 20.00
L10C Nicklas Lidstrom 1.25 3.00

1997-98 Upper Deck Ice Power Shift

Randomly inserted in packs at the rate of 1:23, this 90-card set is a gold foil parallel version of the base set.

*STARS: 6X TO 12X BASIC CARDS
*ROOKIES: 3X TO 6X BASIC CARDS

2000-01 Upper Deck Ice

Released in mid-September, Upper Deck Ice featured a 60-card set comprised of 40 Veterans, 14 Fresh Faces cards die cut and sequentially numbered to 1500, and six Prime Performers cards die cut and sequentially numbered to 1500. Base cards were printed on clear acetate plastic card stock. Ice was released in 18-pack boxes with each pack containing four cards and carried a suggested retail price of $3.99. There was an update set that included an additional 63 cards, which was packaged along with other Upper Deck product updates.

COMPLETE SET (60) 200.00 400.00
COMP.SET w/o SP's (40) 7.50 15.00
COMP.SET w/UPDATE (123) 400.00800.00
1 Paul Kariya .40 1.00
2 Teemu Selanne .40 1.00
3 Patrik Stefan .10 .25
4 Joe Thornton .60 1.50
5 Dominik Hasek .75 2.00
6 Michael Peca .10 .25
7 Valeri Bure .10 .25
8 Ron Francis .30 .75
9 Tony Amonte .30 .75
10 Patrick Roy 2.00 5.00
11 Ray Bourque .75 2.00
12 Milan Hejduk .40 1.00
13 Peter Forsberg .75 2.00
14 Brett Hull .50 1.25
15 Mike Modano .60 1.50
16 Brendan Shanahan .40 1.00
17 Chris Osgood .30 .75
18 Steve Yzerman 1.50 4.00
19 Doug Weight .30 .75
20 Pavel Bure .40 1.00
21 Luc Robitaille .30 .75
22 Jose Theodore .50 1.25
23 David Legwand .30 .75
24 Martin Brodeur 1.00 2.50
25 Scott Gomez .10 .25
26 Tim Connolly .10 .25
27 Mike York .10 .25
28 Marian Hossa .40 1.00
29 Brian Boucher .40 1.00
30 John LeClair .40 1.00
31 Jeremy Roenick .50 1.25
32 Jaromir Jagr .60 1.50
33 Steve Shields .30 .75
34 Chris Pronger .30 .75
35 Roman Turek .30 .75
36 Vincent Lecavalier .40 1.00
37 Curtis Joseph .40 1.00
38 Mats Sundin .40 1.00
39 Mark Messier .40 1.00
40 Olaf Kolzig .30 .75
41 Matt Pettinger RC 2.00 5.00
42 Chris Nielsen RC 2.00 5.00
43 Dany Heatley RC 25.00 60.00
44 Matt Zultek RC 2.00 5.00
45 Dmitri Afanasenkov RC 2.00 5.00
46 Tyler Bouck RC 2.50 6.00
47 Jonas Andersson RC 2.00 5.00
48 Marc-Andre Thinel RC 2.00 5.00
49 Jaroslav Svoboda RC 2.00 5.00
50 Josef Vasicek RC 2.00 5.00
51 Andrew Raycroft RC 5.00 12.00
52 Juraj Kolnik RC 2.00 5.00
53 Zdenek Blatny RC 2.00 5.00
54 Sebastien Caron RC 2.00 5.00
55 Eric Nickulas RC 2.00 5.00
56 Serge Aubin RC 2.00 5.00
57 Steven Reinprecht RC 2.00 5.00
58 David Gosselin RC 2.00 5.00
59 Colin White RC 2.00 5.00
60 Steve Valiquette RC 2.00 5.00
61 Jeff Friesen .10 .25
62 Bill Guerin .30 .75
63 J-P Dumont .10 .25
64 Oleg Saprykin .10 .25
65 Shane Willis .10 .25
66 Josef Vasicek .10 .25
67 Steve Reinprecht .10 .25
68 Marc Denis .30 .75
69 Marty Turco RC 6.00 15.00
70 Sergei Fedorov .60 1.50
71 Adam Deadmarsh .10 .25
72 Keith Tkachuk .40 1.00
73 Mark Messier .40 1.00
74 Alexei Yashin .10 .25
75 Mario Lemieux 2.00 5.00
76 Evgeni Nabakov .30 .75
77 Brad Richards .30 .75
78 Henrik Sedin .10 .25
79 Daniel Sedin .10 .25
80 Matt Pettinger .10 .25
81 Marc Chouinard RC 2.00 5.00
82 Bryan Adams RC 2.00 5.00
83 Martin Brochu RC 2.00 5.00
84 Craig Adams RC 2.00 5.00
85 David Aebischer RC 5.00 12.00
86 Rostislav Klesla RC 2.00 5.00
87 Shawn Horcoff RC 4.00 10.00
88 Mike Comrie RC 4.00 10.00
89 Eric Belanger RC 2.00 5.00
90 Marian Gaborik RC 15.00 40.00
91 Eric Landry RC 2.00 5.00
92 Scott Hartnell RC 4.00 10.00
93 Chris Mason RC 4.00 10.00
94 Rick DiPietro RC 8.00 20.00
95 Martin Havlat RC 8.00 20.00
96 Roman Cechmanek RC 2.00 5.00
97 Justin Williams RC 4.00 10.00
98 Ruslan Fedotenko RC 2.00 5.00
99 Jean-Guy Trudel RC 2.00 5.00
100 Reed Low RC 2.00 5.00
101 Alexei Ponikarovsky RC 2.00 5.00
102 Rob Blake .30 .75
103 Andy McDonald RC 4.00 10.00
104 Petr Tenkrat RC 2.00 5.00
105 Brad Tapper RC 2.00 5.00
106 Darcy Hordichuk RC 2.00 5.00
107 J.P. Vigier RC 2.00 5.00
108 Pavel Kolarik RC 2.00 5.00
109 Jarno Kultanen RC 2.00 5.00
110 Eric Manlow RC 2.00 5.00
111 Eric Boulton RC 2.00 5.00
112 Brian Swanson RC 2.00 5.00
113 Lubomir Sekeras RC 2.00 5.00
114 Greg Classen RC 2.00 5.00
115 Jiri Bicek RC 2.00 5.00
116 Jeff Ulmer RC 2.00 5.00
117 Johan Holmqvist RC 3.00 8.00
118 Shane Hnidy RC 2.00 5.00
119 Ossi Vaananen RC 2.00 5.00
120 Johan Hedberg RC 3.00 8.00
121 Mark Smith RC 2.00 5.00
122 Alexander Khavanov RC 2.00 5.00
123 Bryce Salvador RC 2.00 5.00

2000-01 Upper Deck Ice Immortals

Randomly inserted in packs, this 60-card set parallels the Series I set sequentially numbered to 25.

*STARS: 30X TO 80X BASIC CARDS
*SP's: 2X TO 4X BASIC CARDS
43 Dany Heatley 150.00 300.00

2000-01 Upper Deck Ice Legends

Randomly inserted in packs, this 60-card set parallels the Series I set and is sequentially numbered to 150.

*STARS: 6X TO 15X BASIC CARDS
*SP's: .75X TO 1.5X BASIC CARDS
43 Dany Heatley 75.00 150.00

2000-01 Upper Deck Ice Stars

Randomly inserted in packs, this 60-card set parallels the Series I set enhanced with gold foil stamping and is sequentially numbered to 500.

*STARS STARS: 2X TO 5X BASIC CARDS
*STARS SP's: .5X TO 1.25X BASIC CARDS
43 Dany Heatley 40.00 100.00

2000-01 Upper Deck Ice Champions

COMPLETE SET (6) 15.00 30.00
STATED ODDS 1:18
IC1 Patrick Roy 5.00 12.00
IC2 Mike Modano 2.00 5.00
IC3 Steve Yzerman 5.00 12.00
IC4 Martin Brodeur 2.50 6.00
IC5 John LeClair 1.50 4.00
IC6 Jaromir Jagr 1.50 4.00

2000-01 Upper Deck Ice Clear Cut Autographs

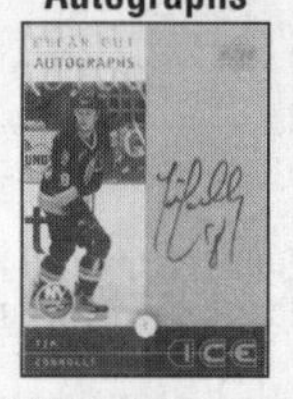

Randomly inserted in packs at the rate of 1:108, this 10-card set features authentic player autographs on the right side of the card on a gray background, and full color player action shots on the right.

BH Brett Hull 15.00 40.00
BL Brian Leetch 8.00 20.00
CJ Curtis Joseph 10.00 25.00
MY Mike York 4.00 10.00
PB Pavel Bure 10.00 25.00
PS Patrik Stefan 4.00 10.00
RT Roman Turek 4.00 10.00
SG Scott Gomez 4.00 10.00
SY Steve Yzerman 30.00 80.00
TC Tim Connolly 4.00 10.00

2000-01 Upper Deck Ice Cool Competitors

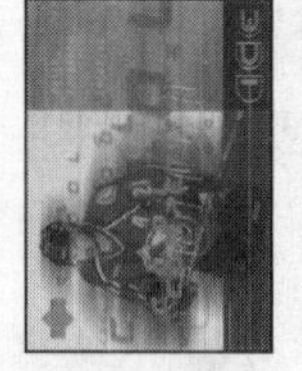

Randomly inserted in packs at the rate of 1:53, this six card set features player action shots on clear acetate plastic card stock with gold foil highlights.

COMPLETE SET (6) 40.00 80.00
CC1 Paul Kariya 4.00 10.00
CC2 Peter Forsberg 10.00 25.00
CC3 Pavel Bure 5.00 12.00
CC4 Scott Gomez 4.00 10.00
CC5 Jaromir Jagr 6.00 15.00
CC6 Curtis Joseph 4.00 10.00

2000-01 Upper Deck Ice Gallery

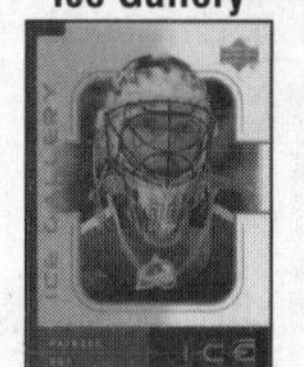

COMPLETE SET (9) 15.00 30.00
STATED ODDS 1:6
IG1 Teemu Selanne .75 2.00
IG2 Patrick Roy 4.00 10.00
IG3 Brendan Shanahan 1.25 3.00
IG4 Pavel Bure 1.00 2.50
IG5 Scott Gomez .75 2.00
IG6 John LeClair 1.00 2.50
IG7 Jaromir Jagr 1.25 3.00
IG8 Vincent Lecavalier .75 2.00
IG9 Curtis Joseph .75 2.00

2000-01 Upper Deck Ice Game Jerseys

Randomly inserted in UD Ice packs at the rate of 1:45 and 1:60 in UD Update packs this 20-card set features swatches of authentic game jerseys on acetate plastic card stock. The backs of these cards are clear as well, so the jersey swatch can be viewed from both sides of the card. Update cards are marked below.

*MULT.COLOR SWATCH: .75X TO 1.5X
JCAC Anson Carter 4.00 10.00
JCBH Brett Hull 5.00 12.00
JCBS Brendan Shanahan 4.00 10.00
JCCO Chris Osgood 4.00 10.00
JCDL David Legwand 4.00 10.00
JCJJ Jaromir Jagr 6.00 15.00
JCJL John LeClair 4.00 10.00
JCJN Joe Nieuwendyk 4.00 10.00
JCMB Martin Brodeur 12.50 30.00
JCMH Michal Handzus 4.00 10.00
JCMM Mike Modano 6.00 15.00
JCMS Miroslav Satan 4.00 10.00
JCPB Pavel Bure 4.00 10.00
JCPD Pavol Demitra 4.00 10.00
JCPK Paul Kariya 4.00 10.00
JCRB Ray Bourque 10.00 25.00
JCSF Sergei Fedorov 5.00 12.00

JCSS Sergei Samsonov 4.00 10.00
JCTC Tim Connolly 4.00 10.00
JCTS Teemu Selanne 4.00 10.00
IFO Peter Forsberg Upd 10.00 25.00
IJT Joe Thornton Upd 5.00 12.00
ILE John LeClair Upd 4.00 10.00
IMO Mike Modano Upd 6.00 15.00
IRO Patrick Roy Upd 15.00 40.00
ISA Joe Sakic Upd 10.00 25.00
ISH Brendan Shanahan Upd 4.00 10.00
ITH Jocelyn Thibault Upd 4.00 10.00
ITK Keith Tkachuk Upd 4.00 10.00

2000-01 Upper Deck Ice Rink Favorites

COMPLETE SET (9) 15.00 30.00
STATED ODDS 1:9
FP1 Paul Kariya 1.00 2.50
FP2 Peter Forsberg 2.00 5.00
FP3 Ray Bourque 1.50 4.00
FP4 Mike Modano 1.25 3.00
FP5 Steve Yzerman 4.00 10.00
FP6 Pavel Bure 1.00 2.50
FP7 Martin Brodeur 2.00 5.00
FP8 John LeClair 1.00 2.50
FP9 Jaromir Jagr 1.25 3.00

2001-02 Upper Deck Ice

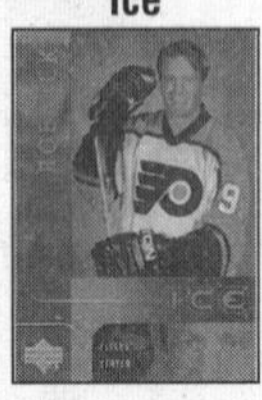

Released in early September 2001, this 151-card set featured all acetate card stock and carried an SRP of $3.99 for a 4-card pack. Ice was originally released as a 84-card set of 44 regular base cards and 40 Fresh Faces redemption cards which entitled the holder to a first year card of a rookie who made his debut during the 2001-02 season. Cards 85-151 were available in random packs of UD Rookie Update. Cards 43-84 were serial-numbered to 1500 and cards 127-151 were serial-numbered to 1000 copies each.

COMPLETE SET w/o SP's 25.00 50.00
1 Paul Kariya .40 1.00
2 Joe Thornton .60 1.50
3 Sergei Samsonov .30 .75
4 Martin Biron .30 .75
5 Jarome Iginla .50 1.25
6 Arturs Irbe .30 .75
7 Tony Amonte .30 .75
8 Patrick Roy 2.00 5.00
9 Peter Forsberg 1.00 2.50
10 Ray Bourque .75 2.00
11 Ron Tugnutt .30 .75
12 Mike Modano .60 1.50
13 Ed Belfour .40 1.00
14 Brett Hull .50 1.25
15 Steve Yzerman 2.00 5.00
16 Dominik Hasek 1.00 2.50
17 Sergei Fedorov .60 1.50
18 Tommy Salo .30 .75
19 Mike Comrie .30 .75
20 Pavel Bure .40 1.00
21 Adam Deadmarsh .10 .25
22 Zigmund Palffy .30 .75
23 Marian Gaborik .75 2.00
24 Manny Fernandez .30 .75
25 Jose Theodore .50 1.25
26 Mike Dunham .30 .75
27 Martin Brodeur 1.00 2.50
28 Patrik Elias .30 .75
29 Rick DiPietro .30 .75
30 Mark Messier .40 1.00
31 Martin Havlat .30 .75
32 Marian Hossa .40 1.00
33 Jeremy Roenick .50 1.25
34 Sean Burke .30 .75
35 Johan Hedberg .40 1.00
36 Mario Lemieux 2.50 6.00
37 Evgeni Nabokov .30 .75
38 Keith Tkachuk .40 1.00
39 Vincent Lecavalier .40 1.00
40 Curtis Joseph .40 1.00
41 Markus Naslund .40 1.00
42 Jaromir Jagr .75 2.00
43 Ilja Bryzgalov RC 4.00 10.00
44 Ilya Kovalchuk RC 15.00 40.00
45 Zdenek Kutlak RC 2.50 6.00
46 Ales Kotalik RC 4.00 10.00
47 Scott Nichol RC 2.50 6.00
48 Erik Cole RC 4.00 10.00
49 Casey Hankinson RC 2.50 6.00
50 Vaclav Nedorost RC 2.50 6.00
51 Martin Spanhel RC 2.50 6.00
52 Niko Kapanen RC 2.50 6.00
53 Pavel Datsyuk RC 8.00 20.00
54 Ty Conklin RC 2.50 6.00
55 Kristian Huselius RC 4.00 10.00
56 Jaroslav Bednar RC 2.50 6.00
57 Nick Schultz RC 2.50 6.00
58 Martti Jarventie RC 2.50 6.00
59 Martin Erat RC 2.50 6.00
60 Andreas Salomonsson RC 2.50 6.00
61 Radek Martinek RC 2.50 6.00
62 Dan Blackburn RC 2.50 6.00
63 Ivan Ciernik RC 2.50 6.00
64 Jiri Dopita RC 2.50 6.00
65 Krys Kolanos RC 2.50 6.00
66 Bill Tibbetts RC 2.50 6.00
67 Jeff Jillson RC 2.50 6.00
68 Mark Rycroft RC 2.50 6.00
69 Nikita Alexeev RC 2.50 6.00
70 Bob Wren RC 2.50 6.00
71 Pat Kavanagh RC 2.50 6.00
72 Brian Sutherby RC 2.50 6.00
73 Timo Parssinen RC 2.50 6.00
74 Kamil Piros RC 2.50 6.00
75 Jukka Hentunen RC 2.50 6.00
76 Niklas Hagman RC 2.50 6.00
77 Travis Roche RC 2.50 6.00
78 Pavel Skrbek RC 2.50 6.00
79 Scott Clemmensen RC 2.50 6.00
80 Chris Neil RC RC 2.50 6.00
81 Vaclav Pletka RC 2.50 6.00
82 Josef Boumedienne RC 2.50 6.00
83 Ryan Tobler RC 2.50 6.00
84 Chris Corrinet RC 2.50 6.00
85 Dany Heatley .50 1.25
86 Glen Murray .10 .25
87 Jozef Stumpel .10 .25
88 Tim Connolly .10 .25
89 Roman Turek .30 .75
90 Joe Sakic .75 2.00
91 Radim Vrbata .30 .75
92 Milan Hejduk .40 1.00
93 Brenden Morrow .30 .75
94 Pierre Turgeon .30 .75
95 Brett Hull .50 1.25
96 Luc Robitaille .30 .75
97 Brendan Shanahan .40 1.00
98 Nicklas Lidstrom .40 1.00
99 Sandis Ozolinsh .10 .25
100 Jason Allison .10 .25
101 Felix Potvin .40 1.00
102 Donald Audette .10 .25
103 Chris Osgood .30 .75
104 Alexei Yashin .10 .25
105 Mark Parrish .10 .25
106 Eric Lindros .40 1.00
107 Theo Fleury .10 .25
108 Barrett Heisten .10 .25
109 Daniel Alfredsson .30 .75
110 Donald Brashear .10 .25
111 Luke Richardson .10 .25
112 John LeClair .40 1.00
113 Brian Boucher .30 .75
114 Alexei Kovalev .30 .75
115 Teemu Selanne .40 1.00
116 Owen Nolan .30 .75
117 Pavol Demitra .30 .75
118 Chris Pronger .30 .75
119 Doug Weight .30 .75
120 Sheldon Keefe .10 .25
121 Nikolai Khabibulin .40 1.00
122 Mats Sundin .40 1.00
123 Jan Hlavac .10 .25
124 Trevor Linden .10 .25
125 Peter Bondra .40 1.00
126 Olaf Kolzig .30 .75
127 Pasi Nurminen RC 2.50 6.00
128 Ivan Huml RC 2.50 6.00
129 Tony Tuzzolino RC 2.50 6.00
130 Steve Montador RC 2.50 6.00
131 Mike Peluso RC 2.50 6.00
132 Steve Poapst RC 2.50 6.00
133 Riku Hahl RC 2.50 6.00
134 Blake Bellefeuille RC 2.50 6.00
135 David Ling RC 2.50 6.00
136 John Erskine RC 2.50 6.00
137 Brad Norton RC 2.50 6.00
138 Nick Smith RC 2.50 6.00
139 Ryan Flinn RC 2.50 6.00
140 Pascal Dupuis RC 2.50 6.00
141 Olivier Michaud RC 2.50 6.00
142 Marcel Hossa RC 4.00 10.00
143 Raffi Torres RC 5.00 12.00
144 Mikael Samuelsson RC 2.50 6.00
145 Christian Berglund RC 2.50 6.00
146 Shane Endicott RC 2.50 6.00
147 Eric Meloche RC 2.50 6.00
148 Steve Bancroft RC 2.50 6.00
149 Martin Cibak RC 2.50 6.00
150 Dean Melanson RC 2.50 6.00
151 Mike Farrell RC 2.50 6.00

2001-02 Upper Deck Ice Autographs

Inserted at 1:179 in UD Ice and 1:180 in UD Update, this 22-card set featured authentic player autographs on acetate card stock. Update cards are marked below.

KNOWN PRINT RUNS LISTED BELOW
AI Arturs Irbe Upd 8.00 20.00
CJ Curtis Joseph Upd/31 20.00 50.00
DH Dany Heatley Upd 15.00 40.00
DS Daniel Sedin 8.00 20.00
HS Henrik Sedin 8.00 20.00
IK Ilya Kovalchuk Upd/10
JI Jarome Iginla Upd 15.00 40.00
KH Kristian Huselius Upd 8.00 20.00
KK Krys Kolanos Upd 8.00 20.00
MB Martin Brodeur 30.00 80.00
MC Mike Comrie Upd 8.00 20.00
MC Mike Comrie 10.00 25.00
MG Marian Gaborik Upd/20
MH Milan Hejduk Upd 8.00 20.00
MK Milan Kraft 8.00 20.00
MM Mike Modano 20.00 50.00
PB Peter Bondra Upd 8.00 20.00
PS Petr Sykora 8.00 20.00
RK Rostislav Klesla Upd 8.00 20.00
RL Roberto Luongo 12.50 30.00
SY Steve Yzerman 40.00 100.00
WG Wayne Gretzky 125.00 250.00

2001-02 Upper Deck Ice Combos

Inserted at 1:179, this 10-card set featured swatches of game-used jerseys coupled with a piece of game-used stick from the featured player. Cards were produced on all acetate stock. A gold parallel was also produced and serial-numbered to just 25 copies each.

*MULT.COLOR SWATCH: 1X TO 1.5X
GOLD: 2X TO 4X BASIC CARDS
C-JJ Jaromir Jagr 12.50 30.00
C-JL John LeClair 8.00 20.00
C-JR Jeremy Roenick 15.00 40.00
C-JS Joe Sakic 12.50 30.00
C-ML Mario Lemieux 30.00 80.00
C-MM Mike Modano 12.50 30.00
C-PK Paul Kariya 10.00 25.00
C-PR Patrick Roy 20.00 50.00
C-SF Sergei Fedorov 12.50 30.00
C-SY Steve Yzerman 20.00 50.00

2001-02 Upper Deck Ice First Rounders

Inserted at 1:36, this 7-card set featured swatches of game-used jersey of former first round draft picks.

*MULT.COLOR SWATCH: .75X TO 1.5X HI
F-JJ Jaromir Jagr 8.00 20.00
F-JR Jeremy Roenick 8.00 20.00
F-JS Joe Sakic 8.00 20.00
F-MM Mike Modano 6.00 15.00
F-PK Paul Kariya 5.00 12.00
F-PS Patrik Stefan 5.00 12.00
F-SY Steve Yzerman 10.00 25.00

2001-02 Upper Deck Ice Jerseys

Inserted at 1:32, this 8-card set featured swatches of game-worn jersey on all acetate card stock.

*MULT.COLOR SWATCH: .75X TO 1.5X HI
J-BH Brett Hull 5.00 12.00
J-DW Doug Weight 6.00 15.00
J-ED Eric Daze 6.00 15.00
J-JL John LeClair 4.00 10.00
J-MS Marc Savard 4.00 10.00
J-PR Patrick Roy 12.50 30.00
J-SA Serge Aubin 4.00 10.00
J-SF Sergei Fedorov 6.00 15.00

2003-04 Upper Deck Ice

Upper Deck Ice was re-introduced in 2003-04 as a 130-card set featuring 90 veteran base cards (1-90); 30 Tier 1 rookie cards (91-120) serial-numbered to 999 and 10 Tier 2 Rookie cards serial-numbered to 99.

COMP.SET w/o SP's (90) 12.50 25.00
1 Sergei Fedorov .30 .75
2 Vaclav Prospal .10 .25
3 J-S Giguere .20 .50
4 Dany Heatley .30 .75
5 Ilya Kovalchuk .30 .75
6 Andrew Raycroft .20 .50
7 Joe Thornton .40 1.00
8 Sergei Samsonov .20 .50
9 Mika Noronen .20 .50
10 Chris Drury .20 .50
11 Daniel Briere .10 .25
12 Roman Turek .20 .50
13 Jarome Iginla .30 .75
14 Justin Williams .10 .25
15 Ron Francis .20 .50
16 Bryan Berard .10 .25
17 Alexei Zhamnov .10 .25
18 Jocelyn Thibault .20 .50
19 Joe Sakic .50 1.25
20 Paul Kariya .25 .60
21 Peter Forsberg .60 1.50
22 David Aebischer .20 .50
23 Todd Marchant .10 .25
24 Rick Nash .30 .75
25 Marc Denis .20 .50
26 Mike Modano .40 1.00
27 Marty Turco .20 .50
28 Bill Guerin .20 .50
29 Brett Hull .30 .75
30 Pavel Datsyuk .25 .60
31 Henrik Zetterberg .25 .60
32 Steve Yzerman 1.25 3.00
33 Adam Oates .20 .50
34 Tommy Salo .20 .50
35 Raffi Torres .10 .25
36 Ales Hemsky .10 .25
37 Olli Jokinen .20 .50
38 Roberto Luongo .30 .75
39 Jay Bouwmeester .10 .25
40 Martin Straka .10 .25
41 Roman Cechmanek .20 .50
42 Zigmund Palffy .20 .50
43 Marian Gaborik .50 1.25
44 Alexandre Daigle .10 .25
45 Manny Fernandez .20 .50
46 Mike Ribeiro .10 .25
47 Saku Koivu .25 .60
48 Jose Theodore .30 .75
49 David Legwand .20 .50
50 Tomas Vokoun .20 .50
51 Patrik Elias .20 .50
52 Martin Brodeur .60 1.50
53 Scott Stevens .20 .50
54 Scott Gomez .10 .25
55 Rick DiPietro .20 .50
56 Alexei Yashin .10 .25
57 Trent Hunter .10 .25
58 Mark Messier .25 .60
59 Eric Lindros .25 .60
60 Jaromir Jagr .40 1.00
61 Patrick Lalime .20 .50
62 Jason Spezza .25 .60
63 Marian Hossa .25 .60
64 Sean Burke .20 .50
65 Jeremy Roenick .30 .75
66 Tony Amonte .20 .50
67 Ladislav Nagy .10 .25
68 Mike Comrie .20 .50
69 Mario Lemieux 1.50 4.00
70 Rico Fata .10 .25
71 Vincent Damphousse .10 .25
72 Patrick Marleau .20 .50
73 Evgeni Nabokov .20 .50
74 Keith Tkachuk .25 .60
75 Chris Osgood .20 .50
76 Doug Weight .20 .50
77 Pavol Demitra .20 .50
78 Vincent Lecavalier .25 .60
79 Nikolai Khabibulin .25 .60
80 Ed Belfour .25 .60
81 Mats Sundin .25 .60
82 Alexander Mogilny .20 .50
83 Owen Nolan .20 .50
84 Todd Bertuzzi .25 .60
85 Ed Jovanovski .20 .50
86 Jason King .10 .25
87 Markus Naslund .25 .60
88 Peter Bondra .20 .50
89 Anson Carter .20 .50
90 Olaf Kolzig .20 .50
91 Pavel Vorobiev RC 2.00 5.00
92 Antti Miettinen RC 2.00 5.00
93 Chris Higgins RC 6.00 15.00
94 Dan Hamhuis RC 2.00 5.00
95 Marek Zidlicky RC 2.00 5.00
96 Mikhail Yakubov RC 2.00 5.00
97 Antoine Vermette RC 2.00 5.00
98 Jiri Hudler RC 5.00 12.00
99 Milan Michalek RC 6.00 15.00
100 Peter Sejna RC 2.00 5.00
101 Matt Stajan RC 6.00 15.00
102 Maxim Kondratiev RC 2.00 5.00
103 Alexander Semin RC 10.00 25.00
104 Sergei Zinovjev RC 2.00 5.00
105 Julien Vauclair RC 2.00 5.00
106 Dominic Moore RC 2.00 5.00
107 Tony Salmelainen RC 2.00 5.00
108 Rastislav Stana RC 2.00 5.00
109 Peter Sarno RC 2.00 5.00
110 Jed Ortmeyer RC 2.00 5.00
111 Nathan Smith RC 2.00 5.00
112 Matthew Lombardi RC 2.00 5.00
113 Dustin Brown RC 4.00 10.00
114 John-Michael Liles RC 2.00 5.00
115 Tim Gleason RC 2.00 5.00
116 Boyd Gordon RC 2.00 5.00
117 Greg Campbell RC 2.00 5.00
118 Ryan Kesler RC 2.00 5.00
119 Trevor Daley RC 2.00 5.00
120 John Pohl RC 2.00 5.00
121 Joffrey Lupul RC 30.00 80.00
122 Patrice Bergeron RC 75.00 150.00
123 Eric Staal RC 100.00 200.00
124 Tuomo Ruutu RC 40.00 80.00
125 Nikolai Zherdev RC 40.00 80.00
126 Nathan Horton RC 60.00 125.00
127 Fredrik Sjostrom RC 15.00 40.00
128 Jordin Tootoo RC 50.00 100.00
129 Joni Pitkanen RC 20.00 50.00
130 Marc-Andre Fleury RC 150.00 300.00
90P Marc-Andre Fleury PROMO .40 1.00

2003-04 Upper Deck Ice Glass Parallel

This 40-card set paralleled the rookie cards in the base set on clear acetate stock cards. Each card was serial-numbered out of 25.

*ROOKIES 91-120: 1.25X TO 3X BASE HI
*121-130: .3X TO .75X

2003-04 Upper Deck Ice Gold

This 90-card set paralleled the first 90 cards in the base set. Each card was serial-numbered out of 40.

*STARS: 4X TO 10X

2003-04 Upper Deck Ice Authentics

This 26-card memorabilia set featured certified autographs and jersey swatches. They were inserted at 1:80.

*MULT.COLOR SWATCH: .5X TO 1.25X
IA-AC Anson Carter 10.00 25.00
IA-AH Ales Hemsky 10.00 25.00
IA-CK Chuck Kobasew 6.00 15.00
IA-DA David Aebischer 15.00 40.00
IA-HA Marcel Hossa 6.00 15.00
IA-HZ Henrik Zetterberg 15.00 40.00
IA-IK Ilya Kovalchuk 25.00 60.00
IA-JI Jarome Iginla 25.00 60.00
IA-JR Jeremy Roenick 15.00 40.00
IA-JS Jason Spezza 15.00 40.00
IA-JT Joe Thornton 25.00 60.00
IA-MB Martin Brodeur 75.00 150.00
IA-MH Gordie Howe 75.00 150.00
IA-MH Marian Hossa 15.00 40.00
IA-MN Markus Naslund 15.00 40.00
IA-MT Marty Turco SP 50.00 125.00
IA-ON Owen Nolan 8.00 20.00
IA-PR Patrick Roy SP 75.00 200.00
IA-RD Rick DiPietro 15.00 40.00
IA-RL Roberto Luongo 20.00 50.00
IA-RN Rick Nash 25.00 60.00
IA-SK Saku Koivu 15.00 40.00
IA-TB Todd Bertuzzi 15.00 40.00
IA-TH Jose Theodore 25.00 60.00
IA-WG Wayne Gretzky 150.00 300.00
IA-ZP Zigmund Palffy 8.00 20.00

2003-04 Upper Deck Ice Breakers

This 42-card set featured swatches of jersey on acetate card stock. Each card was serial-numbered out of 75. A patch parallel was also created and serial-numbered out of 25

*MULT.COLOR SWATCH: .6X TO 1.5X
*PATCHES: 1.5X TO 4X
IB-AH Ales Hemsky 6.00 15.00
IB-BG Bill Guerin 6.00 15.00
IB-BH Brett Hull 8.00 20.00
IB-BL Brian Leetch 6.00 15.00
IB-BS Brendan Shanahan 6.00 15.00
IB-DA David Aebischer 6.00 15.00
IB-DH Dominik Hasek 10.00 25.00
IB-EB Ed Belfour 6.00 15.00
IB-HK Milan Hejduk 4.00 10.00
IB-IK Ilya Kovalchuk 8.00 20.00
IB-JJ Jaromir Jagr 10.00 25.00
IB-JK Jason King 4.00 10.00
IB-JR Jeremy Roenick 8.00 20.00
IB-JS Joe Sakic 12.50 30.00
IB-JT Joe Thornton 8.00 20.00
IB-JSG J-S Giguere 6.00 15.00
IB-KT Keith Tkachuk 6.00 15.00
IB-MB Martin Brodeur 15.00 40.00
IB-MH Marian Hossa 6.00 15.00
IB-ML Mario Lemieux 20.00 50.00
IB-MM Mike Modano 8.00 20.00
IB-MN Markus Naslund 6.00 15.00
IB-MR Mark Messier 8.00 20.00
IB-MS Mats Sundin 6.00 15.00
IB-MT Marty Turco 6.00 15.00
IB-NL Nicklas Lidstrom 4.00 10.00
IB-PF Peter Forsberg 10.00 25.00
IB-PK Paul Kariya 6.00 15.00
IB-PR Patrick Roy 20.00 50.00
IB-RB Rob Blake 4.00 10.00
IB-RF Ron Francis 6.00 15.00
IB-RN Rick Nash 10.00 25.00
IB-RT Raffi Torres 4.00 10.00
IB-SG Scott Gomez 4.00 10.00
IB-SP Jason Spezza 6.00 15.00
IB-SS Sergei Samsonov 6.00 15.00
IB-ST Scott Stevens 4.00 10.00
IB-SY Steve Yzerman 15.00 40.00
IB-TB Todd Bertuzzi 6.00 15.00
IB-TH Jose Theodore 8.00 20.00
IB-VL Vincent Lecavalier 6.00 15.00
IB-ZP Zigmund Palffy 6.00 15.00

2003-04 Upper Deck Ice Clear Cut Winners

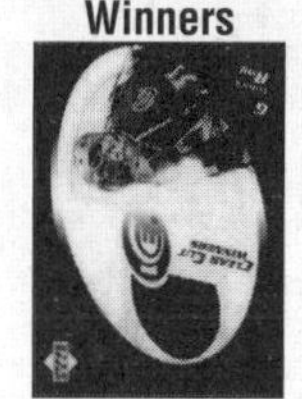

This 20-card set featured jersey swatches on acetate card stock. Cards from this set were inserted at 1:10. A patch parallel was also created and serial-numbered to 25.

*MULT.COLOR SWATCH: .6X TO 1.5X
*PATCHES: 1.5X TO 4X
CC-BH Brett Hull 4.00 10.00
CC-BL Brian Leetch 3.00 8.00
CC-BS Brendan Shanahan 6.00 15.00
CC-DH Dominik Hasek 6.00 15.00
CC-EB Ed Belfour 6.00 15.00
CC-JJ Jaromir Jagr 5.00 12.00
CC-JS Joe Sakic 8.00 20.00
CC-MB Martin Brodeur 12.50 30.00
CC-MH Milan Hejduk 6.00 15.00
CC-ML Mario Lemieux 15.00 40.00
CC-MM Mike Modano 5.00 12.00
CC-MR Mark Messier 6.00 15.00
CC-NL Nicklas Lidstrom 6.00 15.00
CC-PF Peter Forsberg 8.00 20.00
CC-PR Patrick Roy 12.50 30.00
CC-RB Rob Blake 3.00 8.00
CC-RF Ron Francis 3.00 8.00
CC-SG Scott Gomez 3.00 8.00
CC-SS Scott Stevens 3.00 8.00
CC-SY Steve Yzerman 12.50 30.00

2003-04 Upper Deck Ice Frozen Fabrics

This 20-card set featured swatches of jersey on acetate card stock. A patch parallel was also created and serial-numbered to 25.

COMPLETE SET (20)
*MULT.COLOR SWATCH: .6X TO 1.5X
*PATCHES: 2X TO 5X
FF-AH Ales Hemsky 5.00 12.00
FF-BG Bill Guerin 5.00 12.00
FF-DA David Aebischer 5.00 12.00
FF-JK Jason King 8.00 20.00
FF-JR Jeremy Roenick 6.00 15.00
FF-JS Jason Spezza 5.00 12.00
FF-JT Joe Thornton 6.00 15.00
FF-JSG Jean-Sebastien Giguere 5.00 12.00
FF-KT Keith Tkachuk 5.00 12.00
FF-MH Marian Hossa 5.00 12.00
FF-MN Markus Naslund 5.00 12.00
FF-MS Mats Sundin 5.00 12.00
FF-MT Marty Turco 5.00 12.00
FF-PK Paul Kariya 5.00 12.00
FF-RN Rick Nash 6.00 15.00
FF-RT Raffi Torres 5.00 12.00
FF-SS Sergei Samsonov 5.00 12.00
FF-TB Todd Bertuzzi 5.00 12.00
FF-TH Jose Theodore 6.00 15.00
FF-ZP Zigmund Palffy 5.00 12.00

2003-04 Upper Deck Ice Icons

COMPLETE SET (10) 20.00 50.00
STATED ODDS 1:40
I-AM Al MacInnis 2.00 5.00
I-BL Brian Leetch 2.00 5.00
I-EB Ed Belfour 2.00 5.00
I-JR Jeremy Roenick 2.50 6.00
I-JS Joe Sakic 4.00 10.00
I-MB Martin Brodeur 5.00 12.00
I-ML Mario Lemieux 6.00 15.00
I-MM Mike Modano 3.00 8.00
I-SY Steve Yzerman 5.00 12.00
I-TD Tie Domi 2.00 5.00

2003-04 Upper Deck Ice Icons Jerseys

*MULT.COLOR SWATCH: .5X TO 1.25X
STATED ODDS 1:40
I-AM Al MacInnis 4.00 10.00
I-BL Brian Leetch 4.00 10.00
I-EB Ed Belfour 6.00 15.00
I-JR Jeremy Roenick 5.00 12.00
I-MB Martin Brodeur 12.50 30.00
I-ML Mario Lemieux 12.50 30.00
I-MM Mike Modano 5.00 12.00
I-SY Steve Yzerman 12.50 30.00
I-TD Tie Domi 4.00 10.00

2003-04 Upper Deck Ice Under Glass Autographs

This 20-card set featured certified player autographs on thick acetate card stock. Cards in this set were inserted at 1:160.

UG-AH Ales Hemsky 20.00 50.00
UG-BO Bobby Orr 150.00 250.00
UG-DC Don Cherry 25.00 60.00
UG-EL Eric Lindros SP 50.00 100.00
UG-HA Marian Hossa 20.00 50.00
UG-HZ Henrik Zetterberg 25.00 60.00
UG-IK Ilya Kovalchuk 40.00 100.00
UG-JR Jeremy Roenick 25.00 60.00
UG-JS Jason Spezza 50.00 100.00
UG-JT Joe Thornton 30.00 80.00
UG-MB Martin Brodeur 150.00 250.00
UG-MG Marian Gaborik 40.00 100.00
UG-MH Gordie Howe 75.00 200.00
UG-ON Owen Nolan 20.00 50.00
UG-PR Patrick Roy SP 250.00 400.00
UG-RD Rick DiPietro 25.00 60.00
UG-RL Roberto Luongo 30.00 80.00
UG-RN Rick Nash 30.00 80.00
UG-TB Todd Bertuzzi 20.00 50.00
UG-WG Wayne Gretzky 300.00 500.00

2005-06 Upper Deck Ice

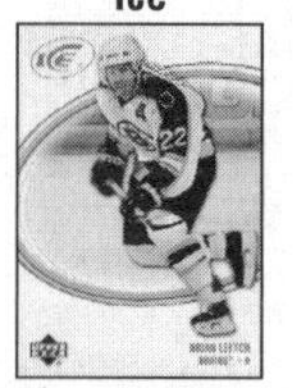

COMP. SET w/o SPs (1-100) 12.50 30.00
101-106 PRINT RUN 99 #'d SETS
107-118 PRINT RUN 999 #'d SETS
119-142 PRINT RUN 1,999 #'d SETS
143-268 PRINT RUN 2,999 #'d SETS
1 Joffrey Lupul .15 .40
2 Scott Niedermayer .15 .40
3 Jean-Sebastien Giguere .25 .60
4 Teemu Selanne .30 .75
5 Ilya Kovalchuk .40 1.00
6 Kari Lehtonen .30 .75
7 Marian Hossa .25 .60
8 Andrew Raycroft .25 .60
9 Patrice Bergeron .30 .75
10 Brian Leetch .30 .75
11 Glen Murray .15 .40
12 Ryan Miller .25 .60
13 Chris Drury .25 .60
14 Jarome Iginla .40 1.00
15 Miikka Kiprusoff .30 .75
16 Jordan Leopold .15 .40
17 Tony Amonte .25 .60
18 Erik Cole .15 .40
19 Eric Staal .25 .60
20 Nikolai Khabibulin .30 .75
21 Tuomo Ruutu .15 .40
22 Joe Sakic .60 1.50
23 Milan Hejduk .30 .75
24 Alex Tanguay .25 .60
25 David Aebischer .25 .60
26 Rick Nash .40 1.00
27 Sergei Fedorov .30 .75
28 Mike Modano .30 .75
29 Marty Turco .25 .60
30 Bill Guerin .15 .40
31 Steve Yzerman 1.25 3.00
32 Pavel Datsyuk .30 .75
33 Brendan Shanahan .30 .75
34 Nicklas Lidstrom .30 .75
35 Henrik Zetterberg .30 .75
36 Chris Pronger .25 .60
37 Ty Conklin .25 .60
38 Ryan Smyth .25 .60
39 Michael Peca .15 .40
40 Roberto Luongo .40 1.00
41 Joe Nieuwendyk .25 .60
42 Jay Bouwmeester .15 .40
43 Stephen Weiss .15 .40
44 Jeremy Roenick .40 1.00
45 Luc Robitaille .25 .60
46 Alexander Frolov .25 .60
47 Marian Gaborik .60 1.50
48 Dwayne Roloson .25 .60
49 Jose Theodore .40 1.00
50 Saku Koivu .30 .75
51 Michael Ryder .25 .60
52 Mike Ribeiro .15 .40
53 Steve Sullivan .15 .40
54 Paul Kariya .30 .75
55 Tomas Vokoun .25 .60
56 Martin Brodeur 1.50 4.00

57 Patrik Elias .25 .60
58 Brian Gionta .15 .40
59 Alexei Yashin .15 .40
60 Miroslav Satan .15 .40
61 Rick DiPietro .25 .60
62 Jaromir Jagr .50 1.25
63 Kevin Weekes .25 .60
64 Tom Poti .15 .40
65 Dany Heatley .40 1.00
66 Dominik Hasek .60 1.50
67 Martin Havlat .25 .60
68 Jason Spezza .30 .75
69 Daniel Alfredsson .25 .60
70 Robert Esche .25 .60
71 Peter Forsberg .50 1.25
72 Keith Primeau .15 .40
73 Simon Gagne .30 .75
74 Shane Doan .15 .40
75 Curtis Joseph .30 .75
76 Mario Lemieux 2.00 5.00
77 Zigmund Palffy .25 .60
78 Mark Recchi .25 .60
79 Marc-Andre Fleury .25 .60
80 Joe Thornton .50 1.25
81 Jonathan Cheechoo .30 .75
82 Evgeni Nabokov .25 .60
83 Patrick Marleau .25 .60
84 Keith Tkachuk .30 .75
85 Doug Weight .25 .60
86 Martin St. Louis .25 .60
87 Brad Richards .25 .60
88 Sean Burke .25 .60
89 Vincent Lecavalier .30 .75
90 Mats Sundin .30 .75
91 Nik Antropov .15 .40
92 Eric Lindros .30 .75
93 Ed Belfour .30 .75
94 Jason Allison .15 .40
95 Markus Naslund .30 .75
96 Todd Bertuzzi .30 .75
97 Brendan Morrison .15 .40
98 Ed Jovanovski .25 .60
99 Jeff Friesen .15 .40
100 Olaf Kolzig .25 .60
101 Gilbert Brule RC 175.00 350.00
102 Thomas Vanek RC 300.00 450.00
103 Alexander Ovechkin RC 500.00 800.00
104 Jeff Carter RC 200.00 400.00
105 Corey Perry RC 175.00 350.00
106 Sidney Crosby RC 2200.00 3000.00
107 Ryan Getzlaf RC 15.00 40.00
108 Hannu Toivonen RC 6.00 15.00
109 Dion Phaneuf RC 20.00 40.00
110 Cam Ward RC 10.00 25.00
111 Wojtek Wolski RC 10.00 25.00
112 Jim Howard RC 8.00 20.00
113 Rostislav Olesz RC 4.00 10.00
114 Alexander Perezhogin RC 6.00 15.00
115 Zach Parise RC 10.00 25.00
116 Mikko Koivu RC 6.00 15.00
117 Mike Richards RC 8.00 20.00
118 Alexander Steen RC 10.00 25.00
119 Braydon Coburn RC 3.00 8.00
120 Andrew Alberts RC 3.00 8.00
121 Eric Nystrom RC 3.00 8.00
122 Kevin Nastiuk RC 3.00 8.00
123 Brent Seabrook RC 3.00 8.00
124 R.J. Umberger RC 5.00 12.00
125 Cam Barker RC 4.00 10.00
126 Peter Budaj RC 5.00 12.00
127 Jussi Jokinen RC 4.00 10.00
128 Johan Franzen RC 3.00 8.00
129 Brad Winchester RC 3.00 8.00
130 Anthony Stewart RC 3.00 8.00
131 Matt Foy RC 3.00 8.00
132 Yann Danis RC 5.00 12.00
133 Ryan Suter RC 4.00 10.00
134 Petteri Nokelainen RC 3.00 8.00
135 Chris Campoli RC 3.00 8.00
136 Al Montoya RC 5.00 12.00
137 Henrik Lundqvist RC 12.00 30.00
138 Ryan Whitney RC 4.00 10.00
139 Andrej Meszaros RC 3.00 8.00
140 Keith Ballard RC 3.00 8.00
141 David Leneveu RC 4.00 10.00
142 Jeff Woywitka RC 3.00 8.00
143 Jim Slater RC 4.00 10.00
144 Adam Berkhoel RC 4.00 10.00
145 Kevin Dallman RC 2.00 5.00
146 Milan Jurcina RC 2.00 5.00
147 Niklas Nordgren RC 2.00 5.00
148 Duncan Keith RC 3.00 8.00
149 Jaroslav Balastik RC 2.00 5.00
150 Brett Lebda RC 2.00 5.00
151 Kyle Brodziak RC 2.00 5.00
152 George Parros RC 2.00 5.00
153 Derek Boogaard RC 3.00 8.00
154 Mark Streit RC 2.00 5.00
155 Raitis Ivanans RC 2.00 5.00
156 Ryan Hollweg RC 2.00 5.00
157 Chris Holt RC 2.00 5.00
158 Petr Prucha RC 5.00 12.00
159 Brian McGrattan RC 2.00 5.00
160 Patrick Eaves RC 4.00 10.00
161 Wade Skolney RC 2.00 5.00
162 Maxime Talbot RC 2.00 5.00
163 Ryane Clowe RC 2.00 5.00
164 Josh Gorges RC 2.00 5.00
165 Andy Roach RC 2.00 5.00
166 Jay McClement RC 2.00 5.00
167 Jeff Hoggan RC 2.00 5.00
168 Lee Stempniak RC 2.00 5.00
169 Colin Hemingway RC 2.00 5.00
170 Timo Helbling RC 2.00 5.00
171 Paul Ranger RC 2.00 5.00
172 Andrew Wozniewski RC 2.00 5.00
173 Robert Nilsson RC 4.00 10.00
174 Rene Bourque RC 2.00 5.00
175 Brandon Bochenski RC 2.00 5.00
176 Steve Bernier RC 4.00 10.00
177 Evgeny Artyukhin RC 2.00 5.00
178 Christoph Schubert RC 2.00 5.00
179 Jakub Klepis RC 2.00 5.00
180 Dimitri Patzold RC 3.00 8.00
181 Vojtech Polak RC 2.00 5.00
182 Rob McVicar RC 3.00 8.00
183 Staffan Kronwall RC 2.00 5.00
184 Jordan Sigalet RC 3.00 8.00
185 Dustin Penner RC 4.00 10.00
186 Michael Wall RC 3.00 8.00
187 Zenon Konopka RC 2.00 5.00
188 Jay Leach RC 2.00 5.00
189 Danny Richmond RC 2.00 5.00
190 Martin St. Pierre RC 2.00 5.00
191 Andrew Penner RC 2.00 5.00
192 Steve Goertzen RC 2.00 5.00
193 Ole-Kristian Tollefsen RC 2.00 5.00
194 Junior Lessard RC 2.00 5.00
195 Danny Syvret RC 2.00 5.00
196 Greg Jacina RC 2.00 5.00
197 Jeff Giuliano RC 2.00 5.00
198 Adam Hauser RC 3.00 8.00
199 Maxim Lapierre RC 2.00 5.00
200 Barry Tallackson RC 2.00 5.00
201 Cam Janssen RC 2.00 5.00
202 Kevin Colley RC 22.00 5.00
203 Jeremy Colliton RC 2.00 5.00
204 Yanick Lehoux RC 2.00 5.00
205 Erik Christensen RC 3.00 8.00
206 Dennis Wideman RC 2.00 5.00
207 Nick Tarnasky RC 2.00 5.00
208 Brian Eklund RC 3.00 8.00
209 Gerald Coleman RC 3.00 8.00
210 Tomas Fleischmann RC 2.00 5.00
211 Brad Richardson RC 2.00 5.00
212 Mark Cullen RC 2.00 5.00
213 Jean-Philippe Cote RC 2.00 5.00
214 Andrei Kostitsyn RC 3.00 8.00
215 Matt Jones RC 2.00 5.00
216 Ben Eager RC 2.00 5.00
217 Andrew Ladd RC 5.00 12.00
218 Bruno Gervais RC 2.00 5.00
219 Jeff Tambellini RC 2.00 5.00
220 Kevin Klein RC 2.00 5.00
221 Kyle Quincey RC 2.00 5.00
222 Chris Thorburn RC 2.00 5.00
223 Doug Murray RC 2.00 5.00
224 Eric Healey RC 2.00 5.00
225 Grant Stevenson RC 2.00 5.00
226 Ryan Ready RC 2.00 5.00
227 Vitaly Kolesnik RC 3.00 8.00
228 Geoff Platt RC 2.00 5.00
229 Chris Beckford-Tseu Rc 4.00 10.00
230 Jon DiSalvatore RC 2.00 5.00
231 Ben Walter RC 2.00 5.00
232 Jonathan Ferland RC 2.00 5.00
233 Kevin Bieksa RC 2.50 6.00
234 Rick Rypien RC 2.00 5.00
235 Alexandre Burrows RC 2.00 5.00
236 David Steckel RC 2.00 5.00
237 Mike Green RC 2.00 5.00
238 Richie Regehr RC 2.00 5.00
239 Josh Gratton RC 2.00 5.00
240 Chad Larose RC 2.00 5.00
241 Petr Kanko RC 4.00 10.00
242 Matt Ryan RC 2.00 5.00
243 Connor James RC 2.00 5.00
244 Richard Petiot RC 2.00 5.00
245 Darren Reid RC 2.00 5.00
246 Ryan Craig RC 2.00 5.00
247 Matt Greene RC 2.00 5.00
248 Rob Globke RC 2.00 5.00
249 Colby Armstrong RC 4.00 10.00
250 Greg Zanon RC 2.00 5.00
251 Pekka Rinne RC 3.00 8.00
252 Valtteri Filppula RC 2.00 5.00
253 Daniel Paille RC 2.00 5.00
254 Nathan Paetsch RC 2.00 5.00
255 Jiri Novotny RC 2.00 5.00
256 Petr Taticek RC 2.00 5.00
257 Alexandre Picard RC 2.00 5.00
258 Keith Aucoin RC 2.00 5.00
259 Alexandre Picard RC 4.00 10.00
260 Corey Crawford RC 3.00 8.00
261 Jason Ryznar RC 2.00 5.00
262 Doug O'Brien RC 2.00 5.00
263 Mike Glumac RC 2.00 5.00
264 Jay Harrison RC 2.00 5.00
265 Ben Guite RC 2.00 5.00
266 Mark Giordano RC 2.00 5.00
267 David Gove RC 2.00 5.00
268 J-F Jacques RC 2.00 5.00

2005-06 Upper Deck Ice Rainbow

RAINBOW: 6X to 15X HI
PRINT RUN 100 SER. #'d SETS
31 Steve Yzerman 12.00 30.00
56 Martin Brodeur 15.00 40.00
76 Mario Lemieux 20.00 50.00

2005-06 Upper Deck Ice Cool Threads

STATED ODDS 1:36
CTAO Alexander Ovechkin 15.00 40.00
CTAP Alexander Perezhogin 3.00 8.00
CTAR Andrew Raycroft 3.00 8.00
CTAS Alexander Steen 3.00 8.00
CTBS Brent Seabrook 3.00 8.00
CTCP Corey Perry 4.00 10.00
CTCW Cam Ward 6.00 15.00
CTDP Dion Phaneuf 6.00 15.00
CTGB Gilbert Brule 4.00 10.00
CTHL Henrik Lundqvist 6.00 15.00
CTHT Hannu Toivonen 3.00 8.00
CTJB Jay Bouwmeester 2.00 5.00
CTJC Jeff Carter 4.00 10.00
CTJJ Jaromir Jagr 4.00 10.00
CTJK Jussi Jokinen 3.00 8.00
CTJO Jose Theodore 3.00 8.00
CTJT Joe Thornton 4.00 10.00
CTMB Martin Brodeur 5.00 12.00
CTMH Milan Hejduk 2.00 5.00
CTML Matthew Lombardi 2.00 5.00
CTMM Mike Modano 2.00 5.00
CTMN Markus Naslund 2.00 5.00
CTMP Michael Peca 2.00 5.00
CTMR Mike Richards 3.00 8.00
CTMV Martin Havlat 2.00 5.00
CTNH Nathan Horton 2.00 5.00
CTNI Robert Nilsson 3.00 8.00
CTPB Patrice Bergeron 3.00 8.00
CTPE Patrik Elias 3.00 8.00
CTRG Ryan Getzlaf 4.00 10.00
CTRL Roberto Luongo 4.00 10.00
CTRN Rick Nash 4.00 10.00
CTRS Ryan Suter 3.00 8.00
CTSC Sidney Crosby 40.00 80.00
CTSG Simon Gagne 3.00 8.00
CTTR Tuomo Ruutu 3.00 8.00
CTTV Thomas Vanek 4.00 10.00
CTVO Tomas Vokoun 3.00 8.00
CTZC Zdeno Chara 2.00 5.00
CTZP Zach Parise 4.00 10.00

2005-06 Upper Deck Ice Cool Threads Autographs

PRINT RUN 35 SER. #'d SETS
ACTAO Alexander Ovechkin 125.00 250.00
ACTAP Alexander Perezhogin 15.00 40.00
ACTAR Andrew Raycroft 20.00 50.00
ACTAS Alexander Steen 50.00 100.00
ACTBS Brent Seabrook 15.00 40.00
ACTCP Corey Perry
ACTCW Cam Ward 30.00 75.00
ACTDP Dion Phaneuf 50.00 100.00
ACTGB Gilbert Brule 30.00 75.00
ACTHL Henrik Lundqvist 50.00 100.00
ACTHT Hannu Toivonen 15.00 40.00
ACTJB Jay Bouwmeester 10.00 25.00
ACTJC Jeff Carter 25.00 60.00
ACTJK Jussi Jokinen
ACTJO Jose Theodore 25.00 60.00
ACTJT Joe Thornton
ACTMB Martin Brodeur 50.00 125.00
ACTMH Milan Hejduk 12.50 30.00
ACTMM Mike Modano 20.00 40.00
ACTMN Markus Naslund 20.00 50.00
ACTMP Michael Peca
ACTMR Mike Richards 20.00 40.00
ACTMV Martin Havlat 20.00 40.00
ACTNH Nathan Horton
ACTNI Robert Nilsson 15.00 40.00
ACTPB Patrice Bergeron
ACTRG Ryan Getzlaf 20.00 50.00
ACTRL Roberto Luongo
ACTRN Rick Nash
ACTRS Ryan Suter 10.00 25.00
ACTSC Sidney Crosby 350.00 500.00
ACTSD Shane Doan 10.00 25.00
ACTSG Simon Gagne 12.00 30.00
ACTTR Tuomo Ruutu 25.00 60.00
ACTTV Thomas Vanek 15.00 40.00
ACTZC Zdeno Chara 12.50 30.00
ACTZP Zach Parise 25.00 60.00

2005-06 Upper Deck Ice Cool Threads Glass

CTAO Alexander Ovechkin 20.00 50.00
CTAP Alexander Perezhogin 6.00 15.00
CTAR Andrew Raycroft 6.00 15.00
CTAS Alexander Steen 6.00 15.00
CTBS Brent Seabrook 6.00 15.00
CTCP Corey Perry 8.00 20.00
CTCW Cam Ward 8.00 20.00
CTDP Dion Phaneuf 12.50 30.00
CTGB Gilbert Brule 8.00 20.00
CTHL Henrik Lundqvist 12.00 30.00
CTHT Hannu Toivonen 6.00 15.00
CTJB Jay Bouwmeester 4.00 10.00
CTJC Jeff Carter 10.00 25.00
CTJJ Jaromir Jagr 12.00 30.00
CTJK Jussi Jokinen 6.00 15.00
CTJO Jose Theodore 8.00 20.00
CTJT Joe Thornton 10.00 25.00
CTMB Martin Brodeur 15.00 40.00
CTMH Milan Hejduk 6.00 15.00
CTML Matthew Lombardi 4.00 10.00
CTMM Mike Modano 6.00 15.00
CTMN Markus Naslund 8.00 20.00
CTMP Michael Peca 6.00 15.00
CTMR Mike Richards 6.00 15.00
CTMV Martin Havlat 6.00 15.00
CTNH Nathan Horton 4.00 10.00
CTNI Robert Nilsson 4.00 10.00
CTPB Patrice Bergeron 8.00 20.00
CTPE Patrik Elias 6.00 15.00
CTRG Ryan Getzlaf 6.00 15.00
CTRL Roberto Luongo 10.00 25.00
CTRN Rick Nash 10.00 25.00
CTRS Ryan Suter 6.00 15.00
CTSC Sidney Crosby 30.00 75.00
CTSD Shane Doan 6.00 15.00
CTSG Simon Gagne 6.00 15.00
CTTR Tuomo Ruutu 6.00 15.00
CTTV Thomas Vanek 10.00 25.00
CTVO Tomas Vokoun 8.00 20.00
CTZC Zdeno Chara 6.00 15.00
CTZP Zach Parise 6.00 15.00

2005-06 Upper Deck Ice Cool Threads Patches

CTPAO Alexander Ovechkin 50.00 125.00
CTPAP Alexander Perezhogin
CTPAR Andrew Raycroft 12.50 30.00
CTPAS Alexander Steen 20.00 50.00
CTPBS Brent Seabrook 20.00 50.00
CTPCP Corey Perry 12.00 30.00
CTPCW Cam Ward 20.00 50.00
CTPDP Dion Phaneuf 30.00 60.00
CTPGB Gilbert Brule 25.00 60.00
CTPHL Henrik Lundqvist 20.00 50.00
CTPHT Hannu Toivonen 20.00 50.00
CTPJB Jay Bouwmeester 15.00 40.00
CTPJC Jeff Carter 15.00 40.00
CTPJJ Jaromir Jagr 25.00 60.00
CTPJK Jussi Jokinen
CTPJO Jose Theodore 15.00 40.00
CTPJT Joe Thornton 25.00 60.00
CTPMB Martin Brodeur 50.00 125.00
CTPMH Milan Hejduk 12.00 30.00
CTPML Matthew Lombardi 10.00 25.00
CTPMM Mike Modano 15.00 40.00
CTPMN Markus Naslund 12.50 30.00
CTPMP Michael Peca 15.00 40.00
CTPMR Mike Richards 15.00 40.00
CTPMV Martin Havlat 20.00 50.00
CTPNH Nathan Horton 20.00 50.00
CTPNI Robert Nilsson 10.00 25.00
CTPPB Patrice Bergeron 20.00 50.00
CTPPE Patrik Elias 10.00 25.00
CTPRG Ryan Getzlaf 12.00 30.00
CTPRL Roberto Luongo 20.00 50.00
CTPRN Rick Nash 25.00 50.00
CTPRS Ryan Suter 12.00 30.00
CTPSC Sidney Crosby 60.00 150.00
CTPSD Shane Doan 10.00 25.00
CTPSG Simon Gagne 10.00 25.00
CTPTR Tuomo Ruutu 15.00 40.00
CTPTV Thomas Vanek 20.00 50.00
CTPVO Tomas Vokoun 30.00 80.00
CTPZC Zdeno Chara 15.00 40.00
CTPZP Zach Parise 12.00 30.00

2005-06 Upper Deck Ice Fresh Ice

FIAF Alexander Frolov 2.00 5.00
FIAH Adam Hall 2.00 5.00
FIAS Anthony Stewart 3.00 8.00
FIBB Brandon Bochenski 3.00 8.00
FIBC Braydon Coburn 3.00 8.00
FIBS Brent Seabrook 3.00 8.00
FIBU Peter Budaj 3.00 8.00
FIBW Brad Winchester 3.00 8.00
FIDB Dustin Brown 2.00 5.00
FIEN Eric Nystrom 3.00 8.00
FIGP George Parros 3.00 8.00
FIHE Ales Hemsky 2.00 5.00
FIHV Martin Havlat 3.00 8.00
FIHZ Henrik Zetterberg 4.00 10.00
FIJB Jay Bouwmeester 2.00 5.00
FIJF Johan Franzen 3.00 8.00
FIJJ Jussi Jokinen 3.00 8.00
FIJL Jordan Leopold 2.00 5.00
FIJP Joni Pitkanen 2.00 5.00
FIKL Kari Lehtonen 3.00 8.00
FILU Joffrey Lupul 2.00 5.00
FIMC Jay McClement 2.00 5.00
FIMH Marcel Hossa 2.00 5.00
FIMJ Milan Jurcina 2.00 5.00
FIMM Milan Michalek 2.00 5.00
FIMR Mike Richards 4.00 10.00
FIMT Maxime Talbot 2.00 5.00
FIPB Patrice Bergeron 4.00 10.00
FIPN Petteri Nokelainen 3.00 8.00
FIPP Petr Prucha 3.00 8.00
FIPS Philippe Sauve 3.00 8.00
FIRC Ryane Clowe 2.00 5.00
FIRG Ryan Getzlaf 4.00 12.00
FIRI Mike Ribeiro 2.00 5.00
FIRK Ryan Kesler 2.00 5.00
FIRM Ryan Miller 4.00 10.00
FIRS Ryan Suter 3.00 8.00
FIRT Raffi Torres 2.00 5.00
FIYD Yann Danis 3.00 8.00
FIZP Zach Parise 4.00 10.00

2005-06 Upper Deck Ice Fresh Ice Glass

FIAF Alexander Frolov 4.00 10.00
FIAH Adam Hall 4.00 10.00
FIAS Anthony Stewart 6.00 15.00
FIBB Brandon Bochenski 6.00 15.00
FIBC Braydon Coburn 6.00 15.00
FIBS Brent Seabrook 6.00 15.00
FIBU Peter Budaj 6.00 15.00
FIBW Brad Winchester 4.00 10.00
FIDB Dustin Brown 4.00 10.00
FIEN Eric Nystrom 6.00 15.00
FIGP George Parros 6.00 15.00
FIHE Ales Hemsky 4.00 10.00
FIHV Martin Havlat 6.00 15.00
FIHZ Henrik Zetterberg 8.00 20.00
FIJB Jay Bouwmeester 4.00 10.00
FIJF Johan Franzen 6.00 15.00
FIJJ Jussi Jokinen 6.00 15.00
FIJL Jordan Leopold 4.00 10.00
FIJP Joni Pitkanen 4.00 10.00
FIKL Kari Lehtonen 6.00 15.00
FILU Joffrey Lupul 4.00 10.00
FIMC Jay McClement 4.00 10.00
FIMH Marcel Hossa 4.00 10.00
FIMJ Milan Jurcina 4.00 10.00
FIMM Milan Michalek 4.00 10.00
FIMR Mike Richards 8.00 20.00
FIMT Maxime Talbot 4.00 10.00
FINH Nathan Horton 4.00 10.00
FIPB Patrice Bergeron 8.00 20.00
FIPN Petteri Nokelainen 6.00 15.00
FIPP Petr Prucha 6.00 15.00
FIPS Philippe Sauve 6.00 15.00
FIRC Ryane Clowe 4.00 10.00
FIRG Ryan Getzlaf 8.00 20.00
FIRI Mike Ribeiro 4.00 10.00
FIRK Ryan Kesler 4.00 10.00
FIRM Ryan Miller 8.00 20.00
FIRS Ryan Suter 6.00 15.00
FIRT Raffi Torres 4.00 10.00
FIYD Yann Danis 6.00 15.00
FIZP Zach Parise 8.00 20.00

2005-06 Upper Deck Ice Fresh Ice Glass Patches

FIPAF Alexander Frolov 15.00 40.00
FIPAH Adam Hall 12.50 30.00
FIPAS Anthony Stewart 12.50 30.00
FIPBB Brandon Bochenski 12.50 30.00
FIPBC Braydon Coburn 12.50 30.00
FIPBS Brent Seabrook 20.00 50.00
FIPBU Peter Budaj 25.00 60.00
FIPBW Brad Winchester 12.50 30.00
FIPDB Dustin Brown 12.50 30.00
FIPEN Eric Nystrom 12.50 30.00
FIPGP George Parros 12.50 30.00
FIPHE Ales Hemsky 12.50 30.00
FIPHV Martin Havlat 15.00 40.00
FIPHZ Henrik Zetterberg 25.00 60.00
FIPJB Jay Bouwmeester 12.50 30.00
FIPJF Johan Franzen 12.50 30.00
FIPJJ Jussi Jokinen 15.00 40.00
FIPJL Jordan Leopold 12.50 30.00
FIPJP Joni Pitkanen 12.50 30.00
FIPKL Kari Lehtonen 15.00 40.00
FIPLU Joffrey Lupul 12.50 30.00
FIPMC Jay McClement/35 12.50 30.00
FIPMH Marcel Hossa 12.50 30.00
FIPMJ Milan Jurcina 12.50 30.00
FIPMM Milan Michalek 12.50 30.00
FIPMR Mike Richards 20.00 40.00
FIPMT Maxime Talbot 15.00 40.00
FIPPB Patrice Bergeron 25.00 60.00
FIPPN Petteri Nokelainen 12.50 30.00
FIPPP Petr Prucha 15.00 40.00
FIPRC Ryane Clowe 12.50 30.00
FIPRG Ryan Getzlaf 15.00 40.00
FIPRI Mike Ribeiro 12.50 30.00
FIPRK Ryan Kesler 12.50 30.00
FIPRM Ryan Miller 25.00 60.00
FIPRS Ryan Suter 12.50 30.00
FIPRT Raffi Torres 12.50 30.00
FIPYD Yann Danis 12.50 30.00
FIPZP Zach Parise 15.00 40.00

2005-06 Upper Deck Ice Frozen Fabrics

FFAT Alex Tanguay 2.50 6.00
FFAY Alexei Yashin 1.50 4.00
FFBS Brendan Shanahan 3.00 8.00
FFCO Chris Osgood 2.50 6.00
FFCP Chris Pronger 2.50 6.00
FFDA Daniel Alfredsson 2.50 6.00
FFDH Dany Heatley 4.00 10.00
FFDW Doug Weight 2.50 6.00
FFEB Ed Belfour 3.00 8.00
FFGM Glen Murray 1.50 4.00
FFIK Ilya Kovalchuk 4.00 10.00
FFJI Jarome Iginla 4.00 10.00
FFJP Joni Pitkanen 1.50 4.00
FFJR Jeremy Roenick 4.00 10.00
FFJS Joe Sakic 5.00 15.00
FFJT Jocelyn Thibault 2.50 6.00
FFKP Keith Primeau 1.50 4.00
FFKT Keith Tkachuk 3.00 8.00
FFMB Martin Brodeur 8.00 20.00
FFMK Miikka Kiprusoff 3.00 8.00
FFML Mario Lemieux 8.00 20.00
FFMM Milan Michalek 1.50 4.00
FFMS Mats Sundin 3.00 8.00
FFMT Marty Turco 2.50 6.00
FFNK Nikolai Khabibulin 3.00 8.00
FFPD Pavel Datsyuk 3.00 8.00
FFPF Peter Forsberg 8.00 20.00
FFPK Paul Kariya 3.00 8.00
FFPM Patrick Marleau 2.50 6.00
FFPR Patrick Roy 8.00 20.00
FFRB Ray Bourque 5.00 12.00
FFRS Ryan Smyth 2.50 6.00
FFSC Sidney Crosby 25.00 60.00
FFSK Saku Koivu 3.00 8.00
FFSL Martin St. Louis 2.50 6.00
FFSP Jason Spezza 3.00 8.00
FFSY Steve Yzerman 8.00 20.00
FFSZ Sergei Zubov 1.50 4.00
FFTB Todd Bertuzzi 3.00 8.00
FFVL Vincent Lecavalier 3.00 8.00
FFZP Zigmund Palffy 2.50 6.00

2005-06 Upper Deck Ice Frozen Fabrics Autographs

PRINT RUN 35 SER. #'d SETS
AFFAT Alex Tanguay
AFFAY Alexei Yashin 12.00 30.00
AFFCO Chris Osgood 15.00 40.00
AFFCP Chris Pronger 15.00 40.00
AFFDA Daniel Alfredsson
AFFDH Dany Heatley
AFFDW Doug Weight
AFFEB Ed Belfour 30.00 80.00
AFFGM Glen Murray 12.00 30.00
AFFIK Ilya Kovalchuk 20.00 50.00
AFFJI Jarome Iginla 20.00 50.00
AFFJP Joni Pitkanen 12.00 30.00
AFFJR Jeremy Roenick 15.00 40.00
AFFJT Jocelyn Thibault
AFFKP Keith Primeau
AFFMB Martin Brodeur 60.00 125.00
AFFMM Milan Michalek
AFFMS Mats Sundin
AFFMT Marty Turco
AFFPR Patrick Roy 75.00 200.00
AFFRB Ray Bourque 40.00 75.00
AFFRS Ryan Smyth 25.00 60.00
AFFSC Sidney Crosby 250.00 400.00
AFFSK Saku Koivu 20.00 50.00
AFFSL Martin St. Louis 12.50 30.00
AFFSP Jason Spezza 15.00 40.00
AFFSZ Sergei Zubov
AFFTB Todd Bertuzzi 15.00 40.00
AFFVL Vincent Lecavalier 40.00 80.00
AFFZP Zigmund Palffy 15.00 40.00

2005-06 Upper Deck Ice Frozen Fabrics Glass

FFAT Alex Tanguay 5.00 12.00
FFAY Alexei Yashin 5.00 12.00
FFBS Brendan Shanahan 5.00 12.00
FFCO Chris Osgood 5.00 12.00
FFCP Chris Pronger 5.00 12.00
FFDA Daniel Alfredsson 5.00 12.00
FFDH Dany Heatley 12.00 30.00
FFDW Doug Weight 5.00 12.00
FFEB Ed Belfour 5.00 12.00
FFGM Glen Murray 5.00 12.00
FFIK Ilya Kovalchuk 10.00 25.00
FFJI Jarome Iginla 10.00 25.00
FFJP Joni Pitkanen 5.00 12.00
FFJR Jeremy Roenick 5.00 12.00
FFJS Joe Sakic 12.00 30.00
FFJT Jocelyn Thibault 5.00 12.00
FFKP Keith Primeau 5.00 12.00
FFKT Keith Tkachuk 5.00 12.00
FFMB Martin Brodeur 12.00 30.00
FFMK Miikka Kiprusoff 10.00 25.00
FFML Mario Lemieux 15.00 40.00
FFMM Milan Michalek 5.00 12.00
FFMS Mats Sundin 5.00 12.00
FFMT Marty Turco 5.00 12.00
FFPD Pavel Datsyuk 5.00 12.00
FFPF Peter Forsberg 8.00 20.00
FFPK Paul Kariya 6.00 15.00
FFPM Patrick Marleau 5.00 12.00
FFPR Patrick Roy 20.00 50.00
FFRB Ray Bourque 8.00 20.00
FFRS Ryan Smyth 5.00 12.00
FFSC Sidney Crosby 75.00 125.00
FFSK Saku Koivu 6.00 15.00
FFSL Martin St. Louis 5.00 12.00
FFSP Jason Spezza 6.00 15.00
FFSY Steve Yzerman 12.00 30.00
FFSZ Sergei Zubov 5.00 12.00
FFTB Todd Bertuzzi 5.00 12.00
FFVL Vincent Lecavalier 6.00 15.00
FFZP Zigmund Palffy 8.00 20.00

2005-06 Upper Deck Ice Frozen Fabrics Patches

FFPAT Alex Tanguay 15.00 40.00
FFPAY Alexei Yashin
FFPBS Brendan Shanahan 20.00 50.00
FFPCO Chris Osgood 12.00 30.00
FFPCP Chris Pronger
FFPDA Daniel Alfredsson 12.00 30.00
FFPDH Dany Heatley 15.00 40.00
FFPDW Doug Weight 10.00 25.00
FFPEB Ed Belfour 20.00 50.00
FFPGM Glen Murray 10.00 25.00
FFPIK Ilya Kovalchuk 25.00 60.00
FFPJI Jarome Iginla 25.00 60.00
FFPJP Joni Pitkanen 10.00 25.00
FFPJR Jeremy Roenick 20.00 50.00
FFPJS Joe Sakic 30.00 75.00
FFPJT Jocelyn Thibault 12.00 30.00
FFPKP Keith Primeau 12.00 30.00
FFPKT Keith Tkachuk 15.00 40.00
FFPMB Martin Brodeur 40.00 100.00
FFPMK Miikka Kiprusoff 25.00 60.00
FFPML Mario Lemieux 50.00 125.00
FFPMM Milan Michalek 12.00 30.00
FFPMS Mats Sundin 15.00 40.00
FFPMT Marty Turco 20.00 50.00
FFPNK Nikolai Khabibulin 20.00 50.00
FFPPD Pavel Datsyuk 20.00 50.00
FFPPF Peter Forsberg 20.00 50.00
FFPPK Paul Kariya
FFPPM Patrick Marleau 12.00 30.00
FFPPR Patrick Roy 60.00 150.00
FFPRB Ray Bourque 30.00 75.00
FFPRS Ryan Smyth
FFPSC Sidney Crosby 100.00 200.00
FFPSK Saku Koivu 15.00 40.00
FFPSL Martin St. Louis 12.00 30.00
FFPSP Jason Spezza 20.00 50.00
FFPSY Steve Yzerman 50.00 125.00
FFPSZ Sergei Zubov 6.00 15.00
FFPTB Todd Bertuzzi 15.00 40.00
FFPVL Vincent Lecavalier 15.00 40.00
FFPZP Zigmund Palffy 10.00 25.00

2005-06 Upper Deck Ice Frozen Fabrics Patch Autographs

PRINT RUN 10 SER. #'d SETS
NOT PRICED DUE TO SCARCITY

2005-06 Upper Deck Ice Glacial Graphs

GGAF Alexander Frolov 4.00 10.00
GGAO Alexander Ovechkin 40.00 80.00
GGAP Alex Perezhogin 6.00 15.00
GGAR Andrew Raycroft 5.00 12.00
GGCB Cam Barker 5.00 12.00
GGCP Corey Perry 8.00 20.00
GGCW Cam Ward 12.00 30.00
GGDP Dion Phaneuf 20.00 50.00
GGEN Eric Nystrom 4.00 10.00
GGGB Gilbert Brule 8.00 20.00
GGGH Gordie Howe SP 75.00 150.00
GGHO Marian Hossa 6.00 15.00
GGHT Hannu Toivonen 6.00 15.00
GGHV Martin Havlat 6.00 15.00
GGIK Ilya Kovalchuk 20.00 50.00
GGJB Jay Bouwmeester 4.00 10.00
GGJC Jeff Carter 8.00 20.00
GGJI Jarome Iginla 15.00 30.00
GGKB Keith Ballard 4.00 10.00
GGMB Martin Brodeur 40.00 80.00
GGMM Mike Modano SP 15.00 40.00
GGMP Michael Peca 6.00 15.00
GGMR Mike Ribeiro 4.00 10.00
GGMS Matt Stajan 4.00 10.00
GGMT Marty Turco 8.00 20.00
GGNA Rick Nash 12.00 30.00
GGRB Rob Blake SP 15.00 40.00
GGRI Mike Richards 6.00 15.00
GGRK Ryan Kesler 4.00 10.00
GGRL Roberto Luongo 20.00 50.00
GGRM Ryan Miller 15.00 30.00
GGRN Robert Nilsson 4.00 10.00
GGSC Sidney Crosby 300.00 500.00
GGSD Shane Doan 4.00 10.00
GGST Alexander Steen 6.00 15.00
GGTA Tyler Arnason 4.00 10.00
GGTH Trent Hunter 4.00 10.00
GGTL Trevor Linden 8.00 20.00
GGTV Thomas Vanek 10.00 25.00
GGWG Wayne Gretzky SP 250.00 400.00
GGWW Wojtek Wolski 8.00 20.00
GGZP Zach Parise 6.00 15.00

2005-06 Upper Deck Ice Glacial Graphs Labels

GGCB Cam Barker 8.00 20.00
GGCW Cam Ward 20.00 50.00
GGEN Eric Nystrom 8.00 20.00
GGHT Hannu Toivonen 12.50 30.00
GGJB Jay Bouwmeester 8.00 20.00
GGKB Keith Ballard 8.00 20.00
GGMS Matt Stajan 8.00 20.00
GGRK Ryan Kesler 8.00 20.00
GGRN Robert Nilsson 8.00 20.00
GGTA Tyler Arnason 8.00 20.00
GGTH Trent Hunter 8.00 20.00
GGTV Thomas Vanek 20.00 50.00
GGWW Wojtek Wolski 20.00 50.00
GGZP Zach Parise 12.50 30.00

2005-06 Upper Deck Ice Premieres Auto Patches

PRINT RUN 10 SER. #'d SETS
NOT PRICED DUE TO SCARCITY
AIPAA Andrew Alberts
AIPAM Andrej Meszaros
AIPAO Alexander Ovechkin
AIPAP Alexander Perezhogin
AIPAS Alexander Steen
AIPAW Andrew Wozniewski
AIPBB Brandon Bochenski
AIPBC Braydon Coburn
AIPBL Brett Lebda
AIPBS Brent Seabrook
AIPBT Barry Tallackson
AIPBW Brad Winchester
AIPCB Cam Barker
AIPCC Chris Campoli
AIPCP Corey Perry
AIPCW Cam Ward
AIPDB Derek Boogaard
AIPDK Duncan Keith
AIPDL David Leneveu
AIPDP Dion Phaneuf
AIPEN Eric Nystrom
AIPGB Gilbert Brule
AIPGP George Parros
AIPHL Henrik Lundqvist
AIPHO Jeff Hoggan
AIPHT Hannu Toivonen
AIPJB Jaroslav Balastik
AIPJC Jeff Carter
AIPJF Johan Franzen
AIPJG Josh Gorges
AIPJH Jim Howard
AIPJJ Jussi Jokinen
AIPJK Jakub Klepis
AIPJM Jay McClement
AIPJS Jim Slater
AIPJW Jeff Woywitka
AIPKB Keith Ballard
AIPKD Kevin Dallman
AIPKN Kevin Nastiuk
AIPMF Matt Foy
AIPMJ Milan Jurcina
AIPMK Mikko Koivu
AIPMO Alvaro Montoya
AIPMR Mike Richards
AIPMT Maxime Talbot
AIPNN Niklas Nordgren
AIPPB Peter Budaj
AIPPE Patrick Eaves
AIPPN Petteri Nokelainen
AIPPP Petr Prucha
AIPRB Rene Bourque
AIPRC Ryane Clowe
AIPRG Ryan Getzlaf
AIPRH Ryan Hollweg
AIPRI Raitis Ivanans
AIPRN Robert Nilsson
AIPRO Rostislav Olesz
AIPRS Ryan Suter
AIPSC Sidney Crosby
AIPST Anthony Stewart
AIPTF Tomas Fleischmann
AIPTH Timo Helbling
AIPTV Thomas Vanek
AIPWW Wojtek Wolski
AIPYD Yann Danis
AIPZP Zach Parise

2005-06 Upper Deck Ice Signature Swatches

SSAO Alexander Ovechkin 90.00 150.00
SSAS Alexander Steen 20.00 50.00
SSAT Alex Tanguay 20.00 50.00
SSBL Brian Leetch 20.00 50.00
SSBO Mike Bossy SP 30.00 80.00
SSCP Chris Pronger 25.00 60.00
SSCW Cam Ward 20.00 50.00
SSDH Dominik Hasek SP 75.00 125.00
SSDW Doug Weight 15.00 40.00
SSEB Ed Belfour SP 25.00 60.00
SSGB Gilbert Brule 20.00 50.00
SSHE Dany Heatley SP 40.00 80.00
SSHZ Henrik Zetterberg 20.00 50.00
SSIK Ilya Kovalchuk /50 SP 40.00 100.00
SSJC Jeff Carter 20.00 50.00
SSJI Jarome Iginla 40.00 75.00
SSJK Jari Kurri /100 SP 30.00 80.00
SSJR Jeremy Roenick SP 25.00 60.00
SSJS Jason Spezza /25 SP 100.00 200.00
SSJT Joe Thornton Sp 30.00 80.00
SSLC Luc Robitaille 20.00 50.00
SSMB Martin Brodeur SP
SSMH Milan Hejduk 15.00 40.00
SSMM Mike Modano /50 SP 50.00 100.00
SSMN Markus Naslund 20.00 50.00
SSMS Martin St. Louis SP 25.00 60.00
SSNZ Nikolai Zherdev 15.00 40.00
SSPB Patrice Bergeron 15.00 40.00
SSPR Patrick Roy /10 SP
SSRB Ray Bourque SP 60.00 125.00
SSRN Rick Nash /25 SP 100.00 200.00
SSSC Sidney Crosby /100 SP 400.00 700.00
SSSG Simon Gagne 20.00 50.00
SSSK Saku Koivu SP 30.00 80.00
SSSU Mats Sundin /15 SP
SSTB Todd Bertuzzi 20.00 50.00
SSTH Jose Theodore 20.00 50.00
SSVL Vincent Lecavalier SP 60.00 125.00
SSZP Zigmund Palffy /55 SP 50.00 100.00

2000-01 Upper Deck Jason Spezza Giveaways

These cards were given away at the Upper Deck booth at the 2000 and 2001 Toronto Expos. The version numbered to 300 was given away at the Fall Expo while the version numbered to 600 was given away at the Spring Expo. In order to receive a card, one had to open a box of Upper Deck product at the booth. Differently numbered and unnumberd varitions have also surfaced fueling speculation that some cards were distributed differently.

1 Jason Spezza AU/300 25.00 60.00
2 Jason Spezza AU/600 15.00 40.00

2000-01 Upper Deck Legends

Released in mid November 2000, Upper Deck Legends features a 135-card set where base design features both color and black and white photos of the greats of hockey. Base cards are enhanced with blue foil highlights and a white border that fades to each respective player's team color along the bottom. Legends was packaged in 24-pack boxes with each pack containing five cards and carried a suggested retail price of $4.99.

COMPLETE SET (135) 25.00 50.00
1 Paul Kariya .15 .40
2 Teemu Selanne .15 .40
3 Paul Kariya .15 .40
Teemu Selanne
4 Patrik Stefan .02 .10
5 Patrik Stefan .02 .10
Damian Rhodes
6 Bobby Orr .60 1.50
7 Phil Esposito .30 .75
8 Johnny Bucyk .12 .30
9 Cam Neely .15 .40
10 Eddie Shore .15 .40
11 Joe Thornton .25 .60
12 Sergei Samsonov .12 .30
13 Cam Neely .25 .60
Joe Thornton
14 Gilbert Perreault .12 .30
15 Pat LaFontaine .20 .50
16 Dominik Hasek .30 .75
17 Doug Gilmour .12 .30
18 Gilbert Perreault .30 .75
Dominik Hasek
19 Lanny McDonald .12 .30
20 Valeri Bure .02 .10
21 Theoren Fleury .02 .10
Valeri Bure
22 Ron Francis .12 .30
23 Arturs Irbe .12 .30
24 Ron Francis .12 .30
Arturs Irbe
25 Bobby Hull .30 .75
26 Stan Mikita .25 .60
27 Tony Esposito .25 .60
28 Glenn Hall .15 .40
29 Tony Amonte .12 .30
30 Bobby Hull .20 .50
Tony Amonte
31 Patrick Roy .75 2.00
32 Ray Bourque .25 .60
33 Chris Drury .12 .30
34 Peter Forsberg .40 1.00
35 Milan Hejduk .15 .40
36 Patrick Roy .75 2.00
Peter Forsberg
37 Brett Hull .20 .50
38 Ed Belfour .15 .40
39 Mike Modano .25 .60
40 M.Modano/E.Belfour .25 .60
41 Gordie Howe .60 1.50
42 Ted Lindsay .15 .40
43 Terry Sawchuk .30 .75
44 Brendan Shanahan .15 .40
45 Chris Osgood .12 .30
46 Steve Yzerman .75 2.00
47 Gordie Howe .75 2.00
Steve Yzerman
48 Grant Fuhr .15 .40
49 Wayne Gretzky 1.00 2.50
50 Jari Kurri .15 .40
51 Mark Messier .15 .40
52 Paul Coffey .15 .40
53 Doug Weight .12 .30
54 Wayne Gretzky 1.00 2.50
Doug Weight
55 Pavel Bure .15 .40
56 Viktor Kozlov .12 .30
57 John Vanbiesbrouck .25 .60
Pavel Bure
58 Marcel Dionne .20 .50
59 Zigmund Palffy .12 .30
60 Luc Robitaille .12 .30
61 Wayne Gretzky .75 2.00
Luc Robitaille
62 Dino Ciccarelli .12 .30
63 Saku Koivu .15 .40
64 Jean Beliveau .15 .40
65 Doug Harvey .25 .60
66 Jacques Plante .20 .50
67 Guy Lafleur .25 .60
68 Serge Savard .15 .40
69 Larry Robinson .15 .40
70 Eric Weinrich .02 .10
71 Bernie Geoffrion .15 .40
72 Jose Theodore .20 .50
73 Guy Lafleur .75 2.00
Patrick Roy
74 David Legwand .12 .30
75 David Legwand .12 .30
Mike Dunham
76 Martin Brodeur* .40 1.00
77 Scott Gomez .02 .10
78 Scott Stevens .12 .30
79 Scott Stevens .40 1.00
Martin Brodeur
80 Denis Potvin .15 .40
81 Mike Bossy .20 .50
82 Bryan Trottier .12 .30
83 Butch Goring .12 .30
84 Bob Nystrom .12 .30
85 Chico Resch .12 .30
86 Clark Gillies .12 .30
87 Tim Connolly .02 .10
88 Bryan Trottier .02 .10
Tim Connolly
89 Ed Giacomin .12 .30
90 Rod Gilbert .15 .40
91 Theo Fleury .02 .10
92 Mark Messier .20 .50
Brian Leetch
93 Marian Hossa .15 .40
94 Radek Bonk .02 .10
95 Radek Bonk .02 .10
Marian Hossa
96 Bobby Clarke .20 .50
97 Bernie Parent .15 .40
98 Eric Lindros .15 .40
99 Brian Boucher .15 .40
100 John LeClair .15 .40
101 Bobby Clarke .20 .50
John LeClair
102 Jeremy Roenick .20 .50
103 Keith Tkachuk .15 .40
104 Jeremy Roenick .15 .40
Keith Tkachuk
105 Mario Lemieux .75 2.00
106 Joe Mullen .12 .30
107 Jaromir Jagr .25 .75
108 Mario Lemieux .40 1.00
Jaromir Jagr
109 Peter Stastny .15 .40
110 Michel Goulet .12 .30
111 Steve Shields .12 .30
112 Jeff Friesen .02 .10
113 Owen Nolan .02 .10
Jeff Friesen
114 Bernie Federko .12 .30
115 Chris Pronger .12 .30
116 Roman Turek .12 .30
117 Brett Hull .20 .50
Pavol Demitra
118 Vincent Lecavalier .15 .40
119 Vincent Lecavalier .15 .40
Paul Mara
120 Frank Mahovlich .15 .40
121 Syl Apps .12 .30
122 Tim Horton .15 .40
123 Eddie Shack .15 .40
124 Curtis Joseph .15 .40
125 Mats Sundin .15 .40
126 Frank Mahovlich .20 .50
Curtis Joseph
127 Richard Brodeur .12 .30
128 Richard Brodeur .02 .10
Markus Naslund
129 Mike Gartner .12 .30
130 Adam Oates .12 .30
131 Olaf Kolzig .12 .30
132 Mike Gartner .12 .30
Olaf Kolzig
133 Dale Hawerchuk .12 .30
134 Wayne Gretzky CL .40 1.00
135 Steve Yzerman CL .30 .75

2000-01 Upper Deck Legends Legendary Collection Bronze

Randomly inserted in packs, this 135-card set parallels the base Legends set enhanced with bronze foil highlights and cards are sequentially numbered to 25.

*BRONZE: 50X TO 120X BASIC CARDS

2000-01 Upper Deck Legends Legendary Collection Gold

Randomly inserted in packs, this 135-card set parallels the base Legends set enhanced with gold foil highlights and cards are sequentially numbered to 375.

*GOLD: 5X TO 12X BASIC CARDS

2000-01 Upper Deck Legends Legendary Collection Silver

Randomly inserted in packs, this 135-card set parallels the base Legends set enhanced with silver foil highlights and cards are sequentially numbered to 100.

*SILVER: 8X TO 20X BASIC CARDS

2000-01 Upper Deck Legends Enshrined Stars

Randomly inserted in packs at the rate of 1:12, this 15-card set features Hall of Famers on a foil bordered card with silver foil highlights.

COMPLETE SET (15) 30.00 60.00
ES1 Wayne Gretzky 6.00 15.00
ES2 Gordie Howe 4.00 10.00
ES3 Mario Lemieux 5.00 12.00
ES4 Bobby Hull 2.50 6.00
ES5 Marcel Dionne 1.50 4.00
ES6 Denis Potvin 1.50 4.00
ES7 Guy Lafleur 2.00 5.00
ES8 Mike Bossy 1.50 4.00
ES9 Bobby Clarke 1.50 4.00
ES10 Frank Mahovlich 1.50 4.00
ES11 Gilbert Perreault 1.50 4.00
ES12 Phil Esposito 2.50 6.00
ES13 Tony Esposito 2.00 5.00
ES14 Stan Mikita 2.00 5.00
ES15 Ted Lindsay 1.50 4.00

2000-01 Upper Deck Legends Epic Signatures

Randomly inserted in packs at the rate of 1:23, this 43-card set features player photography and authentic player autographs.

BC Bobby Clarke 12.50 30.00
BG Bernie Geoffrion 10.00 25.00
BH Brett Hull 12.50 30.00
BO Bobby Orr 75.00 200.00
BT Bryan Trottier 6.00 15.00
CJ Curtis Joseph 10.00 25.00
CN Cam Neely 12.00 30.00
DH Dale Hawerchuk 6.00 15.00
DP Denis Potvin 6.00 15.00
FM Frank Mahovlich 6.00 15.00
GH Gordie Howe 60.00 150.00
GL Guy Lafleur 10.00 25.00
GP Gilbert Perreault 8.00 20.00
JB John Bucyk 6.00 15.00
JK Jari Kurri 10.00 25.00
JL John LeClair 4.00 10.00
JM Joe Mullen 6.00 15.00
JN Joe Nieuwendyk 8.00 20.00
JT Joe Thornton 12.50 30.00
KT Keith Tkachuk 4.00 10.00
LM Lanny McDonald 8.00 20.00
LR Larry Robinson 8.00 20.00
MB Mike Bossy 8.00 20.00
MD Marcel Dionne 6.00 15.00
MG Mike Gartner 6.00 15.00
ML Mario Lemieux 75.00 150.00
MM Mark Messier 60.00 125.00
PB Pavel Bure 6.00 15.00
PE Phil Esposito 25.00 60.00
PL Pat LaFontaine 6.00 15.00
PS Patrik Stefan 4.00 10.00
PV Pat Verbeek 10.00 25.00
SF Sergei Fedorov 20.00 50.00
SM Stan Mikita 10.00 25.00
SS Sergei Samsonov 4.00 10.00
SY Steve Yzerman 30.00 80.00
TE Tony Esposito 12.50 30.00
TL Ted Lindsay 8.00 20.00
WG Wayne Gretzky 100.00 200.00
BHU Bobby Hull 25.00 60.00
JBE Jean Beliveau 10.00 25.00
MBR Martin Brodeur 60.00 100.00
MGO Michel Goulet 6.00 15.00
PBO Peter Bondra 5.00 10.00

2000-01 Upper Deck Legends Essence of the Game

Randomly inserted in packs at the rate of 1:23, this 8-card set combines a star from yesterday with a star from today on this all foil insert card with silver foil highlights.

COMPLETE SET (8) 30.00 60.00
EG1 Guy Lafleur 1.50 4.00
Paul Kariya
EG2 Jaromir Jagr 4.00 10.00
Wayne Gretzky
EG3 Pavel Bure 1.50 4.00
Mike Bossy
EG4 Patrick Roy 5.00 12.00
Terry Sawchuk
EG5 Martin Brodeur 2.50 6.00
Bernie Parent
EG6 Cam Neely 1.50 4.00
Brendan Shanahan
EG7 Raymond Bourque 5.00 12.00
Bobby Orr
EG8 Steve Yzerman 5.00 12.00
Gordie Howe

2000-01 Upper Deck Legends Legendary Game Jerseys

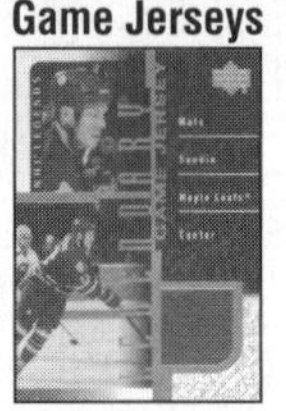

Randomly inserted in packs at the rate of 1:23, this 36-card set features both color and black and white player photos, silver foil highlights, and a swatch of an authentic game jersey in the lower right hand corner of the card front.

JAM Al MacInnis 6.00 15.00
JBG Butch Goring 5.00 12.00
JBH Brett Hull 8.00 20.00
JBN Bob Nystrom 5.00 12.00
JBO Bobby Orr SP 50.00 125.00
JBT Bryan Trottier 6.00 15.00
JCG Clark Gillies 5.00 12.00
JCR Chico Resch 5.00 12.00
JDG Doug Gilmour 6.00 15.00
JDH Dominik Hasek 8.00 20.00
JDP Denis Potvin 6.00 15.00
JGF Grant Fuhr SP 15.00 40.00
JGH Gordie Howe 20.00 50.00
JJJ Jaromir Jagr 6.00 15.00
JJK Jari Kurri SP 10.00 25.00
JJL John LeClair 6.00 15.00
JJS Joe Sakic 8.00 20.00
JKT Keith Tkachuk 6.00 15.00
JLR Larry Robinson SP 6.00 15.00
JMB Mike Bossy 8.00 20.00
JMD Marcel Dionne SP 10.00 25.00
JMG Mike Gartner 6.00 15.00
JML Mario Lemieux 12.50 30.00
JMM Mike Modano 6.00 15.00
JMS Mats Sundin 6.00 15.00
JPB Pavel Bure 6.00 15.00
JPF Peter Forsberg 10.00 25.00
JPK Paul Kariya 6.00 15.00
JPL Pat LaFontaine 5.00 12.00
JPR Patrick Roy 12.50 30.00
JRB Ray Bourque 8.00 20.00
JSF Sergei Fedorov 6.00 15.00
JSY Steve Yzerman 12.50 30.00
JTS Teemu Selanne 6.00 15.00
JWG Wayne Gretzky 30.00 80.00
JMBR Martin Brodeur 10.00 25.00

2000-01 Upper Deck Legends of the Cage

Randomly inserted in packs at the rate of 1:18, this 10-card set showcases the greatest goalies to grace the game of hockey. Base cards feature and all-foil backdrop with player action photography and silver foil highlights.

COMPLETE SET (10) 20.00 40.00
LC1 Patrick Roy 5.00 12.00
LC2 Martin Brodeur 3.00 8.00
LC3 Dominik Hasek 2.50 6.00
LC4 Curtis Joseph 1.25 3.00
LC5 Ed Belfour 1.50 4.00
LC6 Grant Fuhr 1.25 3.00
LC7 Mike Richter 1.25 3.00
LC8 Jacques Plante 1.50 4.00
LC9 Terry Sawchuk 2.50 6.00
LC10 Tony Esposito 2.00 5.00

2000-01 Upper Deck Legends Playoff Heroes

Randomly inserted in packs at the rate of 1:15, this 12-card set showcases NHL players who year after year stepped it up in the playoffs. Cards feature 3 action panels along the center of the card set against an all foil backdrop with a close up photo of the featured player. Cards have silver foil highlights.

COMPLETE SET (12) 30.00 60.00
PH1 Patrick Roy 5.00 12.00
PH2 Steve Yzerman 5.00 12.00
PH3 Jaromir Jagr 1.50 4.00
PH4 Mike Modano 2.00 5.00
PH5 Peter Forsberg 2.50 6.00
PH6 Mark Messier 1.50 4.00
PH7 Wayne Gretzky 6.00 15.00
PH8 Brett Hull 1.50 4.00
PH9 Gordie Howe 4.00 10.00
PH10 Bobby Hull 2.50 6.00
PH11 Bryan Trottier 1.50 4.00
PH12 Phil Esposito 2.50 6.00

2000-01 Upper Deck Legends Supreme Milestones

Randomly inserted in packs at the rate of 1:4, this 15-card set spotlights NHL legends and highlights some of their most significant career achievements on an all holo-foil card with silver foil highlights. Player photos are set against a larger "faded" player photo in the background.

COMPLETE SET (15) 25.00 50.00
SM1 Wayne Gretzky 4.00 10.00
SM2 Gordie Howe 2.50 6.00
SM3 Bobby Hull 1.50 4.00
SM4 Wayne Gretzky 4.00 10.00
SM5 Steve Yzerman 2.50 6.00
SM6 Brett Hull .75 2.00
SM7 Joe Sakic 1.25 3.00
SM8 Mark Messier .75 2.00
SM9 Patrick Roy 3.00 8.00
SM10 Luc Robitaille .75 2.00
SM11 Mario Lemieux 3.00 8.00
SM12 Mike Bossy 1.00 2.50
SM13 Phil Esposito 1.50 4.00
SM14 Tony Esposito 1.25 3.00
SM15 Ray Bourque 1.00 2.50

2001-02 Upper Deck Legends

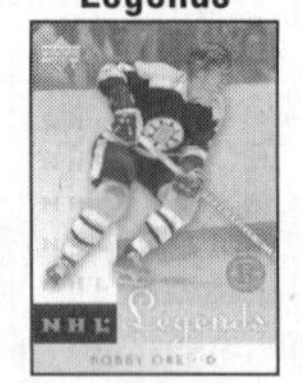
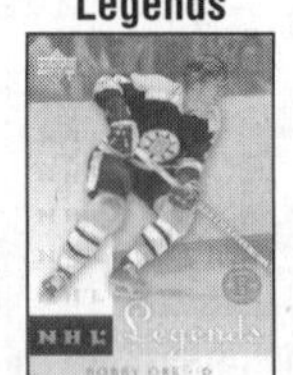

issued in early-December 2001, this 100-card set carried an SRP of $4.99 for a 5-card pack. The set focused on legendary NHL players of the past.

COMPLETE SET (100) 25.00 50.00
1 Bobby Orr 1.25 3.00
2 Eddie Shore .40 1.00
3 Phil Esposito .60 1.50
4 Johnny Bucyk .30 .75
5 Cam Neely .40 1.00
6 Gerry Cheevers .40 1.00
7 Gilbert Perreault .30 .75
8 Rene Robert .10 .25
9 Lanny McDonald .30 .75
10 Al Secord .10 .25
11 Bobby Hull .75 2.00
12 Glenn Hall .40 1.00
13 Stan Mikita .40 1.00
14 Tony Esposito .40 1.00
15 Gordie Howe 1.25 3.00
16 Terry Sawchuk .60 1.50
17 Ted Lindsay .40 1.00
18 Sid Abel .10 .25
19 Red Kelly .40 1.00
20 Alex Delvecchio .40 1.00
21 Glenn Anderson .10 .25
22 Wayne Gretzky 1.50 4.00
23 Jari Kurri .30 .75
24 Grant Fuhr .30 .75
25 Bill Ranford .30 .75
26 Gordie Howe 1.25 3.00
27 Marcel Dionne .30 .75
28 Butch Goring .10 .25
29 Rogie Vachon .10 .25
30 Maurice Richard .75 2.00
31 Jean Beliveau .40 1.00
32 Serge Savard .40 1.00
33 Jacques Plante .60 1.50
34 Guy Lafleur .40 1.00
35 Yvan Cournoyer .40 1.00
36 Steve Shutt .10 .25
37 Rick Green .10 .25
38 Henri Richard .40 1.00
39 Bernie Geoffrion .40 1.00
40 Guy Lapointe .10 .25
41 Denis Potvin .30 .75
42 Mike Bossy .30 .75
43 Bryan Trottier .30 .75
44 Clark Gillies .10 .25
45 Billy Smith .30 .75
46 Ed Giacomin .40 1.00
47 Jean Ratelle .10 .25
48 Lester Patrick .10 .25
49 William Jennings .10 .25
50 Ray Bourque .75 2.00
51 Frank Calder .10 .25
52 Andy van Hellemond .10 .25
53 Bobby Clarke .30 .75
54 Bernie Parent .40 1.00
55 Bill Barber .10 .25
56 Syl Apps .10 .25
57 Bernie Federko .10 .25
58 Frank Mahovlich .40 1.00
59 Darryl Sittler .40 1.00
60 Tim Horton .40 1.00
61 Rick Vaive .10 .25
62 Frank Selke .10 .25
63 Conn Smythe .10 .25
64 King Clancy .10 .25
65 Tony Tanti .10 .25
66 Mike Ridley .10 .25
67 Rod Langway .10 .25
68 Mike Gartner .30 .75
69 Kent Nilsson .10 .25
70 Reggie Leach .10 .25
71 Dennis Maruk .10 .25
72 Wilf Paiement .10 .25
73 Barry Beck .10 .25
74 Simon Nolet .10 .25
75 Don Beaupre .10 .25
76 Peter Stastny .30 .75
77 Michel Goulet .30 .75
78 Dale Hawerchuk .30 .75
79 Gerry Cheevers .40 1.00
80 Glenn Hall .40 1.00
81 Terry Sawchuk .60 1.50
82 Grant Fuhr .30 .75
83 Bernie Parent .40 1.00
84 Jacques Plante .60 1.50
85 Ed Giacomin .40 1.00
86 Bill Ranford .30 .75
87 Billy Smith .30 .75
88 Tony Esposito .40 1.00
89 Bobby Orr 1.25 3.00
90 Bobby Hull .75 2.00
91 Gordie Howe 1.25 3.00
92 Wayne Gretzky 1.50 4.00
93 Marcel Dionne .30 .75
94 Maurice Richard .75 2.00
95 Guy Lafleur .50 1.25
96 Mike Bossy .30 .75
97 Jari Kurri .40 1.00
98 Mike Gartner .40 1.00
99 Gordie Howe CL .60 1.50
100 Wayne Gretzky CL .75 2.00

2001-02 Upper Deck Legends Epic Signatures

Randomly inserted at 1:54 packs, this 18-card set featured authentic autographs of NHL alums.

AD Alex Delvecchio 12.50 30.00
BC Bobby Clarke 12.50 30.00
BH Bobby Hull 20.00 50.00
BO Bobby Orr 100.00 250.00
BT Bryan Trottier 12.50 30.00
CN Cam Neely 15.00 40.00
FM Frank Mahovlich 12.50 30.00
GH Gordie Howe 60.00 150.00
GL Guy Lafleur 15.00 40.00
GP Gilbert Perreault 12.50 30.00
JB Jean Beliveau 15.00 40.00
MB Mike Bossy 12.50 30.00
MD Marcel Dionne 12.50 30.00
PE Phil Esposito 12.50 30.00
SM Stan Mikita 12.50 30.00
TE Tony Esposito 15.00 40.00
TL Ted Lindsay 12.50 30.00
WG Wayne Gretzky 125.00 250.00

2001-02 Upper Deck Legends Fiorentino Collection

Randomly inserted at 1:18, this 15-card set featured reproductions of photographs taken by renowned sports photographer James Fiorentino.

COMPLETE SET (15) 40.00 80.00
FCBC Bobby Clarke 1.50 4.00
FCBH Bobby Hull 2.50 6.00
FCBO Bobby Orr 6.00 15.00
FCBT Bryan Trottier 1.50 4.00
FCGH Gordie Howe 3.00 8.00
FCGL Guy Lafleur 1.50 4.00
FCJP Jacques Plante 1.50 4.00
FCMB Mike Bossy 1.50 4.00
FCMD Marcel Dionne 1.50 4.00
FCMR Maurice Richard 3.00 8.00
FCPE Phil Esposito 1.50 4.00
FCSM Stan Mikita 1.50 4.00
FCTE Tony Esposito 1.50 4.00
FCTS Terry Sawchuk 1.50 4.00
FCWG Wayne Gretzky 6.00 15.00

2001-02 Upper Deck Legends Jerseys

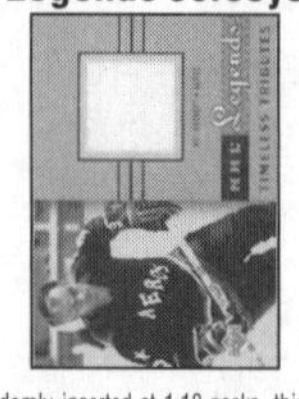

Randomly inserted at 1:18 packs, this 27-card set featured game-worn jersey swatches form the player(s) featured on the card fronts. A platinum parallel was also created and serial-numbered to 100 copies each.

*MULT.COLOR SWATCH: .75X TO 2X HI
*PLATINUM: .5X TO 1.25X HI
TTBB Bill Barber 5.00 12.00
TTBH Bobby Hull 10.00 25.00
TTBR Bill Ranford 5.00 12.00
TTBS Billy Smith 5.00 12.00
TTBT Bryan Trottier 5.00 12.00
TTCG Clark Gillies 5.00 12.00
TTCN Cam Neely 12.50 30.00
TTDP Denis Potvin 5.00 12.00
TTFL Guy Lafleur Que. 5.00 12.00
TTGC Gerry Cheevers 5.00 12.00
TTGH Gordie Howe 12.50 30.00
TTGL Guy Lafleur AS 5.00 12.00
TTGP Gilbert Perreault 5.00 12.00
TTLA Guy Lafleur Mon. 5.00 12.00
TTLF Guy Lafleur NY 5.00 12.00
TTMG Mike Gartner 5.00 12.00
TTPE Phil Esposito 5.00 12.00
TTSM Stan Mikita 5.00 12.00
TTSS Steve Shutt 5.00 12.00
TTVH Andy van Hellemond 5.00 12.00
TTWG Wayne Gretzky 25.00 60.00
TTGU Guy Lafleur Mon./Que. 12.50 30.00
TTGY Guy Lafleur NY/AS 12.50 30.00
TTHM Bobby Hull 20.00 50.00
Stan Mikita
TTSL Steve Shutt 15.00 40.00
Guy Lafleur
TTST Billy Smith 15.00 40.00
Bryan Trottier

2001-02 Upper Deck Legends Milestones

Randomly inserted at 1:18, this 16-card set honored past players and the different career milestones they achieved. Each card carried a swatch of game-used jersey from the featured player. A platinum parallel was also created and serial-numbered to just 25 copies each. The platinum parallel was not priced due to scacrity.

MBB Bill Barber 8.00 20.00
MBC Bobby Clarke 12.50 30.00
MBS Brent Sutter 8.00 20.00
MBT Bryan Trottier 8.00 20.00
MCN Cam Neely 8.00 20.00
MDP Denis Potvin 8.00 20.00
MGP Gilbert Perreault 8.00 20.00
MLM Lanny McDonald 8.00 20.00
MMB Mike Bossy 8.00 20.00
MMG Mike Gartner 8.00 20.00
MNB Neal Broten 8.00 20.00
MSS Steve Shutt 8.00 20.00
MSY Steve Yzerman 12.50 30.00
MWG Wayne Gretzky 25.00 60.00

2001-02 Upper Deck Legends Sticks

Randomly inserted at 1:18, this 29-card set featured a piece of game-used stick from the pictured player.

PHBC Bobby Clarke 12.50 30.00
PHBH Bobby Hull 12.50 30.00
PHBO Bobby Orr 50.00 125.00
PHBS Billy Smith 8.00 20.00
PHBT Bryan Trottier 8.00 20.00
PHDP Denis Potvin 8.00 20.00
PHDS Darryl Sittler 8.00 20.00
PHES Phil Esposito 8.00 20.00
PHFM Frank Mahovlich 8.00 20.00
PHGC Gerry Cheevers 8.00 20.00
PHGH Gordie Howe Det. 15.00 40.00
PHGL Guy Lafleur 8.00 20.00
PHGR Wayne Gretzky LA 40.00 100.00
PHHU Bobby Hull 15.00 40.00
PHJB Jean Beliveau 12.50 30.00
PHJK Jari Kurri 15.00 40.00
PHJP Jacques Plante 15.00 40.00
PHJR Jean Ratelle 8.00 20.00
PHMB Mike Bossy 8.00 20.00
PHMD Marcel Dionne 8.00 20.00
PHMG Mike Gartner 8.00 20.00
PHMH Gordie Howe NE 15.00 40.00
PHMR Maurice Richard 15.00 40.00
PHPE Phil Esposito 8.00 20.00
PHRA Ray Bourque Col. 15.00 40.00
PHRB Ray Bourque Bos. 12.50 30.00
PHSM Stan Mikita 8.00 20.00
PHTE Tony Esposito 8.00 20.00
PHWG Wayne Gretzky Edm. 50.00 125.00

1993 Upper Deck Locker All-Stars

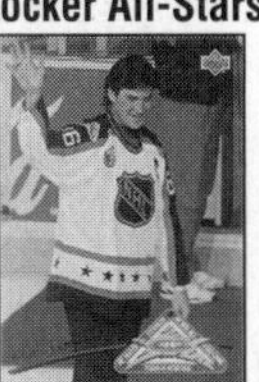

This 60-card standard-size set was issued as the 1992-93 Upper Deck NHL All-Star Locker Series. The set came in a plastic locker box. Personally signed Gordie Howe "Hockey Heroes" cards were randomly inserted throughout the locker boxes; the odds of finding one are one in 120 boxes. The fronts feature full-bleed, color, action player photos. The player's name is printed in gold foil above a blue and gold-foil curving stripe at the bottom. The 44th NHL All-Star game logo overlaps the stripe and is printed in the lower right corner. The backs carry a small, close-up picture within a bright blue rough-edged border that gives the effect of torn paper. This photo overlaps a gray panel with the same rough-edge look. This panel carries player profile information. After presenting the NHL All-Stars by conference, Campbell Conference All-Stars (1-18) and Wales Conference All-Stars (19-36), the set features the following special subsets, All-Star Skills Winners (37-40), All-Star Heroes (41-50), and Future All-Stars (51-60). The card pictures for this set were taken during the 1993 NHL All-Star Weekend in Montreal.

COMPLETE SET (60) 6.00 15.00
1 Peter Bondra .20 .50
2 Steve Duchesne .02 .05
3 Jaromir Jagr .60 1.50
4 Pat LaFontaine .20 .50
5 Brian Leetch .20 .50
6 Mario Lemieux 1.00 2.50
7 Mark Messier .24 .60
8 Alexander Mogilny .10 .25
9 Kirk Muller .02 .05
10 Adam Oates .10 .25
11 Mark Recchi .10 .25
12 Patrick Roy 1.00 2.50
13 Joe Sakic .40 1.00
14 Kevin Stevens .02 .05
15 Scott Stevens .10 .25
16 Rick Tocchet .02 .05
17 Pierre Turgeon .10 .25
18 Zarley Zalapski .02 .05
19 Ed Belfour .20 .50
20 Brian Bradley .02 .05
21 Pavel Bure .40 1.00
22 Chris Chelios .20 .50
23 Paul Coffey .20 .50
24 Doug Gilmour .20 .50
25 Wayne Gretzky 1.20 3.00
26 Phil Housley .10 .25
27 Brett Hull .24 .60
28 Kelly Kisio .02 .05
29 Jari Kurri .20 .50
30 Dave Manson .02 .05
31 Mike Modano .24 .60
32 Gary Roberts .10 .25
33 Luc Robitaille .10 .25
34 Jeremy Roenick .20 .50
35 Teemu Selanne .40 1.00
36 Steve Yzerman .60 1.50
37 Al Iafrate .10 .25
38 Mike Gartner .10 .25
39 Ray Bourque .24 .60
40 Jon Casey .10 .25
41 Bob Gainey .10 .25
42 Gordie Howe .40 1.00
43 Bobby Hull .30 .75
44 Frank Mahovlich .20 .50
45 Lanny McDonald .10 .25
46 Stan Mikita .16 .40
47 Henri Richard .12 .30
48 Larry Robinson .20 .50
49 Glen Sather .10 .25
50 Bryan Trottier .10 .25
51 Tony Amonte .10 .25
52 Pat Falloon .02 .05
53 Joe Juneau .10 .25
54 Alexei Kovalev .10 .25
55 Dmitri Kvartalnov .02 .05
56 Eric Lindros .50 1.25
57 Vladimir Malakhov .02 .05
58 Felix Potvin .20 .50
59 Mats Sundin .20 .50
60 Alexei Zhamnov .10 .25
AU Gordie Howe AU 60.00 125.00
(Certified autograph)

2003 Upper Deck Magazine

As a bonus to buyers of the Upper Deck magazine produced by Krause Publications late in 2003, a nine-card perforated sheet featuring players basically signed to Upper Deck exclusives was included. When the cards were perforated, these cards measured the standard size. Only the hockey card is listed below.

UD9 Wayne Gretzky 2.00

2000-01 Upper Deck Mario Lemieux Return to Excellence

Available in various Upper Deck products, this set features game-used jersey swatches from Mario Lemieux and each card was serial numbered out of 66. Cards ML1-ML3 were randomly available in Upper Deck Pros & Prospects, cards ML4-ML6 were randomly available in SP Authentic, and cards ML7-ML9were randomly available in Upper Deck Rookie Update.

COMMON CARD (ML1-9) 100.00 200.00

1998-99 Upper Deck MVP

The 1998-99 new Upper Deck MVP set was issued in one series totaling 220 cards and distributed in ten-card packs with a suggested retail price of $1.59. The fronts feature color action player photos printed on internally die-cut, double laminated cards with player information on the backs.

COMPLETE SET (220) 15.00 30.00
1 Paul Kariya .10 .30
2 Teemu Selanne .10 .30
3 Tomas Sandstrom .05 .15
4 Johan Davidsson .05 .15
5 Mike Crowley RC .05 .15
6 Guy Hebert .08 .25
7 Marty McInnis .05 .15
8 Steve Rucchin .05 .15
9 Ray Bourque .20 .50
10 Sergei Samsonov .08 .25
11 Cameron Mann .05 .15
12 Joe Thornton .20 .50
13 Jason Allison .05 .15
14 Byron Dafoe .08 .25
15 Kyle McLaren .05 .15
16 Dimitri Khristich .05 .15
17 Hal Gill .05 .15
18 Anson Carter .08 .25
19 Miroslav Satan .08 .25
20 Brian Holzinger .05 .15
21 Dominik Hasek .25 .60
22 Matthew Barnaby .05 .15
23 Erik Rasmussen .05 .15
24 Geoff Sanderson .08 .25
25 Michal Grosek .05 .15
26 Michael Peca .08 .25
27 Rico Fata .05 .15
28 Derek Morris .05 .15
29 Phil Housley .05 .15
30 Valeri Bure .05 .15
31 Ed Ward .05 .15
32 J-S Giguere .08 .25
33 Jeff Shantz .05 .15
34 Jarome Iginla .12 .40
35 Ron Francis .08 .25
36 Trevor Kidd .08 .25
37 Keith Primeau .05 .15
38 Sami Kapanen .05 .15
39 Martin Gelinas .05 .15
40 Jeff O'Neill .05 .15
41 Gary Roberts .05 .15
42 Jocelyn Thibault .08 .25
43 Doug Gilmour .08 .25
44 Chris Chelios .10 .30
45 Tony Amonte .08 .25
46 Bob Probert .05 .15
47 Daniel Cleary .05 .15
48 Eric Daze .08 .25
49 Mike Maneluk RC .05 .15
50 Remi Royer RC .05 .15
51 Peter Forsberg .30 .75
52 Patrick Roy .60 1.50
53 Joe Sakic .25 .60
54 Chris Drury .08 .25
55 Milan Hejduk RC .60 1.50
56 Greg DeVries .05 .15
57 Theo Fleury .05 .15
58 Adam Deadmarsh .05 .15
59 Brett Hull .15 .40
60 Ed Belfour .10 .30
61 Mike Modano .20 .50
62 Darryl Sydor .05 .15
63 Joe Nieuwendyk .08 .25
64 Grant Marshall .05 .15
65 Sergei Zubov .05 .15
66 Derian Hatcher .05 .15
67 Jere Lehtinen .08 .25
68 Sergei Fedorov .20 .50
69 Steve Yzerman .60 1.50
70 Nicklas Lidstrom .10 .30
71 Chris Osgood .08 .25
72 Brendan Shanahan .10 .30
73 Darren McCarty .05 .15
74 Tomas Holmstrom .05 .15
75 Norm Maracle RC .20 .50
76 Doug Brown .05 .15
77 Doug Weight .08 .25
78 Janne Niinimaa .05 .15
79 Tom Poti .05 .15
80 Bill Guerin .08 .25
81 Mike Grier .05 .15
82 Ryan Smyth .08 .25
83 Roman Hamrlik .05 .15
84 Kevin Brown .05 .15
85 Pavel Bure .10 .30
86 Jaroslav Spacek .05 .15
87 Rob Niedermayer .05 .15
88 Robert Svehla .05 .15
89 Ray Whitney .05 .15
90 Peter Worrell RC .15 .40
91 Mark Parrish RC .08 .25
92 Oleg Kvasha RC .10 .30
93 Steve Duchesne .05 .15
94 Rob Blake .08 .25
95 Olli Jokinen .08 .25
96 Donald Audette .05 .15
97 Luc Robitaille .08 .25
98 Josh Green .08 .25
99 Philippe Boucher .05 .15
100 Matt Johnson .05 .15
101 Vincent Damphousse .05 .15
102 Dainius Zubrus .05 .15
103 Terry Ryan .05 .15
104 Saku Koivu .10 .30
105 Brett Clark RC .05 .15
106 Dave Morissette RC .05 .15
107 Eric Weinrich .05 .15
108 Brian Savage .05 .15
109 Shayne Corson .05 .15
110 Mike Dunham .08 .25
111 Greg Johnson .05 .15
112 Cliff Ronning .05 .15
113 Andrew Brunette .08 .25
114 Sergei Krivokrasov .05 .15
115 Sebastien Bordeleau .05 .15
116 Scott Stevens .08 .25
117 Martin Brodeur .30 .75
118 Brendan Morrison .08 .25
119 Patrik Elias .08 .25
120 Scott Niedermayer .05 .15
121 Bobby Holik .05 .15
122 Jason Arnott .05 .15
123 Jay Pandolfo .05 .15
124 Eric Brewer .05 .15
125 Zigmund Palffy .08 .25
126 Felix Potvin .10 .30
127 Robert Reichel .05 .15
128 Mike Watt .05 .15
129 Tommy Salo .08 .25
130 Kenny Jonsson .05 .15
131 Trevor Linden .08 .25
132 Wayne Gretzky .75 2.00
133 Brian Leetch .10 .30
134 Manny Malhotra .05 .15
135 Mike Richter .10 .30
136 Mike Knuble .05 .15
137 Niklas Sundstrom .05 .15
138 Todd Harvey .05 .15
139 Alexei Yashin .05 .15
140 Damian Rhodes .08 .25
141 Daniel Alfredsson .08 .25
142 Magnus Arvedson .05 .15
143 Shawn McEachern .05 .15
144 Chris Phillips .05 .15
145 Vaclav Prospal .05 .15
146 Wade Redden .05 .15
147 Eric Lindros .10 .30
148 John LeClair .10 .30
149 John Vanbiesbrouck .08 .25
150 Keith Jones .08 .25
151 Colin Forbes .08 .25
152 Mark Recchi .08 .25
153 Dan McGillis .05 .15
154 Eric Desjardins .08 .25
155 Rod Brind'Amour .08 .25
156 Keith Tkachuk .10 .30
157 Daniel Briere .05 .15
158 Nikolai Khabibulin .05 .15
159 Brad Isbister .05 .15
160 Jeremy Roenick .15 .40
161 Oleg Tverdovsky .05 .15
162 Rick Tocchet .08 .25
163 Jaromir Jagr .20 .50
164 Tom Barrasso .08 .25
165 Alexei Morozov .08 .25
166 Robert Dome .05 .15
167 Stu Barnes .05 .15
168 Martin Straka .05 .15
169 German Titov .05 .15
170 Patrick Marleau .05 .15
171 Andrei Zyuzin .05 .15
172 Marco Sturm .08 .25
173 Owen Nolan .08 .25
174 Jeff Friesen .05 .15
175 Bob Rouse .05 .15
176 Mike Vernon .08 .25
177 Mike Ricci .05 .15
178 Marty Reasoner .05 .15
179 Al MacInnis .08 .25
180 Chris Pronger .08 .25
181 Pierre Turgeon .08 .25
182 Michal Handzus RC .08 .25
183 Jim Campbell .05 .15
184 Tony Twist .05 .15
185 Pavol Demitra .08 .25
186 Daren Puppa .08 .25
187 Vincent Lecavalier .30 .75
188 Bill Ranford .08 .25
189 Alexandre Daigle .05 .15
190 Wendel Clark .08 .25
191 Rob Zamuner .05 .15
192 Chris Gratton .05 .15
193 Fredrik Modin .05 .15
194 Curtis Joseph .10 .30
195 Mats Sundin .10 .30
196 Steve Thomas .05 .15
197 Tomas Kaberle RC .15 .40
198 Alyn McCauley .05 .15
199 Mike Johnson .05 .15
200 Bryan Berard .05 .15
201 Mark Messier .10 .30
202 Jason Strudwick RC .05 .15
203 Mattias Ohlund .08 .25
204 Alexander Mogilny .08 .25
205 Bill Muckalt RC .05 .15
206 Ed Jovanovski .08 .25
207 Josh Holden .05 .15
208 Peter Schaefer .05 .15
209 Peter Bondra .08 .25
210 Olaf Kolzig .08 .25
211 Sergei Gonchar .05 .15
212 Adam Oates .08 .25
213 Brian Bellows .05 .15
214 Matt Herr RC .05 .15
215 Richard Zednik .05 .15
216 Joe Juneau .05 .15
217 Jaroslav Svejkovski .05 .15
218 Wayne Gretzky CL .40 1.00
219 Wayne Gretzky CL .40 1.00
220 Wayne Gretzky CL .40 1.00
NNO GRETZKY RETIREMENT/99 150.00 400.00

1998-99 Upper Deck MVP Gold Script

Randomly inserted in hobby packs only, this 220-card set is a gold foil hobby parallel version of the base set. Only 100 sequentially numbered sets were produced.

*STARS: 20X TO 50X BASIC CARDS
*ROOKIES: 10X TO 25X BASIC CARDS

1998-99 Upper Deck MVP Silver Script

Randomly inserted into packs at the rate of 1:2, this 220-card set is a silver foil parallel version of the base set.

*STARS: .75X TO 2X BASIC CARD
*ROOKIES: .5X TO 1.25X BASIC CARD

1998-99 Upper Deck MVP Super Script

Randomly inserted into hobby packs only, this 220-card set is a hobby limited edition, holographic foil parallel version of the base set. Only 25 sequentially numbered sets were produced.

*STARS: 40X TO 100X BASIC CARDS
*ROOKIES: 12X TO 30X BASIC CARDS

1998-99 Upper Deck MVP Dynamics

Randomly inserted into packs at a ratio of 1:28, this 15-card set commemorates the brilliant career of Wayne Gretzky.

COMPLETE SET (15) 75.00 150.00
COMMON GRETZKY (D1-D15) 6.00 12.00

1998-99 Upper Deck MVP Game Souvenirs

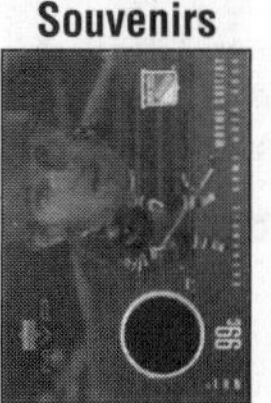

Randomly inserted in hobby packs only at the rate of 1:144, this 10-card set features color action player photos with actual pieces of game used memorabilia right on the cards.

BH Brett Hull 12.50 30.00
BS Brendan Shanahan 8.00 20.00
EL Eric Lindros 8.00 20.00
JL John LeClair 8.00 20.00
MM Mike Modano 15.00 40.00
PR Patrick Roy 25.00 60.00
RB Ray Bourque 15.00 40.00
SF Sergei Fedorov 20.00 50.00
SS Sergei Samsonov 8.00 20.00
SY Steve Yzerman 25.00 60.00
VL Vincent Lecavalier 12.50 30.00
WG Wayne Gretzky 40.00 100.00
SYA S.Yzerman AU/19 500.00 1000.00
VLA V.Lecavalier AU/14 250.00 500.00

1998-99 Upper Deck MVP OT Heroes

COMPLETE SET (15) 20.00 40.00
STATED ODDS 1:9
OT1 Steve Yzerman 4.00 10.00
OT2 Patrick Roy 4.00 10.00
OT3 Jaromir Jagr 1.25 3.00
OT4 Ray Bourque 1.25 3.00
OT5 Wayne Gretzky 5.00 12.00
OT6 Sergei Samsonov .60 1.50
OT7 Dominik Hasek 1.50 4.00
OT8 Peter Forsberg 2.00 5.00
OT9 Paul Kariya .75 2.00
OT10 Eric Lindros .75 2.00
OT11 Pavel Bure .75 2.00
OT12 Keith Tkachuk .75 2.00
OT13 Brendan Shanahan .75 2.00
OT14 John LeClair .75 2.00
OT15 Joe Sakic 1.50 4.00

1998-99 Upper Deck MVP Power Game

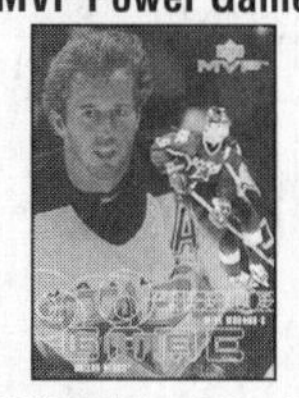

COMPLETE SET (15) 12.00 25.00
STATED ODDS 1:9
PG1 Brendan Shanahan .75 2.00
PG2 Keith Tkachuk .75 2.00
PG3 Eric Lindros .75 2.00
PG4 Mike Modano 1.25 3.00
PG5 Vincent Lecavalier 2.00 5.00
PG6 John LeClair .75 2.00
PG7 Mark Messier .75 2.00
PG8 Mats Sundin .75 2.00
PG9 Peter Forsberg 2.00 5.00
PG10 Jaromir Jagr 1.25 3.00
PG11 Keith Primeau .40 1.00
PG12 Mark Recchi .60 1.50
PG13 Patrick Marleau .40 1.00
PG14 Bill Guerin .60 1.50
PG15 Jeremy Roenick 1.00 2.50

1998-99 Upper Deck MVP ProSign

Randomly inserted in retail packs only at the rate of 1:216, this 23-card set features color action photos of the NHL's superstars with the player's autograph in the wide bottom margin. These cards were among this years toughest autograph pulls.

AM Alyn McCauley 4.00 10.00
BB Brian Bellows 4.00 10.00
BM Brendan Morrison 4.00 10.00
CD Chris Drury 5.00 12.00
DN Dmitri Nabokov 4.00 10.00
DW Doug Weight 5.00 12.00
EB Eric Brewer 4.00 10.00
ER Erik Rasmussen 4.00 10.00
JA Jason Allison 4.00 10.00
JI Jarome Iginla 12.50 30.00
JT Jose Theodore 12.50 30.00
MD Mike Dunham 4.00 10.00
MJ Mike Johnson 4.00 10.00
MM Manny Malhotra 4.00 10.00
MP Mark Parrish 4.00 10.00
OT Oleg Tverdovsky 4.00 10.00
RF Rico Fata 4.00 10.00
RN Rob Niedermayer 4.00 10.00
SY Steve Yzerman 40.00 100.00
VL Vincent Lecavalier 10.00 25.00
WG Wayne Gretzky 125.00 300.00
WR Wade Redden 4.00 10.00
JAR Jason Arnott 4.00 10.00

1998-99 Upper Deck MVP Snipers

COMPLETE SET (12) 10.00 20.00
STATED ODDS 1:6
S1 Vincent Lecavalier 1.00 2.50
S2 Wayne Gretzky 2.50 6.00
S3 Sergei Samsonov .30 .75
S4 Teemu Selanne .40 1.00
S5 Peter Forsberg 1.00 2.50
S6 Paul Kariya .40 1.00
S7 Eric Lindros .40 1.00
S8 Pavel Bure .40 1.00
S9 Peter Bondra .30 .75
S10 Joe Sakic .75 2.00
S11 Steve Yzerman 2.00 5.00
S12 Sergei Fedorov .60 1.50

1998-99 Upper Deck MVP Special Forces

COMPLETE SET (15) 30.00 60.00
STATED ODDS 1:14
F1 Brett Hull 1.25 3.00
F2 Sergei Samsonov .75 2.00
F3 Vincent Lecavalier 2.50 6.00
F4 Dominik Hasek 2.00 5.00
F5 Eric Lindros 1.00 2.50
F6 Paul Kariya 1.00 2.50
F7 Steve Yzerman 5.00 12.00
F8 Brendan Shanahan 1.00 2.50
F9 Martin Brodeur 2.50 6.00
F10 Teemu Selanne 1.00 2.50
F11 Jaromir Jagr 1.50 4.00
F12 Wayne Gretzky 6.00 15.00
F13 Patrick Roy 5.00 12.00
F14 Peter Forsberg 2.50 6.00
F15 Joe Sakic 2.00 5.00

1999-00 Upper Deck MVP

Released as a 220-card set, Upper Deck MVP featured white bordered cards with enhanced bronze foil stamping. The base set is composed of 218 regular cards and two Wayne Gretzky checklist cards. Also released with this set is a special Wayne Gretzky autographed Game Jersey card limited to just 40. MVP was packaged in 28-pack boxes of 10 card packs and carried a suggested retail price of $1.59.

COMPLETE SET (220) 12.50 25.00
1 Wayne Gretzky .75 2.00
2 Damian Rhodes .10 .25
3 Jody Hull .02 .10
4 Paul Kariya .10 .30
5 Teemu Selanne .10 .30
6 Guy Hebert .10 .25
7 Matt Cullen .02 .10
8 Steve Rucchin .02 .10
9 Oleg Tverdovsky .02 .10
10 Johan Davidsson .02 .10
11 Ray Bourque .20 .50
12 Sergei Samsonov .10 .25
13 Joe Thornton .20 .50
14 Anson Carter .10 .25
15 Jason Allison .10 .25
16 Kyle McLaren .02 .10
17 Byron Dafoe .10 .25
18 Shawn Bates .02 .10
19 Jonathan Girard .02 .10
20 Hal Gill .02 .10
21 Dominik Hasek .25 .60
22 Joe Juneau .10 .25
23 Michael Peca .10 .25
24 Cory Sarich .02 .10
25 Martin Biron .10 .25
26 Miroslav Satan .10 .25
27 Dixon Ward .02 .10
28 Michal Grosek .02 .10
29 Valeri Bure .02 .10
30 Phil Housley .02 .10
31 Derek Morris .02 .10
32 Jarome Iginla .15 .40
33 Wade Belak .02 .10
34 Rico Fata .02 .10
35 J-S Giguere .10 .25
36 Rene Corbet .02 .10
37 Arturs Irbe .10 .25
38 Keith Primeau .02 .10
39 Sami Kapanen .02 .10
40 Ron Francis .10 .25
41 Shane Willis .10 .25
42 Gary Roberts .02 .10
43 Bates Battaglia .02 .10
44 J-P Dumont .10 .25
45 Ty Jones .02 .10
46 Tony Amonte .10 .25
47 Jocelyn Thibault .10 .25
48 Doug Gilmour .10 .25
49 Remi Royer .02 .10
50 Alexei Zhamnov .02 .10
51 Joe Sakic .30 .75
52 Peter Forsberg .30 .75
53 Theo Fleury .02 .10
54 Chris Drury .10 .25
55 Patrick Roy .60 1.50
56 Sandis Ozolinsh .02 .10
57 Adam Deadmarsh .02 .10
58 Milan Hejduk .10 .30
59 Mike Modano .20 .50
60 Brett Hull .15 .40
61 Darryl Sydor .02 .10
62 Ed Belfour .10 .30
63 Jere Lehtinen .10 .25
64 Jamie Langenbrunner .02 .10
65 Derian Hatcher .02 .10
66 Jon Sim RC .10 .25
67 Joe Nieuwendyk .10 .25
68 Sergei Fedorov .20 .50
69 Steve Yzerman .60 1.50
70 Brendan Shanahan .10 .30
71 Chris Osgood .10 .25
72 Nicklas Lidstrom .10 .30
73 Chris Chelios .10 .30
74 Igor Larionov .02 .10
75 Tomas Holmstrom .02 .10
76 Vyacheslav Kozlov .10 .25
77 Josef Beranek .02 .10
78 Bill Guerin .02 .10
79 Doug Weight .10 .25
80 Tommy Salo .10 .25
81 Mike Grier .02 .10
82 Tom Poti .02 .10
83 Fredrik Lindquist .02 .10
84 Mark Parrish .02 .10
85 Pavel Bure .10 .30
86 Viktor Kozlov .02 .10
87 Ray Whitney .10 .25
88 Rob Niedermayer .10 .25
89 Oleg Kvasha .02 .10
90 Scott Mellanby .02 .10
91 Chris Allen RC .10 .25
92 Rob Blake .10 .25
93 Pavel Rosa .02 .10
94 Jamie Storr .10 .25
95 Donald Audette .02 .10
96 Luc Robitaille .10 .25
97 Jozef Stumpel .10 .25
98 Vladimir Tsyplakov .02 .10
99 Manny Legace .15 .40
100 Saku Koivu .10 .30
101 Martin Rucinsky .02 .10
102 Vladimir Malakhov .02 .10
103 Eric Weinrich .02 .10
104 Jeff Hackett .10 .25
105 Arron Asham .02 .10
106 Trevor Linden .10 .25
107 Brian Savage .02 .10
108 Cliff Ronning .10 .25
109 Sergei Krivokrasov .02 .10
110 David Legwand .10 .25
111 Kimmo Timonen .02 .10
112 Mark Mowers RC .10 .25
113 Mike Dunham .10 .25
114 Scott Stevens .10 .25
115 Martin Brodeur .30 .75
116 Patrik Elias .10 .25
117 Brendan Morrison .10 .25
118 Scott Niedermayer .02 .10
119 Petr Sykora .02 .10
120 Jason Arnott .02 .10
121 Vadim Sharifijanov .02 .10
122 John Madden RC .25 .60
123 Mariusz Czerkawski .02 .10
124 Felix Potvin .10 .30
125 Mike Watt .02 .10
126 Eric Brewer .10 .25
127 Dmitri Nabokov .02 .10
128 Claude Lapointe .02 .10
129 Kenny Jonsson .02 .10
130 Zdeno Chara .02 .10
131 Wayne Gretzky .75 2.00
132 Brian Leetch .10 .30
133 Mike Richter .10 .30
134 Petr Nedved .02 .10
135 Adam Graves .10 .25
136 Manny Malhotra .02 .10
137 John MacLean .02 .10
138 Alexei Yashin .02 .10
139 Magnus Arvedson .02 .10
140 Daniel Alfredsson .10 .25
141 Wade Redden .10 .25
142 Ron Tugnutt .10 .25
143 Sami Salo .10 .25
144 Marian Hossa .10 .30
145 Shawn McEachern .02 .10
146 Eric Lindros .10 .30
147 Jean-Marc Pelletier .10 .25
148 John LeClair .10 .30
149 Rod Brind'Amour .10 .25
150 Mark Recchi .10 .25
151 Keith Jones .02 .10
152 Eric Desjardins .02 .10
153 Ryan Bast RC .02 .10
154 Brian Wesenberg RC .02 .10
155 John Vanbiesbrouck .10 .25
156 Jeremy Roenick .15 .40
157 Robert Reichel .02 .10
158 Keith Tkachuk .10 .30
159 Rick Tocchet .02 .10
160 Robert Esche RC .10 .30
161 Nikolai Khabibulin .10 .25
162 Daniel Briere .02 .10
163 Greg Adams .02 .10
164 Trevor Letowski .02 .10
165 Jaromir Jagr .20 .50
166 Martin Straka .02 .10
167 German Titov .02 .10
168 Tom Barrasso .10 .25
169 Jan Hrdina .02 .10
170 Alexei Kovalev .02 .10
171 Matthew Barnaby .10 .25
172 Jean-Sebastien Aubin .10 .25
173 Vincent Damphousse .10 .25
174 Owen Nolan .10 .25
175 Jeff Friesen .02 .10
176 Patrick Marleau .10 .25
177 Marco Sturm .02 .10
178 Mike Ricci .02 .10
179 Gary Suter .02 .10
180 Scott Hannan .02 .10
181 Andy Sutton .02 .10
182 Pavol Demitra .10 .25
183 Al MacInnis .10 .25
184 Pierre Turgeon .10 .25
185 Grant Fuhr .10 .25
186 Chris Pronger .10 .25

187 Lubos Bartecko .02 .10
188 Jochen Hecht RC .30 .75
189 Michal Handzus .10 .25
190 Vincent Lecavalier .10 .30
191 Paul Mara .10 .25
192 Darcy Tucker .02 .10
193 Chris Gratton .02 .10
194 Pavel Kubina .02 .10
195 Kevin Hodson .10 .25
196 Mats Sundin .10 .30
197 Daniil Markov .02 .10
198 Curtis Joseph .10 .30
199 Sergei Berezin .10 .25
200 Steve Thomas .02 .10
201 Bryan Berard .10 .25
202 Mike Johnson .10 .25
203 Tomas Kaberle .02 .10
204 Mark Messier .10 .30
205 Bill Muckalt .10 .25
206 Markus Naslund .10 .30
207 Mattias Ohlund .10 .25
208 Kevin Weekes .10 .25
209 Ed Jovanovski .02 .10
210 Alexander Mogilny .10 .25
211 Josh Holden .10 .25
212 Richard Zednik .02 .10
213 Jaroslav Svejkovsky .02 .10
214 Adam Oates .10 .25
215 Peter Bondra .10 .25
216 Sergei Gonchar .02 .10
217 Olaf Kolzig .10 .25
218 Jan Bulis .02 .10
219 Wayne Gretzky CL .40 1.00
220 Wayne Gretzky CL .40 1.00

1999-00 Upper Deck MVP Gold Script

Randomly inserted in packs, this 220-card set parallels the base MVP set on cards enhanced with gold foil highlights and feature a foil facsimile signature of the respective player. For several players, signatures were not available, therefore these cards appear with just the gold foil highlights.
*STARS: 30X TO 80X BASIC CARDS
*ROOKIES: 15X TO 40X BASIC CARDS
1 Wayne Gretzky 30.00 80.00
55 Patrick Roy 25.00 60.00
69 Steve Yzerman 25.00 60.00
131 Wayne Gretzky 30.00 80.00
219 Wayne Gretzky CL 30.00 80.00
220 Wayne Gretzky CL 30.00 80.00

1999-00 Upper Deck MVP Silver Script

Randomly inserted in packs, this 220-card set parallels the base MVP set on cards enhanced with silver foil highlights and feature a foil facsimile signature of the respective player. For several players, signatures were not available, therefore these cards appear with just the silver foil highlights.
*STARS: 1.25X TO 3X BASIC CARDS
*ROOKIES: .75X TO 2X BASIC CARDS

1999-00 Upper Deck MVP Super Script

Randomly inserted in packs, this 220-card set parallels the base MVP set on cards enhanced with holographic foil highlights and feature a holographic foil facsimile signature of the respective player. For several players, signatures were not available, therefore these cards appear with just the holographic foil highlights. Each Super Script card is sequentially numbered to 25.
*STARS: 50X TO 125X BASIC CARDS
*ROOKIES: 20X TO 50X

1999-00 Upper Deck MVP 21st Century NHL

COMPLETE SET (10) 5.00 10.00
STATED ODDS 1:13
1 David Legwand .30 .75
2 Sergei Samsonov .30 .75
3 Paul Kariya .40 1.00
4 Peter Forsberg 1.00 2.50
5 Vincent Lecavalier .40 1.00
6 Jaromir Jagr .60 1.50
7 Paul Mara .30 .75
8 Marian Hossa .40 1.00
9 Pavel Bure .50 1.25
10 Chris Drury .30 .75

1999-00 Upper Deck MVP 90's Snapshots

Randomly inserted in packs at the rate of 1:27, this 10-card set features multiple snapshots on the card front that highlight each player's accomplishments during the '90's.
COMPLETE SET (10) 25.00 50.00
S1 Wayne Gretzky 6.00 15.00
S2 Jaromir Jagr 1.50 4.00
S3 Patrick Roy 5.00 12.00
S4 Eric Lindros 1.50 4.00
S5 Brendan Shanahan 1.50 4.00
S6 Peter Forsberg 2.50 6.00
S7 Steve Yzerman 5.00 12.00
S8 Teemu Selanne 2.50 6.00
S9 Dominik Hasek 2.00 5.00
S10 Pavel Bure 1.25 3.00

1999-00 Upper Deck MVP Draft Report

Randomly inserted in packs at the rate of 1:6, this 10-card set showcases some of the hottest new stars from the 1999 amateur draft. Each card features a top pick on the card front and a brief report about him and three other draftees for the same team on the card back.
COMPLETE SET (10) 4.00 8.00
CHECKLIST REFERS TO PLAYER ON FRONT
DR1 Damian Rhodes .30 .75
DR2 Bill Muckalt .30 .75
DR3 Wayne Gretzky 1.50 4.00
DR4 Eric Brewer .30 .75
DR5 David Legwand .30 .75
DR6 Peter Bondra .40 1.00
DR7 Rico Fata .20 .50
DR8 Mark Parrish .30 .75
DR9 Tom Poti .20 .50
DR10 Jeff Friesen .25 .60

1999-00 Upper Deck MVP Draw Your Own Trading Card

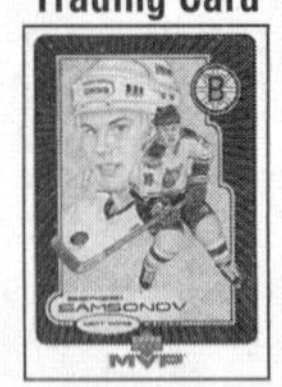

Randomly inserted in packs, this 30-card set features the winning artwork from Upper Deck's Draw Your Own Trading Card contest.
COMPLETE SET (45) 15.00 30.00
W1 Joey Kocur .10 .25
W2 Mike Richter .10 .30
W3 Wayne Gretzky 1.25 3.00
W4 Dominik Hasek .40 1.00
W5 Steve Yzerman 1.00 2.50
W6 Ray Bourque .30 .75
W7 Arturs Irbe .10 .25
W8 Wayne Gretzky 1.25 3.00
W9 Martin Brodeur .50 1.25
W10 Patrick Roy 1.00 2.50
W11 Wayne Gretzky 1.25 3.00
W12 Paul Kariya .20 .50
W13 Wayne Gretzky 1.25 3.00
W14 Jaromir Jagr .30 .75
W15 Wayne Gretzky 1.25 3.00
W16 Felix Potvin .10 .30
W17 Marc Denis .10 .25
W18 Dominik Hasek .40 1.00
W19 Patrick Roy .75 2.00
W20 Robert Svehla .10 .25
W21 Joe Juneau .10 .25
W22 Mattias Ohlund .10 .25
W23 Kirk Muller .10 .25
W24 Peter Forsberg .50 1.25
W25 Stu Barnes .10 .25
W26 Nikolai Khabibulin .10 .25
W27 Sergei Samsonov .10 .25
W28 Jeremy Roenick .15 .40
W29 Wayne Gretzky 1.25 3.00
W30 Sergei Fedorov .40 1.00
W31 Wayne Gretzky .75 2.00
W32 Wayne Gretzky .75 2.00
W33 Wayne Gretzky .75 2.00
W34 Wayne Gretzky .75 2.00
W35 Wayne Gretzky .75 2.00
W36 Wayne Gretzky .75 2.00
W37 Wayne Gretzky .75 2.00
W38 Wayne Gretzky .75 2.00
W39 Wayne Gretzky .75 2.00
W40 Wayne Gretzky .75 2.00
W41 Wayne Gretzky .75 2.00
W42 Wayne Gretzky .75 2.00
W43 Wayne Gretzky .75 2.00
W44 Wayne Gretzky .75 2.00
W45 Wayne Gretzky .75 2.00

1999-00 Upper Deck MVP Game-Used Souvenirs

Randomly inserted in packs at the rate of 1:130, this 30-card set features swatches from game used pucks or game used sticks coupled with an image of the featured player. Autographed cards of Wayne Gretzky and Pavel Bure were limited to a print run of 25.
GU1 Paul Kariya P 6.00 15.00
GU2 Teemu Selanne P 6.00 15.00
GU3 Brett Hull P 8.00 20.00
GU4 Pavel Bure P 6.00 15.00
GU5 Marian Hossa P 6.00 15.00
GU6 Wayne Gretzky P 25.00 60.00
GU7 Brendan Shanahan P 6.00 15.00
GU8 Sergei Samsonov P 6.00 15.00
GU9 Eric Lindros P 6.00 15.00
GU10 Keith Tkachuk P 6.00 15.00
GU11 Steve Yzerman P 20.00 50.00
GU12 Jaromir Jagr P 10.00 25.00
GU13 Alexei Yashin P 6.00 15.00
GU14 Curtis Joseph P 6.00 15.00
GU15 Paul Kariya S 8.00 20.00
GU16 Teemu Selanne S 8.00 20.00
GU17 Dominik Hasek S 15.00 40.00
GU18 Pavel Bure S 8.00 20.00
GU19 Peter Forsberg S 15.00 40.00
GU20 Wayne Gretzky S 30.00 80.00
GU21 Brendan Shanahan S 8.00 20.00
GU22 Joe Sakic S 15.00 40.00
GU23 Eric Lindros S 8.00 20.00
GU24 Keith Tkachuk S 8.00 20.00
GU25 Jeremy Roenick S 10.00 25.00
GU26 Alexei Yashin S 8.00 20.00
GU27 Curtis Joseph S 8.00 20.00
GU28 Steve Yzerman S 25.00 60.00
GUS1 W.Gretzky AU/25 225.00 550.00
GUS2 P.Bure AU/25 125.00 300.00

1999-00 Upper Deck MVP Hands of Gold

COMPLETE SET (10) 12.00 25.00
STATED ODDS 1:9
H1 Wayne Gretzky 4.00 6.00
H2 Brett Hull .75 1.25
H3 Pavel Bure .60 1.50
H4 Teemu Selanne .60 1.50
H5 Sergei Samsonov .30 .75
H6 Peter Forsberg 1.50 2.50
H7 Eric Lindros 1.00 1.50
H8 Paul Kariya .60 1.50
H9 Jaromir Jagr .60 1.50
H10 Steve Yzerman 3.00 5.00
H11 Mike Modano 1.00 1.50

1999-00 Upper Deck MVP Last Line

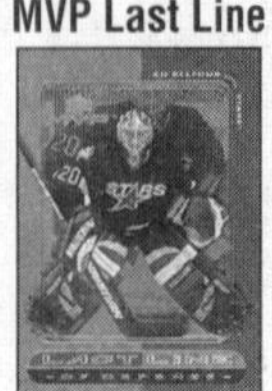

COMPLETE SET (10) 5.00 10.00
STATED ODDS 1:9
LL1 Dominik Hasek .75 2.00
LL2 Martin Brodeur 1.00 2.50
LL3 Patrick Roy 2.00 5.00
LL4 Byron Dafoe .30 .75
LL5 Ed Belfour .40 1.00
LL6 Curtis Joseph .30 .75
LL7 John Vanbiesbrouck .30 .75
LL8 Tom Barrasso .30 .75
LL9 Chris Osgood .30 .75
LL10 Nikolai Khabibulin .30 .75

1999-00 Upper Deck MVP Legendary One

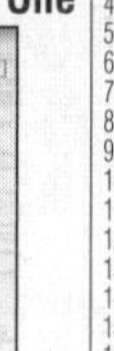

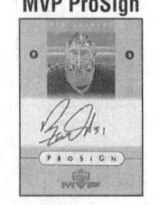

Randomly inserted in packs at the rate of 1:27, this 10-card set pays tribute to Wayne Gretzky and highlights some of the greatest moments of his career. Card backs carry an "LO" prefix.
COMPLETE SET (10) 30.00 60.00
COMMON CARD (LO1-LO10) 4.00 8.00

1999-00 Upper Deck MVP ProSign

Randomly inserted in retail packs at the rate of 1:144, this 30-card set features authentic player autographs coupled with an action photo.
BH Brett Hull 12.00 30.00
BM Bill Muckalt 2.00 5.00
CD Chris Drury 5.00 12.00
DA Donald Audette 2.00 5.00
DM Derek Morris 2.00 5.00
GM Glen Murray 4.00 10.00
IL Igor Larionov 4.00 10.00
JF Jeff Friesen 4.00 10.00
JH Jeff Hackett 5.00 12.00
JR Jeremy Roenick 12.00 30.00
JT Joe Thornton 12.00 30.00
LR Luc Robitaille 6.00 15.00
MC Matt Cullen 2.00 5.00
PB Pavel Bure 8.00 20.00
PD Pavol Demitra 5.00 12.00
RB Ray Bourque 30.00 80.00
RT Ron Tugnutt 5.00 12.00
SG Sergei Gonchar 2.00 5.00
SK Sami Kapanen 2.00 5.00
SY Steve Yzerman 30.00 80.00
TF Theo Fleury 4.00 10.00
TK Tomas Kaberle 2.00 5.00
TL Trevor Linden 4.00 10.00
TP Tom Poti 2.00 5.00
WC Wendel Clark 4.00 10.00
WG Wayne Gretzky 125.00 250.00
JHR Jan Hrdina 2.00 5.00
RBR Rod Brind'Amour 5.00 12.00

1999-00 Upper Deck MVP Talent

Randomly inserted in packs at the rate of 1:13, this 10-card set identifies some of the most likely candidates for the 1999-00 Hart Trophy.
COMPLETE SET (10) 10.00 20.00
MVP1 Wayne Gretzky 2.50 6.00
MVP2 Paul Kariya .75 2.00
MVP3 Dominik Hasek .75 2.00
MVP4 Eric Lindros .60 1.50
MVP5 Ray Bourque .60 1.50
MVP6 Steve Yzerman 2.00 5.00
MVP7 Patrick Roy 2.00 5.00
MVP8 Jaromir Jagr .75 2.00
MVP9 Martin Brodeur 1.25 3.00
MVP10 Mike Modano .60 1.50

2000-01 Upper Deck MVP

Released in late September 2000, Upper Deck MVP features a 220-card base set comprised of 183 veteran player cards and 35 NHL Prospect cards. Base cards are white bordered and have copper foil highlights. MVP was packaged in 28-pack boxes with each pack containing 10 cards and carried a suggested retail price of $1.59.
COMPLETE SET (220) 12.50 25.00
1 Antti Aalto .02 .10
2 Matt Cullen .02 .10
3 Oleg Tverdovsky .02 .10
4 Paul Kariya .10 .30
5 Steve Rucchin .02 .10
6 Teemu Selanne .10 .30
7 Maxim Balmochnyk .02 .10
8 Andrew Brunette .08 .20
9 Damian Rhodes .08 .20
10 Dean Sylvester .02 .10
11 Donald Audette .02 .10
12 Patrik Stefan .02 .10
13 Ray Ferraro .02 .10
14 Brian Rolston .02 .10
15 Sergei Samsonov .08 .20
16 Jason Allison .08 .20
17 Joe Thornton .20 .50
18 Kyle McLaren .02 .10
19 Byron Dafoe .08 .20
20 Hal Gill .02 .10
21 Curtis Brown .02 .10
22 Stu Barnes .02 .10
23 Dominik Hasek .25 .60
24 Doug Gilmour .08 .20
25 Maxim Afinogenov .02 .10
26 Michael Peca .08 .20
27 Miroslav Satan .08 .20
28 Chris Gratton .02 .10
29 Derek Morris .02 .10
30 Fred Brathwaite .08 .20
31 Jarome Iginla .15 .40
32 Marc Savard .08 .20
33 Phil Housley .08 .20
34 Valeri Bure .08 .20
35 Arturs Irbe .08 .20
36 Dave Tanabe .08 .20
37 Jeff O'Neill .02 .10
38 Rod Brind'Amour .08 .20
39 Ron Francis .08 .20
40 Sami Kapanen .02 .10
41 Alexei Zhamnov .08 .20
42 Eric Daze .08 .20
43 Jocelyn Thibault .08 .20
44 Michael Nylander .02 .10
45 Steve Sullivan .02 .10
46 Tony Amonte .08 .20
47 Chris Drury .08 .20
48 Joe Sakic .30 .75
49 Milan Hejduk .10 .30
50 Patrick Roy .60 1.50
51 Peter Forsberg .30 .75
52 Ray Bourque .25 .60
53 Adam Deadmarsh .02 .10
54 Alex Tanguay .08 .20
55 Marc Denis .08 .20
56 Brenden Morrow .08 .20
57 Brett Hull .15 .40
58 Derian Hatcher .02 .10
59 Ed Belfour .10 .30
60 Jamie Langenbrunner .02 .10
61 Mike Modano .20 .50
62 Sergei Zubov .02 .10
63 Joe Nieuwendyk .08 .20
64 Brendan Shanahan .10 .30
65 Chris Chelios .10 .30
66 Chris Osgood .08 .20
67 Nicklas Lidstrom .10 .30
68 Pat Verbeek .02 .10
69 Sergei Fedorov .20 .50
70 Steve Yzerman .60 1.50
71 Darren McCarty .02 .10
72 Tom Poti .02 .10
73 Bill Guerin .08 .20
74 Doug Weight .08 .20
75 Mike Grier .02 .10
76 Ryan Smyth .08 .20
77 Tommy Salo .08 .20
78 Bret Hedican .02 .10
79 Pavel Bure .10 .30
80 Ray Whitney .08 .20
81 Scott Mellanby .02 .10
82 Trevor Kidd .08 .20
83 Viktor Kozlov .08 .20
84 Bryan Smolinski .02 .10
85 Stephane Fiset .08 .20
86 Jozef Stumpel .08 .20
87 Luc Robitaille .08 .20
88 Rob Blake .08 .20
89 Zigmund Palffy .08 .20
90 Brian Savage .02 .10
91 Dainius Zubrus .02 .10
92 Jose Theodore .15 .40
93 Martin Rucinsky .02 .10
94 Saku Koivu .10 .30
95 Sergei Zholtok .02 .10
96 Manny Fernandez .08 .20
97 Cliff Ronning .02 .10
98 David Legwand .08 .20
99 Drake Berehowsky .02 .10
100 Vitali Yachmenev .02 .10
101 Mike Dunham .08 .20
102 Patric Kjellberg .02 .10
103 Alexander Mogilny .08 .20
104 Claude Lemieux .02 .10
105 John Madden .02 .10
106 Martin Brodeur .30 .75
107 Patrik Elias .08 .20
108 Scott Gomez .08 .20
109 Scott Stevens .08 .20
110 Dave Scatchard .02 .10
111 Kenny Jonsson .02 .10
112 Mariusz Czerkawski .02 .10
113 Mathieu Biron .08 .20
114 Tim Connolly .02 .10
115 Claude Lapointe .02 .10
116 Adam Graves .02 .10
117 Brian Leetch .08 .20
118 Mike York .02 .10
119 Mike Richter .10 .30
120 Petr Nedved .08 .20
121 Theo Fleury .02 .10
122 Daniel Alfredsson .08 .20
123 Patrick Lalime .08 .20
124 John LeClair .10 .30
125 Marian Hossa .10 .30
126 Keith Primeau .02 .10
127 Radek Bonk .02 .10
128 Shawn McEachern .02 .10
129 Andreas Dackell .02 .10
130 Brian Boucher .10 .30
131 Mark Recchi .08 .20
132 Simon Gagne .10 .30
133 Eric Desjardins .08 .20
134 Jeremy Roenick .15 .40
135 Keith Tkachuk .10 .30
136 Teppo Numminen .02 .10
137 Eric Lindros .10 .30
138 Shane Doan .02 .10
139 Travis Green .02 .10
140 Trevor Letowski .02 .10
141 Alexei Kovalev .02 .10
142 Jan Hrdina .02 .10
143 Jaromir Jagr .20 .50
144 Jean-Sebastien Aubin .08 .20
145 Martin Straka .02 .10
146 Matthew Barnaby .02 .10
147 Brad Stuart .08 .20
148 Jeff Friesen .02 .10
149 Mike Ricci .08 .20
150 Owen Nolan .08 .20
151 Steve Shields .08 .20
152 Vincent Damphousse .02 .10
153 Al MacInnis .08 .20
154 Chris Pronger .08 .20
155 Jochen Hecht .02 .10
156 Pavol Demitra .08 .20
157 Pierre Turgeon .08 .20
158 Roman Turek .08 .20
159 Dan Cloutier .08 .20
160 Fredrik Modin .02 .10
161 Mike Johnson .02 .10
162 Paul Mara .02 .10
163 Vincent Lecavalier .10 .30
164 Petr Svoboda .02 .10
165 Curtis Joseph .10 .30
166 Darcy Tucker .02 .10
167 Mats Sundin .10 .30
168 Nikolai Antropov .02 .10
169 Sergei Berezin .02 .10
170 Steve Thomas .08 .20
171 Dimitri Yushkevich .02 .10
172 Brendan Morrison .08 .20
173 Ed Jovanovski .02 .10
174 Felix Potvin .10 .30
175 Harold Druken .02 .10
176 Todd Bertuzzi .10 .30
177 Markus Naslund .10 .30
178 Adam Oates .08 .20
179 Chris Simon .02 .10
180 Jeff Halpern .08 .20
181 Olaf Kolzig .08 .20
182 Peter Bondra .10 .30
183 Sergei Gonchar .02 .10
184 Vitali Vishnevsky .02 .10
185 Andreas Karlsson .02 .10
186 Eric Nickulas RC .40 1.00
187 Brandon Smith RC .40 1.00
188 Dimitri Kalinin .02 .10
189 Chris Herperger .02 .10
190 Serge Aubin RC .40 1.00
191 Alan Letang .08 .20
192 Keith Aldridge RC .40 1.00
193 Steven Reinprecht RC .40 1.00
194 Brad Chartrand .02 .10
195 David Gosselin RC .40 1.00
196 Colin White RC .40 1.00
197 Willie Mitchell RC .40 1.00
198 Jason Krog .02 .10
199 Steve Valiquette RC .40 1.00
200 Petr Schastlivy .02 .10
201 Andy Delmore .08 .20
202 Mark Eaton .02 .10
203 Evgeni Nabokov .08 .20
204 Ladislav Nagy .08 .20
205 Kyle Freadrich RC .40 1.00
206 Greg Andrusak RC .40 1.00
207 Alfie Michaud .02 .10
208 Brent Sopel RC .40 1.00
209 Matt Pettinger RC .40 1.00
210 Chris Nielsen RC .40 1.00
211 Dany Heatley RC 6.00 15.00
212 Josef Vasicek RC .40 1.00
213 Matt Zultek RC .40 1.00
214 Dmitri Afanasenkov RC .40 1.00
215 Tyler Bouck RC .40 1.00
216 Jonas Andersson RC .40 1.00
217 Juraj Kolnik RC .40 1.00
218 Andrew Raycroft RC 1.50 4.00
219 Pavel Bure CL .10 .30
220 Steve Yzerman CL .10 .30

2000-01 Upper Deck MVP Excellence

Randomly inserted in packs at the rate of 1:18, this 10-card set pairs up top NHL players on an all foil card with holographic foil highlights. Full color action shots are set side to side on the card front.
COMPLETE SET (10) 15.00 30.00
ME1 Curtis Joseph 1.25 3.00
Roberto Luongo
ME2 Pavel Bure 1.25 3.00
Pavel Brendl
ME3 Sergei Samsonov 1.25 3.00
Oleg Saprykin
ME4 Milan Hejduk 1.25 3.00
Ivan Novoseltsev
ME5 S.Yzerman/P.Verbeek 4.00 10.00
ME6 Roman Turek 1.25 3.00
Martin Biron
ME7 Henrik Sedin 2.00 5.00
Daniel Sedin
ME8 Patrik Stefan 1.25 3.00
Ladislav Nagy
ME9 Manny Malhotra 1.25 3.00
Mike York
ME10 Wayne Gretzky 6.00 15.00
Raymond Bourque

2000-01 Upper Deck MVP First Stars

Randomly inserted in Hobby packs, this 218-card set parallels the base MVP set on cards enhanced with a single star along the right side. Each card is sequentially numbered to 25.
*STARS: 75X TO 200X BASIC CARDS
*ROOKIES: 25X TO 60X BASIC CARDS
211 Dany Heatley 75.00 200.00

2000-01 Upper Deck MVP Game-Used Souvenirs

Randomly inserted in packs at the rate of 1:83, this 29-card set features cards with swatches of game used sticks. Cards with a "C" prefix were found in Canadian hobby packs only.
CGCJ Curtis Joseph 6.00 15.00
CGCO Chris Osgood 6.00 15.00
CGEB Ed Belfour 6.00 15.00
CGFP Felix Potvin 6.00 15.00
CGMB Martin Brodeur 15.00 40.00
CGMS Mats Sundin 6.00 15.00
CGWG Wayne Gretzky 25.00 60.00
GSAI Arturs Irbe 6.00 15.00
GSBS Brendan Shanahan 6.00 15.00
GSCC Chris Chelios 6.00 15.00
GSDH Dominik Hasek 10.00 25.00
GSEL Eric Lindros 6.00 15.00
GSJA Jason Allison 6.00 15.00
GSJJ Jaromir Jagr 10.00 25.00
GSJL John LeClair 6.00 15.00
GSKT Keith Tkachuk 6.00 15.00
GSMM Mark Messier 6.00 15.00
GSMR Mike Richter 10.00 25.00
GSPB Pavel Bure 6.00 15.00
GSPF Peter Forsberg 12.50 30.00
GSPK Paul Kariya 6.00 15.00
GSPR Patrick Roy 15.00 40.00
GSRB Ray Bourque 12.50 30.00
GSRL Roberto Luongo 10.00 25.00
GSSF Sergei Fedorov 10.00 25.00
GSSY Steve Yzerman 15.00 40.00
GSTS Teemu Selanne 6.00 15.00
GSWG Wayne Gretzky 25.00 60.00
GSZP Zigmund Palffy 6.00 15.00

2000-01 Upper Deck MVP Mark of Excellence

Randomly inserted in packs, this 10-card set parallels the base Excellence insert set. Each card is autographed by both players and is sequentially numbered to 50. The original checklist included a Gretzky/Bourque card which does not exist.
SGBB Pavel Bure 25.00 60.00
Pavel Brendl
SGHN Milan Hejduk 25.00 60.00
Ivan Novoseltsev
SGJL Curtis Joseph 40.00 100.00
Roberto Luongo
SGMY Manny Malhotra 25.00 60.00
Mike York
SGSE Henrik Sedin 125.00 300.00
Daniel Sedin
SGSL Patrik Stefan 25.00 60.00
Ladislav Nagy
SGSS Sergei Samsonov 25.00 60.00
Oleg Saprykin
SGTB Roman Turek 25.00 60.00
Martin Biron
SGYV S.Yzerman/P.Verbeek 75.00 200.00

2000-01 Upper Deck MVP Masked Men

COMPLETE SET (10) 15.00 30.00
STATED ODDS 1:18
MM1 Dominik Hasek 2.00 5.00
MM2 Patrick Roy 5.00 12.00
MM3 Ed Belfour 1.00 2.50
MM4 Chris Osgood .75 2.00
MM5 Martin Brodeur 2.50 6.00
MM6 Brian Boucher 1.00 2.50
MM7 Steve Shields .75 2.00

MM8 Roman Turek .75 2.00
MM9 Curtis Joseph 1.00 2.50
MM10 Olaf Kolzig .75 2.00

2000-01 Upper Deck MVP ProSign

Randomly inserted in retail packs, this 18-card set features a small portrait player photo centered that fades into a white-out background and authentic player autographs. The Boucher card has never been confirmed and probably does not exist.

AM Al MacInnis 8.00 20.00
BM Brenden Morrow 8.00 20.00
CB Curtis Brown 6.00 15.00
CJ Curtis Joseph 25.00 50.00
DL David Legwand 8.00 20.00
IV Ivan Novoseltsev 6.00 15.00
LN Ladislav Nagy 6.00 15.00
MJ Mike Johnson 6.00 15.00
MM Manny Malhotra 6.00 15.00
MR Mike Ribeiro 6.00 15.00
MY Mike York 6.00 15.00
OS Oleg Saprykin 6.00 15.00
PB Pavel Bure 10.00 25.00
PS Patrik Stefan 6.00 15.00
RL Roberto Luongo 8.00 20.00
RT Roman Turek 8.00 20.00
SM Steven McCarthy 6.00 15.00
SS Sergei Samsonov 8.00 20.00

2000-01 Upper Deck MVP Second Stars

Randomly inserted in Hobby packs, this 218-card set parallels the base MVP set on cards enhanced with two stars along the right side. Each card is sequentially numbered to 100.

*STARS: 30X TO 80X BASIC CARDS
*ROOKIES: 12.5X TO 30X BASIC CARDS
211 Dany Heatley 40.00 100.00

2000-01 Upper Deck MVP Super Game-Used Souvenirs

Randomly inserted in packs, this 29-card set parallels the base souvenirs set on cards enhanced with both a swatch of a game used stick and a game used puck. Each card is sequentially numbered to 50.

*SUPER: 1.25X TO 2.5X BASIC INSERTS

2000-01 Upper Deck MVP Talent

COMPLETE SET (15) 10.00 20.00
STATED ODDS 1:6
M1 Paul Kariya .30 .75
M2 Teemu Selanne .30 .75
M3 Ray Bourque .60 1.50
M4 Joe Sakic .60 1.50
M5 Patrick Roy 1.50 4.00
M6 Brett Hull .40 1.00
M7 Sergei Fedorov .60 1.50
M8 Pavel Bure .40 1.00
M9 Zigmund Palffy .30 .75
M10 Martin Brodeur .75 2.00
M11 Theo Fleury .30 .75
M12 Eric Lindros .50 1.25
M13 John LeClair .40 1.00
M14 Jaromir Jagr .50 1.25
M15 Jeremy Roenick .40 1.00

2000-01 Upper Deck MVP Third Stars

Randomly inserted in packs at the rate of 1:2, this 218-card set parallels the base MVP set on cards enhanced with a silver border, silver foil stamping, and three white stars along the right edge.

*STARS: 1.25X TO 3X BASIC CARDS
*ROOKIES: .75X TO 2X BASIC CARDS

2000-01 Upper Deck MVP Top Draws

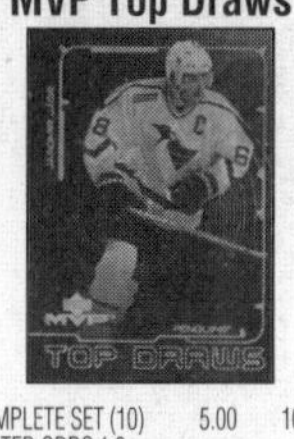

COMPLETE SET (10) 5.00 10.00
STATED ODDS 1:9
TD1 Teemu Selanne .30 .75
TD2 Dominik Hasek .60 1.50
TD3 Peter Forsberg .75 2.00
TD4 Brendan Shanahan .50 1.25
TD5 Pavel Bure .40 1.00
TD6 Scott Gomez .30 .75
TD7 Eric Lindros .50 1.25
TD8 John LeClair .40 1.00
TD9 Keith Tkachuk .30 .75
TD10 Jaromir Jagr .50 1.25

2000-01 Upper Deck MVP Top Playmakers

COMPLETE SET (10) 15.00 30.00
STATED ODDS 1:18
TP1 Paul Kariya .75 2.00
TP2 Dominik Hasek 1.50 4.00
TP3 Peter Forsberg 2.00 5.00
TP4 Mike Modano 1.25 3.00
TP5 Steve Yzerman 4.00 10.00
TP6 Pavel Bure 1.00 2.50
TP7 Scott Gomez .75 2.00
TP8 Eric Lindros 1.25 3.00
TP9 Jaromir Jagr 1.25 3.00
TP10 Jeremy Roenick 1.00 2.50

2000-01 Upper Deck MVP Valuable Commodities

COMPLETE SET (10) 20.00 40.00
STATED ODDS 1:18
VC1 Paul Kariya .75 2.00
VC2 Patrick Roy 4.00 10.00
VC3 Peter Forsberg 2.00 5.00
VC4 Mike Modano 1.25 3.00
VC5 Steve Yzerman 4.00 10.00
VC6 Martin Brodeur 2.00 5.00
VC7 Theo Fleury .75 2.00
VC8 Eric Lindros 1.25 3.00
VC9 Jaromir Jagr 1.25 3.00
VC10 Curtis Joseph .75 2.00

2001-02 Upper Deck MVP

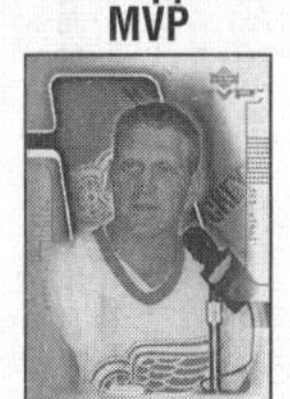

Released in late September, this 233-card set was originally released as a smaller 220-card set. Cards 221-233 were randomly available in UD Rookie Update packs.

COMP.SERIES I SET (220) 15.00 30.00
COMP.SET w/UPDATE (233) 40.00 80.00
1 J-S Giguere .08 .20
2 Paul Kariya .10 .25
3 Jeff Friesen .02 .10
4 Oleg Tverdovsky .02 .10
5 Mike Leclerc .02 .10
6 Milan Hnilicka .08 .20
7 Patrik Stefan .02 .10
8 Ray Ferraro .02 .10
9 Jiri Slegr .02 .10
10 Hnat Domenichelli .02 .10
11 Jason Allison .02 .10
12 Joe Thornton .20 .50
13 Bill Guerin .08 .20
14 Sergei Samsonov .08 .20
15 Kyle McLaren .02 .10
16 Jonathan Girard .02 .10
17 Maxim Afinogenov .02 .10
18 Stu Barnes .02 .10
19 Doug Gilmour .08 .20
20 Chris Gratton .02 .10
21 Martin Biron .08 .20
22 J-P Dumont .02 .10
23 Miroslav Satan .08 .20
24 Craig Conroy .02 .10
25 Jarome Iginla .12 .30
26 Rico Fata .02 .10
27 Derek Morris .02 .10
28 Marc Savard .02 .10
29 Oleg Saprykin .02 .10
30 Arturs Irbe .08 .20
31 Shane Willis .02 .10
32 Rod Brind'Amour .08 .20
33 Jeff O'Neill .02 .10
34 Sami Kapanen .02 .10
35 Ron Francis .08 .20
36 Dave Tanabe .02 .10
37 Steve Sullivan .02 .10
38 Tony Amonte .08 .20
39 Jaroslav Spacek .02 .10
40 Eric Daze .08 .20
41 Michael Nylander .02 .10
42 Alexei Zhamnov .02 .10
43 Joe Sakic .25 .60
44 Peter Forsberg .30 .75
45 Milan Hejduk .10 .25
46 Chris Drury .08 .20
47 Rob Blake .08 .20
48 Ray Bourque .25 .60
49 Patrick Roy .60 1.50
50 Alex Tanguay .08 .20
51 Geoff Sanderson .02 .10
52 Espen Knutsen .02 .10
53 Ray Whitney .02 .10
54 Rostislav Klesla .02 .10
55 Ron Tugnutt .08 .20
56 Tyler Wright .02 .10
57 Mike Modano .20 .50
58 Jere Lehtinen .08 .20
59 Sergei Zubov .02 .10
60 Brenden Morrow .08 .20
61 Ed Belfour .10 .25
62 Joe Nieuwendyk .08 .20
63 Pierre Turgeon .08 .20
64 Steve Yzerman .60 1.50
65 Brendan Shanahan .10 .25
66 Brett Hull .15 .40
67 Luc Robitaille .08 .20
68 Sergei Fedorov .20 .50
69 Dominik Hasek .30 .75
70 Darren McCarty .02 .10
71 Mike Grier .02 .10
72 Ryan Smyth .02 .10
73 Anson Carter .08 .20
74 Tom Poti .08 .20
75 Tommy Salo .08 .20
76 Mike Comrie .08 .20
77 Todd Marchant .02 .10
78 Pavel Bure .10 .25
79 Viktor Kozlov .02 .10
80 Marcus Nilson .02 .10
81 Kevyn Adams .02 .10
82 Roberto Luongo .12 .30
83 Denis Shvidki .02 .10
84 Zigmund Palffy .08 .20
85 Jozef Stumpel .02 .10
86 Adam Deadmarsh .02 .10
87 Mathieu Schneider .02 .10
88 Bryan Smolinski .02 .10
89 Eric Belanger .02 .10
90 Lubomir Visnovsky .02 .10
91 Marian Gaborik .20 .50
92 Lubomir Sekeras .02 .10
93 Wes Walz .02 .10
94 Manny Fernandez .08 .20
95 Roman Simicek .02 .10
96 Stacy Roest .02 .10
97 Saku Koivu .10 .25
98 Oleg Petrov .02 .10
99 Patrice Brisebois .02 .10
100 Jose Theodore .12 .30
101 Richard Zednik .02 .10
102 Martin Rucinsky .02 .10
103 Andrei Markov .02 .10
104 David Legwand .08 .20
105 Cliff Ronning .02 .10
106 Mike Dunham .08 .20
107 Kimmo Timonen .02 .10
108 Scott Walker .02 .10
109 Patric Kjellberg .02 .10
110 Martin Brodeur .30 .75
111 Scott Stevens .08 .20
112 Patrik Elias .08 .20
113 Scott Niedermayer .02 .10
114 Petr Sykora .02 .10
115 Jason Arnott .02 .10
116 Scott Gomez .02 .10
117 Rick DiPietro .08 .20
118 Mark Parrish .02 .10
119 Roman Hamrlik .02 .10
120 Mariusz Czerkawski .02 .10
121 Kenny Jonsson .02 .10
122 Dave Scatchard .02 .10
123 Mark Messier .10 .25
124 Brian Leetch .08 .20
125 Jan Hlavac .02 .10
126 Theo Fleury .02 .10
127 Eric Lindros .10 .25
128 Petr Nedved .02 .10
129 Daniel Alfredsson .08 .20
130 Radek Bonk .02 .10
131 Marian Hossa .10 .25
132 Shawn McEachern .02 .10
133 Patrick Lalime .08 .20
134 Wade Redden .02 .10
135 Magnus Arvedson .02 .10
136 Martin Havlat .08 .20
137 Simon Gagne .10 .25
138 Roman Cechmanek .08 .20
139 Justin Williams .08 .20
140 John LeClair .10 .25
141 Mark Recchi .08 .20
142 Eric Desjardins .02 .10
143 Jeremy Roenick .15 .40
144 Paul Mara .02 .10
145 Shane Doan .02 .10
146 Landon Wilson .02 .10
147 Sean Burke .08 .20
148 Michal Handzus .02 .10
149 Ladislav Nagy .02 .10
150 Mario Lemieux .75 2.00
151 Jan Hrdina .02 .10
152 Johan Hedberg .08 .20
153 Robert Lang .02 .10
154 Alexei Kovalev .08 .20
155 Martin Straka .02 .10
156 Owen Nolan .08 .20
157 Vincent Damphousse .02 .10
158 Brad Stuart .02 .10
159 Teemu Selanne .10 .25
160 Evgeni Nabokov .08 .20
161 Mike Ricci .02 .10
162 Chris Pronger .08 .20
163 Keith Tkachuk .10 .25
164 Scott Young .02 .10
165 Pavol Demitra .08 .20
166 Doug Weight .08 .20
167 Al MacInnis .08 .20
168 Cory Stillman .02 .10
169 Vincent Lecavalier .10 .25
170 Brad Richards .08 .20
171 Nikolai Khabibulin .10 .25
172 Fredrik Modin .02 .10
173 Mats Sundin .10 .25
174 Gary Roberts .02 .10
175 Curtis Joseph .10 .25
176 Nikolai Antropov .02 .10
177 Darcy Tucker .02 .10
178 Jonas Hoglund .02 .10
179 Markus Naslund .10 .25
180 Brendan Morrison .08 .20
181 Todd Bertuzzi .10 .25
182 Daniel Sedin .02 .10
183 Ed Jovanovski .08 .20
184 Peter Bondra .10 .25
185 Sergei Gonchar .02 .10
186 Jeff Halpern .02 .10
187 Olaf Kolzig .08 .20
188 Jaromir Jagr .20 .50
189 Gregg Naumenko .02 .10
190 Dan Snyder RC .50 1.25
191 Zdenek Kutlak RC .50 1.25
192 Niclas Wallin .02 .10
193 Michel Larocque RC .50 1.25
194 Casey Hankinson RC .50 1.25
195 Chris Nielsen .02 .10
196 Martin Spanhel RC .50 1.25
197 Mathieu Darche RC .50 1.25
198 Matt Davidson RC .50 1.25
199 Brad Larsen .02 .10
200 Steve Gainey .02 .10
201 Jason Chimera RC .50 1.25
202 Andrej Podkonicky RC .50 1.25
203 Mike Matteucci RC .50 1.25
204 Pascal Dupuis RC .50 1.25
205 Francis Belanger RC .50 1.25
206 Mike Jefferson RC .50 1.25
207 Stanislav Gron RC .50 1.25
208 Peter Smrek RC .50 1.25
209 Joel Kwiatkowski RC .50 1.25
210 Kirby Law RC .50 1.25
211 Tomas Divisek RC .50 1.25
212 David Cullen RC .50 1.25
213 Billy Tibbetts RC .50 1.25
214 Dan Lacouture .02 .10
215 Jaroslav Obsut RC .50 1.25
216 Dale Clarke RC .50 1.25
217 Thomas Ziegler RC .50 1.25
218 Mike Brown .02 .10
219 Steve Yzerman CL .10 .25
220 Curtis Joseph CL .10 .25
221 Ilya Kovalchuk RC 4.00 10.00
222 Erik Cole RC 1.50 4.00
223 Pavel Datsyuk RC 3.00 8.00
224 Kristian Huselius RC 1.50 4.00
225 Marcel Hossa RC 1.50 4.00
226 Martin Erat RC 1.50 4.00
227 Christian Berglund RC 1.50 4.00
228 Raffi Torres RC 1.50 4.00
229 Dan Blackburn RC 1.50 4.00
230 Jiri Dopita RC 1.50 4.00
231 Krys Kolanos RC 1.50 4.00
232 Brian Sutherby RC 1.50 4.00
233 Olivier Michaud RC 2.00 5.00

2001-02 Upper Deck MVP Goalie Sticks

Randomly inserted in 1:288 hobby and 1:240 retail packs, this 15-card set featured pieces of game-used sticks from the goalie pictured.

G-AI Arturs Irbe 12.50 30.00
G-BD Byron Dafoe 12.50 30.00
G-CJ Curtis Joseph 20.00 50.00
G-CO Chris Osgood 12.50 30.00
G-DH Dominik Hasek 30.00 80.00
G-EB Ed Belfour 20.00 50.00
G-JT Jose Theodore 25.00 60.00
G-MB Martin Brodeur 30.00 80.00
G-MR Mike Richter 20.00 50.00
G-NK Nikolai Khabibulin 20.00 50.00
G-OK Olaf Kolzig 12.50 30.00
G-PR Patrick Roy 40.00 100.00
G-RC Roman Cechmanek 12.50 30.00
G-RD Rick DiPietro 12.50 30.00
G-TS Tommy Salo 12.50 30.00

2001-02 Upper Deck MVP Masked Men

This 14-card set was randomly inserted at 1:12 packs.

COMPLETE SET (14) 10.00 20.00
MM1 Martin Brodeur 1.50 4.00
MM2 Ed Belfour .60 1.50
MM3 Patrick Roy 3.00 8.00
MM4 Jocelyn Thibault .50 1.25
MM5 Tommy Salo .50 1.25
MM6 Olaf Kolzig .50 1.25
MM7 Johan Hedberg .50 1.25
MM8 Evgeni Nabokov .50 1.25
MM9 Patrick Lalime .50 1.25
MM10 Sean Burke .50 1.25
MM11 Curtis Joseph .60 1.50
MM12 Arturs Irbe .50 1.25
MM13 Roman Cechmanek .50 1.25
MM14 Felix Potvin .60 1.50

2001-02 Upper Deck MVP Morning Skate Jerseys

Randomly inserted in 1:96 hobby and 1:120 retail packs, this 15-card set featured swatches of player worn practice jerseys.

*MULT.COLOR SWATCHES: 1X TO 1.5X
J-BB Brian Boucher 4.00 10.00
J-EL Eric Lindros 4.00 10.00
J-JA Jarome Iginla 6.00 15.00
J-JI Jarome Iginla 6.00 15.00
J-JJ Jaromir Jagr 8.00 20.00
J-JL John LeClair 4.00 10.00
J-JO John LeClair 4.00 10.00
J-JS Joe Sakic 8.00 20.00
J-KP Keith Primeau 4.00 10.00
J-MH Milan Hejduk 4.00 10.00
J-MM Mike Modano 6.00 15.00
J-MR Mark Recchi 4.00 10.00
J-PF Peter Forsberg 8.00 20.00
J-RB Rod Brind'Amour 4.00 10.00
J-SG Simon Gagne 4.00 10.00

2001-02 Upper Deck MVP Morning Skate Jersey Autographs

Serial-numbered to 100 copies each, this 10-card set partially paralleled the base morning skate jersey set but included authentic player autographs.

SJ-BB Brian Boucher 15.00 40.00
SJ-JA Jarome Iginla 30.00 60.00
SJ-JI Jarome Iginla 30.00 60.00
SJ-JL John LeClair 15.00 40.00
SJ-KP Keith Primeau 15.00 40.00
SJ-MH Milan Hejduk 15.00 40.00
SJ-MM Mike Modano 30.00 60.00
SJ-MR Mark Recchi 15.00 40.00
SJ-RB Rod Brind'Amour 15.00 40.00
SJ-SG Simon Gagne 15.00 40.00

2001-02 Upper Deck MVP Souvenirs

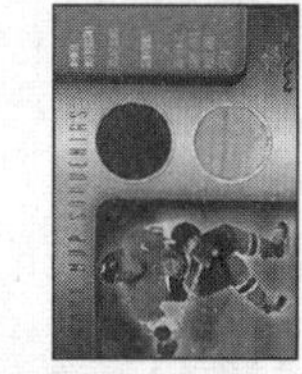

Randomly inserted into hobby packs only, this 30-card set featured game-used swatches of equipment. Cards with a "C" prefix carried two pieces of memorabilia and cards with a "S" prefix carried one. Dual souvenir cards were inserted at 1:288 and single souvenir cards were inserted at 1:96. A gold parallel serial-numbered to 50 copies each was also created.

*GOLD: 2X TO 4X HI BASIC CARDS
C-AM Al MacInnis 10.00 25.00
C-DA Daniel Alfredsson 10.00 25.00
C-JR Jeremy Roenick 12.50 30.00
C-JS Joe Sakic 15.00 40.00
C-MM Mike Modano 15.00 40.00
C-PB Pavel Bure 8.00 20.00
C-SS Sergei Samsonov 10.00 25.00
C-VL Vincent Lecavalier 10.00 25.00
C-WG Wayne Gretzky 75.00 150.00
C-ZP Zigmund Palffy 10.00 25.00
S-AM Alexander Mogilny 6.00 15.00
S-BH Brett Hull 12.50 30.00
S-BS Brendan Shanahan 8.00 20.00
S-JA Jason Allison 6.00 15.00
S-JJ Jaromir Jagr 12.50 30.00
S-JL John LeClair 8.00 20.00
S-KT Keith Tkachuk 8.00 20.00
S-LR Luc Robitaille 6.00 15.00
S-ML Mario Lemieux 40.00 100.00
S-MM Mark Messier 8.00 20.00
S-MR Mark Recchi 6.00 15.00
S-MS Mats Sundin 8.00 20.00
S-PB Peter Bondra 8.00 20.00
S-PF Peter Forsberg 25.00 60.00
S-PS Patrik Stefan 6.00 15.00
S-RB Ray Bourque 12.50 30.00
S-SH Scott Hartnell 6.00 15.00
S-SY Steve Yzerman 20.00 50.00
S-TA Tony Amonte 6.00 15.00
S-TS Teemu Selanne 8.00 20.00

2001-02 Upper Deck MVP Talent

This 14-card set was randomly inserted at 1:12 packs.

COMPLETE SET (14) 15.00 30.00
MT1 Peter Forsberg 1.25 3.00
MT2 Joe Sakic 1.00 2.50
MT3 Mike Modano .75 2.00
MT4 Mario Lemieux 3.00 8.00
MT5 Sergei Fedorov 1.00 2.50
MT6 Steve Yzerman 2.50 6.00
MT7 Pavel Bure .60 1.50
MT8 Paul Kariya .40 1.00
MT9 Teemu Selanne .40 1.00
MT10 Patrik Elias .30 .75
MT11 Zigmund Palffy .30 .75
MT12 John LeClair .60 1.50
MT13 Chris Pronger .30 .75
MT14 Martin Brodeur 1.25 3.00

2001-02 Upper Deck MVP Valuable Commodities

This 7-card set was randomly inserted at 1:24 packs.

COMPLETE SET (7) 15.00 30.00
VC1 Steve Yzerman 3.00 8.00
VC2 Pavel Bure .75 2.00
VC3 Joe Sakic 1.25 3.00
VC4 Martin Brodeur 1.50 4.00
VC5 Mario Lemieux 4.00 10.00
VC6 Peter Forsberg 1.50 4.00
VC7 Mike Modano 1.00 2.50

2001-02 Upper Deck MVP Watch

This 7-card set was randomly inserted at 1:24 packs.

COMPLETE SET (7) 10.00 20.00
MW1 Mario Lemieux 4.00 10.00
MW2 Joe Sakic 1.25 3.00
MW3 Jaromir Jagr 1.00 2.50
MW4 Brett Hull .75 2.00
MW5 Sergei Fedorov 1.25 3.00
MW6 Mark Messier .75 2.00
MW7 Chris Pronger .40 1.00

2002-03 Upper Deck MVP

Released in September, this 220-card set carried an SRP of $1.99 for an 8-card pack, and had 24 packs per box.

COMPLETE SET (220) 20.00 40.00
1 Mike LeClerc .02 .10
2 J-S Giguere .08 .20
3 Matt Cullen .02 .10
4 Andy McDonald .02 .10
5 Jason York .02 .10
6 Paul Kariya .10 .25
7 Frantisek Kaberle .02 .10
8 Dany Heatley .12 .30
9 Pasi Nurminen .02 .10
10 Ilya Kovalchuk .15 .40
11 Patrik Stefan .02 .10
12 Pascal Rheaume .02 .10
13 Sergei Samsonov .08 .20
14 Joe Thornton .20 .50
15 Brian Rolston .02 .10
16 Martin Lapointe .02 .10
17 Nick Boynton .02 .10
18 Jozef Stumpel .02 .10
19 Stu Barnes .02 .10
20 J-P Dumont .02 .10
21 Miroslav Satan .08 .20
22 Tim Connolly .02 .10
23 Maxim Afinogenov .02 .10
24 Martin Biron .08 .20
25 Craig Conroy .02 .10
26 Roman Turek .08 .20
27 Derek Morris .02 .10
28 Marc Savard .02 .10
29 Jarome Iginla .12 .30
30 Igor Kravchuk .02 .10
31 Sami Kapanen .02 .10
32 Bates Battaglia .02 .10
33 Ron Francis .08 .20
34 Erik Cole .02 .10
35 Jeff O'Neill .02 .10
36 Arturs Irbe .08 .20
37 Rod Brind'Amour .08 .20
38 Alexei Zhamnov .02 .10
39 Michael Nylander .02 .10
40 Steve Sullivan .02 .10
41 Jocelyn Thibault .08 .20
42 Kyle Calder .02 .10
43 Eric Daze .08 .20
44 Patrick Roy .60 1.50
45 Milan Hejduk .10 .25
46 Peter Forsberg .30 .75
47 Rob Blake .08 .20
48 Chris Drury .08 .20
49 Joe Sakic .30 .75
50 Steven Reinprecht .02 .10
51 Brad Moran .02 .10
52 Jaroslav Spacek .02 .10
53 Marc Denis .08 .20
54 Ray Whitney .02 .10
55 Rostislav Klesla .02 .10
56 Espen Knutsen .02 .10
57 Marty Turco .08 .20
58 Jere Lehtinen .08 .20
59 Mike Modano .20 .50
60 Derian Hatcher .02 .10
61 Brenden Morrow .08 .20
62 Jason Arnott .02 .10
63 Dominik Hasek .30 .75
64 Brendan Shanahan .10 .25
65 Curtis Joseph .10 .25
66 Brett Hull .15 .40
67 Steve Yzerman .60 1.50
68 Nicklas Lidstrom .10 .25
69 Pavel Datsyuk .10 .25
70 Ryan Smyth .02 .10
71 Anson Carter .08 .20
72 Mike Comrie .08 .20
73 Tommy Salo .08 .20
74 Eric Brewer .02 .10
75 Todd Marchant .02 .10
76 Roberto Luongo .12 .30
77 Kristian Huselius .02 .10
78 Marcus Nilsson .02 .10
79 Viktor Kozlov .02 .10
80 Sandis Ozolinsh .02 .10
81 Valeri Bure .02 .10
82 Jason Allison .02 .10
83 Zigmund Palffy .08 .20
84 Adam Deadmarsh .02 .10
85 Felix Potvin .10 .25
86 Mathieu Schneider .02 .10
87 Bryan Smolinski .02 .10
88 Jim Dowd .02 .10
89 Marian Gaborik .20 .50
90 Manny Fernandez .08 .20
91 Andrew Brunette .02 .10
92 Wes Walz .02 .10
93 Antti Laaksonen .02 .10
94 Yanic Perreault .02 .10
95 Richard Zednik .02 .10
96 Jose Theodore .12 .30
97 Oleg Petrov .02 .10
98 Donald Audette .02 .10
99 Saku Koivu .10 .25
100 Kimmo Timonen .02 .10
101 Stu Grimson .02 .10
102 Denis Arkhipov .02 .10
103 Scott Hartnell .02 .10
104 Mike Dunham .08 .20
105 Andy Delmore .02 .10
106 Brian Rafalski .02 .10
107 John Madden .02 .10
108 Martin Brodeur .30 .75
109 Scott Stevens .08 .20
110 Patrik Elias .08 .20
111 Scott Niedermayer .02 .10
112 Joe Nieuwendyk .08 .20
113 Mark Parrish .02 .10
114 Michael Peca .02 .10
115 Alexei Yashin .02 .10
116 Adrian Aucoin .02 .10
117 Chris Osgood .08 .20
118 Stephen Webb .02 .10
119 Eric Lindros .10 .25
120 Brian Leetch .08 .20
121 Tom Poti .02 .10
122 Pavel Bure .10 .25
123 Petr Nedved .02 .10
124 Dan Blackburn .08 .20
125 Daniel Alfredsson .08 .20
126 Patrick Lalime .08 .20
127 Marian Hossa .10 .25
128 Martin Havlat .08 .20
129 Zdeno Chara .02 .10
130 Radek Bonk .02 .10
131 Wade Redden .02 .10

132 Keith Primeau .02 .10
133 John LeClair .10 .25
134 Mark Recchi .08 .20
135 Eric Desjardins .02 .10
136 Jeremy Roenick .15 .40
137 Justin Williams .02 .10
138 Simon Gagne .10 .25
139 Tony Amonte .08 .20
140 Daniel Briere .02 .10
141 Sean Burke .08 .20
142 Ladislav Nagy .02 .10
143 Shane Doan .02 .10
144 Teppo Numminen .02 .10
145 Alexei Kovalev .08 .20
146 Johan Hedberg .08 .20
147 Jan Hrdina .02 .10
148 Mario Lemieux .75 2.00
149 Martin Straka .02 .10
150 Hans Jonsson .02 .10
151 Vincent Damphousse .02 .10
152 Owen Nolan .08 .20
153 Adam Graves .02 .10
154 Evgeni Nabokov .08 .20
155 Mike Ricci .02 .10
156 Patrick Marleau .08 .20
157 Teemu Selanne .10 .25
158 Brent Johnson .08 .20
159 Doug Weight .08 .20
160 Keith Tkachuk .10 .25
161 Al MacInnis .08 .20
162 Chris Pronger .08 .20
163 Pavol Demitra .02 .10
164 Tyson Nash .02 .10
165 Nikolai Khabibulin .10 .25
166 Vincent Lecavalier .10 .25
167 Martin St. Louis .08 .20
168 Fredrik Modin .02 .10
169 Brad Richards .08 .20
170 Shane Willis .02 .10
171 Alyn McCauley .02 .10
172 Gary Roberts .02 .10
173 Darcy Tucker .02 .10
174 Ed Belfour .10 .25
175 Mats Sundin .10 .25
176 Alexander Mogilny .08 .20
177 Todd Bertuzzi .10 .25
178 Brendan Morrison .08 .20
179 Markus Naslund .10 .25
180 Dan Cloutier .08 .20
181 Daniel Sedin .02 .10
182 Henrik Sedin .02 .10
183 Sergei Gonchar .02 .10
184 Jaromir Jagr .20 .50
185 Peter Bondra .10 .25
186 Olaf Kolzig .08 .20
187 Robert Lang .02 .10
188 Steve Konowalchuk .02 .10
189 Patrick Roy .60 1.50
190 Steve Yzerman .60 1.50
191 Mark Hartigan .02 .10
192 Mike Weaver .02 .10
193 Frederic Cassivi .08 .20
194 Andy Hilbert .02 .10
195 Chris Kelleher .02 .10
196 Henrik Tallinder .02 .10
197 Micki Dupont RC .02 .10
198 Tyler Arnason .08 .20
199 Riku Hahl .02 .10
200 Andrej Nedorost .02 .10
201 Sean Avery .02 .10
202 Stephen Weiss .02 .10
203 Lukas Krajicek .02 .10
204 Kyle Rossiter .02 .10
205 Eric Beaudoin .02 .10
206 Tony Virta .02 .10
207 Marcel Hossa .02 .10
208 Jan Lasak .02 .10
209 Trent Hunter .02 .10
210 Ray Schultz RC .02 .10
211 Martin Prusek .08 .20
212 Chris Bala .02 .10
213 Neil Little .02 .10
214 Guillaume Lefebvre .02 .10
215 Hannes Hyvonen .02 .10
216 Gaetan Royer .02 .10
217 Martin Cibak .02 .10
218 Sebastien Centomo .08 .20
219 Karel Pilar .02 .10
220 Sebastien Charpentier .02 .10

2002-03 Upper Deck MVP Gold

This 220-card hobby only set directly paralleled the base set but was serial-numbered to 100 copies each.
*GOLD: 8X TO 20X BASIC CARDS

2002-03 Upper Deck MVP Classics

This 220-card set paralleled the base set with silver borders and was inserted at odds of 1:2.
*CLASSICS: .75X TO 1.5X BASIC CARDS

2002-03 Upper Deck MVP Golden Classics

This 220-card hobby only set paralleled the base set with gold borders and was serial-numbered to 50 copies each.
*GLDN CLASSICS: 12.5X TO 30X BASIC CARDS

2002-03 Upper Deck MVP Highlight Nights

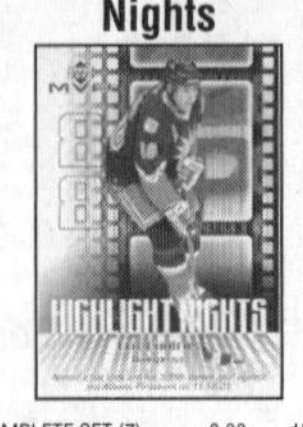

COMPLETE SET (7) 8.00 15.00
STATED ODDS 1:18
HN1 Ilya Kovalchuk .75 2.00
HN2 Joe Thornton 1.00 2.50
HN3 Jarome Iginla .50 1.25
HN4 Brendan Shanahan .75 2.00
HN5 Eric Lindros .40 1.00
HN6 Mario Lemieux 3.00 8.00
HN7 Markus Naslund .40 1.00

2002-03 Upper Deck MVP Masked Men

COMPLETE SET (7) 10.00 20.00
STATED ODDS 1:18
MM1 Patrick Roy 3.00 8.00
MM2 Dominik Hasek 1.50 4.00
MM3 Jose Theodore .75 2.00
MM4 Martin Brodeur 2.00 5.00
MM5 Mike Richter .75 2.00
MM6 Sean Burke .50 1.25
MM7 Olaf Kolzig .50 1.25

2002-03 Upper Deck MVP Overdrive

COMPLETE SET (14) 6.00 12.00
STATED ODDS 1:9
SO1 Paul Kariya .50 1.25
SO2 Ilya Kovalchuk .60 1.50
SO3 Jarome Iginla .60 1.50
SO4 Sami Kapanen .40 1.00
SO5 Chris Drury .40 1.00
SO6 Peter Forsberg 1.00 2.50
SO7 Mike Modano .60 1.50
SO8 Sergei Fedorov .60 1.50
SO9 Sandis Ozolinsh .40 1.00
SO10 Marian Hossa .50 1.25
SO11 Simon Gagne .50 1.25
SO12 Alexei Kovalev .40 1.00
SO13 Markus Naslund .50 1.25
SO14 Peter Bondra .50 1.25

2002-03 Upper Deck MVP Prosign

Inserted at 1:144, this 15-card set featured authentic player autographs. The Henrik Sedin card was originally issued as an exchange card. Known print runs were provided by UD.
BO Bobby Orr 125.00 300.00
CJ Curtis Joseph 25.00 50.00
DH Dany Heatley 10.00 25.00
DS Daniel Sedin 6.00 15.00
GH Gordie Howe 75.00 200.00
HS Henrik Sedin/33 10.00 25.00
KH Kristian Huselius 6.00 15.00
MF Manny Fernandez 6.00 15.00
MO Maxime Ouellet 6.00 15.00
PB Pavel Bure/145 6.00 15.00
PR Patrick Roy 100.00 200.00
RB Ray Bourque 50.00 125.00
SE Teemu Selanne 8.00 20.00
TS Tommy Salo 10.00 25.00
WG Wayne Gretzky 100.00 250.00

2002-03 Upper Deck MVP Skate Around Jerseys

This 57-card set featured swatches of practice-worn jerseys from the players featured alongside color action photos. Single jersey cards were inserted at 1:72, dual jersey cards were inserted at 1:288 and triple jersey cards were serial-numbered out of 100. Dual jersey cards were hobby exclusives.
SAAD Adam Deadmarsh 4.00 10.00
SACD Chris Drury 4.00 10.00
SAEK Espen Knutsen 4.00 10.00
SAEL Eric Lindros 5.00 12.00
SAFP Felix Potvin 5.00 12.00
SAJI Jarome Iginla 6.00 15.00
SAJL John LeClair 4.00 10.00
SAJS Joe Sakic 10.00 25.00
SAJT Joe Thornton 8.00 20.00
SAKP Keith Primeau 4.00 10.00
SAMM Mike Modano 8.00 20.00
SAOK Olaf Kolzig 5.00 12.00
SAPF Peter Forsberg 10.00 25.00
SAPK Paul Kariya 5.00 12.00
SAPR Patrick Roy 12.50 30.00
SDBK Rob Blake 8.00 20.00
Rostislav Klesla
SDBN Rod Brind'Amour 8.00 20.00
Joe Nieuwendyk
SDBP Ed Belfour 10.00 25.00
Felix Potvin
SDCB Roman Cechmanek 8.00 20.00
Brian Boucher
SDDB J-P Dumont 8.00 20.00
Martin Biron
SDDG Chris Drury 10.00 25.00
Simon Gagne
SDDH Chris Drury 10.00 25.00
Milan Hejduk
SDDL Adam Deadmarsh 8.00 20.00
John LeClair
SDFL Peter Forsberg 15.00 40.00
Eric Lindros
SDHP Milan Hejduk 10.00 25.00
Zigmund Palffy
SDHR Dan Hinote 8.00 20.00
Steven Reinprecht
SDJM Jaromir Jagr 12.00 30.00
Mark Messier
SDKC Olaf Kolzig 10.00 25.00
Roman Cechmanek
SDKR Alexei Kovalev 8.00 20.00
Mark Recchi
SDLC John LeClair 8.00 20.00
Roman Cechmanek
SDLF Eric Lindros 10.00 25.00
Theo Fleury
SDLP John LeClair 8.00 20.00
Keith Primeau
SDMS M.Modano/T.Selanne 10.00 25.00
SDMT M.Modano/M.Turco 10.00 25.00
SDNL Joe Nieuwendyk 8.00 20.00
Eric Lindros
SDPO Felix Potvin 15.00 40.00
Chris Osgood
SDPP Zigmund Palffy 8.00 20.00
Felix Potvin
SDRA Patrick Roy 40.00 100.00
David Aebischer
SDRG Mark Recchi 8.00 20.00
Simon Gagne
SDSD Joe Sakic 20.00 50.00
Chris Drury
SDTBE Marty Turco 10.00 25.00
Ed Belfour
SDTBL Alex Tanguay 8.00 20.00
Rob Blake
SDTD Ron Tugnutt 8.00 20.00
Marc Denis
SDWF Justin Williams 8.00 20.00
Ruslan Fedotenko
SDWG Justin Williams 8.00 20.00
Simon Gagne
STDAP Adam Deadmarsh 12.50 30.00
Jason Allison
Zigmund Palffy
STDSB J-P Dumont 12.50 30.00
Miroslav Satan
Martin Biron
STKFS Alexei Kovalev 12.50 30.00
Theo Fleury
Miroslav Satan
STLNT Eric Lindros 15.00 40.00
Joe Nieuwendyk
Joe Thornton
STLPR John LeClair 12.50 30.00
Keith Primeau
Mark Recchi
STMMT Mess./Mdno/Thornton 25.00 60.00
STSFR Joe Sakic 25.00 60.00
Peter Forsberg
Patrick Roy
STSHP Teemu Selanne 12.50 30.00
Milan Hejduk
Zigmund Palffy
STSMJ Teemu Selanne 20.00 50.00
Mike Modano
Jaromir Jagr
STTDG Joe Thornton 12.50 30.00
Chris Drury
Simon Gagne
STTDH Alex Tanguay 12.50 30.00
Chris Drury
Milan Hejduk
STWKT Ray Whitney 12.50 30.00
Rostislav Klesla
Ron Tugnutt

2002-03 Upper Deck MVP Souvenirs

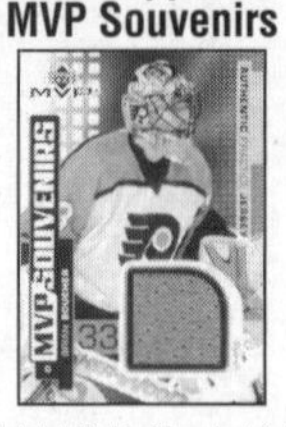

Inserted at 1:48, this 27-card set featured swatches of practice-worn jerseys alongside color action photos of the feaured player.
S-AK Alexei Kovalev 4.00 10.00
S-AT Alex Tanguay 6.00 15.00
S-BB Brian Boucher 4.00 10.00
S-BR Rod Brind'Amour 4.00 10.00
S-CO Chris Osgood 6.00 15.00
S-DH Dan Hinote 4.00 10.00
S-DU Mike Dunham 4.00 10.00
S-EB Ed Belfour 6.00 15.00
S-JJ Jaromir Jagr 10.00 25.00
S-JN Joe Nieuwendyk 4.00 10.00
S-JW Justin Williams 4.00 10.00
S-MB Martin Biron 4.00 10.00
S-MD Marc Denis 4.00 10.00
S-MM Mark Messier 8.00 20.00
S-MO Mike Modano 10.00 25.00
S-MR Mark Recchi 4.00 10.00
S-MS Miroslav Satan 4.00 10.00
S-MT Marty Turco 6.00 15.00
S-RB Rob Blake 4.00 10.00
S-RC Roman Cechmanek 4.00 10.00
S-RK Rostislav Klesla 4.00 10.00
S-RT Ron Tugnutt 4.00 10.00
S-SG Simon Gagne 6.00 15.00
S-TFO Theo Fleury 6.00 15.00
S-TS Teemu Selanne 6.00 15.00
S-VN Ville Nieminen 4.00 10.00
S-ZP Zigmund Palffy 6.00 15.00

2002-03 Upper Deck MVP Vital Forces

COMPLETE SET (14) 15.00 30.00
STATED ODDS 1:9
VF1 Paul Kariya .40 1.00
VF2 Ilya Kovalchuk .60 1.50
VF3 Joe Thornton .60 1.50
VF4 Jarome Iginla .50 1.25
VF5 Patrick Roy 2.00 5.00
VF6 Joe Sakic .75 2.00
VF7 Mike Modano .60 1.50
VF8 Dominik Hasek .75 2.00
VF9 Steve Yzerman 2.00 5.00
VF10 Eric Lindros .40 1.00
VF11 Jeremy Roenick .50 1.25
VF12 Mario Lemieux 2.50 6.00
VF13 Teemu Selanne .40 1.00
VF14 Jaromir Jagr .60 1.50

2003-04 Upper Deck MVP

This 470-card set consisted of 440 base cards and 30 rookie cards that were avaialble only via redemption cards found in packs. Three different redemption cards represented groups of 10 rookies. Groups "A" and "B" were inserted at 1:35 while Group "C" was inserted at 1:72 hobby packs.
COMPLETE SET (470) 30.00 60.00
COMP.SET w/o SP's (440) 20.00 40.00
1 Jason Krog .04 .10
2 Petr Sykora .08 .20
3 Steve Rucchin .04 .10
4 Cam Severson .04 .10
5 Sandis Ozolinsh .04 .10
6 Steve Thomas .04 .10
7 Stanislav Chistov .04 .10
8 Sergei Fedorov .15 .40
9 Rob Niedermayer .04 .10
10 Keith Carney .04 .10
11 Alexei Smirnov .04 .10
12 Kurt Sauer .04 .10
13 Martin Gerber .08 .20
14 J-S Giguere .08 .20
15 Dany Heatley .15 .40
16 Slava Kozlov .04 .10
17 Ilya Kovalchuk .15 .40
18 Marc Savard .04 .10
19 Patrik Stefan .04 .10
20 Yannick Tremblay .04 .10
21 Shawn McEachern .04 .10
22 Frantisek Kaberle .04 .10
23 Andy Sutton .04 .10
24 Lubos Bartecko .04 .10
25 Jeff Odgers .04 .10
26 Pasi Nurminen .08 .20
27 Simon Gamache .04 .10
28 Byron Dafoe .08 .20
29 Garnet Exelby .04 .10
30 Joe DiPenta RC 1.00 2.50
31 Joe Thornton .20 .50
32 Glen Murray .04 .10
33 Mike Knuble .04 .10
34 Brian Rolston .08 .20
35 Ivan Huml .04 .10
36 Bryan Berard .04 .10
37 P-J Axelsson .04 .10
38 Nick Boynton .04 .10
39 Jonathan Girard .04 .10
40 Dan McGillis .04 .10
41 Michal Grosek .04 .10
42 Hal Gill .04 .10
43 Sergei Samsonov .08 .20
44 P.J. Stock .04 .10
45 Martin Lapointe .04 .10
46 Jeff Jillson .04 .10
47 Andrew Raycroft .08 .20
48 Martin Samuelsson .04 .10
49 Krzysztof Oliwa .04 .10
50 Steve Shields .08 .20
51 Miroslav Satan .08 .20
52 Daniel Briere .04 .10
53 Ales Kotalik .04 .10
54 J-P Dumont .04 .10
55 Curtis Brown .04 .10
56 Taylor Pyatt .04 .10
57 Jochen Hecht .04 .10
58 Chris Drury .08 .20
59 Alexei Zhitnik .04 .10
60 Maxim Afinogenov .04 .10
61 Martin Biron .08 .20
62 Mika Noronen .04 .10
63 Ryan Miller .08 .20
64 Milan Bartovic RC 1.00 2.50
65 Jarome Iginla .12 .30
66 Craig Conroy .04 .10
67 Steve Reinprecht .04 .10
68 Martin Gelinas .04 .10
69 Oleg Saprykin .04 .10
70 Dave Lowry .04 .10
71 Dean McAmmond .04 .10
72 Jordan Leopold .04 .10
73 Chuck Kobasew .04 .10
74 Roman Turek .08 .20
75 Jamie McLennan .04 .10
76 Rick Mrozik RC .04 .10
77 Jeff O'Neill .04 .10
78 Ron Francis .08 .20
79 Rod Brind'Amour .08 .20
80 Radim Vrbata .04 .10
81 Sean Hill .04 .10
82 Erik Cole .04 .10
83 Jan Hlavac .04 .10
84 Ryan Bayda .04 .10
85 Jaroslav Svoboda .04 .10
86 Pavel Brendl .04 .10
87 Aaron Ward .04 .10
88 Patrick DesRochers .04 .10
89 Kevin Weekes .08 .20
90 Steve Sullivan .04 .10
91 Alexei Zhamnov .04 .10
92 Eric Daze .04 .10
93 Kyle Calder .04 .10
94 Tyler Arnason .08 .20
95 Mark Bell .04 .10
96 Chris Simon .04 .10
97 Alexander Karpovtsev .04 .10
98 Igor Radulov .04 .10
99 Michael Leighton .08 .20
100 Jocelyn Thibault .08 .20
101 Peter Forsberg .30 .75
102 Milan Hejduk .10 .25
103 Alex Tanguay .08 .20
104 Joe Sakic .30 .75
105 Paul Kariya .10 .25
106 Derek Morris .04 .10
107 Rob Blake .08 .20
108 Adam Foote .04 .10
109 Eric Messier .04 .10
110 Teemu Selanne .10 .25
111 Dan Hinote .04 .10
112 David Aebischer .08 .20
113 Patrick Roy .60 1.50
114 Ray Whitney .04 .10
115 Andrew Cassels .04 .10
116 Geoff Sanderson .04 .10
117 David Vyborny .04 .10
118 Jaroslav Spacek .04 .10
119 Mike Sillinger .04 .10
120 Rick Nash .12 .30
121 Tyler Wright .04 .10
122 Todd Marchant .04 .10
123 Rostislav Klesla .04 .10
124 Jody Shelley .04 .10
125 Marc Denis .08 .20
126 Kent McDonell RC 1.00 2.50
127 Mike Modano .20 .50
128 Sergei Zubov .04 .10
129 Bill Guerin .08 .20
130 Jere Lehtinen .08 .20
131 Jason Arnott .04 .10
132 Brenden Morrow .08 .20
133 Scott Young .04 .10
134 Darryl Sydor .04 .10
135 Niko Kapanen .04 .10
136 Don Sweeney .04 .10
137 Steve Ott .04 .10
138 Jason Bacashihua .08 .20
139 Marty Turco .08 .20
140 Stephane Robidas .04 .10
141 Ron Tugnutt .08 .20
142 Sergei Fedorov .15 .40
143 Brett Hull .15 .40
144 Brendan Shanahan .10 .25
145 Nicklas Lidstrom .10 .25
146 Pavel Datsyuk .10 .25
147 Mathieu Schneider .04 .10
148 Henrik Zetterberg .10 .25
149 Igor Larionov .04 .10
150 Tomas Holmstrom .04 .10
151 Jason Woolley .04 .10
152 Darren McCarty .04 .10
153 Derian Hatcher .04 .10
154 Chris Chelios .10 .25
155 Dominik Hasek .30 .75
156 Steve Yzerman .60 1.50
157 Jiri Fischer .04 .10
158 Manny Legace .08 .20
159 Curtis Joseph .10 .25
160 Ryan Smyth .04 .10
161 Marty Reasoner .04 .10
162 Mike York .04 .10
163 Mike Comrie .08 .20
164 Radek Dvorak .04 .10
165 Ales Hemsky .08 .20
166 Eric Brewer .04 .10
167 Brad Isbister .04 .10
168 Fernando Pisani .04 .10
169 Georges Laraque .04 .10
170 Alexei Semenov .04 .10
171 Raffi Torres .04 .10
172 Jani Rita .04 .10
173 Jarret Stoll .04 .10
174 Cory Cross .04 .10
175 Jason Chimera .04 .10
176 Tommy Salo .08 .20
177 Olli Jokinen .08 .20
178 Viktor Kozlov .04 .10
179 Kristian Huselius .04 .10
180 Marcus Nilson .04 .10
181 Ivan Novoseltsev .04 .10
182 Stephen Weiss .04 .10
183 Jay Bouwmeester .04 .10
184 Valeri Bure .04 .10
185 Denis Shvidki .04 .10
186 Jaroslav Bednar .04 .10
187 Peter Worrell .04 .10
188 Roberto Luongo .12 .30
189 Jani Hurme .08 .20
190 Zigmund Palffy .08 .20
191 Jaroslav Modry .04 .10
192 Eric Belanger .04 .10
193 Alexander Frolov .04 .10
194 Jason Allison .04 .10
195 Lubomir Visnovsky .04 .10
196 Ian Laperriere .04 .10
197 Adam Deadmarsh .04 .10
198 Maxim Kuznetsov .04 .10
199 Joe Corvo .04 .10
200 Mike Cammalleri .04 .10
201 Aaron Miller .04 .10
202 Mattias Norstrom .04 .10
203 Jared Aulin .04 .10
204 Jozef Stumpel .04 .10
205 Roman Cechmanek .08 .20
206 Cristobal Huet .08 .20
207 Marian Gaborik .20 .50
208 Pascal Dupuis .04 .10
209 Cliff Ronning .04 .10
210 Andrew Brunette .04 .10
211 Sergei Zholtok .04 .10
212 Wes Walz .04 .10
213 Filip Kuba .04 .10
214 P-M Bouchard .04 .10
215 Willie Mitchell .04 .10
216 Matt Johnson .04 .10
217 Darby Hendrickson .04 .10
218 Andrei Zyuzin .04 .10
219 Manny Fernandez .08 .20
220 Dwayne Roloson .08 .20
221 Saku Koivu .10 .25
222 Richard Zednik .04 .10
223 Yanic Perreault .04 .10
224 Jan Bulis .04 .10
225 Andrei Markov .04 .10
226 Niklas Sundstrom .04 .10
227 Joe Juneau .04 .10
228 Mike Ribeiro .04 .10
229 Marcel Hossa .04 .10
230 Stephane Quintal .04 .10
231 Jose Theodore .12 .30
232 Michael Komisarek .04 .10
233 Mathieu Garon .08 .20
234 Ron Hainsey .04 .10
235 David Legwand .08 .20
236 Kimmo Timonen .04 .10
237 Andreas Johansson .04 .10
238 Denis Arkhipov .04 .10
239 Darren Haydar .04 .10
240 Scott Hartnell .04 .10
241 Scott Walker .04 .10
242 Adam Hall .04 .10
243 Greg Johnson .04 .10
244 Scottie Upshall .04 .10
245 Tomas Vokoun .08 .20
246 Brian Finley .08 .20
247 Patrik Elias .08 .20
248 Jamie Langenbrunner .04 .10
249 Scott Gomez .04 .10
250 Jeff Friesen .04 .10
251 Joe Nieuwendyk .08 .20
252 John Madden .04 .10
253 Brian Rafalski .04 .10
254 Scott Niedermayer .04 .10
255 Grant Marshall .04 .10
256 Brian Gionta .04 .10
257 Scott Stevens .08 .20
258 Colin White .04 .10
259 Michael Rupp .04 .10
260 Martin Brodeur .30 .75
261 Corey Schwab .08 .20
262 Ken Daneyko .04 .10
263 Alexei Yashin .04 .10
264 Jason Blake .04 .10
265 Mark Parrish .04 .10
266 Dave Scatchard .04 .10
267 Michael Peca .04 .10
268 Roman Hamrlik .04 .10
269 Adrian Aucoin .04 .10
270 Arron Asham .04 .10
271 Janne Niinimaa .04 .10
272 Mattias Weinhandl .04 .10
273 Rick DiPietro .08 .20
274 Garth Snow .08 .20
275 Eric Godard .04 .10
276 Alex Kovalev .08 .20
277 Anson Carter .08 .20
278 Petr Nedved .04 .10
279 Eric Lindros .10 .25
280 Tom Poti .04 .10
281 Bobby Holik .04 .10
282 Matthew Barnaby .04 .10
283 Pavel Bure .10 .25
284 Vladimir Malakhov .04 .10
285 Jamie Lundmark .04 .10
286 Mike Dunham .08 .20
287 Dan Blackburn .08 .20
288 Marian Hossa .10 .25
289 Daniel Alfredsson .08 .20
290 Todd White .04 .10
291 Martin Havlat .08 .20
292 Radek Bonk .08 .20
293 Wade Redden .04 .10
294 Zdeno Chara .04 .10
295 Magnus Arvedson .04 .10
296 Shaun Van Allen .04 .10
297 Karel Rachunek .04 .10
298 Peter Schaefer .04 .10
299 Jason Spezza .10 .25
300 Vaclav Varada .04 .10
301 Anton Volchenkov .04 .10
302 Patrick Lalime .08 .20
303 Ray Emery .08 .20
304 Jody Hull .04 .10
305 Jeremy Roenick .15 .40
306 Mark Recchi .08 .20
307 Tony Amonte .08 .20
308 Keith Primeau .08 .20
309 Michal Handzus .04 .10
310 Kim Johnsson .04 .10
311 Eric Desjardins .04 .10
312 Sami Kapanen .04 .10
313 John LeClair .10 .25
314 Simon Gagne .10 .25
315 Donald Brashear .04 .10
316 Justin Williams .04 .10
317 Eric Weinrich .04 .10
318 Jeff Hackett .08 .20
319 Robert Esche .08 .20
320 Mike Johnson .04 .10
321 Shane Doan .04 .10
322 Ladislav Nagy .04 .10
323 Daymond Langkow .04 .10
324 Chris Gratton .04 .10
325 Jan Hrdina .04 .10
326 Teppo Numminen .04 .10
327 Branko Radivojevic .04 .10
328 Paul Mara .04 .10
329 Tyson Nash .04 .10
330 Jeff Taffe .04 .10
331 Brian Boucher .08 .20
332 Sean Burke .08 .20
333 Mario Lemieux .75 2.00
334 Martin Straka .04 .10
335 Dick Tarnstrom .04 .10
336 Aleksey Morozov .04 .10
337 Mikael Samuelsson .04 .10
338 Ville Nieminen .04 .10
339 Rico Fata .04 .10
340 Dan Focht .04 .10
341 Johan Hedberg .08 .20
342 Sebastien Caron .08 .20
343 Brooks Orpik .04 .10
344 Vincent Damphousse .04 .10
345 Patrick Marleau .08 .20
346 Marco Sturm .04 .10
347 Mike Ricci .04 .10
348 Scott Hannan .04 .10
349 Jim Fahey .04 .10
350 Todd Harvey .04 .10
351 Adam Graves .04 .10
352 Jonathan Cheechoo .05 .12
353 Brad Stuart .04 .10
354 Niko Dimitrakos .04 .10
355 Kyle McLaren .04 .10
356 Miikka Kiprusoff .08 .20
357 Evgeni Nabokov .08 .20
358 Pavol Demitra .08 .20
359 Al MacInnis .08 .20
360 Eric Boguniecki .04 .10
361 Doug Weight .08 .20
362 Scott Mellanby .04 .10
363 Keith Tkachuk .10 .25
364 Petr Cajanek .04 .10
365 Alexander Khavanov .04 .10
366 Barret Jackman .08 .20
367 Steve Martins .04 .10
368 Bryce Salvador .04 .10
369 Dallas Drake .04 .10
370 Ryan Johnson .04 .10
371 Reed Low .04 .10
372 Chris Pronger .08 .20
373 Brent Johnson .08 .20
374 Chris Osgood .08 .20
375 Peter Sejna RC 1.00 2.50
376 Vaclav Prospal .04 .10
377 Vincent Lecavalier .10 .25
378 Brad Richards .08 .20
379 Martin St. Louis .08 .20
380 Dan Boyle .04 .10
381 Fredrik Modin .04 .10
382 Dave Andreychuk .08 .20
383 Pavel Kubina .04 .10
384 Alexander Svitov .04 .10
385 Nikita Alexeev .04 .10
386 Nikolai Khabibulin .10 .25
387 John Grahame .08 .20
388 Chris Dingman .04 .10
389 Tim Taylor .04 .10
390 Alexander Mogilny .08 .20
391 Mats Sundin .10 .25
392 Owen Nolan .08 .20
393 Tomas Kaberle .04 .10
394 Nik Antropov .04 .10
395 Ed Belfour .10 .25
396 Darcy Tucker .04 .10
397 Doug Gilmour .08 .20
398 Tie Domi .08 .20
399 Phil Housley .04 .10
400 Aki Berg .04 .10
401 Bryan McCabe .04 .10
402 Gary Roberts .04 .10
403 Carlo Colaiacovo .04 .10
404 Jyrki Lumme .04 .10
405 Mikael Tellqvist .08 .20
406 Trevor Kidd .08 .20
407 Matt Stajan RC 2.50 6.00
408 Markus Naslund .10 .25
409 Todd Bertuzzi .10 .25
410 Brendan Morrison .08 .20
411 Ed Jovanovski .08 .20
412 Matt Cooke .04 .10
413 Trevor Linden .04 .10
414 Henrik Sedin .04 .10
415 Brent Sopel .04 .10
416 Daniel Sedin .04 .10

417 Mattias Ohlund .04 .10
418 Brandon Reid .04 .10
419 Marek Malik .04 .10
420 Bryan Allen .04 .10
421 Jarkko Ruutu .04 .10
422 Alexander Auld .04 .10
423 Dan Cloutier .08 .20
424 Jaromir Jagr .20 .50
425 Robert Lang .04 .10
426 Sergei Gonchar .04 .10
427 Michael Nylander .04 .10
428 Peter Bondra .08 .20
429 Sergei Berezin .04 .10
430 Jeff Halpern .04 .10
431 Mike Grier .04 .10
432 Steve Konowalchuk .04 .10
433 Ivan Ciernik .04 .10
434 Steve Eminger .04 .10
435 Olaf Kolzig .08 .20
436 Sebastien Charpentier .08 .20
437 Joe Thornton CL .20 .50
438 Martin Brodeur CL .30 .75
439 Dany Heatley CL .12 .30
440 J-S Giguere CL .08 .20
441 Eric Staal RC 5.00 12.00
442 Boyd Gordon RC 1.00 2.50
443 Joni Pitkanen RC 2.00 5.00
444 Christopher Brandner RC 1.00 2.50
445 Joffrey Lupul RC 2.00 5.00
446 Matthew Lombardi RC 1.00 2.50
447 Cody McCormick RC 1.00 2.50
448 Tim Gleason RC 1.00 2.50
449 Jiri Hudler RC 2.50 6.00
450 Antoine Vermette RC 1.00 2.50
451 Alexander Semin RC 1.00 2.50
452 Tuomo Ruutu RC 4.00 10.00
453 Dan Hamhuis RC 1.00 2.50
454 Sean Bergenheim RC 1.00 2.50
455 Brent Burns RC 1.00 2.50
456 Dan Fritsche RC 1.00 2.50
457 Antti Miettinen RC 1.00 2.50
458 Nathan Horton RC 2.50 6.00
459 Maxim Kondratiev RC 1.00 2.50
460 Matthew Spiller RC 1.00 2.50
461 Marc-Andre Fleury RC 8.00 20.00
462 David Hale RC 1.00 2.50
463 Marek Svatos RC 1.00 2.50
464 Milan Michalek RC 1.00 2.50
465 John-Michael Liles RC 1.00 2.50
466 Dustin Brown RC 1.00 2.50
467 Chris Higgins RC 1.00 2.50
468 Patrice Bergeron RC 6.00 15.00
469 Pavel Vorobiev RC 1.00 2.50
470 Jordin Tootoo RC 5.00 12.00

2003-04 Upper Deck MVP Gold Script

COMMON CARD (1-440) 5.00 12.00
*STARS: 30X TO 80X BASIC CARDS
*ROOKIES: 1.5X TO 4X
GOLD PRINT RUN 25 SER.#'d SETS

2003-04 Upper Deck MVP Silver Script

*STARS: 6X TO 15X BASE HI
*ROOKIES: .6X TO 1.5X
STATED PRINT RUN 150 SER.#'d SETS

2003-04 Upper Deck MVP Canadian Exclusives

COMMON CARD (1-440) 6.00 15.00
*STARS: 30X TO 80X BASIC CARDS
*ROOKIES: 1.5X TO 4X
CAN.EXCL.PRINT RUN 25 SER.#'d SETS

2003-04 Upper Deck MVP Clutch Performers

COMPLETE SET (7) 8.00 15.00
STATED ODDS 1:24
CP1 Patrick Roy 2.50 6.00
CP2 Markus Naslund .60 1.50
CP3 Martin Brodeur 2.00 5.00
CP4 Joe Thornton .75 2.00
CP5 Jean-Sebastien Giguere .60 1.50
CP6 Marian Gaborik .75 2.00
CP7 Steve Yzerman 2.00 5.00

2003-04 Upper Deck MVP Lethal Lineups

STAT.PRINT RUN 50 SER.#'d SETS
LL1 Milan Hejduk 60.00 150.00
Joe Sakic
Peter Forsberg
LL2 Tony Amonte 30.00 80.00
Jeremy Roenick
John LeClair
LL3 Joe Thornton 30.00 80.00
Sergei Samsonov
Glen Murray
LL4 Markus Naslund 30.00 80.00
Todd Bertuzzi
Trevor Linden
LL5 Doug Gilmour 30.00 80.00
Mats Sundin
Owen Nolan
LL6 Brendan Shanahan 60.00 150.00
Brett Hull
Steve Yzerman

2003-04 Upper Deck MVP Masked Men

STATED ODDS 1:18
MM1 Martin Brodeur 2.00 5.00
MM2 Patrick Roy 2.50 6.00
MM3 Nikolai Khabibulin .50 1.25
MM4 Jocelyn Thibault .50 1.25
MM5 J-S Giguere .50 1.25
MM6 Patrick Lalime .50 1.25
MM7 Roberto Luongo .60 1.50
MM8 Ed Belfour .50 1.25
MM9 David Aebischer .50 1.25
MM10 Marty Turco .50 1.25

2003-04 Upper Deck MVP ProSign

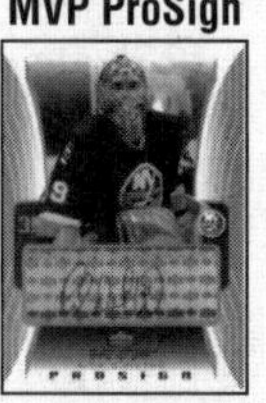

This 19-card set featured certified player autographs on diamond-mirrored stickers affixed to the card fronts. Cards from this set were inserted at a rate of 1:480. Please note that the Gretzky card has been confirmed to exist though there is not significant market information to price it currently; the Joseph card has yet to be confirmed.

PS-BO Bobby Orr 125.00 300.00
PS-CJ Curtis Joseph EXISTS?
PS-DH Dany Heatley 15.00 40.00
PS-EC Erik Cole 6.00 15.00
PS-GH Gordie Howe 100.00 250.00
PS-HZ Henrik Zetterberg 20.00 50.00
PS-JT Joe Thornton 30.00 80.00
PS-MA Maxim Afinogenov 6.00 15.00
PS-MB Martin Brodeur 125.00 300.00
PS-MC Mike Comrie 20.00 50.00
PS-MH Martin Havlat 15.00 40.00
PS-MN Markus Naslund 25.00 60.00
PS-RB Ray Bourque 75.00 200.00
PS-RD Rick DiPietro 15.00 40.00
PS-RM Adam Hall 10.00 25.00
PS-SC Stanislav Chistov 12.50 30.00
PS-SG Simon Gagne 12.50 30.00
PS-SH Scott Hartnell 10.00 25.00
PS-WG Wayne Gretzky 400.00 600.00

2003-04 Upper Deck MVP Souvenirs

This 26-card set featured swatches of practice-worn jerseys. Cards were randomly inserted at 1:24.

S1 Chris Drury 5.00 12.00
S2 Joe Sakic 10.00 25.00
S3 Patrick Roy 15.00 40.00
S4 Rob Blake 5.00 12.00
S5 Ray Whitney 5.00 12.00
S6 Jaromir Jagr 8.00 20.00
S7 Olaf Kolzig 5.00 12.00
S8 Peter Bondra 5.00 12.00
S9 Paul Kariya 5.00 12.00
S10 John LeClair 5.00 12.00
S11 Keith Primeau 5.00 12.00
S12 Mark Recchi 5.00 12.00
S13 Roman Cechmanek 5.00 12.00
S14 Felix Potvin 5.00 12.00
S15 Jason Allison 5.00 12.00
S16 Zigmund Palffy 5.00 12.00
S17 Peter Forsberg 10.00 25.00
S18 Alex Kovalev 5.00 12.00
S19 J-P Dumont 5.00 12.00
S20 Maxim Afinogenov 5.00 12.00
S21 Brett Hull 6.00 15.00
S22 Simon Gagne 5.00 12.00
S23 Brian Boucher 5.00 12.00
S24 Ville Nieminen 5.00 12.00
S25 Eric Lindros 5.00 12.00
S26 Jarome Iginla 6.00 15.00

2003-04 Upper Deck MVP SportsNut

This 91-card set featured a scratch off area that revealed a game code. Collectors could enter the code on the cards at the UD website to accumulate points redeemable for UD merchandise.

SN1 J-S Giguere .50 1.25
SN2 Paul Kariya .60 1.50
SN3 Petr Sykora .50 1.25
SN4 Pasi Nurminen .50 1.25
SN5 Ilya Kovalchuk 1.00 2.50
SN6 Dany Heatley 1.00 2.50
SN7 Jeff Hackett .50 1.25
SN8 Joe Thornton 1.25 3.00
SN9 Glen Murray .25 .60
SN10 Sergei Samsonov .50 1.25
SN11 Martin Biron .50 1.25
SN12 Miroslav Satan .50 1.25
SN13 Maxim Afinogenov .25 .60
SN14 Roman Turek .50 1.25
SN15 Jarome Iginla .75 2.00
SN16 Chris Drury .50 1.25
SN17 Pavel Brendl .25 .60
SN18 Jeff O'Neill .25 .60
SN19 Jocelyn Thibault .50 1.25
SN20 Eric Daze .25 .60
SN21 David Aebischer .50 1.25
SN22 Peter Forsberg 2.00 5.00
SN23 Joe Sakic 2.00 5.00
SN24 Milan Hejduk .60 1.50
SN25 Marc Denis .50 1.25
SN26 Rick Nash .75 2.00
SN27 Marty Turco .50 1.25
SN28 Mike Modano 1.25 3.00
SN29 Bill Guerin .50 1.25
SN30 Dominik Hasek 2.00 5.00
SN31 Steve Yzerman 4.00 10.00
SN32 Sergei Fedorov 1.00 2.50
SN33 Brett Hull 1.00 2.50
SN34 Tommy Salo .50 1.25
SN35 Mike Comrie .50 1.25
SN36 Ryan Smyth .25 .60
SN37 Ales Hemsky .50 1.25
SN38 Roberto Luongo .75 2.00
SN39 Olli Jokinen .50 1.25
SN40 Stephen Weiss .25 .60
SN41 Roman Cechmanek .50 1.25
SN42 Zigmund Palffy .50 1.25
SN43 Dwayne Roloson .50 1.25
SN44 Manny Fernandez .50 1.25
SN45 Marian Gaborik 1.25 3.00
SN46 Jose Theodore .75 2.00
SN47 Saku Koivu .60 1.50
SN48 Marcel Hossa .25 .60
SN49 Tomas Vokoun .50 1.25
SN50 Martin Brodeur 2.00 5.00
SN51 Jamie Langenbrunner .25 .60
SN52 Patrik Elias .50 1.25
SN53 Garth Snow .50 1.25
SN54 Alexei Yashin .25 .60
SN55 Mike Dunham .50 1.25
SN56 Dan Blackburn .50 1.25
SN57 Eric Lindros .60 1.50
SN58 Pavel Bure .60 1.50
SN59 Alex Kovalev .50 1.25
SN60 Patrick Lalime .50 1.25
SN61 Marian Hossa .60 1.50
SN62 Daniel Alfredsson .60 1.50
SN63 Jason Spezza .60 1.50
SN64 Robert Esche .50 1.25
SN65 Jeremy Roenick 1.00 2.50
SN66 John LeClair .60 1.50
SN67 Tony Amonte .50 1.25
SN68 Sean Burke .50 1.25
SN69 Mike Johnson .25 .60
SN70 Johan Hedberg .50 1.25
SN71 Mario Lemieux 5.00 12.00
SN72 Martin Straka .25 .60
SN73 Evgeni Nabokov .50 1.25
SN74 Vincent Damphousse .25 .60
SN75 Chris Osgood .50 1.25
SN76 Keith Tkachuk .60 1.50
SN77 Al MacInnis .50 1.25
SN78 Nikolai Khabibulin .60 1.50
SN79 Vincent Lecavalier .60 1.50
SN80 Martin St. Louis .50 1.25
SN81 Ed Belfour .60 1.50
SN82 Mats Sundin .60 1.50
SN83 Owen Nolan .50 1.25
SN84 Alexander Mogilny .50 1.25
SN85 Alexander Auld .25 .60
SN86 Todd Bertuzzi .60 1.50
SN87 Markus Naslund .60 1.50
SN88 Ed Jovanovski .50 1.25
SN89 Olaf Kolzig .50 1.25
SN90 Jaromir Jagr 1.25 3.00
SN91 Peter Bondra .50 1.25

2003-04 Upper Deck MVP Talent

COMPLETE SET (15) 15.00 30.00
STATED ODDS 1:12
MT1 Mario Lemieux 3.00 8.00
MT2 Martin Brodeur 2.00 5.00
MT3 Markus Naslund .50 1.25
MT4 Marian Gaborik 1.50 4.00
MT5 Dany Heatley 1.00 2.50
MT6 Joe Thornton 1.25 3.00
MT7 Steve Yzerman 2.50 6.00
MT8 Marian Hossa .50 1.25
MT9 Ed Belfour .50 1.25
MT10 Pavel Bure .50 1.25
MT11 Peter Forsberg 2.00 5.00
MT12 Ilya Kovalchuk 1.00 2.50
MT13 Jaromir Jagr 1.25 3.00
MT14 Zigmund Palffy .50 1.25
MT15 Mike Modano 1.25 3.00

2003-04 Upper Deck MVP Threads

STAT.PRINT RUN 100 SER.#'d SETS
TC1 Al MacInnis 12.50 30.00
TC2 Bill Guerin 12.50 30.00
TC3 Brendan Shanahan 15.00 40.00
TC4 Brett Hull 20.00 50.00
TC5 Chris Osgood 12.50 30.00
TC6 Ed Belfour 15.00 40.00
TC7 Jaromir Jagr 20.00 50.00
TC8 Keith Primeau 12.50 30.00
TC9 Patrick Roy 40.00 100.00
TC10 Ray Bourque 25.00 60.00

2003-04 Upper Deck MVP Winning Formula

COMPLETE SET (10) 10.00 20.00
STATED ODDS 1:18
WF1 Rick Nash .60 1.50
WF2 Todd Bertuzzi .50 1.25
WF3 Jeremy Roenick .60 1.50
WF4 Steve Yzerman 2.50 6.00
WF5 Jason Spezza .50 1.25
WF6 Brett Hull 1.00 2.50
WF7 Jean-Sebastien Giguere .50 1.25
WF8 Mike Modano 1.25 3.00
WF9 Paul Kariya .50 1.25
WF10 Henrik Zetterberg .50 1.25

2005-06 Upper Deck MVP

COMPLETE SET (445) 75.00 150.00
1 Sergei Fedorov .15 .40
2 Sandis Ozolinsh .05 .15
3 Scott Niedermayer .05 .15
4 Rob Niedermayer .05 .15
5 Teemu Selanne .10 .30
6 J-S Giguere .10 .25
7 Ruslan Salei .05 .15
8 Joffrey Lupul .05 .15
9 Andy McDonald .05 .15
10 Keith Carney .05 .15
11 Vitali Vishnevsky .05 .15
12 Petr Sykora .05 .15
13 Marian Hossa .10 .30
14 Patrik Stefan .05 .15
15 Kari Lehtonen .10 .30
16 Bobby Holik .05 .15
17 Andy Sutton .05 .15
18 Serge Aubin .05 .15
19 Marc Savard .05 .15
20 Peter Bondra .10 .25
21 Jaroslav Modry .05 .15
22 Niclas Havelid .05 .15
23 Mike Dunham .10 .25
24 Slava Kozlov .05 .15
25 Scott Mellanby .05 .15
26 Ilya Kovalchuk .15 .40
27 Glen Murray .05 .15
28 Joe Thornton .20 .50
29 Andrew Raycroft .10 .25
30 Patrice Bergeron .10 .25
31 Hal Gill .05 .15
32 P.J. Axelsson .05 .15
33 Shawn McEachern .05 .15
34 Brian Leetch .10 .30
35 Alexei Zhamnov .05 .15
36 Nick Boynton .05 .15
37 Brad Isbister .05 .15
38 Jiri Slegr .05 .15
39 Brad Boyes .05 .15
40 Travis Green .05 .15
41 Tom Fitzgerald .05 .15
42 Dave Scatchard .05 .15
43 Chris Drury .10 .25
44 Martin Biron .10 .25
45 Maxim Afinogenov .05 .15
46 Daniel Briere .05 .15
47 Mika Noronen .10 .25
48 Jean-Pierre Dumont .05 .15
49 Derek Roy .05 .15
50 Mike Grier .05 .15
51 Jochen Hecht .05 .15
52 Jeff Jillson .05 .15
53 Teppo Numminen .05 .15
54 Ryan Miller .10 .25
55 Tim Connolly .05 .15
56 Jarome Iginla .15 .40
57 Jordan Leopold .05 .15
58 Tony Amonte .10 .25
59 Chris Simon .05 .15
60 Shean Donovan .05 .15
61 Roman Hamrlik .05 .15
62 Chuck Kobasew .05 .15
63 Darren McCarty .05 .15
64 Robyn Regehr .05 .15
65 Phillippe Sauve .10 .25
66 Stephane Yelle .05 .15
67 Daymond Langkow .05 .15
68 Matthew Lombardi .05 .15
69 Marcus Nilson .05 .15
70 Jason Wiemer .05 .15
71 Erik Cole .05 .15
72 Glen Wesley .05 .15
73 Josef Vasicek .05 .15
74 Radim Vrbata .05 .15
75 Niclas Wallin .05 .15
76 Martin Gerber .10 .25
77 Rod Brind'Amour .10 .25
78 Eric Staal .10 .25
79 Justin Williams .10 .25
80 Ray Whitney .05 .15
81 Oleg Tverdovsky .05 .15
82 Bret Hedican .05 .15
83 Jesse Boulerice .05 .15
84 Cory Stillman .05 .15
85 Nikolai Khabibulin .10 .30
86 Tuomo Ruutu .05 .15
87 Eric Daze .10 .25
88 Kyle Calder .05 .15
89 Matthew Barnaby .05 .15
90 Adrian Aucoin .05 .15
91 Tyler Arnason .10 .25
92 Martin Lapointe .05 .15
93 Jaroslav Spacek .05 .15
94 Curtis Brown .05 .15
95 Mark Bell .05 .15
96 Pavel Vorobiev .05 .15
97 Joe Sakic .25 .60
98 Rob Blake .10 .25
99 Alex Tanguay .10 .25
100 Milan Hejduk .10 .30
101 John-Michael Liles .05 .15
102 Steve Konowalchuk .05 .15
103 David Aebischer .10 .25
104 Brad May .05 .15
105 Patrice Brisebois .05 .15
106 Pierre Turgeon .05 .15
107 Andrew Brunette .05 .15
108 Antti Laaksonen .05 .15
109 Riku Hahl .05 .15
110 Dan Hinote .05 .15
111 Karlis Skrastins .05 .15
112 Rick Nash .15 .40
113 Marc Denis .10 .25
114 Todd Marchant .05 .15
115 David Vyborny .05 .15
116 Manny Malhotra .05 .15
117 Tyler Wright .05 .15
118 Jan Hrdina .05 .15
119 Nikolai Zherdev .10 .25
120 Bryan Berard .05 .15
121 Adam Foote .05 .15
122 Luke Richardson .05 .15
123 Trevor Letowski .05 .15
124 Jody Shelley .05 .15
125 Mike Modano .12 .30
126 Brenden Morrow .10 .25
127 Sergei Zubov .05 .15
128 Marty Turco .10 .25
129 Steve Ott .05 .15
130 Jason Arnott .05 .15
131 Bill Guerin .10 .25
132 Stu Barnes .05 .15
133 Jere Lehtinen .10 .25
134 Jaroslav Svoboda .05 .15
135 Phillippe Boucher .05 .15
136 Johan Hedberg .10 .25
137 Trevor Daley .05 .15
138 Martin Skoula .05 .15
139 Steve Yzerman .50 1.25
140 Chris Chelios .10 .30
141 Robert Lang .05 .15
142 Chris Osgood .10 .25
143 Tomas Holmstrom .05 .15
144 Kris Draper .05 .15
145 Jiri Fischer .05 .15
146 Brendan Shanahan .10 .30
147 Nicklas Lidstrom .10 .30
148 Manny Legace .10 .30
149 Henrik Zetterberg .10 .30
150 Mathieu Schneider .05 .15
151 Pavel Datsyuk .10 .30
152 Ty Conklin .10 .25
153 Ryan Smyth .05 .15
154 Jason Smith .05 .15
155 Ales Hemsky .05 .15
156 Michael Peca .05 .15
157 Chris Pronger .10 .25
158 Radek Dvorak .05 .15
159 Georges Laraque .05 .15
160 Raffi Torres .05 .15
161 Alexei Semenov .05 .15
162 Todd Harvey .05 .15
163 Igor Ulanov .05 .15
164 Jani Rita .05 .15
165 Roberto Luongo .15 .40
166 Jay Bouwmeester .05 .15
167 Olli Jokinen .10 .25
168 Sean Hill .05 .15
169 Nathan Horton .05 .15
170 Stephen Weiss .05 .15
171 Chris Gratton .05 .15
172 Joe Nieuwendyk .10 .25
173 Gary Roberts .05 .15
174 Jamie McLennan .05 .15
175 Mike Van Ryn .05 .15
176 Martin Gelinas .05 .15
177 Jozef Stumpel .05 .15
178 Luc Robitaille .10 .25
179 Mathieu Garon .10 .25
180 Lubomir Visnovsky .05 .15
181 Jeremy Roenick .15 .40
182 Mattias Norstrom .05 .15
183 Dustin Brown .05 .15
184 Alexander Frolov .10 .25
185 Valeri Bure .05 .15
186 Pavol Demitra .10 .25
187 Mike Cammalleri .05 .15
188 Aaron Miller .05 .15
189 Manny Fernandez .10 .25
190 Marian Gaborik .25 .60
191 Brian Rolston .05 .15
192 Filip Kuba .05 .15
193 P-M Bouchard .05 .15
194 Andrei Zyuzin .05 .15
195 Pascal Dupuis .05 .15
196 Alexandre Daigle .05 .15
197 Dwayne Roloson .10 .25
198 Marc Chouinard .05 .15
199 Nick Schultz .05 .15
200 Saku Koivu .10 .30
201 Richard Zednik .05 .15
202 Michael Ryder .10 .25
203 Radek Bonk .05 .15
204 Alexei Kovalev .10 .25
205 Jan Bulis .05 .15
206 Pierre Dagenais .05 .15
207 Mike Ribeiro .05 .15
208 Jose Theodore .15 .40
209 Mike Komisarek .05 .15
210 Sheldon Souray .05 .15
211 Niklas Sundstrom .05 .15
212 Mathieu Dandenault .05 .15
213 Andrei Markov .05 .15
214 Craig Rivet .05 .15
215 Tomas Vokoun .10 .25
216 David Legwand .10 .25
217 Steve Sullivan .05 .15
218 Adam Hall .05 .15
219 Scott Walker .05 .15
220 Martin Erat .05 .15
221 Paul Kariya .10 .30
222 Scott Hartnell .05 .15
223 Scott Nichol .05 .15
224 Randy Robitaille .05 .15
225 Kimmo Timonen .05 .15
226 Danny Markov .05 .15
227 Jordin Tootoo .05 .15
228 Scott Gomez .10 .25
229 Patrik Elias .10 .25
230 Martin Brodeur .50 1.25
231 Sergei Brylin .05 .15
232 John Madden .05 .15
233 Dan McGillis .05 .15
234 Paul Martin .05 .15
235 Alexander Mogilny .10 .25
236 Brian Rafalski .05 .15
237 Brian Gionta .05 .15
238 Viktor Kozlov .05 .15
239 Jamie Langenbrunner .05 .15
240 Jay Pandolfo .05 .15
241 Erik Rasmussen .05 .15
242 Alexei Yashin .05 .15
243 Rick DiPietro .10 .25
244 Alexei Zhitnik .05 .15
245 Brent Sopel .05 .15
246 Jason Blake .05 .15
247 Janne Niinimaa .05 .15
248 Mark Parrish .05 .15
249 Miroslav Satan .10 .25
250 Trent Hunter .05 .15
251 Garth Snow .10 .25
252 Mike York .05 .15
253 Shawn Bates .05 .15
254 Tom Poti .05 .15
255 Martin Straka .05 .15
256 Jaromir Jagr .20 .50
257 Darius Kasparaitis .05 .15
258 Michael Nylander .05 .15
259 Kevin Weekes .10 .25
260 Steve Rucchin .05 .15
261 Fedor Tyutin .05 .15
262 Martin Rucinsky .05 .15
263 Ville Nieminen .05 .15
264 Jason Ward .05 .15
265 Marcel Hossa .05 .15
266 Dany Heatley .15 .40
267 Dominik Hasek .25 .60
268 Wade Redden .05 .15
269 Jason Spezza .10 .30
270 Chris Phillips .05 .15
271 Bryan Smolinski .05 .15
272 Zdeno Chara .10 .25
273 Daniel Alfredsson .10 .25
274 Martin Havlat .10 .25
275 Vaclav Varada .05 .15
276 Peter Schaefer .05 .15
277 Antoine Vermette .05 .15
278 Mike Fisher .05 .15
279 Simon Gagne .10 .30
280 Peter Forsberg .20 .50
281 Keith Primeau .05 .15
282 Derian Hatcher .05 .15
283 Kim Johnsson .05 .15
284 Sami Kapanen .05 .15
285 Mike Knuble .05 .15
286 Eric Desjardins .05 .15
287 Robert Esche .10 .25
288 Donald Brashear .05 .15
289 Joni Pitkanen .05 .15
290 Mike Rathje .05 .15
291 Chris Therien .05 .15
292 Michal Handzus .05 .15
293 Geoff Sanderson .05 .15
294 Curtis Joseph .10 .30
295 Mike Ricci .05 .15
296 Derek Morris .05 .15
297 Mike Johnson .05 .15
298 Petr Nedved .05 .15
299 Oleg Saprykin .05 .15
300 Shane Doan .05 .15
301 Ladislav Nagy .05 .15
302 Tyson Nash .05 .15
303 Mike Comrie .10 .25
304 Brad Ference .05 .15
305 Paul Mara .05 .15
306 Mario Lemieux .75 2.00
307 Zigmund Palffy .10 .25
308 Ryan Malone .05 .15
309 Rico Fata .05 .15
310 John LeClair .10 .30
311 Lasse Pirjeta .05 .15
312 Konstantin Koltsov .05 .15
313 Mark Recchi .10 .25
314 Jocelyn Thibault .10 .25
315 Sergei Gonchar .05 .15
316 Lyle Odelein .05 .15
317 Dick Tarnstrom .05 .15
318 Jonathan Cheechoo .10 .30
319 Marco Sturm .05 .15
320 Evgeni Nabokov .10 .25
321 Alyn McCauley .05 .15
322 Milan Michalek .05 .15
323 Brad Stuart .05 .15
324 Wayne Primeau .05 .15
325 Patrick Marleau .10 .25
326 Scott Thornton .05 .15
327 Vesa Toskala .10 .25
328 Marcel Goc .05 .15
329 Kyle McLaren .05 .15
330 Christian Ehrhoff .05 .15
331 Keith Tkachuk .10 .30
332 Barret Jackman .05 .15
333 Patrick Lalime .10 .25
334 Doug Weight .10 .25
335 Mark Rycroft .05 .15
336 Christian Backman .05 .15
337 Dallas Drake .05 .15
338 Mike Sillinger .05 .15
339 Jamal Mayers .05 .15
340 Eric Brewer .05 .15
341 Scott Young .05 .15
342 Dean McAmmond .05 .15
343 Brad Richards .10 .25
344 Fredrik Modin .05 .15
345 Martin St. Louis .10 .25
346 Ruslan Fedotenko .05 .15
347 Dave Andreychuk .05 .15
348 Pavel Kubina .05 .15
349 Tim Taylor .05 .15
350 Vincent Lecavalier .10 .30
351 Sean Burke .10 .25
352 Darryl Sydor .05 .15
353 Vaclav Prospal .05 .15
354 Mats Sundin .10 .30
355 Tie Domi .10 .25
356 Bryan McCabe .05 .15
357 Darcy Tucker .05 .15
358 Tomas Kaberle .05 .15
359 Kyle Wellwood .05 .15
360 Nikolai Antropov .05 .15
361 Ken Klee .05 .15
362 Ed Belfour .10 .30
363 Matt Stajan .05 .15
364 Eric Lindros .10 .30
365 Jason Allison .05 .15
366 Jeff O'Neill .05 .15
367 Mariusz Czerkawski .05 .15
368 J-S Aubin .05 .15
369 Markus Naslund .10 .30
370 Dan Cloutier .10 .25
371 Trevor Linden .05 .15
372 Anson Carter .10 .25
373 Todd Bertuzzi .10 .30
374 Daniel Sedin .05 .15
375 Sami Salo .05 .15
376 Mattias Ohlund .05 .15
377 Henrik Sedin .05 .15
378 Jarkko Ruutu .05 .15
379 Brendan Morrison .05 .15
380 Ed Jovanovski .10 .25
381 Jason King .05 .15
382 Alex Auld .05 .15
383 Matt Cooke .05 .15
384 Olaf Kolzig .10 .25
385 Brendan Witt .05 .15
386 Jeff Halpern .05 .15
387 Dainius Zubrus .05 .15
388 Alexander Semin .05 .15
389 Jeff Friesen .05 .15
390 Andrew Cassels .05 .15
391 Brian Willsie .05 .15
392 Boyd Gordon .05 .15
393 Sidney Crosby RC 15.00 40.00
394 Alexander Ovechkin RC 8.00 20.00
395 Gilbert Brule RC 2.50 6.00
396 Wojtek Wolski RC 2.50 6.00
397 Rene Bourque RC 1.25 3.00
398 Jeff Woywitka RC 1.25 3.00
399 Hannu Toivonen RC 1.50 4.00
400 Yann Danis RC 1.25 3.00
401 Alexander Perezhogin RC 2.00 5.00
402 David Leneveu RC 1.25 3.00
403 Zach Parise RC 2.50 6.00
404 Dion Phaneuf RC 4.00 10.00
405 Eric Nystrom RC 1.25 3.00
406 Mike Richards RC 1.50 4.00
407 Jeff Carter RC 2.50 6.00
408 Cam Ward RC 3.00 8.00
409 Kevin Nastiuk RC 1.25 3.00
410 Petteri Nokelainen RC 1.25 3.00
411 Robert Nilsson RC 2.00 5.00
412 Andy Wozniewski RC 1.25 3.00
413 Alexander Steen RC 2.50 6.00
414 Ryan Getzlaf RC 3.00 8.00
415 Corey Perry RC 2.50 6.00
416 Rostislav Olesz RC 2.00 5.00
417 Ryan Suter RC 2.00 5.00
418 Henrik Lundqvist RC 4.00 10.00
419 Petr Prucha RC 1.50 4.00
420 Jimmy Howard RC 1.50 4.00
421 Johan Franzen RC 1.25 3.00
422 Thomas Vanek RC 3.00 8.00
423 Brandon Bochenski RC 1.25 3.00
424 Andrej Meszaros RC 1.25 3.00
425 Ryane Clowe RC 1.25 3.00
426 Jussi Jokinen RC 1.50 4.00
427 Braydon Coburn RC 2.00 5.00
428 Jim Slater RC 2.00 5.00
429 Matthew Foy RC 1.25 3.00
430 Peter Budaj RC 1.25 3.00
431 Brent Seabrook RC 1.25 3.00
432 Lee Stempniak RC 1.50 4.00
433 Andrew Alberts RC 1.25 3.00
434 Keith Ballard RC 1.25 3.00
435 Duncan Keith RC 2.00 5.00
436 Milan Jurcina RC 1.25 3.00
437 Chris Campoli RC 1.25 3.00
438 Joe Sakic CL .25 .60
439 Joe Thornton CL .20 .50
440 Jarome Iginla CL .15 .40
441 Steve Yzerman CL .50 1.25
442 Martin Brodeur CL .50 1.25
443 Peter Forsberg CL .20 .50
444 Mario Lemieux CL .75 2.00
445 Martin St. Louis CL .10 .25

2005-06 Upper Deck MVP Gold

*STARS: 10X TO 25X BASE HI
*ROOKIES: 1.25X TO 3X BASE HI
PRINT RUN 100 SER.#'d SETS
393 Sidney Crosby 100.00 250.00
394 Alexander Ovechkin 80.00 200.00

2005-06 Upper Deck MVP Platinum

*STARS: 30X TO 80 BASE HI
*ROOKIES: 4X TO 10X
PRINT RUN 25 SER.#'d SETS

2005-06 Upper Deck MVP Materials

STATED ODDS 1:24
M-AA Aaron Asham 3.00 8.00
M-AF Adam Foote 3.00 8.00
M-AH Adam Hall 3.00 8.00
M-BB Brian Boucher 3.00 8.00
M-BO Brooks Orpik 3.00 8.00
M-CO Chris Osgood 3.00 8.00
M-CS Chris Simon 3.00 8.00
M-DC Dan Cloutier 3.00 8.00
M-DH Derian Hatcher 3.00 8.00
M-DR Derek Roy 3.00 8.00
M-ED Eric Daze 3.00 8.00
M-GM Glen Murray 3.00 8.00
M-JA Jason Arnott 3.00 8.00
M-JB Jason Blake 3.00 8.00
M-JJ Jaromir Jagr 5.00 12.00
M-JL John LeClair 3.00 8.00
M-JR Jarkko Ruutu 3.00 8.00
M-KJ Kenny Jonsson 3.00 8.00
M-LO Lyle Odelein 3.00 8.00
M-MD Marc Denis 3.00 8.00
M-MF Manny Fernandez 3.00 8.00
M-MP Mark Parrish 3.00 8.00
M-MR Mark Recchi 3.00 8.00
M-MS Martin Straka 3.00 8.00
M-PD Pavol Demitra 3.00 8.00
M-PE Patrik Elias 3.00 8.00
M-PL Patrick Lalime 3.00 8.00
M-RB Rob Blake 3.00 8.00
M-RF Ruslan Fedotenko 3.00 8.00
M-RK Ryan Kesler 3.00 8.00
M-RL Robert Lang 3.00 8.00
M-SK Steve Konowalchuk 3.00 8.00
M-SN Scott Niedermayer 3.00 8.00
M-SS Scott Stevens 3.00 8.00
M-SW Stephen Weiss 3.00 8.00
M-SY Steve Yzerman SP 60.00 100.00
M-TA Tony Amonte 3.00 8.00
M-TB Todd Bertuzzi 3.00 8.00
M-TP Tom Poti 3.00 8.00
M-VD Vincent Damphousse 3.00 8.00
M-VK Viktor Kozlov 3.00 8.00
M-ZC Zdeno Chara 3.00 8.00

2005-06 Upper Deck MVP Materials Duals

STATED PRINT RUN 100 SER.#'d SETS
D-CO Zedno Chara 8.00 20.00
Lyle Odelein
D-DR Pavol Demitra 8.00 20.00
Mark Recchi
D-HH M.Havlat/M.Hejduk 12.00 30.00
D-JF E.Jovanovski/A.Foote 8.00 20.00
D-LC T.Linden/D.Cloutier 20.00 50.00
D-LJ Mario Lemieux 30.00 80.00
Jaromir Jagr
D-PB Mike Peca 8.00 20.00
Rob Blake
D-PD Keith Primeau 8.00 20.00
Eric Daze
D-RN Wade Redden 8.00 20.00
Scott Niedermayer
D-SH Joe Sakic 20.00 50.00
Dan Hinote

2005-06 Upper Deck MVP Materials Triples

STATED PRINT RUN 25 SER.#'d SETS
T-GST Wayne Gretzky 100.00 250.00
Joe Sakic
Joe Thornton
T-GPD Gaborik/Palffy/Demitra 40.00 100.00
T-SKF Joe Sakic 50.00 125.00
Paul Kariya
Peter Forsberg
T-TFD Theodore/Fernandez/Denis 40.00 100.00
T-VAN Markus Naslund 40.00 100.00
Trevor Linden
Ed Jovanovski
T-LKF Martin St. Louis 30.00 80.00
Nikolai Khabibulin
Ruslan Fedotenko

2005-06 Upper Deck MVP Monumental Moments

COMPLETE SET (7) 8.00 20.00
STATED ODDS 1:24
MM1 Wayne Gretzky 3.00 8.00
MM2 Gordie Howe 2.50 6.00
MM3 Brett Hull .60 1.50
MM4 Steve Yzerman 2.00 5.00
MM5 Mario Lemieux 3.00 8.00
MM6 Jaromir Jagr .75 2.00
MM7 Dominik Hasek 1.00 2.50

2005-06 Upper Deck MVP ProSign

STATED ODDS 1:480
P-AL Daniel Alfredsson SP 20.00 50.00
P-BG Boyd Gordon 6.00 15.00
P-BM Bryan McCabe 10.00 25.00
P-DA David Aebischer 15.00 40.00
P-DH Dany Heatley SP
P-DM Darren McCarty 15.00 40.00
P-DW Doug Weight 10.00 25.00
P-EC Erik Cole 10.00 25.00
P-ED Eric Daze 6.00 15.00
P-JI Jarome Iginla SP
P-JL John-Michael Liles 10.00 25.00
P-JR Jeremy Roenick 20.00 50.00
P-JT Joe Thornton SP 30.00 80.00
P-MA Maxim Afinogenov
P-MB Martin Biron 10.00 25.00
P-MC Mike Cammalleri 10.00 25.00
P-MH Milan Hejduk SP 15.00 40.00
P-MO Brendan Morrison 10.00 25.00
P-MP Michael Peca 10.00 25.00
P-MW Brenden Morrow 10.00 25.00
P-NA Nikolai Antropov 6.00 15.00
P-OK Olaf Kolzig 10.00 25.00
P-ON Owen Nolan 20.00 50.00
P-PO Mark Popovic 6.00 15.00
P-RB Rob Blake 15.00 40.00
P-RE Robert Esche 10.00 25.00
P-RK Ryan Kesler 6.00 15.00
P-RN Rick Nash SP 40.00 80.00
P-RS Ryan Smyth 10.00 25.00
P-SD Shane Doan 10.00 25.00
P-SG Simon Gagne 15.00 40.00
P-SL Martin St. Louis 20.00 50.00
P-SS Sheldon Souray 6.00 15.00
P-SU Steve Sullivan 6.00 15.00
P-TA Tyler Arnason 6.00 15.00
P-TH Trent Hunter 6.00 15.00
P-TL Trevor Linden 20.00 50.00
P-TP Tom Poti 6.00 15.00
P-TS Tony Salmelainen 6.00 15.00
P-WG Wayne Gretzky SP
P-ZC Zdeno Chara 10.00 25.00
T-MR Mike Ribeiro 6.00 15.00

2005-06 Upper Deck MVP Rising to the Occasion

COMPLETE SET (14) 8.00 20.00
STATED ODDS 1:12
RO1 Joe Sakic .75 2.00
RO2 Mario Lemieux 2.50 6.00
RO3 Martin St. Louis .30 .75
RO4 Jarome Iginla .50 1.25
RO5 Martin Brodeur 2.00 5.00
RO6 Steve Yzerman 1.50 4.00
RO7 Dominik Hasek .75 2.00
RO8 Peter Forsberg .60 1.50
RO9 Mike Modano .40 1.00
RO10 Jose Theodore .50 1.25
RO11 Jaromir Jagr .60 1.50
RO12 Ed Belfour .40 1.00
RO13 Wayne Gretzky 2.50 6.00
RO14 Ilya Kovalchuk .50 1.25

2005-06 Upper Deck MVP Rookie Breakthrough

COMPLETE SET (14) 25.00 60.00
STATED ODDS 1:12
RB1 Sidney Crosby 8.00 20.00
RB2 Alexander Ovechkin 4.00 10.00
RB3 Jeff Carter 2.50 6.00
RB4 Gilbert Brule 2.50 6.00
RB5 Wojtek Wolski 2.50 6.00
RB6 Alexander Perezhogin 2.00 5.00
RB7 Zach Parise 2.00 5.00
RB8 Dion Phaneuf 3.00 8.00
RB9 Corey Perry 2.50 6.00
RB10 Alexander Steen 2.00 5.00
RB11 Thomas Vanek 2.50 6.00
RB12 Hannu Toivonen 2.00 5.00
RB13 Mike Richards 2.00 5.00
RB14 Robert Nilsson 2.00 5.00

2005-06 Upper Deck MVP Tribute to Greatness

COMPLETE SET (7) 10.00 25.00
COMMON CARD (TG1-TG7) 2.00 5.00
STATED ODDS 1:24
TG1 Wayne Gretzky 2.00 5.00
TG2 Wayne Gretzky 2.00 5.00
TG3 Wayne Gretzky 2.00 5.00
TG4 Wayne Gretzky 2.00 5.00
TG5 Wayne Gretzky 2.00 5.00
TG6 Wayne Gretzky 2.00 5.00
TG7 Wayne Gretzky 2.00 5.00

2006-07 Upper Deck MVP

COMPLETE SET (360) 75.00 150.00
1 Chris Pronger .15 .40
2 Ilya Bryzgalov .15 .40
3 Andy McDonald .10 .25
4 Teemu Selanne .20 .50
5 Francois Beauchemin .10 .25
6 Chris Kunitz .10 .25
7 Corey Perry .15 .40
8 Scott Niedermayer .10 .25
9 Ryan Getzlaf .15 .40
10 Jean-Sebastien Giguere .15 .40
11 Ilya Kovalchuk .25 .60
12 Jim Slater .10 .25
13 Slava Kozlov .10 .25
14 Kari Lehtonen .20 .50
15 Bobby Holik .10 .25
16 Marian Hossa .15 .40
17 Niko Kapanen .10 .25
18 Steve Rucchin .10 .25
19 Johan Hedberg .15 .40
20 Brad Boyes .10 .25
21 Hannu Toivonen .20 .50
22 Zdeno Chara .10 .25
23 Tim Thomas .15 .40
24 Marco Sturm .10 .25
25 Patrice Bergeron .20 .50
26 Brad Stuart .10 .25
27 Marc Savard .10 .25
28 Glen Murray .10 .25
29 Paul Mara .10 .25
30 Daniel Briere .10 .25
31 Chris Drury .10 .25
32 Ryan Miller .20 .50
33 Ales Kotalik .10 .25
34 Thomas Vanek .10 .25
35 Jaroslav Spacek .10 .25
36 Maxim Afinogenov .10 .25
37 Jason Pominville .10 .25
38 Derek Roy .10 .25
39 Jochen Hecht .10 .25
40 Martin Biron .15 .40
41 Miikka Kiprusoff .20 .50
42 Alex Tanguay .15 .40
43 Jamie Lundmark .10 .25
44 Jeff Friesen .10 .25
45 Jarome Iginla .25 .60
46 Dion Phaneuf .25 .60
47 Tony Amonte .10 .25
48 Chuck Kobasew .10 .25
49 Kristian Huselius .10 .25
50 Daymond Langkow .10 .25
51 Cam Ward .20 .50
52 Rod Brind'Amour .15 .40
53 Erik Cole .10 .25
54 Mike Commodore .10 .25
55 Andrew Ladd .10 .25
56 Eric Staal .20 .50
57 Cory Stillman .10 .25
58 Justin Williams .10 .25
59 Ray Whitney .10 .25
60 Frantisek Kaberle .10 .25
61 Nikolai Khabibulin .20 .50
62 Michal Handzus .10 .25
63 Pavel Vorobiev .10 .25
64 Rene Bourque .10 .25
65 Martin Havlat .15 .40
66 Duncan Keith .10 .25
67 Bryan Smolinski .10 .25
68 Tuomo Ruutu .10 .25
69 Brandon Bochenski .10 .25
70 Joe Sakic .40 1.00
71 Jose Theodore .20 .50
72 John-Michael Liles .10 .25
73 Marek Svatos .15 .40
74 Brad Richardson .10 .25
75 Wojtek Wolski .10 .25
76 Milan Hejduk .10 .25
77 Pierre Turgeon .10 .25
78 Andrew Brunette .10 .25
79 Peter Budaj .15 .40
80 Patrice Brisebois .10 .25
81 Rick Nash .20 .50
82 Rostislav Klesla .10 .25
83 Gilbert Brule .20 .50
84 Pascal Leclaire .15 .40
85 Bryan Berard .10 .25
86 Fredrik Modin .10 .25
87 David Vyborny .10 .25
88 Sergei Fedorov .20 .50
89 Nikolai Zherdev .10 .25
90 Adam Foote .10 .25
91 Jody Shelley .10 .25
92 Marty Turco .15 .40
93 Brenden Morrow .15 .40
94 Sergei Zubov .10 .25
95 Eric Lindros .20 .50
96 Jussi Jokinen .10 .25
97 Mike Modano .20 .50
98 Jere Lehtinen .10 .25
99 Steve Ott .10 .25
100 Jeff Halpern .10 .25
101 Pavel Datsyuk .15 .40
102 Tomas Holmstrom .10 .25
103 Kris Draper .10 .25
104 Dominik Hasek .30 .75
105 Nicklas Lidstrom .20 .50
106 Henrik Zetterberg .20 .50
107 Robert Lang .10 .25
108 Mikael Samuelsson .10 .25
109 Chris Chelios .15 .40
110 Mathieu Schneider .10 .25
111 Jason Williams .10 .25
112 Dwayne Roloson .15 .40
113 Ales Hemsky .10 .25
114 Fernando Pisani .10 .25
115 Shawn Horcoff .10 .25
116 Jarret Stoll .10 .25
117 Jason Smith .10 .25
118 Ryan Smyth .15 .40
119 Raffi Torres .10 .25
120 Jussi Markkanen .15 .40
121 Joffrey Lupul .10 .25
122 Marc-Andre Bergeron .10 .25
123 Nathan Horton .10 .25
124 Stephen Weiss .10 .25
125 Alex Auld .15 .40
126 Olli Jokinen .10 .25
127 Todd Bertuzzi .15 .40
128 Joe Nieuwendyk .15 .40
129 Ed Belfour .20 .50
130 Jay Bouwmeester .10 .25
131 Rostislav Olesz .10 .25
132 Alexander Frolov .10 .25
133 Dan Cloutier .15 .40
134 Mike Cammalleri .10 .25
135 Rob Blake .15 .40
136 Craig Conroy .10 .25
137 Lubomir Visnovsky .10 .25
138 Mathieu Garon .15 .40
139 Sean Avery .10 .25
140 Dustin Brown .10 .25
141 Marian Gaborik .25 .60
142 Mark Parrish .10 .25
143 Pierre-Marc Bouchard .10 .25
144 Mikko Koivu .10 .25
145 Wes Walz .10 .25
146 Brian Rolston .10 .25
147 Manny Fernandez .15 .40
148 Pavol Demitra .10 .25
149 Kim Johnsson .10 .25
150 Todd White .10 .25
151 Cristobal Huet .25 .60
152 Saku Koivu .20 .50
153 Chris Higgins .10 .25
154 Andrei Markov .10 .25
155 Mike Ribeiro .10 .25
156 David Aebischer .15 .40
157 Alex Kovalev .10 .25
158 Sergei Samsonov .15 .40
159 Michael Ryder .15 .40
160 Sheldon Souray .10 .25
161 Alexander Perezhogin .10 .25
162 Paul Kariya .20 .50
163 Jason Arnott .10 .25
164 Jordin Tootoo .15 .40
165 J.P. Dumont .10 .25
166 Steve Sullivan .10 .25
167 Tomas Vokoun .15 .40
168 Marek Zidlicky .10 .25
169 Martin Erat .10 .25
170 Scott Hartnell .10 .25
171 Martin Brodeur .75 2.00
172 Brian Gionta .10 .25
173 John Madden .10 .25
174 Zach Parise .15 .40
175 Brian Rafalski .10 .25
176 Patrik Elias .10 .25
177 Sergei Brylin .10 .25
178 Scott Gomez .10 .25
179 Jamie Langenbrunner .10 .25
180 Paul Martin .10 .25
181 Miroslav Satan .10 .25
182 Mike Sillinger .10 .25
183 Tom Poti .10 .25
184 Jason Blake .10 .25
185 Trent Hunter .10 .25
186 Alexei Yashin .10 .25
187 Rick DiPietro .15 .40
188 Alexei Zhitnik .10 .25
189 Shawn Bates .10 .25
190 Jeff Tambellini .10 .25
191 Jaromir Jagr .30 .75
192 Brendan Shanahan .20 .50
193 Martin Straka .10 .25
194 Marek Malik .10 .25
195 Petr Prucha .10 .25
196 Henrik Lundqvist .25 .60
197 Sandis Ozolinsh .10 .25
198 Matt Cullen .10 .25
199 Michael Nylander .10 .25
200 Fedor Tyutin .10 .25
201 Jason Spezza .20 .50
202 Ray Emery .15 .40
203 Wade Redden .10 .25
204 Patrick Eaves .10 .25
205 Daniel Alfredsson .15 .40
206 Martin Gerber .15 .40
207 Dany Heatley .25 .60
208 Andrej Meszaros .10 .25
209 Mike Fisher .10 .25
210 Peter Schaefer .10 .25
211 Simon Gagne .20 .50
212 Joni Pitkanen .10 .25
213 Jeff Carter .15 .40
214 R.J. Umberger .10 .25
215 Peter Forsberg .40 1.00
216 Antero Niittymaki .15 .40
217 Mike Richards .15 .40
218 Mike Knuble .10 .25
219 Robert Esche .15 .40
220 Kyle Calder .10 .25
221 Geoff Sanderson .10 .25
222 Shane Doan .10 .25
223 Ed Jovanovski .10 .25
224 Ladislav Nagy .10 .25
225 Curtis Joseph .20 .50
226 Jeremy Roenick .25 .60
227 Keith Ballard .10 .25
228 Mike Comrie .10 .25
229 David Leneveu .15 .40
230 Owen Nolan .15 .40
231 Sidney Crosby 1.25 3.00
232 Mark Recchi .10 .25
233 Nils Ekman .10 .25
234 Ryan Whitney .10 .25
235 Colby Armstrong .10 .25
236 John LeClair .15 .40
237 Marc-Andre Fleury .20 .50
238 Sergei Gonchar .10 .25
239 Ryan Malone .10 .25
240 Joe Thornton .30 .75
241 Vesa Toskala .15 .40
242 Mark Bell .10 .25
243 Steve Bernier .10 .25
244 Christian Ehrhoff .10 .25
245 Jonathan Cheechoo .20 .50
246 Patrick Marleau .15 .40
247 Mike Grier .10 .25
248 Milan Michalek .10 .25
249 Evgeni Nabokov .15 .40
250 Keith Tkachuk .15 .40
251 Manny Legace .15 .40
252 Martin Rucinsky .10 .25
253 Bill Guerin .10 .25
254 Lee Stempniak .10 .25
255 Petr Cajanek .10 .25
256 Doug Weight .10 .25
257 Jay McKee .10 .25
258 Martin St. Louis .15 .40
259 Marc Denis .15 .40
260 Vaclav Prospal .10 .25
261 Brad Richards .15 .40
262 Paul Ranger .10 .25
263 Ruslan Fedotenko .10 .25
264 Vincent Lecavalier .20 .50
265 Filip Kuba .10 .25
266 Ryan Craig .10 .25
267 Dan Boyle .10 .25
268 Mats Sundin .20 .50
269 Michael Peca .10 .25
270 Alexander Steen .15 .40
271 Bryan McCabe .10 .25
272 Tomas Kaberle .10 .25
273 Andrew Raycroft .15 .40
274 Nikolai Antropov .10 .25
275 Kyle Wellwood .10 .25
276 Mikael Tellqvist .15 .40
277 Darcy Tucker .10 .25
278 Matt Stajan .10 .25
279 Jeff O'Neill .10 .25
280 Matt Cooke .10 .25
281 Sami Salo .10 .25
282 Roberto Luongo .25 .60
283 Markus Naslund .20 .50
284 Daniel Sedin .10 .25
285 Mattias Ohlund .10 .25
286 Ryan Kesler .10 .25
287 Henrik Sedin .10 .25
288 Brendan Morrison .10 .25
289 Mika Noronen .15 .40
290 Brian Sutherby .10 .25
291 Steve Eminger .10 .25
292 Alexander Ovechkin 1.00 2.50
293 Olaf Kolzig .20 .50
294 Richard Zednik .10 .25
295 Dainius Zubrus .15 .40
296 Brent Johnson .15 .40
297 Chris Clark .10 .25
298 Patrick O'Sullivan RC 1.50 4.00
299 Phil Kessel RC 2.50 6.00
300 Guillaume Latendresse RC 3.00 8.00
301 Jordan Staal RC 5.00 12.00
302 Paul Stastny RC 2.50 6.00
303 Evgeni Malkin RC 5.00 12.00
304 Luc Bourdon RC 1.50 4.00
305 Alexei Kaigorodov RC 1.25 3.00
306 Anze Kopitar RC 2.50 6.00
307 Travis Zajac RC 2.00 5.00
308 Nigel Dawes RC 1.25 3.00
309 Kristopher Letang RC 1.50 4.00
310 Marc-Edouard Vlasic RC 1.25 3.00
311 Patrick Thoresen RC 1.50 4.00
312 Ladislav Smid RC 1.00 2.50
313 Loui Eriksson RC 1.25 3.00
314 Shane O'Brien RC 1.25 3.00
315 Ryan Shannon RC 1.25 3.00
316 John Oduya RC 1.25 3.00
317 Fredrik Norrena RC 1.50 4.00
318 Niklas Backstrom RC 2.00 5.00
319 D.J. King RC 1.25 3.00
320 Patrick Fischer RC 1.25 3.00
321 Mikko Lehtonen RC 1.25 3.00
322 Roman Polak RC 1.25 3.00
323 Ben Ondrus RC 1.25 3.00
324 Bill Thomas RC 1.25 3.00
325 Billy Thompson RC 1.00 2.50
326 Brendan Bell RC 1.25 3.00
327 Carsen Germyn RC 1.25 3.00
328 Keith Yandle RC 1.25 3.00
329 Dan Jancevski RC 1.25 3.00
330 David Liffiton RC 1.25 3.00
331 David Printz RC 1.25 3.00
332 Dustin Byfuglien RC 1.25 3.00
333 Eric Fehr RC 1.50 4.00
334 Erik Reitz RC 1.25 3.00
335 Filip Novak RC 1.25 3.00
336 Frank Doyle RC 1.50 4.00
337 Ian White RC 1.25 3.00
338 Jarkko Immonen RC 1.00 2.50
339 Jeremy Williams RC 1.25 3.00
340 Joel Perrault RC 1.25 3.00
341 Jonas Johansson RC 1.25 3.00
342 Konstantin Pushkarev RC 1.25 3.00
343 Marc-Antoine Pouliot RC 1.50 4.00
344 Mark Stuart RC 1.25 3.00
345 Masi Marjamaki RC 1.25 3.00
346 Matt Carle RC 1.50 4.00
347 Matt Koalska RC 1.25 3.00
348 Michel Ouellet RC 2.00 5.00
349 Miroslav Kopriva RC 1.00 2.50
350 Noah Welch RC 1.25 3.00
351 Rob Collins RC 1.25 3.00
352 Ryan Caldwell RC 1.25 3.00
353 Ryan Potulny RC 1.50 4.00
354 Shea Weber RC 1.50 4.00
355 Enver Lisin RC 1.25 3.00
356 Tomas Kopecky RC 1.50 4.00
357 Yan Stastny RC 1.25 3.00
358 Joe Thornton CL .30 .75
359 Martin St. Louis CL .15 .40
360 Peter Forsberg CL .40 1.00

2006-07 Upper Deck MVP Gold Script

*GOLD 8X TO 20X BASE HI
*ROOKIES .75X TO 2X BASE HI
PRINT RUN 100 SETS

2006-07 Upper Deck MVP Super Script

*SUPER SCRIPT: 12X TO 30X BASE HI
*RCS: 2X TO 5X BASE HI
STATED PRINT RUN 25 #'d SETS
231 Sidney Crosby 125.00 250.00
303 Evgeni Malkin 100.00 200.00

2006-07 Upper Deck MVP Autographs

STATED ODDS 1:240
OAAT Nikolai Antropov 12.00 30.00
Mikael Tellqvist
OABK Rene Bourque 8.00 20.00
Duncan Keith
OABM Steve Bernier 12.00 30.00
Milan Michalek
OABP Pierre-Marc Bouchard 12.00 30.00
Mark Parrish
OABS Brad Boyes 12.00 30.00
Yan Stastny
OACL Erik Cole 12.00 30.00
Andrew Ladd
OACR Jeff Carter 12.00 30.00
Mike Richards
OACS Zdeno Chara 12.00 30.00
Mark Stuart
OADA Chris Drury 15.00 40.00
Maxim Afinogenov
OADO Kris Draper 15.00 40.00
Chris Osgood
OAEE Robert Esche 8.00 20.00
Ben Eager
OAEG Patrik Elias 12.00 30.00
Brian Gionta
OAFC Alexander Frolov 12.00 30.00
Mike Cammalleri
OAFQ Valtteri Filppula 12.00 30.00
Kyle Quincey
OAGA Martin Gerber 25.00 60.00
David Aebischer SP
OAGL Wayne Gretzky
Mario Lemieux SP
OAHC Dany Heatley 25.00 60.00
Jonathan Cheechoo SP
OAHH Martin Havlat 12.00 30.00
Michal Handzus
OAHT Milan Hejduk 15.00 40.00
Jose Theodore
OAKL Miikka Kiprusoff
Roberto Luongo SP
OALH Joffrey Lupul 8.00 20.00
Shawn Horcoff
OALS David Leneveu 8.00 20.00
Philippe Sauve
OALW Manny Legace 8.00 20.00
Jeff Woywitka
OALZ Nicklas Lidstrom
Henrik Zetterberg SP
OAMC Ryan Malone 15.00 40.00
Erik Christensen
OAMK Andy McDonald 8.00 20.00
Chris Kunitz
OANI Rick Nash 75.00 125.00
Jarome Iginla SP
OANM Markus Naslund 12.00 30.00
Brendan Morrison
OAPK Dion Phaneuf 20.00 50.00
Chuck Kobasew SP
OAPT Michael Peca 20.00 50.00
Darcy Tucker SP
OARK Mike Ribeiro 15.00 40.00
Andrei Kostitsyn SP
OARL Brad Richardson 8.00 20.00
John-Michael Liles
OARS Michael Ryder 12.00 30.00
Sergei Samsonov SP
OASC Miroslav Satan 8.00 20.00
Jeremy Colliton
OATM Joe Thornton 30.00 80.00
Patrick Marleau
OAVV Tomas Vokoun 20.00 50.00
Josef Vasicek SP

2006-07 Upper Deck MVP Clutch Performers

COMPLETE SET (25) 10.00 25.00
STATED ODDS 1:8
CP1 Cam Ward .40 1.00
CP2 Peter Forsberg .75 2.00
CP3 Joe Sakic .75 2.00
CP4 Martin Brodeur 1.50 4.00
CP5 Jarome Iginla .50 1.25
CP6 Jaromir Jagr .60 1.50
CP7 Mats Sundin .40 1.00
CP8 Dany Heatley .50 1.25
CP9 Ryan Miller .40 1.00
CP10 Alexander Ovechkin 2.00 5.00
CP11 Eric Staal .40 1.00
CP12 Mike Modano .40 1.00
CP13 Martin St. Louis .30 .75
CP14 Ryan Smyth .30 .75
CP15 Chris Pronger .30 .75
CP16 Henrik Zetterberg .40 1.00
CP17 Jonathan Cheechoo .40 1.00
CP18 Ilya Kovalchuk .50 1.25
CP19 Marian Gaborik .50 1.25
CP20 Shane Doan .30 .75
CP21 Rick Nash .40 1.00
CP22 Sidney Crosby 2.50 6.00
CP23 Markus Naslund .40 1.00
CP24 Dominik Hasek .60 1.50
CP25 Mario Lemieux 2.00 5.00

2006-07 Upper Deck MVP Gotta Have Hart

COMPLETE SET (25) 10.00 25.00
STATED ODDS 1:8
HH1 Joe Thornton .60 1.50
HH2 Peter Forsberg .60 1.50
HH3 Martin St. Louis .30 .75
HH4 Jose Theodore .40 1.00
HH5 Joe Sakic .75 2.00
HH6 Chris Pronger .30 .75
HH7 Jaromir Jagr .60 1.50
HH8 Mario Lemieux 2.00 5.00
HH9 Wayne Gretzky 3.00 8.00
HH10 Eric Lindros .40 1.00
HH11 Sergei Fedorov .40 1.00
HH12 Alexander Ovechkin 2.00 5.00
HH13 Sidney Crosby 2.50 6.00
HH14 Jarome Iginla .50 1.25
HH15 Eric Staal .40 1.00
HH16 Martin Brodeur 1.50 4.00
HH17 Miikka Kiprusoff .40 1.00
HH18 Rick Nash .40 1.00
HH19 Ilya Kovalchuk .50 1.25
HH20 Dominik Hasek .60 1.50
HH21 Marian Gaborik .50 1.25
HH22 Patrice Bergeron .40 1.00
HH23 Mats Sundin .40 1.00
HH24 Markus Naslund .40 1.00
HH25 Dany Heatley .50 1.25

2006-07 Upper Deck MVP International Icons

COMPLETE SET (25)
STATED ODDS 1:8
II1 Teemu Selanne .40 1.00
II2 Ilya Kovalchuk .50 1.25
II3 Marian Hossa .30 .75
II4 Marco Sturm .20 .50
II5 Milan Hejduk .20 .50
II6 Sergei Fedorov .40 1.00
II7 Mike Modano .40 1.00
II8 Nicklas Lidstrom .30 .75
II9 Dominik Hasek .60 1.50
II10 Olli Jokinen .20 .50
II11 Marian Gaborik .40 1.00
II12 Saku Koivu .30 .75
II13 Tomas Vokoun .30 .75
II14 Martin Brodeur 1.25 3.00
II15 Miroslav Satan .20 .50
II16 Rick DiPietro .30 .75
II17 Jaromir Jagr .75 2.00
II18 Martin Gerber .30 .75
II19 Peter Forsberg .60 1.50
II20 Sidney Crosby 2.00 5.00
II21 Vincent Lecavalier .40 1.00
II22 Mats Sundin .30 .75
II23 Nikolai Antropov .20 .50
II24 Alexander Ovechkin 2.00 5.00
II25 Olaf Kolzig .40 1.00

2006-07 Upper Deck MVP Jerseys

COMPLETE SET (97)
STATED ODDS 1:24
OJAB Alexandre Picard 4.00 10.00
Brandon Bochenski
OJAR David Aebischer 8.00 20.00
Andrew Raycroft
OJBJ Jay Bouwmeester 4.00 10.00
Olli Jokinen
OJBK Pierre-Marc Bouchard 4.00 10.00
Ryan Kesler
OJBL Martin Brodeur 15.00 40.00
Henrik Lundqvist
OJBN Martin Brodeur 12.00 30.00
Antero Niittymaki
OJBR Patrice Bergeron 6.00 15.00
Michael Ryder
OJCF Sidney Crosby 40.00 80.00
Peter Forsberg SP
OJCG Jeff Carter 6.00 15.00
Scott Gomez
OJCJ Chuck Kobasew 4.00 10.00
Jarret Stoll
OJCO Sidney Crosby 75.00 150.00
Alexander Ovechkin SP
OJCR Zdeno Chara 4.00 10.00
Wade Redden
OJCS Jonathan Cheechoo 8.00 20.00
Teemu Selanne
OJDH Pavol Demitra 4.00 10.00
Ales Hemsky
OJDK Chris Drury 4.00 10.00
Alex Kovalev
OJDM Shane Doan 6.00 15.00
Brenden Morrow
OJDP Kris Draper 4.00 10.00
Michael Peca
OJDR Martin Brodeur 15.00 40.00
Jaromir Jagr
OJEP Patrik Elias 4.00 10.00
Petr Prucha
OJER Eric Staal 6.00 15.00
Ryan Smyth
OJES Patrik Elias 4.00 10.00
Miroslav Satan
OJEV Eric Staal 8.00 20.00
Vincent Lecavalier
OJFA Sergei Fedorov 6.00 15.00
Jason Arnott
OJFD Sergei Fedorov 8.00 20.00
Pavel Datsyuk
OJFM Fernando Pisani 4.00 10.00
Matthew Lombardi
OJFN Alexander Frolov 6.00 15.00
Ladislav Nagy
OJFR Manny Fernandez 6.00 15.00
Dwayne Roloson
OJGC Ryan Getzlaf 4.00 10.00
Mike Cammalleri
OJGH Marian Gaborik 10.00 25.00
Martin Havlat
OJGL Wayne Gretzky 150.00 300.00
Mario Lemieux SP
OJHB Dany Heatley 15.00 40.00

Daniel Briere SP
OJHF Marian Hossa 4.00 10.00
Ruslan Fedotenko
OJHH Milan Hejduk 4.00 10.00
Ales Hemsky
OJHL Nathan Horton 4.00 10.00
Andrew Ladd
OJHM Trent Hunter 4.00 10.00
Ryan Malone
OJHS Dany Heatley 10.00 25.00
Alexander Steen
OJHV Dominik Hasek 10.00 25.00
Tomas Vokoun
OJIS Jarome Iginla 10.00 25.00
Ryan Smyth
OJJC Curtis Joseph 6.00 15.00
Dan Cloutier
OJJF Jaromir Jagr 12.00 30.00
Peter Forsberg
OJJJ Jarret Stoll 4.00 10.00
Jeff Friesen
OJJL Ed Jovanovski 4.00 10.00
Jordan Leopold
OJJM Jarret Stoll 4.00 10.00
Marek Svatos
OJJS Jaromir Jagr 10.00 25.00
Miroslav Satan
OJKD Olaf Kolzig 6.00 15.00
Marc Denis
OJKL Miikka Kiprusoff 15.00 40.00
Roberto Luongo
OJKR Mikko Koivu 6.00 15.00
Tuomo Ruutu
OJKS Jason Spezza 6.00 15.00
Saku Koivu
OJKW Paul Kariya 6.00 15.00
Doug Weight
OJKZ Paul Kariya 8.00 20.00
Henrik Zetterberg
OJLD Henrik Lundqvist 10.00 25.00
Rick DiPietro
OJLF Andrew Ladd 4.00 10.00
Tomas Fleischmann
OJLJ Vincent Lecavalier 6.00 15.00
Olli Jokinen
OJLK Kari Lehtonen 6.00 15.00
Olaf Kolzig
OJLM Nicklas Lidstrom 10.00 25.00
Bryan McCabe
OJLS Robert Lang 4.00 10.00
Steve Sullivan
OJLZ Nicklas Lidstrom 6.00 15.00
Sergei Zubov
OJMJ Andrej Meszaros 4.00 10.00
Milan Jurcina
OJMS Martin St. Louis 6.00 15.00
Simon Gagne
OJMT Mike Modano 6.00 15.00
Pierre Turgeon
OJNJ Scott Niedermayer 4.00 10.00
Ed Jovanovski
OJNT Rick Nash 6.00 15.00
Keith Tkachuk
OJOC Chris Osgood 6.00 15.00
Ty Conklin
OJOK Alexander Ovechkin 20.00 50.00
Ilya Kovalchuk
OJOT Jason Spezza 10.00 25.00
Mats Sundin
OJPB Chris Pronger 6.00 15.00
Rob Blake
OJPJ Corey Perry 4.00 10.00
Jussi Jokinen
OJPL Dion Phaneuf 10.00 25.00
John-Michael Liles
OJPN Dion Phaneuf 6.00 15.00
Scott Niedermayer
OJPO Joni Pitkanen 4.00 10.00
Sandis Ozolinsh
OJPR Joni Pitkanen 4.00 10.00
Brian Rafalski
OJRB Brad Richards 6.00 15.00
Rod Brind'Amour
OJRL Jeremy Roenick 8.00 20.00
Eric Lindros
OJRM Roberto Luongo 6.00 15.00
Manny Fernandez
OJRW Brian Rafalski 4.00 10.00
Brendan Witt
OJSA Sergei Samsonov 4.00 10.00
Maxim Afinogenov
OJSC Steve Sullivan 4.00 10.00
Kyle Calder
OJSD Marc Savard 4.00 10.00
Chris Drury
OJSF Teemu Selanne 6.00 15.00
Alexander Frolov
OJSG Brendan Shanahan 8.00 20.00
Simon Gagne
OJSH Martin St. Louis 6.00 15.00
Nathan Horton
OJSK Mats Sundin 6.00 15.00
Saku Koivu
OJSL Brendan Shanahan 15.00 40.00
John LeClair SP
OJSM Joe Sakic 10.00 25.00
Mike Modano
OJSN Sergei Samsonov 4.00 10.00
Nikolai Antropov
OJSS Miroslav Satan 4.00 10.00
Martin Straka
OJST Joe Sakic 12.00 30.00
Joe Thornton
OJSV Marek Svatos 4.00 10.00
Joffrey Lupul
OJTG Marty Turco 8.00 20.00
Jean-Sebastien Giguere
OJTH Keith Tkachuk 4.00 10.00
Martin Havlat
OJTN Alex Tanguay 6.00 15.00
Markus Naslund
OJWA Doug Weight 4.00 10.00
Jason Arnott
OJWC Doug Weight 4.00 10.00
Kyle Calder
OJWD Cam Ward 8.00 20.00
Marc Denis
OJWL Cam Ward 8.00 20.00
Kari Lehtonen
OJWW Justin Williams 4.00 10.00
Stephen Weiss
OJZN Henrik Zetterberg 8.00 20.00
Rick Nash

2006-07 Upper Deck MVP Last Line of Defense

COMPLETE SET (25) 10.00 25.00
STATED ODDS 1:8
LL1 Martin Brodeur 2.00 5.00
LL2 Miikka Kiprusoff .60 1.50
LL3 Henrik Lundqvist .75 2.00
LL4 Marty Turco .50 1.25
LL5 Cristobal Huet .75 2.00
LL6 Marc-Andre Fleury .60 1.50
LL7 Roberto Luongo .75 2.00
LL8 Cam Ward .60 1.50
LL9 Ryan Miller .60 1.50
LL10 Nikolai Khabibulin .60 1.50
LL11 Kari Lehtonen .60 1.50
LL12 Tomas Vokoun .50 1.25
LL13 Dwayne Roloson .50 1.25
LL14 Olaf Kolzig .60 1.50
LL15 Ed Belfour .60 1.50
LL16 Vesa Toskala .50 1.25
LL17 Jose Theodore .60 1.50
LL18 Curtis Joseph .60 1.50
LL19 Manny Fernandez .50 1.25
LL20 Dominik Hasek 1.00 2.50
LL21 Martin Gerber .50 1.25
LL22 Andrew Raycroft .50 1.25
LL23 Rick DiPietro .50 1.25
LL24 Hannu Toivonen .60 1.50
LL25 Manny Legace .50 1.25

1999-00 Upper Deck MVP SC Edition

Released late in the 1999-00 hockey season, the 1999-00 Upper Deck MVP Stanley Cup Edition set features 193 regular cards, 25 CHL Prospects cards, and 2 Checklists to comprise the 220-card set. MVP Stanley Cup Edition was packaged in boxes containing 28-packs with 10-cards per pack, and carried a suggested retail price of $1.59.

COMPLETE SET (220) 20.00 40.00
1 Teemu Selanne .10 .30
2 Paul Kariya .10 .30
3 Guy Hebert .08 .25
4 Oleg Tverdovsky .05 .15
5 Tony Hrkac .05 .15
6 Mike Leclerc .05 .15
7 Ladislav Kohn .05 .15
8 Ray Ferraro .05 .15
9 Ed Ward .05 .15
10 Norm Maracle .08 .25
11 Dean Sylvester RC .08 .25
12 Yannick Tremblay .05 .15
13 Patrik Stefan RC .40 1.00
14 Johan Garpenlov .05 .15
15 Per-Johan Axelsson .05 .15
16 Joe Thornton .20 .50
17 Sergei Samsonov .08 .25
18 Jay Henderson RC .05 .15
19 Byron Dafoe .08 .25
20 Steve Heinze .05 .15
21 Marty McSorley .05 .15
22 Dominik Hasek .25 .60
23 Miroslav Satan .08 .25
24 Curtis Brown .05 .15
25 Martin Biron .08 .25
26 Jason Woolley .05 .15
27 Michael Peca .08 .25
28 Wayne Primeau .05 .15
29 Valeri Bure .05 .15
30 Derek Morris .08 .25
31 Cory Stillman .05 .15
32 Fred Brathwaite .08 .25
33 Jarome Iginla .15 .40
34 Andre Nazarov .05 .15
35 Jeff Shantz .05 .15
36 Ron Francis .05 .15
37 Jeff O'Neill .05 .15
38 Arturs Irbe .08 .25
39 Sami Kapanen .05 .15
40 Sean Hill .05 .15
41 Byron Ritchie RC .08 .25
42 Tommy Westlund RC .08 .25
43 Tony Amonte .08 .25
44 Doug Gilmour .08 .25
45 Blair Atcheynum .05 .15
46 Alexei Zhamnov .05 .15
47 Dean Mcammond .05 .15
48 Michael Nylander .05 .15
49 Aaron Miller .05 .15
50 Milan Hejduk .10 .30
51 Patrick Roy .60 1.50
52 Joe Sakic .30 .75
53 Chris Drury .08 .25
54 Peter Forsberg .30 .75
55 Ray Bourque .20 .50
56 Marc Denis .08 .25
57 Brett Hull .15 .40
58 Mike Modano .20 .50
59 Ed Belfour .10 .30
60 Kirk Muller .05 .15
61 Brenden Morrow .10 .30
62 Mike Keane .05 .15
63 Brad Lukowich RC .05 .15
64 Sergei Fedorov .20 .50
65 Steve Yzerman .60 1.50
66 Chris Osgood .08 .25
67 Brendan Shanahan .10 .30
68 Martin Lapointe .08 .25
69 Pat Verbeek .05 .15
70 Stacy Roest .05 .15
71 Tommy Salo .08 .25
72 Doug Weight .08 .25
73 Alexander Selivanov .05 .15
74 Ryan Smyth .05 .15
75 Boyd Devereaux .05 .15
76 Ethan Moreau .05 .15
77 Pavel Bure .10 .30
78 Viktor Kozlov .05 .15
79 Mike Vernon .08 .25
80 Ivan Novoseltsev RC .25 .60
81 Ray Whitney .08 .25
82 Filip Kuba RC .08 .25
83 Ray Sheppard .05 .15
84 Zigmund Palffy .08 .25
85 Luc Robitaille .08 .25
86 Ryan Smolinski .08 .25
87 Rob Blake .08 .25
88 Jere Karalahti RC .05 .15
89 Marko Tuomainen .05 .15
90 Garry Galley .05 .15
91 Saku Koivu .10 .30
92 Dainius Zubrus .05 .15
93 Jose Theodore .15 .40
94 Karl Dykhuis .05 .15
95 Sergei Zholtok .05 .15
96 Francis Bouillon RC .05 .15
97 David Legwand .08 .25
98 Mike Dunham .08 .25
99 Robert Valicevic RC .05 .15
100 Cliff Ronning .08 .25
101 Drake Berehowsky .05 .15
102 Greg Johnson .05 .15
103 Patric Kjellberg .05 .15
104 Martin Brodeur .30 .75
105 Scott Stevens .08 .25
106 Claude Lemieux .05 .15
107 Scott Gomez .05 .15
108 Partik Elias .08 .25
109 Randy McKay .05 .15
110 Sergei Brylin .05 .15
111 Tim Connolly .05 .15
112 Roberto Luongo .15 .40
113 Dave Scatchard .05 .15
114 Kenny Jonsson .05 .15
115 Vladimir Orszagh RC .05 .15
116 Ted Drury .05 .15
117 Theo Fleury .05 .15
118 Mike Richter .10 .30
119 Mike York .05 .15
120 Brian Leetch .10 .30
121 Petr Nedved .05 .15
122 Radek Dvorak .05 .15
123 Jan Hlavac .05 .15
124 Marian Hossa .10 .30
125 Radek Bonk .05 .15
126 Daniel Alfredsson .08 .25
127 Ron Tugnutt .08 .25
128 Rob Zamuner .05 .15
129 Jason York .05 .15
130 Shaun Van Allen .05 .15
131 Eric Lindros .10 .30
132 John LeClair .10 .30
133 Simon Gagne .10 .30
134 Mark Recchi .08 .25
135 Keith Primeau .05 .15
136 Daymond Langkow .08 .25
137 Brian Boucher .10 .30
138 Luke Richardson .05 .15
139 Keith Tkachuk .10 .30
140 Jeremy Roenick .15 .40
141 Travis Green .05 .15
142 Dallas Drake .05 .15
143 Jyrki Lumme .05 .15
144 Shane Doan .05 .15
145 Sean Burke .08 .25
146 Jaromir Jagr .20 .50
147 Alexei Kovalev .05 .15
148 Tom Barrasso .08 .25
149 Martin Sonnenberg RC .05 .15
150 Robert Lang .05 .15
151 Robert Dome .05 .15
152 Darius Kasparaitis .05 .15
153 Owen Nolan .08 .25
154 Jeff Friesen .05 .15
155 Steve Shields .08 .25
156 Vincent Damphousse .05 .15
157 Mike Rathje .05 .15
158 Alexander Korolyuk .05 .15
159 Todd Harvey .08 .25
160 Pavol Demitra .08 .25
161 Pierre Turgeon .08 .25
162 Roman Turek .08 .25
163 Chris Pronger .08 .25
164 Jochen Hecht RC .50 1.25
165 Todd Reirden RC .05 .15
166 Scott Young .05 .15
167 Vincent Lecavalier .10 .30
168 Dan Cloutier .05 .15
169 Chris Gratton .05 .15
170 Todd Warriner .05 .15
171 Mike Sillinger .05 .15
172 Petr Svoboda .05 .15
173 Mats Sundin .10 .30
174 Curtis Joseph .10 .30
175 Jonas Hoglund .05 .15
176 Sergei Berezin .05 .15
177 Nathan Dempsey RC .05 .15
178 Nikolai Antropov RC .50 1.25
179 Alyn McCauley .05 .15
180 Alexander Karpovtsev .05 .15
181 Steve Kariya RC .30 .75
182 Mark Messier .10 .30
183 Markus Naslund .05 .15
184 Adrian Aucoin .05 .15
185 Andrew Cassels .05 .15
186 Artem Chubarov .05 .15
187 Brad May .08 .25
188 Peter Bondra .10 .30
189 Olaf Kolzig .08 .25
190 Dmitri Mironov .05 .15
191 Jeff Halpern RC .30 .75
192 Andrei Nikolishin .05 .15
193 Terry Yake .08 .25
194 Pavel Brendl RC .50 1.25
195 Sheldon Keefe RC .40 1.00
196 Branislav Mezei RC .08 .25
197 Milan Kraft RC .50 1.25
198 Ryan Jardine RC .30 .75
199 Kristian Kudroc RC .08 .25
200 Alexander Buturlin RC .15 .40
201 Jaroslav Kristek RC .10 .30
202 Andrei Shefer RC .10 .30
203 Brad Moran RC .15 .40
204 Brett Lysak RC .08 .25
205 Michal Sivek RC .15 .40
206 Luke Sellars RC .08 .25
207 Brad Ralph RC .08 .25
208 Bryan Kazarian RC .08 .25
209 Barrett Jackman .08 .25
210 Brian Finley .08 .25
211 Jamie Lundmark .08 .25
212 Denis Shvidki .08 .25
213 Taylor Pyatt .08 .25
214 Kris Beech .05 .15
215 Michael Zigomanis .05 .15
216 Justin Papineau .08 .25
217 Daniel Sedin .05 .15
218 Henrik Sedin .05 .15
219 Checklist .05 .15
220 Checklist .05 .15

1999-00 Upper Deck MVP SC Edition Gold Script

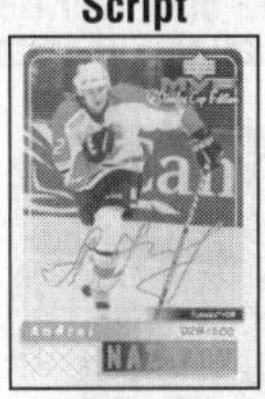

Randomly seeded in packs, this 220-card set parallels the base set and is enhanced with gold foil instead of bronze, and on the regular cards, a gold-foil signature. Cards are serial numbered out of 100.
*STARS: 30X TO 80X BASIC CARDS
*ROOKIES: 15X TO 40X BASIC CARDS

1999-00 Upper Deck MVP SC Edition Silver Script

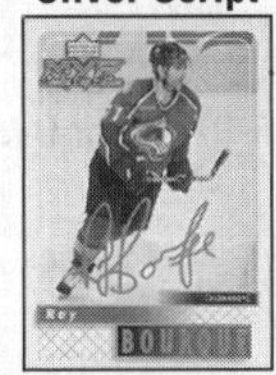

Randomly seeded in packs at 1:2, this 220-card set parallels the base set and is enhanced with silver foil instead of bronze, and on the regular cards, a silver-foil signature.
*STARS: 1.25X TO 3X BASIC CARDS
*ROOKIES: .75X TO 2X BASIC CARDS

1999-00 Upper Deck MVP SC Edition Super Script

Randomly inserted in packs, this 220-card set parallels the base set and features a printed signature on the front of the regular cards. Each card is serial numbered out of 25.
*STARS: 50X TO 125X BASE CARD HI
*ROOKIES: 20X TO 50X

1999-00 Upper Deck MVP SC Edition Clutch Performers

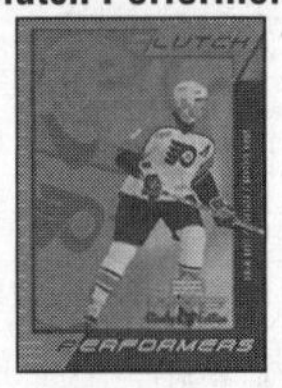

Randomly inserted in packs at 1:28, this 10-card set showcases some of the NHL's key clutch players.
COMPLETE SET (10) 15.00 30.00
CP1 Paul Kariya 1.00 2.50
CP2 Ray Bourque 1.50 4.00
CP3 Joe Sakic 2.00 5.00
CP4 Steve Yzerman 5.00 12.00
CP5 Luc Robitaille .75 2.00
CP6 Martin Brodeur 2.50 6.00
CP7 Theo Fleury .75 2.00
CP8 John LeClair 1.25 3.00
CP9 Jaromir Jagr 1.50 4.00
CP10 Curtis Joseph 1.00 2.50

1999-00 Upper Deck MVP SC Edition Cup Contenders

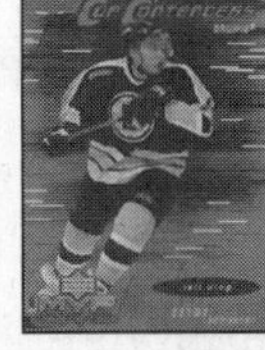

Randomly inserted in packs at 1:9, this 10-card set features emerging NHL superstars.
COMPLETE SET (10) 5.00 10.00
CC1 Patrik Stefan .75 2.00
CC2 Sergei Samsonov .60 1.50
CC3 Milan Hejduk .75 2.00
CC4 Chris Drury .60 1.50
CC5 David Legwand .40 1.00
CC6 Scott Gomez .50 1.25
CC7 Marian Hossa .60 1.50
CC8 Jeff Friesen .50 1.25
CC9 Vincent Lecavalier .50 1.25
CC10 Steve Kariya .50 1.25

1999-00 Upper Deck MVP SC Edition Game-Used Souvenirs

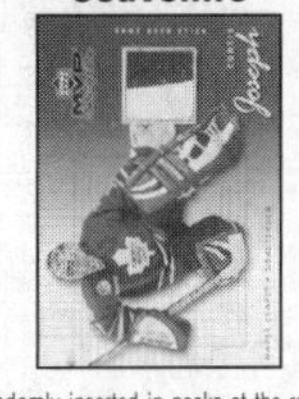

Randomly inserted in packs at the rate of 1:130, this 18-card set features players with swatches of game-used sticks. Super Game Used Souvenirs came inserted into Canadian packs at the rate of 1:130, and feature two swatches of material instead of one.
GUBH Brett Hull 6.00 15.00
GUBJ Barret Jackman 3.00 8.00
GUCJ Curtis Joseph 5.00 12.00
GUDS Denis Shvidki 3.00 8.00
GUEL Eric Lindros 6.00 15.00
GUJC John LeClair 5.00 12.00
GUJS Joe Sakic 10.00 25.00
GUKB Kris Beech 3.00 8.00
GUMK Milan Kraft 3.00 8.00
GUMO Maxime Ouellet 3.00 8.00
GUPB Pavel Brendl 3.00 8.00
GUPF Peter Forsberg 10.00 25.00
GUPV Pavel Bure 6.00 15.00
GURB Ray Bourque 10.00 25.00
GUSK Scott Kelman 3.00 8.00
GUSY Steve Yzerman 12.50 30.00
GUTP Taylor Pyatt 3.00 8.00
GUTS Teemu Selanne 5.00 12.00
SGDS Denis Shvidki Super 4.00 10.00
SGKB Kris Beech Super 4.00 10.00
SGMK Milan Kraft Super 4.00 10.00
SGPB Pavel Brendl Super 4.00 10.00

1999-00 Upper Deck MVP SC Edition Golden Memories

Randomly inserted in packs at 1:14, this 10-card set spotlights outstanding moments in NHL post-season play.
COMPLETE SET (10) 12.00 25.00
GM1 Paul Kariya .50 1.25
GM2 Patrick Roy 2.50 6.00
GM3 Peter Forsberg 1.25 3.00
GM4 Mike Modano .75 2.00
GM5 Steve Yzerman 2.50 6.00
GM6 Martin Brodeur 1.25 3.00
GM7 Theo Fleury .50 1.25
GM8 Eric Lindros .75 2.00
GM9 Jaromir Jagr .75 2.00
GM10 Curtis Joseph .50 1.25

1999-00 Upper Deck MVP SC Edition Great Combinations

Randomly inserted in packs at the rate of 1:196, this 16-card set showcases some of the NHL's most dominating teammates. Parallels numbered to just 25 were also randomly inserted in packs.
*PARALLEL: 1.25X TO 3X BASIC CARDS
GCBK Pavel Bure 10.00 25.00
Viktor Kozlov
GCGL Wayne Gretzky 25.00 60.00
Brian Leetch
GCGR Wayne Gretzky 20.00 50.00
Mike Richter
GCHM B.Hull/M.Modano 12.50 30.00
GCHP Dominik Hasek 8.00 20.00
Michael Peca
GCJS Jaromir Jage 10.00 25.00
Martin Straka
GCKS Paul Kariya 10.00 25.00
Teemu Selanne
GCLL Eric Lindros 10.00 25.00
John LeClair
GCLS Vincent Lecavalier 8.00 20.00
Petr Svoboda
GCRF Patrick Roy 25.00 60.00
Peter Forsberg
GCSF Brendan Shanahan 10.00 25.00
Sergei Fedorov
GCSJ Mats Sundin 8.00 20.00
Curtis Joseph
GCSR Patrik Stefan 8.00 20.00
Damian Rhodes
GCTR Keith Tkachuk 8.00 20.00
Jeremy Roenick
GCTS Joe Thornton 12.50 30.00
Sergei Samsonov
GCYO Steve Yzerman 15.00 40.00
Chris Osgood

1999-00 Upper Deck MVP SC Edition Playoff Heroes

Randomly seeded in packs at the rate of 1:72, this 10-card set pays tribute to the rare superstars who have performed exceptionally in the post season.
COMPLETE SET (10) 40.00 80.00
PH1 Paul Kariya 3.00 8.00
PH2 Dominik Hasek 5.00 12.00
PH3 Patrick Roy 12.50 30.00
PH4 Mike Modano 4.00 10.00
PH5 Sergei Fedorov 5.00 12.00
PH6 Pavel Bure 3.00 8.00
PH7 Martin Brodeur 6.00 15.00
PH8 Eric Lindros 4.00 10.00
PH9 Jaromir Jagr 4.00 10.00
PH10 Mark Messier 3.00 8.00

1999-00 Upper Deck MVP SC Edition ProSign

Randomly inserted in reatil packs at the rate of 1:144, this 24-card set featured an authentic autograph.
AM Al MacInnis 6.00 15.00
AT Alex Tanguay 6.00 15.00
BF Brian Finley 4.00 10.00
BH Brett Hull 15.00 40.00
BJ Barret Jackman 6.00 15.00
BL Brian Leetch 6.00 15.00
CJ Curtis Joseph 20.00 50.00
DA Dave Andreychuk 4.00 10.00
DL David Legwand 4.00 10.00
DS Denis Shvidki 2.00 5.00
JH Jochen Hecht 4.00 10.00
JS Jozef Stumpel 2.00 5.00
KB Kris Beech 2.00 5.00
MB Martin Biron 4.00 10.00
MK Milan Kraft 2.00 5.00
MO Maxime Ouellet 4.00 10.00
PB Pavel Bure 6.00 15.00
PS Patrik Stefan 2.00 5.00
SG Simon Gagne 6.00 15.00
SK Scott Kelman 2.00 5.00
SS Sergei Samsonov 6.00 15.00
SY Steve Yzerman 75.00 150.00
TP Taylor Pyatt 6.00 15.00
PBR Pavel Brendl 4.00 10.00

1999-00 Upper Deck MVP SC Edition Second Season Snipers

Randomly inserted in packs at 1:28, this 12-card set spotlights players that have a knack for scoring clutch goals.
COMPLETE SET (12) 12.00 25.00
SS1 Teemu Selanne 1.00 2.50
SS2 Joe Thornton 1.00 2.50
SS3 Peter Forsberg 2.50 6.00
SS4 Brendan Shanahan 1.00 2.50
SS5 Pavel Bure 1.00 2.50
SS6 Claude Lemieux .75 2.00
SS7 Eric Lindros 1.00 2.50
SS8 John LeClair 1.00 2.50
SS9 Keith Tkachuk 1.00 2.50
SS10 Jaromir Jagr 1.50 4.00
SS11 Mats Sundin 1.00 2.50
SS12 Mark Messier 1.00 2.50

1999-00 Upper Deck MVP SC Edition Stanley Cup Talent

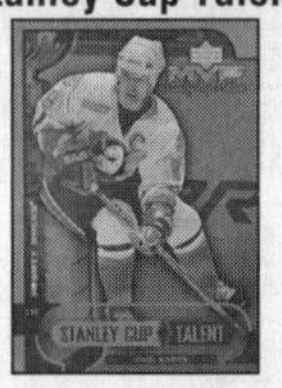

Inserted at a rate of 1:5 packs, this 20-card set features elite players of top teams in full color action photos on the card fronts, and a breakdown of individual stats on card backs.
COMPLETE SET (20) 8.00 15.00
SC1 Paul Kariya .30 .75
SC2 Teemu Selanne .30 .75
SC3 Ray Bourque .50 1.25
SC4 Joe Sakic .60 1.50
SC5 Patrick Roy 1.50 4.00
SC6 Brett Hull .40 1.00
SC7 Sergei Fedorov .50 1.25
SC8 Pave Bure .30 .75
SC9 Zigmund Palffy .25 .60
SC10 Martin Brodeur .75 2.00
SC11 Theo Fleury .20 .50
SC12 Eric Lindros .30 .75
SC13 John LeClair .30 .75
SC14 Jaromir Jagr .50 1.25
SC15 Jeremy Roenick .40 1.00
SC16 Keith Tkachuk .30 .75
SC17 Steve Shields .20 .50
SC18 Mats Sundin .30 .75
SC19 Mark Messier .30 .75
SC20 Peter Bondra .20 .50

2002 Upper Deck National Convention *

COMPLETE SET (3) 40.00
N8 Wayne Gretzky 20.00
N9 Bobby Orr 20.00
N10 Gordie Howe 10.00

2005 Upper Deck National VIP *

Upper Deck produced this set and distributed it to special VIP package members attending the 2005 National Sport Collectors Convention in Chicago. The set includes famous athletes from a variety of sports with the title "The National" printed on the cardfronts along with a "VIP" stamp.
VIP4 Wayne Gretzky

1994 Upper Deck NHLPA/Be A Player

This special 45-card set features the NHL's top players in unique settings. Upper Deck sent three top photographers, including Walter Iooss, to capture on film players in off-ice situations. The first 18 cards bear Iooss' photos (Walter Iooss Collection) and are arranged alphabetically. Cards 19-40 are also arranged alphabetically and carry photos of the other photographers. The final five cards feature Doug Gilmour: A Canadian Hero (41-45).
COMPLETE SET (45) 12.00 30.00
1 Tony Amonte .20 .50
2 Chris Chelios .30 .75
3 Alexandre Daigle .10 .25
4 Dave Ellett .10 .25
5 Sergei Fedorov .60 1.50
6 Chris Gratton .10 .25
7 Wayne Gretzky 2.00 5.00
8 Brett Hull .40 1.00
9 Brian Leetch .30 .75
10 Rob Niedermayer .20 .50
11 Felix Potvin .30 .75
12 Luc Robitaille .20 .50
13 Jeremy Roenick .30 .75
14 Joe Sakic .60 1.50
15 Teemu Selanne .60 1.50
16 Brendan Shanahan .40 1.00
17 Alexei Yashin .20 .50
18 Steve Yzerman 1.60 4.00
Detroit R
19 Jason Arnott .20 .50
20 Pavel Bure .60 1.50
21 Theo Fleury .30 .75
22 Mike Gartner .20 .50
23 Kevin Haller .10 .25
24 Derian Hatcher .10 .25
25 Mark Howe .30 .75
Gordie Howe
26 Al Iafrate .10 .25
27 Joe Juneau .20 .50
28 Pat LaFontaine .20 .50
29 Eric Lindros .60 1.50
30 Dave Manson .10 .25
31 Mike Modano .40 1.00
32 Scott Niedermayer .20 .50

33 Owen Nolan .20 .50
34 Joel Otto .10 .25
35 Chris Pronger .20 .50
36 Scott Stevens .20 .50
37 Pierre Turgeon .20 .50
38 Pat Verbeek .10 .25
39 Doug Weight .20 .50
40 Terry Yake .10 .25
41 Doug Gilmour .30 .75
(Two-Year Old Doug With A Hockey Stick)
42 Doug Gilmour .30 .75
(Nine-Year Old Doug On The Ice)
43 Doug Gilmour .30 .75
(Standing Next To A Little Girl)
44 Doug Gilmour .30 .75
(Sitting On Motorcycle)
45 Doug Gilmour .30 .75
(With Fishing Rod)

2000-01 Upper Deck NHLPA

These cards were produced by UD at the behest of the Players' Association to ensure that every member of the PA earned a card in the 2000-01 season. Approximately 100 copies of each card were produced, with all copies going to the individual player for them to do with as they wish. Therefore, there were no sets available and likely none exist outside of the NHLPA repository. The cards share the same design as the base 2000-01 UD set. Because we have seen so few singles trade hands, the cards are checklisted but not priced. Thanks to collector Aaron Brownley for providing the checklist.

COMPLETE SET (90)
PA1 Mike Crowley
PA2 Ruslan Salei
PA3 Pascal Trepanier
PA4 David Harlock
PA5 Jeff Odgers
PA6 Yves Sarault
PA7 Ken Belanger
PA8 Jay Henderson
PA9 Cameron Mann
PA10 Denis Hamel
PA11 Jason Holland
PA12 Rob Ray
PA13 Dallas Eakins
PA14 Denis Gauthier
PA15 Dwayne Hay
PA16 Dave Karpa
PA17 Darren Langdon
PA18 Tyler Moss
PA19 Kevin Dean
PA20 Mark Janssens
PA21 Rob Tallas
PA22 Chris Dingman
PA23 Greg DeVries
PA24 Dave Reid
PA25 Kevin Dahl
PA26 Frantisek Kucera
PA27 Steve Maltais
PA28 Sami Helenius
PA29 Brad Lukowich
PA30 Kirk Muller
PA31 Yuri Butsayev
PA32 Maxim Kuznetsov
PA33 Aaron Ward
PA34 Rem Murray
PA35 Frank Musil
PA36 Dominic Pittis
PA37 Len Barrie
PA38 Dan Boyle
PA39 John Jakopin
PA40 Philippe Boucher
PA41 Steve Passmore
PA42 Scott Thomas
PA43 J.J. Daigneault
PA44 Matt Johnson
PA45 Stacy Roest
PA46 Francois Bouillon
PA47 Eric Fichaud
PA48 Stephane Robidas
PA49 Cale Hulse
PA50 Ville Peltonen
PA51 Mike Watt
PA52 Ken Daneyko
PA53 Jim McKenzie
PA54 Ed Ward
PA55 Jesse Belanger
PA56 Anders Myrvold
PA57 Steve Webb
PA58 Jason Doig
PA59 Bert Robertsson
PA60 David Wilkie
PA61 John Emmons
PA62 David Oliver
PA63 Jamie Rivers
PA64 Chris McAllister
PA65 Paul Ranheim
PA66 P.J. Stock
PA67 Joel Bouchard
PA68 Landon Wilson
PA69 Juha Ylonen
PA70 Marc Bergevin
PA71 Bob Boughner
PA72 Rene Corbet
PA73 Bobby Dollas
PA74 Tony Granato
PA75 Jim Montgomery
PA76 Vladimir Chebaturkin
PA77 Pascal Rheaume
PA78 Reid Simpson
PA79 Ben Clymer
PA80 Nils Ekman
PA81 Craig Miller
PA82 Donald MacLean
PA83 Alyn McCauley
PA84 Glenn Healy
PA85 Bob Essensa
PA86 Scott Lachance
PA87 Denis Pederson
PA88 Craig Billington
PA89 Dmitri Mironov
PA90 Joe Sacco

1999-00 Upper Deck Ovation

Released as a 90-card set, Ovation was comprised of 60 regular issue base cards and 30 short prints. The short prints were divided up into Premier Prospects seeded at one in three and Superstar Spotlights seeded at one in six packs. Base cards featured an embossed border molded to look like a used ice rink and silver foil stamping.

COMPLETE SET (90) 60.00 125.00
1 Paul Kariya .30 .75
2 Teemu Selanne .30 .75
3 Patrik Stefan RC 1.25 3.00
4 Sergei Samsonov .25 .60
5 Ray Bourque .50 1.25
6 Dominik Hasek .60 1.50
7 Michael Peca .25 .60
8 Miroslav Satan .25 .60
9 Oleg Saprykin RC 1.25 3.00
10 Valeri Bure .10 .25
11 Ron Francis .25 .60
12 Dave Tanabe .10 .25
13 Tony Amonte .25 .60
14 J-P Dumont .25 .60
15 Patrick Roy 1.50 4.00
16 Alex Tanguay .25 .60
17 Joe Sakic .60 1.50
18 Peter Forsberg .75 2.00
19 Mike Modano .50 1.25
20 Ed Belfour .30 .75
21 Brett Hull .40 1.00
22 Sergei Fedorov .50 1.25
23 Chris Osgood .25 .60
24 Steve Yzerman 1.50 4.00
25 Doug Weight .25 .60
26 Tom Poti .10 .25
27 Pavel Bure .30 .75
28 Ivan Novoseltsev RC .60 1.50
29 Luc Robitaille .25 .60
30 Zigmund Palffy .25 .60
31 Mike Ribeiro .25 .60
32 David Legwand .25 .60
33 Martin Brodeur .75 2.00
34 Scott Gomez .10 .25
35 Tim Connolly .10 .25
36 Theo Fleury .10 .25
37 Mike Richter .30 .75
38 Brian Leetch .30 .75
39 Marian Hossa .30 .75
40 Daniel Alfredsson .25 .60
41 Eric Lindros .30 .75
42 John LeClair .30 .75
43 Simon Gagne .30 .75
44 Keith Tkachuk .40 1.00
45 Jeremy Roenick .40 1.00
46 Jaromir Jagr .50 1.25
47 Alexei Kovalev .10 .25
48 Pavol Demitra .25 .60
49 Al MacInnis .25 .60
50 Owen Nolan .25 .60
51 Brad Stuart .25 .60
52 Steve Shields .25 .60
53 Vincent Lecavalier .30 .75
54 Paul Mara .25 .60
55 Curtis Joseph .30 .75
56 Mats Sundin .30 .75
57 Steve Kariya RC .75 2.00
58 Mark Messier .30 .75
59 Peter Bondra .30 .75
60 Olaf Kolzig .25 .60
61 Pavel Brendl PP SP RC 3.00 8.00
62 Daniel Sedin PP SP .75 2.00
63 Henrik Sedin PP SP .75 2.00
64 Sheldon Keefe PP SP RC 1.25 3.00
65 Jeff Heerema PP SP .75 2.00
66 Norm Milley PP SP .75 2.00
67 Branislav Mezei PP SP RC .75 2.00
68 Denis Shvidki PP SP .75 2.00
69 Brian Finley PP SP .75 2.00
70 Taylor Pyatt PP SP .75 2.00
71 Jamie Lundmark PP SP .75 2.00
72 Milan Kraft PP SP RC 3.00 8.00
73 Kris Beech PP SP .75 2.00
74 Alexei Volkov PP SP .75 2.00
75 Mathieu Chouinard PP SP .75 2.00
76 Justin Papineau PP SP .75 2.00
77 Brad Moran PP SP RC .75 2.00
78 Jonathan Cheechoo PP SP .75 2.00
79 Mark Bell PP SP .75 2.00
80 Mattias Weinhandl PP SP .75 2.00
81 Jaromir Jagr SS SP 1.50 4.00
82 Steve Kariya SS SP 1.00 2.50
83 Dominik Hasek SS SP 2.00 5.00
84 Paul Kariya SS SP 1.25 3.00
85 Eric Lindros SS SP 1.00 2.50
86 Patrick Roy SS SP 5.00 12.00
87 Steve Yzerman SS SP 5.00 12.00
88 Pavel Bure SS SP 1.00 2.50
89 Theo Fleury SS SP 1.00 2.50
90 Patrik Stefan SS SP 1.50 4.00

1999-00 Upper Deck Ovation Standing Ovation

Randomly inserted in packs, this 90-card set parallels the base Ovation set. Each card is enhanced with gold foil highlights and is sequentially numbered to 50.

*STARS: 50X TO 120X BASIC CARDS
*PP's: 6X TO 15X BASIC CARDS
*ROOKIES: 10X TO 25X BASIC CARDS
*SS's: 12.5X TO 30X BASIC CARDS
61 Pavel Brendl PP 100.00 175.00
72 Milan Kraft PP 100.00 175.00

1999-00 Upper Deck Ovation A Piece Of History

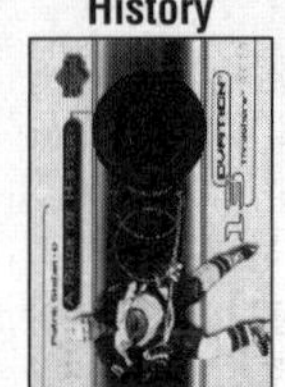

Randomly seeded in packs at the rate of 1:118, and autographs numbered to 25, this 16-card set features swatches of game used memorabilia.

BH Brett Hull 12.50 30.00
CJ Curtis Joseph 8.00 20.00
JJ Jaromir Jagr 12.50 30.00
MB Martin Brodeur 20.00 50.00
MR Mike Ribeiro 8.00 20.00
PB Pavel Bure 8.00 20.00
PK Paul Kariya 8.00 20.00
PR Patrick Roy 20.00 50.00
PS Patrik Stefan 8.00 20.00
SK Steve Kariya 8.00 20.00
SS Sergei Samsonov 8.00 20.00
TC Tim Connolly 8.00 20.00
WG Wayne Gretzky 25.00 60.00
BHS Brett Hull AU/25 150.00 300.00
CJS Curtis Joseph AU/25 125.00 250.00
PBS Pavel Bure AU/25 200.00 400.00
PSS Patrik Stefan AU/25 30.00 75.00

1999-00 Upper Deck Ovation Center Stage

Randomly inserted in packs as a tiered insert set, card numbers 1-10 are seeded at one in nine and feature silver foil highlights, card numbers 11-20 are seeded at one in 39 and feature gold foil highlights, and card numbers 21-30 are seeded at one in 99 and feature rainbow holofoil highlights.

COMPLETE SET (30) 200.00 400.00
COMMON CARD (CS1-CS5) 2.00 5.00
COMMON CARD (CS6-CS10) 1.25 3.00
COMMON CARD (CS11-CS15) 6.00 15.00
COMMON CARD (CS16-CS20) 4.00 10.00
COMMON CARD (CS21) 20.00 50.00
COMMON CARD (CS22-CS25) 20.0050.00
COMMON CARD (CS26-CS27) 12.5030.00
COMMON CARD (CS28-CS30) 25.0060.00

1999-00 Upper Deck Ovation Lead Performers

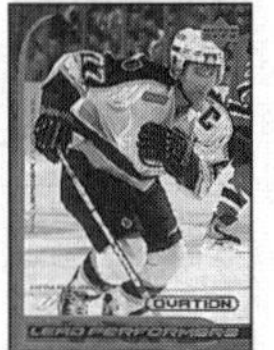

COMPLETE SET (20) 15.00 30.00
STATED ODDS 1:4
LP1 Mike Modano .75 2.00
LP2 Theo Fleury .15 .40
LP3 Paul Kariya .50 1.25
LP4 Peter Forsberg 1.25 3.00
LP5 Pavel Bure .60 1.50
LP6 John LeClair .60 1.50
LP7 Keith Tkachuk .50 1.25
LP8 Jaromir Jagr .75 2.00
LP9 Patrik Stefan .15 .40
LP10 Steve Kariya .15 .40
LP11 Ray Bourque .75 2.00
LP12 Teemu Selanne .50 1.25
LP13 Zigmund Palffy .50 1.25
LP14 Steve Yzerman 2.50 6.00
LP15 Eric Lindros .75 2.00
LP16 Dominik Hasek 1.00 2.50
LP17 Martin Brodeur 1.25 3.00
LP18 Brendan Shanahan .75 2.00
LP19 Ed Belfour .50 1.25
LP20 Patrick Roy 2.50 6.00

1999-00 Upper Deck Ovation Super Signatures

Randomly inserted in packs, this set features Wayne Gretzky and Gordie Howe autographs. Base versions are sequentially numbered to 99, Gold versions are sequentially numbered to 50, Rainbow versions are numbered to 25, and the Rainbow Combination card is numbered to nine. Wayne Gretzky SS1 was issued as a redemption. The Gretzky/Howe card is not priced due to scarcity.

SS1 Wayne Gretzky/99 150.00 400.00
SS2 Gordie Howe/99 60.00 150.00
SSG1 Wayne Gretzky GOLD/50 300.00 600.00
SSG2 Gordie Howe GOLD/50 150.00 400.00
SSR1 Wayne Gretzky RAINBOW/25 500.00 1200.00
SSR2 Gordie Howe RAINBOW/25 300.00 600.00
SSRC Wayne Gretzky Gordie Howe/9

1999-00 Upper Deck Ovation Superstar Theater

COMPLETE SET (10) 10.00 20.00
STATED ODDS 1:9
ST1 Paul Kariya .60 1.50
ST2 Sergei Fedorov 1.00 2.50
ST3 Brett Hull .60 1.50
ST4 Patrick Roy 2.50 6.00
ST5 Dominik Hasek 1.00 2.50
ST6 Eric Lindros .75 2.00
ST7 Jaromir Jagr .75 2.00
ST8 Martin Brodeur 1.25 3.00
ST9 Pavel Bure .60 1.50
ST10 Teemu Selanne .60 1.50

2006-07 Upper Deck Ovation

COMPLETE SET (200) 75.00 125.00
DISTRIBUTED IN FOUR RETAIL TINS
1 Jean-Sebastien Giguere .20 .50
2 Teemu Selanne .25 .60
3 Slava Kozlov .12 .30
4 Brad Boyes .12 .30
5 Hannu Toivonen .25 .60
6 Thomas Vanek .12 .30
7 Ales Kotalik .12 .30
8 Miikka Kiprusoff .25 .60
9 Erik Cole .12 .30
10 Nikolai Khabibulin .25 .60
11 Tuomo Ruutu .12 .30
12 Alex Tanguay .20 .50
13 Jose Theodore .25 .60
14 David Vyborny .12 .30
15 Jason Arnott .12 .30
16 Brendan Shanahan .25 .60
17 Pavel Datsyuk .20 .50
18 Nicklas Lidstrom .25 .60
19 Chris Pronger .20 .50
20 Jarret Stoll .12 .30
21 M-A Pouliot XRC 1.00 2.50
22 Joe Nieuwendyk .20 .50
23 Lubomir Visnovsky .12 .30
24 Manny Fernandez .20 .50
25 Erik Reitz XRC .60 1.50
26 Mike Ribeiro .12 .30
27 Chris Higgins .12 .30
28 Martin Brodeur 1.00 2.50
29 Brian Gionta .12 .30
30 Miroslav Satan .12 .30
31 Jason Blake .12 .30
32 Petr Prucha .12 .30
33 Jason Spezza .30 .75
34 Filip Novak XRC .60 1.50
35 Simon Gagne .25 .60
36 Robert Esche .20 .50
37 Ryan Potulny XRC 1.00 2.50
38 Mike Comrie .12 .30
39 Bill Thomas XRC .60 1.50
40 Marc-Andre Fleury .25 .60
41 Sergei Gonchar .12 .30
42 Evgeni Nabokov .20 .50
43 Keith Tkachuk .20 .50
44 Martin St. Louis .20 .50
45 Mike Commodore .12 .30
46 Bryan McCabe .12 .30
47 Alexander Steen .20 .50
48 Markus Naslund .25 .60
49 Ed Jovanovski .12 .30
50 Dainius Zubrus .12 .30
51 Scott Niedermayer .12 .30
52 Joffrey Lupul .12 .30
53 Ilya Kovalchuk .30 .75
54 Brian Leetch .25 .60
55 Marco Sturm .12 .30
56 Martin Biron .20 .50
57 Dion Phaneuf .30 .75
58 Daymond Langkow .12 .30
59 Cam Ward .25 .60
60 Kyle Calder .12 .30
61 Dustin Byfuglien XRC .60 1.50
62 Milan Hejduk .12 .30
63 Rick Nash .25 .60
64 Sergei Fedorov .25 .60
65 Nikolai Zherdev .12 .30
66 Sergei Zubov .12 .30
67 Henrik Zetterberg .25 .60
68 Kris Draper .12 .30
69 Tomas Kopecky XRC 1.00 2.50
70 Dwayne Roloson .25 .60
71 Roberto Luongo .30 .75
72 Jay Bouwmeester .12 .30
73 Nathan Horton .12 .30
74 Mathieu Garon .20 .50
75 Pierre-Marc Bouchard .12 .30
76 Cristobal Huet .30 .75
77 Steve Sullivan .12 .30
78 Scott Gomez .12 .30
79 Alexei Yashin .12 .30
80 Mike York .12 .30
81 Ryan Caldwell XRC .60 1.50
82 Jaromir Jagr .40 1.00
83 Jason Spezza .25 .60
84 Ray Emery .20 .50
85 Jeff Carter .25 .60
86 Mike Knuble .12 .30
87 Keith Ballard .12 .30
88 Joel Perrault XRC .60 1.50
89 John LeClair .20 .50
90 Joe Thornton .40 1.00
91 Matt Carle XRC 1.00 2.50
92 Scott Young .12 .30
93 Vincent Lecavalier .25 .60
94 Brad Richards .20 .50
95 Vaclav Prospal .12 .30
96 Darcy Tucker .12 .30
97 Ian White XRC .60 1.50
98 Brendan Morrison .12 .30
99 Olaf Kolzig .25 .60
100 Jeff Halpern .12 .30
101 Corey Perry .20 .50
102 Ryan Getzlaf .20 .50
103 Kari Lehtonen .25 .60
104 Marian Hossa .20 .50
105 Tim Thomas .20 .50
106 Mark Stuart XRC .60 1.50
107 Ryan Miller .25 .60
108 Maxim Afinogenov .12 .30
109 Chuck Kobasew .12 .30
110 Carsen Germyn XRC 1.00 2.50
111 Eric Staal .25 .60
112 Rod Brind`Amour .20 .50
113 Mark Bell .12 .30
114 Rob Blake .20 .50
115 Pascal Leclaire .20 .50
116 Mike Modano .25 .60
117 Brenden Morrow .20 .50
118 Jussi Jokinen .12 .30
119 Tomas Holmstrom .12 .30
120 Ryan Smyth .20 .50
121 Raffi Torres .12 .30
122 Alexander Frolov .12 .30
123 Mike Cammalleri .12 .30
124 Konstantin Pushkarev XRC .60 1.50
125 Marian Gaborik .30 .75
126 Brian Rolston .12 .30
127 Alex Kovalev .12 .30
128 Tomas Vokoun .20 .50
129 Scott Hartnell .12 .30
130 Brian Rafalski .12 .30
131 Henrik Lundqvist .30 .75
132 Michael Nylander .12 .30
133 David Liffiton XRC .60 1.50
134 Daniel Alfredsson .20 .50
135 Wade Redden .12 .30
136 Billy Thompson XRC 1.00 2.50
137 Peter Forsberg .40 1.00
138 Keith Primeau .12 .30
139 Ladislav Nagy .12 .30
140 Sidney Crosby 4.00 10.00
141 Jonathan Cheechoo .25 .60
142 Vesa Toskala .20 .50
143 Petr Cajanek .12 .30
144 Fredrik Modin .12 .30
145 Mats Sundin .25 .60
146 Kyle Wellwood .12 .30
147 Alexander Steen .20 .50
148 Brendan Bell .12 .30
149 Daniel Sedin .12 .30
150 Eric Fehr XRC 1.00 2.50
151 Marc Savard .12 .30
152 Patrice Bergeron .25 .60
153 Glen Murray .12 .30
154 Phil Kessel XRC 2.00 5.00
155 Chris Drury .12 .30
156 Daniel Briere .20 .50
157 Jarome Iginla .30 .75
158 Doug Weight .12 .30
159 Justin Williams .12 .30
160 Brent Seabrook .12 .30
161 Joe Sakic .50 1.25
162 Marek Svatos .12 .30
163 Paul Stastny XRC 4.00 10.00
164 Marty Turco .20 .50
165 Jere Lehtinen .12 .30
166 Fernando Pisani .12 .30
167 Ales Hemsky .12 .30
168 Shawn Horcoff .12 .30
169 Olli Jokinen .12 .30
170 Pavol Demitra .12 .30
171 Mikko Koivu .12 .30
172 Guillaume Latendresse XRC 2.50 6.00
173 Saku Koivu .25 .60
174 Michael Ryder .20 .50
175 David Aebischer .20 .50
176 Paul Kariya .25 .60
177 Mike Sillinger .12 .30
178 Shea Weber XRC 1.00 2.50
179 Patrik Elias .12 .30
180 Rick DiPietro .20 .50
181 Steve Regier XRC .60 1.50
182 Masi Marjamaki XRC .60 1.50
183 Martin Straka .12 .30
184 Jarkko Immonen XRC .60 1.50
185 Patrick O'Sullivan XRC 1.00 2.50
186 Martin Havlat .20 .50
187 Antero Niittymaki .20 .50
188 Shane Doan .12 .30
189 Curtis Joseph .25 .60
190 Colby Armstrong .12 .30
191 Jordan Staal XRC 6.00 15.00
192 Evgeni Malkin XRC 8.00 20.00
193 Patrick Marleau .20 .50
194 Steve Bernier .12 .30
195 Curtis Sanford .20 .50
196 Ruslan Fedotenko .12 .30
197 Andrew Raycroft .20 .50
198 Henrik Sedin .12 .30
199 Luc Bourdon XRC 1.00 2.50
200 Alexander Ovechkin 2.00 5.00

2001 Upper Deck Pearson Awards

These three extremely rare cards were handed out only to attendees of the 2001 NHLPA Pearson Awards Banquet. It is commonly believed that most were either thrown out or stashed away, and that very few got into circulation within the hobby.

COMPLETE SET (3) 400.00 700.00
1 Jaromir Jagr 100.00 200.00
2 Mario Lemieux 200.00 400.00
3 Joe Sakic 100.00 200.00

2002 Upper Deck Pearson Awards

Like the set from the previous year, these three cards were available exclusively to attendees of the annual NHLPA Pearson Awards Banquet. Their relative scarcity makes them very unique and desirable.

COMPLETE SET (3) 250.00 500.00
1 Patrick Roy 200.00 400.00
2 Jarome Iginla 75.00 150.00
3 Sean Burke 30.00 75.00

2004 Upper Deck Pearson Awards

Like the sets from previous years, these three cards were available exclusively to attendees of the annual NHLPA Pearson Awards Banquet. Their relative scarcity makes them very unique and desirable.

COMPLETE SET (3) 250.00 400.00
1 Joe Sakic 100.00 200.00
2 Martin St.Louis 30.00 75.00
3 Roberto Luongo 100.00 200.00

1999 Upper Deck PowerDeck Athletes of the Century

4 Wayne Gretzky

1999-00 Upper Deck PowerDeck

The 1999-00 Upper Deck PowerDeck set was released as a 20-card base set featuring digital CD cards. Packaged at four cards per pack and 24-packs per box, PowerDeck carried a suggested retail price of $4.99. Auxiliary parallels were released as a paper parallel to the CD base cards, this 20-card set is randomly inserted in packs. The card backs carry an "AUX" prefix.

COMPLETE SET (20) 25.00 60.00
1 Paul Kariya 1.25 3.00
2 Teemu Selanne 1.25 3.00
3 Patrik Stefan 1.00 2.50
4 Ray Bourque 2.00 5.00
5 Sergei Samsonov 1.25 3.00
6 Dominik Hasek 2.00 5.00
7 Peter Forsberg 2.00 5.00
8 Patrick Roy 5.00 12.00
9 Brett Hull 1.50 4.00
10 Mike Modano 2.00 5.00
11 Steve Yzerman 4.00 10.00
12 Pavel Bure 1.25 3.00
13 David Legwand 1.00 2.50
14 Martin Brodeur 2.50 6.00
15 Theo Fleury 1.25 3.00
16 Eric Lindros 1.25 3.00
17 Jaromir Jagr 1.50 4.00
18 Bobby Orr 6.00 15.00
19 Gordie Howe 4.00 10.00
20 Wayne Gretzky 6.00 15.00

1999-00 Upper Deck PowerDeck Auxiliary

Released as a paper parallel to the CD base cards, this 20-card set is randomly inserted in packs. The card backs carry an "AUX" prefix.

COMPLETE SET (20) 30.00 60.00
*AUXILARY: .2X TO .5X BASE CARD HI

1999-00 Upper Deck PowerDeck Auxiliary 1 of 1

Randomly inserted in packs, this 20-card paper parallel set is serial numbered one of one.

PRINT RUN 1 SER.#'d SET
NOT PRICED DUE TO SCARCITY
1 Paul Kariya
2 Teemu Selanne
3 Patrik Stefan
4 Ray Bourque
5 Sergei Samsonov
6 Dominik Hasek
7 Peter Forsberg
8 Patrick Roy
9 Brett Hull
10 Mike Modano
11 Steve Yzerman
12 Pavel Bure
13 David Legwand
14 Martin Brodeur
15 Theo Fleury
16 Eric Lindros
17 Jaromir Jagr
18 Bobby Orr
19 Gordie Howe
20 Wayne Gretzky

1999-00 Upper Deck PowerDeck Powerful Moments

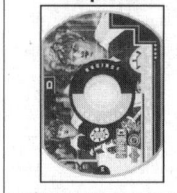

Randomly inserted in packs at 1:23, this 4-card CD set features great moments from Wayne Gretzky's career. The card backs carry a "PM" prefix.

COMPLETE SET (4) 20.00 40.00
COMMON CARD (PM1-PM4) 6.00 15.00
*AUXILIARY: SAME VALUE

1999-00 Upper Deck PowerDeck Time Capsule

Randomly inserted in packs at 1:7, this 8-card CD set features a digital flashback of current players as well as some of yesterday's greats. Card backs carry a "T" prefix. Auxiliary parallels were released as a paper parallels to the CD base cards, and inserted at 1:7.

COMPLETE SET (8) 20.00 50.00
*AUXILARY: SAME VALUE
T1 Jaromir Jagr 2.00 5.00
T2 Paul Kariya 2.00 5.00
T3 Patrick Roy 6.00 15.00
T4 Bobby Orr 8.00 20.00
T5 Dominik Hasek 3.00 8.00
T6 Gordie Howe 4.00 10.00
T7 Brett Hull 2.00 5.00
T8 Steve Yzerman 5.00 12.00

1999-00 Upper Deck Retro

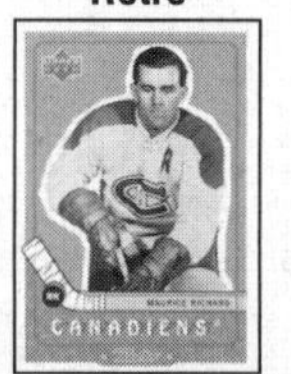

Released as a 109-card set, Upper Deck Retro features players from both today and yesterday on a "throwback" style base card enhanced with bronze foil stamping. Each Retro box was packaged in an actual Wayne Gretzky lunchbox, contained 24-packs per box with six cards per pack and carried a suggested retail price of $4.99. Card number 82 was supposed to be Gordie Howe, but a licensing agreement was never reached. A few of the Howe cards are known to exist with a crimp of Jeff Gordon over Howe's head.

COMPLETE SET (109) 20.00 40.00
1 Paul Kariya .20 .50
2 Teemu Selanne .20 .50
3 Jim McKenzie .02 .10
4 Ray Bourque .20 .50
5 Sergei Samsonov .15 .40
6 Joe Thornton .20 .50
7 Dominik Hasek .40 1.00
8 Miroslav Satan .15 .40
9 Michael Peca .15 .40
10 Todd Simpson .02 .10
11 Valeri Bure .02 .10
12 Jarome Iginla .25 .60
13 Kent Manderville .15 .60
14 Keith Primeau .02 .10
15 Sami Kapanen .02 .10
16 Mark Janssens .02 .10
17 Tony Amonte .15 .40
18 Doug Gilmour .15 .40

19 Peter Forsberg .50 1.25
20 Patrick Roy 1.00 2.50
21 Joe Sakic .40 1.00
22 Theo Fleury .02 .10
23 Chris Drury .15 .40
24 Mike Modano .20 .50
25 Brett Hull .20 .50
26 Ed Belfour .20 .50
27 Steve Yzerman 1.00 2.50
28 Sergei Fedorov .30 .75
29 Brendan Shanahan .20 .50
30 Chris Chelios .20 .50
31 Doug Weight .15 .40
32 Bill Guerin .15 .40
33 Tom Poti .02 .10
34 Gord Murphy .02 .10
35 Pavel Bure .20 .50
36 Mark Parrish .02 .10
37 Rob Blake .15 .40
38 Pavel Rosa .02 .10
39 Luc Robitaille .15 .40
40 Stephane Quintal .02 .10
41 Saku Koivu .20 .50
42 Bob Boughner .02 .10
43 David Legwand .15 .40
44 Mike Dunham .15 .40
45 Martin Brodeur .50 1.25
46 Scott Stevens .15 .40
47 John Madden RC .20 .50
48 Vadim Sharifijanov .02 .10
49 Wayne Gretzky 1.25 3.00
50 Manny Malhotra .02 .10
51 Brian Leetch .15 .40
52 Mike Richter .20 .50
53 Eric Brewer .02 .10
54 Alexei Yashin .02 .10
55 Marian Hossa .20 .50
56 Chris Phillips .02 .10
57 Eric Lindros .20 .50
58 John LeClair .20 .50
59 Mark Recchi .15 .40
60 Jeremy Roenick .30 .75
61 Keith Tkachuk .20 .50
62 Nikolai Khabibulin .15 .40
63 Robert Esche RC .15 .40
64 Jaromir Jagr .30 .75
65 Martin Straka .02 .10
66 Jeff Friesen .02 .10
67 Vincent Damphousse .02 .10
68 Chris Pronger .15 .40
69 Pavol Demitra .15 .40
70 Al MacInnis .15 .40
71 Paul Mara .02 .10
72 Vincent Lecavalier .20 .50
73 Sergei Berezin .02 .10
74 Mats Sundin .20 .50
75 Curtis Joseph .20 .50
76 Markus Naslund .20 .50
77 Mark Messier .20 .50
78 Bill Muckalt .02 .10
79 Peter Bondra .20 .50
80 Adam Oates .15 .40
81 Bobby Orr 1.00 2.50
82 UNLICENSED
83 Mario Lemieux 1.00 2.50
84 Maurice Richard .50 1.25
85 Jean Beliveau .20 .50
86 Bobby Hull .40 1.00
87 Terry Sawchuk .40 1.00
88 Eddie Shore .15 .60
89 Alex Delvecchio .15 .60
90 Jacques Plante .15 .60
91 Stan Mikita .20 .50
92 Gerry Cheevers .40 1.00
93 Glenn Hall .15 .60
94 Phil Esposito .40 1.00
95 Lanny McDonald .15 .60
96 Mike Bossy .15 .60
97 Ted Lindsay .15 .60
98 Red Kelly .15 .60
99 Bobby Clarke .15 .60
100 Larry Robinson .15 .60
101 Ken Dryden .50 1.25
102 Vladislav Tretiak RC .50 1.25
103 Marcel Dionne .15 .60
104 Bernie Geoffrion .20 .50
105 Johnny Bucyk .15 .60
106 Brad Park .15 .60
107 Tony Esposito .20 .50
108 Jari Kurri .15 .60
109 Henri Richard .15 .60
110 Mike Gartner .15 .60

1999-00 Upper Deck Retro Gold

Randomly inserted in packs, this 109-card set parallels the base Retro set and is enhanced with gold foil highlights. Each card is sequentially numbered to 150.
*STARS: 20X TO 50X BASIC CARDS

1999-00 Upper Deck Retro Platinum

Randomly inserted in packs, this 109-card set parallels the base Retro set and is enhanced with platinum silver foil highlights. Each card is numbered one of one.
NOT PRICED DUE TO SCARCITY

1999-00 Upper Deck Retro Distant Replay

Randomly inserted in packs at the rate on 1:11, this 14-card set features black and white photography on a card enhanced with gold foil highlights. Card number DR11 was not released. Level 2 parallels were also released and inserted randomly, these cards were numbered out of 100.
COMPLETE SET (14) 30.00 60.00
*LEVEL 2: 6X TO 15X BASIC CARDS
DR1 Ray Bourque 1.50 4.00
DR2 Martin Brodeur 2.50 6.00
DR3 Jaromir Jagr 1.50 4.00
DR4 Paul Kariya 1.00 2.50
DR5 Steve Yzerman 5.00 12.00
DR6 Mark Messier 1.00 2.50
DR7 Patrick Roy 5.00 12.00
DR8 Dominik Hasek 2.50 5.00
DR9 Wayne Gretzky 6.00 15.00
DR10 Bobby Orr 5.00 12.00
DR11 NOT RELEASED
DR12 Mario Lemieux 5.00 12.00
DR13 Lanny McDonald 1.00 2.50
DR14 Maurice Richard 3.00 8.00
DR15 Vladislav Tretiak 2.00 5.00

1999-00 Upper Deck Retro Epic Gretzky

Randomly inserted in packs at the rate of 1:23, this 10-card set spotlights Wayne Gretzky. Base cards feature action photography set against a blue background with gold foil highlights. Level 2 parallels were also released and inserted randomly, these cards were numbered out of 50.
COMPLETE SET (10) 75.00 150.00
COMMON GRETZKY (EG1-EG10) 8.00 15.00
COMMON LEVEL 2 50.00 125.00

1999-00 Upper Deck Retro Generation

Randomly inserted in packs at the rate of 1:3, this 29-card set features tow players of the past on separate cards paired with another card featuring a player of today who has assumed a modern day role of a legend. Card number G2A was not released. Level 2 parallels were also released and inserted randomly, these cards were numbered out of 500.
COMPLETE SET (29) 20.00 40.00
*LEVEL 2: 1.5X TO 4X BASIC CARDS
G1A Bobby Orr 2.50 6.00
G1B Brian Leetch .40 1.00
G1C Bryan Berard .40 1.00
G2A NOT RELEASED
G2B Bobby Clarke .50 2.00
G2C Keith Tkachuk .50 2.00
G3A Glenn Hall .50 2.00
G3B Patrick Roy 2.50 6.00
G3C Jean-Marc Pelletier .40 1.00
G4A Eddie Shore .50 2.00
G4B Bobby Orr 2.50 6.00
G4C Ray Bourque .50 2.00
G5A Jean Beliveau 1.00 2.50
G5B Mario Lemieux 2.50 6.00
G5C Vincent Lecavalier .50 2.00
G6A Maurice Richard 1.50 4.00
G6B Pavel Bure .50 2.00
G6C Sergei Samsonov .40 1.00
G7A Stan Mikita 1.00 2.50
G7B Theo Fleury .40 1.00
G7C Paul Kariya .50 2.00
G8A Jari Kurri .50 2.00
G8B Teemu Selanne .50 2.00
G8C Olli Jokinen .40 1.00
G9A Phil Esposito 1.25 3.00
G9B Brendan Shanahan .50 2.00
G9C Mark Parrish .40 1.00
G10A Terry Sawchuk 1.25 3.00
G10B Dominik Hasek 1.00 2.50
G10C J-S Giguere .40 1.00

1999-00 Upper Deck Retro Inkredible

Randomly inserted in packs at the rate of 1:23, this 29-card set features authentic player autographs.
AD Alex Delvecchio 8.00 20.00
BC Bobby Clarke 12.50 30.00
BG Bernie Geoffrion 15.00 40.00
BO Bobby Orr 175.00 300.00
BP Brad Park 8.00 20.00
DW Doug Weight 4.00 10.00
GC Gerry Cheevers 12.50 30.00
KP Keith Primeau 4.00 10.00
LM Lanny McDonald 8.00 20.00
MB Mike Bossy 8.00 20.00
MD Marcel Dionne 8.00 20.00
ML Mario Lemieux 150.00 250.00
PE Phil Esposito 15.00 40.00
RB Ray Bourque 30.00 80.00
SM Stan Mikita 10.00 25.00
SS Sergei Samsonov 4.00 10.00
SY Steve Yzerman 50.00 100.00
TA Tony Amonte 4.00 10.00
TE Tony Esposito 10.00 25.00
TL Ted Lindsay 8.00 20.00
VL Vincent Lecavalier 12.50 30.00
VT Vladislav Tretiak 25.00 60.00
WG Wayne Gretzky 200.00 400.00
BOH Bobby Hull 15.00 40.00
BRH Brett Hull 12.00 40.00
JEB Jean Beliveau 15.00 40.00
JOB John Bucyk 8.00 20.00
MAR Maurice Richard 75.00 200.00
PAB Pavel Bure 8.00 20.00

1999-00 Upper Deck Retro Inkredible Level 2

Parallel to the regular Inkredible set, these cards are randomly inserted into packs, and feature a serial number out of 25.
*STARS: 2.5X TO 6X BASIC INSERTS
BO Bobby Orr 250.00 600.00
ML Mario Lemieux 150.00 400.00
SY Steve Yzerman 200.00 400.00
WG Wayne Gretzky 400.00 800.00
MAR Maurice Richard 150.00 400.00

1999-00 Upper Deck Retro Lunchboxes

Each box of Retro was packaged in a Wayne Gretzky lunchbox showcasing the great one in his Kings, Oilers, Ranger jerseys, as well as a special tribute lunchbox.
COMPLETE SET (4) 35.00 70.00
1 Wayne Gretzky Kings 7.50 15.00
2 Wayne Gretzky Oilers 7.50 15.00
3 Wayne Gretzky Rangers 7.50 15.00
4 Wayne Gretzky Tribute 15.00 35.00

1999-00 Upper Deck Retro Memento

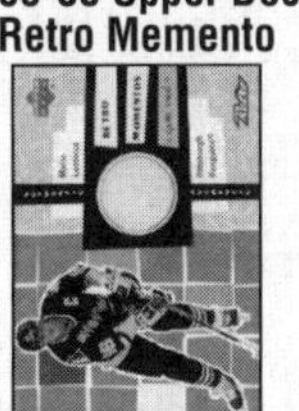

Randomly inserted in packs, this 5-card set features hockey's greats coupled with a swatch of game used memorabilia.
RM1 Wayne Gretzky 75.00 200.00
RM2 Marcel Dionne 12.50 30.00
RM3 Mario Lemieux 50.00 125.00
RM4 Phil Esposito 40.00 100.00
RM5 Ken Dryden 60.00 150.00

1999-00 Upper Deck Retro Turn of the Century

Randomly inserted in packs at the rate of 1:23, this 14-card set features Light F/X holofoil technology and players from the past and present.
COMPLETE SET (14) 40.00 80.00
TC1 Vincent Lecavalier 2.00 5.00
TC2 Martin Brodeur 2.50 6.00
TC3 Jaromir Jagr 1.50 4.00
TC4 Paul Kariya 2.00 5.00
TC5 Steve Yzerman 5.00 12.00
TC6 Ray Bourque 1.50 4.00
TC7 Patrick Roy 5.00 12.00
TC8 Dominik Hasek 2.00 5.00
TC9 Wayne Gretzky 6.00 15.00
TC10 Bobby Clarke .60 1.50
TC11 Larry Robinson .60 1.50
TC12 NOT RELEASED
TC13 Mario Lemieux 5.00 12.00
TC14 Maurice Richard 2.50 6.00
TC15 Bobby Orr 5.00 12.00

2007 Upper Deck Rookie Class

COMPLETE SET (50) 6.00 15.00
1 Shea Weber .30 .75
2 Matt Carle .30 .75
3 Patrick O'Sullivan .40 1.00
4 Phil Kessel .75 2.00
5 Guillaume Latendresse .75 2.00
6 Loui Eriksson .30 .75
7 Luc Bourdon .30 .75
8 Enver Lisin .10 .25
9 Evgeni Malkin 2.00 5.00
10 Dustin Boyd .30 .75
11 Mark Stuart .10 .25
12 Eric Fehr .10 .25
13 Noah Welch .10 .25
14 Anze Kopitar 1.25 3.00
15 Travis Zajac .40 1.00
16 Jordan Staal 1.50 4.00
17 Ladislav Smid .10 .25
18 Alexander Radulov .75 2.00
19 Ryan Potulny .10 .25
20 Marc-Antoine Pouliot .10 .25
21 Jarkko Immonen .10 .25
22 Paul Stastny 1.25 3.00
23 Alexei Kaigorodov .10 .25
24 Dave Bolland .10 .25
25 Nigel Dawes .10 .25
26 Jeremy Williams .10 .25
27 Marc-Edouard Vlasic .10 .25
28 Keith Yandle .10 .25
29 Matt Lashoff .10 .25
30 Ian White .10 .25
31 Alexei Mikhnov .10 .25
32 Tomas Kopecky .20 .50
33 Konstantin Pushkaryov .10 .25
34 Kristopher Letang .10 .25
35 Michael Blunden .10 .25
36 Brandon Prust .10 .25
37 Dustin Byfuglien .10 .25
38 Ben Ondrus .10 .25
39 Brendan Bell .10 .25
40 Janis Sprukts .10 .25
41 Ryan Shannon .10 .25
42 Shane O'Brien .10 .25
43 Patrick Thoresen .10 .25
44 Nathan McIver .10 .25
45 Drew Stafford .60 1.50
46 Alexander Edler .10 .25
47 Yan Stastny .10 .25
48 Kelly Guard .10 .25
49 Nate Thompson .10 .25
50 Adam Burish .10 .25

2000-01 Upper Deck Rookie Update

This product updated several Upper Deck sets. All cards are listed with their parent set.
CARDS LISTED UNDER ORIGINAL BASE SETS

2001-02 Upper Deck Rookie Update

Released in early May 2002, this product updated earlier Upper Deck products and carried an SRP of $4.99 for a 3-card pack.. Updates cards for SPx, Top Shelf, Ice, MVP and Victory were randomly inserted along with various inserts. All cards from this product can be found listed under their original base sets.
CARDS LISTED UNDER ORIGINAL BASE SETS

2001-02 Upper Deck Rookie Update Signs of History

This limited autograph card was randomly inserted into packs of UD Rookie Update. Little is known about the card other than it's serial-numbered out of 33.
STATED PRINT RUN 33 SER.#'d SETS
1 Patrick Roy AU

2002-03 Upper Deck Rookie Update

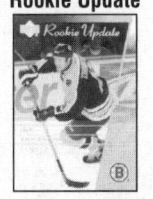

Released in May 2003, Rookie Update consisted of a 176-card base set, a jersey card insert set, an autograph insert set and update cards for SP Authentic, SPx, UD Foundations and UD Classic Portraits. In the base set, cards 101-116 were serial-numbered to 999, cards 117-148 and 173-176 were serial-numbered to 1500, and cards 163-171 were serial-numbered to 199. Cards 163-171 carried dual autographs. Cards 149-162 had three different versions, A, B and C. Each version was serial-numbered with the 'A' cards being serial-numbered from 1 to 400; the 'B' cards being serial-numbered 401-800 and the 'C' versions serial-numbered 801-1200 for a total of 1200 cards. Cards 149-162 carried jersey swatches of each player pictured.
COMP.SET w/o SP's (100) 20.00 40.00
1 Paul Kariya .30 .75
2 Adam Oates .25 .60
3 J-S Giguere .25 .60
4 Sandis Ozolinsh .10 .25
5 Dany Heatley .40 1.00
6 Ilya Kovalchuk .40 1.00
7 Patrik Stefan .10 .25
8 Dan McGillis .10 .25
9 Joe Thornton .50 1.25
10 Sergei Samsonov .25 .60
11 Jeff Hackett .25 .60
12 Glen Murray .10 .25
13 Miroslav Satan .25 .60
14 Martin Biron .25 .60
15 Daniel Briere .10 .25
16 Chris Drury .25 .60
17 Jarome Iginla .40 1.00
18 Roman Turek .25 .60
19 Pavel Brendl .25 .60
20 Rod Brind'Amour .25 .60
21 Ron Francis .25 .60
22 Tyler Arnason .25 .60
23 Jocelyn Thibault .25 .60
24 Bryan Marchment .10 .25
25 Joe Sakic .60 1.50
26 Peter Forsberg .75 2.00
27 Patrick Roy 1.50 4.00
28 Rob Blake .25 .60
29 Geoff Sanderson .10 .25
30 Marc Denis .25 .60
31 Mike Modano .50 1.25
32 Bill Guerin .25 .60
33 Marty Turco .25 .60
34 Steve Yzerman 1.50 4.00
35 Brendan Shanahan .30 .75
36 Brett Hull .40 1.00
37 Curtis Joseph .30 .75
38 Nicklas Lidstrom .30 .75
39 Sergei Fedorov .50 1.25
40 Mathieu Schneider .10 .25
41 Mike Comrie .25 .60
42 Tommy Salo .25 .60
43 Olli Jokinen .25 .60
44 Kristian Huselius .10 .25
45 Roberto Luongo .40 1.00
46 Adam Deadmarsh .25 .60
47 Zigmund Palffy .25 .60
48 Felix Potvin .30 .75
49 Marian Gaborik .60 1.50
50 Gordie Howe 1.50 4.00
51 Pascal Dupuis .10 .25
52 Saku Koivu .30 .75
53 Marcel Hossa .10 .25
54 Jose Theodore .40 1.00
55 David Legwand .25 .60
56 Scott Hartnell .10 .25
57 Tomas Vokoun .25 .60
58 John Madden .10 .25
59 Scott Gomez .10 .25
60 Martin Brodeur .75 2.00
61 Alexei Yashin .10 .25
62 Mark Parrish .10 .25
63 Janne Niinimaa .10 .25
64 Alex Kovalev .25 .60
65 Pavel Bure .30 .75
66 Mike Dunham .25 .60
67 Mark Messier .30 .75
68 Brian Leetch .25 .60
69 Daniel Alfredsson .25 .60
70 Marian Hossa .30 .75
71 Patrick Lalime .25 .60
72 Jeremy Roenick .40 1.00
73 John LeClair .30 .75
74 Tony Amonte .25 .60
75 Gordie Howe 1.50 4.00
76 Roman Cechmanek .25 .60
77 Brian Boucher .25 .60
78 Shane Doan .10 .25
79 Mario Lemieux 2.00 5.00
80 Martin Straka .10 .25
81 Sebastien Caron .25 .60
82 Alexei Morozov .10 .25
83 Doug Weight .30 .75
84 Keith Tkachuk .30 .75
85 Chris Osgood .25 .60
86 Teemu Selanne .30 .75
87 Kyle McLaren .10 .25
88 Evgeni Nabokov .25 .60
89 Martin St. Louis .25 .60
90 Nikolai Khabibulin .30 .75
91 Doug Gilmour .25 .60
92 Mats Sundin .30 .75
93 Owen Nolan .25 .60
94 Ed Belfour .30 .75
95 Todd Bertuzzi .30 .75
96 Markus Naslund .30 .75
97 Dan Cloutier .25 .60
98 Jaromir Jagr .50 1.25
99 Olaf Kolzig .25 .60
100 Michael Nylander .10 .25
101 Gordie Howe RRM 3.00 8.00
102 Wayne Gretzky RRM 4.00 10.00
103 Bobby Orr RRM 8.00 20.00
104 Patrick Roy RRM 3.00 8.00
105 Mario Lemieux RRM 4.00 10.00
106 Joe Thornton RRM 1.00 2.50
107 Martin Brodeur RRM 1.50 4.00
108 Steve Yzerman RRM 3.00 8.00
109 Jaromir Jagr RRM 1.00 2.50
110 Paul Kariya RRM .60 1.50
111 Jarome Iginla RRM 1.00 2.50
112 Joe Sakic RRM 1.25 3.00
113 Mats Sundin RRM .60 1.50
114 Ilya Kovalchuk RRM .75 2.00
115 Marian Gaborik RRM .75 2.00
116 Mike Modano RRM 1.00 2.50
117 Carlo Colaiacovo RC 2.00 5.00
118 Jay Bouwmeester RC 4.00 10.00
119 Ari Ahonen RC 3.00 8.00
120 Patrick Boileau RC 2.00 5.00
121 Mike Komisarek RC 4.00 10.00
122 Cristobal Huet RC 8.00 20.00
123 Josh Harding RC 12.00 30.00
124 Chris Schmidt RC 3.00 5.00
125 Niko Dimitrakos RC 2.00 5.00
126 Ryan Bayda RC 2.00 5.00
127 Radoslav Hecl RC 2.00 5.00
128 Burke Henry RC 2.00 5.00
129 Frederic Cloutier RC 2.00 5.00
130 Tomas Kurka RC 2.00 5.00
131 John Tripp RC 2.00 5.00
132 Francois Beauchemin RC 2.00 5.00
133 Brandon Reid RC 3.00 8.00
134 Tomas Surovy RC 2.00 8.00
135 Chad Wiseman RC 2.00 5.00
136 Jason Bacashihua RC 4.00 10.00
137 Jesse Fibiger RC 2.00 5.00
138 Marc-Andre Bergeron RC 2.00 5.00
139 Ryan Miller RC 12.00 30.00
140 Ryan Kraft RC 2.00 5.00
141 Simon Gamache RC 2.00 5.00
142 Rob Davison RC 2.00 5.00
143 Jason King RC 3.00 8.00
144 Brad Defauw RC 2.00 5.00
145 Miroslav Zalesak RC 2.00 5.00
146 Sean McMorrow RC 2.00 5.00
147 Mike Siklenka RC 2.00 5.00
148 Doug Janik RC 2.00 5.00
149A A.Svitov RC/B.Shanahan 4.00 10.00
149B A.Svitov RC/T.Bertuzzi 4.00 10.00
149C A.Svitov RC/J.LeClair 4.00 10.00
150A A.Smirnov RC/A.Yashin 4.00 10.00
150B A.Smirnov RC/T.Bertuzzi 4.00 10.00
150C A.Smirnov RC/J.LeClair 4.00 10.00
151A B.Orpik RC/R.Blake 4.00 10.00
151B B.Orpik RC/E.Jovanoski 4.00 10.00
151C B.Orpik RC/S.Stevens 4.00 10.00
152A A.Hall RC/J.LeClair 4.00 10.00
152B A.Hall RC/A.Deadmarsh 4.00 10.00
152C A.Hall RC/J.Iginla 6.00 15.00
153A J.Taffe RC/C.Drury 4.00 10.00
153B J.Taffe RC/M.York 4.00 10.00
153C J.Taffe RC/J.Roenick 4.00 10.00
154A S.Eminger RC/N.Lidstrom 6.00 15.00
154B S.Eminger RC/S.Gonchar 4.00 10.00
154C S.Eminger RC/B.Leetch 4.00 10.00
155A J.Leopold RC/A.MacInnis 4.00 10.00
155B J.Leopold RC/B.Leetch 6.00 15.00
155C J.Leopold RC/S.Niedermayer 4.00 10.00
156A P.Sharp RC/S.Reinprecht 4.00 10.00
156B P.Sharp RC/M.Peca 4.00 10.00
156C P.Sharp RC/J.Roenick 6.00 15.00
157A S.Ott RC/P.Kariya 6.00 15.00
157B S.Ott RC/S.Samsonov 4.00 10.00
157C S.Ott RC/T.Fleury 4.00 10.00
158A A.Hemsky RC/J.Jagr 10.00 25.00
158B A.Hemsky RC/M.Hejduk 8.00 20.00
158C A.Hemsky RC/P.Elias 8.00 20.00
159A A.Frolov RC/J.LeClair 6.00 15.00
159B A.Frolov RC/A.Yashin 6.00 15.00
159C A.Frolov RC/J.Jagr 10.00 25.00
160A J.Stoll RC/J.LeClair 6.00 15.00
160B J.Stoll RC/K.Tkachuk 6.00 15.00
160C J.Stoll RC/B.Guerin 8.00 20.00
161A A.Volchenkov RC/R.Blake 4.00 10.00
161B A.Volchenkov RC/S.Stevens 4.00 10.00
161C A.Volchenkov RC/E.Jovanoski 4.00 10.00
162A D.Bykov RC/B.Leetch 4.00 10.00
162B D.Bykov RC/N.Lidstrom 6.00 15.00
162C D.Bykov RC/S.Gonchar 4.00 10.00
163 J.Spezza RC/W.Gretzky 300.00 450.00
164 P.Bouchard RC/S.Samsonov 15.00 40.00
165 R.Hainsey RC/R.Bourque 25.00 60.00
166 S.Chistov RC/P.Bure 15.00 40.00
167 C.Kobasew RC/J.Iginla 20.00 50.00
168 H.Zetterberg RC/G.Howe 100.00 200.00
169 S.Upshall RC/M.Comrie 15.00 40.00
170 P.LeClaire RC/P.Roy 75.00 200.00
171 M.Tellqvist RC/E.Belfour 25.00 60.00
172 R.Nash RC/J.Thornton 100.00 200.00
173 Igor Radulov RC 2.00 5.00
174 Paul Gaustad RC 2.00 5.00
175 Christian Backman RC 2.00 5.00
176 Cam Severson RC 3.00 8.00

2002-03 Upper Deck Rookie Update Autographs

Inserted in packs at 1:144, this 29-card set featured authentic player autographs inset vertically on the card fronts. As of press time, not all cards have been verified. Print run totals below were provided by UD, cards with print runs under 25 are not priced due to scarcity.
STATED ODDS 1:144
BO Bobby Orr/9
BR Pavel Brendl 10.00 25.00
CJ Curtis Joseph 20.00 50.00
CK Chuck Kobasew/24
DH Dany Heatley 15.00 40.00
EC Erik Cole 10.00 25.00
GH Gordie Howe/24
HZ Henrik Zetterberg/24
IK Ilya Kovalchuk 15.00 40.00
JA Jason Spezza/24
JB Jay Bouwmeester/24 15.00 40.00
JI Jarome Iginla 15.00 40.00
JL John LeClair 10.00 25.00
MA Maxim Afinogenov 10.00 25.00
MC Mike Comrie 10.00 25.00
MH Martin Havlat 12.50 30.00
MN Markus Naslund 10.00 25.00
MT Mikael Tellqvist/24 60.00 100.00
PB Pavel Bure 10.00 25.00
PM P-M Bouchard/24 20.00 50.00
PR Patrick Roy/24 100.00 150.00
RB Ray Bourque/24 40.00 80.00
RH Ron Hainsey/24 20.00 40.00
SC Stanislav Chistov/24 10.00 25.00
SG Simon Gagne 10.00 25.00
SO Steve Ott 10.00 25.00
SS Sergei Samsonov 10.00 25.00
SY Steve Yzerman 30.00 80.00
WG Wayne Gretzky 100.00 250.00

2002-03 Upper Deck Rookie Update Jerseys

Randomly insrted in packs, this 42-card set consisted of 36 single jersey cards and 6 dual jersey cards. Single jersey cards were serial-numbered out of 299 and dual cards were serial-numbered out of 99.
*MULT.COLOR SWATCH: .75X TO 1.5X
DAY Alexei Yashin 4.00 10.00
DBG Bill Guerin 4.00 10.00
DBS Brendan Shanahan 5.00 12.00
DCO Chris Osgood 4.00 10.00
DDH Dany Heatley 6.00 15.00
DEL Eric Lindros 6.00 15.00
DFP Felix Potvin 5.00 12.00
DHO Marian Hossa 4.00 10.00
DIK Ilya Kovalchuk 6.00 15.00
DJG J-S Giguere 10.00 25.00
DJI Jarome Iginla 6.00 15.00
DJJ Jaromir Jagr 8.00 20.00
DJR Jeremy Roenick 6.00 15.00
DJS Joe Sakic 8.00 20.00
DJT Joe Thornton 8.00 20.00
DKP Keith Primeau 4.00 10.00
DMD Mike Dunham 4.00 10.00
DMH Milan Hejduk 4.00 10.00
DML Mario Lemieux 12.50 30.00
DMM Mike Modano 6.00 15.00
DMS Mats Sundin 4.00 10.00
DOK Olaf Kolzig 4.00 10.00
DPB Pavel Bure 5.00 12.00
DPD Pavol Demitra 4.00 10.00
DPK Paul Kariya 5.00 12.00
DPR Patrick Roy 12.50 30.00
DRC Roman Cechmanek 4.00 10.00
DRL Roberto Luongo 6.00 15.00
DRT Roman Turek 4.00 10.00
DSK Saku Koivu 4.00 10.00
DSS Sergei Samsonov 4.00 10.00
DSY Steve Yzerman 12.50 30.00
DTB Todd Bertuzzi 4.00 10.00
DTH Jose Theodore 6.00 15.00
DTS Tommy Salo 4.00 10.00
DZP Zigmund Palffy 4.00 10.00
SJK Jaromir Jagr 12.50 30.00
Olaf Kolzig
SKH Ilya Kovalchuk 15.00 40.00
Dany Heatley
SLB Eric Lindros 12.50 30.00
Pavel Bure
SRS Patrick Roy 20.00 50.00
Joe Sakic
STS Joe Thornton 12.50 30.00
Sergei Samsonov
SYS Steve Yzerman 20.00 50.00
Brendan Shanahan

2002-03 Upper Deck Rookie Update Jerseys Gold

This 42-card set directly paralleled the base jersey set but featured gold foil highlights. Single jersey cards were serial-numbered to 125 and dual jersey cards were serial-numbered to 10. Dual jersey cards were not priced due to scarcity.
*SINGLE JSY: .6X TO 1.5X BASIC CARD
DUAL JSY NOT PRICED DUE TO SCARCITY

2003-04 Upper Deck Rookie Update

This 217-card set consisted of 90-veteran base cards, 65 base rookies (91-150 and 166-172) numbered to 999, 10 dual-jersey cards (151-158 and 173-174) numbered to 999 that featured both a rookie and a veteran, 8 dual-autograph cards (159-165 and 175) numbered to 199 that featured a rookie and a veteran and an additional 43 rookie cards (176-217) serial-numbered to 199 that were available only via a redemption card good for all 43 cards.
COMP.SET w/o SP's (90) 25.00 50.00
1 Petr Sykora .10 .25
2 J-S Giguere .25 .60
3 Sergei Fedorov .40 1.00
4 Dany Heatley .40 1.00
5 Ilya Kovalchuk .40 1.00
6 Sergei Samsonov .25 .60
7 Joe Thornton .50 1.25
8 Andrew Raycroft .25 .60
9 Chris Drury .25 .60
10 Daniel Briere .10 .25
11 Mika Noronen .25 .60
12 Jarome Iginla .40 1.00
13 Miikka Kiprusoff .25 .60
14 Justin Williams .10 .25
15 Ron Francis .25 .60

16 Jocelyn Thibault .25 .60
17 Bryan Berard .10 .25
18 Mark Bell .10 .25
19 Joe Sakic .60 1.50
20 Paul Kariya .30 .75
21 Peter Forsberg .60 1.50
22 David Aebischer .25 .60
23 Todd Marchant .10 .25
24 Rick Nash .40 1.00
25 Marc Denis .25 .60
26 Bill Guerin .25 .60
27 Marty Turco .25 .60
28 Mike Modano .40 1.00
29 Pavel Datsyuk .30 .75
30 Henrik Zetterberg .30 .75
31 Brett Hull .40 1.00
32 Steve Yzerman 1.50 4.00
33 Adam Oates .25 .60
34 Tommy Salo .25 .60
35 Raffi Torres .10 .25
36 Ales Hemsky .25 .60
37 Roberto Luongo .40 1.00
38 Jay Bouwmeester .10 .25
39 Olli Jokinen .25 .60
40 Martin Straka .10 .25
41 Roman Cechmanek .25 .60
42 Zigmund Palffy .25 .60
43 Marian Gaborik .60 1.50
44 Alexandre Daigle .10 .25
45 Manny Fernandez .25 .60
46 Jose Theodore .40 1.00
47 Saku Koivu .30 .75
48 Mike Ribeiro .10 .25
49 Steve Sullivan .10 .25
50 Tomas Vokoun .25 .60
51 Patrik Elias .25 .60
52 Scott Gomez .10 .25
53 Martin Brodeur .75 2.00
54 Scott Stevens .25 .60
55 Alexei Yashin .10 .25
56 Trent Hunter .10 .25
57 Rick DiPietro .25 .60
58 Jaromir Jagr .50 1.25
59 Mark Messier .30 .75
60 Peter Bondra .25 .60
61 Jason Spezza .30 .75
62 Marian Hossa .30 .75
63 Patrick Lalime .25 .60
64 Sean Burke .25 .60
65 Jeremy Roenick .40 1.00
66 Alexei Zhamnov .10 .25
67 Brian Boucher .25 .60
68 Mike Comrie .25 .60
69 Mario Lemieux 2.00 5.00
70 Sebastien Caron .25 .60
71 Vincent Damphousse .10 .25
72 Evgeni Nabokov .25 .60
73 Patrick Marleau .25 .60
74 Chris Osgood .25 .60
75 Doug Weight .25 .60
76 Pavol Demitra .25 .60
77 Keith Tkachuk .30 .75
78 Nikolai Khabibulin .30 .75
79 Vincent Lecavalier .30 .75
80 Mats Sundin .30 .75
81 Alexander Mogilny .25 .60
82 Owen Nolan .25 .60
83 Ed Belfour .30 .75
84 Todd Bertuzzi .30 .75
85 Ed Jovanovski .25 .60
86 Markus Naslund .30 .75
87 Jason King .10 .25
88 Dan Cloutier .25 .60
89 Anson Carter .25 .60
90 Olaf Kolzig .25 .60
91 Niklas Kronwall RC 4.00 10.00
92 Doug Doull RC 2.00 5.00
93 Fedor Tyutin RC 2.00 5.00
94 Dwayne Zinger RC 2.00 5.00
95 Jason MacDonald RC 2.00 5.00
96 Ryan Malone RC 3.00 8.00
97 Rob Skrlac RC 2.00 5.00
98 Jame Pollock RC 2.00 5.00
99 Grant McNeill RC 2.00 5.00
100 Noah Clarke RC 2.00 5.00
101 Joey MacDonald RC 2.00 5.00
102 John Pohl RC 2.00 5.00
103 Tony Martensson RC 2.00 5.00
104 Antti Miettinen RC 2.00 5.00
105 Ryan Barnes RC 2.00 5.00
106 Graham Mink RC 2.00 5.00
107 Patrick Leahy RC 2.00 5.00
108 Sergei Zinovjev RC 2.00 5.00
109 Steve McLaren RC 2.00 5.00
110 Seamus Kotyk RC 2.00 5.00
111 Tim Jackman RC 2.00 5.00
112 Andrew Hutchinson RC 2.00 5.00
113 Andy Chiodo RC 2.00 5.00
114 Timofei Shishkanov RC 2.00 5.00
115 Milan Michalek RC 4.00 10.00
116 Trevor Daley RC 2.00 5.00
117 Jeff MacMillan RC 2.00 5.00
118 Jason Pominville RC 4.00 10.00
119 Mikko Luoma RC 2.00 5.00
120 Brad Boyes RC 4.00 10.00
121 Michael Morrison RC 2.00 5.00
122 Tomas Plekanec RC 2.00 5.00
123 Mike Stuart RC 2.00 5.00
124 Tuomas Pihlman RC 2.00 5.00
125 Darcy Verot RC 2.00 5.00
126 Mark Popovic RC 2.00 5.00
127 Erik Westrum RC 2.00 5.00
128 Aaron Johnson RC 2.00 5.00
129 Doug Lynch RC 2.00 5.00
130 Randy Jones RC 2.00 5.00
131 Nathan Smith RC 2.00 5.00
132 Aleksander Suglobov RC 2.00 5.00
133 Kyle Wellwood RC 3.00 8.00
134 Chris Kunitz RC 3.00 8.00
135 Jeff Hamilton RC 2.00 5.00
136 Garth Murray RC 2.00 5.00
137 Peter Sejna RC 2.00 5.00
138 Mike Smith RC 6.00 15.00
139 Antero Niittymaki RC 5.00 12.00
140 Carl Corazzini RC 2.00 5.00
141 Anton Babchuk RC 2.00 5.00
142 Julien Vauclair RC 2.00 5.00
143 Nathan Robinson RC 2.00 5.00
144 Dan Ellis RC 2.00 5.00
145 Colton Orr RC 2.00 5.00
146 Rastislav Stana RC 2.00 5.00
147 Gavin Morgan RC 2.00 5.00
148 Dan Hamhuis RC 3.00 8.00
149 Nolan Schaefer RC 2.00 5.00
150 Pat Rissmiller RC 2.00 5.00
151 Bergeron J RC/Thornton J 8.00 20.00
152 J.Hudler J RC/S.Yzerman J 10.0025.00
153 R.Kesler J RC/T.Bertuzzi J 5.00 12.00
154 A.Semin J RC/P.Bure J 8.00 20.00
155 C.Higgins J RC/S.Koivu J 8.00 20.00
156 J.Lupul J RC/S.Fedorov J 6.00 15.00
157 D. Brown J RC/Z.Palffy J 5.00 12.00
158 J.Pitkanen J RC/J. Roenick J 5.00 12.00
159 M.Fleury AU RC/P.Roy AU 200.00 400.00
160 T.Ruutu AU RC/S.Koivu AU 50.00 100.00
161 E.Staal AU RC/W.Gretzky AU 200.00 400.00
162 N.Horton AU RC/G.Howe AU 100.00 200.00
163 N.Zherdev AU RC/R.Nash AU 60.00 125.00
164 F.Sjostrom RC/M.Naslund AU 15.00 40.00
165 J.Tootoo AU RC/O.Nolan AU 20.00 50.00
166 Zbynek Michalek RC 2.00 5.00
167 Lawrence Nycholat RC 2.00 5.00
168 Fred Meyer RC 2.00 5.00
169 Mike Bishai RC 2.00 5.00
170 Mike Green RC 2.00 5.00
171 Matt Ellison RC 2.00 5.00
172 Joe Motzko RC 2.00 5.00
173 Derek Roy JSY RC 4.00 10.00
Chris Drury JSY
174 D.Fritsche J RC/R.Nash J 6.00 15.00
175 Matt Stajan AU RC 30.00 60.00
Owen Nolan AU
176 Kari Lehtonen RC 30.00 80.00
177 Goran Bezina RC 4.00 10.00
178 Owen Fussey RC 4.00 10.00
179 Josh Olson RC 4.00 10.00
180 Michal Barinka RC 4.00 10.00
181 Bryce Lampman RC 4.00 10.00
182 Matt Hussey RC 4.00 10.00
183 Mike Stutzel RC 4.00 10.00
184 Roman Tvrdon RC 4.00 10.00
185 Matthew Yeats RC 4.00 10.00
186 Thomas Pock RC 4.00 10.00
187 Wade Dubielewicz RC 4.00 10.00
188 Greg Mauldin RC 4.00 10.00
189 Mike Pandolfo RC 4.00 10.00
190 Eric Perrin RC 4.00 10.00
191 Christoph Brandner RC 4.00 10.00
192 Matthew Lombardi RC 6.00 15.00
193 John-Michael Liles RC 6.00 15.00
194 Marek Svatos RC 15.00 40.00
195 Tony Salmelainen RC 4.00 10.00
196 Dominic Moore RC 4.00 10.00
197 Brooks Laich RC 4.00 10.00
198 Cory Larose RC 4.00 10.00
199 Adam Munro RC 4.00 10.00
200 Mikhail Kuleshov RC 4.00 10.00
201 Matt Keith RC 4.00 10.00
202 Denis Grebeshkov RC 4.00 10.00
203 Quintin Laing RC 4.00 10.00
204 Benoit Dusablon RC 4.00 10.00
205 Matt Underhill RC 4.00 10.00
206 Jozef Balej RC 4.00 10.00
207 Robert Scuderi RC 4.00 10.00
208 Libor Pivko RC 4.00 10.00
209 Mikhail Yakubov RC 4.00 10.00
210 Tom Preissing RC 4.00 10.00
211 Cody McCormick RC 4.00 10.00
212 Pavel Vorobiev RC 4.00 10.00
213 Matt Murley RC 4.00 10.00
214 Matthew Spiller RC 4.00 10.00
215 Marek Zidlicky RC 4.00 10.00
216 Christian Ehrhoff RC 4.00 10.00
217 Brent Burns RC 6.00 15.00
RR1 Rookie Redemption

2003-04 Upper Deck Rookie Update All-Star Lineup

This 12-card set featured swatches of game-used jersey and each card was serial-numbered out of 25. As of press time, all cards have not been verified.
*MULT.COLOR SWATCH: .5X TO 1.25X
AS1 Martin Brodeur 25.00 60.00
AS2 Ilya Kovalchuk 15.00 40.00
AS3 Joe Thornton 20.00 50.00
AS4 Marian Hossa 10.00 25.00
AS5 Scott Niedermayer 8.00 20.00
AS6 Zdeno Chara
AS7 Marty Turco 8.00 20.00
AS8 Markus Naslund 10.00 25.00
AS9 Joe Sakic 12.50 30.00
AS10 Brett Hull 20.00 50.00
AS11 Rob Blake 12.50 30.00
AS12 Nicklas Lidström 10.00 25.00

2003-04 Upper Deck Rookie Update Skills

*MULT.COLOR SWATCH: .5X TO 1.25X
PRINT RUN 75 SER.#'d SETS
SKJSG J-S Giguere 3.00 8.00
SKAH Ales Hemsky 3.00 8.00
SKAY Alexei Yashin 3.00 8.00
SKBG Bill Guerin 3.00 8.00
SKBH Brett Hull 5.00 12.00
SKCD Chris Drury 3.00 8.00
SKDA David Aebischer 3.00 8.00
SKDH Dany Heatley 5.00 12.00
SKDW Doug Weight 3.00 8.00
SKEB Ed Belfour 4.00 10.00
SKEL Eric Lindros 4.00 10.00
SKGM Glen Murray 3.00 8.00
SKJJ Jaromir Jagr 6.00 15.00
SKJR Jeremy Roenick 5.00 12.00
SKJS Jason Spezza 4.00 10.00
SKJT Jose Theodore 5.00 12.00
SKMB Martin Brodeur 12.50 30.00
SKMF Manny Fernandez 3.00 8.00
SKMG Marian Gaborik 8.00 20.00
SKMH Marian Hossa 4.00 10.00
SKMK Mark Messier 4.00 10.00
SKML Mario Lemieux 12.50 30.00
SKMM Mike Modano 6.00 15.00
SKMN Markus Naslund 4.00 10.00
SKMS Mats Sundin 4.00 10.00
SKMT Marty Turco 3.00 8.00
SKNK Nikolai Khabibulin 4.00 10.00
SKON Owen Nolan 3.00 8.00
SKPF Peter Forsberg 10.00 25.00
SKPK Paul Kariya 4.00 10.00
SKPL Patrick Lalime 3.00 8.00
SKRN Rick Nash 5.00 12.00
SKSA Joe Sakic 8.00 20.00
SKSB Sean Burke 3.00 8.00
SKSF Sergei Fedorov 6.00 15.00
SKSK Saku Koivu 4.00 10.00
SKSY Steve Yzerman 12.50 30.00
SKTA Tony Amonte 4.00 10.00
SKTB Todd Bertuzzi 4.00 10.00
SKTH Joe Thornton 6.00 15.00
SKVL Vincent Lecavalier 3.00 8.00
SKZP Zigmund Palffy 3.00 8.00

2003-04 Upper Deck Rookie Update Super Stars

*MULT.COLOR SWATCH: .5X TO 1.25X
PRINT RUN 75 SER,#'d SETS
SSHJK Milan Hejduk 4.00 10.00
SSMSL Martin St. Louis 3.00 8.00
SSAF Alexander Frolov 3.00 8.00
SSAM Alexander Mogilny 3.00 8.00
SSBH Brett Hull 5.00 12.00
SSBM Brendan Morrison 3.00 8.00
SSDA David Aebischer 3.00 8.00
SSDH Dany Heatley 5.00 12.00
SSDW Doug Weight 3.00 8.00
SSEB Ed Belfour 4.00 10.00
SSGM Glen Murray 3.00 8.00
SSHZ Henrik Zetterberg 4.00 10.00
SSJB Jay Bouwmeester 3.00 8.00
SSJI Jarome Iginla 5.00 12.00
SSJL John LeClair 4.00 10.00
SSJO Joe Sakic 8.00 20.00
SSJR Jeremy Roenick 6.00 15.00
SSJS Jason Spezza 4.00 10.00
SSJT Joe Thornton 6.00 15.00
SSKT Keith Tkachuk 4.00 10.00
SSLR Luc Robitaille 3.00 8.00
SSMB Martin Brodeur 12.50 30.00
SSMF Manny Fernandez 3.00 8.00
SSMG Marian Gaborik 8.00 20.00
SSMH Marian Hossa 4.00 10.00
SSMK Mark Messier 4.00 10.00
SSML Mario Lemieux 12.50 30.00
SSMM Mike Modano 6.00 15.00
SSMS Mats Sundin 4.00 10.00
SSMT Marty Turco 3.00 8.00
SSON Owen Nolan 3.00 8.00
SSPD Pavol Demitra 3.00 8.00
SSPF Peter Forsberg 10.00 25.00
SSPL Patrick Lalime 3.00 8.00
SSRC Roman Cechmanek 3.00 8.00
SSSD Shane Doan 3.00 8.00
SSSF Sergei Fedorov 6.00 15.00
SSSK Saku Koivu 4.00 10.00
SSSS Sergei Samsonov 3.00 8.00
SSSY Steve Yzerman 12.50 30.00
SSVL Vincent Lecavalier 3.00 8.00
SSZP Zigmund Palffy 3.00 8.00

2003-04 Upper Deck Rookie Update Top Draws

This 20-card autograph set featured "cut" autographs of current stars. Cards in this set were inserted at odds of 1:72.
KNOWN PRINT RUNS LISTED BELOW
PRINT RUNS UNDER 25 NOT
PRICED DUE TO SCARCITY
TD1 Evgeni Nabokov 6.00 15.00
TD2 Teemu Selanne 8.00 20.00
TD3 Todd Bertuzzi SP 20.00 50.00
TD4 Wayne Gretzky/14
TD5 Gordie Howe/14
TD6 Jason Spezza SP 75.00 150.00
TD7 Rick DiPietro EXCH 6.00 15.00
TD8 J-S Giguere 50.00 100.00
TD9 Nikolai Zherdev 6.00 15.00
TD10 Ales Hemsky 6.00 15.00
TD11 Ilya Kovalchuk SP 20.00 50.00
TD12 Pascal Leclaire 6.00 15.00
TD13 Rick Nash 12.50 30.00
TD14 Nikolai Khabibulin SP 25.00 60.00
TD15 Steve Yzerman 30.00 80.00
TD16 John LeClair 8.00 15.00
TD17 Patrick Roy 60.00 150.00
TD18 Jay Bouwmeester 6.00 15.00
TD19 Alexander Svitov 6.00 15.00
TD20 Fredrik Sjostrom 6.00 15.00

2003-04 Upper Deck Rookie Update YoungStars

*MULT.COLOR SWATCH: .5X TO 1.25X
PRINT RUN 99 SER.#'d SETS
YS1 Michael Ryder 8.00 20.00
YS2 Eric Staal 12.00 30.00
YS2A Eric Staal 12.00 30.00
YS3 Patrice Bergeron 12.00 30.00
YS3A Patrice Bergeron 12.00 30.00
YS4 Trent Hunter 4.00 10.00
YS5 Ryan Malone 5.00 12.00
YS6 Derek Roy 4.00 10.00
YS6A Derek Roy 4.00 10.00
YS7 Matt Stajan 6.00 15.00
YS7A Matt Stajan 6.00 15.00
YS8 Joni Pitkanen 5.00 12.00
YS8A Joni Pitkanen 5.00 12.00
YS9 Paul Martin 4.00 10.00
YS10 Brooks Orpik 4.00 10.00
YS11 Andrew Raycroft 8.00 20.00
YS11A Andrew Raycroft 8.00 20.00
YS12 Pierre-Marc Bouchard 4.00 10.00
YS13 Joffrey Lupul 6.00 15.00
YS14 Matthew Lombardi 4.00 10.00
YS15 Tuomo Ruutu 8.00 20.00
YS15A Tuomo Ruutu 8.00 20.00
YS16 Raffi Torres 4.00 10.00
YS17 Nikolai Zherdev 8.00 20.00
YS17A Nikolai Zherdev 8.00 20.00
YS18 Jonathan Cheechoo 12.00 30.00
YS19 Christian Ehrhoff 4.00 10.00
YS20 Dan Hamhuis 5.00 12.00
YS21 Alexei Semenov 4.00 10.00
YS22 Philippe Sauve 4.00 10.00

2005-06 Upper Deck Rookie Update

COMPLETE SET w/o SPs (100) 8.00 20.00
101-195 PRINT RUN 1,999 #'d SETS
196-254 PRINT RUN 999 #'d SETS
255-273 PRINT RUN 499 #'d SETS
274-276 PRINT RUN 199 #'d SETS
1 J-S Giguere .20 .50
2 Teemu Selanne .25 .60
3 Joffrey Lupul .15 .30
4 Ilya Kovalchuk .30 .75
5 Marian Hossa .20 .50
6 Kari Lehtonen .25 .60
7 Andrew Raycroft .20 .50
8 Brian Leetch .25 .60
9 Patrice Bergeron .25 .60
10 Glen Murray .15 .30
11 Chris Drury .20 .50
12 Ryan Miller .20 .50
13 Jarome Iginla .30 .75
14 Miikka Kiprusoff .25 .60
15 Daymond Langkow .15 .30
16 Eric Staal .20 .50
17 Martin Gerber .20 .50
18 Doug Weight .20 .50
19 Erik Cole .15 .30
20 Nikolai Khabibulin .25 .60
21 Tuomo Ruutu .15 .30
22 Jose Theodore .30 .75
23 Alex Tanguay .20 .50
24 Joe Sakic .50 1.25
25 Marek Svatos .15 .30
26 Milan Hejduk .25 .60
27 Rob Blake .20 .50
28 Rick Nash .30 .75
29 Sergei Fedorov .25 .60
30 Mike Modano .25 .60
31 Brenden Morrow .20 .50
32 Marty Turco .20 .50
33 Steve Yzerman 1.00 2.50
34 Pavel Datsyuk .25 .60
35 Henrik Zetterberg .25 .60
36 Brendan Shanahan .25 .60
37 Nicklas Lidstrom .25 .60
38 Ryan Smyth .20 .50
39 Chris Pronger .20 .50
40 Ales Hemsky .15 .30
41 Roberto Luongo .30 .75
42 Nathan Horton .15 .30
43 Olli Jokinen .20 .50
44 Alexander Frolov .20 .50
45 Jeremy Roenick .30 .75
46 Pavol Demitra .20 .50
47 Luc Robitaille .20 .50
48 Marian Gaborik .50 1.25
49 Manny Fernandez .20 .50
50 Saku Koivu .25 .60
51 David Aebischer .20 .50
52 Michael Ryder .20 .50
53 Mike Ribeiro .15 .30
54 Paul Kariya .25 .60
55 Tomas Vokoun .20 .50
56 Martin Brodeur 1.25 3.00
57 Patrik Elias .20 .50
58 Brian Gionta .15 .30
59 Scott Gomez .20 .50
60 Alexei Yashin .15 .30
61 Miroslav Satan .15 .30
62 Rick DiPietro .20 .50
63 Jaromir Jagr .40 1.00
64 Martin Straka .15 .30
65 Dominik Hasek .50 1.25
66 Dany Heatley .30 .75
67 Daniel Alfredsson .20 .50
68 Jason Spezza .25 .60
69 Wade Redden .15 .30
70 Peter Forsberg .40 1.00
71 Simon Gagne .25 .60
72 Antero Niittymaki .20 .50
73 Keith Primeau .12 .30
74 Joni Pitkanen .15 .30
75 Curtis Joseph .25 .60
76 Shane Doan .15 .30
77 Ladislav Nagy .15 .30
78 Mario Lemieux 1.50 4.00
79 Ryan Malone .15 .30
80 Marc-Andre Fleury .20 .50
81 Joe Thornton .40 1.00
82 Patrick Marleau .20 .50
83 Evgeni Nabokov .20 .50
84 Jonathan Cheechoo .25 .60
85 Keith Tkachuk .25 .60
86 Barret Jackman .15 .30
87 Vincent Lecavalier .25 .60
88 Martin St. Louis .20 .50
89 Brad Richards .20 .50
90 Vaclav Prospal .15 .30
91 Mats Sundin .25 .60
92 Ed Belfour .25 .60
93 Jason Allison .15 .30
94 Bryan McCabe .15 .30
95 Eric Lindros .25 .60
96 Markus Naslund .25 .60
97 Alex Auld .15 .30
98 Todd Bertuzzi .25 .60
99 Brendan Morrison .15 .30
100 Olaf Kolzig .20 .50
101 Dustin Penner RC 3.00 8.00
102 Michael Wall RC 2.50 6.00
103 Zenon Konopka RC 1.50 4.00
104 Adam Berkhoel RC 2.50 6.00
105 Jay Leach RC 1.50 4.00
106 Eric Healey RC 1.50 4.00
107 Ben Guite RC 1.50 4.00
108 Ben Walter RC 1.50 4.00
109 Brian Eklund RC 2.50 6.00
110 Nathan Paetsch RC 1.50 4.00
111 Jiri Novotny RC 1.50 4.00
112 Mark Giordano RC 1.50 4.00
113 Richie Regehr RC 1.50 4.00
114 Chad Larose RC 1.50 4.00
115 Keith Aucoin RC 1.50 4.00
116 David Gove RC 1.50 4.00
117 Mark Cullen RC 1.50 4.00
118 Rene Bourque RC 1.50 4.00
119 Martin St. Pierre RC 1.50 4.00
120 Corey Crawford RC 2.50 6.00
121 James Wisniewski RC 1.50 4.00
122 Vitaly Kolesnik RC 2.50 6.00
123 Andrew Penner RC 1.50 4.00
124 Steven Goertzen RC 1.50 4.00
125 Geoff Platt RC 1.50 4.00
126 Joakim Lindstrom RC 1.50 4.00
127 Junior Lessard RC 1.50 4.00
128 Vojtech Polak RC 1.50 4.00
129 Brett Lebda RC 1.50 4.00
130 Kyle Brodziak RC 1.50 4.00
131 Danny Syvret RC 1.50 4.00
132 Matt Greene RC 1.50 4.00
133 J-F Jacques RC 1.50 4.00
134 Mathieu Roy RC 2.50 6.00
135 Greg Jacina RC 1.50 4.00
136 Rob Globke RC 1.50 4.00
137 Petr Taticek RC 1.50 4.00
138 Adam Hauser RC 2.50 6.00
139 George Parros RC 1.50 4.00
140 Yanick Lehoux RC 1.50 4.00
141 Petr Kanko RC 2.50 6.00
142 Jeff Giuliano RC 1.50 4.00
143 Matt Ryan RC 1.50 4.00
144 Connor James RC 1.50 4.00
145 Richard Petiot RC 1.50 4.00
146 Derek Boogaard RC 2.50 6.00
147 Matt Foy RC 1.50 4.00
148 Raitis Ivanans RC 1.50 4.00
149 Mark Streit RC 1.50 4.00
150 Jonathan Ferland RC 1.50 4.00
151 J-P Cote RC 1.50 4.00
152 Kevin Klein RC 1.50 4.00
153 Pekka Rinne RC 2.50 6.00
154 Greg Zanon RC 1.50 4.00
155 Cam Janssen RC 1.50 4.00
156 Jason Ryznar RC 1.50 4.00
157 Bruno Gervais RC 1.50 4.00
158 Kevin Colley RC 1.50 4.00
159 Ryan Hollweg RC 1.50 4.00
160 Chris Holt RC 1.50 4.00
161 Brian McGrattan RC 1.50 4.00
162 Wade Skolney RC 1.50 4.00
163 Josh Gratton RC 1.50 4.00
164 Ryan Ready RC 1.50 4.00
165 Alexandre Picard RC 1.50 4.00
166 Stefan Ruzicka RC 1.50 4.00
167 Matt Jones RC 1.50 4.00
168 Colby Armstrong RC 3.00 8.00
169 Doug Murray RC 1.50 4.00
170 Grant Stevenson RC 1.50 4.00
171 Kevin Dallman RC 1.50 4.00
172 Andy Roach RC 1.50 4.00
173 Jon DiSalvatore RC 1.50 4.00
174 Dennis Wideman RC 1.50 4.00
175 Jeff Hoggan RC 1.50 4.00
176 Colin Hemingway RC 1.50 4.00
177 Chris Beckford-Tseu RC 3.00 8.00
178 Mike Glumac RC 1.50 4.00
179 Timo Helbling RC 1.50 4.00
180 Nick Tarnasky RC 1.50 4.00
181 Gerald Coleman RC 2.50 6.00
182 Paul Ranger RC 1.50 4.00
183 Darren Reid RC 1.50 4.00
184 Doug O'Brien RC 1.50 4.00
185 Staffan Kronwall RC 1.50 4.00
186 Jay Harrison RC 1.50 4.00
187 Rick Rypien RC 1.50 4.00
188 Rob McVicar RC 2.50 6.00
189 Alexandre Burrows RC 1.50 4.00
190 Tomas Mojzis RC 1.50 4.00
191 Prestin Ryan RC
192 David Steckel RC 1.50 4.00
193 Mike Green RC 1.50 4.00
194 Joey Tenute RC 1.50 4.00
195 Louis Robitaille RC 2.50 6.00
196 Braydon Coburn 4.00 10.00
Jay Bouwmeester
197 Jim Slater 4.00 10.00
Kris Draper
198 Milan Jurcina 4.00 10.00
Zdeno Chara
199 Jordan Sigalet 6.00 15.00
Andrew Raycroft
200 Eric Nystrom 4.00 10.00
Tony Amonte
201 Kevin Nastiuk 6.00 15.00
Martin Biron
202 Danny Richmond 4.00 10.00
Brian Rafalski
203 Brent Seabrook 4.00 10.00
Ed Jovanovski
204 Cam Barker 6.00 15.00
Rob Blake
205 Peter Budaj 8.00 20.00
Tomas Vokoun
206 Brad Richardson 10.00 25.00
Joe Sakic
207 Jussi Jokinen 6.00 15.00
Jere Lehtinen
208 Jim Howard 6.00 15.00
Ty Conklin
209 Johan Franzen 10.00 25.00
Henrik Zetterberg
210 Brad Winchester 6.00 15.00
Keith Tkachuk
211 Anthony Stewart 4.00 10.00
Shane Doan
212 Jeff Tambellini 4.00 10.00
Martin St. Louis
213 Yann Danis 6.00 15.00
Jose Theodore
214 Maxim Lapierre 4.00 10.00
Pierre Turgeon
215 Ryan Suter 4.00 10.00
Chris Chelios
216 Zach Parise 6.00 15.00
Jeremy Roenick
217 Barry Tallackson 4.00 10.00
Bill Guerin
218 Petteri Nokelainen 4.00 10.00
Olli Jokinen
219 Robert Nilsson 4.00 10.00
Markus Naslund
220 Chris Campoli 4.00 10.00
Bryan McCabe
221 Al Montoya 6.00 15.00
Robert Esche
222 Christoph Schubert 4.00 10.00
Joni Pitkanen
223 Brandon Bochenski 4.00 10.00
Mark Parrish
224 Patrick Eaves 4.00 10.00
Michael Peca
225 R.J. Umberger 6.00 15.00
Keith Primeau
226 Keith Ballard 4.00 10.00
Scott Niedermayer
227 David Leneveu 6.00 15.00
Curtis Joseph
228 Maxime Talbot 4.00 10.00
Brendan Morrison
229 Ryan Whitney 6.00 15.00
Brian Leetch
230 Steve Bernier 8.00 20.00
Dany Heatley
231 Ryane Clowe 8.00 20.00
Jonathan Cheechoo
232 Jeff Woywitka 4.00 10.00
Adam Foote
233 Lee Stempniak 6.00 15.00
Patrice Bergeron
234 Evgeny Artyukin 6.00 15.00
Jaromir Jagr
235 Andrew Wozniewski 4.00 10.00
Derian Hatcher
236 Jakub Klepis 4.00 10.00
Ales Hemsky
237 Tomas Fleischmann 6.00 15.00
Milan Hejduk
238 Andrew Alberts 4.00 10.00
Nick Boynton
239 Ben Eager 4.00 10.00
Eric Daze
240 Alexandre Picard 6.00 15.00
Luc Robitaille
241 Ole-Kristian Tollefsen 4.00 10.00
Rostislav Klesla
242 Daniel Paille 4.00 10.00
Cory Stillman
243 Erik Christensen 6.00 15.00
Eric Staal
244 Dimitri Patzold 6.00 15.00
Evgeni Nabokov
245 Ryan Craig 6.00 15.00
Vincent Lecavalier
246 Kevin Bieksa 4.00 10.00
Barret Jackman
247 Jeremy Colliton 4.00 10.00
Trent Hunter
248 Jay McClement 4.00 10.00
Jason Arnott
249 Josh Gorges 4.00 10.00
Dan Hamhuis
250 Kyle Quincey 4.00 10.00
Robyn Regehr
251 Chris Thorburn 4.00 10.00
Rod Brind'Amour
252 Niklas Nordgren 4.00 10.00
Tomas Holmstrom
253 Duncan Keith 4.00 10.00
Brad Stuart
254 Jaroslav Balastik 4.00 10.00
Vaclav Prospal
255 Petr Prucha 8.00 20.00
Martin Straka
256 Ryan Getzlaf 25.00 60.00
Jason Spezza
257 Corey Perry 15.00 40.00
Alex Tanguay
258 Hannu Toivonen 20.00 50.00
Miikka Kiprusoff
259 Thomas Vanek 30.00 60.00
Jarome Iginla
260 Alexander Steen 25.00 60.00
Mats Sundin
261 Andrew Ladd 12.00 30.00
Todd Bertuzzi
262 Cam Ward 20.00 50.00
Marty Turco
263 Wojtek Wolski 15.00 40.00
Ryan Smyth
264 Gilbert Brule 20.00 50.00
Simon Gagne
265 Valtteri Filppula 12.00 30.00
Tuomo Ruutu
266 Rostislav Olesz 10.00 25.00
Martin Havlat
267 Mikko Koivu 15.00 40.00
Saku Koivu
268 Alexander Perezhogin 12.00 30.00
Alexei Yashin
269 Andrei Kostitsyn 15.00 40.00
Alexander Frolov
270 Henrik Lundqvist 40.00 80.00
Dominik Hasek
271 Andrej Meszaros 12.00 30.00
Wade Redden
272 Jeff Carter 25.00 60.00
Joe Thornton
273 Mike Richards 20.00 50.00
Mike Modano
274 Dion Phaneuf 125.00 225.00
Chris Pronger SP
275 Alexander Ovechkin 350.00 600.00
Ilya Kovalchuk SP
276 Sidney Crosby RC SP 1600.002200.00

2005-06 Upper Deck Rookie Update Inspirations Patch Rookies

PRINT RUN 25 SER. #'d SETS
NOT PRICED DUE TO SCARCITY

2006-07 Upper Deck Sweet Shot

JSY RCs #'d TO 499
1 Teemu Selanne 1.00 2.50
2 Chris Pronger .75 2.00
3 Jean-Sebastien Giguere .75 2.00
4 Ilya Kovalchuk 1.25 3.00
5 Marian Hossa .75 2.00
6 Kari Lehtonen 1.00 2.50
7 Patrice Bergeron 1.00 2.50
8 Zdeno Chara .50 1.25
9 Cam Neely 1.25 3.00
10 Bobby Orr 8.00 20.00
11 Phil Esposito 1.50 4.00
12 Ray Bourque 2.00 5.00
13 Ryan Miller 1.00 2.50
14 Maxim Afinogenov .50 1.25
15 Chris Drury .50 1.25
16 Gilbert Perreault 1.00 2.50
17 Alex Tanguay .75 2.00
18 Dion Phaneuf 1.25 3.00
19 Jarome Iginla 1.25 3.00
20 Miikka Kiprusoff 1.00 2.50
21 Cam Ward 1.00 2.50
22 Eric Staal 1.00 2.50
23 Nikolai Khabibulin 1.00 2.50
24 Martin Havlat .75 2.00
25 Bobby Hull 1.50 4.00
26 Tony Esposito 1.00 2.50
27 Joe Sakic 2.50 6.00
28 Jose Theodore 1.00 2.50
29 Milan Hejduk .50 1.25
30 Patrick Roy 6.00 15.00
31 Rick Nash 1.00 2.50
32 Sergei Fedorov 1.00 2.50
33 Pascal LeClaire .75 2.00
34 Mike Modano 1.00 2.50
35 Eric Lindros 1.00 2.50
36 Marty Turco .75 2.00
37 Henrik Zetterberg 1.00 2.50
38 Nicklas Lidstrom 1.00 2.50
39 Pavel Datsyuk .75 2.00
40 Dominik Hasek 1.50 4.00
41 Gordie Howe 2.00 5.00
42 Ted Lindsay .50 1.25
43 Ales Hemsky .50 1.25
44 Dwayne Roloson 1.00 2.50
45 Wayne Gretzky 10.00 25.00
46 Jari Kurri 1.00 2.50
47 Grant Fuhr 1.25 3.00
48 Ed Belfour 1.00 2.50
49 Olli Jokinen .50 1.25
50 Rob Blake .75 2.00
51 Alexander Frolov .50 1.25
52 Manny Fernandez .75 2.00
53 Pavol Demitra .50 1.25
54 Marian Gaborik 1.25 3.00
55 Saku Koivu 1.00 2.50
56 Cristobal Huet 1.25 3.00
57 Michael Ryder .75 2.00
58 Guy Lafleur 1.50 4.00
59 Larry Robinson .75 2.00
60 Paul Kariya 1.00 2.50
61 Tomas Vokoun .75 2.00
62 Brian Gionta .50 1.25
63 Martin Brodeur 3.00 8.00
64 Patrik Elias .50 1.25

65 Rick DiPietro .75 2.00
66 Alexei Yashin .50 1.25
67 Mike Bossy .75 2.00
68 Billy Smith 1.00 2.50
69 Denis Potvin .75 2.00
70 Jaromir Jagr 1.50 4.00
71 Henrik Lundqvist 1.25 3.00
72 Brendan Shanahan 1.00 2.50
73 Dany Heatley 1.25 3.00
74 Jason Spezza 1.00 2.50
75 Daniel Alfredsson .75 2.00
76 Peter Forsberg 1.50 4.00
77 Simon Gagne 1.00 2.50
78 Bobby Clarke 1.00 2.50
79 Jeremy Roenick 1.25 3.00
80 Shane Doan .50 1.25
81 Curtis Joseph 1.00 2.50
82 Sidney Crosby 15.00 40.00
83 Marc-Andre Fleury 1.00 2.50
84 Mario Lemieux 6.00 15.00
85 Peter Stastny .50 1.25
86 Joe Thornton 1.50 4.00
87 Patrick Marleau .75 2.00
88 Jonathan Cheechoo 1.00 2.50
89 Doug Weight .50 1.25
90 Brad Richards .75 2.00
91 Vincent Lecavalier 1.00 2.50
92 Martin St. Louis .75 2.00
93 Mats Sundin 1.00 2.50
94 Andrew Raycroft .75 2.00
95 Darcy Tucker .50 1.25
96 Johnny Bower .75 2.00
97 Darryl Sittler 1.00 2.50
98 Roberto Luongo 1.25 3.00
99 Markus Naslund 1.00 2.50
100 Alexander Ovechkin 3.00 8.00
101 Shane O'Brien JSY RC 2.00 5.00
102 Ryan Shannon JSY RC 2.00 5.00
103 David McKee JSY RC 3.00 8.00
104 Phil Kessel JSY RC 8.00 20.00
105 Yan Stastny JSY RC 2.00 5.00
106 Mark Stuart JSY RC 2.00 5.00
107 Matt Lashoff JSY RC 2.00 5.00
108 Clarke MacArthur JSY RC 2.00 5.00
109 Drew Stafford JSY RC 8.00 20.00
110 Masi Marjamaki JSY RC 2.00 5.00
111 Michael Funk JSY RC 2.00 5.00
112 Brandon Prust JSY RC 2.00 5.00
113 Dustin Boyd JSY RC 4.00 10.00
114 Dustin Byfuglien JSY RC 2.00 5.00
115 Dave Bolland JSY RC 2.00 5.00
116 Michael Blunden JSY RC 2.00 5.00
117 Paul Stastny JSY RC 10.00 25.00
118 Fredrik Norrena JSY RC 4.00 10.00
119 Niklas Grossman JSY RC 1.00 2.50
120 Loui Eriksson JSY RC 2.00 5.00
121 Tomas Kopecky JSY RC 4.00 10.00
122 Stefan Liv JSY RC 4.00 10.00
123 Patrick Thoresen JSY RC 4.00 10.00
124 Marc-Antoine Pouliot JSY RC 4.00 10.00
125 Ladislav Smid JSY RC 2.00 5.00
126 Janis Sprukts JSY RC 2.00 5.00
127 Jeff Deslauriers JSY RC 2.00 5.00
128 David Booth JSY RC 2.00 5.00
129 Konstantin Pushkaryov JSY RC 2.00 5.00
130 Anze Kopitar JSY RC 8.00 20.00
131 Patrick O'Sullivan JSY RC 5.00 12.00
132 Benoit Pouliot JSY RC 4.00 10.00
133 Niklas Backstrom JSY RC 5.00 12.00
134 Guillaume Latendresse JSY RC 10.00 25.00
135 Shea Weber JSY RC 4.00 10.00
136 Alexander Radulov JSY RC 6.00 15.00
137 Travis Zajac JSY RC 4.00 10.00
138 Nigel Dawes JSY RC 2.00 5.00
139 Jarkko Immonen JSY RC 2.00 5.00
140 Josh Hennessy JSY RC 2.00 5.00
141 Jussi Timonen JSY RC 2.00 5.00
142 Ryan Potulny JSY RC 4.00 10.00
143 Keith Yandle JSY RC 2.00 5.00
144 Michel Ouellet JSY RC 4.00 10.00
145 Jordan Staal JSY RC 25.00 60.00
146 Evgeni Malkin JSY RC 25.00 60.00
147 Noah Welch JSY RC 2.00 5.00
148 Kristopher Letang JSY RC 3.00 8.00
149 Matt Carle JSY RC 3.00 8.00
150 Marc-Edouard Vlasic JSY RC 2.00 5.00
151 Joe Pavelski JSY RC 3.00 8.00
152 Marek Schwarz JSY RC 3.00 8.00
153 Karri Ramo JSY RC 2.00 5.00
154 Blair Jones JSY RC 2.00 5.00
155 Ian White JSY RC 2.00 5.00
156 Jeremy Williams JSY RC 2.00 5.00
157 Luc Bourdon JSY RC 3.00 8.00
158 Jesse Schultz JSY RC 2.00 5.00
159 Alexander Edler JSY RC 2.00 5.00
160 Eric Fehr JSY RC 3.00 8.00

2006-07 Upper Deck Sweet Shot Endorsed Equipment

STATED PRINT RUN 25 #'d SETS
EEAR Andrew Raycroft 50.00 100.00
EEBR Bill Ranford 50.00 100.00
EEEB Ed Belfour 50.00 100.00
EEGC Gerry Cheevers 60.00 125.00
EEGF Grant Fuhr 50.00 100.00
EEJT Jose Theodore 30.00 80.00
EEMF Marc-Andre Fleury 100.00 200.00
EEMT Marty Turco 50.00 100.00
EEPR Patrick Roy 200.00 350.00
EETE Tony Esposito 60.00 125.00

2006-07 Upper Deck Sweet Shot Rookie Jerseys Autographs

*AUs: 3X to 7X RC HI
STATED PRINT RUN 25 #'d SETS
101 Shane O'Brien 20.00 50.00
102 Ryan Shannon 20.00 50.00
103 David McKee 25.00 60.00
104 Phil Kessel 40.00 100.00
105 Yan Stastny 15.00 40.00
106 Mark Stuart 15.00 40.00
107 Matt Lashoff 15.00 40.00
108 Clarke MacArthur 15.00 40.00
109 Drew Stafford 50.00 125.00
110 Masi Marjamaki 20.00 50.00
111 Michael Funk 15.00 40.00
112 Brandon Prust 15.00 40.00
113 Dustin Boyd 20.00 50.00
114 Dustin Byfuglien 15.00 40.00
115 Dave Bolland 15.00 40.00
116 Michael Blunden 15.00 40.00
117 Paul Stastny 60.00 150.00
118 Fredrik Norrena 20.00 50.00
119 Niklas Grossman 15.00 40.00
120 Loui Eriksson 15.00 40.00
121 Tomas Kopecky 20.00 50.00
122 Stefan Liv 20.00 50.00
123 Patrick Thoresen 20.00 50.00
124 Marc-Antoine Pouliot 20.00 50.00
125 Ladislav Smid 15.00 40.00
126 Janis Sprukts 15.00 40.00
127 Jeff Deslauriers 15.00 40.00
128 David Booth 15.00 40.00
129 Konstantin Pushkaryov 15.00 40.00
130 Anze Kopitar 60.00 150.00
131 Patrick O'Sullivan 20.00 50.00
132 Benoit Pouliot 20.00 50.00
133 Niklas Backstrom 25.00 60.00
134 Guillaume Latendresse 40.00 100.00
135 Shea Weber 20.00 50.00
136 Alexander Radulov 30.00 80.00
137 Travis Zajac 25.00 60.00
138 Nigel Dawes 15.00 40.00
139 Jarkko Immonen 15.00 40.00
140 Josh Hennessy 15.00 40.00
141 Jussi Timonen 15.00 40.00
142 Ryan Potulny 20.00 50.00
143 Keith Yandle 15.00 40.00
144 Michel Ouellet 25.00 60.00
145 Jordan Staal 100.00 200.00
146 Evgeni Malkin 125.00 250.00
147 Noah Welch 15.00 40.00
148 Kristopher Letang 20.00 50.00
149 Matt Carle 20.00 50.00
150 Marc-Edouard Vlasic 15.00 40.00
151 Joe Pavelski 20.00 50.00
152 Marek Schwarz 25.00 60.00
153 Karri Ramo 15.00 40.00
154 Blair Jones 15.00 40.00
155 Ian White 15.00 40.00
156 Jeremy Williams 15.00 40.00
157 Luc Bourdon 25.00 60.00
158 Jesse Schultz 15.00 40.00
159 Alexander Edler 15.00 40.00
160 Eric Fehr 25.00 60.00

2006-07 Upper Deck Sweet Shot Signature Shots/Saves

SSAF Alexander Frolov 3.00 8.00
SSAH Ales Hemsky 3.00 8.00
SSAK Anze Kopitar 15.00 40.00
SSAO Adam Oates 3.00 8.00
SSAR Andrew Raycroft 5.00 12.00
SSAT Alex Tanguay SP 5.00 12.00
SSBB Brad Boyes 3.00 8.00
SSBE Jean Beliveau SP 50.00 100.00
SSBF Bernie Federko 3.00 8.00
SSBG Brian Gionta 8.00 20.00
SSBH Bobby Hull SP 25.00 60.00
SSBI Martin Biron 5.00 12.00
SSBM Brenden Morrow 5.00 12.00
SSBO Pierre-Marc Bouchard 3.00 8.00
SSBR Martin Brodeur SP 40.00 80.00
SSCA Colby Armstrong 3.00 8.00
SSCH Jonathan Cheechoo 6.00 15.00
SSCI Dino Ciccarelli 3.00 8.00
SSCN Cam Neely SP 15.00 30.00
SSCP Corey Perry 5.00 12.00
SSCW Cam Ward 6.00 15.00
SSDC Don Cherry SP 30.00 80.00
SSDH Dominik Hasek 8.00 20.00
SSDI Dick Irvin 8.00 20.00
SSDP Denis Potvin SP 10.00 25.00
SSDR Dwayne Roloson 5.00 12.00
SSDS Drew Stafford 6.00 15.00
SSEM Evgeni Malkin 40.00 100.00
SSES Eric Staal 20.00 50.00
SSGB Gilbert Brule 6.00 15.00
SSGE Martin Gerber 6.00 15.00
SSGF Grant Fuhr SP 15.00 30.00
SSGH Gordie Howe 30.00 80.00
SSGL Guillaume Latendresse 12.00 30.00
SSGO Scott Gomez 6.00 15.00
SSHA Dale Hawerchuk 5.00 12.00
SSHE Dany Heatley SP 12.00 30.00
SSHI Chris Higgins 5.00 12.00
SSHU Cristobal Huet 10.00 25.00
SSHZ Henrik Zetterberg SP 20.00 50.00
SSIK Ilya Kovalchuk 8.00 20.00
SSJB Johnny Bucyk SP 8.00 20.00
SSJC Jeff Carter 6.00 15.00
SSJG Jean-Sebastien Giguere 5.00 12.00
SSJI Jarome Iginla 8.00 20.00
SSJP Joni Pitkanen 3.00 8.00
SSJS Jarret Stoll 8.00 20.00
SSJT Joe Thornton SP 20.00 50.00
SSKD Kris Draper 20.00 50.00
SSKL Kari Lehtonen 6.00 15.00
SSMA Matt Carle SP 5.00 12.00
SSMB Mike Bossy SP 6.00 15.00
SSMC Mike Cammalleri 3.00 8.00
SSME Barry Melrose 10.00 25.00
SSMF Marc-Andre Fleury 10.00 25.00
SSMG Marian Gaborik 10.00 25.00
SSMH Martin Havlat 5.00 12.00
SSMI Milan Hejduk 10.00 25.00
SSMK Miikka Kiprusoff 6.00 15.00
SSML Mario Lemieux SP 90.00 150.00
SSMM Marty McSorley 3.00 8.00
SSMO Mike Modano SP 12.00 30.00
SSMP Michael Peca 3.00 8.00
SSMR Michael Ryder 5.00 12.00
SSMS Marc Savard 8.00 20.00
SSMT Marty Turco 5.00 12.00
SSND Nigel Dawes 3.00 8.00
SSNL Nicklas Lidstrom SP 20.00 40.00
SSNZ Nikolai Zherdev 3.00 8.00
SSOR Bobby Orr 100.00 175.00
SSPB Patrice Bergeron 6.00 15.00
SSPE Patrik Elias 8.00 20.00
SSPK Phil Kessel 6.00 15.00
SSPM Patrick Marleau SP 5.00 12.00
SSPO Patrick O'Sullivan 5.00 12.00
SSPP Petr Prucha 12.00 30.00
SSPS Paul Stastny 12.00 30.00
SSRA Alexander Radulov 10.00 25.00
SSRB Ray Bourque SP 25.00 60.00
SSRH Ron Hextall 8.00 20.00
SSRM Ryan Miller 8.00 20.00
SSRN Rick Nash 6.00 15.00
SSRS Ryan Smyth 10.00 25.00
SSSC Sidney Crosby 100.00 150.00
SSSG Simon Gagne 10.00 25.00
SSST Jordan Staal 30.00 60.00
SSSV Marek Svatos 3.00 8.00
SSTH Jose Theodore SP 12.00 30.00
SSTO Terry O'Reilly 5.00 12.00
SSTV Tomas Vokoun 6.00 15.00
SSVL Vincent Lecavalier SP 25.00 60.00
SSVT Vesa Toskala 5.00 12.00
SSWG Wayne Gretzky SP 150.00 250.00
SSWO Willie O'Ree 8.00 20.00
SSZC Zdeno Chara 3.00 8.00

2006-07 Upper Deck Sweet Shot Signature Shots/Saves Ice Signings

STATED PRINT RUN 100 #'d SETS
SSIAH Ales Hemsky 6.00 15.00
SSIAR Alexander Radulov 25.00 60.00
SSIBB Brad Boyes 6.00 15.00
SSIBO Bobby Orr 150.00 250.00
SSICA Colby Armstrong 12.00 30.00
SSICW Cam Ward 10.00 25.00
SSIDH Dominik Hasek 25.00 60.00
SSIEM Evgeni Malkin 90.00 150.00
SSIES Eric Staal 10.00 25.00
SSIGH Gordie Howe 40.00 80.00
SSIHE Dany Heatley 15.00 40.00
SSIHZ Henrik Zetterberg 12.00 30.00
SSIIK Ilya Kovalchuk 15.00 40.00
SSIJG Jean-Sebastien Giguere 15.00 40.00
SSIJI Jarome Iginla 15.00 40.00
SSIJK Jari Kurri 20.00 50.00
SSIJS Jarret Stoll 6.00 15.00
SSIJT Joe Thornton 25.00 60.00
SSIKL Kari Lehtonen 12.00 30.00
SSILR Larry Robinson 10.00 25.00
SSIMB Martin Brodeur 50.00 100.00
SSIMD Marcel Dionne 10.00 25.00
SSIMG Marian Gaborik 20.00 50.00
SSIMH Martin Havlat 12.00 30.00
SSIMK Miikka Kiprusoff 15.00 40.00
SSIMM Mike Modano 12.00 30.00
SSIMR Michael Ryder 10.00 25.00
SSIMS Marek Svatos 6.00 15.00
SSIMT Marty Turco 15.00 40.00
SSINL Nicklas Lidstrom 20.00 50.00
SSIPE Patrik Elias 6.00 15.00
SSIPK Phil Kessel 25.00 60.00
SSIRB Ray Bourque 30.00 80.00
SSIRK Red Kelly 12.00 30.00
SSIRM Ryan Miller 20.00 50.00
SSIRN Rick Nash 12.00 30.00
SSISC Sidney Crosby 150.00 300.00
SSISG Simon Gagne 10.00 25.00
SSIST Jordan Staal 60.00 125.00
SSITV Tomas Vokoun 10.00 25.00
SSIWG Wayne Gretzky 150.00 300.00

2006-07 Upper Deck Sweet Shot Signature Shots/Saves Sticks

STATED PRINT RUN 25 #'d SETS
SSSAB Andy Bathgate 15.00 40.00
SSSAF Alexander Frolov 15.00 40.00
SSSAH Ales Hemsky 25.00 60.00
SSSAK Anze Kopitar 100.00 200.00
SSSAR Andrew Raycroft 25.00 60.00
SSSBB Brad Boyes 40.00
SSSBC Bobby Clarke 25.00 60.00
SSSBG Brian Gionta 20.00 50.00
SSSBH Bobby Hull 40.00 100.00
SSSBM Brenden Morrow 25.00 60.00
SSSBO Mike Bossy
SSSBP Bernie Parent 50.00 125.00
SSSBR Brent Sutter 15.00 40.00
SSSBS Borje Salming
SSSBU Johnny Bucyk 20.00 50.00
SSSCA Colby Armstrong
SSSCD Chris Drury 25.00 60.00
SSSCH Cristobal Huet 40.00 80.00
SSSCN Cam Neely 30.00 80.00
SSSDC Don Cherry 100.00 200.00
SSSDE Denis Potvin 20.00 50.00
SSSDH Dominik Hasek 50.00 100.00
SSSDP Dion Phaneuf 40.00 80.00
SSSDR Dwayne Roloson 25.00 60.00
SSSDS Denis Savard 15.00 40.00
SSSDT Dave Taylor 20.00 50.00
SSSDW Doug Wilson 15.00 40.00
SSSEM Evgeni Malkin 150.00 300.00
SSSES Eric Staal 25.00 60.00
SSSGB Gilbert Brule 25.00 60.00
SSSGE Martin Gerber
SSSGF Grant Fuhr 30.00 80.00
SSSGH Gordie Howe 60.00 150.00
SSSGL Guillaume Latendresse 60.00 150.00
SSSGP Gilbert Perreault
SSSHE Dany Heatley 40.00 80.00
SSSHZ Henrik Zetterberg 50.00 100.00
SSSIK Ilya Kovalchuk 30.00 80.00
SSSJA Jason Arnott
SSSJB Jean Beliveau 50.00 125.00
SSSJC Jonathan Cheechoo 30.00 60.00
SSSJE Jeff Carter 25.00 60.00
SSSJI Jarome Iginla 40.00 80.00
SSSJK Jari Kurri 30.00 00.00
SSSJO Johnny Bower
SSSJR Jeremy Roenick 30.00 80.00
SSSJS Jordan Staal 125.00 250.00
SSSJT Jose Theodore
SSSKL Kari Lehtonen
SSSLA Guy Lafleur 50.00 100.00
SSSLR Luc Robitaille
SSSMA Matt Carle 15.00 40.00
SSSMB Martin Brodeur 100.00 200.00
SSSMC Mike Cammalleri
SSSMD Marcel Dionne 30.00 60.00
SSSMF Marc-Andre Fleury 40.00 80.00
SSSMG Marian Gaborik 50.00 125.00
SSSMH Martin Havlat 30.00 60.00
SSSMI Milan Hejduk
SSSMK Miikka Kiprusoff 25.00 60.00
SSSML Mario Lemieux 125.00 250.00
SSSMM Mike Modano 40.00 80.00
SSSMP Michael Peca
SSSMR Michael Ryder 25.00 60.00
SSSMS Marek Svatos 20.00 50.00
SSSMT Marty Turco 25.00 60.00
SSSNL Nicklas Lidstrom 25.00 60.00
SSSNZ Nikolai Zherdev 20.00 50.00
SSSOR Bobby Orr 300.00 450.00
SSSPA Patrice Bergeron 25.00 60.00
SSSPB Pierre-Marc Bouchard
SSSPE Patrik Elias 20.00 50.00
SSSPH Phil Esposito 75.00 150.00
SSSPK Phil Kessel 50.00 125.00
SSSPM Patrick Marleau
SSSPO Patrick O'Sullivan 15.00 40.00
SSSPS Paul Stastny 100.00 200.00
SSSRA Alexander Radulov 50.00 125.00
SSSRB Ray Bourque 40.00 100.00
SSSRH Ron Hextall 40.00 100.00
SSSRM Ryan Miller 25.00 60.00
SSSRN Rick Nash 25.00 60.00
SSSRO Larry Robinson 20.00 50.00
SSSRS Ryan Smyth
SSSRV Rick Vaive 25.00 60.00
SSSSC Sidney Crosby 300.00 450.00
SSSSG Scott Gomez 20.00 50.00
SSSSI Darryl Sittler 25.00 60.00
SSSSJ Jarret Stoll 15.00 40.00
SSSSK Saku Koivu 25.00 60.00
SSSST Peter Stastny 30.00 80.00
SSSSU Brian Sutter 15.00 40.00
SSSTE Tony Esposito 25.00 60.00
SSSTH Joe Thornton 40.00 100.00
SSSTL Ted Lindsay
SSSTV Tomas Vokoun 30.00 60.00
SSSVL Vincent Lecavalier 25.00 60.00
SSSWG Wayne Gretzky 300.00 450.00

2006-07 Upper Deck Sweet Shot Signature Sticks

STATED PRINT RUN 15 #'d SETS
STAM Al MacInnis 30.00 80.00
STAO Adam Oates
STAR Andrew Raycroft 25.00 60.00
STBB Bob Bourne 25.00 60.00
STBC Bobby Clarke 60.00 125.00
STBH Bobby Hull 75.00 150.00
STBL Rob Blake 30.00 80.00
STBO Bobby Orr 400.00 600.00
STBP Bernie Parent
STBS Billy Smith 30.00 80.00
STCD Chris Drury 30.00 80.00
STCG Clark Gillies
STCH Cristobal Huet 40.00 100.00
STCW Cam Ward 30.00 80.00
STDA David Aebischer 30.00 80.00
STDB Daniel Briere 40.00 100.00
STDG Doug Gilmour 100.00 175.00
STDH Dominik Hasek 75.00 150.00
STDP Dion Phaneuf 60.00 125.00
STDR Dwayne Roloson 30.00 80.00
STEM Evgeni Malkin
STES Eric Staal 40.00 100.00
STFM Frank Mahovlich 40.00 100.00
STGH Gordie Howe 150.00 250.00
STGL Guy Lafleur 60.00 125.00
STGP Gilbert Perreault 40.00 100.00
STHA Dale Hawerchuk 40.00 80.00
STHE Dany Heatley 60.00 125.00
STHZ Henrik Zetterberg 50.00 125.00
STIK Ilya Kovalchuk 60.00 125.00
STJB Jean Beliveau 75.00 150.00
STJC Jonathan Cheechoo 60.00 125.00
STJG Jean-Sebastien Giguere 40.00 100.00
STJI Jarome Iginla 125.00 250.00
STJK Jari Kurri 50.00 125.00
STJL Joffrey Lupul 25.00 60.00
STJM Joe Mullen 25.00 60.00
STJP Joni Pitkanen 25.00 60.00
STJR Jeremy Roenick 75.00 150.00
STJT Joe Thornton 75.00 150.00
STKL Kari Lehtonen 40.00 100.00
STLE Manny Legace 25.00 60.00
STLM Larry Murphy 25.00 60.00
STLR Luc Robitaille 40.00 100.00
STMB Martin Brodeur 150.00 250.00
STMG Marian Gaborik 100.00 175.00
STMH Milan Hejduk 25.00 60.00
STMI Mike Bossy 30.00 80.00
STMK Miikka Kiprusoff 50.00 125.00
STML Mario Lemieux 250.00 400.00
STMM Mike Modano 50.00 125.00
STMN Markus Naslund 40.00 80.00
STMP Michael Peca 40.00 100.00
STMR Michael Ryder 40.00 100.00
STMS Martin St. Louis 40.00 100.00
STMT Marty Turco 40.00 100.00
STNL Nicklas Lidstrom 40.00 100.00
STNZ Nikolai Zherdev 30.00 80.00
STPB Patrice Bergeron 30.00 80.00
STPE Patrik Elias 25.00 60.00
STPI Pierre-Marc Bouchard 30.00 60.00
STPK Phil Kessel 60.00 125.00
STPM Patrick Marleau 30.00 80.00
STPO Denis Potvin 30.00 80.00
STPR Patrick Roy 300.00 500.00
STRB Ray Bourque 75.00 150.00
STRH Ron Hextall
STRM Ryan Malone 25.00 60.00
STRN Rick Nash 40.00 100.00
STRO Larry Robinson 25.00 60.00
STRY Ryan Miller 40.00 100.00
STSA Denis Savard 25.00 60.00
STSK Saku Koivu 40.00 100.00
STST Jordan Staal 125.00 250.00
STSV Marek Svatos 25.00 60.00
STTE Tony Esposito 30.00 80.00
STTR Tuomo Ruutu 25.00 60.00
STTV Tomas Vokoun 40.00 100.00
STWG Wayne Gretzky 500.00 800.00

2006-07 Upper Deck Sweet Shot Sweet Stitches

STATED PRINT RUN 200 #'d SETS
SSAF Alexander Frolov 2.50 6.00
SSAH Ales Hemsky 2.50 6.00
SSAL Daniel Alfredsson 3.00 8.00
SSAN Antero Niittymaki 3.00 8.00
SSAO Alexander Ovechkin 8.00 20.00
SSAR Andrew Raycroft 3.00 8.00
SSAS Alexander Steen 3.00 8.00
SSAT Alex Tanguay 3.00 8.00
SSBG Brian Gionta 2.50 6.00
SSBL Rob Blake 3.00 8.00
SSBO Pierre-Marc Bouchard 2.50 6.00
SSBR Brendan Shanahan 3.00 8.00
SSBS Billy Smith 3.00 8.00
SSBT Bryan Trottier 3.00 8.00
SSCD Chris Drury 2.50 6.00
SSCH Cristobal Huet 4.00 10.00
SSCN Cam Neely 4.00 10.00
SSCP Chris Pronger 3.00 8.00
SSCW Cam Ward 3.00 8.00
SSDA Dany Heatley 5.00 12.00
SSDH Dominik Hasek 5.00 12.00
SSDP Dion Phaneuf 4.00 10.00
SSDS Darryl Sittler 3.00 8.00
SSDW Doug Weight 2.50 6.00
SSEL Eric Lindros 3.00 8.00
SSES Eric Staal 3.00 8.00
SSFM Frank Mahovlich 3.00 8.00
SSGF Grant Fuhr 4.00 10.00
SSGL Guy Lafleur 4.00 10.00
SSGP Gilbert Perreault 3.00 8.00
SSHA Dale Hawerchuk 2.50 6.00
SSHE Milan Hejduk 2.50 6.00
SSHL Henrik Lundqvist 4.00 10.00
SSHO Marian Hossa 3.00 8.00
SSHZ Henrik Zetterberg 3.00 8.00
SSIK Ilya Kovalchuk 4.00 10.00
SSJC Jonathan Cheechoo 3.00 8.00
SSJG Jean-Sebastien Giguere 3.00 8.00
SSJI Jarome Iginla 5.00 12.00
SSJJ Jaromir Jagr 5.00 12.00
SSJL Joffrey Lupul 2.50 6.00
SSJM Joe Mullen 2.50 6.00
SSJS Joe Sakic 6.00 15.00
SSJT Jose Theodore 3.00 8.00
SSKL Kari Lehtonen 4.00 10.00
SSLR Luc Robitaille 3.00 8.00
SSMA Maxim Afinogenov 2.50 6.00
SSMB Martin Brodeur 8.00 20.00
SSMF Manny Fernandez 3.00 8.00
SSMG Marian Gaborik 5.00 12.00
SSMH Martin Havlat 3.00 8.00
SSMI Mike Bossy 3.00 8.00
SSMK Miikka Kiprusoff 3.00 8.00
SSML Mario Lemieux 12.00 30.00
SSMM Mike Modano 4.00 10.00
SSMN Markus Naslund 3.00 8.00
SSMR Michael Ryder 3.00 8.00
SSMS Marek Svatos 2.50 6.00
SSMT Marty Turco 3.00 8.00
SSNL Nicklas Lidstrom 3.00 8.00
SSOJ Olli Jokinen 2.50 6.00
SSOK Olaf Kolzig 3.00 8.00
SSPB Patrice Bergeron 3.00 8.00
SSPD Pavel Datsyuk 3.00 8.00
SSPE Patrik Elias 2.50 6.00
SSPF Peter Forsberg 5.00 12.00
SSPK Paul Kariya 3.00 8.00
SSPL Pascal LeClaire 3.00 8.00
SSPM Patrick Marleau 3.00 8.00
SSPO Denis Potvin 3.00 8.00
SSPR Patrick Roy 12.00 30.00
SSPS Peter Stastny 2.50 6.00
SSRB Ray Bourque 5.00 12.00
SSRE Mark Recchi 2.50 6.00
SSRH Ron Hextall 4.00 10.00
SSRI Brad Richards 3.00 8.00
SSRL Roberto Luongo 5.00 12.00
SSRM Ryan Miller 3.00 8.00
SSRN Rick Nash 3.00 8.00
SSRO Larry Robinson 3.00 8.00
SSRS Ryan Smyth 3.00 8.00
SSRV Rogie Vachon 3.00 8.00
SSSA Miroslav Satan 2.50 6.00
SSSB Borje Salming 3.00 8.00
SSSC Sidney Crosby 25.00 60.00
SSSD Shane Doan 2.50 6.00
SSSF Sergei Fedorov 3.00 8.00
SSSH Steve Shutt 2.50 6.00
SSSK Saku Koivu 3.00 8.00
SSSP Jason Spezza 3.00 8.00
SSSS Sergei Samsonov 3.00 8.00
SSST Martin St. Louis 3.00 8.00
SSSU Mats Sundin 3.00 8.00
SSSZ Sergei Zubov 2.50 6.00
SSTH Joe Thornton 5.00 12.00
SSTS Teemu Selanne 3.00 8.00
SSTV Tomas Vokoun 3.00 8.00
SSVL Vincent Lecavalier 3.00 8.00
SSWG Wayne Gretzky 20.00 50.00
SSZC Zdeno Chara 2.50 6.00

2006-07 Upper Deck Sweet Shot Sweet Stitches Duals

*DUALS: .75X to 2X SINGLE SWATCH
STATED PRINT RUN 50 #'d SETS
SSAF Alexander Frolov 4.00 10.00
SSAH Ales Hemsky 4.00 10.00
SSAL Daniel Alfredsson 6.00 15.00
SSAN Antero Niittymaki 6.00 15.00
SSAO Alexander Ovechkin 15.00 40.00
SSAR Andrew Raycroft 6.00 15.00
SSAS Alexander Steen 6.00 15.00
SSAT Alex Tanguay 6.00 15.00
SSBG Brian Gionta 4.00 10.00
SSBL Rob Blake 6.00 15.00
SSBO Pierre-Marc Bouchard 4.00 10.00
SSBR Brendan Shanahan 6.00 15.00
SSBS Billy Smith 6.00 15.00
SSBT Bryan Trottier 6.00 15.00
SSCD Chris Drury 5.00 12.00
SSCH Cristobal Huet 8.00 20.00
SSCN Cam Neely 6.00 15.00
SSCP Chris Pronger 6.00 15.00
SSCW Cam Ward 6.00 15.00
SSDA Dany Heatley 6.00 15.00
SSDH Dominik Hasek 10.00 25.00
SSDP Dion Phaneuf 6.00 15.00
SSDS Darryl Sittler 6.00 15.00
SSDW Doug Weight 4.00 10.00
SSEL Eric Lindros 6.00 15.00
SSES Eric Staal 6.00 15.00
SSFM Frank Mahovlich 5.00 12.00
SSGF Grant Fuhr 6.00 15.00
SSGL Guy Lafleur 8.00 20.00
SSGP Gilbert Perreault 6.00 15.00
SSHA Dale Hawerchuk 4.00 10.00
SSHE Milan Hejduk 4.00 10.00
SSHL Henrik Lundqvist 6.00 15.00
SSHO Marian Hossa 6.00 15.00
SSHZ Henrik Zetterberg 6.00 15.00
SSIK Ilya Kovalchuk 6.00 15.00
SSJC Jonathan Cheechoo 6.00 15.00
SSJG Jean-Sebastien Giguere 6.00 15.00
SSJI Jarome Iginla 6.00 15.00
SSJJ Jaromir Jagr 8.00 20.00
SSJL Joffrey Lupul 4.00 10.00
SSJM Joe Mullen 4.00 10.00
SSJS Joe Sakic 10.00 25.00
SSJT Jose Theodore 6.00 15.00
SSKL Kari Lehtonen 6.00 15.00
SSLR Luc Robitaille 6.00 15.00
SSMA Maxim Afinogenov 4.00 10.00
SSMB Martin Brodeur 15.00 40.00
SSMF Manny Fernandez 5.00 12.00
SSMG Marian Gaborik 6.00 15.00
SSMH Martin Havlat 6.00 15.00
SSMI Mike Bossy 6.00 15.00
SSMK Miikka Kiprusoff 8.00 20.00
SSML Mario Lemieux 25.00 60.00
SSMM Mike Modano 6.00 15.00
SSMN Markus Naslund 6.00 15.00
SSMR Michael Ryder 6.00 15.00
SSMS Marek Svatos 4.00 10.00
SSMT Marty Turco 6.00 15.00
SSNL Nicklas Lidstrom 6.00 15.00
SSOJ Olli Jokinen 4.00 10.00
SSOK Olaf Kolzig 6.00 15.00
SSPB Patrice Bergeron 6.00 15.00
SSPD Pavel Datsyuk 6.00 15.00
SSPE Patrik Elias 4.00 10.00
SSPF Peter Forsberg 8.00 20.00
SSPK Paul Kariya 6.00 15.00
SSPL Pascal LeClaire 6.00 15.00
SSPM Patrick Marleau 6.00 15.00
SSPO Denis Potvin 6.00 15.00
SSPR Patrick Roy 25.00 60.00
SSPS Peter Stastny 4.00 10.00
SSRB Ray Bourque 8.00 20.00
SSRE Mark Recchi 4.00 10.00
SSRH Ron Hextall 8.00 20.00
SSRI Brad Richards 6.00 15.00
SSRL Roberto Luongo 6.00 15.00
SSRM Ryan Miller 6.00 15.00
SSRN Rick Nash 6.00 15.00
SSRO Larry Robinson 6.00 15.00
SSRS Ryan Smyth 6.00 15.00
SSRV Rogie Vachon 6.00 15.00
SSSA Miroslav Satan 4.00 10.00
SSSB Borje Salming 6.00 15.00
SSSC Sidney Crosby 30.00 80.00
SSSD Shane Doan 4.00 10.00
SSSF Sergei Fedorov 6.00 15.00
SSSH Steve Shutt 5.00 12.00
SSSK Saku Koivu 6.00 15.00
SSSP Jason Spezza 6.00 15.00
SSSS Sergei Samsonov 6.00 15.00
SSST Martin St. Louis 6.00 15.00
SSSU Mats Sundin 6.00 15.00
SSSZ Sergei Zubov 4.00 10.00
SSTH Joe Thornton 8.00 20.00
SSTS Teemu Selanne 6.00 15.00
SSTV Tomas Vokoun 6.00 15.00
SSVL Vincent Lecavalier 6.00 15.00
SSWG Wayne Gretzky 30.00 80.00
SSZC Zdeno Chara 4.00 10.00

2006-07 Upper Deck Sweet Shot Sweet Stitches Triples

STATED PRINT RUN 25 #'d SETS
NOT PRICED THIS MONTH DUE TO SCARCITY
SSSC Sidney Crosby 60.00 150.00
SSWG Wayne Gretzky 60.00 150.00

2003-04 Upper Deck Trilogy

Released in early December 2003, this 181-card set consisted of 100 veteran base cards; two different rookie subsets and the Crest of Honor subset. Crest cards carried miniature felt emblems on the card fronts. Cards 142-171 were serial-numbered to 999 sets and cards 172-181 were serial-numbered to 499 each. Cards 182-189 were only available in packs of UD Rookie Update and were serial numbered to 999. Please note that two cards carry the number 17 on the cardbacks.

COMP.SET w/o SP's 50.00 100.00
COH 123-141 ODDS 1:9
1 Sergei Fedorov .75 2.00
2 Stanislav Chistov .30 .75
3 J-S Giguere .50 1.25
4 Dany Heatley .75 2.00
5 Ilya Kovalchuk .75 2.00
6 Joe Thornton 1.00 2.50
7 Glen Murray .30 .75
8 Bobby Orr 6.00 15.00
9 Miroslav Satan .50 1.25
10 Maxim Afinogenov .30 .75
11 Chris Drury .50 1.25
12 Jarome Iginla .75 2.00
13 Lanny McDonald .75 2.00
14 Roman Turek .50 1.25
15 Ron Francis .50 1.25
16 Jeff O'Neill .30 .75
17 Kyle Calder .30 .75
17 Alexei Zhamnov .30 .75
19 Jocelyn Thibault .50 1.25
20 Teemu Selanne .60 1.50
21 Peter Forsberg 1.50 4.00
22 Paul Kariya .60 1.50
23 Joe Sakic 1.25 3.00
24 Patrick Roy 3.00 8.00
25 Rick Nash .75 2.00
26 Marc Denis .50 1.25
27 Todd Marchant .30 .75
28 Mike Modano 1.00 2.50
29 Bill Guerin .50 1.25
30 Marty Turco .50 1.25
31 Brendan Shanahan .60 1.50
32 Gordie Howe 3.00 8.00
33 Steve Yzerman 3.00 8.00
34 Dominik Hasek 1.25 3.00
35 Ryan Smyth .30 .75
36 Mike Comrie .50 1.25
37 Ales Hemsky .50 1.25
38 Wayne Gretzky 5.00 12.00
39 Olli Jokinen .50 1.25
40 Stephen Weiss .30 .75
41 Jay Bouwmeester .30 .75
42 Roberto Luongo .75 2.00
43 Zigmund Palffy .50 1.25
44 Alexander Frolov .30 .75
45 Roman Cechmanek .50 1.25
46 Marian Gaborik 1.25 3.00
47 Pierre-Marc Bouchard .30 .75
48 Manny Fernandez .50 1.25
49 Dwayne Roloson .50 1.25
50 Saku Koivu .60 1.50
51 Marcel Hossa .30 .75
52 Jose Theodore .75 2.00
53 Guy Lafleur 1.00 2.50
54 David Legwand .50 1.25
55 Tomas Vokoun .50 1.25
56 Patrik Elias .50 1.25
57 Jamie Langenbrunner .30 .75
58 Scott Stevens .50 1.25
59 Martin Brodeur 1.50 4.00
60 Alexei Yashin .30 .75
61 Rick DiPietro .50 1.25
62 Alex Kovalev .50 1.25
63 Eric Lindros .60 1.50
64 Pavel Bure .60 1.50
65 Mike Dunham .50 1.25
66 Marian Hossa .60 1.50
67 Daniel Alfredsson .50 1.25
68 Jason Spezza .60 1.50
69 Patrick Lalime .50 1.25
70 Jeremy Roenick .75 2.00
71 Tony Amonte .50 1.25
72 John LeClair .60 1.50
73 Bobby Clarke 1.00 2.50
74 Mike Johnson .30 .75
75 Chris Gratton .30 .75
76 Sean Burke .50 1.25
77 Mario Lemieux 4.00 10.00
78 Martin Straka .30 .75
79 Sebastien Caron .50 1.25
80 Mike Ricci .30 .75
81 Niko Dimitrakos .30 .75
82 Evgeni Nabokov .50 1.25
83 Al MacInnis .50 1.25
84 Keith Tkachuk .60 1.50
85 Chris Pronger .50 1.25
86 Chris Osgood .50 1.25
87 Vincent Lecavalier .60 1.50
88 Martin St. Louis .50 1.25
89 Nikolai Khabibulin .60 1.50
90 Alexander Mogilny .50 1.25
91 Mats Sundin .60 1.50
92 Owen Nolan .50 1.25
93 Ed Belfour .60 1.50
94 Alexander Auld .30 .75
95 Markus Naslund .60 1.50
96 Todd Bertuzzi .60 1.50
97 Ed Jovanovski .50 1.25
98 Jaromir Jagr 1.00 2.50
99 Peter Bondra .50 1.25
100 Olaf Kolzig .50 1.25
101 Joe Thornton COH 8.00 20.00
102 Sergei Fedorov COH 5.00 12.00
103 Dany Heatley COH 6.00 15.00
104 Steve Yzerman COH 8.00 20.00
105 Henrik Zetterberg COH 6.00 15.00
106 Patrick Roy COH 12.50 30.00
107 Peter Forsberg COH 8.00 20.00
108 J-S Giguere COH 4.00 10.00
109 Marian Gaborik COH 8.00 20.00
110 Markus Naslund COH 6.00 15.00
111 Jeremy Roenick COH 6.00 15.00
112 Mario Lemieux COH 12.50 30.00
113 Mats Sundin COH 6.00 15.00
114 Ed Belfour COH 4.00 10.00
115 Ilya Kovalchuk COH 8.00 20.00
116 Marian Hossa COH 4.00 10.00
117 Eric Lindros COH 4.00 10.00
118 Jocelyn Thibault COH 4.00 10.00
119 Jose Theodore COH 8.00 20.00
120 Mike Modano COH 8.00 20.00
121 Jason Spezza COH 8.00 20.00
122 Rick Nash COH 8.00 20.00
123 Jean Beliveau COH 6.00 15.00
124 Mike Bossy COH 6.00 15.00
125 Johnny Bucyk COH 4.00 10.00
126 Marcel Dionne COH 4.00 10.00
127 Grant Fuhr COH 10.00 25.00
128 Michel Goulet COH 4.00 10.00
129 Jari Kurri COH 4.00 10.00
130 Guy Lafleur COH 4.00 10.00
131 Ted Lindsay COH 4.00 10.00
132 Scotty Bowman COH 4.00 10.00
133 Lanny McDonald COH 4.00 10.00

134 Stan Mikita COH 6.00 15.00
135 Denis Potvin COH 4.00 10.00
136 Ray Bourque COH 8.00 20.00
137 Don Cherry COH 10.00 25.00
138 Bobby Orr COH 20.00 40.00
139 Gordie Howe COH 12.50 30.00
140 Bobby Clarke COH 8.00 20.00
141 Phil Esposito COH 6.00 15.00
142 Jiri Hudler RC 3.00 8.00
143 Patrice Bergeron RC 8.00 20.00
144 Matthew Lombardi RC 2.00 5.00
145 Lasse Kukkonen RC 2.00 5.00
146 John-Michael Liles RC 2.00 5.00
147 Marek Svatos RC 5.00 12.00
148 Cody McCormick RC 2.00 5.00
149 Dan Fritsche RC 2.00 5.00
150 Antti Miettinen RC 2.00 5.00
151 Esa Pirnes RC 2.00 5.00
152 Tim Gleason RC 2.00 5.00
153 Brent Burns RC 2.00 5.00
154 Christoph Brandner RC 2.00 5.00
155 Chris Higgins RC 5.00 12.00
156 Dan Hamhuis RC 2.00 5.00
157 Marek Zidlicky RC 2.00 5.00
158 Wade Brookbank RC 2.00 5.00
159 David Hale RC 2.00 5.00
160 Paul Martin RC 2.00 5.00
161 Sean Bergenheim RC 2.00 5.00
162 Antoine Vermette RC 4.00 10.00
163 Matthew Spiller RC 2.00 5.00
164 Ryan Malone RC 4.00 10.00
165 Christian Ehrhoff RC 2.00 5.00
166 Alexander Semin RC 6.00 15.00
167 Tom Preissing RC 2.00 5.00
168 Peter Sejna RC 2.00 5.00
169 Maxim Kondratiev RC 2.00 5.00
170 Matt Stajan RC 4.00 10.00
171 Boyd Gordon RC 2.00 5.00
172 Joffrey Lupul RC 5.00 12.00
173 Eric Staal RC 10.00 25.00
174 Tuomo Ruutu RC 6.00 15.00
175 Pavel Vorobiev RC 2.00 5.00
176 Nathan Horton RC 6.00 15.00
177 Dustin Brown RC 5.00 12.00
178 Jordin Tootoo RC 8.00 20.00
179 Joni Pitkanen RC 4.00 10.00
180 Marc-Andre Fleury RC 12.00 30.00
181 Milan Michalek RC 5.00 12.00
182 Mikhail Yakubov RC 2.00 5.00
183 Trevor Daley RC 2.00 5.00
184 Ryan Kesler RC 2.00 5.00
185 Fredrik Sjostrom RC 2.00 5.00
186 Nikolai Zherdev RC 4.00 10.00
187 Timofei Shishkanov RC 2.00 5.00
188 Niklas Kronwall RC 2.50 6.00
189 Fedor Tyutin RC 2.00 5.00

2003-04 Upper Deck Trilogy Authentic Patches

These jersey patch cards were inserted at 1:27.
*SINGLE COLOR SWATCH: .5X TO 1X
AP1 Wayne Gretzky 100.00 250.00
AP2 J-S Giguere 15.00 40.00
AP3 Mike Modano 20.00 50.00
AP4 Jaromir Jagr 20.00 50.00
AP5 Steve Yzerman 30.00 80.00
AP6 Jose Theodore 25.00 60.00
AP7 Joe Sakic 20.00 50.00
AP8 Mario Lemieux 30.00 80.00
AP9 Marian Hossa 15.00 40.00
AP10 Martin Brodeur 25.00 60.00
AP11 Dominik Hasek 15.00 40.00
AP12 Mats Sundin 15.00 40.00
AP13 Milan Hejduk 15.00 40.00
AP14 Jeremy Roenick 20.00 50.00
AP15 Ray Bourque 25.00 60.00
AP16 Markus Naslund 15.00 40.00
AP17 Pavol Demitra 15.00 40.00
AP18 Doug Gilmour 15.00 40.00
AP19 Joe Thornton 20.00 50.00
AP20 Peter Forsberg 25.00 60.00
AP21 Scott Gomez 15.00 40.00
AP22 Sergei Fedorov 20.00 50.00
AP23 Pavel Bure 15.00 40.00
AP24 Dany Heatley 20.00 50.00
AP25 Teemu Selanne 15.00 40.00
AP26 John LeClair 15.00 40.00
AP27 Zigmund Palffy 15.00 40.00
AP28 Guy Lafleur 20.00 50.00
AP29 Ed Belfour 15.00 40.00
AP30 Jari Kurri 25.00 60.00
AP31 Marcel Dionne 15.00 40.00
AP32 Tony Amonte 15.00 40.00
AP33 Patrick Roy 40.00 100.00
AP34 Eric Lindros 15.00 40.00
AP35 Sergei Samsonov 15.00 40.00
AP36 Keith Tkachuk 15.00 40.00
AP37 Grant Fuhr 15.00 40.00
AP38 Guy Lafleur 15.00 40.00
AP39 Wayne Gretzky 100.00 250.00
AP40 Nicklas Lidstrom 15.00 40.00
AP41 Ray Bourque 25.00 60.00
AP42 Patrick Roy 40.00 100.00

2003-04 Upper Deck Trilogy Crest Variations

This parallel to the "Crest of Honor" subset carried different emblems on the card fronts. Cards 101-122 carried the player's jersey number and were limited to that number of copies. Cards 123-141 carried an image of the Stanley Cup, print runs were based on the last year the player won the Cup and are listed below. The cards of Marcel Dionne and Michel Goulet carried alternate team emblems since neither won a Cup during their career. The Don Cherry card carried a cherries emblem.
PRINT RUNS PROVIDED BY UD
101 Joe Thornton JSY#/19
102 Sergei Fedorov JSY#/91 20.00 50.00
103 Dany Heatley JSY#/15
104 Steve Yzerman JSY#/19
105 Henrik Zetterberg JSY#/40 25.00 60.00
106 Patrick Roy JSY#/33 75.00 200.00
107 Peter Forsberg JSY#/21
108 J-S Giguere JSY#/35 30.00 60.00
109 Marian Gaborik JSY#/10
110 Markus Naslund JSY#/19
111 Jeremy Roenick JSY#/97 15.00 40.00
112 Mario Lemieux JSY#/66 40.00 100.00
113 Mats Sundin JSY#/13
114 Ed Belfour JSY#/20 60.00 150.00
115 Ilya Kovalchuk JSY#/17
116 Marian Hossa JSY#/18
117 Eric Lindros JSY#/88 12.50 30.00
118 Jocelyn Thibault JSY#/41 20.00 50.00
119 Jose Theodore JSY#/60 20.00 50.00
120 Mike Modano JSY#/9
121 Jason Spezza JSY#/39 50.00 100.00
122 Rick Nash JSY#/61 15.00 40.00
123 Jean Beliveau SC/72 15.00 40.00
124 Mike Bossy SC/91 12.50 30.00
125 Johnny Bucyk SC/81 15.00 40.00
126 Marcel Dionne DET/92 15.00 40.00
127 Grant Fuhr SC/3
128 Michel Goulet QUE/98
129 Jari Kurri SC/1
130 Guy Lafleur SC/88 15.00 40.00
131 Ted Lindsay SC/66 12.50 30.00
132 Scotty Bowman SC/91 15.00 40.00
133 Lanny McDonald SC/92 12.50 30.00
134 Stan Mikita SC/83 15.00 40.00
135 Denis Potvin SC/91 15.00 40.00
136 Ray Bourque SC/77 20.00 50.00
137 Don Cherry Cherries/99 20.00 50.00
138 Bobby Orr SC/79 50.00 100.00
139 Gordie Howe SC/72 30.00 80.00
140 Bobby Clarke SC/87 12.50 30.00
141 Wayne Gretzky SC/99
141 Phil Esposito SC/84 12.50 30.00

2003-04 Upper Deck Trilogy Limited

*STARS: 8X TO 20X BASE HI
*CRESTS: 2X TO 5X
*ROOKIES: 1.25X TO 3X
STATED PRINT RUN 30 SER.#'d SETS

2003-04 Upper Deck Trilogy Limited Threads

This 30-card set featured a replica felt team logo on one side of the card front and a swatch of game-used jersey on the other. Cards were serial-numbered out of 50.
STATED PRINT RUN 50 SER.#'d SETS
LT1 Jaromir Jagr 25.00 60.00
LT2 Scott Stevens 12.00 30.00
LT3 Mario Lemieux 50.00 125.00
LT4 Jarome Iginla 30.00 80.00
LT5 Roman Turek 12.00 30.00
LT6 Patrick Roy 50.00 125.00
LT7 Steve Yzerman 40.00 100.00
LT8 Mats Sundin 12.00 30.00
LT9 Mike Modano 25.00 60.00
LT10 Zigmund Palffy 12.00 30.00
LT11 Peter Forsberg 25.00 60.00
LT12 Pavel Bure 12.00 30.00
LT13 Todd Bertuzzi 15.00 40.00
LT14 Jason Spezza 20.00 50.00
LT15 Scott Stevens 15.00 40.00
LT16 Jocelyn Thibault 12.00 30.00
LT17 Joe Sakic 30.00 80.00
LT18 Henrik Zetterberg 20.00 50.00
LT19 Joe Thornton 25.00 60.00
LT20 Patrick Lalime 12.00 30.00
LT21 Adam Deadmarsh 12.00 30.00
LT22 Markus Naslund 12.00 30.00
LT23 Ed Belfour 15.00 40.00
LT24 Scott Gomez 12.00 30.00
LT25 Marian Hossa 12.00 30.00
LT26 Alexei Yashin 12.00 30.00
LT27 Sergei Samsonov 12.00 30.00
LT28 Martin Brodeur 30.00 80.00
LT29 Martin Brodeur 30.00 80.00
LT30 Marian Gaborik

2003-04 Upper Deck Trilogy Scripts

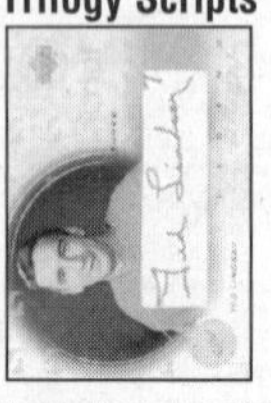

This autographed insert set consisted of 4 distinct subsets. Script 1 cards were rookies and prospects, Script 2 cards were current stars, Script 3 cards were retired greats. The Custom Scripts subset included special "customized" autographs of the featured player. Please note that several of the "Custom" cards on this checklist have yet to be confirmed while different, un-catalogued version appear frequently. Any further information can be sent to hockeymag@beckett.com.-
SCRIPTS 1-3 ODDS 1:4
CUSTOM ODDS 1:45
S1AH Ales Hemsky 4.00 10.00
S1BO Brooks Orpik 3.00 8.00
S1HL Adam Hall 3.00 8.00
S1HZ Henrik Zetterberg 12.50 30.00
S1JA Jared Aulin 3.00 8.00
S1JB Jay Bouwmeester 8.00 20.00
S1JL Jordan Leopold 3.00 8.00
S1JS Jason Spezza 12.50 30.00
S1PB P-M Bouchard 5.00 12.00
S1PL Pascal Leclaire 4.00 10.00
S1RH Ron Hainsey 3.00 8.00
S1SO Steve Ott 5.00 12.00
S2CJ Curtis Joseph 10.00 25.00
S2EC Erik Cole 3.00 8.00
S2IK Ilya Kovalchuk EXCH 15.00 40.00
S2JG J-S Giguere 6.00 15.00
S2JL John LeClair 6.00 15.00
S2JT Jose Theodore 20.00 50.00
S2JT Joe Thornton 25.00 60.00
S2JW Justin Williams 5.00 12.00
S2MA Maxim Afinogenov 5.00 12.00
S2MB Martin Brodeur 75.00 200.00
S2MH Martin Havlat 6.00 15.00
S2MH Marian Hossa 6.00 15.00
S2MN Markus Naslund 6.00 15.00
S2MT Marty Turco 8.00 20.00
S2PR Patrick Roy 75.00 200.00
S2SS Sergei Samsonov 4.00 10.00
S2TB Todd Bertuzzi 6.00 15.00
S3BC Bobby Clarke 12.50 30.00
S3BK Johnny Bucyk AS 8.00 20.00
S3BO Bobby Orr 75.00 200.00
S3BY Mike Bossy AS 10.00 25.00
S3DC Don Cherry 15.00 40.00
S3DP Denis Potvin NYI 6.00 15.00
S3G1 Wayne Gretzky AS 75.00 200.00
S3GF Grant Fuhr 8.00 20.00
S3GH Gordie Howe HAR 30.00 80.00
S3GL Guy Lafleur 12.50 30.00
S3GR Wayne Gretzky AS 75.00 200.00
S3GT Michel Goulet AS 12.00 30.00
S3GY Wayne Gretzky NYR 75.00 200.00
S3JB Jean Beliveau 15.00 40.00
S3JK Jari Kurri 10.00 25.00
S3JK Johnny Bucyk BOS 8.00 20.00
S3LM Lanny McDonald 5.00 12.00
S3MB Mike Bossy NYI 10.00 25.00
S3MD Marcel Dionne 5.00 12.00
S3MG Michel Goulet CHI 5.00 12.00
S3MH Gordie Howe DET 50.00 125.00
S3PE Phil Esposito 15.00 40.00
S3PN Denis Potvin AS 6.00 15.00
S3RB Ray Bourque 15.00 40.00
S3SB Scotty Bowman 15.00 40.00
S3SM Stan Mikita 6.00 15.00
S3TL Ted Lindsay 10.00 25.00
S3WA Wayne Gretzky LA 75.00 200.00
S3WG Wayne Gretzky EDM 75.00 200.00
S399 Wayne Gretzky HOF 75.00 200.00
CSBC Bobby Clarke HOF 20.00 50.00
CSBC2 Bobby Clarke Broad Street Bullies 30.00 80.00
CSBU Jean Beliveau LeGros Bill 25.00 60.00
CSBU2 J.Beliveau HOF 25.00 60.00
CSBU3 J.Beliveau SC
CSBY M.Bossy HOF 10.00 25.00
CSBY2 M.Bossy SC 25.00 60.00
CSDC D.Cherry Grapes 20.00 50.00
CSGH Gordie Howe
CSGL Guy Lafleur HOF 20.00 50.00
CSGL2 G.Lafleur SC
CSJB J.Bucyk Chief 15.00 40.00
CSJG J.Giguere Jiggy 12.50 30.00
CSMC Mike Comrie 8.00 20.00
CSMH G.Howe HOF 50.00 125.00
CSMH2 G.Howe Mr.Elbows 50.00 125.00
CSMH3 G.Howe SC 50.00 125.00
CSMH4 Gordie Howe Production Line 50.00 125.00
CSRN R.Nash #1 Pick 25.00 60.00
CSSB S.Bowman HOF 30.00 80.00
CSSO S.Ott Otter 8.00 20.00
CSTB T.Bertuzzi Bert 20.00 50.00
CSTL T.Lindsay Prod.Line 15.00 40.00
CSTL2 T.Lindsay Art Ross 15.00 40.00
CSTL3 T.Lindsay HOF 15.00 40.00
CSTL4 T.Lindsay SC Winner 15.00 40.00
CSZP Z.Palffy Ziggy 15.00 40.00

2003-04 Upper Deck Trilogy Scripts Limited

This partial-parallel to the basic Sripts set carried a gold foil "Limited" stamp on the card fronts and serial-numbering out of 30.
COMMON GRETZKY 100.00 250.00

2003-04 Upper Deck Trilogy Scripts Red

This unannounced partial-parallel set to the basic Scripts set carried red ink signatures and hand written serial-numbering (listed below). Please note that the Gretzky cards were signed in blue ink, not red and that Gordie Howe signed all of his cards in this product with red ink.
PRINT RUNS UNDER 27
NOT PRICED DUE TO SCARCITY
S1HL Adam Hall/31 15.00 40.00
S1JB Jay Bouwmeester/31 20.00 50.00
S1JL Jordan Leopold/2
S1PL Pascal Leclaire/31 15.00 40.00
S1RH Ron Hainsey/2
S1SO Steve Ott/6
S2CJ Curtis Joseph/30 20.00 50.00
S2IK Ilya Kovalchuk/30 40.00 100.00
S2JT Joe Thornton/7
S2JW Justin Williams/2
S2MN Markus Naslund/30 30.00 80.00
S2MT Marty Turco/13
S2PR Patrick Roy/27 150.00 250.00
S2SS Sergei Samsonov/17
S2TB Todd Bertuzzi/22
S3BC Bobby Clarke/30 20.00 50.00
S3BO Bobby Orr/30 125.00 250.00
S3DC Don Cherry/30 60.00 150.00
S3DP Denis Potvin/30 25.00 60.00
S3GF Grant Fuhr/30 30.00 80.00
S3GL Guy Lafleur/30 30.00 80.00
S3JB Johnny Bucyk/30 15.00 40.00
S3JB Jean Beliveau/30 25.00 60.00
S3JK Jari Kurri/30
S3LM Lanny McDonald/30 15.00 40.00
S3MB Mike Bossy/30 20.00 50.00
S3MD Marcel Dionne/30 20.00 50.00
S3MG Michel Goulet/30 20.00 50.00
S3MH Gordie Howe/30 60.00 125.00
S3RB Ray Bourque/30 40.00 100.00
S3SB Scotty Bowman/30 40.00 100.00
S3SM Stan Mikita/30 30.00 80.00
S3TL Ted Lindsay/30 25.00 60.00
S3WG W.Gretzky EDM Blue/30 300.00 500.00

2005-06 Upper Deck Trilogy

COMP.SET w/o SP's (90) 20.00 40.00
FIT PRINT RUN 599 SER.#'d SETS
RC PRINT RUN 999 SER.#'d SETS
1 J-S Giguere .50 1.25
2 Joffrey Lupul .30 .75
3 Sergei Fedorov .60 1.50
4 Marian Hossa .60 1.50
5 Ilya Kovalchuk .75 2.00
6 Kari Lehtonen .60 1.50
7 Andrew Raycroft .50 1.25
8 Joe Thornton 1.00 2.50
9 Patrice Bergeron .50 1.25
10 Glen Murray .30 .75
11 Brian Leetch .60 1.50
12 Daniel Briere .30 .75
13 Chris Drury .30 .75
14 Maxim Afinogenov .30 .75
15 Jarome Iginla .75 2.00
16 Jordan Leopold .30 .75
17 Miikka Kiprusoff .60 1.50
18 Eric Staal .60 1.50
19 Erik Cole .30 .75
20 Nikolai Khabibulin .60 1.50
21 Tuomo Ruutu .30 .75
22 David Aebischer .50 1.25
23 Joe Sakic 1.25 3.00
24 Rob Blake .50 1.25
25 Milan Hejduk .60 1.50
26 Alex Tanguay .50 1.25
27 Rick Nash .75 2.00
28 Nikolai Zherdev .60 1.50
29 Mike Modano .60 1.50
30 Bill Guerin .50 1.25
31 Marty Turco .50 1.25
32 Manny Legace .60 1.50
33 Pavel Datsyuk .60 1.50
34 Brendan Shanahan .60 1.50
35 Steve Yzerman 2.50 6.00
36 Henrik Zetterberg .60 1.50
37 Ty Conklin .50 1.25
38 Ryan Smyth .30 .75
39 Chris Pronger .50 1.25
40 Roberto Luongo .75 2.00
41 Stephen Weiss .30 .75
42 Luc Robitaille .50 1.25
43 Jeremy Roenick .75 2.00
44 Marian Gaborik 1.25 3.00
45 Mike Ribeiro .30 .75
46 Michael Ryder .50 1.25
47 Jose Theodore .75 2.00
48 Saku Koivu .60 1.50
49 Paul Kariya .60 1.50
50 Steve Sullivan .30 .75
51 Tomas Vokoun .50 1.25
52 Martin Brodeur 3.00 8.00
53 Scott Gomez .50 1.25
54 Patrik Elias .50 1.25
55 Jaromir Jagr 1.00 2.50
56 Kevin Weekes .50 1.25
57 Alexei Yashin .30 .75
58 Miroslav Satan .30 .75
59 Rick DiPietro .50 1.25
60 Daniel Alfredsson .50 1.25
61 Dany Heatley .75 2.00
62 Jason Spezza .60 1.50
63 Martin Havlat .50 1.25
64 Peter Forsberg 1.00 2.50
65 Keith Primeau .30 .75
66 Simon Gagne .60 1.50
67 Robert Esche .50 1.25
68 Ladislav Nagy .30 .75
69 Curtis Joseph .60 1.50
70 Shane Doan .30 .75
71 Zigmund Palffy .50 1.25
72 Mario Lemieux 4.00 10.00
73 Mark Recchi .50 1.25
74 Evgeni Nabokov .50 1.25
75 Patrick Marleau .50 1.25
76 Jonathan Cheechoo .60 1.50
77 Patrick Lalime .50 1.25
78 Doug Weight .50 1.25
79 Keith Tkachuk .60 1.50
80 Brad Richards .50 1.25
81 Sean Burke .50 1.25
82 Martin St. Louis .50 1.25
83 Vincent Lecavalier .60 1.50
84 Ed Belfour .60 1.50
85 Mats Sundin .60 1.50
86 Eric Lindros .60 1.50
87 Kyle Wellwood .30 .75
88 Markus Naslund .60 1.50
89 Ed Jovanovski .50 1.25
90 Olaf Kolzig .50 1.25
91 J-S Giguere FIT 4.00 10.00
92 Sergei Fedorov FIT 5.00 12.00
93 Sergei Fedorov FIT 4.00 10.00
94 Ilya Kovalchuk FIT 5.00 12.00
95 Joe Thornton FIT 6.00 15.00
96 Ray Bourque FIT 5.00 12.00
97 Chris Drury FIT 4.00 10.00
98 Jarome Iginla FIT 5.00 12.00
99 Miikka Kiprusoff FIT 5.00 12.00
100 Eric Staal FIT 4.00 10.00
101 Tuomo Ruutu FIT 2.50 6.00
102 Joe Sakic FIT 6.00 15.00
103 Patrick Roy FIT 12.00 30.00
104 Paul Kariya FIT 4.00 10.00
105 Peter Forsberg FIT 5.00 12.00
106 Nikolai Zherdev FIT 3.00 8.00
107 Rick Nash FIT 4.00 10.00
108 Mike Modano FIT 4.00 10.00
109 Gordie Howe FIT 8.00 20.00
110 Pavel Datsyuk FIT 4.00 10.00
111 Steve Yzerman FIT 10.00 25.00
112 Henrik Zetterberg FIT 4.00 10.00
113 Wayne Gretzky FIT 15.00 40.00
114 Marian Gaborik FIT 5.00 12.00
115 Jose Theodore FIT 4.00 10.00
116 Saku Koivu FIT 4.00 10.00
117 Martin Brodeur FIT 8.00 20.00
118 Jaromir Jagr FIT 6.00 15.00
119 Mark Messier FIT 4.00 10.00
120 Jason Spezza FIT 4.00 10.00
121 Jeremy Roenick FIT 4.00 10.00
122 Marc-Andre Fleury FIT 4.00 10.00
123 Mario Lemieux FIT 12.00 30.00
124 Chris Pronger FIT 3.00 8.00
125 Brad Richards FIT 3.00 8.00
126 Martin St. Louis FIT 3.00 8.00
127 Vincent Lecavalier FIT 4.00 10.00
128 Ed Belfour FIT 4.00 10.00
129 Mats Sundin FIT 4.00 10.00
130 Markus Naslund FIT 4.00 10.00
131 Kari Lehtonen FIT 4.00 10.00
132 Andrew Raycroft FIT 3.00 8.00
133 Patrice Bergeron FIT 3.00 8.00
134 Alex Tanguay FIT 3.00 8.00
135 Milan Hejduk FIT 3.00 8.00
136 Marty Turco FIT 3.00 8.00
137 Bill Guerin FIT 3.00 8.00
138 Brendan Shanahan FIT 3.00 8.00
139 Ryan Smyth FIT 3.00 8.00
140 Roberto Luongo FIT 5.00 12.00
141 Luc Robitaille FIT 3.00 8.00
142 Michael Ryder FIT 3.00 8.00
143 Tomas Vokoun FIT 3.00 8.00
144 Patrik Elias FIT 3.00 8.00
145 Rick DiPietro FIT 3.00 8.00
146 Daniel Alfredsson FIT 3.00 8.00
147 Marian Hossa FIT 3.00 8.00
148 Keith Primeau FIT 2.00 5.00
149 Brett Hull FIT 5.00 12.00
150 Evgeni Nabokov FIT 3.00 8.00
151 Patrick Marleau FIT 3.00 8.00
152 Doug Weight FIT 3.00 8.00
153 Keith Tkachuk FIT 3.00 8.00
154 Todd Bertuzzi FIT 3.00 8.00
155 Olaf Kolzig FIT 3.00 8.00
156 Cam Neely FIT 4.00 10.00
157 Gilbert Perreault FIT 4.00 10.00
158 Denis Savard FIT 3.00 8.00
159 Tony Esposito FIT 3.00 8.00
160 Jari Kurri FIT 3.00 8.00
161 Grant Fuhr FIT 4.00 10.00
162 Mike Ribeiro FIT 3.00 8.00
163 Guy Lafleur FIT 4.00 10.00
164 Mike Bossy FIT 4.00 10.00
165 Alexei Yashin FIT 2.00 5.00
166 Phil Esposito FIT 4.00 10.00
167 Dominik Hasek FIT 6.00 15.00
168 Martin Havlat FIT 3.00 8.00
169 Simon Gagne FIT 4.00 10.00
170 Ed Jovanovski FIT 3.00 8.00
171 Corey Perry RC 5.00 12.00
172 Ryan Getzlaf RC 6.00 15.00
173 Braydon Coburn RC 4.00 10.00
174 Jim Slater RC 3.00 8.00
175 Hannu Toivonen RC 4.00 10.00
176 Milan Jurcina RC 3.00 8.00
177 Andrew Alberts RC 3.00 8.00
178 Thomas Vanek RC 8.00 20.00
179 Dion Phaneuf RC 12.00 30.00
180 Eric Nystrom RC 4.00 10.00
181 Cam Ward RC 8.00 20.00
182 Brent Seabrook RC 3.00 8.00
183 Rene Bourque RC 3.00 8.00
184 Cam Barker RC 4.00 8.00
185 Wojtek Wolski RC 5.00 12.00
186 Peter Budaj RC 3.00 8.00
187 Gilbert Brule RC 5.00 12.00
188 Jussi Jokinen RC 4.00 10.00
189 Jim Howard RC 4.00 10.00
190 Johan Franzen RC 2.50 6.00
191 Brett Lebda RC 2.50 6.00
192 Rostislav Olesz RC 4.00 10.00
193 Anthony Stewart RC 4.00 10.00
194 Alexander Perezhogin RC 4.00 10.00
195 Yann Danis RC 2.50 6.00
196 Mark Streit RC 3.00 8.00
197 Ryan Suter RC 3.00 8.00
198 Zach Parise RC 5.00 12.00
199 Robert Nilsson RC 2.50 6.00
200 Petteri Nokelainen RC 3.00 8.00
201 Chris Campoli RC 3.00 8.00
202 Henrik Lundqvist RC 12.00 30.00
203 Petr Prucha RC 4.00 10.00
204 Al Montoya RC 4.00 10.00
205 Andrej Meszaros RC 5.00 12.00
206 Brandon Bochenski RC 3.00 8.00
207 Jeff Carter RC 6.00 15.00
208 Mike Richards RC 4.00 10.00
209 David Leneveu RC 4.00 10.00
210 Keith Ballard RC 3.00 8.00
211 Sidney Crosby RC 150.00 300.00
212 Maxime Talbot RC 3.00 8.00
213 Ryane Clowe RC 3.00 8.00
214 Jeff Woywitka RC 3.00 8.00
215 Jay McClement RC 3.00 8.00
216 Lee Stempniak RC 4.00 10.00
217 Jeff Hoggan RC 3.00 8.00
218 Alexander Steen RC 3.00 10.00
219 Andrew Wozniewski RC 2.50 6.00
220 Alexander Ovechkin RC 50.00 100.00
221 Dustin Penner RC 4.00 10.00
222 Zenon Konopka RC 3.00 8.00
223 Michael Wall RC 4.00 10.00
224 Adam Berkhoel RC 4.00 10.00
225 Jordan Sigalet RC 4.00 8.00
226 Ben Walter RC 2.50 6.00
227 Chris Thorburn RC 3.00 8.00
228 Daniel Paille RC 2.50 6.00
229 Nathan Paetsch RC 2.50 6.00
230 Jiri Novotny RC 2.50 6.00
231 Richie Regehr RC 2.50 6.00
232 Mark Giordano RC 2.50 6.00
233 Andrew Ladd RC 4.00 8.00
234 Chad Larose RC 2.50 6.00
235 Niklas Nordgren RC 2.50 6.00
236 Danny Richmond RC 2.50 6.00
237 Martin St. Pierre RC 2.50 6.00
238 Corey Crawford RC 4.00 10.00
239 James Wisniewski RC
240 Duncan Keith RC 4.00 10.00
241 Brad Richardson RC 2.50 6.00
242 Vitaly Kolesnik RC 4.00 8.00
243 Andrew Penner RC 2.50 6.00
244 Ole-Kristian Tollefsen RC 2.50 6.00
245 Alexandre Picard RC 3.00 8.00
246 Joakim Lindstrom RC 2.50 6.00
247 Steven Goertzen RC 2.50 6.00
248 Geoff Platt RC 2.50 6.00
249 Jaroslav Balastik RC 2.50 6.00
250 Junior Lessard RC 2.50 6.00
251 Vojtech Polak RC 2.50 6.00
252 Kyle Quincey RC 2.50 6.00
253 Valtteri Filppula RC 3.00 8.00
254 Brad Winchester RC 2.50 6.00
255 Matt Greene RC 2.50 6.00
256 Kyle Brodziak RC 2.50 6.00
257 J-F Jacques RC 2.50 6.00
258 Mathieu Roy RC 2.50 6.00
259 Danny Syvret RC 2.50 6.00
260 Greg Jacina RC 2.50 6.00
261 Rob Globke RC 2.50 6.00
262 Petr Taticek RC 2.50 6.00
263 Jeff Tambellini RC 2.50 6.00
264 Petr Kanko RC 3.00 8.00
265 Yanick Lehoux RC 2.50 6.00
266 Richard Petiot RC 2.50 6.00
267 Matt Ryan RC 2.50 6.00
268 Connor James RC 2.50 6.00
269 Mikko Koivu RC 3.00 8.00
270 Derek Boogaard RC 3.00 8.00
271 Maxim Lapierre RC 2.50 6.00
272 Andrei Kostitsyn RC 3.00 8.00
273 J-P Cote RC 2.50 6.00
274 Jonathan Ferland RC 2.50 6.00
275 Kevin Klein RC 2.50 6.00
276 Pekka Rinne RC 3.00 8.00
277 Barry Tallackson RC 2.50 6.00
278 Cam Janssen RC 2.50 6.00
279 Jason Ryznar RC 2.50 6.00
280 Jeremy Colliton RC 2.50 6.00
281 Bruno Gervais RC 2.50 6.00
282 Ryan Hollweg RC 2.50 6.00
283 Chris Holt RC 2.50 6.00
284 Patrick Eaves RC 3.00 8.00
285 Christoph Schubert RC 2.50 6.00
286 Brian McGrattan RC 2.50 6.00
287 R.J. Umberger RC 3.00 8.00
288 Ben Eager RC 2.50 6.00
289 Alexandre Picard RC 2.50 6.00
290 Stefan Ruzicka RC 2.50 6.00
291 Matt Jones RC 2.50 6.00
292 Ryan Whitney RC 2.50 6.00
293 Erik Christensen RC 3.00 8.00
294 Colby Armstrong RC 3.00 8.00
295 Steve Bernier RC 4.00 10.00
296 Dimitri Patzold RC 3.00 8.00
297 Grant Stevenson RC 2.50 6.00
298 Doug Murray RC 2.50 6.00
299 Josh Gorges RC 2.50 6.00
300 Dennis Wideman RC 2.50 6.00
301 Chris Beckford-Tseu RC 3.00 8.00
302 Colin Hemingway RC 2.50 6.00
303 Jon DiSalvatore RC
304 Evgeny Artyukhin RC
305 Gerald Coleman RC 3.00 8.00
306 Ryan Craig RC
307 Nick Tarnasky RC 2.50 6.00
308 Paul Ranger RC 2.50 6.00
309 Darren Reid RC 2.50 6.00
310 Doug O'Brien RC 2.50 6.00
311 Staffan Kronwall RC 2.50 6.00
312 Jay Harrison RC 2.50 6.00
313 Kevin Bieksa RC 2.50 6.00
314 Rob McVicar RC 3.00 8.00
315 Tomas Mojzis RC 2.50 6.00
316 Tomas Fleischmann RC 2.50 6.00
317 Jakub Klepis RC 2.50 6.00
318 Mike Green RC
319 David Steckel RC 2.50 6.00
320 Joey Tenute RC 2.50 6.00

2005-06 Upper Deck Trilogy Crystal

*STARS: 1.5X TO 4X BASE HI
PRINT RUN 25 SER.#'d SETS

2005-06 Upper Deck Trilogy Crystal Autographs

PRINT RUN 10 SER.#'d SETS
NOT PRICED DUE TO SCARCITY
91 J-S Giguere
93 Dany Heatley
94 Ilya Kovalchuk
95 Joe Thornton
96 Ray Bourque
98 Jarome Iginla
100 Tuomo Ruutu
109 Gordie Howe
111 Henrik Zetterberg
113 Wayne Gretzky
114 Marian Gaborik
115 Jose Theodore
116 Saku Koivu
117 Martin Brodeur
120 Jason Spezza
121 Jeremy Roenick
126 Martin St. Louis
127 Vincent Lecavalier
129 Mats Sundin
130 Markus Naslund

2005-06 Upper Deck Trilogy Honorary Swatches

STATED ODDS 1:3
SCRIPTS PRINT RUN 10 SER.#'d SETS
SCRIPTS NOT PRICED DUE TO SCARCITY
PATCHES PRINT RUN 10 SER.#'d SETS
PATCHES NOT PRICED DUE TO SCARCITY
PATCH SCRIPT PRINT RUN 5 SER.#'d SETS
PATCH SCRIPT NOT PRICED DUE TO SCARCITY
HS-PK Paul Kariya 4.00 10.00
HS-JR Jeremy Roenick 4.00 10.00
HS-JI Jarome Iginla 5.00 12.00
HS-LU Joffrey Lupul 2.00 5.00
HS-WG Wayne Gretzky 30.00 80.00
HS-DC Dan Cloutier 3.00 8.00
HS-TR Tuomo Ruutu 2.00 5.00
HS-RS Ryan Smyth 4.00 10.00
HS-MS Mats Sundin 4.00 10.00
HS-RY Michael Ryder 3.00 8.00
HS-AM Al MacInnis 3.00 8.00
HS-GM Glen Murray 2.00 5.00
HS-SS Scott Stevens 3.00 8.00
HS-AR Andrew Raycroft 3.00 8.00
HS-TK Keith Tkachuk 4.00 10.00
HS-RE Robert Esche 3.00 8.00
HS-MO Mike Modano 5.00 12.00
HS-VL Vincent Lecavalier 4.00 10.00
HS-JW Justin Williams 2.00 5.00
HS-BR Brad Richards SP 3.00 8.00
HS-MP Michael Peca 2.00 5.00
HS-KL Kari Lehtonen 4.00 10.00
HS-SF Sergei Fedorov 5.00 12.00
HS-AF Alexander Frolov 3.00 8.00
HS-JB Jay Bouwmeester 2.00 5.00
HS-IK Ilya Kovalchuk 5.00 12.00
HS-DW Doug Weight 3.00 8.00
HS-JO Jose Theodore 4.00 10.00
HS-DL David Legwand 3.00 8.00
HS-AT Alex Tanguay 3.00 8.00
HS-EL Eric Lindros 3.00 8.00
HS-MN Markus Naslund 4.00 10.00
HS-AH Ales Hemsky 3.00 8.00
HS-CP Chris Pronger 3.00 8.00
HS-JC Jonathan Cheechoo 4.00 10.00
HS-ML Mario Lemieux 15.00 40.00
HS-NZ Nikolai Zherdev 3.00 8.00
HS-BG Bill Guerin 3.00 8.00
HS-KP Keith Primeau 2.00 5.00
HS-SY Steve Yzerman 10.00 25.00
HS-KD Kris Draper 2.00 5.00
HS-MH Milan Hejduk 4.00 10.00
HS-MD Marc Denis 3.00 8.00
HS-HK Dominik Hasek 8.00 20.00
HS-JS Joe Sakic 8.00 20.00
HS-AL Daniel Alfredsson 3.00 8.00
HS-CC Chris Chelios 4.00 10.00
HS-RN Rick Nash 5.00 12.00
HS-SG Simon Gagne 4.00 10.00
HS-MB Martin Brodeur 10.00 25.00
HS-ED Eric Daze 3.00 8.00
HS-MK Miikka Kiprusoff 4.00 10.00
HS-DB Daniel Briere 3.00 8.00
HS-JJ Jaromir Jagr 6.00 15.00
HS-MM Mark Messier 4.00 10.00
HS-OK Olaf Kolzig 3.00 8.00
HS-SP Jason Spezza 4.00 10.00
HS-NL Nicklas Lidstrom 4.00 10.00
HS-HO Marian Hossa 4.00 10.00
HS-JT Joe Thornton 6.00 15.00
HS-TB Todd Bertuzzi 4.00 10.00
HS-JG J-S Giguere 3.00 8.00
HS-SK Saku Koivu 4.00 10.00
HS-MT Marty Turco 3.00 8.00
HS-TC Ty Conklin 3.00 8.00
HS-NK Nikolai Khabibulin 4.00 10.00
HS-CJ Curtis Joseph 4.00 10.00
HS-DA David Aebischer 3.00 8.00
HS-EJ Ed Jovanovski 3.00 8.00
HS-RI Mike Ribeiro 2.00 5.00
HS-SV Sergei Samsonov 3.00 8.00
HS-BL Brian Leetch 4.00 10.00
HS-RL Roberto Luongo 5.00 12.00
HS-PE Patrik Elias 3.00 8.00
HS-ZP Zigmund Palffy 3.00 8.00
HS-PF Peter Forsberg 6.00 15.00
HS-HA Martin Havlat 3.00 8.00

HS-MG Marian Gaborik 3.00 8.00
HS-NH Nathan Horton 2.00 5.00
HS-JL John LeClair 4.00 10.00

2005-06 Upper Deck Trilogy Ice Scripts

STATED ODDS 1:9
IS-AH Ales Hemsky 8.00 20.00
IS-AT Alex Tanguay 8.00 20.00
IS-AR Andrew Raycroft 8.00 20.00
IS-BC Bobby Clarke 30.00 80.00
IS-CN Cam Neely 15.00 40.00
IS-AL Daniel Alfredsson 75.00 200.00
IS-DB Daniel Briere 12.00 30.00
IS-DH Dany Heatley 25.00 60.00
IS-DA David Aebischer 6.00 15.00
IS-DC Don Cherry 20.00 50.00
IS-GC Gerry Cheevers 12.00 30.00
IS-GP Gilbert Perreault 10.00 25.00
IS-HL Glenn Hall 20.00 50.00
IS-GH Gordie Howe 60.00 125.00
IS-IK Ilya Kovalchuk 40.00 100.00
IS-JI Jarome Iginla 20.00 50.00
IS-JT Joe Thornton 20.00 50.00
IS-JO Jose Theodore 15.00 40.00
IS-JG J-S Giguere 8.00 20.00
IS-LR Luc Robitaille 15.00 40.00
IS-MF Marc-Andre Fleury 12.00 30.00
IS-HS Marcel Hossa 6.00 15.00
IS-MG Marian Gaborik 15.00 40.00
IS-HO Marian Hossa 10.00 25.00
IS-MN Markus Naslund 10.00 25.00
IS-MB Martin Brodeur 100.00 200.00
IS-HA Martin Havlat 8.00 20.00
IS-SL Martin St. Louis 12.00 30.00
IS-MT Marty Turco 12.00 30.00
IS-MS Mats Sundin SP 150.00 300.00
IS-BO Mike Bossy 15.00 40.00
IS-MM Mike Modano 15.00 40.00
IS-MH Milan Hejduk 8.00 20.00
IS-RB Ray Bourque SP 50.00 100.00
IS-RN Rick Nash 15.00 40.00
IS-RS Ryan Smyth 15.00 40.00
IS-SK Saku Koivu SP 150.00 400.00
IS-SW Stephen Weiss 6.00 15.00
IS-VL Vincent Lecavalier 60.00 150.00
IS-WG Wayne Gretzky 150.00 300.00

2005-06 Upper Deck Trilogy Legendary Scripts

STATED ODDS 1:45
LEG-BC Bobby Clarke 10.00 25.00
LEG-BH Bobby Hull SP 30.00 80.00
LEG-CG Clark Gillies 6.00 15.00
LEG-CN Cam Neely 10.00 25.00
LEG-DC Don Cherry 15.00 40.00
LEG-DS Denis Savard 6.00 15.00
LEG-GA Glenn Anderson 6.00 15.00
LEG-GC Gerry Cheevers 12.00 30.00
LEG-GH Gordie Howe SP 75.00 150.00
LEG-GL Guy Lafleur SP 100.00 200.00
LEG-GP Gilbert Perreault 12.00 30.00
LEG-JK Jari Kurri 12.00 30.00
LEG-LM Lanny McDonald 6.00 15.00
LEG-MD Marcel Dionne 10.00 25.00
LEG-PE Phil Esposito SP 30.00 80.00
LEG-RB Ray Bourque SP 60.00 150.00
LEG-RR Rene Robert 6.00 15.00
LEG-SM Stan Mikita SP 8.00 20.00
LEG-TE Tony Esposito SP 20.00 50.00
LEG-TL Ted Lindsay 8.00 20.00
LEG-WG Wayne Gretzky SP 250.00 500.00

2005-06 Upper Deck Trilogy Personal Scripts

STATED ODDS 1:90
PER-BC Bobby Clarke SP 20.00 50.00
PER-BH Bobby Hull SP 40.00 100.00
PER-CN Cam Neely SP 25.00 60.00
PER-DS Denis Savard SP 12.00 30.00
PER-GF Grant Fuhr 20.00 50.00
PER-GH Gordie Howe 75.00 200.00
PER-GL Guy Lafleur SP 50.00 100.00
PER-GP Gilbert Perreault SP 25.00 50.00
PER-LM Lanny McDonald 10.00 25.00
PER-MB Martin Brodeur SP 200.00 300.00
PER-MD Marcel Dionne 15.00 40.00
PER-MF Marc-Andre Fleury 20.00 50.00
PER-PE Phil Esposito SP 40.00 80.00
PER-RB Ray Bourque SP 75.00 200.00
PER-RH Ron Hextall 25.00 60.00
PER-RN Rick Nash 15.00 40.00
PER-RR Rene Robert SP 10.00 25.00
PER-SM Stan Mikita SP 25.00 60.00
PER-SP Jason Spezza 12.00 30.00
PER-TE Tony Esposito SP 30.00 60.00
PER-GC1 G.Cheevers No Inscrip. 12.50 30.00
PER-GC2 Gerry Cheevers 20.00 50.00
Cheesy

2005-06 Upper Deck Trilogy Scripts

FS1 ODDS 1:9
CS2 ODDS 1:27
SS3 PRINT RUN 50 SER.#'d SETS
SCS-AY Alexei Yashin 5.00 12.00
SCS-CD Chris Drury 5.00 12.00
SCS-JG J-S Giguere 8.00 20.00
SCS-JL John LeClair 5.00 12.00
SCS-JS Jason Spezza 10.00 25.00
SCS-MN Markus Naslund 6.00 15.00
SCS-MP Mark Parrish 5.00 12.00
SCS-MT Marty Turco 6.00 15.00
SCS-PB Pavel Bure 6.00 15.00
SCS-PE Michael Peca 5.00 12.00
SCS-RL Roberto Luongo 6.00 15.00
SCS-RN Rick Nash 12.50 30.00
SCS-RS Ryan Smyth 8.00 20.00
SCS-TB Todd Bertuzzi 8.00 20.00
SCS-TR Tuomo Ruutu 5.00 12.00
SFS-AF Alexander Frolov 4.00 10.00
SFS-AH Ales Hemsky 3.00 8.00
SFS-AM Antti Miettinen 3.00 8.00
SFS-AR Andrew Raycroft 4.00 10.00
SFS-BB Brad Boyes 3.00 8.00
SFS-BG Boyd Gordon 3.00 8.00
SFS-BM Brenden Morrow 4.00 10.00
SFS-CK Chuck Kobasew 3.00 8.00
SFS-DA David Aebischer 4.00 10.00
SFS-DB Dustin Brown 3.00 8.00
SFS-FS Fredrik Sjostrom 3.00 8.00
SFS-JB Jay Bouwmeester 3.00 8.00
SFS-JL Joffrey Lupul 3.00 8.00
SFS-JP Joni Pitkanen 3.00 8.00
SFS-KL Kari Lehtonen 6.00 15.00
SFS-LN Ladislav Nagy 3.00 8.00
SFS-MA Maxim Afinogenov 3.00 8.00
SFS-MC Mike Cammalleri 3.00 8.00
SFS-MF Marc-Andre Fleury 15.00 40.00
SFS-MH Martin Havlat 4.00 10.00
SFS-MR Mike Ribeiro 3.00 8.00
SFS-MS Matt Stajan 3.00 8.00
SFS-NA Nik Antropov 3.00 8.00
SFS-NH Nathan Horton 3.00 8.00
SFS-NS Nathan Smith 3.00 8.00
SFS-NZ Nikolai Zherdev 4.00 10.00
SFS-PS Philippe Sauve 4.00 10.00
SFS-RF Ruslan Fedotenko 3.00 8.00
SFS-RK Ryan Kesler 3.00 8.00
SFS-RM Ryan Miller 6.00 15.00
SFS-SB Sean Bergenheim 3.00 8.00
SFS-TC Ty Conklin 4.00 10.00
SFS-TH Trent Hunter 3.00 8.00
SFS-TM Travis Moen 3.00 8.00
SFS-TP Tom Poti 3.00 8.00
SSS-DH Dominik Hasek 25.00 60.00
SSS-GL Guy Lafleur 20.00 50.00
SSS-IK Ilya Kovalchuk 25.00 60.00
SSS-JI Jarome Iginla 20.00 50.00
SSS-JO Jose Theodore 12.50 30.00
SSS-JT Joe Thornton 15.00 40.00
SSS-MB Martin Brodeur 75.00 150.00
SSS-MG Marian Gaborik 15.00 40.00
SSS-RB Ray Bourque 40.00 100.00
SSS-WG Wayne Gretzky 150.00 250.00

2006-07 Upper Deck Trilogy

1 Chris Pronger .50 1.25
2 Teemu Selanne .60 1.50
3 Jean-Sebastien Giguere .50 1.25
4 Ilya Kovalchuk .75 2.00
5 Kari Lehtonen .60 1.50
6 Marian Hossa .50 1.25
7 Hannu Toivonen .60 1.50
8 Zdeno Chara .30 .75
9 Patrice Bergeron .60 1.50
10 Brad Boyes .30 .75
11 Ryan Miller .60 1.50
12 Chris Drury .30 .75
13 Daniel Briere .30 .75
14 Miikka Kiprusoff .60 1.50
15 Jarome Iginla .75 2.00
16 Alex Tanguay .30 .75
17 Dion Phaneuf .75 2.00
18 Eric Staal .60 1.50
19 Cam Ward .60 1.50
20 Rod Brind'Amour .50 1.25
21 Martin Havlat .50 1.25
22 Nikolai Khabibulin .60 1.50
23 Tuomo Ruutu .30 .75
24 Joe Sakic 1.25 3.00
25 Jose Theodore .60 1.50
26 Milan Hejduk .30 .75
27 Marek Svatos .30 .75
28 Pascal Leclaire .50 1.25
29 Rick Nash .60 1.50
30 Fredrik Modin .30 .75
31 Sergei Fedorov .60 1.50
32 Mike Modano .60 1.50
33 Marty Turco .50 1.25
34 Eric Lindros .60 1.50
35 Pavel Datsyuk .50 1.25
36 Henrik Zetterberg .60 1.50
37 Nicklas Lidstrom .60 1.50
38 Dominik Hasek 1.00 2.50
39 Ryan Smyth .30 .75
40 Joffrey Lupul .30 .75
41 Ales Hemsky .30 .75
42 Dwayne Roloson .50 1.25
43 Todd Bertuzzi .50 1.25
44 Olli Jokinen .30 .75
45 Ed Belfour .60 1.50
46 Rob Blake .50 1.25
47 Alexander Frolov .30 .75
48 Marian Gaborik .75 2.00
49 Pavol Demitra .30 .75
50 Manny Fernandez .50 1.25
51 Saku Koivu .60 1.50
52 Cristobal Huet .75 2.00
53 Michael Ryder .50 1.25
54 Alex Kovalev .30 .75
55 Tomas Vokoun .50 1.25
56 Paul Kariya .60 1.50
57 Jason Arnott .30 .75
58 Martin Brodeur 1.50 4.00
59 Patrik Elias .30 .75
60 Brian Gionta .30 .75
61 Miroslav Satan .30 .75
62 Rick DiPietro .50 1.25
63 Alexei Yashin .30 .75
64 Jaromir Jagr 1.00 2.50
65 Henrik Lundqvist .75 2.00
66 Brendan Shanahan .60 1.50
67 Daniel Alfredsson .50 1.25
68 Jason Spezza .60 1.50
69 Dany Heatley .75 2.00
70 Martin Gerber .50 1.25
71 Peter Forsberg 1.00 2.50
72 Jeff Carter .50 1.25
73 Simon Gagne .60 1.50
74 Mike Richards .50 1.25
75 Shane Doan .30 .75
76 Curtis Joseph .60 1.50
77 Jeremy Roenick .75 2.00
78 Mark Recchi .30 .75
79 Sidney Crosby 4.00 10.00
80 Marc-Andre Fleury .60 1.50
81 Joe Thornton 1.00 2.50
82 Vesa Toskala .50 1.25
83 Patrick Marleau .50 1.25
84 Jonathan Cheechoo .60 1.50
85 Keith Tkachuk .50 1.25
86 Doug Weight .30 .75
87 Manny Legace .50 1.25
88 Brad Richards .50 1.25
89 Vincent Lecavalier .60 1.50
90 Martin St. Louis .50 1.25
91 Mats Sundin .60 1.50
92 Andrew Raycroft .50 1.25
93 Michael Peca .30 .75
94 Alexander Steen .50 1.25
95 Roberto Luongo .75 2.00
96 Markus Naslund .60 1.50
97 Henrik Sedin .30 .75
98 Daniel Sedin .30 .75
99 Alexander Ovechkin 1.50 4.00
100 Olaf Kolzig .60 1.50
101 Shane O'Brien RC 2.00 5.00
102 Ryan Shannon RC 2.00 5.00
103 Yan Stastny RC 2.00 5.00
104 Mark Stuart RC 2.00 5.00
105 Phil Kessel RC 6.00 15.00
106 Carsen Germyn RC 2.00 5.00
107 Dustin Byfuglien RC 2.00 5.00
108 Paul Stastny RC 10.00 25.00
109 Filip Novak RC 2.00 5.00
110 Fredrik Norrena RC 3.00 8.00
111 Loui Eriksson RC 2.00 5.00
112 Tomas Kopecky RC 3.00 8.00
113 Marc-Antoine Pouliot RC 3.00 8.00
114 Patrick Thoresen RC 3.00 8.00
115 Ladislav Smid RC 2.00 5.00
116 Konstantin Pushkarev RC 2.00 5.00
117 Patrick O'Sullivan RC 3.00 8.00
118 Anze Kopitar RC 8.00 20.00
119 Erik Reitz RC 2.00 5.00
120 Miroslav Kopriva RC 2.00 5.00
121 Niklas Backstrom RC 4.00 10.00
122 Dan Jancevski RC 2.00 5.00
123 Guillaume Latendresse RC 8.00 20.00
124 Shea Weber RC 3.00 8.00
125 Mikko Lehtonen RC 2.00 5.00
126 Frank Doyle RC 3.00 8.00
127 John Oduya RC 2.00 5.00
128 Travis Zajac RC 4.00 10.00
129 Rob Collins RC 2.00 5.00
130 Steve Regier RC 2.00 5.00
131 Matt Koalska RC 2.00 5.00
132 Ryan Caldwell RC 2.00 5.00
133 Masi Marjamaki RC 2.00 5.00
134 Keith Yandle RC 2.00 5.00
135 Enver Lisin RC 2.00 5.00
136 Jarkko Immonen RC 2.00 5.00
137 David Liffiton RC 2.00 5.00
138 Nigel Dawes RC 2.00 5.00
139 Alexei Kaigorodov RC 2.00 5.00
140 Ryan Potulny RC 3.00 8.00
141 David Printz RC 2.00 5.00
142 Bill Thomas RC 2.00 5.00
143 Joel Perrault RC 2.00 5.00
144 Patrick Fischer RC 2.00 5.00
145 Noah Welch RC 2.00 5.00
146 Michel Ouellet RC 3.00 8.00
147 Jordan Staal RC 25.00 60.00
148 Kristopher Letang RC 3.00 8.00
149 Evgeni Malkin RC 30.00 60.00
150 Matt Carle RC 3.00 8.00
151 Marc-Edouard Vlasic RC 2.00 5.00
152 D.J. King RC 2.00 5.00
153 Roman Polak RC 2.00 5.00
154 Ben Ondrus RC 2.00 5.00
155 Brendan Bell RC 2.00 5.00
156 Ian White RC 2.00 5.00
157 Jeremy Williams RC 2.00 5.00
158 Luc Bourdon RC 3.00 8.00
159 Eric Fehr RC 3.00 8.00
160 Jonas Johansson RC 2.00 5.00

2006-07 Upper Deck Trilogy Combo Autographed Jerseys

PRINT RUN 15 #'d SETS
NOT PRICED DUE TO SCARCITY
CJBS Mike Bossy
Billy Smith
CJCL Guy Lafleur
Bobby Clarke
CJGP Marian Gaborik
Mark Parrish
CJHK Ilya Kovalchuk
Marian Hossa
CJHL Ales Hemsky
Joffrey Lupul
CJHN Rick Nash
Dany Heatley
CJHT Jose Theodore
Milan Hejduk
CJIT Jarome Iginla
Alex Tanguay
CJKL Miikka Kiprusoff
Kari Lehtonen
CJKR Saku Koivu
Michael Ryder
CJLG Wayne Gretzky
Mario Lemieux
CJLZ Henrik Zetterberg
Nicklas Lidstrom
CJNB Cam Neely
Patrice Bergeron
CJNL Roberto Luongo
Markus Naslund
CJRB Patrick Roy
Martin Brodeur
CJRD Jeremy Roenick
Shane Doan
CJTC Joe Thornton
Jonathan Cheechoo
CJTM Marty Turco
Brenden Morrow
CJVH Dominik Hasek
Tomas Vokoun

2006-07 Upper Deck Trilogy Combo Autographed Patches

PRINT RUN 5 #'d SETS
NOT PRICED DUE TO SCARCITY
CJBS Mike Bossy
Billy Smith
CJCL Guy Lafleur
Bobby Clarke
CJGP Marian Gaborik
Mark Parrish
CJHK Ilya Kovalchuk
Marian Hossa
CJHL Ales Hemsky
Joffrey Lupul
CJHN Rick Nash
Dany Heatley
CJHT Jose Theodore
Milan Hejduk
CJIT Jarome Iginla
Alex Tanguay
CJKL Miikka Kiprusoff
Kari Lehtonen
CJKR Saku Koivu
Michael Ryder
CJLG Wayne Gretzky
Mario Lemieux
CJLZ Henrik Zetterberg
Nicklas Lidstrom
CJNB Cam Neely
Patrice Bergeron
CJNL Roberto Luongo
Markus Naslund
CJRB Patrick Roy
Martin Brodeur
CJRD Jeremy Roenick
Shane Doan
CJTC Joe Thornton
Jonathan Cheechoo
CJTM Marty Turco
Brenden Morrow
CJVH Dominik Hasek
Tomas Vokoun

2006-07 Upper Deck Trilogy Combo Clearcut Autographs

DOUBLE AU PRINT RUN 100 #'d SETS
TRIPLE AU PRINT RUN 25 #'d SETS
C2AR Ryan Smyth 12.00 30.00
Ales Hemsky
C2BB Brad Boyes 12.00 30.00
Patrice Bergeron
C2CK Kyle Calder 12.00 30.00
Nikolai Khabibulin
C2EE Phil Esposito 30.00 80.00
Tony Esposito
C2GP Scott Gomez 20.00 50.00
Zach Parise
C2HS Milan Hejduk 12.00 30.00
Marek Svatos
C2KK Saku Koivu 20.00 50.00
Mikko Koivu
C2KN Miikka Kiprusoff 20.00 50.00
Antero Niittymaki
C2LJ Roberto Luongo 20.00 50.00
Olli Jokinen
C2LS Vincent Lecavalier 40.00 80.00
Martin St. Louis
C2LZ Manny Legace 20.00 50.00
Henrik Zetterberg
C2MM Lanny McDonald 12.00 30.00
Joe Mullen
C2MV Ryan Miller 25.00 60.00
Thomas Vanek
C2NM Markus Naslund 12.00 30.00
Brendan Morrison
C2PG Corey Perry 25.00 60.00
Ryan Getzlaf
C2PM Patrick Marleau 15.00 40.00
Milan Michalek
C2RC Wade Redden 15.00 40.00
Zdeno Chara
C2SH Billy Smith 25.00 60.00
Ron Hextall
C2VS Tomas Vokoun 20.00 50.00
Steve Sullivan
C3BLS Jean Beliveau 90.00 150.00
Guy Lafleur
Steve Shutt
C3BPS Mike Bossy 60.00 125.00
Denis Potvin
Billy Smith
C3CGS Erik Cole 40.00 80.00
Martin Gerber
Eric Staal
C3CLP Bobby Clarke
Reggie Leach
Bernie Parent
C3FCB Alexander Frolov 50.00 100.00
Mike Cammalleri
Dustin Brown
C3FEC Grant Fuhr 60.00 125.00
Tony Esposito
Gerry Cheevers
C3HTT Milan Hejduk 60.00 125.00
Jose Theodore
Alex Tanguay
C3IKP Jarome Iginla 100.00 200.00
Miikka Kiprusoff
Dion Phaneuf
C3LDZ Manny Legace 100.00 200.00
Kris Draper
Henrik Zetterberg
C3MSS Lanny McDonald
Darryl Sittler
Borje Salming
C3MTC Patrick Marleau
Joe Thornton
Jonathan Cheechoo
C3MTM Mike Modano 50.00 100.00
Marty Turco
Brenden Morrow
C3NOB Cam Neely 75.00 150.00
Terry O'Reilly
Ray Bourque
C3NZB Rick Nash
Nikolai Zherdev
Gilbert Brule
C3PGC Keith Primeau 30.00 60.00
Simon Gagne
Jeff Carter
C3RBH Patrick Roy 300.00 450.00
Martin Brodeur
Dominik Hasek
C3RHH Wade Redden 50.00 100.00
Martin Havlat
Dany Heatley

2006-07 Upper Deck Trilogy Frozen In Time

COMPLETE SET (20) 150.00 250.00
PRINT RUN 999 #'d SETS
FT1 Alexander Ovechkin 8.00 20.00
FT2 Bobby Clarke 4.00 10.00
FT3 Brendan Shanahan 4.00 10.00
FT4 Cam Neely 5.00 12.00
FT5 Dominik Hasek 5.00 12.00
FT6 Gordie Howe 8.00 20.00
FT7 Guy Lafleur 6.00 15.00
FT8 Jaromir Jagr 6.00 15.00
FT9 Jean Beliveau 4.00 10.00
FT10 Joe Sakic 6.00 15.00
FT11 Martin Brodeur 8.00 20.00
FT12 Mats Sundin 4.00 10.00
FT13 Mike Bossy 4.00 10.00
FT14 Mike Modano 4.00 10.00
FT15 Patrick Roy 10.00 25.00
FT16 Ray Bourque 5.00 12.00
FT17 Sidney Crosby 20.00 50.00
FT18 Steve Yzerman 8.00 20.00
FT19 Tony Esposito 4.00 10.00
FT20 Wayne Gretzky 15.00 40.00

2006-07 Upper Deck Trilogy Honorary Scripted Patches

PRINT RUN 10 #'d SETS
NOT PRICED DUE TO SCARCITY
HSAH Ales Hemsky
HSPAF Alexander Frolov
HSPAO Alexander Ovechkin
HSPAR Andrew Raycroft
HSPAT Alex Tanguay
HSPBB Brad Boyes
HSPBG Brian Gionta
HSPBL Rob Blake
HSPBM Brenden Morrow
HSPBO Borje Salming
HSPBR Bill Ranford
HSPBS Billy Smith
HSPCA Jeff Carter
HSPCD Chris Drury
HSPCK Chuck Kobasew
HSPCN Cam Neely
HSPCO Corey Perry
HSPDA David Aebischer
HSPDB Dustin Brown
HSPDC Dan Cloutier
HSPDG Doug Gilmour
HSPDH Dany Heatley
HSPDR Dwayne Roloson
HSPDS Darryl Sittler
HSPDW Doug Weight
HSPEB Ed Belfour
HSPES Eric Staal
HSPGA Simon Gagne
HSPGL Guy Lafleur
HSPHA Dominik Hasek
HSPHE Milan Hejduk
HSPHV Martin Havlat
HSPHZ Henrik Zetterberg
HSPIK Ilya Kovalchuk
HSPJA Jarret Stoll
HSPJB Jay Bouwmeester
HSPJI Jarome Iginla
HSPJL Joffrey Lupul
HSPJP Joni Pitkanen
HSPJR Jeremy Roenick
HSPJS Jason Spezza
HSPJT Joe Thornton
HSPJW Justin Williams
HSPKC Kyle Calder
HSPKD Kris Draper
HSPKL Kari Lehtonen
HSPKP Keith Primeau
HSPLE Mario Lemieux
HSPLM Lanny McDonald
HSPMB Martin Brodeur
HSPMC Mike Cammalleri
HSPMG Martin Gerber
HSPMH Marian Hossa
HSPMK Miikka Kiprusoff
HSPML Manny Legace
HSPMN Markus Naslund
HSPMP Michael Peca
HSPMR Michael Ryder
HSPMS Marek Svatos
HSPMT Marty Turco
HSPNH Nathan Horton
HSPNK Nikolai Khabibulin
HSPNL Nicklas Lidstrom
HSPON Owen Nolan
HSPPB Patrice Bergeron
HSPPE Patrik Elias
HSPPI Pierre-Marc Bouchard
HSPPM Patrick Marleau
HSPPR Patrick Roy
HSPRB Ray Bourque
HSPRE Robert Esche
HSPRL Roberto Luongo
HSPRM Ryan Miller
HSPRN Rick Nash
HSPRS Ryan Smyth
HSPSA Miroslav Satan
HSPSC Sidney Crosby
HSPSD Shane Doan
HSPSG Scott Gomez
HSPSK Saku Koivu
HSPSN Scott Niedermayer
HSPSS Sergei Samsonov
HSPST Martin St. Louis
HSPSU Steve Sullivan
HSPTB Todd Bertuzzi
HSPTV Tomas Vokoun
HSPVL Vincent Lecavalier
HSPWG Wayne Gretzky
HSPWI Doug Wilson

2006-07 Upper Deck Trilogy Honorary Scripted Swatches

STATED PRINT RUN 25 #'d SETS
HSAH Ales Hemsky 12.00 30.00
HSSAF Alexander Frolov 12.00 30.00
HSSAO Alexander Ovechkin 60.00 125.00
HSSAR Andrew Raycroft 15.00 40.00
HSSAT Alex Tanguay 15.00 40.00
HSSBB Brad Boyes 12.00 30.00
HSSBG Brian Gionta 12.00 30.00
HSSBL Rob Blake 15.00 40.00
HSSBM Brenden Morrow 15.00 40.00
HSSBO Borje Salming 15.00 40.00
HSSBR Bill Ranford 20.00 50.00
HSSBS Billy Smith 20.00 50.00
HSSCA Jeff Carter 15.00 40.00
HSSCD Chris Drury 12.00 30.00
HSSCK Chuck Kobasew 12.00 30.00
HSSCN Cam Neely 25.00 60.00
HSSCO Corey Perry 15.00 40.00
HSSDA David Aebischer 15.00 40.00
HSSDB Dustin Brown 12.00 30.00
HSSDC Dan Cloutier 15.00 40.00
HSSDG Doug Gilmour 20.00 50.00
HSSDH Dany Heatley 25.00 60.00
HSSDR Dwayne Roloson 15.00 40.00
HSSDS Darryl Sittler 20.00 50.00
HSSDW Doug Weight 12.00 30.00
HSSEB Ed Belfour 20.00 50.00
HSSES Eric Staal 20.00 50.00
HSSGA Simon Gagne 20.00 50.00
HSSGH Gordie Howe 75.00 200.00
HSSGL Guy Lafleur 60.00 150.00
HSSHA Dominik Hasek 30.00 80.00
HSSHE Milan Hejduk 12.00 30.00
HSSHV Martin Havlat 15.00 40.00
HSSHZ Henrik Zetterberg 20.00 50.00
HSSIK Ilya Kovalchuk 25.00 60.00
HSSJA Jarret Stoll 15.00 40.00
HSSJB Jay Bouwmeester 12.00 30.00
HSSJI Jarome Iginla 25.00 60.00
HSSJL Joffrey Lupul 12.00 30.00
HSSJP Joni Pitkanen 12.00 30.00
HSSJR Jeremy Roenick 25.00 60.00
HSSJS Jason Spezza 20.00 50.00
HSSJT Joe Thornton 50.00 125.00
HSSJW Justin Williams 12.00 30.00
HSSKC Kyle Calder 12.00 30.00
HSSKD Kris Draper 12.00 30.00
HSSKL Kari Lehtonen 20.00 50.00
HSSKP Keith Primeau 12.00 30.00
HSSLE Mario Lemieux 75.00 200.00
HSSLM Lanny McDonald 15.00 40.00
HSSMB Martin Brodeur 60.00 125.00
HSSMC Mike Cammalleri 12.00 30.00
HSSMG Martin Gerber 15.00 40.00
HSSMH Marian Hossa 15.00 40.00
HSSMK Miikka Kiprusoff 20.00 50.00
HSSML Manny Legace 15.00 40.00
HSSMN Markus Naslund 20.00 50.00
HSSMP Michael Peca 12.00 30.00
HSSMR Michael Ryder 15.00 40.00
HSSMS Marek Svatos 15.00 40.00
HSSMT Marty Turco 15.00 40.00
HSSNH Nathan Horton 12.00 30.00
HSSNK Nikolai Khabibulin 20.00 50.00
HSSNL Nicklas Lidstrom 20.00 50.00
HSSON Owen Nolan 15.00 40.00
HSSPB Patrice Bergeron 20.00 50.00
HSSPE Patrik Elias 12.00 30.00
HSSPI Pierre-Marc Bouchard 12.00 30.00
HSSPM Patrick Marleau 15.00 40.00
HSSPR Patrick Roy 75.00 200.00
HSSRB Ray Bourque 40.00 100.00
HSSRE Robert Esche 15.00 40.00
HSSRL Roberto Luongo 25.00 60.00
HSSRM Ryan Miller 20.00 50.00
HSSRN Rick Nash 20.00 50.00
HSSRS Ryan Smyth 15.00 40.00
HSSSA Miroslav Satan 12.00 30.00
HSSSC Sidney Crosby 200.00 350.00
HSSSD Shane Doan 12.00 30.00
HSSSG Scott Gomez 12.00 30.00
HSSSK Saku Koivu 20.00 50.00
HSSSN Scott Niedermayer 12.00 30.00
HSSSS Sergei Samsonov 15.00 40.00
HSSST Martin St. Louis 15.00 40.00
HSSSU Steve Sullivan 12.00 30.00
HSSTB Todd Bertuzzi 15.00 40.00
HSSTV Tomas Vokoun 15.00 40.00
HSSVL Vincent Lecavalier 25.00 60.00
HSSWG Wayne Gretzky 150.00 300.00
HSSWI Doug Wilson 15.00 40.00

2006-07 Upper Deck Trilogy Honorary Swatches

STATED ODDS 1:3
HSAH Ales Hemsky 2.50 6.00
HSAO Alexander Ovechkin 10.00 25.00
HSBM Brenden Morrow 4.00 10.00
HSBO Ray Bourque 6.00 15.00
HSBR Bill Ranford 5.00 12.00
HSBS Borje Salming 4.00 10.00
HSCD Chris Drury 2.50 6.00
HSCN Cam Neely 6.00 15.00
HSCW Cam Ward 4.00 10.00
HSDG Doug Gilmour 5.00 12.00
HSDH Dany Heatley 6.00 15.00
HSDS Darryl Sittler 5.00 12.00
HSEB Ed Belfour 5.00 12.00
HSES Eric Staal 5.00 12.00
HSGH Gordie Howe 12.00 30.00
HSGL Guy Lafleur 10.00 25.00
HSGO Scott Gomez 2.50 6.00
HSHA Dominik Hasek 8.00 20.00
HSHO Marian Hossa 4.00 10.00
HSHZ Henrik Zetterberg 5.00 12.00
HSIK Ilya Kovalchuk 6.00 15.00
HSIM Jarkko Immonen 3.00 6.00
HSJG Jean-Sebastien Giguere 4.00 10.00
HSJI Jarome Iginla 6.00 15.00
HSJS Jason Spezza 5.00 12.00
HSJT Joe Thornton 6.00 15.00
HSJW Justin Williams 2.50 6.00
HSKD Kris Draper 2.50 6.00
HSKL Kari Lehtonen 6.00 15.00
HSKP Keith Primeau 2.50 6.00
HSLE Manny Legace 4.00 10.00
HSLM Lanny McDonald 4.00 10.00
HSMB Martin Brodeur 10.00 25.00
HSMH Milan Hejduk 2.50 6.00
HSMK Miikka Kiprusoff 5.00 12.00
HSML Mario Lemieux 15.00 40.00
HSMN Markus Naslund 5.00 12.00
HSMP Marc-Antoine Pouliot 2.50
HSMR Michael Ryder 4.00 10.00
HSMS Marek Svatos 2.50 6.00
HSMT Marty Turco 4.00 10.00
HSPB Patrice Bergeron 5.00 12.00
HSPR Patrick Roy 10.00 25.00
HSRB Rob Blake 4.00 10.00
HSRL Roberto Luongo 6.00 15.00
HSRM Ryan Miller 5.00 12.00
HSRN Rick Nash 5.00 12.00
HSRS Ryan Smyth 4.00 10.00
HSSA Miroslav Satan 2.50 6.00
HSSC Sidney Crosby 30.00 80.00
HSSG Simon Gagne 5.00 12.00
HSSK Saku Koivu 5.00 12.00
HSSM Billy Smith 5.00 12.00
HSSN Scott Niedermayer 2.50 6.00
HSST Martin St. Louis 4.00 10.00
HSVL Vincent Lecavalier 5.00 12.00
HSWG Wayne Gretzky 40.00 80.00

2006-07 Upper Deck Trilogy Ice Scripts

STATED ODDS 1:9
ISAH Ales Hemsky 8.00 20.00
ISAK Andrei Kostitsyn 6.00 15.00
ISAL Andrew Ladd 6.00 15.00
ISAN Antero Niittymaki 12.00 30.00
ISAO Alexander Ovechkin 60.00 125.00
ISBB Brad Boyes 6.00 15.00
ISBH Bobby Hull 60.00 125.00
ISBR Dustin Brown 6.00 15.00
ISCD Chris Drury 8.00 20.00
ISCK Chuck Kobasew 6.00 15.00
ISCP Chris Pronger 15.00 40.00
ISDA David Aebischer 10.00 25.00
ISDB Daniel Briere 8.00 20.00
ISDC Don Cherry 20.00 50.00
ISDH Dominik Hasek 25.00 60.00
ISDR Dwayne Roloson 12.00 30.00
ISGF Grant Fuhr 20.00 50.00
ISGH Gordie Howe 40.00 80.00
ISGL Guy Lafleur 75.00 150.00
ISHE Dany Heatley 15.00 40.00
ISJB Johnny Bucyk 12.00 30.00
ISJC Jonathan Cheechoo 12.00 30.00
ISJI Jarome Iginla 60.00 125.00
ISJL Joffrey Lupul 6.00 15.00
ISJO Joe Thornton 30.00 80.00
ISJT Jose Theodore 12.00 30.00
ISKD Kris Draper 8.00 20.00
ISMA Martin Brodeur 75.00 150.00
ISMB Mike Bossy 12.00 30.00
ISMC Mike Cammalleri 6.00 15.00
ISMF Marc-Andre Fleury 20.00 50.00
ISMG Marian Gaborik 20.00 50.00
ISMH Milan Hejduk 8.00 20.00
ISMI Miikka Kiprusoff 15.00 40.00
ISMK Mikko Koivu 8.00 20.00
ISMM Milan Michalek 8.00 20.00
ISMN Markus Naslund 12.00 30.00
ISMR Mike Ribeiro 6.00 15.00
ISMS Marek Svatos 8.00 20.00
ISOJ Olli Jokinen 8.00 20.00
ISPB Patrice Bergeron 10.00 25.00
ISPE Phil Esposito 20.00 50.00
ISPR Patrick Roy 150.00 300.00
ISRB Ray Bourque 50.00 100.00
ISRM Ryan Malone 10.00 25.00
ISRY Ryan Miller 15.00 40.00
ISSB Scotty Bowman 60.00 125.00
ISSC Sidney Crosby 200.00 350.00
ISSH Shawn Horcoff 6.00 15.00
ISSK Saku Koivu 25.00 60.00
ISTV Thomas Vanek 15.00 40.00
ISVL Vincent Lecavalier 25.00 60.00
ISVO Tomas Vokoun 10.00 25.00
ISWG Wayne Gretzky 150.00 300.00

2006-07 Upper Deck Trilogy Legendary Scripts

PRINT RUN 50 UNLESS OTHERWISE NOTED
LSBC Bobby Clarke 25.00 60.00
LSBR Richard Brodeur 20.00 50.00
LSBS Billy Smith 15.00 40.00
LSCN Cam Neely 25.00 60.00
LSDC Don Cherry 25.00 60.00
LSDS Denis Savard 10.00 25.00
LSGA Glenn Anderson 6.00 15.00
LSGC Gerry Cheevers 15.00 40.00
LSGF Grant Fuhr 15.00 40.00
LSGH Gordie Howe/25 125.00 225.00
LSGL Guy Lafleur/25 30.00 80.00
LSJB Jean Beliveau 30.00 80.00
LSJM Joe Mullen 6.00 15.00
LSMB Mike Bossy 20.00 50.00
LSML Mario Lemieux/25 150.00 250.00
LSPE Phil Esposito 20.00 50.00
LSRB Ray Bourque/25 40.00 80.00
LSRH Ron Hextall 25.00 60.00
LSRL Reggie Leach 20.00 50.00
LSSB Scotty Bowman 25.00 60.00
LSTE Tony Esposito 15.00 40.00

LSTL Ted Lindsay 8.00 20.00
LSWG Wayne Gretzky/25 200.00 350.00

2006-07 Upper Deck Trilogy Scripts

UNDER 20 NOT LISTED DUE TO SCARCITY
S1AO Alexander Ovechkin/1
S1BC Bobby Clarke/15
S1BR Martin Brodeur/13
S1DH Dany Heatley/4
S1DP Dion Phaneuf/1
S1GC Gerry Cheevers/12
S1GH Gordie Howe/26 75.00 200.00
S1GL Guy Lafleur/17 100.00 200.00
S1HA Dominik Hasek/14
S1IK Ilya Kovalchuk/4
S1JB Jean Beliveau/19
S1KL Kari Lehtonen/2
S1MB Mike Bossy/10
S1MF Marc-Andre Fleury/2
S1MG Marian Gaborik/5
S1ML Mario Lemieux/17 150.00 250.00
S1NL Nicklas Lidstrom/14
S1PB Patrice Bergeron/2
S1PR Patrick Roy/19 150.00 300.00
S1RB Ray Bourque/23 40.00 80.00
S1RL Roberto Luongo/6
S1RN Rick Nash/3
S1SC Sidney Crosby/1
S1VL Vincent Lecavalier/7
S1WG Wayne Gretzky/20 200.00 400.00
S2CH Cristobal Huet/7
S2CN Cam Neely/3
S2DH Dominik Hasek/6
S2DS Darryl Sittler/10
S2ES Eric Staal/28 20.00 50.00
S2GH Gordie Howe/6
S2GL Guy Lafleur/3
S2HZ Henrik Zetterberg/39 20.00 50.00
S2IK Ilya Kovalchuk/27 25.00 60.00
S2JB Jean Beliveau/10
S2JC Jonathan Cheechoo/5
S2JI Jarome Iginla/2
S2JT Jose Theodore/1
S2MB Martin Brodeur/5
S2MK Miikka Kiprusoff/10
S2ML Mario Lemieux/6
S2MS Marek Svatos/9
S2NL Nicklas Lidstrom/4
S2PE Phil Esposito/5
S2PM Patrick Marleau/7
S2PR Patrick Roy/3
S2RB Ray Bourque/5
S2SC Sidney Crosby/3
S2TH Joe Thornton/1
S2WG Wayne Gretzky/9
S3AR Andrew Raycroft/25 20.00 40.00
S3DH Dany Heatley/25 25.00 60.00
S3ES Eric Staal/25 20.00 50.00
S3HA Dominik Hasek/25 40.00 80.00
S3HZ Henrik Zetterberg/25 30.00 60.00
S3IK Ilya Kovalchuk/25 25.00 60.00
S3JC Jonathan Cheechoo/25 25.00 60.00
S3JI Jarome Iginla/25 40.00 80.00
S3JR Jeremy Roenick/25 25.00 60.00
S3JT Joe Thornton/25 40.00 80.00
S3MB Martin Brodeur/25
S3MG Marian Gaborik/25 25.00 60.00
S3MK Miikka Kiprusoff/25 25.00 50.00
S3MN Markus Naslund/25 25.00 50.00
S3MT Marty Turco/25
S3NL Nicklas Lidstrom/25 25.00 60.00
S3PB Patrice Bergeron/25 15.00 40.00
S3RB Rob Blake/25 25.00 50.00
S3RL Roberto Luongo/25 25.00 60.00
S3RN Rick Nash/25 30.00 60.00
S3SC Sidney Crosby/25 250.00 400.00
S3SK Saku Koivu/25 20.00 50.00
S3TH Jose Theodore/25 20.00 40.00
S3TV Tomas Vokoun/25 20.00 50.00
S3VL Vincent Lecavalier/25 40.00 80.00
TSAA Adrian Aucoin 3.00 8.00
TSAF Alexander Frolov 5.00 12.00
TSAH Ales Hemsky 5.00 12.00
TSAL Andrew Ladd 3.00 8.00
TSAN Antero Niittymaki 6.00 15.00
TSAP Alexandre Picard 3.00 8.00
TSBB Brad Boyes 4.00 10.00
TSBR Dustin Brown 4.00 10.00
TSBS Billy Smith SP 10.00 25.00
TSCD Chris Drury 4.00 10.00
TSCK Chuck Kobasew 3.00 8.00
TSCN Cam Neely SP 12.00 30.00
TSDA David Aebischer 8.00 20.00
TSDB Daniel Briere SP 15.00 40.00
TSDC Dan Cloutier 5.00 12.00
TSDL David Leneveu 5.00 12.00
TSDO Doug Wilson 4.00 10.00
TSDP Dion Phaneuf SP 20.00 50.00
TSDR Danny Richmond 3.00 8.00
TSDS Derek Sanderson 8.00 20.00
TSDT Dave Taylor 4.00 10.00
TSDW Doug Weight 3.00 8.00
TSED Eric Daze 3.00 8.00
TSGH Gordie Howe SP 30.00 60.00
TSHO Shawn Horcoff 4.00 10.00
TSHZ Henrik Zetterberg
TSJB Johnny Bucyk 6.00 15.00
TSJC Jonathan Cheechoo 8.00 20.00
TSJH Jeff Halpern 3.00 8.00
TSJI Jarome Iginla SP 15.00 40.00
TSJL Jason Labarbera 4.00 10.00
TSJM Joe Mullen SP 8.00 20.00
TSJP Joni Pitkanen 4.00 10.00
TSJT Jose Theodore SP 10.00 25.00
TSKC Kyle Calder 3.00 8.00
TSKD Kris Draper 4.00 10.00
TSKL Kari Lehtonen SP 15.00 40.00
TSKM Kirk Muller SP 8.00 20.00
TSKU Chris Kunitz 3.00 8.00
TSLI John-Michael Liles 3.00 8.00
TSLN Ladislav Nagy 3.00 8.00
TSLS Lee Stempniak 3.00 8.00
TSLU Joffrey Lupul SP 6.00 15.00
TSMB Martin Biron 5.00 12.00
TSMC Mike Cammalleri 5.00 12.00
TSMF Marc-Andre Fleury SP 25.00 60.00
TSMG Marian Gaborik SP 15.00 40.00
TSMH Marcel Hossa 3.00 8.00
TSMI Ryan Miller 10.00 25.00
TSMK Miikka Kiprusoff SP
TSML Manny Legace 5.00 12.00
TSMM Milan Michalek 4.00 10.00
TSMN Markus Naslund SP 12.00 30.00
TSMP Mark Parrish 3.00 8.00
TSMR Mike Ribeiro 3.00 8.00
TSMS Marc Savard 4.00 10.00
TSMT Mikael Tellqvist 5.00 12.00
TSNA Nikolai Antropov 3.00 8.00
TSPM Patrick Marleau SP 15.00 40.00
TSPO Denis Potvin SP 15.00 40.00
TSPS Philippe Sauve 4.00 10.00
TSRB Richard Brodeur SP 12.00 30.00
TSRF Ruslan Fedotenko 3.00 8.00
TSRG Ryan Getzlaf 8.00 20.00
TSRH Ron Hextall 10.00 25.00
TSRL Reggie Leach SP 15.00 40.00
TSRM Ryan Malone 6.00 15.00
TSRV Rogie Vachon 10.00 25.00
TSRY Michael Ryder 5.00 12.00
TSSA Denis Savard 5.00 12.00
TSSC Sidney Crosby SP 125.00 250.00
TSSG Scott Gomez 3.00 8.00
TSSH Scott Hartnell 3.00 8.00
TSSS Steve Shutt 5.00 12.00
TSSW Stephen Weiss 3.00 8.00
TSTA Jeff Tambellini 3.00 8.00
TSTC Ty Conklin 5.00 12.00
TSTE Tony Esposito SP
TSTL Ted Lindsay SP 15.00 40.00
TSTV Tomas Vokoun 6.00 15.00
TSVA Rick Vaive 4.00 10.00
TSWC Wayne Cashman 5.00 12.00
TSWG Wayne Gretzky SP 125.00 225.00
TSWI Dave Williams 5.00 12.00
TSWR Wade Redden 4.00 10.00
TSZC Zdeno Chara 4.00 10.00

2006 Upper Deck National NHL

COMPLETE SET (3) 25.00 50.00
NHL-1 Sidney Crosby 10.00 25.00
NHL-2 Wayne Gretzky 6.00 15.00
NHL-3 Alexander Ovechkin 6.00 15.00

2006 Upper Deck National NHL Autographs

Randomly inserted in VIP packages at the National Convention. Limited print runs preclude us from giving pricing.

COMPLETE SET (2)
NHL-1 Sidney Crosby
NHL-2 Wayne Gretzky

2006 Upper Deck National NHL VIP

COMPLETE SET (6) 30.00 60.00
1 Alexander Ovechkin 6.00 15.00
2 Wayne Gretzky 6.00 15.00
3 Sidney Crosby 10.00 25.00
4 Martin Brodeur 4.00 10.00
5 Steve Yzerman 4.00 10.00
6 Jean-Sebastian Giguere .75 2.00

2002 Upper Deck USHL Gordie Howe

This rare single was given away at the USHL All-Star Game in Sioux Falls. It commemorated Mr. Howe as the honorary spokesman for Upper Deck.

1 Gordie Howe AU 300.00

1999-00 Upper Deck Victory

Released as a 440-card set, 1999-00 Upper Deck Victory was comprised of 265 regular cards, 12 All Victory team cards showcasing top players, 30 Season Leaders, 40 Victory Prospects, 15 Stacking the Pads cards, 50 Hockey Legacy cards, and 28 Team Checklist cards. Base cards are white bordered with a red "Victory" logo. This brand contains no insert cards. Victory was packaged in 36-pack boxes where packs contained 12 cards and carried a suggested retail price of $.99.

COMPLETE SET (440) 40.00 80.00
1 Paul Kariya CL .10 .30
2 Paul Kariya .10 .30
3 Teemu Selanne .10 .30
4 Matt Cullen .02 .10
5 Steve Rucchin .02 .10
6 Oleg Tverdovsky .02 .10
7 Guy Hebert .08 .25
8 Fredrik Olausson .02 .10
9 Ted Donato .02 .10
10 Marty McInnis .02 .10
11 Damian Rhodes CL .08 .25
12 Jody Hull .02 .10
13 Damian Rhodes .08 .25
14 Kelly Buchberger .02 .10
15 Scott Langkow RC .08 .25
16 Norm Maracle .08 .25
17 Jason Botterill .02 .10
18 Randy Robitaille .02 .10
19 Ray Ferraro .02 .10
20 Ray Bourque CL .08 .25
21 Ray Bourque .20 .50
22 Sergei Samsonov .08 .25
23 Joe Thornton .20 .50
24 Shawn Bates .02 .10
25 Byron Dafoe .08 .25
26 Jonathan Girard .02 .10
27 Jason Allison .02 .10
28 Anson Carter .08 .25
29 Hal Gill .02 .10
30 Kyle McLaren .02 .10
31 Don Sweeney .02 .10
32 Dominik Hasek CL .08 .25
33 Dominik Hasek .25 .60
34 Michael Peca .08 .25
35 Miroslav Satan .08 .25
36 Dixon Ward .02 .10
37 Martin Biron .08 .25
38 Joe Juneau .08 .25
39 Cory Sarich .02 .10
40 Brian Holzinger .02 .10
41 Rhett Warrener .02 .10
42 Alexei Zhitnik .02 .10
43 J-S Giguere CL .08 .25
44 Valeri Bure .02 .10
45 J-S Giguere .08 .25
46 Jarome Iginla .15 .40
47 Rico Fata .02 .10
48 Derek Morris .02 .10
49 Rene Corbet .02 .10
50 Phil Housley .08 .25
51 Tyrone Garner RC .02 .10
52 Marc Savard .02 .10
53 Keith Primeau CL .02 .10
54 Sami Kapanen .02 .10
55 Bates Battaglia .02 .10
56 Arturs Irbe .08 .25
57 Keith Primeau .02 .10
58 Gary Roberts .02 .10
59 Ron Francis .08 .25
60 Paul Coffey .10 .30
61 Martin Gelinas .02 .10
62 Jeff O'Neill .02 .10
63 Glen Wesley .02 .10
64 Tony Amonte CL .02 .10
65 Tony Amonte .08 .25
66 J-P Dumont .08 .25
67 Doug Gilmour .08 .25
68 Ty Jones .02 .10
69 Anders Eriksson .02 .10
70 Remi Royer .02 .10
71 Jocelyn Thibault .08 .25
72 Alexei Zhamnov .02 .10
73 Eric Daze .08 .25
74 Bryan McCabe .02 .10
75 Peter Forsberg CL .08 .25
76 Chris Drury .08 .25
77 Peter Forsberg .30 .75
78 Patrick Roy .60 1.50
79 Joe Sakic .25 .60
80 Milan Hejduk .10 .30
81 Adam Deadmarsh .02 .10
82 Adam Foote .02 .10
83 Sandis Ozolinsh .02 .10
84 Claude Lemieux .02 .10
85 Brett Hull CL .08 .25
86 Ed Belfour .10 .30
87 Brett Hull .15 .40
88 Mike Modano .20 .50
89 Derian Hatcher .02 .10
90 Jamie Langenbrunner .02 .10
91 Joe Nieuwendyk .08 .25
92 Jon Sim RC .08 .25
93 Jere Lehtinen .08 .25
94 Darryl Sydor .02 .10
95 Sergei Zubov .02 .10
96 Steve Yzerman CL .08 .25
97 Brendan Shanahan .10 .30
98 Steve Yzerman .60 1.50
99 Chris Chelios .10 .30
100 Sergei Fedorov .20 .50
101 Vyacheslav Kozlov .02 .10
102 Igor Larionov .02 .10
103 Nicklas Lidstrom .10 .30
104 Tomas Holmstrom .02 .10
105 Chris Osgood .08 .25
106 Kris Draper .02 .10
107 Darren McCarty .02 .10
108 Doug Weight CL .02 .10
109 Bill Guerin .08 .25
110 Tom Poti .02 .10
111 Mike Grier .02 .10
112 Tommy Salo .08 .25
113 Doug Weight .08 .25
114 Josef Beranek .02 .10
115 Fredrik Lindquist .02 .10
116 Roman Hamrlik .02 .10
117 Todd Marchant .02 .10
118 Janne Niinimaa .02 .10
119 Pavel Bure CL .08 .25
120 Pavel Bure .10 .30
121 Mark Parrish .08 .25
122 Scott Mellanby .02 .10
123 Viktor Kozlov .08 .25
124 Oleg Kvasha .02 .10
125 Rob Niedermayer .02 .10
126 Bret Hedican .02 .10
127 Trevor Kidd .08 .25
128 Robert Svehla .02 .10
129 Peter Worrell .02 .10
130 Rob Blake CL .02 .10
131 Rob Blake .08 .25
132 Pavel Rosa .02 .10
133 Donald Audette .02 .10
134 Luc Robitaille .08 .25
135 Vladimir Tsyplakov .02 .10
136 Jozef Stumpel .08 .25
137 Nathan Lafayette .02 .10
138 Glen Murray .02 .10
139 Zigmund Palffy .08 .25
140 Bryan Smolinski .02 .10
141 Jamie Storr .08 .25
142 Saku Koivu CL .10 .30
143 Saku Koivu .10 .30
144 Arron Asham .02 .10
145 Jeff Hackett .08 .25
146 Trevor Linden .02 .10
147 Eric Weinrich .02 .10
148 Vladimir Malakhov .02 .10
149 Martin Rucinsky .02 .10
150 Brian Savage .02 .10
151 Shayne Corson .02 .10
152 Scott Lachance .02 .10
153 Jose Theodore .15 .40
154 David Legwand CL .08 .25
155 Mike Dunham .08 .25
156 David Legwand .08 .25
157 Sergei Krivokrasov .02 .10
158 Cliff Ronning .02 .10
159 Kimmo Timonen .02 .10
160 Bob Boughner .02 .10
161 Mark Mowers RC .02 .10
162 Patrick Cote .02 .10
163 Tomas Vokoun .08 .25
164 Jan Vopat .02 .10
165 Martin Brodeur CL .08 .25
166 Martin Brodeur .30 .75
167 John Madden RC .25 .60
168 Vadim Sharifijanov .02 .10
169 Patrik Elias .08 .25
170 Scott Stevens .08 .25
171 Petr Sykora .02 .10
172 Jason Arnott .02 .10
173 Brendan Morrison .08 .25
174 Scott Niedermayer .02 .10
175 Bobby Holik .02 .10
176 Eric Brewer CL .02 .10
177 Eric Brewer .02 .10
178 Zdeno Chara .02 .10
179 Kenny Jonsson .02 .10
180 Dmitri Nabokov .02 .10
181 Mariusz Czerkawski .02 .10
182 Brad Isbister .02 .10
183 Olli Jokinen .08 .25
184 Felix Potvin .10 .30
185 Mike Watt .02 .10
186 Claude Lapointe .02 .10
187 Brian Leetch CL .02 .10
188 Manny Malhotra .08 .25
189 Mike Richter .10 .30
190 Theo Fleury .02 .10
191 Adam Graves .02 .10
192 Brian Leetch .10 .30
193 Petr Nedved .08 .25
194 Brent Fedyk .02 .10
195 Barry Richter .02 .10
196 Valeri Kamensky .08 .25
197 Kirk McLean .08 .25
198 Kevin Stevens .02 .10
199 Alexei Yashin CL .02 .10
200 Marian Hossa .10 .30
201 Alexei Yashin .02 .10
202 Shawn McEachern .02 .10
203 Sami Salo .02 .10
204 Daniel Alfredsson .08 .25
205 Magnus Arvedson .02 .10
206 Wade Redden .02 .10
207 Ron Tugnutt .08 .25
208 Chris Phillips .02 .10
209 Vaclav Prospal .02 .10
210 Eric Lindros CL .08 .25
211 John LeClair .10 .30
212 Eric Lindros .10 .30
213 Mark Recchi .08 .25
214 Rod Brind'Amour .02 .10
215 Eric Desjardins .08 .25
216 Jean-Marc Pelletier .08 .25
217 Ryan Bast RC .02 .10
218 Keith Jones .02 .10
219 John Vanbiesbrouck .08 .25
220 Brian Wesenberg RC .02 .10
221 Dan McGillis .02 .10
222 Keith Tkachuk CL .08 .25
223 Robert Esche RC .08 .25
224 Keith Tkachuk .10 .30
225 Nikolai Khabibulin .08 .25
226 Trevor Letowski .02 .10
227 Robert Reichel .02 .10
228 Jeremy Roenick .15 .40
229 Greg Adams .02 .10
230 Daniel Briere .02 .10
231 Rick Tocchet .08 .25
232 Stanislav Neckar .02 .10
233 Teppo Numminen .02 .10
234 Jaromir Jagr CL .10 .30
235 Jaromir Jagr .20 .50
236 Matthew Barnaby .02 .10
237 Tom Barrasso .08 .25
238 Jan Hrdina .02 .10
239 Martin Straka .02 .10
240 Jean-Sebastien Aubin .08 .25
241 Alexei Kovalev .02 .10
242 German Titov .02 .10
243 Kevin Hatcher .02 .10
244 Kip Miller .02 .10
245 Alexei Morozov .02 .10
246 Jeff Friesen CL .02 .10
247 Vincent Damphousse .02 .10
248 Jeff Friesen .02 .10
249 Scott Hannan .02 .10
250 Patrick Marleau .10 .30
251 Mike Ricci .02 .10
252 Owen Nolan .08 .25
253 Marco Sturm .02 .10
254 Gary Suter .02 .10
255 Jeff Norton .02 .10
256 Steve Shields .08 .25
257 Mike Vernon .08 .25
258 Al MacInnis CL .08 .25
259 Pavol Demitra .08 .25
260 Al MacInnis .08 .25
261 Lubos Bartecko .02 .10
262 Jochen Hecht RC 1.50 4.00
263 Chris Pronger .08 .25
264 Grant Fuhr .08 .25
265 Michal Handzus .08 .25
266 Pierre Turgeon .08 .25
267 Jim Campbell .02 .10
268 Roman Turek .08 .25
269 Vincent Lecavalier CL .08 .25
270 Vincent Lecavalier .10 .30
271 Paul Mara .02 .10
272 Kevin Hodson .08 .25
273 Dan Cloutier .08 .25
274 Chris Gratton .02 .10
275 Pavel Kubina .02 .10
276 Darcy Tucker .02 .10
277 Alexandre Daigle .02 .10
278 Stephane Richer .02 .10
279 Niklas Sundstrom .02 .10
280 Mats Sundin CL .08 .25
281 Mats Sundin .10 .30
282 Bryan Berard .08 .25
283 Sergei Berezin .02 .10
284 Curtis Joseph .10 .30
285 Tomas Kaberle .02 .10
286 Daniil Markov .02 .10
287 Steve Thomas .02 .10
288 Mike Johnson .02 .10
289 Tie Domi .08 .25
290 Yanic Perreault .02 .10
291 Derek King .02 .10
292 Mark Messier CL .08 .25
293 Mark Messier .10 .30
294 Bill Muckalt .02 .10
295 Josh Holden .02 .10
296 Markus Naslund .10 .30
297 Kevin Weekes .08 .25
298 Ed Jovanovski .02 .10
299 Alexander Mogilny .08 .25
300 Mattias Ohlund .02 .10
301 Todd Bertuzzi .10 .30
302 Peter Schaefer .02 .10
303 Peter Bondra CL .02 .10
304 Peter Bondra .08 .25
305 Adam Oates .08 .25
306 Jan Bulis .02 .10
307 Jaroslav Svejkovsky .02 .10
308 Sergei Gonchar .02 .10
309 Olaf Kolzig .08 .25
310 Richard Zednik .02 .10
311 Benoit Gratton RC .02 .10
312 Matt Herr .02 .10
313 Nolan Baumgartner .02 .10
314 Peter Forsberg .10 .30
315 Jaromir Jagr .10 .30
316 Paul Kariya .10 .30
317 Ray Bourque .10 .30
318 Al MacInnis .08 .25
319 Dominik Hasek .10 .30
320 Steve Yzerman .10 .30
321 Teemu Selanne .10 .30
322 Brett Hull .10 .30
323 Chris Pronger .08 .25
324 Nicklas Lidstrom .10 .30
325 Patrick Roy .10 .30
326 Teemu Selanne .10 .30
327 Tony Amonte .08 .25
328 Jaromir Jagr .10 .30
329 Alexei Yashin .02 .10
330 John LeClair .10 .30
331 Jaromir Jagr .10 .30
332 Peter Forsberg .10 .30
333 Paul Kariya .10 .30
334 Teemu Selanne .10 .30
335 Joe Sakic .10 .30
336 Jaromir Jagr .10 .30
337 Teemu Selanne .10 .30
338 Paul Kariya .10 .30
339 Peter Forsberg .10 .30
340 Joe Sakic .10 .30
341 Al MacInnis .08 .25
342 Nicklas Lidstrom .10 .30
343 Ray Bourque .10 .30
344 Fredrik Olausson .02 .10
345 Brian Leetch .10 .30
346 Martin Brodeur .10 .30
347 Ed Belfour .10 .30
348 Curtis Joseph .10 .30
349 Chris Osgood .08 .25
350 Patrick Roy .10 .30
351 Milan Hejduk .10 .30
352 Brendan Morrison .08 .25
353 Chris Drury .08 .25
354 Jan Hrdina .02 .10
355 Mark Parrish .02 .10
356 Oleg Saprykin RC 1.25 3.00
357 Patrik Stefan RC 1.25 3.00
358 Pavel Brendl RC 2.50 6.00
359 Roberto Luongo .15 .40
360 Scott Gomez .02 .10
361 Sheldon Keefe RC .75 2.00
362 Simon Gagne .10 .30
363 Steve Kariya RC .75 2.00
364 Alex Tanguay .08 .25
365 Brad Stuart .10 .30
366 Branislav Mezei RC .10 .30
367 Brian Campbell RC .08 .25
368 Daniel Sedin .02 .10
369 Henrik Sedin .02 .10
370 Mike Ribiero .10 .30
371 Ivan Novoseltsev RC .60 1.50
372 Nick Boynton .08 .25
373 Nikos Tselios .08 .25
374 Tim Connolly .02 .10
375 J.F. Damphousse RC .10 .30
376 Patrick Roy .10 .30
377 Ed Belfour .10 .30
378 Chris Osgood .08 .25
379 Arturs Irbe .08 .25
380 Nikolai Khabibulin .08 .25
381 Dominik Hasek .10 .30
382 Byron Dafoe .08 .25
383 J-S Giguere .08 .25
384 Olaf Kolzig .08 .25
385 John Vanbiesbrouck .08 .25
386 Martin Brodeur .10 .30
387 Dan Cloutier .08 .25
388 Damian Rhodes .08 .25
389 Curtis Joseph .10 .30
390 Mike Richter .10 .30
391 Wayne Gretzky .30 .75
392 Wayne Gretzky .30 .75
393 Wayne Gretzky .30 .75
394 Wayne Gretzky .30 .75
395 Wayne Gretzky .30 .75
396 Wayne Gretzky .30 .75
397 Wayne Gretzky .30 .75
398 Wayne Gretzky .30 .75
399 Wayne Gretzky .30 .75
400 Wayne Gretzky .30 .75
401 Wayne Gretzky .30 .75
402 Wayne Gretzky .30 .75
403 Wayne Gretzky .30 .75
404 Wayne Gretzky .30 .75
405 Wayne Gretzky .30 .75
406 Wayne Gretzky .30 .75
407 Wayne Gretzky .30 .75
408 Wayne Gretzky .30 .75
409 Wayne Gretzky .30 .75
410 Wayne Gretzky .30 .75
411 Wayne Gretzky .30 .75
412 Wayne Gretzky .30 .75
413 Wayne Gretzky .30 .75
414 Wayne Gretzky .30 .75
415 Wayne Gretzky .30 .75
416 Wayne Gretzky .30 .75
417 Wayne Gretzky .30 .75
418 Wayne Gretzky .30 .75
419 Wayne Gretzky .30 .75
420 Wayne Gretzky .30 .75
421 Wayne Gretzky .30 .75
422 Wayne Gretzky .30 .75
423 Wayne Gretzky .30 .75
424 Wayne Gretzky .30 .75
425 Wayne Gretzky .30 .75
426 Wayne Gretzky .30 .75
427 Wayne Gretzky .30 .75
428 Wayne Gretzky .30 .75
429 Wayne Gretzky .30 .75
430 Wayne Gretzky .30 .75
431 Wayne Gretzky .30 .75
432 Wayne Gretzky .30 .75
433 Wayne Gretzky .30 .75
434 Wayne Gretzky .30 .75
435 Wayne Gretzky .30 .75
436 Wayne Gretzky .30 .75
437 Wayne Gretzky .30 .75
438 Wayne Gretzky .30 .75
439 Wayne Gretzky .30 .75
440 Wayne Gretzky .30 .75

2000-01 Upper Deck Victory

Released as a 330-card set, Upper Deck Victory features 210 regular player cards, 20 Season Highlight cards, 30 Team Checklist cards, 20 NHL Prospect cards, and 50 NHL's Best cards. Victory was released in mid September and was packaged in 36-pack boxes with packs containing 12 cards and carried a suggested retail price of $.99. A contest card was also included in most packs, it allowed the collector to visit the Upper Deck website and enter a contest to win a Pavel Bure autographed jersey.

COMPLETE SET (330) 25.00 50.00
1 Paul Kariya CL .08 .20
2 Ladislav Kohn .02 .10
3 Vitali Vishnevsky .02 .10
4 Steve Rucchin .02 .10
5 Oleg Tverdovsky .02 .10
6 Guy Hebert .08 .20
7 Teemu Selanne .15 .40
8 Paul Kariya .15 .40
9 Patrik Stefan CL .10 .25
10 Andrew Brunette .02 .10
11 Patrik Stefan .02 .10
12 Donald Audette .02 .10
13 Damian Rhodes .08 .20
14 Maxim Galanov .02 .10
15 Dean Sylvester .02 .10
16 Ray Ferraro .02 .10
17 Joe Thornton CL .10 .25
18 Brian Rolston .02 .10
19 Sergei Samsonov .08 .20
20 Joe Thornton .25 .60
21 Byron Dafoe .08 .20
22 Jason Allison .02 .10
23 Anson Carter .08 .20
24 Hal Gill .02 .10
25 Dominik Hasek CL .15 .40
26 Dominik Hasek .30 .75
27 Michael Peca .08 .20
28 Miroslav Satan .08 .20
29 Doug Gilmour .08 .20
30 Chris Gratton .02 .10
31 Curtis Brown .02 .10
32 Maxim Afinogenov .02 .10
33 Jay McKee .02 .10
34 Valeri Bure CL .02 .10
35 Valeri Bure .02 .10
36 Fred Brathwaite .08 .20
37 Jarome Iginla .20 .50
38 Phil Housley .08 .20
39 Derek Morris .02 .10
40 Cory Stillman .02 .10
41 Marc Savard .02 .10
42 Ron Francis CL .02 .10
43 Sami Kapanen .02 .10
44 Arturs Irbe .08 .20
45 Rod Brind'Amour .08 .20
46 Gary Roberts .02 .10
47 Ron Francis .08 .20
48 Paul Coffey .15 .40
49 Jeff O'Neill .02 .10
50 Tony Amonte CL .02 .10
51 Tony Amonte .08 .20
52 Steve Sullivan .02 .10
53 Michal Grosek .08 .20
54 Boris Mironov .02 .10
55 Jocelyn Thibault .08 .20
56 Alexei Zhamnov .02 .10
57 Eric Daze .08 .20
58 Peter Forsberg CL .20 .50
59 Chris Drury .08 .20
60 Peter Forsberg .40 1.00
61 Patrick Roy .75 2.00
62 Joe Sakic .30 .75
63 Ray Bourque .30 .75
64 Adam Deadmarsh .02 .10
65 Milan Hejduk .15 .40
66 Sandis Ozolinsh .02 .10
67 Alex Tanguay .08 .20
68 Adam Foote .02 .10
69 Blue Jackets CL .08 .20
70 Mike Modano CL .12 .30
71 Ed Belfour .15 .40
72 Brett Hull .20 .50
73 Sergei Zubov .02 .10
74 Brenden Morrow .08 .20
75 Jamie Langenbrunner .02 .10
76 Joe Nieuwendyk .08 .20
77 Mike Modano .25 .60
78 Derian Hatcher .02 .10
79 Jere Lehtinen .08 .20
80 Roman Lyashenko .02 .10
81 Steve Yzerman CL .40 1.00
82 Brendan Shanahan .15 .40
83 Steve Yzerman .75 2.00
84 Chris Chelios .15 .40
85 Sergei Fedorov .25 .60
86 Slava Kozlov .02 .10
87 Pat Verbeek .02 .10
88 Nicklas Lidstrom .15 .40
89 Tomas Holmstrom .02 .10
90 Chris Osgood .08 .20
91 Martin Lapointe .08 .20
92 Doug Weight CL .02 .10
93 Bill Guerin .08 .20
94 Tom Poti .02 .10
95 Mike Grier .02 .10
96 Tommy Salo .08 .20
97 Doug Weight .08 .20
98 Ryan Smyth .08 .20
99 Alexander Selivanov .02 .10
100 Pavel Bure CL .12 .30
101 Pavel Bure .15 .40
102 Mark Parrish .02 .10
103 Scott Mellanby .02 .10
104 Viktor Kozlov .08 .20
105 Oleg Kvasha .02 .10
106 Ray Whitney .02 .10
107 Trevor Kidd .08 .20
108 Rob Blake CL .02 .10
109 Rob Blake .08 .20
110 Jere Karalahti .02 .10
111 Luc Robitaille .08 .20
112 Jozef Stumpel .02 .10
113 Glen Murray .02 .10
114 Zigmund Palffy .08 .20
115 Bryan Smolinski .02 .10
116 Wild CL .08 .20
117 Saku Koivu CL .08 .20
118 Saku Koivu .15 .40
119 Sergei Zholtok .02 .10
120 Eric Weinrich .02 .10
121 Jose Theodore .20 .50
122 Martin Rucinsky .02 .10
123 Brian Savage .02 .10
124 Shayne Corson .02 .10
125 Dainius Zubrus .02 .10
126 David Legwand CL .02 .10
127 Mike Dunham .08 .20
128 David Legwand .08 .20
129 Greg Johnson .02 .10
130 Cliff Ronning .02 .10
131 Kimmo Timonen .02 .10
132 Patric Kjellberg .02 .10
133 Drake Berehowsky .02 .10
134 Martin Brodeur CL .20 .50
135 Martin Brodeur .40 1.00
136 John Madden .02 .10
137 Scott Gomez .02 .10
138 Patrik Elias .08 .20
139 Scott Stevens .08 .20
140 Jason Arnott .02 .10
141 Alexander Mogilny .08 .20
142 Tim Connolly CL .02 .10
143 Dave Scatchard .02 .10
144 Tim Connolly .02 .10
145 Kenny Jonsson .02 .10
146 Claude Lapointe .02 .10
147 Mariusz Czerkawski .02 .10
148 Brad Isbister .02 .10
149 Olli Jokinen .08 .20
150 Theo Fleury CL .08 .20
151 Mike Richter .15 .40
152 Theo Fleury .02 .10
153 Adam Graves .02 .10
154 Brian Leetch .08 .20
155 Petr Nedved .02 .10
156 Radek Dvorak .02 .10
157 Mike York .02 .10
158 Marian Hossa CL .02 .10
159 Marian Hossa .15 .40
160 Radek Bonk .02 .10
161 Shawn McEachern .02 .10
162 Vaclav Prospal .02 .10
163 Daniel Alfredsson .08 .20
164 Magnus Arvedson .02 .10
165 Wade Redden .02 .10
166 John LeClair CL .08 .25
167 John LeClair .15 .40
168 Eric Lindros .15 .40
169 Mark Recchi .08 .20
170 Keith Primeau .02 .10
171 Eric Desjardins .02 .10
172 Brian Boucher .08 .20
173 Daymond Langkow .08 .20
174 Simon Gagne .15 .40
175 Jeremy Roenick CL .25 .50
176 Daniel Briere .02 .10
177 Keith Tkachuk .15 .40
178 Sean Burke .08 .20
179 Trevor Letowski .02 .10
180 Shane Doan .02 .10
181 Jeremy Roenick .20 .50
182 Travis Green .02 .10
183 Jaromir Jagr CL .12 .30
184 Jaromir Jagr .25 .60
185 Matthew Barnaby .02 .10
186 Robert Lang .02 .10
187 Jan Hrdina .02 .10
188 Martin Straka .02 .10
189 Ron Tugnutt .08 .20
190 Alexei Kovalev .08 .20
191 Jeff Friesen CL .02 .10
192 Vincent Damphousse .02 .10
193 Jeff Friesen .02 .10
194 Brad Stuart .08 .20
195 Patrick Marleau .08 .20

196 Mike Ricci .02 .10
197 Owen Nolan .08 .20
198 Steve Shields .08 .20
199 Chris Pronger CL .02 .10
200 Pavol Demitra .08 .20
201 Al MacInnis .08 .20
202 Lubos Bartecko .02 .10
203 Jochen Hecht .02 .10
204 Chris Pronger .08 .20
205 Roman Turek .08 .20
206 Michal Handzus .02 .10
207 Pierre Turgeon .08 .20
208 Vincent Lecavalier CL .08 .20
209 Vincent Lecavalier .15 .40
210 Paul Mara .02 .10
211 Mike Johnson .02 .10
212 Dan Cloutier .08 .20
213 Wayne Primeau .02 .10
214 Pavel Kubina .02 .10
215 Fredrik Modin .02 .10
216 Mats Sundin CL .08 .20
217 Mats Sundin .15 .40
218 Darcy Tucker .02 .10
219 Sergei Berezin .02 .10
220 Curtis Joseph .15 .40
221 Jonas Hoglund .02 .10
222 Nikolai Antropov .02 .10
223 Steve Thomas .02 .10
224 Tie Domi .08 .20
225 Mark Messier CL .10 .25
226 Mark Messier .15 .40
227 Andrew Cassels .02 .10
228 Brendan Morrison .08 .20
229 Markus Naslund .15 .40
230 Felix Potvin .15 .40
231 Ed Jovanovski .02 .10
232 Harold Druken .02 .10
233 Olaf Kolzig CL .02 .10
234 Peter Bondra .15 .40
235 Adam Oates .08 .20
236 Jan Bulis .02 .10
237 Jeff Halpern .02 .10
238 Sergei Gonchar .02 .10
239 Olaf Kolzig .08 .20
240 Chris Simon .02 .10
241 P.Bure/V.Bure HL .15 .40
242 P.Kariya/S.Kariya HL .15 .40
243 Dominik Hasek HL .15 .40
244 Patrick Roy HL .40 1.00
245 Joe Sakic HL .15 .40
246 Ray Bourque HL .15 .40
247 Brett Hull HL .10 .25
248 Brendan Shanahan HL .12 .30
249 Steve Yzerman HL .40 1.00
250 Pat Verbeek HL .02 .10
251 Pavel Bure HL .12 .30
252 Scott Gomez HL .02 .10
253 John LeClair HL .08 .25
254 Brian Boucher HL .02 .10
255 Jeremy Roenick HL .25 .50
256 Jaromir Jagr HL .12 .30
257 Chris Pronger HL .02 .10
258 Roman Turek HL .02 .10
259 Curtis Joseph HL .10 .25
260 Wayne Gretzky HL 1.00 2.50
261 Serge Aubin RC .30 .75
Dan Hinote
262 Brandon Smith RC .08 .20
Andre Savage
263 Keith Aldridge RC .08 .20
Ryan Christie
264 Steven Reinprecht RC .75 2.00
Brad Chartrand
265 Petr Mika RC .08 .20
Jason Krog
266 Steve Valiquette RC .15 .40
Vladimir Orszagh
267 Kyle Freadrich RC .08 .20
Corey Sarich
268 Eric Nickulas RC .08 .20
Joel Prpic
269 David Gosselin RC .08 .20
Richard Lintner
270 Greg Andrusak RC .08 .20
Nathan Dempsey
271 Brent Sopel RC .10 .25
Alfie Michaud
272 Jeremy Stevenson RC .08 .20
Maxim Balmochnykh
273 Andreas Karlsson .08 .20
Scott Fankhouser
274 Dave Tanabe .08 .20
Byron Ritchie
275 Steven McCarthy .08 .20
Kyle Calder
276 Petr Schastlivy .08 .20
Mike Fisher
277 Andy Delmore .08 .20
Mark Eaton
278 Evgeni Nabokov .15 .40
Scott Hannan
279 Dany Heatley RC 1.00 2.50
Jaroslav Svoboda RC
280 Matt Pettinger RC .08 .20
Chris Nielsen RC
281 Teemu Selanne NB .08 .20
282 Paul Kariya NB .15 .40
283 Patrik Stefan NB .10 .25
284 Sergei Samsonov NB .08 .20
285 Joe Thornton NB .10 .25
286 Dominik Hasek NB .15 .40
287 Doug Gilmour NB .08 .20
288 Valeri Bure NB .02 .10
289 Ron Francis NB .02 .10
290 Tony Amonte NB .08 .20
291 Peter Forsberg NB .20 .50
292 Patrick Roy NB .40 1.00
293 Joe Sakic NB .15 .40
294 Ray Bourque NB .15 .40
295 Milan Hejduk NB .10 .25
296 Ed Belfour NB .08 .20
297 Brett Hull NB .10 .25
298 Mike Modano NB .12 .30
299 Brendan Shanahan NB .12 .30
300 Steve Yzerman NB .40 1.00
301 Sergei Fedorov NB .15 .40
302 Chris Osgood NB .08 .20
303 Doug Weight NB .02 .10
304 Pavel Bure NB .12 .30
305 Zigmund Palffy NB .08 .20
306 Rob Blake NB .02 .10
307 Saku Koivu NB .08 .20
308 David Legwand NB .02 .10
309 Martin Brodeur NB .20 .50
310 Scott Gomez NB .02 .10
311 Tim Connolly NB .02 .10
312 Theo Fleury NB .08 .20
313 Marian Hossa NB .15 .40
314 John LeClair NB .08 .25
315 Eric Lindros NB .12 .30
316 Keith Tkachuk NB .08 .20
317 Jeremy Roenick NB .25 .50
318 Jaromir Jagr NB .12 .30
319 Jeff Friesen NB .02 .10
320 Owen Nolan NB .02 .10
321 Al MacInnis NB .02 .10
322 Pavol Demitra NB .02 .10
323 Chris Pronger NB .02 .10
324 Roman Turek NB .02 .10
325 Vincent Lecavalier NB .08 .20
326 Mats Sundin NB .08 .20
327 Curtis Joseph NB .10 .25
328 Mark Messier NB .10 .25
329 Peter Bondra NB .15 .40
330 Olaf Kolzig NB .02 .10
WCB Pavel Bure Jer Contest .02 .10

2001-02 Upper Deck Victory

Released in mid-August 2001, this 453-card set carried an SRP of $3.99 for a 10-card pack. The set was originally released as a 440-card set, and cards 441-453 were available in random packs of UD Rookie Update.

COMP.SERIES I SET (440) 30.00 60.00
COMP.SET w/UPDATE (453) 50.00 100.00
1 J-S Giguere CL .02 .10
2 Steve Rucchin .02 .10
3 Oleg Tverdovsky .02 .10
4 Matt Cullen .02 .10
5 Vitali Vishnevsky .02 .10
6 J-S Giguere .08 .20
7 Mike LeClerc .02 .10
8 Petr Tenkrat .02 .10
9 Paul Kariya .12 .30
10 Samuel Pahlsson .02 .10
11 Jeff Friesen .02 .10
12 Milan Hnilicka CL .02 .10
13 Patrik Stefan .02 .10
14 Andrew Brunette .02 .10
15 Hnat Domenichelli .02 .10
16 Jiri Slegr .02 .10
17 Tomi Kallio .02 .10
18 Steve Staios .02 .10
19 Steve Guolla .02 .10
20 Milan Hnilicka .08 .20
21 Ray Ferraro .02 .10
22 Frantisek Kaberle .02 .10
23 Ladislav Kohn .02 .10
24 Byron Dafoe CL .08 .20
25 Sergei Samsonov .08 .20
26 Joe Thornton .25 .60
27 Per Johan Axelsson .02 .10
28 Brian Rolston .02 .10
29 Mikko Eloranta .02 .10
30 Jason Allison .02 .10
31 Mike Knuble .02 .10
32 Eric Weinrich .02 .10
33 Byron Dafoe .08 .20
34 Bill Guerin .08 .20
35 Kyle McLaren .02 .10
36 Dominik Hasek CL .15 .40
37 Curtis Brown .02 .10
38 Miroslav Satan .08 .20
39 Dominik Hasek .30 .75
40 Maxim Afinogenov .02 .10
41 Stu Barnes .02 .10
42 J-P Dumont .02 .10
43 Martin Biron .08 .20
44 Alexei Zhitnik .02 .10
45 Dimitri Kalinin .02 .10
46 Chris Gratton .02 .10
47 Denis Hamel .02 .10
48 Mike Vernon CL .02 .10
49 Jarome Iginla .15 .40
50 Marc Savard .02 .10
51 Jeff Cowan .02 .10
52 Derek Morris .02 .10
53 Dave Lowry .02 .10
54 Craig Conroy .02 .10
55 Robyn Regehr .02 .10
56 Oleg Saprykin .02 .10
57 Clarke Wilm .02 .10
58 Toni Lydman .02 .10
59 Arturs Irbe CL .08 .20
60 Rod Brind'Amour .08 .20
61 Ron Francis .08 .20
62 Sami Kapanen .02 .10
63 Jeff O'Neill .02 .10
64 Sandis Ozolinsh .02 .10
65 Arturs Irbe .08 .20
66 Dave Tanabe .02 .10
67 Shane Willis .02 .10
68 Josef Vasicek .02 .10
69 Tommy Westlund .02 .10
70 Bates Battaglia .02 .10
71 Jocelyn Thibault CL .02 .10
72 Steve Sullivan .02 .10
73 Tony Amonte .08 .20
74 Eric Daze .08 .20
75 Steven McCarthy .02 .10
76 Alexei Zhamnov .02 .10
77 Jaroslav Spacek .02 .10
78 Jocelyn Thibault .08 .20
79 Michael Nylander .02 .10
80 Kyle Calder .02 .10
81 Chris Herperger .02 .10
82 Ryan Vandenbussche .02 .10
83 Patrick Roy CL .40 1.00
84 Peter Forsberg .40 1.00
85 Ray Bourque .30 .75
86 Milan Hejduk .12 .30
87 Alex Tanguay .08 .20
88 David Aebischer .08 .20
89 Chris Drury .08 .20
90 Rob Blake .08 .20
91 Joe Sakic .30 .75
92 Patrick Roy .75 2.00
93 Ville Nieminen .02 .10
94 Steven Reinprecht .02 .10
95 Adam Foote .02 .10
96 Ron Tugnutt CL .02 .10
97 Geoff Sanderson .02 .10
98 Serge Aubin .02 .10
99 David Vyborny .02 .10
100 Ron Tugnutt .08 .20
101 Espen Knutsen .02 .10
102 Tyler Wright .02 .10
103 Lyle Odelein .02 .10
104 Marc Denis .08 .20
105 Blake Sloan .02 .10
106 Jean-Luc Grand-Pierre .02 .10
107 Mike Maneluk .02 .10
108 Ed Belfour CL .08 .20
109 Mike Modano .25 .60
110 Brett Hull .20 .50
111 Brenden Morrow .08 .20
112 Joe Nieuwendyk .08 .20
113 Sergei Zubov .02 .10
114 Ed Belfour .12 .30
115 Derian Hatcher .02 .10
116 Jamie Langenbrunner .02 .10
117 Grant Marshall .02 .10
118 Marty Turco .08 .20
119 Jere Lehtinen .08 .20
120 Darryl Sydor .02 .10
121 Chris Osgood CL .08 .20
122 Sergei Fedorov .25 .60
123 Steve Yzerman .75 2.00
124 Nicklas Lidstrom .12 .30
125 Mathieu Dandenault .02 .10
126 Slava Kozlov .02 .10
127 Chris Osgood .08 .20
128 Darren McCarty .02 .10
129 Kirk Maltby .02 .10
130 Boyd Devereaux .02 .10
131 Manny Legace .08 .20
132 Brendan Shanahan .12 .30
133 Tomas Holmstrom .02 .10
134 Tommy Salo CL .02 .10
135 Anson Carter .08 .20
136 Todd Marchant .02 .10
137 Ryan Smyth .02 .10
138 Tommy Salo .08 .20
139 Doug Weight .08 .20
140 Janne Niinimaa .02 .10
141 Rem Murray .02 .10
142 Daniel Cleary .02 .10
143 Tom Poti .02 .10
144 Georges Laraque .02 .10
145 Mike Grier .02 .10
146 Roberto Luongo CL .02 .10
147 Kevyn Adams .02 .10
148 Viktor Kozlov .08 .20
149 Marcus Nillson .02 .10
150 Robert Svehla .02 .10
151 Pavel Bure .12 .30
152 Anders Eriksson .02 .10
153 Vaclav Prospal .02 .10
154 Roberto Luongo .15 .40
155 Denis Shvidki .02 .10
156 Peter Worrell .02 .10
157 Olli Jokinen .08 .20
158 Felix Potvin CL .08 .20
159 Luc Robitaille .08 .20
160 Zigmund Palffy .08 .20
161 Jozef Stumpel .02 .10
162 Bryan Smolinski .02 .10
163 Glen Murray .02 .10
164 Aaron Miller .02 .10
165 Adam Deadmarsh .02 .10
166 Jaroslav Modry .02 .10
167 Felix Potvin .12 .30
168 Eric Belanger .02 .10
169 Ian Laperriere .02 .10
170 Manny Fernandez CL .02 .10
171 Marian Gaborik .25 .60
172 Stacy Roest .02 .10
173 Wes Walz .02 .10
174 Lubomir Sekeras .02 .10
175 Manny Fernandez .08 .20
176 Darby Hendrickson .02 .10
177 Aaron Gavey .02 .10
178 Roman Simicek .02 .10
179 Jamie McLennan .02 .10
180 Antti Laaksonen .02 .10
181 Andy Sutton .02 .10
182 Jose Theodore CL .12 .30
183 Richard Zednik .02 .10
184 Martin Rucinsky .02 .10
185 Saku Koivu .12 .30
186 Jose Theodore .15 .40
187 Brian Savage .02 .10
188 Oleg Petrov .02 .10
189 Patrice Brisebois .02 .10
190 Chad Kilger .02 .10
191 Craig Darby .02 .10
192 Andrei Markov .02 .10
193 Mike Dunham CL .02 .10
194 Cliff Ronning .02 .10
195 Vitali Yachmenev .02 .10
196 Scott Walker .02 .10
197 Kimmo Timonen .02 .10
198 Patric Kjellberg .02 .10
199 Mike Dunham .08 .20
200 Greg Johnson .02 .10
201 David Legwand .08 .20
202 Scott Hartnell .02 .10
203 Tom Fitzgerald .02 .10
204 Tomas Vokoun .02 .10
205 Martin Brodeur CL .20 .50
206 Scott Stevens .08 .20
207 Patrik Elias .08 .20
208 Randy McKay .02 .10
209 Jason Arnott .02 .10
210 Alexander Mogilny .08 .20
211 Petr Sykora .02 .10
212 Scott Gomez .02 .10
213 Sergei Brylin .02 .10
214 Bobby Holik .02 .10
215 Martin Brodeur .40 1.00
216 John Madden .02 .10
217 Scott Niedermayer .02 .10
218 Rick DiPietro CL .02 .10
219 Mariusz Czerkawski .02 .10
220 Jason Krog .02 .10
221 Roman Hamrlik .02 .10
222 Jason Blake .02 .10
223 Rick DiPietro .08 .20
224 Dave Scatchard .02 .10
225 Brad Isbister .02 .10
226 Mark Parrish .02 .10
227 Kenny Jonsson .02 .10
228 Oleg Kvasha .02 .10
229 Mike Richter CL .08 .20
230 Mark Messier .12 .30
231 Mike York .02 .10
232 Theo Fleury .02 .10
233 Brian Leetch .08 .20
234 Petr Nedved .02 .10
235 Radek Dvorak .02 .10
236 Jan Hlavac .02 .10
237 Mike Richter .12 .30
238 Manny Malhotra .02 .10
239 Tomas Kloucek .02 .10
240 Sandy McCarthy .02 .10
241 Patrick Lalime CL .02 .10
242 Marian Hossa .12 .30
243 Shawn McEachern .02 .10
244 Wade Redden .02 .10
245 Daniel Alfredsson .08 .20
246 Radek Bonk .02 .10
247 Martin Havlat .08 .20
248 Patrick Lalime .08 .20
249 Magnus Arvedson .02 .10
250 Karel Rachunek .02 .10
251 Sami Salo .02 .10
252 Jani Hurme .08 .20
253 Roman Cechmanek CL .02 .10
254 John LeClair .12 .30
255 Daymond Langkow .08 .20
256 Keith Primeau .02 .10
257 Justin Williams .02 .10
258 Simon Gagne .12 .30
259 Roman Cechmanek .08 .20
260 Mark Recchi .08 .20
261 Ruslan Fedotenko .08 .20
262 Dan McGillis .02 .10
263 Eric Desjardins .02 .10
264 Brian Boucher .08 .20
265 Sean Burke CL .02 .10
266 Shane Doan .02 .10
267 Mike Johnson .02 .10
268 Michal Handzus .02 .10
269 Landon Wilson .02 .10
270 Jeremy Roenick .15 .40
271 Mika Alatalo .02 .10
272 Sean Burke .08 .20
273 Daniel Briere .02 .10
274 Trevor Letowski .02 .10
275 Teppo Numminen .02 .10
276 Ladislav Nagy .02 .10
277 Johan Hedberg CL .02 .10
278 Jaromir Jagr .25 .75
279 Jan Hrdina .02 .10
280 Mario Lemieux 1.00 2.50
281 Alexei Kovalev .08 .20
282 Robert Lang .02 .10
283 Martin Straka .02 .10
284 Alexei Morozov .02 .10
285 Janne Laukkanen .02 .10
286 Rene Corbet .02 .10
287 Jean-Sebastien Aubin .02 .10
288 Darius Kasparaitis .02 .10
289 Evgeni Nabokov CL .02 .10
290 Teemu Selanne .12 .30
291 Patrick Marleau .08 .20
292 Owen Nolan .08 .20
293 Marcus Ragnarsson .02 .10
294 Brad Stuart .08 .20
295 Mike Ricci .02 .10
296 Vincent Damphousse .02 .10
297 Scott Thornton .02 .10
298 Mike Rathje .02 .10
299 Marco Sturm .02 .10
300 Evgeni Nabokov .08 .20
301 Alexander Korolyuk .02 .10
302 Brent Johnson CL .08 .20
303 Keith Tkachuk .12 .30
304 Cory Stillman .02 .10
305 Chris Pronger .08 .20
306 Scott Young .02 .10
307 Pavol Demitra .08 .20
308 Al MacInnis .08 .20
309 Jochen Hecht .02 .10
310 Pierre Turgeon .08 .20
311 Tyson Nash .02 .10
312 Jamal Mayers .02 .10
313 Dallas Drake .02 .10
314 Kevin Weekes CL .02 .10
315 Vincent Lecavalier .12 .30
316 Brad Richards .08 .20
317 Brian Holzinger .02 .10
318 Fredrik Modin .02 .10
319 Kevin Weekes .02 .10
320 Pavel Kubina .02 .10
321 Andrei Zyuzin .02 .10
322 Martin St. Louis .08 .20
323 Matthew Barnaby .02 .10
324 Nikolai Khabibulin .12 .30
325 Curtis Joseph CL .10 .25
326 Mats Sundin .12 .30
327 Gary Roberts .02 .10
328 Bryan McCabe .02 .10
329 Curtis Joseph .12 .30
330 Tomas Kaberle .02 .10
331 Jonas Hoglund .02 .10
332 Darcy Tucker .02 .10
333 Nikolai Antropov .02 .10
334 Tie Domi .08 .20
335 Aki Berg .02 .10
336 Dimitri Yushkevich .02 .10
337 Dan Cloutier CL .10 .25
338 Markus Naslund .12 .30
339 Donald Brashear .02 .10
340 Andrew Cassels .02 .10
341 Todd Bertuzzi .12 .30
342 Ed Jovanovski .02 .10
343 Brendan Morrison .08 .20
344 Daniel Sedin .02 .10
345 Henrik Sedin .02 .10
346 Dan Cloutier .08 .20
347 Peter Schaefer .02 .10
348 Harold Druken .02 .10
349 Olaf Kolzig CL .02 .10
350 Peter Bondra .12 .30
351 Sergei Gonchar .02 .10
352 Steve Konowalchuk .02 .10
353 Chris Simon .02 .10
354 Adam Oates .08 .20
355 Olaf Kolzig .08 .20
356 Jeff Halpern .02 .10
357 Trevor Linden .02 .10
358 Calle Johansson .02 .10
359 Dainius Zubrus .02 .10
360 Andrei Nikolishin .02 .10
361 Glen Naumenko .02 .10
362 Brad Tapper .08 .20
J.P. Vigier
Dan Snyder RC
363 Zdenek Kutlak RC .08 .20
Lee Goren
Pavel Kolarik
364 Mika Noronen .08 .20
365 Marty Murray .08 .20
Rico Fata
Ronald Petrovicky
366 Casey Hankinson RC .08 .20
Michel Larocque RC
Mark Bell
367 Yuri Babenko .08 .20
Rob Shearer
368 Steve Gainey .02 .10
369 Jason Williams .08 .20
Maxim Kuznetsov
370 Jason Chimera .08 .20
Mike Comrie
Chris Hajt
371 Jody Shelley RC .08 .20
Martin Spanhel RC
Rostislav Klesla
372 Mathieu Darche .08 .20
Matt Davidson
373 Andrej Podkonicky RC .08 .20
Rocky Thompson
374 Travis Scott .08 .20
Andreas Lilja
375 Pascal Dupuis RC .02 .10
376 Mike Matteucci RC .08 .20
Derek Gustafson
377 Francis Belanger RC .08 .20
378 Chris Mason .08 .20
Pavel Skrbek RC
379 Pierre Dagenais .08 .20
Mike Jefferson RC
380 Juraj Kolnik .02 .10
381 Peter Smrek .08 .20
Jeff Ulmer
Vitali Yeremeyev
382 Joel Kwiatkowski RC .08 .20
383 Maxime Ouellet .08 .20
384 David Cullen RC .02 .10
385 Bill Tibbetts RC .12 .30
Greg Crozier
Johan Hedberg
386 Miikka Kiprusoff .08 .20
Mikael Samuelsson RC
387 Jaroslav Obsut .08 .20
Mike Van Ryn
388 Thomas Ziegler RC .08 .20
Dmitri Afanasenkov
389 Alexei Ponikarovsky .08 .20
Jeff Farkas
390 Kris Beech .02 .10
Matt Pettinger
391 Mario Lemieux MHG 1.25 3.00
392 Jaromir Jagr MHG .30 .75
393 Chris Pronger MHG .10 .25
394 Peter Forsberg MHG .50 1.25
395 Pavel Bure MHG .25 .60
396 Patrick Roy MHG 1.00 2.50
397 Joe Sakic MHG .40 1.00
398 Dominik Hasek MHG .40 1.00
399 John Leclair MHG .25 .60
400 Sergei Fedorov MHG .40 1.00
401 Nicklas Lidstrom MHG .15 .40
402 Martin Brodeur MHG .50 1.25
403 Ed Belfour MHG .15 .40
404 Steve Yzerman MHG .50 1.25
405 Owen Nolan MHG .10 .25
406 Keith Tkachuk MHG .15 .40
407 Olaf Kolzig MHG .10 .25
408 Rob Blake MHG .10 .25
409 Brett Hull MHG .25 .60
410 Brian Leetch MHG .15 .40
411 Ray Bourque MHG .40 1.00
412 Pierre Turgeon MHG .10 .25
413 Alexei Yashin MHG .05 .15
414 Mike Modano MHG .30 .80
415 Curtis Joseph MHG .15 .40
416 Alexei Kovalev MHG .10 .25
417 Marian Hossa MHG .15 .40
418 Milan Hejduk MHG .15 .40
419 Markus Naslund MHG .15 .40
420 Theo Fleury MHG .05 .15
421 Bill Guerin MHG .10 .25
422 Doug Weight MHG .10 .25
423 Luc Robitaille MHG .10 .25
424 Zigmund Palffy MHG .10 .25
425 Jeremy Roenick MHG .20 .50
426 Mats Sundin MHG .15 .40
427 Alexander Mogilny MHG .10 .25
428 Ed Jovanovski MHG .05 .15
429 Adam Foote MHG .05 .15
430 Peter Bondra MHG .15 .40
431 Mark Recchi MHG .10 .25
432 Radek Bonk MHG .05 .15
433 Simon Gagne MHG .15 .40
434 Scott Stevens MHG .10 .25
435 Steve Sullivan MHG .05 .15
436 Martin Straka MHG .05 .15
437 Evgeni Nabokov MHG .10 .25
438 Keith Primeau MHG .05 .15
439 Brendan Shanahan MHG .30 .80
440 Vincent Lecavalier MHG .15 .40
441 Ilya Kovalchuk RC 3.00 8.00
442 Erik Cole RC 1.50 4.00
443 Pavel Datsyuk RC 2.50 6.00
444 Kristian Huselius RC 1.50 4.00
445 Marcel Hossa RC 1.50 4.00
446 Martin Erat RC 1.50 4.00
447 Christian Berglund RC 1.50 4.00
448 Raffi Torres RC 1.50 4.00
449 Dan Blackburn RC 1.50 4.00
450 Jiri Dopita RC 1.50 4.00
451 Krys Kolanos RC 1.50 4.00
452 Brian Sutherby RC 1.50 4.00
453 Olivier Michaud RC 1.50 4.00

2001-02 Upper Deck Victory Gold

Randomly inserted at 1:2 packs, this 440-card set paralleled the Series I base set but was printed on gold card stock.
*STARS: .75X TO 1.5X BASIC CARDS

2002-03 Upper Deck Victory

Released in late-July 2002, this 220-card set had an SRP of $.99 for a 10-card pack. A bronze bordered parallel was also created and inserted in 1:2 packs.
COMPLETE SET (220) 20.00 40.00
*BRONZE: .5X to 1.25 X BASIC CARD
1 Vitali Vishnevsky .02 .10
2 Paul Kariya .12 .30
3 Jeff Friesen .02 .10
4 J-S Giguere .08 .20
5 Oleg Tverdovsky .02 .10
6 Matt Cullen .02 .10
7 Mike LeClerc .02 .10
8 Pasi Nurminen .02 .10
9 Dany Heatley .15 .40
10 Ilya Kovalchuk .20 .50
11 Pascal Rheaume .02 .10
12 Lubos Bartecko .02 .10
13 Mark Hartigan .02 .10
14 Frederic Cassivi .08 .20
15 Jozef Stumpel .02 .10
16 Sergei Samsonov .08 .20
17 P.J. Stock .02 .10
18 Joe Thornton .25 .60
19 Nick Boynton .02 .10
20 Brian Rolston .02 .10
21 Martin Lapointe .02 .10
22 Maxim Afinogenov .02 .10
23 Martin Biron .08 .20
24 J-P Dumont .02 .10
25 Stu Barnes .02 .10
26 Tim Connolly .02 .10
27 Miroslav Satan .08 .20
28 Taylor Pyatt .02 .10
29 Craig Conroy .02 .10
30 Roman Turek .08 .20
31 Jarome Iginla .15 .40
32 Dean McAmmond .02 .10
33 Marc Savard .02 .10
34 Derek Morris .02 .10
35 Micki Dupont RC .02 .10
36 Sami Kapanen .02 .10
37 Jeff O'Neill .02 .10
38 Ron Francis .08 .20
39 Rod Brind'Amour .08 .20
40 Erik Cole .02 .10
41 Bates Battaglia .02 .10
42 Arturs Irbe .08 .20
43 Alexei Zhamnov .02 .10
44 Jocelyn Thibault .08 .20
45 Eric Daze .08 .20
46 Steve Sullivan .02 .10
47 Phil Housley .02 .10
48 Kyle Calder .02 .10
49 Bob Probert .02 .10
50 Patrick Roy .75 2.00
51 Radim Vrbata .02 .10
52 Chris Drury .08 .20
53 Joe Sakic .30 .75
54 Milan Hejduk .12 .30
55 Alex Tanguay .08 .20
56 Peter Forsberg .40 1.00
57 Rob Blake .08 .20
58 Ray Whitney .02 .10
59 Espen Knutsen .02 .10
60 Marc Denis .08 .20
61 Rostislav Klesla .02 .10
62 Ron Tugnutt .08 .20
63 Mike Sillinger .02 .10
64 Chris Nielsen .02 .10
65 Jason Arnott .02 .10
66 Marty Turco .08 .20
67 Jere Lehtinen .08 .20
68 Sergei Zubov .02 .10
69 Mike Modano .25 .60
70 Brenden Morrow .08 .20
71 Pierre Turgeon .08 .20
72 Derian Hatcher .02 .10
73 Brendan Shanahan .12 .30
74 Dominik Hasek .30 .75
75 Sergei Fedorov .25 .60
76 Pavel Datsyuk .12 .30
77 Steve Yzerman .75 2.00
78 Brett Hull .20 .50
79 Chris Chelios .12 .30
80 Luc Robitaille .08 .20
81 Mike Comrie .08 .20
82 Anson Carter .08 .20
83 Ryan Smyth .02 .10
84 Tommy Salo .08 .20
85 Jochen Hecht .02 .10
86 Eric Brewer .02 .10
87 Mike York .02 .10
88 Kristian Huselius .02 .10
89 Stephen Weiss .02 .10
90 Roberto Luongo .15 .40
91 Sandis Ozolinsh .02 .10
92 Valeri Bure .02 .10
93 Marcus Nilsson .02 .10
94 Niklas Hagman .02 .10
95 Adam Deadmarsh .02 .10
96 Felix Potvin .12 .30
97 Jason Allison .02 .10
98 Eric Belanger .02 .10
99 Zigmund Palffy .08 .20
100 Cliff Ronning .02 .10
101 Mathieu Schneider .02 .10
102 Andrew Brunette .02 .10
103 Sylvain Blouin RC .02 .10
104 Marian Gaborik .25 .60
105 Wes Walz .02 .10
106 Filip Kuba .02 .10
107 Manny Fernandez .08 .20
108 Tony Virta .02 .10
109 Jose Theodore .15 .30
110 Saku Koivu .12 .30
111 Mike Ribeiro .02 .10
112 Yanic Perreault .02 .10
113 Oleg Petrov .02 .10
114 Joe Juneau .02 .10
115 Marcel Hossa .02 .10
116 Denis Arkhipov .02 .10
117 Scott Hartnell .02 .10
118 David Legwand .08 .20
119 Mike Dunham .08 .20
120 Kimmo Timonen .02 .10
121 Greg Johnson .02 .10
122 Andy Delmore .02 .10
123 Petr Sykora .02 .10
124 Scott Stevens .08 .20
125 Brian Gionta .02 .10
126 Scott Niedermayer .02 .10
127 Martin Brodeur .40 1.00
128 Patrik Elias .08 .20
129 Joe Nieuwendyk .08 .20
130 Scott Gomez .02 .10
131 Ray Schultz RC .02 .10
132 Mark Parrish .02 .10
133 Raffi Torres .02 .10
134 Alexei Yashin .02 .10
135 Chris Osgood .08 .20
136 Michael Peca .02 .10
137 Shawn Bates .02 .10
138 Pavel Bure .12 .30
139 Mark Messier .12 .30
140 Eric Lindros .12 .30
141 Brian Leetch .08 .20
142 Petr Nedved .02 .10
143 Tom Poti .02 .10
144 Dan Blackburn .08 .20
145 Mike Richter .12 .30
146 Martin Havlat .08 .20
147 Patrick Lalime .08 .20
148 Daniel Alfredsson .08 .20
149 Marian Hossa .12 .30
150 Radek Bonk .02 .10
151 Wade Redden .02 .10
152 Magnus Arvedson .02 .10
153 Todd White .02 .10
154 Roman Cechmanek .08 .20
155 Mark Recchi .08 .20
156 Simon Gagne .12 .30
157 Jeremy Roenick .15 .40
158 John LeClair .12 .30
159 Keith Primeau .02 .10
160 Justin Williams .02 .10
161 Brian Boucher .08 .20
162 Krys Kolanos .02 .10
163 Sean Burke .08 .20
164 Teppo Numminen .02 .10
165 Shane Doan .02 .10
166 Ladislav Nagy .02 .10
167 Daymond Langkow .08 .20
168 Daniel Briere .02 .10
169 Kris Beech .02 .10
170 Johan Hedberg .08 .20
171 Martin Straka .02 .10
172 Mario Lemieux 1.00 2.50
173 Alexei Kovalev .08 .20
174 Jan Hrdina .02 .10
175 Alexei Morozov .02 .10
176 Vincent Damphousse .02 .10
177 Owen Nolan .08 .20
178 Patrick Marleau .08 .20
179 Evgeni Nabokov .08 .20
180 Brad Stuart .02 .10
181 Mike Ricci .02 .10
182 Scott Thornton .02 .10
183 Al MacInnis .08 .20
184 Pavol Demitra .08 .20
185 Chris Pronger .08 .20
186 Brent Johnson .08 .20
187 Doug Weight .08 .20
188 Keith Tkachuk .12 .30
189 Scott Young .02 .10
190 Cory Stillman .02 .10
191 Sheldon Keefe .02 .10
192 Brad Richards .08 .20
193 Nikolai Khabibulin .12 .30
194 Martin St. Louis .08 .20
195 Vincent Lecavalier .12 .30
196 Fredrik Modin .02 .10
197 Pavel Kubina .02 .10
198 Alexander Mogilny .08 .20
199 Tomas Kaberle .02 .10

200 Mats Sundin .12 .30
201 Gary Roberts .02 .10
202 Mikael Renberg .02 .10
203 Tie Domi .08 .20
204 Darcy Tucker .02 .10
205 Brendan Morrison .08 .20
206 Brent Sopel .02 .10
207 Trevor Linden .02 .10
208 Dan Cloutier .08 .20
209 Todd Bertuzzi .12 .30
210 Ed Jovanovski .08 .20
211 Markus Naslund .12 .30
212 Sergei Gonchar .02 .10
213 Jaromir Jagr .25 .60
214 Peter Bondra .08 .20
215 Steve Konowalchuk .02 .10
216 Dainius Zubrus .02 .10
217 Brian Sutherby .02 .10
218 Olaf Kolzig .08 .20
219 Patrick Roy CL .40 1.00
220 Pavel Bure CL .12 .30

2002-03 Upper Deck Victory Bronze

This 220-card set paralleled the base set with bronze trim and was inserted at 1:2 packs.
*BRONZE: X TO X BASIC CARD

2002-03 Upper Deck Victory Gold

This 220-card set paralleled the base set with gold trim. Each card was serial-numbered to 100.
*GOLD: 8X TO 20X BASIC CARD

2002-03 Upper Deck Victory Silver

This 220-card set paralleled the base set with silver trim and was inserted at 1:36.
*SILVER: 4X TO 10X BASIC CARD

2002-03 Upper Deck Victory National Pride

Inserted at 1:4, this 60-card set featured small color player photos over larger silhouettes.
COMPLETE SET 20.00 40.00
NP1 Ruslan Salei .15 .40
NP2 Paul Kariya .30 .75
NP3 Jarome Iginla .40 1.00
NP4 Joe Sakic .60 1.50
NP5 Rob Blake .25 .60
NP6 Steve Yzerman 1.50 4.00
NP7 Brendan Shanahan .50 1.25
NP8 Martin Brodeur .75 2.00
NP9 Eric Lindros .30 .75
NP10 Simon Gagne .30 .75
NP11 Mario Lemieux 2.00 5.00
NP12 Chris Pronger .25 .60
NP13 Curtis Joseph .30 .75
NP14 Milan Hejduk .30 .75
NP15 Dominik Hasek .60 1.50
NP16 Patrik Elias .25 .60
NP17 Petr Sykora .15 .40
NP18 Martin Rucinsky .15 .40
NP19 Martin Havlat .25 .60
NP20 Robert Lang .15 .40
NP21 Jaromir Jagr .50 1.25
NP22 Sami Kapanen .15 .40
NP23 Ville Nieminen .15 .40
NP24 Jere Lehtinen .25 .60
NP25 Jani Hurme .25 .60
NP26 Teppo Numminen .15 .40
NP27 Teemu Selanne .30 .75
NP28 Jochen Hecht .15 .40
NP29 Marco Sturm .15 .40
NP30 Olaf Kolzig .25 .60
NP31 Ilya Kovalchuk .40 1.00
NP32 Sergei Samsonov .25 .60
NP33 Alexei Zhamnov .15 .40
NP34 Sergei Fedorov .60 1.50
NP35 Pavel Bure .50 1.25
NP36 Alexei Yashin .15 .40
NP37 Alexei Kovalev .25 .60
NP38 Nikolai Khabibulin .30 .75
NP39 Sergei Gonchar .15 .40
NP40 Miroslav Satan .25 .60
NP41 Zigmund Palffy .25 .60
NP42 Marian Hossa .30 .75
NP43 Pavol Demitra .25 .60
NP44 Nicklas Lidstrom .30 .75
NP45 Tomas Holmstrom .15 .40
NP46 Tommy Salo .25 .60
NP47 Daniel Alfredsson .25 .60
NP48 Kim Johnsson .15 .40
NP49 Mats Sundin .30 .75
NP50 Markus Naslund .30 .75
NP51 Bill Guerin .25 .60
NP52 Tony Amonte .25 .60
NP53 Chris Drury .25 .60
NP54 Mike Modano .50 1.25
NP55 Chris Chelios .30 .75
NP56 Mike Dunham .25 .60
NP57 Mike Richter .30 .75
NP58 Jeremy Roenick .40 1.00
NP59 Keith Tkachuk .30 .75
NP60 Doug Weight .25 .60

2003-04 Upper Deck Victory

Released in September, this 210-card set featured 200 base cards and a 10-card rookie redemption set. The rookie redemption exchange card was inserted to 1:72. Please note that card #15 does not exist and card #27 was duplicated.
COMP.SET w/o ROOK.RED (200) 25.00 50.00
COMMON RC (201-210) 1.50 4.00
1 Paul Kariya .12 .30
2 Petr Sykora .02 .10
3 Adam Oates .08 .20
4 Stanislav Chistov .02 .10
5 J-S Giguere .08 .20
6 Dany Heatley .15 .40
7 Ilya Kovalchuk .20 .50
8 Marc Savard .02 .10
9 Patrik Stefan .02 .10
10 Simon Gamache .02 .10
11 Joe DiPenta RC .60 1.50
12 Joe Thornton .25 .60
13 Glen Murray .02 .10
14 Bryan Berard .02 .10
16 P.J. Stock .02 .10
17 Jeff Hackett .02 .10
18 Steve Shields .08 .20
19 Miroslav Satan .08 .20
20 Daniel Briere .02 .10
21 Ales Kotalik .02 .10
22 Milan Bartovic RC .60 1.50
23 Maxim Afinogenov .02 .10
24 Martin Biron .08 .20
25 Ryan Miller .08 .20
26 Rick Mrozik RC .02 .10
27 Sergei Samsonov .08 .20
27 Jarome Iginla .15 .40
28 Chris Drury .08 .20
29 Jordan Leopold .02 .10
30 Roman Turek .08 .20
31 Jamie McLennan .02 .10
32 Jeff O'Neill .02 .10
33 Ron Francis .08 .20
34 Rod Brind'Amour .08 .20
35 Erik Cole .02 .10
36 Pavel Brendl .02 .10
37 Steve Sullivan .02 .10
38 Alexei Zhamnov .02 .10
39 Eric Daze .02 .10
40 Kyle Calder .02 .10
41 Igor Radulov .02 .10
42 Jocelyn Thibault .08 .20
43 Peter Forsberg .40 1.00
44 Milan Hejduk .12 .30
45 Alex Tanguay .08 .20
46 Joe Sakic .30 .75
47 Rob Blake .08 .20
48 David Aebischer .08 .20
49 Patrick Roy .75 2.00
50 Ray Whitney .02 .10
51 Andrew Cassels .02 .10
52 Geoff Sanderson .02 .10
53 Rick Nash .15 .40
54 Marc Denis .08 .20
55 Kent McDonell RC .40 1.00
56 Mike Modano .25 .60
57 Bill Guerin .08 .20
58 Jere Lehtinen .08 .20
59 Jason Arnott .02 .10
60 Steve Ott .02 .10
61 Marty Turco .08 .20
62 Sergei Fedorov .15 .40
63 Brett Hull .15 .40
64 Brendan Shanahan .12 .30
65 Nicklas Lidstrom .12 .30
66 Pavel Datsyuk .12 .30
67 Henrik Zetterberg .12 .30
68 Steve Yzerman .75 2.00
69 Manny Legace .08 .20
70 Curtis Joseph .12 .30
71 Ryan Smyth .02 .10
72 Todd Marchant .02 .10
73 Mike Comrie .08 .20
74 Ales Hemsky .08 .20
75 Eric Brewer .02 .10
76 Fernando Pisani .02 .10
77 Tommy Salo .08 .20
78 Olli Jokinen .08 .20
79 Viktor Kozlov .02 .10
80 Stephen Weiss .02 .10
81 Jay Bouwmeester .02 .10
82 Roberto Luongo .15 .40
83 Zigmund Palffy .08 .20
84 Alexander Frolov .02 .10
85 Jason Allison .02 .10
86 Adam Deadmarsh .02 .10
87 Jamie Storr .08 .20
88 Cristobal Huet .08 .20
89 Marian Gaborik .30 .75
90 Pascal Dupuis .02 .10
91 P-M Bouchard .02 .10
92 Manny Fernandez .08 .20
93 Dwayne Roloson .08 .20
94 Wes Walz .02 .10
95 Saku Koivu .12 .30
96 Richard Zednik .02 .10
97 Marcel Hossa .02 .10
98 Jose Theodore .15 .40
99 Michael Komisarek .02 .10
100 Mathieu Garon .08 .20
101 Ron Hainsey .02 .10
102 David Legwand .08 .20
103 Denis Arkhipov .02 .10
104 Scott Hartnell .02 .10
105 Scottie Upshall .02 .10
106 Tomas Vokoun .08 .20
107 Patrik Elias .08 .20
108 Jamie Langenbrunner .02 .10
109 Scott Gomez .02 .10
110 Joe Nieuwendyk .08 .20
111 John Madden .02 .10
112 Scott Stevens .08 .20
113 Martin Brodeur .75 2.00
114 Alexei Yashin .02 .10
115 Jason Blake .02 .10
116 Dave Scatchard .02 .10
117 Michael Peca .02 .10
118 Janne Niinimaa .02 .10
119 Rick DiPietro .08 .20
120 Garth Snow .02 .10
121 Alex Kovalev .08 .20
122 Anson Carter .08 .20
123 Eric Lindros .12 .30
124 Tom Poti .02 .10
125 Mark Messier .12 .30
126 Pavel Bure .12 .30
127 Brian Leetch .08 .20
128 Mike Dunham .08 .20
129 Dan Blackburn .08 .20
130 Marian Hossa .12 .30
131 Daniel Alfredsson .08 .20
132 Todd White .02 .10
133 Zdeno Chara .02 .10
134 Jason Spezza .12 .30
135 Patrick Lalime .08 .20
136 Ray Emery .08 .20
137 Jeremy Roenick .15 .40
138 Mark Recchi .08 .20
139 Tony Amonte .08 .20
140 Keith Primeau .02 .10
141 John LeClair .12 .30
142 Simon Gagne .12 .30
143 Robert Esche .08 .20
144 Mike Johnson .02 .10
145 Shane Doan .02 .10
146 Ladislav Nagy .02 .10
147 Chris Gratton .02 .10
148 Sean Burke .08 .20
149 Mario Lemieux 1.00 2.50
150 Martin Straka .02 .10
151 Rico Fata .02 .10
152 Johan Hedberg .08 .20
153 Sebastien Caron .08 .20
154 Brooks Orpik .02 .10
155 Teemu Selanne .12 .30
156 Vincent Damphousse .02 .10
157 Patrick Marleau .08 .20
158 Jim Fahey .02 .10
159 Niko Dimitrakos .02 .10
160 Kyle McLaren .02 .10
161 Evgeni Nabokov .08 .20
162 Peter Sejna RC 1.50 4.00
163 Pavol Demitra .08 .20
164 Al MacInnis .08 .20
165 Doug Weight .08 .20
166 Keith Tkachuk .12 .30
167 Chris Pronger .08 .20
168 Chris Osgood .08 .20
169 Barret Jackman .08 .20
170 Vaclav Prospal .02 .10
171 Vincent Lecavalier .12 .30
172 Martin St. Louis .08 .20
173 Alexander Svitov .02 .10
174 Nikolai Khabibulin .12 .30
175 Matt Stajan RC 1.00 2.50
176 Alexander Mogilny .08 .20
177 Mats Sundin .12 .30
178 Owen Nolan .08 .20
179 Nik Antropov .02 .10
180 Doug Gilmour .08 .20
181 Tie Domi .08 .20
182 Gary Roberts .02 .10
183 Ed Belfour .12 .30
184 Carlo Colaiacovo .02 .10
185 Alexander Auld .02 .10
186 Markus Naslund .12 .30
187 Todd Bertuzzi .12 .30
188 Brendan Morrison .08 .20
189 Ed Jovanovski .08 .20
190 Matt Cooke .02 .10
191 Trevor Linden .02 .10
192 Henrik Sedin .02 .10
193 Daniel Sedin .02 .10
194 Dan Cloutier .08 .20
195 Jaromir Jagr .25 .60
196 Sergei Gonchar .02 .10
197 Michael Nylander .02 .10
198 Peter Bondra .08 .20
199 Mike Grier .02 .10
200 Olaf Kolzig .08 .20
201 Joffrey Lupul RC 2.00 5.00
202 Eric Staal RC 2.50 6.00
203 Tuomo Ruutu RC 2.00 5.00
204 Nathan Horton RC 2.00 5.00
205 Dustin Brown RC 1.50 4.00
206 Jordin Tootoo RC 2.00 5.00
207 Joni Pitkanen RC 1.50 4.00
208 Milan Michalek RC 1.50 4.00
209 Sean Bergenheim RC 1.50 4.00
210 Marc-Andre Fleury RC 1.50 4.00

2003-04 Upper Deck Victory Bronze

*STARS: 2X TO 5X BASIC CARDS
*ROOKIES: .4X TO 1X
STATED PRINT RUN 199 SER.#'d SETS

2003-04 Upper Deck Victory Gold

*STARS: 12X TO 30X BASIC CARDS
*ROOKIES: 1.5X TO 4X
STATED PRINT RUN 25 SER.#'d SETS

2003-04 Upper Deck Victory Silver

*STARS: 8X TO 20X BASIC CARDS
*ROOKIES: .75X TO 2X
STATED PRINT RUN 50 SER.#'d SETS

2003-04 Upper Deck Victory Freshman Flashback

COMPLETE SET (50) 15.00 30.00
STATED ODDS 1:2
FF1 Paul Kariya .20 .50
FF2 Stanislav Chistov .15 .40
FF3 Ilya Kovalchuk .40 1.00
FF4 Dany Heatley .30 .75
FF5 Joe Thornton .50 1.25
FF6 Sergei Samsonov .15 .40
FF7 Ryan Miller .15 .40
FF8 Jarome Iginla .25 .60
FF9 Jordan Leopold .15 .40
FF10 Jocelyn Thibault .15 .40
FF11 Igor Radulov .15 .40
FF12 Peter Forsberg .75 2.00
FF13 Joe Sakic .60 1.50
FF14 Patrick Roy 1.50 4.00
FF15 Rick Nash .25 .60
FF16 Mike Modano .50 1.25
FF17 Henrik Zetterberg .20 .50
FF18 Brett Hull .40 1.00
FF19 Brendan Shanahan .20 .50
FF20 Dmitri Bykov .15 .40
FF21 Roberto Luongo .25 .60
FF22 Jay Bouwmeester .15 .40
FF23 Zigmund Palffy .15 .40
FF24 Cristobal Huet .15 .40
FF25 Marian Gaborik .60 1.50
FF26 Mike Komisarek .15 .40
FF27 Martin Brodeur .75 2.00
FF28 Alex Kovalev .15 .40
FF29 Pavel Bure .20 .50
FF30 Marian Hossa .20 .50
FF31 Jason Spezza .20 .50
FF32 Ray Emery .15 .40
FF33 John LeClair .20 .50
FF34 Tony Amonte .15 .40
FF35 Jeremy Roenick .25 .60
FF36 Mario Lemieux 2.00 5.00
FF37 Teemu Selanne .20 .50
FF38 Jim Fahey .15 .40
FF39 Niko Dimitrakos .15 .40
FF40 Chris Pronger .15 .40
FF41 Keith Tkachuk .20 .50
FF42 Vincent Lecavalier .20 .50
FF43 Owen Nolan .15 .40
FF44 Mats Sundin .20 .50
FF45 Alexander Mogilny .15 .40
FF46 Jaromir Jagr .50 1.25
FF47 Bobby Orr 2.00 5.00
FF48 Ray Bourque .60 1.50
FF49 Wayne Gretzky 2.00 5.00
FF50 Gordie Howe 1.50 4.00

2003-04 Upper Deck Victory Game Breakers

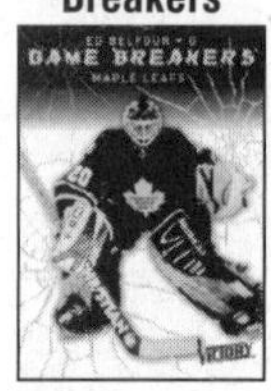

COMPLETE SET (50) 12.50 25.00
STATED ODDS 1:2
GB1 Peter Forsberg .75 2.00
GB2 Paul Kariya .20 .50
GB3 Ilya Kovalchuk .25 .60
GB4 Martin Brodeur 1.00 2.50
GB5 Sean Burke .15 .40
GB6 Bill Guerin .15 .40
GB7 Owen Nolan .15 .40
GB8 Alexei Yashin .15 .40
GB9 Marty Turco .15 .40
GB10 Dany Heatley .25 .60
GB11 Joe Sakic .40 1.00
GB12 Mike Comrie .15 .40
GB13 Jason Blake .15 .40
GB14 Nikolai Khabibulin .20 .50
GB15 Ed Belfour .20 .50
GB16 Chris Pronger .15 .40
GB17 Rick Nash .25 .60
GB18 Jaromir Jagr .30 .75
GB19 Vincent Lecavalier .20 .50
GB20 Olli Jokinen .15 .40
GB21 Alex Kovalev .15 .40
GB22 Mike Modano .30 .75
GB23 Henrik Zetterberg .20 .50
GB24 Roberto Luongo .25 .60
GB25 Teemu Selanne .20 .50
GB26 John LeClair .20 .50
GB27 Tie Domi .15 .40
GB28 Todd Bertuzzi .20 .50
GB29 Pavel Bure .20 .50
GB30 Mario Lemieux 1.25 3.00
GB31 Al MacInnis .15 .40
GB32 Joe Thornton .30 .75
GB33 Mats Sundin .20 .50
GB34 Keith Tkachuk .20 .50
GB35 Alexander Mogilny .15 .40
GB36 Marian Hossa .20 .50
GB37 Brett Hull .25 .60
GB38 Marian Gaborik .40 1.00
GB39 Tony Amonte .15 .40
GB40 Zigmund Palffy .15 .40
GB41 Patrick Roy 1.00 2.50
GB42 Sergei Samsonov .15 .40
GB43 Sergei Fedorov .25 .60
GB44 Markus Naslund .20 .50
GB45 Brendan Shanahan .20 .50
GB46 Saku Koivu .20 .50
GB47 Jarome Iginla .25 .60
GB48 Jocelyn Thibault .15 .40
GB49 Jason Spezza .20 .50
GB50 Jeremy Roenick .25 .60

2005-06 Upper Deck Victory

Victory was released in late-summer 2005, this 300-card set was one of the first of the 2005-06 season. The final 100 cards in the series were found in Upper Deck Series 2 packs.
COMP.SET w/o UPDATE (200) 15.00 30.00
COMP.UPDATE SET (100) 40.00 80.00
UPDATE FOUND IN UDII PACKS
1 J-S Giguere .10 .30
2 Joffrey Lupul .10 .20
3 Sergei Fedorov .20 .50
4 Stanislav Chistov .10 .20
5 Sandis Ozolinsh .10 .20
6 Steve Rucchin .10 .20
7 Dany Heatley .20 .50
8 Ilya Kovalchuk .20 .50
9 Kari Lehtonen .15 .40
10 Shawn McEachern .10 .20
11 Marc Savard .10 .20
12 Patrik Stefan .10 .20
13 Glen Murray .10 .20
14 Patrice Bergeron .15 .40
15 Andrew Raycroft .10 .30
16 Nick Boynton .10 .20
17 Sergei Gonchar .10 .20
18 Sergei Samsonov .10 .30
19 Joe Thornton .25 .60
20 Miroslav Satan .10 .30
21 Chris Drury .10 .20
22 Martin Biron .10 .30
23 Jochen Hecht .10 .20
24 Daniel Briere .10 .20
25 Maxim Afinogenov .10 .20
26 Mike Grier .10 .20
27 Jarome Iginla .20 .50
28 Martin Gelinas .10 .20
29 Jordan Leopold .10 .20
30 Miikka Kiprusoff .15 .40
31 Chris Simon .10 .20
32 Ville Nieminen .10 .20
33 Jeff O'Neill .10 .20
34 Martin Gerber .10 .30
35 Rod Brind'Amour .10 .30
36 Erik Cole .10 .20
37 Eric Staal .10 .30
38 Josef Vasicek .10 .20
39 Bryan Berard .10 .20
40 Eric Daze .10 .30
41 Jocelyn Thibault .10 .30
42 Tyler Arnason .10 .20
43 Mark Bell .10 .20
44 Tuomo Ruutu .10 .20
45 Joe Sakic .30 .75
46 Peter Forsberg .40 1.00
47 David Aebischer .10 .30
48 Rob Blake .10 .30
49 Milan Hejduk .15 .40
50 Alex Tanguay .10 .30
51 Paul Kariya .15 .40
52 Adam Foote .10 .20
53 Teemu Selanne .15 .40
54 Rick Nash .20 .50
55 Rostislav Klesla .10 .20
56 Geoff Sanderson .10 .20
57 Nikolai Zherdev .10 .30
58 Marc Denis .10 .30
59 Pascal LeClaire .10 .30
60 Mike Modano .15 .40
61 Bill Guerin .10 .20
62 Marty Turco .10 .30
63 Brenden Morrow .10 .30
64 Jere Lehtinen .10 .30
65 Jason Arnott .10 .20
66 Sergei Zubov .10 .20
67 Steve Yzerman .60 1.50
68 Brendan Shanahan .15 .40
69 Chris Chelios .15 .40
70 Pavel Datsyuk .15 .40
71 Henrik Zetterberg .15 .40
72 Robert Lang .10 .20
73 Nicklas Lidstrom .15 .40
74 Kris Draper .10 .20
75 Curtis Joseph .10 .30
76 Gordie Howe .75 2.00
77 Wayne Gretzky 1.00 2.50
78 Raffi Torres .10 .20
79 Ty Conklin .10 .30
80 Ryan Smyth .10 .30
81 Jason Smith .10 .20
82 Georges Laraque .10 .20
83 Mike York .10 .20
84 Stephen Weiss .10 .20
85 Roberto Luongo .20 .50
86 Olli Jokinen .10 .20
87 Mike Van Ryn .10 .20
88 Kristian Huselius .10 .20
89 Jay Bouwmeester .10 .20
90 Eric Belanger .10 .20
91 Luc Robitaille .10 .30
92 Mathieu Garon .10 .30
93 Zigmund Palffy .10 .30
94 Lubomir Visnovsky .10 .20
95 Mike Cammalleri .10 .20
96 Marian Gaborik .30 .75
97 Pascal Dupuis .10 .20
98 Andrew Brunette .10 .20
99 Brian Rolston .10 .20
100 Manny Fernandez .10 .30
101 Dwayne Roloson .10 .30
102 Jose Theodore .20 .50
103 Saku Koivu .15 .40
104 Michael Ryder .10 .30
105 Mike Ribeiro .10 .20
106 Sheldon Souray .10 .20
107 Richard Zednik .10 .20
108 Yanic Perreault .10 .20
109 David Legwand .10 .30
110 Scott Walker .10 .20
111 Tomas Vokoun .10 .30
112 Steve Sullivan .10 .20
113 Kimmo Timonen .10 .20
114 Martin Erat .10 .20
115 Martin Brodeur .75 2.00
116 Scott Stevens .10 .30
117 Scott Gomez .10 .30
118 Brian Rafalski .10 .20
119 Scott Niedermayer .10 .20
120 Patrik Elias .10 .30
121 Rick DiPietro .10 .30
122 Alexei Yashin .10 .30
123 Mark Parrish .10 .30
124 Michael Peca .10 .20
125 Trent Hunter .10 .20
126 Adrian Aucoin .10 .20
127 Bobby Holik .10 .20
128 Mark Messier .15 .40
129 Mike Dunham .10 .30
130 Jaromir Jagr .25 .60
131 Jamie Lundmark .10 .20
132 Tom Poti .10 .20
133 Daniel Alfredsson .10 .30
134 Martin Havlat .10 .30
135 Dominik Hasek .30 .75
136 Jason Spezza .15 .40
137 Marian Hossa .10 .30
138 Peter Bondra .10 .30
139 Wade Redden .10 .20
140 Jeremy Roenick .20 .50
141 Simon Gagne .15 .40
142 Keith Primeau .10 .25
143 John LeClair .15 .40
144 Robert Esche .10 .30
145 Tony Amonte .10 .30
146 Donald Brashear .10 .20
147 Michal Handzus .10 .20
148 Brett Hull .20 .50
149 Shane Doan .10 .20
150 Ladislav Nagy .10 .20
151 Brian Boucher .10 .30
152 Mike Comrie .10 .20
153 Mike Ricci .10 .30
154 Milan Kraft .10 .20
155 Mario Lemieux 1.00 2.50
156 Marc-Andre Fleury .10 .30
157 Mark Recchi .10 .30
158 Dick Tarnstrom .10 .20
159 Ryan Malone .10 .20
160 Patrick Marleau .10 .30
161 Nils Ekman .10 .20
162 Jonathan Cheechoo .15 .40
163 Evgeni Nabokov .10 .30
164 Marco Sturm .10 .20
165 Alyn McCauley .10 .20
166 Doug Weight .10 .30
167 Keith Tkachuk .15 .40
168 Chris Pronger .10 .30
169 Al MacInnis .10 .30
170 Patrick Lalime .10 .30
171 Pavol Demitra .10 .30
172 Barret Jackman .10 .20
173 Brad Richards .10 .30
174 Vincent Lecavalier .15 .40
175 Fredrik Modin .10 .20
176 Nikolai Khabibulin .15 .40
177 Ruslan Fedotenko .10 .20
178 Cory Stillman .10 .20
179 Martin St. Louis .10 .30
180 Dan Boyle .10 .20
181 Mats Sundin .15 .40
182 Bryan McCabe .10 .20
183 Joe Nieuwendyk .10 .30
184 Gary Roberts .10 .25
185 Tie Domi .10 .30
186 Ed Belfour .15 .40
187 Brian Leetch .15 .40
188 Darcy Tucker .10 .20
189 Markus Naslund .15 .40
190 Brendan Morrison .10 .20
191 Dan Cloutier .10 .20
192 Ed Jovanovski .10 .30
193 Matt Cooke .10 .20
194 Brent Sopel .10 .20
195 Trevor Linden .10 .20
196 Olaf Kolzig .10 .30
197 Jeff Halpern .10 .20
198 Alexander Semin .10 .20
199 Rastislav Stana .10 .30
200 Brendan Witt .10 .20
201 Teemu Selanne .15 .40
202 Scott Niedermayer .10 .30
203 Marian Hossa .10 .30
204 Peter Bondra .10 .30
205 Brian Leetch .15 .40
206 Brad Boyes .10 .20
207 Ryan Miller .10 .30
208 Tony Amonte .10 .30
209 Justin Williams .10 .30
210 Nikolai Khabibulin .15 .40
211 Pavel Vorobiev .10 .20
212 Pierre Turgeon .10 .30
213 Sergei Fedorov .15 .40
214 Antti Miettinen .10 .20
215 Niko Kapanen .10 .20
216 Manny Legace .15 .40
217 Jason Williams .10 .30
218 Chris Pronger .10 .30
219 Ales Hemsky .10 .30
220 Joe Nieuwendyk .10 .30
221 Nathan Horton .10 .30
222 Jeremy Roenick .20 .50
223 Pavol Demitra .10 .30
224 Pierre-Marc Bouchard .10 .20
225 Alex Kovalev .10 .30
226 Paul Kariya .15 .40
227 Scott Hartnell .10 .20
228 Brian Gionta .10 .20
229 Jamie Langenbrunner .10 .20
230 Miroslav Satan .10 .20
231 Alexei Zhitnik .10 .20
232 Steve Rucchin .10 .20
233 Kevin Weekes .10 .30
234 Dany Heatley .20 .50
235 Zdeno Chara .10 .30
236 Peter Forsberg .30 .75
237 Joni Pitkanen .10 .20
238 Curtis Joseph .15 .40
239 Geoff Sanderson .10 .20
240 Sergei Gonchar .10 .20
241 John LeClair .15 .40
242 Milan Michalek .10 .20
243 Petr Cajanek .10 .20
244 Sean Burke .10 .30
245 Vaclav Prospal .10 .20
246 Eric Lindros .15 .40
247 Jason Allison .10 .20
248 Jeff O'Neill .10 .20
249 Todd Bertuzzi .15 .40
250 Jeff Friesen .10 .20
251 Peter Budaj RC .40 1.00
252 Wojtek Wolski RC 1.00 2.50
253 Brent Seabrook RC .40 1.00
254 Cam Barker RC .60 1.50
255 Gilbert Brule RC 1.00 2.50
256 Jay McClement RC .40 1.00
257 Jeff Woywitka RC .40 1.00
258 Andrew Alberts RC .40 1.00
259 Hannu Toivonen RC .75 2.00
260 Yann Danis RC .40 1.00
261 Alexander Perezhogin RC .75 2.00
262 Brad Winchester RC .40 1.00
263 Kyle Brodziak RC .40 1.00
264 Alexander Ovechkin RC 5.00 12.00
265 Jakub Klepis RC .40 1.00
266 Keith Ballard RC .40 1.00
267 David Leneveu RC .60 1.00
268 Zach Parise RC .75 2.00
269 Dion Phaneuf RC 1.50 4.00
270 Eric Nystrom RC .40 1.50
271 Mike Richards RC 1.00 2.50
272 Jeff Carter RC 1.00 2.50
273 R.J. Umberger RC .60 1.50
274 Cam Ward RC 1.50 4.00
275 Robert Nilsson RC .60 1.50
276 Chris Campoli RC .40 1.00
277 George Parros RC .40 1.00
278 Evgeny Artyukhin RC .40 1.00
279 Alexander Steen RC 1.00 2.50
280 Ryan Getzlaf RC 1.00 2.50
281 Corey Perry RC 1.00 2.50
282 Rostislav Olesz RC .60 1.50
283 Anthony Stewart RC .60 1.50
284 Ryan Whitney RC .40 1.00
285 Sidney Crosby RC 12.00 30.00
286 Maxime Talbot RC .40 1.00
287 Ryan Suter RC .60 1.50
288 Henrik Lundqvist RC 1.50 4.00
289 Alvaro Montoya RC .75 2.00
290 Jim Howard RC .75 2.00
291 Johan Franzen RC .40 1.00
292 Thomas Vanek RC 1.25 3.00
293 Andrej Meszaros RC .40 1.00
294 Christoph Schubert RC .40 1.00
295 Patrick Eaves RC .60 1.50
296 Steve Bernier RC .75 2.00
297 Jussi Jokinen RC .75 2.00
298 Braydon Coburn RC .60 1.50
299 Matt Foy RC .40 1.00
300 Mikko Koivu RC .75 2.00

2005-06 Upper Deck Victory Black

PRINT RUN 5 SER.#'d SETS
NOT PRICED DUE TO SCARCITY

2005-06 Upper Deck Victory Gold

*GOLD: 6X TO 15X BASE HI
*ROOKIES: 3X TO 8X BASE HI
PRINT RUN 100 SER.#'d SETS
264 Alexander Ovechkin 30.00 80.00
269 Dion Phaneuf 10.00 25.00
285 Sidney Crosby 125.00 250.00

2005-06 Upper Deck Victory Silver

*SILVER: 3X TO 8X BASE HI
PRINT RUN 250 SER.#'d SETS

2005-06 Upper Deck Victory Game Breakers

COMPLETE SET (45) 6.00 12.00
STATED ODDS 1:2
GB1 Sergei Fedorov .25 .60
GB2 Dany Heatley .25 .60
GB3 Ilya Kovalchuk .25 .60
GB4 Glen Murray .15 .40
GB5 Joe Thornton .30 .75
GB6 Chris Drury .15 .40
GB7 Eric Daze .15 .40
GB8 Tuomo Ruutu .15 .40
GB9 Peter Forsberg .75 2.00
GB10 Joe Sakic .40 1.00
GB11 Milan Hejduk .20 .50
GB12 Paul Kariya .20 .50
GB13 Rick Nash .25 .60
GB14 Mike Modano .30 .75
GB15 Bill Guerin .15 .40
GB16 Brendan Shanahan .20 .50

B17 Steve Yzerman 1.00 2.50
B18 Kris Draper .15 .40
B19 Henrik Zetterberg .20 .50
B20 Ryan Smyth .15 .40
B21 Olli Jokinen .15 .40
B22 Zigmund Palffy .15 .40
B23 Marian Gaborik .30 .75
B24 Michael Ryder .15 .40
B25 Saku Koivu .20 .50
B26 Steve Sullivan .15 .40
B27 Alexei Yashin .15 .40
B28 Jaromir Jagr .30 .75
B29 Marian Hossa .20 .50
B30 Martin Havlat .15 .40
B31 Peter Bondra .15 .40
B32 Keith Primeau .15 .40
B33 Simon Gagne .20 .50
B34 Brett Hull .25 .60
B35 Shane Doan .15 .40
B36 Mario Lemieux 1.25 3.00
B37 Patrick Marleau .15 .40
B38 Pavol Demitra .15 .40
B39 Keith Tkachuk .20 .50
B40 Martin St. Louis .15 .40
B41 Vincent Lecavalier .20 .50
B42 Brad Richards .15 .40
B43 Alexander Mogilny .15 .40
B44 Mats Sundin .20 .50
B45 Markus Naslund .20 .50

2005-06 Upper Deck Victory Stars on Ice

COMPLETE SET (45) 6.00 12.00
S1 J-S Giguere .15 .40
S2 Dany Heatley .25 .60
S3 Ilya Kovalchuk .25 .60
S4 Joe Thornton .30 .75
S5 Andrew Raycroft .15 .40
S6 Miroslav Satan .15 .40
S7 Jarome Iginla .25 .60
S8 Miikka Kiprusoff .15 .40
S9 Jeff O'Neill .15 .40
S10 Jocelyn Thibault .15 .40
S11 Joe Sakic .40 1.00
S12 Peter Forsberg .75 2.00
S13 Alex Tanguay .15 .40
S14 Rob Blake .15 .40
S15 David Aebischer .15 .40
S16 Rick Nash .25 .60
S17 Marty Turco .15 .40
S18 Sergei Zubov .15 .40
S19 Mike Modano .30 .75
S20 Nicklas Lidstrom .20 .50
S21 Steve Yzerman 1.00 2.50
S22 Robert Lang .15 .40
S23 Roberto Luongo .25 .60
S24 Luc Robitaille .15 .40
S25 Jose Theodore .25 .60
S26 Martin Brodeur 1.00 2.50
S27 Scott Stevens .15 .40
S28 Eric Lindros .20 .50
S29 Dominik Hasek .40 1.00
S30 Daniel Alfredsson .15 .40
S31 Jason Spezza .20 .50
S32 Jeremy Roenick .25 .60
S33 John LeClair .20 .50
S34 Brett Hull .25 .60
S35 Mario Lemieux 1.25 3.00
S36 Evgeni Nabokov .15 .40
S37 Keith Tkachuk .20 .50
S38 Doug Weight .15 .40
S39 Martin St. Louis .15 .40
S40 Nikolai Khabibulin .20 .50
S41 Ed Belfour .20 .50
S42 Brian Leetch .20 .50
S43 Mats Sundin .20 .50
S44 Markus Naslund .20 .50
S45 Ed Jovanovski .15 .40

2006-07 Upper Deck Victory

COMPLETE SET (230) 15.00 40.00
COMPLETE UDATE SET (100)
231-330 FOUND IN UD2 PACKS
1 Jean-Sebastien Giguere .15 .40
2 Joffrey Lupul .10 .25
3 Teemu Selanne .20 .50
4 Andy McDonald .10 .25
5 Scott Niedermayer .10 .25
6 Corey Perry .15 .40
7 Ilya Kovalchuk .25 .60
8 Kari Lehtonen .20 .50
9 Marian Hossa .15 .40
10 Marc Savard .10 .25
11 Slava Kozlov .10 .25
12 Patrice Bergeron .20 .50
13 Tim Thomas .15 .40
14 Brian Leetch .20 .50
15 Glen Murray .10 .25
16 Brad Boyes .10 .25
17 Marco Sturm .10 .25
18 Brad Stuart .10 .25
19 Andrew Raycroft .15 .40
20 Chris Drury .10 .25
21 Ryan Miller .15 .40
22 Thomas Vanek .10 .25
23 Tim Connolly .10 .25
24 Maxim Afinogenov .10 .25
25 Martin Biron .15 .40
26 Ales Kotalik .10 .25
27 Daniel Briere .10 .25
28 Miikka Kiprusoff .20 .50
29 Jarome Iginla .25 .60
30 Dion Phaneuf .25 .60
31 Daymond Langkow .10 .25
32 Chuck Kobasew .10 .25
33 Kristian Huselius .10 .25
34 Cam Ward .20 .50
35 Eric Staal .20 .50
36 Mark Recchi .10 .25
37 Doug Weight .10 .25
38 Justin Williams .10 .25
39 Erik Cole .10 .25
40 Rod Brind'Amour .15 .40
41 Tuomo Ruutu .10 .25
42 Nikolai Khabibulin .20 .50
43 Kyle Calder .10 .25
44 Brent Seabrook .10 .25
45 Mark Bell .10 .25
46 Pavel Vorobiev .10 .25
47 Joe Sakic .40 1.00
48 Jose Theodore .20 .50
49 Marek Svatos .10 .25
50 Milan Hejduk .15 .40
51 Alex Tanguay .15 .40
52 Rob Blake .15 .40
53 Andrew Brunette .10 .25
54 Rick Nash .20 .50
55 David Vyborny .10 .25
56 Marc Denis .15 .40
57 Nikolai Zherdev .10 .25
58 Sergei Fedorov .20 .50
59 Pascal Leclaire .15 .40
60 Mike Modano .20 .50
61 Marty Turco .15 .40
62 Jussi Jokinen .15 .40
63 Brenden Morrow .15 .40
64 Sergei Zubov .10 .25
65 Jere Lehtinen .10 .25
66 Bill Guerin .10 .25
67 Jason Arnott .10 .25
68 Steve Yzerman .75 2.00
69 Pavel Datsyuk .15 .40
70 Brendan Shanahan .20 .50
71 Manny Legace .15 .40
72 Nicklas Lidstrom .20 .50
73 Henrik Zetterberg .20 .50
74 Tomas Holmstrom .10 .25
75 Kris Draper .10 .25
76 Ryan Smyth .15 .40
77 Shawn Horcoff .10 .25
78 Ales Hemsky .10 .25
79 Chris Pronger .15 .40
80 Dwayne Roloson .15 .40
81 Michael Peca .10 .25
82 Raffi Torres .25 .60
83 Roberto Luongo .25 .60
84 Nathan Horton .10 .25
85 Olli Jokinen .10 .25
86 Jay Bouwmeester .10 .25
87 Mike Van Ryn .10 .25
88 Joe Nieuwendyk .15 .40
89 Mathieu Garon .15 .40
90 Dustin Brown .10 .25
91 Alexander Frolov .10 .25
92 Pavol Demitra .10 .25
93 Craig Conroy .10 .25
94 Mike Cammalleri .10 .25
95 Lubomir Visnovsky .10 .25
96 Marian Gaborik .25 .60
97 Manny Fernandez .15 .40
98 Brian Rolston .10 .25
99 Pierre-Marc Bouchard .10 .25
100 Wes Walz .10 .25
101 Mikko Koivu .10 .25
102 David Aebischer .15 .40
103 Saku Koivu .20 .50
104 Alex Kovalev .10 .25
105 Michael Ryder .15 .40
106 Chris Higgins .15 .40
107 Mike Ribeiro .10 .25
108 Cristobal Huet .25 .60
109 Paul Kariya .20 .50
110 Tomas Vokoun .15 .40
111 Steve Sullivan .10 .25
112 Martin Erat .10 .25
113 Kimmo Timonen .10 .25
114 Scott Hartnell .10 .25
115 David Legwand .10 .25
116 Martin Brodeur 1.00 2.50
117 Brian Gionta .10 .25
118 Scott Gomez .10 .25
119 Patrik Elias .10 .25
120 Brian Rafalski .10 .25
121 Zach Parise .15 .40
122 Alexei Yashin .10 .25
123 Rick DiPietro .15 .40
124 Miroslav Satan .10 .25
125 Jason Blake .10 .25
126 Mike York .10 .25
127 Alexei Zhitnik .10 .25
128 Trent Hunter .10 .25
129 Henrik Lundqvist .25 .60
130 Jaromir Jagr .30 .75
131 Martin Straka .10 .25
132 Petr Prucha .10 .25
133 Michael Nylander .10 .25
134 Fedor Tyutin .10 .25
135 Jason Spezza .20 .50
136 Dany Heatley .25 .60
137 Dominik Hasek .30 .75
138 Daniel Alfredsson .15 .40
139 Zdeno Chara .10 .25
140 Wade Redden .10 .25
141 Martin Havlat .15 .40
142 Ray Emery .15 .40
143 Peter Forsberg .40 1.00
144 Antero Niittymaki .15 .40
145 Simon Gagne .20 .50
146 Joni Pitkanen .10 .25
147 Keith Primeau .10 .25
148 Jeff Carter .15 .40
149 Mike Richards .15 .40
150 Robert Esche .15 .40
151 Shane Doan .10 .25
152 Curtis Joseph .20 .50
153 Ladislav Nagy .10 .25
154 Mike Comrie .10 .25
155 Geoff Sanderson .10 .25
156 Keith Ballard .10 .25
157 Sidney Crosby 1.25 3.00
158 Ryan Malone .10 .25
159 Marc-Andre Fleury .15 .40
160 Sergei Gonchar .10 .25
161 Colby Armstrong .10 .25
162 Ryan Whitney .10 .25
163 Joe Thornton .30 .75
164 Evgeni Nabokov .15 .40
165 Patrick Marleau .15 .40
166 Jonathan Cheechoo .20 .50
167 Vesa Toskala .15 .40
168 Steve Bernier .10 .25
169 Curtis Sanford .15 .40
170 Lee Stempniak .10 .25
171 Keith Tkachuk .20 .50
172 Scott Young .10 .25
173 Petr Cajanek .10 .25
174 Barret Jackman .10 .25
175 Evgeni Artyukhin .10 .25
176 Vaclav Prospal .10 .25
177 Martin St. Louis .15 .40
178 Vincent Lecavalier .20 .50
179 Sean Burke .15 .40
180 Brad Richards .15 .40
181 Fredrik Modin .10 .25
182 Tie Domi .10 .25
183 Mats Sundin .20 .50
184 Ed Belfour .20 .50
185 Eric Lindros .20 .50
186 Bryan McCabe .10 .25
187 Alexander Steen .15 .40
188 Darcy Tucker .10 .25
189 Jason Allison .10 .25
190 Henrik Sedin .10 .25
191 Alex Auld .15 .40
192 Markus Naslund .20 .50
193 Brendan Morrison .10 .25
194 Ed Jovanovski .10 .25
195 Mattias Ohlund .10 .25
196 Daniel Sedin .10 .25
197 Jeff Halpern .10 .25
198 Dainius Zubrus .10 .25
199 Alexander Ovechkin 1.00 2.50
200 Olaf Kolzig .20 .50
201 Tomas Kopecky RC .60 1.50
202 Billy Thompson RC .40 1.00
203 Dustin Byfuglien RC .40 1.00
204 Yan Stastny RC .40 1.00
205 Eric Fehr RC .60 1.50
206 Ben Ondrus RC .40 1.00
207 Rob Collins RC .40 1.00
208 Brendan Bell RC .40 1.00
209 Frank Doyle RC .75 2.00
210 Noah Welch RC .40 1.00
211 Filip Novak RC .40 1.00
212 Ian White RC .40 1.00
213 Konstantin Pushkaryov RC .40 1.00
214 Dan Jancevski RC .40 1.00
215 Shea Weber RC .60 1.50
216 Michel Ouellet RC .75 2.00
217 Marc-Antoine Pouliot RC .60 1.50
218 Carsen Germyn RC .40 1.00
219 Matt Carle RC .60 1.50
220 Steve Regier RC .40 1.00
221 Mark Stuart RC .40 1.00
222 Bill Thomas RC .40 1.00
223 Jarkko Immonen RC .40 1.00
224 Erik Reitz RC .40 1.00
225 Joel Perrault RC .40 1.00
226 Ryan Potulny RC .60 1.50
227 Jeremy Williams RC .40 1.00
228 Masi Marjamaki RC .40 1.00
229 Miroslav Kopriva RC .40 1.00
230 Matt Koalska RC .40 1.00
231 Chris Pronger .20 .50
232 Zdeno Chara .40
233 Marc Savard .10 .25
234 Hannu Toivonen .20 .50
235 Alex Tanguay .15 .40
236 Martin Havlat .15 .40
237 Michal Handzus .10 .25
238 Wojtek Wolski .10 .25
239 Jordan Leopold .10 .25
240 Fredrik Modin .10 .25
241 Gilbert Brule .20 .50
242 Anson Carter .10 .25
243 Mike Ribeiro .10 .25
244 Eric Lindros .20 .50
245 Patrik Stefan .10 .25
246 Jeff Halpern .10 .25
247 Dominik Hasek .30 .75
248 Joffrey Lupul .20 .50
249 Petr Sykora .10 .25
250 Todd Bertuzzi .15 .40
251 Ed Belfour .20 .50
252 Alexander Auld .15 .40
253 Rob Blake .15 .40
254 Dan Cloutier .10 .25
255 Pavol Demitra .10 .25
256 Mark Parrish .10 .25
257 Sergei Samsonov .15 .40
258 Jason Arnott .10 .25
259 Mike Sillinger .10 .25
260 Brendan Shanahan .20 .50
261 Matt Cullen .10 .25
262 Martin Gerber .15 .40
263 Kyle Calder .10 .25
264 Geoff Sanderson .10 .25
265 Owen Nolan .15 .40
266 Ed Jovanovski .10 .25
267 Jeremy Roenick .25 .60
268 Mark Recchi .10 .25
269 Nils Ekman .10 .25
270 Mark Bell .10 .25
271 Mike Grier .10 .25
272 Doug Weight .10 .25
273 Bill Guerin .10 .25
274 Manny Legace .15 .40
275 Marc Denis .15 .40
276 Andrew Raycroft .15 .40
277 Michael Peca .10 .25
278 Kyle Wellwood .10 .25
279 Roberto Luongo .25 .60
280 Alexander Semin .15 .40
281 Shane O'Brien RC .40 1.00
282 Jonas Johansson RC .40 1.00
283 Ryan Shannon RC .40 1.00
284 Patrick O'Sullivan RC .60 1.50
285 Anze Kopitar RC 1.50 4.00
286 John Oduya RC .40 1.00
287 Travis Zajac RC .75 2.00
288 Fredrik Norrena RC .60 1.50
289 Phil Kessel RC 1.50 4.00
290 Guillaume Latendresse RC 1.50 4.00
291 Nigel Dawes RC .40 1.00
292 Jordan Staal RC 3.00 8.00
293 Kristopher Letang RC .60 1.50
294 Paul Stastny RC 2.00 5.00
295 Niklas Backstrom RC .75 2.00
296 D.J. King RC .40 1.00
297 Marc-Edouard Vlasic RC .40 1.00
298 Patrick Thoresen RC .60 1.50
299 Ladislav Smid RC .40 1.00
300 Loui Eriksson RC .40 1.00
301 Patrick Fischer RC .40 1.00
302 Mikko Lehtonen RC .40 1.00
303 Roman Polak RC .40 1.00
304 Evgeni Malkin RC 3.00 8.00
305 Luc Bourdon RC .60 1.50
306 Alexei Kaigorodov RC .40 1.00
307 Alex Brooks RC .40 1.00
308 Nate Thompson RC .40 1.00
309 Janis Sprukts RC .40 1.00
310 Alexander Radulov RC 1.25 3.00
311 Keith Yandle RC .40 1.00
312 Enver Lisin RC .40 1.00
313 Cole Jarrett RC .40 1.00
314 Ryan Caldwell RC .40 1.00
315 David Printz RC .40 1.00
316 David Liffiton RC .40 1.00
317 Adam Burish RC .40 1.00
318 Dave Bolland RC .40 1.00
319 Michael Blunden RC .40 1.00
320 Matt Lashoff RC .40 1.00
321 Alexei Mikhnov RC .40 1.00
322 Jan Hejda RC .40 1.00
323 Lars Jonsson RC .40 1.00
324 Triston Grant RC .40 1.00
325 Alexander Edler RC .40 1.00
326 Brandon Prust RC .40 1.00
327 Dustin Boyd RC .60 1.50
328 Drew Stafford RC 1.50 4.00
329 Kelly Guard RC .40 1.00
330 Nathan McIver RC .40 1.00

2006-07 Upper Deck Victory Black

STATED ODDS 1:720
NOT PRICED DUE TO SCARCITY

2006-07 Upper Deck Victory Gold

COMMON CARD 2.00 5.00
*STARS: 5X to 12X HI
* ROOKIES: 1.5X to 4X HI
68 Steve Yzerman 10.00 25.00
116 Martin Brodeur 10.00 25.00
157 Sidney Crosby 12.00 30.00
199 Alexander Ovechkin 10.00 25.00

2006-07 Upper Deck Victory GameBreakers

ODDS 1:4 PACKS
GB1 Jean-Sebastien Giguere .75 2.00
GB2 Ilya Kovalchuk 1.25 3.00
GB3 Marian Hossa .75 2.00
GB4 Patrice Bergeron 1.00 2.50
GB5 Jarome Iginla 1.25 3.00
GB6 Miikka Kiprusoff 1.00 2.50
GB7 Eric Staal 1.00 2.50
GB8 Martin Gerber .75 2.00
GB9 Nikolai Khabibulin 1.00 2.50
GB10 Joe Sakic 2.00 5.00
GB11 Alex Tanguay .75 2.00
GB12 Marek Svatos .50 1.25
GB13 Rick Nash 1.00 2.50
GB14 Mike Modano 1.00 2.50
GB15 Marty Turco .75 2.00
GB16 Henrik Zetterberg 1.00 2.50
GB17 Pavel Datsyuk .75 2.00
GB18 Brendan Shanahan 1.00 2.50
GB19 Roberto Luongo 1.25 3.00
GB20 Olli Jokinen .50 1.25
GB21 Alexander Frolov .50 1.25
GB22 Marian Gaborik 1.25 3.00
GB23 Saku Koivu 1.00 2.50
GB24 Alex Kovalev .50 1.25
GB25 Michael Ryder .75 2.00
GB26 Paul Kariya 1.00 2.50
GB27 Tomas Vokoun .75 2.00
GB29 Patrik Elias .50 1.25
GB30 Jaromir Jagr 1.50 4.00
GB31 Henrik Lundqvist 2.00 5.00
GB32 Jason Spezza 1.00 2.50
GB33 Dany Heatley 1.25 3.00
GB34 Daniel Alfredsson .75 2.00
GB35 Dominik Hasek 1.50 4.00
GB36 Simon Gagne 1.00 2.50
GB37 Jeff Carter .75 2.00
GB38 Peter Forsberg 2.00 5.00
GB39 Shane Doan .50 1.25
GB40 Sidney Crosby 4.00 10.00
GB41 Marc-Andre Fleury .75 2.00
GB42 Joe Thornton 1.50 4.00
GB43 Patrick Marleau .75 2.00
GB44 Jonathan Cheechoo 1.00 2.50
GB45 Martin St. Louis .75 2.00
GB46 Vincent Lecavalier 1.00 2.50
GB47 Ed Belfour 1.00 2.50
GB48 Mats Sundin 1.00 2.50
GB49 Markus Naslund 1.00 2.50
GB50 Alexander Ovechkin 3.00 8.00

2006-07 Upper Deck Victory Next In Line

ODDS 1:4
NL1 Corey Perry .75 2.00
NL2 Joffrey Lupul .75 2.00
NL3 Ryan Getzlaf .75 2.00
NL4 Ilya Kovalchuk 1.25 3.00
NL5 Kari Lehtonen 1.00 2.50
NL6 Patrice Bergeron 1.00 2.50
NL7 Andrew Raycroft .75 2.00
NL8 Brad Boyes .60 1.50
NL9 Thomas Vanek .60 1.50
NL10 Ryan Miller .75 2.00
NL11 Dion Phaneuf 1.50 4.00
NL12 Eric Staal .75 2.00
NL13 Cam Ward 1.00 2.50
NL14 Tuomo Ruutu .60 1.50
NL15 Marek Svatos .60 1.50
NL16 Rick Nash 1.25 3.00
NL17 Nikolai Zherdev .60 1.50
NL18 Gilbert Brule 1.25 3.00
NL19 Jussi Jokinen .60 1.50
NL20 Henrik Zetterberg 1.00 2.50
NL21 Ales Hemsky .60 1.50
NL22 Jarret Stoll .60 1.50
NL23 Nathan Horton .60 1.50
NL24 Rostislav Olesz .60 1.50
NL25 Alexander Frolov .60 1.50
NL26 Mike Cammalleri .60 1.50
NL27 Marian Gaborik 1.00 2.50
NL28 Mikko Koivu .75 2.00
NL29 Yann Danis .75 2.00
NL30 Alexander Perezhogin .75 2.00
NL31 Zach Parise .75 2.00
NL32 Rick DiPietro .75 2.00
NL33 Henrik Lundqvist 2.00 5.00
NL34 Petr Prucha .60 1.50
NL35 Jason Spezza 1.00 2.50
NL36 Dany Heatley 1.25 3.00
NL37 Jeff Carter .75 2.00
NL38 Mike Richards .75 2.00
NL39 Joni Pitkanen .60 1.50
NL40 Marc-Andre Fleury .75 2.00
NL41 Sidney Crosby 4.00 10.00
NL42 Jonathan Cheechoo 1.00 2.50
NL43 Evgeni Artyukhin .60 1.50
NL44 Matt Stajan .60 1.50
NL45 Alexander Steen .75 2.00
NL46 Ryan Kesler .60 1.50
NL47 Alex Auld .75 2.00
NL48 Alexander Ovechkin 3.00 8.00
NL49 Erik Cole .60 1.50
NL50 Kyle Wellwood .60 1.50

2000-01 Upper Deck Vintage

Released in mid January 2001, Upper Deck Vintage is a 400-card set comprised of 340 regular cards, 30 prospect cards and 30 triple player team checklists. Base cards are thick cardboard with a throwback vintage design. Backgrounds are white with a colored nameplate along the bottom. Vintage was packaged in 24-pack boxes with packs containing 10 cards and carried a suggested retail price of $1.99. NOTE: The Curtis Joseph promo was handed out as a single to announce the upcoming arrival of the product. It is numbered 31 (the P was added on our end as a database sorter) and has the word sample written across the back.

COMPLETE SET (400) 30.00 60.00
1 German Titov .08 .20
2 Teemu Selanne .25 .60
3 Matt Cullen .08 .20
4 Oleg Tverdovsky .08 .20
5 J-S Giguere .20 .50
6 Guy Hebert .08 .20
7 Mike Leclerc .08 .20
8 Jason Marshall .08 .20
9 Paul Kariya .25 .60
10 Steve Rucchin .08 .20
11 Paul Kariya .25 .60
Guy Hebert
Teemu Selanne
12 Paul Kariya .25 .60
Guy Hebert
13 Patrik Stefan .08 .20
14 Damian Rhodes .08 .20
15 Donald Audette .08 .20
16 Yannick Tremblay .08 .20
17 Hnat Domenichelli .08 .20
18 Dean Sylvester .08 .20
19 Steve Guolla .08 .20
20 Petr Buzek .08 .20
21 Andrew Brunette .08 .20
22 Ray Ferraro .08 .20
23 Patrik Stefan .08 .20
Damian Rhodes
Denny Lambert
24 Patrik Stefan .08 .20
Damian Rhodes
25 Joe Thornton .40 1.00
26 Brian Rolston .08 .20
27 Kyle McLaren .08 .20
28 Sergei Samsonov .20 .50
29 Paul Coffey .25 .60
30 Andrei Kovalenko .08 .20
31 Jason Allison .08 .20
31P Curtis Joseph PROMO
32 Bill Guerin .20 .50
33 Byron Dafoe .08 .20
34 Mikko Eloranta .08 .20
35 Don Sweeney .08 .20
36 Joe Thornton .08 .20
Byron Dafoe
Kyle McLaren
37 Joe Thornton .08 .20
Byron Dafoe
38 Miroslav Satan .20 .50
39 Dominik Hasek .50 1.25
40 Stu Barnes .08 .20
41 Chris Gratton .08 .20
42 Doug Gilmour .20 .50
43 Curtis Brown .08 .20
44 James Patrick .08 .20
45 Alexei Zhitnik .08 .20
46 Rhett Warrener .08 .20
47 Dave Andreychuk .20 .50
48 Maxim Afinogenov .08 .20
49 Miroslav Satan .25 .60
Dominik Hasek
Rob Ray
50 Miroslav Satan .30 .75
Dominik Hasek
51 Valeri Bure .08 .20
52 Mike Vernon .20 .50
53 Marc Savard .08 .20
54 Clarke Wilm .08 .20
55 Phil Housley .08 .20
56 Fred Brathwaite .20 .50
57 Cory Stillman .08 .20
58 Derek Morris .08 .20
59 Robyn Regehr .08 .20
60 Jarome Iginla .30 .75
61 Valeri Bure .08 .20
Fred Brathwaite
Jason Wiemer
62 Valeri Bure .08 .20
Fred Brathwaite
63 Bates Battaglia .08 .20
64 Sandis Ozolinsh .08 .20
65 Jeff O'Neill .08 .20
66 Ron Francis .20 .50
67 Sami Kapanen .08 .20
68 Martin Gelinas .08 .20
69 Arturs Irbe .20 .50
70 Dave Tanabe .08 .20
71 Rod Brind'Amour .20 .50
72 Glen Wesley .08 .20
73 Jeff O'Neill .08 .20
Arturs Irbe
Ron Francis
74 Ron Francis .08 .20
Arturs Irbe
75 Tony Amonte .20 .50
76 Steve Sullivan .08 .20
77 Eric Daze .20 .50
78 Boris Mironov .08 .20
79 Jocelyn Thibault .20 .50
80 Jean-Yves Leroux .08 .20
81 Valeri Zelepukin .08 .20
82 Alexei Zhamnov .08 .20
83 Josef Marha .08 .20
84 Michael Nylander .08 .20
85 Tony Amonte .08 .20
Jocelyn Thiabault
Bob Probert
86 Tony Amonte .08 .20
Jocelyn Thibault
87 Patrick Roy 1.25 3.00
88 Joe Sakic .50 1.25
89 Jon Klemm .08 .20
90 Adam Deadmarsh .08 .20
91 Ray Bourque .50 1.25
92 Peter Forsberg .60 1.50
93 Milan Hejduk .25 .60
94 Chris Drury .20 .50
95 Alex Tanguay .20 .50
96 Adam Foote .08 .20
97 Dave Reid .08 .20
98 Joe Sakic .60 1.50
Patrick Roy
Raymond Bourque
99 Joe Sakic .60 1.50
Patrick Roy
100 Marc Denis .20 .50
101 Geoff Sanderson .08 .20
102 Ron Tugnutt .20 .50
103 Lyle Odelein .08 .20
104 Krzysztof Oliwa .08 .20
105 Kevyn Adams .08 .20
106 Steve Heinze .08 .20
107 Jamie Pushor .08 .20
108 Bruce Gardiner .08 .20
109 Jan Caloun .08 .20
110 Kevyn Adams .08 .20
Marc Denis
Krzysztof Oliwa
111 Geoff Sanderson .08 .20
Ron Tugnutt
112 Mike Modano .40 1.00
113 Jere Lehtinen .20 .50
114 Brett Hull .30 .75
115 Sergei Zubov .08 .20
116 Jamie Langenbrunner .08 .20
117 Shaun Van Allen .08 .20
118 Ed Belfour .25 .60
119 Brenden Morrow .20 .50
120 Darryl Sydor .08 .20
121 Joe Nieuwendyk .20 .50
122 Derian Hatcher .08 .20
123 Mike Modano .08 .20
Ed Belfour
Derian Hatcher
124 M.Modano/E.Belfour .25 .60
125 Steve Yzerman 1.25 3.00
126 Nicklas Lidstrom .25 .60
127 Sergei Fedorov .40 1.00
128 Chris Osgood .20 .50
129 Brendan Shanahan .25 .60
130 Larry Murphy .08 .20
131 Darren McCarty .08 .20
132 Chris Chelios .25 .60
133 Kris Draper .08 .20
134 Tomas Holmstrom .08 .20
135 Slava Kozlov .08 .20
136 Steve Yzerman 1.00 2.50
Chris Osgood
Brendan Shanahan
137 Steve Yzerman 1.00 2.50
Chris Osgood
138 Doug Weight .20 .50
139 Todd Marchant .08 .20
140 Eric Brewer .08 .20
141 Mike Grier .08 .20
142 Tom Poti .08 .20
143 Ryan Smyth .08 .20
144 Tommy Salo .20 .50
145 Janne Niinimaa .08 .20
146 Daniel Cleary .08 .20
147 Bill Guerin .20 .50
148 Doug Weight .08 .20
Tommy Salo
Georges Laraque
149 Doug Weight .08 .20
Tommy Salo
150 Pavel Bure .25 .60
151 Ray Whitney .08 .20
152 Viktor Kozlov .20 .50
153 Igor Larionov .08 .20
154 Scott Mellanby .08 .20
155 Trevor Kidd .20 .50
156 Rob Niedermayer .20 .50
157 Robert Svehla .08 .20
158 Roberto Luongo .30 .75
159 Mike Sillinger .08 .20
160 Pavel Bure .25 .60
Roberto Luongo
Peter Worrell
161 Pavel Bure .25 .60
Trevor Kidd
162 Zigmund Palffy .20 .50
163 Luc Robitaille .20 .50
164 Stephane Fiset .08 .20
165 Rob Blake .20 .50
166 Bryan Smolinski .08 .20
167 Glen Murray .08 .20
168 Mattias Norstrom .08 .20
169 Jamie Storr .20 .50
170 Craig Johnson .08 .20
171 Nelson Emerson .08 .20
172 Zigmund Palffy .08 .20
Jamie Storr
Rob Blake
173 Luc Robitaille .08 .20
Stephane Fiset
174 Stacy Roest .08 .20
175 Manny Fernandez .20 .50
176 Jim Dowd .08 .20
177 Curtis Leschyshyn .08 .20
178 Jeff Nielsen .08 .20
179 Aaron Gavey .08 .20
180 Sergei Krivokrasov .08 .20
181 Brad Bombardir .08 .20
182 Cam Stewart .08 .20
183 Scott Pellerin .08 .20
184 Pellerin/Frnandz/Gaborik CL .20
.50
185 Sergei Krivokrasov .08 .20
Manny Fernandez
186 Saku Koivu .25 .60
187 Eric Weinrich .08 .20
188 Sergei Zholtok .08 .20
189 Dainius Zubrus .08 .20
190 Brian Savage .08 .20
191 Jeff Hackett .08 .20
192 Patrick Poulin .08 .20
193 Jose Theodore .30 .75
194 Christian Laflamme .08 .20
195 Martin Rucinsky .08 .20
196 Linden/Theodore/Koivu CL .25 .60
197 S.Koivu/J.Theodore .25 .60
198 Greg Johnson .08 .20
199 Cliff Ronning .08 .20
200 Drake Berehowsky .08 .20
201 Mike Dunham .08 .20
202 David Legwand .20 .50
203 Tom Fitzgerald .08 .20
204 Patric Kjellberg .08 .20
205 Scott Walker .08 .20
206 Kimmo Timonen .08 .20
207 Bill Houlder .08 .20
208 David Legwand .08 .20
Mike Dunham
Todd Fitzgerald
209 David Legwand .08 .20
Mike Dunham
210 Scott Stevens .20 .50
211 Martin Brodeur .60 1.50
212 Jason Arnott .08 .20
213 Patrik Elias .20 .50
214 Alexander Mogilny .20 .50
215 Scott Gomez .08 .20
216 John Madden .08 .20
217 Bobby Holik .08 .20
218 Petr Sykora .08 .20
219 Ken Sutton .08 .20
220 Randy McKay .08 .20
221 Scott Gomez .25 .60
Martin Brodeur
Scott Stevens
222 Scott Gomez .30 .75
Martin Brodeur
223 Tim Connolly .08 .20
224 Kevin Haller .08 .20
225 Brad Isbister .20 .50
226 Mariusz Czerkawski .08 .20
227 Roman Hamrlik .08 .20
228 Claude Lapointe .08 .20
229 Bill Muckalt .08 .20
230 John Vanbiesbrouck .20 .50
231 Kenny Jonsson .08 .20
232 Mark Parrish .08 .20
233 Tim Connolly .08 .20
John Vanbiesbrouck
Kenny Jonsson
234 Tim Connolly .08 .20
John Vanbiesbrouck
235 Theo Fleury .08 .20
236 Brian Leetch .20 .50
237 Mark Messier .25 .60
238 Adam Graves .08 .20
239 Mike Richter .25 .60
240 Vladimir Malakhov .08 .20

241 Mike York .08 .20
242 Radek Dvorak .08 .20
243 Petr Nedved .08 .20
244 Jan Hlavac .08 .20
245 Tim Taylor .08 .20
246 Mark Messier .25 .60
Mike Richter
Adam Graves
247 Mark Messier .25 .60
Mike Richter
248 Radek Bonk .08 .20
249 Marian Hossa .25 .60
250 Jason York .08 .20
251 Wade Redden .08 .20
252 Patrick Lalime .20 .50
253 Daniel Alfredsson .20 .50
254 Shawn McEachern .08 .20
255 Sami Salo .08 .20
256 Petr Schastlivy .08 .20
257 Vaclav Prospal .08 .20
258 Alexei Yashin .10 .30
Patrick Lalime
Marian Hossa
259 Marian Hossa .10 .30
Patrick Lalime
260 John LeClair .25 .60
261 Rick Tocchet .08 .20
262 Daymond Langkow .20 .50
263 Simon Gagne .25 .60
264 Keith Primeau .08 .20
265 Eric Desjardins .20 .50
266 Brian Boucher .25 .60
267 Andy Delmore .08 .20
268 Mark Recchi .20 .50
269 Keith Jones .08 .20
270 Chris Therien .08 .20
271 John LeClair .25 .60
Brian Boucher
Rick Tocchet
272 John LeClair .20 .50
Brian Boucher
273 Jeremy Roenick .30 .75
274 Teppo Numminen .08 .20
275 Brad May .08 .20
276 Keith Tkachuk .25 .60
277 Trevor Letowski .08 .20
278 Shane Doan .08 .20
279 Jyrki Lumme .08 .20
280 Joe Juneau .08 .20
281 Sean Burke .20 .50
282 Travis Green .08 .20
283 Jeremy Roenick .10 .30
Sean Burke
Keith Tkachuk
284 Keith Tkachuk .10 .30
Sean Burke
285 Jean-Sebastien Aubin .20 .50
286 Jaromir Jagr .40 1.00
287 Alexei Morozov .08 .20
288 Josef Beranek .08 .20
289 Jan Hrdina .08 .20
290 Milan Kraft .08 .20
291 Alexei Kovalev .20 .50
292 Robert Lang .08 .20
293 Janne Laukkanen .08 .20
294 Martin Straka .08 .20
295 Jaromir Jagr .25 .60
Jean-Sebastien Aubin
Darius Kasparaitis
296 Jaromir Jagr .20 .50
Jean-Sebastien Aubin
297 Niklas Sundstrom .08 .20
298 Owen Nolan .20 .50
299 Jeff Friesen .08 .20
300 Vincent Damphousse .08 .20
301 Brad Stuart .20 .50
302 Marco Sturm .08 .20
303 Alexander Korolyuk .08 .20
304 Mike Ricci .08 .20
305 Patrick Marleau .20 .50
306 Steve Shields .20 .50
307 Jeff Friesen .08 .20
Steve Shields
Owen Nolan
308 Jeff Friesen .08 .20
Steve Shields
309 Chris Pronger .20 .50
310 Pavol Demitra .20 .50
311 Marty Reasoner .08 .20
312 Jochen Hecht .08 .20
313 Michal Handzus .08 .20
314 Al MacInnis .20 .50
315 Roman Turek .20 .50
316 Lubos Bartecko .08 .20
317 Jamal Mayers .08 .20
318 Dallas Drake .08 .20
319 Pierre Turgeon .20 .50
320 Pavol Demitra .08 .20
Roman Turek
Chris Pronger
321 Chris Pronger .08 .20
Roman Turek
322 Vincent Lecavalier .25 .60
323 Mike Johnson .08 .20
324 Brad Richards .08 .20
325 Dan Cloutier .08 .20
326 Paul Mara .08 .20
327 Fredrik Modin .08 .20
328 Bryan Muir .08 .20
329 Jassen Cullimore .08 .20
330 Todd Warriner .08 .20
331 Petr Svoboda .08 .20
332 Vincent Lecavalier .10 .30
Dan Cloutier
Petr Svoboda
333 Vincent Lecavalier .10 .30
Dan Cloutier
334 Mats Sundin .25 .60
335 Sergei Berezin .08 .20
336 Nikolai Antropov .08 .20
337 Steve Thomas .08 .20
338 Curtis Joseph .25 .60
339 Jonas Hoglund .08 .20
340 Dimitri Yushkevich .08 .20
341 Darcy Tucker .08 .20
342 Gary Roberts .08 .20
343 Jeff Farkas .08 .20
344 Tie Domi .20 .50
345 Mats Sundin .15 .40
Curtis Joseph
Tie Domi
346 Mats Sundin .15 .40
Curtis Joseph
347 Markus Naslund .25 .60
348 Brendan Morrison .20 .50
349 Todd Bertuzzi .25 .60
350 Adrian Aucoin .08 .20
351 Donald Brashear .08 .20
352 Murray Baron .08 .20
353 Daniel Sedin .08 .20
354 Andrew Cassels .08 .20
355 Henrik Sedin .08 .20
356 Mattias Ohlund .08 .20
357 Markus Naslund .08 .20
Felix Potvin
Donald Brashear
358 Markus Naslund .08 .20
Felix Potvin
359 Chris Simon .08 .20
360 Olaf Kolzig .20 .50
361 Jeff Halpern .08 .20
362 Andrei Nikolishin .08 .20
363 Steve Konowalchuk .08 .20
364 Peter Bondra .25 .60
365 Adam Oates .20 .50
366 Richard Zednik .08 .20
367 Sergei Gonchar .08 .20
368 Brendan Witt .08 .20
369 Peter Bondra .08 .20
Olaf Kolzig
Chris Simon
370 Adam Oates .08 .20
Olaf Kolzig
371 Rostislav Klesla RC .60 1.50
372 Jonas Ronnqvist RC .40 1.00
373 Eric Nickulas RC .40 1.00
374 Andrew Raycroft RC 2.00 5.00
375 Jeff Cowan RC .40 1.00
376 Reto Von Arx RC .40 1.00
377 Serge Aubin RC .40 1.00
378 Tyler Bouck RC .40 1.00
379 Michel Riesen RC .40 1.00
380 Eric Belanger RC .40 1.00
381 Marian Gaborik RC 2.50 6.00
382 Scott Hartnell RC .60 1.50
383 Greg Classen RC .40 1.00
384 Willie Mitchell RC .40 1.00
385 Colin White RC .40 1.00
386 Steve Valiquette RC .40 1.00
387 Jani Hurme RC .60 1.50
388 Martin Havlat RC 2.00 5.00
389 Justin Williams RC .60 1.50
390 Petr Hubacek RC .40 1.00
391 Roman Simicek RC .40 1.00
392 Matt Elich RC .40 1.00
393 Brent Sopel RC .40 1.00
394 Marc-Andre Thinel RC .40 1.00
395 Zdenek Blatny RC .40 1.00
396 Michael Ryder RC 5.00 12.00
397 Jason Jaspers RC .40 1.00
398 Jordan Krestanovich RC .40 1.00
399 Fedor Fedorov RC .40 1.00
400 Jeff Bateman RC .40 1.00

2000-01 Upper Deck Vintage All UD Team

COMPLETE SET (10) 6.00 15.00
STATED ODDS 1:23
UD1 Patrick Roy 2.00 5.00
UD2 Martin Brodeur 1.00 2.50
UD3 Chris Pronger .25 .60
UD4 Ray Bourque .75 2.00
UD5 Paul Kariya .25 .60
UD6 John LeClair .50 1.25
UD7 Steve Yzerman 2.00 5.00
UD8 Peter Forsberg 1.00 2.50
UD9 Jaromir Jagr .60 1.50
UD10 Pavel Bure .50 1.25

2000-01 Upper Deck Vintage Dynasty: A Piece of History

Randomly inserted in packs at the rate of 1:72, this 11-card set features two swatches of game worn jerseys from some of the NHL's most dominating teams and player combinations. Two player photos are pictured in the middle of the card's horizontal design with jersey swatches on the outside. Gold parallels to this set were also created and inserted randomly, these cards were numbered to just 50.

*MULTI-COLOR SWATCH: 1X TO 1.5X
*GOLD: 1X TO 1.5X BASIC CARDS
BG Bob Bourne 8.00 20.00
Clark Gillies
BK Mike Bossy 8.00 20.00
Anders Kallur
GC Butch Goring 8.00 20.00
Billy Carroll
GH Clark Gillies 8.00 20.00
Mats Hallin
GK Wayne Gretzky 60.00 150.00
Mark Messier
LJ Mario Lemieux 25.00 60.00
Jaromir Jagr
LL Pat Lafontaine 8.00 20.00
Dave Langevin
NS Bobby Nystrom 8.00 20.00
Brent Sutter
PR Denis Potvin 12.50 30.00
Chico Resch
TP Bryan Trottier 8.00 20.00
Stefan Persson
YO Steve Yzerman 15.00 40.00
Chris Osgood

2000-01 Upper Deck Vintage Great Gloves

COMPLETE SET (20) 4.00 10.00
STATED ODDS 1:12
GG1 Guy Hebert .40 1.00
GG2 Byron Dafoe .40 1.00
GG3 Dominik Hasek 1.25 2.50
GG4 Fred Brathwaite .40 1.00
GG5 Arturs Irbe .40 1.00
GG6 Patrick Roy 2.50 6.00
GG7 Ed Belfour .50 1.25
GG8 Chris Osgood .40 1.00
GG9 Tommy Salo .40 1.00
GG10 Trevor Kidd .40 1.00
GG11 Jose Theodore .60 1.50
GG12 Mike Richter .40 1.00
GG13 Brian Boucher .40 1.00
GG14 Jean-Sebastien Aubin .40 1.00
GG15 Steve Shields .40 1.00
GG16 Roman Turek .40 1.00
GG17 Dan Cloutier .40 1.00
GG18 Curtis Joseph .50 1.25
GG19 Felix Potvin .50 1.25
GG20 Olaf Kolzig .40 1.00

2000-01 Upper Deck Vintage Messier Heroes of Hockey

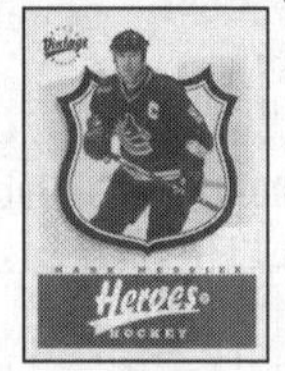

Randomly inserted in packs at the rate of 1:23, this 10-card set pays tribute to Mark Messier. Base cards are white bordered with an action photo set inside the NHL logo shield. The bottom of the card features a blue box containing the Mark Messier Heroes of Hockey logo.

COMPLETE SET (10) 10.00 20.00
COMMON MESSIER 1.25 3.00

2000-01 Upper Deck Vintage National Heroes

Randomly inserted in packs at the rate of 1:4, this 20-card set features top NHL players in action on a card with each respective player's home country flag set against a yellow background.

COMPLETE SET (20) 6.00 15.00
NH1 Paul Kariya .25 .60
NH2 Teemu Selanne .25 .60
NH3 Patrik Stefan .20 .50
NH4 Sergei Samsonov .20 .50
NH5 Dominik Hasek .50 1.25
NH6 Valeri Bure .20 .50
NH7 Tony Amonte .20 .50
NH8 Patrick Roy 1.25 3.00
NH9 Peter Forsberg .60 1.50
NH10 Mike Modano .40 1.00
NH11 Steve Yzerman 1.25 3.00
NH12 Pavel Bure .30 .75
NH13 Saku Koivu .25 .60
NH14 Martin Brodeur .60 1.50
NH15 Scott Gomez .20 .50
NH16 Mark Messier .30 .75
NH17 John LeClair .30 .75
NH18 Jeremy Roenick .30 .75
NH19 Jaromir Jagr .40 1.00
NH20 Mats Sundin .25 .60

2000-01 Upper Deck Vintage Original 6: A Piece of History

Randomly inserted in packs at the rate of 1:72, this six card set features six top players from yesterday and today, each representing one of the NHL's original six teams. Cards have player action shots and a circular jersey swatch in the middle of the number six on the right side of the card front. Gold parallels to this set were also created and inserted randomly, these cards were limited to just 67 sets.

*MULTI-COLOR SWATCH: 1X TO 1.5X
STATED ODDS 1:72
*GOLD: 1.5X TO 3X BASIC CARDS
OCJ Curtis Joseph 6.00 15.00
OJT Jose Theodore 8.00 20.00
OMY Mike York 6.00 15.00
OSS Sergei Samsonov 6.00 15.00
OSY Steve Yzerman 12.50 30.00
OTE Tony Esposito 10.00 25.00

2000-01 Upper Deck Vintage Star Tandems

COMPLETE SET (10) 10.00 20.00
STATED ODDS 1:23
S1A Paul Kariya .50 1.25
S1B Teemu Selanne .50 1.25
S2A Joe Sakic .75 2.00
S2B Patrick Roy 2.00 5.00
S3A Steve Yzerman 2.00 5.00
S3B Brendan Shanahan .60 1.50
S4A Scott Gomez .50 1.25
S4B Martin Brodeur 1.00 2.50
S5A John LeClair .50 1.25
S5B Brian Boucher .50 1.25

2001-02 Upper Deck Vintage

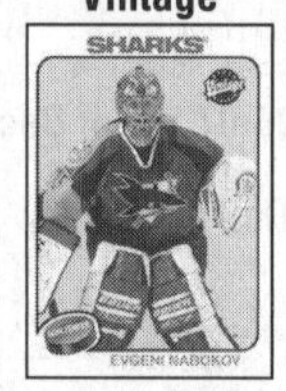

Issued in late-December 2001, this 300-card set carried an SRP of $1.99 for a 10-card pack.

COMPLETE SET (300) 40.00 80.00
1 J-S Giguere .20 .50
2 Jeff Friesen .08 .20
3 Paul Kariya .25 .60
4 Oleg Tverdovsky .08 .20
5 Steve Rucchin .08 .20
6 Mike Leclerc .08 .20
7 Dan Bylsma .08 .20
8 Paul Kariya .25 .60
9 Paul Kariya .08 .20
Mike Leclerc
Oleg Tverdovsky
Marty McInnis
10 Patrik Stefan .08 .20
11 Tomi Kallio .08 .20
12 Chris Tamer .08 .20
13 Milan Hnilicka .20 .50
14 Ray Ferraro .08 .20
15 Stephen Guolla .08 .20
16 Ray Ferraro .08 .20
17 Patrik Stefan .08 .20
Ray Ferraro
Milan Hnilicka
Tommi Kallio
18 Kyle McLaren .08 .20
19 Brian Rolston .08 .20
20 Byron Dafoe .20 .50
21 Mikko Eloranta .08 .20
22 Sergei Samsonov .20 .50
23 Joe Thornton .40 1.00
24 Bill Guerin .20 .50
25 Joe Thornton .40 1.00
26 Bill Guerin .08 .20
Joe Thornton
Sergei Samsonov
Byron Dafoe
27 Martin Biron .20 .50
28 Maxim Afinogenov .08 .20
29 J-P Dumont .08 .20
30 Chris Gratton .08 .20
31 Rhett Warrener .08 .20
32 Miroslav Satan .20 .50
33 Curtis Brown .08 .20
34 Miroslav Satan .20 .50
35 Chris Gratton .08 .20
Miroslav Satan
J.P. Dumont
Curtis Brown
36 Marc Savard .08 .20
37 Jarome Iginla .30 .75
38 Derek Morris .08 .20
39 Oleg Saprykin .08 .20
40 Jeff Shantz .08 .20
41 Craig Conroy .08 .20
42 Jarome Iginla .30 .75
43 Marc Savard .25 .60
Derek Morris
Jarome Iginla
Oleg Saprykin
44 Jeff O'Neill .08 .20
45 Arturs Irbe .20 .50
46 Shane Willis .08 .20
47 Dave Tanabe .08 .20
48 Rod Brind'Amour .20 .50
49 Sami Kapanen .08 .20
50 Ron Francis .20 .50
51 Jeff O'Neill .08 .20
52 Arturs Irbe .08 .20
Sami Kapanen
Jeff O'Neill
Rod Brind'Amour
53 Eric Daze .20 .50
54 Alexei Zhamnov .08 .20
55 Jaroslav Spacek .08 .20
56 Michael Nylander .08 .20
57 Tony Amonte .20 .50
58 Steve Sullivan .08 .20
59 Kevin Dean .08 .20
60 Steve Sullivan .08 .20
61 Tony Amonte .08 .20
Eric Daze
Alexei Zhamnov
Steve Sullivan
62 Chris Drury .20 .50
63 Rob Blake .20 .50
64 Joe Sakic .50 1.25
65 Peter Forsberg .60 1.50
66 Ray Bourque .50 1.25
67 Milan Hejduk .25 .60
68 Patrick Roy 1.25 3.00
69 Joe Sakic .50 1.25
70 Patrick Roy .25 .60
Joe Sakic
Peter Forsberg
Milan Hejduk
71 Ron Tugnutt .20 .50
72 Geoff Sanderson .08 .20
73 Espen Knutsen .08 .20
74 Tyler Wright .08 .20
75 Rostislav Klesla .08 .20
76 Jamie Heward .08 .20
77 Geoff Sanderson .08 .20
78 Ron Tugnutt .08 .20
Espen Knutsen
Geoff Sanderson
Rostislav Klesla
79 Mike Modano .40 1.00
80 Ed Belfour .25 .60
81 Pierre Turgeon .20 .50
82 Joe Nieuwendyk .20 .50
83 Sergei Zubov .08 .20
84 Jere Lehtinen .20 .50
85 Donald Audette .08 .20
86 Mike Modano .40 1.00
87 Mike Modano .08 .20
Ed Belfour
Joe Nieuwendyk
Sergei Zubov
88 Steve Yzerman 1.25 3.00
89 Brendan Shanahan .25 .60
90 Sergei Fedorov .40 1.00
91 Luc Robitaille .20 .50
92 Dominik Hasek .50 1.25
93 Nicklas Lidstrom .25 .60
94 Darren McCarty .08 .20
95 Brendan Shanahan .40 1.00
96 Steve Yzerman .25 .60
Nicklas Lidstrom
Brendan Shanahan
Tomas Holmstrom
97 Tommy Salo .20 .50
98 Mike Comrie .20 .50
99 Tom Poti .08 .20
100 Mike Grier .08 .20
101 Janne Niinimaa .08 .20
102 Ryan Smyth .08 .20
103 Anson Carter .20 .50
104 Ryan Smyth .08 .20
105 Tommy Salo .08 .20
Mike Comrie
Ryan Smyth
Tom Poti
106 Pavel Bure .25 .60
107 Viktor Kozlov .08 .20
108 Marcus Nilsson .08 .20
109 Denis Shvidki .08 .20
110 Bret Hedican .08 .20
111 Roberto Luongo .30 .75
112 Pavel Bure .40 1.00
113 Pavel Bure .25 .60
Roberto Luongo
Viktor Kozlov
Marcus Nilsson
114 Zigmund Palffy .20 .50
115 Felix Potvin .25 .60
116 Adam Deadmarsh .08 .20
117 Glen Murray .08 .20
118 Eric Belanger .08 .20
119 Jason Holland .08 .20
120 Jozef Stumpel .08 .20
121 Zigmund Palffy .20 .50
122 Felix Potvin .08 .20
Zigmund Palffy
Adam Deadmarsh
Jozef Stumpel
123 Marian Gaborik .50 1.25
124 Manny Fernandez .20 .50
125 Brad Bombardir .08 .20
126 Lubomir Sekeras .08 .20
127 Wes Walz .08 .20
128 Antti Laaksonen .08 .20
129 Marian Gaborik .50 1.25
130 Wild CL .08 .20
131 Saku Koivu .25 .60
132 Oleg Petrov .08 .20
133 Martin Rucinsky .08 .20
134 Jose Theodore .30 .75
135 Brian Savage .08 .20
136 Andrei Markov .08 .20
137 Richard Zednik .08 .20
138 Saku Koivu .25 .60
139 Andre Savage .25 .60
Jose Theodore
Martin Rucinsky
Saku Koivu
140 David Legwand .20 .50
141 Mike Dunham .20 .50
142 Scott Walker .08 .20
143 Cliff Ronning .08 .20
144 Patric Kjellberg .08 .20
145 Greg Johnson .08 .20
146 Vitali Yachmenev .08 .20
147 Cliff Ronning .08 .20
148 Mike Dunham .08 .20
David Legwand
Scott Walker
Cliff Ronning
149 Martin Brodeur .60 1.50
150 Patrik Elias .20 .50
151 Jason Arnott .08 .20
152 Scott Niedermayer .08 .20
153 Petr Sykora .08 .20
154 Scott Gomez .08 .20
155 Scott Stevens .20 .50
156 Patrik Elias .20 .50
157 Martin Brodeur .08 .20
Scott Stevens
Jason Arnott
Bobby Holik
158 Michael Peca .08 .20
159 Rick DiPietro .20 .50
160 Mariusz Czerkawski .08 .20
161 Roman Hamrlik .08 .20
162 Dave Scatchard .08 .20
163 Brad Isbister .08 .20
164 Mark Parrish .08 .20
165 Rick DiPietro .08 .20
Mariusz Czerkawski
Roman Hamrlik
Dave Scatchard
166 Mark Messier .25 .60
167 Theo Fleury .08 .20
168 Mike Richter .25 .60
169 Brian Leetch .20 .50
170 Kim Johnsson .08 .20
171 Radek Dvorak .08 .20
172 Theo Fleury .08 .20
173 Mark Messier .08 .20
Brian Leetch
Mike Richter
Theo Fleury
174 Marian Hossa .25 .60
175 Radek Bonk .08 .20
176 Martin Havlat .20 .50
177 Daniel Alfredsson .20 .50
178 Magnus Arvedson .08 .20
179 Patrick Lalime .20 .50
180 Shawn McEachern .08 .20
181 Radek Bonk .08 .20
182 Marian Hossa .08 .20
Daniel Alfredsson
Radek Bonk
Magnus Arvedson
183 Jeremy Roenick .30 .75
184 Roman Cechmanek .20 .50
185 Keith Primeau .08 .20
186 John LeClair .25 .60
187 Kent Manderville .08 .20
188 Mark Recchi .20 .50
189 Eric Desjardins .08 .20
190 Mark Recchi .20 .50
191 Keith Primeau .08 .20
John LeClair
Roman Cechmanek
Mark Recchi
192 Sean Burke .20 .50
193 Shane Doan .08 .20
194 Michal Handzus .08 .20
195 Teppo Numminen .08 .20
196 Ladislav Nagy .08 .20
197 Landon Wilson .08 .20
198 Sean Burke .20 .50
199 Michal Handzus .08 .20
Sean Burke
Shane Doan
Teppo Numminen
200 Alexei Kovalev .20 .50
201 Mario Lemieux 1.50 4.00
202 Johan Hedberg .20 .50
203 Robert Lang .08 .20
204 Martin Straka .08 .20
205 Andrew Ference .08 .20
206 Kevin Stevens .08 .20
207 Alexei Kovalev .20 .50
208 Mario Lemieux .08 .20
Alexei Kovalev
Martin Straka
Johan Hedberg
209 Evgeni Nabokov .20 .50
210 Teemu Selanne .25 .60
211 Owen Nolan .20 .50
212 Mike Ricci .08 .20
213 Scott Thornton .08 .20
214 Vincent Damphousse .08 .20
215 Brad Stuart .08 .20
216 Evgeni Nabokov .20 .50
217 Owen Nolan .08 .20
Teemu Selanne
Vincent Damphousse
Brad Stuart
218 Chris Pronger .20 .50
219 Keith Tkachuk .25 .60
220 Doug Weight .20 .50
221 Pavol Demitra .20 .50
222 Cory Stillman .08 .20
223 Al MacInnis .20 .50
224 Bryce Salvador .08 .20
225 Scott Young .08 .20
226 Chris Pronger .08 .20
Pavol Demitra
Keith Tkachuk
Al MacInnis
227 Brad Richards .20 .50
228 Vincent Lecavalier .25 .60
229 Nikolai Khabibulin .25 .60
230 Fredrik Modin .08 .20
231 Martin St. Louis .20 .50
232 Pavel Kubina .08 .20
233 Brad Richards .20 .50
234 Vincent Lecavalier .08 .20
Brad Richards
Fredrik Modin
Nikolai Khabibulin
235 Curtis Joseph .25 .60
236 Mats Sundin .25 .60
237 Shayne Corson .08 .20
238 Darcy Tucker .08 .20
239 Nikolai Antropov .08 .20
240 Gary Roberts .08 .20
241 Bryan McCabe .08 .20
242 Mats Sundin .25 .60
243 Curtis Joseph .08 .20
Darcy Tucker
Mats Sundin
Gary Roberts
244 Markus Naslund .25 .60
245 Daniel Sedin .08 .20
246 Peter Schaefer .08 .20
247 Andrew Cassels .08 .20
248 Brendan Morrison .20 .50
249 Todd Bertuzzi .25 .60
250 Markus Naslund .25 .60
251 Marcus Naslund .08 .20
Daniel Sedin
Henrik Sedin
Todd Bertuzzi
252 Steve Konowalchuk .08 .20
253 Sergei Gonchar .08 .20
254 Calle Johansson .08 .20
255 Peter Bondra .25 .60
256 Jaromir Jagr .40 1.00
257 Olaf Kolzig .20 .50
258 Andrei Nikolishin .08 .20
259 Olaf Kolzig .20 .50
260 Peter Bondra .08 .20
Olaf Kolzig
Sergei Gonchar
Steve Konowalchuk
261 Pavel Bure .40 1.00
Joe Sakic
Jaromir Jagr
262 Jaromir Jagr .40 1.00
Adam Oates
Martin Straka
263 Jaromir Jagr .40 1.00
Joe Sakic
Patrik Elias
264 Peter Bondra .40 1.00
Pavel Bure
Joe Sakic
265 Joe Sakic .40 1.00
Patrik Elias
Scott Stevens
266 Matthew Barnaby .40 1.00
Peter Worrell
Stu Grimson
267 M.Brodeur/P.Roy/D.Hasek 1.50 4.00
268 Roman Cechmanek .40 1.00
Manny Legace
Marty Turco
269 Mike Dunham .40 1.00
SeanBurke
Marty Turco
270 Dominik Hasek .40 1.00
Roman Cechmanek
Martin Brodeur
271 Timo Parssinen RC 1.50 4.00
272 Ilja Bryzgalov RC 1.50 4.00
273 Kevin Sawyer RC 1.50 4.00
274 Kamil Piros RC 1.50 4.00
275 Ilya Kovalchuk RC 2.00 5.00
276 Brian Pothier RC 1.50 4.00
277 Zdenek Kutlak RC 1.50 4.00
278 Vaclav Nedorost RC 1.50 4.00
279 Jaroslav Obsut RC 1.50 4.00
280 Niko Kapanen RC .40 1.00
281 Kristian Huselius RC 1.50 4.00
282 Jaroslav Bednar RC 1.50 4.00
283 Martin Erat RC 1.50 4.00
284 Josef Boumedienne RC 1.50 4.00
285 Scott Clemmensen RC 1.50 4.00
286 Andreas Salomonsson RC 1.50 4.00
287 Radek Martinek RC 1.50 4.00
288 Mikael Samuelsson RC 1.50 4.00
289 Peter Smrek RC 1.50 4.00
290 Ivan Ciernik RC 1.50 4.00
291 Chris Neil RC 1.50 4.00
292 Jiri Dopita RC 1.50 4.00
293 David Cullen RC 1.50 4.00
294 Krys Kolanos RC 1.50 4.00
295 Jeff Jillson RC 1.50 4.00
296 Mark Rycroft RC 1.50 4.00
297 Nikita Alexeev RC 1.50 4.00
298 Thomas Ziegler RC 1.50 4.00
299 Bob Wren RC 1.50 4.00
300 Brian Sutherby RC 1.50 4.00

2001-02 Upper Deck Vintage Jerseys

Randomly inserted at 1:144 packs, this 16-card set featured swatches of game-worn jerseys of the featured players. The set consisted of three subsets: Golden Goalies (denoted by a "GG" prefix), Stars of the Decades (denoted by a "SD" prefix), and Stanley Cup Stars (denoted by a "SC" prefix).

GGAM Andy Moog 10.00 25.00
GGBS Billy Smith 12.50 30.00
GGGC Gerry Cheevers 10.00 25.00
GGGF Grant Fuhr 10.00 25.00
GGRV Rogie Vachon 12.50 30.00
SCBS Billy Smith 10.00 25.00

SCBT Bryan Trottier 10.00 25.00
SCMB Mike Bossy 10.00 25.00
SCSY Steve Yzerman 10.00 25.00
SCWG Wayne Gretzky 40.00 100.00
SDBC Bobby Clarke 15.00 40.00
SDGH Gordie Howe 12.50 30.00
SDGL Guy Lafleur 10.00 25.00
SDGP Gilbert Perreault 10.00 25.00
SDMB Mike Bossy 10.00 25.00
SDPE Phil Esposito 10.00 25.00

2001-02 Upper Deck Vintage Next In Line

Serial-numbered to just 50-copies each, this 6-card set featured game-worn jersey swatches of NHL legends and their heir-apparents.

NLBL Ray Bourque 60.00 125.00
Nicklas Lidstrom
NLCO Gerry Cheevers 25.00 60.00
Maxime Ouellet
NLGS Wayne Gretzky 125.00 250.00
Joe Sakic
NLHY Gordie Howe 150.00 300.00
Steve Yzerman
NLLK Guy Lafleur 25.00 60.00
Paul Kariya
NLSC Billy Smith 25.00 60.00
Roman Cechmanek

2001-02 Upper Deck Vintage Sweaters of Honor

Inserted randomly in 1:96 hobby packs, this 4-card set featured game-used jersey swatches of the pictured players.

SHGL Guy Lafleur 8.00 20.00
SHLA Guy Lapointe 8.00 20.00
SHML Michel Larocque 6.00 15.00
SHSS Steve Shutt 6.00 15.00

2002-03 Upper Deck Vintage

This 350-card set consisted of 305 base cards (1-260, 291-305 and 321-350); 30 checklist cards (261-290) and 15 statistical leaders cards (306-320). SP's were inserted at 1:5.

COMPLETE SET (350) 60.00 125.00
1 Vitali Vishnevski .08 .20
2 Paul Kariya SP .20 .50
3 Samuel Pahlsson .08 .20
4 Mike LeClerc .08 .20
5 Matt Cullen .08 .20
6 Ruslan Salei .08 .20
7 J-S Giguere .15 .40
8 Andy McDonald .08 .20
9 Patrik Stefan .08 .20
10 Milan Hnilicka .15 .40
11 Lubos Bartecko .08 .20
12 Jeff Cowan .08 .20
13 Ilya Kovalchuk .25 .60
14 Frantisek Kaberle .08 .20
15 Dany Heatley .25 .60
16 Daniel Tjarnqvist .08 .20
17 Sergei Samsonov .15 .40
18 P.J. Stock .08 .20
19 Nick Boynton .08 .20
20 Martin Lapointe .08 .20
21 Jozef Stumpel .08 .20
22 John Grahame .15 .40
23 Joe Thornton SP .50 1.25
24 Glen Murray .08 .20
25 Brian Rolston .08 .20
26 Hal Gill .08 .20
27 Stu Barnes .08 .20
28 Tim Connolly .08 .20
29 Miroslav Satan .15 .40
30 Maxim Afinogenov .08 .20
31 Martin Biron .15 .40
32 Jay McKee .08 .20
33 J-P Dumont .08 .20
34 Curtis Brown .08 .20
35 Alexei Zhitnik .08 .20
36 Roman Turek .15 .40
37 Rob Niedermayer .08 .20
38 Marc Savard .08 .20
39 Jarome Iginla SP .30 .75
40 Derek Morris .08 .20
41 Denis Gauthier .08 .20
42 Dave Lowry .08 .20
43 Craig Conroy .08 .20
44 Sami Kapanen .08 .20
45 Ron Francis .15 .40
46 Rod Brind'Amour .15 .40
47 Niclas Wallin .08 .20
48 Josef Vasicek .08 .20
49 Jeff O'Neill .08 .20
50 Erik Cole .08 .20
51 Dave Tanabe .08 .20
52 Arturs Irbe .15 .40
53 Steve Sullivan .08 .20
54 Ryan VandenBussche .08 .20
55 Michael Nylander .08 .20
56 Mark Bell .08 .20
57 Kyle Calder .08 .20
58 Jocelyn Thibault .15 .40
59 Eric Daze .15 .40
60 Alexei Zhamnov .08 .20
61 Steve Reinprecht .08 .20
62 Stephane Yelle .08 .20
63 Rob Blake .15 .40
64 Peter Forsberg .50 1.25
65 Patrick Roy SP 1.50 4.00
66 Milan Hejduk .20 .50
67 Joe Sakic SP .60 1.50
68 Greg DeVries .08 .20
69 Chris Drury .15 .40
70 Alex Tanguay .15 .40
71 Adam Foote .08 .20
72 David Vyborny .08 .20
73 Rostislav Klesla .08 .20
74 Marc Denis .15 .40
75 Ray Whitney .08 .20
76 Jody Shelley .08 .20
77 Jean-Luc Grand-Pierre .08 .20
78 Geoff Sanderson .08 .20
79 Espen Knutsen .08 .20
80 Pierre Turgeon .15 .40
81 Mike Modano SP .50 1.25
82 Marty Turco .15 .40
83 Bill Guerin .15 .40
84 Jere Lehtinen .15 .40
85 Jason Arnott .08 .20
86 Derian Hatcher .08 .20
87 Brenden Morrow .15 .40
88 Steve Yzerman SP 1.50 4.00
89 Sergei Fedorov .30 .75
90 Pavel Datsyuk .20 .50
91 Nicklas Lidstrom .20 .50
92 Luc Robitaille .15 .40
93 Kris Draper .08 .20
94 Curtis Joseph .20 .50
95 Dominik Hasek SP .60 1.50
96 Brett Hull .25 .60
97 Brendan Shanahan .20 .50
98 Boyd Devereaux .08 .20
99 Tommy Salo .15 .40
100 Ryan Smyth .08 .20
101 Mike York .08 .20
102 Mike Comrie SP .25 .60
103 Georges Laraque .08 .20
104 Ethan Moreau .08 .20
105 Daniel Cleary .08 .20
106 Anson Carter .15 .40
107 Viktor Kozlov .08 .20
108 Valeri Bure .08 .20
109 Olli Jokinen .15 .40
110 Sandis Ozolinsh .08 .20
111 Roberto Luongo .25 .60
112 Peter Worrell .08 .20
113 Niklas Hagman .08 .20
114 Kristian Huselius .08 .20
115 Zigmund Palffy .15 .40
116 Mattias Norstrom .08 .20
117 Mathieu Schneider .08 .20
118 Jason Allison .08 .20
119 Felix Potvin .20 .50
120 Bryan Smolinski .08 .20
121 Adam Deadmarsh .08 .20
122 Aaron Miller .08 .20
123 Richard Park .08 .20
124 Nick Schultz .08 .20
125 Marian Gaborik SP .50 1.25
126 Jim Dowd .08 .20
127 Hnat Domenichelli .08 .20
128 Filip Kuba .08 .20
129 Manny Fernandez .15 .40
130 Andrew Brunette .08 .20
131 Yanic Perreault .08 .20
132 Saku Koivu .20 .50
133 Richard Zednik .08 .20
134 Jose Theodore SP .40 1.00
135 Donald Audette .08 .20
136 Craig Rivet .08 .20
137 Andrei Markov .08 .20
138 Andreas Dackell .08 .20
139 Stu Grimson .08 .20
140 Scott Hartnell .08 .20
141 Mike Dunham .15 .40
142 Martin Erat .08 .20
143 Kimmo Timonen .08 .20
144 Denis Arkhipov .08 .20
145 David Legwand .15 .40
146 Andy Delmore .08 .20
147 Sergei Brylin .08 .20
148 Scott Stevens .15 .40
149 Scott Niedermayer .08 .20
150 John Madden .08 .20
151 Patrik Elias .15 .40
152 Martin Brodeur SP .75 2.00
153 Joe Nieuwendyk .15 .40
154 Brian Rafalski .08 .20
155 Roman Hamrlik .08 .20
156 Raffi Torres .08 .20
157 Michael Peca .08 .20
158 Mark Parrish .08 .20
159 Oleg Kvasha .08 .20
160 Eric Cairns .08 .20
161 Dave Scatchard .08 .20
162 Chris Osgood .15 .40
163 Alexei Yashin SP .08 .20
164 Tom Poti .08 .20
165 Sandy McCarthy .08 .20
166 Radek Dvorak .08 .20
167 Petr Nedved .08 .20
168 Pavel Bure SP .20 .50
169 Matthew Barnaby .08 .20
170 Mark Messier .20 .50
171 Eric Lindros .20 .50
172 Dan Blackburn .15 .40
173 Brian Leetch .15 .40
174 Wade Redden .15 .40
175 Radek Bonk .08 .20
176 Patrick Lalime .15 .40
177 Mike Fisher .08 .20
178 Martin Havlat .15 .40
179 Marian Hossa .20 .50
180 Magnus Arvedson .08 .20
181 Daniel Alfredsson .15 .40
182 Simon Gagne SP .30 .75
183 Kim Johnsson .08 .20
184 Roman Cechmanek .15 .40
185 Mark Recchi .15 .40
186 Keith Primeau .08 .20
187 Justin Williams .08 .20
188 John LeClair .20 .50
189 Jeremy Roenick .25 .60
190 Eric Weinrich .08 .20
191 Donald Brashear .08 .20
192 Teppo Numminen .08 .20
193 Shane Doan .08 .20
194 Sean Burke .15 .40
195 Ladislav Nagy .08 .20
196 Daymond Langkow .08 .20
197 Daniel Briere .08 .20
198 Claude Lemieux .08 .20
199 Tony Amonte .15 .40
200 Ville Nieminen .08 .20
201 Martin Straka .08 .20
202 Mario Lemieux SP 2.00 5.00
203 Johan Hedberg .15 .40
204 Jan Hrdina .08 .20
205 Andrew Ference .08 .20
206 Alexei Kovalev .15 .40
207 Alexei Morozov .08 .20
208 Vincent Damphousse .08 .20
209 Scott Thornton .08 .20
210 Patrick Marleau .15 .40
211 Owen Nolan .15 .40
212 Mike Ricci .08 .20
213 Marcus Ragnarsson .08 .20
214 Marco Sturm .08 .20
215 Evgeni Nabokov SP .25 .60
216 Brad Stuart .08 .20
217 Tyson Nash .08 .20
218 Shjon Podein .08 .20
219 Pavol Demitra .15 .40
220 Keith Tkachuk SP .25 .60
221 Doug Weight .15 .40
222 Cory Stillman .08 .20
223 Chris Pronger .15 .40
224 Brent Johnson .15 .40
225 Al MacInnis .15 .40
226 Vincent Lecavalier .20 .50
227 Vaclav Prospal .08 .20
228 Shane Willis .08 .20
229 Pavel Kubina .08 .20
230 Nikolai Khabibulin .20 .50
231 Martin St. Louis .15 .40
232 Fredrik Modin .08 .20
233 Brad Richards .15 .40
234 Tomas Kaberle .08 .20
235 Tie Domi .15 .40
236 Shayne Corson .08 .20
237 Mats Sundin SP .30 .75
238 Gary Roberts .08 .20
239 Darcy Tucker .08 .20
240 Ed Belfour .20 .50
241 Bryan McCabe .08 .20
242 Alyn McCauley .08 .20
243 Alexander Mogilny .15 .40
244 Trevor Linden .08 .20
245 Todd Bertuzzi .20 .50
246 Markus Naslund .20 .50
247 Henrik Sedin .08 .20
248 Ed Jovanovski .15 .40
249 Daniel Sedin .08 .20
250 Dan Cloutier .15 .40
251 Brendan Morrison .15 .40
252 Brendan Witt .08 .20
253 Steve Konowalchuk .08 .20
254 Sergei Gonchar .08 .20
255 Peter Bondra .15 .40
256 Olaf Kolzig .15 .40
257 Jeff Halpern .08 .20
258 Jaromir Jagr SP .50 1.25
259 Andrei Nikolishin .08 .20
260 Robert Lang .08 .20
261 Paul Kariya .15 .40
Vitali Vishnevski
J-S Giguere
Mike LeClerc
262 Ilya Kovalchuk .15 .40
Dany Heatley
Milan Hnilicka
Patrik Stefan
263 Sergei Samsonov .15 .40
Joe Thornton
Nick Boynton
Glen Murray
264 Tim Connolly .15 .40
Stu Barnes
Miroslav Satan
Martin Biron
265 Jarome Iginla .15 .40
Roman Turek
Marc Savard
Derek Morris
266 Jeff O'Neill .15 .40
Ron Francis
Arturs Irbe
Erik Cole
267 Eric Daze .15 .40
Kyle Calder
Jocelyn Thibault
Alexei Zhamnov
268 Joe Sakic .20 .50
Peter Forsberg
Patrick Roy
Rob Blake
269 Geoff Sanderson .15 .40
Rostislav Klesla
Marc Denis
Jody Shelley
270 Pierre Turgeon .15 .40
Mike Modano
Marty Turco
Derian Hatcher
271 Steve Yzerman .15 .40
Sergei Fedorov
Brendan Shanahan
Nicklas Lidstrom
272 Mike Comrie .15 .40
Ryan Smyth
Tommy Salo
Georges Laraque
273 Viktor Kozlov .15 .40
Stephen Weiss
Roberto Luongo
Peter Worrell
274 Zigmund Palffy .15 .40
Jason Allison
Felix Potvin
Adam Deadmarsh
275 Wild CL .15 .40
276 Saku Koivu .15 .40
Donald Audette
Jose Theodore
Yanic Perreault
277 Scott Hartnell .15 .40
Martin Erat
Mike Dunham
Stu Grimson
278 Patrik Elias .15 .40
Brian Rafalski
Martin Brodeur
Scott Stevens
279 Mike Peca .15 .40
Alexei Yashin
Chris Osgood
Eric Cairns
280 Pavel Bure .15 .40
Eric Lindros
Mike Richter
Mark Messier
281 Marian Hossa .15 .40
Daniel Alfredsson
Patrick Lalime
Martin Havlat
282 Simon Gagne .15 .40
Jeremy Roenick
Roman Cechmanek
Donald Brashear
283 Daniel Briere .15 .40
Teppo Numminen
Sean Burke
Tony Amonte
284 Penguins CL .15 .40
285 Patrick Marleau .15 .40
Owen Nolan
Evgeni Nabokov
Mike Ricci
286 Pavol Demitra .15 .40
Chris Pronger
Brent Johnson
Tyson Nash
287 Vincent Lecavalier .20 .50
Brad Richards
Nikolai Khabibulin
Pavel Kubina
288 Mats Sundin .15 .40
Alexander Mogilny
Ed Belfour
Tie Domi
289 Todd Bertuzzi .15 .40
Markus Naslund
Dan Cloutier
Trevor Linden
290 Peter Bondra .15 .40
Jaromir Jagr
Olaf Kolzig
Sergei Gonchar
291 Joe Sakic .40 1.00
292 Patrick Roy 1.00 2.50
293 Mike Modano .30 .75
294 Brendan Shanahan .20 .50
295 Steve Yzerman 1.00 2.50
296 Detroit Red Wings .20 .50
297 Joe Nieuwendyk .15 .40
298 Martin Brodeur .50 1.25
299 Pavel Bure .20 .50
300 Brian Leetch .15 .40
301 Jeremy Roenick .25 .60
302 Mark Recchi .15 .40
303 Mario Lemieux 1.25 3.00
304 Teemu Selanne .20 .50
305 Peter Bondra .15 .40
306 Jarome Iginla .15 .40
Glen Murray
Mats Sundin
307 Adam Oates .15 .40
Jason Allison
Joe Sakic
308 Jarome Iginla .15 .40
Markus Naslund
Todd Bertuzzi
309 Peter Bondra .15 .40
Jarome Iginla
Alexei Yashin
310 Sergei Gonchar .15 .40
Nicklas Lidstrom
Rob Blake
311 Brian Rolston .15 .40
Mike Peca
Miroslav Satan
312 Chris Chelios .15 .40
Jeremy Roenick
Simon Gagne
313 Peter Worrell .15 .40
Brad Ference
Chris Neil
314 Daniel Briere .15 .40
Jan Hrdina
Adam Deadmarsh
315 Dany Heatley .25 .60
Ilya Kovalchuk
Kristian Huselius
316 Dominik Hasek .20 .50
Martin Brodeur
Evgeni Nabokov
317 Patrick Roy .20 .50
Roman Cechmanek
Marty Turco
318 Jose Theodore .20 .50
Patrick Roy
Roman Cechmanek
319 Patrick Roy .25 .60
Jose Theodore
Nikolai Khabibulin
320 Dan Blackburn .15 .40
Mikka Kiprusoff
Mika Noronen
321 Pasi Nurminen .08 .20
322 Mark Hartigan .08 .20
323 Henrik Tallinder .08 .20
324 Micki Dupont RC .40 1.00
325 Jaroslav Svoboda .08 .20
326 Jordan Krestanovich .08 .20
327 Kelly Fairchild .08 .20
328 Riku Hahl .08 .20
329 Andrej Nedorost .08 .20
330 Blake Bellefeuille .08 .20
331 Ales Pisa .08 .20
332 Jani Rita .08 .20
333 Stephen Weiss .08 .20
334 Lukas Krajicek .08 .20
335 Sylvain Blouin RC .40 1.00
336 Marcel Hossa .08 .20
337 Adam Hall RC .40 1.00
338 Jonas Andersson .08 .20
339 Jan Lasak .08 .20
340 Ray Schultz RC .40 1.00
341 Trent Hunter .08 .20
342 Martin Prusek .15 .40
343 Branko Radivojevic .08 .20
344 Shane Endicott .08 .20
345 Sebastien Centomo .15 .40
346 Karel Pilar .08 .20
347 Sebastien Charpentier .08 .20
348 Jean-Francois Fortin .08 .20
349 Ales Kotalik .08 .20
350 Kyle Rossiter .08 .20

2002-03 Upper Deck Vintage Jerseys

OS STAT.ODDS 1:96 RETAIL
SO/EE/HS ODDS 1:96 HBBY/RETAIL
FS STAT.ODDS 1:96 HOBBY
EEBB Brian Boucher 4.00 10.00
EEDA David Aebischer 4.00 10.00
EEFP Felix Potvin 6.00 15.00
EEMB Martin Biron 4.00 10.00
EEMD Mike Dunham 4.00 10.00
EEMO Maxime Ouellet 4.00 10.00
EEMT Marty Turco 6.00 15.00
EEOK Olaf Kolzig 6.00 15.00
EERC Roman Cechmanek 4.00 10.00
EERT Ron Tugnutt 4.00 10.00
FSBM Brenden Morrow 6.00 15.00
FSCD Chris Drury 6.00 15.00
FSJJ Jaromir Jagr 8.00 20.00
FSKP Keith Primeau 4.00 10.00
FSMH Milan Hejduk 4.00 10.00
FSSY Steve Yzerman 12.00 30.00
HSJD J-P Dumont 4.00 10.00
HSJW Justin Williams 4.00 10.00
HSMD Marc Denis 4.00 10.00
HSPB Peter Bondra 6.00 15.00
HSRB Ray Bourque 8.00 20.00
HSRF Ruslan Fedotenko 4.00 10.00
HSRK Rostislav Klesla 4.00 10.00
HSSG Simon Gagne 6.00 15.00
HSSK Steve Konowalchuk 4.00 10.00
HSVN Ville Nieminen 4.00 10.00
OSED Eric Daze 4.00 10.00
OSGM Glen Murray 4.00 10.00
OSJT Jose Theodore SP 8.00 20.00
OSMS Mats Sundin 6.00 15.00
OSRD Radek Dvorak 4.00 10.00
OSSY Steve Yzerman 12.00 30.00
SOCD Chris Drury 6.00 15.00
SOEL Eric Lindros 6.00 15.00
SOJH Jeff Halpern 4.00 10.00
SOJI Jarome Iginla SP 8.00 20.00
SOJJ Jaromir Jagr SP 10.00 25.00
SOJL John LeClair 4.00 10.00
SOKP Keith Primeau 4.00 10.00
SOMR Mark Recchi 4.00 10.00
SOPF Peter Forsberg 8.00 20.00
SOPK Paul Kariya 6.00 15.00

2002-03 Upper Deck Vintage Jerseys Gold

*GOLD: 1.25X TO 3X BASIC CARDS
GOLD PRINT RUN 50 SER.#'d SETS

2002-03 Upper Deck Vintage Tall Boys

Inserted 2 per hobby box, this 70-card set partially paralleled the base set on oversized cards. A gold version numbered out of 99 was also created.

COMPLETE SET (70) 40.00 100.00
*GOLD: 1.25X TO 3X BASE HI
T1 Paul Kariya .75 2.00
T2 J-S Giguere .60 1.50
T3 Dany Heatley 1.00 2.50
T4 Ilya Kovalchuk 1.00 2.50
T5 Joe Thornton 1.25 3.00
T6 Sergei Samsonov .60 1.50
T7 Miroslav Satan .60 1.50
T8 Maxim Afinogenov .60 1.50
T9 Roman Turek .60 1.50
T10 Jarome Iginla 1.00 2.50
T11 Arturs Irbe .60 1.50
T12 Ron Francis .60 1.50
T13 Eric Daze .60 1.50
T14 Jocelyn Thibault .60 1.50
T15 Patrick Roy 4.00 10.00
T16 Peter Forsberg 2.00 5.00
T17 Joe Sakic 1.50 4.00
T18 Chris Drury .60 1.50
T19 Alex Tanguay .60 1.50
T20 Espen Knutsen .60 1.50
T21 Rostislav Klesla .60 1.50
T22 Mike Modano 1.25 3.00
T23 Jason Arnott .60 1.50
T24 Steve Yzerman 4.00 10.00
T25 Brendan Shanahan .75 2.00
T26 Sergei Fedorov 1.25 3.00
T27 Curtis Joseph .75 2.00
T28 Mike Comrie .60 1.50
T29 Tommy Salo .60 1.50
T30 Roberto Luongo 1.00 2.50
T31 Stephen Weiss, .60 1.50
T32 Jason Allison .60 1.50
T33 Zigmund Palffy .60 1.50
T34 Marian Gaborik 1.50 4.00
T35 Jose Theodore 1.00 2.50
T36 Saku Koivu .75 2.00
T37 Mike Dunham .60 1.50
T38 Scott Hartnell .60 1.50
T39 Martin Brodeur 2.00 5.00
T40 Patrik Elias .60 1.50
T41 Michael Peca .60 1.50
T42 Chris Osgood .60 1.50
T43 Eric Lindros .75 2.00
T44 Pavel Bure .75 2.00
T45 Daniel Alfredsson .60 1.50
T46 Marian Hossa .75 2.00
T47 Jeremy Roenick 1.00 2.50
T48 Simon Gagne .75 2.00
T49 Sean Burke .60 1.50
T50 Daniel Briere .60 1.50
T51 Tony Amonte .60 1.50
T52 Mario Lemieux 5.00 12.00
T53 Johan Hedberg .60 1.50
T54 Owen Nolan .60 1.50
T55 Evgeni Nabokov .60 1.50
T56 Keith Tkachuk .75 2.00
T57 Chris Pronger .60 1.50
T58 Vincent Lecavalier .75 2.00
T59 Nikolai Khabibulin .75 2.00
T60 Mats Sundin .75 2.00
T61 Alexander Mogilny .60 1.50
T62 Markus Naslund .75 2.00
T63 Todd Bertuzzi .75 2.00
T64 Jaromir Jagr 1.25 3.00
T65 Olaf Kolzig .60 1.50
T66 Gordie Howe 5.00 12.00
T67 Gordie Howe 5.00 12.00
T68 Gordie Howe 5.00 12.00
T69 Gordie Howe 5.00 12.00
T70 Gordie Howe 5.00 12.00
with Coleen Howe

2000 Upper Deck Wayne Gretzky Master Collection

Released as a box set limited in production to 300 total sets (150 US and 150 Canada) the Upper Deck Wayne Gretzky Collection includes an 18-card base set where each card is sequentially numbered to 150, eight insert cards consisting of jersey cards and signed jersey cards sequentially numbered to 50, and one mystery pack containing an autograph, memorabilia card, or an autographed memorabilia card. Canadian versions are differentiated by the maple leaf they carry along the side of the card. US and Canadian versions carry the same value.

COMPLETE SET (18) 240.00 600.00
COMMON GRETZKY (1-18) 16.00 40.00

2000 Upper Deck Wayne Gretzky Master Collection Inserts

Three versions of each card were released. Each Master Collection contains one of each of these three versions: One Edmonton autographed jersey card in Canadian issues and one unautographed Edmonton jersey card in USA sets, one Los Angeles jersey card, one All-Star jersey card, and one New York jersey card in Canadian sets and one autographed New York jersey card in American sets. Each card is sequentially numbered to 50. As of press time, not all cards have been verified for pricing.

1 Gretzky Ed.AU/50 Can 320.00 800.00
2 Gretzky Ed.AU/50 Can 320.00 800.00
3 Gretzky Ed.AU/50 Can 320.00 800.00
4 Gretzky Ed/50 USA 120.00 300.00
5 Gretzky Ed/50 USA 120.00 300.00
6 Gretzky Ed/50 USA 120.00 300.00
7 Gretzky LA/50 120.00 300.00
8 Gretzky LA/50 120.00 300.00
9 Gretzky LA/50 120.00 300.00
10 Gretzky AS/50 120.00 300.00
11 Gretzky AS/50 120.00 300.00
12 Gretzky AS/50 120.00 300.00
13 Gretzky NY AU/50 USA 300.00 750.00
14 Gretzky NY AU/50 USA 300.00 750.00
15 Gretzky NY AU/50 USA 300.00 750.00
16 Gretzky NY/50 Can 120.00 300.00
17 Gretzky NY/50 Can 120.00 300.00
18 Gretzky NY/50 Can 120.00 300.00

2000 Upper Deck Wayne Gretzky Master Collection Mystery Pack

One Mystery Pack was inserted into each Wayne Gretzky Master Collection which contained one of the following: one of 18 different Ultimate Gretzky Autograph 1/1's, one Great Gretzky Jersey card sequentially numbered to 99 , one Great Gretzky Signed Jersey card, one Great Gretzky Patch card, or one Great Gretzky Signed Patch card. Lower print runs are not priced due to scarcity.

ULTIMATE AU's #'D 1/1
US AND CANADA SAME VALUE
19 Gretzky Jersey/99 200.00 500.00
20 Gretzky Jersey AU/9
21 Gretzky Patch/15
22 Gretzky Patch AU/9

2000 Upper Deck Wayne Gretzky Retirement Set

Released by Upper Deck Authenticated as a tribute to Wayne Gretzky, this 16-card set features 3 1/2" X 5" cards highlighting Wayne's career. Cards contain gold foil highlights and the date of Gretzky's retirement. Card number 16 is printed on black and gold card stock and lists the Grand total of Gretzky's NHL goals. This set was offered at retail price of $19.99.

COMPLETE SET (16) 12.00 30.00
COMMON GRETZKY (1-16) .80 2.00

2005-06 Upper Deck Where's Sidney?

We have no pricing information on this card.

NNO Sidney Crosby
Redemption Card

1924 V-122

This set features athletes from a variety of sports and was inserted along with Willard's Chocolates. The cards measure 1 3/8 by 3 7/8 and feature black and white photography. The four hockey players in the set, all members of the 1924 gold medal-winning Canadian Olympic team, are listed below. Although the set is designated as a 1923-24 issue by the ACC, our research suggests it was not released until the summer of 1924.

COMPLETE SET (4) 375.00 750.00
43 Harry Watson 125.00 250.00
45 Ernie Collett RC 75.00 150.00
47 Hooley Smith 125.00 250.00
52 Dunc Munro RC 100.00 200.00

1923-24 V128-1 Paulin's Candy

This 70-card set was issued during the 1923-24 season and featured players from the WCHL. The horizontal back explains how to obtain either a hockey stick or a box of Paulin's chocolates by collecting and sending in the complete Famous Hockey Players set. The cards were to be returned to the collector with the hockey stick or chocolates. The cards are in black and white and measure approximately 1 3/8" by 2 3/4".

COMPLETE SET (70) 4500.00 9000.00
1 Bill Borland 75.00 150.00
2 Pete Speirs 50.00 100.00
3 Jack Hughes 50.00 100.00
4 Errol Gillis 50.00 100.00
5 Cecil Browne 50.00 100.00
6 W. Roberts 50.00 100.00
7 Howard Brandon 50.00 100.00
8 Fred Comfort 50.00 100.00
9 Cliff O'Meara 50.00 100.00
10 Leo Benard 50.00 100.00
11 Lloyd Harvey 50.00 100.00
12 Bobby Connors 50.00 100.00
13 Daddy Dalman 50.00 100.00
14 Dub Mackie 50.00 100.00
15 Lorne Chabot 150.00 300.00
16 Phat Wilson 62.50 125.00
17 Wilf L'Heureux 50.00 100.00
18 Danny Cox 50.00 100.00
19 Bill Brydge 50.00 100.00
20 Alex Gray. 50.00 100.00
21 Albert Pudas 50.00 100.00
22 Jack Irwin 50.00 100.00
23 Puss Traub 50.00 100.00
24 Red McCusker 62.50 125.00
25 Jack Asseltine 62.50 125.00
26 Duke Dutkowski 50.00 100.00

27 Charley McVeigh 50.00 100.00
28 George Hay 125.00 250.00
29 Amby Moran 50.00 100.00
30 Barney Stanley 150.00 300.00
31 Art Gagne 50.00 100.00
32 Louis Berlinquette 50.00 100.00
33 P.C. Stevens 50.00 100.00
34 W.D. Elmer 50.00 100.00
35 Bill Cook 175.00 350.00
36 Leo Reise 50.00 100.00
37 Curly Headley 125.00 250.00
38 Newsy Lalonde 300.00 600.00
39 George Hainsworth 300.00 600.00
40 Laurie Scott 50.00 100.00
41 Joe Simpson 175.00 350.00
42 Bob Trapp 50.00 100.00
43 Joe McCormick 50.00 100.00
44 Ty Arbour 50.00 100.00
45 Duke Keats 62.50 125.00
46 Hal Winkler 50.00 100.00
47 Johnny Sheppard 50.00 100.00
48 Crutchy Morrison 50.00 100.00
49 Spunk Sparrow 50.00 100.00
50 Percy McGregor 50.00 100.00
51 Harry Tuckwell 50.00 100.00
52 Chubby Scott 50.00 100.00
53 Scotty Fraser 50.00 100.00
54 Bob Davis 50.00 100.00
55 Clucker White 50.00 100.00
56 Bob Armstrong 50.00 100.00
57 Doc Longtry 50.00 100.00
58 Darb Sommers 50.00 100.00
59 Frank Hacquoil 50.00 100.00
60 Stan Evans 50.00 100.00
61 Ed Oatman 50.00 100.00
62 Mervyn(Red) Dutton 200.00 400.00
63 Herb Gardiner 125.00 250.00
64 Bernie Morris 50.00 100.00
65 Bobbie Benson 50.00 100.00
66 Ernie Anderson 50.00 100.00
67 Cully Wilson 50.00 100.00
68 Charlie Reid 62.50 125.00
69 Harry Oliver 125.00 250.00
70 Rusty Crawford 100.00 200.00

1928-29 V128-2 Paulin's Candy

This scarce set of 90 black and white cards was produced and distributed in Western Canada and features Western Canadian teams and players. The cards are numbered on the back and measure approximately 1 3/8" by 2 5/8". The card back details an offer (expiring June 1st, 1929) of a hockey stick prize (or box of chocolates for girls) if someone could bring in a complete set of 90 cards. Players on the Calgary Jimmies are not explicitly identified on the card so they are listed below without a specific player name.

COMPLETE SET (90) 2750.00 5500.00
1 Univ. of Man. Girls Hockey Team 50.00 100.00
2 Elgin Hockey Team 40.00 80.00
3 Brandon Schools Boy Champions 40.00 80.00
4 Port Arthur Hockey Team 40.00 80.00
5 Enderby Hockey Team 40.00 80.00
6 Humboldt High School Team 40.00 80.00
7 Regina Collegiate Hockey Team 40.00 80.00
8 Weyburn Beavers 40.00 80.00
9 Moose Jaw College Junior Hockey Team 50.00 100.00
10 M.A.C. Junior Hockey 40.00 80.00
11 Vermillion Agricultural School 40.00 80.00
12 Rovers& Cranbrook B.C. 40.00 80.00
13 Empire School& Moose Jaw 40.00 80.00
14 Arts Senior Hockey 40.00 80.00
15 Juvenile Varsity Hockey 40.00 80.00
16 St. Peter's College Hockey 40.00 80.00
17 Arts Girls Hockey 50.00 100.00
18 Swan River Hockey Team 40.00 80.00
19 U.M.S.U. Junior Hockey Team 40.00 80.00
20 Campion College Hockey Team 50.00 100.00
21 Drinkwater Hockey Team 40.00 80.00
22 Elks Hockey Team Biggar, Saskatchewan 40.00 80.00
23 South Calgary High School 40.00 80.00
24 Meota Hockey 40.00 80.00
25 Chartered Accountants 50.00 100.00
26 Nutana Collegiate Hockey Team 40.00 80.00
27 MacLeod Hockey Team 50.00 100.00
28 Arts Junior Hockey 40.00 80.00
29 Fort William Juniors 40.00 80.00
30 Swan Lake Hockey Team 40.00 80.00
31 Dauphin Hockey Team 40.00 80.00
32 Mount Royal Hockey Team 40.00 80.00
33 Port Arthur W. End Junior Hockey 40.00 80.00
34 Hanna Hockey Club 40.00 80.00
35 Vermillion Junior Hockey 40.00 80.00
36 Smithers Hockey Team 40.00 80.00
37 Lloydminster High School 40.00 80.00
38 Winnipeg Rangers 50.00 100.00
39 Delisle Intermediate Hockey 40.00 80.00
40 Moose Jaw College Senior Hockey 40.00 80.00
41 Art Bonneyman 25.00 50.00
42 Jimmy Graham 25.00 50.00
43 Pat O'Hunter 25.00 50.00
44 Leo Moret 25.00 50.00
45 Blondie McLennen 25.00 50.00
46 Red Beattie 40.00 80.00
47 Frank Peters 40.00 80.00
48 Lloyd McIntyre 25.00 50.00
49 Art Somers 40.00 80.00
50 Ikey Morrison 25.00 50.00
51 Calgary Jimmies 25.00 50.00
52 Don Cummings 25.00 50.00
53 Calgary Jimmies 25.00 50.00
54 P. Gerlitz 25.00 50.00
55 A. Kay 25.00 50.00
56 Paul Runge 40.00 80.00
57 J. Gerlitz 25.00 50.00
58 H. Gerlitz 25.00 50.00
59 C. Biles 25.00 50.00
60 Jimmy Evans 25.00 50.00
61 Ira Stuart 25.00 50.00
62 Berg Irving 50.00 100.00
63 Cecil Browne 40.00 80.00
64 Nick Wasnie 40.00 80.00
65 Gordon Teal 40.00 80.00
66 Jack Hughes 40.00 80.00
67 D. Yeatman 40.00 80.00
68 Connie Johanneson 25.00 50.00
69 S. Walters 25.00 50.00
70 Harold McMunn 40.00 80.00
71 Smokey Harris 25.00 50.00
72 Calgary Jimmies 25.00 50.00
73 Bernie Morris 25.00 50.00
74 J. Fowler 40.00 80.00
75 Calgary Jimmies 25.00 50.00
76 Pete Spiers 25.00 50.00
77 Bill Borland 40.00 80.00
78 Cliff O'Meara 40.00 80.00
79 F. Porteous 40.00 80.00
80 W. Brooks 40.00 80.00
81 Everett McGowan 25.00 50.00
82 Calgary Jimmies 25.00 50.00
83 George Dame 25.00 50.00
84 Calgary Jimmies 25.00 50.00
85 Calgary Jimmies 25.00 50.00
86 Calgary Jimmies 25.00 50.00
87 Heck Fowler 40.00 80.00
88 Jimmy Hoyle 25.00 50.00
89 Charlie Gardiner 75.00 150.00
90 Calgary Jimmies 40.00 80.00

1933-34 V129

This 50-card set was issued anonymously during the 1933-34 season. Recent research may link the cards' distribution to British Consul Cigarettes. This has yet to be confirmed. The cards are sepia toned and measure approximately 1 5/8" by 2 7/8". The cards are numbered on the back with the capsule biography both in French and in English. Card number 39 is now known to exist but is quite scarce as it was the card that the company (allegedly) short-printed in order to make it difficult to complete the set. The short-printed Oliver card is not included in the complete set price below.

COMPLETE SET (49) 7500.00 15000.00
1 Red Horner RC 250.00 500.00
2 Hap Day 175.00 350.00
3 Ace Bailey RC 250.00 500.00
4 Buzz Boll RC 75.00 150.00
5 Charlie Conacher RC 500.00 1000.00
6 Busher Jackson RC 250.00 500.00
7 Joe Primeau RC 250.00 500.00
8 King Clancy 500.00 1000.00
9 Alex Levinsky RC 100.00 200.00
10 Bill Thoms RC 75.00 150.00
11 Andy Blair RC 75.00 150.00
12 Harold Cotton RC 100.00 200.00
13 George Hainsworth 250.00 500.00
14 Ken Doraty RC 75.00 150.00
15 Fred Robertson RC 75.00 150.00
16 Charlie Sands RC 75.00 150.00
17 Hec Kilrea RC 75.00 150.00
18 John Roach RC 100.00 200.00
19 Larry Aurie RC 75.00 150.00
20 Ebbie Goodfellow RC 150.00 300.00
21 Normie Himes RC 100.00 200.00
22 Bill Brydge RC 75.00 150.00
23 Mervyn (Red) Dutton RC 150.00 300.00
24 Cooney Weiland RC 200.00 400.00
25 Bill Beveridge RC 100.00 200.00
26 Frank Finnigan 100.00 200.00
27 Albert Leduc RC 100.00 200.00
28 Babe Siebert RC 200.00 400.00
29 Murray Murdoch RC 75.00 150.00
30 Butch Keeling RC 75.00 150.00
31 Bill Cook 150.00 300.00
32 Cecil Dillon RC 75.00 150.00
33 Ching Johnson RC 200.00 400.00
34 Ott Heller RC 75.00 150.00
35 Red Beattie RC 75.00 150.00
36 Dit Clapper 300.00 600.00
37 Eddie Shore RC 1000.00 2000.00
38 Marty Barry RC 150.00 300.00
39 Harry Oliver RC SP 7500.00 15000.00
40 Bob Gracie RC 75.00 150.00
41 Howie Morenz 1500.00 3000.00
42 Pit Lepine RC 75.00 150.00
43 Johnny Gagnon RC 75.00 150.00
44 Armand Mondou RC 75.00 150.00
45 Lorne Chabot RC 150.00 300.00
46 Bun Cook RC 150.00 300.00
47 Alex Smith RC 75.00 150.00
48 Danny Cox RC 75.00 150.00
49 Baldy Northcott RC UER 100.00 200.00
50 Paul Thompson RC 100.00 200.00

1924-25 V130 Maple Crispette

This 30-card set was issued during the 1924-25 season in the Montreal area. The cards are in black and white and measure approximately 1 3/8" by 2 3/8". There was a prize offer detailed on the reverse of every card offering a pair of hockey skates for a complete set of the cards. Card number 15 apparently was the "impossible" card that prevented most collectors of that day from ever getting the skates. The cards are numbered on the front in the lower right hand corner. The set is considered complete without the short-printed Cleghorn.

COMPLETE SET (29) 4000.00 8000.00
1 Capt. Dunc Munro 100.00 200.00
2 Clint Benedict 200.00 400.00
3 Norman Fowler 100.00 200.00
4 Curly Headley 75.00 150.00
5 Alf Skinner 75.00 150.00
6 Bill Cook 150.00 300.00
7 Smokey Harris 75.00 150.00
8 Jim Herberts 75.00 150.00
9 Carson Cooper 75.00 150.00
10 Red Green 75.00 150.00
11 Billy Boucher 75.00 150.00
12 Howie Morenz 1000.00 2000.00
13 Georges Vezina 700.00 1400.00
14 Aurel Joliat 400.00 800.00
15 Sprague Cleghorn SP 6000.0012000.00
16 Dutch Cain 75.00 150.00
17 Charlie Dinsmore 75.00 150.00
18 Punch Broadbent 150.00 300.00
19 Sam Rothschild 75.00 150.00
20 George Carroll 75.00 150.00
21 Billy Burch 150.00 300.00
22 Shorty Green 150.00 300.00
23 Mickey Roach 75.00 150.00
24 Ken Randall 75.00 150.00
25 Vernon Forbes 100.00 200.00
26 Charlie Langlois 75.00 150.00
27 Newsy Lalonde 300.00 600.00
28 Fred (Frock) Lowrey 75.00 150.00
29 Ganton Scott 75.00 150.00
30 Louis Berlinguette 100.00 200.00

1923-24 V145-1

This relatively unattractive 40-card set is printed in sepia tone. The cards measure approximately 2" by 3 1/4". The cards have blank backs. The cards are numbered on the front in the lower left corner. The player's name, team, and National Hockey League are at the bottom of each card. The issuer of the set is not indicated in any way on the card, although speculation suggests it was William Patterson, Ltd, a Canadian confectioner. This set is easily confused with the other V145 set. Except for the tint and size differences and the different card name/number correspondence, these sets are essentially the same. Thankfully the only player with the same number in both sets is number 3 King Clancy. The Bert Corbeau card (#25) is extremely difficult to find in any condition, as it most likely was short printed. It is not included in the complete set price below.

COMPLETE SET (40) 6000.00 12000.00
1 Eddie Gerard 125.00 250.00
2 Frank Nighbor RC 175.00 350.00
3 King Clancy RC 900.00 1800.00
4 Jack Darragh 100.00 200.00
5 Harry Helman RC 50.00 100.00
6 George (Buck) Boucher RC 100.00200.00
7 Clint Benedict 150.00 300.00
8 Lionel Hitchman RC 100.00 200.00
9 Punch Broadbent 125.00 250.00
10 Cy Denneny RC 200.00 400.00
11 Sprague Cleghorn 150.00 300.00
12 Sylvio Mantha RC 125.00 250.00
13 Joe Malone 200.00 400.00
14 Aurel Joliat RC 650.00 1300.00
15 Howie Morenz RC 1500.00 3000.00
16 Billy Boucher RC 60.00 125.00
17 Billy Coutu RC 60.00 125.00
18 Odie Cleghorn 60.00 125.00
19 Georges Vezina 750.00 1500.00
20 Amos Arbour RC 50.00 100.00
21 Lloyd Andrews RC 50.00 100.00
22 Red Stuart RC 60.00 125.00
23 Cecil (Babe) Dye RC 150.00 300.00
24 Jack Adams RC 200.00 400.00
25 Bert Corbeau RC SP 10000.0020000.00
26 Reg Noble RC 150.00 300.00
27 Stan Jackson RC 50.00 100.00
28 John Roach 60.00 125.00
29 Vernon Forbes RC 60.00 125.00
30 Shorty Green RC 100.00 200.00
31 Red Green RC 50.00 100.00
32 Goldie Prodgers 50.00 100.00
33 Leo Reise RC 50.00 100.00
34 Ken Randall RC 50.00 100.00
35 Billy Burch RC 100.00 200.00
36 Jesse Spring RC 50.00 100.00
37 Eddie Bouchard RC 50.00 100.00
38 Mickey Roach RC 50.00 100.00
39 Chas. Fraser RC 50.00 100.00
40 Corbett Denneny RC 100.00 200.00

1924-25 V145-2

This 60-card set was issued anonymously during the 1924-25 season. The cards have a green-black tint and measure approximately 1 3/4" by 3 1/4". Cards are numbered in the lower left corner and have a blank back. The player's name, team, and National Hockey League are at the bottom of each card. The issuer of the set is not indicated in any way on the card, although speculation points to William Patterson, Ltd., a Canadian confectioner. This set is easily confused with the V145 set. Except for the tint and size differences and the different card name/number correspondence, these sets are essentially the same. Thankfully the only player with the same number in both sets is number 3 King Clancy.

COMPLETE SET (60) 6000.00 12000.00
1 Joe Ironstone RC 125.00 250.00
2 George (Buck) Boucher 100.00 200.00
3 King Clancy 750.00 1500.00
4 Lionel Hitchman 75.00 150.00
5 Hooley Smith RC 125.00 250.00
6 Frank Nighbor 100.00 200.00
7 Cy Denneny 125.00 250.00
8 Spiff Campbell RC 50.00 100.00
9 Frank Finnigan RC 75.00 150.00
10 Alex Connell RC 125.00 250.00
11 Vernon Forbes 60.00 125.00
12 Ken Randall 50.00 100.00
13 Billy Burch 100.00 200.00
14 Shorty Green 100.00 200.00
15 Red Green 50.00 100.00
16 Alex McKinnon RC 50.00 100.00
17 Charlie Langlois RC 50.00 100.00
18 Mickey Roach 50.00 100.00
19 Eddie Bouchard 50.00 100.00
20 Jesse Spring 50.00 100.00
21 Carson Cooper RC 50.00 100.00
22 Smokey Harris RC 50.00 100.00
23 Gopher Headley RC 50.00 100.00
24 Bill Cook RC 200.00 400.00
25 Jim Herberts RC 50.00 100.00
26 Werner Schnarr RC 50.00 100.00
27 Alf Skinner RC 50.00 100.00
28 George Redding RC 50.00 100.00
29 Herbie Mitchell RC 50.00 100.00
30 Hek Fowler RC 60.00 125.00
31 Red Stuart 50.00 100.00
32 Clint Benedict 100.00 200.00
33 Gerald Munro RC 50.00 100.00
34 Dunc Munro RC 60.00 125.00
35 Dutch Cain RC 50.00 100.00
36 Fred (Frock) Lowrey RC 50.00 100.00
37 Sam Rothschild RC 50.00 100.00
38 Ganton Scott RC 50.00 100.00
39 Punch Broadbent 125.00 250.00
40 Charlie Dinsmore RC 50.00 100.00
41 Louis Berlinquette RC 50.00 100.00
42 George Carroll RC 50.00 100.00
43 Georges Vezina 600.00 1200.00
44 Billy Coutu 50.00 100.00
45 Odie Cleghorn 60.00 125.00
46 Billy Boucher 75.00 150.00
47 Howie Morenz 1000.00 2000.00
48 Aurel Joliat 500.00 1000.00
49 Sprague Cleghorn 125.00 250.00
50 Billy Mantha RC 75.00 150.00
51 Reg Noble 100.00 200.00
52 John Roach 60.00 125.00
53 Jack Adams 100.00 200.00
54 Cecil (Babe) Dye 100.00 200.00
55 Reg Reid RC 50.00 100.00
56 Albert Holway RC 50.00 100.00
57 Bert McCaffery RC 50.00 100.00
58 Bert Corbeau 100.00 200.00
59 Lloyd Andrews 50.00 100.00
60 Stan Jackson 75.00 150.00

1933-34 V252 Canadian Gum

This unnumbered set of 50 cards was designated V252 by the American Card Catalog. Cards are black and white pictures with a red border. Backs are written in both French and English. Cards measure approximately 2 1/2" by 3 1/4" including a 3/4" tab at the bottom describing a premium (contest) offer and containing one large letter. When enough of these letters were saved so that the collector could spell out the names of five NHL teams, they could be redeemed for a free home hockey game according to the details given on the card backs. The cards are checklisted in alphabetical order.

COMPLETE SET (50) 4500.00 9000.00
1 Clarence Abel RC 75.00 150.00
2 Larry Aurie RC 50.00 100.00
3 Ace Bailey RC 200.00 400.00
4 Helge Bostrom RC 50.00 100.00
5 Bill Brydge RC 50.00 100.00
6 Glyn Brydson RC 50.00 100.00
7 Marty Burke RC 50.00 100.00
8 Gerald Carson 50.00 100.00
9 Lorne Chabot RC 200.00 400.00
10 King Clancy 450.00 800.00
11 Dit Clapper RC 200.00 400.00
12 Charlie Conacher RC 400.00 750.00
13 Lionel Conacher RC 200.00 400.00
14 Alex Connell 100.00 175.00
15 Bun Cook RC 100.00 175.00
16 Danny Cox RC 50.00 100.00
17 Hap Day 100.00 200.00
18 Cecil Dillon RC 50.00 100.00
19 Lorne Duguid RC 60.00 125.00
20 Duke Dutkowski RC 50.00 100.00
21 Mervyn (Red) Dutton RC 100.00 175.00
22 Hap Emms RC 60.00 125.00
23 Frank Finnigan 60.00 125.00
24 Chuck Gardiner RC 100.00 175.00
25 Ebbie Goodfellow RC 100.00 175.00
26 Johnny Gottselig RC 60.00 125.00
27 Bob Gracie RC 50.00 100.00
28 George Hainsworth 200.00 400.00
29 Ott Heller RC 50.00 100.00
30 Normie Himes RC 60.00 125.00
31 Red Horner RC 150.00 300.00
32 Busher Jackson RC 200.00 400.00
33 Walter (Red) Jackson RC 50.00 100.00
34 Aurel Joliat 400.00 750.00
35 Dave Kerr RC 60.00 125.00
36 Pit Lepine RC 50.00 100.00
37 Georges Mantha RC 50.00 100.00
38 Howie Morenz 1000.00 2000.00
39 Murray Murdoch RC 50.00 100.00
40 Baldy Northcott RC 60.00 125.00
41 John Roach RC 60.00 125.00
42 Johnny Sheppard 50.00 100.00
43 Babe Siebert RC 125.00 250.00
44 Alex Smith RC 50.00 100.00
45 John Sorrell RC 50.00 100.00
46 Nelson Stewart RC 200.00 400.00
47 Dave Trottier RC 50.00 100.00
48 Bill Touhey RC 50.00 100.00
49 Jimmy Ward RC 50.00 100.00
50 Nick Wasnie RC 50.00 100.00

1933-34 V288 Hamilton Gum

This skip-numbered set of 21 cards was designated V288 by the American Card Catalog. Cards are black and white pictures with a beige, blue, green, or orange background. Backs are written in both French and English. Cards measure approximately 2 3/8" by 2 3/4".

COMPLETE SET (21) 3000.00 6000.00
1 Nick Wasnie 62.50 125.00
2 Joe Primeau 200.00 400.00
3 Marty Burke 50.00 100.00
7 Bill Thoms 50.00 100.00
8 Howie Morenz 1000.00 2000.00
9 Andy Blair 50.00 100.00
11 Ace Bailey 175.00 350.00
14 Wildor Larochelle 50.00 100.00
17 King Clancy 400.00 800.00
18 Sylvio Mantha 87.50 175.00
21 Red Horner 150.00 300.00
23 Pit Lepine 50.00 100.00
27 Aurel Joliat 400.00 800.00
29 Harvey(Busher) Jackson 175.00 350.00
30 Lorne Chabot 100.00 200.00
33 Clarence(Hap) Day 100.00 200.00
36 Alex Levinsky 62.50 125.00
39 Harold Cotton 75.00 150.00
42 Ebbie Goodfellow 87.50 175.00
44 Larry Aurie 50.00 100.00
49 Charlie Conacher 400.00 800.00

1937-38 V356 Worldwide Gum

These rather crude greenish-gray cards feature the player's name and card number on the front and the card number, the player's name, his position and biographical data (in both English and French) on the back. Cards are approximately 2 3/8" by 2 7/8". Although the backs of the cards state that the cards were printed in Canada, no mention of the issuer, World Wide Gum, is apparent anywhere on the card.

COMPLETE SET (135) 11000.00 22000.00
1 Charlie Conacher 500.00 1000.00
2 Jimmy Ward 50.00 100.00
3 Babe Siebert 175.00 350.00
4 Marty Barry 100.00 200.00
5 Eddie Shore 750.00 1500.00
6 Paul Thompson 50.00 100.00
7 Roy Worters 150.00 300.00
8 Red Horner 100.00 200.00
9 Wilfred Cude 75.00 150.00
10 Lionel Conacher 175.00 350.00
11 Ebbie Goodfellow 125.00 250.00
12 Tiny Thompson 150.00 300.00
13 Harold(Mush) March RC 62.50 125.00
14 Mervyn (Red) Dutton 100.00 200.00
15 Butch Keeling 50.00 100.00
16 Frank Boucher 100.00 200.00
17 Tommy Gorman RC 50.00 100.00
18 Howie Morenz 1250.00 2500.00
19 Marvin Wentworth 75.00 150.00
20 Hooley Smith 100.00 200.00
21 Ching Johnson RC 150.00 300.00
22 Baldy Northcott 75.00 150.00
23 Syl Apps 400.00 800.00
24 Hec Kilrea 50.00 100.00
25 John Sorrell 50.00 100.00
26 Lorne Carr RC 50.00 100.00
27 Charlie Sands 50.00 100.00
28 Nick Metz 50.00 100.00
29 King Clancy 500.00 1000.00
30 Russ Blinco 50.00 100.00
31 Pete Martin RC 50.00 100.00
32 Walter Buswell RC 50.00 100.00
33 Paul Haynes 50.00 100.00
34 Wildor Larochelle 62.50 125.00
35 Harold Cotton 62.50 125.00
36 Dit Clapper 200.00 400.00
37 Joe Lamb 50.00 100.00
38 Bob Gracie 50.00 100.00
39 Jack Shill 50.00 100.00
40 Buzz Boll 50.00 100.00
41 John Gallagher 50.00 100.00
42 Art Chapman 50.00 100.00
43 Tom Cook RC 50.00 100.00
44 Bill MacKenzie 50.00 100.00
45 Georges Mantha 50.00 100.00
46 Herb Cain 62.50 125.00
47 Mud Bruneteau RC 75.00 150.00
48 Bob Davidson 50.00 100.00
49 Doug Young 50.00 100.00
50 Paul Drouin 50.00 100.00
51 Busher Jackson 200.00 400.00
52 Hap Day 150.00 300.00
53 Dave Kerr 100.00 200.00
54 Al Murray 50.00 100.00
55 Johnny Gottselig 62.50 125.00
56 Andy Blair 50.00 100.00
57 Lynn Patrick 200.00 400.00
58 Sweeney Schriner 125.00 250.00
59 Hap Emms 62.50 125.00
60 Allan Shields 50.00 100.00
61 Alex Levinsky 62.50 125.00
62 Flash Hollett 50.00 100.00
63 Peggy O'Neil 50.00 100.00
64 Herbie Lewis RC 100.00 200.00
65 Aurel Joliat 400.00 800.00
66 Carl Voss 100.00 200.00
67 Stew Evans 50.00 100.00
68 Bun Cook 125.00 250.00
69 Cooney Weiland 125.00 250.00
70 Dave Trottier 50.00 100.00
71 Louis Trudel 50.00 100.00
72 Marty Burke 50.00 100.00
73 Leroy Goldsworthy 50.00 100.00
74 Normie Smith RC 50.00 100.00
75 Syd Howe 150.00 300.00
76 Gordon Pettinger RC 50.00 100.00
77 Jack McGill 50.00 100.00
78 Pit Lepine 50.00 100.00
79 Sammy McManus RC 50.00 100.00
80 Phil Watson 75.00 150.00
81 Paul Runge 50.00 100.00
82 Bill Beveridge 62.50 125.00
83 Johnny Gagnon 50.00 100.00
84 Bucko MacDonald 62.50 125.00
85 Earl Robinson 50.00 100.00
86 Pep Kelly 50.00 100.00
87 Ott Heller 50.00 100.00
88 Murray Murdoch 50.00 100.00
89 Mac Colville RC 50.00 100.00
90 Alex Shibicky 75.00 150.00
91 Neil Colville 125.00 250.00
92 Normie Himes 62.50 125.00
93 Charley McVeigh 50.00 100.00
94 Lester Patrick 200.00 400.00
95 Connie Smythe 200.00 400.00
96 Art Ross 200.00 400.00
97 Cecil M.Hart RC 125.00 250.00
98 Dutch Gainor RC 50.00 100.00
99 Jack Adams 150.00 300.00
100 Howie Morenz Jr. 150.00 300.00
101 Buster Mundy RC 50.00 100.00
102 Johnny Wing 50.00 100.00
103 Morris Croghan 50.00 100.00
104 Pete Jotkus RC 50.00 100.00
105 Doug MacQuisten RC 50.00 100.00
106 Lester Brennan RC 50.00 100.00
107 Jack O'Connell RC 50.00 100.00
108 Ray Malenfant RC 50.00 100.00
109 Ken Murray RC 50.00 100.00
110 Frank Stangle RC 50.00 100.00
111 Dave Neville RC 50.00 100.00
112 Claude Burke 50.00 100.00
113 Herman Murray RC 50.00 100.00
114 Buddy O'Connor RC 125.00 250.00
115 Albert Perreault RC 50.00 100.00
116 Johnny Taugher 50.00 100.00
117 Rene Boudreau RC 50.00 100.00
118 Kenny McKinnon RC 50.00 100.00
119 Alex Bolduc 50.00 100.00
120 Jimmy Keiller RC 50.00 100.00
121 Lloyd McIntyre RC 50.00 100.00
122 Emile Fortin RC 50.00 100.00
123 Mike Karakas 62.50 125.00
124 Art Wiebe 50.00 100.00
125 Louis St. Denis RC 50.00 100.00
126 Stan Pratt 50.00 100.00
127 Jules Cholette RC 50.00 100.00
128 Jimmy Muir RC 50.00 100.00
129 Pete Morin RC 50.00 100.00
130 Jimmy Heffernan RC 50.00 100.00
131 Morris Bastien RC 50.00 100.00
132 Tuffy Griffiths RC 50.00 100.00
133 Johnny Mahaffey RC 50.00 100.00
134 Trueman Donnelly RC 50.00 100.00
135 Bill Stewart 75.00 150.00

1933-34 V357 Ice Kings

This interesting and attractive set of 72 cards features black and white photos on the front, upon which the head of the player portrayed has been tinted in flesh tones. The cards measure approximately 2 3/8" by 2 7/8". The player's name appears on the front of the card. The card number, position, team and player's name is listed on the back as are brief biographies in both French and English. Some cards appear with the resumes in English only. Printed in Canada and issued by World Wide Gum, the catalog designation for this set is V357.

COMP.SET (72) 9000.00 15000.00
1 Dit Clapper RC 350.00 600.00
2 Bill Brydge RC 50.00 100.00
3 Aurel Joliat UER 500.00 800.00
4 Andy Blair 50.00 100.00
5 Earl Robinson RC 50.00 100.00
6 Paul Haynes RC 50.00 100.00
7 Ronnie Martin RC 50.00 100.00
8 Babe Siebert RC 175.00 300.00
9 Archie Wilcox RC 50.00 100.00
10 Clarence(Hap) Day 150.00 250.00
11 Roy Worters RC 200.00 350.00
12 Nels Stewart RC 350.00 600.00
13 King Clancy 600.00 1000.00
14 Marty Burke RC 125.00 200.00
15 Cecil Dillon RC 50.00 100.00
16 Red Horner RC 175.00 300.00
17 Armand Mondou RC 50.00 100.00
18 Paul Raymond RC 50.00 100.00
19 Dave Kerr RC 75.00 125.00
20 Butch Keeling RC 50.00 100.00
21 Johnny Gagnon RC 50.00 100.00
22 Ace Bailey RC 300.00 500.00
23 Harry Oliver RC 150.00 250.00
24 Gerald Carson RC 50.00 100.00
25 Mervyn (Red) Dutton RC 150.00 250.00
26 Georges Mantha RC 50.00 100.00
27 Marty Barry RC 150.00 250.00
28 Wildor Larochelle RC 75.00 125.00
29 Red Beattie RC 50.00 100.00
30 Bill Cook 150.00 250.00
31 Hooley Smith 150.00 250.00
32 Art Chapman RC 50.00 100.00
33 Harold Cotton RC 125.00 200.00
34 Lionel Hitchman 125.00 200.00
35 George Patterson RC 50.00 100.00
36 Howie Morenz 1200.00 2000.00
37 Jimmy Ward RC 50.00 100.00
38 Charley McVeigh RC 75.00 125.00
39 Glen Brydson RC 75.00 125.00
40 Joe Primeau RC 300.00 500.00
41 Joe Lamb RC 90.00 150.00
42 Sylvio Mantha 125.00 200.00
43 Cy Wentworth RC 75.00 125.00
44 Normie Himes RC 75.00 125.00
45 Doug Brennan RC 50.00 100.00
46 Pit Lepine RC 50.00 100.00
47 Alex Levinsky RC 75.00 125.00
48 Baldy Northcott RC 75.00 125.00
49 Ken Doraty RC 75.00 125.00
50 Bill Thoms RC 75.00 125.00
51 Vernon Ayres RC 75.00 125.00
52 Lorne Duguid RC 75.00 125.00
53 Wally Kilrea RC 75.00 125.00
54 Vic Ripley RC 75.00 125.00
55 Hap Emms RC 75.00 125.00
56 Duke Dutkowski RC 75.00 125.00
57 Tiny Thompson RC 300.00 500.00
58 Charlie Sands RC 75.00 125.00
59 Larry Aurie RC 75.00 125.00
60 Bill Beveridge RC 75.00 125.00
61 Bill McKenzie RC 75.00 125.00
62 Earl Roche RC 75.00 125.00
63 Bob Gracie RC 75.00 125.00
64 Hec Kilrea RC 75.00 125.00
65 Cooney Weiland RC 250.00 400.00
66 Bun Cook RC 200.00 350.00
67 John Roach RC 90.00 150.00
68 Murray Murdoch RC 75.00 125.00
69 Danny Cox RC 75.00 125.00
70 Desse Roche RC 75.00 125.00
71 Lorne Chabot RC 175.00 300.00
72 Syd Howe RC 250.00 400.00

1933-34 V357-2 Ice Kings Premiums

These six black-and-white large cards are actually premiums. The cards measure approximately 7" by 9". The cards are unnumbered and rather difficult to find now.

COMPLETE SET (6) 2000.00 4000.00
1 King Clancy 500.00 1000.00
2 Clarence(Hap) Day 175.00 350.00
3 Aurel Joliat 400.00 800.00
4 Howie Morenz 1000.00 2000.00
5 Allan Shields 87.50 175.00
6 Reginald(Hooley) Smith 125.00 250.00

1983-84 Vachon

his set of 140 standard-size cards was ssued by Vachon Foods as panels of two ards. The set includes players from the even Canadian NHL teams. The cards were lso available as a set directly from Vachon. he first printing contained an error in that umber 96 pictures Peter Ihnacek instead of Valt Poddubny. The error was corrected for he second printing. The card backs are ritten in French and English. The Vachon ogo is on the front of every card in the lower ight corner. The set is difficult to collect in ncut panels of two; the prices below are for ndividual cards, the panel prices are 50 ercent greater than the prices listed below.

COMPLETE SET (140) 80.00 200.00
Paul Baxter .30 .75
Ed Beers .20 .50
Steve Bozek .20 .50
Mike Eaves .20 .50
Don Edwards .40 1.00
Kari Eloranta .20 .50
Dave Hindmarch .20 .50
Jamie Hislop .20 .50
Steve Konroyd .20 .50
0 Reggie Lemelin .40 1.00
1 Hakan Loob .80 2.00
2 Jamie Macoun .20 .50
3 Lanny McDonald 1.20 3.00
4 Kent Nilsson .80 2.00
5 Colin Patterson .20 .50
6 Jim Peplinski .40 1.00
7 Paul Reinhart .40 1.00
8 Doug Risebrough .40 1.00
9 Steve Tambellini .20 .50
0 Mickey Volcan .20 .50
1 Glenn Anderson 1.60 4.00
2 Paul Coffey 4.80 12.00
3 Lee Fogolin .20 .50
4 Grant Fuhr 2.00 5.00
5 Randy Gregg .20 .50
6 Wayne Gretzky 20.00 50.00
7 Charlie Huddy .30 .75
8 Pat Hughes .20 .50
9 Dave Hunter .20 .50
0 Don Jackson .20 .50
1 Jari Kurri 3.20 8.00
2 Willy Lindstrom .20 .50
3 Ken Linseman .30 .75
4 Kevin Lowe .60 1.50
5 Dave Lumley .20 .50
6 Mark Messier 10.00 25.00
7 Andy Moog 2.00 5.00
8 Jaroslav Pouzar .20 .50
9 Tom Roulston .20 .50
0 Dave Semenko .30 .75
1 Guy Carbonneau 1.20 3.00
2 Kent Carlson .20 .50
3 Gilbert Delorme .20 .50
4 Bob Gainey .80 2.00
5 Jean Hamel .20 .50
6 Mark Hunter .20 .50
7 Guy Lafleur 2.40 6.00
8 Craig Ludwig .20 .50
9 Pierre Mondou .20 .50
0 Mats Naslund .80 2.00
1 Chris Nilan .40 1.00
2 Greg Paslawski .20 .50
3 Larry Robinson .80 2.00
4 Richard Sevigny .40 1.00
5 Steve Shutt .80 2.00
6 Bobby Smith .40 1.00
7 Mario Tremblay .30 .75
8 Ryan Walter .30 .75
9 Rick Wamsley .40 1.00
0 Doug Wickenheiser .20 .50
1 Bo Berglund .20 .50
2 Dan Bouchard .40 1.00
3 Alain Cote .20 .50
4 Brian Ford .20 .50
5 Michel Goulet 1.00 2.50
6 Dale Hunter .80 2.00
7 Mario Marois .30 .75
8 Tony McKegney .30 .75
9 Randy Moller .20 .50
0 Wilf Paiement .40 1.00
1 Pat Price .20 .50
2 Normand Rochefort .20 .50
3 Andre Savard .20 .50
4 Louis Sleigher .20 .50
5 Anton Stastny .30 .75
6 Marian Stastny .30 .75
7 Peter Stastny 2.40 6.00
8 John Van Boxmeer .20 .50
9 Wally Weir .20 .50
0 Blake Wesley .20 .50
1 John Anderson .30 .75
2 Jim Benning .20 .50
3 Dan Daoust .20 .50
4 Bill Derlago .30 .75
5 Dave Farrish .20 .50
6 Miroslav Frycer .20 .50
7 Stewart Gavin .30 .75
8 Gaston Gingras .20 .50
9 Billy Harris .20 .50
0 Peter Ihnacek .40 1.00
1 Jim Korn .20 .50
2 Terry Martin .20 .50
3 Dale McCourt .20 .50
4 Gary Nylund .20 .50
5 Mike Palmateer .80 2.00
96A Walt Poddubny ERR 4.00 10.00
(Photo actually
Peter Ihnacek
no mustache)
96B Walt Poddubny COR 1.00 2.50
(With mustache)
97 Borje Salming 1.20 3.00
98 Rick St.Croix .40 1.00
99 Greg P. Terrion .20 .50
100 Rick Vaive .40 1.00
101 Richard Brodeur .60 1.50
102 Jiri Bubla .20 .50
103 Garth Butcher .20 .50
104 Ron Delorme .20 .50
105 John Garrett .60 1.50
106 Jere Gillis .20 .50
107 Thomas Gradin .40 1.00
108 Doug Halward .20 .50
109 Mark Kirton .20 .50
110 Rick Lanz .20 .50
111 Gary Lupul .20 .50
112 Kevin McCarthy .20 .50
113 Lars Molin .20 .50
114 Jim Nill .20 .50
115 Darcy Rota .20 .50
116 Stan Smyl .40 1.00
117 Harold Snepsts .60 1.50
118 Patrik Sundstrom .40 1.00
119 Tony Tanti .40 1.00
120 Dave(Tiger) Williams .80 2.00
121 Scott Arniel .20 .50
122 Dave Babych .40 1.00
123 Laurie Boschman .20 .50
124 Wade Campbell .20 .50
125 Lucien DeBlois .20 .50
126 Dale Hawerchuk 3.00 7.50
127 Brian Hayward .40 1.00
128 Jim Kyte .30 .75
129 Morris Lukowich .20 .50
130 Bengt Lundholm .20 .50
131 Paul MacLean .40 1.00
132 Moe Mantha .20 .50
133 Andrew McBain .20 .50
134 Brian Mullen .20 .50
135 Robert Picard .20 .50
136 Doug Smail .40 1.00
137 Doug Soetaert .40 1.00
138 Thomas Steen .60 1.50
139 Tim Watters .20 .50
140 Tim Young .30 .75

1973-74 Vancouver Blazers

This set features the Blazers of the WHA. The cards are actually oversized black and white photos and were issued as a promotional item by the team. The Archambault and Cardiff cards were recently confirmed by collector M.R. LaFleche. No pricing information is available for these singles at this time.

COMPLETE SET (21) 25.00 50.00
1 Jim Adair 1.50 3.00
2 Yves Archambault
3 Don Burgess 2.00 4.00
4 Bryan Campbell 2.00 4.00
5 Colin Campbell 2.50 5.00
6 Jim Cardiff
7 Mike Chernoff 1.50 3.00
8 Peter Donnelly 1.50 3.00
9 George Gardner 1.50 3.00
10 Sam Gellard 1.50 3.00
11 Ed Hatoum 1.50 3.00
12 Dave Hutchison 2.00 4.00
13 Danny Lawton 1.50 3.00
14 Ralph MacSweyn 1.50 3.00
15 Denis Meloche 1.50 3.00
16 John Migneault 1.50 3.00
17 Murray Myers 1.50 3.00
18 Michel Plante 1.50 3.00
19 Ron Plumb 2.00 4.00
20 Claude St. Sauveur 1.50 3.00
21 Irv Spencer 2.00 4.00

2000-01 Vanguard

In 2000-01 Pacific Vanguard was released as a 151-card set with cards 101-150 released as short-printed cards. The base set design consisted of card fronts that featured laser-etched technology to silhouette the player with silver blending into a team color. The short printed cards were serial numbered to 390.

COMP.SET w/o SP's (101) 15.00 40.00
1 Guy Hebert .50 1.25
2 Paul Kariya .60 1.50
3 Teemu Selanne .60 1.50
4 Ray Ferraro .20 .50
5 Damian Rhodes .20 .50
6 Patrik Stefan .20 .50
7 Jason Allison .20 .50
8 Bill Guerin .50 1.25
9 Sergei Samsonov .50 1.25
10 Joe Thornton 1.00 2.50
11 Maxim Afinogenov .20 .50
12 Doug Gilmour .50 1.25
13 Dominik Hasek 1.25 3.00
14 Miroslav Satan .50 1.25
15 Valeri Bure .20 .50
16 Jarome Iginla .75 2.00
17 Marc Savard .20 .50
18 Rod Brind'Amour .50 1.25
19 Ron Francis .50 1.25
20 Arturs Irbe .50 1.25
21 Sami Kapanen .20 .50
22 Tony Amonte .50 1.25
23 Jocelyn Thibault .50 1.25
24 Alexei Zhamnov .20 .50
25 Ray Bourque 1.25 3.00
26 Chris Drury .50 1.25
27 Peter Forsberg 1.25 3.00
28 Milan Hejduk .60 1.50
29 Patrick Roy 3.00 6.00
30 Joe Sakic 1.25 3.00
31 Geoff Sanderson .20 .50
32 Ron Tugnutt .50 1.25
33 Ed Belfour .60 1.50
34 Brett Hull .75 2.00
35 Mike Modano 1.00 2.50
36 Joe Nieuwendyk .50 1.25
37 Sergei Fedorov 1.00 2.50
38 Nicklas Lidstrom .60 1.50
39 Chris Osgood .50 1.25
40 Brendan Shanahan .60 1.50
41 Steve Yzerman 3.00 6.00
42 Anson Carter .50 1.25
43 Tommy Salo .50 1.25
44 Doug Weight .50 1.25
45 Pavel Bure .60 1.50
46 Viktor Kozlov .50 1.25
47 Ray Whitney .20 .50
48 Ziggy Palffy .50 1.25
49 Luc Robitaille .50 1.25
50 Sergei Krivokrasov .20 .50
51 Saku Koivu .60 1.50
52 Trevor Linden .50 1.25
53 Jose Theodore .75 2.00
54 David Legwand .50 1.25
55 Randy Robitaille .20 .50
56 Jason Arnott .20 .50
57 Martin Brodeur 1.50 4.00
58 Patrik Elias .50 1.25
59 Scott Gomez .20 .50
60 Alexander Mogilny .50 1.25
61 Tim Connolly .20 .50
62 Mariusz Czerkawski .20 .50
63 John Vanbiesbrouck .50 1.25
64 Theo Fleury .20 .50
65 Brian Leetch .50 1.25
66 Mark Messier .60 1.50
67 Mike Richter .60 1.50
68 Daniel Alfredsson .50 1.25
69 Marian Hossa .60 1.50
70 Alexei Yashin .20 .50
71 Brian Boucher .60 1.50
72 Simon Gagne .60 1.50
73 John LeClair .60 1.50
74 Eric Lindros .60 1.50
75 Shane Doan .20 .50
76 Jeremy Roenick .75 2.00
77 Keith Tkachuk .60 1.50
78 Jean-Sebastien Aubin .50 1.25
79 Jan Hrdina .20 .50
80 Jaromir Jagr 1.00 2.50
81 Martin Straka .20 .50
82 Al MacInnis .50 1.25
83 Chris Pronger .50 1.25
84 Roman Turek .50 1.25
85 Pierre Turgeon .50 1.25
86 Vincent Damphousse .20 .50
87 Jeff Friesen .20 .50
88 Owen Nolan .50 1.25
89 Mike Johnson .20 .50
90 Vincent Lecavalier .60 1.50
91 Nik Antropov .20 .50
92 Tie Domi .50 1.25
93 Curtis Joseph .60 1.50
94 Mats Sundin .60 1.50
95 Andrew Cassels .20 .50
96 Markus Naslund .60 1.50
97 Felix Potvin .60 1.50
98 Peter Bondra .60 1.50
99 Olaf Kolzig .50 1.25
100 Adam Oates .50 1.25
101 Samuel Pahlsson SP 1.50 4.00
102 Jonas Ronnqvist RC 1.50 4.00
103 Milan Hnilicka SP 1.50 4.00
104 Andrew Raycroft RC 10.00 25.00
105 Dimitri Kalinin SP 1.50 4.00
106 Mika Noronen SP 1.50 4.00
107 Oleg Saprykin SP 1.50 4.00
108 Josef Vasicek RC 2.50 6.00
109 Shane Willis SP 1.50 4.00
110 Steve McCarthy SP 1.50 4.00
111 David Aebischer RC 8.00 20.00
112 Serge Aubin RC 1.50 4.00
113 Marc Denis SP 2.50 6.00
114 Rostislav Klesla RC 2.50 6.00
115 David Vyborny SP 1.50 4.00
116 Tyler Bouck RC 1.50 4.00
117 Marty Turco RC 10.00 25.00
118 Joaquin Gage SP 1.50 4.00
119 Michel Riesen RC 1.50 4.00
120 Brian Swanson RC 1.50 4.00
121 Roberto Luongo SP 2.50 6.00
122 Ivan Novoseltsev SP 1.50 4.00
123 Eric Belanger RC 1.50 4.00
124 Steven Reinprecht RC 1.50 4.00
125 Lubomir Visnovsky RC 1.50 4.00
126 Manny Fernandez SP 1.50 4.00
127 Marian Gaborik RC 12.00 30.00
128 Filip Kuba SP 1.50 4.00
129 Mathieu Garon SP 1.50 4.00
130 Andrei Markov SP 1.50 4.00
131 Scott Hartnell RC 2.50 6.00
132 Colin White RC 1.50 4.00
133 Rick DiPietro RC 10.00 25.00
134 Taylor Pyatt SP 1.50 4.00
135 Martin Havlat RC 10.00 25.00
136 Jani Hurme RC 2.50 6.00
137 Roman Cechmanek RC 1.50 4.00
138 Justin Williams RC 6.00 15.00
139 Robert Esche SP 1.50 4.00
140 Wyatt Smith SP 1.50 4.00
141 Ossi Vaananen RC 1.50 4.00
142 Milan Kraft SP 1.50 4.00
143 Brent Johnson SP 1.50 4.00
144 Ladislav Nagy SP 2.50 6.00
145 Evgeni Nabokov SP 2.50 6.00
146 Sheldon Keefe SP 1.50 4.00
147 Brad Richards SP 1.50 4.00
148 Petr Svoboda RC 1.50 4.00
149 Daniel Sedin SP 1.50 4.00
150 Henrik Sedin SP 1.50 4.00
151 Mario Lemieux 4.00 10.00

2000-01 Vanguard Premiere Date

These cards were random inserts in 2000-01 Pacific Vanguard. This parallel set had the serial numbers on the bottom right corner on the front of the card. The cards were serial numbered to 100.

*STARS: 3X TO 6X BASIC CARDS

2000-01 Vanguard Cosmic Force

Randomly inserted in packs at a rate of 1:73, this 10-card set featured some of the top players from the NHL. The card design had a foilboard card front and used 30-point styrene. There was a photo of the players head over laying a full body photo faintly seen in the background.

COMPLETE SET (10) 30.00 80.00
1 Paul Kariya 2.50 6.00
2 Dominik Hasek 4.00 10.00
3 Peter Forsberg 4.00 10.00
4 Patrick Roy 10.00 25.00
5 Steve Yzerman 8.00 20.00
6 Pavel Bure 2.50 6.00
7 Martin Brodeur 6.00 15.00
8 Eric Lindros 2.50 6.00
9 Jaromir Jagr 4.00 10.00
10 Curtis Joseph 2.50 6.00

2000-01 Vanguard Dual Game-Worn Jerseys

These cards were inserted into packs of Pacific Vanguard at a rate of 2 per box. The 20-card set featured the some of the top players from the NHL. The cards featured 2 jersey swatches per card, one on the front and one on the back. The cards were highlighted with silver-foil markings. The cards were serial numbered and the print runs vary, please see below for actual print runs.

*MULT.COLOR SWATCH: 1X TO 2X
1 Joe Thornton 6.00 15.00
Sergei Samsonov/1500
2 Peter Forsberg 25.00 60.00
Mats Sundin/125
3 Joe Sakic 15.00 40.00
Eric Lindros/250
4 Derian Hatcher 6.00 15.00
Mike Modano/1500
5 Brendan Shanahan 6.00 15.00
Chris Chelios/1500
6 Sergei Fedorov 8.00 20.00
Chris Osgood/400
7 Doug Weight 6.00 15.00
Ryan Smyth/1500
8 Bobby Holik 6.00 15.00
Mariusz Czerkawski/1500
9 John Vanbiesbrouck 25.00 60.00
Mike Richter/50
10 Alexei Zhamnov 6.00 15.00
Cory Stillman/1500
11 Cliff Ronning 6.00 15.00
Vitali Yachmenev/1500
12 Tom Fitzgerald 6.00 15.00
Kimmo Timonen/1400
13 Byron Dafoe 6.00 15.00
Darren McCarty/1400
14 Kyle McLaren 6.00 15.00
Don Sweeney/1400
15 Jere Lehtinen 6.00 15.00
Jamie Langenbrunner/400
16 Eric Daze 6.00 15.00
Marty McInnis/300
17 Andreas Dackell 6.00 15.00
Ulf Dahlen/400
18 Shayne Corson 6.00 15.00
Jeff Hackett/400
19 Chris Terreri 6.00 15.00
Guy Hebert/400
20 Scott Niedermayer 6.00 15.00
Claude Lapointe/400

2000-01 Vanguard Dual Game-Worn Patches

The 20-card set featured the some of the top players from the NHL. The cards featured 2 jersey-patch swatches per card, one on the front and one on the back. The cards were highlighted with silver-foil markings. The cards were serial numbered and the print runs vary, please see below for actual print runs. Note that card 9 does not exist. Lower print run cards not priced due to scarcity.

1 Joe Thornton 20.00 50.00
Sergei Samsonov/300
2 Peter Forsberg 50.00 125.00
Mats Sundin/100
3 Joe Sakic 25.00 60.00
Eric Lindros/100
4 Derian Hatcher 15.00 40.00
Mike Modano/300
5 Brendan Shanahan 25.00 60.00
Chris Chelios/125
6 Sergei Fedorov
Chris Osgood/25
7 Doug Weight 10.00 25.00
Ryan Smyth/300
8 Bobby Holik 10.00 25.00
Mariusz Czerkawski/300
10 Alexei Zhamnov 10.00 25.00
Cory Stillman/300
11 Cliff Ronning 10.00 25.00
Vitali Yachmenev/300
12 Tom Fitzgerald 10.00 25.00
Kimmo Timonen/300
13 Byron Dafoe 10.00 25.00
Darren McCarty/300
14 Kyle McLaren 10.00 25.00
Don Sweeney/300
15 Jere Lehtinen 10.00 25.00
Jamie Langenbrunner/100
16 Eric Daze
Marty McInnis/15
17 Andreas Dackell 10.00 25.00
Ulf Dahlen/75
18 Shayne Corson 10.00 25.00
Jeff Hackett/75
19 Chris Terreri 10.00 25.00
Guy Hebert/75
20 Scott Niedermayer 10.00 25.00
Claude Lapointe/100

2000-01 Vanguard High Voltage

These cards were randomly inserted in 2000-01 Pacific Vanguard at a rate of 1:1. The set consisted of 36 cards that featured some of the most prolific player from the NHL. Four different colored parallels were also created and randomly inserted. Parallel values can be found by using the multipliers below. Red parallels were serial numbered out of 299, gold parallels were serial numbered out of 199, green parallels were serial numbered out of 99, and silver parallels were serial numbered to just 10. Silver parallels are not priced due to scarcity.

COMPLETE SET (36) 10.00 20.00
*RED: 2X TO 4X BASIC CARDS
*GOLD: 3X TO 6X BASIC CARDS
*GREEN: 4X TO 8X BASIC CARDS
1 Paul Kariya .30 .75
2 Teemu Selanne .30 .75
3 Joe Thornton .40 1.00
4 Jason Allison .25 .60
5 Dominik Hasek .60 1.50
6 Ray Bourque .60 1.50
7 Peter Forsberg .75 2.00
8 Patrick Roy 1.50 4.00
9 Joe Sakic .60 1.50
10 Ed Belfour .30 .75
11 Brett Hull .40 1.00
12 Mike Modano .50 1.25
13 Brendan Shanahan .30 .75
14 Steve Yzerman 1.50 4.00
15 Doug Weight .25 .60
16 Pavel Bure .30 .75
17 Zigmund Palffy .25 .60
18 Marian Gaborik 2.00 5.00
19 Martin Brodeur .75 2.00
20 Scott Gomez .25 .60
21 Rick DiPietro 2.00 5.00
22 Theo Fleury .25 .60
23 Mark Messier .30 .75
24 Marian Hossa .30 .75
25 John LeClair .30 .75
26 Eric Lindros .30 .75
27 Jeremy Roenick .40 1.00
28 Keith Tkachuk .30 .75
29 Jaromir Jagr .50 1.25
30 Pierre Turgeon .25 .60
31 Vincent Lecavalier .30 .75
32 Curtis Joseph .30 .75
33 Mats Sundin .30 .75
34 Daniel Sedin .25 .60
35 Henrik Sedin .25 .60
36 Peter Bondra .30 .75

2000-01 Vanguard Holographic Gold

These cards were randomly inserted into packs of 2000-01 Pacific Vanguard retail at a rate of 1:25. These 100 cards were a parallel to the base set of Vanguard, and they were serial numbered to 60.

*STARS: 10X TO 20X BASIC CARDS

2000-01 Vanguard Holographic Purple

These cards were randomly inserted into packs of 2000-01 Pacific Vanguard hobby at a rate of 1:24. These 100 cards were a parallel to the base set of Vanguard, and they were serial numbered to 105.

*STARS: 3X TO 6X BASIC CARDS

2000-01 Vanguard In Focus

COMPLETE SET (20) 20.00 40.00
STATED ODDS 1:25
1 Paul Kariya .60 1.50
2 Teemu Selanne .60 1.50
3 Jason Allison .50 1.25
4 Ray Bourque 1.25 3.00
5 Peter Forsberg 1.50 4.00
6 Patrick Roy 3.00 8.00
7 Brett Hull .75 2.00
8 Sergei Fedorov 1.25 3.00
9 Steve Yzerman 3.00 8.00
10 Pavel Bure .75 2.00
11 Marian Gaborik 3.00 8.00
12 Martin Brodeur 1.50 4.00
13 Theo Fleury .50 1.25
14 John LeClair .75 2.00
15 Jaromir Jagr 1.00 2.50
16 Vincent Lecavalier .60 1.50
17 Curtis Joseph .60 1.50
18 Mats Sundin .60 1.50
19 Daniel Sedin .50 1.25
20 Henrik Sedin .50 1.25

2000-01 Vanguard Press East/West

Randomly inserted in packs of 2000-01 Pacific Vanguard, this 20-card set featured some of the top players from the NHL split into hobby-only cards and retail-only cards. The split was done on an East/West basis, the West players are hobby-only and the East players were retail-only. They were found in packs at a rate of 2:25 for either distribution channel.

COMPLETE SET (20) 30.00 60.00
1 Paul Kariya .60 1.50
2 Teemu Selanne .60 1.50
3 Peter Forsberg 1.50 4.00
4 Patrick Roy 3.00 8.00
5 Brett Hull .75 2.00
6 Sergei Fedorov 1.25 3.00
7 Steve Yzerman 3.00 8.00
8 Zigmund Palffy .50 1.25
9 Jeremy Roenick .75 2.00
10 Pierre Turgeon .50 1.25
11 Joe Thornton 2.50 6.00
12 Dominik Hasek 3.00 8.00
13 Pavel Bure 2.00 5.00
14 Martin Brodeur 4.00 10.00
15 Mark Messier 2.00 5.00
16 Alexei Yashin 1.50 4.00
17 Eric Lindros 1.50 4.00
18 Jaromir Jagr 2.50 6.00
19 Vincent Lecavalier 1.50 4.00
20 Curtis Joseph 1.50 4.00

2001-02 Vanguard

Released in early-February 2002, this 130-card set consisted of 100 regular base cards and 30 cards of first year players serial-numbered to 404 copies each.

COMP.SET w/o SP's (100) 20.00 50.00
1 Jeff Friesen .20 .50
2 Paul Kariya .40 1.00
3 Dany Heatley .75 2.00
4 Milan Hnilicka .30 .75
5 Byron Dafoe .30 .75
6 Glen Murray .20 .50
7 Sergei Samsonov .30 .75
8 Joe Thornton .75 2.00
9 Martin Biron .30 .75
10 Tim Connolly .20 .50
11 J-P Dumont .20 .50
12 Jarome Iginla .75 2.00
13 Marc Savard .20 .50
14 Roman Turek .30 .75
15 Ron Francis .30 .75
16 Arturs Irbe .30 .75
17 Jeff O'Neill .20 .50
18 Tony Amonte .30 .75
19 Mark Bell .20 .50
20 Kyle Calder .20 .50
21 Eric Daze .30 .75
22 Jocelyn Thibault .30 .75
23 Rob Blake .30 .75
24 Chris Drury .30 .75
25 Milan Hejduk .40 1.00
26 Patrick Roy 2.50 6.00
27 Joe Sakic 1.25 3.00
28 Alex Tanguay .30 .75
29 Rostislav Klesla .20 .50
30 Ron Tugnutt .30 .75
31 Ed Belfour .40 1.00
32 Mike Modano .75 2.00
33 Pierre Turgeon .30 .75
34 Sergei Fedorov .60 1.50
35 Dominik Hasek 1.25 3.00
36 Brett Hull .60 1.50
37 Brendan Shanahan .40 1.00
38 Steve Yzerman 2.50 6.00
39 Mike Comrie .30 .75
40 Tommy Salo .30 .75
41 Ryan Smyth .20 .50
42 Pavel Bure .40 1.00
43 Roberto Luongo .75 2.00
44 Jason Allison .20 .50
45 Zigmund Palffy .30 .75
46 Felix Potvin .40 1.00
47 Manny Fernandez .30 .75
48 Marian Gaborik .75 2.00
49 Doug Gilmour .30 .75
50 Yanic Perreault .20 .50
51 Brian Savage .20 .50
52 Jose Theodore .60 1.50
53 Mike Dunham .30 .75
54 David Legwand .30 .75
55 Jason Arnott .20 .50
56 Martin Brodeur 1.50 4.00
57 Patrik Elias .30 .75
58 Rick DiPietro .30 .75
59 Chris Osgood .30 .75
60 Mark Parrish .20 .50
61 Michael Peca .20 .50
62 Alexei Yashin .20 .50
63 Brian Leetch .30 .75
64 Eric Lindros .40 1.00
65 Mark Messier .40 1.00
66 Mike Richter .40 1.00
67 Daniel Alfredsson .30 .75
68 Martin Havlat .30 .75
69 Marian Hossa .40 1.00
70 Patrick Lalime .30 .75
71 Pavel Brendl .30 .75
72 Roman Cechmanek .30 .75
73 John LeClair .40 1.00
74 Jeremy Roenick .60 1.50
75 Sean Burke .30 .75
76 Shane Doan .20 .50
77 Daymond Langkow .20 .50
78 Kris Beech .20 .50
79 Johan Hedberg .30 .75
80 Mario Lemieux 3.00 8.00
81 Brent Johnson .30 .75
82 Chris Pronger .30 .75
83 Keith Tkachuk .40 1.00
84 Doug Weight .30 .75
85 Patrick Marleau .30 .75
86 Evgeni Nabokov .30 .75
87 Owen Nolan .30 .75
88 Teemu Selanne .40 1.00
89 Vincent Lecavalier .40 1.00
90 Brad Richards .30 .75
91 Martin St. Louis .30 .75
92 Curtis Joseph .40 1.00
93 Alexander Mogilny .30 .75
94 Mats Sundin .40 1.00
95 Dan Cloutier .30 .75
96 Brendan Morrison .30 .75
97 Markus Naslund .40 1.00
98 Peter Bondra .40 1.00
99 Jaromir Jagr 1.00 2.50
100 Olaf Kolzig .30 .75
101 Ilja Bryzgalov RC 4.00 10.00
102 Timo Parssinen RC 2.00 5.00
103 Ilya Kovalchuk RC 15.00 40.00
104 Brian Pothier RC 2.00 5.00
105 Jukka Hentunen RC 2.00 5.00
106 Erik Cole RC 4.00 10.00
107 Vaclav Nedorost RC 2.00 5.00
108 Niko Kapanen RC 2.00 5.00
109 Pavel Datsyuk RC 8.00 20.00
110 Jason Chimera RC 2.00 5.00
111 Ty Conklin RC 2.00 5.00
112 Jussi Markkanen SP 2.00 5.00
113 Niklas Hagman RC 2.00 5.00
114 Kristian Huselius RC 4.00 10.00
115 Jaroslav Bednar RC 2.00 5.00
116 Pascal Dupuis RC 2.00 5.00
117 Nick Schultz RC 2.00 5.00
118 Martin Erat RC 2.00 5.00
119 Andreas Salomonsson RC 2.00 5.00
120 Radek Martinek RC 2.00 5.00
121 Raffi Torres RC 4.00 10.00
122 Dan Blackburn RC 2.00 5.00
123 Chris Neil RC 2.00 5.00
124 Jiri Dopita RC 2.00 5.00
125 David Cullen RC 2.00 5.00
126 Krystofer Kolanos RC 2.00 5.00
127 Mark Rycroft RC 2.00 5.00
128 Jeff Jillson RC 2.00 5.00
129 Nikita Alexeev RC 2.00 5.00
130 Brian Sutherby RC 2.00 5.00

2001-02 Vanguard Blue

Inserted in 1:49 hobby and 1:25 retail packs, this 130-card set paralleled the base set with blue foil highlights replacing the silver. Each card was serial-numbered out of 89.

*STARS: 4X TO 8X BASIC CARD
*SP's: .25X TO .75X BASIC CARD

2001-02 Vanguard Red

Randomly inserted at 1:96 hobby and retail packs, this 130-card set paralleled the base set with red foil replacing the silver. Cards in this set were serial-numbered out of 38.

*STARS: 5X TO 12X BASIC CARD
*SP's: .5X TO 1X BASIC CARD

2001-02 Vanguard East Meets West

This 10-card set was randomly inserted at 1:97 packs.

COMPLETE SET (10) 20.00 50.00
1 M.Lemieux/J.Jagr 5.00 12.00
2 Patrick Roy 5.00 12.00
Dominik Hasek
3 Joe Sakic 4.00 10.00
Peter Forsberg
4 Martin Brodeur 4.00 10.00
Johan Hedberg
5 Eric Lindros 2.00 5.00
Alexei Yashin
6 Paul Kariya 2.00 5.00
Teemu Selanne
7 Steve Yzerman 4.00 10.00
Sergei Fedorov
8 Brendan Shanahan 2.00 5.00
Pavel Bure
9 Jarome Iginla 2.50 6.00
Mats Sundin
10 Chris Pronger 2.00 5.00
Nicklas Lidstrom

2001-02 Vanguard In Focus

This 10-card set was randomly inserted at a rate of 1:481 hobby packs. Each card was serial-numbered to 55 copies each,

1 Patrick Roy 20.00 50.00
2 Joe Sakic 12.50 30.00
3 Dominik Hasek 12.50 30.00
4 Brendan Shanahan 10.00 25.00
5 Steve Yzerman 20.00 50.00
6 Pavel Bure 8.00 20.00
7 Martin Brodeur 15.00 40.00
8 Mario Lemieux 25.00 60.00
9 Mats Sundin 8.00 10.00
10 Jaromir Jagr 10.00 25.00

2001-02 Vanguard Memorabilia

This 50-card set featured pieces of game-used equipment. Cards 1-41 and 43-44 carried dual swatches of game jerseys. Card #42 carried a swatch of jersey and a piece of game-used stick. Cards 45-50 carried a piece of the goal net from the NHL All-Star game. Cards 1-44 were inserted at 2:25 hobby and 1:25 retail. Cards 45-50 were inserted at 1:97 hobby packs only.

*MULT.COLOR SWATCH: 1X TO 1.5X HI
1 Paul Kariya 3.00 8.00
Oleg Tverdovsky
2 Paul Kariya 3.00 8.00
Guy Hebert
3 Sergei Samsonov 2.00 5.00
Don Sweeney
4 Jarome Iginla 3.00 8.00
Marc Savard
5 Fred Brathwaite 2.00 5.00
Roman Turek
6 Craig Stillman 2.00 5.00
Cory Conroy
7 Boris Mironov 2.00 5.00
Michael Nylander
8 Tony Amonte 5.00 12.00
Steve Sullivan SP
9 Joe Sakic 10.00 20.00
Peter Forsberg
10 Patrick Roy 15.00 40.00
Joe Sakic
11 Mike Modano 4.00 10.00
Derian Hatcher
12 Jamie Langenbrunner 2.00 5.00
Darryl Sydor
13 Steve Yzerman 12.00 30.00
Chris Chelios
14 Niklas Lidstrom 12.00 30.00
Sergei Fedorov SP
15 Saku Koivu 6.00 15.00
Teemu Selanne
16 Cliff Ronning 2.00 5.00
Vitali Yachmenev
17 Bobby Holik 2.00 5.00
Scott Niedermayer
18 Mariusz Czerkawski 2.00 5.00
Shawn Bates
19 Eric Lindros 3.00 8.00
Pavel Brendl
20 Mike Richter 12.00 30.00
Mike York
21 Jeremy Roenick 5.00 12.00
Eric Weinrich
22 Jeremy Lehtinen 2.00 5.00
Jyrki Lumme
23 Martin Straka 2.00 5.00
Josef Beranek
24 Jan Hrdina 2.00 5.00
Bob Boughner
25 Alexei Kovalev 2.00 5.00
Darius Kasparaitis
26 M.Lemieux/R.Lang 15.00 40.00
27 Martin Straka 2.00 5.00
Rich Parent
28 Dallas Drake 2.00 5.00
Mike Eastwood
29 Jochen Hecht 2.00 5.00
Jamie McLennan
30 Pierre Turgeon 4.00 10.00
Vincent Lecavalier
31 J-P Dumont 2.00 5.00
Scott Young
32 Curtis Joseph 12.00 30.00
Jose Theodore
33 Jaromir Jagr 10.00 25.00
Peter Bondra
34 Mats Sundin 3.00 8.00
Andrew Cassels
35 Olaf Kolzig 5.00 12.00
Dan Cloutier
36 Claude Lapointe 2.00 5.00
Mats Lindgren
37 Greg DeVries 5.00 12.00
Eric Messier
38 Steve Yzerman 20.00 50.00
Eric Lindros
39 Alexei Kovalev 2.00 5.00
Kip Miller
40 Lyle Odelein 2.00 5.00
Andre Savage
41 Marc Savard 2.00 5.00
Roman Turek
42 Jaromir Jagr 15.00 40.00
Ilya Kovalchuk STK/200
43 Patrick Roy 15.00 40.00
Jose Theodore
44 M.Lemieux/M.Sundin 15.00 40.00
45 Theo Fleury 10.00 25.00
Marian Hossa NET
46 Brett Hull 25.00 60.00
Pavel Bure NET
47 Doug Weight 10.00 25.00
Peter Forsberg NET
48 Jason Allsion 10.00 25.00
Zigmund Palffy NET
49 Rob Blake 12.00 30.00
Milan Hejduk NET
50 Martin Brodeur 30.00 80.00
Dominik Hasek NET

2001-02 Vanguard Patches

Randomly inserted at 1:97 hobby packs, this 16-card set partially paralleled the base memorabilia set but featured swatches of jersey patches. The set is skip-numbered.

3 Sergei Samsonov 12.50 30.00
Don Sweeney/35
5 Fred Brathwaite 12.50 30.00
Roman Turek/181
6 Cory Stillman 12.50 30.00
Craig Conroy
10 Patrick Roy 30.00 80.00
Joe Sakic/55
12 Jamie Langenbrunner 12.50 30.00
Darryl Sydor
21 Jeremy Roenick 20.00 50.00
Eric Weinrich
22 Jeremy Lehtinen 12.50 30.00
Jyrki Lumme
23 Martin Straka 12.50 30.00
Josef Beranek
25 Alexei Kovalev 12.50 30.00
Darius Kasparaitis
27 Martin Straka 12.50 30.00
Rich Parent
28 Dallas Drake 12.50 30.00
Mike Eastwood
33 Jaromir Jagr 25.00 60.00
Peter Bondra
37 Greg DeVries 12.50 30.00
Eric Messier
38 Steve Yzerman 30.00 80.00
Eric Lindros/25
39 Alexei Kovalev 12.50 30.00
Kip Miller
41 Marc Savard 12.50 30.00
Roman Turek

2001-02 Vanguard Premiere Date

Randomly inserted into hobby packs, this 130-card set paralleled the base set but each card carried a "Premier Date" stamp on the card front. Cards from this set were serial-numbered to 83 copies each.

*STARS: 4X TO 10X BASIC CARD
*SP's: .25X TO .75X BASIC CARD

2001-02 Vanguard Prime Prospects

This 20-card set was randomly inserted at 1:25 packs.

COMPLETE SET (20) 30.00 60.00
1 Dany Heatley 3.00 8.00
2 Ilya Kovalchuk 4.00 10.00
3 Vaclav Nedorost .75 2.00
4 Rostislav Klesla .75 2.00
5 Pavel Datsyuk 3.00 8.00
6 Mike Comrie 1.25 3.00
7 Kristian Huselius .75 2.00
8 Jaroslav Bednar .75 2.00
9 Marian Gaborik 3.00 8.00
10 Martin Erat .75 2.00
11 Rick DiPietro 2.00 5.00
12 Dan Blackburn .75 2.00
13 Martin Havlat 2.00 5.00
14 Pavel Brendl .75 2.00
15 Krystofer Kolanos .75 2.00
16 Brent Johnson 1.25 3.00
17 Jeff Jillson .75 2.00
18 Nikita Alexeev .75 2.00
19 Daniel Sedin 2.00 5.00
20 Henrik Sedin 2.00 5.00

2001-02 Vanguard Quebec Tournament Heroes

Cards from this 20-card set were split distributed. Cards 1-10 were found in packs at 1:25. Cards11-20 were distributed as giveaways to fans attending the Quebec Tournament in Feb, 2002.

COMPLETE HOBBY SET (10) 20.00 40.00
1 Brett Hull 1.25 3.00
2 Mario Lemieux 5.00 12.00
3 Patrick Roy 4.00 10.00
4 Steve Yzerman 4.00 10.00
5 Mike Modano 1.50 4.00
6 Jeremy Roenick 1.25 3.00
7 Brendan Shanahan 1.50 4.00
8 Felix Potvin 1.00 2.50
9 Doug Weight 1.00 2.50
10 Eric Lindros 1.50 4.00
11 Jocelyn Thibault 4.00 10.00
12 Jason Allison 2.00 5.00
13 Chris Drury 2.00 5.00
14 Jeff O'Neill 2.00 5.00
15 Sergei Samsonov 10.00 25.00
16 Alex Tanguay 4.00 10.00
17 Marian Hossa 10.00 25.00
18 Simon Gagne 10.00 25.00
19 Vincent Lecavalier 6.00 15.00
20 Rick DiPietro 6.00 15.00

2001-02 Vanguard Stonewallers

This 20-card set was randomly inserted at 1:49 packs.

COMPLETE SET (20) 40.00 80.00
1 Milan Hnilicka 1.25 3.00
2 Byron Dafoe 1.25 3.00
3 Martin Biron 1.25 3.00
4 Roman Turek 1.25 3.00
5 Patrick Roy 6.00 15.00
6 Ed Belfour 1.50 4.00
7 Dominik Hasek 3.00 8.00
8 Tommy Salo 1.25 3.00
9 Roberto Luongo 2.00 5.00
10 Jose Theodore 2.00 5.00
11 Martin Brodeur 4.00 10.00
12 Chris Osgood 1.25 3.00
13 Mike Richter 1.50 4.00
14 Patrick Lalime 1.25 3.00
15 Roman Cechmanek 1.25 3.00
16 Johan Hedberg 1.25 3.00
17 Evgeni Nabokov 1.25 3.00
18 Nikolai Khabibulin 1.50 4.00
19 Curtis Joseph 1.50 4.00
20 Olaf Kolzig 1.25 3.00

2001-02 Vanguard V-Team

This 20-card set was randomly inserted at 1:25 hobby and retail packs. Cards 1-10 were hobby exclusives and cards 11-20 were retail exclusives.

COMPLETE SET (20) 40.00 80.00
1 Roman Turek .60 1.50
2 Patrick Roy 4.00 10.00
3 Ed Belfour .75 2.00
4 Dominik Hasek 1.50 4.00
5 Martin Brodeur 2.00 5.00
6 Chris Osgood .60 1.50
7 Roman Cechmanek .60 1.50
8 Johan Hedberg .60 1.50
9 Evgeni Nabokov .60 1.50
10 Curtis Joseph .75 2.00
11 Jarome Iginla 1.00 2.50
12 Joe Sakic 1.50 4.00
13 Brendan Shanahan 1.25 3.00
14 Steve Yzerman 4.00 10.00
15 Pavel Bure 1.00 2.50
16 Eric Lindros 1.25 3.00
17 Mario Lemieux 5.00 12.00
18 Teemu Selanne .75 2.00
19 Mats Sundin .75 2.00
20 Jaromir Jagr 1.25 3.00

2002-03 Vanguard

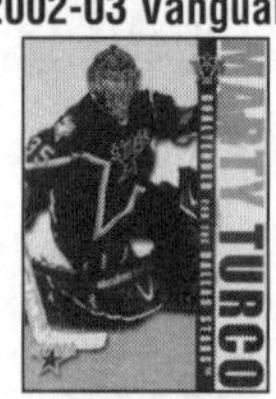

Released in March, this 136-card set consisted of 100 veteran base cards and 36 shortprinted rookie cards. Rookies were serial-numbered out of 1650. There were 6 cards per pack and 24 packs per box.

COMPLETE SET (136) 75.00 200.00
COMP.SET w/o SP's (100) 15.00 40.00
1 J-S Giguere .20 .50
2 Paul Kariya .30 .75
3 Steve Rucchin .10 .25
4 Byron Dafoe .20 .50
5 Dany Heatley .40 1.00
6 Ilya Kovalchuk .40 1.00
7 Glen Murray .10 .25
8 Brian Rolston .20 .50
9 Steve Shields .20 .50
10 Joe Thornton .75 2.00
11 Martin Biron .20 .50
12 Chris Gratton .10 .25
13 Jochen Hecht .10 .25
14 Chris Drury .20 .50
15 Jarome Iginla .40 1.00
16 Roman Turek .20 .50
17 Rod Brind'Amour .20 .50
18 Ron Francis .20 .50
19 Jeff O'Neill .10 .25
20 Kevin Weekes .20 .50
21 Tyler Arnason .20 .50
22 Eric Daze .20 .50
23 Theo Fleury .10 .25
24 Jocelyn Thibault .20 .50
25 Peter Forsberg 1.50 4.00
26 Milan Hejduk .30 .75
27 Patrick Roy 2.00 5.00
28 Joe Sakic 1.00 2.50
29 Andrew Cassels .10 .25
30 Marc Denis .20 .50
31 Geoff Sanderson .10 .25
32 Bill Guerin .20 .50
33 Mike Modano .75 2.00
34 Marty Turco .20 .50
35 Sergei Fedorov .75 2.00
36 Brett Hull .40 1.00
37 Curtis Joseph .30 .75
38 Nicklas Lidstrom .30 .75
39 Brendan Shanahan .30 .75
40 Steve Yzerman 2.00 5.00
41 Anson Carter .20 .50
42 Mike Comrie .20 .50
43 Tommy Salo .20 .50
44 Kristian Huselius .20 .50
45 Olli Jokinen .20 .50
46 Roberto Luongo .40 1.00
47 Jason Allison .10 .25
48 Adam Deadmarsh .10 .25
49 Ziggy Palffy .20 .50
50 Felix Potvin .30 .75
51 Andrew Brunette .10 .25
52 Marian Gaborik .75 2.00
53 Dwayne Roloson .20 .50
54 Jeff Hackett .20 .50
55 Saku Koivu .30 .75
56 Yanic Perreault .10 .25
57 Jose Theodore .40 1.00
58 Andreas Johansson .10 .25
59 David Legwand .20 .50
60 Martin Brodeur 1.50 4.00
61 Patrik Elias .20 .50
62 Jamie Langenbrunner .10 .25
63 Mark Parrish .10 .25
64 Michael Peca .10 .25
65 Alexei Yashin .10 .25
66 Dan Blackburn .20 .50
67 Pavel Bure .30 .75
68 Eric Lindros .30 .75
69 Daniel Alfredsson .20 .50
70 Marian Hossa .30 .75
71 Patrick Lalime .20 .50
72 Roman Cechmanek .20 .50
73 Simon Gagne .30 .75
74 John LeClair .30 .75
75 Jeremy Roenick .40 1.00
76 Tony Amonte .20 .50
77 Brian Boucher .20 .50
78 Mike Johnson .10 .25
79 Johan Hedberg .20 .50
80 Alexei Kovalev .20 .50
81 Mario Lemieux 2.50 6.00
82 Eric Boguniecki .10 .25
83 Cory Stillman .10 .25
84 Doug Weight .20 .50
85 Evgeni Nabokov .20 .50
86 Owen Nolan .20 .50
87 Teemu Selanne .30 .75
88 Nikolai Khabibulin .30 .75
89 Vincent Lecavalier .30 .75
90 Martin St. Louis .20 .50
91 Ed Belfour .30 .75
92 Alexander Mogilny .20 .50
93 Mats Sundin .30 .75
94 Todd Bertuzzi .30 .75
95 Dan Cloutier .20 .50
96 Brendan Morrison .20 .50
97 Markus Naslund .30 .75
98 Peter Bondra .20 .50
99 Jaromir Jagr .75 2.00
100 Olaf Kolzig .20 .50
101 Stanislav Chistov RC 1.50 4.00
102 Martin Gerber RC 1.50 4.00
103 Alexei Smirnov RC 1.00 2.50
104 Tim Thomas RC 1.50 4.00
105 Ryan Miller RC 4.00 10.00
106 Chuck Kobasew RC 1.50 4.00
107 Jordan Leopold RC 1.50 4.00
108 Pascal Leclaire RC 2.00 5.00
109 Rick Nash RC 8.00 20.00
110 Lasse Pirjeta RC 1.00 2.50
111 Steve Ott RC 1.50 4.00
112 Dmitri Bykov RC 1.00 2.50
113 Henrik Zetterberg RC 6.00 15.00
114 Ales Hemsky RC 2.00 5.00
115 Jay Bouwmeester RC 2.00 5.00
116 Mike Cammalleri RC 1.50 4.00
117 Alexander Frolov RC 2.00 5.00
118 P-M Bouchard RC 2.00 5.00
119 Stephane Veilleux RC 1.00 2.50
120 Sylvain Blouin RC 1.00 2.50
121 Ron Hainsey RC 1.00 2.50
122 Adam Hall RC 1.50 4.00
123 Scottie Upshall RC 1.50 4.00
124 Jason Spezza RC 6.00 15.00
125 Anton Volchenkov RC 1.50 4.00
126 Dennis Seidenberg RC 1.00 2.50
127 Patrick Sharp RC 1.00 2.50
128 Radovan Somik RC 1.00 2.50
129 Jeff Taffe RC 1.00 2.50
130 Dick Tarnstrom RC 1.00 2.50
131 Tom Koivisto RC 1.00 2.50
132 Curtis Sanford RC 1.50 4.00
133 Lynn Loyns RC 1.00 2.50
134 Alexander Svitov RC 1.00 2.50
135 Carlo Colaiacovo RC 1.00 2.50
136 Steve Eminger RC 1.50 4.00

2002-03 Vanguard LTD

Inserted at 1:5 hobby, this 136-card set paralleled the base set but each card was serial-numbered to 450.

*STARS: 3X TO 8X BASIC CARDS
*ROOKIES: .5X TO 1.25X

2002-03 Vanguard East Meets West

COMPLETE SET (10) 15.00 30.00
STATED ODDS 1:13
1 Ilya Kovalchuk 2.00 5.00
Markus Naslund
2 Joe Thornton 2.50 6.00
Jarome Iginla
3 M.Lemieux/S.Yzerman 4.00 10.00
4 Pavel Bure 2.00 5.00
Sergei Fedorov
5 J.LeClair/M.Modano 2.00 5.00
6 Mats Sundin 2.00 5.00
Peter Forsberg
7 Vincent Lecavalier 2.00 5.00
Joe Sakic
8 M.Hossa/M.Gaborik 2.00 5.00
9 M.Brodeur/P.Roy 4.00 10.00
10 Ed Belfour 2.50 6.00
Marty Turco

2002-03 Vanguard In Focus

COMPLETE SET (10) 20.00 40.00
STATED ODDS 1:25
1 Paul Kariya 1.25 3.00
2 Ilya Kovalchuk 2.00 5.00
3 Peter Forsberg 2.00 5.00
4 Joe Sakic 2.00 5.00
5 Rick Nash 3.00 8.00
6 Steve Yzerman 4.00 10.00
7 Marian Gaborik 2.00 5.00
8 Jason Spezza 3.00 8.00
9 Mario Lemieux 4.00 10.00
10 Jaromir Jagr 1.50 4.00

2002-03 Vanguard Jerseys

*MULT.COLOR SWATCH: .5X TO 1.25X
STATED ODDS 3:25
1 Adam Oates 2.00 5.00
2 Dany Heatley 5.00 12.00
3 Ilya Kovalchuk 5.00 12.00
4 Patrik Stefan 2.00 5.00
5 Joe Thornton 6.00 15.00
6 J-P Dumont 2.00 5.00
7 Chris Drury 2.00 5.00
8 Jamie McLennan 2.00 5.00
9 Rod Brind'Amour 2.00 5.00
10 Sergei Berezin 2.00 5.00
11 Theo Fleury 3.00 8.00
12 Alexei Zhamnov SP 3.00 8.00
13 Joe Sakic 6.00 15.00
14 Rostislav Klesla 2.00 5.00
15 Mike Modano 6.00 15.00
16 Pierre Turgeon 2.00 5.00
17 Sergei Fedorov 4.00 10.00
18 Brett Hull 4.00 10.00
19 Curtis Joseph 3.00 8.00
20 Ryan Smyth 3.00 8.00
21 Kristian Huselius 2.00 5.00
22 Ziggy Palffy 3.00 8.00
23 Yanic Perreault 2.00 5.00
24 Jose Theodore 4.00 10.00
25 Scott Walker 2.00 5.00
26 Martin Brodeur 10.00 25.00
27 Scott Gomez 2.00 5.00
28 Michael Peca 2.00 5.00
29 Pavel Bure 3.00 8.00
30 Mark Messier 3.00 8.00
31 Daniel Alfredsson 3.00 8.00
32 Patrick Lalime 2.00 5.00
33 John LeClair 2.00 5.00
34 Tomi Kallio 2.00 5.00
35 Krystofer Kolanos 2.00 5.00
36 Johan Hedberg 2.00 5.00
37 Mario Lemieux 12.50 30.00
38 Pavol Demitra 2.00 5.00
39 Keith Tkachuk 2.00 5.00
40 Patrick Marleau 3.00 8.00
41 Evgeni Nabokov 3.00 8.00
42 Nikolai Khabibulin 3.00 8.00
43 Alexander Mogilny 2.00 5.00
44 Gary Roberts 2.00 5.00
45 Darcy Tucker 2.00 5.00
46 Dan Cloutier 2.00 5.00
47 Brendan Morrison 2.00 5.00
48 Markus Naslund 3.00 8.00
49 Peter Bondra 3.00 8.00
50 Jaromir Jagr 6.00 15.00

2002-03 Vanguard Jerseys Gold

*GOLD: 1X TO 2.5X BASE HI
GOLD PRINT RUN 50 SER.#'d SETS

2002-03 Vanguard Prime Prospects

COMPLETE SET (20) 15.00 40.00
STATED ODDS 1:7
1 Stanislav Chistov .75 2.00
2 Alexei Smirnov .75 2.00
3 Ivan Huml .75 2.00
4 Ryan Miller 2.00 5.00
5 Chuck Kobasew 1.25 3.00
6 Jordan Leopold .75 2.00
7 Tyler Arnason .75 2.00
8 Rick Nash 4.00 10.00
9 Henrik Zetterberg 3.00 8.00
10 Ales Hemsky 1.50 4.00
11 Jay Bouwmeester 1.50 4.00
12 Stephen Weiss .75 2.00
13 Alexander Frolov 1.50 4.00
14 P-M Bouchard 1.50 4.00
15 Scottie Upshall .75 2.00
16 Justin Mapletoft .75 2.00
17 Jamie Lundmark .75 2.00
18 Jason Spezza 3.00 8.00
19 Petr Cajanek .75 2.00
20 Barret Jackman .75 2.00

2002-03 Vanguard Stonewallers

COMPLETE SET (12) 10.00 20.00
STATED ODDS 1:9
1 Patrick Roy 4.00 10.00
2 Marty Turco .60 1.50
3 Curtis Joseph .75 2.00
4 Roberto Luongo 1.00 2.50
5 Felix Potvin .75 2.00
6 Jose Theodore 1.00 2.50
7 Martin Brodeur 2.00 5.00
8 Mike Richter .75 2.00
9 Patrick Lalime .60 1.50
10 Roman Cechmanek .60 1.50
11 Nikolai Khabibulin .75 2.00
12 Ed Belfour .75 2.00

2002-03 Vanguard V-Team

Inserted at odds of 1:25, this 12-card set had split insertion. Cards 1-6 were found in hobby packs while cards 7-12 were found in retail packs.

COMPLETE SET (12) 20.00 40.00
1 Patrick Roy 4.00 10.00
2 Marty Turco .60 1.50
3 Curtis Joseph .75 2.00
4 Jose Theodore 1.00 2.50
5 Martin Brodeur 2.00 5.00
6 Ed Belfour .75 2.00
7 Ilya Kovalchuk 1.00 2.50
8 Joe Thornton 1.25 3.00
9 Joe Sakic 1.50 4.00
10 Steve Yzerman 4.00 10.00
11 Mario Lemieux 5.00 12.00
12 Jaromir Jagr 1.25 3.00

1999-00 Wayne Gretzky Hockey

This Upper Deck-produced set features the top players in the NHL. Company spokesman Gretzky offered comments on each player on the card back. The product was packaged in 24-pack boxes with packs containing eight cards and carried a suggested retail price of $2.49. Please note that although card #GM1 was supposed to carry a piece of game-used puck, there have been several singles found with stick pieces instead. The error does not affect the value.

COMPLETE SET (181) 20.00 40.00
1 Paul Kariya .20 .50
2 Guy Hebert .15 .40
3 Steve Rucchin .15 .40
4 Teemu Selanne .20 .50
5 Oleg Tverdovsky .15 .40
6 Matt Cullen .08 .25
7 Jeff Nielsen .08 .25
8 Patrik Stefan RC .50 1.25
9 Kelly Buchberger .08 .25
10 Andrew Brunette .15 .40
11 Ray Ferraro .08 .25
12 Nelson Emerson .08 .25
13 Damian Rhodes .15 .40
14 Sergei Samsonov .15 .40
15 John Grahame RC .50 1.25
16 Joe Thornton .30 .75
17 Jason Allison .08 .25
18 Kyle McLaren .08 .25
19 Rob DiMaio .08 .25
20 Ray Bourque .30 .75
21 Dominik Hasek .40 1.00
22 Miroslav Satan .15 .40
23 Alexei Zhitnik .08 .25
24 Stu Barnes .08 .25
25 Curtis Brown .08 .25
26 Brian Campbell RC .08 .25
27 Michael Peca .15 .40
28 Marc Savard .08 .25
29 Valeri Bure .08 .25
30 Phil Housley .08 .25
31 Grant Fuhr .15 .40
32 Cory Stillman .08 .25
33 Oleg Saprykin RC .50 1.25
34 Sami Kapanen .08 .25
35 Bates Basttaglia .08 .25
36 Dave Tanabe .15 .40
37 Ron Francis .15 .40
38 Arturs Irbe .15 .40

39 Keith Primeau .08 .25
40 Doug Gilmour .15 .40
41 J-P Dumont .15 .40
42 Eric Daze .15 .40
43 Tony Amonte .15 .40
44 Alexei Zhamnov .15 .40
45 Kyle Calder RC .20 .50
46 Joe Sakic .40 1.00
47 Chris Drury .15 .40
48 Milan Hejduk .20 .50
49 Adam Deadmarsh .08 .25
50 Patrick Roy 1.00 2.50
51 Peter Forsberg .50 1.25
52 Alex Tanguay .15 .40
53 Mike Modano .30 .75
54 Brett Hull .25 .60
55 Ed Belfour .20 .50
56 Jamie Langenbrunner .08 .25
57 Pavel Patera RC .08 .25
58 Joe Nieuwendyk .15 .40
59 Jere Lehtinen .15 .40
60 Steve Yzerman 1.00 2.50
61 Jiri Fischer .08 .25
62 Brendan Shanahan .20 .50
63 Chris Osgood .15 .40
64 Chris Chelios .20 .50
65 Sergei Fedorov .30 .75
66 Nicklas Lidstrom .20 .50
67 Doug Weight .15 .40
68 Mike Grier .08 .25
69 Ryan Smyth .15 .40
70 Jason Smith .08 .25
71 Tom Poti .08 .25
72 Pavel Bure .20 .50
73 Mark Parrish .08 .25
74 Ivan Novoseltsev RC .40 1.00
75 Trevor Kidd .08 .25
76 Viktor Kozlov .15 .40
77 Scott Mellanby .08 .25
78 Rob Blake .15 .40
79 Ian Lapperiere .08 .25
80 Zigmund Palffy .15 .40
81 Luc Robitaille .15 .40
82 Jozef Stumpel .15 .40
83 Aki Berg .08 .25
84 Stephane Fiset .15 .40
85 Saku Koivu .20 .50
86 Brian Savage .08 .25
87 Trevor Linden .08 .25
88 Jeff Hackett .15 .40
89 Eric Weinrich .08 .25
90 David Legwand .15 .40
91 Sergei Krivokrasov .08 .25
92 Randy Robitaille .08 .25
93 Kimmo Timonen .08 .25
94 Mike Dunham .15 .40
95 Brendan Morrison .15 .40
96 Scott Stevens .15 .40
97 Sheldon Souray .08 .25
98 Petr Sykora .08 .25
99 Wayne Gretzky 1.25 3.00
100 Martin Brodeur .50 1.25
101 Scott Niedermayer .08 .25
102 Patrik Elias .15 .40
103 Tim Connolly .08 .25
104 Jorgen Jonsson RC .08 .25
105 Mathieu Biron .15 .40
106 Claude Lapointe .08 .25
107 Kenny Jonsson .08 .25
108 Roberto Luongo .25 .60
109 Theo Fleury .08 .25
110 Petr Nedved .15 .40
111 Valeri Kamensky .15 .40
112 Adam Graves .08 .25
113 Manny Malhotra .15 .40
114 Brian Leetch .20 .50
115 Mike Richter .20 .50
116 Marian Hossa .20 .50
117 Radek Bonk .08 .25
118 Joe Juneau .08 .25
119 Wade Redden .08 .25
120 Ron Tugnutt .15 .40
121 Daniel Alfredsson .15 .40
122 Eric Lindros .20 .50
123 John LeClair .20 .50
124 Marc Bureau .08 .25
125 Simon Gagne .20 .50
126 Mark Recchi .15 .40
127 Rod Brind'Amour .15 .40
128 John Vanbiesbrouck .15 .40
129 Keith Tkachuk .20 .50
130 Jeremy Roenick .25 .60
131 Daniel Briere .08 .25
132 Bob Essensa .15 .40
133 J.J. Daigneault .08 .25
134 Mika Alatalo RC .15 .40
135 Travis Green .08 .25
136 Jaromir Jagr .30 .75
137 Martin Straka .08 .25
138 Alexei Morozov .15 .40
139 Jan Hrdina .08 .25
140 Alexei Kovalev .08 .25
141 Peter Skudra .08 .25
142 John Slaney .08 .25
143 Pierre Turgeon .15 .40
144 Roman Turek .15 .40
145 Pavol Demitra .15 .40
146 Al MacInnis .15 .40
147 Chris Pronger .15 .40
148 Jochen Hecht RC 1.00 2.50
149 Jeff Friesen .08 .25
150 Steve Shields .15 .40
151 Patrick Marleau .15 .40
152 Vincent Damphousse .08 .25
153 Marco Sturm .15 .40
154 Brad Stuart .15 .40
155 Darcy Tucker .08 .25
156 Vincent Lecavalier .20 .50
157 Andrei Zyuzin .08 .25
158 Chris Gratton .08 .25
159 Fredrik Modin .08 .25
160 Mats Sundin .20 .50
161 Steve Thomas .08 .25
162 Sergei Berezin .15 .40
163 Mike Johnson .15 .40
164 Dimitri Khristich .08 .25
165 Bryan Berard .08 .25
166 Curtis Joseph .20 .50
167 Mark Messier .20 .50
168 Alexander Mogilny .15 .40
169 Garth Snow .15 .40
170 Markus Naslund .20 .50
171 Steve Kariya RC .50 1.25
172 Peter Schaefer .08 .25
173 Peter Bondra .20 .50
174 Joe Sacco .08 .25
175 Adam Oates .15 .40
176 Olaf Kolzig .15 .40
177 Jan Bulis .08 .25
178 Alexander Volchkov RC .15 .40
179 Wayne Gretzky CL .08 .25
180 Curtis Joseph CL .08 .25
GM1 W.Gretzky PUCK or STICK 30.00 80.00

1999-00 Wayne Gretzky Hockey Changing The Game

Randomly inserted in packs at the rate of 1:27, this 10-card set highlights 10 top NHL stars who have left their mark on hockey. Each card is enhanced with silver foil stamping.

COMPLETE SET (10) 15.00 30.00
CG1 Peter Forsberg 2.50 6.00
CG2 Eric Lindros 1.00 2.50
CG3 Paul Kariya 1.00 2.50
CG4 Jaromir Jagr 1.50 4.00
CG5 Dominik Hasek 2.00 5.00
CG6 Sergei Samsonov .75 2.00
CG7 Theo Fleury .75 2.00
CG8 Al MacInnis .75 2.00
CG9 Pavel Bure 1.00 2.50
CG10 Patrick Roy 5.00 12.00

1999-00 Wayne Gretzky Hockey Elements of the Game

Randomly seeded in packs at the rate of 1:6, this 15-card set showcases top players on a card with purple foil borders with enhanced silver foil highlights.

COMPLETE SET (15) 8.00 15.00
EG1 Teemu Selanne .40 1.00
EG2 Mike Peca .30 .75
EG3 Sergei Samsonov .30 .75
EG4 Sergei Fedorov .60 1.50
EG5 Peter Forsberg 1.00 2.50
EG6 Brett Hull .50 1.25
EG7 Eric Lindros .40 1.00
EG8 Pavel Bure .40 1.00
EG9 Theo Fleury .30 .75
EG10 Martin Brodeur 1.00 2.50
EG11 Jaromir Jagr .60 1.50
EG12 Keith Tkachuk .40 1.00
EG13 Peter Bondra .40 1.00
EG14 Joe Sakic .75 2.00
EG15 Curtis Joseph .40 1.00

1999-00 Wayne Gretzky Hockey Great Heroes

Randomly inserted in packs at the rate of 1:27, this 10-card set showcases modern day heroes on a card with silver and purple foil borders and silver foil stamping.

COMPLETE SET (10) 20.00 40.00
GH1 Jaromir Jagr 1.50 4.00
GH2 Paul Kariya 2.00 5.00
GH3 Joe Sakic 2.00 5.00
GH4 Dominik Hasek 2.00 5.00
GH5 Patrick Roy 5.00 12.00
GH6 Steve Yzerman 5.00 12.00
GH7 Eric Lindros 1.50 4.00
GH8 Patrik Stefan 1.50 4.00
GH9 Teemu Selanne 2.00 5.00
GH10 Pavel Bure 1.25 3.00

1999-00 Wayne Gretzky Hockey Hall of Fame Career

Inserted one per pack this 30-card set traced Wayne Gretzky's career on a card with purple foil borders and silver foil stamping.

COMPLETE SET (30) 12.00 25.00
COMMON GRETZKY .40 1.00

1999-00 Wayne Gretzky Hockey Signs of Greatness

Randomly inserted in Retail packs at the rate of 1:15, this 15-card set features portrait photography and authentic player signatures.

AI Arturs Irbe 6.00 15.00
BH Brett Hull SP 30.00 60.00
CD Chris Drury 6.00 15.00
CJ Curtis Joseph SP 40.00 80.00
CO Chris Osgood 6.00 15.00
DL David Legwand 6.00 15.00
MP Mark Parrish 6.00 15.00
NK Nikolai Khabibulin 10.00 25.00
PB Pavel Bure SP 25.00 60.00
PM Paul Mara 6.00 15.00
PS Patrik Stefan 6.00 15.00
RB Ray Bourque 25.00 60.00
SS Sergei Samsonov SP 10.00 25.00
VS Vadim Sharifijanov 6.00 15.00
WG Wayne Gretzky SP 200.00 400.00

1999-00 Wayne Gretzky Hockey Tools of Greatness

Randomly inserted in Hobby packs at the rate of 1:139, this 20-card set features action player photography coupled with a swatch of a game used stick.

TGAI Arturs Irbe 10.00 25.00
TGBH Brett Hull 12.50 30.00
TGBS Brendan Shanahan 10.00 25.00
TGCJ Curtis Joseph 10.00 25.00
TGDW Doug Weight 10.00 25.00
TGEB Ed Belfour 10.00 25.00
TGEL Eric Lindros 10.00 25.00
TGLR Luc Robitaille 10.00 25.00
TGMR Mike Richter 10.00 25.00
TGMS Mats Sundin 10.00 25.00
TGNK Nikolai Khabibulin 10.00 25.00
TGPB Pavel Bure 10.00 25.00
TGPF Peter Forsberg 20.00 50.00
TGPK Paul Kariya 10.00 25.00
TGPR Patrick Roy 20.00 50.00
TGRB Ray Bourque 15.00 40.00
TGSS Sergei Samsonov 10.00 25.00
TGTA Tony Amonte 10.00 25.00
TGTS Teemu Selanne 10.00 25.00

1999-00 Wayne Gretzky Hockey Visionary

Randomly inserted in packs at the rate of 1:167, this 10-card set features none other than the Great One on an acetate holofoil insert card. Cards carry a "V" prefix

COMPLETE SET (10) 75.00 150.00
COMMON GRETZKY (V1-V10) 10.00 25.00

1999-00 Wayne Gretzky Hockey Will to Win

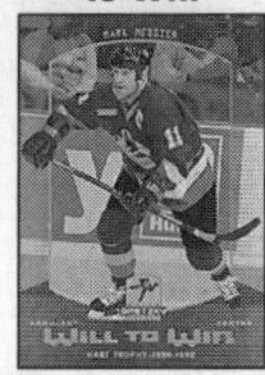

Randomly seeded in packs at the rate of 1:13, this 10-card set features ten of the most dominant stars of the NHL. Cards are enhanced with silver foil highlights.

COMPLETE SET (10) 12.00 25.00
W1 Paul Kariya .60 1.50
W2 Steve Yzerman 3.00 8.00
W3 Jaromir Jagr 1.00 2.50
W4 Dominik Hasek 1.25 3.00
W5 Patrick Roy 3.00 8.00
W6 Jeremy Roenick .75 2.00
W7 Ray Bourque 1.00 2.50
W8 John LeClair .75 2.00
W9 Mats Sundin .60 1.50
W10 Mark Messier .75 2.00

1999 Wayne Gretzky Living Legend

Released as a 99-card set, Wayne Gretzky Living Legend traces The Great One's course of life from beginning to New York. Base cards feature both portrait and action photography with enhanced gold foil stamping. Wayne Gretzky Living Legend was packaged in 24-pack boxes with packs containing six cards and carried a suggested retail price of $1.99. One Wayne Gretzky bonus pack was inserted in every box.

COMMON GRETZKY (1-99) .20 .50

1999 Wayne Gretzky Living Legend A Leader by Example

Randomly inserted in Wayne Gretzky bonus packs at the rate of 1:23, this 6-card set photos Gretzky in each of his NHL as well as some All-Star jerseys.

COMPLETE SET (6) 15.00 30.00
COMMON GRETZKY (L1-L6) 2.00 5.00

1999 Wayne Gretzky Living Legend Authentics

Randomly inserted in packs at the rate of 1:288 for pucks, 1:1196 for sticks, and jerseys autographed and sequentially numbered to 99, this 10-card set features swatches of game used items.

COMMON WG PUCK (P1-P6) 15.00 40.00
COMMON WG STICK (S1-S2) 25.00 60.00
C1 W.Gretzky Collection/99 AU 150.00 300.00
GJ1 Wayne Gretzky Jersey/99 AU 150.00 300.00

1999 Wayne Gretzky Living Legend Goodwill Ambassador

Randomly inserted in packs at the rate of 1:11, this nine card set showcases Wayne Gretzky not just as a player of the game, but as a spokesman and ambassador of hockey. Cards are enhanced with holofoil borders and gold foil stamping.

COMMON GRETZKY (GW1-GW9) 1.50 4.00

1999 Wayne Gretzky Living Legend Great Accolades

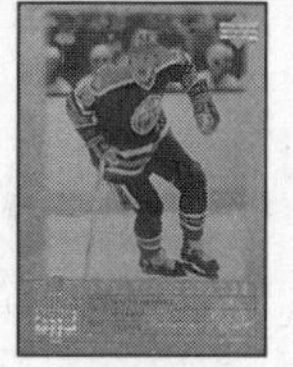

Randomly seeded in packs at the rate of 1:6, this 45-card set highlights some of Wayne Gretzky's greatest achievements. Cards are enhanced with silver foil stamping.

COMMON GRETZKY (GA1-GA45) 2.50 6.00

1999 Wayne Gretzky Living Legend Great Stats

Randomly inserted in Wayne Gretzky bonus packs at the rate of 1:23, this six card set features Wayne in all of his professional Hockey and All-Star jerseys. Cards are enhanced with holofoil borders and gold foil highlights.

COMMON GRETZKY (GS1-GS6) 2.00 5.00

1999 Wayne Gretzky Living Legend Magic Moments

Randomly inserted in Wayne Gretzky bonus packs at the rate of 1:23, this six card set highlights some of Wayne Gretzky's greatest NHL achievements. Cards are enhanced with holofoil borders and gold foil stamping.

COMMON GRETZKY (MM1-MM6) 2.00 5.00

1999 Wayne Gretzky Living Legend More Than a Number

Randomly inserted in packs, this 99-card set parallels the base Wayne Gretzky Living Legend set on cards that are sequentially numbered to 99.

COMMON GRETZKY (1-99) 25.00 60.00

1999 Wayne Gretzky Living Legend Only One 99

Randomly inserted in packs, this 99-card set parallels the base Wayne Gretzky Living Legend set. As the cards are each one-of-ones, they are not priced below.

NOT PRICED DUE TO SCARCITY

1999 Wayne Gretzky Living Legend The Great One

Randomly inserted in packs at the rate of 1:2, this 9-card set highlights Wayne Gretzkys impact on the sport of hockey. Cards are enhanced with holofoil borders and gold foil stamping.

COMMON GRETZKY (GO1-GO9) .75 2.00

1999 Wayne Gretzky Living Legend Wearing the Leaf

Randomly inserted in Wayne Gretzky bonus packs at the rate of 1:23, this six card holofoil set features Gretzky in his Team Canada jersey. Cards are enhanced with holofoil borders and gold foil stamping.

COMMON GRETZKY (WL1-WL6) 2.00 5.00

1999 Wayne Gretzky Living Legend Year of the Great One

Randomly inserted in packs, this 99-card set parallels the base Wayne Gretzky Living Legend set on die cut cards. Each card is serial numbered out of 1999.

COMMON GRETZKY (1-99) 1.50 4.00

1927 Werner and Mertz Field Hockey

Cards measure approximately 2 1/2 x 4 1/2 and feature full color drawings of field hockey action shots. Produced in Germany by Werner & Mertz Aktiengesellschaft, Mainz.

COMPLETE SET (6) 62.50 125.00
1 Womens Field Hockey 12.50 25.00
2 Womens Field Hockey 12.50 25.00
3 Mens Field Hockey 12.50 25.00
Scrum at midfield
4 Mens Field Hockey 12.50 25.00
Chasing the ball
5 Mens Field Hockey 12.50 25.00
Pileup
6 Mens Field Hockey 12.50 25.00
Goalie action shot

1982-83 Whalers Junior Hartford Courant

Sponsored by the Hartford Courant, this 23-card set measures approximately 3 1/4" by 6 3/8". The fronts feature borderless color action player photos. and the sponsor's name. The white backs carry a black-and-white headshot, player's name, jersey number, biography and statistics. The cards are unnumbered and checklisted below in alphabetical order. The card of Ron Francis appears in his Rookie Card year.

COMPLETE SET (22) 14.00 75.00
1 Greg Adams 1.00 4.00
2 Russ Anderson .40 2.00
3 Ron Francis 4.00 25.00
4 Michel Galarneau .40 2.00
5 Dan Fridgen .40 2.00
6 Archie Henderson .40 2.00
7 Ed Hospodar .40 2.00
8 Mark Johnson .80 3.00
9 Chris Kotsopoulos .40 2.00
10 Pierre Larouche 1.00 4.00
11 George Lyle .40 2.00
12 Greg Millen 1.20 5.00
13 Warren Miller .40 2.00
14 Ray Neufeld .60 3.00
15 Mark Renaud .40 2.00
16 Risto Siltanen .60 3.00
17 Stuart Smith .40 2.00
18 Blaine Stoughton 1.00 4.00
19 Doug Sulliman .40 2.00
20 Bob Sullivan .40 2.00
21 Mike Veisor .60 3.00
22 Mickey Volcan .40 2.00
23 Blake Wesley .40 2.00

1983-84 Whalers Junior Hartford Courant

Sponsored by the Hartford Courant, this 22-card set measures approximately 3 3/4" by 8 1/4". The fronts feature color action player photos and the sponsor's name. The white backs carry a black-and-white headshot, player's name, jersey number, biography and statistics. The cards are unnumbered and checklisted below in alphabetical order.

COMPLETE SET (22) 10.00 25.00
1 Bob Crawford .40 1.00
2 Mike Crombeen .40 1.00
3 Richie Dunn .40 1.00
4 Normand Dupont .40 1.00
5 Ron Francis 3.20 8.00
6 Ed Hospodar .40 1.00
7 Marty Howe .80 2.00
8 Mark Johnson .60 1.50
9 Chris Kotsopoulos .40 1.00
10 Pierre Lacroix .60 1.50
11 Greg Malone .60 1.50
12 Greg Malone .60 1.50
13 Ray Neufeld .40 1.00
14 Joel Quenneville .60 1.50
15 Torrie Robertson .60 1.50
16 Risto Siltanen .40 1.00
17 Blaine Stoughton .80 2.00
18 Steve Stoyanovich .40 1.00
19 Doug Sulliman .40 1.00
20 Sylvain Turgeon .60 1.50
21 Mike Veisor .60 1.50
22 Mike Zuke .40 1.00

1984-85 Whalers Junior Wendy's

This 22-card set was sponsored by Wendy's and The Civic Center Mall. The cards measure approximately 3 3/4" by 8 1/4" and feature color action player photos. The backs have a black and white head shot, biography, 1983-84 season summary, career summary, miscellaneous player information, and statistics. The cards are unnumbered and checklisted below in alphabetical order.

COMPLETE SET (22) 10.00 25.00
1 Jack Brownschidle .40 1.00
2 Sylvain Cote .40 1.00
3 Bob Crawford .40 1.00
4 Mike Crombeen .40 1.00
5 Tony Currie .40 1.00
6 Ron Francis 2.40 6.00
7 Mark Fusco .40 1.00
8 Dave Jensen .40 1.00
9 Mark Johnson .60 1.50
10 Chris Kotsopoulos .40 1.00
11 Greg Malone .60 1.50
12 Greg Millen .80 2.00
13 Ray Neufeld .40 1.00
14 Randy Pierce .40 1.00
15 Joel Quenneville .60 1.50
16 Torrie Robertson .60 1.50
17 Ulf Samuelsson 1.60 4.00
18 Risto Siltanen .40 1.00
19 Dave Tippett .40 1.00
20 Sylvain Turgeon .40 1.00
21 Steve Weeks .80 2.00
22 Mike Zuke .60 1.50

1985-86 Whalers Junior Wendy's

Sponsored by Wendy's, this 23-card set measures approximately 3 3/4" by 8 1/4". The fronts feature full-bleed color action player photos, along with the sponsor's name. The white backs carry a black-and-white headshot, biography, 1984-85 season summary, career summary, personal information, and statistics. The cards were issued to members of the team's Kid's Club. Since they are unnumbered, the cards are checklisted below in alphabetical order.

COMPLETE SET (23) 12.00 30.00
1 Jack Brownschidle .40 1.00
2 Sylvain Cote .40 1.00
3 Bob Crawford .40 1.00
4 Kevin Dineen 1.60 4.00

5 Paul Fenton	.40	1.00
6 Ray Ferraro	1.20	3.00
7 Ron Francis	2.00	5.00
8 Scott Kleinendorst	.40	1.00
9 Paul Lawless	.40	1.00
10 Mike Liut	1.20	3.00
11 Paul MacDermid	.40	1.00
12 Greg Malone	.40	1.00
13 Dana Murzyn	.40	1.00
14 Ray Neufeld	.40	1.00
15 Jorgen Pettersson	.40	1.00
16 Joel Quenneville	.40	1.00
17 Torrie Robertson	.60	1.50
18 Ulf Samuelsson	1.20	3.00
19 Risto Siltanen	.40	1.00
20 Dave Tippett	.40	1.00
21 Sylvain Turgeon	.60	1.50
22 Steve Weeks	.60	1.50
23 Mike Zuke	.40	1.00

1986-87 Whalers Junior Thomas'

Sponsored by Thomas', this 23-card set measures approximately 3 3/4" by 8 1/4". The cards were issued only to members of the team's Kid's Club. The fronts feature color action player photos, along with the team and sponsor name. The white backs carry a black-and-white headshot, player's name, jersey number, biography, 1985-86 season summary, career summary, personal information, and statistics. The cards are unnumbered and checklisted below in alphabetical order.

COMPLETE SET (23)	12.00	30.00
1 John Anderson	.40	1.00
2 Dave Babych	.80	2.00
3 Wayne Babych	.40	1.00
4 Sylvain Cote	.40	1.00
5 Kevin Dineen	1.20	3.00
6 Dean Evason	.40	1.00
7 Ray Ferraro	.40	1.00
8 Ron Francis	2.40	6.00
9 Bill Gardner	.40	1.00
10 Stewart Gavin	.40	1.00
11 Doug Jarvis	.40	1.00
12 Scot Kleinendorst	.40	1.00
13 Paul Lawless	.40	1.00
14 Mike Liut	1.20	3.00
15 Paul MacDermid	.40	1.00
16 Mike McEwen	.40	1.00
17 Dana Murzyn	.40	1.00
18 Joel Quenneville	.40	1.00
19 Torrie Robertson	.50	1.25
20 Ulf Samuelsson	1.20	3.00
21 Dave Tippett	.40	1.00
22 Sylvain Turgeon	.40	1.00
23 Steve Weeks	.60	1.50

1987-88 Whalers Jr. Burger King/Pepsi

This 21-card set was sponsored by Burger King restaurants and Pepsi Cola and measures approximately 3 3/4" by 8 1/4". The fronts feature color action player photos with the team name and sponsors' logos at the bottom. The backs carry a small headshot, biography, season summary, career summary, miscellaneous player information, and statistics. The cards, which were issued only to members of the team's Kid's Club, are unnumbered and checklisted below in alphabetical order.

COMPLETE SET (21)	10.00	25.00
1 John Anderson	.40	1.00
2 Dave Babych	.80	2.00
3 Sylvain Cote	.40	1.00
4 Kevin Dineen	1.00	2.50
5 Dean Evason	.40	1.00
6 Ray Ferraro	1.00	2.50
7 Ron Francis	1.60	4.00
8 Stew Gavin	.40	1.00
9 Doug Jarvis	.40	1.00
10 Scott Kleinendorst	.40	1.00
11 Randy Ladouceur	.40	1.00
12 Paul Lawless	.40	1.00
13 Mike Liut	1.00	2.50
14 Paul MacDermid	.40	1.00
15 Dana Murzyn	.40	1.00
16 Joel Quenneville	.40	1.00
17 Torrie Robertson	.40	1.00
18 Ulf Samuelsson	.80	2.00
19 Dave Tippett	.40	1.00
20 Sylvain Turgeon	.40	1.00
21 Steve Weeks	.60	1.50

1988-89 Whalers Junior Ground Round

This 18-card set of Hartford Whalers was sponsored by Ground Round restaurants. The cards measure approximately 3 11/16" by 8 1/4". The front features a borderless full color photo of the player. The team logo and a Ground Round advertisement appear in the blue and green stripes that cut across the bottom of the card face. The back has a black and white head shot of the player at the upper left hand corner as well as extensive player information and career statistics. Another Ground Round advertisement and a Ground Round Drug Tip (an anti-drug and alcohol message) appear at the bottom of the card. The cards were issued to members of the team's Kid's Club. They are unnumbered and hence are checklisted below in alphabetical order.

COMPLETE SET (18)	8.00	20.00
1 John Anderson	.40	1.00
2 Dave Babych	.60	1.50
3 Sylvain Cote	.40	1.00
4 Kevin Dineen	.80	2.00
5 Dean Evason	.40	1.00
6 Ray Ferraro	.80	2.00
7 Ron Francis	1.40	3.50
8 Scott Kleinendorst	.40	1.00
9 Randy Ladouceur	.40	1.00
10 Mike Liut	.80	2.00
11 Paul MacDermid	.40	1.00
12 Brent Peterson	.40	1.00
13 Joel Quenneville	.40	1.00
14 Torrie Robertson	.40	1.00
15 Ulf Samuelsson	.80	2.00
16 Dave Tippett	.40	1.00
17 Sylvain Turgeon	.40	1.00
18 Carey Wilson	.40	1.00

1989-90 Whalers Junior Milk

This 23-card set of Hartford Whalers was sponsored by Milk and issued to members of the team's Kid's Club. The cards measure approximately 3 11/16" by 8 1/4". The front features a borderless full color photo of the player. The team logo and a Milk advertisement appear in the blue and green stripes that cut across the bottom of the card face. The back has a black and white head shot of the player at the upper left hand corner as well as extensive player information and career statistics. A Junior Whaler Nutrition Tip and another Milk advertisement appear at the bottom of the card's reverse. The cards are unnumbered and hence are checklisted below in alphabetical order. Three cards (11, 12, 21) were added to the set at the end of the season and are marked as SP in the checklist below.

COMPLETE SET (23)	8.00	20.00
1 Mikael Andersson	.20	.50
2 Dave Babych	.30	.75
3 Sylvain Cote	.20	.50
4 Randy Cunneyworth	.20	.50
5 Kevin Dineen	.60	1.50
6 Dean Evason	.20	.50
7 Ray Ferraro	.40	1.00
8 Ron Francis	1.20	3.00
9 Jody Hull	.20	.50
10 Grant Jennings	.20	.50
11 Ed Kastelic SP	.80	2.00
12 Todd Krygier SP	.80	2.00
13 Randy Ladouceur	.20	.50
14 Mike Liut	.60	1.50
15 Paul MacDermid	.20	.50
16 Joel Quenneville	.20	.50
17 Ulf Samuelsson	.60	1.50
18 Brad Shaw	.30	.75
19 Peter Sidorkiewicz	.30	.75
20 Dave Tippett	.20	.50
21 Mike Tomlak SP	.80	2.00
22 Pat Verbeek	.60	1.50
23 Scott Young	.40	1.00

1990-91 Whalers Jr. 7-Eleven

This 27-card set of Hartford Whalers was issued by 7-Eleven and sent out as a premium to all members of the Hartford Junior Whalers. This set features full-color photographs on the front while the backs contain the same information about the players that is available in the media guides. The set has been checklisted alphabetically for convenient reference. The set measures approximately 3 3/4" by 8 1/4" and has the players of the Hartford Whalers along with a special Gordie Howe card. Four cards (3, 12, 19, 20) were added to the set at the end of the season and their backs are blank.

COMPLETE SET (27)	8.00	20.00
1 Mikael Andersson	.20	.50
2 Dave Babych	.30	.75
3 Rob Brown SP	.80	2.00
4 Yvon Corriveau	.20	.50
5 Sylvain Cote	.20	.50
6 Doug Crossman	.20	.50
7 Randy Cunneyworth	.20	.50
8 Paul Cyr	.20	.50
9 Kevin Dineen	.40	1.00
10 Dean Evason	.20	.50
11 Ron Francis	.80	2.00
12 Chris Govedaris SP	.80	2.00
13 Bobby Holik	.40	1.00
14 Gordie Howe	2.00	5.00
15 Grant Jennings	.20	.50
16 Ed Kastelic	.20	.50
17 Todd Krygier	.20	.50
18 Randy Ladouceur	.20	.50
19 Jim McKenzie SP	.80	2.00
20 Daryl Reaugh SP	1.00	2.50
21 Ulf Samuelsson	.40	1.00
22 Brad Shaw	.30	.75
23 Peter Sidorkiewicz	.30	.75
24 Mike Tomlak	.20	.50
25 Pat Verbeek	.60	1.50
26 Carey Wilson	.20	.50
27 Scott Young	.30	.75

1991-92 Whalers Jr. 7-Eleven

This 28-card set of Hartford Whalers was issued by 7-Eleven and sent out as a premium to all members of the Hartford Junior Whalers. This set features full-color photographs on the front while the backs contain the same information about the players that is available in the media guides. The set has been checklisted alphabetically for convenient reference. The set measures approximately 3 3/4" by 8 1/4" and contains the players of the Hartford Whalers. Six cards (3, 6, 10, 12, 18, 19) were issued late in the season and their backs are blank.

COMPLETE SET (28)	8.00	20.00
1 Mikael Andersson	.20	.50
2 Marc Bergevin	.20	.50
3 James Black SP	.60	1.50
4 Rob Brown	.24	.60
5 Adam Burt	.20	.50
6 Andrew Cassels SP	1.20	3.00
7 Murray Craven	.30	.75
8 John Cullen	.40	1.00
9 Randy Cunneyworth	.20	.50
10 Paul Cyr SP	.60	1.50
11 Joe Day	.20	.50
12 Paul Gillis SP	.60	1.50
13 Mark Greig	.20	.50
14 Bobby Holik	.30	.75
15 Doug Houda	.20	.50
16 Mark Hunter	.20	.50
17 Ed Kastelic	.20	.50
18 Dan Keczmer SP	.80	2.00
19 Steve Konroyd SP	.60	1.50
20 Randy Ladouceur	.20	.50
21 Jim McKenzie	.20	.50
22 Michel Picard	.20	.50
23 Geoff Sanderson	2.00	5.00
24 Brad Shaw	.24	.60
25 Peter Sidorkiewicz	.30	.75
26 Pat Verbeek	.60	1.50
27 Kay Whitmore	.30	.75
28 Zarley Zalapski	.30	.75

1992-93 Whalers Dairymart

Sponsored by Dairymart, this 26-card set was issued to members of the team's Kid's Club. Each features a white-bordered glossy color studio head shot on a card that measures approximately 2 3/8" by 3 1/2". The Dairymart and Whalers logos are displayed above the player photo, and the player's name and position, along with "1992-93 Hartford Whalers," appear beneath his image. The white horizontal back carries the player's name, uniform number, position, and biography above a stat table. The cards are unnumbered and checklisted below in alphabetical order.

COMPLETE SET (26)	7.20	18.00
1 Jim Agnew	.20	.50
2 Sean Burke	.60	1.50
3 Adam Burt	.20	.50
4 Andrew Cassels	.40	1.00
5 Murray Craven	.24	.60
6 Randy Cunneyworth	.20	.50
7 Paul Gillis	.20	.50
8 Paul Holmgren CO	.20	.50
9 Doug Houda	.20	.50
10 Mark Janssens	.20	.50
11 Tim Kerr	.30	.75
12 Steve Konroyd	.20	.50
13 Nick Kypreos	.20	.50
14 Randy Ladouceur	.20	.50
15 Jim McKenzie	.20	.50
16 Michael Nylander	.40	1.00
17 Allen Pedersen	.20	.50
18 Robert Petrovicky	.20	.50
19 Frank Pietrangelo	.30	.75
20 Patrick Poulin	.20	.50
21 Geoff Sanderson	1.60	4.00
22 Pat Verbeek	.60	1.50
23 Eric Weinrich	.20	.50
24 Terry Yake	.20	.50
25 Zarley Zalapski	.20	.50
26 Junior Whalers Member Card	.10	.25

1993-94 Whalers Coke

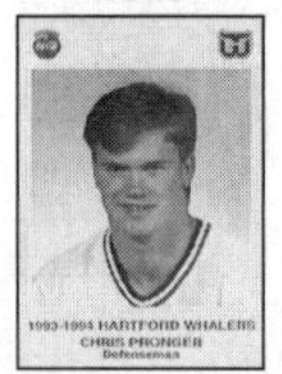

Sponsored by Coca-Cola, this 24-card set features white-bordered color studio head shots on cards that measure approximately 2 3/8" by 3 1/2". The white horizontal backs carry the player's name, uniform number, position, and biography above a stat table. The cards were issued to members of the Junior Whalers club, and as they are unnumbered, they are checklisted below in alphabetical order.

COMPLETE SET (24)	7.20	18.00
1 Sean Burke	.80	2.00
2 Adam Burt	.20	.50
3 Andrew Cassels	.40	1.00
4 Randy Cunneyworth	.20	.50
5 Alexander Godynyuk	.20	.50
6 Mark Greig	.20	.50
7 Mark Janssens	.20	.50
8 Robert Kron	.20	.50
9 Bryan Marchment	.20	.50
10 Brad McCrimmon	.20	.50
11 Pierre McGuire CO	.10	.25
12 Michael Nylander	.30	.75
13 James Patrick	.20	.50
14 Frank Pietrangelo	.30	.75
15 Marc Potvin	.20	.50
16 Chris Pronger	1.20	3.00
17 Brian Propp	.30	.75
18 Jeff Reese	.30	.75
19 Geoff Sanderson	.80	2.00
20 Jim Sandlak	.20	.50
21 Jim Storm	.20	.50
22 Darren Turcotte	.30	.75
23 Pat Verbeek	.60	1.50
24 Zarley Zalapski	.20	.50

1995-96 Whalers Bob's Stores

This set features the Whalers of the NHL. The standard-sized cards were issued to members of the team's Junior Whalers kid's club. The cards are unnumbered, and so are listed below in alphabetical order.

COMPLETE SET (27)	4.80	12.00
1 Sean Burke	.30	.75
2 Adam Burke	.16	.40
3 Andrew Cassels	.16	.40
4 Kelly Chase	.16	.40
5 Scott Daniels	.16	.40
6 Gerald Diduck	.16	.40
7 Nelson Emerson	.24	.60
8 Glen Featherstone	.16	.40
9 Brian Glynn	.16	.40
10 Mark Janssens	.16	.40
11 Robert Kron	.16	.40
12 Frantisek Kucera	.16	.40
13 Jocelyn Lemieux	.16	.40
14 Marek Malik	.16	.40
15 Steve Martins	.16	.40
16 Paul Maurice CO	.10	.25
17 Brad McCrimmon	.16	.40
18 Jason Muzzatti	.16	.40
19 Andrei Nikolishin	.16	.40
20 Jeff O'Neill	.16	.40
21 Paul Ranheim	.16	.40
22 Steven Rice	.16	.40
23 Geoff Sanderson	.24	.60
24 Brendan Shanahan	1.20	3.00
25 Kevin Smyth	.16	.40
26 Glen Wesley	.24	.60
27 Kids Club Discount Card	.04	.10

1996-97 Whalers Kid's Club

This set features the Whalers of the NHL. The cards were produced by the team for distribution to members of its Kid's Club. The cards of Steve Chiasson and Kent Manderville were available only in sets issued late in the season. The Kevin Brown card is not necessary for the complete set. The photo features him with the Springfield Falcons, the Whalers' farm team, the background is a different color, and the stock is noticeably thinner.

COMPLETE SET (28)	14.00	35.00
1 Sean Burke	.80	2.00
2 Jason Muzzatti	.60	1.50
3 Kevin Dineen	.60	1.50
4 Geoff Sanderson	.60	1.50
5 Keith Primeau	.80	2.00
6 Jeff O'Neill	.80	2.00
7 Marek Malik	.40	1.00
8 Paul Ranheim	.40	1.00
9 Alexander Godynyuk	.40	1.00
10 Robert Kron	.40	1.00
11 Gerald Diduck	.40	1.00
12 Kelly Chase	.40	1.00
13 Glen Wesley	.40	1.00
14 Andrew Cassels	.60	1.50
15 Hnat Domenichelli	.40	1.00
16 Sami Kapanen	.80	2.00
17 Nelson Emerson	.60	1.50
18 Mark Janssens	.40	1.00
19 Stu Grimson	.80	2.00
20 Nolan Pratt	.40	1.00
21 Glen Featherstone	.40	1.00
22 Curtis Leschyshyn	.40	1.00
23 Jeff Brown	.40	1.00
24 Adam Burt	.40	1.00
25 Steven Rice	.40	1.00
26 Kevin Brown	1.20	3.00
27 Steve Chiasson	1.20	3.00
28 Kent Manderville	1.20	3.00

1960-61 Wonder Bread Labels

Similar to Wonder Bread Premium Photos, these are the actual labels that were wrapped around the Wonder Bread packages. Little is known about them, and few are confirmed to exist, so no prices have been established.

1 Gordie Howe
2 Bobby Hull
3 Dave Keon
4 Maurice Richard

1960-61 Wonder Bread Premium Photos

Produced and issued in Canada, the 1960-61 Wonder Bread set features four hockey stars. This set of premium photos measure approximately 5" by 7" and are unnumbered. There were actually two sets produced: Bread Labels and Premium Photos. The bread labels are valued at 50 to 100 percent of the values listed below. Reportedly the premium photo was inside the bread package and there was also a small picture of the player on the end of the bread wrapper. Keon's photo is noteworthy for preceding his RC by one year.

COMPLETE SET (4)	300.00	600.00
1 Gordie Howe	150.00	300.00
2 Bobby Hull	100.00	200.00
3 Dave Keon	40.00	80.00
4 Maurice Richard	100.00	200.00

2001-02 Wild Crime Prevention

These eight cards are part of a larger 24-card set that also features players from the Minnesota Twins and Vikings. The cards are standard sized and were issued by local police.

COMPLETE SET (8)	4.00	20.00
17 Willie Mitchell	.40	1.00
18 Marian Gaborik	2.00	15.00
19 Darby Hendrickson	.40	1.00
20 Andrew Brunette	.40	1.00
21 Sergei Zholtok	.40	1.00
22 Jim Dowd	.40	1.00
23 Manny Fernandez	.60	1.50
24 Nick Schultz	.40	1.00

2001-02 Wild Team Issue

These oversized (5X8) team issues feature player photos on the front and stats on the back. The sponsor (SBC) appears on all three, but just two (Fernandez and Mitchell) have text reading Limited Edition, 1 of 2,500. It's not known whether these cards actually are from the same set (which is assumed) or not. The checklist is far from complete -- if you know of additional cards, please email us at hockeymag@beckett.com.

COMPLETE SET (?)	
1 Manny Fernandez	2.00
2 Stacy Roest	1.00
3 Willie Mitchell	1.00

2003-04 Wild Law Enforcement Cards

These cards were handed out by local police in the St. Paul area. They are unnumbered and listed below in alphabetical order. It's quite likely that more cards exist. Please contact us at hockeymag@beckett.com if you can confirm.

COMPLETE SET (11)	
1 Brad Bombardir	1.00
2 Pierre-Marc Bouchard	3.00
3 Marian Gaborik	3.00
4 Filip Kuba	1.00
5 Willie Mitchell	1.00
6 Richard Park	1.00
7 Dwayne Roloson	2.00
8 Nick Schultz	1.00
9 Wes Walz	1.00
10 Sergei Zholtok	1.00
11 McGruff the Crime Dog	.10

2006-07 Wild Crime Prevention

1 Pavol Demitra	.40	1.00
2 Kim Johnsson	.40	1.00
3 Keith Carney	.40	1.00
4 Mark Parrish	.40	1.00
5 Brian Rolston	.40	1.00
6 Kurtis Foster	.40	1.00
7 Mikko Koivu	.75	2.00
8 Marian Gaborik	2.00	5.00
9 McGruff the Crime Dog	.10	.25

1960-61 York Photos

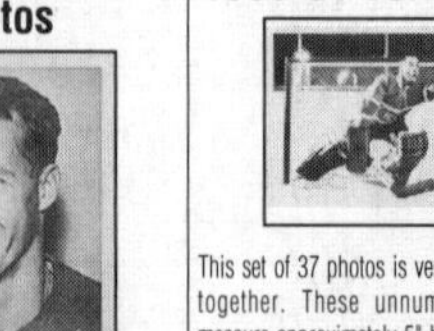

This set of 37 photos is very difficult to put together. These unnumbered photos measure approximately 5" by 7" and feature members of the Montreal Canadiens (MC) and Toronto Maple Leafs (TML). The checklist below is ordered alphabetically. These large black and white cards were supposedly available from York Peanut Butter as a mail-in premium in return for two proofs of purchase; unfortunately there are no identifying marking on the photo that indicate the producer or the year of issue. The photos are action shots with a facsimile autograph of the player on the photo. The cards were apparently issued very late in the 1960-61 season since the set includes Eddie Shack as a Maple Leaf (he was acquired by Toronto from the Rangers during the 1960-61 season), Gilles Tremblay (his first NHL season was 1960-61 with the Canadiens), and several players (Jean-Guy Gendron, Larry Regan, Bob Turner) who were with other teams for the 1961-62 season.

COMPLETE SET (37)	1200.00	2400.00
1 George Armstrong TML	30.00	60.00
2 Ralph Backstrom MC	25.00	50.00
3 Bob Baun TML	30.00	60.00
4 Jean Beliveau MC	87.50	175.00
5 Marcel Bonin MC	17.50	35.00
6 Johnny Bower TML	62.50	125.00
7 Carl Brewer TML	25.00	50.00
8 Dick Duff TML	25.00	50.00
9 Jean-Guy Gendron MC	17.50	35.00
10 Boom Boom Geoffrion MC	62.50	125.00
11 Phil Goyette MC	17.50	35.00
12 Billy Harris TML	17.50	35.00
13 Doug Harvey MC	50.00	100.00
14 Bill Hicke MC	17.50	35.00
15 Larry Hillman TML	17.50	35.00
16 Charlie Hodge MC	25.00	50.00
17 Tim Horton TML	87.50	175.00
18 Tom Johnson MC	25.00	50.00
19 Red Kelly TML	30.00	60.00
20 Dave Keon TML	62.50	125.00
21 Albert Langlois MC	17.50	35.00
22 Frank Mahovlich TML	62.50	125.00
23 Don Marshall MC	25.00	50.00
24 Dickie Moore MC	30.00	60.00
25 Bob Nevin TML	17.50	35.00
26 Bert Olmstead TML	30.00	60.00
27 Jacques Plante MC	175.00	350.00
28 Claude Provost MC	25.00	50.00
29 Bob Pulford TML	30.00	60.00
30 Larry Regan TML	17.50	35.00
31 Henri Richard MC	62.50	125.00
32 Eddie Shack TML	50.00	100.00
33 Allan Stanley TML	30.00	60.00
34 Ron Stewart TML	17.50	35.00
35 Jean-Guy Talbot MC	25.00	50.00
36 Gilles Tremblay MC	25.00	50.00
37 Bob Turner MC	17.50	35.00

1961-62 York Yellow Backs

This set of 42 octagonal cards was issued by York Peanut Butter. The cards are numbered on the backs at the top. An album was originally available as a send-in offer or at certain food stores for 25 cents. The cards measure approximately 2 1/2" in diameter. The set can be dated as a 1961-62 set by referring to the career totals given on the back of each player's cards. The card backs were written in both French and English. The set is considered complete without the album.

COMPLETE SET (42)	300.00	600.00
1 Bob Baun	7.50	15.00
2 Dick Duff	6.00	12.00
3 Frank Mahovlich	12.50	25.00
4 Gilles Tremblay	5.00	10.00
5 Dickie Moore	7.50	15.00
6 Don Marshall	5.00	10.00
7 Tim Horton	15.00	30.00
8 Johnny Bower	10.00	20.00
9 Allan Stanley	7.50	15.00
10 Jean Beliveau	20.00	40.00
11 Tom Johnson	7.50	15.00
12 Jean-Guy Talbot	6.00	12.00
13 Carl Brewer	5.00	10.00
14 Bob Pulford	7.50	15.00
15 Billy Harris	5.00	10.00
16 Bill Hicke	5.00	10.00
17 Claude Provost	6.00	12.00
18 Henri Richard	12.50	25.00
19 Bert Olmstead	7.50	15.00
20 Ron Stewart	5.00	10.00
21 Red Kelly	7.50	15.00
22 Hector(Toe) Blake CO	7.50	15.00
23 Jacques Plante	25.00	50.00
24 Ralph Backstrom	6.00	12.00
25 Eddie Shack	10.00	20.00
26 Bob Nevin	5.00	10.00
27 Dave Keon	20.00	40.00
28 Boom Boom Geoffrion	10.00	20.00
29 Marcel Bonin	5.00	10.00
30 Phil Goyette	5.00	10.00
31 Larry Hillman	5.00	10.00
32 Larry Keenan	5.00	10.00
33 Al Arbour	7.50	15.00
34 J.C. Tremblay	6.00	12.00
35 Bobby Rousseau	5.00	10.00
36 Al McNeil	5.00	10.00
37 George Armstrong	7.50	15.00
38 Punch Imlach CO	6.00	12.00
39 King Clancy	10.00	20.00
40 Lou Fontinato	5.00	10.00
41 Cesare Maniago	7.50	15.00
42 Jean Gauthier	5.00	10.00
xx Album	20.00	40.00

1962-63 York Iron-On Transfers

These iron-on transfers are very difficult to find. They measure approximately 2 1/4" by 4 1/4". There is some dispute with regard to the year of issue but the 1962-63 season seems to be a likely date based on the careers of the players included in the set. These transfers are numbered at the bottom.

COMPLETE SET (36)	900.00	1800.00
1 Johnny Bower	25.00	50.00
2 Jacques Plante	75.00	150.00
3 Tim Horton	50.00	100.00
4 Jean-Guy Talbot	15.00	30.00
5 Carl Brewer	15.00	30.00
6 J.C. Tremblay	15.00	30.00
7 Dick Duff	15.00	30.00
8 Jean Beliveau	50.00	100.00
9 Dave Keon	25.00	50.00
10 Henri Richard	40.00	80.00
11 Frank Mahovlich	40.00	80.00
12 BoomBoom Geoffrion	25.00	50.00
13 Kent Douglas	12.50	25.00
14 Claude Provost	15.00	30.00
15 Bob Pulford	15.00	30.00
16 Ralph Backstrom	15.00	30.00
17 George Armstrong	20.00	40.00
18 Bobby Rousseau	12.50	25.00
19 Gordie Howe	125.00	250.00
20 Red Kelly	20.00	40.00
21 Alex Delvecchio	20.00	40.00
22 Dickie Moore	20.00	40.00
23 Marcel Pronovost	15.00	30.00
24 Doug Barkley	12.50	25.00
25 Terry Sawchuk	50.00	100.00
26 Billy Harris	12.50	25.00
27 Parker MacDonald	12.50	25.00
28 Don Marshall	12.50	25.00
29 Norm Ullman	25.00	50.00
30A Andre Pronovost	12.50	25.00
30B Vic Stasiuk	12.50	25.00
31 Bill Gadsby	15.00	30.00
32 Eddie Shack	25.00	50.00
33 Larry Jeffrey	12.50	25.00
34 Gilles Tremblay	12.50	25.00
35 Howie Young	12.50	25.00
36 Bruce MacGregor	12.50	25.00

1963-64 York White Backs

This set of 54 octagonal cards was issued with York Peanut Butter and York Salted Nuts. The cards are numbered on the backs at the top. The cards measure approximately 2 1/2" in diameter. The set can be dated as a 1963-64 set by referring to the career totals given on the back of each player's cards. The card backs were written in both French and English. An album was originally available for holding the set; the set is considered complete without the album.

COMPLETE SET (54)	375.00	750.00
1 Tim Horton	20.00	40.00
2 Johnny Bower	12.50	25.00
3 Ron Stewart	7.50	15.00
4 Eddie Shack	12.50	25.00
5 Frank Mahovlich	15.00	30.00
6 Dave Keon	15.00	30.00
7 Bob Baun	7.50	15.00
8 Bob Nevin	7.50	15.00
9 Dick Duff	7.50	15.00
10 Billy Harris	7.50	15.00
11 Larry Hillman	7.50	15.00
12 Red Kelly	10.00	20.00
13 Kent Douglas	7.50	15.00
14 Allan Stanley	7.50	15.00
15 Don Simmons	7.50	15.00
16 George Armstrong	10.00	20.00
17 Carl Brewer	7.50	15.00
18 Bob Pulford	7.50	15.00
19 Henri Richard	15.00	30.00
20 BoomBoom Geoffrion	12.50	25.00
21 Gilles Tremblay	7.50	15.00
22 Gump Worsley	12.50	25.00
23 Jean-Guy Talbot	7.50	15.00
24 J.C. Tremblay	7.50	15.00
25 Bobby Rousseau	7.50	15.00
26 Jean Beliveau	20.00	40.00
27 Ralph Backstrom	7.50	15.00
28 Claude Provost	7.50	15.00
29 Jean Gauthier	7.50	15.00
30 Bill Hicke	7.50	15.00
31 Terry Harper	7.50	15.00
32 Marc Reaume	7.50	15.00
33 Dave Balon	7.50	15.00
34 Jacques Laperriere	10.00	20.00
35 John Ferguson	10.00	20.00
36 Red Berenson	7.50	15.00
37 Terry Sawchuk	25.00	50.00
38 Marcel Pronovost	7.50	15.00
39 Bill Gadsby	10.00	20.00
40 Parker MacDonald	7.50	15.00
41 Larry Jeffrey	7.50	15.00
42 Floyd Smith	7.50	15.00
43 Andre Pronovost	7.50	15.00
44 Art Stratton	7.50	15.00
45 Gordie Howe	50.00	100.00
46 Doug Barkley	7.50	15.00
47 Norm Ullman	10.00	20.00
48 Eddie Joyal	7.50	15.00
49 Alex Faulkner	15.00	30.00
50 Alex Delvecchio	10.00	20.00
51 Bruce MacGregor	7.50	15.00
52 Ted Hampson	7.50	15.00
53 Pete Goegan	7.50	15.00
54 Ron Ingram	7.50	15.00
xx Album	20.00	40.00

1967-68 York Action Octagons

This 36-card set was issued by York Peanut Butter. Only cards 13-36 are numbered. The twelve unnumbered cards have been assigned the numbers 1-12 based on alphabetizing the names of the first player listed on each card. Each card shows an action scene involving two or three players. Uniform numbers are also given on the cards. The card backs give the details of a send-in contest ending June 30, 1968. Collecting four cards spelling "YORK" entitled one to receive a Bobby Hull Hockey Game. These octagonal cards measure approximately 2 7/8" in diameter. The card backs were written in both French and English.

COMPLETE SET (36)	300.00	600.00
1 Brian Conacher 22	7.50	15.00
Allan Stanley 26		
Leon Rochefort 25		
2 Terry Harper 19	10.00	20.00
Gump Worsley 30		
Mike Walton 16		
3 Tim Horton 7	20.00	40.00
George Armstrong 10		
Jean Beliveau 4		
4 Dave Keon 14	10.00	20.00
George Armstrong 10		
Claude Provost 14		
5 Jacques Laperriere 2	10.00	20.00
Rogatien Vachon 29		
Bob Pulford 20		
6 Bob Pulford 20	6.00	12.00
Brian Conacher 22		
Claude Provost 14		
7 Bob Pulford 20	6.00	12.00
Jim Pappin 18		
Terry Harper 19		
8 Pete Stemkowski 12	6.00	12.00
Jim Pappin 18		
Harris 10		
9 J.C. Tremblay 3	7.50	15.00
Rogatien Vachon 29		
Pete Stemkowski 12		
10 Rogatien Vachon 29	10.00	20.00
Ralph Backstrom 6		
Bob Pulford 20		
11 Rogatien Vachon 29	10.00	20.00
Jacques Laperriere 2		
Mike Walton 16		
12 Mike Walton 16	6.00	12.00
Pete Stemkowski 12		
J.C. Tremblay 3		
13 Dave Keon 14	7.50	15.00
Mike Walton 16		
J.C. Tremblay 3		
14 Pete Stemkowski 12	5.00	10.00
Ralph Backstrom 6		
Rogatien Vachon 29		
15 Rogatien Vachon 29	7.50	15.00
Bob Pulford 20		
16 Johnny Bower 1	7.50	15.00
Ron Ellis 8		
John Ferguson 22		
17 Ron Ellis 8	7.50	15.00
Gump Worsley 30		
18 Gump Worsley 30	12.50	25.00
Jacques Laperriere 2		
Frank Mahovlich 27		
19 J.C. Tremblay 3	7.50	15.00
Dave Keon 14		
20 Claude Provost 14	10.00	20.00
Frank Mahovlich 27		
21 John Ferguson 22	10.00	20.00
Tim Horton 7		
22 Gump Worsley 30	7.50	15.00
Ron Ellis 8		
23 Johnny Bower 1	10.00	20.00
Mike Walton 16		
Jean Beliveau 4		
24 J.C. Tremblay 3	7.50	15.00
Gump Worsley 30		
Bob Pulford 20		
25 Tim Horton 7	15.00	30.00
Johnny Bower 1		
Jean Beliveau 4		
26 Allan Stanley 26	7.50	15.00
Johnny Bower 1		
Dick Duff 8		
27 Ralph Backstrom 6	7.50	15.00
Johnny Bower 1		
28 Yvan Cournoyer 12	20.00	40.00
Jean Beliveau 4		
Frank Mahovlich 27		
29 Johnny Bower 1	10.00	20.00
Larry Hillman 2		
Yvan Cournoyer 12		
30 Johnny Bower 1	10.00	20.00
Yvan Cournoyer 12		
31 Tim Horton 7	10.00	20.00
Rogatien Vachon 29		
32 Jim Pappin 18	7.50	15.00
Bob Pulford 20		
Rogatien Vachon 29		
33 Terry Harper 19	5.00	10.00
Bobby Rousseau 15		
Pronovost 3		
34 Johnny Bower 1	6.00	12.00
Pronovost 3		
Ralph Backstrom 6		
35 Frank Mahovlich 27	12.50	25.00
Gump Worsley 30		
36 Claude Provost 14	6.00	12.00
Johnny Bower 1		

1992-93 Zeller's Masters of Hockey

This seven-card "Signature Series" standard-size set, featuring former NHL greats, was a promotion by Zeller's. According to the certificate of authenticity, the production run was 1,000 sets. The cards have posed color player photos inside white borders. A blue stripe above the picture carries the player's name and is accented by a thin mustard stripe. A silver foil facsimile signature is inscribed across the picture. The backs have the blue and mustard stripes running down the left side and carrying the player's jersey number. In English and French, biography, career highlights, and statistics are included on a white background. A close-up color player photo with a shadow border partially overlaps the stripe near the top. The cards are unnumbered and checklisted below in alphabetical order. There was also a large Marcel Dionne card reportedly given out at various store signings.

COMPLETE SET (7)	8.00	20.00
1 Johnny Bower	1.20	3.00
2 Rod Gilbert	1.20	3.00
3 Ted Lindsay	1.20	3.00
4 Frank Mahovlich	1.60	4.00
5 Stan Mikita	1.60	4.00
6 Maurice Richard	2.40	6.00
7 Certificate of Authenticity		.01

1992-93 Zeller's Masters of Hockey Signed

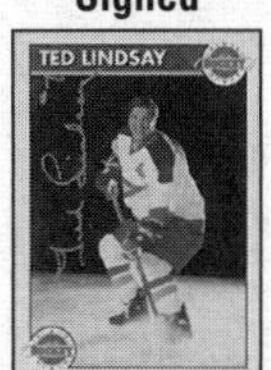

This set features cards signed by former NHL greats and was distributed by Canadian retailing giant Zeller's. It is believed that approximately 1,000 copies exist of each card. We cannot confirm exactly how they were distributed at this point, although it is believed they could be acquired through a Zeller's customer loyalty program. Any further information can be forwarded to hockeymag@beckett.com.

COMPLETE SET (7)	50.00	125.00
1 Johnny Bower	6.00	15.00
2 Rod Gilbert	6.00	15.00
3 Ted Lindsay	6.00	15.00
4 Frank Mahovlich	0.00	20.00
5 Stan Mikita	8.00	20.00
6 Maurice Richard	24.00	60.00
7 Certificate of Authenticity		.01

1993-94 Zeller's Masters of Hockey

Featuring former NHL greats, this 8-card "Signature Series" marks the second consecutive year a promotion was issued by Zellers. The cards measure the standard size and have posed color player photos inside white borders. A blue stripe above the picture carries the player's name and is accented by a thin mustard stripe. A silver foil facsimile signature is inscribed across the picture. The backs have the blue and mustard stripes running down the left side and carrying the player's jersey number. In English and French, biography, career highlights, and statistics are included on a white background. A close-up color player photo with a shadow border partially overlaps the stripe near the top. The cards are unnumbered and checklisted below in alphabetical order.

COMPLETE SET (8)	6.00	15.00
1 Andy Bathgate	.40	1.00
2 Johnny Bucyk	.80	2.00
3 Yvan Cournoyer	.80	2.00
4 Marcel Dionne	.80	2.00
5 Bobby Hull	1.60	4.00
6 Brad Park	.80	2.00
7 Jean Ratelle	.80	2.00
8 Gump Worsley	1.00	2.50
NNO Marcel Dionne Large	.40	1.00

1993-94 Zeller's Masters of Hockey Signed

This set features cards signed by former NHL greats and was distributed by Canadian retailing giant Zeller's. It is believed that approximately 2,000 copies exist of each card. We cannot confirm exactly how they were distributed at this point, although it is believed they could be acquired through a Zeller's customer loyalty program. Any further information can be forwarded to hockeymag@beckett.com.

COMPLETE SET (8)	60.00	150.00
1 Andy Bathgate	6.00	15.00
2 Johnny Bucyk	10.00	25.00
3 Yvan Cournoyer	10.00	25.00
4 Marcel Dionne	10.00	25.00
5 Bobby Hull	16.00	40.00
6 Brad Park	10.00	25.00
7 Jean Ratelle	6.00	15.00
8 Gump Worsley	10.00	25.00
NNO Marcel Dionne Large		

1994-95 Zeller's Masters of Hockey

For the third consecutive year, Zeller's issued an 8-card "Signature Series" set, featuring former NHL greats. The cards measure the standard size and have posed color player photos inside white borders. A blue stripe above the picture carries the player's name and is accented by a thin mustard stripe. A silver foil facsimile signature is inscribed across the picture. The backs have the blue and mustard stripes running down the left side and carrying the player's jersey number. In English and French, biography, career highlights, and statistics are included on a white background. A close-up color player photo with a shadow border partially overlaps the stripe near the top. The cards are unnumbered and checklisted below in alphabetical order.

COMPLETE SET (8)	4.00	10.00
1 Jean Beliveau	1.60	4.00
2 Gerry Cheevers	.80	2.00
3 Red Kelly	.80	2.00
4 Dave Keon	.80	2.00
5 Lanny McDonald	.40	1.00
6 Pierre Pilote	.40	1.00
7 Henri Richard	.80	2.00
8 Norm Ullman	.80	2.00
NNO Jean Beliveau Large	.80	2.00

1994-95 Zeller's Masters of Hockey Signed

This set features cards signed by former NHL greats and was distributed by Canadian retailing giant Zeller's. It is believed that approximately 1,100 copies exist of each card. We cannot confirm exactly how they were distributed at this point, although it is believed they could be acquired through a Zeller's customer loyalty program. Any further information can be forwarded to hockeymag@beckett.com.

COMPLETE SET (8)	50.00	125.00
1 Jean Beliveau	12.00	30.00
2 Gerry Cheevers	6.00	15.00
3 Red Kelly	6.00	15.00
4 Dave Keon	6.00	15.00
5 Lanny McDonald	6.00	15.00
6 Pierre Pilote	6.00	15.00
7 Henri Richard	8.00	20.00
8 Norm Ullman	6.00	15.00

1995-96 Zeller's Masters of Hockey Signed

This set features cards signed by former NHL greats and was distributed by Canadian retailing giant Zeller's. It is believed that approximately 3,500 copies exist of each card. Unlike previous years, it is thought that there were no un-signed versions released. We cannot confirm exactly how they were distributed at this point, although it is believed they could be acquired through a Zeller's customer loyalty program. Any further information can be forwarded to hockeymag@beckett.com.

COMPLETE SET (8)	70.00	175.00
1 Mike Bossy	10.00	25.00
2 Eddie Giacomin	6.00	15.00
3 Gordie Howe	20.00	50.00
4 Jacques Laperriere	6.00	15.00
5 Gilbert Perreault	8.00	20.00
6 Serge Savard	6.00	15.00
7 Steve Shutt	6.00	15.00
8 Darryl Sittler	8.00	20.00

1995-96 Zenith

The 1995-96 Zenith set was issued in one series totaling 150 standard-size cards. The 6-card packs had a suggested retail of $3.99. The set features 24-point card stock with exclusive Dufex all-foil printing.

COMPLETE SET (150)	15.00	40.00
1 Brett Hull	.30	.75
2 Paul Coffey	.25	.60
3 Jaromir Jagr	.40	1.00
4 Joe Murphy	.08	.25
5 Jim Carey	.15	.40
6 Eric Lindros	.25	.60
7 Ulf Dahlen	.08	.25
8 Mark Recchi	.15	.40
9 Pavel Bure	.25	.60
10 Adam Oates	.15	.40
11 Theo Fleury	.08	.25
12 Martin Brodeur	.75	2.00
13 Wayne Gretzky	2.00	5.00
14 Geoff Sanderson	.08	.25
15 Chris Gratton	.08	.25
16 Owen Nolan	.15	.40
17 Paul Kariya	.25	.60
18 Mark Messier	.25	.60
19 Mats Sundin	.25	.60
20 Brian Savage	.08	.25
21 Mathieu Schneider	.08	.25
22 Alexandre Daigle	.08	.25
23 Jason Arnott	.08	.25
24 Mike Modano	.40	1.00
25 Scott Mellanby	.08	.25
26 Alexei Zhamnov	.15	.40
27 Scott Niedermayer	.08	.25
28 Chris Pronger	.25	.60
29 Ray Bourque	.30	.75
30 Sergei Fedorov	.60	1.50
31 Alexander Mogilny	.15	.40
32 Brian Leetch	.15	.40
33 Adam Graves	.08	.25
34 Jocelyn Thibault	.25	.60
35 Ron Francis	.15	.40
36 John Vanbiesbrouck	.15	.40
37 Chris Chelios	.25	.60
38 Pierre Turgeon	.15	.40
39 Stephane Richer	.15	.40
40 Al MacInnis	.15	.40
41 Dave Andreychuk	.15	.40
42 Mikael Renberg	.15	.40
43 Nelson Emerson	.08	.25
44 Kevin Hatcher	.08	.25
45 Kirk Muller	.08	.25
46 Bernie Nicholls	.08	.25
47 Bill Ranford	.15	.40
48 Luc Robitaille	.15	.40
49 Peter Bondra	.15	.40
50 Jari Kurri	.25	.60
51 Dino Ciccarelli	.15	.40
52 Kevin Stevens	.08	.25
53 Mike Richter	.25	.60
54 Doug Gilmour	.15	.40
55 Kelly Hrudey	.15	.40
56 Dave Gagner	.08	.25
57 Kirk McLean	.15	.40
58 Geoff Courtnall	.08	.25
59 John LeClair	.25	.60
60 Mike Vernon	.15	.40
61 Cam Neely	.25	.60
62 Mike Gartner	.15	.40
63 Igor Korolev	.08	.25
64 Joe Sakic	.60	1.50
65 Jeff Friesen	.08	.25
66 Sergei Zubov	.08	.25
67 Trevor Kidd	.15	.40
68 Rod Brind'Amour	.15	.40
69 John MacLean	.15	.40
70 Peter Forsberg	.60	1.50
71 Oleg Tverdovsky	.08	.25
72 Jeremy Roenick	.30	.75
73 Gary Suter	.08	.25
74 Keith Tkachuk	.25	.60
75 Todd Harvey	.15	.40
76 Felix Potvin	.25	.60
77 Vincent Damphousse	.08	.25
78 Blaine Lacher	.15	.40
79 Tomas Sandstrom	.08	.25
80 Chris Osgood	.15	.40
81 Arturs Irbe	.15	.40
82 Pat Verbeek	.08	.25
83 Keith Primeau	.08	.25
84 Brett Lindros	.08	.25
85 Pat LaFontaine	.25	.60
86 Brendan Shanahan	.25	.60
87 Trevor Linden	.15	.40
88 Rob Blake	.15	.40
89 Scott Stevens	.15	.40
90 Tom Barrasso	.15	.40
91 Mike Ricci	.15	.40
92 Ray Sheppard	.08	.25
93 Steve Yzerman	1.00	2.50
94 Wendel Clark	.15	.40
95 Ed Belfour	.25	.60
96 Joe Juneau	.08	.25
97 Ron Hextall	.15	.40
98 Shayne Corson	.08	.25
99 Guy Hebert	.15	.40
100 Sean Burke	.15	.40
101 Sandis Ozolinsh	.08	.25
102 Teemu Selanne	.25	.60
103 Petr Nedved	.15	.40
104 Phil Housley	.15	.40
105 Andy Moog	.25	.60
106 Larry Murphy	.15	.40
107 Grant Fuhr	.25	.60
108 Mario Lemieux	1.25	3.00
109 Dominik Hasek	.60	1.50
110 Rob Niedermayer	.15	.40
111 Steve Duchesne	.08	.25
112 Joe Nieuwendyk	.15	.40
113 Yanic Perreault	.08	.25
114 Steve Thomas	.15	.40
115 Russ Courtnall	.08	.25
116 Claude Lemieux	.08	.25
117 Patrick Roy	1.25	3.00
118 Rick Tocchet	.15	.40
119 Stephane Fiset	.15	.40
120 Daren Puppa	.15	.40
121 Ed Jovanovski	.25	.60
122 Eric Daze	.15	.40
123 Cory Stillman RC	.08	.25
124 Brendan Witt	.08	.25
125 Valeri Bure	.08	.25
126 Brian Holzinger RC	.15	.40
127 Kyle McLaren RC	.08	.25
128 Niklas Sundstrom	.15	.40
129 Jamie Langenbrunner	.15	.40
130 Jeff O'Neill	.08	.25
131 Vitali Yachmenev	.08	.25
132 Shane Doan RC	1.25	3.00
133 Byron Dafoe RC	.15	.40
134 Corey Hirsch	.15	.40
135 Antti Tormanen RC	.08	.25
136 Jason Bonsignore	.08	.25
137 Ryan Smyth	.15	.40
138 Bryan McCabe RC	.08	.25
139 Chad Kilger RC	.08	.25
140 Todd Bertuzzi RC	1.25	3.00
141 Marcus Ragnarsson RC	.15	.40
142 Marty Murray	.25	.60
143 Daymond Langkow RC	.25	.60
144 Saku Koivu	.25	.60
145 Jere Lehtinen	.15	.40
146 Aki-Petteri Berg RC	.15	.40
147 Radek Dvorak RC	.25	.60
148 Robert Svehla RC	.08	.25
149 Daniel Alfredsson RC	1.25	3.00
150 Miroslav Satan RC	.40	1.00

1995-96 Zenith Gifted Grinders

Randomly inserted in packs at a rate of 1:6, this 18-card set showcases some of the best tough-play wingers in the game.

COMPLETE SET (18)	10.00	20.00
1 Keith Tkachuk	1.00	2.50
2 Kevin Stevens	.40	1.00
3 Wendel Clark	.60	1.50
4 Claude Lemieux	.40	1.00
5 Rick Tocchet	.60	1.50
6 Trevor Linden	.60	1.50
7 John LeClair	1.00	2.50
8 Mikael Renberg	.60	1.50
9 Owen Nolan	.60	1.50
10 Todd Harvey	.60	1.50
11 Dave Gagner	.40	1.00
12 Dale Hunter	.40	1.00
13 Dave Andreychuk	.60	1.50
14 Mark Recchi	.60	1.50
15 Jason Arnott	.40	1.00
16 Dino Ciccarelli	.60	1.50
17 Adam Graves	.40	1.00
18 Steve Thomas	.60	1.50

1995-96 Zenith Rookie Roll Call

Randomly inserted in packs at a rate of 1:24, this 18-card set features the hottest 1995-96 rookies highlighted by the Dufex technology. A note on the card backs alluded to the total production run of these cards being no greater than 1,200 total sets.

COMPLETE SET (18)	15.00	40.00
1 Saku Koivu	1.25	3.00
2 Radek Dvorak	.40	1.00
3 Brendan Witt	.40	1.00
4 Antti Tormanen	.40	1.00
5 Brian Holzinger	.40	1.00
6 Aki-Petteri Berg	.40	1.00
7 Ed Jovanovski	.75	2.00
8 Marcus Ragnarsson	.40	1.00
9 Todd Bertuzzi	2.00	5.00
10 Daniel Alfredsson	2.00	5.00
11 Vitali Yachmenev	.40	1.00
12 Chad Kilger	.40	1.00
13 Eric Daze	.40	1.00
14 Niklas Sundstrom	.40	1.00
15 Shane Doan	2.00	5.00
16 Cory Stillman	.40	1.00
17 Kyle McLaren	.40	1.00
18 Jeff O'neill	.40	1.00

1995-96 Zenith Z-Team

Randomly inserted in packs at a rate of 1:72, this 18-card set depicts the best players in hockey, using a modified Dufex-type foil style. Based on stated insertion odds and the information given on the backs of the Rookie Roll Call singles, it is believed that no more than 400 of each Z-Team card is in existence.

COMPLETE SET (18)	75.00	150.00
STATED ODDS 1:72		
1 Patrick Roy	10.00	25.00
2 Martin Brodeur	6.00	15.00
3 Mario Lemieux	10.00	25.00
4 Wayne Gretzky	12.00	30.00
5 Mark Messier	4.00	10.00
6 Jeremy Roenick	3.00	8.00
7 Eric Lindros	2.00	5.00
8 Peter Forsberg	5.00	12.00
9 Sergei Fedorov	3.00	8.00
10 Mike Modano	5.00	12.00
11 Jaromir Jagr	5.00	12.00
12 Pavel Bure	4.00	10.00
13 Joe Sakic	6.00	15.00
14 Paul Kariya	2.00	5.00
15 Drett Hull	3.00	0.00
16 Brendan Shanahan	2.00	5.00
17 Felix Potvin	2.00	5.00
18 Jim Carey	1.00	2.50
S2 Martin Brodeur-SAMPLE	2.00	5.00

1996-97 Zenith

The 1996-97 Zenith set was issued in one series totaling 150 cards and was distributed in six-card packs. Printed on thick card stock, the fronts feature color action player images on a gold foil background. The backs carry in-depth player statistics. Dainius Zubrus and Sergei Berezin are the key rookies in the set.

COMPLETE SET (150) 12.00 30.00
1 Mike Modano .30 .75
2 Martin Brodeur .75 2.00
3 Pavel Bure .20 .50
4 Ray Bourque .30 .75
5 Steve Yzerman 1.25 3.00
6 Keith Tkachuk .20 .50
7 Jim Carey .20 .50
8 Valeri Kamensky .10 .25
9 Valeri Bure .05 .15
10 Ron Francis .10 .25
11 Trevor Kidd .10 .25
12 Doug Weight .10 .25
13 Wayne Gretzky 2.00 5.00
14 Todd Gill .05 .15
15 Dominik Hasek .60 1.50
16 Scott Mellanby .10 .25
17 John LeClair .20 .50
18 Al MacInnis .10 .25
19 Derian Hatcher .05 .15
20 Stephane Fiset .10 .25
21 Alexander Selivanov .05 .15
22 Vyacheslav Kozlov .05 .15
23 Alexei Yashin .05 .15
24 Wendel Clark .10 .25
25 Ed Belfour .20 .50
26 Travis Green .10 .25
27 Joe Juneau .05 .15
28 Teemu Selanne .20 .50
29 Jeff O'Neill .05 .15
30 Jeremy Roenick .30 .75
31 Felix Potvin .20 .50
32 Bernie Nicholls .05 .15
33 Steve Thomas .05 .15
34 Alexander Mogilny .10 .25
35 Patrick Roy 1.50 4.00
36 Luc Robitaille .10 .25
37 Owen Nolan .10 .25
38 Sergei Zubov .05 .15
39 Pierre Turgeon .10 .25
40 Nikolai Khabibulin .10 .25
41 Adam Oates .10 .25
42 Stephane Richer .10 .25
43 Daren Puppa .10 .25
44 Joe Sakic .60 1.50
45 Ed Jovanovski .10 .25
46 Ron Hextall .10 .25
47 Doug Gilmour .10 .25
48 Paul Coffey .20 .50
49 Craig Janney .10 .25
50 Brendan Witt .05 .15
51 Jere Lehtinen .05 .15
52 Vitali Yachmenev .05 .15
53 Damian Rhodes .10 .25
54 Petr Nedved .10 .25
55 Theo Fleury .05 .15
56 Petr Sykora .05 .15
57 Kelly Hrudey .10 .25
58 Saku Koivu .20 .50
59 Brian Bradley .05 .15
60 Arturs Irbe .10 .25
61 Eric Lindros .20 .50
62 Michal Pivonka .05 .15
63 Joe Nieuwendyk .10 .25
64 Mats Sundin .20 .50
65 Jason Arnott .05 .15
66 Mike Richter .20 .50
67 Brett Hull .30 .75
68 Chris Chelios .20 .50
69 Jocelyn Thibault .20 .50
70 Oleg Tverdovsky .10 .25
71 Peter Bondra .10 .25
72 Bill Ranford .10 .25
73 Scott Stevens .10 .25
74 Jaromir Jagr .50 1.25
75 Corey Hirsch .10 .25
76 Peter Forsberg .60 1.50
77 Brendan Shanahan .20 .50
78 Antti Tormanen .05 .15
79 Marcus Ragnarsson .05 .15
80 Sergei Fedorov .30 .75
81 Todd Bertuzzi .20 .50
82 Grant Fuhr .10 .25
83 Pat LaFontaine .20 .50
84 Rob Niedermayer .10 .25
85 Brian Leetch .20 .50
86 Yanic Perreault .05 .15
87 Dino Ciccarelli .10 .25
88 Dimitri Khristich .05 .15
89 Jeff Friesen .05 .15
90 Paul Kariya .20 .50
91 John Vanbiesbrouck .10 .25
92 Roman Hamrlik .10 .25
93 Pat Verbeek .05 .15
94 Mark Messier .20 .50
95 Trevor Linden .10 .25
96 Igor Larionov .05 .15
97 Zigmund Palffy .10 .25
98 Tom Barrasso .10 .25
99 Eric Daze .10 .25
100 Vincent Damphousse .05 .15
101 Keith Primeau .05 .15
102 Claude Lemieux .05 .15
103 Daniel Alfredsson .10 .25
104 Ryan Smyth .20 .50
105 Chris Osgood .10 .25
106 Bill Guerin .05 .15
107 Shayne Corson .05 .15
108 Alexei Zhamnov .10 .25
109 Mikael Renberg .10 .25
110 Andy Moog .10 .25
111 Larry Murphy .10 .25
112 Curtis Joseph .20 .50
113 Cory Stillman .05 .15
114 Mario Lemieux 1.50 4.00
115 Scott Young .05 .15
116 Eric Fichaud .10 .25
117 Jonas Hoglund .05 .15
118 Tomas Holmstrom RC .75 2.00
119 Jarome Iginla .40 1.00
120 Richard Zednik RC .30 .75
121 Andreas Dackell RC .05 .15
122 Anson Carter .10 .25
123 Dainius Zubrus RC .60 1.50
124 Janne Niinimaa .20 .50
125 Jason Allison .05 .15
126 Bryan Berard .20 .50
127 Sergei Berezin RC .30 .75
128 Wade Redden .05 .15
129 Jim Campbell .05 .15
130 Darcy Tucker .05 .15
131 Harry York RC .20 .50
132 Brandon Convery .05 .15
133 Ethan Moreau RC .20 .50
134 Mattias Timander RC .05 .15
135 Christian Dube .05 .15
136 Kevin Hodson RC .20 .50
137 Anders Eriksson .05 .15
138 Chris O'Sullivan .05 .15
139 Jamie Langenbrunner .05 .15
140 Steve Sullivan RC .30 .75
141 Daymond Langkow .10 .25
142 Landon Wilson .05 .15
143 Scott Bailey RC .05 .15
144 Terry Ryan RC .05 .15
145 Curtis Brown .05 .15
146 Rem Murray RC .05 .15
147 Jamie Pushor .05 .15
148 Daniel Goneau RC .05 .15
149 Mike Prokopec RC .05 .15
150 Brad Smyth RC .05 .15

1996-97 Zenith Artist's Proofs

Randomly inserted in packs at a rate of 1:48, this 150-card set is parallel to the regular set and is similar in design. The difference is found in the gold, rainbow holographic foil stamp on each card.

*STARS: 20X TO 50X BASIC CARDS
*ROOKIES: 8X TO 20X BASIC CARDS

1996-97 Zenith Assailants

Randomly inserted in packs at a rate of 1:10, this 15-card set features color photos of some of the NHL's most deadly snipers (as well as a couple of guys who couldn't hit water from the beach) and is printed on silver, micro-etched, poly-laminate card stock.

COMPLETE SET (15) 15.00 30.00
1 Alexei Yashin .75 2.00
2 Mike Modano 2.00 5.00
3 Jason Arnott .75 2.00
4 Mikael Renberg .75 2.00
5 Saku Koivu 1.25 3.00
6 Todd Bertuzzi 1.25 3.00
7 Zigmund Palffy 1.25 3.00
8 Eric Lindros 2.00 5.00
9 Pat LaFontaine .75 2.00
10 John LeClair .75 2.00
11 Theo Fleury .75 2.00
12 Pierre Turgeon .75 2.00
13 Petr Nedved .75 2.00
14 Owen Nolan 1.25 3.00
15 Valeri Bure .75 2.00

1996-97 Zenith Champion Salute

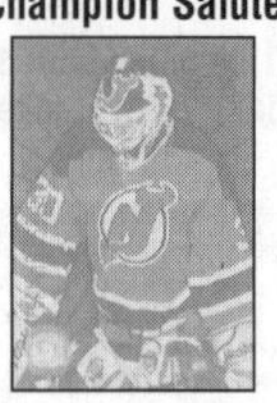

Randomly inserted in packs at a rate of 1:23, this special commemorative insert set honors superstar veteran players who have played on a Stanley Cup championship team. The fronts feature color player photos printed on micro-etched, silver poly-laminate card stock, along with a faux "diamond" chip embedded in the Stanley Cup ring icon. A parallel to this set, entitled Champion Salute Extra, included an actual diamond chip.

*DIAMONDS: 2.5X TO 6X BASIC INSERTS
1 Mark Messier .75 2.00
2 Wayne Gretzky 5.00 12.00
3 Grant Fuhr .75 2.00
4 Paul Coffey .75 2.00
5 Mario Lemieux 4.00 10.00
6 Jaromir Jagr 1.25 3.00
7 Ron Francis .75 2.00
8 Joe Sakic 1.50 4.00
9 Peter Forsberg 2.00 5.00
10 Claude Lemieux .75 2.00
11 Patrick Roy 3.00 8.00
12 Chris Chelios .75 2.00
13 Doug Gilmour .75 2.00
14 Mike Richter .75 2.00
15 Martin Brodeur 2.00 5.00
P3 Grant Fuhr PROMO 1.50 4.00
P9 Peter Forsberg PROMO 3.00 8.00
P15 Martin Brodeur PROMO 4.00 10.00

1996-97 Zenith Z-Team

Randomly inserted packs at a rate of 1:71, this 18-card set honors some of the NHL superstars by combining embossing, micro-etching, rainbow holographic and gold foil stamping on clear plastic card stock.

1 Eric Lindros 4.00 10.00
2 Paul Kariya 4.00 10.00
3 Teemu Selanne 4.00 10.00
4 Brendan Shanahan 4.00 10.00
5 Sergei Fedorov 4.00 10.00
6 Steve Yzerman 15.00 40.00
7 Brett Hull 6.00 15.00
8 Pavel Bure 4.00 10.00
9 Alexander Mogilny 2.00 5.00
10 Jeremy Roenick 4.00 10.00
11 Jocelyn Thibault 2.00 5.00
12 Keith Tkachuk 2.00 5.00
13 Daniel Alfredsson 2.00 5.00
14 Eric Daze 2.00 5.00
15 Jim Carey 2.00 5.00
16 Felix Potvin 4.00 10.00
17 John Vanbiesbrouck 2.00 5.00
18 Chris Osgood 2.00 5.00

1997-98 Zenith

The 1997-98 Zenith set was issued in one series totaling 100 cards and was distributed in packs of three 5" by 7" cards with one regular size card inside each of the jumbo cards. The jumbo cards had to be torn open to get to the regular cards inside. The fronts feature action color player photos. The backs carry player information and another photo.

COMPLETE SET (100) 60.00 150.00
1 Jarome Iginla .60 1.50
2 Peter Forsberg .60 1.50
3 Brendan Shanahan .50 1.25
4 Wayne Gretzky 2.00 5.00
5 Steve Yzerman 1.25 3.00
6 Eric Lindros .50 1.25
7 Keith Tkachuk .50 1.25
8 John LeClair .50 1.25
9 John Vanbiesbrouck .30 .75
10 Patrick Roy 1.25 3.00
11 Ray Bourque .60 1.50
12 Theo Fleury .20 .50
13 Brian Leetch .50 1.25
14 Chris Chelios .50 1.25
15 Paul Kariya .50 1.25
16 Mark Messier .50 1.25
17 Curtis Joseph .50 1.25
18 Mike Richter .50 1.25
19 Jeremy Roenick .60 1.50
20 Dominik Hasek .75 2.00
21 Martin Brodeur 1.00 2.50
22 Sergei Fedorov .60 1.50
23 Pierre Turgeon .30 .75
24 Teemu Selanne .50 1.25
25 Brett Hull .60 1.50
26 Saku Koivu .50 1.25
27 Owen Nolan .30 .75
28 Jozef Stumpel .20 .50
29 Joe Sakic .75 2.00
30 Zigmund Palffy .30 .75
31 Jaromir Jagr .75 2.00
32 Adam Oates .30 .75
33 Jeff Friesen .20 .50
34 Pavel Bure .50 1.25
35 Chris Osgood .30 .75
36 Mark Recchi .30 .75
37 Mike Modano .60 1.50
38 Felix Potvin .50 1.25
39 Vincent Damphousse .20 .50
40 Byron Dafoe .20 .50
41 Luc Robitaille .30 .75
42 Peter Bondra .30 .75
43 Daniel Alfredsson .30 .75
44 Pat LaFontaine .20 .50
45 Mikael Renberg .20 .50
46 Doug Gilmour .30 .75
47 Dino Ciccarelli .20 .50
48 Mats Sundin .50 1.25
49 Ed Belfour .50 1.25
50 Ron Francis .30 .75
51 Miroslav Satan .30 .75
52 Cory Stillman .20 .50
53 Bryan Berard .20 .50
54 Keith Primeau .20 .50
55 Eric Daze .30 .75
56 Chris Gratton .30 .75
57 Claude Lemieux .30 .75
58 Nicklas Lidstrom .50 1.25
59 Olaf Kolzig .30 .75
60 Grant Fuhr .30 .75
61 Jamie Langenbrunner .20 .50
62 Doug Weight .30 .75
63 Joe Nieuwendyk .20 .50
64 Yanic Perreault .20 .50
65 Jocelyn Thibault .30 .75
66 Guy Hebert .20 .50
67 Shayne Corson .20 .50
68 Bobby Holik .20 .50
69 Sami Kapanen .20 .50
70 Robert Reichel .20 .50
71 Ryan Smyth .20 .50
72 Alexei Yashin .20 .50
73 Trevor Linden .20 .50
74 Rod Brind'Amour .30 .75
75 Dave Gagner .20 .50
76 Nikolai Khabibulin .30 .75
77 Tom Barrasso .30 .75
78 Tony Amonte .30 .75
79 Alexander Mogilny .30 .75
80 Jason Allison .20 .50
81 Patrik Elias RC 1.50 4.00
82 Mike Johnson RC .30 .75
83 Richard Zednik .30 .75
84 Patrick Marleau .30 .75
85 Mattias Ohlund .30 .75
86 Sergei Samsonov .30 .75
87 Marco Sturm RC .75 2.00
88 Alyn McCauley .30 .75
89 Chris Phillips .30 .75
90 Brendan Morrison RC .75 2.00
91 Vaclav Prospal RC .40 1.00
92 Joe Thornton 1.50 4.00
93 Boyd Devereaux .30 .75
94 Alexei Morozov .30 .75
95 Vincent Lecavalier RC 15.00 40.00
96 Manny Malhotra RC .40 1.00
97 Roberto Luongo RC 20.00 50.00
98 Mathieu Garon .30 .75
99 Alex Tanguay RC 4.00 10.00
UER front Tanquay
100 Josh Holden .30 .75

1997-98 Zenith Z-Gold

Randomly inserted in packs, this 100-card set is a parallel version of the base set printed on gold-foil card stock and sequentially numbered to 100.

*STARS: 15X TO 40X BASIC CARDS
*YNG.STARS: 12.5X TO 30X BASIC CARDS
*ROOKIES: 1.5X TO 3X BASIC CARDS
2 Peter Forsberg 30.00 80.00
4 Wayne Gretzky 50.00 125.00
5 Steve Yzerman 40.00 100.00
10 Patrick Roy 40.00 100.00
11 Ray Bourque 25.00 60.00
15 Paul Kariya 20.00 50.00
19 Jeremy Roenick 20.00 50.00
20 Dominik Hasek 25.00 60.00
21 Martin Brodeur 40.00 100.00
22 Sergei Fedorov 25.00 60.00
24 Teemu Selanne 25.00 60.00
25 Brett Hull 25.00 50.00
29 Joe Sakic 25.00 60.00
31 Jaromir Jagr 20.00 50.00
37 Mike Modano 20.00 50.00
95 Vincent Lecavalier 125.00 250.00
97 Roberto Luongo 150.00 300.00
99 Alex Tanguay 75.00 200.00
UER front Tanquay

1997-98 Zenith Z-Silver

Randomly inserted in packs at the rate of 1:7, this 100-card set is a parallel version of the base set printed on silver-foil board.

*STARS: 2X TO 5X BASIC CARDS
*YOUNG STARS: 2X TO 4X
*RC's/PROSPECTS: 1.25X TO 2.5X
95 Vincent Lecavalier 20.00 50.00
97 Roberto Luongo 25.00 60.00

1997-98 Zenith 5 x 7

This 80-card set measuring 5" by 7" was distributed in three-card packs with a regular size card inside each jumbo card. The fronts feature color action player photos with another photo and player information on the backs.

COMPLETE SET (80) 75.00 150.00
1 Wayne Gretzky 4.00 10.00
2 Eric Lindros .60 1.50
3 Patrick Roy 3.00 8.00
4 John Vanbiesbrouck .50 1.25
5 Martin Brodeur 1.50 4.00
6 Teemu Selanne .60 1.50
7 Joe Sakic 1.25 3.00
8 Jaromir Jagr 1.00 2.50
9 Brendan Shanahan .60 1.50
10 Ed Belfour .60 1.50
11 Guy Hebert .50 1.25
12 Doug Gilmour .50 1.25
13 Keith Primeau .25 .60
14 Grant Fuhr .50 1.25
15 Joe Nieuwendyk .50 1.25
16 Ryan Smyth .50 1.25
17 Chris Osgood .50 1.25
18 Keith Tkachuk .60 1.50
19 Peter Forsberg 1.50 4.00
20 Jarome Iginla .75 2.00
21 Steve Yzerman 3.00 8.00
22 Jeremy Roenick .75 2.00
23 Jozef Stumpel .50 1.25
24 Mark Recchi .50 1.25
25 Daniel Alfredsson .50 1.25
26 Pat LaFontaine .60 1.50
27 Zigmund Palffy .50 1.25
28 Jason Allison .25 .60
29 Yanic Perreault .25 .60
30 Olaf Kolzig .50 1.25
31 Mikael Renberg .50 1.25
32 Bryan Berard .50 1.25
33 Jocelyn Thibault .50 1.25
34 Shayne Corson .50 1.25
35 Dave Gagner .25 .60
36 Claude Lemieux .25 .60
37 Saku Koivu .60 1.50
38 Curtis Joseph .60 1.50
39 Chris Chelios .60 1.50
40 Ray Bourque 1.00 2.50
41 Adam Oates .50 1.25
42 Felix Potvin .60 1.50
43 Peter Bondra .50 1.25
44 Sergei Fedorov 1.00 2.50
45 Paul Kariya .60 1.50
46 Theo Fleury .25 .60
47 John LeClair .60 1.50
48 Brett Hull .75 2.00
49 Rod Brind'Amour .50 1.25
50 Doug Weight .50 1.25
51 Jamie Langenbrunner .25 .60
52 Mats Sundin .60 1.50
53 Ron Francis .50 1.25
54 Eric Daze .50 1.25
55 Nicklas Lidstrom .60 1.50
56 Luc Robitaille .50 1.25
57 Vincent Damphousse .25 .60
58 Mike Modano 1.00 2.50
59 Pavel Bure .60 1.50
60 Owen Nolan .50 1.25
61 Pierre Turgeon .50 1.25
62 Dominik Hasek 1.25 3.00
63 Mike Richter .60 1.50
64 Mark Messier .60 1.50
65 Brian Leetch .60 1.50
66 Sergei Samsonov .30 .75
67 Alexei Morozov .30 .75
68 Marco Sturm RC 1.50 3.00
69 Patrik Elias RC 1.00 2.50
70 Eric Messier RC .30 .75
71 Alyn McCauley .30 .75
72 Richard Zednik .30 .75
73 Mattias Ohlund .30 .75
74 Joe Thornton 1.50 4.00
75 Vincent Lecavalier RC 8.00 20.00
76 Manny Malhotra RC .75 2.00
77 Roberto Luongo RC 10.00 25.00
78 Mathieu Garon .30 .75
79 Alex Tanguay RC 2.50 6.00
80 Josh Holden .30 .75

1997-98 Zenith 5 x 7 Gold Impulse

Randomly inserted in packs, this 80-card set is a gold foil parallel version of the base set and is sequentially numbered to 100.

*STARS: 10X TO 25X BASIC CARDS
*RC's: 2X TO 5X BASIC CARDS

1997-98 Zenith 5 x 7 Silver Impulse

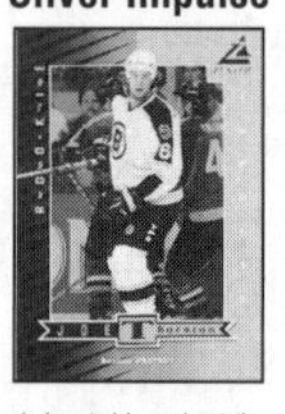

Randomly inserted in packs at the rate of 1:7, this 80-card set is a silver foil parallel version of the base set.

*STARS: 2.5X TO 5X BASIC CARDS
*RC's: .25X TO .75X

1997-98 Zenith Chasing The Cup

Randomly inserted in packs at the rate of 1:25, this 15-card set features color photos of top players printed on rainbow-hued holographic foil with an image of the trophy in the background.

COMPLETE SET (15) 50.00 125.00
1 Patrick Roy 12.00 30.00
2 Wayne Gretzky 15.00 40.00
3 Jaromir Jagr 4.00 10.00
4 Eric Lindros 2.00 5.00
5 Mike Modano 4.00 10.00
6 Brendan Shanahan 2.00 5.00
7 Brett Hull 3.00 8.00
8 John LeClair 1.25 3.00
9 Jocelyn Thibault 1.25 3.00
10 Ed Belfour 2.00 5.00
11 Martin Brodeur 8.00 20.00
12 Peter Forsberg 6.00 15.00
13 Saku Koivu 2.00 5.00
14 Pat LaFontaine 1.25 3.00
15 Steve Yzerman 12.00 30.00

1997-98 Zenith Rookie Reign

Randomly inserted in packs at the rate of 1:25, this 15-card set features color photos of top young players printed on holographic foil.

COMPLETE SET (15) 30.00 60.00
1 Sergei Samsonov 4.00 10.00
2 Joe Thornton 8.00 20.00
3 Erik Rasmussen 1.25 3.00
4 Brendan Morrison 2.00 5.00
5 Magnus Arvedson 1.25 3.00
6 Vaclav Prospal 1.25 3.00
7 Brad Isbister 1.25 3.00
8 Alexei Morozov 1.25 3.00
9 Marco Sturm 2.00 5.00
10 Patrick Marleau 4.00 10.00
11 Alyn McCauley 2.00 5.00
12 Mike Johnson 1.25 3.00
13 Mattias Ohlund 1.25 3.00
14 Patrik Elias 2.00 5.00
15 Richard Zednik 1.25 3.00

1997-98 Zenith Z-Team

Randomly inserted in packs at the rate of 1:35 for cards #1-9 and 1:58 for #10-18, this 18-card set features color action photos of top NHL players and rookies in white, black, and colored borders. The backs carry player information.

COMPLETE SET (18) 100.00 200.00
1 Teemu Selanne 3.00 8.00
2 Wayne Gretzky 20.00 50.00
3 Patrick Roy 15.00 40.00
4 Eric Lindros 3.00 8.00
5 Peter Forsberg 8.00 20.00
6 Paul Kariya 3.00 8.00
7 John LeClair 3.00 8.00
8 Martin Brodeur 8.00 20.00
9 Brendan Shanahan 3.00 8.00
10 Joe Thornton 8.00 20.00
11 Mattias Ohlund 2.50 6.00
12 Mike Johnson 2.50 6.00
13 Vaclav Prospal 2.50 6.00
14 Sergei Samsonov 2.50 6.00
15 Marco Sturm 2.50 6.00
16 Patrik Elias 8.00 20.00
17 Richard Zednik 2.50 6.00
18 Alexei Morozov 2.50 6.00

1997-98 Zenith Z-Team 5x7

Randomly inserted in packs at the rate of 1:35, this nine-card set features color action photos of top NHL players printed on jumbo 5" by 7" cards.

*5X7s: .5X TO 1.2X BASIC INSERTS

1997-98 Zenith Z-Team Gold

Randomly inserted in packs at the rate of 1:175, this 18-card set is a gold parallel version of the regular Z-Team set printed on gold micro-etched foil.

*GOLDS: 1X TO 2.5X BASIC INSERTS

Minors, Juniors & European

1995-96 Austrian National Team

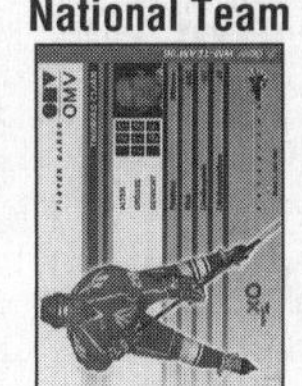

This 24-card set of the Austrian national team was sold at the 1996 World Championships in Vienna. The cards measure approximately 2 7/8" by 4" and feature color player cut-outs on the left with a head shot and player information printed on the right. The backs are blank. The cards are unnumbered and checklisted below in alphabetical order.

COMPLETE SET (28) 6.00 15.00
1 Christoph Brander .20 1.00
2 Thomas Cijan .20 .50
3 Claus Dalpiaz .30 .75
4 Reinhard Divis .20 3.00
5 Konrad Dorn .20 .50
6 Robin Doyle .20 .50
7 Michael Guntner .20 .50
8 Karl Heinzle .20 .50
9 Herbert Hohenberger .40 .75
10 Dieter Kalt .20 .50
11 Peter Kasper .20 .50
12 Werner Kerth .20 .50
13 Martin Krainz .20 .50
14 Gunter Lanzinger .20 .50
15 Engelbert Linder .20 .50
16 Arthur Marczell .20 .50
17 Manfred Muhr .20 .50
18 Rick Nasheim .20 .50
19 Kraig Nienhuis .30 1.00
20 Christian Perthaler .20 .50
21 Michael Puschacher .20 .50
22 Gerhard Puschnik .20 .50
23 Andreas Puschnig .20 .50
24 Gerald Ressmann .20 .50
25 Mario Schaden .20 .50
26 Michael Shea .20 .50
27 Wolfgang Strauss .20 .50
28 Martin Ulrich .20 .50

1937 British Sporting Personalities

Card features black and white front with biographical information on back.

37 Joe Beaton 10.00 20.00

1932 Bulgaria Zigaretten Sport Photos

Cards measure approximately 1 1/2 x 2 1/2 and are black and white photos. Cards were meant to be glued onto strips along with the appropriate caption. There were 272 cards in this multi-sport set.

142 Field Hockey 5.00 10.00
143 Field Hockey 5.00 10.00
144 Field Hockey 5.00 10.00
148 Ice Hockey 12.50 25.00
149 Dr. B. Watson Canada 10.00 20.00
150 Ice Hockey Goalie 12.50 25.00

1994-95 Czech APS Extraliga

This 303-card set measures the standard size and features the players of the Czech Elite League. Several prominent NHLers, including Jaromir Jagr and Martin Straka appear in this set. They returned to their homeland to play for their old club teams during the 1994 NHL lockout.

COMPLETE SET (303) 60.00 150.00

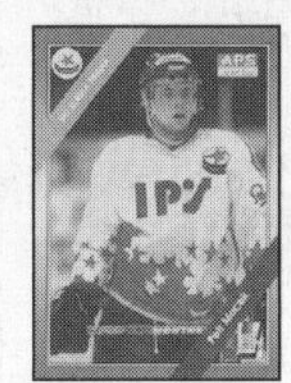

1 Pavel Cagas .20 .75
2 Ladislav Blazek .20 .50
3 Ales Flasar .10 .25
4 Petr Tejkl .10 .25
5 Jaromir Latal .10 .25
6 Ales Tomasek .10 .25
7 Jiri Kuntos .10 .25
8 Jan Vavrecka .10 .25
9 Martin Smetak .10 .25
10 Patrik Rimmel .10 .25
11 Michal Slavik .10 .25
12 Milan Navratil .10 .25
13 Petr Fabian .16 .40
14 Zdenek Eichenmann .10 .25
15 Miroslav Chalanek .10 .25
16 Pavel Nohel .10 .25
17 Radim Radevic .10 .25
18 Tomas Martinec .10 .25
19 Ales Zima .10 .25
20 Ivo Hrstka .10 .25
21 Richard Brancik .10 .25
22 Martin Jenacek .10 .25
23 Robert Holy .10 .25
24 Radovan Biegl .20 .50
25 Dusan Salficky .20 .75
26 Jiri Malinsky .10 .25
27 Jan Filip .10 .25
28 Jaroslav Spelda .10 .25
29 Petr Jancarik .10 .25
30 Robert Kostka .10 .25
31 Kamil Toupal .10 .25
32 Tomas Pacal .10 .25
33 Ales Pisa .16 .40
34 Milan Hejduk 14.00 35.00
35 Josef Zajic .20 .50
36 Stanislav Prochazka .10 .25
37 Jiri Sejba .20 .50
38 Marek Zadina .10 .25
39 Milan Filipi .10 .25
40 David Pospisil .10 .25
41 Tomas Blazek .30 .50
42 Patrik Weber .16 .40
43 Richard Kral .16 .40
44 Martin Sekera .10 .25
45 Ladislav Lubina .10 .25
46 Jiri Provaznik .10 .25
47 Martin Chlad .20 .50
48 Tomas Vokoun 2.00 10.00
49 Pavel Trnka .30 .75
50 Petr Kuda .10 .25
51 Frantisek Kaberle .30 .75
52 Libor Prochazka .30 .75
53 Jan Dlouhy .10 .25
54 Otakar Cerny .10 .25
55 Martin Ancicka .10 .25
56 Marek Zidlicky .10 2.00
57 Martin Prochazka .20 .50
58 Pavel Patera .30 .75
59 Otakar Vejvoda .30 .75
60 Jan Blaha .10 .25
61 David Cermak .16 .40
62 Petr Ton .10 .25
63 Miroslav Mach .10 .25
64 Patrik Elias 6.00 15.00
65 Martin Stepanek .10 .25
66 Tomas Mikolasek .10 .25
67 Milan Ruchar .16 .40
68 Jaromir Jagr 20.00 50.00
69 Milos Kajer .10 .25
70 Jaromir Sindel .40 1.00
71 Ivo Capek .20 .50
72 Jan Bohacek .10 .25
73 Zdenek Touzimsky .10 .25
74 Jan Krulis .10 .25
75 Frantisek Musil .20 .50
76 Jaroslav Nedved .16 .25
77 Frantisek Ptacek .10 .25
78 Pavel Taborsky .10 .25
79 Frantisek Kucera .20 .50
80 Pavel Srek .10 .25
81 Martin Simek .10 .25
82 Zbynek Kukacka .10 .25
83 Jiri Zelenka .16 .40
84 Jan Hlavac .80 2.00
85 Patrik Martinec .10 .25
86 David Bruk .10 .25
87 Pavel Geffert .20 .50
88 Michal Sup .10 .25
89 Jaromir Kverka .10 .25
90 Miroslav Hlinka .10 .25
91 Milan Kastner .20 .50
92 Andrej Potajcuk .10 .25
93 Roman Turek 2.00 5.00
94 Ladislav Gula .20 .50
95 Robert Slavik .20 .50
96 Jiri Hala .10 .25
97 Jaroslav Modry .20 .50
98 Petr Sedy .10 .25
00 Petr Hodek .10 .25
100 Petr Mainer .10 .25
101 Michael Kubicek .10 .25
102 Milan Nedoma .20 .50
103 Rudolf Suchanek .10 .25
104 Libor Zabransky .30 .50
105 Jaroslav Brabec .10 .25
106 Lubos Rob .16 .40
107 Zdenek Sperger .10 .25
108 Ondrej Vosta .10 .25
109 Filip Turek .10 .25
110 Radek Belohlav .20 .50
111 Frantisek Sevcik .10 .25
112 Roman Bozek .16 .40
113 Roman Horak .20 .50
114 Pavel Pycha .10 .25
115 Arpad Gyori .10 .25
116 Tomas Vasicek .20 .50
117 Michal Hlinka .20 .50
118 Daniel Kysela .10 .25
119 Rudolf Wolf .10 .25
120 Antonin Planovsky .10 .25
121 Tomas Kramny .10 .25
122 Vitezslav Skuta .20 .50
123 Pavel Marecek .10 .25
124 Miroslav Javin .10 .25
125 Kamil Pribyla .10 .25
126 Michal Cerny .10 .25
127 Juris Opulskis .10 .25
128 Richard Smehlik .40 .75
129 Ales Badal .10 .25
130 Robert Simicek .10 .25
131 Vladimir Vujtek .20 .50
132 Tomas Chlubna .10 .25
133 Michal Piskor .16 .40
134 Petr Folta .16 .40
135 Roman Kadera .16 .40
136 Lumir Kotala .10 .25
137 Jan Peterek .16 .40
138 Roman Rysanek .10 .25
139 Rudolf Pejchar .20 .50
140 Jiri Kucera .20 .50
141 Stanislav Benes .10 .25
142 Karel Smid .20 .50
143 Martin Kovarik .10 .25
144 Jiri Jonak .10 .25
145 Alexander Savickij .10 .25
146 Vaclav Ruprecht .10 .25
147 Ivan Vlcek .10 .25
148 Jaroslav Spacek .20 .50
149 Peter Veselovsky .10 .25
150 Milan Cerny .10 .25
151 Milan Volak .10 .25
152 Dusan Huml .10 .25
153 Tomas Kucharcik .10 .25
154 Martin Zivny .10 .25
155 Martin Straka 1.20 2.00
156 Michal Straka .10 .25
157 Jiri Beranek .16 .40
158 Ondrej Steiner .20 .50
159 Josef Rybar .20 1.00
160 Jaroslav Kreuzmann .10 .25
161 David Trachta .10 .25
162 Marek Novotny .20 .50
163 Pavel Falta .20 .50
164 Antonin Necas .10 .25
165 Roman Cech .10 .25
166 Pavel Zmrhal .10 .25
167 Petr Buzek .40 .50
168 Jaroslav Benak .20 .50
169 Michael Vyhlidal .10 .25
170 Petr Kuchyna .10 .25
171 Josef Marha .40 1.00
172 Leos Pipa .10 .25
173 Jiri Poukar .10 .25
174 Libor Dolana .10 .25
175 Viktor Ujcik .30 .75
176 Ladislav Prokupek .20 .50
177 Jiri Cihlar .20 .50
178 Patrik Fink .10 .25
179 Oldrich Valek .10 .25
180 Zdenek Cely .10 .25
181 Jaroslav Kames .20 .75
182 Pavel Malac .20 .50
183 Martin Maskarinec .10 .25
184 Pavel Rajnoha .16 .40
185 Pavel Kowalczyk .10 .25
186 Miloslav Guren .20 .50
187 Radim Tesarik .10 .25
188 Jan Krajicek .10 .25
189 Patrik Hucko .10 .25
190 Roman Kankovsky .10 .25
191 Jaroslav Hub .10 .25
192 Petr Kankovsky .10 .25
193 Pavel Janku .20 .50
194 Miroslav Okal .10 .25
195 Zdenek Okal .10 .25
196 Roman Mejzlik .16 .40
197 Juraj Jurik .10 .25
198 Roman Meluzin .10 .25
199 Josef Straub .20 .50
200 Martin Kotasek .10 .25
201 Zdenek Sedlak .10 .25
202 Petr Cajanek .20 3.00
203 Zdenek Orct .20 1.00
204 Petr Franek .20 .50
205 Petr Svoboda .40 1.00
206 Angel Nikolov .20 .50
207 Petr Molnar .10 .25
208 Kamil Prachar .20 .50
209 Jiri Slegr .40 1.00
210 Radek Mrazek .10 .25
211 Jan Vopat .20 .50
212 Ondrej Zetek .10 .25
213 Martin Stelcich .10 .25
214 Zdenek Skorepa .10 .25
215 Stanislav Rosa .10 .25
216 Radek Sip .20 .50
217 Martin Rousek .10 .25
218 Tomas Vlasak .20 .50
219 Radim Piroutek .10 .25
220 Robert Kysela .20 .50
221 Martin Rucinsky .40 1.00
222 Robert Lang .40 2.00
223 Ivo Prorok .10 .25
224 Jan Alinc .16 .40
225 Vladimir Machulda .10 .25
226 Kamil Kolacek .10 .25
227 David Balazs .10 .25
228 Roman Cechmanek 6.00 10.00
229 Ivo Pesat .20 .50
230 Antonin Stavjana .20 .50
231 Pavel Augusta .10 .25
232 Daniel Vrla .10 .25
233 Alexej Jaskin .10 .25
234 Radek Mesicek .10 .25
235 Marek Tichy .10 .25
236 Stanislav Pavelec .10 .25
237 Jan Srdinko .10 .25
238 Zbynek Marak .10 .25
239 Andrej Galkin .10 .25
240 Miroslav Stavjana .10 .25
241 Libor Forch .10 .25
242 Roman Stantien .10 .25
243 Josef Beranek .40 .75
244 Lubos Jenacek .10 .25
245 Michal Tomek .10 .25
246 Rostislav Vlach .10 .25
247 Miroslav Barus .10 .25
248 Josef Podlaha .10 .25
249 Pavel Rohlik .10 .25
250 Martin Altrichter .20 .50
251 Radek Toth .20 .75
252 Vladimir Hudacek .20 .50
253 Miloslav Horava .20 .50
254 Petr Macek .10 .25
255 Pavel Blaha .10 .25
256 Radomir Brazda .10 .25
257 Jiri Hes .10 .25
258 Tomas Arnost .10 .25
259 Miroslav Hosek .10 .25
260 Jan Penk .10 .25
261 Tomas Jelinek .20 .50
262 Jiri Hlinka .10 .25
263 Lubos Pazler .10 .25
264 Roman Blazek .10 .25
265 Vladimir Ruzicka .40 1.00
266 Tomas Kupka .10 .25
267 Lubos Dopita .10 .25
268 Ladislav Slizek .10 .25
269 Milan Antos .10 .25
270 Vadim Kulabuchov .10 .25
271 Anatolij Najda .10 .25
272 Tomas Hyka .10 .25
273 Vaclav Eiselt .10 .25
274 Tomas Placatka .10 .25
275 Jan Nemecek .20 .50
276 Josef Augusta CO .10 .25
277 Lubomir Fischer CO .10 .25
278 Jaromir Precechtel CO .10 .25
279 Marek Sykora CO .10 .25
280 Petr Hemsky CO .10 .25
281 Jan Neliba CO .10 .25
282 Zdenek Muller CO .10 .25
283 Frantisek Vyborny CO .10 .25
284 Stanislav Berger CO .10 .25
285 Karel Prazak CO .10 .25
286 Vladimir Caldr CO .10 .25
287 Alois Hadamczik CO .10 .25
288 Bretislav Bochensky CO .10 .25
289 Karel Trachta CO .10 .25
290 Jindrich Setikovsky CO .10 .25
291 Jaroslav Holik CO .10 .25
292 Jan Hrbaty CO .10 .25
293 Vladimir Vujtek CO .10 .25
294 Zdenek Cech CO .10 .25
295 Frantisek Vorlicek CO .10 .25
296 Ondrej Weissmann CO .10 .25
297 Horst Valasek CO .10 .25
298 Zdislav Tabara CO .10 .25
299 Pavel Richter CO .10 .25
300 Bretislav Kopriva CO .10 .25
NNO Checklist 1 .10 .10
NNO Checklist 2 .10 .10
NNO Checklist 3 .10 .10

1995-96 Czech APS Extraliga

This 400-card set features color action player photos of members of the Czech Republic's Extraliga.

COMPLETE SET (400) 50.00 125.00
1 Horst Valasek CO .10 .25
2 Zdislav Tabara CO .10 .25
3 Roman Cechmanek 2.00 4.00
4 Ivo Pesat .30 .75
5 Alexej Jaskin .10 .25
6 Stanislav Pavelec .10 .25
7 Jan Srdinko .10 .25
8 Antonin Stavjana .30 .50
9 Pavel Taborsky .10 .25
10 Jiri Veber .10 .25
11 Daniel Vrla .10 .25
12 Miroslav Barus .10 .25
13 Ivan Padelek .10 .25
14 Libor Forch .10 .25
15 Andrej Galkin .10 .25
16 Lubos Jenacek .10 .25
17 Tomas Srsen .16 .25
18 Rostislav Vlach .10 .25
19 Zbynek Marak .10 .25
20 Jiri Dopita .80 1.00
21 Ales Polcar .30 .75
22 Roman Stantien .10 .25
23 Michal Tomek .10 .25
24 Jiri Zadrazil .10 .25
25 Pavel Augusta .10 .25
26 Tomas Jakes .10 .25
27 Vladimir Vujtek CO .20 .50
28 Zdenek Cech CO .10 .25
29 Jaroslav Kames .30 .75
30 Pavel Malac .30 .75
31 Jan Vavrecka .10 .25
32 Miroslav Javin .10 .25
33 Stanislav Medrik .10 .25
34 Pavel Kowalczyk .10 .25
35 Miloslav Guren .30 .50
36 Radim Tesarik .10 .25
37 Jan Krajicek .10 .25
38 Jiri Marusak .10 .25
39 Josef Straub .30 .75
40 Pavel Janku .30 .25
41 Roman Meluzin .30 .75
42 Miroslav Okal .10 .25
43 Zdenek Okal .10 .25
44 David Bruk .10 .25
45 Jaroslav Hub .10 .25
46 Petr Cajanek .60 1.00
47 Tomas Nemcicky .10 .25
48 Martin Kotasek .10 .25
49 Zdenek Sedlak .10 .25
50 Petr Leska .10 .25
51 Vladimir Caldr CO .10 .25
52 Jaroslav Liska .10 .25
53 Oldrich Svoboda .10 .25
54 Robert Slavik .20 .50
55 Rudolf Suchanek .10 .25
56 Milan Nedoma .30 .75
57 Lukas Zib .10 .25
58 Karel Soudek .10 .25
59 Petr Sedy .10 .25
60 Libor Zabransky .30 .50
61 Kamil Toupal .10 .25
62 Michal Kubicek .10 .25
63 Martin Masak .10 .25
64 Radek Belohlav .20 .50
65 Radek Toupal .16 .40
66 Pavel Pycha .10 .25
67 Lubos Rob .16 .40
68 Filip Turek .10 .25
69 Ondrej Vosta .10 .25
70 Roman Bozek .16 .40
71 Jaroslav Brabec .10 .25
72 Petr Sailer .10 .25
73 Martin Strba .10 .25
74 Zdenek Sperger .10 .25
75 Jan Neliba CO .10 .25
76 Zdenek Muller CO .10 .25
77 Martin Chlad .30 .75
78 Jiri Kucera .10 .25
79 Jan Dlouhy .10 .25
80 Tomas Kaberle .80 2.00
81 Petr Kasik .10 .25
82 Jan Krulis .10 .25
83 Petr Kuda .10 .25
84 Libor Prochazka .30 .50
85 Martin Stepanek .10 .25
86 Marek Zidlicky .10 1.00
87 Jiri Beranek .16 .40
88 Jiri Burger .10 .25
89 David Cermak .10 .25
90 Milos Kajer .10 .25
91 Miroslav Mach .10 .25
92 Tomas Mikolasek .10 .25
93 Pavel Patera .30 .75
94 Martin Prochazka .30 .75
95 Petr Ton .10 .25
96 Otakar Vejvoda .30 .75
97 Josef Zajic .30 .75
98 Josef Augusta CO .10 .25
99 Lubomir Fischer CO .10 .25
100 Jaromir Precechtel CO .10 .25
101 Pavel Cagas .30 .50
102 Ladislav Blazek .30 .50
103 Jaromir Latal .10 .25
104 Jiri Latal .16 .40
105 Petr Tejkl .10 .25
106 Jiri Kuntos .10 .25
107 Patrik Rimmel .10 .25
108 Robert Machalek .10 .25
109 Jiri Polak .10 .25
110 Martin Bakula .10 .25
111 Michal Slavik .10 .25
112 Pavel Nohel .10 .25
113 Igor Cikl .10 .25
114 Zdenek Eichenmann .10 .25
115 Milan Navratil .10 .25
116 Ales Zima .10 .25
117 Tomas Martinec .16 .40
118 Richard Brancik .10 .25
119 Ondrej Kratena .30 .75
120 Michal Bros .20 .50
121 Juraj Jurik .10 .25
122 Jan Tomajko .10 .25
123 Richard Farda .16 .40
124 Dretislav Kopriva CO .10 .25
125 Martin Altrichter .30 .75
126 Radek Toth .30 .50
127 Miloslav Horava .30 .75
128 Martin Maskarinec .10 .25
129 Jakub Ficenec .20 .50
130 Jiri Hes .10 .25
131 Andrej Jakovenko .16 .40
132 Petr Macek .10 .25
133 Jan Penk .10 .25
134 Robert Kostka .10 .25
135 Vladimir Ruzicka .30 .75
136 Viktor Ujcik .30 .75
137 Ivo Prorok .10 .25
138 Tomas Jelinek .20 .50
139 Michal Sup .10 .25
140 Milan Antos .10 .25
141 Roman Blazek .10 .25
142 Jiri Hlinka .10 .25
143 Tomas Kupka .10 .25
144 Vaclav Eiselt .10 .25
145 Jaroslav Bednar .80 2.00
146 Ladislav Svoboda .10 .25
147 Ladislav Kudrna .10 .25
148 Josef Beranek .30 .50
149 Vladimir Kyhos .10 .25
150 Zdenek Orct .30 .75
151 Petr Franek .30 .75
152 Kamil Prachar .16 .40
153 Angel Nikolov .20 .50
154 Ondrej Zetek .10 .25
155 Tomas Arnost .10 .25
156 Normunds Sejejs .10 .25
157 Petr Kratky .10 .25
158 Sergej Butko .10 .25
159 Petr Molnar .10 .25
160 Radek Mrazek .10 .25
161 Radim Piroutek .10 .25
162 David Balazs .10 .25
163 Jindrich Kotrla .10 .25
164 Jaroslav Buchal .10 .25
165 Josef Straka .30 .75
166 Michail Fadejev .10 .25
167 Radek Sip .10 .25
168 Martin Rousek .10 .25
169 Tomas Vlasak .30 .50
170 Robert Kysela .30 .75
171 Jan Alinc .16 .40
172 Vladimir Machulda .10 .25
173 Vladimir Jerabek .10 .25
174 Frantisek Vorlicek CO .10 .25
175 Jan Hrbaty CO .10 .25
176 Marek Novotny .30 .50
177 Lukas Sablik .10 .25
178 Roman Kankovsky .10 .25
179 Michael Vyhlidal .10 .25
180 Jan Bohacek .10 .25
181 Roman Cech .30 .75
182 Zdenek Touzimsky .10 .25
183 Marek Posmyk .40 .50
184 Pavel Rajnoha .16 .40
185 Martin Tupa .10 .25
186 Libor Dolana .10 .25
187 Petr Vlk .16 .40
188 Petr Kankovsky .10 .25
189 Jiri Cihlar .30 .75
190 Jiri Poukar .10 .25
191 Jaromir Kverka .10 .25
192 Leos Pipa .10 .25
193 Ladislav Prokupek .30 .75
194 Patrik Fink .10 .25
195 Marek Melenovsky .30 .75
196 Jiri Holik .10 .25
197 Miroslav Bruna .10 .25
198 Jaroslav Walter .10 .25
199 Otto Zelezny .10 .25
200 Libor Barta .10 .25
201 Pavel Nestak .10 .25
202 Leo Gudas .10 .25
203 Karel Beran .10 .25
204 Richard Adam .10 .25
205 Pavel Zubicek .10 .25
206 Alexandr Elsner .10 .25
207 Robert Kantor .10 .25
208 Ladislav Tresl .20 .50
209 Frantisek Sevcik .20 .50
210 Michal Konecny .10 .25
211 Richard Sebestu .10 .25
212 Roman Mejzlik .16 .40
213 Zdenek Cely .10 .25
214 Jiri Vitek .10 .25
215 Radek Haman .10 .25
216 Tomas Krasny .10 .25
217 Jiri Suhrada .10 .25
218 Jaroslav Smolik .10 .25
219 Alois Hadamczik CO .10 .25
220 Karel Suchanek .10 .25
221 Michal Hlinka .30 .75
222 Josef Lucak .10 .25
223 Karel Pavlik CO .10 .25
224 Stanislav Meciar .30 .75
225 Petr Mainer .10 .25
226 Petr Pavlas .10 .25
227 Lubomir Sekeras .40 1.00
228 Roman Sindel .20 .50
229 Vaclav Slaby .10 .25
230 Miroslav Cihal .10 .25
231 Martin Palinek .10 .25
232 Petr Zajonc .10 .25
233 Michal Piskor .16 .40
234 Roman Kadera .30 .75
235 Marek Zadina .10 .25
236 Richard Kral .16 .40
237 Miroslav Skovira .10 .25
238 Vladimir Michalek .10 .25
239 Libor Zatopek .10 .25
240 Dusan Adamcik .10 .25
241 Jiri Novotny .10 .25
242 Karel Trachta CO .10 .25
243 Jindrich Setikovsky CO .10 .25
244 Rudolf Pejchar .30 .75
245 Michal Marik .10 .25
246 Karel Smid .30 .75
247 Martin Kovarik .10 .25
248 Jiri Hanzlik .10 .25
249 Jaroslav Spacek .30 .50
250 Stanislav Benes .10 .25
251 Robert Jindrich .20 .50
252 Vaclav Ruprecht .10 .25
253 Tomas Kucharcik .10 .25
254 Michal Straka .10 .25
255 Ondrej Steiner .20 .50
256 Tomas Klimt .20 .50
257 Martin Zivny .10 .25
258 Milan Volak .10 .25
259 Pavel Metlicka .10 .25
260 Josef Rybar .20 .75
261 Jaroslav Kreuzmann .10 .25
262 David Trachta .10 .25
263 Anatolij Najda .10 .25
264 Tomas Ruprecht .10 .25
265 Dalibor Sanda .10 .25
266 Jaroslav Brabec .10 .25
267 Frantisek Vyborny CO .10 .25
268 Stanislav Berger CO .10 .25
269 Ivo Capek .30 .75
270 David Volek .30 .75
271 Jiri Vykoukal .20 .50
272 Vaclav Burda .10 .25
273 Petr Kuchyna .20 .25
274 Pavel Srek .10 .25
275 Frantisek Ptacek .10 .25
276 Radek Hamr .16 .40
277 Jiri Krocak .10 .25
278 Jaroslav Nedved .16 .25
279 Jiri Zelenka .16 .40
280 David Vyborny .30 .75
281 Checklist 1 .10 .10
282 Checklist 2 .10 .10
283 Checklist 3 .10 .10
284 Checklist 4 .10 .10
285 Zbynek Kukacka .10 .25
286 Miroslav Hlinka .10 .25
287 Jaroslav Hlinka .10 .25
288 Jan Hlavac .80 1.00
289 Andrej Potajcuk .10 .25
290 Richard Zemlicka .30 1.00
291 Vladimir Stransky .10 .25
292 Ladislav Svozil .10 .25
293 Martin Prusek .80 10.00
294 Vladimir Hudacek .10 .50
295 Pavel Marecek .10 .25
296 Rudolf Wolf .10 .25
297 Tomas Kramny .10 .25
298 Pavel Kubina .80 3.00
299 Rene Sevecek .10 .25
300 Filip Kuba .30 .75
301 Ales Tomasek .10 .25
302 Roman Rysanek .10 .25
303 Vladimir Vujtek .20 .50
304 Petr Folta .10 .25
305 Jan Peterek .10 .25
306 Roman Simicek .40 .50
307 Pavel Zdrahal .10 .25
308 Pavel Sebesta .10 .25
309 David Moravec .40 1.00
310 Tomas Chlubna .10 .25
311 Ludek Krayzel .10 .25
312 Waldemar Klisiak .10 .25
313 Petr Fabian .10 .25
314 Josef Palacek .10 .25
315 Florian Strida .10 .25
316 Radovan Biegl .10 .25
317 Dusan Salficky .80 .75
318 Petr Jancarik .10 .25
319 Tomas Pacal .10 .25
320 Radomir Brazda .10 .25
321 Radek Mesicek .10 .25
322 Jiri Antonin .10 .25
323 Alexander Terechov .10 .25
324 Milan Beranek .10 .25
325 Ladislav Lubina .10 .25
326 David Pospisil .10 .25
327 Milan Kastner .10 .25
328 Stanislav Prochazka .10 .25
329 Patrik Weber .10 .25
330 Milan Hejduk 10.00 20.00
331 Tomas Blazek .20 .25
332 Jiri Jantovsky .10 .25
333 Jaroslav Kudrna .10 .25
334 Tomas Pisa .10 .25
335 Ales Pisa .10 .25
336 Ivan Vasilev .10 .25
337 Milan Hnilicka 2.00 5.00
338 Ales Flasar .10 .25
339 Martin Smetak .10 .25
340 Libor Polasek .20 .50
341 Vitezslav Skuta .10 .25
342 Ladislav Benysek .40 1.00
343 Jaroslav Smolik .10 .25
344 Igor Cikl .10 .25
345 Jan Czerlinski .10 .25
346 Marek Vorel .10 .25
347 Martin Ancicka .10 .25
348 Pavel Skrbek .40 .50
349 Petr Kadlec .10 .25
350 Tomas Kucharcik .10 .25
351 Ludek Bukac .30 .75
352 Zdenek Uher .10 .25
353 Roman Cechmanek 2.00 4.00
354 Roman Turek .75 2.00
355 Petr Briza .80 2.00
356 Jaroslav Kames .40 .75
357 Antonin Stavjana .30 .50

358 Bedrich Scerban .30 .75
359 Petr Kuchyna .10 .25
360 Jiri Vykoukal .30 .75
361 Frantisek Kaberle .40 .75
362 Jan Vopat .30 .75
363 Libor Prochazka .20 .50
364 Jiri Kucera .20 .50
365 Tomas Jelinek .20 .50
366 Richard Zemlicka .40 1.00
367 Martin Hostak .20 .50
368 Tomas Srsen .10 .25
369 Jiri Dopita .80 1.00
370 Martin Prochazka .30 .75
371 Pavel Patera .40 .50
372 Otakar Vejvoda .30 .75
373 Roman Horak .10 .25
374 Radek Belohlav .30 .50
375 Pavel Geffert .10 .25
376 Jan Alinc .10 .25
377 Roman Kadera .10 .25
378 Viktor Ujcik .30 .75
379 Roman Meluzin .20 .50
380 Pavel Janku .10 .25
381 Tomas Kucharcik .10 .25
382 Zbynek Marak .10 .25
383 Ales Zima .10 .25
384 Jaromir Jagr 10.00 25.00
385 Pavel Patera .30 .75
386 Martin Prochazka .30 .75
387 Pavel Janku .10 .25
388 Roman Cechmanek 2.00 4.00
389 Antonin Stavjana .30 .50
390 Rostislav Vlach .10 .25
391 Lubos Jenacek .10 .25
392 Dominik Hasek 6.00 15.00
393 Jiri Holik .10 .25
394 Frantisek Pospisil .10 .25
395 Ivan Hlinka .30 .75
396 Vladimir Martinec .10 .25
397 Jaroslav Pouzar .10 .25
398 Karel Gut .10 .25
399 Jan Benda .30 .75
400 unknown .10 .25

1996-97 Czech APS Extraliga

This 350-card set features the players of the top division in the Czech Republic, the Extraliga. They were produced by APS cards and sponsored by Fuji Film. Key cards in the set include Roman Turek, Marek Posmyk and Robert Reichel.

COMPLETE SET (350) 36.00 90.00
1 Marek Sykora CO .10 .10
2 Vladimir Kolek .10 .10
3 Rudolf Pejchar .12 .35
4 Ladislav Kudrna .12 .35
5 Miroslav Horava .25
6 Petr Kadlec .10 .25
7 Jaromir Latal .10 .25
8 Jiri Hes .25
9 Andrei Jakovenko .10 .25
10 Martin Maskarinec .25
11 Jaroslav Horacek .10 .25
12 Robert Kostka .25
13 Jiri Dolezal .10 .25
14 Tomas Kucharcik .25
15 Ivo Prorok .10 .25
16 Roman Kadera .25
17 Jiri Hlinka .10 .25
18 Tomas Kupka .25
19 Viktor Ujcik .30 .75
20 Vladimir Ruzicka .12 .35
21 Ladislav Slizek .10 .25
22 Jaroslav Bednar .40 1.00
23 Michal Sup .25
24 Radek Matejovsky .10 .25
25 Horst Valasek .10 .10
26 Jiri Vodak .10 .10
27 Jaroslav Kames .30 .75
28 Petr Kubena .12 .35
29 Petr Kuchyna .25
30 Jiri Marusak .10 .25
31 Radim Tesarik .25
32 Vadim Podrezov .10 .25
33 Stanislav Medrik .25
34 Jan Krajicek .10 .25
35 Pavel Kowalczyk .10 .25
36 David Bruk .25
37 Tomas Nemcicky .10 .25
38 Zdenek Sedlak .25
39 Ales Zima .10 .25
40 Zbynek Marak .25
41 Ales Polcar .10 .25
42 Roman Meluzin .10 .25
43 Pavel Janku .25
44 Miroslav Okal .10 .25
45 Petr Cajanek .40 1.00
46 Martin Kotasek .25
47 Petr Leska .10 .25
48 Alois Hadamczik CO .10 .10
49 Ales Mach .10 .25
50 Radovan Biegl .20 .50
51 Josef Lukac .20 .50
52 Petr Jancarik .25
53 Lubomir Sekeras .40 1.00
54 Jiri Kuntos .10 .25
55 Stanislav Pavelec .25
56 Patrik Hucko .10 .25
57 Miroslav Cihal .25
58 Karel Pavlik .25
59 Ondrej Zetek .10 .25
60 Richard Kral .25
61 Petr Folta .10 .25
62 Josef Straub .25
63 Petr Zajonc .10 .25
64 Roman Kontsek .25
65 Marek Zadina .10 .25
66 Roman Blazek .25
67 Michal Piskor .10 .25
68 Jozef Dano .10 .25
69 Vladimir Machulda .25
70 Jiri Novotny .10 .25
71 Petr Lipina .10 .25
72 Jan Novotny CO .10 .10
73 Lubomir Bauer .10 .10
74 Milan Hnilicka 2.00 5.00
75 Martin Chlad .20 .50
76 Petr Kasik .10 .25
77 Jan Krulis .10 .25
78 Libor Prochazka .20 .50
79 Jan Dlouhy .10 .25
80 Marek Zidlicky .40 1.00
81 Tomas Kaberle .60 1.50
82 Pavel Skrbek .20 .50
83 Tomas Trachta .10 .25
84 Zdenek Eichenmann .10 .25
85 Josef Zajic .20 .50
86 David Cermak .10 .25
87 Ladislav Svoboda .10 .25
88 Tomas Mikolasek .10 .25
89 Petr Ton .10 .25
90 Jiri Beranek .15 .40
91 Vaclav Eiselt .10 .25
92 Jiri Burger .10 .25
93 Petr Tenkrat .30 .75
94 Petr Vogeltanz .10 .25
95 Filip Klapac .10 .25
96 Karel Suchanek .10 .25
97 Kamil Konecny .10 .25
98 Rostislav Haas .10 .25
99 Roman Slupina .10 .25
100 Milos Hrubes .10 .25
101 Petr Tejkl .10 .25
102 Martin Bakula .10 .25
103 Radek Mesicek .10 .25
104 Karel Frydl .10 .25
105 David Galvas .10 .25
106 Denis Tsygurov .15 .40
107 Juraj Jurik .10 .25
108 Petr Fabian .10 .25
109 Radim Radevic .10 .25
110 Jiri Zadrazil .10 .25
111 Martin Filip .10 .25
112 Karel Horny .10 .25
113 Zdenek Pavelek .10 .25
114 Eduard Gorbachev .12 .35
115 Valerij Belov .10 .25
116 Dalibor Rimsky .10 .25
117 Marek Harazim .10 .25
118 David Dostal .10 .25
119 Slavomir Lener CO .12 .35
120 Vaclav Sykora .10 .25
121 Robert Schistad .12 .35
122 Martin Cinibulk .10 .25
123 Jiri Vykoukal .20 .50
124 Jan Bohacek .10 .25
125 Jaroslav Nedved .10 .25
126 Jiri Krocak .10 .25
127 Vaclav Burda .10 .25
128 Radek Hamr .12 .35
129 Frantisek Ptacek .10 .25
130 Roman Horak .10 .25
131 Pavel Geffert .10 .25
132 Richard Zemlicka .20 .50
133 Jiri Zelenka .12 .35
134 Patrik Martinec .10 .25
135 David Vyborny .20 .50
136 Miroslav Hlinka .10 .25
137 Martin Hostak .12 .35
138 Jan Hlavac .40 1.00
139 Jaroslav Hinka .10 .25
140 Jan Benda .12 .35
141 Josef Palecek .10 .25
142 Milos Riha CO .10 .25
143 Libor Barta .10 .25
144 Dusan Salficky .30 .75
145 Radomir Brazda .10 .25
146 Pavel Augusta .10 .25
147 Jiri Malinsky .10 .25
148 Tomas Pacal .10 .25
149 Ales Pisa .10 .25
150 Pavel Kriz .12 .35
151 Alexander Tsyplakov .20 .50
152 Petr Mudroch .10 .25
153 Ladislav Lubina .10 .25
154 David Pospisil .10 .25
155 Stanislav Prochazka .10 .25
156 Tomas Martinec .10 .25
157 Milan Hejduk 8.00 15.00
158 Tomas Martinec .10 .25
159 Jiri Jantovsky .10 .25
160 Martin Koudelka .10 .25
161 Pavel Kabrt .10 .25
162 Petr Sykora .20 .50
163 Milan Prochazka .12 .35
164 Karel Plasek .10 .25
165 Josef Beranek .20 .50
166 Vladimir Kyhos .10 .25
167 Zdenek Orct .30 .75
168 Richard Hrazdira .10 .25
169 Kamil Prachar .12 .35
170 Radek Mrazek .10 .25
171 Roman Cech .20 .50
172 Angel Nikolov .20 .50
173 Martin Stepanek .10 .25
174 Sergej Butko .10 .25
175 Normunds Sejejs .10 .25
176 Petr Kratky .10 .25
177 Vladimir Jerabek .10 .25
178 Kamil Kastak .12 .35
179 Robert Kysela .10 .25
180 Petr Hrbek .10 .25
181 Martin Rousek .10 .25
182 Tomas Krasny .10 .25
183 Tomas Vlasak .20 .50
184 David Balazs .10 .25
185 Jindrich Kotrla .10 .25
186 Josef Straka .20 .50
187 Jaroslav Buchal .10 .25
188 Kamil Piros .60 1.50
189 Vladimir Vujtek CO .10 .25
190 Ladislav Svozil .10 .25
191 Martin Prusek 2.00 5.00
192 Tomas Vasicek .10 .25
193 Jiri Jonak .10 .25
194 Ales Tomasek .10 .25
195 Daniel Kysela .10 .25
196 Vitezslav Skuta .10 .25
197 Tomas Kramny .10 .25
198 Rene Sevecek .10 .25
199 Dmitrij Jerofejev .10 .25
200 Pavel Kumstat .10 .25
201 Roman Rysanek .10 .25
202 Roman Simicek .20 .50
203 Martin Smetak .10 .25
204 Tomas Chlubna .10 .25
205 Ludek Krayzel .10 .25
206 David Moravec .20 .50
207 Alexander Prokopjev .10 .25
208 Ales Kratoska .10 .25
209 Libor Pavlis .10 .25
210 Radek Klauda .10 .25
211 Libor Polasek .12 .35
212 Jan Neliba CO .10 .25
213 Zdislav Tabara CO .10 .25
214 Roman Cechmanek .75 2.00
215 Ivo Pesat .20 .50
216 Antonin Stavjana .20 .50
217 Bedrich Scerban .12 .35
218 Jiri Veber .10 .25
219 Alexej Jaskin .10 .25
220 Jan Srdinko .10 .25
221 Tomas Jakes .10 .25
222 Petr Kubox .10 .25
223 Michal Divisek .10 .25
224 Rostislav Vlach .10 .25
225 Michal Tomek .10 .25
226 Oto Hascak .20 .50
227 Tomas Kapusta .20 .50
228 Tomas Srsen .10 .25
229 Roman Stantien .10 .25
230 Jiri Dopita .30 .75
231 Ivan Padelek .10 .25
232 Andrej Galkin .10 .25
233 Ondrej Kratena .20 .50
234 David Hruska .10 .25
235 Daniel Tesarik .10 .25
236 Lukas Duba .10 .25
237 Vladimir Caldr CO .10 .25
238 Jaroslav Liska .10 .25
239 Oldrich Svoboda .10 .25
240 Robert Slavik .20 .50
241 Rudolf Suchanek .10 .25
242 Karel Soudek .10 .25
243 Milan Nedoma .20 .50
244 Kamil Toupal .10 .25
245 Petr Sedy .10 .25
246 Lukas Zib .10 .25
247 Martin Masak .10 .25
248 Radek Martinek .40 1.00
249 Vladimir Antipin .10 .25
250 Radek Toupal .12 .35
251 Pavel Pycha .10 .25
252 Lubos Rob .12 .35
253 Filip Turek .10 .25
254 Arpad Gyori .10 .25
255 Radek Belohlav .20 .50
256 Ondrej Vosta .10 .25
257 Milan Navratil .10 .25
258 Frantisek Sevcik .10 .25
259 Petr Sailer .10 .25
260 Michal Horak .10 .25
261 Kamil Brabenec .15 .40
262 Miroslav Barus .10 .25
263 Jiri Latal .12 .35
264 Miroslav Venkrbec .10 .25
265 Ladislav Blazek .20 .50
266 Robert Horyna .12 .35
267 Petr Pavlas .10 .25
268 Roman Veber .10 .25
269 Marek Tichy .10 .25
270 Jergus Baca .12 .35
271 Ladislav Benysek .20 .50
272 Jiri Polak .10 .25
273 Marek Cernosek .10 .25
274 Michal Slavik .10 .25
275 Pavel Nohel .10 .25
276 Radek Sip .10 .25
277 Jan Tomajko .10 .25
278 Michal Bros .12 .35
279 Radek Prochazka .10 .25
280 Radek Svoboda .10 .25
281 Michal Dvorak .10 .25
282 Ales Lipensky .20 .50
283 Filip Dvorak .10 .25
284 Milan Jurak .10 .25
285 Adam Drabek .10 .25
286 Bohuslav Ebermann .10 .25
287 Radim Rulik .10 .25
288 Martin Altrichter .20 .50
289 Michal Marik .10 .25
290 Ivan Vlcek .10 .25
291 Josef Reznicek .10 .25
292 Karel Smid .10 .25
293 Vaclav Ruprecht .20 .50
294 Jaroslav Spacek .20 .50
295 Jiri Hanzlik .10 .25
296 Robert Jindrich .20 .50
297 Tomas Jelinek .10 .25
298 Milan Volak .10 .25
299 Radek Kampf .10 .25
300 Miroslav Mach .12 .35
301 Petr Korinek .20 .50
302 Jiri Kucera .15 .40
303 Michal Straka .10 .25
304 Tomas Klimt .20 .50
305 Josef Rybar .20 .50
306 Dalibor Sanda .10 .25
307 Jiri Novotny .10 .25
308 Pavel Vostrak .10 .25
309 Frantisek Vorlicek CO .10 .25
310 Jan Hrbaty CO .10 .25
311 Ivo Capek .20 .50
312 Marek Novotny .10 .25
313 Roman Kankovsky .10 .25
314 Miroslav Javin .10 .25
315 Michael Vyhlidal .10 .25
316 Zdenek Touzimsky .10 .25
317 Martin Tupa .20 .50
318 Marian Morava .10 .25
319 Filip Vanecek .20 .50
320 Marek Posmyk .20 .50
321 Libor Dolana .10 .25
322 Petr Vlk .15 .40
323 Petr Kankovsky .10 .25
324 Jaroslav Hub .10 .25
325 Jiri Poukar .10 .25
326 Leos Pipa .10 .25
327 Ladislav Prokupek .20 .50
328 Patrik Fink .10 .25
329 Marek Melenovsky .15 .40
330 Milan Antos .10 .25
331 Jiri Holik .10 .25
332 Miroslav Bruna .10 .25
333 Michail Fadejev .10 .25
334 Ludek Bukac CO .15 .40
335 Slavomir Lener CO .12 .35
336 Zdenek Uher .10 .25
337 Roman Cechmanek .75 2.00
338 Roman Turek .75 2.00
339 Robert Sysela .10 .25
340 Jiri Veber .10 .25
341 Pavel Patera .20 .50
342 Radek Bonk .40 1.00
343 Radek Belohlav .20 .50
344 Drahomir Kadlec .15 .40
345 Michal Sykora .20 .50
346 Jiri Vykoukal .20 .50
347 Viktor Ujcik .20 .50
348 Stanislav Neckar .20 .50
349 Robert Reichel .30 .75
350 Roman Meluzin .12 .35

1997-98 Czech APS Extraliga

This standard-sized set features the players of the Czech Republic's Extraliga and was produced by APS. The set features early or even first cards of several top NHLers including Milan Hejduk, Patrik Stefan and Roman Cechmanek.

COMPLETE SET (380) 50.00 125.00
1 Slavomir Lener CO .20 .50
2 Vaclav Sykora CO .10 .25
3 Milan Hnilicka 2.00 5.00
4 Martin Cinibulk .10 .25
5 Frantisek Ptacek .10 .25
6 Frantisek Kucera .10 .25
7 Jaroslav Nedved .10 .25
8 Jiri Krocak .10 .25
9 Martin Holy .10 .25
10 Jaromir Kverka .10 .25
11 Jiri Zelenka .10 .25
12 Richard Zemlicka .20 .50
13 Jaroslav Hlinka .10 .25
14 Jaroslav Bednar .40 1.00
15 Ivo Novotny .10 .25
16 Radek Duda .20 .50
17 Michal Sivek .75 2.00
18 Jan Hlavac .40 1.00
19 Miroslav Hlinka .10 .25
20 Patrik Stefan ERC 1.25 3.00
21 Vaclav Burda .10 .25
22 Patrik Martinec .10 .25
23 Ladislav Benysek .20 .50
24 Jiri Vykoukal .20 .50
25 Petr Nedved .80 2.00
26 Jan Neliba CO .10 .25
27 Zdislav Tabara CO .10 .25
28 Roman Cechmanek 2.00 5.00
29 Ivo Pesat .30 .75
30 Radim Tesarik .10 .25
31 Antonin Stavjana .20 .50
32 Jiri Veber .10 .25
33 Michal Bros .10 .25
34 Alexej Jaskin .10 .25
35 Andrej Galkin .10 .25
36 Rostislav Vlach .10 .25
37 Ivan Padelek .10 .25
38 Tomas Srsen .10 .25
39 Jiri Dopita .30 .75
40 Ondrej Kratena .20 .50
41 Tomas Kapusta .10 .25
42 Pavel Zubicek .10 .25
43 Radek Belohlav .20 .50
44 Tomas Demel .10 .25
45 Michal Divisek .10 .25
46 Michal Safarik .10 .25
47 Josef Beranek .20 .50
48 Jan Tomajko .10 .25
49 Jan Srdinko .10 .25
50 Roman Stantien .10 .25
51 Eduard Novak CO .10 .25
52 Zdenek Cech CO .10 .25
53 Jaroslav Kames .40 1.00
54 Robert Hamrla .10 .25
55 Pavel Kowalczyk .10 .25
56 Jan Krajicek .10 .25
57 Petr Kuchyna .10 .25
58 Pavel Rajnoha .10 .25
59 Martin Hamrlik .10 .25
60 Jiri Marusak .10 .25
61 Karel Rachunek .40 1.00
62 Roman Meluzin .20 .50
63 Ales Zima .10 .25
64 Pavel Janku .20 .50
65 Tomas Nemcicky .10 .25
66 Petr Cajanek .30 .75
67 Miroslav Okal .10 .25
68 Zdenek Sedlak .10 .25
69 Ales Polcar .10 .25
70 Petr Leska .10 .25
71 Martin Spanhel .30 .75
72 Branislav Janos .10 .25
73 Marek Vorel .10 .25
74 Tomas Zizka .10 .25
75 Ondrej Weissman CO .10 .25
76 Vladimir Jerabek CO .10 .25
77 Zdenek Orct .30 .75
78 Richard Hrazdira .10 .25
79 Angel Nikolov .10 .25
80 Drahomir Kadlec .30 .75
81 Frantisek Prochazka .10 .25
82 Radek Mrazek .10 .25
83 Petr Molnar .10 .25
84 Martin Stepanek .10 .25
85 Roman Cech .10 .25
86 Vladimir Gyna .10 .25
87 Tomas Vlasak .10 .25
88 Robert Kysela .10 .25
89 Martin Rousek .10 .25
90 Petr Hrbek .10 .25
91 Vladimir Petrovka .10 .25
92 Ivo Prorok .10 .25
93 Tomas Krasny .10 .25
94 David Balazs .10 .25
95 Josef Straka .10 .25
96 Kamil Piros .40 1.00
97 Denis Afinogenov .20 .50
98 Rail Muftijev .10 .25
99 Dmitrij Denisov .10 .25
100 Karel Franek CO .10 .25
101 Petr Pelucha CO .10 .25
102 Rostislav Haas .10 .25
103 Pavel Nestak .10 .25
104 Martin Maskarinec .10 .25
105 David Galvas .10 .25
106 Milos Hrubes .10 .25
107 Pavel Sebesta .10 .25
108 Tomas Kramny .10 .25
109 Pavel Marecek .10 .25
110 Vaclav Slaby .10 .25
111 Petr Suchanek .10 .25
112 Zbynek Marak .10 .25
113 Michal Tomek .10 .25
114 Michal Piskor .10 .25
115 Juraj Jurik .10 .25
116 Karel Horny .10 .25
117 Jiri Zurek .10 .25
118 Martin Sychra .10 .25
119 Zdenek Pavelek .10 .25
120 Richard Brancik .10 .25
121 Milan Ministr .10 .25
122 Martin Sekera .10 .25
123 Vladimir Vujtek CO .20 .50
124 Ladislav Svozil CO .10 .25
125 Martin Prusek 1.50 4.00
126 Zdenek Dobes .10 .25
127 Jiri Jonak .10 .25
128 Vitezslav Skuta .10 .25
129 Dmitrij Jerofejev .10 .25
130 Petr Jurecka .10 .25
131 Pavel Kumstat .10 .25
132 Roman Simicek .20 .50
133 Roman Rysanek .10 .25
134 David Moravec .30 .75
135 Alexander Prokopjev .10 .25
136 Alexander Cherbajev .10 .25
137 Libor Pavlis .10 .25
138 Jan Matejny .10 .25
139 Libor Polasek .10 .25
140 Martin Kotasek .10 .25
141 Petr Zajonc .10 .25
142 Martin Lamich .10 .25
143 Daniel Vilasek .10 .25
144 Martin Tomasek .10 .25
145 Ales Kratoska .10 .25
146 Richard Farda CO .10 .25
147 Ladislav Slizek CO .10 .25
148 Martin Altrichter .10 .25
149 Ladislav Blazek .20 .50
150 Robert Kostka .10 .25
151 Jiri Hes .10 .25
152 Andrej Jakovenko .10 .25
153 Pavel Kolarik .20 .50
154 Martin Bakula .10 .25
155 Petr Kadlec .10 .25
156 Jan Novak .10 .25
157 Jan Hejda .10 .25
158 Vladimir Ruzicka .20 .50
159 Viktor Ujcik .20 .50
160 Jiri Dolezal .10 .25
161 Jiri Poukar .10 .25
162 Tomas Kucharcik .10 .25
163 Michal Sup .10 .25
164 Jiri Hlinka .10 .25
165 Tomas Kupka .10 .25
166 Radek Matejovsky .10 .25
167 Robert Kucera .10 .25
168 Jan Fadrny .10 .25
169 Jan Sochor .10 .25
170 Marek Sykora CO .10 .25
171 Radim Rulik CO .10 .25
172 Michal Marik .10 .25
173 Dusan Salficky .40 1.00
174 Josef Reznicek .10 .25
175 Ivan Vlcek .10 .25
176 Robert Jindrich .20 .50
177 Jiri Hanzlik .10 .25
178 Pavel Srek .10 .25
179 Ondrej Zetek .10 .25
180 Pavel Geffert .10 .25
181 David Pospisil .10 .25
182 Martin Filip .10 .25
183 Tomas Jelinek .10 .25
184 Michal Straka .10 .25
185 Milan Volak .10 .25
186 Pavel Vostrak .10 .25
187 Dalibor Sanda .10 .25
188 Milan Navratil .10 .25
189 Mojmir Musil .10 .25
190 Milan Kraft 2.00 5.00
191 Jiri Jelen .10 .25
192 Martin Cech .10 .25
193 Jan Novotny CO .10 .25
194 Lubomir Bauer CO .10 .25
195 Radek Toth .10 .25
196 Martin Bilek .10 .25
197 Jan Krulis .10 .25
198 Marek Zidlicky .10 .25
199 Tomas Kaberle 1.20 3.00
200 Pavel Skrbek .20 .50
201 Jan Penk .10 .25
202 Jan Dlouhy .10 .25
203 Jan Hranac .10 .25
204 Josef Zajic .10 .25
205 Zdenek Eichenmann .10 .25
206 Petr Ton .10 .25
207 Jiri Beranek .10 .25
208 Ladislav Svoboda .10 .25
209 Vaclav Eiselt .10 .25
210 Jiri Burger .10 .25
211 Petr Tenkrat .30 .75
212 Jiri Kuchler .10 .25
213 Tomas Trachta .10 .25
214 Jiri Holsan .10 .25
215 Milan Novy .10 .25
216 Jiri Kloboucek .10 .25
217 Tomas Mikolasek .10 .25
218 Milan Kasparek CO .10 .25
219 Karel Trachta CO .10 .25
220 Vladimir Hudacek .10 .25
221 Robert Horyna CO .10 .25
222 Petr Pavlas .10 .25
223 Petr Mainer .10 .25
224 Ales Tomasek .10 .25
225 Pavel Blaha .10 .25
226 Jiri Polak .10 .25
227 Martin Richter .10 .25
228 Martin Rejthar .10 .25
229 Michal Cerny .10 .25
230 Zbynek Kukacka .10 .25
231 Ondrej Steiner .10 .25
232 Pavel Metlicka .10 .25
233 Martin Streit .10 .25
234 Radek Prochazka .10 .25
235 Radek Svoboda .10 .25
236 Michal Porak .10 .25
237 Michal Horak .10 .25
238 Jan Lipiansky .10 .25
239 Jaroslav Buchal .10 .25
240 Tomas Klimt .20 .50
241 Petr Fical .10 .25
242 Milos Riha CO .10 .25
243 Josef Palecek CO .10 .25
244 Libor Barta .10 .25
245 Adam Svoboda .40 1.00
246 Patrik Rozsival .10 .25
247 Jiri Malinsky .10 .25
248 Ales Pisa .10 .25
249 Tomas Pacal .10 .25
250 Pavel Kriz .20 .50
251 Pavel Augusta .10 .25
252 Petr Murdoch .10 .25
253 Robert Pospisil .10 .25
254 Tomas Blazek .20 .50
255 Milan Hejduk 8.00 20.00
256 Jiri Jantovsky .10 .25
257 Stanislav Prochazka .10 .25
258 Tomas Martinec .10 .25
259 Pavel Kabrt .10 .25
260 Jaroslav Kudrna .20 .50
261 Karel Plasek .10 .25
262 Petr Sykora 2.00 5.00
263 Lukas Palecek .10 .25
264 Vladimir Caldr CO .10 .25
265 Jaroslav Liska CO .10 .25
266 Oldrich Svoboda .40 1.00
267 Robert Slavik .10 .25
268 Rudolf Suchanek .10 .25
269 Karel Soudek .10 .25
270 Milan Nedoma .10 .25
271 Kamil Toupal .10 .25
272 Lukas Zib .10 .25
273 Jan Bohacek .10 .25
274 Filip Vanecek .10 .25
275 Radek Martinek .30 .75
276 Radek Toupal .10 .25
277 Lubos Rob .10 .25
278 Pavel Pycha .10 .25
279 David Bruk .10 .25
280 Filip Turek .10 .25
281 Ondrej Vosta .10 .25
282 Arpad GyÃ¶ri .10 .25
283 Petr Sailer .10 .25
284 Martin Strba .10 .25
285 Petr Sachl .10 .25
286 Miroslav Barus .10 .25
287 Vaclav Kral .10 .25
288 Ales Kotalik ERC 2.00 5.00
289 Josef Augusta CO .20 .50
290 Karel Dvorak CO .20 .50
291 Marek Novotny .20 .50
292 Lukas Sablik .10 .25
293 Michael Vyhlidal .10 .25
294 Miroslav Javin .10 .25
295 Martin Tupa .10 .25
296 Marian Morava .10 .25
297 Jaroslav Horacek .10 .25
298 Tomas Jakes .10 .25
299 Daniel Zapotocny .10 .25
300 Miroslav Duben .10 .25
301 Petr Vlk .10 .25
302 Roman Mejzlik .10 .25
303 Jiri Cihlar .10 .25
304 Jaroslav Hub .10 .25
305 Leos Pipa .10 .25
306 Ladislav Prokupek .10 .25
307 Marek Melenovsky .10 .25
308 Milan Antos .10 .25
309 Vaclav Adamec .10 .25
310 Ales Sochorec .10 .25
311 Ales Polcar .10 .25
312 Daniel Hodek .10 .25
313 Alois Hadamczik CO .10 .25
314 Kamil Konecny CO .10 .25
315 Radovan Biegl .20 .50
316 Vlastimil Lakosil .10 .25
317 Lubomir Sekeras .30 .75
318 Miroslav Cihal .10 .25
319 Petr Jancarik .10 .25
320 Stanislav Pavelec .10 .25
321 Jiri Kuntos .10 .25
322 Patrik Hucko .10 .25
323 Petr Gregorek .10 .25
324 Filip Stefanka .10 .25
325 Vladimir Machulda .10 .25
326 Marek Zadina .10 .25
327 Richard Kral .10 .25
328 Jozef Dano .10 .25
329 Ladislav Lubina .10 .25
330 Tomas Chlubna .10 .25
331 Jan Peterek .10 .25
332 Petr Folta .10 .25
333 Josef Straub .10 .25
334 Roman Kadera .10 .25
335 Marian Kacir .10 .25
336 Robert Kantor .10 .25
337 Roman Kontsek .10 .25
338 Miroslav Horava .10 .25
339 Ladislav Kudrna .10 .25
340 Ivan Hlinka CO .30 .75
341 Slavomir Lener CO .10 .25
342 Roman Cechmanek 2.00 5.00
343 Milan Hnilicka 2.00 5.00
344 Martin Prusek 1.50 4.00
345 Frantisek Kaberle .20 .50
346 Jiri Slegr .20 .50
347 Jiri Vykoukal .20 .50
348 Jiri Veber .10 .25
349 Ladislav Benysek .20 .50
350 Frantisek Kucera .10 .25
351 Libor Prochazka .10 .25
352 Jaroslav Spacek .20 .50
353 Vlastimil Kroupa .10 .25
354 Robert Reichel .30 .75
355 Robert Lang .40 1.00
356 Pavel Patera .20 .50
357 Martin Prochazka .20 .50
358 Jiri Dopita .30 .75
359 Josef Beranek .20 .50
360 Viktor Ujcik .20 .50
361 David Vyborny .20 .50
362 Vladimir Vujtek .20 .50
363 Roman Simicek .20 .50
364 Jan Alinc .10 .25
365 Rostislav Vlach .10 .25
366 Ondrej Kratena .10 .25
367 Richard Zemlicka .20 .50
368 Dominik Hasek POY 4.00 10.00
369 Jiri Dopita .30 .75
370 Roman Cechmanek 2.00 5.00
371 Roman Horak .10 .25
372 Richard Zemlicka .20 .50
373 Antonin Stavjana .20 .50
374 Ondrej Kratena .10 .25
375 Richard Farda .10 .25
376 Frantisek Cernik .10 .25
377 Ludek Cajka .10 .25
378 Vlastimil Bubnik .10 .25
379 Josef Mikolas .10 .25
380 Stanislav Konopasek .10 .25

1997-98 Czech DS Extraliga

This set features the top players of the Czech Extraliga. The first 13 cards are short printed. Card No. 1, Roman Cechmanek Super Chase, was issued 1:48, while the Golden All-Stars cards No. 2-12 came 1:4.

COMPLETE SET (120) 20.00 75.00
1 Roman Cechmanek 4.00 10.00
2 Milan Hnilicka 4.00 10.00
3 Josef Beranek .40 .75
4 Milan Nedoma .40 1.00
5 Lubomir Sekeras .80 1.00
6 Jiri Vykoukal .80 2.00
7 Jiri Dopita .75 2.00
8 Robert Kysela .40 1.00
9 Roman Meluzin .80 2.00
10 Roman Simicek .20 .50
11 Petr Ton .40 1.00
12 Viktor Ujcik .80 2.00
13 Vladimir Hudacek .10 .50
14 Petr Pavlas .10 .25
15 Ales Tomasek .10 .25
16 Pavel Blaha .10 .25
17 Pavel Nohel .10 .25
18 Tomas Klimt .20 .50
19 Radek Prochazka .10 .25
20 Rostislav Haas .10 .25
21 Karel Smid .20 .50
22 Milos Hrubes .10 .25
23 Martin Maskarinec .10 .25
24 Zbynek Marak .10 .25
25 Michal Tomek .10 .25
26 Juraj Jurik .10 .25
27 Oldrich Svoboda .40 1.00
28 Rudolf Suchanek .10 .25
29 Karel Soudek .10 .25
30 Radek Martinek .30 .75
31 Radek Toupal .10 .25
32 Lubos Rob .10 .25
33 Pavel Pycha .10 .25
34 Marek Novotny .10 .25
35 Michael Vyhlidal .10 .25
36 Petr Vlk .10 .25
37 Roman Mejzlik .10 .25
38 Jiri Cihlar .10 .25
39 Jaroslav Hub .10 .25
40 Marek Melenovsky .10 .25
41 Zdenek Orct .30 .75
42 Angel Nikolov .20 .50
43 Frantisek Prochazka .10 .25
44 Martin Stepanek .10 .25
45 Tomas Vlasak .10 .25
46 Martin Rousek .10 .25
47 Petr Hrbek .10 .25
48 Ivo Prorok .10 .25
49 Dusan Salficky .40 .75
50 Josef Reznicek .10 .25
51 Ivan Vlcek .10 .25
52 Robert Jindrich .20 .50
53 Pavel Geffert .10 .25
54 Tomas Jelinek .10 .25
55 David Pospisil .10 .25
56 Milan Volak .10 .25
57 Antonin Stavjana .20 .50
58 Radim Tesarik .10 .25
59 Alexej Jaskin .10 .25
60 Tomas Srsen .10 .25
61 Tomas Kapusta .10 .25
62 Radek Belohlav .20 .50
63 Ondrej Kratena .10 .25
64 Jan Tomajko .10 .25
65 Michal Bros .10 .25
66 Rostislav Vlach .10 .25
67 Libor Barta .10 .25
68 Pavel Augusta .10 .25
69 Tomas Blazek .20 .25
70 Milan Hejduk 4.00 10.00
71 Stanislav Prochazka .10 .25
72 Tomas Martinec .10 .25
73 Jaroslav Kudrna .20 .50

74 Ladislav Blazek .10 .25
75 Martin Bakula .10 .25
76 Vladimir Ruzicka .20 .50
77 Jiri Dolezal .10 .25
78 Jiri Poukar .10 .25
79 Tomas Kucharcik .10 .25
80 Frantisek Kucera .10 .25
81 Vaclav Burda .10 .25
82 Jaroslav Nedved .10 .25
83 Richard Zemlicka .20 .50
84 Jiri Zelenka .10 .25
85 Patrik Martinec .10 .25
86 Jan Hlavac .80 1.00
87 Patrik Stefan ERC .75 2.00
88 Jaroslav Bednar .40 1.00
89 Radek Toth .10 .25
90 Jan Krulis .10 .25
91 Pavel Skrbek .20 .50
92 Josef Zajic .10 .25
93 Zdenek Eichenmann .10 .25
94 Ladislav Svoboda .10 .25
95 Martin Prusek .75 2.00
96 Jiri Jonak .10 .25
97 Vitezslav Skuta .10 .25
98 Dmitri Jerofejev .10 .25
99 Roman Rysanek .10 .25
100 David Moravec .30 .50
101 Alexander Prokopjev .10 .25
102 Jaroslav Kames .40 .75
103 Pavel Kowalczyk .10 .25
104 Petr Kuchyna .10 .25
105 Ales Zima .10 .25
106 Pavel Janku .20 .25
107 Tomas Nemcicky .10 .25
108 Petr Cajanek .30 1.00
109 Branislav Janos .10 .25
110 Radovan Biegl .20 .50
111 Richard Kral .10 .25
112 Roman Kontsek .10 .25
113 Jozef Dano .10 .25
114 Ladislav Lubina .10 .25
115 Tomas Chlubna .10 .25
116 Jozef Straub .10 .25
117 Roman Kadera .10 .25
118 Marek Zadina .10 .25
119 Checklist .10 .10
120 Premium card

1997-98 Czech DS Stickers

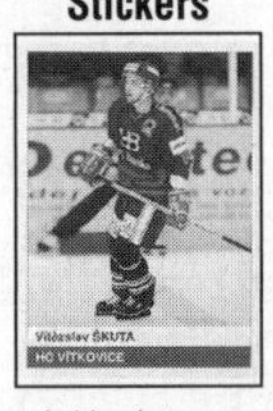

This set of stickers features many of the players in the Czech Republic Extraliga. The stickers are about 1/3 the size of a standard card. Because many of them were placed into sticker albums, they are difficult to find in their original condition.

COMPLETE SET (283) 35.00 90.00
1 Roman Cechmanek .60 1.50
2 Jiri Veber .10 .25
3 Jiri Vykoukal .20 .50
4 Miloslav Horava .10 .25
5 Martin Stepanek .10 .25
6 Antonin Stavjana .20 .50
7 Bedrich Scerban .10 .25
8 Radek Belohlav .20 .50
9 League Logo .10 .25
10 Jiri Dopita .30 .75
11 David Vyborny .20 .50
12 Josef Beranek .20 .50
13 Vladimir Jerabek .10 .25
14 Viktor Ujcik .20 .50
15 Roman Meluzin .20 .50
16 Jiri Kucera .10 .25
17 Robert Lang .40 1.00
18 Roman Cechmanek .60 1.50
19 Antonin Stavjana .20 .50
20 Tomas Jakes .10 .25
21 Alexej Jaskin .10 .25
22 Jan Srdinko .10 .25
23 Jiri Veber .10 .25
24 Bedrich Scerban .10 .25
25 Ivan Padelek .10 .25
26 HC Petra Vsetin Logo .10 .25
27 HC Petra Vsetin Team Card .10 .25
28 HC Petra Vsetin Team Card .10 .25
29 Rostislav Vlach .10 .25
30 Josef Beranek .20 .50
31 Ondrej Kratena .10 .25
32 Jiri Dopita .30 .75
33 Tomas Kapusta .10 .25
34 Tomas Srsen .10 .25
35 Andrej Galkin .10 .25
36 Oto Hascak .10 .25
37 Zdenek Orct .30 .75
38 Martin Stepanek .10 .25
39 Normunds Sejejs .10 .25
40 Sergej Butko .10 .25
41 Roman Cech .10 .25
42 Radek Mrazek .10 .25
43 Angel Nikolov .20 .50
44 Robert Kysela .10 .25
45 HC Litvinov Logo .10 .25
46 HC Litvinov Team Card .10 .25
47 HC Litvinov Team Card .10 .25
48 Vladimir Jerabek .10 .25
49 Martin Rousek .10 .25
50 Jaroslav Buchal .10 .25
51 Petr Hrbek .10 .25
52 Tomas Vlasak .10 .25
53 Tomas Krasny .10 .25
54 Josef Straka .10 .25
55 Kamil Kastak .10 .25
56 Robert Schistad .10 .25
57 Radek Hamr .10 .25
58 Jaroslav Nedved .10 .25
59 Jan Bohacek .10 .25
60 Vaclav Burda .10 .25
61 Jiri Vykoukal .10 .50
62 Frantisek Ptacek .10 .25
63 Jan Benda .10 .25
64 HC Sparta Praha Logo .10 .25
65 HC Sparta Praha Team Card .10 .25
66 HC Sparta Praha Team Card .10 .25
67 Richard Zemlicka .20 .50
68 Roman Horak .20 .50
69 Patrik Martinec .20 .50
70 Martin Hostak .10 .25
71 David Vyborny .20 .50
72 Pavel Geffert .10 .25
73 Robert Lang .40 1.00
74 Andrej Potajcuk .10 .25
75 Oldrich Svoboda .40 1.00
76 Karel Soudek .10 .25
77 Kamil Toupal .10 .25
78 Milan Nedoma .10 .25
79 Radek Martinek .40 .50
80 Vladimir Antipin .10 .25
81 Rudolf Suchanek .10 .25
82 Pavel Pycha .10 .25
83 HC Ceske Budejovice Logo .10 .25
84 HC Ceske Budejovice Team .10 .25
85 HC Ceske Budejovice Team .10 .25
86 Radek Toupal .10 .25
87 Lubos Rob .10 .25
88 Milan Navratil .10 .25
89 Filip Turek .10 .25
90 Radek Belohlav .20 .50
91 Miroslav Barus .10 .25
92 Frantisek Sevcik .10 .25
93 Arpad GyÃ¶ri .10 .25
94 Jaroslav Kames .40 .75
95 Petr Kuchyna .10 .25
96 Pavel Kowalczyk .10 .25
97 Stanislav Medrik .10 .25
98 Jan Krajicek .10 .25
99 Radim Tesarik .10 .25
100 Jiri Marusak .10 .25
101 Pavel Janku .20 .25
102 HC ZPS Zlin Logo .10 .25
103 HC ZPS Zlin Team Card .10 .25
104 HC ZPS Zlin Team Card .10 .25
105 Ales Polcar .10 .25
106 David Bruk .10 .25
107 Zbynek Marak .10 .25
108 Ales Zima .10 .25
109 Roman Meluzin .20 .50
110 Miroslav Okal .10 .25
111 Petr Cajanek .30 1.00
112 Tomas Nemcicky .10 .25
113 Rudolf Pejchar .10 .25
114 Jaromir Latal .10 .25
115 Robert Kostka .10 .25
116 Jiri Hes .10 .25
117 Petr Kadlec .10 .25
118 Martin Maskarinec .10 .25
119 Miloslav Horava .10 .25
120 Roman Kadera .10 .25
121 HC Slavia Praha Logo .10 .25
122 HC Slavia Praha Team Card .10 .25
123 HC Slavia Praha Team Card .10 .25
124 Tomas Kucharcik .10 .25
125 Jiri Dolezal .10 .25
126 Jaroslav Bednar .40 1.00
127 Ladislav Slizek .10 .25
128 Tomas Kupka .10 .25
129 Viktor Ujcik .20 .50
130 Vladimir Ruzicka .20 .50
131 Ivo Prorok .10 .25
132 Milan Hnilicka .60 1.50
133 Jan Krulis .10 .25
134 Jan Dlouhy .10 .25
135 Libor Prochazka .10 .25
136 Tomas Kaberle .60 1.50
137 Marek Zidlicky .10 1.00
138 Petr Kasik .10 .25
139 Jiri Beranek .10 .25
140 HC Poldi Kladno Logo .10 .25
141 HC Poldi Kladno Team Card .10 .25
142 HC Poldi Kladno Team Card .10 .25
143 Josef Zajic .10 .25
144 Tomas Mikolasek .10 .25
145 Ladislav Svoboda .10 .25
146 Zdenek Eichenmann .10 .25
147 Vaclev Eiselt .10 .25
148 Petr Ton .10 .25
149 Jiri Burger .10 .25
150 David Cermak .10 .25
151 Ivo Capek .10 .25
152 Marian Morava .10 .25
153 Michael Vyhlidal .10 .25
154 Roman Kankovsky .10 .25
155 Zdenek Touzimsky .10 .25
156 Marek Posmyk .10 .25
157 Miroslav Javin .10 .25
158 Miroslav Bruna .10 .25
159 HC Dukla Jihlava Logo .10 .25
160 HC Dukla Jihlava Team Card .10 .25
161 HC Dukla Jihlava Team Card .10 .25
162 Jaroslav Hub .10 .25
163 Petr Vlk .10 .25
164 Jiri Poukar .10 .25
165 Petr Kankovsky .10 .25
166 Ladislav Prokupek .10 .25
167 Milan Antos .10 .25
168 Leos Pipa .10 .25
169 Michail Fadejev .10 .25
170 Ladislav Blazek .10 .25
171 Petr Pavlas .20 .50
172 Marek Cernosek .10 .25
173 Ladislav Benysek .20 .50
174 Jergus Baca .10 .25
175 Marek Tichy .10 .25
176 Roman Veber .10 .25
177 Martin Streit .10 .25
178 Hockey Olomouc Logo .10 .25
179 Hockey Olomouc Team Card .10 .25
180 Hockey Olomouc Team Card .10 .25
181 Michal Bros .10 .25
182 Radek Svoboda .10 .25
183 Pavel Nohel .10 .25
184 Radek Prochazka .10 .25
185 Jan Tomajko .10 .25
186 Michal Slavik .10 .25
187 Radek Sip .10 .25
188 Filip Dvorak .10 .25
189 Martin Prusek .60 1.50
190 Jiri Jonak .10 .25
191 Pavel Kumstat .10 .25
192 Vitezslav Skuta .10 .25
193 Dmitri Jerofejev .10 .25
194 Rene Sevecek .10 .25
195 Ales Tomasek .10 .25
196 Roman Simicek .20 .50
197 HC Vitkovice Logo .10 .25
198 HC Vitkovice Team Card .10 .25
199 HC Vitkovice Team Card .10 .25
200 Alexander Prokopjev .10 .25
201 Jan Peterek .10 .25
202 David Moravec .30 .50
203 Tomas Chlubna .10 .25
204 Libor Polasek .10 .25
205 Ales Kratoska .10 .25
206 Roman Rysanek .10 .25
207 Martin Smetak .10 .25
208 Martin Altrichter .10 .25
209 Karel Smid .20 .50
210 Josef Reznicek .10 .25
211 Jaroslav Spacek .20 .50
212 Ivan Vlcek .10 .25
213 Jiri Hanzlik .10 .25
214 Robert Jindrich .20 .50
215 Milan Volak .10 .25
216 HC ZKZ Plzen Logo .10 .25
217 HC ZKZ Plzen Team Card .10 .25
218 HC ZKZ Plzen Team Card .10 .25
219 Jiri Kucera .10 .25
220 Tomas Klimt .20 .50
221 Tomas Jelinek .20 .25
222 Michal Straka .10 .25
223 Miroslav Mach .10 .25
224 Pavel Vostrak .10 .25
225 Petr Korinek .10 .25
226 Radek Kampf .10 .25
227 Radovan Biegl .20 .50
228 Jiri Kuntos .10 .25
229 Lubomir Sekeras .30 .75
230 Petr Jancarik .10 .25
231 Stanislav Pavelec .10 .25
232 Ondrej Zetek .10 .25
233 Patrik Hucko .10 .25
234 Vladimir Machulda .10 .25
235 HC Zelezarny Trinec Logo .10 .25
236 HC Zelezarny Trinec Team .10 .25
237 HC Zelezarny Trinec Team .10 .25
238 Jozef Dano .10 .25
239 Roman Blazek .10 .25
240 Marek Zadina .10 .25
241 Richard Kral .10 .25
242 Petr Folta .10 .25
243 Michal Piskor .10 .25
244 Josef Straub .10 .25
245 Petr Zajonc .10 .25
246 Dusan Salficky .40 .75
247 Pavel Augusta .10 .25
248 Tomas Pacal .10 .25
249 Jiri Malinsky .10 .25
250 Pavel Kriz .10 .25
251 Radomir Brazda .10 .25
252 Ales Pisa .10 .25
253 Ladislav Lubina .10 .25
254 HC IB Pardubice Logo .10 .25
255 HC IB Pardubice Team .10 .25
256 HC IB Pardubice Team .10 .25
257 Tomas Blazek .20 .25
258 Jiri Jantovsky .10 .25
259 Milan Hejduk 4.00 10.00
260 Tomas Martinec .10 .25
261 David Pospisil .10 .25
262 Stanislav Prochazka .10 .25
263 Milan Prochazka .10 .25
264 Milan Kastner .10 .25
265 Rostislav Haas .10 .25
266 Denis Tsygurov .10 .25
267 Martin Bakula .10 .25
268 David Galvas .10 .25
269 Petr Tejkl .10 .25
270 Radek Mesicek .10 .25
271 Milos Hrubes .10 .25
272 Eduard Gorbachev .10 .25
273 HC Slezan Opava Logo .10 .25
274 HC Slezan Opava Team .10 .25
275 HC Slezan Opava Team .10 .25
276 Petr Fabian .10 .25
277 Zdenek Pavelek .10 .25
278 Karel Horny .10 .25
279 Martin Filip .10 .25
280 Juraj Jurik .10 .25
281 Radim Radevic .10 .25
282 Jan Zurek .10 .25
283 Valerij Belov .10 .25

1998-99 Czech DS

This set features the top players of the Czech Republic's Extraliga. The set features several short prints. Card no. 1 is 1:125, cards no. 2-11 are 1:30 and cards no. 12-25 are 1:20.

COMPLETE SET (125) 75.00 150.00
1 Jiri Dopita 10.00 25.00
2 Pavel Patera 2.00 5.00
3 Martin Prochazka 2.00 5.00
4 Martin Rucinsky 2.00 5.00
5 Vladimir Vujtek 2.00 5.00
6 David Moravec 2.00 5.00
7 Libor Prochazka 2.00 5.00
8 Viktor Ujcik 2.00 5.00
9 Vladimir Ruzicka 2.00 5.00
10 Frantisek Kucera 2.00 5.00
11 David Vyborny 2.00 5.00
12 Rudolf Pejchar 4.00 10.00
13 Oldrich Svoboda 2.00 5.00
14 Marek Novotny 2.00 5.00
15 Zdenek Orct 2.00 5.00
16 Libor Barta 2.00 5.00
17 Dusan Salficky 2.00 5.00
18 Pavel Cagas 2.00 5.00
19 Ladislav Blazek 2.00 5.00
20 Roman Cechmanek 2.00 5.00
21 Milan Hnilicka 2.00 5.00
22 Martin Cinibulk 2.00 5.00
23 Martin Prusek 2.00 5.00
24 Jaroslav Kames 2.00 5.00
25 Radovan Biegl 2.00 5.00
26 Petr Pavlas .10 .25
27 Ondrej Steiner .10 .25
28 Pavel Janku .10 .25
29 Jaromir Kverka .10 .25
30 Martin Rousek .10 .25
31 Milan Nedoma .10 .25
32 Radek Martinek .20 .50
33 Rudolf Suchanek .10 .25
34 Radek Toupal .15 .40
35 Filip Turek .14 .25
36 Miroslav Barus .10 .25
37 Miroslav Duben .10 .25
38 Petr Vlk .10 .25
39 Marek Melenovsky .10 .25
40 Jiri Cihlar .10 .25
41 Roman Mejzlik .10 .25
42 Ales Polcar .10 .25
43 Angel Nikolov .20 .50
44 Martin Stepanek .10 .25
45 Petr Hrbek .10 .25
46 Ivo Prorok .10 .25
47 Vladimir Petrovka .10 .25
48 Robert Kysela .10 .25
49 Josef Straka .10 .25
50 Ales Pisa .10 .25
51 Pavel Kriz .10 .25
52 Tomas Blazek .10 .25
53 Tomas Martinec .10 .25
54 Jiri Jantovsky .10 .25
55 Stanislav Prochazka .10 .25
56 Jaroslav Kudrna .10 .25
57 Josef Reznicek .10 .25
58 Pavel Geffert .10 .25
59 Petr Korinek .15 .40
60 Pavel Vostrak .10 .25
61 Michal Straka .10 .25
62 David Pospisil .10 .25
63 Milan Volak .10 .25
64 Milan Navratil .10 .25
65 Vitezslav Skuta .10 .25
66 Michael Vyhlidal .10 .25
67 Petr Kuchyna .10 .25
68 Drahomir Kadlec .10 .25
69 Petr Kadlec .10 .25
70 Martin Bakula .10 .25
71 Andrej Jakovenko .10 .25
72 Marian Kacir .20 .50
73 Vladimir Machulda .10 .25
74 Michal Sup .10 .25
75 Jiri Dolezal .15 .40
76 Tomas Kucharcik .10 .25
77 Jiri Veber .10 .25
78 Jan Srdinko .10 .25
79 Radim Tesarik .10 .25
80 Ondrej Kratena .10 .25
81 Michal Bros .10 .25
82 Jan Tomajko .10 .25
83 Tomas Srsen .10 .25
84 Zbynek Marak .10 .25
85 Radek Belohlav .15 .40
86 Roman Stantien .10 .25
87 Alexej Jaskin .10 .25
88 Vaclav Burda .10 .25
89 Ladislav Benysek .20 .50
90 Frantisek Ptacek .10 .25
91 Roman Horak .10 .25
92 Richard Zemlicka .20 .50
93 Jan Hlavac .40 1.00
94 Jiri Zelenka .10 .25
95 Patrik Martinec .10 .25
96 Jaroslav Bednar .40 1.00
97 Marek Zidlicky .40 1.00
98 Ladislav Svoboda .10 .25
99 Vaclav Eiselt .10 .25
100 Zdenek Eichenmann .10 .25
101 Jiri Burger .10 .25
102 Ales Tomasek .10 .25
103 Tomas Jelinek .10 .25
104 Rene Sevecek .10 .25
105 Pavel Kowalczyk .10 .25
106 Alexander Cherbajev .10 .25
107 Martin Kotasek .10 .25
108 Ales Kratoska .10 .25
109 Martin Hamrlik .10 .25
110 Roman Meluzin .10 .25
111 Petr Cajanek .40 1.00
112 Tomas Nemcicky .15 .40
113 Josef Straub .10 .25
114 Miroslav Okal .10 .25
115 Lubomir Sekeras .30 .75
116 Jiri Kuntos .10 .25
117 Stanislav Pavelec .10 .25
118 Richard Kral .10 .25
119 Ladislav Lubina .10 .25
120 Roman Kadera .10 .25
121 Jozef Dano .10 .25
122 Tomas Chlubna .10 .25
123 Ales Zima .10 .25
124 Branislav Janos .10 .25
125 Checklist .02 .10

1998-99 Czech DS Stickers

This set features many of the top stars of the Czech Extraliga in fun sticker form. The stickers are approximately 1-by-1 1/2 inches and feature color fronts and blank backs.

COMPLETE SET 30.00 60.00
1 HC Petra Vsetin .10 .25
2 HC Petra Vsetin .10 .25
3 HC Petra Vsetin .10 .25
4 HC Petra Vsetin .10 .25
5 HC Petra Vsetin .10 .25
6 HC Petra Vsetin .10 .25
7 League Logo .10 .25
8 Roman Cechmanek .40 1.00
9 unknown
10 Antonin Stavjana .15 .40
11 Milan Nedoma .10 .25
12 Jiri Vykoukal .20 .50
13 unknown
14 Martin Stepanek .10 .25
15 Vitezslav Skuta .10 .25
16 Jiri Zelenka .10 .25
17 Robert Lang .40 1.00
18 Ondrej Kratena .10 .25
19 Viktor Ujcik .15 .40
20 unknown
21 unknown
22 unknown
23 unknown
24 Team Logo .10 .10
25 Team Photo .10 .25
26 Team Photo .10 .25
27 Vladimir Hudacek .20 .50
28 Robert Horyna .10 .25
29 Petr Pavlas .10 .25
30 Ales Tomasek .10 .25
31 Pavel Blaha .10 .25
32 Jiri Polak .10 .25
33 Martin Richter .10 .25
34 Marek Cernosek .10 .25
35 Pavel Nohel .10 .25
36 Michal Cerny .10 .25
37 Tomas Klimt .20 .50
38 Ondrej Steiner .10 .25
39 Zbynek Kukacka .10 .25
40 Martin Streit .10 .25
41 Radek Prochazka .10 .25
42 Radek Svoboda .10 .25
43 Jan Lipiansky .10 .25
44 Team Logo .10 .10
45 Team Photo .10 .25
46 Team Photo .10 .25
47 Rostislav Haas .10 .25
48 Pavel Nestak .10 .25
49 Martin Maskarinec .10 .25
50 David Galvas .10 .25
51 Milos Hrubes .10 .25
52 Karel Smid .20 .50
53 Tomas Kramny .10 .25
54 Pavel Marecek .10 .25
55 Zbynek Marak .10 .25
56 Michal Tomek .10 .25
57 Juraj Jurik .10 .25
58 Michal Piskor .10 .25
59 Karel Horny .10 .25
60 Pavel Sebesta .10 .25
61 Martin Sychra .10 .25
62 Zdenek Pavelek .10 .25
63 Milan Kubis .10 .25
64 Team Logo .10 .10
65 Team Photo .10 .25
66 Team Photo .10 .25
67 Oldrich Svoboda .20 .50
68 Rudolf Suchanek .10 .25
69 Karel Soudek .10 .25
70 Milan Nedoma .10 .25
71 Radek Martinek .20 .50
72 Jan Bohacek .10 .25
73 Kamil Toupal .10 .25
74 Radek Toupal .10 .25
75 Lubos Rob .10 .25
76 Pavel Pycha .10 .25
77 Filip Turek .10 .25
78 David Bruk .10 .25
79 Ondrej Vosta .10 .25
80 Arpad GyÃ¶ri .10 .25
81 Miroslav Barus .10 .25
82 Petr Sailer .10 .25
83 Petr Sachl .10 .25
84 Team Logo .10 .10
85 Team Photo .10 .25
86 Team Photo .10 .25
87 Zdenek Orct .30 .75
88 Richard Hrazdira .10 .25
89 Frantisek Prochazka .10 .25
90 Angel Nikolov .20 .50
91 Martin Stepanek .10 .25
92 Roman Cech .10 .25
93 Radek Mrazek .10 .25
94 Robert Kysela .10 .25
95 Tomas Vlasak .10 .25
96 Martin Rousek .10 .25
97 Petr Hrbek .10 .25
98 Vladimir Petrovka .10 .25
99 Ivo Prorok .10 .25
100 Denis Afinogenov .20 .50
101 Rail Muftijev .10 .25
102 Dmitrij Denisov .10 .25
103 Kamil Piros .40 1.00
104 Team Logo .10 .10
105 Team Photo .10 .25
106 Team Photo .10 .25
107 Marek Novotny .20 .25
108 Lukas Sablik .10 .25
109 Michael Vyhlidal .10 .25
110 Miroslav Javin .10 .25
111 Martin Tupa .10 .25
112 Marian Morava .10 .25
113 Tomas Jakes .10 .25
114 Miroslav Duben .10 .25
115 Petr Vlk .10 .25
116 Roman Mejzlik .10 .25
117 Jiri Cihlar .10 .25
118 Jaroslav Hub .10 .25
119 Leos Pipa .10 .25
120 Ladislav Prokupek .10 .25
121 Marek Melenovsky .10 .25
122 Milan Antos .10 .25
123 Miroslav Stavjana .10 .25
124 Team Logo .10 .10
125 Team Photo .10 .25
126 Team Photo .10 .25
127 Libor Barta .10 .25
128 Adam Svoboda .30 .75
129 Michal Sykora .15 .40
130 Pavel Augusta .10 .25
131 Tomas Pacal .10 .25
132 Ales Pisa .10 .25
133 Petr Mudroch .10 .25
134 Alexander Cypljakov .10 .25
135 Jiri Malinsky .10 .25
136 Milan Hejduk 4.00 10.00
137 Tomas Blazek .20 .25
138 Jaroslav Kudrna .10 .25
139 Tomas Maskarinec .10 .25
140 Stanislav Prochazka .10 .25
141 Jiri Jantovsky .10 .25
142 Pavel Kabrt .10 .25
143 Martin Koudelka .10 .25
144 Team Logo .10 .10
145 Team Photo .10 .25
146 Team Photo .10 .25
147 Dusan Salficky .30 .75
148 Michal Marik .10 .25
149 Josef Reznicek .10 .25
150 Ivan Vlcek .10 .25
151 Robert Jindrich .20 .50
152 Martin Cech .10 .25
153 Jiri Hanzlik .10 .25
154 Pavel Srek .10 .25
155 Tomas Jelinek .10 .25
156 Pavel Geffert .10 .25
157 David Pospisil .10 .25
158 Martin Filip .10 .25
159 Milan Volak .10 .25
160 Michal Straka .10 .25
161 Milan Navratil .10 .25
162 Mojmir Musil .10 .25
163 Pavel Vostrak .10 .25
164 Team Logo .10 .10
165 Team Photo .10 .25
166 Team Photo .10 .25
167 Roman Cechmanek .40 1.00
168 Antonin Stavjana .15 .40
169 Jan Srdinko .10 .25
170 Radim Tesarik .10 .25
171 Alexej Jaskin .10 .25
172 Michal Divisek .10 .25
173 Pavel Zubicek .10 .25
174 Rostislav Vlach .10 .25
175 Jiri Dopita .30 .75
176 Tomas Srsen .10 .25
177 Radek Belohlav .15 .40
178 Tomas Kapusta .10 .25
179 Ondrej Kratena .10 .25
180 Michal Bros .10 .25
181 Jan Tomajko .10 .25
182 Andrej Galkin .10 .25
183 Josef Beranek .20 .50
184 Team Logo .10 .10
185 Team Photo .10 .25
186 Team Photo .10 .25
187 Ladislav Blazek .20 .50
188 Martin Altrichter .10 .25
189 Robert Kostka .10 .25
190 Andrej Jakovenko .10 .25
191 Pavel Kolarik .20 .50
192 Martin Bakula .10 .25
193 Petr Kadlec .10 .25
194 Jan Hejda .10 .25
195 Vladimir Ruzicka .20 .50
196 Viktor Ujcik .15 .40
197 Jiri Dolezal .15 .40
198 Jiri Poukar .10 .25
199 Tomas Kucharcik .10 .25
200 Michal Sup .10 .25
201 Jiri Hlinka .10 .25
202 Tomas Kupka .10 .25
203 Radek Matejovsky .10 .25
204 Team Logo .10 .10
205 Team Photo .10 .25
206 Team Photo .10 .25
207 Milan Hnilicka .75 2.00
208 Martin Cinibulk .10 .25
209 Jiri Vykoukal .20 .50
210 Vaclav Burda .10 .25
211 Frantisek Kucera .10 .25
212 Jaroslav Nedved .10 .25
213 Frantisek Ptacek .10 .25
214 Richard Zemlicka .20 .50
215 Jiri Zelenka .10 .25
216 Patrik Martinec .10 .25
217 Jaroslav Bednar .40 1.00
218 Jaromir Kverka .10 .25
219 Jan Hlavac .40 1.00
220 Miroslav Hlinka .10 .25
221 Jaroslav Hlinka .10 .25
222 Patrik Stefan .75 2.00
223 Petr Nedved .40 1.00
224 Team Logo .10 .10
225 Team Photo .10 .25
226 Team Photo .10 .25
227 Radek Toth .10 .25
228 Martin Bilek .20 .50
229 Jan Krulis .10 .25
230 Marek Zidlicky .40 1.00
231 Tomas Kaberle .40 1.00
232 Pavel Skrbek .20 .50
233 Jan Penk .10 .25
234 Jan Dlouhy .10 .25
235 Josef Zajic .10 .25
236 Zdenek Eichenmann .10 .25
237 Petr Ton .10 .25
238 Jiri Beranek .10 .25
239 Tomas Mikolasek .10 .25
240 Ladislav Svoboda .10 .25
241 Vaclav Eiselt .10 .25
242 Jiri Burger .10 .25
243 Petr Tenkrat .40 1.00
244 Team Logo .10 .10
245 Team Photo .10 .25
246 Team Photo .10 .25
247 Martin Prusek .75 2.00
248 Zdenek Dobes .10 .25
249 Vitezslav Skuta .10 .25
250 Pavel Kumstat .10 .25
251 Jiri Jonak .10 .25
252 Rene Sevecek .10 .25
253 Dmitrij Jerofejev .10 .25
254 Petr Jurecka .10 .25
255 Roman Simicek .20 .50
256 Roman Rysanek .10 .25
257 David Moravec .20 .50
258 Alexander Prokopjev .10 .25
259 Libor Polasek .10 .25
260 Martin Kotasek .10 .25
261 Alexander Cherbajev .10 .25
262 Libor Pavlis .10 .25
263 Petr Zajonc .10 .25
264 Team Logo .10 .10
265 Team Photo .10 .25
266 Team Photo .10 .25
267 Radovan Biegl .20 .50
268 Lubomir Sekeras .30 .75
269 Jiri Kuntos .10 .25
270 Stanislav Pavelec .10 .25
271 Patrik Hucko .10 .25
272 Petr Jancarik .10 .25
273 Robert Kantor .10 .25
274 Richard Kral .10 .25
275 Ladislav Lubina .10 .25
276 Tomas Chlubna .10 .25
277 Roman Kadera .10 .25
278 Josef Straub .10 .25
279 Jozef Dano .10 .25
280 Roman Kontsek .10 .25
281 Marek Zadina .10 .25
282 Petr Folta .10 .25
283 Jan Peterek .10 .25
284 Team Logo .10 .10
285 Team Photo .10 .25
286 Team Photo .10 .25
287 Jaroslav Kames .30 .75
288 Pavel Kowalczyk .10 .25
289 Jan Krajicek .10 .25
290 Petr Kuchyna .10 .25
291 Martin Hamrlik .10 .25
292 Pavel Rajnoha .10 .25
293 Jiri Marusak .10 .25
294 Roman Meluzin .20 .50
295 Pavel Janku .10 .10
296 Ales Zima .10 .25
297 Miroslav Okal .10 .25
298 Petr Cajanek .40 1.00
299 Tomas Nemcicky .10 .25
300 Branislav Janos .10 .25
301 Ales Polcar .10 .25
302 Zdenek Sedlak .10 .25
303 Petr Leska .10 .25

1998-99 Czech OFS

This expansive set covers the entire Czech Extraliga. Cards 1-249 comprise Series I, while cards 250-490 make up Series II. Each series also has four NNO checklists. The set is noteworthy for including early cards of Martin Havlat and Roman Cechmanek, among others.

COMPLETE SET (490) 60.00 150.00
1 Ondrej Weissmann .10 .25
2 Zdenek Orct .20 .50
3 Angel Nikolov .20 .50
4 Radek Mrazek .10 .25
5 Martin Stepanek .10 .25
6 Sergej Butko .10 .25
7 Oleg Romanov .10 .25
8 Marian Menhart .20 .50
9 Vladimir Petrovka .10 .25
10 Ivo Prorok .10 .25
11 Jindrich Kotrla .10 .25
12 Josef Straka .10 .25
13 Vadim Bekbulatov .10 .25
14 Daniel Branda .10 .25
15 Vojtech Kubincak .10 .25
16 Michal Travnicek .20 .50
17 Zdenek Venera .10 .25
18 Jaroslav Kames .30 .75
19 Pavel Augusta .10 .25
20 Patrik Hucko .10 .25
21 Martin Hamrlik .10 .25
22 Jiri Marusak .10 .25
23 Pavel Mojzis .10 .25
24 Tomas Zizka .10 .25
25 Roman Meluzin .10 .25
26 Michal Tomek .10 .25
27 Josef Straub .10 .25
28 Tomas Nemcicky .15 .40
29 Petr Cajanek .40 1.00
30 Miroslav Okal .10 .25
31 Petr Leska .10 .25
32 Petr Vala .10 .25
33 Radim Rulik .10 .25
34 Dusan Salficky .30 .75
35 Josef Reznicek .10 .25
36 Robert Jindrich .20 .50
37 Jiri Hanzlik .10 .25
38 Ondrej Kriz .10 .25
39 Vladimir Zajic .10 .25
40 Pavel Geffert .10 .25
41 David Pospisil .10 .25
42 Milan Antos .10 .25
43 Petr Korinek .15 .40
44 Michal Straka .10 .25
45 Milan Volak .10 .25
46 Pavel Vostrak .10 .25
47 Milan Navratil .10 .25
48 Martin Spanhel .40 1.00
49 Josef Augusta .10 .25
50 Jaroslav Suchan .10 .25
51 Martin Tupa .10 .25
52 Marian Morava .10 .25
53 Michal Divisek .10 .25
54 Petr Svoboda .15 .40
55 Zdenek Fuksa .10 .25
56 Petr Vlk .10 .25
57 Jiri Cihlar .10 .25
58 Leos Pipa .10 .25
59 Marek Melenovsky .10 .25
60 Miroslav Bruna .10 .25
61 Petr Mokrejs .10 .25
62 Vaclav Adamec .10 .25
63 Richard [illegible] .10 .25
64 Jan Kloboucek .10 .25
65 Stanislav Nevesely .10 .25
66 Radek Masny .10 .25
67 Jan Krajicek .10 .25
68 Ales Tomasek .10 .25

69 Vladimir Holik .10 .25
70 Tomas Jelinek .10 .25
71 Pavel Nohel .10 .25
72 Jaroslav Hub .10 .25
73 Robert Kucera .10 .25
74 Andrej Galkin .10 .25
75 Pavel Selingr .10 .25
76 Pavel Bacho .10 .25
77 Jiri Zurek .10 .25
78 Pavel Zdrahal .10 .25
79 Bogdan Savenko .10 .25
80 Zdenek Sedlak .10 .25
81 Karel Trachta .10 .25
82 Rudolf Pejchar .20 .50
83 Petr Pavlas .10 .25
84 Pavel Blaha .10 .25
85 Martin Richter .10 .25
86 Jan Snopek .15 .40
87 Martin Filip .10 .25
88 Jaromir Kverka .10 .25
89 Pavel Janku .10 .25
90 Martin Rousek .10 .25
91 Ondrej Steiner .10 .25
92 Pavel Metlicka .10 .25
93 Streit Martin .10 .25
94 Ladislav Prokupek .10 .25
95 Richard Richter .10 .25
96 Martin Maskarinec .10 .25
97 Zdislav Tabara .10 .25
98 Miroslav Venkrbec .10 .25
99 Roman Cechmanek .40 1.00
100 Jiri Veber .10 .25
101 Radim Tesarik .10 .25
102 Jan Srdinko .10 .25
103 Alexej Jaskin .10 .25
104 Pavel Zubicek .10 .25
105 Jiri Dopita .30 .75
106 Martin Prochazka .20 .50
107 Pavel Patera .20 .50
108 Radek Belohlav .15 .40
109 Ondrej Kratena .10 .25
110 Michal Bros .10 .25
111 Jan Tomajko .10 .25
112 Roman Stantien .10 .25
113 Ladislav Svozil .10 .25
114 Jiri Trvaj .10 .25
115 Rene Sevecek .10 .25
116 Vitezslav Skuta .10 .25
117 Pavel Kowalczyk .10 .25
118 Radek Philipp .10 .25
119 Vladimir Vujtek .20 .50
120 Alexander Cherbajev .10 .25
121 Libor Pavlis .10 .25
122 Libor Polasek .10 .25
123 Martin Kotasek .10 .25
124 Zdenek Pavelek .10 .25
125 Martin Lamich .10 .25
126 Igor Varickij .10 .25
127 Petr Hubacek .10 .25
128 Zbynek Irgl .10 .25
129 Julius Supler .10 .25
130 Milan Hnilicka .40 1.00
131 Frantisek Ptacek .10 .25
132 Ladislav Benysek .20 .50
133 Richard Adam .10 .25
134 Frantisek Kucera .10 .25
135 Pavel Srek .10 .25
136 Jiri Zelenka .10 .25
137 David Vyborny .20 .50
138 Patrik Martinec .10 .25
139 Jaroslav Bednar .40 1.00
140 Jan Hlavac .40 1.00
141 Miroslav Hlinka .10 .25
142 Jaroslav Hlinka .10 .25
143 Martin Chabada .10 .25
144 Vaclav Novak .10 .25
145 Michal Chalupa .10 .25
146 Adam Svoboda .30 .75
147 Jiri Malinsky .10 .25
148 Ales Pisa .10 .25
149 Tomas Pacal .10 .25
150 Pavel Kriz .10 .25
151 Petr Jancarik .10 .25
152 Petr Mudroch .10 .25
153 Tomas Blazek .10 .25
154 Jiri Jantovsky .10 .25
155 Stanislav Prochazka .10 .25
156 Tomas Martinec .10 .25
157 Pavel Kabrt .10 .25
158 Jaroslav Kudrna .20 .50
159 Karel Plasek .10 .25
160 Michal Mikeska .10 .25
161 Zdenek Sindler .10 .25
162 Martin Cinibulk .10 .25
163 Marek Zidlicky .40 1.00
164 Jan Dlouhy .10 .25
165 Pavel Taborsky .10 .25
166 Michal Madl .10 .25
167 Jiri Jelinek .10 .25
168 Tomas Mikolasek .10 .25
169 Ladislav Svoboda .10 .25
170 Jiri Burger .10 .25
171 Petr Tenkrat .40 1.00
172 Tomas Kupka .10 .25
173 Marke Vorel .10 .25
174 Michal Kanka .10 .25
175 Tomas Horna .10 .25
176 Zdenek Mraz .10 .25
177 Kamil Konecny .10 .25
178 Radovan Biegl .20 .50
179 Stanislav Pavelec .10 .25
180 Jiri Kuntos .10 .25
181 Petr Gregorek .10 .25
182 Miroslav Cihal .10 .25
183 Robert Prochazka .10 .25
184 Viktor Ujcik .20 .50
185 Ladislav Lubina .10 .25
186 Jan Peterek .10 .25
187 Petr Folta .10 .25
188 Ales Zima .10 .25
189 Roman Kadera .10 .25
190 Vaclav Pletka .20 .50
191 Patrik Moskal .10 .25
192 David Appel .10 .25
193 Jaroslav Parizek CO .10 .25
194 Michal Marik .10 .25
195 Rudolf Suchanek .10 .25
196 Milan Nedoma .10 .25
197 Kamil Toupal .10 .25
198 Roman Cech .10 .25
199 Radek Martinek .20 .50
200 Vladimir Sicak .10 .25
201 Radek Toupal .15 .40
202 Filip Turek .14 .25
203 Petr Sailer .10 .25
204 Martin Strba .10 .25
205 Miroslav Barus .10 .25
206 Vaclav Kral .10 .25
207 Milan Filipi .10 .25
208 Peter Bartos .10 .25
209 Richard Farda .10 .25
210 Roman Malek .10 .25
211 Robert Kostka .10 .25
212 Pavel Kolarik .20 .50
213 Martin Bakula .10 .25
214 Petr Kadlec .10 .25
215 Jan Novak .10 .25
216 Vladimir Ruzicka .20 .50
217 Jiri Dolezal .15 .40
218 Tomas Kucharcik .10 .25
219 Michal Sup .10 .25
220 Vladimir Machulda .10 .25
221 Petr Mika .30 .75
222 Tomas Divisek .30 .75
223 Jan Kopecky .10 .25
224 Jiri Polak .10 .25
225 Ivan Hlinka OLY .30 .75
226 Slavomir Lener OLY .15 .40
227 Dominik Hasek OLY 4.00 10.00
228 Roman Cechmanek OLY .40 1.00
229 Milan Hnilicka OLY .40 1.00
230 Richard Smehlik OLY .15 .40
231 Petr Svoboda OLY .15 .40
232 Roman Hamrlik OLY .30 .75
233 Jiri Slegr OLY .15 .40
234 Frantisek Kucera OLY .10 .25
235 Libor Prochazka OLY .20 .50
236 Jaroslav Spacek OLY .20 .50
237 Robert Reichel OLY .40 1.00
238 Robert Lang OLY .40 1.00
239 Pavel Patera OLY .30 .75
240 Martin Prochazka OLY .20 .50
241 Jiri Dopita OLY .30 .75
242 Josef Beranek OLY .20 .50
243 David Moravec OLY .30 .75
244 Jan Caloun OLY .20 .50
245 Martin Rucinsky OLY .30 .75
246 Martin Straka OLY .40 1.00
247 Jaromir Jagr OLY 8.00 20.00
248 Vladimir Ruzicka OLY .20 .50
249 Milan Hejduk OLY 4.00 10.00
250 Ladislav Slizek .10 .25
251 Ladislav Blazek .20 .25
252 Andrej Jakovenko .10 .25
253 Jan Hejda .10 .25
254 Marian Kacir .20 .50
255 Robin Bacul .10 .25
256 Jan Sochor .10 .25
257 Petr Hrbek .10 .25
258 Jan Sebor .10 .25
259 Michal Slavik .10 .25
260 Vladimir Jerabek .10 .25
261 Marek Pinc .10 .25
262 Vladimir Gyna .10 .25
263 Martin Znojemsky .10 .25
264 Robert Kysela .10 .25
265 Petr Hrbek .10 .25
266 Kamil Piros .40 1.00
267 Viktor Hubl .10 .25
268 Marian Kacir .20 .50
269 Miloslav Horava .10 .25
270 Michal Pinc .10 .25
271 Zdenek Skorepa .10 .25
272 Vaclav Sykora .10 .25
273 Antonin Stavjana .15 .40
274 Richard Hrazdira .10 .25
275 Karel Rachunek .40 1.00
276 David Brezik .10 .25
277 Marek Zadina .10 .25
278 Jaroslav Balastik .10 .25
279 Martin Ambruz .10 .25
280 Ondrej Vesely .10 .25
281 Tomas Kapusta .10 .25
282 Tomas Martinek .10 .25
283 Ivan Rachunek .20 .50
284 Karel Sefcik .10 .25
285 Marek Sykora .10 .25
286 Vladimir Hudacek .20 .50
287 Ivan Vlcek .10 .25
288 Martin Cech .10 .25
289 Michal Vasicek .10 .25
290 Michal Jelinek .10 .25
291 Vladimir Bednar .10 .25
292 Pavel Augusta .10 .25
293 Ladislav Slizek .10 .25
294 Karel Dvorak .10 .25
295 Marek Novotny .10 .25
296 Lukas Sablik .10 .25
297 Daniel Zapotocny .10 .25
298 Miroslav Duben .10 .25
299 Ales Polcar .10 .25
300 Roman Mejzlik .10 .25
301 Radek Matejovsky .10 .25
302 Daniel Hodek .10 .25
303 Ales Padelek .10 .25
304 Ivan Padelek .10 .25
305 Pavel Rajnoha .10 .25
306 Richard Adam .10 .25
307 Vladimir Caldr .10 .25
308 Jiri Dobrovolny .10 .25
309 Lukas Novak .10 .25
310 Ivo Novotny .10 .25
311 Jan Smarda .10 .25
312 Lubomir Oslizlo .10 .25
313 Pavel Cagas .20 .50
314 Petr Kuchyna .10 .25
315 Drahomir Kadlec .10 .25
316 Michael Vyhlidal .10 .25
317 Miroslav Javin .10 .25
318 Petr Suchanek .10 .25
319 Vitezslav Skuta .10 .25
320 Libor Polasek .10 .25
321 Jiri Poukal .10 .25
322 Michal Cech .10 .25
323 Lukas Fiala .10 .25
324 Milota Florian .10 .25
325 Milan Kubis .10 .25
326 Jiri Latal .10 .25
327 Libor Pavlis .10 .25
328 Ivan Puncochar .10 .25
329 Rostislav Vlach .10 .25
330 Tomas Zapletal .10 .25
331 Josef Beranek .20 .50
332 Robert Hamrla .15 .40
333 Marek Cernosek .10 .25
334 Normunds Sejejs .10 .25
335 Tomas Klimt .10 .25
336 Radek Prochazka .10 .25
337 Radek Svoboda .10 .25
338 Michal Horak .10 .25
339 Jakub Kraus .10 .25
340 Ivo Pesat .10 .25
341 Tomas Jakes .10 .25
342 Michal Safarik .10 .25
343 Tomas Srsen .10 .25
344 Zbynek Marak .10 .25
345 Tomas Demel .10 .25
346 Ondrej Kavulic .10 .25
347 Petr Suchy .10 .25
348 Libor Zabransky .15 .40
349 Vladimir Vujtek .20 .50
350 Martin Prusek .40 1.00
351 Lukas Galvas .10 .25
352 Petr Jurecka .10 .25
353 Vadim Brezgunov .10 .25
354 Lukas Zatopek .10 .25
355 David Moravec .20 .50
356 Ludek Krayzel .10 .25
357 Ales Kratoska .10 .25
358 Ales Tomasek .10 .25
359 Milos Holan .15 .40
360 Roman Kelner .10 .25
361 Frantisek Vyborny .10 .25
362 Petr Prikryl .10 .25
363 Zdenek Touzimsky .10 .25
364 Vaclav Burda .10 .25
365 Vaclav Benak .10 .25
366 Michal Dobron .10 .25
367 Richard Zemlicka .10 .25
368 Roman Horak .10 .25
369 Michal Sivek .40 1.00
370 Jaroslav Kalla .10 .25
371 Pavel Richter .10 .25
372 Jaroslav Roubik .10 .25
373 Michal Sykora .15 .40
374 Milos Riha .10 .25
375 Libor Barta .10 .25
376 Alexander Cypljakov .10 .25
377 Robert Pospisil .10 .25
378 Petr Caslava .10 .25
379 Martin Koudelka .10 .25
380 Patrik Rozsival .10 .25
381 Michal Tvrdik .10 .25
382 Tomas Vak .10 .25
383 Alois Hadamczik CO .10 .25
384 Vlastimil Lakosil .10 .25
385 Lubomir Sekeras .20 .50
386 Libor Prochazka .20 .50
387 Robert Kantor .10 .25
388 Mario Cartelli .10 .25
389 Richard Kral .10 .25
390 Jozef Dano .10 .25
391 Branislav Janos .10 .25
392 Tomas Chlubna .10 .25
393 Martin Havlat 15.00 30.00
394 Jaroslav Jagr .20 .50
395 Lubomir Bauer .10 .25
396 Martin Bilek .20 .50
397 Lubos Horcicka .10 .25
398 Jiri Krocak .10 .25
399 Martin Taborsky .10 .25
400 Zdenek Eichenmann .10 .25
401 Vaclav Eiselt .10 .25
402 Premysl Sedlak .10 .25
403 Jiri Holsan .10 .25
404 Jiri Kames .10 .25
405 Jiri Habacek .10 .25
406 Stanislav Lapacek .10 .25
407 Lukas Poznik .10 .25
408 Otakar Vejvoda .15 .40
409 Jaroslav Liska .10 .25
410 Oldrich Svoboda .20 .50
411 Lukas Zib .10 .25
412 Michal Klimes .10 .25
413 Kamil Brabenec .10 .25
414 Ales Kotalik 1.00 2.50
415 Jiri Broz .10 .25
416 Zdenek Kutlak .20 .50
417 Vaclav Nedorost .40 1.00
418 Lubos Rob .10 .25
419 Martin Prusek .40 1.00
420 Frantisek Kaberle .20 .50
421 Jiri Vykoukal .20 .50
422 Jiri Veber .10 .25
423 Ladislav Benysek .20 .50
424 Martin Stepanek .10 .25
425 Jan Srdinko .10 .25
426 Radek Belohlav .15 .40
427 David Vyborny .20 .50
428 Viktor Ujcik .20 .50
429 Roman Meluzin .10 .25
430 Vladimir Vujtek .20 .50
431 Ondrej Kratena .10 .25
432 Michal Bros .10 .25
433 Marian Kacir .20 .50
434 Jan Hlavac .40 1.00
435 Richard Kral .10 .25
436 Roman Kadera .10 .25
437 Ivan Hlinka .40 1.00
438 Roman Cechmanek .40 1.00
439 Milan Hnilicka .40 1.00
440 Libor Prochazka .20 .50
441 Pavel Patera .20 .50
442 Martin Prochazka .20 .50
443 Josef Augusta .10 .25
444 Pavel Richter .20 .50
445 Marek Sykora .10 .25
446 Milan Hnilicka .40 1.00
447 Dusan Salficky .30 .75
448 Frantisek Kucera .10 .25
449 Ladislav Benysek .20 .50
450 Josef Reznicek .10 .25
451 Martin Richter .10 .25
452 Ales Pisa .10 .25
453 Ivan Vlcek .10 .25
454 Martin Stepanek .10 .25
455 Petr Jancarik .10 .25
456 David Vyborny .20 .50
457 Jan Hlavac .40 1.00
458 Jiri Zelenka .10 .25
459 Petr Tenkrat .40 1.00
460 Vaclav Kral .10 .25
461 David Pospisil .10 .25
462 Vaclav Eiselt .10 .25
463 Tomas Kucharcik .10 .25
464 Petr Korinek .15 .40
465 Pavel Janku .10 .25
466 Radek Toupal .15 .40
467 Ivo Prorok .10 .25
468 Zdislav Tabara .10 .25
469 Jaroslav Jagr .20 .50
470 Roman Cechmanek .40 1.00
471 Libor Prochazka .20 .50
472 Jiri Veber .10 .25
473 Milos Holan .15 .40
474 Jan Srdinko .10 .25
475 Robert Kantor .10 .25
476 Ales Tomasek .10 .25
477 Miroslav Duben .10 .25
478 Jiri Dopita .30 .75
479 Martin Prochazka .20 .50
480 Pavel Patera .20 .50
481 Radek Belohlav .15 .40
482 David Moravec .20 .50
483 Roman Meluzin .10 .25
484 Jiri Poukar .10 .25
485 Andrej Galkin .10 .25
486 Ivo Padelek .10 .25
487 Marek Zadina .10 .25
488 Petr Cajanek .40 1.00
489 Miroslav Javin .10 .25
490 Ondrej Kratena .10 .25
NNO Checklist .10 .25
NNO Checklist .10 .10
NNO Checklist .10 .10
NNO Checklist .10 .10
NNO Checklist .10 .10
NNO Checklist .10 .10
NNO Checklist .10 .10
NNO Checklist .10 .10

1998-99 Czech OFS Legends

This series of insert cards honoring some of the greatest players in Czech history were randomly included in series II packs.

COMPLETE SET (20) 12.00 30.00
1 Vaclav Nedomansky .80 2.00
2 Miroslav Horava .80 2.00
3 Peter Stastny 4.00 10.00
4 Jiri Sejba .40 1.00
5 Ivan Hlinka 1.20 3.00
6 Vladimir Martinec .40 1.00
7 Jaroslav Pouzar .40 1.00
8 Jiri Holecek .40 1.00
9 Ludek Cajka .40 1.00
10 Ludek Bukac .40 1.00
11 Milan Novy .80 2.00
12 Jiri Kralik .40 1.00
13 Jiri Hrdina .40 1.00
14 Frantisek Cernik .40 1.00
15 Frantisek Pospisil .40 1.00
16 Jiri Lala .40 1.00
17 Antonin Stavjana .80 2.00
18 Jaromir Sindel .80 2.00
19 Vincent Lukac .40 1.00
20 Dusan Pasek 1.20 3.00

1998-99 Czech OFS Olympic Winners

This insert series commemorates the members of the Czech Republic's gold medal-winning Olympic squad. Cards 1-10 were found in Series I packs, while cards 11-20 were found in Series II.

COMPLETE SET (20) 30.00 75.00
1 Jiri Dopita 1.20 2.00
2 Dominik Hasek 8.00 20.00
3 Jaromir Jagr 16.00 40.00
4 Frantisek Kucera .80 2.00
5 Pavel Patera .80 2.00
6 Robert Reichel 1.20 2.00
7 Martin Rucinsky .80 2.00
8 Vladimir Ruzicka .80 2.00
9 Jiri Slegr .80 2.00
10 Petr Svoboda .80 2.00
11 David Moravec .80 2.00
12 Richard Smehlik .80 2.00
13 Jaroslav Spacek .80 2.00
14 Martin Prochazka .80 2.00
15 Roman Hamrlik .80 2.00
16 Ivan Hlinka .80 2.00
17 Roman Cechmanek 1.20 3.00
18 Josef Beranek .80 2.00
19 Robert Lang 1.20 3.00
20 Martin Straka 1.20 3.00

1998 Czech Bonaparte

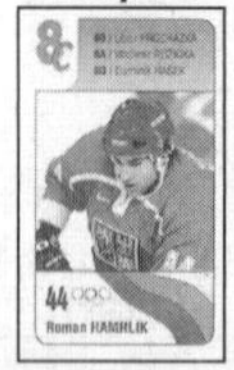

This unusual set features many members of the 1998 Czech Gold medal winning Olympic team. The cards are the size of playing cards, feature a photo on the front, and the word Bonaparte on the back. The numbering assigned to each is found on the front of the cards.

COMPLETE SET (33) 14.00 35.00
1A Martin Prochazka .20 .50
1B Robert Reichel .20 .50
1C Robert Lang .20 .50
1D Milan Hejduk 1.20 4.00
2A Martin Rucinsky .20 .50
2B Jaromir Jagr 2.00 5.00
2C Richard Smehlik .20 .50
2D Dominik Hasek 1.20 3.00
3A Josef Beranek .20 .50
3B Jaroslav Spacek .20 .50
3C Jaromir Jagr 2.00 5.00
3D Jiri Slegr .20 .50
4A Vladimir Ruzicka .20 .50
4B Roman Cechmanek .80 1.00
4C Jan Caloun .20 .50
4D Milan Hnilicka .80 2.00
5A Jiri Dopita .30 .75
5B Frantisek Kucera .20 .50
5C Jaromir Jagr 2.00 5.00
5D Petr Svoboda .20 .50
6A Petr Svoboda .20 .50
6B Ivan Hlinka .20 .50
6C Slavomir Lener .20 .50
6D Jaromir Jagr 2.00 5.00
7A Jiri Slegr .20 .50
7B Martin Straka .20 .50
7C Pavel Patera .20 .50
7D David Moravec .20 .50
8A Vladimir Ruzicka .20 .50
8B Libor Prochazka .20 .50
8C Roman Hamrlik .20 .50
8D Dominik Hasek 1.20 3.00
HOKEJ Jaromir Jagr

1998 Czech Bonaparte Tall

These Tall Boy-type cards feature Czech's Olympic champs from 1998. The cards have a small colour photo surrounded by plenty of white space, a large Czech flag and the Bonaparte 1998. Only three cards are confirmed to exist to this point. Please forward additional information to hockeymag@beckett.com.

COMPLETE SET ?
1 Dominik Hasek
2 Jaromir Jagr
3 Robert Reichel

1998 Czech Pexeso

This set of undersized cards features members of the Olympic Gold medal-winning Czech squad. It is believed that the cards were issued as a premium with some sort of food item.

COMPLETE SET (28) 8.00 20.00
1 Martin Prochazka .10 .25
2 Robert Reichel .20 .50
3 Robert Lang .20 .50
4 Milan Hejduk 1.20 4.00
5 Martin Rucinsky .10 .25
6 Richard Smehlik .10 .25
7 Dominik Hasek .80 3.00
8 Josef Beranek .10 .25
9 Jaroslav Spacek .10 .25
10 Jaromir Jagr 2.00 5.00
11 Roman Cechmanek .40 1.00
12 Martin Rucinsky .10 .25
13 Jiri Slegr .10 .25
14 Jan Caloun .10 .25
15 Milan Hnilicka .40 2.00
16 Jiri Dopita .20 .50
17 Jiri Kucera .10 .25
18 Jaromir Jagr 2.00 5.00
19 Petr Svoboda .10 .25
20 Ivan Hlinka .10 .25
21 Slavomir Lener .10 .25
22 Jiri Slegr .10 .25
23 Martin Straka .10 .25
24 Pavel Patera .10 .25
25 David Moravec .10 .25
26 Libor Prochazka .10 .25
27 Roman Hamrlik .10 .25
28 Dominik Hasek .80 3.00

1998 Czech Spaghetti

This undersized set honors the members of the Czech team that won the Olympic Gold medal. The cards were issued as a premium on boxes of pasta products, and were licensed by the NHLPA.

COMPLETE SET (12) 8.00 20.00
1 Jaromir Jagr 4.00 10.00
2 Dominik Hasek 2.00 5.00
3 Josef Beranek .40 1.00
4 Roman Hamrlik .40 1.00
5 Robert Lang .60 1.50
6 Martin Straka .60 1.50
7 Robert Reichel .60 1.50
8 Martin Rucinsky .60 1.50
9 Jiri Slegr .40 1.00
10 Petr Svoboda .40 1.00
11 Richard Smehlik .40 1.00
12 Martin Prochazka .40 1.00

1999-00 Czech DS

This set features the stars of the Czech Republic's top league. The set includes cards of NHLers Patrik Elias and Brendan Morrison, who began that season in the Czech league whilst in the midst of a contract dispute. Checklist courtesy of Hockey Heaven.

COMPLETE SET (196) 30.00 75.00
1 Richard Hrazdira .20 .50

2 Vladimir Hudacek .10 .50
3 Roman Hamrlik .40 .75
4 Martin Hamrlik .10 .25
5 Jiri Marusak .10 .25
6 Tomas Zizka .10 .50
7 Petr Cajanek .20 .75
8 Miroslav Okal .10 .25
9 Josef Straub .10 .25
10 Petr Leska .10 .25
11 Michal Tomek .10 .25
12 Martin Kotasek .10 .25
13 Ondrej Vesely .10 .25
14 Petr Vala .10 .25
15 Rudolf Pejchar .10 .25
16 Zdenek Smid .30 .75
17 Martin Richter .10 .25
18 Petr Pavlas .10 .25
19 Martin Maskarinec .10 .25
20 Jan Snopek .10 .25
21 Michal Divisek .10 .25
22 Pavel Janku .10 .25
23 Jaromir Kverka .10 .25
24 Martin Rousek .10 .25
25 Miroslav Barus .10 .25
26 Martin Streit .10 .25
27 Martin Filip .10 .25
28 Radek Prochazka .10 .25
29 Ivo Capek .20 .50
30 Michal Marik .10 .25
31 Milan Nedoma .10 .25
32 Radek Martinek .30 .50
33 Rudolf Suchanek .20 .50
34 Roman Cech .10 .25
35 Vaclav Kral .10 .25
36 Filip Turek .10 .25
37 Petr Sailer .10 .25
38 Radek Toupal .10 .25
39 Lubos Rob .10 .25
40 Martin Strba .10 .25
41 Petr Sailer .10 .25
42 Kamil Brabenec .10 .25
43 Pavel Cagas .20 .50
44 Robert Horyna .10 .25
45 Michael Vyhlidal .10 .25
46 Miroslav Javin .10 .25
47 Libor Pivko .10 .25
48 Ales Tomasek .10 .25
49 Roman Horak .20 .50
50 Pavel Nohel .10 .25
51 Ales Alma .10 .25
52 Marek Melanovsky .10 .25
53 Jaroslav Hub .10 .25
54 Pavel Zdrahal .10 .25
55 Bogdan Savenko .10 .25
56 Robert Kantor .10 .25
57 Zdenek Orct .20 .50
58 Marek Pinc .10 .25
59 Miloslav Horava .10 .25
60 Angel Nikolov .20 .50
61 Petr Kratky .10 .25
62 Radek Mrazek .10 .25
63 Robert Reichel .30 .50
64 Robert Kysela .10 .25
65 Ivo Prorok .10 .25
66 Jan Alinc .20 .50
67 Jindrich Kotrla .10 .25
68 Zdenek Skorepa .20 .50
69 Josef Straka .10 .25
70 Michal Travnicek .20 .50
71 Libor Barta .20 .25
72 Adam Svoboda .30 .75
73 Ales Pisa .10 .25
74 Tomas Pacal .10 .25
75 Jiri Malinsky .10 .25
76 Petr Jancarik .10 .25
77 Patrik Elias 1.60 2.00
78 Brendan Morrison .80 3.00
79 Radek Bonk .40 1.00
80 Jaroslav Kudrna .20 .50
81 Tomas Blazek .20 .25
82 Ladislav Lubina .10 .25
83 Stanislav Prochazka .10 .25
84 Jiri Jantovsky .10 .25
85 Dusan Salficky .40 .75
86 Radek Masny .10 .25
87 Josef Reznicek .10 .25
88 Ivan Vlcek .10 .25
89 Martin Cech .10 .25
90 Jiri Hanzlik .10 .25
91 Martin Spanhel .40 .75
92 Michal Straka .10 .25
93 Zdenek Sedlak .10 .25
94 Pavel Vostrak .10 .25
95 Petr Korinek .20 .50
96 Pavel Geffert .10 .25
97 David Pospisil .10 .25
98 Milan Volak .10 .25
99 Vlastimil Lakosil .20 .50
100 Marek Novotny .10 .25
101 Jiri Kuntos .10 .25
102 Petr Gregorek .10 .25
103 Milos Holan .10 .25
104 Lubomir Sekeras .40 .50
105 Richard Kral .10 .25
106 Marek Zadina .10 .25
107 Martin Havlat 8.00 15.00
108 Roman Dadera .10 .25
109 Tomas Chlubna .10 .25
110 Petr Folta .10 .25
111 Ondrej Zetek .10 .25
112 Branislav Janos .10 .25
113 Ladislav Blazek .20 .25
114 Roman Malek .10 .25
115 Vitezslav Skuta .10 .25
116 Jan Krajicek .10 .25
117 Pavel Kolarik .20 .50
118 Martin Bakula .10 .25
119 Vladimir Ruzicka .20 .50
120 Tomas Kucharcik .10 .25
121 Michal Sup .10 .25
122 Jiri Dolezal .10 .25
123 Jan Kopecky .10 .25
124 Petr Hrbek .10 .25
125 Radek Matejovsky .10 .25
126 Vladimir Machulda .10 .25
127 Roman Cechmanek 2.00 1.00
128 Ivo Pesat .10 .25
129 Jan Srdinko .10 .25
130 Libor Zabransky .20 .25
131 Jiri Veber .10 .25
132 Radim Tesarik .10 .25
133 Jiri Dopita .40 .50
134 Radek Belohlav .20 .35
135 Jan Tomajko .10 .25
136 Jan Pardavy .10 .25
137 Roman Stantien .10 .25
138 Zbynek Marak .10 .25
139 Alexej Jaskin .10 .25
140 Pavel Zubicek .10 .25
141 Petr Briza .40 .75
142 Petr Prikryl .10 .25
143 Frantisek Kucera .20 .20
144 Ladislav Benysek .30 .50
145 Michal Sykora .20 .50
146 Jaroslav Nedved .10 .25
147 David Vyborny .20 .50
148 Patrik Martinec .10 .25
149 Jaroslav Hlinka .10 .25
150 Ondrej Kratena .10 .25
151 Michal Bros .20 .25
152 Richard Zemlicka .20 .50
153 Jiri Zelenka .10 .25
154 Vaclav Eiselt .10 .25
155 Martin Bilek .20 .50
156 Lubos Horcicka .10 .25
157 Michal Madl .10 .25
158 Jan Krulis .10 .25
159 Jiri Krocak .10 .25
160 Jan Dlouhy .10 .25
161 Tomas Horna .10 .25
162 Ladislav Svoboda .10 .25
163 Zdenek Eichenmann .10 .25
164 Jiri Burger .10 .25
165 Tomas Kupka .10 .25
166 Jiri Kames .20 .50
167 Juri Holdan .10 .25
168 Ondrej Kriz .10 .25
169 Martin Prusek .80 2.00
170 Jiri Trvaj .10 .25
171 Dmitrij Jerofejev .10 .25
172 Lukas Galvas .10 .25
173 Pavel Kowalczyk .10 .25
174 Petr Jurecka .10 .25
175 Ludik Krayzel .10 .25
176 Libor Polasek .20 .25
177 Martin Lamich .10 .25
178 Petr Hubacek .10 .25
179 Serej Petrenko .10 .25
180 Zdenik Pavelek .10 .25
181 Martin Tomasek .10 .25
182 Zbynik Irgi .10 .25
183 Ladislav Kudrna .20 .50
184 Pavol Rybar .20 .50
185 Pavel Kumstat .10 .25
186 Tomas Jakes .10 .25
187 Karel Soudek .10 .25
188 Jiri Hes .10 .25
189 Petr Kankovsky .10 .25
190 Milan Kastner .10 .25
191 Jiri Poukar .10 .25
192 Peter Pucher .10 .25
193 Marek Vorel .10 .25
194 Radek Haman .10 .25
195 Karel Plasek .10 .25
196 Milan Prochazka .10 .25
GC Jaromir Jagr Gold 20.00 50.00

1999-00 Czech DS Goalies

This set, featuring the top goalies of the Czech league, were random inserts in packs. The set includes a key pre-NHL card of Roman Cechmanek.

COMPLETE SET (14) 16.00 40.00
G1 Richard Hrazdira 1.20 3.00
G2 Rudolf Pejchar 1.20 3.00
G3 Ivo Capek 1.20 3.00
G4 Pavel Cagas 1.20 3.00
G5 Zdenek Orct 1.20 3.00
G6 Libor Barta 1.20 3.00
G7 Dusan Salficky 2.00 4.00
G8 Vlastimil Lakosil 1.20 3.00
G9 Ladislav Blazek 1.20 3.00
G10 Roman Cechmanek 4.00 4.00
G11 Petr Briza 2.00 4.00
G12 Martin Bilek 1.20 3.00
G13 Martin Prusek 2.00 10.00
G14 Pavol Rybar 1.20 3.00

1999-00 Czech DS National Stars

These cards, featuring the members of the Czech Republic's gold medal winning team, were randomly inserted in packs.

COMPLETE SET (23) 50.00 125.00
NS1 Dominik Hasek 8.00 20.00
NS2 Milan Hnilicka 3.20 5.00
NS3 Jaromir Jagr 15.00 40.00
NS4 Jiri Slegr 1.20 3.00
NS5 Jaroslav Spacek 1.20 3.00
NS6 Frantisek Kucera 1.20 3.00
NS7 Roman Hamrlik 2.00 4.00
NS8 Petr Svoboda 2.00 4.00
NS9 Viktor Ujcik 1.20 3.00
NS10 Frantisek Kaberle 1.20 3.00
NS11 Libor Prochazka 1.20 3.00
NS12 Robert Reichel 2.00 3.00
NS13 Martin Rucinsky 1.20 3.00
NS14 Martin Straka 2.00 4.00
NS15 Martin Prochazka 1.20 3.00
NS16 Pavel Patera 1.20 3.00
NS17 Vladimir Ruzicka 1.20 3.00
NS18 Josef Beranek 1.20 3.00
NS19 David Moravec 1.20 3.00
NS20 Jan Hlavac 2.00 4.00
NS21 David Vyborny 1.20 3.00

NS22 Jiri Dopita 2.00 3.00
NS23 Petr Sykora 3.20 5.00

1999-00 Czech DS Premium

This insert set features the top Czech-born players and was randomly seeded into packs. The cards were limited to 150 copies each.

COMPLETE SET (12) 36.00 75.00
P1 Dominik Hasek 10.00 25.00
P2 Roman Turek 3.20 4.00
P3 Roman Cechmanek 4.00 4.00
P4 Milan Hnilicka 4.00 5.00
P5 Martin Prochazka .80 3.00
P6 Jaromir Jagr 20.00 50.00
P7 Jiri Slegr .80 3.00
P8 Jaroslav Spacek .80 3.00
P9 Pavel Patera .80 3.00
P10 Jiri Dopita 2.00 3.00
P11 Robert Reichel 1.20 3.00
P12 Martin Rucinsky 1.20 4.00

1999-00 Czech OFS

This set features every player from the Czech Elite League.

COMPLETE SET (560) 30.00 75.00
1 Libor Barta .20 .25
2 Martin Bilek .20 .50
3 Ladislav Blazek .20 .25
4 Petr Briza .30 .75
5 Ivo Capek .20 .50
6 Roman Cechmanek 1.20 1.00
7 Robert Horyna .20 .50
8 Vladimir Hudacek .20 .50
9 Ladislav Kudrna .20 .50
10 Vlastimil Lakosil .20 .50
11 Michal Marik .20 .50
12 Zdenek Orct .20 .50
13 Rudolf Pejchar .20 .50
14 Martin Prusek .80 2.00
15 Dusan Salficky .30 .75
16 Richard Farda .08 .20
17 Marian Jelinek .08 .20
18 Josef Beranek .08 .20
19 Leo Gudas .08 .20
20 Milan Hnilicka 1.20 1.00
21 Milos Holan .08 .20
22 Jan Hrdina .80 2.00
23 Jaromir Jagr 4.00 10.00
24 Frantisek Kaberle .08 .50
25 Tomas Kaberle .30 .75
26 Pavel Kubina .30 1.00
27 Marek Malik .08 .20
28 Pavel Patera .08 .50
29 Martin Prochazka .08 .20
30 Vaclav Prospal .20 .50
31 Robert Reichel .20 .50
32 Martin Rucinsky .20 .50
33 Vladimir Ruzicka .20 .50
34 Pavel Skrbek .20 .50
35 Jiri Slegr .20 .50
36 Jaroslav Spacek .20 .50
37 Martin Straka .40 1.00
38 Vaclav Varada .20 .50
39 David Volek .20 .50
40 Jan Vopat .20 .50
41 Vladimir Caldr .08 .20
42 Martin Bakula .08 .20
43 Miroslav Hajek .08 .20
44 Petr Hrbek .08 .20
45 Petr Kadlec .08 .20
46 Jan Kopecky .08 .20
47 Jan Krajicek .08 .20
48 Angel Krstev .08 .20
49 Radek Matejovsky .08 .20
50 Jan Novak .08 .20
51 Vladimir Pojkar .08 .20
52 Vladimir Ruzicka .08 .50
53 Jan Slavik .08 .20
54 Jan Sochor .08 .20
55 Michal Sup .08 .20
56 Zdislav Tabara .08 .20
57 Jiri Dopita .80 .50
58 Ondrej Kavulic .08 .20
59 Petr Kubos .08 .20
60 Radim Kucharczyk .08 .20
61 Marko Palo .08 .20
62 Jukka Seppo .08 .20
63 Lukas Slaby .08 .20
64 Roman Stantien .08 .20
65 Petr Suchy .08 .20
66 Radim Tesarik .08 .20
67 Jan Tomajko .08 .20
68 Martin Vozdecky .08 .20
69 Petr Zajgla .08 .20
70 Pavel Zubicek .08 .20
71 Pavel Pazourek .08 .20
72 Petr Belohlavek .08 .20
73 Radim Freibauer .08 .20
74 Radek Haman .08 .20
75 David Havir .08 .20
76 Jiri Hes .08 .20
77 Jiri Hradecky .08 .20
78 Jan Kloboucek .08 .20
79 David Pazourek .08 .20
80 David Petlak .08 .20
81 Karel Plasek .08 .20
82 Jiri Poukar .08 .20
83 Milan Prochazka .08 .20
84 Peter Pucher .08 .20
85 Marek Vorel .08 .20
86 Pavel Marek .08 .20
87 Martin Barek .08 .20
88 Tomas Blazek .08 .20
89 Jan Dusanek .08 .20
90 Patrik Elias .80 2.00
91 Petr Jancarik .08 .20
92 Jaroslav Kudrna .08 .50
93 Tomas Martinec .08 .20
94 Brendan Morrison .40 1.00
95 Andrej Novotny .08 .20
96 Tomas Pacal .08 .20
97 Rastislav Palov .08 .20
98 Patrik Rozsival .08 .20
99 Michael Tvrdik .08 .20
100 Tomas Vak .08 .20
101 Pavel Richter .08 .20
102 Michal Bros .20 .25
103 Vaclav Eiselt .08 .20
104 Petr Havelka .08 .20
105 Martin Holy .08 .20
106 Pavel Kasparik .08 .20
107 Ondrej Kratena .20 .25
108 Frantisek Kucera .08 .20
109 Jaroslav Nedved .08 .20
110 Frantisek Ptacek .08 .20
111 Miha Rebolj .08 .20
112 Pavel Srek .08 .20
113 David Vyborny .08 .20
114 Jiri Zelenka .08 .20
115 Richard Zemlicka .20 .50
116 Marek Sykora .08 .20
117 Milan Antos .08 .20
118 Martin Cech .08 .20
119 Marek Cernosek .08 .20
120 Petr Chvojka .08 .20
121 Pavel Geffert .08 .20
122 Jiri Hanzlik .08 .20
123 Jiri Jelen .08 .20
124 Michal Jelinek .08 .20
125 Petr Korinek .20 .50
126 Josef Reznicek .08 .20
127 Radek Svoboda .08 .20
128 Petr Ulehla .08 .20
129 Ivan Vlcek .08 .20
130 Pavel Vostrak .08 .20
131 Martin Pesout .08 .20
132 Michal Dobron .08 .20
133 Martin Filip .08 .20
134 Pavel Janku .08 .20
135 Jaroslav Kalla .08 .20
136 Jan Kostal .08 .20
137 Jaromir Kverka .08 .20
138 Petr Macek .08 .20
139 Martin Maskarinec .08 .20
140 Petr Pavlas .08 .20
141 Josef Podlaha .08 .20
142 Michal Porak .08 .20
143 Martin Richter .08 .20
144 Jan Snopek .08 .20
145 Martin Streit .08 .20
146 Vaclav Sykora .08 .20
147 David Balazs .08 .20
148 Viktor Hubl .08 .20
149 Petr Kratky .08 .20
150 Vojtech Kubincak .08 .20
151 Robert Kysela .08 .20
152 Marian Menhart .20 .50
153 Radek Mrazek .08 .20
154 Angel Nikolov .20 .50
155 Karel Pilar .80 1.00
156 Ivo Prorok .08 .20
157 Robert Reichel .20 .50
158 Zdenek Skorepa .20 .50
159 Josef Straka .08 .20
160 Martin Strbak .08 .20
161 Otakar Vejvoda .08 .20
162 Jan Dlouhy .08 .20
163 Zdenek Eichenmann .08 .20
164 Jiri Holsan .08 .20
165 Tomas Horna .08 .20
166 Ondrej Kriz .08 .20
167 Jiri Krocak .08 .20
168 Tomas Kupka .08 .20
169 Michal Madl .08 .20
170 Milan Novy .08 .20
171 Tomas Polansky .08 .20
172 Lukas Poznik .08 .20
173 Ladislav Svoboda .08 .20
174 Tomas Ullrych .08 .20
175 Martin Vejvoda .08 .20
176 Jaroslav Liska .08 .20
177 Kamil Brabenec .08 .20
178 Roman Cech .08 .20
179 Milan Filipi .08 .20
180 Stanislav Jasecko .08 .20
181 Josef Jindra .08 .20
182 Michal Klimes .08 .20
183 Zdenek Kutlak .08 .50
184 Milan Nedoma .08 .20
185 David Nedorost .08 .20
186 Lubos Rob .08 .20
187 Petr Sailer .08 .20
188 Jiri Simanek .08 .20
189 Rudolf Suchanek .08 .20
190 Radek Toupal .08 .20
191 Alois Hadamczik CO .08 .20
192 Mario Cartelli .08 .20
193 Petr Gregorek .08 .20
194 Martin Havlat 6.00 15.00
195 Branislav Janos .08 .20
196 Roman Kadera .08 .20
197 Richard Kral .08 .20
198 Jiri Kuntos .08 .20
199 David Nosek .08 .20
200 Vaclav Pletka .40 .50
201 Pavel Selinger .08 .20
202 Petr Svoboda .08 .35
203 Viktor Ujcik .08 .35
204 Marek Zadina .08 .20
205 Jiri Zurek .08 .20
206 Antonin Stavjana .08 .20
207 Jaroslav Balastik .08 .20
208 Roman Hamrlik .30 .75
209 Lubomir Korhon .08 .20
210 Martin Kotasek .08 .20
211 Petr Leska .08 .20
212 Patrik Luza .08 .20
213 Jiri Marusak .08 .20
214 Pavel Mojzis .08 .20
215 Milan Navratil .08 .20
216 Miroslav Okal .08 .20
217 Michal Tomek .08 .20
218 Petr Vala .08 .20
219 Pavol Valko .08 .20
220 Tomas Zizka .08 .20
221 Vladimir Vujtek .08 .20
222 Lukas Galvas .08 .20
223 Dmitrij Gogolev .08 .20
224 Zbynek Irgl .08 .20
225 Dmitri Jerofejev .08 .20
226 Petr Jurecka .08 .20
227 Ludek Krayzel .08 .20
228 Daniel Kysela .08 .20
229 Zdenek Pavelek .08 .20
230 Sergei Petrenko .08 .20
231 Daniel Seman .08 .20
232 Lukas Smolka .08 .20
233 Vaclav Varada .20 .50
234 Jan Vytisk .08 .20
235 Lukas Zatopek .08 .20
236 Richard Farda .08 .20
237 Michal Cech .08 .20
238 Vladimir Holik .08 .20
239 Andrei Yakovenko .08 .20
240 Marek Melenovsky .08 .20
241 Martin Miklik .08 .20
242 Pavel Nohel .08 .20
243 Libor Pivko .08 .20
244 Bogdan Savenko .08 .20
245 Petr Suchanek .08 .20
246 Kamil Suchanek .08 .20
247 Petr Tejkl .08 .20
248 Petr Vlasanek .08 .20
249 Michael Vyhlidal .08 .20
250 Tomas Zapletal .08 .20
251 Josef Augusta .08 .20
252 Ivan Hlinka .08 .50
253 Vladimir Martinec .08 .20
254 Roman Cechmanek 1.20 1.00
255 Martin Prusek .80 2.00
256 Radek Belohlav .08 .35
257 Ladislav Benysek .30 .50
258 Petr Cajanek .08 .75
259 Jan Caloun .20 .50
260 Jiri Dopita .80 .50
261 Vaclav Kral .08 .20
262 Frantisek Kucera .08 .20
263 Tomas Kucharcik .08 .20
264 Radek Martinek .30 .50
265 Ales Pisa .08 .20
266 Robert Reichel .20 .50
267 Martin Richter .08 .20
268 Roman Simicek .30 .50
269 Jan Srdinko .08 .20
270 Martin Stepanek .08 .20
271 Petr Tenkrat .30 .75
272 Jan Tomajko .08 .20
273 Viktor Ujcik .08 .35
274 Tomas Vlasak .08 .20
275 David Vyborny .08 .20
276 Jiri Vykoukal .08 .20
277 Jaroslav Parizek CO .08 .20
278 Peter Bartos .08 .20
279 Jiri Broz .08 .20
280 Ales Kotalik .30 3.00
281 Lukas Zib .08 .20
282 Vaclav Kral .08 .20
283 Radek Martinek .30 .50
284 Vaclav Nedorost 6.00 2.00
285 Martin Strba .08 .20
286 Filip Turek .08 .20
287 Ivo Pestuka CO .08 .20
288 Jaroslav Hub .08 .20
289 Miroslav Javin .08 .20
290 Roman Kontsek .08 .20
291 Rostislav Pilavka .08 .20
292 Ivan Puncochar .08 .20
293 Roman Rysanek .08 .20
294 Petr Sykora .08 .20
295 Ales Tomasek .08 .20
296 Daniel Vilasek .08 .20
297 David Kriz .08 .20
298 Michal Mikeska .08 .20
299 Pavol Pekarik .08 .20
300 Jan Peterek .08 .20
301 Radek Philipp .08 .20
302 Pavel Zdrahal .08 .20
303 Ales Zima .08 .20
304 Filip Stefanka .08 .20
305 Tomas Sykora .08 .20
306 Marcel Hanzal .08 .20
307 Roman Horak .08 .20
308 Milos Riha CO .08 .20
309 Ladislav Prokupek .08 .20
310 Roman Prosek .08 .20
311 Martin Rousek .08 .20
312 Miroslav Barus .08 .20
313 Michal Divisek .08 .20
314 David Hruska .08 .20
315 Pavel Metlicka .08 .20
316 Radek Prochazka .08 .20
317 Tomas Martinec .08 .20
318 Zdenek Pavelek .08 .20
319 Jiri Polak .08 .20
320 Tomas Chlubna .08 .20
321 Jiri Malinsky .08 .20
322 Petr Fiala .08 .20
323 Eduard Novak CO .08 .20
324 Lubomir Bauer .08 .20
325 Petr Bohunicky .08 .20
326 Jiri Burger .08 .20
327 Jiri Hubacek .08 .20
328 Jiri Kames .08 .20
329 Michal Kanka .08 .20
330 Petr Kounovsky .08 .20
331 Jan Krulis .08 .20
332 Radim Skuhrovec .08 .20
333 Martin Taborsky .08 .20
334 Ladislav Vlcek .08 .20
335 Radek Gardon .08 .20
336 Vladimir Jerabek CO .08 .20
337 Jan Alinc .08 .20
338 Vladimir Gyna .08 .20
339 Jindrich Kotrla .08 .20
340 Michal Travnicek .08 .20
341 Lukas Bednarik .08 .20
342 Daniel Branda .08 .20
343 Marek Cernosek .08 .20
344 Jan Liska .08 .20
345 Kamil Piros .40 1.00
346 Petr Rosol .08 .20
347 Josef Palecek CO .08 .20
348 Petr Hemsky CO .08 .20
349 Milan Chalupa CO .08 .20
350 Ales Hemsky 4.00 20.00
351 Jiri Jantovsky .08 .20
352 Robert Kantor .08 .20
353 Marek Cernosek .08 .20
354 Jiri Malinsky .08 .20
355 Miroslav Mosnar .08 .20
356 Ales Pisa .08 .20
357 Stanislav Prochazka .08 .20
358 Petr Sykora .08 .20
359 Jan Archalous .08 .20
360 Martin Filip .08 .20
361 Pavel Kabrt .08 .20
362 Jan Kolar .08 .20
363 Martin Koudelka .08 .20
364 Radek Matejovsky .08 .20
365 Michal Mikeska .08 .20
366 Petr Mudroch .08 .20
367 Petr Caslava .08 .20
368 Radim Rulik CO .08 .20
369 Jiri Dobrovolny .08 .20
370 Mojmir Musil .08 .20
371 David Pospisil .08 .20
372 Martin Spanhel .40 1.00
373 Jaroslav Spelda .08 .20
374 Michal Straka .08 .20
375 Milan Volak .08 .20
376 Zdenek Sedlak .08 .20
377 Jan Fiala .08 .20
378 Petr Kadlec .08 .20
379 Josef Straka .08 .20
380 Jiri Kalous CO .08 .20
381 Josef Beranek CO .08 .20
382 Jiri Dolezal .08 .20
383 Jan Hejda .08 .20
384 Pavel Kolarik .20 .50
385 Tomas Kucharcik .08 .20
386 Vladimir Machulda .08 .20
387 Jan Bohac .08 .20
388 Pavel Geffert .08 .20
389 Jiri Jantovsky .08 .20
390 Zdenek Skorepa .08 .20
391 Vitezslav Skuta .08 .20
392 Robin Bacul .08 .20
393 Marek Tomica .08 .20
394 Frantisek Vyborny CO .08 .20
395 Ladislav Benysek .30 .50
396 Jaroslav Hlinka .08 .20
397 Vaclav Novak .08 .20
398 Patrik Martinec .08 .20
399 Vaclav Novak .08 .20
400 Josef Slanec .08 .20
401 Michal Sykora .20 .50
402 Vladimir Vujtek .20 .50
403 Kamil Konecny CO .08 .20
404 Jozef Dano .08 .20
405 Petr Folta .08 .20
406 Tomas Chlubna .08 .20
407 Robert Kantor .08 .20
408 Jan Marek .08 .20
409 Lubomir Sekeras .30 .50
410 Ondrej Zetek .08 .20
411 David Appel .08 .20
412 Pavel Janku .08 .20
413 Dmitrij Jerofejev .08 .20
414 David Nosek .08 .20
415 Vladimir Vlk .08 .20
416 Kamil Konecny .08 .20
417 Jan Sterbak CO .08 .20
418 Mojmir Trlicik .08 .20
419 Pavel Bacho .08 .20
420 Ondrej Zetek .08 .20
421 Roman Kadera .08 .20
422 Petr Hubacek .08 .20
423 Roman Kelner .08 .20
424 Pavel Kowalczyk .08 .20
425 Martin Lamich .08 .20
426 Jan Matejny .08 .20
427 Libor Pavlis .08 .20
428 Radek Philipp .08 .20
429 Libor Polasek .08 .20
430 Martin Tomasek .08 .20
431 Libor Gelacek .08 .20
432 Martin Louzek .08 .20
433 Martin Maskarinec .08 .20
434 David Moravec .08 .20
435 Ivan Padelek .08 .20
436 Martin Streit .08 .20
437 Miroslav Venkrbec .08 .20
438 Radek Belohlav .08 .35
439 Alexej Jaskin .08 .20
440 Zbynek Marak .08 .20
441 Oleg Antonenko .08 .20
442 Josef Mikes .08 .20
443 Jan Pardavy .08 .20
444 Jan Srdinko .08 .20
445 Jiri Veber .08 .20
446 Libor Zabransky .08 .20
447 Pavel Patera .20 .50
448 Martin Prochazka .08 .20
449 Zbynek Spitzer .08 .20
450 S. Prikryl CO .08 .20
451 Petr Cajanek .08 .75
452 Jiri David .08 .20
453 Martin Hamrlik .08 .20
454 Marek Ivan .08 .20
455 Josef Straub .08 .20
456 Ondrej Vesely .08 .20
457 Martin Ambruz .08 .20
458 Jan Homer .08 .20
459 Rostislav Malena .08 .20
460 S. Barada CO .08 .20
461 Pavol Valko .08 .20
462 Marek Uram .08 .20
463 Patrik Fink .08 .20
464 Tomas Hradecky .08 .20
465 Tomas Jakes .08 .20
466 Petr Kankovsky .08 .20
467 Milan Kastner .08 .20
468 David Kudelka .08 .20
469 Pavel Kumstat .08 .20
470 Karel Soudek .08 .20
471 Jan Kopecky .08 .20
472 Michal Bros .08 .25
473 Martin Cech .08 .20
474 Petr Gregorek .08 .20
475 Jiri Hanzlik .08 .20
476 Jaroslav Hlinka .08 .20
477 Petr Korinek .08 .20
478 Ludek Krayzel .08 .20
479 David Moravec .08 .20
480 Angel Nikolov .08 .20
481 Pavel Patera .20 .50
482 Kamil Piros .40 1.00
483 Vaclav Pletka .40 .50
484 Martin Spanhel .40 1.00
485 Radim Tesarik .08 .20
486 Libor Zabransky .08 .20
487 Petr Briza .20 .75
488 Dusan Salficky .20 .75
489 Roman Cechmanek 1.20 1.00
490 Vladimir Hudacek .08 .50
491 Peter Bartos .08 .20
492 Vladimir Vujtek .08 .20
493 David Vyborny .08 .20
494 Ladislav Benysek .30 .50
495 Tomas Blazek .20 .25
496 Frantisek Kucera .08 .20
497 Jiri Burger .08 .20
498 Jan Kopecky .08 .20
499 Vaclav Kral .08 .20
500 Jan Krulis .08 .20
501 Ivo Prorok .08 .20
502 Radek Martinek .30 .50
503 Jaroslav Nedved .08 .20
504 Petr Pavlas .08 .20
505 Ales Pisa .08 .20
506 Michal Sykora .08 .25
507 Robert Reichel .20 .50
508 Miroslav Buras .08 .20
509 Martin Spanhel .40 1.00
510 Michal Sup .08 .20
511 Petr Cajanek .08 1.00
512 Jiri Dopita .80 .50
513 Martin Hamrlik .08 .20
514 Roman Horak .08 .20
515 Zbynek Irgl .08 .20
516 Tomas Jakes .08 .20
517 Ludek Krayzel .08 .20
518 Jiri Kuntos .08 .20
519 Petr Leska .08 .20
520 Jiri Marusak .08 .20
521 David Moravec .08 .50
522 Jan Pardavy .08 .20
523 Pavel Patera .20 .50
524 Jan Peterek .08 .20
525 Martin Prochazka .08 .20
526 Karel Soudek .08 .20
527 Jan Srdinko .08 .20
528 Radim Tesarik .08 .20
529 Viktor Ujcik .08 .35
530 Libor Zabransky .08 .20
531 Pavel Cagas .20 .50
532 Zdenek Smid .20 .75
533 Lubos Horcicka .20 .50
534 Pavel Krizek .20 .50
535 Marek Pinc .20 .50
536 Petr Jez .20 .25
537 Radek Masny .20 .50
538 Roman Malek .20 .50
539 Tomas Duba .20 .50
540 Petr Prikryl .20 .50
541 Jiri Kratochvil .20 .50
542 Marek Novotny .20 .25
543 Jiri Trvaj .20 .50
544 Ivo Pesat .20 .50
545 Richard Hrazdira .20 .50
546 Petr Kubena .20 .50
547 Pavol Rybar .20 .50
548 Adam Svoboda .20 .75
549 Radek Masny .20 .50
550 Petr Tucek .20 .50
551 Vladimir Hudacek .20 .50
552 Dusan Salficky .20 .75
NNO Petr Briza CL .40 .75
NNO Martin Prusek CL .60 1.00
NNO Ladislav Blazek CL .40 .25
NNO Rudolf Pejchar CL .40 1.00
NNO Vladimir Hudacek CL .40 .50
NNO Roman Cechmanek CL .80 1.00
NNO Zdenek Orct CL .40 1.00
NNO Dusan Salficky CL .40 .75

1999-00 Czech OFS All-Star Game Blue

A blue-foil enhanced parallel to the 44-card All-Star Game subset. These cards were random inserts in packs.

COMPLETE SET (44) 15.00 25.00
487 Petr Briza .40 1.00
488 Dusan Salficky .40 1.00
489 Roman Cechmanek .75 2.00
490 Vladimir Hudacek .20 .50
491 Peter Bartos .20 .50
492 Vladimir Vujtek .20 .50
493 David Vyborny .20 .50
494 Ladislav Benysek .40 1.00
495 Tomas Blazek .40 1.00
496 Frantisek Kucera .20 .50
497 Jiri Burger .20 .50
498 Jan Kopecky .20 .50
499 Vaclav Kral .20 .50
500 Jan Krulis .20 .50
501 Ivo Prorok .20 .50
502 Radek Martinek .40 1.00
503 Jaroslav Nedved .20 .50
504 Petr Pavlas .20 .50
505 Ales Pisa .20 .50
506 Michal Sykora .20 .50
507 Robert Reichel .40 1.00
508 Miroslav Buras .20 .50
509 Martin Spanhel .30 .75
510 Michal Sup .20 .50
511 Petr Cajanek 1.25 3.00
512 Jiri Dopita .40 1.00
513 Martin Hamrlik .20 .50
514 Roman Horak .20 .50
515 Zbynek Irgl .20 .50
516 Tomas Jakes .20 .50
517 Ludek Krayzel .20 .50
518 Jiri Kuntos .20 .50
519 Petr Leska .20 .50
520 Jiri Marusak .20 .50
521 David Moravec .20 .50
522 Jan Pardavy .20 .50
523 Pavel Patera .20 .50
524 Jan Peterek .20 .50
525 Martin Prochazka .20 .50
526 Karel Soudek .20 .50
527 Jan Srdinko .20 .50
528 Radim Tesarik .20 .50
529 Viktor Ujcik .20 .50
530 Libor Zabransky .30 .75

1999-00 Czech OFS Goalie Die-Cuts

These randomly inserted cards parallel the first 15 cards in the base set and feature a distinctive die-cutting.

COMPLETE SET (15) 40.00 80.00
1 Libor Barta 2.00 5.00
2 Martin Bilek 2.00 5.00
3 Ladislav Blazek 2.00 5.00
4 Petr Briza 3.00 8.00
5 Ivo Capek 2.00 5.00
6 Roman Cechmanek 4.00 10.00
7 Robert Horyna 2.00 5.00
8 Vladimir Hudacek 2.00 5.00
9 Ladislav Kudrna 2.00 5.00
10 Vlastimil Lakosil 2.00 5.00
11 Michal Marik 2.00 5.00
12 Zdenek Orct 2.00 5.00
13 Rudolf Pejchar 2.00 5.00
14 Martin Prusek 8.00 20.00
15 Dusan Salficky 3.00 8.00

1999-00 Czech OFS Jagr Team Embossed

This set parallels cards #16-40 of the base OFS set, which features the Jagr Team subset. The cards are distinguishable from base cards by an embossed feature.

COMPLETE SET (25) 15.00 30.00
16 Richard Farda .20 .50
17 Marian Jelinek .20 .50
18 Josef Beranek .20 .50
19 Leo Gudas .20 .50
20 Milan Hnilicka 1.25 3.00
21 Milos Holan .20 .50
22 Jan Hrdina .75 2.00
23 Jaromir Jagr 8.00 20.00
24 Frantisek Kaberle .20 .50
25 Tomas Kaberle .60 1.50
26 Pavel Kubina .75 2.00
27 Marek Malik .20 .50
28 Pavel Patera .20 .50
29 Martin Prochazka .20 .50
30 Vaclav Prospal .40 1.00
31 Robert Reichel .40 1.00
32 Martin Rucinsky .40 1.00
33 Vladimir Ruzicka .40 1.00
34 Pavel Skrbek .40 1.00
35 Jiri Slegr .40 1.00
36 Jaroslav Spacek .40 1.00
37 Martin Straka .75 2.00
38 Vaclav Varada .40 1.00
39 David Volek .40 1.00
40 Jan Vopat .40 1.00

1999-00 Czech Score Blue 2000

This set features players from the Czech second division. The set is noteworthy for the inclusion of cards of NHLers Brendan Morrison and Patrik Elias, who were holding out from the New Jersey Devils at the time. A parallel version of the set, Red Ice 2000, also exists. At this time, we believe there is no price difference between the two versions.

COMPLETE SET (165) 20.00 50.00
1 Roman Malek .30 .75
2 Roman Hrubes .20 .50
3 Ladislav Slizek .20 .50
4 Jaroslav Roubik .20 .50
5 Jiri Kuchler .20 .50
6 Petr Mudroch .20 .50
7 Jiri Cmunt .20 .50
8 Lukas Palecek .20 .50
9 Pavel Malecek .20 .50
10 Vaclav Drabek .20 .50
11 Dalibor Sanda .20 .50
12 Jiri Novotny .20 .50
13 Dalimil Svoboda .20 .50
14 Petr Kubena .20 .50
15 Martin Svetlik .20 .50
16 Jakub Ziska .20 .50
17 Richard Kolacek .20 .50
18 Tomas Trachta .20 .50
19 Patrik Weber .20 .50
20 Ales Sochorec .20 .50
21 Alexandr Elsner .20 .50
22 Michal Safarik .20 .50
23 Michal Safarik .20 .50
24 Tomas Mikolasek .20 .50
25 Pavel Malac .20 .50
26 Kamil Jarina .20 .50
27 Petr Martinek .20 .50
28 Ladislav Bousek .20 .50
29 Kamil Kolacek .20 .50
30 Jiri Gombar .20 .50
31 David Hajek .20 .50
32 Martin Tupa .20 .50
33 Stanislav Slavensky .20 .50
34 Martin Stelcich .20 .50
35 Radek Sip .20 .50
36 Petr Altrichter .20 .50
37 Lukas Stabl .20 .50
38 Lukas Sablik .20 .50
39 Marian Morava .20 .50
40 Zdenek Fuksa .20 .50
41 Petr Mokrejs .20 .50
42 Miroslav Duben .20 .50
43 Jiri Cihlar .20 .50
44 Vaclav Adamec .20 .50
45 Daniel Hodek .20 .50
46 Ales Polcar .20 .50
47 Daniel Zapotocny .20 .50
48 Richard Cachnin .20 .50
49 Roman Spiler .20 .50
50 Filip Sindelar .20 .50
51 Petr Jaros .20 .50
52 Marek Dvorak .20 .50
53 Jaroslav Mares .20 .50
54 Robert Vavroch .20 .50
55 Vratislav Hreben .20 .50
56 Petr Cerveny .20 .50
57 Jaroslav Kocar .20 .50
58 Ales Skokan .20 .50
59 Michal Horak .20 .50
60 Jakub Kraus .20 .50
61 Marcel Kucera .20 .50
62 Miroslav Sedlacek .20 .50
63 Richard Richter .20 .50
64 Rudolf Mudra .20 .50
65 Jaroslav Muller .20 .50
66 Evzen Gal .20 .50
67 Petr Spojcar .20 .50
68 Jaroslav Kreuzman .20 .50
69 Premysl Sedlak .20 .50
70 Martin Nosek .20 .50
71 Tomas Vyskocil .20 .50
72 Michal Lanicek .20 .50
73 Pavel Malac .20 .50
74 Ales Vala .20 .50
75 Martin Vyborny .20 .50
76 Tomas Vozka .20 .50
77 Petr Hocicka .20 .50
78 Jan Plodek .20 .50
79 Oldrich Nyc .20 .50
80 Filip Pesan .20 .50
81 Milan Plodek .20 .50
82 Jiri Matousek .20 .50
83 Vitezslav Jankovych .20 .50
84 Petr Kus .20 .50
85 Martin Chlad .20 .50
86 Hiroyuki Murakami .20 .50
87 Lukas Bednarik .20 .50
88 Michal Oliverius .20 .50
89 Tomas Pisa .20 .50
90 Jan Hranac .20 .50
91 Jan Bohacek .20 .50
92 Tomas Klimt .20 .50
93 Martin Zivny .20 .50
94 Michal Havel .20 .50
95 Martin Rejthar .20 .50
96 Karl Rakovsky .20 .50
97 Martin Vojtek .20 .50
98 Robert Prochazka .20 .50
99 Daniel Vilasek .20 .50
100 Jan Kasik .20 .50
101 Jevgenij Alipov .20 .50
102 Ales Kretinsky .20 .50
103 Pavel Sebesta .20 .50
104 David Kostelnak .20 .50
105 Karel Harazim .20 .50
106 Richard Brancik .20 .50
107 Petr Rozum .20 .50
108 Michal Pinkas .20 .50
109 Robert Slavik .20 .50
110 Josef Vachulka .20 .50
111 Lubos Pindiak .20 .50
112 Robert Zak .20 .50
113 David Mika .20 .50
114 Jiri Kudrna .20 .50
115 Vaclav Benak .20 .50
116 Roman Bezpalec .20 .50
117 Pavel Hejl .20 .50
118 Michal Janiga .20 .50
119 Vladimir Mizera .20 .50
120 David Plsek .20 .50
121 Petr Tucek .20 .50
122 Martin Palinek .20 .50
123 Jiri Polak .20 .50
124 Michal Cerny .20 .50
125 Milan Ministr .20 .50
126 Tomas Hradecky .20 .50
127 David Svec .20 .50
128 Filip Janecek .20 .50
129 Tomas Hradecky .20 .50
130 Radomir Brazda .20 .50
131 Petr Hrachovina .20 .50
132 Martin Altrichter .20 .50
133 Jaromir Pichal .20 .50
134 Jiri Bures .20 .50
135 Jiri Mifek .20 .50
136 Jaroslav Smolik .20 .50
137 Milota Florian .20 .50
138 Robert Holy .20 .50
139 Josef Drabek .20 .50
140 Michal Slavik .20 .50
141 Tomas Kramny .20 .50
142 Jan Konecny .20 .50
143 Radek Lukes .20 .50
144 Robert Hamrla .20 .50
145 Petr Lustinec .20 .50
146 Radek Kucera .20 .50
147 Petr Sakarov .20 .50
148 Pavel Kormunda .20 .50
149 Petr Suchy .20 .50
150 David Brezik .20 .50
151 Michal Nohejl .20 .50
152 Martin Jenacek .20 .50
153 Dusan Barica .20 .50
154 Zdenek Kucirek .20 .50
155 Stanislav Neruda .20 .50
156 Robert Pospisil .20 .50
157 Brendan Morrison .75 2.00
158 Frantisek Sevcik .20 .50
159 Roman Hloush .20 .50
160 Patrik Elias .75 2.00
161 Oldrich Bakus .20 .50
162 Jiri Oliva .20 .50
163 Karel Sefcik .20 .50
164 Marcel Hrbacek .20 .50
165 Rostislav Malena .20

2000-01 Czech DS Extraliga

This set features the top players of the Czech Elite league. The cards feature an action photo on the front surrounded by a white border, with two more photos and stats on the back.

COMPLETE SET (168) 25.00 60.00
1 Petr BrizaÂ .40 1.00
2 Petr PrikrylÂ .20 .50

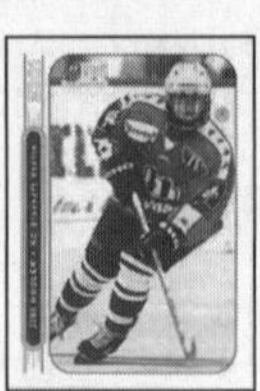

3 Libor ZabranskyÂ .20 .50
4 Vlastimil KroupaÂ .20 .50
5 Frantisek PtacekÂ .20 .50
6 Michal DobronÂ .20 .50
7 Vladimir VujtekÂ .20 .50
8 Jaroslav HlinkaÂ .20 .50
9 Martin ChabadaÂ .20 .50
10 Ondrej KratenaÂ .20 .50
11 Michal BrosÂ .20 .50
12 Richard ZemlickaÂ .30 .75
13 Jaroslav KamesÂ .40 1.00
14 Ivo PesatÂ .20 .50
15 Jan SrdinkoÂ .20 .50
16 Milan NedomaÂ .20 .50
17 Martin StrbakÂ .20 .50
18 Radim TesarikÂ .20 .50
19 Jan PardavyÂ .20 .50
20 Jiri DopitaÂ .40 1.00
21 Jan SochorÂ .20 .50
22 Jan LipianskyÂ .20 .50
23 Jiri HudlerÂ 6.00 15.00
24 Ondrej VeselyÂ .20 .50
25 Dusan SalfickyÂ .40 1.00
26 Petr KusÂ .20 .50
27 Josef ReznicekÂ .20 .50
28 Martin CechÂ .20 .50
29 Ivan VlcekÂ .20 .50
30 Jiri HanzlikÂ .20 .50
31 Pavel VostrakÂ .20 .50
32 Petr KorinekÂ .20 .50
33 Milan VolakÂ .20 .50
34 Michal StrakaÂ .20 .50
35 David PospisilÂ .20 .50
36 Milan AntosÂ .20 .50
37 Zdenek OrctÂ .40 1.00
38 Michal PodolkaÂ .40 1.00
39 Angel NikolovÂ .30 .75
40 Karel PilarÂ .40 1.00
41 Radek MrazekÂ .20 .50
42 Vladimir GynaÂ .20 .50
43 Robert ReichelÂ .30 .75
44 Petr RosolÂ .20 .50
45 Vojtech KubincakÂ .20 .50
46 Kamil PirosÂ .40 1.00
47 Vesa KarjalainenÂ .20 .50
48 Robert KyselaÂ .20 .50
49 Vladimir HudacekÂ .40 1.00
50 Richard HrazdiraÂ .20 .50
51 Tomas ZizkaÂ .40 1.00
52 Jiri MarusakÂ .20 .50
53 Martin HamrlikÂ .20 .50
54 Miroslav BarusÂ .20 .50
55 Miroslav OkalÂ .20 .50
56 Petr CajanekÂ .30 .75
57 Jaroslav BalastikÂ .20 .50
58 Petr ValaÂ .20 .50
59 Martin AmbruzÂ .20 .50
60 Petr LeskaÂ .20 .50
61 Marek NovotnyÂ .20 .50
62 Vlastimil LakosilÂ .40 1.00
63 Marek ZadinaÂ .20 .50
64 Mario CartelliÂ .20 .50
65 Vladimir VlkÂ .20 .50
66 Jiri KuntosÂ .20 .50
67 Richard KralÂ .20 .50
68 Viktor UjcikÂ .30 .75
69 Jozef DanoÂ .20 .50
70 Petr GregorekÂ .20 .50
71 Richard KapusÂ .20 .50
72 Pavel JankuÂ .20 .50
73 Michal MarikÂ .20 .50
74 Ivo CapekÂ .40 1.00
75 Radek MartinekÂ .40 1.00
76 Rudolf SuchanekÂ .20 .50
77 Stanislav JaseckoÂ .20 .50
78 Vaclav KralÂ .20 .50
79 Filip TurekÂ .20 .50
80 Lubos RobÂ .20 .50
81 Radek BelohlavÂ .30 .75
82 Jiri SimanekÂ .20 .50
83 Ales KotalikÂ .20 .50
84 Kamil BrabenecÂ .20 .50
85 Libor BartaÂ .20 .50
86 Adam SvobodaÂ .40 1.00
87 Ales PisaÂ .40 1.00
88 Jiri MalinskyÂ .20 .50
89 Petr JancarikÂ .20 .50
90 Otakar JaneckyÂ .30 .75
91 Ladislav LubinaÂ .20 .50
92 Tomas BlazekÂ .20 .50
93 Jaroslav KudrnaÂ .30 .75
94 Michal MikeskaÂ .20 .50
95 Stanislav ProchazkaÂ .20 .50
96 Michal TvrdikÂ .20 .50
97 Oldrich SvobodaÂ .40 1.00
98 Ladislav KudrnaÂ .20 .50
99 Tomas JakesÂ .20 .50
100 Jiri HesÂ .20 .50
101 Pavel KumstatÂ .20 .50
102 Karel SoudekÂ .20 .50
103 Peter PucherÂ .20 .50
104 David HavirÂ .20 .50
105 Zbynek MarakÂ .20 .50
106 Milan ProchazkaÂ .20 .50
107 Radek HamanÂ .20 .50
108 David PazourekÂ .20 .50
109 Ladislav BlazekÂ .20 .50
110 Roman MalekÂ .40 1.00
111 Petr KadlecÂ .20 .50
112 Jan NovakÂ .20 .50
113 Angel KrstevÂ .20 .50
114 Jan SnopekÂ .20 .50
115 Daniel BrandaÂ .20 .50
116 Jan AlincÂ .20 .50
117 Viktor HublÂ .20 .50
118 Petr HrbekÂ .20 .50
119 Jan BohacÂ .20 .50
120 Zdenek SkorepaÂ .20 .50
121 Petr FranekÂ .20 .50
122 Zdenek SmidÂ .40 1.00
123 Libor ProchazkaÂ .20 .50
124 Normunds SejejsÂ .20 .50
125 Jiri PolakÂ .20 .50
126 Roman ZakÂ .20 .50
127 Jaromir KverkaÂ .20 .50
128 Tomas ChlubnaÂ .20 .50
129 Radek ProchazkaÂ .20 .50
130 David HruskaÂ .20 .50
131 Robert TomikÂ .20 .50
132 Pavel KasparikÂ .20 .50
133 Lubos HorcickaÂ .20 .50
134 Marek PincÂ .30 .75
135 Jan KrulisÂ .20 .50
136 Michal MadlÂ .20 .50
137 Radek GardonÂ .20 .50
138 Jan BohacekÂ .20 .50
139 Ladislav SvobodaÂ .20 .50
140 Tomas HornaÂ .20 .50
141 Jiri HolsanÂ .20 .50
142 Ondrej KrizÂ .20 .50
143 Ladislav VlcekÂ .20 .50
144 Jozef VoskarÂ .20 .50
145 Radovan BieglÂ .30 .75
146 Radek MasnyÂ .20 .50
147 Michael VyhlidalÂ .20 .50
148 Miroslav JavinÂ .20 .50
149 Petr PavlasÂ .20 .50
150 Tomas SrsenÂ .20 .50
151 Petr FoltaÂ .20 .50
152 Libor PivkoÂ .20 .50
153 Daniel BohacÂ .20 .50
154 Roman HorakÂ .20 .50
155 Jan PeterekÂ .20 .50
156 Richard PavlikovskyÂ .20 .50
157 Martin PrusekÂ .40 1.00
158 Jiri TrvajÂ .20 .50
159 Zdenek PavelekÂ .20 .50
160 Vitezslav SkutaÂ .20 .50
161 Dimitri JerofejevÂ .20 .50
162 David MoravecÂ .40 1.00
163 Roman KaderaÂ .20 .50
164 Zbynek IrglÂ .20 .50
165 Marek IvanÂ .20 .50
166 Martin ProchazkaÂ .30 .75
167 Josef StraubÂ .20 .50
168 Ivan PadelekÂ .20 .50

2000-01 Czech DS Extraliga Best of the Best

This insert set features the two best Czech-born players ever. The autograph cards are serial numbered out of 200.

COMPETE SET (4) 25.00 60.00
PRINT RUN 200 SER.#'d SETS
BBH1 Dominik Hasek 4.00 10.00
BBH2 Dominik Hasek 4.00 10.00
BBJ1 Jaromir Jagr 6.00 15.00
BBJ2 Jaromir Jagr 6.00 15.00
BBH1 D.Hasek AU/200 40.00 100.00
BBJ2 J.Jagr AU/200 60.00 150.00

2000-01 Czech DS Extraliga Goalies

This insert set features the top stoppers in the Czech Extraliga.

COMPLETE SET (14) 25.00 60.00
G1 Petr BrizaÂ 3.00 8.00
G2 Jaroslav KamesÂ 2.00 5.00
G3 Dusan SalfickyÂ 2.00 5.00
G4 Zdenek OrctÂ 2.00 5.00
G5 Vladimir HudacekÂ 2.00 5.00
G6 Vlastimil LakosilÂ 2.00 5.00
G7 Ivo CapekÂ 2.00 5.00
G8 Adam SvobodaÂ 2.00 5.00
G9 Oldrich SvobodaÂ 2.00 5.00
G10 Roman MalekÂ 2.00 5.00
G11 Zdenek SmidÂ 2.00 5.00
G12 Marek PincÂ 2.00 5.00
G13 Radovan BieglÂ 2.00 5.00
G14 Martin PrusekÂ 4.00 10.00

2000-01 Czech DS Extraliga National Team

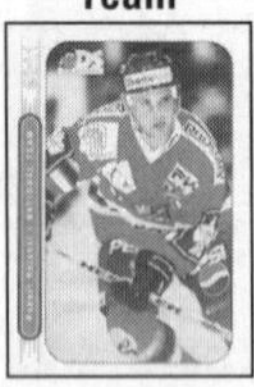

This insert set features members of the Czech Republic's gold medal-winning World Championships team.

COMPLETE SET (10) 25.00 60.00
NT1 Dusan SalfickyÂ 2.00 5.00
NT2 Roman CechmanekÂ 3.00 7.50
NT3 Martin StepanekÂ 1.25 3.00
NT4 Vladimir VujtekÂ 1.25 3.00
NT5 Robert ReichelÂ 2.00 5.00
NT6 Jiri DopitaÂ 2.00 5.00
NT7 Martin RucinskyÂ 2.00 5.00
NT8 Martin HavlatÂ 10.00 25.00
NT9 Tomas VlasakÂ 1.25 3.00
NT10 Michal BrosÂ 1.25 3.00

2000-01 Czech DS Extraliga Team Jagr

This players for this insert set were chosen by Jagr himself as his favorite Czech stars. The cards are slightly thicker than the base cards of this season.

COMPETE SET (16) 40.00 80.00
JT1 Roman TurekÂ 2.00 5.00
JT2 Milan HnilickaÂ 2.00 5.00
JT3 Petr SykoraÂ 1.50 4.00

JT4 Roman HamrlikÂ 1.25 3.00
JT5 Martin StrakaÂ 1.50 4.00
JT6 Pavel KubinaÂ 1.25 3.00
JT7 Petr NedvedÂ 1.50 4.00
JT8 Martin ProchazkaÂ 1.25 3.00
JT9 Vaclav ProspalÂ 1.25 3.00
JT10 David VolekÂ 1.25 3.00
JT11 Milan HejdukÂ 6.00 15.00
JT12 Jaromir JagrÂ 8.00 25.00
JT13 Jan HlavacÂ 1.50 4.00
JT14 Pavel PateraÂ 1.25 3.00
JT15 Tomas VlasakÂ 1.25 3.00
JT16 Vaclav VaradaÂ 1.25 3.00

2000-01 Czech DS Extraliga Team Jagr Parallel

This partial parallel set features Jagr's favorite Czech players in the NHL. The cards were serial numbered out of 300.

COMPLETE SET (9) 50.00 125.00
STATED PRINT RUN 300 SER.#'d SETS
JT1 Roman TurekÂ 8.00 20.00
JT2 Milan HnilickaÂ 4.00 10.00
JT3 Petr SykoraÂ 4.00 15.00
JT4 Roman HamrlikÂ 4.00 10.00
JT5 Martin StrakaÂ 4.00 10.00
JT6 Petr NedvedÂ 4.00 10.00
JT7 Milan HejdukÂ 12.50 30.00
JT8 Jaromir JagrÂ 20.00 50.00
JT9 Jan HlavacÂ 4.00 10.00

2000-01 Czech DS Extraliga Top Stars

This set features the first All-Star team of the Czech Extraliga.

TS1 Petr BrizaÂ 3.00 8.00
TS2 Radek MartinekÂ 2.00 5.00
TS3 Petr CajanekÂ 2.00 5.00
TS4 Jiri DopitaÂ 3.00 8.00
TS5 Robert ReichelÂ 3.00 8.00
TS6 Martin ProchazkaÂ 2.00 5.00

2000-01 Czech DS Extraliga Valuable Players

Yet another insert set featuring the Extraliga's top stars.

COMPLETE SET (6) 12.00 20.00
VP1 Vladimir HudacekÂ 2.00 5.00
VP2 Frantisek KuceraÂ 1.00 3.00
VP3 Michal SykoraÂ 1.00 3.00
VP4 Robert ReichelÂ 2.00 5.00
VP5 Jiri DopitaÂ 2.00 5.00
VP6 Petr CajanekÂ 1.00 3.00

2000-01 Czech DS Extraliga World Champions

This insert set features more members of the Czech World Championship team.

COMPLETE SET (11) 30.00 75.00
WCH1 Roman CechmanekÂ 6.00 8.00
WCH2 Dusan SalfickyÂ 2.00 5.00
WCH3 Radek MartinekÂ 2.00 5.00
WCH4 Martin StepanekÂ 2.00 5.00
WCH5 Frantisek KuceraÂ 2.00 5.00
WCH6 Michal SykoraÂ 2.00 5.00
WCH7 Martin HavlatÂ 10.00 25.00
WCH8 Robert ReichelÂ 2.00 5.00
WCH9 Tomas VlasakÂ 2.00 5.00
WCH10 David VybornyÂ 2.00 5.00
WCH11 Michal BrosÂ 2.00 5.00

2000-01 Czech OFS

This set was released in pack form in the Czech Republic and features every member of that country's elite league.

COMPLETE SET (421) 32.00 80.00
1 Team Logo .04 .10
2 Jaroslav Liska CO .04 .10
3 Jaroslav Parizek CO .04 .10
4 Jan Tlacil CO .04 .10
5 Jaroslav Pouzar CO .04 .10
6 Michal Marik .10 .25
7 Ivo Capek .20 .50
8 Radek Martinek .30 .50
9 Rudolf Suchanek .20 .50
10 Stanislav Jasecko .10 .25
11 Pavel Mojzis .10 .25
12 Vaclav Benak .10 .25
13 Ladislav Cierny .20 .50
14 Josef Jindra .10 .25
15 Vaclav Kral .10 .25
16 Filip Turek .10 .25
17 Lubos Rob .10 .25
18 Radek Belohlav .15 .40
19 Ales Kotalik .75 2.00
20 Kamil Brabenec .10 .25
21 Jiri Simanek .10 .25
22 Martin Strba .10 .25
23 Petr Sailer .10 .25
24 Milan Filipi .04 .25
25 Jiri Broz .10 .25
26 Jiri Novotny .20 .50
27 Michal Vondrka .10 .25
28 Team Logo .04 .10
29 Josef Palacek CO .04 .10
30 Petr Hemsky CO .04 .10
31 Libor Barta .20 .25
32 Adam Svoboda .30 .75
33 Martin Barek .10 .25
34 Ales Pisa .10 .25
35 Jiri Malinsky .10 .25
36 Petr Jancarik .10 .25
37 Miroslav Duben .10 .25
38 Tomas Pacal .10 .25
39 Michal Divisek .10 .25
40 Andrej Novotny .10 .25
41 Petr Mudroch .10 .25
42 Otakar Janecky .20 .50
43 Ladislav Lubina .10 .25
44 Tomas Blazek .20 .25
45 Jaroslav Kudrna .20 .50
46 Michal Mikeska .10 .25
47 Stanislav Prochazka .10 .25
48 Michal Tvrdik .10 .25
49 Martin Filip .10 .25
50 Martin Koudelka .10 .25
51 Pavel Kabrt .10 .25
52 Petr Sykora .20 .50
53 Tomas Rolinek .10 .25
54 Jan Kolar .10 .25
55 Team Logo .04 .10
56 Marek Sykora CO .04 .10
57 Dusan Salficky .30 .75
58 Petr Kus .10 .25
59 Josef Reznicek .10 .25
60 Martin Cech .10 .25
61 Ivan Vlcek .10 .25
62 Jiri Hanzlik .10 .25
63 Jaroslav Spelda .10 .25
64 Zdenek Touzimsky .10 .25
65 Jiri Dobrovolny .10 .25
66 Jan Choteborsky .10 .25
67 Pavel Vostrak .10 .25
68 Petr Korinek .20 .50
69 Milan Volak .10 .25
70 Michal Straka .10 .25
71 David Pospisil .10 .25
72 Josef Straka .10 .25
73 Milan Antos .10 .25
74 Andrej Nedorost .40 1.00
75 Vaclav Eiselt .10 .25
76 Jiri Jelen .10 .25
77 Michal Dvorak .10 .25
78 Jiri Zurek .10 .25
79 Dusan Andrasovsky .10 .25
80 Team Logo .04 .10
81 Jaromir Šindel CO .10 .25
82 Ondrej Weissmann CO .04 .10
83 Ladislav Blazek .20 .25
84 Roman Malek .10 .25
85 Petr Kadlec .10 .25
86 Jan Novak .10 .25
87 Angel Krstev .10 .25
88 Jan Snopek .10 .25
89 Jan Kloboucek .10 .25
90 Jan Hejda .10 .25
91 Petr Martinek .10 .25
92 Jan Slavik .10 .25
93 Daniel Branda .10 .25
94 Jan Alinc .20 .50
95 Viktor Hubl .10 .25
96 Jan Kopecky .10 .25
97 Jan Bohac .10 .25
98 Zdenek Skorepa .20 .50
99 Michal Sup .10 .25
100 Radek Matejovsky .10 .25
101 Robin Bacul .10 .25
102 Leos Cermak .10 .25
103 Petr Jira .10 .25
104 Marek Tomica .10 .25
105 Petr Hrbek .10 .25
106 Team Logo .04 .10
107 Eduard Novak CO .04 .10
108 Petr Fiala CO .04 .10
109 Lubos Horcicka .10 .25
110 Marek Pinc .10 .25
111 Jan Pospisil .10 .25
112 Jan Krulis .10 .25
113 Michal Madl .10 .25
114 Ondrej Kriz .10 .25
115 Jan Bohacek .10 .25
116 David Hajek .10 .25
117 Jan Dlouhy .10 .25
118 Martin Taborsky .10 .25
119 Jiri Kames .20 .50
120 Ladislav Svoboda .10 .25
121 Pavel Geffert .10 .25
122 Tomas Horna .10 .25
123 Jiri Holsan .10 .25
124 Radek Gardon .10 .25
125 Ladislav Vlcek .10 .25
126 Jozef Voskar .10 .25
127 Tomas Klimt .20 .50
128 Premysl Sedlak .10 .25
129 Tomas Plekanec ERC .10 .25
130 Michal Havel .10 .25
131 Vaclav Skuhravy .10 .25
132 Team Logo .04 .10
133 Vaclav Sykora CO .04 .10
134 Otakar Vejvoda CO .04 .10
135 Zdenek Orct .20 .50
136 Michal Podolka .30 .75
137 Angel Nikolov .20 .50
138 Karel Pilar .40 1.00
139 Radek Mrazek .10 .25
140 Marek Cernosek .10 .25
141 Vladimir Gyna .10 .25
142 Martin Tupa .10 .25
143 Jan Hranac .10 .25
144 Petr Suchy .10 .25
145 Robert Reichel .31 .50
146 Petr Rosol .10 .25
147 Vojtech Kubincak .10 .25
148 Kamil Piros .40 1.00
149 Jindrich Kotrla .10 .25
150 Vesa Karjalainen .10 .25
151 Robert Kysela .10 .25
152 Stanislav Stavensky .10 .25
153 Tomas Martinec .10 .25
154 Zdenek Zak .10 .25
155 Martin Tvrznik .10 .25
156 Lukas Bednarik .10 .25
157 Team Logo .04 .10
158 Radim Rulik CO .04 .10
159 Martin Pesout CO .04 .10
160 Petr Franek .10 .25
161 Zdenek Smid .30 .75
162 Pavel Csipka .10 .25
163 Libor Prochazka .10 .25
164 Robert Kantor .10 .25
165 Jiri Polak .10 .25
166 Normunds Sejejs .10 .25
167 Roman Prosek .10 .25
168 Roman Zak .10 .25
169 Ivan Puncochar .10 .25
170 Petr Puncochar .10 .25
171 Jakub Grof .10 .25
172 Jaromir Kverka .10 .25
173 Tomas Chlubna .10 .25
174 Radek Prochazka .10 .25
175 David Hruska .10 .25
176 Robert Tomik .10 .25
177 Pavel Kasparik .10 .25
178 Martin Rousek .10 .25
179 Jaroslav Kalla .10 .25
180 Peter Bohunicky .10 .25
181 Jan Kostal .10 .25
182 Petr Domin .10 .25
183 Petr Sinagl .10 .25
184 Team Logo .04 .10
185 Milan Chalupa CO .10 .25
186 Pavel Pazourek CO .04 .10
187 Oldrich Svoboda .10 .25
188 Ladislav Kudrna .20 .50
189 Miloslav Bahensky .10 .25
190 Tomas Jakes .10 .25
191 Jiri Hes .10 .25
192 Pavel Kumstat .10 .25
193 Karel Soudek .10 .25
194 Pavol Valko .10 .25
195 David Havir .10 .25
196 David Petlak .10 .25
197 Vladimir Holik .10 .25
198 Peter Pucher .10 .25
199 Marek Uram .10 .25
200 Karel Plasek .10 .25
201 Zbynek Marak .10 .25
202 Milan Prochazka .10 .25
203 Patrik Fink .10 .25
204 David Pazourek .10 .25
205 Marek Vorel .10 .25
206 Radek Haman .10 .25
207 Petr Lipina .10 .25
208 Petr Kumstat .10 .25
209 Team Logo .04 .10
210 Vladimir Vujtek CO .04 .10
211 Ales Mach CO .04 .10
212 Marek Novotny .10 .25
213 Vlastimil Lakosil .20 .50
214 Mario Cartelli .10 .25
215 Vladimir Vlk .10 .25
216 Jiri Kuntos .10 .25
217 Petr Gregorek .10 .25
218 Robert Prochazka .10 .25
219 Ondrej Zetek .10 .25
220 David Nosek .10 .25
221 Tomas Houdek .10 .25
222 Tomas Harant .10 .25
223 Richard Kral .10 .25
224 Viktor Ujcik .15 .40
225 Jozef Dano .10 .25
226 Richard Kapus .10 .25
227 Pavel Janku .20 .25
228 Marek Zadina .10 .25
229 Branislav Janos .10 .25
230 Tomas Nemcicky .10 .25
231 Patrik Moskal .10 .25
232 David Appel .10 .25
233 Jan Marek .10 .25
234 Jiri Hasek .10 .25
235 Team Logo .04 .10
236 Alois Hadamczik CO .04 .10
237 Kamil Konecny CO .04 .10
238 Mojmir Trlicik CO .04 .10
239 Martin Prusek .75 2.00
240 Jiri Trvaj .10 .25
241 Lukas Smolka .10 .25
242 Vitezslav Skuta .10 .25
243 Dmitrij Jerofejev .10 .25
244 Daniel Kapotocny .10 .25
245 Petr Jurecka .10 .25
246 Radek Philipp .10 .25
247 Lukas Zatopek .10 .25
248 Daniel Seman .10 .25
249 Jan Vytisk .10 .25
250 David Moravec .20 .50
251 Martin Prochazka .10 .25
252 Ivan Padelek .10 .25
253 Josef Straub .10 .25
254 Roman Kadera .10 .25
255 Marek Ivan .10 .25
256 Zdenek Pavelek .10 .25
257 Martin Tomasek .10 .25
258 Pavel Selinger .10 .25
259 Jan Pleva .10 .25
260 Ales Padelek .10 .25
261 Team Logo .04 .10
262 Ivo Pestuka CO .04 .10
263 Jiri Reznar CO .04 .10
264 Radovan Biegl .10 .25
265 Radek Masny .10 .25
266 Michael Vyhlidal .10 .25
267 Miroslav Javin .10 .25
268 Richard Pavlikovsky .10 .25
269 Petr Pavlas .10 .25
270 Patrik Rimmel .10 .25
271 Ales Tomasek .10 .25
272 Petr Suchanek .10 .25
273 Tomas Srsen .10 .25
274 Petr Folta .10 .25
275 Libor Pivko .10 .25
276 Daniel Bohac .10 .25
277 Roman Horak .20 .50
278 Jan Peterek .10 .25
279 Marek Melenovsky .10 .25
280 Pavel Zdrahal .10 .25
281 Roman Kontsek .10 .25
282 Michal Cech .10 .25
283 Tomas Sykora .10 .25
284 Martin Streit .10 .25
285 Milos Melicherik .10 .25
286 Team Logo .04 .10
287 Milos Riha CO .04 .10
288 Frantisek Vyborny CO .04 .10
289 Pavel Hynek CO .04 .10
290 Petr Briza .30 .75
291 Petr Prikryl .10 .25
292 Tomas Duba .10 .25
293 Libor Zabransky .20 .25
294 Vlastimil Kroupa .20 .50
295 Frantisek Ptacek .10 .25
296 Michal Dobron .10 .25
297 Pavel Srek .10 .25
298 Jaroslav Nedved .10 .25
299 Martin Holy .10 .25
300 Miha Rebolj .10 .25
301 Jan Hanzlik .10 .25
302 Vladimir Vujtek .20 .50
303 Jaroslav Hlinka .10 .25
304 Martin Chabada .10 .25
305 Ondrej Kratena .10 .25
306 Michal Bros .20 .25
307 Patrik Martinec .10 .25
308 Richard Zemlicka .20 .50
309 Jiri Zelenka .10 .25
310 Vaclav Novak .10 .25
311 Petr Havelka .10 .25
312 Michal Sivek .60 1.50
313 Petr Hrbek .10 .25
314 Radek Duda .10 .25
315 Josef Slanec .10 .25
316 Petr Kanko .75 2.00
317 Team Logo .04 .10
318 Zdislav Tabara CO .04 .10
319 Miroslav Venkrbec CO .04 .10
320 Jaroslav Kames .30 .75
321 Ivo Pesat .10 .25
322 Lukas Plsek .10 .25
323 Jan Srdinko .10 .25
324 Milan Nedoma .10 .25
325 Martin Strbak .10 .25
326 Radim Tesarik .10 .25
327 Pavel Zubicek .10 .25
328 Alexej Jaskin .10 .25
329 Petr Kubos .10 .25
330 Zbynek Spitzer .10 .25
331 Michal Safarik .10 .25
332 Pavel Augusta .10 .25
333 Jan Pardavy .10 .25
334 Jiri Dopita .20 .50
335 Jan Tomajko .10 .25
336 Roman Stantien .10 .25
337 Jan Sochor .10 .25
338 Martin Paroulek .10 .25
339 Jan Lipiansky .10 .25
340 Jiri Hudler ERC 6.00 15.00
341 Ondrej Vesely .10 .25
342 Jiri Jantovsky .10 .25
343 Petr Zajgla .10 .25
344 Tomas Demel .10 .25
345 Petr Vampola .10 .25
346 Team Logo .04 .10
347 Antonin Stavjana CO .10 .25
348 Zdenek Venera CO .04 .10
349 Vladimir Hudacek .20 .50
350 Richard Hrazdira .20 .50
351 Petr Tucek .10 .25
352 Tomas Zizka .10 .25
353 Jiri Marusak .10 .25
354 Martin Hamrlik .10 .25
355 Patrik Luza .10 .25
356 Rostislav Malena .08 .20
357 Jan Homer .10 .25
358 Lukas Zib .10 .25
359 Boris Zabka .10 .25
360 Miroslav Okal .08 .20
361 Petr Cajanek .30 .75
362 Jaroslav Balastik .10 .25
363 Petr Vala .10 .25
364 Martin Ambruz .10 .25
365 Petr Leska .10 .25
366 Miroslav Barus .10 .25
367 Martin Kotasek .10 .25
368 Lubomir Korhon .20 .50
369 Ivan Rachunek .40 1.00
370 Radovan Somik .10 .25
371 Filip Cech .10 .25
372 Martin Jenacek .10 .25
373 Pavel Mojzis .10 .25
374 Milan Navratil .10 .25
375 Michal Safarik .10 .25
376 Miroslav Blatak .10 .25
377 Team Logo .04 .10
378 Roman Turek .40 1.00
379 Milan Hnilicka .40 1.00
380 Tomas Kaberle .30 .75
381 Frantisek Kaberle .20 .50
382 Roman Hamrlik .30 .75
383 Pavel Kubina .40 1.00
384 Jaromir Jagr 2.00 5.00
385 Patrik Elias .75 2.00
386 Milan Hejduk 2.00 5.00
387 Radek Dvorak .40 1.00
388 Petr Nedved .30 .75
389 Vaclav Prospal .40 1.00
390 Pavel Patera .20 .50
391 Petr Sykora 1.25 3.00
392 Vaclav Varada .20 .50
393 Martin Straka .40 1.00
394 Jan Hrdina .40 1.00
395 David Volek .20 .50
396 Tomas Vlasak .10 .25
397 Michal Rozsival .30 .75
398 Team Logo .04 .10
399 Ladislav Blazek .20 .25
400 Miloslav Horava .10 .25
401 Frantisek Kucera .20 .20
402 Lubomir Sekeras .20 .50
403 Petr Kadlec .10 .25
404 Jaroslav Spacek .20 .50
405 Frantisek Prochazka .20 .50
406 Antonin Stavjana .10 .25
407 Vladimir Ruzicka .20 .50
408 Petr Rosol .10 .25
409 Robert Reichel .31 .50
410 Martin Rucinsky .20 .50
411 Josef Beranek .20 .50
412 Viktor Ujcik .15 .40
413 Michal Sup .10 .25
414 Ivo Prorok .10 .25
415 Zdeno Ciger .20 .50
416 Jiri Hrdina .10 .25
417 J.Jagr/V.Ruzicka 2.00 5.00
418 Checklist .04 .10
419 Checklist .04 .10
420 Checklist .04 .10
421 Checklist .04 .10

2000-01 Czech OFS Star Emerald

This is one of three versions of this insert set, found exclusively in packs of Czech OFS. The Emerald version was found 1:2 packs. The Violet parallels were found 1:3 packs and the Pink parallels were found 1:6 packs.

COMPLETE SET (36) 10.00 25.00
EMERALD ODDS 1:2
VIOLET PARALLELS: 1X to 2X
VIOLET ODDS 1:3
PINK PARALLELS : 2X to 3X
PINK ODDS 1:6
1 Jaroslav Kames .40 1.00
2 Jiri Dopita .40 1.00
3 Jan Pardavy .20 .50
4 Vladimir Hudacek .20 .50
5 Petr Cajanek .75 2.00
6 Richard Hrazdira .40 1.00
7 Petr Briza .75 2.00
8 Jiri Zelenka .20 .50
9 Richard Zemlicka .40 1.00
10 Libor Barta .40 1.00
11 Adam Svoboda .40 1.00
12 Otakar Janecky .40 1.00
13 Vaclav Kral .20 .50
14 Rudolf Suchanek .40 1.00
15 Michal Marik .20 .50
16 Dusan Salficky .60 1.50
17 Petr Korinek .40 1.00
18 Ivan Vlcek .20 .50
19 Zdenek Orct .40 1.00
20 Robert Reichel .40 1.00
21 Petr Franek .20 .50
22 Libor Prochazka .20 .50
23 Vlastimil Lakosil .40 1.00
24 Richard Kral .20 .50
25 Viktor Ujcik .20 .50
26 Martin Prusek 1.00 2.50
27 Martin Prochazka .20 .50
28 Josef Straub .20 .50
29 Radek Gardon .20 .50
30 Lubos Horcicka .20 .50
31 Tomas Srsen .20 .50
32 Radovan Biegl .20 .50
33 Oldrich Svoboda .20 .50
34 Marek Uram .20 .50
35 Ladislav Blazek .40 1.00
36 Roman Malek .20 .50

2000 Czech Stadion

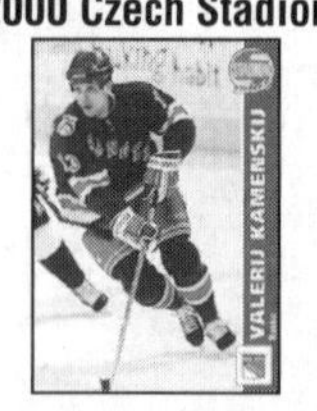

This set was issued in conjunction with Stadion, a Czech sports magazine. It was released in two series totaling 216 cards and featuring athletes of several different sports. The hockey cards from the set are listed below in checklist order.

COMPLETE SET (216) 100.00 200.00
5 Dominik Hasek 2.00 3.00
13 Roman Turek 1.20 .50
57 Jaromir Jagr 2.00 5.00
61 Mike Ricci .20 .50
64 Marty McSorley .20 .50
65 Martin Brodeur 2.00 10.00
66 Olaf Kolzig 1.20 1.50
67 Mark Messier 1.60 4.00
68 Eric Lindros 2.00 3.00
69 Robert Lang .20 .50
71 Milan Hejduk 1.60 3.00
72 Alexei Yashin .40 .50
74 Owen Nolan 1.20 1.00
75 Patrick Roy 6.00 15.00
76 Petr Svoboda .10 .25
77 Martin Straka .20 .50
79 Mario Lemieux 6.00 15.00
80 Petr Nedved .40 .50
81 Mats Sundin 1.20 3.00
82 Wayne Gretzky 8.00 25.00
83 Jaromir Jagr 2.00 5.00
84 Saku Koivu 1.20 3.00
85 Steve Yzerman 6.00 15.00
87 Mike Modano 1.60 3.00
90 Brian Leetch 1.20 2.00
91 Patrik Stefan 1.20 .50
92 Ed Belfour 1.60 4.00
93 Curtis Joseph 1.60 3.00
94 Brett Hull 1.60 4.00
95 Scott Stevens .80 1.00
96 Patrik Elias 1.20 1.00
99 Pavel Bure 2.00 3.00
109 Roman Turek .80 .50
110 Arturs Irbe 1.20 .50
111 Radek Dvorak .20 .50
112 Valeri Kamensky .20 .50
113 Jiri Slegr .20 .50
114 Alexander Mogilny .40 1.00
115 Peter Forsberg 3.20 5.00
116 Martin Havlat 4.00 10.00
117 Daniel Alfredsson .40 1.00
118 Theo Fleury 1.20 2.00
119 Sergei Brylin .10 .25
120 Patrick Roy 6.00 15.00
121 Patrick Lalime .80 1.50
122 Tomas Vokoun .40 1.50
123 Marian Hossa 1.20 3.00

124 Zigmund Palffy .80 1.00
125 Evgeni Nabokov 2.00 2.00
126 Jaroslav Modry .10 .25
145 Rob Blake 1.20 1.00
146 Jaromir Jagr 2.00 5.00
147 Mario Lemieux 6.00 15.00
148 Mario Lemieux 6.00 15.00
149 Al MacInnis .80 1.00
150 Mark Messier 1.60 4.00
151 Chris Pronger 1.20 2.00
152 Mike Richter 1.20 3.00
153 Brian Savage .20 .50
154 Maxim Afinogenov .40 1.00
155 Martin Biron 1.20 2.00
156 Martin Brodeur 2.00 10.00
157 Paul Coffey 1.20 2.00
158 Mariusz Czerkawski .20 .50
159 Wayne Gretzky 8.00 25.00
160 Michal Grosek .10 .25
161 Adam Graves .20 .50
162 J.Jagr/M.Lemieux 6.00 15.00
190 Dominik Hasek 2.00 3.00
191 Milan Hnilicka .80 1.00
192 Joe Sakic 2.00 5.00
193 Jocelyn Thibault 1.20 2.00
194 Vladimir Chebaturkin .10 .25
195 Bill Guerin 1.20 1.00
196 Krzysztof Oliwa .80 1.00
197 Bob Probert .80 2.00
198 Rick Tocchet .80 1.00

2001-02 Czech DS

COMPLETE SET (61) 15.00 30.00
1 Dominik Hasek 2.00 5.00
2 Vladimir Hudacek .20 .50
3 Roman Malek .10 .25
4 Mario Cartelli .10 .25
5 Tomas Kaberle .30 .75
6 Petr Kadlec .10 .25
7 Angel Nikolov .20 .50
8 Radek Philipp .10 .25
9 Libor Prochazka .10 .25
10 Michal Sykora .10 .25
11 Libor Zabransky .10 .25
12 Kamil Brabenec .10 .25
13 Michal Bros .10 .25
14 Jiri Burger .10 .25
15 Petr Cajanek .30 .75
16 Jaroslav Hlinka .10 .25
17 Viktor Hubl .10 .25
18 David Moravec .20 .50
19 Martin Prochazka .10 .25
20 Petr Sykora .10 .25
21 Jan Tomajko .10 .25
22 Viktor Ujcik .15 .35
23 Pavel Vostrak .10 .25
24 Jaroslav Bednar .20 .50
25 Martin Rucinsky .20 .50
26 Tomas Vokoun 1.25 3.00
27 Milan Hnilicka .20 .50
28 Josef Melichar .20 .50
29 Michal Rozsival .20 .50
30 Karel Pilar .20 .50
31 Jan Horacek .10 .25
32 Robert Schnabel .20 .50
33 Pavel Kolarik .20 .50
34 Petr Mika .20 .50
35 Petr Tenkrat .20 .50
36 Jaromir Jagr 2.00 5.00
37 Pavel Patera .20 .50
38 Josef Beranek .20 .50
39 Martin Straka .30 .75
40 Petr Nedved .30 .75
41 Martin Rucinsky .20 .50
42 Robert Reichel .20 .50
43 David Vyborny .40 1.00
44 Roman Hamrlik .30 .75
45 Milan Hejduk 1.25 3.00
46 Patrik Elias .75 2.00
47 Vaclav Prospal .20 .50
48 Vaclav Varada .20 .50
49 Petr Sykora .10 .25
50 Dusan Salficky .30 .75
51 Petr Briza .30 .75
52 Martin Prusek .40 1.00
53 Radek Martinek .20 .50
54 Karel Pilar .20 .50
55 Viktor Ujcik .15 .35
56 Vaclav Nedorost .40 1.00
57 Ales Kotalik .60 1.50
58 Jiri Dopita .20 .50
59 Robert Reichel .20 .50
60 Petr Cajanek .30 .75
61 David Moravec .20 .50

2001-02 Czech DS Best of the Best

COMPLETE SET (9) 5.00 10.00
STATED ODDS 1:3
BB1 Dominik Hasek 2.00 5.00
BB2 Tomas Kaberle .60 1.50
BB3 Michal Sykora .20 .50
BB4 Petr Cajanek .60 1.50
BB5 David Moravec .40 1.00
BB6 Martin Prochazka .20 .50
BB7 Martin Rucinsky .40 1.00
BB8 Robert Reichel .40 1.00
BB9 Jiri Dopita .40 1.00

2001-02 Czech DS Goalies

COMPLETE SET (5) 6.00 15.00
STATED ODDS 1:4
G1 Dominik Hasek 4.00 10.00
G2 Milan Hnilicka .75 2.00
G3 Petr Briza .75 2.00
G4 Roman Cechmanek .75 2.00
G5 Roman Malek .75 2.00

2001-02 Czech DS Ice Heroes

COMPLETE SET (10) 8.00 15.00
STATED ODDS 1:2
IH1 Tomas Vokoun 2.00 5.00
IH2 Jaromir Jagr 3.00 8.00
IH3 Pavel Patera .40 1.00
IH4 Josef Beranek .40 1.00
IH5 Martin Straka .75 2.00
IH6 Petr Nedved .60 1.50
IH7 Martin Rucinsky .40 1.00
IH8 Robert Reichel .40 1.00
IH9 David Vyborny .20 .50
IH10 Petr Tenkrat .60 1.50

2001-02 Czech DS Legends

COMPLETE SET (12) 3.00 6.00
STATED ODDS 1:2
L1 Jiri Holocek .40 1.00
L2 Jiri Kralik .20 .50
L3 Vlastimil Bubnik .40 1.00
L4 Vaclav Rozinak .20 .50
L5 Vladimir Zabrodsky .40 1.00
L6 Vladimir Martinec .40 1.00
L7 Ivan Hlinka .40 1.00
L8 Jan Havel .20 .50
L9 Frantisek Pospisil .20 .50
L10 Jaroslav Holik .20 .50
L11 Milan Novy .40 1.00
L12 Jiri Lala .20 .50

2001-02 Czech DS Top Gallery

COMPLETE SET (2) 8.00 15.00
STATED ODDS 1:10
1 Jaromir Jagr 4.00 10.00
2 Jaromir Jagr 4.00 10.00

2001-02 Czech National Team Postcards

COMPLETE SET (16) 20.00 40.00
1 Josef Beranek .75 2.00
2 Petr Briza .75 2.00
3 Josef Beranek .75 2.00
4 Radek Duda .75 2.00
5 Jiri Hudler 2.00 5.00
6 Jaromir Jagr 4.00 10.00
7 Richard Kral .75 2.00
8 Frantisek Kucera .75 2.00
9 David Moravec .75 2.00
10 Karel Rachunek .75 2.00
11 Martin Richter .75 2.00
12 Dusan Salficky .75 2.00
13 Michal Sykora .75 2.00
14 Viktor Ujcik .75 2.00
15 Tomas Vlasak .75 2.00
16 Vladimir Vujtek .75 2.00

2001-02 Czech OFS

This set features the top players of the Czech Elite League. The cards were sold in pack form. The set is noteworthy for including an early card of Jiri Hudler.

COMPLETE SET (284) 25.00 50.00
1 Lukas Hronek .08 .20
2 Petr Martinek .08 .20
3 Petr Kadlec .08 .20
4 Roman Malek .08 .20
5 Jan Alinc .20 .50
6 Josef Beranek .20 .50
7 Viktor Hubl .08 .20
8 Martin Rousek .08 .20
9 Radek Matejovsky .08 .20
10 Jan Kloboucek .08 .20
11 Daniel Brandl .08 .20
12 Viktor Ujcik .20 .50
13 Milan Antos .08 .20
14 Radek Belohlav .08 .20
15 Michal Bros .20 .50
16 Petr Briza .20 .50
17 Radek Hamr .08 .20
18 Jaroslav Hlinka .08 .20
19 Martin Chabada .08 .20
20 Pavel Kasparik .08 .20
21 Marek Ivan .08 .20
22 Lukas Galvas .08 .20
23 Radek Simicek .08 .20
24 Robert Tomanek .08 .20
25 Jan Tomajko .08 .20
26 Ivan Padelek .08 .20
27 Zdenek Pavelek .08 .20
28 Radek Philipp .08 .20
29 Pavel Srek .08 .20
30 David Moravec .20 .50
31 Jan Srdinko .08 .20
32 Marek Melenovsky .20 .50
33 Frantisek Ptacek .08 .20
34 Vaclav Novak .08 .20
35 Jaroslav Nedved .20 .50
36 Ludek Krayzel .08 .20
37 Roman Kadera .08 .20
38 Petr Jurecka .08 .20
39 Lukas Smolka .08 .20
40 Vitezslav Skuta .08 .20
41 Josef Straub .08 .20
42 Jiri Trvaj .08 .20
43 Jan Vytisk .08 .20
44 Daniel Zapotocny .08 .20
45 Pavel Selingr .08 .20
46 Martin Prochazka .20 .50
47 Vlastimil Lakosil .08 .20
48 Petr Gregorek .08 .20
49 Mario Cartelli .08 .20
50 Miloslav Guren .08 .20
51 Petr Jancarik .08 .20
52 Libor Prochazka .20 .50
53 Jan Slavik .08 .20
54 Pavel Janku .08 .20
55 Branislav Janos .08 .20
56 Marek Zadina .08 .20
57 Jiri Polak .08 .20
58 Ondrej Nemec .08 .20
59 Petr Kubos .08 .20
60 Slavomir Hrina .08 .20
61 Ivo Pesat .08 .20
62 Radovan Biegl .20 .50
63 Zdenek Skorepa .20 .50
64 Roman Meluzin .08 .20
65 Jan Marek .08 .20
66 Richard Kral .08 .20
67 Rostislav Vlach .08 .20
68 Ondrej Vetchy .08 .20
69 Petr Vampola .08 .20
70 Lukas Valko .08 .20
71 Michal Sararcik .08 .20
72 Martin Streit .08 .20
73 Radim Kucharczyk .08 .20
74 Jiri Hudler 8.00 20.00
75 Jiri Burger .08 .20
76 Martin Strbak .08 .20
77 Martin Ambruz .08 .20
78 Jakub Blazek .08 .20
79 Pavel Mojzis .08 .20
80 Jiri Marusak .08 .20
81 Rostislav Malena .08 .20
82 Jan Homer .08 .20
83 Martin Hamrlik .08 .20
84 Petr Tucek .08 .20
85 Vladimir Hubacek .08 .20
86 Ales Zacha .08 .20
87 Radovan Somik .08 1.00
88 Ivan Rachunek .08 .20
89 Libor Pivko .08 .20
90 Milan Ministr .08 .20
91 Petr Leska .08 .20
92 Martin Jenacek .08 .20
93 Petr Cajanek .30 .75
94 Karol Bartanus .20 .50
95 Jaroslav Balastik .08 .20
96 Petr Havelka .08 .20
97 Jan Hanzlik .08 .20
98 Petr Prikryl .08 .20
99 Libor Zabransky .20 .50
100 David Hnat .08 .20
101 David Pazourek .08 .20
102 Zbynek Marak .08 .20
103 Radek Haman .08 .20
104 Karel Soudek .08 .20
105 Pavel Kumstat .08 .20
106 Tomas Jakes .08 .20
107 Vladimir Holik .08 .20
108 Jiri Hes .08 .20
109 David Havir .08 .20
110 Oldrich Svoboda .20 .50
111 Ladislav Kudrna .20 .50
112 Valdemar Jirus .08 .20
113 Miroslav Okal .08 .20
114 Peter Bohunicky .08 .20
115 Patrik Hucko .08 .20
116 Miroslav Blatak .08 .20
117 Tomas Netik .08 .20
118 Richard Zemlicka .20 .50
119 Marek Uram .08 .20
120 Peter Pucher .08 .20
121 Lukas Krajicek ERC .75 2.00
122 Michal Klimes .08 .20
123 Josef Jindra .08 .20
124 Ladislav Cierny .08 .20
125 Michal Marik .08 .20
126 Josef Kucera .08 .20
127 Michal Kolarik .08 .20
128 Jiri Hasek .08 .20
129 David Nosek .08 .20
130 Martin Vojtek .08 .20
131 Milan Nedoma .08 .20
132 Rudolf Suchanek .08 .20
133 Filip Vanecek .08 .20
134 Pavel Zubicek .08 .20
135 Kamil Brabenec .08 .20
136 Jiri Broz .08 .20
137 Dan Hlavka .08 .20
138 Stepan Hrebejk .08 .20
139 Roman Horak .08 .20
140 Milan Michalek ERC 6.00 15.00
141 Peter Bartos .20 .50
142 Michal Vondrka .08 .20
143 Jiri Simanek .08 .20
144 Petr Sailer .08 .20
145 Lubos Rob .08 .20
146 Jan Rehor .08 .20
147 Martin Strba .08 .20
148 Marek Pinc .08 .20
149 Vladimir Gyna .08 .20
150 Jan Hranac .08 .20
151 Martin Nosek .08 .20
152 Lukas Pozivil .08 .20
153 Vojtech Kubincak .08 .20
154 Anton Lezo .08 .20
155 Martin Tupa .08 .20
156 Vlastimil Kroupa .20 .50
157 Jindrich Kotrla .08 .20
158 David Hruska .08 .20
159 Petr Jira .08 .20
160 Michal Oliverius .08 .20
161 Lukas Havel .08 .20
162 Jaroslav Buchal .08 .20
163 Jan Sulc .08 .20
164 Pavol Rieciciar .08 .20
165 Petr Klima .20 .50
166 Jiri Gombar .08 .20
167 Tomas Kaberle .20 .50
168 Ladislav Svoboda .08 .20
169 Pavel Geffert .08 .20
170 Tomas Horna .08 .20
171 Zdenek Orct .20 .50
172 Robert Kysela .08 .20
173 Radek Gardon .08 .20
174 Ondrej Kriz .20 .50
175 Tomas Klimt .20 .50
176 Jan Bohacek .20 .50
177 Michal Havel .08 .20
178 David Hajek .08 .20
179 Vaclav Skuhravy .08 .20
180 Radim Skuhrovec .08 .20
181 Tomas Plekanec .08 .20
182 Jan Dlouhy .08 .20
183 David Patera .08 .20
184 Jan Krulis .08 .20
185 Jan Pospisil .08 .20
186 David Appel .08 .20
187 Jakub Kraus .08 .20
188 Petr Machulda .08 .20
189 Petr Franek .08 .20
190 Jaromir Kverka .08 .20
191 Michal Madl .08 .20
192 Marcel Kucera .08 .20
193 Jakub Grof .08 .20
194 Michal Dobron .08 .20
195 Jan Kopecky .08 .20
196 Dmitrij Rodine .08 .20
197 David Balasz .08 .20
198 Roman Prosek .08 .20
199 Jan Kostal .08 .20
200 Petr Domin .08 .20
201 Jan Choteborsky .08 .20
202 Vaclav Benak .08 .20
203 Miroslav Simonovic .08 .20
204 Jiri Hanzlik .08 .20
205 Josef Reznicek .08 .20
206 Ivan Vlcek .08 .20
207 Libor Barta .08 .20
208 Ondrej Steiner .08 .20
209 Dusan Andrasovsky .08 .20
210 Martin Vyborny .08 .20
211 Juraj Stefanka .08 .20
212 Radek Duda .08 .20
213 Josef Slanec .08 .20
214 Michal Dvorak .08 .20
215 Libor Pavlis .08 .20
216 Vaclav Eiselt .08 .20
217 Tomas Nemcicky .08 .20
218 Petr Mudroch .08 .20
219 Patrik Moskal .08 .20
220 Zdenek Sedlak .08 .20
221 Pavel Vostrak .08 .20
222 Milan Volak .08 .20
223 Petr Mudroch .08 .20
224 Jiri Malinsky .08 .20
225 Jan Svik .08 .20
226 Petr Caslava .08 .20
227 Michal Straka .08 .20
228 Adam Svoboda .20 .50
229 Josef Straka .20 .50
230 Patrik Rimmel .08 .20
231 Petr Pavlas .08 .20
232 Michael Prochazka .20 .50
233 Miroslav Javin .08 .20
234 Robin Bacul .08 .20
235 Marek Cernosek .08 .20
236 Petr Folta .08 .20
237 Pavel Malac .08 .20
238 Radek Krestan .08 .20
239 Lubomir Korhon .08 .20
240 Pavel Cagas .20 .50
241 Radoslav Kropac .20 .50
242 Dusan Pohorelec .08 .20
243 Petr Vala .08 .20
244 Pavel Zdrahal .08 .20
245 Otakar Janecky .20 .50
246 Tomas Blazek .20 .50
247 Michael Vyhlidal .20 .50
248 Michal Sykora .20 .50
249 Tomas Pacal .08 .20
250 Andrej Novotny .08 .20
251 Tomas Rolinek .08 .20
252 Stanislav Prochazka .08 .20
253 David Pospisil .08 .20
254 Michal Mikeska .08 .20
255 Ladislav Lubina .08 .20
256 Jaroslav Kudrna .20 .50
257 Tomas Vak .08 .20
258 Michal Tvrdik .08 .20
259 Petr Sykora .20 .50
260 Jan Bokoc .08 .20
261 Milan Prochazka .08 .20
262 Patrik Fink .08 .20
263 Richard Kuckrek .08 .20
264 Marek Vorel .08 .20
265 Tomas Klimes .08 .20
266 Premysl Sedlak .08 .20
267 David Hajek .08 .20
268 Ladislav Vlcek .08 .20
269 Jiri Kames .20 .50
270 Radek Krestan .08 .20
271 Jan Hejda .08 .20
272 Borek Stagma .08 .20
273 Leos Cermak .08 .20
274 Jan Novak .08 .20
275 Zbynek Tuma .08 .20
276 Daniel Bohac .08 .20
277 Michal Sup .08 .20
278 Jan Snopek .08 .20
279 Adam Saffer .08 .20
280 David Pojkar .08 .20
281 Marek Tomica .08 .20
282 Petr Jurecka .08 .20
283 Lukas Krenzelok .08 .20
284 Michael Prochazka .20 .50

2001-02 Czech OFS All Stars

These cards were randomly inserted into packs of Czech OFS.

COMPLETE SET (41) 17.78 44.44
1 Martin Hamrlik .40 1.00
2 Petr Gregorek .40 1.00
3 Oldrich Svoboda .80 2.00
4 Radim Tesarik .40 1.00
5 Jiri Dopita 1.20 3.00
6 Petr Cajanek .80 2.00
7 Marek Uram .40 1.00
8 Michael Vyhlidal .40 1.00
9 Mario Cartelli .40 1.00
10 Pavel Zdrahal .40 1.00
11 Libor Prochazka .80 2.00
12 Ales Pisa .80 2.00
13 Robert Reichel .80 2.00
14 Josef Reznicek .40 1.00
15 Karel Pilar 1.20 3.00
16 Dusan Salficky .80 2.00
17 Patrik Martinec .40 1.00
18 Rudolf Suchanek .40 1.00
19 Jaromir Kverka .40 1.00
20 Ladislav Svoboda .40 1.00
21 Daniel Branda .40 1.00
22 Jan Pardavy .40 1.00
23 David Moravec .80 2.00
24 Zbynek Marak .40 1.00
25 Petr Leska .40 1.00
26 Jiri Marusak .40 1.00
27 Roman Stantien .40 1.00
28 Jan Srdinko .40 1.00
29 Martin Prusek 2.00 5.00
30 Libor Pivko .40 1.00
31 Zdenek Pavelek .40 1.00
32 Jaroslav Hlinka .40 1.00
33 Otakar Janecky .80 2.00
34 Petr Kadlec .80 2.00
35 Ales Kotalik 1.20 3.00
36 Jan Krulis .40 1.00
37 Robert Tomik .40 1.00
38 Petr Sykora .80 2.00
39 Ivan Vlcek .40 1.00
40 Pavel Vostrak .40 1.00
41 Vladimir Vujtek .40 1.00

2001-02 Czech OFS Gold Inserts

These cards were randomly inserted into packs of Czech OFS. We have no confirmation on insertion rate.

COMPLETE SET (11) 20.00 40.00
G1 Roman Malek 2.00 5.00
G2 Petr Franek 2.00 5.00
G3 Petr Prikryl 2.00 5.00
G4 Vlastimil Lakosil 2.00 5.00
G5 Radovan Biegl 2.00 5.00
G6 Vladimir Hudacek 2.00 5.00
G7 Oldrich Svoboda 2.00 5.00
G8 Josef Kucera 2.00 5.00
G9 Michal Marik 2.00 5.00
G10 Miroslav Simonovic 2.00 5.00
G11 Pavel Malac 2.00 5.00

2001-02 Czech OFS H Inserts

These cards were randomly inserted into packs of Czech OFS. We have no confirmation on insertion rate.

COMPLETE SET (15) 25.00 50.00
H1 Lukas Hronek 1.50 4.00
H2 Marcel Kucera 1.50 4.00
H3 Zdenek Orct 2.00 5.00
H4 Martin Vojtek 1.50 4.00
H5 Jan Pospisil 1.50 4.00
H6 Lukas Smolka 1.50 4.00
H7 Jiri Trvaj 1.50 4.00
H8 Ivo Pesat 1.50 4.00
H9 Petr Tucek 1.50 4.00
H10 Ladislav Kudrna 1.50 4.00
H11 Marek Pinc 1.50 4.00
H12 Pavel Cagas 1.50 4.00
H13 Adam Svoboda 2.00 5.00
H14 Libor Barta 1.50 4.00
H15 Petr Briza 2.50 6.00

2001-02 Czech OFS Red Inserts

These cards were randomly inserted into packs of Czech OFS. We have no confirmation on insertion rate.

COMPLETE SET (24) 50.00
RE1D Viktor Ujcik .75 2.00
RE2D Josef Beranek .75 2.00
RE3D Tomas Plekanec .75 2.00
RE4D Tomas Kaberle 1.25 3.00
RE5D Jiri Zelenka .75 2.00
RE6D Martin Prochazka .75 2.00
RE7D David Moravec .75 2.00
RE8D Petr Klima .75 2.00
RE9D Rudolf Suchanek .75 2.00
RE10D Frantisek Kucera .75 2.00
RE11D Michal Sykora .75 2.00
RE12D Otakar Janecky .75 2.00
RE13D Pavel Zdrahal .75 2.00
RE14D Radoslav Kropac .75 2.00
RE15D Rostislav Vlach .75 2.00
RE16D Marek Uram .75 2.00
RE17D Petr Leska .75 2.00
RE18D Petr Cajanek 1.25 3.00
RE19D Ondrej Kratena 1.25 3.00
RE20D Petr Korinek .75 2.00
RE21D Jiri Hudler 6.00 15.00
RE22D Pavel Janku 2.00
RE23D Richard Kral 2.00
RE24D Miloslav Guren 2.00

2001 Czech Stadion

This set was issued in conjunction with the Czech sports magazine Stadion. It is a multi-sport issue. We have only included hockey players, so it is listed below in skip-numbered form.

COMPLETE SET (45) 30.00 60.00
217 Ray Bourque 2.00 5.00
218 Patrik Elias .75 2.00
219 Milan Hejduk .75 2.00
220 Bobby Holik .40 1.00
221 Tomas Kaberle .40 1.00
222 Nick Lidstrom 1.25 3.00
223 Petr Sykora .40 1.00
224 Martin Skoula .40 1.00
225 Alex Tanguay .75 2.00
226 Daniel Alfredsson .75 2.00
227 Jason Allison .40 1.00
228 Adam Deadmarsh .40 1.00
229 Chris Drury .75 2.00
230 Bob Essensa .40 1.00
231 Scott Gomez .40 1.00
233 Tomas Holmstrom .75 2.00
234 Darius Kasparaitis .40 1.00
235 Pavel Brendl .40 1.00
236 Eric Lindros 1.25 3.00
237 Rostislav Klesla .40 1.00
238 Scott Niedermayer .40 1.00
239 Brett Hull 1.25 3.00
240 Paul Kariya 1.25 3.00
241 Chris Gratton .40 1.00
242 Doug Gilmour .75 2.00
243 Alexei Yashin .40 1.00
244 Saku Koivu .75 2.00
245 Randy McKay .40 1.00
246 Markus Naslund .75 2.00
247 Keith Primeau .40 1.00
248 Dainius Zubrus .40 1.00
249 Dominik Hasek 1.50 4.00
250 Frantisek Kaberle .40 1.00
251 Jaromir Jagr 2.00 5.00
252 Jaromir Jagr (Tennis) 2.00 5.00
253 Rob Blake .40 1.00
254 Adam Oates .40 1.00
255 Joe Sakic 2.00 5.00
256 Alexei Kovalev .40 1.00
257 Ivan Hlinka .40 1.00
258 Martin Straka .40 1.00
259 Milan Hnilicka .40 1.00
260 Miroslav Satan .40 1.00
261 Peter Bondra .40 1.00
324 John Leclair .40 1.00

2002-03 Czech DS

This set features the top Czech players in the world. The first 40 cards in the set are base cards. 41-54 are Young Heroes (1:2); 55-75 are Jagr Team base cards; 76-82 are Goalies (1:3); 83-89 are Best Shooters (1:3); 90-96 are Power Stars (1:3) and 97-100 are Stanley Cup Champs (1:7).

COMPLETE SET (100) 30.00 60.00
41-54 ODDS 1:2
55-96 ODDS 1:3
97-100 ODDS 1:7
1 Milan Hnilicka .40 1.00
2 Dusan Salficky .30 .75
3 Petr Briza .30 .75
4 Adam Svoboda .30 .75
5 Frantisek Kucera .10 .25
6 Petr Kadlec .10 .25
7 Karel Rachunek .30 .75
8 Richard Kral .10 .25
9 Josef Beranek .20 .50
10 Radek Duda .10 .25
11 Petr Mudroch .10 .25
12 Milan Michalek 2.00 5.00
13 Tomas Kucharcik .10 .25
14 Frantisek Kaberle .10 .25
15 Rostislav Klesla .75 2.00
16 Filip Kuba .20 .50
17 Pavel Kubina .30 .75
18 Jaroslav Spacek .20 .50
19 Michal Sykora .10 .25
20 Martin Richter .10 .25
21 Michal Bros .10 .25
22 Petr Cajanek .30 .75
23 Jaroslav Hlinka .10 .25
24 Jan Hrdina .40 1.00
25 Jaromir Jagr 2.00 5.00
26 David Moravec .20 .50
27 Pavel Patera .20 .50
28 Martin Prochazka .10 .25
29 Zdenek Sedlak .10 .25
30 Viktor Ujcik .20 .50
31 Tomas Vlasak .10 .25
32 Ondrej Kratena .10 .25
33 David Vyborny .10 .25
34 Vladimir Vujtek .20 .50
35 Petr Leska .10 .25
36 Marek Zidlicky .30 .75
37 Jaroslav Balastik .10 .25
38 Libor Pivko .10 .25
39 David Hruska .10 .25
40 Jiri Marusak .10 .25
41 Milan Hnilicka 2.00 5.00
42 Tomas Vokoun .20 .50
43 Jaroslav Spacek .10 .25
44 Jaroslav Bednar .10 .25
45 Martin Rucinsky .10 .25
46 Jaromir Jagr .20 .50
47 Karel Pilar 2.00 5.00
48 David Vyborny .10 .25
49 Frantisek Kaberle .20 .50
50 Tomas Kaberle .10 .25
51 Vaclav Prospal .40 1.00
52 Jan Hrdina .10 .25
53 Robert Reichel .20 .50
54 Josef Melichar .10 .25
55 Jan Hlavac .40 1.00
56 Jiri Fischer .75 2.00
57 Milan Hejduk .20 .50
58 Jiri Dopita .40 1.00
59 Vaclav Varada .20 .50
60 Patrik Stefan 2.00 5.00
61 Milan Kraft .20 .50
62 Jiri Hudler .10 .25
63 Libor Ustrnul .10 .25
64 Lukas Hronek .30 .75
65 Miroslav Blatak .20 .50
66 Jan Hanzlik .40 1.00
67 Jiri Novotny .20 .50
68 Ales Hemsky .20 .50
69 Tomas Plekanec .20 .50
70 Filip Novak .75 2.00
71 Miloslav Horava 1.50 4.00
72 Lukas Krajicek .20 .50
73 Tomas Mojzis .20 .50
74 Jiri Jakes .40 1.00
75 Jan Bohac .40 1.00
76 Milan Hnilicka .40 1.00
77 Dusan Salficky .30 .75
78 Roman Malek .10 .25
79 Tomas Vokoun .75 2.00
80 Lukas Hronek .10 .25
81 Petr Briza .20 .50
82 Adam Svoboda .30 .75
83 Viktor Ujcik .20 .50
84 Martin Prochazka .10 .25
85 Petr Cajanek .30 .75
86 Pavel Patera .20 .50
87 Radek Duda .10 .25
88 Tomas Vlasak .10 .25
89 Jaromir Jagr 2.00 5.00
90 Jaromir Jagr 2.00 5.00
91 Robert Reichel .20 .50
92 Frantisek Kaberle .10 .25
93 Jaroslav Spacek .20 .50
94 Jan Hlavac .20 .50
95 Martin Rucinsky .20 .50
96 Tomas Kaberle .30 .75
97 Dominik Hasek 1.25 3.00
98 Dominik Hasek 1.25 3.00
99 Dominik Hasek 1.25 3.00
100 Checklist .10 .25

2002-03 Czech OFS Plus

COMPLETE SET (369) 75.00 125.00
1 Daniel Branda .20 .50
2 Michal Bros .20 .50
3 Petr Briza .30 .75
4 Jan Hanzlik .20 .50
5 Petr Havelka .20 .50
6 Valdemar Jirus .20 .50
7 Pavel Kasparik .20 .50
8 Ondrej Kratena .20 .50
9 Petr Leska .20 .50
10 Patrik Martinec .20 .50
11 Jaroslav Nedved .20 .50
12 Petr Prikryl .20 .50
13 Frantisek Ptacek .20 .50
14 Martin Richter .20 .50
15 Jan Srdinko .20 .50
16 Martin Spanhel .20 .50
17 Pavel Srek .20 .50
18 Jan Tomajko .20 .50
19 Robert Tomik .20 .50
20 Roman Vondracek .20 .50
21 Jiri Zelenka .20 .50
22 Richard Zemlicka .20 .50
23 Jaroslav Balastik .60 1.50
24 Miroslav Blatak .20 .50
25 Martin Cech .20 .50
26 Lukas Galvas .20 .50
27 Martin Hamrlik .20 .50
28 Jan Homer .20 .50
29 Slavomir Hrina .20 .50
30 Petr Hubacek .20 .50
31 Patrik Hucko .20 .50
32 Martin Jenacek .20 .50
33 Jiri Marusak .20 .50
34 Milan Ministr .20 .50
35 Petr Mokrejs .20 .50
36 Miroslav Okal .20 .50
37 Ivo Pesat .20 .50
38 Libor Pivko .20 .50
39 Ivan Rachunek .20 .50
40 Petr Tucek .20 .50
41 Ondrej Vesely .20 .50
42 Rostislav Vlach .20 .50
43 Ladislav Vlcek .20 .50
44 Martin Zahorovsky .20 .50
45 Pavel Zubicek .20 .50
46 Jiri Burger .20 .50
47 Marek Cernosek .20 .50
48 Martin Falter .20 .50
49 Stanislav Gron .40 1.00
50 Jakub Hulva .20 .50
51 Lukas Chmelir .20 .50
52 Zbynek Irgl .30 .75
53 Petr Jurecka .20 .50
54 Roman Kadera .20 .50

55 Ludek Krayzel .20 .50
56 Leszek Laszkiewicz .20 .50
57 Marek Melenovsky .20 .50
58 David Moravec .20 .50
59 Ales Padelek .20 .50
60 Ivan Padelek .20 .50
61 Radek Philipp .20 .50
62 Martin Ambruz .20 .50
63 Peter Bartek .20 .50
64 Radovan Biegl .30 .75
65 Tomas Demel .20 .50
66 Marek Dubec .20 .50
67 Jiri Hudler 10.00 25.00
68 Alexej Jaskin .20 .50
69 Petr Kubos .20 .50
70 Radim Kucharczyk .20 .50
71 Patrik Luza .20 .50
72 Ondrej Nemec .20 .50
73 Lukas Plsek .20 .50
74 Jiri Polak .20 .50
75 Bohuslav Ptacek .20 .50
76 Jan Sochor .20 .50
77 Roman Stantien .20 .50
78 Martin Streit .20 .50
79 Tomas Vak .20 .50
80 Lukas Valko .20 .50
81 Petr Vampola .20 .50
82 Jiri Hasek .20 .50
83 Lubos Horcicka .20 .50
84 Tomas Houdek .20 .50
85 Jiri Hunkes .20 .50
86 Marek Ivan .20 .50
87 Petr Jancarik .20 .50
88 Pavel Janku .20 .50
89 Richard Kral .20 .50
90 Vlastimil Lakosil .20 .50
91 Jiri Malinsky .20 .50
92 Jan Marek .20 .50
93 Rostislav Martynek .20 .50
94 Roman Meluzin .20 .50
95 Marian Morava .20 .50
96 David Nosek .20 .50
97 Zdenek Pavelek .20 .50
98 Gregor Poloncic .20 .50
99 Libor Prochazka .20 .50
100 Marek Zadina .20 .50
101 Tomas Zboril .20 .50
102 Boris Zabka .20 .50
103 Martin Altrichter .20 .50
104 Miroslav Barus .20 .50
105 Vaclav Benak .20 .50
106 Roman Erat .20 .50
107 Radek Haman .20 .50
108 David Havir .20 .50
109 Ales Kretinsky .20 .50
110 Pavel Kumstat .20 .50
111 Petr Kumstat .20 .50
112 David Ludvik .20 .50
113 Jan Mikulik .20 .50
114 Karel Plasek .20 .50
115 Jan Plch .20 .50
116 Milan Prochazka .20 .50
117 Peter Pucher .20 .50
118 Jaroslav Sklenar .20 .50
119 Jan Snopek .20 .50
120 Karel Soudek .20 .50
121 Oldrich Svoboda .20 .50
122 Milan Toman .20 .50
123 Marek Uram .20 .50
124 Marek Vorel .20 .50
125 Lukas Bednarik .20 .50
126 Daniel Bohac .20 .50
127 Jakub Cech .20 .50
128 Michal Cech .20 .50
129 Vratislav Cech .20 .50
130 Ales Cerny .20 .50
131 Juraj Durco .20 .50
132 Martin Filip .20 .50
133 Petr Folta .20 .50
134 Tomas Harant .20 .50
135 Martin Holy .20 .50
136 Jan Kopecky .20 .50
137 Jiri Kucera .20 .50
138 Michal Marik .20 .50
139 Petr Pavlas .20 .50
140 Albin Podstavek .20 .50
141 Radek Prochazka .20 .50
142 Rene Pucher .20 .50
143 Tomas Srsen .20 .50
144 Ales Stanek .20 .50
145 Vaclav Studeny .20 .50
146 Filip Stefanka .20 .50
147 Milan Beranek .20 .50
148 Martin Cakajik .20 .50
149 Pavel Falta .20 .50
150 Miroslav Hajek .20 .50
151 Jan Holub .20 .50
152 Vitezslav Jankovych .20 .50
153 Pavel Kabrt .20 .50
154 Vaclav Koci .20 .50
155 Radoslav Kropac .20 .50
156 Angel Krstev .20 .50
157 Vojtech Kubincak .20 .50
158 Jiri Kudrna .20 .50
159 Pavel Malecek .20 .50
160 Jiri Moravec .20 .50
161 Mojmir Musil .20 .50
162 Vaclav Novak .20 .50
163 Jan Plodek .20 .50
164 Robert Pospisil .20 .50
165 Stanislav Prochazka .20 .50
166 Patrik Rozsival .20 .50
167 Michal Straka .20 .50
168 Daniel Babka .20 .50
169 Michal Barinka .20 .50
170 Peter Bartos .20 .50
171 Jiri Broz .20 .50
172 Petr Gregorek .20 .50
173 Stepan Hrebejk .20 .50
174 Vladimir Hudacek .20 .50
175 Josef Jindra .20 .50
176 Ivo Kotaska .20 .50
177 Josef Kucera .20 .50
178 Milan Michalek 4.00 10.00
179 Frantisek Mrazek .20 .50
180 Jan Mucha .20 .50
181 Milan Nedoma .20 .50
182 Zdenek Ondrej .20 .50
183 Lubos Rob .20 .50
184 Petr Sailer .20 .50
185 Rudolf Suchanek .20 .50
186 Jiri Simanek .20 .50
187 Martin Strba .20 .50
188 Filip Turek .20 .50
189 Michal Vondrka .20 .50
190 Jan Alinc .20 .50
191 Jiri Gombar .20 .50
192 Vladimir Gyna .20 .50
193 Lukas Havel .20 .50
194 Jan Hranac .20 .50
195 Petr Klima .20 .50
196 Jan Kloboucek .20 .50
197 Jindrich Kotrla .20 .50
198 Vlastimil Kroupa .20 .50
199 Jiri Kuntos .20 .50
200 Petr Macholda .20 .50
201 Tomas Martinec .20 .50
202 Marek Pinc .20 .50
203 Michal Podolka .20 .50
204 Lukas Pozivil .20 .50
205 Ivo Prorok .20 .50
206 Lukas Riha .20 .50
207 Stanislav Stavensky .20 .50
208 Jiri Slegr .20 .50
209 Jan Sulc .20 .50
210 Martin Tupa .20 .50
211 Martin Barek .20 .50
212 Jakub Barton .20 .50
213 Tomas Blazek .20 .50
214 Tomas Divisek .40 1.00
215 Miroslav Duben .20 .50
216 Otakar Janecky .20 .50
217 Jan Kolar .20 .50
218 Petr Koukal .20 .50
219 Ladislav Lubina .20 .50
220 Michal Mikeska .20 .50
221 Petr Mocek .20 .50
222 Petr Mudroch .20 .50
223 Andrej Novotny .20 .50
224 Lubomir Pistek .20 .50
225 David Pospisil .20 .50
226 Petr Prucha ERC 6.00 15.00
227 Tomas Rolinek .20 .50
228 Petr Caslava .20 .50
229 Adam Svoboda .30 .75
230 Michal Sykora .20 .50
231 Petr Sykora .20 .50
232 Michael Vyhlidal .20 .50
233 Milan Antos .20 .50
234 Josef Beranek .20 .50
235 Dominik Granak .20 .50
236 Jan Hejda .40 1.00
237 Lukas Hronek .20 .50
238 David Hruska .20 .50
239 Petr Jaros .20 .50
240 Petr Kadlec .20 .50
241 Jakub Klepis ERC 1.25 3.00
242 Pavel Kolarik .20 .50
243 Frantisek Kucera .20 .50
244 Roman Malek .20 .50
245 Petr Mika .30 .75
246 Jan Novak .20 .50
247 Marek Posmyk .20 .50
248 Ondrej Steiner .20 .50
249 Michal Sup .20 .50
250 Adam Saffer .20 .50
251 Josef Straub .20 .50
252 Marek Tomica .20 .50
253 Viktor Ujcik .20 .50
254 Dusan Andrasovsky .20 .50
255 Libor Barta .20 .50
256 Michal Dobron .20 .50
257 Radek Duda .20 .50
258 Michal Dvorak .20 .50
259 Robert Hamrla .20 .50
260 Jiri Hanzlik .20 .50
261 Petr Chvojka .20 .50
262 Vaclav Kral .20 .50
263 Ales Kratoska .20 .50
264 Radek Matejovsky .20 .50
265 Josef Reznicek .20 .50
266 Josef Straka .20 .50
267 Jaroslav Spelda .20 .50
268 Juraj Stefanka .20 .50
269 Jan Svik .20 .50
270 Ivan Vlcek .20 .50
271 Milan Voboril .20 .50
272 Milan Volak .20 .50
273 Josef Voskar .20 .50
274 Martin Vyborny .20 .50
275 Robin Bacul .20 .50
276 David Balasz .20 .50
277 Richard Bauer .20 .50
278 Petr Franek .20 .50
279 Jakub Grof .20 .50
280 Martin Hlavacka .20 .50
281 Jan Kostal .20 .50
282 Lukas Krajicek .60 1.50
283 Jakub Kraus .20 .50
284 Marcel Kucera .20 .50
285 Jaromir Kverka .20 .50
286 Michal Madl .20 .50
287 Tomas Nemcicky .20 .50
288 Martin Opatovsky .20 .50
289 Libor Pavlis .20 .50
290 Petr Puncochar .20 .50
291 Dmitri Rodine .20 .50
292 Vaclav Skuhravy .20 .50
293 Ladislav Svoboda .20 .50
294 Petr Sinagl .20 .50
295 Marek Topoli .20 .50
296 Kamil Tvrdek .20 .50
297 Pavel Selinger .20 .50
298 Radim Tesarik .20 .50
299 Jiri Trvaj .20 .50
300 Jan Vytisk .20 .50
301 Danniel Zapotocny .20 .50
302 Michal Divisek .20 .50
303 Jiri Dobrovolny .20 .50
304 Michal Kello .20 .50
305 Radek Krestan .20 .50
306 Tomas Micka .20 .50
307 Petr Mika .20 .50
308 Jan Dresler .20 .50
309 Rostislav Olesz ERC 4.00 10.00
310 Lukas Zatopek .20 .50
311 Vaclav Pletka .30 .75
312 Lukas Krenzelok .20 .50
313 Lukas Smolka .20 .50
314 Jaroslav Sklenar .20 .50
315 Richard Bordowski .20 .50
316 Mario Cartelli .20 .50
317 Tomas Horna .20 .50
318 Petr Hrbek .20 .50
319 Martin Kotasek .20 .50
320 Jan Korotvicka .20 .50
321 Michal Tvrdik .20 .50
322 David Pojkar .20 .50
323 Martin Adamsky .20 .50
324 Jaroslav Kracik .20 .50
325 Miloslav Topol .20 .50
326 Vojtech Polak .20 .50
327 Lukas Pech .20 .50
328 Jaroslav Hasek .20 .50
329 Jan Kudrna .20 .50
330 Jan Visek .20 .50
331 Patrik Moskal .20 .50
332 Zdenek Smid .20 .50
333 Michal Travnicek .20 .50
334 Martin Nosek .20 .50
335 Zdenek Skorepa .20 .50
336 Jan Horacek .20 .50
337 David Appel .20 .50
338 Petr Svoboda .20 .50
339 Jan Nemecek .20 .50
340 Jan Kotatko .20 .50
341 Ales Vala .20 .50
342 Radek Mrazek .20 .50
343 Viktor Hubl .20 .50
344 Jaroslav Kudrna .20 .50
345 Tomas Pacal .20 .50
346 David Mazanec .20 .50
347 Radek Prochazka .20 .50
348 Ales Kratoska .20 .50
349 Michal Marik .20 .50
350 Ladislav Vlcek .20 .50
351 Jiri Hanzlik .20 .50
352 Jaroslav Hubl .20 .50
353 Martin Tuma .20 .50
354 Petr Martinek .20 .50
355 Michal Divisek .20 .50
356 Lubomir Hurtaj .20 .50
357 Jakub Koreis ERC .75 2.00
358 Ondrej Kubes .20 .50
359 Viktor Ujcik .20 .50
360 Radek Dlouhy .20 .50
361 Radek Duda .20 .50
362 Milan Kopecky .20 .50
363 Patrik Stejskal .20 .50
364 Vaclav Pletka .30 .75
365 Radek Masny .20 .50
366 Zbynek Spitzer .20 .50
367 Tomas Frolo .20 .50
368 Martin Filip .20 .50
369 Ivan Rachunek .20 .50
370 Tomas Klimes .20 .50

2002-03 Czech OFS Plus All-Star Game

COMPLETE SET (43) 30.00 75.00
H1 Jaroslav Balastik 2.00 5.00
H2 Jiri Burger .75 2.00
H3 Petr Cajanek 1.25 3.00
H4 Petr Gregorek .75 2.00
H5 Miloslav Guren .75 2.00
H6 Martin Hamrlik .75 2.00
H7 Vladimir Hudacek .75 2.00
H8 Jiri Hudler 4.00 10.00
H9 Tomas Jakes .75 2.00
H10 Miroslav Javin .75 2.00
H11 Lubomir Korhon .75 2.00
H12 Richard Kral .75 2.00
H13 Petr Leska .75 2.00
H14 Jiri Marusak .75 2.00
H15 Marek Melenovsky .75 2.00
H16 David Moravec .75 2.00
H17 David Nosek .75 2.00
H18 Karel Soudek .75 2.00
H19 Jiri Trvaj .75 2.00
H20 Marek Uram .75 2.00
H21 Petr Vala .75 2.00
H22 Ondrej Vesely .75 2.00
H23 Peter Bartos .75 2.00
H24 Petr Briza 1.25 3.00
H25 Vladimir Gyna .75 2.00
H26 Martin Hlavacka .75 2.00
H27 Jaroslav Hlinka .75 2.00
H28 Otakar Janecky .75 2.00
H29 Petr Kadlec .75 2.00
H30 Ladislav Lubina .75 2.00
H31 Jaroslav Nedved .75 2.00
H32 Tomas Nemcicky .75 2.00
H33 Josef Reznicek .75 2.00
H34 Vaclav Skuhravy .75 2.00
H35 Jan Srdinko .75 2.00
H36 Josef Straka .75 2.00
H37 Adam Svoboda 1.25 3.00
H38 Ladislav Svoboda .75 2.00
H39 Michal Sykora .75 2.00
H40 Viktor Ujcik .75 2.00
H41 Unknown .75 2.00
H42 Jiri Zelenka .75 2.00
H43 Daniel Branda .75 2.00

2002-03 Czech OFS Plus Checklists

COMPLETE SET (12) 5.00 10.00
C1 Jakub Cech .40 1.00
C2 Marek Pinc .40 1.00
C3 Pavel Falta .40 1.00
C4 Petr Prikril .40 1.00
C5 Lukas Hronek .40 1.00
C6 Robert Hamrla .40 1.00
C7 Adam Svoboda .75 2.00
C8 Petr Franek .40 1.00
C9 Petr Tucek .40 1.00
C10 Lubos Horcicka .40 1.00
C11 Jiri Trvaj .40 1.00
C12 Radovan Biegl .75 2.00

2002-03 Czech OFS Plus Masks

COMPLETE SET (?)
M1 Unknown
M2 Ivo Pesat 4.00 10.00
M3 Petr Tucek 4.00 10.00
M4 Jiri Trvaj 4.00 10.00
M5 Lukas Plsek 4.00 10.00
M6 Radovan Biegl 4.00 10.00
M7 Marek Pinc 4.00 10.00
M8 Petr Prikril 4.00 10.00
M9 Lukas Hronek 4.00 10.00
M10 Roman Malek 4.00 10.00
M11 Pavel Falta 4.00 10.00
M12 Unknown
M13 Unknown
M14 Vladimir Hudacek 4.00 10.00
M15 Unknown
M16 Adam Svoboda 6.00 15.00
M17 Robert Hamrla 4.00 10.00
M18 Marcel Kucera 4.00 10.00
M19 Unknown
M20 Unknown
M21 Unknown
M22 Unknown
M23 Unknown
M24 Jakub Cech 4.00 10.00

2002-03 Czech OFS Plus Trios

We have no pricing information on this series.

COMPLETE SET (25)
STATED ODDS 1:8
T1 Vladimir Hudacek
Rudolf Suchanek
Peter Bartos
T2 Michal Marik
Filip Stefanka
Michal Cech
T3 Jakub Cech
Tomas Harant
Daniel Bohac
T4 Petr Franek
Dmitri Rodine
TomasNemcicky
T5 Pavel Falta
Angel Krstev
Vitezslav Jankovych
T6 Marek Pinc
Jiri Slegr
Martin Rucinsky
T7 Michal Podolka
{ Petr Martinek
Petr Klima
T8 Adam Svoboda
Michal Sykora
Petr Sykora
T9 Tomas Maly
Michael Vyhlidal
Ladislav Lubina
T10 Libor Barta
Josef Reznicek
Radek Duda
T11 Robert Hamrla
Ivan Vlcek
Josef Straka
T12 Roman Malek
Frantisek Kucera
Josef Beranek
T13 Lukas Hronek
Petr Kadlec
Viktor Ujcik
T14 Petr Briza
Jaroslav Nedved
Richard Zemlicka
T15 Petr Prikril
Jan Srdinko
Petr Leska
T16 Vlastimil Lakosil
Libor Prochazka
Richard Kral
T17 Lubos Horcicka
David Nosek
Vaclav Pletka
T18 Jiri Trvaj
Radim Tesarik
David Moravec
T19 Martin Falter
Marek Cernosek
Roman Kadera
T20 Radovan Biegl
Alexej Jaskin
Jiri Hudler
T21 Radek Masny
Petr Kubos
Radim Kucharczyk
T22 Ivo Pesat
Martin Hamrlik
Miroslav Okal
T23 Petr Tucek
Jirin Marusak
Ladislav Vlach
T24 Petr Svoboda
Jan Snopek
Peter Pucher
T25 Martin Altrichter
Karel Soudek
Marek Uram

2002-03 Czech OFS Plus Znaky Klubu

COMPLETE SET (14) 5.00 10.00
Z1 Ceske Budejovice .40 1.00
Z2 Havirov Panthers .40 1.00
Z3 Energie Karlovy Vary .40 1.00
Z4 Bili Tygri Liberec .40 1.00
Z5 Chemopetrol Litvinov .40 1.00
Z6 IPB Pojistovna Pardubice .40 1.00
Z7 Keramika Plzen .40 1.00
Z8 Slavia Praha .40 1.00
Z9 Sparta Praha .40 1.00
Z10 Ocelari Trinec .40 1.00
Z11 Vitkovice .40 1.00
Z12 Vsetin .40 1.00
Z13 Hame Zlin .40 1.00
Z14 ME Znojemsti Orli .40 1.00

2002-03 Czech OFS Plus Duos

COMPLETE SET (25) 40.00 80.00
STATED ODDS 1:8
D1 Radovan Biegl 6.00 15.00
Jiri Hudler
D2 Petr Briza 2.00 5.00
Jiri Zelenka
D3 Martin Richter 2.00 5.00
Jan Tomajko
D4 Josef Beranek 2.00 5.00
Roman Malek
D5 Frantisek Kucera 2.00 5.00
Viktor Ujcik
D6 Jiri Trvaj 2.00 5.00
David Moravec
D7 Jiri Burger 2.00 5.00
Roman Kadera
D8 Libor Prochazka 2.00 5.00
Richard Kral
D9 Vaclav Pletka 2.00 5.00
Vlastimil Lakocil
D10 Adam Svoboda 2.00 5.00
Michal Vyhlidal
D11 Michal Sykora 2.00 5.00
Ladislav Lubina
D12 Oldrich Svoboda 3.00 8.00
Marek Uram
D13 Peter Pucher 2.00 5.00
Martin Altrichter
D14 Martin Vyborny 2.00 5.00
Libor Barta
D15 Radek Duda 2.00 5.00
Robert Hamrla
D16 Martin Hamrlik 2.00 5.00
Jiri Marusak
D17 Rostislav Vlach 2.00 5.00
Petr Tucek
D18 Petr Ranek 2.00 5.00
Robin Bacul
D19 Vladimir Hudacek 2.00 5.00
Milan Nedoma
D20 Vlastimil Kroupa 2.00 5.00
Marek Pinc
D21 Martin Rucinsky 2.00 5.00
Jiri Slegr
D22 Radoslav Kropac 2.00 5.00
Pavel Falta
D23 Angel Krstev 2.00 5.00
Vitezslav Jankovych
D24 Tomas Srsen 2.00 5.00
Jakub Cech
D25 Jan Kopecky 2.00 5.00
Michal Marik

2002 Czech IQ Sports Blue

We have no pricing information on these cards, but present the complete checklist for you below.

COMPLETE SET (29)
1 Dominik Hasek
2 Josef Beranek
3 Jan Caloun
4 Roman Cechmanek
5 Jiri Dopita
6 Roman Hamrlik
7 Dominik Hasek
8 Dominik Hasek
9 Dominik Hasek
10 Milan Hejduk
11 Roman Simicek
12 Jaromir Jagr
13 Frantisek Kaberle
14 Frantisek Kucera
15 Frantisek Kucera
16 Robert Lang
17 David Moravec
18 Pavel Patera
19 Libor Prochazka
20 Martin Prochazka
21 Robert Reichel
22 Martin Rucinsky
23 Vladimir Ruzicka
24 Vladimir Ruzicka
25 Jiri Slegr
26 Richard Smehlik
27 Jaroslav Spacek
28 Martin Straka
29 Petr Svoboda

2002 Czech IQ Sports Yellow

We have no pricing information for these cards, but present the complete checklist for you below.

COMPLETE SET (29)
1 Jaromir Jagr
2 Josef Beranek
3 Jan Caloun
4 Roman Cechmanek
5 Jiri Dopita
6 Roman Hamrlik
7 Roman Hamrlik
8 Milan Hnilicka
9 Dominik Hasek
10 Dominik Hasek
11 Dominik Hasek
12 Milan Hejduk
13 Jaromir Jagr
14 Jaromir Jagr
15 Petr Sykora
16 Frantisek Kucera
17 Robert Lang
18 David Moravec
19 Pavel Patera
20 Martin Prochazka
21 Libor Prochazka
22 Robert Reichel
23 Martin Rucinsky
24 Vladimir Ruzicka
25 Jiri Slegr
26 Jiri Slegr
27 Richard Smehlik
28 Jaroslav Spacek
29 Petr Svoboda

2002 Czech National Team Postcards

COMPLETE SET (15) 10.00 20.00
1 Jaroslav Balastik .75 2.00
2 Jaroslav Bednar .75 2.00
3 Petr Briza .75 2.00
4 Jan Hlavac .75 2.00
5 Jindrich Kotrla .40 1.00
6 Tomas Kucharcik .40 1.00
7 Jan Marek .40 1.00
8 Zbynek Michalek 1.25 3.00
9 Jaroslav Modry .40 1.00
10 Vaclav Pletka .40 1.00
11 Jaroslav Spacek .40 1.00
12 Petr Tenkrat .40 1.00
13 Radim Tesarik .40 1.00
14 Marek Vorel .40 1.00
15 David Vyborny .75 2.00

2002 Czech Stadion Cup Finals

This set features stars from the World Cup and Stanley Cup. Only hockey players are listed below.

COMPLETE SET (9)
484 Scotty Bowman .75 2.00
485 Jiri Fischer .75 2.00
486 Ron Francis .75 2.00
487 Dominik Hasek 2.00 5.00
488 Arturs Irbe .75 2.00
489 Marek Malik .40 1.00
490 Jaroslav Svoboda .40 1.00
491 Jiri Slegr .40 1.00
492 Josef Vasicek .40 1.00

2002 Czech Stadion Olympics

This set was issued in conjunction with the Czech sports magazine Stadion. It features athletes who represented the Czech Republic at the 2002 Winter Olympics. We only include hockey players, so the set is listed in skip-number form below.

325 Petr Cajanek .75 2.00
326 Roman Cechmanek .40 1.00
327 Jiri Dopita .40 1.00
328 Radek Dvorak .40 1.00
329 Patrik Elias 1.25 3.00
330 Roman Hamrlik .40 1.00
331 Milan Hejduk 1.25 3.00
332 Martin Havlat 2.00 5.00
333 Dominik Hasek 2.00 5.00
334 Jan Hrdina .40 1.00
335 Jaromir Jagr 2.00 5.00
336 Tomas Kaberle .75 2.00
337 Pavel Patera .40 1.00
338 Robert Lang .40 1.00
339 Pavel Kubina .40 1.00
340 Petr Sykora .40 1.00
341 Martin Rucinsky .40 1.00
342 Robert Reichel .40 1.00
347 Roman Turek .40 1.00
348 Jaroslav Spacek .40 1.00
349 Richard Smehlik .40 1.00
350 Martin Skoula .40 1.00
351 Michal Sykora .40 1.00

2003-04 Czech National Team

This partial checklist represents what appears to be a set produced by World Sport of the 2003-04 Czech National Team. If anyone has additional information, please forward it to hockeymag@beckett.com

COMPLETE SET (?)
1 Dusan Salficky .40 1.00
2 Jan Hejda .20 .50
3 Martin Cech .20 .50
4 Pavel Patera .20 .50

2003-04 Czech OFS Plus

COMPLETE SET (398) 40.00 80.00
1 Jiri Burger .20 .50
2 Marek Cernosek .20 .50
3 Jan Dresler .20 .50
4 Martin Falter .20 .50
5 Petr Hubacek .20 .50
6 Jakub Hulva .20 .50
7 Lukas Chmelir .20 .50
8 Zbynek Irgl .20 .50
9 Roman Kadera .20 .50
10 Rostislav Olesz 1.25 3.00
11 Lukas Krayzel .20 .50
12 Lukas Krenzelok .20 .50
13 Pavel Kumstat .20 .50
14 Jiri Trvaj .20 .50
15 Petr Vala .20 .50
16 Ales Padelek .20 .50
17 Ivan Padelek .20 .50
18 Tomas Ficenc .20 .50
19 Pavel Kowalczyk .20 .50
20 Petr Mika .20 .50
21 Daniel Zapotocny .20 .50
22 Daniel Seman .20 .50
23 Martin Tomasek .20 .50
24 Martin Ambruz .20 .50
25 Marek Dubec .20 .50
26 Radovan Biegl .30 .75
27 Michal Horak .20 .50
28 Tomas Demel .20 .50
29 Radim Hruska .20 .50
30 Petr Kubos .20 .50
31 Alexej Jaskin .20 .50
32 Ondrej Nemec .20 .50
33 Jiri Polak .20 .50
34 Roman Stantien .20 .50
35 Jan Sochor .20 .50
36 Radek Masny .20 .50
37 Tomas Vak .20 .50
38 Petr Vampola .20 .50
39 Pavel Selinger .20 .50
40 Jiri Hasek .20 .50
41 Michal Hudec .20 .50
42 Lubomir Stach .20 .50
43 Martin Vyrubalik .20 .50
44 Patrik Luza .20 .50
45 Otakar Janecky .20 .50
46 Martin Barek .20 .50
47 Tomas Blazek .20 .50
48 Petr Caslava .20 .50
49 Tomas Divisek .20 .50
50 Miroslav Duben .20 .50
51 Petr Koukal .20 .50
52 Jaroslav Kudrna .20 .50
53 Frantisek Mrazek .20 .50
54 Petr Mudroch .20 .50
55 Andrej Novotny .20 .50
56 Tomas Pacal .20 .50
57 Lubomir Pistek .20 .50
58 Petr Prucha 2.00 5.00
59 Adam Svoboda .30 .75
60 Jan Kolar .20 .50
61 Michal Sykora .20 .50
62 Petr Sykora .20 .50
63 Jiri Dopita .20 .50
64 Peter Podhradsky .20 .50
65 Tomas Razingar .20 .50
66 Jan Alinc .20 .50
67 Robin Bacul .20 .50
68 Richard Bauer .20 .50
69 Lukas Bednarik .20 .50
70 Jakub Kraus .20 .50
71 Lukas Galvas .20 .50
72 Jan Kostal .20 .50
73 Lukas Krajicek .40 1.00
74 Petr Kumstat .20 .50
75 Tomas Mencicky .20 .50
76 Rudolf Pejchar .20 .50
77 Dmitrij Rodin .20 .50
78 Vaclav Skuhravy .20 .50
79 Frantisek Ptacek .20 .50
80 Vojtech Polak .20 .50
81 Ladislav Svoboda .20 .50
82 Michal Tvrdik .20 .50
83 Lukas Sablik .20 .50
84 Tomas Netik .20 .50
85 Miroslav Vantroba .20 .50
86 Martin Kivon .20 .50
87 Jan Lipansky .20 .50
88 David Balaze .20 .50
89 Frantisek Bojnic .20 .50
90 Viktor Hubl .20 .50
91 Jan Hranac .20 .50
92 Jiri Gombar .20 .50
93 Lukas Havel .20 .50
94 Marian Kacir .20 .50
95 Lukas Kaspar .20 .50
96 Jan Kloboucek .20 .50
97 Vlastimil Kroupa .20 .50
98 Vojtech Kubincak .20 .50
99 Tomas Martinec .20 .50
100 Petr Martinek .20 .50
101 Lukas Riha .20 .50
102 Richard Zemlicka .20 .50
103 Tomas Rolinek .20 .50
104 Miha Rebolj .20 .50
105 Michal Travnicek .20 .50
106 Marek Pinc .20 .50
107 Lukas Pozivil .20 .50
108 Ivo Prorok .20 .50
109 Martin Cakajik .20 .50
110 Miroslav Hajek .20 .50
111 Jan Holub .20 .50
112 Richard Jares .20 .50
113 Waldemar Jirus .20 .50
114 Pavel Kasparik .20 .50
115 Vaclav Koci .20 .50
116 Radoslav Kropac .20 .50
117 Angel Krstev .20 .50
118 Vaclav Novak .20 .50
119 Jiri Moravec .20 .50
120 Lukas Pabiska .20 .50
121 Mojmir Musil .20 .50
122 Jan Plodek .20 .50
123 Stanislav Prochazka .20 .50
124 Patrik Rozsival .20 .50
125 Michal Straka .20 .50
126 Oldrich Svoboda .20 .50
127 Ladislav Smid ERC 2.00 5.00
128 Lubomir Korhon .20 .50
129 Rudolf Vercik .20 .50
130 Jaroslav Balastik .40 1.00
131 Miroslav Blatak .20 .50
132 Martin Cech .20 .50
133 Martin Cech .20 .50
134 Martin Hamrlik .20 .50
135 Martin Jenacek .20 .50
136 Petr Leska .20 .50
137 Petr Macholda .20 .50
138 Petr Mokrejs .20 .50
139 Martin Nosek .20 .50
140 Miroslav Okal .20 .50
141 Martin Altrichter .20 .50
142 Radim Tesarik .20 .50
143 Petr Tucek .20 .50
144 Ondrej Vesely .20 .50
145 Rostislav Vlach .20 .50
146 Martin Zahorovsky .20 .50
147 Pavel Zubicek .20 .50
148 Peter Barinka .20 .50
149 Erik Weissemann .20 .50
150 Pavel Zavrtalek .20 .50
151 Michal Bros .20 .50
152 Petr Briza .30 .75
153 Jan Hanzlik .20 .50
154 Jaroslav Mrazek .20 .50
155 Jakub Sindel .20 .50
156 Ondrej Kratena .30 .75
157 Jan Marek .20 .50
158 Martin Paroulek .20 .50
159 Petr Ton .20 .50
160 David Vrbata .20 .50
161 Libor Prochazka .20 .50
162 Josef Reznicek .20 .50
163 Marek Schwarz ERC 2.00 5.00
164 Jan Srdinko .20 .50
165 Jan Tomajko .20 .50
166 Roman Vondracek .20 .50
167 Jan Vytisk .20 .50
168 Karel Hromas .20 .50
169 Jiri Jakes .20 .50

170 Radek Mika .20 .50
171 Milan Antos .20 .50
172 Josef Beranek .20 .50
173 Radek Dlouhy .20 .50
174 Jan Fadrny .20 .50
175 Dominik Granak .20 .50
176 Lukas Hronek .20 .50
177 David Hruska .20 .50
178 Jiri Kuntos .20 .50
179 Roman Malek .20 .50
180 Patrik Martinec .20 .50
181 Petr Jaros .20 .50
182 Jakub Klepis .40 1.00
183 Pavel Kolarik .20 .50
184 Milan Kopecky .20 .50
185 Frantisek Kucera .20 .50
186 Jan Novak .20 .50
187 David Pojkar .20 .50
188 Ondrej Stanek .20 .50
189 Michal Sup .20 .50
190 Adam Saffer .20 .50
191 Stanislav Gron .40 1.00
192 Petr Kadlec .20 .50
193 Marek Tomica .20 .50
194 Leos Cermak .20 .50
195 Ivan Dropa .20 .50
196 Martin Adamsky .20 .50
197 Michal Dobron .20 .50
198 Michal Dvorak .20 .50
199 Libor Barta .20 .50
200 Mario Cartelli .20 .50
201 Jiri Hanzlik .20 .50
202 Ales Kratoska .20 .50
203 Ondrej Kubes .20 .50
204 Josef Straka .20 .50
205 Radek Matejovsky .20 .50
206 Jan Svik .20 .50
207 Milan Voboril .20 .50
208 Milan Volak .20 .50
209 Zdenek Smid .20 .50
210 David Pospisil .20 .50
211 Roman Bilek .20 .50
212 Jiri Dobrovolny .20 .50
213 Michal Duraz .20 .50
214 Patrik Rimmel .20 .50
215 Zdenek Sedlak .20 .50
216 Vitezslav Bilek .20 .50
217 Jakub Evan .20 .50
218 Martin Frolik .20 .50
219 Radek Gardon .20 .50
220 Tomas Horna .20 .50
221 Miloslav Horava .20 .50
222 Vitezslav Jankovych .20 .50
223 Jaroslav Kalla .20 .50
224 David Pazourek .20 .50
225 Jan Pospisil .20 .50
226 Tomas Klimt .20 .50
227 Jan Krulis .20 .50
228 Robert Kysela .20 .50
229 Rostislav Malena .20 .50
230 Zdenek Orct .20 .50
231 Jiri Zeman .20 .50
232 Jan Dlouhy .20 .50
233 Petr Horava .20 .50
234 Petr Kasik .20 .50
235 Miroslav Lazo .20 .50
236 Martin Prochazka .20 .50
237 Juraj Stefanka .20 .50
238 Miroslav Barus .20 .50
239 Vaclav Benak .20 .50
240 Roman Erat .20 .50
241 Radek Haman .20 .50
242 David Havir .20 .50
243 Ales Kretinsky .20 .50
244 David Ludvik .20 .50
245 Roman Nemecek .20 .50
246 Karel Plasek .20 .50
247 Jan Snopek .20 .50
248 Milan Prochazka .20 .50
249 Peter Pucher .20 .50
250 Robert Slavik .20 .50
251 Pavel Mojzis .20 .50
252 Tomas Duba .20 .50
253 Igor Rataj .20 .50
254 Jan Pardavy .20 .50
255 Lukas Vomela .20 .50
256 Daniel Babka .20 .50
257 Radek Belohlav .20 .50
258 Stepan Hrebejk .20 .50
259 Vladimir Hudacek .20 .50
260 Stanislav Jasecko .20 .50
261 Josef Jindra .20 .50
262 Vaclav Koci .20 .50
263 Jaroslav Kristek .20 .50
264 Josef Kucera .20 .50
265 Lukas Kveton .20 .50
266 Jan Mucha .20 .50
267 Zbynek Neckar .20 .50
268 Zdenek Ondrej .20 .50
269 Ivan Rachunek .20 .50
270 Lubos Rob .20 .50
271 Petr Sailer .20 .50
272 Jiri Simanek .20 .50
273 Vladimir Skoda .20 .50
274 Rudolf Suchanek .20 .50
275 Filip Turek .20 .50
276 Michal Vondra .20 .50
277 Robert Prochazka .20 .50
278 Marek Schwarz 2.00 5.00
279 Zdenek Skorepa .20 .50
280 Filip Stefanka .20 .50
281 Richard Bordowski .20 .50
282 Michal Holes .20 .50
283 Lubos Horcicka .20 .50
284 Tomas Houdek .20 .50
285 Jiri Hunkes .20 .50
286 Marek Ivan .20 .50
287 Petr Jancarik .20 .50
288 Pavel Janku .20 .50
289 Richard Kral .20 .50
290 Jan Kudrna .20 .50
291 Vlastimil Lakosil .20 .50
292 Marek Melenovsky .20 .50
293 Jiri Malinsky .20 .50
294 Rostislav Martynek .20 .50
295 Roman Meluzin .20 .50
296 Zdenek Pavelek .20 .50
297 Vaclav Pletka .20 .50
298 Michal Podolka .20 .50
299 Jiri Polansky .20 .50
300 Gregor Poloncic .20 .50
301 Josef Vitek .20 .50
302 Boris Zabka .20 .50
303 Marek Zadina .20 .50
304 Tomas Zboril .20 .50
305 Tomas Frolo .20 .50
306 Martin Vyborny .20 .50
307 Marek Posmyk .20 .50
308 Milan Nedoma .20 .50
309 Dusan Andrasovsky .20 .50
310 Ladislav Lubina .20 .50
311 Alexandr Hylak .20 .50
312 Jaroslav Nedved .20 .50
313 Pavel Falta .20 .50
314 Leos Cermak .20 .50
315 Tomas Vlcek .20 .50
316 Igor Murin .20 .50
317 Tomas Karny .20 .50
318 Patrik Hucko .20 .50
319 Michal Mikeska .20 .50
320 Pavel Srek .20 .50
321 Gabriel Spilar .20 .50
322 Petr Havelka .20 .50
323 Martin Richter .20 .50
324 Radovan Sloboda .20 .50
325 Peter Bartos .20 .50
326 Vladimir Gyna .20 .50
327 Jan Chabera .20 .50
328 Andrej Mezin .20 .50
329 Jan Rehor .20 .50
330 Martin Strba .20 .50
331 Miroslav Durak .20 .50
332 Kamil Jarina .20 .50
333 Roman Kadera .20 .50
334 Angel Krstev .20 .50
335 Michal Marik .20 .50
336 Jakub Petruzalek .20 .50
337 Lubos Bartecko .20 .50
338 Petr Buzek .20 .50
339 Vaclav Eiselt .20 .50
340 Martin Chabada .20 .50
341 Tomas Popperle .20 .50
342 Zdenek Sedlak .20 .50
343 Ladislav Svoboda .20 .50
344 Roman Simicek .20 .50
345 Martin Havlat 2.00 5.00
346 Martin Vojtek .20 .50
347 Martin Jurecka .20 .50
348 Petr Jurecka .20 .50
349 David Mocek .20 .50
350 Patrik Rimmel .20 .50
351 Juraj Stefanka .20 .50
352 Filip Turek .20 .50
353 Pavel Zdrahal .20 .50
354 Daniel Mracka .20 .50
355 Libor Pavlis .20 .50
356 Tomaz Razingar .20 .50
357 Pavel Sebesta .20 .50
358 Dalibor Sochorek .20 .50
359 Radim Tesarik .20 .50
360 Juraj Prokop .20 .50
361 Josef Hrabal .20 .50
362 Stefan Zigardy .20 .50
363 Jan Kudrna .20 .50
364 Vaclav Skuhravy .20 .50
365 Ivan Droppa .20 .50
366 Michal Hreus .20 .50
367 Radim Skuhrovec .20 .50
368 Jiri Veber .20 .50
369 Jan Dlouhy .20 .50
370 Marek Dubec .20 .50
371 Miroslav Hlinka .20 .50
372 Jiri Beroun .20 .50
373 Tomas Duba .20 .50
374 Tomas Hradecky .20 .50
375 Jaroslav Mares .20 .50
376 Petr Puncochar .20 .50
377 Michal Straka .20 .50
378 Marek Uram .20 .50
379 Jakub Kindl .20 .50
380 Libor Zabransky .20 .50
381 Lubomir Jurtaj .20 .50
382 Petr Jez .20 .50
383 Robert Jindrich .20 .50
384 Roman Malek .20 .50
385 Martin Paroulek .20 .50
386 Adam Saffer .20 .50
387 Michal Straka .20 .50
388 Martin Klaus .20 .50
389 Tomas Kapusta .20 .50
390 Lubomir Vosatko .20 .50
391 Jiri Hanzlik .20 .50
392 Jiri Hasek .20 .50
393 Ctibor Jech .20 .50
394 Ctirad Ovcacik .20 .50
395 Tomas Rolinek .20 .50
396 Martin Tupa .20 .50
397 Libor Barta .20 .50
398 Jiri Jantovsky .20 .50
399 Petr Jares .20 .50
400 Martin Havlat CL .75 2.00

2003-04 Czech OFS Plus All-Star Game

COMPLETE SET (45) 30.00 75.00
H1 Miroslav Simonovic .75 2.00
H2 Normunds Sejejs .75 2.00
H3 Jiri Hes .75 2.00
H4 Marcel Hanzal .75 2.00
H5 Roman Kukumberg .75 2.00
H6 Arne Krotak .75 2.00
H7 Karol Krizan .75 2.00
H8 Juraj Kledrowetz .75 2.00
H9 Miroslav Vantroba .75 2.00
H10 Miroslav Skovira .75 2.00
H11 Jaroslav Kmit .75 2.00
H12 Lubomir Kolnik .75 2.00
H13 Pavel Kowalczyk .75 2.00
H14 Martin Ivicic .75 2.00
H15 Branislav Janos .75 2.00
H16 Zdeno Ciger .75 2.00
H17 Petr Korinek .75 2.00
H18 Tomas Starosta .75 2.00
H19 Tomas Nadazdi .75 2.00
H20 Igor Rataj .75 2.00
H21 Richard Kapus .75 2.00
H22 Erik Weissmann .75 2.00
H23 Adam Svoboda 1.25 3.00
H24 Michal Sykora .75 2.00
H25 Petr Sykora .75 2.00
H26 Roman Malek 1.25 3.00
H27 Petr Kadlec .75 2.00
H28 Jan Hejda .75 2.00
H29 Michal Sup .75 2.00
H30 Frantisek Kucera .75 2.00
H31 Frantisek Ptacek .75 2.00
H32 Ondrej Kratena .75 2.00
H33 Libor Prochazka .75 2.00
H34 Richard Kral .75 2.00
H35 Marek Zadina .75 2.00
H36 Jan Marek .75 2.00
H37 Vaclav Pletka .75 2.00
H38 Martin Hlavacka .75 2.00
H39 Jan Vytisk .75 2.00
H40 David Moravec .75 2.00
H41 Jiri Burger .75 2.00
H42 Jiri Hudler 6.00 15.00
H43 Marek Uram .75 2.00
H44 Peter Pucher .75 2.00
H45 A.Svoboda/M.Sykora CL .75 2.00

2003-04 Czech OFS Plus Checklists

COMPLETE SET (14) 15.00 30.00
1 Jiri Trvaj 1.25 3.00
2 Radovan Biegl 1.25 3.00
3 Adam Svoboda 1.25 3.00
4 Petr Franek 1.25 3.00
5 Marek Pinc 1.25 3.00
6 Oldrich Svoboda 1.25 3.00
7 Petr Tucek 1.25 3.00
8 Petr Briza 1.25 3.00
9 Roman Malek 1.25 3.00
10 Libor Barta 1.25 3.00
11 Josef Kucera 1.25 3.00
12 Martin Altrichter 1.25 3.00
13 Josef Kucera 1.25 3.00
14 Vlastimil Lakosil 1.25 3.00

2003-04 Czech OFS Plus Insert B

We have no pricing information on this series.
B1 Roman Malek
B2 Petr Briza
B3 Adam Svoboda
B4 Marek Pinc
B5 Jiri Trvaj
B6 Vlastomil Lakosil
B7 Petr Franek
B8 Martin Altrichter
B9 Vladimir Hudacek
B10 Radovan Biegl
B11 Petr Tucek
B12 Libor Barta
B13 Lubos Horcicka
B14 Pavel Falta
B15 Petr Briza
Zdenek Orct CL

2003-04 Czech OFS Plus Insert C

We have no pricing information on this series.
C1 Lubos Rob
C2 Ladislav Svoboda
C3 Radek Gardon
C4 Michal Straka
C5 Richard Zemlicka
C6 Jiri Dopita
C7 Jiri Hanzlik
C8 Josef Beranek
C9 Ondrej Kratena
C10 Richard Kral
C11 Roman Kadera
C12 Josef Straub
C13 Miroslav Okal
C14 Rene Pucher

2003-04 Czech OFS Plus Insert G

We have no pricing information on this series.
G1 Lubos Rob
G2 Michal Sup
G3 Radoslav Kropac
G4 Marek Zadina
G5 Jan Marek
G6 Roman Kadera
G7 Viktor Ujcik
G8 Richard Kral
G9 Marek Uram
G10 Pavel Janku

2003-04 Czech OFS Plus Insert H

We have no pricing information on this series.
H1 Josef Kucera
H2 Jiri Trvaj
H3 Roman Kadera
H4 Pavel Falta
H5 Jaroslav Nedved
H6 Igor Murin
H7 Jan Pardavy
H8 Jan Snopek
H9 Richard Kral
H10 Vaclav Pletka
H11 Zdenek Pavelek
H12 Roman Stantien
H13 Richard Zemlicka
H14 Marek Pinc
H15 Tomas Horna
H16 Michal Mikeska
H17 Adam Svoboda
H18 Michal Sykora
H19 Petr Briza
H20 Dusan Andrasovsky
H21 Marek Posmyk
H22 Radovan Sloboda
H23 Lukas Hronek
H24 Michal Sup
H25 David Hruska

2003-04 Czech OFS Plus Insert M

We have no pricing information on this series.
M1 Josef Straka
M2 Jiri Dopita
M3 Ladislav Lubina
M4 Petr Sykora
M5 Josef Beranek
M6 Jakub Klepis
M7 Roman Malek
M8 Tomas Klimt
M9 Zdenek Orct
M10 Jiri Hasek
M11 Tomas Martinec
M12 Jan Marek
M13 Ondrej Kratena
M14 Zdenek Skorepa
M15 Rostislav Martynek
M16 Martin Cakajik
M17 Martin Altrichter
M18 Martin Hamrlik
M19 Tomas Duba
M20 Peter Pucher
M21 Jiri Burger
M22 Ivan Padelek
M23 Lukas Sablik
M24 Jan Alinc
M25 Jaroslav Kristek
M26 Jiri Dopita CL

2003-04 Czech OFS Plus Insert P

We have no pricing information on this series.
P1 Roman Malek
P2 Petr Briza
P3 Petr Franek
P4 Adam Svoboda
P5 Marek Pinc
P6 Jiri Trvaj
P7 Vlastomil Lakosil
P8 Martin Altrichter
P9 Radovan Biegl
P10 Libor Barta
P11 Lubos Horcicka
P12 Petr Tucek
P13 Vladimir Hudacek
P14 Pavel Falta
P15 Roman Malek
Jiri Trvaj CL

2003-04 Czech OFS Plus Insert S

We have no pricing information on this series.
S1 Richard Kral
S2 Jan Marek
S3 Jiri Burger
S4 David Moravec
S5 Zdenek Pavelek
S6 Lubos Rob
S7 Marek Zadina
S8 Radoslav Kropac
S9 Jiri Hudler
S10 Roman Kadera

2003-04 Czech OFS Plus MS Praha

COMPLETE SET (50) 30.00 75.00
SE1 Martin Havlat 4.00 10.00
SE2 Roman Simicek .75 2.00
SE3 Petr Briza 1.25 3.00
SE4 Jan Marek .75 2.00
SE5 Petr Buzek .75 2.00
SE6 Ondrej Kratena .75 2.00
SE7 Michal Sykora .75 2.00
SE8 Petr Sykora .75 2.00
SE9 Adam Svoboda 1.25 3.00
SE10 Jiri Dopita .75 2.00
SE11 Michal Mikeska .75 2.00
SE12 Petr Prucha 4.00 10.00
SE13 Martin Prochazka .75 2.00
SE14 Zdenek Orct 1.25 3.00
SE15 Petr Leska .75 2.00
SE16 Jaroslav Balastik 1.25 3.00
SE17 Jan Snopek .75 2.00
SE18 Jiri Burger .75 2.00
SE19 Rostislav Olesz 4.00 10.00
SE20 Jiri Trvaj .75 2.00
SE21 Zdenek Pavelek .75 2.00
SE22 Frantisek Ptacek .75 2.00
SE23 Roman Malek .75 2.00
SE24 Marek Posmyk .75 2.00
SE25 Petr Kadlec .75 2.00
SE26 Oldrich Svoboda .75 2.00
SE27 Josef Beranek .75 2.00
SE28 Michal Travnicek .75 2.00
SE29 Lukas Havel .75 2.00
SE30 Jiri Hudler 4.00 10.00
SE31 David Moravec .75 2.00
SE32 Radim Tesarik .75 2.00
SE33 Jan Hejda .75 2.00
SE34 Vlastimil Lakosil .75 2.00
SE35 Martin Chabada .75 2.00
SE36 Petr Franek .75 2.00
SE37 Radovan Biegl 1.25 3.00
SE38 Tomas Duba .75 2.00
SE39 Lukas Hronek .75 2.00
SE40 Jan Novak .75 2.00
SE41 Martin Altrichter .75 2.00
SE42 Marek Schwarz 2.00 5.00
SE43 Josef Kucera .75 2.00
SE44 Tomas Divisek .75 2.00
SE45 Jakub Klepis 2.00 5.00
SE46 Michal Sup .75 2.00
SE47 Michal Marik .75 2.00
SE48 Richard Kral .75 2.00
SE49 Marek Pinc .75 2.00
SE50 Pavel Falta .75 2.00

2003-04 Czech Pardubice Postcards

This team-issued set features postcard sized (4X6) collectibles of the Pardubice squad from the Czech Elite League. They are listed below in alphabetical order.

COMPLETE SET (16) 8.00 15.00
1 Martin Barek .40 1.00
2 Tomas Blazek .40 1.00
3 Tomas Divisek .40 1.00
4 Jiri Dopita .40 1.00
5 Otakar Janecky .40 1.00
6 Petr Koukal .40 1.00
7 Jaroslav Kudrna .40 1.00
8 Ladislav Lubina .40 1.00
9 Michal Mikeska .40 1.00
10 Frantisek Mrazek .40 1.00
11 Andrej Novotny .40 1.00
12 Tomas Pacal .40 1.00
13 Petr Prucha 2.00 5.00
14 Tomaz Razingar .40 1.00
15 Adam Svoboda .75 2.00
16 Michal Sykora .40 1.00

2003-04 Czech Stadion

These cards were issued as part of a multi-sport set by a Czech athletic magazine.

601 Scott Stevens .75 2.00
603 Patrik Elias .75 2.00
604 Jeff Friesen .40 1.00
605 Grant Marshall .40 1.00
606 Jamie Langenbrunner .40 1.00
607 Martin Brodeur 4.00 10.00
608 Scott Niedermayer .40 1.00
609 Mike Rupp .40 1.00
610 Ruslan Salei .40 1.00
611 Guy Lafleur 1.50 4.00
612 Petr Sykora .40 1.00
613 Steve Rucchin .40 1.00
614 J-S Giguere 1.25 3.00
615 Adam Oates .40 1.00
616 Paul Kariya 1.50 4.00
617 Steve Thomas .40 1.00
618 Rob Niedermayer .40 1.00
622 Vladimir Zabrodsky .40 1.00
637 Vsevolod Bobrov .40 1.00
638 Vlastimil Bubnik .40 1.00
639 Leif Holmqvist .40 1.00
640 Vladimir Dzurilla .75 2.00
641 Anatoli Firsov .40 1.00
642 Josef Golonka .40 1.00
643 Jiri Holecek .40 1.00
644 Jaroslav Holik .40 1.00
645 Jiri Holik .40 1.00
646 Bobby Hull 2.00 5.00
647 Alexander Yakushev .75 2.00
648 Sven Tumba Johansson .40 1.00
649 Alexander Maltsev .75 2.00
650 Vaclav Nedomansky .40 1.00
651 Alexander Ragulin .75 2.00
652 Maurice Richard 2.00 5.00
653 Vladimir Martinek .40 1.00
654 Frantisek Pospisil .40 1.00

2003 Czech National Team Postcards

This postcard-sized issue features members of the Czech team from the 2003 World Championships.

COMPLETE SET (17) 20.00 40.00
1 Jaroslav Balastik 1.25 3.00
2 Jan Hejda .75 2.00
3 Milan Hejduk 2.00 5.00
4 Jan Hlavac .75 2.00
5 Ivan Hlinka CO .40 1.00
6 Jiri Hudler 4.00 10.00
7 Frantisek Kaberle .75 2.00
8 Jindrich Kotrla .75 2.00
9 Jaroslav Modry .75 2.00
10 Robert Reichel .75 2.00
11 Martin Straka .75 2.00
12 Radek Sup .75 2.00
13 Martin Tomasek .75 2.00
14 Josef Vasicek .75 2.00
15 Tomas Vokoun 2.00 5.00
16 Radim Vrbata 1.25 3.00
17 David Vyborny 1.25 3.00

2003 Czech Stadion

This multi-sport set was issued in conjunction with the Czech magazine Stadion. It is listed below in skip-numbered form.

COMPLETE SET 15.00 40.00
529 Anson Carter .40 1.00
530 Peter Bondra .40 1.00
531 Magnus Arvedson .40 1.00
532 Sandy McCarthy .40 1.00
533 Mikko Eloranta .40 1.00
534 Tie Domi .75 2.00
534 Bates Battaglia .40 1.00
536 Jaromir Jagr 4.00 10.00
Mario Lemieux
537 Darcy Tucker .40 1.00
538 Brian Rafalski .40 1.00
539 Jozef Stumpel .40 1.00
540 Marco Sturm .40 1.00
541 Eric Lindros 1.25 3.00
542 Ed Jovanovski .40 1.00
543 Darren McCarty .40 1.00
544 Zigmund Palffy .40 1.00
545 Luc Robitaille 1.25 3.00
546 Keith Primeau .40 1.00
547 Bobby Clarke .40 1.00
548 Marcel Dionne .40 1.00
549 Ken Dryden 2.00 5.00
550 Frank Mahovlich .75 2.00
551 Valeri Kharlamov .75 2.00
552 Phil Esposito 2.00 5.00
553 Boris Mikhailov .75 2.00
554 Stan Mikita .75 2.00
555 Bobby Orr 4.00 10.00
556 Vladimir Petrov .40 1.00
557 Vladislav Tretiak 1.25 3.00
562 Chuck Kobasew
565 Bobby Holik .40 1.00

2004-05 Czech HC Plzen Postcards

This postcard issue features members of HC Plzen, one of the top teams in the Czech Extraliga. The set is noteworthy for the inclusion of several NHLers who joined the team during the 2004-05 lockout.

COMPLETE SET (23) 10.00 20.00
1 Martin Adamsky .40 1.00
2 Dusan Andrasovsky .40 1.00
3 Mario Cartelli .40 1.00
4 Martin Cibak .60 1.50
5 Tomas Duba .40 1.00
6 Michal Duras .40 1.00
7 Robert Jindrich .60 1.50
8 Jaroslav Kracik .40 1.00
9 Jaroslav Kucera .40 1.00
10 Radek Matejovsky .40 1.00
11 Frank Mrazek .40 1.00
12 Milan Nedoma .40 1.00
13 Martin Paroulek .40 1.00
14 Rudolf Pejchar .40 1.00
15 David Pospisil .40 1.00
16 Jaroslav Spacek .40 1.00
17 Pavel Srek .40 1.00
18 Josef Straka .40 1.00
19 Martin Straka .60 1.50
20 Michal Straka .40 1.00
21 Pavel Trnka .40 1.00
22 Martin Vyborny .40 1.00
23 Jan Vytisk .40 1.00

2004-05 Czech HC Slavia Praha Postcards

This postcard issue features HC Slavia Praha from the Czech Extraliga. The set is noteworthy for the inclusion of several well-known NHL stars who played with the team during the 2004-05 lockout. but if you know of others, please contact us via email at hockeymag@beckett.com.

COMPLETE SET (12) 15.00 25.00
1 Milan Antos .40 1.00
2 Radek Duda .40 1.00
3 Petr Franek .40 1.00
4 Petr Kadlec .40 1.00
5 Tomas Kloucek .60 1.50
6 Zigmund Palffy 1.50 4.00
7 Vladimir Ruzicka .40 1.00
8 Jozef Stumpel .60 1.50
9 Radek Sup .40 1.00
10 Josef Vasicek .60 1.50
11 Tomas Vlasak .40 1.00
12 Team Card .60 1.50
13 Josef Beranek .40 1.00
14 Jan Novak .40 1.00
15 Pavel Kolarik .40 1.00
16 David Hruska .40 1.00
17 Michal Sup .40 1.00
18 Jaroslav Spacek .40 1.00
19 Dominik Granak .40 1.00
20 Lukas Havel .40 1.00
21 Zdenek Smid .40 1.00
22 Tomas Zizka .40 1.00

2004-05 Czech HC Sparta Praha Postcards

This postcard issue features Sparta Praha, a top team in the Czech Extraliga. It features a number of well-known NHLers who ventured overseas during the lockout of 2004-05.

COMPLETE SET (24) 15.00 30.00
1 Petr Briza .75 2.00
2 Michal Bros .40 1.00
3 Martin Chabada .40 1.00
4 Michal Dobron .40 1.00
5 Michal Dragoun .40 1.00
6 Jan Hanzlik .40 1.00
7 Jan Hlavac .75 2.00
8 Pavel Kasparik .40 1.00
9 Jindrich Kotrla .40 1.00
10 Ondrej Kratena .40 1.00
11 Jan Marek .40 1.00
12 Petr Nedved .75 2.00
13 Tomas Netik .40 1.00
14 Rostislav Olesz 1.25 3.00
15 Karel Pilar .75 2.00
16 Tomas Popperle .40 1.00
17 Libor Prochazka .40 1.00
18 Jozef Reznicek .40 1.00
19 Martin Richter .40 1.00
20 Robert Schnabel .40 1.00
21 Jakub Sindel .40 1.00
22 Michal Sivek .75 2.00
23 Petr Ton .40 1.00
24 David Vyborny .75 2.00

2004-05 Czech NHL ELH Postcards

This series of 16 postcards features NHL players who spent all or part of the 2004-05 season in the Czech Extraliga. The cards feature full-colour photos on the fronts showing the players in their Czech sweaters. The cards are unnumbered and listed below alphabetically.

COMPLETE SET (16) 15.00 30.00
1 Jan Bulis .75 2.00
2 Petr Cajanek .75 2.00
3 Roman Hamrlik .75 2.00
4 Milan Hejduk 1.50 4.00
5 Ales Hemsky 1.50 4.00
6 Jan Hlavac .75 2.00
7 Jaromir Jagr 2.00 5.00
8 Ales Kotalik .75 2.00
9 Petr Nedved .75 2.00
10 Karel Pilar .75 2.00
11 Robert Reichel .75 2.00
12 Martin Rucinsky .75 2.00
13 Jiri Slegr .75 2.00
14 Jaroslav Spacek .75 2.00
15 Martin Straka .75 2.00
16 David Vyborny .75 2.00

2004-05 Czech OFS

COMPLETE SET (372) 40.00 100.00
1 Petr Altrichter .08 .20
2 Oldrich Bakus .08 .20
3 Petr Buzek .08 .20
4 Tomas Cachotsky .08 .20
5 Dusan Devecka .08 .20
6 Jiri Dobrovolny .08 .20
7 Tomas Ficenc .08 .20
8 Marian Havel .08 .20
9 Roman Hlouch .08 .20
10 Lukas Hronek .08 .20
11 Jiri Jantovsky .08 .20
12 Petr Kuchyna .08 .20
13 Rostislav Malena .08 .20
14 Jaroslav Mares .08 .20
15 Ales Padelek .08 .20
16 Vojtech Polak .08 .20
17 Petr Puncochar .08 .20
18 Ladislav Rytnauer .08 .20
19 Jaroslav Suchan .08 .20
20 Petr Vala .08 .20
21 Rudolf Vercik .08 .20
22 Martin Zajac .08 .20
23 Richard Bauer .08 .20
24 Michal Dvorak .08 .20
25 Martin Hlavacka .08 .20
26 Martin Kivon .08 .20
27 Jan Kostal .08 .20
28 Petr Kumstat .08 .20
29 Edgars Masalskis .08 .20
30 Petr Mika .08 .20
31 Lukas Pech .08 .20
32 Milan Prochazka .08 .20
33 Frantisek Ptacek .08 .20
34 Vaclav Skuhravy .08 .20
35 Zdenek Smid .08 .20
36 Dmitrij Suur .08 .20
37 Robert Tomik .08 .20
38 Jiri Polak .08 .20
39 Lukas Krajicek .40 1.00
40 Lukas Bednarik .08 .20
41 Jakub Kraus .08 .20
42 Jan Alinc .08 .20
43 Jan Lipansky .08 .20
44 Lubomir Hurtaj .08 .20
45 Zdenek Kutlak .08 .20
46 Lukas Mensator .20 .50
47 Vitezslav Bilek .08 .20
48 Vratislav Cech .08 .20
49 Jakub Evan .08 .20
50 Martin Frolik .08 .20
51 Michael Frolik 2.00 5.00
52 Radek Gardon .08 .20
53 Miloslav Horava .08 .20
54 Petr Horava .08 .20
55 Tomas Horna .08 .20
56 Jaromir Jagr 2.00 5.00
57 Jiri Jelinek .08 .20
58 Tomas Kaberle .20 .50
59 Jaroslav Kalla .08 .20
60 Tomas Klimt .08 .20
61 Jakub Lev .08 .20
62 Zdenek Orct .20 .50
63 Pavel Patera .08 .20
64 Martin Prochazka .08 .20
65 Martin Sevc .08 .20
66 Jaroslav Spelda .08 .20
67 Josef Zajic .08 .20
68 Jan Holub .08 .20
69 Richard Jares .08 .20
70 Valdemar Jirus .08 .20
71 Ales Kotalik .60 1.50
72 Jiri Moravec .08 .20
73 Vaclav Nedorost .40 1.00
74 Vaclav Novak .08 .20
75 Jan Plodek .08 .20
76 Andrej Podkonicky .08 .20
77 Stanislav Prochazka .08 .20
78 Igor Rataj .08 .20
79 Patrik Rozsival .08 .20
80 Ladislav Smid ERC .75 2.00

81 Jan Tomajko .08 .20
82 Lubomir Vaic .20 .50
83 Radim Vrbata .40 1.00
84 Pavel Falta .08 .20
85 Leos Cermak .08 .20
86 Miroslav Duben .08 .20
87 Milan Hnilicka .40 1.00
88 Jiri Hanzlik .08 .20
89 David Balaze .08 .20
90 Frantisek Bombic .08 .20
91 Daniel Branda .08 .20
92 Jiri Gombar .08 .20
93 Lukas Havel .08 .20
94 Viktor Hubl .08 .20
95 Kamil Jarina .08 .20
96 Jan Kloboucek .08 .20
97 Vlastimil Kroupa .08 .20
98 Vojtech Kubincak .08 .20
99 Tomas Kurka .08 .20
100 Michal Marik .08 .20
101 Lukas Pozivil .08 .20
102 Robert Reichel .20 .50
103 Lukas Riha .08 .20
104 Martin Rucinsky .20 .50
105 Zbynek Sklenicka .08 .20
106 Martin Skoula .20 .50
107 Radim Skuhrovec .08 .20
108 Jiri Slegr .08 .20
109 Michal Travnicek .08 .20
110 Martin Tupa .08 .20
111 Tomas Blazek .08 .20
112 Jan Bulis .08 .20
113 Petr Caslava .08 .20
114 Tomas Divisek .20 .50
115 Jiri Dopita .20 .50
116 David Havir .08 .20
117 Milan Hejduk .75 2.00
118 Alexandr Hylak .08 .20
119 Jaroslav Kames .20 .50
120 Jan Kolar .08 .20
121 Petr Koukal .08 .20
122 Tomas Linhart .08 .20
123 Ladislav Lubina .08 .20
124 Michal Mikeska .08 .20
125 Petr Mudroch .08 .20
126 Andrej Novotny .08 .20
127 Tomas Pacal .08 .20
128 Petr Prucha .75 2.00
129 Tomaz Razingar .08 .20
130 Tomas Rolinek .08 .20
131 Jan Snopek .08 .20
132 Petr Sykora .40 1.00
133 Jan Lasak .75 2.00
134 Ales Hemsky 1.25 3.00
135 Michal Tvrdik .08 .20
136 Lubomir Korhon .08 .20
137 Martin Adamsky .08 .20
138 Dusan Andrasovsky .08 .20
139 Mario Cartelli .08 .20
140 Tomas Duba .08 .20
141 Michal Duraz .08 .20
142 Petr Havelka .08 .20
143 Robert Jindrich .20 .50
144 Josef Straka .08 .20
145 Jaroslav Kracik .08 .20
146 Milan Kraft .40 1.00
147 Martin Straka .40 1.00
148 Radek Matejovsky .08 .20
149 Michal Straka .08 .20
150 Milan Nedoma .08 .20
151 Rudolf Pejchar .08 .20
152 David Pospisil .08 .20
153 Adam Saffer .08 .20
154 Jaroslav Spacek .08 .20
155 Pavel Trnka .08 .20
156 Martin Vyborny .08 .20
157 Jan Vytisk .08 .20
158 Milan Antos .08 .20
159 Radek Dlouhy .08 .20
160 Radek Duda .08 .20
161 Petr Franek .08 .20
162 Dominik Granak .08 .20
163 David Hruska .08 .20
164 Petr Kadlec .08 .20
165 Tomas Kloucek .20 .50
166 Pavel Kolarik .08 .20
167 Milan Kopecky .08 .20
168 Ales Kratoska .08 .20
169 Frantisek Kucera .08 .20
170 Lukas Musil .08 .20
171 Jan Novak .08 .20
172 Zigmund Palffy .75 2.00
173 Jozef Stumpel .20 .50
174 Michal Sup .08 .20
175 Marek Tomica .08 .20
176 Josef Vasicek .20 .50
177 Michal Vondrka .08 .20
178 Boris Zabka .08 .20
179 Petr Jaros .08 .20
180 David Pojkar .08 .20
181 Patrik Martinec .08 .20
182 Vladimir Sobotka .08 .20
183 Petr Briza .20 .50
184 Michal Dobron .08 .20
185 Jan Hanzlik .08 .20
186 Jan Hlavac .20 .50
187 Martin Chabada .08 .20
188 Pavel Kasparik .08 .20
189 Jindrich Kotrla .08 .20
190 Jan Marek .08 .20
191 Petr Nedved .20 .50
192 Tomas Netik .08 .20
193 Rostislav Olesz 1.25 3.00
194 Karel Pilar .20 .50
195 Tomas Popperle .08 .20
196 Libor Prochazka .08 .20
197 Josef Reznicek .08 .20
198 Martin Richter .08 .20
199 Robert Schnabel .08 .20
200 Jakub Sindel .08 .20
201 Michal Sivek .08 .20
202 Petr Ton .08 .20
203 David Vyborny .20 .50
204 Radek Bonk .20 .50
205 Richard Bordowski .08 .20
206 Martin Cakajik .08 .20
207 Miroslav Durak .08 .20
208 Jiri Hasek .08 .20
209 Pavel Janku .08 .20
210 Vladislav Koutsky .08 .20
211 Richard Kral .08 .20
212 Vlastimil Lakosil .08 .20
213 Jiri Malinsky .08 .20
214 Rostislav Martynek .08 .20
215 Marek Melenovsky .08 .20
216 Zdenek Pavelek .08 .20
217 Jan Peterek .08 .20
218 Vaclav Pletka .20 .50
219 Peter Podhradsky .08 .20
220 Jiri Polansky .08 .20
221 Michal Rozsival .20 .50
222 Zdenek Skorepa .08 .20
223 Filip Stefanka .08 .20
224 Jiri Burger .08 .20
225 Marek Cernosek .08 .20
226 Petr Hubacek .08 .20
227 Stanislav Hudec .08 .20
228 Jakub Hulva .08 .20
229 Zbynek Irgl .08 .20
230 Martin Krayzel .08 .20
231 Lukas Krenzelok .08 .20
232 Pavel Kumstat .08 .20
233 Marek Malik .08 .20
234 David Moravec .08 .20
235 Ivan Padelek .08 .20
236 Radek Philipp .08 .20
237 Marek Pinc .08 .20
238 Martin Prusek .40 1.00
239 Patrik Rimmel .08 .20
240 Martin Tomasek .08 .20
241 Filip Turek .08 .20
242 Vaclav Varada .20 .50
243 Kamil Brabenec .08 .20
244 Roman Cechmanek .20 .50
245 Tomas Demel .08 .20
246 Marek Dubec .08 .20
247 Tomas Frolo .08 .20
248 Ladislav Gengel .08 .20
249 Josef Hrabal .08 .20
250 Alexej Jaskin .08 .20
251 Rostislav Klesla .40 1.00
252 Robin Kovar .08 .20
253 Pavel Kowalczyk .08 .20
254 Radek Masny .08 .20
255 Ondrej Nemec .08 .20
256 Libor Pavlis .08 .20
257 Lukas Plsek .08 .20
258 Branko Radivojevic .40 1.00
259 Pavel Selingr .08 .20
260 Roman Stantien .08 .20
261 Tomas Vak .08 .20
262 Martin Vasut .08 .20
263 Rostislav Vlach .08 .20
264 Marek Zadina .08 .20
265 Robert Horak .08 .20
266 Radovan Somik .08 .20
267 Jan Koroptvicka .08 .20
268 Ondrej Vesely .08 .20
269 Martin Altrichter .08 .20
270 Martin Ambruz .08 .20
271 Jaroslav Balastik .40 1.00
272 Peter Barinka .20 .50
273 Miroslav Blatak .08 .20
274 Petr Cajanek .20 .50
275 Martin Cech .08 .20
276 Martin Erat .40 1.00
277 Lukas Galvas .08 .20
278 Roman Hamrlik .20 .50
279 Martin Jenacek .08 .20
280 Miroslav Kovacik .08 .20
281 Jaroslav Kristek .08 .20
282 Tomas Kudelka .08 .20
283 Petr Leska .08 .20
284 Petr Mokrejs .08 .20
285 Igor Murin .08 .20
286 David Nosek .08 .20
287 Miroslav Okal .08 .20
288 Radim Tesarik .08 .20
289 Martin Vosatko .08 .20
290 Martin Zahorovsky .08 .20
291 Pavel Zubicek .08 .20
292 Vaclav Benak .08 .20
293 Radim Bicanek .08 .20
294 Roman Erat .08 .20
295 Radek Haman .08 .20
296 Tomas Kucharcik .20 .50
297 Branislav Kvetan .08 .20
298 Zdenek Ondrej .08 .20
299 Jan Pardavy .08 .20
300 Peter Pucher .08 .20
301 Ivan Rachunek .08 .20
302 Milan Toman .08 .20
303 Marek Vorel .08 .20
304 Marek Uram .08 .20
305 Karel Plasek .08 .20
306 Ales Kretinsky .08 .20
307 Miroslav Barus .08 .20
308 David Ludvik .08 .20
309 Robert Slavik .08 .20
310 Pavel Mojzis .08 .20
311 Tomas Vokoun 1.25 3.00
312 Patrik Elias .40 1.00
313 Martin Havlat .75 2.00
314 David Vsetecka .08 .20
315 Josef Vitek .08 .20
316 Jiri Hunkes .08 .20
317 Radim Kucharczyk .08 .20
318 Branislav Mezei .20 .50
319 Karel Rachunek .20 .50
320 Ivan Majesky .20 .50
321 David Vrbata .08 .20
322 Jaroslav Kasik .08 .20
323 Ondrej Malinsky .08 .20
324 Michal Dragoun .08 .20
325 Michal Bros .08 .20
326 Ondrej Kratena .08 .20
327 Petr Kasik .08 .20
328 Jiri Zeman .08 .20
329 Miroslav Kopriva .08 .20
330 Robert Kysela .08 .20
331 Frantisek Kaberle .20 .50
332 Jan Hrdina .20 .50
333 Jiri Jelinek .08 .20
334 Milan Hluchy .08 .20
335 Jiri Stejskal .20 .50
336 Jiri Fischer .20 .50
337 Angel Krstev .08 .20
338 Tomas Klimenta .08 .20
339 Lukas Pabiska .08 .20
340 Petr Vampola .08 .20
341 Jan Visek .08 .20
342 Jaroslav Modry .20 .50
343 Martin Strba .08 .20
344 David Stich .08 .20
345 Jakub Korinek .08 .20
346 Martin Paroulek .08 .20
347 Frantisek Mrazek .08 .20
348 Martin Cibak .20 .50
349 David Moravec .08 .20
350 Lukas Pulpan .08 .20
351 Josef Beranek .08 .20
352 Tomas Vlasak .08 .20
353 Tomas Zizka .08 .20
354 Vladimir Vujtek .08 .20
355 Daniel Seman .08 .20
356 Roman Simicek .08 .20
357 Juraj Stefanka .08 .20
358 Tomas Dolana .08 .20
359 Pavel Vostrak .08 .20
360 Radovan Biegl .20 .50
361 Karol Sloboda .08 .20
362 Vladimir Gyna .08 .20
363 Petr Gregorek .08 .20
364 Jiri Hudler 1.50 4.00
365 Pavel Kubina .40 1.00
366 Ludek Krayzel .08 .20
367 Martin Hamrlik .08 .20
368 Michal Hrazdira .08 .20
369 Connor Dunlop .40 1.00
370 Miroslav Hanuljak .08 .20
371 Miroslav Zalesak .40 1.00
372 Radovan Biegl .20 .50
373 Martin Vojtek .08 .20
374 TomÃ¡Å¡ Zboril .08 .20
375 TomÃ¡Å¡ Kloucek .20 .50
376 TomÃ¡Å¡ PospÃ-Å¡il .20 .50
377 Jaroslav Kudrna .20 .50
378 TomÃ¡Å¡ Harant .20 .50
379 Milan Kraft .20 .50
380 Radim Kucharczyk .08 .20
381 Roman MÃ¡lek .20 .50
382 Andrej Nedorost .20 .50
383 Vojtech PolÃ¡k .30 .75
384 FrantiÅ¡ek MrÃ¡zek .08 .20
385 Jan Caloun .08 .20
386 Radek Fiala .08 .20
387 Martin Heinisch .08 .20
388 Peter Jansky .08 .20
389 Jindrich Kotrla .08 .20
390 Jaroslav Å pacek .08 .20
391 Matej Badiura .08 .20
392 Å tepÃ¡n Hrebejk .08 .20
393 Radek HubÃ¡cek .08 .20
394 Radek HubÃ¡cek .08 .20
395 MojmÃ-r Musil .08 .20
396 Robert Najdek .08 .20
397 Michal NedbÃ¡lek .08 .20
398 Michal Å afarÃ-k .08 .20
399 Radek Bonk .20 .50
400 Ondrej VeselÃ½ .08 .20
401 Martin Ambruz .08 .20
402 JirÃ- Beroun .08 .20
403 Martin CakajÃ-k .08 .20
404 Petr KuboÅ¡ .08 .20
405 Milan MikulÃ-k .08 .20
406 Roman Nemecek .08 .20
407 Ondrej Å mach .08 .20
408 Josef Straka .08 .20
409 RÃ³bert Filc .08 .20
410 Pavel MojzÃ-Å¡ .08 .20
411 Jan Peterek .08 .20
412 Radek ProchÃ¡zka .08 .20
NNO Frantisek Kaberle CL .08 .20

2004-05 Czech OFS Assist Leaders

COMPLETE SET (15) 15.00 35.00
1 Josef Beranek 1.25 3.00
2 Petr Leska 1.25 3.00
3 Peter Pucher 1.25 3.00
4 Josef Straka 1.25 3.00
5 Jan Marek 1.25 3.00
6 Zdenek Pavelek 1.25 3.00
7 Jiri Dopita 1.25 3.00
8 Jiri Burger 1.25 3.00
9 Martin Hamrlik 1.25 3.00
10 Michal Bros 1.25 3.00
11 Pavel Janku 1.25 3.00
12 Marek Uram 1.25 3.00
13 Tomas Divisek 1.25 3.00
14 Dusan Andrasovsky 1.25 3.00
15 Petr Sykora 1.25 3.00

2004-05 Czech OFS Checklist Cards

COMPLETE SET 10.00 25.00
1 Petr Buzek .75 2.00
2 Frantisek Ptacek .75 2.00
3 Jaromir Jagr 2.00 5.00
4 Patrik Rozsival .75 2.00
5 Martin Skoula .75 2.00
6 Milan Hejduk 1.25 3.00
7 Jaroslav Spacek .75 2.00
8 Zigmund Palffy 1.25 3.00
9 Petr Nedved .75 2.00
10 Radek Bonk .75 2.00
11 David Moravec .75 2.00
12 Rostislav Klesla .75 2.00
13 Petr Cajanek .75 2.00
14 Patrik Elias 1.25 3.00

2004-05 Czech OFS Czech/Slovak

COMPLETE SET (46) 20.00 40.00
1 Jaroslav Balastik .75 2.00
2 Jiri Burger .40 1.00
3 Tomas Demel .40 1.00
4 Michal Dobron .40 1.00
5 Jiri Dopita .40 1.00
6 Tomas Duba .40 1.00
7 Martin Chabada .40 1.00
8 Waldemar Jirus .40 1.00
9 Jiri Malinsky .40 1.00
10 Jan Novak .40 1.00
11 Frantisek Ptacek .40 1.00
12 Peter Pucher .40 1.00
13 Petr Sailer .40 1.00
14 Jan Srdinko .40 1.00
15 Josef Straka .40 1.00
16 Michal Sup .40 1.00
17 Adam Svoboda .75 2.00
18 Michal Sykora .40 1.00
19 Petr Sykora .40 1.00
20 Michal Travnicek .40 1.00
21 Marek Uram .40 1.00
22 Libor Zabransky .40 1.00
23 Daniel Babka .40 1.00
24 Martin Bartek .40 1.00
25 Zdeno Ciger .40 1.00
26 Peter Fabus .40 1.00
27 Miroslav Hala .40 1.00
28 Juraj Halaj .40 1.00
29 Richard Hartmann .40 1.00
30 Jiri Hes .40 1.00
31 Martin Ivicic .40 1.00
32 Juraj Kledrowetz .40 1.00
33 Jaroslav Kmit .40 1.00
34 Arne Krotak .40 1.00
35 Roman Kukumberg .40 1.00
36 Igor Majesky .40 1.00
37 Petr Pavlas .40 1.00
38 Slavomir Pavlicko .40 1.00
39 Pavol Rybar .40 1.00
40 Michal Segla .40 1.00
41 Richard Sechny .40 1.00
42 Marcel Simurda .40 1.00
43 Tomas Starosta .40 1.00
44 Rastislav Stork .40 1.00
45 Adam Svoboda CL .75 2.00
46 Pavol Rybar CL .40 1.00

2004-05 Czech OFS Defence Points

COMPLETE SET (15) 15.00 25.00
1 Martin Hamrlik 1.00 2.50
2 David Havir 1.00 2.50
3 Jan Novak 1.00 2.50
4 Stanislav Jasecko 1.00 2.50
5 Michal Sykora 1.00 2.50
6 Josef Reznicek 1.00 2.50
7 Frantisek Ptacek 1.00 2.50
8 Alexej Jaskin 1.00 2.50
9 Valdemar Jirus 1.00 2.50
10 Petr Kadlec 1.00 2.50
11 Jiri Malinsky 1.00 2.50
12 Patrik Luza 1.00 2.50
13 Radim Tesarik 1.00 2.50
14 Pavel Kowalczyk 1.00 2.50
15 Petr Jancarik 1.00 2.50

2004-05 Czech OFS Goals-Against Leaders

COMPLETE SET (16) 25.00 60.00
1 Igor Murin 2.00 5.00
2 Adam Svoboda 2.50 6.00
3 Petr Briza 2.00 5.00
4 Jiri Trvaj 2.00 5.00
5 Roman Malek 2.00 5.00
6 Petr Franek 2.00 5.00
7 Radovan Biegl 2.00 5.00
8 Tomas Duba 2.00 5.00
9 Zdenek Orct 2.00 5.00
10 Lukas Hronek 2.00 5.00
11 Martin Vojtek 2.00 5.00
12 Martin Altrichter 2.00 5.00
13 Oldrich Svoboda 2.00 5.00
14 Michal Marik 2.00 5.00
15 Marek Pinc 2.00 5.00
NNO Altrichter/Murin CL 2.00 5.00

2004-05 Czech OFS Goals Leaders

COMPLETE SET (15) 12.00 30.00
1 Jaroslav Balastik 1.50 4.00
2 Michal Sup 1.00 2.50
3 Marek Uram 1.00 2.50
4 Josef Straka 1.00 2.50
5 Jiri Burger 1.00 2.50
6 Petr Sykora 1.00 2.50
7 Marek Melenovsky 1.00 2.50
8 Jan Marek 1.00 2.50
9 Lukas Havel 1.00 2.50
10 Jiri Dopita 1.00 2.50
11 Tomas Divisek 1.00 2.50
12 Peter Barinka 1.00 2.50
13 Zbynek Irgl 1.00 2.50
14 David Hruska 1.00 2.50
15 Ondrej Vesely 1.00 2.50

2004-05 Czech OFS Jaromir Jagr

COMPLETE SET (6) 20.00 50.00
JO1 Jaromir Jagr 4.00 10.00
JO2 Jaromir Jagr 4.00 10.00
JO3 Jaromir Jagr 4.00 10.00
JO4 Jaromir Jagr 4.00 10.00
JO5 Jaromir Jagr 4.00 10.00
JO6 Jaromir Jagr 4.00 10.00

2004-05 Czech OFS Points Leaders

COMPLETE SET (15) 20.00 40.00
1 Josef Beranek 1.25 3.00
2 Petr Leska 1.25 3.00
3 Josef Straka 1.25 3.00
4 Peter Pucher 1.25 3.00
5 Jan Marek 1.25 3.00
6 Marek Uram 1.25 3.00
7 Jiri Burger 1.25 3.00
8 Jiri Dopita 1.25 3.00
9 Jaroslav Balastik 1.25 3.00
10 Petr Sykora 1.25 3.00
11 Michal Sup 1.25 3.00
12 Tomas Divisek 1.25 3.00
13 Marek Melenovsky 1.25 3.00
14 Zdenek Pavelek 1.25 3.00
15 Michal Bros 1.25 3.00

2004-05 Czech OFS Save Percentage Leaders

COMPLETE SET (15) 25.00 60.00
1 Igor Murin 2.00 5.00
2 Petr Briza 2.00 5.00
3 Zdenek Orct 2.00 5.00
4 Petr Franek 2.00 5.00
5 Roman Malek 2.00 5.00
6 Jiri Trvaj 2.00 5.00
7 Adam Svoboda 2.50 6.00
8 Radovan Biegl 2.00 5.00
9 Martin Vojtek 2.00 5.00
10 Tomas Duba 2.00 5.00
11 Martin Altrichter 2.00 5.00
12 Marek Pinc 2.00 5.00
13 Lukas Hronek 2.00 5.00
14 Libor Barta 2.00 5.00
15 Michal Marik 2.00 5.00

2004-05 Czech OFS Stars

COMPLETE SET (51) 30.00 60.00
1 Tomas Kaberle .75 2.00
2 Jaromir Jagr 4.00 10.00
3 Radim Vrbata 1.25 3.00
4 Vaclav Nedorost .75 2.00
5 Tomas Kurka .40 1.00
6 Martin Rucinsky .40 1.00
7 Martin Skoula .40 1.00
8 Robert Reichel .40 1.00
9 Jiri Slegr .40 1.00
10 Jan Bulis .40 1.00
11 Milan Hejduk 1.50 4.00
12 Ales Hemsky 2.00 5.00
13 Jiri Dopita .40 1.00
14 Jan Lasak .75 2.00
15 Martin Straka .40 1.00
16 Jaroslav Spacek .40 1.00
17 Milan Kraft .75 2.00
18 Zigmund Palffy 1.25 3.00
19 Josef Stumpel .40 1.00
20 Josef Vasicek .40 1.00
21 Tomas Kloucek .40 1.00
22 Radek Duda .40 1.00
23 Jan Hlavac .40 1.00
24 Karel Pilar .40 1.00
25 David Vyborny .75 2.00
26 Petr Nedved .40 1.00
27 Michal Rozsival .40 1.00
28 Radek Bonk .40 1.00
29 Branislav Mezei .40 1.00
30 Martin Prusek .75 2.00
31 Marek Malik .40 1.00
32 Pavel Kubina .40 1.00
33 Vaclav Varada .40 1.00
34 Rostislav Klesla .40 1.00
35 Roman Cechmanek .40 1.00
36 Branko Radivojevic .40 1.00
37 Radovan Somik .40 1.00
38 Martin Erat .40 1.00
39 Roman Hamrlik .40 1.00
40 Petr Cajanek .40 1.00
41 Patrik Elias .75 2.00
42 Martin Havlat 1.50 4.00
43 Karel Rachunek .40 1.00
44 Tomas Vokoun 2.00 5.00
45 Petr Buzek .40 1.00
46 David Moravec .40 1.00
47 Martin Hlavacka .40 1.00
48 Ales Kotalik 1.25 3.00
49 Robert Schnabel .40 1.00
50 Michal Sivek .40 1.00
51 Jaromir Jagr CL 4.00 10.00

2004-05 Czech OFS Stars II

COMPLETE SET (8) 20.00 50.00
1 Frantisek Kaberle 1.50 4.00
2 Jan Hrdina 1.50 4.00
3 Ivan Majesky 1.50 4.00
4 Jiri Hudler 6.00 15.00
5 Connor Dunlop 1.50 4.00
6 Vladimir Vujtek 1.50 4.00
7 Josef Beranek 1.50 4.00
8 Tomas Vlasak 1.50 4.00
9 Roman Malek 1.50 4.00
10 Jan Caloun 1.50 4.00
11 JirÃ- Fischer 2.00 5.00
12 Jaroslav Modry 1.50 4.00
13 Roman Simicek 1.50 4.00
14 Tomas Harant 1.50 4.00
15 Martin Hamrlik 1.50 4.00
16 Pavel Kubina CL 1.50 4.00

2004-05 Czech OFS Team Cards

COMPLETE SET (14) 6.00 15.00
1 Jaroslav Suchan .40 1.00
2 Zdenek Smid .40 1.00
3 Zdenek Orct .75 2.00
4 Milan Hnilicka .75 2.00
5 Michal Marik .40 1.00
6 Jan Lasak 1.25 3.00
7 Tomas Duba .40 1.00
8 Petr Franek .40 1.00
9 Petr Briza .75 2.00
10 Vlastimil Lakosil .40 1.00
11 Martin Prusek .75 2.00
12 Roman Cechmanek .75 2.00
13 Martin Altrichter .40 1.00
14 Robert Slavik .40 1.00

2004 Czech World Championship Postcards

This series was issued to commemorate the 2004 World Championships, which were held in Prague and Ostrava, Czech Republic. They are postcard sized and unnumbered.

COMPLETE SET (24) 10.00 25.00
1 Josef Beranek .40 1.00
2 Roman Cechmanek .60 1.50
3 Jiri Dopita .40 1.00
4 Radek Dvorak .40 1.00
5 Radek Hamr .40 1.00
6 Roman Hamrlik .40 1.00
7 Jan Hejda .40 1.00
8 Jan Hlavac .40 1.00
9 Jaroslav Hlinka .40 1.00
10 Jaromir Jagr 2.00 5.00
11 Frantisek Kaberle .40 1.00
12 Milan Kraft .40 1.00
13 Jan Novak .40 1.00
14 Vaclav Prospal .40 1.00
15 Petr Prucha 1.50 4.00
16 Martin Rucinsky .40 1.00
17 Dusan Salficky .60 1.50
18 Jiri Slegr .40 1.00
19 Jaroslav Spacek .40 1.00
20 Martin Straka .40 1.00
21 Michal Sup .40 1.00
22 Tomas Vokoun 1.50 4.00
23 David Vyborny .60 1.50

2005 Czech World Champions Postcards

Standard postcard-sized issue was released to commemorate the Czech Republic's victory at the 2005 WC. The cards are unnumbered.

COMPLETE SET (23)
1 Frantisek Kaberle .40 1.00
2 Jiri Slegr .40 1.00
3 David Vyborny .40 1.00
4 Jiri Fischer .40 1.00
5 Jan Hlavac .40 1.00
6 Josef Vasicek .40 1.00
7 Vaclav Prospal .40 1.00
8 Vaclav Varada .40 1.00
9 Pavel Kubina .40 1.00
10 Radek Dvorak .40 1.00
11 Ales Hemsky 1.50 4.00
12 Radim Vrbata .75 2.00
13 Martin Rucinsky .40 1.00
14 Martin Straka .40 1.00
15 Jaromir Jagr 4.00 10.00
16 Marek Zidlicky .40 1.00
17 Milan Hnilicka .75 2.00
18 Petr Sykora .40 1.00
19 Tomas Kaberle .40 1.00
20 Petr Cajanek .40 1.00
21 Tomas Vokoun 2.00 5.00
22 Jaroslav Spacek .40 1.00
23 Jan Hejda .40 1.00

2005 Czech Stadion

673 Jaromir Jagr 2.00 5.00
675 Martin Havlat .40 1.00
676 Robert Reichel .40 1.00
677 Tomas Vokoun .75 2.00
678 Martin Brodeur 2.00 5.00
679 Mario Lemieux 4.00 10.00
680 Keith Tkachuk .40 1.00
681 Teemu Selanne .75 2.00
682 Ruslan Fedotenko .40 1.00
683 Nikolai Khabibulin 1.00 2.50
684 Jarome Iginla 2.00 5.00
685 Mikka Kiprusoff 1.25 3.00
686 Pavel Kubina .40 1.00
687 Vincent Lecavalier 1.50 4.00
688 Robyn Regehr .40 1.00
689 Brad Richards .75 2.00
690 Martin St. Louis .75 2.00

2005-06 Czech HC Ceski Budejovice

COMPLETE SET (16) 8.00 20.00
1 Kamil Brabenec .60 1.50
2 Petr Gregorek .60 1.50
3 Tomas Harant .60 1.50
4 Stepan Hrebejk .60 1.50
5 Viktor Hubl .60 1.50
6 Michal Hudec .60 1.50
7 Milan Kopecky .60 1.50
8 Jindrich Kotrla .60 1.50
9 Ales Kratoska .60 1.50
10 Zdenek Kutlak .60 1.50
11 Jan Moucha .60 1.50
12 Marek Posmyk .60 1.50
13 Petr Sailer .60 1.50
14 Roman Turek .75 2.00
15 Tomas Vak .60 1.50
16 Rene Vydareny .60 1.50

2005-06 Czech HC Hame Zlin

COMPLETE SET (16) 8.00 20.00
1 Martin Altrichter .60 1.50
2 Petr Barinka .60 1.50
3 Jan Benda .60 1.50
4 Miroslav Blatak .60 1.50
5 Lukas Galvas .60 1.50
6 Martin Hamrlik .60 1.50
7 Richard Kral .60 1.50
8 Petr Leska .60 1.50
9 Marek Melenovsky .60 1.50
10 Petr Mokrejs .60 1.50
11 Igor Murin .60 1.50
12 David Nosek .60 1.50
13 Miroslav Okal .60 1.50
14 Ivan Rachunek .60 1.50
15 Michal Travnicek .60 1.50
16 Martin Zahorovsky .60 1.50

2005-06 Czech HC Karlovy Vary

COMPLETE SET (16) 8.00 20.00
1 Jan Alinc .60 1.50
2 Roman Cechmanek .75 2.00
3 Miroslav Duben .60 1.50
4 Michal Dvorak .60 1.50
5 Lubomir Hurtaj .60 1.50
6 Jan Kostal .60 1.50
7 Lukas Krajicek .60 1.50
8 Petr Kumstat .60 1.50
9 Lukas Mensator .60 1.50
10 Andrej Nedorost .60 1.50
11 Ondrej Nemec .60 1.50
12 Lukas Pech .60 1.50
13 Frantisek Ptacek .60 1.50
14 Josef Reznicek .60 1.50
15 Vaclav Skuhravy .60 1.50
16 Libor Ustrnul .60 1.50

2005-06 Czech HC Kladno

COMPLETE SET (15) 109.00 25.00
1 Jan Besser .60 1.50
2 Martin Frolik .60 1.50
3 Michael Frolik 2.00 5.00
4 Radek Gardon .60 1.50
5 Tomas Horna .60 1.50
6 Ivan Huml 1.00 2.50
7 Jaroslav Kalla .60 1.50
8 Jakub Lev .60 1.50
9 Zdenek Orct .75 2.00
10 Libor Prochazka .60 1.50
11 Martin Prochazka .60 1.50
12 Jaroslav Spelda .60 1.50
13 Ladislav Vlcek .60 1.50
14 Josef Zajic .60 1.50
15 Jiri Zeman .60 1.50

2005-06 Czech HC Liberec

COMPLETE SET (16) 8.00 20.00
1 Leos Cermak .60 1.50
2 Pavel Falta .60 1.50
3 Jiri Hanzlik .60 1.50
4 Milan Hnilicka .75 2.00
5 Valdemar Jirus .60 1.50
6 Angel Krstev .60 1.50
7 Lukas Pabiska .60 1.50
8 Andrej Podkonicky .60 1.50
9 Stanislav Prochazka .60 1.50
10 Igor Rataj .60 1.50
11 Martin Richtr .60 1.50
12 Patrik Rozsival .60 1.50
13 Martin Rygl .60 1.50
14 Jan Tomajko .60 1.50
15 Lubomir Vaic .60 1.50
16 Petr Vampola .60 1.50

2005-06 Czech HC Pardubice

COMPLETE SET (16) 8.00 20.00
1 Tomas Blazek .60 1.50
2 Jan Caloun .60 1.50
3 Petr Caslava .60 1.50
4 David Havir .60 1.50
5 Robert Kantor .60 1.50
6 Jan Kolar .60 1.50
7 Lubomir Korhon .60 1.50
8 Jan Lasak 1.25 3.00
9 Ladislav Lubina .60 1.50
10 Michal Mikeska .60 1.50
11 Frantisek Mrazek .60 1.50
12 Petr Mudroch .75 2.00
13 Andrej Novotny .75 2.00
14 Tomas Rolinek .60 1.50
15 Jan Snopek .60 1.50
16 Michal Tvrdik .60 1.50

2005-06 Czech HC Plzen

COMPLETE SET (16) 8.00 20.00
1 Martin Adamsky .60 1.50
2 Mario Cartelli .60 1.50
3 Michal Duras .60 1.50
4 Petr Jez .60 1.50
5 Robert Jindrich .60 1.50
6 Jaroslav Kracik .60 1.50
7 Roman Malek .60 1.50
8 Radek Matejovsky .60 1.50
9 David Moravec .60 1.50
10 Martin Stepanek .60 1.50
11 Josef Straka .60 1.50
12 Michal Straka .60 1.50
13 Pavel Trnka .60 1.50
14 Matej Trojovsky .60 1.50
15 Roman Tvrdon .60 1.50
16 Marek Vorel .60 1.50

2005-06 Czech HC Slavia Praha

COMPLETE SET (16) 8.00 20.00
1 Jaroslav Bednar .60 1.50
2 Josef Beranek .60 1.50
3 Roman Cervenka .60 2.00
4 Radek Dlouhy .60 1.50
5 Jiri Drtina .60 1.50
6 Radek Duda .60 1.50
7 Petr Franek .60 1.50
8 David Hruska .60 1.50
9 Petr Kadlec .60 1.50
10 Pavel Kolarik .60 1.50
11 Jan Novak .60 1.50
12 Michal Sup .60 1.50
13 Tomas Vlasak .60 1.50
14 Michal Vondrka .60 1.50
15 Boris Zabka .60 1.50
16 Tomas Zizka .60 1.50

2005-06 Czech HC Sparta Praha

COMPLETE SET (16) 8.00 20.00
1 Petr Briza 1.25 3.00
2 Marek Cernosek .60 1.50
3 Michal Dobron .60 1.50
4 Jan Hanzlik .60 1.50
5 Martin Hlavacka .60 1.50
6 Martin Chabada .60 1.50
7 Ondrej Kratena .60 1.50
8 Jan Marek .60 1.50
9 Jakub Sindel .60 1.50
10 Michal Sivek .75 2.00
11 Martin Spanhel .75 2.00
12 Josef Straka .60 1.50
13 Milan Toman .60 1.50

14 Petr Ton	.60	1.50
15 Roman Vopat	.60	1.50
16 Jiri Vykoukal	.60	1.50

2005-06 Czech HC Trinec

COMPLETE SET (15)	8.00	20.00
1 Richard Bordowski	.60	1.50
2 Lukas Danecek	.60	1.50
3 Jiri Hasek	.60	1.50
4 Jiri Hunkes	.60	1.50
5 Tomas Jurdic	.60	1.50
6 Jaroslav Kudrna	.60	1.50
7 Tomas Pacal	.60	1.50
8 Jan Peterek	.60	1.50
9 Lubomir Pistek	.60	1.50
10 Vaclav Pletka	1.00	2.50
11 Jiri Polansky	.60	1.50
12 Radim Tesarik	.60	1.50
13 David Vsetecka	.60	1.50
14 Martin Vojtek	.60	1.50
15 Tomas Zboril	.60	1.50

2005-06 Czech HC Vitkovice

COMPLETE SET (16)	8.00	20.00
1 Jiri Burger	.60	1.50
2 Jan Dresler	.60	1.50
3 Petr Hubacek	.60	1.50
4 Stanislav Hudec	.60	1.50
5 Jakub Hulva	.60	1.50
6 Zbynek Irgl	.60	1.50
7 Petr Jurecka	.60	1.50
8 Jaroslav Kames	.75	2.00
9 Bedrich Kohler	.60	1.50
10 Lukas Krenzelok	.60	1.50
11 Radoslav Kropac	.60	1.50
12 Radek Philipp	.60	1.50
13 Marek Pinc	.75	2.00
14 Radek Prochazka	.60	1.50
15 Roman Simicek	.60	1.50
16 Martin Tomasek	.60	1.50

2005-06 Czech HC Vsetin

COMPLETE SET (15)	8.00	20.00
1 Richard Bauer	.60	1.50
2 Tomas Demel	.60	1.50
3 Roman Gorev	.60	1.50
4 Michal Horak	.60	1.50
5 Josef Hrabal	.60	1.50
6 Ondrej Hruska	.60	1.50
7 Radim Hruska	.60	1.50
8 Josef Kucera	.60	1.50
9 David Kveton	.60	1.50
10 Havi Sasu	.60	1.50
11 Zdenek Spitzer	.60	1.50
12 Roman Stantien	.60	1.50
13 Filip Stefanka	.60	1.50
14 Ondrej Steiner	.60	1.50
15 Patrik Luza	.60	1.50

2005-06 Czech HC Znojmo

COMPLETE SET (14)	8.00	20.00
1 Radim Bicanek	.60	1.50
2 Martin Cakajik	.60	1.50
3 Jiri Dopita	.60	1.50
4 Roman Erat	.60	1.50
5 Radek Haman	.60	1.50
6 Richard Jares	.60	1.50
7 Ales Kretinsky	.60	1.50
8 Milan Ministr	.60	1.50
9 Pavel Mojzis	.60	1.50
10 Zdenek Ondrej	.60	1.50
11 Karel Plasek	.60	1.50
12 Peter Pucher	.60	1.50
13 Jiri Trvaj	.60	1.50
14 Marek Uram	.60	1.50

2006-07 Czech CP Cup Postcards

COMPLETE SET (23)	20.00	40.00
1 Miroslav Blatak	.75	2.00
2 Jiri Burger	.75	2.00
3 Radek Hamr	.75	2.00
4 Jaroslav Hlinka	.75	2.00
5 Milan Hnilicka	1.25	3.00
6 Miloslav Horava	.75	2.00
7 Petr Hubacek	.75	2.00
8 Jiri Hunkes	.75	2.00
9 Martin Chabada	.75	2.00
10 Zbynek Irgl	.75	2.00
11 Zdenek Kutlak	.75	2.00
12 Roman Malek	.75	2.00
13 Jan Marek	.75	2.00
14 Josef Marha	.75	2.00
15 Vaclav Pletka	.75	2.00
16 Tomas Rolinek	.75	2.00
17 Michal Sivek	.75	2.00
18 Vaclav Skuhravy	.75	2.00
19 Petr Sykora	.75	2.00
20 Martin Sevc	.75	2.00
21 Ivan Rachunek	.75	2.00
22 Lukas Zib	.75	2.00
23 Tomas Zizka	.75	2.00

2006-07 Czech HC Ceske Budejovice Postcards

COMPLETE SET (14)	15.00	25.00
1 Petr Gregorek	.75	2.00
2 Viktor Hubl	.75	2.00
3 Michal Hudec	.75	2.00
4 Jindrich Kotrla	.75	2.00
5 Jan Mucha	.75	2.00
6 Vaclav Nedorost	1.25	3.00
7 Petr Sailer	.75	2.00
8 Jiri Simanek	.75	2.00
9 Milan Toman	.75	2.00
10 Roman Turek	1.25	3.00
11 Martin Vagner	.75	2.00
12 Tomas Vak	.75	2.00
13 Ondrej Vesely	.75	2.00
14 Rene Vydareny	.75	2.00

2006-07 Czech HC Kladno Postcards

It is quite likely that this checklist is incomplete. If you know if additional postcards, please email us at hockeymag@beckett.com.

COMPLETE SET (11)	10.00	20.00
1 Ales Pavlas	.75	2.00
2 Jakub Lev	.75	2.00
3 Jaroslav Kalla	.75	2.00
4 Martin Frolik	.75	2.00
5 Martin Prochazka	.75	2.00
6 Martin Sevc	.75	2.00
7 Michal Havel	.75	2.00
8 Milan Hluchy	.75	2.00
9 Pavel Patera	.75	2.00
10 Radek Gardon	.75	2.00
11 Zdenek Orct	1.25	3.00

2006-07 Czech HC Liberec Postcards

It is likely this checklist is incomplete. Please forward additional information to hockeymag@beckett.com.

COMPLETE SET (12)	10.00	20.00
1 Jakub Cutta	.75	2.00
2 Ondrej Hruska	.75	2.00
3 Waldemar Jirus	.75	2.00
4 Angel Krstev	.75	2.00
5 Michal Nedvidek	.75	2.00
6 Vaclav Novak	.75	2.00
7 Vaclav Pletka	.75	2.00
8 Filip Sindelar	.75	2.00
9 Jan Tomajko	.75	2.00
10 Lubomir Vaic	.75	2.00
11 Jan Visek	.75	2.00
12 Lukas Zib	.75	2.00

2006-07 Czech HC Pardubice Postcards

COMPLETE SET (23)	20.00	40.00
1 Dusan Andrasovsky	.75	2.00
2 Tomas Blazek	1.25	3.00
3 Jan Caloun	1.25	3.00
4 Petr Caslava	.75	2.00
5 David Havir	.75	2.00
6 Miroslav Hlinka	.75	2.00
7 Jan Kolar	.75	2.00
8 Jaroslav Koma	.75	2.00
9 Petr Koukal	.75	2.00
10 Vladislav Koutsky	.75	2.00
11 Jan Lasak	1.25	3.00
12 Tomas Linhart	.75	2.00
13 Frantisek Mrazek	.75	2.00
14 Andrej Novotny	.75	2.00
15 Ales Pisa	.75	2.00
16 Libor Pivko	.75	2.00
17 Tomas Rolinek	.75	2.00
18 Michal Seda	.75	2.00
19 Jan Snopek	.75	2.00
20 Adam Svoboda	1.25	3.00
21 Petr Sykora	.75	2.00
22 Michal Tvrdik	.75	2.00
23 Jan Stary	.75	2.00

2006-07 Czech HC Plzen Postcards

COMPLETE SET (16)	15.00	30.00
1 Adam Saffer	.75	2.00
2 Ales Padelek	.75	2.00
3 David Ludvik	.75	2.00
4 Jiri Malinsky	.75	2.00
5 Jiri Zelenka	.75	2.00
6 Lukas Derner	.75	2.00
7 Lukas Pulpan	.75	2.00
8 Roman Malek	1.25	3.00
9 Martin Adamsky	.75	2.00
10 Michal Duras	.75	2.00
11 Milan Nedoma	.75	2.00
12 Peter Fabus	.75	2.00
13 Petr Jez	.75	2.00
14 Tomas Divisek	.75	2.00
15 Tomas Kubalik	.75	2.00
16 Vaclav Benak	.75	2.00

2006-07 Czech HC Slavia Praha Postcards

COMPLETE SET (16)	15.00	30.00
1 Jaroslav Bednar	.75	2.00
2 Josef Beranek	.75	2.00
3 Leos Cermak	.75	2.00
4 Roman Cervenka	.75	2.00
5 Radek Dlouhy	.75	2.00
6 Jiri Drtina	.75	2.00
7 Dominik Granak	.75	2.00
8 Martin Hlavacka	.75	2.00
9 David Hruska	.75	2.00
10 Pavel Kolarik	.75	2.00
11 Igor Rataj	.75	2.00
12 Vladimir Sobotka	.75	2.00
13 Michal Sup	.75	2.00
14 Adam Svoboda	1.25	3.00
15 Tomas Vlasak	.75	2.00
16 Tomas Zizka	.75	2.00

2006-07 Czech HC Sparta Praha Postcards

COMPLETE SET (15)	15.00	30.00
1 Ladislav Benysek	.75	2.00
2 Marek Cernosek	.75	2.00
3 David Vrbata	.75	2.00
4 Dusan Salficky	1.25	3.00
5 Frantisek Ptacek	.75	2.00
6 Jan Hanzlik	.75	2.00
7 Jan Hlavac	1.25	3.00
8 Jaroslav Hlinka	.75	2.00
9 Jakub Langhammer	.75	2.00
10 Michal Sivek	1.25	3.00
11 Ondrej Kratena	.75	2.00
12 Petr Ton	.75	2.00
13 Martin Strba	.75	2.00
14 Tomas Netik	.75	2.00
15 Tomas Protivny	.75	2.00

2006-07 Czech HC Vsetin Postcards

This set is likely to be incomplete. If you have additional information, please email hockeymag@beckett.com.

COMPLETE SET (12)	10.00	
1 Lukas Bolf	.75	2.00
2 Guntis Galvins	.75	2.00
3 Josef Hrabal	.75	2.00
4 Jiri Kucny	.75	2.00
5 Lukas Duba	.75	2.00
6 Lubos Rob	.75	2.00
7 Lubomir Sabol	.75	2.00
8 Vladimir Skoda	.75	2.00
9 Lubomir Stach	.75	2.00
10 Roman Stantien	.75	2.00
11 Martin Stefl	.75	2.00
12 Tomas Demel	.75	2.00

2006-07 Czech HC Zlin Hame Postcards

COMPLETE SET (15)	15.00	30.00
1 Martin Cech	.75	2.00
2 Martin Hamrlik	.75	2.00
3 Jan Horacek	.75	2.00
4 Robin Kovar	.75	2.00
5 Jaroslav Kristek	.75	2.00
6 Pavel Kubis	.75	2.00
7 Petr Leska	.75	2.00
8 Marek Melenovsky	1.25	3.00
9 Igor Murin	.75	2.00
10 Roman Psurny	.75	2.00
11 Ivan Rachunek	.75	2.00
12 Robert Tomik	.75	2.00
13 Lubomir Sekeras	.75	2.00
14 Martin Zahorovsky	.75	2.00
15 Pavel Zubicek	.75	2.00

2006-07 Czech IIHF World Championship Postcards

COMPLETE SET (23)	20.00	40.00
1 Jaroslav Balastik	.75	2.00
2 Jaroslav Bednar	.60	1.50
3 Jan Bulis	.60	1.50
4 Martin Erat	.60	1.50
5 Jan Hejda	.60	1.50
6 Jan Hlavac	.60	1.50
7 Jaroslav Hlinka	.60	1.50
8 Milan Hnilicka	.75	2.00
9 Petr Hubacek	.60	1.50
10 Zbynek Irgl	.60	1.50
11 Tomas Kaberle	.75	2.00
12 Lukas Krajicek	.75	2.00
13 Zdenek Kutlak	.60	1.50
14 Zbynek Michalek	.60	1.50
15 Tomas Plekanec	1.25	3.00
16 Ivo Prorok	.60	1.50
17 Martin Richter	.60	1.50
18 Tomas Rolinek	.60	1.50
19 Martin Skoula	.60	1.50
20 Patrik Stefan	.60	1.50
21 Adam Svoboda	.60	1.50
22 Petr Tenkrat	.60	1.50
23 David Vyborny	.75	2.00

2006-07 Czech LG Hockey Games Postcards

COMPLETE SET (22)	15.00	30.00
1 Jaroslav Balastik	.75	2.00
2 Jaroslav Bednar	.40	1.00
3 Miroslav Blatak	.40	1.00
4 Petr Hubacek	.40	1.00
5 Jiri Hunkes	.40	1.00
6 Zbynek Irgl	.75	2.00
7 Jaroslav Kracik	.40	1.00
8 Lukas Krajicek	.75	2.00
9 Jaroslav Kudrna	.75	2.00
10 Zdenek Kutlak	.40	1.00
11 Jan Marek	.40	1.00
12 Zbynek Michalek	.40	1.00
13 Jan Novak	.40	1.00
14 Jan Peterek	.40	1.00
15 Tomas Popperle	.75	2.00
16 Ivo Prorok	.40	1.00
17 Tomas Rolinek	.40	1.00
18 Martin Sevc	.40	1.00
19 Martin Skoula	.40	1.00
20 Patrik Stefan	.40	1.00
21 Adam Svoboda	.75	2.00
22 Petr Tenkrat	.40	1.00

2006-07 Czech OFS

COMPLETE SET (326)	75.00	125.00
1 Kamil Brabenec	.20	.50
2 Petr Gregorek	.20	.50
3 Milan Gulas	.20	.50
4 Stepan Hrebejk	.20	.50
5 Viktor Hubl	.20	.50
6 Michal Hudec	.20	.50
7 Jan Chabera	.30	.75
8 Jindrich Kotrla	.20	.50
9 Zdenek Kutlak	.30	.75
10 Lukas Kveton	.20	.50
11 Petr Machacek	.20	.50
12 Jan Mucha	.20	.50
13 Vaclav Nedorost	.40	1.00
14 Marek Posmyk	.30	.75
15 Petr Sailer	.20	.50
16 Jiri Simanek	.20	.50
17 Milan Toman	.20	.50
18 Roman Turek	.40	1.00
19 Martin Vagner	.30	.75
20 Tomas Vak	.20	.50
21 Ondrej Vesely	.20	.50
22 Rene Vydareny	.20	.50
23 David Balasz	.20	.50
24 Michal Borovansky	.20	.50
25 Michal Dobron	.20	.50
26 Miroslav Duben	.20	.50
27 Michal Dvorak	.20	.50
28 Jiri Hanzlik	.20	.50
29 Vojtech Kloz	.20	.50
30 Jan Kostal	.20	.50
31 Milan Kraft	.40	1.00
32 Petr Kumstat	.20	.50
33 Vladimir Machulda	.20	.50
34 Lukas Mensator	.30	.75
35 Petr Mudroch	.20	.50
36 Ondrej Nemec	.20	.50
37 Lukas Pech	.20	.50
38 Milan Prochazka	.20	.50
39 Josef Reznicek	.20	.50
40 Lukas Sablik	.30	.75
41 Frantisek Skladany	.20	.50
42 Vaclav Skuhravy	.20	.50
43 Kamil Tvrdek	.20	.50
44 Libor Ustrnul	.30	.75
45 Jiri Burger	.20	.50
46 Jan Dresler	.20	.50
47 Michal Gulasi	.20	.50
48 Petr Hubacek	.20	.50
49 Stanislav Hudec	.20	.50
50 Lukas Chmelir	.20	.50
51 Zbynek Irgl	.30	.75
52 Stanislav Jasecko	.20	.50
53 Petr Jurecka	.20	.50
54 Tomas Kana	.20	.50
55 Bedrich Kohler	.20	.50
56 Lukas Krenzelok	.20	.50
57 Radoslav Kropac	.20	.50
58 Petr Kubos	.20	.50
59 Milan Mikulik	.20	.50
60 Marek Pinc	.30	.75
61 Radek Prochazka	.20	.50
62 Filip Seman	.20	.50
63 Roman Simicek	.20	.50
64 Jakub Stepanek	.30	.75
65 Martin Tomasek	.20	.50
66 Lukas Klimek	.20	.50
67 Jiri Vykoukal	.20	.50
68 David Vrbata	.20	.50
69 Petr Ton	.20	.50
70 Jan Tabacek	.20	.50
71 Michal Sivek	.40	1.00
72 Dusan Salficky	.60	1.50
73 Frantisek Ptacek	.20	.50
74 Petr Prikryl	.30	.75
75 Tomas Protivny	.20	.50
76 Martin Podlesak	.20	.50
77 Tomas Netik	.20	.50
78 Jaroslav Mrazek	.20	.50
79 Jakub Langhammer	.20	.50
80 Ondrej Kratena	.30	.75
81 Karel Hromas	.20	.50
82 Jaroslav Hlinka	.20	.50
83 Jan Hlavac	.40	1.00
84 Jan Hanzlik	.20	.50
85 Michal Dragoun	.20	.50
86 Marek Cernosek	.20	.50
87 Ladislav Benysek	.20	.50
88 Jan Holub	.20	.50
89 Ondrej Hruska	.20	.50
90 Ctibor Jech	.20	.50
91 Valdemar Jirus	.20	.50
92 Tomas Klimenta	.20	.50
93 Vaclav Koci	.20	.50
94 Angel Krstev	.20	.50
95 Jiri Moravec	.20	.50
96 Michal Nedvidek	.30	.75
97 Lukas Pabiska	.20	.50
98 Rok Pajic	.20	.50
99 Vaclav Pletka	.30	.75
100 Jan Plodek	.20	.50
101 Andrej Podkonicky	.20	.50
102 Stanislav Prochazka	.20	.50
103 Jiri Stejskal	.30	.75
104 Petr Sachl	.20	.50
105 Lubomir Vaic	.20	.50
106 Petr Vampola	.20	.50
107 Jan Visek	.20	.50
108 Lukas Zib	.20	.50
109 Boris Zabka	.20	.50
110 Dusan Andrasovsky	.20	.50
111 Tomas Blazek	.20	.50
112 Jan Caloun	.30	.75
113 Petr Caslava	.20	.50
114 David Havir	.20	.50
115 Miroslav Hlinka	.20	.50
116 Jan Kolar	.20	.50
117 Jaroslav Koma	.20	.50
118 Petr Koukal	.20	.50
119 Vladislav Koutsky	.30	.75
120 Jan Lasak	.75	2.00
121 Tomas Linhart	.20	.50
122 Andrej Novotny	.20	.50
123 Zdenek Ondrej	.20	.50
124 Tomas Rolinek	.20	.50
125 Jan Snopek	.20	.50
126 Petr Sykora	.20	.50
127 Michal Seda	.20	.50
128 Lukas Bednarik	.20	.50
129 Jan Benda	.20	.50
130 Frantisek Bombic	.20	.50
131 Daniel Branda	.20	.50
132 Jakub Cerny	.20	.50
133 Vladimir Gyna	.20	.50
134 Jan Hranac	.20	.50
135 Jaroslav Hubl	.30	.75
136 Peter Jansky	.20	.50
137 Martin Jenacek	.20	.50
138 Milan Kopecky	.20	.50
139 Vojtech Kubincak	.20	.50
140 Frantisek Lukes	.20	.50
141 Marian Morava	.20	.50
142 Angel Nikolov	.20	.50
143 Lukas Pozivil	.20	.50
144 Ivo Prorok	.20	.50
145 Robert Reichel	.40	1.00
146 Zbynek Sklenicka	.20	.50
147 Radim Skuhrovec	.20	.50
140 Jiri Slcgr	.30	.75
149 Michal Travnicek	.20	.50
150 Michal Podolka	.40	1.00
151 Jaroslav Barton	.20	.50
152 Radovan Biegl	.30	.75
153 Jan Danecek	.20	.50
154 Lukas Danecek	.40	1.00
155 Tomas Frolo	.20	.50
156 Jiri Hasek	.20	.50
157 Alexandr Hegegy	.20	.50
158 Marcin Kolusz	.20	.50
159 Lubomir Korhon	.20	.50
160 Vlastimil Kroupa	.20	.50
161 Jaroslav Kudrna	.20	.50
162 Rostislav Martynek	.20	.50
163 Tomas Pacal	.20	.50
164 Jan Peterek	.20	.50
165 Jiri Polansky	.20	.50
166 Tomaz Razingar	.20	.50
167 Zdenek Skorepa	.20	.50
168 Radim Tesarik	.20	.50
169 Roman Tomas	.20	.50
170 Tomas Vrba	.20	.50
171 Jan Vytisk	.20	.50
172 Stefan Zigardy	.30	.75
173 Armands Berzins	.20	.50
174 Lukas Bolf	.20	.50
175 Martin Davidek	.20	.50
176 Tomas Demel	.20	.50
177 Lukas Duba	.20	.50
178 Marek Dubec	.20	.50
179 Guntis Galvins	.20	.50
180 Marek Grill	.20	.50
181 Michal Horak	.20	.50
182 Josef Hrabal	.20	.50
183 Jakub Kraus	.20	.50
184 Jiri Kucny	.20	.50
185 David Kveton	.20	.50
186 Radim Ostrcil	.20	.50
187 Lubos Rob	.20	.50
188 Lubomir Sabol	.20	.50
189 Petr Sakrajda	.20	.50
190 Roman Stantien	.20	.50
191 Matej Stritesky	.20	.50
192 Vladimir Skoda	.20	.50
193 Lubomir Stach	.20	.50
194 Martin Stefl	.20	.50
195 Simo Vehvilainen	.30	.75
196 Dusan Brincko	.20	.50
197 Waldemar Pelikovsky	.20	.50
198 Jiri Beroun	.20	.50
199 Radim Bicanek	.20	.50
200 Martin Cakajik	.20	.50
201 Jiri Dopita	.30	.75
202 Roman Erat	.20	.50
203 Radek Haman	.20	.50
204 Christoph Harand	.20	.50
205 Richard Jares	.20	.50
206 Ivo Kotaska	.20	.50
207 Radim Kucharczyk	.20	.50
208 Pavel Mojzis	.20	.50
209 Roman Nemecek	.20	.50
210 Karel Plasek	.20	.50
211 Peter Pucher	.20	.50
212 Martin Ruzicka	.20	.50
213 Pavel Selingr	.20	.50
214 Jaroslav Svoboda	.20	.50
215 Ondrej Smach	.20	.50
216 Jiri Trvaj	.30	.75
217 David Turon	.20	.50
218 Lubomir Vaskovic	.20	.50
219 David Adamec	.30	.75
220 Stanislav Balan	.20	.50
221 Jakub Cech	.30	.75
222 Martin Cech	.20	.50
223 Lukas Galvas	.20	.50
224 Martin Hamrlik	.20	.50
225 Jan Horacek	.20	.50
226 Pavel Kasparik	.20	.50
227 Robin Kovar	.20	.50
228 Jaroslav Kristek	.20	.50
229 Pavel Kubis	.20	.50
230 Petr Leska	.20	.50
231 Martin Lucka	.20	.50
232 Jiri Marusak	.20	.50
233 Marek Melenovsky	.20	.50
234 Pavel Mokrejs	.20	.50
235 Igor Murin	.30	.75
236 David Nosek	.20	.50
237 Miroslav Okal	.20	.50
238 Michal Psurny	.20	.50
239 Roman Psurny	.20	.50
240 Ivan Rachunek	.20	.50
241 Dalibor Sedlar	.30	.75
242 Lubomir Sekeras	.20	.50
243 Robert Tomik	.20	.50
244 Lubomir Vosatko	.20	.50
245 Martin Zahorovsky	.20	.50
246 Pavel Zubicek	.20	.50
247 Vitezslav Bilek	.20	.50
248 Vratislav Cech	.20	.50
249 Marek Curilla	.20	.50
250 Richard Divis	.20	.50
251 Martin Frolik	.20	.50
252 Radek Gardon	.20	.50
253 David Hajek	.20	.50
254 Michal Havel	.20	.50
255 Milan Hluchy	.20	.50
256 Tomas Horna	.20	.50
257 Petr Jaros	.20	.50
258 Jaroslav Kalla	.20	.50
259 Jiri Kuchler	.20	.50
260 Jakub Lev	.30	.75
261 Zdenek Orct	.30	.75
262 Pavel Patera	.20	.50
263 Ales Pavlas	.20	.50
264 Libor Prochazka	.20	.50
265 Martin Prochazka	.20	.50
266 Martin Sevc	.20	.50
267 Martin Stepanek	.20	.50
268 Jiri Zeman	.20	.50
269 Vaclav Benak	.20	.50
270 Mario Cartelli	.20	.50
271 Michal Duraz	.20	.50
272 Jan Herman	.20	.50
273 Petr Jez	.30	.75
274 Richard Kepl	.20	.50
275 Richard Kral	.20	.50
276 Roman Malek	.30	.75
277 Jiri Malinsky	.20	.50
278 Radek Matejovsky	.20	.50
279 David Mazanec	.20	.50
280 Milan Nedoma	.20	.50
281 Ales Padelek	.20	.50
282 Igor Rataj	.20	.50
283 Adam Saffer	.20	.50
284 Jakub Sindel	.20	.50
285 Pavel Trnka	.20	.50
286 Milan Voboril	.20	.50
287 Jiri Zelenka	.20	.50
288 Jaroslav Bednar	.40	1.00
289 Josef Beranek	.20	.50
290 Roman Cervenka	.20	.50
291 Tomas Divisek	.40	1.00
292 Radek Dlouhy	.20	.50
293 Jiri Drtina	.20	.50
294 Petr Franek	.30	.75
295 Dominik Granak	.20	.50
296 Lukas Hronek	.30	.75
297 David Hruska	.20	.50
298 Jiri Jebavy	.20	.50
299 Petr Kadlec	.20	.50
300 David Pojkar	.20	.50
301 Vladimir Ruzicka	.20	.50
302 Jakub Sklenar	.20	.50
303 Vladimir Sobotka	.20	.50
304 Michal Sup	.20	.50
305 Tomas Spila	.20	.50
306 Tomas Vlasak	.20	.50
307 Michal Vondrka	.20	.50
308 Tomas Zizka	.20	.50
309 Radek Hubacek	.20	.50
310 Petr Tucek	.30	.75
311 Andrej Novotny	.20	.50
312 Petr Puncochar	.20	.50
313 Jan Stary	.20	.50
314 Michal Tvrdik	.20	.50
315 Libor Pivko	.20	.50
316 Jan Kolar	.20	.50
317 Martin Cech	.20	.50
318 Jan Kana	.20	.50
319 Tomas Voracek	.20	.50
320 Marek Novotny	.20	.50
321 Tomas Brnak	.20	.50
322 Martin Zatovic	.30	.75
323 Tomas Chrenko	.20	.50
324 Ales Pisa	.20	.50
325 Frantisek Mrazek	.20	.50
326 Josef Kucera	.20	.50

2006-07 Czech OFS All Stars

1 Milan Hnilicka	2.00	5.00
2 Roman Malek	2.00	5.00
3 Jan Novak	1.50	4.00
4 Miroslav Blatak	1.50	4.00
5 Frantisek Ptacek	1.50	4.00
6 Josef Reznicek	1.50	4.00
7 Radim Tesarik	1.50	4.00
8 Stanislav Hudec	1.50	4.00
9 Valdemar Jirus	1.50	4.00
10 Martin Richter	1.50	4.00
11 Ivan Rachunek	1.50	4.00
12 Lubomir Vaic	1.50	4.00
13 Petr Sykora	1.50	4.00
14 Michal Mikeska	1.50	4.00
15 Jan Marek	1.50	4.00
16 Marek Tomica	1.50	4.00
17 Jiri Burger	1.50	4.00
18 Michal Travnicek	1.50	4.00
19 Radek Gardon	1.50	4.00
20 David Moravec	1.50	4.00
21 Jan Peterek	1.50	4.00
22 Ales Kretinsky	1.50	4.00

2006-07 Czech OFS Brothers

1 Martin Herman Jan Herman	2.00	5.00
2 Jan Kana Tomas Kana	2.00	5.00
3 Lukas Danecek Jan Danecek	2.00	5.00
4 Radek Hubacek Petr Hubacek	2.00	5.00
5 Michal Psurny Roman Psurny	2.00	5.00

2006-07 Czech OFS Coaches

1 Ernest Bokros	.40	1.00
2 Milos Holan	.40	1.00
3 Miloslav Horava	.40	1.00
4 Josef Jandac	.40	1.00
5 Jiri Jurik	.40	1.00
6 Zdenek MÃ¼ller	.40	1.00
7 Josef Palecek	.40	1.00
8 Vladimir Ruzicka	.40	1.00
9 Milos Riha	.40	1.00
10 Marek Sykora	.40	1.00
11 Vaclav Sykora	.40	1.00
12 Zdenek Venera	.40	1.00
13 Rostislav Vlach	.40	1.00
14 Frantisek Vyborny	.40	1.00

2006-07 Czech OFS Defenders

1 Martin Hamrlik	.75	2.00
2 Jan Novak	.75	2.00
3 Stanislav Hudec	.75	2.00
4 Martin Richter	.75	2.00
5 Valdemar Jirus	.75	2.00
6 Petr Gregorek	.75	2.00
7 Marek Posmyk	.75	2.00
8 Martin Sevc	.75	2.00
9 Josef Reznicek	.75	2.00
10 Miroslav Blatak	.75	2.00
11 Petr Kadlec	.75	2.00
12 Radim Tesarik	.75	2.00
13 Angel Krstev	.75	2.00
14 Radim Bicanek	.75	2.00
15 Frantisek Ptacek	.75	2.00

2006-07 Czech OFS Goalies I

1 Igor Murin	2.00	5.00
2 Lukas Mensator	2.00	5.00
3 Petr Franek	2.00	5.00
4 Milan Hnilicka	2.00	5.00
5 Jiri Trvaj	2.00	5.00
6 Marek Pinc	2.00	5.00
7 Roman Malek	2.00	5.00
8 Jan Chabera	2.00	5.00
9 Radek Fiala	2.00	5.00
10 Sasu Hovi	2.00	5.00
11 Jan Lasak	2.50	6.00
12 Kamil Jarina	2.00	5.00
13 Petr Briza	2.50	6.00
14 Martin Altrichter	2.00	5.00
15 Roman Turek	2.00	5.00

2006-07 Czech OFS Goalies II

1 Milan Hnilicka	2.00	5.00
2 Igor Murin	2.00	5.00
3 Petr Franek	2.00	5.00
4 Jan Chabera	2.00	5.00
5 Jiri Trvaj	2.00	5.00
6 Lukas Mensator	2.00	5.00
7 Marek Pinc	2.00	5.00
8 Roman Turek	2.00	5.00
9 Radek Fiala	2.00	5.00
10 Roman Malek	2.00	5.00
11 Kamil Jarina	2.00	5.00
12 Martin Altrichter	2.00	5.00
13 Jan Lasak	2.50	6.00
14 Petr Briza	2.50	6.00
15 Radovan Biegl	2.00	5.00

2006-07 Czech OFS Goals Leaders

1 Petr Ton	1.25	3.00
2 Michal Sup	1.25	3.00
3 Jan Marek	1.25	3.00
4 Jaroslav Kudrna	1.25	3.00
5 Jaroslav Bednar	1.25	3.00
6 Ales Padelek	1.25	3.00
7 Lubomir Vaic	1.25	3.00
8 Jan Caloun	1.25	3.00
9 Igor Rataj	1.25	3.00
10 Peter Pucher	1.25	3.00
11 Radek Duda	1.25	3.00
12 Petr Hubacek	1.25	3.00
13 Ondrej Kratena	1.25	3.00
14 Jiri Zelenka	1.25	3.00
15 Jan Benda	1.25	3.00

2006-07 Czech OFS Jagr Team

1 Marek Schwarz	4.00	10.00
2 Jaroslav Kames	1.25	3.00
3 Jiri Tlusty	4.00	10.00
4 Petr Taticek	1.25	3.00
5 Jakub Koreis	2.00	5.00
6 Jiri Novotny	1.25	3.00
7 Lukas Krajicek	1.25	3.00
8 Martin Richter	1.25	3.00
9 Rostislav Klesla	1.25	3.00
10 Josef Melichar	1.25	3.00
11 Michal Rozsival	1.25	3.00
12 Petr Tenkrat	1.25	3.00
13 Tomas Plekanec	2.50	6.00
14 Jaroslav Hlinka	1.25	3.00
15 Jan Hrdina	1.25	3.00
16 Ales Kotalik	2.00	5.00
17 Tomas Kaberle	2.00	5.00
18 David Vyborny	1.25	3.00
19 Martin Straka	1.25	3.00
20 Martin Rucinsky	1.25	3.00
21 Jaromir Jagr	4.00	10.00
22 Jaroslav Svoboda	1.25	3.00
23 Jiri Hudler	2.50	6.00

2006-07 Czech OFS Points Leaders

1 Jan Marek	1.25	3.00
2 Lubomir Vaic	1.25	3.00
3 Josef Beranek	1.25	3.00
4 Petr Ton	1.25	3.00
5 Jaroslav Kudrna	1.25	3.00
6 Jaroslav Bednar	1.25	3.00
7 Radek Duda	1.25	3.00
8 Jan Peterek	1.25	3.00
9 Peter Pucher	1.25	3.00
10 Jan Benda	1.25	3.00
11 Petr Hubacek	1.25	3.00
12 Jan Caloun	1.25	3.00
13 Tomas Vlasak	1.25	3.00
14 Martin Strba	1.25	3.00
15 Michal Sup	1.25	3.00

2006-07 Czech OFS Stars

1 Jiri Stejskal	1.25	3.00
2 Andrej Podkonicky	1.25	3.00
3 Daniel Branda	1.25	3.00
4 Lukas Mensator	1.25	3.00
5 Milan Kraft	1.25	3.00
6 Igor Murin	1.25	3.00
7 Petr Leska	1.25	3.00
8 Martin Hamrlik	1.25	3.00
9 Roman Malek	1.25	3.00
10 Richard Kral	1.25	3.00
11 Petr Sykora	1.25	3.00
12 Miroslav Hlinka	1.25	3.00
13 Roman Turek	1.50	4.00
14 Vaclav Nedorost	1.25	3.00
15 Jiri Polansky	1.25	3.00
16 Zdenek Orct	1.50	4.00
17 Jaroslav Bednar	1.25	3.00
18 Dusan Salficky	1.50	4.00
19 Jiri Vykoukal	1.25	3.00
20 Tomas Demel	1.25	3.00
21 Martin Stefl	1.25	3.00
22 Roman Erat	1.25	3.00
23 Pavel Mojzis	1.25	3.00
24 Jiri Trvaj	1.50	4.00
25 Zbynek Irgl	1.50	4.00

2006-07 Czech OFS Team Cards

1 Roman Turek Vaclav Nedorost	1.50	4.00
2 Lukas Mansator Petr Kumstat	1.50	4.00

3 Pavel Patera 1.50 4.00
Zdenek Orct
4 Jiri Stejskal 1.50 4.00
Jan Plodek
5 Robert Reichel 1.50 4.00
Jaroslav HÃ¼bl
6 Petr Sykora 2.00 5.00
Jan Lasak
7 Jiri Zelenka 1.50 4.00
Roman Malek
8 Tomas Vlasak 1.50 4.00
Petr Franek
9 Dusan Salficky 1.50 4.00
Jaroslav Hlinka
10 Radovan Biegl 1.50 4.00
Jan Vytisk
11 Marek Pinc 1.50 4.00
Jiri Burger
12 Martin Stefl 1.50 4.00
Roman Stantien
13 Igor Murin 1.50 4.00
Petr Leska
14 Jiri Trvaj 1.50 4.00
Jiri Dopita

2006-07 Czech NHL ELH Postcards

COMPLETE SET (15) 15.00 30.00
1 Martin Havlat .75 2.00
2 Milan Hnilicka .75 2.00
3 Jan Hrdina .75 2.00
4 Milan Kraft .75 2.00
5 Pavel Kubina .75 2.00
6 Jason Marshall .75 2.00
7 Vaclav Nedorost .75 2.00
8 Zigmund Palffy 1.25 3.00
9 Michal Rozsival .75 2.00
10 Jaroslav Spacek .75 2.00
11 Josef Stumpel .75 2.00
12 Pavel Trnka .75 2.00
13 Vaclav Varada .75 2.00
14 Radim Vrbata .75 2.00
15 Josef Vasicek .75 2.00

2006-07 Czech Super Six Postcards

1 Niklas Backstrom 2.00 5.00
2 Michal Bros .75 2.00
3 Mikhail Grabovskij 1.25 3.00
4 David Havir .75 2.00
5 Miroslav Hlinka .75 2.00
6 Robert Kantor .75 2.00
7 Jan Lasak 1.25 3.00
8 Michal Mikeska .75 2.00
9 Vaclav Pletka .75 2.00
10 Tomasz Razingar 1.25 3.00
11 Tomas Rolinek .75 2.00
12 Pavel Rosa .75 2.00
13 Maxim Susinskij .75 2.00
14 Petr Tenkrat .75 2.00
15 Viktor Ujcik .75 2.00
16 Jari Viuhkola .75 2.00

1998-99 Danish Hockey League

We know little about this set, beyond the checklist provided by collector Vinnie Montalbano. As a result, we have no pricing. If you have additional information, please contact us at hockeymag@beckett.com.

COMPLETE SET (239)
1 Ola Persson
2 Kenneth Jensen
3 Jesper Skov
4 Henrik Benjaminsen
5 Mikkel Bjerrum
6 Keld Frederiksen
7 Kristian Lodberg
8 Jukka Vilander
9 Jesper Pedersen
10 Oleg Starkov
11 Soren Jensen
12 Andreas Andreasen
13 Magnus Sorensen
14 Ken Peters
15 Kasper Kristensen
16 Torbin Benjaminsen
17 Thomas Bjerrum
18 Bjorn Eden
19 Jesper Madsen
20 Thomas Kjogx
21 Preben Bertram
22 Anders Johansson
23 Alexei Salomatin
24 Daniel Jardemyr
25 Rolf Nilsson
26 Morten Evensen
27 Jens Terkelsen
28 Anders V. Jensen
29 Morten Dahlmann
30 Randy Maxwell
31 Soren Tresler
32 Leonid Truhno
33 Mads True
34 Morten Green
35 Nikolai Clausen
36 Alexander Alexeev
37 Pavel Kostichkin
38 Thomas Johansen
39 Jens Johansson
40 Nicklas Monberg
41 Jesper Gram
42 Mikkel Schmidt
43 Kent Aalborg
44 Christian Mourier
45 Ole Valipirtti
46 G. Karlstrom
47 Jiri Podesva
48 Michael Thomsen
49 Not produced?
50 Thomas Pedersen
51 Bo Nordby Andersen
52 Jan Jakobsen
53 Nick Lamia
54 Karel Krecek
55 Kasper Sorensen
56 Johan Moller Jensen
57 Tomas Klima
58 Tomas Pedersen
59 Rico Larsen
61 Jacek Nowakowski
62 Kasper Haslund Knudsen
63 Martin Struzinski
64 Michael Steffensen
65 Gert Andreasen
66 Jens Christian Gregersen
67 Rasmus Christiansen
68 Kristian L. Hansen
69 Henning Ludvigsen
69 Mads Moller
70 Valeri Shilov
71 Christian De Brass
72 Mikkel Quistgaard Lund
73 Rasmus Aradsson
74 Peter Hjort
75 Morten Ahlberg
76 Steen Bengtson
77 Andreas Mattsson
78 Brian Holse
79 Jeppe Ahlberg
80 Alexander Sundberg
81 Rasmus Olsen
82 Poul B. Andersen
83 Simon Petersen
84 Claus Esmark
85 Markku Tiemonen
86 Jens Maribo
87 Claus Tauson
88 Dennis Olsson
89 Andre Clausen
90 Johan Allringer
91 Casper Nilsson
92 Soren Tranholm
93 David Moore
94 Rene B. Madsen
95 Jens Hellsten
96 Lars Oxholm
97 Marten Rasten
98 Randy Murphy
99 Henrik Oxholm
100 Jonas Hansson
101 Rene Jensen
102 Per Apollo
103 Flemming Jensen
104 Marku Kyllonen
105 Peter Skraem
106 Dmitri Lavrentiev
107 Ntsika Shange
108 Curt Regnier
109 David Moore
110 Rasmus Holst
111 Hans Hansson
112 Not produced?
113 Andrejs Zinkovs
114 Thomas Ingvordsen
115 Konstantins Grigorjevs
116 Morten Rasmussen
117 Rasmus Jacobsen
118 Thor Dresler
119 Tom Dibbern
120 Ronni Thomassen
121 Christian Fabricius
122 Brian Schultz
123 Filip Faurholm
124 Sergejs Cubars
125 Peter F. Hansen
126 Johan Marklund
127 Dennis Olsson
128 Torben Schultz
129 Kenneth Madsen
130 Ulrich Hansen
131 Rene Sloth
132 Jesper Andersen
133 Aigars Razgals
134 Yuri Agureikin
135 Johan Westermark
136 Mads Johnsen
137 Rasmus Norgaard
138 Christian Schioldan
139 Karel Smid
140 Jesper Pedersen
141 Klaus Nielsen
142 Rasmus Christiansen
143 Soren Jensen
144 Martin E. Andersen
145 Niklas Rinaldo
146 Andreas Borup
147 Thomas Englund
148 Jorn Ole Bertelsen
149 Thomas Reinert
150 Bent Christensen
151 Anders Thomsen
152 Sergejs Senins
153 Soren Pedersen
154 Ilya Dubkov
155 Mike Grey
156 Jimmy Nielsson
157 Tomas Placatka
158 Jan Justra
159 Peter Therkildsen
160 Kim Fonnesbech
161 Rasmus Pander
162 Claus Mortensen
163 Jan Phillipsen
164 Jesper Molby
165 Lars Molgaard
166 Ulrik Thomsen
167 Petri Skriko
168 Martin Kristiansen
169 Lasse Degn
170 Daniel Nielsen
171 Erkki Makela
172 Henrik Toft
173 Todd Bjorkstrand
174 Claus Damgaard
175 Anders Pyndt
176 Dan Jensen
177 Rasmus Hartung
178 Kasper Degn
179 Jarmo Makitalo
180 Jarmo Kuusisto
181 Seppo Repo
182 Not produced?
183 Dan Jensen
184 Ulrick Nielsen
185 Claus Jensen
186 Mikael Wiklander
187 Kim Foder
188 Mats Diberius
189 Ole Christiansen
190 Brian Foder
191 Dennis Blom
192 Soren Gerber
193 Lars Bach
194 Kim Jensen
195 Rasmus Kubel
196 Jan Jensen
197 Soren Nielsen
198 Todd Sparks
199 Morten Callesen
200 Ian Hebert
201 Jesper Gaarde
202 Henrik Lundin
203 Mika Nyqvist
204 Daniel Ullbors
205 Bill Morrison
206 Michael Senderovitz
207 Igor A. Knyazev
208 Lars Bundgaard
209 Jens Edmund
210 Ruby Flomo
211 Magnus Sundquist
212 Morten Ovesen
213 Boris Bykovsky
214 Martin Sorensen
215 Lars Eller
216 Bo Larsen
217 Soren Koziol
218 Martin Skygge
219 Rasmus Edmund
220 Michael Thomsen
221 Soren Lykke-Jorgensen
222 Mathies Stengaard
223 Henrik Borner
224 Jannik Sonderby
225 Sergei Solomatov
226 Ulrick Sinding Olsen
227 Anatoli Chistyakov
228 Olaf Eller
229 Ken Ruddick
NNO Vojens Lions
NNO Rungsted Cobras
NNO Odense Bulldogs
NNO Herning Blue Fox
NNO Gentofte
NNO Rodovre
NNO Aalborg
NNO Frederikshavn Hawks
NNO Esbjerg Pirates
NNO Hvidovre

1999-00 Danish Hockey League

Little is known about this set beyond the checklist and thus it is not priced. Several cards are marked below as unknown. If you have information about the identities of these cards or have sales information, write hockeymag@beckett.com.

COMPLETE SET (225)
1 Jan Jensen
2 Kenneth Jensen
3 Torben Schultz
4 Michael Pedersen
5 Henrik Benjaminsen
6 Mikkel Bjerrum
7 Todd Sparks
8 Keld Frederiksen
9 Alexander Weinrich
10 Kristian Lodberg
11 Lars T. Pedersen
12 Oleg Starkov
13 Andreas Andreasen
14 Mikko Suvanto
15 Anders Skov
16 Jacques Joubert
17 Thomas Bjerrum
18 Bjorn Eden
19 Jesper Madsen
20 Thomas Kjogx
21 Anders Johansson
22 Mats Diberius
23 Bill Stewart
24 Robert Nordberg
25 Peter Nordstrom
26 Rasmus Aradsson
27 Ole Valipirtti
28 Mathias Frelin
29 Bo Larsen
30 Mikko Niemi
31 Michel Olsen
32 Rasmus Jacobsen
33 Jens Maribo
34 Brian Jensen
35 Claus Esmark
36 Rasmus Olsen
37 Brian Schultz
38 Christian Jorgensen
39 Johan Marklund
40 Rene Sloth
41 Ronni Dahlsten
42 Ronni Thomassen
43 Thor Dresler
44 Poul B. Andersson
45 Steen Bengtson
46 Peter Therkildsen
47 unknown
48 Claus Mortensen
49 Daniel Nielsen
50 Jan Philipsen
51 Kasper Degn
52 Martin Kristiansen
53 Jarmo Kuusisto
54 unknown
55 Rasmus Hartung
56 Todd Bjorkstrand
57 Rico Larsen
58 unknown
59 Martin Struzinski
60 Christian Kjaergaard
61 Jesper Molby
62 Rasmus Pander
63 Dan Jensen
64 Lasse Degn
65 Sami Wikstrom
66 unknown
67 Michael Madsen
68 Mikael Wiklander
69 Lars Bach
70 Christian Erntgaard
71 unknown
72 Claus Jensen
73 Henrik Lundin
74 Mikko Honkonen
75 Morten Callesen
76 Ray Podloski
77 Sami Simonen
78 Stefan Nyman
79 Soren Nielsen
80 Valeri Chierny
81 Brian Foder
82 Rasmus Kubel
83 Jan Jensen
84 Ole Christiansen
85 Kim Foder
86 Dan Jensen
87 Thomas Carlsson
88 Jiri Podesva
89 Jens Sonny Thomsen
90 Alexanders Shishkovich
91 Jesper Pedersen
92 Carsten Ronnest
93 Alexanders Macijevskis
94 Jacek Nowakowski
95 Mads Moller
96 unknown
97 Ronnie Sorensen
98 Thomas Englund
99 Tomas Placatka
100 unknown
101 Kasper Haslund Knudsen
102 Thomas Mortensen
103 Bo Nordby Andersen
104 Rasmus Kristiansen
105 Jens Christian Gregersen
106 Jesper Pedersen
107 Thomas Pedersen
108 Johan Allringer
109 Casper Nilsson
110 Peter Skraem
111 Henrik B. Madsen
112 Curt Regnier
113 Dean Seymour
114 Mario Simioni
115 Jens Hellsten
116 Hernik Oxholm
117 Ntsika Shange
118 Dmitri Lavrentiev
119 Marku Kyllonen
120 Lars Oxholm
121 Pavel Tolstik
122 Anders Holst
123 Rasmus Holst
124 Pierre Dufour
125 Soren Tranholm
126 unknown
127 Rene B. Madsen
128 Rene Jensen
129 Bill Morrison
130 Michael Senderovitz
131 Michael Sauffaus
132 Christian Fabricius
133 Pavel Lazerev
134 unknown
135 Soren Koziol
136 Boris Bykovsky
137 Igor A. Knyazev
138 Henrik Borner
139 Jannik Sonderby
140 Michael Thomsen
141 Magnus Sorensen
142 Anatoli Chistyakov
143 Filip Faurholm
144 Ulrich Hansen
145 Magnus Sundquist
146 Soren Lykke-Jorgensen
147 unknown
148 Ulrick Sinding Olsen
149 Martin Skygge
150 Rasmus Nielsen
151 Lars Bundgaard
152 Johan Westermark
153 Mads Johnsen
154 Mike Grey
155 Anders Thomsen
156 Kasper Kristensen
157 Lars Molgaard
158 Karel Smid
159 Soren Jensen
160 Martin E. Andersen
161 Ilja Dubkov
162 Mads Brandt
163 Radim Piroutek
164 Thomas Reinert
165 Christian Schioldan
166 Bent Christensen
167 Sergejs Senins
168 Hasse Olsen
169 Simon Pedersen
170 Klaus Nielsen
171 Torbin Benjaminsen
172 Andreas Borup
173 Henrik Bjerring
174 unknown
175 Anders V. Jensen
176 Michael Widenborg
177 Ruby Flomo
178 unknown
179 Marco Poulsen
180 unknown
181 Sergejs Cubars
182 Andreas Sabroe
183 Christian Dall-Hansen
184 unknown
185 Lars-Peter Drewsen
186 Michael Lauridsen
187 Morten Ovesen
188 Thomas Hansen
189 Dan Vollertzen
190 unknown
191 Casper Brandis
192 Casper Skovby
193 unknown
194 Thomas Wahlgren
195 Dan Jensen
196 Thomas Robbert
197 Benny Nielsen
198 Troels Biltoft
199 unknown
200 Jimmy Nielsson
201 Mikkel Schmidt
202 Anders Hansen
203 unknown
204 Morten Hagen
205 unknown
206 Morten Dahlmann
207 Nicklas Plampeck
208 Randy Maxwell
209 Soren True
210 Leronid Truhno
211 Mads True
212 Nikolai Clausen
213 Alexander Alexeev
214 Pavel Kostichkin
215 Thomas Johansen
216 Jens Johansson
217 Jesper Gram
218 Alexander Sundberg
219 Christian Mourier
220 Kristian Just Petersen
221 Dennis Olsson
222 Andreas Mattsson
223 Andre Clausen
224 Hakan Falkenhall
225 Nicklas Monberg

2005-06 Dutch Vadeko Flyers

COMPLETE SET (20) 8.00 15.00
1 Kevin Bruijsten .30 .75
2 Andriy Butochnov .30 .75
3 Anton Butochnov .30 .75
4 Sander Dijkstra .30 .75
5 James Easter .30 .75
6 Brent Janssen .30 .75
7 Matt Korthuis .30 .75
8 Petr Kratky .30 .75
9 Hans Kroon .30 .75
10 Paul Kroon .30 .75
11 Jacco Landman .30 .75
12 Don Nichols .30 .75
13 Marcel Nijland .30 .75
14 Tyler Palmiscno .30 .75
15 Marco Postma .30 .75
16 Brad Smulders .30 .75
17 Ruud vander Holst .30 .75
18 Jeroen van Olphen .30 .75
19 Stanislav Vernikov .30 .75
20 Brain de Bruijn HC .10 .25

1965-66 Finnish Hellas

This vintage set is the earliest confirmed to feature members of the Finnish SM-Liiga. The cards were apparently issued in packs by a company named Hellas, which is the parent company for Leaf. Because of the age and limited availability of these cards, we have no pricing information and are presenting them below for checklisting purposes only.

COMPLETE SET (160)
1 Lasse Kiili
2 Ilkka Mesikammen
3 Jorma Laapas
4 Esko Reijonen
5 Juhani Iso Eskeli
6 Pertti Nieminen
7 Kari Aro
8 Juhani Wahlsten
9 Rauno Heinonen
10 Kalevi Leppanen
11 Pertti Karelius
12 Pekka Oikkonen
13 Kari Sillanpaa
14 Jarmo Rantanen
15 Heikki Heimo
16 Jorma Valtonen
17 Risto Kaitala
18 Kalevi Virkku
19 Heikko Stenvall
20 Teppo Rastio
21 Seppo Vainio
22 Pentti Jokinen
23 Matti Keinonen
24 Matti Koivunen
25 Esa Isaksson
26 Juhani Jylha
27 Pentti Rautalin
28 Simo Saimo
29 Hannu Torma
30 Olli Malmivuori
31 Matti Saurio
32 Mikko Erholm
33 Anto Virtanen
34 Juha Rantasila
35 Jaakko Honkanen
36 Antti Heikkila
37 Lasse Heikkila
38 Veli-Pekka Ketola
39 Keijo Koistinen
40 Mikko Myllyniemi
41 Matti Salmi
42 Tuomo Pirskanen
43 Matti Jansson
44 Erkki Saine
45 Erkki Harju
46 Kaj Matalamaki
47 Seppo Nystrom
48 Timo Jussila
49 Jorma Rikala
50 Tapio Raunio
51 Pekka Korjakoff
52 Jorma Borgstrom
53 Jorma Kyntola
54 Jyrki Malmio
55 Aarno Heikkaranta
56 Kalevi Salo
57 Martti Kuokkanen
58 Seppo Ikola
59 Hannu Kyllastinen
60 Pentti Katainen
61 Harri Linnonmaa
62 Kyosti Wall
63 Kari Kinnunen
64 Martti Kallionpaa
65 Pekka Kuusisto
66 Johannes Karttunen
67 Heikki Veravainen
68 Pentti Riitahaara
69 Lauri Lehtonen
70 Matti Harju
71 Pertti Kontto
72 Timo Makela
73 Tapio Rautalammi
74 Kimmo Kivela
75 Raimo Maattanen
76 Kari Rajala
77 Tapani Suominen
78 Heimo Tervo
79 Raimo Kilpio
80 Matti Lampainen
81 Raimo Helppolainen
82 Esko Nenonen
83 Lalli Partinen
84 Leo Haakana
85 Hannu Lemander
86 Leevi Ryhanen
87 Yrjo Hakala
88 Pauli Hyvari
89 Jorma Hietanen
90 Juhani Pyyhtia
91 Timo Vaatamoinen
92 Heikki Juselius
93 Pentti Hyvari
94 Antti Ravi
95 Markku Eiskonen
96 Martti Sinkkonen
97 Tapio Majaniemi
98 Matti Reunamaki
99 Rauno Heinonen
100 Rauno Lehtio
101 Risto Lehtio
102 Juhani Tamminen
103 Matti Kautto
104 Pekka Lehtolainen
105 Markku Pulli
106 Eero Hopalainen
107 Aaro Nurminen
108 Kalevi Pulli
109 Jorma Suokko
110 Erkki Suokko
111 Heino Pulli
112 Seppo Nikkila
113 Pentti Pynnonen
114 Lasse Oksanen
115 Olli Wirzenius
116 Pentti Uotila
117 Jaakko Jaskari
118 Markku Hakanen
119 Illka Halme
120 Pekka Alfors
121 Tauno Niemi
122 Erkan Nasib
123 Veikko Ukkonen
124 Jarmo Wasama
125 Juhani Lahtinen
126 Jorma Peltonen
127 Kari Palooja
128 Reijo Hakanen
129 Esko Kaonpaa
130 Kimmo Heino
131 Jaako Siren
132 Seppo Naukkarinen
133 Rainer Kolehmainen
134 Henrik Granholm
135 Erkki Partanen
136 Heikki Jarn
137 Jerry Sullivan
138 Jaakko Marttinen
139 Ulf Lindholm
140 Pentti Lindegren
141 Pentti Kotkas
142 Pekka Perttula
143 Esko Rekomaa
144 Christer Thun
145 Matti Kaski
146 Pekka Marjamaki
147 Antti Virtanen
148 Matti Peltonen
149 Reijo Ojanen
150 Timo Ahlqvist
151 Seppo Makinen
152 Jouni Seistamo
153 Harri Harvela
154 Kari Makinen
155 Heikki Koskimies
156 Timo Jussila
157 Pertti Ansakorpi
158 Hannu Elo
159 Mikko Holopainen
160 Kalevi Numminen

1966 Finnish Jaakiekkosarja

This early Finnish set is presented for checklisting purposes only. We have no confirmed sales info and thus the set is unpriced. If you have additional info on this series, please forward it to hockeymag@beckett.com.

COMPLETE SET (220)
COMMON CARD (1-220)
1 Jukka Haapala
2 Simo Saimo
3 Hannu Torma
4 Jukka Savunen
5 Tenho Lotila
6 Tapani Koskimaki
7 Matti Saurio
8 Risto Kaitala
9 Raimo Tiainen
10 Esa Isaksson
11 Pentti Rautalin
12 Heikko Stenvall
13 Teppo Rastio
14 Jorma Vehmanen
15 Raimo Kilpio
16 Veikko Ukkonen
17 Lauri Lehtonen
18 Heikki Veravainen
19 Pentti Riitahaara
20 Pekka Kuusisto
21 Tapio Rautalammi
22 Raimo Tuli
23 Matti Paivinen
24 Matti Harju
25 Kari Sillanpaa
26 Matti Keinonen
27 Pekka Lahti
28 Johannes Karttunen
29 Sakari Isomaki
30 Samu Leikko
31 Tapani Suominen
32 Esa Vesslin
33 Pekka Jalava
34 Pertti Makela
35 Juha Rantasila
36 Jukka Haanpaa
37 Teuvo Helenius
38 Anto Virtanen
39 Kimmo Nokikuru
40 Jaakko Honkanen
41 Seppo Nystrom
42 Tuomo Pirskainen
43 Matti Jansson
44 Alpo Suhonen
45 Matti Varpela
46 Kaj Matalamaki
47 Antti Heikkila
48 Jaakko Jaskari
49 Jouko Ojansuu
50 Mikko Myllyniemi
51 Veli-Pekka Ketola
52 Matti Salmi
53 Pentti Vihanto
54 Hannu Luojola
55 Seppo Parikka
56 Martti Salonen
57 Risto Forss
58 Hannu Niittoaho
59 Kari Johansson
60 Henry Leppa
61 Jarmo Rantanen
62 Kari Torkkel
63 Seppo Vikstrom
64 Veijo Saarinen
65 Pekka Lahtela
66 Risto Vainio
67 Reijo Paksal
68 Erkan Nasib
69 Martti Heino
70 Voitto Soini
71 Urpo Ylonen
72 Rauno Heinonen
73 Heikki Heino
74 Lasse Killi
75 Ilkka Mesikammen
76 Timo Nummelin
77 Pertti Kuismanen
78 Juhani Wahlsten
79 Rauli Ottila
80 Pentti Karelius
81 Teuvo Andelmin
82 Kari Varjanen
83 Kalevi Leppanen
84 Juhani Iso-Eskeli
85 Hannu Koivunen
86 Yrjo Hakala
87 Kari Ruontimo
88 Raimo Lohko
89 Markku Eiskonen
90 Hannu Lemander
91 Timo Vaatamoinen
92 Pekka Moisio
93 Martti Makia
94 Risto Heinvirta
95 Taisto Jahma
96 Veikko Makia
97 Raimo Helppolainen
98 Lalli Partinen
99 Keijo Sinkkonen
100 Antti Ravi
101 Martti Sinkkonen
102 Heikki Juselius
103 Timo Rantala
104 Heikki Mikkola
105 Jaakko Siren
106 Matti Korhonen
107 Erkki Mononen
108 Pertti Valkonen
109 Ilpo Koskela
110 Bengt Wilenius
111 Hannu Lindberg
112 Kristen Bertell
113 Veikko Kuusisto
114 Tapio Majaniemi
115 Leo Vankka
116 Pentti Harju
117 Ari Myllymaki
118 Matti Koskinen
119 Pentti Andersson
120 Pertti Heikkinen
121 Pekka Peltoniemi
122 Jouko Jarvinen
123 Matti Vartiainen
124 Esko Reijonen
125 Erkki Rasanen
126 Timo Viskari
127 Raimo Turkulainen
128 Paavo Tirkkonen
129 Orvo Paatero
130 Juhani Leirivaara
131 Jyrki Turunen
132 Timo Tuomainen
133 Pentti Karkkainen
134 Jussi Piuhola
135 Pentti Pihlapuro
136 Pentti Pennanen
137 Esa Viskari
138 Timo Luostarinen
139 Seppo Iivonen
140 Risto Alho
141 Esko Kiuru
142 Jaakko Hovinheimo
143 Jaakko Koikkalainen
144 Juhani Sodervik
145 Seppo Makinen
146 Teuvo Peltola
147 Antti Alenius
148 Kalevi Numminen
149 Esko Kaonpaa
150 Lauri Salomaa
151 Risto Pirttiaho
152 Antti Leppanen
153 Kari Makinen

154 Jorma Oksala
155 Pekka Marjamaki
156 Jouni Seistamo
157 Pertti Ansakorpi
158 Erkki Jarkko
159 Juhani Peltola
160 Erkki Mannikko
161 Keijo Mannisto
162 Matti Peltonen
163 Hannu Heikkonen
164 Pentti Hyytiainen
165 Antti Virtanen
166 Seppo Nurmi
167 Matti Reunamaki
168 Mikko Raikkonen
169 Esko Rantanen
170 Eero Holopainen
171 Juhani Ruohonen
172 Veikko Savolainen
173 Heikki Sivonen
174 Markku Pulli
175 Pekka Uitus
176 Heikki Keinonen
177 Jorma Saarikorpi
178 Rauno Lehtio
179 Kalevi Toivonen
180 Jorma Vilen
181 Pentti Kuusinen
182 Olavi Haapalainen
183 Seppo Nikkila
184 Jorma Suokko
185 Heino Pulli
186 Risto Lehtio
187 Pekka Lehtolainen
188 Timo Hirsimaki
189 Kari Palo-Oja
190 Pekka Leimu
191 Ali Saadetin
192 Erkki Jarvinen
193 Markku Hakanen
194 Jorma Kallio
195 Vaino Kolkka
196 Timo Saari
197 Jorma Peltonen
198 Pentti Pynnonen
199 Pentti Uotila
200 Timo Lahtinen
201 Juhani Lahtinen
202 Reijo Hakanen
203 Lasse Oksanen
204 Juhani Aromaki
205 Jukka Alkula
206 Pekka Olkkonen
207 Tapani Salo
208 Vesa Kartsalo
209 Antti Komsi
210 Asko Sallamaa
211 Juhani Tarkiainen
212 Antero Hakala
213 Ulf Slotte
214 Raimo Savolainen
215 Matias Savolainen
216 Risto Savolainen
217 Keijo Makinen
218 Tapio Makinen
219 Ossi Peltoniemi
220 Matti Valikangas

1970-71 Finnish Jaakiekko

This early Finnish set is presented for checklisting purposes only. We have no confirmed sales information at this time.

COMPLETE SET (384)
1 Vitali Davydov
2 Anatoli Firsov
3 Valeri Kharlamov
4 Aleksandr Yakushev
5 Viktor Konovalenko
6 Vladimir Lutshenko
7 Aleksandr Maltsev
8 Boris Mikhailov
9 Jevgeni Mishakov
10 Valeri Nikitin
11 Vladimir Petrov
12 Jevgeni Paladjev
13 Viktor Polupanov
14 Aleksandr Ragulin
15 Igor Romishevski
16 Vladimir Shadrin
17 Vjatjeslav Starsinov
18 Vladislav Tretjak
19 Valeri Vasiljev
20 Vladimir Vikulov
21 Tommy Abrahamsson
22 Gunnar Backman
23 Arne Carlsson
24 Anders Hagstrom
25 Anders Hedberg
26 Leif Holmqvist
27 Nils Johansson
28 Stig-Goran Johansson
29 Stefan Karlsson
30 Hans Lindberg
31 Tord Lundstrom
32 Kjell-Rune Milton
33 Lars-Goran Nilsson
34 Anders Nordin
35 Roger Olsson
36 Bjorn Palmqvist
37 Lars-Erik Sjoberg
38 Ulf Sterner
39 Lennart Svedberg
40 Hakan Wickberg
41 Vladimir Bednar
42 Josef Cerny
43 Vladimir Dzurilla
44 Richard Farda
45 Julius Haas
46 Ivan Hlinka
47 Jaroslav Holik
48 Jiri Holik
49 Josef Horesovsky
50 Jan Hrbaty
51 Jiri Kochta
52 Miroslav Lacky
53 Oldrich Machac
54 Vladislav Martinec
55 Vaclav Nedomansky
56 Frantisek Pospisil
57 Stanislav Pryl
58 Frantisek Sevcik
59 Jan Suchy
60 Lubomir Ujvary
61 Matti Keinonen
62 Veli-Pekka Ketola
63 Vaino Kolkka
64 Ilpo Koskela
65 Pekka Leimu
66 Seppo Lindstrom
67 Harri Linnonmaa
68 Pekka Marjamaki
69 Lauri Mononen
70 Matti Murto
71 Lasse Oksanen
72 Lalli Partinen
73 Esa Peltonen
74 Jorma Peltonen
75 Juha Rantasila
76 Heikki Riihiranta
77 Juhani Tamminen
78 Jorma Valtonen
79 Jorma Vehmanen
80 Urpo Ylonen
81 Rolf Bielas
82 Frank Braun
83 Dieter Dewitz
84 Lothar Fuchs
85 Bernd Hiller
86 Klaus Hirche
87 Reinhard Karger
88 Bernd Karrenbauer
89 Hartmut Nickel
90 Rudiger Noack
91 Helmut Novy
92 Rainer Patschinski
93 Dietmar Peters
94 Wolfgang Plotka
95 Peter Prusa
96 Dieter Purschel
97 Wilfried Rohrbach
98 Dieter Rohl
99 Peter Slapke
100 Joachim Ziesche
101 Juhani Bostrom
102 Henrik Granholm
103 Matti Harju
104 Kimmo Heino
105 Esa Isaksson
106 Juhani Jylha
107 Heikki Riihiranta
108 Mauri Kaukokari
109 Vaino Kolkka
110 Harri Linnonmaa
111 Matti Murto
112 Lalli Partinen
113 Juha Rantasila
114 Heikki Riihiranta
115 Jorma Rikala
116 Jorma Thusberg
117 Matti Vaisanen
118 Sakari Ahlberg
119 Jorma Aro
120 Esko Eriksson
121 Markku Hakanen
122 Matti Hakanen
123 Reijo Hakanen
124 Pentti Hartin
125 Timo Hirsimaki
126 Jorma Kallio
127 Pekka Kuusisto
128 Juhani Lahtinen
129 Timo Lahtinen
130 Pekka Leimu
131 Jukka Mattila
132 Esko Makinen
133 Lasse Oksanen
134 Kari Palo-oja
135 Jorma Peltonen
136 Ali Saadetdin
137 Timo Saari
138 Heikki Hurme
139 Matti Jakonen
140 Kari Johansson
141 Keijo Jarvinen
142 Reijo Leppanen
143 Seppo Lindstrom
144 Hannu Luojola
145 Hannu Niitoaho
146 Reijo Paksal
147 Seppo Parikka
148 Jarmo Rantanen
149 Martti Salonen
150 Voitto Soini
151 Kari Torkkel
152 Risto Vainio
153 Pentti Vihanto
154 Urpo Ylonen
155 Rauno Heinonen
156 Lauri Jamsen
157 Lasse Kiili
158 Hannu Koivunen
159 Jarmo Koivunen
160 Pertti Kuismanen
161 Pekka Lahtela
162 Harry Luoto
163 Jaakko Marttinen
164 Timo Nummelin
165 Rauli Ottila
166 Matti Rautee
167 Pekka Rautee
168 Jouni Samuli
169 Rauli Tammelin
170 Juhani Tamminen
171 Kari Varjanen
172 Pertti Ahokas
173 Pertti Hiirros
174 Eero Holopainen
175 Veli-Pekka Ketola
176 Kari Kinnunen
177 Ilpo Koskela
178 Osmo Kuusisto
179 Timo Kyntola
180 Henry Leppa
181 Erkki Mononen
182 Lauri Mononen
183 Pertti Nurmi
184 Antti Perttula
185 Seppo Peraoja
186 Timo Relas
187 Alpo Suhonen
188 Timo Turunen
189 Tapio Flinck
190 Jaakko Honkanen
191 Antti Heikkila
192 Matti Jansson
193 Esa Kari
194 Raimo Kilpio
195 Tapio Koskinen
196 Kaj Matalamaki
197 Ilkka Mesikammen
198 Pertti Makela
199 Jaakko Nurminen
200 Pekka Rautakallio
201 Tapio Rautalammi
202 Markku Riihimaki
203 Matti Salmi
204 Kari-Pekka Toivonen
205 Jorma Valtonen
206 Anto Virtanen
207 Erkki Vakiparta
208 Pertti Ansakorpi
209 Pertti Koivulahti
210 Ilpo Kuisma
211 Harri Lappalainen
212 Pekka Marjamaki
213 Mikko Mynttinen
214 Kari Makinen
215 Pekka Makinen
216 Seppo Makinen
217 Keijo Mannisto
218 Jorma Oksala
219 Matti Peltonen
220 Tuomo Rautiainen
221 Lauri Salomaa
222 Risto Seesvuori
223 Jorma Siitarinen
224 Teemu Sistonen
225 Lasse Aaltonen
226 Mikko Erholm
227 Jukka Haapala
228 Veikko Ihalainen
229 Matti Keinonen
230 Tapani Koskimaki
231 Arto Laine
232 Hannu Lunden
233 Pentti Rautalin
234 Paavo Riekkinen
235 Kai Rosvall
236 Matti Saurio
237 Jukka Savunen
238 Hannu Siivonen
239 Heikko Stenvall
240 Jorma Vanhanen
241 Hannu Haapalainen
242 Timo Jarvinen
243 Heikki Keinonen
244 Heimo Keinonen
245 Rauno Lehtio
246 Tapio Nummela
247 Seppo Nurmi
248 Markku Pulli
249 Esko Rantanen
250 Juhani Ruohonen
251 Mikko Raikkonen
252 Jorma Saarikorpi
253 Veikko Savolainen
254 Leo Seppanen
255 Pertti Sihvonen
256 Pekka Uitus
257 Jorma Vilen
258 Tapio Virhimo
259 Jaakko Koikkalainen
260 Jorma Muikku
261 Ossi Oksala
262 Pekka Parikka
263 Pentti Pennanen
264 Jussi Piuhola
265 Seppo Repo
266 Erkki Rasanen
267 Juhani Sodervik
268 Heikki Tirkkonen
269 Paavo Tirkkonen
270 Timo Tuomainen
271 Raimo Turkulainen
272 Jyrki Turunen
273 Martti Turunen
274 Timo Viskari
275 Antero Vaatamoinen
276 Juhani Aaltonen
277 Matti Ahvenharju
278 Hannu Auvinen
279 Jorma Borgstrom
280 Seppo Laakkio
281 Jarmo Laukkanen
282 Hannu Lindberg
283 Reijo Myyrylainen
284 Raimo Maattanen
285 Esa Peltonen
286 Keijo Puhakka
287 Antti Ravi
288 Erkki Suni
289 Henrik Wahl
290 Stig Wetzell
291 Olli Viilma
292 Esa Willberg
293 Kauko Fomin
294 Risto Forss
295 Rauno Karlsson
296 Jarmo Kiprusoff
297 Matti Koivunen
298 Timo Kokkonen
299 Timo Lehtonen
300 Kalevi Leppanen
301 Hans Martin
302 Timo Nurminen
303 Jari Rosberg
304 Veijo Saarinen
305 Simo Suoknuuti
306 Veikko Suominen
307 Seppo Wikstrom
308 Juha-Pekka Aho
309 Seppo Aro
310 Kari Jokinen
311 Pekka Karhunen
312 Pertti Kettunen
313 Lauri Kosonen
314 Jyrki Kahonen
315 Marko Lepaus
316 Matti Lisko
317 Marko Niemi
318 Hannu Pohja
319 Jarmo Ronkainen
320 Mikko Silvasti
321 Jari Suokas
322 Kimmo Turunen
323 Jari Viitala
324 Mikko Vilonen
325 Jaakko Virtanen
326 Jarmo Viteli
327 Kari Anttila
328 Harri Hiltunen
329 Arto Javanainen
330 Tapio Jylhasaari
331 Jorma Korkeamaki
332 Kari Koskinen
333 Martti Lunden
334 Petri Niskanen
335 Jari Nystrom
336 Ari Peltola
337 Jari Peltonen
338 Petri Salminen
339 Juha Salo
340 Esa Salosensaari
341 Rauli Siimes
342 Esa Suvanto
343 Jukka Tuli
344 Jukka Virtanen
345 Pertti Vaisanen
346 Timo Hyrsky
347 Jorma Jokinen
348 Jari Kokkola
349 Pentti Kuosmanen
350 Pekka Laukkanen
351 Tom Lund
352 Jouni Niemela
353 Kari Rantanen
354 Pekka Reimola
355 Teijo Salminen
356 Veli-Matti Tammi
357 Juha Tamminen
358 Risto Vaihinen
359 Antti Vanne
360 Ari Vanne
361 Hannu Vehmanen
362 Heikki Virta
363 Hannu Virtanen
364 Jyrki Valimaki
365 Pekka Anttila
366 Jouni Honkanen
367 Kari Jalonen
368 Ari Kaikkonen
369 Timo Kajula
370 Jorma Kinnunen
371 Esa Kontio
372 Tapio Kuiri
373 Pekka Kyllonen
374 Ari Mustaniemi
375 Jukka Pajala
376 Pentti Perhomaa
377 Reijo Raatesalmi
378 Markku Ruotsalainen
379 Reijo Ruotsalainen ERC
380 Jarmo Tauriainen
381 Ari Timosaari
382 Pekka Tuomisto
383 Timo Vahanen
384 Sakari Valiharju

1971-72 Finnish Suomi Stickers

COMPLETE SET (384) 200.00 400.00
1 Vitaly Davydov .30 .75
2 Anatoli Firsov 2.00 5.00
3 Valeri Kharlamov 6.00 15.00
4 Viktor Konovalenko .30 .75
5 Viktor Kuzkin .30 .75
6 Yuri Liapkin .40 1.00
7 Vladimir Lutchenko .30 .75
8 Alexander Maltsev 2.00 5.00
9 Alexander Martiniuk .40 1.00
10 Boris Mikhailov 2.00 5.00
11 Evgeni Mishakov .30 .75
12 Vladimir Petrov 2.00 5.00
13 Alexander Ragulin .75 2.00
14 Igor Romishevski .30 .75
15 Vladimir Shadrin .40 1.00
16 Viatjeslav Starshinov .40 1.00
17 Vladislav Tretiak 10.00 20.00
18 Gennady Tsygankov .40 1.00
19 Vladimir Vikulov .40 1.00
20 Evgeni Zimin .40 1.00
21 Bedrich Brunschk .20 .50
22 Jiri Bubla .75 2.00
23 Josef Cerny .30 .75
24 Richard Farda .20 .50
25 Jan Havel .20 .50
26 Ivan Hnlicka .20 .50
27 Jiri Holecek .40 1.00
28 Jiri Holik .30 .75
29 Josef Horesovsky .20 .50
30 Jiri Kochta .20 .50
31 Oldrich Machac .20 .50
32 Vladimir Martinec .20 .50
33 Vaclav Nedomansky .75 2.00
34 Eduard Novak .20 .50
35 Frantisek Panchartek .20 .50
36 Frantisek Pospisil .30 .75
37 Marcel Sakac .20 .50
38 Bohuslav Stastny .40 1.00
39 Jan Suchy .30 .75
40 Christer Abrahamsson .75 2.00
41 Thommy Abrahamsson .40 1.00
42 Thommie Bergman 1.25 3.00
43 Arne Carlsson .20 .50
44 Inge Hammarstrom 4.00 10.00
45 Anders Hedberg 3.00 8.00
46 Leif Holmqvist .75 2.00
47 Stig-Goran Johansson .40 1.00
48 Stefan Karlsson .20 .50
49 Hans Lindberg .20 .50
50 Tord Lundstrom .20 .50
51 William Lofqvist .40 1.00
52 Kjell-Rune Milton .20 .50
53 Lars-Goran Nilsson .20 .50
54 Bert-Ola Nordlander .40 1.00
55 Hakan Nygren .20 .50
56 Bjorn Palmqvist .20 .50
57 Hakan Pettersson .20 .50
58 Ulf Sterner .20 .50
59 Lennart Svedberg .40 1.00
60 Hakan Wickberg .20 .50
61 Esa Isaksson .20 .50
62 Heikki Jarn .20 .50
63 Veli-Pekka Ketola .75 2.00
64 Ilpo Koskela .20 .50
65 Seppo Lindstrom .20 .50
66 Harri Linnonmaa .20 .50
67 Hannu Luojola .20 .50
68 Pekka Mononen .20 .50
69 Erkki Mononen .20 .50
70 Lauri Mononen .20 .50
71 Matti Murto .40 1.00
72 Lasse Oksanen .20 .50
73 Esa Peltonen .20 .50
74 Seppo Repo .20 .50
75 Tommi Salmelainen .20 .50
76 Juhani Tamminen .20 .50
77 Jorma Valtonen .40 1.00
78 Jorma Vehmanen .20 .50
79 Urpo Ylonen .40 1.00
80 Jouko Oystila .20 .50
81 Tapio Flinck .20 .50
82 Antti Heikkila .20 .50
83 Reijo Heinonen .20 .50
84 Jaakko Honkanen .20 .50
85 Veli-Pekka Ketola .75 2.00
86 Raimo Kilpio .20 .50
87 Tapio Koskinen .20 .50
88 Kaj Matalamaki .20 .50
89 Pertti Makela .20 .50
90 Pekka Rautakallio .20 .50
91 Markku Riihimaki .20 .50
92 Matti Salmi .20 .50
93 Jorma Valtonen .40 1.00
94 Anto Virtanen .20 .50
95 Erkki Vakiparta .20 .50
96 Pertti Ahokas .20 .50
97 Pertti Arvaja .20 .50
98 Olli Hietanen .20 .50
99 Pentti Hiiros .20 .50
100 Eero Holopainen .20 .50
101 Kari Kinnunen .20 .50
102 Ilpo Koskela .20 .50
103 Timo Kyntola .20 .50
104 Henry Leppa .20 .50
105 Erkki Mononen .20 .50
106 Pertti Nurmi .20 .50
107 Timo Relas .20 .50
108 Timo Sutinen .20 .50
109 Timo Turunen .20 .50
110 Jouko Oystila .20 .50
111 Juhani Bostrom .20 .50
112 Kimmo Heino .20 .50
113 Esa Isaksson .20 .50
114 Juhani Jylha .20 .50
115 Heikki Jarn .20 .50
116 Mauri Kaukorari .20 .50
117 Vaino Kolkka .20 .50
118 Harri Linnonmaa .20 .50
119 Jaakko Marttinen .20 .50
120 Matti Murto .40 1.00
121 Lalli Partinen .20 .50
122 Juha Rantasila .20 .50
123 Heikki Riihiranta .20 .50
124 Jorma Rikala .20 .50
125 Tommi Salmelainen .20 .50
126 Jorma Thusberg .20 .50
127 Matti Vaisanen .20 .50
128 Jukka Alkula .20 .50
129 Pertti Ansakorpi .20 .50
130 Keijo Jarvinen .20 .50
131 Pertti Koivulahti .20 .50
132 Ilpo Kuisma .20 .50
133 Antti Leppanen .20 .50
134 Pekka Marjamaki .20 .50
135 Mikko Myntyinen .20 .50
136 Pekka Makinen .20 .50
137 Seppo Makinen .20 .50
138 Keijo Mannisto .20 .50
139 Antti Perttula .20 .50
140 Tuomo Rautiainen .20 .50
141 Juhani Saarelainen .20 .50
142 Jorma Saarikorpi .20 .50
143 Risto Seesvuori .20 .50
144 Jorma Siitarinen .20 .50
145 Raimo Suoniemi .20 .50
146 Juhani Aaltonen .20 .50
147 Matti Ahvenharju .20 .50
148 Hannu Auvinen .20 .50
149 Jorma Borgstrom .20 .50
150 Martti Immonen .20 .50
151 Matti Keinonen .20 .50
152 Seppo Laakkio .20 .50
153 Timo Lahtinen .20 .50
154 Esa Peltonen .20 .50
155 Keijo Puhakka .20 .50
156 Antti Ravi .20 .50
157 Timo Saari .20 .50
158 Esa Siren .20 .50
159 Erkki Suni .20 .50
160 Seppo Suoraniemi .20 .50
161 Juhani Tamminen .20 .50
162 Jorma Vehmanen .20 .50
163 Stig Wetzell .20 .50
164 Olli Viilma .20 .50
165 Leo Aikas .20 .50
166 Sakari Ahlberg .20 .50
167 Seppo Ahokainen .20 .50
168 Jorma Aro .20 .50
169 Esko Eriksson .20 .50
170 Markku Hakanen .20 .50
171 Matti Hakanen .20 .50
172 Reijo Hakanen .20 .50
173 Martti Helle .20 .50
174 Timo Hirsimaki .20 .50
175 Jorma Kallio .20 .50
176 Esko Kaonpaa .20 .50
177 Pentti Koskela .20 .50
178 Pekka Kuusisto .20 .50
179 Pekka Leimu .20 .50
180 Jukka Mattila .20 .50
181 Lasse Oksanen .20 .50
182 Kari Palooja .20 .50
183 Jorma Peltonen .40 1.00
184 Tuomo Sillman .20 .50
185 Jaakko Siren .20 .50
186 Veikkoi Suominen .20 .50
187 Matti Jakonen .20 .50
188 Kari Johansson .20 .50
189 Arto Kaunonen .20 .50
190 Arto Kaunonen .20 .50
191 Timo Kokkonen .20 .50
192 Reijo Leppanen .20 .50
193 Seppo Lindstrom .20 .50
194 Hannu Luojola .20 .50
195 Hannu Niittoaho .20 .50
196 Reijo Paksal .20 .50
197 Seppo Parikka .20 .50
198 Jarmo Rantanen .20 .50
199 Veijo Saarinen .20 .50
200 Martti Salonen .20 .50
201 Voitto Soini .20 .50
202 Kari Torkkel .20 .50
203 Risto Vainio .20 .50
204 Pentti Vihanto .20 .50
205 Seppo Wikstrom .20 .50
206 Urpo Ylonen .40 1.00
207 Hannu Haapalainen .20 .50
208 Jukka-Pekka Jarvenpaa .20 .50
209 Timo Jarvinen .20 .50
210 Heikki Keinonen .20 .50
211 Heimo Keinonen .20 .50
212 Rauno Lehtio .20 .50
213 Markku Moisio .20 .50
214 Seppo Nurmi .20 .50
215 Esko Rantanen .20 .50
216 Juhani Ruohonen .20 .50
217 Mikko Raikkonen .20 .50
218 Lauri Salomaa .20 .50
219 Veikko Savolainen .20 .50
220 Leo Seppanen .20 .50
221 Pekka Uitus .20 .50
222 Jorma Vilen .20 .50
223 Tapio Virhimo .20 .50
224 Kauko Fomin .20 .50
225 Heikki Hurme .20 .50
226 Eero Juntunen .20 .50
227 Lauri Jamsen .20 .50
228 Lasse Kiili .20 .50
229 Hannu Koivunen .20 .50
230 Jarmo Koivunen .20 .50
231 Pekka Lahtela .20 .50
232 Ilkka Mesikammen .20 .50
233 Timo Nummelin .20 .50
234 Rauli Ottila .20 .50
235 Matti Rautee .20 .50
236 Pekka Rautee .20 .50
237 Jari Rosberg .20 .50
238 Jouni Samuli .20 .50
239 Harry Silver .20 .50
240 Rauli Tammelin .20 .50
241 Bengt Wilenius .20 .50
242 Mikko Erholm .20 .50
243 Veikko Ihalainen .20 .50
244 Heikki Kauhanen .20 .50
245 Tapani Koskimaki .20 .50
246 Antti Laine .20 .50
247 Arto Laine .20 .50
248 Timo Lehtorinne .20 .50
249 Hannu Lunden .20 .50
250 Teppo Rastio .20 .50
251 Pentti Rautalin .20 .50
252 Kai Rosvall .20 .50
253 Ilkka Saarikko .20 .50
254 Jari Sarronlahti .20 .50
255 Matti Saurio .20 .50
256 Hannu Siivonen .20 .50
257 Erkki Sundelin .20 .50
258 Simo Suoknuuti .20 .50
259 Martti Haapala .20 .50
260 Yrjo Hakulinen .20 .50
261 Pentti Hirvonen .20 .50
262 Antero Honkanen .20 .50
263 Pekka Lavkainen .20 .50
264 Pentti Lavkainen .20 .50
265 Pentti Martikainen .20 .50
266 Pentti Martikainen .20 .50
267 Seppo Nevalainen .20 .50
268 Tapio Pohtinen .20 .50
269 Kari Puustinen .20 .50
270 Markku Rouhiainen .20 .50
271 Jarmo Sahlmann .20 .50
272 Seppo Saros .20 .50
273 Juha Silvennoinen .20 .50
274 Unto Turpeinen .20 .50
275 Kari Viitakahti .20 .50
276 Erkki Airaksinen .20 .50
277 Kauko Alkunen .20 .50
278 Jarmo Gummerus .20 .50
279 Bjorn Herbert .20 .50
280 Jarmo Jaakkola .20 .50
281 Hannu Kapanen .20 .50
282 Martti Koskinen .20 .50
283 Martti Kuokkanen .20 .50
284 Juhani Laine .20 .50
285 Heikki Leppik .20 .50
286 Juhani Langstrom .20 .50
287 Osmo Lotjonen .20 .50
288 Lauri Mononen .20 .50
289 Christer Nordblad .20 .50
290 Juha Poikolainen .20 .50
291 Kimmo Rantanen .20 .50
292 Seppo Repo .20 .50
293 Ilpo Ruokosalmi .20 .50
294 Arto Siisala .20 .50
295 Bo Sjostedt .20 .50
296 Pertti Viitanen .20 .50
297 Pekka Arbelius .40 1.00
298 Olli Enqvist .20 .50
299 Hannu Hiltunen .20 .50
300 Paavo Holopainen .20 .50
301 Juha Huikari .20 .50
302 Ari Jalonen .20 .50
303 Kari Jalonen .20 .50
304 Ari Kaikkonen .20 .50
305 Ari Kalmokoski .20 .50
306 Arto Lehtinen .20 .50
307 Markku Narhi .20 .50
308 Ilkka Okkonen .20 .50
309 Matti Perhomaa .20 .50
310 Juha-Pekka Porvari .20 .50
311 Arto Ruotanen .20 .50
312 Reijo Ruotsalainen .20 .50
313 Matti Ruutti .20 .50
314 Pertti Raisanen .20 .50
315 Ari Timosaari .20 .50
316 Janno Oro .20 .50
317 Anssi Eronen .20 .50
318 Seppo Hirvonen .20 .50
319 Jari Hannu Hamalainen .20 .50
320 Jari Pekka Hamalainen .20 .50
321 Timo Harkonen .40 1.00
322 Jouko Ikonen .20 .50
323 Lasse Kaiponen .20 .50
324 Jyri Kemppinen .20 .50
325 Jouni Kostiainen .20 .50
326 Kai Kulhoranta .20 .50
327 Olli Lemola .20 .50
328 Jari Lopponen .20 .50
329 Pasi Makkonen .20 .50
330 Vesa Massinen .20 .50
331 Timo Minkkila .20 .50
332 Petri Pellinen .20 .50
333 Juhan Rasanen .20 .50
334 Pasi Sallinen .20 .50
335 Kauko Tamminen .20 .50
336 Olli Teijonmaa .20 .50
337 Ismo Tolvanen .20 .50
338 Timo Vaahtoluoto .20 .50
339 Kari Heikkila .20 .50
340 Pekka Helander .20 .50
341 Jari Hirsimaki .20 .50
342 Jari Huotari .20 .50
343 Ilkka Huura .20 .50
344 Tero Juojarvi .20 .50
345 Jari Jarvinen .20 .50
346 Mika Laine .20 .50
347 Marko Lepaus .20 .50
348 Pertti Lundberg .20 .50
349 Tino Minetti .20 .50
350 Jarom Partanen .20 .50
351 Olli-Pekka Perala .20 .50
352 Ari Ruuska .20 .50
353 Kai Saario .20 .50
354 Olli-Pekka Turunen .20 .50
355 Veli-Matti Uusimaa .20 .50
356 Mauri Viita .20 .50
357 Timo Virtanen .20 .50
358 Jarmo Viteli .20 .50
359 Petri Viteli .20 .50
360 Ari Havukainen .20 .50
361 Ismo Heinonen .20 .50
362 Riku Hoyden .20 .50
363 Jari Jokinen .20 .50
364 Timo Joutsenvuori .20 .50
365 Jyrki Jantti .20 .50
366 Kimmo Jantti .20 .50
367 Toni Ketola .20 .50
368 Juha Korhonen .20 .50
369 Ari Laine .20 .50
370 Kari Lainio .20 .50
371 Juha Makinen .20 .50
372 Reima Numminen .20 .50
373 Mika Pirila .20 .50
374 Kai Pulli .20 .50
375 Tero Tommila .20 .50
376 Harri Tuohimaa .20 .50
377 Pasi Tuohimaa .20 .50
378 Ari Veijalainen .20 .50
379 Jean Beliveau 10.00 25.00
380 Phil Esposito 15.00 40.00
381 Tony Esposito 15.00 40.00
382 Gordie Howe 30.00 60.00
383 Bobby Hull 15.00 40.00
384 Bobby Orr 50.00 100.00

1972-73 Finnish Jaakiekko

COMPLETE SET (360) 100.00 200.00
1 Vladimir Bednar .40 1.00
2 Jiri Bubla .40 1.00
3 Vladimir Dzurilla 1.25 3.00
4 Richard Farda .20 .50
5 Julius Haas .20 .50
6 Ivan Hlinka .75 2.00
7 Jiri Holecek .75 2.00
8 Jaroslav Holik .40 1.00
9 Jiri Holik .40 1.00
10 Josef Horesovsky .20 .50
11 Jan Klapac .20 .50
12 Jiri Kochta .20 .50
13 Milan Kuzela .20 .50
14 Oldrich Machac .20 .50
15 Vladimir Martinec .20 .50
16 Vaclav Nedomansky 2.00 5.00
17 Josef Palecek .20 .50
18 Frantisek Pospisil .20 .50
19 Bohuslav Stastny .20 .50
20 Rudolf Tajcnar .20 .50
21 Vjatsjeslav Anisin .40 1.00
22 Juri Blinov .40 1.00
23 Aleksandr Gusev .75 2.00
24 Valeri Kharlamov 6.00 15.00
25 Aleksandr Yakushev 4.00 10.00
26 Viktor Kuzkin .40 1.00
27 Vladimir Lutshenko .40 1.00
28 Aleksandr Maltsev 2.00 5.00
29 Boris Mikhailov 2.00 5.00
30 Jevgeni Mishakov .75 2.00
31 Vladimir Petrov 2.00 5.00
32 Aleksandr Ragulin .75 2.00
33 Igor Romishevski .40 1.00
34 Vladimir Shadrin .75 2.00
35 Vladimir Shepovalov .40 1.00
36 Vjatsjeslav Solodukhin .40 1.00
37 Vladislav Tretjak 8.00 20.00
38 Gennadi Tsigankov .40 1.00
39 Valeri Vasiljev 2.00 5.00
40 Vladimir Vikulov .40 1.00
41 Christer Abrahamsson 1.25 3.00
42 Tommy Abrahamsson 1.25 3.00
43 Thommie Bergman 2.00 5.00
44 Inge Hammarstrom 3.00 8.00
45 Anders Hedberg 3.00 8.00
46 Leif Holmqvist .75 2.00
47 Bjorn Johansson .20 .50
48 Stig-Goran Johansson .40 1.00
49 Stefan Karlsson .20 .50
50 Stig Larsson .20 .50
51 Mats Lind .20 .50
52 Tord Lundstrom .20 .50
53 Lars-Goran Johansson .20 .50
54 Bjorn Palmqvist .20 .50
55 Hakan Pettersson .20 .50
56 Borje Salming 8.00 20.00
57 Lars-Erik Sjoberg 1.25 3.00
58 Carl Sundqvist .20 .50
59 Hakan Wickberg .20 .50
60 Stig Ostling .20 .50
61 Seppo Ahokainen .20 .50
62 Matti Keinonen .20 .50

1972-73 Finnish Jaakiekko

63 Veli-Pekka Ketola 1.25 3.00
64 Harri Linnonmaa .20 .50
65 Pekka Marjamaki .20 .50
66 Lauri Mononen .20 .50
67 Matti Murto .20 .50
68 Timo Nummelin .20 .50
69 Lasse Oksanen .20 .50
70 Esa Peltonen .20 .50
71 Juha Rantasila .20 .50
72 Pekka Rautakallio 1.25 3.00
73 Seppo Repo .20 .50
74 Heikki Riihiranta .20 .50
75 Juhani Tamminen .40 1.00
76 Timo Turunen .20 .50
77 Pertti Valkeapaa .20 .50
78 Jorma Valtonen .20 .50
79 Stig Wetzell .20 .50
80 Jouko Oystila .20 .50
81 Juhani Bostrom .20 .50
82 Kimmo Heino .20 .50
83 Pentti Karlsson .20 .50
84 Mauri Kaukokari .20 .50
85 Jarmo Koivunen .20 .50
86 Heikki Kojola .20 .50
87 Vaino Kolkka .20 .50
88 Harri Linnonmaa .20 .50
89 Jaakko Marttinen .20 .50
90 Matti Murto .20 .50
91 Lalli Partinen .20 .50
92 Juha Rantasila .20 .50
93 Heikki Riihiranta .20 .50
94 Jorma Rikala .20 .50
95 Henry Saleva .20 .50
96 Tommi Salmelainen .20 .50
97 Jorma Thusberg .20 .50
98 Jorma Virtanen .20 .50
99 Matti Vaisanen .20 .50
100 Juhani Aaltonen .20 .50
101 Jorma Immonen .20 .50
102 Martti Immonen .20 .50
103 Heikki Jarn .20 .50
104 Matti Keinonen .20 .50
105 Seppo Laakkio .20 .50
106 Timo Lahtinen .20 .50
107 Esa Peltonen .20 .50
108 Keijo Puhakka .20 .50
109 Seppo Railio .20 .50
110 Antti Ravi .20 .50
111 Timo Saari .20 .50
112 Esa Siren .20 .50
113 Seppo Suoraniemi .20 .50
114 Juhani Tamminen .20 .50
115 Jorma Vehmanen .20 .50
116 Stig Wetzell .20 .50
117 Leo Aikas .20 .50
118 Sakari Ahlberg .20 .50
119 Seppo Ahokainen .20 .50
120 Jorma Aro .20 .50
121 Esko Eriksson .20 .50
122 Markku Hakanen .20 .50
123 Timo Hirsimaki .20 .50
124 Jorma Kallio .20 .50
125 Esko Kaonpaa .20 .50
126 Pentti Koskela .20 .50
127 Pekka Kuusisto .20 .50
128 Pekka Leimu .20 .50
129 Len Lunde .20 .50
130 Jukka Mattila .20 .50
131 Lasse Oksanen .20 .50
132 Hannu Palmu .20 .50
133 Kari Palo-oja .20 .50
134 Jorma Peltonen .20 .50
135 Tuomo Sillman .20 .50
136 Veikko Suominen .20 .50
137 Pertti Ahokass .20 .50
138 Pertti Arvaja .20 .50
139 Christer Bergenheim .20 .50
140 Jorma Borgstrom .20 .50
141 Olli Hietanen .20 .50
142 Pentti Hiiros .20 .50
143 Eero Holopainen .20 .50
144 Kari Kinnunen .20 .50
145 Keijo Koivunen .20 .50
146 Ilpo Koskela .20 .50
147 Timo Kyntola .20 .50
148 Henry Leppa .20 .50
149 Erkki Mononen .20 .50
150 Pertti Nurmi .20 .50
151 Tero Raty .20 .50
152 Timo Sutinen .20 .50
153 Timo Turunen .20 .50
154 Jouko Oystila .20 .50
155 Hannu Haapalainen .20 .50
156 Olavi Haapalainen .20 .50
157 Jukka-Pekka Jarvenpaa .20 .50
158 Heimo Keinonen .20 .50
159 Markku Moisio .20 .50
160 Heikki Nurmi .20 .50
161 Seppo Nurmi .20 .50
162 Olva Oijennus .20 .50
163 Reino Pulkkinen .20 .50
164 Esko Rantanen .20 .50
165 Juhani Ruohonen .20 .50
166 Mikko Raikkonen .20 .50
167 Lauri Salomaa .20 .50
168 Leo Seppanen .20 .50
169 Pekka Uitus .20 .50
170 Jorma Vilen .20 .50
171 Tapio Virhimo .20 .50
172 Leo Haakana .20 .50
173 Seppo Hyvonen .20 .50
174 Heikki Juselius .20 .50
175 Hannu Lemander .20 .50
176 Kyosti Lahde .20 .50
177 Ari Mikkola .20 .50
178 Martti Makia .20 .50
179 Martti Narinen .20 .50
180 Pekka Nieminen .20 .50
181 Teijo Rasanen .20 .50
182 Timo Sartiala .20 .50
183 Pekka Sartjarvi .20 .50
184 Keijo Sinkkonen .20 .50
185 Martti Sinkkonen .20 .50
186 Arto Summanen .20 .50
187 Erkki Suni .20 .50
188 Seppo Urpalainen .20 .50
189 Matti Vaatamoinen .20 .50
190 Timo Vaatamoinen .20 .50
191 Jukka Alkula .20 .50
192 Pertti Ansakorpi .20 .50
193 Keijo Jarvinen .20 .50
194 Pertti Koivulahti .20 .50
195 Ilpo Kuisma .20 .50
196 Vesa Lehtoranta .20 .50
197 Antti Leppanen .20 .50
198 Pekka Marjamaki .20 .50
199 Mikko Mynttinen .20 .50
200 Pekka Makinen .20 .50
201 Seppo Makinen .20 .50
202 Antti Perttula .20 .50
203 Tuomo Rautiainen .20 .50
204 Jorma Saarikorpi .20 .50
205 Jorma Siitarinen .20 .50
206 Raimo Suoniemi .20 .50
207 Pertti Valkeapaa .20 .50
208 Kari Horkko .20 .50
209 Eero Juntunen .20 .50
210 Lauri Jamsen .20 .50
211 Kari Kauppila .20 .50
212 Lasse Kiili .20 .50
213 Olli Kokkonen .20 .50
214 Pekka Lahtela .20 .50
215 Robert Lamoureux .20 .50
216 Ilkka Mesikammen .20 .50
217 Timo Nummelin .20 .50
218 Rauli Ottila .20 .50
219 Matti Rautee .20 .50
220 Pekka Rautee .20 .50
221 Jari Rosberg .20 .50
222 Jouni Samuli .20 .50
223 Harri Silver .20 .50
224 Rauli Tammelin .20 .50
225 Bengt Wilenius .20 .50
226 Pertti Hasanen .20 .50
227 Kari Johansson .20 .50
228 Arto Kaunonen .20 .50
229 Timo Kokkonen .20 .50
230 Reijo Leppanen .20 .50
231 Seppo Lindstrom .20 .50
232 Hannu Luojola .20 .50
233 Hannu Niittoaho .20 .50
234 Reijo Paksal .20 .50
235 Seppo Parikka .20 .50
236 Jarmo Rantanen .20 .50
237 Kari Salonen .20 .50
238 Tapani Sura .20 .50
239 Kari Torkkel .20 .50
240 Risto Vainio .20 .50
241 Pentti Vihanto .20 .50
242 Seppo Wikstrom .20 .50
243 Urpo Ylonen .20 .50
244 Tapio Flinck .20 .50
245 Antti Heikkila .20 .50
246 Reijo Heinonen .20 .50
247 Jaakko Honkanen .20 .50
248 Veli-Pekka Ketola 1.25 3.00
249 Raimo Kilpio .20 .50
250 Tapio Koskinen .20 .50
251 Jarkko Levonen .20 .50
252 Kaj Matalamaki .20 .50
253 Pertti Makela .20 .50
254 Hannu Pulkkinen .20 .50
255 Pekka Rautakallio 1.25 3.00
256 Markku Riihimaki .20 .50
257 Matti Salmi .20 .50
258 Jorma Valtonen .20 .50
259 Anto Virtanen .20 .50
260 Erkki Vakiparta .20 .50
261 Martti Jarkko .20 .50
262 Torsti Jarvenpaa .20 .50
263 Tapio Kallio .20 .50
264 Jussi Kiansten .20 .50
265 Kimmo Korpela .20 .50
266 Jarmo Kuisma .20 .50
267 Antero Lehtonen .20 .50
268 Mikko Leinonen .20 .50
269 Tuomas Leinonen .20 .50
270 Lasse Litma .20 .50
271 Seppo Makinen .20 .50
272 Heikki Niemi .20 .50
273 Reijo Narvanen .20 .50
274 Kalevi Paakkonen .20 .50
275 Reijo Rossi .20 .50
276 Seppo Sevon .20 .50
277 Jorma Siren .20 .50
278 Risto Sirkkola .20 .50
279 Risto Hevonkorpi .20 .50
280 Veijo Hukkanen .20 .50
281 Timo Hyyti .20 .50
282 Kalle Impola .20 .50
283 Pertti Jarvenpaa .20 .50
284 Rauno Jarvinen .20 .50
285 Antti Kaivola .20 .50
286 Jorma Karvonen .20 .50
287 Pekka Karvonen .20 .50
288 Seppo Kettunen .20 .50
289 Kari Niemi .20 .50
290 Timo Niiniviita .20 .50
291 Jari Nurminen .20 .50
292 Pentti Poussu .20 .50
293 Matti Rautiainen .20 .50
294 Vesa Ronkainen .20 .50
295 Mauri Salminen .20 .50
296 Kari Silius .20 .50
297 Kimo Turtiainen .20 .50
298 Juha Wikman .20 .50
299 Juha-Pekka Aho .20 .50
300 Matti Estola .20 .50
301 Markku Heinonen .20 .50
302 Mauri Heinonen .20 .50
303 Jukka Hirsimaki .20 .50
304 Jarmo Huhtala .20 .50
305 Harri Huotari .20 .50
306 Kari Jarvinen .20 .50
307 Jari Kaarela .20 .50
308 Kai Lehto .20 .50
309 Jari Leppanen .20 .50
310 Jarmo Lilius .20 .50
311 Markus Matsson .20 .50
312 Jari Niinimaki .20 .50
313 Hannu Oksanen .20 .50
314 Sakari Pehu .20 .50
315 Mika Rajala .20 .50
316 Risto Siltanen .20 .50
317 Jarmo Siro .20 .50
318 Jukka Siro .20 .50
319 Jari Uusikartano .20 .50
320 Seppo Vartiainen .20 .50
321 Mika Weissman .20 .50
322 Seppo Aro .20 .50
323 Jari Huotari .20 .50
324 Ilkka Huura .20 .50
325 Jari Hytti .20 .50
326 Jarmo Jamalainen .20 .50
327 Jari Jokinen .20 .50
328 Tero Juojarvi .20 .50
329 Jari Jarvinen .20 .50
330 Lauri Kosonen .20 .50
331 Aki Laakso .20 .50
332 Ismo Laine .20 .50
333 Matti Lisko .20 .50
334 Dale Lunde .20 .50
335 Markku Pirkkalanniemi .20 .50
336 Rauno Saarnio .20 .50
337 Jukka Silander .20 .50
338 Olli-Pekka Turunen .20 .50
339 Mauri Unkila .20 .50
340 Jarmo Viteli .20 .50
341 Jukka Ahonen .20 .50
342 Jari Hallila .20 .50
343 Jari Helle .20 .50
344 Jari Hirsimaki .20 .50
345 Petri Jokinen .20 .50
346 Kari Jarvinen .20 .50
347 Arto Laine .20 .50
348 Ari Leinonen .20 .50
349 Jukka Oksanen .20 .50
350 Sten Pakarinen .20 .50
351 Jyrki Seppa .20 .50
352 Jari Simola .20 .50
353 Olli Sarkilahti .20 .50
354 Kari-Pekka Tarko .20 .50
355 Timo Toivonen .20 .50
356 Veli-Matti Uusimaa .20 .50
357 Risto Viljanen .20 .50
358 Timo Virtanen .20 .50
359 Teppo Valimaki .20 .50
360 Juha Yrjola .20 .50

1972 Finnish Hellas

This vintage Finnish set appears to feature players who appeared in the previous World Championships.

COMPLETE SET (99) 50.00 125.00
1 Seppo Ahokainen .20 .50
2 Veli-Pekka Ketola .60 1.50
3 Henry Leppa .20 .50
4 Harri Linnonmaa .20 .50
5 Pekka Marjamaki .20 .50
6 Lauri Mononen .20 .50
7 Matti Murto .20 .50
8 Timo Nummelin .20 .50
9 Lasse Oksanen .20 .50
10 Esa Peltonen .20 .50
11 Pekka Rautakallio .60 1.50
12 Seppo Repo .20 .50
13 Heikki Riihiranta .40 1.00
14 Tommi Salmelainen .20 .50
15 Leo Seppanen .20 .50
16 Juhani Tamminen .40 1.00
17 Timo Turunen .20 .50
18 Pertti Valkeapaa .20 .50
19 Jorma Valtonen .40 1.00
20 Jouko Oystila .20 .50
21 Timo Saari .20 .50
22 Seppo Suoraniemi .20 .50
23 Leif Holmqvist .40 1.00
24 Thommy Abrahamsson .40 1.00
25 Thommie Bergman .75 2.00
26 Stig Ostling .40 1.00
27 Lars Sjoberg .75 2.00
28 Carl Sundqvist .20 .50
29 Bjorn Johansson .20 .50
30 Tord Lundstrom .20 .50
31 Stig-Goran Johansson .20 .50
32 Stefan Karlsson .20 .50
33 Lars-Goran Nilsson .20 .50
34 Stig Larsson .20 .50
35 Mats Lindh .20 .50
36 Bjorn Palmqvist .20 .50
37 Inge Hammarstrom 4.00 10.00
38 Anders Hedberg 2.00 5.00
39 Kurt Larsson .20 .50
40 Hakan Pettersson .20 .50
41 Hakan Wickberg .20 .50
42 Borje Salming 6.00 15.00
43 Franz Funk .20 .50
44 Otto Schneitberger .20 .50
45 Josef Volk .20 .50
46 Rudolph Thanner .20 .50
47 Paul Langner .20 .50
48 Harald Kadow .20 .50
49 Anton Pohl .20 .50
50 Karl-Heinz Egger 2.00 5.00
51 Lorenz Funk .20 .50
52 Alois Schloder .20 .50
53 Gustav Hanig .20 .50
54 Philips Reiner .20 .50
55 Bernd Kuhn .20 .50
56 Johan Eimansberger .20 .50
57 Rainer Makatsch .20 .50
58 Michael Eibl .20 .50
59 Hans Schichti .20 .50
60 Anrton Hoffher .20 .50
61 Valdimir Lutchenko .40 1.00
62 Aleksandr Gusev .30 .75
63 Vladimir Lutchenko .40 1.00
64 Viktor Kuzkin .20 .50
65 Aleksandr Ragulin .40 1.00
66 Igor Romishevski .20 .50
67 Gennadi Tsigankov .40 1.00
68 Valeri Vasiliev .40 1.00
69 Yuri Blinov .20 .50
70 Alexander Maltsev 2.00 5.00
71 Evgeny Mishakov .30 .75
72 Boris Mikhailov 2.00 5.00
73 Vjatseslav Anisin .20 .50
74 Alexander Yakushev 2.00 5.00
75 Vladimir Petrov 1.25 3.00
76 Valeri Kharlamov 4.00 10.00
77 Vladimir Vikulov .30 .75
78 Vladimir Shadrin .30 .75
79 Vladislav Tretiak 6.00 15.00
80 Vladimir Dzurilla .60 1.50
81 Jiri Holecek .40 1.00
82 Josef Horesovsky .20 .50
83 Oldrich Machac .20 .50
84 Jaroslav Holik .30 .75
85 Rudolf Tajcnar .20 .50
86 Frantisek Pospisil .30 .75
87 Jiri Kochta .20 .50
88 Jan Klapac .20 .50
89 Vladimir Martinec .20 .50
90 Richard Farda .30 .75
91 Bohuslav Stastny .30 .75
92 Vaclav Nedomansky .60 1.50
93 Julius Haas .20 .50
94 Josef Palecek .20 .50
95 Jiri Bubla .40 1.00
96 Milan Kuzela .20 .50
97 Vladimir Bednar .20 .50
98 Jiri Holik .40 1.00
99 Ivan Hlinka .30 .75

1972 Finnish Panda Toronto

COMPLETE SET (118) 50.00 100.00
1 Juhani Bostrom .40 1.00
2 Gary Engberg .40 1.00
3 Kimmo Heino .40 1.00
4 Mauri Kaukokari .40 1.00
5 Vaino Kolkka .40 1.00
6 Harri Linnonmaa .40 1.00
7 Jaakko Marttinen .40 1.00
8 Matti Murto .40 1.00
9 Lalli Partinen .40 1.00
10 Juha Rantasila .40 1.00
11 Heikki Riihiranta .40 1.00
12 Jorma Rikala .40 1.00
13 Tommi Salmelainen .40 1.00
14 Jorma Thusberg .40 1.00
15 Jorma Virtanen .40 1.00
16 Matti Vaisanen .40 1.00
17 Sakari Ahlberg .40 1.00
18 Jorma Aro .40 1.00
19 Esko Eriksson .40 1.00
20 Markku Hakanen .40 1.00
21 Matti Hakanen .40 1.00
22 Reijo Hakanen .40 1.00
23 Timo Hirsimaki .40 1.00
24 Jorma Kallio .40 1.00
25 Esko Kaonpaa .40 1.00
26 Pentti Koskela .40 1.00
27 Pekka Kuusisto .40 1.00
28 Pekka Leimu .40 1.00
29 Lasse Oksanen .40 1.00
30 Kari Palo-oja .40 1.00
31 Jorma Peltonen .40 1.00
32 Veikko Suominen .40 1.00
33 Tapio Flinck .40 1.00
34 Pentti Hakamaki .40 1.00
35 Antti Heikkila .40 1.00
36 Reijo Heinonen .40 1.00
37 Jaakko Honkanen .40 1.00
38 Veli-Pekka Ketola .40 1.00
39 Raimo Kilpio .40 1.00
40 Tapio Koskinen .40 1.00
41 Kaj Matalamaki .40 1.00
42 Pekka Rautakallio .40 1.00
43 Matti Salmi .40 1.00
44 Kari-Pekka Toivonen .40 1.00
45 Jorma Valtonen .40 1.00
46 Anto Virtanen .40 1.00
47 Erkki Vakiparta .40 1.00
48 Vitaly Davydov .75 2.00
49 Anatoly Firsov .75 2.00
50 Valeri Kharlamov 8.00 20.00
51 Victor Konovalenko .75 2.00
52 Victor Kuzkin .75 2.00
53 Yuri Liapkin .75 2.00
54 Vladimir Lutchenko .75 2.00
55 Alexander Maltsev 2.00 5.00
56 Alexander Martyniuk .75 2.00
57 Boris Mikhailov 2.00 5.00
58 Aleksander Ragulin .75 2.00
59 Igor Romishevskyi .75 2.00
60 Vladimir Shadrin .75 2.00
61 Viacheslav Starshinov .75 2.00
62 Vladislav Tretiak 8.00 20.00
63 Evgenyi Zimin .75 2.00
64 Christer Abrahamsson .75 2.00
65 Tommy Abrahamsson .75 2.00
66 Arne Carlsson .40 1.00
67 Inge Hammarstrom 2.00 5.00
68 Leif Holmqvist .75 2.00
69 Stig-Goran Johansson .40 1.00
70 Stefan Karlsson .40 1.00
71 Hans Lindberg .40 1.00
72 Tord Lundstrom .40 1.00
73 Lars-Goran Nilsson .40 1.00
74 Bert-Ola Nordlander .40 1.00
75 Hakan Nygren .40 1.00
76 Bjorn Palmqvist .40 1.00
77 Ulf Sterner .40 1.00
78 Lennart Svedberg .40 1.00
79 Hakan Wickberg .40 1.00
80 Josef Cerny .40 1.00
81 Richard Farda .40 1.00
82 Ivan Hlinka .40 1.00
83 Jiri Holecek .40 1.00
84 Jiri Holik .40 1.00
85 Josef Horesovsky .40 1.00
86 Milan Kuzela .40 1.00
87 Oldrich Machac .40 1.00
88 Vladimir Martinec .40 1.00
89 Vladimir Nadrchal .40 1.00
90 Vaclav Nedomansky 1.50 4.00
91 Frantisek Panchartek .40 1.00
92 Frantisek Pospisil .40 1.00
93 Marcel Sakac .40 1.00
94 Bohuslav Stastny .40 1.00
95 Rudolf Tajcnar .40 1.00
96 Esa Isaksson .40 1.00
97 Heikki Jarn .40 1.00
98 Veli-Pekka Ketola 1.50 4.00
99 Ilpo Koskela .40 1.00
100 Seppo Lindstrom .40 1.00
101 Harri Linnonmaa .40 1.00
102 Pekka Marjamaki .40 1.00
103 Erkki Mononen .40 1.00
104 Lauri Mononen .40 1.00
105 Matti Murto .40 1.00
106 Lasse Oksanen .40 1.00
107 Esa Peltonen .40 1.00
108 Seppo Repo .40 1.00
109 Tommi Salmelainen .40 1.00
110 Jorma Valtonen .40 1.00
111 Urpo Ylonen .40 1.00
112 Jouko Oystila .40 1.00
113 Sovjet - Finland .40 1.00
114 Sverige - Tjeckoslovakien .40 1.00
115 Finland - Svergie .40 1.00
116 Tjeckoslovakien - Sovjet .40 1.00
117 USA - Sovjet .40 1.00
118 Hockey Sticks .40 1.00

1973-74 Finnish Jaakiekko

COMPLETE SET (325) 125.00 250.00
1 Vjatsjeslav Anisin .75 2.00
2 Aleksandr Bodunov .75 2.00
3 Aleksandr Gusev .75 2.00
4 Valeri Kharlamov 6.00 15.00
5 Aleksandr Yakushev 2.00 5.00
6 Juri Lebedev .75 2.00
7 Juri Liapkin .75 2.00
8 Vladimir Lutshenko .75 2.00
9 Aleksandr Maltsev 2.00 5.00
10 Aleksandr Martiniuk .75 2.00
11 Boris Mikhailov 2.00 5.00
12 Jevgeni Paladiev .75 2.00
13 Vladimir Petrov 2.00 5.00
14 Aleksandr Ragulin .75 2.00
15 Vladimir Shadrin .75 2.00
16 Aleksandr Sidelnikov .75 2.00
17 Vladislav Tretiak 8.00 20.00
18 Gennadi Tsigankov .75 2.00
19 Valeri Vasiljev 2.00 5.00
20 Vladimir Vikulov .75 2.00
21 Aleksandr Voltshkov .75 2.00
22 Christer Abrahamsson 1.25 3.00
23 Thommy Abrahamsson 1.25 3.00
24 Roland Bond .40 1.00
25 Arne Carlsson .40 1.00
26 Inge Hammarstrom 2.00 5.00
27 Anders Hedberg 2.00 5.00
28 Bjorn Johansson .40 1.00
29 Stefan Karlsson .40 1.00
30 Curt Larsson .40 1.00
31 Tord Lundstrom .40 1.00
32 William Lofqvist .40 1.00
33 Ulf Nilsson 2.00 5.00
34 Borje Salming 6.00 15.00
35 Lars-Erik Sjoberg 1.25 3.00
36 Ulf Sterner .40 1.00
37 Karl-Johan Sundqvist .40 1.00
38 Dan Soderstrom .40 1.00
39 Hakan Wickberg .40 1.00
40 Kjell-Arne Wickstrom .40 1.00
41 Dick Yderstrom .40 1.00
42 Mats Ahlberg .40 1.00
43 Peter Adamik .40 1.00
44 Jiri Bubla .40 1.00
45 Jiri Crha 1.25 3.00
46 Richard Farda .40 1.00
47 Ivan Hlinka .75 2.00
48 Jiri Holecek .75 2.00
49 Jaroslav Holik .40 1.00
50 Jiri Holik .40 1.00
51 Josef Horesovsky .40 1.00
52 Jan Klapac .40 1.00
53 Jiri Kochta .40 1.00
54 Milan Kuzela .40 1.00
55 Oldrich Machac .40 1.00
56 Vladimir Martinec .40 1.00
57 Vaclav Nedomansky 1.25 3.00
58 Jiri Novak .40 1.00
59 Josef Palecek .40 1.00
60 Frantisek Pospisil .40 1.00
61 Bohuslav Stastny .40 1.00
62 Karel Vohralik .40 1.00
63 Seppo Ahokainen .40 1.00
64 Matti Keinonen .40 1.00
65 Veli-Pekka Ketola 1.25 3.00
66 Ilpo Koskela .40 1.00
67 Ilpo Kuisma .40 1.00
68 Pekka Kuusisto .40 1.00
69 Henry Leppa .40 1.00
70 Antti Leppanen .40 1.00
71 Seppo Lindstrom .40 1.00
72 Lauri Mononen .40 1.00
73 Timo Nummelin .40 1.00
74 Lalli Partinen .40 1.00
75 Esa Peltonen .40 1.00
76 Pekka Rautakallio 1.25 3.00
77 Seppo Repo .40 1.00
78 Heikki Riihiranta .40 1.00
79 Timo Sutinen .40 1.00
80 Juhani Tamminen .40 1.00
81 Timo Turunen .40 1.00
82 Jorma Valtonen .40 1.00
83 Jorma Vehmanen .40 1.00
84 Jouko Oystila .40 1.00
85 Josef Batkiewicz .40 1.00
86 Krzysztof Bialynicki .40 1.00
87 Stefan Chowaniec .40 1.00
88 Ludwik Czachovski .40 1.00
89 Andrzej Czczepaniec .40 1.00
90 Stanislav Fryzlewicz .40 1.00
91 Robert Goralczyk .40 1.00
92 Mieczyslaw Jaskierski .40 1.00
93 Tadeusz Kacik .40 1.00
94 Adam Kopczynski .40 1.00
95 Valery Kosyl .40 1.00
96 Tadeusz Obloj .40 1.00
97 Jerzy Potz .40 1.00
98 Andrzej Slowakiewicz .40 1.00
99 Josef Slowakiewicz .40 1.00
100 Jan Szeja .40 1.00
101 Leszek Tokarz .40 1.00
102 Wieslav Tokarz .40 1.00
103 Henryk Vojtynek .40 1.00
104 Walenty Zietara .40 1.00
105 Pertti Arvaja .40 1.00
106 Olli J. Hietanen .40 1.00
107 Olli T. Hietanen .40 1.00
108 Pentti Hiiros .40 1.00
109 Eero Holopainen .40 1.00
110 Kari Kinnunen .40 1.00
111 Ilpo Koskela .40 1.00
112 Timo Kyntola .40 1.00
113 Henry Leppa .40 1.00
114 Jan Lindberg .40 1.00
115 Lauri Mononen .40 1.00
116 Mika Rajala .40 1.00
117 Pertti Nurmi .40 1.00
118 Jyrki Seivo .40 1.00
119 Jorma Siitarinen .40 1.00
120 Seppo Suoraniemi .40 1.00
121 Timo Sutinen .40 1.00
122 Timo Turunen .40 1.00
123 Jorma Valtonen .40 1.00
124 Seppo Vartiainen .40 1.00
125 Jouko Oystila .40 1.00
126 Juhani Bostrom .40 1.00
127 Matti Hagman 1.25 3.00
128 Kimmo Heino .40 1.00
129 Jorma Immonen .40 1.00
130 Pentti Karlsson .40 1.00
131 Mauri Kaukokari .40 1.00
132 Jarmo Koivunen .40 1.00
133 Vaino Kolkka .40 1.00
134 Harri Linnonmaa .40 1.00
135 Jaakko Marttinen .40 1.00
136 Matti Murto .40 1.00
137 Lalli Partinen .40 1.00
138 Esa Peltonen .40 1.00
139 Juha Rantasila .40 1.00
140 Heikki Riihiranta .40 1.00
141 Jorma Rikala .40 1.00
142 Tommi Salmelainen .40 1.00
143 Henry Saleva .40 1.00
144 Juhani Tamminen .75 2.00
145 Jorma Thusberg .40 1.00
146 Jorma Virtanen .40 1.00
147 Matti Vaisanen .40 1.00
148 Stig Wetzell .40 1.00
149 Jukka Alkula .40 1.00
150 Pertti Ansakorpi .40 1.00
151 Hannu Haapalainen .40 1.00
152 Martti Jarkko .40 1.00
153 Keijo Jarvinen .40 1.00
154 Pertti Koivulahti .40 1.00
155 Ilpo Kuisma .40 1.00
156 Antero Lehtonen .40 1.00
157 Antti Leppanen .40 1.00
158 Lasse Litma .40 1.00
159 Pekka Marjamaki .40 1.00
160 Mikko Mynttinen .40 1.00
161 Pekka Makinen .40 1.00
162 Seppo I. Makinen .40 1.00
163 Seppo S. Makinen .40 1.00
164 Keijo Mannisto .40 1.00
165 Antti Perttula .40 1.00
166 Tuomo Rautiainen .40 1.00
167 Jorma Saarikorpi .40 1.00
168 Juha Silvennoinen .40 1.00
169 Jorma Siren .40 1.00
170 Raimo Suoniemi .40 1.00
171 Pertti Valkeapaa .40 1.00
172 Sakari Ahlberg .40 1.00
173 Seppo Ahokainen .40 1.00
174 Jorma Aro .40 1.00
175 Esko Eriksson .40 1.00
176 Markku Hakanen .40 1.00
177 Reijo Hakanen .40 1.00
178 Martti Helle .40 1.00
179 Erkki Jarvinen .40 1.00
180 Jorma Kallio .40 1.00
181 Erkki Kesalainen .40 1.00
182 Pekka Kuusisto .40 1.00
183 Pekka Leimu .40 1.00
184 Jukka Mattila .40 1.00
185 Esko Makinen .40 1.00
186 Lasse Oksanen .40 1.00
187 Kari Palo-oja .40 1.00
188 Jorma Peltonen .40 1.00
189 Pekka Rampa .40 1.00
190 Heikki Salminen .40 1.00
191 Tuomo Sillman .40 1.00
192 Veikko Suominen .40 1.00
193 Tapio Virhimo .40 1.00
194 Juhani Aaltonen .40 1.00
195 Bjorn Herbert .40 1.00
196 Hannu Kapanen .40 1.00
197 Matti Keinonen .40 1.00
198 Lasse Kiili .40 1.00
199 Matti Koskinen .40 1.00
200 Martti Kuokkanen .40 1.00
201 Urpo Kuukauppi .40 1.00
202 Seppo Laakkio .40 1.00
203 Timo Lahtinen .40 1.00
204 Juhani Laine .40 1.00
205 Heikki Leppik .40 1.00
206 Osmo Lotjonen .40 1.00
207 Kyosti Majava .40 1.00
208 Keijo Puhakka .40 1.00
209 Antti Ravi .40 1.00
210 Seppo Repo .40 1.00
211 Timo Saari .40 1.00
212 Arto Siissala .40 1.00
213 Jorma Vehmanen .40 1.00
214 Pentti Viitanen .40 1.00
215 Leo Aikas .40 1.00
216 Raine Heinonen .40 1.00
217 Vladimir Jursinov .40 1.00
218 Jukka-Pekka Jarvenpaa .40 1.00
219 Pertti Jarvenpaa .40 1.00
220 Heimo Keinonen .40 1.00
221 Seppo Kettunen .40 1.00
222 Veikko Kirveskoski .40 1.00
223 Reijo Laksola .40 1.00
224 Raimo Majapuro .40 1.00
225 Markku Moisio .40 1.00
226 Heikki Nurmi .40 1.00
227 Seppo Nurmi .40 1.00
228 Olva Oijennus .40 1.00
229 Esko Rantanen .40 1.00
230 Matti Rautiainen .40 1.00
231 Juhani Ruohonen .40 1.00
232 Mikko Raikkonen .40 1.00
233 Lauri Salomaa .40 1.00
234 Veikko Savolainen .40 1.00
235 Leo Seppanen .40 1.00
236 Veikko Seppanen .40 1.00
237 Pekka Uitus .40 1.00
238 Kari Viitalahti .40 1.00
239 Jorma Vilen .40 1.00
240 Asko Ahonen .40 1.00
241 Tapio Flinck .40 1.00
242 Martti Hakanen .40 1.00
243 Antti Heikkila .40 1.00
244 Reijo Heinonen .40 1.00
245 Jaakko Honkanen .40 1.00
246 Jari Kaski .40 1.00
247 Veli-Pekka Ketola .40 1.00
248 Raimo Kilpio .40 1.00
249 Tapio Koskinen .40 1.00
250 Jarkko Levonen .40 1.00
251 Kaj Matalamaki .40 1.00
252 Pertti Makela .40 1.00
253 Jaakko Niemi .40 1.00
254 Hannu Pulkkinen .40 1.00
255 Pekka Rautakallio .40 1.00
256 Markku Riihimaki .40 1.00
257 Anto Virtanen .40 1.00
258 Erkki Vakiparta .40 1.00
259 Pertti Hasanen .40 1.00
260 Rainer Holmroos .40 1.00
261 Kari Johansson .40 1.00
262 Arto Kaunonen .40 1.00
263 Timo Kokkonen .40 1.00
264 Reijo Leppanen .40 1.00
265 Seppo Lindstrom .40 1.00
266 Hannu Luojola .40 1.00
267 Hannu Niittoaho .40 1.00
268 Reijo Paksal .40 1.00
269 Seppo Parikka .40 1.00
270 Jarmo Rantanen .40 1.00
271 Kari Hyokki .40 1.00
272 Kari Salonen .40 1.00
273 Tapani Sura .40 1.00
274 Kari Torkkel .40 1.00
275 Risto Vainio .40 1.00
276 Pentti Vihanto .40 1.00
277 Urpo Ylonen .40 1.00
278 Lars Elifolk .40 1.00
279 Kari Horkko .40 1.00
280 Hannu Jortikka .40 1.00
281 Eero Juntunen .40 1.00
282 Lauri Jamsen .40 1.00
283 Jari Kapanen .40 1.00
284 Jari Kauppila .40 1.00
285 Matti Kauppila .40 1.00
286 Jukka Koskilahti .40 1.00
287 Jukka Koivu .40 1.00
288 Ilkka Laaksonen .40 1.00
289 Robert Lamoureux .40 1.00
290 Hannu Lunden .40 1.00
291 Ilkka Mesikammen .40 1.00
292 Timo Nummelin .40 1.00
293 Timo Nurminen .40 1.00
294 Rauli Ottila .40 1.00
295 Matti Rautee .40 1.00
296 Pekka Rautee .40 1.00
297 Jari Rosberg .40 1.00
298 Tarmo Saarni .40 1.00
299 Asko Salminen .40 1.00
300 Jouni Samuli .40 1.00
301 Rauli Tammelin .40 1.00
302 Veijo Wahlsten .40 1.00
303 Bengt Wilenius .40 1.00
304 Denis Bavaudin .40 1.00
305 Mikko Erholm .40 1.00
306 Matti Fors .40 1.00
307 Esa Hakkarainen .40 1.00
308 Veikko Ihalainen .40 1.00
309 Esa Isaksson .40 1.00
310 Juhani Jylha .40 1.00
311 Heikki Kauhanen .40 1.00
312 Jari Laiho .40 1.00
313 Arto Laine .40 1.00
314 Jouni Peltonen .40 1.00
315 Jouni Rinne .40 1.00
316 Kai Rosvall .40 1.00
317 Seppo Santala .40 1.00
318 Jari Sarronlahti .40 1.00
319 Matti Saurio .40 1.00
320 Ari Sjoman .40 1.00
321 Erkki Sundelin .40 1.00
322 Ismo Villa .40 1.00
323 Mikko Ylaja .40 1.00
324 Veijo Ylanen .40 1.00
NNO Album 25.00 50.00

1974 Finnish Jenkki

COMPLETE SET (120) 50.00 100.00
1 Sakari Ahlberg .30 .75
2 Seppo Ahokainen .30 .75
3 Jukka Alkula .30 .75
4 Jorma Aro .30 .75
5 Hannu Haapalainen .30 .75
6 Veli-Pekka Ketola 1.25 3.00
7 Tapio Koskinen .30 .75
8 Henry Leppa .30 .75
9 Antti Leppanen .30 .75
10 Reijo Leppanen .30 .75
11 Pekka Marjamaki .30 .75
12 Matti Murto .30 .75
13 Esa Peltonen .30 .75
14 Pekka Rautakallio 1.25 3.00
15 Leo Seppanen .30 .75
16 Juha Silvennoinen .30 .75
17 Raimo Suoniemi .30 .75
18 Seppo Suoraniemi .30 .75
19 Timo Sutinen .30 .75
20 Juhani Tamminen .75 2.00
21 Pertti Valkeapaa .30 .75
22 Christer Abrahamsson 1.25 3.00
23 Thommie Bergman 1.25 3.00
24 Roland Bond .30 .75
25 Anders Hedberg 2.00 5.00
26 Bjorn Johansson .30 .75
27 Stefan Karlsson .30 .75
28 Mats Lind .30 .75
29 Tord Lundstrom .30 .75
30 William Lofqvist .30 .75
31 Ulf Nilsson 2.00 5.00
32 Bjorn Palmqvist .30 .75
33 Hakan Pettersson .30 .75
34 Lars-Erik Sjoberg .75 2.00
35 Ulf Sterner .30 .75
36 Karl-Johan Sundqvist .30 .75
37 Hakan Wickberg .30 .75
38 Kjell-Arne Wickstrom .30 .75
39 Dick Yderstrom .30 .75
40 Mats Ahlberg .30 .75
41 Stig Ostling .30 .75
42 Vjatseslav Anisin .40 1.00
43 Aleksandr Bodunov .40 1.00
44 Aleksandr Gusev .40 1.00
45 Valeri Kharlamov 6.00 15.00
46 Aleksandr Yakushev 2.00 5.00
47 Juri Liapkin .40 1.00
48 Vladimir Lutshenko .40 1.00
49 Aleksandr Maltsev 2.00 5.00
50 Aleksandr Martiniuk .40 1.00
51 Boris Mikhailov 2.00 5.00
52 Jevgeni Paladiev .40 1.00
53 Vladimir Petrov 2.00 5.00
54 Aleksandr Ragulin .40 1.00

55 Vladimir Shadrin .40 1.00
56 Aleksandr Sidelnikov .40 1.00
57 Vladislav Tretiak 6.00 15.00
58 Gennadi Tsigankov .40 1.00
59 Valeri Vasiljev 2.00 5.00
60 Vladimir Vikulov .40 1.00
61 Aleksandr Voltshkov .40 1.00
62 Julij Blinov .40 1.00
63 Vladimir Sepovalov .40 1.00
64 Josef Horesovsky .30 .75
65 Peter Adamik .30 .75
66 Vladimir Bednar .30 .75
67 Jiri Bubla .75 2.00
68 Richard Farda .30 .75
69 Julius Haas .30 .75
70 Ivan Hlinka .75 2.00
71 Jiri Holecek .75 2.00
72 Jaroslav Holik .30 .75
73 Jiri Holik .30 .75
74 Jan Klapac .30 .75
75 Jiri Kochta .30 .75
76 Milan Kuzela .30 .75
77 Oldrich Machac .30 .75
78 Vladimir Martinec .30 .75
79 Vaclav Nedomansky 1.50 4.00
80 Josef Palecek .30 .75
81 Frantisek Pospisil .30 .75
82 Bohuslav Stastny .30 .75
83 Rudolf Tajcnar .30 .75
84 Karl Vohralik .30 .75
85 Jerzy Potz .30 .75
86 Andrzej Slowakiewicz .30 .75
87 Josef Slowakiewicz .30 .75
88 Leszek Tokarz .30 .75
89 Wieslaw Tokarz .30 .75
90 Henryk Vojtynek .30 .75
91 Walenty Zietara .30 .75
92 Josef Batkiewicz .30 .75
93 Stefan Chowaniec .30 .75
94 Ludvik Czachovski .30 .75
95 Andrzej Czczepaniec .30 .75
96 Robert Goralczyk .30 .75
97 Mieczyslaw Jaskierski .30 .75
98 Tadeusz Kacik .30 .75
99 Adam Kopczynski .30 .75
100 Valery Kosyl .30 .75
101 Tadeusz Obloj .30 .75
102 Joachim Stasche .30 .75
103 Roland Peters .30 .75
104 Dietmar Peters .30 .75
105 Bernd Karrenbauer .30 .75
106 Peter Prusa .30 .75
107 Rainer Patschinski .30 .75
108 Hartmut Nickel .30 .75
109 Dieter Dewitz .30 .75
110 Harald Felber .30 .75
111 Joachim Hurbanek .30 .75
112 Wolfgang Fischer .30 .75
113 Frank Braun .30 .75
114 Dieter Huschto .30 .75
115 Ruediger Hoack .30 .75
116 Dieter Simon .30 .75
117 Hartwig Schur .30 .75
118 Jochen Philip .30 .75
119 Rolf Bielas .30 .75
120 Peter Slapke .30 .75

1974 Finnish Typotor

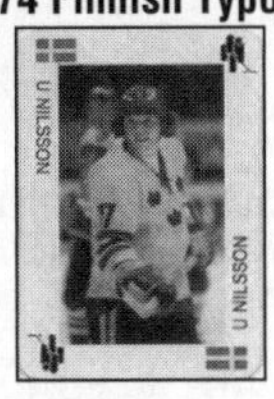

COMPLETE SET (120)
1 Matti Murto .40 1.00
2 Esa Peltonen .20 .50
3 Juha Rantasila .40 1.00
4 Heikki Riihiranta .75 2.00
5 Juhani Tamminen .75 2.00
6 Jorma Virtanen .40 1.00
7 Seppo Ahokainen .40 1.00
8 Jorma Kallio .20 .50
9 Ari Kankaanpera .20 .50
10 Lasse Oksanen .20 .50
11 Jorma Peltonen .40 1.00
12 Tapio Virhimo .20 .50
13 Ilpo Kokela .20 .50
14 Henry Leppa .20 .50
15 Seppo Suoraniemi .20 .50
16 Timo Sutinen .20 .50
17 Timo Turunen .20 .50
18 Jorma Valtonen .40 1.00
19 Mikko Erholm .20 .50
20 Esa Isaksson .20 .50
21 Juhani Jylha .20 .50
22 Tapani Koskimaki .20 .50
23 Hannu Siivonen .20 .50
24 Jorma Vehmanen .40 1.00
25 Jukka Alkula .20 .50
26 Hannu Haapalainen .20 .50
27 Martti Jarkko .20 .50
28 Antti Leppannen .20 .50
29 Pekka Marjamaki .20 .50
30 Raimo Suoniemi .20 .50
31 Lasse Kiili .20 .50
32 Timo Nummelin .20 .50
33 Matti Rautee .20 .50
34 Pekka Rautee .20 .50
35 Seppo Repo .20 .50
36 Jouko Oystila .20 .50
37 Kari Johansson .20 .50
38 Reijo Leppanen .20 .50
39 Seppo Lindstrom .20 .50
40 Hannu Niittoaho .20 .50
41 Pentti Vihanto .20 .50
42 Urpo Ylonen .20 .50
43 Antti Heikkila .20 .50
44 Reijo Heinonen .20 .50
45 Veli-Pekka Ketola .60 1.50
46 Raimo Kilpio .20 .50
47 Tapio Koskinen .20 .50
48 Pekka Rautakallio .75 2.00
49 Seppo Ahokainen .20 .50
50 Henry Leppa .20 .50
51 Antti Leppanen .20 .50
52 Pekka Marjamaki .20 .50
53 Matti Murto .20 .50
54 Esa Peltonen .20 .50
55 Heikki Riihiranta .40 1.00
56 Timo Sutinen .20 .50
57 Juhani Tamminen .75 2.00
58 Rolf Bielas .20 .50
59 Joachim Hurbanek .20 .50
60 Reinhard Karger .20 .50
61 Hartmut Nickel .20 .50
62 Rudiger Noack .20 .50
63 Helmut Novy .20 .50
64 Dietmar Peters .20 .50
65 Peter Prusa .20 .50
66 Peter Slapke .20 .50
67 Vakeri Kharlamov 4.00 10.00
68 Alexander Yakushev 1.50 4.00
69 Alexander Maltsev 1.50 4.00
70 Boris Mikhailov 1.50 4.00
71 Vladimir Petrov 1.50 4.00
72 Vladimir Shadrin .40 1.00
73 Vladislav Tretiak 6.00 15.00
74 Gennady Tsygankov .40 1.00
75 Valeri Vasilijev 1.25 3.00
76 Per-Erik Ingier .20 .50
77 Morten Johansen .20 .50
78 Hakan Lundenes .20 .50
79 N. Nilsen .20 .50
80 Morten Sethereng .20 .50
81 T. Skar .20 .50
82 J-E. Solberg .20 .50
83 K. Thorkildsen .20 .50
84 T. Troymark .20 .50
85 J. Borovicz .20 .50
86 L. Czachovski .20 .50
87 Michael Jaskierski .20 .50
88 Tadeusz Kacik .20 .50
89 Adam Kopczynski .20 .50
90 Tadeusz Obtoj .20 .50
91 Jan Szeja .20 .50
92 Leszek Tokarz .20 .50
93 Walenty Zietara .20 .50
94 Christer Abrahamsson .50 1.50
95 Tommy Abrahamsson .75 2.00
96 Anders Hedberg 1.50 4.00
97 Stefan Karlsson .20 .50
98 Kjell-Rune Milton .20 .50
99 Ulf Nilsson 1.50 4.00
100 Bjorn Palmqvist .20 .50
101 Dan Soderstrom .20 .50
102 Mats Ahlberg .30 .75
103 Guy Dubois .40 1.00
104 C. Friedrich .20 .50
105 Charly Henzen .20 .50
106 Ueli Hofmann .20 .50
107 Mirco Horisberger .20 .50
108 M. Lindenmann .20 .50
109 Alfio Molina .20 .50
110 Tony Neininger .20 .50
111 U. Williman .20 .50
112 Richard Farda .20 .50
113 Ivan Hlinka .40 1.00
114 Jiri Holecek .40 1.00
115 Jiri Holik .40 1.00
116 Josef Horesovsky .20 .50
117 Jiri Kochta .20 .50
118 Oldrich Machac .20 .50
119 Vladimir Martinec .20 .50
120 Bohuslav Stastny .30 .75

1977-79 Finnish Sportscasters

This set mirrors the North American version in many ways in that the series features personalities from many sports and that only the hockey players are listed. Card front and back text is entirely in Finnish. The checklist may not be complete. Additional information can be forwarded to us via hockeymag@beckett.com.

12-279 MM-Kilpailut .50 1.00
14-335 Suomen Maajoukkue .50 1.00
16-364 Antti Leppanen 2.50 5.00
Jorma Valtonen
17-397 Veli-Pekka Ketola 2.50 5.00
19-436 Pekka Marjamaki 1.50 3.00
19-447 MM-Kilpailut .50 1.00
20-469 Vaclav Nedomansky 2.50 5.00
21-492 Pelaajien Varusteet .50 1.00
23-532 Hat Trick 1.50 3.00
26-673 Valeri Kharlamov 2.50 5.00
Boris Mikhailov
Vladimir Petrov
26-692 Brad Park 4.00 8.00
31-736 NHL 1.50 3.00
32-747 Matti Hagman 2.50 5.00
33-775 Porin Assat .50 1.00
33-785 Jean Beliveau 6.00 12.00
36-845 Lalli Partinen 1.00 2.00
37-869 Phil Esposito 7.50 15.00
38-891 Bobby Clarke 4.00 8.00
38-895 Guy Lafleur 5.00 10.00
40-937 Matti Keinonen 1.00 2.00
40-945 The Stanley Cup 2.50 5.00
41-961 Matti Murto 1.00 2.00
42-1008 Viivoja Jaasa .50 1.00
43-1009 HIFK 1.50 3.00
43-1031 Tommy Abrahamsson 5.00 10.00
Christer Abrahamsson
45-1057 Lasse Oksanen 1.50 3.00
45-1075 Ilves Tampere 1.50 3.00
45-1069 Jaroslav Jirik 1.00 2.00
46-1084 Juhani Tamminen 1.50 3.00
47-1125 TPS .50 1.00
47-1113 Helmut Balderis 1.50 3.00
47-1106 Pekka Rautakallio 2.50 5.00
48-1152 Timo Nummelin 1.50 3.00
48-1145 Ken Dryden 10.00 20.00
49-1174 Gerry Cheevers 5.00 10.00
49-1197 Bryan Trottier 4.00 8.00
49-1176 Esa Peltonen 2.50 5.00
50-1178 Steve Shutt 2.50 5.00
50-1197 Rogie Vachon 4.00 8.00
50-1199 Teppo Rastio 1.50 3.00
50-1188 Izvestia Tournament .50 1.00
50-1190 Laman .50 1.00
51-1218 Jiri Holik 1.50 3.00
Jaroslav Holik
51-1214 Jokerit 1.50 3.00
51-1212 Rangaistukset .50 1.00
51-1224 Stan Mikita 6.00 12.00
51-1201 Markus Mattsson 1.00 2.00
52-1243 Ilpo Koskela 2.50 5.00
52-1235 Oulun Karpat .50 1.00
52-1230 Nurkkapeli .50 1.00
52-1232 Garry Unger 2.50 5.00
53-1265 Darryl Sittler 6.00 12.00
54-1273 Antero Lehtonen 2.50 5.00
54-1290 Bryan Trottier 5.00 10.00
Clark Gillies
Mike Bossy
56-1324 Denis Potvin 4.00 8.00
57-1364 Kasvosuojukset 1.00 2.00
57-1358 Bobby Hull 10.00 20.00
57-1356 Guy Lafleur 5.00 10.00
58-1392 Yvan Cournoyer 4.00 8.00
58-1381 Bobby Hull 10.00 20.00
66-1566 Montreal Forum 6.00 12.00
68-1623 Pete Stemkowski 2.50 5.00
69-1649 Bobby Clarke 4.00 8.00
70-1663 Borje Salming 5.00 10.00
70-1670 Gordie Howe 15.00 30.00
Mark Howe
Marty Howe
71-1686 Alexander Yakushev 2.50 5.00
71-1699 Soviet Union 1.00 2.00
72-1716 Lester Patrick 1.50 3.00
72-1705 Jukka Porvari 1.50 3.00
74-1758 Ed Giacomin 4.00 8.00
74-1760 Seppo Repo 1.50 3.00
75-1796 Risto Siltanen 2.50 5.00
75-1800 Kalevi Numminen 1.00 2.00
76-1801 Pertti Koivulahti 1.00 2.00
76-1821 Mikko Leinonen 1.00 2.00
77-1848 Jari Kurri 7.50 15.00
78-1861 Vladislav Tretiak 7.50 15.00
78-1849 Tapio Levo 1.50 3.00
79-1896 Rauman Luokko .50 1.00
79-1973 Koovee .50 1.00
80-1911 Ulf Nilsson 4.00 8.00
Anders Hedberg
81-1922 NHL and Soviet Union 1.50 3.00
81-1931 Tssekoslovakia .50 1.00
82-1949 Hannu Haapalainen 2.50 5.00
82-1955 Markku Hakulinen 1.00 2.00
Yrjo Hakulinen
83-1983 Jiri Holecek 1.50 3.00
83-1982 Seppo Lindstrom 1.50 3.00
83-1970 Reijo Leppanen 1.50 3.00
84-2015 Alexander Yakushev 2.50 5.00
84-2016 Lasse Litma 1.00 2.00
84-2006 Canada 5.00 10.00
85-2017 Seppo Suoraniemi 1.50 3.00
85-2024 Dave Dryden 4.00 8.00
85-2035 Jacques Lemaire 6.00 12.00
86-2064 Hannu Koskinen 2.50 5.00
86-2041 Reijo Ruotsalainen 2.50 5.00
87-2072 Jouni Rinne 1.50 3.00
88-2103 HIFK 1.50 3.00
89-2127 Wayne Gretzky 200.00 400.00
90-2169 Timo Susi 1.50 3.00
90-2148 Antero Kivela 2.50 5.00
90-2152 Jarmo Makitalo 1.50 3.00
90-2139 Real Cloutier 2.50 5.00
90-2150 Markku Kimmalainen 1.00 2.00
90-2162 Scotty Bowman 12.50 25.00
90-2160 NHL and WHA 1.50 3.00
90-2165 Ismo Villa 1.50 3.00
103-2455 Ivan Hlinka 1.50 3.00
105-2513 Soviet Union 1.00 2.00
107-2559 Jorma Valtonen 1.00 2.00
108-2573 Henry Leppa 1.50 3.00
108-2583 Suomen Jaahallit .50 1.00
02-27 Tsekkoslovakia .50 1.00
02-39 Stanley Cup .50 1.00
03-71 Olympiakiekkoilu 1960 .50 1.00
04-83 Bobby Orr 20.00 50.00
05-105 Phil Esposito 10.00 20.00
Tony Esposito
05-115 Tappara 1976-77 .50 1.00
07-152 Soviet Union 1976 1.50 3.00
07-168 Gordie Howe 12.50 25.00
08-181 Bobby Hull 10.00 20.00
UK-327 Suomen Jaakiekkoilu .50 1.00

1978-79 Finnish SM-Liiga

This set features the top players from Finland's elite league. These odd-sized cards measure 2 X 2 3/8. The set is noteworthy for including the first known card of Hall of Famer Jari Kurri. It is believed the cards were issued in pack form, but that cannot be ascertained at this point.

COMPLETE SET (240) 50.00 125.00
1 Hannu Kamppuri .40 1.00
2 Pekka Rautakallio .75 2.00
3 Timo Nummelin .20 .50
4 Pertti Valkeapaa .20 .50
5 Risto Siltanen .40 1.00
6 Hannu Haapalainen .20 .50
7 Markku Kiimalainen .20 .50
8 Tapio Levo .40 1.00
9 Lasse Litma .20 .50
10 Reijo Ruotsalainen .75 2.00
11 Jukka Porvari .20 .50
12 Matti Rautiainen .20 .50
13 Veli-Pekka Ketola .75 2.00
14 Antero Lehtonen .20 .50
15 Martti Jarkko .20 .50
16 Juhani Tamminen .75 2.00
17 Pertti Koivulahti .20 .50
18 Kari Makkonen .20 .50
19 Antero Kivela .20 .50
20 Veli-Matti Ruisma .20 .50
21 Stig Wetzell .20 .50
22 Kyosti Majava .20 .50
23 Seppo Pakelo .20 .50
24 Reijo Laksola .20 .50
25 Heikki Riihiranta .20 .50
26 Raimo Hirvonen .20 .50
27 Jorma Immonen .20 .50
28 Terry Ball .20 .50
29 Pentti Lehtonen .20 .50
30 Jaakko Marttinen .20 .50
31 Esa Peltonen .40 1.00
32 Lauri Mononen .40 1.00
33 Tommi Salmelainen .20 .50
34 Hannu Kapanen .20 .50
35 Matti Forss .20 .50
36 Harri Linnonmaa .20 .50
37 Matti Murto .20 .50
38 Juhani Bostrom .20 .50
39 Matti Hagman .40 1.00
40 Ilkka Sinisalo .75 2.00
41 Tomi Taimio .20 .50
42 Ari Lahteenmaki .20 .50
43 Tapio Virhimo .20 .50
44 Jukka Airaksinen .20 .50
45 Hannu Helander .20 .50
46 Jorma Aro .20 .50
47 Jouko Urvikko .20 .50
48 Hannu Pulkkinen .20 .50
49 Olli Pennanen .20 .50
50 Ari Kankaanpera .20 .50
51 Risto Siltanen .40 1.00
52 Jari Jarvinen .20 .50
53 Sakari Ahlberg .20 .50
54 Keijo Kivela .20 .50
55 Lasse Oksanen .20 .50
56 Risto Kankaanpera .20 .50
57 Kari Jarvinen .20 .50
58 Pekka Orimus .20 .50
59 Jarmo Huhtala .20 .50
60 Hannu Oksanen .20 .50
61 Jari Viitala .20 .50
62 Veikko Suominen .20 .50
63 Antti Heikkila .20 .50
64 Seppo Hiitela .20 .50
65 Hannu Kamppuri .40 1.00
66 Patrik Wainio .20 .50
67 Timo Blomqvist .40 1.00
68 Ilmo Uotila .20 .50
69 Pertti Savolainen .20 .50
70 Jussi Lepisto .20 .50
71 Jorma Piisinen .20 .50
72 Robert Barnes .20 .50
73 Ari Makinen .20 .50
74 David Conte .40 1.00
75 Juha Jyrkkio .20 .50
76 Jari Kurri 20.00 40.00
77 Matti Heikkila .20 .50
78 Henry Leppa .20 .50
79 Pekka Kaski .20 .50
80 Jari Kapanen .20 .50
81 Ari Mikkola .20 .50
82 Vesa Rajaniemi .20 .50
83 Ari Blomqvist .20 .50
84 Erkki Korhonen .20 .50
85 Rainer Risku .20 .50
86 Henry Saleva .20 .50
87 Leo Seppanen .20 .50
88 Rauli Sohlman .20 .50
89 Juhani Ruohonen .20 .50
90 Tuomo Martin .20 .50
91 Reijo Mansikka .20 .50
92 Reino Pulkkinen .20 .50
93 Mauri Kultakuusi .20 .50
94 Kari Saarikko .20 .50
95 Kari Viitalahti .20 .50
96 Barry Salovaara .20 .50
97 Auvo Vaananen .20 .50
98 Pauli Pyykko .20 .50
99 Ari Jortikka .20 .50
100 Jukka-Pekka Jarvenpaa .20 .50
101 Seppo Sevon .20 .50
102 Pekka Koskela .20 .50
103 Arto Jokinen .20 .50
104 Timo Niinivirta .20 .50
105 Matti Rautiainen .20 .50
106 Pertti Jarvenpaa .20 .50
107 Reima Pullinen .20 .50
108 Jukka-Pekka Vuorinen .20 .50
109 Petteri Kanerva .20 .50
110 Kalevi Rantanen .20 .50
111 Jorma Virtanen .20 .50
112 Matti Kaario .20 .50
113 Frank Neal .20 .50
114 Eero Mantere .20 .50
115 Harri Nyman .20 .50
116 Olli Saarinen .20 .50
117 Juha Saarela .20 .50
118 Pasi Virta .20 .50
119 Dave Chalk .20 .50
120 Hannu Koskinen .20 .50
121 Harri Toivonen .20 .50
122 Jarmo Makitalo .20 .50
123 Kari Makitalo .20 .50
124 Olavi Niemenranta .20 .50
125 Pekka Laine .20 .50
126 Markku Hakulinen .20 .50
127 Pekka Nissinen .20 .50
128 Yrjo Hakulinen .20 .50
129 Timo Heino .20 .50
130 Hannu Savolainen .20 .50
131 Ari Hellgren .20 .50
132 Matti Saikkonen .20 .50
133 Ilpo Kukkola .20 .50
134 Pentti Karlsson .20 .50
135 Pekka Karjala .20 .50
136 Juha Tuohimaa .20 .50
137 Pekka Makinen .20 .50
138 Reijo Ruotsalainen .75 2.00
139 Seppo Tenhunen .20 .50
140 Hannu Jalonen .20 .50
141 Jari Virtanen .20 .50
142 Juha Huikuri .20 .50
143 Veikko Torkkeli .20 .50
144 Markku Kiimalainen .20 .50
145 Kalevi Hongisto .20 .50
146 Eero Vartiainen .20 .50
147 Jouko Kamarainen .20 .50
148 Kai Suikkanen .20 .50
149 Ilkka Alatalo .20 .50
150 Markku Perkkio .20 .50
151 Jorma Torkkeli .20 .50
152 Kari Jalonen .20 .50
153 Hannu Siivonen .20 .50
154 Kari Kaupinsalo .20 .50
155 Teppo Mattsson .20 .50
156 Esa Hakkarainen .20 .50
157 Jouni Peltonen .20 .50
158 Timo Pentila .20 .50
159 Hannu Luojola .20 .50
160 Tapani Koskimaki .20 .50
161 Tuomo Jormakka .20 .50
162 Mika Rajala .20 .50
163 Pekka Santanen .20 .50
164 Jorma Vehmanen .20 .50
165 Olli Tuominen .20 .50
166 Hannu Kemppainen .20 .50
167 Ismo Villa .20 .50
168 Matti Tynkkynen .20 .50
169 Jouni Rinne .20 .50
170 Jari Rastio .20 .50
171 Harri Tuohimaa .20 .50
172 Jari Laiho .20 .50
173 Juhani Wallenius .20 .50
174 Pekka Strander .20 .50
175 Pertti Hasanen .20 .50
176 Petri Karjalainen .20 .50
177 Jorma Kallio .20 .50
178 Pekka Marjamaki .20 .50
179 Hannu Haapalainen .20 .50
180 Pertti Valkeapaa .20 .50
181 Lasse Litma .20 .50
182 Jukka Hirsimaki .20 .50
183 Oiva Oijennus .20 .50
184 Jukka Alkula .20 .50
185 Timo Susi .20 .50
186 Jukka Porvari .20 .50
187 Erkki Lehtonen .20 .50
188 Antero Lehtonen .20 .50
189 Juha Solvennoinen .20 .50
190 Pertti Koivulahti .20 .50
191 Keijo Mannisto .20 .50
192 Jorma Sevon .20 .50
193 Martti Jarkko .20 .50
194 Jari Lindgren .20 .50
195 Tapio Kallio .20 .50
196 Tero Kapynen .20 .50
197 Urpo Ylonen .20 .50
198 Jorma Valtonen .20 .50
199 Harri Kari .20 .50
200 Hannu Jortikka .20 .50
201 Timo Nummelin .20 .50
202 Seppo Suoraniemi .20 .50
203 Ilkka Mesikammen .20 .50
204 Pertti Ahokas .20 .50
205 Hannu Niitoaho .20 .50
206 Arto Kaunonen .20 .50
207 Pekka Rautee .20 .50
208 Juhani Tamminen .20 .50
209 Timo Viljanen .20 .50
210 Kari Kauppila .20 .50
211 Bengt Willenius .20 .50
212 Reijo Leppanen .20 .50
213 Rauli Tammelin .20 .50
214 Jukka Koskilahti .20 .50
215 Markku Haapaniemi .20 .50
216 Kari Horkko .20 .50
217 Kalevi Aho .20 .50
218 Hakan Hjerpe .20 .50
219 Antero Kivela .20 .50
220 Pertti Lehti .20 .50
221 Antti Heikkila .20 .50
222 Tapio Flinck .20 .50
223 Pekka Rautakallio .75 2.00
224 Jaakko Niemi .20 .50
225 Tapio Levo .40 1.00
226 Jyrki Levonen .20 .50
227 Harry Nikander .20 .50
228 Arto Javanainen .20 .50
229 Pekka Makela .20 .50
230 Tapio Koskinen .20 .50
231 Pekka Stenfors .20 .50
232 Ari Peltola .20 .50
233 Veli-Pekka Ketola .75 2.00
234 Erkki Vakiparta .20 .50
235 Rauli Levonen .20 .50
236 Martti Nenonen .20 .50
237 Jouni Makitalo .20 .50
238 Veli-Matti Ruisma .20 .50
239 Tauno Makela .20 .50
240 Kari Makkonen .20 .50

1980 Finnish Mallasjuoma

We have no pricing information for this series and present it only for checklisting purposes.

COMPLETE SET (220)
1 Stig Wetzell
2 Seppo Pakola
3 Frank Neal
4 Heikki Riihiranta
5 Esa Peltonen
6 Tommi Salmelainen
7 Matti Forss
8 Olli Ignatius
9 Raimo Hirvonen
10 Harri Linnonmaa
11 Jorma Immonen
12 Arto Sirvio
13 Matti Murto
14 Jari Kapanen
15 Ilkka Sinisalo
16 Arto Jokinen
17 Pertti Lehtonen
18 Timo Ukkola
19 Rainer Risku
20 Ari Lahteenmaki
21 Hannu Riihimaki
22 Jarmo Vuorinen
23 Jukka Airaksinen
24 Reijo Laksola
25 Jorma Aro
26 Jari Jarvinen
27 Jouko Urvikko
28 Ari Jokinen
29 Kari Heikkila
30 Auvo Vaananen
31 Risto Jalo
32 Lasse Oksanen
33 Lasse Tasala
34 Kari Jarvinen
35 Jarmo Lilius
36 Jyrki Seppa
37 Jorma Huhtala
38 Jari Viitala
39 Antti Heikkila
40 Matti Rautiainen
41 Pertti Jarvenpaa
42 Seppo Sevon
43 Henry Lehvonen
44 Tapio Virhimo
45 Rauli Sohlman
46 Martti Tuomisto
47 Pekka Rasanen
48 Aarre Kourula
49 Timo Saari
50 Arto Laine
51 Anssi Melametsa
52 Veli-Pekka Kinnunen
53 Matti Heikkila
54 Tony Arima
55 Ismo Lehkonen
56 Matti Virmanen
57 Sakari Petajaaho
58 Antti Lehto
59 Pasi Mustonen
60 Erkki Korhonen
61 Ilmo Uotila
62 Jussi Lepisto
63 Hannu Nykvist
64 Ari Blomqvist
65 Henry Leppa
66 Ari Makinen
67 Jari Vuorio
68 Olli Saarinen
69 Matti Kaario
70 Timo Blomqvist
71 Petteri Kanerva
72 Timo Harkonen
73 Keijo Koivisto
74 Eero Mantere
75 Harri Nyman
76 Harri Toivonen
77 Harri Laine
78 Olavi Niemenranta
79 Pekka Laine
80 Harri Haapaniemi
81 Juha Silvennoinen
82 Pekka Lumela
83 Yrjo Hakulinen
84 Tom Regnier
85 Richard Regnier
86 Jukka Holtari
87 Timo Heino
88 Hannu Koskinen
89 Ari Hellgren
90 Arto Ruotanen
91 Hannu Jalonen
92 Kari Suoraniemi
93 Hannu Hiltunen
94 Juha Tuohimaa
95 Pentti Perhomaa
96 Reijo Ruotsalainen
97 Seppo Tenhunen
98 Kari Jalonen
99 Markku Kiimalainen
100 Juha Huikari
101 Pekka Tuomisto
102 Jouni Koutuaniemi
103 Veikko Torkkeli
104 Jouko Kamarainen
105 Kai Suikkanen
106 Jorma Torkkeli
107 Mikko Leinonen
108 Ari Timosaari
109 Jarmo Tauriainen
110 Pekka Arbelius
111 Teppo Mattsson
112 Esa Hakkarainen
113 Jouni Peltonen
114 Jarmo Kuusisto
115 Timo Peltonen
116 Ari-Pekka Strander
117 Jorma Vehmanen
118 Pasi Tuohimaa
119 Olli Tuominen
120 Hannu Kemppainen
121 Ismo Villa
122 Esa Wallin
123 Matti Tynkkynen
124 Jari Rastio
125 Kari Kaupinsalo
126 Lasse Lindberg
127 Olli-Pekka Rajala
128 Harri Tuohimaa
129 Hannu Vierimaa
130 Jari Laiho
131 Juhani Wallenius
132 Jarmo Kaistakari
133 Jukka Peitsoma
134 Tuomo Martin
135 Keijo Taskula
136 Martti Immonen
137 Ilkka Kaarna
138 Pertti Ahokas
139 Ari Lehikoinen
140 Jyrki Paakkarinen
141 Jouko Kukko
142 Harri Poyhia
143 Pentti Matikainen
144 Juha Sokkanen
145 Antero Vaatamoinen
146 Pertti Heikkeri
147 Esko Heikkeri
148 Heikki Malkia
149 Tuomo Laukkanen
150 Kari Weckstrom
151 Seppo Urpalainen
152 Kari Saarikko
153 Tuomo Jormakka
154 Juha Henttonen
155 Lasse Schultz
156 Mikko Vilonen
157 Hannu Helander
158 Pertti Valkeapaa
159 Lasse Litma
160 Timo Jutila
161 Oiva Oijennus
162 Timo Susi
163 Jukka Porvari
164 Erkki Lehtonen
165 Esa Valioja
166 Pertti Koivulahti
167 Juha Nurmi
168 Hannu Kamppuri
169 Petri Karjalainen
170 Timo Penttila
171 Jari Lindgren
172 Seppo Virta
173 Jukka Hirsimaki
174 Petri Niukkanen
175 Seppo Ahokainen
176 Antero Lehtonen
177 Hannu Jortikka
178 Timo Nummelin
179 Seppo Suoraniemi
180 Pasi Virta
181 Kari Vaihinen
182 Henry Saleva
183 Jari Hytti
184 Kari Kauppila
185 Reijo Leppanen
186 Rauli Tammelin
187 Markku Haapaniemi
188 Kari Horkko
189 Martti Jarkko
190 Juhani Tamminen
191 Kalevi Aho
192 Reima Pullinen
193 Hukan Hjerppe
194 Rauno Sjoroos
195 Hannu Niitoaho
196 Jari Paavola
197 Petteri Lehto
198 Jim Bedard
199 Antero Kivela
200 Antti Heikkila
201 Tapio Flinck
202 Arto Javanainen
203 Jukka Virtanen
204 Risto Tuomi
205 Tapio Koskinen
206 Juha Jyrkkio
207 Ari Peltola
208 Tapio Levo
209 Veli-Pekka Ketola
210 Erkki Vakiparta
211 Simo Ketola
212 Rauli Levonen
213 Jari Nystrom
214 Matti Ruisma
215 Tauno Makela
216 Kari Makkonen
217 Harry Nikander
218 Pentti Rautakallio
219 Martti Nenonen
220 Kari Takko

1982 Finnish Skopbank

Little is known about this sticker set beyond the checklist and values, provided by Finnish collector Janne Harvula. The cards are unnumbered and are checklisted below in alphabetical order.

COMPLETE SET (8) 24.00 60.00
1 Pekka Arbelius 2.00 5.00
2 Ari Hellgren 2.00 5.00
3 Raimo Hirvonen 2.00 5.00
4 Hannu Kamppuri 2.80 7.00
5 Markku Kiimalainen 2.00 5.00
6 Pertti Koivulahti 2.00 5.00
7 Hannu Koskinen 2.00 5.00
8 Mikko Leinonen 2.00 5.00
9 Reijo Leppanen 2.00 5.00
10 Tapio Levo 2.00 5.00
11 Timo Nummelin 2.00 5.00
12 Jukka Porvari 2.00 5.00
13 Reijo Ruotsalainen 2.80 7.00
14 Seppo Suoraniemi 2.00 5.00
15 Timo Susi 2.00 5.00
16 Juhani Tamminen 2.80 7.00

1989 Finnish Pelimiehen

Little is known about this six-sticker set beyond the accuracy of the checklist, which was provided by collector Ray Bayless. Any additional information can be forwarded to hockeymag@beckett.com.

COMPLETE SET (6) 12.00 30.00
1 Kari Eloranta 1.20 3.00
2 Jari Kurri 6.00 15.00
3 Reijo Ruotsalainen 1.20 3.00
4 Christian Ruuttu 1.20 3.00
5 Kari Takko 2.00 5.00
6 Esa Tikkanen 3.20 8.00

1990-91 Finnish Jyvas-Hyva Stickers

Size about 1 2/3 X 4 1/6. These stickers were inserted inside chocolate bar wrappers (one sticker per bar).

COMPLETE SET (12) 10.00 25.00
NNO JypHT Jyvaskyla .75 2.00
NNO Saipa Lappeenranta .75 2.00
NNO Tappara Tampere .75 2.00
NNO Hockey Reipas Lahti .75 2.00
NNO HPK Hameenlinna .75 2.00
NNO Ilves Tampere .75 2.00
NNO Kalpa Kuopio .75 2.00
NNO HIFK .75 2.00
NNO TPS Turku .75 2.00
NNO Lukko Rauma 1.25 3.00
NNO Assat Pori .75 2.00
NNO Jokerit .75 2.00

1991 Finnish Semic World Championship Stickers

These hockey stickers, which measure approximately 2 1/8" by 2 7/8", were sold five to a packet. Also an album was available to display all 250 stickers. The fronts display color posed player shots framed by a red inner border studded with yellow miniature stars and a white outer border. The team flag, the player's name, and the sticker number appear in the white border below the picture. The backs were different based on distribution; blank backs were sold in Czechoslovakia; Marabou Chocolate ads were on the backs of cards sold in Finland and Milky Way ads were on the back of cards sold in Sweden. The stickers are grouped according to country. Teemu

Selanne and Nicklas Lidstrom each appears in his Rookie Card year.

COMPLETE SET (250) 50.00 100.00
1 Finnish Emblem .02 .10
2 Markus Ketterer .20 .50
3 Sakari Lindfors .20 .50
4 Jukka Tammi .20 .50
5 Timo Jutila .10 .25
6 Hannu Virta .10 .25
7 Simo Saarinen .10 .25
8 Jukka Marttila .10 .25
9 Ville Siren .10 .25
10 Pasi Huura .10 .25
11 Hannu Henriksson .10 .25
12 Arto Ruotanen .10 .25
13 Ari Haanpaa .10 .25
14 Pauli Jarvinen .10 .25
15 Teppo Kivela .10 .25
16 Risto Kurkinen .10 .25
17 Mika Nieminen .10 .25
18 Jari Kurri .75 2.00
19 Esa Keskinen .10 .25
20 Raimo Summanen .10 .25
21 Teemu Selanne 4.00 10.00
22 Jari Torkki .10 .25
23 Hannu Jarvenpaa .10 .25
24 Raimo Helminen .10 .25
25 Timo Peltomaa .10 .25
26 Swedish Emblem .02 .10
27 Peter Lindmark .20 .50
28 Rolf Ridderwall .20 .50
29 Tommy Soderstrom .20 .50
30 Thomas Eriksson .10 .25
31 Nicklas Lidstrom 4.00 10.00
32 Tomas Jonsson .10 .25
33 Tommy Samuelsson .10 .25
34 Fredrik Stillman .10 .25
35 Peter Andersson .10 .25
36 Peter Andersson .10 .25
37 Kenneth Kennholt .10 .25
38 Hakan Loob .40 1.00
39 Thomas Rundqvist .10 .25
40 Hakan Ahlund .10 .25
41 Jan Viktorsson .10 .25
42 Charles Berglund .10 .25
43 Mikael Johansson .10 .25
44 Robert Burakovsky .10 .25
45 Bengt-Ake Gustafsson .10 .25
46 Patrik Carnback .10 .25
47 Patrik Erickson .10 .25
48 Anders Carlsson .10 .25
49 Mats Naslund .75 2.00
50 Kent Nilsson .75 2.00
51 Canadian Emblem .40 1.00
52 Patrick Roy 10.00 25.00
53 Ed Belfour 2.00 5.00
54 Daniel Berthiaume .40 1.00
55 Ray Bourque 4.00 10.00
56 Scott Stevens .40 1.00
57 Al MacInnis .75 2.00
58 Paul Coffey .75 2.00
59 Paul Cavallini .40 1.00
60 Zarley Zalapski .40 1.00
61 Steve Duchesne .40 1.00
62 Dave Ellett .40 1.00
63 Mark Messier 4.00 10.00
64 Wayne Gretzky 12.00 30.00
65 Steve Yzerman 8.00 20.00
66 Pierre Turgeon .40 1.00
67 Bernie Nicholls .40 1.00
68 Cam Neely 2.00 5.00
69 Joe Nieuwendyk .40 1.00
70 Luc Robitaille 2.00 5.00
71 Kevin Dineen .40 1.00
72 John Cullen .40 1.00
73 Steve Larmer .40 1.00
74 Mark Recchi .75 2.00
75 Joe Sakic 4.00 10.00
76 Soviet Emblem .02 .10
77 Arturs Irbe .40 1.00
78 Alexei Marin .20 .50
79 Mikhail Shtalenkov .20 .50
80 Vladimir Malakhov .10 .25
81 Vladimir Konstantinov 1.25 3.00
82 Igor Kravchuk .10 .25
83 Ilya Byakin .10 .25
84 Dimitri Mironov .10 .25
85 Vladimir Turikov .10 .25
86 Vjatjeslav Uvajev .10 .25
87 Vladimir Fedosov .10 .25
88 Valeri Kamensky .10 .25
89 Pavel Bure 2.00 5.00
90 Vyacheslav Butsayev .10 .25
91 Igor Maslennikov .10 .25
92 Evgeny Davydov .10 .25
93 Andrei Kovalev .10 .25
94 Alexander Semak .10 .25
95 Alexei Zhamnov .10 .25
96 Sergei Nemchinov .10 .25
97 Viktor Gordijuk .10 .25
98 Vyacheslav Kozlov .10 .25
99 Andrei Khomotov .10 .25
100 Vyacheslav Bykov .10 .25
101 Czech Emblem .02 .10
102 Petr Briza .20 .50
103 Dominik Hasek 4.00 10.00
104 Eduard Hartmann .20 .50
105 Bedrich Scerban .10 .25
106 Jiri Slegr .10 .25
107 Josef Reznicek .10 .25
108 Petr Pavlas .10 .25
109 Peter Slanina .10 .25
110 Martin Maskarinec .10 .25
111 Antonin Stavjana .10 .25
112 Stanislav Medrik .10 .25
113 Dusan Pasek .10 .25
114 Jiri Lala .10 .25
115 Darius Rusnak .10 .25
116 Oto Hascak .10 .25
117 Radek Toupal .10 .25
118 Pavel Pycha .10 .25
119 Lubomir Kolnik .10 .25
120 Libor Dolana .10 .25
121 Ladislav Lubina .10 .25
122 Tomas Jelinek .10 .25
123 Petr Vlk .10 .25
124 Vladimir Petrovka .10 .25
125 Richard Zemlicka .10 .25
126 U.S.A. Emblem .02 .10
127 John Vanbiesbrouck .75 2.00
128 Mike Richter .75 2.00
129 Chris Terreri .40 1.00
130 Chris Chelios 2.00 5.00
131 Brian Leetch 1.25 3.00
132 Gary Suter .40 1.00
133 Phil Housley .40 1.00
134 Mark Howe .40 1.00
135 Al Iafrate .40 1.00
136 Kevin Hatcher .40 1.00
137 Mathieu Schneider .40 1.00
138 Pat LaFontaine .75 2.00
139 Darren Turcotte .40 1.00
140 Neal Broten .75 2.00
141 Mike Modano 2.00 5.00
142 Dave Christian .40 1.00
143 Craig Janney .40 1.00
144 Brett Hull 2.00 5.00
145 Kevin Stevens .40 1.00
146 Joe Mullen .40 1.00
147 Tony Granato .40 1.00
148 Ed Olczyk .40 1.00
149 Jeremy Roenick 2.00 5.00
150 Jimmy Carson .40 1.00
151 West German Emblem .02 .10
152 Helmut De Raaf .20 .50
153 Josef Heiss .20 .50
154 Karl Friesen .20 .50
155 Uli Hiemer .10 .25
156 Harold Kreis .10 .25
157 Udo Kiessling .10 .25
158 Michael Schmidt .10 .25
159 Michael Heidt .10 .25
160 Andreas Pokorny .10 .25
161 Bernd Wagner .10 .25
162 Uwe Krupp .10 .25
163 Gerd Truntschka .10 .25
164 Bernd Truntschka .10 .25
165 Thomas Brandl .10 .25
166 Peter Draisaitl .10 .25
167 Andreas Brockmann .10 .25
168 Ulrich Liebsch .10 .25
169 Ralf Hantschke .10 .25
170 Thomas Schinko .10 .25
171 Anton Krinner .10 .25
172 Thomas Werner .10 .25
173 Dieter Hegen .10 .25
174 Helmut Steiger .10 .25
175 Georg Franz .10 .25
176 Swiss Emblem .02 .10
177 Renato Tosio .20 .50
178 Reto Pavoni .20 .50
179 Dino Stecher .20 .50
180 Sven Leuenberger .10 .25
181 Rick Tschumi .10 .25
182 Patrice Brasey .10 .25
183 Didier Massy .10 .25
184 Sandro Bertaggia .10 .25
185 Samuel Balmer .10 .25
186 Martin Rauch .10 .25
187 Marc Leuenberger .10 .25
188 Jorg Eberle .10 .25
189 Fredy Luthi .10 .25
190 Andy Ton .10 .25
191 Raymond Walder .10 .25
192 Manuele Celio .10 .25
193 Roman Wager .10 .25
194 Felix Hollenstein .10 .25
195 Andre Rotheli .10 .25
196 Christian Weber .10 .25
197 Peter Jaks .10 .25
198 Gil Montandon .10 .25
199 Oliver Hoffmann .10 .25
200 Thomas Vrabec .10 .25
201 Teppo Numminen .10 .25
202 Jyrki Lumme .10 .25
203 Esa Tikkanen .10 .25
204 Petri Skriko .10 .25
205 Christian Ruutu .10 .25
206 Ilkka Sinisalo .10 .25
207 Calle Johansson .10 .25
208 Tomas Sandstrom .10 .25
209 Thomas Steen .10 .25
210 Per-Erik Eklund .10 .25
211 Mats Sundin 1.25 3.00
212 Johan Garpenlov .10 .25
213 Slava Fetisov .10 .25
214 Alexei Kasatonov .10 .25
215 Mikhail Tatarinov .10 .25
216 Sergei Makarov .20 .50
217 Igor Larionov .40 1.00
218 Alexander Mogilny .40 1.00
219 Sergei Fedorov 1.25 3.00
220 Petr Klima .10 .25
221 David Volek .10 .25
222 Michal Pivonka .10 .25
223 Robert Reichel .10 .25
224 Robert Holik .10 .25
225 Jaromir Jagr 4.00 10.00
226 Urpo Ylonen .10 .25
227 Ilpo Koskela .10 .25
228 Pekka Rautakallio .20 .50
229 Lasse Oksanen .20 .50
230 Veli-Pekka Ketola .20 .50
231 Leif Holmqvist .20 .50
232 Lennart Svedberg .10 .25
233 Sven Tumba Johansson .10 .25
234 Ulf Sterner .10 .25
235 Anders Hedberg .20 .50
236 Ken Dryden 2.00 5.00
237 Bobby Orr 10.00 25.00
238 Gordie Howe 4.00 10.00
239 Bobby Hull 3.00 8.00
240 Phil Esposito 2.00 5.00
241 Vladislav Tretiak 4.00 10.00
242 Alexander Ragulin .10 .25
243 Anatoli Firsov .10 .25
244 Valeri Kharlamov 2.00 5.00
245 Alexander Maltsev .75 2.00
246 Jiri Holecek .10 .25
247 Jan Suchy .10 .25
248 Jozef Golonka .10 .25
249 Vaclav Nedomansky .10 .25
250 Ivan Hlinka .10 .25

1991-92 Finnish Jyvas-Hyva Stickers

This set features the players of Finland's SM-Liiga. The stickers were inserted as premiums in candy products. They measured 1 2/3 X 4 1/6. The set is noteworthy for the inclusion of a sticker of Teemu Selanne in his RC year. A poster on which to place the stickers was also issued for this set.

COMPLETE SET (84) 20.00 50.00
1 Sakari Lindfors .40 1.00
2 Jukka Seppo .10 .25
3 Pekka Tuomisto .06 .15
4 Harri Tuohimaa .06 .15
5 Pertti Lehtonen .06 .15
6 Simo Saarinen .06 .15
7 Timo Lehkonen .06 .15
8 Teppo Kivela .06 .15
9 Markku Piikkila .06 .15
10 Pekka Peltola .06 .15
11 Hannu Henriksson .06 .15
12 Jari Haapamaki .06 .15
13 Jukka Tammi .40 1.00
14 Risto Jalo .06 .15
15 Timo Peltomaa .06 .15
16 Raimo Summanen .40 1.00
17 Ville Siren .20 .50
18 Risto Siltanen .40 1.00
19 Markus Ketterer .30 .75
20 Pekka Jarvela .06 .15
21 Teemu Selanne 15.00 40.00
22 Keijo Sailynoja .06 .15
23 Mika Stromberg .10 .25
24 Waltteri Immonen .06 .15
25 Ari-Pekka Siekkinen .10 .25
26 Jari Lindroos .10 .25
27 Ari Haanpaa .06 .15
28 Jiri Dolezal .10 .25
29 Harri Laurila .06 .15
30 Leo Gudas .10 .25
31 Mika Rautio .06 .15
32 Pekka Tirkkonen .06 .15
33 Jarmo Kekalainen .20 .50
34 Juha Jokiharju .06 .15
35 Juha Tuohimaa .06 .15
36 Erik Hamalainen .10 .25
37 Juha Jaaskelainen .06 .15
38 Rostislav Vlach .06 .15
39 Jouni Mustonen .06 .15
40 Markku Kyllonen .06 .15
41 Antonin Stavjana .10 .25
42 Ossi Piitulainen .06 .15
43 Petr Briza .40 1.00
44 Mika Nieminen .20 .50
45 Jari Torkki .06 .15
46 Tommi Pullola .06 .15
47 Jarmo Kuusisto .06 .15
48 Pasi Huura .06 .15
49 Jaromir Sindel .20 .50
50 Marko Jantunen .10 .25
51 Erkki Laine .06 .15
52 Erkki Makela .06 .15
53 Niko Marttila .06 .15
54 Erik Kakko .06 .15
55 Jari Halme .06 .15
56 Kari Heikkinen .06 .15
57 Jiri Kucera .10 .25
58 Vesa Viitakoski .20 .50
59 Jukka Marttila .06 .15
60 Pekka Laksola .06 .15
61 Jouni Rokama .10 .25
62 Esa Keskinen .20 .50
63 Jukka Vilander .06 .15
64 Jari Pulliainen .06 .15
65 Jouko Narvanmaa .06 .15
66 Hannu Virta .10 .25
67 Kari Takko .40 1.00
68 Janne Virtanen .06 .15
69 Arto Javanainen .06 .15
70 Oleg Znarok .10 .25
71 Tapio Levo .06 .15
72 Harry Nikander .06 .15
NNO Assat Pori .06 .15
NNO HIFK Helsinki .06 .15
NNO KaiPa Kupio .06 .15
NNO Joensuun Kiekkopojat .06 .15
NNO JyPHT Jyvaskyla .06 .15
NNO Rauman Luoko .06 .15
NNO Turun Palloseura .06 .15
NNO Tappara Tampere .06 .15
NNO Jokerit Helsinki .10 .25
NNO HPK Hameenlinna .06 .15
NNO Hockey Reipat Lahti .06 .15
NNO Ilves Tampere .06 .15

1992-93 Finnish Jyvas-Hyva Stickers

This sticker set features the players of the SM-Liiga. The odd-sized stickers (about 2 x 3 1/3) were inserted as premiums with candy products and came in strips of three. The set is noteworthy for early appearances of Saku Koivu and Sami Kapanen.

COMPLETE SET (204) 19.56 48.89
1 Harri Rindell .06 .15
2 Sakari Lindfors .40 1.00
3 Simo Saarinen .06 .15
4 Pertti Lehtonen .06 .15
5 Kari Laitinen .06 .15
6 Teppo Kivela .06 .15
7 Darren Boyko .20 .50
8 Kai Rautio .06 .15
9 Drahomir Kadlec .10 .25
10 Mika Kortelainen .06 .15
11 Jukka Seppo .10 .25
12 Pekka Tuomisto .06 .15
13 Pasi Sormunen .06 .15
14 Kai Tervonen .06 .15
15 Ville Peltonen .40 1.00
16 Valeri Krykov .06 .15
17 Iiro Jarvi .20 .50
18 Hannu Jortikka .06 .15
19 Timo Lehkonen .06 .15
20 Timo Nykopp .06 .15
21 Janne Laukkanen .40 1.00
22 Marko Palo .10 .25
23 Juha Ylonen 1.20 3.00
24 Jarkko Varvio .20 .50
25 Marko Allen .06 .15
26 Marko Tuulola .06 .15
27 Jarkko Nikander .10 .25
28 Radek Toupal .06 .15
29 Tommi Varjonen .06 .15
30 Niko Marttila .06 .15
31 Jari Haapamaki .06 .15
32 Pasi Kivela .06 .15
33 Tony Virta .06 .15
34 Markku Piikkila .06 .15
35 Anatoli Bogdanov .06 .15
36 Jukka Tammi .40 1.00
37 Jani Nikko .10 .25
38 Jukka Ollila .06 .15
39 Tommi Kiiski .06 .15
40 Mikko Luovi .10 .25
41 Juha Jarvenpaa .06 .15
42 Juha Lampinen .06 .15
43 Janne Siva .06 .15
44 Timo Peltomaa .10 .25
45 Mika Arvaja .06 .15
46 Esa Tommila .06 .15
47 Kristian Taubert .06 .15
48 Jarkko Glad .06 .15
49 Hannu Mattila .06 .15
50 Pasi Maattanen .06 .15
51 Petri Sullamaa .06 .15
52 Boris Majorov .06 .15
53 Markus Ketterer .40 1.00
54 Waltteri Immonen .06 .15
55 Mika Stromberg .10 .25
56 Keijo Sailynoja .06 .15
57 Otakar Janecky .10 .25
58 Jiri Sejba .10 .25
59 Kari Martikainen .06 .15
60 Erik Hamalainen .10 .25
61 Timo Norppa .06 .15
62 Pekka Jarvela .06 .15
63 Juha Salo .06 .15
64 Heikki Riihijarvi .06 .15
65 Ari Salo .06 .15
66 Hannu Jarvenpaa .20 .50
67 Jali Wahlsten .06 .15
68 Juha Jokiharju .06 .15
69 Hannu Aravirta .06 .15
70 Ari-Pekka Siekkinen .10 .25
71 Jarmo Jokilahti .06 .15
72 Harri Laurila .06 .15
73 Juha Riihijarvi .20 .50
74 Jari Lindroos .10 .25
75 Marko Virtanen .06 .15
76 Jari Munck .06 .15
77 Markku Heikkinen .06 .15
78 Lasse Nieminen .06 .15
79 Tero Lehikoinen .06 .15
80 Ari Haanpaa .06 .15
81 Jarmo Rantanen .06 .15
82 Veli-Pekka Hard .06 .15
83 Mika Paananen .06 .15
84 Joni Lius .10 .25
85 Risto Kurkinen .06 .15
86 Juha Junno .06 .15
87 Pasi Kuivalainen .20 .50
88 Jari Jarvinen .06 .15
89 Vesa Salo .06 .15
90 Vesa Karjalainen .06 .15
91 Darius Rusnak .06 .15
92 Arto Sirvio .06 .15
93 Vesa Ruotsalainen .06 .15
94 Juha Tuohimaa .06 .15
95 Jari Hamalainen .06 .15
96 Pekka Tirkkonen .06 .15
97 Jari Laukkanen .06 .15
98 Antti Tuomenoksa .06 .15
99 Janne Leppanen .06 .15
100 Marko Jantunen .06 .15
101 Dusan Pasek .40 1.00
102 Sami Kapanen 1.20 3.00
103 Martti Merra .06 .15
104 Sami Aikaa .06 .15
105 Teemu Sillanpaa .06 .15
106 Sami Nuutinen .06 .15
107 Jere Lehtinen 3.20 8.00
108 Jan Langbacka .06 .15
109 Tero Lehtera .10 .25
110 Robert Salo .06 .15
111 Jimi Helin .06 .15
112 Sami Kokko .06 .15
113 Riku Kuusisto .06 .15
114 Markku Tiinus .06 .15
115 Pasi Heinisto .06 .15
116 Petri Pulkkinen .06 .15
117 Tom Laaksonen .06 .15
118 Jarmo Muukkonen .06 .15
119 Petro Koivunen .10 .25
120 Matti Keinonen .06 .15
121 Petr Briza .40 1.00
122 Timo Kulonen .06 .15
123 Allan Measures .06 .15
124 Harri Suvanto .06 .15
125 Timo Saarikoski .06 .15
126 Mika Alatalo .80 2.00
127 Kari-Pekka Friman .06 .15
128 Jarmo Kuusisto .06 .15
129 Mika Valila .06 .15
130 Jari Torkki .06 .15
131 Pekka Peltola .06 .15
132 Pasi Huura .06 .15
133 Matti Forss .06 .15
134 Kalle Sahlstedt .10 .25
135 Tommi Pullola .06 .15
136 Tero Arkiomaa .06 .15
137 Esko Nokelainen .06 .15
138 Petri Engman .06 .15
139 Timo Kahelin .06 .15
140 Pasi Ruponen .06 .15
141 Petteri Sihvonen .06 .15
142 Toni Sihvonen .06 .15
143 Sami Wikstrom .06 .15
144 Erik Kakko .06 .15
145 Jari Parviainen .06 .15
146 Jonni Vauhkonen .10 .25
147 Jari Kauppila .06 .15
148 Erkki Makela .06 .15
149 Jarkko Hamalainen .06 .15
150 Petri Koski .06 .15
151 Sami Lekkerimaki .06 .15
152 Toni Koivunen .06 .15
153 Jani Uski .06 .15
154 Pertti Hasanen .06 .15
155 Jaromir Sindel .20 .50
156 Tommi Haapsaari .06 .15
157 Jukka Marttila .06 .15
158 Jarmo Kekalainen .20 .50
159 Tommi Pohja .06 .15
160 Pauli Jarvinen .06 .15
161 Timo Jutila .20 .50
162 Janne Gronvall .10 .25
163 Jussi-Pekka Jarvinen .06 .15
164 Kari Heikkinen .06 .15
165 Marko Ek .06 .15
166 Veli-Pekka Kautonen .06 .15
167 Pekka Laksola .06 .15
168 Pasi Forsberg .06 .15
169 Marko Lapinkoski .06 .15
170 Mikko Peltola .06 .15
171 Vladimir Jursinov .06 .15
172 Jouni Rokama .10 .25
173 Mikko Haapakoski .06 .15
174 Kari Harila .06 .15
175 Kari Kanervo .06 .15
176 Esa Keskinen .20 .50
177 Saku Koivu 6.00 15.00
178 Jouko Narvanmaa .06 .15
179 Alexander Smirnov .06 .15
180 Reijo Mikkolainen .06 .15
181 Mikko Makela .30 .75
182 Raimo Summanen .20 .50
183 Hannu Virta .10 .25
184 Jukka Virtanen .06 .15
185 German Titov .20 .50
186 Jukka Vilander .06 .15
187 Ari Vuori .06 .15
188 Vasili Tikhonov .20 .50
189 Kari Takko .40 1.00
190 Sami Saarinen .06 .15
191 Marko Sten .06 .15
192 Arto Javanainen .06 .15
193 Janne Virtanen .06 .15
194 Arto Heiskanen .06 .15
195 Jouni Vento .06 .15
196 Olli Kaski .06 .15
197 Vyacheslav Fandul .06 .15
198 Jokke Hainanen .06 .15
199 Petri Varis .20 .50
200 Harry Nikander .06 .15
201 Jarno Miikkulainen .06 .15
202 Jari Korpisalo .10 .25
203 Rauli Raitanen .06 .15
204 Jari Levonen .06 .15

1992 Finnish Semic

COMPLETE SET (288) 50.00 100.00
1 Finland .02 .10
2 Pentti Matikainen .20 .50
3 Markus Ketterer .20 .50
4 Sakari Lindfors .20 .50
5 Teppo Numminen .10 .25
6 Jyrki Lumme .10 .25
7 Janne Laukkanen .10 .25
8 Ville Siren .10 .25
9 Mikko Haapakoski .10 .25
10 Simo Saarinen .10 .25
11 Teemu Selanne 2.00 5.00
12 Petri Skriko .10 .25
13 Iiro Jarvi .10 .25
14 Esa Tikkanen .10 .25
15 Christian Ruuttu .10 .25
16 Raimo Summanen .10 .25
17 Jari Kurri .75 2.00
18 Timo Peltomaa .10 .25
19 Mika Nieminen .10 .25
20 Mikko Makela .10 .25
21 Janne Ojanen .10 .25
22 Jarmo Kekalainen .10 .25
23 Keijo Sailynoja .10 .25
24 Esa Keskinen .10 .25
25 Norge .02 .10
26 Bengt Ohlsson .20 .50
27 Jim Marthinsen .20 .50
28 Steve Allman .20 .50
29 Petter Salsten .10 .25
30 Age Ellingsen .10 .25
31 Kim Sogaard .10 .25
32 Jan Roar Fagerli .10 .25
33 Tommy Jakobsen .10 .25
34 Cato Tom Andersen .10 .25
35 Arne Billkvam .10 .25
36 Oystein Olsen .10 .25
37 Geir Hoff .10 .25
38 Erik Kristiansen .10 .25
39 Orjan Lovdal .10 .25
40 Espen Knutsen .75 2.00
41 Ole Eskild Dahlstrom .10 .25
42 Rune Gulliksen .10 .25
43 Marius Rath .10 .25
44 Petter Thoresen .10 .25
45 Tom Johansen .10 .25
46 Stephen Foyn .10 .25
47 Stig Johansen .10 .25
48 Per Christian Knold .10 .25
49 Sverige .02 .10
50 Conny Evensson .02 .10
51 Tommy Soderstrom .20 .50
52 Fredrik Andersson .20 .50
53 Thomas Eriksson .10 .25
54 Peter Andersson .10 .25
55 Peter Andersson .10 .25
56 Nicklas Lidstrom 2.00 5.00
57 Calle Johansson .10 .25
58 Ulf Samuelsson .10 .25
59 Fredrik Olausson .10 .25
60 Borje Salming .40 1.00
61 Hakan Loob .10 .25
62 Thomas Rundqvist .10 .25
63 Mats Naslund .10 .25
64 Mikael Johansson .10 .25
65 Bengt-Ake Gustavsson .10 .25
66 Peter Ottosson .10 .25
67 Markus Naslund .10 .25
68 Daniel Rydmark .10 .25
69 Tomas Sandstrom .10 .25
70 Thomas Steen .10 .25
71 Per-Erik Eklund .10 .25
72 Mats Sundin .75 2.00
73 Kanada .20 .50
74 Dave King .02 .10
75 Bill Ranford .75 2.00
76 Ed Belfour 1.25 3.00
77 Al MacInnis .75 2.00
78 Scott Stevens .40 1.00
79 Steve Smith .40 1.00
80 Ray Bourque 3.00 8.00
81 Paul Coffey .75 2.00
82 Larry Murphy .40 1.00
83 Mark Tinordi .40 1.00
84 Wayne Gretzky 10.00 25.00
85 Mark Messier 3.00 8.00
86 Mario Lemieux 8.00 20.00
87 Steve Yzerman 6.00 15.00
88 Eric Lindros 1.25 3.00
89 Luc Robitaille 1.25 3.00
90 Theoren Fleury .75 2.00
91 Steve Larmer .40 1.00
92 Brent Sutter .40 1.00
93 Shayne Corson .40 1.00
94 Dale Hawerchuk .75 2.00
95 Russ Courtnall .40 1.00
96 Rick Tocchet .40 1.00
97 Soviet .02 .10
98 Victor Tikhonov .02 .10
99 Andrei Trefilov .20 .50
100 Mikhail Shtalenkov .20 .50
101 Alexei Kasatonov .10 .25
102 Mikhail Tatarinov .10 .25
103 Igor Kravchuk .10 .25
104 Vladimir Malakhov .10 .25
105 Alex Gusarov .10 .25
106 Dimitri Filimonov .10 .25
107 Dimitri Mironov .10 .25
108 Vladimir Konstantinov .75 2.00
109 Sergei Fedorov 1.25 3.00
110 Alexei Zhamnov .10 .25
111 Vyatcheslav Kozlov .10 .25
112 Valery Kamesky .10 .25
113 Alexander Semak .10 .25
114 Vjatcheslav Butsayev .10 .25
115 Andrei Lomakin .10 .25
116 Pavel Bure 2.00 5.00
117 Andrei Kovalenko .10 .25
118 Ravil Khaidarov .10 .25
119 Victor Gordiuk .10 .25
120 Vitali Prokhorov .10 .25
121 Tjeckoslovakien .02 .10
122 Ivan Hlinka .02 .10
123 Oldrich Svoboda .20 .50
124 Dominik Hasek 4.00 10.00
125 Leo Gudas .10 .25
126 Frantisek Musil .10 .25
127 Kamil Prachar .10 .25
128 Frantisek Kucera .10 .25
129 Richard Smehlik .10 .25
130 Jergus Baca .10 .25
131 Jiri Slegr .10 .25
132 Petr Hrbek .10 .25
133 Kamil Kastak .10 .25
134 Richard Zemlicka .10 .25
135 Jaromir Jagr 3.00 8.00
136 Martin Rucinsky .10 .25
137 Josef Beranek .10 .25
138 Michael Pivonka .10 .25
139 Robert Kron .10 .25
140 Zigmund Palffy .75 2.00
141 Tomas Jelinek .10 .25
142 Robert Reichel .10 .25
143 Lubomir Kolnik .10 .25
144 Zdeno Ciger .10 .25
145 USA .02 .10
146 Tim Taylor .02 .10
147 John Vanbiesbrouck .75 2.00
148 Mike Richter .75 2.00
149 Phil Housley .10 .25
150 Brian Leetch .40 1.00
151 Kevin Hatcher .10 .25
152 Gary Suter .10 .25
153 Chris Chelios .75 2.00
154 Eric Weinrich .10 .25
155 Jim Johnson .10 .25
156 Brett Hull 2.00 5.00
157 Mike Modano 2.00 5.00
158 Jeremy Roenick 2.00 5.00
159 Pat LaFontaine .40 1.00
160 Craig Janney .10 .25
161 Ed Olczyk .10 .25
162 Tony Granato .10 .25
163 Joe Mullen .10 .25
164 Dave Christian .10 .25
165 Doug Brown .10 .25
166 Kevin Miller .10 .25
167 Joel Otto .10 .25
168 Randy Wood .10 .25
169 Tyskland .02 .10
170 Ludek Bukac .10 .25
171 Klaus Merk .10 .25
172 Josef Heiss .10 .25
173 Harold Kreiss .10 .25
174 Michael Heidt .10 .25
175 Jorg Mayr .10 .25
176 Marco Rentzsch .10 .25
177 Heinrich Schiffel .10 .25
178 Stefan Steinecker .10 .25
179 Torsten Kienass .10 .25
180 Raimund Hilger .10 .25
181 Ernst Kopf .10 .25
182 Peter Draisatl .10 .25
183 Axel Kammerer .10 .25
184 Michael Rumrich .10 .25
185 Jurgen Rumrich .10 .25
186 Georg Holzmann .10 .25
187 Lorenz Funk .10 .25
188 Thomas Schinko .10 .25
189 Andreas Lupzig .10 .25
190 Tobias Abstreiter .10 .25
191 Michael Pohl .10 .25
192 Antony Vogel .10 .25
193 Schweiz .02 .10
194 Juhani Tamminen .02 .10
195 Renato Tosio .20 .50
196 Reto Pavoni .20 .50
197 Rick Tschumi .10 .25
198 Patrice Brasey .10 .25
199 Didier Massy .10 .25
200 Sandro Bertaggia .10 .25
201 Sven Leuenberger .10 .25
202 Samuel Palmer .10 .25
203 Martin Rauch .10 .25
204 Dino Kessler .10 .25
205 Raymond Walder .10 .25
206 Peter Jaks .10 .25
207 Andy Ton .10 .25
208 Jorg Eberle .10 .25
209 Felix Hollenstein .10 .25
210 Fredy Luthi .10 .25
211 Manuele Celio .10 .25
212 Christian Weber .10 .25
213 Andre Rotheli .10 .25
214 Gil Montandon .10 .25
215 Thomas Vrabec .10 .25
216 Patrick Howald .10 .25
217 Frankrike .02 .10
218 Kjell Larsson .02 .10
219 Jean-Marc Djian .20 .50
220 Petri Ylonen .20 .50
221 Stephane Botteri .10 .25
222 Michel Leblanc .10 .25
223 Jean-Philippe Lemoine .10 .25
224 Denis Perez .10 .25
225 Bruno Saunier .10 .25
226 Steven Woodburn .10 .25
227 Serge Poudrier .10 .25
228 Michael Babin .10 .25
229 Stephane Barin .10 .25
230 Philippe Bozon .40 1.00
231 Arnaud Briand .10 .25
232 Yves Crettenand .10 .25
233 Patrick Dunn .10 .25
234 Yannick Goicoechea .10 .25
235 Benoit Laporte .10 .25
236 Christian Pouget .10 .25
237 Antoine Richer .10 .25
238 Christophe Ville .10 .25
239 Peter Almasy .10 .25
240 Pierre Pousse .10 .25
241 Italien .02 .10
242 Gene Ubriaco .02 .10
243 David Delfino .40 1.00
244 Mike Zanier .40 1.00
245 Erwin Kostner .10 .25
246 Roberto Oberrauch .10 .25
247 Jim Camazzola .10 .25
248 Anthony Circelli .10 .25
249 Michael de Angelis .10 .25
250 Giovanni Marchetti .10 .25
251 Alessandro Batiani .10 .25
252 Georg Comploi .10 .25
253 Gaetano Orlando .10 .25
254 Bruno Zarrillo .10 .25
255 Emilio Iovio .10 .25
256 Frank Nigro .10 .25
257 Marco Scapinello .10 .25
258 Giuseppe Foglietta .10 .25
259 Rick Morocco .10 .25
260 Santino Pellegrino .10 .25
261 Lucio Topatigh .10 .25
262 Mario Simioni .10 .25
263 Ivano Cloch .10 .25
264 Martino Soracreppa .10 .25
265 Polen .02 .10
266 Leszek Lejcyk .10 .25
267 Andrzej Hanisz .20 .50
268 Mariusz Kieca .20 .50
269 Henryk Gruth .10 .25
270 Janusz Syposz .10 .25
271 Robert Szopinski .10 .25
272 Mark Cholewa .10 .25
273 Jacek Zamojski .10 .25
274 Rafal Stroka .10 .25
275 Dariusz Garbocz .10 .25
276 Stanislaw Cyrwus .10 .25
277 Janusz Adamiec .10 .25
278 Miloslaw Copija .10 .25
279 Piotr Zdunek .10 .25
280 Krzysztof Bujar .10 .25
281 Ludwik Czapka .10 .25
282 Andrzej Kotonski .10 .25
283 Janusz Hajnos .10 .25
284 Slawomir Wieloch .10 .25
285 Wojciech Matczak .10 .25
286 Jedrzej Kasperczyk .10 .25
287 Wojciech Tkacs .10 .25
288 Mariusz Czerkawski .20 .50

1993-94 Finnish Jyvas-Hyva Stickers

This 349-sticker set features the players of Finland's SM-Liiga. The odd-sized stickers (1 X 1 1/2") were inserted as premiums with candy products. The set skips the following numbers: 30, 60, 90, 120, 150, 180, 210, 240, 270, 300, 330. There are no spaces for these cards in the binder produced to store the set, and the cards were never issued. The set is noteworthy for early appearances of Saku Koivu and Janne Niinimaa.

COMPLETE SET (359) 24.00 60.00
1 HIFK Team Photo .04 .10
2 HIFK Team Photo .04 .10
3 HIFK Team Photo .04 .10
4 HIFK Team Photo .04 .10
5 HIFK Team Photo .04 .10
6 HIFK Team Photo .04 .10
7 HIFK Team Photo .04 .10
8 HIFK Team Photo .04 .10
9 HIFK Team Photo .04 .10
10 HIFK Team Photo .04 .10
11 HIFK Team Photo .04 .10
12 HIFK Team Photo .04 .10
13 Harri Rindell CO .06 .15
14 Sakari Lindfors .40 1.00
15 Simo Saarinen .06 .15
16 Pertti Lehtonen .06 .15
17 Jari Laukkanen .06 .15
18 Valeri Krykov .06 .15
19 Iiro Jarvi .20 .50
20 Jari Munck .06 .15
21 Pasi Sormunen .06 .15
22 Pekka Peltola .06 .15
23 Teppo Kivela .06 .15
24 Pekka Tuomisto .06 .15
25 Kai Tervonen .06 .15
26 Dan Lambert .20 .50
27 Marco Poulsen .06 .15
28 Ville Peltonen .40 1.00
29 Kim Ahlroos .06 .15
31 HPK Team Photo .04 .10
32 HPK Team Photo .04 .10
33 HPK Team Photo .04 .10
34 HPK Team Photo .04 .10
35 HPK Team Photo .04 .10
36 HPK Team Photo .04 .10
37 HPK Team Photo .04 .10
38 HPK Team Photo .04 .10
39 HPK Team Photo .04 .10
40 HPK Team Photo .04 .10
41 HPK Team Photo .04 .10
42 HPK Team Photo .04 .10
43 Pentti Matikainen .06 .15

44 Kari Rosenberg .10 .25
45 Mikko Myllykoski .06 .15
46 Janne Laukkanen .40 1.00
47 Jarkko Nikander .10 .25
48 Tomas Kapusta .06 .15
49 Mika Lartama .06 .15
50 Niko Marttila .06 .15
51 Jari Haapamaki .06 .15
52 Tommi Varjonen .06 .15
53 Tony Virta .06 .15
54 Marko Palo .10 .25
55 Marko Allen .06 .15
56 Miikka Ruokonen .06 .15
57 Jani Hassinen .06 .15
58 Pasi Kivila .06 .15
59 Markku Piikkila .06 .15
61 Ilves Team Photo .04 .10
62 Ilves Team Photo .04 .10
63 Ilves Team Photo .04 .10
64 Ilves Team Photo .04 .10
65 Ilves Team Photo .04 .10
66 Ilves Team Photo .04 .10
67 Ilves Team Photo .04 .10
68 Ilves Team Photo .04 .10
69 Ilves Team Photo .04 .10
70 Ilves Team Photo .04 .10
71 Ilves Team Photo .04 .10
72 Ilves Team Photo .04 .10
73 Jukka Jalonen CO .06 .15
74 Jukka Tammi .40 1.00
75 Jani Nikko .10 .25
76 Hannu Henriksson .06 .15
77 Juha Jarvenpaa .06 .15
78 Hannu Mattila .06 .15
79 Timo Peltomaa .10 .25
80 Jukka Ollila .06 .15
81 Juha-Matti Marijarvi .06 .15
82 Mikko Louvi .10 .25
83 Jarno Peltonen .06 .15
84 Pasi Maattanen .06 .15
85 Juha Lampinen .06 .15
86 Allan Measures .06 .15
87 Janne Seva .06 .15
88 Risto Jalo .06 .15
89 Esa Tommila .06 .15
91 Jokerit Team Photo .04 .10
92 Jokerit Team Photo .04 .10
93 Jokerit Team Photo .04 .10
94 Jokerit Team Photo .04 .10
95 Jokerit Team Photo .04 .10
96 Jokerit Team Photo .04 .10
97 Jokerit Team Photo .04 .10
98 Jokerit Team Photo .04 .10
99 Jokerit Team Photo .04 .10
100 Jokerit Team Photo .04 .10
101 Jokerit Team Photo .04 .10
102 Jokerit Team Photo .04 .10
103 Alpo Suhonen CO .20 .50
104 Ari Sulander .40 1.00
105 Kari Martikainen .10 .25
106 Erik Hamalainen .10 .25
107 Juha Jokiharju .06 .15
108 Otakar Janecky .10 .25
109 Petri Varis .20 .50
110 Waltteri Immonen .06 .15
111 Mika Stromberg .10 .25
112 Keijo Sailynoja .06 .15
113 Timo Saarikoski .06 .15
114 Juha Ylonen .80 2.00
115 Ari Salo .06 .15
116 Heikki Riihijarvi .06 .15
117 Timo Norppa .06 .15
118 Jali Wahlsten .06 .15
119 Rami Koivisto .06 .15
121 JYP HT Team Photo .04 .10
122 JYP HT Team Photo .04 .10
123 JYP HT Team Photo .04 .10
124 JYP HT Team Photo .04 .10
125 JYP HT Team Photo .04 .10
126 JYP HT Team Photo .04 .10
127 JYP HT Team Photo .04 .10
128 JYP HT Team Photo .04 .10
129 JYP HT Team Photo .04 .10
130 JYP HT Team Photo .04 .10
131 JYP HT Team Photo .04 .10
132 JYP HT Team Photo .04 .10
133 Kari Savolainen CO .06 .15
134 Ari-Pekka Siekkinen .10 .25
135 Harri Laurila .06 .15
136 Markku Heikkinen .06 .15
137 Jari Lindroos .10 .25
138 Lasse Nieminen .06 .15
139 Risto Kurkinen .06 .15
140 Jarmo Jokilahti .06 .15
141 Veli-Pekka Hard .06 .15
142 Joni Lius .10 .25
143 Jyrki Jokinen .06 .15
144 Mika Arvaja .06 .15
145 Vesa Ponto .06 .15
146 Jarmo Rantanen .06 .15
147 Mika Paananen .06 .15
148 Marko Virtanen .10 .25
149 Marko Ek .06 .15
151 Kalpa Team Photo .04 .10
152 Kalpa Team Photo .04 .10
153 Kalpa Team Photo .04 .10
154 Kalpa Team Photo .04 .10
155 Kalpa Team Photo .04 .10
156 Kalpa Team Photo .04 .10
157 Kalpa Team Photo .04 .10
158 Kalpa Team Photo .04 .10
159 Kalpa Team Photo .04 .10
160 Kalpa Team Photo .04 .10
161 Kalpa Team Photo .04 .10
162 Kalpa Team Photo .04 .10
163 Hannu Kapanen .06 .15
164 Pasi Kuivalainen .20 .50
165 Kimmo Timonen .60 1.50
166 Vesa Salo .06 .15
167 Jani Rautio .06 .15
168 Pekka Tirkkonen .06 .15
169 Dimitri Zinine .06 .15
170 Antti Tuomenoksa .06 .15
171 Jari Jarvinen .06 .15
172 Tuomas Kalliomaki .06 .15
173 Tommi Miettinen .10 .25
174 Sami Kapanen .80 2.00
175 Vesa Ruotsalainen .06 .15
176 Mikko Tavi .06 .15
177 Sami Mettovaara .06 .15
178 Veli-Pekka Pekkarinen .06 .15
179 Arto Sirvio .06 .15
181 Kiekko-Espoo Team Photo .04 .10
182 Kiekko-Espoo Team Photo .04 .10
183 Kiekko-Espoo Team Photo .04 .10
184 Kiekko-Espoo Team Photo .04 .10
185 Kiekko-Espoo Team Photo .04 .10
186 Kiekko-Espoo Team Photo .04 .10
187 Kiekko-Espoo Team Photo .04 .10
188 Kiekko-Espoo Team Photo .04 .10
189 Kiekko-Espoo Team Photo .04 .10
190 Kiekko-Espoo Team Photo .04 .10
191 Kiekko-Espoo Team Photo .04 .10
192 Kiekko-Espoo Team Photo .04 .10
193 Martti Merra .06 .15
194 Timo Maki .06 .15
195 Sami Nuutinen .06 .15
196 Teemu Sillanpaa .06 .15
197 Tero Lehtera .10 .25
198 Jan Langbacka .06 .15
199 Jukka Tiilikainen .06 .15
200 Petri Pulkkinen .06 .15
201 Robert Salo .06 .15
202 Petro Koivunen .10 .25
203 Juha Ikonen .06 .15
204 Mikko Lempiainen .06 .15
205 Marko Halonen .06 .15
206 Jimi Helin .06 .15
207 Timo Hirvonen .06 .15
208 Mikko Halonen .06 .15
209 Kimmo Maki-Kokkila .06 .15
211 Lukko Team Photo .04 .10
212 Lukko Team Photo .04 .10
213 Lukko Team Photo .04 .10
214 Lukko Team Photo .04 .10
215 Lukko Team Photo .04 .10
216 Lukko Team Photo .04 .10
217 Lukko Team Photo .04 .10
218 Lukko Team Photo .04 .10
219 Lukko Team Photo .04 .10
220 Lukko Team Photo .04 .10
221 Lukko Team Photo .04 .10
222 Lukko Team Photo .04 .10
223 Vaclav Sykora .06 .15
224 Jarmo Myllys .40 1.00
225 Kari-Pekka Friman .06 .15
226 Timo Kulonen .06 .15
227 Pasi Saarela .06 .15
228 Kalle Sahlstedt .10 .25
229 Kimmo Rintanen .20 .50
230 Jarmo Kuusisto .06 .15
231 Tuomas Gronman .10 .25
232 Tero Arkiomaa .06 .15
233 Petr Korinek .10 .25
234 Mika Alatalo .60 1.50
235 Marko Tuulola .06 .15
236 Pasi Huura .06 .15
237 Tommi Pullola .06 .15
238 Mika Valila .06 .15
239 Jari Sundell .06 .15
241 Reipas Lahti Team Photo .04 .10
242 Reipas Lahti Team Photo .04 .10
243 Reipas Lahti Team Photo .04 .10
244 Reipas Lahti Team Photo .04 .10
245 Reipas Lahti Team Photo .04 .10
246 Reipas Lahti Team Photo .04 .10
247 Reipas Lahti Team Photo .04 .10
248 Reipas Lahti Team Photo .04 .10
249 Reipas Lahti Team Photo .04 .10
250 Reipas Lahti Team Photo .04 .10
251 Reipas Lahti Team Photo .04 .10
252 Reipas Lahti Team Photo .04 .10
253 Kari Makinen CO .06 .15
254 Oldrich Svoboda .06 .15
255 Timo Kahelin .06 .15
256 Pasi Ruponen .06 .15
257 Tommy Kiviaho .06 .15
258 Jari Multanen .06 .15
259 Erkki Makela .06 .15
260 Jarj Parviainen .06 .15
261 Petri Koski .06 .15
262 Jouni Vauhkonen .10 .25
263 Toni Koivunen .06 .15
264 Sami Wikstrom .06 .15
265 Jarkko Hamalainen .06 .15
266 Sami Helenius .20 .50
267 Sami Lekkerimaki .06 .15
268 Jari Kauppila .06 .15
269 Jani Uski .06 .15
271 Tappara Team Photo .04 .10
272 Tappara Team Photo .04 .10
273 Tappara Team Photo .04 .10
274 Tappara Team Photo .04 .10
275 Tappara Team Photo .04 .10
276 Tappara Team Photo .04 .10
277 Tappara Team Photo .04 .10
278 Tappara Team Photo .04 .10
279 Tappara Team Photo .04 .10
280 Tappara Team Photo .04 .10
281 Tappara Team Photo .04 .10
282 Tappara Team Photo .04 .10
283 Boris Majorov .06 .15
284 Timo Hankela .06 .15
285 Timo Jutila .20 .50
286 Samuli Rautio .06 .15
287 Ari Haanpaa .06 .15
288 Mikko Peltola .06 .15
289 Pauli Jarvinen .06 .15
290 Pekka Laksola .06 .15
291 Janne Gronvall .10 .25
292 Kari Heikkinen .06 .15
293 Tommi Pohja .06 .15
294 Petri Aaltonen .06 .15
295 Petri Kalteva .06 .15
296 Tommi Haapsaari .06 .15
297 Teemu Numminen .06 .15
298 Pasi Forsberg .06 .15
299 Veli-Pekka Kautonen .06 .15
301 TPS Team Photo .04 .10
302 TPS Team Photo .04 .10
303 TPS Team Photo .04 .10
304 TPS Team Photo .04 .10
305 TPS Team Photo .04 .10
306 TPS Team Photo .04 .10
307 TPS Team Photo .04 .10
308 TPS Team Photo .04 .10
309 TPS Team Photo .04 .10
310 TPS Team Photo .04 .10
311 TPS Team Photo .04 .10
312 TPS Team Photo .04 .10
313 Vladimir Jursinov CO .06 .15
314 Jouni Rokama .10 .25
315 Hannu Virta .10 .25
316 Erik Kakko .06 .15
317 Jukka Vilander .06 .15
318 Esa Keskinen .20 .50
319 Ari Vuori .06 .15
320 Jouko Narvanmaa .06 .15
321 Marko Kiprusoff .10 .25
322 Jere Lehtinen 2.00 5.00
323 Saku Koivu 4.00 10.00
324 Marko Jantunen .10 .25
325 Kari Harila .06 .15
326 Alexander Smirnov .06 .15
327 Toni Sihvonen .06 .15
328 Harri Sillgren .06 .15
329 Kai Nurminen .40 1.00
331 Assat Team Photo .04 .10
332 Assat Team Photo .04 .10
333 Assat Team Photo .04 .10
334 Assat Team Photo .04 .10
335 Assat Team Photo .04 .10
336 Assat Team Photo .04 .10
337 Assat Team Photo .04 .10
338 Assat Team Photo .04 .10
339 Assat Team Photo .04 .10
340 Assat Team Photo .04 .10
341 Assat Team Photo .04 .10
342 Assat Team Photo .04 .10
343 Veli-Pekka Ketola CO .10 .25
344 Kari Takko .40 1.00
345 Olli Kaski .06 .15
346 Karri Kivi .06 .15
347 Arto Heiskanen .06 .15
348 Janne Virtanen .06 .15
349 Mikael Kotkaniemi .06 .15
350 Stanislav Meciar .06 .15
351 Jarno Miikkulainen .06 .15
352 Jokke Heinanen .06 .15
353 Vjatseslav Fandul .10 .25
354 Ari Saarinen .06 .15
355 Jouni Vento .06 .15
356 Arto Javanainen .06 .15
357 Jari Korpisalo .10 .25
358 Rauli Raitanen .06 .15
359 Jari Levonen .06 .15
NNO Binder 4.00 10.00

1993-94 Finnish SISU

The 396 standard-size cards comprising this first series of players from the Finnish Hockey League feature on-ice color player photos on their fronts. The photos are bordered in a gray lithic, and each carries the player's name, uniform number, and team logo near the bottom. The gray lithic design continues on the horizontal back, which carries the player's team name in a yellow stripe across the top, followed below by his name, position, biography, and statistics. With a few exceptions, all text is in Finnish. Cards 301-396 differ from the others in that the design is orange lithic instead of gray, and some have horizontal fronts. The cards are numbered on the front. There are several new errors and variations in this edition, as provided by Finnish collector Heikki Silvennoinen.

COMPLETE SET (396) 20.00 50.00
1 Jokerit Team Card .10 .25
2 Alpo Suhonen .20 .50
3 Ari Sulander .40 1.00
4 Marko Rantanen .06 .15
5 Ari Salo .04 .10
6 Kalle Koskinen .04 .10
7 Sebastian Sulku .04 .10
8 Waltteri Immonen .06 .15
9 Mika Stromberg .10 .25
10 Heikki Riihijarvi .04 .10
11 Kari Martikainen .06 .15
12 Erik Hamalainen .10 .25
13 Juha Jokiharju .04 .10
14 Timo Norppa .04 .10
15 Rami Koivisto .04 .10
16 Antti Tormanen .30 .75
17 Keijo Sailynoja .06 .15
18 Jere Keskinen .06 .15
19 Jali Wahlsten .04 .10
20 Mikko Kontilla .04 .10
21 Juha Ylonen .60 1.50
22 Jussi Vienonen ERR .04 .10
(wrong photo
22B Jussi Vienonen COR .25
23 Petri Varis .20 .50
24 Juha Lind .40 1.00
25 Timo Saarikoski .04 .10
26 Otakar Janecky .10 .25
27 TPS Team Card .06 .15
28 Vladimir Jursinov CO .06 .15
29 Jouni Rokama .04 .10
30 Kimmo Lecklin .04 .10
31 Jouko Narvanmaa .04 .10
32 Petteri Nummelin .06 .15
33 Erik Kakko .04 .10
34 Tom Koivisto .04 .10
35 Marko Kiprusoff .10 .25
36 Kari Harila .04 .10
37 Hannu Virta .10 .25
38 Aki Berg .40 1.00
39 Aleksander Smirnov .04 .10
40 Esa Keskinen .10 .25
41 Saku Koivu 4.00 10.00
42 Jukka Vilander .04 .10
43 Antti Aalto .40 1.00
44 Mika Karapuu ERR .04 .10
(wrong photo
44B Mika Karapuu COR .25
45 Toni Sihvonen .04 .10
46 Pavel Torgajev .10 .25
47 Jere Lehtinen 1.20 3.00
48 Kai Nurminen .20 .50
49 Harri Sillgren .04 .10
50 Niko Mikkola .04 .10
51 Ari Vuori .04 .10
52 Lasse Pirjeta .04 .10
53 Reijo Mikkolainen .04 .10
54 Marko Jantunen .10 .25
55 Mikko Virolainen ERR .04 .10
(wrong photo
55B Mikko Virolainen COR .25
56 Tappara Team Card .06 .15
57 Boris Majorov CO .06 .15
58 Jaromir Sindel .10 .25
59 Timo Hankela .04 .10
60 Teemu Kivinen .04 .10
61 Petri Kalteva .04 .10
62 Jari Harjumaki .04 .10
63 Timo Jutila .10 .25
64 Janne Gronvall .10 .25
65 Jari Gronstrand .06 .15
66 Pekka Laksola .04 .10
67 Tommi Haapsaari .04 .10
68 Veli-Pekka Kautonen .04 .10
69 Mikko Peltola .04 .10
70 Kari Heikkinen .04 .10
71 Teemu Numminen .04 .10
72 Jiri Kucera .06 .15
73 Pauli Jarvinen .04 .10
74 Pasi Forsberg .04 .10
75 Tero Toivola .04 .10
76 Ari Haanpaa .06 .15
77 Tommi Pohja .04 .10
78 Samuli Rautio .04 .10
79 Markus Oijennus .04 .10
80 Petri Aaltonen .04 .10
81 HIFK Team Card .06 .15
82 Harri Rindell CO .04 .10
83 Sakari Lindfors .10 .25
84 Mikael Granlund .04 .10
85 Kimmo Hyttinen .04 .10
86 Jere Karalahti .20 .50
87 Dan Lambert .20 .50
88 Simo Saarinen .04 .10
89 Pasi Sormunen .04 .10
90 Tommi Hamalainen .04 .10
91 Pertti Lehtonen .04 .10
92 Jari Munck .04 .10
93 Kai Tervonen .04 .10
94 Kim Ahlroos .04 .10
95 Teppo Kivela .04 .10
96 Darren Boyko .06 .15
97 Pekka Peltola .04 .10
98 Marco Poulsen .04 .10
99 Valeri Krykov .04 .10
100 Jari Laukkanen .04 .10
101 Ville Peltonen .40 1.00
102 Pekka Tuomisto .04 .10
103 Miro Haapaniemi .04 .10
104 Mika Kortelainen .04 .10
105 Marko Ojanen .04 .10
106 Iiro Jarvi .06 .15
107 Ilves Tampere Team Card .06 .15
108 Jukka Jalonen CO .04 .10
109 Jukka Tammi .20 .50
110 Mika Manninen .06 .15
111 Jani Nikko .10 .25
112 Jukka Ollila .04 .10
113 Juha Lampinen .04 .10
114 Hannu Henriksson .04 .10
115 Sami Lehtonen .04 .10
116 Mikko Niemi .04 .10
117 Juha-Matti Marijarvi .04 .10
118 Jarkko Glad .04 .10
119 Allan Measures .04 .10
120 Mikko Luovi .06 .15
121 Risto Jalo .06 .15
122 Juha Jarvenpaa .06 .15
123 Jarno Peltonen .04 .10
124 Matti Kaipainen .04 .10
125 Timo Peltomaa .06 .15
126 Esa Tommila .04 .10
127 Hannu Mattila .04 .10
128 Jari Neuvonen .04 .10
129 Pasi Maattanen .04 .10
130 Juha Hautamaa .04 .10
131 Janne Seva .04 .10
132 Sami Ahlberg .04 .10
133 Jari Virtanen .04 .10
134 JyP HT Team Card .06 .15
135 Kari Savolainen CO .04 .10
136 Ari-Pekka Siekkinen .06 .15
137 Marko Leinonen .04 .10
138 Jan Latvala .04 .10
139 Markku Heikkinen .04 .10
140 Jarmo Jokilahti .04 .10
141 Veli-Pekka Hard .04 .10
142 Kalle Koskinen .04 .10
143 Vesa Ponto .04 .10
144 Petri Kujala .04 .10
145 Jarmo Rantanen .04 .10
146 Harri Laurila .04 .10
147 Lasse Nieminen .04 .10
148 Mika Paananen .04 .10
149 Mika Arvaja .04 .10
150 Marko Virtanen .06 .15
151 Marko Ek .04 .10
152 Joni Lius .04 .10
153 Teemu Kohvakka .04 .10
154 Jari Lindroos .06 .15
155 Marko Kupari .04 .10
156 Markku Ikonen .04 .10
157 Jyrki Jokinen .04 .10
158 Risto Kurkinen .04 .10
159 KalPa Team Card .06 .15
160 Hannu Kapanen CO .04 .10
161 Pasi Kuivalainen .06 .15
162 Kimmo Kapanen .04 .10
163 Kimmo Timonen .40 1.00
164 Jari Jarvinen .04 .10
165 Mikko Tavi .04 .10
166 Jermu Pisto .04 .10
167 Antti Tuomenoksa .04 .10
168 Vesa Ruotsalainen .04 .10
169 Vesa Salo .04 .10
170 Veli-Pekka Pekkarinen .04 .10
171 Tuomas Kalliomaki .04 .10
172 Dimitri Zinine .04 .10
173 Jani Rautio .04 .10
173B Marko Virtanen ERR .25
(incorrect numbering
174 Janne Kekalainen .04 .10
174B Marko Ek ERR .25
(incorrect numbering
175 Arto Sirvio .04 .10
176 Sami Mettovaara .04 .10
177 Sami Simonen .04 .10
178 Pekka Tirkkonen .06 .15
179 Sami Kapanen .80 2.00
180 Jussi Tarvainen .04 .10
181 Lukko Team Card .06 .15
182 Vaclav Sykora .04 .10
183 Jarmo Myllys .40 1.00
183B Petri Kujala ERR .25
(incorrect numbering
184 Kimmo Vesa .04 .10
185 Mika Yli-Maenpaa .06 .15
185B Jarmo Rantanen ERR .25
(incorrect numbering
186 Jarmo Kuusisto .04 .10
187 Marko Tuulola .04 .10
188 Tuomas Gronman .10 .25
189 Timo Kulonen .04 .10
189B Mika Arvaja ERR .25
(incorrect numbering
190 Kari-Pekka Friman VAR .04 .10
(name on front smaller font size
190B Kari-Pekka Friman VAR .25
(name on front larger font size
191 Pasi Huura .06 .15
192 Harri Suvanto .04 .10
193 Kamil Kastak .04 .10
194 Jari Torkki .06 .15
195 Kalle Sahlstedt .06 .15
196 Tommi Pullola .04 .10
197 Mika Valila .04 .10
198 Tero Arkiomaa .04 .10
199 Pasi Saarela .04 .10
200 Matti Forss .04 .10
201 Jussi Kiuru ERR .04 .10
(wrong photo
201B Jussi Kiuru COR .25
202 Mika Alatalo .80 2.00
203 Kimmo Rintanen .10 .25
204 Petri Latti ERR .04 .10
(wrong photo
204B Petri Latti COR .25
205 Petr Korinek .06 .15
206 Assat Team Card .06 .15
207 Veli-Pekka Ketola CO .06 .15
208 Kari Takko .10 .25
209 Timo Jarvinen .04 .10
210 Marko Sten .04 .10
211 Pasi Peltonen .04 .10
212 Olli Kaski .04 .10
213 Jarno Miikkulainen .04 .10
214 Jouni Vento .04 .10
215 Karri Kivi .06 .15
215B HIFK Team Card ERR .25
(incorrect numbering
215C Jouni Vento ERR .25
(incorrect numbering
216 Stanislav Meciar .04 .10
217 Nemo Nokkosmaki .04 .10
218 Arto Javanainen .04 .10
219 Janne Virtanen .04 .10
220 Vjatseslav Fandul .06 .15
221 Jari Levonen .04 .10
222 Jarno Levonen .04 .10
223 Jari Korpisalo .10 .25
224 Jokke Heinanen .04 .10
225 Harri Lonnberg .04 .10
226 Ari Saarinen .04 .10
227 Kari Syvasalmi .04 .10
228 Jarno Makela .04 .10
229 Rauli Raitanen .04 .10
230 Arto Heiskanen .04 .10
231 Mikael Kotkaniemi .04 .10
232 HPK Team Card .06 .15
233 Pentti Matikainen .04 .10
234 Kari Rosenberg .06 .15
235 Petri Vilen .04 .10
236 Marko Allen .04 .10
237 Mikko Myllykoski .04 .10
238 Kim Vahanen .04 .10
239 Janne Laukkanen .30 .75
240 Jari Haapamaki .04 .10
241 Niko Marttila .04 .10
242 Esa Sateri .04 .10
243 Toni Virta .04 .10
244 Marko Palo .06 .15
245 Markku Piikkila .04 .10
246 Jani Hassinen .04 .10
247 Jarkko Nikander .06 .15
248 Pasi Kivila .04 .10
249 Mika Lartama .04 .10
250 Tomas Kapusta .06 .15
251 Tommi Varjonen .04 .10
252 Teemu Tamminen .04 .10
253 Jukka Seppo .06 .15
254 Kiekko-Espoo Team Card .06 .15
255 Martti Merra .04 .10
256 Scott Brower .20 .50
257 Timo Maki .04 .10
258 Petri Pulkkinen .04 .10
259 Robert Salo .04 .10
260 Sami Nuutinen .04 .10
261 Teemu Sillanpaa .04 .10
262 Marko Halonen .04 .10
263 Jimi Helin .04 .10
264 Kari Haakana .04 .10
265 Jukka Tiilikainen .04 .10
266 Jan Langbacka .04 .10
267 Jarmo Muukkonen .04 .10
268 Timo Hirvonen .04 .10
269 Pasi Heinisto .04 .10
270 Kimmo Maki-Kokkila .04 .10
271 Mikko Lempiainen .04 .10
272 Tero Lehtera .04 .10
273 Hannu Jarvenpaa .06 .15
274 Riku Kuusisto .04 .10
275 Mikko Halonen .04 .10
276 Markku Takala .04 .10
277 Petro Koivunen .04 .10
278 Reipas Lahti Team Card .06 .15
279 Kari Makinen CO .04 .10
280 Oldrich Svoboda .04 .10
281 Pekka Ilmivalta .04 .10
282 Matti Vuorio .04 .10
283 Jari Parviainen .04 .10
284 Timo Kahelin .04 .10
285 Ville Skinnari .04 .10
286 Petri Koski .04 .10
287 Jarkko Hamalainen .04 .10
288 Pasi Ruponen .04 .10
289 Oldrich Valek .04 .10
290 Juha Nurminen .04 .10
291 Erkki Laine .04 .10
292 Sami Lekkerimaki .04 .10
293 Tommy Kiviaho .04 .10
293B Ville Skinnari ERR .25
(incorrect numbering
294 Jyrki Poikolainen .04 .10
295 Sami Wikstrom .04 .10
296 Jonni Vauhkonen .10 .25
297 Erkki Laine .04 .10
298 Jani Uski .04 .10
299 Jari Multanen .04 .10
300 Toni Koivunen .04 .10
301 Runkosarjan 1 .04 .10
302 Runkosarjan 2 .04 .10
303 Runkosarjan 3 .04 .10
304 Runkosarjan 4 .04 .10
305 Runkosarjan 5 .04 .10
306 Runkosarjan 6 .04 .10
307 Runkosarjan 7 .04 .10
308 Runkosarjan 8 .04 .10
309 Runkosarjan 9 .04 .10
310 Runkosarjan 10 .04 .10
311 Runkosarjan 11 .04 .10
312 Runkosarjan 12 .04 .10
313 Runkosarjan 13 .04 .10
314 Runkosarjan 14 .04 .10
315 Runkosarjan 15 .04 .10
316 Runkosarjan 16 .04 .10
317 Runkosarjan 17 .04 .10
318 Runkosarjan 18 .04 .10
319 Runkosarjan 19 .04 .10
320 Runkosarjan 20 .04 .10
321 Runkosarjan 21 .04 .10
322 Runkosarjan 22 .04 .10
323 Runkosarjan 23 .04 .10
324 Runkosarjan 24 .04 .10
325 Runkosarjan 25 .04 .10
326 Runkosarjan 26 .04 .10
327 Runkosarjan 27 .04 .10
328 Runkosarjan 28 .04 .10
329 Runkosarjan 29 .04 .10
330 Runkosarjan 30 .04 .10
331 Runkosarjan 31 .04 .10
332 Runkosarjan 32 .04 .10
333 Runkosarjan 33 .04 .10
334 Runkosarjan 34 .04 .10
335 Runkosarjan 35 .04 .10
336 Runkosarjan 36 .04 .10
337 Runkosarjan 37 .04 .10
338 Runkosarjan 38 .04 .10
339 Runkosarjan 39 .04 .10
340 Runkosarjan 40 .04 .10
341 Runkosarjan 41 .04 .10
342 Runkosarjan 42 .04 .10
343 Runkosarjan 43 .04 .10
344 Runkosarjan 44 .04 .10
345 Paikallisottelut .04 .10
(HIFK/Jokerit/K-Espoo)
346 Paikallisottelut .04 .10
(Lukko/TPS/Assat)
347 Paikallisottelut .04 .10
(HPK/Ilves/Tappara)
348 Paikallisottelut .04 .10
(JyP HT/KalPa/Reipas)
349 Puolivaliera .04 .10
(HPK/Lukko)
350 Puolivaliera .04 .10
(Jokerit/Assat)
351 Puolivaliera .04 .10
(Jokerit/Assat)
352 Puolivaliera .04 .10
(TPS/Ilves)
353 Valiera .04 .10
(HPK/JyP HT)
354 Valiera .04 .10
(TPS/Assat)
355 Pronssiottelu .04 .10
356 1.Finaali .04 .10
(TPS 9& HPK 3)
357 2. Finalli .04 .10
358 3.Finaali .04 .10
(TPS 3& HPK 2)
360 Esa Keskinen LL .10 .25
361 Tomas Kapusta LL .04 .10
362 Erik Hamalainen LL .06 .15
363 Brian Tutt LL .04 .10
364 Otakar Janecky LL ERR .06 .15
364B Otakar Janecky LL COR .25
365 Ville Peltonen LL .40 1.00
366 Petr Briza AS .40 1.00
367 Janne Laukkanen AS .20 .50
368 Timo Jutila AS .10 .25
369 Juha Riihijarvi AS ERR .10 .25
(card back from 384
369B Juha Riihijarvi AS COR .50
370 Esa Keskinen AS ERR .10 .25
(card back from 372
370B Esa Keskinen AS COR
371 Jarkko Varvio AS .06 .15
372 Esa Keskinen AW ERR .10 .25
(card back from 370
372B Esa Keskinen AW COR .50
373 Vladimir Jursinov AW .04 .10
374 Erik Hamalainen AW .06 .15
375 Timo Lehkonen AW .06 .15
376 German Titov AW .10 .25
377 Raimo Summanen AW .06 .15
378 Mikko Haapakoski AW .04 .10
379 Marko Palo AW .04 .10
380 Seppo Makela AW .04 .10
381 TPS, Turku Team Card .04 .10
382 HPK Hameenlinna .04 .10
383 JyP HT Jyvaskyla .04 .10
384 Juha Riihijarvi MVP ERR .06 .15
(card back from 369
384B Juha Riihijarvi MVP COR .25
385 Jukka Virtanen .04 .10
386 Kari Jalonen .06 .15
387 Matti Forss .04 .10
388 Arto Javanainen .04 .10
389 Saku Koivu 4.00 10.00
390 Janne Niinimaa .40 1.00
391 Ville Peltonen .40 1.00
392 Jonni Vauhkonen .10 .25
393 Petri Varis .20 .50
394 Antti Aalto .40 1.00
395 Jere Karalahti .20 .50
396 Kimmo Timonen .40 1.00

1993-94 Finnish SISU Autographs

These cards were issued as random inserts in packs of 1993-94 SISU. Essentially, they are the same as the base cards, save for the autograph and serial numbering. We do not have confirmed serial numbers for any of these cards. If you can provide them, please contact us at hockeymag@beckett.com. Thanks to collector Heikki Silvennoinen for providing the checklist.

COMPLETE SET (12) 90.00 150.00
8 Waltteri Immonen 10.00
41 Saku Koivu 50.00
73 Pauli Jarvinen 10.00
83 Sakari Lindfors 25.00
121 Risto Jalo 10.00
173 Marko Virtanen 10.00
178 Pekka Tirkkonen 15.00
203 Kimmo Rintanen 10.00
223 Jari Korpisalo 10.00
239 Janne Laukkanen 15.00
260 Sami Nuutinen 10.00
296 Jonni Vauhkonen 10.00

1993-94 Finnish SISU Promos

Produced by Leaf, this 12-card promo set was handed out to members of the Finnish media before the 1993-94 season to introduce North American style hockey cards to the fanatical hockey followers of Finland. The card design mirrors that of the base cards, but the cards are not numbered on the back.

COMPLETE SET (12) 4.00 125.00
NNO Timo Jutila .30 10.00
NNO Rami Koivisto .20 10.00
NNO Petri Skriko .40 15.00
NNO Rauli Raitanen .20 10.00
NNO German Titov .40 10.00
NNO Simo Saarinen .20 10.00
NNO Janne Laukkanen .75 15.00
NNO Mika Alatalo .75 15.00
NNO Pasi Ruponen .20 10.00
NNO Jari Lindroos .20 10.00
NNO Timo Peltomaa .20 10.00
NNO Pekka Tirkkonen .20 15.00

1994-95 Finnish SISU

Manufactured by Leaf in Turku, Finland, this set consists of 400 standard-size cards and features Finnish Hockey League players. The cards were sold in eight-card foil packs. The Canada Bowl Super Chase Card was inserted in first series foil packs. The Saku Koivu Super Chase Card was randomly inserted in second series foil packs at a rate of one in 192 packs. Several notable NHLers, including Teemu Selanne, Jari Kurri and Esa Tikkanen returned to Finland during the 1994 NHL lockout and thus appear in the second series.

COMPLETE SET (400) 20.00 50.00
COMPLETE SERIES 1 (200) 6.00 15.00
COMPLETE SERIES 2 (200) 14.00 35.00
1 Pasi Kuivalainen .08 .20
2 Jere Karalahti .20 .50
3 Markku Heikkinen .04 .10
4 Marko Allen .04 .10
5 Jarmo Kuusisto .04 .10
6 Marko Tuulola .04 .10
7 Marko Kiprusoff 3.00 .25
8 Vesa Ponto .04 .10
9 Tero Lehtera .08 .20
10 Darren Boyko .04 .10
11 Kari Heikkinen .04 .10
12 Niko Marttila .04 .10
13 Jari Torkki .04 .10
14 Jiri Kucera .08 .20
15 Jari Levonen .04 .10
16 Juha Ikonen .04 .10
17 Joni Lius .04 .10
18 Pekka Tuomisto .04 .10
19 Petri Kokku .04 .10
20 Jere Lehtinen 1.20 3.00
21 Janne Kekalainen .04 .10
22 Ari Haanpaa .04 .10
23 Hannu Jarvenpaa .08 .20
24 Waltteri Immonen .04 .10
25 Jari Lindroos .08 .20
26 Jan Langbacka .04 .10
27 Kari Takko .20 .50
28 Pasi Maattanen .04 .10
29 Jan Latvala .04 .10
30 Arto Heiskanen .04 .10
31 Iiro Jarvi .10 .25
32 Igor Boldin .04 .10
33 Sami Simonen .04 .10
34 Kari Rosenberg .08 .20
35 Sakari Lindfors .20 .50
36 Veli-Pekka Hard .04 .10
37 Jari Halme .10 .25
38 Jukka Tammi .20 .50
39 Kalle Koskinen .04 .10
40 Pekka Tirkkonen .04 .10
41 Ari Sulander .20 .50
42 Joni Hassinen .04 .10
43 Timo Peltomaa .04 .10
44 Sami Mettovaara .04 .10
45 Mika Yli-Maenpaa .10 .25
46 Toni Virta .04 .10
47 Kimmo Lecklin .08 .20
48 Rauli Raitanen .04 .10
49 Juha Lind .20 .50
50 Ari-Pekka Siekkinen .08 .20
51 Kim Ahlroos .04 .10
52 Jarkko Nikander .04 .10
53 Jouni Vento .04 .10
54 Juha Lampinen .04 .10
55 Kalle Sahlstedt .04 .10

1994-95 Finnish SISU

56 Teemu Sillanpaa .04 .10
57 Lasse Nieminen .04 .10
58 Janne Niinimaa .40 1.00
59 Timo Jutila .08 .20
60 Tommi Haapsaari .04 .10
61 Allan Measures .04 .10
62 Petteri Nummelin .04 .10
63 Antti Tormanen .10 .25
64 Pekka Laksola .04 .10
65 Esa Sateri .04 .10
66 Petro Koivunen .04 .10
67 Janne Virtanen .04 .10
68 Pekka Peltola .04 .10
69 Matti Kaipainen .04 .10
70 Semi Pekki .04 .10
71 Jussi Tarvainen .04 .10
72 Jari Virtanen .04 .10
73 Kimmo Salminen .04 .10
74 Tommi Varjonen .04 .10
75 Pauli Jarvinen .04 .10
76 Hannu Mattila .04 .10
77 Aleksander Smirnov .04 .10
78 Arto Kulmala .04 .10
79 Roland Carlsson .04 .10
80 Jarma Miikkulainen .04 .10
81 Jarmo Muukkonen .04 .10
82 Mika Paananen .04 .10
83 Pasi Kivila .04 .10
84 Jari Laukkanen .04 .10
85 Tero Arkiomaa .04 .10
86 Tommi Miettinen .08 .20
87 Juha Jarvenpaa .04 .10
88 Niko Mikkola .04 .10
89 Antti Tuomenoksa .04 .10
90 Ilkka Sinisalo .10 .25
91 Otakar Janecky .08 .20
92 Arto Sirvio .04 .10
93 Robert Salo .04 .10
94 Ari Saarinen .04 .10
95 Kari Martikainen .04 .10
96 Miro Haapaniemi .04 .10
97 Fredrik Norrena .08 .20
98 Erik Hamalainen .08 .20
99 Simo Saarinen .04 .10
100 Harri Suvanto .04 .10
101 Kai Nurminen .20 .50
102 Rami Koivisto .04 .10
103 Pasi Peltonen .04 .10
104 Kari-Pekka Friman .04 .10
105 Mika Kortelainen .08 .20
106 Timo Hirvanen .04 .10
107 Jari Haapamaki .04 .10
108 Mika Manninen .04 .10
109 Ari Vuori .04 .10
110 Markku Ikonen .04 .10
111 Mikko Konttila .04 .10
112 Harri Sillgren .04 .10
113 Mikko Teui .04 .10
114 Markus Oijennus .04 .10
115 Kimmo Hyttinen .04 .10
116 Jokke Heinanen .04 .10
117 Sami Ahlberg .04 .10
118 Mika Rautio .08 .20
119 Ari Salo .08 .20
120 Juha Hautamaa .04 .10
121 Kari Haakana .04 .10
122 Sami Nuutinen .04 .10
123 Lasse Pirjeta .04 .10
124 Koijo Sailynoja .08 .20
125 Mikael Kotkaniemi .04 .10
126 Samuli Rautio .04 .10
127 Veli-Pekka Pekkarinen .04 .10
128 Hannu Henriksson .04 .10
129 Antti Aalto .26 .65
130 Jyrki Jokinen .04 .10
131 Marko Ek .04 .10
132 Marko Ojanen .04 .10
133 Mika Arvaja .04 .10
134 Karri Kivi .04 .10
135 Timo Saarikoski .04 .10
136 Toni Sihvonen .04 .10
137 Mika Laaksonen .04 .10
138 HIFK Helsinki Team Card .04 .10
139 HPK Team Card .04 .10
140 Ilves Team Card .04 .10
141 Jokerit Team Card .10 .25
142 JyP HT Team Card .04 .10
143 KalPa Team Card .04 .10
144 Kiekko-Espoo Team Card .04 .10
145 Lukko Team Card .04 .10
146 Tappara Team Card .04 .10
147 TPS Turku Team Card .04 .10
148 TuTo Turku Team Card .04 .10
149 Assat Team Card .04 .10
150 Petteri Nummelin CL .04 .10
151 Kari Takko CL .10 .25
152 Vladimir Jursinov CL .04 .10
153 Juha Lind CL .10 .25
154 Marko Jantunen LL .08 .20
155 Jere Lehtinen LL .80 2.00
156 Esa Keskinen LL .10 .25
157 Jere Lehtinen LL .80 2.00
158 Timo Peltomaa LL .10 .25
159 Janne Gronval LL .10 .25
160 Jarmo Myllys AS .20 .50
161 Markko Kiprusoff AS .10 .25
162 Timo Jutila AS .08 .20
163 Sami Kapanen AS .40 1.00
164 Esa Keskinen AS .10 .25
165 Mika Alatalo AS .20 .50
166 Ville Peltonen .20 .50
167 Igor Boldin .04 .10
168 Sami Lehtonen .04 .10
169 Juha Jokiharju .04 .10
170 Harri Laurila .04 .10
171 Pekka Tirkkonen .04 .10
172 Mikko Halonen .04 .10
173 Tero Arkiomaa .04 .10
174 Jonni Vauhkonen .10 .25
175 Janne Gronvall .10 .25
176 Marko Jantunen .04 .10
177 Jouni Vento .08 .20
178 HIFK .04 .10
179 HPK .04 .10
180 Ilves Tampere .04 .10
181 JyP HT .04 .10
182 Jokerit .04 .10
183 KalPa .04 .10
184 Kiekko-Espoo .04 .10
185 Lukko .04 .10
186 Tappara .04 .10
187 TPS .04 .10
188 Reipas .04 .10
189 Assat .04 .10
190 Jokerit Champions .10 .25
191 Lukko 2nd Place .04 .10
192 TPS Euro Champs 1994 .10 .25
193 TPS Euro Cup Champs .10 .25
194 Playoffs .04 .10
195 Playoffs .04 .10
196 Playoffs .04 .10
197 Finals Game 1 .04 .10
198 Finals Game 2 .04 .10
199 Finals Game 3 .04 .10
200 Finals Game 4 .04 .10
201 Jouni Rokama .08 .20
202 Sami Leinonen .04 .10
203 Jani Nikko .10 .25
204 Arto Vuoti .04 .10
205 Petr Pavlas .04 .10
206 Reijo Mikkolainen .04 .10
207 Jari Kurri .80 2.00
208 Janne Ojanen .20 .50
209 Sami Kapanen .80 2.00
210 Teppo Kivela .04 .10
211 Saku Koivu 2.00 5.00
212 Pekka Virta .04 .10
213 Risto Jalo .08 .20
214 Sergei Prjakhin .10 .25
215 Aleksander Barkov .04 .10
216 Ville Peltonen .30 .75
217 Jari Korpisalo .08 .20
218 Jari Liikkanen .04 .10
219 Timo Lehkonen .08 .20
220 Juha Ylonen .20 .50
221 Harri Lonnberg .04 .10
222 Teemu Vuorinen .04 .10
223 Pertti Lehtonen .04 .10
224 Tommi Pullola .04 .10
225 Tomas Kapusta .08 .20
226 Joonas Jaaskelainen .04 .10
227 Jukka Tiilikainen .04 .10
228 Jarno Kultanen .20 .50
229 Kimmo Kapanen .10 .25
230 Jari Kauppila .04 .10
231 Jarkko Glad .04 .10
232 Nemo Nokkosmaki .04 .10
233 Petri Matikainen .04 .10
234 Christian Ruutu .20 .50
235 Martti Jarventie .30 .75
236 Sami Salo .20 .50
237 Timo Kulonen .04 .10
238 Pasi Sormunen .04 .10
239 Timo Nurmberg .04 .10
240 Jari Hirsimaki .04 .10
241 Tommi Hamalainen .04 .10
242 Vesa Salo .10 .25
243 Juha Nurminen .04 .10
244 Petr Korinek .04 .10
245 Kimmo Vesa .08 .20
246 Jukka Seppo .04 .10
247 Jarno Makela .04 .10
248 Petri Varis .20 .50
249 Marko Virtanen .04 .10
250 Risto Siltanen .10 .25
251 Juha Jarvenpaa .04 .10
252 Raimo Summanen .10 .25
253 Markus Hatinen .04 .10
254 Kimmo Nurro .04 .10
255 Timo Salonen .04 .10
256 Jari Munck .04 .10
257 Kimmo Rintanen .10 .25
258 Jarno Levonen .04 .10
259 Jarno Peltonen .04 .10
260 Valeri Krykov .04 .10
261 Kai Rautio .04 .10
262 Timo Blomqvist .10 .25
263 Teemu Selanne 2.00 5.00
264 Juha Virtanen .04 .10
265 Veli-Pekka Kautonen .04 .10
266 Mikko Koivunoro .04 .10
267 Mikko Luovi .10 .25
268 Jaroslav Otevrel .04 .10
269 Erik Kakko .04 .10
270 Peter Ahola .08 .20
271 Miikka Kemppi .04 .10
272 Toni Makiaho .04 .10
273 Pekka Poikolainen .04 .10
274 Timo Norppa .04 .10
275 Sebastian Sulku .04 .10
276 Esa Tikkanen .40 1.00
277 Pasi Saarela .04 .10
278 Ilpo Kauhanen .20 .50
279 Mika Alatalo .20 .50
280 Jukka Suomalainen .04 .10
281 Tony Arima .04 .10
282 Mika Puhakka .04 .10
283 Jussi Kiuru .04 .10
284 Jarkko Isotalo .04 .10
285 Esa Tommila .04 .10
286 Jouni Loponen .04 .10
287 Jermu Pisto .04 .10
288 Pasi Heinisto .04 .10
289 Toni Porkka .04 .10
290 Juha Vuorivirta .10 .25
291 Vesa Karjalainen .04 .10
292 Tom Koivisto .04 .10
293 Markku Hurme .04 .10
294 Mika Kannisto .04 .10
295 Marko Rantanen .08 .20
296 Petri Kalteva .04 .10
297 Pasi Huura .04 .10
298 Miikka Ruokonen .04 .10
299 Tuomo Raty .04 .10
300 Vadim Shaidullin .04 .10
301 Juha Riihijarvi .08 .20
302 Brad Turner .04 .10
303 Marko Toivola .04 .10
304 Kimmo Timonen .30 .75
305 Kai Nurminen .20 .50
306 Vesa Lehtonen .04 .10
307 Mika Niittymaki .04 .10
308 Sami Wahlsten .04 .10
309 Pavel Torgajev .10 .25
310 Pasi Kemppainen .04 .10
311 Markku Kallio .04 .10
312 Timo Maki .08 .20
313 Mika Stromberg .10 .25
314 Tuomas Gronman .10 .25
315 Tommi Rajamaki .10 .25
316 Juri Kuznetsov .08 .20
317 Mikko Myllykoski .04 .10
318 Brian Tutt .04 .10
319 Teemu Numminen .08 .20
320 Juha Jokiharju .04 .10
321 Mika Lehtinen .04 .10
322 Jari Pulliainen .04 .10
323 Kimmo Maki-Kokkila .04 .10
324 Mikko Peltola .04 .10
325 Risto Kurkinen .04 .10
326 Harri Laurila .04 .10
327 Vjatcheslav Fandul .04 .10
328 Niklas Hede .04 .10
329 Boris Rousson .20 .50
330 Jukka Ollila .10 .25
331 Jouni Tuominen .04 .10
332 Marko Harkonen .08 .20
333 Petri Engman .08 .20
334 Mikko Halonen .04 .10
335 Aki Berg .30 .75
336 Kristian Fagerstrom .04 .10
337 Jiri Veber .04 .10
338 Tommy Kiviaho .04 .10
339 Konstantin Astrahantsev .04 .10
340 Jukka Makitalo .08 .20
341 Timo Nykopp .04 .10
342 Sami Lehtonen .04 .10
343 Joni Lehto .08 .20
344 Jouko Myrra .04 .10
345 Mikko Makela .20 .50
346 Marco Poulsen .04 .10
347 Janne Seva .04 .10
348 Shawn McEachern .20 .50
349 Jarkko Varvio .08 .20
350 Mikko Konttila .04 .10
351 Veli-Pekka Ahonen .04 .10
352 Michael Nylander .30 .75
353 Kristian Taubert .04 .10
354 Ismo Kuoppala .04 .10
355 Kimmo Hyttinen .04 .10
356 Petri Latti .04 .10
357 Ted Donato .20 .50
358 Jari Harjumaki .04 .10
359 Teppo Numminen .20 .50
360 Jyrki Lumme .20 .50
361 German Titov .20 .50
362 Kari Eloranta .10 .25
363 Raimo Helminen .10 .25
364 Marko Jantunen .10 .25
365 Olli Kaski .04 .10
366 Jarmo Kekalainen .08 .20
367 Esa Keskinen .10 .25
368 Jarmo Makitalo .04 .10
369 Mika Nieminen .10 .25
370 Marko Palo .04 .10
371 Ville Siren .10 .25
372 Kari Suoraniemi .04 .10
373 Otakar Janecky PM .10 .25
374 Jari Lindroos PM .04 .10
375 Teppo Kivela PM .04 .10
376 Petri Varis PM .10 .25
377 Pekka Laksola PM .04 .10
378 Jari Korpisalo PM .08 .20
379 Iiro Jarvi PM .10 .25
380 Timo Saarikoski PM .04 .10
381 Rauli Raitanen PM .04 .10
382 Juha Riihijarvi PM .04 .10
383 Juha Jokiharju PM .04 .10
384 Vesa Salo PM .04 .10
385 Mika Nieminen CL .10 .25
386 Marko Jantunen CL .04 .10
387 Jere Lehtinen CL .40 1.00
388 Ari Sulander CL .10 .25
389 Hannu Kapanen CO .04 .10
390 Hannu Savolainen CO .04 .10
391 Heikki Vesala CO .04 .10
392 Hannu Aravirta CO .04 .10
393 Kari Savolainen CO .04 .10
394 Anatoli Bogdanov CO .04 .10
395 Harri Rindell CO .04 .10
396 Vaclav Sykora CO .04 .10
397 Boris Majorov CO .04 .10
398 Vladimir Jursinov CO .06 .15
399 Seppo Suoraniemi CO .04 .10
400 Veli-Pekka Ketola CO .10 .25
NNO1 Canada Bowl Super Chase COR 8.00 20.00
NNO1B Canada Bowl Super Chase ERR {card back text not fully printed
NNO2 Saku Koivu Super Chase 20.0050.00

1994-95 Finnish SISU Fire On Ice

This 20-card set highlights players who had multiple games of three or more points during the 1993-94 Finnish season. The cards were randomly inserted in first series packs.

COMPLETE SET (20) 12.00 30.00
1 Tero Arkiomoa .40 1.00
2 Igor Boldin .40 1.00
3 Vjatseslav Fandul .40 1.00
4 Otakar Janecky .80 2.00
5 Marko Jantunen .80 2.00
6 Timo Jutila .40 1.00
7 Pauli Jarvinen .40 1.00
8 Sami Kapanen 1.20 3.00
9 Tomas Kapusta .40 1.00
10 Esa Keskinen .80 2.00
11 Saku Koivu 4.00 10.00
12 Petro Koivunen .40 1.00
13 Petr Korinek .40 1.00
14 Jari Karpisolo .40 1.00
15 Risto Kurkinen .40 1.00
16 Tero Lehtera .80 2.00
17 Juha Nurminen .40 1.00
18 Kai Nurminen .80 2.00
19 Janne Ojanen .80 2.00
20 Jari Torkki .40 1.00

1994-95 Finnish SISU Guest Specials

Randomly inserted at a rate of one in thirteen series two foil packs, this 12-card standard-size set focuses on NHL stars who signed on to play in the Finnish league during the 1994 NHL lockout.

COMPLETE SET (12) 16.00 30.00
1 Ted Donato 1.20 2.00
2 Jari Kurri 2.00 5.00
3 Jyrki Lumme .80 2.00
4 Shawn McEachern 1.20 2.00
5 Mikko Makela .80 2.00
6 Teppo Numminen .80 2.00
7 Michael Nylander 1.20 2.00
8 Christian Ruuttu .80 2.00
9 Teemu Selanne 10.00 20.00
10 Esa Tikkanen 1.20 2.00
11 German Titov .80 1.00
12 Jarkko Varvio .80 1.00

1994-95 Finnish SISU Horoscopes

Randomly inserted at a rate of one in four second series foil packs, this 20-card standard-size set describes the players' personalities according to the astrological signs they were born under.

COMPLETE SET (20) 4.80 12.00
1 Juha Lind .40 1.00
2 Jukka Seppo .40 1.00
3 Antti Tuomenoksa .20 .50
4 Tuomas Gronman .40 1.00
5 Peter Ahola .20 .50
6 Ville Peltonen .80 2.00
7 Timo Saarikoski .20 .50
8 Timo Peltomaa .40 1.00
9 Jari Levonen .20 .50
10 Teppo Kivela .20 .50
11 Valeri Krykov .20 .50
12 Juha Riihijarvi .20 .50
13 Kai Nurminen .40 1.00
14 Mikko Luovi .20 .50
15 Raimo Summanen .40 1.00
16 Tommy Kiviaho .20 .50
17 Hannu Jarvenpaa .20 .50
18 Marko Virtanen .20 .50
19 Sami Lehtonen .20 .50
20 Mika Alatalo .80 2.00

1994-95 Finnish SISU Junior

These standard size cards feature ten of Finland's brightest young stars as they appeared as youth hockey players. The cards were randomly inserted into series I packs.

COMPLETE SET (10) 6.00 15.00
1 Saku Koivu 3.20 8.00
2 Jekke Heimanen .40 1.00
3 Tommi Miettinen .40 1.00
4 Jere Karalahti .80 2.00
5 Kalle Koskinen .40 1.00
6 Kari Rosenberg .40 1.00
7 Mika Manninen .40 1.00
8 Jussi Tarvainen .40 1.00
9 Mika Stromberg .40 1.00
10 Kalle Sahlstedt .40 1.00

1994-95 Finnish SISU Magic Numbers

This ten-card standard-size set was randomly inserted at a rate of one in eight second series foil packs.

COMPLETE SET (10) 4.80 12.00
STATED ODDS 1:8 SERIES 2
1 Pasi Kuivalainen .40 1.00
2 Petteri Nummelin .80 2.00
3 Jarmo Kuusisto .40 1.00
4 Janne Ojanen .40 1.00
5 Sami Kapanen 1.20 3.00
6 Pekka Virta .40 1.00
7 Antti Tormanen .40 1.00
8 Jari Korpisalo .40 1.00
9 Kimmo Salminen .40 1.00
10 Jukka Tammi 1.20 3.00

1994-95 Finnish SISU NHL Draft

Randomly inserted at a rate of one in twenty foil second series packs, this eight-card standard-size set spotlights seven Finns who were drafted by NHL teams in 1994.

COMPLETE SET (8) 2.00 5.00
STATED ODDS 1:20 SERIES 2
1 Title Card .20 .50
2 Marko Kiprusoff .40 1.00
3 Jussi Tarvainen .40 1.00
4 Arto Kuki .40 1.00
5 Tommi Rajamaki .40 1.00
6 Tero Lehtera .40 1.00
7 Tommi Miettinen .40 1.00
8 Antti Tormanen .40 1.00

1994-95 Finnish SISU NIL Phenoms

These standard size cards feature ten goaltenders who posted multiple shutouts during the 1993-94 Finnish campaign. The cards show the netminder cutout photo of the netminder over a brown backdrop.

COMPLETE SET (10) 12.00 30.00
1 Mika Manninen 1.20 3.00
2 Kari Takko 2.00 5.00
3 Ari Sulander 2.00 5.00
4 Jouni Rokama 1.20 3.00
5 Kari Rosenberg 1.20 3.00
6 Mika Rautio 1.20 3.00
7 Ari-Pekka Siekkinen 1.20 3.00
8 Allain Roy 1.20 3.00
9 Pasi Kuivalainen 1.20 3.00
10 Sakari Lindfors 1.20 3.00

1994-95 Finnish SISU Specials

These ten standard sized cards were random inserts in Leaf first series packs and showcase winners of the player of the month award, among other titles. The main cards are white. The B cards are black. The B suffix does not appear on the actual card: it is included here for checklisting purposes only. The Koivu Jumbo was available as a redemption to those who sent in the Koivu Super Bonus card. It mirrors the white version of the Koivu card.

COMPLETE SET (10) 8.00 20.00
1 Mika Alatalo .80 2.00
1B Mika Alatalo
2 Jari Korpisalo .40 1.00
2B Jari Korpisalo
3 Petteri Nummelin .80 2.00
3B Petteri Nummelin
4 Janne Ojanen .40 1.00
4B Janne Ojanen
5 Sami Kapanen 1.20 3.00
5B Sami Kapanen
6 Kari Takko .80 2.00
6B Kari Takko
7 Esa Keskinen .40 1.00
7B Esa Keskinen
8 Ari Sulander .80 2.00
8B Ari Sulander
9 Jarmo Myllys .80 2.00
9B Jarmo Myllys
10 Saku Koivu 4.00 10.00
10B Saku Koivu
10J Saku Koivu JUMBO

1994 Finnish Jaa Kiekko

This 360-card set was issued in Finland by Semic in conjunction with the 1994 World Championships. The set includes players from the traditional hockey powers, as well as Great Britain, Austria, Norway and France, shown in action for their countries. A number of NHL players who had participated in previous Canada Cups or World Championships are also pictured. The cards were distributed in 5-card packets. A binder also was available to house the collection.

COMPLETE SET (360) 30.00 50.00
1 Jarmo Myllys .10 .25
2 Pasi Kuivalainen .04 .10
3 Jukka Tammi .08 .20
4 Markus Ketterer .10 .25
5 Timo Jutila .06 .15
6 Mikko Haapakoski .04 .10
7 Marko Tuulola .04 .10
8 Jyrki Lumme .10 .25
9 Kari Harila .04 .10
10 Teppo Numminen .10 .25
11 Pasi Sormunen .04 .10
12 Petteri Nummelin .04 .10
13 Harri Laurila .04 .10
14 Mika Stromberg .06 .15
15 Ville Siren .06 .15
16 Pekka Laksola .04 .10
17 Janne Laukkanen .08 .20
18 Marko Kiprusoff .06 .15
19 Waltteri Immonen .06 .15
20 Teemu Selanne .80 1.50
21 Mika Alatalo .10 .25
22 Vesa Viitakoski .06 .15
23 Tero Arkiomaa .04 .10
24 Jari Kurri .20 .50
25 Pekka Tirkkonen .04 .10
26 Jarmo Kekalainen .06 .15
27 Saku Koivu .40 1.00
28 Antti Tormanen .08 .20
29 Jere Lehtinen .20 .50
30 Raimo Helminen .06 .15
31 Mikko Makela .06 .15
32 Marko Jantunen .06 .15
33 Ville Peltonen .10 .25
34 Esa Tikkanen .10 .25
35 Janne Ojanen .06 .15
36 Mika Nieminen .04 .10
37 Marko Palo .04 .10
38 Rauli Raitanen .04 .10
39 Sami Kapanen .40 1.00
40 Juha Riihijarvi .04 .10
41 Esa Keskinen .04 .10
42 Jari Korpisalo .04 .10
43 Christian Ruuttu .06 .15
44 Jarkko Varvio .06 .15
45 Sami Wahlsten .04 .10
46 Petri Varis .10 .25
47 Timo Saarikoski .04 .10
48 Timo Norppa .04 .10
49 Marko Virtanen .04 .10
50 Pauli Jarvinen .04 .10
51 Hakan Algotsson .08 .20
52 Tommy Soderstrom .10 .25
53 Rolf Ridderwall .06 .15
54 Tomas Jonsson .06 .15
55 Christian Due-Boje .04 .10
56 Peter Popovic .06 .15
57 Fredrik Stillman .04 .10
58 Magnus Svensson .08 .20
59 Fredrik Nilsson .04 .10
60 Tommy Albelin .06 .15
61 Joacim Esbjors .04 .10
62 Roger Johansson .06 .15
63 Stefan Nilsson .04 .10
64 Hakan Loob .10 .25
65 Peter Ottosson .04 .10
66 Daniel Rydmark .04 .10
67 Mikael Renberg .10 .25
68 Patrik Juhlin .08 .20
69 Thomas Rundqvist .06 .15
70 Andreas Johansson .10 .25
71 Stefan Ornskog .06 .15
72 Nillas Eriksson .04 .10
73 Jonas Bergqvist .10 .25
74 Mats Sundin .40 1.00
75 Peter Forsberg 1.20 2.00
76 Stefan Elvenes .04 .10
77 Tomas Forslund .06 .15
78 Patric Kjellberg .10 .25
79 Bill Ranford .20 .50
80 Corey Hirsch .10 .25
81 Larry Murphy .10 .25
82 Mark Tinordi .06 .15
83 Scott Stevens .20 .50
84 Al Macinnis .40 1.00
85 Steve Smith .10 .25
86 Paul Coffey .40 1.00
87 Eric Desjardins .10 .25
88 Eric Lindros .80 1.50
89 Dale Hawerchuk .20 .50
90 Steve Larmer .10 .25
91 Brent Sutter .08 .20
92 Luc Robitaille .40 1.00
93 Shayne Corson .10 .25
94 Mark Messier .60 1.50
95 Rick Tocchet .20 .50
96 Theo Fleury .40 1.00
97 Dirk Graham .10 .25
98 Russ Courtnall .10 .25
99 Wayne Gretzky 4.00 5.00
100 Brendan Shanahan .80 1.50
101 Mark Recchi .40 1.00
102 David Harlock .06 .15
103 Craig Woodcroft .04 .10
104 Paul Kariya 1.60 2.00
105 Jason Marshall .06 .15
106 Brett Lindros .10 .25
107 Mike Richter .40 1.00
108 Mike Dunham .20 .50
109 Craig Wolanin .06 .15
110 Jim Johnson .06 .15
111 Chris Chelios .40 1.00
112 Eric Weinrich .06 .15
113 Brian Leetch .40 1.00
114 Kevin Hatcher .10 .25
115 Ed Olczyk .10 .25
116 Kevin Miller .08 .20
117 Doug Brown .04 .10
118 Joe Mullen .10 .25
119 Craig Janney .10 .25
120 Pat LaFontaine .20 .50
121 Gary Suter .10 .25
122 Jeremy Roenick .40 1.00
123 Brett Hull .60 1.50
124 Joel Otto .10 .25
125 Mike Modano .60 1.50
126 Tony Granato .10 .25
127 Dave Christian .08 .20
128 Brian Mullen .06 .15
129 Chris Ferraro .08 .20
130 John Lilley .06 .15
131 Jeff Lazaro .06 .15
132 Peter Ferraro .10 .25
133 Brian Rolston .10 .25
134 David Roberts .06 .15
135 Nikolai Khabibulin .40 1.00
136 Andrei Trefilov .10 .25
137 Vladimir Malakhov .10 .25
138 Alexander Karpovtsev .08 .20
139 Alexander Kmirnov .04 .10
140 Sergei Zubov .10 .25
141 Sergei Seljanin .04 .10
142 Sergei Shendelev .04 .10
143 Alexei Kasatonov .08 .20
144 Sergei Sorokin .04 .10
145 Vjatseslav Bykov .04 .10
146 Sergei Fedorov .80 1.50
147 Alexei Yashin .10 .25
148 Vjatseslav Butsajev .06 .15
149 Konstantin Astrahantsev .04 .10
150 Alexei Zhamnov .10 .25
151 Dimitri Frolov .04 .10
152 Slava Kozlov .10 .25
153 Sergei Pushkov .04 .10
154 Andrei Khomutov .04 .10
155 Sergei Makarov .10 .25
156 Igor Larionov .20 .50
157 Valeri Kamenski .10 .25
158 Alexander Semak .06 .15
159 Alexei Gusarov .06 .15
160 Andrei Lomakin .06 .15
161 Igor Korolev .06 .15
162 Ravil Haidarov .04 .10
163 Dominik Hasek .80 1.50
164 Oldrich Svoboda .04 .10
165 Petr Briza .10 .25
166 Leo Gudas .04 .10
167 Kamil Prachar .04 .10
168 Richard Smehlik .08 .20
169 Frantisek Kucera .06 .15
170 Drahomir Kadlec .06 .15
171 Jan Vopat .04 .10
172 Frantisek Prochazka .04 .10
173 Antonin Stavjana .04 .10
174 Bedrich Scerban .04 .10
175 Kamil Kastak .04 .10
176 Josef Beranek .10 .25
177 Martin Rucinsky .10 .25
178 Michal Pivonka .10 .25
179 Tomas Jelinek .04 .10
180 Richard Zemlicka .04 .10
181 Robert Kron .08 .20
182 Jiri Slegr .10 .25
183 Jaromir Jagr 1.20 2.00
184 Robert Reichel .10 .25
185 David Vyborny .06 .15
186 Robert Lang .10 .25
187 Petr Rosol .04 .10
188 Otakar Janecky .06 .15
189 Martin Hostak .04 .10
190 Jiri Kucera .06 .15
191 Eduard Hartmann .10 .25
192 Lubomir Sekeras .04 .10
193 Marian Smerciak .04 .10
194 Jan Varholik .04 .10
195 Lubomir Rybovic .04 .10
196 Miroslav Marcinko .04 .10
197 Stanislav Medrik .04 .10
198 Zdeno Ciger .08 .20
199 Jergus Baca .06 .15
200 Peter Stastny .10 .25
201 Peter Veselovsky .04 .10
202 Anton Stastny .08 .20
203 Lubomir Kolnik .06 .15
204 Roman Kontsek .04 .10
205 Rene Pucher .04 .10
206 Slavomir Ilvasky .04 .10
207 Zigmund Palffy .40 1.00
208 Vlastimil Plavucha .04 .10
209 Dusan Pohorelec .04 .10
210 Robert Petrovicky .06 .15
211 Michel Valliere .04 .10
212 Petri Ylonen .10 .25
213 Jean-Philippe Lemoine .04 .10
214 Christophe Moyon .04 .10
215 Denis Perez .04 .10
216 Bruno Saunier .04 .10
217 Stephane Botteri .04 .10
218 Michel Breistroff .04 .10
219 Geralf Guennelon .04 .10
220 Serge Poudrier .04 .10
221 Benjamin Agnel .04 .10
222 Stephane Arcangeloni .04 .10
223 Pierrick Maia .04 .10
224 Antoine Richer .04 .10
225 Christoph Ville .04 .10
226 Michael Babin .04 .10
227 Lionel Orsolini .04 .10
228 Stephane Barin .04 .10
229 Arnaud Briand .04 .10
230 Franck Pajonkowski .08 .20
231 Claus Dalpiaz .08 .20
232 Brian Stankiewicz .04 .10
233 Rob Doyle .04 .10
234 Michael Guntner .04 .10
235 Martin Krainz .04 .10
236 Michael Shea .04 .10
237 Martin Ulrich .04 .10
238 Erich Solderer .04 .10
239 Wayne Groulx .04 .10
240 Andreas Puschnig .04 .10
241 Dieter Kalt .04 .10
242 Gerhard Puschnik .04 .10
243 Werner Kerth .04 .10
244 Richard Nasheim .04 .10
245 Arno Maier .04 .10
246 Mario Schaden .04 .10
247 Reinhard Lampert .04 .10
248 Karl Heinzle .04 .10
249 Wolfgang Kromp .04 .10
250 Marty Dallman .04 .10
251 Jim Marthinsen .08 .20
252 Rob Schistad .04 .10
253 Tom Cato Andersen .04 .10
254 Anders Myrvold .08 .20
255 Svein Enok Norstebo .04 .10
256 Tommy Jakobsen .04 .10
257 Pal Kristiansen .04 .10
258 Petter Salsten .04 .10
259 Ole Eskild Dahlstrom .04 .10
260 Morten Finstad .04 .10
261 Espen Knutsen .10 .25
262 Erik Kristiansen .04 .10
263 Geir Hoff .04 .10
264 Roy Johansen .04 .10
265 Trond Magnussen .04 .10
266 Marius Rath .04 .10
267 Vegar Barlie .04 .10
268 Arne Billkvam .04 .10
269 Tom Johansen .04 .10
270 Petter Thoresen .04 .10
271 Klaus Merk .10 .25
272 Josef Heiss .08 .20
273 Rikhard Amann .04 .10
274 Torsten Kienass .04 .10
275 Mirco Ludemann .04 .10
276 Jason Meyer .04 .10
277 Uli Hiemer .04 .10
278 Karsten Mende .04 .10
279 Andreas Niederberger .04 .10
280 Thomas Brandl .04 .10
281 Benoit Doucet .06 .15
282 Robert Hock .04 .10
283 Georg Franz .04 .10
284 Ernst Kopf, Jr. .04 .10
285 Reemt Pyka .06 .15
286 Jurgen Rumrich .04 .10
287 Dieter Hegen .04 .10
288 Raimund Hilger .04 .10
289 Thomas Schinko .04 .10
290 Leo Stefan .04 .10
291 David Delfino .08 .20
292 Elmar Parth .04 .10
293 Luigi Da Corte .04 .10
294 Phil De Gaetano .04 .10
295 Ralph Di Fiore .04 .10
296 Giorgio Comploi .04 .10
297 Alexander Thaler .04 .10
298 Giovanni Marchetti .04 .10
299 Gaetano Orlando .06 .15
300 Frank Di Muzio .04 .10
301 Giuseppe Foglietta .04 .10
302 Stefano Figliuzzi .04 .10
303 John Vecchiarelli .04 .10
304 Maurizio Mansi .04 .10
305 Santino Pellegrino .04 .10
306 Lino De Toni .04 .10
307 Mario Chitarroni .04 .10
308 Bruno Zarillo .04 .10
309 Armando Chelodi .04 .10
310 Carmine Vani .04 .10
311 Martin McKay .04 .10
312 Scott O'Connor .04 .10
313 John McCrone .04 .10
314 Stephen Cooper .04 .10
315 Mike O'Connor .04 .10
316 Chris Kelland .04 .10
317 Graham Waghorn .04 .10
318 Nicky Chinn .04 .10
319 Damian Smith .04 .10
320 Tim Cranston .04 .10
321 Scott Morrisson .04 .10
322 Antony Johnson .04 .10
323 Tony Hand .06 .15
324 Kevin Conway .04 .10
325 Rick Fera .04 .10
326 Doug McEwen .04 .10
327 Scott Neil .04 .10
328 John Iredale .04 .10
329 Iain Robertson .04 .10
330 Ian Cooper .04 .10
331 Bill Ranford DT .10 .25
332 Jarmo Myllys DT .10 .25
333 Dominik Hasek DT .80 1.50
334 Tommy Soderstrom DT .10 .25
335 Teppo Numminen DT .10 .25
336 Mihail Tatarinov DT .06 .15

337 Paul Coffey DT .40 1.00
338 Chris Chelios DT .40 1.00
339 Brian Leetch DT .40 1.00
340 Al MacInnis DT .40 1.00
341 Vladimir Malakhov DT .10 .25
342 Kevin Hatcher DT .10 .25
343 Jiri Slegr DT .06 .15
344 Wayne Gretzky DT 4.00 5.00
345 Teemu Selanne DT .80 1.50
346 Jari Kurri DT .20 .50
347 Brett Hull DT .60 1.50
348 Sergei Fedorov DT .80 1.50
349 Esa Tikkanen DT .10 .25
350 Mark Messier DT .60 1.50
351 Jaromir Jagr DT 1.20 2.00
352 Jeremy Roenick DT .40 1.00
353 Luc Robitaille DT .40 1.00
354 Tomas Sandstrom DT .10 .25
355 Peter Forsberg DT 1.20 2.00
356 Alexei Zhamnov DT .10 .25
357 Theo Fleury DT .40 1.00
358 Rick Tocchet DT .20 .50
359 Pat LaFontaine DT .20 .50
360 Eric Lindros DT .80 1.50
NNO Album 4.00 10.00

1995-96 Finnish Beckett Ad Cards

This eight-card set features color action player photos on a perforated sheet which measures approximately 3" by 9". The top half of the sheet contains the photo while the bottom half is a form to subscribe to the Finnish Beckett Hockey Monthly magazine. The backs are blank. Although these look like cards, they actually were meant to be folded in half and used as a protective covering for trading cards which were dispensed through vending machines in Finland during the 1995-96 season. The cards were not manufactured by Beckett, but by Semic, the company which produced the Finnish and Swedish versions of Beckett Hockey Monthly.

COMPLETE SET (8) 10.00 25.00
1 Saku Koivu 4.00 10.00
2 Jere Lehtinen 2.00 5.00
3 Ville Peltonen .80 2.00
4 Erik Hamalainen .80 2.00
5 Sami Kapanen 2.00 5.00
6 Marko Kiprusoff .80 2.00
7 Mika Stromberg .80 2.00
8 Marko Palo .80 2.00

1995-96 Finnish Jaa Kiekko Lehti Ad Cards

This eight-card set features color action photos on a perforated sheet which measures approximately 3" by 9". The top half of the sheet contains the photo of a popular Finnish national team member, while the bottom half is a form to subscribe to Jaa Kiekko Lehti, the leading hockey magazine in that country. The backs are blank. Although these look like cards when separated, they actually were meant to be folded in half and used as a protective barrier for trading cards which were dispensed through vending machines in Finland during the 1995-96 season. The cards were produced by Semic, and were numbered out of 8 on the front.

COMPLETE SET (8) 14.00 35.00
1 Jarmo Myllys 1.20 3.00
2 Jari Kurri 1.60 4.00
3 Saku Koivu 3.20 8.00
4 Teemu Selanne 6.00 15.00
5 Esa Tikkanen 1.20 3.00
6 Christian Ruuttu .80 2.00
7 Mika Nieminen .80 2.00
8 Timo Jutila .80 2.00

1995-96 Finnish SISU

This 400-card set features the players of Finland's top hockey circuit, the SM-Liiga. The cards were distributed in two series of 200 cards each, and in packs of eight cards. The fronts feature a full-bleed photo with the player's name ghosted along the bottom. The Saku Koivu Super Chase card was randomly inserted in series 1 packs at a rate of 1:600. The Koivu Super Bonus and Niinimaa Super Chase cards were found in series 2 packs at a rate of 1:480. The latter Koivu card could be redeemed to Leaf in Finland for an exclusive Koivu SISU Specials jumbo card. If redeemed, the Super Bonus card was returned with a punch hole. These cards trade for about half the unpunched.

COMPLETE SET (400) 20.00 50.00
COMPLETE SERIES 1 (200) 12.00 30.00
COMPLETE SERIES 2 (200) 8.00 20.00
1 HIFK, Team Card .04 .10
2 Kimmo Kapanen .04 .10
3 Juri Kuznetsov .04 .10
4 Simo Saarinen .04 .10
5 Roland Carlsson .04 .10
6 Veli-Pekka Fagerstrom .04 .10
7 Kristian Fagerstrom .04 .10
8 Mika Kortelainen .04 .10
9 Jari Laukkanen .04 .10
10 Juha Nurminen .04 .10
11 Markku Hurme .04 .10
12 Sami Kapanen .40 1.00
13 Darren Boyko .04 .10
14 Marko Ojanen .04 .10
15 HPK, Team Card .04 .10
16 Kari Rosenberg .10 .25
17 Petri Engman .04 .10
18 Niko Marttila .04 .10
19 Jari Haapamaki .04 .10
20 Marko Allen .04 .10
21 Erik Kakko .04 .10
22 Mikko Myllykoski .04 .10
23 Jani Hassinen .04 .10
24 Risto Jalo .10 .25
25 Juha Jarvenpaa .04 .10
26 Jari Kauppila .04 .10
27 Toni Makiaho .04 .10
28 Ilves, Team Card .04 .10
29 Mika Manninen .10 .25
30 Hannu Henriksson .04 .10
31 Petri Kokko .04 .10
32 Martti Jarventie .20 .50
33 Allan Measures .04 .10
34 Pasi Huura .04 .10
35 Janne Seva .04 .10
36 Tommy Kiviaho .04 .10
37 Reijo Mikkolainen .04 .10
38 Hannu Mattila .04 .10
39 Jari Virtanen .04 .10
40 Sami Ahlberg .04 .10
41 Juha Hautamaa .04 .10
42 Jokerit, Team Card .04 .10
43 Ari Sulander .20 .50
44 Santeri Immonen .04 .10
45 Pasi Sormunen .04 .10
46 Waltteri Immonen .04 .10
47 Mika Stromberg .10 .25
48 Kari Martikainen .04 .10
49 Tommi Sova .10 .25
50 Juha Lind .20 .50
51 Niko Halttunen .04 .10
52 Keijo Sailynoja .10 .25
53 Otakar Janecky .10 .25
54 Timo Saarikoski .04 .10
55 JYP HT, Team Card .04 .10
56 Ari-Pekka Siekkinen .10 .25
57 Vesa Ponto .04 .10
58 Kalle Koskinen .04 .10
59 Jouni Loponen .04 .10
60 Miska Kangasniemi .10 .25
61 Mika Paananen .04 .10
62 Markku Ikonen .04 .10
63 Kimmo Salminen .04 .10
64 Joni Lius .04 .10
65 Lasse Nieminen .04 .10
66 Janne Kurjenniemi .04 .10
67 Marko Virtanen .04 .10
68 KalPa, Team Card .04 .10
69 Jarkko Kortesoja .04 .10
70 Petri Matikainen .04 .10
71 Mika Laaksonen .04 .10
72 Kai Rautio .04 .10
73 Jarno Kultanen .20 .50
74 Miikka Ruokonen .04 .10
75 Jussi Tarvainen .04 .10
76 Mikko Honkonen .04 .10
77 Sami Simonen .04 .10
78 Petr Korinek .04 .10
79 Veli-Pekka Pekkarinen .04 .10
80 Pekka Tirkkonen .04 .10
81 Kiekko-Espoo, Team Card .04 .10
82 Iiro Itamies .10 .25
83 Tommi Nyyssonen .04 .10
84 Robert Salo .04 .10
85 Sami Nuutinen .04 .10
86 Timo Blomqvist .04 .10
87 Ismo Kuoppala .04 .10
88 Mikko Koivunoro .04 .10
89 Petro Koivunen .10 .25
90 Jarmo Muukkonen .04 .10
91 Sergei Prjahin .04 .10
92 Teemu Riihijarvi .10 .25
93 Juha Ikonen .04 .10
94 Lukko, Team Card .04 .10
95 Boris Rousson .20 .50
96 Vesa Salo .10 .25
97 Toni Porkka .04 .10
98 Mika Yli-Maenpaa .10 .25
99 Juha Riihijarvi .10 .25
100 Petri Latti .04 .10
101 Veli-Pekka Ahonen .04 .10
102 Mikko Peltola .04 .10
103 Kalle Sahlstedt .10 .25
104 Jari Torkki .04 .10
105 Jussi Kiuru .04 .10
106 Sakari Palsola .04 .10
107 Tappara, Team Card .04 .10
108 Ilpo Kauhanen .20 .50
109 Sami Lehtonen .04 .10
110 Pasi Petrilainen .04 .10
111 Pekka Laksola .04 .10
112 Tommi Haapsaari .04 .10
113 Ville Nieminen 2.00 3.00
114 Arto Kulmala .04 .10
115 Valeri Krykov .04 .10
116 Timo Nurmberg .04 .10
117 Aleksander Barkov .04 .10
118 Miikka Kemppi .04 .10
119 Marko Toivola .04 .10
120 Juha Vuorivirta .10 .25
121 TPS, Team Card .04 .10
122 Miikka Kiprusoff 4.00 10.00
123 Kimmo Timonen .20 .50
124 Sami Salo .04 .10
125 Kari Harila .04 .10
126 Tuomas Gronman .10 .25
127 Vjatsheslav Fandul .04 .10
128 Mika Alatalo .20 .50
129 Jukka Tiilikainen .04 .10
130 Kimmo Rintanen .16 .40
131 Hannes Hyvonen .20 .50
132 Simo Rouvali .04 .10
133 Harri Sillgren .04 .10
134 Harri Suvanto .04 .10
135 TuTo, Team Card .04 .10
136 Markus Korhonen .04 .10
137 Sebastian Sulku .04 .10
138 Jukka Suomalainen .04 .10
139 Timo Kulonen .04 .10
140 Risto Siltanen .10 .25
141 Sami Leinonen .04 .10
142 Juha Virtanen .04 .10
143 Jari Hirsimaki .04 .10
144 Jouni Tuominen .04 .10
145 Vesa Karjalainen .04 .10
146 Pekka Virta .04 .10
147 Jouko Myrra .04 .10
148 Assat, Team Card .04 .10
149 Kari Takko .20 .50
150 Timo Nykopp .04 .10
151 Harri Laurila .04 .10
152 Jarno Miikkulainen .04 .10
153 Pasi Peltonen .04 .10
154 Jari Korpisalo .04 .10
155 Teppo Kivela .04 .10
156 Jari Levonen .04 .10
157 Janne Virtanen .04 .10
158 Jarno Makela .04 .10
159 Mikael Kotkaniemi .04 .10
160 Ari Saarinen .04 .10
161 Boris Rousson AS .20 .50
162 Joni Lehto AS .06 .15
163 Marko Kiprusoff AS .10 .25
164 Jere Lehtinen AS .40 1.00
165 Saku Koivu AS 1.20 3.00
166 Kai Nurminen AS .20 .50
167 Ari Sulander AS .20 .50
168 Mika Stromberg AS .10 .25
169 All Stars/Kuusisto .04 .10
170 All Stars/Arkiomaa .04 .10
171 Otakar Janecky AS .10 .25
172 Ville Peltonen AS .20 .50
173 Milestones/Arima .04 .10
174 Milestones/Boyko .04 .10
175 Milestones/Friman .04 .10
176 Milestones/Heiskanen .04 .10
177 Milestones/Henriksson .04 .10
178 Milestones/Hamalainen .04 .10
179 Milestones/Jalo .04 .10
180 Timo Jutila AS .08 .20
181 Milestones/Jarvenpaa .04 .10
182 Milestones/Kuusisto .04 .10
183 Milestones/Laksola .04 .10
184 Milestones/Laurila .04 .10
185 Milestones/Lehtonen .04 .10
186 Milestones/Lindroos .04 .10
187 Milestones/Mikkolainen .04 .10
188 Milestones/Tommila .04 .10
189 Milestones/Torkki .04 .10
190 Milestones/Tuomenoksa .04 .10
191 Milestones/Vuori .04 .10
192 TPS, SM-kultaa .04 .10
193 Jokerit, SM-hopeaa .04 .10
194 Assat, SM-pronssia .04 .10
195 Jokerit, EM-kultaa .04 .10
196 TPS, EM-pronssia .04 .10
197 Kai Nurminen CL .16 .40
198 Veli-Pekka Kautonen CL .04 .10
199 Koivu Checklist .40 1.00
200 Kiprusoff Checklist .10 .25
201 HIFK, Fan Card .04 .10
202 Sakari Lindfors .20 .50
203 Lauri Puolanne .04 .10
204 Pertti Lehtonen .04 .10
205 Peter Ahola .04 .10
206 Jere Karalahti .20 .50
207 Kimmo Maki-Kokkila .04 .10
208 Tom Laaksonen .04 .10
209 Tero Hamalainen .04 .10
210 Miro Haapaniemi .04 .10
211 Toni Sihvonen .04 .10
212 Sami Laine .04 .10
213 Iiro Jarvi .10 .25
214 Pekka Tuomisto .04 .10
215 HPK, Fan Card .04 .10
216 Mika Pietila .10 .25
217 Tom Koivisto .04 .10
218 Tommi Hamalainen .04 .10
219 Kai Rautio .04 .10
220 Jani Nikko .10 .25
221 Mika Kannisto .04 .10
222 Jason Miller .04 .10
223 Niklas Hede .04 .10
224 Tony Virta .04 .10
225 Aleksander Andrijevski .04 .10
226 Mika Puhakka .04 .10
227 Timo Peltomaa .04 .10
228 Toni Saarinen .04 .10
229 Ilves, Fan Card .04 .10
230 Vesa Toskala 1.50 3.00
231 Pekka Kangasalusta .04 .10
232 Juha Lampinen .04 .10
233 Pasi Saarinen .04 .10
234 Teemu Vuorinen .04 .10
235 Jarno Peltonen .04 .10
236 Matti Kaipainen .04 .10
237 Semi Pekki .04 .10
238 Sami Karjalainen .04 .10
239 Juoni Lahtinen .04 .10
240 Pasi Maatanen .04 .10
241 Petri Murtovaara .04 .10
242 Tomi Hirvonen .04 .10
243 Mikko Eloranta .20 .50
244 Mika Arvaja .04 .10
245 Juha Jarvenpaa .10 .25
246 Jokerit, Fan Card .04 .10
247 Marko Rantanen .04 .10
248 Marko Tuulola .04 .10
249 Jani-Matti Loikala .04 .10
250 Antti-Jussi Niemi .20 .50
251 Janne Niinimaa .30 .75
252 Jari Lindroos .04 .10
253 Paso Saarela .04 .10
254 Juha Ylonen .30 .75
255 Mika Asikainen .10 .25
256 Eero Somervuori .40 1.00
257 Tero Lehtera .04 .10
258 Jukka Penttinen .04 .10
259 Petri Varis .20 .50
260 JyP HT, Fan Card .04 .10
261 Marko Leinonen .04 .10
262 Jan Latvala .04 .10
263 Jukka Laamanen .04 .10
264 Pekka Poikolainen .04 .10
265 Thomas Sjogren .04 .10
266 Pasi Kangas .10 .25
267 Tini Koivunen .04 .10
268 Lasse Jamsen .04 .10
269 Petri Kujala .04 .10
270 Mikko Inkinen .04 .10
271 Kalpa, Fan Card .04 .10
272 Pasi Kuivalainen .20 .50
273 Pasi Kolehmainen .04 .10
274 Reijo Ruotsalainen .10 .25
275 Jarkko Glad .04 .10
276 Ivan Vlzek .04 .10
277 Jarmo Levonen .04 .10
278 Janne Kekalainen .04 .10
279 Veli-Pekka Nutikka .20 .50
280 Mikko Konttila .10 .25
281 Janne Virtanen .04 .10
282 Pasi Kemppainen .04 .10
283 Kiekko-Espoo, Fan Card .04 .10
284 Mika Rautio .10 .25
285 Kari Haakana .04 .10
286 Teemu Sillanpaa .04 .10
287 Timo Nykopp .04 .10
288 Miikka Teimonen .04 .10
289 Tero Tiainen .04 .10
290 Joonas Jaaskelainen .04 .10
291 Lubomir Kolnik .10 .25
292 Arto Sirvio .04 .10
293 Iikka Sinisalo .10 .25
294 Timo Hirvonen .04 .10
295 Arto Kuki .04 .10
296 Timo Norppa .04 .10
297 Lukko, Fan Card .04 .10
298 Timo Kauharren .04 .10
299 Joni Lehto .04 .10
300 Jarno Miikkulainen .04 .10
301 Kimmo Lotvonen .04 .10
302 Robert Nordmark .04 .10
303 Riku Kallioniemi .04 .10
304 Matti Raunio .04 .10
305 Tommi Turunen .04 .10
306 Jarkko Varvio .06 .15
307 Tero Arkiomaa .04 .10
308 Harri Lonnberg .10 .25
309 Mikko Luovi .04 .10
310 Tappara, Fan Card .04 .10
311 Jussi Markkanen .80 2.00
312 Timo Jutila .04 .10
313 Jukka Ollila .04 .10
314 Antti Rahkonen .04 .10
315 Derek Mayer .04 .10
316 Petri Kalteva .04 .10
317 Jarkko Nikander .04 .10
318 Pauli Jarvinen .04 .10
319 Mikko Helisten .04 .10
320 Ari Haanpaa .04 .10
321 Markus Oijennus .04 .10
322 Janne Ojanen .16 .40
323 TPS, Fan Card .04 .10
324 Fredrik Norrena .16 .40
325 Mika Lehtinen .04 .10
326 Karlis Skrastins .20 .50
327 Marru Laapas .04 .10
328 Antti Aalto .20 .50
329 Teemu Numminen .04 .10
330 Tommi Miettinen .04 .10
331 Lasse Pirjeta .04 .10
332 Miikka Rousu .04 .10
333 Marko Makinen .04 .10
334 Mikko Markkanen .40 1.00
335 Tommi Kallio .40 1.00
336 Miika Elomo .20 .50
337 Sami Mettovaara .04 .10
338 TuTo, Fan Card .04 .10
339 Jukka Tammi .16 .40
340 Kari-Pekka Friman .04 .10
341 Veli-Pekka Hard .04 .10
342 Antti Tirkkonen .04 .10
343 Jukka Seppo .04 .10
344 Kim Ahlroos .04 .10
345 Marto Poulsen .04 .10
346 Juha Kuusisaari .04 .10
347 Mikko Laaksonen .04 .10
348 Tuomas Jalava .04 .10
349 Timo Pullola .10 .25
350 Tuomas Kalliomaki .04 .10
351 Assat, Fan Card .04 .10
352 Karri Kivi .04 .10
353 Olli Kaski .04 .10
354 Jouni Vento .04 .10
355 Tommi Rajamaki .10 .25
356 Jokke Heinanen .04 .10
357 Tomas Kapusta .04 .10
358 Jaroslav Otevrel .04 .10
359 Timo Salonen .04 .10
360 Pekka Virta .04 .10
361 Vesa Goman .04 .10
362 Pekka Peltola .04 .10
363 Rauli Raitanen .04 .10
364 Pasi Tuominen .04 .10
365 Kari Syvasalmi .04 .10
366 Timo Hakanen .04 .10
367 Foreigners/Andrijevski .04 .10
368 Foreigners/Barkov .04 .10
369 Foreigners/Boyko .04 .10
370 Foreigners/Fandul .04 .10
371 Foreigners/Janecky .04 .10
372 Foreigners/Kapusta .04 .10
373 Foreigners/Kolnik .04 .10
374 Foreigners/Korinek .04 .10
375 Foreigners/Mayer .04 .10
376 Foreigners/Measures .04 .10
377 Foreigners/Miller .04 .10
378 Foreigners/Nordmark .04 .10
379 Foreigners/Otevrel .04 .10
380 Foreigners/Prjahin .04 .10
381 Foreigners/Rousson .10 .25
382 Foreigners/Sjogren .04 .10
383 Foreigners/Skrastins .04 .10
384 Foreigners/Vlzek .04 .10
385 Vladimir Jursinov CO .04 .10
386 Hannu Aravirta CO .04 .10
387 Veli-Pekka Ketola CO .10 .25
388 Vaclav Sykora CO .04 .10
389 Hannu Kapanen CO .04 .10
390 Kari Savolainen CO .04 .10
391 Harri Rindell CO .04 .10
392 Anatoli Bogdanov .04 .10
393 Sakari Pietilla .04 .10
394 Jukka Rautakorpi .04 .10
395 Harri Jalava .04 .10
396 Vladimir Jursinov Jr. .04 .10
397 Jere Lehtinen CL .20 .50
398 Checklist 251-300 .04 .10
399 Checklist 301-350 .04 .10
400 Koivu Checklist .40 1.00
NNOA Saku Koivu Super Bonus 10.00 20.00
(SISU logo upper right
NNOB Saku Koivu Super Bonus
(SISU logo upper left
NNO Saku Koivu Jumbo 2.00 5.00
NNO Janne Niinimaa Super Chase 6.00 10.00
NNO Saku Koivu Super Chase 15.00 25.00

1995-96 Finnish SISU Double Trouble

This eight-card set features action shots of the top two players from the teams of the SM-Liiga. The cards were randomly inserted at a rate of 1:17 series 2 packs.

COMPLETE SET (8) 8.00 20.00
STATED ODDS 1:17 SERIES 2
1 Tuomas Gronman 1.20 3.00
Kimmo Timonen
2 Waltteri Immonen 1.20 3.00
Mika Stromberg
3 Olli Kaski 1.20 3.00
Karri Kivi
4 Joni Lehto 1.20 3.00
Robert Nordmark
5 Peter Ahola 1.20 3.00
Pertti Lehtonen
6 Timo Blomqvist 1.20 3.00
Sami Nuutinen
7 Reijo Ruotsalainen 1.20 3.00
Ivan Vizek
8 Timo Jutila 1.20 3.00
Pekka Laksola

1995-96 Finnish SISU Drafted Dozen

Randomly inserted at a rate of 1:19 series 2 packs, this set depicts a dozen players from the SM-Liiga who were selected in the NHL Entry Draft.

COMPLETE SET (12) 8.00 25.00
STATED ODDS 1:19 SERIES 2
1 Aki Berg .80 2.00
2 Teemu Riihijarvi .40 1.00
3 Miika Elomo .80 2.00
4 Marko Makinen .40 1.00
5 Tomi Kallio 1.25 3.00
6 Sami Kapanen 1.60 4.00
7 Vesa Toskala 2.80 5.00
8 Miikka Kiprusoff 6.00 15.00
9 Timo Hakanen .40 1.00
10 Juha Vuorivirta .40 1.00
11 Tomi Hirvonen .40 1.00
12 Mikko Markkanen .40 1.00

1995-96 Finnish SISU Ghost Goalies

This 10-card set focuses on the top netminders of the SM-Liiga. The cards were randomly inserted at a rate of 1:24 series 1 packs.

COMPLETE SET (10) 16.00 40.00
STATED ODDS 1:24 SERIES 1
1 Sakari Lindfors 2.00 5.00
2 Boris Rousson 1.60 4.00
3 Ari Sulander 2.00 5.00
4 Kari Takko 1.60 4.00
5 Fredrik Norrena 1.60 4.00
6 Kari Rosenberg 1.60 4.00
7 Ari-Pekka Siekkinen 1.60 4.00
8 Jukka Tammi 1.60 4.00
9 Pasi Kuivalainen 1.60 4.00
10 Ilpo Kauhanen 1.60 4.00

1995-96 Finnish SISU Gold Cards

This 24-card set celebrates the players who earned Finland's first major title by winning the 1995 World Championship. The cards were distributed over both series in a scattered (i.e., not 1-12 and 13-24) fashion. The cards were randomly inserted at a rate of 1:10 series 1 packs and 1:9 series 2 packs.

COMPLETE SET (24) 24.00 60.00
STATED ODDS 1:10 SERIES 1/1:9 SERIES 2
1 Title Card .80 2.00
2 Jarmo Myllys 1.60 4.00
3 Ari Sulander 1.60 4.00
4 Jukka Tammi 1.60 4.00
5 Erik Hamalainen .80 2.00
6 Timo Jutila .80 2.00
7 Marko Kiprusoff .80 2.00
8 Janne Niinimaa 1.60 4.00
9 Petteri Nummelin .80 2.00
10 Mika Stromberg .80 2.00
11 Hannu Virta .80 2.00
12 Raimo Helminen .80 2.00
13 Sami Kapanen 2.00 5.00
14 Esa Keskinen .80 2.00
15 Saku Koivu 6.00 15.00
16 Tero Lehtera .80 2.00
17 Jere Lehtinen 3.20 8.00
18 Mika Nieminen .80 2.00
19 Janne Ojanen .80 2.00
20 Marko Palo .80 2.00
21 Ville Peltonen 1.20 3.00
22 Raimo Summanen .80 2.00
23 Antti Tormanen .80 2.00
24 Juha Ylonen 1.20 3.00

1995-96 Finnish SISU Limited

This 108-card set is the first super-premium issue released in Europe. The cards are printed on 24-point stock and picture the elite athletes of the Finnish SM-Liiga. Production was announced as 7,500 individually numbered boxes. Each box contained 18, 5-card "packs". These packs were actually boxes themselves, and pictured either Saku Koivu, Teemu Selanne or Esa Tikkanen. The card fronts have a color photo of the player over his ghosted close-up in the background. The back contains another photo as well as a brief bio in Finnish and the Leaf trademark. Several NHLers who played here during the 1994 lockout are featured, including Selanne, Jari Kurri, and Koivu. The Koivu Line super chase card was randomly inserted 1:219 and was serial numbered out of 720.

COMPLETE SET (108) 20.00 40.00
1 Fredrik Norrena .20 .50
2 Hannu Virta .16 .40
3 Petteri Nummelin .08 .20
4 Tuomas Gronman .16 .40
5 Marko Kiprusoff .16 .40
6 Saku Koivu 2.00 5.00
7 Raimo Summanen .16 .40
8 Esa Keskinen .16 .40
9 Jere Lehtinen 1.20 3.00
10 Ari Sulander .30 .75
11 Waltteri Immonen .08 .20
12 Mika Stromberg .08 .20
13 Janne Niinimaa .40 1.00
14 Otakar Janecky .16 .40
15 Teemu Selanne 4.00 10.00
16 Jari Kurri 1.20 3.00
17 Antti Tormanen .16 .40
18 Petri Varis .30 .75
19 Kari Takko .30 .75
20 Olli Kaski .08 .20
21 Rauli Raitanen .08 .20
22 Jari Korpisalo .08 .20
23 Teppo Kivela .08 .20
24 Jokke Heinanen .08 .20
25 Arto Javanainen .08 .20
26 Jari Levonen .08 .20
27 Arto Heiskanen .08 .20
28 Jarmo Myllys .40 1.00
29 Boris Rousson .20 .50
30 Jarmo Kuusisto .08 .20
31 Joni Lehto .08 .20
32 Robert Nordmark .08 .20
33 Tero Arkiomaa .08 .20
34 Jari Torkki .08 .20
35 Juha Riihijarvi .16 .40
36 Matti Forss .08 .20
37 Sakari Lindfors .30 .75
38 Pertti Lehtonen .08 .20
39 Simo Saarinen .08 .20
40 Esa Tikkanen .40 1.00
41 Ville Peltonen .16 .40
42 Christian Ruuttu .16 .40
43 Mika Kortelainen .08 .20
44 Darren Boyko .08 .20
45 Iiro Jarvi .16 .40
46 Ari-Pekka Siekkinen .20 .50
47 Harri Laurila .08 .20
48 Jouni Loponen .08 .20
49 Joni Lius .08 .20
50 Jari Lindroos .08 .20
51 Risto Kurkinen .08 .20
52 Thomas Sjogren .08 .20
53 Marko Virtanen .08 .20
54 Michael Nylander .30 1.00
55 Mika Rautio .20 .50
56 Sami Nuutinen .08 .20
57 Peter Ahola .08 .20
58 Timo Blomqvist .08 .20
59 Ikka Sinisalo .16 .40
60 Petro Koivunen .16 .40
61 Sergei Prjahin .08 .20
62 Tero Lehtera .08 .20
63 Mariusz Czerkawski .40 1.00
64 Pasi Kuivalainen .30 .75
65 Kimmo Timonen .40 1.00
66 Reijo Ruotsalainen .16 .40
67 Vesa Salo .16 .40
68 Petr Korinek .08 .20
69 Marko Jantunen .16 .40
70 Pekka Tirkkonen .08 .20
71 Janne Kekalainen .08 .20
72 Sami Kapanen .80 2.00
73 Timo Jutila .08 .20
74 Pekka Laksola .08 .20
75 Janne Gronvall .16 .40
76 Jiri Kucera .08 .20
77 Janne Ojanen .20 .50
78 Pauli Jarvinen .08 .20
79 Ari Haanpaa .08 .20
80 Aleksander Barkov .08 .20
81 Theo Fleury 1.20 3.00
82 Kari Rosenberg .16 .40
83 Janne Laukkanen .20 .50
84 Jani Nikko .16 .40
85 Mika Lartama .08 .20
86 Kai Nurminen .30 .75
87 Tomas Kapusta .08 .20
88 Marko Palo .08 .20
89 Jarkko Varvio .16 .40
90 Risto Jalo .16 .40
91 Jukka Tammi .20 .50
92 Risto Siltanen .16 .40
93 Teppo Numminen .30 .75
94 Marco Poulsen .08 .20
95 Jukka Seppo .08 .20
96 Vesa Karjalainen .08 .20
97 Ted Donato .16 .40
98 Juha Virtanen .08 .20
99 Jari Hirsimaki .08 .20
100 Vesa Toskala 2.50 5.00
101 Jyrki Lumme .40 1.00
102 Hannu Henriksson .08 .20
103 Allan Measures .08 .20
104 Timo Peltomaa .08 .20
105 Juha Hautamaa .08 .20
106 Mikko Makela .16 .40
107 Juha Jarvenpaa .08 .20
108 Semi Pekki .08 .20
NNO Koivu Line Super Chase 15.00 25.00

1995-96 Finnish SISU Limited Leaf Gallery

The nine cards in this set were randomly inserted at a rate of 1 in 6 packs of SISU Limited. The fronts feature a dynamic action photo surrounded by a refractive holofoil border. The cards are numbered of 9 on the front. The backs display a gold-foil etched portrait of the player.

COMPLETE SET (9) 10.00 15.00
STATED ODDS 1:6
1 Jyrki Lumme 1.20 2.00
2 Janne Laukkanen 1.20 2.00
3 Michael Nylander 1.20 3.00
4 Janne Ojanen 1.20 2.00
5 Peter Ahola 1.20 2.00
6 Kari Takko 2.00 3.00
7 Hannu Virta 1.20 2.00
8 Juha Lind 1.20 2.00
9 Sakari Lindfors 2.00 3.00

1995-96 Finnish SISU Limited Signed and Sealed

The nine cards in this set were randomly inserted at a rate of 1 in 9 SISU Limited packs. The set features a number of current and former NHLers. The cards feature an action photo printed on a silver foil background. The player's "signature" is embossed in gold foil across the bottom of the photo. The backs feature another photo and are numbered out of 9.

COMPLETE SET (9) 20.00 25.00
STATED ODDS 1:9
1 Sami Kapanen 2.00 3.00
2 Christian Ruuttu .80 2.00
3 Teemu Selanne 12.00 15.00
4 Aki Berg .80 2.00
5 Joni Lehto .80 2.00
6 Teppo Numminen 1.20 2.00
7 Jari Kurri 4.00 5.00
8 Esa Tikkanen 2.00 3.00
9 Theo Fleury 4.00 5.00

1995-96 Finnish SISU Painkillers

Randomly inserted in series 1 packs at a rate of 1:15, these eight cards highlight some of the dominant snipers of the SM-Liiga.

COMPLETE SET (8) 3.20 8.00
STATED ODDS 1:15 SERIES 1
1 Jokke Heinanen .40 1.00
2 Mika Alatalo .40 1.00
3 Joni Lehto .40 1.00
4 Harri Lonnberg .40 1.00
5 Ville Peltonen .80 2.00
6 Harri Sillgren .40 1.00
7 Petri Varis .80 2.00
8 Marko Virtanen .40 1.00

1995-96 Finnish SISU Specials

Randomly inserted at a rate of 1:24 series 1 packs, these cards picture some of the most popular players in the SM-Liiga, including several NHLers who played there during the 1994 lockout.

COMPLETE SET (10) 16.00 40.00
STATED ODDS 1:24 SERIES 1
1 Petri Varis 1.20 3.00
2 Boris Rousson 1.20 3.00
3 Saku Koivu 6.00 15.00
4 Jari Kurri 3.20 8.00
5 Jarmo Kuusisto .80 2.00
6 Janne Ojanen .80 2.00
7 Jere Lehtinen 3.20 8.00
8 Peter Ahola .80 2.00
9 Jukka Seppo .80 2.00
10 Michael Nylander .80 3.00

1995-96 Finnish SISU Spotlights

This eight-card series shines the -- yes -- spotlight on some of the most offensively gifted players in the SM-Liiga. The cards were randomly inserted in series 2 packs at a rate of 1:8.

COMPLETE SET (8) 2.00 5.00
STATED ODDS 1:8 SERIES 2
1 Otakar Janecky .40 1.00
2 Jari Korpisalo .40 1.00
3 Juha Riihijarvi .40 1.00
4 Iiro Jarvi .40 1.00
5 Thomas Sjogren .40 1.00
6 Risto Jalo .40 1.00
7 Jari Hirsimaki .40 1.00
8 Juha Hautamaa .40 1.00

1995 Finnish Karjala World Championship Labels

This unusual set is comprised of 24 odd-sized (2 1/2 by 2 1/2") labels that were issued on the front of Karjala beer bottles in Finland to commemorate that country's first World Championship. Each label features an action photo of the player superimposed over the gold medal, with his name underneath. The Finnish national team logo is in the upper left corner, and World Champions, 1995 (in Finnish) is in the right. The labels are blank backed. As they are unnumbered, the labels are listed below in alphabetical order.

COMPLETE SET (24) 16.00 40.00
1 Erik Hamalainen .40 1.00
2 Raimo Helminen .40 1.00
3 Timo Jutila .60 1.50
4 Sami Kapanen .80 2.00
5 Esa Keskinen .40 1.00
6 Marko Kiprusoff .40 1.00
7 Saku Koivu 2.00 5.00
8 Tero Lehtera .40 1.00
9 Jere Lehtinen 1.20 3.00
10 Curt Lindstrom .40 1.00
11 Jarmo Myllys .80 2.00
12 Mika Nieminen .40 1.00
13 Janne Niinimaa .80 2.00
14 Petteri Nummelin .40 1.00
15 Janne Ojanen .40 1.00
16 Marko Palo .40 1.00
17 Ville Peltonen .60 1.50
18 Mika Stromberg .40 1.00
19 Ari Sulander .80 2.00
20 Raimo Summanen .40 1.00
21 Jukka Tammi .80 2.00
22 Antti Tormanen .40 1.00
23 Hannu Virta .60 1.50
24 Juha Ylonen .60 1.50

1995 Finnish Kellogg's

This six-card set was issued as a one-card-per-box premium in Kellogg's cereals in Finland. The cards are about half the size of a standard card.

COMPLETE SET (6) 12.00 30.00
1 Jarmo Myllys 2.00 5.00
2 Marko Kiprusoff 1.20 3.00
3 Hannu Virta 1.20 3.00
4 Ville Peltonen 1.20 3.00
5 Saku Koivu 6.00 15.00
6 Sami Kapanen 2.00 5.00

1995 Finnish Semic World Championships

This 240 standard-size card set features players from Finland and other countries who have taken part in international competition. Subsets include All Stars, Maalivahti Extra and Future Stars.

COMPLETE SET (240) 20.00 50.00
1 Pasi Kuivalainen .08 .20
2 Marko Kiprusoff .06 .15
3 Tuomas Gronman .06 .15
4 Erik Hamalainen .04 .10
5 Timo Jutila .06 .15
6 Pasi Sormunen .04 .10
7 Waltteri Immonen .06 .15
8 Janne Ojanen .06 .15
9 Esa Keskinen .06 .15
10 Kimmo Timonen .10 .25
11 Saku Koivu .40 1.00
12 Janne Laukkanen .10 .25
13 Marko Palo .04 .10
14 Raimo Helminen .06 .15
15 Mika Alatalo .10 .25
16 Ville Peltonen .16 .40
17 Jari Kurri .30 .75
18 Jari Korpisalo .06 .15
19 Kimmo Rintanen .06 .15
20 Jere Lehtinen .40 1.00
21 Kalle Sahlstedt .06 .15
22 Christian Ruuttu .06 .15
23 Hannu Virta .06 .15
24 Sami Kapanen .20 .50
25 Marko Tuulola .04 .10
26 Mika Stromberg .06 .15
27 Tero Lehtera .06 .15
28 Petri Varis .06 .15
29 Mikko Peltola .04 .10
30 Jukka Tammi .10 .25
31 Tero Arkiomaa .04 .10
32 Olli Kaski .04 .10
33 Pekka Laksola .04 .10
34 Mika Valila .04 .10
35 Jarmo Myllys .10 .25
36 Harri Laurila .04 .10
37 Teppo Numminen .10 .25
38 Jyrki Lumme .08 .20
39 Petteri Nummelin .04 .10
40 Mika Nieminen .10 .25
41 Teemu Selanne .80 1.50
42 Mikko Makela .06 .15
43 Esa Tikkanen .16 .40
44 Jarkko Varvio .06 .15
45 Vesa Viitakoski .06 .15
46 Juha Riihijarvi .06 .15
47 Markus Ketterer .10 .25
48 Mikko Haapakoski .04 .10
49 Antti Tormanen .06 .15
50 Timo Peltomaa .04 .10
51 Rauli Raitanen .04 .10
52 Roger Nordstrom .04 .10
53 Tommy Salo .20 .50
54 Tommy Soderstrom .20 .50
55 Magnus Svensson .06 .15
56 Fredrik Stillman .04 .10
57 Nicklas Lidstrom .80 1.00
58 Roger Johansson .04 .10
59 Kenny Jonsson .20 .50
60 Peter Andersson .04 .10
61 Tommy Sjodin .06 .15
62 Mats Sundin .40 1.00
63 Jonas Bergqvist .06 .15
64 Peter Forsberg 1.20 2.00
65 Roger Hansson .04 .10
66 Jorgen Jonsson .04 .10
67 Charles Berglund .04 .10
68 Mikael Johansson .06 .15
69 Tomas Forslund .06 .15
70 Andreas Dackell .10 .25
71 Stefan Ornskog .04 .10
72 Mikael Andersson .06 .15
73 Jan Larsson .04 .10
74 Patrik Carnback .06 .15
75 Hakan Loob .10 .25
76 Patrik Juhlin .10 .25
77 Bill Ranford .20 .50
78 Ed Belfour .60 1.50
79 Rob Blake .20 .50
80 Yves Racine .06 .15
81 Steve Smith .06 .15
82 Paul Coffey .40 1.00
83 Larry Murphy .20 .50
84 Mark Tinordi .06 .15
85 Al MacInnis .40 1.00
86 Paul Kariya 1.60 2.00
87 Joe Sakic 1.20 2.00
88 Brendan Shanahan .80 1.50
89 Luc Robitaille .40 1.00
90 Rod Brind'Amour .30 .75
91 Shayne Corson .10 .25
92 Mike Ricci .10 .25
93 Mario Lemieux ERR Name 3.20 5.00
94 Eric Lindros 1.20 2.00
95 Russ Courtnall .10 .25
96 Theo Fleury .40 1.00
97 Mark Messier .60 1.50
98 Rick Tocchet .20 .50
99 Wayne Gretzky 4.00 5.00
100 Steve Larmer .10 .25
101 Brett Lindros .10 .25
102 John Vanbiesbrouck .40 1.00
103 Craig Wolanin .06 .15
104 Chris Chelios .40 1.00
105 Brian Leetch .40 1.00
106 Kevin Hatcher .08 .20
107 Craig Janney .10 .25
108 Tim Sweeney .06 .15
109 Shawn Chambers .06 .15
110 Scott Young .10 .25
111 John Lilley .06 .15
112 Joe Sacco .06 .15
113 Brett Hull .80 1.50
114 Pat LaFontaine .20 .50
115 Joel Otto .10 .25
116 Mike Modano .60 1.50
117 Tony Granato .06 .15
118 Jeremy Roenick .60 1.50
119 Jeff Lazaro .06 .15
120 Brian Mullen .06 .15
121 Mihail Shtalenkov .20 .50
122 Valeri Ivannikov .04 .10
123 Andrei Nikolishin .10 .25
124 Ilya Byakin .06 .15
125 Alexander Smirnov .04 .10
126 Dimitri Yushkevich .10 .25
127 Sergei Shendelev .04 .10
128 Alexei Zhitnik .06 .15
129 Igor Ulanov .06 .15
130 Dmitri Frolov .04 .10
131 Valeri Kamensky .16 .40
132 Igor Fedulov .04 .10
133 Andrei Kovalenko .10 .25
134 Valeri Bure .20 .50
135 Sergei Berezin .16 .40
136 Alexei Yashin .20 .50
137 Vyatcheslav Kozlov .16 .40
138 Vyatcheslav Bykov .10 .25
139 Andrei Khomutov .10 .25
140 Petr Briza .10 .25
141 Dominik Hasek .80 1.50
142 Roman Turek .30 .75
143 Jan Vopat .06 .15
144 Drahomir Kadlec .06 .15
145 Petr Pavlas .04 .10
146 Frantisek Kucera .06 .15
147 Jiri Veber .04 .10
148 David Vyborny .06 .15
149 Radek Toupal .06 .15
150 Jiri Kucera .06 .15
151 Richard Zemlicka .06 .15
152 Martin Rucinsky .10 .25
153 Jiri Dolezal .04 .10
154 Josef Beranek .06 .15
155 Martin Prochazka .04 .10
156 Tomas Srsen .06 .15
157 David Bruk .04 .10
158 Jaromir Jagr 1.60 2.00
159 Jan Caloun .06 .15
160 Martin Straka .20 .50
161 Roman Horak .04 .10
162 Frantisek Musil .06 .15
163 Petr Hrbek .04 .10
164 Jan Alino .04 .10
165 Joseph Heiss .08 .20
166 Peter Gulda .04 .10
167 Jayson Meyer .04 .10
168 Ernst Kopf .04 .10
169 Raimund Hilger .04 .10
170 Richard Bohm .04 .10
171 Michael Rosati .10 .25
172 Michael DeAngelis .04 .10
173 Anthony Circelli .04 .10
174 Gaetano Orlando .04 .10
175 Lucio Topatigh .04 .10
176 Martin Pavlu .04 .10
177 Jim Marthinsen .10 .25
178 Petter Salsten .04 .10
179 Tommy Jacobson .04 .10
180 Morten Finsted .04 .10
181 Tom Andersen .04 .10
182 Manus Rath .04 .10
183 Michael Puschacher .06 .15
184 James Burton .04 .10
185 Michael Shea .04 .10
186 Dieter Kalt .04 .10
187 Manfred Muhr .04 .10
188 Andreas Puschnig .04 .10
189 Renato Tosio .04 .10
190 Doug Honneger .04 .10
191 Felix Hollenstein .04 .10
192 Jorg Eberle .04 .10
193 Gil Montandon .04 .10
194 Roberto Triulzi .04 .10
195 Petri Ylonen .06 .15
196 Bruno Maynort .04 .10
197 Michel LeBlanc .04 .10
198 Benoit Laborte .04 .10
199 Christophe Ville .04 .10
200 Antoine Richer .04 .10
201 Bill Ranford AS .20 .50
202 Timo Jutila AS .06 .15
203 Magnus Svensson AS .06 .15
204 Jari Kurri AS .30 .75
205 Saku Koivu AS .40 1.00
206 Paul Kariya AS 1.60 2.00
207 Jarmo Myllys ME .10 .25
208 Bill Ranford ME .20 .50
209 Roger Nordstrom ME .04 .10
210 Guy Hebert ME .30 .75
211 Mihail Shtalenkov ME .20 .50
212 Tommy Soderstrom ME .20 .50
213 Petr Briza ME .10 .25
214 Dominik Hasek ME .80 1.50
215 Tom Barrasso ME .16 .40
216 Jukka Tammi ME .06 .15
217 John Vanbiesbrouck ME .40 1.00
218 Mike Richter ME .40 1.00
219 Saku Koivu Special .40 1.00
220 Saku Koivu Special .40 1.00
221 Saku Koivu Special .40 1.00
222 Saku Koivu Special .40 1.00
223 Saku Koivu Special .40 1.00
224 Saku Koivu Special .40 1.00
225 Tuomas Gronman FS .06 .15
226 Jani Nikko FS .04 .10
227 Janne Niinimaa FS .40 1.00
228 Jukka Tiilikainen FS .04 .10
229 Kimmo Rintanen FS .06 .15
230 Ville Peltonen FS .16 .40
231 Sami Kapanen FS .30 .75
232 Jere Lehtinen FS .40 1.00
233 Kimmo Timonen FS .06 .15
234 Jonni Vauhkonen FS .06 .15
235 Juha Lind FS .10 .25
236 Tommi Miettinen FS .06 .15
237 Jere Karalahti FS .10 .25
238 Antti Aalto FS .10 .25
239 Teemu Kohvakka FS .04 .10
240 Niko Mikkola FS .04 .10

1996-97 Finnish SISU Redline

This set featuring players of Finland's SM-Liiga is complete at 200 cards; although a second series was intended, it was not produced as a result of disappointing sales for the first series. The Super Chase and Super Bonus cards were randomly inserted at the rate of 1:240 packs. If found, they could be exchanged by mail with Leaf for one of five Silver Signature goalie cards that were limited to 400 copies. We have no further information on these Silver Signature cards. Anyone who can provide photocopies or other documentation of these cards is asked to email hockeymag@beckett.com.

COMPLETE SET (200) 8.00 20.00
1 Checklist (1-50) .04 .10
2 Sakari Lindfors .20 .50
3 Peter Ahola .06 .15
4 Jere Karalahti .20 .50
5 Pertti Lehtonen .04 .10
6 Lauri Puolanne .04 .10
7 Sami Laine .10 .25
8 Tommy Kiviaho .04 .10
9 Markku Hurme .04 .10
10 Jari Laukkanen .04 .10
11 Tero Nyman .04 .10
12 Toni Sihvonen .04 .10
13 Mika Kortelainen .06 .15
14 Tero Hamalainen .04 .10
15 Mika Pietila .10 .25
16 Erik Kakko .04 .10
17 Tom Koivisto .04 .10
18 Jani Nikko .10 .25
19 Risto Jalo .10 .25
20 Aleksander Andrievski .06 .15
21 Jari Kaupila .04 .10
22 Jarkko Savijoki .04 .10
23 Toni Makiaho .04 .10
24 Mika Kannisto .04 .10
25 Mika Puhakka .04 .10
26 Toni Saarinen .04 .10
27 Vesa Toskala 1.20 1.00
28 Teemu Vuorinen .04 .10
29 Petri Kokko .04 .10
30 Pekka Kangasalusta .04 .10
31 Tommi Kahiluoto .04 .10
32 Jarno Peltonen .04 .10
33 Mika Arvaja .04 .10
34 Matti Kaipainen .04 .10
35 Hannu Mattila .04 .10
36 Tomi Hirvonen .04 .10
37 Jouni Lahtinen .04 .10
38 Jari Suorsa .04 .10
39 Juha Jarvenpaa .08 .20
40 Semi Pekki .04 .10
41 Ari Sulander .20 .50
42 Mika Stromberg .10 .25
43 Marko Tuulola .04 .10
44 Pasi Sormunen .04 .10
45 Waltteri Immonen .06 .15
46 Jukka Penttinen .04 .10
47 Petri Varis .20 .50
48 Keijo Sailynoja .10 .25
49 Tero Lehtera .06 .15
50 Checklist (51-100) .04 .10
51 Jari Lindroos .06 .15
52 Ismo Kuoppala .04 .10
53 Juha Ylonen .20 .50
54 Pasi Saarela .06 .15
55 Marko Leinonen .04 .10
56 Kalle Koskinen .04 .10
57 J-P Laamanen .04 .10
58 Jouni Loponen .04 .10
59 Pekka Poikolainen .04 .10
60 Jan Latvala .04 .10
61 Timo Ahmaoja .04 .10
62 Mika Paananen .04 .10
63 Kimmo Salminen .04 .10
64 Lasse Jamsen .04 .10
65 Thomas Sjogren .08 .20
66 Juha Viinikainen .04 .10
67 Mikko Inkinen .04 .10
68 Toni Koivunen .04 .10
69 Pasi Kuivalainen .10 .25
70 Tommi Kovanen .04 .10
71 Jermu Pisto .04 .10
72 Ivan Vlzek .04 .10
73 Mika Laaksonen .04 .10
74 Miikka Ruokonen .04 .10
75 Sami Simonen .04 .10
76 Mikko Honkonen .04 .10
77 Veli-Pekka Nutikka .20 .50
78 Arto Sirvio .04 .10
79 Janne Kekalainen .04 .10
80 Jarno Levonen .04 .10
81 Jussi Tarvainen .04 .10
82 Iiro Itamies .10 .25
83 Tommi Nyyssonen .04 .10
84 Kari Haakana .04 .10
85 Jarmo Muukkonen .04 .10
86 Tero Nissinen .04 .10
87 Tero Tiainen .04 .10
88 Joonas Jaaskelainen .04 .10
89 Juha Ikonen .04 .10
90 Timo Norppa .04 .10
91 Teemu Riihijarvi .10 .25
92 Mikko Koivunoro .04 .10
93 Sergei Priakhin .06 .15
94 Timo Hirvonen .04 .10
95 Boris Rousson .20 .50
96 Kimmo Lotvonen .04 .10
97 Riku Kallioniemi .04 .10
98 Martti Jarventie .14 .35
99 Mikko Luovi .08 .20
100 Checklist (101-150) .04 .10
101 Kalle Sahlstedt .10 .25
102 Sakari Palsola .04 .10
103 Tommi Turunen .04 .10
104 Petri Latti .04 .10
105 Jonni Vauhkonen .06 .15
106 Veli-Pekka Ahonen .04 .10
107 Jari Torkki .06 .15
108 Jarkko Varvio .06 .15
109 Matti Viitakoski .04 .10
110 Mikko Myllykoski .04 .10
111 Petri Peronmaa .04 .10
112 Vesa Ruotsalainen .04 .10
113 Timo Lohko .04 .10
114 Simo Liukka .04 .10
115 Juha-Pekka Rinkinen .04 .10
116 Timo Makinen .04 .10
117 Marko Ek .06 .15
118 Matti Nevalainen .04 .10
119 Ari Santanen .04 .10
120 Jonas Hemming .04 .10
121 Mika Karapuu .04 .10
122 Ilpo Kauhanen .20 .50
123 Sami-Ville Salomaa .04 .10
124 Antti Rahkonen .04 .10
125 Harri Laurilla .04 .10
126 Sami Lehtonen .04 .10
127 Pasi Petrilainen .10 .25
128 Arto Kulmala .04 .10
129 Jarkko Nikander .04 .10
130 Timo Nurmberg .04 .10
131 Tuomas Reijonen .04 .10
132 Aleksander Barkov .04 .10
133 Mika Niittymaki .04 .10
134 Valeri Krykov .04 .10
135 Fredrik Norrena .20 .50
136 Mika Lehtinen .04 .10
137 Sami Salo .20 .50
138 Riku-Petteri Lehtonen .04 .10
139 Mikko Sokka .04 .10
140 Manu Laapas .04 .10
141 Hannes Hyvonen .14 .35
142 Miikka Rousu .04 .10
143 Simo Rouvali .04 .10
144 Tommi Miettinen .04 .10
145 Kimmo Rintanen .20 .50
146 Tomi Kallio .20 .50
147 Antti Aalto .20 .50
148 Miika Elomo .20 .50
149 Kari Takko .20 .50
150 Checklist (151-200) .04 .10
151 Tommi Rajamaki .10 .25
152 Pasi Peltonen .04 .10
153 Karri Kivi .08 .20
154 Jokke Heinanen .04 .10
155 Teppo Kivela .04 .10
156 Vesa Goman .04 .10
157 Pekka Virta .04 .10
158 Pasi Tuominen .04 .10
159 Timo Hakanen .04 .10
160 Jari Levonen .04 .10
161 Jari Korpisalo .06 .15
162 Timo Salonen .04 .10
163 Jokerit .10 .25
164 Jokerit .04 .10
165 Jokerit .04 .10
166 Jokerit .04 .10
167 Jokerit .04 .10
168 Jokerit .04 .10
169 Jokerit .04 .10
170 Jokerit .04 .10
171 Jokerit .04 .10
172 Jokerit .04 .10
173 Jokerit .04 .10
174 Jokerit .04 .10
175 Ari Sulander .20 .50
176 Joni Lehto .06 .15
177 Timo Jutila .06 .15
178 Mikko Peltola .04 .10
179 Juha Riihijarvi .10 .25
180 Petri Varis .20 .50
181 Boris Rousson .20 .50
182 Kimmo Timonen .20 .50
183 Mika Stromberg .10 .25
184 Jari Korpisalo .06 .15
185 Otakar Janecky .10 .25
186 Juha Lind .10 .25
187 Aarne Honkavaara .20 .50
188 Esko Niemi .04 .10
189 Raimo Kilpio .04 .10
190 Jarmo Wasama .04 .10
191 Lalli Partinen .04 .10
192 Urpo Ylonen .10 .25
193 Ilpo Koskela .20 .50
194 Jorma Vehmanen .04 .10
195 Pekka Marjamaki .04 .10
196 Veli-Pekka Ketola .10 .25
197 Matti Murto .04 .10
198 Juhani Tamminen .10 .25
199 Matti Hagman .08 .20
200 Mask CL .10 .25
NNO Kari Takko Super Bonus 4.00 5.00
NNO Juha Riihijarvi Chase 4.00 5.00

1996-97 Finnish SISU Redline At The Gala

This set of inserts showcases the 1995-96 award winners from the SM-Liiga. The cards were randomly inserted at a rate of 1:6 packs. The card fronts display the players in the tuxedos accepting the awards, while the backs show the player in action.

COMPLETE SET (8) 5.00 10.00
STATED ODDS 1:6
1 Petri Varis .75 2.00
2 Juha Riihijarvi .40 1.00
3 Waltteri Immonen .40 1.00
4 Jani Hurme 4.00 3.00
5 Pasi Kuivalainen .75 2.00
6 Mika Stromberg .40 1.00
7 Sakari Pietila .40 1.00
8 Ari Sulander .75 2.00

1996-97 Finnish SISU Redline Foil Parallels

Little is known about these cards beyond the confirmed checklist below. The skip numbering, and the odd player selection, suggests that a complete set might exist. Any additional information can be forwarded to hockeymag@beckett.com.

COMPLETE SET (25)
1 Checklist
2 Sakari Lindfors
27 Vesa Toskala
41 Ari Sulander
50 Checklist
69 Pasi Kuivalainen
95 Timo Hirvonen
100 Checklist
122 Ilpo Kauhanen
135 Fredrik Norrena
149 Kari Takko
150 Checklist
163 Jokerit
164 Jokerit
165 Jokerit
166 Jokerit
167 Jokerit
168 Jokerit
169 Jokerit
170 Jokerit
171 Jokerit
172 Jokerit
173 Jokerit
174 Jokerit
200 Mask Checklist

1996-97 Finnish SISU Redline Keeping It Green

This most difficult of the SISU inserts (1:60) features four top netminders in a set promoting environmental awareness, as well as keeping the light behind their nets from turning red.

COMPLETE SET (4) 15.00 30.00
STATED ODDS 1:60
1 Ari Sulander 4.00 10.00
2 Jani Hurme 10.00 15.00
3 Boris Rousson 4.00 10.00
4 Mika Pietila 4.00 10.00

1996-97 Finnish SISU Redline Mighty Adversaries

This 9-card set with a two-front format was inserted at a rate of 1:8 packs. Each side featured either a forward or a goalie, with the ghosted image of the counterpart's face in the background. Each side also had text addressing their adversarial relationship.

COMPLETE SET (9) 10.00 25.00
STATED ODDS 1:8
1 K.Takko/K.Rintanen 1.20 3.00
2 B.Rousson/P.Saarela 1.20 3.00
3 I.Kauhanen/A.Andrijevski 1.20 3.00
4 A.Sulander/M.Kortelainen 1.20 3.00
5 P.Kuivalainen/T.Sjogren 1.20 3.00
6 V.Toskala/J.Ojanen 4.00 5.00
7 F.Norrena/O.Janecky 1.20 3.00
8 S.Lindfors/J.Korpisalo 1.20 3.00
9 A.Siekkinen/J.Lindroos 1.20 3.00

1996-97 Finnish SISU Redline Promos

These cards were handed out at a hockey event in Finland to promote the upcoming series. Checklist courtesy of collector Heikki Silvenoinen.

COMPLETE SET (12) 15.00
1 Mika Kortelainen 1.00
2 Alexander Andrievski 1.00
3 Vesa Toskala 3.00
4 Jari Lindroos 1.00
5 Thomas Sjogren 1.00
6 Pasi Kuivalainen 2.00
7 Iiro Itamies 2.00
8 Kalle Sahlstedt 2.00
9 Mika Karapuu 1.00
10 Valeri Krykov 1.00
11 Miikka Rintanen 1.00
12 Jari Levonen 1.00

1996-97 Finnish SISU Redline Rookie Energy

This 9-card set features the top rookies from the SM-Liiga's 95-96 campaign. The cards were randomly inserted into packs at a rate of 1:6. The card fronts feature an image of the player over a colored sky highlighted by lightning bolts. The backs include a head shot as well as some text relating the player's fine season.

COMPLETE SET (9) 8.00 15.00
STATED ODDS 1:6
1 Jani Hurme 4.00 5.00
2 Mikko Eloranta .80 2.00
3 Sami Salo .80 2.00
4 Tero Hamalainen .40 1.00
5 Miika Elomo .80 2.00
6 Mika Pietila .40 1.00
7 Arto Kuki .40 1.00
8 Vesa Toskala 2.00 5.00
9 Miikka Rousu .40 1.00

1996-97 Finnish SISU Redline Silver Signatures

These cards were available as a redemption only to those who mailed in their Kari Takko Super Bonus card. Thanks to collector Heikki Silvennoinen for providing the checklist.

COMPLETE SET (5) 60.00 125.00
1 Jani Hurme 12.00 30.00
2 Pasi Kuivalainen 8.00 20.00
3 Boris Rousson 12.00 30.00
4 Ari Sulander 12.00 30.00
5 Vesa Toskala 15.00 40.00

1996-97 Finnish SISU Redline Sledgehammers

These 9 cards were randomly inserted into packs at a rate of 1:6. The cards are essentially double-fronted, with both sides picturing the player in action, superimposed over a Sledgehammer logo.

COMPLETE SET (9) 2.00 5.00
STATED ODDS 1:6
1 Hannu Henriksson .40 1.00
2 Robert Nordmark .40 1.00
3 Pasi Sormunen .40 1.00
4 Tuomas Gronman .40 1.00
5 Derek Mayer .40 1.00
6 Toni Porkka .40 1.00
7 Timo Peltomaa .40 1.00
8 Iiro Jarvi .40 1.00
9 Joni Lehto .40 1.00

1998-99 Finnish Kerailysarja

This set features many of the players of Finland's SM-Liiga. The cards feature a colour action photo on the front, while the backs feature another photo and stats.

COMPLETE SET (270) 16.00 40.00
1 Checklist 1-60 .08 .20
2 Checklist 61-120 .08 .20
3 Checklist 121-180 .08 .20
4 Checklist 181-240 .08 .20
5 Checklist 241-270 .08 .20
6 Inserts Checklist .08 .20
7 Ari-Pekka Siekkinen .14 .35
8 Jani Riihinen .08 .20
9 Riku Varjamo .08 .20
10 Jiri Vykoukal .08 .20
11 Jonas Andersson-Junkka .14 .35
12 Riku-Petteri Lehtonen .08 .20
13 Pasi Sormunen .08 .20
14 Robert Salo .08 .20
15 Juha Gustafsson .14 .35
16 Christian Ruuttu .14 .35
17 Teemu Hamalainen .08 .20
18 Juha Ikonen .08 .20
19 Hannes Hyvonen .20 .50
20 Timo Hirvonen .20 .50
21 Petr Ton .08 .20
22 Nils Ekman .20 .75
23 Joonas Jaaskelainen .08 .20
24 Tommy Kiviaho .08 .20
25 Tomas Kapusta .08 .20
26 Tero Tiainen .08 .20
27 Teemu Riihijarvi .14 .35
28 Jan Lundell .08 .20
29 Niklas Backstrom .08 .20
30 Ville Siren .08 .20

31 Marko From .08 .20
32 Brian Rafalski .40 1.00
33 Jarno Kultanen .20 .50
34 Toni Lydman .20 .50
35 Jani Nikko .14 .35
36 Jere Karalahti .14 .35
37 Kari Rajala .08 .20
38 Kari Kalto .08 .20
39 Kimmo Kuhta .08 .20
40 Jan Caloun .14 .35
41 Markku Hurme .08 .20
42 Tom Laaksonen .08 .20
43 Niklas Hagman 1.20 1.00
44 Luciano Borsato .08 .20
45 Toni Sihvonen .08 .20
46 Mika Kortelainen .14 .35
47 Toni Makiaho .08 .20
48 Mika Nieminen .14 .35
49 Jarkko Ruutu .14 .75
50 Marko Tuomainen .14 .35
51 Pasi Nurminen .80 4.00
52 Kari Rosenberg .08 .20
53 Aki Heino .08 .20
54 Erik Kakko .08 .20
55 Tom Koivisto .08 .20
56 Ari Vallin .08 .20
57 Tomi Kallarsson .08 .20
58 Jaroslav Nedved .08 .20
59 Kai Rautio .08 .20
60 Mikko Kuparinen .14 .35
61 Mika Kannisto .08 .20
62 Juha Virtanen .08 .20
63 Jani Keinanen .08 .20
64 Jyrki Louhi .08 .20
65 Roman Simicek .20 .50
66 Semi Pekki .08 .20
67 Timo Parssinen .08 .20
68 Jarkko Savijoki .08 .20
69 Marko Palo .08 .20
70 Antti Virtanen .08 .20
71 Niko Kapanen .08 2.00
72 Tomas Vlasak .14 .35
73 Riku Hahl 1.20 1.00
74 Vesa Toskala 1.20 2.00
75 Markus Korhonen .08 .20
76 Timo Willman .08 .20
77 Veli-Pekka Hard .08 .20
78 Pekka Kangasalusta .08 .20
79 Oscar Ackestrom .08 .20
80 Allan Measures .08 .20
81 Pasi Puistola .08 .20
82 Pasi Saarinen .14 .35
83 Mikko Haapakoski .08 .20
84 Martti Jarventie .20 .50
85 Mika Arvaja .08 .20
86 Juha Hautamaa .08 .20
87 Raimo Helminen .14 .35
88 Tomi Hirvonen .08 .20
89 Matti Kaipainen .08 .20
90 Peter Larsson .08 .20
91 Vesa Viitakoski .14 .35
92 Mikko Peltola .08 .20
93 Timo Peltomaa .08 .20
94 Hannu Mattila .08 .20
95 Sami Ahlberg .08 .20
96 Juha Jarvenpaa .08 .20
97 Markus Ketterer .14 .35
98 Ari Kumpula .08 .20
99 Waltteri Immonen .08 .20
100 Antti-Jussi Niemi .14 .35
101 Sami Nuutinen .08 .20
102 Yves Racine .14 .35
103 Rami Alanko .08 .20
104 Mika Stromberg .14 .35
105 Ossi Vaananen .40 1.00
106 Jani Rita 1.20 1.00
107 Sami Mettovaara .08 .20
108 Fredrik Nilsson .08 .20
109 Kimmo Rintanen .14 .35
110 Jari Kauppila .08 .20
111 Pasi Saarela .14 .35
112 Timo Saarikoski .08 .20
113 Eero Somervuori .14 .35
114 Jukka Tiilikainen .08 .20
115 Jarkko Vaananen .08 .20
116 Otakar Janecky .14 .35
117 Patrik Juhlin .14 .35
118 Juha Lind .20 .50
119 Marko Leinonen .08 .20
120 Tommi Satosaari .08 .20
121 Mikko Luoma .08 .20
122 Jan Latvala .08 .20
123 Kevin Wortman .08 .20
124 Kalle Koskinen .08 .20
125 Jyrki Valivaara .08 .20
126 Markus Kankaanpera .08 .20
127 Jarkko Glad .08 .20
128 Marko Kauppinen .08 .20
129 Robert Nordberg .08 .20
130 Juha Viinikainen .08 .20
131 Marko Ojanen .08 .20
132 Toni Koivunen .08 .20
133 Mikko Rantala .08 .20
134 Jussi Tarvainen .08 .20
135 Tommi Turunen .08 .20
136 Timo Vertala .08 .20
137 Veli-Pekka Nutikka .14 .35
138 Stefan Ornskog .08 .20
139 Marko Virtanen .08 .20
140 Lasse Jamsen .08 .20
141 Kimmo Kapanen .08 .20
142 Ari Luostarinen .08 .20
143 Tobias Ablad .08 .20
144 Derry Menard .08 .20
145 Jermu Pisto .08 .20
146 Sebastian Sulku .08 .20
147 Timo Ahmaoja .08 .20
148 Teemu Tuomainen .08 .20
149 Pekka Poikolainen .08 .20
150 Aki Korhonen .08 .20
151 Pekka Tirkkonen .08 .20
152 Petro Koivunen .08 .20
153 Marko Levanen .08 .20
154 Janne Kekalainen .08 .20
155 Antti Riekkinen .08 .20
156 Mikko Honkonen .08 .20
157 Timo Sikkula .08 .20
158 Sami Simonen .08 .20
159 Mikko Konttila .08 .20
160 Jaakko Uhlback .08 .20
161 Lubos Rob .08 .20
162 Kimmo Vesa .08 .20
163 Sinuhe Wallinheimo .08 .20
164 Jaakko Harikkala .14 .35
165 Atvars Tribuntsovs .08 .20
166 Ismo Kuoppala .08 .20
167 Kimmo Lotvonen .08 .20
168 Marko Toivonen .08 .20
169 Erik Hamalainen .14 .35
170 Mikael Tjallden .08 .20
171 Roland Carlsson .08 .20
172 Niko Halttunen .08 .20
173 Jouni Vauhkonen .08 .20
174 Matti Raunio .08 .20
175 Ville Mikkonen .08 .20
176 Petri Pakaslahti .08 .20
177 Janne Seva .08 .20
178 Harri Sillgren .08 .20
179 Leonids Tambijevs .08 .20
180 Jari Hyvarinen .08 .20
181 Patrik Wallenberg .08 .20
182 Jarkko Nikander .08 .20
183 Aigars Cipruss .08 .20
184 Jussi Markkanen .40 1.50
185 Pasi Hakkinen .08 .20
186 Harri Tikkanen .08 .20
187 Juri Kuznetsov .08 .20
188 Riku Kallioniemi .08 .20
189 Jussi Pekkala .08 .20
190 Mikko Myllykoski .08 .20
191 Vesa Ruotsalainen .08 .20
192 Tommi Sova .08 .20
193 Dale McTavish .08 .20
194 Pasi Maattanen .08 .20
195 Aleksander Matsijevski .08 .20
196 Sami Kaartinen .08 .20
197 Ari Saarinen .08 .20
198 Joel Salonen .08 .20
199 Ari Santanen .08 .20
200 Mika Skytta .08 .20
201 Mika Kauppinen .08 .20
202 Keijo Sailynoja .08 .20
203 Eric Weilleux .08 .20
204 Ville Immonen .08 .20
205 Mika Noronen 2.00 5.00
206 Iiro Itamies .08 .20
207 Josef Boumedienne .20 .50
208 Miska Kangasniemi .14 .35
209 Mikko Tamminen .08 .20
210 Timo Jutila .08 .20
211 Janne Gronvall .14 .35
212 Sami-Ville Salomaa .08 .20
213 Janne Vuorela .08 .20
214 Pasi Petrilainen .14 .35
215 Pasi Tuominen .08 .20
216 Jani Hassinen .08 .20
217 Valeri Krykov .08 .20
218 Juha Vuorivirta .08 .20
219 Aleksander Barkov .08 .20
220 Harri Lonnberg .08 .20
221 Arto Kumala .08 .20
222 Janne Ojanen .14 .35
223 Lasse Pirjeta .08 .20
224 Sami Salonen .08 .20
225 Johannes Alanen .08 .20
226 Mikko Makela .14 .35
227 Fredrik Norrena .14 .35
228 Miikka Kiprusoff 2.00 5.00
229 Kimmo Eronen .08 .20
230 Marko Kiprusoff .08 .20
231 Jouni Loponen .08 .20
232 Ilkka Mikkola .14 .35
233 Aki Berg .20 .50
234 Tommi Rajamaki .14 .35
235 Peter Ahola .08 .20
236 Mika Lehtinen .08 .20
237 Tony Virta .08 .20
238 Joni Lius .08 .20
239 Mikko Eloranta .20 .50
240 Marco Tuokko .08 .20
241 Juha Joninen .08 .20
242 Tomi Kallio .14 .35
243 Mikko Rautio .08 .20
244 Jani Kiviharju .08 .20
245 Tommi Miettinen .20 .50
246 Simo Rouvali .08 .20
247 Kalle Sahlstedt .14 .35
248 Teemu Elomo .14 .35
249 Mika Alatalo .20 .50
250 Miika Elomo .14 .35
251 Pasi Kuivalainen .14 .35
252 Mika Lehto .08 .20
253 Joachim Esbjors .08 .20
254 Mikko Sokka .08 .20
255 Pasi Peltonen .14 .35
256 Vesa Goman .08 .20
257 Mika Laaksonen .08 .20
258 Santeri Immonen .08 .20
259 Jonas Esbjors .08 .20
260 Vjatcheslav Fandul .08 .20
261 Kimmo Salminen .08 .20
262 Jokke Heinanen .08 .20
263 Jari Levonen .08 .20
264 Niko Mikkola .08 .20
265 Andrei Potaitshuk .08 .20
266 Rauli Raitanen .08 .20
267 Timo Hakanen .08 .20
268 Jan Benda .08 .20
269 Tero Arkiomaa .14 .35
270 Marko Kivenmaki .08 .20

1998-99 Finnish Kerailysarja 90's Top 12

These inserts honor the decade's best Finnish players. They were randomly inserted into packs. Unfortunately, the wrappers do not reveal the insertion odds.

COMPLETE SET (12) 16.00 30.00
1 Jere Lehtinen 2.00 3.00
2 Pertti Lehtonen .80 2.00
3 Janne Laukkanen 1.20 2.00
4 Jukka Tammi 1.20 2.00
5 Teemu Selanne 8.00 10.00
6 Jari Lindroos .80 2.00
7 Sami Kapanen 2.00 3.00
8 Jarmo Kuusisto .80 2.00
9 Ari Santanen .80 2.00
10 Timo Jutila .80 2.00
11 Saku Koivu 4.00 5.00
12 Kari Takko 1.20 2.00

1998-99 Finnish Kerailysarja Dream Team

These inserts honor the best of Finland's current talent pool. The cards were randomly inserted into packs. Unfortunately, the packs do not reveal the insertion odds.

COMPLETE SET (7) 16.00 20.00
1 Jari Kurri 2.00 5.00
2 Ari Sulander 1.20 3.00
3 Jyrki Lumme .80 2.00
4 Janne Niinimaa .80 2.00
5 Jere Lehtinen 2.00 4.00
6 Saku Koivu 4.00 5.00
7 Teemu Selanne 8.00 10.00

1998-99 Finnish Kerailysarja Leijonat

These inserts honor players who have performed for The Lions, the nickname of Finland's national team. The cards were randomly inserted into packs. Unfortunately, the packs do not reveal the insertion odds.

COMPLETE SET (47) 6.00 15.00
1 Markus Ketterer .20 .50
2 Jarmo Myllys .20 .50
3 Jukka Tammi .20 .50
4 Peter Ahola .10 .25
5 Erik Hamalainen .10 .25
6 Timo Jutila .10 .25
7 Jere Karalahti .20 .50
8 Marko Kiprusoff .10 .25
9 Janne Laukkanen .20 .50
10 Joni Lehto .10 .25
11 Kaj Linna .10 .25
12 Jouni Loponen .10 .25
13 Toni Lydman .14 .35
14 Antti-Jussi Niemi .20 .50
15 Petteri Nummelin .10 .25
16 Mika Stromberg .10 .25
17 Kimmo Timonen .20 .50
18 Hannu Virta .10 .25
19 Mika Alatalo .20 .50
20 Mikko Eloranta .20 .50
21 Raimo Helminen .10 .25
22 Juha Ikonen .10 .25
23 Marko Jantunen .10 .25
24 Olli Jokinen .75 2.00
25 Joonas Jaaskelainen .10 .25
26 Sami Kapanen .80 2.00
27 Esa Keskinen .10 .25
28 Jari Korpisalo .10 .25
29 Tero Lehtera .10 .25
30 Juha Lind .10 .25
31 Joni Lius .10 .25
32 Toni Makiaho .10 .25
33 Mika Nieminen .20 .50
34 Janne Ojanen .10 .25
35 Marko Palo .10 .25
36 Ville Peltonen .30 .75
37 Juha Riihijarvi .10 .25
38 Kimmo Rintanen .10 .25
39 Christian Ruuttu .14 .35
40 Jarkko Ruutu .10 .25
41 Jukka Seppo .10 .25
42 Raimo Summanen .10 .25
43 Esa Tikkanen .40 1.00
44 Marko Tuomainen .10 .25
45 Antti Tormanen .10 .25
46 Jarkko Varvio .10 .25
47 Juha Ylonen .20 .50

1998-99 Finnish Kerailysarja Mad Masks

These inserts honor the best goalies in Finland. The cards were randomly inserted into packs. Unfortunately, the packs do not reveal the insertion odds.

COMPLETE SET (12) 24.00 75.00
1 Ari-Pekka Siekkinen 2.00 5.00
2 Jan Lundell 2.00 5.00
3 Pasi Nurminen 4.00 15.00
4 Vesa Toskala 4.00 10.00
5 Markus Ketterer 2.00 5.00
6 Marko Leinonen 2.00 5.00
7 Kimmo Kapanen 2.00 5.00
8 Sinuhe Wallinheimo 2.00 5.00
9 Jussi Markkanen 4.00 10.00
10 Mika Noronen 6.00 15.00
11 Fredrik Norrena 2.00 5.00
12 Pasi Kuivalainen 2.00 5.00

1998-99 Finnish Kerailysarja Off Duty

These inserts show players away from the ice. The cards were randomly inserted into packs. Unfortunately, the packs do not reveal the insertion odds.

COMPLETE SET (12) 8.00 20.00
1 Juha Ikonen .80 2.00
2 Toni Sihvonen .80 2.00
3 Tom Koivisto .80 2.00
4 Juha Hautamaa .80 2.00
5 Kimmo Rintanen .80 2.00
6 Marko Leinonen .80 2.00
7 Sami Simonen .80 2.00
8 Sinuhe Wallinheimo 1.20 3.00
9 Jussi Markkanen 1.60 4.00
10 Arto Kulmala .80 2.00
11 Marko Kiprusoff .80 2.00
12 Pasi Kuivalainen .80 2.00

1999-00 Finnish Cardset

This set features the top players of the Finnish SM-Liiga. It was issued in foil packs over two series. The cards feature action photos over a computer generated background. Cards #158-177 comprise a Sharpshooters subset while cards #178-200 form a Flaming Patriots subset. The Jere Lehtinen Triple Threat card was a long-odds insert that was hand serial numbered out of 1,000 copies. The Teemu Selanne Global Glory card was a long-odds insert that was hand serial numbered out of 1,000 copies as well. Neither card is considered part of the complete set.

COMPLETE SET (346) 30.00 75.00
1 Checklist 1-40 .08 .20
2 Checklist 41-80 .08 .20
3 Checklist 81-120 .08 .20
4 Checklist 121-160 .08 .20
5 Checklist 161-200 .08 .20
6 Inserts Checklist .08 .20
7 Ari-Pekka Siekkinen .14 .35
8 Jiri Vykoukal .08 .20
9 Riku Varjamo .08 .20
10 Riku-Petteri Lehtonen .08 .20
11 Juha Gustafsson .14 .35
12 Arto Laatikainen .30 .75
13 Hannes Hyvonen .20 .50
14 Timo Hirvonen .20 .50
15 Tommy Kiviaho .08 .20
16 Tero Tiainen .08 .20
17 Joonas Jaaskelainen .08 .20
18 Teemu Riihijarvi .14 .35
19 Olli Ahonen .08 .20
20 Santeri Heiskanen .08 .20
21 Jarno Kultanen .20 .50
22 Marko From .08 .20
23 Kimmo Kuhta .08 .20
24 Tom Laaksonen .08 .20
25 Kari Kalto .08 .20
26 Jan Caloun .14 .35
27 Markku Hurme .08 .20
28 Toni Makiaho .08 .20
29 Mika Nieminen .14 .35
30 Luciano Borsato .08 .20
31 Aki Heino .08 .20
32 Jonas Andersson-Junkka .14 .35
33 Tomi Kallarsson .08 .20
34 Roman Simicek .20 .50
35 Juha Virtanen .08 .20
36 Antti Virtanen .08 .20
37 Jyrki Louhi .08 .20
38 Jarkko Savijoki .08 .20
39 Jukka Hentunen .20 .50
40 Timo Parssinen .40 1.00
41 Niko Kapanen .40 1.00
42 Tomas Vlasak .14 .35
43 Kristian Antila .08 .20
44 Pasi Puistola .08 .20
45 Pasi Saarinen .14 .35
46 Pekka Kangasalusta .08 .20
47 Martti Jarventie .08 .20
48 Sami Karjalainen .08 .20
49 Riku Niemela .08 .20
50 Mikko Peltola .08 .20
51 Juha Hautamaa .08 .20
52 Raimo Helminen .14 .35
53 Tomi Hirvonen .08 .20
54 Sami Ahlberg .08 .20
55 Vesa Viitakoski .08 .20
56 Mika Arvaja .08 .20
57 Rami Alanko .08 .20
58 Antti-Jussi Niemi .14 .35
59 Antti Hulkkonen .12 .30
60 Jani Rita 1.60 1.00
61 Jarkko Vaananen .08 .20
62 Fredrik Nilsson .08 .20
63 Jari Kauppila .08 .20
64 Eero Somervuori .20 .50
65 Jukka Tiilikainen .08 .20
66 Patrik Juhlin .14 .35
67 Tommi Satosaari .08 .20
68 Jarkko Glad .08 .20
69 Jyrki Valivaara .08 .20
70 Markus Kankaanpera .08 .20
71 Kalle Koskinen .08 .20
72 Juha Viinikainen .08 .20
73 Marko Ojanen .08 .20
74 Toni Koivunen .08 .20
75 Veli-Pekka Nutikka .14 .35
76 Stefan Ornskog .08 .20
77 Marko Virtanen .08 .20
78 Lasse Jamsen .08 .20
79 Petri Vehanen .08 .20
80 Kimmo Lotvonen .08 .20
81 Jaakko Harikkala .14 .35
82 Ismo Kuoppala .08 .20
83 Erik Hamalainen .14 .35
84 Zdenek Nedved .08 .20
85 Harri Suvanto .08 .20
86 Jouni Vauhkonen .08 .20
87 Ville Mikkonen .08 .20
88 Janne Seva .08 .20
89 Petri Latti .08 .20
90 Harri Sillgren .08 .20
91 Leonids Tambijevs .08 .20
92 Sami Lehtinen .08 .20
93 Jussi-Antti Reimari .08 .20
94 Marko Ahonen .08 .20
95 Veli-Pekka Laitinen .08 .20
96 Mika Niskanen .08 .20
97 Jan Latvala .08 .20
98 Mika Asikainen .08 .20
99 Aigars Cipruss .08 .20
100 Michael Johansson .08 .20
101 Tomi-Pekka Kolu .08 .20
102 Jarkko Ollikainen .08 .20
103 Toni Saarinen .08 .20
104 Jussi Vienonen .08 .20
105 Jouko Mytta .08 .20
106 Jussi Markkanen .40 1.00
107 Harri Tikkanen .08 .20
108 Riku Kallioniemi .08 .20
109 Jussi Pekkala .08 .20
110 Mikko Myllykoski .08 .20
111 Vesa Ruotsalainen .08 .20
112 Tommi Sova .08 .20
113 Ari Santanen .08 .20
114 Pasi Maattanen .08 .20
115 Tero Hamalainen .08 .20
116 Mika Skytta .08 .20
117 Ville Immonen .08 .20
118 Keijo Sailynoja .08 .20
119 Miska Kangasniemi .14 .35
120 Josef Boumedienne .20 .50
121 Janne Vuorela .08 .20
122 Janne Gronvall .14 .35
123 Valeri Krykov .08 .20
124 Arto Kumala .08 .20
125 Aleksander Barkov .08 .20
126 Johannes Alanen .08 .20
127 Jani Hassinen .08 .20
128 Janne Ojanen .14 .35
129 Tuomas Reijonen .08 .20
130 Sami Salonen .08 .20
131 Fredrik Norrena .14 .35
132 Kimmo Eronen .08 .20
133 Marko Kiprusoff .10 .25
134 Jouni Loponen .08 .20
135 Ilkka Mikkola .14 .35
136 Jani Kiviharju .08 .20
137 Tony Virta .08 .20
138 Kalle Sahlstedt .14 .35
139 Tomi Kallio .60 1.00
140 Joni Lius .08 .20
141 Teemu Elomo .14 .35
142 Ville Vahalahti .08 .20
143 Marco Tuokko .08 .20
144 Kai Nurminen .14 .35
145 Petr Kuchyna .08 .20
146 Tuomo Kyha .08 .20
147 Pasi Peltonen .14 .35
148 Santeri Immonen .08 .20
149 Pauli Levokari .08 .20
150 Vesa Salo .08 .20
151 Timo Salonen .08 .20
152 Marko Kivenmaki .08 .20
153 Niko Mikkola .08 .20
154 Andrei Potaitshuk .08 .20
155 Tero Arkiomaa .14 .35
156 Timo Hakanen .08 .20
157 Jan Peterek .08 .20
158 Jan Caloun .14 .35
159 Pasi Saarela .14 .35
160 Tomas Vlasak .14 .35
161 Brian Rafalski .40 1.00
162 Peter Larsson .08 .20
163 Roman Simicek .08 .20
164 Raimo Helminen .14 .35
165 Leonids Tambijevs .08 .20
166 Mika Nieminen .14 .35
167 Janne Ojanen .14 .35
168 Otakar Janecky .14 .35
169 Juha Ikonen .08 .20
170 Jari Kauppila .08 .20
171 Jan Benda .08 .20
172 Tony Virta .08 .20
173 Niko Kapanen .40 1.00
174 Aleksander Barkov .08 .20
175 Hannes Hyvonen .20 .50
176 Lasse Pirjeta .08 .20
177 Jussi Tarvainen .08 .20
178 Miikka Kiprusoff 2.00 5.00
179 Ari Sulander .30 .75
180 Vesa Toskala 2.00 2.00
181 Aki Berg .20 .50
182 Jere Karalahti .20 .50
183 Marko Kiprusoff .10 .25
184 Toni Lydman .20 .50
185 Kari Martikainen .08 .20
186 Antti-Jussi Niemi .14 .35
187 Petteri Nummelin .14 .35
188 Kimmo Timonen .30 .75
189 Mikko Eloranta .20 .50
190 Raimo Helminen .14 .35
191 Olli Jokinen .40 1.00
192 Tomi Kallio .60 1.00
193 Saku Koivu 1.20 3.00
194 Juha Lind .20 .50
195 Ville Peltonen .20 .50
196 Kimmo Rintanen .14 .35
197 Teemu Selanne 2.00 5.00
198 Toni Sihvonen .08 .20
199 Marko Tuomainen .08 .20
200 Antti Tormanen .20 .50
201 Tom Draper .14 .35
202 Timo Leinonen .08 .20
203 Pasi Nurminen 1.20 3.00
204 Tommi Satosaari .08 .20
205 Mika Oksa .08 .20
206 Jermu Pisto .08 .20
207 Niclas Hedberg .14 .35
208 Peter Ahola .08 .20
209 Aki Korhonen .08 .20
210 Mikko Kaukokari .08 .20
211 Esa Pirnes .08 .20
212 Arto Kuki .08 .20
213 Dale McTavish .14 .35
214 Ari Katavisto .08 .20
215 Teemu Siren .08 .20
216 Mikael Jamsanen .08 .20
217 Otakar Janecky .14 .35
218 Niklas Backstrom .08 .20
219 Ari Ahonen ERC 2.00 3.00
220 Jere Karalahti .20 .50
221 Marek Zidlicky .08 .20
222 Toni Lydman .08 .20
223 Pekka Kangasalusta .08 .20
224 Kari Rajala .08 .20
225 Mike Gaffney .08 .20
226 Timo Ahmaoja .08 .20
227 Aki Tuominen .08 .20
228 Aki Uusikartano .08 .20
229 Mika Kortelainen .14 .35
230 Toni Sihvonen .08 .20
231 Pasi Nielikainen .08 .20
232 Lasse Pirjeta .08 .20
233 Kimmo Kapanen .08 .20
234 Ari Kumpula .08 .20
235 Kimmo Peltonen .08 .20
236 Sebastian Sulku .08 .20
237 Harri Laurila .08 .20
238 Teemu Aalto .08 .20
239 Oscar Ackestrom .08 .20
240 Antti Miettinen ERC .08 .75
241 Marko Palo .08 .20
242 Riku Hahl 2.00 1.00
243 Petr Tenkrat .40 .75
244 Pasi Kuivalainen .14 .35
245 Arto Tukio .08 .20
246 Hannu Henriksson .08 .20
247 Teemu Kesa .08 .20
248 Antti Bruun .08 .20
249 Tomi Pettinen .08 .20
250 Tapio Sammalkangas .08 .20
251 Rodrigo Lavins .14 .35
252 Ilkka Laitinen .08 .20
253 Tommi Miettinen .14 .35
254 Jarkko Nikander .08 .20
255 Daniel Marois .14 .35
256 Antti Hilden .08 .20
257 Kimmo Vesa .08 .20
258 Pasi Nurminen 1.20 3.00
259 Ossi Vaananen .40 1.00
260 Sean Gagnon .14 .35
261 Marko Kauppinen .14 .35
262 Tuomas Gronman .08 .20
263 Tom Koivisto .08 .20
264 Tomek Valtonen .08 .20
265 Esa Tikkanen .40 1.00
266 Jan Benda .08 .20
267 Tommi Santala .08 .20
268 Petri Varis .14 .35
269 Tuomas Eskelinen .08 .20
270 Tero Lehtera .14 .35
271 Markus Hatinen .08 .20
272 Pekka Poikolainen .08 .20
273 Mikko Luoma .08 .20
274 Vesa Ponto .08 .20
275 Nik Zupancic .08 .20
276 Pasi Kangas .14 .35
277 Topi Riutta .08 .20
278 Jussi Pesonen .08 .20
279 Petr Ton .08 .20
280 Jaroslav Bednar .60 .75
281 Tom Draper .20 .50
282 Mika Laaksonen .08 .20
283 Allan Measures .08 .20
284 Martin Stepanek .08 .20
285 Marko Toivonen .08 .20
286 Petteri Lotila .08 .20
287 Jari Hyvarinen .08 .20
288 Timo Peltomaa .08 .20
289 Petri Pakaslahti .08 .20
290 Jokke Heinanen .08 .20
291 Matti Kaipainen .08 .20
292 Ville Koivula .08 .20
293 Veli-Pekka Kautonen .08 .20
294 Daniel Johansson .08 .20
295 Tommi Kovanen .08 .20
296 Roland Carlsson .08 .20
297 Jani Keinanen .08 .20
298 Mikko Juutilainen .08 .20
299 Aki Kaskinen .08 .20
300 Tommi Turunen .08 .20
301 Mathias Bosson .08 .20
302 Teemu Riihijarvi .08 .20
303 Pasi Hakkinen .08 .20
304 Jani-Matti Loikala .08 .20
305 Juri Kuznetsov .14 .35
306 Mikko Jokela .08 .20
307 Ville Hamalainen .08 .20
308 Joel Salonen .08 .20
309 Timo Saarikoski .08 .20
310 Pekka Tirkkonen .08 .20
311 Mika Kauppinen .14 .35
312 Sami Kaartinen .08 .20
313 Timo Jarvinen .08 .20
314 Jason Muzzatti .20 .50
315 Per Lofstrom .08 .20
316 Ari Vallin .08 .20
317 Asko Rantanen .08 .20
318 Tuukka Mantyla .08 .20
319 Pasi Petrilainen .20 .50
320 Pasi Tuominen .20 .50
321 Roman Meluzin .08 .20
322 Miikka Mannikko .08 .20
323 Jussi Tarvainen .08 .20
324 Timo Vertala .08 .20
325 Jaakko Uhlback .08 .20
326 Antero Niittymaki ERC 1.20 3.00
327 Kimmo Lecklin .08 .20
328 Tommi Rajamaki .08 .20
329 Mika Lehtinen .08 .20
330 Kari Harila .08 .20
331 Petri Tahtisalo .08 .20
332 Esa Keskinen .08 .20
333 Kimmo Rintanen .14 .35
334 Michael Holmkvist .20 .50
335 Mikko Rautee .08 .20
336 Mika Lehto .08 .20
337 Timo Leinonen .08 .20
338 Timo Willman .08 .20
339 Olli Kaski .08 .20
340 Samu Wesslin .08 .20
341 Mika Kannisto .08 .20
342 Ales Kratoska .08 .20
343 Marko Luomala .08 .20
344 Jaakko Makela .08 .20
345 Ondrej Steiner .08 .20
346 Markku Tahtinen .08 .20
NNO Teemu Selanne GG 20.00 25.00
NNO Jere Lehtinen TT 6.00 10.00

1999-00 Finnish Cardset Aces High

This insert set was created in the form of playing cards. Several great stars of Finland's past, as well as four cheerleaders from the SM-Liiga are featured alongside today's heroes. The fronts feature action photos with symbols in the corners of typical playing cards. As the cards are not traditionally numbered, they have been listed below according to their suits. C stands for Clubs, D for Diamonds, H for Hearts and S for Spades.

COMPLETE SET (54) 0.00 25.00
J1 Jari Kurri .80 2.00
J2 Teemu Selanne 2.00 5.00
C-2 Peter Ahola .08 .20
C-3 Teppo Numminen .20 .50
C-4 Janne Laukkanen .08 .20
C-5 Risto Siltanen .08 .20
C-6 Iiro Jarvi .08 .20
C-7 Antti Aalto .08 .20
C-8 Theo Fleury .80 2.00
C-9 Ilkka Sinsalo .08 .20
C-10 Michael Nylander .08 .20
D-2 Timo Blomqvist .08 .20
D-3 Sami Salo .08 .20
D-4 Marko Kiprusoff .08 .20
D-5 Aki Berg .20 .50
D-6 Jan Caloun .08 .20
D-7 Olli Jokinen .20 1.00
D-8 Patrik Juhlin .08 .20
D-9 Dale McTavish .08 .20
D-10 Sami Kapanen .40 1.00
H-2 Hannu Virta .08 .20
H-3 Tuomas Gronman .08 .20
H-4 Timo Jutila .08 .20
H-5 Jyrki Lumme .20 .50
H-6 Juha Ylonen .30 .75
H-7 Janne Ojanen .08 .20
H-8 Juha Lind .20 .50
H-9 Antti Tormanen .08 .20
H-10 Jarkko Varvio .08 .20
S-2 Reijo Ruotsalainen .08 .20
S-3 Janne Niinimaa .20 .50
S-4 Brian Rafalski .20 .50
S-5 Kimmo Timonen .20 .50
S-6 Kai Nurminen .08 .20
S-7 Raimo Helminen .08 .20
S-8 Raimo Summanen .08 .20
S-9 Petri Varis .14 .35
S-10 Christian Ruuttu .08 .20
C-A Jani Hurme 1.20 1.00
C-J Mika Alatalo .20 .50
C-K Ville Peltonen .14 .35
C-Q Paivi Ylitite .20 1.00
D-A Jarmo Myllys .20 .50
D-J Mikko Eloranta .20 .50
D-K Jere Lehtinen .40 1.50
D-Q Carissa Chan .20 1.00
H-A Boris Rousson .20 .50
H-J Jan Benda .08 .20
H-K Saku Koivu 1.20 4.00
H-Q Ann Bjorklof .20 1.00
S-A Kari Takko .20 .50
S-J Marko Tuomainen .08 .20
S-K Esa Tikkanen .40 1.00
S-Q Satu Jokinen .20 1.00

1999-00 Finnish Cardset Blazing Patriots

This insert set is a partial parallel of the Flaming Patriots subset and features the top performers for Finland's national team. The cards were inserted at a rate of 1:10 packs.

COMPLETE SET (6) 20.00 30.00
STATED ODDS 1:10
1 Miikka Kiprusoff 4.00 10.00
2 Jere Karalahti 1.20 3.00
3 Kimmo Timonen 1.20 3.00
4 Teemu Selanne 12.00 10.00
5 Saku Koivu 4.00 8.00
6 Marko Tuomainen 1.20 3.00

1999-00 Finnish Cardset Jere Lehtinen Triple Threat

This is a single card tribute to Finnish hockey hero Jere Lehtinen. The card is hand numbered on the back out of 1,000.

1 Jere Lehtinen 4.00 10.00

1999-00 Finnish Cardset Most Wanted

This insert set features the players drafted earliest in the NHL draft. The cards were inserted at a rate of 1:4 packs.

COMPLETE SET (12) 20.00 30.00
STATED ODDS 1:4
1 Aki Berg .80 2.00
2 Olli Jokinen .80 2.00
3 Teemu Selanne 8.00 10.00
4 Teemu Riihuarvi .40 1.00
5 Jani Rita 1.60 2.00
6 Saku Koivu 4.00 8.00
7 Mika Noronen 4.00 5.00
8 Miika Elomo .80 2.00
9 Jukka Seppo .40 1.00
10 Ari Ahonen 3.20 5.00
11 Tuomas Gronman .40 1.00
12 Ville Siren .40 1.00

1999-00 Finnish Cardset Par Avion

This insert set focuses on some of the best Finnish players who have moved on to play in North America. The cards were inserted 1:4 packs.

COMPLETE SET (12) 14.00 25.00
STATED ODDS 1:4
1 Mika Alatalo 1.20 2.00
2 Toni Lydman .80 2.00
3 Brian Rafalski 1.20 2.00
4 Jere Karalahti .80 2.00
5 Juha Lind .80 2.00
6 Mikko Kuparinen .40 1.00
7 Marko Tuomainen .40 1.00
8 Miikka Kiprusoff 4.00 10.00
9 Mika Noronen 4.00 5.00
10 Vesa Toskala 2.80 5.00
11 Mikko Eloranta 1.20 2.00
12 Jarkko Ruutu .80 2.00

1999-00 Finnish Cardset Puck Stoppers

This six-card set features the top netminders in the SM-Liiga. The cards were inserted at a

rate of 1:10.
COMPLETE SET (6) 12.00 25.00
STATED ODDS 1:10
1 Antero Niittymaki 6.00 10.00
2 Ari-Pekka Siekkinen 2.00 5.00
3 Pasi Kuivalainen 2.00 5.00
4 Sami Lehtinen 2.00 5.00
5 Jason Muzzatti 2.00 5.00
6 Kimmo Kapanen 2.00 5.00

1999 Finnish Valio World Championships

Little is known about this Finnish issued set other than the confirmed checklist. Any additional information can be forwarded to hockeymag@beckett.com.

COMPLETE SET (6) 6.00 15.00
1 Kari Eloranta .80 2.00
2 Jari Kurri 3.20 8.00
3 Tapio Levo .80 2.00
4 Markus Mattsson 1.20 3.00
5 Jukka Porvari .80 2.00
6 Pekka Rautakallio .80 2.00

2000-01 Finnish Cardset

This brand features the players from Finland's tip league, the SM-Liiga. It was issued in foil packs across three separate series. The cards are brightly colored with an action photo on the front, another on the back, and a bizarre ranking system on the back which tabulates how great the player is. The brand is noteworthy for including cards of several prominent Finnish players currently in the NHL, as well as several 2001 draft picks such as Mikko Koivu and Tuomo Ruutu. There were three special cards hand numbered to 1,000 copies available: Saku Koivu Millennium Thunder was found in series 1 packs, Pasi Nurminen Masked Marvel was found in series 2, and Ari Ahonen Masked Marvel card was inserted into series 3 packs.

COMPLETE SET (360) 30.00 60.00
COMMON CARD (1-360) .04 .10
SEMISTARS/GOALIES .08 .20
UNLISTED STARS .20 .50
1 Checklist .04 .10
2 Checklist .04 .10
3 Checklist .04 .10
4 Mika Oksa .04 .10
5 Peter Ahola .04 .10
6 Jermu Pisto .04 .10
7 Jiri Vykoukal .04 .10
8 Niclas Hedberg .04 .10
9 Teemu Siren .04 .10
10 Joonas Jaaskelainen .20 .50
11 Timo Hirvonen .04 .10
12 Mikko Kaukokari .04 .10
13 Ari Ahonen 1.25 3.00
14 Marek Zidlicky .04 .10
15 Jarno Kultanen .08 .20
16 Toni Sihvonen .04 .10
17 Aki Uusikartano .04 .10
18 Pasi Nielikainen .04 .10
19 Hannes Hyvonen .20 .50
20 Mika Nieminen .20 .50
21 Mika Kortelainen .04 .10
22 Kimmo Kapanen .04 .10
23 Jonas Andersson-Junkka .08 .20
24 Kimmo Peltonen .04 .10
25 Sebastian Sulku .04 .10
26 Teemu Aalto .04 .10
27 Antti Miettinen .30 .75
28 Riku Hahl .40 1.00
29 Marko Palo .04 .10
30 Juha Pitkamaki .04 .10
31 Arto Tukio .20 .50
32 Tapio Sammalkangas .04 .10
33 Tomi Pettinen .04 .10
34 Jarkko Nikander .04 .10
35 Raimo Helminen .08 .20
36 Juha Hautamaa .04 .10
37 Sami Karjalainen .04 .10
38 Pasi Nurminen .75 2.00
39 Ossi Vaananen .30 .75
40 Marko Kauppinen .20 .50
41 Tom Koivisto .20 .50
42 Rami Alanko .04 .10
43 Petri Varis .20 .50
44 Jan Benda .08 .20
45 Jani Rita .40 1.00
46 Markus Kankaanpera .20 .50
47 Jarkko Glad .04 .10
48 Jyrki Valivaara .04 .10
49 Tuomas Pihlman ERC .04 .10
50 Jussi Pesonen .04 .10
51 Petr Ton .04 .10
52 Markus Korhonen .20 .50
53 Harri Aho .04 .10
54 Karri Kivi .08 .20
55 Mikko Haapakoski .04 .10
56 Jakko Niskavaara .08 .20
57 Niklas Hagman .40 1.00
58 Sakari Palsola .04 .10
59 Jari Laukkanen .04 .10
60 Petri Isotalus .20 .50
61 Jari Viuhkola .04 .10
62 Allan Measures .04 .10
63 Mika Laaksonen .04 .10
64 Marko Toivonen .04 .10
65 Matti Kaipainen .04 .10
66 Petri Latti .04 .10
67 Sami Torkki .04 .10
68 Jokke Hainanen .04 .10
69 Sami Lehtinen .20 .50
70 Veli-Pekka Laitinen .04 .10
71 Kaj Lindstrom .04 .10
72 Mika Niskanen .04 .10
73 Jani Keinanen .04 .10
74 Tommi Turunen .04 .10
75 Mikko Juutilainen .04 .10
76 Veli-Pekka Nutikka .08 .20
77 Mikko Jokela .20 .50
78 Martin Richter .04 .10
79 Pekka Tirkkonen .08 .20
80 Vladimir Machulda .04 .10
81 Ville Hamalainen .04 .10
82 Mika Skytta .04 .10
83 Ville Immonen .04 .10
84 Sami Kaartinen .04 .10
85 Tuukka Mantyla .20 .50
86 Miska Kangasniemi .08 .20
87 Janne Gronvall .08 .20
88 Jussi Tarvainen .08 .20
89 Janne Ojanen .04 .10
90 Jaakko Uhlback .04 .10
91 Johannes Alanen .04 .10
92 Jani Hassinen .04 .10
93 Fredrik Norrena .20 .50
94 Jouni Loponen .04 .10
95 Tommi Rajamaki .04 .10
96 Kimmo Eronen .04 .10
97 Kimmo Rintanen .04 .10
98 Tony Virta .04 .10
99 Jani Kiviharju .04 .10
100 Teemu Elomo .04 .10
101 Mikko Rautee .04 .10
102 Jim Hrivnak .20 .50
103 Pasi Peltonen .04 .10
104 Timo Willman .04 .10
105 Pauli Levokari .04 .10
106 Tuomo Kyha .04 .10
107 Janne Laitila .04 .10
108 Janne Makela .04 .10
109 Samu Wesslin .04 .10
110 Hannu Tala .04 .10
111 Vesa Toskala .40 1.00
112 Aki Berg .20 .50
113 Antti-Jussi Niemi .08 .20
114 Janne Niinimaa .20 .50
115 Ville Peltonen .30 .75
116 Olli Jokinen .40 1.00
117 Teemu Selanne 1.25 3.00
118 Marko Tuomainen .08 .20
119 Juha Lind .20 .50
120 Niko Kapanen .40 1.00
121 Checklist 1 .04 .10
122 Checklist 2 .04 .10
123 Checklist 3 .04 .10
124 Arto Laatikainen .20 .50
125 Tero Maatta .30 .50
126 Juha Gustafsson .04 .10
127 Toni Koivunen .04 .10
128 Teemu Virkkunen .04 .10
129 Valeri Krykov .04 .10
130 Frank Banham .20 .50
131 Semir Ben-Amor .04 .10
132 Jiri Burger .04 .10
133 Aki Tuominen .04 .10
134 Ray Giroux .08 .20
135 Mikko Kurvinen .04 .10
136 Patrik Hucko .04 .10
137 Jari Kauppila .04 .10
138 Tony Salmelainen .04 .10
139 Kimmo Kuhta .04 .10
140 Jaroslav Bednar .40 .50
141 Ari Vallin .04 .10
142 Sami Nuutinen .04 .10
143 Jani Virtanen .04 .10
144 Timo Ahmaoja .04 .10
145 Tomi Suoniemi .04 .10
146 Jari Kesti .04 .10
147 Tommi Santala .04 .10
148 Pavel Rosa .20 .50
149 Eero Somervuori .08 .20
150 Mika Pietila .04 .10
151 Ivan Majesky ERC .04 .10
152 Antti Bruun .04 .10
153 Matt Smith .08 .20
154 Jari-Pekka Pajula .04 .10
155 Kimmo Vaha-Ruohola .04 .10
156 Toni Dahlman .04 .10
157 Antti Hilden .04 .10
158 Timo Koskela .04 .10
159 Vesa Viitakoski .08 .20
160 Kari Haakana .04 .10
161 Pasi Saarinen .08 .20
162 Santeri Heiskanen .04 .10
163 Antti Tormanen .08 .20
164 Juha Virtanen .04 .10
165 Tuomo Ruutu ERC 4.00 10.00
166 Niko Mikkola .04 .10
167 Aigars Cipruss .04 .10
168 Mika Lehto .04 .10
169 Chris MacKenzie .08 .20
170 Pekka Poikolainen .04 .10
171 Riku Varjamo .04 .10
172 Markku Paukkunen .04 .10
173 Mika Paananen .04 .10
174 Juha-Pekka Hytonen .04 .10
175 Janne Hauhtonen .04 .10
176 Jouni Kulonen .04 .10
177 Antti Virtanen .04 .10
178 Kristian Taubert .04 .10
179 Mikko Lehtonen .20 .50
180 Lasse Kukkonen ERC .04 .10
181 Kimmo Koskenkorva .04 .10
182 Tuomo Harjula .04 .10
183 Juha Joenvaara .04 .10
184 Brett Lievers .04 .10
185 Miikka Rousu .04 .10
186 Bruce Racine .20 .50
187 Ismo Kuoppala .04 .10
188 Topi Lehtonen .04 .10
189 Toni Koivisto .04 .10
190 Jouni Vauhkonen .08 .20
191 Jimmy Provencher .04 .10
192 Pasi Saarela .04 .10
193 Pasi Kuivalainen .20 .50
194 Jussi-Antti Reimari .04 .10
195 Jan Latvala .04 .10
196 Roman Vopat .08 .20
197 Janne Sinkkonen .04 .10
198 Ales Kratoska .04 .10
200 Niklas Backstrom .04 .10
201 Oleg Romanov .04 .10
202 Riku Kallioniemi .04 .10
203 Petri Kokko .04 .10
204 Juha Pursiainen .04 .10
205 Joni Yli-Torkko .04 .10
206 Pasi Tuominen .04 .10
207 Ludek Krayzel .04 .10
208 Mika Kauppinen .08 .20
209 Jussi Markkanen .40 1.00
210 Alain Cote .08 .20
211 Pekka Saravo .04 .10
212 Niki Siren .04 .10
213 Timo Vertala .04 .10
214 Tero Lehtera .08 .20
216 Henrik Tallinder .20 .50
217 Martti Jarventie .30 .50
218 Marco Tuokko .04 .10
219 Joni Lius .04 .10
220 Jarkko Varvio .08 .20
222 Mikko Koivu ERC 6.00 15.00
223 Ari Vapola .04 .10
224 Curtis Sheptak .04 .10
225 Marcus Kristoffersson .40 1.00
226 Jari Korpisalo .04 .10
227 Gabriel Karlsson .20 .50
228 Sami Salonen .04 .10
229 Jarkko Vaananen .04 .10
230 Niklas Hede .04 .10
231 Ari Sulander .20 .50
232 Jere Karalahti .20 .50
233 Toni Lydman .20 .50
234 Petteri Nummelin .20 .50
235 Raimo Helminen .20 .50
236 Tomi Kallio .30 .50
237 Toni Sihvonen .04 .10
238 Jukka Hentunen .20 .50
239 Tony Virta .04 .10
240 Esa Tikkanen .20 .50
241 Checklist 1 .04 .10
242 Checklist 2 .04 .10
243 Checklist 3 .04 .10
244 Tom Draper .20 .50
245 Timo Willman .04 .10
246 Asko Rantanen .04 .10
247 Jukka Tiilikainen .04 .10
248 Mikael Jamsanen .04 .10
249 Kari Kalto .04 .10
250 Esa Pirnes .04 .10
251 Johan Davidsson .20 .50
252 Shayne Toporowski .20 .50
253 Sakari Lindfors .20 .50
254 Tomi Nyman .04 .10
255 Kari Rajala .04 .10
256 Martin Stepanek .04 .10
257 Veli-Pekka Kautonen .04 .10
258 Toni Makiaho .04 .10
259 Lasse Pirjeta .04 .10
260 Markku Hurme .04 .10
261 Erkki Rajamaki .04 .10
262 Jan Caloun .20 .50
263 Joonas Vihko .04 .10
264 Jan Lundell .04 .10
265 Dan Ratushny .08 .20
266 Darcy Werenka .08 .20
267 Timo Parssinen .30 .50
268 Tomas Vlasak .04 .10
269 Jyrki Louhi .04 .10
270 Pasi Maattanen .04 .10
271 Petr Kuchyna .04 .10
272 Jani Nikko .04 .10
273 Tommi Miettinen .30 .50
274 Jesse Welling .04 .10
275 Oliver Setzinger .04 .50
276 Jarno Peltonen .04 .10
277 Tony Salmelainen .04 .10
278 Kari Lehtonen ERC 8.00 20.00
279 Pauli Levokari .04 .10
280 Thomas Johansson .04 .10
281 Lee Sorochan .20 .50
282 Tomek Valtonen .04 .10
283 Jukka Hentunen .20 .50
284 Mikko Ruutu .20 .50
285 Timo Saarikoski .04 .10
286 Teemu Sainomaa .04 .10
287 Ari-Pekka Siekkinen .04 .10
288 Tomi Hirvonen .04 .10
289 Jarno Tiilikainen .04 .10
290 Radoslav Kropac .04 .10
291 Zdenek Sedlak .04 .10
292 Tuomo Jaaskelainen .04 .10
293 Antti Kangas .04 .10
294 Steve Shierreffs .04 .10
295 Pekka Kangasalusta .04 .10
296 Vjatsheslav Fandul .04 .10
297 Kimmo Salminen .04 .10
298 Sami Alalauri .04 .10
299 Andrei Potaitshuk .04 .10
300 Petri Vehanen .04 .10
301 Erik Hamalainen .04 .10
302 Tuomas Gronman .04 .10
303 Kimmo Lotvonen .04 .10
304 Janne Siivonen .04 .10
305 Marko Kivenmaki .04 .10
306 Zdenek Nedved .04 .10
307 Petri Pakaslahti .04 .10
308 Harri Sillgren .04 .10
309 Samu Isosalo .04 .10
310 Henri Laurila .04 .10
311 Jussi Salminen .04 .10
312 Kalle Koskinen .04 .10
313 Jarkko Ollikainen .04 .10
314 Toni Saarinen .04 .10
315 Teemu Riihijarvi .08 .20
316 Lasse Jamsen .04 .10
317 Jouko Myrra .04 .10
318 Pasi Hakkinen .04 .10
319 Juha Kuokkanen .04 .10
320 Roland Carlsson .04 .10
321 Harri Tikkanen .04 .10
322 Juri Kuznetsov .20 .50
323 Ville Kiiskinen .04 .10
324 Olli Sipilainen .04 .10
325 Tuomas Reijonen .04 .10
326 Joel Salonen .04 .10
327 Sami Ahlberg .04 .10
328 Sasu Hovi .04 .10
329 Janne Vourela .04 .10
330 Mikko Luoma .04 .10
331 Miro Laitinen .04 .10
332 Sami Venalainen .04 .10
333 Marko Ojanen .04 .10
334 Marko Makinen .04 .10
335 Aleksander Barkov .04 .10
336 Antero Niittymaki 1.25 3.00
337 Markus Seikola .04 .10
338 Ilkka Mikkola .04 .10
339 Mika Lehtinen .04 .10
340 Niko Kapanen .40 1.00
341 Ville Vahalahti .04 .10
342 Kalle Sahlstedt .20 .50
343 Kristian Antila .04 .10
344 Pasi Puistola .04 .10
345 Vesa Salo .04 .10
346 Veli-Pekka Hard .04 .10
347 Eric Perrin .04 .10
348 Tomas Kucharcik .04 .10
349 Markku Tahtinen .04 .10
350 Mikko Konttila .04 .10
351 Pasi Nurminen .75 2.00
352 Kimmo Timonen .20 .50
353 Jyrki Lumme .20 .50
354 Janne Laukkanen .20 .50
355 Kimmo Rintanen .20 .50
356 Saku Koivu .75 2.00
357 Jere Lehtinen .40 1.00
358 Sami Kapanen .40 1.00
359 Antti Aalto .20 .50
360 Mika Alatalo .20 .50
NNO Ari Ahonen MM 8.00 20.00
NNO Pasi Nurminen MM 10.00 25.00
NNO Saku Koivu MT 10.00 25.00

2000-01 Finnish Cardset Masquerade

These singles feature the masks of the top netminders of the SM-Liiga. They were inserted approximately 1:5 packs in series three only.

COMPLETE SET (9) 24.00 40.00
STATED ODDS 1:5 SERIES 3
1 Mika Pietila 2.00 5.00
2 Bruce Racine 4.00 10.00
3 Sami Lehtinen 2.00 5.00
4 Niklas Backstrom 2.00 5.00
5 Antero Niittymaki 6.00 15.00
6 Markus Korhonen 2.00 5.00
7 Jussi Markkanen 6.00 15.00
8 Tom Draper 4.00 10.00
9 Kristian Antila 2.00 5.00

2000-01 Finnish Cardset Master Blasters

This nine-card set honors the Finnish league's top snipers. The cards were inserted 1:5 packs in series one.

COMPLETE SET (9) 12.50 20.00
STATED ODDS 1:5 SERIES 1
1 Kai Nurminen 1.20 3.00
2 Jan Caloun 1.20 3.00
3 Petr Tenkrat 2.00 5.00
4 Jaroslav Bednar 2.00 5.00
5 Dale McTavish .80 2.00
6 Kalle Sahlstedt 1.20 3.00
7 Zdenek Nedved .80 2.00
8 Tomi Kallio 2.00 5.00
9 Timo Parssinen 2.00 5.00

2000-01 Finnish Cardset Next Generation

This set features the top newcomers to the Finnish Elite League. The cards were inserted at a rate of 1:5 packs in series two only.

COMPLETE SET (9) 30.00 30.00
STATED ODDS 1:5 SERIES 2
1 Mikko Koivu 8.00 10.00
2 Tuukka Mantyla 1.20 1.00
3 Tuomo Ruutu 3.00 8.00
4 Jani Rita 6.00 3.00
5 Ari Ahonen 8.00 5.00
6 Arto Tukio 1.20 1.00
7 Antti Miettinen 2.00 4.00
8 Markus Kankaanpera 1.20 1.00
9 Antero Niittymaki 4.00 5.00

2001-02 Finnish Cardset

This set features the top players of the Finnish SM-Liiga. The series was divided into two sets, with 180 cards in the first series, and 200 in the second. The set is noteworthy for containing early cards of first-rounders such as Mikko Koivu, Tuomo Ruutu and Hannu Toivonen. The autographs of Koivu and Ruutu, along with the American Dream card of Ville Nieminen, were random inserts in series 1 packs. The Niittymaki and Lehtonen autographs, along with the Kurri insert, were found in series 2 packs. There were 200 copies of each autograph, and 999 copies of the Nieminen and Kurri inserts.

COMPLETE SET (380) 35.00 70.00
1 Espoo Blues .04 .10
2 Mika Oksa .08 .20
3 Tero Maatta .20 .50
4 Jermu Pisto .08 .20
5 Niclas Hedberg .08 .20
6 Arto Laatikainen .20 .50
7 Valeri Krykov .08 .20
8 Teemu Virkkunen .08 .20
9 Teemu Siren .08 .20
10 Timo Hirvonen .08 .20
11 Mikael Jamsanen .08 .20
12 Kari Kalto .08 .20
13 HIFK Helsinki .04 .10
14 Sakari Lindfors .20 .50
15 Marek Zidlicky .40 1.00
16 Tuomas Eskelinen .08 .20
17 Aki Tuominen .08 .20
18 Mikko Kurvinen .08 .20
19 Hannes Hyvonen .20 .50
20 Kimmo Kuhta .08 .20
21 Toni Happola .08 .20
22 Pasi Nielikainen .08 .20
23 Mika Nieminen .20 .50
24 Toni Makiaho .08 .20
25 Jaroslav Bednar .20 .50
26 HPK Hameenlinna .04 .10
27 Kimmo Peltonen .08 .20
28 Teemu Aalto .08 .20
29 Eero Somervuori .08 .20
30 Riku Hahl .20 .50
31 Antti Miettinen .75 2.00
32 Tommi Santala .08 .20
33 Kasper Kenig .08 .20
34 Pasi Maattanen .08 .20
35 Ilves Tampere .04 .10
36 Mika Pietila .08 .20
37 Jani Nikko .08 .20
38 Antti Bruun .08 .20
39 Tomi Pettinen .08 .20
40 Matt Smith .08 .20
41 Oliver Setzinger .20 .50
42 Toni Dahlman .08 .20
43 Timo Koskela .08 .20
44 Kimmo Vaha-Ruohola .08 .20
45 Jarkko Nikander .08 .20
46 Jari-Pekka Pajula .08 .20
47 Antti Hilden .08 .20
48 Jokerit Helsinki .04 .10
49 Pasi Nurminen .60 1.50
50 Kari Haakana .20 .50
51 Rami Alanko .08 .20
52 Tomek Valtonen .08 .20
53 Teemu Sainomaa .08 .20
54 Antti Tormanen .08 .20
55 Timo Saarikoski .08 .20
56 Teemu Laine .20 .50
57 Mikko Ruutu .08 .20
58 Tuomo Ruutu 1.50 4.00
59 Niko Mikkola .08 .20
60 JYP Jyvaskala .04 .10
61 Mika Lehto .08 .20
62 Pekka Poikolainen .08 .20
63 Jarkko Glad .08 .20
64 Tuomo Jaaskelainen .08 .20
65 Juha-Pekka Hytonen .08 .20
66 Tuomas Pihlman .20 .50
67 Janne Hauhtonen .08 .20
68 Jouni Kulonen .08 .20
69 Tomi Hirvonen .08 .20
70 Antti Virtanen .08 .20
71 Oulun Karpat .04 .10
72 Antti Kangas .08 .20
73 Lasse Kukkonen .20 .50
74 Joni Pitkanen ERC .75 2.00
75 Harri Aho .08 .20
76 Kristian Taubert .08 .20
77 Mikko Lehtonen .20 .50
78 Kimmo Koskenkorva .08 .20
79 Jari Laukkanen .08 .20
80 Juha Joenvaara .08 .20
81 Brett Lievers .08 .20
82 Jari Viuhkola .08 .20
83 Andrei Potaitshuk .08 .20
84 Rauman Lukko .04 .10
85 Mika Laaksonen .08 .20
86 Topi Lehtonen .08 .20
87 Marko Toivonen .08 .20
88 Tuomas Gronman .08 .20
89 Petteri Lotila .08 .20
90 Toni Koivisto .08 .20
91 Sami Torkki .08 .20
92 Samu Isosalo .08 .20
93 Petri Latti .08 .20
94 Janne Siivonen .08 .20
95 Matti Kaipainen .08 .20
96 Lahden Pelicans .04 .10
97 Pasi Kuivalainen .20 .50
98 Mika Niskanen .08 .20
99 Jan Latvala .08 .20
100 Kaj Lindstrom .08 .20
101 Mikko Peltola .08 .20
102 Teemu Riihijarvi .08 .20
103 Jani Keinanen .08 .20
104 Lasse Jamsen .08 .20
105 Toni Saarinen .08 .20
106 Veli-Pekka Nutikka .08 .20
107 SaiPa Lappeenranta .04 .10
108 Harri Tikkanen .08 .20
109 Riku Kallioniemi .08 .20
110 Juri Kuznetsov .20 .50
111 Petri Kokko .08 .20
112 Mikko Jokela .20 .50
113 Ville Hamalainen .08 .20
114 Pasi Tuominen .08 .20
115 Pekka Tirkkonen .08 .20
116 Mika Kauppinen .08 .20
117 Vladimir Machulda .20 .50
118 Olli Sipilainen .08 .20
119 Joni Yli-Torkko .08 .20
120 Tappara Tampere .04 .10
121 Jussi Markkanen .40 1.00
122 Miska Kangasniemi .08 .20
123 Miikko Luoma .08 .20
124 Pekka Saravo .08 .20
125 Miro Laitinen .08 .20
126 Aleksander Barkov .08 .20
127 Jussi Tarvainen .08 .20
128 Marko Ojanen .08 .20
129 Johannes Alanen .08 .20
130 Timo Vertala .08 .20
131 Jaakko Uhlback .08 .20
132 Arto Kuki .08 .20
133 TPS Turku .04 .10
134 Antero Niittymaki .75 2.00
135 Tuomo Karjalainen .08 .20
136 Mika Lehtinen .08 .20
137 Henrik Tallinder .20 .50
138 Markus Seikola .08 .20
139 Kimmo Eronen .08 .20
140 Martti Jarventie .20 .50
141 Mikko Rautee .08 .20
142 Mikko Koivu 2.00 5.00
143 Marco Tuokko .08 .20
144 Michael Holmqvist .40 1.00
145 Ville Vahalahti .08 .20
146 Porin Assat .04 .10
147 Kristian Antila .08 .20
148 Pasi Peltonen .08 .20
149 Curtis Sheptak .08 .20
150 Sami Karjalainen .08 .20
151 Jari Korpisalo .08 .20
152 Mikko Konttila .08 .20
153 Juha Viinikainen .08 .20
154 Eric Perrin .08 .20
155 Markku Tahtinen .08 .20
156 Finnish National Team .04 .10
157 Pasi Nurminen .60 1.50
158 Miikka Kiprusoff .75 2.00
159 Jarmo Myllys .20 .50
160 Marko Kiprusoff .08 .20
161 Petteri Nummelin .20 .50
162 Kimmo Timonen .20 .50
163 Sami Salo .20 .50
164 Ossi Vaananen .20 .50
165 Aki Berg .20 .50
166 Antti-Jussi Niemi .08 .20
167 Janne Gronvall .08 .20
168 Raimo Helminen .08 .20
169 Antti Laaksonen .20 .50
170 Tomi Kallio .20 .50
171 Niko Kapanen .40 1.00
172 Sami Kapanen .40 1.00
173 Jukka Hentunen .20 .50
174 Timo Parssinen .20 .50
175 Juha Lind .20 .50
176 Toni Sihvonen .08 .20
177 Kimmo Rintanen .08 .20
178 Tony Virta .08 .20
179 Juha Ylonen .20 .50
180 Jarkko Ruutu .20 .50
181 Espoo Blues .04 .10
182 Jarmo Myllys .20 .50
183 Juha Gustafsson .08 .20
184 Matti Kuusisto .08 .20
185 Jani Virtanen .08 .20
186 Jiri Vykoukal .08 .20
187 Jan Caloun .20 .50
188 Markku Hurme .08 .20
189 Jiri Zelenka .08 .20
190 Tero Lehtera .08 .20
191 Janne Seva .08 .20
192 Teemu Elomo .08 .20
193 Filip Turek .08 .20
194 HIFK Helsinki .04 .10
195 Mikko Stromberg .08 .20
196 Antti-Pekka Lamberg .08 .20
197 Robert Kantor .08 .20
198 Jonas Junkka .08 .20
199 Mikko Ilkka .08 .20
200 Pauli Levokari .08 .20
201 Kari Rajala .08 .20
202 Joonas Vihko .08 .20
203 Carlo Grunn .08 .20
204 Jonni Vauhkonen .20 .50
205 Mika Kortelainen .08 .20
206 Kimmo Salminen .08 .20
207 Aigars Cipruss .08 .20
208 Ilkka Pikkarainen .08 .20
209 Andrej Podkonicky .20 .50
210 Kim Hirschovits .08 .20
211 HPK Hameenlinna .04 .10
212 Zdenek Smid .20 .50
213 Hannu Toivonen ERC 1.25 3.00
214 Joni Puurula .08 .20
215 Vladimir Sicak .08 .20
216 Janne Juppo .08 .20
217 Sebastian Sulku .08 .20
218 Markus Kankaanpera .20 .50
219 Marko Tuulola .08 .20
220 Tuukka Makela .40 1.00
221 Erkki Rajamaki .08 .20
222 Olli Sillanpaa .08 .20
223 Vladimir Vujtek .08 .20
224 Tomas Kucharcik .08 .20
225 Harri Suutarinen .08 .20
226 Jarkko Savijoki .08 .20
227 Zdenek Nedved .08 .20
228 Janne Lahti .08 .20
229 Ilves Tampere .04 .10
230 Bruce Racine .20 .50
231 Juha Pitkamaki .08 .20
232 Kari Takko .20 .50
233 Ville Koistinen .08 .20
234 Arto Tukio .20 .50
235 Teemu Jaaskelainen .08 .20
236 Ivan Majesky .20 .50
237 Roman Vopat .08 .20
238 Tommi Miettinen .20 .50
239 Riku Rahikainen .08 .20
240 Ville Hirvonen .08 .20
241 Tony Salmelainen .08 .20
242 Vesa Viitakoski .08 .20
243 Mika Nieminen .20 .50
244 Raimo Helminen .08 .20
245 Jokerit Helsinki .04 .10
246 Markus Helanen .08 .20
247 Jamie Ram .20 .50
248 Kari Lehtonen 4.00 10.00
249 Ari Vallin .08 .20
250 Pasi Saarinen .08 .20
251 Tuomas Luotonen .08 .20
252 Ilkka Mikkola .08 .20
253 Tom Koivisto .08 .20
254 Olli Malmivaara .08 .20
255 Rob Cowie .20 .50
256 Alex Brooks .08 .20
257 Sean Bergenheim ERC .60 1.50
258 Antti Aalto .20 .50
259 Ville Peltonen .20 .50
260 Petri Pakaslahti .08 .20
261 Petri Varis .20 .50
262 Jussi Pesonen .08 .20
263 Frank Banham .20 .50
264 Pavel Rosa .20 .50
265 JYP Jyvaskyla .04 .10
266 Tero Leinonen .08 .20
267 Jani-Matti Loikala .08 .20
268 Martin Cech .08 .20
269 Sami Siltavirta .08 .20
270 Jyri Marttinen .08 .20
271 Petri Virolainen .08 .20
272 Angel Nikolov .20 .50
273 Olli Ahonen .08 .20
274 Jari Jaaskelainen .08 .20
275 Harri Sillgren .08 .20
276 Petr Ton .08 .20
277 Tomas Chlubna .08 .20
278 Oulun Karpat .04 .10
279 Markus Korhonen .20 .50
280 Kimmo Lotvonen .08 .20
281 Mikko Myllykoski .08 .20
282 Pekka Saarenheimo .08 .20
283 Mika Pyorala .08 .20
284 Tuomo Harjula .08 .20
285 Harri Korpela .08 .20
286 Janne Pesonen .08 .20
287 Juha-Pekka Haataja .08 .20
288 Sakari Palsola .08 .20
289 Lasse Pirjeta .08 .20
290 Jussi Jokinen ERC 2.00 5.00
291 Rauman Lukko .04 .10
292 Petri Vehanen .08 .20
293 Jaakko Harikkala .08 .20
294 Mikko Purontakanen .08 .20
295 Ville Piekkola .20 .50
296 Janne Niskala .08 .20
297 Teemu Kesa .08 .20
298 Jaakko Hagelberg .08 .20
299 Jari Hyvarinen .08 .20
300 Mika Viinanen .08 .20
301 Joel Salonen .08 .20
302 Teemu Normio .08 .20
303 Hermani Vidman .08 .20
304 Aki Uusikartano .08 .20
305 Pasi Saarela .08 .20
306 Markus Jamsa .08 .20
307 Lahden Pelicans .04 .10
308 Mikko Ramo .08 .20
309 Kalle Koskinen .08 .20
310 Jussi-Antti Reimari .08 .20
311 Veli-Pekka Laitinen .08 .20
312 Henri Laurila .08 .20
313 Teemu Viherva .08 .20
314 Jussi Saarinen .08 .20
315 Olli Sinkkonen .08 .20
316 Jarkko Vaananen .08 .20
317 Jarkko Ollikainen .08 .20
318 Joonas Jaaskelainen .20 .50
319 Niki Siren .08 .20
320 Tommi Turunen .08 .20
321 Toni Koivunen .08 .20
322 SaiPa Lappeenranta .04 .10
323 Juha Kuokkanen .08 .20
324 Sami Lehtinen .20 .50
325 Tomas Duba .08 .20
326 Antti Hulkkonen .08 .20
327 Juha Pursiainen .08 .20
328 Jan Huokko .08 .20
329 Ville Immonen .08 .20
330 Mikko Kinnunen .08 .20
331 Mika Skytta .08 .20
332 Juuso Vakkilainen .08 .20
333 Jesse Welling .08 .20
334 Ville Koho .08 .20
335 Tappara Tampere .04 .10
336 Tom Draper .20 .50
337 Tuukka Mantyla .20 .50
338 Pasi Puistola .08 .20
339 Jyrki Valivaara .08 .20
340 Janne Gronvall .08 .20
341 Esa Pirnes .08 .20
342 Christian Sjogren .08 .20
343 Marko Makinen .08 .20
344 Sami Venalainen .08 .20
345 Janne Ojanen .08 .20
346 Tuomas Reijonen .08 .20
347 Jani Hassinen .08 .20
348 TPS Turku .04 .10
349 Fredrik Norrena .20 .50
350 Matti Tahkapaa .08 .20
351 Marko Kauppinen .20 .50
352 Pasi Petrilainen .08 .20
353 Pekka Kangasalusta .08 .20
354 Markku Paukkunen .08 .20
355 Chris Joseph .20 .50
356 Peter Schaefer .20 .50
357 Kai Nurminen .20 .50
358 Miika Elomo .20 .50
359 Janne Jokila .08 .20
360 Mikko Kankaanpera .08 .20
361 Tommi Hannus .08 .20
362 Mika Alatalo .20 .50
363 Rob Shearer .20 .50
364 Jani Kiviharju .08 .20
365 Porin Assat .04 .10
366 Tommi Satosaari .08 .20
367 Matti Jarvinen .08 .20
368 Mika Rontti .08 .20
369 Timo Willman .08 .20
370 Stanislav Jasecko .08 .20
371 Jukka-Pekka Laamanen .08 .20
372 Timo Ahmaoja .08 .20
373 Tapio Sammalkangas .08 .20
374 Jan Lipiansky .08 .20
375 Jani Vaananen .08 .20
376 Jarkko Immonen .08 .20
377 Sandy Moger .20 .50
378 Marko Palo .08 .20
379 Semir Ben-Amor .08 .20
380 Samu Wesslin .08 .20
NNO Mikko Koivu AU 30.00 80.00
NNO Kari Lehtonen AU 50.00 125.00
NNO Ville Nieminen DREAM 2.00 5.00
NNO Antero Niittymaki AU 12.50 30.00
NNO Tuomo Ruutu AU 25.00 60.00
NNO Jari Kurri HOF 8.00 20.00

2001-02 Finnish Cardset Adrenaline Rush

This set features some of the top young talent in Finland's SM-Liiga. The odds for these series 1 inserts is not confirmed at this time.

COMPLETE SET (6) 16.00 35.00
RANDOM INSERTS IN SERIES 1 PACKS
1 Kari Lehtonen 6.00 15.00
2 Tero Maatta 2.00 3.00

3 Tuukka Mantyla 2.00 3.00
4 Tony Salmelainen 2.00 3.00
5 Mikko Koivu 4.00 10.00
6 Tuomo Ruutu 4.00 10.00

2001-02 Finnish Cardset Dueling Aces

This set features a pair of arch-enemies from the Finnish SM-Liiga. The cards were random inserts in series 2 packs. The exact odds of insertion are not confirmed at this time.

COMPLETE SET (8) 6.00 15.00
RANDOM INSERTS IN SERIES 2 PACKS
1 Joonas Jaaskelainen .80 2.00
Vladimir Machulda
2 Ville Peltonen 1.20 3.00
Janne Ojanen
3 Jan Caloun .80 2.00
Kai Nurminen
4 Toni Happola .80 2.00
Mika Viinanen
5 Vladimir Vujtek .80 2.00
Raimo Helminen
6 Petr Ton .80 2.00
Pavel Rosa
7 Marek Zidlicky .80 2.00
Jiri Vykoukal
8 Tom Draper 1.20 3.00
Jari Korpisalo

2001-02 Finnish Cardset Haltmeisters

This set features the top Finnish-born goaltenders, many of whom were employed in North America during this season. The odds on these series 1 inserts are unconfirmed at this time.

COMPLETE SET (12) 30.00 75.00
RANDOM INSERTS IN SERIES 1 PACKS
1 Pasi Nurminen 4.00 10.00
2 Miikka Kiprusoff 6.00 15.00
3 Jani Hurme 4.00 10.00
4 Vesa Toskala 6.00 10.00
5 Mika Noronen 6.00 10.00
6 Jarmo Myllys 2.00 5.00
7 Ari Sulander 2.00 5.00
8 Ari Ahonen 6.00 10.00
9 Jussi Markkanen 4.00 10.00
10 Fredrik Norrena 2.00 5.00
11 Sakari Lindfors 2.00 5.00
12 Pasi Kuivalainen 2.00 5.00

2001-02 Finnish Cardset Salt Lake City

This set features 12 members of Finland's Olympic team. The cards were inserted in series 2 packs. The odds of insertion cannot be confirmed at this time.

COMPLETE SET (12) 20.00 30.00
RANDOM INSERTS IN SERIES 2 PACKS
1 Jani Hurme 2.00 3.00
2 Miikka Kiprusoff 2.00 8.00
3 Teppo Numminen .80 2.00
4 Kimmo Timonen .80 2.00
5 Janne Niinimaa .80 2.00
6 Jyrki Lumme .80 2.00
7 Teemu Selanne 6.00 10.00
8 Juha Ylonen .80 2.00
9 Jere Lehtinen 2.00 3.00
10 Tomi Kallio .80 2.00
11 Raimo Helminen .80 2.00
12 Sami Kapanen 2.00 3.00

2001 Finnish Cardset Teemu Selanne

NNO Teemu Selanne 8.00 20.00

2002-03 Finnish Cardset

This set was issued in two series and features the top players of the SM-Liiga.

COMPLETE SET (300) 30.00 80.00
1 Peter Ahola .08 .20
2 Mika Alatalo .08 .20
3 Kristian Antila .08 .20
4 Frank Banham .25 .60
5 Jaroslav Bednar .25 .60
6 Jan Benda .08 .20
7 Frantisek Bombic .08 .20
8 Jan Caloun .08 .20
9 Martin Cech .08 .20
10 Tomas Chlubna .08 .20
11 Toni Dahlman .08 .20
12 Johan Davidsson .08 .20
13 Tom Draper .25 .60
14 Tomas Duba .08 .20
15 Miika Elomo .25 .60
16 Mikko Eloranta .25 .60
17 Vjatsheslav Fandul .08 .20
18 Theo Fleury .40 1.00
19 Janne Gronvall .08 .20
20 Kari Haakana .08 .20
21 Niklas Hagman .25 .60
22 Riku Hahl .40 1.00
23 Jaakko Harikkala .25 .60
24 Jani Hassinen .08 .20
25 Timo Hirvonen .08 .20
26 Sasu Hovi .08 .20
27 Markku Hurme .08 .20
28 Ville Immonen .08 .20
29 Otakar Janecky .25 .60
30 Olli Jokinen .25 .60
31 Martti Jarventie .25 .60
32 Erik Kakko .08 .20
33 Tomi Kallio .25 .60
34 Kimmo Kapanen .08 .20
35 Niko Kapanen .25 .60
36 Sami Kapanen .25 .60
37 Jari Kauppila .08 .20
38 Markus Ketterer .25 .60
39 Marko Kiprusoff .08 .20
40 Miikka Kiprusoff .40 1.00
41 Tom Koivisto .25 .60
42 Markus Korhonen .25 .60
43 Jari Korpisalo .08 .20
44 Mika Kortelainen .08 .20
45 Kimmo Koskenkorva .08 .20
46 Valeri Krykov .08 .20
47 Kimmo Kuhta .08 .20
48 Pasi Kuivalainen .25 .60
49 Jarno Kultanen .08 .20
50 Mikko Kuparinen .08 .20
51 Jari Kurri .40 1.00
52 Jarmo Kuusisto .08 .20
53 Juri Kuznetsov .08 .20
54 Arto Laatikainen .25 .60
55 Veli-Pekka Laitinen .08 .20
56 Peter Larsson .08 .20
57 Mikko Lehtonen .08 .20
58 Pertti Lehtonen .08 .20
59 Jari Levonen .08 .20
60 Brett Lievers .08 .20
61 Juha Lind .08 .20
62 Sakari Lindfors .25 .60
63 Kimmo Lotvonen .08 .20
64 Jyrki Lumme .25 .60
65 Petri LÃ¤tti .08 .20
66 Vladimir Machulda .08 .20
67 Ivan Majesky .25 .60
68 Olli Malmivaara .08 .20
69 Jussi Markkanen .25 .60
70 Kari Martikainen .08 .20
71 Dale McTavish .08 .20
72 Sami Mettovaara .08 .20
73 Antti Miettinen 3.00 8.00
74 Niko Mikkola .08 .20
75 Cory Murphy .08 .20
76 Jason Muzzatti .25 .60
77 Tuukka Makela .25 .60
78 Marko MÃ¤kinen .25 .60
79 David Nemirovsky .08 .20
80 Ville Nieminen .25 .60
81 Antero Niittymaki .40 1.00
82 Angel Nikolov .08 .20
83 Janne Niskala .25 .60
84 Fredrik Norrena .25 .60
85 Petteri Nummelin .25 .60
86 Kai Nurminen .25 .60
87 Janne Ojanen .08 .20
88 Mika Oksa .08 .20
89 Petri Pakaslahti .08 .20
90 Mikko Peltola .08 .20
91 Kimmo Peltonen .08 .20
92 Pasi Peltonen .08 .20
93 Tomi Pettinen .08 .20
94 Tuomas Pihlman .40 1.00
95 Ilkka Pikkarainen .08 .20
96 Lasse Pirjeta .08 .20
97 Esa Pirnes .08 .20
98 Andrei Potaitshuk .08 .20
99 Pasi Puistola .08 .20
100 Joni Puurula .40 1.00
101 Timo Parssinen .08 .20
102 Bruce Racine .25 .60
103 Brian Rafalski .25 .60
104 Jamie Ram .25 .60
105 Martin Richter .25 .60
106 Juha Riihijarvi .08 .20
107 Teemu Riihijarvi .08 .20
108 Kimmo Rintanen .08 .20
109 Pavel Rosa .08 .20
110 Boris Rousson .25 .60
111 Christian Ruuttu .08 .20
112 Pasi Saarela .08 .20
113 Peter Schaefer .08 .20
114 Markus Seikola .08 .20
115 Teemu Selanne .75 2.00
116 Oliver Setzinger .25 .60
117 Vladimir Sicak .08 .20
118 Ari-Pekka Siekkinen .08 .20
119 Toni Sihvonen .08 .20
121 Ari Sulander .25 .60
122 Sebastian Sulku .08 .20
123 Mike Stapleton .08 .20
123 Kari Takko .25 .60
124 Jussi Tarvainen .08 .20
125 Esa Tikkanen .25 .60
126 Harri Tikkanen .08 .20
127 Petr Ton .08 .20
128 Vesa Toskala .25 .60
129 Arto Tukio .08 .20
130 Tommi Turunen .08 .20
131 Marko Tuulola .08 .20
132 Markku TÃ¤htinen .08 .20
133 Antti Tormanen .08 .20
134 Ville Vahalahti .08 .20
135 Ari Vallin .08 .20
136 Petri Varis .25 .60
137 Timo Vertala .08 .20
138 Joonas Vihko .08 .20
139 Mika Viinanen .08 .20
140 Vesa Viitakoski .08 .20
141 Tony Virta .08 .20
142 Tomas Vlasak .08 .20
143 Pavel Vostrak .08 .20
144 Vladimir Vujtek .08 .20
145 Jiri Vykoukal .08 .20
146 Marek Zidlicky .08 .20
147 Kari Lehtonen CL 2.50 6.00
148 Niklas Backstrom CL .08 .20
149 Petri Vehanen CL .08 .20
150 Tomas Duba CL .08 .20
151 Antti Aalto .25 .60
152 Teemu Aalto .08 .20
153 Ari Ahonen .75 2.00
154 Rami Alanko .08 .20
155 Drew Bannister .08 .20
156 Aleksander Barkov .08 .20
157 Aki Berg .25 .60
158 Sean Bergenheim .25 .60
159 Tom Bissett .25 .60
160 Niklas Backstrom .08 .20
161 Aigars Cipruss .08 .20
162 Parris Duffus .25 .60
163 Jason Elliott .25 .60
164 Teemu Elomo .08 .20
165 Jarkko Glad .08 .20
166 Carlo Grunn .08 .20
167 Tuomas Gronman .08 .20
168 Juha Gustafsson .08 .20
169 Timo Hakanen .08 .20
170 Quinn Hancock .08 .20
171 Markus Helanen .08 .20
172 Raimo Helminen .08 .20
173 Jukka Hentunen .08 .20
174 Michael Holmkvist .25 .60
175 Antti Hulkkonen .08 .20
176 Jani Hurme .40 1.00
177 Hannes Hyvonen .25 .60
178 Erik Hamalainen .08 .20
179 Toni Happola .08 .20
180 Juha Ikonen .08 .20
181 Jarkko Immonen .08 .20
182 Mikko Jokela .25 .60
183 Jussi Jokinen .40 1.00
184 Timo Jutila .08 .20
185 Lasse Jamsen .08 .20
186 Joonas Jaaskelainen .08 .20
187 Matti Kaipainen .08 .20
188 Robert Kantor .08 .20
189 Jere Karalahti .08 .20
190 Marko Kauppinen .08 .20
191 Mika Kauppinen .08 .20
192 Jani Keinanen .08 .20
193 Max Kenig .08 .20
194 Esa Keskinen .08 .20
195 Jani Kiviharju .08 .20
196 Toni Koivisto .08 .20
197 Mikko Koivu 2.00 5.00
198 Saku Koivu 1.25 3.00
199 Toni Koivunen .08 .20
200 Tomas Kucharcik .08 .20
201 Arto Kuki .08 .20
202 Lasse Kukkonen .08 .20
203 Juha Kuokkanen .08 .20
204 Janne Laakkonen .08 .20
205 Antii Laaksonen .25 .60
206 Jukka-Pekka Laamanen .08 .20
207 Scott Langkow .25 .60
208 Jan Latvala .08 .20
209 Janne Laukkanen .08 .20
210 Jari Laukkanen .08 .20
211 Tero Lehtera .25 .60
212 Jere Lehtinen .40 1.00
213 Mika Lehto .08 .20
214 Kari Lehtonen 5.00 12.00
215 Tero Leinonen .08 .20
216 Pauli Levokari .08 .20
217 Joni Lius .08 .20
218 Jouni Loponen .08 .20
219 Mikko Luoma .08 .20
220 Toni Lydman .08 .20
221 Jyri Marttinen .08 .20
222 Ilkka Mikkola .08 .20
223 Mikko Myllykoski .08 .20
224 Jere Myllyniemi .08 .20
225 Jarmo Myllys .25 .60
226 Toni Makiaho .08 .20
227 Tuuka Mantyla .08 .20
228 Tero Maatta .25 .60
229 Antti-Jussi Niemi .08 .20
230 Mika Nieminen .08 .20
231 Janne Niinimaa .25 .60
232 Jesse Niinimaki .40 1.00
233 Tuomas Nissinen .08 .20
234 Mika Noronen .40 1.00
235 Teppo Numminen .25 .60
236 Pasi Nurminen .25 .60
237 Michael Nylander .25 .60
238 Matti Naatanen .08 .20
239 Marko Ojanen .08 .20
240 Marko Palo .08 .20
241 Sakari Palsola .08 .20
242 Jan Pardavy .08 .20
243 Timo Peltomaa .08 .20
244 Ville Peltonen .08 .20
245 Eric Perrin .08 .20
246 Jussi Pesonen .08 .20
247 Pasi Petrilainen .08 .20
248 Juha Pitkamaki .08 .20
249 Joni Pitkanen 1.25 3.00
250 Toni Porkka .08 .20
251 Mika Pyorala .08 .20
252 Erkki Rajamaki .08 .20
253 Jani Rita .25 .60
254 Jarkko Ruutu .25 .60
255 Mikko Ruutu .40 1.00
256 Tuomo Ruutu 1.00 2.50
257 Mikko Ramo .08 .20
258 Timo Saarikoski .08 .20
259 Pasi Saarinen .08 .20
260 Kalle Sahlstedt .08 .20
261 Teemu Sainomaa .08 .20
262 Tony Salmelainen .08 .20
263 Sami Salo .25 .60
264 Timo Salonen .08 .20
265 Tommi Santala .08 .20
266 Peter Sarno .25 .60
267 Tommi Satosaari .08 .20
268 Steve Shirreffs .08 .20
269 Harri Sillgren .08 .20
270 Roman Simicek .08 .20
271 Eero Somervuori .25 .60
272 Dave Stathos .08 .20
273 Mika Stromberg .25 .60
274 Raimo Summanen .25 .60
275 Henrik Tallinder .25 .60
276 Petr Tenkrat .25 .60
277 Tim Thomas .25 .60
278 Kimmo Timonen .08 .20
279 Pekka Tirkkonen .08 .20
280 Hannu Toivonen 1.25 3.00
281 Sami Torkki .08 .20
282 Marco Tuokko .08 .20
283 Marko Tuomainen .08 .20
284 Aki Uusikartano .08 .20
285 Lubomir Vaic .08 .20
286 Tomek Valtonen .08 .20
287 Petri Vehanen .08 .20
288 Samu Wesslin .08 .20
289 Hannu Virta .08 .20
290 Antii Virtanen .08 .20
291 Jari Viuhkola .08 .20
292 Roman Vopat .08 .20
293 Julkka Voutilainen .08 .20
294 Jyrki Valivaara .08 .20
295 Ossi Vaananen .25 .60
296 Juha Ylonen .25 .60
297 Dave Stathos .08 .20
298 Scott Langkow .25 .60
299 Tero Leinonen .08 .20
300 Mika Lehto .08 .20

2002-03 Finnish Cardset Bound for Glory

Random inserts in series two packs. Insertion odds unknown.

COMPLETE SET (10) 12.00 30.00
1 Sean Bergenheim .75 2.00
2 Jussi Jokinen 1.50 4.00
3 Mikko Koivu 3.00 8.00
4 Kari Lehtonen 4.00 10.00
5 Jesse Niinimaki .40 1.00
6 Joni Pitkanen 1.25 3.00
7 Tuomo Ruutu 2.00 5.00
8 Oliver Setzinger .40 1.00
9 Jussi Timonen .75 2.00
10 Hannu Toivonen 2.00 5.00

2002-03 Finnish Cardset Dynamic Duos

Randomly inserted in series 2 packs. Insertion ratios unknown.

COMPLETE SET (10) 15.00 40.00
1 Saku Koivu 4.00 10.00
Mikko Koivu
2 Pasi Nurminen 4.00 10.00
Kari Lehtonen
3 Sami Kapanen 2.00 5.00
Tuomo Ruutu
4 Janne Niinimaa 1.25 3.00
Joni Pitkanen
5 Olli Jokinen 1.25 3.00
Jukka Voutilainen
6 Ville Nieminen 1.25 3.00
Tuukka Mantyla
7 Tomi Kallio 1.25 3.00
Tuomas Pihlman
8 Jani Hurme 1.25 3.00
Tomas Duba
9 Niko Kapanen 2.00 5.00
Antti Miettinen
10 Teemu Selanne 4.00 10.00
Sean Bergenheim

2002-03 Finnish Cardset Kari Lehtonen Honors

Random inserts in series 2 packs. Odds unconfirmed, but believed to be 1:64.

COMPLETE SET (3) 10.00 25.00
1 Kari Lehtonen 4.00 10.00
U-18 top goalie
2 Kari Lehtonen 4.00 10.00
U-18 All-Stars
3 Kari Lehtonen 4.00 10.00
(U-20 top goalie

2002-03 Finnish Cardset Kari Lehtonen Trophies

Random inserts in series 1 packs. Odds were 1:64.

COMPLETE SET (3) 10.00 25.00
1 Kari Lehtonen 4.00 10.00
2 Kari Lehtonen 4.00 10.00
3 Kari Lehtonen 4.00 10.00

2002-03 Finnish Cardset Signatures

STATED ODDS 1:128 SERIES 1
STATED PRINT RUN 120 SER.#'d SETS
1 Sean Bergenheim 10.00 25.00
2 Jussi Jokinen 15.00 40.00
3 Mikko Koivu 20.00 50.00
4 Kari Lehtonen 75.00 200.00
5 Jesse Niinimaki 10.00 25.00
6 Joni Pitkanen 20.00 50.00
7 Tuomo Ruutu 25.00 60.00
8 Oliver Setzinger 10.00 25.00
9 Jussi Timonen 10.00 25.00
10 Hannu Toivonen 15.00 40.00

2002-03 Finnish Cardset Solid Gold

COMPLETE SET (6) 15.00
STATED ODDS 1:16 SERIES 1
1 Pasi Nurminen 2.00
2 Janne Niinimaa 2.00
3 Sami Salo 2.00
4 Sami Kapanen 2.00
5 Saku Koivu 5.00
6 Teemu Selanne 5.00

2002-03 Finnish Cardset Solid Gold Six-Pack

Randomly inserted in series 2 packs. Insertion ratios unknown.

COMPLETE SET (6) 8.00
1 Jussi Markkanen 3.00
2 Toni Lydman 1.00
3 Ossi Vaananen 1.00
4 Niklas Hagman 1.00
5 Olli Jokinen 3.00
6 Niko Kapanen 3.00

2003-04 Finnish Cardset

COMPLETE SET (182) 20.00 40.00
1 Jere Myllyniemi .20 .50
2 Sami Heinonen .20 .50
3 Sebastien Sulku .08 .20
4 Tero Maatta .08 .20
5 Rami Alanko .08 .20
6 Arto Laatikainen .08 .20
7 Jan Caloun .08 .20
8 Markku Hurme .08 .20
9 Jukka Tiilikainen .08 .20
10 Ladislav Kohn .08 .20
11 Miika Elomo .08 .20
12 Bruce Gardiner .20 .50
13 Marko Tuomainen .08 .20
14 Teemu Elomo .08 .20
15 Dave Stathos .30 .75
16 Ladislav Benysek .08 .20
17 Jere Karalahti .08 .20
18 Jarno Kultanen .08 .20
19 Toni Soderholm .08 .20
20 Pasi Saarinen .08 .20
21 Kim Hirschovits .08 .20
22 Kimmo Kuhta .08 .20
23 Joonas Vihko .08 .20
24 Toni Happola .08 .20
25 Carlo Grunn .08 .20
26 Timo Parssinen .20 .50
27 Brett Harkins .20 .50
28 Martin Spanhel .08 .20
29 Joni Puurula .20 .50
30 Rob Tallas .20 .50
31 Vladimir Sicak .08 .20
32 Aki Heino .08 .20
33 Tomas Eskeleinen .08 .20
34 Marko Tuulola .08 .20
35 Teemu Aalto .08 .20
36 Jyrki Louhi .08 .20
37 Tony Virta .08 .20
38 Vladimir Vujtek .08 .20
39 Tomas Kucharcik .08 .20
40 Janne Laakkonen .08 .20
41 Janne Lahti .08 .20
42 Anders Burstrom .08 .20
43 Juha Pitkamaki .20 .50
44 Tuomas Nissinen .20 .50
45 Cory Murphy .08 .20
46 Ismo Siren .08 .20
47 Martin Hlavacka .08 .20
48 Jukka-Pekka Laamanen .08 .20
49 Jesse Niinimaki .30 .75
50 Ville Snellman .08 .20
51 Toni Dahlman .08 .20
52 Erkki Rajamaki .08 .20
53 Marek Vorel .08 .20
54 Mikko Suvanto .08 .20
55 Vesa Viitakoski .08 .20
56 Raimo Helminen .08 .20
57 Markus Helanen .20 .50
58 Pasi Hakkinen .20 .50
59 Sami Helenius .20 .50
60 Jan Latvala .08 .20
61 Martti Jarventie .20 .50
62 Arto Tukio .08 .20
63 Tomek Valtonen .08 .20
64 Petri Pakaslahti .08 .20
65 Jussi Pesonen .08 .20
66 Timo Vertala .08 .20
67 Tommi Turunen .08 .20
68 Glen Metropolit .30 .75
69 Marko Jantunen .08 .20
70 Teemu Laine .08 .20
71 Tero Leinonen .20 .50
72 Tommi Nikkila .20 .50
73 Tuomo Kortelainen .08 .20
74 Tommi Kovanen .08 .20
75 Jari Korhonen .08 .20
76 Jyri Marttinen .08 .20
77 Ilari Filppula .08 .20
78 Tuomo Jaaskelainen .08 .20
79 Alexandre Tremblay .08 .20
80 Jari Jaaskelainen .08 .20
81 Jarkko Immonen .08 .20
82 Jaakko Uhlback .08 .20
83 Antti Virtanen .08 .20
84 P.C. Drouin .20 .50
85 Niklas Backstrom .30 .75
86 Ari Vallin .08 .20
87 Ilkka Mikkola .08 .20
88 Martin Stepanek .08 .20
89 Mikko Lehtonen .08 .20
90 Kimmo Lotvonen .08 .20
91 Mikko Myllykoski .08 .20
92 Jussi Jokinen .08 .20
93 Lasse Jamsen .08 .20
94 Mika Pyorala .08 .20
95 Janne Pesonen .08 .20
96 Brett Lievers .08 .20
97 Jari Viuhkola .08 .20
98 Sakari Palsola .08 .20
99 Antti Jokela .20 .50
100 Petri Vehanen .20 .50
101 Jaakko Harikkala .08 .20
102 Toni Porkka .08 .20
103 Janne Niskala .08 .20
104 Erik Hamalainen .08 .20
105 Mikko Luovi .08 .20
106 Mika Viinanen .08 .20
107 Toni Koivisto .08 .20
108 Sami Torkki .08 .20
109 Joe Murphy .20 .50
110 Markku Tahtinen .08 .20
111 Quinn Hancock .20 .50
112 Pasi Saarela .08 .20
113 Mikko Ramo .08 .20
114 Martin Cech .08 .20
115 Tero Paappanen .08 .20
116 Santeri Heiskanen .08 .20
117 Jermu Pisto .08 .20
118 Radek Philipp .08 .20
119 Tommi Hannus .08 .20
120 Daniel Widing .08 .20
121 Jari Kauppila .08 .20
122 Ville Hirvonen .08 .20
123 Toni Saarinen .08 .20
124 Toni Makiaho .08 .20
125 Shayne Toporowski .20 .50
126 Oliver Setzinger .20 .50
127 Juha Kuokkanen .08 .20
128 Jarmo Myllys .20 .50
129 Jussi Pekkala .08 .20
130 Petri Kokko .08 .20
131 Antti Bruun .08 .20
132 Sami Kaartinen .08 .20
133 Ville Immonen .08 .20
134 Kalle Kerman .08 .20
135 Mika Kauppinen .08 .20
136 Vladimir Machulda .08 .20
137 Pasi Nielikainen .08 .20
138 Petr Sachl .08 .20
139 Aki Uusikartano .08 .20
140 Timo Hirvonen .08 .20
141 Sasu Hovi .20 .50
142 Mika Lehto .20 .50
143 Pekka Saravo .08 .20
144 Pasi Puistola .08 .20
145 Pasi Petrilainen .08 .20
146 Miska Kangasniemi .08 .20
147 Janne Ojanen .08 .20
148 Alexander Barkov .08 .20
149 Petri Varis .08 .20
150 Marko Ojanen .08 .20
151 Marko Makinen .08 .20
152 Sami Venalainen .08 .20
153 Stefan Ohman .08 .20
154 Arto Kuki .08 .20
155 Teemu Lassila .20 .50
156 Tuomo Karjalainen .20 .50
157 Kimmo Peltonen .08 .20
158 Marko Kauppinen .08 .20
159 David Schneider .08 .20
160 Jiri Vykoukal .08 .20
161 Antti Hulkkonen .08 .20
162 Mikko Koivu 1.25 3.00
163 Marko Tuokko .08 .20
164 Antti Aalto .08 .20
165 Kai Nurminen .08 .20
166 Ville Vahalahti .08 .20
167 Mikko Eloranta .08 .20
168 Niko Mikkola .08 .20
169 Scott Langkow .30 .75
170 Steve Shierreffs .20 .50
171 Pasi Peltonen .08 .20
172 Oleg Sorokin .08 .20
173 Jarkko Glad .08 .20
174 Samu Wesslin .08 .20
175 Vyacheslav Fandul .08 .20
176 Jari Korpisalo .08 .20
177 Pasi Tuominen .08 .20
178 Marko Kivenmaki .08 .20
179 Tomi Pollanen .08 .20
180 Timo Salonen .08 .20
181 Juha Kiilholma .08 .20
182 Martin Bergeron .20 .50

2003-04 Finnish Cardset D-Day

Featuring Finnish prospects drafted highly by the NHL, these cards were inserted 1:8 packs.

COMPLETE SET (16) 15.00 40.00
DD1 Sean Bergenheim .75 2.00
DD2 Mikael Holmqvist .75 2.00
DD3 Lasse Kukkonen .75 2.00
DD4 Kari Lehtonen 5.00 12.00
DD5 Mikko Luoma .40 1.00
DD6 Antti Miettinen .75 2.00
DD7 Eric Perrin 1.25 3.00
DD8 Tuomas Pihlman .75 2.00
DD9 Ilkka Pikkarainen .40 1.00
DD10 Esa Pirnes .40 1.00
DD11 Joni Pitkanen 1.25 3.00
DD12 Tuomo Ruutu 3.00 8.00
DD13 Tomi Santala .40 1.00
DD14 Eero Somervuori .40 1.00
DD15 Hannu Toivonen 3.00 8.00
DD16 Marek Zidlicky 1.25 3.00

2003-04 Finnish Cardset Globetrotters

These cards were inserted 1:16.

COMPLETE SET (9) 6.00 15.00
GR1 Toni Dahlman .75 2.00
GR2 Mikko Eloranta .75 2.00
GR3 Sami Helenius .75 2.00
GR4 Marko Jantunen .75 2.00
GR5 Jere Karalahti .75 2.00
GR6 Martin Stepanek .75 2.00
GR7 Petri Varis .75 2.00
GR8 Tony Virta .75 2.00
GR9 Vladimir Vujtek .75 2.00

2003-04 Finnish Cardset Vintage 1983

Featuring three top prospects born in 1983, these cards were inserted 1:32.

COMPLETE SET (3) 10.00 25.00
V1 Mikko Koivu 6.00 15.00
V2 Joni Pitkanen 2.00 5.00
V3 Tuomo Ruutu 4.00 10.00

2004-05 Finnish Cardset

Includes cards from a 200-card main set plus a 117-card update series.

COMPLETE SET (317) 30.00 60.00
1 Jere Myllyniemi .20 .50
2 Mika Oksa .20 .50
3 Kari Haakana .08 .20
4 Arto Laatikainen .08 .20
5 Mika Lehtinen .08 .20
6 Landon Wilson .20 .50
7 Donald MacLean .20 .50
8 Krystofer Kolanos .20 .50
9 Joni Toykkala .08 .20
10 Olli Ahonen .08 .20
11 Ladislav Kohn .08 .20
12 Lauri Tukonen ERC 1.25 3.00
13 Teemu Elomo .08 .20
14 Dave Stathos .20 .50
15 Marek Zidlicky .20 .50
16 Jere Karalahti .08 .20
17 Jarno Kultanen .08 .20
18 Toni Soderholm .08 .20
19 Pasi Saarinen .08 .20
20 Kim Hirschovits .08 .20
21 Kimmo Kuhta .08 .20
22 Joonas Vihko .08 .20
23 Jarkko Ruutu .20 .50
24 Timo Parssinen .08 .20
25 Arttu Luttinen .08 .20
26 Lennart Petrell .08 .20
27 Brett Harkins .20 .50
28 Eetu Holma .08 .20
29 Roman Vopat .08 .20
30 Miika Wiikman .20 .50
31 Vladimir Sicak .20 .50
32 Tuomas Eskelinen .08 .20
33 Mikko Jokela .08 .20
34 Veli-Pekka Laitinen .08 .20
35 Tuukka Makela .08 .20
36 Jyrki Louhi .08 .20
37 Jani Hassinen .08 .20
38 Hannu Vaisanen .08 .20
39 Riku Hahl .20 .50
40 Jani Keinanen .08 .20
41 Janne Laakkonen .08 .20
42 Jani Rita .20 .50
43 Jukka Voutilainen .08 .20
44 Toni Makiaho .08 .20
45 Oliver Setzinger .20 .50
46 Juha Pitkamaki .08 .20
47 Tuukka Rask ERC 2.00 5.00
48 Ville Koistinen .08 .20
49 Cory Murphy .08 .20
50 Sami Helenius .20 .50
51 Ismo Kuoppala .08 .20
52 Jesse Niinimaki .20 .50
53 Marko Luomala .08 .20
54 Timo Peltomaa .08 .20
55 Ville Leino .08 .20
56 Steve Kariya .40 1.00
57 Patrik Stefan .20 .50
58 Jussi Pesonen .08 .20
59 Tommi Turunen .08 .20
60 Raimo Helminen .08 .20
61 Simo Vidgren .08 .20
62 Pasi Hakkinen .20 .50
63 Tim Thomas .40 1.00
64 Kevin Kantee .08 .20
65 Kari Martikainen .08 .20
66 Jan Latvala .08 .20
67 Sami Lepisto .08 .20
68 Martti Jarventie .08 .20
69 Marko Jantunen .08 .20
70 Tomek Valtonen .08 .20
71 Toni Dahlman .08 .20
72 Petri Pakaslahti .08 .20
73 Petri Varis .08 .20
74 Juha Lind .08 .20
75 Timo Vertala .08 .20
76 Quinn Hancock .08 .20
77 Glen Metropolit .20 .50
78 Valtteri Filppula ERC .40 1.00
79 Tommi Nikkila .20 .50
80 Sinuhe Wallinheimo .20 .50
81 Tommi Kovanen .08 .20
82 Duvie Westcott .20 .50
83 Jari Korhonen .08 .20
84 Ilari Filppula .08 .20
85 Arsi Piispanen .08 .20
86 Steve Martins .20 .50
87 Jarkko Immonen .20 .50
88 Janne Hauhtonen .08 .20
89 Jaakko Uhlback .08 .20
90 Antti Virtanen .08 .20
91 Niklas Backstrom .40 1.00
92 Oskari Korpikari .08 .20
93 Lasse Kukkonen .20 .50
94 Ari Vallin .08 .20
95 Mikko Lehtonen .20 .50
96 Janne Niinimaa .08 .20
97 Jussi Jokinen .40 1.00
98 Viktor Ujcik .08 .20
99 Pekka Saarenheimo .08 .20
100 Mika Pyorala .08 .20
101 Janne Pesonen .08 .20
102 Jari Viuhkola .08 .20
103 Toni Sihvonen .08 .20
104 Sakari Palsola .08 .20
105 Petr Tenkrat .08 .20
106 Eero Somervuori .08 .20
107 Michael Nylander .20 .50
108 Dwayne Roloson .75 2.00
109 Petri Vehanen .08 .20
110 Toni Porkka .08 .20
111 Tomi Pettinen .08 .20

112 Janne Niskala .08 .20
113 Otto Honkaheimo .08 .20
114 Erik Hamalainen .08 .20
115 Steve Larouche .20 .50
116 Esa Pirnes .08 .20
117 Ville Snellman .08 .20
118 Shayne Toporowski .08 .20
119 Martin Bartek .08 .20
120 Toni Koivisto .08 .20
121 Sami Torkki .08 .20
122 Markku Tahtinen .08 .20
123 Pasi Saarela .08 .20
124 Pasi Nurminen .20 .50
125 Santeri Heiskanen .08 .20
126 Topi Lehtonen .08 .20
127 Erik Kakko .08 .20
128 Daniel Widing .08 .20
129 Sami Salonen .08 .20
130 Lasse Jamsen .08 .20
131 Ville Hirvonen .08 .20
132 Toni Saarinen .08 .20
133 Jesse Saarinen .08 .20
134 Jesse Welling .08 .20
135 Toni Koivunen .08 .20
136 Jarmo Myllys .20 .50
137 Jussi Pekkala .08 .20
138 Jussi Timonen .08 .20
139 Olli Malmivaara .08 .20
140 Petri Kokko .08 .20
141 Justin D. Forrest .08 .20
142 Eetu Qvist .08 .20
143 Kalle Kerman .08 .20
144 Mika Kauppinen .08 .20
145 Petr Sachl .08 .20
146 Petteri Nokelainen ERC 1.25 3.00
147 Timo Hirvonen .08 .20
148 Frank Banham .20 .50
149 Ville Viitaluoma .08 .20
150 Mika Lehto .20 .50
151 Anssi Salmela .08 .20
152 Pekka Saravo .08 .20
153 Juha Gustafsson .08 .20
154 Pasi Puistola .08 .20
155 Robert Kantor .08 .20
156 Mikko Myllykoski .08 .20
157 Janne Ojanen .08 .20
158 Johannes Alanen .08 .20
159 Mika Viinanen .08 .20
160 Marko Ojanen .08 .20
161 Petri Kontiola .08 .20
162 Ville Nieminen .20 .50
163 Sami Venalainen .08 .20
164 Stefan Ohman .08 .20
165 Tomas Chlubna .08 .20
166 Teemu Laine .08 .20
167 Teemu Lassila .20 .50
168 Tuomo Karjalainen .08 .20
169 Marko Kiprusoff .08 .20
170 Kimmo Eronen .08 .20
171 Markus Seikola .08 .20
172 David Schneider .08 .20
173 Jiri Vykoukal .08 .20
174 Antti Hulkkonen .08 .20
175 Marco Tuokko .08 .20
176 Antti Aalto .08 .20
177 Joni Lius .08 .20
178 Kai Nurminen .08 .20
179 Ville Vahalahti .08 .20
180 Lauri Korpikoski ERC 1.25 3.00
181 Mika Alatalo .08 .20
182 Jari Kauppila .08 .20
183 Arttu Virtanen .08 .20
184 Tuomas Nissinen .08 .20
185 Scott Langkow .20 .50
186 Pasi Peltonen .08 .20
187 Olegs Sorokins .08 .20
188 Pauli Levokari .08 .20
189 Greg Classen .20 .50
190 Samu Wesslin .08 .20
191 Mika Niemi .08 .20
192 Jari Korpisalo .08 .20
193 Jesse Joensuu .08 .20
194 Pasi Tuominen .08 .20
195 Marko Kivenmaki .08 .20
196 Teemu Virkkunen .08 .20
197 Pasi Nielikainen .08 .20
198 Jason Williams .20 .50
199 Aki Uusikartano .08 .20
200 Juha Kiilholma .08 .20
201 Janne Jalasvaara .08 .20
202 Tommi Pelkonen .08 .20
203 Tero Maatta .08 .20
204 Antti Pihlstrom .08 .20
205 Miika Elomo .08 .20
206 Jarkko Almmonen .08 .20
207 Mike Ribeiro .20 .50
208 Matti Naatanen .08 .20
209 Jani Nieminen .08 .20
210 Tomas Vokoun .75 2.00
211 Mikko Turunen .08 .20
212 Mikko Kurvinen .08 .20
213 Hannu Pikkarainen .08 .20
214 Lasse Pirjeta .08 .20
215 Juha Fagerstedt .08 .20
216 Jermu PorthÃ¨n .08 .20
217 Mikko Laine .08 .20
218 Mika Noronen .20 .50
219 Jarno Virkki .08 .20
220 Tuomas Immonen .08 .20
221 Jukka-Pekka Laamanen .08 .20
222 Josh Holden .08 .20
223 Petteri Virtanen .08 .20
224 Joni Lappalainen .08 .20
225 Joni Lindlof .08 .20
226 Juha-Pekka Loikas .08 .20
227 Janne Lahti .08 .20
228 Juuso Riksman .08 .20
229 Teemu Jaaskelainen .08 .20
230 Henri Laurila .08 .20
231 Ossi Pellinen .08 .20
232 Antti Miettinen .40 1.00
233 Hannes Hyvonen .08 .20
234 Jukka Tiilikainen .08 .20
235 Tommi Jaminki .08 .20
236 Mikko Suvanto .08 .20
237 Samuli Jalkanen .08 .20
238 Brian Campbell .20 .50
239 Mikko Kalteva .08 .20
240 Markus Kankaanpera .08 .20
241 Tero Konttinen .08 .20
242 Ossi Vaananen .08 .20
243 Tomi Maki .08 .20
244 Arto Koivisto .08 .20
245 Arto Kuki .08 .20
246 Roni Andersson .08 .20
247 Teemu Kuusisto .08 .20
248 Petri Virolainen .08 .20
249 Ilkka Vaarasuo .08 .20
250 Carlo GrÃ¼nn .08 .20
251 Juha-Pekka Hytonen .08 .20
252 Jari Jaaskelainen .08 .20
253 Ossi Louhivaara .08 .20
254 Tuomas Mikkonen .08 .20
255 Eero Hyvarinen .08 .20
256 Jody Shelley .40 1.00
257 Pekka Rinne .40 1.00
258 Ilkka Mikkola .08 .20
259 Topi Jaakola .08 .20
260 Kimmo Lotvonen .08 .20
261 Josef Boumedienne .08 .20
262 Juha-Pekka Haataja .08 .20
263 Antti Aarnio .08 .20
264 Mikael Vuorio .08 .20
265 Jaakko Harikkala .08 .20
266 Antti Bruun .08 .20
267 Ilkka Saarela .08 .20
268 Jarkko Kauvosaari .08 .20
269 Teemu Normio .08 .20
270 Janne Siivonen .08 .20
271 Juhamatti Yli-Junnila .08 .20
272 Joni Yli-Torkko .08 .20
273 Jaakko Suomalainen .08 .20
274 Karri Ramo .08 .20
275 Markus Helanen .08 .20
276 Olli Korkeavuori .08 .20
277 Antti-Pekka Lamberg .08 .20
278 Mikko Niinikoski .08 .20
279 Petri Koskinen .08 .20
280 Tommi Hannus .08 .20
281 Tuomas Santavuori .08 .20
282 Juha Kuokkanen .08 .20
283 Thomas Innerwinkler .08 .20
284 Harri Tikkanen .08 .20
285 Matti Hana .08 .20
286 Ossi-Petteri Gronholm .08 .20
287 Mike Gabinet .08 .20
288 Kalle Kaijomaa .08 .20
289 Ville Koho .08 .20
290 Mika Skytta .08 .20
291 Tuomas Vanttinen .08 .20
292 Andrew Raycroft .60 1.50
293 Sasu Hovi .08 .20
294 Mikko Pukka .08 .20
295 Kimmo Koskenkorva .08 .20
296 Teemu Nurmi .08 .20
297 Robert Tomik .08 .20
298 Jarkko Pyymaki .08 .20
299 Marko Makinen .08 .20
300 Timo Vertala .08 .20
301 Juho Santanen .08 .20
302 Simon Backman .08 .20
303 Markku Paukkunen .08 .20
304 Craig Rivet .08 .20
305 Tomi Sykko .08 .20
306 Saku Koivu .75 2.00
307 Matias Metsaranta .08 .20
308 Markus Ojala .08 .20
309 Tyler Bouck .20 .50
310 Matti Aho .08 .20
311 Marko Toivonen .08 .20
312 Mika Rontti .08 .20
313 Atte Pentikainen .08 .20
314 Aki Heino .08 .20
315 Kristian Kuusela .08 .20
316 Matti Kuparinen .08 .20
317 Juha-Pekka Ketola .08 .20

2004-05 Finnish Cardset Parallel

2X to 5X BASE CARD VALUE

2004-05 Finnish Cardset Saku Koivu Golden Signatures

Random inserts in series II packs.
COMPLETE SET (3) 10.00 25.00
1 Saku Koivu 4.00 10.00
2 Saku Koivu 4.00 10.00
3 Saku Koivu 4.00 10.00

2004-05 Finnish Cardset Signatures

Random inserts in series II packs. Inserted approximately one per box.
1 Joni Toykkala 8.00 20.00
2 Ladislav Kohn 8.00 20.00
3 Lauri Tukonen 12.00 30.00
4 Marek Zidlicky 12.00 30.00
5 Jere Karalahti 8.00 20.00
6 Jarno Kultanen 8.00 20.00
7 Brett Harkins 8.00 20.00
8 Vladimir Sicak 8.00 20.00
9 Tuomas Eskelinen 8.00 20.00
10 Riku Hahl 8.00 20.00
11 Jani Rita 8.00 20.00
12 Tuukka Rask 25.00 60.00
13 Jussi Pesonen 8.00 20.00
14 Simo Vidgren 8.00 20.00
15 Toni Dahlman 8.00 20.00
16 Valtteri Filppula 12.00 30.00
17 Duvie Westcott 12.00 30.00
18 Arsi Piispanen 8.00 20.00
19 Steve Martins 8.00 20.00
20 Jarkko Immonen 12.00 30.00
21 Niklas Backstrom 15.00 40.00
22 Jussi Jokinen 60.00
23 Dwayne Roloson 15.00 40.00
24 Esa Pirnes 8.00 20.00
25 Erik Kakko 8.00 20.00
26 Jarmo Myllys 8.00 20.00
27 Petteri Nokelainen 12.00 30.00
28 Frank Banham 12.00 30.00
29 Pekka Saravo 8.00 20.00
30 Pasi Puistola 8.00 20.00
31 Mikko Myllykoski 8.00 20.00
32 Petri Kontiola 8.00 20.00
33 Ville Nieminen 8.00 20.00
34 Marko Kiprusoff 8.00 20.00
35 David Schneider 8.00 20.00
36 Lauri Korpikoski 12.00 30.00
37 Olegs Sorokins 8.00 20.00
38 Mika Niemi 8.00 20.00
39 Jesse Joensuu 8.00 20.00
40 Teemu Virkkunen 8.00 20.00
41 Jason Williams 12.00 30.00

2004-05 Finnish Cardset Stars of the Game

COMPLETE SET (14) 25.00
1 Riku Hahl 3.00
2 Hannes Hyvonen 1.00
3 Jarkko Immonen 3.00
4 Scott Langkow 2.00
5 Teemu Lassila 1.00
6 Ville Nieminen 2.00
7 Janne Niinimaa 2.00
8 Mika Noronen 3.00
9 Pasi Nurminen 3.00
10 Michael Nylander 2.00
11 Jarkko Ruutu 2.00
12 Patrik Stefan 2.00
13 Tim Thomas 3.00
14 Marek Zidlicky 2.00

2004-05 Finnish Cardset Tribute to Koivu

Random inserts in series II packs.
COMPLETE SET (3) 25.00
1 Saku Koivu 10.00
2 Saku Koivu 10.00
3 Saku Koivu 10.00

2005 Finnish Tappara Legendat

COMPLETE SET (32) 10.00 25.00
1 Antti Leppanen .40 1.00
2 Seppo Liitsola .40 1.00
3 Aleksander Barkov .40 1.00
4 Jukka Porvari .40 1.00
5 Mikko Leinonen .40 1.00
6 Martti Jarkko .40 1.00
7 Kiira Korpi .40 1.00
8 Ville Nieminen .40 1.00
9 Esko Niemi .40 1.00
10 Teppo Numminen .40 1.00
11 Erkki Lehtonen .40 1.00
12 Jarl Ohlson .40 1.00
13 Timo Susi .40 1.00
14 Kiira Korpi .40 1.00
15 Timo Jutila .40 1.00
16 Hannu Kamppuri .75 2.00
17 Lasse Litma .40 1.00
18 Pertti Valkeapaa .40 1.00
19 Yrjo Hakala .40 1.00
20 Jouni Seistamo .40 1.00
21 Kiira Korpi .40 1.00
22 Pekka Marjamaki .40 1.00
23 Markus Mattsson .40 1.00
24 Seppo Ahokainen .40 1.00
25 Hannu Haapalainen .40 1.00
26 Esko Luostarinen .40 1.00
27 Pertti Koivulahti .40 1.00
28 Kiira Korpi .40 1.00
29 Janne Ojanen .40 1.00
30 Kalevi Numminen .40 1.00
31 Jukka Rautakorpi .40 1.00
32 Rauno Korpi .40 1.00

2005-06 Finnish Cardset

COMPLETE SET (352) 25.00 60.00
1 Janne Jalasvaara .10 .25
2 Kari Haakana .10 .25
3 Arto Laatikainen .10 .25
4 Joni Toykkala .10 .25
5 Olli Ahonen .10 .25
6 Ladislav Kohn .10 .25
7 Lauri Tukonen .20 .50
8 Mike Ribeiro .20 .50
9 Niko Nieminen .10 .25
10 Jan Lundell .10 .25
11 Marek Zidlicky .20 .50
12 Mikko Turunen .10 .25
13 Toni Lydman .10 .25
14 Mikko Kurvinen .10 .25
15 Pasi Saarinen .10 .25
16 Kim Hirschovits .10 .25
17 Joonas Vihko .10 .25
18 Toni Happola .10 .25
19 Juha Fagerstedt .10 .25
20 Turo Jarvinen .10 .25
21 Arttu Luttinen .10 .25
22 Eetu Holma .10 .25
23 Olli Jokinen .20 .50
24 Mika Noronen .20 .50
25 Miika Wiikman .10 .25
26 Tuomas Immonen .10 .25
27 Mikko Jokela .10 .25
28 Veli-Pekka Laitinen .10 .25
29 Jyrki Louhi .10 .25
30 Petteri Wirtanen .10 .25
31 Joni Lappalainen .10 .25
32 Hannu Vaisanen .10 .25
33 Riku Hahl .10 .25
34 Jani Keinanen .10 .25
35 Juha-Pekka Loikas .10 .25
36 Janne Lahti .10 .25
37 Oliver Setzinger .10 .25
38 Juha Pitkamaki .10 .25
39 Vesa Toskala .40 1.00
40 Tuukka Rask 1.25 3.00
41 Joonas Ronnberg .10 .25
42 Ville Koistinen .20 .50
43 Ossi Pellinen .10 .25
44 Marko Anttila .10 .25
45 Marko Luomala .10 .25
46 Patrik Stefan .10 .25
47 Jussi Pesonen .10 .25
48 Raimo Helminen .10 .25
49 Simo Vidgren .10 .25
50 Pasi Hakkinen .10 .25
51 Tim Thomas .75 2.00
52 Brian Campbell .20 .50
53 Markus Kankaanpera .10 .25
54 Kevin Kantee .10 .25
55 Kari Martikainen .10 .25
56 Ossi Vaananen .10 .25
57 Martti Jarventie .10 .25
58 Tomi Maki .10 .25
59 Toni Dahlman .10 .25
60 Petri Pakaslahti .10 .25
61 Petri Varis .10 .25
62 Teemu Kuusisto .10 .25
63 Tommi Nikkila .10 .25
64 Tommi Kovanen .10 .25
65 Duvie Westcott .20 .50
66 Ilkka Vaarasuo .10 .25
67 Carlo Crunn .10 .25
68 Juha-Pekka Hytonen .10 .25
69 Arsi Piispanen .10 .25
70 Jari Jaaskelainen .10 .25
71 Ossi Louhivaara .10 .25
72 Tuomas Mikkonen .10 .25
73 Jarkko Immonen .20 .50
74 Antti Virtanen .10 .25
75 Ari Luostarinen .10 .25
76 Jermu Pisto .10 .25
77 Mikko Saavinen .10 .25
78 Samuli Suhonen .10 .25
79 Ville Hamalainen .10 .25
80 Tuomas Kiiskinen .10 .25
81 Henri Huohvanainen .10 .25
82 Sami Salonen .10 .25
83 Max Kenig .10 .25
84 Saku Kekalainen .10 .25
85 Sami Kaartinen .10 .25
86 Timo Kuuluvainen .10 .25
87 Pekka Rinne .40 1.00
88 Oskari Korpikari .10 .25
89 Lasse Kukkonen .10 .25
90 Ilkka Mikkola .10 .25
91 Topi Jaakola .10 .25
92 Janne Niinimaa .10 .25
93 Jussi Jokinen .40 1.00
94 Viktor Ujcik .10 .25
95 Pekka Saarenheimo .10 .25
96 Mika Pyorala .10 .25
97 Juha-Pekka Haataja .10 .25
98 Petr Tenkrat .10 .25
99 Antti Jokela .10 .25
100 Dwayne Roloson .40 1.00
101 Toni Porkka .10 .25
102 Antti Bruun .10 .25
103 Otto Honkaheimo .10 .25
104 Ilkka Heikkinen .10 .25
105 Tommi Hannus .10 .25
106 Ville Snellman .10 .25
107 Jarkko Kauvosaari .10 .25
108 Jaakko Hagelberg .10 .25
109 Teemu Normio .10 .25
110 Markku Tahtinen .10 .25
111 Juhamatti Yli-Junnila .10 .25
112 Pasi Nurminen .15 .40
113 Olli Korkeavuori .10 .25
114 Kimmo Pikkarainen .10 .25
115 Santeri Heiskanen .10 .25
116 Matias Loppi .10 .25
117 Tuomas Santavuori .10 .25
118 Toni Sihvonen .10 .25
119 Henri Heino .10 .25
120 Marcus Paulsson .10 .25
121 Tommi Turunen .10 .25
122 Ville-Matti Koponen .10 .25
123 Jesse Saarinen .10 .25
124 Jussi Timonen .10 .25,
125 Harri Tikkanen .10 .25
126 Olli Malmivaara .10 .25
127 Ossi-Petteri Gronholm .10 .25
128 Petri Kokko .10 .25
129 Kalle Kaijomaa .10 .25
130 Ville Koho .10 .25
131 Teemu Paakkarinen .10 .25
132 Mika Skytta .10 .25
133 Tuomas Vanttinen .10 .25
134 Eetu Qvist .10 .25
135 Ville Viitaluoma .10 .25
136 Mikko Silvennoinen .10 .25
137 Mika Lehto .10 .25
138 Anssi Salmela .10 .25
139 Ville Mantymaa .10 .25
140 Pasi Puistola .10 .25
141 Mikko Pukka .10 .25
142 Janne Ojanen .10 .25
143 Mika Viinanen .10 .25
144 Marko Ojanen .10 .25
145 Petri Kontiola .10 .25
146 Marko Makinen .10 .25
147 Ville Nieminen .10 .25
148 Sami Venalainen .10 .25
149 Stefan Ã–hman .10 .25
150 Teemu Laine .10 .25
151 Juho Santanen .10 .25
152 Tuomo Karjalainen .10 .25
153 Marko Kiprusoff .10 .25
154 Kimmo Eronen .10 .25
155 Antti Hulkkonen .10 .25
156 Saku Koivu .40 1.00
157 Antti Aalto .10 .25
158 Kai Nurminen .10 .25
159 Ville Vahalahti .10 .25
160 Lauri Korpikoski .40 1.00
161 Jari Kauppila .10 .25
162 Arttu Virtanen .10 .25
163 Matti Aho .10 .25
164 Tuomas Nissinen .10 .25
165 Pasi Peltonen .10 .25
166 Marko Toivonen .10 .25
167 Kristian Kuusela .10 .25
168 Mika Niemi .10 .25
169 Matti Kuparinen .10 .25
170 Marko Kivenmaki .10 .25
171 Pasi Nielikainen .10 .25
172 Jason Williams .40 1.00
173 Aki Uusikartano .10 .25
174 Juha Kiilholma .10 .25
175 Neil Little .40 1.00
176 Matti Kaltiainen .10 .25
177 Tuomas Eskelinen .10 .25
178 Tero Maatta .10 .25
179 Kimmo Peltonen .10 .25
180 Joakim Eriksson .10 .25
181 Esa Pirnes .10 .25
182 Markku Hurme .10 .25
183 Pentti Noyranen .10 .25
184 Steve Kariya .40 1.00
185 Timo Hirvonen .10 .25
186 Jaakko Uhlback .10 .25
187 Kari Kalto .10 .25
188 Tom Askey .20 .50
189 Robert Schnabel .10 .25
190 Jere Karalahti .10 .25
191 Hannu Pikkarainen .10 .25
192 Patrik Lostedt .10 .25
193 Tony Salmelainen .20 .50
194 Miika Jouhkimainen .10 .25
195 Jermu Porthen .10 .25
196 Janne Hauhtonen .10 .25
197 Tobias Salmelainen .10 .25
198 Lennart Petrell .10 .25
199 Pasi Salonen .10 .25
200 Heikki Laine .10 .25
201 Juha Toivonen .10 .25
202 David Schneider .10 .25
203 Juuso Hietanen .10 .25
204 Jukka-Pekka Laamanen .10 .25
205 Kaspars Astashenko .10 .25
206 Jani Hassinen .10 .25
207 Jari Sailio .10 .25
208 Mikko Laine .10 .25
209 Antti Hilden .10 .25
210 Jukka Voutilainen .10 .25
211 Janis Sprukts .10 .25
212 Ville Leino .10 .25
213 Toni Niemi .10 .25
214 Jyrki Lumme .10 .25
215 Juha Alen .10 .25
216 Mikko Kuukka .10 .25
217 Jonas Andersson .10 .25
218 Perttu Lindgren .40 1.00
219 Ville Korhonen .10 .25
220 Tommi Huhtala .10 .25
221 Toni Koivisto .10 .25
222 Jason Guerriero .10 .25
223 Tomi Hirvonen .10 .25
224 Henrik Juntunen .10 .25
225 Vesa Viitakoski .10 .25
226 Joonas Hallikainen .10 .25
227 Samuli Jalkanen .10 .25
228 Mikko Kalteva .10 .25
229 Jan Latvala .10 .25
230 Sami Lepisto .10 .25
231 Tero Konttinen .10 .25
232 Tony Virta .10 .25
233 Marko Jantunen .10 .25
234 Tomek Valtonen .10 .25
235 Jesse Niinimaki .10 .25
236 Arto Koivisto .10 .25
237 Ilari Filppula .10 .25
238 Tommi Santala .10 .25
239 Arto Kuki .10 .25
240 Sinuhe Wallinheimo .20 .50
241 Miika Huczkowski .10 .25
242 Jaako Niskavaara .10 .25
243 Eerikki Koivu .10 .25
244 Juha Salmu .10 .25
245 Jyri Marttinen .10 .25
246 Johannes Alanen .10 .25
247 Filip Riska .10 .25
248 Miikka Mannikko .10 .25
249 Valtteri Tenkanen .10 .25
250 Lucas Lawson .10 .25
251 Tero Koponen .10 .25
252 Miika Lahti .10 .25
253 Juha Jaaskelainen .10 .25
254 Kimmo Kapanen .10 .25
255 Juha Alastalo .10 .25
256 Juho Kuronen .10 .25
257 Jussi Savolainen .10 .25
258 Matti Kuusisto .10 .25
259 Mikko Hakkarainen .10 .25
260 Jani Tuppurainen .10 .25
261 Tomi Pollanen .10 .25
262 Kasper Kenig .10 .25
263 Tomas Kurka .10 .25
264 Matti Tiihonen .10 .25
265 Niklas Backstrom .75 2.00
266 Mika Pietila .10 .25
267 Antti Ylonen .10 .25
268 Ari Vallin .10 .25
269 Mikko Lehtonen .15 .40
270 Jouni Loponen .10 .25
271 Janne Pesonen .10 .25
272 Tommi Paakkolanvaara .10 .25
273 Jari Viuhkola .10 .25
274 Mikko Alikoski .10 .25
275 Michal Bros .10 .25
276 Kalle Sahlstedt .10 .25
277 Juhamatti Aaltonen .10 .25
278 Tomi Mustonen .10 .25
279 Scott Langkow .20 .50
280 Topi Lehtonen .10 .25
281 Markku Paukkunen .10 .25
282 Tuukka Makela .10 .25
283 Pauli Levokari .10 .25
284 Erik Hamalainen .10 .25
285 Jamie Wright .10 .25
286 Petri Lammassaari .10 .25
287 Shayne Toporowski .10 .25
288 Miikka Tuomainen .10 .25
289 Pasi Saarela .10 .25
290 Joni Yli-Torkko .10 .25
291 Antti Niemi .10 .25
292 Esa Saksinen .10 .25
293 Sami Helenius .10 .25
294 Jarkko Glad .10 .25
295 Erik Kakko .10 .25
296 Kari Sihvonen .10 .25
297 Toni Koivunen .10 .25
298 Olli Julkunen .10 .25
299 Jussi Saarinen .10 .25
300 Lasse Jamsen .10 .25
301 Mikko Stromberg .10 .25
302 Rob Zepp .20 .50
303 Mikko Palomaki .10 .25
304 Juha Jokiraita .10 .25
305 Joni Tuominen .10 .25
306 Kristian Kudroc .10 .25
307 Antti Pihlstrom .10 .25
308 Kimmo Koskenkorva .10 .25
309 Jaska Vilen .10 .25
310 Morten Ask .10 .25
311 Jarkko Immonen .20 .50
312 Peter Nylander .10 .25
313 Janne Kolehmainen .10 .25
314 Teemu Seppanen .10 .25
315 Pekka Tuokkola .10 .25
316 Brian White .10 .25
317 Marko Kauppinen .10 .25
318 Tuukka Mantyla .10 .25
319 Jussi Halme .10 .25
320 Greg Hawgood .20 .50
321 Janne Gronvall .10 .25
322 Teemu Nurmi .10 .25
323 Jarkko Pyymaki .10 .25
324 Teemu Virkkunen .10 .25
325 Timo Vertala .10 .25
326 Quinn Hancock .10 .25
327 Mika Lehtinen .10 .25
328 Henri Palmroth .10 .25
329 Simon Backman .10 .25
330 Markus Seikola .10 .25
331 Tomi Sykko .10 .25
332 Joni Lius .10 .25
333 Jussi Makkonen .10 .25
334 Mika Alatalo .10 .25
335 Jarmo Jokila .10 .25
336 Daniel Widing .10 .25
337 Andreas Jamtin .10 .25
338 Tuukka Pulliainen .10 .25
339 Juuso Riksman .10 .25
340 Jussi Rynnas .10 .25
341 Justin Forrest .10 .25
342 Atte Pentikainen .10 .25
343 Matt Nickerson .20 .50
344 Jesse Saarinen .10 .25
345 Mikko Rautee .10 .25
346 Jesse Joensuu .20 .50
347 Tuomas Takala .10 .25
348 Rob Hisey .10 .25
349 Patrik Forsbacka .10 .25
350 Petteri Tasku .10 .25
351 Leo Komarov .10 .25
352 Matti Kaipainen .10 .25

2005-06 Finnish Cardset Magicmakers

COMPLETE SET (18) 15.00 40.00
STATED ODDS 1:4
1 Mike Ribeiro .75 2.00
2 Toni Lydman .75 2.00
3 Olli Jokinen 1.25 3.00
4 Jarkko Ruutu .75 2.00
5 Riku Hahl .75 2.00
6 Josh Holden .75 2.00
7 Steve Kariya 1.25 3.00
8 Patrik Stefan .75 2.00
9 Sami LepistÃ¶ .75 2.00
10 Ossi VÃ¤Ã¤nÃ¤nen .75 2.00
11 Valtteri Filppula 2.00 5.00
12 Jarkko Immonen 1.50 4.00
13 Jussi Jokinen 2.00 5.00
14 Jari Viuhkola .75 2.00
15 Ville Nieminen .75 2.00
16 Saku Koivu 2.00 5.00
17 Craig Rivet .75 2.00
18 Jason Williams 1.50 4.00

2005-06 Finnish Cardset Super Snatchers

COMPLETE SET (18) 20.00 50.00
STATED ODDS 1:4
1 Jan Lundell 1.25 3.00
2 Tomas Vokoun 2.50 6.00
3 Mika Noronen 1.25 3.00
4 Miika Wiikman 1.25 3.00
5 Juha PitkÃ¤mÃ¤ki 1.25 3.00
6 Vesa Toskala 2.50 6.00
7 Tim Thomas 2.50 6.00
8 Sinuhe Wallinheimo 1.25 3.00
9 Kimmo Kapanen 1.25 3.00
10 Niklas BÃ¤ckstrÃ¶m 1.50 4.00
11 Dwayne Roloson 1.50 4.00
12 Pasi Nurminen 1.25 3.00
13 Jarmo Myllys 1.25 3.00
14 Andrew Raycroft 2.00 5.00
15 Mika Lehto 1.25 3.00
16 Tuomo Karjalainen 1.25 3.00
17 Teemu Lassila 1.25 3.00
18 Tuomas Nissinen 1.25 3.00

2006-07 Finnish Cardset

COMPLETE SERIES 1 (180) 40.00 80.00
1 Juha Gustafsson .20 .50
2 Tuomas Eskelinen .20 .50
3 Arto Laatikainen .20 .50
4 Kimmo Peltonen .20 .50
5 Jari Korhonen .20 .50
6 Markku Hurme .20 .50
7 Olli Ahonen .20 .50
8 Ladislav Kohn .20 .50
9 Erkki RajamÃ¤ki .20 .50
10 Mikko Lehtonen .20 .50
11 Pentti NÃ¶yrÃ¤nen .20 .50
12 Kari Kalto .20 .50
13 Jan Lundell .30 .75
14 Teemu Laakso .20 .50
15 Jere Karalahti .20 .50
16 Mikko Turunen .20 .50
17 Hannu Pikkarainen .20 .50
18 Tony Salmelainen .20 .50
19 Turo JÃ¤rvinen .20 .50
20 Jermu PorthÃ©n .20 .50
21 Janne Hauhtonen .20 .50
22 Arttu Luttinen .20 .50
23 Pasi Salonen .20 .50
24 Heikki Laine .20 .50
25 Karri RÃ¤mÃ¶ .75 2.00
26 Juha Toivonen .20 .50
27 David Schneider .20 .50
28 Juuso Hietanen .20 .50
29 Mikko Jokela .20 .50
30 Veli-Pekka Laitinen .20 .50
31 Jani Hassinen .20 .50
32 Jari Sailio .20 .50
33 Petteri Wirtanen .20 .50
34 Iivo Hokkanen .20 .50
35 Joni Lappalainen .20 .50
36 Hannu VÃ¤isÃ¤nen .20 .50
37 Juha-Pekka Loikas .20 .50
38 Ville Leino .20 .50
39 Tuukka Rask 2.00 5.00
40 Toni Niemi .20 .50
41 Jyrki Lumme .20 .50
42 Ville Koistinen .20 .50
43 Juha AlÃ©n .20 .50
44 Juho Mielonen .20 .50
45 Perttu Lindgren .60 1.50
46 Marko Anttila .20 .50
47 Ville Korhonen .20 .50
48 Toni Koivisto .20 .50
49 Jussi Pesonen .20 .50
50 Tomi Hirvonen .20 .50
51 Vesa Viitakoski .20 .50
52 Raimo Helminen .20 .50
53 Joonas Hallikainen .20 .50
54 Mikko Kalteva .20 .50
55 Markus KankaanperÃ¤ .20 .50
56 Kevin Kantee .20 .50
57 Jan Latvala .20 .50
58 Sami LepistÃ¶ .20 .50
59 Tony Virta .20 .50
60 Tomek Valtonen .20 .50
61 Arto Koivisto .20 .50
62 Petri Pakaslahti .20 .50
63 Tommi Santala .20 .50
64 Petri Varis .20 .50
65 Jesse Uronen .20 .50
66 Roni Andersson .20 .50
67 Sinuhe Wallinheimo .30 .75
68 Miika Huczkowski .20 .50
69 Jaako Niskavaara .20 .50
70 Erkka LeppÃ¤nen .20 .50
71 Eerikki Koivu .20 .50
72 Juha Salmu .20 .50
73 Jyrki Marttinen .20 .50
74 Carlo GrÃ¼nn .20 .50
75 Johannes Alanen .20 .50
76 Miikka MÃ¤nnikkÃ¶ .20 .50
77 Juha-Pekka HytÃ¶nen .20 .50
78 Arsi Piispanen .20 .50
79 Jari JÃ¤Ã¤skelÃ¤inen .20 .50
80 Ossi Louhivaara .20 .50
81 Kimmo Kapanen .30 .75
82 Jermu Pisto .20 .50
83 Matti Kuusisto .20 .50
84 Juha Alastalo .20 .50
85 Ville HÃ¤mÃ¤lÃ¤inen .20 .50
86 Jani Tuppurainen .20 .50
87 Kasper Kenig .20 .50
88 Henri Huohvanainen .20 .50
89 Sami Salonen .20 .50
90 Tuomas Kiiskinen .20 .50
91 Sami Kaartinen .20 .50
92 Niklas BÃ¤ckstrÃ¶m 1.50 4.00
93 Oskari Korpikari .20 .50
94 Ari Vallin .20 .50
95 Ilkka Mikkola .20 .50
96 Mikko Lehtonen .20 .50
97 Jouni Loponen .20 .50
98 Viktor Ujcik .20 .50
99 Janne Pesonen .20 .50
100 Tommi Paakkolanvaara .20 .50
101 Jyri Junnila .20 .50
102 Jari Viuhkola .20 .50
103 Michal Bros .20 .50
104 Kalle Sahlstedt .20 .50
105 Tomi Mustonen .20 .50
106 Markus Nordlund .20 .50
107 Otto Honkaheimo .20 .50
108 Tuukka MÃ¤kelÃ¤ .20 .50
109 Ilkka Heikkinen .20 .50
110 Pauli Levokari .20 .50
111 Erik HÃ¤mÃ¤lÃ¤inen .20 .50
112 Tommi Hannus .20 .50
113 Ville-Vesa Vainiola .20 .50
114 Petri Lammassaari .20 .50
115 Shayne Toporowski .20 .50
116 Jarkko Kauvosaari .20 .50
117 Miikka Tuomainen .20 .50
118 Juhamatti Yli-Junnila .20 .50
119 Antti Niemi .30 .75
120 Esa Saksinen .20 .50
121 Olli Korkeavuori .20 .50
122 Sami Helenius .20 .50
123 Jarkko Glad .20 .50
124 Erik Kakko .20 .50
125 Matias Loppi .20 .50
126 Olli Julkunen .20 .50
127 Jesse Saarinen .20 .50
128 Jussi Saarinen .20 .50
129 Tuomas Santavuori .20 .50
130 Henri Heino .20 .50
131 Ville-Matti Koponen .20 .50
132 Toni Koivunen .20 .50
133 Mikko StrÃ¶mberg .20 .50
134 Jussi Timonen .30 .75
135 Harri Tikkanen .20 .50
136 Mikko PalomÃ¤ki .20 .50
137 Ossi-Petteri GrÃ¶nholm .20 .50
138 Ville Koho .20 .50
139 Kimmo Koskenkorva .20 .50
140 Teemu Paakkarinen .20 .50
141 Jaska Vilen .20 .50
142 Jarkko Immonen .30 .75
143 Janne Kolehmainen .20 .50
144 Mika Lehto .30 .75
145 Marko Kauppinen .20 .50
146 Ville MÃ¤ntymaa .20 .50
147 Tuukka MÃ¤ntylÃ¤ .20 .50
148 Mikko Pukka .20 .50
149 Janne GrÃ¶nvall .20 .50
150 Teemu Nurmi .20 .50
151 Mika Viinanen .20 .50
152 Petri Kontiola .20 .50
153 Sami VenÃ¤lÃ¤inen .20 .50
154 Stefan Ã–hman .20 .50
155 Quinn Hancock .20 .50
156 Teemu Laine .20 .50
157 Marko Kiprusoff .20 .50
158 Simon Backman .20 .50
159 Tomi SykkÃ¶ .20 .50
160 Kai Nurminen .20 .50
161 Jussi Makkonen .20 .50
162 Ville Vahalahti .20 .50
163 Lauri Korpikoski .60 1.50
164 Mika Alatalo .20 .50

165 Arttu Virtanen .20 .50
166 Matti Aho .20 .50
167 Tuukka Pulliainen .20 .50
168 Jussi RynnÃ¤s .20 .50
169 Pasi Peltonen .20 .50
170 Marko Toivonen .20 .50
171 Mika Rontti .20 .50
172 Juhamatti HietamÃ¤ki .20 .50
173 Matt Nickerson .40 1.00
174 Kristian Kuusela .20 .50
175 Jesse Joensuu .20 .50
176 Marko KivenmÃ¤ki .20 .50
177 Matti Kuparinen .20 .50
178 Tuomas Takala .20 .50
179 Rob Hisey .20 .50
180 Patrik Forsbacka .20 .50
181 Bernd BrÃ¼ckler .30 .75
182 Ari Ahonen .40 1.00
183 Tomi KÃ¤llarsson .20 .50
184 Kimmo Pikkarainen .20 .50
185 Ismo Kuoppala .20 .50
186 Samuli Suhonen .20 .50
187 Tomas Sinisalo .20 .50
188 Joni TÃ¶ykkÃ¤lÃ¤ .20 .50
189 Jari Tolsa .20 .50
190 Semir Ben-Amor .20 .50
191 Ville Viitaluoma .20 .50
192 Mikko Laine .20 .50
193 Martin Kariya .20 .50
194 Toni KÃ¤hkÃ¶nen .20 .50
195 Aleksis Ahlqvist .30 .75
196 Robert Schnabel .20 .50
197 Cory Murphy .20 .50
198 Patrik Lostedt .20 .50
199 Pasi Saarinen .20 .50
200 Kimmo Kuhta .20 .50
201 Miikka Jouhkimainen .20 .50
202 Raymond Murray .20 .50
203 Juha Fagerstedt .20 .50
204 Janne Laakkonen .20 .50
205 Lennart Petrell .20 .50
206 Ilkka Pikkarainen .20 .50
207 Jan Hrdina .20 .50
208 Pasi NielikÃ¤inen .20 .50
209 Mika Oksa .30 .75
210 Miika Wiikman .30 .75
211 Risto Korhonen .20 .50
212 Mikko MÃ¤enpÃ¤Ã¤ .20 .50
213 Philippe Seydoux .20 .50
214 Mika StrÃ¶mberg .30 .75
215 Fredrik Svensson .20 .50
216 Jani KeinÃ¤nen .20 .50
217 Janne Lahti .20 .50
218 Joonas Vihko .20 .50
219 Aki Uusikartano .20 .50
220 Antti PihlstrÃ¶m .20 .50
221 Jonas Andersson .20 .50
222 Toni MÃ¤kiaho .20 .50
223 Riku Helenius .60 1.50
224 Teemu JÃ¤Ã¤skelÃ¤inen .20 .50
225 Mikko Kuukka .20 .50
226 Teppo Tuomanen .20 .50
227 Kristian Kudroc .20 .50
228 Pasi PetrilÃ¤inen .20 .50
229 Mikko Peltola .20 .50
230 Sami Sandell .20 .50
231 Tommi Huhtala .20 .50
232 Pasi MÃ¤Ã¤ttÃ¤nen .20 .50
233 Lauris Darzins .20 .50
234 Tomas Kurka .20 .50
235 Niko Hovinen .30 .75
236 Juuso Riksman .30 .75
237 Mikko Kuparinen .20 .50
238 Marko Tuulola .20 .50
239 Martti JÃ¤rventie .20 .50
240 Tim Stapleton .20 .50
241 Jyrki Louhi .20 .50
242 Jani Rita .20 .50
243 Arto Kuki .20 .50
244 Kim Hirschovits .20 .50
245 Ryan VandenBussche .40 1.00
246 Jori LehterÃ¤ .20 .50
247 Samuli Jalkanen .20 .50
248 Pekka Tuokkola .20 .50
249 Miska Kangasniemi .20 .50
250 Henrik Forsberg .20 .50
251 Valtteri Tenkanen .20 .50
252 Miika Lahti .20 .50
253 Tuomas VÃ¤nttinen .20 .50
254 Samuli Piiroinen .20 .50
255 Olli SipilÃ¤inen .20 .50
256 Riku Rahikainen .20 .50
257 Ilari Filppula .20 .50
258 Tuomas Nissinen .30 .75
259 Janne Jalasvaara .20 .50
260 Kyle Peto .20 .50
261 Mats Hansson .20 .50
262 Mikko Purontakanen .20 .50
263 Eetu Qvist .20 .50
264 Timo Koskela .20 .50
265 Martin Sonnenberg .20 .50
266 Matt Davidson .20 .50
267 Aatu HÃ¤mÃ¤lÃ¤inen .20 .50
268 Jaakko Suomalainen .30 .75
269 Tuomas Tarkki .30 .75
270 Tommi Leinonen .20 .50
271 Topi Jaakola .20 .50
272 Ivan Majesky .20 .50
273 Atvars Tribuncovs .20 .50
274 Jukka-Pekka Laamanen .20 .50
275 Antti YlÃ¶nen .20 .50
276 Teemu Normio .20 .50
277 Veikko Karppinen .20 .50
278 Mika PyÃ¶rÃ¤lÃ¤ .20 .50
279 Antti Aarnio .20 .50
280 Juhamatti Aaltonen .20 .50
281 Markus Korhonen .30 .75
282 Petri TÃ¤htisalo .20 .50
283 Kari Martikainen .20 .50
284 Jiri Hunkes .20 .50
285 Otto Honkaheimo .20 .50
286 Jan Platil .20 .50
287 Pekka Saarenheimo .20 .50
288 Toni Dahlman .20 .50
289 Juha-Pekka Haataja .20 .50
290 Henrik Juntunen .20 .50
291 Marko Luomala .20 .50
292 Josef Straka .20 .50
293 Tommi Satosaari .20 .50
294 Jani ForsstrÃ¶m .20 .50
295 Mikko Heiskanen .20 .50
296 Anssi Salmela .20 .50
297 Ville Uusitalo .20 .50
298 Vili Sopanen .20 .50
299 Karo Koivunen .20 .50
300 Toni Sihvonen .20 .50
301 Kari Sihvonen .20 .50
302 Leo Komarov .20 .50
303 Marko Jantunen .20 .50
304 Rob Zepp .30 .75
305 Jarno Virkki .20 .50
306 Joonas RÃ¶nnberg .20 .50
307 Pauli Levokari .20 .50
308 Kalle Kaijomaa .20 .50
309 Henrik PetrÃ© .20 .50
310 Sami RyhÃ¤nen .20 .50
311 Petri Koskinen .20 .50
312 Mikko Hakkarainen .20 .50
313 Janne Jokila .20 .50
314 Eetu Holma .20 .50
315 Emil Lundberg .20 .50
316 Ville Snellman .20 .50
317 Jens BergenstrÃ¶m .20 .50
318 Tommi NikkilÃ¤ .30 .75
319 Burke Henry .20 .50
320 Matti Koistinen .20 .50
321 Harri Ilvonen .20 .50
322 Dale Clarke .20 .50
323 Teemu Aalto .20 .50
324 Janne Ojanen .20 .50
325 Niko Nieminen .20 .50
326 Jarkko PyymÃ¤ki .20 .50
327 Marko Ojanen .20 .50
328 Jonas Enlund .20 .50
329 Antti HÃ¶lli .20 .50
330 Teemu Virkkunen .20 .50
331 Juho Santanen .20 .50
332 Jani Hurme .40 1.00
333 Juho Jokinen .20 .50
334 Aki Berg .20 .50
335 Vladimir Sicak .20 .50
336 Jesse Saarinen .20 .50
337 Mikko Rautee .20 .50
338 Tommi Laine .20 .50
339 Layne Ulmer .20 .50
340 Tuomas Suominen .20 .50
341 Ivan Huml .30 .75
342 Teemu Ramstedt .20 .50
343 Joni Yli-Torkko .20 .50
344 Matti Kaltiainen .30 .75
345 Eero KilpelÃ¤inen .30 .75
346 Peter Aston .20 .50
347 Anssi Tieranta .20 .50
348 Eetu Heikkinen .20 .50
349 Ilkka TÃ¶rnvall .20 .50
350 Tapio Sammalkangas .20 .50
351 Toni HÃ¤ppÃ¶lÃ¤ .20 .50
352 Tom Wandell .20 .50
353 Aleksandr Naurov .20 .50
354 Joonas Kemppainen .20 .50
355 Ville Hirvonen .20 .50
356 Brandon Crombeen .30 .75

2006-07 Finnish Cardset Between the Pipes

1 Ari Ahonen 3.00 8.00
2 Bernd BrÃ¼ckler 2.00 5.00
3 Aleksis Ahlqvist 2.00 5.00
4 Jan Lundell 2.00 5.00
5 Mika Oksa 2.00 5.00
6 Miika Wiikman 2.00 5.00
7 Riku Helenius 4.00 10.00
8 Tuukka Rask 8.00 20.00
9 Niko Hovinen 2.00 5.00
10 Juuso Riksman 2.00 5.00
11 Sinuhe Wallinheimo 2.00 5.00
12 Kimmo Kapanen 2.00 5.00
13 Tuomas Nissinen 2.00 5.00
14 Jaakko Suomalainen 2.00 5.00
15 Tuomas Tarkki 2.00 5.00
16 Markus Korhonen 2.00 5.00
17 Antti Niemi 2.00 5.00
18 Mikko StrÃ¶mberg 2.00 5.00
19 Rob Zepp 2.00 5.00
20 Mika Lehto 2.00 5.00
21 Tommi NikkilÃ¤ 2.00 5.00
22 Jani Hurme 3.00 8.00
23 Matti Kaltiainen 2.00 5.00
24 Eero KilpelÃ¤inen 2.00 5.00

2006-07 Finnish Cardset Enforcers

1 Sami Helenius 1.25 3.00
2 Kristian Kudroc 1.25 3.00
3 Ryan VandenBussche 2.00 5.00
4 Robert Schnabel 1.25 3.00
5 Burke Henry 1.25 3.00
6 Jan Platil 1.25 3.00
7 Toni MÃ¤kiaho 1.25 3.00
8 Markus KankaanperÃ¤ 1.25 3.00
9 Aki Berg 1.25 3.00
10 Pasi Peltonen 1.25 3.00
11 Pasi NielikÃ¤inen 1.25 3.00
12 Jere Karalahti 1.25 3.00

2006-07 Finnish Cardset Playmakers Rookies

1 Perttu Lindgren 2.00 5.00
2 Juhamatti Aaltonen 1.25 3.00
3 Jussi Makkonen 1.25 3.00
4 Pasi Salonen 1.25 3.00
5 Juuso Hietanen 1.25 3.00
6 Petteri Wirtanen 1.25 3.00
7 Petri Lammassaari 1.25 3.00
8 Patrick Forsbacka 1.25 3.00
9 Juha AlÃ©n 1.25 3.00
10 Miika Lahti 1.25 3.00
11 Jari Sailio 1.25 3.00
12 Leo Komarov 1.25 3.00

2006-07 Finnish Cardset Playmakers Rookies Gold

COMPLETE SET (12)
STATED PRINT RUN 100 SETS
1 Perttu Lindgren 6.00 15.00
2 Juhamatti Aaltonen 4.00 10.00
3 Jussi Makkonen 4.00 10.00
4 Pasi Salonen 4.00 10.00
5 Juuso Hietanen 4.00 10.00
6 Petteri Wirtanen 4.00 10.00
7 Petri Lammassaari 4.00 10.00
8 Patrick Forsbacka 4.00 10.00
9 Juha AlÃ©n 4.00 10.00
10 Miika Lahti 4.00 10.00
11 Jari Sailio 4.00 10.00
12 Leo Komarov 4.00 10.00

2006-07 Finnish Cardset Playmakers Rookies Silver

COMPLETE SET (12)
STATED PRINT RUN 200 SETS
1 Perttu Lindgren 4.00 10.00
2 Juhamatti Aaltonen 2.00 5.00
3 Jussi Makkonen 2.00 5.00
4 Pasi Salonen 2.00 5.00
5 Juuso Hietanen 2.00 5.00
6 Petteri Wirtanen 2.00 5.00
7 Petri Lammassaari 2.00 5.00
8 Patrick Forsbacka 2.00 5.00
9 Juha AlÃ©n 2.00 5.00
10 Miika Lahti 2.00 5.00
11 Jari Sailio 2.00 5.00
12 Leo Komarov 2.00 5.00

2006-07 Finnish Cardset Signature Sensations

1 Mikko Lehtonen 15.00 40.00
2 Erkki RajamÃ¤ki 15.00 40.00
3 Miika Wiikman 15.00 40.00
4 Juuso Hietanen 15.00 40.00
5 Petteri Wirtanen 15.00 40.00
6 Tuukka Rask 40.00 100.00
7 Ville Koistinen 15.00 40.00
8 Perttu Lindgren 25.00 60.00
9 Joonas Hallikainen 15.00 40.00
10 Sami LepistÃ¶ 15.00 40.00
11 Tommi Santala 15.00 40.00
12 Sinuhe Wallinheimo 15.00 40.00
13 Miika Lahti 15.00 40.00
14 Arsi Piispanen 15.00 40.00
15 Kimmo Kapanen 15.00 40.00
16 Tuomas Kiiskinen 15.00 40.00
17 Mikko Alikoski 15.00 40.00
18 Lasse Kukkonen 15.00 40.00
19 Juhamatti Aaltonen 15.00 40.00
20 Otto Honkaheimo 15.00 40.00
21 Petri Lammassaari 15.00 40.00
22 Miikka Tuomainen 15.00 40.00
23 Antti Niemi 15.00 40.00
24 Jesse Saarinen 15.00 40.00
25 Mikko StrÃ¶mberg 15.00 40.00
26 Jarkko Immonen 15.00 40.00
27 Mika Lehto 15.00 40.00
28 Petri Kontiola 15.00 40.00
29 Juho Santanen 15.00 40.00
30 Jussi Makkonen 15.00 40.00
31 Tuukka Pulliainen 15.00 40.00
32 Kristian Kuusela 15.00 40.00
33 Jesse Joensuu 15.00 40.00
34 Marko KivenmÃ¤ki 15.00 40.00
35 Patrick Forsbacka 15.00 40.00

2006-07 Finnish Cardset Superior Snatchers

1 Niklas BÃ¤ckstrÃ¶m 4.00 10.00
2 Joonas Hallikainen 2.00 5.00
3 Kimmo Kapanen 2.00 5.00
4 Mika Lehto 2.00 5.00
5 Jan Lundell 2.00 5.00
6 Antti Niemi 2.00 5.00
7 Tuukka Rask 6.00 15.00
8 Juuso Riksman 2.00 5.00
9 Karri RÃ¤mÃ¶ 3.00 8.00
10 Sinuhe Wallinheimo 2.00 5.00
11 Miika Wiikman 2.00 5.00
12 Rob Zepp 2.00 5.00

2006-07 Finnish Cardset Superior Snatchers Gold

COMPLETE SET (12)
STATED PRINT RUN 100 SETS
1 Niklas BÃ¤ckstrÃ¶m 12.00 30.00
2 Joonas Hallikainen 6.00 15.00
3 Kimmo Kapanen 6.00 15.00
4 Mika Lehto 6.00 15.00
5 Jan Lundell 6.00 15.00
6 Antti Niemi 6.00 15.00
7 Tuukka Rask 15.00 40.00
8 Juuso Riksman 6.00 15.00
9 Karri RÃ¤mÃ¶ 8.00 20.00
10 Sinuhe Wallinheimo 6.00 15.00
11 Miika Wiikman 6.00 15.00
12 Rob Zepp 6.00 15.00

2006-07 Finnish Cardset Superior Snatchers Silver

COMPLETE SET (12)
STATED PRINT RUN 200 SETS
1 Niklas BÃ¤ckstrÃ¶m 8.00 20.00
2 Joonas Hallikainen 4.00 10.00
3 Kimmo Kapanen 4.00 10.00
4 Mika Lehto 4.00 10.00
5 Jan Lundell 4.00 10.00
6 Antti Niemi 4.00 10.00
7 Tuukka Rask 12.00 30.00
8 Juuso Riksman 4.00 10.00
9 Karri RÃ¤mÃ¶ 6.00 15.00
10 Sinuhe Wallinheimo 4.00 10.00
11 Miika Wiikman 4.00 10.00
12 Rob Zepp 4.00 10.00

2006-07 Finnish Cardset Trophy Winners

COMPLETE SET (7)
1 Jukka Jalonen 1.25 3.00
2 Perttu Lindgren 2.00 5.00
3 Esa Pirnes 1.25 3.00
4 Juuso Riksman 1.25 3.00
5 Lasse Kukkonen 1.25 3.00
6 Miika Wiikman 1.25 3.00
7 Tony Salmelainen 1.25 3.00

2006-07 Finnish Ilves Team Set

1 Juha Alen .20 .50
2 Juuso Antonen .20 .50
3 Marko Anttila .20 .50
4 Lauris Darzins .20 .50
5 Riku Helenius .75 2.00
6 Tomi Hirvonen .20 .50
7 Tommi Huhtala .20 .50
8 Teemu Jaaskelainen .20 .50
9 Toni Koivisto .20 .50
10 Ville Korhonen .20 .50
11 Kristian Kudroc .20 .50
12 Tomas Kurka .20 .50
13 Mikko Kuukka .20 .50
14 Jarno Laitinen .20 .50
15 Joonas Lehtivuori .20 .50
16 Perttu Lindgren .60 1.50
17 Juho Mielonen .20 .50
18 Pasi Maattanen .20 .50
19 Toni Niemi .20 .50
20 Mikko Peltola .20 .50
21 Jussi Pesonen .20 .50
22 Pasi Petrilainen .20 .50
23 Tuukka Rask 4.00 10.00
24 Sami Sandell .20 .50
25 Teppo Tuomainen .20 .50
26 Vesa Viitakoski .20 .50
27 Kari Eloranta CO .10 .25
28 Petteri Hirvonen CO .10 .25

2006-07 Finnish Porin Assat Pelaajakortit

COMPLETE SET (32) 10.00 25.00
1 Matti Kaltiainen .30 .75
2 Eero Kilpelainen .60 1.50
3 Jussi Rynnas .30 .75
4 Pasi Peltonen .30 .75
5 Marko Toivonen .30 .75
6 Mika Rontti .30 .75
7 Peter Aston .30 .75
8 Tero Konttinen .30 .75
9 Juhamatti Hietamaki .30 .75
10 Anssi Tieranta .30 .75
11 Eetu Heikkinen .30 .75
12 Iikka Tornvall .30 .75
13 Tapio Samalkangas .30 .75
14 Toni Happola .30 .75
15 Kristian Kuusela .30 .75
16 Tom Wandell .30 .75
17 Tuomas Huhtanen .30 .75
18 Jesse Joensuu .30 .75
19 Marko Kivenmaki .30 .75
20 Matti Kuparinen .30 .75
21 Tuomas Takala .30 .75
22 Patrick Forsbacka .30 .75
23 Petteri Tasku .30 .75
24 Alexander Naurov .30 .75
25 Joonas Kemppainen .30 .75
26 Jussi Peltomaa .30 .75
27 Ville Hirvonen .30 .75
28 Brandon BJ Crombeen .40 1.00
29 Teemu Kesa .30 .75
30 Tobias Salmelainen .30 .75
31 David Bararuk .30 .75
32 Jari Harkala .30 .75

1994-95 French National Team

These standard-size cards were made available to fans at venues where the national team was appearing in France. The cards feature simulated action photography, surrounded by red, white and blue borders. The player's name is at the top of the card, while the words "Equipe de France 94-95" line the bottom. Card backs contain a color headshot, and international statistics. The cards are unnumbered and checklisted below in alphabetical order.

COMPLETE SET (35) 8.00 20.00
1 Benjamin Agnel .20 .50
2 Richard Aimonetto .20 .50
3 Stephane Arcangeloni .20 .50
4 Mickael Babin .20 .50
5 Alain Beaule .20 .50
6 J. Francois Bonnard .20 .50
7 Arnaud Briand .20 .50
8 Karl DeWolf .20 .50
9 Serge Djelloul .20 .50
10 Roger Dube .20 .50
11 Patrick Dunn .20 .50
12 J. Christophe Filippin .20 .50
13 Michel Galarneau .20 .50
14 Gerald Guennelon .20 .50
15 Eric Lemarque .20 .50
16 J. Philippe Lemoine .20 .50
17 Fabrice L'Henry .30 .75
18 Pierrick Maia .20 .50
19 Antoine Mindjimba .80 2.00
20 Christophe Moyon .20 .50
21 Lionel Orsolini .20 .50
22 Franck Pajonkowski .30 .75
23 Denis Perez .20 .50
24 Eric Pinard .20 .50
25 Serge Poudrier .30 .75
26 Christian Pouget .20 .50
27 Pierre Pousse .20 .50
28 Antoine Richer .20 .50
29 Franck Saunier .20 .50
30 J. Marc Soghomonian .20 .50
31 Juhani Tamminen .30 .75
32 Michel Valliere .30 .75
33 Andre Vittenberg .20 .50
34 Steven Woodburn .20 .50
35 Petri Ylonen .60 1.50

1932 German Margarine Sanella

Cards measure 2 3/4 x 4 1/8 and feature full color fronts. Backs are in German.

NNO Field Hockey Goalie 5.00 10.00
NNO Ice Hockey 25.00 50.00
NNO Field Hockey Scrum 5.00 10.00

1936 German Jaszmatzi

Full color card from the Deutscher Sports series of Germany. Thin paper stock, with back in German.

208 Ice Hockey 15.00 30.00

1994-95 German DEL

This 440-card set of the German hockey league was produced (apparently) by International Hockey Archives. The cards feature an action photo on the front, with player and team name along the borders. The back contain a space for autographing, as well as another photo and player bio in German. The set includes NHL prospects Florian Keller and Jochen Hecht, as well as several ex-NHL players.

COMPLETE SET (440) 20.00 50.00
1 Int'l Hockey Association .04 .10
2 DEL 1994/95 .04 .10
3 Season 1994-95 .04 .10
4 Augsburger Panther Team .04 .10
5 Gunnar Leidborg .04 .10
6 Gary Prior .10 .25
7 Scott Campbell .04 .10
8 Dieter Medicus .04 .10
9 Duanne Moeser .04 .10
10 Daniel Naud .04 .10
11 Andy Romer .04 .10
12 Thomas Groger .04 .10
13 Sven Zywitza .04 .10
14 Fritz Meyer .04 .10
15 Christian Curth .04 .10
16 Toni Krinner .04 .10
17 Patrik Pysz .04 .10
18 Heinrich Romer .04 .10
19 Ales Polcar .04 .10
20 Philip Kukuk .04 .10
21 Dietrich Adam .04 .10
22 Tim Schnobrich .04 .10
23 Tim Ferguson .10 .25
24 Robert Heidt .04 .10
25 Alfred Burkhard .04 .10
26 Charly Fliegauf .04 .10
27 Robert Paclik .04 .10
28 Stefan Mayer .04 .10
29 Reinhard Haider .04 .10
30 Dennis Schrapp .04 .10
31 Eisbaren Berlin Team Card .04 .10
32 Walter Jaroslav .04 .10
33 Klaus Schroder .04 .10
34 Andre Dietzsch .04 .10
35 Juri Stumpf .04 .10
36 Torsten Deutscher .04 .10
37 Frank Kannewurf .04 .10
38 Thomas Graul .04 .10
39 Sven Felski .04 .10
40 Moritz Schmidt .04 .10
41 Marco Swibenko .04 .10
42 Holger Mix .04 .10
43 Jiri Dopita .40 1.00
44 Dirk Perschau .04 .10
45 Guido Hiller .04 .10
46 Daniel Held .04 .10
47 Richard Zemlicka .10 .25
48 Jan Schertz .04 .10
49 Mike Losch .04 .10
50 Patrick Solf .04 .10
51 Rupert Meister .04 .10
52 BSC Preussen Team Card .04 .10
53 Billy Flynn .10 .25
54 Tony Tanti .10 .25
55 Jochen Molling .04 .10
56 Andreas Schubert .04 .10
57 Stefan Steinecker .04 .10
58 Josef Lehner .04 .10
59 Tom O'Regan .10 .25
60 Gaetan Malo .04 .10
61 Michael Komma .04 .10
62 Marco Schinko .04 .10
63 Marco Rentzsch .04 .10
64 Georg Holzmann .04 .10
65 Mark Kosturik .04 .10
66 Jurgen Rumrich .04 .10
67 John Chabot .20 .50
68 Harald Windler .04 .10
69 Mark Teevens .10 .25
70 Klaus Merk .10 .25
71 Stephan Sinner .04 .10
72 Mark Gronau .04 .10
73 Bruce Hardy .10 .25
74 Fabian Brannstrom .04 .10
75 Daniel Poudrier .10 .25
76 Dusseldorfer EG Team Card .04 .10
77 Hans Zach .04 .10
78 Helmut DeRaaf .04 .10
79 Markus Kehle .04 .10
80 Christian Schmitz .04 .10
81 Lorenz Funk .04 .10
82 Chris Valentine .20 .50
83 Rafael Jedamzik .04 .10
84 Torsten Kienass .10 .25
85 Christopher Kreutzer .04 .10
86 Benoit Doucet .10 .25
87 Bernd Kuhnhauser .04 .10
88 Andreas Niederberger .04 .10
89 Rick Amann .10 .25
90 Thorsten Van Leyen .04 .10
91 Bruce Eakin .04 .10
92 Pierre Rioux .10 .25
93 Andreas Brockmann .04 .10
94 Uli Hiemer .04 .10
95 Bernd Truntschka .10 .25
96 Wolfgang Kummer .04 .10
97 Carsten Gossmann .04 .10
98 Ernst Kopf .10 .25
99 Robert Sterflinger .04 .10
100 Kevin LaVallee .10 .25
101 Rainer Zerwesz .04 .10
102 Frankfurt Lions Team Card .04 .10
103 Pjotr Vorobjev .04 .10
104 Peter Obresa .04 .10
105 Vladimir Quapp .04 .10
106 Florian Storf .04 .10
107 Alexander Wedl .04 .10
108 Olaf Scholz .04 .10
109 Ilya Vorobjev .04 .10
110 Ladislav Strompf .04 .10
111 Udo Dohler .04 .10
112 Alexander Wunsch .04 .10
113 Jiri Lala .04 .10
114 Andrej Jaufmann .04 .10
115 Thomas Muhlbauer .04 .10
116 Markus Kempf .04 .10
117 Igor Schultz .04 .10
118 Martin Schultz .04 .10
119 Michael Raubal .04 .10
120 Rudi Gorgenlander .04 .10
121 Jurgen Schaal .04 .10
122 Patrick Vozar .04 .10
123 Rochus Schneider .04 .10
124 Toni Raubal .04 .10
125 Stefan Koniger .04 .10
126 EC Hannover Team Card .04 .10
127 Hartmut Nickel .04 .10
128 Joachim Lempio .04 .10
129 Torsten Hanusch .04 .10
130 Thomas Jungwirth .04 .10
131 David Reierson .04 .10
132 Friedhelm Bogelsack .04 .10
133 Thomas Werner .04 .10
134 Dirk Rohrbach .04 .10
135 Harald Kuhnke .04 .10
136 Florian Funk .04 .10
137 Mark Maroste .04 .10
138 Anton Maidl .04 .10
139 Rene Reuter .04 .10
140 Rene Ledock .04 .10
141 Marco Herbst .04 .10
142 Milos Vanik .04 .10
143 Gunther Preuss .04 .10
144 Troy Tumbach .04 .10
145 Marc Wittbrock .04 .10
146 Roger Mede .04 .10
147 Craig Topolnisky .04 .10
148 Josef Schlickenrieder .04 .10
149 Marcus Bleicher .04 .10
150 EC Kassel Team Card .04 .10
151 Ross Yates .04 .10
152 Josef Kontny .04 .10
153 Milan Mokros .04 .10
154 Alexander Engel .04 .10
155 Greg Johnston .10 .25
156 Jedrzej Kasperczyk .04 .10
157 Dave Morrison .04 .10
158 Jaro Mucha .04 .10
159 Mike Millar .10 .25
160 Ireneusz Pacula .04 .10
161 Vitalij Grossmann .04 .10
162 Murray McIntosh .04 .10
163 Manfred Ahne .04 .10
164 Peter Kwasigroch .04 .10
165 Georg Guttler .04 .10
166 Falk Ozellis .04 .10
167 Mario Naster .04 .10
168 Sergej Wikulow .04 .10
169 Gerhard Hegen .04 .10
170 Brian Hannon .04 .10
171 Tino Boos .04 .10
172 Kaufbeurer Adler Team Card .04 .10
173 Peter Kathan .04 .10
174 Kenneth Karpuk .04 .10
175 Michael Olbrich .04 .10
176 Drahomir Kadlec .10 .25
177 Christian Seeberger .04 .10
178 Elmar Boiger .04 .10
179 Oto Hascak .04 .10
180 Thorsten Rau .04 .10
181 Tomas Martinec .04 .10
182 Norbert Zabel .04 .10
183 Daniel Kunce .04 .10
184 Hans-Jorg Mayer .04 .10
185 Manfred Jorde .04 .10
186 Roland Timoschuk .04 .10
187 Jim Hoffmann .04 .10
188 Andreas Volland .04 .10
189 Rolf Hammer .04 .10
190 Manuel Hess .04 .10
191 Timo Gschwill .04 .10
192 Marc Pethke .04 .10
193 Axel Kammerer .04 .10
194 Jurgen Simon .04 .10
195 Patrick Lange .04 .10
196 Ronny Martin .04 .10
197 Kolner EC Team Card .04 .10
198 Vladimir Vassiliev .04 .10
199 Bernd Haake .04 .10
200 Joseph Heiss .30 .75
201 Jorg Mayr .04 .10
202 Thomas Brandl .04 .10
203 Stephan Mann .04 .10
204 Tonny Reddo .04 .10
205 Mirco Ludemann .10 .25
206 Leo Stefan .10 .25
207 Andreas Pokorny .04 .10
208 Peter Draisaitl .10 .25
209 Ralf Dobrzynski .04 .10
210 Andreas Lupzig .04 .10
211 Karsten Mende .04 .10
212 Frank Hohenadl .04 .10
213 Marco Heinrichs .04 .10
214 Michael Rumrich .04 .10
215 Martin Ondrejka .04 .10
216 Herbert Hohenberger .10 .25
217 Thorsten Sendt .04 .10
218 Thorsten Koslowski .04 .10
219 Olaf Grundmann .04 .10
220 Franz Demmel .04 .10
221 Sergej Berezin .80 2.00
222 Krefelder EV Team Card .04 .10
223 Michael Zettel .04 .10
224 Frank Brunsing .04 .10
225 Karel Lang .04 .10
226 Markus Kranwinkel .04 .10
227 Earl Spry .04 .10
228 Andre Grein .04 .10
229 Greg Evtushevski .10 .25
230 Herberts Vasiljevs .04 .10
231 Ken Petrash .04 .10
232 Greg Thomson .04 .10
233 Reemt Pyka .10 .25
234 Brad Bergen .10 .25
235 Chris Lindberg .10 .25
236 Markus Kranwinkel .04 .10
237 Martin Gebel .04 .10
238 Francois Sills .04 .10
239 Klaus Micheller .04 .10
240 Peter Ihnacak .20 .50
241 Marek Stebnicki .04 .10
242 Johnny Walker .04 .10
243 Gunter Oswald .04 .10
244 James Hanlon .04 .10
245 Rene Bielke .04 .10
246 EV Landshut Team Card .04 .10
247 Bernhard Johnston .04 .10
248 Mark Stuckey .04 .10
249 Michael Bresagk .04 .10
250 Bernd Wagner .04 .10
251 Eduard Uvria .04 .10
252 Mike Smazal .04 .10
253 Jacek Plachta .04 .10
254 Georg Franz .04 .10
255 Stephan Retzer .04 .10
256 Henri Marcoux .04 .10
257 Andreas Loth .04 .10
258 Mike Bullard .04 .10
259 Markus Berwanger .04 .10
260 Petr Briza .40 1.00
261 Wally Schreiber .20 .50
262 Peter Gulda .04 .10
263 Ralf Hantschke .04 .10
264 Steve McNeil .04 .10
265 Christian Kunast .04 .10
266 Jorg Hendrick .04 .10
267 Helmut Steiger .04 .10
268 Udo Kiessling .04 .10
269 Mike Lay .04 .10
270 Adler Mannheim Team Card .04 .10
271 Lance Nethery .10 .25
272 Marcus Kuhl .04 .10
273 Joachim Appel .04 .10
274 Harold Kreis .04 .10
275 Mike Heidt .04 .10
276 Mario Gehrig .04 .10
277 Pavel Gross .04 .10
278 Steffen Michel .04 .10
279 Daniel Korber .04 .10
280 Robert Cimetta .10 .25
281 Dale Krentz .10 .25
282 Jochen Hecht 4.00 10.00
283 Till Feser .04 .10
284 Lars Bruggemann .04 .10
285 Toni Plattner .04 .10
286 Alexander Schuster .04 .10
287 Dieter Willmann .04 .10
288 Markus Flemming .04 .10
289 Rick Goldmann .20 .50
290 Damian Adamus .04 .10
291 Frederik Ledlin .04 .10
292 David Musial .04 .10
293 Michael Gabler .04 .10
294 Sven Valenti .04 .10
295 Maddogs Munchen Team Card .04 .10
296 Robert Murdoch .04 .10
297 Alexander Genze .04 .10
298 Greg Muller .04 .10
299 Mike Schmidt .04 .10
300 Zdenek Travnicek .04 .10
301 Christian Lukes .04 .10
302 Gordon Sherven .10 .25
303 Anthony Vogel .04 .10
304 Michael Hreuss .04 .10
305 Dale Derkatch .10 .25
306 Sergej Schendelew .04 .10
307 Christian Brittig .04 .10
308 Harald Waibel .04 .10

309 Rainer Lutz .04 .10
310 Ewald Steiger .04 .10
311 Didi Hegen .04 .10
312 Ralf Reisinger .04 .10
313 Henrik Holscher .04 .10
314 Karl Friesen .20 .50
315 Christian Frutel .04 .10
316 Tobias Abstreiter .04 .10
317 Christopher Sandner .04 .10
318 Harald Birk .04 .10
319 Chris Strausse .04 .10
320 EHC 80 Numberg Team Card .04 .10
321 Josef Golonka .04 .10
322 Christian Gerum .04 .10
323 Paul Geddes .04 .10
324 Ian Young .04 .10
325 Stefan Steinbock .04 .10
326 Doug Irwin .04 .10
327 Christian Flugge .04 .10
328 Klaus Birk .04 .10
329 Jurgen Lechl .04 .10
330 Thomas Popiesch .04 .10
331 Miroslav Maly .04 .10
332 Stephan Eder .04 .10
333 Arno Brux .04 .10
334 Jiri Dolezal .04 .10
335 Reiner Vorderbruggen .04 .10
336 Thomas Sterflinger .04 .10
337 Bernhard Engelbrecht .04 .10
338 Michael Weinfurther .04 .10
339 Sepp Wassermann .04 .10
340 Stephan Bauer .04 .10
341 Otto Sykora .04 .10
342 Ratingen Die Lowen Team Card .04 .10
343 Bill Lochead .10 .25
344 Pavel Mann .04 .10
345 Christian Kohmann .04 .10
346 Sven Prusa .04 .10
347 Otto Kereszies .04 .10
348 Frank Kovacs .04 .10
349 Jiri Smicek .04 .10
350 Richard Brodnicke .04 .10
351 Andrej Fuchs .04 .10
352 Oliver Kasper .04 .10
353 Michael Kratz .04 .10
354 Klaus Striemitzer .04 .10
355 Oliver Schwarz .04 .10
356 Boris Fuchs .04 .10
357 Christian Althoff .04 .10
358 Waldemar Novosjolov .04 .10
359 Thomas Imdahl .04 .10
360 Helmut Elters .04 .10
361 Andrej Hanisz .04 .10
362 Peter Lutter .04 .10
363 Martem Janov .04 .10
364 Mark Bassen .04 .10
365 Udo Schmid .04 .10
366 Mark Bassen .10 .25
367 Rosenheim Star Bulls Team Card .04 .10
368 Ernst Hofner .04 .10
369 Ludek Bukac .04 .10
370 Markus Wieland .04 .10
371 Andreas Schneider .04 .10
372 Raphael Kruger .04 .10
373 Michael Tattner .04 .10
374 Rick Boehm .04 .10
375 Robert Hock .04 .10
376 Joachim Reil .04 .10
377 Radek Toupal .04 .10
378 Martin Reichel .04 .10
379 Ron Fischer .04 .10
380 Raimund Hilger .10 .25
381 Petr Hrbek .04 .10
382 Oliver Hausler .04 .10
383 Christian Gegenfurther .04 .10
384 Marc Seliger .10 .25
385 Venci Sebek .04 .10
386 Florian Keller .10 .25
387 Heinrich Schiffl .04 .10
388 Michael Pohl .04 .10
389 Fuchse Sachsen Team Card .04 .10
390 Jiri Kochta .04 .10
391 Boris Capla .04 .10
392 Matthias Kliemann .04 .10
393 Josef Rednicek .04 .10
394 Branjo Heisig .04 .10
395 Jens Schwabe .10 .25
396 Frank Peschke .04 .10
397 Thomas Schubert .04 .10
398 Torsten Eisebitt .04 .10
399 Marcel Lichnovsky .04 .10
400 Jari Gronstrand .10 .25
401 Thomas Knobloch .04 .10
402 Falk Herzig .04 .10
403 Thomas Wagner .04 .10
404 Jan Tabor .04 .10
405 Sebastian Klenner .04 .10
406 Peter Hofmann .04 .10
407 Terry Cambell .10 .25
408 Antonio Fonso .04 .10
409 Thomas Bresagk .04 .10
410 Petr Franke .04 .10
411 Andreas Ott .04 .10
412 Michael Flemming .04 .10
413 Janusz Janikowski .04 .10
414 Schwenningen Wild Wings Team Card .04 .10
415 Miroslav Berek .04 .10
416 Bob Burns .04 .10
417 Thomas Gaus .04 .10
418 Richard Trojan .04 .10
419 Ilmar Toman .04 .10
420 Alan Young .04 .10
421 Michael Pastika .04 .10
422 Thomas Schadler .04 .10
423 Andrei Kovalev .04 .10
424 Alexander Horn .04 .10
425 Petr Kopta .04 .10
426 Robert Brezina .04 .10
427 Wayne Hynes .10 .25
428 Frantisek Frosch .04 .10
429 Carsten Solbach .04 .10
430 George Fritz .04 .10
431 Mike Bader .04 .10
432 Thomas Deiter .04 .10
433 Daniel Nowak .10 .25
434 Peter Heinold .04 .10
435 Matthias Hoppe .04 .10
436 Grant Martin .10 .25
437 Roger Bruns .04 .10
438 Andreas Renz .04 .10
439 Karsten Schulz .04 .10
440 Alfie Turcotte .10 .25

1994-95 German First League

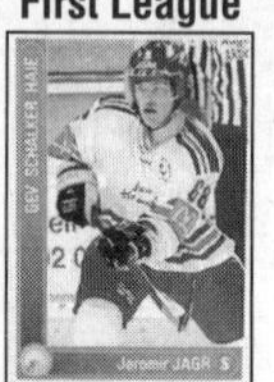

This set features players of the German First League, a division one lower than the DEL. The set is noteworthy for the inclusion of several NHLers who performed briefly on this circuit during the 1994 NHL lockout, including Jaromir Jagr, Petr Klima and Vladimir Konstantinov.

COMPLETE SET (665) 30.00 80.00
33 Jorn Seuthe .10 .25
34 Pietro Vacca .10 .25
35 Gunther Eisenhut .10 .25
36 Thomas Kulzer .10 .25
37 Christian Zessak .10 .25
38 Peter Sterz .10 .25
39 Michael Maass .10 .25
40 Thomas Brandl .10 .25
41 Thomas Daffner .10 .25
42 Volker Kollmeder .10 .25
43 Thomas Haiti .10 .25
44 Hans Eberhard .10 .25
45 Enrico Kock .10 .25
46 Peter Hampl .10 .25
47 German Wolgin .10 .25
48 Andrej Balandin .10 .25
49 Rainer Wohlmann .10 .25
50 Teamcard/Checklist .10 .25
51 Michael Eibl .10 .25
52 Sven Schubert .10 .25
53 Franz Steer .10 .25
54 Ottmar Schluttenhofer .10 .25
55 Wolfgang Oswald .10 .25
56 John Samanski .10 .25
57 Marty Irvine .10 .25
58 Herbert Schadler .10 .25
59 Jeff Vaive .10 .25
60 Markus Neumuller .10 .25
61 Norbert Arians .10 .25
62 Alfred Weiss .10 .25
63 Gert Heubach .10 .25
64 Hans-Georg Eder .10 .25
65 Hansi Bader .10 .25
66 Franz Futtner .10 .25
67 Klaus Pillmaier .10 .25
68 Donar Dotzauer .10 .25
69 Bertil Filgis .10 .25
70 Roman Zaborowski .10 .25
71 Thomas Dahlem .10 .25
72 Markus Faistenhammer .10 .25
73 Teamcard/Checklist .10 .25
74 Thomas Dolak .10 .25
75 Oliver Kratt .10 .25
76 Klaus Muller .10 .25
77 Ralf Lux .10 .25
78 Igor Dorochin .10 .25
79 Ravil Khaidarov .10 .25
80 Peter Hejma .10 .25
81 Thomas Geldreich .10 .25
82 Christian Helber .10 .25
83 Marc Schonfeld .10 .25
84 Christian Wolfgramm .10 .25
85 Leos Zajic .10 .25
86 Rick Laycock .10 .25
87 Stefan Lahn .10 .25
88 Thomas Steinberg .10 .25
89 Jan Repka .10 .25
90 Joseph Peroutka .10 .25
91 Andreas Mockl .10 .25
92 Peter Salmik .10 .25
93 Jorg Lettgen .10 .25
94 Frank Furderer .10 .25
95 Christian Ott .10 .25
96 Teamcard/Checklist .10 .25
97 Rodion Pauels .10 .25
98 Aaron Strasser .10 .25
99 Ernst Messthaler .10 .25
100 Juri Starkhov .10 .25
101 Nikolai Varianov .10 .25
102 Tomas Krejcir .10 .25
103 Stefan Zellhuber .10 .25
104 Markus Gmeiner .10 .25
105 Richard Schnetz .10 .25
106 Wolfgang Koziol .10 .25
107 Christian Hauserer .10 .25
108 Gerhard Dittrich .10 .25
109 Christopher Zweng .10 .25
110 Peter Hartung .10 .25
111 Robert Scharpf .10 .25
112 Florian Schneider .10 .25
113 Tauno Zobel .10 .25
114 Matthias Sanger .10 .25
115 Peter Asanger .10 .25
116 Christian Ganseneder .10 .25
117 Hans-Jorg Stetter .10 .25
118 Thomas Frohlich .10 .25
119 Karl Streit .10 .25
120 Stefan Bardzinski .10 .25
121 Teamcard/Checklist .10 .25
122 Josef Capla .10 .25
123 Jorg Zinnecker .10 .25
124 Peter Harrer .10 .25
125 Heinrich Korph .10 .25
126 Martin Kirsch .10 .25
127 Michael Freissmann .10 .25
128 Peter Rappold .10 .25
129 Daniel Piechaczek .10 .25
130 Bernd Gessinger .10 .25
131 Michael Hogl .10 .25
132 Hubert Jellen .10 .25
133 Hans Hansch .10 .25
134 Steven Schafer .10 .25
135 Harald Wust .10 .25
136 Jean-Claude Brehm .10 .25
137 Olaf Bjorner .10 .25
138 Dusan Canik .10 .25
139 Martin Gessinger .10 .25
140 Martin Tschichoflos .10 .25
141 Ullich Liebsch .10 .25
142 Svyatoslav Khalizov .10 .25
143 Michael Pescheck .10 .25
144 Roland Seckler .10 .25
145 Teamcard/Checklist .10 .25
146 Gerd Wittmann .10 .25
147 Vladimir Macholda .10 .25
148 Sascha Bernhardt .10 .25
149 Michael Thurner .10 .25
150 Norbert Haslach .10 .25
151 Vitus ner Mitterfell .10 .25
152 Thorsten Haaf .10 .25
153 Michael Stejskal .10 .25
154 Klaus Jansen .10 .25
155 Oliver Hackert .10 .25
156 Ladislav Svozil .10 .25
157 Karsten Neumann .10 .25
158 Alexander Ulmer .10 .25
159 Joseph West .10 .25
160 Oliver Weissenberger .10 .25
161 Manfred Schuster .10 .25
162 Oliver Vost .10 .25
163 Peter Stankovic .10 .25
164 Uwe Geisert .10 .25
165 Peter Holdschick .10 .25
166 Ralf Hartfuss .10 .25
167 Bernhard Kopf .10 .25
168 Teamcard/Checklist .10 .25
169 Kim Collins .10 .25
170 Josef Wieser .10 .25
171 Frank Fischer .10 .25
172 Peter Geier .10 .25
173 Glenn Goodall .40 1.00
174 Patrick Fertich .10 .25
175 Mathias Wieser .10 .25
176 Maximilian Schindler .10 .25
177 Bastian Kammerloher .10 .25
178 James Quinlan .10 .25
179 Dirk Heick .10 .25
180 Walter Deisenberger .10 .25
181 Christoph Sauter .10 .25
182 Christian Walleitner .10 .25
183 Martin Sauter .10 .25
184 Oliver Mayer .10 .25
185 Roland Floss .10 .25
186 Maximilian Ahammer .10 .25
187 Robert Schumacher .10 .25
188 Ludvik Kopecky .10 .25
189 Florian Eder .10 .25
190 Teamcard/Checklist .10 .25
191 Ewalds Grabowskis .10 .25
192 Gerhard Petrussek .10 .25
193 Robert Bockler .10 .25
194 Markus Epple .10 .25
195 Mivhael Weisenbach .10 .25
196 Michael Billmaier .10 .25
197 Joachim Ried .10 .25
198 Holger Micheller .10 .25
199 Igor Pavlov .10 .25
200 Rudiger Weis .10 .25
201 Alexander Zittlau .10 .25
202 Michael Schaeufl .10 .25
203 Oleg Znarok .10 .25
204 Armin Fohry .10 .25
205 Franz-Xaver Ibelherr .10 .25
206 Karl Sajdl .10 .25
207 Daniel Schury .10 .25
208 Manfred Korb .10 .25
209 Christian Baier .10 .25
210 Christian Reuter .10 .25
211 Paul Haringer .10 .25
212 Erwin Haiusa .10 .25
213 Roland Hanemann .10 .25
214 Joachim Jais .10 .25
215 Teamcard/Checklist .10 .25
216 Eduard Giblak .10 .25
217 Robert Bohm .10 .25
218 Paul Greiter .10 .25
219 Max Ostermeier .10 .25
220 Florian Schmid .10 .25
221 Alexander Meyer .10 .25
222 Michael Lehmann .10 .25
223 Andi Ostermeier .10 .25
224 Manfred Braun .10 .25
225 Franz Daxner .10 .25
226 Michael Hock .10 .25
227 Oliver Kleininger .10 .25
228 Chris Clarke .10 .25
229 Andreas Paukner .10 .25
230 Florian Jager .10 .25
231 Patrick Gerber .10 .25
232 Karl Huttl .10 .25
233 Brad Belland .10 .25
234 Christian Lex .10 .25
235 Anton Hager .10 .25
236 Uli Stadler .10 .25
237 Teamcard/Checklist .10 .25
238 Florian Strida .10 .25
239 Peter Freissl .10 .25
240 Peter Engel .10 .25
241 Georg Weckerle .10 .25
242 Reiner Bauerle .10 .25
243 Johann Fischer .10 .25
244 Christian Kratzmeir .10 .25
245 Martin Strida .10 .25
246 Wolfgang Obermeier .10 .25
247 Franz Bruckl .10 .25
248 Robert Schmidt .10 .25
249 Jiri Jiroutek .10 .25
250 Bjorn Lehner .10 .25
251 Florian Rohde .10 .25
252 Paul Ruzicka .10 .25
253 Andreas Kraus .10 .25
254 Oliver Ciganovic .10 .25
255 Christian Steidl .10 .25
256 Klaus Strobl .10 .25
257 Robert Hauck .10 .25
258 Thomas Reitmeir .10 .25
259 Joachim Hagelsperger .10 .25
260 Florian Steidl .10 .25
261 Teamcard/Checklist .10 .25
262 Alexej Sulak .10 .25
263 Markus Mayer .10 .25
264 Thomas Brenzig .10 .25
265 Sven Erhart .10 .25
266 Holger Lieb .10 .25
267 Josef Maier .10 .25
268 Paul Huber .10 .25
269 Rainer Hain .10 .25
270 Peter Kothmayr .10 .25
271 Denis Hanko .10 .25
272 Manfred Muhlegger .10 .25
273 James Johannsen .10 .25
274 Michael Kteitl .10 .25
275 Reiner Sangl .10 .25
276 Rainer Hirschvogel .10 .25
277 Markus Weiss .10 .25
278 Herbert Gmeinder .10 .25
279 Gunther Hartmann .10 .25
280 Jorg Peters .10 .25
281 Sergej Boldavesko .10 .25
282 Peter Dorn .10 .25
283 Markus Kothmayr .10 .25
284 Teamcard/Checklist .10 .25
285 Georg Kink .10 .25
286 Gerhard Stranka .10 .25
287 Michael Pump .10 .25
288 Tom Gobel .10 .25
289 Vladimir Fedossov .10 .25
290 Andreas Oswald .10 .25
291 Andreas Ludwig .10 .25
292 Martin Leuthner .10 .25
293 Jurgen Reindl .10 .25
294 Karl Ostler .10 .25
295 Martin Holzer .10 .25
296 Peter Fischer .10 .25
297 Jens Feller .10 .25
298 Henry Domke .10 .25
299 Markus Kossig .10 .25
300 Andreas Maurer .10 .25
301 Georg Grunauer .10 .25
302 Andreas Wittig .10 .25
303 Andreas Gebauer .10 .25
304 Hubert Buchwieser .10 .25
305 Andreas Raubal .10 .25
306 Christian Winkler .10 .25
307 Brett Stewart .10 .25
308 Christoph Sandner .10 .25
309 Rainer Lutz .10 .25
310 Alfred Burkhard .10 .25
311 Dale Derkatch .20 .50
312 Teamcard/Checklist .10 .25
313 Rudolf Sindelar .10 .25
314 Thomas Hobek .10 .25
315 Jason Hall .10 .25
316 Jochen Hordler .10 .25
317 Mark Armstrong .10 .25
318 Peter Netsch .10 .25
319 Armin Hanke .10 .25
320 Jaroslav Peska .10 .25
321 Steve Neumann .10 .25
322 Markus Trendl .10 .25
323 Daniel Gardner .10 .25
324 Marek Kurowski .10 .25
325 Markus Albrecht .10 .25
326 Sascha Groger .10 .25
327 Stefan Leuschner .10 .25
328 Andreas Kimker .10 .25
329 Roland Schneider .10 .25
330 Elko Porzi .10 .25
331 Stefan Wegmann .10 .25
332 Holger Cecco .10 .25
333 Ralf Gaess .10 .25
334 EHC Straubing .10 .25
335 Franz Hejcik .10 .25
336 Christoph Reitz .10 .25
337 Achim Sipmeier .10 .25
338 Christian Penzkofer .10 .25
339 Thomas Schambeck .10 .25
340 Douglas Kirton .10 .25
341 Rainer Schuster .10 .25
342 Vaclav Mandous .10 .25
343 Christian Knott .10 .25
344 Edward Zawatsky .10 .25
345 Christian Heitzer .10 .25
346 RÃ¼diger Metsch .10 .25
347 Christian Setz .10 .25
348 Sascha Werner .10 .25
349 Martin Ebenburger .10 .25
350 Daniel Vogl .10 .25
351 Stephan Meier .10 .25
352 Sven Barnet .10 .25
353 Robert Steinmann .10 .25
354 1. EV Weiden .10 .25
355 Wilbert Duszenko .10 .25
356 Alexander Becker .10 .25
357 Frank Gentges .10 .25
358 Anton Doll .10 .25
359 Stefan Peschek .10 .25
360 Oliver Hecht .10 .25
361 Dirk Salinger .10 .25
362 Yuri Chipitsyn .10 .25
363 Marco Zimmermann .10 .25
364 Christian Martin .10 .25
365 Lubos Thur .10 .25
366 Andreas Frysztacki .10 .25
367 Sergej Agejkin .10 .25
368 Roman Bartosch .10 .25
369 Ales Volek .10 .25
370 Josef PreuÃŸ .10 .25
371 Thomas Pokorny .10 .25
372 Roman Zilka .10 .25
373 Dietmar Habnitt .10 .25
374 Horst BÃ¤rnreuther .10 .25
375 Stefan Breitner .10 .25
376 Teamcard/Checklist .10 .25
377 Ricki Alexander .10 .25
378 Ingo Schwarz .10 .25
379 Serge Lajoie .10 .25
380 Thomas Barczikowski .10 .25
381 Rik Schaefer .10 .25
382 Markus Reiter .10 .25
383 Todd Goodwin .10 .25
384 Thorsten Wolf .10 .25
385 Volker Lindenzweig .10 .25
386 Sven Paschek .10 .25
387 Markus Jehner .10 .25
388 Jurgen Engels .10 .25
389 Martin Prada .10 .25
390 Norbert Scholz .10 .25
391 Gregory Pruden .10 .25
392 Oliver Vieten .10 .25
393 Robert Vozar .10 .25
394 Martin Williams .10 .25
395 Jan Schier .10 .25
396 Michael Eckert .10 .25
397 Thomas Krebs .10 .25
398 Teamcard/Checklist .10 .25
399 Gerald Mull .10 .25
400 Juris Kruminsch .10 .25
401 Frank Strauss .10 .25
402 Peter Kaluza .10 .25
403 Dirk Sobottka .10 .25
404 Alwin Wever .10 .25
405 Jerzey Christ .10 .25
406 Andreas Kemper .10 .25
407 Andre Wilmshofer .10 .25
408 Olaf Busch .10 .25
409 Rico Petrick .10 .25
410 Kurt Wickenheiser .20 .50
411 Marc Muller .20 .50
412 Steffen Klau .10 .25
413 Zsolt Heffler .10 .25
414 Martin Bergeron .10 .25
415 Willi Tesch .10 .25
416 Frank Fischoder .10 .25
417 Darius Wonschewski .10 .25
418 Teamcard/Checklist .10 .25
419 Eduard Nocak .10 .25
420 Stephan Schafer .10 .25
421 Michael Schmitz .10 .25
422 Jochen Hecker .10 .25
423 Axel Gesser .10 .25
424 Heinz-Gerd Albers .10 .25
425 Markus Bak .10 .25
426 Bernd Deske .10 .25
427 Ron Noak .10 .25
428 Darren Colbourne .10 .25
429 Frank Pribil .10 .25
430 Holger Rimroth .10 .25
431 Lars Tannhof .10 .25
432 Ulrik Kuhnekath .10 .25
433 Jorg Deske .10 .25
434 Guy Phillips .10 .25
435 Jorg Bohme .10 .25
436 Udo Sofan .10 .25
437 Matthias Starke .10 .25
438 Oliver Walde .10 .25
439 Teamcard/Checklist .10 .25
440 Dieter Bruggemann .10 .25
441 Julian Binavince .10 .25
442 Kai Kemper .10 .25
443 Raimund Peschke .10 .25
444 Frank Besser .10 .25
445 Frank Blanke .10 .25
446 John Neeld .10 .25
447 Alexander Knoff .10 .25
448 Brad Scott .10 .25
449 Bodo Mischer .10 .25
450 Jiri Kovarik .10 .25
451 Markus Kolloch .10 .25
452 Carsten Plate .10 .25
453 Thomas Hesse .10 .25
454 Jorg Loschek .10 .25
455 Dirk Voss .10 .25
456 Detlev Eltermann .10 .25
457 Volker Loscheck .10 .25
458 Richard Drewniak .10 .25
459 Teamcard/Checklist .10 .25
460 Erwin Materna .10 .25
461 Ingmar Kracht .10 .25
462 Michael Meixner .10 .25
463 Dirk Rossbach .10 .25
464 Karsten Scherping .10 .25
465 Mark Mahon .10 .25
466 Wolfgang Hofbauer .10 .25
467 Uwe Geiselmann .10 .25
468 Sean Krakivsky .10 .25
469 Douglas Murray .10 .25
470 Marek Gajewski .10 .25
471 Mario Feigl .10 .25
472 Frank Liebert .10 .25
473 Miroslav Mago .10 .25
474 Mirsolav Sakmirda .10 .25
475 Dirk Nieleck .10 .25
476 Jan Furd .10 .25
477 Ralf Kubiak .10 .25
478 Marek Adamec .10 .25
479 Douglas Murray .10 .25
480 Teamcard/Checklist .10 .25
481 Sergej Svetlov .10 .25
482 Christian Berlin .10 .25
483 Marek Adamek .10 .25
484 Ralf Cassebaum .10 .25
485 Ingo Rdurch .10 .25
486 Sergej Hatkevitsch .10 .25
487 Thomas Otto .10 .25
488 Riccardo Siegert .10 .25
489 Willy Reinhard .10 .25
490 Jorn Sigmansky .10 .25
491 Guido Drongowski .10 .25
492 Carsten Boss .10 .25
493 Jacek Piechutta .10 .25
494 Thorsten Peters .10 .25
495 Lutz Bongers .10 .25
496 Armin Schnitzler .10 .25
497 Teamcard/Checklist .10 .25
498 Walter Koberle .10 .25
499 Carsten Lange .10 .25
500 Jurgen Schultz .10 .25
501 Jan Raspel .10 .25
502 Christoph Gelzinus .10 .25
503 Markus Kamman .10 .25
504 Markus Buchhart .10 .25
505 Holger Schmitz .10 .25
506 Ladislav Kolda .10 .25
507 Arndt Kons .10 .25
508 Boris Morsch .10 .25
509 Darius Wonschewski .10 .25
510 Benedikt Kons .10 .25
511 James Dressler .10 .25
512 Dirk Scholz .10 .25
513 Marco Scharf .10 .25
514 Mike van Hauten .10 .25
515 Max Bander .10 .25
516 Gilbert Schroder .10 .25
517 Teamcard/Checklist .10 .25
518 Alexander Wolkow .10 .25
519 Sven Schmitz .10 .25
520 Andrej Ovtschinnikov .10 .25
521 Boguslav Kuta .10 .25
522 Sergej Zaitsev .10 .25
523 Rene Naroska .10 .25
524 Markus Menschig .10 .25
525 Milos Piperski .10 .25
526 Andreas Halfmann .10 .25
527 Marcus Golabek .10 .25
528 Peter Kraus .10 .25
529 Peter Juchem .10 .25
530 Marius Cissewski .10 .25
531 Falk Elzner .10 .25
532 Jens Herget .10 .25
533 Fabian Dahlem .10 .25
534 Jurgen Trattner .10 .25
535 Daniel Walther .10 .25
536 Peter Burfant .10 .25
537 Eduard Lorer .10 .25
538 Andreas Keiler .10 .25
539 Haie Schalker GEV .10 .25
540 Charly Stenner CO .10 .25
541 Thomas Blasche .10 .25
542 Dietmar Schramm .10 .25
543 Achim Blaar .10 .25
544 Graischa Pietsch .10 .25
545 Robert Simon .10 .25
546 Bruce Bonner .10 .25
547 Ladislav Hospodar .10 .25
548 Martin Jilek .10 .25
549 Michael Scanu .10 .25
550 Phil Berger .10 .25
551 Christoph Kleckers .10 .25
552 Patrick Schmitz .10 .25
553 Gregor Wilk .10 .25
554 Jens Casten .10 .25
555 Andre Jucknischke .10 .25
556 Vladimir Kames .10 .25
557 Petr Fiala .10 .25
558 Marco Blazyczek .10 .25
559 Trajan Cazacu .10 .25
560 Robert Schutz .10 .25
561 Jaromir Jagr 20.00 50.00
562 ETC Timmendorf .10 .25
563 Jeff Pyle .10 .25
564 Gerd Vogel .10 .25
565 Andrzej Bielenink .10 .25
566 Marvin Glaser .10 .25
567 Harald Bolke .10 .25
568 Christian Spaan .10 .25
569 Henry Thom .10 .25
570 Matthias Schnabel .10 .25
571 Mike Bukowski .10 .25
572 Jeff Tomlinson .20 .50
573 Steffen Thau .10 .25
574 Mark MacKay .20 .50
575 Olaf Broll .10 .25
576 Moe Lemay .40 1.00
577 Michael Mai .10 .25
578 Peter Hiller .10 .25
579 Christoph Hadraschek .10 .25
580 Mike Wehrmann .10 .25
581 Lars Wunsche .10 .25
582 Maj Boguslaw .10 .25
583 Sven Rampf .10 .25
584 Teamcard/Checklist .10 .25
585 Helmut Bauer .10 .25
586 Guido Titzhoff .10 .25
587 Lubomir Lang .10 .25
588 Guy Rouleau .10 .25
589 Andreas Naumann .20 .50
590 Marc Otten .10 .25
591 Kenneth Filgis .10 .25
592 Dimitri Matuschow .10 .25
593 Markus Pollock .10 .25
594 Mario Plack .10 .25
595 Herbert Plattner .10 .25
596 Roman Sindelar .20 .50
597 Herbert Ott .10 .25
598 Reik Blasche .10 .25
599 Vladimir Lukscheider .10 .25
600 Christof Grunthal .10 .25
601 Hermann Retzer .10 .25
602 Adam Gedyk .10 .25
603 Ralf Lamberty .10 .25
604 Teamcard/Checklist .10 .25
605 Kevin Gaudet .10 .25
606 Dale Reinig .10 .25
607 Jorg Meyer .10 .25
608 Bruce Keller .10 .25
609 Laszlo Csata .10 .25
610 Douglas Morton .10 .25
611 Garry Schwindt .10 .25
612 Fred Carroll .10 .25
613 Len Soccio .20 .50
614 Michail Lemmer .10 .25
615 Dieter Reiss .10 .25
616 Jirko Seib .10 .25
617 Matthias Kuhnel .10 .25
618 Heinrich Synowietz .10 .25
619 Paul Synowietz .10 .25
620 Justyn Denisiuk .10 .25
621 Slawomir Osinski .10 .25
622 Jari Pasanen .10 .25
623 Marcus Beeck .10 .25
624 Vladimir Konstantinov 4.00 10.00
625 Teamcard/Checklist .10 .25
626 Josef Vimmer .10 .25
627 Torsten Kluin .10 .25
628 Dieter Frenzel .10 .25
629 Harald Hebig .10 .25
630 Jorg Volkle .10 .25
631 Alexander Gorsdorf .10 .25
632 Roman Slezak .10 .25
633 Jan Baron .10 .25
634 Sergej Jaschin .10 .25
635 Robert Eylert .10 .25
636 Anatoli Antipov .10 .25
637 Heiko Tabor .10 .25
638 Jan-Hans Pokorny .10 .25
639 Roman Blazek .10 .25
640 Alexander Purschel .10 .25
641 Bernd Timmer .10 .25
642 Tomasz Mieszkowski .10 .25
643 Vaclav Drobny .10 .25
644 Teamcard/Checklist .10 .25
645 Nikolai Besprosvannych .10 .25
646 Dimitri Ritthaler .10 .25
647 Dimitri Konjuchov .10 .25
648 Erwin Forster .10 .25
649 Olaf-Bjorn Kolle .10 .25
650 Gary Cummins .10 .25
651 Garth Bannatyne .10 .25
652 Jamie Hartnett .10 .25
653 Cory Holden .10 .25
654 Andreas Henkel .10 .25
655 Janusz Wielgus .10 .25
656 Douglas Morton .10 .25
657 Kebin McGibney .10 .25
658 Daniel Poudrier .20 .50
659 Peter Just .10 .25
660 Lumir Mikesz .10 .25
661 Kenneth Filbey .10 .25
662 Richard Jelsovsky .10 .25
663 Petr Klima .40 1.00
664 Jiri Jiroutek .10 .25
665 Mark MacKay .20 .50

1995-96 German DEL

This 450-card set features the players of Germany's top hockey division, the DEL. The cards measure the standard size, and were issued in six-card packs for 2.5 marks. The card fronts feature action photography with the player name, position and team logo along the bottom. The back includes another photo along with stats. The set is highlighted by the inclusion of several NHLers who played in the DEL during the 1994 lockout including Pavel Bure, Jeremy Roenick and Brendan Shanahan. The hologram chase card was randomly inserted in 1:375 packs. A collector's album to house the cards was available through a wrapper offer for 45 marks.

COMPLETE SET (450) 50.00 125.00
1 Gary Prior .06 .15
2 Rupert Meister .04 .10
3 Dennis Schrapp .04 .10
4 Scott Campbell .04 .10
5 Fritz Meyer .04 .10
6 Rob Mendel .04 .10
7 Ken Collins .06 .15
8 Stefan Mayer .04 .10
9 Torsten Fendt .04 .10
10 Andrei Skopintsev .06 .15
11 Bob Wilkie .04 .10
12 Duanne Moeser .04 .10
13 Martin Nagler .04 .10
14 Sven Zywitza .04 .10
15 Marc Habscheid .10 .25
16 Daniel Held .04 .10
17 Heinrich Romer .04 .10
18 Rick Laycock .04 .10
19 Robert Francz .04 .10
20 Tim Ferguson .04 .10
21 Robert Heidt .06 .15
22 Eric Dylla .04 .10
23 Harald Birk .04 .10
24 Rochus Schneider .04 .10
25 Billy Flynn .04 .10
26 Andre Dietzsch .04 .10
27 Udo Dohler .04 .10
28 Juri Stumpf .04 .10
29 Torsten Deutscher .04 .10
30 Frank Kannewurf .04 .10
31 Thomas Graul .04 .10
32 Dirk Perschau .04 .10
33 Patrick Solf .04 .10
34 Daniel Poudrier .04 .10
35 Bernhard Kaminski .04 .10
36 Christoph Hadraschek .04 .10
37 Sven Felski .04 .10
38 Marco Swibenko .04 .10
39 Holger Mix .04 .10
40 Mark Maroste .04 .10
41 Troy Tumbach .04 .10
42 Jan Schertz .04 .10
43 Mike Losch .04 .10
44 Andreas Naumann .06 .15
45 Marc Garthe .04 .10
46 Igor Dorochin .04 .10
47 Thomas Mitew .04 .10
48 Claes Lundmark .04 .10
49 Chris Straube .04 .10
50 Klaus Merk .20 .50
51 Mark Gronau .04 .10
52 Stefan Steinecker .04 .10
53 Josef Lehner .04 .10
54 Tom O'Regan .06 .15
55 Fredrik Stillmann .04 .10
56 Marco Rentzsch .04 .10
57 Stephan Sinner .04 .10
58 Andreas Schubert .06 .15
59 Tony Tanti .10 .25
60 Gaeten Malo .04 .10
61 Michael Komma .04 .10
62 Thomas Schinko .04 .10
63 Georg Holzmann .04 .10
64 Mark Kosturik .04 .10
65 Christian Brittig .04 .10
66 Jurgen Rumrich .04 .10
67 John Chabot .20 .50
68 Andreas Dimbat .04 .10
69 Ulrich Liebsch .04 .10
70 Mark Teevens .06 .15
71 Fabian Brannstom .04 .10
72 Dennis Meyer .04 .10
73 Lars Hoffmann .04 .10
74 Hardy Nilsson CO .04 .10
75 Marcus Karlsson .04 .10
76 Helmut De Raaf .10 .25
77 Kai Fischer .30 .75
78 Carsten Gossmann .04 .10
79 Torsten Kienass .10 .25
80 Christopher Kreutzer .04 .10
81 Brad Bergen .04 .10
82 Andreas Niederberger .06 .15
83 Rick Amann .04 .10
84 Uli Hiemer .06 .15
85 Sergei Sorokin .06 .15
86 Robert Sterflinger .04 .10
87 Lorenz Funk .04 .10
88 Chris Valentine .20 .50
89 Gord Sherven .06 .15
90 Boris Lingemann .04 .10
91 Benoit Doucet .10 .25
92 Bernd Kuhnhauser .04 .10
93 Bruce Eakin .06 .15
94 Dieter Hegen .10 .25
95 Andreas Brockmann .04 .10
96 Bernd Truntschka .10 .25
97 Wolfgang Kummer .04 .10
98 Mikko Makela .10 .25
99 Nikolaus Mondt .04 .10
100 Piotr Vorobjew .06 .15
101 Peter Obresa .04 .10
102 Thierry Mayer .04 .10
103 Marc Seliger .40 1.00

104 Florian Storf .04 .10
105 Ladislav Strompf .04 .10
106 Greg Thompson .04 .10
107 Sergei Schendelev .04 .10
108 Martin Duris .04 .10
109 Rudi Gorgenlander .04 .10
110 Andreas Raubal .04 .10
111 Stephan Ziesche .06 .15
112 Petr Kopta .04 .10
113 Thomas Popiesch .04 .10
114 Francois Sills .04 .10
115 Jiri Lala .06 .15
116 Robert Reichel .40 1.00
117 Markus Kempf .04 .10
118 Igor Schultz .04 .10
119 Martin Schultz .04 .10
120 Brian Hannon .04 .10
121 Jurgen Schaal .04 .10
122 Patrick Vozar .04 .10
123 Ron Kennedy .04 .10
124 Friedhelm Bogelsack .06 .15
125 Marco Herbst .04 .10
126 Josef Schlickenrieder .04 .10
127 Torsten Hanusch .04 .10
128 Thomas Jungwirth .04 .10
129 David Reierson .04 .10
130 Christian Curth .04 .10
131 Anton Maidl .04 .10
132 Marc Wittbrock .04 .10
133 Brad Schlegel .10 .25
134 Thomas Werner .04 .10
135 Dirk Rohrbach .04 .10
136 Bruce Hardy .04 .10
137 Harald Kuhnke .04 .10
138 Florian Funk .04 .10
139 Rene Reuter .04 .10
140 Milos Vanik .04 .10
141 Gunther Preuss .04 .10
142 Kevin LaVallee .06 .15
143 Marcus Bleicher .04 .10
144 Anton Krinner .04 .10
145 Harald Waibel .04 .10
146 Hans Zach .04 .10
147 Josef Kontny .04 .10
148 Gerhard Hegen .04 .10
149 Milan Mokros .04 .10
150 Venci Sebek .04 .10
151 Alexander Engel .04 .10
152 Alexander Wedl .04 .10
153 Jaro Mucha .04 .10
154 Murray McIntosh .04 .10
155 Georg Guttler .04 .10
156 Greg Johnston .06 .15
157 Jederzej Kasperczyk .04 .10
158 Dave Morrison .04 .10
159 Mike Millar .06 .15
160 Ireneusz Pacula .04 .10
161 Vitalij Grossmann .04 .10
162 Igor Varitsky .04 .10
163 Peter Kwasigroch .04 .10
164 Branjo Heisig .04 .10
165 Greg Evtushevski .06 .15
166 Falk Ozellis .04 .10
167 Tino Boos .04 .10
168 Jarmo Tolvanen .04 .10
169 Dieter Medicus .04 .10
170 Michael Olbrich .04 .10
171 Marc Pethke .04 .10
172 Drahomir Kadlec .06 .15
173 Christian Seeberger .04 .10
174 Georg Kunce .04 .10
175 Daniel Kunce .04 .10
176 Timo Gschwill .04 .10
177 Marco Eltner .04 .10
178 Jurgen Simon .04 .10
179 Alexander Herbst .04 .10
180 Elmar Boiger .04 .10
181 Otto Hascak .10 .25
182 Tim Schnobrich .04 .10
183 Anthony Vogel .04 .10
184 Tomas Martinec .04 .10
185 Hans-Jorg Mayer .06 .15
186 Roland Timoschuk .04 .10
187 Jim Hoffmann .04 .10
188 Andreas Volland .04 .10
189 Rolf Hammer .04 .10
190 Manuel Hess .04 .10
191 Dale Derkatch .20 .50
192 Sebastian Schwele .04 .10
193 Bob Murdoch .10 .25
194 Bernd Haake .04 .10
195 Joseph Heiss .30 .75
196 Olaf Grundmann .04 .10
197 Alexander Genze .04 .10
198 A. von Trzcinski .04 .10
199 Jorg Mayr .06 .15
200 Mirco Ludemann .10 .25
201 Andreas Pokorny .04 .10
202 Jayson Meyer .04 .10
203 Karsten Mende .04 .10
204 Herbert Hohenberger .20 .50
205 Thomas Brandl .04 .10
206 Stefan Mann .04 .10
207 Luciano Borsato .10 .25
208 Leo Stefan .10 .25
209 Peter Draisaitl .10 .25
210 Andreas Lupzig .10 .25
211 Ralf Reisinger .04 .10
212 Rainer Zerwesz .04 .10
213 Michael Rumrich .04 .10
214 Martin Ondrejka .04 .10
215 Tobias Abstreiter .04 .10
216 Franz Demmel .04 .10
217 Sergei Berezin .80 1.00
218 Miroslav Berek CO .04 .10
219 Karel Lang .04 .10
220 Rene Bielke .04 .10
221 Markus Krawinkel .04 .10
222 Kenneth Karpuk .04 .10
223 Klaus Micheller .04 .10
224 Earl Spry .04 .10
225 Andreas Ott .04 .10
226 Petri Limatainen .04 .10
227 Andre Grein .04 .10
228 Ken Petrash .04 .10
229 James Hanlon .04 .10
230 Reemt Pyka .10 .25
231 Thomas Imdahl .04 .10
232 Chris Lindberg .10 .25
233 Jay Luknowsky .04 .10
234 Peter Ihnacak .10 .25
235 Marek Stebnicki .04 .10
236 Johnny Walker .04 .10
237 Arno Brux .04 .10
238 Robert Busch .04 .10
239 Mark Bassen .04 .10
240 Martin Gebel .04 .10
241 Bernhard Johnston .04 .10
242 Petr Briza .30 .75
243 Christian Kunast .04 .10
244 Michael Bresagk .04 .10
245 Eduard Uvria .04 .10
246 Michael Heidt .04 .10
247 Peter Gulda .04 .10
248 Udo Kiessling .10 .25
249 Dieter Bloem .04 .10
250 Thomas Vogl .04 .10
251 Jacek Plachta .04 .10
252 Georg Franz .04 .10
253 Stephan Retzer .04 .10
254 Henri Marcoux .04 .10
255 Andreas Loth .04 .10
256 Mike Bullard .10 .25
257 Jose Charbonneau .10 .25
258 Wally Schreiber .10 .25
259 Jorg Handrick .04 .10
260 Holger Steiger .04 .10
261 Marco Sturm 6.00 15.00
262 Lance Nethery .06 .15
263 Marcus Kuhl .04 .10
264 Joachim Appel .04 .10
265 Markus Flemming .04 .10
266 Harold Kreis .04 .10
267 Paul Stanton .10 .25
268 Christian Lukes .04 .10
269 Steffen Michel .04 .10
270 Stephane J.G. Richer .06 .15
271 Jorg Hanft .04 .10
272 Erich Goldmann .04 .10
273 Mario Gehrig .04 .10
274 Pavel Gross .04 .10
275 Daniel Korber .04 .10
276 Rob Cimetta .10 .25
277 Jochen Hecht 4.00 3.00
278 Till Feser .04 .10
279 Alexander Serikow .80 1.00
280 Patrik Pysz .06 .15
281 Darian Adamus .04 .10
282 David Musial .04 .10
283 Michael Hreus .04 .10
284 Chris Strausse .04 .10
285 Sven Valenti .04 .10
286 Sebastien Thivierge .04 .10
287 Jan Eysselt CO .04 .10
288 Richard Neubauer .04 .10
289 Roman Turek 4.00 1.00
290 Stefan Lahn .04 .10
291 Christian Gerum .04 .10
292 Heiko Smazal .04 .10
293 Miroslav Maly .04 .10
294 Thomas Sterflinger .04 .10
295 Michael Weinfurter .04 .10
296 Stephan Bauer .04 .10
297 Lars Bruggemann .04 .10
298 Markus Kehle .04 .10
299 Paul Geddes .04 .10
300 Ian Young .04 .10
301 Stefan Steinbock .04 .10
302 Jurgen Lechl .04 .10
303 Markus Goerlitz .04 .10
304 Jiri Dolezal .10 .25
305 Henrik Holscher .04 .10
306 Sepp Wassermann .04 .10
307 Otto Sykora .04 .10
308 Bil Lochead .06 .15
309 Patrick Lange .04 .10
310 Ian Wood .04 .10
311 H. Thorn .04 .10
312 Doug Irwin .04 .10
313 Christian Schmitz .04 .10
314 Alexander Wunsch .04 .10
315 Cory Holden .04 .10
316 Jamie Bartman .04 .10
317 Peter Lutter .04 .10
318 Pavel Mann .04 .10
319 Greg Muller .04 .10
320 Christian Kohmann .04 .10
321 Paul Beraldo .06 .15
322 Thomas Groger .04 .10
323 Andrej Fuchs .04 .10
324 Klaus Birk .04 .10
325 Dave Rich .04 .10
326 Boris Fuchs .04 .10
327 Thomas Muhlbauer .04 .10
328 Axel Kammerer .04 .10
329 Jeff Lazaro .20 .50
330 Olaf Scholz .04 .10
331 Bobby Reynolds .04 .10
332 Jaroslav Sevcik .10 .25
333 P.M. Arnholt .04 .10
334 Gerhard Stranka .04 .10
335 Vincent Riendeau .20 .50
336 Michael Schmidt .04 .10
337 T. Gobel .04 .10
338 Vladimir Fedosov .04 .10
339 R. Jadamzik .04 .10
340 Frank Hohenadl .04 .10
341 Anton Raubal .04 .10
342 C. Schonmoser .04 .10
343 Andreas Ludwig .04 .10
344 Karl Ostler .04 .10
345 Markus Berwanger .04 .10
346 Martin Holzer .04 .10
347 Jens Feller .04 .10
348 Henry Domke .04 .10
349 Andreas Maurer .04 .10
350 Andreas Gebauer .04 .10
351 Guntar Oswald .04 .10
352 Hubert Buchwieser .04 .10
353 Brett Stewart .04 .10
354 Christopher Sandner .04 .10
355 Joachim Hagelsperger .04 .10
356 Robert Hock .04 .10
357 Mark Jooris .04 .10
358 Ernst Hofner .04 .10
359 Gary Clark CO .04 .10
360 Karl Friesen .30 .75
361 Klaus Dalpiaz .10 .25
362 Markus Wieland .04 .10
363 Chris Clarke .04 .10
364 Markus Pottinger .04 .10
365 Raphael Kruger .04 .10
366 Ron Fischer .04 .10
367 Christian Gegenfurter .04 .10
368 Heinrich Schiffl .04 .10
369 Andreas Schneider .04 .10
370 Vitus Mitterfellner .04 .10
371 Richard Bohm .04 .10
372 Dale Krentz .10 .25
373 Tobias Schraven .04 .10
374 Florian Keller .40 1.00
375 Doug Derraugh .04 .10
376 Martin Reichel .06 .15
377 Markus Draxler .04 .10
378 Raimund Hilger .06 .15
379 Michael Pohl .04 .10
380 Martin Kropf .04 .10
381 Joel Savage .20 .50
382 J. Eckmaier .04 .10
383 R.R. Burns .04 .10
384 Gunnar Leidborg .04 .10
385 Carsten Solbach .04 .10
386 Matthias Hoppe .04 .10
387 Gord Hynes .10 .25
388 Thomas Gaus .04 .10
389 Zdenek Travnicek .04 .10
390 Richard Trojan .04 .10
391 Frantisek Frosch .04 .10
392 Daniel Nowak .04 .10
393 Andreas Renz .04 .10
394 Alan Young .04 .10
395 Robert Brezina .04 .10
396 Wayne Hynes .04 .10
397 George Fritz .04 .10
398 Mike Bader .04 .10
399 Grant Martin .04 .10
400 Karsten Schulz .04 .10
401 Mike Lay .04 .10
402 Jackson Penney .06 .15
403 Rich Chernomaz .06 .15
404 Mark MacKay .30 .75
405 Sana Hassan .04 .10
406 Jiri Kochta .04 .10
407 Thomas Bresagk .04 .10
408 Peter Franke .04 .10
409 Jochen Molling .04 .10
410 Frantisek Prochazka .04 .10
411 Josef Reznicek .04 .10
412 Thomas Schubert .04 .10
413 Ronny Martin .04 .10
414 Marcel Lichnovsky .04 .10
415 Matthias Kliemann .04 .10
416 Ronny Reddo .04 .10
417 Frank Peschke .04 .10
418 Torsten Eisebitt .04 .10
419 Janusz Janikowski .04 .10
420 Thomas Knobloch .04 .10
421 Falk Herzig .04 .10
422 Thomas Wagner .04 .10
423 Jan Tabor .06 .15
424 Jorg Pohling .04 .10
425 Pavel Vit .04 .10
426 Vadim Kulabuchov .04 .10
427 D. Cup Meister 1995 .10 .25
428 Kingston/Kuhnhauser/Genze .10 .25
429 Heiss/Lupzig .10 .25
430 Brandl/Mann .10 .25
431 Doucet/Nowak .10 .25
432 Meyer/Pyka .10 .25
433 Hegen/Kunce .10 .25
434 Rumrich/Ludemann .10 .25
435 Benda/Kosturik .10 .25
436 Kienass/Brockmann/Hanft .06 .15
437 Draisaitl/Simon/Schneider .10 .25
438 Andreas Niederberger .10 .25
439 Martin Reichel .06 .15
440 Klaus Merk .20 .50
441 Glenn Anderson 1.20 3.00
442 Pavel Bure 14.00 30.00
443 Vincent Damphousse 2.00 5.00
444 Uwe Krupp .20 .50
445 Robert Reichel .40 1.00
446 Jeremy Roenick 8.00 30.00
447 Brendan Shanahan 12.00 30.00
448 Jozef Stumpel 1.20 2.00
449 Doug Weight 4.00 5.00
450 Scott Young .80 2.00
NNO Hologram Karte 4.00 10.00

1996-97 German DEL

This 360-card set features the players of Germany's top division, the DEL. The cards measure the standard size and were issued in six-card packs. The card fronts feature full-bleed action photography, along with the player's name, team logo and logo of the manufacturer. The back includes another photo, affiliated logos, and stats for the '95-96 season, along with career totals and, in some cases, NHL totals. In a few instances, no stats are provided in the case of those players making their debuts in the DEL.

COMPLETE SET (360) 16.00 40.00
1 Gary Prior CO .06 .15
2 Bruno Campese .10 .25
3 Leonardo Conti .06 .15
4 Scott Campbell .06 .15
5 Robert Mendel .06 .15
6 Serge Poudrier .06 .15
7 Torsten Fendt .06 .15
8 Shawn Rivers .06 .15
9 Stefan Mayer .06 .15
10 Michael Bakos .06 .15
11 Tommy Jakobsen .06 .15
12 Duanne Moeser .06 .15
13 Tero Arkiomaa .06 .15
14 Sven Zywitza .06 .15
15 Craig Streu .06 .15
16 Terry Campbell .06 .15
17 Timothy Ferguson .06 .15
18 Yves Heroux .06 .15
19 Max Boldt .06 .15
20 Andre Faust .06 .15
21 Rochus Schneider .06 .15
22 Ron Kennedy CO .06 .15
23 Barry Lewis ACO .06 .15
24 Mario Brunetta .20 .50
25 Udo Dohler .06 .15
26 Dirk Perschau .06 .15
27 Darren Durdle .06 .15
28 Greg Andrusak .10 .25
29 Leif Carlsson .06 .15
30 Derek Mayer .10 .25
31 Rob Leask .06 .15
32 Chad Biafore .06 .15
33 Thomas Steen .06 .15
34 Lorenz Funk .06 .15
35 Florian Funk .06 .15
36 Sven Felski .06 .15
37 Peter Lee .10 .25
38 Andrew McKim .20 .50
39 Andrei Lomakin .10 .25
40 Pelle Svensson .06 .15
41 Jan Schertz .06 .15
42 Kraig Nienhuis .20 .50
43 Niklas Hede .06 .15
44 Mario Chitarroni .10 .25
45 Chris Govedaris .20 .50
46 Pentti Matikainen CO .06 .15
47 Jukka Tammi .10 .25
48 Rupert Meister .06 .15
49 Florian Storf .06 .15
50 Greg Thomson .06 .15
51 Toni Porkka .06 .15
52 Sergej Schendelev .06 .15
53 Kai Rautio .06 .15
54 Rudi Gorgenlander .06 .15
55 Petr Kopta .06 .15
56 Tony Virta .10 .25
57 Ilja Vorobjev .06 .15
58 Thomas Popiesch .06 .15
59 Francois Sills .06 .15
60 Iiro Jarvi .06 .15
61 Jurgen Schaal .06 .15
62 Pavel Vit .06 .15
63 Timo Peltomaa .06 .15
64 Igor Schultz .06 .15
65 Dave Archibald .10 .25
66 Joni Lehto .06 .15
67 Brad Jones .06 .15
68 Miroslav Berek CO .06 .15
69 Karel Lang .06 .15
70 Peter Franke .06 .15
71 Markus Krawinkel .06 .15
72 Zdenek Travnicek .06 .15
73 Martin Gebel .06 .15
74 Klaus Micheller .06 .15
75 Earl Spry .06 .15
76 Frantisek Frosch .06 .15
77 Petri Liimatainen .06 .15
78 Andre Grein .06 .15
79 Ken Petrash .06 .15
80 James Hanlon .06 .15
81 Andrej Kovalev .06 .15
82 Reemt Pyka .06 .15
83 Chris Lindberg .10 .25
84 Jay Luknowsky .06 .15
85 Peter Ihnacak .10 .25
86 Marek Stebnicki .06 .15
87 Johnny Walker .06 .15
88 Danton Cole .10 .25
89 Michael Hreus .06 .15
90 Damian Adamus .06 .15
91 Bill Lochead CO .10 .25
92 Joakim Persson .10 .25
93 Ian Wood .06 .15
94 Pierre Jonsson .06 .15
95 Juha Lampinen .06 .15
96 Christian Schmitz .06 .15
97 Cory Holden .06 .15
98 Peter Lutter .06 .15
99 Dieter Bloem .06 .15
100 Maurizio Catenacci .06 .15
101 Andrej Fuchs .06 .15
102 Mark Montanari .06 .15
103 Boris Fuchs .06 .15
104 Andreas Salomonsson .06 .15
105 Robert Reynolds .06 .15
106 Axel Kammerer .06 .15
107 Jeffrey Lazaro .10 .25
108 Olaf Scholz .06 .15
109 Tony Cimellaro .06 .15
110 Kenneth Hodge .10 .25
111 Gregory Burke .06 .15
112 Tom Coolen CO .06 .15
113 Marc Pethke .06 .15
114 Christian Kunast .06 .15
115 Drahomir Kadlec .10 .25
116 Florian Kuhn .10 .25
117 Erich Goldmann .06 .15
118 Jurgen Simon .06 .15
119 Jeff Winstanley .06 .15
120 Stefano Figliuzzi .06 .15
121 Maurice Mansi .06 .15
122 Agostino Casale .06 .15
123 Hans-Jorg Mayer .06 .15
124 Dino Felicetti .06 .15
125 Roland Timoschuk .06 .15
126 Jim Hoffmann .06 .15
127 John Porco .06 .15
128 Rolf Hammer .06 .15
129 Manuel Hess .06 .15
130 Andy Rymsha .10 .25
131 Wolfgang Kummer .06 .15
132 Trevor Burgess .06 .15
133 Daniel Kunce .06 .15
134 Timo Sutinen CO .06 .15
135 Petr Briza .30 .75
136 Markus Nachtmann .06 .15
137 Markus Wieland .06 .15
138 Mike Heidt .06 .15
139 Peter Gulda .06 .15
140 Jacek Plachta .06 .15
141 Georg Franz .06 .15
142 Stephan Retzer .06 .15
143 Henry Marcoux .06 .15
144 Mike Bullard .30 .75
145 Jose Charbonneau .10 .25
146 Wally Schreiber .10 .25
147 Jorg Handrick .06 .15
148 Helmut Steiger .06 .15
149 Marco Sturm 4.00 10.00
150 Jonas Johnsson .06 .15
151 Vesa Salo .06 .15
152 Gino Cavallini .10 .25
153 Lars Hurtig .06 .15
154 Olli Kaski .06 .15
155 007 Charly .06 .15
156 Lance Nethery CO .06 .15
157 Ross Yates ACO .06 .15
158 Joachim Appel .06 .15
159 Mike Rosati .20 .50
160 Harold Kreis .06 .15
161 Paul Stanton .10 .25
162 Christian Lukes .06 .15
163 Robert Nardella .06 .15
164 Alexander Erdmann .06 .15
165 Stephane J.G. Richer .10 .25
166 Martin Ulrich .06 .15
167 Mike Pellegrims .06 .15
168 Mario Gehrig .06 .15
169 Pavel Gross .06 .15
170 Dave Tomlinson .10 .25
171 Daniel Korber .06 .15
172 Francois Guay .06 .15
173 Jochen Hecht 2.00 3.00
174 Florian Keller .20 .50
175 Till Feser .06 .15
176 Alexander Serikow .20 .50
177 Christian Pouget .06 .15
178 Dieter Kalt .06 .15
179 Paul Beraldo .06 .15
180 Steven Thornton .06 .15
181 Robert Cimetta .20 .50
182 Gary Clark CO .06 .15
183 Bjorn Leonhardt .06 .15
184 Claus Dalpiaz .10 .25
185 Jesper Duus .06 .15
186 Manuel Hiemer .06 .15
187 Markus Pottinger .06 .15
188 Chris Bartolone .06 .15
189 Christian Gegenfurther .06 .15
190 Heinrich Schiffl .06 .15
191 Per Lundell .06 .15
192 Joel Savage .10 .25
193 Josef Muller .06 .15
194 Jari Torkki .06 .15
195 James Hiller .06 .15
196 Doug Derraugh .06 .15
197 Pekka Tirkkonen .06 .15
198 Martin Reichel .06 .15
199 Raimond Hilger .10 .25
200 Michael Schneidawind .06 .15
201 Scott Beattie .06 .15
202 Paris Proft .06 .15
203 Kevin Gaudet CO .06 .15
204 Wayne Cowley .06 .15
205 Marco Herbst .06 .15
206 Andreas Schubert .06 .15
207 Stephan Sinner .06 .15
208 Heinrich Synowietz .06 .15
209 Paul Synowietz .06 .15
210 Dimitri Frolov .06 .15
211 Andrej Saposhnikov .06 .15
212 Jedrzej Kasperczyk .06 .15
213 Joseph West .06 .15
214 Fabian Ahrens .06 .15
215 Maurice Lemay .06 .15
216 Mark Kosturik .06 .15
217 Mark Jooris .06 .15
218 Len Soccio .06 .15
219 Mark Mahon .06 .15
220 Frank LaScala .06 .15
221 Jari Pasanen .06 .15
222 Ralph Vos .06 .15
223 Anthony Cirelli .06 .15
224 Emilio Iovio .06 .15
225 Gerhard Brunner CO .06 .15
226 Pavel Cagas .06 .15
227 Jonas Eriksson .06 .15
228 Alexander Engel .06 .15
229 Gregory Johnston .10 .25
230 Alexander Wedl .06 .15
231 Jouni Vento .06 .15
232 Roger Ohman .06 .15
233 David Morrison .06 .15
234 Bruce Eakin .06 .15
235 Michael Millar .06 .15
236 Roger Hansson .04 .10
237 Peter Kwasigroch .06 .15
238 Branjo Heisig .06 .15
239 Jukka Seppo .06 .15
240 Greg Evtushevski .06 .15
241 Falk Ozellis .06 .15
242 Daniel Larin .06 .15
243 Tino Boos .06 .15
244 Toni Krinner .06 .15
245 Milan Mokros .06 .15
246 Peter Ustorf CO .06 .15
247 Klaus Merk .10 .25
248 David Berge .06 .15
249 Georg Holzmann .06 .15
250 Tom O'Regan .06 .15
251 Jochen Molling .06 .15
252 Joseph Lehner .06 .15
253 Marco Rentzsch .06 .15
254 Pekka Laksola .06 .15
255 Petri Matikainen .06 .15
256 Tony Tanti .30 .75
257 Gaetan Malo .06 .15
258 Thomas Schinko .06 .15
259 Vitali Karamnov .06 .15
260 Gunther Oswald .06 .15
261 Christian Brittig .06 .15
262 Jurgen Rumrich .06 .15
263 John Chabot .20 .50
264 Andreas Dimbat .06 .15
265 Mark Teevens .06 .15
266 Veli-Pekka Kautonen .06 .15
267 Jarno-Sakari Peltonen .06 .15
268 Hardy Nilsson CO .06 .15
269 Martin Karlsson ACO .06 .15
270 Ake Lilljebjorn .06 .15
271 Kai Fischer .10 .25
272 Brad Bergen .06 .15
273 Andreas Niederberger .06 .15
274 Sergej Sorokin .06 .15
275 Robert Sterflinger .06 .15
276 Peter Andersson .06 .15
277 Viktor Gordiouk .10 .25
278 Gordon Sherven .10 .25
279 Benoit Doucet .20 .50
280 Bernd Kuhnhauser .10 .25
281 Dieter Hegen .06 .15
282 Andreas Brockmann .06 .15
283 Ernst Kopf .06 .15
284 Alexej Kudashov .06 .15
285 Bernd Truntschka .10 .25
286 Mikko Makela .06 .15
287 Nikolaus Mondt .06 .15
288 Boris Lingemann .06 .15
289 Thomas Brandl .10 .25
290 Leo Stefan .10 .25
291 Bob Burns CO .06 .15
292 Carsten Solbach .06 .15
293 Matthias Hoppe .06 .15
294 Sascha Goc .20 .50
295 Gordon Hynes .20 .50
296 Thomas Gaus .06 .15
297 Brian Tutt .06 .15
298 Richard Trojan .06 .15
299 Daniel Nowak .06 .15
300 Andreas Renz .06 .15
301 Sana Hassan .06 .15
302 Alan Young .06 .15
303 Mike Bader .06 .15
304 Robert Brezina .06 .15
305 Wayne Hynes .06 .15
306 Mark Bassen .06 .15
307 Andrew Clark .06 .15
308 Grant Martin .06 .15
309 Michael Lay .06 .15
310 Jackson Penney .06 .15
311 Rich Chernomaz .14 .35
312 Mark MacKay .20 .50
313 Vladimir Fedosov .06 .15
314 Emanuel Viveiros .10 .25
315 Jan Eysselt CO .06 .15
316 Michel Valliere .06 .15
317 Stefan Lahn .06 .15
318 Christian Gerum .06 .15
319 Heiko Smazal .06 .15
320 Christian Curth .06 .15
321 Miroslav Maly .06 .15
322 Torsten Kienass .06 .15
323 Thomas Sterflinger .06 .15
324 Lars Bruggemann .06 .15
325 Paul Geddes .06 .15
326 Rolan Ramoser .06 .15
327 Martin Jiranek .06 .15
328 Stefan Steinbock .06 .15
329 Martin Ekrt .06 .15
330 Jurgen Lechl .06 .15
331 Dion Del Monte .06 .15
332 Markus Welz .06 .15
333 Henrik Holscher .06 .15
334 Otto Sykora .06 .15
335 Milos Vanik .06 .15
336 Robert Murdoch CO .06 .15
337 Bernd Haake ACO .06 .15
338 Joseph Heiss .10 .25
339 Olaf Grundmann .06 .15
340 Alexander Genze .06 .15
341 Jorg Mayr .06 .15
342 Mirco Ludemann .06 .15
343 Jayson Meyer .06 .15
344 Karsten Mende .06 .15
345 Herbert Hohenberger .10 .25
346 Joe Cirella .10 .25
347 Peter Nilsson .06 .15
348 Jim Montgomery .20 .50
349 Stefan Mann .06 .15
350 Luciano Borsato .10 .25
351 Dwayne Norris .10 .25
352 Bruno Zarrillo .06 .15
353 Peter Draisaitl .10 .25
354 Joe Busillo .06 .15
355 Andreas Lupzig .06 .15
356 Rainer Zerwesz .06 .15
357 Thomas Forslund .10 .25
358 Tobias Abstreiter .06 .15
359 Patrick Carnback .10 .25
360 Franz Demmel .06 .15

1998-99 German DEL

This set features members of Germany's top hockey circuit. The card stock is very thin, and the words Schirner Edition appear on the front. The backs feature sponsor information (including Eishockey News), stats, and a reproduced signature.

COMPLETE SET (344) 20.00 50.00
1 Burke Murphy .08 .20
2 Marc Seliger .20 .50
3 Jason Clark .08 .20
4 Mike McNeill .08 .20
5 Norm Matherson .08 .20
6 Jeff Sebastien .08 .20
7 Phil Huber .08 .20
8 Todd Wtzel .08 .20
9 Jesper Morin .08 .20
10 Marc Pethke .08 .20
11 Jacek Plachta .08 .20
12 Marcus Adolfson .08 .20
13 Christian Schmitz .08 .20
14 Bob Marshall .08 .20
15 Peter Lutter .08 .20
16 Stefan Mayer .08 .20
17 Daniel Korber .08 .20
18 Carsten Gosdeck .08 .20
19 Jiri Kochta .08 .20
20 Petri Liimatainen .08 .20
21 Thomas Brandl .08 .20
22 Andrej Kovalev .10 .25
23 Johnny Walker .08 .20
24 Neil Eisenhut .20 .50
25 Karel Lang .08 .20
26 Marek Stebnicki .08 .20
27 Chris Bartolone .08 .20
28 John Van Kessel .08 .20
29 Lars Bruggemann .08 .20
30 Jason Meyer .08 .20
31 Reemt Pyka .08 .20
32 Mark Pederson .08 .20
33 Veli-Pekka Kautonen .08 .20
34 Tommie Hartogs .08 .20
35 Frantisek Frosch .08 .20
36 Leo van den Thillart .08 .20
37 Vitali Karamnov .10 .25
38 Stephane Barin .08 .20
39 Roger Nordstrom .08 .20
40 Robert Ouellet .08 .20
41 Doug Mason .08 .20
42 Francois Guay .08 .20
43 Greg Johnston .20 .50
44 Greg Evtushevski .08 .20
45 Shane Peacock .08 .20
46 Chris Rogles .30 .75
47 Gunter Oswald .08 .20
48 Jukka Seppo .08 .20
49 Jurgen Rumrich .08 .20
50 Roger Hansson .08 .20
51 Stephane Robitaille .08 .20
52 Orjan Lindmark .08 .20
53 Jeff MacLeod .08 .20
54 Alexander Wedl .08 .20
55 Jochen Molling .08 .20
56 Paul Cohen .08 .20
57 Daniel Kreutzer .08 .20
58 Nikolaus Mondt .08 .20
59 John Lilley .20 .50
60 Roland Ramoser .08 .20
61 Thomas Dolak .08 .20
62 Tino Boos .08 .20
63 Tobias Abstreiter .08 .20
64 Hans Zach .08 .20
65 Petr Briza .30 .75
66 Wally Schreiber .20 .50
67 Chris Luongo .20 .50
68 Dean Evason .20 .50
69 David Bruce .20 .50
70 Peter Douris .20 .50
71 Jason Herter .20 .50
72 Jorg Hendrick .08 .20
73 Rob Murphy .20 .50
74 Mike Casselmann .08 .20
75 Steve Junker .08 .20
76 Zbynek Kukacka .08 .20
77 Mark Krys .08 .20
78 Markus Wieland .08 .20
79 Evan Marble .08 .20
80 Jari Korpisalo .08 .20
81 Peter Gulda .08 .20
82 Bob Joyce .20 .50
83 Johan Rosen .08 .20
84 Christian Kunast .08 .20
85 Olli Kaski .08 .20
86 Chris Valentine .30 .75
87 Corey Millen .20 .50
88 Tomas Forslund .14 .35
89 Bruno Zarrillo .20 .50
90 Igor Alexandrov .08 .20
91 Bob Halkidis .20 .50
92 Petri Varis .20 .50
93 Joseph Heiss .20 .50
94 Greg Brown .20 .50
95 Dwayne Norris .20 .50
96 Mirko Ludemann .08 .20
97 John Miner .08 .20
98 Boris Rousson .30 .75
99 Craig Woodcroft .08 .20
100 Jorg Mayr .08 .20
101 Steve Wilson .08 .20
102 Rainer Zerwesz .08 .20
103 Brian McReynolds .08 .20
104 Andreas Lupzig .08 .20
105 Giuseppe Busillo .08 .20
106 Jeff Ricciardi .08 .20
107 Mike Hartman .20 .50
108 Timo Lahtinen .08 .20
109 Stephane Morin .20 .50
110 Paul Broten .20 .50
111 Robert Guillet .08 .20
112 Clayton Beddoes .14 .35
113 Robert Cimetta .20 .50
114 Dave MacIntyre .08 .20
115 Johan Norgren .08 .20
116 Todd Nelson .08 .20
117 Guy Phillips .08 .20
118 Craig Martin .20 .50
119 Parris Duffus .30 .75
120 Christian Brittig .08 .20
121 Thomas Schinko .08 .20
122 Mario Gehrig .08 .20
123 Fredrik Ytfeldt .08 .20
124 Lawrence Rucchin .08 .20
125 Heinz Ehlers .08 .20
126 Heinrich Schiffl .08 .20
127 Sylvain Couturier .10 .25
128 Hakan Galiamoutsas .08 .20
129 David Berge .08 .20
130 Marc Savard .08 .20
131 Dale McCourt .20 .50
132 Jukka Tammi .20 .50
133 Chris Snell .20 .50
134 John Chabot .20 .50
135 Len Barrie .20 .50
136 Lija Vorobjev .08 .20
137 Steve Palmer .08 .20
138 Fabrice L'Henry .08 .20
139 Rob Doyle .08 .20
140 Victor Gervais .08 .20
141 Jose Charbonneau .10 .25
142 Thorsten Apel .08 .20
143 Michael Bresagk .08 .20
144 Rick Hayward .10 .25
145 Phil von Steffenelli .08 .20
146 Martin Williams .08 .20
147 Toni Porkka .08 .20
148 Jean-Marc Richard .08 .20
149 Douglas Kirton .08 .20
150 Joel Savage .20 .50
151 Ralf Hantschke .08 .20
152 Ken Quinney .14 .35
153 Marcus Bleicher .08 .20
154 Bob Manno .10 .25
155 Rob Cowie .08 .20

156 Mike Bullard .30 .75
157 Maren Valenti .08 .20
158 Sven Felski .08 .20
159 Andrew McKim .20 .50
160 Derek Mayer .10 .25
161 Niklas Hede .08 .20
162 Thomas Steen .20 .50
163 Mario Brunetta .20 .50
164 Marc Fortier .20 .50
165 Thomas Rhodin .08 .20
166 Nico Pyka .08 .20
167 Chris Govedaris .10 .25
168 Lorenz Funk .08 .20
169 Florian Funk .08 .20
170 Yvon Corriveau .20 .50
171 Mikael Wahlberg .08 .20
172 Darren Durdle .08 .20
173 Pelle Svensson .08 .20
174 Greg Andrusak .10 .25
175 Leif Carlsson .08 .20
176 Andreas Brockmann .08 .20
177 Robert Leask .08 .20
178 Mario Chitaroni .08 .20
179 Chad Biafore .08 .20
180 Peter John Lee .08 .20
181 Len Soccio .20 .50
182 Jason Lafreniere .20 .50
183 Joe West .08 .20
184 Brent Tully .20 .50
185 Mark Kosturik .08 .20
186 David Haas .08 .20
187 Darcy Martini .08 .20
188 Gary Leeman .20 .50
189 Lee Davidson .08 .20
190 Scott Metcalfe .20 .50
191 Tom Pederson .20 .50
192 Francois Gravel .08 .20
193 Bjorn Leonhardt .08 .20
194 Mike Johnson .08 .20
195 Claudio Scremin .08 .20
196 Mike Ware .08 .20
197 Jurgen Trattner .08 .20
198 Dan Currie .20 .50
199 Patrick Curcio .08 .20
200 Patrick Senger .08 .20
201 Frank Di Muzio .08 .20
202 Kevin Gaudet .08 .20
203 Mark MacKay .20 .50
204 Claude Vilgrain .20 .50
205 Rich Chernomaz .08 .20
206 Daniel Laperriere .20 .50
207 Wayne Hynes .08 .20
208 Todd Harkins .08 .20
209 Scott McCrory .20 .50
210 Andrew Rymsha .14 .35
211 Daniel Nowak .08 .20
212 Andy Schneider .14 .35
213 David Marcinshyn .08 .20
214 Marc Laniel .08 .20
215 Guy Lehoux .08 .20
216 Matthias Vater .08 .20
217 Jens Stramkowski .08 .20
218 Alexander Dexheimer .08 .20
219 Mark Bassen .08 .20
220 Steffen Karg .08 .20
221 Randy Perry .08 .20
222 Robert Schistad .20 .50
223 Andreas Renz .08 .20
224 Matthias Hoppe .08 .20
225 Ron Ivany .08 .20
226 Phillippe Bozon .30 1.00
227 Dave Tomlinson .20 .50
228 Stephane Richer .08 .20
229 Paul Stanton .20 .50
230 Pavel Gross .08 .20
231 Christian Pouget .08 .20
232 Jackson Penney .08 .20
233 Gordon Hynes .20 .50
234 Jason Young .08 .20
235 Alexander Serikow .20 .50
236 Mike Stevens .08 .20
237 Mike Pellegrims .08 .20
238 Reid Simonton .08 .20
239 Christian Lukes .08 .20
240 Ron Pasco .08 .20
241 Mike Hudson .30 .75
242 Denis Perez .08 .20
243 Svan Rampf .08 .20
244 Danny Lorenz .20 .50
245 Brian Tutt .08 .20
246 Jan Alston .08 .20
247 Lance Nethery .08 .20
248 Sergio Momesso .20 .50
249 Andrej Mezin .30 1.00
250 Jarno Peltonen .08 .20
251 Martin Reichel .08 .20
252 Sergej Stas .08 .20
253 Martin Jiranek .08 .20
254 Jason Miller .08 .20
255 Jozef Cierny .08 .20
256 Liam Garvey .08 .20
257 Kevin Grant .08 .20
258 Chris Strausse .08 .20
259 Heiko Smazal .08 .20
260 Vadim Shakhraichuk .08 .20
261 Leszek Laszkiewicz .08 .20
262 Sven Valenti .08 .20
263 Michel Valliere .08 .20
264 Per Lundell .08 .20
265 Dimitri Dudik .08 .20
266 Daniel Kunce .08 .20
267 Ivan Droppa .08 .20
268 Peter Ihnacak .20 .50
269 Harald Birk .08 .20
270 Bradley Bergen .08 .20
271 Pierre Rioux .08 .20
272 Jim Camazzola .08 .20
273 Klaus Merk .20 .50
274 Rick Girard .08 .20
275 Andre Faust .08 .20
276 Hakan Ahlund .08 .20
277 Kyosti Karjalainen .20 .50
278 Leonardo Conti .08 .20
279 Leo Gudas .08 .20
280 Mathias Ahxner .08 .20
281 Francois Groleau .08 .20
282 Michael Bakos .08 .20
283 Alan Reader .08 .20
284 Nordin Harfaoui .08 .20
285 Dale Craigwell .20 .50
286 Dimitri Gromling .08 .20
287 Duanne Moeser .08 .20
288 Tommy Jakobsen .08 .20
289 Patrik Degerstedt .08 .20
290 Greg Bullock .08 .20
291 Gunnar Leidborg .08 .20
292 Dieter Hegen .08 .20
293 Derek Cormier .08 .20
294 Jim Hiller .08 .20
295 Gordon Sherven .10 .25
296 Eric Murana .08 .20
297 Robert Muller .08 .20
298 Klaus Kathan .08 .20
299 Raimond Hilger .08 .20
300 Christian Due-Boje .08 .20
301 Jesper Duus .08 .20
302 Michael Pohl .08 .20
303 Bernd Kuhnhauser .14 .35
304 Frank Hohenadl .08 .20
305 Alexander Jansen .08 .20
306 Teemu Sillanpaa .08 .20
307 Hans Abranamsson .08 .20
308 Claus Dalpiaz .10 .25
309 Kari Haakana .08 .20
310 Christian Gegenfurtner .08 .20
311 Peter Ottosson .08 .20
312 Wolfgang Kummer .08 .20
313 Beppi Eckmaier .08 .20
314 Gerhard Brunner .08 .20
315 Mirko Ludemann .10 .25
316 Sven Felski .08 .20
317 Reemt Pyka .08 .20
318 Jorg Mayr .08 .20
319 Michael Bresagk .08 .20
320 Andraes Lupzig .08 .20
321 Jurgen Rumrich .08 .20
322 Josef Lehner .08 .20
323 Peter Draisaitl .08 .20
324 Leo Stefan .08 .20
325 Joseph Heiss .10 .25
326 Klaus Kathan .08 .20
327 Klaus Merk .10 .25
328 Peter Gulda .08 .20
329 Daniel Nowak .08 .20
330 Bradley Bergen .08 .20
331 Thomas Dolak .08 .20
332 Martin Reichel .08 .20
333 Alexander Serikow .20 .50
334 Harold Birk .08 .20
335 Michael Bakos .08 .20
336 Mario Gehrig .08 .20
337 Mark Mackay .20 .50
338 Dieter Hegen .14 .35
339 Hans Zach .08 .20
340 Erich Kuhnackl .14 .35
341 Ernst Hofner .08 .20
NNO Gerhard Leinauer CL .08 .20
NNO Robert Muller CL .08 .20
NNO Rick Amann CL .10 .25

1999-00 German DEL

This 434-card set features the players of Germany's elite hockey league. The regulation-sized cards feature a color photo on the front, along with two photos and stats on the back. The set was sponsored by Eishockey News and Skoda and may have been produced by a company named Eberswalder.

COMPLETE SET (434) 24.00 60.00
1 Mannheim .06 .15
2 Gordon Hynes .20 .50
3 Paul Stanton .20 .50
4 Christian Lukes .06 .15
5 Clayton Beddoes .20 .50
6 Shawn McCosh .06 .15
7 Dave Tomlinson .20 .50
8 Patrice Lefebvre .20 .50
9 Steve Junker .20 .50
10 Ralph Intranuovo .20 .50
11 Joel Savage .20 .50
12 Stephane J.G. Richer .20 .50
13 Rainer Zerwesz .06 .15
14 Yves Racine .20 .50
15 Mike Stevens .20 .50
16 Markus Wieland .06 .15
17 Bjorn Leonhardt .06 .15
18 Mike Rosati .20 .50
19 Philip Schumacher .06 .15
20 Jan Alston .06 .15
21 Kevin Grant .06 .15
22 Chris Straube .06 .15
23 Dennis Seidenberg .06 .15
24 Chris Valentine TR .20 .50
25 NÃ¼rnberg .06 .15
26 Stefan Mann .06 .15
27 Vadim Shakhraichuk .06 .15
28 Roland Ramoser .06 .15
29 Martin Jiranek .20 .50
30 Hannes KÃ¶rber .06 .15
31 Jarno Peltonen .06 .15
32 Dimitri Dudik .06 .15
33 Viktors Ignatjevs .06 .15
34 Alexander Cherbayev .10 .25
35 Martin Reichel .06 .15
36 Russ Romaniuk .10 .25
37 Jason Miller .06 .15
38 Sergej Bautin .06 .15
39 Jozef Cierny .06 .15
40 Marc Seliger .30 1.00
41 Daniel Kunce .06 .15
42 Pasi Sormunen .06 .15
43 Christian SchÃ¶nmoser .06 .15
44 Stefan Mayer .06 .15
45 Alain Cote .10 .25
46 Liam Garvey .06 .15
47 John Craighead .06 .15
48 Petr Franek .06 .15
49 Peter Ihnacak TR .20 .50
50 Eisbaren .06 .15
51 Nico Pyka .06 .15
52 Robert Leask .20 .50
53 Alexander Godynyuk .10 .25
54 Lorenz Funk .06 .15
55 Sven Felski .06 .15
56 Giuseppe Busillo .06 .15
57 Yvon Corriveau .20 .50
58 Mikael Wahlberg .06 .15
59 Udo Dohler .06 .15
60 Sandy Smith .20 .50
61 Jaroslav Kames .06 .15
62 Rob Murphy .10 .25
63 Marc Fortier .20 .50
64 Mario Chitaroni .06 .15
65 Leif Carlsson .06 .15
66 Derek Mayer .20 .50
67 Sebastian Elwing .06 .15
68 Thomas Schinko .06 .15
69 Rob Cowie .06 .15
70 Thomas Rhodin .06 .15
71 Peter Hammarstrom .06 .15
72 Chris Govedaris .20 .50
73 Mike Bullard .20 .50
74 Peter John Lee TR .06 .15
75 Frankfurt .06 .15
76 Michael Bresagk .06 .15
77 Joachim Appel .06 .15
78 Rick Hayward .20 .50
79 Robin Doyle .06 .15
80 Christian Langer .06 .15
81 Bob Bassen .20 .50
82 John Chabot .20 .50
83 Devin Edgerton .06 .15
84 Toni Porkka .06 .15
85 Jean-Marc Richard .06 .15
86 Jose Charbonneau .10 .25
87 Douglas Kirton .06 .15
88 Andrej Vasilyev .06 .15
89 Ralf Hantschke .06 .15
90 Steve Palmer .06 .15
91 Jason Ruff .20 .50
92 Bastian Niedermeier .06 .15
93 Chris Hynes .06 .15
94 Victor Gervais .06 .15
95 Ken Quinney .20 .50
96 Mark Bassen .06 .15
97 Chris Snell .20 .50
98 Eldon Reddick .20 .50
99 Peter Obresa TR .06 .15
100 Koln .06 .15
101 Joseph Heiss .20 .50
102 Steve Wilson .06 .15
103 Mario Doyon .20 .50
104 Jorg Mayr .06 .15
105 Marty Murray .20 .50
106 Mirko Ludemann .06 .15
107 Dwayne Norris .20 .50
108 Christoph Paepke .06 .15
109 Bruno Zarrillo .20 .50
110 Dan Lambert .20 .50
111 Anders Huusko .06 .15
112 George Zajankala .06 .15
113 Andreas Lupzig .06 .15
114 Jean-Yves Roy .20 .50
115 Tomas Forslund .10 .25
116 Jason Young .10 .25
117 Todd Hlushko .20 .50
118 Andrew Verner .20 .50
119 Corey Millen .20 .50
120 Greg Brown .06 .15
121 John Miner .10 .25
122 Sergio Momesso .20 .50
123 Lance Nethery TR .06 .15
124 Krefeld .06 .15
125 Karel Lang .06 .15
126 Andy Roach .06 .15
127 Tomas Brandl .06 .15
128 Neil Eisenhut .20 .50
129 Ilja Vorobjev .06 .15
130 Andrey Kovalev .06 .15
131 Mark Pederson .10 .25
132 Shayne Wright .06 .15
133 Reemt Pyka .06 .15
134 Andrew Rymsha .06 .15
135 Lars Bruggemann .06 .15
136 Tommie Hartogs .06 .15
137 Marek Stebnicki .06 .15
138 Johnny Walker .06 .15
139 Chris Bartolone .06 .15
140 Stephane Barin .06 .15
141 Mickey Elick .06 .15
142 Phil von Stefenelli .10 .25
143 Jean-Francois Jomphe .20 .50
144 Robert Ouellet .06 .15
145 Roger Nordstrom .06 .15
146 Martin Lindman .06 .15
147 Doug Mason TR .06 .15
148 Augsburg .06 .15
149 Vladislav Boulin .06 .15
150 Leo Gudas .06 .15
151 Duane Moeser .06 .15
152 Sergej Vostrikov .06 .15
153 Igor Maslennikov .06 .15
154 Kyosti Karjalainen .06 .15
155 Kurtis Miller .06 .15
156 Bradley Bergen .06 .15
157 Scott Allison .06 .15
158 Hakan Ahlund .06 .15
159 Peter Larsson .06 .15
160 Brian Loney .06 .15
161 Michael Bakos .06 .15
162 Sven Rampf .06 .15
163 Jim Camazzola .06 .15
164 Andre Faust .06 .15
165 Harald Birk .06 .15
166 Tommy Jakobsen .06 .15
167 Sergej Klimovich .06 .15
168 Klaus Merk .20 .50
169 Bob Manno TR .10 .25
170 Kassel .06 .15
171 Jochen Molling .06 .15
172 David Cooper .20 .50
173 Thomas Dolak .06 .15
174 Stephane Robitaille .06 .15
175 Jeff MacLeod .10 .25
176 Roger Hansson .06 .15
177 Francois Guay .06 .15
178 Nikolaus Mondt .06 .15
179 Andreas Loth .06 .15
180 Ron Pasco .06 .15
181 Jurgen Rumrich .06 .15
182 Greg Evtushevski .06 .15
183 Daniel Kreutzer .06 .15
184 Brent Tully .06 .15
185 Ivan Droppa .06 .15
186 Tobias Abstreiter .06 .15
187 Sylvain Turgeon .20 .50
188 Chris Rogles .20 .50
189 Leonardo Conti .06 .15
190 Tino Boos .06 .15
191 Benjamin Hinterstocker .06 .15
192 Craig Woodcroft .20 .50
193 Orjan Lindmark .06 .15
194 Hans Zach TR .06 .15
195 Schwenningen .06 .15
196 Kevin Wortman .06 .15
197 Marc Laniel .20 .50
198 Daniel Laperriere .20 .50
199 Marcel Goc 2.00 3.00
200 Guy Lehoux .06 .15
201 Steffen Oder .06 .15
202 Jens Stramkowski .06 .15
203 Mark Kolesar .14 .35
204 Scott McCrory .20 .50
205 John Lilley .20 .50
206 Patrik Augusta .06 .15
207 Randy Perry .06 .15
208 Daniel Nowak .06 .15
209 Todd Harkins .06 .15
210 Robert Schistad .06 .15
211 Andreas Renz .06 .15
212 Stephane Beauregard .20 .50
213 Rick Girard .06 .15
214 Iain Fraser .20 .50
215 Andy Schneider .20 .50
216 Mark Mackay .20 .50
217 Rich Chernomaz TR .20 .50
218 Hannover .06 .15
219 Lars Jansson .06 .15
220 Tom Pederson .20 .50
221 Juri Gunko .06 .15
222 Mattias Loof .06 .15
223 Joseph West .06 .15
224 Egor Bashkatov .10 .25
225 Grigori Panteleyev .20 .50
226 Mark Kosturik .06 .15
227 Len Soccio .06 .15
228 Dominic Lavoie .20 .50
229 Peter Willmann .06 .15
230 Wally Schreiber .20 .50
231 Scott Metcalfe .20 .50
232 David Haas .06 .15
233 Ildar Mukhometov .20 .50
234 Igor Chibirev .10 .25
235 Michael Thurner .06 .15
236 Jan Munster .06 .15
237 Jacob Karlsson .06 .15
238 David Sulkovsky .06 .15
239 Brian Tutt .06 .15
240 Igor Alexandrov .06 .15
241 Kevin Gaudet TR .06 .15
242 Rosenheim .06 .15
243 Hakan Algotsson .20 .50
244 Trevor Burgess .06 .15
245 Christian Due-Boje .06 .15
246 Teemu Sillanpaa .06 .15
247 Curtis Fry .06 .15
248 Gordon Sherven .20 .50
249 Frank Hohenadl .06 .15
250 Bernd Kuhnhauser .06 .15
251 Michael Pohl .06 .15
252 Derek Cormier .06 .15
253 Jean-Francois Quintin .20 .50
254 Dieter Hegen .06 .15
255 Peter Ottosson .06 .15
256 Raimond Hilger .10 .25
257 Niklas Brannstrom .06 .15
258 Wolfgang Kummer .06 .15
259 Kari Haakana .06 .15
260 Paul Weismann .06 .15
261 Klaus Kathan .06 .15
262 Sami Nuutinen .06 .15
263 Patrik Hucko .06 .15
264 Robert Muller .06 .15
265 Gerhard Brunner TR .06 .15
266 Capitals .06 .15
267 Andrej Mezin .80 1.00
268 Fredrik Stillman .20 .50
269 Fredrik Ytfeldt .06 .15
270 Markus Pottinger .06 .15
271 Niklas Hede .06 .15
272 Alexander Kuzminski .06 .15
273 Thomas Sjogren .06 .15
274 Dennis Meyer .06 .15
275 Robert Cimetta .20 .50
276 Jim Hiller .06 .15
277 Doug Derraugh .06 .15
278 Patrick Senger .06 .15
279 Pavel Gross .06 .15
280 Robert Guillet .06 .15
281 Sylvain Couturier .06 .15
282 Heinrich Schiffl .06 .15
283 Heinz Ehlers .06 .15
284 Larry Rucchin .06 .15
285 Gregory Johnston .20 .50
286 David Berge .06 .15
287 Johan Norgren .06 .15
288 Martin Ulrich .06 .15
289 Benjamin Hecker .06 .15
290 Mike Pellegrims .06 .15
291 Michael Komma TR .06 .15
292 Oberhausen .06 .15
293 Peter Gulda .06 .15
294 Jergus Baca .06 .15
295 Bob Marshall .06 .15
296 Mike Sullivan .20 .50
297 Jacek Plachta .06 .15
298 Andrej Fuchs .06 .15
299 Mike McNeill .20 .50
300 Aleksandrs Kerch .06 .15
301 Robert Hock .06 .15
302 Albert Malgin .06 .15
303 Kai Fischer .20 .50
304 Burke Murphy .06 .15
305 Jeff Sebastian .06 .15
306 Sergej Stas .06 .15
307 Sebastian Klenner .06 .15
308 Boris Fuchs .06 .15
309 Ivo Jan .06 .15
310 Francois Gravel .06 .15
311 Alexander Makritzky .06 .15
312 Viktor Karatchun .06 .15
313 Gunnar Leidborg TR .06 .15
314 Munchen .06 .15
315 Boris Rousson .20 .50
316 Hans Lodin .06 .15
317 Chris Luongo .20 .50
318 Mike Casselman .20 .50
319 Heiko Smazal .06 .15
320 Peter Abstreiter .06 .15
321 Simon Wheeldon .20 .50
322 Phil Huber .06 .15
323 Peter Douris .20 .50
324 Jari Korpisalo .06 .15
325 Kent Fearns .06 .15
326 Markus Jocher .06 .15
327 Pelle Svensson .06 .15
328 Sven Wiele .06 .15
329 Wayne Hynes .06 .15
330 Bill McDougall .20 .50
331 Alexander Serikow .20 .50
332 Robert Joyce .20 .50
333 Jorg Handrick .06 .15
334 Jason Herter .10 .25
335 Johan Rosen .06 .15
336 Mike Kennedy .20 .50
337 Christian Kunast .06 .15
338 Shane Peacock .06 .15
339 Sean Simpson TR .06 .15
340 Essen .06 .15
341 Oldrich Svoboda .06 .15
342 Bodo Mueller-Boenigk .06 .15
343 Vlastimil Kroupa .06 .15
344 Zdenek Touzimsky .06 .15
345 Pavel Augusta .06 .15
346 Christian Kohmann .06 .15
347 Martin Sychra .06 .15
348 Torsten Kienass .10 .25
349 Peter Draisaitl .06 .15
350 Marian Kacir .06 .15
351 Terry Campbell .06 .15
352 Roland Verwey .06 .15
353 Radek Toth .06 .15
354 Josef Zajic .06 .15
355 Jochen Vollmer .06 .15
356 Jiri Sejba .06 .15
357 Jukka Seppo .06 .15
358 Marc Savard .20 .50
359 Enrico Ciccone .10 .25
360 Michael Dvorak .06 .15
361 Tomas Nemcicky .06 .15
362 Andrej Nederost .40 1.00
363 Tomas Srsen .06 .15
364 Bedrich Scerban .06 .15
365 Jan Benda TR .14 .35
366 3fi National .06 .15
367 Robert Muller .06 .15
368 Torsten Kienass .10 .25
369 Markus Pottinger .06 .15
370 Lorenz Funk .06 .15
371 Nico Pyka .06 .15
372 Sven Felski .06 .15
373 Jochen Molling .06 .15
374 Christian Langer .06 .15
375 Nikolaus Mondt .06 .15
376 Bernd Kuhnhauser .06 .15
377 Jurgen Rumrich .06 .15
378 Lars Bruggemann .06 .15
379 Alexander Serikow .20 .50
380 Klaus Kathan .06 .15
381 Terry Campbell .06 .15
382 Tino Boos .06 .15
383 Michael Bresagk .06 .15
384 Christian Lukes .06 .15
385 Heiko Smazal .06 .15
386 Tobias Abstreiter .06 .15
387 Thomas Dolak .06 .15
388 Udo Dohler .06 .15
389 Andreas Loth .06 .15
390 David Berge .06 .15
391 Mark MacKay .20 .50
392 Hans Zach TR .06 .15
393 Moderatoren .06 .15
394 Marc Hindelang .06 .15
395 Peter Kohl .06 .15
396 Sven Kukulies .06 .15
397 Claus Muller .06 .15
398 Gerhard Leinauer .06 .15
399 Michael Leopold .06 .15
400 Rick Amann .06 .15
401 Schiris .06 .15
402 Holger Gerstberger .06 .15
403 Ralph Dimmers .06 .15
404 Harald Deubert .06 .15
405 Petr Chvatal .06 .15
406 Frank Awizus .06 .15
407 Axel Rademaker .06 .15
408 Wolfgang Hellwig .06 .15
409 Gerhard Muller .06 .15
410 Gerhard Lichtnecker .06 .15
411 Rainer Kluge .06 .15
412 Stefan TR .06 .15
413 Richard SchÃ¼tz .06 .15
414 Willi Schimm .06 .15
415 Peter Slapke .06 .15
416 TW 1 .06 .15
417 TW 2 .06 .15
418 TW 3 .06 .15
419 TW 4 .06 .15
420 TW 5 .06 .15
421 TW 6 .06 .15
422 TW 7 .06 .15
423 TW 8 .06 .15
424 TW 9 .06 .15
425 RS 1 .06 .15
426 RS 2 .06 .15
427 RS 3 .06 .15
428 RS 4 .06 .15
429 RS 5 .06 .15
430 RS 6 .06 .15
431 RS 7 .06 .15
432 RS 8 .06 .15
433 RS 9 .06 .15
434 SK .06 .15

1999-00 German Bundesliga 2

COMPLETE SET (330) 30.00 60.00
1 EC Bad Nauheim Team Card .02 .10
2 Darryl Olsen .20 .50
3 Sven Gerbig .10 .25
4 Gaetan Malo .10 .25
5 Steffen Michel .10 .25
6 Dennis Cardona .10 .25
7 Marco Rentzsch .10 .25
8 Dino Felicetti .10 .25
9 David Matsos .10 .25
10 Sven Paschek .10 .25
11 Marco Heinrichs .10 .25
12 Larry Mitchell .10 .25
13 Ingo Schwarz .10 .25
14 Dale Jago .10 .25
15 Claus Dalpiaz .20 .50
16 Marc West .10 .25
17 Christian Seeberger .10 .25
18 Olaf Scholz .10 .25
19 Carsten Gosdeck .10 .25
20 Dan Olsen .10 .25
21 EC Bad TÃ¶lz Team Card .02 .10
22 Christian Proulx .20 .50
23 Michael Teltscher .10 .25
24 Florian Keller .10 .25
25 Christian Curth .10 .25
26 Yanick Dube .20 .50
27 Markus Witting .10 .25
28 Axel Kammerer .10 .25
29 Dave Flanagan .10 .25
30 Ilpo Kauhanen .20 .50
31 Johan SÃ¤lle .10 .25
32 Ambrosius Fichtner .10 .25
33 David St. Pierre .10 .25
34 Mathias Hart .10 .25
35 Franz Demmel .10 .25
36 Markus Feierabend .10 .25
37 Florian Zeller .10 .25
38 Sven Valenti .10 .25
39 Christian Gegenfurtner .10 .25
40 Josef Schlickenrieder .10 .25
41 SC Bietigheim-Bissingen Team Card .02 .10
42 David Belitski .20 .50
43 Frank Appel .10 .25
44 Markus Rohde .10 .25
45 Milos Vanik .10 .25
46 Marc Mundil .10 .25
47 Ulrich Liebsch .10 .25
48 Darren Ritchie .10 .25
49 Mike Bader .10 .25
50 Daniel Held .10 .25
51 Andrej Jaufmann .10 .25
52 Tim Leahy .10 .25
53 Martin Ancicka .10 .25
54 Christian Baader .10 .25
55 Craig Teeple .10 .25
56 Ralf StÃ¤rk .10 .25
57 Andreas Naumann .10 .25
58 Stephan Sinner .10 .25
59 Timo Nykopp .10 .25
60 Vaclav Drobny .10 .25
61 Thomas Mieszkowski .10 .25
62 Tom Pokel .10 .25
63 Braunlager EHC/Harz Team Card .02 .10
64 Jarno Miikkulainen .20 .50
65 Peter Lundmark .20 .50
66 Josef Beppi Eckmair .10 .25
67 Douglas Murray .10 .25
68 Chris Clarke .10 .25
69 Ron Gaudet .10 .25
70 Sven Gerike .10 .25
71 Marek Gajewski .10 .25
72 Markus Draxler .10 .25
73 Frederik Andersson .10 .25
74 Timo Gschwill .10 .25
75 Georg Gailer .10 .25
76 Frank Richardt .10 .25
77 Johan Silfwerplatz .10 .25
78 Marcus Bleicher .10 .25
79 Anton Krinner .10 .25
80 Sebastian Buchwieser .10 .25
81 Bastian Niedermeier .10 .25
82 Anton Raubal .10 .25
83 Peter Gailer .10 .25
84 DÃ¼sseldorfer EG Team Card .02 .10
85 Chad Biafore .20 .50
86 Fabian BrÃ¤nnstrÃ¶m .20 .50
87 Zdenek Travnicek .10 .25
88 Victor Gordiouk .10 .25
89 Leo Stefan .10 .25
90 Till Feser .10 .25
91 Andreas Pokorny .10 .25
92 Andreas Brockmann .10 .25
93 Ralf Reisinger .10 .25
94 Marc Dillmann .10 .25
95 Sergej Sorokin .10 .25
96 Peter Franke .10 .25
97 Udo Schmid .10 .25
98 Rafael Jedamzik .10 .25
99 Jouni Vento .10 .25
100 Torsten Kunz .10 .25
101 Sebastian Odenthal .10 .25
102 Anders Gozzi .10 .25
103 Maurizio Mansi .10 .25
104 Boris Lingemann .10 .25
105 Czeslaw Panek .10 .25
106 EHC Freiburg Team Card .02 .10
107 Rostislav Haas .20 .50
108 Alexander Semak .10 .25
109 Oleg Znarok .10 .25
110 David Danner .10 .25
111 Igor Dorochin .10 .25
112 Tobias Samendinger .10 .25
113 Ravil Khaidarov .10 .25
114 Evgeni Sultanowitsch .10 .25
115 Thomas Jetter .10 .25
116 Rudolf GorgenlÃ¤nder .10 .25
117 Andrej Strakhov .10 .25
118 Vitalij Grossmann .10 .25
119 Max Bauer .10 .25
120 Peter Mares .10 .25
121 Josef Peroutka .10 .25
122 Peter Precan .10 .25
123 Michael Vasicek .10 .25
124 Patrick Vozar .10 .25
125 Frantisek Frosch .10 .25
126 Thomas Dolak sen. .10 .25
127 Grefrather EV Team Card .02 .10
128 Frank Gentges .20 .50
129 Jochen Hecker .10 .25
130 Dirk Kuhnekath .10 .25
131 Bill Trew .10 .25
132 Thomas Popiesch .10 .25
133 Christoph Kleckers .10 .25
134 Henrik HÃ¶lscher .10 .25
135 Arno Brux .10 .25
136 Ashlin Halfnight .10 .25
137 Nolan McDonald .10 .25
138 Gilbert SchrÃ¶der .10 .25
139 Nicklas Norlander .10 .25
140 Steve Smillie .10 .25
141 Tobias Grossecker .10 .25
142 Marcel Sakac .10 .25
143 Elmar Schmitz .10 .25
144 Hamburg Crocodiles Team Card .02 .10
145 Alexander Genze .10 .25
146 Derek Booth .10 .25
147 Alexander Engel .10 .25
148 John Johnson .10 .25
149 Jason Dunham .10 .25
150 Mike Millar .10 .25
151 Jay Luknowsky .10 .25
152 Andy Pritchard .10 .25
153 Mark Mahon .10 .25
154 Patrick Pysz .10 .25
155 Karsten Mende .10 .25
156 Phil Bourque .20 .50
157 JÃ¼rgen Trattner .10 .25
158 Carsten Solbach .10 .25
159 Maurice Lemay .30 .75
160 Jayson Meyer .10 .25
161 Marius Cissewski .10 .25
162 Christoph Sandner .10 .25
163 Harald Waibel .10 .25
164 Mario Gehrig .10 .25
165 Ross Yates .10 .25
166 Heilbronner EC Team Card .02 .10
167 Mikael Granlund .20 .50
168 Alexander Schuster .10 .25
169 Niklas Rinaldo .10 .25
170 Todd Sparks .10 .25
171 Thomas SchÃ¤dler .10 .25
172 Martin Williams .10 .25
173 Kenneth Filbey .10 .25
174 Ronny Martin .10 .25
175 Henri Marcoux .10 .25
176 Christian Martin .10 .25
177 Felix Feeser .10 .25
178 Brad Scott .10 .25
179 Alexander Semjonov .10 .25
180 Michael Rumrich .10 .25
181 Layne Roland .10 .25
182 BjÃ¶rn Barta .10 .25
183 Markus Eberl .10 .25
184 Rainer Suchan .10 .25
185 Johan Lindh .10 .25
186 Gary Prior .10 .25
187 ERC Ingolstadt Team Card .02 .10
188 Marco Thommes .10 .25
189 Stephane Julien .10 .25
190 Agostino Casale .10 .25
191 Kevin Ryan .10 .25
192 Harald SchÃ¤fler .10 .25
193 Markus Welz .10 .25
194 Wolfgang Fries .10 .25
195 Petr Bares .10 .25
196 Thomas Daffner .10 .25
197 Clayton Young .10 .25
198 Samuel Groleau .10 .25
199 Philippe DeRouville .30 .75
200 Cory Holden .10 .25
201 Sven Zywitza .10 .25
202 Frank Kannewurf .10 .25
203 Fabian Dahlem .10 .25
204 JÃ¼rgen Simon .10 .25
205 Roland Timoschuk .10 .25
206 Glenn Goodall .40 1.00
207 Giacinto Boni .10 .25
208 Iserlohner EC Team Card .02 .10
209 Cory Laylin .10 .25
210 Oliver Bernhardt .10 .25
211 Robert Gratza .10 .25
212 Collin Danielsmeier .10 .25
213 Pat Mikesch .10 .25
214 Tomas Martinec .10 .25
215 Teal Fowler .10 .25
216 Michael Hackert .10 .25
217 Mike Muller .10 .25
218 Oliver Hackert .10 .25
219 Peter Hellmann .10 .25
220 Steve Potvin .10 .25
221 Torsten Fendt .10 .25
222 Manuel Kofler .10 .25
223 Lars MÃ¼ller .10 .25
224 Elvis Beslagic .10 .25
225 Ronny Arendt .10 .25
226 Christian Franz .10 .25
227 Ian Wood .20 .50
228 Greg Poss .10 .25
229 EHC Neuwied Team Card .02 .10
230 Juri Stumpf .10 .25
231 Dean Fedorchuk .10 .25
232 Andrej Teljukin .10 .25
233 Alexander Andrievsky .10 .25
234 Ladislav Strompf .10 .25
235 Richard Baptist .10 .25
236 Otto Keresztes .10 .25
237 Klaus Micheller .10 .25
238 Todd Johnson .10 .25
239 Mario Naster .10 .25
240 Jens Hergt .10 .25
241 Falk Ozellis .10 .25
242 Craig Streu .10 .25
243 Marc Gronau .10 .25
244 Ole Kopitz .10 .25
245 Vitalij Semenchenko .10 .25
246 Radek Vit .10 .25
247 Sinuhe Wallinheimo .30 .75
248 Michael Weinfurter .10 .25
249 Petteri Lehmussaari .10 .25
250 GEC Nordhorn Team Card .02 .10
251 Christian von Trzcinski .10 .25
252 Jedrzej Kasperczyk .10 .25
253 Peter Kwasigroch .10 .25
254 Christian Spaan .10 .25
255 Gabriel KrÃ¼ger .10 .25
256 Moritz Schmidt .10 .25
257 Alexej Pogodin .10 .25

258 Markus Kempf .10 .25
259 Sergej Zvyagin .10 .25
260 Christian Brittig .10 .25
261 Juris Opulskis .10 .25
262 Andreas Morczinietz .10 .25
263 Andrej Hanisz .10 .25
264 Sami Leinonen .10 .25
265 Sergej Tchoudinov .10 .25
266 Mikka Kemppi .10 .25
267 Anton Weissgerber .10 .25
268 SC Riessersee Team Card .02 .10
269 Michael Pump .10 .25
270 Georg GÃ¼ttler .10 .25
271 Christoph Klotz .10 .25
272 Tim Regan .10 .25
273 Alexander Wedl .10 .25
274 Mika Puhakka .10 .25
275 Martin Holzer .10 .25
276 Hubert Buchwieser .10 .25
277 Michael Raubal .10 .25
278 Josef Lehner .10 .25
279 Christian Mayr .10 .25
280 Tobias Netter .10 .25
281 Tom O´Grady .10 .25
282 Samuli Peltosara .10 .25
283 Leonhard Wild .10 .25
284 Florian Brandl .10 .25
285 Duane Dennis .10 .25
286 Mark Zdan .10 .25
287 Florian Storf .10 .25
288 Ron Chyzowski .10 .25
289 ES Weisswasser Team Card .02 .10
290 Torsten Hanusch .10 .25
291 Daniel Sikorski .10 .25
292 Alexej Jefimov .10 .25
293 Alexandre Vinogradov .10 .25
294 Ronny Reddo .10 .25
295 Frank Peschke .10 .25
296 Ronny Glaser .10 .25
297 JÃ¶rgen Hermansson .10 .25
298 Robert Brezina .10 .25
299 Sven Steinecke .10 .25
300 David Musial .10 .25
301 Pekka Virta .10 .25
302 Thomas Knobloch .10 .25
303 Daniel Bartell .10 .25
304 Falk Herzig .10 .25
305 Dimitri Alekhin .10 .25
306 Joakim Wiberg .10 .25
307 Martin Wiita .10 .25
308 JÃ¶rg Pohling .10 .25
309 Bror Hansson .10 .25
310 EC Wilhelmshaven-Stickhausen Team Card .02 .10
311 Vadim Finko .10 .25
312 Harald Hebig .10 .25
313 Kai Ahlroth .10 .25
314 Boris Blank .10 .25
315 Eduard Lewandowski .10 .25
316 Alexander Rusch .10 .25
317 Dimitry Dudarev .10 .25
318 Vitali Janke .10 .25
319 Ilja Stachenkov .10 .25
320 JÃ¼rgen Schaal .10 .25
321 Andrej Dmitriev .10 .25
322 Iiro ItÃ¤mies .10 .25
323 Sergej Jaschin .10 .25
324 Martin Ekrt .10 .25
325 Marian Horvarth .10 .25
326 Mario SchÃ¼ssel .10 .25
327 Alexander Herbst .10 .25
328 Andrej Naumann .10 .25
329 Peter Kalinowski .10 .25
330 Anatoli Antipov .10 .25

2000-01 German Berlin Polar Bears Postcards

This team-issued set is standard postcard size. Cards are unnumbered and listed below in alphabetical order. Thanks to collector Andy Hatzos for this and other Polar Bears checklist.

COMPLETE SET (22) 10.00 20.00
1 John Chabot .40 1.00
2 Derek Cormier .40 1.00
3 Rob Cowie .40 1.00
4 Uli Egen .40 1.00
5 Sven Felski .40 1.00
6 Marc Fortier .40 1.00
7 Alexander Godynyuk .40 1.00
8 Rich Gosselin .40 1.00
9 Peter Hammarstrom .40 1.00
10 Todd Harkins .40 1.00
11 Alex Hicks .40 1.00
12 Alexander Jung .40 1.00
13 Daniel Laperriere .40 1.00
14 Rob Leask .40 1.00
15 Martin Lindman .40 1.00
16 Derek Mayer .40 1.00
17 Klaus Merk .40 1.00
18 Nico Pyka .40 1.00
19 Sandy Smith .40 1.00
20 Jeff Tomlinson .40 1.00
21 Lubomir Vaic .40 1.00
22 Steve Walker .40 1.00

2000-01 German DEL

This set features the top players in Germany's elite league. The cards were produced by Upper Deck and feature an action photo on the front, with a head shot and stats on the back.

COMPLETE SET (240) 15.00 40.00
1 Gordon Hynes .10 .25
2 Dave Tomlinson .20 .50
3 Stephane Richer .05 .15
4 Steve Junker .05 .15
5 Wayne Hynes .05 .15
6 Bradley Bergen .05 .15
7 Devin Edgerton .05 .15
8 Ron Pasco .05 .15
9 Francois Groleau .05 .15
10 Todd Hlushko .20 .50
11 Mike Rosati .20 .50
12 Chris Straube .05 .15
13 Jean-Francois Jomphe .20 .50
14 Jan Alston .05 .15
15 Sven Rampf .05 .15
16 Sergej Vostrikov .05 .15
17 Igor Maslennikov .05 .15
18 Reemt Pyka .05 .15
19 Dave Chyzowski .20 .50
20 Arnaud Briand .05 .15
21 Sergej Stas .05 .15
22 Sebastian Klenner .05 .15
23 Vasily Pankov .05 .15
24 Duane Moeser .05 .15
25 Jason Muzzatti .40 1.00
26 Herbert Hohenberger .20 .50
27 Ryan Savoia .05 .15
28 Jim Camazzola .05 .15
29 Tommy Jakobsen .05 .15
30 Andrei Mezin .40 1.00
31 Markus Pottinger .05 .15
32 Thomas Sjogren .05 .15
33 Jim Hiller .05 .15
34 Pavel Gross .05 .15
35 Robert Guillet .05 .15
36 Udo Dohler .05 .15
37 Anders Huusko .05 .15
38 Heinz Ehlers .05 .15
39 Gregory Johnston .20 .50
40 Petri Liimatainen .05 .15
41 Johan Norgren .05 .15
42 Martin Ulrich .05 .15
43 Iain Fraser .10 .25
44 Gary Shuchuk .10 .25
45 Torsten Kienass .05 .15
46 Niki Mondt .05 .15
47 Bernd Kuhnhauser .05 .15
48 Craig Reichert .10 .25
49 Niclas Sundblad .10 .25
50 Sergey Sorokin .05 .15
51 Peter Franke .05 .15
52 Ivan Droppa .05 .15
53 Christopher Bartolone .05 .15
54 Leo Stefan .05 .15
55 Victor Gordiouk .10 .25
56 Lorenz Funk .05 .15
57 Boris Lingemann .05 .15
58 Andrei Trefilov .20 .50
59 Nico Pyka .05 .15
60 Alexander Jung .05 .15
61 Alexander Godynyuk .10 .25
62 Derek Mayer .05 .15
63 Sven Felski .05 .15
64 Marc Fortier .10 .25
65 John Chabot .20 .50
66 Derek Cormier .05 .15
67 Steve Walker .05 .15
68 Lubomir Vaic .05 .15
69 Klaus Merk .20 .50
70 Dan Laperriere .20 .50
71 Rob Cowie .05 .15
72 Martin Lindman .05 .15
73 Chris Govedaris .20 .50
74 Michael Bresagk .05 .15
75 Leonardo Conti .05 .15
76 Robin Doyle .05 .15
77 Toni Porkka .05 .15
78 John Walker .05 .15
79 Jean-Marc Richard .05 .15
80 Jason Ruff .10 .25
81 Jason Cirone .10 .25
82 Jose Charbonneau .10 .25
83 Victor Gervais .05 .15
84 Patrice Lefebvre .20 .50
85 Martin Gendron .20 .50
86 Ken Quinney .20 .50
87 Keith Aldridge .20 .50
88 Eldon Reddick .20 .50
89 Oscar Ackestrom .05 .15
90 Mattias Loof .05 .15
91 Egor Bashkatov .10 .25
92 Mark Kosturik .05 .15
93 Wallace Schreiber .20 .50
94 Dominic Lavoie .10 .25
95 Rob Murphy .10 .25
96 Pavel Cagas .05 .15
97 Igor Chibirev .10 .25
98 Kevin Grant .05 .15
99 Jan Munster .05 .15
100 Chris Snell .10 .25
101 Patrik Zetterberg .05 .15
102 Colin Beardsmore .05 .15
103 Calle Carlsson .05 .15
104 Tomas Martinec .05 .15
105 Teal Fowler .05 .15
106 Alexander Kuzminski .05 .15
107 Terence Campbell .05 .15
108 Duane Derksen .20 .50
109 Peter Roed .05 .15
110 Torsten Fendt .05 .15
111 Shawn Anderson .05 .15
112 Manuel Kofler .05 .15
113 Radek Toth .05 .15
114 Steve Potvin .05 .15
115 Brent Tully .05 .15
116 Ted Crowley .05 .15
117 Pat Mikesch .05 .15
118 Stephane Robitaille .05 .15
119 Francois Guay .05 .15
120 Andreas Loth .05 .15
121 Patrice Tardif .20 .50
122 Scott Levins .05 .15
123 Joachim Appel .05 .15
124 Chris Rogles .20 .50
125 Thomas Daffner .05 .15
126 Klaus Kathan .05 .15
127 Sylvain Turgeon .10 .25
128 Andrew Verner .20 .50
129 Bruno Zarrillo .05 .15
130 Dwayne Norris .20 .50
131 Christoph Paepke .05 .15
132 Mirko Ludemann .05 .15
133 Andreas Lupzig .05 .15
134 Jason Young .10 .25
135 Joseph Heiss .20 .50
136 Tomas Forslund .10 .25
137 Andre Faust .05 .15
138 Tino Boos .05 .15
139 John Miner .10 .25
140 Dave McIlwain .20 .50
141 Dieter Kalt .05 .15
142 Corey Millen .20 .50
143 Marc Hussey .05 .15
144 Brent Severyn .20 .50
145 Christian Ehrhoff .05 .15
146 Neil Eisenhut .10 .25
147 Ilja Vorobjev .05 .15
148 Shayne Wright .05 .15
149 Dan Lambert .20 .50
150 Brad Purdie .05 .15
151 Christoph Brandner .05 .15
152 Roger Nordstrom .05 .15
153 Jeff Christian .10 .25
154 Karel Lang .05 .15
155 Thomas Brandl .05 .15
156 Martin Sychra .05 .15
157 Jason McBain .05 .15
158 Ralph Intranuovo .20 .50
159 Jarkko Savijoki .05 .15
160 Marc Savard .20 .50
161 Roman Meluzin .05 .15
162 Todd Simon .10 .25
163 Jean-Francois Quintin .10 .25
164 Scott Pearson .20 .50
165 Kevin Wortman .05 .15
166 Geoff Sarjeant .20 .50
167 Leonard Wild .05 .15
168 Erich Goldmann .20 .50
169 Marc Laniel .20 .50
170 Esa Tikkanen .75 2.00
171 Hans Lodin .05 .15
172 Rick Girard .05 .15
173 Christian Kunast .05 .15
174 Simon Wheeldon .15 .40
175 Shane Peacock .05 .15
176 Christoph Schubert .05 .15
177 Peter Douris .10 .25
178 Alexander Serikow .20 .50
179 Peter Larsson .05 .15
180 Thomas Dolak .05 .15
181 Jorg Handrick .05 .15
182 Jason Herter .10 .25
183 Andrew Schneider .10 .25
184 Parris Duffus .20 .50
185 Luciano Borsato .10 .25
186 Jurgen Rumrich .05 .15
187 Dimitri Dudik .05 .15
188 Alexander Cherbayev .10 .25
189 Martin Jiranek .05 .15
190 Martin Reichel .05 .15
191 Mario Chitarroni .05 .15
192 Jason Miller .05 .15
193 Bjorn Nord .05 .15
194 Kevin Miehm .10 .25
195 Marc Seliger .20 .50
196 Daniel Kunce .05 .15
197 Paul Stanton .10 .25
198 Peter Gulda .05 .15
199 Christian Kohmann .05 .15
200 Mika Arvaja .05 .15
201 Carsten Gosdeck .05 .15
202 Aleksandrs Kercs .05 .15
203 Alexandre Andrievski .10 .25
204 Robert Hock .05 .15
205 Josef Zajic .05 .15
206 Marek Stebnicki .05 .15
207 Andrej Kovalev .05 .15
208 Ladislav Karabin .05 .15
209 Peter Draisaitl .05 .15
210 Sinuhe Wallinheimo .10 .25
211 Jergus Baca .05 .15
212 Peter Allen .05 .15
213 Alexander Duck .05 .15
214 Marcel Goc .60 1.50
215 Jens Stramkowski .05 .15
216 Mark MacKay .10 .25
217 Vadym Slivchenko .05 .15
218 Jacek Plachta .05 .15
219 Alexei Yegorov .20 .50
220 Patrik Augusta .05 .15
221 Brad Schlegel .10 .25
222 Andreas Renz .05 .15
223 Thomas Greilinger .05 .15
224 Ian Gordon .10 .25
225 Mike Bullard .20 .50
226 Robert Muller .05 .15
227 Mike Pellegrims .05 .15
228 Mike Casselman .05 .15
229 Leonardo Soccio .05 .15
230 Andreas Pokorny .10 .25
231 Tim Schnelle .05 .15
232 Daniel Kreutzer .05 .15
233 Tobias Abstreiter .05 .15
234 Tomas Hartogs .05 .15
235 Stephane Barin .05 .15
236 Boris Rousson .20 .50
237 Mike Kennedy .10 .25
238 John Craighead .05 .15
239 Marc Pethke .05 .15
240 Markus Janka .05 .15

2000-01 German DEL All-Star Class

This series was an insert found in the 2000-01 German DEL set and features the league's top scorers. They were inserted at a rate of 1:17.

COMPLETE SET (10) 8.00 20.00
STATED ODDS 1:17
A1 Martin Jiranek .80 2.00
A2 Patrice Lefebvre 1.60 4.00
A3 Peter Douris .80 2.00
A4 Sergej Vostrikov .80 2.00
A5 Gregory Johnston 1.20 3.00
A6 Chris Govedaris .80 2.00
A7 Mike Casselman .80 2.00
A8 Corey Millen 1.20 3.00
A9 Shawn Anderson 1.20 3.00
A10 Sylvain Turgeon 1.20 3.00

2000-01 German DEL Game Jersey

This insert set features a swatch of actual game-worn jersey on each card. Because the jerseys in the DEL are laden with ads, multi-colored swatches are plentiful. As such, they do not draw significant premiums as similar swatches might earn in North American sets. The cards were inserted 1:144 packs.

COMPLETE SET (16) 160.00 400.00
STATED ODDS 1:144
BZ Bruno Zarrillo 16.00 40.00
DM Duane Moeser 10.00 25.00
JB Jergus Baca 12.00 30.00
JR Jurgen Rumrich 10.00 25.00
LE Leonard Soccio 12.00 30.00
LS Leo Stefan 12.00 30.00
MF Marc Fortier 12.00 30.00
MM Mark MacKay 12.00 30.00
MS Marc Savard 20.00 50.00
PG Pavel Gross 12.00 30.00
SR Stephane Richer 12.00 30.00
SW Simon Wheeldon 16.00 40.00
TA Tobias Abstreiter 16.00 40.00
TF Teal Fowler 12.00 30.00
TH Tomas Hartogs 12.00 30.00
TP Toni Porkka 10.00 25.00

2000-01 German DEL Profiles

Inserted 1:8 packs of German DEL, these cards picture the league's top performers.

COMPLETE SET (11) 8.00 20.00
STATED ODDS 1:8
P1 Jan Alston .80 2.00
P2 Andrei Mezin 2.00 5.00
P3 John Chabot 1.20 3.00
P4 Wallace Schreiber 1.20 3.00
P5 Shane Peacock .80 2.00
P6 Mike Bullard 1.20 3.00
P7 Mirko Ludemann .80 2.00
P8 Boris Rousson 1.20 3.00
P9 Andrej Kovalev .80 2.00
P10 Mike Pellegrims .40 1.00
P11 Andrei Trefilov .80 2.00

2000-01 German DEL Star Attractions

This set profiles the most popular players in the German DEL. The cards were inserted 1:17 packs.

COMPLETE SET (10) 10.00 25.00
STATED ODDS 1:17
S1 Ivan Droppa 1.20 3.00
S2 Gordon Hynes 1.20 3.00
S3 Marek Stebnicki 1.20 3.00
S4 Daniel Kreutzer 1.20 3.00
S5 Thomas Brandl 1.20 3.00
S6 Esa Tikkanen 2.00 5.00
S7 Bob Sweeney 1.20 3.00
S8 Paul Stanton 1.20 3.00
S9 Dave Tomlinson 1.20 3.00
S10 Brent Severyn 2.00 5.00

2001-02 German Berlin Polar Bears Postcards

COMPLETE SET (27) 10.00 25.00
1 Keith Aldridge .40 1.00
2 Alex Barta .40 1.00
3 Boris Blank .40 1.00
4 David Cooper .40 1.00
5 Patrick Czajka .40 1.00
6 Uli Egen .40 1.00
7 Sven Felski .40 1.00
8 Marc Fortier .40 1.00
9 Daniel Laperriere .40 1.00
10 Steve Larouche .40 1.00
11 Rob Leask .40 1.00
12 Scott Levins .40 1.00
13 Eduard Lewandoski .40 1.00
14 Martin Lindman .40 1.00
15 Chris Marinucci .40 1.00
16 Klaus Merk .40 1.00
17 Hartmut Nickel .40 1.00
18 Fabio Patrzek .40 1.00
19 Ed Patterson .40 1.00
20 Nico Pyka .40 1.00
21 David Roberts .40 1.00
22 Jan Schertz .40 1.00
23 Richard Shulmistra .40 1.00
24 Tom Skinner .40 1.00
25 Lee Sorochan .40 1.00
26 Jeff Tomlinson .40 1.00
27 Steve Walker .40 1.00

2001-02 German Upper Deck

This set features the top players of the German DEL. The cards were produced by Upper Deck and sold only in Germany. The design mirrors that of the base 2001-02 Upper Deck series.

COMPLETE SET (268) 16.00 40.00
1 Igor Alexandrov .08 .20
2 Marc Beaucage .16 .40
3 Eric Dylla .20 .50
4 Mickey Elick .16 .40
5 Magnus Eriksson .08 .20
6 Jakub Ficenec .20 .50
7 Robert Guillet .08 .20
8 Tommy Jakobsen .08 .20
9 Christian Lukes .08 .20
10 Igor Maslennikov .08 .20
11 Duanne Moeser .16 .40
12 Vasily Pankov .08 .20
13 Reemt Pyka .08 .20
14 Reid Simonton .16 .40
15 Sergej Vostrikov .08 .20
16 Alexander Cherbayev .08 .20
17 Heinz Ehlers .08 .20
18 Ronny Arendt .08 .20
19 Andrej Vassilyev .08 .20
20 Francois Leroux .20 .50
21 Andrei Mezin .40 1.00
22 Jan MÃ¼nster .08 .20
23 Markus PÃ¶ttinger .08 .20
24 Patrick Senger .08 .20
25 Aleksandrs Kercs .08 .20
26 Gordon Hynes .20 .50
27 Greg Andrusak .20 .50
28 Vjatcheslav Fanduls .08 .20
29 Yvon Corriveau .20 .50
30 Frederik Ã–berg .08 .20
31 Keith Aldridge .20 .50
32 David Cooper .16 .40
33 Sven Felski .20 .50
34 Marc Fortier .20 .50
35 Dan Laperriere .20 .50
36 Steve LaRouche .20 .50
37 Scott Levins .20 .50
38 Chris Marinucci .20 .50
39 Klaus Merk .20 .50
40 Nico Pyka .08 .20
41 David Roberts .20 .50
42 Jan Schertz .08 .20
43 Richard Shulmistra .20 .50
44 Lee Sorochan .20 .50
45 Steve Walker .16 .40
46 Chris Bartolone .16 .40
47 Jan Alston .08 .20
48 Ivan Droppa .16 .40
49 Neil Eisenhut .16 .40
50 Tore Vikingstad .08 .20
51 Torsten Kienass .08 .20
52 Bernd KÃ¼hnhauser .08 .20
53 Trond Magnussen .08 .20
54 Mike Pellegrims .16 .40
55 Jean-Francois Quintin .16 .40
56 Ralf Reisinger .08 .20
57 Leo Stefan .08 .20
58 Andrej Trefilov .20 .50
59 Martin Ulrich .08 .20
60 Rainer Zerwesz .08 .20
61 Frank Appel .16 .40
62 Lars BrÃ¼ggemann .08 .20
63 Mike Casselman .16 .40
64 Ted Crowley .16 .40
65 Liam Garvey .08 .20
66 Erich Goldmann .20 .50
67 Todd Hawkins .16 .40
68 Ralph Intranuovo .20 .50
69 Martin Sychra .08 .20
70 Riku-Petteri Lehtonen .08 .20
71 Doug MacDonald .16 .40
72 Marc Savard .20 .50
73 Todd Simon .16 .40
74 Jimmy Waite .30 .75
75 Craig Woodcroft .16 .40
76 Michael Bresagk .08 .20
77 Brent Cullaton .16 .40
78 Rob Doyle .08 .20
79 Greg Evtushevski .16 .40
80 Victor Gervais .16 .40
81 Rick Girard .16 .40
82 Stewart Malgunas .16 .40
83 Rob Pearson .20 .50
84 Eldon Reddick .20 .50
85 Ian Fraser .16 .40
86 Alexander Selivanov .08 .20
87 Vadim Slivchenko .08 .20
88 Chris Snell .16 .40
89 Brent Tully .16 .40
90 John Walker .16 .40
91 Oscar AckestrÃ¶m .08 .20
92 Egor Bashkatov .08 .20
93 Igor Chibirev .08 .20
94 Kevin Grant .16 .40
95 David Haas .16 .40
96 Peter Jakobsson .08 .20
97 Dominic Lavoie .20 .50
98 Mattias LÃ¶Ã¶f .08 .20
99 Rob Murphy .16 .40
100 Mark Pederson .16 .40
101 Wally Schreiber .16 .40
102 Len Soccio .20 .50
103 Andrew Verner .20 .50
104 Steve Wilson .16 .40
105 Patrik Zetterberg .08 .20
106 Doug Ast .16 .40
107 Colin Beardsmore .16 .40
108 Guy Dupuis .16 .40
109 Oliver Bernhardt .08 .20
110 Rusty Fitzgerald .20 .50
111 Terry Hollinger .20 .50
112 Kimmo Kapanen .08 .20
113 Dmitrij Kotschnew .08 .20
114 Cory Laylin .16 .40
115 Paul Dyck .20 .50
116 Tomas Martinec .08 .20
117 Colin Danielsmeier .08 .20
118 David Musial .08 .20
119 Andreas Pokorny .08 .20
120 Sean Tallaire .16 .40
121 Tobias Abstreiter .20 .50
122 Thomas Daffner .08 .20
123 Doug Derraugh .16 .40
124 Leonid Fatikov .08 .20
125 Tommie Hartogs .08 .20
126 Klaus Kathan .08 .20
127 Ilpo Kauhanen .20 .50
128 Ã–rjan Lindmark .08 .20
129 Andreas Loth .08 .20
130 Jeff MacLeod .16 .40
131 Pat Mikesch .08 .20
132 Jochen Molling .08 .20
133 Brent Peterson .20 .50
134 Shayne Wright .16 .40
135 Jeff Tory .16 .40
136 Tino Boos .08 .20
137 AndrÃ© Faust .08 .20
138 Alex Hicks .08 .20
139 Petri Liimatainen .08 .20
140 Mirko LÃ¼demann .20 .50
141 JÃ¶rg Mayr .08 .20
142 Dave McIlwain .20 .50
143 Corey Millen .20 .50
144 John Miner .16 .40
145 Dwayne Norris .16 .40
146 Toni Porkka .08 .20
147 Andreas Renz .08 .20
148 Chris Rogles .20 .50
149 Niklas Sundblad .20 .50
150 Jason Young .16 .40
151 Patrik Augusta .08 .20
152 StÃ©phane Barin .08 .20
153 Thomas Brandl .08 .20
154 Steffen Ziesche .08 .20
156 Jeff Christian .16 .40
157 Gilbert Dionne .20 .50
158 Mario Doyon .20 .50
159 Daniel Kunce .08 .20
160 Dan Lambert .30 .75
161 Roger NordstrÃ¶m .08 .20
162 Brad Purdie .20 .50
163 Gary Shuchuk .20 .50
164 Sergej Stas .08 .20
165 Phil von Stefenelli .20 .50
166 Brad Bergen .16 .40
167 Fabian BrÃ¤nnstrÃ¶m .08 .20
168 Devin Edgerton .16 .40
169 Todd Hlushko .20 .50
170 Wayne Hynes .16 .40
171 FranÃ§ois Groleau .16 .40
172 Michel Picard .20 .50
173 Yves Racine .20 .50
174 StÃ©phane Richer .16 .40
175 Andy Roach .16 .40
176 Mike Rosati .30 .75
177 Mike Stevens .16 .40
178 Dave Tomlinson .16 .40
179 Steve Junker .16 .40
180 Stefan Ustorf .20 .50
181 Kent Fearns .16 .40
182 Jason Herter .16 .40
183 Mike Kennedy .20 .50
184 Derek King .20 .50
185 Christian KÃ¼nast .08 .20
186 Hans Lodin .08 .20
187 David Oliver .16 .40
188 Shane Peacock .16 .40
189 Derek PlantÃ© .20 .50
190 Johan RosÃ©n .08 .20
191 Boris Rousson .20 .50
192 Andy Schneider .16 .40
193 Peter Douris .20 .50
194 Heiko Smazal .08 .20
195 Simon Wheeldon .20 .50
196 Shawn Anderson .16 .40
197 Luciano Borsato .20 .50
198 Frederic Chabot .40 1.50
199 Mario Chitarroni .20 .50
200 Kevin Dahl .16 .40
201 David Emma .20 .50
202 Martin Jiranek .08 .20
203 Chris Luongo .20 .50
204 Guy Lehoux .20 .50
205 Jacek Plachta .08 .20
206 Martin Reichel .08 .20
207 JÃ¼rgen Rumrich .08 .20
208 Christian SchÃ¶nmoser .08 .20
209 Jan Nemecek .08 .20
210 Bruno Zarrillo .20 .50
211 Andreas Lupzig .08 .20
212 Jergus Baca .08 .20
213 Derek Cormier .16 .40
214 John Craighead .16 .75
215 Jesper Damgaard .08 .20
216 Peter Gulda .08 .20
217 Robert Hock .08 .20
218 Martin Hohenberger .08 .20
219 Ladislav Karabin .08 .20
220 Christian Kohmann .08 .20
221 Andrej Kovalev .16 .40
222 Jason McBain .16 .40
223 Andrei Teljukin .08 .20
224 Sinuhe Wallinheimo .20 .50
225 Josef Zajic .08 .20
226 Micah Alvazoff .30 .75
227 Peter Allen .16 .40
228 Mike Bullard .20 .50
229 Dave Chyzowski .20 .50
230 Eric Dubois .16 .40
231 Ian Gordon .16 .40
232 Markus Janka .08 .20
233 Mark MacKay .16 .40
234 Neal Martin .16 .40
235 Jeff Nelson .16 .40
236 Jackson Penney .16 .40
237 Kent Simpson .16 .40
238 Jason Deleurme .16 .40
239 Gerhard Unterluggauer .08 .20
240 Darcy Werenka .20 .50
241 Andreas Morczinietz .08 .20
242 Christian Rohde .08 .20
243 Jonas Lanier .08 .20
244 Boris Blank .08 .20
245 Eduard Lewandowski .08 .20
246 Niki Mondt .08 .20
247 Leonard Wild .08 .20
248 Leonardo Conti .08 .20
249 Philip Schumacher .08 .20
250 BjÃ¶rn Leonhardt .20 .50
251 Christian Franz .20 .50
252 Manuel Kofler .20 .50
253 Daniel Kreutzer .20 .50
254 Markus Guggemos .20 .50
255 Dimitri PÃ¤tzold .20 .50
256 Benjamin Hinterstocker .20 .50
257 Christian Ehrhoff .20 1.00
258 Adrian Grygiel .20 .50
259 Benjamin Voigt .20 .50
260 Robert MÃ¼ller .20 .50
261 Dennis Seidenberg .20 1.50
262 Peter Abstreiter .20 .50
263 Christoph Schubert .20 .50
264 Andrej Strakhov .20 .50
265 Benjamin Hecker .20 .50
266 Vitalij Aab .20 .50
267 Carsten Gosdeck .20 .50
268 Lasse Kopitz .20 .50
269 Marcel Goc 1.20 2.00
270 Alexander DÃ¼ck .20 .50

2001-02 German Upper Deck Gate Attractions

This set features the most exciting players in the DEL. The cards were inserted one in every 17 packs.

COMPLETE SET (10) 10.00 25.00
STATED ODDS 1:17
GA1 Sergej Vostrikov 1.20 3.00
GA2 Aleksandrs Kercs 1.20 3.00
GA3 Sven Felski 1.20 3.00
GA4 Mark MacKay 1.20 3.00
GA5 Alexander Selivanov 1.20 3.00
GA6 Len Soccio 2.00 5.00
GA7 Ivan Droppa 1.20 3.00
GA8 Gilbert Dionne 2.00 5.00
GA9 Stefan Ustorf 1.20 3.00
GA10 Jason Miller 1.20 3.00

2001-02 German Upper Deck Goalies in Action

This set features the top stoppers in the DEL. The cards were inserted one in every 17 packs

COMPLETE SET (10) 20.00 40.00
STATED ODDS 1:17
G1 Andrei Mezin 3.20 6.00
G2 Klaus Merk 2.00 5.00
G3 Andrej Trefilov 3.20 6.00
G4 Andrew Verner 2.00 5.00
G5 Chris Rogles 2.00 5.00
G6 Roger Nordstrom 2.00 5.00
G7 Mike Rosati 2.00 5.00
G8 Christian Kunast 2.00 5.00
G9 Marc Seliger 4.00 8.00
G10 Sinuhe Wallinheimo 2.00 5.00

2001-02 German Upper Deck Jersey Cards

The cards in this set feature a swatch of a jersey worn in an actual DEL game. Singles were inserted one in every 144 packs. Cards that display multi-colour swatches are valued at 1X to 2X the prices below.

COMPLETE SET (6) 160.00 400.00
AM-J Andrei Mezin 20.00 50.00
AT-J Andrej Trefilov 16.00 30.00
AV-J Andrew Verner 16.00 30.00
CK-J Christian Kunast 10.00 20.00
CR-J Chris Rogles 16.00 30.00
ER-J Eldon Reddick 16.00 30.00
FC-J Frederic Chabot 20.00 50.00
IG-J Ian Gordon 10.00 20.00
JW-J Jimmy Waite 20.00 50.00
KK-J Kimmo Kapanen 10.00 20.00
LF-J Leonid Fatikov 10.00 20.00
ME-J Magnus Eriksson 10.00 20.00
MR-J Mike Rosati 16.00 30.00
RN-J Roger Nordstrom 10.00 20.00
RS-J Richard Shulmistra 16.00 30.00
SW-J Sinuhe Wallinheimo 16.00 30.00

2001-02 German Upper Deck Skilled Stars

This series features some of the DEL's top players. The cards were inserted one in every eight packs.

COMPLETE SET (11) 6.00 15.00
SS1 Robert Hock .80 2.00
SS2 David Cooper 1.20 3.00
SS3 Brad Purdie 1.20 3.00
SS4 Todd Simon .80 2.00
SS5 Oscar Ackestrom .80 2.00
SS6 Tomas Martinec .80 2.00
SS7 Pat Mikesch .80 2.00
SS8 Mirko Ludemann .80 2.00
SS9 Stephane Richer .80 2.00
SS10 Shane Peacock .80 2.00
SS11 Paul Stanton .80 2.00

2002-03 German Berlin Polar Bears Postcards

COMPLETE SET (28) 10.00 25.00
1 Keith Aldridge .40 1.00
2 Alex Barta .40 1.00
3 Marc Beaufait .40 1.00
4 Brad Bergen .40 1.00
5 Boris Blank .40 1.00
6 David Cooper .40 1.00
7 Yvon Corriveau .40 1.00
8 Kelly Fairchild .40 1.00
9 Sven Felski .40 1.00
10 John Gruden .40 1.00
11 Thorsten Heine .40 1.00
12 Martin Hoffmann .40 1.00
13 Oliver Jonas .40 1.00
14 Florian Katz .40 1.00
15 Florian Keller .40 1.00
16 Mark Kosick .40 1.00
17 Rob Leask .40 1.00
18 Klaus Merk .40 1.00
19 Hartmut Nickel .40 1.00
20 Pierre Page CO .40 1.00
21 Ricard Persson .40 1.00
22 Daniel Pyka .40 1.00
23 Nico Pyka .40 1.00
24 David Roberts .40 1.00
25 Rob Shearer .40 1.00
26 Richard Shulmistra .40 1.00
27 Jeff Tomlinson .40 1.00
28 Steve Walker .40 1.00

2002-03 German DEL City Press

Please note that cards #58-64 are not on the below checklist and are not known to exist. Please send any info to the contrary to hockeymag@beckett.com.

COMPLETE SET (290) 50.00 100.00
1 Ronny Arendt .20 .50
2 Philippe Audet .20 .50
3 Bjorn Barta .20 .50
4 Frederic Bouchard .20 .50
6 Shawn Carter .20 .50
7 Igor Dorochin .20 .50
8 P.C. Drouin .40 1.00
9 Magnus Eriksson .20 .50
10 Thorsten Fendt .20 .50
11 Maxim Galanov .20 .50
12 Patrick Koslow .20 .50
13 Greg Leeb .40 1.00
14 Christian Lukes .20 .50
15 Shayne McCosh .20 .50
16 Duanne Moeser .20 .50
17 Christopher Oravec .20 .50
18 Reid Simonton .20 .50
19 Andrej Strakhov .20 .50
20 Chris Straube .20 .50
21 Sergej Vostrikov .20 .50
22 Keith Aldridge .20 .50
23 Alexander Barta .20 .50
24 Mark Beaufait .20 .50
25 Bradley Bergen .20 .50
26 Boris Blank .20 .50
27 David Cooper .20 .50
28 Yvon Corriveau .20 .50
29 Kelly Fairchild .20 .50
30 Sven Felski .20 .50
31 John Gruden .20 .50
32 Oliver Jonas .20 .50
33 Florian Keller .20 .50
34 Robert Leask .20 .50
35 Ricard Persson .20 .50
36 Nico Pyka .20 .50
37 David Roberts .20 .50
38 Rob Shearer .20 .50
39 Richard Shulmistra .20 .50
40 Jeff Tomlinson .20 .50
41 Steve Walker .20 .50
42 Marc Beaucage .20 .50
43 Fabian Brannstrom .20 .50
44 Jeff Christian .20 .50
45 Neil Eisenhut .20 .50
46 Jakub Ficenec .40 1.00
47 Michael Hackert .20 .50
48 Mathias Hart .20 .50
49 Tommy Jakobsen .20 .50
50 Alexander Jung .20 .50
51 Torsten Kienass .20 .50
52 Daniel Kreutzer .20 .50
53 Bernd Kuhnhauser .20 .50
54 Trond Magnussen .20 .50
55 Nikolaus Mondt .20 .50
56 Mike Pellegrims .20 .50
57 Markus Pottinger .20 .50
58 Jean-Francois Quintin .20 .50
65 Greg Adams .20 .50
66 Pascal Appel .20 .50
67 Michael Bresagk .20 .50
68 Robert Busch .20 .50
69 Collin Danielsmeier .20 .50
70 Jason Dunham .20 .50
71 Rusty Fitzgerald .20 .50
73 Robert Francz .20 .50
74 Matthias Frenzel .20 .50
75 Victor Gervais .20 .50
76 Rick Girard .20 .50
77 Cory Laylin .20 .50
78 Stewart Malgunas .20 .50
79 Jackson Penney .20 .50
80 Marc Pethke .20 .50
81 Stephane Richer .20 .50
82 Dominic Roussel .40 1.00
83 Christoph Sandner .20 .50
84 Chris Snell .20 .50
85 Paul Stanton .20 .50
86 Jonas Stopfgeshoff .20 .50
87 Peter Abstreiter .20 .50
88 Greg Andrusak .20 .50
89 Ted Crowley .20 .50
90 Thomas Dolak .20 .50
91 Ted Drury .20 .50
92 Bobby House .20 .50
93 Manuel Kofler .20 .50
94 Patrick Koppchen .20 .50
95 Christian Kunast .20 .50
96 Bob Lachance .20 .50
97 Jason Miller .20 .50
98 Jacek Plachta .20 .50
99 Boris Rousson .40 1.00
100 Andrew Schneider .20 .50
101 Heiko Smazal .20 .50
102 Mike Stevens .20 .50
103 David Sulkovsky .20 .50
104 Jeff Tory .20 .50
105 Christian Volk .20 .50
106 Phil von Stefenelli .20 .50
107 Gilbert Dionne .20 .50
108 Patrick Ehelechner .20 .50
109 Edvin Frylen .20 .50
110 Lorenz Funk Jr. .20 .50
111 Todd Hawkins .20 .50
112 Stefan Hellkvist .20 .50
113 Peter Jakobsson .20 .50
114 Peter Johansson .20 .50
115 Torbjorn Johansson .20 .50
116 Jakob Karlsson .20 .50
117 Sebastian Klenner .20 .50
118 Mattias Loof .20 .50
119 Rob Murphy .20 .50
120 Fredrik Oberg .20 .50
121 Daniel Reiss .20 .50
122 Wallace Schreiber .20 .50
123 Patrick Senger .20 .50
124 Leonard Soccio .20 .50
125 Andrew Verner .20 .50
126 Steve Wilson .20 .50
127 Chad Allan .20 .50
128 Mike Bales .40 1.00
129 Petr Bares .20 .50
130 Francois Bouchard .20 .50
131 Brad Burym .20 .50
132 Terry Campbell .20 .50
133 Kent Fearns .20 .50
134 Alexander Genze .20 .50
135 Erich Goldman .20 .50
136 Glen Goodall .40 1.00
137 Samuel Groleau .20 .50
138 Jean-Francois Jomphe .20 .50
139 Ilpo Kauhanen .20 .50
140 Steve Lingren .20 .50
141 Christoph Melischko .20 .50
142 Neville Rautert .20 .50
143 Jason Ruff .20 .50
144 Reiner Suchan .20 .50
145 Sean Tallaire .20 .50
146 Shayne Toporowski .20 .50
147 Jason Young .20 .50
148 Igor Alexandrov .20 .50
149 Doug Ast .20 .50
150 Christopher Bartolone .20 .50
151 Colin Beardsmore .20 .50
152 Oliver Bernhardt .20 .50
153 Lars Bruggemann .20 .50
154 Markus Draxler .20 .50
155 Jorgen Eriksson .20 .50
156 Petr Fical .20 .50
157 Christian Franz .20 .50
158 Carsten Gosdeck .20 .50
159 Justin Harney .20 .50
160 Christian Hommel .20 .50
161 Scott King .20 .50
162 Lasse Kopitz .20 .50
163 Dimitrij Kotschnew .20 .50
164 Chris Lipsett .20 .50
165 Andrej Podkonicky .20 .50
166 Roland Verwey .20 .50
167 Jimmy Waite .40 1.00
168 Steve Washburn .20 .50
169 Tobias Abstreiter .20 .50
170 Gert Acker .20 .50
171 Frank Appel .20 .50
172 Alexander Cherbayev .20 .50
173 Thomas Daffner .20 .50
174 Doug Deraugh .20 .50
175 Markus Janka .20 .50
176 Lars Jansson .20 .50
177 Orjan Lindmark .20 .50
178 Andreas Loth .20 .50
179 Jeffrey John MacLeod .20 .50
180 Pat Mikesch .20 .50
181 Zdenek Nedved .20 .50
182 Rich Parent .40 1.00
183 Brent Peterson .20 .50
184 Stephan Retzer .20 .50
185 StÃ©phane Robitaille .20 .50
186 Alexander Serikow .20 .50
187 Andrej Teljukin .20 .50
188 Sven Valenti .20 .50
189 Mikael Wahlberg .20 .50
190 Shayne Wright .20 .50
191 Tino Boos .20 .50
192 Mickey Elick .20 .50
193 Sebastian Furchner .20 .50
194 Alex Hicks .20 .50
195 Robert Hock .20 .50
196 Markus Jocher .20 .50
197 Eduard Lewandowski .20 .50
198 Mirko Ludemann .20 .50
199 Dave McLlwain .20 .50
200 Andreas Morczinietz .20 .50
201 Frederik Nilsson .20 .50
202 Dwayne Norris .20 .50
203 Ron Pasco .20 .50
204 Shane Peacock .20 .50
205 Andreas Renz .20 .50
206 Chris Rogles .40 1.00
207 Stefan Schauer .20 .50
208 Brad Schlegel .20 .50
209 Niklas Sundblad .20 .50
210 Christoph Ullmann .20 .50
211 Darcy Werenka .20 .50
212 Leonard Wild .20 .50
213 Patrick Augusta .20 .50
214 Stephane Barin .20 .50
215 Thomas Brandl .20 .50
216 Christoph Brandner .20 .50
217 Mario Doyon .20 .50
218 Paul Dyck .20 .50
219 Christian Ehrhoff 1.25 3.00
220 Adrian Grygiel .20 .50
221 Daniel Kunce .20 .50
222 Dan Lambert .20 .50
223 Jonas Lanier .20 .50
224 Sandy Moger .20 .50
225 Robert Muller .20 .50
226 David Musial .20 .50
227 Roger Nordstrom .20 .50
228 Gunther Oswald .20 .50
229 Brad Purdie .20 .50
230 Andreas Raubal .20 .50
231 Darryl Shannon .20 .50
232 Gary Shuchuk .20 .50
233 Sergej Stas .20 .50
234 Steffen Ziesche .20 .50
235 Michael Bakos .20 .50
236 Rene Corbet .20 .50
237 Devin Edgerton .20 .50
238 Sascha Goc .20 .50
239 Marcel Goc .75 2.00
240 Francois Groleau .20 .50
241 Todd Hlushko .20 .50
242 Wayne Hynes .20 .50
243 Chris Joseph .20 .50
244 Steve Junker .20 .50
245 Klaus Kathan .20 .50
246 Mike Kennedy .20 .50
247 Tomas Martinec .20 .50
248 Anders Myrvold .20 .50
249 Nick Naumenko .20 .50
250 Dimitri Patzold .75 2.00
251 Jason Podollan .20 .50
252 Yves Racine .20 .50
253 Andy Roach .40 1.00
254 Mike Rosati .40 1.00
255 Yannic Seidenberg .20 .50
256 Stefan Ustorf .20 .50
257 Ilja Vorobiev .20 .50
258 Vitalij Aab .20 .50
259 Shawn Anderson .20 .50
260 Frederic Chabot .75 2.00
261 Kevin Dahl .20 .50
262 Ivan Droppa .20 .50
263 Thomas Greilinger .20 .50
264 Robert Guillet .20 .50
265 Martin Jiranek .20 .50
266 Steve Larouche .20 .50
267 Guy Lehoux .20 .50
268 Christopher Luongo .20 .50
269 Martin Reichel .20 .50
270 Jurgen Rumrich .20 .50
271 Marc Savard .20 .50
272 Thomas Schinko .20 .50
273 Christian Schonmoser .20 .50
274 Marc Seliger .20 .50
275 Martin Sychra .20 .50
276 Dave Tomlinson .20 .50
277 Terry Yake .20 .50
278 Paul Brousseau .20 .50
279 Markus Busch .20 .50
280 Dave Chyzowski .20 .50
281 Alexander Duck .20 .50
282 Mark Etz .20 .50
283 Francois Fortier .20 .50
284 Ian Gordon .20 .50
285 Eric Houde .20 .50
286 Ladislav Karabin .20 .50
287 Steffen Karg .20 .50
288 Rainer Kosttstorfer .20 .50
289 Christian Kohmann .20 .50
290 Alexander Kuzminski .20 .50
291 Neal Martin .20 .50
292 Jochen Molling .20 .50
293 Curtis Sheptak .20 .50
294 Vadim Slivchenko .20 .50
295 Ralf Stark .20 .50
296 Jens Stramkowski .20 .50
297 Mathias Svedberg .20 .50
298 Lukas Zib .20 .50

2002-03 German DEL City Press All-Stars

We have no pricing information on this series.

COMPLETE SET (16)
AS1 Alex Hicks
AS2 Vitalij Aab
AS3 David Cooper
AS4 Magnus Eriksson
AS5 Robert Muller
AS6 Mike Pellegrims
AS7 Stephane Richer
AS8 Chris Snell
AS9 Jeff Tory
AS10 Robert Hock
AS11 Thomas Martinec
AS12 Frederik Oberg
AS13 Brad Purdie
AS14 Andrew Schneider
AS15 Paul Stanton
AS16 Terry Yake

2002-03 German DEL City Press Top Scorers

We have no pricing information on this series.

COMPLETE SET (10)
TS1 Christoph Brandner
TS2 Vadim Slivchenko
TS3 Robert Guillet
TS4 Andreas Morczinietz
TS5 Leonard Soccio
TS6 Marc Fortier
TS7 Sean Tallaire
TS8 David Roberts
TS9 Trond Magnussen
TS10 Stefan Ustorf

2002-03 German DEL City Press Top Stars

We have no pricing information on this series.

COMPLETE SET (10)
GT1 Marc Seliger
GT2 Tobias Abstreiter
GT3 Christian Ehrhoff
GT4 Jurgen Rumrich
GT5 Mirko Ludemann
GT6 Christian Kunast
GT7 Sven Felski
GT8 Daniel Kreutzer
GT9 Wayne Hynes
GT10 Klaus Kathan

2003-04 German Berlin Polar Bears Postcards

COMPLETE SET (31) 10.00 25.00
1 Keith Aldridge .40 1.00
2 Nils Antons .40 1.00
3 Alex Barta .40 1.00
4 Jens Baxmann .40 1.00
5 Mark Beaufait .40 1.00
6 Brad Bergen .40 1.00
7 Florian Busch .40 1.00
8 Yvon Corriveau .40 1.00
9 Tobias Draxinger .40 1.00
10 Micki DuPont .40 1.00
11 Kelly Fairchild .40 1.00
12 Sven Felski .40 1.00
13 Tom Fiedler .40 1.00
14 Patrick Flynn .40 1.00
15 Mathias Forster .40 1.00
16 Martin Hoffmann .40 1.00
17 Frank Hordler .40 1.00
18 Oliver Jonas .40 1.00
19 Florian Keller .40 1.00
20 Rob Leask .40 1.00
21 Hartmut Nickel .40 1.00
22 Pierre Page CO .40 1.00
23 Rich Parent .75 2.00
24 Denis Pederson .40 1.00
25 Ricard Persson .40 1.00
26 Andre Rankel .40 1.00
27 David Roberts .40 1.00
28 Darryl Shannon .40 1.00
29 Rob Shearer .40 1.00
30 Jeff Tomlinson .40 1.00
31 Steve Walker .40 1.00

2003-04 German Deg Metro Stars

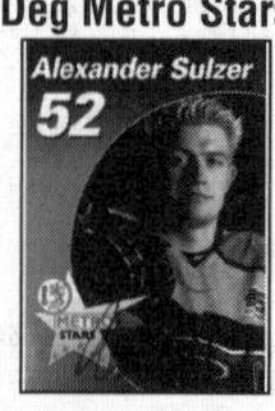

This was a team-issued set featuring a club from the top German league.

COMPLETE SET (23) 10.00 20.00
1 Fabian Brannstrom .40 1.00
2 Christian Brittig .40 1.00
3 Mathias Hart .40 1.00
4 Tommy Jakobsen .40 1.00
5 Thomas Jorg .40 1.00
6 Alexander Jung .40 1.00
7 Florian Jung .40 1.00
8 Walter Koberle .40 1.00
9 Michael Komma .40 1.00
10 Daniel Kreutzer .40 1.00
11 Bobo Kuhnhauser .40 1.00
12 Trond Magnussen .40 1.00
13 Pat Mikesch .40 1.00
14 Johan Molin .40 1.00
15 Mike Pellegrims .40 1.00
16 Markus Pottinger .40 1.00
17 Alexander Sulzer .40 1.00
18 Jeff Tory .40 1.00
19 Andrej Trefilov .40 1.00
20 Martin Ulrich .40 1.00
21 Gerhard Unterluggauer .40 1.00
22 Tore Vikingstad .40 1.00
23 Clayton Young .40 1.00

2003-04 German DEL

COMPLETE SET (210) 15.00 40.00
1 Rene Corbet .10 .25
2 Devin Edgerton .10 .25
3 Sascha Goc .10 .25
4 Francois Groleau .10 .25
5 Robert Hock .10 .25
6 Chris Joseph .10 .25
7 Klaus Kathan .10 .25
8 Tomas Martinec .10 .25
9 Jochen Molling .10 .25
10 Derek Plante .10 .25
11 Jason Podollan .10 .25
12 Andy Roach .20 .50
13 Marc Seliger .10 .25
14 Richard Shulmistra .10 .25
15 Christoph Ullmann .10 .25
16 Ronny Arendt .10 .25
17 Bjorn Barta .10 .25
18 Colin Beardsmore .10 .25
19 Shawn Carter .10 .25
20 Eric Dandenault .10 .25
21 Xavier Delisle .10 .25
22 Magnus Eriksson .10 .25
23 Francois Fortier .10 .25
24 Rick Girard .10 .25
25 John Miner .10 .25
26 Duanne Moeser .10 .25
27 Arvids Rekis .10 .25
28 Marc Savard .10 .25
29 Andrej Strakhov .10 .25
30 Bob Wren .10 .25
31 Fabian Brannstrom .10 .25
32 Christian Brittig .10 .25
33 Tommy Jakobsen .10 .25
34 Alexander Jung .10 .25
35 Daniel Kreutzer .10 .25
36 Trond Magnussen .10 .25
37 Pat Mikesch .10 .25
38 Mike Pellegrims .10 .25
39 Marcus Thuresson .10 .25
40 Jeff Tory .10 .25
41 Andrej Trefilov .10 .25
42 Martin Ulrich .10 .25
43 Gerhard Unterluggauer .10 .25
44 Tore Vikingstad .10 .25
45 Clayton Young .10 .25
46 Peter Boon .10 .25
47 Dany Bousquet .10 .25
48 Olivier Coqueux .10 .25
49 David Danner .10 .25
50 Juraj Faith .10 .25
51 Dusan Frosch .10 .25
52 Rudolf Gorgenlander .10 .25
53 Rostislav Haas .10 .25
54 Henrik Holscher .10 .25
55 Thomas Jetter .10 .25
56 Ravil Khaidarov .10 .25
57 Vadim Slivchenko .10 .25
58 Sergej Stas .10 .25
59 Bastian Steingross .10 .25
60 Jiri Zelenka .10 .25
61 Keith Aldridge .10 .25
62 Alexander Barta .10 .25
63 Mark Beaufait .10 .25
64 Micki Dupont .10 .25
65 Kelly Fairchild .10 .25
66 Sven Felski .10 .25
67 Oliver Jonas .10 .25
68 Florian Keller .10 .25
69 Robert Leask .10 .25
70 Rich Parent .40 1.00
71 Denis Pederson .10 .25
72 Ricard Persson .10 .25
73 David Roberts .10 .25
74 Rob Shearer .10 .25
75 Steve Walker .10 .25
76 Doug Ast .10 .25
77 Craig Ferguson .10 .25
78 Jakub Ficenec .20 .50
79 Glenn Goodall .40 1.00
80 Samuel Groleau .10 .25
81 Justin Harney .10 .25
82 Cameron Mann .40 1.00
83 Nikolaus Mondt .10 .25
84 Gunther Oswald .10 .25
85 Yves Racine .10 .25
86 Thomas Schinko .10 .25
87 Ken Sutton .10 .25
88 Sean Tallaire .10 .25
89 Phil von Stefenelli .10 .25
90 Jimmy Waite .40 1.00
91 Christian Kohmann .10 .25
92 Jesse Belanger .10 .25
93 Francois Bouchard .10 .25
94 Michael Bresagk .10 .25
95 Ian Gordon .10 .25
96 David Gosselin .10 .25
97 Michael Hackert .10 .25
98 Mike Harder .10 .25
99 Sebastian Klenner .10 .25
100 Patrick Lebeau .40 1.00
101 Dwayne Norris .10 .25
102 Peter Ratchuk .10 .25
103 Martin Reichel .10 .25
104 Paul Stanton .10 .25
105 Jason Young .10 .25
106 Darren van Impe .10 .25
107 Mark Greig .10 .25
108 Robert House .10 .25
109 Wayne Hynes .10 .25
110 Christian Kunast .10 .25
111 Patrick Koppchen .10 .25
112 Dan Lambert .10 .25
113 Paul Manning .10 .25
114 Shane Peacock .10 .25
115 Jacek Plachta .10 .25
116 Brad Purdie .10 .25
117 Boris Rousson .40 1.00
118 Andrew Schneider .10 .25
119 Heiko Smazal .10 .25
120 Dave Tomlinson .10 .25
121 Patrik Augusta .10 .25
122 Bjorn Bombis .10 .25
123 Jeff Christian .10 .25
124 Gordon Borberg .10 .25
125 Edvin Frylen .10 .25
126 Lorenz Funk .10 .25
127 David Haas .10 .25
128 Peter Jakobsson .10 .25
129 Ilpo Kauhanen .10 .25
130 Mattias Loof .10 .25
131 Zdenek Nedved .10 .25
132 Frederik Oberg .10 .25
133 Leonard Soccio .10 .25
134 Andrej Teljukin .10 .25
135 Steve Wilson .10 .25
136 David Cooper .10 .25
137 Bryan Adams .10 .25
138 Chris Bartolone .10 .25
139 James Black .10 .25
140 Lars Bruggemann .10 .25
141 Jason Cipolla .10 .25
142 Michael Fountain .10 .25
143 Erich Goldmann .10 .25
144 Matt Henderson .10 .25
145 Matt Higgins .10 .25
146 Christian Hommel .10 .25
147 Scott King .10 .25
148 Dimitrij Kotschnew .10 .25
149 Rob Sandrock .10 .25
150 Roland Verwey .10 .25
151 Tobias Abstreiter .10 .25
152 Paul Brousseau .10 .25
153 Ted Crowley .10 .25
154 Josh DeWolf .10 .25
155 Ted Drury .10 .25
156 Joaquin Gage .10 .25
157 Orjan Lindmark .10 .25
158 Andreas Loth .10 .25
159 Jeff MacLeod .10 .25
160 Brent Peterson .10 .25
161 Stephan Retzer .10 .25
162 Stephane Robitaille .10 .25
163 Alexander Serikow .10 .25
164 Matthias Trattnig .10 .25
165 Mikael Wahlberg .10 .25
166 Jeremy Adduono .10 .25
167 Tino Boos .10 .25
168 Jeff Dessner .10 .25
169 Mickey Elick .10 .25
170 Sebastian Furchner .10 .25
171 Alex Hicks .10 .25
172 Mirko Ludemann .10 .25
173 Eduard Lewandowski .10 .25
174 Dave McLlwain .10 .25
175 Andreas Morczinietz .10 .25
176 Andreas Renz .10 .25
177 Chris Rogles .10 .25
178 Jean-Yves Roy .10 .25
179 Brad Schlegel .10 .25
180 Leo Stefan .10 .25
181 Pascal Appel .10 .25
182 Marc Beaucage .10 .25
183 Eric Bertrand .10 .25
184 Adrian Grygiel .10 .25
185 Robert Guillet .10 .25
186 Christopher Kelleher .10 .25
187 Daniel Kunce .10 .25
188 Justin Kurtz .10 .25
189 Chris Luongo .10 .25
190 Robert Muller .10 .25
191 Alexander Selivanov .10 .25
192 Stefan Ustorf .10 .25
193 Shayne Wright .10 .25
194 Terry Yake .10 .25
195 Steffen Ziesche .10 .25
196 Vitalij Aab .10 .25
197 Frederic Chabot .40 1.00
198 Marian Cisar .10 .25
199 Petr Fical .10 .25
200 Liam Garvey .10 .25
201 Thomas Greilinger .10 .25
202 Martin Jiranek .10 .25
203 Stephane Julien .10 .25
204 Lasse Kopitz .10 .25
205 Steve Larouche .10 .25
206 Greg Leeb .20 .50
207 Guy Lehoux .10 .25
208 Alfie Michaud .10 .25
209 Yan Stastny ERC 1.25 3.00
210 Robert Tomik .10 .25

2003-04 German DEL All-Stars

COMPLETE SET (22) 15.00 30.00
AS1 Jimmy Waite 1.25 3.00
AS2 Andrej Trefilov 1.25 3.00
AS3 Chris Rogles 1.25 3.00
AS4 Justin Harney .75 2.00
AS5 Paul Stanton .75 2.00
AS6 Andy Roach 1.25 3.00
AS7 Christoph Brandner .75 2.00
AS8 Dwayne Norris .75 2.00
AS9 Francois Fortier .75 2.00
AS10 Philippe Audet .75 2.00
AS11 Doug Ast .75 2.00
AS12 Brad Purdie .75 2.00
AS13 Kelly Fairchild .75 2.00
AS14 Wally Schreiber .75 2.00
AS15 Terry Yake .75 2.00
AS16 Jean-Francois Jomphe .75 2.00
AS17 Andrew Schneider .75 2.00
AS18 Tommy Jakobsen .75 2.00
AS19 Dave McLlwain .75 2.00
AS20 Trond Magnussen .75 2.00
AS21 Shawn Anderson .75 2.00
AS22 Jeff Tory .75 2.00

2003-04 German Mannheim Eagles Postcards

These 4X6 postcards were issued by the team in set form. All cards are autographed by the players, although the Sachar Blank autograph was scratched out in our set. Perhaps the auto was determined to have been signed by someone else???

COMPLETE SET (29) 30.00 75.00
1 Richard Shulmistra 1.50 4.00
2 Marc Seliger 1.50 4.00
3 Marco Schutz 1.50 4.00
4 Sachar Blank .40 1.00
5 Yannic Seidenberg 1.50 4.00
6 Bill Stewart 1.50 4.00
7 Christoph Ullmann 1.50 4.00
8 Stefan Ustorf 1.50 4.00
9 Rico Rossi 1.50 4.00
10 Andy Roach 2.50 6.00
11 Yves Racine 1.50 4.00
12 Nico Pyka 1.50 4.00
13 Jason Podollan 2.50 6.00
14 Derek Plante 2.50 6.00
15 Jochen Molling 1.50 4.00
16 Tomas Martinec 1.50 4.00
17 Mike Kennedy 1.50 4.00
18 Klaus Kathan 1.50 4.00
19 Steve Junker 1.50 4.00
20 Chris Joseph 1.50 4.00
21 Robert Hock 1.50 4.00
22 Todd Hlushko 1.50 4.00
23 Francois Groleau 1.50 4.00
24 Sascha Goc 1.50 4.00
25 Devin Edgerton 1.50 4.00
26 Rene Corbet 1.50 4.00
27 Fabio Carciola 1.50 4.00
28 Michael Bakos 1.50 4.00
29 Danny Aus Den Birken 1.50 4.00
30 Marc Bruns 1.50 4.00
31 Markus Koch 1.50 4.00
32 Andy Roach 2.50 6.00
33 Christoph Ullmann 1.50 4.00

2003-04 German Nuremberg Ice Tigers Postcards

These 4X6 postcards were issued in set form by the team. They are unnumbered and listed below in alphabetical order.

COMPLETE SET (26) 10.00 25.00
1 Vitalij Aab .40 1.00
2 Benjamin Barz .40 1.00
3 Frederic Chabot 1.25 3.00
4 Marian Cisar .40 1.00
5 Kevin Dahl .40 1.00
6 Jon DiSalvatore .40 1.00
7 Petr Fical .40 1.00
8 Konstantin Firsanov .40 1.00
9 Liam Garvey .40 1.00
10 Thomas Greilinger .40 1.00
11 Tobias Guttner .40 1.00
12 Martin Jiranek .40 1.00
13 Stephane Julien .40 1.00
14 Lasse Kopitz .40 1.00
15 Steve Larouche .40 1.00
16 Greg Leeb .75 2.00
17 Guy Lehoux .40 1.00
18 Josef Menauer .40 1.00
19 Alfie Michaud .40 1.00
20 Sebastian Osterloh .40 1.00
21 Felix Petermann .40 1.00
22 Greg Poss .40 1.00
23 Jurgen Rumrich .40 1.00
24 Christian Schonmoser .40 1.00
25 Otto Sykora GM .40 1.00
26 Robert Tomik .40 1.00

2004-05 German Augsburg Panthers Postcards

These cards are unnumbered and so are listed below in alphabetical order.

COMPLETE SET (27) 10.00 25.00
1 Pascal Appel .40 1.00
2 Ronny Arendt .40 1.00
3 Steve Bancroft .40 1.00
4 Bjorn Barta .40 1.00
5 Rich Brennan .40 1.00
6 Robert Brezina .40 1.00
7 Marc Brown .40 1.00
8 Robert Busch .40 1.00
9 Shawn Carter .40 1.00
10 David Danner .40 1.00
11 Dennis Endras .40 1.00
12 Brian Felsner .40 1.00
13 Torsten Fendt .40 1.00
14 Francois Fortier .40 1.00
15 Rick Girard .40 1.00
16 Manuel Kopfler .40 1.00
17 Jean-Francois Labbe .75 2.00
18 Benoit Laporte CO .20 .50
19 Roland Mayr .40 1.00
20 Francois Methot .40 1.00
21 John Miner .40 1.00
22 Duanne Moeser .40 1.00
23 Mike Pudlick .40 1.00
24 Daniel Rau .40 1.00
25 Arvids Rekis .40 1.00
26 Steffen Tolzer .40 1.00
27 Benjamin Voigt .40 1.00

2004-05 German Berlin Eisbarens 50th Anniversary

Standard-sized card set features top players from the past and present of Germany's most famous team.

COMPLETE SET (75) 15.00 30.00
1 Header .02 .10
2 Mike Losch .20 .50
3 Dave Morrison .20 .50
4 Roland Peters .20 .50
5 Mario Plack .20 .50
6 Joachim Stasche .20 .50
7 Detlef Radant .20 .50
8 Pelle Svensson .20 .50
9 Egon Schmeisser .20 .50
10 Klaus Merk .20 .50
11 Rainer Patschinski .20 .50
12 Franz Steer .20 .50
13 Sergej Jaschin .20 .50
14 Steffen Ziesche .20 .50
15 Wolfgang Kraske .20 .50
16 Torsten Deutscher .20 .50
17 Magnus Roupe .20 .50
18 Heinz Pohland .20 .50
19 Mark Jooris .20 .50
20 Wolfgang Beuthner .20 .50
21 Uwe Geisert .20 .50
22 Rene Bielke .20 .50
23 Reinhard Fengler .20 .50
24 Dietmar Peters .20 .50
25 Helmut Senftleben .20 .50
26 Peter Prusa .20 .50
27 Thomas Swibenko .20 .50
28 Marc Fortier .20 .50
29 Andre Dietzch .20 .50
30 Holger Mix .20 .50
31 Werner Thomas .20 .50
32 Hanne Frenzel .20 .50
33 Thomas Mitew .20 .50
34 Jeff Tomlinson .20 .50
35 Fred Freitag .20 .50
36 Bernd Karrenbauer .20 .50
37 Friedhelm Bogelsack .20 .50
38 Thomas Graul .20 .50
39 Sven Felski .20 .50
40 Dirk Perschau .20 .50
41 Gerhard Muller .20 .50
42 Jurgen Schmutzler .20 .50
43 Wilhelm Kopatz .20 .50

44 Dieter Janke .20 .50
45 Jurgen Geisert .20 .50
46 Rob Cowie .20 .50
47 Dieter Dewitz .20 .50
48 Joachim Lempio .20 .50
49 Leif Carlsson .20 .50
50 Joachim Hurbanek .20 .50
51 Gerhard Klugel .20 .50
52 Udo Dohler .20 .50
53 Frank Proske .20 .50
54 Wolfgang Plotka .20 .50
55 Hartmut Nickel .20 .50
56 Andrew McKim .20 .50
57 Jens Ziesche .20 .50
58 Wilfried Rohrbach .20 .50
59 Dieter Frenzel .20 .50
60 Jurgen Breitschuh .20 .50
61 Peter-John Lee .20 .50
62 Mike Bullard .20 .50
63 Guido Hiller .20 .50
64 Gunther Katzur .20 .50
65 Peter Lehnigk .20 .50
66 Matthias Dietz .20 .50
67 Harald Kuhnke .20 .50
68 Frank Krause .20 .50
69 Joachim Ziesche .20 .50
70 Dieter Voigt .20 .50
71 Thomas Steen .20 .50
72 Daniel Held .20 .50
73 Derek Mayer .20 .50
74 Nico Pyka .20 .50
75 Checklist .02 .10

2004-05 German Berlin Polar Bears Postcards

These cards are unnumbered and are listed below in alphabetical order.

COMPLETE SET (32) 10.00 25.00
1 Alexander Barta .30 .75
2 Jens Baxmann .30 .75
3 Mark Beaufait .30 .75
4 Florian Busch .30 .75
5 Erik Cole .75 2.00
6 Nathan Dempsey .40 1.00
7 Tobias Draxinger .30 .75
8 Danier Dshunussow .30 .75
9 Micki Dupont .40 1.00
10 Kelly Fairchild .40 1.00
11 Sven Felski .30 .75
12 Christoph Gawlik .30 .75
13 Shawn Heins .40 1.00
14 Martin Hoffmann .30 .75
15 Frank Hordler .30 .75
16 Kay Hurbanek .30 .75
17 Oliver Jonas .30 .75
18 Florian Keller .30 .75
19 Olaf Kolzig 2.00 5.00
20 Rob Loask .30 .75
21 Hartmut Nickel ACO .10 .25
22 Pierre Page CO .10 .25
23 Denis Pederson .40 1.00
24 Ricard Persson .30 .75
25 Andre Rankel .30 .75
26 Rob Shearer .30 .75
27 Stefan Ustorf .30 .75
28 Steve Walker .30 .75
29 Derrick Walser .40 1.00
30 Yourri Ziffzer .30 .75
31 Bully MASCOT .10 .25
32 Team Photo .10 .25

2004-05 German Cologne Sharks Postcards

The cards are unnumbered, so they are listed below alphabetically.

COMPLETE SET (28) 10.00 25.00
1 Jeremy Adduono .40 1.00
2 Colin Beardsmore .40 1.00
3 Markus Berwanger CO .10 .25
4 Dan Bjornlie .40 1.00
5 Boris Blank .40 1.00
6 Tino Boos .40 1.00
7 Jon Coleman .40 1.00
8 Thomas Fischer .40 1.00
9 Sebastian Furchner .40 1.00
10 Philip Gogulla .40 1.00
11 Thomas Greiss .40 1.00
12 Mattias Hart .40 1.00
13 Alex Hicks .40 1.00
14 Kai Hospelt .40 1.00
15 Michael Hrstka .40 1.00
16 Stephane Julien .40 1.00
17 Eduard Lewandowski .40 1.00
18 Mirko Ludemann .40 1.00
19 Dave McLlwain .40 1.00
20 Rupert Meister ACO .10 .25
21 Moritz Muller .40 1.00
22 Andreas Renz .40 1.00
23 Chris Rogles .60 1.50
24 Jean-Yves Roy .40 1.00
25 Brad Schlegel .40 1.00
26 Yannic Seidenberg .40 1.00
27 Paul Traynor .40 1.00
28 Hans Zach CO .10 .25

2004-05 German DEL

COMPLETE SET (283) 25.00 50.00
1 Vitalij Aab .10 .25
2 Danny aus den Birken .10 .25
3 Michael Bakos .10 .25
4 Sven Butenschon .10 .25
5 Rene Corbet .20 .50
6 Andy Delmore .20 .50
7 Devin Edgerton .10 .25
8 Sascha Goc .20 .50
9 Francois Groleau .10 .25
10 Eric Healey .20 .50
11 Jochen Hecht .40 1.00
12 Christopher Joseph .10 .25
13 Steve Kelly .10 .25
14 Markus Kink .10 .25
15 Derek Plante .10 .25
16 Jason Podollan .10 .25
17 Nico Pyka .10 .25
18 John Tripp .10 .25
19 Cristobal Huet 1.25 3.00
20 Thomas Greilinger .10 .25
21 Christoph Ullmann .10 .25
22 Ronny Arendt .10 .25
23 Bjorn Barta .10 .25
24 Robert Brezina .10 .25
25 Marc Brown .10 .25
26 Shawn Carter .10 .25
27 Brian Felsner .10 .25
28 Thorsten Fendt .10 .25
29 Francois Fortier .10 .25
30 Rick Girard .10 .25
31 Manuel Kofler .10 .25
32 Jean Francois Labbe .20 .50
33 Roland Mayr .10 .25
34 Francois Methot .10 .25
35 John Miner .10 .25
36 Duanne Moeser .10 .25
37 Arvids Rekis .10 .25
38 Steve Bancroft .10 .25
39 Mike Pudlick .10 .25
40 David Danner .10 .25
41 Daniel Rau .10 .25
42 Christian Brittig .10 .25
43 Fabian Brannstrom .10 .25
44 Eric Dandenault .10 .25
45 Matt Davidson .10 .25
46 Matt Herr .20 .50
47 Tommy Jakobsen .10 .25
48 Alexander Jung .10 .25
49 Klaus Kathan .10 .25
50 Bernd Kuhnhauser .10 .25
51 Daniel Kreutzer .10 .25
52 Trond Magnussen .10 .25
53 Mike Pellegrims .10 .25
54 Andrew Schneider .10 .25
55 Jeff Tory .10 .25
56 Andrej Trefilov .20 .50
57 Martin Ulrich .10 .25
58 Tore Vikingstad .10 .25
59 Clayton Young .10 .25
60 Florian Jung .10 .25
61 Alexander Sulzer .10 .25
62 Jens Baxmann .10 .25
63 Mark Beaufait .10 .25
64 Tobias Draxinger .10 .25
65 Micki DuPont .20 .50
66 Kelly Fairchild .20 .50
67 Sven Felski .10 .25
68 Shawn Heins .20 .50
69 Frank Hordler .10 .25
70 Oliver Jonas .10 .25
71 Florian Keller .10 .25
72 Robert Leask .10 .25
73 Denis Pederson .10 .25
74 Ricard Persson .10 .25
75 Rob Shearer .10 .25
76 Stefan Ustorf .10 .25
77 Steve Walker .10 .25
78 Derrick Walser .20 .50
79 Youri Ziffzer .10 .25
80 Alexander Barta .10 .25
81 Florian Busch .10 .25
82 Chris Armstrong .10 .25
83 Doug Ast .20 .50
84 Brad Burym .20 .50
85 Craig Ferguson .10 .25
86 Jakub Ficenec .20 .50
87 Glenn Goodall .20 .50
88 Justin Harney .10 .25
89 Martin Jiranek .10 .25
90 Andreas Loth .10 .25
91 Cameron Mann .40 1.00
92 Nikolaus Mondt .10 .25
93 Gunther Oswald .10 .25
94 Aleksander Polaczek .10 .25
95 Marco Sturm .40 1.00
96 Ken Sutton .10 .25
97 Phil von Stefenelli .10 .25
98 Jimmy Waite .20 .50
99 Andy McDonald .40 1.00
100 Daniel Hilpert .10 .25
101 Christoph Melischko .10 .25
102 Boris Ackers .10 .25
103 Marc Beaucage .10 .25
104 Francois Bouchard .10 .25
105 Mihael Bresagk .10 .25
106 Ian Gordon .10 .25
107 Markus Jocher .10 .25
108 Sebastian Klenner .10 .25
109 Christian Kohmann .10 .25
110 Patrick Lebeau .20 .50
111 Mikael Magnusson .10 .25
112 Dwayne Norris .10 .25
113 Sean Pronger .10 .25
114 Peter Ratchuk .10 .25
115 Martin Reichel .10 .25
116 Andrej Strakhov .10 .25
117 David Sulkovsky .10 .25
118 Jason Young .10 .25
119 Stephane Robidas .20 .50
120 Michael Hackert .10 .25
121 Neville Rautert .10 .25
122 Nils Antons .10 .25
123 Robert Francz .10 .25
124 Robert House .10 .25
125 Wayne Hynes .10 .25
126 Craig Johnson .10 .25
127 Alan Letang .10 .25
128 Paul Manning .10 .25
129 Jochen Molling .10 .25
130 Shane Peacock .10 .25
131 Jacek Plachta .10 .25
132 Brad Purdie .10 .25
133 Brandon Reid .40 1.00
134 Boris Rousson .40 1.00
135 Jurgen Rumrich .10 .25
136 Heiko Smazal .10 .25
137 Dave Tomlinson .10 .25
138 Darren van Impe .10 .25
139 Leonhard Wild .10 .25
140 Jim Dowd .20 .50
141 Christopher Oravec .10 .25
142 Martin Walter .10 .25
143 Peter Abstreiter .10 .25
144 Patrick Augusta .10 .25
145 Gordon Borberg .10 .25
146 Lars Bruggemann .10 .25
147 Jason Cipolla .10 .25
148 Thomas Dolak .10 .25
149 Edvin Frylen .10 .25
150 Robert Hock .10 .25
151 Christian Kunast .10 .25
152 Lipo Kauhanen .10 .25
153 Patrick Koppchen .10 .25
154 Dan Lambert .10 .25
155 Andreas Morczienitz .10 .25
156 Frederik Oberg .10 .25
157 Len Soccio .10 .25
158 Andrej Teljukin .10 .25
159 Steve Wilson .10 .25
160 Michael Nemirovski .10 .25
161 Rene Rothke .10 .25
162 Benedikt Schopper .10 .25
163 Bryan Adams .10 .25
164 Igor Alexandrov .10 .25
165 Oliver Bernhardt .10 .25
166 Leonardo Conti .10 .25
167 Collin Danielsmeier .10 .25
168 Sven Gerbig .10 .25
169 Erich Goldmann .10 .25
170 Rhett Gordon .10 .25
171 Matt Higgins .20 .50
172 Ralph Intrnuovo .20 .50
173 Martin Knold .10 .25
174 Dimitij Kotschew .10 .25
175 Brett Lysak .10 .25
176 Mike Martin .10 .25
177 Kevin Mitchell .10 .25
178 Roland Verwey .10 .25
179 Brian White .10 .25
180 Mike York .20 .50
181 Mark Etz .10 .25
182 Franz Fritzmeier .10 .25
183 Tobias Abstreiter .10 .25
184 Gert Acker .10 .25
185 Dany Bousquet .20 .50
186 Daniel Corso .20 .50
187 Kirk Furey .10 .25
188 Joaquin Gage .20 .50
189 David Gosselin .10 .25
190 Christian Hommel .10 .25
191 Sebastian Jones .10 .25
192 Mark Greig .10 .25
193 Christian Laflamme .10 .25
194 Jan Munster .10 .25
195 Dean Melanson .10 .25
196 Alexander Serikow .10 .25
197 Brian Swanson .10 .25
198 Martin Sychra .10 .25
199 Sven Valent .10 .25
200 Nick Schultz .20 .50
201 Stephan Retzer .10 .25
202 Petr Macholda .10 .25
203 Christian Retzer .10 .25
204 Jeremy Adduono .20 .50
205 Colin Beardsmore .10 .25
206 Dan Bjornlie .10 .25
207 Boris Blank .10 .25
208 Tino Boos .10 .25
209 Thomas Fischer .10 .25
210 Thomas Greiss .10 .25
211 Matthias Hart .10 .25
212 Alex Hicks .10 .25
213 Stephane Julien .10 .25
214 Mirko Ludemann .10 .25
215 Eduard Lewandowski .10 .25
216 Dave McLlwain .10 .25
217 Andreas Renz .10 .25
218 Chris Rogles .20 .50
219 Jean-Yves Roy .10 .25
220 Brad Schlegel .10 .25
221 Leo Stefan .10 .25
222 Yannic Seidenberg .10 .25
223 Sebastian Furchner .10 .25
224 Steve Brule .10 .25
225 Alexander Dueck .10 .25
226 Paul Dyck .10 .25
227 Carsten Gosdeck .10 .25
228 Robert Guillet .10 .25
229 Chris Herperger .10 .25
230 Christian Rhode .10 .25
231 Ivo Jan .10 .25
232 Markus Janka .10 .25
233 Scott King .10 .25
234 Daniel Kunce .10 .25
235 Justin Kurtz .10 .25
236 Guy Lehoux .10 .25
237 Robert Muller .10 .25
238 Florian Schnitzer .10 .25
239 Alexander Selivanov .10 .25
240 Shayne Wright .10 .25
241 Steffen Ziesche .10 .25
242 Adrian Grygiel .10 .25
243 Rainer Kottstorfer .10 .25
244 Drew Bannister .10 .25
245 Benjamin Barz .10 .25
246 Petr Fical .10 .25
247 Konstantin Firsanov .10 .25
248 Christian Franz .10 .25
249 Mike Green .10 .25
250 Lasse Kopitz .10 .25
251 Greg Leeb .10 .25
252 Tomas Martinec .10 .25
253 Ulrich Maurer .10 .25
254 Josef Menauer .10 .25
255 Stefan Schauer .10 .25
256 Lubomir Sekeras .10 .25
257 Yan Stastny 1.25 3.00
258 Adam Svoboda .20 .50
259 Sean Tallaire .10 .25
260 Brad Tapper .20 .50
261 Pascal Trepanier .10 .25
262 Bjorn Bombis .10 .25
263 Felix Petermann .10 .25
264 Ivan Ciernik .10 .25
265 Dale Clarke .10 .25
266 Xavier Delisle .10 .25
267 Alexander Genze .10 .25
268 Ladislav Karabin .10 .25
269 Andrej Kaufmann .10 .25
270 Boris Lingemann .10 .25
271 Per-Anton Lundstrom .10 .25
272 Marek Mastic .10 .25
273 David Musial .10 .25
274 Christoph Paepke .10 .25
275 Richard Pavlikovsky .10 .25
276 Marc Seliger .10 .25
277 Todd Simon .10 .25
278 Peter Smrek .10 .25
279 Rainer Suchan .10 .25
280 Roman Veber .10 .25
281 Jan Zurek .10 .25
282 Markus Guggemos .10 .25
283 Tobias Samendinger .10 .25
NNO Deutscher Meister 2004 Frankfurt Lions 4.00 10.00

2004-05 German DEL All-Stars

COMPLETE SET (19) 15.00 30.00
AS1 Jimmy Waite 2.00 5.00
AS2 Andrej Trefilov .75 2.00
AS3 Stephane Julien .75 2.00
AS4 Ricard Persson .75 2.00
AS5 Peter Ratchuk .75 2.00
AS6 Jakub Ficenec 1.25 3.00
AS7 Mike Pellegrims .75 2.00
AS8 John Miner .75 2.00
AS9 Cameron Mann 1.25 3.00
AS10 Marian Cisar .75 2.00
AS11 Ted Drury .75 2.00
AS12 Rene Corbet .75 2.00
AS13 Kelly Fairchild .75 2.00
AS14 Danny Bousquet .75 2.00
AS15 Patrick Augusta .75 2.00
AS16 Alexander Selivanov .75 2.00
AS17 Dave McLlwain .75 2.00
AS18 Brad Purdie .75 2.00
AS19 Scott King .75 2.00

2004-05 German DEL Global Players

COMPLETE SET (5) 10.00 20.00
GP1 Olaf Kolzig 4.00 10.00
GP2 Christian Ehrhoff 1.25 3.00
GP3 Jochen Hecht 1.25 3.00
GP4 Marco Sturm 1.25 3.00
GP5 Dennis Seidenberg 1.25 3.00
GP6 Checklist .40 1.00

2004-05 German DEL Superstars

COMPLETE SET (23) 20.00 40.00
SU01 Sven ButenschÃ¶n .75 2.00
SU02 Jochen Hecht 1.25 3.00
SU03 Cristobal Huet 2.00 5.00
SU04 Yannick Tremblay .75 2.00
SU05 Erik Cole 1.25 3.00
SU06 Olaf KÃ¶lzig 2.00 5.00
SU07 Nathan Dempsey .75 2.00
SU08 Stephane Robidas .75 2.00
SU09 Doug Weight .75 2.00
SU10 Andy McDonald .75 2.00
SU11 Marco Sturm 1.25 3.00
SU12 Jamie Langenbrunner .75 2.00
SU13 Aaron Ward .75 2.00
SU14 Mike York .75 2.00
SU15 John-Michael Liles .75 2.00
SU16 Jean-Sebastian Giguere .75 2.00
SU17 Paul Mara .75 2.00
SU18 Nick Schultz .75 2.00
SU19 Tom Preissing .75 2.00
SU20 Krys Kolanos .75 2.00
SU21 Ty Conklin 1.25 3.00
SU22 Kevyn Adams .75 2.00
SU23 Superstars Checklist .40 1.00

2004-05 German DEL Update

We only have a partial checklist at this time. Please forward additional information to hockeymag@beckett.com.

COMPLETE SET (?)
289 Markus Pottinger .10 .25
290 Patrick Reimer .10 .25
291 Thomas Jorg .10 .25
292 DEG Metro Stars CL .02 .10
321A Paul Traynor .10 .25
322A John Coleman .10 .25
323A Kai Hospelt .10 .25
324A Andreas Loth .10 .25
325A Marquis Mathieu .40 1.00
334 Stefan Schroder .10 .25
335 Martin Hyun .10 .25
336 Martin Schymainski .10 .25
337 Vadim Slivchenko .10 .25
338 Krefeld Checklist .02 .10
339 Herbert Vasiljievs .10 .25
340 Lukas Lang .10 .25
341 Robert Tomik .10 .25
342 Nuremberg Checklist .02 .10
284 Fabio Carciola .10 .25
285 Steven Passmore .20 .50
286 Adler Manheim CL .02 .10
287 Richard Brennan .10 .25
288 Augsburger Panther CL .02 .10
293 Andre Rankel .10 .25
294 Norman Martens .10 .25
295 Christoph Gawlik .10 .25
296 Daniar Dshunussov .10 .25
297 Richard Mueller .10 .25
298 Marcus Sommerfeld .10 .25
299 Ehc EisBaren Berlin CL .02 .10
300 Mike Harder .10 .25
301 Markus Schroder .10 .25
302 Steffen Karg .10 .25
303 ERC Ingolstadt CL .02 .10
305 Chad Bassen .10 .25
306 Frankfurt Lions CL .02 .10
307 Sasha Martinovic .10 .25
308 Clayton Young .10 .25
309 Hamburg Freezers CL .02 .10
310 Todd Hlushko .10 .25
311 Marian Cisar .10 .25
312 Bastian Steingrog .02 .10
313 Alexander Serikow .10 .25
314 Jonas Lanier .10 .25
316 Wayne Hynes .10 .25
317 Rich Parent .40 1.00
318 Hannover Scorpions CL .02 .10
319 Tobias Schwab .10 .25
320 Iserluhn Roosters CL .02 .10
326 Manuel Klinge .10 .25
327 Kassel Huskies CL .02 .10
343 Sebastian Osterloh .10 .25
344 Lars Bruggemann .10 .25
345 Artjom Kostyrev .10 .25
346 Eric Wolfsburg CL .02 .10
304 Joseph Murray .10 .25
315 Michael Kozhenikov .10 .25
322B Ted Drury .20 .50
323B Corey Hirsch .20 .50
324B Peter Abstreiter .10 .25
325B Mark Kosick .10 .25
326A Manuel Klinge .10 .25
326b Kolner Haie CL .02 .10
NNO Kolner Haie Checklist .02 .10

2004-05 German Dusseldorf Metro Stars Postcards

COMPLETE SET (25) 10.00 20.00
1 Fabian Brannstrom .40 1.00
2 Christian Brittig .40 1.00
3 Eric Dandenault .40 1.00
4 Matt Davidson .40 1.00
5 Matt Herr .75 2.00
6 Tommy Jakobsen .40 1.00
7 Thomas Jorg .40 1.00
8 Alexander Jung .40 1.00
9 Florian Jung .40 1.00
10 Klaus Kathan .40 1.00
11 Walter Koberle CO .10 .25
12 Daniel Kreutzer .40 1.00
13 Bernd Kuhnhauser .40 1.00
14 Trond Magnussen .40 1.00
15 Mike Pellegrims .40 1.00
16 Markus Pottinger .40 1.00
17 Patrick Reimer .40 1.00
18 Andy Schneider .40 1.00
19 Alexander Sulzer .40 1.00
20 Jeff Tory .40 1.00
21 Andrei Trefilov .60 1.50
22 Martin Ulrich .40 1.00
23 Tore Vikingstad .40 1.00
24 Clayton Young .40 1.00
25 Dussi MASCOT .02 .10

2004-05 German Hamburg Freezers Postcards

The cards are unnumbered and so are listed below in alphabetical order.

COMPLETE SET (22) 10.00 20.00
1 Nils Antons .40 1.00
2 Robert Francz .40 1.00
3 Jean-Sebastien Giguere 2.00 5.00
4 Bobby House .40 1.00
5 Craig Johnson .40 1.00
6 Alan Letang .40 1.00
7 Paul Manning .40 1.00
8 Sasha Martinovic .40 1.00
9 Jochen Molling .40 1.00
10 Christopher Oravec .40 1.00
11 Shane Peacock .40 1.00
12 Jacek Plachta .40 1.00
13 Brad Purdie .40 1.00
14 Brandon Reid .75 2.00
15 Boris Rousson .75 2.00
16 Jorgen Rumrich .40 1.00
17 Mike Schmidt CO .40 1.00
18 Mike Smazal .40 1.00
19 Dave Tomlinson .40 1.00
20 Darren Van Impe .40 1.00
21 Martin Walter .40 1.00
22 Clayton Young .40 1.00

2004-05 German Hannover Scorpions Postcards

Cards are unnumbered and so are listed below alphabetically.

COMPLETE SET (29) 10.00 25.00
1 Peter Abstreiter .40 1.00
2 Patrik Augusta .40 1.00
3 Gordon Borberg .40 1.00
4 Lars Bruggemann .40 1.00
5 Jason Cipolla .40 1.00
6 Marian Cisar .40 1.00
7 Thomas Dolak .40 1.00
8 Edvin Frylen .40 1.00
9 Axel Hackert .40 1.00
10 Todd Hlushko .40 1.00
11 Robert Hock .40 1.00
12 Wayne Hynes .40 1.00
13 Ilpo Kauhanen .75 2.00
14 Patrick Koppchen .40 1.00
15 Mikhail Kozhevnikov .40 1.00
16 Christian Kunast .40 1.00
17 Dan Lambert .40 1.00
18 Jonas Lanier .40 1.00
19 Paul Mara .75 2.00
20 Andreas Morczinietz .40 1.00
21 Fredrik Oberg .40 1.00
22 Andy Reiss .40 1.00
23 Rene Rothke .40 1.00
24 Benedikt Schopper .40 1.00
25 Alexander Serikow .40 1.00
26 Lenny Soccio .40 1.00
27 Bastian Steingross .40 1.00
28 Andrei Teljukin .40 1.00
29 Steve Wilson .40 1.00

2004-05 German Ingolstadt Panthers

Cards are unnumbered and are listed below alphabetically.

COMPLETE SET (27) 10.00 25.00
1 Chris Armstrong .30 .75
2 Doug Ast .30 .75
3 Jamie Bartman CO .10 .25
4 Brad Burym .30 .75
5 Craig Ferguson .30 .75
6 Jakub Ficenec .30 .75
7 Glen Goodall .30 .75
8 Mike Harder .30 .75
9 Justin Harney .30 .75
10 Daniel Hilpert .30 .75
11 Martin Jiranek .30 .75
12 Steffen Karg .30 .75
13 Ron Kennedy CO .10 .25
14 Jamie Langenbrunner .30 .75
15 Cameron Mann .75 2.00
16 Andy McDonald .75 2.00
17 Christoph Melischko .30 .75
18 Nikolaus Mondt .30 .75
19 Gunther Oswald .30 .75
20 Alexander Polaczek .30 .75
21 Markus Schroder .30 .75
22 Marco Sturm 1.25 3.00
23 Ken Sutton .30 .75
24 Phil von Stefenelli .30 .75
25 Jimmy Waite .75 2.00
26 Aaron Ward .75 2.00
27 Xavier MASCOT .02 .10
28 Drew Omicioli .30 .75
29 Andreas Loth .30 .75

2004-05 German Krefeld Penguins Postcards

COMPLETE SET (24) 30.00
1 Steve Brule .60 1.50
2 Alexander Duck .60 1.50
3 Paul Dyck .60 1.50
4 Franz Fritzmeier CO .10 .25
5 Carsten Gosdeck .60 1.50
6 Adrien Grygiel .60 1.50
7 Robert Guillet .60 1.50
8 Chris Herperger .60 1.50
9 Martin Hyun .60 1.50
10 Ivo Jan .60 1.50
11 Markus Janka .60 1.50
12 Scott King .60 1.50
13 Rainer Kottstorfer .60 1.50
14 Daniel Kunce .60 1.50
15 Justin Kurtz .60 1.50
16 Guy Lehoux .60 1.50
17 Robert Muller .60 1.50
18 Christian Rohde .60 1.50
19 Florian Schnitzer .60 1.50
20 Alexander Selivanov .60 1.50
21 Mario Simioni CO .10 .25
22 Ferdinand Stradter MD .10 .25
23 Shayne Wright .60 1.50
24 Steffen Ziesche .60 1.50

2004-05 German Nuremburg Ice Tigers Postcards

Set is unnumbered and cards are listed below alphabetically.

COMPLETE SET (19) 25.00
1 Drew Bannister .60 1.50
2 Benjamin Barz .60 1.50
3 Bjorn Bombis .60 1.50
4 Robert Dietrich .60 1.50
5 Petr Fical .60 1.50
6 Konstantin Firsanov .60 1.50
7 Christian Franz .60 1.50
8 Mike Green .60 1.50
9 Lasse Kopitz .60 1.50
10 Lukas Lang .60 1.50
11 Tomas Martinec .60 1.50
12 Ulrich Maurer .60 1.50
13 Felix Petermann .60 1.50
14 Greg Poss CO .10 .25
15 Stefan Schauer .60 1.50
16 Yan Stastny 1.25 3.00
17 Adam Svoboda 1.25 3.00
18 Otto Sykora MG .10 .25
19 Brad Tapper .60 1.50

2004-05 German Weiden Blue Devils

Team-issued set from the German Second Division.

COMPLETE SET (27) 10.00 20.00
1 Florian Bartels .30 .75
2 Michal Bartosch .30 .75
3 J.F. Boutin .30 .75
4 Christian Franz .30 .75
5 Roman Goeldner .30 .75
6 Christian Grosch .30 .75
7 Peter Gruhle .30 .75
8 Benjamin Grunwald .30 .75
9 Stephan Hagn .30 .75
10 Reinhard Haider .30 .75
11 Alexander Herbst .30 .75
12 Michael Hoeck .30 .75
13 Thomas Kastner .30 .75
14 Stefan Keski-Kungas .30 .75
15 Christian Kinateder .30 .75
16 Holger Koenig .30 .75
17 Christian Meiler .30 .75
18 Florian Ondruschka .30 .75
19 Jan Penk .30 .75
20 Michal Piskor .30 .75
21 Daniel Rappl .30 .75
22 Samuel St. Pierre .30 .75
23 Damiel Strom .30 .75
24 Sebastian Wolsch .30 .75
25 Florian Zellner .30 .75
26 Josef Hefner ACO .10 .25
27 Leos Sulak CO .10 .25

2005-06 German DEL

COMPLETE SET (381) 30.00 60.00
1 Patrick Aufiero .10 .25
2 Christian Eklund .10 .25
3 Dennis Endrass .10 .25
4 Thorsten Fendt .10 .25
5 Rick Girard .10 .25
6 Scott King .20 .50
7 Manuel Kofler .10 .25
8 Martin Lindmann .10 .25
9 Roland Mayr .10 .25
10 Josef Menauer .10 .25
11 Steve Potvin .10 .25
12 Daniel Rau .10 .25
13 Arvids Rekis .10 .25
14 Rainer Suchan .10 .25
15 Jayme Filipowicz .10 .25
16 Rolf Wanhainen .10 .25
17 Stefan Endrass .10 .25
18 Brendan Yarema .10 .25
19 David Danner .10 .25
20 Konstantin Firsanov .10 .25
21 Jens Baxmann .10 .25
22 Mark Beaufait .10 .25
23 Tobias Draxinger .10 .25
24 Daniar Dshunussow .10 .25
25 Micki DuPont .20 .50
26 Kelly Fairchild .20 .50
27 Sven Felski .10 .25
28 Steve Walker .10 .25
29 Christoph Gawlik .10 .25
30 Frank HÃ¶rdler .10 .25
31 Rob Leask .10 .25
32 Norman Martens .10 .25
33 Richard Mueller .10 .25
34 Rene Kramer .10 .25
35 Stefan Ustorf .10 .25
36 Derrick Walser .20 .50
37 Denis Pederson .20 .50
38 Youri Ziffzer .10 .25
39 Florian Busch .10 .25
40 Andre Rankel .10 .25
41 Steve Brule .10 .25
42 Mathieu Darche .20 .50
43 Robert Francz .10 .25
44 Thorsten Kienass .10 .25
45 Patrick Koslow .10 .25
46 Petri Kujala .10 .25
47 Trond Magnussen .10 .25
48 Shawn McNeill .20 .50
49 Stephane Robitaille .10 .25
50 Christian Rohde .10 .25
51 Martin Schymainski .10 .25
52 Niklas Sundblad .10 .25
53 Andrej Teljukin .10 .25
54 Michael Waginger .10 .25
55 Jean-Luc Grand-Pierre .20 .50
56 Radek Vit .10 .25
57 Francois Groleau .10 .25
58 Mika Puhakka .10 .25
59 BjÃ¶rn Reiser .10 .25
60 Anton Bader .10 .25
61 Alexander Jung .10 .25
62 Marian Bazany .10 .25
63 Fabian BrÃ¤nnstrÃ¶m .10 .25
64 Chris Ferraro .20 .50
65 Florian Jung .10 .25
66 Thomas JÃ¶rg .10 .25
67 Craig Johnson .20 .50
68 Klaus Kathan .10 .25
69 Daniel Kreutzer .10 .25
70 Peter Ferraro .20 .50
71 Mike Pellegrims .10 .25
72 Chris Schmidt .10 .25
73 Andrew Schneider .20 .50
74 Jeff Tory .10 .25
75 Andrej Trefilov .20 .50
76 Tore Vikingstad .10 .25
77 Todd Reirden .10 .25
78 Tommy Jakobsen .10 .25
79 Patrick Reimer .10 .25
80 Alexander Sulzer .10 .25
81 Patrick Boileau .10 .25
82 Francois Bouchard .10 .25
83 Michael Bresagk .10 .25
84 Daniel Corso .20 .50
85 Ian Gordon .20 .50
86 David Gosselin .20 .50
87 Markus Jocher .10 .25
88 Sebastian Klenner .10 .25
89 Christian Kohmann .10 .25
90 Patrick Lebeau .20 .50
91 Dwayne Norris .10 .25
92 Philippe Plante .10 .25
93 Neville Rautert .10 .25
94 Jonas StÃ¶pfgeshoff .10 .25
95 David Sulkovsky .10 .25
96 Jason Young .10 .25
97 Boris Ackers .10 .25
98 Chad Bassen .10 .25
99 Simon Danner .10 .25
100 Jan Barta .10 .25
101 Marc Beaucage .10 .25
102 BjÃ¶rn Bombis .10 .25
103 Francois Fortier .10 .25
104 Benoit Gratton .20 .50
105 Tobias GÃ¼ttner .10 .25
106 Benjamin Hinterstocker .10 .25
107 Martin Hinterstocker .10 .25
108 Christian Hommel .10 .25
109 Alan Letang .10 .25
110 Paul Manning .10 .25
111 Sasa Martinovic .10 .25
112 Shane Peacock .10 .25
113 Jacek Plachta .10 .25
114 Boris Rousson .20 .50
115 Heiko Smazal .10 .25
116 Christopher Oravec .10 .25
117 Jeff Ulmer .10 .25
118 Darren van Impe .10 .25
119 Alexander Barta .10 .25
120 Martin Walter .10 .25
121 Patrick Augusta .10 .25
122 Brad Burym .10 .25
123 Jason Cipolla .10 .25
124 Thomas Dolak .10 .25
125 Sascha Goc .20 .50
126 Mike Green .20 .50

127 Shawn Heins .20 .50
128 Robert Hock .10 .25
129 Marcel Juhasz .10 .25
130 Trevor Kidd .20 .50
131 Patrick KÃ¶ppchen .10 .25
132 Christian KÃ¼nast .10 .25
133 Dan Lambert .20 .50
134 Andreas Morczinietz .10 .25
135 Brad Tapper .20 .50
136 Todd Warriner .20 .50
137 Jeff Finley .10 .25
138 Steve Guolla .20 .50
139 Rene RÃ¶thke .10 .25
140 Michael HÃ¶ck .10 .25
141 Chris Armstrong .10 .25
142 Doug Ast .10 .25
143 BjÃ¶rn Barta .10 .25
144 Craig Ferguson .10 .25
145 Jakub Ficenec .20 .50
146 Glenn Goodall .20 .50
147 Daniel Hilpert .10 .25
148 Jason Holland .10 .25
149 Martin Jiranek .10 .25
150 Florian Keller .10 .25
151 Cameron Mann .20 .50
152 Christoph Melischko .10 .25
153 GÃ¼nther Oswald .10 .25
154 Sebastian Vogl .10 .25
155 Ken Sutton .10 .25
156 Sean Tallaire .10 .25
157 Phil von Stefenelli .20 .50
158 Jimmy Waite .20 .50
159 Christoph HÃ¶henleitner .10 .25
160 Yannic Seidenberg .10 .25
161 Vitalij Aab .10 .25
162 Bryan Adams .10 .25
163 Collin Danielsmeier .10 .25
164 Mark Etz .10 .25
165 Linus Fagemo .10 .25
166 Kirk Furey .10 .25
167 Erich Goldmann .10 .25
168 Michael Wolf .10 .25
169 Matt Higgins .20 .50
170 Raffaele Intranuovo .20 .50
171 Sebastian Jonas .10 .25
172 Ladislav Karabin .10 .25
173 Martin Knold .10 .25
174 Leonardo Conti .10 .25
175 Dimitrij Kotschnew .10 .25
176 Markus PÃ¶ttinger .10 .25
177 Bruce Richardson .10 .25
178 Mats Trygg .10 .25
179 Tobias Schwab .10 .25
180 Alexej Dmitriev .10 .25
181 Tobias Abstreiter .10 .25
182 Drew Bannister .20 .50
183 Eric Bertrand .10 .25
184 Joaquin Gage .20 .50
185 Sven Gerbig .10 .25
186 Domminik Hammer .10 .25
187 Justin Harney .10 .25
188 Guy Lehoux .10 .25
189 Alexander Serikow .10 .25
190 Martin Sychra .10 .25
191 Sven Valenti .10 .25
192 Steffen Ziesche .10 .25
193 Dale Clarke .10 .25
194 Danny Groulx .10 .25
195 Ryan Kraft .10 .25
196 Adam Ondraschek .10 .25
197 Jason Ulmer .10 .25
198 Alexander Heinrich .10 .25
199 Manuel Klinge .10 .25
200 Tobias WÃ¶rle .10 .25
201 Jeremy Adduono .10 .25
202 Tino Boos .10 .25
203 Ivan Ciernik .10 .25
204 Sebastian Furchner .10 .25
205 Thomas Greiss .10 .25
206 Kai Hospelt .10 .25
207 Oliver Jonas .10 .25
208 Stephane Julien .10 .25
209 Lasse Kopitz .10 .25
210 Eduard Lewandowski .10 .25
211 Mirko LÃ¼demann .10 .25
212 Dave McLlwain .10 .25
213 Nikolaus Mondt .10 .25
214 Andreas Renz .10 .25
215 Jean-Yves Roy .10 .25
216 Paul Traynor .10 .25
217 Brad Schlegel .10 .25
218 Alex Hicks .10 .25
219 Philip Gogulla .10 .25
220 Moritz MÃ¼ller .10 .25
221 Boris Blank .10 .25
222 Alexander DÃ¼ck .10 .25
223 Franz Fritzmeier .10 .25
224 Robert Guillet .10 .25
225 Chris Herperger .10 .25
226 Andre Huebscher .10 .25
227 Ivo Jan .10 .25
228 Rainer KÃ¶ttsdorfer .10 .25
229 Daniel Kunce .10 .25
230 Richard Pavlikovski .10 .25
231 Ken Passmann .10 .25
232 Alexander Selivanov .10 .25
233 Herberts Vasiljevs .10 .25
234 Roland Verwey .10 .25
235 Markus Witting .10 .25
236 Robert MÃ¼ller .10 .25
237 Philip Hendle .10 .25
238 Andy Hedlund .10 .25
239 Adrian Grygiel .10 .25
240 Daniel Pietta .10 .25
241 Ronny Arendt .10 .25
242 Patrick Ehelechner .20 .50
243 Michael Bakos .10 .25
244 Lonny Bohonos .10 .25
245 Shawn Carter .10 .25
246 Karl Dykhuis .10 .25
247 Devin Edgerton .10 .25
248 Pierre Hedin .10 .25
249 Steve Kelly .20 .50
250 Marcus Kink .10 .25
251 Peter Ratchuk .10 .25
252 Sefan Retzer .10 .25
253 Jeff Shantz .10 .25
254 John Tripp .10 .25
255 Marco SchÃ¼tz .10 .25
256 Sachar Blank .10 .25
257 Fredrik Chabot .20 .50
258 Rene Corbet .20 .50
259 Fabio Carciola .10 .25
260 Christoph Ullmann .10 .25
261 Benjamin Barz .10 .25
262 Colin Beardsmore .10 .25
263 Rich Brennan .10 .25
264 Matt Davidson .20 .50
265 Robert DÃ¶me .20 .50
266 Petr Fical .10 .25
267 Christian Franz .10 .25
268 Lukas Lang .10 .25
269 Jean-Francois Labbe .20 .50
270 Christian Laflamme .10 .25
271 Greg Leeb .10 .25
272 Thomas Martinec .10 .25
273 Francois Methot .10 .25
274 Michel Periard .10 .25
275 Alexander Polaczek .10 .25
276 Jame Pollock .10 .25
277 Christian Retzer .10 .25
278 Brian Swanson .10 .25
279 Felix Petermann .10 .25
280 Stefan Schauer .10 .25
281 Olaf KÃ¶lzig 2.00 5.00
282 Alexander Jung .10 .25
283 Rob Leask .10 .25
284 Christian Erhoff .30 .75
285 Chritoph Schubert .10 .25
286 Andreas Renz .10 .25
287 Lasse Kopitz .10 .25
288 Dennis Seidenberg .20 .50
289 Sven Felski .10 .25
290 Jochen Hecht .40 1.00
291 Marco Sturm .40 1.00
292 Stefan Ustorf .10 .25
293 Daniel Kreutzer .10 .25
294 Alexander Barta .10 .25
295 Thomas Martinec .10 .25
296 Klaus Kathan .10 .25
297 Michael Hackert .10 .25
298 Tino Boos .10 .25
299 Andreas Morczinietz .10 .25
300 Jan Benda .10 .25
301 Patrick Buzas .10 .25
302 Jay Henderson .20 .50
303 Marc Savard .10 .25
304 Steffen TÃ¶lzer .10 .25
305 Drake Berehowsky .10 .25
306 Constantin Braun .10 .25
307 Sean Fischer .10 .25
308 Patrick Jarrett .20 .50
309 TomÃ¡s PÃ¶pperle .10 .25
310 Deron Quint .20 .50
311 Thomas Schenkel .10 .25
312 Hugo Boisvert .10 .25
313 Patrick Ehelechner .20 .50
314 Kari Haakana .10 .25
315 Martin Hamann .10 .25
316 Michael Henrich .10 .25
317 Markus Schmidt .10 .25
318 Chris Bright .10 .25
319 Michael Hackert .10 .25
320 Steve Kelly .10 .25
321 James Patrick .10 .25
322 Martin Reichel .10 .25
323 Andrej Strakhov .10 .25
324 Roman Cechmanek .20 .50
325 Matthias Forster .10 .25
326 Niklas Hede .10 .25
327 Ryan Jardine .10 .25
328 Steffen Karg .10 .25
329 Max Lingemann .10 .25
330 Florian Schnitzer .10 .25
331 Lukas Slavetinsky .10 .25
332 BjÃ¶rn Bombis .10 .25
333 Dominik Hammer .10 .25
334 Jonas Lanier .10 .25
335 Marty Murray .10 .25
336 AndrÃ© Reiss .10 .25
337 Benedikt Schopper .10 .25
338 Wally Schreiber .10 .25
339 Matt Kinch .10 .25
340 Bastian Steingrog .10 .25
341 Rob Valicevic .20 .50
342 Mark Greig .10 .25
343 Brad Purdie .10 .25
344 Rich Parent .40 1.00
345 Steve Brule .10 .25
346 Brad Burym .10 .25
347 Martin Hlinka .10 .25
348 Sinsa Martinovic .10 .25
349 Chris Nielsen .10 .25
350 Sebastian Osterloh .10 .25
351 Torsten Ankert .10 .25
352 Daniel Hatterscheid .10 .25
353 William Lindsay .10 .25
354 Henry Martens .10 .25
355 Ted Drury .10 .25
356 Mike Pudlick .10 .25
357 Igor Alexandrov .10 .25
358 Anthony Aquino .10 .25
359 David Cespiva .10 .25
360 Daniel Del Monte .10 .25
361 Ilpo Kauhanen .20 .50
362 Stefan Langwieder .10 .25
363 Thomas Pielmeier .10 .25
364 Yannick Tremblay .10 .25
365 Gert Acker .10 .25
366 Ulrich Maurer .10 .25
367 Florian Ondruschka .10 .25
368 BjÃ¶rn Barta .10 .25
369 Michael Bresagk .10 .25
370 Petr Fical .10 .25
371 Sebastian Furchner .10 .25
372 Marcel Goc .20 .50
373 Dimitrij Kotschnew .10 .25
374 Eduard Lewandowski .10 .25
375 Robert MÃ¼ller .10 .25
376 Alexander Sulzer .10 .25
377 Christoph Ullmann .10 .25
378 Thomas Greiss .10 .25
379 Nico Pyka .10 .25
NNO EisbÃ¤ren Berlin Deutscher Meister 2005 4.00 10.00
NNO DEG Metro Stars DEB Pokalsieger 2006 4.00 10.00

2005-06 German DEL All-Star Jerseys

AS01 Andy Delmore 8.00 20.00
AS02 Micki DuPont 8.00 20.00
AS03 Jakub Ficenec 8.00 20.00
AS04 Darren van Impe 8.00 20.00
AS05 Stephane Julien 8.00 20.00
AS06 Ladislav Karabin 8.00 20.00
AS07 Ivan Ciernik 8.00 20.00
AS08 Patrick Lebeau 8.00 20.00
AS09 Dave McLlwain 8.00 20.00
AS10 Francois Methot 8.00 20.00
AS11 Duanne Moeser 8.00 20.00
AS12 Dwayne Norris 8.00 20.00
AS13 Mike Pellegrims 8.00 20.00
AS14 Brad Purdie 8.00 20.00
AS15 Chris Rogles 8.00 20.00
AS16 Boris Rousson 10.00 25.00
AS17 Alexander Selivanov 8.00 20.00
AS18 Yan Stastny 12.00 30.00
AS19 Steve Walker 8.00 20.00
AS20 Pascal Trepanier 8.00 20.00
AS21 All Star Game 2006 20.00 50.00

2005-06 German DEL DEB-Jerseys

TR01 Jan Benda 8.00 20.00
TR02 Jochen Hecht 12.00 30.00
TR03 Olaf KÃ¶lzig 20.00 50.00
TR04 Marco Sturm 12.00 30.00

2005-06 German DEL Defender

We have no pricing data on this set.
DF01 Drew Bannister
DF02 Francois Bouchard
DF03 Micki DuPont
DF04 Karl Dykhuis
DF05 Jakub Ficenec
DF06 Francois Groleau
DF07 Andy Hedlund
DF08 Shawn Evans
DF09 Tommy Jakobsen
DF10 Stephane Julien
DF11 Martin Knold
DF12 Shane Peacock
DF13 Jame Pollock
DF14 Arvids Rekis

2005-06 German DEL Defender Promos

We have no pricing information on this set. The skip-numbered checklist is believed to be complete.
DF02 Francois Bouchard
DF03 Micki DuPont
DF04 Karl Dykhuis
DF05 Jakub Ficenec
DF10 Stephane Julien
DF12 Shane Peacock
DF13 Jame Pollock

2005-06 German DEL Goalies

COMPLETE SET (14) 20.00 40.00
G01 Roman Cechmanek 1.25 3.00
G02 Patrick Ehelechner 2.00 5.00
G03 Joaquin Gage 1.25 3.00
G04 Ian Gordon 1.25 3.00
G05 Thomas Greiss 1.25 3.00
G06 Trevor Kidd 2.00 5.00
G07 Alexander Jung 1.25 3.00
G08 Ilpo Kauhanen 1.25 3.00
G09 Jean-Francois LabbÃ© 1.25 3.00
G10 Robert MÃ¼ller 1.25 3.00
G11 Rich Parent 2.00 5.00
G12 TomÃ¡s PÃ¶pperle 1.25 3.00
G13 Jimmy Waite 2.00 5.00
G14 Rolf Wanhainen 1.25 3.00

2005-06 German DEL Star Attack

COMPLETE SET (10) 8.00 20.00
ST01 Ivan Ciernik .75 2.00
ST02 Jochen Hecht 1.25 3.00
ST03 Daniel Kreutzer .75 2.00
ST04 Patrick Lebeau .75 2.00
ST05 Dwayne Norris .75 2.00
ST06 Yan Stastny 1.50 4.00
ST07 Brad Tapper .75 2.00
ST08 Pascal Trepanier .75 2.00
ST09 Mike York 1.25 3.00
ST10 Jason Young .75 2.00

2005-06 German DEL Team Checklists

COMPLETE SET (20) 6.00 15.00
CL01 Augsburger Panther Checklist .40 1.00
CL02 EisbÃ¤ren Berlin Checklist .40 1.00
CL03 DEG Metro Stars Checklist .40 1.00
CL04 EV Duisburg Checklist .40 1.00
CL05 Frankfurt Lions Checklist .40 1.00
CL06 Hamburg Freezers Checklist .40 1.00
CL07 Hannover Scorpions Checklist .40 1.00
CL08 ERC Ingolstadt Checklist .40 1.00
CL09 Iserlohn Roosters Checklist .40 1.00
CL10 Kassel Huskies Checklist .40 1.00
CL11 KÃ¶lner Haie Checklist .40 1.00
CL12 Krefeld Pinguine Checklist .40 1.00
CL13 Adler Mannheim Checklist .40 1.00
CL14 NÃ¼rnberg Ice Tigers Checklist .40 1.00
CL15 Nationalmannschaft Checklist .40 1.00
CL16 Defender Checklist .40 1.00
CL17 Star Attack Checklist .40 1.00
CL18 Allstars ™05 Checklist .40 1.00
CL19 Goalies Checklist .40 1.00
CL20 Trikotkarten DEB Checklist .40 1.00

2006-07 German DEL

1 Travis Brigley .20 .50
2 Jesper Damgaard .20 .50
3 Craig Darby .30 .75
4 Patrick Buzas .20 .50
5 Thorsten Fendt .20 .50
6 Jay Henderson .30 .75
7 Manuel Kofler .20 .50
8 Kevin Lavallee .30 .75
9 Roland Mayr .20 .50
10 Josef Menauer .20 .50
11 Arvids Rekis .20 .50
12 Rainer Suchan .20 .50
13 Rolf Wanhainen .20 .50
14 Mark Beaufait .30 .75
15 Florian Busch .20 .50
16 Cole Jarrett .30 .75
17 Kelly Fairchild .30 .75
18 Sven Felski .20 .50
19 Frank Hordler .20 .50
20 Patrick Jarrett .30 .75
21 Deron Quint .30 .75
22 Andre Rankel .20 .50
23 Andy Roach .30 .75
24 Stefan Ustorf .20 .50
25 Steve Walker .30 .75
26 Youri Ziffzer .20 .50
27 Anton Bader .20 .50
28 Martin Bartek .20 .50
29 Calle Bergstrom .20 .50
30 Daniel Del Monte .20 .50
31 Johan Forsander .20 .50
32 Robert Francz .20 .50
33 Stanislav Gron .20 .50
34 Torsten Kienass .20 .50
35 Artjom Kostyrev .20 .50
36 Christopher Oravec .20 .50
37 Thomas Schenkel .20 .50
38 Alexander Engel .20 .50
39 Levente Szuper .40 1.00
40 Marian Bazany .20 .50
41 Rob Collins .30 .75
42 Jean Luc Grand Pierre .30 .75
43 Thomas Jorg .20 .50
44 Craig Johnson .30 .75
45 Klaus Kathan .20 .50
46 Daniel Kreutzer .20 .50
47 Jeff Panzer .20 .50
48 Charlie Stephens .30 .75
49 Jamie Storr .40 1.00
50 Alexander Sulzer .20 .50
51 Darren Van Impe .30 .75
52 Tore Vikingstad .20 .50
53 Chris Armstrong .30 .75
54 Michael Bresagk .20 .50
55 Ian Gordon .30 .75
56 Steve Kelly .30 .75
57 Patrick Lebeau .40 1.00
58 Michael Hackert .20 .50
59 Dwayne Norris .30 .75
60 Shane Peacock .30 .75
61 Peter Podhradsky .20 .50
62 Martin Reichel .20 .50
63 Chris Taylor .30 .75
64 Jeff Ulmer .30 .75
65 Jason Young .20 .50
66 Vitalij Aab .20 .50
67 Alexander Barta .20 .50
68 Marc Beaucage .20 .50
69 Patrick Boileau .30 .75
70 Cory Cross .30 .75
71 Francois Fortier .30 .75
72 Alan Letang .30 .75
73 Paul Manning .30 .75
74 Jacek Plachta .20 .50
75 Boris Rousson .40 1.00
76 Florian Schnitzer .20 .50
77 Brad Smyth .30 .75
78 Christoph Brandner .20 .50
79 Thomas Dolak .20 .50
80 Rob Hisey .30 .75
81 Martin Hlinka .20 .50
82 Alexander Jung .20 .50
83 Dan Lambert .30 .75
84 Andreas Morczinietz .20 .50
85 Eric Nickulas .30 .75
86 Stephane Robitaille .30 .75
87 Brad Schlegel .30 .75
88 Eric Schneider .20 .50
89 Sascha Goc .30 .75
90 Jason Ulmer .30 .75
91 Todd Warriner .30 .75
92 Doug Ast .20 .50
93 Michael Bakos .20 .50
94 Bjorn Barta .20 .50
95 Jakub Ficenec .40 1.00
96 Glen Goodall .30 .75
97 Matt Higgins .30 .75
98 Jason Holland .20 .50
99 Florian Keller .20 .50
100 Yannic Seidenberg .20 .50
101 Jeff Tory .30 .75
102 Rob Valicevic .40 1.00
103 Michael Waginger .20 .50
104 Jimmy Waite .40 1.00
105 Jeremy Adduono .30 .75
106 Kirk Furey .20 .50
107 Erich Goldmann .20 .50
108 Mark Greig .30 .75
109 Robert Hock .20 .50
110 Jens Karlsson .20 .50
111 Dmitrij Kotschnew .20 .50
112 Brad Purdie .30 .75
113 Jimmy Roy .30 .75
114 David Sulkovsky .20 .50
115 Brad Tiley .30 .75
116 Paul Traynor .20 .50
117 Michael Wolf .20 .50
118 Tino Boos .20 .50
119 Ivan Ciernik .20 .50
120 Sebastian Furchner .20 .50
121 Philip Gogulla .40 1.00
122 Adam Hauser .40 1.00
123 Kai Hospelt .20 .50
124 Stephane Julien .20 .50
125 Lasse Kopitz .20 .50
126 Mirko Ludemann .20 .50
127 Jason Marshall .30 .75
128 Dave McLlwain .30 .75
129 Sean Tallaire .30 .75
130 Bryan Adams .30 .75
131 Boris Blank .20 .50
132 Raymond Dilauro .20 .50
133 Ted Drury .30 .75
134 Franz Fritzmeier .20 .50
135 Rainer Kottstorfer .20 .50
136 Dusan Milo .20 .50
137 Richard Pavlikovsky .20 .50
138 Reto Pavoni .30 .75
139 Daniel Pietta .20 .50
140 Alexander Selivanov .20 .50
141 Herberts Vasilijevs .20 .50
142 Roland Verwey .20 .50
143 Jan Alinc .20 .50
144 Francois Bouchard .20 .50
145 Sven Butenschon .20 .50
146 Rene Corbet .30 .75
147 Colin Forbes .30 .75
148 Jason Jaspers .30 .75
149 Eduard Lewandowski .20 .50
150 Tomas Martinec .20 .50
151 Francois Methot .20 .50
152 Robert Muller .20 .50
153 Nathan Robinson .30 .75
154 Pascal Trepanier .20 .50
155 Christoph Ullmann .20 .50
156 Martin Ancicka .20 .50
157 Rich Brennan .30 .75
158 Shawn Carter .30 .75
159 Petr Fical .20 .50
160 Adrian Grygiel .20 .50
161 Martin Jiranek .20 .50
162 Scott King .40 1.00
163 Jean-Francois Labbe .40 1.00
164 Greg Leeb .30 .75
165 Michel Periard .20 .50
166 Alexander Polaczek .20 .50
167 Jame Pollock .30 .75
168 Stefan Schauer .20 .50
169 Colin Beardsmore .30 .75
170 Peter Casparsson .20 .50
171 Jason Dunham .30 .75
172 Per Eklund .20 .50
173 Peter Abstreiter .20 .50
174 Trevor Gallant .30 .75
175 Markus Jocher .20 .50
176 Matt Kinch .30 .75
177 Josef Lehner .20 .50
178 Christoffer Norgren .20 .50
179 Gunther Oswald .20 .50
180 Cam Severson .30 .75
181 William Trew .30 .75
182 Mike Bales .40 1.00
183 Florian Busch .20 .50
184 Petr Fical .20 .50
185 Sascha Goc .30 .75
186 Thomas Greiss .40 1.00
187 Jochen Hecht .60 1.50
188 Daniel Kreutzer .20 .50
189 Uwe Krupp .20 .50
190 Robert Muller .20 .50
191 Andreas Renz .20 .50
192 Stefan Schauer .20 .50
193 Marco Sturm .60 1.50
194 Alexander Sulzer .20 .50
195 Alexander Barta .20 .50

2006-07 German DEL All-Star Jerseys

AS1 Doug Ast 10.00 25.00
AS2 Francois Bouchard 10.00 25.00
AS3 Ivan Ciernik 10.00 25.00
AS4 Ted Drury 10.00 25.00
AS5 Jakub Ficenec 15.00 40.00
AS6 Andy Hedlund 10.00 25.00
AS7 Matt Higgins 10.00 25.00
AS8 Martin Hlinka 10.00 25.00
AS9 Stephane Julien 10.00 25.00
AS10 Trevor Kidd 15.00 40.00

2006-07 German DEL German Forwards

GF1 Tomas Martinec 1.25 3.00
GF2 Michael Hackert 1.25 3.00
GF3 Andreas Morczinietz 1.25 3.00
GF4 Daniel Kreutzer 1.25 3.00
GF5 Manuel Kofler 1.25 3.00
GF6 Sven Felski 1.25 3.00
GF7 Markus Jocher 1.25 3.00
GF8 Robert Hock 1.25 3.00
GF9 Robert Francz 1.25 3.00
GF10 Petr Fical 1.25 3.00
GF11 Tino Boos 1.25 3.00
GF12 Boris Blank 1.25 3.00
GF13 Alexander Barta 1.25 3.00
GF14 Michael Waginger 1.25 3.00

2006-07 German DEL New Arrivals

NA1 Travis Brigley 1.25 3.00
NA2 Cory Cross 1.25 3.00
NA3 Per Eklund 1.25 3.00
NA4 Scott King 1.25 3.00
NA5 Jason Marshall 1.25 3.00
NA6 Dusan Milo 1.25 3.00
NA7 Eric Nickulas 2.00 5.00
NA8 Andy Roach 2.00 5.00
NA9 Nathan Robinson 2.00 5.00
NA10 Jamie Storr 1.50 4.00
NA11 Levente Szuper 1.50 4.00
NA12 Chris Taylor 1.25 3.00
NA13 Brad Tiley 1.25 3.00
NA14 Daniel Tkaczuk 1.25 3.00

2006-07 German DEL Sonderkarten Diverse

We have no pricing information for this card.
MK1 Deutscher Meister 2006

2006-07 German DEL Team Leaders

TL1 Craig Darby 1.25 3.00
TL2 Ted Drury 1.25 3.00
TL3 Glen Goodall 2.00 5.00
TL4 Torsten Kienass 1.25 3.00
TL5 Alan Letang 1.25 3.00
TL6 Greg Leeb 1.25 3.00
TL7 Dave McIlwain 1.25 3.00
TL8 Jimmy Roy 1.25 3.00
TL9 William Trew 1.25 3.00
TL10 Stefan Ustorf 1.25 3.00
TL11 Todd Warriner 1.50 4.00
TL12 Pascal Trepanier 1.25 3.00
TL13 Craig Johnson 1.25 3.00
TL14 Jason Young 1.25 3.00

1994-95 Italian Milano

These 2 1/4 by 3 1/2 cards were apparently issued as part of a perforated sheet. The complete set size is unknown, and we have no pricing information on the cards. They are presented for checklisting purposes only. They are unnumbered and listed below in alphabetical order. If you have any additional info, please contact us at hockeymag@beckett.com.
COMPLETE SET (?)
1 Massimo Ansoldi
2 Scott Beattie
3 Georg Comploi
4 Andrea Mosele
5 Carmine Vani
6 Kim Gellert CO#]Conny Priondolo GM

1992-93 Norwegian Elite Series

COMPLETE SET (242) 20.00 50.00
1 Jim Marthinsen .20 .50
2 Jarl Eriksen .08 .20
3 Erik Tveten .08 .20
4 Carl Gunnar Gundersen .08 .20
5 Nick Carone .08 .20
6 Jaromir Latal .08 .20
7 Tom Johansen .08 .20
8 Asgaut Moe .08 .20
9 Oystein Olsen .08 .20
10 Atle Olsen .08 .20
11 Roy Johansen .08 .20
12 Marius Rath .08 .20
13 Svenn Erik Bjornstad .08 .20
14 Jon Magne Karlstad .08 .20
15 Pal Kristiansen .08 .20
16 Espen Knutsen 2.00 5.00
17 Stig Johansen .08 .20
18 Geir Myhre .08 .20
19 Remo Martinsen .08 .20
20 Jan Tore Ronningen .08 .20
21 Jon Hroar Nordstrom .08 .20
22 Tom Erik Olsen .08 .20
23 Peter Madach .08 .20
24 Rune Gulliksen .08 .20
25 Carl Oscar Boe Andersen .08 .20
26 Martin Ahlberg .08 .20
27 Erik Kristiansen .08 .20
28 Tommy Larsen .08 .20
29 Age Ellingsen .08 .20
30 Patric Eide .08 .20
31 Svein Harald Arnesen .08 .20
32 Petter Thoresen .08 .20
33 Pal Marthinsen .08 .20
34 Ole Eskild Dahlstrom .08 .20
35 Nikolai Davydkin .08 .20
36 Lennart Ahlberg .08 .20
37 Tommie Eriksen .08 .20
38 Jan Roar Fagerli .08 .20
39 Erik Nerell .08 .20
40 Knut Walbye .08 .20
41 Pal Dahlstrom .08 .20
42 Martin Andresen .08 .20
43 Geir Hoff .08 .20
44 Cato Andersen .08 .20
45 Per Oddvar Walbye .08 .20
46 Cato Tom Andersen .08 .20
47 Frode Hansen .20 .50
48 Petter Salsten .08 .20
49 Arne Billkvam .08 .20
50 Jarle Friis .08 .20
51 Steve Allmann .08 .20
52 Torbjorn Orskau .08 .20
53 Christian Kjeldsberg .08 .20
54 Bjorn Mathisrud .08 .20
55 Pal Gjermundsen .08 .20
56 Ketil Martinsen .08 .20
57 Vidar Andersen .08 .20
58 Rene Hansen .08 .20
59 Martin Friis .08 .20
60 Orjan Lovdal .08 .20
61 Lars Hakon Andersen .08 .20
62 Robert Sundt .08 .20
63 Henrik Buskoven .08 .20
64 Morten Finstad .20 .50
65 Magnus Christoffersen .08 .20
66 Roar Larsen .08 .20
67 Zdenek Albrecht .08 .20
68 Oldrich Valek .08 .20
69 Fredrik Jacobsen .08 .20
70 Rune Hansen .08 .20
71 Lars Jacobsen .08 .20
72 Staffan Tholsson .08 .20
73 Lase Syversen .08 .20
74 Kim Sogaard .08 .20
75 Jan Erik Thoresen .08 .20
76 Pal Andre Eriksen .08 .20
77 Bjorn Freddy Bekkerud .08 .20
78 Kjell Erik Myreng .08 .20
79 Lars Eilertsen .08 .20
80 Reino Johansen .08 .20
81 Igor Mishukov .08 .20
82 Ole Petter Dalene .08 .20
83 Jon Gundersen .08 .20
84 Pal Raab Lien .08 .20
85 Vadim Tunikov .08 .20
86 Tommy Skaarberg .08 .20
87 Per Christian Knold .08 .20
88 Stephen Foyn .08 .20
89 Glenn Asland .08 .20
90 Bjorte Olsson .08 .20
91 Gorm Gundersen .08 .20
92 Morgan Andersen .08 .20
93 Vegar Barlie .08 .20
94 Oystein Tronrud .08 .20
95 Kim Fagerhoi .08 .20
96 Tor Nilsen .08 .20
97 Arne Bergseng .08 .20
98 Timo Laituri .08 .20
99 Sjur Robert Nilsen .08 .20
100 Mattis Haakensen .08 .20
101 Lars Bergseng .08 .20
102 Svein Enok Norstebo .20 .50
103 Tor Anders Jacobsen .08 .20
104 Jorgen Salsten .08 .20
105 Tommy Jakobsen .08 .20
106 Tim Budy .08 .20
107 Martin Wiita .08 .20
108 Lenny Eriksson .08 .20
109 Stale Berg .08 .20
110 Bjorn Anders Dahl .08 .20
111 Geir Tore Dahl .08 .20
112 Dallas Gaume .08 .20
113 Geir Haugen .08 .20
114 Roar Husby .08 .20
115 Robert Nielsen .08 .20
116 Lars Erik Lunde .08 .20
117 Kare Nordnes .08 .20
118 Magne Nordnes .08 .20
119 Geir Leknes .08 .20
120 Rob Doroshuk .08 .20
121 Roger Olsen .08 .20
122 Oyvind Sorli .08 .20
123 Gunnar Bye .08 .20
124 Per Kristian Vellan .08 .20
125 Marc Laniel .20 .50
126 Dallas Gaume .08 .20
127 Robert Schistad .08 .20
128 Jan Petter Loschbrandt .08 .20
129 Tore Kristensen .08 .20
130 Eskil Eide .08 .20
131 Erik Brodahl .08 .20
132 Morten Nordhus .08 .20
133 Erik Pettersen .08 .20
134 Hans Bekken .08 .20
135 Jan Bekken .08 .20
136 Jon Erik Haaland .08 .20
137 Richard Little .08 .20
138 Eivind Olsen .08 .20
139 Morten Gilje .08 .20
140 Sverre Hogemark .08 .20
141 Eirik Paulsen .08 .20
142 Kyle McDonough .08 .20
143 Steffen Trettenes .08 .20
144 Richard David .08 .20
145 Odd Nilsen .08 .20
146 Per Marthinsen .08 .20
147 Johnny Nilsen .08 .20
148 Per Christian Fjeldstad .08 .20
149 Christian Hafsmoe .08 .20
150 Raymond Lunde .08 .20
151 Rene Lemire .08 .20
152 Thomas Kristiansen .08 .20
153 Vidar Wold .08 .20
154 Hans Petter Halla .08 .20
155 Michael Smithurst .08 .20
156 Lars Erik Solberg .08 .20
157 Kenneth Fjell .08 .20
158 Morten Hem .08 .20
159 Dag Hoyem .08 .20
160 Vince Guidotti .08 .20
161 Glen Engevik .08 .20
162 Joe Clarke .08 .20
163 Lars Erik Kjaer .08 .20
164 Gorm Laursen .08 .20
165 Per Reidar Johansen .08 .20
166 Anders Martinsen .08 .20
167 Jorn Arild Flatha .08 .20
168 Rune Hansen .08 .20
169 Stian Kraft .08 .20
170 Geir Svendsberget .08 .20
171 Andre Aas .08 .20
172 Erik Skoglund Nilsen .08 .20
173 Frode Sletner .08 .20
174 Petter Syversne .08 .20
175 Jarle Gundersen .08 .20
176 Terje Wikstrom .08 .20
177 Steve MacDonald .08 .20
178 Sjur Kinder .08 .20
179 Morten Fjeldstad .08 .20
180 George Tower .08 .20
181 Espen Knutsen 2.00 5.00
182 Jon Magne Karlstad .08 .20
183 Tommy Jakobsen .08 .20
184 Valerengen .02 .10
185 Trondheim .02 .10
186 Dallas Gaume .20 .50
187 Bjorn Anders Dahl .02 .10
188 Jarl Eriksen .02 .10
189 Mark Fioretti .02 .10
190 Brian Tutt .20 .50
191 Jim Marthinsen .20 .50
192 Brian Tutt .20 .50
193 Jaromir Latal .08 .20
194 Espen Knutsen 2.00 5.00
195 Dallas Gaume .20 .50
196 Oldrich Valek .08 .20
197 Bjorn Skaare .08 .20
198 Knut Walbye .08 .20
199 Age Ellingsen .08 .20
200 Espen Knutsen 2.00 5.00
201 Ole Eskild Dahlstrom .08 .20
202 Tommie Eriksen .08 .20
203 Vegar Barlie .08 .20
204 Glenn Jessesen .08 .20
205 Tor Arne Alseth .08 .20
206 Per Kristian Vellan .08 .20
207 Jone Hatteland .08 .20
208 Henrik Aaby .08 .20
209 Johnny Nilsen .08 .20
210 Geir Svendsberget .08 .20
211 Pal Kristian Eggen .08 .20
212 Andreas Brunvoll .08 .20
213 Andre Manscov Hansen .08 .20
214 Frode Christiansen .08 .20
215 Jan Morten Dahl .08 .20
216 Stian Kraft .08 .20
217 Lubos Sikela .08 .20
218 Rune Fjeldstad .08 .20
219 Sven Arild Olsen .08 .20

220 Kent Inge Kristiansen .08 .20
221 Sjur Rakstad Larsen .08 .20
222 Borre Ostvang .08 .20
223 Harald Bastiansen .08 .20
224 Jon Warset .08 .20
225 Jo Espen Leibnitz .08 .20
226 Arild Syversen .08 .20
227 Terje Haukali .08 .20
228 Geir Dalene .08 .20
229 Jonas Larsen .08 .20
230 Thomas Hansen .08 .20
231 Stig Olsen .08 .20
232 Lars Hansen .08 .20
233 Hans M. Anonsen .08 .20
234 Ketil Kristiansen .08 .20
235 Bjornar Sorensen .08 .20
236 Tom Jostne .08 .20
237 John Klears .08 .20
238 Arve Jansen .08 .20
239 Orjan Gjertsen .08 .20
240 Checklist (1-81) .02 .10
241 Checklist (82-162) .02 .10
242 Checklist (163-242) .02 .10

1999-00 Norwegian National Team

COMPLETE SET (24) 10.00 25.00
1 Robert Schistad .75 2.00
2 Geir Svensberget .40 1.00
3 Henrik Aaby .40 1.00
4 Tommy Jacobsen .40 1.00
5 Tommy Jacobsen .40 1.00
6 Andre Manskov Hansen .40 1.00
7 Morten Fjeldstad .40 1.00
8 Lars Hakon Andersen .40 1.00
9 Marius Trygg .40 1.00
10 Svein Enok Norstebo .75 2.00
11 Carl Oscar Boe Andersen .40 1.00
12 Ole Eskild Dalstrom .40 1.00
13 Per Age Skroder .40 1.00
14 Pal Johnsen .40 1.00
15 Trond Vegar Magnussen .40 1.00
16 Mats Trygg .40 1.00
17 Ketil Wold .40 1.00
18 Sjur Robert Nilsen .40 1.00
19 Anders Myrvold .75 2.00
20 Tore Vikingstad .40 1.00
21 Bjorge Josefsen .40 1.00
22 Oyvind Sorli .40 1.00
23 Bard Sorlie .40 1.00
24 Leif Boork CO .20 .50

1969-70 Russian National Team Postcards

COMPLETE SET (27) 75.00 150.00
1 Viktor Zinger 1.50 4.00
2 Vitali Davydov 1.50 4.00
3 Vladimir Lutchenko 1.50 4.00
4 Viktor Kuzkin 1.50 4.00
5 Alexander Ragulin 4.00 10.00
6 Igor Romishevski 1.50 4.00
7 Boris Mikhailov 6.00 15.00
8 Viacheslav Starshinov 1.50 4.00
9 Evgeny Zimin 1.50 4.00
10 Alexander Maltsev 6.00 15.00
11 Anatoli Firsov 4.00 10.00
12 Evgeny Paladiev 1.50 4.00
13 Alexander Yakushev 6.00 15.00
14 Vladimir Petrov 6.00 15.00
15 Valeri Kharlamov 10.00 25.00
16 Evgeny Mishakov 1.50 4.00
17 Vladimir Vikulov 1.50 4.00
18 Vladimir Yursinov 1.50 4.00
19 Viktor Pushkov 1.50 4.00
20 Arkady Chernishev 1.50 4.00
21 Anatoli Tarasov 4.00 10.00
22 USSR vs Sweden .75 2.00
23 USSR vs Sweden .75 2.00
24 USSR vs Sweden .75 2.00
25 USSR vs Finland, Sweden .75 2.00
26 USSR vs Canada, Sweden 1.50 4.00
27 Team Photo 1.50 4.00

1970-71 Russian National Team Postcards

This set measures 3 1/2" by 5 3/4". The horizontal fronts feature a color head shot and a preprint blue ink autograph on the left, and a black and white action photo on the right. The backs look like standard postcards. A protective sleeve featuring Russia in action against Sweden is usually found with the set.

COMPLETE SET (20) 100.00 150.00
1 Viktor Konovalenko 2.00 5.00
2 Vitali Davydov 2.00 5.00
3 Vladimir Lutchenko 2.00 5.00
4 Valeri Nikitin 2.00 5.00
5 Alexander Ragulin 4.00 10.00
6 Igor Romishevski 2.00 5.00
7 Evgeni Paladiev 2.00 5.00
8 Viacheslav Starshinov 2.00 5.00
9 Viktor Polupanov 2.00 5.00
10 Alexander Maltsev 6.00 15.00
11 Anatoli Firsov 6.00 15.00
12 Evgeni Mishakov 2.00 5.00
13 Boris Mikhailov 6.00 15.00
14 Valeri Vasiliev 4.00 10.00
15 Alexander Yakushev 6.00 15.00
16 Vladimir Petrov 6.00 15.00
17 Valeri Kharlamov 10.00 25.00
18 Vladimir Vikulov 2.00 5.00
19 Vladimir Shadrin 2.00 5.00
20 Vladislav Tretiak 10.00 25.00

1973-74 Russian National Team

This set comes in a commemorative folder and features "cards" that are 4 1/16 by 5 3/4.

COMPLETE SET (25) 60.00 125.00
1 Team Photo 1.50 4.00
2 Vladislav Tretiak 8.00 20.00
3 Alexander Sidelnikov 1.50 4.00
4 Alexander Gusev 1.50 4.00
5 Valeri Vasiliev 3.00 8.00
6 Boris Mikhailov 3.00 8.00
7 Vladimir Petrov 3.00 8.00
8 Valeri Kharlamov 6.00 15.00
9 Kharlamov, Petrov, Mikhailov 4.00 10.00
10 Vladimir Lutchenko 1.50 4.00
11 Gennady Tsygankov 1.50 4.00
12 Alexander Ragulin 1.50 4.00
13 Alexander Volchkov 1.50 4.00
14 Viacheslav Anisin 1.50 4.00
15 Yuri Lebedev 1.50 4.00
16 Alexander Bodunov 1.50 4.00
17 Alexander Martinyuk 1.50 4.00
18 Vladimir Shadrin 1.50 4.00
19 Alexander Yakushev 3.00 8.00
20 Alexander Maltsev 3.00 8.00
21 Evgeny Paladiev 1.50 4.00
22 Yuri Liapkin 1.50 4.00
23 Vsevolod Bobrov CO#Boris Kulagin CO
.75 2.00
24 Boris Mikhailov 3.00 8.00
25 Viktor Kuzkin 1.50 4.00

1974 Russian National Team

Unusually sized (8.25 X 3.5) postcard-type collectibles feature members of the powerful CCCP club. Often found in a folder.

COMPLETE SET (25) 50.00 100.00
1 Vyacheslav Anisin 1.50 4.00
2 Vsevolod Bobrov CO 1.50 4.00
3 Alexander Bodunov 1.50 4.00
4 Alexander Gusev 1.50 4.00
5 Sergei Kapustin 1.50 4.00
6 Valeri Kharlamov 5.00 12.00
7 Boris Kulagin CO 1.50 4.00
8 Viktor Kuzkin 1.50 4.00
9 Yuri Lebedev 1.50 4.00
10 Yuri Liapkin 1.50 4.00
11 Vladimir Lutchenko 1.50 4.00
12 Alexander Maltsev 3.00 8.00
13 Boris Mikhailov 3.00 8.00
14 Boris Mikhailov 3.00 8.00
15 Vladimir Petrov 3.00 8.00
16 Vladimir Repneev 1.50 4.00
17 Vladimir Shadrin 1.50 4.00
18 Yuri Shatalov 1.50 4.00
19 Alexander Sidelnikov 1.50 4.00
20 Vladislav Tretiak 6.00 15.00
21 Gennady Tsygankov 1.50 4.00
22 Valeri Vasiliev 3.00 8.00
23 Alexander Yakushev 3.00 8.00
24 USSR .40 1.00
25 USSR .40 1.00

1979 Russian National Team

This set features the Soviet National Team. The cards measure 8 1/4 by 5 7/8 and were issued in a folder.

COMPLETE SET (24) 37.50 100.00
1 Team Photo .50 1.00
2 Viktor Tikhonov CO 1.00 2.00
3 Vladimir Yursinov CO .50 2.00
4 Vladislav Tretiak 5.00 15.00
5 Alexander Pashkov 1.50 3.00
6 Vladimir Lutchenko 1.00 3.00
7 Valeri Vasiliev 1.00 5.00
8 Gennady Tsygankov 1.00 3.00
9 Yuri Fedorov 1.00 2.00
10 Slava Fetisov 5.00 15.00
11 Zinetula Bilyaletinov 2.50 5.00
12 Vasili Pervukhin 1.00 3.00
13 Boris Mikhailov 2.50 8.00
14 Vladimir Petrov 2.50 8.00
15 Valeri Kharlamov 5.00 15.00
16 Alexander Maltsev 2.50 8.00
17 Sergei Kapustin 1.00 3.00
18 Yuri Lebedev 1.00 2.00
19 Viktor Zhluktov 1.00 3.00
20 Helmut Balderis 1.50 5.00
21 Alexander Golikov 1.00 2.00
22 Sergei Makarov 4.00 15.00
23 Vladimir Golikov 1.00 2.00
24 Team Photo .50 1.00

1984 Russian National Team

This 23-card set presents Russian hockey players. The cards were packaged in a cardboard sleeve that displays a photo of the 1983 Russian national team. The cards measure approximately 5 1/2" by 7" and feature full-bleed head and shoulders shots of the players dressed in civilian clothing. On the left portion, the backs carry three action shots in a filmstrip format while the right portion has player information in Russian. The cards are unnumbered and checklisted below in alphabetical order.

COMPLETE SET (23) 40.00 80.00
1 Sergei Babinov .80 2.00
2 Helmut Balderis 1.20 3.00
3 Zinetula Bilyaletinov 1.20 3.00
4 Vyacheslav Bykov 2.00 5.00
5 Slava Fetisov 4.00 10.00
6 Irek Gimaev .80 2.00
7 Sergei Kapustin .80 2.00
8 Alexei Kasatonov 2.00 5.00
9 Andrei Khomotov 2.00 5.00
10 Vladimir Krutov 3.20 10.00
11 Igor Larionov 6.00 15.00
12 Sergei Makarov 3.20 10.00
13 Alexander Maltsev 2.00 5.00
14 Vladimir Myshkin 5.00
15 Vasily Pervukhin .80 2.00
16 Sergei Shepelev .80 2.00
17 Alexander Skvorstsov .80 2.00
18 Sergei Starikov 1.20 3.00
19 Viktor Tikhonov CO 2.00 2.00
20 Vladislav Tretiak 6.00 10.00
21 Mikhael Vasiliev .80 2.00
22 Vladimir Yursinov CO .80 1.00
23 Viktor Zhluktov .80 2.00
24 Vladimir Zubkov .80 2.00

1987 Russian National Team

This 24-card set presents Russian hockey players and is subtitled "The USSR 1987 National Hockey Team." The cards were printed in the USSR, released by Panorama Publishers (USSR), and distributed in North America by Tri-Globe International, Inc. The production run was reportedly 25,000 sets. The cards were packaged in a cardboard sleeve that displays a team photo from the world championships. The cards measure approximately 4 1/8" by 5 13/16" and feature full-bleed head and shoulders shots of the players dressed in coat and tie. The player's autograph and uniform number are printed on the lower portion of the picture in gold lettering. The backs are in Russian and present player profile and statistics. The cards are unnumbered and checklisted below in alphabetical order.

COMPLETE SET (24) 18.00 45.00
1 Sergei Ageikin .40 1.00
2 Evgeny Belosheikin .80 2.00
3 Zinetula Belyaletdinov .40 1.00
4 Viacheslav Bykov .80 2.00
5 Slava Fetisov 2.00 5.00
6 Alexei Gusarov .60 1.50
7 Valeri Kamensky 1.20 3.00
8 Alexei Kasatonov .80 2.00
9 Yuri Khmylev .60 1.50
10 Andrei Khomutov .80 2.00
11 Vladimir Konstantinov 2.00 5.00
12 Vladimir Krutov 1.20 3.00
13 Igor Larionov 2.00 5.00
14 Sergei Makarov 1.20 3.00
15 Sergei Mylnikov .80 2.00
16 Vasili Pervukhin .40 1.00
17 Sergei Starikov .40 1.00
18 Igor Stelnov .40 1.00
19 Sergei Svetlov .40 1.00
20 Viktor Tikhonov CO .80 2.00
21 Viktor Tjumenev .40 1.00
22 Michael Varnakov .40 1.00
23 Sergei Yashin .40 1.00
24 Vladimir Yursinov CO .40 1.00

1989 Russian National Team

This set of 24 postcards was released by Plakat Publishers, USSR. The cards measure approximately 4 1/8" by 5 13/16" and features some of the best Russian players of modern years. The set features 22 player cards and two coach cards. The cards were packaged in a cardboard sleeve that displays an action photo of Valeri Kamensky. Reportedly 100,000 sets were printed but most were sold in the USSR and fewer sets made it to the U.S. and Canada. The fronts have head and shoulder shots of Russian Team players in coat and tie (street clothes) with a superimposed facsimile autograph while the backs contain biographical information in Russian. An unauthorized reprint of the set was issued in 1991, but the size was reduced to 2 1/2" by 3 1/2". The players in the reprint set who had since played in the NHL were given English biographies on labels added to the back. The cards are listed below alphabetically since they are unnumbered.

COMPLETE SET (24) 14.00 35.00
1 Ilya Byakin .30 .75
2 Viacheslav Bykov .40 1.00
3 Alexandr Chernik .20 .50
4 Igor Dmitriev CO .20 .50
5 Sergei Fedorov 3.20 8.00
6 Slava Fetisov 1.20 3.00
7 Alexei Gusarov .30 .75
8 Arturs Irbe 2.00 5.00
9 Valeri Kamensky .80 2.00
10 Alexei Kasatonov .60 1.50
11 Svatoslav Khalizov .20 .50
12 Yuri Khmylev .30 .75
13 Andrei Khomutov .40 1.00
14 Vladimir Konstantinov 2.00 5.00
15 Vladimir Krutov .80 2.00
16 Dimitri Kvartalnov .40 1.00
17 Igor Larionov 1.60 4.00
18 Sergei Makarov .80 2.00
19 Vladimir Mishkin .40 1.00
20 Sergei Mylnikov .40 1.00
21 Sergei Nemchinov .40 1.00
22 Valeri Shirjaev .20 .50
23 Viktor Tikhonov CO .40 1.00
24 Sergei Yashin .20 .50

1991-92 Russian Stars Red Ace

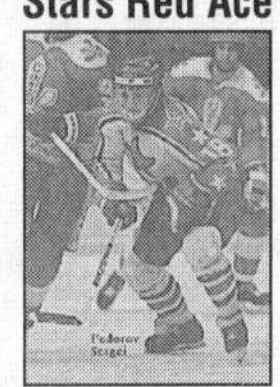

This 17-card standard-size set, featuring Russian stars in the NHL, was produced by Red Ace. The cards were packaged in a box, on which it is claimed that the production run was limited to 50,000 sets. The fronts feature borderless action shots with the player's name. Printed on white cover stock, the horizontal backs feature a close-up photograph as well as biographical and statistical information in Russian and English. The cards are unnumbered and checklisted below in alphabetical order.

COMPLETE SET (17) 4.00 10.00
1 Pavel Bure 1.20 3.00
2 Evgeny Davydov .10 .25
3 Sergei Fedorov 1.20 3.00
4 Slava Fetisov .40 1.00
5 Alexei Gusarov .10 .25
6 Valeri Kamensky .30 .75
7 Alexei Kasatonov .20 .50
8 Ravil Khaidarov .10 .25
9 Vladimir Konstantinov .40 1.00
10 Igor Kravchuk .16 .40
11 Igor Larionov .40 1.00
12 Andrei Lomakin .10 .25
13 Sergei Makarov .30 .75
14 Alexander Mogilny .40 1.00
15 Sergei Nemchinov .16 .40
16 Anatoli Semenov .10 .25
17 Mikhail Tatarinov .10 .25

1991-92 Russian Tri-Globe Bure

This standard-size five-card set was produced by Tri-Globe as part of the "The Magnificent Five" series. These sets spotlight five Russian hockey stars currently playing in the NHL, with set 2 featuring Pavel Bure. It is claimed that 5,000 numbered display boxes were produced, each containing 40 sets (ten for each player). Printed in Russia on heavy laminated textured stock, card fronts feature full-color action shots in various formats and accented predominantly in green. Each set includes a checklist on the back of a Sergei Fedorov promo card.

COMPLETE SET (6) 2.80 7.00
COMMON CARD (6-10) .60 1.50
NNO Sergei Fedorov .20 .50
Checklist

1991-92 Russian Tri-Globe Fedorov

This five-card set honoring Sergei Fedorov is the product of a joint venture between Tri-Globe International, Inc. and Ivan Fiodorov Press. The cards measure approximately 2 1/2" by 3 3/4" and are printed on a grainy cardboard stock. The fronts feature color action game shots. The cards are numbered on the back. According to Tri-Globe, 600 uncut, numbered sheets were printed, producing the equivalent of 3,000 sets, as well as 1,000 uncut, numbered five-card strips. Moreover, 100,000 five-card sets were reportedly produced.

COMPLETE SET (5) 2.40 6.00
COMMON CARD (1-5) .50 1.25

1991-92 Russian Tri-Globe Irbe

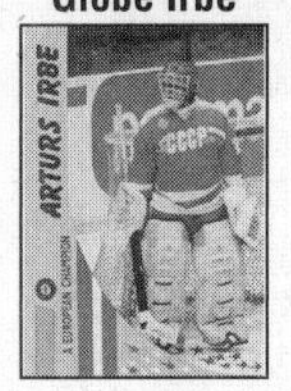

This standard-size five-card set was produced by Tri-Globe as part of the "The Magnificent Five" series. These sets spotlight five Russian hockey stars currently playing in the NHL, with set four featuring Arturs Irbe.

COMPLETE SET (6) 1.60 4.00
COMMON CARD (16-20) .30 .75
NNO Sergei Fedorov .20 .50
Checklist

1991-92 Russian Tri-Globe Kamensky

This standard-size five-card set was produced by Tri-Globe as part of the "The Magnificent Five" series. These sets spotlight five Russian hockey stars currently playing in the NHL, with set 1 featuring Valeri Kamensky.

COMPLETE SET (6) .60 1.50
COMMON CARD (1-5) .30 .75
NNO Sergei Fedorov .20 .50
Checklist

1991-92 Russian Tri-Globe Semenov

This standard-size five-card set was produced by Tri-Globe as part of the "The Magnificent Five" series. These sets spotlight five Russian hockey stars currently playing in the NHL, with set three featuring Anatoli Semenov.

COMPLETE SET (6) .60 1.50
COMMON CARD (11-15) .10 .25
NNO Sergei Fedorov .20 .50
Checklist

1991 Russian Sports Unite Hearts

A boxed set of standard-sized cards of Russian players in the NHL, this issue was limited to 50,000 sets produced.

COMPLETE SET (10) 6.00 15.00
1 Sergei Fedorov 2.00 5.00
2 Slava Kozlov .80 2.00
3 Alexei Gusarov .40 1.00
4 Alexei Kasatonov .40 1.00
5 Vladimir Konstantinov .80 2.00
6 Igor Larionov .80 2.00
7 Sergei Makarov .40 1.00
8 Alexander Mogilny .80 2.00
9 Mikhail Tatarinov .40 1.00
10 Vladislav Tretiak 1.20 3.00

1991 Russian Stars in NHL

This 11-card standard-size set was reportedly printed in Leningrad by Ivan Fiodorov Press as a special limited edition; it is claimed that there were only 50,000 sets issued. The cards essentially feature Russian players in the NHL. The front has a full-color player photo, bordered on the two sides by hockey sticks (with hockey gloves below). A red banner is draped across the top of the picture, with the player's name in between USSR (sickle and hammer) and USA (US flag) emblems. In contrast to the dark purple background, the bottom is light purple and presents the message "Sports Unites Hearts" in English and Russian. The horizontally-oriented back provide player information in two colored panels (English and Russian) and has a head shot of the player as well.

COMPLETE SET (11) 3.20 8.00
1 Sergei Fedorov 1.60 4.00
2 Slava Fetisov .40 1.00
3 Alexei Gusarov .10 .25
4 Alexei Kasatonov .20 .50
5 Vladimir Konstantinov .40 1.00
6 Igor Larionov .40 1.00
7 Sergei Makarov .40 1.00
8 Alexander Mogilny .60 1.50
9 Mikhail Tatarinov .10 .25
10 Vladislav Tretiak .80 2.00
11 Team Photo .16 .40
USSR National Team

1992-93 Russian Stars Red Ace

This 37-card, standard-size set features action color player photos bordered in white. The player's name and the Red Ace logo appear in a gradated violet stripe at the bottom. A red triangle at the upper left corner of the picture carries a white star outline. In a red box with rounded corners, the back provides biography in Cyrillic (Russian) and English. The top portion of the back has a yellow background and displays a close-up photo in a circular format and the player's name in Russian and English. The cards are numbered on the back essentially alphabetically.

COMPLETE SET (37) 3.20 5.00
1 Alexander Barkov .04 .10
2 Sergei Bautin .04 .10
3 Igor Boldin .04 .10
4 Nikolai Borchevsky .10 .25
5 Sergei Brylin .10 .25
6 Viacheslav Butsayev .04 .10
7 Alexander Cherbajev .04 .10
8 Evgeny Garanin .04 .10
9 Sergei Gonchar .20 .50
10 Alexander Karpovtsev .10 .25
11 Darius Kasparaitis .10 .25
12 Alexander Kharlamov .10 .25
13 Yuri Khmylev .10 .25
14 Sergei Klimovich .04 .10
15 Igor Korolev .10 .25
16 Andrei Kovalenko .10 .25
17 Alexei Kovalev UER .30 .75
(Back photo is
Igor Korolev)
18 Dmitri Kvartalnov .10 .25
19 Vladimir Malakhov .10 .25
20 Maxim Mikhailovsky .04 .10
21 Boris Mironov .10 .25
22 Dmitri Mironov .10 .25
23 Andrei Nazarov .10 .25
24 Roman Oksyuta .04 .10
25 Artur Oktyabrev .04 .10
26 Sergei Petrenko .04 .10
27 Oleg Petrov .10 .25
28 Andrei Potaichuk .04 .10
29 Vitali Prokhorov .04 .10
30 Alexander Semak .10 .25
31 Dmitri Starostenko .04 .10
32 Ravil Yakubov .04 .10
33 Alexei Yashin .20 .50
34 Dmitri Yushkevich .10 .25
35 Alexei Zhamnov .20 .25
36 Alexei Zhitnik .10 .25
NNO Checklist Card .04 .01

1992 Russian Stars Red Ace

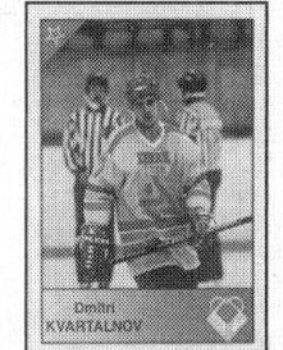

The 1992 Red Ace Russian Hockey Stars boxed set was co-sponsored by the World of Hockey Magazine and World Sport. The cards were sold in a light blue box with production limited supposedly to 25,000 sets. The cards are printed on thin card stock and measure approximately 2 1/2" by 3 3/8". The light blue bordered fronts feature color action player photos. The player's name appears on a light green diagonal stripe in an upper corner, accented with a red triangle containing a white star. The Red Ace logo is printed in a lower corner of the picture. The white backs display a small head shot next to the player's name on a green bar. In a pale pink panel below is the player's biography and career highlights in Russian and English. The cards are numbered on the back.

COMPLETE SET (36) 4.00 5.00
1 Darius Kasparaitis .20 .25
2 Alexei Zhamnov .20 .25
3 Dimitri Khristich .20 .50
4 Andrei Trefilov .20 .50
5 Vitali Prokhorov .06 .10
6 Dmitri Filimonov .06 .10
7 Valeri Zelepukin .10 .25
8 Alexei Kovalev .30 .75
9 Dmitri Kvartalnov .10 .25
10 Igor Korolev .10 .25
11 Nikolai Borschevsky .10 .25
12 Igor Boldin .06 .10
13 Arturs Irbe .30 .75
14 Viacheslav Butsayev .10 .10
15 Boris Mironov .10 .25
16 Sergei Bautin .06 .10
17 Alexander Kharlamov .10 .25
18 Viacheslav Kozlov .30 .50
19 Mikhail Shtalenkov .20 .50
20 Roman Oksyuta .10 .10
21 Sandis Ozolinsh .20 .50
22 Dmitri Mironov .10 .25
23 Sergei Brylin .20 .25
24 Vladimir Grachev .06 .10
25 Dmitri Starostenko .06 .10
26 Andrei Nazarov .20 .25
27 Alexei Yashin .20 .50
28 Vladimir Malakhov .10 .25
29 Ravil Jakubov .06 .10
30 Sergei Klimovich .06 .10
31 Artur Oktjabrev .06 .10
32 Lev Berdichevski .06 .10
33 Ian Kaminski .10 .25
34 Andrei Kovalenko .10 .25
35 Dmitri Yushkevich .20 .25
36 Checklist .04 .01

1992 Russian Tri-Globe From Russia With Puck

Twelve Russian hockey stars who are currently playing in the NHL are featured in this 24-card boxed standard-size set, with two cards devoted to each player. The production run was reportedly 50,000 sets. The fronts of all cards display color action player photos. On the player's first card (i.e., an odd-numbered card), his name appears at the top in a silver stripe, and red, white, and blue stripes accent the picture on three sides. On his second card (i.e., an even-numbered card), black-and-white speckled stripes edge the picture above and below. The back of the player's first card carries a second color action photo and biographical information, while the back of his second card has a close-up color photo and career statistics. All text is in French and English.

COMPLETE SET (24) 4.00 10.00
1 Igor Larionov .20 .50
2 Igor Larionov .20 .50
3 Andrei Lomakin .10 .25
4 Andrei Lomakin .10 .25
5 Pavel Bure .80 2.00
6 Pavel Bure .80 2.00
7 Alexei Zhamnov .10 .25
8 Alexei Zhamnov .10 .25
9 Sergei Krivokrasov .10 .25
10 Sergei Krivokrasov .10 .25
11 Valeri Kamensky .10 .25
12 Valeri Kamensky .10 .25
13 Viacheslav Kozlov .20 .50
14 Viacheslav Kozlov .20 .50
15 Valeri Zelepukin .10 .25
16 Valeri Zelepukin .10 .25
17 Igor Kravchuk .10 .25
18 Igor Kravchuk .10 .25
19 Vladimir Malakhov .10 .25
20 Vladimir Malakhov .10 .25
21 Boris Mironov .10 .25
22 Boris Mironov .10 .25
23 Arturs Irbe .20 .50
24 Arturs Irbe .20 .50

1998-99 Russian Hockey League

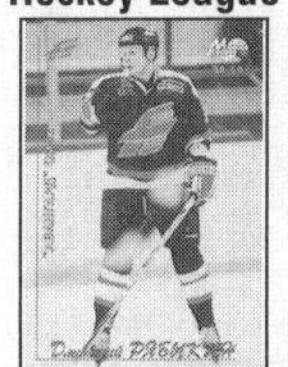

This set features the elite of the Russian Hockey League. The cards feature blue borders around action shots. The set is notable for featuring 2001 first-overall draft pick Ilya Kovalchuk.

COMPLETE SET (167) 24.00 60.00
1 Sergei Gomolyako .20 .50
2 Sergei Zemchenok .20 .50
3 Oleg Mikulchik .20 .50
4 Evgueni Koreshkov .20 .50
5 Andrei Razin .20 .50
6 Ravil Gusmanov .20 .50
7 Dmitri Popov .20 .50
8 Valeri Karpov .30 .75
9 Andrei Sokolov .20 .50
10 Makhail Borodulin .20 .50
11 Konstantin Shafranov .30 .75
12 Vladimir Antipin .20 .50
13 Igor Zemlyanoi .20 .50
14 Sergei Tertyshny .20 .50
15 Vadim Glovatski .20 .50
16 AlexanderÂ Golts .30 .75
17 AlexanderÂ Koreshkov .20 .50
18 Boris Tortunov .20 .50
19 Valeri Nikulin .20 .50
20 Andrei Sapoznikov .20 .50
21 Dmitri Maksimov .20 .50
22 Dmitri Mylnikov .40 2.00
23 Maxim Sushinski .40 1.00
24 Yuri Panov .20 .50

25 AlexanderÂ Terekhov .20 .50
26 Vladimir Zorkin .20 .50
27 Eduard Gorbachev .20 .50
28 Leonid Kanarekin .20 .50
29 AlexanderÂ Savchenkov .20 .50
30 Maxim Chukanov .20 .50
31 Evgueni Fedorov .20 .50
32 Yaroslav Lyuzenkov .20 .50
33 Oleg Leontiev .20 .50
34 Sergei Osipov .20 .50
35 Andrei Kudinov .20 .50
36 Dmitri Krasotkin .20 .50
37 Ravil Yakubov .80 1.00
38 Dmitri Zatonski .20 .50
39 Konstantin Maslyukov .20 .50
40 Andrei Subbotin .30 .75
41 Pavel Kamentsev .20 .50
42 Evgueni Tarasov .20 .50
43 Oleg Kryazhev .20 .50
44 Igor Nikitin .20 .50
45 Denis Arkhipov 2.00 3.00
46 Albert Loginov .20 .50
47 Andrei Samokhvalov .20 .50
48 Igor Dorofeev .20 .50
49 Sergei Bautin .20 .50
50 Evgueni Varlamov .20 .50
51 Sergei Korobkin .20 .50
52 Rafik Yakubov .20 .50
53 Alexei Chupin .20 .50
54 Dmitri Ryabikin .20 .50
55 Alexei Kudashov .20 .50
56 AlexanderÂ Trofimov .20 .50
57 Igor Andryushchenko .20 .50
58 Igor Gorbenko .20 .50
59 Dmitri Gorenko .20 .50
60 AlexanderÂ Kazakov .20 .50
61 Evgueni Kuveko .20 .50
62 Igor Nikolaev .20 .50
63 Mikhail Pereyaslov .20 .50
64 AlexanderÂ Filippov .20 .50
65 Igor Mikhailov .20 .50
66 Roman Shipulin .20 .50
67 Dmitri Shpakovski .20 .50
68 Dmitri Shulakov .20 .50
69 Konstantin Golokhvastov .20 .50
70 Yuri Fimin .20 .50
71 Sergei Yasakov .20 .50
72 Oleg Filimonov .20 .50
73 Anatoli Ustyugov .20 .50
74 Andrei Skabelka .30 .75
75 Sergei Zolotov .20 .50
76 Dmitri Bezrukov .20 .50
77 Dmitri Vanyasov .20 .50
78 Evgueni Zakharov .20 .50
79 Arat Kadyekin .20 .50
80 Evgueni Mlinchenko .20 .50
81 Leonid Labzov .20 .50
82 Andrei Mazhugin .20 .50
83 Vladislav Makarov .20 .50
84 Remir Khaidarov .20 .50
85 Pavel Agarkov .20 .50
86 Igor Belyavski .20 .50
87 Dmitri Dubrovski .20 .50
88 Vyacheslav Zavalnyuk .20 .50
89 Yuri Zuev .20 .50
90 Andrei Evstafiev .20 .50
91 Vadim Epanchintsev .40 1.00
92 Igor Zelenchev .20 .50
93 Dmitri Klevakin .20 .50
94 Alexei Koledaev .20 .50
95 Nikolai Kurochkin .20 .50
96 Boris Kuzmin .20 .50
97 Roman Kukhtinov .20 .50
98 Sergei Moskalev .20 .50
99 Evgueni Pupkov .20 .50
100 Alexei Tkachuk .20 .50
101 Rinat Khasanov .20 .50
102 Sergei Shalamai .20 .50
103 Vadim Tarasov 1.60 2.00
104 Vladislav Morozov .20 .50
105 Almaz Garifullin .30 .75
106 Ilnur Gizatullin .20 .50
107 AlexanderÂ Zavyalov .20 .50
108 Oleg Vevcherenko .20 .50
109 AlexanderÂ Savitski .20 .50
110 Mikhail Sarmatin .20 .50
111 Igor Stepanov .20 .50
112 Konstantin Butsenko .20 .50
113 Alexei Murzin .20 .50
114 Andrei Nikolaev .20 .50
115 Dmitri Plekhanov .20 .50
116 Roman Salnikov .20 .50
117 Vyacheslav Timchenko .20 .50
118 Anitoli Stepanishev .20 .50
119 Roman Baranov .20 .50
120 Artem Anisimov .20 .50
121 Yuri Guniko .20 .50
122 Eduard Kudermetov .20 .50
123 Dmitri Balmin .20 .50
124 Igor Dyakiv .20 .50
125 Ramil Saifullin .20 .50
126 AlexanderÂ Vyukhin .20 .50
127 Oleg Leontiev .20 .50
128 Evgueni Koreshkov .20 .50
129 Sergei Gomolyako .20 .50
130 Oleg Mikulchik .20 .50
131 Andrei Petrakov .20 .50
132 Alexei Stepanov .20 .50
133 Dmitri Verzhinin .20 .50
134 Artem Ostroushko .20 .50
135 Sergei Berdnikov .20 .50
136 Konstantin Koltsov .20 .50
137 Vladimir Tarasov .20 .50
138 Sergei Shimkovski .20 .50
139 Oleg Pchelyakov .20 .50
140 Oleg Burlutski .20 .50
141 Oleg Bratash .20 .50
142 Sergei Voronov .20 .50
143 Uldar Mukhometov .30 .75
144 Alexei Egorov .40 1.00
145 Vladimir Kopat .20 .50
146 Vladimir Kochin .20 .50
147 Alexei Putilin .20 .50
148 Andrei Rasolko .20 .50
149 Vadim Molotilov .20 .50
150 Dmitri Nazarov .20 .50
151 Igor Vyazmikin .20 .50
152 Alexei Kalyukhny .20 .50
153 Denis Kartsev .20 .50
154 AlexanderÂ Kuvaldin .20 .50
155 Alexei Troschinsky .20 .50
156 AlexanderÂ Kharitonov .80 1.00
157 Valeri Cherny .20 .50
158 Yuri Dobrishkin .20 .50
159 Evgueni Pavlov .20 .50
160 Nikolai Antropov 1.60 3.00
161 AlexanderÂ Zhurik .20 .50
162 Valeri Belousov .20 .50
163 Artem Chubarov .40 1.00
164 Boris Zelenko .20 .50
165 Dmitri Frolov .40 1.00
166 Vladimir Kirik .20 .50
167 Alexei Danilov .20 .50

1999-00 Russian Dynamo Moscow

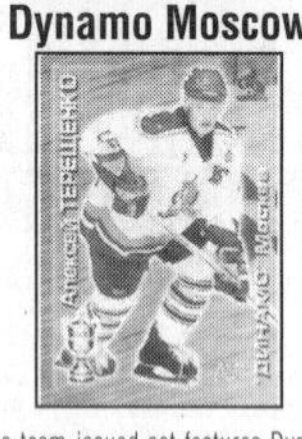

This team-issued set features Dynamo Moscow of the Russian League. The cards were sold by the team at its souvenir stands.

COMPLETE SET (27) 6.00 15.00
1 Alexei Tereshenko .20 .50
2 Igor Shadilov .20 .50
3 Alexei Ponikarovski .30 .75
4 Alexei Litvinenko .20 .50
5 Roman Zolotov .20 .50
6 Andrei Markov .40 1.00
7 Alexander Khavanov .40 .75
8 Vitali Proshkin .20 .50
9 Alexei Troschinsky .20 .50
10 Oleg Orekhovski .20 .50
11 Marat Davydov .20 .50
12 Dmitri Kokorev .20 .50
13 Alexander Kharitonov .40 .75
14 Alexander Prokopiev .20 .50
15 Mikhail Ivanov .20 .50
16 Alexei Kudashov .30 .75
17 Alexander Kuvaldin .20 .50
18 Denis Kartsev .20 .50
19 Stanislav Romanov .20 .50
20 Alexander Savchenkov .20 .50
21 Lev Berdichevski .20 .50
22 Alexei Kalyuzhni .20 .50
23 Alexander Stepanov .20 .50
24 Boris Zelenko .20 .50
25 Vitali Yeremeev .60 1.50
26 Alexei Yegorov .40 1.00
NNO Team Photo .20 .50

1999-00 Russian Hockey League

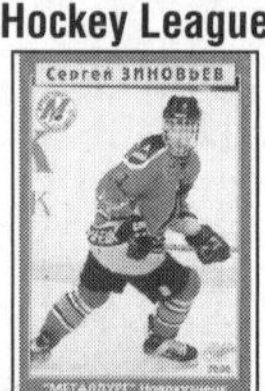

This set features the top players of the sprawling Russian Hockey League. The cards feature a color action photo on the front and player information on the back in Cyrillic. The set is noteworthy for featuring the first ever card of 2001 first overall pick, Ilya Kovalchuk.

COMPLETE SET (270) 60.00 100.00
1 Valeri Karpov .40 1.00
2 Igor Zemlyanoi .10 .25
3 Mikhail Borodulin .10 .25
4 Vladimir Antipin .10 .25
5 Vadim Glovatskin .10 .25
6 Alexei Stepanov .10 .25
7 Sergei Gomolyako .10 .25
8 Andrei Sokolov .10 .25
9 Andrei Razin .10 .25
10 Dmitri Popov .10 .25
11 Valeri Nikulin .10 .25
12 Andrei Petrakov .10 .25
13 Evgueni Koreshkov .10 .25
14 Alexander Koreshkov .10 .25
15 Andrei Sapozhnikov .20 .50
16 Oleg Mikulchik .40 1.00
17 Ravil Gusmanov .30 .75
18 Vitali Prokhorov .20 .50
19 Boris Tortunov .10 .25
20 Sergei Zemchenok .10 .25
21 Sergei Tertyshny .10 .25
22 Yuri Kuznetsov .10 .25
23 Maxim Bets .40 1.00
24 Sergei Osipov .10 .25
25 Oleg Leontiev .10 .25
26 Andrei Kudinov .10 .25
27 Konstantin Bezborodov .10 .25
28 Maxim Stepanov .10 .25
29 Alexei Lazarenko .10 .25
30 Vladimir Tyurikov .10 .25
31 Alexei Komarov .10 .25
32 Oleg Polkovinkov .10 .25
33 Dmitri Vershinin .10 .25
34 Vladimir Dumnov .10 .25
35 Oleg Smirnov .10 .25
36 Denis Ivanov .10 .25
37 Alexander Grishin .10 .25
38 Sergei Luchinkin .10 .25
39 Sergei Reshetnikov .10 .25
40 Denis Martiniuk .10 .25
41 Igor Boldin .10 .25
42 Nikolai Semin .10 .25
43 Alexander Zhdan .30 .75
44 Denis Metliuk .10 .25
45 Sergei Zolotov .10 .25
46 Yuri Dobryshkin .10 .25
47 Sergei Mylnikov, Jr. .40 1.00
48 Anton Ulyanov .10 .25
49 Yakov Deev .10 .25
50 Dmitri Bykov .10 .25
51 Dmitri Milnikov .40 1.00
52 Rinat Kasyanov .10 .25
53 Dmitri Balmin .10 .25
54 Alexei Chupin .10 .25
55 Artem Anisimov .10 .25
56 Sergei Smirnov .10 .25
57 Ivan Andriyashev .10 .25
58 Sergei Shilov .10 .25
59 Vladislav Makarov .10 .25
60 Dmitri Mylnikov .75 2.00
(Sergei Mylnikov Jr.
61 Rafik Yakubov .10 .25
62 Dmitri Shandurov .10 .25
63 Vladimir Pozdnyakov .10 .25
64 Alexei Ivashkin .10 .25
65 Valeri Ivannikov .10 .25
66 Egor Mikhailov .10 .25
67 Alexander Zibin .10 .25
68 Igor Averchenkov .10 .25
69 Alexei Sheblanov .10 .25
70 Dmitri Yachanov .10 .25
71 Oleg Romanov .10 .25
72 Denis Arkhipov 2.00 3.00
73 Almaz Garifullin .10 .25
74 Evgueni Varlamov .10 .25
75 Igor Stepanov .10 .25
76 Alexander Zavyalov .10 .25
77 Ilinur Gizhatullin .10 .25
78 Alexander Trofimov .10 .25
79 Eduard Kudermetov .10 .25
80 Remir Khaidarov .10 .25
81 Nikolai Pronin .10 .25
82 Andrei Glebov .10 .25
83 Andrei Savchenko .10 .25
84 Andrei Mukhachev .10 .25
85 Maxim Ossipov .20 .50
86 Sergei Mozyakin .10 .25
87 Alexei Gubarev .10 .25
88 Oleg Filimonov .30 .75
89 Igor Nikolaev .10 .25
90 Eduard Polyakov .10 .25
91 Konstantin Tatarintsev .10 .25
92 Anitoli Ustyugov .10 .25
93 Victor Dronov .10 .25
94 Sergei Yasakov .10 .25
95 Oleg Gorbenko .10 .25
96 Igor Andryushenko .10 .25
97 Alexei Plotinkov .10 .25
98 Igor Bakhmutov .10 .25
99 Dmitri Shandurov .10 .25
100 Dmitri Bezrukov .10 .25
101 Airat Kadeikin .10 .25
102 Leonid Labzov .10 .25
103 Alexei Vakhrushev .10 .25
104 Denis Tsigurov .10 .25
105 Roman Baranov .10 .25
106 Vladimir Zorkin .10 .25
107 Dmitri Maksimov .10 .25
108 Dmitri Kulikov .10 .25
109 Alexander Guskov .10 .25
110 Dmitri Khomutov .10 .25
111 Alexander Skugarev .10 .25
112 Mikhail Pereyaslov .10 .25
113 Artem Argokov .10 .25
114 Alexei Strakhov .10 .25
115 Dmitri Shulakov .10 .25
116 Oleg Vevcherenko .10 .25
117 Yuri Fimin .10 .25
118 Ruslan Bernikov .10 .25
119 Alexander Titov .10 .25
120 Dmitri Gorenko .10 .25
121 Alexander Filippov .10 .25
122 Konstantin Mitroshkin .10 .25
123 Alexander Zevakhin .10 .25
124 Steve Plouffe .40 1.00
125 Nikolai Tsulgin .30 .75
126 Alexei Tertyshny .10 .25
127 Nikolai Zavarykhin .30 .75
128 Evgueni Zakharov .10 .25
129 Sergei Klimentiev .20 .50
130 Pavel Duma .30 .75
131 Maxim Vasyuchkov .10 .25
132 Rustem Amirov .10 .25
133 Matvei Belousov .10 .25
134 AlexanderÂ Schev .10 .25
135 Evgueni Muratov .10 .25
136 Andrei Buldakov .10 .25
137 Andrei Tsareev .10 .25
138 Vladimir Zavyalov .10 .25
139 Andrei Pchelyakov .10 .25
140 Igor Knyazev 1.20 3.00
141 Ilya Kovalchuk 25.00 50.00
142 Alexei Chervyakov .10 .25
143 Vladimir Kulikov .10 .25
144 Andrei Bushan .10 .25
145 Ravil Yakubov .20 .50
146 Sergei Shitkovski .10 .25
147 Sergei Berdnikov .10 .25
148 Ramil Saifullin .10 .25
149 Konstantin Golokhvastov .10 .25
150 Konstantin Maslyukov .10 .25
151 Alexei Bulatov .10 .25
152 Dmitri Kirilenko .10 .25
153 Sergei Makarov .10 .25
154 Rustem Kamaletdinov .10 .25
155 Maxim Mikhailovski .30 .75
156 Denis Khlopotnov .40 1.00
157 Albert Loginov .10 .25
158 Dmitri Nazarov .10 .25
159 Alexei Miroshnikov .10 .25
160 Sergei Zimakov .10 .25
161 Valeri Belov .10 .25
162 Alexei Kochegarov .10 .25
163 Alexei Pogonin .10 .25
164 Andrei Rasolko .10 .25
165 Dmitri Denisov .20 .50
166 Dmitri Tarasov .10 .25
167 Vadim Pokotilo .10 .25
168 Evgueni Fedorov .10 .25
169 Maxim Sushinski .30 .75
170 Alexander Popov .10 .25
171 Dmitri Parkhomenko .10 .25
172 Oleg Kryazhev .10 .25
173 Vitali Lyutkevich .10 .25
174 Dmitri Zatonski .10 .25
175 Oleg Ugolnikov .10 .25
176 Alexander Svitov 1.50 4.00
177 Dmitri Ryabkin .10 .25
178 Nikolai Babenko .10 .25
179 Yuri Panov .10 .25
180 Andrei Samokhvalov .10 .25
181 Alexander Ermakov .10 .25
182 Sergei Kagaikin .10 .25
183 Anvar Gatiyatulin .10 .25
184 Vladimir Tarasov .10 .25
185 Igor Varitskin .10 .25
186 Oleg Bolkov .10 .25
187 Rail Muftiev .10 .25
188 Vitali Yeremeev 1.20 3.00
189 Vladislav Brizgalov .30 .75
190 Dmitri Teplyakov .10 .25
191 Vladimir Kopat .10 .25
192 Denis Kuzmenko .10 .25
193 Evgueni Petrochinin .10 .25
194 Sergei Arekaev .10 .25
195 Pavel Agarkov .10 .25
196 Evgueni Pupkov .10 .25
197 Vadim Tarasov .40 1.00
198 Andrei Smirnov .10 .25
199 Alexander Maksimov .10 .25
200 Vitali Valui .10 .25
201 Sergei Petrenko .10 .25
202 Alexei Chistyakov .10 .25
203 Alexei Murzin .10 .25
204 Oleg Komissarov .10 .25
205 Mikhail Buturlin .10 .25
206 Konstantin Frolov .10 .25
207 Igor Zhelenchev .10 .25
208 Oleg Shargorodski .40 1.00
209 Sergei Selyutin .10 .25
210 Alexei Kupreenkov .10 .25
211 Roman Kukhtinov .10 .25
212 Vladislav Morozov .10 .25
213 Igor Belyavski .10 .25
214 Sergei Moskalev .10 .25
215 Alexei Tkachuk .10 .25
216 Sergei Chernyavski .10 .25
217 Vitali Kabanov .10 .25
218 Dmitri Klevakin .10 .25
219 Alexei Koledaev .10 .25
220 Oleg Glebov .10 .25
221 Georgi Evtyukhin .10 .25
222 Alexei Koznev .10 .25
223 Alexei Rubov .10 .25
224 Sergei Zinovjev .80 5.00
225 Evgueni Petrochinin .10 .25
226 Valeri Pokrovski .10 .25
227 Sergei Fedotov .10 .25
228 Vyacheslav Kurochkin .10 .25
229 Oleg Boltunov .10 .25
230 Alexei Baranov .10 .25
231 Igor Emeleev .10 .25
232 Roman Krivomazov .10 .25
233 Sergei Tikhonov .10 .25
234 Vladislav Brizgalov .30 .75
235 Dmitri Dubrovski .10 .25
236 Stepan Mokhov .10 .25
237 Dmitri Gogolev .10 .25
238 Evgueni Filinov .10 .25
239 Alexander Yudin .20 .50
240 Alexander Drozdetskin .10 .25
241 Sergei Shalamai .10 .25
242 Timofei Shishkanov .40 1.00
243 Alexander Sivov .10 .25
244 Vadim Musatov .10 .25
245 Andrei Chernoskutov .10 .25
246 Ruslan Shafikov .10 .25
247 Maxim Sokolov .20 .50
248 Alexander Matvichuk .10 .25
249 Andrei Evstafiev .10 .25
250 Vyacheslav Zavalnyuk .10 .25
251 Andrei Korolev .10 .25
252 Alexander Yudin .20 .50
253 Dmitri Mikhailov .10 .25
254 Artem Ostroushko .10 .25
255 Rinat Khasanov .10 .25
256 Vadim Epanchintsev .30 .75
257 Pavel Komarov .10 .25
258 Alexander Vyukhin .10 .25
259 Alfred Fatkullin .10 .25
260 Danis Zaripov .10 .25
261 Andrei Zubkov .10 .25
262 Marat Askarov .10 .25
263 Alexei Myagkikh .10 .25
264 Alexander Yudin .20 .50
265 Eduard Dmitriev .10 .25
266 Oleg Saltikov .10 .25
267 Oleg Grachev .10 .25
268 Valeri Oleinik .10 .25
269 Konstantin Koltsov .40 1.00
NNO Andrei Raiski .10 .25
NNO I.Koreshkov .20 .50
Alexander Koreshkov
Evgeni Koreshkov

1999-00 Russian Metallurg Magnetogorsk

This team set features Metallurg of the Russian Hockey League. The cards are numbered sequentially to those in the Dynamo Moscow set.

COMPLETE SET 6.00 15.00
27 Sergei Gomolyako .20 .50
28 Vadim Glovatski .20 .50
29 Sergei Tertyshny .20 .50
30 Igor Zemlyanoi .20 .50
31 Valeri Nikulin .20 .50
32 Andrei Sapozhnikov .30 .75
33 Boris Tortunov .20 .50
34 Sergei Zemchenok .20 .50
35 Oleg Mikulchuk .30 .75
36 Andrei Razin .30 .75
37 Ravil Gusmanov .30 .75
38 Maxim Bets .30 .75
39 Andrei Petrakov .20 .50
40 Andrei Kudinov .20 .50
41 Mikhail Borodulin .20 .50
42 Sergei Osipov .20 .50
43 Valeri Karpov .30 .75
44 Evgeni Koreshkov .20 .50
45 Alexander Koreshkov .20 .50
46 Dmitri Popov .20 .50
47 Andrei Sokolov .20 .50
48 Oleg Leontiev .20 .50
49 Vladimir Antipin .20 .50
50 Alexei Stelanov .20 .50
51 Vitali Prokhorov .30 .75
52 Alexander Golts .20 .50
53 Konstantin Shafranov .40 1.00
54 Team Card .20 .50

1999-00 Russian Stars of Hockey

This 42-card set was issued in May of 2000 in conjunction with the Russian Championship tournament. It was created to commemorate stars of past championship tournaments.

COMPLETE SET (42) 12.00 30.00
1 Alexei Chupin .10 .25
2 Alexander Prokopiev .10 .25
3 Alexei Kudashov .10 .25
4 Alexander Khavanov .20 .50
5 Andrei Markov .20 .50
6 Maxim Sushinski .10 .25
7 Dmitri Krasotkin .10 .25
8 Sergei Petrenko .10 .25
9 Valeri Karpov .10 .25
10 Sergei Tertyshny .10 .25
11 Ravil Gusmanov .10 .25
12 Egor Podomatski .20 .50
13 Alexei Chervyakov .10 .25
14 Valeri Ivannikov .10 .25
15 Maxim Mikhailovski .10 .25
16 Alexander Kharitonov .20 .50
17 Denis Arkhipov .30 .75
18 Yuri Dobryshkin .10 .25
19 Alexander Kuvaldin .10 .25
20 Dmitri Vlasenkov .10 .25
21 Evgeny Petrochinin .10 .25
22 Alexei Koznev .10 .25
23 Oleg Shargorodski .10 .25
24 Maxim Bets .10 .25
25 Dmitri Filimonov .10 .25
26 Alexei Yashin .20 .50
27 Pavel Bure 1.00 2.50
28 Sergei Fedorov 1.25 3.00
29 Alexander Mogilny .40 1.00
30 Alexei Kovalev .40 1.00
31 Maxim Sokolov .10 .25
32 Vyacheslav Kozlov .30 .75
33 Alexander Yakushev .40 1.00
34 Valeri Kharlamov 1.00 2.50
35 Alexei Kasatonov .20 .50
36 Vladislav Tretiak 2.00 5.00
37 Vyacheslav Fetisov .75 2.00
38 Valeri Vasiliev .40 1.00
39 Boris Mikhailov .40 1.00
40 Vyacheslav Anisin .10 .25
41 Vladimir Petrov .40 1.00
42 Alexander Maltsev .40 1.00

1999-00 Russian Stars Postcards

These postcards picture Russian stars with their club teams. It's likely that the listing below is not complete. The cards feature only the player's jersey number, so they are listed below in alphabetical order.

COMPLETE SET (32)
1 Maxim Afinogenov .75 2.00
2 Maxim Balmochnykh .40 1.00
3 Maxim Bets .40 1.00
4 Alexander Boikov .40 1.00
5 Victor Chistov .40 1.00
6 Marat Davydov .40 1.00
7 Kirill Golubev .40 1.00
8 Alexei Gorshkov .40 1.00
9 Airat Kadeikin .40 1.00
10 Svyatoslav Khalizov .40 1.00
11 Igor Khatsej .40 1.00
12 Viacheslav Kurochkin .40 1.00
13 Evgeny Kuveko .40 1.00
14 Albert Lecshev .40 1.00
15 Egor Mikhailov .75 2.00
16 Ildar Mukhametov .75 2.00
17 Andrei Pchelyakov .40 1.00
18 Sergey Petrenko .40 1.00
19 Alexander Prokopiev .40 1.00
20 Maxim Rybin .40 1.00
21 Vener Safin .40 1.00
22 Evgeny Shtepa .40 1.00
23 Dmitry Starostenko .40 1.00
24 Maxim Stepanov .40 1.00
25 Andrei Subbotin .40 1.00
26 Vadim Tarasov .75 2.00
27 Alexei Tkachuk .40 1.00
28 Andrei Tsarev .40 1.00
29 Vasily Turkovsky .40 1.00
30 Vladimir Tyurikov .40 1.00
31 Alexander Vyukhin .40 1.00
32 Sergei Yasakov .40 1.00

1999 Russian Fetisov Tribute

This set commemorates a game held in Russia in tribute of Slava Fetisov, perhaps the most important Russian-born player ever. It featured both Russian and NHL stars.

COMPLETE SET (41) 6.00 15.00
1 Alexander Korolyuk .08 .20
2 Pavel Bure .75 2.00
3 Alexei Morozov .08 .20
4 Viktor Kozlov .08 .20
5 Sergei Makarov .20 .50
6 Valeri Kamensky .08 .20
7 Maxim Afinogenov .20 .50
8 Slava Fetisov .20 .50
9 Maxim Sokolov .20 .50
10 Vladimir Malakhov .08 .20
11 Alexei Yashin .08 .20
12 Sergei Vyshedkevich .08 .20
13 Oleg Tverdovsky .08 .20
14 Sergei Brylin .08 .20
15 Vladimir Krutov .20 .50
16 Gennadi Tsygankov .08 .20
17 Egor Podomatski .20 .50
18 Vitali Vishnevski .08 .20
19 Sergei Nemchinov .08 .20
20 Daniil Markov .08 .20
21 Alexander Kharitonov .08 .20
22 Slava Bykov .08 .20
23 Bobby Carpenter .08 .20
24 Scott Stevens .20 .50
25 Ken Daneyko .08 .20
26 Jari Kurri .75 2.00
27 Slava Kozlov .20 .50
28 Anders Eriksson .08 .20
29 Darius Kasparaitis .08 .20
30 Doug Brown .08 .20
31 Ilkka Sinisalo .08 .20
32 Valeri Shiryaev .08 .20
33 Martin Brodeur 2.00 5.00
34 Christian Ruuttu .08 .20
35 Randy McKay .08 .20
36 Gino Odjick .20 .50
37 Igor Larionov .20 .50
38 Martin Lapointe .08 .20
39 Larry Robinson CO .20 .50
40 Viktor Tikhonov CO .08 .20
41 Scotty Bowman CO .20 .50

2000 Russian Champions

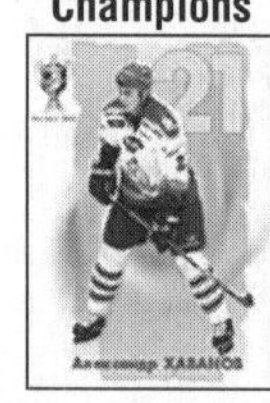

This Russian-produced set features players who have won the big one back in the ol' USSR.

COMPLETE SET (6) 4.00 10.00
1 Alexander Khavanov .80 2.00
2 Alexei Troschinsky .80 2.00
3 Andrei Markov .80 2.00
4 Alexander Kharitonov .80 2.00
5 Alexander Prokopiev .40 1.00
6 Vitali Yeremeyev 1.20 3.00

2000-01 Russian Dynamo Moscow

This set features players from the top Russian club team, Dynamo Moscow. The cards were produced in Russia and apparently were sold at home games. Some sets made their way to North America via the Internet.

COMPLETE SET (33) 6.00 15.00
1 Alexey Yegorov .30 .75
2 Oleg Shevtsov .20 .50
3 Alexander Yeremenko .30 .75
4 Mikhail Shtalenkov .40 1.00
5 Roman Zolotov .20 .50
6 Oleg Orekhovsky .20 .50
7 Igor Stchadilov .20 .50
8 Oleg Polkovnikov .20 .50
9 Ilya Nikulin .30 .75
10 Evgeny Gribko .20 .50
11 Marat Davydov .20 .50
12 Mikhail Donika .20 .50
13 Andrei Kuzmin .20 .50
14 Mikhail Ivanov .20 .50
15 Alexander Kuvaldin .20 .50
16 Sergei Klimovich .20 .50
17 Alexander Kharlamov .30 .75
18 Alexander Savchenkov .20 .50
19 Alexei Smirnov .40 1.00
20 Oleg Smirnov .20 .50
21 Stanislav Romanov .20 .50
22 Alexei Kudashov .30 .75
23 Boris Zelenko .20 .50
24 Alexei Tereshenko .20 .50
25 Alexander Stepanov .20 .50
26 Dmitri Dudarev .20 .50
27 Denis Kartsev .20 .50
28 Dmitri Subbotin .20 .50
29 Igor Bakhmutov .20 .50
30 Alexander Karpovtsev .30 .75
31 Alexander Klebnikov .20 .50
32 Dmitri Semenov .20 .50
33 Dmitriy Kokorev .30 .75

2000-01 Russian Dynamo Moscow Blue-White

Little is known about this Russian-produced set beyond the checklist. Additional information can be forwarded to hockeymag@beckett.com

COMPLETE SET (5) 2.50 6.00
1 Mikhail Shtalenkov 1.25 3.00
2 Alexei Kudashov .75 2.00
3 Oleg Orekhovsky .40 1.00
4 Mikhail Ivanov .40 1.00
5 Dmitri Subbotin .40 1.00

2000-01 Russian Goalkeepers

As the title suggests, this Russian-produced set features top stoppers from the RHL. Any additional information can be forwarded to hockeymag@beckett.com.

COMPLETE SET (9) 5.00 12.00
1 Maxim Sokolov .40 1.00
2 Mikhail Shtalenkov .75 2.00
3 Ilja Bryzgalov 1.50 4.00
4 Andrei Tsareev .40 1.00
5 Oleg Shevtsov .40 1.00
6 Andrei Malkov .40 1.00
7 Sergey Nikolaev .40 1.00
8 Alexei Yegorov .40 1.00
9 Maxim Mikhailovsky .40 1.00

2000-01 Russian Hockey League

This set features the top players in Russia's elite league. The set is noteworthy for including early or first cards of top Russian prospects Ilya Kovalchuk, Stan Chistov, Alexander Svitov, Andrei Medvedev, Pavel Datsyuk, etc. It is worth noting that card #260 is misnumbered at #199.

COMPLETE SET (394) 75.00 175.00
COMMON CARD (1-394) .10 .25
SEMISTARS/GOALIES .20 .50
UNLISTED STARS .30 .75
1 Oleg Filimonov .10 .25
2 Alexei Lazarenko .10 .25
3 Sergei Yasakov .10 .25
4 Steve Plouffe .30 .75
5 Alexander Tichkin .10 .25
6 Igor Boldin .10 .25
7 Vitali Evdokimov .10 .25
8 Igor Andryiotshenko .10 .25
9 Alexander Grishin .10 .25
10 Andrei Kyselev .10 .25
11 Dmitri Tarasov .10 .25
12 Anatoli Ustyugov .10 .25
13 Ruslan Bernikov .10 .25
14 Oleg Naumenko .10 .25
15 Igor Nikolaev .10 .25
16 Renat Khairetdinov .10 .25
17 Vadim Pokotilo .10 .25
18 Vladimir Tyorikov .10 .25
19 Dmitri Uchaikin .10 .25
20 Konstantin Mitroshkin .10 .25
21 Alexei Plotnikov .10 .25
22 Oleg Vevcherenko .10 .25
23 Dmitri Shulakov .10 .25
24 Sergei Butko .10 .25
25 Dmitri Levinski .10 .25
26 Vladimir Gusev .30 .75
27 Denis Martiniuk .10 .25
28 Ross Harris .10 .25
29 Nikolai Pronin .10 .25
30 Sergei Zholotov .10 .25
31 Dmitri Bykov .75 2.00
32 Remir Khaidarov .10 .25
33 Eduard Kudermetov .10 .25
34 Dmitri Yachanov .10 .25
35 Dmitri Balmin .10 .25
36 Alexander Zhdan .30 .75
37 Alexei Chupin .10 .25
38 Almaz Gariffillin .10 .25
39 Alexander Zavyalov .10 .25
40 Ilnur Gizhatullin .10 .25
41 Alexei Tertyshny .10 .25
42 Evgeni Varlamov .10 .25
43 Oleg Glebov .10 .25
44 Sergei Mylnikov Jr. .30 .75
45 Leonid Kanaryekin .10 .25
46 Ildar Yobin .10 .25
47 Anton Volchenkov ERC 2.00 5.00
48 Andrei Loginov .10 .25
49 Vitali Drindeyen .10 .25
50 Pavel Khanarski .10 .25
51 Vladimir Kramskoy .10 .25
52 Oleg Mikulchik .10 .25
53 Vyacheslav Zhavaliuk .10 .25
54 Sergei Soin ERC .75 2.00
55 Andrei Galkin .10 .25
56 Valeri Cherni .10 .25
57 Andrei Posnov .10 .25
58 Alexander Ardashev .10 .25
59 Roman Salnikov .10 .25
60 Eduard Gorbachev .10 .25
61 Sergei Martinov .10 .25
62 Dmitri Perozhkov .10 .25
63 Alexander Frolov ERC 6.00 15.00
64 Vladimir Zhavyalov .10 .25
65 Lev Berdischevski .10 .25
66 Andrei Maximenko .10 .25
67 Dmitri Teplyakov .10 .25
68 Boris Kuzmin .10 .25
69 Nikolai Ruzhenikov .10 .25
70 Maxim Ossipov .20 .50
71 Vladimir Loginov .10 .25
72 Andrei Kuzmin .20 .50
73 Ilya Dokshin .10 .25

Card	Low	High
74 Sergei Yakimovich	.10	.25
75 Oleg Kuzmin	.10	.25
76 Yuri Truvacheev	.10	.25
77 Fedor Tjutin ERC	.10	.25
78 Alexei Tsvetkov	.10	.25
79 Alexander Shenkar	.10	.25
80 Gyori Kabanov	.10	.25
81 Vitali Chumicheev	.10	.25
82 Artem Chernov	.30	.75
83 Dmitri Khramchenko	.20	.50
84 Andrei Sharapov	.10	.25
85 Oleg Antonenko	.10	.25
86 Oleg Namestnikov	.10	.25
87 Andrei Poddyakon	.10	.25
88 Vasili Smirnov	.10	.25
89 Vitali Novopashin	.10	.25
90 Roman Malov	.10	.25
91 Vadim Averkin	.10	.25
92 Nikolai Voevodin	.10	.25
93 Vladimir Fedosov	.10	.25
94 Vasili Chestokletov	.10	.25
95 Anatoli Filatov	.10	.25
96 Igor Safonov	.10	.25
97 Mikhail Belobragin	.10	.25
98 Maxim Ovchinikov	.10	.25
99 Alexei Vorobiev	.10	.25
100 Igor Shevtsov	.10	.25
101 Sergei Fadeyev	.10	.25
102 Dmitri Pankov	.10	.25
103 Sergei Berdnikov	.10	.25
104 Georgi Evtyiokhin	.10	.25
105 Sergei Voronov	.10	.25
106 Alexei Kaliozhni	.10	.25
107 Yuri Kuznetsov	.10	.25
108 Alexander Golts	.20	.50
109 Sergei Klyshin	.10	.25
110 Igor Melyakov	.10	.25
111 Sergei Kiseleev	.10	.25
112 Igor Karpenko	.30	.75
113 Igor Karpenko	.30	.75
114 Sergei Nikolayev	.10	.25
115 Igor Sipchenko	.10	.25
116 Valeri Pokrovski	.10	.25
117 Sergei Gubernatorov	.10	.25
118 Igor Samoylov	.10	.25
119 Alexander Urakin	.10	.25
120 Oleg Eremeyev	.10	.25
121 Paolo Della Bella	.20	.50
122 Slava Bezhukladnikov	.10	.25
123 Alexei Troschinsky	.20	.50
124 Vladimir Antipin	.10	.25
125 Alexander Yudin	.10	.25
126 Vitali Proshkin	.10	.25
127 Ilya Kovalchuk	6.00	15.00
128 Dmitri Ryabikin	.10	.25
129 Alexander Zhurik	.10	.25
130 Igor Shastin	.10	.25
131 Mikhail Shukaev	.10	.25
132 Anvar Gatiyatulin	.10	.25
133 Andrei Anisimov	.10	.25
134 Maxim Solovev	.10	.25
135 Konstantin Bezborodov	.10	.25
136 Ravil Yakubov	.10	.25
137 Alexander Prokopiev	.10	.25
138 Oleg Shargorodsky	.20	.50
139 Ruslan Batyrshin	.20	.50
140 Alexei Kypreyenkov	.10	.25
141 Pavel Komarov	.10	.25
142 Alexei Sharnin	.10	.25
143 Sergei Fedotov	.10	.25
144 Denis Khlistov	.10	.25
145 Mikhail Potapov	.10	.25
146 Alexander Semak	.20	.50
147 Andrei Vasilevski	.30	.75
148 Azhat Sharipov	.10	.25
149 Andrei Sidyakin	.10	.25
150 Sergei Shikhanov	.10	.25
151 Sergei Gomolyako	.10	.25
152 Dmitri Nabokov	.20	.50
153 Valentin Morozov	.10	.25
154 Denis Metliuk	.20	.50
155 Ilja Bryzgalov ERC	2.00	5.00
156 Alexander Lyubimov	.20	.50
157 Ilya Byakin	.20	.50
158 Sergei Tertyshny	.10	.25
159 Valeri Karpov	.20	.50
160 Andrei Tarasenko	.10	.25
161 Alexander Yudin	.20	.50
162 Nikolai Zavarukin	.20	.50
163 Oleg Belkin	.10	.25
164 Andrei Skabelka	.10	.25
165 Leonid Fatikov	.10	.25
166 Oleg Khmylev	.10	.25
167 Denis Afinogenov	.10	.25
168 Alexander Nesterov	.10	.25
169 Andrei Kruchinin	.10	.25
170 Andrei Petrunin	.20	.50
171 Vladimir Malenkikh	.10	.25
172 Sergei Shabanov	.10	.25
173 Vadim Tarasov	.30	.75
174 Igor Zhelenchev	.10	.25
175 Sergei Shalamai	.10	.25
176 Yuri Zhuev	.10	.25
177 Artem Argokov	.10	.25
178 Evgeni Pupkov	.10	.25
179 Sergei Moskaleev	.10	.25
180 Alexander Filippov	.10	.25
181 Igor Dyakiv	.10	.25
182 Stanislav Pinevski	.10	.25
183 Alexander Agnevtshikov	.10	.25
184 Sergei Sherevtsov	.10	.25
185 Roman Kuhtinov	.10	.25
186 Evgeni Lapin	.10	.25
187 Nikolai Kurochkin	.10	.25
188 Alexei Alekeev	.10	.25
189 Alexei Koledaev	.10	.25
190 Sergei Berenikin	.10	.25
191 Denis Tyurin	.10	.25
192 Rail Rozakov	.10	.25
193 Vladimir Pozdnyakov	.10	.25
194 Pavel Desyatkov	.10	.25
195 Alexei Krovopuskov	.10	.25
196 Sergei Sevastyanov	.10	.25
197 Mikhail Yakubov ERC	1.50	4.00
198 Mikhail Sevastyanov	.10	.25
199 Pavel Torgaev	.10	.25
200 Denis Tyulyapkin	.10	.25
201 Dmitri Altareev	.10	.25
202 Maxim Savosin	.10	.25
203 Leonid Toropchenko	.10	.25
204 Stanislav Timakov	.10	.25
205 Valeri Emelyanov	.10	.25
206 Igor Gracheev	.10	.25
207 Stanislav Udyachski	.10	.25
208 Yuris Ozols	.10	.25
209 Alexander Galkin	.10	.25
210 Sergei C. Makarov	.10	.25
211 Sergei Seliutin	.10	.25
212 Alexander Popov	.10	.25
213 Sergei Zhadeleyenov	.10	.25
214 Alexei Litvinenko	.10	.25
215 Dmitri Shulga	.10	.25
216 Denis Sokolov	.10	.25
217 Maxim Krayev	.10	.25
218 Renat Hasanov	.10	.25
219 Boris Tortunov	.10	.25
220 Dmitri Krasotkin	.10	.25
221 Maxim Velikov	.10	.25
222 Yuri Panov	.10	.25
223 Alexander Vyukhin	.10	.25
224 Vadim Shakhraichuk	.10	.25
225 Alexei Badyukov	.10	.25
226 Alexander Korobolin	.10	.25
227 Dmitri Zatonski	.10	.25
228 Kirill Koltsov	.75	2.00
229 Alexander Svitov	1.25	3.00
230 Ilya Gorbushin	.10	.25
231 Andrei Samokhvalov	.10	.25
232 Igor Nikitin	.10	.25
233 Ramil Saifullin	.10	.25
234 Viktor Chistov	.10	.25
235 Vladimir Vorobiev	.10	.25
236 Igor Niklulin	.10	.25
237 Alexander Sidorovski	.10	.25
238 Oleg Polkovnikov	.10	.25
239 Dmitri Dudarev	.10	.25
240 Andrei Sapozhnikov	.10	.25
241 Andrei Kudinov	.10	.25
242 Alik Gareev	.10	.25
243 Ruslan Nurtdinov	.10	.25
244 Alexander Ageev	.10	.25
245 Andrei Yakhanov	.10	.25
246 Vener Safin	.10	.25
247 Sergei Komarov	.10	.25
248 Nail Shayakhmetov	.10	.25
249 Vladislav Ozolin	.10	.25
250 Nikolai Tsuligin	.10	.25
251 Albert Letsvheyev	.10	.25
252 Stanislav Shalnov	.10	.25
253 Maxim Orlov	.10	.25
254 Alexei Chernikov	.10	.25
255 Sergei B. Makarov	.10	.25
256 Sergei Zimakov	.20	.50
257 Gennady Savilov	.10	.25
258 Vasili Turkovski	.10	.25
259 Igor Mikhailov	.10	.25
260 Vadim Glovatskin	.10	.25
261 Alexei Tkachuk	.10	.25
262 Mikhail Volkov	.10	.25
263 Dmitri Gogolev	.10	.25
264 Pavel Agarkov	.10	.25
265 Vladimir Korsunov	.10	.25
266 Andrei Medvedev	1.50	4.00
267 Dmitri Bykov	.75	2.00
268 Ruslan Zainullin	.20	.50
269 Dmitri Starostenko	.10	.25
270 Alexander Schev	.10	.25
271 Andrei Petrakov	.10	.25
272 Sergei Klimentiev	.10	.25
273 Yuri Kuznetsov	.10	.25
274 Igor Knyazev	.60	1.50
275 Vladimir Tikhomirov	.10	.25
276 Vladimir Repneev	.10	.25
277 Alexander Boikov	.10	.25
278 Sergei Voronov	.10	.25
279 Rustem Kamaletdinov	.10	.25
280 Konstantin Molodstov	.10	.25
281 Andrei Frolkin	.10	.25
282 Vladimir Terekhov	.10	.25
283 Dmitri Klevakin	.10	.25
284 Denis Denisov	.20	.50
285 Vladislav Korneev	.20	.50
286 Evgeni Muratov	.20	.50
287 Pavel Duma	.30	.75
288 Egor Shastin	.75	2.00
289 Artem Chernov	.30	.75
290 Rail Rozakov	.30	.75
291 Alexander Chagodaev	.30	.75
292 Alexander Buturlin	.75	2.00
293 Mikhail Yakubov	1.50	4.00
294 Alexei Petrov	.30	.75
295 Pavel Vorobiev ERC	1.50	4.00
296 Ilya Kovalchuk	6.00	15.00
297 Vladimir Tikhomirov	.20	.50
298 Igor Bakhmutov	.20	.50
299 Sergei Zholotov	.20	.50
300 Vadim Tarasov	.30	.75
301 Andrei Medvedev	1.50	4.00
302 Anton Volchenkov ERC	2.00	5.00
303 Denis Grebeshkov ERC	.40	1.00
304 Andrei Shefer	.75	2.00
305 Alexander Seluyanov	.20	.50
306 Ivan Nepryaev	.30	.75
307 Stanislav Chistov ERC	2.00	5.00
308 Alexander Barkunov	.30	.75
309 Alexander Svitov	1.25	3.00
310 Igor Boriskov	.20	.50
311 Alexander Zhdan	.30	.75
312 Ilya Nikulin	.20	.50
313 Mikhail Donika	.20	.50
314 Andrei Kuzmin	.20	.50
315 Alexei Smirnov	.75	2.00
316 Vadim Brezhgunov	.75	2.00
317 Mikhail Shtalenkov	.30	.75
318 Sergei Klimovich	.20	.50
319 Alexander Kharlamov	.20	.50
320 Dmitri Subbotin	.20	.50
321 Alexander Karpovstev	.10	.25
322 Oleg Shevtsov	.10	.25
323 Evgeni Gribko	.10	.25
324 Denis Khlopotnov	.30	.75
325 Pavel Boichenko	.10	.25
326 Alexander Stepanov	.10	.25
327 Nikolai Ignatov	.10	.25
328 Alexander Skoptsov	.10	.25
329 Mikhail Mikhailovski	.10	.25
330 Sergei Semin	.10	.25
331 Pavel Trakhanov	.10	.25
332 Dmitri Riabkin	.10	.25
333 Ravil Yakubov	.10	.25
334 Pavel Datsyuk ERC	15.00	40.00
335 Andrei Evstafiev	.10	.25
336 Andrei Razin	.10	.25
337 Denis Afinogenov	.10	.25
338 Oleg Orekhovsky	.10	.25
339 Ilya Gorbushin	.10	.25
340 Viktor Tchistov	.10	.25
341 Valeri Oleinik	.10	.25
342 Sergei Shumykin	.10	.25
343 Oleg Romashko	.10	.25
344 Yuri Bogusevich	.10	.25
345 Nikolai Koptin	.10	.25
346 Vladislav Pustovalov	.10	.25
347 Andrei Gavrylin	.10	.25
348 Dmitri Chikin	.10	.25
349 Evgeni Letov	.10	.25
350 Vadim Navrotskin	.10	.25
351 Vitali Chumichev	.10	.25
352 Sergei Mozyakin	.10	.25
353 Alexei Simakov	.10	.25
354 Vadim Gusev	.10	.25
355 Sergei Kutyavin	.10	.25
356 Lev Trifonov	.10	.25
357 Roman Oksiuta	.10	.25
358 Alexei Chervyakov	.10	.25
359 Sergei Erkovich	.10	.25
360 Oleg Volkov	.10	.25
361 Sergei Gomolyako	.10	.25
362 Evgeni Bobariko	.10	.25
363 Evgeni Bobariko	.10	.25
364 Igor Boldin	.10	.25
365 Oleg Komissarov	.10	.25
366 Yuri Zlov	.10	.25
367 Andrei Pchelyakov	.10	.25
368 Oleg Boltunov	.10	.25
369 Nikolai Babenko	.10	.25
370 Igor Varitskin	.10	.25
371 Andrei Rasolko	.10	.25
372 Dmitri Denisov	.10	.25
373 Konstantin Maslyukov	.10	.25
374 Vadim Epanchintsev	.20	.50
375 Alexei Krivchenkov	.10	.25
376 Maksim Sokolov	.10	.25
377 Alexei Koznev	.10	.25
378 Evgeni Petrochinin	.10	.25
379 Vladislav Luchkin	.10	.25
380 Artur Oktyabriev	.10	.25
381 Vladimir Kopat	.10	.25
382 Vladimir Kochin	.10	.25
383 Igor Emeleev	.10	.25
384 Sergei Shitkovski	.10	.25
385 Andrei Kozrev	.10	.25
386 Alexander Smagin	.10	.25
387 Rafik Yakubov	.10	.25
388 Ildar Mukhometov	.30	.75
389 Ivan Tkachenko	.10	.25
390 Evgeni Akhmetov	.10	.25
391 Vitali Lyutkevich	.10	.25
392 Alexander Vinogradov	.10	.25
393 Evgeni Artyukhin	.10	.25
394 Andrei Tsareev	.10	.25

2001-02 Russian Dynamo Moscow

This set features the players of Moscow's top team, Dynamo. The cards were sold in set form, apparently at home games.

Card	Low	High
COMPLETE SET (22)	15.00	35.00
1 Oleg Orekhovskiy	.20	.50
2 Alexei Troschinsky	.30	.75
3 Andrey Razin	.20	.50
4 Dmitriy Starostenko	.20	.50
5 Andrey Skopintsev	.20	.50
6 Evgeniy Gribko	.20	.50
7 Alexey Kudashov	.20	.50
8 Evgeniy Lapin	.20	.50
9 Iliy Nikulin	.20	.50
10 Valeriy Karpov	.20	.50
11 Alexander Kuvaldin	.20	.50
12 Ravil Yakubov	.20	.50
13 Alexander Nizivij	.20	.50
14 Dmitriy Semenov	.20	.50
15 Alexander Ovechkin	.20	25.00
16 Marat Davydov	.20	.50
17 Mikhail Shtalenkov	.30	.75
18 Vladimir Korolkov	.20	.50
19 Igor Mirnov	.20	.50
20 Vitaliy Yeremeev	.40	1.00
21 Alexander Savchenkov	.30	.75
22 Sergei Vishedkevich	.30	.75

2001-02 Russian Dynamo Moscow Mentos

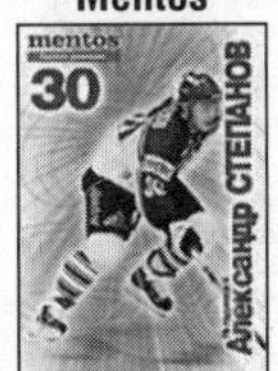

This set also features Dynamo Moscow and is distinguishable from the other set by the prominent placement of the Mentos trademark. Little else is known about this set; additional information can be forwarded to hockeymag@beckett.com.

Card	Low	High
COMPLETE SET (16)	3.00	8.00
1 Sergey Vishedkevich	.20	.50
2 Evgeniy Lapin	.20	.50
3 Alexander Savtchenkov	.20	.50
4 Alexander Stepanov	.20	.50
5 Mikhail Ivanov	.20	.50
6 Mikhail Shtalenkov	.30	.75
7 Dmitriy Starostenko	.20	.50
8 Alexei Troschinsky	.20	.50
9 Ravil Yakubov	.20	.50
10 Oleg Orekhovskiy	.20	.50
11 Andrey Skopintsev	.20	.50
12 Andrey Razin	.20	.50
13 Marat Davydov	.20	.50
14 Iliy Nikulin	.20	.50
15 Alexander Yudin	.20	.50
16 Evgeniy Gribko	.20	.50

2001-02 Russian Hockey League

Card	Low	High
COMPLETE SET (173)	30.00	60.00
1 Dmitri Spirin	.08	.20
2 Alexander Yakovenko	.08	.20
3 Ivan Sakharov	.08	.20
4 Andrei Mukhachev	.08	.20
5 Anatoli Stepanov	.08	.20
6 Nikolai Pronin	.08	.20
7 Igor Boiko	.08	.20
8 Alexander Borovkov	.08	.20
9 Dmitri Sergeev	.08	.20
10 Stepanov Brothers	.08	.20
11 Renat Kharetdinov	.08	.20
12 Alexander Andrievsky	.08	.20
13 Evgeni Bobariko	.08	.20
14 Andrei Galkin	.08	.20
15 Evgeni Gamalei	.08	.20
16 Oleg Grachev	.08	.20
17 Dmitri Yevdokimov	.08	.20
18 Andrei Yershov	.08	.20
19 Sergei Kiselev	.08	.20
20 Maxim Korobov	.08	.20
21 Denis Kuzmenko	.08	.20
22 Denis Makarov	.08	.20
23 Sergei Makarov	.08	.20
24 Oleg Mikulchik	.08	.20
25 Roman Oksiuta	.08	.20
26 Slava Polikarkin	.08	.20
27 Andrei Ponomarev	.08	.20
28 Dmitri Popov	.08	.20
29 Vitali Prokhorov	.08	.20
30 Alexander Romanov	.08	.20
31 Sergei Selyutin	.08	.20
32 Alexander Smirnov	.75	2.00
33 Sergei Sorokin	.08	.20
34 Mikhail Strelkov	.08	.20
35 Stanislav Timakov	.08	.20
36 Dmitri Timofeev	.08	.20
37 Vladimir Fedossov	.08	.20
38 Alexei Chrevyakov	.08	.20
39 Vitali Chinakhov	.08	.20
40 Oleg Yashin	.08	.20
41 Sergei Gomolyako	.08	.20
42 Vasili Chistokletov	.08	.20
43 Alexander Yudin	.08	.20
44 Alexander Yudin	.08	.20
45 Alexander Yudin	.08	.20
46 Artem Anisimov	.08	.20
47 Sergei Shikhanov	.08	.20
48 Evgeni Akhmetov	.08	.20
49 Igor Varitsky	.08	.20
50 Vladimir Antipin	.08	.20
51 Vadim Sharifjanov	.20	.50
52 Rail Muftiev	.08	.20
53 Maxim Bets	.20	.50
54 Viktor Ignatiev	.20	.50
55 Yuri Trubachev	.08	.20
56 Igor Shadilov	.08	.20
57 Sergei Gusev	.08	.20
58 Viktor Chistov	.20	.50
59 Maxim Sokolov	.40	1.00
60 Alexander Semak	.08	.20
61 Ruslan Akhmadullin	.08	.20
62 Igor Volkov	.08	.20
63 Sergei Shalamai	.08	.20
64 Vitali Karamnov	.08	.20
65 Vladislav Ozolin	.08	.20
66 Vladislav Makarov	.08	.20
67 Igor Karpenko	.40	1.00
68 Parris Duffus	.75	2.00
69 Igor Shastin	.08	.20
70 Evgeny Muratov	.08	.20
71 Nikolai Bardin	.08	.20
72 Roman Baranov	.08	.20
73 Artem Chernov	.08	.20
74 Konstantin Mikhailov	.08	.20
75 Dmitri Parkhomenko	.08	.20
76 Igor Mikhailov	.08	.20
77 Vladimir Korsunov	.08	.20
78 Alexei Livinenko	.08	.20
79 Alexander Vyukhin	.20	.50
80 Dmitri Zatonski	.08	.20
81 Kirill Koltsov	.75	2.00
82 Alexander Kharitonov	.08	.20
83 Renat Kharetdinov	.08	.20
84 Alexander Levenyuk	.08	.20
85 Alexei Volkov	.40	1.00
86 Sergei Yasakov	.08	.20
87 Andrei Dylevsky	.08	.20
88 Sergei Kutyavin	.08	.20
89 Sergei Yerkovich	.08	.20
90 Sergei Berdnikov	.08	.20
91 Oleg Shargorodsky	.20	.50
92 Oleg Vevchenko	.08	.20
93 Stanislav Shalnov	.08	.20
94 Alexei Gorshkov	.08	.20
95 Andrei Subbotin	.60	1.50
96 Ramil Saifullin	.08	.20
97 Ilya Gorbushin	.08	.20
98 Alexander Svitov	1.25	3.00
99 Sergei Tertyshny	.08	.20
100 Alexander Popov	.08	.20
101 Alexander Korobolin	.08	.20
102 Denis Zaripov	.08	.20
103 Sergei Klimentiev	.08	.20
104 Dmitri Kirilenko	.08	.20
105 Maxim Rybin	.08	.20
106 Konstantin Gorovikov	.08	.20
107 Denis Khlystov	.08	.20
108 Andrei Tsareev	.20	.50
109 Alexei Chupin	.08	.20
110 unknown		
111 Alexander Drozdetski	.08	.20
112 unknown		
113 Vadim Brezgunov	.08	.20
114 Alexei Podalinski	.08	.20
115 Konstantin Shafronov	.08	.20
116 Alexander Golts	.08	.20
117 Ilya Gorokhov	.08	.20
118 Dmitri Zatonski	.08	.20
119 Vadim Epanchinsev	.08	.20
120 Dmitri Gogolev	.08	.20
121 Alexander Yudin	.08	.20
122 Maxim Sokolov	.40	1.00
123 Boris Tortunov	.20	.50
124 Vladimir Antipov	.08	.20
125 Vladimir Kretchin	.08	.20
126 Sergei Zinovjev	1.25	3.00
127 Andrei Kruchinin	.08	.20
128 Sergei Zhukov	.08	.20
129 Yuri Kuznetsov	.08	.20
130 Anton But	.08	.20
131 Denis Khlopotnov	.20	.50
132 Yuri Kuznetsov	.08	.20
133 Oleg Shvetsov	.20	.50
134 Andrei Loginov	.08	.20
135 Stanislav Udiansky	.08	.20
136 Denis Baev	.08	.20
137 Sergei Semin	.08	.20
138 Maxim Soloviev	.08	.20
139 Dmitri Dubrovsky	.08	.20
140 Vitali Drynin	.08	.20
141 Lev Berdischevski	.08	.20
142 Alexei Sergievsky	.08	.20
143 Evgeni Artyukhin	.08	.20
144 Alexei Kochegarov	.08	.20
145 Evgeny Lapenkov	.08	.20
146 Alexander Borozenko	.08	.20
147 Dmitri Vershinin	.08	.20
148 Yaroslav Lyuzenkov	.08	.20
149 Artem Rybin	.08	.20
150 Alexander Skoptsev	.08	.20
151 Alexei Pogonin	.08	.20
152 Vladislav Poperechny	.08	.20
153 Dmitri Plekhanov	.08	.20
154 Alexei Krovopuskov	.08	.20
155 Alexei Yegorov	.20	.50
156 Oleg Voschenikin	.08	.20
157 Vitali Trigubov	.20	.50
158 Jan Benda	.08	.20
159 Patrik Martinec	.08	.20
160 Dmitri Yachanov	.20	.50
161 Almaz Garifullin	.08	.20
162 Alexei Murzin	.08	.20
163 Vladimir Loginov	.08	.20
164 Khalim Nigmatullin	.08	.20
165 Alexander Dolishnya	.08	.20
166 Igor Fadeev	.08	.20
167 Dmitri Kulikov	.08	.20
168 Andrei Yemelin	.08	.20
169 Oleg Yashin	.08	.20
170 Andrei Zabolotnev	.08	.20
171 Alexander Semak	.08	.20
172 Sergei Askimov	.08	.20
173 Rinat Khasanov	.08	.20

2001-02 Russian Legions

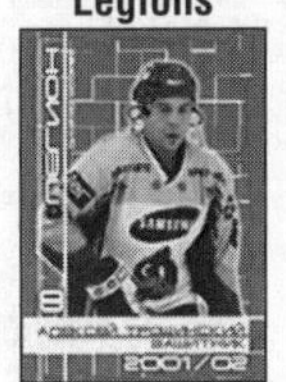

Little is known about this set, which features top Russian players. It is believed that the checklist below is incomplete. Any additional information can be forwarded to hockeymag@beckett.com.

Card	Low	High
COMPLETE SET (3)	.80	2.00
1 Alexei Troschinsky	.40	1.00
2 Dmitriy Starostenko	.40	1.00
3 Vladimir Tsiplakov	.40	1.00

2001-02 Russian Lightnings

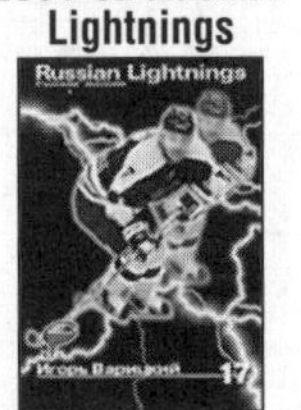

Little is known about this Russian set, which features top players of the RHL. Any additional information can be forwarded to hockeymag@beckett.com.

Card	Low	High
COMPLETE SET (8)	2.00	5.00
1 Maxim Sushinskiy	.40	1.00
2 Igor Varitskiy	.40	1.00
3 Alexey Kudashov	.40	1.00
4 Andrey Razin	.40	1.00
5 Dmitriy Gogolev	.40	1.00
6 Dmitriy Kvartalnov	.40	1.00
7 Denis Metlyuk	.40	1.00
8 Andrei Kovalenko	.40	1.00

2001-02 Russian Ultimate Line

Little is known about this Russian set, which features top goaltenders of the RHL. Any additional information can be forwarded to hockeymag@beckett.com.

Card	Low	High
COMPLETE SET (5)		
1 Vitaliy Yeremeev	.80	2.00
2 Egor Podomatskiy	.80	2.00
3 Mike Fountain	.80	2.00
4 Jaroslav Kamesh	.40	1.00
5 Alexander Yeremenko	.40	1.00

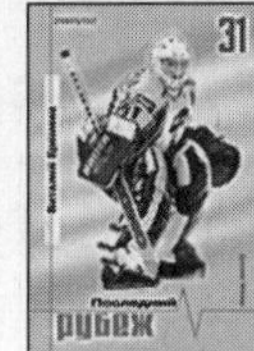

2001-02 Russian Young Lions

Little is known about this Russian set, which features top players of the RHL. Any additional information can be forwarded to hockeymag@beckett.com.

Card	Low	High
COMPLETE SET (11)	10.00	40.00
1 Ilya Kovalchuk	4.00	15.00
2 Alexander Svitov	1.20	2.00
3 Alexander Ovechkin	.40	15.00
4 Igor Grigorenko	1.20	4.00
5 Kirill Koltsov	.80	2.00
6 Anton Babchuk	.80	2.00
7 Alexander Frolov	1.20	3.00
8 Nikolai Zherdev	1.25	3.00
9 Alexander Perezhogin	.40	1.00
10 Ilya Nikulin	.40	1.00
11 Maxim Sheviev	.40	1.00

2002-03 Russian Future Stars

This Russian-produced set features many of that country's top young stars.

Card	Low	High
COMPLETE SET (20)	10.00	25.00
1 Alexander Ovechkin	6.00	15.00
2 Igor Grigorenko	1.25	3.00
3 Vladislav Evseev	.75	2.00
4 Konstantin Glazachev	.40	1.00
5 Fedor Tyutin	.40	1.00
6 Denis Grebeshkov	.40	1.00
7 Alexander Perezhogin	.75	2.00
8 Kiril Koltsov	.40	1.00
9 Yuri Trubachev	.20	.50
10 Andrei Taratukhin	.20	.50
11 Igor Mirnov	.20	.50
12 Dmitri Chernykh	.20	.50
13 Dmitri Shitikov	.20	.50
14 Dmitri Semin	.20	.50
15 Andrei Medvedev	.40	1.00
16 Alexei Volkov	.30	.75
17 Sergei Zinovjev	.75	2.00
18 Sergei Soin	.40	1.00
19 Alexei Mikhnov	.20	.50
20 Ilya Nikulin	.20	.50

2002-03 Russian Hockey League

This set, produced by World Sport, features the top players in the Russian circuit. Many players have multiple cards in the set from a variety of subsets including All-Stars, Team Russia and World Juniors. Card #184 appears twice.

Card	Low	High
COMPLETE SET (273)	75.00	150.00
COMMON CARD (1-273)	.08	.20
SEMISTARS/GOALIES	.20	.50
UNLISTED STARS	.40	1.00
1 Evgeni Krutov	.08	.20
2 Sergei Zhurikov	.08	.20
3 Alexei Medvedev	.08	.20
4 Juri Bogusevich	.08	.20
5 Gleb Klimenko	.08	.20
6 Alexei Petrov	.08	.20
7 Andrei Tsarev	.20	.50
8 Victor Lee	.08	.20
9 Slava Zavalnyuk ENG	.20	.50
10 Slava Zavalnyuk RUS	.20	.50
11 Dmitri Klevakin	.20	.50
12 Dmitri Semin	.08	.20
13 Evgeny Fedorov	.08	.20
14 Evgeny Fedorov	.08	.20
15 Dmitri Yachanov	.20	.50
16 Dmitri Balmin	.08	.20
17 Konstantin Maslyukov	.08	.20
18 Vitali Atyushov	.08	.20
19 Denis Metliuk	.08	.20
20 Andrei Kudinov	.08	.20
21 Anton Babchuk ERC	1.25	3.00
22 Alexei Badyukov	.08	.20
23 Dmitri Gogolev	.08	.20
24 Alexei Chupin	.08	.20
25 Denis Platonov	.08	.20
26 Sergei Zolotov	.08	.20
27 Jan Benda	.08	.20
28 Steve Plouffe	.75	2.00
29 Artem Chernov	.08	.20
30 Dmitri Khomutov	.20	.50
31 Sergei Zvyagin	.20	.50
32 Vladimir Malenjkih	.08	.20
33 Oleg Minakov	.08	.20
34 Stanislav Yasechko	.08	.20
35 Mike Fountain	.75	2.00
36 Oleg Volkov	.08	.20
37 Maxim Mikhailovsky	.20	.50
38 Oleg Belkin	.08	.20
39 Alexander Buturlin	.08	.20
40 Alexander Bobkin	.08	.20
41 Sergei Sevostjanov	.08	.20
42 Andrei Frolkin	.08	.20
43 Alexander Boikov	.08	.20
44 Richard Shekhny	.08	.20
45 Petr Vorobiev CO		.05
46 Andrei Esipov	.08	.20
47 Mikhail Sevostjanov	.08	.20
48 Alexander Semin ERC	6.00	15.00
49 Alexander Yudin	.08	.20
50 Rail Rozakov	.08	.20
51 Sergei Berdnikov	.08	.20
52 Philip Metliuk	.08	.20
53 Vadim Averkin	.08	.20
54 Alexander Gutov	.08	.20
55 Ilya Gorokov	.20	.50
56 Maxim Kondratiev	.20	.50
57 Alexander Nesterov	.08	.20
58 Igor Grigorenko ERC	5.00	12.00
59 Vladislav Boulin	.08	.20
60 Artur Oktyabrev	.08	.20
61 Ladislav Chierny	.08	.20
62 Alexander Yudin	.08	.20
63 Alex Westlund	.75	2.00
64 Alexander Fomitchev	.40	1.00
65 David MacIsaac	.20	.50
66 Andrei Tsarev	.20	.50
67 Maxim Spiridonov	.08	.20
68 Vadim Pokotilo	.08	.20
69 Konstantin Chaschukhin	.20	.50
70 Evgeni Safronov	.08	.20
71 Albert Vishnyakov	.08	.20
72 Christian Bronsard	.75	2.00
73 Alexei Mikhnov	.20	.50
74 Askhat Rakhmatullin	.08	.20
75 Andrei Tarasenko	.08	.20
76 Alexei Korshkov	.08	.20
77 Leo Chermak	.08	.20
78 Kirill Sidorenko	.08	.20
79 Sergei Gomolyako	.08	.20
80 Ildar Mukhometov	.20	.50
81 Dmitri Dudarev	.08	.20
82 Artem Ternavsky	.08	.20
83 Igor Kamaev	.08	.20
84 Sergei Rozin	.08	.20
85 Roman Gorev	.08	.20
86 Dmitri Kokorev	.08	.20
87 Martin Tomasek	.08	.20
88 Roman Popov	.08	.20
89 Vladimir Antipin	.08	.20
90 Vadim Tarasov	.20	.50
91 Sergei Mikhailev CO		.05
92 Nikolai Zherdev ERC	6.00	15.00
93 Andrei Mukhachev	.08	.20
94 Ilya Byakin	.08	.20
95 Miroslav Guren	.08	.20
96 Nikolai Pronin	.08	.20
97 Sergei Mozyakin	.08	.20
98 Maxim Ossipov	.08	.20
99 Alexei Kolkunov	.08	.20
100 Albert Leschev	.08	.20
101 Alexander Polushin ERC	2.00	5.00
102 Igor Emeleev	.08	.20
103 Sergei Luchinkin	.08	.20
104 Rail Muftiev	.08	.20
105 Nikolai Semin	.08	.20
106 Sergei Anshakov	.20	.50
107 Vadim Khomitsky	.08	.20
108 Pavel Trakhanov	.08	.20
109 Yan Golubovsky	.20	.50
110 Dusan Salficky	.40	1.00
111 Dmitri Kosmachev	.08	.20
112 Vladimir Kramskoy	.08	.20
113 Alexander Drozdetsky	.08	.20
114 Alexei Shotkov	.08	.20
115 Maxim Velikov	.08	.20
116 Evgeni Akhmetov	.08	.20
117 Vladimir Gorbunov	.08	.20
118 Pavel Patera	.08	.20
119 Maxim Sokolov	.40	1.00
120 Martin Prochazka	.08	.20
121 Tomas Vlasak	.08	.20
122 Alexander Perezhogin	.75	2.00
123 Dmitri Zatonsky	.08	.20
124 Andrei Subbotin	.40	1.00
125 Ravil Yakubov	.08	.20
126 Valeri Pokrovsky	.08	.20
127 Kirill Koltsov	1.25	3.00
128 Ramil Saifullin	.08	.20
129 Maxim Sokolov	.40	1.00
130 Igor Varitsky	.08	.20
131 Maxim Balmochnykh	.20	.50
132 Marcel Cousineau	.75	2.00
133 Yuri Kuznetsov	.08	.20
134 Ruslan Nurtdinov	.08	.20
135 Andrei Sidyakin	.08	.20
136 Sergei Zvyagin	.20	.50
137 Patrik Guchko	.08	.20
138 Andrei Yakhanov	.08	.20
139 Evgeni Muratov	.08	.20
140 Alexei Simakov	.08	.20
141 Roman Baranov	.08	.20
142 Alexander Zavyalov	.08	.20
143 Evgeni Varlamov	.08	.20
144 Alexei Tertyshny	.08	.20
145 Danis Zaripov	.08	.20
146 Vasili Turkovsky	.08	.20
147 Alexander Guskov	.08	.20
148 Alexander Zhurik	.08	.20
149 Yuri Kuznetsov	.08	.20
150 Maxim Balmochnykh	.20	.50
151 Marat Davydov	.08	.20
152 Alexei Koznev	.08	.20
153 Valeri Karpov	.08	.20
154 Oleg Shargorodsky	.20	.50
155 Sergei Gomolyako	.08	.20
156 Vladimir Tikhomirov	.20	.50
157 Alexei Yegorov	.20	.50
158 Konstantin Simchuk	.20	.50
159 Sergei Shalamai	.20	.50
160 Alexei Danilov	.08	.20
161 Vadim Epanchintsev	.08	.20
162 Vasily Tikhonov ACO		.05

163 Viktor Tikhonov CO .08 .20
164 Andrei Sapozhnikov .08 .20
165 Yuri Dobryshkin .08 .20
166 Vasili Turkovsky .08 .20
167 Evgeni Petrochinin .08 .20
168 Sergei Gimaev .08 .20
169 Alexander Yudin .08 .20
170 Alexander Shinin .08 .20
171 Yuri Trubachev .08 .20
172 Evgeny Isakov .08 .20
173 Andrei Nikitenko .08 .20
174 Alexander Shinkar .08 .20
175 Viktor Chistov .20 .50
176 Andrei Shefer .20 .50
177 Igor Shadilov .08 .20
178 Martin Brochu .75 2.00
179 Alexei Kalyuzhny .08 .20
180 Alexander Shinin .08 .20
181 Maxim Balmochnykh .20 .50
182 Vladimir Antipov .08 .20
183 Boris Tortunov .08 .20
184 Vadim Epanchintsev .08 .20
184B Yuri Trubachev .08 .20
185 Fedor Tjutin 1.25 3.00
186 Sergei Anshakov .20 .50
187 Timofei Shishkanov 2.00 5.00
188 Igor Grigorenko ERC 6.00 15.00
189 Maxim Kondratiev ERC .20 .50
190 Kirill Koltsov .75 2.00
191 Evgeny Artyukhin .08 .20
192 Konstantin Barulin ERC .40 1.00
193 Andrei Taratukhin .08 .20
194 Dmitri Fakhrutdinov .08 .20
195 Dmitri Pestunov .08 .20
196 Andrei Medvedev .75 2.00
197 Nikolai Zherdev ERC 6.00 15.00
198 Alexander Ovechkin ERC 25.00 60.00
199 Alexander Polushin ERC 2.00 5.00
200 Alexei Kaigorodov .08 .20
201 Alexander Perezhogin ERC .75 2.00
202 Mikhail Lyubushin .08 .20
203 Konstantin Korneev .20 .50
204 Denis Grebeshkov 1.25 3.00
205 Konstantin Gorovikov .08 .20
206 Vitali Proshkin .20 .50
207 Alexander Suglobov ERC .40 1.00
208 Alexei Chupin .08 .20
209 Sergei Soin .20 .50
210 Andrei Subbotin .40 1.00
211 Dmitri Vlasenkov .08 .20
212 Sergei Gusev .08 .20
213 Vladimir Vujtek .08 .20
214 Vasily Turkovsky .08 .20
215 Igor Shadilov .08 .20
216 Yuri Dobryshin .08 .20
217 Igor Podomatski .40 1.00
218 Alexander Semak .08 .20
219 Ilya Byakin .08 .20
220 Alexander Guskov .08 .20
221 Alexander Guskov .08 .20
222 Nikolai Zavarukhin .08 .20
223 Andrei Petrunin .08 .20
224 Konstantin Gorovikov .08 .20
225 Alexei Gorshkov .08 .20
226 Rustem Kamaletdinov .08 .20
227 Alexander Zavakhin .08 .20
228 Vladislav Ozolin .08 .20
229 Dmitri Krasotkin .08 .20
230 Sergei Nemchinov .20 .50
231 Alexei Chupin .08 .20
232 Andrei Kovalenko .08 .20
233 Sergei Gomolyako .08 .20
234 Vitali Yeremeyev .40 1.00
235 Sergei Zholotov .08 .20
236 Dmitri Kirilenko .08 .20
237 Sergei Askimov .08 .20
238 Ruslan Berdnikov .08 .20
239 Yuri Butsayev .08 .20
240 Sergei Zinovjev 2.00 5.00
241 Radim Tesarik .08 .20
242 Dmitri Zatonsky .08 .20
243 Konstantin Baranov .08 .20
244 Vladimir Popov CO .05
245 Sergei Piskunov .08 .20
246 Vladimir Antipin .08 .20
247 Alexander Drozdetsky .08 .20
248 Sergei Vyshedkevich .20 .50
249 Timofei Shishkanov 2.00 5.00
250 Alexander Kharitonov .08 .20
251 Dmitri Fakhrutdinov .08 .20
252 Vladimir Tsyplakov .08 .20
253 Evgeni Namestnikov .20 .50
254 Vitali Atyushov .08 .20
255 Dmitri Erofeev .08 .20
256 Sergei Korolev .08 .20
257 Dmitri Erofeev .08 .20
258 Vladislav Gushin .08 .20
259 Vadim Glovatskin .08 .20
260 Renat Khasanov .08 .20
261 Nikolai Zherdev ERC 6.00 15.00
262 Dmitri Zatonsky .08 .20
263 Yan Peterik .08 .20
264 Alexei Petrov .08 .20
265 Lev Trifonov .08 .20
266 Almaz Garifullin .08 .20
267 Mikhail Sarmatin .08 .20
268 Rail Rozakov .08 .20
269 Patrick Labrecque .75 2.00
270 Oleg Khmyl .08 .20
271 Alexander Blokhin .08 .20
272 Leonid Labzov .08 .20

2002-03 Russian Lightnings

COMPLETE SET (3) 6.00 15.00
1 Alexander Ovechkin 6.00 15.00
2 Alexander Polushin .75 2.00
3 Alexander Stepanov .20 .50

2002-03 Russian SL

Little is known about the background of this set. If you have any information, please forward it to hockeymag@beckett.com.

COMPLETE SET (52) 20.00 40.00
1 Andrei Razin .20 .50
2 Dusan Salficky .40 1.00
3 Alexander Polushin .75 2.00
4 Alexander Guskov .20 .50
5 Vladimir Vujtek CO .02 .10

6 Evgeni Varlamov .20 .50
7 Andrei Skopintsev .20 .50
8 Vladimir Plyustchev CO .02 .10
9 Valeri Karpov .20 .50
10 Igor Mirnov .20 .50
11 Egor Podomatskiy .30 .75
12 Mike Fountain .30 .75
13 Mikhail Donika .20 .50
14 Vyacheslav Butsaev .20 .50
15 Andrei Esipov .20 .50
16 Igor Grigorenko 1.25 3.00
17 Yuri Moiseev CO .02 .10
18 Alexander Zhdan .20 .50
19 Maxim Sokolov .20 .50
20 Alexander Selivanov .20 .50
21 Mikhail Ivanov .20 .50
22 Ivan Hlinka CO .08 .25
23 Andrei Tsareev .20 .50
24 Dmitri Ryabykin .20 .50
25 Jiri Slegr .20 .50
26 Sergei Soin .30 .75
27 Anton But .20 .50
28 Alexander Ovechkin 10.00 25.00
29 Vladimir Antipov .20 .50
30 Evgeni Makarov .20 .50
31 Sergei Naumov .20 .50
32 Andrei Pyatanov CO .02 .10
33 Sergei Gusev .20 .50
34 Viktor Tikhonov CO .02 .10
35 Mikhail Lyubushin .20 .50
36 Dmitri Yachanov .20 .50
37 Tomas Vlasak .20 .50
38 Alex Westlund .40 1.00
39 Vladislav Boulin .20 .50
40 Jan Peterek .20 .50
41 Vladimir Vorobiev .20 .50
42 Petr Vorobiev CO .02 .10
43 Vasily Turkovski .20 .50
44 Nikolai Zherdev 1.50 4.00
45 Andrei Taratukhin .20 .50
46 Viktor Aleksandrov .20 .50
47 Yuri Dobryshkin .20 .50
48 Alexander Savchenkov .20 .50
49 Sergei Voronov .20 .50
50 Alexei Terestchenko .20 .50
51 Alexei Shkotov .20 .50
52 Alexander Zevakhin .20 .50

2002-03 Russian Transfert

COMPLETE SET (31) 6.00 15.00
1 Alexander Semin .40 1.00
2 Alexander Golts .20 .50
3 Georgi Evtyukhin .20 .50
4 Alexander Korolyuk .20 .50
5 Marcel Cousineau .30 .75
6 Sergei Bautin .20 .50
7 Vitali Lutkevich .20 .50
8 Valeri Zelepukin .20 .50
9 Nikolai Zherdev 1.25 3.00
10 Vladimir Vorobiev .20 .50
11 Sergei Petrenko .20 .50
12 Osmo Soutukorva .20 .50
13 Sergei Korolev .20 .50
14 Alex Westlund .20 .50
15 Denis Afinogenov .20 .50
16 Vadim Tarasov .40 1.00
17 Alexander Zhdan .20 .50
18 Alexander Selivanov .20 .50
19 Vladislav Boulin .20 .50
20 Maxim Sokolov .20 .50
21 Dmitri Gogolev .20 .50
22 Alexei Volkov .30 .75
23 Ravil Yakubov .20 .50
24 Mikhail Ivanov .20 .50
25 Alexei Egorov .20 .50
26 Viktor Gordiyuk .20 .50
27 Alexander Semak .20 .50
28 Bruce Gardiner .20 .50
29 Rodrigo Lavins .20 .50
30 Steve Plouffe .30 .75
31 Sergei Krivokrasov .20 .50

2002-03 Russian Transfert Promos

COMPLETE SET (6) 2.00 5.00
1 Vladimir Vorobiev .40 1.00
2 Osmo Soutukorvo .40 1.00
3 Vitali Lutkevich .40 1.00
4 Denis Afinogenov .40 1.00
5 Alexei Volkov .75 2.00
6 Maxim Sokolov .75 2.00

2002-03 Russian Ultimate Line

COMPLETE SET (13) 6.00 15.00
1 Sergei Zvyagin .40 1.00
2 Dusan Salficky .75 2.00
3 Alexander Yeremenko .40 1.00
4 Sergei Nikolaev .40 1.00
5 Mike Fountain 1.25 3.00
6 Steve Plouffe 1.25 3.00
7 Igor Karpenko .75 2.00
8 Oleg Glebov .40 1.00
9 Patrick Labrecque 1.25 3.00
10 Alexei Volkov .75 2.00
11 Vadim Tarasov .75 2.00
12 Andrei Medvedev .75 2.00
13 Vitali Yeremeyev .75 2.00

2002-03 Russian Young Lions

COMPLETE SET (17) 10.00 25.00
1 Dmitri Kazionov .20 .50
2 Alexander Ovechkin 6.00 15.00
3 Igor Mirnov .20 .50
4 Alexander Semin .40 1.00
5 Igor Grigorenko 1.25 3.00
6 Sergei Soin .30 .75
7 Denis Grebeshkov .40 1.00
8 Alexei Kaigorodov .20 .50
9 Dmitry Pestunov .20 .50
10 Alexander Polushin .75 2.00
11 Konstantin Mikhailov .20 .50
12 Iliy Nikulin .20 .50
13 Alexander Perezhogin .75 2.00
14 Alexei Mikhnov .20 .50
15 Nikolai Zherdev 1.25 3.00
16 Fedor Tyutin .40 1.00
NNO Alexander Ovechkin PROMO 6.00 15.00

2002 Russian Olympic Faces

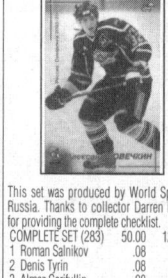

This set was released in Russia to celebrate key players on the Russian Olympic club. It is believed that the list below is incomplete. Please forward additional information to hockeymag@beckett.com.

COMPLETE SET (4) 2.76 6.89
1 Nikolai Khabibulin .80 2.00
2 Nikolai Khabibulin .80 2.00
3 Sergei Fedorov 1.20 2.50
4 Sergei Fedorov 1.20 2.50

2002 Russian Olympic Team

This set was released in Russia to celebrate members of its Olympic Team. It is believed that the listing below could be incomplete. Please forward information of additional cards to hockeymag@beckett.com.

COMPLETE SET (9) 6.00 15.00
1 Sergei Samsonov .80 2.00
2 Sergei Fedorov 1.25 3.00
3 Pavel Bure 1.00 2.50
4 Ilya Kovalchuk 3.00 8.00
5 Valeri Bure .20 .50
6 Alexei Kovalev .20 .50
7 Nikolai Khabibulin .80 2.00
8 Maxim Afinogenov .75 2.00
9 Darius Kasparaitis .10 .25

2002 Russian World Championships

This Russian-produced set honors members of that country's World Championship team.

COMPLETE SET (20) 3.00 8.00
1 Egor Podomatski .40 1.00
2 Alexander Yudin .20 .50
3 Maxim Sushinski .20 .50
4 Maxim Sokolov .40 1.00
5 Ivan Tkachenko .20 .50
6 Vladimir Antipov .20 .50
7 Roman Lyashenko .30 .75
8 Maxim Afinogenov .75 2.00
9 Alexander Guskov .20 .50
10 Alexei Koznev .20 .50
11 Sergei Gusev .20 .50
12 Slava Butsayev .20 .50
13 Ravil Gusmanov .20 .50
14 Dmitri Kalinin .20 .50
15 Valeri Karpov .20 .50
16 Andrei Kovalenko .20 .50
17 Alexander Prokopiev .20 .50
18 Sergei Vyshedkevich .20 .50
19 Dmitri Zatonsky .20 .50
20 Sergei Zhukov .20 .50

2003-04 Russian Avangard Omsk

This 28-card set honours the 2002-03 champions of the Russian league. It was produced by World Sport.

COMPLETE SET (28) 4.00 10.00
1 Maxim Sokolov .20 .50
2 Konstantin Baranov .10 .25
3 Maxim Sushinski .10 .25
4 Dmitri Zatonsky .10 .25
5 Tomas Vlasak .10 .25
6 Oleg Tverdovsky .10 .25
7 Sergei Krivokrasov .10 .25
8 Stanislav Shalnov .10 .25
9 Dmitri Subbotin .10 .25
10 Dmitri Ryabikin .10 .25
11 Valeri Belousov CO .02 .10
12 Igor Nikitin .10 .25
13 Pavel Patera .10 .25
14 Alexander Popov .10 .25
15 Ramil Saifullin .10 .25
16 Yuri Yermolin .10 .25
17 Alexander Golovin .10 .25
18 Alexander Prokopiev .10 .25
19 Evgeni Khatsei .10 .25
20 Oleg Grachev .10 .25
21 Jaroslav Bednar .20 .50
22 Oleg Orekhovsky .10 .25
23 Yuri Panov .10 .25
24 Anton Kuzmin .10 .25
25 Vladimir Antipin .10 .25
26 Vitali Semenchenko .20 .50
27 Anatoli Bardin GM .02 .10
28 Checklist .02 .10

2003-04 Russian Hockey League

This set was produced by World Sport in Russia. Thanks to collector Darren Morris for providing the complete checklist.

COMPLETE SET (283) 50.00 125.00
1 Roman Salnikov .08 .20
2 Denis Tyrin .08 .20
3 Almaz Garifullin .08 .20
4 Sergei Shalamai .08 .20
5 Andrei Evstafiev .08 .20
6 Nikolai Zherdev 2.00 5.00
7 Mikhail Sarmatin .08 .20
8 Dusan Salficky .40 1.00
9 Sergei Mozyakin .08 .20
10 Andrei Razin .08 .20
11 Yuri Butsayev .08 .20
12 Oleg Romashko .20 .50
13 Evgeny Fedorov .08 .20
14 Danis Zaripov .08 .20
15 Gennady Razin .08 .20
16 Oleg Filimonov .20 .50
17 Dmitri Tarasov .08 .20
18 Vitali Shulakov .08 .20
19 Oleg Minakov .08 .20
20 Jan Benda .08 .20
21 Alexander Zevakhin .08 .20
22 Alexander Yudin .08 .20
23 Alexander Yudin .08 .20
24 SKA St. Pete's .02 .05
25 Dynamo Moscow .02 .05
26 Vitali Yeremeev .20 .50
27 Alexei Volkov .20 .50
28 Alexander Yeremenko .20 .50
29 Mikhail Lyubishin .08 .20
30 Ilya Nikulin .08 .20
31 Alexei Troschinsky .08 .20
32 Igor Mirnov .08 .20
33 Alexander Kuvaldin .08 .20
34 Igor Schyadilov .08 .20
35 Andrei Skopintsev .08 .20
36 Alexander Kharitonov .08 .20
37 Alexei Chupin .08 .20
38 Vadim Shakhrajchuk .08 .20
39 Alexander Savchenkov .08 .20
40 Vladislav Boulin .08 .20
41 Alexei Kudashov .08 .20
42 Alexander Zhdan .08 .20
43 Alexei Tereschenko .08 .20
44 Alexander Stepanov .08 .20
45 Alexander Ovechkin 10.00 25.00
46 Sergei Vyshedkevich .20 .50
47 Miroslav Hlinka .08 .20
48 Dmitri Starostenko .08 .20
49 Alexander Stepanov .08 .20
50 Alexander Ovechkin 10.00 25.00
51 Tomas Garant .20 .50
52 Vladimir Vorobiev .08 .20
53 Yuri Babenko .08 .20
54 Ruslan Zainullin .20 .50
55 Robert Kantor .08 .20
56 Denis Kartsev .08 .20
57 Vladislav Evseev .40 1.00
58 Zinatula Bilyaletdinov CO .08 .20
59 Alexei Yegorov .20 .50
60 Sergei Naumov .40 1.00
61 Sergei Semin .08 .20
62 Valeri Pokrovski .08 .20
63 Torbjorn Johansson .08 .20
64 Artem Ostroushko .08 .20
65 Andrei Spiridonov .08 .20
66 Marat Davydov .08 .20
67 Nikolai Syrtsov .08 .20
68 Vyacheslav Zavalnyuk .08 .20
69 Andrei Kozyrev .08 .20
70 Yan Golubovsky .20 .50
71 Jan Lasak .75 2.00
72 Konstantin Kasjyanchuk .08 .20
73 Egor Bashkatov .08 .20
74 Andrei Potaichuk .08 .20
75 Egor Mikhailov .08 .20
76 Andrei Galushkin .08 .20
77 Mike Watt .20 .50
78 Alexei Akifjev .08 .20
79 Andrei Pchelyakov .08 .20
80 Evgeni Tunik .08 .20
81 Pavel Boichenko .08 .20
82 Valeri Zelepukin .08 .20
83 Oleg Boltunov .08 .20
84 Alexei Tsvetkov .08 .20
85 Boris Mikhailov CO .20 .50
86 Eduard Kudermetov .08 .20
87 Sergei Berdnikov .08 .20
88 Vladimir Antipin .08 .20
89 Oleg Tverdovsky .08 .20
90 Denis Khlopotnov .08 .20
91 Fedor Tjutin .40 1.00
92 Andrei Shurupov .08 .20
93 Evgeny Koronov .08 .20
94 Albert Leschev .08 .20
95 Sergei Yerkovich .08 .20
96 Vladimir Tyurikov .08 .20
97 Dmitri Vershinin .08 .20
98 Alexei Krutov .08 .20
99 German Titov .08 .20
100 Igor Nikolaev .08 .20
101 Maxim Shevyev .08 .20
102 Andrei Ershov .08 .20
103 Ilya Krikunov .08 .20
104 Peter Skudra .40 1.00
105 Andrei Galkin .08 .20
106 Andei Dylevski .08 .20
107 Ondrej Steiner .08 .20
108 Vadim Brezgunov .08 .20
109 Roman Oksiuta .08 .20
110 Oleg Belkin .08 .20
111 Alexander Boikov .08 .20
112 Dmitri Kazionov .08 .20
113 Vladimir Malenkikh .08 .20
114 Ruslan Bernikov .08 .20
115 Alexander Buturlin .08 .20
116 Andrei Esipov .08 .20
117 Maxim Semenov .08 .20
118 Yakov Rachinsky .08 .20
119 Mikhail Balandin .08 .20
120 Dmitri Vorobiev .08 .20
121 J.F. Labbe .40 1.00
122 Rinat Khasanov .08 .20
123 Vladimir Loginov .08 .20
124 Alexei Deev .08 .20
125 Alexander Grishin .08 .20
126 Sergei Gomolyako .08 .20
127 Anatoli Filatov .08 .20
128 Vasili Koshechkin .20 .50
129 Alexander Seluyanov .08 .20
130 Ladislav Cherny .08 .20
131 Igor Varitski .08 .20
132 Maxim Yakutsenya .08 .20
133 Alexander Gutov .08 .20
134 Stanislav Zhmakin .08 .20
135 Mikhail Sevostjanov .08 .20
136 Alexander Skugarev .08 .20
137 Sergei Sevostjanov .08 .20
138 Petr Vorobiev CO .02 .05
139 Yevgeni Safronov .08 .20
140 Ilya Vorobiev .08 .20
141 Alexander Titov .08 .20
142 Ruslan Nurtdinov .08 .20
143 Alexander Zavjalov .08 .20
144 Vadim Epanchinsev .08 .20
145 Jamie Ram .75 2.00
146 Viktor Chistov CO .02 .05
147 Tomas Hlubna .08 .20
148 Alexander Semak .08 .20
149 Sergei Gimaev .08 .20
150 Nikolai Makarov CO .02 .05
151 Atvars Tribuntsovs .08 .20
152 Vladislav Ozolin .08 .20
153 Nikolai Semin .08 .20
154 Vitali Proshkin .08 .20
155 Vassiliy Turkovsky .08 .20
156 Denis Platonov .08 .20
157 Radek Duda .08 .20
158 Sergei Korolev .08 .20
159 Konstantin Korneev .20 .50
160 Sergei Arakaev .08 .20
161 Denis Denisov .08 .20
162 Alexander Drozdetsky .08 .20
163 Alexander Cherbayev .08 .20
164 Maxim Mikhailovsky .20 .50
165 Mikhail Tyulyapkin .08 .20
166 Valeri Kamensky .08 .20
167 Vladimir Vujtek .08 .20
168 Konstantin Glazachev .20 .50
169 Konstantin Mikhailov .08 .20
170 Egor Shastin .08 .20
171 Alexei Mikhnov .40 1.00
172 Alexander Fomitchev .30 .75
173 Daniel Branda .08 .20
174 Eric Charron .08 .20
175 Miroslav Guren .08 .20
176 Ravil Yakubov .08 .20
177 Dmitri Dudarev .08 .20
178 Ruslan Batyrshin .08 .20
179 Ruslan Shafikov .08 .20
180 Martin Cech .08 .20
181 Tero Lehtera .08 .20
182 Egor Mikhailov .08 .20
183 Valeri Pokrovsky .08 .20
184 Vadim Sharifjanov .20 .50
185 David Pospisil .08 .20
186 Yan Golubovsky .08 .20
187 Angel Nikolov .20 .50
188 Viktor Alexandrov .20 .50
189 Dmitri Pankov .08 .20
190 Jiri Marushak .08 .20
191 Oleg Gross CO .02 .05
192 Sergei Moskalev .08 .20
193 Alexei Medvedev .08 .20
194 Vadim Tarasov .30 .75
195 Evgeny Shtaiger .08 .20
196 Nikolai Soloviev CO .02 .05
197 Evgeny Lapin .08 .20
198 Mikhail Chernov .08 .20
199 Zdenek Skorepa .08 .20
200 Sergei Mikhailev CO .02 .05
201 Sergei Naumov .40 1.00
202 Evgeny Korolev .08 .20
203 Rail Rozakov .08 .20
204 Yuri Kuznetsov .20 .50
205 Sergei Berdnikov .08 .20
206 Yuri Kuznetsov .20 .50
207 Andrei Sapozhnikov .08 .20
208 Andrei Nikitenko .08 .20
209 Andrei Petrunin .08 .20
210 Yuri Dobryshkin .08 .20
211 Sergei Gimaev .08 .20
212 Alexander Astashev CO .02 .05
213 Vadim Khomitsky .08 .20
214 Maxim Yakutsenya .08 .20
215 Martin Richter .08 .20
216 Sergei Anshakov .20 .50
217 Denis Parshin .20 .50
218 Sergei Berezin .08 .20
219 Jan Hejda .08 .20
220 Dmitri Levinsky .08 .20
221 Norm Maracle .75 2.00
222 Pavel Patera .08 .20
223 Tomas Vlasak .08 .20
224 Jaroslav Bednar .20 .50
225 Konstantin Baranov .08 .20
226 Maxim Sokolov .30 .75
227 Dennis Kuzmenko .20 .50
228 Oleg Burlitsky .08 .20
229 Alexei Potemkin .08 .20
230 Alexander Zhukov .08 .20
231 Ilnaz Zagitov .08 .20
232 Dmitri Yushkevich .08 .20
233 Martin Hlavacka .08 .20
234 Alexander Guskov .08 .20
235 Robert Kantor .08 .20
236 Marat Vailullin .08 .20
237 Zdenek Orct .20 .50
238 David Nemirovsky .20 .50
239 Jiri Hudler 2.00 5.00
240 Maxim Krivonozhkin .08 .20
241 Yuri Butsayev .20 .50
242 Andrei Esipov .08 .20
243 Rudolf Guna .08 .20
244 Philip Metliuk .08 .20
245 Alexander Lyubimov .08 .20
246 Jiri Trvaj .20 .50
247 Dmitri Cherhukh .08 .20
248 Renat Khairetdinov .08 .20
249 Artem Vostrikov .08 .20
250 Peter Skudra .40 1.00
251 Evgeny Malkin 15.00 40.00
252 Nikolai Tsulygin .08 .20
253 Andrei Kostitsyn 4.00 10.00
254 Denis Belsky .08 .20
255 Andrei Davletov .08 .20
256 Sergei Konkov .08 .20
257 Denis Loginov .08 .20
258 Michael Martin .08 .20
259 David Moravec .08 .20
260 Yan Peterik .08 .20
261 Lubomir Sekeras .08 .20
262 Toivo Suursoo .08 .20
263 Marat Salimov .08 .20
264 Sergei Fadeev .08 .20
265 Mikhail Shukaev .08 .20
266 Dmitri Yachanov .20 .50
267 Lukas Zib .08 .20
268 Butsayev Brothers .08 .20
269 Sergei Sevostjanov .08 .20
270 Mikhail Sevostjanov .08 .20
271 Ruslan Nurtdinov .08 .20
272 Frank Banham .20 .50
273 Herbert Vasiliev .08 .20
274 Dave Karpa .20 .50
275 Kirill Lyamin .08 .20
276 Mikhail Chernov .08 .20
277 Ildar Mukhometov .20 .50
278 Ilya Zubov .08 .20
279 Sergei Shinkar .08 .20
280 Sergei Voronov .08 .20
281 Sergei Borisov .20 .50
282 Yuri Trubachev .08 .20
283 Sergei Bernatsky .08 .20

2003-04 Russian Metallurg Magnitogorsk

COMPLETE SET (9) 3.00 8.00
1 Vitali Atyushov .40 1.00
2 Alexander Boikov .40 1.00
3 Evgeni Gladskikh .40 1.00
4 Oleg Davydov .40 1.00
5 Nikolia Ignatov .40 1.00
6 Dmitri Pestunov .40 1.00
7 Ivan Sidorov .40 1.00
8 Martin Cech .40 1.00
9 Lubomir Vaic .40 1.00

2003-04 Russian National Team

Produced by World Sport, this set highlights 36 players who wore the jersey of Russia's various national teams over the 2003-04 season.

COMPLETE SET (36) 10.00 25.00
1 Alexei Badyukov .20 .50
2 Danis Zaripov .20 .50
3 Sergei Mozyakin .20 .50
4 Andrei Mukhachev .20 .50
5 Igor Emeleev .20 .50
6 Denis Gusmanov .20 .50
7 Maxim Spiridonov .20 .50
8 Alexei Yegorov .20 .50
9 Alexander Stepanov .20 .50
10 Nikolai Semin .20 .50
11 Alexander Drozdetsky .20 .50
12 Alexander Skugarev .20 .50
13 Sergei Korolev .20 .50
14 Vladimir Chebaturkin .20 .50
15 Andrei Kovalenko .20 .50
16 Vitali Yachmenev .20 .50
17 Igor Volkov .20 .50
18 Alexander Boikov .20 .50
19 Yuri Dobryshkin .20 .50
20 Alexander Ryazantsev .20 .50
21 Maxim Sushinsky .30 .75
22 Alexander Prokopiev .20 .50
23 Oleg Tverdovsky .20 .50
24 Alexander Ovechkin 6.00 15.00
25 Viktor Tikhonov .20 .50
26 Vladimir Malenkikh .20 .50
27 Valeri Zelepukin .20 .50
28 Dmitri Yushkevich .20 .50
29 Andrei Bashkirov .20 .50
30 Alexander Buturlin .20 .50
31 Leonid Kanareikin .20 .50
32 Artur Oktyabrev .20 .50
33 Maxim Kondratiev .20 .50
34 Vyacheslav Butsayev .20 .50
35 Alexander Savchenkov .20 .50
36 Sergei Krivokrasov .20 .50

2003-04 Russian Postcards

This postcard-sized set features 12 members of Russia's national team. The cards feature only jersey numbers, so they are listed below alphabetically.

COMPLETE SET (12) 8.00 20.00
1 Viacheslav Butsayev .75 2.00
2 Alexander Guskov .75 2.00
3 Andrei Kovalenko .75 2.00
4 Sergei Mozyakin .75 2.00
5 Egor Podomatsky .75 2.00
6 Alexander Prokopiev .75 2.00
7 Maxim Sokolov .75 2.00
8 Maxim Sushinsky .75 2.00
9 Oleg Tverdovsky .75 2.00
10 Igor Volkov .75 2.00
11 Vitali Yachmenev .75 2.00
12 Dmitry Zatonsky .75 2.00

2003-04 Russian SL

COMPLETE SET (40) 15.00 30.00
1 Alexei Chupin .20 .50
2 Radek Duda .20 .50
3 Alexei Yegorov .40 1.00
4 Tomas Harant .20 .50
5 Miroslav Hlinka .20 .50
6 Tomas Hlubna .20 .50
7 J.F. Labbe .30 .75
8 Oleg Orekhovsky .20 .50
9 Alexander Ovechkin 4.00 10.00
10 Andrei Razin .20 .50
11 Dmitri Ryabykin .20 .50
12 Konstantin Simchuk .40 1.00
13 Andrei Subbotin .20 .50
14 Yuri Trubachev .20 .50
15 Ravil Yakubov .20 .50
16 Nikolai Zherdev 1.25 3.00
17 Vadim Tarasov .40 1.00
18 Sergei Naumovs .40 1.00
19 Christian Bronsard .40 1.00
20 Dmitri Kazionov .20 .50
21 Sergei Gomolyako .20 .50
22 Alexander Kuvaldin .20 .50
23 Peter Skudra .40 1.00
24 Alex Westlund .40 1.00
25 Sergei Shalamai .20 .50
26 Atvars Tribuntsovs .20 .50
27 Alexei Kudashov .20 .50
28 Ruslan Nurtdinov .20 .50
29 David Moravec .20 .50
30 Alexei Tertyshny .20 .50
31 Mikhail Shukaev .40 1.00
32 Alexei Vasiliev .20 .50
33 Kirill Lyamin .40 1.00
34 Daniel Branda .20 .50
35 Vadim Khomitsky .20 .50
36 Vitali Yeremeev .40 1.00
37 Lubomir Vaic .20 .50
38 Ruslan Zainullin .20 .50
39 Alexander Savchenkov .20 .50
40 Sergei Mozyakin .20 .50

2003-04 Russian Young Lions

COMPLETE SET (7) 5.00 12.00
1 Dmitri Chernykh .40 1.00
2 Alexander Semin .60 1.50
3 Alexander Ovechkin 4.00 10.00
4 Maxim Shevjev .40 1.00
5 Dmitri Pestunov .40 1.00
6 Maxim Krivonozhkin .40 1.00
7 Kirill Lyamin .40 1.00

2003 Russian Under-18 Team

COMPLETE SET (22) 15.00 35.00
1 Grigori Shafigulin .20 .50
2 Dmitri Petrov .20 .50
3 Alexei Ivanov .20 .50
4 Evgeni Malkin 6.00 15.00
5 Dmitri Pestunov .20 .50
6 Vitali Anikienko .20 .50
7 Dmitri Chernykh .20 .50
8 Anton Dubinin .20 .50
9 Rustan Sidikov .30 .75
10 Alexander Naurov .20 .50
11 Denis Pervyshin .20 .50
12 Alexander Ovechkin 6.00 15.00
13 Denis Ezhov .20 .50
14 Georgi Misharin .20 .50
15 Anton Belov .20 .50
16 Artem Nosov .20 .50
17 Denis Loginov .20 .50
18 Dmitri Kosmachev .20 .50
19 Konstantin Makarov .20 .50
20 Sergei Gorelov .30 .75
21 Konstantin Glazachev .60 1.50
22 Dmitri Shitikov .20 .50

2003 Russian World Championship Stars

COMPLETE SET (35) 10.00 25.00
1 Jan Benda .10 .25
2 Leonid Tambievs .10 .25

3 Jan Lasak .30 .75
4 Miroslav Hlinka .10 .25
5 Sergei Naumov .20 .50
6 Atvars Tribuntsovs .10 .25
7 Peter Forsberg 1.25 3.00
8 Tommy Salo .30 .75
9 Mats Sundin .60 1.50
10 Henrik Zetterberg .60 1.50
11 Mikael Tellqvist .60 1.50
12 Dany Heatley .75 2.00
13 Sean Burke .40 1.00
14 Mike Comrie .30 .75
15 Kris Draper .40 1.00
16 Roberto Luongo 1.25 3.00
17 Anson Carter .40 1.00
18 Miroslav Satan .40 1.00
19 Peter Bondra .40 1.00
20 Zigmund Palffy .40 1.00
21 Robert Svehla .10 .25
22 Richard Zednik .10 .25
23 Arturs Irbe .40 1.00
24 Milan Hejduk .60 1.50
25 Jiri Hudler .75 2.00
26 Robert Reichel .10 .25
27 Martin Straka .20 .50
28 Radek Duda .10 .25
29 Alexander Khavanov .10 .25
30 Ilya Kovalchuk 1.00 2.50
31 Maxim Sokolov .20 .50
32 Tomas Vokoun .60 1.50
33 Ryan Smith .60 1.50
34 Rodrigo Lavins .10 .25
35 Eric Brewer .20 .50

2003 Russian World Championship Team 2003

COMPLETE SET (24) 6.00 15.00
1 Maxim Sokolov .20 .50
2 Igor Podomatski .20 .50
3 Alexander Frolov .75 2.00
4 Alexander Semin 1.00 2.50
5 Pavel Datsyuk 1.00 2.50
6 Ivan Novoseltsev .10 .25
7 Sergei Zinovjev .40 1.00
8 Vladimir Antipov .10 .25
9 Dmitri Kalinin .10 .25
10 Vitali Proshkin .10 .25
11 Sergei Soin .10 .25
12 Alexander Suglobov .20 .50
13 Alexander Zhdan .10 .25
14 Sergei Vyshedkevich .10 .25
15 Sergei Gusev .10 .25
16 Oleg Saprykin .20 .50
17 Denis Arkhipov .20 .50
18 Dmitri Erofeev .10 .25
19 Igor Grigorenko .75 2.00
20 Alexander Guskov .10 .25
21 Vasily Turkovsky .10 .25
22 Alexander Khavanov .10 .25
23 Ilya Kovalchuk 2.00 5.00
24 Alexei Kaigorodov .40 1.00

2003 Russian World Championships Preview

COMPLETE SET (5) 6.00 15.00
1 Alexander Ovechkin 6.00 15.00
2 Pavel Datsyuk .75 2.00
3 Denis Loginov .20 .50
4 Denis Arkhipov .20 .50
5 Ilya Kovalchuk 1.50 4.00

2004-05 Russian Back to Russia

COMPLETE SET (41) 12.00 30.00
1 Alexander Frolov .75 2.00
2 Pavel Datsyuk 1.50 4.00
3 Konstantin Koltsov .20 .50
4 Andrei Markov .40 1.00
5 Slava Kozlov .40 1.00
6 Dmitri Afanasenkov .20 .50
7 Igor Korolev .20 .50
8 Ilya Kovalchuk 4.00 10.00
9 Artem Chubarov .20 .50
10 Nikolai Zherdev 1.00 2.50
11 Alexander Semin 1.50 4.00
12 Maxim Kuznetsov .20 .50
13 Andrei Nikolishin .20 .50
14 Alexei Ponikarovsky .40 1.00
15 Maxim Afinogenov .75 2.00
16 Oleg Saprykin .20 .50
17 Viktor Kozlov .40 1.00
18 Andrei Nazarov .20 .50
19 Fedor Fedorov .40 1.00
20 Maxim Kondratiev .20 .50
21 Alexei Morozov .20 .50
22 Dmitry Kalinin .20 .50
23 Alexander Karpovtsev .20 .50
24 Nikolai Khabibulin .75 2.00
25 Oleg Kvasha .20 .50
26 Vitaly Vishnevsky .40 1.00
27 Sergei Gonchar .40 1.00
28 Darius Kasparaitis .20 .50
29 Alexander Perezhogin .40 1.00
30 Kirill Safronov .20 .50
31 Fedor Tyutin .20 .50
32 Nikolai Antropov .40 1.00
33 Evgeny Nabokov 1.00 2.50
34 Sergei Brylin .20 .50
35 Alexei Kovalev .40 1.00
36 Alexei Yashin .40 1.00
37 Ruslan Salei .20 .50
38 Sergei Samsonov 1.00 2.50
39 Alexei Zhitnik .20 .50
40 Igor Radulov .20 .50
41 Denis Arkhipov .40 1.00

2004-05 Russian Hope

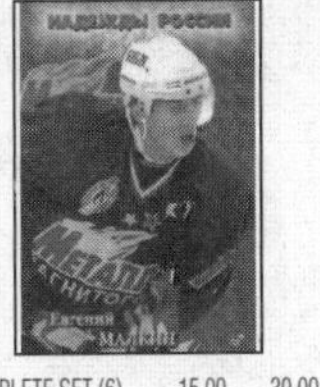

COMPLETE SET (6) 15.00 30.00
1 Alexander Ovechkin 8.00 20.00
2 Evgeni Malkin 8.00 20.00
3 Enver Lisin .40 1.00
4 Anton Belov .40 1.00
5 Yakov Rylov .40 1.00
6 Viacheslav Seluyanov .40 1.00

2004-05 Russian Legion

COMPLETE SET (41) 15.00 40.00
1 Pavel Rosa .20 .50
2 Jaromir Jagr 6.00 15.00
3 Lubomir Bartecko .20 .50
4 Martin Strbak .20 .50
5 Martin Havlat 1.50 4.00
6 Fred Brathwaite .75 2.00
7 Tomas Harant .20 .50
8 Vladimir Tsyplakov .20 .50
9 Joni Puurula .20 .50
10 Dainius Zubrus .20 .50
11 Vadim Shakhraichuk .20 .50
12 Jussi Markkanen .40 1.00
13 Vladimir Hudacek .20 .50
14 Curtis Murphy .20 .50
15 Roman Tomas .20 .50
16 Jiri Trvaj .20 .50
17 Jaroslav Bednar .20 .50
18 Miroslav Lipovsky .20 .50
19 Martin Cech .20 .50
20 Jaroslav Hlinka .20 .50
21 Lukas Zib .20 .50
23 Jan Hejda .20 .50
24 Vincent Lecavalier 6.00 15.00
25 Miroslav Guren .20 .50
27 Petr Sykora .40 1.00
28 Kamil Piros .20 .50
29 Patrik Elias .40 1.00
30 Petr Kubos .20 .50
31 Marc Lamothe .40 1.00
32 Roman Malek .20 .50
33 Aigars Cipruss .20 .50
34 Markus Korhonen .20 .50
35 Jan Benda .20 .50
36 Dusan Salficky .40 1.00
37 Dany Heatley 6.00 15.00
38 Mika Pietila .20 .50
39 Pauli Jaks .20 .50
41 Atvars Tribuntsovs .20 .50

2004-05 Russian Moscow Dynamo

COMPLETE SET (36) 15.00 35.00
1 Maxim Afinogenov .75 2.00
2 Yuri Babenko .20 .50
3 Lubomir Bartecko .20 .50
4 Vladislav Boulin .20 .50
5 Albert Vishnyakov .20 .50
6 Vladimir Vorobiev .20 .50
7 Sergey Vyshedkevich .20 .50
8 Martin Havlat 1.50 4.00
9 Tomas Harant .20 .50
10 Pavel Datsyuk 1.25 3.00
11 Vladislav Evseev .20 .50
12 Vitaly Yeremeev .40 1.00
13 Alexander Yeremenko .40 1.00
14 Vladimir Karpov .20 .50
15 Denis Kartsev .20 .50
16 Alexei Komarov .20 .50
17 Alexei Kudashov .20 .50
18 Maxim Kuznetsov .20 .50
19 Andrei Markov .20 .50
20 Igor Mirnov .20 .50
21 Ilya Nikulin .20 .50
22 Alexander Ovechkin 8.00 20.00
23 Oleg Orekhovsky .20 .50
24 Konstantin Romanov .20 .50
25 Pavel Rosa .20 .50
26 Yakov Rylov .20 .50
27 Alexander Savchenkov .20 .50
28 Andrei Skopintsev .20 .50
29 Alexander Stepanov .20 .50
30 Alexei Tereschenko .20 .50
31 Alexei Troschinsky .20 .50
32 Alexander Radulov .20 .50
33 Artem Chubarov .20 .50
34 Alexei Chupin .20 .50
35 Igor Shadilov .20 .50
36 Vladimir Krikunov CO .20 .50

2004-05 Russian RHL

COMPLETE SET (22) 15.00 30.00
1 Sergey Borisov .20 .50
2 Andrei Kovalenko .20 .50
3 Maxim Potapov .20 .50
4 Roman Sychev .20 .50
5 Andrei Taratukhin .20 .50
6 Maxim Ovchinikov .20 .50
7 Denis Mashanov .20 .50
8 Alexander Zavyzlov .20 .50
9 Andrei Petrunin .20 .50
10 Mikhail Varnakov .20 .50
11 Sergey Zhurikov .20 .50
12 Evgeni Malkin 10.00 25.00
13 Igor Grigorenko 1.25 3.00
14 Vladimir Popov .20 .50
15 Ruslan Khasanshin .20 .50
16 Dmitry Dudarev .20 .50
17 Valery Pokrovsky .20 .50
18 Andrei Tsareev .20 .50
19 Roman Malov .20 .50
20 Sergey Korolev .20 .50
21 Maxim Ossipov .20 .50
22 Vladimir Antipin .20 .50

2004 Russian Super League All-Stars

COMPLETE SET (31) 6.00 15.00
1 Egor Podomatsky .40 1.00
2 Viktor Chistov .40 1.00
3 Dmitry Krasotkin .20 .50
4 Alexei Troschinsky .20 .50
5 Vladimir Tyurikov .20 .50
6 Alexander Yudin .20 .50
7 Alexander Semak .20 .50
8 Marat Davydov .20 .50
9 Dmitry Gogolev .20 .50
10 Andrei Razin .20 .50
11 Valeri Zelepukin .20 .50
12 Egor Mikhailov .20 .50
13 Pavel Boichenko .20 .50
14 Vladimir Samylin .20 .50
15 Vladimir Vorobiev .20 .50
16 Alexei Chupin .20 .50
17 Konstantin Simchuk .40 1.00
18 Alexander Fomitchev .40 1.00
19 Sergei Klimentiev .20 .50
20 Andrei Evstafiev .20 .50
21 Jiri Marushak .20 .50
22 Nikolai Tsulygin .20 .50
23 Oleg Khmylev .20 .50
24 Jan Benda .20 .50
25 Sergei Gomolyako .20 .50
26 Igor Varitsky .20 .50
27 Andrei Skabelka .20 .50
28 Evgeny Koreshkov .20 .50
29 Sergei Moskalev .20 .50
30 Dmitri Kvartalnov .20 .50
31 Vadim Epanchintsev .20 .50

2004 Russian Under-18 Team

COMPLETE SET (23) 15.00 40.00
1 Adgur Dzhugelia .20 .50
2 Evgeni Biryukov .20 .50
3 Sergei Salnikov .20 .50
4 Kirill Lyamin .30 .75
5 Dmitri Shitikov UER .20 .50
(first name listed as Sergei
6 Rinat Ibragimov .20 .50
7 Anton Belov .20 .50
8 Sergei Shirokov .20 .50
9 Nikolai Kulemin .20 .50
10 Ivan Kasutin .30 .75
11 Evgeni Malkin 10.00 25.00
12 Roman Voloshenko .40 1.00
13 Alexander Aksenenko .20 .50
14 Sergei Karetin .20 .50
15 Enver Lisin .40 1.00
16 Denis Parshin .20 .50
17 Alexander Plyuschev .20 .50
18 Mikhail Yunkov .20 .50
19 Sergei Ogorodnikov .20 .50
20 Anton Khudobin .30 .75
21 Alexei Yemelin .20 .50
22 Alexander Radulov 4.00 10.00
NNO Checklist .02 .10

2004 Russian World Championship Team

This set, produced by World Sport, features the 2004 World Championship team.

COMPLETE SET (25) 15.00 30.00
1 Maxim Afinogenov .60 1.50
2 Alexei Yashin .20 .50
3 Nikolai Pronin .20 .50
4 Maxim Kondratiev .20 .50
5 Andrei Skopintsev .20 .50
6 Alexander Prokopiev .20 .50
7 Alexei Morozov .20 .50
8 Alexander Ovechkin 8.00 20.00
9 Maxim Sushinski .20 .50
10 Alexander Guskov .20 .50
11 Alexander Skugarev .20 .50
12 Vasili Turkovski .20 .50
13 Alexander Fomitchev .30 .75
14 Andrei Bashkirov .20 .50
15 Valeri Zelepukin .20 .50
16 Vitali Proshkin .20 .50
17 Ilya Kovalchuk 2.00 5.00
18 Maxim Sokolov .20 .50
19 Dmitri Bykov .20 .50
20 Oleg Tverdovsky .20 .50
21 Slava Butsayev .20 .50
22 Dmitri Yushkevich .20 .50
23 Dmitri Kalinin .20 .50
24 Vladimir Antipov .20 .50
25 Egor Podomatski .30 .75

2004 Russian World Junior Team

This team set was sold in Russia after the team won the WJC Gold medal in Finland. Produced by World Sport.

COMPLETE SET (22) 15.00 40.00
1 Konstantin Korneev .20 .50
2 Denis Grot .20 .50
3 Alexander Ovechkin 8.00 20.00
4 Dmitry Pestunov .20 .50
5 Alexei Shkotov .20 .50
6 Sergei Gimaev .20 .50
7 Andrei Spiridonov .20 .50
8 Ilya Krikunov .20 .50
9 Yevgeny Malkin 8.00 20.00
10 Sergei Anshakov .20 .50
11 Mikhail Tyulyapkin .20 .50
12 Sergei Karpov .20 .50
13 Grigory Shafigulin .20 .50
14 Alexander Kozhevnikov .20 .50
15 Yuri Ermolin .20 .50
16 Dmitry Kosmachev .20 .50
17 Denis Ezhov .20 .50
18 Evgeny Tunik .20 .50
19 Dmitry Kazionov .20 .50
20 Alexander Semin 1.25 3.00
21 Konstantin Barulin .40 1.00
22 Denis Khudyakov .40 1.00

2005 Russian Avangard Omsk Calendars

These oversized cards (4X3) feature players from the 2003-04 Russian champs on the front, and a calendar on the back. It's possible other cards exist in this series.

COMPLETE SET (5) 4.00 8.00
1 Alexander Prokopiev .75 2.00
2 Dmitry Subbotin .75 2.00
3 Maxim Sushinsky .75 2.00
4 Oleg Tverdovsky .75 2.00
5 Team photo .75 2.00

2005-06 Russian Hockey League RHL

COMPLETE SET (60) 20.00 40.00
1 Denis Kulyash .20 .50
2 Alexander Bumagin .20 .50
3 Alexei Kaigorodov .40 1.00
4 Anton Krysanov .20 .50
5 Alexander Budkin .20 .50
6 Denis Bodrov .20 .50
7 Stanislav Chistov .30 .75
8 Mikhail Grabovsky .30 .75
9 Nikita Alexeev .30 .75
10 Dmitri Shitikov .20 .50
11 Igor Ignatushkin .20 .50
12 Vladislav Bouljin .20 .50
13 Fred Brathwaite .40 1.00
14 Alexander Korolyuk .30 .75
15 Alexei Troschinsky .20 .50
16 Alexei Shkotov .20 .50
17 Eugeni Birukov .20 .50
18 Alexei Chupin .20 .50
19B Alexander Ryazantsev .20 .50
20 Vadim Epanchintsev .20 .50
21 Milan Kraft .30 .75
22 Andrei Mukhachev .20 .50
23 Eugeni Fedorov .30 .75
24 Alexander Semin 1.25 3.00
25 Vladimir Vorobiev .20 .50
26 Eugeni Ryasenski .20 .50
27 Did Not Issue/Unknown
28 Travis Scott .40 1.00
29 Did Not Issue/Unknown
30 Maxim Sushinsky .30 .75
31 David Nemirovsky .30 .75
32 David Ling .30 .75
33 Vyacheslav Buravchikov .20 .50
34 Sergei Zvyagin .20 .50
35 Raymond Giroux .30 .75
36 Kirill Koltsov .40 1.00
37 Eugeni Malkin 8.00 20.00
38 Atrem Bikkinyaev .20 .50
39 Ilya Zubov .40 1.00
40 Nikolai Kulemin .40 1.00
41 Oleg Romashko .20 .50
42 Alexander Rybakov .20 .50
43 Dusan Sakficky .40 1.00
44 Maxim Yakutsenya .20 .50
45 Boris Tortunov .20 .50
46 Ilya Nikulin .20 .50
47 Did Not Issue/Unknown
48 Radik Zakiyev .20 .50
49 Ruslan Nurtdinov .20 .50
50 Tyler Moss .40 1.00
51 Dmitri Obukhov .20 .50
52 Andrei Nikolishin .20 .50
53 Alexander Yunkov|#Mikhail Yunkov .20 .50
54 Alexander Yudin .20 .50
55 Eugeni Konstantinov .40 1.00
C1 Milos Rziga .20 .50
C2 Jan Zachurla .20 .50
C3 Vladimir Kapulovsky .20 .50

2006 Russian Sport Collection Olympic Stars

1 Maxim Afinogenov 1.00 2.50
2 Ilya Bryzgalov 1.00 2.50
3 Anton Volchenkov 1.00 2.50
4 Sergei Gonchar 1.00 2.50
5 Pavel Datsyuk 2.00 5.00
6 Darius Kasparaitis 1.00 2.50
7 Alexei Kovalev 1.00 2.50
8 Ilya Kovalchuk 4.00 10.00
9 Evgeny Malkin 8.00 20.00
10 Andrei Markov 1.00 2.50
11 Evgeny Nabokov 2.00 5.00
12 Alexander Ovechkin 8.00 20.00
13 Maxim Sokolov 1.00 2.50
14 Fedor Tyutin 1.00 2.50
15 Alexei Yashin 1.00 2.50
16 Daniel Alfredson 2.00 5.00
17 Henrik Zetterberg 2.00 5.00
18 Nicklas Lidstrom 2.00 5.00
19 Henrik Lundqvist 4.00 10.00
20 Mats Sundin 2.00 5.00
21 Peter Forsberg 4.00 10.00
22 Jussi Jokinen 1.00 2.50
23 Saku Koivu 2.00 5.00
24 Jere Lehtinen 2.00 5.00
25 Antero Niittymaki 2.00 5.00
26 Ville Peltonen 1.00 2.50
27 Teemu Selanne 4.00 10.00
28 Tomas Vokoun 2.00 5.00
29 Tomas Kaberle 1.00 2.50
30 Martin Straka 1.00 2.50
31 Milan Hejduk 2.00 5.00
32 Ales Hemsky 2.00 5.00
33 Jaromir Jagr 4.00 10.00
34 Martin Brodeur 6.00 15.00
35 Jarome Iginla 4.00 10.00
36 Vincent Lecavalier 4.00 10.00
37 Rick Nash 4.00 10.00
38 Brad Richards 2.00 5.00
39 Joe Sakic 6.00 15.00
40 Joe Thornton 4.00 10.00
41 Dany Heatley 4.00 10.00
42 Peter Bondra 1.00 2.50
43 Peter Budaj 1.00 2.50
44 Marian Gaborik 4.00 10.00
45 Pavol Demitra 1.00 2.50
46 Richard Zednik 1.00 2.50
47 Zdeno Chara 1.00 2.50
48 Marian Hossa 2.00 5.00
49 Miroslav Satan 1.00 2.50
50 Rick Dipietro 2.00 5.00
51 Mike Modano 3.00 8.00
52 Keith Tkachuk 2.00 5.00
53 Vitali Yeremeyev 1.00 2.50

2006 Russian Torino Olympic Team

COMPLETE SET (26) 15.00 25.00
1 Alexander Ovechkin 4.00 10.00
2 Evgeny Malkin 4.00 10.00
3 Maxim Sokolov .20 .50
4 Ilya Bryzgalov .40 1.00
5 Fedor Tyutin .20 .50
6 Vitaly Vishnevsky .20 .50
7 Maxim Sushinski .20 .50
8 Alexei Yashin .20 .50
9 Alexei Kovalev .40 1.00
10 Alexander Korolyuk .20 .50
11 Ilya Kovalchuk 1.25 3.00
12 Maxim Afinogenov .40 1.00
13 Alexander Kharitonov .20 .50
14 Pavel Datsyuk .75 2.00
15 Viktor Kozlov .20 .50
16 Ivan Nepryaev .20 .50
17 Andrei Markov .20 .50
18 Alexander Frolov .40 1.00
19 Sergei Zhukov .20 .50
20 Evgeny Nabokov .40 1.00
21 Darius Kasparaitis .20 .50
22 Andrei Taratukhin .20 .50
23 Sergei Gonchar .20 .50
24 Anton Volchenkov .20 .50
25 Daniil Markov .20 .50
26 Russian Team CL .02 .10

1995-96 Slovakian APS National Team

This set of 28-cards features the 1996 Slovakian national team. The cards were sold in team set form at home games. The cards feature an action photo complemented by national and federation logos. The card backs reprise the front photo along with international statistics. The set is notable for the inclusion of sniper Peter Bondra, among other NHLers.

COMPLETE SET (28) 20.00 40.00
1 Dr. Jan Mitosinka CO .10 .25
2 Dusan Pasek CO .10 .25
3 Julius Supler CO .10 .25
4 Jan Selvek .10 .25
5 Jaromir Dragan .10 .25
6 Eduard Hartmann .10 .25
7 Roman Cunderlik .10 .25
8 Stanislav Jasecko .10 .25
9 Lubomir Sekeras .40 1.00
10 Stanislav Medrik .10 .25
11 Jan Varholik .10 .25
12 Marian Smerciak .10 .25
13 Robert Svehla .40 1.00
14 Slavomir Vorobel .20 .50
15 Vlastimil Plavucha .10 .25
16 Oto Hascak .20 .50
17 Peter Bondra 6.00 15.00
18 Rene Pucher .10 .25
19 Miroslav Satan 6.00 15.00
20 Branislav Janos .10 .25
21 Lubomir Kolnik .20 .50
22 Peter Stastny 2.00 5.00
23 Zdeno Ciger .20 .50
24 Zigmund Palffy 6.00 15.00
25 Josef Dano .10 .25
26 Robert Petrovicky .20 .50
27 Dusan Pohorelec .10 .25
28 Jozef Stumpel .80 2.00

1995 Slovakian-Quebec Pee-Wee Tournament

This 29-card set features the group of youngsters who represented Slovakia at the 1995 Quebec Pee Wee Tournament. The cards were sold at the tournament to help finance the team's trip. The cards have color player photos with red inside and faded purple outside borders. The backs carry player information. The cards are unnumbered and checklisted below in alphabetical order.

COMPLETE SET (29) 3.20 8.00
1 Jozef Balej .40 3.00
2 Patrik Behan .10 .25
3 Michal Bela .10 .25
4 Ivan Dobry .10 .25
5 Milan Dornic CO .10 .10
6 Vladimir Dubek .10 .25
7 Ladislav Gero CO .10 .10
8 Marian Hutyra .10 .25
9 Peter Hutyra .10 .25
10 Dr. Leopold Karafiat MG .10 .10
11 Miroslav Karafiat CO .10 .10
12 Vladimir Kulich .10 .25
13 Marek Laco .10 .25
14 Michal Loksa .10 .25
15 Igor Martak .10 .25
16 Branislav Medzihorsky .10 .25
17 Miroslav Micuda .10 .25
18 Tomas Mihalik .10 .25
19 Stanislav Mistrik .10 .25
20 Andrej Mrena .10 .25
21 Marian Nemeth .10 .25
22 Vladimir Polacek .10 .25
23 Rastislav Sendrey .10 .25
24 Norbert Skorvaga .10 .25
25 Tomas Surovy .10 1.50
26 Michal Turcer .10 .25
27 Sponsor Card .10 .01
28 Team Card .10 .10
29 Title Card .10 .01

1996 Slovakian Quebec Pee-Wee Tournament Team

This 30-card set features color player photos with red inside and faded purple outside borders. The backs carry player information. The cards are unnumbered and checklisted below in alphabetical order.

COMPLETE SET (30) 5.60 15.00
1 Jozef Balej .30 2.00
2 Michal Baranka .20 .50
3 Jan Behan CO .20 .10
4 Martin Bonda .20 .50
5 Robert Cerny .20 .50
6 Peter Duris .20 .50
7 Jan Frkan .20 .50
8 Milan Fujerik CO .20 .10
9 Michal Gunis .20 .50
10 Stefan Hlusek .20 .50
11 Peter Holecko .20 .50
12 Dr. Leopold Karafial GM .20 .10
13 Lukas Krejci .20 .50
14 Miroslav Kristin .20 .50
15 Andrej Kucko .20 .50
16 Roman Kyndl .20 .50
17 Michal Macho .20 .50
18 Tomas Mikus .30 .75
19 Juraj Nemcak .30 .75
20 Viliam Ondrejik .20 .50
21 Miroslav Pistek .20 .50
22 Marek Pollak .30 .75
23 Tomas Psenka .20 .50
24 Milan Sitar CO .20 .10
25 Frantisek Skladany .20 1.00
26 Peter Steklac .20 .50
27 Richard Svrbik .20 .50
28 Michal Sykora .20 .50
29 Martin Wala .20 .50
30 Team Picture .20 .10

1998-99 Slovakian Eurotel

This set of cards was released in Slovakia to promote Eurotel. The slightly undersized issues feature a number of NHL stars -- primarily of European origin.

COMPLETE SET (29) 32.00 80.00
1 Peter Bondra 1.20 3.00
2 Sergei Fedorov 2.00 5.00
3 Peter Forsberg 3.00 7.50
4 Wayne Gretzky 8.00 20.00
5 Bill Guerin 1.20 2.00
6 Brett Hull 1.60 4.00
7 Jaromir Jagr 3.00 5.00
8 Saku Koivu 1.20 3.00
9 Jari Kurri .80 2.00
10 Pat Lafontaine .80 2.00
11 Janne Laukkanen .40 1.00
12 Robert Lang .40 1.00
13 John LeClair 1.20 2.00
14 Eric Lindros 2.00 4.00
15 Al MacInnis .80 2.00
16 Joe Nieuwendyk .80 2.00
17 Zigmund Palffy .80 2.00
18 Mike Richter 1.20 3.00
19 Patrick Roy 6.00 15.00
20 Joe Sakic 3.00 5.00
21 Tommy Salo .80 2.00
22 Miroslav Satan .80 2.00
23 Teemu Selanne 2.00 4.00
24 Mikhail Shtalenkov .40 1.00
25 Martin Straka .40 1.00
26 Mats Sundin .80 2.00
27 Alexei Yashin .40 1.00
28 Steve Yzerman 6.00 15.00
29 Alexei Zhamnov .40 1.00

1999-00 Slovakian Challengers

This odd-sized set was produced as a promotional incentive by a Slovakian candy bar manufacturer. The checklist for this set provided by www.hockeyheaven.com.

COMPLETE SET (30) 30.00 60.00
1 Rob Niedermayer .20 .50
2 Robert Svehla .20 .50
3 Richard Zednik .20 .50
4 Steve Sullivan .20 .50
5 Alexei Yashin .20 .50
6 Alexander Mogilny .30 .75
7 Zigmund Palffy .40 1.00
8 Martin Brodeur 6.00 15.00
9 Sandis Ozolinsh .20 .50
10 Adam Deadmarsh .30 .75
11 Peter Forsberg 2.50 6.00
12 Martin Rucinsky .20 .50
13 Shayne Corson .20 .50
14 Grant Fuhr .75 2.00
15 Al MacInnis .75 2.00
16 Paul Kariya 2.00 5.00
17 Teemu SelÃonne 2.00 5.00
18 Steve Yzerman 8.00 20.00
19 Chris Osgood .75 2.00
20 Brendan Shanahan 1.25 3.00
21 Vaclav Varada .20 .50
22 Brian Holzinger .20 .50
23 Dominik Hasek 2.50 6.00
24 Michael Peca .30 .75
25 Ed Belfour 1.25 3.00
26 Jere Lehtinen .75 2.00
27 Jaromir Jagr 3.00 8.00
28 Kevin Hatcher .20 .50
29 John LeClair .75 2.00
30 Alexei Zhamnov .20 .50

2001 Slovakian Kvarteto

This set features players who routinely suit up for Slovakia in key international events. The cards are shaped like playing cards, with a photo on front and the words Kvarteto on the back.

COMPLETE SET (33) 10.00 25.00
1A Jergus Baca .20 .50
1B Josef Dano .20 .50
1C Peter Bondra .40 2.00
1D Jaromir Dragan .40 1.00
2A Zdeno Ciger .20 .50
2B Peter Bondra .60 2.00
2C Pavol Demitra .60 2.00
2D Stanislav Jasecko .20 .50
3A Ivan Droppa .20 .50
3B Otto Hascak .20 .50
3C Branislav Janos .20 .50
3D Peter Bondra .60 2.00
4A Stanislav Jasecko .20 .50
4B Lubomir Kolnik .20 .50
4C Zigmund Palffy .60 2.00
4D Roman Kontsek .20 .50
5A Igor Murin .20 .50
5B Lubomir Visnovsky .30 .75
5C Lubomir Kolnik .20 .50
5D Jan Pardavy .20 .50
6A Robert Petrovicky .20 .50
6B Vlastimil Plavucha .20 .50
6C Peter Pucher .20 .50
6D Rene Pucher .20 .50
7A Pavol Rybar .20 .75
7B Miroslav Satan .60 2.00
7C Lubomir Sekeras .30 .75
7D Roman Stantien .20 .50
8A Roman Stantien .20 .50
8B Jozef Stumpel .30 .75
8C Robert Svehla .20 .50
8D Marian Varolik .20 .50
HOKEJ Peter Bondra 2.00 5.00

2002 Slovakian Kvarteto

This set features the world champion Slovaks. They look like playing cards with a player photo on the front and the word Kvarteto on the back. We have a complete

list of players, but the numbering was randomly assigned. If you have the correct numbering, please get in touch.
COMPLETE SET (32) 8.00 20.00
1 Miroslav Satan .75 2.00
2 Peter Bondra .75 2.00
3 Zigmund Palffy .75 2.00
4 Jan Lasak .40 1.00
5 Rastislav Stana .40 1.00
6 Radoslav Hecl .20 .50
7 Richard Lintner .20 .50
8 Dusan Milo .20 .50
9 Peter Smrek .20 .50
10 Martin Strbak .20 .50
11 Lubomir Visnovsky .20 .50
12 Jergus Baca .20 .50
13 Michael Handzus .20 .50
14 Rastislav Pavlikovsky .20 .50
15 Robert Petrovicky .20 .50
16 Jozef Stumpel .20 .50
17 Radovan Somik .20 .50
18 Robert Tomik .20 .50
19 Miroslav Hlinka .20 .50
20 Lubos Bartecko .20 .50
21 Ladislav Nagy .40 1.00
22 Vladimir Orszagh .20 .50
23 Peter Stastny GM .20 .50
24 Samuel Petras .20 .50
25 Dalimir Jancovic .20 .50
26 Ernest Bokros .20 .50
27 Marek Uram .20 .50
28 Peter Pucher .20 .50
29 Ladislav Cierny .20 .50
30 Vladimir Stastny .20 .50
31 Miroslav Simonovic .20 .50
32 Jan Filc .20 .50

2004-05 Slovakian Poprad Team Set

COMPLETE SET (30) 10.00 25.00
1 Ladislav Svozil .30 .75
2 Vladimir Klinga .30 .75
3 Stanislav Kozuch .30 .75
4 Radovan Hurajt .30 .75
5 Miroslav Javin .30 .75
6 Stefan Rusnak .30 .75
7 Miroslav Turan .30 .75
8 Lukas Bambuch .30 .75
9 Stefan Fabian .30 .75
10 Ridvan Sadiki .30 .75
11 Tomas Jurco .30 .75
12 Radoslav Suchy .30 .75
13 Tomas Valecko .30 .75
14 Pavol Gurcik .30 .75
15 Peter Bondra 1.25 3.00
16 Miroslav Skovira .30 .75
17 Slavomir Pavlicko .30 .75
18 Juraj Halaj .30 .75
19 Pavol Zavacky .30 .75
20 Miroslav Ihnacak .30 .75
21 Juraj Faith .30 .75
22 Peter Misal .30 .75
23 Ludovit Jurinyi .30 .75
24 Jozef Slaninak .30 .75
25 Richard Zemlicka .30 .75
26 Stefan Rusnak .30 .75
27 Miroslav Stolc .30 .75
28 Viktor Kubenko .30 .75
29 Erik Piatak .30 .75
30 Roman Soltys .30 .75

2004-05 Slovakian Skalica Team Set

COMPLETE SET (28) 10.00 25.00
1 Martin Kucera .40 1.00
2 Matej Bukna .40 1.00
3 Tibor Visnovsky .40 1.00
4 Josef Mrena .40 1.00
5 Jaroslav Prosvic .40 1.00
6 Roman Chatrnuch .40 1.00
7 Milan Carsky .40 1.00
8 Miroslav Zalesak .60 1.50
9 Davis Galvas .40 1.00
10 Rene Jarolin .40 1.00
11 Richard Hartmann .40 1.00
12 Peter Kocak .40 1.00
13 Roman Kelner .40 1.00
14 Milan Malik .40 1.00
15 Marek Grill .40 1.00
16 Robert Liscak .40 1.00
17 Zigmund Palffy 1.25 3.00
18 Ladislav Paciga .40 1.00
19 Jozef Liska .40 1.00
20 Radovan Sloboda .40 1.00
21 Boris Flamik .40 1.00
22 Juraj Mikus .40 1.00
23 Peter Ivicic .40 1.00
24 Richard Stehlik .40 1.00
25 Martin Ivicic .40 1.00
26 Petr Tucek .40 1.00
27 Lukas Komarek .40 1.00
28 Martin Skadra .40 1.00

2004-05 South Surrey Eagles

COMPLETE SET (30) 15.00
1 Tyson Angus .50
2 Tim Crowder .50
3 Chris Defrancescanto .50
4 Korey Diehl .50
5 Korey Diehl PROMO 1.00
6 Tyler Eckford .50
7 Tyler Eckford PROMO 1.00
8 Matthew Girling .50
9 Daniel Idema .50
10 Andrew Kozek .50
11 Andrew Kozek PROMO 1.00
12 Kyle Kuehner .50
13 Aaron McKenzie .50
14 Brock Meadows .50
15 T.J. Miller .50
16 David Moncur .50
17 Tyrell Moulton .50
18 T.J. Mulock .50
19 T.J. Mulock PROMO 1.00
20 Kyle Nason .50
21 Blake Rielly PROMO 1.00
22 Blake Rielly PROMO 1.00
23 David Rutherford .50
24 David Rutherford PROMO 1.00
25 Cody Rymut .50
26 Dustin Slade .50
27 Stewart Thiessen .50
28 Matt Wiest .50
29 Rick Hillier HC .10
30 Team Card .10

1932-33 Swedish Marabou

This multi-sport Swedish issue is believed to contain just six hockey players. The singles are very small, measuring about 1/2" by 1". It is believed that two versions of the set exist, one with white borders and another without. The fronts feature a photo, while the backs have the player's name, history, and the set name, Marabou-Sportserie. If anyone knows of other hockey players in this set, please contact us at hockeymag@beckett.com
Hockey players in set (6)
4 C. Abrahamsson
146 Herman Carlsson
147 Folke Wohlin
148 Carl-Erik Furst
149 Bertil Linde
150 Olof Johansson

1938-39 Swedish Liv's Magazine

Hockey Players In Set (2)
56 Vilhelm Petersen
57 Axel Nilsson

1955-56 Swedish Alfabilder

We have no pricing information on this early Swedish set.
COMPLETE SET (36)
COMMON CARD (1-36)
1 Lars Bjorn
2 Sven Tumba Johansson
3 Sven Lill-Cacka Andersson
4 Bertz Zetterberg
5 Yngve Johansson
6 Yngve Carlsson
7 Bengt Bingen Larsson
8 Torsten Totte Magnusson
9 Arne Boman
10 Gote Vicke Hallon Blomquist
11 Stig Carlsson
12 Erik Epa Johansson
13 Borje Lofgren
14 Birger Bigge Nilsson
15 Rune Mankan Magnusson
16 Thord Flodqvist
17 Sven Thunman
18 Lars Erik Lundvall
19 Lars Henrik Johansson
20 Arne Jern
21 Kalle Lilja
22 Yngve Casslind
23 Nisse Nilsson
24 Patrik Linder
25 Lars-Erik Soderberg
26 Per Rockstrom
27 Ake Blomberg
28 Holger Numela
29 Sune Rakan Holmgren
30 Karl-Harry Engstrom
31 Kurt Andersson
32 Hans Bjargestad
33 Ake Plutten Andersson
34 Rolf Pettersson
35 Lars Lasse Svensson
36 Ake Elgstrom

1956-57 Swedish Alfabilder

We have no pricing information on this early Swedish set.
COMPLETE SET (72)
37 Carl Gustav Gustafsson
38 Gunnar Nilas Brundin
39 Runar Soderstrom
40 Gert Blome
41 Egon Hillgren
42 Carl-Goran Lill-Stoveln Oberg
43 Bertil Bomben Carlbaum
44 Hans Stoveln Oberg
45 Sven Wikman
46 Valter Ahlen
47 Bernt Eriksson
48 Einar Granath
49 Uno Ohrlund
50 Nils-Olov Fredriksson
51 Karl-Erik Olsson
52 Jarl Sjoberg
53 Gote Almqvist
54 Stig Wallner
55 Roland Granberg
56 Folke Aronsson
57 Anders Andersson
58 Haldor Jonsson
59 Olle Larsson
60 Soren Hedlund
61 Ivan Aronsson
62 Ake Lundmark
63 Hjalle Sundqvist
64 Lennart Markgren
65 Harry Granberg
66 Gunnar Segerman
67 Lasse Pettersson
68 Torsten Pettersson
69 Sven Svard
70 Jan Gustafsson
71 Birger Adrian
72 Bertil Svard
73 Anders Fernstrom
74 Ake Nilsson
75 Bjorn Johansson
76 Sune Johansson
77 Bo Hultin
78 Sven Gote Andersson
79 Hans Pfeiffer
80 S.A. Nilsson
81 Pelle Jansson
82 Sven Ake Sahlin
83 Sven Erik Sundqvist
84 Hasse Andersson
85 Folke Gustafsson
86 Kjell Eklind
87 Rune Blomberg
88 Arne Kuben Lang
89 Mas-Ake Larsson
90 Bo Olsson
91 Evert Tysk
92 Erik Pettersson
93 Sven Kristoffersson
94 Ingvar Mattsson
95 Ake Alfvendahl
96 Jan-Erik Johansson
97 Bo Hessel
98 Lennart Astrom
99 Torsten Osterberg
100 Yngve Feldt
101 Gunnar Svensson
102 Olle Linder
103 Sven-Erik Ekdahl
104 Jan Hjelm
105 Karl-Erik Jansson
106 Nils Nord
107 Bernt Sjoqvist
108 Hans Saker

1957-58 Swedish Alfabilder

COMPLETE SET (72)
73 Eje Lindstrom
74 Lennart Andersson
75 Soren Bostrom
76 Berndt Arvidsson
77 Gote Wiklund
78 Alf Skonberg
79 Bo Eriksson
80 Ingvar Lillen Naslund
81 Lars Soderblom
82 Sune Bojan Bolin
83 Arne Pandel
84 Bert-Ola Nordlander
85 Stig Pafvels
86 Gunnar Hedbys
87 Gunnar Jonses
88 Knut Knutsson
89 Vilgot Larsson
90 Per-Agne Karlstrom
91 Ingemar Lysen
92 Ake Lassas
93 Goran Lysen
94 Ingemar Brandstrom
95 Karl-Gerhard Juhlin
96 Erik Holmgren
97 Rune Holmgren
98 Arne Holmgren
99 Sune Johansson
100 Lars-Erik Jansson
101 Olsten Johansson
102 Sune Wretling
103 Anders Hemmingsson
104 Ove Dahlberg
105 Hans-Ove Norrman
106 Ake Johansson
107 Arne Fallkvist
108 Olle Groning
109 Kjell Andersson
110 Ove Andersson
111 Nisse Edholm
112 Fred Andersson
113 Hans-Ove Lindberg
114 Roland Hellgren
115 Lars Andersson
116 Tor Horstad
117 Bernt-Ola Stenlund
118 Campbell Fuhrberg
119 Lennart Skarp
120 Hjalle Sundkvist
121 Rune Holmstrom
122 Kurt Lovgren
123 Kjell Adrian
124 Rickard Fagerlund
125 Bengt Nilsson
126 Sten Lindqvist
127 Roland Skarm
128 Lars Rosenstam
129 Rolf Ek
130 Bertil Andersson
131 Arne Lund
132 Sigge Broms
133 Bert-Ola Nordlander
134 Sonny Fernstrom
135 Bertil Hasselqvist
136 Bertil Carlbaum
137 Goran Wallin
138 Olle Stenar
139 Berndt Karlsson
140 Olle Westlund
141 Bertil Masen Karlsson
142 Ulf Gronberg
143 Rolf Gardin
144 Lars Jansson

1964 Swedish Coralli ISHockey

These tiny cards (1 7/8" by 1 1/4") feature players from the Swedish national team, Tre Kroner, as well as many club teams. The cards apparently were distributed as premiums in chocolate bars. According to reports, such sets existed in Sweden as far back as 1955. The card fronts have a posed player photo, name and card number. The backs offer a brief biography in Swedish. An album to hold these cards is believed to exist; this, however, has not been confirmed.
COMPLETE SET (165) 150.00 300.00
1 Sven Johansson 1.50 3.00
2 Ove Malmberg 1.00 2.00
3 Bjorn Larsson 1.00 2.00
4 Ulf Sterner 1.00 2.00
5 Bertil Karlsson 1.00 2.00
6 Leif Holmqvist 5.00 10.00
7 Uno Ohrlund 1.00 2.00
8 Mats Lonn 1.00 2.00
9 Bjorn Palmqvist 1.00 2.00
10 Nils Johansson 1.00 2.00
11 Anders Andersson 1.00 2.00
12 Lennart Haggroth 2.00 4.00
13 Hans Svedberg 1.00 2.00
14 Ronald Pettersson 1.00 2.00
15 Lars Eric Lundvall 1.00 2.00
16 Gert Blome 1.00 2.00
17 Bo Englund 1.00 2.00
18 Folke Bengtsson 1.00 2.00
19 Nils Nilsson 1.00 2.00
20 Lennart Johansson 1.00 2.00
21 Lennart Svedberg 2.50 5.00
22 Lars Ake Sivertsson 1.00 2.00
23 Hakan Wickberg 1.00 2.00
24 Tord Lundstrom 1.00 2.00
25 Ove Andersson 1.00 2.00
26 Bert Ola Nordlander 1.50 3.00
27 Jan Erik Nilsson 1.00 2.00
28 Eilert Maatta 1.00 2.00
29 Roland Stoltz 1.00 2.00
30 Kurt Thulin 1.00 2.00
31 Ove Andersson 1.00 2.00
32 Ingemar Johansson 1.00 2.00
33 Rune Lind 1.00 2.00
34 Bert-Ola Nordlander 1.50 3.00
35 Hans Eriksson 1.00 2.00
36 Antik Johansson 1.00 2.00
37 Bo Hansson 1.00 2.00
38 Jan Back 1.00 2.00
39 Lennart Soderberg 1.00 2.00
40 Benny Soderling 1.00 2.00
41 Anders Parmstrom 1.00 2.00
42 Lennart Selinder 1.00 2.00
43 Bjorn Larsson 1.00 2.00
44 Jorma Salmi 1.00 2.00
45 Berndt Arvidsson 1.00 2.00
46 P.A. Karlstrom 1.00 2.00
47 Lars Erik Sjoberg 5.00 10.00
48 Vilgot Larsson 1.00 2.00
49 Gunnar Andersson 1.00 2.00
50 Roland Bond 1.00 2.00
51 Goran Lysen 1.00 2.00
52 Bosse Englund 1.00 2.00
53 Stig Pavels 1.00 2.00
54 Bengt Bornstrom 1.00 2.00
55 Nisse Nilsson 1.00 2.00
56 Lennart Lange 1.00 2.00
57 Des Moroney 1.00 2.00
58 Folke Bengtsson 1.00 2.00
59 Olle Sjogren 1.00 2.00
60 Knut Knutsson 1.00 2.00
61 Kjell Svensson 1.00 2.00
62 Rickard Fagerlund 2.50 5.00
63 Arne Loong 1.00 2.00
64 Stig Carlsson 1.00 2.00
65 Lars Hagg 1.00 2.00
66 Olle Stenar 1.00 2.00
67 Einar Granath 1.00 2.00
68 Leif Andersson 1.00 2.00
69 Hans Soderstrom 1.00 2.00
70 Kalle Lilja 1.00 2.00
71 Soren Maatta 1.00 2.00
72 Sven Bystrom 1.00 2.00
73 Hans Karlsson 1.00 2.00
74 Stig Goran Johansson 1.50 3.00
75 Jan Allinger 1.00 2.00
76 Kjell Larsson 1.00 2.00
77 Hakan Wickberg 1.00 2.00
78 Tord Lundstrom 1.00 2.00
79 Lennart Svedberg 2.50 5.00
80 Jan Erik Lyck 1.00 2.00
81 Hans Eriksson 1.00 2.00
82 Kjell Jonsson 1.00 2.00
83 Lars Hedenstrom 1.00 2.00
84 Lars Ake Sivertsson 1.00 2.00
85 Lennart Johansson 1.00 2.00
86 Hans Sjoberg 1.00 2.00
87 Hans Dahllof 1.00 2.00
88 Leif Jansson 1.00 2.00
89 Lars Byling 1.00 2.00
90 Bertil Lindstrom 1.00 2.00
91 Arne Eriksson 1.00 2.00
92 Gert Blomer 1.00 2.00
93 Kjell Adrian 1.00 2.00
94 Jan Olsen 1.00 2.00
95 Benny Karlsson 1.00 2.00
96 Tommy Carlsson 1.00 2.00
97 Ulf Sterner 1.00 2.00
98 Kjell-Ove Gustafsson 1.00 2.00
99 Lars Erik Lundvall 1.00 2.00
100 Kjell-Ronny Pettersson 1.00 2.00
101 Ronald Pettersson 1.00 2.00
102 Kjell Jonsson 1.00 2.00
103 Gote Hansson 1.00 2.00
104 Rolf Eklof 1.00 2.00
105 Eine Olsson 1.00 2.00
106 Hans-Erik Fernstrom 1.00 2.00
107 Leif Holmqvist 1.00 2.00
108 Bo Zetterberg 1.00 2.00
109 Ake Zattlin 1.00 2.00
110 Bengt-Olov Andreasson 1.00 2.00
111 Borje Mohlander 1.00 2.00
112 Sture Sundin 1.00 2.00
113 Bertil Karlsson 1.00 2.00
114 Lars Molander 1.00 2.00
115 Benno Persson 1.00 2.00
116 Gert Nystrom 1.00 2.00
117 Sune Bohlin 1.00 2.00
118 Olle Westlund 1.00 2.00
119 Goran Wallin 1.00 2.00
120 Ingemar Persson 1.00 2.00
121 Tommy Bjorkman 1.00 2.00
122 Eddie Wingren 1.00 2.00
123 Lars Bjorn 1.00 2.00
124 Roland Stoltz 1.00 2.00
125 Sven Johansson 1.50 3.00
126 Leif Skold 1.00 2.00
127 Hans Mild 1.00 2.00
128 Kurt Thulin 1.00 2.00
129 Ake Rydberg 1.00 2.00
130 Ove Malmberg 1.00 2.00
131 Lars Lundqvist 1.00 2.00
132 Kurt Svensson 1.00 2.00
133 Gosta Westerlund 1.00 2.00
134 Lars Andersson 1.00 2.00
135 Ulf Rydin 1.00 2.00
136 Lennart Haggroth 2.00 4.00
137 Jan Hedberg 1.00 2.00
138 Karl Soren Hedlund 1.00 2.00
139 Hans Svedberg 1.00 2.00
140 Sture Hoverberg 1.00 2.00
141 Anders Ronnblom 1.00 2.00
142 Ulf Eriksson 1.00 2.00
143 Anders Andersson 1.00 2.00
144 Henrik Hedlund 1.00 2.00
145 Per Lundstrom 1.00 2.00
146 Hakan Nygren 1.00 2.00
147 Bo Berglund, Sr 2.00 4.00
148 Lars Ake Warning 1.00 2.00
149 Sven-Olov Johansson 1.00 2.00
150 Ove Stenlund 1.00 2.00
151 Ivar Larsson 1.00 2.00
152 Nils Johansson 1.00 2.00
153 Sten Olsen 1.00 2.00
154 Lars Gidlund 1.00 2.00
155 Tor Haarstad 1.00 2.00
156 Kjell-Olav Barrefjord 1.00 2.00
157 Bjorn Palmqvist 1.00 2.00
158 Soren Lindstrom 1.00 2.00
159 Henna Svensson 1.00 2.00
160 Lars Hagstrom 1.00 2.00
161 Ake Eklof 1.00 2.00
162 Ulf Lundstrom 1.00 2.00
163 Ronny Nordstrom 1.00 2.00
164 Paul Stahl 1.00 2.00
165 Kenneth Sahlen 1.50 3.00

1965 Swedish Coralli ISHockey

These tiny (1 7/8" by 1 1/4") feature players from the Swedish National Team, Tre Kroner, as well as many club teams. The cards apparently were issued as premiums with chocolate bars. The card fronts have a posed player photo, name and card number. The backs offer a brief biography in Swedish.
COMPLETE SET (214) 125.00 300.00
1 Sven Johansson 1.25 3.00
2 Ove Malmberg .75 2.00
3 Bjorn Larsson .75 2.00
4 Ulf Sterner .75 2.00
5 Bertil Karlsson 1.00 3.00
6 Leif Holmqvist 4.00 8.00
7 Uno Ohrlund .75 2.00
8 Mats Lonn .75 2.00
9 Bjorn Palmqvist .75 2.00
10 Nils Johansson .75 2.00
11 Anders Andersson .75 2.00
12 Lennart Haggroth 1.50 4.00
13 Hans Svedberg .75 2.00
14 Ronald Pettersson .75 2.00
15 Lars Eric Lundvall .75 2.00
16 Gert Blome .75 2.00
17 Bo Englund .75 2.00
18 Folke Bengtsson .75 2.00
19 Nils Nilsson .75 2.00
20 Lennart Johansson .75 2.00
21 Lennart Svedberg 1.75 4.00
22 Lars Ake Sivertsson .75 2.00
23 Hakan Wickberg .75 2.00
24 Tord Lundstrom .75 2.00
25 Ove Andersson .75 2.00
26 Bert Ola Nordlander 1.25 3.00
27 Jan Erik Nilsson .75 2.00
28 Eilert Maatta .75 2.00
29 Roland Stoltz .75 2.00
30 Kurt Thulin .75 2.00
31 Leif Holmquist 4.00 8.00
32 Ingemar Johansson 1.00 3.00
33 Rune Lind .75 2.00
34 Bert-Ola Nordlander 1.25 3.00
35 Hans Eriksson .75 2.00
36 Antik Johansson .75 2.00
37 Bo Hansson .75 2.00
38 Hans-Ake Carlsson .75 2.00
39 Lennart Soderberg .75 2.00
40 Benny Soderling .75 2.00
41 Anders Parmstrom .75 2.00
42 Lennart Selinder .75 2.00
43 Bjorn Larsson .75 2.00
44 Ove Hedberg .75 2.00
45 Berndt Arvidsson .75 2.00
46 P.A. Carlstrom .75 2.00
47 Lars Erik Sjoberg 4.00 8.00
48 Kjell Fhinn .75 2.00
49 Gunnar Andersson .75 2.00
50 Roland Bond .75 2.00
51 Goran Lysen .75 2.00
52 Bosse Englund .75 2.00
53 Stig Pavels .75 2.00
54 Bengt Bornstrom .75 2.00
55 Nisse Nilsson .75 2.00
56 Lennart Lange .75 2.00
57 Tommy Abrahamsson 4.00 8.00
58 Folke Bengtsson .75 2.00
59 Olle Sjogren .75 2.00
60 Knut Knutsson .75 2.00
61 Kjell Svensson .75 2.00
62 Rickard Fagerlund 1.75 4.00
63 Eilert Maatta .75 2.00
64 Stig Carlsson .75 2.00
65 Lars Hagg .75 2.00
66 Olle Stenar .75 2.00
67 Einar Andersson .75 2.00
68 Leif Andersson .75 2.00
69 Percy Lind .75 2.00
70 Gunnar Tallberg .75 2.00
71 Soren Maatta .75 2.00
72 Sven Bystrom .75 2.00
73 Hans Carlsson .75 2.00
74 Stig Goran Johansson 1.25 3.00
75 Thomas Warming .75 2.00
76 Kjell Larsson .75 2.00
77 Hakan Wickberg .75 2.00
78 Tord Lundstrom .75 2.00
79 Lennart Svedberg 2.00 4.00
80 Jan Erik Lyck .75 2.00
81 Stefan Carlsson .75 2.00
82 Kjell Jonsson .75 2.00
83 Lars Hedenstrom .75 2.00
84 Lars Ake Sivertsson .75 2.00
85 Lennart Johansson .75 2.00
86 Hans Sjoberg .75 2.00
87 Hans Dahllof .75 2.00
88 Hans Lindberg .75 2.00
89 Lars Bylund .75 2.00
90 Sten Edqvist .75 2.00
91 Arne Ericsson .75 2.00
92 Gert Blomer .75 2.00
93 Kjell Adrian .75 2.00
94 Jan Olsen .75 2.00
95 Berny Karlsson .75 2.00
96 Jorma Salmi .75 2.00
97 Ulf Sterner .75 2.00
98 Kjell-Ove Gustafsson .75 2.00
99 Lars Erik Lundvall .75 2.00
100 Kjell-Ronny Pettersson 1.00 3.00
101 Ronald Pettersson .75 2.00
102 Kjell Jonsson .75 2.00
103 Gote Hansson .75 2.00
104 Ove Sterner .75 2.00
105 Eine Olsson .75 2.00
106 Hans-Erik Fernstrom .75 2.00
107 Per-Olov Hardin .75 2.00
108 Bo Zetterberg .75 2.00
109 Ake Zettlin .75 2.00
110 Bengt-Olov Andreasson .75 2.00
111 Borje Molander .75 2.00
112 Sture Sundin .75 2.00
113 Bertil Karlsson 1.00 3.00
114 Lars Molander .75 2.00
115 Benno Persson .75 2.00
116 Rolf Larsson .75 2.00
117 Ronny Francis .75 2.00
118 Olle Westlund .75 2.00
119 Goran Wallin .75 2.00
120 Ingemar Persson .75 2.00
121 Tommy Bjorkman .75 2.00
122 Eddie Wingren .75 2.00
123 Lars Bjorn .75 2.00
124 Roland Stoltz .75 2.00
125 Sven Johansson 1.25 3.00
126 Arne Loong .75 2.00
127 Hans Mild .75 2.00
127 Per Lundstrom 5.00
128 Kurt Thulin .75 2.00
129 Ake Rydberg .75 2.00
130 Ove Malmberg .75 2.00
131 Lars Lundqvist .75 2.00
132 Kurt Svensson .75 2.00
133 Gosta Westerlund .75 2.00
134 Lars Andersson .75 2.00
135 Ulf Rydin .75 2.00
136 Lennart Haggroth 1.50 4.00
137 Jan Hedberg .75 2.00
138 Anders Carlberg .75 2.00
139 Hans Svedberg .75 2.00
140 Sture Hofverberg .75 2.00
141 Anders Ronnblom .75 2.00
142 Ulf Eriksson .75 2.00
143 Anders Andersson .75 2.00
144 Henrik Hedlund .75 2.00
145 Roger Boman .75 2.00
146 Bo Astrom .75 2.00
147 Bo Berglund 1.50 3.00
148 Lars Ake Warning .75 2.00
149 Sven-Olov Johansson .75 2.00
150 Ove Stenlund .75 2.00
151 Ivar Larsson .75 2.00
152 Nicke Johansson .75 2.00
153 Sten Olsen .75 2.00
154 Lars Gidlund .75 2.00
155 Tor Haarstad .75 2.00
156 Hakan Nygren .75 2.00
157 Bjorn Palmqvist .75 2.00
158 Soren Lindstrom .75 2.00
159 Henry Svensson .75 2.00
160 Lars Hagstrom .75 2.00
161 Ake Eklof .75 2.00
162 Ulf Lundstrom .75 2.00
163 Ronny Nordstrom .75 2.00
164 Paul Stahl .75 2.00
165 Kenneth Sahlen 1.25 3.00
166 Anders Hedlund .75 2.00
167 Ingemar Caris .75 2.00
168 Arne Carlsson .75 2.00
169 Gote Bostrom .75 2.00
170 Roger Olsson .75 2.00
171 Ole Jacobson .75 2.00
172 Curt Edenvik .75 2.00
173 Goran Svensson .75 2.00
174 Eje Lindstrom .75 2.00
175 Curt Larsson 2.50 5.00
176 Gunnar Backman .75 2.00
177 Anders Nordin .75 2.00
178 Ulf Torstensson .75 2.00
179 Kent Lindgren .75 2.00
180 Kent Sjalin .75 2.00
181 Lars Goran Nilsson .75 2.00
182 Heimo Klockare .75 2.00
183 Lars Sattare .75 2.00
184 Lars-Ake Lundell .75 2.00
185 Kjell Savstrom .75 2.00
186 Carl-Goran Oberg .75 2.00
187 Bjorn Larsson .75 2.00
188 Leif Eriksson .75 2.00
189 Dag Olsson .75 2.00
190 Lars Lohman .75 2.00
191 unknown .75 2.00
192 unknown .75 2.00
193 unknown .75 2.00
194 unknown .75 2.00
195 unknown .75 2.00
196 unknown .75 2.00
197 unknown .75 2.00
198 unknown .75 2.00
199 unknown .75 2.00
200 Hans Aleblad .75 2.00
201 Karl Soren Hedlund .75 2.00
202 Clarence Carlsson .75 2.00
203 Bjorn Johansson .75 2.00
204 Kent Persson .75 2.00
205 Goran Thelin .75 2.00
206 Leif Ohrlund .75 2.00
207 Mats Davidsson .75 2.00
208 Leif Arturssson .75 2.00
209 Karl Gunnar Backman .75 2.00
210 Hans Mellinger .75 2.00
211 Hans Inge Lund .75 2.00
212 Kent Jansson .75 2.00
213 Anders Ronnkvist .75 2.00
214 Bo Olofsson .75 2.00

1967-68 Swedish Hockey

This 300-card set features the skaters from the Swedish first and second division teams from the 1967-68 season, as well as the national team, Tre Kronor. The cards measure 2" by 3 1/8" and feature posed color photos on the front. The national team cards have the words Tre Kronor and the three crown logo across the top. The backs have the card number, player stats and an invitation to purchase a collectors album, all in Swedish. The album for the set includes numerous pages of text and photos about Swedish hockey, and is valued at $35. Although short on widely recognizable names, the set does include early -- if not first -- cards of Inge Hammarstrom and Christer Abrahamsson.
COMPLETE SET (300) 62.50 150.00
1 Christer Abrahamsson 2.00 4.00
2 Tommy Abrahamsson 1.00 2.00
3 Folke Bengtsson .25 1.00
4 Arne Carlsson .25 1.00
5 Bengt-Ake Gustavsson .25 1.00
6 Anders Hagstrom .25 1.00
7 Inge Hammarstrom 2.50 5.00
8 Leif Henriksson .25 1.00
9 Leif Holmqvist 1.00 2.00
10 Per-Arne Hubinette .25 1.00
11 Mats Hysing .25 1.00
12 Nils Johansson .25 1.00
13 Stig-Goran Johansson .25 1.00
14 Hans Lindberg .25 1.00
15 Tord Lundstrom .25 1.00
16 Lars-Goran Nilsson .25 1.00
17 Anders Nordin .25 1.00
18 Bert-Ola Nordlander .25 1.00
19 Roger Olsson .25 1.00
20 Bjorn Palmqvist .25 1.00
21 Kjell Sundstrom .25 1.00
22 Lennart Svedberg .50 2.00
23 Hakan Wickberg .25 1.00
24 Carl-Goran Oberg .25 1.00
25 Lasse Ohman .25 1.00
26 Curt Edenvik .25 1.00
27 Hans Eriksson .25 1.00
28 Rolf Hallgren .25 1.00
29 Bo Hansson .25 1.00
30 Ove Hedberg .25 1.00
31 Kjell Hedman .50 2.00
32 Leif Holmqvist 1.00 2.00
33 Anders Johansson .25 1.00
34 Bengt Larsson .25 1.00
35 Bjorn Larsson .25 1.00
36 Rune Lindh .25 1.00
37 Borje Molander .25 1.00
38 Kjell Nilsson .25 1.00
39 Bert-Ola Nordlander .25 1.00
40 Anders Parmstrom .25 1.00
41 Lennart Sellinder .25 1.00
42 Kjell Savstrom .25 1.00
43 Lars Bylund .25 1.00
44 Hans Dahllof .50 2.00
45 Lennart Gustafsson .25 1.00
46 Lars Hedenstrom .25 1.00
47 Lennart Johansson .25 1.00
48 Kjell Johnsson .25 1.00
49 Stefan Karlsson .25 1.00
50 Nisse Larsson .25 1.00
51 Lennart Lind .25 1.00
52 Hans Lindberg .25 1.00
53 Tord Lundstrom .25 1.00
54 Jan-Erik Lyck .25 1.00
55 Lars-Goran Nilsson .25 1.00
56 Anders Sahlin .50 2.00
57 Lars-Ake Sivertsson .25 1.00
58 Hans Sjoberg .25 1.00
59 Hakan Wickberg .25 1.00
60 Tommy Bjorkman .50 2.00
61 Lasse Bjorn .25 1.00
62 Thomas Carlsson .25 1.00
63 Roland Einarsson .50 2.00
64 Kjell Keijser .25 1.00
65 Stig Larsson .25 1.00
66 Kent Lindgren .25 1.00
67 Tommie Lindgren .25 1.00
68 Lars-Ake Lundell .25 1.00
69 Per Lundstrom .25 1.00
70 Bjorn Palmquist .25 1.00
71 Ulf Rydin .25 1.00
72 Lars-Eric Sjoberg 2.00 4.00
73 Lars Starck .25 1.00
74 Roland Stoltz .25 1.00
75 Henry Svensson .25 1.00
76 Kurt Thulin .25 1.00
77 Gosta Westerlund .25 1.00
78 Eddie Wingren .25 1.00
79 Carl-Goran Oberg .25 1.00
80 Anders Andersson .25 1.00
81 Hasse Andersson .25 1.00
82 Hakan Andersson .25 1.00
83 Anders Asplund .25 1.00
84 Hans Bergqvist .25 1.00
85 Hans Bostrom .25 1.00
86 Kjell Eriksson .50 2.00
87 Conny Evensson .50 2.00
88 Bjorn Fagerlund .50 2.00
89 Ingemar Magnusson .25 1.00
90 Hans-Ake Nilsson .25 1.00

91 Rune Nilsson .25 1.00
92 Kent Olsson .25 1.00
93 Lars Stalberg .25 1.00
94 Christer Sundquist .25 1.00
95 Christer Abrahamsson 2.00 4.00
96 Tommy Abrahamsson 1.00 2.00
97 Bosse Andersson .25 1.00
98 Gunnar Andersson .25 1.00
99 Lars Andersson .25 1.00
100 Folke Bengtsson .25 1.00
101 Roland Bond .25 1.00
102 Kjell Fihnn .25 1.00
103 Jan-Olof Kroon .25 1.00
104 Lennart Lange .25 1.00
105 Sture Leksell .50 2.00
106 Goran Lysen .25 1.00
107 Ulf Martensson .25 1.00
108 Nisse Nilsson .25 1.00
109 Dag Ohlsson .25 1.00
110 Olle Sjogren .25 1.00
111 Ake Sunesson .25 1.00
112 Dan Soderstrom .25 1.00
113 Goran Winge .25 1.00
114 Mats Ahlberg .25 1.00
115 Olle Ost .25 1.00
116 Gunnar Backman .50 2.00
117 Lage Edin .25 1.00
118 Ake Eklof .25 1.00
119 Torbjorn Hubinette .25 1.00
120 Nils Johansson .25 1.00
121 Ulf Kroon .25 1.00
122 Ivar Larsson .50 2.00
123 Christer Nilsson .25 1.00
124 Anders Nordin .25 1.00
125 Hakan Nygren .25 1.00
126 Sten Olsen .25 1.00
127 Paul Stahl .25 1.00
128 Gunnar Safsten .25 1.00
129 Ulf Torstensson .25 1.00
130 Ulf Wigren .25 1.00
131 Lars Ohman .25 1.00
132 Tore Ohman .25 1.00
133 Bengt Andersson .25 1.00
134 Nils Carlsson .25 1.00
135 Kjell Eklind .25 1.00
136 Allan Fernstrom .25 1.00
137 Bengt Gustavsson .25 1.00
138 Bengt-Ake Gustavsson .50 2.00
139 Gote Hansson .25 1.00
140 Per-Arne Hubinette .25 1.00
141 Sven-Ake Jakobsson .25 1.00
142 Goran Johansson .50 2.00
143 Mats Lind .25 1.00
144 Mats Lonn .25 1.00
145 Ulf Nises .25 1.00
146 Bo Olsson .25 1.00
147 Lennart Svedberg .50 2.00
148 Evert Tysk .25 1.00
149 Stig Ostling .25 1.00
150 Ulf Berglund .25 1.00
151 Clarence Carlsson .25 1.00
152 Arne Ekenberg .25 1.00
153 Kenneth Ekman .25 1.00
154 Tom Haugh .50 2.00
155 Rolf Joelsson .25 1.00
156 Bjorn Johanesson .25 1.00
157 Arne Johansson .25 1.00
158 Bengt-Goran Karlsson .25 1.00
159 Kjell Larsson .25 1.00
160 Lasse Larsson .25 1.00
161 Barry Murman .25 1.00
162 Klas Goran Nilsson .25 1.00
163 Rolf Norell .25 1.00
164 Lennart Skordaker .25 1.00
165 Ulf Sterner .50 2.00
166 Arne Wickstrom .25 1.00
167 Bengt-Olov Andreasson .50 2.00
168 Leif Eriksson .25 1.00
169 Ove Evaldson .25 1.00
170 Hans-Erik Fernstrom .25 1.00
171 Kenneth Hillgren .25 1.00
172 Per-Olof Hardin .25 1.00
173 Bertil Karlsson .25 1.00
174 Torsten Karlsson .25 1.00
175 Rolf Larsson .25 1.00
176 William Lofqvist 1.00 2.00
177 Lars Mollander .25 1.00
178 Gert Nystrom .25 1.00
179 Olle Westlund .25 1.00
180 Bo Zetterberg .25 1.00
181 Leif Andersson .25 1.00
182 Borje Burlin .25 1.00
183 Hans Carlsson .25 1.00
184 Stig Carlsson .25 1.00
185 Einar Granath .25 1.00
186 Kjell-Ake Hedstrom .25 1.00
187 Mats Hysing .25 1.00
188 Stig-Goran Johansson .25 1.00
189 Curt Larsson 1.25 2.50
190 Eilert Maatta .25 1.00
191 Soren Maatta .25 1.00
192 Nils-Olof Schilstrom .25 1.00
193 Jan Schullstrom .25 1.00
194 Kjell Svensson .50 2.00
195 Gunnar Tallberg .25 1.00
196 Dick Yderstrom .25 1.00
197 Sten Andersson .50 2.00
198 Lars Arne Bergkvist .25 1.00
199 Anders Edstrom .25 1.00
200 Lars Bertil Eriksson .25 1.00
201 Charles Gustavsson .25 1.00
202 Ake Johansson .25 1.00
203 Lars Karestal .25 1.00
204 Rolf Karlsson .25 1.00
205 Erik Lindahl .25 1.00
206 Freddy Lindfors .50 2.00
207 Lennart Lindkvist .25 1.00
208 Kjell Rune Milton .25 1.00
209 Olle Nilsater .25 1.00
210 Birger Nordlund .25 1.00
211 Inge Tornlund .25 1.00
212 Jan Roger Oberg .25 1.00
213 Kjell Sture Oberg .25 1.00
214 Tommy Andersson .25 1.00
215 Soren Bostrom .25 1.00
216 Anders Bryner .25 1.00
217 Anders Claesson .50 2.00
218 Svante Granholm .25 1.00
219 Inge Hammarstrom 2.50 5.00
220 Borje Holmstrom .25 1.00
221 Jan Johansson .25 1.00
222 Antero Jonasson .25 1.00
223 Ove Jonsson .25 1.00
224 Lennart Lind .50 2.00
225 Jan-Erik Nilsson .25 1.00
226 Kurt Olofsson .25 1.00
227 Gosta Sjokvist .25 1.00
228 Jan Stolpe .25 1.00
229 Kjell Westerlund .25 1.00
230 Olle Ahman .25 1.00
231 Jan-Ivar Bergqvist .25 1.00
232 Lars-Ake Brannlund .50 2.00
233 Hans Bohlmark .25 1.00
234 Jan Christiansson .25 1.00
235 Bengt Eriksson .25 1.00
236 Arne Grenemo .25 1.00
237 Lars-Olof Henriksson .25 1.00
238 Kurt Jakobsson .25 1.00
239 Leif Jakobsson .25 1.00
240 Lars-Goran Johansson .25 1.00
241 Kimo Kivela .25 1.00
242 Borje Maatta .25 1.00
243 Anders Rapp .25 1.00
244 Tommy Sahlsten .25 1.00
245 Stig-Olof Zetterbrg .25 1.00
246 Lennart Abrahamsson .25 1.00
247 John Andersson .25 1.00
248 Ove Andersson .50 2.00
249 Kjell-olov Barrefjord .25 1.00
250 Ulf Barrefjord .25 1.00
251 Kent Bjork .25 1.00
252 Lars Dahlgren .25 1.00
253 Karl-Ove Eriksson .25 1.00
254 Osten Folkesson .25 1.00
255 Anders Hagstrom .25 1.00
256 Eric Jarvholm .25 1.00
257 Ulf Larsson .25 1.00
258 Bengt Lovgren .25 1.00
259 Roger Nilsson .25 1.00
260 Bengt Persson .50 2.00
261 Kjell Sundstrom .25 1.00
262 Roger Osterlund .25 1.00
263 Hans Aleblad .50 2.00
264 Ake Bolander .25 1.00
265 Karl-Gunnar Backman .25 1.00
266 Mats Davidsson .25 1.00
267 Bosse Englund .25 1.00
268 Tommy Eriksson .25 1.00
269 Karl-Soren Hedlund .25 1.00
270 Don Hughes .25 1.00
271 Krister Lindgren .25 1.00
272 Hans Mellinger .25 1.00
273 Des Moroney .25 1.00
274 Bo Olofsson .25 1.00
275 Hakan Olsson .25 1.00
276 Kent Persson .25 1.00
277 Ove Stenlund .25 1.00
278 Goran Thelin .25 1.00
279 Ove Thelin .25 1.00
280 Leif Ohrlund .25 1.00
281 Uno Ohrlund .25 1.00
282 Jan Ostling .25 1.00
283 Gert Blome .25 1.00
284 Ingemar Caris .50 2.00
285 Arne Carlsson .25 1.00
286 Kjell-Ove Gustafsson .25 1.00
287 Henric Hedlund .25 1.00
288 Leif Henriksson .25 1.00
289 Kjell Jonsson .25 1.00
290 Berny Karlsson .25 1.00
291 Goran Lindberg .25 1.00
292 Bernt Lundqvist .25 1.00
293 Lars Eric Lundvall .25 1.00
294 Carl-Fredrik Montan .25 1.00
295 Eine Ohlsson .50 2.00
296 Jan Olsen .25 1.00
297 Roger Olsson .25 1.00
298 Kjell-Ronnie Pettersson .50 2.00
299 Ronald Pettersson .25 1.00
300 Ronald Sarnholm .25 1.00

1969-70 Swedish Hockey

This 384-card set was released in Sweden by Williams Forlags AB to commemorate the players and nations competing in the World Championships, as well as club teams from Sweden. The cards measured 1 7/8" by 2 1/2" and featured a small portrait on the front, along with team name and emblem. The backs gave the player's name, vital stats (in Swedish) and sticker number. Early (first?) appearances by many legends make this set notable: look for Valeri Kharlamov, Alexander Yakushev and Ulf Nilsson. An album was available which not only housed the set, but offered stories, photos and stats to wrap up the previous season. This album is valued at $50.

COMPLETE SET (384) 200.00 400.00
1 Valerij Charlamov 7.50 15.00
2 Vitalij Davydov .75 1.50
3 Anatolij Firsov 3.00 6.00
4 Alexander Jakusjev 5.00 10.00
5 Vladimir Jursinov 1.00 2.00
6 Victor Kuzkin .38 .75
7 Vladimir Lutjenko 1.00 2.00
8 Alexander Maltsev 5.00 10.00
9 Boris Michailov 5.00 10.00
10 Jevgenij Misjakov 1.50 3.00
11 Vladimir Petrov 5.00 10.00
12 Jevgenij Poladjev .38 .75
13 Victor Putjkov .50 1.00
14 Alexander Ragulin 1.50 3.00
15 Igor Romisjevskij .38 .75
16 Vjatjeslav Starsjinov 1.25 2.50
17 Vladimir Vikulov .75 1.50
18 Jevgenij Zimin .75 1.50
19 Victor Zinger .50 1.00
20 Josef Augusta .38 .75
21 Vladimir Bednar .38 .75
22 Josef Cerny .50 1.00
23 Vladimir Dzurilla 5.00 10.00
24 Richard Farda .38 .75
25 Josef Golonka .75 1.50
26 Jan Havel .38 .75
27 Jaroslav Holik .75 1.50
28 Jiri Holik .50 1.00
29 Josef Horesovsky .38 .75
30 Jan Hrbaty .38 .75
31 Jaroslav Jirik .38 .75
32 Jan Klapac .38 .75
33 Miroslav Lacky .75 1.50
34 Oldrich Machac .38 .75
35 Vaclav Nedomansky 2.50 5.00
36 Frantisek Pospisil 1.00 2.00
37 Frantisek Sevcik .50 1.00
38 Jan Suchy .50 1.00
39 Ake Carlsson .38 .75
40 Curt Edenvik .38 .75
41 Hans Eriksson .38 .75
42 Bo Hansson .38 .75
43 Ove Hedberg .38 .75
44 Kjell Hedman .75 1.50
45 Leif Holmqvist 1.50 3.00
46 Anders Johansson .38 .75
47 Bjorn Larsson .38 .75
48 Borje Molander .38 .75
49 Ulf Nilsson 10.00 20.00
50 Bert-Ola Nordlander .50 1.00
51 Bo Olofsson .38 .75
52 Anders Parmstrom .38 .75
53 Lennart Selinder .38 .75
54 Hans Stromberg .38 .75
55 Kjell Savstrom .38 .75
56 Lars-Ake Warning .38 .75
57 Lars Bylund .38 .75
58 Inge Hammarstrom 2.50 5.00
59 Hans Dahllof .75 1.50
60 Lars Hedenstrom .38 .75
61 Kjell Johnsson .38 .75
62 Lennart Johansson .38 .75
63 Bertil Karlsson .38 .75
64 Stefan Karlsson .38 .75
65 Lennart Lind .38 .75
66 Hans Lindberg .38 .75
67 Tord Lundstrom .38 .75
68 Jan-Erik Lyck .38 .75
69 William Lovqvist 1.00 2.00
70 Lars-Goran Nilsson .38 .75
71 Stig Salming .50 1.00
72 Lars-Ake Sivertsson .38 .75
73 Lars-Goran Tano .38 .75
74 Hakan Wickberg .38 .75
75 Rolf Berglund .38 .75
76 Lars Alserydh .75 1.50
77 Tage Blom .38 .75
78 Alf Granstrom .38 .75
79 Lennart Haggroth .75 1.50
80 Bertil Karlsson .38 .75
81 Sven-Bertil Lindstrom .38 .75
82 Anders Lundberg .38 .75
83 Goran Lundmark .75 1.50
84 Sven-Erik Lundqvist .38 .75
85 Hans Lundstrom .38 .75
86 Kjell Lang .38 .75
87 Borje Lofstedt .38 .75
88 Olle Nilsson .38 .75
89 Jan-Olof Nordin .38 .75
90 Kjell Rehnstrom .38 .75
91 Peder Rehnstrom .38 .75
92 Leif Tjernstrom .38 .75
93 Kjell-Arne Wikstrom .38 .75
94 Anders Andren .38 .75
95 Thomas Carlsson .38 .75
96 Roland Einarsson 1.00 2.00
97 Lars Granlund .38 .75
98 Stig Larsson .38 .75
99 Lars-Ake Lundell .38 .75
100 Per Lundstrom .38 .75
101 Bjorn Palmquist .38 .75
102 Ult Rydin .38 .75
103 Christer Sehlstedt .75 1.50
104 Lars Starck .38 .75
105 Roland Stoltz .38 .75
106 Billy Sundstrom .38 .75
107 Henry Svensson .38 .75
108 Ove Svensson .38 .75
109 Ulf Torstensson .38 .75
110 Christer Abrahamsson 2.50 5.00
111 Tommy Abrahamsson 1.00 2.00
112 Gunnar Andersson .38 .75
113 Folke Bengtsson .38 .75
114 Kjell Brus .38 .75
115 Ake Danielsson .38 .75
116 Bo Englund .38 .75
117 Lennart Gustavsson .38 .75
118 Hans Jax .38 .75
119 Jan-Olov Kroon .38 .75
120 Roger Lindqvist .38 .75
121 Gunnar Mars .75 1.50
122 Ulf Martensson .38 .75
123 Nisse Nilsson .38 .75
124 Lars-Erik Sjoberg 2.50 5.00
125 Olle Sjogren .38 .75
126 Dan Soderstrom .38 .75
127 Mats Ahlberg .38 .75
128 Gunnar Backman 1.00 2.00
129 Ulf Croon .38 .75
130 Lage Edin .38 .75
131 Ake Eklof .38 .75
132 Anders Hedberg 10.00 20.00
133 Torbjorn Hubinette .38 .75
134 Nils Johansson .38 .75
135 Ivar Larsson 1.00 2.00
136 Christer Nilsson .38 .75
137 Lennart Norberg .38 .75
138 Anders Nordin .38 .75
139 Hakan Nygren .38 .75
140 Sten Olsen .38 .75
141 Anders Schahlin .38 .75
142 Gunnar Safsten .38 .75
143 Ulf Wigren .38 .75
144 Lars Ohman .38 .75
145 Tore Ohman .38 .75
146 Nils Carlsson .38 .75
147 Kjell Eklund .38 .75
148 Bengt Gustavsson .38 .75
149 Bengt-Ake Gustavsson 1.00 2.00
150 Gote Hansson .38 .75
151 Hans Hansson .38 .75
152 Per-Arne Hubinette .38 .75
153 Sven-Ake Jakobsson .38 .75
154 Goran Johansson .75 1.50
155 Mats Lind .38 .75
156 Mats Lonn .38 .75
157 Borje Marcus .38 .75
158 Lars Mjoberg .38 .75
159 Ulf Nises .38 .75
160 Bo Olsson .38 .75
161 Erling Sundblad .38 .75
162 Lennart Svedberg 1.00 2.00
163 Evert Tysk .38 .75
164 Stig Ostling .38 .75
165 Magnus Andersson .38 .75
166 Erling Bergmark .38 .75
167 Kenneth Hellman .38 .75
168 Bjorn Johansson .38 .75
169 Ulf Johansson .38 .75
170 Berny Karlsson .38 .75
171 Nils-Erik Karlsson .38 .75
172 Rolf Larsson .38 .75
173 Tore Larsson .38 .75
174 Roland Lestander .75 1.50
175 Lennart Lindgren .38 .75
176 Finn Lundstrom .38 .75
177 Kenneth Manberg .38 .75
178 Lars Molander .38 .75
179 Lennart Rudby .38 .75
180 Sven-Ake Rudby .38 .75
181 Curt Svensson .38 .75
182 Sverker Torstensson .38 .75
183 Gunnar Backman 1.00 2.00
184 Arne Carlsson .38 .75
185 Leif Henriksson .38 .75
186 Leif Holmqvist 1.50 3.00
187 Mats Hysing .38 .75
188 Nils Johansson .38 .75
189 Stig-Goran Johansson .75 1.50
190 Stefan Karlsson .38 .75
191 Tord Lundstrom .38 .75
192 Kjell-Rune Milton .38 .75
193 Lars-Goran Nilsson .38 .75
194 Bert-Ola Nordlander .50 1.00
195 Hakan Nygren .38 .75
196 Roger Olsson .38 .75
197 Bjorn Palmquist .38 .75
198 Lars-Erik Sjoberg 2.00 4.00
199 Ulf Sterner .38 .75
200 Lennart Svedberg .75 1.50
201 Dick Yderstrom .38 .75
202 Lennart Abrahamsson .38 .75
203 Anders Bengtsson .75 1.50
204 Agne Bylund .38 .75
205 Jan Edlund .38 .75
206 Goran Hedberg .38 .75
207 Christer Johansson .38 .75
208 Rolf Jager .38 .75
209 Per-Erik Kall .38 .75
210 Anders Norberg .38 .75
211 Janne Pettersson .75 1.50
212 Bo Sjostrom .38 .75
213 Dick Sjostrom .38 .75
214 Lasse Sjostrom .38 .75
215 Ulf Stecksen .38 .75
216 Lennart Strohm .38 .75
217 Kurt Tillander .38 .75
218 Roger Osterlund .38 .75
219 Hans-Ake Andersson .38 .75
220 Hans Bejbom .38 .75
221 Carl-Axel Berglund .38 .75
222 Goran Borell .38 .75
223 Bjarne Brostrom .38 .75
224 Per Backman .38 .75
225 Kennet Calen .38 .75
226 Lennart Carlsson .38 .75
227 Mats Davidsson .38 .75
228 Curt Ferding .38 .75
229 Lars-Olof Granstrom .38 .75
230 Rolf Hansson .38 .75
231 Rune Holmgren .38 .75
232 Rune Norrstrom .38 .75
233 Bert-Ake Olsson .38 .75
234 Olle Olsson .38 .75
235 Jan Svedman .38 .75
236 Walter Winsth .38 .75
237 Goran Akerlund .38 .75
238 Borje Burlin .38 .75
239 Hans Carlsson .38 .75
240 Stig Carlsson .38 .75
241 Gunnar Granberg .38 .75
242 Allan Helenefors .38 .75
243 Mats Hysing .38 .75
244 Bertil Jacobsson .38 .75
245 Stig-Goran Johansson .75 1.50
246 Curt Larsson 1.25 2.50
247 Eilert Maatta .38 .75
248 Soren Maatta .38 .75
249 Tommy Bergman .38 .75
250 Nils-Olof Schilstrom .38 .75
251 Jan Schullstrom .38 .75
252 Kjell Svensson .75 1.50
253 Gunnar Tallberg .38 .75
254 Borje Ulweback .38 .75
255 Dick Yderstrom .38 .75
256 Tommy Andersson .38 .75
257 Bulla Berggren .38 .75
258 Anders Bryner .38 .75
259 Anders Claesson .75 1.50
260 Jan Johansson .38 .75
261 Ove Jonsson .38 .75
262 Lennart Lind .38 .75
263 Arne Lundstrom .38 .75
264 Ake Lundstrom .38 .75
265 Jan-Erik Nilsson .38 .75
266 Lennart Norberg .38 .75
267 Sten-Olov Olsson .38 .75
268 Hakan Pettersson .38 .75
269 Stefan Pettersson .38 .75
270 Gosta Sjokvist .38 .75
271 Jan Stolpe .38 .75
272 Ake Soderberg .38 .75
273 Kjell Westerlund .38 .75
274 Olle Ahman .38 .75
275 Krister Andersson .75 1.50
276 Bert Danielsson .38 .75
277 Gert Danielsson .38 .75
278 Bengt Eriksson .38 .75
279 Lars-Anders Gustavsson .38 .75
280 Curt Jacobsson .38 .75
281 Leif Jacobsson .38 .75
282 Lars-Erik Jakobsson .38 .75
283 Lars-Goran Johansson .38 .75
284 Des Moroney .38 .75
285 Borje Maatta .38 .75
286 Lars-Ake Nordin .38 .75
287 Kenneth Pedersen .38 .75
288 Anders Rapp .38 .75
289 Benny Runesson .38 .75
290 Jonny Ryman .38 .75
291 Ake Ryman .38 .75
292 Goran Ahstrom .75 1.50
293 John Andersson .38 .75
294 Kjell-Olov Barrefjord .38 .75
295 Ulf Barrefjord .38 .75
296 Kent Bjork .38 .75
297 Lars Dahlgren .38 .75
298 Karl-Olof Eriksson .38 .75
299 Osten Folkesson .38 .75
300 Anders Hagstrom .38 .75
301 Eric Jarvholm .38 .75
302 Ulf Larsson .38 .75
303 Bo Leong .75 1.50
304 Bengt Lofgren .38 .75
305 Roger Nilsson .38 .75
306 Bengt Persson .75 1.50
307 Ulf Stromsoe .38 .75
308 Kjell Sundstrom .38 .75
309 Leif Andersson .38 .75
310 Bernt Augustsson .38 .75
311 Kjell Augustsson .38 .75
312 Tommy Eriksson 1.00 2.00
313 Lars-Olof Feltendahl .38 .75
314 Karl-Soren Hedlund .38 .75
315 Penti Hyytiainen .38 .75
316 Arne Johansson .38 .75
317 Bengt-Goran Karlsson .38 .75
318 Curt Lundmark 1.00 2.00
319 Hakan Olsson .75 1.50
320 Kent Persson .38 .75
321 Ove Stenlund .38 .75
322 Goran Thelin .38 .75
323 Ove Thelin .38 .75
324 Bo Astrom .38 .75
325 Hasse Mellinger .38 .75
326 Uno Ohrlund .38 .75
327 Jan Ostling .38 .75
328 Kjell Andersson .38 .75
329 Ronny Andersson 1.00 2.00
330 Gert Blome .38 .75
331 Ingemar Caris 1.00 2.00
332 Arne Carlsson .38 .75
333 Svante Granholm .38 .75
334 Henric Hedlund .38 .75
335 Leif Henriksson .38 .75
336 Anders Johansson .38 .75
337 Kjell Jonsson .38 .75
338 Bjorn Lindberg .38 .75
339 Goran Lindberg .38 .75
340 Carl-Fredrik Montan .38 .75
341 Leif Nilsson .38 .75
342 Kurt Olofsson .38 .75
343 Jan Olsen .38 .75
344 Roger Olsson .38 .75
345 Kjell-Ronnie Petterson .38 .75
346 Ulf Sterner .38 .75
347 Rickie Bayes 1.25 2.50
348 Gary Begg .75 1.50
349 Roger Bourbonnais 1.00 2.00
350 Jack Bownass 1.00 2.00
351 Terry Caffery 1.25 2.50
352 Steve Carlyle 1.25 2.50
353 Ab Demarco 1.50 3.00
354 Ted Hargreaves 1.00 2.00
355 Bill Heindl 1.25 2.50
356 Fran Huck .75 1.50
357 Steve King 1.25 2.50
358 Chuck Lefley 2.00 4.00
359 Morris Mott 1.25 2.50
360 Terry O'Malley 1.00 2.00
361 Kevin O'Shea 1.25 2.50
362 Gerry Pinder 2.00 4.00
363 Steve Rexe 1.50 3.00
364 Ken Stephenson 1.25 2.50
365 Wayne Stephenson 5.00 10.00
366 Matti Harju .38 .75
367 Esa Isaksson .38 .75
368 Kari Johansson .38 .75
369 Juhani Jylha .38 .75
370 Matti Keinonen .38 .75
371 Veli-Pekka Ketola 1.50 3.00
372 Lasse Kiili .75 1.50
373 Ilpo Koskela .38 .75
374 Pekka Leimu .38 .75
375 Seppo Lindstrom .38 .75
376 Pekka Marjamaki .38 .75
377 Lauri Mononen .38 .75
378 Lasse Oksanen .38 .75
379 Lalli Partanen .38 .75
380 Esa Peltonen .38 .75
381 Jorma Peltonen .38 .75
382 Juhani Rantasila .38 .75
383 Juhani Wahlsten .38 .75
384 Urpo Ylonen .75 1.50

1970-71 Swedish Hockey

This set of 384-cards was issued by Williams Forlags AB and printed by Panini in Italy. The cards, which measure approximately 2 1/2" by 1 3/4", feature teams from the Swedish first and second divisions, as well as national team members from Tre Kroner, Russia, Czechoslovakia, Finland and East Germany. The card fronts feature a small player portrait along with the team emblem. The backs give player name, a brief bio and card number. The set includes many well known international stars, most prominently the first appearance of HOFer Borje Salming. An album to house the stickers was available as well; it also included text and photos to give a brief history of the teams involved. It is valued at approximately $40. Note: Spellings are as they appear on the cards and, in the case of Russian players, are not necessarily the spellings typically used for these players.

COMPLETE SET (384) 200.00 400.00
1 Leif (Honken) Holmqvist 1.25 2.50
2 Kjell Hedman .75 1.50
3 Lars Danielsson .38 .75
4 Ake Fagerstrom .38 .75
5 Per-Arne Hubinette .38 .75
6 Hakan Lindgren .38 .75
7 Bert-Ola Nordlander .50 1.00
8 Rolf (Rattan) Edberg .38 .75
9 Bo Hansson .38 .75
10 Jan-Olov Kroon .38 .75
11 Ulf Nilsson 5.00 10.00
12 Bosse Olofsson .38 .75
13 Lennart Selinder .38 .75
14 Hans Stromberg .38 .75
15 Kjell Savstrom .38 .75
16 Lars-Ake Warning .38 .75
17 Lars-Goran Nilsson .75 1.50
Alexander Yakushev
18 William Lofqvist .75 1.50
19 Hans Dahllof .75 1.50
20 Lars Bylund .38 .75
21 Lars Hedenstrom .38 .75
22 Kjell Johnsson .38 .75
23 Borje Salming 12.50 25.00
24 Stig Salming .38 .75
25 Stig Ostling .38 .75
26 Inge Hammarstrom 2.50 5.00
27 Lennart Johansson .38 .75
28 Stefan Karlsson .38 .75
29 Lennart Lind .38 .75
30 Hans (Virus) Lindberg .38 .75
31 Tord Lundstrom .38 .75
32 Jan-Erik Lyck .38 .75
33 Lars-Goran Nilsson .38 .75
34 Lars-Ake Sivertsson .38 .75
35 Hakan Wickberg .38 .75
36 puzzle .38 .75
37 puzzle .38 .75
38 puzzle .38 .75
39 puzzle .38 .75
40 puzzle .38 .75
41 puzzle .38 .75
42 puzzle .50 .75
43 puzzle .50 .75
44 puzzle .38 .75
45 puzzle .38 .75
46 puzzle .50 .75
47 puzzle .50 .75
48 Roland Einarsson .75 1.50
49 Ake Eklof .38 .75
50 Christer Ahlstrand .38 .75
51 Thomas Carlsson .38 .75
52 Anders Rylin .38 .75
53 Billy Sundstrom .38 .75
54 Folke Bengtsson .38 .75
55 Stig Larsson .38 .75
56 Lars-Ake Lundell .38 .75
57 Per Lundstrom .38 .75
58 Bjorn Palmqvist .38 .75
59 Ulf Rydin .38 .75
60 Ove Svensson .38 .75
61 Jan Zabrodsky .38 .75
62 Leif Holmqvist PUZ 1.00 2.00
63 Leif Holmqvist PUZ 1.00 2.00
64 Leif Holmqvist PUZ 1.00 2.00
65 Leif Holmqvist PUZ 1.00 2.00
66 Christer Abrahamsson 1.50 3.00
67 Christer Sterner .75 1.50
68 Thommy Abrahamsson .75 1.50
69 Karl-Gustaf Alander .38 .75
70 Gunnar Andersson .38 .75
71 Roland Bond .38 .75
72 Ake Danielsson .38 .75
73 Per-Olov Brasar 1.50 3.00
74 Kjell Brus .38 .75
75 Hans Jax .38 .75
76 Dan Labraaten 1.50 3.00
77 Roger Lindqvist .38 .75
78 Ulf Martensson .38 .75
79 Olle Sjogren .38 .75
80 Ingemar Snis .38 .75
81 Dan Soderstrom .38 .75
82 Mats Ahlberg .38 .75
83 Gunnar Backman .75 1.50
84 Ivar Larsson .75 1.50
85 Lage Edin .38 .75
86 Kjell-Rune Milton .38 .75
87 Ulf Torstensson .38 .75
88 Ulf Wigren .38 .75
89 Ulf Croon .38 .75
90 Hakan Dahllof .38 .75
91 Anders Hedberg 5.00 10.00
92 Torbjorn Hubinette .38 .75
93 Christer Nilsson .38 .75
94 Lennart Norberg .38 .75
95 Anders Nordin .38 .75
96 Hakan Nygren .38 .75
97 Per-Olof Uusitalo .38 .75
98 Lars Ohman .38 .75
99 Tore Ohman .38 .75
100 V. Dzurilla PUZ .75 1.50
101 V. Dzurilla PUZ .75 1.50
102 V. Dzurilla PUZ .75 1.50
103 V. Dzurilla PUZ .75 1.50
104 V. Dzurilla PUZ .75 1.50
105 V. Dzurilla PUZ .75 1.50
106 V. Dzurilla PUZ .75 1.50
107 V. Dzurilla PUZ .75 1.50
108 V. Dzurilla PUZ .75 1.50
109 V. Dzurilla PUZ .75 1.50
110 V. Dzurilla PUZ .75 1.50
111 V. Dzurilla PUZ .75 1.50
112 Bengt-Ake Gustavsson .75 1.50
113 Lars Gustavsson .75 1.50
114 Tommy Andersson .38 .75
115 Hans-Olov Ernlund .38 .75
116 Lars Mjoberg .38 .75
117 Gote Hansson .38 .75
118 L. Svedberg PUZ .50 1.00
119 B. Mikhailov PUZ 1.50 3.00
120 Leif Holmqvist PUZ 1.00 2.00
121 Hans Hansson .38 .75
122 Sven-Ake Jakobsson .38 .75
123 Mats Lind .38 .75
124 Mats Lonn .38 .75
125 Borje Marcus .38 .75
126 Ulf Nises .38 .75
127 Borje Skoog .38 .75
128 Erling Sundblad .38 .75
129 Kent Sundkvist .38 .75
130 Curt Larsson 1.00 2.00
131 Torbjorn Hellsing .75 1.50
132 Tommie Bergman 2.00 4.00
133 Arne Carlsson .38 .75
134 Allan Helenefors .38 .75
135 Eilert Maatta .38 .75
136 Jan Schullstrom .38 .75
137 Hans Carlsson .38 .75
138 Tommy Carlsson .38 .75
139 Gunnar Granberg .38 .75
140 Mats Hysing .38 .75
141 Bertil Jacobsson .38 .75
142 Stig-Goran Johansson .38 .75
143 Soren Maatta .38 .75
144 Nils-Olov Schilstrom .38 .75
145 Dick Yderstrom .38 .75
146 Carl-Goran Oberg .38 .75
147 Lennart Svedberg .50 1.00
148 Anders Claesson .75 1.50
149 Kent Othberg .75 1.50
150 Jan Johansson .38 .75
151 Jan-Erik Nilsson .38 .75
152 Stefan Pettersson .38 .75
153 Lennart Svedberg .75 1.50
154 Bo Berggren .38 .75
155 Arne Lundstrom .38 .75
156 Finn Lundstrom .38 .75
157 I. Romisjevskij PUZ .38 .75
158 I. Romisjevskij PUZ .50 1.00
159 Ake Lundstrom .38 .75
160 V. Tretiak PUZ 4.00 8.00
161 V. Tretiak PUZ 4.00 8.00
162 Lennart Norberg .38 .75
163 Hakan Pettersson .38 .75
164 Ake Soderberg .50 1.00
165 Olle Ahman .38 .75
166 puzzle .38 .75
167 puzzle .38 .75
168 puzzle .38 .75
169 puzzle .38 .75
170 puzzle .38 .75
171 puzzle .38 .75
172 puzzle .38 .75
173 puzzle .38 .75
174 puzzle .38 .75
175 puzzle .38 .75
176 puzzle .38 .75
177 puzzle .38 .75
178 Christer Andersson .75 1.50
179 Goran Astrom .75 1.50
180 Kenneth Ekman .38 .75
181 Lars Erik Jakobsson .38 .75
182 Des Moroney .38 .75
183 Borje Maatta .38 .75
184 Kenneth Pedersen .38 .75
185 Anders Rapp .38 .75
186 Sven Crabo .38 .75
187 Lars Anders Gustavsson .38 .75
188 Kurt Jacobsson .38 .75
189 Leif Jacobsson .38 .75
190 Lars Goran Johansson .38 .75
191 Bernt Karlsson .38 .75
192 Benny Runesson .38 .75
193 Jonny Ryman .38 .75
194 Ake Ryman .38 .75
195 Christer Grahn .75 1.50
196 Ronny Sandstrom .38 .75
197 John Andersson .38 .75
198 Karl-Olof Eriksson .38 .75
199 Anders Hagstrom .38 .75
200 Rolf Jager .38 .75
201 Erik Jarvholm .38 .75
202 Lars Nordin .38 .75
203 Ulf Barrefjord .38 .75
204 Lars Dahlgren .38 .75
205 Ulf Ingvarsson .38 .75
206 Ulf Larsson .38 .75
207 Jan Lundqvist .38 .75
208 Ulf Lundstrom .38 .75
209 Bengt Lovgren .38 .75
210 Lars SJostrom .38 .75
211 Kjell Sundstrom .38 .75
212 Ulf Stromsoe .38 .75
213 Hakan Olsson .75 1.50
214 Leif Andersson .38 .75
215 Tommy Eriksson .75 1.50
216 Karl-Soren Hedlund .38 .75
217 Curt Lundmark .75 1.50
218 Ove Nystrom .38 .75
219 Gote Gustavsson .38 .75
220 Hans Hjelm .38 .75
221 Pennti Hyytiainen .38 .75
222 Arne Johansson .38 .75
223 Bengt-Goran Karlsson .38 .75
224 Kent Persson .38 .75
225 Ove Stenlund .38 .75
226 Goran Thelin .38 .75
227 Ove Thelin .38 .75
228 Bo Astrom .38 .75
229 Jan Ostling .38 .75
230 V. Tretiak action 10.00 20.00
231 V. Konovalenko PUZ .38 .75
232 V. Konovalenko PUZ .38 .75
233 V. Konovalenko PUZ .38 .75
234 V. Konovalenko PUZ .38 .75
235 V. Konovalenko PUZ .38 .75
236 V. Konovalenko PUZ .38 .75
237 V. Konovalenko PUZ .38 .75
238 V. Konovalenko PUZ .38 .75
239 V. Konovalenko PUZ .38 .75
240 V. Konovalenko PUZ .38 .75
241 V. Konovalenko PUZ .38 .75
242 V. Konovalenko PUZ .38 .75
243 Ingemar Caris .75 1.50
244 Ronny Andersson .75 1.50
245 Gert Blome .38 .75
246 Anders Johansson .38 .75
247 Goran Lindberg .38 .75
248 Jan Olsen .38 .75
249 Lars-Erik Sjoberg 2.00 4.00

250 Kjell Andersson .38 .75
251 Svante Granholm .38 .75
252 Henrik Hedlund .38 .75
253 Leif Henriksson .38 .75
254 Bjorn Lindberg .38 .75
255 Billy Lindstrom .38 .75
256 Carl-Fredrik Montan .38 .75
257 Leif Nilsson .38 .75
258 Kurt Olofsson .38 .75
259 Roger Olsson .38 .75
260 Kjell-Ronnie Pettersson .38 .75
261 Soviet team PUZ .38 .75
262 Soviet team PUZ .38 .75
263 Soviet team PUZ .38 .75
264 Soviet team PUZ .38 .75
265 Soviet team PUZ .38 .75
266 Soviet team PUZ .38 .75
267 Soviet team PUZ .38 .75
268 Soviet team PUZ .38 .75
269 Soviet team PUZ .38 .75
270 Soviet team PUZ .38 .75
271 Soviet team PUZ .38 .75
272 Soviet team PUZ .38 .75
273 Leif Holmqvist 1.00 2.00
274 Gunnar Backman .75 1.50
275 Christer Abrahamsson 1.50 3.00
276 Thommy Abrahamsson .75 1.50
277 Arne Carlsson .38 .75
278 Nils Johansson .38 .75
279 Ljell-Rune Milton .38 .75
280 Lars-Erik Sjoberg 2.00 4.00
281 Lennart Svedberg .75 1.50
282 Anders Hedberg 5.00 10.00
283 Stig-Goran Johansson .38 .75
284 Stefan Karlsson .38 .75
285 Hans Lindberg .38 .75
286 Tord Lundstrom .38 .75
287 Lars-Goran Nilsson .38 .75
288 Anders Nordin .38 .75
289 Roger Olsson .38 .75
290 Bjorn Palmqvist .38 .75
291 Ulf Sterner .38 .75
292 Hakan Wickberg .38 .75
293 Urpo Ylonen 1.00 2.00
294 Jorma Valtonen .75 1.50
295 Ilpo Koskela .38 .75
296 Seppo Lindstrom .38 .75
297 Pekka Marjamaki .38 .75
298 Lalli Partinen .38 .75
299 Juha Rantasila .38 .75
300 Heikki Riihiranta 1.00 2.00
301 Pekka Keimu .38 .75
302 Matti Keinonen .38 .75
303 Veli-Pekka Ketola 1.50 3.00
304 Vaino Kolkka .38 .75
305 Harri Linnonmaa .38 .75
306 Lauri Mononen .38 .75
307 Matti Murto .75 1.50
308 Lasse Oksanen .38 .75
309 Esa Peltonen .38 .75
310 Jorma Peltonen .38 .75
311 Juhani Tamminen .75 1.50
312 Jorma Vehmanen .38 .75
313 Viktor Konovalenko .75 1.50
314 Vladislav Tretjak 20.00 40.00
315 Vitalij Davidov .75 1.50
316 Vladimir Lutjenko .75 1.50
317 Jevgenij Paladjev .38 .75
318 Alexander Ragulin 1.50 3.00
319 Igor Romisjevskij .50 1.00
320 Valerij Vasiljev 2.50 5.00
321 Valerij Nikitin .50 1.00
322 Valerij Kharlamov 7.50 15.00
323 Anatolij Firsov 4.00 8.00
324 Alexander Jakusjev 4.00 8.00
325 Alexander Maltsev 4.00 8.00
326 Boris Michailov 4.00 8.00
327 Jevgenij Misjakov 1.25 2.50
328 Vladimir Petrov 2.50 5.00
329 Viktor Polupanov .38 .75
330 Vladimir Sjadrin 1.50 3.00
331 Vjatjeslav Starsinov 1.25 2.50
332 Vladimir Vikulov .50 1.00
333 puzzle .38 .75
334 puzzle .38 .75
335 puzzle .38 .75
336 puzzle .38 .75
337 puzzle .38 .75
338 puzzle .38 .75
339 puzzle .38 .75
340 puzzle .38 .75
341 puzzle .38 .75
342 puzzle .38 .75
343 puzzle .38 .75
344 puzzle .38 .75
345 Vladimir Dzurilla 2.50 5.00
346 Miroslav Lacky .75 1.50
347 Vladimir Bednar .38 .75
348 Josef Horesovsky .38 .75
349 Oldrich Machac .38 .75
350 Frantisek Pospisil .75 1.50
351 Jan Suchy .50 1.00
352 Lubomir Ujvary .38 .75
353 Josef Cerny .50 1.00
354 Richard Farda .38 .75
355 Julius Haas .38 .75
356 Ivan Hlinka .75 1.50
357 Jaroslav Holik .50 1.00
358 Jiri Holik .50 1.00
359 Jan Hrbaty .38 .75
360 Jiri Kochta .38 .75
361 Vladislav Martinec .38 .75
362 Vaclav Nedomansky 1.50 3.00
363 Stanislav Pryl .38 .75
364 Frantisek Sevcik .38 .75
365 Klaus Hirche .75 1.50
366 Diter Purschel .75 1.50
367 Frank Braun .38 .75
368 Dieter Dewitz .38 .75
369 Bernd Karrenbauer .38 .75
370 Helmut Novy .38 .75
371 Dietmar Peters .38 .75
372 Wolfgang Plotka .38 .75
373 Peter Slapke .38 .75
374 Rolf Bielas .38 .75
375 Lothar Fuchs .38 .75
376 Bernd Hiller .38 .75
377 Reinhard Karger .38 .75
378 Hartmut Nickel .38 .75
379 Rudiger Noack .38 .75
380 Rainer Patschinski .38 .75
381 Peter Prusa .38 .75
382 Wilfried Rohrbach .38 .75
383 Dieter Rohl .38 .75
384 Joachim Ziesche .38 .75

1970 Swedish Masterserien

This 200-card set was released in Sweden to commemorate the 1970 World Championships held in Bern and Geneva, Switzerland. The cards in the set are inconsistent in their appearance. Cards 1-50 measure approximately 2 3/4" by 3 3/4". Cards 51-100 are 3" by 4". Cards 101-200 are 3" by 3 3/4". All feature color action photos on the front, but only the first and third groupings have numbers on the front. Cards 51-100 were not numbered on the cards but only in the collector's album. The cards were distributed in 5-card, clear plastic packages. The key cards in the set are two of HOFer Ken Dryden as a member of Team Canada. The cards precede his RC by two years. An album was available to store the cards; it is valued at $30.

COMPLETE SET (200) 175.00 350.00
1 Vladimir Dzurila 4.00 8.00
2 Jozef Golonka .50 1.00
3 Jiri Holik .38 .75
4 Vaclav Nedomansky 1.25 2.50
5 Vaclav Nedomansky 1.25 2.50
6 Jaroslav Holik .50 1.00
7 Jozef Golonka .50 1.00
8 Vaclav Nedomansky 1.25 2.50
9 Vladimir Bednar .25 .50
10 Jan Havel .25 .50
11 Jan Hrbaty .25 .50
12 Jan Suchy .38 .75
13 Lasse Oksanen .25 .50
14 Urpo Ylonen .50 1.00
15 Michael Curran .75 1.50
16 Gary Begg .50 1.00
17 Carl Lackey .50 1.00
18 Terry O'Malley .75 1.50
19 Gary Gamucci .50 1.00
20 Seppo Lindstrom .25 .50
21 Vladimir Lucenko .75 1.50
Yevgeny Misjakov
Vitalij Davidov
Alexandr Ragulin
Vladimir Petrov
Igor Romisjevsky
Victor Putjkov
Valerij Charlamov
Vladimir Jursinov
Anatolij Firsov
22 Victor Putjkov .38 .75
23 Alexandr Ragulin 1.00 2.00
24 Gerry Pinder 1.25 2.50
25 Fran Huck .50 1.00
26 Ken Dryden 50.00 100.00
27 Viktor Zinger .38 .75
28 Vladimir Petrov 2.50 5.00
29 Igor Romisjevsky .50 1.00
Viktor Zinger
30 Valerij Charlamov 5.00 10.00
31 Alexandr Ragulin 1.00 2.00
32 Ab Demarco 1.00 2.00
33 Morris Mott .75 1.50
34 Fran Huck .50 1.00
35 Vjatjeslav Starsinov .75 1.50
36 Lars-Goran Nilsson .50 1.00
Roger Bourbonnais
37 Stig-Goran Johansson .50 1.00
38 Leif "Honken" Holmqvist 1.00 2.00
39 Hakan Nygren .25 .50
40 Tord Lundstrom .25 .50
41 Ulf Sterner .25 .50
42 Lars-Erik Sjoberg 1.50 3.00
43 Kjell-Rune Milton .25 .50
44 Leif "Honken" Holmqvist 1.00 2.00
45 Stefan Karlsson .25 .50
46 Lennart Svedberg .50 1.00
47 Tord Lundstrom .25 .50
48 Ulf Sterner .25 .50
49 Tord Lundstrom .25 .50
50 Lennart Svedberg .50 1.00
51 Sverige (12 st) .25 .50
52 Bert-Ola Nordlander .38 .75
53 Leif "Honken" Holmqvist 1.00 2.00
54 Lars-Erik Sjoberg 1.50 3.00
55 Lars-Erik Sjoberg 1.50 3.00
56 Nils Johansson .25 .50
57 Ulf Sterner .25 .50
58 Ulf Sterner .25 .50
Leif Henriksson
59 Tord Lundstrom .25 .50
60 Mats Hysing .25 .50
Nils Johansson
61 Lars-Goran Nilsson .25 .50
62 Hakan Nygren .25 .50
63 Gerry Pinder 1.25 2.50
Anatolij Firsov
64 Evgenij Misjakov .50 1.00
65 Vjatjeslav Starsinov .75 1.50
66 Alexandr Ragulin 1.00 2.00
67 Alexandr Maltsev 2.50 5.00
68 Anatolij Firsov 2.00 4.00
69 Vladimir Lucenko .75 1.50
70 Vladimir Petrov 2.50 5.00
71 Vladimir Petrov 2.50 5.00
72 Vjatjeslav Starsinov .75 1.50
73 Vladimir Vikulov .50 1.00
74 Vitaly Davidov .50 1.00
75 Evgenij Zimin .38 .75
76 Vladimir Bednar 1.25 2.50
Vladimir Dzurilla
77 Jan Suchy .38 .75
78 Jaroslav Holik .50 1.00
79 Josef Horesovsky .25 .50
80 Jozef Golonka .50 1.00
81 Richard Farda .25 .50
82 Frantisek Pospisil .50 1.00
Oldrich Machac
83 Ilpo Koskela .25 .50
84 Juhani Jylha .25 .50
85 Esa Peltonen .25 .50
86 Lasse Oksanen .25 .50
87 Juhani Wahlsten .25 .50
88 Juha Rantasila .25 .50
89 Bob Paradise .50 1.00
90 Bob Paradise .50 1.00
91 Tim Sheehy .50 1.00
92 Michael Curran .75 1.50
93 Ken Dryden 50.00 100.00
94 Morris Mott .75 1.50
95 Fran Huck .50 1.00
96 unknown .25 .50
97 unknown .25 .50
98 unknown .25 .50
99 unknown .25 .50
100 unknown .25 .50
101 Arne Carlsson .25 .50
102 Nils Johansson .25 .50
103 Leif Holmqvist 1.00 2.00
104 Leif Henriksson .25 .50
105 Lennart Svedberg .50 1.00
106 Hakan Wickberg .25 .50
107 Gennar Backman .25 .50
108 Roger Olsson .25 .50
109 Kjell-Rune Milton .25 .50
110 Mats Hysing .25 .50
111 Lars-Erik Sjoberg 1.50 3.00
112 Anders Hedberg 5.00 10.00
113 Bjorn Palmqvist .25 .50
114 Tord Lundstrom .25 .50
115 Ulf Sterner .25 .50
116 Stig-Goran Johansson .50 1.00
117 Lars-Goran Nilsson .25 .50
118 Stefan Karlsson .25 .50
119 Anders Nordin .25 .50
120 Hans Lindberg .25 .50
121 Vitalij Davidov .50 1.00
Vjatjeslav Starsinov
Victor Polupanov
Alexandr Jakusjev
Alexandr Maltsev
Anatolij Firsov
122 Vitaly Davidov .50 1.00
123 Alexandr Jakusjev 2.50 5.00
Valtonen O. Rantasila
124 Alexandr Maltsev 2.50 5.00
125 Valerij Charlamov 5.00 10.00
126 Alexandr Ragulin 1.00 2.00
127 Igor Romisjevskij .25 .50
128 Boris Michailov 2.50 5.00
129 Vyatcheslav Starsinov .50 1.00
Victor Polupanov
Alexander Ragulin
Vladimir Lucenko
130 Victor Konovalenko .25 .50
131 Alexandr Jakusjev 2.00 4.00
Vitaly Davidov
Boris Michailov
Vladislav Tretjak
Alexandr Maltsev
Evgenij Paladjev
132 Vladimir Lucenko 1.50 3.00
Vladimir Petrov
Anatolij Firsov
Valerij Nikitin
Igor Romisjevskij
Vladimir Vikulov
Alexandr Jakusjev
133 Alexandr Maltsev 2.50 5.00
134 Valerij Nikitin .25 .50
135 Vladimir Vikulov .50 1.00
136 Vjatjeslav Starsinov .75 1.50
137 Evgenij Paladjev .25 .50
138 Vladimir Shapovalov .25 .50
139 Anatolij Firsov 2.00 4.00
140 Victor Polupanov .25 .50
141 Jaroslav Jirik .25 .50
142 Miroslav Lacky .50 1.00
143 Jan Suchy .38 .75
144 Lubomir Ujvary .25 .50
145 Vladimir Bednar .25 .50
146 Richard Farda .25 .50
147 Josef Cernyh .38 .75
148 Vaclav Nedomansky 1.25 2.50
149 Jaroslav Holik .75 1.50
150 Jiri Holik .38 .75
151 Julius Haas .38 .75
Vladislav Martinec
152 Vaclav Nedomansky 1.25 2.50
153 Josef Horesovsky .25 .50
154 Oldrich Machac .25 .50
155 Tommy Abrahamsson .50 1.00
Jiri Kochta
156 Vladimir Dzurila 2.00 4.00
Jan Suchy
Vladimir Bednar
157 Jorma Valtonen .50 1.00
158 Veli-Pekka Ketola 1.00 2.00
159 Matti Murto .25 .50
Lauri Mononen
160 Heikki Riihiranta .50 1.00
161 Pekka Leimu .25 .50
162 Lasse Oksanen .25 .50
163 Jorma Valtonen .25 .50
Vaino Kolkka
Pekka Marjamaki
164 Urpo Ylonen .50 1.00
165 Matti Keinonen .25 .50
166 Juha Rantasila .75 1.50
Anatolij Firsov
167 Jorma Vehmanen .25 .50
168 Matti Murto .25 .50
169 Peter Slapke .25 .50
170 Claus Hirche .25 .50
171 Frank Braun .25 .50
172 Rolf Bielas .25 .50
173 Reinhard Kargar .25 .50
Hiller
Ziesche
Frank Braun
174 Rolf Beilas .25 .50
Frank Braun
Claus Hirche
Jim Kolbe
175 Wilfried Rohrbach .25 .50
Hartmut Nickel
176 Wolfgang Plotka .25 .50
Bernd Karrenbauer
Wilfried Rohrbach
Rainer Patschinski
177 John Mayasich .25 .50
(James Branch
178 Larry Skime .50 1.00
179 Paul Coppo .50 1.00
180 Larry Pleau .50 1.00
181 Bruce Riutta .50 1.00
Ron Naslund
John Lothrop
182 Jerry Lackey .50 1.00
Larry Skime
Tim Sheehy
Larry Stordahl
183 Bob Paradise .75 1.50
Michael Curran
Carl Lackey
184 Paul Coppo .50 1.00
Peter Markle
185 Roger Bourbonnais .75 1.50
186 Ted Hargreaves .75 1.50
187 Fran Huck .50 1.00
188 Wayne Stephenson 2.50 5.00
189 Morris Mott .75 1.50
190 Gerry Pinder 1.25 2.50
191 Gary Begg .50 1.00
192 Ken Dryden 50.00 100.00
Blank Back
193 Felix Goralczyk .25 .50
194 Andrzej Tkacz .25 .50
195 Jan Modzelewski .25 .50
196 Marian Kajzerek .25 .50
197 Josef Stefaniak .25 .50
198 Walery Kosyl .25 .50
199 Jan Modzelewski .25 .50
200 Pajerski .25 .50
(Felix Goralczyk
Chachowski
Polen

1971-72 Swedish Hockey

This set of 400 cards was printed by Panini and released in Sweden by Williams Forlags AB. The cards-- which measure approximately 2 1/2" by 1 3/4" -- feature players from Sweden's top league, as well as from several national teams and NHL clubs. The fronts offer a simple player portrait; the backs contain sticker number and a brief player bio in Swedish. An album to house the set can be found; it is valued approximately at $40. Key stars in this loaded set include Bobby Orr, Gordie Howe and Vladislav Tretiak. NOTE: Spellings used are those found on the sticker. In the case of the Russian players, these spellings may differ from those in common usage.

COMPLETE SET (400) 225.00 450.00
1 Christer Abrahamsson 1.00 2.00
2 Leif Holmqvist .50 1.00
3 William Lofqvist .50 1.00
4 Thommy Abrahamsson .50 1.00
5 Gunnar Andersson .25 .50
6 Thommie Bergman 1.50 3.00
7 Arne Carlsson .25 .50
8 Kjell-Rune Milton .25 .50
9 Bert-Ola Nordlander .50 1.00
10 Lennart Svedberg .50 1.00
11 Lars-Erik Sjoberg 1.00 2.00
12 Stig Ostling .25 .50
13 Inge Hammarstrom 1.50 10.00
14 Anders Hedberg 4.00 8.00
15 Stig-Goran Johansson .50 1.00
16 Stefan Karlsson .25 .50
17 Dan Labraaten 1.00 2.00
18 Hans Lindberg .25 .50
19 Tord Lundstrom .25 .50
20 Lars-Goran Nilsson .25 .50
21 Hakan Nygren .25 .50
22 Bjorn Palmqvist .25 .50
23 Hakan Pettersson .25 .50
24 Ulf Sterner .25 .50
25 Hakan Wickberg .25 .50
26 Viktor Konovalenko .30 .75
27 Vladislav Tretjak 10.00 20.00
28 Gennadij Tsigankov .30 .75
29 Vitalij Davidov .30 .75
30 Victor Kuskin .25 .50
31 Vladimir Lutjenko .30 .75
32 Alexander Ragulin .50 1.00
33 Igor Romisjevskij .30 .75
34 Valerij Kharlamov 5.00 15.00
35 Anatolij Firsov 2.50 5.00
36 Alexander Maltsev 2.50 5.00
37 Boris Mikhailov 2.50 5.00
38 Jevgenij Misjakov .50 1.00
39 Vladimir Petrov 2.50 5.00
40 Vjatjeslav Starshinov .50 1.00
41 Vladimir Vikulov .30 .75
42 Evgenij Zimin .50 1.00
43 Jiri Holecek .50 1.00
44 Josef Horesovsky .25 .50
45 Oldrich Machac .25 .50
46 Frantisek Panchartek .25 .50
47 Frantisek Pospisil .30 .75
48 Jan Suchy .30 .75
49 Josef Cerny .30 .75
50 Richard Farda .25 .50
51 Jan Havel .25 .50
52 Ivan Hlinka .50 1.00
53 Jiri Holik .30 .75
54 Jiri Kochta .25 .50
55 Vladimir Martinec .50 1.00
56 Vaclav Nedomansky 1.00 2.00
57 Eduard Novak .25 .50
58 Bohuslav Stastny .50 1.00
59 Jorma Valtonen .50 1.00
60 Urpo Ylonen .50 1.00
61 Ilpo Koskela .25 .50
62 Seppo Lindstrom .25 .50
63 Hannu Luojola .25 .50
64 Pekka Marjamaki .25 .50
65 Esa Isaksson .25 .50
66 Veli-Pekka Ketola 1.00 2.00
67 Harri Linnonmaa .25 .50
68 Erkki Mononen .25 .50
69 Lauri Mononen .25 .50
70 Matti Murto .50 1.00
71 Lasse Oksanen .25 .50
72 Esa Peltonen .25 .50
73 Juhanni Tamminen .50 1.00
74 Jorma Vehmanen .25 .50
75 Leif Holmqvist .50 1.00
76 Bert Jattne .50 1.00
77 Lars Danielsson .25 .50
78 Ake Fagerstrom .25 .50
79 Per-Arne Hubinette .25 .50
80 Hakan Lindgren .25 .50
81 Bert-Ola Nordlander .50 1.00
82 Lennart Pettersson .25 .50
83 Rolf Edberg .25 .50
84 Bo Hansson .25 .50
85 Jan-Olov Kroon .25 .50
86 Gunnar Lindkvist .25 .50
87 Christer Lundberg .25 .50
88 Ulf Nilsson 4.00 8.00
89 Bo Olofsson .25 .50
90 Jan Olsson .25 .50
91 Lennart Selinder .25 .50
92 Soren Sjogren .25 .50
93 Hans Stromberg .25 .50
94 Jan Ostling .25 .50
95 Kjell Helling .50 1.00
96 William Lofqvist .50 1.00
97 Lars Bylund .25 .50
98 Kjell Johnsson .25 .50
99 Par Malmstrom .25 .50
100 Borje Salming 5.00 10.00
101 Stig Salming .25 .50
102 Stig Ostling .25 .50
103 Inge Hammarstrom 1.50 10.00
104 Lennart Johansson .25 .50
105 Stefan Karlsson .25 .50
106 Lennart Lind .25 .50
107 Hans Lindberg .25 .50
108 Tord Lundstrom .25 .50
109 Jan-Erik Lyck .25 .50
110 Lars-Goran Nilsson .25 .50
111 Leif Olsson .25 .50
112 Lars-Ake Sivertsson .25 .50
113 Hakan Wickberg .25 .50
114 Lars Oberg .25 .50
115 Roland Einarsson .50 1.00
116 Peder Nilsson .50 1.00
117 Kent Olsson .50 1.00
118 Thomas Carlsson .25 .50
119 Lars-Ake Lundell .25 .50
120 Jorgen Palm .25 .50
121 Anders Rylin .25 .50
122 Billy Sundstrom .25 .50
123 Kent Soderlund .25 .50
124 Folke Bengtsson .25 .50
125 Ake Eklof .25 .50
126 Stig Larsson .25 .50
127 Sven-Bertil Lindstrom .25 .50
128 Thomas Palm .25 .50
129 Bjorn Palmqvist .25 .50
130 Ulf Rydin .25 .50
131 Ove Svensson .25 .50
132 Per-Allan Wikstrom .25 .50
133 Anders Andren .25 .50
134 Per Lundstrom .25 .50
135 Lennart Andersson .50 1.00
136 Kent Bodin .50 1.00
137 Bjorn Fagerlund .50 1.00
138 Ake Carlsson .25 .50
139 Nils Johansson .25 .50
140 Lars-Goran Nilsson .25 .50
141 Kent Olsson .50 1.00
142 Hans-Ake Rosendahl .25 .50
143 Karl-Johan Sundqvist .25 .50
144 Benny Andersson .25 .50
145 Hasse Andersson .25 .50
146 Kent-Erik Andersson .25 .50
147 Berndt Augustsson .25 .50
148 Kjell Augustsson .25 .50
149 Per-Ole Backman .25 .50
150 Conny Evensson .50 1.00
151 Sten Johansson .25 .50
152 Leif Labraaten .25 .50
153 Sven-Ove Olsson .25 .50
154 Ulf Sterner .25 .50
155 Christer Abrahamsson 1.00 2.00
156 Krister Sterner .50 1.00
157 Thommy Abrahamsson .50 1.00
158 Karl-Gustaf Alander .25 .50
159 Gunnar Andersson .25 .50
160 Roland Bond .25 .50
161 Ake Danielsson .25 .50
162 Ulf Weinstock .25 .50
163 Per-Olov Brasar 1.00 2.00
164 Kjell Brus .25 .50
165 Hans Jax .25 .50
166 Dan Labraaten 1.00 2.00
167 Roger Lindqvist .25 .50
168 Ulf Martensson .25 .50
169 Stig Nordin .25 .50
170 Olle Sjogren .25 .50
171 Ingemar Snis .25 .50
172 Dan Soderstrom .25 .50
173 Bo Theander .30 .75
174 Mats Ahlberg .25 .50
175 Gunnar Backman .25 .50
176 Ivar Larsson .50 1.00
177 Sture Andersson .25 .50
178 Lage Edin .25 .50
179 Kjell-Rune Milton .25 .50
180 Per-Olof Uusitalo .25 .50
181 Ulf Wigren .25 .50
182 Hakan Dahlof .25 .50
183 Anders Hedberg 4.00 8.00
184 Torbjorn Hubinette .25 .50
185 Assar Lundgren .25 .50
186 Per Lundqvist .25 .50
187 Christer Nilsson .25 .50
188 Kenneth Nordenberg .25 .50
189 Anders Nordin .25 .50
190 Hakan Nygren .25 .50
191 Ulf Thors .25 .50
192 Ulf Torstensson .25 .50
193 Lars Ohman .25 .50
194 Tore Ohman .25 .50
195 Tony Esposito 17.50 35.00
196 Bobby Orr 50.00 100.00
197 Jean Beliveau 12.50 35.00
198 Gordie Howe 40.00 75.00
199 Phil Esposito 12.50 35.00
200 Bobby Hull 20.00 40.00
201 Bengt-Ake Gustavsson .50 1.00
202 Lars Gustavsson .50 1.00
203 Tommy Andersson .25 .50
204 Hans-Olov Ernlund .50 1.00
205 Tord Johansson .25 .50
206 Lars Mjoberg .25 .50
207 Per-Erik Olsson .25 .50
208 Tord Svensson .25 .50
209 Jan Danielsson .25 .50
210 Tommy Eriksson .50 1.00
211 Gote Hansson .25 .50
212 Hans Hansson .25 .50
213 Sven-Ake Jacobsson .25 .50
214 Mats Lonn .25 .50
215 Borje Marcus .25 .50
216 Lars Munther .25 .50
217 Ulf Nises .25 .50
218 Anders Rosen .25 .50
219 Borje Skogs .25 .50
220 Kent Sundkvist .25 .50
221 Mikael Collin .50 1.00
222 Bjorn Jansson .50 1.00
223 Curt Larsson .50 1.00
224 Thommie Bergman 1.50 3.00
225 Arne Carlsson .25 .50
226 Christer Karlsson .25 .50
227 Eilert Maatta .25 .50
228 Jan Schullstrom .25 .50
229 Borje (Poppen) Burlin .25 .50
230 Hans Carlsson .25 .50
231 Tommy Carlsson .25 .50
232 Mats Hysing .25 .50
233 Bertil Jacobsson .25 .50
234 Stig-Goran Johansson .50 1.00
235 Dan Landegren .25 .50
236 Kjell Landstrom .25 .50
237 Soren Maatta .25 .50
238 Nils-Olov Schilstrom .25 .50
239 Dick Yderstrom .25 .50
240 Carl Goran Oberg .25 .50
241 Anders Claesson .50 1.00
242 Kent Othberg .50 1.00
243 Jan Johansson .25 .50
244 Jan-Erik Nilsson .25 .50
245 Stefan Pettersson .25 .50
246 Tord Salomonsson .25 .50
247 Lennart Svedberg .50 1.00
248 Bo Berggren .25 .50
249 Bjorn Broman .25 .50
250 Lennart Broman .25 .50
251 Ove Larsson .25 .50
252 Rolf Larsson .25 .50
253 Orjan Lindstrom .25 .50
254 Arne Lundstrom .25 .50
255 Fhinn Lundstrom .25 .50
256 Ake Lundstrom .25 .50
257 Lennart Norberg .25 .50
258 Hakan Pettersson .25 .50
259 Ake Soderberg .25 .50
260 Olle Ahman .25 .50
261 Christer Andersson .50 1.00
262 Bengt Gustavsson .25 .50
263 Goran Astrom .25 .50
264 Anders Brostrom .25 .50
265 Kenneth Ekman .25 .50
266 Soren Gunnarsson .25 .50
267 Lars-Erik Jacobsson .25 .50
268 Des Moroney .25 .50
269 Borje Maatta .25 .50
270 Tommy Pettersson .25 .50
271 Bengt Alm .25 .50
272 Sven Crabo .25 .50
273 Bengt Eriksson .25 .50
274 Kurt Jakobsson .25 .50
275 Leif Jakobsson .25 .50
276 Lars-Goran Johansson .25 .50
277 Bert Karlsson .25 .50
278 Benny Runesson .25 .50
279 Ake Ryman .25 .50
280 Jan Roger Strand .25 .50
281 Christer Grahn .30 .75
282 Ronny Sandstrom .25 .50
283 John Andersson .25 .50
284 Karl-Olov Eriksson .25 .50
285 Anders Hagstrom .25 .50
286 Ulf Ingvarsson .25 .50
287 Rolf Jager .25 .50
288 Erik Jarvholm .25 .50
289 Bo Westling .25 .50
290 Ulf Barrefjord .25 .50
291 Kent Bjork .25 .50
292 Lars Dahlgren .25 .50
293 Ulf Larsson .25 .50
294 Jan Lundqvist .25 .50
295 Ulf Lundstrom .25 .50
296 Bengt Lovgren .25 .50
297 Leif Martensson .25 .50
298 Lars-Ake Nordin .25 .50
299 Lars Sjostrom .25 .50
300 Kjell Sundstrom .25 .50
301 Ronny Andersson .50 1.00
302 Ingemar Caris .50 1.00
303 Anders Johansson .25 .50
304 Hakan Norstrom .25 .50
305 Jan Olsen .25 .50
306 Lars-Erik Sjoberg .50 1.00
307 Bengt Sjoholm .25 .50
308 Kjell Andersson .25 .50
309 Svante Granholm .25 .50
310 Kjell-Ove Gustavsson .25 .50
311 Henrik Hedlund .25 .50
312 Leif Henriksson .25 .50
313 Lars-Erik Johansson .25 .50
314 Bjorn Lindberg .25 .50
315 Evert Lindstrom .25 .50
316 Willy Lindstrom 1.00 2.00
317 Leif Nilsson .25 .50
318 Kurt Olofsson .25 .50
319 Roger Olsson .25 .50
320 Kjell-Ronnie Pettersson .25 .50
321 Kenneth Holmstedt .50 1.00
322 Lars-Erik Larsson .25 .50
323 Lennart Eriksson .25 .50
324 Lennart Gustavsson .25 .50
325 Jan-Ake Karlsson .25 .50
326 Rolf Karlsson .25 .50
327 Bengt Lundberg .25 .50
328 Anders Thelander .25 .50
329 Kent Bengtsson .25 .50
330 Gunnar Backman .50 1.00
331 Stefan Canderyd .25 .50
332 Curt Edenvik .25 .50
333 Per Edenvik .25 .50
334 Weine Gullberg .25 .50
335 Nils-Arne Hedqvist .25 .50
336 Bengt-Ake Karlsson .25 .50
337 Christer Kihlstrom .25 .50
338 Stig-Olof Persson .25 .50
339 Christer Sjoberg .25 .50
340 Roddy Skyllqvist .25 .50
341 Lars Blomqvist .50 1.00
342 Bjorn Forsberg .50 1.00
343 Anders Hedlund .25 .50
344 Lennart Johansson .25 .50
345 Martin Kruger .25 .50
346 Harry Namd .25 .50
347 Lennart Strohm .25 .50
348 Peter Bejemark .25 .50
349 Bertil Bond .25 .50
350 Nils Carlsson .25 .50
351 Ulf Pilo .25 .50
352 Claes-Ove Fjallby .25 .50
353 Lars Granlund .25 .50
354 Kjell Keijser .25 .50
355 Lennart Lange .25 .50
356 Bo Mellbin .25 .50
357 Lars Starck .25 .50
358 Leif Svensson .25 .50
359 Kjell Ahlen .25 .50
360 Henry Svensson .25 .50
361 Sven-Allan Ellstrom .50 1.00
362 Tommy Eriksson .50 1.00
363 Walter Winsth .50 1.00
364 Hans-Ake Andersson .25 .50
365 Jan Andersson .25 .50
366 Hans Bejbom .25 .50
367 Goran Borell .25 .50
368 Bo Schilstrom .25 .50
369 Bjarne Brostrom .25 .50
370 Kenneth Calen .25 .50
371 Lennart Carlsson .50 1.00
372 Mats Davidsson .50 1.00
373 Rolf Hansson .25 .50
374 Rune Norrstrom .25 .50
375 Gunther Rauch .25 .50
376 Jan Vestberg .25 .50
377 Bengt Wistling .50 1.00
378 Kent Zetterberg .25 .50
379 Goran Akerlund .25 .50
380 Uno Ohrlund .25 .50
381 Goran Hogosta .60 1.50
382 Juha Raninen .50 1.00
383 Bert Backman .25 .50
384 Christer Collin .25 .50
385 Dag Olsson .25 .50
386 Bjorn Resare .25 .50
387 Lars Thoreus .25 .50
388 Stig Andersson .25 .50
389 Borje Engblom .25 .50
390 Christer Englund .25 .50
391 Bo Eriksson .25 .50
392 Mats Eriksson .25 .50
393 Roland Eriksson .25 .50
394 Olle Henriksson .25 .50
395 Yngve Hindrikes .25 .50
396 Kjell Jansson .25 .50
397 Jan Johansson .25 .50
398 Jan Karlsson .25 .50
399 Agne Norberg .25 .50
400 Christian Reuthie .25 .50

1972-73 Swedish Stickers

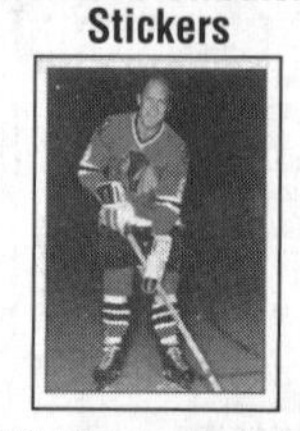

This 300-sticker set was issued in Sweden by Williams Forlags AB for the 1972-73 season. While the majority of the set is taken up by players from the Swedish Elitserien, there also are stickers featuring stars from Russia, Czechoslovakia, Finland and the NHL. Key stickers include pre-NHL appearances from Anders Hedberg, Borje Salming and Ulf Nilsson. NHL stars such as Bobby Orr, Ken Dryden and Bobby Hull also are featured, along with Soviet greats such as Tretiak and Kharlamov. The card fronts feature a posed color photo, while the backs have the sticker number and player information in Swedish. A book to hold the stickers was available at the time for 3.5 kroner, or about fifty cents. It is filled with stories about the teams, league schedules and photos, along with spaces for the stickers. It is valued now at $25. The prices below are for unused stickers; because it was the habit then to put them in the album, relatively few remain in their original state.

COMPLETE SET (300) 150.00 300.00
1 Christer Abrahamsson 1.00 2.00
2 Leif Holmqvist .50 1.00
3 Tommy Abrahamsson .50 1.00
4 Thommie Bergman 1.00 2.00
5 Bjorn Johansson .25 .50
6 Kjell-Rune Milton .25 .50
7 Borje Salming 5.00 10.00
8 Lars-Erik Sjoberg 1.00 2.00
9 Karl-Johan Sundqvist .25 .50
10 Stig Ostling .25 .50
11 Inge Hammarstrom 1.00 2.00
12 Anders Hedberg 2.50 5.00
13 Stig-Goran Johansson .25 .50
14 Stefan Karlsson .25 .50
15 Hans Lindberg .25 .50
16 Mats Lindh .25 .50

17 Tord Lundstrom .25 .50
18 Lars-Goran Nilsson .25 .50
19 Bjorn Palmqvist .25 .50
20 Hakan Wickberg .25 .50
21 Jiri Holecek .50 1.00
22 Josef Horesovsky .25 .50
23 Frantisek Pospisil .38 .75
24 Jaroslav Holik .25 .50
25 Jiri Holik .38 .75
26 Vaclav Nedomansky 1.00 2.00
27 Vladislav Tretiak 10.00 20.00
28 Gennadi Tsigankov .38 .75
29 Igor Romisjevskij .38 .75
30 Valeri Kharlamov 5.00 10.00
31 Alexander Maltsev 2.50 5.00
32 Vladimir Vikulov .38 .75
33 Jorma Valtonen .38 .75
34 Pekka Marjamaki .25 .50
35 Matti Keinonen .25 .50
36 Veli-Pekka Ketola 1.00 2.00
37 Lauri Mononen .25 .50
38 Lasse Oksanen .25 .50
39 Krister Sterner .50 1.00
40 Sten-Ake Bark .25 .50
41 Jan-Erik Silfverberg .25 .50
42 Steffan Andersson .25 .50
43 Roland Eriksson .25 .50
44 Gunnar Johansson .25 .50
45 Jiri Holecek .50 1.00
46 Thommie Bergman 1.00 2.00
47 Josef Horesovsky .25 .50
48 Vladimir Vikulov .38 .75
49 Alexander Maltsev 2.50 5.00
50 Valeri Kharlamov 5.00 10.00
51 Leif Holmqvist .50 1.00
52 Lars Danielsson .25 .50
53 Ake Fagerstrom .25 .50
54 Per-Arne Hubinette .25 .50
55 Hakan Lindgren .25 .50
56 Bert-Ola Nordlander .25 .50
57 Bo Olofsson .25 .50
58 Soren Sjogren .25 .50
59 Jan Olsson .25 .50
60 Lennart Selinder .25 .50
61 Jan Olof Kroon .25 .50
62 Rolf Edberg .25 .50
63 Ulf Nilsson 2.50 5.00
64 Leif Holmgren .25 .50
65 Jan Ostling .25 .50
66 Christer Grahn .50 1.00
67 Karl-Olov Grahn .50 1.00
68 Anders Hagstrom .25 .50
69 Erik Jarvholm .25 .50
70 Bo Westling .25 .50
71 Ulf Ingvarsson .25 .50
72 Bengt Lovgren .25 .50
73 Kjell Sundstrom .25 .50
74 Kent Bjork .25 .50
75 Ulf Lundstrom .25 .50
76 Mats Lundmark .25 .50
77 Ulf Barrefjord .25 .50
78 Lars Dahlgren .25 .50
79 Olle Nilsson .25 .50
80 Roger Nilsson .25 .50
81 Willie Lofqvist .50 1.00
82 Jan-Erik Silfverberg .25 .50
83 Kjell Johnsson .25 .50
84 Jan-Olof Svensson .25 .50
85 Stig Salming .25 .50
86 Borje Salming 5.00 10.00
87 Stig Ostling .25 .50
88 Tord Lundstrom .25 .50
89 Inge Hammarstrom 1.00 2.00
90 Lars-Goran Nilsson .25 .50
91 Hans Lindberg .25 .50
92 Hakan Wickberg .25 .50
93 Jan-Erik Lyck .25 .50
94 Stefan Karlsson .25 .50
95 Lars Oberg .25 .50
96 Roland Einarsson .50 1.00
97 Billy Sundstrom .25 .50
98 Anders Rylin .25 .50
99 Tomas Carlsson .25 .50
100 Ulf Ojerklint .25 .50
101 L-A Gustavsson .50 1.00
102 Jorgen Palm .25 .50
103 Lars-Ake Lundell .25 .50
104 Ake Eklof .25 .50
105 Bengt-Ake Karlsson .25 .50
106 Bjorn Palmqvist .25 .50
107 Per-Allan Wickstrom .25 .50
108 Sven-Bertil Lindstrom .25 .50
109 Totte Bengtsson .25 .50
110 Stig Larsson .25 .50
111 Ken Dryden 20.00 40.00
112 Jacques Laperriere 1.50 3.00
113 Bobby Orr 37.50 75.00
114 Brad Park 2.50 5.00
115 Phil Esposito 10.00 20.00
116 Rod Gilbert 2.50 5.00
117 Vic Hadfield 1.50 3.00
118 Bobby Hull 15.00 30.00
119 Frank Mahovlich 5.00 10.00
120 Jean Ratelle 2.50 5.00
121 Lennart Andersson .50 1.00
122 Karl-Johan Sundqvist .25 .50
123 Nicke Johansson .25 .50
124 Lars-Goran Nilsson .25 .50
125 Ake Carlsson .25 .50
126 Hans-Ake Rosendahl .25 .50
127 Sten-Ake Bark .25 .50
128 Par Backman .25 .50
129 Leif Labraaten .25 .50
130 Berndt Augustsson .25 .50
131 Uffe Sterner .25 .50
132 Benny Andersson .25 .50
133 Conny Evensson .50 1.00
134 Kjell Augustsson .25 .50
135 Hans Andersson .25 .50
136 Kenneth Holmstedt .50 1.00
137 Lennart Gustavsson .25 .50
138 Lennart Eriksson .25 .50
139 Rolf Carlsson .25 .50
140 Bengt Lundberg .25 .50
141 Jan-Ake Karlsson .25 .50
142 Curt Edenvik .25 .50
143 Per Edenvik .25 .50
144 Weine Gullberg .25 .50
145 Gunnar Backman .50 1.00
146 Roddy Skyllqvist .25 .50
147 Stefan Canderyd .25 .50
148 Christer Kihlstrom .25 .50
149 Nils-Arne Hedqvist .25 .50
150 Stig-Olof Persson .25 .50
151 Christer Abrahamsson 1.00 2.00
152 Thommy Abrahamsson .50 1.00
153 Roland Bond .25 .50
154 Gunnar Andersson .25 .50
155 Ulf Weinstock .25 .50
156 Ake Danielsson .25 .50
157 Peter Gudmundsson .25 .50
158 Olle Sjogren .25 .50
159 Hans Jax .25 .50
160 Mats Ahlberg .25 .50
161 Dan Labraaten 1.00 2.00
162 Ulf Martensson .25 .50
163 Kjell Brus .25 .50
164 Dan Soderstrom .25 .50
165 Per Olof Brasar 1.00 2.00
166 Ivar Larsson .50 1.00
167 Sture Andersson .25 .50
168 Lage Edin .25 .50
169 Kjell Rune Milton .25 .50
170 Ulf Wigren .25 .50
171 Hakan Dahllof .25 .50
172 Anders Hedberg 2.50 5.00
173 Assar Lundgren .25 .50
174 Christer Nilsson .25 .50
175 Anders Nordin .25 .50
176 Hakan Nygren .25 .50
177 Ulf Thors .25 .50
178 Ulf Torstensson .25 .50
179 Lasse Ohman .25 .50
180 Tore Ohman .25 .50
181 Bengt Ake Gustafsson .38 .75
182 Tommy Andersson .25 .50
183 Hans-Olof Ernlund .25 .50
184 Tord Johansson .25 .50
185 Tord Svensson .25 .50
186 Jan Danielsson .25 .50
187 Tommy Eriksson .50 1.00
188 Gote Hansson .25 .50
189 Hans Hansson .25 .50
190 Sven-Ake Jacobsson .25 .50
191 Mats Lonn .25 .50
192 Lars Mjoberg .25 .50
193 Lars Munther .25 .50
194 Ulf Nises .25 .50
195 Borje Skogs .25 .50
196 Roland Lestander .25 .50
197 Bosse Andersson .25 .50
198 Hakan Dahlin .25 .50
199 Martin Johansson .25 .50
200 Anders Lindberg .25 .50
201 Lars-Fredrik Nystrom .25 .50
202 Hans Gunnar Skarin .25 .50
203 Jerry Aberg .25 .50
204 Anders Almqvist .25 .50
205 Christer Johansson .25 .50
206 Per Johansson .25 .50
207 Martin Karlsson .25 .50
208 Lars-Gunnar Lundberg .25 .50
209 Hardy Nilsson .25 .50
210 Kjell-Arne Wikstrom .25 .50
211 Mikael Collin .50 1.00
212 Curt Larsson .50 1.00
213 Arne Carlsson .25 .50
214 Bjorn Johansson .25 .50
215 Nils-Olov Schilstrom .25 .50
216 Jan Schullstrom .25 .50
217 Borje Burlin .25 .50
218 Hans Carlsson .25 .50
219 Mats Hysing .25 .50
220 Bertil Jacobsson .25 .50
221 Stisse Johansson .25 .50
222 Dan Landegren .25 .50
223 Kjell Landstrom .25 .50
224 Dick Yderstrom .25 .50
225 Carl-Goran Oberg .25 .50
226 Christer Sehlstedt .25 .50
227 Tommie Lindgren .25 .50
228 Jan-Erik Nilsson .25 .50
229 Stefan Pettersson .25 .50
230 Tord Nansen .25 .50
231 Bo Berggren .25 .50
232 Bjorn Broman .25 .50
233 Ove Larsson .25 .50
234 Kent Lindgren .25 .50
235 Orjan Lindstrom .25 .50
236 Lennart Norberg .25 .50
237 Arne Lundstrom .25 .50
238 Hakan Pettersson .25 .50
239 Ake Soderberg .25 .50
240 Olle Ahman .25 .50
241 Christer Andersson 1.00 2.00
242 Anders Brostrom .25 .50
243 Kenneth Ekman .25 .50
244 Soren Gunnarsson .25 .50
245 Borje Maatta .25 .50
246 Tommy Pettersson .25 .50
247 Kurt Jakobsson .25 .50
248 Leif Jakobsson .25 .50
249 Lars-Goran Johansson .25 .50
250 Bengt-Goran Karlsson .25 .50
251 Berndt Karlsson .25 .50
252 Tadeusz Niedomyst .25 .50
253 Benny Runesson .25 .50
254 Ake Ryman .25 .50
255 Jan-Roger Strand .25 .50
256 Goran Hogosta .50 1.00
257 Bert Backman .25 .50
258 Christer Collin .25 .50
259 Bo Eriksson .25 .50
260 Hakan Norstrom .25 .50
261 Lars Thoreus .25 .50
262 Stig Andersson .25 .50
263 Mats Eriksson .25 .50
264 Roland Eriksson .25 .50
265 Kjell Fhinn .25 .50
266 Olle Henriksson .25 .50
267 Yngve Hindrikes .25 .50
268 Jan Karlsson .25 .50
269 Kjell Jansson .25 .50
270 Ingemar Snis .25 .50
271 Christer Stahl .25 .50
272 Leif Andersson .25 .50
273 Tommy Eriksson .50 1.00
274 Christer Holmstrom .25 .50
275 Curt Lundmark 1.00 2.00
276 Dennis Pettersson .25 .50
277 Ove Thelin .25 .50
278 Bo Wahlberg .25 .50
279 Gote Gustavsson .25 .50
280 Christer Lindgren .25 .50
281 Kent Persson .25 .50
282 Par Marts .25 .50
283 Ove Stenlund .25 .50
284 Bo Olsson .25 .50
285 Bo Astrom .25 .50
286 Ronny Andersson .50 1.00
287 Roger Bergman .25 .50
288 Thommie Bergman 1.00 2.00
289 Anders Johansson .25 .50
290 Jan Olsen .25 .50
291 Lars Erik Sjoberg 1.00 2.00
292 Kjell Andersson .25 .50
293 Svante Granholm .25 .50
294 Henrik Hedlund .25 .50
295 Leif Henriksson .25 .50
296 Mats Lindh .25 .50
297 Evert Lindstrom .25 .50
298 Willy Lindstrom 1.00 2.00
299 Roger Olsson .25 .50
300 Kjell-Ronnie Pettersson .25 .50

1972 Swedish Semic World Championship

Printed in Italy by Semic Press, the 233 cards comprising this set measure 1 7/8" by 2 1/2" and feature posed color player photos on their white-bordered fronts. The white back carries the player's name and text in Swedish. The cards are numbered on the back and arranged by national teams as follows: Soviet Union (1-20), Czechoslovakia (21-41), Sweden (42-70), Finland (71-92), Germany (93-117), United States (118-137), France (138-162), and Canada (163-233).

COMPLETE SET (233) 200.00 400.00
1 Viktor Konovalenko .38 .75
2 Vitalij Davydov .38 .75
3 Vladimir Lutjenko .38 .75
4 Viktor Kuskin .38 .75
5 Alexander Ragulin .75 3.00
6 Igor Romitjevskij .38 .75
7 Gennadij Tsigankov .38 .75
8 Vjatsjeslav Starsjinov .75 1.50
9 Evgenij Zimin .50 1.00
10 Alexander Maltsev 2.50 5.00
11 Anatolij Firsov 1.25 2.00
12 Evgenij Misjakov .38 .75
13 Boris Michailov 2.00 4.00
14 Juri Ljapkin .50 1.00
15 Alexander Martinyk .38 .75
16 Vladimir Petrov 2.00 4.00
17 Valeri Kharlamov 5.00 10.00
18 Vladimir Vikulov .38 .75
19 Vladimir Sjadrin .50 1.00
20 Vladislav Tretiak 10.00 20.00
21 Marcel Sakac .25 .50
22 Jiri Holecek .50 1.00
23 Josef Horesovsky .25 .50
24 Oldrich Machac .25 .50
25 Rudolf Tajcnar .25 .50
26 Frantisek Panchartek .25 .50
27 Frantisek Pospisil .38 .75
28 Jiri Kochta .25 .50
29 Jan Havel .25 .50
30 Vladimir Martinec .50 1.00
31 Richard Farda .25 .50
32 Bohuslav Stastny .38 .75
33 Vaclav Nedomansky .75 1.50
34 Josef Cerny .25 .50
35 Bedrich Brunchk .25 .50
36 Jan Suchy .25 .50
37 Eduard Novak .25 .50
38 Jiri Bubla .75 1.50
39 Jiri Holik .38 .75
40 Ivan Hlinka 1.00 2.00
41 Vladimir Bednar .25 .50
42 Leif Holmqvist .50 1.00
43 Christer Abrahamsson 1.00 2.00
44 Christer Andersson .50 1.00
45 Lars-Erik Sjoberg .75 1.50
46 Lennart Svedberg .50 1.00
47 Stig-Goran Johansson .25 .50
48 Bert-Ola Nordlander .25 .50
49 Thommy Abrahamsson .50 1.00
50 Arne Carlsson .25 .50
51 Stefan Karlsson .25 .50
52 Hakan Wickberg .25 .50
53 Hakan Nygren .25 .50
54 Lars-Goran Nilsson .25 .50
55 Thommie Bergman 1.00 2.00
56 Ulf Sterner .38 .75
57 Hans Lindberg .25 .50
58 Tord Lundstrom .25 .50
59 Gunnar Andersson .25 .50
60 Bjorn Palmqvist .25 .50
61 Inge Hammarstrom 1.00 2.00
62 Kjell-Rune Milton .25 .50
63 Kjell Brus .25 .50
64 Kenneth Ekman .25 .50
65 Bengt-Goran Karlsson .25 .50
66 Hakan Pettersson .25 .50
67 Dan Labraaten .75 1.50
68 Dan Soderstrom .25 .50
69 Anders Hedberg 2.50 5.00
70 Ake Soderberg .25 .50
71 Urpo Ylonen .25 .50
72 Ilpo Koskela .25 .50
73 Seppo Lindstrom .25 .50
74 Hannu Luojola .25 .50
75 Pekka Marjamaki .25 .50
76 Jouko Oystila .25 .50
77 Heikki Jarn .25 .50
78 Esa Isaksson .25 .50
79 Veli-Pekka Ketola .75 1.50
80 Harri Linnonmaa .25 .50
81 Erkki Mononen .25 .50
82 Lauri Mononen .25 .50
83 Matti Murto .25 .50
84 Lasse Oksanen .25 .50
85 Esa Peltonen .25 .50
86 Seppo Repo .25 .50
87 Tommi Salmelainen .25 .50
88 Juhani Tamminen .25 .50
89 Jorma Vehmanen .25 .50
90 Jorma Valtonen .38 .75
91 Matti Keinonen .25 .50
92 Juha Rantasila .25 .50
93 Toni Kehle .25 .50
94 Josef Schramm .25 .50
95 Walter Stadler .25 .50
96 Josef Volk .25 .50
97 Hans Schichtl .25 .50
98 Erwin Riedmeier .25 .50
99 Werner Modes .25 .50
100 Johann Eimannsberger .25 .50
101 Karlheinz Egger .25 .50
102 Lorenz Funk, Sr. .25 .50
103 Klaus Ego .25 .50
104 Anton Hofherr .25 .50
105 Otto Schneitberger .25 .50
106 Heinz Weisenbach .25 .50
107 Alois Schloder .25 .50
108 Gustav Hanig .25 .50
109 Rainer Philipp .25 .50
110 Bernd Kuhn .25 .50
111 Paul Langner .25 .50
112 Franz Hofherr .25 .50
113 Reinhold Bauer .25 .50
114 Johann Rotkirch .25 .50
115 Walter Koberle .25 .50
116 Rainer Makatsch .25 .50
117 Carl Wetzel .38 .75
118 Mike Curran .38 .75
119 Jim McElmury .38 .75
120 Bruce Riutta .38 .75
121 Tom Mellor .38 .75
122 Don Ross .38 .75
123 Gary Gambucci .38 .75
124 Keith Christiansen .38 .75
125 Len Lilyholm .38 .75
126 Henry Boucha .75 3.00
127 Craig Falkman .38 .75
128 Tim Sheehy .38 .75
129 Kevin Ahearn .38 1.00
130 Craig Patrick 1.00 2.00
131 Pete Fichuk .38 1.00
132 George Konik .38 1.00
133 Dick McGlynn .38 1.00
134 Dick Toomey .38 1.00
135 Paul Schilling .38 1.00
136 Bob Lindberg .38 1.00
137 Dick Tomasoni .38 1.00
138 Nando Mathieu .25 .50
139 Francis Reinhard .25 .50
140 Gaston Furrer .25 .50
141 Bruno Wittwer .25 .50
142 Andre Berra .25 .50
143 Hans Keller .25 .50
144 Peter Luthi .25 .50
145 Peter Aeschlimann .25 .50
146 Werner Kuenzi .25 .50
147 Tony Neininger .25 .50
148 Jacques Pousaz .25 .50
149 Roger Chappot .25 .50
150 Charly Henzen .25 .50
151 Paul Probst .25 .50
152 Guy Dubois .25 .50
153 Rene Sgualdo .25 .50
154 Rene Huegenin .25 .50
155 Gaston Pelletier .25 .50
156 Beat Kaufmann .25 .50
157 Alfio Molina .25 .50
158 Gerald Rigolet .25 .50
159 Harald Jones .25 .50
160 Gilbert Mathieu .25 .50
161 Michel Turler .25 .50
162 Reto Taillens .25 .50
163 Norm Ullman 1.50 5.00
164 Dave Keon 2.50 10.00
165 Roger Crozier 2.50 5.00
166 Ron Ellis 1.50 5.00
167 Paul Henderson 2.50 10.00
168 Jim Dorey .50 1.00
169 Jacques Plante 15.00 30.00
170 Jean-Guy Gendron .50 1.00
171 Gary Smith 1.50 3.00
172 Dennis Hextall .50 2.00
173 Norm Ferguson .50 1.00
174 Simon Nolet .50 1.00
175 Bernie Parent 5.00 10.00
176 Ted Hampson .50 1.00
177 Earl Ingarfield .50 1.00
178 Larry Hillman .50 2.00
179 Gary Dornhoefer 1.00 3.00
180 Gary Croteau .50 1.00
181 Carol Vadnais .50 2.00
182 Jim Roberts .50 2.00
183 Red Berenson 1.50 5.00
184 Phil Esposito 12.50 25.00
185 John McKenzie 1.00 3.00
186 Barclay Plager 1.00 3.00
187 Glenn Hall 7.50 15.00
188 Gerry Cheevers 7.50 15.00
189 Jim McKenny .50 1.00
190 Gordie Howe 25.00 50.00
191 Garry Unger 1.00 3.00
192 Roy Edwards 1.50 5.00
193 Alex Delvecchio 2.50 5.00
194 Brad Park 2.50 10.00
195 Frank Mahovlich 5.00 10.00
196 Phil Goyette .50 1.00
197 Don Marshall .50 1.00
198 Henri Richard 5.00 10.00
199 Claude Larose .50 1.00
200 Bobby Rousseau .50 1.00
201 Lorne Worsley 5.00 10.00
202 Gilles Marotte .75 1.50
203 Bob Pulford 1.50 5.00
204 Yvan Cournoyer 2.50 5.00
205 Eddie Joyal .50 1.00
206 Ross Lonsberry .50 1.00
207 Jean Beliveau 10.00 20.00
208 Jacques Lemaire 2.50 5.00
209 Orland Kurtenbach .75 1.50
210 Andre Boudrias .50 1.00
211 Jim Neilson .50 2.00
212 Walter Tkaczuk 1.00 3.00
213 Ed Giacomin 5.00 10.00
214 Jean Ratelle 2.50 5.00
215 Les Binkley 1.50 5.00
216 Jean Pronovost .50 1.00
217 Bryan Watson .50 2.00
218 Dean Prentice .50 1.00
219 Jean-Paul Parise 1.00 3.00
220 Bill Goldsworthy .75 3.00
221 Wayne Maki .50 2.00
222 Dale Tallon .75 3.00
223 Bobby Orr 37.50 75.00
224 Pit Martin .50 2.00
225 Jacques Laperriere 1.50 3.00
226 Bill Flett .50 2.00
227 Stan Mikita 7.50 15.00
228 Bobby Hull 15.00 30.00
229 Larry Pleau .50 2.00
230 Keith Magnuson 1.00 2.00
231 Tony Esposito 7.50 15.00
232 Rogatien Vachon 4.00 10.00
233 Mickey Redmond 7.50 15.00

1973-74 Swedish Stickers

This 243-sticker set was produced in Sweden by Williams Forlags AB. It features players from the top Swedish league, as well as several Russian teams. The set includes such legendary figures as Valeri Kharlamov, Vladislav Tretiak and a rare card of notorious head coach Vselvolod Bobrov. The fronts feature a color player photo, while the backs have sticker number and information in Swedish. There was an album available to store the set; it currently retails for around $20.

COMPLETE SET (243) 100.00 175.00
1 Christer Abrahamsson 1.00 2.00
2 William Lofqvist .50 1.00
3 Arne Karlsson .25 .50
4 Lars-Erik Sjoberg 1.00 2.00
5 Bjorn Johansson .25 .50
6 Thommy Abrahamsson .50 1.00
7 Borje Salming 5.00 10.00
8 Karl Johan Sundqvist .25 .50
9 Ulf Sterner .25 .50
10 Ulf Nilsson 2.50 5.00
11 Kjell-Arne Wickstrom .25 .50
12 Inge Hammarstrom 2.50 5.00
13 Hakan Wickberg .25 .50
14 Tord Lundstrom .25 .50
15 Dan Soderstrom .25 .50
16 Mats Ahlberg .50 1.00
17 Anders Hedberg 2.50 5.00
18 Dick Yderstrom .30 .75
19 Stefan Karlsson .25 .50
20 Roland Bond .25 .50
21 Kjell-Rune Milton .25 .50
22 Willy Lindstrom .75 1.50
23 Kurt Carlsson .30 .75
24 Mats Walltin .25 .50
25 Roland Eriksson .25 .50
26 Martin Karlsson .25 .50
27 Jiri Holecek .50 1.00
28 Josef Horesovsky .25 .50
29 Oldrich Machac .25 .50
30 Vladimir Martinec .50 1.00
31 Vaclav Nedomansky .75 1.50
32 Jiri Kochta .25 .50
33 Jorma Waltonen .25 .50
34 Heikki Riihiranta .50 1.00
35 Lauri Mononen .25 .50
36 Timo Turunen .25 .50
37 Matti Keinonen .25 .50
38 Seppo Repo .25 .50
39 Christer Abrahamsson .75 1.50
40 Lars Stenvall .25 .50
41 Per Karlsson .25 .50
42 Roland Bond .25 .50
43 Thommy Abrahamsson .50 1.00
44 Ulf Weinstock .25 .50
45 Gunnar Andersson .25 .50
46 Hans Eriksson .25 .50
47 Peter Gudmundsson .25 .50
48 Mats Ahlberg .50 1.00
49 Per-Olov Brasar .75 1.50
50 Roger Lindqvist .25 .50
51 Dan Soderstrom .25 .50
52 Ulf Martensson .25 .50
53 Kjell Brus .25 .50
54 Hans Jax .25 .50
55 Dan Labraaten .75 1.50
56 Nils-Olov Olsson .25 .50
57 Stig Nordin .25 .50
58 Bo Theander .25 .50
59 Curt Larsson .50 1.00
60 Mikael Collin .50 1.00
61 Arne Carlsson .25 .50
62 Leif Svensson .25 .50
63 Sverker Torstensson .25 .50
64 Bjorn Johansson .25 .50
65 Stisse Johansson .25 .50
66 Carl-Goran Oberg .25 .50
67 Mats Hysing .25 .50
68 Mats Walltin .25 .50
69 Hans Carlsson .25 .50
70 Nils-Olov Schilstrom .25 .50
71 Kjell-Arne Wickstrom .25 .50
72 Jan Schullstrom .25 .50
73 Borje Burlin .25 .50
74 Dick Yderstrom .30 .75
75 Dan Landegren .25 .50
76 Kjell Landstrom .25 .50
77 Vladislav Tretjak 10.00 20.00
78 Alexander Sidelnikov 1.00 2.00
79 Alexander Ragulin 1.25 2.50
80 Vladimir Luttjenko 1.00 2.00
81 Gennadij Tsygankov .75 1.50
82 Alexander Gusev .50 1.00
83 Jevgenij Poladiev .30 .75
84 Jurij Liapkin .75 1.50
85 Valerij Vasiljev 1.50 3.00
86 Boris Michailov 2.50 5.00
87 Valeri Kharlamov 5.00 10.00
88 Vladimir Petrov 2.50 5.00
89 Alexander Maltsev 2.50 5.00
90 Vladimir Sjadrin 1.25 2.50
91 Alexander Yakusjev 2.50 5.00
92 Alexander Martynjuk .30 .75
93 Vjateslav Anissin .50 1.00
94 Jurij Lebedev 1.00 2.00
95 Alexander Bodunov .50 1.00
96 Alexander Volchkov 1.00 2.00
97 Vsevolod Bobrov 2.00 4.00
98 Konstantin Loktev .25 .50
99 Anatolij Firsov 1.50 3.00
100 Viktor Kuzkin .50 1.00
101 Jurij Blochin .25 .50
102 Vladimir Vikulov .50 1.00
103 Jurij Blinov .50 1.00
104 Jevgenij Misjakov 1.00 2.00
105 Vladimir Trunov .25 .50
106 Sergej Glazov .25 .50
107 Vladimir Popov .75 1.50
108 Viktor Zinger .50 1.00
109 Viktor Krivolapov .30 .75
110 Jevgenij Kazatjkin .25 .50
111 Viktor Korotkov .75 1.50
112 Valentin Markov .25 .50
113 Alexander Sapjolkin .25 .50
114 Leonid Borzov .25 .50
115 Gennadij Krylov .25 .50
116 Konstantin Klimov .25 .50
117 Jevgenij Zimin .50 1.00
118 Vladimir Gurejev .25 .50
119 Viktor Jaroslavtsev .25 .50
120 Alexander Pasjkov .30 .75
121 Vladimir Polupanov .50 1.00
122 Vitalij Davydov .75 1.50
123 Michail Alexeenko .25 .50
124 Alexander Filippov .50 1.00
125 Valerij Nazarov .25 .50
126 Vladimir Orlov .25 .50
127 Stanislav Sitjegolev .25 .50
128 Anatolij Bjelonozjkin .25 .50
129 Alexander Devjatov .25 .50
130 Jevgenij Kotlov .25 .50
131 Anatolij Motovilov .25 .50
132 Jurij Reps .25 .50
133 Igor Samotjernov .25 .50
134 Alexander Sevidov .25 .50
135 Viktor Sjilov .25 .50
136 Jurij Tjitjurin .30 .75
137 Sune Odling .25 .50
138 Lars-Erik Sjoberg 1.00 2.00
139 Bengt Sjoholm .25 .50
140 Leif Henriksson .25 .50
141 Henric Hedlund .25 .50
142 Roger Olsson .25 .50
143 Kjell-Rune Milton .25 .50
144 Kjell-Ronnie Pettersson .25 .50
145 Svante Granholm .25 .50
146 Kjell Andersson .25 .50
147 Lars-Erik Esbjorn .25 .50
148 Bjorn Lindberg .25 .50
149 Willy Lindstrom .75 1.50
150 Evert Lindstrom .25 .50
151 Lars-Erik Johansson .25 .50
152 Krister Sterner .30 .75
153 Mats Lindh .25 .50
154 Roger Bergman .25 .50
155 Willie Lofqvist .50 1.00
156 Jan Olov Svensson .25 .50
157 Jan Erik Silfverberg .25 .50
158 Stig Ostling .50 1.00
159 Kjell Johansson .25 .50
160 Borje Salming 5.00 10.00
161 Stig Salming .50 1.00
162 Tord Lundstrom .25 .50
163 Hakan Wickberg .25 .50
164 Inge Hammarstrom 2.50 5.00
165 Lars Goran Nilsson .25 .50
166 Jan Erik Lyck .25 .50
167 Stefan Karlsson .25 .50
168 Lennart Lind .50 1.00
169 Hans Ake Persson .25 .50
170 Lars Oberg .25 .50
171 Lars Erik Eriksson .25 .50
172 Bjorn Fagerlund .30 .75
173 Nicke Johansson .25 .50
174 Lars Goran Nilsson .25 .50
175 Hans Erik Jansson .25 .50
176 Per Backman .25 .50
177 Jorgen Palm .25 .50
178 Conny Evensson .30 .75
179 Ulf Sterner .25 .50
180 Sven Ake Rudby .25 .50
181 Lennart Andersson .30 .75
182 Kent Erik Andersson .25 .50
183 Hans Ake Rosendahl .25 .50
184 Karl Johan Sundqvist .25 .50
185 Hasse Andersson .25 .50
186 Benny Andersson .25 .50
187 Gunnar Johansson .25 .50
188 Sten Ake Bark .25 .50
189 Lasse Zetterstrom .25 .50
190 Leif Holmqvist .50 1.00
191 Bert Jattne .50 1.00
192 Lars Danielsson .25 .50
193 Hakan Lindgren .25 .50
194 Ake Fagerstrom .25 .50
195 Bert-Ola Nordlander .30 .75
196 Leif Holmgren .25 .50
197 Soren Sjogren .25 .50
198 Hans Lindberg .25 .50
199 Jan-Olov Kroon .25 .50
200 Rolf Edberg .25 .50
201 Lennart Selinder .25 .50
202 Ulf Nilsson 2.50 5.00
203 Jan Olsson .25 .50
204 Jan Ostling .25 .50
205 Christer Lundberg .25 .50
206 Christer Englund .25 .50
207 Bo Olofsson .25 .50
208 Roland Einarsson .25 .50
209 Ake Danielsson .25 .50
210 Billy Sundstrom .25 .50
211 Thomas Carlsson .25 .50
212 Stig Larsson .25 .50
213 Lars Ake Gustavsson .50 1.00
214 Bjorn Palmqvist .25 .50
215 Anders Hedberg 2.50 5.00
216 Anders Rylin .25 .50
217 Sven Bertil Lindstrom .25 .50
218 Kjell Nilsson .25 .50
219 Claes Goran Wallin .25 .50
220 Ake Eklof .25 .50
221 Peder Nilsson .30 .75
222 Lars Ake Lundell .25 .50
223 Bengt Ake Karlsson .25 .50
224 Ove Svensson .25 .50
225 Soren Johansson .25 .50
226 Christer Sehlstedt .30 .75
227 Lage Edin .25 .50
228 Tommy Andersson .25 .50
229 Janerik Nilsson .25 .50
230 Tommie Lindgren .25 .50
231 Bo Bergman .25 .50
232 Lennart Norberg .25 .50
233 Olle Ahman .25 .50
234 Arne Lundstrom .30 .75
235 Kent Lindgren .25 .50
236 Orjan Lindstrom .25 .50
237 Kent Othberg .30 .75
238 Finn Lundstrom .25 .50
239 Ake Soderberg .25 .50
240 Jan Kock .25 .50
241 Ove Larsson .25 .50
242 Hakan Pettersson .25 .50
243 Stefan Pettersson .25 .50

1974-75 Swedish Stickers

This set of 324 stickers commemorates the competitors on the 1974-75 World Championship, along with players from club teams across Europe. The stickers -- which measure approximately 3" by 2" -- feature action photography on the front, with player name and card number along the bottom. The backs have the set logo, a reprise of the card number and encouragement in Swedish to build the entire set. The last six cards were recently identified by Swedish collector Per Vedin.

COMPLETE SET (324) 100.00 175.00
1 Vladislav Tretiak 7.50 15.00
2 Gennadij Tsigannkov .50 1.00
3 Valerij Vasiljev 1.50 3.00
4 Alexander Gusev .50 1.00
5 Valeri Kharlamov 3.00 10.00
6 Vladimir Petrov 2.00 4.00
7 Boris Michailov 2.00 4.00
8 Alexander Maltsev 2.00 4.00
9 Alexander Yakusjev 2.00 4.00
10 Jiri Chra 1.50 3.00
11 Jiri Bubla .50 1.00
12 Milan Kuzela .25 .50
13 Oldrich Machac .25 .50
14 Ivan Hlinka .50 1.00
15 Vaclav Nedomansky .75 1.50
16 Boshulav Stastny .75 1.50
17 Vladimir Martinec .50 1.00
18 Richard Farda .25 .50
19 Curt Larsson .30 .75
20 Lars-Erik Sjoberg 1.00 2.00
21 Thommy Abrahamsson .50 1.00
22 Kjell-Rune Milton .25 .50
23 Anders Hedberg 2.00 4.00
24 Mats Ahlberg .30 .75
25 Dan Soderstrom .25 .50
26 Ulf Nilsson 2.00 4.00
27 Per-Olof Brassar .75 1.50
28 Stig Wetzell .25 .50
29 Juha Rantasila .25 .50
30 Heikki Riihiranta .50 1.00
31 Timo Saari .25 .50
32 Seppo Repo .25 .50
33 Esa Peltonen .25 .50
34 Juhani Tamminen .50 1.00
35 Matti Murto .25 .50
36 Harri Linnonmaa .25 .50
37 Gennadij Lapsjenkov .50 1.00
38 Pjotr Zjulin .25 .50
39 Vladimir Merinov .25 .50
40 Sergej Tyznych 1.00 2.00
41 Valerij Kostin .25 .50
42 Valerij Nikitin .50 1.00
43 Sergej Gusev .50 1.00
44 Valentin Kozin .25 .50
45 Viktor Liksiutkin .25 .50
46 Alexander Golikov .50 1.00
47 Viktor Zhluktov .50 1.00
48 Anatolij Frolov .75 1.50
49 Vladimir Golikov 1.00 2.00
50 Nikolaj Epstein .25 .50
51 Alexander Kasjajev .25 .50
52 Alexander Sidelnikov 1.00 2.00
53 Valerij Kuzmin .50 1.00
54 Viktor Kuznetsov .50 1.00
55 Jurij Terechin .30 .75
56 Jurij Tjitjurin .30 .75
57 Jurij Sjatavalov .30 .75
58 Vjatjeslav Anissin .30 .75
59 Alexander Bodunov .50 1.00
60 Jurij Lebedev .75 1.50
61 Igor Dmitriev 2.00 4.00
62 Konstantin Klimov .30 .75
63 Sergej Kapustin .30 .75
64 Vladimir Repnjov .30 .75
65 Jevgenij Kucharzj .30 .75
66 Boris Kulagin 1.00 2.00
67 Viktor Afonin .25 .50

68 Juris Liberts .30 .75
69 Igor Kobzev .30 .75
70 Valerij Odintsov .30 .75
71 Vjatjeslav Nazarov .50 1.00
72 Andris Hendelis .30 .75
73 Alexander Sokolovskij .30 .75
74 Michail Denisov .30 .75
75 Helmut Balderis 2.00 4.00
76 Vladimir Sorokin .25 .50
77 Vladimir Sernjajev .25 .50
78 Viktor Verizjnikov .25 .50
79 Vladimir Markov .25 .50
80 Viktor Tichonov 2.50 5.00
81 Edgar Rosenberg .25 .50
82 Alexander Kotomkin .25 .50
83 Vladimir Astafjev .50 1.00
84 Alexander Kulikov .25 .50
85 Sergej Mosjkarov .25 .50
86 Vjatjeslav Usjmakov .25 .50
87 Jurij Fjodorov .50 1.00
88 Victor Dobrochotov .25 .50
89 Vitalij Krajov .25 .50
90 Alexej Masjin .25 .50
91 Vladimir Orlov .25 .50
92 Vladimir Smagin .25 .50
93 Alexander Usov .25 .50
94 Alexander Fedotov .50 1.00
95 Alexander Prilepskij .25 .50
96 Alexander Rogov .25 .50
97 Seppo Ahokainen .25 .50
98 Lasse Oksanen .25 .50
99 Jorma Peltonen .50 1.00
100 Henry Leppa .25 .50
101 Seppo Suoraniemi .25 .50
102 Timi Sutinen .25 .50
103 Jorma Valtonen .50 1.00
104 Antti Leppanen .25 .50
105 Pekka Marjamaki .25 .50
106 Juoko Oystila .25 .50
107 Seppo Lindstrom .25 .50
108 Veli-Pekka Ketola .75 1.50
109 Jiri Holecek .50 1.00
110 Jiri Kochta .25 .50
111 Josef Horesovsky .25 .50
112 Jaroslav Sima .25 .50
113 Frantisek Vorlicek .25 .50
114 Vladimir Kostka .25 .50
115 Jaroslav Holik .30 .75
116 Jiri Holik .50 1.00
117 Jan Suchy .30 .75
118 Josef Augusta, .25 .50
119 Miroslav Dvorak .50 1.00
120 Jan Hrbaty .25 .50
121 AIK .25 .50
122 If Bjorkloven .25 .50
123 Brynas IF .25 .50
124 Djurgardens IF .25 .50
125 Farjestads BK .25 .50
126 IF Karlskoga .25 .50
127 Leksands IF .25 .50
128 MoDo .25 .50
129 Mora IK .25 .50
130 Skelleftea AIK .25 .50
131 Sodertalje SK .25 .50
132 Timra IK .25 .50
133 Tingsryds AIF .25 .50
134 V. Frolunda IF .25 .50
135 Vasteras IK .25 .50
136 Orebro IK .25 .50
137 Christer Abrahamsson .75 1.50
138 Christer Andersson .25 .50
139 Mikael Collin .50 1.00
140 Bjorn Fagerlund .25 .50
141 Christer Grahn .50 1.00
142 Kenneth Holmstedt .25 .50
143 Goran Hogosta .50 1.00
144 Bert Jattne .25 .50
145 Curt Larsson .30 .75
146 Ivar Larsson .25 .50
147 Wille Lofqvist .50 1.00
148 Peder Nilsson .25 .50
149 Christer Sehlstedt .25 .50
150 Krister Sterner .30 .75
151 Christer Stahl .25 .50
152 Sune Odling .25 .50
153 Thommy Abrahamsson .50 1.00
154 Gunnar Andersson .25 .50
155 Jan Andersson .25 .50
156 Leif Andersson .25 .50
157 Sture Andersson .25 .50
158 Tommy Andersson .25 .50
159 Sten Ake Bark .25 .50
160 Roger Bergman .25 .50
161 Roland Bond .25 .50
162 Arne,Carlsson .25 .50
163 Thomas Carlsson .25 .50
164 Lasse Danielsson .25 .50
165 Ake Danielsson .25 .50
166 Kenneth Ekman .25 .50
167 Lars Erik Esbjors .25 .50
168 Soren Gunnarsson .25 .50
169 Mats Hysing .25 .50
170 Bjorn Johansson .25 .50
171 Martin Johansson .25 .50
172 Jan Kock .25 .50
173 Hakan Lindgren .25 .50
174 Larsake Lundell .25 .50
175 Mats Lundmark .25 .50
176 Kjell-Rune Milton .25 .50
177 Jan Erik Nilsson .25 .50
178 Lars Goran Nilsson .25 .50
179 Hakan Nygren .25 .50
180 Jan Olsson .25 .50
181 Jorgen Palm .25 .50
182 Dennis Pettersson .25 .50
183 Stefan Pettersson .25 .50
184 Anders Rylin .25 .50
185 Stig Salming .30 .75
186 Nils-Olof Schilstrom .25 .50
187 Jan Erik Silfverberg .25 .50
188 Lars Erik Sjoberg 1.50 3.00
189 Karl-Johan Sundqvist .25 .50
190 Jan-Olof Svensson .25 .50
191 Leif Svensson .25 .50
192 Tord Svensson .25 .50
193 Sverker Torstensson .25 .50
194 Mats Walltin .25 .50
195 Ulf Weinstock .25 .50
196 Jan Ove Wiberg .25 .50
197 Lars Zetterstrom .25 .50
198 Stig Ostling .30 .75
199 Hans Andersson .25 .50
200 Kent-Erik Andersson .25 .50
201 Kjell Andersson .25 .50
202 Ulf Barrefjord .25 .50
203 Kent Bengtsson .25 .50
204 Bo Berggren .25 .50
205 Kjell Brus .25 .50
206 Per-Olof Brasar .75 1.50
207 Borje Burlin .25 .50
208 Per Backman .25 .50
209 Stefan Canderyd .25 .50
210 Hans Carlsson .25 .50
211 Hakan Dahlov .25 .50
212 Rolf Edberg .25 .50
213 Ake Eklof .25 .50
214 Roland Eriksson .25 .50
215 Conny Evensson .50 1.00
216 Svante Granholm .25 .50
217 Peter Gudmundsson .25 .50
218 Hans Hansson .25 .50
219 Anders Hedberg 2.00 4.00
220 Henric Hedlund .25 .50
221 Nils Arne Hedqvist .25 .50
222 Leif Henriksson .25 .50
223 Leif Holmgren .25 .50
224 Sven-Ake Jacobsson .25 .50
225 Hans Jax .25 .50
226 Christer Johansson .25 .50
227 Gunnar Johansson .25 .50
228 Lars Erik Johansson .25 .50
229 Stig-Goran Johansson .25 .50
230 Soren Johansson .25 .50
231 Bengt Goran Karlsson .25 .50
232 Bengt-Ake Karlsson .25 .50
233 Martin Karlsson .25 .50
234 Stefan Karlsson .25 .50
235 Jan-Olov Kroon .25 .50
236 Dan Labraaten .75 1.50
237 Dan Landegren .25 .50
238 Kjell Landstrom .25 .50
239 Ove Larsson .25 .50
240 Stig Larsson .25 .50
241 Hans Lindberg .25 .50
242 Mats Lindh .25 .50
243 Willy Lindstrom .50 1.00
244 Orjan Lindstrom .25 .50
245 Christer Lundberg .25 .50
246 Lars-Gunnar Lundberg .25 .50
247 Per Lundqvist .25 .50
248 Arne Lundstrom .50 1.00
249 Fhinn Lundstrom .25 .50
250 Bengt Lovgren .25 .50
251 Ulf Martensson .25 .50
252 Par Marts .25 .50
253 Tadeusz Niedomysl .25 .50
254 Hardy Nilsson .25 .50
255 Lars Goran Nilsson .25 .50
256 Ulf Nilsson 2.00 4.00
257 Anders Nordin .25 .50
258 Nils-Olof Olsson .25 .50
259 Bjorn Palmqvist .25 .50
260 Kent Persson .25 .50
261 Hakan Pettersson .25 .50
262 Sven-Ake Rudby .25 .50
263 Benny Runesson .25 .50
264 Jan Roger Strand .25 .50
265 Ake Soderberg .50 1.00
266 Dan Soderstrom .25 .50
267 Ulf Torstensson .25 .50
268 Claes Goran Wallin .25 .50
269 Hakan Wickberg .25 .50
270 Kjell Arne Wickstrom .25 .50
271 Per Allan Wickstrom .25 .50
272 Dick Yderstrom .25 .50
273 Mats Ahlberg .30 .75
274 Olle Ahman .25 .50
275 Lars Oberg .25 .50
276 Jan Ostling .25 .50
277 Akning .25 .50
278 Akning .25 .50
279 Akning .25 .50
280 Skott .25 .50
281 Skott .25 .50
282 Skott .25 .50
283 Puckforing .25 .50
284 Tekning .25 .50
285 Malvaktsspel .50 1.00
286 Malvaktsspel .50 1.00
287 Forsvarsspel .25 .50
288 Forsvarsspel .25 .50
289 Forsvarsspel .25 .50
290 Forsvarsspel .25 .50
291 Forsvarsspel .25 .50
292 Forsvarsspel .25 .50
293 Forsvarsspel .25 .50
294 Forsvarsspel .25 .50
295 Forsvarsspel .25 .50
296 Forsvarsspel .25 .50
297 Forsvarsspel .25 .50
298 Forsvarsspel .25 .50
299 Forsvarsspel .25 .50
300 Forsvarsspel .25 .50
301 Forsvarsspel .25 .50
302 Forsvarsspel .25 .50
303 Anfallsspel .25 .50
304 Anfallsspel .25 .50
305 Anfallsspel .25 .50
306 Anfallsspel .25 .50
307 Anfallsspel .25 .50
308 Anfallsspel .25 .50
309 Anfallsspel .25 .50
310 Anfallsspel .25 .50
311 Anfallsspel .25 .50
312 Anfallsspel .25 .50
313 Inge Hammarstrom 1.00 2.00
314 Borje Salming 3.00 6.00
315 Thommie Bergman 1.25 2.50
316 Leif Holmqvist .50 1.00
317 Ulf Sterner .25 .50
318 Tord Lundstrom .25 .50
319 Tre Kroner puzzle .25 .50
320 Tre Kroner puzzle .25 .50
321 Tre Kroner puzzle .25 .50
322 Tre Kroner puzzle .25 .50
323 Tre Kroner puzzle .25 .50
324 Tre Kroner puzzle .25 .50

1974 Swedish Semic World Championship Stickers

This 100-sticker set featuring World Championship players was produced by Semic of Sweden. The stickers measure approximately 2" by 3", and were designed to be placed on one of four team-specific posters. The cards were issued in sheets of two.

COMPLETE SET (100) 40.00 80.00
1 Christer Abrahamsson .75 1.50
2 William Lofqvist .50 1.00
3 Arne Carlsson .25 .50
4 Lars-Erik Sjoberg 1.00 2.00
5 Bjorn Johansson .25 .50
6 Tommy Abrahamsson .50 1.00
7 Karl-Johan Sundqvist .25 .50
8 Ulf Nilsson 2.00 4.00
9 Hakan Wickberg .25 .50
10 Dan Soderstrom .25 .50
11 Mats Ahlberg .30 .75
12 Anders Hedberg 2.00 4.00
13 Dick Yderstrom .25 .50
14 Stefan Karlsson .25 .50
15 Roland Bond .25 .50
16 Kjell-Rune Milton .25 .50
17 Willy Lindstrom .50 1.00
18 Mats Waltin .25 .50
19 Lars-Goran Nilsson .25 .50
20 Bjorn Palmquist .25 .50
21 Stig-Goran Johansson .25 .50
22 Bo Berggren .25 .50
23 Dan Labraaten .75 1.50
24 Curt Larsson .30 .75
25 Mats Lindh .25 .50
26 Vladislav Tretiak 7.50 15.00
27 Alexander Ragulin .50 1.00
28 Vladimir Luttjenko .50 1.00
29 Gennadij Tsygankov .50 1.00
30 Alexander Gusev .50 1.00
31 Jevgenij Poladiev .25 .50
32 Jurij Ljapkin .50 1.00
33 Boris Michailov 2.00 4.00
34 Valeri Kharlamov 3.00 10.00
35 Vladimir Petrov 2.00 3.00
36 Alexander Maltsev 2.00 4.00
37 Vladimir Sjadrin .30 .75
38 Alexander Yakusjev 2.00 4.00
39 Alexander Martynjuk .30 .75
40 Jurij Lebedev .75 1.50
41 Alexander Bodunov .50 1.00
42 Anatolij Firsov .75 1.50
43 Vitalij Davydov .30 .75
44 Vjateslav Starsjinov .30 .75
45 Viktor Kuzkin .25 .50
46 Igor Romitjevskij .25 .50
47 Jevgenij Zimin .30 .75
48 Jevgenij Misjakov .50 1.00
49 Vladimir Vikulov .30 .75
50 Viktor Konovalenko .50 1.00
51 Jiri Holecek .50 1.00
52 Frantisek Pospisil .30 .75
53 Jiri Bubla .50 1.00
54 Josef Horesovsky .25 .50
55 Oldrich Machac .25 .50
56 Vladimir Martinec .25 .50
57 Vaclav Nedomansky .75 1.50
58 Jiri Kochta .25 .50
59 Milan Novy .50 1.00
60 Jaroslav Holik .30 .75
61 Jiri Holik .50 1.00
62 Jiri Klapac .25 .50
63 Richard Farda .30 .75
64 Bohuslav Stastny .30 .75
65 Jiri Novak .25 .50
66 Ivan Hlinka .30 .75
67 Jan Suchy .30 .75
68 Vladimir Bednar .25 .50
69 Rudolf Tajcnar .25 .50
70 Josef Cerny .25 .50
71 Jan Havel .30 .75
72 Marcel Sakac .25 .50
73 Frantisek Pancharek .25 .50
74 Bedrich Brunchk .25 .50
75 Edvard Novak .25 .50
76 Jorma Valtonen .50 1.00
77 Seppo Lindstrom .25 .50
78 Pekka Marjamaki .25 .50
79 Pekka Rautakallio .75 1.50
80 Heikki Riihiranta .50 1.00
81 Seppo Suoraniemi .25 .50
82 Jouko Oystila .25 .50
83 Veli-Pekka Ketola .75 1.50
84 Henry Leppa .25 .50
85 Harri Linnonmaa .25 .50
86 Matti Murto .25 .50
87 Lasse Oksanen .25 .50
88 Esa Peltonen .25 .50
89 Seppo Repo .25 .50
90 Raimo Suoniemi .25 .50
91 Timo Sutinen .25 .50
92 Juhani Tamminen .50 1.00
93 Leo Seppanen .25 .50
94 Hannu Haapalainen .25 .50
95 Pertti Valkeapaa .25 .50
96 Sakari Ahlberg .25 .50
97 Antti Leppanen .25 .50
98 Kalevi Numminen .25 .50
99 Lauri Mononen .25 .50
100 Ilpo Koskela .30 .75
NNO Ulf Nilsson poster
NNO Valeri Kharlamov poster
NNO Timo Sutinen poster
NNO Vaclav Nedomansky poster

1981 Swedish Semic Hockey VM Stickers

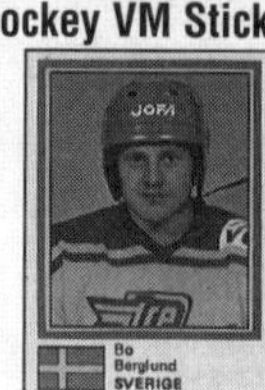

This 144-sticker set was released in conjunction with the 1981 World Championships. The stickers, which measure 3" by 2 1/8", feature a color photo on the front along with the player name, country and national flag. The backs contain the card number and a remainder to place the stickers in the special set album (which retails now in the $25 range). The set is notable for the inclusion of Glenn Anderson in his RC year, as well as Mats Naslund and Neal Broten prior to their RCs. The set also features members of the American "Miracle On Ice" Olympic team; in some cases, these are the only "legitimate" card-like elements of players such as Mike Eruzione, Buzz Schneider, etc.

COMPLETE SET (144) 50.00 125.00
1 Goran Hogosta .20 .50
2 Tomas Jonsson .20 .50
3 Ulf Weinstock .10 .25
4 Goran Nilsson .10 .25
5 Jan Eriksson .10 .25
6 Tommy Samuelsson .10 .25
7 Mats Waltin .10 .25
8 Peter Helander .10 .25
9 Per Lundqvist .10 .25
10 Conny Silfverberg .10 .25
11 Mats Naslund 2.00 5.00
12 Lennart Norberg .10 .25
13 Bengt Lundholm .40 1.00
14 Leif Holmgren .10 .25
15 Bo Berglund .40 1.00
16 Dan Soderstrom .10 .25
17 Lars Molin .30 .75
18 Tore Oqvist .10 .25
19 Ari Hellgren .10 .25
20 Hannu Lassila .10 .25
21 Kari Eloranta .40 1.00
22 Lasse Litma .10 .25
23 Seppo Suoraniemi .10 .25
24 Tapio Levo .20 .50
25 Timo Nummelin .10 .25
26 Reijo Ruotsalainen .60 1.50
27 Markku Kiimalainen .10 .25
28 Mikko Leinonen .30 .75
29 Reijo Leppanen .10 .25
30 Hannu Koskinen .10 .25
31 Timo Susi .10 .25
32 Jukka Porvari .10 .25
33 Arto Javanainen .10 .25
34 Juhanni Tamminen .40 1.00
35 Pertti Koivulahti .10 .25
36 Antero Lehtonen .10 .25
37 Vladislav Tretiak 4.00 10.00
38 Vladimir Mysjkin .60 1.50
39 Slava Fetisov 2.50 6.00
40 Vladimir Luttjenko .30 .75
41 Sergei Babinov .20 .50
42 Vasilij Pervuchin .30 .75
43 Sergej Starikov .30 .75
44 Zinetula Biljaletdinov .30 .75
45 Vladimir Krutov 2.00 5.00
46 Alexander Maltsev 1.25 3.00
47 Jurij Lebedev .30 .75
48 Viktor Tiumenev .20 .50
49 Nikolaj Drozdetskij .10 .25
50 Valeri Kharlamov 2.50 6.00
51 Sergej Makarov 2.00 5.00
52 Vladimir Golikov .30 .75
53 Alexander Skvortsov .20 .50
54 Michail Varnakov .30 .75
55 Jiri Kralik .20 .50
56 Jaromir Sindel .60 1.50
57 Miroslav Dvorak .30 .75
58 Frantisek Kaberle .20 .50
59 Arnold Kadlec .20 .50
60 Jan Neliba .10 .25
61 Radoslav Svoboda .10 .25
62 Jaroslav Lycka .10 .25
63 Milan Novy .40 1.00
64 Jaroslav Pouzar .40 1.00
65 Miroslav Frycer .60 1.50
66 Karel Holy .10 .25
67 Ladislav Svozil .10 .25
68 Marian Bezak .10 .25
69 Jindrich Kokrment .10 .25
70 Jiri Lala .30 .75
71 Ludos Penicka .10 .25
72 Ivan Hlinka .75 2.00
73 Wayne Stephenson .75 2.00
74 Ron Paterson .30 .75
75 Warren Anderson .30 .75
76 Brad Pirie .30 .75
77 Randy Gregg .60 1.50
78 Tim Watters .40 1.00
79 Joe Grant .30 .75
80 Don Spring .30 .75
81 Ron Davidson .30 .75
82 Glenn Anderson 4.00 10.00
83 Kevin Maxwell .30 .75
84 Jim Nill .40 1.00
85 John Devaney .30 .75
86 Paul MacLean .60 1.50
87 Dan D'Alvise .30 .75
88 Ken Berry .30 .75
89 David Hindmarch .30 .75
90 Kevin Primeau .40 1.00
91 Steve Janaszak 2.00 5.00
92 Bob Suter 2.00 5.00
93 Ken Morrow 2.00 5.00
94 Mike Ramsey 2.00 5.00
95 Bill Baker 2.00 5.00
96 Dave Christian 2.00 5.00
97 Les Auge .40 1.00
98 Dave Silk 2.00 5.00
99 Neal Broten 2.00 5.00
100 Mark Johnson 2.00 5.00
101 Steve Christoff 1.25 5.00
102 Mark Pavelich 1.25 5.00
103 Eric Strobel 1.25 5.00
104 Mike Eruzione 10.00 25.00
105 Rob McClanahan 2.00 5.00
106 Buzz Schneider 2.00 5.00
107 Phil Verchota 2.00 5.00
108 John Harrington 2.00 5.00
109 Leif Holmqvist .40 1.00
110 Kjell Svensson .30 .75
111 Roland Stoltz .10 .25
112 Bert-Ola Nordlander .10 .25
113 Nils Johansson .10 .25
114 Lennart Svedberg .20 .50
115 Ulf Sterner .10 .25
116 Hakan Wickberg .10 .25
117 Tord Lundstrom .10 .25
118 Carl-Goran Oberg .10 .25
119 Eilert Maatta .10 .25
120 Lars-Goran Nilsson .10 .25
121 Nils Nilsson .10 .25
122 Hans Oberg .10 .25
123 Lars-Erik Lundvall .10 .25
124 Sven Tumba Johansson .20 .50
125 Lars Bjorn .10 .25
126 Ronald Pettersson .10 .25
127 World Championships 1981 .10
.25
128 Sweden .10 .25
129 Finland .10 .25
130 Soviet Union .10 .25
131 CSSR .10 .25
132 Canada .30 .75
133 U.S.A. .30 .75
134 West Germany .10 .25
135 Holland .10 .25
136 Referee's Signs .10 .25
137 Referee's Signs .10 .25
138 Referee's Signs .10 .25
139 Referee's Signs .10 .25
140 Referee's Signs .10 .25
141 Referee's Signs .10 .25
142 Referee's Signs .10 .25
143 Referee's Signs .10 .25
144 Referee's Signs .10 .25

1982 Swedish Semic VM Stickers

This 162-sticker set was released in 1982 to commemorate the World Championships held in Helsinki and Tampere, Finland. The stickers measure 3" by 2 1/8" and feature color photos along with the player's name and emblem (national or NHL) on the front. The backs have the sticker number, along with text in both Finnish and Swedish. The set does not include any North American-born NHLers, but does have several prominent Swedish NHL stars, including Hakan Loob, Mats Naslund, and Kent Nilsson.

COMPLETE SET (162) 24.00 60.00
1 Peter Lindmark .40 1.00
2 Gote Walitalo .10 .25
3 Gunnar Leidborg .10 .25
4 Goran Lindblom .10 .25
5 Thomas Eriksson .10 .25
6 Mats Waltin .10 .25
7 Jan Eriksson .10 .25
8 Mats Thelin .30 .75
9 Peter Helander .10 .25
10 Tommy Samuelsson .10 .25
11 Bo Ericsson .10 .25
12 Peter Andersson .20 .50
13 Mats Naslund 2.00 5.00
14 Ulf Isaksson .10 .25
15 Patrik Sundstrom .75 2.00
16 Peter Sundstrom .60 1.50
17 Thomas Rundqvist .30 .75
18 Mats Ulander .10 .25
19 Tommy Morth .10 .25
20 Ove Olsson .10 .25
21 Rolf Edberg .10 .25
22 Hakan Loob 1.50 4.00
23 Leif Holmgren .40 1.00
24 Jan Erixon .60 1.50
25 Harald Luckner .10 .25
26 Hannu Kamppuri .40 1.00
27 Hannu Issila .20 .50
28 Kari Heikkila .10 .25
29 Timo Nummelin .10 .25
30 Pertti Lehtonen .10 .25
31 Raimo Hirvonen .10 .25
32 Seppo Suoraniemi .10 .25
33 Juha Huikari .10 .25
34 Hannu Helander .10 .25
35 Lasse Litma .10 .25
36 Hakan Hjerpe .10 .25
37 Kari Jalonen .20 .50
38 Arto Javanainen .10 .25
39 Jari Lindgren .10 .25
40 Markku Kiimalainen .10 .25
41 Jarmo Makitalo .10 .25
42 Jorma Sevon .10 .25
43 Erkki Laine .10 .25
44 Hannu Koskinen .10 .25
45 Reijo Leppanen .10 .25
46 Pekka Arbelius .10 .25
47 Markku Hakulinen .10 .25
48 Timo Susi .10 .25
49 Esa Peltonen .10 .25
50 Juhani Tamminen .40 1.00
51 Vladislav Tretiak 4.00 10.00
52 Vladimir Mysjkin .30 .75
53 Slava Fetisov 2.00 5.00
54 Sergej Babinov .20 .50
55 Vasilij Pervuchin .20 .50
56 Valerij Vasiljev .30 .75
57 Alexei Kasatonov .75 2.00
58 Zinetula Biljaletdinov .40 1.00
59 Sergej Starikov .30 .75
60 Sergej Makarov 1.25 3.00
61 Sergej Sjepelev .30 .75
62 Vladimir Krutov 1.25 3.00
63 Nikolaj Drozdetskij .30 .75
64 Viktor Zjluktov .20 .50
65 Viktor Sjalimov .20 .50
66 Vladimir Golikov .20 .50
67 Aleksandr Maltsev 1.00 2.50
68 Andrej Khomutov .75 2.00
69 Sergej Svetlov .20 .50
70 Helmut Balderis .30 .75
71 Sergej Kapustin .20 .50
72 Vladimir Zubkov .20 .50
73 Aleksandr Kozjevnikov .20 .50
74 Jurij Lebedev .20 .50
75 Nikolaj Makarov .20 .50
76 Jiri Kralik .20 .50
77 Karel Lang .20 .50
78 Jaromir Sindel .40 1.00
79 Miroslav Horava .20 .50
80 Milan Chalupa .20 .50
81 Stanislav Hajdusek .10 .25
82 Arnold Kadlec .20 .50
83 Miroslav Dvorak .20 .50
84 Jan Neliba .10 .25
85 Petr Misek .10 .25
86 Eduard Uvira .10 .25
87 Milan Novy .20 .50
88 Frantisek Cerny .20 .50
89 Jiri Lala .20 .50
90 Jindrich Kokrment .10 .25
91 Frantisek Cernik .20 .50
92 Darius Rusnak .10 .25
93 Dusan Pasek .20 .50
94 Lubomir Penicka .10 .25
95 Jaroslav Korbela .10 .25
96 Peter Ihnacak .40 1.00
97 Jaroslav Hrdina .10 .25
98 Igor Liba .20 .50
99 Peter Slania .10 .25
100 Vincent Lukac .10 .25
101 Erich Weishaupt .20 .50
102 Bernhard Engelbrecht .20 .50
103 Robert Murray .20 .50
104 Peter Gailer .10 .25
105 Udo Kiessling .20 .50
106 Harold Kreis .20 .50
107 Joachim Reil .10 .25
108 Harald Krull .10 .25
109 Ulrich Egen .10 .25
110 Marcus Kuhl .10 .25
111 Peter Schiller .10 .25
112 Erich Kuhnhackl .20 .50
113 Holger Meitinger .10 .25
114 Ernst Hofner .10 .25
115 Vladimir Vacatko .10 .25
116 Manfred Wolf .10 .25
117 Johann Morz .10 .25
118 Franz Reindl .10 .25
119 Helmut Steiger .10 .25
120 Georg Holzmann .10 .25
121 Roy Roedger .10 .25
122 Jim Corsi .40 1.00
123 Nick Sanza .10 .25
124 Guido Tenisi .10 .25
125 Erwin Kostner .10 .25
126 Mike Amodeo .20 .50
127 John Bellio .10 .25
128 Dave Tomassoni .10 .25
129 Daniel Pupillo .10 .25
130 Giulio Francella .10 .25
131 Fabio Polloni .10 .25
132 Adolf Insam .10 .25
133 Patrick Dell'Jannone .10 .25
134 Rick Bragnalo .10 .25
135 Michael Mair .10 .25
136 Alberto DiFazio .10 .25
137 Cary Farelli .10 .25
138 Tom Milani .10 .25
139 Martin Pavlu .10 .25
140 Bob De Piero .10 .25
141 Grant Goegan .10 .25
142 Jerry Ciarcia .10 .25
143 Borje Salming 2.00 5.00
144 Lars Lindgren .20 .50
145 Ulf Nilsson .75 2.00
146 Bengt-Ake Gustavsson .60 1.50
147 Kent Nilsson 1.50 4.00
148 Thomas Gradin 1.25 3.00
149 Lars Molin .30 .75
150 Thomas Steen 1.25 3.00
151 Bengt Lundholm .30 .75
152 Jorgen Pettersson .30 .75
153 Jukka Porvari .20 .50
154 Tapio Levo .20 .50
155 Reijo Ruotsalainen .30 .75
156 Matti Hagman .30 .75
157 Risto Siltanen .30 .75
158 Ilkka Sinisalo .40 1.00
159 Markus Mattsson .30 .75
160 Mikko Leinonen .20 .50
161 Pekka Rautakallio .40 1.00
162 Veli-Pekka Ketola .40 1.00

1983-84 Swedish Semic Elitserien

Card fronts feature action photos from players in the Swedish Elite League. Many players have cards in this set that predate their NHL Rookie Cards, which make for unique and challenging collectibles.

COMPLETE SET (243) 24.00 60.00
1 Gunnar Leidborg .20 .50
2 Peter Aslin .40 1.00
3 Mats Thelin .40 1.00
4 Jan Eriksson .10 .25
5 Hans Cederholm .10 .25
6 Bo Ericsson .10 .25
7 Bjorn Hellman .10 .25
8 Tomas Nord .10 .25
9 Anders Wallin .10 .25
10 Mats Alba .10 .25
11 Ronny Jansson .10 .25
12 Roger Lindstrom .10 .25
13 Mats Hessel .10 .25
14 Peter Gradin .10 .25
15 Mats Ulander .10 .25
16 Per-Erik Eklund 1.25 3.00
17 Ulf Isaksson .10 .25
18 Rolf Eriksson .10 .25
19 Michael Wikstrom .10 .25
20 Leif Holmgren .10 .25
21 Per Martinelle .10 .25
22 Tommy Lehmann .30 .75
23 Hans Norberg .10 .25
24 Jan Ericsson .10 .25
25 Per Backman .10 .25
26 Gote Walitalo .10 .25
27 Jakob Gustavsson .10 .25
28 Staffan Andersson .10 .25
29 Torbjorn Andersson .10 .25
30 Anders Bostrom .10 .25
31 Jan Lindholm .10 .25
32 Ulf Nilsson 2.00 5.00
33 Par Sjolander .10 .25
34 Lennart Dahlberg .10 .25
35 Rolf Berglund .10 .25
36 Patrik Aberg .10 .25
37 Tom Eklund .10 .25
38 Stefan Nilsson .10 .25
39 Matti Pauna .10 .25
40 Jan Lundstrom .10 .25
41 Mikael Andersson 1.25 3.00
42 Hans Edlund .10 .25
43 Jon Lundstrom .10 .25
44 Tony Lundgren .10 .25
45 Ulf Wikgren .10 .25
46 Tomas Hedin .10 .25
47 Lars-Gunnar Pettersson .10 .25
48 Peter Edstrom .10 .25
49 Tore Okvist .10 .25
50 Tommy Sandlin .30 .75
51 Lars Eriksson .10 .25
52 Ake Lilljebjorn .20 .50
53 Anders Backstrom .10 .25
54 Goran Grundstrom .10 .25
55 Jan Kock .10 .25
56 Gunnar Persson .10 .25
57 Torbjorn Mattsson .10 .25
58 Stig Ostling .10 .25
59 Hans Johansson .10 .25
60 Robert Nordmark .40 1.00
61 Mikael Sandstrom .10 .25
62 Anders Carlsson .10 .25
63 Christer Andersson .10 .25
64 Per Hedenstrom .10 .25
65 Bjorn Akerblom .10 .25
66 Conny Silfverberg .10 .25
67 Jonny Stridh .10 .25
68 Goran Sjoberg .10 .25
69 Kenneth Andersson .10 .25
70 Fredrik Lundstrom .10 .25
71 Henrik Cedergren .10 .25
72 Tomas Sandstrom 1.25 3.00
73 Anders Huss .10 .25
74 Stig Salming .20 .50
75 Rolf Ridderwall .40 1.00
76 Bo Larsson .10 .25
77 Mikael Westling .10 .25
78 Tord Nansen .10 .25
79 Tommy Albelin 1.25 3.00
80 Orvar Stambert .10 .25
81 Karl-Erik Lilja .10 .25
82 Mats Waltin .10 .25
83 Stefan Perlstrom .10 .25
84 Michael Thelven .20 .50
85 Stefan Jansson .10 .25
86 Jens Ohling .10 .25
87 Peter Nilsson .10 .25
88 Hakan Eriksson .10 .25
89 Jorgen Holmberg .10 .25
90 Tommy Morth .10 .25
91 Jan Claesson .10 .25
92 Per Goransson .10 .25
93 Martin Linse .10 .25
94 Bjorn Carlsson .10 .25
95 Hakan Sodergren .10 .25
96 Anders Johnsson .10 .25
97 Jan Viktorsson .20 .50
98 Jeff Hallegard .10 .25
99 Leif Boork .10 .25
100 Hakan Hermansson .10 .25
101 Thomas Blom .10 .25
102 Christer Dalgard .10 .25
103 Tommy Samuelsson .10 .25
104 Lars-Goran Nilsson .10 .25
105 Peter Andersson .40 1.00
106 Mats Lusth .10 .25
107 Tommy Moller .10 .25
108 Leif Carlsson .10 .25
109 Urban Larsson .10 .25
110 Hakan Nordin .10 .25
111 Harald Luckner .10 .25
112 Thomas Rundqvist .60 1.50
113 Kjell Dahlin .75 2.00
114 Robin Eriksson .10 .25
115 Jan Ingman .10 .25
116 Stefan Persson .10 .25
117 Peter Berndtsson .10 .25
118 Anders Steen .10 .25
119 Claes-Henrik Silfver .10 .25
120 Magnus Roupe .40 1.00
121 Jan Wickberg .10 .25
122 Dan Mohlin .10 .25
123 Kent Olsson .10 .25
124 Stefan Lunner .10 .25
125 Niklas Holmberg .10 .25
126 Anders Alverud .10 .25
127 Stefan Svensson .10 .25
128 Lars Karlsson .10 .25

29 Ulf Weinstock .10 .25
30 Kjell Samuelsson 1.25 3.00
31 Magnus Svensson .40 1.00
32 Ove Pettersson .10 .25
33 Hans Eriksson .10 .25
34 Ulf Samuelsson .25 3.00
35 Roland Eriksson .10 .25
36 Kjell Bond .10 .25
37 Per Nordlinder .10 .25
38 Ivan Hansen .10 .25
39 Sivert Andersson .10 .25
40 Jonas Bergkvist .40 1.00
41 Per-Olof Carlsson .10 .25
42 Dan Labraaten .60 1.50
43 Ulf Skoglund .10 .25
44 Ove Olsson .10 .25
45 Mikael Leek .10 .25
46 Mats Loov .10 .25
47 Lennart Ahlberg .10 .25
48 Hardy Astrom 2.00 5.00
49 Anders Bergman .10 .25
50 Per Forsberg .10 .25
51 Sture Andersson .10 .25
52 Mikael Good .10 .25
53 Jan Nyman .10 .25
54 Roger Eliasson .10 .25
55 Jan Karlsson .10 .25
56 Lennart Jonsson .10 .25
57 Robert Frestadius .10 .25
58 Juha Tuohimaa .10 .25
59 Jerry Lundberg .10 .25
160 Tommy Sjalin .10 .25
161 Ulf Norberg .10 .25
162 Michael Hjalm .10 .25
163 Per Nilsson .10 .25
164 Lars Nyberg .10 .25
165 Ulf Odmark .10 .25
166 Ingemar Strom .10 .25
167 Erik Holmberg .10 .25
168 Lars Bystrom .10 .25
169 Lars Hellstrom .10 .25
170 Henry Saleva .10 .25
171 Hardy Nilsson .10 .25
172 Mats Abrahamsson .10 .25
173 Ulf Nilsson 2.00 5.00
174 Jens Johansson .10 .25
175 Lars Marklund .10 .25
176 Robert Ohman .10 .25
177 Goran Lindblom .10 .25
178 Ola Stenlund .10 .25
179 Ulf Agren .10 .25
180 Thomas Ahlen .10 .25
181 Tomas Jonsson .75 2.00
182 Mikael Granstedt .10 .25
183 Mats Lundstrom .10 .25
184 Per Andersson .10 .25
185 Johnny Forsman .10 .25
186 Lars Nystrom .10 .25
187 Niklas Mannberg .10 .25
188 Peter Lundmark .75 2.00
189 Claes Lindblom .10 .25
190 Leif Hedlund .10 .25
191 Roland Stoltz .10 .25
192 Martin Pettersson .10 .25
193 Jorgen Marklund .10 .25
194 Mats Lundstrom .10 .25
195 Tommy Andersson .10 .25
196 Ake Andersson .10 .25
197 Lars Fernqvist .10 .25
198 Anders Eldebrink .40 1.00
199 Ulf Borg .10 .25
200 Mats Kihlstrom .30 .75
201 Bo Andersson .10 .25
202 Peter Ekroth .10 .25
203 Jukka Hirsimaki .10 .25
204 Stefan Jonsson .10 .25
205 Peter Loob .20 .50
206 Tomas Jernberg .10 .25
207 Dan Hermansson .10 .25
208 Glenn Johansson .10 .25
209 Leif R. Carlsson .10 .25
210 Johan Mellstrom .10 .25
211 Tomas Gustavsson .10 .25
212 Olof Johansson .10 .25
213 Peter Wallin .10 .25
214 Hans Sarkijarvi .10 .25
215 Reine Karlsson .10 .25
216 Conny Jansson .10 .25
217 Jarmo Makitalo .10 .25
218 Mikael Johansson .10 .25
219 Timo Lahtinen .10 .25
220 Goran Nilsson .10 .25
221 Joakim Hokegard .10 .25
222 Peter Pettersson .10 .25
223 Goran Nilsson .10 .25
224 Jan Carlsson .10 .25
225 Soren Johansson .10 .25
226 Thomas Lundin .10 .25
227 Calle Johansson .75 2.00
228 Anders Brostrom .10 .25
229 Stefan Larsson .10 .25
230 Thomas Karrbrandt .10 .25
231 Roger Hagglund .10 .25
232 Christer Kellgren .10 .25
233 Kent Eriksson .10 .25
234 Mikael Andersson 1.25 3.00
235 Ove Karlsson .10 .25
236 Peter Elander .10 .25
237 Hans Jonsson .10 .25
238 Hasse Sjoo .10 .25
239 Ulf Labraaten .10 .25
240 Jens Hellgren .10 .25
241 Roger Ahsberg .10 .25
242 Kurt Carlsson .10 .25
243 Peter Gustavsson .10 .25

1983 Swedish Semic VM Stickers

COMPLETE SET (162) 40.00 80.00
1 Peter Lindmark .40 1.00
2 Gote Walitalo .10 .25
3 Lars Eriksson .10 .25
4 Roger Hagglund .10 .25
5 Thomas Eriksson .30 .75
6 Mats Waltin .10 .25
7 Jan Eriksson .10 .25
8 Mats Thelin .30 .75
9 Michael Thelven .20 .50
10 Peter Andersson .40 1.00
11 Bo Ericson .10 .25
12 Bo Berglund .20 .50
13 Tomas Sandstrom 1.25 3.00
14 Per-Erik Eklund .75 2.00
15 Roland Eriksson .10 .25
16 Peter Sundstrom .40 1.00
17 Thomas Rundqvist .60 1.50
18 Mats Ulander .10 .25
19 Tommy Morth .10 .25
20 Ove Olsson .10 .25
21 HÃ¥kan Sodergren .10 .25
22 HÃ¥kan Loob 2.00 5.00
23 Leif Holmgren .10 .25
24 Jan Erixon .40 1.00
25 Tom Eklund .10 .25
26 Hannu Kamppuri .40 1.00
27 Rauli Sohlman .10 .25
28 Kari Takko .40 1.00
29 Pekka Rautakallio .40 1.00
30 Pertti Lehtonen .10 .25
31 Hannu Haapalainen .10 .25
32 Markus Lehto .10 .25
33 Juha Huikari .10 .25
34 Hannu Helander .10 .25
35 Lasse Litma .10 .25
36 Arto Routanen .10 .25
37 Raimo Summanen .20 .50
38 Arto Javanainen .10 .25
39 Jari Lindgren .10 .25
40 Risto Jalo .20 .50
41 Petri Skriko .10 .25
42 Juha Nurmi .10 .25
43 Erkki Laine .20 .50
44 Anssi Melametsa .10 .25
45 Reijo Leppanen .10 .25
46 Matti Hagman .40 1.00
47 Kari Makkonen .10 .25
48 Timo Susi .10 .25
49 Harri Touhimaa .10 .25
50 Arto Jokinen .10 .25
51 Vladislav Tretiak 6.00 15.00
52 Vladimir Mysjkin .40 1.00
53 Vjatjeslav Fetisov 2.00 5.00
54 Sergej Babinov .10 .25
55 Vasilij Pervuchin .30 .75
56 Sergej Gimajev .10 .25
57 Aleksej Kasatonov .40 1.00
58 Zinetula Biljaletdinov .20 .50
59 Sergej Starikov .10 .25
60 Sergej Makarov 2.00 5.00
61 Sergej Sjepelev .10 .25
62 Vladimir Krutov 2.00 5.00
63 Nikolaj Drozdetskij .10 .25
64 Viktor Zjluktov .10 .25
65 Viktor Sjalimov .10 .25
66 Vladimir Golikov .10 .25
67 Aleksandr Maltsev 1.25 3.00
68 Andrej Chomutov .40 1.00
69 Vjatjeslav Bykov .30 .75
70 Michail Vasiljev .10 .25
71 Sergej Kapustin .20 .50
72 Aleksandr Gerasimov .10 .25
73 Aleksandr Kozjevnikov .10 .25
74 Igor Larionov 4.00 10.00
75 Vladimir Zubkov .10 .25
76 Jiri Kralik .10 .25
77 Karel Lang .20 .50
78 Jaromir Sindel .20 .50
79 Miroslav Horava .20 .50
80 Milan Chalupa .20 .50
81 Stanislav Hajdusek .10 .25
82 Arnold Kadlec .20 .50
83 Ladislav Kolda .10 .25
84 Jaroslav Benak .10 .25
85 Radoslav Svoboda .10 .25
86 Eduard Uvira .10 .25
87 Antonin Planovsky .10 .25
88 Petr Slanina .10 .25
89 Jiri Lala .20 .50
90 Jindrich Kokrment .10 .25
91 Frantisek Cernik .10 .25
92 Darius Rusnak .10 .25
93 Dusan Pasek .30 .75
94 Pavel Richtr .10 .25
95 Jaroslav Korbela .10 .25
96 Ivan Dornic .10 .25
97 Jiri Hrdina .10 .25
98 Igor Liba .20 .50
99 Jiri Dudacek .20 .50
100 Vincent Lukac .10 .25
101 Erich Weishaupt .10 .25
102 Bernhard Engelbrecht .10 .25
103 Karl-Heinz Friesen .30 .75
104 Ignaz Berndaner .10 .25
105 Udo Kiessling .20 .50
106 Harold Kreis .10 .25
107 Joachim Reil .10 .25
108 Gerd Truntschka .20 .50
109 Ulrich Egen .10 .25
110 Marcus Kuhl .10 .25
111 Peter Schiller .10 .25
112 Erich KÃ¼hnhackl .20 .50
113 Holger Meitinger .10 .25
114 Ernst Hofner .10 .25
115 Dieter Hegen .10 .25
116 Manfred Wolf .10 .25
117 Johann Morz .10 .25
118 Franz Reindl .10 .25
119 Helmut Steiger .10 .25
120 Horst-Peter Kretschmer .10 .25
121 Roy Roedger .10 .25
122 Jim Corsi .10 .25
123 Nick Sanza .10 .25
124 Guido Tenisi 8.00 20.00
125 Erwin Kostner .10 .25
126 Mike Amodeo .20 .50
127 John Bellio .10 .25
128 Dave Tomassoni .10 .25
129 Bob Manno .30 .75
130 Gino Pasqualotto .10 .25
131 Fabio Polloni .10 .25
132 Adolf Insam .10 .25
133 Constant Priondolo .10 .25
134 Rick Bragnalo .10 .25
135 Michael Mair .10 .25
136 Alberto Di Fazio .10 .25
137 Cary Farelli .10 .25
138 Tom Milani .10 .25
139 Martin Pavlu .10 .25
140 Bob De Piero .10 .25
141 Grant Goegan .10 .25
142 Jerry Ciarcia .10 .25
143 Rene Bielke .10 .25
144 Ingolf Spantig .10 .25
145 Frank Braun .10 .25
146 Joachim Lempio .10 .25
147 Reinhardt Fengler .10 .25
148 Dieter Frenzel .10 .25
149 Klaus Schroder .10 .25
150 Dietmar Peters .10 .25
151 Dieter Simon .10 .25
152 Andreas Ludwig .10 .25
153 Detlef Radant .10 .25
154 Friedhelm Bogelsack .10 .25
155 Thomas Graul .10 .25
156 Roland Peters .10 .25
157 Frank Proske .10 .25
158 Fred Bartell .10 .25
159 Harald Kuhnke .10 .25
160 Gerhard MÃ¼ller .10 .25
161 Harald Bolke .10 .25
162 Dieter Kinzel .10 .25

1984-85 Swedish Semic Elitserien

This 243-sticker set captures the top players in the Swedish Elitserien. The stickers were produced by Semic Press AB, and measure approximately 3" by 2 1/4". The fronts display a color portrait along with player name, card number and team emblem. The backs have ordering information for the set album (valued at $10) and more stickers.

COMPLETE SET (243) 20.00 50.00
1 Gunnar Leidborg .20 .50
2 Thomas Ostlund .80 2.00
3 Jan Eriksson .10 .25
4 Tomas Nord .10 .25
5 Bjorn Hellman .10 .25
6 Hans Cederholm .10 .25
7 Mats Alba .10 .25
8 Roger Hellgren .10 .25
9 Peter Zetterholm .10 .25
10 Tony Barthelsson .10 .25
11 Roger Lindstrom .10 .25
12 Mats Hessel .10 .25
13 Peter Gradin .10 .25
14 Per-Erik Eklund .80 2.00
15 Ulf Isaksson .10 .25
16 Harri Tiala .10 .25
17 Michael Wikstrom .10 .25
18 Per Backe .10 .25
19 Per Martinelle .10 .25
20 Tommy Lehmann .20 .50
21 Hans Norberg .10 .25
22 Odd Nilsson .10 .25
23 Henrik Cedergren .10 .25
24 Stefan Sandin .10 .25
25 Per Backman .10 .25
26 Gote Walitalo .10 .25
27 Jakob Gustavsson .10 .25
28 Torbjorn Andersson .10 .25
29 Anders Bostrom .10 .25
30 Jan Lindholm .10 .25
31 Lars Karlsson .10 .25
32 Rolf Berglund .10 .25
33 Lennart Dahlberg .10 .25
34 Patric Aberg .10 .25
35 Ulf Nilsson 1.60 4.00
36 Mats Jacobsson .10 .25
37 Michael Hjalm .10 .25
38 Stefan Nilsson .10 .25
39 Matti Pauna .10 .25
40 Jan Lundstrom .10 .25
41 Mikael Andersson .40 1.00
42 Hans Edlund .10 .25
43 Jon Lundstrom .10 .25
44 Tony Lundgren .10 .25
45 Ulf Wikgren .10 .25
46 Thomas Hedin .10 .25
47 Lars-Gunnar Pettersson .10 .25
48 Peter Edstrom .10 .25
49 Tommy Sandlin .20 .50
50 Lars Eriksson .10 .25
51 Ake Lilljebjorn .20 .50
52 Mats Kihlstrom .20 .50
53 Anders Backstrom .10 .25
54 Lars Ivarsson .40 1.00
55 Jan Kock .10 .25
56 Gunnar Persson .10 .25
57 Torbjorn Mattsson .10 .25
58 Per Jarnberg .10 .25
59 Hans Johansson .10 .25
60 Anders Huss .10 .25
61 Per Nilsson .10 .25
62 Owe Eriksson .10 .25
63 Christer Andersson .10 .25
64 Per Hedenstrom .10 .25
65 Jan Larsson .10 .25
66 Conny Silfverberg .10 .25
67 Jonny Stridh .10 .25
68 Erik Holmberg .10 .25
69 Kenneth Andersson .10 .25
70 Fredrik Lundstrom .10 .25
71 Peter Eriksson .10 .25
72 Peter Eriksson .10 .25
73 Stig Salming .20 .50
74 Rolf Ridderwall .40 1.00
75 Mats Ytter .10 .25
76 Michael Thelven .30 .75
77 Stefan Perlstrom .10 .25
78 Tord Nansen .10 .25
79 Tommy Albelin .80 2.00
80 Orvar Stambert .10 .25
81 Karl-Erik Lilja .10 .25
82 Kristian Henriksson .10 .25
83 Arto Blomsten .30 .75
84 Anders Johnsson .10 .25
85 Pontus Molander .10 .25
86 Jens Ohling .10 .25
87 Peter Nilsson .10 .25
88 Hakan Sodergren .10 .25
89 Jorgen Holmberg .10 .25
90 Tommy Morth .10 .25
91 Jan Claesson .10 .25
92 Per Goransson .10 .25
93 Jan Viktorsson .20 .50
94 Bjorn Carlsson .10 .25
95 Erik Ahlstrom .10 .25
96 Peter Schank .10 .25
97 Ake Eksell .10 .25
98 Gunnar Svensson .10 .25
99 Peter Lindmark .10 .25
100 Christer Dalgard .10 .25
101 Hakan Nordin .10 .25
102 Fredrik Olausson 1.20 3.00
103 Tommy Samuelsson .10 .25
104 Anders Svensson .10 .25
105 Peter Andersson .30 .75
106 Mats Lusth .10 .25
107 Tommy Moller .10 .25
108 Leif Carlsson .10 .25
109 Kent-Erik Andersson .10 .25
110 Erkki Laine .10 .25
111 Harald Luckner .10 .25
112 Staffan Lundh .10 .25
113 Kjell Dahlin .80 2.00
114 Dan Mohlin .10 .25
115 Jan Ingman .10 .25
116 Stefan Persson .40 1.00
117 Peter Berndtsson .10 .25
118 Lars Karlsson .10 .25
119 Claes-Henrik Silfver .10 .25
120 Magnus Roupe .30 .75
121 Conny Evensson .30 .75
122 Bo Larsson .10 .25
123 Hans-Goran Elo .10 .25
124 Carsten Bokstrom .10 .25
125 Claes Norstrom .10 .25
126 Alf Tornqvist .10 .25
127 Bruno Ohlzon .10 .25
128 Peter Lindgren .10 .25
129 Christian Due-Boije .20 .50
130 Tony Landeskog .10 .25
131 Tomas Lunden .10 .25
132 Lars Lindskog .10 .25
133 Anders Karlsson .10 .25
134 Morgan Craas .10 .25
135 Ulf Andersson .10 .25
136 Timo Salomaa .10 .25
137 Ulf Radbjer .10 .25
138 Hans Segerberg .10 .25
139 Roger Melin .10 .25
140 Rolf Edberg .10 .25
141 Lasse Bjork .10 .25
142 Robin Eriksson .10 .25
143 Thomas Jagenstedt .10 .25
144 Jan Lindberg .10 .25
145 Bjorn Berggren .10 .25
146 Tommy Nilsson .10 .25
147 Stefan Lunner .10 .25
148 Niklas Holmberg .10 .25
149 Anders Alverud .10 .25
150 Stefan Svensson .10 .25
151 Jussi Lepisto .10 .25
152 Kjell Samuelsson .80 2.00
153 Magnus Svensson .30 .75
154 Ove Pettersson .10 .25
155 Stefan Nilsson .10 .25
156 Jens Christiansson .10 .25
157 Orjan Lindmark .10 .25
158 Tomas Gustafsson .10 .25
159 Jan Segersten .10 .25
160 Jonas Bergqvist .40 1.00
161 Per-Olof Carlsson .10 .25
162 Hannu Oksanen .10 .25
163 Dan Labraaten .60 1.50
164 Ulf Skoglund .10 .25
165 Ove Olsson .10 .25
166 Mats Loov .10 .25
167 Hakan Olsson .10 .25
168 Carl-Erik Larsson .10 .25
169 Dan Soderstrom .10 .25
170 Mats Blomqvist .10 .25
171 Robert Skoog .10 .25
172 Lars Lindgren .10 .25
173 Robert Nordmark .30 .75
174 Kjell-Ake Johansson .10 .25
175 Kari Heikkila .10 .25
176 Torbjorn Wirf .10 .25
177 Lars Modig .10 .25
178 Bo Eriksson .10 .25
179 Roger Ohman .30 .75
180 Mats Ohman .10 .25
181 Matti Ruisma .10 .25
182 Erik Stalnacke .10 .25
183 Jari Lindgren .10 .25
184 Jens Hellgren .10 .25
185 Lars-Goran Niemi .10 .25
186 Tore Okvist .10 .25
187 Ingemar Mikko .10 .25
188 Roger Mikko .10 .25
189 Rolf Karlsson .10 .25
190 Petter Antti .10 .25
191 Johan Stromvall .10 .25
192 Tomas Backstrom .10 .25
193 Jan Nilsson .10 .25
194 Freddy Lindfors .10 .25
195 Mats Abrahamsson .10 .25
196 Ulf Nilsson 1.60 4.00
197 Goran Lindblom .10 .25
198 Thomas Ahlen .10 .25
199 Jens Johansson .10 .25
200 Lars Marklund .10 .25
201 Ola Stenlund .10 .25
202 Ulf Lindblom .10 .25
203 Olle Haggstrom .10 .25
204 Ulf Agren .10 .25
205 Mikael Granstedt .10 .25
206 Hans Nilsson .10 .25
207 Per Andersson .10 .25
208 Jonny Forsman .10 .25
209 Lars Nystrom .10 .25
210 Niklas Mannberg .10 .25
211 Peter Lundmark .40 1.00
212 Claes Lindblom .10 .25
213 Leif Hedlund .10 .25
214 Roland Stoltz .10 .25
215 Martin Pettersson .10 .25
216 Jorgen Marklund .10 .25
217 Mats Lundstrom .10 .25
218 Tommy Andersson .10 .25
219 Hardy Astrom 1.20 3.00
220 Sam Lindstahl .30 .75
221 Jari Luoma .10 .25
222 Anders Eldebrink .30 .75
223 Ulf Borg .10 .25
224 Bo Ericson .10 .25
225 Tomas Jernberg .10 .25
226 Peter Ekroth .10 .25
227 Stefan Jonsson .10 .25
228 Niklas Gallstedt .10 .25
229 Jonas Heed .10 .25
230 Jarmo Makitalo .10 .25
231 Thom Eklund .10 .25
232 Dan Hermansson .10 .25
233 Glenn Johansson .10 .25
234 Leif R. Carlsson .10 .25
235 Johan Mellstrom .10 .25
236 Niclas Lindgren .10 .25
237 Peter Wallin .10 .25
238 Hans Sarkijarvi .10 .25
239 Anders Carlsson .10 .25
240 Reine Karlsson .10 .25
241 Conny Jansson .10 .25
242 Stefan Karlsson .10 .25
243 Timo Lahtinen .10 .25

1985-86 Swedish Panini Stickers

This set of 240 stickers was produced by Panini Italy for distribution in Sweden. The stickers feature the top players of the Swedish elite league and were packaged five per pack. The 2 1/2" by 2" stickers feature a player portrait on the front. An album for housing the stickers also was available; it now trades in the $10 range. North American collectors may not rave about the player selection, but some of Sweden's best are represented including Peter Lindmark, Tomas Rundqvist and Anders Eldebrink. Some sticker are half of a larger image -- these are designated by U (upper), L (lower or left) and R (right).

COMPLETE SET (240) 25.00 60.00
1 AIK Team Emblem .10 .25
2 Per Backman .10 .25
3 Tomas Ostlund .80 2.00
4 Gunnar Leidborg .10 .25
5 Jari Munck .10 .25
6 Jan Eriksson .10 .25
7 Hans Cederholm .10 .25
8 Bjorn Hellman .10 .25
9 Tomas Ahlen .10 .25
10 Roger Hellgren .10 .25
11 Mats Alba .10 .25
12 Roger Lindstrom .10 .25
13 Team Picture Left .10 .25
14 Team Picture Right .10 .25
15 Mats Hessel .10 .25
16 Peter Gradin .10 .25
17 Thomas Bjuhr .10 .25
18 Per Martinelle .10 .25
19 Tommy Lehman .20 .50
20 Thomas Jagenstedt .10 .25
21 Hans Segerberg .10 .25
22 Odd Nilsson .10 .25
23 Bjorkloven Team Picture L .10 .25
24 Bjorkloven Team Picture U .10 .25
25 Jakob Gustavsson .10 .25
26 Gote Walitalo .10 .25
27 Torbjorn Andersson .10 .25
28 Jan Lindholm .10 .25
29 Lars Karlsson .10 .25
30 Calle Johansson .80 2.00
31 Ulf Nilsson 1.20 3.00
32 Rolf Berglund .10 .25
33 Matti Pauna .10 .25
34 Mikael Andersson .80 2.00
35 Tommy Sandlin .10 .25
36 Team Emblem .10 .25
37 Hans Edlund .10 .25
38 Ulf Dahlen 1.20 3.00
39 Mikael Hjalm .10 .25
40 Jon Lundstrom .10 .25
41 Lars-Gunnar Pettersson .10 .25
42 Peter Edstrom .10 .25
43 Tore Oqvist .10 .25
44 Par Edlund .10 .25
45 Brynas Team Emblem .10 .25
46 Stig Salming .10 .25
47 Lars Eriksson .10 .25
48 Ake Lilljebjorn .10 .25
49 Anders Backstrom .10 .25
50 Lars Ivarsson .10 .25
51 Mats Kihlstrom .10 .25
52 Jan Ove Mettavainio .10 .25
53 Gunnar Persson .10 .25
54 Torbjorn Mattsson .10 .25
55 Christer Andersson .10 .25
56 Per Hedenstrom .10 .25
57 Team Picture L .10 .25
58 Team Picture R .10 .25
59 Per Nilsson .10 .25
60 Conny Silfverberg .10 .25
61 Jonny Stridh .10 .25
62 Owe Eriksson .10 .25
63 Kenneth Andersson .10 .25
64 Erik Holmberg .10 .25
65 Joakim Pehrson .10 .25
66 Anders Huss .20 .50
67 Djurgarden Team Picture L .10 .25
68 Djurgarden Team Picture R .10 .25
69 Rolf Ridderwall .40 1.00
70 Mats Ytter .20 .50
71 Orvar Stambert .10 .25
72 Karl-Erik Lilja .10 .25
73 Arto Blomsten .20 .50
74 Stefan Perlstrom .10 .25
75 Peter Lindgren .10 .25
76 Tommy Albelin .30 .75
77 Jens Ohling .10 .25
78 Peter Nilsson .10 .25
79 Gunnar Svenson .10 .25
80 Team Emblem .10 .25
81 Jorgen Holmberg .10 .25
82 Tommy Morth .10 .25
83 Bjorn Carlsson .10 .25
84 Hakan Sodergren .20 .50
85 Anders Johnson .10 .25
86 Mikael Johansson .10 .25
87 Jan Viktorsson .10 .25
88 Erik Ahlstrom .10 .25
89 Farjestad Team Emblem .10 .25
90 Conny Evensson .20 .50
91 Peter Lindmark .60 1.50
92 Christer Dalgard .10 .25
93 Tommy Samuelsson .10 .25
94 Peter Andersson .30 .75
95 Mats Lusth .10 .25
96 Leif Karlsson .10 .25
97 Fredrik Olausson .80 2.00
98 Hakan Nordin .10 .25
99 Harald Luckner .10 .25
100 Tomas Rundqvist .20 .50
101 Team Picture L .10 .25
102 Team Picture R .10 .25
103 Jan Ingman .10 .25
104 Erkki Laine .10 .25
105 Stefan Persson .40 1.00
106 Claes-Henrik Silfver .10 .25
107 Magnus Roupe .30 .75
108 Mikael Holmberg .10 .25
109 Kent-Erik Andersson .10 .25
110 Staffan Lundh .10 .25
111 Kjell Dahlin U .20 .50
112 Kjell Dahlin L .20 .50
113 Kjell Samuelsson U .40 1.00
114 Kjell Samuelsson L .40 1.00
115 Peter Lindmark U .20 .50
116 Peter Lindmark L .20 .50
117 Pelle Lindberg U 4.00 10.00
118 Pelle Lindberg L 4.00 10.00
119 Per-Erik Eklund U .30 .75
120 Per-Erik Eklund L .30 .75
121 Anders Eldebrink L .14 .35
122 Anders Eldebrink R .14 .35
123 Michael Thelven U .14 .35
124 Michael Thelven L .14 .35
125 Dan Labraaten L .20 .50
126 Dan Labraaten R .20 .50
127 Ove Olsson L .10 .25
128 Ove Olsson R .10 .25
129 Kent-E Andersson L .10 .25
130 Kent-E Andersson R .10 .25
131 Leksand Team Emblem .10 .25
132 Dan Soderstrom .10 .25
133 Stefan Lunner .10 .25
134 Peter Aslin .40 1.00
135 Jussi Lepisto .10 .25
136 Magnus Svensson .30 .75
137 Owe Pettersson .10 .25
138 Stefan Nilsson .10 .25
139 Orjan Lindmark .10 .25
140 Tomas Nord .10 .25
141 Robert Burakovsky .20 .50
142 Jan Segersten .10 .25
143 Team Picture L .10 .25
144 Team Picture R .10 .25
145 Jonas Bergkvist .30 .75
146 Per-Olof Carlsson .10 .25
147 Dan Labraaten .40 1.00
148 Ulf Skoglund .10 .25
149 Ove Olsson .10 .25
150 Heinz Ehlers .10 .25
151 Mats Loov .10 .25
152 Jarmo Makitalo .10 .25
153 Lulea Team Picture L .10 .25
154 Lulea Team Picture R .10 .25
155 Mats Blomqvist .10 .25
156 Robert Skoog .10 .25
157 Lars Modig .10 .25
158 Kjell-Ake Johansson .10 .25
159 Bo Eriksson .10 .25
160 Robert Nordmark .20 .50
161 Kari Heikkila .10 .25
162 Lars Lindgren .10 .25
163 Roger Mikko .10 .25
164 Kari Jaako .10 .25
165 Hans Lindberg .10 .25
166 Team Emblem .10 .25
167 Petter Antti .10 .25
168 Johan Stromvall .10 .25
169 Juha Nurmi .10 .25
170 Erik Stalnacke .10 .25
171 Lars Hurtig .10 .25
172 Jari Lindgren .10 .25
173 Jens Hellgren .10 .25
174 Hans Norberg .10 .25
175 HV 71 Team Emblem .10 .25
176 Curt Lundmark .40 1.00
177 Kenneth Johansson .10 .25
178 Tomas Javeblad .10 .25
179 Nils-G Svensson .10 .25
180 Bert-Roland Naslund .10 .25
181 Kevan Beaton .10 .25
182 Jan Hedell .10 .25
183 Fredrik Stillman .14 .35
184 Kari Eloranta .30 .75
185 Klas Heed .10 .25
186 Hans Sallin .10 .25
187 Team Picture L .10 .25
188 Team Picture R .10 .25
189 Ove Tornberg .10 .25
190 Thomas Ljungberg .10 .25
191 Bengt Kinell .10 .25
192 Roland Eriksson .10 .25
193 Uno Johansson .10 .25
194 Ivan Hansen .10 .25
195 Thomas Lindster .10 .25
196 Per Martinsson .10 .25
197 MoDo Team Picture L .10 .25
198 MoDo Team Picture R .10 .25
199 Anders Bergman .10 .25
200 Goran Arnmark .10 .25
201 Thomas Olofsson .10 .25
202 Jorgen Palm .10 .25
203 Ulf Agren .10 .25
204 Roger Eliasson .10 .25
205 Juha Tuohimaa .10 .25
206 Jan Karlsson .10 .25
207 Lennart Jonsson .10 .25
208 Ulf Norberg .10 .25
209 Hakan Nygren .10 .25
210 Team Emblem .10 .25
211 Hakan Hjerpe .10 .25
212 Anders Wikberg .10 .25
213 P-A Alexandersson .10 .25
214 Ingemar Strom .10 .25
215 Tommy Eriksson .10 .25
216 Lars Molin .20 .50
217 Lars Bystrom .10 .25
218 Pekka Arbelius .10 .25
219 Sodertalje Team Emblem .10 .25
220 Kjell Larsson .10 .25
221 Sam Lindstal .10 .25
222 Hardy Astrom 1.20 3.00
223 Anders Eldebrink .30 .75
224 Niklas Gallstedt .10 .25
225 Jonas Heed .10 .25
226 Peter Ekroth .10 .25
227 Bo Eriksson .10 .25
228 Stefan Jonsson .10 .25
229 Thom Eklund .10 .25
230 Glenn Johansson .10 .25
231 Team Picture L .10 .25
232 Team Picture R .10 .25
233 Leif Carlsson .10 .25
234 Jan Claesson .10 .25
235 Niclas Lindgren .10 .25
236 Peter Wallin .10 .25
237 Hans Sarkijarvi .10 .25
238 Reine Karlsson .10 .25
239 Conny Jansson .10 .25
240 Anders Carlsson .10 .25

1986-87 Swedish Panini Stickers

This 270-sticker set features the top players in Sweden for the '86-87 season. The stickers -- which measure approximately 2 1/2" by 2" -- were produced by Panini in Italy. The fronts feature a portrait along with name and team logo. The backs are numbered and include information about completing the set and the available album (valued at $10). The set is short on recognizable names, but does include early appearances by Ulf Dahlen and Calle Johansson, among others.

COMPLETE SET (270) 20.00 50.00
1 Bjorkloven Team Emblem .10 .25
2 Hans Lindberg .10 .25
3 Gote Walitalo .10 .25
4 Jakob Gustavsson .10 .25
5 Torbjorn Andersson .10 .25
6 Lars Karlsson .10 .25
7 Calle Johansson .40 1.00
8 Rolf Berglund .10 .25
9 Patrik Aberg .10 .25
10 Niclas Holmgren .10 .25
11 Roger Hagglund .10 .25
12 Team Picture Left .10 .25
13 Team Picture Right .10 .25
14 Peter Andersson .30 .75
15 Tore Oqvist .10 .25
16 Johan Tornqvist .10 .25
17 Par Edlund .10 .25
18 Stefan Nilsson .10 .25
19 Matti Pauna .10 .25
20 Lars-Gunnar Pettersson .10 .25
21 Mikael Hjalm .10 .25
22 Hans Edlund .10 .25
23 Peter Sundstrom .40 1.00
24 Jon Lundstrom .10 .25
25 Peter Edstrom .10 .25
26 Mikael Andersson .40 1.00
27 Ulf Dahlen .80 2.00
28 Brynas Team Emblem .10 .25
29 Stig Salming .10 .25
30 Ake Lilljebjorn .10 .25
31 Lars Eriksson .10 .25
32 Christer Lundqvist .10 .25
33 Lars Ivarsson .10 .25
34 Torbjorn Mattsson .10 .25
35 Gunnar Persson .10 .25
36 Anders Backstrom .10 .25
37 Team Picture L .10 .25
38 Team Picture R .10 .25
39 Jan Ove Mettavainio .10 .25
40 Par Djoos .20 .50
41 Tommy Sjodin .40 1.00
42 Conny Silfverberg .10 .25
43 Christer Andersson .10 .25
44 Kenneth Andersson .10 .25
45 Lars Andersson .10 .25
46 Anders Huss .10 .25
47 Joakim Pehrson .10 .25
48 Jonny Stridh .10 .25
49 Patrik Eriksson .10 .25

50 Anders Ivarsson .10 .25
51 Mikael Lindholm .10 .25
52 Jan Larsson .10 .25
53 Peter Eriksson .10 .25
54 Jan Gronberg .10 .25
55 Djurgarden Team Emblem .10 .25
56 Leif Boork .10 .25
57 Rolf Ridderwall .40 1.00
58 Hans-Goran Elo .10 .25
59 Tommy Albelin .40 1.00
60 Orvar Stambert .10 .25
61 Tomas Eriksson .10 .25
62 Stefan Perlstrom .10 .25
63 Arto Blomsten .20 .50
64 Christian Due-Boije .20 .50
65 Kalle Lilja .10 .25
66 Team Picture L .10 .25
67 Team Picture R .10 .25
68 Stefan Jansson .10 .25
69 Hakan Sodergren .10 .25
70 Jens Ohling .10 .25
71 Peter Nilsson .10 .25
72 Tommy Morth .10 .25
73 Bjorn Carlsson .10 .25
74 Per Goransson .10 .25
75 Pontus Molander .10 .25
76 Jeff Hallegard .10 .25
77 Tomaz Eriksson .10 .25
78 Mikael Johansson .10 .25
79 Anders Johnson .10 .25
80 Jan Viktorsson .10 .25
81 Johan Garpenlov .40 1.00
82 Farjestad Team Emblem .10 .25
83 Conny Evensson .20 .50
84 Peter Lindmark .40 1.00
85 Christer Dalgard .10 .25
86 Tommy Samuelsson .10 .25
87 Mats Lusth .10 .25
88 Peter Andersson .10 .25
89 Hakan Nordin .10 .25
90 Leif Carlsson .10 .25
91 Team Picture L .10 .25
92 Team Picture R .10 .25
93 Patrik Lundback .10 .25
94 Anders Berglund .10 .25
95 Roger Johansson .10 .25
96 Thomas Rundqvist .20 .50
97 Harald Luckner .10 .25
98 Erkki Laine .10 .25
99 Jan Ingman .10 .25
100 Staffan Lund .10 .25
101 Claes-Henrik Silfver .10 .25
102 Magnus Roupe .20 .50
103 Stefan Persson .40 1.00
104 Daniel Rydmark .10 .25
105 Bo Svanberg .10 .25
106 Mikael Holmberg .10 .25
107 Tomas Tallberg .10 .25
108 Kjell Augustsson .10 .25
109 HV 71 Team Emblem .10 .25
110 Curt Lundmark .20 .50
111 Thomas Javeblad .10 .25
112 Kenneth Johansson .10 .25
113 Kari Eloranta .30 .75
114 Jan Hedell .10 .25
115 Arto Routanen .10 .25
116 Klas Heed .10 .25
117 Bert-Roland Naslund .10 .25
118 Nils-Gunnar Svensson .10 .25
119 Fredrik Stillman .10 .25
120 Team Picture L .10 .25
121 Team Picture R .10 .25
122 Nicklas Carlsson .10 .25
123 Ivan Hansen .10 .25
124 Thomas Ljungberg .10 .25
125 Peter Eriksson .10 .25
126 Hans Wallin .10 .25
127 Ove Thornberg .10 .25
128 Per Martinsson .10 .25
129 Mats Loov .10 .25
130 Stefan Nilsson .10 .25
131 Peter Eriksson .10 .25
132 Thomas Lindster .10 .25
133 Boo Peterzen .10 .25
134 Stefan Falk .10 .25
135 Torgny Karlsson .10 .25
136 Leksand Team Emblem .10 .25
137 Kalle Alander .10 .25
138 Peter Aslin .30 .75
139 Bengt-Ake Pers .10 .25
140 Magnus Svensson .20 .50
141 Ove Pettersson .10 .25
142 Stefan Nilsson .10 .25
143 Jens Christiansson .10 .25
144 Leif Eriksson .10 .25
145 Team Picture L .10 .25
146 Team Picture R .10 .25
147 Orjan Lindmark .10 .25
148 Thomas Nord .10 .25
149 Peter Imhauser .10 .25
150 Dan Labraaten .40 1.00
151 Ulf Skoglund .10 .25
152 Jarmo Makitalo .10 .25
153 Per-Olof Carlsson .10 .25
154 Ove Olsson .10 .25
155 Heinz Ehlers .10 .25
156 Jonas Bergqvist .20 .50
157 Robert Burakovsky .20 .50
158 Carl-Erik Larsson .10 .25
159 Cenneth Soderlund .10 .25
160 Ola Sundberg .10 .25
161 Ronny Reichenberg .10 .25
162 Hans Jax .10 .25
163 Lulea Team Emblem .10 .25
164 Freddy Lindfors .10 .25
165 Mats Blomqvist .10 .25
166 Robert Skoog .10 .25
167 Robert Nordmark .20 .50
168 Lars Lindgren .10 .25
169 Lars Modig .10 .25
170 Bo Eriksson .10 .25
171 Kjell-Ake Johansson .10 .25
172 Roger Akerstrom .10 .25
173 Juha Tuohimaa .10 .25
174 Team Picture L .10 .25
175 Team Picture R .10 .25
176 Mats Ohman .10 .25
177 Erik Stalnacke .10 .25
178 Juha Nurmi .10 .25
179 Lars-Goran Niemi .10 .25
180 Hans Norberg .10 .25
181 Jari Lindgren .10 .25
182 Roger Mikko .10 .25
183 Lars Hurtig .10 .25
184 Johan Stromvall .10 .25
185 Jens Hellgren .10 .25
186 Kari Jaako .10 .25
187 Stefan Nilsson .10 .25
188 Ulf Taavola .10 .25
189 Tomas Edstrom .10 .25
190 MoDo Team Emblem .10 .25
191 Hakan Nygren .10 .25
192 Anders Bergman .10 .25
193 Fredrik Andersson .10 .25
194 Robert Frestadius .10 .25
195 Jouko Narvanmaa .10 .25
196 Jan Asplund .10 .25
197 Ulf Agren .10 .25
198 Jorgen Palm .10 .25
199 Team Picture L .10 .25
200 Team Picture R .10 .25
201 Per Forsberg .10 .25
202 Jens Johansson .10 .25
203 Hans Lodin .10 .25
204 Lars Molin .10 .25
205 Per-Arne Alexandersson .10 .25
206 Pecka Arbelius .10 .25
207 Per Nilsson .10 .25
208 Anders Wikberg .10 .25
209 Lars Bystrom .10 .25
210 Ulf Odmark .10 .25
211 Robert Tedenby .10 .25
212 Kent Lantz .10 .25
213 Ulf Sandstrom .10 .25
214 Mikael Pettersson .10 .25
215 Peter Smedberg .10 .25
216 Mikael Stahl .10 .25
217 Skelleftea Team Emblem .10 .25
218 Christer Abrahamsson .40 1.00
219 Mats Abrahamsson .10 .25
220 Ulf Nilsson 1.00 2.50
221 Goran Lindblom .10 .25
222 Lars Marklund .10 .25
223 Ola Stenlund .10 .25
224 Serge Roy .20 .50
225 Mikael Lindman .10 .25
226 Robert Larsson .10 .25
227 Stefan Svensson .10 .25
228 Team Picture L .10 .25
229 Team Picture R .10 .25
230 Roland Stoltz .10 .25
231 Martin Pettersson .10 .25
232 Jonny Forsman .10 .25
233 Tomas Hedin .10 .25
234 Mikael Granstedt .10 .25
235 Randy Heath .10 .25
236 Peter Lundmark .30 .75
237 Niklas Mannberg .10 .25
238 Claes Lindblom .20 .50
239 Mats Lundmark .10 .25
240 Jorgen Marklund .10 .25
241 Daniel Pettersson .10 .25
242 Mats Lundstrom .10 .25
243 Hans Hjalmar .10 .25
244 Sodertalje Team Emblem .10 .25
245 Dan Hober .10 .25
246 Sam Lindstahl .10 .25
247 Reino Sundberg .10 .25
248 Anders Eldebrink .20 .50
249 Mats Kihlstrom .10 .25
250 Ulf Borg .10 .25
251 Bo Ericsson .10 .25
252 Peter Ekroth .10 .25
253 Team Picture L .10 .25
254 Team Picture R .10 .25
255 Jonas Heed .10 .25
256 Stefan Jonsson .10 .25
257 Hans Pettersson .10 .25
258 Hans Sarkijarvi .10 .25
259 Thom Eklund .10 .25
260 Glenn Johansson .10 .25
261 Peter Loob .10 .25
262 Niklas Lindgren .10 .25
263 Conny Jansson .10 .25
264 Tomas Jernberg .10 .25
265 Reine Karlsson .10 .25
266 Anders Frykbo .10 .25
267 Jan Loob .10 .25
268 Peter Larsson .10 .25
269 Erik Holmberg .10 .25
270 Jorgen Winborg .10 .25

1987-88 Swedish Panini Stickers

This 270-sticker set features the top players from the Elitserien. The stickers -- which measure approximately 2 1/2" by 2" -- were produced by Panini in Italy. The fronts feature a portrait along with player name and team logo. The backs are numbered and contain information about completing the set and acquiring a collector's album (valued now at about $10).

COMPLETE SET (270) 20.00 50.00
1 AIK Team Emblem .10 .25
2 AIK Team Picture Left .10 .25
3 AIK Team Picture Right .10 .25
4 Lars-Gunnar Jansson .10 .25
5 Ake Liljebjorn .10 .25
6 Thomas Ostlund .40 1.00
7 Jan Eriksson .10 .25
8 Hans Cederholm .10 .25
9 Rickard Franzen .10 .25
10 Thomas Ahlen .10 .25
11 Mats Thelin .20 .50
12 Bjorn Hellman .10 .25
13 Peter Gradin .20 .50
14 Bjorn Carlsson .10 .25
15 Anders Gozzi .10 .25
16 Per Martinelle .10 .25
17 Bo Berglund .20 .50
18 Thomas Gradin .40 1.00
19 Hans Segerberg .10 .25
20 Odd Nilsson .10 .25
21 Mats Hessel .10 .25
22 IF Bjorkloven Team Emblem .10 .25
23 IF Bjorkloven .10 .25
Team Picture Left
24 IF Bjorkloven .10 .25
Team Picture Right
25 Rolf Jager .10 .25
26 Gote Walitalo .10 .25
27 Staffan Andersson .10 .25
28 Torbjorn Andersson .10 .25
29 Lars Karlsson .10 .25
30 Roger Hagglund .10 .25
31 Rolf Berglund .10 .25
32 Peter Andersson .10 .25
33 Age Ellingsen .10 .25
34 Matti Pauna .10 .25
35 Tore Oqvist .10 .25
36 Mikael Andersson .40 1.00
37 Hans Edlund .10 .25
38 Johan Tornqvist .10 .25
39 Peter Edstrom .10 .25
40 Par Edlund .10 .25
41 Erik Kristiansen .10 .25
42 Ulf Andersson .10 .25
43 Brynas IF Team Emblem .10 .25
44 Brynas IF Team Picture Left .10 .25
45 Brynas IF Team Picture Right .10 .25
46 Tord Lundstrom .10 .25
47 Lars Eriksson .10 .25
48 Michael Sundlov .40 1.00
49 Lars Ivarsson .10 .25
50 Par Djoos .20 .50
51 Jan Ove Mettavainio .10 .25
52 Anders Backstrom .10 .25
53 Gunnar Persson .10 .25
54 Christer Andersson .10 .25
55 Conny Silfverberg .10 .25
56 Jonny Stridh .10 .25
57 Kyosti Karjalainen .20 .50
58 Willy Lindstrom .30 .75
59 Joakim Pehrson .10 .25
60 Patrik Erickson .10 .25
61 Anders Huss .10 .25
62 Peter Eriksson .10 .25
63 Jan Larsson .10 .25
64 Djurgardens IF Team Emblem .10 .25
65 Djurgardens IF .10 .25
Team Picture Left
66 Djurgardens IF .10 .25
Team Picture Right
67 Ingvar Karlsson .10 .25
68 Rolf Ridderwall .40 1.00
69 Hans-Goran Elo .10 .25
70 Orvar Stambert .10 .25
71 Kalle Lilja .10 .25
72 Arto Blomsten .20 .50
73 Stefan Jansson .10 .25
74 Tomas Eriksson .10 .25
75 Christian Due-Boije .20 .50
76 Jens Ohling .10 .25
77 Pontus Molander .10 .25
78 Tommy Morth .10 .25
79 Johan Garpenlov .40 1.00
80 Hakan Sodergren .10 .25
81 Anders Johnson .10 .25
82 Mikael Johansson .10 .25
83 Jan Viktorsson .10 .25
84 Peter Nilsson .10 .25
85 Farjestads BK Team Emblem .10 .25
86 Farjestads BK .10 .25
Team Picture Left
87 Farjestads BK .10 .25
Team Picture Right
88 Per Backman .10 .25
89 Peter Lindmark .40 1.00
90 Christer Dalgard .10 .25
91 Tommy Samuelsson .10 .25
92 Peter Andersson .10 .25
93 Mats Lusth .10 .25
94 Leif Carlsson .10 .25
95 Jesper Duus .10 .25
96 Hakan Nordin .10 .25
97 Thomas Rundqvist .20 .50
98 Staffan Lund .10 .25
99 Harald Luckner .10 .25
100 Erkki Laine .10 .25
101 Stefan Persson .30 .75
102 Bo Svanberg .10 .25
103 Claes-Henrik Silfver .10 .25
104 Mikael Holmberg .10 .25
105 Roger Johansson .10 .25
106 HV 71 Team Emblem .10 .25
107 HV 71 Team Picture Left .10 .25
108 HV 71 Team Picture Right .10 .25
109 Curt Lundmark .40 1.00
110 Kenneth Johansson .10 .25
111 Boo Peterzen .10 .25
112 Arto Routanen .10 .25
113 Jan Hedell .10 .25
114 Fredrik Stillman .10 .25
115 Reijo Ruotsalainen .40 1.00
116 Bert-Roland Naslund .10 .25
117 Peter Eriksson .10 .25
118 Hans Wallin .10 .25
119 Peter Berndtsson .10 .25
120 Mats Loov .10 .25
121 Thomas Lindster .10 .25
122 Peter Eriksson .10 .25
123 Hasse Sjoo .10 .25
124 Stefan Nilsson .10 .25
125 Stefan Falk .10 .25
126 Ove Thornberg .10 .25
127 Wash Out .10 .25
128 Butt-Ending .10 .25
129 Fordrojd Signal .10 .25
130 Hakning .10 .25
131 Charging .10 .25
132 Olampligt Upptradande .10 .25
133 Fasthallning .10 .25
134 Hog Klubba .10 .25
135 Tripping .10 .25
136 Cross Checking .10 .25
137 Armbagstackling .10 .25
138 Icing .10 .25
139 Icing .10 .25
140 Boarding .10 .25
141 Slashing .10 .25
142 Roughing .10 .25
143 Spearing .10 .25
144 Interference .10 .25
145 Leksands IF Team Emblem .10 .25
146 Leksands IF Team Picture Left .10 .25
147 Leksands IF .10 .25
Team Picture Right
148 Christer Abrahamsson .40 1.00
149 Peter Aslin .20 .50
150 Bengt-Ake Pers .10 .25
151 Magnus Svensson .20 .50
152 Stefan Nilsson .10 .25
153 Orjan Lindmark .10 .25
154 Thomas Nord .10 .25
155 Peter Imhauser .10 .25
156 Stefan Larsson .10 .25
157 Robert Burakovsky .20 .50
158 Jonas Bergqvist .20 .50
159 Heinz Ehlers .10 .25
160 Ivan Hansen .10 .25
161 Jarmo Makitalo .10 .25
162 Dan Labraaten .30 .75
163 Per-Olof Carlsson .10 .25
164 Carl-Erik Larsson .10 .25
165 Ulf Skoglund .10 .25
166 Lulea Hockey Team Emblem .10 .25
167 Lulea Hockey .10 .25
Team Picture Left
168 Lulea Hockey .10 .25
Team Picture Right
169 Freddy Lindfors .10 .25
170 Tomas Javeblad .10 .25
171 Robert Skoog .10 .25
172 Juha Tuohimaa .10 .25
173 Bo Eriksson .10 .25
174 Roger Akerstrom .10 .25
175 Lars Lindgren .10 .25
176 Lars Modig .10 .25
177 Erik Stalnacke .10 .25
178 Johan Stromvall .10 .25
179 Juha Nurmi .10 .25
180 Lars-Goran Niemi .10 .25
181 Jari Lindgren .10 .25
182 Lars-Gunnar Pettersson .10 .25
183 Hans Norberg .10 .25
184 Kari Jaako .10 .25
185 Lars Hurtig .10 .25
186 Jens Hellgren .10 .25
187 MoDo Hockey Team Emblem .10 .25
188 MoDo Hockey .10 .25
Team Picture Left
189 MoDo Hockey .10 .25
Team Picture Right
190 Anders Nordin .10 .25
191 Anders Bergman .10 .25
192 Fredrik Andersson .10 .25
193 Hans Lodin .10 .25
194 Jens Johansson .10 .25
195 Juouko Narvanmaa .10 .25
196 Robert Frestadius .10 .25
197 Per Forsberg .10 .25
198 Mikael Hjalm .10 .25
199 Ulf Sandstrom .10 .25
200 Ulf Odmark .10 .25
201 Per Nilsson .10 .25
202 Anders Wikberg .10 .25
203 Lars Molin .20 .50
204 Per-Arne Alexandersson .10 .25
205 Lars Bystrom .10 .25
206 Mikael Stahl .10 .25
207 Ove Pettersson .10 .25
208 Skelleftea Hockey Team .10 .25
Emblem
209 Skelleftea Hockey Team .10 .25
Picture Left
210 Skelleftea Hockey Team .10 .25
Picture Right
211 Tommie Bergman .40 1.00
212 Ulf Nilsson .80 2.00
213 Sam Lindstahl .10 .25
214 Lars Marklund .10 .25
215 Goran Lindblom .10 .25
216 Ola Stenlund .10 .25
217 Stefan Svensson .10 .25
218 Kari Suoraniemi .10 .25
219 Hans Hjalmar .10 .25
220 Mikael Granstedt .10 .25
221 Mats Lundstrom .10 .25
222 Jonny Forsman .10 .25
223 Kari Jalonen .20 .50
224 Claes Lindblom .20 .50
225 Tomas Hedin .10 .25
226 Martin Pettersson .10 .25
227 Jorgen Marklund .10 .25
228 Niklas Mannberg .10 .25
229 Sodertalje SK Team Emblem .10 .25
230 Sodertalje SK .10 .25
Team Picture Left
231 Sodertalje SK .10 .25
Team Picture Right
232 John Pettersson .10 .25
233 Reino Sundberg .10 .25
234 Jari Luoma .10 .25
235 Anders Eldebrink .20 .50
236 Mats Kihlstrom .10 .25
237 Jonas Heed .10 .25
238 Bo Ericsson .10 .25
239 Ulf Borg .10 .25
240 Stefan Jonsson .10 .25
241 Mats Hallin .10 .25
242 Glenn Johansson .10 .25
243 Thomas Ljungberg .10 .25
244 Hans Sarkijarvi .10 .25
245 Thom Eklund .10 .25
246 Peter Larsson .10 .25
247 Conny Jansson .10 .25
248 Niklas Lindgren .10 .25
249 Reine Karlsson .10 .25
250 Vasby IK Team Emblem .10 .25
251 Vasby IK Team Picture Left .10 .25
252 Vasby IK Team Picture Right .10 .25
253 Anders Jacobsen .10 .25
254 Jorgen Larsson .10 .25
255 Stefan Sohlin .10 .25
256 Torbjorn Mattsson .10 .25
257 Hakan Persson .10 .25
258 Kenneth Lindqvist .10 .25
259 Jens Mackegard .10 .25
260 Anders Lindberg .10 .25
261 Mats Edholm .10 .25
262 Mats Poppler .10 .25
263 Claes Gustafsson .10 .25
264 Per Bergman .10 .25
265 Peter Wallen .10 .25
266 Hans-Rickard Andersson .10 .25
267 Arto Heinola .10 .25
268 Mats Lindberg .10 .25
269 Urban Jakobsson .10 .25
270 Stefan Sandin .10 .25

1989-90 Swedish Semic Elitserien Stickers

This 285-sticker set captures the excitement of the Elitserien in thrilling posed color photos. The 3" by 2 1/8" sticker fronts are complemented by player name, sticker number and team emblem. the backs contain an ad for Pripp's Energy drink. The set is notable for the first "card" appearances of Mats Sundin and Nicklas Lidstrom.

COMPLETE SET (285) 20.00 50.00
1 AIK .10 .25
2 Ake Lilljebjorn .10 .25
3 Thomas Ostlund .30 .75
4 Mats Thelin .10 .25
5 Thomas Ahlen .10 .25
6 Petri Liimatainen .10 .25
7 Roger Ohman .10 .25
8 Rikard Franzen .10 .25
9 Stefan Claesson .10 .25
10 Tommy Hedlund .10 .25
11 Stefan Jansson .10 .25
12 Peter Gradin .10 .25
13 Thomas Gradin .20 .50
14 Bo Berglund .10 .25
15 Heinz Ehlers .10 .25
16 Robert Burakovsky .10 .25
17 Alexander Kozjevnikov .10 .25
18 Peter Hammarstrom .10 .25
19 Anders Gozzi .10 .25
20 Thomas Bjuhr .10 .25
21 Patric Englund .10 .25
22 Odd Nilsson .10 .25
23 Mats Lindberg .10 .25
24 Peter Johansson .10 .25
25 Patric Kjellberg .30 .75
26 Brynas IF .10 .25
27 Lars Eriksson .10 .25
28 Michael Sundlov .10 .25
29 Par Djoos .10 .25
30 Tommy Sjodin .10 .25
31 Nikolaj Davydkin .10 .25
32 Niklas Gallstedt .10 .25
33 Mikael Lindman .10 .25
34 Jan-Erik Stormqvist .10 .25
35 Tommy Melkersson .10 .25
36 Mikael Enander .10 .25
37 Anders Huss .10 .25
38 Anders Carlsson .10 .25
39 Willy Lindstrom .20 .50
40 Kyosti Karjalainen .10 .25
41 Jan Larsson .10 .25
42 Patrik Erickson .10 .25
43 Joakim Pehrson .10 .25
44 Johan Brummer .10 .25
45 Peter Eriksson .10 .25
46 Peter Gustafsson .10 .25
47 Tomas Olund .10 .25
48 Magnus Asberg .10 .25
49 Djurgardens IF .10 .25
50 Rolf Ridderwall .20 .50
51 Tommy Soderstrom .60 1.50
52 Thomas Eriksson .10 .25
53 Arto Blomsten .10 .25
54 Orvar Stambert .10 .25
55 Christian Due-Boje .10 .25
56 Kenneth Kennholt .10 .25
57 Mats Waltin .10 .25
58 Karl-Erik Lilja .10 .25
59 Marcus Ragnarsson .20 .50
60 Hakan Sodergren .10 .25
61 Mikael Johansson .10 .25
62 Jens Ohling .10 .25
63 Jan Viktorsson .10 .25
64 Peter Nilsson .10 .25
65 Charles Berglund .10 .25
66 Kent Johansson .10 .25
67 Johan Garpenlov .20 .50
68 Ola Andersson .10 .25
69 Anders Johnson .10 .25
70 Bengt Akerblom .10 .25
71 Ola Josefsson .10 .25
72 Mats Sundin 4.00 10.00
73 Farjestads BK .10 .25
74 Anders Bergman .10 .25
75 Jorgen Ryden .10 .25
76 Tommy Samuelsson .10 .25
77 Fredrik Olausson .30 .75
78 Peter Hasselblad .10 .25
79 Jesper Duus .10 .25
80 Anders Berglund .10 .25
81 Mattias Andersson .10 .25
82 Mattias Olsson .10 .25
83 Greger Artursson .10 .25
84 Jacob Karlsson .10 .25
85 Thomas Rundqvist .10 .25
86 Staffan Lundh .10 .25
87 Jan Ingman .10 .25
88 Kjell Dahlin .10 .25
89 Bengt-Ake Gustafsson .20 .50
90 Magnus Roupe .10 .25
91 Hakan Loob .40 1.00
92 Mikael Holmberg .10 .25
93 Daniel Rydmark .10 .25
94 Lars Karlsson .10 .25
95 Peter Ottosson .10 .25
96 HV 71 .10 .25
97 Kenneth Johansson .10 .25
98 Claes Heljemo .10 .25
99 Lars Ivarsson .10 .25
100 Arto Ruotanen .10 .25
101 Fredrik Stillman .10 .25
102 Klas Heed .10 .25
103 Nils-Gunnar Svensson .10 .25
104 Per Gustafsson .10 .25
105 Tommy Fritz .10 .25
106 Mats Nilsson .10 .25
107 Hasse Sjoo .10 .25
108 Mats Loov .10 .25
109 Ove Thornberg .10 .25
110 Eddy Ericsson .10 .25
111 Ivan Avdejev .10 .25
112 Stefan Persson .20 .50
113 Rick Erdall .10 .25
114 Stefan Nilsson .10 .25
115 Stefan Ornskog .10 .25
116 Patrik Ross .10 .25
117 Stefan Falk .10 .25
118 Claes Roupe .10 .25
119 Peter Ekelund .10 .25
120 Leksands IF .10 .25
121 Peter Aslin .30 .75
122 Olow Sundstrom .10 .25
123 Jonas Leven .10 .25
124 Tomas Jonsson .20 .50
125 Magnus Svensson .10 .25
126 Ricard Persson .20 .50
127 Per Lundell .10 .25
128 Tomas Nord .10 .25
129 Peter Wallin .10 .25
130 Orjan Lindmark .10 .25
131 Henric Bjorkman .10 .25
132 Anders Pettersson .10 .25
133 Per-Olof Carlsson .10 .25
134 Tomas Forslund .20 .50
135 Niklas Eriksson .10 .25
136 Richard Kromm .10 .25
137 Jarmo Makitalo .10 .25
138 Peter Lundmark .30 .75
139 Ronny Reichenberg .10 .25
140 Cenneth Soderlund .10 .25
141 Jens Nielsen .10 .25
142 Marcus Thuresson .10 .25
143 Anders Broms .10 .25
144 Joakim Backlund .10 .25
145 Lulea HF .10 .25
146 Robert Skoog .10 .25
147 Tomas Javeblad .10 .25
148 Lars Modig .10 .25
149 Jan-Ove Mettavainio .10 .25
150 Osmo Soutokorva .10 .25
151 Torbjorn Lindberg .10 .25
152 Timo Jutila .20 .50
153 Roger Akerstrom .10 .25
154 Per Ljusterang .10 .25
155 Tomas Lilja .10 .25
156 Johan Stromvall .10 .25
157 Lars-Gunnar Pettersson .10 .25
158 Lars Hurtig .10 .25
159 Morgan Samuelsson .10 .25
160 Stefan Nilsson .10 .25
161 Vesa Kangas .10 .25
162 Kari Jaako .10 .25
163 Juha Nurmi .10 .25
164 Jens Hellgren .10 .25
165 Tomas Berglund .10 .25
166 Lars Edstrom .10 .25
167 Petter Antti .10 .25
168 MoDo HK .10 .25
169 Fredrik Andersson .10 .25
170 Goran Arnmark .10 .25
171 Timo Blomqvist .10 .25
172 Hakan Stromqvist .10 .25
173 Robert Frestadius .10 .25
174 Lars Jansson .10 .25
175 Hans Lodin .10 .25
176 Ove Pettersson .10 .25
177 Tony Olofsson .10 .25
178 Jorgen Eriksson .10 .25
179 Ulf Sandstrom .10 .25
180 Michael Hjalm .10 .25
181 Urban Nordin .10 .25
182 Lars Bystrom .10 .25
183 Jens Ohman .10 .25
184 Ulf Odmark .10 .25
185 Mikael Stahl .10 .25
186 Per Nilsson .10 .25
187 Ingemar Strom .10 .25
188 Kent Lantz .10 .25
189 Kent Norberg .10 .25
190 Patrik Soderholm .10 .25
191 Skelleftea HC .10 .25
192 Sam Lindstahl .10 .25
193 Dick Andersson .10 .25
194 Kari Suoraniemi .10 .25
195 Robert Larsson .10 .25
196 Kari Yli-Maenpaa .10 .25
197 Ola Stenlund .10 .25
198 Tony Barthelson .10 .25
199 Lars Marklund .10 .25
200 Glenn Hedman .10 .25
201 Dick Burlin .10 .25
202 Michael Granstedt .10 .25
203 Pekka Jarvela .10 .25
204 Hans Hjalmar .10 .25
205 Mats Lundstrom .10 .25
206 Martin Pettersson .10 .25
207 Johnny Forsman .10 .25
208 Daniel Pettersson .10 .25
209 Niklas Mannberg .10 .25
210 Niklas Brannstrom .10 .25
211 Jan Johansson .10 .25
212 Jorgen Wannstrom .10 .25
213 Leif Johansson .10 .25
214 Par Mikaelsson .10 .25
215 Fredrik Andersson .10 .25
216 Sodertalje SK .10 .25
217 Reino Sundberg .10 .25
218 Jari Luoma .10 .25
219 Anders Eldebrink .10 .25
220 Mats Kilstrom .10 .25
221 Jonas Heed .10 .25
222 Hans Pettersson .10 .25
223 Jan Bergman .10 .25
224 Thomas Carlsson .10 .25
225 Stefan Jonsson .10 .25
226 Thom Eklund .10 .25
227 Ola Rosander .10 .25
228 Bjorn Carlsson .10 .25
229 Thomas Sjogren .10 .25
230 Thomas Ljungbergh .10 .25
231 Stefan Olsson .10 .25
232 Reine Landgren .10 .25
233 Anders Frykbo .10 .25
234 Conny Jansson .10 .25
235 Peter Larsson .10 .25
236 Tomaz Eriksson .10 .25
237 Erik Holmberg .10 .25
238 Patrik Lindh .10 .25
239 Vasteras IK .10 .25
240 Mats Ytter .10 .25
241 Par Hellenberg .10 .25
242 Jan Eriksson .10 .25
243 Peter Popovic .20 .50
244 Tore Lindgren .10 .25
245 Leif Rohlin .20 .50
246 Henrik Andersson .10 .25
247 Nicklas Lidstrom 4.00 10.00
248 Jan Karlsson .10 .25
249 Peter Jacobsson .10 .25
250 Patrik Juhlin .20 .50
251 Goran Sjoberg .10 .25
252 Fredrik Nilsson .10 .25
253 Stefan Hellkvist .10 .25
254 Tomas Strandberg .10 .25
255 Anders Berglund .10 .25
256 Claes Lindblom .10 .25
257 Magnus Wallin .10 .25
258 Bjorn Akerblom .10 .25
259 Joakim Lundholm .10 .25
260 Jorgen Holmberg .10 .25
261 Ronny Hansen .10 .25
262 Misjat Fachrutdinov .10 .25
263 Vastra Frolunda HC .10 .25
264 Hakan Algotsson .30 .75
265 Per Lundbergh .10 .25
266 Jan Karlsson .10 .25
267 Joacim Esbjors .10 .25
268 Leif Carlsson .10 .25
269 Stefan Axelsson .10 .25
270 Peter Ekroth .10 .25
271 Jorgen Palm .10 .25
272 Hakan Nordin .10 .25
273 Stefan Larsson .10 .25
274 Mikael Andersson .20 .50
275 Terho Koskela .10 .25
276 Patrik Carnback .20 .50
277 Serge Boisvert .10 .25
278 Arto Sirvio .10 .25
279 Peter Berndtsson .10 .25
280 Jorgen Pettersson .10 .25
281 Niklas Andersson .10 .25
282 Peter Gustavsson .10 .25
283 Paul Andersson .10 .25
284 Mats Graesen .10 .25
285 Kent Orrgren .10 .25

1989 Swedish Semic World Championship Stickers

This 200-sticker set captures some of the players who have represented their country at the World Championships. The stickers, which came in packs of five, measure 3" by 2 1/8" and feature color photos, along with player name, card number and national flag. The backs contain an ad for Pepsi. The NHL players are pictured in their team sweaters, including stars such as Wayne Gretzky and Patrick Roy. An album to house the set also was available; it retails for about $10.

COMPLETE SET (200) 60.00 125.00
1 Sweden National Emblem .04 .10
2 Tommy Sandlin .10 .25
3 Peter Lindmark .10 .25
4 Rolf Ridderwall .10 .25
5 Tomas Jonsson .10 .25
6 Tommy Albelin .10 .25
7 Mats Kihlstrom .04 .10
8 Tommy Samuelsson .04 .10
9 Anders Eldebrink .06 .15
10 Fredrik Olausson .10 .25
11 Peter Andersson .06 .15
12 Thomas Eriksson .04 .10
13 Thom Eklund .04 .10
14 Bo Berglund .06 .15
15 Thomas Steen .16 .40
16 Ulf Sandstrom .04 .10
17 Jonas Bergkvist .10 .25
18 Thomas Rundqvist .06 .15
19 Per-Erik Eklund .20 .50
20 Bengt-Ake Gustavsson .06 .15
21 Patrik Sundstrom .16 .40
22 Mikael Johansson .06 .15
23 Hakan Sodergren .04 .10
24 Kent Nilsson .20 .50
25 Lars-Gunnar Pettersson .04 .10
26 Finland National Emblem .04 .10
27 Pentti Matikainen .10 .25
28 Jukka Tammi .10 .25
29 Sakari Lindfors .10 .25
30 Reijo Ruotsalainen .10 .25
31 Kari Eloranata .10 .25
32 Timo Blomqvist .10 .25
33 Simo Saarinen .04 .10
34 Hannu Virta .10 .25
35 Jouko Narvanmaa .04 .10
36 Jarmo Kuusisto .04 .10
37 Kari Suoraniemi .04 .10
38 Reijo Mikkolainen .04 .10
39 Raimo Helminen .10 .25

40 Raimo Summanen .10 .25
41 Mikko Makela .10 .25
42 Kari Jalonen .04 .10
43 Kari Laitinen .04 .10
44 Petri Skriko .16 .40
45 Erkki Laine .04 .10
46 Pauli Jarvinen .04 .10
47 Jukka Vilander .04 .10
48 Esa Keskinen .16 .40
49 Ari Vuori .04 .10
50 Mika Nieminen .16 .40
51 Canada National Emblem .10 .25
52 Dave King .10 .25
53 Grant Fuhr .75 2.00
54 Patrick Roy 12.00 30.00
55 Ron Hextall .75 2.00
56 Al MacInnis .60 1.50
57 Ray Bourque 4.00 10.00
58 Scott Stevens .20 .50
59 Paul Coffey 1.25 3.00
60 Zarley Zalapski .16 .40
61 James Patrick .16 .40
62 Kevin Lowe .16 .40
63 Brad McCrimmon .16 .40
64 Mario Lemieux 12.00 30.00
65 Wayne Gretzky 20.00 50.00
66 Denis Savard .30 .75
67 Dale Hawerchuk .40 1.00
68 Luc Robitaille .75 2.00
69 Mark Messier 4.00 10.00
70 Michel Goulet .20 .50
71 Cam Neely 2.00 5.00
72 Steve Yzerman 10.00 25.00
73 Bernie Nicholls .30 .75
74 Joe Nieuwendyk .40 1.00
75 Mike Gartner .40 1.00
76 USSR National Emblem .10 .25
77 Viktor Tichonov .08 .20
78 Jevgenij Belosjejkin .20 .50
79 Sergei Mylnikov .20 .50
80 Sergei Golosjumov .10 .25
81 Alexei Kasatonov .20 .50
82 Aleksej Gusarov .10 .25
83 Andrej Smirnov .06 .15
84 Valerij Sjirjajev .06 .15
85 Igor Stelnov .06 .15
86 Vladimir Konstantinov 1.25 3.00
87 Slava Fetisov .40 1.00
88 Sergei Jasjin .06 .15
89 Vladimir Krutov .20 .75
90 Igor Larionov .75 2.00
91 Valerij Kamenskij .20 .50
92 Vjatjeslav Bykov .20 .50
93 Andrej Chomutov .20 .50
94 Yuri Khmylev .20 .50
95 Sergei Nemchinov .20 .50
96 Sergei Makarov .40 1.00
97 Igor Jesmantovitj .06 .15
98 Andrei Lomakin .08 .20
99 Anatolij Semjonov .10 .25
100 Aleksandr Tjernych .06 .15
101 West Germany .04 .10
(National Emblem
102 Xaver Unsinn .10 .25
103 Karl Friesen .10 .25
104 Josef Schlickenrieder .04 .10
105 Matthias Hoppe .04 .10
106 Andreas Niederberger .04 .10
107 Udo Kiessling .06 .15
108 Uli Hiemer .06 .15
109 Harold Kreis .06 .15
110 Manfred Schuster .04 .10
111 Jorg Hanft .04 .10
112 Ron Fischer .04 .10
113 Michael Heidt .06 .15
114 Dieter Hegen .06 .15
115 Gerd Truntschka .06 .15
116 Helmut Steiger .04 .10
117 Georg Franz .04 .10
118 Georg Holzmann .04 .10
119 Peter Obresa .04 .10
120 Bernd Truntschka .06 .15
121 Manfred Wolf .04 .10
122 Roy Roedger .04 .10
123 Axel Kammerer .04 .10
124 Peter Draisaitl .08 .20
125 Daniel Held .04 .10
126 Poland National Emblem .04 .10
127 Leszek Lejczyk .08 .20
128 Jerzy Mruk .08 .20
129 Andrezej Hanisz .04 .10
130 Dariusz Wieczorek .04 .10
131 Jacek Zamojski .04 .10
132 Marek Cholewa .04 .10
133 Henryk Gruth .04 .10
134 Robert Szopinski .04 .10
135 Jerzy Potz .04 .10
136 Andrzej Swiatek .04 .10
137 Ludvik Czapka .04 .10
138 Piotr Zdunek .04 .10
139 Jedrzej Kasperczyk .04 .10
140 Krzysztof Podsiadlo .04 .10
141 Miroslaw Copija .04 .10
142 Krzysztof Bujar .04 .10
143 Janusz Adamiec .04 .10
144 Jacek Solinski .04 .10
145 Roman Steblecki .04 .10
146 Adam Fraszko .04 .10
147 Leszek Minge .04 .10
148 Piotr Kwasigroch .04 .10
149 Ireneusz Pacula .04 .10
150 1989 World Championship .04 .10
Emblem
151 USA National Emblem .10 .25
152 Art Berglund .04 .10
153 Tom Barrasso .20 .50
154 John Vanbiesbrouck 1.25 3.00
155 Gary Suter .20 .50
156 Phil Housley .20 .50
157 Chris Chelios 1.25 3.00
158 Mike Ramsey .10 .25
159 Rod Langway .10 .25
160 Mark Howe .16 .40
161 Brian Leetch .75 2.00
162 Al Iafrate .16 .40
163 Jimmy Carson .06 .15
164 Pat LaFontaine .40 1.00
165 Neal Broten .20 .50
166 Dave Christian .16 .40
167 Brett Hull 4.00 10.00
168 Bob Carpenter .10 .25
169 Ed Olczyk .10 .25
170 Joe Mullen .20 .50
171 Bob Brooke .06 .15
172 Brian Lawton .06 .15
173 Craig Janney .20 .50
174 Mark Johnson .10 .25
175 Chris Nilan .10 .25
176 CSSR National Emblem .04 .10
177 Pavel Wohl .10 .25
178 Dominik Hasek 6.00 15.00
179 Jaromir Sindel .10 .25
180 Petr Briza .40 1.00
181 Antonin Stavjana .10 .25
182 Bedrich Scerban .08 .20
183 Petr Slanina .04 .10
184 Frantisek Kucera .08 .20
185 Jergus Baca .06 .15
186 Leo Gudas .06 .15
187 Drahomir Kadlec .06 .15
188 Mojmir Bozik .04 .10
189 Petr Vlk .04 .10
190 Vladimir Ruzicka .10 .25
191 Otakar Janecky .10 .25
192 Jan Vodila .04 .10
193 Jiri Dolezal .04 .10
194 Rostislav Vlach .04 .10
195 Jiri Kucera .08 .20
196 Jiri Sejba .06 .15
197 Oldrich Valek .04 .10
198 Jiri Lala .06 .15
199 Robert Kron .10 .25
200 Petr Rosol .06 .15

1990-91 Swedish Semic Elitserien Stickers

This 294-sticker set features the players of the Swedish Elitserien. The stickers measure 3" by 2 1/8" and utilize posed color player photos on the front, along with sticker number, name and club emblem. The backs feature consumer ads. The set includes the first "card" of players such as Mikael Renberg and Markus Naslund.

COMPLETE SET (294) 16.00 40.00
1 MoDo Hockey Team .04 .10
Team Emblem
2 MoDo Hockey .04 .10
Team Picture
3 Fredrik Andersson .10 .25
4 Goran Armmark .10 .25
5 Ari Salo .04 .10
6 Anders Berglund .04 .10
7 Lars Jansson .04 .10
8 Hans Lodin .04 .10
9 Ove Pettersson .04 .10
10 Jorgen Eriksson .04 .10
11 Tony Olofsson .04 .10
12 Tomas Nanzen .04 .10
13 Michael Hjalm .04 .10
14 Erik Holmberg .04 .10
15 Urban Nordin .04 .10
16 Kent Lantz .04 .10
17 Lars Bystrom .04 .10
18 Jens Ohman .04 .10
19 Ulf Odmark .04 .10
20 Mikael Stahl .04 .10
21 Ingemar Strom .04 .10
22 Tommy Pettersson .04 .10
23 Markus Naslund 2.00 5.00
24 Per Wallin .06 .15
25 Vastra Frolunda HC .04 .10
Team Emblem
26 Vastra Frolunda HC .04 .10
(Team Picture
27 Ake Lilljebjorn .20 .50
28 Hakan Algotsson .20 .50
29 Leif Carlsson .04 .10
30 Jonas Heed .04 .10
31 Hakan Nordin .04 .10
32 Joacim Esbjors .06 .15
33 Stefan Axelsson .16 .40
34 Stefan Larsson .06 .15
35 Jorgen Palm .04 .10
36 Oscar Ackerstrom .04 .10
37 Patrik Carnback .20 .50
38 Mats Lundstrom .04 .10
39 Niklas Andersson .10 .25
40 Serge Boisvert .08 .20
41 Arto Sirvio .04 .10
42 Terho Koskela .04 .10
43 Kari Jaako .04 .10
44 Peter Berndtsson .04 .10
45 Mikael Andersson .10 .25
46 Par Edlund .04 .10
47 Jonas Andersson .04 .10
48 Johan Witehall .20 .50
49 Sodertalje SK .04 .10
Team Emblem
50 Sodertalje SK .04 .10
Team Picture
51 Reino Sundberg .10 .25
52 Jari Luoma .10 .25
53 Mats Kilstrom .04 .10
54 Stefan Jonsson .04 .10
55 Peter Ekroth .04 .10
56 Mats Waltin .04 .10
57 Jan Bergman .04 .10
58 Hans Pettersson .04 .10
59 Stefan Nyman .04 .10
60 Conny Jansson .04 .10
61 Thom Eklund .04 .10
62 Otakar Hascak .08 .20
63 Morgan Samuelsson .06 .15
64 Reine Landgren .04 .10
65 Bjorn Carlsson .04 .10
66 Ola Andersson .04 .10
67 Tomaz Eriksson .04 .10
68 Bert-Olav Karlsson .04 .10
69 Ola Rosander .04 .10
70 Stefan Olsson .04 .10
71 Scott Moore .04 .10
72 Anders Frykbo .04 .10
73 AIK .04 .10
Team Emblem
74 AIK .04 .10
Team Picture
75 Thomas Ostlund .20 .50
76 Sam Lindstahl .10 .25
77 Borje Salming 1.20 3.00
78 Mats Thelin .10 .25
79 Petter Salsten .04 .10
80 Petri Liimatainen .04 .10
81 Rikard Franzen .06 .15
82 Stefan Claesson .04 .10
83 Torbjorn Mattsson .04 .10
84 Daniel Jardemyr .04 .10
85 Robert Burakovsky .08 .20
86 Peter Gradin .04 .10
87 Thomas Bjuhr .04 .10
88 Heinz Ehlers .04 .10
89 Tommy Lehmann .08 .20
90 Peter Hammarstrom .04 .10
91 Patric Kjellberg .40 1.00
92 Patric Englund .04 .10
93 Mats Lindberg .04 .10
94 Peter Johansson .04 .10
95 Kristian Gahn .08 .20
96 Niklas Sundblad .10 .25
97 Erik Andersson .04 .10
98 HV 71 .04 .10
Team Emblem
99 HV 71 .04 .10
Team Picture
100 Peter Aslin .20 .50
101 Kenneth Johansson .10 .25
102 Arto Ruotanen .10 .25
103 Fredrik Stillman .06 .15
104 Lars Ivarsson .04 .10
105 Klas Heed .04 .10
106 Per Gustafsson .20 .50
107 Mathias Svedberg .04 .10
108 Tommy Fritz .04 .10
109 Mats Nilsson .04 .10
110 Peter Eriksson .04 .10
111 Risto Kurkinen .04 .10
112 Thomas Ljungbergh .04 .10
113 Ove Thornberg .04 .10
114 Mats Loov .04 .10
115 Eddy Ericsson .04 .10
116 Stefan Ornskog .10 .25
117 Patrik Ross .04 .10
118 Stefan Persson .10 .25
119 Dennis Strom .04 .10
120 Peter Ekelund .04 .10
121 Jonas Jonsson .04 .10
122 Torbjorn Persson .04 .10
123 Malmo IF .04 .10
(Team Emblem
124 Malmo IF .04 .10
Team Picture
125 Peter Lindmark .20 .50
126 Roger Nordstrom .10 .25
127 Timo Blomqvist .10 .25
128 Peter Andersson .10 .25
129 Mats Lusth .04 .10
130 Johan Salle .04 .10
131 Roger Ohman .06 .15
132 Anders Svensson .04 .10
133 Peter Imhauser .04 .10
134 Johan Norgren .04 .10
135 Raimo Helminen .20 .50
136 Peter Sundstrom .10 .25
137 Mats Hallin .04 .10
138 Matti Pauna .04 .10
139 Patrik Gustavsson .04 .10
140 Hakan Ahlund .04 .10
141 Daniel Rydmark .06 .15
142 Lennart Hermansson .04 .10
143 Carl-Erik Larsson .04 .10
144 Rick Erdall .04 .10
145 Bo Svanberg .04 .10
146 Fredrik Johansson .04 .10
147 Jens Hemstrom .04 .10
148 Vasteras IK .04 .10
Team Emblem
149 Vasteras IK .04 .10
Team Picture
150 Mats Ytter .10 .25
151 Par Hellenberg .10 .25
152 Nicklas Lidstrom 2.00 5.00
153 Leif Rohlin .16 .40
154 Peter Popovic .20 .50
155 Jan Karlsson .04 .10
156 Henrik Andersson .04 .10
157 Tore Lindgren .04 .10
158 Peter Jacobsson .04 .10
159 Pierre Ivarsson .04 .10
160 Jan Eriksson .04 .10
161 Goran Sjoberg .04 .10
162 Misjat Fachrutdinov .06 .15
163 Anders Berglund .04 .10
164 Claes Lindblom .04 .10
165 Jorgen Holmberg .04 .10
166 Stefan Hellkvist .04 .10
167 Tomas Strandberg .04 .10
168 Bjorn Akerblom .04 .10
169 Ronny Hansen .04 .10
170 Fredrik Nilsson .06 .15
171 Patrik Juhlin .20 .50
172 Henrik Nilsson .04 .10
173 Brynas IF .04 .10
Team Emblem
174 Brynas IF .04 .10
Team Picture
175 Michael Sundlov .20 .50
176 Lars Eriksson .10 .25
177 Tommy Sjodin .10 .25
178 Brad Berry .04 .10
179 Niklas Gallstedt .04 .10
180 Mikael Lindman .04 .10
181 Urban Molander .04 .10
182 Jan-Erik Stormqvist .04 .10
183 Stefan Klockare .08 .20
184 Tommy Melkersson .04 .10
185 Anders Carlsson .04 .10
186 Patrik Erickson .04 .10
187 Anders Huss .04 .10
188 Jan Larsson .04 .10
189 Peter Larsson .04 .10
190 Anders Gozzi .06 .15
191 Joakim Pehrson .06 .15
192 Peter Gustafsson .04 .10
193 Peter Eriksson .04 .10
194 Johan Brummer .04 .10
195 Tomas Olund .04 .10
196 Kenneth Andersson .04 .10
197 Leksands IF .04 .10
Team Emblem
198 Leksands IF .04 .10
Team Picture
199 Olow Sundstrom .10 .25
200 Lars-Erik Lord .10 .25
201 Jonas Leven .04 .10
202 Tomas Jonsson .10 .25
203 Ricard Persson .10 .25
204 Per Lundell .04 .10
205 Tomas Nord .04 .10
206 Mattias Andersson .04 .10
207 Henric Bjorkman .04 .10
208 Orjan Lindmark .04 .10
209 Tomas Forslund .10 .25
210 Niklas Eriksson .04 .10
211 Peter Lundmark .06 .15
212 Per-Olof Carlsson .04 .10
213 Marcus Thuresson .04 .10
214 Jens Nielsen .04 .10
215 Cenneth Soderlund .04 .10
216 Markus Akerblom .06 .15
217 Ronny Reichenberg .04 .10
218 Fredrik Olsson .04 .10
219 Niklas Hillblom .04 .10
220 Magnus Gustafsson .04 .10
221 Fredrik Jax .06 .15
222 Lulea HF .04 .10
Team Emblem
223 Lulea HF .04 .10
Team Picture
224 Robert Skoog .10 .25
225 Tomas Javeblad .10 .25
226 Timo Jutila .10 .25
227 Per Ljusterang .04 .10
228 Lars Modig .04 .10
229 Torbjorn Lindberg .04 .10
230 Tomas Lilja .20 .50
231 Osmo Soutokorva .04 .10
232 Jan-Ove Mettavainio .04 .10
233 Roger Akerstrom .04 .10
234 Johan Stromvall .04 .10
235 Ulf Sandstrom .04 .10
236 Lars-Gunnar Pettersson .04 .10
237 Pauli Jarvinen .04 .10
238 Lars Hurtig .04 .10
239 Tomas Berglund .04 .10
240 Stefan Nilsson .04 .10
241 Mikael Renberg .80 2.00
242 Hans Hjalmar .04 .10
243 Jens Hellgren .04 .10
244 Lars Edstrom .04 .10
245 Robert Nordberg .10 .25
246 Farjestads BK .04 .10
Team Emblem
247 Farjestads BK .04 .10
Team Picture
248 Anders Bergman .10 .25
249 Jorgen Ryden .10 .25
250 Patrik Haltia .20 .50
251 Tommy Samuelsson .10 .25
252 Jim Leavins .04 .10
253 Peter Hasselblad .04 .10
254 Jesper Duus .04 .10
255 Mattias Olsson .04 .10
256 Greger Artursson .04 .10
257 Jacob Karlsson .04 .10
258 Thomas Rhodin .04 .10
259 Bengt-Ake Gustafsson .16 .40
260 Hakan Loob .40 1.00
261 Thomas Rundqvist .10 .25
262 Kjell Dahlin .10 .25
263 Magnus Roupe .04 .10
264 Jan Ingman .04 .10
265 Lars Karlsson .04 .10
266 Mikael Holmberg .04 .10
267 Staffan Lundh .04 .10
268 Peter Ottosson .04 .10
269 Jonas Hoglund 1.20 3.00
270 Clas Eriksson .04 .10
271 Djurgardens IF .04 .10
Team Emblem
272 Djurgardens IF .04 .10
Team Picture
273 Tommy Soderstrom .40 1.00
274 Joakim Persson .20 .50
275 Thomas Eriksson .04 .10
276 Arto Blomsten .10 .25
277 Kenneth Kennholt .06 .15
278 Christian Due-Boje .08 .20
279 Orvar Stambert .04 .10
280 Per Nygards .04 .10
281 Marcus Ragnarsson .20 .50
282 Thomas Johansson .04 .10
283 Ronnie Pettersson .04 .10
284 Charles Berglund .04 .10
285 Jan Viktorsson .08 .20
286 Jens Ohling .06 .15
287 Ola Josefsson .04 .10
288 Peter Nilsson .04 .10
289 Andres Johnson .04 .10
290 Hakan Sodergren .04 .10
291 Stefan Gustavson .04 .10
292 Magnus Jansson .04 .10
293 Mikael Johansson .04 .10
294 Johan Lindstedt .04 .10

1991-92 Swedish Semic Elitserien Stickers

This 360-sticker series captures the players of the Swedish Elitserien. The sticker, which measure 3" by 2 1/8", have posed color photos on the front, along with player name, team emblem and sticker number. The backs note the set's sponsor "Cloetta" -- a Swedish confectioner. The set includes early appearances by Mats Sundin, Peter Forsberg and Mikael Renberg. An album was available to house the sticker collection; it is valued at $10.

COMPLETE SET (360) 20.00 50.00
1 AIK .04 .10
Team Emblem
2 Thomas Ostlund .10 .25
3 Sam Lindstahl .10 .25
4 Borje Salming .30 .75
5 Petri Liimatainen .04 .10
6 Mats Thelin .10 .25
7 Rikard Franzen .06 .15
8 Petter Sahlsten .04 .10
9 Daniel Jardemyr .04 .10
10 Thomas Nilsson .04 .10
11 Niclas Havelid .04 .10
12 Mattias Norstrom .10 .25
13 Peter Gradin .04 .10
14 Peter Hammarstrom .04 .10
15 Patrik Erickson .06 .15
16 Thomas Bjuhr .04 .10
17 Thomas Strandberg .04 .10
18 Tommy Lehmann .08 .20
19 Mats Lindberg .04 .10
20 Patric Kjellberg .20 .50
21 Michael Nylander .40 1.00
22 Patric Englund .04 .10
23 Niclas Sundblad .20 .50
24 Kristian Gahn .10 .25
25 Erik Andersson .04 .10
26 Bjorn Ahlstrom .04 .10
27 Brynas .04 .10
Team Emblem
28 Michael Sundlov .10 .25
29 Lars Eriksson .10 .25
30 Lars Karlsson .04 .10
31 Tommy Sjodin .08 .20
32 Nikolaj Davydkin .04 .10
33 Niklas Gallstedt .04 .10
34 Mikael Lindman .04 .10
35 Tommy Melkersson .04 .10
36 Mikael Enander .04 .10
37 Urban Molander .04 .10
38 Stefan Klockare .06 .15
39 Anders Huss .06 .15
40 Mikael Lindholm .06 .15
41 Jan Larsson .04 .10
42 Anders Gozzi .06 .15
43 Peter Larsson .04 .10
44 Thomas Tallberg .06 .15
45 Peter Gustafsson .04 .10
46 Joakim Persson .20 .50
47 Peter Eriksson .04 .10
48 Ove Mohlin .06 .15
49 Jonas Johnsson .06 .15
50 Johan Schillgard .04 .10
51 Andreas Dackell .10 .25
52 Tom Bissett .06 .15
53 Djurgarden .04 .10
Team Emblem
54 Tommy Soderstrom .30 .75
55 Joakim Persson .30 .75
56 Petter Ronnqvist .10 .25
57 Thomas Eriksson .04 .10
58 Kenneth Kennholt .06 .15
59 Arto Blomsten .08 .20
60 Orvar Stambert .04 .10
61 Christian Due-Boje .06 .15
62 Marcus Ragnarsson .20 .50
63 Per Nygards .04 .10
64 Thomas Johansson .04 .10
65 Mikael Johansson .04 .10
66 Charles Berglund .06 .15
67 Jan Viktorsson .06 .15
68 Ola Josefsson .04 .10
69 Jens Ohling .06 .15
70 Magnus Jansson .04 .10
71 Peter Nilsson .04 .10
72 Fredrik Lindquist .10 .25
73 Mariusz Czerkawski .60 1.50
74 Johan Lindstedt .04 .10
75 Stefan Ketola .10 .25
76 Erik Huusko .06 .15
77 Anders Huusko .06 .15
78 Farjestad .04 .10
Team Emblem
79 Anders Bergman .10 .25
80 Jorgen Ryden .10 .25
81 Patrik Haltia .16 .40
82 Tommy Samuelsson .04 .10
83 Per Lundell .04 .10
84 Leif Carlsson .04 .10
85 Jesper Duus .04 .10
86 Mattias Olsson .04 .10
87 Thomas Rhodin .04 .10
88 Jacob Karlsson .04 .10
89 Greger Artursson .04 .10
90 Thomas Rundqvist .06 .15
91 Bengt-Ake Gustafsson .10 .25
92 Hakan Loob .40 1.00
93 Lars Karlsson .04 .10
94 Magnus Roupe .08 .20
95 Kjell Dahlin .10 .25
96 Staffan Lundh .04 .10
97 Peter Ottosson .04 .10
98 Niklas Brannstrom .04 .10
99 Jonas Hoglund .80 2.00
100 Clas Eriksson .04 .10
101 Andreas Johansson .20 .50
102 Mathias Johansson .04 .10
103 HV 71 .04 .10
Team Emblem
104 Peter Aslin .16 .40
105 Boo Ahl .20 .50
106 Stefan Magnusson .10 .25
107 Fredrik Stillman .08 .20
108 Lars Ivarsson .04 .10
109 Klas Heed .04 .10
110 Arto Ruotanen .04 .10
111 Per Gustafsson .04 .10
112 Tommy Fritz .04 .10
113 Mathias Svedberg .04 .10
114 Kristian Pedersen .04 .10
115 Peter Eriksson .04 .10
116 Risto Kurkinen .04 .10
117 Ove Thornberg .04 .10
118 Stefan Ornskog .10 .25
119 Thomas Ljungberg .04 .10
120 Patrik Ross .04 .10
121 Eddy Ericsson .04 .10
122 Dennis Strom .04 .10
123 Torbjorn Persson .04 .10
124 Jonas Jonsson .04 .10
125 Peter Ekelund .04 .10
126 Stefan Falk .10 .25
127 Ronny Nilsson .04 .10
128 Leksand .04 .10
Team Emblem
129 Olow Sundstrom .10 .25
130 Jonas Leven .10 .25
131 Tomas Jonsson .10 .25
132 Ricard Persson .10 .25
133 Magnus Svensson .16 .40
134 Mattias Andersson .04 .10
135 Henric Bjorkman .04 .10
136 Orjan Lindmark .04 .10
137 Orjan Nilsson .04 .10
138 Tomas Ring .04 .10
139 Roger Johansson .04 .10
140 Marcus Thuresson .04 .10
141 Per-Olof Carlsson .04 .10
142 Jens Nielsen .04 .10
143 Cenneth Soderlund .04 .10
144 Markus Akerblom .08 .20
145 Fredrik Jax .08 .20
146 Reine Rauhala .06 .15
147 Niklas Eriksson .04 .10
148 Martin Wiita .04 .10
149 Jonas Bergqvist .08 .20
150 Hannu Jarvenpaa .10 .25
151 Lulea .04 .10
Team Emblem
152 Robert Skoog .10 .25
153 Erik Granqvist .10 .25
154 Timo Jutila .10 .25
155 Tomas Lilja .04 .10
156 Lars Modig .04 .10
157 Per Ljusterang .04 .10
158 Jari Gronstrand .04 .10
159 Torbjorn Lindberg .04 .10
160 Patrik Hoglund .08 .20
161 Petter Nilsson .04 .10
162 Daniel Behm .04 .10
163 Johan Stromvall .04 .10
164 Pauli Jarvinen .04 .10
165 Lars Edstrom .04 .10
166 Lars-Gunnar Pettersson .04 .10
167 Stefan Nilsson .04 .10
168 Lars Hurtig .04 .10
169 Tomas Berglund .04 .10
170 Robert Nordberg .10 .25
171 Mikael Renberg .80 2.00
172 Ulf Sandstrom .04 .10
173 Jens Hellgren .04 .10
174 Mikael Engstrom .04 .10
175 Malmo .04 .10
Team Emblem
176 Peter Lindmark .16 .40
177 Roger Nordstrom .16 .40
178 Johan Mansson .04 .10
179 Timo Blomqvist .16 .40
180 Peter Andersson .10 .25
181 Mats Lusth .04 .10
182 Roger Ohman .04 .10
183 Johan Salle .04 .10
184 Anders Svensson .04 .10
185 Johan Norgren .04 .10
186 Raimo Helminen .16 .40
187 Mats Hallin .10 .25
188 Mats Naslund .40 1.00
189 Robert Burakovsky .10 .25
190 Hakan Ahlund .04 .10
191 Peter Sundstrom .16 .40
192 Daniel Rydmark .08 .20
193 Matti Pauna .04 .10
194 Roger Hansson .04 .10
195 Patrik Gustavsson .04 .10
196 Rick Erdall .04 .10
197 Bo Svanberg .04 .10
198 Jesper Mattsson .20 .50
199 Jonas Hakansson .04 .10
200 MoDo .04 .10
Team Emblem
201 Fredrik Andersson .10 .25
202 Goran Armark .10 .25
203 Miroslav Horava .10 .25
204 Hans Lodin .04 .10
205 Lars Jansson .04 .10
206 Jorgen Eriksson .04 .10
207 Anders Berglund .04 .10
208 Osmo Soutokorva .04 .10
209 Tomas Nanzen .04 .10
210 Hans Jonsson .20 .50
211 Fredrik Bergqvist .04 .10
212 Erik Holmberg .04 .10
213 Peter Forsberg 4.00 10.00
214 Markus Naslund 1.20 3.00
215 Magnus Wernblom .04 .10
216 Lars Bystrom .04 .10
217 Kent Lantz .04 .10
218 Per Wallin .08 .20
219 Lennart Henriksson .04 .10
220 Ingemar Strom .04 .10
221 Ulf Odmark .04 .10
222 Jens Ohman .04 .10
223 Tommy Pettersson .04 .10
224 Andreas Salomonsson .06 .15
225 Sodertalje .04 .10
Team Emblem
226 Reino Sundberg .10 .25
227 Stefan Dernestal .10 .25
228 Mats Kihlstrom .04 .10
229 Stefan Jonsson .04 .10
230 Jan Bergman .04 .10
231 Peter Ekroth .04 .10
232 Stefan Nyman .04 .10
233 Thomas Carlsson .04 .10
234 Stefan Claesson .04 .10
235 Oto Hascak .08 .20
236 Morgan Samuelsson .04 .10
237 Tomaz Eriksson .04 .10
238 Thom Eklund .04 .10
239 Conny Jansson .04 .10
240 Bjorn Carlsson .04 .10
241 Scott Moore .04 .10
242 Reine Landgren .04 .10
243 Ola Rosander .04 .10
244 Stefan Olsson .04 .10
245 Anders Frykbo .04 .10
246 Ola Andersson .04 .10
247 Joe Tracy .04 .10
248 Christer Ljungberg .04 .10
249 Patrik Nyberg .04 .10
250 Joakim Skold .04 .10
251 Vasteras .04 .10
Team Emblem
252 Mats Ytter .10 .25
253 Par Hellenberg .10 .25
254 Tommy Salo 1.60 4.00
255 Nicklas Lidstrom 1.60 4.00
256 Robert Nordmark .10 .25
257 Leif Rohlin .16 .40
258 Roger Akerstrom .06 .15
259 Peter Popovic .10 .25
260 Jan Karlsson .04 .10
261 Tore Lindgren .04 .10
262 Peter Jacobsson .04 .10
263 Pierre Ivarsson .04 .10
264 Misjat Fachrutdinov .04 .10
265 Paul Andersson .04 .10
266 Patrik Juhlin .20 .50
267 Henrik Nilsson .04 .10
268 Anders Berglund .04 .10
269 Claes Lindblom .04 .10
270 Jorgen Holmberg .04 .10
271 Stefan Hellkvist .04 .10
272 Fredrik Nilsson .10 .25
273 Johan Brummer .04 .10
274 Micael Karlberg .04 .10
275 Niclas Lundberg .04 .10
276 Vastra Frolunda .04 .10
Team Emblem
277 Ake Lilljebjorn .10 .25
278 Hakan Algotsson .16 .40
279 Hakan Nordin .04 .10
280 Jonas Heed .04 .10
281 Joacim Esbjors .06 .15
282 Stefan Larsson .04 .10
283 Stefan Axelsson .10 .25
284 Oscar Ackestrom .04 .10
285 Jerk Hogstrom .04 .10
286 Patric Aberg .04 .10
287 Patrik Carnback .10 .25
288 Serge Boisvert .10 .25
289 Mats Lundstrom .04 .10
290 Mikael Andersson .20 .50
291 Kari Jaako .04 .10
292 Terho Koskela .04 .10
293 Lars Dahlstrom .04 .10
294 Jerry Persson .04 .10
295 Peter Berndtsson .04 .10
296 Thomas Sjogren .06 .15
297 Par Edlund .04 .10
298 Christian Lechtaler .04 .10
299 Jonas Esbjors .06 .15
300 Dennis Fredriksson .04 .10
301 Mats Hjalmarsson .04 .10
302 Leif Holmgren CO .04 .10
303 Tommy Sandlin CO .04 .10
304 Lars Falk CO .04 .10
305 Harald Luckner CO .04 .10
306 Lars-Erik Lundstrom CO .04 .10
307 Staffan Tholson CO .04 .10
308 Freddy Lindfors CO .04 .10
309 Timo Lahtinen CO .04 .10
310 Jan-Ake Andersson CO .04 .10
311 Claes-Goran Wallin CO .04 .10
312 Mikael Lundstrom CO .04 .10
313 Leif Boork CO .04 .10
314 Thomas Rundqvist .10 .25
315 Hakan Loob .40 1.00
316 Tommy Soderstrom .30 .75
317 Niklas Andersson .10 .25
318 Hakan Loob .40 1.00
319 Tomas Sandstrom .20 .50
320 Rolf Ridderwall .10 .25
321 Thomas Eriksson .04 .10
322 Nicklas Lidstrom 1.60 4.00
323 Mats Sundin 1.60 4.00
324 Thomas Rundqvist .10 .25
325 Hakan Loob .40 1.00
326 Marcus Karlsson .04 .10
327 Anders Eriksson .04 .10
328 Mats Lindgren .20 .50
329 Mikael Hakansson .10 .25
330 Mathias Johansson .04 .10
331 Niclas Sundstrom .40 1.00
332 Jesper Mattsson .20 .50
333 Anders Soderberg .20 .50
334 Swedish IHF Emblem .04 .10
335 1991 World Champions .04 .10
336 Rolf Ridderwall .10 .25
337 Peter Lindmark .16 .40
338 Tommy Soderstrom .30 .75
339 Kjell Samuelsson .10 .25
340 Calle Johansson .20 .50
341 Nicklas Lidstrom 1.60 4.00
342 Tomas Jonsson .10 .25
343 Peter Andersson .10 .25
344 Kenneth Kennholt .06 .15
345 Fredrik Stillman .08 .20
346 Thomas Rundqvist .10 .25
347 Hakan Loob .40 1.00
348 Bengt-Ake Gustafsson .10 .25
349 Mats Naslund .40 1.00
350 Mikael Johansson .04 .10
351 Charles Berglund .06 .15
352 Jan Viktorsson .06 .15
353 Johan Garpenlov .04 .10
354 Anders Carlsson .04 .10
355 Patrik Ericksson .06 .15
356 Jonas Bergqvist .08 .20
357 Mats Sundin 1.60 4.00
358 Per-Erik Eklund .04 .10
359 Conny Evensson .04 .10
360 Curt Lundmark .04 .10

1991 Swedish Semic World Championship Stickers

These hockey stickers, which measure approximately 2 1/8" by 2 7/8", were sold five to a packet. Also an album was available to display all 250 stickers. The fronts display color posed player shots framed by a red inner border studded with yellow miniature stars and a white outer border. The team flag, the player's name, and the sticker number appear in the white border below the picture. The backs were different based on distribution; blank backs were sold in Czechoslovakia; Marabou Chocolate ads were on the backs of cards sold in Finlands and Milky Way ads were on the back of cards sold in Sweden. The stickers are grouped according to country. Teemu Selanne appears in his Rookie Card year.

COMPLETE SET (250) 50.00 125.00
1 Finnish Emblem .04 .10
2 Markus Ketterer .20 .50
3 Sakari Lindfors .10 .25
4 Jukka Tammi .10 .25
5 Timo Jutila .06 .15
6 Hannu Virta .06 .15
7 Simo Saarinen .04 .10
8 Jukka Marttila .04 .10
9 Ville Siren .06 .15
10 Pasi Huura .06 .15
11 Hannu Henriksson .04 .10
12 Arto Ruotanen .04 .10
13 Ari Haanpaa .04 .10
14 Pauli Jarvinen .04 .10
15 Teppo Kivela .04 .10
16 Risto Kurkinen .04 .10
17 Mika Nieminen .06 .15
18 Jari Kurri .40 1.00
19 Esa Keskinen .10 .25
20 Raimo Summanen .04 .10
21 Teemu Selanne 3.00 8.00
22 Jari Torkki .04 .10
23 Hannu Jarvenpaa .06 .15
24 Raimo Helminen .06 .15
25 Timo Peltomaa .06 .15
26 Swedish Emblem .04 .10
27 Peter Lindmark .10 .25
28 Rolf Ridderwall .06 .15
29 Tommy Soderstrom .20 .50
30 Thomas Eriksson .06 .15
31 Nicklas Lidstrom 2.00 5.00
32 Tomas Jonsson .06 .15
33 Tommy Samuelsson .04 .10
34 Fredrik Stillman .06 .15
35 Peter Andersson .06 .15
36 Peter Andersson .06 .15
37 Kenneth Kennholt .06 .15
38 Hakan Loob .10 .25
39 Thomas Rundqvist .06 .15
40 Hakan Ahlund .04 .10
41 Jan Viktorsson .04 .10
42 Charles Berglund .06 .15
43 Mikael Johansson .04 .10
44 Robert Burakovsky .04 .10
45 Bengt-Ake Gustafsson .06 .15
46 Patrik Carnback .04 .10
47 Patrik Erickson .04 .10
48 Anders Carlsson .04 .10
49 Mats Naslund .16 .40
50 Kent Nilsson .16 .40
51 Canadian Emblem .40 1.00
52 Patrick Roy 6.00 15.00
53 Ed Belfour .75 2.00
54 Daniel Berthiaume .06 .15
55 Ray Bourque 2.00 5.00
56 Scott Stevens .30 .75
57 Al MacInnis .60 1.50
58 Paul Coffey .75 2.00
59 Paul Cavallini .06 .15
60 Zarley Zalapski .06 .15
61 Steve Duchesne .06 .15
62 Dave Ellett .06 .15
63 Mark Messier 1.50 4.00
64 Wayne Gretzky 10.00 25.00
65 Steve Yzerman 6.00 15.00
66 Pierre Turgeon .60 1.50
67 Bernie Nicholls .20 .50
68 Cam Neely 1.50 4.00
69 Joe Nieuwendyk .30 .75
70 Luc Robitaille .60 1.50
71 Kevin Dineen .06 .15
72 John Cullen .06 .15
73 Steve Larmer .08 .20
74 Mark Recchi .60 1.50
75 Joe Sakic 2.00 5.00
76 Soviet Emblem .20 .50
77 Arturs Irbe .40 1.00
78 Alexei Marin .04 .10
79 Mikhail Shtalenkov .10 .25
80 Vladimir Malakhov .10 .25
81 Vladimir Konstantinov .40 1.00
82 Igor Kravchuk .06 .15
83 Ilya Byakin .06 .15
84 Dimitri Mironov .08 .20
85 Vladimir Turikov .04 .10
86 Vjatjeslav Uvajev .04 .10
87 Vladimir Fedosov .04 .10
88 Valeri Kamensky .20 .50
89 Pavel Bure 1.50 4.00
90 Vyacheslav Butsayev .06 .15
91 Igor Maslennikov .04 .10
92 Evgeny Davydov .06 .15
93 Andrei Kovalev .06 .15
94 Alexander Semak .06 .15
95 Alexei Zhamnov .16 .40
96 Sergei Nemchinov .06 .15
97 Viktor Gordijuk .04 .10
98 Vyacheslav Kozlov .30 .75
99 Andrei Khomotov .20 .50
100 Vyacheslav Bykov .16 .40
101 Czech Emblem .04 .10
102 Petr Briza .10 .25
103 Dominik Hasek 2.00 5.00
104 Eduard Hartmann .06 .15
105 Bedrich Scerban .06 .15
106 Jiri Slegr .08 .20
107 Josef Reznicek .04 .10
108 Petr Pavlas .04 .10
109 Peter Slanina .04 .10
110 Martin Maskarinec .04 .10
111 Antonin Stavjana .06 .15
112 Stanislav Medrik .04 .10
113 Dusan Pasek .08 .20
114 Jiri Lala .06 .15
115 Darius Rusnak .04 .10
116 Oto Hascak .06 .15
117 Radek Toupal .06 .15
118 Pavel Pycha .04 .10
119 Lubomir Kolnik .04 .10
120 Libor Dolana .04 .10
121 Ladislav Lubina .06 .15
122 Tomas Jelinek .04 .10
123 Petr Vlk .04 .10
124 Vladimir Petrovka .04 .10
125 Richard Zemlicka .06 .15
126 U.S.A. Emblem .20 .50
127 John Vanbiesbrouck .75 2.00
128 Mike Richter .75 2.00
129 Chris Terreri .10 .25
130 Chris Chelios .75 2.00
131 Brian Leetch .40 1.00
132 Gary Suter .08 .20
133 Phil Housley .10 .25
134 Mark Howe .06 .15
135 Al Iafrate .10 .25
136 Kevin Hatcher .10 .25
137 Mathieu Schneider .10 .25
138 Pat LaFontaine .30 .75
139 Darren Turcotte .06 .15
140 Neal Broten .08 .20
141 Mike Modano 1.50 4.00
142 Dave Christian .06 .15
143 Craig Janney .16 .40
144 Brett Hull 1.50 4.00
145 Kevin Stevens .16 .40
146 Joe Mullen .10 .25
147 Tony Granato .08 .20
148 Ed Olczyk .06 .15
149 Jeremy Roenick 1.50 4.00
150 Jimmy Carson .06 .15
151 West German Emblem .04 .10
152 Helmut De Raaf .04 .10
153 Josef Heiss .08 .20
154 Karl Friesen .08 .20
155 Uli Hiemer .06 .15
156 Harold Kreis .04 .10
157 Udo Kiessling .06 .15
158 Michael Schmidt .04 .10
159 Michael Heidt .06 .15
160 Andreas Pokorny .04 .10
161 Bernd Wagner .04 .10
162 Uwe Krupp .10 .25
163 Gerd Truntschka .06 .15
164 Bernd Truntschka .06 .15
165 Thomas Brandl .04 .10
166 Peter Draisaitl .04 .10
167 Andreas Brockmann .04 .10
168 Ulrich Liebsch .04 .10
169 Ralf Hantschke .04 .10
170 Thomas Schinko .04 .10
171 Anton Krinner .04 .10
172 Thomas Werner .04 .10
173 Dieter Hegen .06 .15
174 Helmut Steiger .04 .10
175 Georg Franz .04 .10
176 Swiss Emblem .04 .10
177 Renato Tosio .04 .10
178 Reto Pavoni .06 .15
179 Dino Stecher .04 .10
180 Sven Leuenberger .04 .10
181 Rick Tschumi .04 .10
182 Patrice Brasey .04 .10
183 Didier Massy .04 .10
184 Sandro Bertaggia .04 .10
185 Samuel Balmer .04 .10
186 Martin Rauch .04 .10
187 Marc Leuenberger .04 .10
188 Jorg Eberle .04 .10
189 Fredy Luthi .04 .10
190 Andy Ton .04 .10
191 Raymond Walder .04 .10
192 Manuele Celio .04 .10
193 Roman Wager .04 .10
194 Felix Hollenstein .04 .10
195 Andre Rotheli .04 .10
196 Christian Weber .04 .10
197 Peter Jaks .04 .10
198 Gil Montandon .04 .10
199 Oliver Hoffmann .04 .10
200 Thomas Vrabec .04 .10
201 Teppo Numminen .08 .20
202 Jyrki Lumme .06 .15
203 Esa Tikkanen .16 .40
204 Petri Skriko .06 .15
205 Christian Ruutu .08 .20
206 Ilkka Sinisalo .08 .20
207 Calle Johansson .08 .20
208 Tomas Sandstrom .08 .20
209 Thomas Steen .08 .20
210 Per-Erik Eklund .08 .20
211 Mats Sundin .60 1.50
212 Johan Garpenlov .08 .20
213 Slava Fetisov .40 1.00
214 Alexei Kasatonov .16 .40
215 Mikhail Tatarinov .04 .10
216 Sergei Makarov .20 .50
217 Igor Larionov .40 1.00
218 Alexander Mogilny .60 1.50
219 Sergei Fedorov 1.50 4.00
220 Petr Klima .06 .15
221 David Volek .08 .20
222 Michal Pivonka .10 .25
223 Robert Reichel .10 .25
224 Robert Holik .20 .50
225 Jaromir Jagr 3.00 5.00
226 Urpo Ylonen .04 .10
227 Ilpo Koskela .04 .10
228 Pekka Rautakallio .08 .20
229 Lasse Oksanen .04 .10
230 Veli-Pekka Ketola .08 .20
231 Leif Holmqvist .06 .15
232 Lennart Svedberg .04 .10
233 Sven Tumba Johansson .04 .10
234 Ulf Sterner .04 .10
235 Anders Hedberg .10 .25
236 Ken Dryden 2.00 5.00
237 Bobby Orr 6.00 15.00
238 Gordie Howe 2.00 5.00
239 Bobby Hull 1.25 3.00
240 Phil Esposito 1.50 4.00
241 Vladislav Tretiak 1.50 4.00
242 Alexander Ragulin .10 .25
243 Anatoli Firsov .10 .25
244 Valeri Kharlamov .40 1.00
245 Alexander Maltsev .20 .50
246 Jiri Holecek .08 .20
247 Jan Suchy .04 .10
248 Jozef Golonka .04 .10
249 Vaclav Nedomansky .08 .20
250 Ivan Hlinka .08 .20

1992-93 Swedish Semic Elitserien Stickers

Börje Salming

This 356-sticker set covers the Swedish Elitserien. The stickers, which measure 3" by 2 1/8", feature posed color photos and player name on the front. The back has card number, and a cartoon ad for Buster, a sports magazine for Swedish boys. The set is highlighted by the pre-NHL appearances of Peter Forsberg, Mikael Renberg and Tommy Salo, as well as former greats such as Borje Salming and Hakan Loob.

COMPLETE SET (356) 30.00 75.00
1 AIK Team Picture .04 .10
2 AIK Team Picture .04 .10
3 Brynas Team Picture .04 .10
4 Brynas Team Picture .04 .10
5 Djurgarden Team Picture .04 .10
6 Djurgarden Team Picture .04 .10
7 Farjestad Team Picture .04 .10
8 Farjestad Team Picture .04 .10
9 HV 71 Team Picture .04 .10
10 HV 71 Team Picture .04 .10
11 Leksand Team Picture .04 .10
12 Leksand Team Picture .04 .10
13 Lulea Team Picture .04 .10
14 Lulea Team Picture .04 .10
15 Malmo Team Picture .04 .10
16 Malmo Team Picture .04 .10
17 MoDo Team Picture .04 .10
18 MoDo Team Picture .04 .10
19 Rogle Team Picture .04 .10
20 Rogle Team Picture .04 .10
21 Vasteras Team Picture .04 .10
22 Vasteras Team Picture .04 .10
23 Vastra Frolunda Team .04 .10
24 Vastra Frolunda Team .04 .10
25 AIK Team Emblem .04 .10
26 Rolf Ridderwall .10 .25
27 Sam Lindstahl .08 .20
28 Ronnie Karlsson .04 .10
29 Mats Thelin .10 .25
30 Mattias Norstrom .30 .75
31 Dick Tarnstrom .10 .25
32 Petri Liimatainen .04 .10
33 Rikard Franzen .06 .15
34 Daniel Jardemyr .04 .10
35 Niclas Havelid .40 1.00
36 Borje Salming .80 2.00
37 Thomas Bjuhr .04 .10
38 Peter Hammarstrom .04 .10
39 Thomas Strandberg .04 .10
40 Mats Lindberg .04 .10
41 Anders Bjork .04 .10
42 Anders Johnson .04 .10
43 Patrik Erickson .06 .15
44 Torbjorn Ohrlund .04 .10
45 Bjorn Ahlstrom .04 .10
46 Niclas Sundblad .06 .15
47 Patric Englund .04 .10
48 Kristian Gahn .04 .10
49 Morgan Samuelsson .06 .15
50 Brynas Team Emblem .04 .10
51 Michael Sundlov .20 .50
52 Lars Karlsson .10 .25
53 Bedrich Scerban .06 .15
54 Mikael Lindman .04 .10
55 Tommy Melkersson .04 .10
56 Stefan Klockare .06 .15
57 Mikael Enander .04 .10
58 Roger Karlsson .04 .10
59 Niklas Gallstedt .04 .10
60 Christer Olsson .20 .50
61 Anders Carlsson .04 .10
62 Thomas Tallberg .06 .15
63 Tom Bissett .06 .15
64 Andreas Dackell .40 1.00
65 Mikael Wahlberg .04 .10
66 Jan Larsson .04 .10
67 Anders Gozzi .04 .10
68 Ove Molin .04 .10
69 Anders Huss .06 .15
70 Peter Gustafsson .04 .10
71 Jonas Johnsson .04 .10
72 Peter Larsson .04 .10
73 Mikael Lindholm .04 .10
74 Djurgarden Team Emblem .04 .10
75 Thomas Ostlund .20 .50
76 Petter Ronnquist .08 .20
77 Christian Due-Boje .06 .15
78 Arto Blomsten .06 .15
79 Kenneth Kennholt .08 .20
80 Marcus Ragnarsson .20 .50
81 Thomas Johansson .04 .10
82 Joakim Lundberg .04 .10
83 Thomas Eriksson .04 .10
84 Bjorn Nord .10 .25
85 Mikael Magnusson .04 .10
86 Charles Berglund .04 .10
87 Erik Huusko .06 .15
88 Anders Huusko .04 .10
89 Tony Skopac .04 .10
90 Jens Ohling .08 .20
91 Peter Nilsson .04 .10
92 Magnus Jansson .04 .10
93 Kent Nilsson .30 .75
94 Mikael Hakansson .04 .10
95 Ola Josefsson .04 .10
96 Jerry Friman .04 .10
97 Fredrik Lindquist .16 .40
98 Mathias Hallback .04 .10
99 Jan Viktorsson .04 .10
100 Farjestad .04 .10
Team Emblem
101 Anders Bergman .10 .25
102 Jonas Eriksson .08 .20
103 Patrik Haltia .20 .50
104 Tommy Samuelsson .04 .10
105 Jesper Duus .04 .10
106 Leif Carlsson .04 .10
107 Per Lundell .04 .10
108 Jacob Karlsson .04 .10
109 Thomas Rhodin .04 .10
110 Mattias Olsson .04 .10
111 Hakan Loob .40 1.00
112 Thomas Rundqvist .04 .10
113 Andreas Johansson .20 .50
114 Staffan Lundh .04 .10
115 Jonas Hoglund .40 1.00
116 Bengt-Ake Gustafsson .16 .40
117 Mattias Johansson .04 .10
118 Clas Eriksson .04 .10
119 Peter Ottosson .04 .10
120 Niklas Brannstrom .04 .10
121 Lars Karlsson .10 .25
122 Peter Hagstrom .04 .10
123 Kjell Dahlin .16 .40
124 HV 71 .04 .10
Team Emblem
125 Peter Aslin .10 .25
126 Boo Ahl .20 .50
127 Antonin Stavjana .08 .20
128 Klas Heed .04 .10
129 Tommy Fritz .04 .10
130 Kristian Pedersen .04 .10
131 Per Gustafsson .20 .50
132 Mathias Svedberg .04 .10
133 Niclas Rahm .04 .10
134 Martin Danielsson .04 .10
135 Fredrik Stillman .04 .10
136 Lars Ivarsson .04 .10
137 Ove Thornberg .04 .10
138 Peter Ekelund .04 .10
139 Eddy Eriksson .04 .10
140 Stefan Ornskog .08 .20
141 Patrik Ross .04 .10
142 Torbjorn Persson .04 .10
143 Kamil Kastak .08 .20
144 Dennis Strom .04 .10
145 Peter Eriksson .04 .10
146 Magnus Axelsson .08 .20
147 Stefan Falk .08 .20
148 Thomas Ljungberg .04 .10
149 Leksand .04 .10
Team Emblem
150 Ake Lilljebjorn .10 .25
151 Jonas Leven .10 .25
152 Johan Hedberg 1.25 3.00
153 Tomas Jonsson .16 .40
154 Henric Bjorkman .04 .10
155 Mattias Andersson .04 .10
156 Rickard Persson .10 .25
157 Orjan Nilsson .04 .10
158 Magnus Svensson .10 .25
159 Orjan Lindmark .04 .10
160 Jan Huokko .04 .10
161 Reine Rauhala .04 .10
162 Emil Skoglund .04 .10
163 Jens Nielsen .04 .10
164 Marcus Thuresson .04 .10
165 Niklas Eriksson .04 .10
166 Tomas Srsen .06 .15
167 Jonas Bergqvist .10 .25
168 Per-Olof Carlsson .04 .10
169 Markus Akerblom .04 .10
170 Greg Parks .06 .15
171 Mattias Loof .04 .10
172 Cenneth Soderlund .04 .10
173 Jarmo Makitalo .04 .10
174 Lulea .04 .10
Team Emblem
175 Robert Skoog .08 .20
176 Erik Grankvist .08 .20
177 Lars Modig .04 .10
178 Patrik Hoglund .04 .10
179 Niklas Bjornfot .04 .10
180 Torbjorn Lindberg .04 .10
181 Ville Siren .10 .25
182 Petter Nilsson .04 .10
183 Joakim Gunler .04 .10
184 Tomas Lilja .04 .10
185 Stefan Jonsson .04 .10
186 Stefan Nilsson .08 .20
187 Johan Stromvall .04 .10
188 Robert Nordberg .06 .15
189 Tomas Berglund .06 .15
190 Mikael Renberg .80 2.00
191 Lars-Gunnar Pettersson .04 .10
192 Lars Edstrom .04 .10
193 Kyosti Karjalainen .08 .20
194 Lars Hurtig .04 .10
195 Fredrik Oberg .04 .10
196 Mikael Engstrom .04 .10
197 Mika Nieminen .20 .50
198 Malmo .04 .10
Team Emblem
199 Peter Lindmark .20 .50
200 Roger Nordstrom .10 .25
201 Johan Mansson .04 .10
202 Anders Svensson .04 .10
203 Timo Blomqvist .10 .25
204 Johan Norgren .04 .10
205 Mats Lusth .04 .10
206 Peter Hasselblad .04 .10
207 Robert Svehla .20 .50
208 Johan Salle .04 .10
209 Roger Ohman .04 .10
210 Raimo Helminen .20 .50
211 Roger Hansson .08 .20
212 Per Rosenqvist .04 .10
213 Bo Svanberg .04 .10
214 Daniel Rydmark .08 .20
215 Patrik Sylvegard .04 .10
216 Jonas Hakansson .04 .10
217 Jesper Mattsson .20 .50
218 Hakan Ahlund .04 .10
219 Peter Sundstrom .16 .40
220 Mats Naslund .80 2.00
221 Robert Burakovsky .06 .15
222 MoDo .04 .10
Team Emblem
223 Fredrik Andersson .08 .20
224 Anders Nasstrom .08 .20
225 Anders Berglund .04 .10
226 Miroslav Horava .06 .15
227 Hans Lodin .04 .10
228 Lars Jansson .04 .10
229 Jorgen Eriksson .04 .10
230 Anders Eriksson .40 1.00
231 Hans Jonsson .04 .10
232 Tomas Nanzen .04 .10
233 Mattias Timander .20 .50
234 Fredrik Bergqvist .04 .10
235 Magnus Wernblom .08 .20
236 Martin Hostak .06 .15
237 Mikael Pettersson .04 .10
238 Lennart Hermansson .04 .10
239 Tommy Lehmann .08 .20
240 Markus Naslund .40 1.00
241 Ulf Odmark .04 .10
242 Peter Forsberg 6.00 15.00
243 Andreas Salomonsson .04 .10
244 Niklas Sundstrom .40 1.00
245 Lars Bystrom .04 .10
246 Erik Holmberg .04 .10
247 Henrik Gradin .04 .10
248 Rogle .04 .10
Team Emblem
249 Kenneth Johansson .10 .25
250 Billy Nilsson .10 .25
251 Orjan Jacobsson .04 .10
252 Daniel Johansson .20 .50
253 Kenny Jonsson .60 1.50
254 Kari Eloranta .10 .25
255 Kari Suoraniemi .04 .10
256 Hakan Persson .04 .10
257 Rikard Gronborg .04 .10
258 Stefan Nilsson .04 .10
259 Per Ljusterang .04 .10
260 Igor Stelnov .04 .10
261 Peter Lundmark .10 .25
262 Heinz Ehlers .04 .10
263 Michael Hjalm .04 .10
264 Jan Ericson .04 .10
265 Pelle Svensson .04 .10
266 Mats Loov .06 .15
267 Stefan Elvenes .06 .15
268 Roger Elvenes .08 .20
269 Peter Wennberg .04 .10
270 Per Wallin .10 .25
271 Torgny Lowgren .04 .10
272 Jorgen Jonsson .04 .10
273 Vasteras .04 .10
Team Emblem
274 Mats Ytter .10 .25
275 Tommy Salo .75 2.00
276 Erik Bergstrom .04 .10
277 Pierre Ivarsson .04 .10
278 Peter Popovic .20 .50
279 Sergei Fokin .04 .10
280 Edvin Frylen .10 .25
281 Leif Rohlin .16 .40
282 Peter Karlsson .04 .10
283 Peter Jacobsson .04 .10
284 Roger Akerstrom .06 .15
285 Robert Nordmark .08 .20
286 Patrik Juhlin .20 .50
287 Mishat Fahrutdinov .06 .15
288 Henrik Nilsson .04 .10
289 Mikael Pettersson .04 .10
290 Fredrik Nilsson .06 .15
291 Stefan Hellkvist .04 .10
292 Henrik Pettersson .04 .10
293 Micael Karlberg .04 .10
294 Anders Berglund .04 .10
295 Claes Lindblom .06 .15
296 Johan Brummer .04 .10
297 Patrik Ulin .04 .10
298 Paul Andersson .04 .10
299 Vastra Frolunda .04 .10
Team Emblem
300 Hakan Algotsson .20 .50
301 Mikael Sandberg .10 .25
302 Patric Aberg .04 .10
303 Joacim Esbjors .06 .15
304 Oscar Ackestrom .04 .10
305 Jonas Heed .04 .10
306 Stefan Axelsson .10 .25
307 Ronnie Sundin .20 .50
308 Stefan Larsson .04 .10
309 Jonathan Hagrenius .04 .10
310 Serge Boisvert .06 .15
311 Jerry Persson .04 .10
312 Trond Magnussen .04 .10
313 Terho Koskela .04 .10
314 Peter Berndtsson .04 .10
315 Mikael Persson .04 .10
316 Mats Hjalmarsson .04 .10
317 Henrik Lundin .04 .10
318 Jonas Esbjors .04 .10
319 Daniel Alfredsson 1.00 2.50
320 Stefan Ketola .04 .10
321 Lars Dahlstrom .04 .10
322 Par Edlund .04 .10
323 Thomas Sjogren .06 .15
324 Leif Holmgren CO .04 .10
325 Tommy Sandlin CO .04 .10
326 Lars Falk CO .04 .10
327 Harald Luckner CO .04 .10
328 Lars-Erik Lundstrom CO .04 .10
329 Wayne Fleming CO .04 .10
330 Freddy Lindfors CO .04 .10
331 Timo Lahtinen CO .04 .10
332 Kent Forsberg CO .10 .25
333 Christer Abrahamsson CO .10 .25
334 Mikael Lundstrom CO .04 .10
335 Leif Boork CO .04 .10
336 Tommy Sjodin .10 .25
337 Hakan Loob .40 1.00
338 Michael Nylander .40 1.00
339 Michael Nylander .40 1.00
340 Hakan Loob .40 1.00
341 Calle Johansson .20 .50
342 Tommy Sandlin CO .04 .10
343 Tommy Soderstrom .40 1.00
344 Tommy Sjodin .10 .25
345 Peter Andersson .06 .15
346 Hakan Loob .40 1.00
347 Peter Forsberg 6.00 15.00
348 Mats Sundin 2.00 5.00
349 Jonas Forsberg .20 .50
350 Stefan Bjork .06 .15
351 Edvin Frylen .10 .25
352 Mikael Tjallden .06 .15
353 Johan Davidsson .20 .50
354 Markus Eriksson .06 .15
355 Fredrik Lindh .06 .15
356 Peter Nylander .06 .15

1993-94 Swedish Semic Elitserien

This 320-sticker set was the collectible to own for fans of the Elitserien. This comprehensive issue had a posed player photo and name on the front, with card number and a cartoon ad for the whimsical boy's sports magazine, "Buster" on the back.

COMPLETE SET (320) 24.00 60.00
1 Bjorkloven Team Emblem .04 .10
2 Patrik Hofbauer .04 .10
3 Jorgen Wikstrom .04 .10
4 Mattias Hedlund .04 .10
5 Yuri Kuznetsov .08 .20
6 Ulf Odling .04 .10
7 Jorgen Eriksson .04 .10
8 Jorgen Hermansson .04 .10
9 Peter Andersson .04 .10
10 Joakim Lindgren .04 .10
11 Glenn Hedman .04 .10
12 Roger Kyro .04 .10
13 Niklas Norberg .04 .10
14 Alexander Belyavsky .06 .15
15 Anders Nejdsater .04 .10
16 Stefan Olofsson .04 .10
17 Mikael Andersson .10 .25
18 Ulf Andersson .04 .10
19 Patrik Sundstrom .10 .25
20 Hakan Hermansson .04 .10
21 Micael Karlberg .04 .10
22 Peder Bejegard .04 .10
23 Johan Boman .04 .10
24 Joakim Lindgren .04 .10
25 Brynas Team Emblem .04 .10
26 Michael Sundlov .08 .20
27 Lars Karlsson .08 .20
28 Bedrich Scerban .20 .50
29 Mikael Lindman .04 .10
30 Johan Tornberg .04 .10
31 Tommy Melkersson .04 .10
32 Stefan Klockare .06 .15
33 Mikael Enander .04 .10
34 Mikael Wiklander .04 .10
35 Christer Olsson .10 .25
36 Thomas Tallberg .06 .15
37 Andreas Dackell .40 1.00
38 Mikael Wahlberg .04 .10
39 Anders Gozzi .04 .10
40 Niklas Gallstedt .04 .10
41 Per-Johan Johansson .04 .10
42 Joakim Persson .10 .25
43 Branislav Janos .04 .10
44 Ove Molin .04 .10
45 Anders Huss .04 .10
46 Jonas Johnsson .04 .10
47 Peter Larsson .04 .10
48 Anders Carlsson .04 .10
49 Djurgarden Team Emblem .04 .10
50 Thomas Ostlund .10 .25
51 Petter Ronnquist .06 .15
52 Christian Due-Boje .06 .15
53 Marcus Ragnarsson .20 .50
54 Joakim Musakka .04 .10
55 Thomas Johansson .04 .10
56 Thomas Eriksson .04 .10
57 Bjorn Nord .10 .25
58 Mikael Magnusson .04 .10
59 Robert Nordmark .06 .15
60 Charles Berglund .04 .10
61 Erik Huusko .06 .15
62 Anders Huusko .04 .10
63 Jens Ohling .06 .15
64 Peter Nilsson .04 .10
65 Magnus Jansson .04 .10
66 Mikael Hakansson .04 .10
67 Ola Josefsson .04 .10
68 Jerry Friman .04 .10
69 Mariusz Czerkawski .40 1.00
70 Fredrik Lindquist .08 .20
71 Mattias Hallback .04 .10
72 Patrik Erickson .04 .10
73 Farjestad Team Emblem .04 .10
74 Anders Bergman .10 .25
75 Jonas Eriksson .08 .20
76 Tommy Samuelsson .04 .10
77 Jesper Duus .04 .10
78 Leif Carlsson .04 .10
79 Per Lundell .04 .10
80 Brian Tutt .06 .15
81 Jacob Karlsson .04 .10
82 Thomas Rhodin .04 .10
83 Mattias Olsson .04 .10
84 Hakan Loob .30 .75
85 Andreas Johansson .20 .50
86 Magnus Arvedsson .40 1.00
87 Anders Oberg .04 .10
88 Mattias Johansson .04 .10
89 Mats Lindgren .20 .50
90 Clas Eriksson .04 .10
91 Patrik Degerstedt .04 .10
92 Peter Ottosson .04 .10
93 Niklas Brannstrom .04 .10
94 Lars Karlsson .08 .20
95 Kjell Dahlin .10 .25
96 Jonas Hoglund .40 1.00
97 HV 71 Team Emblem .04 .10
98 Peter Aslin .10 .25
99 Boo Ahl .10 .25
100 Antonin Stavjana .08 .20
101 Kenneth Kennholt .06 .15
102 Hans Abrahamsson .04 .10
103 Andreas Schultz .04 .10
104 Per Gustafsson .10 .25
105 Mathias Svedberg .04 .10
106 Niklas Rahm .04 .10
107 Fredrik Stillman .04 .10
108 Owe Thornberg .04 .10
109 Thomas Gustavsson .04 .10
110 Stefan Ornskog .06 .15
111 Peter Hammarstrom .04 .10
112 Torbjorn Persson .04 .10
113 John Byce .06 .15
114 Peter Eriksson .04 .10
115 Magnus Axelsson .06 .15
116 Stefan Falk .06 .15
117 Patric Kjellberg .08 .20
118 Johan Davidsson .20 .50
119 Thomas Ljungberg .04 .10
120 Patrik Ross .04 .10
121 Leksand Team Emblem .04 .10
122 Johan Hedberg .75 2.00
123 Ake Lilljebjorn .06 .15
124 Tomas Jonsson .10 .25
125 Stefan Bergkvist .06 .15
126 Henric Bjorkman .04 .10
127 Hans Lodin .04 .10
128 Magnus Svensson .06 .15
129 Orjan Lindmark .04 .10
130 Jan Huokko .04 .10
131 Roger Johansson .04 .10
132 Per Widmark .04 .10
133 Marcus Thuresson .04 .10
134 Niklas Eriksson .04 .10
135 Peter Ciavaglia .06 .15
136 Jonas Bergkvist .10 .25
137 Martin Wiita .04 .10
138 Markus Akerblom .04 .10
139 Greg Parks .06 .15
140 Mattias Loof .04 .10
141 Andreas Karlsson .04 .10
142 Markus Eriksson .04 .10
143 Tomas Forslund .10 .25
144 Jarmo Makitalo .04 .10
145 Lulea Team Emblem .04 .10
146 Robert Skoog .06 .15
147 Erik Grankvist .08 .20
148 Lars Modig .04 .10
149 Patrik Hoglund .04 .10
150 Niklas Bjornfot .04 .10
151 Torbjorn Lindberg .04 .10
152 Ville Siren .08 .20
153 Petter Nilsson .04 .10
154 Tomas Lilja .04 .10
155 Stefan Jonsson .04 .10
156 Stefan Nilsson .04 .10
157 Joakim Gunler .04 .10
158 Johan Stromvall .04 .10
159 Kyosti Karjalainen .08 .20
160 Robert Nordberg .04 .10
161 Tomas Berglund .04 .10
162 Lars-Gunnar Pettersson .04 .10
163 Lars Edstrom .04 .10
164 Lars Hurtig .04 .10
165 Fredrik Oberg .04 .10
166 Mikael Engstrom .04 .10
167 Johan Rosen .04 .10
168 Mika Nieminen .10 .25
169 Malmo Team Emblem .04 .10
170 Peter Lindmark .10 .25
171 Roger Nordstrom .06 .15
172 Daniel Granqvist .06 .15
173 Johan Norgren .04 .10
174 Johan Salle .04 .10
175 Petri Liimatainen .04 .10
176 Peter Hasselblad .04 .10
177 Robert Svehla .10 .25
178 Ricard Persson .10 .25
179 Roger Ohman .04 .10
180 Raimo Helminen .10 .25
181 Marcus Magnertoft .04 .10
182 Mattias Bosson .04 .10
183 Roger Hansson .04 .10
184 Bo Svanberg .04 .10
185 Daniel Rydmark .08 .20
186 Patrik Sylvegard .04 .10
187 Jens Hemstrom .04 .10
188 Jesper Mattsson .10 .25
189 Hakan Ahlund .04 .10
190 Peter Sundstrom .10 .25
191 Mats Naslund .40 1.00
192 Mikko Makela .08 .20
193 MoDo Team Emblem .04 .10
194 Henrik Arvsell .04 .10
195 Fredrik Andersson .06 .15
196 Anders Berglund .04 .10
197 Mattias Timander .10 .25
198 Miroslav Horava .06 .15
199 Lars Jansson .04 .10
200 Anders Eriksson .20 .50
201 Hans Jonsson .20 .50
202 Tomas Nanzen .04 .10
203 Fredrik Bergqvist .04 .10
204 Magnus Wernblom .06 .15
205 Anders Soderberg .10 .25
206 Martin Hostak .06 .15
207 Lennart Hermansson .04 .10
208 Ulf Odmark .04 .10
209 Peter Forsberg 4.00 10.00
210 Per Svartvadet .20 .50
211 Andreas Salomonsson .04 .10
212 Niklas Sundstrom .40 1.00

213 Lars Bystrom .04 .10
214 Mats Lundstrom .04 .10
215 Erik Holmberg .04 .10
216 Henrik Gradin .04 .10
217 Rogle Team Emblem .04 .10
218 Kenneth Johansson .08 .20
219 Magnus Swardh .04 .10
220 Daniel Johansson .10 .25
221 Kari Suoraniemi .04 .10
222 Pierre Johnsson .04 .10
223 Kenny Jonsson .40 1.00
224 Per Ljusterang .04 .10
225 Arto Ruotanen .04 .10
226 Daniel Tjarnquist .10 .25
227 Kari Eloranta .06 .15
228 Per Wallin .10 .25
229 Peter Lundmark .06 .15
230 Roger Elvenes .06 .15
231 Michael Hjalm .04 .10
232 Mattias Olvestedt .04 .10
233 Jan Ericsson .04 .10
234 Tomas Srsen .04 .10
235 Pelle Svensson .04 .10
236 Jorgen Jonsson .04 .10
237 Stefan Elvenes .06 .15
238 Fredrik Moller .04 .10
239 Tord Elvenes .04 .10
240 Mats Loov .04 .10
241 Vasteras Team Emblem .04 .10
242 Mats Ytter .08 .20
243 Tommy Salo .40 1.00
244 Sergei Fokin .04 .10
245 Edvin Frylen .08 .20
246 Leif Rohlin .10 .25
247 Peter Karlsson .04 .10
248 Peter Jacobsson .04 .10
249 Thomas Carlsson .04 .10
250 Lars Ivarsson .04 .10
251 Roger Akerstrom .06 .15
252 Patrik Juhlin .10 .25
253 Alexei Salomatin .06 .15
254 Mishat Fahrutdinov .06 .15
255 Henrik Nilsson .04 .10
256 Mikael Pettersson .04 .10
257 Stefan Hellkvist .04 .10
258 Jens Nielsen .04 .10
259 Hans Huczkowski .04 .10
260 Claes Lindblom .04 .10
261 Johan Brummer .04 .10
262 Dejan Kostic .04 .10
263 Paul Andersson .04 .10
264 Henrik Nordfeldt .04 .10
265 V.Frolunda Team Emblem .04 .10
266 Hakan Algotsson .10 .25
267 Mikael Sandberg .08 .20
268 Stefan Nyman .04 .10
269 Joacim Esbjors .06 .15
270 Oscar Ackestrom .04 .10
271 Vladimir Kramskoy .04 .10
272 Richard Sohrman .04 .10
273 Stefan Axelsson .06 .15
274 Ronnie Sundin .10 .25
275 Stefan Larsson .04 .10
276 Thomas Sjogren .04 .10
277 Serge Boisvert .06 .15
278 Jerry Persson .04 .10
279 Terho Koskela .04 .10
280 Peter Strom .04 .10
281 Peter Berndtsson .04 .10
282 Henrik Lundin .04 .10
283 Jonas Esbjors .04 .10
284 Daniel Alfredsson 1.00 2.50
285 Stefan Ketola .04 .10
286 Lars Dahlstrom .04 .10
287 Par Edlund .04 .10
288 Oto Hascak .06 .15
289 Lars-Gunnar Jansson CO .04 .10
290 Tommy Sandlin CO .04 .10
291 Tommy Boustedt CO .04 .10
292 Jorgen Palm CO .04 .10
293 Hakan Nygren CO .04 .10
294 Wayne Fleming CO .04 .10
295 Sakari Pietila CO .04 .10
296 Timo Lahtinen CO .04 .10
297 Kent Forsberg CO .08 .20
298 Christer Abrahamsson CO .10 .25
299 Mikael Lundstrom CO .04 .10
300 Leif Boork CO .04 .10
301 Peter Forsberg 4.00 10.00
302 Peter Forsberg 4.00 10.00
303 Hakan Loob .30 .75
304 Kenny Jonsson .40 1.00
305 Peter Forsberg 4.00 10.00
306 Mats Sundin 1.50 4.00
307 Micheal Sundlov AS .08 .20
308 Roger Akerstrom AS .06 .15
309 Fredrik Stillman AS .04 .10
310 Mikael Renberg AS .40 1.00
311 Peter Forsberg AS 4.00 10.00
312 Ulf Dahlen AS .10 .25
313 Pal Grotnes FS .08 .20
314 Daniel Tjarnquist FS .10 .25
315 Henrik Rehnberg FS .06 .15
316 Mattias Ohlund FS .40 1.00
317 Jan Labraaten FS .10 .25
318 Patrik Wallenberg FS .08 .20
319 Niklas Wallin FS .08 .20
320 Tobias Thermell FS .08 .20

1993 Swedish Semic World Championships Stickers

This 1993 issue of 288-stickers was issued in Sweden to commemorate the 1993 World Championships. The stickers measure 3" by 2 1/8" and feature players from ten nations, mostly in action shots in their national team garb. The NHL players (#169-208) are shown in the club team sweaters. The backs bear the sticker number, as well as player information in Swedish. An album to hold the stickers is valued at about $10.

COMPLETE SET (288) 24.00 60.00
1 Peter Aslin .10 .25
2 Hakan Algotsson .10 .25
3 Kenneth Kennholt .04 .10
4 Arto Blomsten .06 .15
5 Tomas Jonsson .04 .10
6 Fredrik Stillman .04 .10
7 Stefan Larsson .04 .10
8 Peter Popovic .10 .25
9 Hakan Loob .10 .25
10 Thomas Rundqvist .04 .10
11 Patrik Juhlin .10 .25
12 Mikael Renberg .20 .50
13 Peter Forsberg 2.00 5.00
14 Markus Naslund .60 1.50
15 Bengt-Ake Gustafsson .10 .25
16 Jan Larsson .04 .10
17 Fredrik Nilsson .04 .10
18 Roger Hansson .04 .10
19 Tommy Soderstrom .10 .25
20 Anders Eldebrink .06 .15
21 Ulf Samuelsson .10 .25
22 Kjell Samuelsson .10 .25
23 Nicklas Lidstrom 1.25 3.00
24 Tommy Sjodin .06 .15
25 Calle Johansson .10 .25
26 Fredrik Olausson .10 .25
27 Peter Andersson .06 .15
28 Tommy Albelin .06 .15
29 Roger Johansson .06 .15
30 Par Djoos .06 .15
31 Mikael Johansson .04 .10
32 Tomas Sandstrom .10 .25
33 Mats Sundin .60 1.50
34 Ulf Dahlen .10 .25
35 Jan Erixon .06 .15
36 Thomas Steen .10 .25
37 Mikael Andersson .06 .15
38 Johan Garpenlov .10 .25
39 Per-Erik Eklund .10 .25
40 Michael Nylander .10 .25
41 Tomas Forslund .04 .10
42 Patric Kjellberg .20 .50
43 Patrik Carnback .04 .10
44 Niclas Andersson .04 .10
45 Markus Ketterer .10 .25
46 Sakari Lindfors .10 .25
47 Jarmo Myllys .20 .50
48 Peter Ahola .06 .15
49 Mikko Haapakoski .04 .10
50 Kai Harila .04 .10
51 Pasi Huura .06 .15
52 Waltteri Immonen .06 .15
53 Timo Jutila .04 .10
54 Janne Laukkanen .10 .25
55 Harri Laurila .04 .10
56 Jyrki Lumme .10 .25
57 Teppo Numminen .10 .25
58 Sami Nuutinen .04 .10
59 Ville Siren .06 .15
60 Pasi Sormunen .04 .10
61 Mika Stromberg .06 .15
62 Mika Alatalo .20 .50
63 Raimo Helminen .04 .10
64 Pauli Jarvinen .04 .10
65 Jarmo Kekalainen .06 .15
66 Jari Korpisalo .06 .15
67 Jari Kurri .40 1.00
68 Mikko Makela .10 .25
69 Mika Nieminen .06 .15
70 Timo Norppa .04 .10
71 Janne Ojanen .04 .10
72 Timo Peltomaa .04 .10
73 Rauli Raitanen .04 .10
74 Juha Riihijarvi .10 .25
75 Christian Ruuttu .10 .25
76 Timo Saarikoski .04 .10
77 Teemu Selanne 2.00 5.00
78 Jukka Seppo .06 .15
79 Petri Skriko .10 .25
80 Esa Tikkanen .20 .50
81 Pekka Tuomisto .04 .10
82 Petri Varis .10 .25
83 Jarkko Varvio .06 .15
84 Vesa Viitakoski .06 .15
85 Marko Virtanen .04 .10
86 Jali Wahlsten .04 .10
87 Sami Wahlsten .04 .10
88 Pentti Matikainen .04 .10
89 Petr Briza .10 .25
90 Roman Turek .40 1.00
91 Milos Holan .04 .10
92 Drahomir Kadlec .06 .15
93 Bedrick Scerban .06 .15
94 Frantisek Prochazka .04 .10
95 Richard Zemlicka .06 .15
96 Roman Horak .40 1.00
97 Lubos Rob .04 .10
98 Jiri Kucera .06 .15
99 Tomas Kapusta .04 .10
100 Roman Rysanek .04 .10
101 Roman Hamrlik .10 .25
102 Robert Svehla .10 .25
103 Tomas Jelinek .06 .15
104 Petr Klima .10 .25
105 Josef Beranek .08 .20
106 Robert Petrovicky .06 .15
107 Kamil Kastak .06 .15
108 David Volek .06 .15
109 Renato Tosio .04 .10
110 Patrick Schopf .04 .10
111 Samuel Balmer .04 .10
112 Andreas Beutler .04 .10
113 Patrice Brasey .04 .10
114 Rick Tschumi .04 .10
115 Sven Leuenberger .04 .10
116 Sandro Bertaggia .04 .10
117 Patrick Howald .04 .10
118 Andy Ton .04 .10
119 Keith Fair .04 .10
120 Mario Brodmann .04 .10
121 Fredy Luthi .04 .10
122 Jorg Eberle .06 .15
123 Roman Wager .04 .10
124 Manuele Celio .04 .10
125 Christian Weber .04 .10
126 Roger Thony .04 .10
127 Felix Hollenstein .04 .10
128 Gil Montandon .04 .10
129 Nikolai Khabibulin .60 1.50
130 Alexei Cherviakov .04 .10
131 Ilja Biakin .06 .15
132 Dmitri Filimonov .06 .15
133 Alexander Karpovtsev .10 .25
134 Sergei Sorokin .06 .15
135 Andrei Sapozhnikov .04 .10
136 Alexei Yashin .20 .50
137 Alexander Cherbayev .04 .10
138 Konstantin Astrakhantsev .06 .15
139 Sergei Petrenko .06 .15
140 Viktor Kozlov .10 .25
141 Roman Oksyuta .04 .10
142 Vladimir Malakhov .10 .25
143 Andrei Lomakin .06 .15
144 Dimitri Yushkevich .10 .25
145 Igor Korolev .04 .10
146 Darius Kasparaitis .10 .25
147 Vyacheslav Bykov .10 .25
148 Andrei Khomutov .10 .25
149 Helmut De Raaf .04 .10
150 Klaus Merk .10 .25
151 Michael Heidt .10 .25
152 Michael Schmidt .04 .10
153 Uli Hiemer .06 .10
154 Andreas Niederberger .04 .10
155 Rick Amann .04 .10
156 Andreas Brockmann .04 .10
157 Gerd Truntschka .06 .15
158 Dieter Hegen .06 .15
159 Stefan Ustorf .06 .15
160 Georg Holzmann .04 .10
161 Ernst Kopf Jr. .06 .15
162 Bernd Truntschka .06 .15
163 Raimund Hilger .06 .10
164 Wolfgang Kummer .04 .10
165 Georg Franz .04 .10
166 Thomas Brandl .04 .10
167 Michael Rumrich .04 .10
168 Uwe Krupp .10 .25
169 Tom Barrasso .20 .50
170 Mike Richter .60 1.50
171 Brian Leetch .60 1.50
172 Chris Chelios .60 1.50
173 Al Iafrate .10 .25
174 Phil Housley .10 .25
175 Kevin Hatcher .10 .25
176 Gary Suter .10 .25
177 Mathieu Schneider .10 .25
178 Joe Mullen .10 .25
179 Kevin Stevens .10 .25
180 Jeremy Roenick 1.50 4.00
181 Tony Granato .10 .25
182 Mike Modano 1.25 3.00
183 Pat LaFontaine .30 .75
184 Ed Olczyk .06 .15
185 Brett Hull 1.50 4.00
186 Craig Janney .10 .25
187 Jimmy Carson .06 .15
188 Tony Amonte .40 1.00
189 Patrick Roy 5.00 12.00
190 Kirk McLean .20 .50
191 Larry Murphy .20 .50
192 Ray Bourque 2.00 5.00
193 Al MacInnis .60 1.50
194 Steve Duchesne .10 .25
195 Eric Desjardins .20 .50
196 Scott Stevens .30 .75
197 Paul Coffey .60 1.50
198 Mario Lemieux 5.00 12.00
199 Wayne Gretzky 6.00 15.00
200 Rick Tocchet .20 .50
201 Eric Lindros 1.25 3.00
202 Mark Messier 1.25 3.00
203 Steve Yzerman 4.00 10.00
204 Luc Robitaille .60 1.50
205 Mark Recchi .60 1.50
206 Joe Sakic 2.00 5.00
207 Owen Nolan .40 1.00
208 Gary Roberts .20 .50
209 David Delfino .10 .25
210 Mike Rosati .10 .25
211 Robert Oberrauch .04 .10
212 Jim Camazzola .04 .10
213 Bill Stewart .04 .10
214 Mike DeAngelis .04 .10
215 Anthony Circelli .04 .10
216 Georg Comploy .04 .10
217 Frank DiMuzio .04 .10
218 Gates Orlando .06 .15
219 John Vecchiarelli .04 .10
220 Joe Foglietta .04 .10
221 Lucio Topatigh .04 .10
222 Carmine Vani .06 .15
223 Lino DeToni .04 .10
224 Mario Chitarroni .04 .10
225 Bruno Zarrillo .04 .10
226 Maurizio Mansi .04 .10
227 Stefan Figliuzzi .04 .10
228 Santino Pellegrino .04 .10
229 Jim Marthinsen .10 .25
230 Rob Schistad .10 .25
231 Petter Salsten .04 .10
232 Cato Tom Andersen .04 .10
233 Tommy Jakobsen .04 .10
234 Svein E Norstebo .04 .10
235 Jon Magne Karlstad .04 .10
236 Kim Sogaard .04 .10
237 Geir Hoff .04 .10
238 Erik Kristiansen .04 .10
239 Petter Thoresen .04 .10
240 Ole Eskild Dahlstrom .04 .10
241 Espen Knutsen .20 .50
242 Oystein Olsen .04 .10
243 Roy Johansen .04 .10
244 Trond Magnussen .04 .10
245 Arne Billkvam .04 .10
246 Marius Rath .04 .10
247 Tom Erik Olsen .04 .10
248 Morten Finstad .04 .10
249 Petri Ylonen .10 .25
250 Michel Valliere .10 .25
251 Stephane Botteri .04 .10
252 Serge Poudrier .06 .15
253 Eric Durand .04 .10
254 Jean-Philippe Lemoine .06 .15
255 Denis Perez .06 .15
256 Sebastien Marquet .04 .10
257 Michael Babin .04 .10
258 Stephane Barin .04 .10
259 Arnaud Briand .04 .10
260 Yves Crettenand .04 .10
261 Laurent Deschaume .04 .10
262 Roger Dube .04 .10
263 Patrick Dunn .04 .10
264 Franck Pajonkowski .06 .15
265 Pierre Pousse .04 .10
266 Antoine Richer .04 .10
267 Christophe Ville .04 .10
268 Philippe Bozon .40 1.00
269 Brian Stankiewicz .04 .10
270 Claus Dalpiaz .10 .25
271 Michael Shea .10 .25
272 Robin Doyle .04 .10
273 Martin Ulrich .04 .10
274 Martin Krainz .04 .10
275 Erich Solderer .04 .10
276 Michael Guntner .04 .10
277 Friedrich Ganster .04 .10
278 Wayne Groulx .04 .10
279 Dieter Kalt .04 .10
280 Werner Kerth .04 .10
281 Arno Maier .04 .10
282 Richard Nasheim .04 .10
283 Christian Perthaler .04 .10
284 Andreas Puschnig .04 .10
285 Gerhard Puschnik .04 .10
286 Walter Putnik .04 .10
287 Reinhard Lampert .04 .10
288 Mario Schaden .04 .10

1994-95 Swedish Leaf

The 1994-95 Leaf Swedish hockey set consists of 320 standard-size cards that were issued in two series. The fronts feature color action player photos that are full-bleed except on the left, where a team color-coded stripe carries the player's name and his team's name. Leaf's logo in gold-foil appears in one of the corners. The team color-coded backs carry a color player close-up with a short biography, career stats and the team logo. Each series closes with team cards (135-158, 307-318) and checklists (159-160, 319-320).

COMPLETE SET (320) 26.00 65.00
COMPLETE SERIES 1 (1-160) 10.00 25.00
COMPLETE SERIES 2 (161-320) 16.00 40.00
1 Thomas Tallberg .04 .10
2 Hakan Algotsson .10 .25
3 Mikael Magnusson .04 .10
4 Per Lundell .04 .10
5 Kenneth Kennholt .04 .10
6 Jan Huokko .04 .10
7 Petter Nilsson .04 .10
8 Johan Norgren .04 .10
9 Anders Berglund .04 .10
10 Kari Eloranta .08 .20
11 Sam Lindstahl .04 .10
12 Johan Rosen .04 .10
13 Jonas Johnsson .04 .10
14 Erik Huusko .08 .20
15 Thomas Rhodin .04 .10
16 Patric Kjellberg .15 .40
17 Fredrik Andersson .04 .10
18 Stefan Nilsson .04 .10
19 Petri Liimatainen .04 .10
20 Lars Jansson .04 .10
21 Per Wallin .04 .10
22 Mika Nieminen .15 .40
23 Lars Ivarsson .04 .10
24 Ronnie Sundin .15 .40
25 Bedrich Scerban .04 .10
26 Anders Huusko .04 .10
27 Erik Grankvist .04 .10
28 Stefan Ornskog .08 .20
29 Marcus Thuresson .04 .10
30 Johan Stromvall .04 .10
31 Peter Hasselblad .04 .10
32 Anders Eriksson .20 .50
33 Roger Elvenes .04 .10
34 Stefan Larsson .04 .10
35 Alexei Salomatin .04 .10
36 Niclas Havelid .40 1.00
37 Mikael Lindman .04 .10
38 Jens Ohling .04 .10
39 Hakan Loob .30 .75
40 Johan Hedberg .60 1.50
41 Niklas Eriksson .04 .10
42 Robert Nordberg .04 .10
43 Robert Svehla .40 1.00
44 Hans Jonsson .30 .75
45 Thomas Srsen .04 .10
46 Thomas Sjogren .04 .10
47 Mishat Fahrutdinov .04 .10
48 Thomas Strandberg .04 .10
49 Andreas Dackell .40 .75
50 Peter Nilsson .04 .10
51 Andreas Johansson .30 .75
52 Stefan Falk .04 .10
53 Marcus Akerblom .04 .10
54 Peter Aslin .10 .25
55 Ricard Persson .15 .40
56 Tomas Nanzen .04 .10
57 Per-Johan Svensson .04 .10
58 Terho Koskela .04 .10
59 Henrik Nilsson .04 .10
60 Mats Lindberg .04 .10
61 Anders Huss .04 .10
62 Magnus Jansson .04 .10
63 Mats Lindgren .20 .50
64 Thomas Ljungberg .04 .10
65 Tomas Forslund .10 .25
66 Thomas Ostlund .15 .40
67 Raimo Helminen .10 .25
68 Magnus Wernblom .04 .10
69 Jorgen Jonsson .04 .10
70 Peter Berndtsson .04 .10
71 Stefan Hellkvist .04 .10
72 Tommy Lehmann .08 .20
73 Stefan Klockare .04 .10
74 Ola Josefsson .04 .10
75 Peter Lindmark .10 .25
76 Owe Thornberg .04 .10
77 Jarmo Makitalo .04 .10
78 Tomas Berglund .04 .10
79 Bo Svanberg .04 .10
80 Lennart Hermansson .04 .10
81 Stefan Elvenes .04 .10
82 Daniel Alfredsson 1.60 4.00
83 Claes Lindblom .04 .10
84 Bjorn Ahlstrom .04 .10
85 Ove Molin .04 .10
86 Fredrik Lindquist .20 .50
87 Clas Eriksson .04 .10
88 Peter Hammarstrom .04 .10
89 Magnus Swardh .04 .10
90 Lars Hurtig .04 .10
91 Daniel Rydmark .04 .10
92 Lars Bystrom .04 .10
93 Mats Loov .04 .10
94 Lars Dahlstrom .04 .10
95 Johan Brummer .04 .10
96 Patric Englund .04 .10
97 Christer Olsson .15 .40
98 Patrik Erickson .04 .10
99 Peter Ottosson .04 .10
100 Tomas Jonsson .10 .25
101 Lars Modig .04 .10
102 Ake Lilljebjorn .04 .10
103 Patrick Sylvegard .04 .10
104 Daniel Johansson .20 .50
105 Edvin Frylen .10 .25
106 Par Edlund .04 .10
107 Paul Andersson .04 .10
108 Rikard Franzen .04 .10
109 Christian Due-Boje .10 .25
110 Tommy Samuelsson .04 .10
111 Mathias Svedberg .04 .10
112 Hans Lodin .04 .10
113 Jonas Eriksson .10 .25
114 Mikael Engstrom .04 .10
115 Hakan Ahlund .04 .10
116 Kari Suoraniemi .04 .10
117 Peter Jacobsson .04 .10
118 Kristian Gahn .04 .10
119 Tommy Melkersson .04 .10
120 Oscar Ackestrom .04 .10
121 Thomas Johansson .04 .10
122 Jesper Duus .04 .10
123 Hans Abrahamsson .04 .10
124 Orjan Lindmark .04 .10
125 Torbjorn Lindberg .04 .10
126 Michael Sundlov .10 .25
127 Peter Sundstrom .10 .25
128 Pierre Johnsson .04 .10
129 Thomas Carlsson .04 .10
130 Stefan Axelsson .04 .10
131 Robert Nordmark .08 .20
132 Torbjorn Persson .04 .10
133 Bjorn Nord .04 .10
134 Mats Ytter .04 .10
135 AIK
Team Statistics
136 Brynas IF .04 .10
Team Statistics
137 Djurgardens IF .04 .10
Team Statistics
138 Vastra Frolunda .04 .10
Team Statistics
139 Farjestad BK .04 .10
Team Statistics
140 HV-71 .04 .10
Team Statistics
141 Leksand IF .04 .10
Team Statistics
142 Lulea HF .04 .10
Team Statistics
143 Malmo IF .04 .10
Team Statistics
144 MoDo Hockey .04 .10
Team Statistics
145 Rogle BK .04 .10
Team Statistics
146 Varsteras IK .04 .10
Team Statistics
147 AIK Logo .04 .10
148 Brynas IF Logo .04 .10
149 Djurgardens IF .04 .10
150 Vastra Frolunda Logo .04 .10
151 Farjestads BK .04 .10
152 HV-71 Logo .04 .10
153 Leksands IF Logo .04 .10
154 Lulea HF .04 .10
155 Malmo IF .04 .10
156 MoDo Hockey .04 .10
157 Rogle BK .04 .10
158 Vasteras IK .04 .10
159 Checklist 1-80 .04 .10
160 Checklist 81-160 .04 .10
161 Kenneth Johansson .10 .25
162 Stefan Jonsson .04 .10
163 Mikael Wahlberg .04 .10
164 Per Djoos .10 .25
165 Andreas Schultz .04 .10
166 Sacha Molin .04 .10
167 Marcus Ramen .04 .10
168 Jergus Baca .04 .10
169 Erik Bergstrom .04 .10
170 Jonas Forsberg .15 .40
171 Olli Kaski .04 .10
172 Morgan Samuelsson .04 .10
173 Anders Burstrom .04 .10
174 Stanislav Meciar .04 .10
175 Leif Rohlin .15 .40
176 Lars Edstrom .04 .10
177 Esa Keskinen .10 .25
178 Daniel Casselstahl .04 .10
179 Mattias Timander .20 .50
180 Peter Nordstrom .04 .10
181 Patric Aberg .04 .10
182 Mikael Enander .04 .10
183 Charles Berglund .10 .25
184 Jonas Andersson-Junkka .15 .40
185 Sergei Fokin .04 .10
186 Boo Ahl .15 .40
187 Jiri Kucera .10 .25
188 Roger Nordstrom .04 .10
189 Peter Forsberg 6.00 15.00
190 Arto Ruotanen .04 .10
191 Mikael Wiklander .04 .10
192 Joakim Persson .10 .25
193 Peter Larsson .04 .10
194 Per Eklund .15 .40
195 Joacim Esbjors .04 .10
196 Magnus Arvedsson .60 1.50
197 Marko Palo .04 .10
198 Mikael Holmberg .04 .10
199 Mikael Renberg .75 2.00
200 Tero Lehtera .15 .40
201 Fredrik Lindh .04 .10
202 Johan Finnstrom .04 .10
203 Peter Popovic .10 .25
204 Tony Barthelson .04 .10
205 Stefan Polla .04 .10
206 Jonas Esbjors .04 .10
207 Roger Hansson .04 .10
208 Mikael Hakansson .04 .10
209 Daniel Tjarnqvist .15 .40
210 Anders Carlsson .10 .25
211 Dick Tarnstrom .15 .40
212 Johan Tornberg .04 .10
213 Joakim Lundberg .04 .10
214 Marko Jantunen .15 .40
215 Patrik Haltia .04 .10
216 Fredrik Stillman .04 .10
217 Andy Schneider .04 .10
218 Thomas Holmstrom ERC 2.00 5.00
219 Jens Hemstrom .04 .10
220 Anders Soderberg .20 .50
221 Peter Lundmark .04 .10
222 Patrik Juhlin .15 .40
223 Anders Gozzi .04 .10
224 Marcus Ragnarsson .30 .75
225 Mattias Olsson .04 .10
226 Andreas Karlsson .20 .50
227 Tomas Lilja .04 .10
228 Stefan Ohman .04 .10
229 Jarmo Kekalainen .10 .25
230 Tony Skopac .04 .10
231 Lars Karlsson .10 .25
232 Mats Sundin 1.00 2.50
233 Peter Strom .04 .10
234 Mattias Johansson .04 .10
235 Johan Lindbom .04 .10
236 Mats Lusth .04 .10
237 Marcus Magnertoft .04 .10
238 Martin Hostak .04 .10
239 Mikael Pettersson .04 .10
240 Johan Akerman .04 .10
241 Mathias Hallback .04 .10
242 Johan Davidsson .20 .50
243 Per-Erik Eklund .15 .40
244 Johan Salle .04 .10
245 Per Svartvadet .20 .50
246 Ville Siren .10 .25
247 Mattias Loof .04 .10
248 Per-Johan Axelsson .60 1.50
249 Peter Gerhardsson .04 .10
250 Jonas Bergqvist .10 .25
251 Per-Johan Johansson .40 1.00
252 Mattias Bosson .04 .10
253 Andreas Olsson .04 .10
254 Patrik Zetterberg .04 .10
255 Michael Johansson .04 .10
256 Stefan Gustavson .04 .10
257 Jerry Persson .04 .10
258 Stefan Nilsson .04 .10
259 Roger Johansson .04 .10
260 Jarmo Myllys .20 .50
261 Kyosti Karjalainen .04 .10
262 Thomas Eriksson .04 .10
263 Michael Hjalm .04 .10
264 Espen Knutsen .40 1.00
265 Andreas Salomonsson .04 .10
266 Patrik Hoglund .04 .10
267 Peter Andersson .04 .10
268 Brett Hauer .10 .25
269 Stefan Ketola .04 .10
270 Patrik Carnback .10 .25
271 Petter Ronnqvist .04 .10
272 Roger Ohman .04 .10
273 Fredrik Modin .75 2.00
274 Alexander Beliavski .04 .10
275 Niklas Brannstrom .04 .10
276 Per Gustafsson .15 .40
277 Nicklas Nordqvist .04 .10
278 Roger Akerstrom .04 .10
279 Jiri Vykoukal .10 .25
280 Jesper Mattsson .15 .40
281 Henrik Nordfeldt .04 .10
282 Joakim Musakka .04 .10
283 Anders Johnson .04 .10
284 Niklas Sundstrom .40 1.00
285 Nicklas Lidstrom 1.00 2.50
286 Tomas Sandstrom .40 1.00
287 Jens Nielsen .04 .10
288 Mattias Ohlund .75 2.00
289 Markus Eriksson .04 .10
290 Mikael Sandberg .10 .25
291 Sergeij Pushkov .04 .10
292 Jonas Hoglund .40 1.00
293 Peter Ekelund .04 .10
294 Fredrik Bergqvist .04 .10
295 Torgny Bendelin .04 .10
296 Tommy Sandlin CO .04 .10
297 Tommy Boustedt CO .04 .10
298 Conny Evensson CO .04 .10
299 Sune Bergman CO .04 .10
300 Wayne Fleming CO .04 .10
301 Lars Bergstrom CO .04 .10
302 Hannu Jortikka CO .04 .10
303 Leif Boork CO .04 .10
304 Christer Abrahamsson CO .10 .25
305 Randy Edmonds CO .04 .10
306 Ulf Labraaten CO .04 .10
307 AIK .04 .10
308 Brynas IF .04 .10
309 Djurgardens IF .04 .10
310 Farjestads BK .04 .10
311 HV 71 .04 .10
312 Leksands IF .04 .10
313 Lulea HF .04 .10
314 Malmo IF .04 .10
315 MoDo .04 .10
316 Rogle BK .04 .10
317 Vasteras IK .04 .10
318 Vastra Frolunda .04 .10
319 Checklist 161-240 .04 .10
320 Checklist 241-320 .04 .10
NNO1 Malmo IF SuperChase 10.00 25.00
NNO2 M.Lindgren SuperChase 6.00 15.00

1994-95 Swedish Leaf Clean Sweepers

This 10-card standard size set highlights 10 of the top goalies in the Swedish Elitserien. The cards were randomly inserted into series one packs. The fronts have a color photo with the player's name in yellow on a red background at the bottom. The word "Cleansweepers" is at the top in gold-foil as are the words "Elit Set" in the bottom right corner. The backs have player information in green with a blue background. The cards are numbered "X of 10."

COMPLETE SET (10) 10.00 25.00
1 Peter Lindmark 1.25 3.00
2 Michael Sundlov 1.25 3.00
3 Thomas Ostlund 1.25 3.00
4 Jonas Eriksson 1.25 3.00
5 Peter Aslin 1.25 3.00
6 Ake Lilljebjorn 1.25 3.00
7 Johan Hedberg 2.00 5.00
8 Henrik Arvsell 1.25 3.00
9 Fredrik Andersson 1.25 3.00
10 Hakan Algotsson 1.25 3.00

1994-95 Swedish Leaf Foreign Affairs

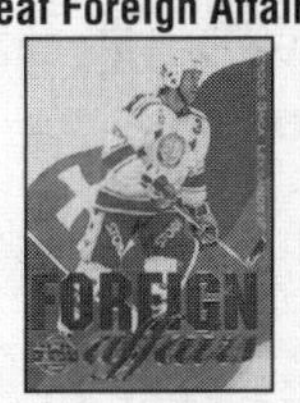

Featuring foreign-born players competing in the Elitserien, this ten-card set was inserted in series two foil packs. The fronts feature a color player cutout superimposed over his country's flag. The words "Foreign Affairs" in foil letters are printed on the bottom, while the player's name and his team's name appear vertically on the right. The backs carry player profile. All information is printed in Swedish.

COMPLETE SET (10) 8.00 20.00
1 Espen Knutsen 2.00 5.00
2 Esa Keskinen .80 2.00
3 Marko Jantunen .80 2.00
4 Jarmo Myllys 1.20 3.00
5 Jiri Kucera .80 2.00
6 Jiri Vykoukal .80 2.00
7 Jarmo Kekalainen .80 2.00
8 Olli Kaski .80 2.00
9 Jergus Baca .80 2.00
10 Tero Lehtera .80 2.00

1994-95 Swedish Leaf Gold Cards

This 24-card standard size set commemorates the members of Sweden's 1994 Olympic gold medal team. The cards were randomly inserted into series one packs. The fronts have a full-color photo ghosted over an image of the gold medal with the player's name at the bottom. The words "Gold Cards" are at the bottom in gold-foil as are the words "Elit Set" in the top right corner. The backs have the player's name and information with a stick figure playing hockey numerous times being the background. The cards are numbered "X of 24."

COMPLETE SET (24) 30.00 75.00
1 Title Card 2.00 5.00
2 Andreas Dackell 1.20 3.00
3 Charles Berglund .80 2.00
4 Christian Due-Boje .80 2.00
5 Daniel Rydmark .80 2.00
6 Fredrik Stillman .80 2.00
7 Hakan Algotsson 1.20 3.00
8 Hakan Loob 1.20 3.00
9 Jonas Bergqvist .80 2.00
10 Jorgen Jonsson .80 2.00
11 Kenny Jonsson 1.20 3.00
12 Leif Rohlin .80 2.00
13 Magnus Svensson .80 2.00

14 Mats Naslund 1.20 3.00
15 Michael Sundlov 1.20 3.00
16 Niklas Eriksson .80 2.00
17 Patric Kjellberg .80 2.00
18 Patrick Juhlin .80 2.00
19 Peter Forsberg 14.00 35.00
20 Roger Hansson .80 2.00
21 Roger Johansson .80 2.00
22 Stefan Ornskog .80 2.00
23 Tomas Jonsson .80 2.00
24 Tommy Salo 2.00 5.00

1994-95 Swedish Leaf Guest Special

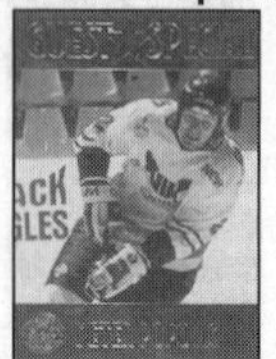

Featuring players who joined the Elitserien during the 1994 NHL lockout, this eight card set was inserted in second-series foil packs. The fronts feature a color player action shot. The words "Guest Special" appear in a foil bar above the photo, while the player's name is printed in a foil bar below. The horizontal backs carry a color player cut-out superimposed over a drawing of the world.

COMPLETE SET (8) 16.00 40.00
1 Mats Sundin 4.00 10.00
2 Tomas Sandstrom .80 2.00
3 Peter Forsberg 10.00 25.00
4 Nicklas Lidstrom 4.00 10.00
5 Mikael Renberg 1.20 3.00
6 Roger Johansson .40 1.00
7 Peter Popovic .40 1.00
8 Patrick Juhlin .40 1.00

1994-95 Swedish Leaf NHL Draft

This ten-card standard-size set featuring players drafted by NHL teams in 1994 was inserted in second-series foil packs. The fronts feature a color player action shot. The year 1994 is separated by the NHL draft logo. The backs contain information in Swedish about the player's selection in the 1994 NHL draft.

COMPLETE SET (10) 12.00 30.00
1 Mattias Ohlund 1.60 4.00
2 Johan Davidsson .80 1.00
3 Fredrik Modin 1.60 4.00
4 Johan Finnstrom .40 1.00
5 Edvin Frylen .40 1.00
6 Daniel Alfredsson 3.20 8.00
7 Patrik Haltia 1.20 3.00
8 Peter Strom .40 1.00
9 Thomas Holmstrom 4.00 10.00
10 Dick Tarnstrom .40 2.00

1994-95 Swedish Leaf Playmakers

This six-card standard size set shines the spotlight on five of the top goal scorers in the Swedish Elitserien. The cards were randomly inserted into series one packs. The fronts have a full-color photo with an orange and black background. The words "Play Makers" are on the left side and the words "Elit Set" is in the bottom right corner in gold-foil. The backs have "Play Makers" at the top in silver with an orange background. The player's name and number of assists he had in each of the previous three seasons with a black background. Card #1 is different in that it is a title card and has a picture of all five players in the set. The cards are numbered "X of 6."

COMPLETE SET (6) 2.00 5.00
1 Title Card .80 2.00
2 Stefan Nilsson .40 1.00
3 Mika Nieminen .40 1.00
4 Raimo Helminen .40 1.00
5 Peter Larsson .40 1.00
6 Hakan Loob .80 2.00

1994-95 Swedish Leaf Rookie Rockets

Inserted in second-series foil packs, this 10-card set features rookies in the Swedish league. Borderless horizontal fronts feature a color player cut-out along with "Rookie" in big foil letters. The player's name and his

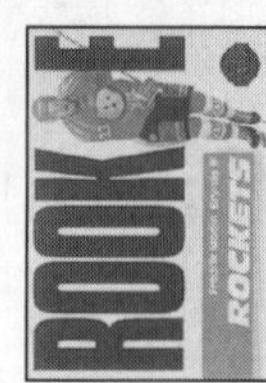

team's name appears in a red bar on the bottom. The horizontal back carry another color player cut-out along with player profile.

COMPLETE SET (10) 8.00 20.00
1 Fredrik Modin 1.20 3.00
2 Jonas Andersson-Junkka .80 2.00
3 Thomas Holmstrom 4.00 10.00
4 Mattias Ohlund 1.20 3.00
5 Per Eklund .40 1.00
6 Daniel Tjarnqvist .40 1.00
7 Joakim Persson .80 2.00
8 Patrik Haltia .80 2.00
9 Andreas Karlsson .40 1.00
10 Stefan Nilsson .40 1.00

1994-95 Swedish Leaf Studio Signatures

This 12-card standard-size set was inserted in second-series foil packs. The fronts feature borderless color studio photos. The player's facsimile autograph in foil letters appears at the bottom. The backs carry a drawing of the player in close-up.

COMPLETE SET (12) 4.00 10.00
1 Rikard Franzen .40 1.00
2 Anders Huss .40 1.00
3 Jens Ohling .40 1.00
4 Tommy Samuelsson .40 1.00
5 Fredrik Stillman .40 1.00
6 Jonas Bergqvist .40 1.00
7 Johan Stromvall .40 1.00
8 Roger Nordstrom .40 1.00
9 Lars Bystrom .40 1.00
10 Roger Elvenes .40 1.00
11 Leif Rohlin .80 2.00
12 Tero Koskela .40 1.00

1994-95 Swedish Leaf Top Guns

This 10-card standard size set consists of some of the top goal scorers in the Swedish Elitserien. The cards were randomly inserted into series one packs. The fronts have a full-color photo with a background that looks like fire works. In one of the top corners the words "Top Gun" are in gold-foil as are the words "Elit Set" in the bottom right corner. The backs have "Top Gun" in red at the top as if it were underneath rippling water. At the bottom is the number of goals they scored each of the previous three seasons. The cards are numbered "X of 10."

COMPLETE SET (10) 4.80 12.00
1 Thomas Srsen .40 1.00
2 Hakan Loob 1.20 3.00
3 Lars Hurtig .40 1.00
4 Stefan Elvenes .40 1.00
5 Jorgen Jonsson .40 1.00
6 Robert Svehla 1.20 3.00
7 Daniel Rydmark .40 1.00
8 Owe Thornberg .40 1.00
9 Patric Kjellberg .80 2.00
10 Mats Loov .40 1.00

1994 Swedish Olympics Lillehammer*

This listing includes only the hockey cards from a larger Swedish issue that was released to commemorate the 1994 Olympic Games, which were held in Lillehammar.

COMPLETE HOCKEY SET (56) 15.00 30.00
273 Ice Hockey Logo .02 .10
274 Russian Team Puzzle .08 .20
275 Russian Team Puzzle .08 .20
276 Russian Team Puzzle .08 .20
277 Russian Team Puzzle .08 .20
278 Russian Team Puzzle .08 .20
279 Russian Team Puzzle .08 .20
280 Konstantin Astrakhantsev .20 .50
281 Viacheslav Bykov .20 .50
282 Sergei Sorokin .20 .50
283 Alexander Smirnov .20 .50
284 Swedish Team Sticker .08 .20
285 Swedish Team Sticker .08 .20
286 Swedish Team Sticker .08 .20
287 Swedish Team Sticker .08 .20
288 Swedish Team Sticker .08 .20
289 Swedish Team Sticker .08 .20
290 Markus Naslund .75 2.00
291 Peter Forsberg 4.00 10.00
292 Mats Sundin 1.50 4.00
293 Mikael Renberg .20 .50
294 Tommy Soderstrom .20 .50
295 Finnish Team Puzzle .08 .20
296 Finnish Team Puzzle .08 .20
297 Finnish Team Puzzle .08 .20
298 Finnish Team Puzzle .08 .20
299 Finnish Team Puzzle .08 .20
300 Finnish Team Puzzle .08 .20
301 Markus Ketterer .20 .50
302 Vesa Viitakoski .08 .20
303 Esa Tikkanen .20 .50
304 Erik Hamalainen .08 .20
305 Norwegian Team Puzzle .08 .20
306 Norwegian Team Puzzle .08 .20
307 Norwegian Team Puzzle .08 .20
308 Norwegian Team Puzzle .08 .20
309 Norwegian Team Puzzle .08 .20
310 Norwegian Team Puzzle .08 .20
311 Jim Marthinsen .20 .50
312 Erik Kristiansen .08 .20
313 Petter Salsten .08 .20
314 Eric Lindros 1.50 4.00
315 Greg Johnson .20 .50
316 Allain Roy .20 .50
317 Hank Lammens .30 .75
318 Leo Gudas .20 .50
319 Petr Briza .30 .75
320 Petr Rosol .20 .50
321 Otakar Janecky .20 .50
322 Mike Richter .75 2.00
323 Brett Hull 2.00 5.00
324 Chris Chelios .75 2.00
325 Pat Lafontaine .75 2.00
326 Claus Dalpiaz .20 .50
327 Stephane Barin .08 .20
328 Gerd Truntschka .08 .20

1995-96 Swedish Leaf

The 1995-96 Leaf Elit set was issued in two series (150 and 160 cards, respectively) and featured the players of Sweden's top league, the Elitserien. The cards feature a beautiful full-bleed design, with the player's name ghosted along the bottom. The set was distributed in 8-card packs. The NNO Per-Erik (Pelle) Eklund card was randomly inserted in series 1 packs, while the HV71 card, commemorating the team's 1994-95 championship, could be found in series 2 packs.

COMPLETE SET (310) 16.00 40.00
COMPLETE SERIES 1 (150) 8.00 20.00
COMPLETE SERIES 2 (160) 8.00 20.00
1 Hakan Loob .20 .50
2 AIK .10 .25
3 AIK, Season Stats .06 .15
4 Joakim Persson .10 .25
5 Niclas Havelid .30 .75
6 Tony Barthelson .06 .15
7 Patric Aberg .06 .15
8 Johan Akerman .06 .15
9 Dick Tarnstrom .10 .25
10 Stefan Gustavson .06 .15
11 Anders Gozzi .06 .15
12 Morgan Samuelsson .10 .25
13 Brynas IF .06 .15
14 Brynas, Season Stats .06 .15
15 Michael Sundlov .10 .25
16 Stefan Klockare .10 .25
17 Bedrich Scerban .06 .15
18 Andreas Dackell .30 .75
19 Fredrik Modin .80 2.00
20 Ove Molin .06 .15
21 Mikael Wahlberg .06 .15
22 Thomas Tallberg .06 .15
23 Peter Larsson .06 .15
24 Stefan Ketola .10 .25
25 Djurgardens IF .10 .25
26 Djurgarden, Season Stats .06 .15
27 Jonas Forsberg .16 .40
28 Christian Due-Boje .10 .25
29 Mikael Magnusson .06 .15
30 Thomas Johansson .06 .15
31 Joakim Musakka .06 .15
32 Erik Hussko .10 .25
33 Jens Ohling .06 .15
34 Per Eklund .10 .25
35 Espen Knutsen .40 1.00
36 Patrik Erickson .06 .15
37 Farjestads BK .06 .15
38 Farjestad, Season Stats .06 .15
39 Patrik Haltia .10 .25
40 Sergei Fokin .06 .15
41 Thomas Rhodin .06 .15
42 Stefan Nilsson .06 .15
43 Magnus Arvedsson .30 .75
44 Mattias Johansson .06 .15
45 Clas Eriksson .06 .15
46 Peter Ottosson .06 .15
47 HV 71 .06 .15
48 HV 71, Season Stats .06 .15
49 Boo Ahl .16 .40
50 Kenneth Kennholt .06 .15
51 Hans Abrahamsson .06 .15
52 Peter Hammarstrom .06 .15
53 Johan Davidsson .20 .50
54 Stefan Falk .06 .15
55 Johan Lindbom .06 .15
56 Esa Keskinen .10 .25
57 Stefan Ornskog .10 .25
58 Peter Ekelund .06 .15
59 Leksands IF .06 .15
60 Leksand, Season Stats .06 .15
61 Johan Hedberg 4.00 4.00
62 Tomas Jonsson .10 .25
63 Hans Lodin .06 .15
64 Orjan Lindmark .06 .15
65 Jan Huokko .06 .15
66 Markus Eriksson .06 .15
67 Andreas Karlsson .06 .15
68 Mikael Holmberg .06 .15
69 Jonas Bergqvist .10 .25
70 Niklas Eriksson .06 .15
71 Per-Erik Eklund .10 .25
72 Lulea HF .06 .15
73 Lulea, Season Stats .06 .15
74 Jarmo Myllys .20 .50
75 Mattias Ohlund .40 1.00
76 Lars Modig .06 .15
77 Torbjorn Lindberg .06 .15
78 Roger Akerstrom .06 .15
79 Stefan Jonsson .06 .15
80 Johan Rosen .06 .15
81 Tomas Berglund .06 .15
82 Robert Nordberg .06 .15
83 Jiri Kucera .10 .25
84 Tomas Holmstrom .80 2.00
85 Malmo IF .06 .15
86 Malmo, Season Stats .06 .15
87 Peter Andersson .06 .15
88 Roger Ohman .06 .15
89 Marcus Magnertoft .06 .15
90 Patrik Sylvegard .06 .15
91 Hakan Ahlund .06 .15
92 Jesper Mattsson .10 .25
93 Roger Hansson .06 .15
94 Mattias Bosson .06 .15
95 Bo Svanberg .06 .15
96 Raimo Helminen .10 .25
97 MoDo Hockey .10 .25
98 MoDo, Season Stats .06 .15
99 Petter Ronnqvist .10 .25
100 Lars Jansson .06 .15
101 Mattias Timander .20 .50
102 Hans Jonsson .06 .15
103 Anders Soderberg .16 .40
104 Martin Hostak .06 .15
105 Kyosti Karjalainen .10 .25
106 Mikael Hakanson .06 .15
107 Per Svartvadet .16 .40
108 Andreas Salomonsson .40 1.00
109 Lars Bystrom .06 .15
110 Magnus Wernblom .06 .15
111 Rogle BK .06 .15
112 Rogle, Season Stats .06 .15
113 Magnus Swardh .10 .25
114 Arto Ruotanen .06 .15
115 Johan Finnstrom .10 .25
116 Daniel Tjarnqvist .20 .50
117 Pierre Johnsson .06 .15
118 Per Wallin .10 .25
119 Michael Johansson .06 .15
120 Per-Johan Svensson .06 .15
121 Roger Elvenes .06 .15
122 Mats Loov .06 .15
123 Michael Hjalm .10 .25
124 Vasteras IK .06 .15
125 Vasteras, Season Stats .06 .15
126 Mats Ytter .10 .25
127 Erik Bergstrom .10 .25
128 Lars Ivarsson .06 .15
129 Mishat Fahrutdinov .06 .15
130 Claes Lindblom .06 .15
131 Paul Andersson .06 .15
132 Henrik Nordfeldt .06 .15
133 Alexei Salomatin .06 .15
134 Mikael Pettersson .06 .15
135 Vastra Frolunda HC .06 .15
136 Frolunda, Season Stats .06 .15
137 Hakan Algotsson .10 .25
138 Jonas Andersson-Junkka .10 .25
139 Stefan Larsson .06 .15
140 Par Djoos .10 .25
141 Ronnie Sundin .10 .25
142 Par Edlund .10 .25
143 Peter Berndtsson .06 .15
144 Joacim Esbjors .06 .15
145 Alexander Beliavski .06 .15
146 Jonas Esbjors .06 .15
147 Marko Jantunen .10 .25
148 Peter Strom .06 .15
149 Checklist 1-75 .06 .15
150 Checklist 76-150 .06 .15
151 AIK .10 .25
152 AIK, Captains .06 .15
153 Mikael Nilsson .06 .15
154 Juha Jokiharju .10 .25
155 Stefan Andersson .06 .15
156 Thomas Strandberg .06 .15
157 Mats Lindberg .06 .15
158 Peter Gerhardsson .06 .15
159 Tommy Lehmann .10 .25
160 Tommy Hedlund .06 .15
161 Peter Wallin .10 .25
162 Bjorn Ahlstrom .06 .15
163 Erik Hamalainen .10 .25
164 Patric Englund .06 .15
165 Rikard Franzen .06 .15
166 Brynas IF .06 .15
167 Brynas, Captains .06 .15
168 Lars Karlsson .06 .15
169 Jonas Lofstrom .06 .15
170 Stefan Polla .06 .15
171 Mikael Lind .06 .15
172 Brian Rafalski .80 2.00
173 Roger Kyro .06 .15
174 Per-Johan Johansson .06 .15
175 Greg Parks .06 .15
176 Per Lofstrom .06 .15
177 Jonas Johnsson .06 .15
178 Mikael Lindman .06 .15
179 Mikael Wiklander .06 .15
180 Tommy Melkersson .06 .15
181 Djurgardens IF .10 .25
182 Djurgarden, Captains .06 .15
183 Thomas Ostlund .20 .50
184 Patrik Hofbauer .06 .15
185 Magnus Jansson .06 .15
186 Niklas Falk .06 .15
187 Ola Josefsson .06 .15
188 Joakim Lundberg .06 .15
189 Fredrik Lindquist .16 .40
190 Patrik Kjellberg .20 .50
191 Jan Viktorsson .10 .25
192 Bjorn Nord .06 .15
193 Tommy Jacobsen .06 .15
194 Anders Huusko .06 .15
195 Kristofer Ottosson .06 .15
196 Vastra Frolunda HC .06 .15
197 Frolunda, Captains .06 .15
198 Mikael Sandberg .06 .15
199 Jerry Persson .06 .15
200 Peter Hogardh .06 .15
201 Stefan Axelsson .10 .25
202 Lars Edstrom .06 .15
203 Lars-Goran Wiklander .10 .25
204 Per-Johan Axelsson .40 1.00
205 Henrik Nilsson .06 .15
206 Petteri Nummelin .10 .25
207 Christian Ruuttu .20 .50
208 Oscar Ackestrom .06 .15
209 Farjestads BK .06 .15
210 Farjestad, Captains .06 .15
211 Markus Ketterer .10 .25
212 Bjorn Eriksson .06 .15
213 Jonas Hoglund .40 1.00
214 Peter Nordstrom .06 .15
215 Jorgen Jonsson .06 .15
216 Greger Artursson .06 .15
217 Jesper Duus .06 .15
218 Roger Johansson .06 .15
219 Leif Carlsson .06 .15
220 Per Lundell .06 .15
221 Vitali Prokhorov .10 .25
222 HV 71 .06 .15
223 HV 71, Captains .06 .15
224 Kenneth Johansson .06 .15
225 Thomas Gustavsson .06 .15
226 Marcus Thuresson .06 .15
227 Vesa Salo .10 .25
228 Kai Nurminen .20 .50
229 Johan Brummer .06 .15
230 Daniel Johansson .10 .25
231 Per Gustafsson .10 .25
232 Niklas Rahm .06 .15
233 Leksands IF .06 .15
234 Leksand, Captains .06 .15
235 Per-Ragnar Bergkvist .10 .25
236 Anders Carlsson .06 .15
237 Micael Karlberg .06 .15
238 Torgny Lowgren .06 .15
239 Stefan Hellkvist .06 .15
240 Markus Akerblom .06 .15
241 Joakim Lidgren .06 .15
242 Tomas Forslund .10 .25
243 Torbjorn Johansson .06 .15
244 Nicklas Nordqvist .06 .15
245 Lulea HF .06 .15
246 Lulea, Captains .06 .15
247 Erik Grankvist .06 .15
248 Mikael Lindholm .06 .15
249 Johan Stromvall .06 .15
250 Anders Burstrom .06 .15
251 Lars Hurtig .06 .15
252 Stefan Nilsson .06 .15
253 Jan Mertzig .10 .25
254 Petter Nilsson .06 .15
255 Malmo IF .06 .15
256 Malmo IF, Captains .06 .15
257 Peter Lindmark .10 .25
258 Roger Nordstrom .10 .25
259 Andreas Lilja .06 .15
260 Brian McReynolds .06 .15
261 Ilja Byakin .10 .25
262 Robert Burakovsky .06 .15
263 Mikael Burakovsky .06 .15
264 Stefan Elvenes .10 .25
265 Johan Salle .06 .15
266 Kim Johnsson .06 .15
267 Peter Hasselblad .06 .15
268 Marko Palo .06 .15
269 MoDo Hockey .10 .25
270 MoDo, Captains .10 .25
271 Fredrik Andersson .06 .15
272 Frantisek Kaberle .10 .25
273 Samuel Pahlsson .30 .75
274 Jan Larsson .06 .15
275 Per-Anton Lundstrom .10 .25
276 Tomas Nansen .06 .15
277 Marcus Karlsson .06 .15
278 Jan-Axel Alavaara .10 .25
279 Kristian Gahn .10 .25
280 Rogle BK .06 .15
281 Rogle, Captains .06 .15
282 Patrik Backlund .06 .15
283 Peter Lundmark .06 .15
284 Anders Berglund .06 .15
285 Harijs Vitolins .06 .15
286 Jens Nielsen .06 .15
287 Greg Brown .10 .25
288 Bjorn Linden .06 .15
289 Vasteras IK .06 .15
290 Vasteras, Captains .06 .15
291 Jacob Karlsson .06 .15
292 Patrik Zetterberg .06 .15
293 Mattias Loof .06 .15
294 Johan Tornberg .06 .15
295 Andrei Korolev .06 .15
296 Mattias Olsson .06 .15
297 Roger Rosen .06 .15
298 Andrei Lulin .06 .15
299 Edvin Fylen .10 .25
300 Mats Lusth .06 .15
301 Fredrik Oberg .06 .15
302 Jarmo Myllys AS .20 .50
303 Tomas Jonsson AS .10 .25
304 All Stars Andersson .10 .25
305 Hakan Loob AS .20 .50
306 Esa Keskinen AS .10 .25
307 Christian Ruuttu AS .10 .25
308 Checklist 151-230 .06 .15
309 Checklist 231-310 .06 .15
310 Checklist Insert Cards .06 .15
NNO HV71, Svenska Mastare 4.00 10.00
NNO Per-Erik Eklund 4.00 10.00

1995-96 Swedish Leaf Champs

Randomly inserted in series 1 packs at a rate of 1:11, this 15-card set celebrates members of Sweden's championship team. The cards are individually serially numbered on the back. It is believed that 1,000 of each were produced.

COMPLETE SET (15) 10.00 25.00
1 Tomas Jonsson .80 2.00
2 Patrik Kjellberg 1.20 3.00
3 Hakan Loob 1.20 3.00
4 Peter Lindmark 1.20 3.00
5 Anders Carlsson .80 2.00
6 Raimo Helminen 1.20 3.00
7 Esa Keskinen .80 2.00
8 Jan Larsson .80 2.00
9 Roger Johansson .80 2.00
10 Andreas Dackell 1.20 3.00
11 Stefan Ornskog .80 2.00
12 Michael Sundlov 1.20 3.00
13 Per-Erik Eklund .80 2.00
14 Kenneth Kennholt .80 2.00
15 Jan Viktorsson .80 2.00

1995-96 Swedish Leaf Face to Face

Randomly inserted in series two packs at a rate of 1:5, this 15-card set features the top two talents on each of the Elitserien teams.

COMPLETE SET (15) 6.00 15.00
1 Morgan Samuelsson / Tomas Strandberg .40 1.00
2 Bedrich Scerban / Greg Parks .40 1.00
3 Erik Huusko / Anders Hussko .40 1.00
4 Stefan Larsson / Marko Jantunen .40 1.00
5 Hakan Loob / Roger Johansson .80 2.00
6 Kenneth Kennholt / Per Gustafsson .40 1.00
7 Stefan Hellkvist / Tomas Forslund .40 1.00
8 Tomas Holmstrom / Roger Akerstrom 2.00 5.00
9 Stefan Elvenes / Robert Burakovsky .40 1.00
10 Martin Hostak / Mattias Timander .40 1.00
11 Mats Loov / Michael Hjalm .40 1.00
12 Alexei Salomatin / Fredrik Oberg .40 1.00
13 Patrik Erickson / Espen Knutsen 1.20 3.00
14 Peter Andersson / Peter Hasselblad .40 1.00
15 Tomas Jonsson / Markus Akerblom .40 1.00

1995-96 Swedish Leaf Goldies

Randomly inserted in series 1 packs at a rate of 1:14, this 10-card set captures some of the top young scorers in Sweden.

COMPLETE SET (10) 6.00 15.00
1 Morgan Samuelsson .80 2.00
2 Ove Molin .80 2.00
3 Fredrik Lindquist .80 2.00
4 Peter Strom .80 2.00
5 Mattias Johansson .80 2.00
6 Stefan Ornskog .80 2.00
7 Niklas Eriksson .80 2.00
8 Johan Rosen .80 2.00
9 Roger Ohman .80 2.00
10 Anders Soderberg .80 2.00

1995-96 Swedish Leaf Mega

The fifteen cards in this set were randomly inserted at a rate of 1:20 series 1 packs.

COMPLETE SET (15) 12.00 30.00
1 Michael Sundlov 1.20 3.00
2 Jonas Bergqvist 1.20 3.00
3 Marko Jantunen .80 2.00
4 Thomas Ostlund 1.20 3.00
5 Tomas Jonsson .80 2.00
6 Esa Keskinen .80 2.00
7 Roger Nordstrom .80 2.00
8 Mattias Ohlund 1.60 4.00
9 Hakan Loob 1.20 3.00
10 Raimo Helminen .80 2.00
11 Per-Erik Eklund 1.20 3.00
12 Jarmo Myllys 1.60 4.00
13 Rikard Franzen .80 2.00
14 Christer Olsson .80 2.00
15 Per Gustafsson .80 2.00

1995-96 Swedish Leaf Rookies

Randomly inserted in series one packs at a rate of 1:6, this nine card set reveals Leaf's picks as the top frosh in the Elitserien.

COMPLETE SET (9) 6.00 15.00
1 Peter Wallin .80 2.00
2 Jan-Axel Alavaara .80 2.00
3 Niklas Falk .80 2.00
4 Lars-Goran Wiklander .80 2.00
5 Torbjorn Johansson .80 2.00
6 Jan Mertzig .80 2.00
7 Mikael Burakovsky .80 2.00
8 Marcus Karlsson .80 2.00
9 Roger Rosen .80 2.00

1995-96 Swedish Leaf Spidermen

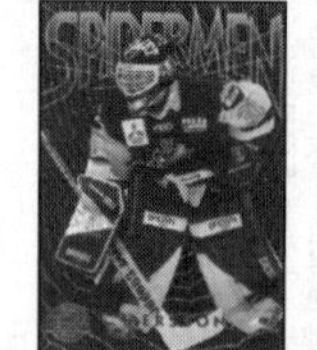

The stingiest netminders in Sweden are the focus of this 14-card set. The cards were randomly inserted at the rate of 1:8 series one packs.

COMPLETE SET (14) 20.00 40.00
1 Joakim Persson 1.25 3.00
2 Michael Sundlov 1.25 3.00
3 Thomas Ostlund 1.50 4.00
4 Hakan Algotsson 1.25 3.00
5 Patrik Haltia 1.25 3.00
6 Boo Ahl 1.50 4.00
7 Johan Hedberg 2.00 5.00
8 Jarmo Myllys 1.50 4.00
9 Jonas Forsberg 1.50 4.00
10 Petter Ronnqvist 1.25 3.00
11 Magnus Swardh 1.25 3.00
12 Mats Ytter 1.25 3.00
13 Mikael Sandberg 1.25 3.00
14 Roger Nordstrom 1.25 3.00

1995-96 Swedish Upper Deck

The 1995-96 Upper Deck Swedish Elit set was issued in one series totaling 260 cards. The set was issued in 10-card packs and features players from the Swedish Elitserien and was endorsed by its Players Association (SICO). The highlight is the subset Where Are They Now? (234-248) which showcases a number of former Swedish stars now in the NHL.

COMPLETE SET (260) 16.00 40.00
1 Joakim Persson .10 .25
2 Erik Hamalainen .10 .25
3 Dick Tarnstrom .10 .25
4 Rikard Franzen .02 .10
5 Niclas Havelid .30 .75
6 Tony Barthelson .02 .10
7 Tommy Hedlund .02 .10
8 Patric Aberg .02 .10
9 Stefan Gustavson .02 .10

10 Anders Gozzi .02 .10
11 David Engblom .02 .10
12 Stefan Andersson .02 .10
13 Tomas Strandberg .02 .10
14 Mats Lindberg .02 .10
15 Tommy Lehmann .10 .25
16 Bjorn Ahlstrom .02 .10
17 Patrik Englund .02 .10
18 Morgan Samuelsson .10 .25
19 Michael Sundlov .20 .50
20 Bedrich Scerban .02 .10
21 Mikael Lindman .02 .10
22 Mikael Wiklander .02 .10
23 Tommy Melkersson .02 .10
24 Stefan Klockare .10 .25
25 Per Lofstrom .02 .10
26 Jonas Johnsson .02 .10
27 Roger Kyro .02 .10
28 Jonas Lofstrom .02 .10
29 Stefan Ketola .10 .25
30 Mikael Wahlberg .02 .10
31 Stefan Polla .02 .10
32 Greg Parks .02 .10
33 Ove Molin .02 .10
34 Peter Larsson .02 .10
35 Fredrik Modin .40 1.00
36 Andreas Dackell .30 .75
37 Thomas Ostlund .20 .50
38 Tommy Jakobsen .02 .10
39 Christian Due-Boje .10 .25
40 Thomas Johansson .02 .10
41 Joakim Lundberg .02 .10
42 Bjorn Nord .02 .10
43 Mikael Magnusson .02 .10
44 Erik Huusko .10 .25
45 Anders Huusko .02 .10
46 Kristofer Ottosson .02 .10
47 Magnus Jansson .02 .10
48 Niklas Falk .10 .25
49 Ola Josefsson .02 .10
50 Per Eklund .10 .25
51 Espen Knutsen .40 1.00
52 Jens Ohling .02 .10
53 Patric Kjellberg .30 .75
54 Patrik Erickson .02 .10
55 Jan Viktorsson .10 .25
56 Markus Ketterer .20 .50
57 Jesper Duus .02 .10
58 Sergei Fokin .02 .10
59 Per Lundell .02 .10
60 Thomas Rhodin .02 .10
61 Henrik Rehnberg .02 .10
62 Roger Johansson .02 .10
63 Leif Carlsson .02 .10
64 Hakan Loob .20 .50
65 Stefan Nilsson .02 .10
66 Vitali Prokhorov .10 .25
67 Magnus Arvedsson .02 .10
68 Jonas Hoglund .40 1.00
69 Mathias Johansson .02 .10
70 Patrik Wallenberg .02 .10
71 Claes Eriksson .02 .10
72 Jorgen Jonsson .02 .10
73 Peter Nordstrom .02 .10
74 Peter Ottosson .02 .10
75 Boo Ahl .15 .40
76 Per Gustafsson .10 .25
77 Niklas Rahm .02 .10
78 Hans Abrahamsson .02 .10
79 Kenneth Kennholt .02 .10
80 Daniel Johansson .10 .25
81 Vesa Salo .10 .25
82 Thomas Gustavsson .02 .10
83 Stefan Ornskog .10 .25
84 Stefan Falk .02 .10
85 Peter Hammarstrom .02 .10
86 Johan Davidsson .20 .50
87 Peter Ekelund .02 .10
88 Johan Lindbom .02 .10
89 Esa Keskinen .10 .25
90 Kai Nurminen .20 .50
91 Magnus Eliasson .02 .10
92 Marcus Thuresson .02 .10
93 Johan Brummer .02 .10
94 Johan Hedberg .40 1.00
95 Tomas Jonsson .10 .25
96 Torbjorn Johansson .02 .10
97 Hans Lodin .02 .10
98 Orjan Lindmark .02 .10
99 Jan Huokko .02 .10
100 Joakim Lidgren .02 .10
101 Per-Erik Eklund .10 .25
102 Anders Carlsson .02 .10
103 Niklas Eriksson .02 .10
104 Mikael Karlberg .02 .10
105 Jonas Bergqvist .10 .25
106 Torgny Lowgren .02 .10
107 Stefan Hellkvist .02 .10
108 Markus Akerblom .02 .10
109 Mikael Holmberg .02 .10
110 Andreas Karlsson .02 .10
111 Markus Akerblom .02 .10
112 Tomas Forslund .10 .25
113 Jarmo Myllys .20 .50
114 Lars Modig .02 .10
115 Patrik Hoglund .02 .10
116 Torbjorn Lindberg .02 .10
117 Jan Mertzig .10 .25
118 Petter Nilsson .02 .10
119 Mattias Ohlund .40 1.00
120 Roger Akerstrom .02 .10
121 Stefan Jonsson .02 .10
122 Stefan Nilsson .02 .10
123 Tomas Holmstrom .75 2.00
124 Mikael Lindholm .02 .10
125 Johan Stromvall .02 .10
126 Jiri Kucera .10 .25
127 Joakim Backlund .02 .10
128 Robert Nordberg .02 .10
129 Tomas Berglund .02 .10
130 Frederik Johansson .02 .10
131 Lars Hurtig .02 .10
132 Johan Rosen .02 .10
133 Roger Nordstrom .10 .25
134 Kim Johnsson .40 1.00
135 Peter Hasselblad .02 .10
136 Ilya Byakin .10 .25
137 Johan Salle .02 .10
138 Peter Andersson .02 .10
139 Roger Ohman .02 .10
140 Marko Palo .02 .10
141 Raimo Helminen .10 .25
142 Mattias Bosson .02 .10
143 Markus Magnertoft .02 .10
144 Roger Hansson .02 .10
145 Bo Svanberg .02 .10
146 Patrik Sylvegard .02 .10
147 Brian McReynolds .02 .10
148 Hakan Ahlund .02 .10
149 Robert Burakovsky .02 .10
150 Stefan Elvenes .10 .25
151 Patrik Boij .02 .10
152 Petter Ronnqvist .10 .25
153 Mattias Timander .20 .50
154 Lars Jansson .02 .10
155 Frantisek Kaberle .20 .50
156 Hans Jonsson .02 .10
157 Tomas Nansen .02 .10
158 Marcus Karlsson .02 .10
159 Kristian Gahn .02 .10
160 Magnus Wernblom .02 .10
161 Anders Soderberg .15 .40
162 Martin Hostak .02 .10
163 Kyosti Karjalainen .10 .25
164 Mikael Hakanson .02 .10
165 Jan Larsson .02 .10
166 Per Svartvadet .15 .40
167 Andreas Salomonsson .40 1.00
168 Samuel Pahlsson .60 1.50
169 Lars Bystrom .02 .10
170 Magnus Swardh .10 .25
171 Anders Berglund .02 .10
172 Pierre Johnsson .02 .10
173 Johan Finnstrom .10 .25
174 Arto Ruotanen .02 .10
175 Daniel Tjarnqvist .20 .50
176 Greg Brown .10 .25
177 Per Wallin .10 .25
178 Peter Lundmark .02 .10
179 Roger Elvenes .02 .10
180 Michael Hjalm .10 .25
181 Jens Hemstrom .02 .10
182 Pelle Svensson .02 .10
183 Harijs Vitolins .02 .10
184 Jens Nielsen .02 .10
185 Mats Loov .02 .10
186 Mats Ytter .10 .25
187 Lars Ivarsson .02 .10
188 Edvin Frylen .10 .25
189 Andrei Lyulin .02 .10
190 Johan Tornberg .02 .10
191 Mattias Olsson .02 .10
192 Mats Lusth .02 .10
193 Fredrik Oberg .02 .10
194 Alexei Salomatin .02 .10
195 Mishat Fahrutdinov .02 .10
196 Mikael Pettersson .02 .10
197 Andrei Korolev .02 .10
198 Mattias Loof .02 .10
199 Claes Lindblom .02 .10
200 Paul Andersson .02 .10
201 Roger Rosen .02 .10
202 Hakan Algotsson .10 .25
203 Par Djoos .10 .25
204 Mikael Sandberg .02 .10
205 Joachim Esbjors .02 .10
206 Stefan Axelsson .10 .25
207 Ronnie Sundin .15 .40
208 Stefan Larsson .02 .10
209 Petteri Nummelin .10 .25
210 Christian Ruuttu .20 .50
211 Marko Jantunen .10 .25
212 Peter Strom .02 .10
213 Peter Berndtsson .02 .10
214 Lars Edstrom .10 .25
215 Peter Hogardh .02 .10
216 Par Edlund .02 .10
217 Lars-Goran Wiklander .10 .25
218 Henrik Nilsson .02 .10
219 Rikard Franzen .02 .10
220 Fredrik Modin .30 .75
221 Anders Soderberg .15 .40
222 Per Eklund .10 .25
223 Hakan Loob .20 .50
224 Markus Ketterer .20 .50
225 Esa Keskinen .10 .25
226 Per Gustafsson .10 .25
227 Tomas Jonsson .10 .25
228 Per-Erik Eklund .10 .25
229 Mattias Ohlund .40 1.00
230 Jarmo Myllys .20 .50
231 Peter Andersson .02 .10
232 Raimo Helminen .10 .25
233 Christian Ruuttu .20 .50
234 Peter Forsberg 3.00 8.00
235 Mikael Renberg .20 .50
236 Mats Sundin 1.00 2.50
237 Michael Nylander .20 .50
238 Tommy Soderstrom .20 .50
239 Nicklas Lidstrom .75 2.00
240 Kenny Jonsson .30 .75
241 Patrik Carnback .02 .10
242 Johan Garpenlov .20 .50
243 Magnus Svensson .15 .40
244 Patrik Juhlin .15 .40
245 Markus Naslund .75 2.00
246 Tommy Salo .40 1.00
247 Fredrik Olausson .20 .50
248 Tommy Albelin .10 .25
249 Rikard Franzen .02 .10
250 Jonas Johnsson .02 .10
251 Thomas Ostlund .20 .50
252 Hakan Loob .20 .50
253 Per Gustafsson .10 .25
254 Per-Erik Eklund .10 .25
255 Tomas Jonsson .10 .25
256 Mattias Ohlund .40 1.00
257 Peter Andersson .02 .10
258 Christian Ruuttu .20 .50
259 Checklist .02 .10
260 Checklist .02 .10

1995-96 Swedish Upper Deck 1st Division Stars

This 20-card insert series, which was included in packs at indeterminate odds (estimated at 1:8) features players from the Swedish First Division, a league one step below the Elitserien.

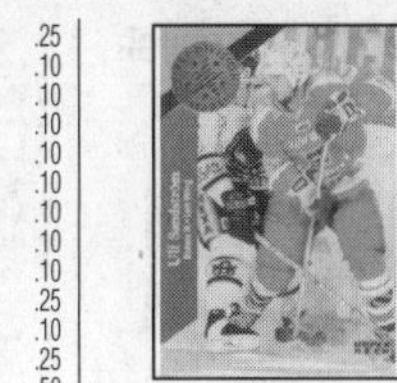

COMPLETE SET (20) 6.00 15.00
DS1 Anders Huss .40 1.00
DS2 Igor Vlasov .40 1.00
DS3 Ulf Sandstrom .40 1.00
DS4 Hans Huczkowski .40 1.00
DS5 Johan Ramstedt .40 1.00
DS6 Anders Eldebrink .40 1.00
DS7 Niklas Brannstrom .40 1.00
DS8 Peter Nilsson .40 1.00
DS9 Sam Lindstahl .40 1.00
DS10 Tony Skopac .40 1.00
DS11 Jonas Eriksson .40 1.00
DS12 Anders Lonn .40 1.00
DS13 Peter Hagstrom .40 1.00
DS14 Magnus Roupe .40 1.00
DS15 Peter Pettersson .40 1.00
DS16 Peter Eriksson .40 1.00
DS17 Fredrik Bergqvist .40 1.00
DS18 Larry Pilut .40 1.00
DS19 Peter Olsson .40 1.00
DS20 Staffan Lundh .40 1.00

1995-96 Swedish Upper Deck Ticket to North America

This 20-card set was randomly inserted in packs at indeterminate odds (estimated at 1:10) and features athletes whose strong play has led to them being selected in the draft and may earn them a shot at the NHL.

COMPLETE SET (20) 12.00 30.00
NA1 Joakim Persson .80 2.00
NA2 Dick Tarnstrom .80 2.00
NA3 Andreas Dackell .80 2.00
NA4 Fredrik Modin 1.20 3.00
NA5 Per Eklund .40 1.00
NA6 Espen Knutsen 1.20 3.00
NA7 Fredrik Lindquist .40 1.00
NA8 Jonas Hoglund .80 2.00
NA9 Jorgen Jonsson .40 1.00
NA10 Johan Davidsson .80 2.00
NA11 Per Gustafsson .40 1.00
NA12 Johan Lindbom .40 1.00
NA13 Markus Akerblom .40 1.00
NA14 Jan Huokko .40 1.00
NA15 Tomas Holmstrom 4.00 10.00
NA16 Mattias Ohlund 1.20 3.00
NA17 Johan Rosen .40 1.00
NA18 Frantisek Kaberle .80 2.00
NA19 Mattias Timander .80 2.00
NA20 Magnus Wernblom .40 1.00

1995 Swedish Globe World Championships

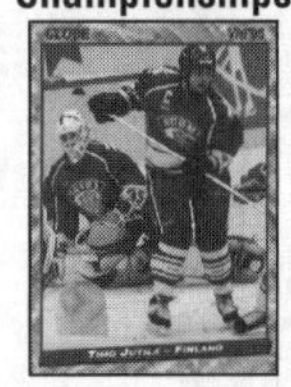

This 270-card set was produced by Semic Press to commemorate the 1995 World Championships, which were held in Stockholm. The players pictured have represented their countries at some point in international competition, and thus are shown wearing their national team garb. Card fronts feature a variegated yellow-orange border, with the Globe and World Championships logo (VM '95) along the top. Player name and country are listed in a blue bar and in Swedish text, along the bottom. A silver foil Globe '95 icon is set in the lower left corner. Card backs include a small reprise of the front photo, along with personal information, including all statistics from major international tournaments. No card number 85 is in the set - Mike Gartner was misnumbered 86. An NNO two-sided card of Peter Forsberg and Mats Sundin was randomly inserted in packs. It is believed that there are less than 2,000 of these cards in circulation. A special binder was released to store the set; it is valued at $5.

COMPLETE SET (270) 20.00 50.00
1 Tommy Soderstrom .10 .25
2 Roger Nordstrom .04 .10
3 Tommy Salo .40 1.00
4 Hakan Algotsson .08 .20
5 Thomas Ostlund .10 .25
7 Ulf Samuelsson .08 .20
8 Calle Johansson .08 .20
9 Nicklas Lidstrom .60 1.50
10 Tommy Albelin .06 .15
11 Peter Andersson .04 .10
12 Magnus Svensson .06 .15
13 Mats Sundin .40 1.00
14 Tomas Jonsson .06 .15
15 Kenny Jonsson .10 .25
16 Tommy Sjodin .06 .15
17 Fredrik Stillman .04 .10
18 Marcus Ragnarsson .10 .25
19 Peter Popovic .06 .15
20 Arto Blomsten .04 .10
21 Peter Forsberg 1.20 3.00
22 Roger Johansson .04 .10
23 Leif Rohlin .06 .15
24 Bjorn Nord .04 .10
25 Stefan Larsson .04 .10
26 Fredrik Olausson .06 .15
27 Kjell Samuelsson .06 .15
28 Tomas Sandstrom .10 .25
29 Mikael Renberg .10 .25
30 Mikael Johansson .04 .10
31 Patrik Juhlin .06 .15
32 Roger Hansson .04 .10
33 Daniel Rydmark .06 .15
34 Jonas Bergqvist .06 .15
35 Michael Nylander .10 .25
36 Johan Garpenlov .06 .15
37 Charles Berglund .04 .10
38 Jorgen Jonsson .04 .10
39 Stefan Ornskog .04 .10
40 Thomas Steen .06 .15
41 Patrik Carnback .04 .10
42 Mikael Andersson .06 .15
43 Markus Naslund .30 .75
44 Andreas Dackell .10 .25
45 Erik Huusko .04 .10
46 Tomas Forslund .06 .15
47 Daniel Alfredsson .20 .50
48 Ulf Dahlen .10 .25
49 Anders Huusko .04 .10
50 Tomas Holmstrom .40 1.00
51 Niklas Andersson .04 .10
52 Hakan Loob .10 .25
53 Per-Erik Eklund .06 .15
54 Patrik Erickson .04 .10
55 Jonas Forsberg .10 .25
56 Daniel Johansson .06 .15
57 Mattias Ohlund .10 .25
58 Anders Eriksson .10 .25
59 Fredrik Modin .20 .50
60 Niklas Sundstrom .10 .25
61 Jesper Mattson .10 .25
62 Johan Davidsson .10 .25
63 Mats Lindgren .10 .25
64 Leif Holmqvist .04 .10
65 Pelle Lindbergh .40 1.00
66 Lennart Svedberg .04 .10
67 Borje Salming .10 .25
68 Sven Tumba Johansson .04 .10
69 Ulf Sterner .04 .10
70 Anders Hedberg .10 .25
71 Kent Nilsson .10 .25
72 Mats Naslund .10 .25
73 Patrick Roy 2.40 6.00
74 Ed Belfour .60 1.50
75 Bill Ranford .20 .50
76 Paul Coffey .40 1.00
77 Ray Bourque .80 2.00
78 Steve Smith .06 .15
79 Al MacInnis .30 .75
80 Mark Tinordi .06 .15
81 Scott Stevens .10 .25
82 Rob Blake .30 .75
83 Theo Fleury .40 1.00
84 Mark Messier .60 1.50
85 Mike Gartner UER .20 .50
card numbered #86
86 Brendan Shanahan .60 1.50
87 Mario Lemieux 2.40 6.00
88 Eric Lindros 1.20 3.00
89 Steve Yzerman 2.40 6.00
90 Adam Oates .20 .50
91 Paul Kariya 1.60 4.00
92 Rick Tocchet .20 .50
93 Doug Gilmour .40 1.00
94 Luc Robitaille .30 .75
95 Jason Arnott .20 .50
96 Adam Graves .20 .50
97 Petr Nedved .10 .25
98 Mark Recchi .30 .75
99 Wayne Gretzky 3.20 8.00
100 Mike Richter .60 1.50
101 John Vanbiesbrouck .40 1.00
102 Tom Barrasso .10 .25
103 Brian Leetch .30 .75
104 Gary Suter .10 .25
105 Kevin Hatcher .06 .15
106 Phil Housley .10 .25
107 Chris Chelios .40 1.00
108 Eric Weinrich .06 .15
109 Derian Hatcher .10 .25
110 Craig Wolanin .06 .15
111 Mike Modano .60 1.50
112 Joe Mullen .10 .25
113 Joel Otto .10 .25
114 Doug Brown .10 .25
115 Brett Hull .60 1.50
116 Pat LaFontaine .20 .50
117 Jeremy Roenick .60 1.50
118 Craig Janney .10 .25
119 Kevin Miller .06 .15
120 Tony Granato .10 .25
121 Tony Amonte .30 .75
122 Kevin Stevens .10 .25
123 Darren Turcotte .06 .15
124 Scott Young .20 .50
125 Doug Weight .30 .75
126 Phil Bourque .06 .15
127 Markus Ketterer .06 .15
128 Jarmo Myllys .20 .50
129 Jyrki Lumme .10 .25
130 Timo Jutila .06 .15
131 Marko Kiprusoff .06 .15
132 Hannu Virta .06 .15
133 Teppo Numminen .10 .25
134 Janne Laukkanen .10 .25
135 Mika Nieminen .10 .25
136 Janne Ojanen .06 .15
137 Jari Kurri .20 .50
138 Esa Tikkanen .10 .25
139 Saku Koivu .40 1.00
140 Teemu Selanne .80 2.00
141 Raimo Helminen .06 .15
142 Mikko Makela .06 .15
143 Christian Ruuttu .06 .15
144 Esa Keskinen .06 .15
145 Dominik Hasek .60 1.50
146 Petr Briza .10 .25
147 Richard Smehlik .06 .15
148 Leo Gudas .04 .10
149 Roman Hamrlik .10 .25
150 Antonin Stavjana .06 .15
151 Jiri Slegr .06 .15
152 Jiri Vykoukal .06 .15
153 Tomas Jelinek .06 .15
154 Richard Zemlicka .06 .15
155 Robert Lang .10 .25
156 Michal Pivonka .10 .25
157 Jaromir Jagr 1.60 3.00
158 Josef Beranek .06 .15
159 Robert Reichel .06 .15
160 Petr Hrbek .04 .10
161 Jiri Kucera .06 .15
162 Kamil Kastak .04 .10
163 Andrei Trefilov .10 .25
164 Mikhail Shtalenkov .10 .25
165 Sergei Zubov .10 .25
166 Vladimir Malakhov .06 .15
167 Igor Kravchuk .06 .15
168 Alexei Gusarov .06 .15
169 Alexei Zhitnik .10 .25
170 Alexander Smirnov .04 .10
171 Dimitri Yushkevich .10 .25
172 Alexei Yashin .16 .40
173 Alexei Zhamnov .10 .25
174 Pavel Bure .80 2.00
175 Sergei Fedorov .80 2.00
176 Andrei Kovalenko .10 .25
177 Alexei Kovalev .20 .50
178 Andrei Khomutov .06 .15
179 Valeri Kamensky .10 .25
180 Viacheslav Bykov .08 .20
181 Claus Dalpiaz .06 .15
182 Michael Puschacher .06 .15
183 Ken Strong .04 .10
184 Martin Ulrich .04 .10
185 Andreas Puschnik .04 .10
186 Herbert Hohenberger .10 .25
187 Marty Dallmann .04 .10
188 James Burton .04 .10
189 Michael Shea .04 .10
190 Jim Marthinsen .10 .25
191 Orjan Lovdal .04 .10
192 Cato Tom Andersen .04 .10
193 Geir Hoff .04 .10
194 Tommy Jakobsen .04 .10
195 Marius Rath .04 .10
196 Trond Magnussen .04 .10
197 Svein Enok Norstebo .04 .10
198 Espen Knutsen .20 .50
199 Petri Ylonen .06 .15
200 Michel Valliere .06 .15
201 Franck Pajonkowski .06 .15
202 Pierrick Maia .04 .10
203 Christophe Ville .04 .10
204 Serge Poudrier .04 .10
205 Philippe Bozon .06 .15
206 Gerald Guennelon .04 .10
207 Antoine Richer .04 .10
208 Reto Pavoni .06 .15
209 Renato Tosio .06 .15
210 Jorg Eberle .06 .15
211 Fredy Luthi .04 .10
212 Christian Weber .04 .10
213 Sandro Bertaggia .04 .10
214 Patrick Howald .04 .10
215 Gil Montandon .04 .10
216 Rick Tschumi .04 .10
217 Klaus Merk .08 .20
218 Josef Heiss .10 .25
219 Rick Amann .04 .10
220 Michael Rumrich .04 .10
221 Thomas Brandl .04 .10
222 Andreas Niederberger .04 .10
223 Leo Stefan .04 .10
224 Stefan Ustorf .04 .10
225 Dieter Hegen .06 .15
226 Michael Rosati .06 .15
227 Bruno Campese .06 .15
228 Roberto Oberrauch .04 .10
229 Anthony Circelli .04 .10
230 Bill Stewart .04 .10
231 Bruno Zarillo .04 .10
232 Gaetano Orlando .04 .10
233 Stefan Figliuzzi .04 .10
234 Jimmy Carnazzola .04 .10
235 Vladislav Tretiak .40 1.00
236 Slava Fetisov .20 .50
237 Alexei Kasatonov .10 .25
238 Sergei Makarov .10 .25
239 Igor Larionov .30 .75
240 Vladimir Krutov .10 .25
241 Valeri Kharlamov .10 .25
242 Vladimir Petrov .06 .15
243 Boris Mikhailov .10 .25
244 Sweden Olympic Gold 94 .10 .25
245 Sweden Olympic Hakan Loob .10 .25
246 Sweden Olympic Gold .10 .25
247 Canada World Champs 94 Team .30 .75
248 Canada Steve Thomas .10 .25
249 Canada Luc Robitaille .20 .50
250 Manon Rheaume 1.20 3.00
251 Sundin and Andersson .20 .50
252 Brolin and Knutsen .10 .25
253 Peter Forsberg Special 1.20 3.00
254 Peter Forsberg Special 1.20 3.00
255 Peter Forsberg Special 1.20 3.00
256 Mats Sundin Special .40 1.00
257 Mats Sundin Special .40 1.00
258 Mats Sundin Special .40 1.00
259 Mikael Renberg Special .10 .25
260 Mikael Renberg Special .10 .25
261 Mikael Renberg Special .10 .25
262 Eric Lindros Special 1.20 3.00
263 Eric Lindros Special 1.20 3.00
264 Eric Lindros Special 1.20 3.00
265 Wayne Gretzky Special 3.20 8.00
266 Wayne Gretzky Special 3.20 8.00
267 Wayne Gretzky Special 3.20 8.00
268 Checklist 1-90 Renberg .10 .25
269 Checklist 91-180 Sundin .40 1.00
270 Checklist 181-270 Forsberg 1.20 3.00
XX Binder 2.00 5.00
NNO Peter Forsberg 12.00 20.00
Mats Sundin

1995 Swedish World Championships Stickers

This set recently was confirmed by collector Per Vedin. We have no pricing information at this point, and thus are listing the set below for checklisting purposes only.

COMPLETE SET (300) 75.00
1 Bill Ranford .02 .10
2 Stephane Fiset .20 .50
3 Steve Duchesne .10 .25
4 Brad Schlegel .02 .10
5 Luke Richardson .02 .10
6 Darryl Sydor .02 .10
7 Yves Racine .02 .10
8 Rob Blake .20 .50
9 Marc Bergevin .02 .10
10 Paul Coffey .60 1.50
11 Jason Arnott .20 .50
12 Geoff Sanderson .20 .50
13 Shayne Corson .20 .50
14 Mike Ricci .20 .50
15 Kelly Buchberger .20 .50
16 Brendan Shanahan .75 2.00
17 Patrick Verbeek .20 .50
18 Nelson Emerson .20 .50
19 Rod Brindâ ™Amour .20 .50
20 Joe Sakic 2.00 5.00
21 Luc Robitaille .60 1.50
22 Stephen Thomas .10 .25
23 Paul Kariya 1.50 4.00
24 Theo Fleury .40 1.00
25 Dave Gagner .20 .50
26 Valeri Ivannikov .02 .10
27 Mikhail Shtalenkov .20 .50
28 Nikolai Tsulygin .02 .10
29 Dmitri Krasotkin .02 .10
30 Morat Davydov .02 .10
31 Andrei Sklopintsev .02 .10
32 Oleg Davydov .02 .10
33 Evgeni Gribko .02 .10
34 Andrei Yakhanov .02 .10
35 Igor Nikulin .02 .10
36 Valeri Kamensky .02 .10
37 Boris Timofeev .02 .10
38 Dmitri Denisov .02 .10
39 Rail Muftiev .02 .10
40 Andrei Tarasenko .02 .10
41 Oleg Belov .02 .10
42 Andrei Kovalenko .02 .10
43 Igor Varitski .02 .10
44 Ravil Yakubov .02 .10
45 Viacheslav Kozlov .20 .50
46 Alexander Vinogradov .02 .10
47 Yuri Tsyplakov .02 .10
48 Stanislav Romanov .02 .10
49 Slava Bykov .10 .25
50 Andrei Khomutov .10 .25
51 Joseph Heiss .02 .10
52 Klaus Merk .10 .25
53 Mirko LÃ¼demann .02 .10
54 Ulrich Hiemer .02 .10
55 Torsten Kienass .02 .10
56 Jayson Meyer .02 .10
57 Josef Lehner .02 .10
58 Ron Fischer .10 .25
59 Michael Bresagk .02 .10
60 Andreas Niederberger .02 .10
61 Peter Gulda .02 .10
62 Jan Benda .10 .25
63 Thomas Brandl .02 .10
64 Andreas Lupzig .02 .10
65 Michael Rumrich .02 .10
66 Benoit Doucet .10 .25
67 Raimond Hilger .02 .10
68 Georg Franz .02 .10
69 Jorg Handrick .02 .10
70 Dieter Hegen .10 .25
71 Ernst Kopf .02 .10
72 Gunter Oswald .02 .10
73 Georg Holzmann .02 .10
74 JÃ¼rgen Rumrich .02 .10
75 Leo Stefan .02 .10
76 Bruno Campese .10 .25
77 Michael Rosati .20 .50
78 Giovanni Marchetti .02 .10
79 Georg Comploj .02 .10
80 Luigi da Corte .02 .10
81 Robert Oberrauch .02 .10
82 Anthony Circelli .02 .10
83 Alex Thaler .02 .10
84 Carlo Lorenzi .02 .10
85 Michael de Angelis .02 .10
86 Emilio Iovio .02 .10
87 Gaetano Orlando .10 .25
88 Lucio Topatigh .02 .10
89 Stefano Figliuzzi .02 .10
90 Bruno Zarrillo .02 .10
91 Mark Montanari .02 .10
92 Armando Chelodi .02 .10
93 Mirko Moroder .02 .10
94 Alex Gschliesser .02 .10
95 Maurizio Mansi .02 .10
96 Petri YlÃ¶nen .10 .25
97 Michel Valliere .10 .25
98 Serge Djelloul .02 .10
99 Christophe Moyon .02 .10
100 Gerald Guennelon .02 .10
101 Philippe Lemoine .02 .10
102 Denis Perez .10 .25
103 Serge Poudrier .10 .25
104 Steven Woodburn .02 .10
105 Michael Babin .02 .10
106 Benjamin Agnel .02 .10
107 Stephane Arcangeloni .02 .10
108 Laurent Deschaume .02 .10
109 Pierre Pousse .02 .10
110 Patrick Dunn .02 .10
111 Pierrick Maia .02 .10
112 Philippe Bozon .40 1.00
113 Christian Pouget .02 .10
114 Antoine Richer .02 .10
115 Richard Aimonetto .02 .10
116 Reto Pavoni .02 .10
117 Renato Tosio .02 .10
118 Marco Bayer .02 .10
119 Sandro Bertaggia .02 .10
120 Fredy Bobillier .02 .10
121 Dino Kessler .02 .10
122 Sven Leuenberger .02 .10
123 Martin Steinegger .02 .10
124 Andreas Zehnder .02 .10
125 Misko Antisin .02 .10
126 Gian-Marco Crameri .10 .25
127 JÃ¶rg Eberle .10 .25
128 Patrick Fischer .02 .10
129 Patrick Howald .02 .10
130 Marcel Jenni .02 .10
131 Gil Montandon .02 .10
132 Pascal Schaller .02 .10
133 Andy Ton .02 .10
134 Roberto Triulzi .02 .10
135 Theo Wittman .02 .10
136 Roger Nordstrom .02 .10
137 Thomas Ostlund .10 .25
138 Magnus Svensson .02 .10
139 Tommy Sjodin .10 .25
140 Fredrik Stillman .02 .10
141 Tomas Jonsson .02 .10
142 Stefan Larsson .02 .10
143 Leif Rohlin .02 .10
144 Marcus Ragnarsson .02 .10
145 Christer Olsson .02 .10
146 Morgan Samuelsson .02 .10
147 Andreas Dackell .02 .10
148 Jonas Johnsson .02 .10
149 Charles Berglund .02 .10
150 Erik Huusko .02 .10
151 Daniel Rydmark .02 .10
152 Patrik CarnbÃ¤ck .02 .10
153 Mats Lindgren .02 .10
154 Jonas Bergkvist .02 .10
155 Stefan Ornskog .02 .10
156 Per-Erik Eklund .10 .25
157 Thomas Forslund .02 .10
158 Roger Hansson .02 .10
159 Hakan Ahlund .02 .10
160 Daniel Alfredsson .20 .50
161 Jarmo Myllys .20 .50
162 Jukka Tammi .10 .25
163 Mika Stromberg .10 .25
164 Erik Hamalainen .02 .10
165 Karri Kivi .02 .10
166 Timo Jutila .02 .10
167 Petteri Nummelin .02 .10
168 Hannu Virta .02 .10
169 Marko Kiprusov .02 .10
170 Waltteri Immonen .10 .25
171 Janne Ojanen .02 .10
172 Esa Keskinen .02 .10
173 Marko Jantunen .02 .10
174 Saku Koivu .40 1.00
175 Marko Palo .02 .10
176 Tero Lehtera .02 .10
177 Mika Alatalo .20 .50
178 Ville Peltonen .10 .25
179 Raimo Helminen .02 .10
180 Petri Varis .10 .25
181 Jokke HeinÃ¤nen .02 .10
182 Timo Saarikoski .02 .10
183 Sami Kapanen .20 .50
184 Tero Arkiomaa .02 .10
185 Mika Nieminen .10 .25
186 Peter Briza .20 .50
187 Roman Turek .20 .50
188 Milos Holan .02 .10
189 Drahomir Kadlec .10 .25
190 Frantisek Kaberle .02 .10
191 Bedrich Scerban .10 .25
192 Roman Hamrlik .10 .25
193 Jan Vopat .02 .10
194 Antonin Stavjana .02 .10
195 Jiri Vykoukal .02 .10
196 Jiri Veber .02 .10
197 Frantisek Musil .02 .10
198 Richard Zemlicka .10 .25
199 Kamil Kastak .10 .25
200 Jiri Kucera .10 .25
201 Roman Horak .02 .10
202 Martin Rucinsky .10 .25
203 Josef Beranek .10 .25
204 Bobby Holik .10 .25
205 Otakar Janecky .10 .25
206 Jiri Dolezal .02 .10
207 Martin Straka .10 .25
208 Martin HostakÂ .02 .10
209 Radek Toupal .02 .10
210 Tomas Kapusta .02 .10
211 Guy Hebert .40 1.00
212 Mike Richter .60 1.50
213 Shawn Chambers .02 .10
214 Sean Hill .02 .10
215 Don McSween .02 .10
216 Pat Neaton .02 .10
217 Barry Richter .02 .10
218 Craig Wolanin .02 .10
219 Gary Suter .10 .25
220 Robert Beers .10 .25
221 Brett Hauer .02 .10
222 Peter Ciavaglia .02 .10
223 Phil Bourque .02 .10
224 Shjon Podein .10 .25
225 John Lilley .10 .25
226 Tim Sweeney .10 .25
227 Scott Young .10 .25
228 Craig Janney .10 .25
229 Joe Sacco .10 .25
230 Jeffrey Lazaro .10 .25
231 Doug Weight .40 1.00
232 Thomas Bissett .20 .50
233 James Campbell .10 .25
234 Mark Beaufait .10 .25
235 Peter Ferraro .10 .25
236 Jim Marthinsen .10 .25

237 Robert Schistad .10 .25
238 Jan Roar Fagerli .02 .10
239 Petter Salsten .02 .10
240 Carl Oscar Boe Andersen .02 .10
241 Svein Enok Norstebo .02 .10
242 Tommie Eriksen .02 .10
243 Tom Erik Olsen .02 .10
244 Geir Hoff .02 .10
245 Bjorn Anders Dahl .02 .10
246 Trond Magnussen .02 .10
247 Orjan Lovdahl .02 .10
248 Espen Knutsen .20 .50
249 Rune Gulliksen .02 .10
250 Eirik Paulsen .02 .10
251 Sjur Robert Nilsen .02 .10
252 Petter Thoresen .02 .10
253 Rune Fjeldstad .02 .10
254 Erik Tveten .02 .10
255 Henrik Aaby .02 .10
256 Michael Puschacher .02 .10
257 Claus Dalpiaz .10 .25
258 Michael Guntner .02 .10
259 Martin Ulrich .02 .10
260 Peter Kasper .02 .10
261 Engelbert Linder .02 .10
262 Herbert Hohenberger .02 .10
263 Gerhard Unterluggauer .02 .10
264 Martin Krainz .02 .10
265 Helmut Karel .02 .10
266 Werner Kerth .02 .10
267 Dieter Kalt .02 .10
268 Patrick Pilloni .02 .10
269 Mario Schaden .02 .10
270 Wolfgang Kromp .02 .10
271 Gunter Lanzinger .02 .10
272 Manfred Muhr .02 .10
273 Gerald Ressman .02 .10
274 Siegfried Haberl .02 .10
275 Christoph Brandner .02 .10
276 Wayne Gretzky 6.00 15.00
277 Mario Lemieux 5.00 12.00
278 Eric Lindros 1.50 4.00
279 Mark Messier 1.25 3.00
280 Steve Yzerman 4.00 10.00
281 Pavel Bure 1.00 2.50
282 Sergei Fedorov 1.25 3.00
283 Igor Larionov .40 1.00
284 Sergei Makarov .40 1.00
285 Alexander Mogilny .40 1.00
286 Ulf Dahlen .10 .25
287 Peter Forsberg 2.00 5.00
288 Mikael Renberg .20 .50
289 Ulf Samuelsson .10 .25
290 Tomas SandstrÃ¶m .10 .25
291 Thomas Steen .10 .25
292 Mats Sundin .60 1.50
293 Jari Kurri .40 1.00
294 Teemu Selanne 2.00 5.00
295 Esa Tikkanen .20 .50
296 Dominik Hasek 1.25 3.00
297 Jaromir Jagr 1.50 4.00
298 Robert Reichel .02 .10
299 Brett Hull 1.50 4.00
300 Brian Leetch .60 1.50

1996 Swedish Semic Wien

The 1996 Semic Wien set was issued in one series totaling 240 cards to commemorate the 1996 World Championships held in Vienna. The set features players who have competed for their countries in various tournaments, including the Olympics. Many top NHLers are featured, including Wayne Gretzky, Eric Lindros and Ray Bourque. The cards were distributed in ten-card packs.

COMPLETE SET (240) 16.00 40.00
1 Jarmo Myllys .10 .25
2 Marko Kiprusoff .06 .15
3 Petteri Nummelin .04 .10
4 Erik Hamalainen .04 .10
5 Timo Jutila .06 .15
6 Janne Ninimaa .10 .25
7 Raimo Summanen .06 .15
8 Janne Ojanen .06 .15
9 Esa Keskinen .06 .15
10 Ari Sulander .10 .25
11 Saku Koivu .20 .50
12 Jukka Tammi .10 .25
13 Marko Palo .04 .10
14 Raimo Helminen .06 .15
15 Antti Tormanen .08 .20
16 Ville Peltonen .10 .25
17 Tero Lehtera .06 .15
18 Mika Stromberg .06 .15
19 Sami Kapanen .14 .35
20 Jere Lehtinen .14 .35
21 Juha Ylonen .08 .20
22 Mika Nieminen .08 .20
23 Hannu Virta .06 .15
24 Jari Kurri .14 .35
25 Christian Ruuttu .06 .15
26 Jyrki Lumme .06 .15
27 Teppo Numminen .10 .25
28 Esa Tikkanen .10 .25
29 Janne Laukkanen .08 .20
30 Aki Berg .10 .25
31 Teemu Selanne .80 1.50
32 Markus Ketterer .10 .25
33 Joni Lehto .04 .10
34 Juha Riihijarvi .06 .15
35 Sakari Lindfors .10 .25
36 Kai Nurminen .10 .25
37 Huey, Dewey, Louie .20 .50
38 Tommy Soderstrom .10 .25
39 Tommy Salo .30 .50
40 Thomas Ostlund .08 .20
41 Boo Ahl .08 .20
42 Calle Johansson .08 .20
43 Tommy Albelin .06 .15
44 Ulf Samuelsson .06 .15
45 Nicklas Lidstrom .40 1.00
46 Magnus Svensson .06 .15
47 Tomas Jonsson .06 .15
48 Tommy Sjodin .06 .15
49 Marcus Ragnarsson .10 .25
50 Christer Olsson .04 .10
51 Rikard Franzen .04 .10
52 Mattias Ohlund .10 .25
53 Kenny Jonsson .10 .25
54 Roger Johansson .04 .10
55 Anders Eriksson .10 .25
56 Mats Sundin .30 .75
57 Peter Forsberg .80 2.00
58 Mikael Renberg .10 .25
59 Tomas Sandstrom .08 .20
60 Ulf Dahlen .06 .15
61 Michael Nylander .06 .15
62 Patrik Juhlin .06 .15
63 Patrik Carnback .06 .15
64 Andreas Johansson .08 .20
65 Mikael Johansson .04 .10
66 Per-Erik Eklund .06 .15
67 Tomas Forslund .06 .15
68 Andreas Dackell .08 .20
69 Per Eklund .06 .15
70 Tomas Holmstrom .20 .50
71 Jonas Bergqvist .06 .15
72 Daniel Alfredsson .14 .35
73 Fredrik Modin .10 .25
74 Magic Moment .40 1.00
75 Ed Belfour .40 1.00
76 Bill Ranford .10 .25
77 Sean Burke .10 .25
78 Ray Bourque .60 1.50
79 Paul Coffey .20 .50
80 Scott Stevens .20 .50
81 Al MacInnis .20 .50
82 Larry Murphy .10 .25
83 Eric Desjardins .10 .25
84 Steve Duchesne .08 .20
85 Mario Lemieux 1.60 4.00
86 Mark Messier .40 1.00
87 Theo Fleury .30 .75
88 Eric Lindros .80 1.50
89 Rick Tocchet .14 .35
90 Brendan Shanahan .60 1.00
91 Claude Lemieux .14 .35
92 Joe Juneau .10 .25
93 Luc Robitaille .30 .75
94 Paul Kariya 1.20 2.00
95 Joe Sakic .80 2.00
96 Mark Recchi .20 .50
97 Jason Arnott .14 .35
98 Rod Brind'Amour .14 .35
99 Wayne Gretzky 2.00 5.00
100 Adam Oates .20 .50
101 Steve Yzerman 1.60 4.00
102 Roman Turek .30 .50
103 Dominik Hasek .60 1.00
104 Petr Briza .10 .25
105 Antonin Stavjana .06 .15
106 Frantisek Kaberle .08 .20
107 Jiri Vykoukal .06 .15
108 Jan Vopat .08 .20
109 Libor Prochazka .04 .10
110 Petr Kuchyna .06 .15
111 Frantisek Musil .06 .15
112 Leo Gudas .04 .10
113 Jiri Slegr .08 .20
114 Pavel Patera .10 .25
115 Otakar Vejvoda .10 .25
116 Martin Prochazka .10 .25
117 Jiri Kucera .04 .10
118 Pavel Janku .08 .20
119 Roman Meluzin .04 .10
120 Richard Zemlicka .04 .10
121 Martin Hostak .04 .10
122 Jiri Dopita .08 .20
123 Radek Belohlav .08 .20
124 Roman Horak .04 .10
125 Jaromir Jagr .80 1.50
126 Michal Pivonka .10 .25
127 Josef Beranek .06 .15
128 Robert Reichel .10 .25
129 Nikolai Khabibulin .20 .50
130 Sergei Abramov .08 .20
131 Yevgeny Tarasov .04 .10
132 Igor Kravchuk .08 .20
133 Dmitri Mironov .10 .25
134 Alexei Zhitnik .10 .25
135 Vladimir Malakhov .08 .20
136 Sergei Zubov .10 .25
137 Dimitri Yushkevich .10 .25
138 Ilya Byakin .04 .10
139 Alexander Smirnov .04 .10
140 Andrei Skopintsev .04 .10
141 Sergei Fedorov .60 1.50
142 Pavel Bure 1.20 2.00
143 Alexei Zhamnov .10 .25
144 Andrei Kovalenko .10 .25
145 Igor Korolev .06 .15
146 Slava Kozlov .14 .35
147 Viktor Kozlov .10 .25
148 Alexei Yashin .14 .35
149 Valeri Kamensky .10 .25
150 Stanislav Romanov .04 .10
151 Viacheslav Bykov .08 .20
152 Andrei Khomutov .10 .25
153 Sergei Berezin .14 .35
154 German Titov .10 .25
155 Dmitri Denisov .04 .10
156 John Vanbiesbrouck .20 .50
157 Jim Carey .10 .25
158 Mike Richter .30 .75
159 Chris Chelios .30 .75
160 Brian Leetch .30 .75
161 Phil Housley .10 .25
162 Gary Suter .08 .20
163 Kevin Hatcher .08 .20
164 Brett Hull .40 1.00
165 Pat LaFontaine .14 .35
166 Mike Modano .40 1.00
167 Jeremy Roenick .30 1.00
168 Keith Tkachuk .30 .75
169 Joe Mullen .08 .20
170 Craig Janney .10 .25
171 Joel Otto .08 .20
172 Doug Weight .20 .50
173 Scott Young .10 .25
174 Michael Rosati .06 .15
175 Bruno Campese .06 .15
176 Robert Oberrauch .04 .10
177 Robert Nardella .04 .10
178 Stefano Figfuzzi .04 .10
179 Maurizio Mansi .04 .10
180 Gaetano Orlando .04 .10
181 Mario Chitarroni .04 .10
182 Martin Pavlu .04 .10
183 Petri Ylonen .08 .20
184 Michel Valliere .04 .10
185 Serge Poudrier .04 .10
186 Denis Perez .04 .10
187 Antoine Richer .04 .10
188 Philippe Bozon .06 .15
189 Christian Pouget .04 .10
190 Franck Pajonkowski .06 .15
191 Stephane Barin .04 .10
192 Klaus Merk .08 .20
193 Marc Seliger .06 .15
194 Mirco Ludermann .04 .10
195 Jayson Meyer .04 .10
196 Benoit Doucet .06 .15
197 Thomas Brandl .04 .10
198 Dieter Hegen .06 .15
199 Martin Reichel .04 .10
200 Leo Stefan .04 .10
201 Robert Schistad .04 .10
202 Jim Marthinsen .08 .20
203 Tommy Jakobsen .04 .10
204 Petter Salsten .04 .10
205 Svein Norstebo .04 .10
206 Espen Knutsen .10 .25
207 Trond Magnussen .04 .10
208 Henrik Aaby .04 .10
209 Marius Rath .04 .10
210 Claus Dalpiaz .06 .15
211 Michael Puschacher .06 .15
212 Robin Doyle .04 .10
213 James Burton .04 .10
214 Herbert Hohenberger .04 .10
215 Andreas Pusnik .04 .10
216 Richard Nasheim .04 .10
217 Deiter Kalt .04 .10
218 Werner Kerth .04 .10
219 Eduard Hartmann .06 .15
220 Jaromir Dragan .10 .25
221 Robert Svehla .10 .25
222 Lubomir Sekeras .10 .25
223 Marian Smerciak .04 .10
224 Jergus Baca .06 .15
225 Stanslav Medrik .04 .10
226 Miroslav Marcinko .04 .10
227 Peter Stastny .10 .25
228 Peter Bondra .20 .50
229 Zdeno Ciger .10 .25
230 Jozef Stumpel .10 .25
231 Miroslav Satan .20 .50
232 Lubomir Kolnik .08 .20
233 Robert Petrovicky .06 .15
234 Zigmund Palffy .20 .50
235 Oto Hascak .06 .15
236 Jozef Dano .04 .10
237 Checklist .10 .25
238 Checklist .10 .25
239 Checklist .10 .25
240 Checklist .10 .25
NNO Mikael Renberg 14.00 25.00
Saku Koivu Super Chase

1996 Swedish Semic Wien All-Stars

Randomly inserted in packs at a rate of 1:20, this 6-card , double-sided set acknowledges the first and second team all-stars from the 1995 WC. Both sides share similar designs; the player on the side with the gold foil stars across the top was the first team selection.

COMPLETE SET (6) 8.00 8.00
AS1 Roman Turek 2.00 2.00
Jarmo Myllys
AS2 Timo Jutila .40 .50
Christer Olsson
AS3 Tommy Sjodin .40 .50
Marko Kiprusoff
AS4 Jere Lehtinen 2.00 2.00
Sergei Berezin
AS5 Saku Koivu 4.00 5.00
Pelle Eklund
AS6 Ville Peltonen .80 1.00
Andrew McKim

1996 Swedish Semic Wien Coca-Cola Dream Team

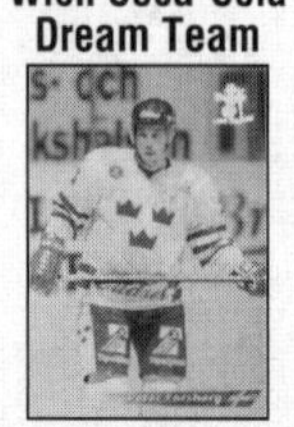

This 12-card set was created as a promotion to tie in with the World Championships and the Semic Wien set. The cards were issued four to a pack at participating Shell gas stations in Sweden with the purchase of a Coca-Cola product. The cards mirror their counterparts in the regular Semic Wien set, save for the numbering and the silver Dream Team icon on the upper corner of each.

COMPLETE SET (12) 20.00 50.00
1 Tommy Soderstrom .80 2.00
2 Boo Ahl .80 2.00
3 Tomas Jonsson .40 1.00
4 Rikard Franzen .40 1.00
5 Mattias Ohlund 1.20 3.00
6 Roger Johansson .40 1.00
7 Mats Sundin 4.00 10.00
8 Peter Forsberg 12.00 30.00
9 Mikael Renberg 1.20 3.00
10 Per-Erik Eklund .40 1.00
11 Andreas Dackell 1.20 3.00
12 Jonas Bergqvist .80 2.00

1996 Swedish Semic Wien Hockey Legends

Randomly inserted in packs at a rate of 1:6, this 18-card set recalls some of the best to lace 'em up on either side of the pond. The card front features a period action photo, with the Hockey Legends logo above in gold foil. The backs display another vintage photo, along with career notes and international play totals. The cards are numbered with an HL prefix.

COMPLETE SET (18) 14.00 35.00
HL1 Ken Dryden 4.00 10.00
HL2 Guy Lafleur 2.00 5.00
HL3 Mike Bossy 1.60 4.00
HL4 Valeri Vasiliev .40 1.00
HL5 Anatoli Firsov .40 1.00
HL6 Alexander Maltsev .80 2.00
HL7 Tony Esposito 2.00 5.00
HL8 Rod Langway .40 1.00
HL9 Bryan Trottier 1.20 3.00
HL10 Lennart Haggroth .40 1.00
HL11 Ulf Nilsson .80 2.00
HL12 Lars-Gunnar Lundberg .40 1.00
HL13 Veli-Pekka Ketola .40 1.00
HL14 Lasse Oksanen .40 1.00
HL15 Pekka Rautakallio .40 1.00
HL16 Jiri Holecek .80 2.00
HL17 Jan Suchy .40 1.00
HL18 Vaclav Nedomansky .80 2.00

1996 Swedish Semic Wien Nordic Stars

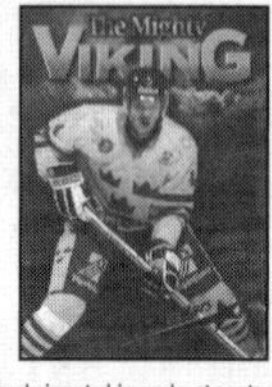

Randomly inserted in packs at a rate of 1:48, this 6-card set heaps praise on Scandinavia's best. Card fronts utilize an action photo over a stylized background with an apt description of the player prominently featured. The backs display international totals, with a brief bio in English. The cards are numbered with an NS prefix.

COMPLETE SET (6) 10.00 25.00
NS1 Peter Forsberg 4.00 10.00
NS2 Teemu Selanne 2.50 6.00
NS3 Mats Sundin 2.00 5.00
NS4 Jari Kurri 2.00 5.00
NS5 Nicklas Lidstrom 2.00 5.00
NS6 Esa Tikkanen .75 2.00

1996 Swedish Semic Wien Super Goalies

Randomly inserted in packs at a rate of 1:12, this 9-card set captures the last line of defense of some elite hockey nations. The fronts have an action photo over a ghosted, maskless image. The back has another photo and a brief bio in English. The cards are numbered with an SG prefix out of 9. The key card is a rare shot of Patrick Roy from a Team Canada training camp session.

COMPLETE SET (9) 15.00 30.00
SG1 Dominik Hasek 4.00 8.00
SG2 Ed Belfour 2.00 5.00
SG3 Jarmo Myllys .75 2.00
SG4 Tommy Soderstrom .75 2.00
SG5 Jim Carey .75 2.00
SG6 Roman Turek .75 2.00
SG7 Patrick Roy 8.00 20.00
SG8 Markus Ketterer .75 2.00
SG9 Tommy Salo .75 2.00

1997-98 Swedish Alfabilder Autographs

These cards are part of a larger multi-sport set of autographs issued within Sweden. We have listed just the hockey players in the set, below. If anyone has information on other hockey players in this set, or on the set itself, please forward it to hockeymag@beckett.com.

1 Sven Tumba Johansson 8.00 20.00
2 Roland Stoltz 4.00 10.00
3 Eilert Maatta 4.00 10.00
4 Lennart Haggroth 6.00 15.00
5 Nisse Nilsson 4.00 10.00
6 Ulf Sterner 8.00 20.00
7 Leif Holmqvist 8.00 20.00
8 Tord Lundstrom 4.00 10.00
9 Borje Salming 20.00 50.00
10 Anders Hedberg 12.00 30.00
11 Anders Kallur 6.00 15.00
12 Stefan Persson 6.00 15.00
13 Goran Hogosta 4.00 10.00
14 Bengt-Ake Gustafsson 8.00 20.00
15 Mats Naslund 12.00 30.00
16 Kent Nilsson 12.00 30.00
17 Hakan Loob 12.00 30.00
18 Peter Lindmark 10.00 25.00

1997-98 Swedish Collector's Choice

This set was produced by Upper Deck for the Swedish SEL. The cards came in 10-card packs for about $1.50 per pack. It is noteworthy for featuring early cards of Daniel and Henrik Sedin.

COMPLETE SET (225) 10.00 25.00
1 Miikka Kiprusoff 1.25 3.00
2 Karri Kivi .04 .10
3 Erik Hamalainen .08 .20
4 Libor Prochazka .04 .10
5 Dick Tarnstrom .20 .50
6 Niclas Havelid .20 .50
7 Tomas Strandberg .04 .10
8 Stefan Gustavsson .04 .10
9 Anders Gozzi .04 .10
10 Pavel Patera .14 .35
11 David Engblom .04 .10
12 Peter Hammarstrom .04 .10
13 Mats Lindberg .04 .10
14 Fredrik Krekula .04 .10
15 Otakar Vejvoda .04 .10
16 Bjorn Ahlstrom .04 .10
17 Michael Sundlov .10 .25
18 PÅor Djoos .04 .10
19 Tommy Melkersson .04 .10
20 Stefan Klockare .04 .10
21 Johan Hansson .04 .10
22 Per Lofstrom .04 .10
23 Tommy Westlund .10 .25
24 Teppo Kivela .04 .10
25 Niclas Wallin .30 .75
26 Roger Kyro .04 .10
27 Ove Molin .04 .10
28 Mikko Luovi .04 .10
29 Evgenij Davydov .04 .10
30 Anders Huss .04 .10
31 Peter Nylander .04 .10
32 Jan Larsson .04 .10
33 Tommy Soderstrom .20 .50
34 Marcus Matthiasson .04 .10
35 Daniel Carlsson .04 .10
36 Ronnie Pettersson .04 .10
37 Kenneth Kennholt .04 .10
38 Bjorn Nord .08 .20
39 Mikael Hakansson .08 .20
40 Daniel Tjarnqvist .20 .50
41 Charles Berglund .04 .10
42 Mikael Johansson .04 .10
43 Marcus Nilsson .20 .50
44 Nichlas Falk .10 .25
45 Fredrik Lindqvist .10 .25
46 Patric Kjellberg .20 .50
47 Patrik Erickson .04 .10
48 Jan Viktorsson .04 .10
49 Niklas Anger .10 .25
50 Boris Rousson .10 .25
51 Peter Jakobsson .04 .10
52 Peter Nordstrom .10 .25
53 Fredrik Sjokvist .04 .10
54 Niklas Sjokvist .04 .10
55 Jaroslav Spacek .10 .25
56 Greger Artursson .04 .10
57 Roger Johansson .04 .10
58 Stefan Nilsson .04 .10
59 Pelle Prestberg .04 .10
60 Kristian Huselius .75 2.00
61 Mathias Johansson .04 .10
62 Trond Magnussen .04 .10
63 Claes Eriksson .04 .10
64 Jorgen Jonsson .14 .35
65 Atle Olsen .04 .10
66 Patrik Wallenberg .04 .10
67 Lars-Goran Wiklander .04 .10
68 Mikael Sandberg .10 .25
69 Christer Olsson .04 .10
70 Joachim Esbjors .04 .10
71 Henrik Nilsson .04 .10
72 Arto Blomsten .04 .10
73 Magnus Johansson .04 .10
74 Stefan Larsson .04 .10
75 Par Edlund .04 .10
76 Marko Jantunen .04 .10
77 Joni Lius .04 .10
78 Patrik Carnback .08 .20
79 Ville Peltonen .20 .50
80 Peter Berndtsson .04 .10
81 Kai Nurminen .08 .20
82 Jonas Esbjors .04 .10
83 Peter Strom .04 .10
84 Kari Takko .10 .25
85 Johan Forsander .10 .25
86 Jouni Loponen .04 .10
87 David Petrasek .04 .10
88 Daniel Johansson .08 .20
89 Fredrik Stillman .04 .10
90 Anatoly Fedotov .04 .10
91 Stefan Ornskog .04 .10
92 Stefan Falk .04 .10
93 Peter Ekelund .04 .10
94 Esa Keskinen .04 .10
95 Patrik Lundback .04 .10
96 Anders Huusko .04 .10
97 Magnus Svensson .04 .10
98 Alexei Salomatin .04 .10
99 Patrik Englund .04 .10
100 Ake Lilljebjorn .10 .25
101 Tomas Jonsson .04 .10
102 Torbjorn Johansson .04 .10
103 Hans Lodin .04 .10
104 Magnus Svensson .04 .10
105 Andreas Karlsson .20 .50
106 Joakim Lidgren .04 .10
107 Fredrik Jonsson .04 .10
108 Per-Erik Eklund .04 .10
109 Anders Carlsson .04 .10
110 Johan Witehall .04 .10
111 Jens Nielsen .04 .10
112 Niklas Eriksson .04 .10
113 Jonas Bergqvist .08 .20
114 Stefan Hellkvist .04 .10
115 Markus Akerblom .08 .20
116 Anders Lonn .04 .10
117 Jarmo Myllys .10 .25
118 Johan Finnstrom .08 .20
119 Sergei Bautin .04 .10
120 Jan Mertzig .08 .20
121 Osmo Soutokorva .04 .10
122 Roger Akerstrom .04 .10
123 Stefan Jonsson .08 .20
124 Stefan Nilsson .04 .10
125 Jonas Ronnqvist .10 .25
126 Joakim Backlund .04 .10
127 Robert Nordberg .04 .10
128 Mikael Lovgren .04 .10
129 Anders Burstrom .04 .10
130 Fredrik Johansson .04 .10
131 Mika Alatalo .20 .50
132 Fredrik Nilsson .04 .10
133 Roger Nordstrom .10 .25
134 Andrew Verner .10 .25
135 Marko Kiprusoff .10 .25
136 Kim Johnsson .20 .50
137 Magnus Nilsson .04 .10
138 Jesper Damgaard .04 .10
139 Marek Malik .08 .20
140 Mats Lusth .04 .10
141 Janne Ojanen .08 .20
142 Mikko Peltola .04 .10
143 Mathias Bosson .04 .10
144 Daniel Rydmark .04 .10
145 Patrik Sylvegard .04 .10
146 Juha Riihijarvi .08 .20
147 Fredrik Oberg .04 .10
148 Mikael Burakovsky .04 .10
149 Petter Ronnqvist .10 .25
150 Pierre Hedin .14 .35
151 Jan-Axel Alavaara .04 .10
152 Frantisek Kaberle .20 .50
153 Hans Jonsson .20 .50
154 Jonas Junkka .08 .20
155 Marcus Karlsson .04 .10
156 Kristian Gahn .10 .25
157 Magnus Wernblom .10 .25
158 Anders Soderberg .10 .25
159 Daniel Sedin 1.25 3.00
160 Henrik Sedin 1.25 3.00
161 Samuel Pahlsson .30 .75
162 Per Svartvadet .14 .35
163 Andreas Salomonsson .20 .50
164 Ravil Yakubov .04 .10
165 David Vyborny .20 .50
166 Magnus Lindqvist .10 .25
167 Anders Eldebrink .04 .10
168 Johan Norgren .04 .10
169 Christian Due-Boje .04 .10
170 Jonas Heed .04 .10
171 Josef Boumedienne .14 .35
172 Marko Virtanen .04 .10
173 Kyosti Karjalainen .04 .10
174 Jorgen Bemstrom .04 .10
175 Joakim Ericsson .04 .10
176 Jens Ohling .04 .10
177 Martin Hostak .04 .10
178 Lars Dahlstrom .04 .10
179 Niklas Brannstrom .04 .10
180 Mikko Makela .04 .10
181 Petr Korinek .08 .20
182 Joakim Persson .10 .25
183 Tobias Lilja .08 .20
184 Edvin Frylen .08 .20
185 Jacob Karlsson .08 .20
186 Johan Tornberg .04 .10
187 Patrik Hoglund .04 .10
188 Mattias Loof .04 .10
189 Mikael Pettersson .04 .10
190 Johan Molin .04 .10
191 Fredrik Eriksson .04 .10
192 Henrik Nordfeldt .04 .10
193 Jonas Olsson .04 .10
194 Roger Jonsson .04 .10
195 Roger Rosen .04 .10
196 Henric Bjorkman .04 .10
197 Harri Sillgren .04 .10
198 Paul Andersson-Everberg .04 .10
199 Tommy Soderstrom .20 .50
200 Stefan Nilsson .04 .10
201 Tomas Jonsson .04 .10
202 Jonas Bergqvist .08 .20
203 Christer Olsson .04 .10
204 Per Svartvadet .14 .35
205 Anders Huss .04 .10
206 Roger Johansson .04 .10
207 Stefan Ornskog .04 .10
208 Anders Eldebrink .04 .10
209 Niclas Havelid .20 .50
210 Charles Berglund .04 .10
211 Kai Nurminen .08 .20
212 Stefan Nilsson .04 .10
213 Per-Erik Eklund .04 .10
214 Janne Ojanen .08 .20
215 Per Svartvadet .14 .35
216 Michael Sundlov .10 .25
217 Roger Johansson .04 .10
218 Stefan Ornskog .04 .10
219 Kyosti Karjalainen .04 .10
220 Roger Rosen .04 .10
221 Jonas Bergqvist .08 .20
222 Esa Keskinen .04 .10
223 Christer Olsson .04 .10
224 Checklist .05
225 Checklist .05

1997-98 Swedish Collector's Choice Crash the Game Exchange

Mirroring the chase program first used in North America, these interactive cards allowed fans a chance to redeem them for specially foiled complete Crash sets. The cards were inserted 1:8 packs.

COMPLETE SET (30) 10.00 25.00
C1 Patric Kjellberg .40 1.00
C2 Mikael Johansson .40 1.00
C3 Daniel Tjarnqvist .40 1.00
C4 Christer Olsson .40 1.00
C5 Ville Peltonen .40 1.00
C6 Kai Nurminen .40 1.00
C7 Stefan Nilsson .40 1.00
C8 Jan Mertzig .40 1.00
C9 Anders Carlsson .40 1.00
C10 Jonas Bergqvist .40 1.00
C11 Magnus Svensson .40 1.00
C12 Janne Ojanen .40 1.00
C13 Marko Kiprusoff .40 1.00
C14 Juha Riihijarvi .40 1.00
C15 Daniel Sedin 2.00 5.00
C16 Henrik Sedin 2.00 5.00
C17 Evgenij Davydov .40 1.00
C18 Anders Huss .40 1.00
C19 Jan Larsson .40 1.00
C20 Roger Johansson .40 1.00
C21 Jorgen Jonsson .40 1.00
C22 Kristian Huselius 1.25 3.00
C23 Stefan Ornskog .40 1.00
C24 Anders Huusko .40 1.00
C25 Esa Keskinen .40 1.00
C26 Joakim Eriksson .40 1.00
C27 Anders Eldebrink .40 1.00
C28 Mikko Makela .40 1.00
C29 Henric Bjorkman .40 1.00
C30 Roger Rosen .40 1.00

1997-98 Swedish Collector's Choice Crash the Game Redemption

These cards were issued in complete set form in exchange for a winning Crash the Game insert card. They feature gold foil fronts, and backs which feature information on the winner.

COMPLETE SET (30) 10.00 20.00
R1 Patric Kjellberg .60 1.50
R2 Mikael Johansson .20 .50
R3 Daniel Tjarnqvist .30 .75
R4 Christer Olsson .20 .50
R5 Ville Peltonen 1.00 1.50
R6 Kai Nurminen .30 .75
R7 Stefan Nilsson .20 .50
R8 Jan Mertzig .20 .50
R9 Anders Carlsson .20 .50
R10 Jonas Bergqvist .20 .50
R11 Magnus Svensson .20 .50
R12 Janne Ojanen .30 .75
R13 Marko Kiprusoff .60 1.50
R14 Juha Riihijarvi .20 .50
R15 Daniel Sedin 2.00 4.00
R16 Henrik Sedin 2.00 4.00
R17 Evgenij Davydov .20 .50
R18 Anders Huss .20 .50
R19 Jan Larsson .20 .50
R20 Roger Johansson .20 .50
R21 Jorgen Jonsson .30 .75
R22 Kristian Huselius 3.20 3.00
R23 Stefan Ornskog .20 .50
R24 Anders Huusko .20 .50
R25 Esa Keskinen .20 .50
R26 Joakim Eriksson .20 .50
R27 Anders Eldebrink .20 .50
R28 Mikko Makela .20 .50
R29 Henric Bjorkman .20 .50
R30 Roger Rosen .20 .50

1997-98 Swedish Collector's Choice Select

This chase set features elite players from the past and present of the SEL. The cards were inserted 1:8 packs.
COMPLETE SET (15) 40.00 80.00
UD1 Peter Forsberg 12.00 30.00
UD2 Daniel Sedin 6.00 10.00
UD3 Nichlas Falk .80 2.00
UD4 Marko Jantunen .40 1.00
UD5 Ville Peltonen 1.60 3.00
UD6 Jorgen Jonsson .80 2.00
UD7 Roger Johansson .40 1.00
UD8 Stefan Ornskog .80 2.00
UD9 Henrik Sedin 4.80 10.00
UD10 Jonas Bergqvist .40 1.00
UD11 Tomas Jonsson .40 1.00
UD12 Stefan Nilsson .40 1.00
UD13 Janne Ojanen .40 1.00
UD14 Magnus Wernblom .40 1.00
UD15 Edvin Frylen .40 1.00
NNO Peter Forsberg Elite 20.00 50.00

1997-98 Swedish Collector's Choice Stick'Ums

These stickers were inserted 1:4 packs and feature top players of the SEL.
COMPLETE SET (15) 4.00 10.00
S1 Miikka Kiprusoff 2.00 3.00
S2 Marcus Nilsson .40 1.00
S3 Christer Olsson .10 .25
S4 Jorgen Jonsson .20 .50
S5 Fredrik Stillman .10 .25
S6 Per-Erik Eklund .20 .50
S7 Jarmo Myllys .20 .50
S8 Daniel Rydmark .10 .25
S9 Henric Bjorkman .10 .25
S10 Henrik Sedin 1.00 2.50
S11 Daniel Sedin 1.00 2.50
S12 Anders Huss .10 .25
S13 Patrik Carnback .10 .25
S14 Daniel Tjarnqvist .20 .50
S15 Jonas Bergqvist .20 .50

1998-99 Swedish UD Choice

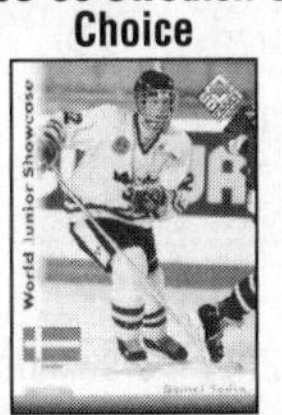

This Upper Deck-produced issue features the players of the Swedish Elitserien. The design mimics that of the 1998-99 North American UD Choice set. It is noteworthy for featuring early cards of Daniel and Henrik Sedin, along with Johan Hedberg and Mattias Karlin. The final two cards in the listing are the first-ever memorabilia cards issued in Sweden. Both feature a pair of swatches from the jerseys of the Sedin Twins, but the second also is graced by the autograph of both players on the jersey swatches.
COMPLETE SET (225) 10.00 25.00
1 Jonas Forsberg .10 .25
2 Rikard Franzen .04 .10
3 Mathias Svedberg .04 .10
4 Dick Tarnstrom .20 .50
5 Jan Sandstrom .04 .10
6 Johan Silfwerplatz .04 .10
7 Henrik Tallinder .20 .50
8 Stefan Gustavson .04 .10
9 Kristian Gahn .20 .50
10 Bjorn Ahlstrom .04 .10
11 Peter Hammarstrom .04 .10
12 Anders Gozzi .04 .10
13 Fredrik Krekula .04 .10
14 Erik Norback .04 .10
15 Niklas Anger .20 .50
16 Mats Lindberg .04 .10
17 Jorgen Wikstrom .04 .10
18 Per-Anton Lundstrom .10 .25
19 Mattias Hedlund .04 .10
20 Jorgen Hermansson .04 .10
21 Fredrik Bergqvist .04 .10
22 Joakim Lidgren .04 .10
23 Robert Karlsson .04 .10
24 Christian Lechtaler .04 .10
25 Aleksandrs Beljavskis .04 .10
26 Jens Ohman .04 .10
27 Stefan Ohman .04 .10
28 Martin Wiita .04 .10
29 Johan Ramstedt .10 .25
30 Per Ledin .04 .10
31 Jukka Penttinen .04 .10
32 Aleksandrs Semjonovs .04 .10
33 Johan Holmqvist .60 1.50
34 Tommy Melkersson .04 .10
35 Marko Tuulola .04 .10
36 Johan Hansson .04 .10
37 Par Djoos .04 .10
38 Per Lofstrom .04 .10
39 Niclas Wallin .20 .50
40 Roger Kyro .04 .10
41 Ove Molin .04 .10
42 Stefan Lundqvist .04 .10
43 Peter Nylander .04 .10
44 Jan Larsson .04 .10
45 Teppo Kivela .04 .10
46 Tom Bissett .10 .25
47 Anders Huss .04 .10
48 Mikko Luovi .10 .25
49 Tommy Soderstrom .30 .75
50 Bjorn Nord .10 .25
51 Ronnie Pettersson .04 .10
52 Thomas Johansson .04 .10
53 Daniel Tjarnqvist .20 .50
54 Anders Myrvold .10 .25
55 Mikael Magnusson .04 .10
56 Mikael Johansson .04 .10
57 Nichlas Falk .10 .25
58 Mikael Hakanson .04 .10
59 Charles Berglund .10 .25
60 Lars-Goran Wiklander .04 .10
61 Per Eklund .08 .20
62 Jan Viktorsson .04 .10
63 Patrik Erickson .04 .10
64 Espen Knutsen .80 1.00
65 Jimmie Olvestad .20 .50
66 Mikael Sandberg .04 .10
67 Christer Olsson .04 .10
68 Petter Nilsson .04 .10
69 Magnus Johansson .04 .10
70 Ronnie Sundin .10 .25
71 Radek Hamr .04 .10
72 Stefan Larsson .04 .10
73 Mattias Nilimaa .04 .10
74 Linus Fagemo .04 .10
75 Marko Jantunen .04 .10
76 Patrik Carnback .04 .10
77 Peter Berndtsson .04 .10
78 Mikael Samuelsson .30 .75
79 Peter Strom .04 .10
80 Par Edlund .04 .10
81 Henrik Nilsson .20 .50
82 Jonas Johnsson .04 .10
83 Kimmo Lecklin .04 .10
84 Roger Johansson .04 .10
85 Sergei Fokin .04 .10
86 Greger Artursson .04 .10
87 Jonas Elofsson .20 .50
88 Peter Jakobsson .04 .10
89 Dimitri Erofeev .04 .10
90 Patrik Zetterberg .04 .10
91 Niklas Sjokvist .04 .10
92 Trond Magnussen .04 .10
93 Peter Hagstrom .04 .10
94 Pelle Prestberg .04 .10
95 Mathias Johansson .10 .25
96 Michael Holmqvist .20 .50
97 Clas Eriksson .04 .10
98 Kristian Huselius 1.00 2.50
99 Jorgen Jonsson .20 .50
100 Kari Takko .10 .25
101 David Petrasek .04 .10
102 Daniel Johansson .20 .50
103 Per Gustafsson .04 .10
104 Fredrik Stillman .04 .10
105 Nicklas Rahm .04 .10
106 Mikael Lindman .04 .10
107 Jerry Persson .04 .10
108 Esa Keskinen .04 .10
109 Peter Ekelund .04 .10
110 Antti Tormanen .10 .25
111 Marcus Kristoffersson .20 .50
112 Anders Huusko .04 .10
113 Erik Huusko .04 .10
114 Johan Lindbom .10 .25
115 Jarkko Varvio .04 .10
116 Ulf Dahlen .10 .25
117 Johan Hedberg 4.00 1.00
118 Jan Huokko .04 .10
119 Torbjorn Johansson .04 .10
120 Hans Lodin .04 .10
121 Nicklas Nordqvist .04 .10
122 Stefan Bergqvist .04 .10
123 Magnus Svensson .04 .10
124 Andreas Karlsson .20 .50
125 Per-Erik Eklund .10 .25
126 Anders Carlsson .04 .10
127 Niklas Eriksson .04 .10
128 Stefan Hellkvist .04 .10
129 Jens Nielsen .04 .10
130 Anders Lonn .04 .10
131 Markus Akerblom .04 .10
132 Mikael Karlberg .04 .10
133 Jarmo Myllys .10 .25
134 Stefan Jonsson .04 .10
135 Osmo Soutokorva .04 .10
136 Johan Finnstrom .04 .10
137 Roger Akerstrom .10 .25
138 Igor Matushkin .04 .10
139 Jonas Ronnqvist .20 .50
140 Thomas Sjogren .04 .10
141 Tomas Berglund .04 .10
142 Mikael Lovgren .04 .10
143 Anders Burstrom .04 .10
144 Jorgen Bemstrom .04 .10
145 Martin Hostak .04 .10
146 Bert-Olav Karlsson .04 .10
147 Lars Edstrom .04 .10
148 Jiri Kucera .04 .10
149 Andrew Verner .10 .25
150 Kim Johnsson .10 .25
151 Kari Harila .04 .10
152 Niclas Havelid .40 1.00
153 Jesper Damgaard .04 .10
154 Johan Tornberg .04 .10
155 Mats Lusth .04 .10
156 Jan Hammar .04 .10
157 Marcus Magnertoft .04 .10
158 Marcus Thuresson .10 .25
159 Magnus Nilsson .04 .10
160 Mikael Lindholm .10 .25
161 Patrik Sylvegard .04 .10
162 Juha Riihijarvi .10 .25
163 Jesper Mattsson .10 .25
164 Niklas Sundblad .04 .10
165 Toivo Suursoo .04 .10
166 Petter Ronnquist .10 .25
167 Pierre Hedin .20 .50
168 Per Hallberg .04 .10
169 Jan-Axel Alavaara .04 .10
170 Hans Jonsson .20 .50
171 Lars Jansson .04 .10
172 Frantisek Kaberle .20 .50
173 Andreas Salomonsson .04 .25
174 Magnus Wernblom .10 .25
175 Mikael Pettersson .04 .10
176 Per Svartvadet .20 .50
177 Daniel Sedin .75 2.00
178 Henrik Sedin .75 2.00
179 Jan Alinc .04 .10
180 Samuel Pahlsson .40 1.00
181 Anders Soderberg .20 .50
182 Magnus Eriksson .04 .10
183 Andrei Lulin .04 .10
184 Jakob Karlsson .10 .25
185 Patrik Hoglund .04 .10
186 Joakim Lundberg .04 .10
187 Arto Blomsten .04 .10
188 Mattias Loof .04 .10
189 Mikael Pettersson .04 .10
190 Joakim Backlund .04 .10
191 Daniel Rydmark .04 .10
192 Johan Molin .04 .10
193 Paul Andersson-Everberg .04 .10
194 Henrik Nordfeldt .04 .10
195 Jonas Olsson .04 .10
196 Fredrik Oberg .04 .10
197 Roger Rosen .04 .10
198 Roland Stoltz .04 .10
199 Lars Bjorn .04 .10
200 Ulf Sterner .04 .10
201 Leif Holmqvist .10 .25
202 Hans Mild .04 .10
203 Bert-Ola Nordlander .04 .10
204 Eilert Maatta .04 .10
205 Ronald Pettersson .04 .10
206 Tord Lundstrom .04 .10
207 Lennart Svedberg .10 .25
208 Roland Stoltz .04 .10
209 Eilert Maatta .04 .10
210 Lennart Svedberg .10 .25
211 Tord Lundstrom .04 .10
212 Leif Holmqvist .10 .25
213 Magnus Nilsson .20 .50
214 Mikael Holmqvist .20 .50
215 Mattias Karlin .20 .50
216 Pierre Hedin .20 .50
217 Henrik Petre .20 .50
218 Johan Forsander .10 .25
219 Daniel Sedin .75 2.00
220 Henrik Sedin .75 2.00
221 Markus Nilsson .40 1.00
222 Checklist .04 .10
223 Checklist .04 .10
224 Checklist .04 .10
225 Checklist .04 .10
GJ1 D.Sedin/H.Sedin 20.00 50.00
GJA1 D.Sedin/H.Sedin 75.00 200.00

1998-99 Swedish UD Choice Day in the Life

This insert set captures moments in the regular lives of the SEL's biggest stars.
COMPLETE SET (10) 4.00 10.00
1 Rikard Franzen .40 1.00
2 Par Djoos .40 1.00
3 Tommy Soderstrom .80 2.00
4 Pelle Prestberg .40 1.00
5 Esa Keskinen .40 1.00
6 Johan Hedberg .75 2.00
7 Jarmo Myllys .75 2.00
8 Marcus Thuresson .40 1.00
9 Samuel Pahlsson 1.00 2.50
10 Christer Olsson .40 1.00

1999-00 Swedish Upper Deck

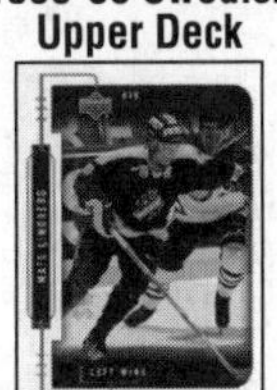

This 220-card set captures the heroes of Sweden's Elitserien. The cards were produced by Upper Deck and mirror the UD MVP set produced earlier in the year for NHL fans.
COMPLETE SET (220) 10.00 25.00
1 Mattias Pettersson .08 .20
2 Rikard Franzen .10 .25
3 Mathias Svedberg .08 .20
4 Dick Tarnstrom .30 .75
5 Jan Sandstrom .08 .20
6 Anders Myrvold .10 .25
7 Henrik Tallinder .20 .50
8 Per-Anton Lundstrom .08 .20
9 Kristian Gahn .08 .20
10 BjÃ¶rn Ahlstrom .08 .20
11 Stefan Gustavsson .08 .20
12 Jarkko Varvio .10 .25
13 Fredrik Krekula .08 .20
14 Erik Norback .08 .20
15 Niklas Anger .14 .35
16 Mats Lindberg .08 .20
17 Erik Andersson .08 .20
18 Johan Holmqvist .60 1.50
19 Tommy Sjodin .10 .25
20 Marko Tuulola .08 .20
21 Henrik Petre .14 .35
22 Par Djoos .10 .25
23 Niclas Wallin .40 1.00
24 Roger Kyro .08 .20
25 Ove Molin .08 .20
26 Stefan Lundqvist .08 .20
27 Goran Hermansson .08 .20
28 Jan Larsson .08 .20
29 Daniel RudslÃ¤tt .08 .20
30 Tom Bisset .14 .35
31 Kenneth Bergqvist .08 .20
32 Mikko Luovi .08 .20
33 Johan Lindstrom .08 .20
34 Daniel Olsson .08 .20
35 Tommy Soderstrom .20 .50
36 Bjorn Nord .14 .35
37 Niklas Kronwall 1.00 2.50
38 Thomas Johansson .08 .20
39 Daniel Tjarnqvist .20 .50
40 Mikael Magnusson .08 .20
41 Mikael Johansson .08 .20
42 Niklas Falk .14 .35
43 Mikael Hakansson .14 .35
44 Charles Berglund .10 .25
45 Lars-Goran Wiklander .08 .20
46 Per Eklund .10 .25
47 Kristofer Johansson .08 .20
48 Mathias Tjarnqvist .14 .35
49 Espen Knutsen .40 1.00
50 Jimmie Olvestad .20 .50
51 Mikko Konttila .08 .20
52 Vesa Toskala .75 2.00
53 Roger Johansson .08 .20
54 Sergei Fokin .08 .20
55 Greger Artursson .08 .20
56 Jonas Elofsson .14 .35
57 Radek Hamr .08 .20
58 Henrik Rehnberg .08 .20
59 Peter Nordstrom .10 .25
60 Niklas Sjokvist .08 .20
61 Trond Magnussen .08 .20
62 Peter Hagstrom .08 .20
63 Pelle Prestberg .08 .20
64 Mathias Johansson .14 .35
65 Tore Vikingstad .08 .20
66 Clas Eriksson .08 .20
67 Marko Jantunen .08 .20
68 Christian Berglund .20 .50
69 Mario Brunetta .14 .35
70 Petter Nilsson .08 .20
71 Magnus Johansson .08 .20
72 Ronnie Sundin .14 .35
73 Stefan Larsson .08 .20
74 Christian Backman .14 .35
75 Par Edlund .10 .25
76 Reid Simonton .08 .20
77 Kristian Huselius .40 1.00
78 Pasi Saarela .08 .20
79 Juha Ikonen .08 .20
80 Linus Fagemo .08 .20
81 Patrik Carnback .10 .25
82 Peter Berndtsson .08 .20
83 Peter Strom .08 .20
84 Henrik Nilsson .08 .20
85 Jonas Johnsson .08 .20
86 Kari Takko .14 .35
87 David Petrasek .08 .20
88 Joacim Esbjors .08 .20
89 Per Gustafsson .10 .25
90 Jani Nikko .08 .20
91 Mikael Lindman .08 .20
92 Oleg Belov .10 .25
93 Jonas Esbjors .08 .20
94 Jonas Forsander .14 .35
95 Peter Ekelund .08 .20
96 Antti Tormanen .10 .25
97 Anders Lonn .08 .20
98 Gabriel Karlsson .08 .20
99 Johan Hult .08 .20
100 Mattias Remstam .08 .20
101 Daniel Wallin .08 .20
102 Johan Lindbom .08 .20
103 Reinhard Divis .40 1.00
104 Jan Huokko .08 .20
105 Torbjorn Johansson .08 .20
106 Per Lundell .08 .20
107 David Ytfeldt .08 .20
108 Stefan Bergkvist .08 .20
109 Patrik Allvin .08 .20
110 Niklas Persson .08 .20
111 Martin Jansson .08 .20
112 Anders Carlsson .08 .20
113 Niklas Eriksson .08 .20
114 Stefan Hellkvist .08 .20
115 Jens Nielsen .08 .20
116 Morten Green .08 .20
117 Markus Akerblom .08 .20
118 Mikael Karlberg .08 .20
119 Mattias Elm .08 .20
120 Edvin Frylen .08 .20
121 Martin Knold .08 .20
122 Erkki Saramaa .08 .20
123 Nicklas Nordqvist .08 .20
124 Jesper Andersson .08 .20
125 Henrik Andersson .08 .20
126 Henrik Nordfeldt .08 .20
127 Ulf Soderstrom .08 .20
128 Ragnar Karlsson .08 .20
129 Fredrik Elmvall .08 .20
130 Peter Casparsson .08 .20
131 Dennis Ejdeholm .08 .20
132 Mattias Nilimaa .08 .20
133 Mike Helber .08 .20
134 Johan Bylow .08 .20
135 Jarmo Myllys .14 .35
136 Vaclav Burda .08 .20
137 Osmo Soutokorva .08 .20
138 Johan Finnstrom .10 .25
139 Roger Akerstrom .08 .20
140 Torbjorn Lindberg .08 .20
141 Jonas Ronnqvist .40 1.00
142 Jonathan Hedstrom .14 .35
143 Tomas Berglund .08 .20
144 Mikael Lovgren .08 .20
145 Anders Burstrom .08 .20
146 JÃ¶rgen Bemstrom .08 .20
147 Martin Hostak .08 .20
148 Hans Huczkowski .08 .20
149 Lars Edstrom .08 .20
150 Jiri Kucera .10 .25
151 Andreas Hadelov .08 .20
152 Johan Tornberg .08 .20
153 Mats Lusth .08 .20
154 Andreas Lilja .08 .20
155 Peter Jakobsson .08 .20
156 Henrik Malmstrom .08 .20
157 Tomas Sandstrom .20 .50
158 Kim Staal .08 .20
159 Jan Hammar .08 .20
160 Marcus Magnertoft .08 .20
161 Marcus Thuresson .08 .20
162 Magnus Nilsson .08 .20
163 Mikael Lindholm .08 .20
164 Juha Riihijarvi .08 .20
165 Jesper Mattsson .10 .25
166 Niklas Sundblad .10 .25
167 Toivo Suursoo .08 .20
168 Tobias Lundstrom .08 .20
169 Pierre Hedin .14 .35
170 Per Hallberg .08 .20
171 Jan-Axel Alavaara .08 .20
172 Jesper Duus .08 .20
173 Francois Bouchard .08 .20
174 Andreas Pihl .08 .20
175 Andreas Salomonsson .30 .75
176 Magnus Wernblom .08 .20
177 Mikael Pettersson .08 .20
178 Mattias Weinhandl .30 .75
179 Daniel Sedin .60 1.50
180 Henrik Sedin .60 1.50
181 Tommy Pettersson .08 .20
182 Samuel Pahlsson .40 1.00
183 Anders Soderberg .14 .35
184 Mattias Karlin .14 .35
185 Magnus Eriksson .08 .20
186 Andrei Lulin .08 .20
187 Denis Chervyakov .08 .20
188 Dimitri Chikin .08 .20
189 Joakim Lundberg .08 .20
190 Henric Bjorkman .08 .20
191 Roger Jonsson .08 .20
192 Peter Nylander .08 .20
193 Mikael Pettersson .08 .20
194 Patrik Zetterberg .08 .20
195 Daniel Rydmark .10 .25
196 Johan Molin .08 .20
197 Paul Andersson-Everberg .08 .20
198 Jonas Finn-Olsson .08 .20
199 Fredrik Oberg .08 .20
200 Roger Rosen .08 .20
201 Henrik Tallinder .14 .35
202 Kenneth Bergqvist .08 .20
203 Mathias Tjarnqvist .14 .35
204 Jimmie Olvestad .30 .75
205 Jonas Elofsson .14 .35
206 Christian Berglund .30 .75
207 Johan Forsander .14 .35
208 David Ytfeldt .08 .20
209 Niklas Persson .08 .20
210 Henrik Andersson .08 .20
211 Jonathan HedstrÃ¶m .14 .50
212 Kim Staal .08 .20
213 Pierre Hedin .14 .35
214 Mattias Weinhandl .30 .75
215 Rikard Ekstrom .08 .20
216 Christian Backman .20 .50
217 Daniel Sedin CL .60 .50
218 Peter Ekelund CL .08 .20
219 Tommy Soderstrom CL .14 .35
220 Henrik Sedin CL .40 .50

1999-00 Swedish Upper Deck Hands of Gold

This set, featuring the top snipers in the Elitserien, was randomly inserted into packs of 1999-2000 UD SHL.
COMPLETE SET (15) 12.00 30.00
1 Mats Lindberg .80 2.00
2 Daniel Sedin 2.00 5.00
3 Jan Larsson 2.00 5.00
4 Per Eklund 1.25 3.00
5 Thomas Johansson .80 2.00
6 Per Eklund 1.25 3.00
7 Peter Ekelund .80 2.00
8 Anders Carlsson .80 2.00
9 Peter Ekelund .80 2.00
10 Jonas Ronnqvist .75 2.00
11 Marcus Thuresson .75 2.00
12 Daniel Sedin 1.25 3.00
13 Henrik Sedin 1.25 3.00
14 Daniel Rydmark .75 2.00
15 Kristian Huselius 2.00 5.00

1999-00 Swedish Upper Deck Lasting Impressions

This insert set features a number of Sweden's top young stars and veterans.
COMPLETE SET (12) 12.00 30.00
1 Rikard Franzen 1.20 3.00
2 Par Djoos 1.20 3.00
3 Charles Berglund 1.20 3.00
4 Roger Johansson 1.20 3.00
5 Kari Takko 1.60 4.00
6 Anders Carlsson 1.20 3.00
7 Mike Helber 1.20 3.00
8 Jiri Kucera 1.20 3.00
9 Juha Riihijarvi 1.20 3.00
10 Samuel Pahlsson 2.00 5.00
11 Magnus Eriksson 1.20 3.00
12 Patrik Carnback 1.20 3.00

1999-00 Swedish Upper Deck PowerDeck

Like the NHL versions that preceded them, these small CD-ROMs offer video action, still shots and statistics when loaded onto your home PC.
COMPLETE SET (2) 6.00 8.00
1 SHL 2.00 5.00
2 Daniel Sedin 6.00 5.00
Henrik Sedin

1999-00 Swedish Upper Deck SHL Signatures

These sweet inserts feature a genuine autograph from a star of the Swedish Elitserien.
COMPLETE SET (20) 70.00 150.00
1 Stefan Gustavsson 2.00 5.00
2 Rikard Franzen 2.00 5.00
3 Johan Holmqvist 6.00 12.00
4 Espen Knutsen 6.00 12.00
5 Peter Nordstrom 2.00 5.00
6 Marko Jantunen 2.00 5.00
7 Kristian Huselius 8.00 20.00
8 Jonas Johnsson 2.00 5.00
9 Per Gustafsson 2.00 5.00
10 Johan Lindbom 4.00 10.00
11 Stefan Hellkvist 2.00 5.00
12 Ulf Soderstrom 2.00 5.00
13 Jarmo Myllys 4.00 10.00
14 Johan Tornberg 2.00 5.00
15 Daniel Sedin 16.00 20.00
16 Henrik Sedin 12.00 20.00
17 Magnus Eriksson 2.00 5.00
18 Tommy Sjodin 2.00 5.00
19 Tommy Soderstrom 4.00 10.00
20 Tomas Sandstrom 4.00 10.00

1999-00 Swedish Upper Deck Snapshots

This insert set features more of the top performers of the SHL.
COMPLETE SET (15) 12.00 30.00
1 Anders Myrvold .80 2.00
2 Johan Holmqvist 1.20 3.00
3 Ove Molin .40 1.00
4 Tommy Soderstrom 1.20 3.00
5 Espen Knutsen 1.60 4.00
6 Peter Nordstrom .40 1.00
7 Per Gustafsson .40 1.00
8 Stefan Bergkvist .40 1.00
9 Mattias Elm .40 1.00
10 Jarmo Myllys 1.60 4.00
11 Tomas Sandstrom 1.60 4.00
12 Magnus Wernblom .40 1.00
13 Mattias Weinhandl 1.60 4.00
14 Denis Chervyakov .40 1.00
15 Kristian Huselius 4.00 10.00

2000-01 Swedish Upper Deck

This set was produced by Upper Deck for distribution in the Swedish market and features the top players of the SHL. The design for the set mimics the one used for 2000-01 UD MVP in North America.
COMPLETE SET (220) 15.00 40.00
1 Tim Thomas .60 1.50
2 Per-Anton Lundstrom .15 .40
3 Dick Tarnstrom .20 .50
4 Rikard Franzen .04 .10
5 Rikard Ekstrom .04 .10
6 Jan Sandstrom .04 .10
7 Stefan Gustavson .04 .10
8 Anders Gozzi .04 .10
9 Stefan Hellkvist .04 .10
10 Mats Lindberg .04 .10
11 Bjorn Danielsson .04 .10
12 Erik Andersson .04 .10
13 Bjorn Ahlstrom .04 .10
14 Kristian Gahn .04 .10
15 Petter Sandstrom .04 .10
16 Mattias Hedlund .04 .10
17 Tommi Hamalainen .04 .10
18 Jorgen Hermansson .04 .10
19 Jesper Jager .04 .10
20 Christian Lechtaler .04 .10
21 Aleksanders Beliavskis .04 .10
22 Johan Ramstedt .04 .10
23 Lars Briell .04 .10
24 Johan Boman .04 .10
25 Aleksanders Semjonovs .04 .10
26 Mathias Bosson .04 .10
27 Niko Halttunen .04 .10
28 Fredrik Nasvall .04 .10
29 Johan Asplund .15 .40
30 Henrik Petre .04 .10
31 Par Djoos .04 .10
32 Tommy Sjodin .04 .10
33 Christer Olsson .04 .10
34 Marko Tuulola .04 .10
35 Johan Molin .04 .10
36 Tony Martensson .04 .10
37 Tom Bissett .15 .40
38 Roger Kyro .04 .10
39 Ove Molin .04 .10
40 Mikko Luovi .04 .10
41 Daniel Rudslatt .04 .10
42 Kenneth Bergqvist .04 .10
43 Jan Larsson .04 .10
44 Mikael Tellqvist .75 2.00
45 Niklas Kronwall 1.00 2.50
46 Francois Bouchard .04 .10
47 Edvin Frylen .04 .10
48 Mikael Magnusson .04 .10
49 Daniel Tjarnqvist .20 .50
50 Charles Berglund .04 .10
51 Kristofer Ottosson .04 .10
52 Kyosti Karjalainen .04 .10
53 Nichlas Falk .04 .10
54 Mathias Tjarnqvist .15 .40
55 Jimmie Olvestad .20 .50
56 Johan Garpenlov .04 .10
57 Andreas Salomonsson .20 .50
58 Mikael Johansson .04 .10
59 Vladimir Orszagh .15 .40
60 Henrik Lundqvist 8.00 20.00
61 Magnus Johansson .04 .10
62 Christian Backman .04 .10
63 Nicklas Rahm .04 .10
64 Ronnie Sundin .04 .10
65 Par Edlund .04 .10
66 Magnus Kahnberg .04 .10
67 Pelle Prestberg .04 .10
68 Patrik Carnback .04 .10
69 Juha Ikonen .04 .10
70 Jari Tolsa .04 .10
71 Kristian Huselius .40 1.00
72 Peter Strom .04 .10
73 Henrik Nilsson .04 .10
74 Jonas Johnsson .04 .10
75 Mikael Andersson .04 .10
76 Magnus Eriksson .04 .10
77 Sergei Fokin .04 .10
78 Jonas Frogren .04 .10
79 Thomas Rhodin .04 .10
80 Greger Artursson .04 .10
81 Radek Hamr .04 .10
82 Roger Johansson .04 .10
83 Marko Jantunen .04 .10
84 Ulf Soderstrom .04 .10
85 Christian Berglund .04 .10
86 Mathias Johansson .04 .10
87 Trond Magnussen .04 .10
88 Peter Nordstrom .15 .40
89 Clas Eriksson .04 .10
90 Jorgen Jonsson .04 .10
91 Marcel Jenni .04 .10
92 Stefan Liv .60 1.50
93 Joacim Esbjors .04 .10
94 Per Gustafsson .04 .10
95 Fredrik Stillman .04 .10
96 Mikael Lindman .04 .10
97 Peter Ottosson .04 .10
98 Oleg Belov .04 .10
99 Peter Ekelund .04 .10
100 Johan Hult .04 .10
101 Johan Lindbom .04 .10
102 Jonas Esbjors .04 .10
103 Johan Forsander .04 .10
104 Mattias Remstam .04 .10
105 Fredrik Oberg .04 .10
106 Reinhard Divis .40 1.00
107 Magnus Svensson .04 .10
108 Jan Huokko .04 .10
109 Stefan Bergkvist .04 .10
110 Lars Jonsson .20 .50
111 Per Lofstrom .04 .10
112 Jens Nielsen .04 .10
113 Niklas Eriksson .04 .10
114 Daniel Widing .04 .10
115 Niklas Persson .04 .10
116 Henrik Nordfeldt .04 .10
117 Tore Vikingstad .15 .40
118 Mikael Karlberg .04 .10
119 Robert Burakovsky .04 .10
120 Jarmo Myllys .20 .50
121 Torbjorn Lindberg .04 .10
122 Petter Nilsson .04 .10
123 Osmo Soutokorva .04 .10
124 Roger Akerstrom .04 .10
125 Johan Finnstrom .04 .10
126 Jiri Kucera .04 .10
127 Jonathan Hedstrom .20 .50
128 Tomas Berglund .04 .10
129 Mikael Renberg .20 .50
130 Anders Burstrom .04 .10
131 Hans Huczkowski .04 .10
132 Martin Hostak .04 .10
133 Lars Edstrom .04 .10
134 Sami Mettovaara .04 .10
135 Andreas Hadelov .04 .10

136 David Petrasek .04 .10
137 Peter Jakobsson .04 .10
138 Joakim Lundberg .04 .10
139 Christian Due-Boje .04 .10
140 Johan Tornberg .04 .10
141 Henrik Malmstrom .04 .10
142 Marcus Thuresson .04 .10
143 Daniel Rydmark .04 .10
144 Juha Riihijarvi .04 .10
145 Jesper Mattsson .04 .10
146 Fredrik Lindquist .04 .10
147 Tomas Sandstrom .04 .10
148 Kim Staal .04 .10
149 Jan Hammar .04 .10
150 Tobias Lundstrom .04 .10
151 Andreas Pihl .04 .10
152 Pierre Hedin .04 .10
153 Jan-Axel Alavaara .04 .10
154 Lars Jansson .04 .10
155 Per Hallberg .04 .10
156 Jesper Duus .04 .10
157 Magnus Wernblom .04 .10
158 Anders Soderberg .15 .40
159 Tommy Pettersson .04 .10
160 Mattias Weinhandl .40 1.00
161 Peter Hogardh .04 .10
162 Patrik Wallenberg .04 .10
163 Jorgen Bemstrom .04 .10
164 Stefan Ohman .04 .10
165 Boo Ahl .15 .40
166 Pasi Petrilainen .15 .40
167 Stefan Klockare .04 .10
168 Daniel Casselstahl .04 .10
169 Marcus Karlsson .04 .10
170 Robert Carlsson .04 .10
171 Per Hallin .04 .10
172 Nik Zupancic .04 .10
173 Timo Peltomaa .04 .10
174 Linus Fagemo .04 .10
175 Henrik Zetterberg 4.00 10.00
176 Mikael Lind .04 .10
177 Anders Huss .04 .10
178 Markus Matthiasson .04 .10
179 Stefan Hellkvist SS .04 .10
180 Kristian Gahn SS .04 .10
181 Bjorn Ahlstrom SS .04 .10
182 Aleksanders Beliavskis SS .04 .10
183 Tom Bissett SS .15 .40
184 Tommy Sjodin SS .04 .10
185 Ove Molin SS .04 .10
186 Mikael Tellqvist SS .75 2.00
187 Mikael Johansson SS .04 .10
188 Vladimir Orszagh SS .15 .40
189 Johan Garpenlov SS .04 .10
190 Christian Berglund SS .04 .10
191 Jorgen Jonsson SS .04 .10
192 Radek Hamr SS .04 .10
193 Kristian Huselius SS .40 1.00
194 Mikael Andersson SS .04 .10
195 Patrik Carnback SS .04 .10
196 Per Gustafsson SS .04 .10
197 Johan Lindbom SS .04 .10
198 Oleg Belov SS .04 .10
199 Robert Burakovsky SS .04 .10
200 Mikael Renberg SS .20 .50
201 Petter Nilsson SS .04 .10
202 Jarmo Myllys SS .20 .50
203 Tomas Sandstrom SS .15 .40
204 Marcus Thuresson SS .04 .10
205 Fredrik Lindquist SS .04 .10
206 Magnus Wernblom SS .04 .10
207 Mattias Weinhandl SS .20 .50
208 Henrik Zetterberg SS 4.00 10.00
209 Mats Lindberg CL .04 .10
210 Jorgen Hermansson CL .04 .10
211 Par Djoos CL .04 .10
212 Jimmie Olvestad CL .15 .40
213 Christian Backman CL .04 .10
214 Radek Hamr CL .04 .10
215 Peter Ekelund CL .04 .10
216 Lars Jonsson CL .20 .50
217 Mikael Renberg CL .20 .50
218 Fredrik Lindquist CL .04 .10
219 Mattias Weinhandl CL .20 .50
220 Marcus Karlsson CL .04 .10

2000-01 Swedish Upper Deck Game Jerseys

This pair of memorabilia cards featuring Sweden's top young prospects were randomly inserted in packs at a rate of 1:216.

COMPLETE SET (2) 40.00 50.00
DS Daniel Sedin 20.00 30.00
HS Henrik Sedin 20.00 30.00

2000-01 Swedish Upper Deck Masked Men

This set features the top goaltenders in the Swedish Elitserien. The cards were randomly inserted at a rate of 1:24 packs.

COMPLETE SET (7) 20.00 40.00
M1 Tim Thomas 3.00 8.00
M2 Mikael Tellqvist 6.00 15.00
M3 Magnus Eriksson 2.50 6.00
M4 Reinhard Divis 4.00 10.00
M5 Jarmo Myllys 2.50 6.00
M6 Andreas Hadelov 2.00 5.00
M7 Boo Ahl 2.00 5.00

2000-01 Swedish Upper Deck SHL Excellence

This set honors two players on the same team who achieved excellence in the SHL. The cards were inserted 1:24 packs.

COMPLETE SET (5) 15.00 30.00
S1 V.Orszagh/J.Garpenlov 2.00 5.00
S2 C.Berglund/J.Jonsson 2.00 5.00
S3 P.Carnback/K.Huselius 4.00 10.00
S4 M.Renberg/J.Myllys 2.50 6.00
S5 M.Weinhandl/M.Wernblom 3.00 8.00

2000-01 Swedish Upper Deck SHL Signatures

This set of signed cards featuring the top stars of the Swedish Elite League were inserted 1:17 packs. The cards ape the design used earlier in the year in Upper Deck's MVP Pro Sign issue.

COMPLETE SET (42) 225.00 450.00
AB Alexander Beliavski 4.00 10.00
AG Anders Gozzi 4.00 10.00
AH Andreas Hadelov 4.00 10.00
AS Alexander Semjonovs 4.00 10.00
BA Boo Ahl 4.00 10.00
CB Christian Backman 4.00 10.00
CH Christian Berglund 4.00 10.00
DR Daniel Rydmark 4.00 10.00
FL Fredrik Lindquist 4.00 10.00
GA Greger Artursson 4.00 10.00
HZ Henrik Zetterberg 25.00 60.00
JE Jonas Esbjors 4.00 10.00
JG Johan Garpenlov 4.00 10.00
JH Jorgen Hermansson 4.00 10.00
JJ Jorgen Jonsson 4.00 10.00
JL Jan Larsson 4.00 10.00
JN Jens Nielsen 4.00 10.00
JO Jonathan Hedstrom 8.00 20.00
KG Kristian Gahn 4.00 10.00
KH Kristian Huselius 12.50 30.00
MA Mikael Andersson 4.00 10.00
ME Mikael Tellqvist 12.50 30.00
MH Martin Hostak 4.00 10.00
MI Mattias Weinhandl 8.00 20.00
MJ Mikael Johansson 4.00 10.00
ML Mats Lindberg 4.00 10.00
MN Mikael Renberg 8.00 20.00
MR Mattias Remstam 4.00 10.00
MS Magnus Svensson 4.00 10.00
MT Marcus Thuresson 4.00 10.00
MW Magnus Wernblom 4.00 10.00
NK Niklas Kronwall 20.00 50.00
OB Oleg Belov 4.00 10.00
OM Ove Molin 4.00 10.00
PC Patrik Carnback 4.00 10.00
PD Par Djoos 4.00 10.00
PN Petter Nilsson 4.00 10.00
RD Reinhard Divis 10.00 25.00
RJ Roger Johansson 4.00 10.00
SH Stefan Hellkvist 4.00 10.00
TB Tom Bissett 4.00 10.00
TL Tobias Lundstrom 4.00 10.00

2000-01 Swedish Upper Deck Top Draws

This set highlights the most popular players in the SHL. Singles were inserted 1:8 packs.

COMPLETE SET (11) 7.50 15.00
T1 Bjorn Ahlstrom .40 1.00
T2 Ove Molin .40 1.00
T3 Mikael Tellqvist 2.00 5.00
T4 Patrik Carnback .40 1.00
T5 Roger Johansson .40 1.00
T6 Oleg Belov .40 1.00
T7 Jens Nielsen .40 1.00
T8 Jonathan Hedstrom .40 1.00
T9 Fredrik Lindquist .40 1.00
T10 Mattias Weinhandl .75 2.00
T11 Anders Huss .40 1.00

2000-01 Swedish Upper Deck Top Playmakers

This insert set honors athletes who consistently top the SHL scoring charts. Cards were inserted at a rate of 1:24 packs.

COMPLETE SET (8) 15.00 30.00
P1 Mats Lindberg 1.50 4.00
P2 Jan Larsson 1.50 4.00
P3 Mikael Johansson 1.50 4.00
P4 Jonas Johnsson 1.50 4.00
P5 Jorgen Jonsson 1.50 4.00
P6 Martin Hostak 1.50 4.00
P7 Juha Riihijarvi 1.50 4.00
P8 Mattias Weinhandl 2.50 6.00

2001-02 Swedish Alfabilder

COMPLETE SET (18) 10.00 25.00
1 Sven Tumba Johansson .40 1.00
2 Roland Rolle Stoltz .40 1.00
3 Eilert Mattaa .40 1.00
4 Lennart Klimpen Haggroth .40 1.00
5 Nisse Nilsson .40 1.00
6 Ulf Sterner .40 1.00
7 Leif Honken Holmqvist .75 2.00
8 Tord Lundstrom .40 1.00
9 Borje Salming 2.00 5.00
10 Anders Hedberg 1.25 3.00
11 Anders Kallur .75 2.00
12 Stefan Persson .75 2.00
13 Goran Hogosta .40 1.00
14 Bengt-Ake Gustavsson .40 1.00
15 Mats Naslund 1.25 3.00
16 Kent Nilsson 1.25 3.00
17 Hakan Loob 1.25 3.00
18 Peter Lindmark .75 2.00

2001-02 Swedish Brynas Tigers

This set features the Tigers of the Swedish Elite League. The set is postcard-styled and sized, with a posed photo on the front, and a b/w head shot and brief stats on the back.

COMPLETE SET (27) 10.00 25.00
1 Adam Andersson .40 1.00
2 Johan Asplund .80 2.00
3 Kenneth Bergqvist .40 1.00
4 Tom Bissett .40 1.50
5 Bjorn Danielsson .40 1.00
6 Par Djoos .40 1.00
7 Jonas Floberg .40 1.00
8 Kristoffer Jobs .40 1.00
9 Daniel Johansson .40 1.00
10 Roger Kyro .40 1.00
11 Jan Larsson .40 1.00
12 Mikko Luovi .40 1.00
13 Per Mars .40 1.00
14 Tony Martensson .40 1.00
15 Roger Melin .40 1.00
16 Ove Molin .40 1.00
17 Christer Olsson .40 1.00
18 Jussi Pekkala .40 1.00
19 Gunnar Persson .40 1.00
20 Henrik Petre .40 1.00
21 Mattias Pettersson .40 1.00
22 Henrik Rehnberg .40 1.00
23 Daniel Rudslatt .40 1.00
24 Tommy Sjodin .40 1.00
25 Jonas Soling .40 1.00
26 Daniel Wagstrom .40 1.00
27 Team Card .40 1.00

2002-03 Swedish SHL

This set features the top players of the Swedish Elite league.

COMPLETE SET (292) 20.00 50.00
1 Johan Asplund .20 .50
2 Par Djoos .08 .20
3 Tommy Sjodin .08 .20
4 Henrik Rehnberg .08 .20
5 Adam Andersson .08 .20
6 Tony Martensson .08 .20
7 Roger Kyro .08 .20
8 Ove Molin .08 .20
9 Bjorn Danielsson .08 .20
10 Jan Larsson .08 .20
11 Jonas Soling .08 .20
12 Sergei Naumov .20 .50
13 Ronnie Pettersson .08 .20
14 Bjorn Nord .08 .20
15 Mikael Magnusson .08 .20
16 Tomas Strandberg .08 .20
17 Peter Lindelof .08 .20
18 Mikael Johansson .08 .20
19 Christian Eklund .08 .20
20 Johan Forsander .08 .20
21 Mikael Hakanson .08 .20
22 Nils Ekman .20 .50
23 Martin Gerber .40 1.00
24 Mats Trygg .08 .20
25 Jonas Frogren .08 .20
26 Thomas Rhodin .08 .20
27 Greger Artursson .08 .20
28 Marko Jantunen .08 .20
29 Claes Eriksson .08 .20
30 Rickard Wallin .08 .20
31 Marcel Jenni .08 .20
32 Mathias Johansson .08 .20
33 Peter Hammarstrom .08 .20
34 Boo Ahl .20 .50
35 Daniel Ljungqvist .08 .20
36 Per Gustafsson .08 .20
37 Jouni Loponen .08 .20
38 Richard Pavlikovsky .08 .20
39 Peter Ekelund .08 .20
40 Anders Huusko .08 .20
41 Mattias Remstam .08 .20
42 Johan Hult .08 .20
43 Bjorn Melin .08 .20
44 Kalle Sahlstedt .08 .20
45 Fredrik Jensen .08 .20
46 Mathias Ahxner .08 .20
47 Martin Knold .08 .20
48 Christoffer Norgren .08 .20
49 Johan Bulow .08 .20
50 Fredrik Johansson .08 .20
51 Henrik Andersson .08 .20
52 Fredrik Emvall .08 .20
53 Per Eklund .08 .20
54 Stefan Pettersson .08 .20
55 Magnus Gastrin .08 .20
56 Daniel Henriksson .20 .50
57 Jonas Andersson-Junkka .08 .20
58 Jan Sandstrom .08 .20
59 Petter Nilsson .08 .20
60 Roger Akerstrom .08 .20
61 Stefan Nilsson .08 .20
62 Jonathan Hedstrom .08 .20
63 Per Ledin .08 .20
64 Anders Burstrom .08 .20
65 Hans Huczkowski .08 .20
66 Emil Lundberg .08 .20
67 Andreas Hadelov .20 .50
68 Peter Hasselblad .08 .20
69 Peter Andersson .08 .20
70 Roger Ohman .08 .20
71 Henrik Malmstrom .08 .20
72 Marcus Thuresson .08 .20
73 Daniel Rydmark .08 .20
74 Juha Riihijarvi .08 .20
75 Marcus Magnertoft .08 .20
76 Mika Hannula .08 .20
77 Jesper Mattsson .08 .20
78 Peter Hirsch .20 .50
79 Pierre Hedin .08 .20
80 Jan Oberg .08 .20
81 Magnus Wernblom .08 .20
82 Tommy Pettersson .08 .20
83 Peter Hogardh .20 .50
84 Petter Oberg .08 .20
85 Joakim Lindstrom .08 .20
86 Magnus Hedlund .08 .20
87 Mattias Wennerberg .08 .20
88 Stefan Ohman .08 .20
89 Rolf Wanhainen .20 .50
90 Ola Mollerstedt .08 .20
91 Stefan Bernstrom .08 .20
92 Peter Popovic .08 .20
93 Peter Ahola .08 .20
94 Jesper Bjorck .08 .20
95 Jukka Tiilikainen .08 .20
96 Erik Norback .08 .20
97 Juha Lind .20 .50
98 Peter Gerhardsson .08 .20
99 Jorgen Bernstrom .08 .20
100 Fredrik Andersson .08 .20
101 Tommi Rajamaki .08 .20
102 David Halvardsson .08 .20
103 Daniel Casselstahl .08 .20
104 Niklas Nordgren .08 .20
105 Markus Matthiasson .20 .50
106 Robert Carlsson .08 .20
107 Per Hallin .08 .20
108 Henrik Zetterberg 1.00 2.50
109 Mikael Lind .08 .20
110 Ed Ward .08 .20
111 Henrik Lundqvist 2.00 5.00
112 Jan-Axel Alavaara .08 .20
113 Christian Backman .08 .20
114 Ronnie Sundin .08 .20
115 Magnus Kahnberg .08 .20
116 Jens Karlsson .08 .20
117 Juha Ikonen .08 .20
118 Jari Tolsa .08 .20
119 Niklas Andersson .08 .20
120 Jonas Johnsson .08 .20
121 Peter Strom .08 .20
122 Brynas IF Logo .08 .20
123 Djurgardens Logo .08 .20
124 Farjestads Logo .08 .20
125 HV 71 Logo .08 .20
126 Leksands Logo .08 .20
127 Linkopings Logo .08 .20
128 Lulea Logo .08 .20
129 Malmo Logo .08 .20
130 MoDo Logo .08 .20
131 Sodertalje Logo .08 .20
132 Timra Logo .08 .20
133 Vastra Frolunda Logo .08 .20
134 Christer Olsson CL .08 .20
135 Thomas Ostlund CL .08 .20
136 Jorgen Jonsson CL .08 .20
137 Johan Davidsson CL .08 .20
138 Mikael Sandberg CL .15 .40
139 Tomas Berglund CL .08 .20
140 Tomas Sandstrom CL .08 .20
141 Richard Lintner CL .08 .20
142 Peter Larsson CL .08 .20
143 Henrik Zetterberg CL .75 2.00
144 Joel Lundqvist CL .08 .20
145 Jamie Ram .20 .50
146 Daniel Johansson .08 .20
147 Jussi Pekkala .08 .20
148 Veli-Pekka Laitinen .08 .20
149 Kristoffer Jobs .08 .20
150 Jonas Floberg .08 .20
151 Simon Ostlund .08 .20
152 Tommi Miettinen .08 .20
153 Niklas Anger .15 .40
154 Daniel Wagstrom .08 .20
155 Joaquin Gage .15 .40
156 Bjorn Bjurling .08 .20
157 Niklas Kronwall .40 1.00
158 Per-Anton Lundstrom .20 .50
159 Kristofer Ottosson .08 .20
160 Joakim Eriksson .08 .20
161 Daniel Rudslatt .08 .20
162 Nichlas Falk .08 .20
163 Matthias Trattnig .08 .20
164 Fredrik Lindquist .08 .20
165 Johan Lindstrom .08 .20
166 Mikael Gerden .08 .20
167 Sinuhe Wallinheimo .08 .20
168 Per Lundell .08 .20
169 Per Hallberg .08 .20
170 Radek Hamr .08 .20
171 Ulf Soderstrom .08 .20
172 Marius Trygg .08 .20
173 Peter Nordstrom .08 .20
174 Jorgen Jonsson .08 .20
175 Par Backer .08 .20
176 Pelle Prestberg .08 .20
177 Dieter Kalt .08 .20
178 Stefan Liv .60 1.50
179 Mika Niskanen .08 .20
180 Timmy Pettersson .08 .20
181 Daniel Josefsson .08 .20
182 Jani Hassinen .08 .20
183 Sebastian Meijer .08 .20
184 Niklas Brannstrom .08 .20
185 Par Arlbrandt .08 .20
186 Pasi Maattanen .08 .20
187 Johan Davidsson .15 .40
188 Jonas Fransson .08 .20
189 Sean Gauthier .15 .40
190 Christer Olsson .08 .20
191 Niklas Gallstedt .08 .20
192 Hans Lodin .08 .20
193 Per Lofstrom .08 .20
194 Mike Stapleton .08 .20
195 Jens Nielsen .08 .20
196 Niklas Eriksson .08 .20
197 Mikael Karlberg .08 .20
198 Mikael Pettersson .08 .20
Robert Nilsson
199 Tobias Holm .08 .20
200 Niklas Persson .08 .20
201 Goran Hermansson .08 .20
202 Tomas Forslund .08 .20
203 Henrik Nordfeldt .08 .20
204 Johan Rosen .08 .20
205 Joel Davis .08 .20
206 Mikael Sandberg .15 .40
207 Andreas Pihl .08 .20
208 Jan Mertzig .08 .20
209 Thomas Johansson .08 .20
210 Andreas Holmqvist .08 .20
211 Barry Richter .15 .40
212 Stefan Gustavson .08 .20
213 Brian Felsner .15 .40
214 Johan Franzen .08 .20
215 Tim Eriksson .08 .20
216 Mikael Hakanson .08 .20
217 Gusten Tornqvist .08 .20
218 Pavel Skrbek .08 .20
219 Patrik Bjaarnhjelm .08 .20
220 Johan Finnstrom .20 .50
221 Fredrik Svensson .08 .20
222 Linus Fagemo .08 .20
223 Patrik Tano .08 .20
224 Kamil Brabenec .08 .20
225 Thomas Berglund .08 .20
226 Jonas Hagerback .08 .20
227 Magnus Nilsson .08 .20
228 Robert Borgqvist .08 .20
229 Joakim Lundberg .08 .20
230 David Petrasek .08 .20
231 Petri Liimatainen .08 .20
232 Johan Norgren .08 .20
233 Jan Hammar .08 .20
234 Frans Nielsen .08 .20
235 Mikael Wahlberg .08 .20
236 Toivo Suursoo .08 .20
237 Juuso Riksman .08 .20
238 Tobias Enstrom .08 .20
239 Jesper Damgaard .08 .20
240 Erik Leverstrom .08 .20
241 Dusan Milo .08 .20
242 Martin Johansson .08 .20
243 Anders Soderberg .15 .40
244 Jonas Almtorp .08 .20
245 Fredrik Warg .08 .20
246 Joakim Lindstrom .08 .20
247 Morten Green .08 .20
248 Miroslav Hlinka .08 .20
249 Magnus Lindquist .08 .20
250 Alexander Blomqvist .08 .20
251 Anders Back .08 .20
252 Leif Rohlin .08 .20
253 Robert Carlsson .08 .20
254 Antti Tormanen .08 .20
255 David Svee .08 .20
256 Gabriel Karlsson .08 .20
257 Mattias Carlsson .08 .20
258 Peter Larsson .08 .20
259 Patrik Zetterberg .08 .20
260 Kristian Gahn .08 .20
261 Kimmo Kapanen .08 .20
262 Martin Lindman .08 .20
263 Kalle Koskinen .08 .20
264 Robert Jindrich .08 .20
265 Par Styf .08 .20
266 Patrik Wallenberg .08 .20
267 Christian Soderstrom .08 .20
268 Henrik Eriksson .08 .20
269 Valeri Krykov .08 .20
270 Toni Koivunen .08 .20
271 Markus Akerblom .08 .20
272 Fredrik Norrena .40 1.00
273 Magnus Johansson .08 .20
274 Kimmo Eronen .08 .20
275 Oscar Ackestrom .08 .20
276 Erik Kakko .08 .20
277 Mattias Luukkonen .08 .20
278 Patrik Carnback .08 .20
279 Alexander Steen ERC 1.50 4.00
280 Joel Lundqvist .08 .20
281 Jonas Esbjors .08 .20
282 Mikael Andersson .08 .20
283 Jamie Ram .20 .50
284 Joaquin Gage .20 .50
285 Sinuhe Wallinheimo .20 .50
286 Stefan Liv .60 1.50
287 Sean Gauthier .15 .40
288 Mikael Sandberg .08 .20
289 Daniel Henriksson .08 .20
290 Andreas Hadelov .08 .20
291 Peter Hirsch .20 .50
292 Magnus Lindquist .08 .20
293 Kimmo Kapanen .08 .20
294 Fredrik Norrena .40 1.00

2002-03 Swedish SHL Dynamic Duos

These cards were randomly inserted at a rate of 1:16 series two packs.

COMPLETE SET (9) 6.00 15.00
1 Par Djoos .75 2.00
Tommy Sjodin
2 Mikael Johansson .75 2.00
Kristofer Ottosson
3 Par Backer .75 2.00
Jorgen Jonsson
4 Lars Jonsson 1.25 3.00
Daniel Widing
5 Petr Nilsson .75 2.00
Stefan Nilsson
6 Mika Hannula .75 2.00
Juha Riihijarvi
7 Juha Lind .75 2.00
Antti Tormanen
8 Markus Matthiasson .75 2.00
Markus Akerblom
9 Joel Lundqvist 2.00 5.00
Alexander Steen

2002-03 Swedish SHL Masks

These cards were randomly inserts in series 2 packs at a rate of 1:32.

COMPLETE SET (9) 25.00 50.00
1 Sinuhe Wallinheimo 3.00 8.00
2 Stefan Liv 4.00 10.00
3 Sean Gauthier 3.00 8.00
4 Mikael Sandberg 3.00 8.00
5 Andreas Hadelov 3.00 8.00
6 Peter Hirsch 3.00 8.00
7 Magnus Lindquist 3.00 8.00
8 Kimmo Kapanen 3.00 8.00
9 Fredrik Norrena 4.00 10.00

2002-03 Swedish SHL Netminders

This set features top Swedish goalies and was inserted 1:8 series one packs.

COMPLETE SET (9) 15.00 20.00
NM1 Martin Gerber 2.00 5.00
NM2 Sergei Naumov 2.00 2.00
NM3 Stefan Liv 2.00 5.00
NM4 Rolf Wanhainen 2.00 2.00
NM5 Peter Hirsch 2.00 2.00
NM6 Daniel Henriksson 2.00 2.00
NM7 Mikael Sandberg 2.00 2.00
NM8 Johan Asplund 2.00 2.00
NM9 Andreas Hadelov 2.00 2.00

2002-03 Swedish SHL Next Generation

This set features the top young players in the SHL and was inserted 1:16 series one packs.

COMPLETE SET (9) 15.00 30.00
NG1 Joel Lundqvist 1.50 4.00
NG2 Par Backer 1.50 4.00
NG3 Magnus Hedlund 1.50 4.00
NG4 Adam Andersson 1.50 4.00
NG5 Henrik Lundqvist 1.50 4.00
NG6 Joakim Lindstrom 1.50 4.00
NG7 Jonas Johansson 1.50 8.00
NG8 Bjorn Melin 1.50 4.00
NG9 Jens Karlsson 2.00 5.00

2002-03 Swedish SHL Parallel

These cards were issued as random inserts in packs.

*PARALLEL: 2X TO 5X BASIC CARDS

2002-03 Swedish SHL Promos

This 11-card set was created to promote the new series of SHL cards, produced by Sweden's The Card Cabinet. The cards feature different photos and numbering than those of the same players in the base set.

COMPLETE SET (11) 8.00 20.00
TCC1 Tommy Sjodin .40 1.00
TCC2 Christian Eklund .40 1.00
TCC3 Martin Gerber .80 2.00
TCC4 Stefan Liv .80 2.00
TCC5 Per Eklund .40 1.00
TCC6 Jonas Andersson-Junkka .40 1.00
TCC7 Mika Hannula .40 1.00
TCC8 Mattias Weinhandl .80 2.00
TCC9 Peter Popovic .40 1.00
TCC10 Henrik Zetterberg 6.00 15.00
TCC11 Jan-Axel Alavaara .40 1.00

2002-03 Swedish SHL Sharpshooters

This set features the best snipers in the SHL and was inserted 1:8 series one packs.

COMPLETE SET (9) 20.00 40.00
SS1 Peter Hogardh 1.50 4.00
SS2 Jorgen Jonsson 1.50 4.00
SS3 Dieter Kalt 1.50 4.00
SS4 Per-Age Skroder 2.50 6.00
SS5 Juha Riihijarvi 1.50 4.00
SS6 Peter Larsson 1.50 4.00
SS7 Markus Matthiasson 1.50 4.00
SS8 Mattias Weinhandl 2.50 6.00
SS9 Nils Ekman 2.50 6.00

2002-03 Swedish SHL Signatures

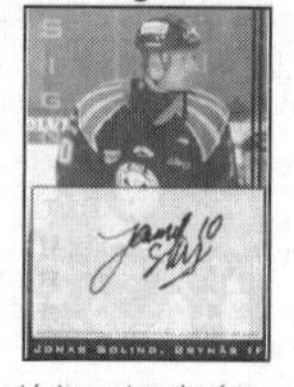

This set features autographs of many of the top stars of the SHL. The cards were inserted 1:32 series one packs.

STATED ODDS 1:32
1 Jonas Soling 4.00 10.00
2 Ove Molin 4.00 10.00
3 Nils Ekman 6.00 15.00
4 Kristofer Ottosson 4.00 10.00
5 Jorgen Jonsson 6.00 15.00
6 Rickard Wallin 6.00 15.00
7 Johan Davidsson 6.00 15.00
8 Mikael Sandberg 6.00 15.00
9 Stefan Nilsson 4.00 10.00
10 Andreas Hadelov 6.00 15.00
11 Jesper Mattsson 4.00 10.00
12 Peter Hogardh 6.00 15.00
13 Rolf Wanhainen 6.00 15.00
14 Juha Lind 6.00 15.00
15 Henrik Zetterberg 30.00 75.00
16 Per Hallin 4.00 10.00
17 Niklas Andersson 4.00 10.00
18 Alexander Steen 15.00 40.00

2002-03 Swedish SHL Signatures Series II

Inserted at a rate of 1:32 series 2 packs. The cards are unnumbered and listed below in checklist order.

STATED ODDS 1:32 SERIES II PACKS
1 Stefan Pettersson 6.00 15.00
2 Daniel Henriksson 6.00 15.00
3 Erik Nordback 6.00 15.00
4 Bjorn Nord 6.00 15.00
5 Ulf Soderstrom 6.00 15.00
6 Stefan Liv 10.00 25.00
7 Mikael Hakansson 6.00 15.00
8 Joel Lundqvist 10.00 25.00
9 Robert Carlsson 6.00 15.00
10 Peter Popovic 6.00 15.00
11 Magnus Wernblom 6.00 15.00
12 Juha Riihijarvi 6.00 15.00
13 Jonathan Hedstrom 8.00 20.00
14 Marcus Thuresson 6.00 15.00
15 Per Eklund 6.00 15.00
16 Antti Tormanen 6.00 15.00
17 Fredrik Lindqvist 6.00 15.00
18 Jens Nielsen 6.00 15.00
19 Sean Gauthier 6.00 15.00
20 Niklas Eriksson 6.00 15.00

21 Leif Rohlin 6.00 15.00
22 Lars Jonsson 8.00 20.00
23 Kalle Sahlstedt SP 15.00 40.00
24 Per-Age Skroder SP 15.00 40.00
25 Dieter Kalt 6.00 15.00
26 Johan Asplund 8.00 20.00

2002-03 Swedish SHL Team Captains

Inserted in series two at a rate of 1:8 packs.
COMPLETE SET (9) 6.00 15.00
1 Jan Larsson .75 2.00
2 Nichlas Falk .75 2.00
3 Jorgen Jonsson .75 2.00
4 Johan Davidsson .75 2.00
5 Christer Olsson .75 2.00
6 Stefan Gustavson .75 2.00
7 Roger Akerstrom .75 2.00
8 Pierre Hedin .75 2.00
9 Peter Popovic .75 2.00

2003-04 Swedish Elite

Sold in two series, with each containing 144 cards.
COMPLETE SET (288) 20.00 40.00
COMMON CARD (1-144) .02 .05
SEMISTARS/GOALIES .08 .20
UNLISTED STARS .20 .50

2003-04 Swedish Elite Enforcers

COMPLETE SET (12) 5.00 10.00
STATED ODDS 1:8 SERIES 2
EF1 Hannes Hyvonen .40 1.00
EF2 Oscar Ackestrom .40 1.00
EF3 Thomas Berglund .40 1.00
EF4 Andreas Pihl .40 1.00
EF5 Joel Lundqvist .75 2.00
EF6 Par Styf .40 1.00
EF7 Bert Robertsson .40 1.00
EF8 Bjorn Nord .40 1.00
EF9 Henrik Nordfeldt .40 1.00
EF10 Christian Sjogren .40 1.00
EF11 Niklas Sundblad .40 1.00
EF12 Magnus Wernblom .40 1.00

2003-04 Swedish Elite Global Impact

COMPLETE SET (12) 6.00 15.00
STATED ODDS 1:8 SERIES 2
GI1 Markus Korhonen .75 2.00
GI2 Richard Lintner .40 1.00
GI3 Tomi Kallio .75 2.00
GI4 Sinuhe Wallinheimo .75 2.00
GI5 Per-age Skroder .40 1.00
GI6 Mike Bales 1.25 3.00
GI7 Brian Felsner 1.00 2.50
GI8 Kamil Brabenec .40 1.00
GI9 Toivo Suursoo .40 1.00
GI10 Jesper Damgaard .40 1.00
GI11 Juha Lind .40 1.00
GI12 Jan Nemecek .40 1.00

2003-04 Swedish Elite Hot Numbers

COMPLETE SET (12) 8.00 20.00
STATED ODDS 1:16 SERIES 2
HN1 Stefan Liv 1.50 4.00
HN2 Robert Nilsson .75 2.00
HN3 Nicklas Falk .40 1.00
HN4 Alexander Steen 3.00 8.00
HN5 Jorgen Jonsson .40 1.00
HN6 Rolf Wanhainen .75 2.00
HN7 Markus Matthiasson .40 1.00
HN8 Thomas Johansson .40 1.00
HN9 Daniel Henriksson .75 2.00
HN10 Mikael Lind .40 1.00
HN11 Petri Liimatainen .40 1.00
HN12 Per Svartvadet .75 2.00

2003-04 Swedish Elite Jerseys

COMPLETE SET (5) 25.00 60.00
1 Kimmo Kapanen 4.00 10.00
2 Sinuhe Wallinheimo 8.00 20.00
3 Daniel Henriksson 4.00 10.00
4 Henrik Lundqvist 8.00 20.00
5 Magnus Johansson 4.00 10.00

2003-04 Swedish Elite Masks

COMPLETE SET (4) 15.00 30.00
1 Sinuhe Wallinheimo 4.00 10.00
2 Stefan Liv 5.00 12.00
3 Andreas Hadelov 4.00 10.00
4 Kimmo Kapanen 4.00 10.00

2003-04 Swedish Elite Masks II

COMPLETE SET (4) 15.00 30.00
STATED ODDS 1:32 SERIES 2
1 Stefan Liv 5.00 12.00
2 Kimmo Kapanen 4.00 10.00
3 Andreas Hadelov 4.00 10.00
4 Sinuhe Wallinheimo 4.00 10.00

2003-04 Swedish Elite Rookies

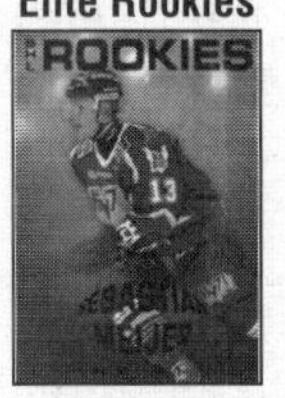

These cards were inserted at a rate of 1:8 packs.
COMPLETE SET (9) 6.00 15.00
STATED ODDS 1:8
1 Adam Andersson .40 1.00
2 Joakim Lundstrom .40 1.00
3 Nicklas Eckerblom .40 1.00
4 Alexander Steen 3.00 8.00
5 Sebastian Meijer .40 1.00
6 Robert Nilsson 1.00 2.50
7 Frans Nielsen 1.00 2.50
8 Tobias Enstrom .40 1.00
9 Joakim Lindstrom .40 1.00

2003-04 Swedish Elite Signatures

These authentic signatures were inserted at a rate of 1:32 Series 1 packs.
COMPLETE SET (16) 50.00 125.00
STATED ODDS 1:32 SERIES 1
1 Antti Tormanen 4.00 10.00
2 Tommy Sjodin 4.00 10.00
3 Joel Lundqvist 8.00 20.00
4 Daniel Henriksson 4.00 10.00
5 Tobias Enstrom 4.00 10.00
6 Jonas Johnsson 4.00 10.00
7 Mika Lehtinen 4.00 10.00
8 Tommi Miettinen 4.00 10.00
9 Peter Popovic 4.00 10.00
10 Fredrik Norrena 8.00 20.00
11 Jonas Andersson-Junkka 4.00 10.00
12 Magnus Wernblom 4.00 10.00
13 Niklas Anger 4.00 10.00
14 Patrik Bjaarnhjelm 4.00 10.00
15 Mattias Wennerberg 4.00 10.00
16 Robert Nilsson SP 10.00 25.00

2003-04 Swedish Elite Signatures II

STATED ODDS 1:32 SERIES 2
1 Sinuhe Wallinheimo 6.00 15.00
2 Per Hallberg 4.00 10.00
3 Par Backer 4.00 10.00
4 Jorgen Jonsson 4.00 10.00
5 Par Styf 4.00 10.00
6 Markus Matthiasson 4.00 10.00
7 Kimmo Kapanen 6.00 15.00
8 Niklas Kronwall 15.00 40.00
9 Bjorn Nord 4.00 10.00
10 Daniel Rudslatt 4.00 10.00
11 Per Eklund 4.00 10.00
12 Pasi Maatanen 4.00 10.00
13 Peter Ekelund 4.00 10.00
14 Stefan Liv 12.00 30.00
15 Johan Davidsson SP 20.00 50.00
16 Daniel Rydmark 4.00 10.00
17 Petri Liimatainen 4.00 10.00
18 Andreas Hadelov 6.00 15.00
19 Christer Olsson 4.00 10.00
20 Niklas Eriksson 4.00 10.00
21 Jens Nielsen 4.00 10.00

2003-04 Swedish Elite Stars of the Game

COMPLETE SET (9) 8.00 20.00
STATED ODDS 1:32
1 Kristofer Ottosson 1.25 3.00
2 Niklas Andersson 1.25 3.00
3 Jorgen Jonsson 1.25 3.00
4 Johan Davidsson 1.25 3.00
5 Per Eklund 1.25 3.00
6 Jonas Ronnqvist 1.25 3.00
7 Juha Riihijarvi 1.25 3.00
8 Antti Tormanen 1.25 3.00
9 Niklas Nordgren 1.25 3.00

2003-04 Swedish Elite Zero Hero

COMPLETE SET (9) 15.00 40.00
STATED ODDS 1:16
1 Henrik Lundqvist 5.00 12.00
2 Rolf Wanhainen 2.00 5.00
3 Andreas Hadelov 2.00 5.00
4 Joaquin Gage 2.00 5.00
5 Sinuhe Wallinheimo 2.00 5.00
6 Stefan Liv 2.50 6.00
7 Sean Gauthier 2.00 5.00
8 Juuso Riksman 2.00 5.00
9 Kimmo Kapanen 2.00 5.00

2003-04 Swedish MoDo Postcards

We have confirmed a handful of singles from this set, thanks to collector Vinnie Montalbano. There are very likely many more yet to be confirmed. If you have any other information about this set, please email us at hockeymag@beckett.com.
COMPLETE SET (?)
1 Jonas Almtorp
2 Kari Haakana
3 Andreas Salomonsson
4 Mattias Wennerberg

2004-05 Swedish Alfabilder Alfa Stars

COMPLETE SET (54) 10.00 25.00
1 Johan Hedberg .20 .50
2 Mattias Ohlund .20 .50
3 Kim Johnsson .20 .50
4 Kenny Jonsson .20 .50
5 Nicklas Lidstrom .40 1.00
6 Mikael Renberg .20 .50
7 Stefan Liv .40 1.00
8 Christian Backman .20 .50
9 Magnus Kahnberg .20 .50
10 Andreas Johansson .20 .50
11 Daniel Alfredsson .40 1.00
12 Daniel Sedin .40 1.00
13 Mats Sundin .75 2.00
14 Mattias Norstrom .20 .50
15 Johan Davidsson .20 .50
16 Tomas Holmstrom .40 1.00
17 Marcus Ragnarsson .20 .50
18 Marcus Nilson .20 .50
19 Markus Naslund .75 2.00
20 Henrik Sedin .40 1.00
21 Peter Forsberg 2.00 5.00
22 Per-Johan Axelsson .20 .50
23 Kristian Huselius .20 .50
24 Michael Nylander .20 .50
25 Mattias Weinhandl .20 .50
26 Samuel Pahlsson .20 .50
27 Jorgen Jonsson .20 .50
28 Dick Tarnstrom .20 .50
29 Nils Ekman .20 .50
30 Henrik Lundqvist 3.00 8.00
31 Fredrik Olausson .20 .50
32 Mikael Tellqvist .40 1.00
33 Fredrik Modin .20 .50
34 Niklas Sundstrom .20 .50
35 Tommy Salo .20 .50
36 Daniel Tjarnqvist .20 .50
37 Fredrik Sjostrom .20 .50
38 Robert Nilsson .20 .50
39 Alexander Steen 2.00 5.00
40 Henrik Zetterberg .75 2.00
41 Tomas Sandstrom .20 .50
42 Tomas Jonsson .20 .50
43 Jonas Bergqvist .20 .50
44 Magnus Svensson .20 .50
45 Challe Berglund .20 .50
46 Leif Holmqvist .20 .50
47 Borje Salming .40 1.00
48 Sven Tumba Johansson .20 .50
49 Ulf Sterner .20 .50
50 Anders Kallur .20 .50
51 Mats Naslund .20 .50
52 Hakan Loob .20 .50
53 Kent Nilsson .20 .50
54 Pekka Lindmark .20 .50

2004-05 Swedish Alfabilder Alfa Stars Golden Ice

COMPLETE SET (12) 10.00 25.00
1 Jonas Bergqvist .75 2.00
2 Sven Tumba .75 2.00
3 Hakan Loob .75 2.00
4 Peter Forsberg 4.00 10.00
5 Pekka Lindmark .75 2.00
6 Tomas Jonsson .75 2.00
7 Challe Berglund .75 2.00
8 Tommy Salo .75 2.00
9 Jorgen Jonsson .75 2.00
10 M.Renberg/N.Sundstrom 1.25 3.00
11 M.Norstrom/M.Ohlund 1.25 3.00
12 F.Modin/K.Johnsson 1.25 3.00

2004-05 Swedish Alfabilder Autographs

Random inserts in Swedish product, limited to 200 copies each.
COMPLETE SET (28) 150.00 300.00
101 Markus Naslund 12.00 30.00
102 Henrik Zetterberg 12.00 30.00
103 Peter Forsberg 25.00 60.00
104 Per-Johan Axelsson 3.00 8.00
105 Henrik Sedin 4.00 10.00
106 Mikael Renberg 3.00 8.00
107 Nicklas Lidstrom 12.00 30.00
108 Tomas Sandstrom 4.00 10.00
109 Johan Hedberg 4.00 10.00
110 Tomas Jonsson 3.00 8.00
111 Michael Nylander 4.00 10.00
112 Mikael Tellqvist 10.00 25.00
113 Nils Ekman 4.00 10.00
114 Mattias Ohlund 3.00 8.00
115 Fredrik Modin 3.00 8.00
116 Jonas Bergqvist 3.00 8.00
117 Tommy Salo 44.00 10.00
118 Dick Tarnstrom 3.00 8.00
119 Niklas Sundstrom 3.00 8.00
120 Tomas Holmstrom 8.00 20.00
121 Charles Berglund 3.00 8.00
122 Christian Backman 3.00 8.00
123 Magnus Svensson 3.00 8.00
124 Marcus Nilson 4.00 10.00
125 Samuel Pahlsson 4.00 10.00
126 Daniel Tjarnqvist 3.00 8.00
127 Kristian Huselius 4.00 10.00
128 Mattias Weinhandl 3.00 8.00

2004-05 Swedish Alfabilder Limited Autographs

Parallel to the basic autographs, these cards are limited to just 50 copies.
COMPLETE SET (28) 500.00 700.00
101 Markus Naslund 20.00 50.00
102 Henrik Zetterberg 20.00 50.00
103 Peter Forsberg 75.00 200.00
104 Per-Johan Axelsson 8.00 20.00
105 Henrik Sedin 8.00 20.00
106 Mikael Renberg 8.00 20.00
107 Nicklas Lidstrom 20.00 50.00
108 Tomas Sandstrom 8.00 20.00
109 Johan Hedberg 8.00 20.00
110 Tomas Jonsson 8.00 20.00
111 Michael Nylander 8.00 20.00
112 Mikael Tellqvist 15.00 40.00
113 Nils Ekman 8.00 20.00
114 Mattias Ohlund 8.00 20.00
115 Fredrik Modin 12.00 30.00
116 Jonas Bergqvist 8.00 20.00
117 Tommy Salo 8.00 20.00
118 Dick Tarnstrom 8.00 20.00
119 Niklas Sundstrom 8.00 20.00
120 Tomas Holmstrom 15.00 40.00
121 Charles Berglund 8.00 20.00
122 Christian Backman 8.00 20.00
123 Magnus Svensson 8.00 20.00
124 Marcus Nilson 8.00 20.00
125 Samuel Pahlsson 8.00 20.00
126 Daniel Tjarnqvist 8.00 20.00
127 Kristian Huselius 8.00 20.00
128 Mattias Weinhandl 8.00 20.00

2004-05 Swedish Alfabilder Next In Line

COMPLETE SET (6) 15.00 40.00
1 Leif Holmqvist 2.00 5.00
Tommy Salo
2 Borje Salming 4.00 10.00
Nick Lidstrom
3 Sven Johansson 6.00 15.00
Peter Forsberg
4 Ulf Sterner 4.00 10.00
Henrik Zetterberg
5 Hakan Loob 4.00 10.00
Mats Naslund
6 Kent Nilsson 2.00 5.00
Robert Nilsson

2004-05 Swedish Alfabilder Proof Parallels

COMPLETE SET (54)
3X to 5X BASE CARD

2004-05 Swedish Djurgardens Postcards

These standard postcard-sized collectibles were issued by the team. All copies we've seen have been signed, so it's likely that's the only way they were made available. It's also likely that more singles exist than listed below. If you have information, contact us at hockeymag@beckett.com.
COMPLETE SET (?)
1 Mariusz Czerkawski .75 2.00
2 Daniel Fernholm .75 2.00
3 Espen Knutsen 1.25 3.00
4 Marcus Kristofferson .75 2.00
5 Staffan Kronwall 1.25 3.00
6 Robert Nilsson 1.25 3.00
7 Jimmie Olvestad .75 2.00
8 Kristofer Ottosson .75 2.00
9 Mika Stromberg .75 2.00
10 Daniel Tjarnqvist .75 2.00

2004-05 Swedish Elitset

COMPLETE SET (288) 15.00 40.00
1 Markus Korhonen .08 .20
2 Daniel Johansson .08 .20
3 Tommy Sjodin .08 .20
4 Daniel Casselstahl .08 .20
5 Henrik Malmstrom .08 .20
6 Jakob Johansson .08 .20
7 Patrik Ronnqvist .08 .20
8 Roger Kyro .08 .20
9 Ove Molin .08 .20
10 Bjorn Danielsson .08 .20
11 Tommi Miettinen .08 .20
12 Bjorn Bjurling .08 .20
13 Staffan Kronwall .08 .20
14 Johnny Oduya .20 .50
15 Daniel Rudslatt .08 .20
16 Nichlas Falk .08 .20
17 Tomas Kollar .08 .20
18 Christian Eklund .08 .20
19 Fredrik Bremberg .08 .20
20 Mikael Johansson .08 .20
21 Marcus Kristoffersson .20 .50
22 Kenneth Bergqvist .08 .20
23 Johan Jonfeldt .08 .20
24 Jan-Axel Alavaara .08 .20
25 Antti-Jussi Niemi .08 .20
26 Ronnie Sundin .08 .20
27 Magnus Kahnberg .08 .20
28 Alexander Steen 1.50 4.00
29 Jari Tolsa .08 .20
30 Jonas Esbjors .08 .20
31 Niklas Andersson .08 .20
32 Peter Strom .08 .20
33 Jonas Johnson .30 .75
34 Jens Karlsson .08 .20
35 Fredrik Eriksson .08 .20
36 Martin Lindman .08 .20
37 Jonas Frogren .08 .20
38 Greger Artursson .08 .20
39 Radek Hamr .08 .20
40 Janne Gronvall .08 .20
41 Hannes Hyvonen .08 .20
42 Peter Nordstrom .08 .20
43 Par Backer .08 .20
44 Marcel Jenni .08 .20
45 Peter Hammarstrom .08 .20
46 Dieter Kalt .08 .20
47 Stefan Liv .40 1.00
48 Fredrik Olausson .08 .20
49 Ola Thorwalls .08 .20
50 Jouni Loponen .08 .20
51 Stefan Hellkvist .08 .20
52 Per-Age Skroder .08 .20
53 Peter Ekelund .08 .20
54 Martin Thornberg .08 .20
55 Anders Huusko .08 .20
56 Kalle Sahlstedt .08 .20
57 Pasi Maattanen .08 .20
58 Mattias Remstam .08 .20
59 Johan Davidsson .08 .20
60 Fredrik Norrrena .20 .50
61 Peter Casparsson .08 .20
62 Martin Knold .08 .20
63 Jyrki Valivaara .08 .20
64 Mikko Peltola .08 .20
65 Tim Eriksson .08 .20
66 Fredrik Emvall .08 .20
67 Jussi Tarvainen .08 .20
68 Mikael Hakanson .08 .20
69 Per Eklund .08 .20
70 Gusten Tornqvist .08 .20
71 Jonas Andersson-Junkka .08 .20
72 Jan Sandstrom .08 .20
73 Tuukka Mantyla .08 .20
74 Stefan Nilsson .08 .20
75 Linus Fagemo .08 .20
76 Emil Lundberg .08 .20
77 Thomas Berglund .08 .20
78 Hans Huczkowski .08 .20
79 Per Ledin .08 .20
80 Johan Tellstrom .08 .20
81 Pierre Berggren .08 .20
82 Robert Borgqvist .08 .20
83 David Petrasek .08 .20
84 Magnus Osterby .08 .20
85 Petri Liimatainen .08 .20
86 Johan Norgren .08 .20
87 Peter Andersson .08 .20
88 Marcus Magnertoft .08 .20
89 Frans Nielsen .08 .20
90 Daniel Rydmark .08 .20
91 Mikael Wahlberg .08 .20
92 Kim Staal .08 .20
93 Jan Oberg .08 .20
94 Martin Johansson .08 .20
95 Lars Jansson .08 .20
96 Anders Soderberg .08 .20
97 Tommy Pettersson .08 .20
98 Fredrik Warg .08 .20
99 Magnus Hedlund .08 .20
100 Morten Green .08 .20
101 Magnus Gastrin .08 .20
102 Bengt Hoglund .08 .20
103 Adam Andersson .08 .20
104 Henrik Petre .08 .20
105 Daniel Back .08 .20
106 Hakan Bogg .08 .20
107 Jonas Westerling .08 .20
108 Magnus Sandberg .08 .20
109 Magnus Lindquist .08 .20
110 Bert Robertsson .08 .20
111 Jonathan Ericsson .08 .20
112 Stefan Bemstrom .08 .20
113 Erik Norback .08 .20
114 Joakim Eriksson .08 .20
115 Robert Dome .08 .20
116 Robert Carlsson .08 .20
117 Teemu Riihijarvi .08 .20
118 Gabriel Karlsson .08 .20
119 Jorgen Bemstrom .08 .20
120 Peter Larsson .08 .20
121 Kimmo Kapanen .20 .50
122 Tommi Rajamaki .08 .20
123 Jesper Jager .08 .20
124 Sanny Lindstrom .08 .20
125 Kalle Koskinen .08 .20
126 Par Styf .08 .20
127 Christian Soderstrom .08 .20
128 Niklas Nordgren .08 .20
129 Valeri Krykov .08 .20
130 Per Hallin .08 .20
131 Christian Sjogren .08 .20
132 Fredrik Sundin .08 .20
133 Peter Andersson .08 .20
134 Ove Molin .08 .20
135 Daniel Rydmark .08 .20
136 Johan Davidsson .08 .20
137 Thomas Berglund .08 .20
138 Pelle Prestberg .08 .20
139 Mathias Johansson .08 .20
140 Roger Kyro .08 .20
141 Kristofer Ottosson .08 .20
142 Nichlas Falk .08 .20
143 Dieter Kalt .08 .20
144 Tomi Kallio .20 .50
145 Johan Holmqvist .20 .50
146 Niklas Andersson .08 .20
147 Mikko Kuparinen .08 .20
148 Mattias Karlsson .08 .20
149 Sebastian Sulku .08 .20
150 Jonas Soling .08 .20
151 Nicklas Danielsson .08 .20
152 Andreas Dackell .20 .50
153 Mikko Luovi .08 .20
154 Mikael Lind .08 .20
155 Vesa Viitakoski .08 .20
156 Rolf Wanhainen .08 .20
157 Mika Stromberg .08 .20
158 Daniel Fernholm .08 .20
159 Daniel Tjarnqvist .08 .20
160 Rikard Franzen .08 .20
161 Nils Ekman .20 .50
162 Kristofer Ottosson .08 .20
163 Robert Nilsson .08 .20
164 Johannes Salmonsson .08 .20
165 Marcus Nilson .30 .75
166 Jimmie Olvestad .08 .20
167 Espen Knutsen .30 .75
168 Mariusz Czerkawski .20 .50
169 Henrik Lundqvist 2.00 5.00
170 Tom Koivisto .08 .20
171 Arto Tukio .08 .20
172 Christian Backman .08 .20
173 Peter Hogardh .08 .20
174 Joel Lundqvist .08 .20
175 Loui Eriksson .60 .75
176 Samuel Pahlsson .20 .50
177 Martin Pluss .08 .20
178 Per-Johan Axelsson .20 .50
179 Tomi Kallio .20 .50
180 Daniel Henriksson .20 .50
181 Robin Jonsson .08 .20
182 Per Hallberg .08 .20
183 Mats Trygg .08 .20
184 Pelle Prestberg .08 .20
185 Jesper Mattsson .08 .20
186 Christian Berglund .08 .20
187 Jonas Hoglund .20 .50
188 Mathias Johansson .08 .20
189 Jorgen Jonsson .08 .20
190 Fredrik Eriksson .08 .20
191 Calle Steen .08 .20
192 Boo Ahl .20 .50
193 Daniel Ljungqvist .08 .20
194 Per Gustafsson .08 .20
195 Johan Halvardsson .08 .20
196 Kimmo Peltonen .08 .20
197 Mathias Tjarnqvist .20 .50
198 Andreas Karlsson .08 .20
199 Andreas Jamtin .08 .20
200 Stefan Pettersson .08 .20
201 Daniel Sperrle .08 .20
202 Magnus Johansson .08 .20
203 Henrik Tallinder .20 .50
204 Christoffer Norgren .08 .20
205 Jakob Karlsson .08 .20
206 Johan Franzen .40 1.00
207 Tony Martensson .08 .20
208 Ulf Soderstrom .08 .20
209 Brendan Morrison .20 .50
210 Kristian Huselius .20 .50
211 Mike Knuble .20 .50
212 Johan Lindstrom .08 .20
213 Kristian Antila .08 .20
214 Johan Fransson .20 .50
215 Niclas Wallin .08 .20
216 Roger Akerstrom .08 .20
217 Jaroslav Obsut .08 .20
218 Jonas Ronnqvist .08 .20
219 Thomas Koch .08 .20
220 Justin Williams .20 .50
221 Jonas Nordquist .08 .20
222 Fredrik Hynning .08 .20
223 Karl Fabritius .08 .20
224 Tomas Holmstrom .40 1.00
225 Andreas Hadelov .20 .50
226 Christopher Nilstorp .20 .50
227 Miska Kangasniemi .08 .20
228 Bjorn Melin .08 .20
229 Jan Hammar .08 .20
230 Jason Deleurme .08 .20
231 Carl Soderberg .60 1.50
232 Andreas Valdix .08 .20
233 Mika Hannula .08 .20
234 Peter Hammarstrom .08 .20
235 Markus Matthiasson .08 .20
236 Tommy Salo .20 .50
237 Mattias Timander .08 .20
238 Hans Jonsson .08 .20
239 Tobias Enstrom .08 .20
240 Jesper Damgaard .08 .20
241 Oscar Hedman .08 .20
242 Pierre Hedin .08 .20
243 Daniel Sedin .40 1.00
244 Mattias Weinhandl .20 .50
245 Andreas Salomonsson .20 .50
246 Peter Oberg .08 .20
247 Henrik Sedin .40 1.00
248 Peter Forsberg 1.25 3.00
249 Alexander Steen .75 4.00
250 Per Svartvadet .20 .50
251 Tero Leinonen .08 .20
252 Andreas Lilja .08 .20
253 Marko Kauppinen .08 .20
254 Pavel Skrbek .08 .20
255 Calle Bergstrom .08 .20
256 Peter Nolander .08 .20
257 Jonathan Granstrom .08 .20
258 Marcus Eriksson .08 .20
259 Shawn Horcoff .20 .50
260 Kenneth Bergqvist .08 .20
261 Anders Nilsson .08 .20
262 Martin Jansson .08 .20
263 Mikael Simons .08 .20
264 Peter Nylander .08 .20
265 Rastislav Stana .30 .75
266 Niclas Havelid .08 .20
267 Dick Tarnstrom .20 .50
268 Peter Popovic .08 .20
269 Petri Liimatainen .08 .20
270 Timmy Pettersson .08 .20
271 Jan Huokko .08 .20
272 Anders Burstrom .08 .20
273 Nicklas Bergfors .40 1.00
274 Jonas Andersson .08 .20
275 Peter Ferraro .20 .50
276 Chris Ferraro .20 .50
277 Miikka Kiprusoff .75 2.00
278 Jimmy Danielsson .08 .20
279 Johan Svedberg .08 .20
280 Mats Hansson .08 .20
281 Lars Jonsson .20 .50
282 Teemu Aalto .08 .20
283 Robert Carlsson .08 .20
284 Kristian Gahn .08 .20
285 Yared Hagos .20 .50
286 Henrik Zetterberg .75 2.00
287 Magnus Nilsson .08 .20
288 Jonathan Hedstrom .20 .50

2004-05 Swedish Elitset Dominators

Inserted at a rate of 1:16 series 2 packs.
COMPLETE SET (9) 25.00 50.00
STATED ODDS 1:16 SERIES 2
1 Magnus Kahnberg 1.25 3.00
Pelle Prestberg
Joakim Eriksson
2 Peter Forsberg 6.00 15.00
Henrik Zetterberg
Kristian Huselius
3 Miikka Kiprusoff 6.00 15.00
Tommy Salo
Johan Holmqvist
4 Johan Fransson 4.00 10.00
Alexander Steen
Henrik Lundqvist
5 Brendan Morrison 3.00 8.00
Justin Williams
Shawn Horcoff
6 Henrik Tallinder 3.00 8.00
Tomas Holmstrom
Andreas Lilja
7 Espen Knutsen 1.25 3.00
Martin Pluss
Tomi Kallio
8 Dick Tarnstrom 1.25 3.00
Fredrik Olausson
Daniel Tjarnqvist
9 Henrik Sedin 6.00 15.00
Daniel Sedin
Peter Forsberg

2004-05 Swedish Elitset Forsberg Tribute

Inserted 1:8 series 1 packs.
COMPLETE SET (6) 10.00 25.00
STATED ODDS 1:8
1 Peter Forsberg 2.00 5.00
2 Peter Forsberg 2.00 5.00
3 Peter Forsberg 2.00 5.00
4 Peter Forsberg 2.00 5.00
5 Peter Forsberg 2.00 5.00
6 Peter Forsberg 2.00 5.00

2004-05 Swedish Elitset Future Stars

Inserted 1:8 series 1 packs.
COMPLETE SET (12) 15.00 30.00
STATED ODDS 1:8 SERIES 1
1 Carl Soderberg 1.50 4.00
2 Loui Eriksson 2.00 5.00
3 Linus Videll .75 2.00
4 Johan Fransson 2.00 5.00
5 Robert Nilsson 2.00 5.00
6 Nicklas Danielsson .75 2.00
7 Andreas Valdix .75 2.00
8 Alexander Steen 4.00 10.00
9 Joakim Lundstrom .75 2.00
10 Daniel Fernholm .75 2.00
11 Joakim Lindstrom .75 2.00
12 Mats Hansson .75 2.00

2004-05 Swedish Elitset Gold

3X to 5X BASE CARD VALUE

2004-05 Swedish Elitset High Expectations

Inserted 1:16 in series 1 packs.
COMPLETE SET (10) 10.00 25.00
STATED ODDS 1:16 SERIES 1
1 Jonas Soling .75 2.00
2 Tomas Kollar .75 2.00
3 Henrik Lundqvist 6.00 15.00
4 Mathias Johansson .75 2.00
5 Bjorn Melin .75 2.00
6 Tim Eriksson .75 2.00
7 Jonas Ronnqvist .75 2.00
8 Mattias Wennerberg .75 2.00
9 Peter Popovic .75 2.00
10 Yared Hagos 1.25 3.00

2004-05 Swedish Elitset In The Crease

Inserted 1:32 series 1 packs.
COMPLETE SET (10) 15.00 40.00
STATED ODDS 1:32 SERIES 1
1 Markus Korhonen 1.25 3.00
2 Bjorn Bjurling 1.25 3.00
3 Henrik Lundqvist 10.00 25.00
4 Sinuhe Wallinheimo 1.25 3.00
5 Stefan Liv 2.00 5.00
6 Fredrik Norrena 2.00 5.00
7 Daniel Henriksson 1.25 3.00
8 Andreas Hadelov 1.25 3.00
9 Rolf Wanhainen 1.25 3.00
10 Kimmo Kapanen 1.25 3.00

2004-05 Swedish Elitset Jerseys Series 1

STATED PRINT RUN 35 SETS
1 Markus Korhonen 12.00 30.00
2 Kimmo Kapanen 12.00 30.00
3 Sinuhe Wallinheimo 12.00 30.00
4 Henrik Lundqvist 30.00 75.00
5 Per Gustavsson 12.00 30.00

2004-05 Swedish Elitset Jerseys Series 2

STATED PRINT RUN 35 SETS
AH Andreas Hadelov 12.00 30.00
PP Peter Popovic 12.00 30.00
SL Stefan Liv 20.00 50.00
TJ Thomas Johansson 12.00 30.00

2004-05 Swedish Elitset Limited Signatures

Random inserts in series 2 packs, limited to 50 copies each.
COMPLETE SET (6)
STATED PRINT RUN 50 SETS
INSERTED RANDOMLY SERIES 2
1 Daniel Henriksson 10.00 25.00
2 Jorgen Jonsson 10.00 25.00
3 Per Gustavsson 10.00 25.00
4 Andreas Lilja 10.00 25.00
5 Niclas Havelid 10.00 25.00
6 Jonas Ronnqvist 10.00 25.00

2004-05 Swedish Elitset Masks

Inserted 1:32 series 2 packs.
COMPLETE SET (8) 50.00 100.00
STATED ODDS 1:32 SERIES 2
1 Johan Holmqvist 4.00 10.00
2 Bjorn Bjurling 4.00 10.00
3 Henrik Lundqvist 12.00 30.00
4 Stefan Liv 6.00 15.00
5 Andreas Hadelov 4.00 10.00
6 Gusten Tornqvist 4.00 10.00
7 Rastislav Stana 6.00 15.00
8 Miikka Kiprusoff 12.00 30.00

2004-05 Swedish Elitset Signatures

Inserted 1:32 series 1 packs.
COMPLETE SET (15) 100.00 175.00
STATED ODDS 1:32 SERIES 1
1 Andreas Hadelov 6.00 15.00
2 Andreas Valdix 6.00 15.00
3 Joakim Eriksson 6.00 15.00
4 Rolf Wanhainen 6.00 15.00
5 Jonas Ronnqvist 6.00 15.00
6 Johan Fransson 10.00 25.00
7 Per Svartvadet 6.00 15.00
8 Bjorn Bjurling 6.00 15.00
9 Niklas Falk 6.00 15.00
10 Robert Carlsson 6.00 15.00
11 Yared Hagos 6.00 15.00
12 Joakim Lundstrom 6.00 15.00
13 Mikael Lind 6.00 15.00
14 Pelle Prestberg 6.00 15.00
15 Hannes Hyvonen 6.00 15.00

2004-05 Swedish Elitset Signatures Series A

STATED ODDS 1:32 SERIES 2
1 Frans Nielsen 4.00 10.00
2 Kim Staal 4.00 10.00
3 Per Eklund 4.00 10.00
4 Fredrik Norrena 6.00 15.00
5 Mikko Peltola 4.00 10.00
6 Tim Eriksson 4.00 10.00
7 Roger Akerstrom 4.00 10.00
8 Daniel Henriksson 4.00 10.00
9 Mats Hansson 4.00 10.00
10 Kimmo Kapanen 6.00 15.00
11 Tommi Miettinen 4.00 10.00
12 Bjorn Danielsson 4.00 10.00
13 Marcel Jenni 4.00 10.00
14 Henrik Lundqvist 20.00 50.00
15 Tomi Kallio 4.00 10.00
16 Niklas Andersson 4.00 10.00
17 Antti-Jussi Niemi 4.00 10.00

2004-05 Swedish Elitset Signatures Series B

STATED ODDS 1:32 SERIES 2
1 Andreas Dackell 4.00 10.00
2 Johan Holmqvist 6.00 15.00
3 Daniel Henriksson 4.00 10.00
4 Jonas Hoglund 4.00 10.00
5 Jorgen Jonsson 4.00 10.00
6 Mathias Johansson 4.00 10.00
7 Kimmo Peltonen 4.00 10.00
8 Mathias Tjarnqvist 6.00 15.00
9 Stefan Pettersson 4.00 10.00
10 Andreas Lilja 6.00 15.00
11 Mikael Simons 4.00 10.00
12 Peter Nylander 4.00 10.00
13 Dick Tarnstrom 4.00 10.00
14 Niclas Havelid 6.00 15.00
15 Peter Forsberg 30.00 75.00
16 Tommy Salo 6.00 15.00
17 Tomas Holmstrom 10.00 25.00

2004-05 Swedish HV71 Postcards

We have confirmed a handful of cards from this Swedish issue, thanks to collector Vinnie Montalbano. It's a certainty that others exist. If you know of others, please email hockeymag@beckett.com.

COMPLETE SET (?)
1 Brian Boucher 1.25 3.00
2 Andreas Jamtin .75 2.00
3 Simon Skoog .75 2.00
4 David Fredriksson .75 2.00
5 Fredrik Olausson .75 2.00
6 Per Gustafsson .75 2.00
7 Peter Ekelund .75 2.00
8 Anders Huusko .75 2.00

2004-05 Swedish MoDo Postcards

These 5X7 postcards were issued by the team, apparently in set form. They are unnumbered and feature more than a dozen moonlighting NHLers.

COMPLETE SET (30) 20.00 40.00
1 Peter Forsberg 4.00 10.00
2 Henrik Sedin 2.00 5.00
3 Daniel Sedin 2.00 5.00
4 Mattias Weinhandl .75 2.00
5 Adrian Aucoin .75 2.00
6 Mattias Timander .75 2.00
7 Per Svartvadet .75 2.00
8 Alexander Steen 4.00 10.00
9 Tommy Salo .75 2.00
10 Markus Naslund 2.00 5.00
11 Andreas Salomonsson .75 2.00
12 Frantisek Kaberle .75 2.00
13 Hans Jonsson .40 1.00
14 Joakim Lindstrom .40 1.00
15 Pierre Hedin .40 1.00
16 Dan Hinote .75 2.00
17 Lars Jansson .40 1.00
18 Magnus Gastrin .40 1.00
19 Mattias Hellstrom .40 1.00
20 Tobias Viklund .40 1.00
21 Michael Zajkowski .40 1.00
22 Morten Green .40 1.00
23 Mattias Wennerberg .40 1.00
24 Magnus Hedlund .40 1.00
25 Peter Oberg .40 1.00
26 Fredrik Warg .40 1.00
27 Oscar Hedman .40 1.00
28 Tobias Enstrom .40 1.00
29 Jan Oberg .40 1.00
30 Jesper Damgaard .40 1.00

2004-05 Swedish Pure Skills

COMPLETE SET (144) 20.00 50.00
1 Johan Holmqvist .20 .50
2 Chris Phillips .08 .20
3 Tommy Sjodin .08 .20
4 Andreas Dackell .08 .20
5 Tommi Miettinen .08 .20
6 Ronald Petrovicky .08 .20
7 Mikael Lind .08 .20
8 Jose Theodore 1.25 3.00
9 Daniel Tjarnqvist .08 .20
10 Dan Boyle .08 .20
11 Nils Ekman .08 .20
12 Marcus Nilson .08 .20
13 Espen Knutsen .08 .20
14 Mariusz Czerkawski .08 .20
15 Henrik Lundqvist 1.50 4.00
16 Tom Koivisto .08 .20
17 Sami Salo .08 .20
18 Christian Backman .08 .20
19 Daniel Alfredsson .40 1.00
20 Niklas Andersson .08 .20
21 Samuel Pahlsson .20 .50
22 Martin Pluss .08 .20
23 Jonas Johnson .08 .20
24 Tomi Kallio .08 .20
25 Martin Gerber .30 .75
26 Zdeno Chara .30 .75
27 Sheldon Souray .08 .20
28 Pelle Prestberg .08 .20
29 Christian Berglund .08 .20
30 Jonas Hoglund .08 .20
31 Peter Nordstrom .08 .20
32 Jorgen Jonsson .08 .20
33 Marian Gaborik 1.25 3.00
34 Stefan Liv .40 1.00
35 Anders Eriksson .08 .20
36 Per Gustafsson .08 .20
37 Manny Malhotra .08 .20
38 Andreas Karlsson .08 .20
39 Jonathan Cheechoo .60 1.50
40 Johan Davidsson .08 .20
41 Fredrik Norrena .40 1.00
42 Magnus Johansson .08 .20
43 Thomas Johansson .08 .20
44 Mikko Peltola .08 .20
45 Tony Martensson .08 .20
46 Brendan Morrison .20 .50
47 Michael Knuble .20 .50
48 Kristian Antila .20 .50
49 Niclas Wallin .08 .20
50 Roger Akerstrom .08 .20
51 Jaroslav Obsut .08 .20
52 Jonas Ronnqvist .08 .20
53 Justin Williams .20 .50
54 Per Ledin .08 .20
55 Tomas Holmstrom .40 1.00
56 Andreas Hadelov .20 .50
57 David Petrasek .08 .20
58 Peter Andersson .08 .20
59 Bjorn Melin .08 .20
60 Carl Soderberg .40 1.00
61 Mika Hannula .08 .20
62 Tommy Salo .20 .50
63 Mattias Timander .08 .20
64 Adrian Aucoin .20 .50
65 Daniel Sedin .30 .75
66 Mattias Weinhandl .08 .20
67 Markus Naslund .75 2.00
68 Henrik Sedin .30 .75
69 Peter Forsberg 2.00 5.00
70 Alexander Steen .75 2.00
71 Per Svartvadet .08 .20
72 Dan Hinote .20 .50
73 Tero Leinonen .20 .50
74 Pavel Skrbek .08 .20
75 Daniel Cleary .08 .20
76 Rastislav Pavlikovsky .20 .50
77 Marian Hossa .75 2.00
78 Shawn Horcoff .30 .75
79 Ladislav Nagy .30 .75
80 Marcel Hossa .30 .75
81 Rastislav Stana .30 .75
82 Dick Tarnstrom .20 .50
83 Peter Popovic .08 .20
84 Joakim Eriksson .08 .20
85 Kyle Calder .20 .50
86 Mikael Samuelsson .20 .50
87 Scott Thornton .20 .50
88 Dragan Umicevic .08 .20
89 Miikka Kiprusoff .75 2.00
90 Aki-Petteri Berg .08 .20
91 Teemu Aalto .08 .20
92 Niklas Nordgren .20 .50
93 Yared Hagos .20 .50
94 Henrik Zetterberg .75 2.00
95 Kent Manderville .20 .50
96 Jonathan Hedstrom .20 .50
97 Landon Wilson .20 .50
98 Ladislav Kohn .20 .50
99 Mike Ribeiro .20 .50
100 Tomas Vokoun .75 2.00
101 Marek Zidlicky .20 .50
102 Jere Karalahti .20 .50
103 Jarno Kultanen .08 .20
104 Lasse Pirjeta .20 .50
105 Jarkko Ruutu .20 .50
106 Timo Parssinen .08 .20
107 Brett Harkins .20 .50
108 Mika Noronen .20 .50
109 Josh Holden .20 .50
110 Riku Hahl .20 .50
111 Jani Rita .20 .50
112 Juuso Riksman .08 .20
113 Sami Helenius .08 .20
114 Steve Kariya .40 1.00
115 Patrik Stefan .20 .50
116 Hannes Hyvonen .08 .20
117 Tim Thomas .40 1.00
118 Ossi Vaananen .20 .50
119 Marko Jantunen .08 .20
120 Toni Dahlman .08 .20
121 Glen Metropolit .20 .50
122 Sinuhe Wallinheimo .20 .50
123 Steve Martins .20 .50
124 Jarkko Immonen .20 .50
125 Jody Shelley .40 1.00
126 Niklas Backman 1.00 2.50
127 Janne Niinimaa .20 .50
128 Josef Boumedienne .08 .20
129 Petr Tenkrat .08 .20
130 Michael Nylander .20 .50
131 Dwayne Roloson .75 2.00
132 Erik Hamalainen .08 .20
133 Esa Pirnes .08 .20
134 Pasi Nurminen .20 .50
135 Jarmo Myllys .20 .50
136 Andrew Raycroft 1.00 2.50
137 Ville Nieminen .20 .50
138 Stefan Ohman .08 .20
139 Teemu Lassila .20 .50
140 Craig Rivet .20 .50
141 Saku Koivu .60 1.50
142 Antti Aalto .08 .20
143 Scott Langkow .20 .50
144 Jason Williams .30 .75

2004-05 Swedish Pure Skills Jerseys

Limited to 35 copies each.
COMPLETE SET (4) 30.00 80.00
JR Jarkko Ruutu 10.00 25.00
PS Per Svartvadet 10.00 25.00
TS Tommy Salo 10.00 25.00
VN Ville Nieminen 10.00 25.00

2004-05 Swedish Pure Skills Parallel

Inserted at a rate of 1:4 packs and limited to just 100 copies.
5X to 8X BASE CARD VALUE

2004-05 Swedish Pure Skills Professional Power

COMPLETE SET (25) 30.00 75.00
AB Aki-Petteri Berg .75 2.00
CR Craig Rivet 1.25 3.00
DA Daniel Alfredsson 2.00 5.00
DS Daniel Sedin 1.25 3.00
DT Dick Tarnstrom 1.25 3.00
DT Daniel Tjarnqvist .75 2.00
HS Henrik Sedin 1.25 3.00
HZ Henrik Zetterberg 4.00 10.00
JN Janne Niinimaa .75 2.00
MC Mariusz Czerkawski .75 2.00
MG Marian Gaborik 6.00 15.00
MH Marian Hossa 4.00 10.00
MN Michael Nylander 1.25 3.00
MN Markus Naslund 4.00 10.00
MN Marcus Nilson .75 2.00
MZ Marek Zidlicky .75 2.00
OV Ossi Vaananen .75 2.00
PF Peter Forsberg 10.00 25.00
PS Patrik Stefan .75 2.00
RH Raimo Helminen .75 2.00
SK Saku Koivu 4.00 10.00
SP Samuel Pahlsson .75 2.00
SS Sami Salo .75 2.00
VN Ville Nieminen .75 2.00
ZC Zdeno Chara 1.25 3.00

2004-05 Swedish Pure Skills Signatures Limited

Limited to just 50 copies each.
PRINT RUN 50 SER.#'d SETS 100.00200.00
1 Andreas Dackell 10.00 25.00
2 Peter Forsberg 50.00 125.00
3 Henrik Zetterberg 20.00 50.00
4 Miikka Kiprusoff 20.00 50.00

2004-05 Swedish Pure Skills The Wall

Inserted at a rate of 1:40.
COMPLETE SET (10) 40.00 100.00
AR Andrew Raycroft 8.00 20.00
FN Fredrik Norrena 2.00 5.00
HL Henrik Lundqvist 8.00 20.00
JT Jose Theodore 10.00 25.00
MG Martin Gerber 4.00 10.00
MK Miikka Kiprusoff 10.00 25.00
MN Mika Noronen 2.00 5.00
NB Niklas Backstrom 4.00 10.00
TS Tommy Salo 2.00 5.00
TT Tim Thomas 6.00 15.00

2005-06 Swedish SHL Elitset

COMPLETE SET (288) 25.00 60.00
1 Johan Holmqvist .40 1.00
2 Niklas Andersson .20 .50
3 Mikko Kuparinen .10 .25
4 Tommy Sjodin .10 .25
5 Sebastian Sulku .10 .25
6 Henrik Malmstrom .10 .25
7 Andreas Dackell .10 .25
8 Ove Molin .10 .25
9 BjÃ¶rn Danielsson .10 .25
10 Tommi Miettinen .10 .25
11 Mikael Lind .10 .25
12 Vesa Viitakoski .10 .25
13 Jose Theodore 1.25 3.00
14 Ronnie Pettersson .10 .25
15 Daniel Tjarnqvist .20 .50
16 Christopher Thorn .10 .25
17 Robert Nilsson .75 2.00
18 Daniel Rudslat .10 .25
19 Nichlas Falk .10 .25
20 Marcus Nilson .20 .50
21 Jimmie Ã–lvestad .10 .25
22 Patrick Thoresen .40 1.00
23 Tom Koivisto .10 .25
24 Antti-Jussi Niemi .10 .25
25 Sami Salo .10 .25
26 Daniel Alfredsson .75 2.00
27 Magnus Kahnberg .10 .25
28 Peter Hogardh .10 .25
29 Jari Tolsa .10 .25
30 Joel Lundqvist .20 .50
31 Jonas Esbjors .10 .25
32 Niklas Andersson .10 .25
33 Samuel Pahlsson .20 .50
34 Martin Pluss .10 .25
35 Jonas Johnson .10 .25
36 Tomi Kallio .10 .25
37 Martin Gerber .40 1.00
38 Daniel Henriksson .10 .25
39 Robin Jonsson .10 .25
40 Jonas Frogren .10 .25
41 Radek Hamr .10 .25
42 Zdeno Chara .75 2.00
43 Pelle Prestberg .10 .25
44 Jesper Mattsson .10 .25
45 Jonas Hoglund .10 .25
46 Mathias Johansson .10 .25
47 Peter Nordstrom .10 .25
48 Fredrik Eriksson .10 .25
49 Par Backer .10 .25
50 Stefan Liv .40 1.00
51 Anders Eriksson .10 .25
52 Daniel Ljungqvist .10 .25
53 Per Gustafsson .10 .25
54 Simon Skoog .10 .25
55 Ola Svanberg .10 .25
56 Johan Halvardsson .10 .25
57 Anders Huusko .10 .25
58 Andreas Karlsson .10 .25
59 Pasi Maattanen .10 .25
60 Stefan Pettersson .10 .25
61 Johan Davidsson .10 .25
62 Johan Backlund .10 .25
63 Stefan Bemstrom .10 .25
64 Ã–rjan Lindmark .10 .25
65 Jens Bergenstrom .10 .25
66 Niklas Eriksson .10 .25
67 Niklas Persson .10 .25
68 Johan Rosen .10 .25
69 Fredrik Norrena .40 1.00
70 Magnus Johansson .10 .25
71 Thomas Johansson .10 .25
72 Christoffer Norgren .10 .25
73 Jyrki Valivaara .10 .25
74 Mikko Peltola .10 .25
75 Ulf Soderstrom .10 .25
76 Johan Andersson .10 .25
77 Tim Eriksson .10 .25
78 Michael Knuble .20 .50
79 Fredrik Emvall .10 .25
80 Jussi Tarvainen .10 .25
81 Mikael Hakanson .10 .25
82 Gusten Tornqvist .10 .25
83 Johan Fransson .10 .25
84 Jan SandstrÃ¶m .10 .25
85 Jaroslav Obsut .10 .25
86 Jonas Ronnqvist .10 .25
87 Thomas Koch .10 .25
88 Emil Lundberg .10 .25
89 Jonas Nordquist .10 .25
90 Fredrik Hynning .10 .25
91 Karl Fabricius .10 .25
92 Michael Zajkowski .10 .25
93 Hans Jonsson .10 .25
94 Tobias Enstrom .10 .25
95 Jesper Damgaard .10 .25
96 Oscar Hedman .10 .25
97 Daniel Sedin .40 1.00
98 Mattias Weinhandl .10 .25
99 Andreas Salomonsson .10 .25
100 Markus Naslund .75 2.00
101 Henrik Sedin .40 1.00
102 Peter Forsberg 2.00 5.00
103 Morten Green .10 .25
104 Per Svartvadet .10 .25
105 Magnus Gastrin .10 .25
106 Calle Bergstrom .10 .25
107 Peter Nolander .10 .25
108 Johnathan Granstrom .10 .25
109 Hakan Bogg .10 .25
110 Shawn Horcoff .40 1.00
111 Jonas Westerling .10 .25
112 Marian Hossa .75 2.00
113 Marcus Eriksson .10 .25
114 Magnus Sandberg .10 .25
115 Kenneth Bergkvist .10 .25
116 Anders Nilsson .10 .25
117 Magnus Simons .10 .25
118 Magnus Lindquist .10 .25
119 Bert Robertsson .10 .25
120 Nicklas Grossman .10 .25
121 Dick Tarnstrom .10 .25
122 Petri Liimatainen .10 .25
123 Timmy Pettersson .10 .25
124 Jan Huokko .10 .25
125 Anders Burstrom .10 .25
126 Robert Carlsson .10 .25
127 Nicklas Bergfors .40 1.00
128 Erik Norback .10 .25
129 Gabriel Karlsson .10 .25
130 JÃ¶rgen Bemstrom .10 .25
131 Miikka Kiprusoff 1.25 3.00
132 Johan Svedberg .10 .25
133 Sanny Lindstrom .10 .25
134 Kalle Koskinen .10 .25
135 Mats Hansson .10 .25
136 Teemu Aalto .10 .25
137 Christian Soderstrom .10 .25
138 Robert Carlsson .10 .25
139 Niklas Nordgren .20 .50
140 Per Hallin .10 .25
141 Kristian Gahn .10 .25
142 Henrik Zetterberg .75 2.00
143 Magnus Nilsson .10 .25
144 Johnathan Hedstrom .10 .25
145 Markus Korhonen .10 .25
146 Daniel Johansson .10 .25
147 Martin Ã–hrstedt .10 .25
148 JÃ¶rgen Sundqvist .10 .25
149 Daniel Casselstahl .10 .25
150 Rodrigo Lavins .10 .25
151 Antti Aarnio .20 .50
152 Jonas Almtorp .10 .25
153 Mathias Mansson .10 .25
154 Nicklas Backstrom 2.00 5.00
155 Lars-Erik Spets .10 .25
156 Mikael Wahlberg .10 .25
157 Petter Ronnquist .10 .25
158 Teemu Lassila .10 .25
159 AndrÃ© Mattsson .10 .25
160 Jonas Liwing .10 .25
161 Erik Ryman .10 .25
162 Adam Andersson .10 .25
163 Jesper Bjorck .10 .25
164 Henrik Nordfeldt .10 .25
165 Johan Enequist .10 .25
166 Christofer Lofberg .10 .25
167 Patric Hornqvist .10 .25
168 Fredrik Bremberg .10 .25
169 Marcus Kristofersson .10 .25
170 Per Eklund .10 .25
171 Mikael Sandberg .10 .25
172 Tommy Salo .20 .50
173 Jan-Axel Alavaara .10 .25
174 Arto Tukio .10 .25
175 Richard DemÃ©n-Willaume .10 .25
176 Ronnie Sundin .10 .25
177 Johnny Oduya .20 .50
178 Sebastian Karlsson .10 .25
179 Kirill Starkov .10 .25
180 Johan Witehall .10 .25
181 Christopher Heino-Lindberg .10 .25
182 Rami Alanko .10 .25
183 Per Hallberg .10 .25
184 Thomas Rhodin .10 .25
185 Mikael Johansson .10 .25
186 Rickard Wallin .10 .25
187 JÃ¶rgen Jonsson .10 .25
188 Fredrik Eriksson .10 .25
189 Johan Olsson .10 .25
190 Emil KÃ¥berg .10 .25
191 Per Ledin .10 .25
192 Erik Ersberg .10 .25
193 Fredrik Olausson .10 .25
194 Lars Jonsson .20 .50
195 Mika Niskanen .10 .25
196 David Petrasek .10 .25
197 Martin Thornberg .10 .25
198 David Fredriksson .10 .25
199 BjÃ¶rn Melin .10 .25
200 Jens Karlsson .10 .25
201 Mattias Remstam .10 .25
202 Mika Hannula .10 .25
203 Tomas Duba .10 .25
204 Elias Granat .10 .25
205 Magnus Osterby .10 .25
206 Yan Golubovsky .10 .25
207 Jan Srdinko .10 .25
208 Patrik Hucko .10 .25
209 Patrik Wallenberg .10 .25
210 Mike Watt .10 .25
211 Sebastian Meijer .10 .25
212 Jesper Ollas .10 .25
213 Niklas Broms .10 .25
214 Magnus Hedlund .10 .25
215 Oscar Steen .10 .25
216 Jimmie Ericsson .10 .25
217 Jukka Tiilikainen .10 .25
218 Jiri Bicek .10 .25
219 Jonas Fransson .10 .25
220 Andreas Pihl .10 .25
221 Mikko Luoma .10 .25
222 Victor Ringberg .10 .25
223 Tony Martensson .10 .25
224 Jonas Soling .10 .25
225 Sami Torkki .10 .25
226 Johan Lindstrom .10 .25
227 Patric Blomdahl .10 .25
228 David Rautio .10 .25
229 Mattias Modig .10 .25
230 Erik Lindberg .10 .25
231 Pekka Saravo .10 .25
232 Pavel Skrbek .10 .25
233 Per Savilahti-Nagander .10 .25
234 Johan Harju .10 .25
235 Mikael Renberg .20 .50
236 Ragnar Karlsson .10 .25
237 Vladimir Machulda .10 .25
238 Lubomir Bartecko .10 .25
239 Magnus Isaksson .10 .25
240 Christopher KÃ¶nigsson .10 .25
241 Karol Krizan .10 .25
242 Mattias Timander .10 .25
243 Vladimir Sicak .10 .25
244 Tobias Viklund .10 .25
245 Mattias Hellstrom .10 .25
246 Pasi Tuominen .10 .25
247 Rastislav Pavlikovsky .10 .25
248 Peter Ã–berg .10 .25
249 Mikael Pettersson .10 .25
250 Miloslav Horava .10 .25
251 Jan Pardavy .10 .25
252 Daniel Sperrle .10 .25
253 Petri Vehanen .10 .25
254 Peter Smrek .10 .25
255 Atvars Tribuntsovs .10 .25
256 Ross Lupaschuk .10 .25
257 Pierre Johnsson .10 .25
258 Jarno Kultanen .10 .25
259 Thomas Skogs .10 .25
260 Jordan Krestanovich .10 .25
261 Marco Tuokko .10 .25
262 Eric Johansson .10 .25
263 Kalle Kerman .10 .25
264 Peter Fabus .10 .25
265 Teemu Elomo .10 .25
266 Martin Jansson .10 .25
267 Rastislav Stana .20 .50
268 Stanislav Neckar .10 .25
269 Henrik Petre .10 .25
270 Jonathan Ericsson .10 .25
271 Daniel Ljungqvist .10 .25
272 Pasi Petrilainen .10 .25
273 Per-Ã…ke Skroder .10 .25
274 Christoph Brandner .10 .25
275 Anze Kopitar 6.00 15.00
276 Tomas Kollar .10 .25
277 Dragan Umicevic .10 .25
278 Petr Leska .10 .25
279 Johan Asplund .10 .25
280 Mika Oksa .10 .25
281 Par Styf .10 .25
282 Carl-Johan Johansson .10 .25
283 Peter Regin .10 .25
284 Frans Nielsen .40 1.00
285 Mattias Wennerberg .10 .25
286 Peter Strom .10 .25
287 Valeri Krykov .10 .25
288 Fredrik Warg .10 .25

2005-06 Swedish SHL Elitset Autographed Jerseys

These cards are not priced due to lack of market activity.
GWAKO Kristofer Ottosson
GWAMK Marcus Kristoffersson

2005-06 Swedish SHL Elitset Catchers

COMPLETE SET (12) 40.00 80.00
STATED ODDS 1:16 SER. 2 PACKS
1 Johan Holmqvist 3.00 8.00
2 Teemu Lassila 3.00 8.00
3 Tommy Salo 3.00 8.00
4 Daniel Henriksson 3.00 8.00
5 Stefan Liv 4.00 10.00
6 Johan Backlund 3.00 8.00
7 Fredrik Norrena 4.00 10.00
8 David Rautio 3.00 8.00
9 Karol Krizan 3.00 8.00
10 Petri Vehanen 3.00 8.00
11 Rastislav Stana 4.00 10.00
12 Mika Oksa 3.00 8.00

2005-06 Swedish SHL Elitset Catchers Gold

These parallel cards are not priced due to lack of market information.
COMPLETE SET (12)
STATED ODDS 1:120 SER. 2 PACKS

2005-06 Swedish SHL Elitset Icons

COMPLETE SET (9) 15.00 30.00
STATED ODDS 1:32 SER. 2 PACKS
1 Peter HammarstrÃ¶m 2.00 5.00
2 JÃ¶rgen JÃ¶nsson 2.00 5.00
3 Mathias Johansson 2.00 5.00
4 Thomas Johansson 2.00 5.00
5 Jonas Johnsson 2.00 5.00
6 Kristian Gahn 2.00 5.00
7 Ove Molin 2.00 5.00
8 Per Gustafsson 2.00 5.00
9 Fredrik Bremberg 2.00 5.00

2005-06 Swedish SHL Elitset Playmakers

COMPLETE SET (12) 25.00 60.00
STATED ODDS 1:32 SER. 1 PACKS
1 Mikael Lind 2.00 5.00
2 Marcus Nilson 2.00 5.00
3 Niklas Andersson 2.00 5.00
4 Daniel Alfredsson 4.00 10.00
5 JÃ¶rgen JÃ¶nsson 2.00 5.00
6 Johan Davidsson 2.00 5.00
7 Brendan Morrison 2.00 5.00
8 Daniel Sedin 3.00 8.00
9 Henrik Sedin 3.00 8.00
10 Marian Hossa 6.00 15.00
11 Scott Thornton 2.00 5.00
12 Henrik Zetterberg 6.00 15.00

2005-06 Swedish SHL Elitset Rookies

COMPLETE SET (9) 12.00 30.00
STATED ODDS 1:32 SER. 2 PACKS
1 Alexander Ribbenstrand 1.50 4.00
2 Anton Axelsson 1.50 4.00
3 Christopher Heino-Lindberg 1.50 4.00
4 Erik Andersson 1.50 4.00
5 Mattias Ritola 1.50 4.00
6 Robin Lindqvist 1.50 4.00
7 Tommy EnstrÃ¶m 1.50 4.00
8 Jens Jakobs 1.50 4.00
9 Anton StrÃ¥lman 2.50 6.00

2005-06 Swedish SHL Elitset Series One Jerseys

COMPLETE SET (4)
STATED PRINT RUN 35 #'d SETS
NOT PRICED DUE TO SCARCITY
1 Stefan Liv
2 Per Svartvadet
3 Thomas Johansson
4 Henrik Lundqvist

2005-06 Swedish SHL Elitset Series One Signatures

COMPLETE SET (15) 100.00 200.00
RANDOM INSERTS IN PACKS
1 Ulf SoderstrÃ¶m 6.00 15.00
2 Tim Eriksson 6.00 15.00
3 Petri Liimatainen 6.00 15.00
4 Nicklas Grossman 6.00 15.00
5 Oscar Hedman 6.00 15.00
6 Tobias Viklund 6.00 15.00
7 Johan Davidsson 6.00 15.00
8 Ola Svanberg 6.00 15.00
9 Anders Huusko 6.00 15.00
10 Jonas Hoglund 6.00 15.00
11 Daniel Henriksson 6.00 15.00
12 Johan Fransson 6.00 15.00
13 Karl Fabricius 6.00 15.00
14 Gusten Tornqvist 6.00 15.00
15 Christopher Thorn 6.00 15.00

2005-06 Swedish SHL Elitset Series Two Jerseys

COMPLETE SET (4)
PRINT RUN 35 SER.#'d SETS
NOT PRICED DUE TO SCARCITY
GWFN Fredrik Norrena
GWJD Johan Davidsson
GWJJ Jorgen Jonsson
GWKO Kristofer Ottosson

2005-06 Swedish SHL Elitset Series Two Signatures

The short printed autographs are not priced due to a lack of market activity.
1 Mathias Mansson SP
2 Mikael Wahlberg SP
3 Adam Andersson 6.00 15.00
4 Patrick Thoresen 8.00 20.00
5 Niklas Andersson 6.00 15.00
6 Magnus Kahnberg 6.00 15.00
7 Tomi Kallio 8.00 20.00
8 Mathias Johansson 6.00 15.00
9 Jesper Mattson 6.00 15.00
10 Thomas Rhodin 6.00 15.00

11 Per Gustafsson 6.00 15.00
12 Stefan Liv 10.00 25.00
13 Stefan Pettersson 6.00 15.00
14 Tomas Duba 6.00 15.00
15 Orjan Lindmark 6.00 15.00
16 Niklas Persson 6.00 15.00
17 Fredrik Emwall 6.00 15.00
18 Tony Martensson 6.00 15.00
19 Fredrik Norrena 8.00 20.00
20 Lubomir Bartecko 6.00 15.00
21 David Rautio 6.00 15.00
22 Mikael Renberg 10.00 25.00
23 Christoph Brandner 6.00 15.00
24 Anze Kopitar 75.00 125.00
25 Jan Huokko 6.00 15.00
26 Peter Strom 6.00 15.00
27 Christian Soderstrom 6.00 15.00
28 Mattias Wennerberg 6.00 15.00
29 Mats Hansson SP
30 Henrik Lundqvist SP
31 JÃ¶rgen Jonsson SP
32 Joel Lundqvist SP

2005-06 Swedish SHL Elitset Star Potential

COMPLETE SET (18) 15.00 40.00
STATED ODDS 1:8 SER. 1 PACKS
1 Niklas Andersson .75 2.00
2 Nicklas Backstrom 2.50 6.00
3 Robert Nilsson .75 2.00
4 Christopher Thorn 1.50 4.00
5 Loui Eriksson 1.50 4.00
6 Henrik Lundqvist 4.00 10.00
7 Robin Jonsson .75 2.00
8 Ola Svanberg .75 2.00
9 Tony Martensson .75 2.00
10 Johan Fransson .75 2.00
11 Tobias Enstrom .75 2.00
12 Oscar Hedman .75 2.00
13 Jonathan Granstrom .75 2.00
14 Nicklas Bergfors 1.50 4.00
15 Dragan Umicevic .75 2.00
16 Linus Videll .75 2.00
17 Yared Hagos .75 2.00
18 Mats Hansson .75 2.00

2005-06 Swedish SHL Elitset Stoppers

COMPLETE SET (12) 30.00 75.00
STATED ODDS 1:16 SER. 1 PACKS
1 Johan Holmqvist 3.00 8.00
2 Jose Theodore 6.00 15.00
3 Rolf Wanhainen 2.00 5.00
4 Henrik Lundqvist 6.00 15.00
5 Martin Gerber 3.00 8.00
6 Daniel Henriksson 2.00 5.00
7 Stefan Liv 3.00 8.00
8 Fredrik Norrena 3.00 8.00
9 Tommy Salo 2.00 5.00
10 Tero Leinonen 2.00 5.00
11 Rastislav Stana 2.00 5.00
12 Miikka Kiprusoff 6.00 15.00

2005-06 Swedish SHL Elitset Teammates

COMPLETE SET (12) 8.00 20.00
STATED ODDS 1:8 SER. 2 PACKS
1 Andreas Dackell .75 2.00
Mikael Lind
2 Nichlas Falk .75 2.00
Patrick Thoresen
3 Jonas HÃ¶glund .75 2.00
Pelle Prestberg
4 Niklas Andersson .75 2.00
Tomi Kallio
5 Johan Davidsson .75 2.00
Mattias Remstam
6 Niklas Person .75 2.00
Patrik Wallenberg
7 Fredrik Emwall .75 2.00
Ulf SÃ¶derstrÃ¶m
8 Karl Fabricius 1.25 3.00
Mikael Renberg
9 Andreas Salomonsson .75 2.00
Per Svartvadet
10 Anders Nilsson .75 2.00
Kalle Kerman
11 JÃ¶rgen BemstrÃ¶m .75 2.00
Timmy Pettersson
12 Robert Carlsson .75 2.00
Valeri Krykov

2006-07 Swedish SHL Elitset

COMPLETE SET (288) 25.00 50.00
1 Johan Holmqvist .40 1.00
2 Daniel Johansson .10 .25
3 Tommy SÃ¶din .10 .25
4 JÃ¶rgen Sundqvist .10 .25
5 Rodrigo Lavins .10 .25
6 Henrik MalmstrÃ¶m .10 .25
7 Jonas Almtorp .10 .25
8 Andreas Dackel .10 .25
9 Mathias MÃ¥nsson .10 .25
10 Ove Molin .10 .25
11 Lars-Erik Spets .10 .25
12 Mikael Lind .10 .25
13 Petter RÃ¶nnquist .10 .25
14 Ronnie Pettersson .10 .25
15 Alexander Ribbenstrand .10 .25
16 Jonas Liwing .10 .25
17 Jesper BjÃ¶rck .10 .25
18 Henrik Nordfeldt .10 .25
19 Johan Eneqvist .10 .25
20 Nichlas Falk .10 .25
21 Christofer LÃ¶fberg .10 .25
22 Patric HÃ¶rnqvist .10 .25
23 Jimmie Olvestad .10 .25
24 Patrick Thoresen .60 1.50
25 Per Eklund .10 .25
26 Mikael Sandberg .10 .25
27 Tom Koivisto .10 .25
28 Antti-Jussi Niemi .10 .25
29 Arto Tukio .10 .25
30 Richard Demen-Willaume .10 .25
31 Johnny Oduya .30 .75
32 Magnus Kahnberg .10 .25
33 Peter HÃ¶gardh .10 .25
34 Kirill Starkov .10 .25
35 Joel Lundqvist .60 1.50
36 Jonas EsbjÃ¶rs .10 .25
37 Niklas Andersson .10 .25
38 Martin Plass .10 .25
39 Tomi Kallio .10 .25
40 Daniel Henriksson .10 .25
41 Rami Alanko .10 .25
42 Robin Jonsson .10 .25
43 Jonas FrÃ¶gren .10 .25
44 Thomas Rhodin .10 .25
45 Jesper Mattsson .10 .25
46 Jonas HÃ¶glund .20 .50
47 Rickard Wallin .10 .25
48 Mathias Johansson .10 .25
49 Peter NordstrÃ¶m .10 .25
50 JÃ¶rgen JÃ¶nsson .10 .25
51 Per Ledin .10 .25
52 Pelle Prestberg .10 .25
53 Stefan Liv .40 1.00
54 Fredrik Olausson .10 .25
55 Per Gustafsson .10 .25
56 Ola Svanberg .10 .25
57 David Petrasek .10 .25
58 Johan Halvardsson .10 .25
59 Martin ThÃ¶rnberg .10 .25
60 Erik Andersson .10 .25
61 Daniel Fredriksson .10 .25
62 Andreas Karlsson .10 .25
63 BjÃ¶rn Melin .10 .25
64 Mattias Remstam .10 .25
65 Johan Davidsson .10 .25
66 Stefan Pettersson .10 .25
67 Mika Hannula .10 .25
68 Jonas Fransson .10 .25
69 Mikko Luoma .10 .25
70 Magnus Johansson .10 .25
71 Christoffer Norgren .10 .25
72 Jyrki VÃ¤livaara .10 .25
73 Tony MÃ¥rtensson .10 .25
74 Jonas Soling .10 .25
75 Ulf SÃ¶derstrÃ¶m .10 .25
76 Tim Eriksson .10 .25
77 Sami Torkki .10 .25
78 Fredrik Emwall .10 .25
79 Jussi Tarvainen .10 .25
80 Johan LindstrÃ¶m .10 .25
81 Mikael HÃ¥kansson .10 .25
82 David Rautio .10 .25
83 Johan Fransson .10 .25
84 Erik Lindberg .10 .25
85 Jan SandstrÃ¶m .10 .25
86 Pekka Saravo .10 .25
87 Thomas Koch .10 .25
88 Emil Lundberg .10 .25
89 Fredrik Hynning .10 .25
90 Mikael Renberg .20 .50
91 Ragnar Karlsson .10 .25
92 Vladimir Machulda .10 .25
93 Lubomir Bartecko .10 .25
94 Robin Lindqvist .10 .25
95 Gustaf Wesslau .10 .25
96 Edvin Frylen .10 .25
97 Jan Ã–berg .10 .25
98 Juha RiihijÃ¤rvi .10 .25
99 Mikael Wahlberg .10 .25
100 Robert Tomik .10 .25
101 Markus Matthiasson .10 .25
102 Karol Krizan .10 .25
103 Mattias Timander .10 .25
104 Hans Jonsson .10 .25
105 Tobias EnstrÃ¶m .10 .25
106 Jesper Damgaard .10 .25
107 Oscar Hedman .10 .25
108 Tobias Viklund .10 .25
109 Pasi Tuominen .10 .25
110 Morten Green .10 .25
111 Andreas Salomonsson .10 .25
112 Peter Ã–berg .10 .25
113 Mikael Pettersson .10 .25
114 Per Svartvadet .10 .25
115 Magnus GÃ¥strin .10 .25
116 Petri Vehanen .10 .25
117 Atvars Tribuntsovs .10 .25
118 Jarno Kultanen .10 .25
119 Thomas Skogs .10 .25
120 Calle BergstrÃ¶m .10 .25
121 Eric Johansson .10 .25
122 Kenneth Bergqvist .10 .25
123 Andreas Nilsson .10 .25
124 Teemu Elomo .10 .25
125 Martin Jansson .10 .25
126 Mikael Simons .10 .25
127 Andreas HadelÃ¶v .10 .25
128 Fredrik Bergqvist .10 .25
129 Libor Prochazka .10 .25
130 Johan Ramstedt .10 .25
131 Pontus PetterstrÃ¶m .10 .25
132 Daniel Welser .10 .25
133 Brett Harkins .10 .25
134 Johan Asplund .10 .25
135 Anton StrÃ¥lman .40 1.00
136 Carl-Johan Johansson .10 .25
137 Peter Regin .10 .25
138 Frans Nielsen .40 1.00
139 Per Hallin .10 .25
140 Kristian Gahn .10 .25
141 Magnus Nilsson .10 .25
142 Mattias Wennerberg .10 .25
143 Peter StrÃ¶m .10 .25
144 Fredrik Warg .10 .25
145 Robert Kristan .10 .25
146 Daniel Sperrle .20 .50
147 Antti Hulkkonen .10 .25
148 Nicholas Angell .10 .25
149 Peter Nolander .10 .25
150 Daniel CasselstÃ¥hl .10 .25
151 Daniel Hermansson .10 .25
152 Nicklas BÃ¤ckstrÃ¶m 2.00 5.00
153 Johannes Salmonsson .10 .25
154 BjÃ¶rn Danielsson .10 .25
155 Mads Hansen .10 .25
156 Sebastian Karlsson .10 .25
157 Jiri Bicek .10 .25
158 Daniel Larsson .10 .25
159 Teemu Lassila .20 .50
160 Martin Lindman .10 .25
161 Thomas Johansson .10 .25
162 Timmy Pettersson .10 .25
163 Fredrik Ericson .10 .25
164 Kristofer Ottosson .10 .25
165 Christian Eklund .10 .25
166 Fredrik Bremberg .10 .25
167 PÃ¤r BÃ¤cker .10 .25
168 Morten Ask .10 .25
169 Nicklas Danielsson .10 .25
170 Dragan Umicevic .10 .25
171 Tommy Salo .20 .50
172 Jan-Axel Alavaara .10 .25
173 Markus Seikola .10 .25
174 Ronnie Sundin .10 .25
175 Tomi Pettinen .10 .25
176 Jonas AhnelÃ¶v .10 .25
177 Johan Fransson .10 .25
178 Fredrik Johansson .10 .25
179 Karl Fabricius .10 .25
180 Anton Axelsson .10 .25
181 Steve Kariya .40 1.00
182 Johan Ryno .10 .25
183 Christopher Heino-Lindberg .20
.50
184 Atte PentikÃ¤inen .10 .25
185 Janne Niskala .10 .25
186 Esa Pirnes .10 .25
187 Per Ã…slund .10 .25
188 Emil KÃ¥berg .10 .25
189 Christian SÃ¶derstrÃ¶m .10 .25
190 Mikael Johansson .10 .25
191 Erik Ersberg .10 .25
192 Scott Langkow .20 .50
193 Johan Ã…kerman .10 .25
194 Daniel Grillfors .10 .25
195 Pasi Puistola .10 .25
196 Lance Ward .10 .25
197 Erik Andersson .10 .25
198 Andreas Falk .10 .25
199 Jari Kauppila .10 .25
200 Timo Vertala .10 .25
201 Jukka Voutilainen .10 .25
202 Andreas JÃ¤mtin .10 .25
203 Roman Cechmanek .20 .50
204 Christopher Kelleher .10 .25
205 Carl Gunnarsson .10 .25
206 Andreas Holmqvist .10 .25
207 Oscar AckestrÃ¶m .10 .25
208 Joakim Eriksson .10 .25
209 Martin Samuelsson .20 .50
210 Niklas Olausson .10 .25
211 Patric Blomdahl .10 .25
212 Tero Leinonen .10 .25
213 Pavel Skrbek .10 .25
214 Roger Ã…kerstrÃ¶m .10 .25
215 Per Savilahti-Nagander .10 .25
216 Jaroslav Obsut .10 .25
217 Tomas Wallgren .10 .25
218 Martin Chabada .10 .25
219 Jesse NiinimÃ¤ki .10 .25
220 Anders BurstrÃ¶m .10 .25
221 Kalle Kerman .10 .25
222 Johan Harju .10 .25
223 Viktor Lindgren .10 .25
224 Tomas Surovy .20 .50
225 Rastislav Stana .10 .25
226 Patrik Hersley .10 .25
227 Johan BjÃ¶rk .10 .25
228 Ross Lupaschuk .10 .25
229 Simon Skoog .10 .25
230 Andreas Thuresson .10 .25
231 Lasse PirjetÃ¤ .10 .25
232 Milan Bartovic .10 .25
233 Nicklas Jadeland .10 .25
234 Marcus Paulsson .10 .25
235 Mikael Johansson .10 .25
236 David Moravec .10 .25
237 Linus Fagemo .10 .25
238 Michal Zajkowski .10 .25
239 Tommy Wargh .10 .25
240 Adam Andersson .10 .25
241 Mattias HellstrÃ¶m .10 .25
242 Per-Ã…ke SkrÃ¶der .10 .25
243 Oscar Steen .10 .25
244 Niklas SundstrÃ¶m .10 .25
245 Miloslav Horava .10 .25
246 Johan Nilsson .10 .25
247 Robert DÃ¶me .10 .25
248 Juha PitkÃ¤mÃ¤ki .10 .25
249 Mikko RÃ¤mÃ¶ .10 .25
250 Tomas Slovak .10 .25
251 Pierre Johnsson .10 .25
252 Antti Bruun .10 .25
253 Mikko Kurvinen .10 .25
254 Miroslav Blatek .10 .25
255 HÃ¥kan Bogg .10 .25
256 Anders Bastiansen .10 .25
257 Marco Tuokko .10 .25
258 Ryan Jardine .10 .25
259 Eric Beaudoin .10 .25
260 Pavel Brendl .20 .50
261 Dave Stathos .10 .25
262 Per Helmersson .10 .25
263 Per-Anton LundstrÃ¶m .10 .25
264 Fredrik Lindgren .10 .25
265 Daniel Sondell .10 .25
266 Kari Haakana .10 .25
267 Richard Lintner .10 .25
268 Magnus Wernblom .10 .25
269 Fredrik Krekula .10 .25
270 Jason King .10 .25
271 Jimmie Eriksson .10 .25
272 Anders SÃ¶derberg .10 .25
273 Marcus Kristoffersson .10 .25
274 Markku TÃ¤htinen .10 .25
275 Fredrik Oberg .10 .25
276 Johan Backlund .10 .25
277 Sanny LindstrÃ¶m .10 .25
278 Kalle Koskinen .10 .25
279 Kimmo Lotvonen .10 .25
280 Petri Kokko .10 .25
281 PÃ¤r Styf .10 .25
282 Oscar Sundh .10 .25
283 Peter Nylander .10 .25
284 Robert Carlsson .10 .25
285 Johan Andersson .10 .25
286 Timo PÃ¤rssinen .10 .25
287 Riku Hahl .20 .50
288 Jonathan HedstrÃ¶m .10 .25

2006-07 Swedish SHL Elitset Goal Patrol

1 Johan Holmqvist 5.00 12.00
2 Markus Korhonen 4.00 10.00
3 Teemu Lassila 4.00 10.00
4 Tommy Salo 4.00 10.00
5 Mikael Sandberg 4.00 10.00
6 Christopher Heino-Lindberg 4.00 10.00
7 Daniel Henriksson 4.00 10.00
8 Stefan Liv 5.00 12.00
9 Tomas Duba 4.00 10.00
10 Jonas Fransson 4.00 10.00
11 Fredrik Norrena 6.00 15.00
12 Mattias Modig 4.00 10.00
13 David Rautio 4.00 10.00
14 Karol Krizan 4.00 10.00
15 Daniel Sperrle 4.00 10.00
16 Petri Vehanen 4.00 10.00
17 Magnus Lindquist 4.00 10.00
18 Mika Oksa 4.00 10.00

2006-07 Swedish SHL Elitset In The Crease

1 Johan Holmqvist 5.00 12.00
2 Teemu Lassila 4.00 10.00
3 Tommy Salo 4.00 10.00
4 Daniel Henriksson 4.00 10.00
5 Stefan Liv 5.00 12.00
6 Fredrik Norrena 6.00 15.00
7 Mattias Modig 4.00 10.00
8 Karol Krizan 4.00 10.00
9 Petri Vehanen 4.00 10.00

2006-07 Swedish SHL Elitset Performers

1 Nicklas BÃ¤ckstrÃ¶m 6.00 15.00
2 Dragan Umicevic 1.50 4.00
3 Niklas Andersson 1.50 4.00
4 Tomi Kallio 1.50 4.00
5 Mathias Johansson 1.50 4.00
6 Mika Hannula 1.50 4.00
7 Johan Davidsson 1.50 4.00
8 Tony MÃ¥rtensson 1.50 4.00
9 Mikael HÃ¥kansson 1.50 4.00
10 Mikael Renberg 2.00 5.00
11 Lasse PirjetÃ¤ 1.50 4.00
12 Juha RiihijÃ¤rvi 1.50 4.00
13 Per Svartvadet 1.50 4.00
14 Pavel Brendl 1.50 4.00
15 Magnus Wernblom 1.50 4.00
16 Anders SÃ¶derberg 1.50 4.00
17 Timo PÃ¤rssinen 1.50 4.00
18 Jonathan HedstrÃ¶m 1.50 4.00

2006-07 Swedish SHL Elitset Playmakers

1 Mikael Lind 1.50 4.00
2 Fredrik Bremberg 1.50 4.00
3 Niklas Andersson 1.50 4.00
4 Joel Lundqvist 2.50 6.00
5 JÃ¶rgen JÃ¶nsson 1.50 4.00
6 Rickard Wallin 1.50 4.00
7 Andreas Karlsson 1.50 4.00
8 Tony MÃ¥rtensson 1.50 4.00
9 Lubomir Bartecko 1.50 4.00
10 Andreas Salomonsson 1.50 4.00
11 HÃ¥kan Bogg 1.50 4.00
12 Frans Nielsen 2.50 6.00

1993-94 Swiss HNL

This large set, released by Jurg Ochsner and sponsored by Ford and Sport newspaper, appears to include everyone who performed in the Swiss National League in 1992-93. The set is highlighted by bright, team-color coordinated design elements and sharp photography, as well as the presence of several ex-NHLers. The set appears to use three languages on the card fronts, varying as to the main language in the team's home locale. All coaches cards below are marked TR (the abbreviation for the French "traineur"). A limited number of factory sets were available; each was serially numbered out of 3,000 and registered to the person making the purchase. A collectible binder to hold the set is valued at $5.

COMPLETE SET (510) 24.00 60.00
1 Title Card .06 .15
2 Title Card .06 .15
3 Title Card .06 .15
4 EHC-Kloten .06 .15
5 EHC-Kloten .06 .15
6 Conny Evensson CO .08 .20
7 Ernst Bruderer ACO .06 .15
8 Reto Pavoni .20 .50
9 Claudio Bayer .20 .50
10 Martin Bruderer .06 .15
11 Anders Eldebrink .10 .25
12 Marco Kloti .06 .15
13 Marco Knecht .06 .15
14 Martin Kout .06 .15
15 Fausto Mazzoleni .06 .15
16 Daniel Sigg .06 .15
17 Daniel Weber .06 .15
18 Manuele Celio .06 .15
19 Patric Della Rossa .20 .50
20 Michael Diener .06 .15
21 Bruno Erni .06 .15
22 Oliver Hoffmann .06 .15
23 Felix Hollenstein .10 .25
24 Mikael Johansson .10 .25
25 Daniel Knecht .06 .15
26 Roger Meier .06 .15
27 Sacha Ochsner .06 .15
28 Peter Schlagenhauf .06 .15
29 Roman Wager .10 .25
30 HC Fribourg-Gotteron .06 .15
31 HC Fribourg-Gotteron .06 .15
32 Paul-Andre Cadieux CO .06 .15
33 Francois Huppe ACO .06 .15
34 Dino Stecher .20 .50
35 Marc Gygli .20 .50
36 Patrice Brasey .06 .15
37 Fredy Bobillier .06 .15
38 Antoine Descloux .06 .15
39 Christian Hofstetter .06 .15
40 Doug Honegger .06 .15
41 Olivier Keller .06 .15
42 David Leibzig .06 .15
43 Didier Princi .06 .15
44 Joel Aeschlimann .06 .15
45 Christophe Brown .06 .15
46 Slava Bykov .20 .50
47 Stefan Grogg .06 .15
48 Andrej Khomutov .20 .50
49 Marc Leuenberger .06 .15
50 Bruno Maurer .06 .15
51 Frank Monnier .06 .15
52 Alain Reymond .06 .15
53 Mario Rottaris .06 .15
54 Pascal Schaller .06 .15
55 Chad Silver .06 .15
56 SC Bern .06 .15
57 SC Bern .06 .15
58 Hannu Jortikka CO .06 .15
59 Jim Koleff ACO .06 .15
60 Renato Tosio .20 .50
61 Roland Meyer .20 .50
62 Raoul Baumgartner .06 .15
63 Andreas Beutler .06 .15
64 Martin Brich .06 .15
65 Mikko Haapakoski .06 .15
66 Martin Rauch .06 .15
67 Jorg Reber .06 .15
68 Daniel Rutschi .06 .15
69 Gaetan Voisard .10 .25
70 Peter Bartschi .06 .15
71 Michael Buhler .06 .15
72 Rene Friedli .06 .15
73 Regis Fuchs .06 .15
74 Gregor Horak .06 .15
75 Michael Meier .06 .15
76 Gil Montandon .06 .15
77 Dan Quinn .20 .50
78 Harry Rogenmoser .06 .15
79 Roberto Triulzi .06 .15
80 Thomas C. Vrabec .06 .15
81 HC Lugano .06 .15
82 HC Lugano .06 .15
83 John Slettvoll CO .06 .15
84 Bruno Rogger ACO .06 .15
85 Lars Weibel .20 .50
86 Christophe Wahl .20 .50
87 Samuel Balmer .06 .15
88 Sandro Bertaggia .20 .50
89 Per Djoos .10 .25
90 Claudio Ghillioni .06 .15
91 Davide Jelmini .06 .15
92 Sven Leuenberger .06 .15
93 Ruedi Niderost .06 .15
94 Patrick Sutter .06 .15
95 Jean-Jacques Aeschlimann .10 .25
96 Jorg Eberle .10 .25
97 Ruben Fontana .06 .15
98 Axel Heim .06 .15
99 Christian Hofstetter .06 .15
100 Patrick Howald .10 .25
101 Marcel Jenni .06 .15
102 Andreas Keller .06 .15
103 Jan Larsson .06 .15
104 Andre Rotheli .06 .15
105 Matthias Schenkel .06 .15
106 Raymond Walder .06 .15
107 EV Zug .06 .15
108 EV Zug .06 .15
109 Bjorn Kinding CO .06 .15
110 Sean Simpson ACO .06 .15
111 Patrick Schopf .20 .50
112 Tony Koller .20 .50
113 Jakub Horak .06 .15
114 Dino Kessler .10 .25
115 Andre Kunzi .06 .15
116 Thomas Kunzi .06 .15
117 Andreas Ritsch .06 .15
118 Bill Schafhauser .06 .15
119 Pat Schafhauser .06 .15
120 Misko Antisin .10 .25
121 Mario Brodmann .06 .15
122 Tom Fergus .20 .50
123 Andreas Fischer .06 .15
124 Patrick Fischer .06 .15
125 Daniel Giger .06 .15
126 Daniel Meier .06 .15
127 Colin Muller .06 .15
128 Philipp Neuenschwander .06 .15
129 Daniel Schaltegger .06 .15
130 Franz Steffen .06 .15
131 Ken Yaremchuk .20 .50
132 HC Ambri-Piotta .06 .15
133 HC Ambri-Piotta .06 .15
134 Perry Pearn CO .10 .25
135 Dale McCourt ACO .10 .25
136 Markus Bachschmied .20 .50
137 Marco Baron .20 .50
138 Mark Astley .10 .25
139 Brenno Celio .06 .15
140 Filippo Celio .06 .15
141 Ivan Gazzaroli .06 .15
142 Tiziano Gianini .10 .25
143 Blair Muller .06 .15
144 Luigi Riva .06 .15
145 Rick Tschumi .06 .15
146 Nicola Celio .10 .25
147 Keith Fair .06 .15
148 Igor Fedulov .06 .15
149 Mathias Holzer .06 .15
150 Peter Jaks .06 .15
151 Vincent Lechenne .06 .15
152 Juri Leonov .06 .15
153 Petr Malkov .06 .15
154 Markus Studer .06 .15
155 Stefano Togni .06 .15
156 Luca Vigano .06 .15
157 Theo Wittmann .06 .15
158 Zurcher SC .06 .15
159 Zurcher SC .06 .15
160 Arno Del Curto CO .06 .15
161 Ueli Hofmann ACO .06 .15
162 Daniel Riesen .20 .50
163 Rolf Simmen .20 .50
164 Marco Bayer .10 .25
165 Jiri Faic .06 .15
166 Yvan Griga .06 .15
167 Noel Guyaz .06 .15
168 Edgar Salis .06 .15
169 Christian Sigrist .06 .15
170 Bruno Vollmer .06 .15
171 Andreas Zehnder .06 .15
172 Matthias Baechler .06 .15
173 Vjeran Ivankovic .06 .15
174 Peter Kobel .06 .15
175 Ronnie Leuthold .06 .15
176 Claudio Micheli .06 .15
177 Patrizio Morger .06 .15
178 Sergei Priakhin .10 .25
179 Roger Thony .06 .15
180 Andy Ton .06 .15
181 Christian Weber .06 .15
182 Vladimir Yeremin .06 .15
183 Michel Zeiter .06 .15
184 EHC Biel-Bienne .06 .15
185 EHC Biel-Bienne .06 .15
186 Jakob Kolliker CO .06 .15
187 Beat Lautenschlager ACO .06 .15
188 Oliver Anken .20 .50
189 Christian Cretin .20 .50
190 Beat Cattaruzza .06 .15
191 Jean-Michel Clavien .06 .15
192 Sven Dick .06 .15
193 Daniel Dubois .06 .15
194 Leo Gudas .10 .25
195 Bjorn Schneider .06 .15
196 Martin Steinegger .06 .15
197 Gaetan Boucher .06 .15
198 Thomas Burillo .06 .15
199 Reynald De Ritz .06 .15
200 Patrick Glanzmann .06 .15
201 Freddy Luthi .06 .15
202 Beat Nuspliger .06 .15
203 Cyrill Pasche .06 .15
204 Robert Yannick .06 .15
205 Andre Rufener .06 .15
206 Bernhard Schuemperli .10 .25
207 Marc Weber .10 .25
208 Ramil Yuldashev .06 .15
209 HC Davos .06 .15
210 HC Davos .06 .15
211 Mats Waltin CO .06 .15
212 Marcus Theus ACO .06 .15
213 Nando Wieser .20 .50
214 Marino Buriola .20 .50
215 Thomi Derungs .06 .15
216 Andy Egli .20 .50
217 Beat Equilino .06 .15
218 Marc Gianola .06 .15
219 Andrea Haller .06 .15
220 Didier Massy .06 .15
221 Roland Ruedi .06 .15
222 Roger Sigg .06 .15
223 Mica Blaha .10 .25
224 Gian Marco Crameri .06 .15
225 Remo Gross .06 .15
226 Martin Hanggi .06 .15
227 Markus Morf .06 .15
228 Rene Muller .06 .15
229 Andi Naser .06 .15
230 Oliver Roth .06 .15
231 Rato Schneider .06 .15
232 Serge Soguel .06 .15
233 Gilles Thibaudeau .20 .50
234 Steve Tsujiura .10 .25
235 EHC Olten .06 .15
236 EHC Olten .06 .15
237 Dick Decloe CO .06 .15
238 Beat Aebischer .20 .50
239 Sascha Friedli .20 .50
240 Matthias Aregger .06 .15
241 Eric Bourquin .06 .15
242 Fabian Gull .06 .15
243 Urs Hirschi .06 .15
244 Alessandro Reinhart .06 .15
245 Christian Schuster .06 .15
246 Christian Silling .06 .15
247 Richard Stucki .06 .15
248 Adrian Bachofner .06 .15
249 Markus Butler .06 .15
250 Ralph Donghi .06 .15
251 Guido Egli .06 .15
252 Paul Gagne .20 .50
253 Thomas Loosli .06 .15
254 Steve Metzger .06 .15
255 Viktor Muller .06 .15
256 Mike Richard .20 .50
257 Kevin Schlapfer .06 .15
258 Peter Trummer .06 .15
259 Andre Von Rohr .06 .15
260 HC Ajoie .06 .15
261 HC Ajoie .06 .15
262 Michael McNamara CO .06 .15
263 Claude Fugere ACO .20 .50
264 Nicola Fraschina .20 .50
265 Didier Tosi .06 .15
266 Dave Baechler .06 .15
267 Sandro Capaul .06 .15
268 Romain Fleury .06 .15
269 Carl Lapointe .06 .15
270 John Miner .06 .15
271 Daniel Rohrbach .06 .15
272 Ralph Tanner .06 .15
273 Yvan Voillat .06 .15
274 Mauro Bornet .06 .15
275 Kalle Furer .06 .15
276 Thomas Griga .06 .15
277 Patrice Heiz .06 .15
278 Willy Kohler .06 .15
279 Daniel Lamminger .06 .15
280 Francois Marquis .06 .15
281 Marco Mozzini .06 .15
282 Giovanni Pestrin .06 .15
283 Ken Priestlay .10 .25
284 Frederic Rothen .06 .15
285 EHC Chur .06 .15
286 EHC Chur .06 .15
287 Bernd Ericsson CO .06 .15
288 Roberto Lavoie ACO .06 .15
289 Peter Martin .20 .50
290 Thomas Liesch .20 .50
291 Marco Capaul .06 .15
292 Marco Gazzola .06 .15
293 Bruno Habisreutinger .06 .15
294 Markus Knobel .06 .15
295 Thomas Locher .06 .15
296 Roger Schnoz .06 .15
297 Roland Simonet .06 .15
298 Ivo Stoffel .06 .15
299 Rene Ackermann .06 .15
300 Patrice Bosch .06 .15
301 Harry Derungs .06 .15
302 Marco Ferrari .06 .15
303 Miguel Fondado .06 .15
304 Claudio Kalser .06 .15
305 Claudio Krattli .06 .15
306 Zbysek Kurylowski .06 .15
307 Andrei Kwartalnov .06 .15
308 Albert Malgin .06 .15
309 Wayne Manley .06 .15
310 Riccardo Signorell .06 .15
311 HC Martigny .06 .15
312 HC Martigny .06 .15
313 Bob Mongrain CO .06 .15
314 Thierry Andrey .20 .50
315 Florian Garnier .20 .50
316 Thierry Evequoz .06 .15
317 Alexandre Formaz .06 .15
318 Tom Jaeggi .06 .15
319 Adrian Jezzone .06 .15
320 Jaques Mauron .06 .15
321 Patrick Neukom .06 .15
322 Brian Rueger .06 .15
323 Bruno Steck .06 .15
324 Steve Aebersold .06 .15
325 Nicolas Baumann .06 .15
326 Alain Bernard .06 .15
327 Jean-Daniel Bonito .06 .15
328 Olivier Ecoeur .06 .15
329 Kelly Glowa .06 .15
330 Thomas Heldner .06 .15
331 Thierry Moret .06 .15
332 Stefan Nussberger .06 .15
333 Petr Rosol .10 .25
334 Gabriel Taccoz .06 .15
335 SC Herisau .06 .15
336 SC Herisau .06 .15
337 Mike McParland CO .06 .15
338 Mark McGregor ACO .06 .15
339 Stephan Mort .20 .50
340 Stefan Allenspach .20 .50
341 Urs Balzarek .06 .15
342 Sascha Bleiker .06 .15
343 Damian Freitag .06 .15
344 Karl Knopf .06 .15
345 Andy Krapf .06 .15
346 Andreas Maag .06 .15
347 Paul Summermatter .06 .15
348 Markus Wetter .06 .15
349 Marco Beer .06 .15
350 Bernhard Blochliger .06 .15
351 Libor Dolana .06 .15
352 Philipp Egli .06 .15
353 Marco Fischer .06 .15
354 Reto Germann .06 .15
355 Urs Hartmann .06 .15
356 Markus Keller .06 .15
357 Trevor Meier .06 .15
358 Roger Nater .06 .15
359 Petr Vlk .10 .25
360 Gerd Zenhausern .06 .15
361 SC Rapperswil-Jona .06 .15
362 SC Rapperswil-Jona .06 .15
363 Pekka Rautakallio CO .20 .50
364 Ueli Scheidegger ACO .06 .15
365 Marius Boesch .06 .15
366 Michael Habig .10 .25
367 Armin Berchtold .06 .15
368 Daniel Bunzli .06 .15
369 Erich Frey .06 .15
370 Patrick Gotz .06 .15
371 Marc Haueter .06 .15
372 Christian Langer .06 .15
373 Markus Naef .06 .15
374 Daniel Aeschbacher .06 .15
375 Ray Allison .06 .15
376 Tom Bissett .20 .50
377 Warren Bruetsch .06 .15
378 Turi Camenzind .06 .15
379 Jean-Noel Honegger .06 .15
380 Roman Kessler .06 .15
381 Hans Kossman .06 .15
382 Marco Seeholzer .06 .15
383 Laurent Stehlin .06 .15
384 Marco Werder .06 .15
385 EHC Bulach .06 .15
386 EHC Bulach .06 .15
387 Lars-Erik Lundstrom CO .06 .15
388 Urs Liljequist ACO .06 .15
389 Ronnie Rueger .20 .50
390 Carlo Buriola .20 .50
391 Rolf Bunter .06 .15
392 David Erny .06 .15
393 Urs Gull .06 .15
394 Thomas Jaggli .06 .15
395 Stefan Meier .06 .15
396 Marco Schellenberg .06 .15
397 Marcel Schonhaar .06 .15
398 Robin Bauer .06 .15
399 Daniele Celio .06 .15
400 Peter Ekelund .06 .15
401 Urs Luthi .06 .15
402 Don McLaren .10 .25
403 Kim Pedersen .06 .15
404 Matthias Pittet .06 .15
405 Ercan Sahin .06 .15
406 Thomas Studer .06 .15
407 Markus Suter .06 .15
408 Martin Caretta .06 .15
409 Mike Tschumi .06 .15
410 Lausanne HC .06 .15
411 Lausanne HC .06 .15

412 Jean Lussier CO .06 .15
413 Beat Kindler .10 .25
414 Michel Pilet .06 .15
415 Urs Burkart .06 .15
416 Jean Gagnon .06 .15
417 Nicolas Goumaz .06 .15
418 Fabian Guignard .06 .15
419 Benedict Sapin .06 .15
420 Raymond Wyssen .06 .15
421 Laurent Bucher .06 .15
422 Olivier Chenuz .06 .15
423 Alain Comte .06 .15
424 Martin Desjardins .06 .15
425 Gaby Epiney .06 .15
426 Stephane Gasser .06 .15
427 Nicolas Gauch .06 .15
428 Gilles Guyaz .06 .15
429 Dan Hodgson .20 .50
430 Maxime Lapointe .06 .15
431 Laurent Pasquini .06 .15
432 Gilles Prince .06 .15
433 Yannick Theler .06 .15
434 HC Thurgau .06 .15
435 HC Thurgau .06 .15
436 Anders Sorensen CO .06 .15
437 Max Baumann .06 .15
438 Martin Studer .20 .50
439 Thomas Berger .20 .50
440 Andy Gasser .06 .15
441 Patrick Henry .06 .15
442 Reto Muller .06 .15
443 Ralph Ott .06 .15
444 Mike Posma .06 .15
445 Hadrian Rosenberg .06 .15
446 Marcel Stocker .06 .15
447 Robert Wiesmann .06 .15
448 Gianni Dalla Vecchia .06 .15
449 Dan Daoust .20 .50
450 Matthias Keller .06 .15
451 Roger Keller .06 .15
452 Peter Kostli .06 .15
453 Bernhard Lauber .06 .15
454 Benjamin Mueller .06 .15
455 Silvio Schai .06 .15
456 Rolf Schrepfer .06 .15
457 Robert Slehofer .06 .15
458 Thomas Steger .06 .15
459 Cuno Weisser .06 .15
460 Grasshoppers-Club Zurich .06 .15
461 Grasshoppers-Club Zurich .06 .15
462 Esa Siren CO .06 .15
463 Bruno Aegerter ACO .06 .15
464 Marcel Kohli .20 .50
465 Olivier Leuenberger .20 .50
466 Giorgio Giacomelli .06 .15
467 Roman Honegger .06 .15
468 Sandro Just .06 .15
469 Mats Lusth .06 .15
470 Marcel Wick .06 .15
471 Lukas Zehnder .06 .15
472 Rolf Ziegler .06 .15
473 Jerry Zuurmond .06 .15
474 Alain Ayer .06 .15
475 Leo Cadisch .06 .15
476 Pascal Fah .06 .15
477 Roman Furrer .06 .15
478 Marco Hagmann .06 .15
479 Peter Hofmann .06 .15
480 Adrian Hotz .06 .15
481 Patrick Looser .06 .15
482 Oliver Muffler .06 .15
483 Keith Osborne .10 .25
484 Thierry Paterlini .06 .15
485 Markus Schellenberg .06 .15
486 HC La Chaux-de-Fonds .06 .15
487 HC LaChaux-de-Fonds .06 .15
488 Ricardo Fuhrer CO .06 .15
489 Jean-Luc Schnegg .10 .25
490 Thierry Loup .10 .25
491 Thierry Baume .06 .15
492 Jean-Luc Christen .06 .15
493 Thierry Murisier .06 .15
494 Danny Ott .06 .15
495 Guido Pfosi .06 .15
496 Rene Raess .06 .15
497 Valeri Shirajev .10 .25
498 Frank Vuillemin .06 .15
499 Marco Dick .06 .15
500 Michael Ferrari .06 .15
501 Olivier Gazzaroli .06 .15
502 Sandy Jeannin .06 .15
503 Lane Lambert .10 .25
504 Guido Laczko .06 .15
505 Boris Leimgruber .06 .15
506 Claude Luthi .06 .15
507 Patrick Oppliger .06 .15
508 Jean-Luc Rod .06 .15
509 Gabriel Rohrbach .06 .15
510 Yvan Zimmermann .06 .15

1995-96 Swiss HNL

This very large set, released by Jurg Ochsner and sponsored by the Swiss Bank Society appears to include everyone who performed in the Swiss national hockey league in 1994-95. They were distributed in 6-card packs for 2 francs. The set is highlighted by marvelous color action photography, a subset of six NNO referee cards, and the inclusion of six NHLers who played in Switzerland during the NHL lockout including Doug Gilmour and Chris Chelios. Of interest is the usage of three languages (French, German and Italian) on the card fronts, which varies by the main language in the team's home locale. Note: the TR suffix in this case is the direct translation of coach (traineur). A collector's album also was available by mail. It is valued at $5.00.

COMPLETE SET (545) 30.00 75.00
1 Kloten .04 .10
2 Kloten .04 .10
3 Alpo Suhonen CO .20 .50
4 Ernst Bruderer ACO .04 .10
5 Matthias Muller .10 .25
6 Reto Pavoni .20 .50
7 Marco Bayer .04 .10
8 Martin Bruderer .04 .10
9 Marco Kloti .04 .10
10 Michael Kress .04 .10
11 Marc Ochsner .04 .10
12 Bjorn Schneider .04 .10
13 Daniel Sigg .04 .10
14 Daniel Weber .04 .10
15 Charles Berglund .04 .10
16 Manuele Celio .04 .10
17 Patrik Della Rossa .04 .10
18 Michael Diener .04 .10
19 Bruno Erni .04 .10
20 Oliver Hoffmann .04 .10
21 Felix Hollenstein .04 .10
22 Mathias Holzer .04 .10
23 Mikael Johansson .04 .10
24 Roger Meier .04 .10
25 Sacha Oscsner .04 .10
26 Frederic Rothen .04 .10
27 Roman Wager .04 .10
28 ZSC .04 .10
29 ZSC .04 .10
30 Larry Huras CO .04 .10
31 Ted Snell ACO .04 .10
32 Thomas Papp .14 .35
33 Dino Stecher .14 .35
34 Patrick Hager .04 .10
35 Martin Kout .04 .10
36 Didier Princi .04 .10
37 Edgar Salis .04 .10
38 Bruno Steck .04 .10
39 Nicholas Steiger .04 .10
40 Andreas Zehnder .04 .10
41 Mario Brodmann .04 .10
42 Marc Fortier .10 .25
43 Nicholas Gauch .04 .10
44 Vjeran Ivankovic .04 .10
45 Sandy Jeannin .04 .10
46 Patrick Lebeau .20 .50
47 Phillipp Luber .04 .10
48 Don McLaren .10 .25
49 Claudio Micheli .04 .10
50 Patrizio Morger .04 .10
51 Marco Seeholzer .04 .10
52 Bruno Vollmer .04 .10
53 Michel Zeiter .04 .10
54 Fribourg .04 .10
55 Fribourg .04 .10
56 Kjell Larsson CO .04 .10
57 Ueli Hofmann ACO .04 .10
58 David Aebischer ERC 10.00 40.00
59 Thomas Berger .14 .35
60 Steve Meuwly .08 .20
61 Johan Bertholet .04 .10
62 Fredy Bobillier .04 .10
63 Patrice Brasey .04 .10
64 Antoine Descloux .04 .10
65 Andy Egli .04 .10
66 Christian Hofstetter .04 .10
67 Olivier Keller .04 .10
68 Andrei Lomakin .10 .25
69 Mark Streit .04 .10
70 Christophe Brown .04 .10
71 Slava Bykov .20 .50
72 Matthias Bachler .04 .10
73 Axel Heim .04 .10
74 Andrei Khomutov .20 .50
75 Marc Leuenberger .04 .10
76 Alfred Luthi .04 .10
77 Daniel Meier .04 .10
78 Mario Rottaris .04 .10
79 Pascal Schaller .04 .10
80 Sacha Schneider .04 .10
81 Joel Aeschlimann .04 .10
82 Bern .04 .10
83 Bern .04 .10
84 Brian Lefley CO .04 .10
85 Ueli Schwarz ACO .04 .10
86 Reto Schurch .14 .35
87 Renato Tosio .14 .35
88 Mikko Haapakoski .04 .10
89 Christian Langer .04 .10
90 Sven Leuenberger .04 .10
91 Phillippe Portner .04 .10
92 Martin Rauch .04 .10
93 Pascal Sommer .04 .10
94 Martin Steinegger .04 .10
95 Gaeton Voisard .04 .10
96 Rene Friedli .04 .10
97 Regis Fuchs .04 .10
98 Patrick Howald .04 .10
99 Andy Keller .04 .10
100 Vincent Lechenne .04 .10
101 Lars Leuenberger .04 .10
102 Trevor Meier .04 .10
103 Gilles Montandon .04 .10
104 Philippe Muller .04 .10
105 Gaetano Orlando .10 .25
106 Roberto Triuizi .04 .10
107 Thomas Vrabec .04 .10
108 Davos .04 .10
109 Davos .04 .10
110 Mats Waltin CO .04 .10
111 Evgeni Popichin ACO .04 .10
112 Ivo Kleeb .14 .35
113 Nando Wiesser .14 .35
114 Samuel Balmer .04 .10
115 Martin Brich .04 .10
116 Beat Equilino .04 .10
117 Ivan Gazzaroli .04 .10
118 Marc Gianola .04 .10
119 Andrea Haeller .04 .10
120 Doug Honegger .04 .10
121 Andrej Kovalev .04 .10
122 Jan Alston .04 .10
123 Gian-Marco Crameri .04 .10
124 Dan Hodgson .20 .50
125 Rene Muller .04 .10
126 Andy Naser .04 .10
127 Oliver Roth .04 .10
128 Ivo Ruthemann .04 .10
129 Reto Stirnimann .04 .10
130 Reto Von Arx .04 .10
131 Christian Weber .04 .10
132 Lugano .04 .10
133 Lugano .04 .10
134 John Slettvoll CO .04 .10
135 Nicola Fraschina .14 .35
136 Lars Weibel .30 .75
137 Sandro Bertaggia .08 .20
138 Francesco Bizzozero .04 .10
139 Michel Kamber .04 .10
140 Ruedi Niderost .04 .10
141 Pat Schafhauser .04 .10
142 Tommy Sjodin .10 .25
143 Patrick Sutter .04 .10
144 Rick Tschumi .04 .10
145 J. Jacques Aeschlimann .04 .10
146 Markus Butler .04 .10
147 Jorg Eberle .04 .10
148 Keith Fair .04 .10
149 Marcel Jenni .04 .10
150 Stephan Lebeau .40 1.00
151 Patrick Looser .04 .10
152 Stefano Togni .04 .10
153 Andy Ton .04 .10
154 Remo Walder .04 .10
155 EVZ .04 .10
156 EVZ .04 .10
157 Jim Koleff CO .04 .10
158 Bob Lesley ACO .04 .10
159 Sacha Friedli .14 .35
160 Patrick Schopf .14 .35
161 Livio Fazio .04 .10
162 Stefan Grauwiler .04 .10
163 Dino Kessler .04 .10
164 Andre Kunzi .04 .10
165 Thomas Kunzi .04 .10
166 Fausto Mazzoleni .04 .10
167 John Miner .04 .10
168 Bill Schafhauser .04 .10
169 Steve Aebersold .04 .10
170 Misko Antisin .04 .10
171 Patrick Fischer .04 .10
172 Daniel Giger .04 .10
173 Mathias Keller .04 .10
174 Marco Koppel .04 .10
175 Colin Muller .04 .10
176 Philipp Neuenschwander .04 .10
177 Andre Rotheli .04 .10
178 Chad Silver .04 .10
179 Franz Steffen .04 .10
180 Ken Yaremchuk .20 .50
181 Ambri Piotta .04 .10
182 Ambri Piotta .04 .10
183 Alexander Yakushev CO .10 .25
184 Petr Malkov ACO .04 .10
185 Markus Bachschmied .14 .35
186 Paolo Della Bella .14 .35
187 Pauli Jaks .20 .50
188 Brenno Celio .04 .10
189 Tiziano Gianini .08 .20
190 Fabian Gull .04 .10
191 Noel Guyaz .04 .10
192 Jakub Horak .04 .10
193 Alessandro Reinhart .04 .10
194 Luigi Riva .04 .10
195 Gianni Sanese .04 .10
196 Oskar Szczepaniec .04 .10
197 Mattia Baldi .04 .10
198 Nicola Celio .04 .10
199 Dmitri Denisov .04 .10
200 Gaby Epiney .04 .10
201 John Fritsche .04 .10
202 Patrick Glanzmann .04 .10
203 Thomas Heldner .04 .10
204 Paolo Imperatori .04 .10
205 Peter Jaks .04 .10
206 Dimitri Kvartalnov .20 .50
207 Omar Tognini .04 .10
208 Nicola Pini .04 .10
209 Luca Vigano .04 .10
210 Theo Wittmann .04 .10
211 Rapperswil .04 .10
212 Rapperswil .04 .10
213 Pekka Rautakallio CO .10 .25
214 Ueli Scheidegger ACO .04 .10
215 Claudio Bayer .14 .35
216 Christian Cretin .14 .35
217 Daniel Bunzli .04 .10
218 Marco Capaul .04 .10
219 Roland Kradolfer .04 .10
220 Blair Muller .04 .10
221 Andreas Ritsch .04 .10
222 Daniel Rutschi .04 .10
223 Roger Sigg .04 .10
224 Adrian Bachofner .04 .10
225 Arthur Camenzind .04 .10
226 Christian Hofstetter .04 .10
227 Michael Meier .04 .10
228 Mike Richard .08 .20
229 Harry Rogenmoser .04 .10
230 Andy Rufener .04 .10
231 Sergio Soguel .04 .10
232 Gilles Thibaudeau .10 .25
233 Roger Thony .04 .10
234 Marc Weber .04 .10
235 Marco Werder .04 .10
236 Lausanne HC .04 .10
237 Jean Lussier CO .04 .10
238 Thierry Andrey .14 .35
239 Beat Kindler .14 .35
240 Jean Gagnon .04 .10
241 Fabian Guignard .04 .10
242 Philippe Marquis .04 .10
243 Stephan Schneider .04 .10
244 Roland Simonet .04 .10
245 Ivo Stoffel .04 .10
246 Marcel Wick .04 .10
247 Raymond Wyssen .04 .10
248 Martin Desjardins .04 .10
249 Maxime Lapointe .04 .10
250 Bruno Maurer .04 .10
251 Frank Monnier .04 .10
252 Cyrill Pasche .04 .10
253 Laurent Pasquini .04 .10
254 Alain Reymond .04 .10
255 Yannick Robert .04 .10
256 Kevin Schlapfer .04 .10
257 Gabriel Taccoz .04 .10
258 Claude Verret .04 .10
259 Gerd Zenhausern .04 .10
260 Biel .04 .10
261 Biel .04 .10
262 Barry Jenkins CO .04 .10
263 Sacha Devaux .14 .35
264 Christoph Wahl .14 .35
265 Beat Cattaruzza .04 .10
266 Sven Dick .04 .10
267 Claudio Ghillioni .04 .10
268 Stefan Lutz .04 .10
269 Guido Pfosi .04 .10
270 Sven Schmid .04 .10
271 Daniel Schneider .04 .10
272 Frank Aeschlimann .04 .10
273 Thomas Burillo .04 .10
274 Stefan Choffat .04 .10
275 Reynald DeRitz .04 .10
276 Marco Dick .04 .10
277 Ralph Donghi .04 .10
278 Stefan Groff .04 .10
279 Andrei Kvartalnov .04 .10
280 Albert Malgin .04 .10
281 Oliver Muller .04 .10
282 Michel Riesen 4.00 2.00
283 Bernhard Schumperli .10 .25
284 Mike Tschumi .04 .10
285 Grasshoppers .04 .10
286 Grasshoppers .04 .10
287 Bruno Aegerter CO .04 .10
288 Matti Alatalo ACO .04 .10
289 Marcel Kohli .14 .35
290 Stephan Morf .14 .35
291 Michel Faeh .04 .10
292 Marc Haueter .04 .10
293 Roman Honegger .04 .10
294 Arne Ramholt .04 .10
295 Hannu Virta .10 .25
296 Rolf Ziegler .04 .10
297 Jerry Zuurmond .04 .10
298 Alain Ayer .04 .10
299 Andre Baumann .04 .10
300 Warren Bruetsch .04 .10
301 Pascal Faeh .04 .10
302 Roman Furrer .04 .10
303 Marco Hagmann .04 .10
304 Dominik Jenny .04 .10
305 Mika Nieminen .04 .10
306 Fabio Obrist .04 .10
307 Thierry Paterlini .04 .10
308 Marco Schellenberg .04 .10
309 Mathias Schenkel .04 .10
310 Peter Schlagenhauf .04 .10
311 Markus Studer .04 .10
312 Thomas Ziegler .04 .10
313 Thurgau .04 .10
314 Thurgau .04 .10
315 Mike McParland CO .04 .10
316 Fritz Lanz ACO .04 .10
317 Roger Hugentobler .14 .35
318 Peter Martin .14 .35
319 Dominik Schmid .04 .10
320 Andrea Baumgartner .04 .10
321 Nicolas Goumaz .04 .10
322 Martin Granicher .04 .10
323 Ralph Ott .04 .10
324 Henry Patrick .04 .10
325 Mike Posma .04 .10
326 Marcel Schmid .04 .10
327 Robert Wiesmann .04 .10
328 Dan Daoust .20 .50
329 Slaven Imhof .04 .10
330 Roger Keller .04 .10
331 Martin Knopfli .04 .10
332 Guido Laczko .04 .10
333 Bernhard Lauber .04 .10
334 Gery Othman .04 .10
335 Rolf Schrepfer .04 .10
336 Thomas Seitz .04 .10
337 Robert Slehofer .04 .10
338 Rene Stussi .04 .10
339 Cuno Weisser .04 .10
340 Benjamin Winkler .04 .10
341 Langnau .04 .10
342 Langnau .04 .10
343 Paul Andre Cadieux CO .04 .10
344 Jakob Kolliker ACO .04 .10
345 Thomas Dreier .14 .35
346 Toni Koller .14 .35
347 Daniel Aegerter .04 .10
348 Raoul Baumgartner .04 .10
349 Andreas Beutler .04 .10
350 Urs Hirschi .04 .10
351 Stefan Probst .04 .10
352 Raphael Schneider .04 .10
353 Pascal Stoller .04 .10
354 Rolf Badertscher .04 .10
355 Peter Bartschi .04 .10
356 Beat Friedrich .04 .10
357 Walter Gerber .04 .10
358 Kelly Glowa .04 .10
359 Alan Hirschi .04 .10
360 Markus Hirschi .04 .10
361 Gregor Horak .04 .10
362 Lane Lambert .10 .25
363 Beat Nuspliger .04 .10
364 Stefan Tschiemer .04 .10
365 Chaux De Fonds .04 .10
366 Chaux De Fonds .04 .10
367 Riccardo Fuhrer CO .04 .10
368 Roland Meyer .14 .35
369 Jean-Luc Schnegg .14 .35
370 Eric Bourquin .04 .10
371 Daniel Dubois .04 .10
372 Andres Egger .04 .10
373 Daniel Elsener .04 .10
374 Thierry Murisier .04 .10
375 Daniel Ott .04 .10
376 Jorg Reber .04 .10
377 Valeri Chiriaev .04 .10
378 Michele Bizzozero .04 .10
379 Philippe Bozon .40 1.00
380 Jean-Marc Brunner .04 .10
381 Florian Chappot .04 .10
382 Gilles Dubois .04 .10
383 Willy Kohler .04 .10
384 Boris Leimgruber .04 .10
385 Patrick Oppliger .04 .10
386 Benoit Pont .04 .10
387 Laurent Stehlin .04 .10
388 Olivier Wuthrich .04 .10
389 Herisau .04 .10
390 Herisau .04 .10
391 Mark McGregor CO .04 .10
392 Reto Roveda ACO .04 .10
393 Michael Habig .14 .35
394 Ronald Rueger .14 .35
395 Urs Balzarek .04 .10
396 Thomas Derungs .04 .10
397 Damian Freitag .04 .10
398 Roland Habisreutinger .04 .10
399 Marco Knecht .04 .10
400 Karl Knopf .04 .10
401 Andy Maag .04 .10
402 Krister Cantoni .04 .10
403 Rico Enzler .04 .10
404 John Fust .04 .10
405 Remo Gastaldo .04 .10
406 Reto German .04 .10
407 Frank Guay .04 .10
408 Daniel Knecht .04 .10
409 Andy Krapf .04 .10
410 Roger Nater .04 .10
411 Marco Tanner .04 .10
412 Claude Vilgrain .40 1.00
413 Chur .04 .10
414 Chur .04 .10
415 Juri Voshakov CO .04 .10
416 Thomas Liesch .14 .35
417 Reto Zuccolini .14 .35
418 Sacha Bleiker .04 .10
419 Patrick Fischer .04 .10
420 Bruno Habisreutinger .04 .10
421 Jurg Hardegger .04 .10
422 Dominic Meier .04 .10
423 Lois Papa .04 .10
424 Robert Papp .04 .10
425 Valery Belov .04 .10
426 Valery Cherny .04 .10
427 Miguel Fondado .04 .10
428 Oliver Gazzaroli .04 .10
429 Claudio Krattli .04 .10
430 Claudio Peer .04 .10
431 Michael Putzi .04 .10
432 Roger Rieder .04 .10
433 Riccardo Signorell .04 .10
434 Peter Thoma .04 .10
435 Patrick Werthan .04 .10
436 Olten .04 .10
437 Olten .04 .10
438 Milan Mrukvia ACO .04 .10
439 Beat Aebischer .14 .35
440 Thierry Loup .14 .35
441 Ralph Gugelmann .04 .10
442 Roland Ruedi .04 .10
443 Andre Schneeberger .04 .10
444 Richard Stucki .04 .10
445 Thomas Studer .04 .10
446 Ville Siren .10 .25
447 Pius Weber .04 .10
448 Rene Ackermann .04 .10
449 Lars Aebi .04 .10
450 Andreas Fischer .04 .10
451 Marcel Franzi .04 .10
452 Paul Gagne .20 .50
453 Stephane Gasser .04 .10
454 Pirmin Keller .04 .10
455 Claude Luthi .04 .10
456 Patrick Siegwart .04 .10
457 Patrik Traber .04 .10
458 Andre Van Rohr .04 .10
459 HCM .04 .10
460 Kent Ruhnke CO .04 .10
461 Patrick Grand .14 .35
462 Didier Tosi .14 .35
463 Pascal Avanthay .04 .10
464 Bernard Bauer .04 .10
465 Ayocholos Escher .04 .10
466 Thierry Evequoz .04 .10
467 David Jelmini .04 .10
468 Xavier Kappeler .04 .10
469 Patrik Neukom .04 .10
470 Pierre-Alain Ancay .04 .10
471 Florian Andenmatten .04 .10
472 J-Daniel Bonito .04 .10
473 Alain Darbellay .04 .10
474 Olivier Ecoeur .04 .10
475 Igor Fedulov .04 .10
476 Nicolas Gastaldo .04 .10
477 Thierry Moret .04 .10
478 Stephan Nussberger .04 .10
479 Achim Pleschberger .04 .10
480 Petr Rosol .04 .10
481 Fabrizio Silietti .04 .10
482 Yannick Theler .04 .10
483 Geneve .04 .10
484 Geneve .04 .10
485 Francois Huppe CO .04 .10
486 Gary Shennan ACO .04 .10
487 Jean-Philippe Challande .14 .35
488 Jerome Hagmann .14 .35
489 Claude Cienciala .04 .10
490 Chris Felix .04 .10
491 Romain Fleury .04 .10
492 Daniel Herlea .04 .10
493 Camille Meylan .04 .10
494 Toni Nelli .04 .10
495 Christian Serena .04 .10
496 David Leibzig .04 .10
497 Antoine Cloux .04 .10
498 Nicolas Corthay .04 .10
499 Marc Hinni .04 .10
500 Olivier Honsberger .04 .10
501 Gael Kertudo .04 .10
502 Jorg Ledermann .04 .10
503 Andrew McKim .20 .50
504 Benjamin Muller .04 .10
505 Martin Stastny .04 .10
506 Michel Wicky .04 .10
507 Swiss National Team .10 .25
508 C. Weber/J. Eberle .20 .50
509 J.J Aeschlimann/T.Vrabec .10 .25
510 S.Bertaggia/L.Weibel .20 .50
511 Lars Weibel .20 .50
512 Tommy Sjodin .10 .25
513 Andrei Khomutov .20 .50
514 Lars Weibel .20 .50
515 Anders Eldebrink .10 .25
516 Ken Yaremchuk .20 .50
517 Reto Pavoni .20 .50
518 Dino Kessler .04 .10
519 Fausto Mazzoleni .04 .10
520 Andy Ton .04 .10
521 Dan Hodgson .20 .50
522 Roman Wager .04 .10
523 Reto Pavoni .20 .50
524 Reijo Ruotsalainen .20 .50
525 Tommy Sjodin .10 .25
526 Andrei Kvartalnov .04 .10
527 Mikael Johansson .04 .10
528 Ken Yaremchuk .40 1.00
529 Reto Pavoni .20 .50
530 Dino Kessler .04 .10
531 Marco Bayer .04 .10
532 Misko Antisin .04 .10
533 Sacha Ochsner .04 .10
534 Roman Wager .04 .10
535 Reto Pavoni .20 .50
536 Reijo Ruotsalainen .20 .50
537 Andreas Eldebrink .10 .25
538 Ken Yaremchuk .40 1.00
539 Mikael Johansson .04 .10
540 Tom Fergus .40 1.00
541 Dan Quinn .20 .50
542 Valeri Kamenski .40 1.00
543 Phil Housley .40 1.00
544 Chris Chelios 6.00 15.00
545 Doug Gilmour 6.00 15.00
NNO Roland Stadler .04 .10
NNO Beat Eichmann .04 .10
NNO Danny Kurmann .04 .10
NNO Reto Bertolotti .04 .10
NNO Beat Eichmann .04 .10

1996-97 Swiss HNL

This set features the players from both the A and B leagues from Switzerland. We've been unable to identify all of the players completely. If you can provide additional information, please forward it to hockeymag@beckett.com

COMPLETE SET (588) 40.00 80.00
1 EHC Kloten .02 .10
2 Fleming CO .02 .10
3 Schumacher .02 .10
4 Reto Pavoni .02 .10
5 Walter .02 .10
6 Marco Bayer .02 .10
7 Greg Brown .02 .10
8 Martin Bruderer .02 .10
9 Marco Kloti .02 .10
10 Marco Knecht .02 .10
11 Michael Kress .02 .10
12 Bjorn Schneider .02 .10
13 Daniel Weber .02 .10
14 Robin Bauer .02 .10
15 Charles Berglund .02 .10
16 Matthias Bachler .02 .10
17 Manuele Celio .02 .10
18 Patrick Della Rossa .02 .10
19 Jorg Eberle .02 .10
20 Felix Hollenstein .02 .10
21 Mathias Holzer .02 .10
22 Mikael Johansson .02 .10
23 Martin Pluss .02 .10
24 Frederic Rothen .02 .10
25 Roman Wager .02 .10
26 SC Bern .02 .10
27 Chuck Lefley CO .02 .10
28 Schwarz .02 .10
29 Renato Tosio .02 .10
30 Alex Reinhard .02 .10
31 Timo Jutila .02 .10
32 Christian Langer .02 .10
33 Sven Leuenberger .02 .10
34 Martin Rauch .02 .10
35 Ville Siren .02 .10
36 Martin Steinegger .02 .10
37 Gaetan Voisard .02 .10
38 Rene Friedli .02 .10
39 Regis Fuchs .02 .10
40 Patrick Howald .02 .10
41 Vincent Lechenne .02 .10
42 Stefan Moser .02 .10
43 Trevor Meier .02 .10
44 Gil Montandon .02 .10
45 Michael Mouther .02 .10
46 Laurent Muller .02 .10
47 Philippe Mueller .02 .10
48 Gates Orlando .20 .50
49 Thierry Paterlini .02 .10
50 Roberto Triulzi .02 .10
51 EV Zug .02 .10
52 Jim Koleff CO .02 .10
53 Simpson .02 .10
54 Patrick Schopf .02 .10
55 Ronnie Rueger .02 .10
56 Livio Fazio .02 .10
57 Stefan Grauwiler .02 .10
58 Dino Kessler .02 .10
59 Andre Kunzi .02 .10
60 Thomas Kunzi .02 .10
61 John Miner .02 .10
62 Patrick Sutter .02 .10
63 Steve Aebersold .02 .10
64 Misko Antisin .02 .10
65 Patrick Fischer .02 .10
66 Daniel Giger .02 .10
67 Stephen Grogg .02 .10
68 Bill McDougall .02 .10
69 Colin Muller .02 .10
70 Phil Neuenschwander .02 .10
71 Philipp Orlandi .02 .10
72 Andre Rotheli .02 .10
73 Chad Silver .02 .10
74 Franz Steffen .02 .10
75 Wes Walz .75 2.00
76 HC Ambri Piotta .02 .10
77 Alexander Jakushev CO .20 .50
78 Pauli Jaks .20 .50
79 Paolo Della Bella .02 .10
80 Brenno Celio .02 .10
81 Ivan Gazzaroli .02 .10
82 Tiziano Gianini .02 .10
83 Noel Guyaz .02 .10
84 Jakub Horak .02 .10
85 Alessandro Reinhart .02 .10
86 Oskar Szczepaniec .02 .10
87 Dmitri Tsygurov .02 .10
88 Mattia Baldi .02 .10
89 Nicola Celio .02 .10
90 John Fritsche .02 .10
91 Patrick Glanzmann .02 .10
92 Thomas Heldner .02 .10
93 Peter Jaks .02 .10
94 Dmitri Kvartalnov .20 .50
95 Oleg Petrov .02 .10
96 Omar Tognini .02 .10
97 Igor Chibirev .02 .10
98 Luca Vigano .02 .10
99 Theo Wittmann .02 .10
100 HC Davos .02 .10
101 Del Curto CO .02 .10
102 Evgeni Popichin ACO .02 .10
103 Nando Wieser .02 .10
104 Thomas Berger .02 .10
105 Samuel Balmer .02 .10
106 Beat Equilino .02 .10
107 Marc Gianola .02 .10
108 Malier .02 .10
109 Valeri Shiryaev .02 .10
110 Daniel Sigg .02 .10
111 Mark Streit .40 1.00
112 Jan Von Arx .02 .10
113 Dan Hodgson .02 .10
114 Philipp Luber .02 .10
115 Rene Mueller .02 .10
116 Andy Naser .02 .10
117 Sergei Petrenko .02 .10
118 Oliver Roth .02 .10
119 Ivo Ruthemann .02 .10
120 Mario Schocher .02 .10
121 Reto Stirnimann .02 .10
122 Reto Von Arx .20 .50
123 Christian Weber .02 .10
124 Ken Yaremchuk .20 .50
125 SC Rapperswil Jona .02 .10
126 Pekka Rautakallio CO .02 .10
127 Ueli Scheidegger .02 .10
128 Claudio Bayer .02 .10
129 Remo Wehrli .02 .10
130 Daniel Buenzli .02 .10
131 Marko Capaul .02 .10
132 Kari Martikainen .02 .10
133 Dominic Meier .02 .10
134 Blair Muller .02 .10
135 Mathias Seger .02 .10
136 Roger Sigg .02 .10
137 Adrian Bachofner .02 .10
138 Arthur Camenzind .02 .10
139 Daniel Bunzli .02 .10
139 Oliver Hoffmann .02 .10
140 Christian Hofstetter .02 .10
141 Michael Meier .02 .10
142 Mike Richard .02 .10
143 Harry Rogenmoser .02 .10
144 Sergio Soguel .02 .10
145 Gilles Thibaudeau .02 .10
146 Roger Thony .02 .10
147 Mark Weber .02 .10
148 Christian Wolhwend .02 .10
149 HC Lugano .02 .10
150 Mats Waltin CO .02 .10
151 Gunnar Leidborg .02 .10
152 Lars Weibel .20 .50
153 Davide Gislimberti .02 .10
154 Sandro Bertaggia .02 .10
155 Fabian Guignard .02 .10
156 David Jelmini .02 .10
157 Rudi Niderost .02 .10
158 Luigi Riva .02 .10
159 Tommy Sjodin .02 .10
160 Rick Tschumi .02 .10
161 Jerry Zuurmond .02 .10
162 J.-J. Aeschlimann .02 .10
163 Markus Butler .02 .10
164 Gian-Marco Crameri .02 .10
165 Bruno Erni .02 .10
166 Keith Fair .02 .10
167 Marcel Jenni .02 .10
168 Marcel Franzi .02 .10
169 Stephan Lebeau .20 .50
170 Stefano Togni .02 .10
171 Andy Ton .02 .10
172 Raymond Walder .02 .10
173 Marco Werder .02 .10
174 Michael Nylander .20 .50
175 Zurcher SC .02 .10
176 Alpo Suhonen CO .02 .10
177 Frutiger .02 .10
178 Thomas Papp .02 .10
179 M. Muller .02 .10
180 Patrick Hager .02 .10
181 Martin Kout .02 .10
182 Robert Nordmark .02 .10
183 Didier Princi .02 .10
184 Edgar Salis .02 .10
185 Bruno Steck .02 .10
186 Nicolas Steiger .02 .10
187 Andreas Zehnder .02 .10
188 Mario Brodmann .02 .10
189 Marc Fortier .02 .10
190 Axel Heim .02 .10
191 Vjeran Ivankovic .02 .10
192 Sandy Jeannin .02 .10
193 Peter Kobel .02 .10
194 Patrick Lebeau .20 .50
195 Claudio Micheli .02 .10
196 Patrizio Morger .02 .10
197 Bruno Vollmer .02 .10
198 Michel Zeiter .02 .10
199 Gerd Zenhausern .02 .10
200 HC Fribourg .02 .10
201 Larsson CO .02 .10
202 Courvoisier .02 .10
203 Thomas Ostlund .02 .10
204 Steve Meuwly .02 .10
205 David Aebischer 4.00 10.00
206 Fredy Bobillier .02 .10
207 Patrice Brasey .02 .10
208 Antoine Descloux .02 .10
209 Andi Egli .02 .10
210 Christian Hofstetter .02 .10
211 Olivier Keller .02 .10
212 Philippe Marquis .02 .10
213 Marc Werlen .02 .10
214 Christophe Brown .02 .10
215 Slava Bykov .20 .50
216 David Dousse .02 .10
217 Stefan Choffat .02 .10
218 Andrei Khomutov .20 .50
219 Daniel Meier .02 .10
220 Patrick Oppliger .02 .10
221 Mario Rottaris .02 .10
222 Pascal Schaller .02 .10

223 Didier Schafer .02 .10
224 Al Raymond .02 .10
225 HC La Chaux De Fonds .02 .10
226 Ricardo Fuhrer CO .02 .10
227 Jean-Luc Schnegg .02 .10
228 Roland Meyer .02 .10
229 Eric Bourquin .02 .10
230 Rob Cowie .02 .10
231 Daniel Dubois .02 .10
232 Dan Eisener .02 .10
233 Thierry Murisier .02 .10
234 Dany Ott .02 .10
235 Jorg Reber .02 .10
236 Pascal Sommer .02 .10
237 Jan Alston .40 1.00
238 Florian Andenmatten .02 .10
239 Loic Burkhalter .02 .10
240 Christer Cantoni .02 .10
241 Florian Chappot .02 .10
242 Michael Diener .02 .10
243 Gilles Dubois .02 .10
244 Rob Gaudreau .02 .10
245 Boris Liemgruber .02 .10
246 Benoit Pont .02 .10
247 Bernhard Schumperli .02 .10
248 Michel Wicky .02 .10
249 HC Lausanne .02 .10
250 Johnston .02 .10
251 Beat Kindler .02 .10
252 Bernhard Lauber .02 .10
253 Sebastien De Allegri .02 .10
254 Thierry Evequoz .02 .10
255 Nicolas Goumaz .02 .10
256 Cull .02 .10
257 Ivo Stoffel .02 .10
258 Turcotte .02 .10
259 Philippe Bozon .40 1.00
260 Johan Bertholet .02 .10
261 Andre Doll .02 .10
262 Rolf Ziegler .02 .10
263 Horvath .02 .10
264 Bruno Maurer .02 .10
265 Alfie Michaud .20 .50
266 Frank Monnier .02 .10
267 Patrice Pellet .02 .10
268 Mario Seeholzer .02 .10
269 Robert Slehofer .02 .10
270 Laurent Stehlin .02 .10
271 Grasshoppers .02 .10
272 Bruno Aegerter .02 .10
273 Alatalo .02 .10
274 Marcel Kohli .02 .10
275 Olivier Wissmann .02 .10
276 Martin Brich .02 .10
277 Marc Haueter .02 .10
278 FahM. .02 .10
279 Roman Honegger .02 .10
280 Arne Ramholt .02 .10
281 Daniel Rutschi .02 .10
282 Alain Ayer .02 .10
283 Andre Baumann .02 .10
284 Warren Brutsch .02 .10
285 Roman Furrer .02 .10
286 Marco Hagmann .02 .10
287 Patrick Looser .02 .10
288 Lasse Nieminen .02 .10
289 Andy Rufener .02 .10
290 Christian Ruuttu .20 .50
291 Mathias Schenkel .02 .10
292 Peter Schlagenhauf .02 .10
293 HC Thurgau .02 .10
294 Mike McParland .02 .10
295 Peter Martin .02 .10
296 Sutter .02 .10
297 Martin Granicher .02 .10
298 Henry .02 .10
299 Ralph Ott .02 .10
300 Mike Posma .02 .10
301 Marcel Schmid .02 .10
302 Christian Schuster .02 .10
303 Robert Wiesmann .02 .10
304 Dan Daoust .02 .10
305 Slaven Imhof .02 .10
306 Matthias Keller .02 .10
307 Ronny Keller .02 .10
308 Guido Laczko .02 .10
309 Don McLaren .02 .10
310 Gery Othman .02 .10
311 Rolf Schrepfer .02 .10
312 Rene Stussi .02 .10
313 Cuno Weisser .02 .10
314 Benjamin Winkler .02 .10
315 SC Langnau .02 .10
316 Paul-Andre Cadieux .02 .10
317 Jakub Kolliker .02 .10
318 Martin Gerber ERC 4.00 10.00
319 Thomas Dreier .02 .10
320 Daniel Aegerter .02 .10
321 Raoul Baumgartner .02 .10
322 Andreas Beutler .02 .10
323 Mario Doyon .02 .10
324 Roland Kradolfer .02 .10
325 Raphael Schneider .02 .10
326 Pascal Stoller .02 .10
327 Rolf Badertscher .02 .10
328 Bruno Brechbuhl .02 .10
329 Peter Bartschi .02 .10
330 Walter Gerber .02 .10
331 Markus Hirschi .02 .10
332 Jakub Horak .02 .10
333 Andreas Keller .02 .10
334 Beat Nuspliger .02 .10
335 Greg Parks .02 .10
336 Kevin Schlapfer .02 .10
337 Stefan Tschiemer .02 .10
338 SC Herisau .02 .10
339 McGregor .02 .10
340 Markus Bachschmied .02 .10
341 Schiess .02 .10
342 Urs Balzarek .02 .10
343 Damien Freitag .02 .10
344 Fritz .02 .10
345 Thomas Jaggli .02 .10
346 Karl Knopf .02 .10
347 Andy Krapf .02 .10
348 Andy Maag .02 .10
349 Devin Edgerton .02 .10
350 Rico Enzler .02 .10
351 John Fust .02 .10
352 Martin Hanggi .02 .10
353 Francois Marquis .02 .10
354 Ludwig Marek .02 .10
355 Pinelli .02 .10
356 Ivo Ruthemann .02 .10
357 Scheiwiller .02 .10
358 Claude Vilgrain .40 1.00
359 Sacha Weibel .02 .10
360 HC Martigny .02 .10
361 Steve Pochon .02 .10
362 Patrick Grand .02 .10
363 Didier Tosi .02 .10
364 Pascal Avanthay .02 .10
365 Jean-Michel Clavien .02 .10
366 Ayocholos Escher .02 .10
367 Alan Hirschi .02 .10
368 Patrik Neukom .02 .10
369 Benedikt Sapin .02 .10
370 Marc Zurbriggen .02 .10
371 Jean-Daniel Bonito .02 .10
372 Igor Fedulov .02 .10
373 Nicolas Gastaldo .02 .10
374 Paolo Imperatori .02 .10
375 Thierry Moret .02 .10
376 Stephan Nussberger .02 .10
377 Petr Rosol .02 .10
378 Fabrizio Silietti .02 .10
379 Yannick Theler .02 .10
380 Natal Zurbriggen .02 .10
381 EHC Biel-Bienne .02 .10
382 Michael Zettel .02 .10
383 Christoph Wahl .02 .10
384 Devaux .02 .10
385 Sven Dick .02 .10
386 Romain Fleury .02 .10
387 Claudio Ghillioni .02 .10
388 Urs Hirschi .02 .10
389 Sven Schmid .02 .10
390 Daniel Schneider .02 .10
391 Alain Villard .02 .10
392 Thomas Burillo .02 .10
393 Reynald De Ritz .02 .10
394 Marco Dick .02 .10
395 Paul Gagne .02 .10
396 Gabriel Taccoz .02 .10
397 Shawn Heaphy .02 .10
398 Maxime Lapointe .02 .10
399 Luthi .02 .10
400 Serge Meyer .02 .10
401 Cyrill Pasche .02 .10
402 Michel Riesen .20 .50
403 HC Geneve-Servette .02 .10
404 Huppe .02 .10
405 Hagmann .02 .10
406 Michel Pilet .02 .10
407 Francesco Bizzozero .02 .10
408 Daniel Herlea .02 .10
409 Pascal Lamprecht .02 .10
410 Thevoz .02 .10
411 Daniel Zieri .02 .10
412 Christian Serena .02 .10
413 Nicolas Studer .02 .10
414 Joel Aeschlimann .02 .10
415 Antoine Cloux .02 .10
416 Claude Verret .02 .10
417 Martin Desjardins .02 .10
418 Olivier Ecoeur .02 .10
419 Gaby Epiney .02 .10
420 Laurent Faller .02 .10
421 Nicholas Gauch .02 .10
422 Olivier Honsberger .02 .10
423 Gael Kertudo .02 .10
424 Jorg Ledermann .02 .10
425 EHC Olten .02 .10
426 Hoffmann .02 .10
427 Beat Aebischer .02 .10
428 Thierry Loup .02 .10
429 Ralph Gugelmann .02 .10
430 Bruno Habisreutinger .02 .10
431 Phillippe Portner .02 .10
432 Gianni Sanese .02 .10
433 Schonauer .02 .10
434 Richard Stucki .02 .10
435 Thomas Studer .02 .10
436 Dobler .02 .10
437 Yannick Dube .02 .10
438 Mario Koppel .02 .10
439 Luthi .02 .10
440 Muller .02 .10
441 Nicola Pini .02 .10
442 Thomas Seitz .02 .10
443 Patrick Siegwart .02 .10
444 Pirmin Keller .02 .10
445 Andre Von Rohr .02 .10
446 Andre Von Rohr .02 .10
447 EHC Chur .02 .10
448 Voschakov .02 .10
449 Thomas Liesch .02 .10
450 Reto Zuccolini .02 .10
451 Armin Berchtold .02 .10
452 Sacha Bleiker .02 .10
453 Sandro Capaul .02 .10
454 Patrick Fischer .02 .10
455 Andreas Ritsch .02 .10
456 Stefan Schneider .02 .10
457 Roland Simonet .02 .10
458 Rene Ackermann .02 .10
459 Andreas Fischer .02 .10
460 Miguel Fondado .02 .10
461 Claudio Peer .02 .10
462 Reto Germann .02 .10
463 Albert Malgin .02 .10
464 Roger Rieder .02 .10
465 Michael Rosenast .02 .10
466 Riccardo Signorell .02 .10
467 Harijs Vitolinsh .02 .10
468 Patrick Werthan .02 .10
469 Nussle .02 .10
470 SC Luzern .02 .10
471 Hansson .02 .10
472 Beat Lautenschlager .02 .10
473 Patrice Bosch .02 .10
474 Rosset .02 .10
475 Alain Comte .02 .10
476 Dominik Jenny .02 .10
477 Samuelsson .02 .10
478 Ron Stillhardt .02 .10
479 Marco Tanner .02 .10
480 Markus Wetter .02 .10
481 Martin Bahnik .02 .10
482 Baiada .02 .10
483 Buchel .02 .10
484 Marco Fischer .02 .10
485 P. Giger .02 .10
486 Daniel Lamminger .02 .10
487 M. Ledermann .02 .10
488 Daniel Mares .02 .10
489 P. Mares .02 .10
490 Marco Mozzini .02 .10
491 Mario Schocher .02 .10
492 Ramil Yuldaschev .02 .10
493 Ron Stillhardt .02 .10
494 HC Ajoie .02 .10
495 Hans Kossmann .02 .10
496 Christian Cretin .02 .10
497 Rosado .02 .10
498 Rapheal Berger .02 .10
499 Matthias Bachler .02 .10
500 Erich Frey .02 .10
501 Heusler .02 .10
502 M. Reinhard .02 .10
503 Julien Vauclair ERC .40 1.00
504 Yann Voillat .02 .10
505 Patrick Adami .02 .10
506 Denis Chalifoux .02 .10
507 Guyaz .02 .10
508 Alexandre Von Arb .02 .10
509 Holmberg .02 .10
510 Honegger .02 .10
511 Herve Meyer .02 .10
512 Marc Fritsche .02 .10
513 Migy .02 .10
514 Giovanni Pestrin .02 .10
515 Geoffrey Vauclair .02 .10
516 Reto Pavoni .02 .10
517 Gaeten Voisard .02 .10
518 Martin Bruderer .02 .10
519 Felix Hollenstein .02 .10
520 Gil Montandon .02 .10
521 Patrick Howald .02 .10
522 National Team .02 .10
523 Schenk .02 .10
524 Paul-Andre Cadieux .02 .10
525 Jakub Kolliker .02 .10
526 Reto Pavoni .02 .10
527 Pauli Jaks .20 .50
528 Samuel Balmer .02 .10
529 Marco Bayer .02 .10
530 Sandro Bertaggia .02 .10
531 Martin Bruderer .02 .10
532 Tiziano Gianini .02 .10
533 Sven Leuenberger .02 .10
534 Gaetan Voisard .02 .10
535 Andreas Zehnder .02 .10
536 Manuele Celio .02 .10
537 Nicola Celio .02 .10
538 Patrick Fischer .02 .10
539 Felix Hollenstein .02 .10
540 Peter Jaks .02 .10
541 Sandy Jeannin .02 .10
542 Marcel Jenni .02 .10
543 Harry Rogenmoser .02 .10
544 Frederic Rothen .02 .10
545 Reto Von Arx .20 .50
546 Christian Weber .02 .10
547 Michel Zeiter .02 .10
548 SIHL .02 .10
549 Swiss National Inline Team .02 .10
550 Alan Wittwer .02 .10
551 Markus Bachschmied .02 .10
552 Waber .02 .10
553 Ochsner .02 .10
554 Mueller .02 .10
555 Bauer .02 .10
556 Ivo Ruthemann .02 .10
557 Sven Lindemann .02 .10
558 Alexandre Von Arb .02 .10
559 Ronnie Rueger .02 .10
561 Klaus .02 .10
562 Guido Lindemann .02 .10
563 Rico Enzler .02 .10
564 Andres Egger .02 .10
565 Kuendig .02 .10
566 Wild .02 .10
567 Johansson .02 .10
568 Patrick Howald .02 .10
569 Muller .02 .10
570 Tschibirev .02 .10
571 Jan Alston .40 1.00
572 Mike Richard .02 .10
573 Stephan Lebeau .20 .50
574 Marc Fortier .02 .10
575 Slava Bykov .20 .50
576 Frank Monnier .02 .10
577 Patrick Oppliger .02 .10
578 Lasse Nieminen .02 .10
579 Dan Daoust .20 .50
580 Glowa .02 .10
581 Claude Vilgrain .40 1.00
582 Petr Rosol .02 .10
583 Dmitri Kvartalnov .20 .50
584 Andrew McKim .20 .50
585 Rene Ackermann .02 .10
586 Valery Cherny .02 .10
587 Referees .02 .10
588 Referees .02 .10

1998-99 Swiss Power Play Stickers

COMPLETE SET (382) 40.00 80.00
1 Team Ambri Left .08 .20
2 Team Ambri Right .08 .20
3 Larry Hurras .08 .20
4 Pauli Jaks .08 .20
5 Peter Martin .08 .20
6 Fredy Bobillier .08 .20
7 Ivan Gazzaroli .08 .20
8 Tiziano Gianini .08 .20
9 Giordano Guidotti .08 .20
10 Leif Rohlin .08 .20
11 Edgar Salis .08 .20
12 Bruno Steck .08 .20
13 Oliver Tschanz .08 .20
14 Mattia Baldi .08 .20
15 Krister Cantoni .08 .20
16 Manuele Celio .08 .20
17 Nicola Celio .08 .20
18 Paul DiPietro .20 .50
19 John Fritsche .08 .20
20 Vjeran Ivankovic .08 .20
21 Oleg Petrov .08 .20
22 Franz Steffen .08 .20
23 Omar Tognini .08 .20
24 Theo Wittmann .08 .20
25 Thomas Ziegler .08 .20
26 Team Bern Left .08 .20
27 Team Bern Right .08 .20
28 Ueli Schwarz .08 .20
29 Renato Tosio .08 .20
30 Reto Schurch .08 .20
31 Alexander Godynyuk .08 .20
32 Sven Leuenberger .08 .20
33 Martin Rauch .08 .20
34 Bjorn Schneider .08 .20
35 Stefan Schneider .08 .20
36 Pascal Sommer .08 .20
37 Martin Steinegger .08 .20
38 Gregor Thommen .08 .20
39 Bjorn Christen .08 .20
40 David Jobin .08 .20
41 Patrick Howald .08 .20
42 Boris Leimgruber .08 .20
43 Lars Leuenberger .08 .20
44 Dave McLlwain .08 .20
45 Gil Montandon .08 .20
46 Daniel Marois .08 .20
47 Michel Mouther .08 .20
48 Thierry Paterlini .08 .20
49 Roberto Triulzi .08 .20
50 Marc Weber .08 .20
51 Team Davos Left .08 .20
52 Team Davos Right .08 .20
53 Arno Del Curto .08 .20
54 Stephane Beauregard .20 .50
55 Marco Wegmuller .08 .20
56 Beat Equilino .08 .20
57 Marc Gianola .08 .20
58 Andrea Haller .08 .20
59 Michael Kress .08 .20
60 Pettri Nummelin .08 .20
61 Mark Streit .40 1.00
62 Jan Von Arx .08 .20
63 Andre Baumann .08 .20
64 Sandy Jeannin .08 .20
65 Rene Muller .08 .20
66 Kai Nurminen .08 .20
67 Peter Kobel .08 .20
68 Sandro Rizzi .08 .20
69 Oliver Roth .08 .20
70 Ivo Ruthemann .08 .20
71 Mario Schocher .08 .20
72 Reto Stirnimann .08 .20
73 Reto Von Arx .20 .50
74 Beat Helbstab .08 .20
75 Timo Helbling .20 .50
76 Team Fribourg Left .08 .20
77 Team Fribourg Right .08 .20
78 Andre Peloffy .08 .20
79 David Aebischer 2.00 5.00
80 Thomas Ostlund .20 .50
81 Alain Sansonnens .08 .20
82 Patrice Brasey .08 .20
83 Antoine Descloux .08 .20
84 Livio Fazio .08 .20
85 Romain Fleury .08 .20
86 Olivier Keller .08 .20
87 Philippe Marquis .08 .20
88 Marc Werlen .08 .20
89 Igor Chibirev .08 .20
90 Flavien Conne .08 .20
91 David Dousse .08 .20
92 Rene Furler .08 .20
93 Daniel Giger .08 .20
94 Goran Bezina .08 .20
95 Philipp Orlandi .08 .20
96 Mario Rottaris .08 .20
97 Pascal Schaller .08 .20
98 Robert Slehofer .08 .20
99 Pavel Torgajev .08 .20
100 Gerd Zenhausern .08 .20
101 Team Kloten Left .08 .20
102 Team Kloten Right .08 .20
103 Reto Pavoni .08 .20
104 Marco Buhrer .08 .20
105 Samuel Balmer .08 .20
106 Marco Bayer .08 .20
107 Martin Bruderer .08 .20
108 Marco Kloti .08 .20
109 Beat Meier .08 .20
110 Tommy Sjodin .08 .20
111 Daniel Weber .08 .20
112 Benjamin Winkler .08 .20
113 Philipp Folghera .08 .20
114 Thomas Heldner .08 .20
115 Felix Hollenstein .08 .20
116 Sven Lindemann .08 .20
117 Bill McDougall .08 .20
118 Martin Pluss .08 .20
119 Frederic Rothen .08 .20
120 Andy Rufener .08 .20
121 Matthias Schenkel .08 .20
122 Rene Stussi .08 .20
123 Chris Tancill .08 .20
124 Adrian Wichser .08 .20
125 Team Langnau Left .08 .20
126 Team Langnau Right .08 .20
127 Jakob Kolliker .08 .20
128 Martin Gerber 2.00 5.00
129 Ivo Kleeb .08 .20
130 Daniel Aegerter .08 .20
131 Mario Doyon .08 .20
132 Marco Knecht .08 .20
133 Pascal Muller .08 .20
134 Wesley Snell .08 .20
135 Oskar Szczepaniec .08 .20
136 Markus Wuthrich .08 .20
137 Alexis Vacheron .08 .20
138 Rolf Bradertscher .08 .20
139 Peter Bartschi .08 .20
140 Bruno Brechbuhl .08 .20
141 Marc Buhlmann .08 .20
142 Todd Elik .08 .20
143 Marco Fischer .08 .20
144 John Fust .08 .20
145 Andy Keller .08 .20
146 Michael Liniger .08 .20
147 Greg Parks .08 .20
148 Benoit Pont .08 .20
149 Stefan Tschiemer .08 .20
150 Team Lugano Left .08 .20
151 Team Lugano Right .08 .20
152 Jim Koleff CO .08 .20
153 Cristobal Huet 6.00 15.00
154 Lars Weibel .08 .20
155 Peter Andersson .08 .20
156 Mark Astley .08 .20
157 Sandro Bertaggia .08 .20
158 Fabian Guignard .08 .20
159 Rick Tschumi .08 .20
160 Julien Vauclair .20 .50
161 GaÃ«tan Voisard .08 .20
162 Rolf Ziegler .08 .20
163 Jean Jacques Aeschlimann .08 .20
164 Misko Antisin .08 .20
165 Gian Marco Crameri .08 .20
166 Andre Doll .08 .20
167 Keith Fair .08 .20
168 Patrick Fischer .08 .20
169 Regis Fuchs .08 .20
170 Marcel Jenni .08 .20
171 Trevor Meier .08 .20
172 Andy Naser .08 .20
173 Gaetano Orlando .20 .50
174 Geoffrey Vauclair .08 .20
175 Team Rapperswil Left .08 .20
176 Team Rapperswil Right .08 .20
177 Mark McGregor .08 .20
178 Claudio Bayer .08 .20
179 Remo Wehrli .08 .20
180 Marco Capaul .08 .20
181 Christian Langer .08 .20
182 Dominic Meier .08 .20
183 Jorg Reber .08 .20
184 Matthias Seger .08 .20
185 Daniel Sigg .08 .20
186 Roger Sigg .08 .20
187 Adrian Bachofner .08 .20
188 Markus Butler .08 .20
189 Rene Friedli .08 .20
190 Oliver Hoffmann .08 .20
191 Christian Hofstetter .08 .20
192 Chris Lindberg .08 .20
193 Frank Monnier .08 .20
194 Mark Ouimet .08 .20
195 Mike Richard .08 .20
196 Harry Rogenmoser .08 .20
197 Bernhard Schumperli .08 .20
198 Ken Yaremchuk .08 .20
199 Team EVZ Left .08 .20
200 Team EVZ Right .08 .20
201 Sean Simpson .08 .20
202 Ronald Rueger .08 .20
203 Patrick Schopf .08 .20
204 RaphaÃ«l Berger .08 .20
205 Matthias Holzer .08 .20
206 Jakub Horak .08 .20
207 Dino Kessler .08 .20
208 Reto Kobach .08 .20
209 Andre Kunzi .08 .20
210 Thomas Kunzi .08 .20
211 Patrick Sutter .08 .20
212 Christoph Brown .08 .20
213 Jorg Eberle .08 .20
214 Devin Edgerton .08 .20
215 Stefan Grogg .08 .20
216 Daniel Meier .08 .20
217 Colin Muller .08 .20
218 Patrick Oppliger .08 .20
219 Andre Rotheli .08 .20
220 Sacha Schneider .08 .20
221 Kevin Todd .08 .20
222 Samuel Villiger .08 .20
223 Wes Walz .40 1.00
224 Team ZSC Left .08 .20
225 Team ZSC Right .08 .20
226 Kent Ruhnke .08 .20
227 Thomas Papp .08 .20
228 Ari Sulander .20 .50
229 Martin Brich .08 .20
230 Marc Haueter .08 .20
231 Michel Kamber .08 .20
232 Martin Kout .08 .20
233 Kari Martikainen .08 .20
234 Adrien Plavsic .08 .20
235 Pascal Stoller .08 .20
236 Andreas Zehnder .08 .20
237 Patrik Della Rossa .08 .20
238 Axel Heim .08 .20
239 Dan Hodgson .08 .20
240 Peter Jaks .08 .20
241 Claudio Micheli .08 .20
242 Patrizio Morger .08 .20
243 Laurent Muller .08 .20
244 Rolf Schrepfer .08 .20
245 Chad Silver .08 .20
246 Christian Weber .08 .20
247 Michel Zeiter .08 .20
248 National Team Left .08 .20
249 National Team Right .08 .20
250 Raphael Kruger .08 .20
251 David Aebischer 2.00 5.00
252 Misko Antisin .08 .20
253 Mattia Baldi .08 .20
254 Gian Marco Crameri .08 .20
255 Patrick Fischer .08 .20
256 Peter Jaks .08 .20
257 Sandy Jeannin .08 .20
258 Marcel Jenni .08 .20
259 Dino Kessler .08 .20
260 Claudio Micheli .08 .20
261 Reto Pavoni .08 .20
262 Martin Pluss .08 .20
263 Martin Rauch .08 .20
264 Ivo Ruthemann .08 .20
265 Edgar Salis .08 .20
266 Matthias Seger .08 .20
267 Franz Steffen .08 .20
268 Martin Steinegger .08 .20
269 Mark Streit .20 .50
270 Patrick Sutter .08 .20
271 Reto Von Arx .20 .50
272 Michel Zeiter .08 .20
273 Bill Gilligan .08 .20
274 Marco Buhrer .08 .20
275 Ralph Bundi .08 .20
276 Alex Chatelain .08 .20
277 Bjorn Christen .08 .20
278 Flavien Conne .08 .20
279 Patrick Fischer .08 .20
280 Sven Lindemann .08 .20
281 Michel Mouther .08 .20
282 Laurent Muller .08 .20
283 Marc Reichert .08 .20
284 Alain Reist .08 .20
285 Michel Riesen .20 .50
286 Sandro Rizzi .08 .20
287 Mario Schocher .08 .20
288 Rene Stussi .08 .20
289 Julien Vauclair .20 .50
290 Jan Von Arx .08 .20
291 Marc Werlen .08 .20
292 Adrian Wichser .08 .20
293 Markus Wuthrich .08 .20
294 Thomas Ziegler .08 .20
295 Team Biel Left .08 .20
296 Team Biel Right .08 .20
297 Christian Cretin .08 .20
Alain Reist
298 Sven Schmid .08 .20
Paul Gagne
299 Paul-Andre Cadieux .08 .20
300 Shawn Heaphy .08 .20
Cyrill Pasche
301 Team La Chaux de Fonds Left .08 .20
302 Team La Chaux de Fonds Right .08 .20
303 Thomas Berger .08 .20
Valeri Schirjaev
304 Lugio Riva .08 .20
Steve Aebersold
305 Riccardo Fuhrer .08 .20
306 Stephan Lebeau .08 .20
Stefano Togni
307 Team Chur Left .08 .20
308 Team Chur Right .08 .20
309 Thomas Liesch .08 .20
Patrick Fischer
310 Mike Posma .08 .20
Mario Brodmann
311 Mike McParland .08 .20
312 Harijs Vitolinsh .08 .20
Reymond Walder
313 Team GC Left .08 .20
314 Team GC Right .08 .20
315 Olivier Wissmann .08 .20
Arne Ramholt
316 Marco Schellenberg .08 .20
Domenic Amodeo
317 Dave Tietzen .08 .20
318 Mark Kaufman .08 .20
Riccardo Signorell
319 Team Servette Left .08 .20
320 Team Servette Right .08 .20
321 Steve Meuwly .08 .20
David Leibzig
322 Maxime Lapointe .08 .20
Christian Serena
323 Jean Perron CO .08 .20
324 Mark Jorris .08 .20
Sandy Smith
325 Team Herisau Left .08 .20
326 Team Herisau Right .08 .20
327 Fabian Gull .08 .20
Robert Burakowsky
328 Markus Bachschmied .08 .20
Urs Balzarek
329 Evgeny Popichin .08 .20
330 Alain Fraser .08 .20
Cuno Weisser
331 Team Lausanne Left .08 .20
332 Team Lausannne Right .08 .20
333 Beat Kindler .08 .20
Serge Poudrier
334 Andy Krapf .08 .20
Jorg Ledermann
335 Benoit Laporte .08 .20
336 Slava Bykov .08 .20
Daniel Nakaoka
337 Team Martigny Left .08 .20
338 Team Martigny Right .08 .20
339 Didier Tosi .08 .20
Jean-Michel Clavien
340 Benedict Sapin .08 .20
Jean-Daniel Bonito
341 Petr Rosol .08 .20
342 Nicolas Gastaldo .08 .20
Thierry Moret
343 Team Olten Left .08 .20
344 Team Olten Right .08 .20
345 Beat Aebischer .08 .20
Richard Stucki
346 Igor Boriskov .08 .20
Albert Malgin
347 Markus Graf .08 .20
348 Luca Vigano .08 .20
Andre Von Rohr
349 Team Sierre Left .08 .20
350 Team Sierre Right .08 .20
351 Matthias Lauber .08 .20
Michel Fah
352 Philippe Faust .08 .20
Bruno Erni
353 Christian Wittwer .08 .20
354 Marco Poulsen .08 .20
Gilles Thibaudeau
355 Team Thurgau Left .08 .20
356 Team Thurgau Right .08 .20
357 Marius Bosch .08 .20
Patrick Henry
358 Ralph Ott .08 .20
Scott Beattie
359 Henryk Gruth .08 .20
360 Kevin Miehm .08 .20
Roman Wager
A SEHV / LSHG .08 .20
B HC Ambri Piotta .08 .20
C SC Bern .08 .20
D HC Davos .08 .20
E HC Fribourg Gotteron .08 .20
F EHC Kloten .08 .20
G SC Langnau .08 .20
H HC Lugano .08 .20
I SC Rapperswil-Jona .08 .20
J EV Zug .08 .20
K ZSC Lions .08 .20
L EHC Biel-Bienne .08 .20
M HC La Chaux De Fonds .08 .20
N EHC Chur .08 .20
O Grasshoppers .08 .20
P HC Geneve Servette .08 .20
Q SC Herisau .08 .20
R HC Lausanne .08 .20
S EHC Martigny .08 .20
T EHC Olten .08 .20
U HC Sierre .08 .20
V HC Thurgau .08 .20

1999-00 Swiss Panini Stickers

COMPLETE SET (380) 40.00 80.00
1 Team Ambri Left .08 .20
2 Team Ambri Right .08 .20
3 Larry Huras .08 .20
4 Pauli Jaks .08 .20
5 Peter Martin .08 .20
6 Fredy Bobillier .08 .20
7 Ivan Gazzaroli .08 .20
8 Tiziano Gianini .08 .20
9 John Gobbi .08 .20
10 Thomas Kunzi .08 .20
11 Leif Rohlin .08 .20
12 Bruno Steck .08 .20
13 Krister Cantoni .08 .20
14 Manuele Celio .08 .20
15 Nicola Celio .08 .20
16 Luca Cereda .20 .50
17 Alain Demuth .08 .20
18 Paolo Duca .08 .20
19 John Fritsche .08 .20
20 Ryan Gardner .08 .20
21 Vitaly Lakhmatov .08 .20
22 Stephan Lebeau .20 .50
23 Patrick Lebeau .20 .50
24 Franz Steffen .08 .20
25 Thomas Ziegler .08 .20
26 Team Bern Left .08 .20
27 Team Bern Right .08 .20
28 Pekka Rautakallio CO .08 .20
29 Martin Kilchor .08 .20
30 Renato Tosio .08 .20
31 David Jobin .08 .20
32 Sven Leuenberger .08 .20
33 Petri Liimatainen .08 .20
34 Martin Rauch .08 .20
35 Pascal Sommer .08 .20
36 Martin Steinegger .08 .20
37 Fabian Stephan .08 .20
38 Gregor Thommen .08 .20
39 Alex Chatelain .08 .20
40 Bjorn Christen .08 .20
41 Patrick Howald .08 .20
42 Roland Kaser .08 .20
43 Boris Leimgruber .08 .20
44 Lars Leuenberger .08 .20
45 Dave McLlwain .08 .20
46 Thierry Paterlini .08 .20
47 Jackson Penney .08 .20
48 Marc Reichert .08 .20
49 Ivo Ruthemann .08 .20
50 Marc Weber .08 .20
51 Team Davos Left .08 .20
52 Team Davos Right .08 .20
53 Arno Del Curto .08 .20
54 Petter Ronnqvist .08 .20
55 Marco Wegmuller .08 .20
56 Beat Equilino .08 .20
57 Marc Gianola .08 .20
58 Andreas Haller .08 .20
59 Timo Helbling .20 .50
60 Beat Heldstab .08 .20
61 Petteri Nummelin .08 .20
62 Jan Von Arx .08 .20
63 Andre Baumann .08 .20
64 Patrick Fischer .08 .20
65 Marc Heberlein .08 .20
66 Sandy Jeannin .08 .20
67 Michael Kress .08 .20
68 Fredrik Lindquist .08 .20
69 Rene Muller .08 .20
70 Claudio Neff .08 .20
71 Sandro Rizzi .08 .20
72 Oliver Roth .08 .20
73 Frederic Rothen .08 .20
74 Mario Schocher .08 .20
75 Reto Von Arx .20 .50
76 Team Fribourg Left .08 .20
77 Team Fribourg Right .08 .20
78 Ueli Schwarz .08 .20
79 Thomas Ostlund .20 .50
80 Alain Sansonnens .08 .20
81 Goran Bezina .08 .20
82 Livio Fazio .08 .20
83 Romain Fleury .08 .20
84 Fabian Guignard .08 .20
85 Philippe Marquis .08 .20
86 Mika Stromberg .08 .20
87 Marc Werlen .08 .20
88 Rolf Ziegler .08 .20
89 Robert Burakowski .08 .20
90 Flavien Conne .08 .20
91 Rene Furler .08 .20
92 Daniel Giger .08 .20
93 Gil Montandon .08 .20
94 Colin Muller .08 .20
95 Michael Neininger .08 .20
96 Real Raemy .08 .20
97 Mario Rottaris .08 .20
98 Pascal Schaller .08 .20
99 Robert Slehofer .08 .20
100 Gerd Zenhausern .08 .20
101 Team Kloten Left .08 .20
102 Team Kloten Right .08 .20
103 Vladimir Jursinov CO .08 .20
104 Reto Pavoni .08 .20
105 Samuel Balmer .08 .20
106 Andre Bielmann .08 .20
107 Martin Bruderer .08 .20
108 Martin Hohener .08 .20
109 Marco Kloti .08 .20
110 Arne Ramholt .08 .20
111 Oskar Szczepaniec .08 .20
112 Benjamin Winkler .08 .20
113 Mathias Wuest .08 .20
114 Thomas Heldner .08 .20
115 Felix Hollenstein .08 .20
116 Peter Kobel .08 .20
117 Sven Lindemann .08 .20
118 Andrew McKim .20 .50
119 Andreas Nauser .08 .20
120 Martin Pluss .08 .20
121 Sebastien Reuille .08 .20
122 Andy Rufener .08 .20
123 Matthias Schenkel .08 .20
124 Tomas Strandberg .08 .20
125 Adrian Wichser .08 .20
126 Team Langnau Left .08 .20

127 Team Langnau Right .08 .20
128 Bengt-Ake Gustafsson .08 .20
129 Alfred Bohren .08 .20
130 Martin Gerber 2.00 5.00
131 Adrian Hunziker .08 .20
132 Daniel Aegeter .08 .20
133 Antoine Descloux .08 .20
134 Steve Hirschi .08 .20
135 Erik Kakko .08 .20
136 Pascal Muller .08 .20
137 Markus Wuthrich .08 .20
138 Rolf Badertscher .08 .20
139 Daniel Bieri .08 .20
140 Bruno Brechbuhl .08 .20
141 Marc Buhlmann .08 .20
142 Todd Elik .08 .20
143 John Fust .08 .20
144 Daniel Gauthier .08 .20
145 Bjorn Guazzini .08 .20
146 Matthias Holzer .08 .20
147 Michael Liniger .08 .20
148 Benoit Pont .08 .20
149 Stefan Tschiemer .08 .20
150 Team Lugano Left .08 .20
151 Team Lugano Right .08 .20
152 Jim Koleff CO .08 .20
153 Cristobal Huet 4.00 10.00
154 Lars Weibel .20 .50
155 Peter Andersson .08 .20
156 Mark Astley .08 .20
157 Sandro Bertaggia .08 .20
158 Olivier Keller .08 .20
159 Rick Tschumi .08 .20
160 Julien Vauclair .20 .50
161 GaÃ«tan Voisard .20 .50
162 J.Jacques Aeschlimann .08 .20
163 Misko Antisin .08 .20
164 Philippe Bozon .40 1.00
165 Gian Marco Crameri .08 .20
166 Andre Doll .08 .20
167 Christian Dube .08 .20
168 Keith Fair .08 .20
169 Igor Fedulov .08 .20
170 Regis Fuchs .08 .20
171 Marcel Jenni .08 .20
172 Trevor Meier .08 .20
173 Andy Naser .08 .20
174 Geoffrey Vauclair .08 .20
175 Team Rapperswil Left .08 .20
176 Team Rapperswil Right .08 .20
177 Evgeny Popichin .08 .20
178 Claudio Bayer .08 .20
179 Remo Wehrli .08 .20
180 Marco Capaul .08 .20
181 Dominic Meier .08 .20
182 Jorg Reber .08 .20
183 Alain Reist .08 .20
184 Daniel Sigg .08 .20
185 Roger Sigg .08 .20
186 Magnus Svensson .08 .20
187 Loic Burkhalter .08 .20
188 Markus Butler .08 .20
189 Rene Friedli .08 .20
190 Sandro Haberlin .08 .20
191 Axel Heim .08 .20
192 Oliver Hoffmann .08 .20
193 Vjeran Ivankovic .08 .20
194 Frank Monnier .08 .20
195 Mark Ouimet .08 .20
196 Mike Richard .08 .20
197 Bernhard Schumperli .08 .20
198 Marcel Sommer .08 .20
199 Paul Ysebaert .08 .20
200 Team EVZ Left .08 .20
201 Team EVZ Right .08 .20
202 Rauno Korpi .08 .20
203 Ronnie Rueger .08 .20
204 Patrick Schopf .08 .20
205 Marco Bayer .08 .20
206 Raphael Berger .08 .20
207 Patrick Fischer .08 .20
208 Jakub Horak .08 .20
209 Dino Kessler .08 .20
210 Reto Kobach .08 .20
211 Andre Kunzi .08 .20
212 Patrick Sutter .08 .20
213 Christophe Brown .08 .20
214 Paul Di Pietro .20 .50
215 Stefan Grogg .08 .20
216 Daniel Meier .08 .20
217 Stefan Niggli .08 .20
218 Patrick Oppliger .08 .20
219 Andre Rotheli .08 .20
220 Sascha Schneider .08 .20
221 Rene Stussi .08 .20
222 Chris Tancill .08 .20
223 Samuel Villiger .08 .20
224 Dave Roberts .08 .20
225 Team ZSC Left .08 .20
226 Team ZSC Right .08 .20
227 Kent Ruhnke .08 .20
228 Thomas Papp .08 .20
229 Ari Sulander .20 .50
230 Ronny Keller .08 .20
231 Martin Kout .08 .20
232 Kari Martikainen .08 .20
233 Adrien Plavsic .08 .20
234 Edgar Salis .08 .20
235 Mathias Seger .08 .20
236 Pascal Stoller .08 .20
237 Andreas Zehnder .08 .20
238 Mattia Baldi .08 .20
239 Robin Bauer .08 .20
240 Patric Della Rossa .08 .20
241 Dan Hodgson .08 .20
242 Peter Jaks .08 .20
243 Claudio Micheli .08 .20
244 Patrizio Morger .08 .20
245 Laurent Muller .08 .20
246 Rolf Schrepfer .08 .20
247 Reto Stirnimann .08 .20
248 Christian Weber .08 .20
249 Michel Zeiter .08 .20
250 Ralph Krueger .08 .20
251 National Team Left .08 .20
252 National Team Right .08 .20
253 David Aebischer 2.00 5.00
254 Pauli Jaks .20 .50
255 Reto Pavoni .08 .20
256 Olivier Keller .08 .20
257 Philippe Marquis .08 .20
258 Ivo Ruthemann .08 .20
259 Mathias Seger .08 .20
260 Martin Steinegger .08 .20
261 Mark Streit .20 .50
262 Patrick Sutter .08 .20
263 Benjamin Winkler .08 .20
264 Mattia Baldi .08 .20
265 Gian Marco Crameri .08 .20
266 Patric Della Rossa .08 .20
267 Patrick Fischer .08 .20
268 Sandy Jeannin .08 .20
269 Marcel Jenni .08 .20
270 Laurent Muller .08 .20
271 Martin Pluss .08 .20
272 Sandro Rizzi .08 .20
273 Geoffrey Vauclair .08 .20
274 Reto Von Arx .20 .50
275 Michel Zeiter .08 .20
276 John Slettvoll .08 .20
277 National U20 TeamLeft .08 .20
278 National U20 Team Right .08 .20
279 Marco Buhrer .08 .20
280 Oliver Wissmann .08 .20
281 Goran Bezina .08 .20
282 David Jobin .08 .20
283 Pascal Muller .08 .20
284 Alain Reist .08 .20
285 Gregor Thommen .08 .20
286 Alex Vacheron .08 .20
287 Julien Vauclair .20 .50
288 Fabio Beccarelli .08 .20
289 Luca Cereda .20 .50
290 Bjorn Christen .08 .20
291 Flavien Conne .08 .20
292 Alain Demuth .08 .20
293 Philipp Folghera .08 .20
294 Roland Kaser .08 .20
295 Cornel Prinz .08 .20
296 Marc Reichert .08 .20
297 Michel Riesen .20 .50
298 Sandro Tschour .08 .20
299 Adrian Wichser .08 .20
300 Team Biel Left .08 .20
301 Team Biel Right .08 .20
302 Paul Gagne .08 .20
303 Sebastien Kohler .08 .20
Sven Schmid
304 Gilles Dubois .08 .20
Michel Mongeau
305 Cyrill Pasche .20 .50
Claude Vilgrain
306 La Chaux De Fonds Left .08 .20
307 La Chaux De Fonds Right .08 .20
308 Jaroslav Jagr .08 .20
309 Thomas Berger .08 .20
Ruedi Niderost
310 Luigi Riva .08 .20
Valeri Shiryayev
311 Steve Aebersold .08 .20
Christian Pouget
312 Team Chur Left .08 .20
313 Team Chur Right .08 .20
314 Mike McParland .08 .20
315 Nando Wieser .08 .20
Matthias Bachler
316 Michael Meier .08 .20
Roger Rieder
317 Sandro Tschour .08 .20
Theo Wittmann
318 Team GC Left .08 .20
319 Team GC Right .08 .20
320 Riccardo Fuhrer .08 .20
321 Oliver Wissmann .08 .20
Pascal Fah
322 David Fehr .08 .20
Oliver Kamber
323 Patrick Looser .08 .20
Riccardo Signorell
324 Team Lausanne Left .08 .20
325 Team Lausanne Right .08 .20
326 Benoit Laporte .08 .20
327 Beat Kindler .08 .20
Slava Bykov
328 Patrick Giove .08 .20
Maxime Lapointe
329 Jorg Ledermann .08 .20
Valentin Wirz
330 Team Olten Left .08 .20
331 Team Olten Right .08 .20
332 Markus Graf .08 .20
333 Beat Aebischer .08 .20
Andy Egli
334 Richard Stucki .08 .20
Evgeny Davydov
335 Michel Mouther .08 .20
Mikhail Volkov
336 Team Servette Left .08 .20
337 Team Servette Right .08 .20
338 Francois Huppe .08 .20
339 David Bochy .08 .20
Christian Serena
340 Sott Beatti .08 .20
Shawn Heaphy
341 Paul Savary .08 .20
Michel Wicky
342 Team Sierre Left .08 .20
343 Team Sierre Right .08 .20
344 Kevin Primeau .08 .20
345 Matthias Lauber .08 .20
Adrian Jezzone
346 Patrick Neukom .08 .20
Philipp Luber
347 Dimitri Shamolin .08 .20
Gilles Thibaudeau
348 Team Thurgau Left .08 .20
349 Team Thurgau Right .08 .20
350 Robert Wiesmann .08 .20
351 Marco Buhrer .08 .20
Stefan Grauwiler
352 Domenic Amodeo .08 .20
Matthias Keller
353 Patrick Meier .08 .20
Morgan Samuelsson
354 Team Visp Left .08 .20
355 Team Visp Right .08 .20
356 Bruno Zenhausern .08 .20
357 Reiner Karlen .08 .20
Wesley Snell
358 Marc Zurbriggen .08 .20
Franziskus Heinzmann
359 Andy Egli .08 .20
Gabriel Taccoz
A SEHV / LSHG .08 .20
B HC Ambri Piotta .08 .20
C SC Bern .08 .20
D HC Davos .08 .20
E HC Fribourg Gotteron .08 .20
F EHC Kloten .08 .20
G SC Langnau .08 .20
H HC Lugano .08 .20
I SC Rapperswil-Jona .08 .20
J EV Zug .08 .20
K ZSC Lions .08 .20
L EHC Biel-Bienne .08 .20
M HC La Chaux De Fonds .08 .20
N EHC Chur .08 .20
O Grasshoppers .08 .20
P HC Lausanne .08 .20
Q EHC Olten .08 .20
R HC Geneve Servette .08 .20
S HC Sierre .08 .20
T HC Thurgau .08 .20
U Visp .08 .20

2000-01 Swiss Panini Stickers

COMPLETE SET (322) 20.00 50.00
1 Logo Swiss Hockey Federation .08 .20
2 Ambri Team Card .08 .20
3 Ambri Team Card .08 .20
4 Ambri Logo .08 .20
5 Pietre Page .08 .20
6 Pauli Jaks .08 .20
7 Gianluca Mona .08 .20
8 Fredy Bobillier .08 .20
9 Ivan Gazzaroli .08 .20
10 Tiziano Gianini .08 .20
11 Thomas Kunzi .08 .20
12 Leif Rohlin .08 .20
13 Krister Cantoni .08 .20
14 Manuele Celio .08 .20
15 Nicola Celio .08 .20
16 Alain Demuth .08 .20
17 Paolo Duca .08 .20
18 John Fritsche .08 .20
19 Ryan Gardner .08 .20
20 Paolo Imperatori .08 .20
21 Vitaly Lakhmatov .08 .20
22 Stephan Lebeau .08 .20
23 Dan Marois .08 .20
24 Omar Tognini .08 .20
25 Thomas Ziegler .08 .20
26 Logo SCB .08 .20
27 Team Card SCB .08 .20
28 Team Card SCB .08 .20
29 Pekka Rautakallio .08 .20
30 Renato Tosio .08 .20
31 David Jobin .08 .20
32 Marc Leuenberger .08 .20
33 Sven Leuenberger .08 .20
34 Dominic Meier .08 .20
35 Frederik Olausson .08 .20
36 Martin Steinegger .08 .20
37 Fabian Stephan .08 .20
38 Rolf Ziegler .08 .20
39 Alex Chatelain .08 .20
40 Bjorn Christen .08 .20
41 Patrick Howald .08 .20
42 Andreas Johansson .08 .20
43 Patrick Juhlin .08 .20
44 Rolan Kasar .08 .20
45 Boris Leimgruber .08 .20
46 Marc Reichert .08 .20
47 Ivo Ruthemann .08 .20
48 Franz Steffen .08 .20
49 Marc Weber .08 .20
50 La Chaux De Fonds Logo .08 .20
51 Chaux Fonds Team Card .08 .20
52 Chaux Fonds Team Card .08 .20
53 Dan Hober .08 .20
54 Thomas Berger .08 .20
55 Gilles Cattela .08 .20
56 Pascal Avanthay .08 .20
57 Raphael Brusa .08 .20
58 Fabian Guignard .08 .20
59 Ruedi Niderost .08 .20
60 Roger Ohmann .08 .20
61 Valery Schirjaev .08 .20
62 Alexis Vacheron .08 .20
63 Steve Aebersold .08 .20
64 Thomas Derungs .08 .20
65 Claude Luthi .08 .20
66 Fabrice Maillat .08 .20
67 Thibaut Monnet .08 .20
68 Daniel Nakaota .08 .20
69 Stefan Nilsson .08 .20
70 Steve Pochon .08 .20
71 Philippe Halmann .08 .20
72 Julien Turler .08 .20
73 Sami Villiger .08 .20
74 Chur Logo .08 .20
75 Chur Team Card .08 .20
76 Chur Team Card .08 .20
77 Mike McParland .08 .20
78 Marco Buhrer .08 .20
79 Nando Wieser .08 .20
80 Noel Guyaz .08 .20
81 Christian Langer .08 .20
82 Ivo Stoffel .08 .20
83 Pasi Sormunen .08 .20
84 Mika Stromberg .08 .20
85 Matthias Bachler .08 .20
86 Fabio Beccarelli .08 .20
87 Patrick Kruger .08 .20
88 Michael Meier .08 .20
89 Daniel Peer .08 .20
90 Roger Rieder .08 .20
91 Michael Rosenast .08 .20
92 Oliver Roth .08 .20
93 Rene Stussi .08 .20
94 Sandro Tschuor .08 .20
95 Harijs Vitolinsh .08 .20
96 Raymond Walder .08 .20
97 Theo Wittmann .08 .20
98 HC Davos Logo .08 .20
99 HC Davos Team Card .08 .20
100 HC Davos Team Card .08 .20
101 Arno Del Curto .08 .20
102 Petter Ronnquist .08 .20
103 Lars Weibel .08 .20
104 Beat Equilino .08 .20
105 Marc Gianola .08 .20
106 Andrea Haller .08 .20
107 Michael Kress .08 .20
108 Kevin Miller .08 .20
109 Ralph Ott .08 .20
110 Jan Von Arx .08 .20
111 Andre Baumann .08 .20
112 Lonny Bohonos .08 .20
113 Pat Falloon .08 .20
114 Patrick Fischer .08 .20
115 Marc Heberlein .08 .20
116 Rene Muller .08 .20
117 Claudio Neff .08 .20
118 Thierry Paterlini .08 .20
119 Sandro Rizzi .08 .20
120 Frederic Rothen .08 .20
121 Mario Schocher .08 .20
122 Gotteron Logo .08 .20
123 Gotteron Team Card .08 .20
124 Gotteron Team Card .08 .20
125 Serge Pelletier .20 .50
126 Thomas Ostlund .20 .50
127 Alain Sansonnens .08 .20
128 Raphael Berger .08 .20
129 Goran Bezina .08 .20
130 Christoph Decurtins .08 .20
131 Antoine Descloux .08 .20
132 Livio Fazio .08 .20
133 Philippe Marquis .08 .20
134 Martin Rauch .08 .20
135 Marc Werlen .08 .20
136 Craig Ferguson .08 .20
137 Lars Leuenberger .08 .20
138 Silvan Lussy .08 .20
139 Gil Montandon .08 .20
140 Michel Mouther .08 .20
141 Mario Rottaris .08 .20
142 Jean Yves Roy .08 .20
143 Pascal Schaller .08 .20
144 Robert Slehofer .08 .20
145 Gerd Zenhausern .08 .20
146 Kloten Logo .08 .20
147 Kloten Team Card .08 .20
148 Kloten Team Card .08 .20
149 Vladimir Yursinov CO .08 .20
150 Reto Pavoni .20 .50
151 Martin Hohener .08 .20
152 Ronny Keller .08 .20
153 Marko Kiprusoff .08 .20
154 Marco Kloti .08 .20
155 Dejan Lozanov .08 .20
156 Oskar Szczepaniec .08 .20
157 Beni Winkler .08 .20
158 Sven Helfenstein .08 .20
159 Felix Hollenstein .08 .20
160 Andy Keller .08 .20
161 Sven Lindemann .08 .20
162 Andreas Nauser .08 .20
163 Fredrik Nilsson .08 .20
164 Martin Pluss .08 .20
165 Sebastian Reuille .08 .20
166 Andy Rufener .08 .20
167 Adi Wichser .08 .20
168 Thomas Widmer .08 .20
169 Mathias Wust .08 .20
170 Langnau Logo .08 .20
171 Langnau Team Card .08 .20
172 Langnau Team Card .08 .20
173 Bengt Ake Gustafsson .08 .20
174 Martin Gerber .75 2.00
175 Martin Zerzuben .08 .20
176 Daniel Aegerter .08 .20
177 Samuel Balmer .08 .20
178 Steve Hirschi .08 .20
179 Erik Kakko .08 .20
180 Pascal Muller .08 .20
181 Pascal Stoller .08 .20
182 Florian Andenmatten .08 .20
183 Rolf Badertscher .08 .20
184 Bruno Brechbuhl .08 .20
185 John Fust .08 .20
186 Daniel Gauthier .08 .20
187 Thomas Heldner .08 .20
188 Matthias Holzer .08 .20
189 Michael Neininger .08 .20
190 Benoit Pont .08 .20
191 Vlastimil Plavucha .08 .20
192 Daniel Steiner .08 .20
193 Stefan Tschiemer .08 .20
194 Lugano Logo .08 .20
195 Lugano Team Card .08 .20
196 Lugano Team Card .08 .20
197 Jim Koleff .08 .20
198 Cristobal Huet .08 5.00
199 Peter Martin .08 .20
200 Peter Andersson .08 .20
201 Mark Astley .08 .20
202 Sandro Bertaggia .08 .20
203 Olivier Keller .08 .20
204 Rick Tschumi .08 .20
205 Gaetan Voisard .08 .20
206 Jean-Jacques Aeschlimann .08 .20
207 Misko Antisin .08 .20
208 Philippe Bozon .40 1.00
209 Flavien Conne .08 .20
210 Christian Dube .08 .20
211 Keith Fair .08 .20
212 Igor Fedulov .08 .20
213 Regis Fuchs .08 .20
214 Sandy Jeannin .08 .20
215 Trevor Meier .08 .20
216 Andy Naser .08 .20
217 Geoffrey Vauclair .08 .20
218 Rapperswil Logo .08 .20
219 Rapperswil Team Card .08 .20
220 Rapperswil Team Card .08 .20
221 Evgeny Popikhin .08 .20
222 Claudio Bayer .08 .20
223 Matthias Lauber .08 .20
224 Marco Capaul .08 .20
225 Jakub Horak .08 .20
226 Kari Martikainen .08 .20
227 Jorg Reber .08 .20
228 Alain Reist .08 .20
229 Roger Sigg .08 .20
230 Loic Burkhalter .08 .20
231 Markus Butler .08 .20
232 Rene Friedli .08 .20
233 Rene Furler .08 .20
234 Dani Giger .08 .20
235 Sandro Haberlin .08 .20
236 Axel Heim .08 .20
237 Philppe Luber .08 .20
238 Dale McTavish .08 .20
239 Patrizio Morger .08 .20
240 Mike Richard .08 .20
241 Bernhard Schumperli .08 .20
242 EVZ Logo .08 .20
243 EVZ Team Card .08 .20
244 EVZ Team Card .08 .20
245 Andre Peloffy .08 .20
246 Ronnie Rueger .08 .20
247 Patrick Schopf .08 .20
248 Marco Bayer .08 .20
249 Ralph Bundi .08 .20
250 Patrick Fischer .08 .20
251 Dino Kessler .08 .20
252 Andre Kunzi .08 .20
253 Reto Kobach .08 .20
254 Patrick Sutter .08 .20
255 Christophe Brown .08 .20
256 Paul Di Pietro .20 .50
257 Todd Elik .08 .20
258 Stefan Grogg .08 .20
259 Vjeran Ivankovic .08 .20
260 Daniel Meier .08 .20
261 Stefan Niggli .08 .20
262 Patrick Oppliger .08 .20
263 Andre Rotheli .08 .20
264 Sascha Schneider .08 .20
265 Chris Tancill .08 .20
266 ZSC Logo .08 .20
267 ZSC Team Card .08 .20
268 ZSC Team Card .08 .20
269 Larry Hurras .08 .20
270 Thomas Papp .08 .20
271 Ari Sulander .20 .50
272 Martin Kout .08 .20
273 Adrien Plavsic .08 .20
274 Edgar Salis .08 .20
275 Mathias Seger .08 .20
276 Bruno Seck .08 .20
277 Andreas Zehnder .08 .20
278 Mattia Baldi .08 .20
279 Gian Marco Crameri .08 .20
280 Partric Della Rossa .08 .20
281 Daniel Hodgson .08 .20
282 Peter Jaks .08 .20
283 Andrew McKim .20 .50
284 Claudio Micheli .08 .20
285 Laurent Muller .08 .20
286 Mark Ouimet .08 .20
287 Rolf Schrepfer .08 .20
288 Reto Stirnimann .08 .20
289 Michel Zeiter .08 .20
290 HC Ajoie Logo .08 .20
291 Yann Voillat .08 .20
292 Chris Belanger .08 .20
293 EHC Basel Logo .08 .20
294 Todd Wetzel .08 .20
295 Patrick Girard .08 .20
296 EHC Biel Logo .08 .20
297 Sven Schmid .08 .20
298 Kevin Schlapfer .08 .20
299 GCK Lions Logo .08 .20
300 Patrick Looser .08 .20
301 Mikko Myllykoski .08 .20
302 HC Geneve Logo .08 .20
303 Patrice Brasey .08 .20
304 Scott Beattie .08 .20
305 SC Herisau Logo .08 .20
306 Andy Karpf .08 .20
307 Patrick Amann .08 .20
308 HC Lausanne Logo .08 .20
309 Beat Kindler .08 .20
310 Serge Poudrier .08 .20
311 EHC Olten Logo .08 .20
312 Beat Aebischer .08 .20
313 Richard Stucki .08 .20
314 HC Sierre Logo .08 .20
315 Jean Michel Clavien .08 .20
316 Gaby Epiney .08 .20
317 HC Thurgau Logo .08 .20
318 Martin Bruderer .08 .20
319 Morgan Samuelsson .08 .20
320 EHC Visp Logo .08 .20
321 Stefan Ketola .08 .20
322 Gabriel Taccoz .08 .20

2000-01 Swiss Slapshot Mini-Cards

COMPLETE SET (192) 20.00 40.00
LT1 Martin Gerber 2.00 5.00
LT2 Daniel Aegerter .10 .25
LT3 Samuel Balmer .10 .25
LT4 Beat Gerber .10 .25
LT5 Steve Hirschi .10 .25
LT6 Erik Kakko .10 .25
LT7 Pascal Muller .10 .25
LT8 Pascal Stoller .10 .25
LT9 Rolf Badertscher .10 .25
LT10 Bruno Brechbuhl .10 .25
LT11 John Fust .10 .25
LT12 Daniel Gauthier .10 .25
LT13 Thomas Heldner .10 .25
LT14 Matthias Holzer .10 .25
LT15 Vlastimil Plavucha .10 .25
LT16 Benoit Pont .10 .25
RJ1 Claudio Bayer .10 .25
RJ2 Marco Capaul .10 .25
RJ3 Kari Martikainen .10 .25
RJ4 Roger Sigg .10 .25
RJ5 Jorg Reber .10 .25
RJ6 LoÃ¯c Burkhalter .10 .25
RJ7 Markus Butler .10 .25
RJ8 Rene Friedli .10 .25
RJ9 Rene Furler .10 .25
RJ10 Daniel Giger .10 .25
RJ11 Axel Heim .10 .25
RJ12 Philipp Luber .10 .25
RJ13 Dale McTavish .10 .25
RJ14 Patrizio Morger .10 .25
RJ15 Mike Richard .10 .25
RJ16 Bernhard Schumperli .10 .25
EVZ1 Ronnie Rueger .10 .25
EVZ2 Patrick Schopf .10 .25
EVZ3 Marco Bayer .10 .25
EVZ4 Patrick Fischer .10 .25
EVZ5 Dino Kessler .10 .25
EVZ6 Andre Kunzi .10 .25
EVZ7 Patrick Sutter .10 .25
EVZ8 Paul Di Pietro .20 .50
EVZ9 Todd Elik .20 .50
EVZ10 Stefan Grogg .10 .25
EVZ11 Vjeran Ivankovic .10 .25
EVZ12 Daniel Meier .10 .25
EVZ13 Patrick Oppliger .10 .25
EVZ14 Andre Rotheli .10 .25
EVZ15 Sascha Schneider .10 .25
EVZ16 Chris Tancill .10 .25
HCD1 Lars Weibel .20 .50
HCD2 Beat Equilino .10 .25
HCD3 Marc Gianola .10 .25
HCD4 Andreas HÃ¤ller .10 .25
HCD5 Ralph Ott .10 .25
HCD6 Jan Von Arx .10 .25
HCD7 Andre Baumann .10 .25
HCD8 Lonny Bohonos .20 .50
HCD9 Patrick Fischer .10 .25
HCD10 Kevin Miller .20 .50
HCD11 Rene Muller .10 .25
HCD12 Thierry Paterlini .10 .25
HCD13 Sandro Rizzi .10 .25
HCD14 Frederic Rothen .10 .25
HCD15 Mario Schocher .10 .25
HCD16 Pat Falloon .20 .50
HCL1 Cristobal Huet 2.00 5.00
HCL2 Peter Anderson .10 .25
HCL3 Igor Fedulov .10 .25
HCL4 Sandro Bertaggia .10 .25
HCL5 Olivier Keller .10 .25
HCL6 Julien Vauclair .10 .25
HCL7 Gaetan Voisard .10 .25
HCL8 J.-Jacques Aeschlimann .10 .25
HCL9 Misko Antisin .10 .25
HCL10 Philippe Bozon .40 1.00
HCL11 Jan-Philippe Cadieux .10 .25
HCL12 Flavien Conne .10 .25
HCL13 Christian Dube .10 .25
HCL14 Regis Fuchs .10 .25
HCL15 Sandy Jeannin .10 .25
HCL16 Keith Fair .10 .25
SCB1 Renato Tosio .10 .25
SCB2 David Jobin .10 .25
SCB3 Sven Leuenberger .10 .25
SCB4 Dominic Meier .10 .25
SCB5 Frederik Olausson .10 .25
SCB6 Martin Steinegger .10 .25
SCB7 Rolf Ziegler .10 .25
SCB8 Bjorn Christen .10 .25
SCB9 Patrick Howald .10 .25
SCB10 Andreas Johansson .10 .25
SCB11 Patrick Juhlin .10 .25
SCB12 Alex Chatelain .10 .25
SCB13 Boris Leimgruber .10 .25
SCB14 Ivo Ruthemann .10 .25
SCB15 Franz Steffen .10 .25
SCB16 Marc Weber .10 .25
EHCC1 Nando Wieser .10 .25
EHCC2 Noel Guyaz .10 .25
EHCC3 Christian Langer .10 .25
EHCC4 Ivo Stoffel .10 .25
EHCC5 Mika Stromberg .10 .25
EHCC6 Pasi Sormunen .10 .25
EHCC7 Matthias Bachler .10 .25
EHCC8 Patrick Kruger .10 .25
EHCC9 Michael Meier .10 .25
EHCC10 Michael Rosenast .10 .25
EHCC11 Oliver Roth .10 .25
EHCC12 Marc Haueter .10 .25
EHCC13 Sandro Tschuor .10 .25
EHCC14 Raymond Walder .10 .25
EHCC15 Theo Wittmann .10 .25
EHCC16 UNKNOWN .10 .25
EHCK1 Reto Pavoni .10 .25
EHCK2 Martin Hohener .10 .25
EHCK3 Marko Kiprusoff .10 .25
EHCK4 Marco Kloti .10 .25
EHCK5 Oskar Szcepaniec .10 .25
EHCK6 UNKNOWN .10 .25
EHCK7 Fredrik Nilsson .10 .25
EHCK8 Sven Helfenstein .10 .25
EHCK9 Felix Hollenstein .10 .25
EHCK10 Andy Keller .10 .25
EHCK11 Sven Lindemann .10 .25
EHCK12 Martin Pluss .10 .25
EHCK13 Sebastien Reuille .10 .25
EHCK14 Andre Rufener .10 .25
EHCK15 Steve Washburn .10 .25
EHCK16 Adrian Wichser .10 .25
HCAP1 Pauli Jaks .10 .25
HCAP2 Fredy Bobillier .10 .25
HCAP3 Ivan Gazzaroli .10 .25
HCAP4 Tiziano Gianini .10 .25
HCAP5 Thomas Kunzi .10 .25
HCAP6 Leif Rohlin .10 .25
HCAP7 Krister Cantoni .10 .25
HCAP8 Manuele Celio .10 .25
HCAP9 Nicola Celio .10 .25
HCAP10 Alain Demuth .10 .25
HCAP11 Paolo Duca .10 .25
HCAP12 John Fritsche .10 .25
HCAP13 Ryan Gardner .10 .25
HCAP14 Paolo Imperatori .10 .25
HCAP15 Stephan Lebeau .20 .50
HCAP16 Daniel Marois .20 .50
HCCF1 Thomas Berger .10 .25
HCCF2 Raphael Brusa .10 .25
HCCF3 Fabian Guignard .10 .25
HCCF4 Valeri Shiryaev .10 .25
HCCF5 Ruedi Niderost .10 .25
HCCF6 Roger Ohmann .10 .25
HCCF7 Alexis Vacheron .10 .25
HCCF8 Steve Aebersold .10 .25
HCCF9 Thomas Derungs .10 .25
HCCF10 Claude Luthi .10 .25
HCCF11 Fabrice Maillat .10 .25
HCCF12 Daniel Nakaoka .10 .25
HCCF13 Stefan Nilsson .10 .25
HCCF14 Julien Turler .10 .25
HCCF15 Samuel Villiger .10 .25
HCCF16 Thibaut Monnet .10 .25
HCFG1 Thomas Ostlund .20 .50
HCFG2 Goran Bezina .10 .25
HCFG3 Antonie Descloux .10 .25
HCFG4 Livio Fazio .10 .25
HCFG5 Philippe Marquis .10 .25
HCFG6 Martin Rauch .10 .25
HCFG7 Marc Werlen .10 .25
HCFG8 Craig Ferguson .10 .25
HCFG9 Lars Leuenberger .10 .25
HCFG10 Gil Montandon .10 .25
HCFG11 Mario Rottaris .10 .25
HCFG12 Jean-Yves Roy .10 .25
HCFG13 Pascal Schaller .10 .25
HCFG14 Robert Slehofer .10 .25
HCFG15 Gerd ZenhÃ¤usern .10 .25
HCFG16 Michel Mouther .10 .25
ZSCL1 Ari Sulander .20 .50
ZSCL2 Adrien Plavsic .10 .25
ZSCL3 Edgar Salis .10 .25
ZSCL4 Matthias Seger .10 .25
ZSCL5 Mark Streit .20 .50
ZSCL6 Andreas Zehnder .10 .25
ZSCL7 Mattia Baldi .10 .25
ZSCL8 Gian Marco Crameri .10 .25
ZSCL9 Patric Della Rossa .10 .25
ZSCL10 Dan Hodgson .10 .25
ZSCL11 Peter Jaks .10 .25
ZSCL12 Andrew McKim .20 .50
ZSCL13 Claudio Micheli .10 .25
ZSCL14 Laurent Muller .10 .25
ZSCL15 Rolf Schrepfer .10 .25
ZSCL16 Michel Zeiter .10 .25

2001-02 Swiss EV Zug Postcards

These unnumbered 4X6 postcards were issued by the team and feature stylized action photos.

COMPLETE SET (27) 10.00 25.00
1 Team photo .40 1.00
2 Doug Mason .40 1.00
3 Richmond Gosselin .40 1.00
4 Patrick Schopf .40 1.00
5 Ronnie Rueger .40 1.00
6 Ruedi Niderost .40 1.00
7 Ralf Bundi .40 1.00
8 Patrick Fischer .40 1.00
9 Fabio Schumacher .40 1.00
10 Pascal Muller .40 1.00
11 Arne Ramholt .40 1.00
12 Kevin Gloor .40 1.00
13 Andre Kunzi .40 1.00
14 Reto Kobach .40 1.00
15 Thomas Nussli .40 1.00
16 Stefan Voegele .40 1.00
17 Stefan Niggli .40 1.00
18 Duri Camichel .40 1.00
19 Vjeran Ivankovic .40 1.00
20 Patrick Oppliger .40 1.00
21 Frederic Rothen .40 1.00
22 Stefan Grogg .40 1.00
23 Christoph Brown .40 1.00
24 Chris Tancill .75 2.00
25 Todd Elik .75 2.00
26 Joel Savage .75 2.00
27 Paul DiPietro .75 2.00

2001-02 Swiss HNL

This series features the top players in the Swiss Elite League, one of the top European circuits.

COMPLETE SET (480) 30.00 75.00
1 Larry Huras .10 .25
2 Thomas Papp .10 .25
3 Ari Sulander .40 1.00
4 Martin Kout .10 .25
5 Adrian Plavsic .10 .25
6 Tim Ramholt .60 1.50
7 Edgar Salis .10 .25
8 Mathias Seger .10 .25
9 Bruno Steck .10 .25
10 Mark Streit .10 .25
11 Jan Alston .20 .50
12 Mattia Baldi .10 .25
13 Gian-Marco Crameri .10 .25
14 Patric Della Rossa .10 .25
15 Paolo Duca .10 .25
16 Dan Hodgson .20 .50
17 Peter Jaks .10 .25
18 Claudio Micheli .10 .25
19 Mark Ouimet .20 .50
20 Morgan Samuelsson .10 .25
21 Stefan Schnyder .10 .25
22 Reto Stirnimann .10 .25
23 Petri Varis .20 .50
24 Michel Zeiter .10 .25
25 Zinetoula Bilyaletdinov .10 .25
26 Paolo Della Bella .10 .25
27 Cristobal Huet ERC 1.60 5.00
28 Mark Astley .20 .50
29 Sandro Bertaggia .10 .25
30 Olivier Keller .10 .25
31 Petteri Nummelin .10 .25
32 Patrick Sutter .10 .25
33 Rick Tschumi .10 .25
34 Gaetan Voisard .10 .25
35 Jean-Jacques Aeschlimann .10 .25
36 Jan Cadieux .10 .25
37 Gregory Christen .10 .25
38 Flavien Conne .10 .25
39 Christian Dube .10 .25
40 Keith Fair .10 .25
41 Regis Fuchs .10 .25
42 Ryan Gardner .20 .50
43 Sandy Jeannin .10 .25
44 Mike Maneluk .20 .50
45 Andy Naser .10 .25
46 Andre Rotheli .10 .25
47 Raffaele Sannitz .30 .75
48 Geoffrey Vauclair .10 .25
49 Kloten-Flyers .10 .25
50 Vladimir Jursinov .10 .25
51 Flavio Ludke .10 .25
52 Reto Pavoni .20 .50
53 Severin Blindenbacher .10 .25
54 Manuel Gossweiler .10 .25
55 Fabian Guignard .10 .25
56 Roman Hardmeier .10 .25
57 Martin Hohener .10 .25
58 Ronny Keller .10 .25
59 Chris O'Sullivan .20 .50
60 Gregor Thommen .10 .25
61 Mathias Wust .10 .25
62 Andre Bielmann .10 .25
63 Patrik Bartschi .10 .25
64 Andreas Cellar .10 .25
65 Felix Hollenstein .10 .25

66 Andy Keller .10 .25
67 Dario Kostovic .10 .25
68 Sven Lindemann .10 .25
69 Fredrik Nilsson .10 .25
70 Emanuel Peter .10 .25
71 Martin Pluss .10 .25
72 Kimmo Rintanen .10 .25
73 Adrian Wichser .30 .75
74 Thomas Widmer .10 .25
75 Riccardo Fuhrer .10 .25
76 Marco Buhrer .20 .50
77 Andreas Schweizer .10 .25
78 Rikard Franzen .10 .25
79 David Jobin .10 .25
80 Sven Leuenberger .10 .25
81 Marc Leuenberger .10 .25
82 Dominic Meier .10 .25
83 Martin Steinegger .10 .25
84 Rolf Ziegler .10 .25
85 Derek Armstrong .20 .50
86 Andre Baumann .10 .25
87 Alex Chatelain .10 .25
88 Sven Helfenstein .10 .25
89 Patrik Juhlin .20 .50
90 Laurent Muller .10 .25
91 Philippe Muller .10 .25
92 Marc Reichert .10 .25
93 Ivo Ruthemann .10 .25
94 Rolf Schrepfer .10 .25
95 Franz Steffen .10 .25
96 Fabian Sutter .10 .25
97 Marc Weber .10 .25
98 Arno Del Curto .10 .25
99 Jonas Hiller .10 .25
100 Lars Weibel .20 .50
101 Beat Equilino .10 .25
102 Beat Forster .10 .25
103 Marc Gianola .10 .25
104 Andrea Haller .10 .25
105 Michael Kress .10 .25
106 Ralph Ott .10 .25
107 Jan von Arx .10 .25
108 Benjamin Winkler .10 .25
109 Andres Ambuhl .10 .25
110 Lonny Bohonos .20 .50
111 Andreas Camenzind .10 .25
112 Bjorn Christen .10 .25
113 Patrick Fischer .10 .25
114 Joel Frohlicher .10 .25
115 Stefan Gahler .10 .25
116 Marc Heberlein .10 .25
117 Josef Marha .10 .25
118 Kevin Miller .20 .50
119 Rene Muller .10 .25
120 Sandro Rizzi .10 .25
121 Serge Pelletier .10 .25
122 Matthias Lauber .20 .50
123 Gianluca Mona .20 .50
124 RaphaÃ«l Berger .10 .25
125 Antoine Descloux .10 .25
126 Mike Gaul .20 .50
127 Lukas Gerber .10 .25
128 Philippe Marquis .10 .25
129 Martin Rauch .10 .25
130 Marc Werlen .10 .25
131 Craig Ferguson .20 .50
132 Gilbert Flueler .10 .25
133 Christof Hiltebrand .10 .25
134 Patrick Howald .10 .25
135 Lars Leuenberger .10 .25
136 Silvan Lussy .10 .25
137 David Maurer .10 .25
138 Thibaut Monnet .10 .25
139 Gil Montandon .10 .25
140 Michel Mouther .10 .25
141 Mario Rottaris .10 .25
142 Jean-Yves Roy .20 .50
143 Robert Slehofer .10 .25
144 Colin Muller .10 .25
145 Evgeni Popichin .10 .25
146 Thomas Berger .20 .50
147 Simon Zuger .20 .50
148 Marco Capaul .10 .25
149 Livio Fazio .10 .25
150 Jakub Horak .10 .25
151 Kari Martikainen .10 .25
152 Alain Reist .10 .25
153 Marc Schefer .10 .25
154 Fabian Stephan .10 .25
155 Markus Butler .10 .25
156 Rene Friedli .10 .25
157 Daniel Giger .10 .25
158 Axel Heim .10 .25
159 Philipp Luber .10 .25
160 Dale McTavish .20 .50
161 Claudio Moggi .10 .25
162 Sandro Moggi .10 .25
163 Patrizio Morger .10 .25
164 Sebastien Reuille .10 .25
165 Mike Richard .10 .25
166 Morgan Samuelsson .10 .25
167 Doug Mason .10 .25
168 Ronnie Rueger .20 .50
169 Patrick Schopf .20 .50
170 Ralf Bundi .10 .25
171 Patrick Fischer .10 .25
172 Reto Kobach .10 .25
173 Andre Kunzi .10 .25
174 Pascal Muller .10 .25
175 Ruedi Niderost .10 .25
176 Arne Ramholt .10 .25
177 Fabio Schumacher .10 .25
178 Christophe Brown .10 .25
179 Duri Camichel .10 .25
180 Paul Di Pietro .20 .50
181 Todd Elik .20 .50
182 Stefan Grogg .10 .25
183 Vjeran Ivankovic .10 .25
184 Stefan Niggli .10 .25
185 Thomas Nussli .10 .25
186 Patrick Oppliger .10 .25
187 Frederic Rothen .10 .25
188 Joel Savage .20 .50
189 Chris Tancill .20 .50
190 Vassily Tikhonov .10 .25
191 Claudio Bayer .20 .50
192 Marco Streit .20 .50
193 Daniel Aegerter .10 .25
194 Samuel Balmer .10 .25
195 Beat Gerber .10 .25
196 Steve Hirschi .10 .25
197 Erik Hamalainen .10 .25
198 Thomas Kunzi .10 .25
199 Pascal Stoller .10 .25
200 Rolf Badertscher .10 .25
201 Brian Bonin .20 .50
202 Bruno Brechbuhl .10 .25
203 John Fust .10 .25
204 Daniel Gauthier .10 .25
205 Thomas Heldner .10 .25
206 Matthias Holzer .10 .25
207 Benjamin Pluss .10 .25
208 Benoit Pont .10 .25
209 Bernhard Schumperli .10 .25
210 Daniel Steiner .10 .25
211 Rostislav Cada .10 .25
212 Lorenzo Barenco .10 .25
213 Pauli Jaks .20 .50
214 Marco Bayer .10 .25
215 Nicola Celio .10 .25
216 Ivan Gazzaroli .10 .25
217 Tiziano Gianini .10 .25
218 John Gobbi .10 .25
219 Andreas Hanni .10 .25
220 Martin Stepanek .10 .25
221 LoÃ¯c Burkhalter .10 .25
222 Corsin Camichel .10 .25
223 Krister Cantoni .10 .25
224 Manuele Celio .10 .25
225 Alain Demuth .10 .25
226 John Fritsche .10 .25
227 Paolo Imperatori .10 .25
228 Roland Kaser .10 .25
229 Vitaly Lakhmatov .10 .25
230 Michel Liniger .10 .25
231 Robert Petrovicky .10 .25
232 Omar Tognini .10 .25
233 Tomas Vlasak .10 .25
234 Niklas Wikegard .10 .25
235 Tobias Stephan .80 3.00
236 Nando Wieser .10 .25
237 Rene Back .10 .25
238 Cyrill Geyer .10 .25
239 Noel Guyaz .10 .25
240 Marc Haueter .10 .25
241 Ivo Stoffel .10 .25
242 Mika Stromberg .10 .25
243 Andreas Zehnder .10 .25
244 Fabio Beccarelli .10 .25
245 Matthias Bachler .10 .25
246 Kristian Gahn .10 .25
247 Patrick Kruger .10 .25
248 Michael Meier .10 .25
249 Daniel Peer .10 .25
250 Roger Rieder .10 .25
251 Oliver Roth .10 .25
252 Ivo Simeon .10 .25
253 Rene Stussi .10 .25
254 Sandro Tschuor .10 .25
255 Johan Witehall .10 .25
256 Theo Wittmann .10 .25
257 HC Lausanne .10 .25
258 Mike McParland .10 .25
259 Beat Kindler .20 .50
260 Reto Schurch .20 .50
261 Malik Benturqui .10 .25
262 Michel Kamber .10 .25
263 Dejan Lozanov .10 .25
264 Michel N'Goy .10 .25
265 Serge Poudrier .10 .25
266 Roger Sigg .10 .25
267 Thomas Studer .10 .25
268 Oliver Tschanz .10 .25
269 Florian Andenmatten .10 .25
270 Andrei Bashkirov .20 .50
271 Daniel Bieri .10 .25
272 Thierry Bornand .10 .25
273 Sandro Haberlin .10 .25
274 Oliver Kamber .10 .25
275 Trevor Meier .10 .25
276 Philippe Orlandi .10 .25
277 Dmitri Shamolin .10 .25
278 Samuel Villiger .10 .25
279 Sacha Weibel .20 .50
280 Gerd Zenhausern .10 .25
281 Michel Lussier .10 .25
282 Gilles Cattela .10 .25
283 Thierry Noel .10 .25
284 Oliver Amadio .10 .25
285 Pascal Avanthay .10 .25
286 Nicolas Bernasconi .10 .25
287 RaphaÃ«l Brusa .10 .25
288 Valeri Chiriaev .10 .25
289 Marc Tschudy .10 .25
290 Alexis Vacheron .10 .25
291 Steve Aebersold .10 .25
292 Jesse Belanger .20 .50
293 Thomas Deruns .10 .25
294 Jamie Heinrich .10 .25
295 Vincent Lechenne .10 .25
296 Claude Luethi .10 .25
297 Fabrice Maillat .10 .25
298 Daniel Nakaoka .10 .25
299 Michael Neininger .10 .25
300 Philippe Thalmann .10 .25
301 Markus Graf .10 .25
302 Marco Wegmuller .20 .50
303 Martin Zerzuben .10 .25
304 Sven Dick .10 .25
305 Serge Meyer .10 .25
306 Jorg Reber .10 .25
307 Sven Schmid .10 .25
308 Bjorn Schneider .10 .25
309 Pascal Sommer .10 .25
310 Mauro Beccarelli .10 .25
311 Philipp Folghera .10 .25
312 Rene Furler .10 .25
313 Stefan Moser .10 .25
314 Andreas Nauser .10 .25
315 Cyrill Pasche .10 .25
316 Reggie Savage .20 .50
317 Ryan Savoia .20 .50
318 Kevin Schlapfer .10 .25
319 Marco Signer .10 .25
320 Stefan Tschiemer .10 .25
321 Chris McSorley .10 .25
322 David Bochy .20 .50
323 Flavio Streit .10 .25
324 Fredy Bobillier .10 .25
325 Patrice Brasey .10 .25
326 Fabian Gull .10 .25
327 David Leibzig .10 .25
328 Todd Richards .20 .50
329 Nicolas Studer .10 .25
330 Misko Antisin .10 .25
331 Philippe Bozon .40 2.00
332 Igor Fedulov .10 .25
333 Marco Fischer .10 .25
334 Xavier Gattuso .10 .25
335 Maxime Lapointe .10 .25
336 Boris Leimgruber .10 .25
337 Paul Savary .10 .25
338 Didier Schafer .10 .25
339 Pascal Schaller .10 .25
340 Mario Schocher .10 .25
341 Bruno Aegerter .10 .25
342 Rainer Karlen .10 .25
343 Marc Zimmermann .20 .50
344 Beat Heldstab .10 .25
345 Karl Knopf .10 .25
346 Philipp Portner .10 .25
347 Francis Reichmuth .10 .25
348 Marco Schupbach .10 .25
349 Marc Zurbriggen .10 .25
350 Patrick Aeberli .10 .25
351 Sergio Biner .10 .25
352 Marc Buhlmann .10 .25
353 Nicolas Gastaldo .10 .25
354 Stefan Ketola .10 .25
355 Swen Kohler .10 .25
356 Richard Laplante .10 .25
357 Cedric Metrailler .10 .25
358 Detlef Prediger .10 .25
359 Gabriel Taccoz .10 .25
360 Ken Zurfluh .10 .25
361 Arnold Lortscher .10 .25
362 Beat Aebischer .10 .25
363 Rainer Kalin .10 .25
364 Francesco Bizzozero .10 .25
365 Christoph Decurtins .10 .25
366 Mark Emmenegger .10 .25
367 Ruedi Forster .10 .25
368 Jurg Hardegger .10 .25
369 Richard Stucki .10 .25
370 Stefan Wuthrich .10 .25
371 Alain Ayer .10 .25
372 Yanick Dube .10 .25
373 Reto Germann .10 .25
374 Patrick Giroud .10 .25
375 Bjorn Guazzini .10 .25
376 Albert Malgin .10 .25
377 Oliver Muller .10 .25
378 Patrick Siegwart .10 .25
379 Andre von Rohr .10 .25
380 Matti Alatalo .10 .25
381 Christian Weber .10 .25
382 Marc Eichmann .10 .25
383 Matthias Schoder .20 .50
384 Stefan Badrutt .10 .25
385 Chris Belanger .10 .25
386 Thomi Derungs .10 .25
387 Michael Hofer .10 .25
388 Andri Stoffel .10 .25
389 Andreas Furrer .10 .25
390 Lukas Grauwiler .10 .25
391 Rolf Hildebrand .10 .25
392 Alex Krstic .10 .25
393 Patrick Landolt .10 .25
394 Patrick Looser .10 .25
395 Dean Seymour .10 .25
396 Riccardo Signorell .10 .25
397 Pascal Tiegermann .10 .25
398 Thomas Walser .10 .25
399 Simon Wanner .10 .25
400 Merlin Malinowski .10 .25
401 Olivier Gigon .10 .25
402 Sebastien Kohler .20 .50
403 Ludovic Aubry .10 .25
404 Eric Bourquin .10 .25
405 Dany Ott .10 .25
406 Christian Schuster .10 .25
407 Wes Snell .10 .25
408 Markus Wuthrich .10 .25
409 Steven Barras .10 .25
410 Martin Bergeron .10 .25
411 Scott Biser .10 .25
412 Florian Conz .10 .25
413 Real Gerber .10 .25
414 Sacha Guerne .10 .25
415 Shawn Heaphy .10 .25
416 JerÃ´me Kohler .10 .25
417 Jean-Charles Lapaire .10 .25
418 Boe Leslie .10 .25
419 Steve Pochon .10 .25
420 Yann Voillat .10 .25
421 Didier Massy .10 .25
422 Gregory Berclaz .10 .25
423 Roland Meyer .10 .25
424 Johan Bertholet .10 .25
425 Lionel D'Urso .10 .25
426 Cedric Favre .10 .25
427 Jonathan Lussier .10 .25
428 Pietro Ottini .10 .25
429 Emmanuel Tacchini .10 .25
430 Beat Brantschen .10 .25
431 Elvis Clavien .10 .25
432 Gaby Epiney .10 .25
433 Kelly Glowa .10 .25
434 Pietro Juri .10 .25
435 Daniel Mares .10 .25
436 Cedric Melly .10 .25
437 Thierry Metrailler .10 .25
438 Fabrizio Silietti .10 .25
439 Daniel Wobmann .10 .25
440 Raymond Zahnd .10 .25
441 Christian Ruegg .10 .25
442 Matthias Muller .10 .25
443 Pascal Sievert .10 .25
444 Claude Amstutz .10 .25
445 Roland Kradolfer .10 .25
446 Pascal Lamprecht .10 .25
447 Patrick Mader .10 .25
448 Michael Marki .10 .25
449 Alessandro Sellitto .10 .25
450 Daniel Sigg .10 .25
451 Rico Beltrame .10 .25
452 Marius Brugger .10 .25
453 Joel Camenzind .10 .25
454 Michael Diener .10 .25
455 Timmy Hoppe .10 .25
456 Roland Korsch .10 .25
457 Real Raemy .10 .25
458 Marco Seeholzer .10 .25
459 Harijs Vitolinsch .10 .25
460 Jacques Zimmermann .10 .25
461 Beat Lautenschlager .10 .25
462 Davide Gislimberti .10 .25
463 Peter Mettler .20 .50
464 Marc Gautschi .10 .25
465 Zbynek Hybler .10 .25
466 Stephane Julien .10 .25
467 Kim Scheidegger .10 .25
468 Olivier Schaublin .10 .25
469 Dominik Z'berg .10 .25
470 Philipp Dornbierer .10 .25
471 Patrick Girod .10 .25
472 Marco Graf .10 .25
473 Andreas Haner .10 .25
474 Michael Murer .10 .25
475 Robert Othmann .10 .25
476 Steve Potvin .10 .25
477 David Raissle .10 .25
478 Jarkko Schaublin .10 .25
479 Lovis Schonenberger .10 .25
480 Marcel Sommer .10 .25

2002-03 Swiss EV Zug Postcards

These unnumbered 4X6 postcards were issued by the team and feature stylized action photos on the front.

COMPLETE SET (26) 10.00 25.00
1 Team photo .40 1.00
2 Doug Mason .40 1.00
3 Chris Tancill .75 2.00
4 Paul DiPietro .75 2.00
5 Richmond Gosselin .40 1.00
6 Patrick Schopf .40 1.00
7 Peter Mettler .40 1.00
8 Ruedi Niderost .40 1.00
9 Ralf Bundi .40 1.00
10 Charles Simard .40 1.00
11 Patrick Fischer .40 1.00
12 Fabio Schumacher .40 1.00
13 Pascal Muller .40 1.00
14 Gaetan Voisard .40 1.00
15 Lovis Schonenberger .40 1.00
16 Stefan Voegele .40 1.00
17 Stefan Niggli .40 1.00
18 Duri Camichel .40 1.00
19 Patrick Oppliger .40 1.00
20 Paolo Duca .40 1.00
21 Andre Rufener .40 1.00
22 Alain Demuth .40 1.00
23 Oliver Kamber .40 1.00
24 Frederic Rothen .40 1.00
25 Joel Savage .75 2.00
26 Chris Armstrong .40 1.00

2002-03 Swiss HNL

This series features the top players in the Swiss Elite League, one of the top European circuits. The set features top prospects Tobias Stephan and Tim Ramholt.

COMPLETE SET (499) 30.00 75.00
1 Lars Weibel .20 .50
2 Andrea Haller .10 .25
3 Jonas Hiller .10 .25
4 Jan von Arx .10 .25
5 Lonny Bohonos .20 .50
6 Marco Gruber .10 .25
7 Marc Gianola .10 .25
8 Josef Marha .10 .25
9 Michel Riesen .80 1.00
10 Reto von Arx .20 .50
11 Ralph Ott .10 .25
12 Ari Sulander .40 1.00
13 Martin Kout .10 .25
14 Edgar Salis .10 .25
15 Andres Ambuhl .10 .25
16 Jan Alston .20 .50
17 Gian-Carlo Hendry .10 .25
18 Peter Jaks .10 .25
19 Patrick Fischer .10 .25
20 Mark Ouimet .20 .50
21 Reto Stirnimann .10 .25
22 Davide Gislimberti .10 .25
23 Marc Heberlein .10 .25
24 Sandro Bertaggia .10 .25
25 Olivier Keller .10 .25
26 Jean-Jacques Aeschlimann .10 .25
27 Thierry Paterlini .10 .25
28 Flavien Conne .10 .25
29 Ryan Gardner .20 .50
30 Corey Millen .20 .50
31 Fabian Sutter .10 .25
32 Andre Rotheli .10 .25
33 Vladimir Jursinov .10 .25
34 Lukas Baumgartner .10 .25
35 Matthias Schoder .20 .50
36 Martin Hohener .10 .25
37 Alain Reist .10 .25
38 Deny Bartschi .10 .25
39 Jakub Horak .10 .25
40 Jaroslav Hlinka .10 .25
41 Sven Lindemann .10 .25
42 Marc Reichert .10 .25
43 Tim Ramholt .40 1.00
44 Thomas Widmer .10 .25
45 Gianluca Mona .20 .50
46 Mike Gaul .20 .50
47 Mark Streit .10 .25
48 Philippe Marquis .10 .25
49 Patrick Howald .10 .25
50 David Maurer .10 .25
51 Patric Della Rossa .10 .25
52 Michel Mouther .10 .25
53 Robert Slehofer .10 .25
54 Pauli Jaks .20 .50
55 Dan Hodgson .20 .50
56 Ivan Gazzaroli .10 .25
57 Martin Rauch .10 .25
58 LoÃ¯c Burkhalter .10 .25
59 Claudio Micheli .10 .25
60 Nicola Celio .10 .25
61 Paolo Imperatori .10 .25
62 Robert Petrovicky .10 .25
63 Raeto Raffainer .10 .25
64 Doug Mason .10 .25
65 Chris Armstrong .10 .25
66 Ruedi Niderost .10 .25
67 Jim Koleff .10 .25
68 Duri Camichel .10 .25
69 Paolo Duca .10 .25
70 Patrick Oppliger .10 .25
71 Mark Astley .20 .50
72 Joel Savage .20 .50
73 Stefan Voegele .10 .25
74 Marc Eichmann .10 .25
75 Andreas Hanni .10 .25
76 Marc Leuenberger .10 .25
77 Martin Steinegger .10 .25
78 Alex Chatelain .10 .25
79 Patrick Sutter .10 .25
80 Patrik Juhlin .20 .50
81 Laurent Muller .10 .25
82 Rolf Schrepfer .10 .25
83 Krister Cantoni .10 .25
84 Beat Kindler .20 .50
85 Fredy Bobillier .10 .25
86 Serge Poudrier .10 .25
87 Regis Fuchs .10 .25
88 Florian Andenmatten .10 .25
89 Thierry Bornand .10 .25
90 Philipp Orlandi .10 .25
91 Mike Maneluk .20 .50
92 Sacha Weibel .20 .50
93 Kari Eloranta .20 .50
94 Livio Fazio .10 .25
95 Andy Naser .10 .25
96 Kari Martikainen .10 .25
97 Patrick Aeberli .10 .25
98 Axel Heim .10 .25
99 Adrian Wichser .20 .50
100 Patrizio Morger .10 .25
101 Jarno Peltonen .10 .25
102 Thomas Walser .10 .25
103 Tobias Stephan .60 2.00
104 Marco Streit .20 .50
105 Beat Gerber .10 .25
106 Pascal Stoller .10 .25
107 Fabian Guignard .10 .25
108 Bruno Brechbuhl .10 .25
109 Todd Elik .20 .50
110 Benjamin Pluss .10 .25
111 Marco Kloti .10 .25
112 Bernhard Schumperli .10 .25
113 Fabien Hecquet .10 .25
114 Brett Hauer .20 .50
115 Cyrill Buhler .10 .25
116 Wes Snell .10 .25
117 Misko Antisin .10 .25
118 Gian-Marco Crameri .10 .25
119 Andreas Camenzind .10 .25
120 Daniel Meier .10 .25
121 Paul Savary .10 .25
122 Dario Kostovic .10 .25
123 Michel Lussier .10 .25
124 Romano Lemm .10 .25
125 Oliver Amadio .10 .25
126 Dejan Lozanov .10 .25
127 Emanuel Peter .10 .25
128 Steve Aebersold .10 .25
129 Martin Pluss .10 .25
130 Boris Leimgruber .10 .25
131 Daniel Nakaoka .10 .25
132 Roger Rieder .10 .25
133 Julien Turler .10 .25
134 Kimmo Rintanen .10 .25
135 Martin Zerzuben .10 .25
136 Sven Dick .10 .25
137 Colin Muller .10 .25
138 Bjorn Schneider .10 .25
139 Matthias Lauber .20 .50
140 Mauro Beccarelli .10 .25
141 Stefan Moser .10 .25
142 Raphael Berger .10 .25
143 Kevin Schlapfer .10 .25
144 Alain Birbaum .10 .25
145 Thomas Papp .10 .25
146 Michael Hofer .10 .25
147 Lukas Gerber .10 .25
148 Andri Stoffel .10 .25
149 Tiziano Gianini .10 .25
150 Sandro Moggi .10 .25
151 Riccardo Signorell .10 .25
152 Oliver Tschanz .10 .25
153 Simon Wanner .10 .25
154 Craig Ferguson .20 .50
155 Rainer Karlen .10 .25
156 Beat Heldstab .10 .25
157 Vjeran Ivankovic .10 .25
158 Marco Schupbach .10 .25
159 Silvan Lussy .10 .25
160 Michael Gerber .10 .25
161 Cedric Metrailler .10 .25
162 Thibaut Monnet .10 .25
163 Stephane Roy .10 .25
164 Gil Montandon .10 .25
165 Merlin Malinowski .10 .25
166 Olivier Devaux .10 .25
167 Mario Rottaris .10 .25
168 Dany Ott .10 .25
169 Jean-Yves Roy .20 .50
170 Markus Wuthrich .10 .25
171 Florian Conz .10 .25
172 Valentin Wirz .10 .25
173 Jerome Kohler .10 .25
174 Rostislav Cada .10 .25
175 Yann Voillat .10 .25
176 Rainer Kalin .10 .25
177 Simon Zuger .20 .50
178 Jurg Hardegger .10 .25
179 Robin Breitbach .10 .25
180 Richard Stucki .10 .25
181 Reto Germann .10 .25
182 John Gobbi .10 .25
183 Claude Luethi .10 .25
184 Reto Kobach .10 .25
185 Robert Othmann .10 .25
186 Matthias Muller .10 .25
187 Martin Stepanek .10 .25
188 Pascal Lamprecht .10 .25
189 Alan Tallarini .10 .25
190 Andre Nussbaum .10 .25
191 Michael Diener .10 .25
192 Corsin Camichel .10 .25
193 Timmy Hoppe .10 .25
194 Manuele Celio .10 .25
195 Marco Signer .10 .25
196 Beat Lautenschlager .10 .25
197 John Fritsche .10 .25
198 Marco Knecht .10 .25
199 John Fust .10 .25
200 Alexis Vacheron .10 .25
201 Martin Bergeron .10 .25
202 Vitaly Lakhmatov .10 .25
203 Andreas Haner .10 .25
204 Michel Liniger .10 .25
205 Marco Seeholzer .10 .25
206 Samuel Villiger .10 .25
207 Zdenek Sedlak .10 .25
208 Roland Meyer .10 .25
209 Egor Shastin .10 .25
210 Cedric Favre .10 .25
211 Roland Kradolfer .10 .25
212 Peter Mettler .20 .50
213 Severin Cavegn .10 .25
214 Patrick Schopf .20 .50
215 Antoine Lussier .10 .25
216 Oleg Siritsa .10 .25
217 Patrick Fischer .10 .25
218 Sascha Friedli .10 .25
219 Pascal Muller .10 .25
220 Rolf Diethelm .10 .25
221 Alan Hirschi .10 .25
222 Charles Simard .10 .25
223 Mario Heiniger .10 .25
224 Gaetan Voisard .10 .25
225 Marco Pistolato .10 .25
226 Mischa von Gunten .10 .25
227 Alain Demuth .10 .25
228 Ralph Krueger .10 .25
229 Paul Di Pietro .20 .50
230 Flavien Conne .10 .25
231 Alain Demuth .10 .25
232 Oliver Kamber .10 .25
233 Martin Hohener .10 .25
234 Stefan Niggli .10 .25
235 David Jobin .10 .25
236 Marc Reichert .10 .25
237 Frederic Rothen .10 .25
238 Mathias Seger .10 .25
239 Andre Rufener .10 .25
240 Patrick Sutter .10 .25
241 Winners Pluss .10 .25
242 Lovis Schonenberger .10 .25
243 Lonny Bohonos .20 .50
244 Chris Tancill .20 .50
245 Mike Maneluk .20 .50
246 Martin Pluss .10 .25
247 Kent Ruhnke .10 .25
248 Arno Del Curto .10 .25
249 Marco Buhrer .20 .50
250 Florian Blatter .10 .25
251 Michael Kress .10 .25
252 Rikard Franzen .10 .25
253 Benjamin Winkler .10 .25
254 David Jobin .10 .25
255 Bjorn Christen .10 .25
256 Steivan Hasler .10 .25
257 Sven Leuenberger .10 .25
258 Kevin Miller .20 .50
259 Dominic Meier .10 .25
260 Sandro Rizzi .10 .25
261 Pekka Rautakallio .20 .50
262 Rolf Ziegler .10 .25
263 Rene Back .10 .25
264 Sebastien Bordeleau .20 .50
265 Arne Ramholt .10 .25
266 Mathias Seger .10 .25
267 Christian Dube .10 .25
268 Mattia Baldi .10 .25
269 Sven Helfenstein .10 .25
270 Rolf Hildebrand .10 .25
271 Christian Matte .20 .50
272 Andy Keller .10 .25
273 Derek Plante .20 .50
274 Lars Leuenberger .10 .25
275 Michel Zeiter .10 .25
276 Ronnie Rueger .20 .50
277 Philippe Muller .10 .25
278 Noel Guyaz .10 .25
279 Ivo Ruthemann .10 .25
280 Petteri Nummelin .10 .25
281 Jan Cadieux .10 .25
282 Thomas Ziegler .10 .25
283 Keith Fair .10 .25
284 Mike McParland .10 .25
285 Sandy Jeannin .10 .25
286 Mirko Murovic .20 .50
287 Reto Schurch .20 .50
288 Raffaele Sannitz .20 .50
289 Malik Benturqui .10 .25
290 Flavio Ludke .10 .25
291 Severin Blindenbacher .10 .25
292 Ronny Keller .10 .25
293 Marko Kiprusoff .10 .25
294 Michel N'Goy .10 .25
295 Gregor Thommen .10 .25
296 Patrik Bartschi .10 .25
297 Thomas Studer .10 .25
298 Marc Werlen .10 .25
299 Andrei Bashkirov .20 .50
300 Daniel Bieri .10 .25
301 Mathias Holzer .10 .25
302 Trevor Meier .10 .25
303 Dmitri Shamolin .10 .25
304 Jarrod Skalde .20 .50
305 Michel Wicky .10 .25
306 Gerd Zenhausern .10 .25
307 Thomas Berger .20 .50
308 Marco Capaul .10 .25
309 Cyrill Geyer .10 .25
310 Michel Kamber .10 .25
311 Marc Schefer .10 .25
312 Fabian Stephan .10 .25
313 Markus Butler .10 .25
314 Daniel Giger .10 .25
315 Philipp Luber .10 .25
316 Dale McTavish .20 .50
317 Thomas Nussli .10 .25
318 Mikko Peltola .10 .25
319 Sebastien Reuille .10 .25
320 Niki Siren .10 .25
321 Alfred Bohren .10 .25
322 Claudio Bayer .20 .50
323 Daniel Aegerter .10 .25
324 Samuel Balmer .10 .25
325 Steve Hirschi .10 .25
326 Thomas Kunzi .10 .25
327 Mathias Wust .10 .25
328 Brian Bonin .20 .50
329 Marc Buhlmann .10 .25
330 Mike Craig .20 .50
331 Stefan Grogg .10 .25
332 Thomas Heldner .10 .25
333 Benoit Pont .10 .25
334 Sascha Schneider .10 .25
335 Daniel Steiner .10 .25
336 Chris McSorley .10 .25
337 Reto Pavoni .20 .50
338 Patrice Brasey .10 .25
339 Jamie Heward .20 .50
340 Dino Kessler .10 .25
341 Nicolas Studer .10 .25
342 Pierre-Alain Ancay .10 .25
343 Yvan Benoit .10 .25
344 Philippe Bozon .40 1.00
345 Thomas Derungs .10 .25
346 Igor Fedulov .10 .25
347 Michael Neininger .10 .25
348 Kevin Romy .10 .25
349 Pascal Schaller .10 .25
350 Theo Wittmann .10 .25
351 Florien Bruegger .10 .25
352 Gilles Cattela .10 .25
353 Nicolas Bernasconi .10 .25
354 Valeri Chiriaev .10 .25
355 Jonathan Pan .10 .25
356 Marc Tschudy .10 .25
357 Philippe Fontana .10 .25
358 Jamie Heinrich .10 .25
359 Fabrice Maillat .10 .25
360 Damien Micheli .10 .25
361 Philippe Thalmann .10 .25
362 Omar Tognini .10 .25
363 Bror Hansson .10 .25
364 Simon Rytz .10 .25
365 Fabian Beck .10 .25
366 Chris Belanger .10 .25
367 Serge Meyer .10 .25
368 Jorg Reber .10 .25
369 Remo Altorfer .10 .25
370 Fabio Beccarelli .10 .25
371 Rene Furler .10 .25
372 Vincent Lechenne .10 .25
373 Steve Pochon .10 .25
374 Ryan Savoia .20 .50
375 Christian Weber .10 .25
376 Yves Burlimann .10 .25
377 Marco Baumann .10 .25
378 Andreas Furrer .10 .25
379 Patrick Meichtry .10 .25
380 Daniel Schnyder .10 .25
381 Lukas Grauwiler .10 .25
382 Claudio Moggi .10 .25
383 Andreas Nauser .10 .25
384 Mike Richard .10 .25
385 Pascal Tiegermann .10 .25
386 Petri Varis .20 .50
387 Alexis Weber .10 .25
388 Bruno Aegerter .10 .25
389 Marc Zimmermann .20 .50
390 Stefan Badrutt .10 .25
391 Philipp Portner .10 .25
392 Kim Scheidegger .10 .25
393 Marc Zurbriggen .10 .25
394 Nicolas Gastaldo .10 .25
395 Stefan Gahler .10 .25
396 Stefan Ketola .10 .25
397 Marcel Moser .10 .25
398 Detlef Prediger .10 .25
399 Adrian Witschi .10 .25
400 Ken Zurfluh .10 .25
401 Michael Fluckiger .10 .25
402 Ludovic Aubry .10 .25
403 John Miner .10 .25
404 Jonathan Miner .10 .25
405 Christian Schuster .10 .25
406 Martin Schupbach .10 .25
407 Steven Barras .10 .25
408 Elvis Clavien .10 .25
409 Gilbert Flueler .10 .25
410 Sacha Guerne .10 .25
411 Christoph Lindberg .10 .25
412 Cyrill Pasche .10 .25
413 Arnold Lortscher .10 .25
414 Beat Aebischer .10 .25
415 Francesco Bizzozero .10 .25
416 Ruedi Forster .10 .25
417 Karl Knopf .10 .25
418 Francis Reichmuth .10 .25
419 Stefan Wuthrich .10 .25
420 Martin Gendron .20 .50
421 Kevin Gloor .10 .25
422 Bjorn Guazzini .10 .25
423 Albert Malgin .10 .25
424 Oliver Muller .10 .25
425 Patrick Siegwart .10 .25
426 Christian Ruegg .10 .25
427 Pasqual Sievert .10 .25
428 Christoph Decurtins .10 .25
429 Patrick Mader .10 .25
430 Michael Marki .10 .25
431 Raphael Schoop .10 .25
432 Daniel Sigg .10 .25
433 Philipp Dornbierer .10 .25
434 Curdin Grischott .10 .25
435 Roland Korsch .10 .25
436 Mikko Liukonnen .10 .25
437 Christian Strasser .10 .25
438 Harijs Vitolinsch .10 .25
439 Flavio Streit .10 .25
440 Stephane Julien .10 .25
441 Roland Kaser .10 .25
442 Olivier Schaublin .10 .25
443 Andreas Zehnder .10 .25
444 Rolf Badertscher .10 .25
445 Marco Fischer .10 .25
446 Marco Graf .10 .25
447 Cornel Prinz .10 .25
448 David Raissle .10 .25
449 Marcel Sommer .10 .25
450 Rene Stussi .10 .25
451 Kim Collins .10 .25
452 Thomas Baumle .10 .25
453 Lionel D'Urso .10 .25
454 Philippe Faust .10 .25
455 Fabian Gull .10 .25
456 Terry Hollinger .10 .25
457 Andre Bielmann .10 .25
458 Joel Camenzind .10 .25
459 Derek Cormier .10 .25
460 Maxime Lapointe .10 .25

461 Thierry Metrailler .10 .25
462 Didier Schafer .10 .25
463 Daniel Wobmann .10 .25
464 Ernst Bruderer .10 .25
465 Andreas Schweizer .10 .25
466 Simon Born .10 .25
467 Bernhard Fankhauser .10 .25
468 Marcel Habisreutinger .10 .25
469 Reto Klay .10 .25
470 Lars Sommer .10 .25
471 Eric Lecompte .20 .50
472 Martin Meyer .10 .25
473 Tassilo Schwarz .10 .25
474 Zeno Schwarz .10 .25
475 Martin Wuthrich .10 .25
476 Bruno Zarrillo .20 .50
477 Jean-Jacques Aeschlimann .10 .25
478 Reto von Arx .20 .50
479 Gian-Marco Crameri .10 .25
480 Patric Della Rossa .10 .25
481 Patrick Fischer .10 .25
482 Martin Gerber 4.00 5.00
483 Sandy Jeannin .10 .25
484 Marcel Jenni .10 .25
485 Olivier Keller .10 .25
486 Martin Pluss .10 .25
487 Michel Riesen .80 1.00
488 Ivo Ruthemann .10 .25
489 Martin Steinegger .10 .25
490 Mark Streit .10 .25
491 Lars Weibel .20 .50
492 Rolf Ziegler .10 .25
493 Cristobal Huet .80 3.00
494 Mark Streit .10 .25
495 Charly Oppliger .10 .25
496 Fredy Pargatzi .10 .25
497 Lonny Bohonos .20 .50
498 Patrik Juhlin .20 .50
499 Felix Hollenstein .10 .25

2002-03 Swiss SCL Tigers

COMPLETE SET (?)
1 Johan Fransson .75 2.00
2 Pavel Skrbek .75 2.00
3 Jonas Ronnqvist .75 2.00
4 Magnus Nilsson .75 2.00
5 Gusten Tornqvist .75 2.00
6 Daniel Henriksson .75 2.00
7 Todd Elik .75 2.00

2003-04 Swiss EV Zug Postcards

These unnumbered 4X6 postcards were issued by the team and feature a colour headshot on the front. The two Patrick Fischers are different players with the same name. The Claude Lemieux single was issued as an update later in the season and so the set is considered complete without it.

COMPLETE SET (27) 10.00 25.00
1 Team Photo .40 1.00
2 Silvan Anthamatten .40 1.00
3 Duri Camichel .40 1.00
4 Corsin Casutt .40 1.00
5 Alain Demuth .40 1.00
6 Rafael Diaz .40 1.00
7 Paul Dipietro .40 1.00
8 Thomas Dommen .40 1.00
9 Paolo Duca .40 1.00
10 Livio Fazio .40 1.00
11 Patrick Fischer .40 1.00
12 Patrick Fischer .40 1.00
13 Daniel Giger .40 1.00
14 Andreas Kung .40 1.00
15 Colin Muller .40 1.00
16 Pascal Muller .40 1.00
17 Patrick Oppliger .40 1.00
18 Barry Richter .40 1.00
19 Frederic Rothen .40 1.00
20 Joel Savage .40 1.00
21 Lovis Schonenberger .40 1.00
22 Patrick Schopf .40 1.00
23 Fabio Schumacher .40 1.00
24 Sean Simpson .40 1.00
25 Chris Tancill .40 1.00
26 Michael Tobler .40 1.00
27 Gaetan Voisard .40 1.00
28 Claude Lemieux 4.00 10.00

2003-04 Swiss HNL

We know this card exists and that's about it. Rumours from the Swiss collecting underground suggest that these cards were not sold in packs but in set form only. It's obviously a huge set since this is card #427. Any additional info would be much appreciated. Email us at hockeymag@beckett.com.

COMPLETE SET (?)
427 Bryan Lundbohm

2004-05 Swiss Davos Postcards

Cards measure 4X6 and feature a head shot on the front. All cards are autographed except for the group cards. Set is noteworthy for the inclusion of Joe Thornton and Rick Nash.

COMPLETE SET (30) 40.00 80.00
1 Team photo .40 1.00
2 Team history .40 1.00
3 Andres Ambuhl 1.25 3.00
4 Thomas Baumle 1.25 3.00

5 Florian Blatter 1.25 3.00
6 Daniell Boss 1.25 3.00
7 Bjorn Christen 1.25 3.00
8 Franco Collenberg 1.25 3.00
9 Arno Del Curto 1.25 3.00
10 Beat Forster 1.25 3.00
11 Marc Gianola 1.25 3.00
12 Peter Guggisberg 1.25 3.00
13 Niklas Hagman 2.00 5.00
14 Andreas Haller 1.25 3.00
15 Stevan Hasler 1.25 3.00
16 Marc Heberlein 1.25 3.00
17 Jonas Hiller 1.25 3.00
18 Michael Kress 1.25 3.00
19 Josef Marha 1.25 3.00
20 Laurent Muller 1.25 3.00
21 Rick Nash 12.00 30.00
22 Claudio Neff 1.25 3.00
23 Arne Ramholt 1.25 3.00
24 Michel Riesen 1.25 3.00
25 Sandro Rizzi 1.25 3.00
26 Fabian Sutter 1.25 3.00
27 Joe Thornton 15.00 40.00
28 Jan Von Arx 1.25 3.00
29 Reto Von Arx 1.25 3.00
30 Benjamin Winkler 1.25 3.00

2004-05 Swiss EV Zug Postcards

The cards are approximately 4X6. We've seen signed versions of the cards as well, but it's not known whether they were issued that way officially, or signed afterwards.

COMPLETE SET (28) 10.00 25.00
1 Brett Hauer .75 2.00
2 Niko Kapanen .75 2.00
3 Mike Fisher 1.25 3.00
4 Barry Richter .40 1.00
5 Oleg Petrov .40 1.00
6 Lars Weibel .40 1.00
7 Rafael Walter .40 1.00
8 Jan Feldmann .40 1.00
9 Livio Fazio .40 1.00
10 Pascal Muller .40 1.00
11 Rafael Diaz .40 1.00
12 Rene Back .40 1.00
13 Gaetan Voisard .40 1.00
14 Silvan Anthamatten .40 1.00
15 Patric Della Rosa .40 1.00
16 Gian-Marco Crameri .40 1.00
17 Patrick Fisher .40 1.00
18 Duri Camichel .40 1.00
19 Patrick Oppliger .40 1.00
20 Duca Paolo .40 1.00
21 Fabian Schnyder .40 1.00
22 Corsin Casutt .40 1.00
23 Daniel Giger .40 1.00
24 Frederic Rothen .40 1.00
25 Beat Schuler .40 1.00
26 Sean Simpson CO .40 1.00
27 Colin Muller ACO .40 1.00
28 Team Photo .40 1.00

2004-05 Swiss Lausanne HC Postcards

Standard postcard-sized collectibles were sold by the team in set form. The series in noteworthy for the inclusion of reigning NHL scoring champ Martin St. Louis. The cards are unnumbered. Checklist courtesy of collector Vincent Montalbano.

COMPLETE SET (25) 25.00
1 Pascal Schaller .40 1.00
2 Robert Slehofer .40 1.00
3 Alain Reist .40 1.00
4 Bruno Steck .40 1.00
5 Andy Roach .75 2.00
6 Thomas Berger .40 1.00
7 Patrick Boileau .75 2.00
8 Florian Andenmatten .40 1.00
9 Sunshine Romerio .40 1.00
10 Julien Turler .40 1.00
11 Gerd Zenhausern .40 1.00
12 Loic Merz .40 1.00
13 Martin St. Louis 4.00 10.00
14 Christophe Brown .40 1.00
15 Michael Ngoy .40 1.00
16 Mathias Holzer .40 1.00
17 Laurent Emery .40 1.00
18 Florian Conz .40 1.00
19 Marko Tuomainen .40 1.00
20 Michael Kamber .40 1.00
21 Lovis Schonenberger .40 1.00
22 Sacha Weibel .40 1.00
23 Eric Landry .40 1.00
24 Bill Stewart CO .10 .25
25 Gary Sheehan ACO .10 .25

1954 UK A and BC Chewing Gum

The cards listed below were part of a multi-sport set issued in England, possibly with packs of A and BC Chewing Gum. They feature b&w headshots and blank backs. The players appear to be from an early English league. It's quite possible that other hockey players were featured. If you can address this checklist, please contact us at hockeymag@beckett.com.

COMPLETE SET (?)
35 Chick Zamick 8.00 20.00
36 Cliff Ryan 8.00 20.00
37 Sonny Rost 8.00 20.00
38 Malcolm Davidson 8.00 20.00
39 Ray Gariepy 12.00 30.00
40 George Beach 8.00 20.00
41 Lefty Wilmot 8.00 20.00
74 Bill Johnson 8.00 20.00
75 Joe Shack 8.00 20.00
76 Tony Licari 8.00 20.00

1998-99 UK Basingstoke Bison

This set features the Bison of the British Hockey League. The set was produced by Armchair Sports, an English card shop, and was sold by that store and the team. The print run has been confirmed at 200 sets.

COMPLETE SET (24) 4.00 10.00
1 Rick Strachan .25 .60
2 Joe Baird .25 .60
3 Chris Crombie .25 .60
4 Steve Smillie .25 .60
5 Chris Bailey .25 .60
6 Bjarne Levison .25 .60
7 Mike Ellis .25 .60
8 Chris Chard .25 .60
9 Anthony Page .25 .60
10 Adam Cathcart .25 .60
11 Rick Fera .25 .60
12 Gary Clark .25 .60
13 Tony Redmond .25 .60
14 Alec Field .25 .60
15 Hakan Klys .25 .60
16 Mitch Grant .25 .60
17 Jake Armstrong .25 .60
18 Don Deopoe CO .04 .10
19 Garfunkel's MASCOT .04 .10
20 The Puck .04 .10
21 The Goal .04 .10
22 Penalty Shots .04 .10
23 Team CL .04 .10
NNO Competition .04 .10

1999-00 UK Basingstoke Bison

This set features the Bison of Britain's top hockey league. The set was produced by Armchair Sports, a card shop in the UK, and was sold by the team. The print run has been confirmed at 200 sets.

COMPLETE SET (22) 4.00 10.00
1 Rick Strachan .20 .50
2 Dru Burgess .20 .50
3 Danny Meyers .20 .50
4 Gary Clark .20 .50
5 Peter Romeo .20 .50
6 Mike Ellis .20 .50
7 Joey Baird .20 .50
8 Charlie Colon .20 .50
9 Wayne Crawford .20 .50
10 Alec Field .20 .50
11 Tony Redmond .20 .50
12 Mitch Grant .20 .50
13 Duncan Paterson .20 .50
14 Dwayne Newman .20 .50
15 Mark Barrow .20 .50
16 Adam Greener .20 .50
17 Face Off .10 .25
18 Goal Mouth Scramble .10 .25
19 Joe Watkins .20 .50
20 Michael Knights .20 .50
21 Jeff Daniels .20 .50
22 Team CL .04 .10

2003-04 UK Basingstoke Bison

COMPLETE SET (21) 4.00 10.00
1 Curtis Cruickshank .30 .75
2 Dean Skinns .30 .75
3 David Geris .30 .75
4 James Hutchinson .20 .50
5 Phil Roy .20 .50
6 Doug Schueller .20 .50
7 Kim Vahanen .20 .50
8 Joe Ciccarello .20 .50
9 Martin Filip .20 .50
10 Richard Hargreaves .20 .50
11 Darren Hurley .20 .50
12 Jaromir Kverka .20 .50
13 Steve Moria .20 .50
14 Blake Sorensen .20 .50
15 Shaun Thompson .20 .50
16 Nicky Watt .30 .75
17 Christian Widauer .20 .50
18 Chris Slater .20 .50
19 Luc Chabot .20 .50
20 Matt Reid .20 .50
21 Checklist .01 .01

2001-02 UK Belfast Giants

This 35-card set featured the Belfast Giants of the British Ice Hockey Superleague for the seasons of 2001-02 and 2002-03. Please note that card #13 was not produced. This set was produced by Armchair Sports in England.

COMPLETE SET (35) 8.00 20.00
1 Mike Bales .40 1.00
2 Terran Sandwith .30 .75
3 Dave Whistle CO .04 .10
4 Shane Johnson .30 .75
5 Colin Ward .30 .75
6 Kevin Riehl .30 .75
7 Rob Stewart .30 .75
8 Jason Ruff .30 .75
9 Sean Berens .30 .75
10 Jeff Hoad .30 .75
11 David Matsos .30 .75
12 Curtis Bowen .30 .75
14 Chad Allan .30 .75
15 Rod Stevens .30 .75
16 Paxton Schulte .40 1.00
17 Jason Bowen .40 1.00
18 Mark Cavallin .30 .75
19 Todd Kelman .30 .75
20 Checklist .01
21 Tom Blatchford TR .04 .10
22 Redemption Card .01
23 Shayne Toporowski .40 1.00
24 Derek Wilkinson .30 .75
25 Paul Ferone .30 .75
26 Todd Goodwin .30 .75
27 Kory Karlander .30 .75
28 Doug Searle .30 .75
29 Jerry Keefe .30 .75
30 Jason Wright .30 .75
31 Steve Roberts .30 .75
32 Mark Cavallin .30 .75
33 Mike Bales NM .40 1.00
34 Front Office .04 .10
35 Checklist .01

2003-04 UK Belfast Giants

Unnumbered cards, listed in alphabetical order.

COMPLETE SET (19) 5.00 10.00
1 Sean Berens .20 .50
2 Curt Bowen .30 .75
3 Jason Bowen .20 .50
4 Mark Finney .20 .50
5 Leigh Jamieson .20 .50
6 Shane Johnson .20 .50
7 Todd Kelman .20 .50
8 Brad Kenny .20 .50
9 Gareth Martin .20 .50
10 Chris McGimpsey .30 .75
11 Mark Morrison .20 .50
12 Jason Ruff .20 .50
13 Colin Ryder .30 .75
14 Paul Sample .20 .50
15 Paxton Schulte .20 .50
16 Rob Stewart .20 .50
17 Grant Taylor .20 .50
18 Graeme Walton .20 .50
19 Colin Ward .20 .50

2004-05 UK Brent Bobyck Testimonial

COMPLETE SET (12) 2.00 5.00
COMMON CARD (1-12)
1 Brent Bobyck 1994-95 .20 .50
2 Brent Bobyck 1995-96 .20 .50
3 Brent Bobyck 1996-97 .20 .50
4 Brent Bobyck 1997-98 .20 .50
5 Brent Bobyck 1998-99 .20 .50
6 Brent Bobyck 1999-00 .20 .50
7 Brent Bobyck 2000-01 .20 .50
8 Brent Bobyck 2001-02 .20 .50
9 Brent Bobyck 2002-03 .20 .50
10 Brent Bobyck 2003-04 .20 .50
11 Brent Bobyck 2004-05 .20 .50
12 Brent Bobyck CL .20 .10

2000-01 UK Cardiff Devils

This set features the Devils of the British league. It is believed that this is an incomplete checklist and so is not priced in set form. If you know of additional singles, please contact us at hockeymag@beckett.com.

COMPLETE SET (14)
1 Derek Herlofsky .20 .50
2 Alan Schuler .20 .50
3 Vezio Sacratini .20 .50
4 Clayton Norris .20 .50
5 Rick Strachan .20 .50
6 John Parco .20 .50
7 Kip Noble .20 .50
8 Steve Thornton .20 .50
9 Denis Chasse .20 .50
10 Mike Ware .20 .50
11 Steve Moria .20 .50
12 Frank Evans .20 .50
13 Jonathan Phillips .20 .50
14 Ian McIntyre .20 .50

2001-02 UK Cardiff Devils

This set was produced by Armchair Sports in England.

COMPLETE SET (19) 5.00 10.00
1 Clayton Norris .30 .75
2 Rick Strachan .20 .50
3 Alan Schuler .20 .50
4 Kim Ahlroos .20 .50
5 John Parco .20 .50
6 Frank Evans .20 .50
7 Denis Chasse .40 1.00
8 Steve Thornton .30 .75
9 Dwight Parrish .20 .50
10 Steve Moria .20 .50
11 Jonathan Phillips .20 .50
12 Ian McIntyre .20 .50
13 Ivan Matulik .20 .50
14 Mike Ware .30 .75
15 Vezio Sacratini .20 .50
16 Steve Lyle .30 .75
17 Derek Herlofsky .40 1.00
18 Kip Noble .20 .50
19 Checklist .02 .10

2002-03 UK Cardiff Devils

This 19-card set featured the Cardiff Devils of the British Ice Hockey Superleague. Each card was numbered at the bottom of the card back. This set was available during home games.

COMPLETE SET (19) 5.00 10.00
1 Clayton Norris .20 .50
2 Rick Strachan .20 .50
3 Alan Schuler .20 .50
4 Kim Ahlroos .20 .50
5 John Parco .20 .50
6 Frank Evans .20 .50
7 Denis Chasse .40 1.00
8 Steve Thornton .30 .75
9 Dwight Parrish .20 .50
10 Steve Moria .20 .50
11 Jonathan Phillips .20 .50
12 Ian McIntyre .20 .50
13 Ivan Matulik .20 .50
14 Mike Ware .30 .75
15 Vezio Sacratini .20 .50
16 Stevie Lyle .30 .75
17 Derek Herlofsky .30 .75
18 Kip Noble .20 .50
19 Checklist .01 .01

2003-04 UK Cardiff Devils

COMPLETE SET (21) 5.00 10.00
1 Jason Cugnet .30 .75
2 Jeff Burgoyne .20 .50
3 Matt Myers .20 .50
4 Jason Stone .20 .50
5 David James .20 .50
6 Phil Manny .20 .50
7 Russ Romaniuk .40 1.00
8 Phil Hill .20 .50
9 Jonathan Phillips .20 .50
10 Jeff Brown .20 .50
11 Ivan Matulik .20 .50
12 Ed Patterson .20 .50
13 Mike Ware .30 .75
14 Vezio Sacratini .20 .50
15 Neil Francis .20 .50
16 James Manson .20 .50
17 Jason Becker .20 .50
18 Dennis Maxwell .20 .50
19 Doug McEwen .20 .50
20 Dave Whistle CO .02 .10
21 Checklist .01 .01

2002-03 UK Coventry Blaze

This 24-card set featured the Coventry Blaze of the Findus British National League. They were available at home games. Cards were unnumbered and are listed below in checklist order.

COMPLETE SET (24) 5.00 12.00
1 Greg Rockman .20 .50
2 Jody Lehman .20 .50
3 Steve Carpenter .20 .50
4 Alan Levers .20 .50
5 James Pease .20 .50
6 Andreas Moborg .20 .50
7 Mathias Soderstrom .20 .50
8 Adam Radmall .20 .50
9 Ron Shudra .30 .75
10 Shaun Johnson .20 .50
11 Steve Chartrand .20 .50
12 Kurt Irvine .20 .50
13 Russ Cowley .20 .50
14 Tom Watkins .20 .50
15 Ashley Tait .30 .75
16 Gareth Owens .20 .50
17 Joel Poirier .30 .75
18 Hilton Ruggles .20 .50
19 Lee Richardson .20 .50
20 Michael Tasker .20 .50
21 Paul Thompson CO .02 .10
22 Steve Small .02 .10
Phil Hadley
John Crook
23 Blaze Dancers .20 .50
24 Checklist .01 .01

2003-04 UK Coventry Blaze

COMPLETE SET (18) 5.00 12.00
1 Alan Levers .25 .60
2 Mathias Soderstrom .25 .60
3 Steve Carpenter .30 .75
4 Jody Lehman .25 .60
5 Steve O'Brien .25 .60
6 Steve Gallace .25 .60
7 Adam Radmall .25 .60
8 Shaun Johnson .25 .60
9 Graham Schlender .25 .60
10 Steve Chartrand .25 .60
11 Russ Cowley .25 .60
12 Tom Watkins .25 .60
13 Ashley Tait .30 .75
14 Gareth Owen .25 .60
15 Joel Poirier .30 .75
16 Hilton Ruggles .25 .60
17 Lee Richardson .25 .60
18 Michael Tasker .25 .60

2003-04 UK Coventry Blaze Calendars

COMPLETE SET (12) 5.00 10.00
1 Mathias Soderstrom .40 1.00
2 Ashley Tait .40 1.00
3 Steve Carpenter .40 1.00
4 Steve Chartrand .40 1.00
Shaun Johnson
5 Russ Cowley .40 1.00
Tom Watkins
6 Graham Schlender .40 1.00
7 Jody Lehman .40 1.00
8 Michael Tasker .40 1.00
Hilton Ruggles
9 Lee Richardson .40 1.00
Alan Levers
10 Joel Poirier .40 1.00
11 Garth Owen .40 1.00
Adam Radmall
12 Steve Gallace .40 1.00
Steve O'Brien

2003-04 UK Coventry Blaze History

COMPLETE SET (18) 5.00 10.00
1 Steve Chartrand .20 .50
2 Kurt Irvine .20 .50
3 Mathias Soderstrom .20 .50
4 Michael Tasker .20 .50
5 A.J. Kelham .20 .50
6 Hilton Ruggles .20 .50
7 Luc Chabot .20 .50
8 Paul Thompson .20 .50
9 Steve Carpenter .30 .75
10 Shaun Johnson .20 .50
11 Andrew McNiven .20 .50
12 Jody Lehman .30 .75
13 Justin George .20 .50
14 Claude Dumas .20 .50
15 Craig Chapman .20 .50
16 Stephen Cooper .30 .75
17 Mike Shewan .20 .50
18 Ron Shudra .30 .75

2004-05 UK Coventry Blaze

Produced by Cardtraders.co.UK.

COMPLETE SET (25) 5.00 10.00
1 Wade Belak .30 .75
2 Adam Brittle .20 .50
3 Adam Calder .20 .50
4 Tom Carlon .20 .50
5 Dan Carlson .20 .50
6 Luc Chabot ACO .02 .10
7 Russ Cowley .20 .50
8 Jody Lehman .20 .50
9 Neal Martin .20 .50
10 Chris McNamara .20 .50
11 Pavol Mihalik .20 .50
12 Andre Payette .20 .50
13 James Pease .20 .50
14 Joel Poirier .20 .50
15 Graham Schlender .20 .50
16 Doug Schueller .20 .50
17 Dan Shea .20 .50
18 Ashley Tait .30 .75
19 Paul Thompson CO .02 .10
20 Michal Vrabel .20 .50
21 Tom Watkins .20 .50
22 Nathanael Williams .20 .50
23 S.Small/A.Henry .20 .50
24 A.Buxton/M.Cowley .20 .50
25 Kix Kat MASCOT .01 .01

2004-05 UK Coventry Blaze Champions

COMPLETE SET (20) 5.00 10.00
1 Jody Lehman .30 .75
2 Dan Shea .20 .50
3 Wade Belak .40 1.00
4 Neal Martin .20 .50
5 Doug Schueller .20 .50
6 Pavol Mahalik .20 .50
7 Jozef Lukac .20 .50
8 James Pease .20 .50
9 Andre Payette .20 .50
10 Dan Carlson .20 .50
11 Graham Schlender .20 .50
12 Adam Calder .20 .50
13 Ashley Tait .30 .75
14 Joel Poirier .20 .50
15 Russ Cowley .20 .50
16 Chris McNamara .20 .50
17 Nathanael Williams .20 .50
18 Tom Watkins .20 .50
19 Card List .01 .01
20 Paul Thompson .20 .50

2006-07 UK Coventry Blaze

COMPLETE SET (20) 8.00 15.00
1 Neal Martin .30 .75
2 Joe Henry .30 .75
3 Reid Simonton .30 .75
4 Samy Nasreddine .30 .75
5 Tom Pease .30 .75
6 Barrie Moore .30 .75
7 Tom Watkins .30 .75
8 Ashley Tait .30 .75
9 James Pease .30 .75
10 Tom Carlon .30 .75
11 Adam Calder .30 .75
12 Dan Carlson .30 .75
13 Steve Fone .30 .75
14 Gareth Owen .30 .75
15 Trevor Koenig .30 .75
16 Danny Stewart .30 .75
17 Michael Wales .30 .75
18 Rumun Ndur .30 .75
19 Sylvain Cloutier .30 .75
20 Paul Thompson .30 .75

2001-02 UK Dundee Stars

This set was produced by Armchair Sports in England.

COMPLETE SET (18) 5.00 10.00
1 Checklist .02 .10
2 Nate Leslie .25 .60
3 Scott Young .25 .60
4 Tony Hand .30 .75
5 Paul Berrington .25 .60
6 Gary Dowd .25 .60
7 Teeder Wynne .25 .60
8 Mikko Inkinen .25 .60
9 Andrew Finlay .25 .60
10 Jan Mikel .25 .60
11 Craig Nelson .25 .60
12 Dominic Hopkins .25 .60
13 Stewart Rugg .25 .60
14 Patrick Lochi .25 .60
15 Stephen Murphy .25 .60
16 Slava Koulikov .25 .60
17 Martin Wiita .25 .60
18 Scott Kirton .25 .60

2002-03 UK Dundee Stars

This 18-card set was produced by cardtraders.co.uk to commerorate the champions of the 2001-02 British National League, the Dundee Stars. The sets were limited to a production run of 495 total.

COMPLETE SET (18) 5.00 10.00
1 Checklist .01
2 Nate Leslie .25 .60

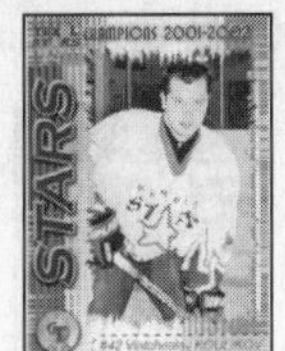

3 Scott Young .25 .60
4 Tony Hand .30 .75
5 Paul Berrington .25 .60
6 Gary Dowd .25 .60
7 Teeder Wynne .25 .60
8 Mikko Inkinen .25 .60
9 Andy Finlay .25 .60
10 Jan Mikel .25 .60
11 Craig Nelson .25 .60
12 Dominic Hopkins .25 .60
13 Stewart Rugg .25 .60
14 Patric Lochi .25 .60
15 Stephen Murphy .25 .60
16 Viatcheslav Koulikov .25 .60
17 Martin Wiita .25 .60
18 Scott Kirton .25 .60

2004-05 UK Edinburgh Capitals

Produced by Cardtraders.co.UK.
COMPLETE SET (18) 5.00 12.00
1 Jan Krajicek .30 .75
2 Mindraugas Kieras .40 1.00
3 Laurie Dunbar .30 .75
4 Steven Francey .30 .75
5 Marty Johnston .30 .75
6 Craig Wilson .30 .75
7 David Beatson .30 .75
8 Ross Hay .30 .75
9 Steven Lynch .30 .75
10 Daniel McIntyre .30 .75
11 Neil Hay .30 .75
12 Martin Cingel .30 .75
13 Dino Bauba .30 .75
14 David Trofimenkoff .40 1.00
15 Rastislav Bohme .30 .75
16 Miroslav Droppa .30 .75
17 Ryan Ford .40 1.00
18 Checklist .02 .10

2004-05 UK EIHL All-Stars

COMPLETE SET (18) 5.00 12.00
1 Jody Lehman .30 .75
2 Wade Belak .40 1.00
3 Neal Martin .20 .50
4 Tony Hand .40 1.00
5 Adam Calder .20 .50
6 Jon Cullen .20 .50
7 Martin Klempa .20 .50
8 Rob Davison .40 1.00
9 Dion Darling .20 .50
10 Dan Carlson .20 .50
11 George Awarda .20 .50
12 Vezio Sacratini .20 .50
13 Curtis Cruickshank .30 .75
14 Eric Cairns .40 1.00
15 Nick Boynton .40 1.00
16 Shawn Maltby .40 1.00
17 David Clarke .20 .50
18 Scott Nichol .40 1.00

1996-97 UK Fife Flyers

This set features the Flyers of Britain's top league. It was produced by the team and sold at home games.
COMPLETE SET (20) 5.00 12.00
1 Gavin Fleming .30 .75
2 John Reid .30 .75
3 Russ Parent .30 .75
4 Derek E. King .30 .75
5 Colin Grubb .30 .75
6 Colin Hamilton .30 .75
7 Andy Finlay .30 .75
8 Richard Dingwall .30 .75
9 Andy Samuel .30 .75
10 Wayne Maxwell .30 .75
11 Craig Wilson .30 .75
12 Daryl Venters .30 .75
13 Gordon Latto .30 .75
14 Richard Danskin .30 .75
15 Martin McKay .30 .75
16 Kyle Horne .30 .75
17 Mark Morrison CO .20 .50
18 Frank Morris .30 .75
19 Steven E. King .30 .75
20 Lee Mercer .30 .75

1997-98 UK Fife Flyers

This set features the Flyers of the British Ice Hockey League. The sets were sold by the team at its souvenir stands on game nights.
COMPLETE SET (20) 4.80 12.00
1 Team Photo .20 .50
2 Bernie McCrone .30 .75
3 Wayne Maxwell .30 .75
4 Derek E. King .30 .75
5 Mark Slater .30 .75
6 Bill Moody .30 .75
7 Lee Cowmedow .30 .75
8 Richard Charles .30 .75
9 Andy Finlay .30 .75
10 Daryl Venters .30 .75
11 Steven E. King .30 .75
12 Andy Samuel .30 .75
13 Gordon Latto .30 .75
14 Mark Morrison CO .20 .50
15 John Haig .30 .75
16 Lee Mercer .30 .75
17 Gary Wishart .30 .75
18 Colin Hamilton .30 .75
19 Frank Morris .30 .75
20 David Smith .30 .75

2001-02 UK Fife Flyers

This 12-card sticker set featured the Fife Flyers of the British National League. Each sticker was approximately 2"x 2" and were issued one per week during the season. A limited edition wall chart to affix the stickers to was also available. The stickers are not numbered and are listed below in order of the player's jersey number.
COMPLETE SET (12) 5.00 10.00
1 Shawn Silver .40 1.00
2 Derek King .40 1.00
3 Kyle Horner .40 1.00
4 Todd Dutiaume .40 1.00
5 Steven King .40 1.00
6 Mark Morrison .40 1.00
7 Mark Dutiaume .40 1.00
8 Gary Wishart .40 1.00
9 Iain Robertson .40 1.00
10 Karry Biette .40 1.00
11 Russell Monteith .40 1.00
12 Frank Morris .40 1.00

1994-95 UK Guildford Flames

This set features the Flames of the British Hockey League. The set was produced by Armchair Sports, an English card shop, and was sold by that store and the team on game nights.
COMPLETE SET (25) 4.00 10.00
1 Ben Challice .20 .50
2 Wayne Trunchion .20 .50
3 Terry Kurtenbach .20 .50
4 Fred Perlini .20 .50
5 Andy Sparks .20 .50
6 Rob Friesen .20 .50
7 Drew Chapman .20 .50
8 Kevin Parish .20 .50
9 John Noctor .20 .50
10 Ron Charbonneau GM .04 .10
11 Peter Morley .20 .50
12 Andy Allan .20 .50
13 Ryan Campbell .20 .50
14 Ronnie Evans-Harvey .20 .50
15 Paul Thompson .20 .50
16 Bill Rawles .20 .50
17 Nicky Landoli .20 .50
18 Elliott Andrews .20 .50
19 Dean Russell-Samways .20 .50
20 Home Kit .04 .10
21 Away Kit .04 .10
22 5 Imports .20 .50
23 3 Letters .04 .10
24 Spectrum .04 .10
25 Checklist .04 .10

1995-96 UK Guildford Flames

This set features the Flames of the British Hockey League. The set was produced by Armchair Sports, an English card shop, and was sold by that store and the team on game nights.
COMPLETE SET (30) 6.00 15.00
1 Dave Gregory .20 .50
2 Wayne Trunchion .20 .50
3 Andy Allan .20 .50
4 Terry Kurtenbach .20 .50
5 Ryan Campbell .20 .50
6 Fred Perlini .20 .50
7 Ronnie Evans-Harvey .20 .50
8 Andy Sparks .20 .50
9 Paul Thompson .20 .50
10 Nick Rothwell .20 .50
11 Drew Chapman .20 .50
12 Troy Kennedy .20 .50
13 Barrie Aisbitt .20 .50
14 Elliott Andrews .20 .50
15 Darrin Zinger .20 .50
16 Dean Russell-Samways .20 .50
17 Dave Graham .20 .50
18 Ivan Brown .20 .50
19 Home Kit .20 .50
20 Away Kit .20 .50
21 Spectrum .20 .50
22 Checklist .20 .50
23 Home Action .20 .50
24 Away Action .20 .50
25 P.C. Jim Bennett .20 .50
26 Terry Kurtenbach GOLD .20 .50
27 Paul Thompson GOLD .20 .50
28 Fred Perlini GOLD .20 .50
29 Future GOLD .20 .50
30 Celebration GOLD .20 .50

1996-97 UK Guildford Flames

This set features the Flames of the British Hockey League. The set was produced by Armchair Sports, an English card shop, and was sold by that store and the team on game nights.
COMPLETE SET (30) 5.00 12.00
1 John Wolfe .20 .50
2 Rob Lamey .20 .50
3 Wayne Crawford .20 .50
4 Terry Kurtenbach .20 .50
5 Ryan Campbell .20 .50
6 Fred Parlini .20 .50
7 Paul Thompson .20 .50
8 Mike Bettens .20 .50
9 Mark Finney .20 .50
10 Ryan Ferster .20 .50
11 Nick Cross .20 .50
12 Damian Smith .20 .50
13 Mike Mowbray .20 .50
14 Elliott Andrews .20 .50
15 Darrin Zinger .20 .50
16 Brad Kirkwood .20 .50
17 Derek DeCosty .20 .50
18 Mark Hazelhurst .20 .50
19 Lee Saunders .20 .50
20 Barrie Aisbitt .20 .50
21 Paul McCallion .20 .50
22 Valeri Vasie .20 .50
23 Goalies .20 .50
24 Capt. & Ast.Capt. .20 .50
25 Celebration .10 .25
26 Pep Talk .10 .25
27 Home Kit .10 .25
28 Away Kit .10 .25
29 Spectrum .10 .25
30 Training Staff .10 .25

1997-98 UK Guildford Flames

This set features the Flames of the British Hockey League. The set was produced by Armchair Sports, an English card shop, and was sold by that store and the team on game nights.
COMPLETE SET (30) 4.80 12.00
1 Peter Morley .20 .50
2 Rob Lamey .30 .75
3 Andrew Hannah .30 .75
4 Joe Johnson .30 .75
5 Terry Kurtenbach .30 .75
6 Ryan Campbell .20 .50
7 Scott Adair .20 .50
8 Paul Thompson .20 .50
9 Ricky Plant .20 .50
10 Pete Kasowski .20 .50
11 Andrew Einhorn .20 .50
12 Bobby Brown .20 .50
13 Anthony Page .20 .50
14 Nick Rothwell .20 .50
15 Mike Harding .20 .50
16 Darrin Zinger .30 .75
17 Jamie Organ .20 .50
18 Barcley Pearce .20 .50
19 Simon Smith .20 .50
20 Russ Plant .20 .50
21 Stan Marple CO .04 .10
22 Home Kit .04 .10
23 Away Kit .04 .10
24 Dressing Room .04 .10
25 Capt. & Ast. Capt. .04 .10
26 Celebration .04 .10
27 Checklist .04 .10
28 Spectrum .04 .10
29 Sizzler .04 .10
30 Training Staff .04 .10

1998-99 UK Guildford Flames

This set features the Flames of the British Hockey League. The set was produced by Armchair Sports, an English card shop, and was sold by that store and the team on game nights.
COMPLETE SET (30) 4.00 10.00
1 Team CL .04 .10
2 Ryan Campbell .20 .50
3 Robin Davison .20 .50
4 Derek DeCosty .20 .50
5 Dominic Hopkins .20 .50
6 Simon Howard .20 .50
7 Kirk Humphreys .20 .50
8 Andy Johnston .20 .50
9 Rob Johnston .20 .50
10 Peter Kasowski .20 .50
11 Terry Kurtenbach .20 .50
12 Rob Lamey .20 .50
13 Adrian Lomonaco .20 .50
14 Sam Mager .20 .50
15 Stan Marple CO .04 .10
16 Brian Mason .20 .50
17 Peter Morley .20 .50
18 Jamey Organ .20 .50
19 Barcley Pearce .20 .50
20 Andy Pickles .20 .50
21 Greg Randall .20 .50
22 Sizzler MASCOT .04 .10
23 Simon Smith .20 .50
24 Scott Stephenson .20 .50
25 Paul Thompson .20 .50
26 Captain & Assistants .04 .10
27 GB Uniform .04 .10
28 Trophies .04 .10
29 Home Kit .04 .10
30 Away Kit .04 .10

1999-00 UK Guildford Flames

This set features the Flames of the British Hockey League. The set was produced by Armchair Sports, an English card shop, and was sold by that store and the team on game nights.
COMPLETE SET (30) 4.00 10.00
1 Team CL .04 .10
2 Biette, Crombie, Dixon .20 .50
3 Team Photo (home) .04 .10
4 Team Photo (away) .20 .50
5 Celebration .04 .10
6 Karry Biette .20 .50
7 Tom Brown .20 .50
8 Ryan Campbell .20 .50
9 Gary Clark .20 .50
10 Chris Crombie .20 .50
11 Derek Decosty .20 .50
12 Paul Dixon .20 .50
13 GB Uniform .04 .10
14 Patrick Flanagan .20 .50
15 Dominic Hopkins .20 .50
16 Simon Howard .20 .50
17 Adrian Jenkinson TR .04 .10
18 Peter Kasowski .20 .50
19 Grant King .20 .50
20 Rob Lamey .20 .50
21 James Manson .20 .50
22 Stan Marple CO .04 .10
23 Stan Marple CO .04 .10
24 Jamey Organ .20 .50
25 Barcley Pearce .20 .50
26 Rick Plant .20 .50
27 Russ Plant .20 .50
28 Sizzlers MASCOT .04 .10
29 Jamie Thompson .20 .50
30 Mike Urquhart ACO .04 .10

2000-01 UK Guildford Flames

This set features the Bison of the British Hockey League. The set was produced by Armchair Sports, an English card shop, and was sold by that store and the team.
COMPLETE SET (30) 4.00 10.00
1 Karry Biette .14 .35
2 Tom Brown .14 .35
3 Ryan Campbell .14 .35
4 Scott Campbell .14 .35
5 Wayne Crawford .14 .35
6 Chris Crombie .14 .35
7 Derek DeCosty .14 .35
8 Paul Dixon .14 .35
9 John Haig .14 .35
10 Adrian Jenkinson TR .10 .25
11 Jason Jennings .14 .35
12 Grant King .14 .35
13 Rob Lamey .14 .35
14 Stan Marple CO .10 .25
15 Stan Marple CO .10 .25
16 Mark McArthur .20 .50
17 Tyrone Miller .14 .35
18 Jason Moses .14 .35
19 Barcley Pearce .14 .35
20 Ricky Plant .14 .35
21 Sizzler MASCOT .10 .25
22 Jason Stone .14 .35
23 David Smith .14 .35
24 Mike Urquhart .14 .35
25 Team Photo (home) .14 .35
26 Team Photo (away) .14 .35
27 Captain & Assistants .14 .35
28 Home Grown .14 .35
29 Celebration .10 .25
30 Logo Card .10 .25

2001-02 UK Guildford Flames

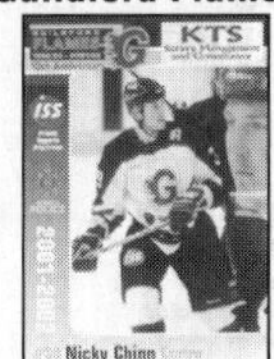

This team set was produced to honor Guildford's tenth anniversary season. The set was co-sponsored by the Surrey Police Department and was available at Flames' home games. The cards were unnumbered and are listed below in checklist order.
COMPLETE SET (30) 5.00 12.00
1 Checklist .04 .10
2 Mark McArthur .30 .75
3 Michael Plenty .20 .50
4 Stan Marple .20 .50
5 Regan Stocco .20 .50
6 Derek DeCosty .20 .50
7 Todd Wetzel .20 .50
8 Ricky Plant .20 .50
9 John Haig .20 .50
10 Tony Redmond .20 .50
11 Paul Dixon .20 .50
12 Grant King .30 .75
13 Greg Burke .20 .50
14 Scott Campbell .20 .50
15 Nicky Chinn .30 .75
16 Mark Galazzi .20 .50
17 David Smith .20 .50
18 Jason Dailey .20 .50
19 Michael Timms .20 .50
20 Mikko Koivunoro .20 .50
21 Stan Marple HCO .04 .10
22 Mike Urquhart ACO .04 .10
23 Adrian Jenkinson TR .04 .10
24 Paul Dixon .20 .50
Derek DeCosty
Nicky Chinn
25 Team Photo Home .20 .50
26 Team Photo Away .20 .50
27 Sizzler MASCOT .04 .10
28 Jason Dailey .20 .50
Celebration
29 Trophies .04 .10
30 Mark McArthur .20 .50
Grant King

2002-03 UK Guildford Flames

This 30-card set featured players from the Guildford Flames of the British National League. The cards were available at home games. The cards were not numbered and were listed below in checklist order.

COMPLETE SET (30) 5.00 12.00
1 Ian Herbers .20 .50
2 Stan Marple HCO .20 .50
3 David Clarke .20 .50
4 Derek DeCosty .20 .50
5 Craig Lyons .20 .50
6 Ricky Plant .20 .50
7 Tony Redmond .20 .50
8 Paul Dixon .20 .50
9 Jason Lafreniere .30 .75
10 Jason Bowen .20 .50
11 Grant King .20 .50
12 Mike Torchia .30 .75
13 Corey Lyons .20 .50
14 Nicky Chinn .30 .75
15 Jeff White .20 .50
16 Mark Galazzi .20 .50
17 Ricky Skene .20 .50
18 Mike Urquhart ACO .02 .10
19 Stan Marple HCO .02 .10
20 Adrian Jenkinson TR .02 .10
21 Paul Dixon .20 .50
Corey Lyons
Jason Lafreniere
22 Team Photo .20 .50
Home
23 Team Photo .20 .50
Away
24 Team Photo .20 .50
Alternate
25 Sizzler MASCOT .02 .10
26 Grant King .30 .75
Mike Torchia
27 Ricky Plant GB .20 .50
28 David Clarke GB .20 .50
29 Andy Sparks .20 .50
Fred Perlini
Ryan Campbell
Retired Numbers
30 Checklist .01 .01

2003-04 UK Guildford Flames

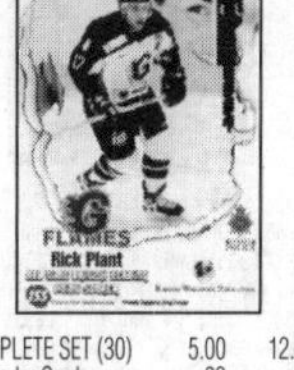

COMPLETE SET (30) 5.00 12.00
1 Header Card .02 .10
2 Peter Michnac .20 .50
3 Stan Marple .20 .50
4 Marian Smerciak .20 .50
5 Neil Liddiard .20 .50
6 Ryan Vince .20 .50
7 Ricky Plant .30 .75
8 Michael Timms .20 .50
9 Tony Redmond .20 .50
10 Milos Melicherik .20 .50
11 Paul Dixon .20 .50
12 Rastislav Palov .20 .50
13 Jozef Kohut .20 .50
14 Joe Dollin .20 .50
15 Stevie Lyle .40 1.00
16 Peter Konder .20 .50
17 Mark Galazzi .20 .50
18 Nick Cross .20 .50
19 Paul Dixon ACO .02 .10
20 Stan Marple HCO .02 .10
21 Dave Wiggins AM .02 .10
22 Captains & Assistants .20 .50
23 Home Kit .02 .10
24 Away Kit .02 .10
25 Mascot .02 .10
26 Action Card .02 .10
27 Flames Goalies .30 .75
28 Flames Eastern Europeans .20 .50
29 British Line .30 .75
30 Ricky Plant .20 .50
Leading British Points

2004-05 UK Guildford Flames

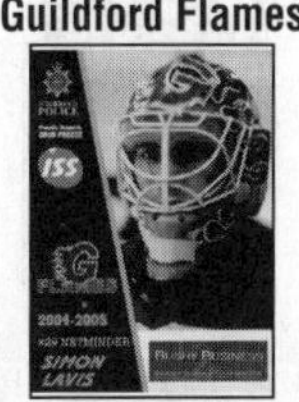

Produced by the team and available through the team's store and Armchair Sports.
COMPLETE SET (30) 5.00 12.00
1 Guildford Flames .02 .10
2 Peter Michnac .20 .50
3 Neil Liddiard .20 .50
4 Marian Smerciak .20 .50
5 David Savage .20 .50
6 Jason Reilly .20 .50
7 Stuart Potts .20 .50
8 Adam Walker .20 .50
9 Milos Melicherik .20 .50
10 Paul Dixon .20 .50
11 Andrew Hemmings .20 .50
12 Rastislav Palov .20 .50
13 Dusan Pohorelec .20 .50
14 Jozef Kohut .20 .50
15 Simon Lavis .20 .50
16 Miroslav Bielik .20 .50
17 Tom Annetts .20 .50
18 Peter Konder .20 .50
19 Nick Cross .20 .50
20 Paul Dixon .02 .10
21 Stan Marple CO .02 .10
22 Dave Wiggin ACO .02 .10
23 Captains and Assistants .20 .50
24 Home Jersey Team Photo .02 .10
25 Away Jersey Team Photo .02 .10
26 Sizzler MASCOT .01 .01
27 Celebration .02 .10
28 Netminders .30 .75
29 Playoff Trophy .01 .01
30 Terry Kurtenbach JSY RET .20 .50

2006-07 UK Guildford Flames

COMPLETE SET (24) 8.00 15.00
1 Neil Liddiard .25 .60
2 Marian Smerciak .25 .60
3 David Savage .25 .60
4 Ben Johnson .25 .60
5 Rob Lamey .25 .60
6 Stuart Potts .25 .60
7 Andrew Hemmings .25 .60
8 Rick Plant .25 .60
9 Robert Young .25 .60
10 Ben Duggan .25 .60
11 Milos Melicherik .25 .60
12 Paul Dixon .25 .60
13 Vaclav Zavoral .25 .60
14 Simon James .25 .60
15 Joe Watkins .40 1.00
16 Tom Annetts .40 1.00
17 Chris Wiggins .25 .60
18 Ben Austin .25 .60
19 Jozef Kohut .25 .60
20 Adam Hyman .25 .60
21 Rick Skene .25 .60
22 Ollie Bronniman .25 .60
23 Stan Marple .25 .60
24 Paul Dixon .25 .60

1999-00 UK Hull Thunder

This set features the Thunder of the British league. The set was produced by card shop Armchair Sports and was sold at the store and at home games. The print run has been confirmed at 500 sets.
COMPLETE SET (20) 4.00 10.00
1 Team CL .04 .10
2 Don Depoe CO .10 .25
3 Ian Defty .20 .50
4 Simon Greaves .20 .50
5 Mark Florence .20 .50
6 Dan Carney .20 .50
7 Stephen Johnson .20 .50
8 Anthony Johnson .20 .50
9 Scott Stephenson .20 .50
10 Tam Watkins .20 .50
11 Paul Thompson .20 .50
12 Jason Tatarnic .20 .50
13 Mark Pallister .20 .50
14 Ron Shudra .20 .50
15 Pasi Raitanen .30 .75
16 Steve Morden .20 .50
17 Slava Koulikov .20 .50
18 Steve Brown .20 .50
19 Chris Douglas .20 .50
20 Chris Bailey .20 .50

2001-02 UK Hull Thunder

Produced and sold by Armchair Sports, a British card shop, this 25-card set was sold at that shop and also at Thunder home games. The total print run has been confirmed at only just sets.
COMPLETE SET (25) 4.00 10.00
1 Checklist .04 .10
2 Mike Bishop CO .04 .10
3 Stephen Foster .20 .50
4 Andy Moffat .20 .50
5 Mike Bishop .20 .50
6 Corey Lyons .20 .50
7 Andy Munroe .20 .50
8 Mark Florence .20 .50
9 Stephen Johnson .20 .50
10 Anthony Johnson .20 .50
11 Anthony Payne .20 .50
12 Ryan Lake .20 .50
13 Karl Hopper UER .20 .50
14 Michael Bowman .20 .50
15 Stephen Wallace .20 .50
16 Ian Defty .20 .50
17 Oleg Synkov .20 .50
18 Steve Smillie .20 .50
19 Rob McCaig .20 .50
20 Darren Houghton .20 .50
21 Daryl Lavoie .20 .50
22 Eric Lavigne .20 .50
23 Mike O'Connor GM .04 .10
24 Terry Ward ACO .04 .10
25 Vanessa Brown TR .04 .10

2002-03 UK Hull Thunder

This 25-card set featured the Hull Thunder of the British National League. This set was produced by Armchair Sports and was available through them or the club shops on game nights.
COMPLETE SET (25) 5.00 12.00
1 Checklist .01 .01
2 Mike Bishop HCO .02 .10
3 Stephen Foster .20 .50
4 Keith Leyland .20 .50
5 Anthony Payne .20 .50
6 Scott Young .20 .50
7 Nathan Hunt .20 .50
8 Paul Ferone .20 .50
9 Andy Munroe .20 .50
10 Mark Florence .20 .50
11 Paul Wallace .20 .50
12 Mike Morin .20 .50
13 Ryan Lake .20 .50
14 Karl Hopper .20 .50
15 Mark Bultje .20 .50
16 Jonathan Weaver .20 .50
17 Steve Smillie .20 .50
18 Dominic Parlatore .20 .50
19 Dan Currie .30 .75
20 Sam Roberts .20 .50
21 Eoin McInerney .40 1.00
22 Marc West .20 .50
23 Mike Bishop .20 .50
24 Eric Lavigne .30 .75
25 Mike O'Connor GM .02 .10

1993-94 UK Humberside Hawks

This postcard set commemorates a now-defunct club in the British Ice Hockey League. The set was sponsored by BAE Aerospace and was given away during the season on game nights.
COMPLETE SET (18) 6.00 15.00
1 Kenny Johnson .40 1.00
2 Gavin De Jonge .40 1.00
3 Chris Hobson .40 1.00
4 Mike Bishop .40 1.00
6 Paul Simpson .40 1.00
7 Stewart Carvil .40 1.00
8 Shaun Johnson .40 1.00
9 Arren Burn .40 1.00
10 Stephen Johnson .40 1.00
12 Anthony Johnson .40 1.00
15 Anthony Payne .40 1.00
16 Andy Giles .40 1.00
17 Mike O'Conner .40 1.00
19 Andy Steel .40 1.00
20 Frank Killen .40 1.00
21 Dan Dorian .40 1.00
23 Alexander Koulikov .40 1.00
NNO Peter Johnson CO .40 1.00

1994-95 UK Humberside Hawks

This postcard set commemorates a now-defunct club in the British Ice Hockey League. The set was sponsored by BAE Aerospace and was given away during the season on game nights.
COMPLETE SET (20) 8.00 20.00
2 Malcolm Bell .40 1.00
4 Mike Bishop .40 1.00
5 Scott Young .40 1.00
6 Paul Simpson .40 1.00
8 Shaun Johnson .40 1.00
9 Wayne Anchikoski .60 1.50
10 Stephen Johnson .40 1.00
12 Anthony Johnson .40 1.00
14 Tony Saxby .40 1.00
15 Darcy Cahill .40 1.00
16 Chris Hobson .40 1.00
17 Danny Parkin .40 1.00
19 Scott Morrison .40 1.00
20 Danny Thompson .40 1.00
21 Paul Cast .40 1.00
22 Andy Port .40 1.00
23 Dominik Love .40 1.00
NNO Gavin De Jonge .40 1.00
NNO David Standling .40 1.00
NNO Peter Johnson CO .20 .50

2002-03 UK Ivan Matulik Testimonial

Set features prominent UK star Ivan Matulik, with one card for each season he played in England.
COMPLETE SET (12) 2.00 5.00
1 Header .20 .50
2 Sheffield Steelers .20 .50
3 Murrayfield Racers .20 .50
4 Cardiff Devils .20 .50
5 Cardiff Devils .20 .50
6 Cardiff Devils .20 .50
7 Cardiff Devils .20 .50
8 Cardiff Devils .20 .50
9 Cardiff Devils .20 .50
10 Manchester Storm .20 .50
11 Manchester Storm .20 .50
12 Cardiff Devils .20 .50

1998-99 UK Kingston Hawks

This set features the Hawks of the British league. The set was produced by Armchair Sports, a local card shop, and sold at that store and at home games. The print run has been confirmed at 500 sets.

COMPLETE SET (25) 4.00 10.00
1 Dale Lambert CO .16 .40
2 Ian Defty .16 .40
3 Mikka Pynnonen .20 .50
4 Simon Greaves .16 .40
5 Kelly Reed .16 .40
6 Dominic Love .20 .50
7 Bjorn Widmark .20 .50
8 Steve Nemeth .20 .50
9 Christer Widmark .20 .50
10 Stephen Johnson .16 .40
11 Mark Florence .16 .40
12 Anthony Payne .16 .40
13 Chris Hobson .16 .40
14 Mark McCoy .20 .50
15 Andy Steel .16 .40
16 Paddy O'Conner .16 .40
17 Ashley Tait .16 .40
18 Matt Staunton .16 .40
19 Pasi Raitanen .20 .50
20 Jason Coles .16 .40
21 Simon Leach .16 .40
22 Lucas Miller .16 .40
23 Michael Tasker .16 .40
24 Keith Milhench GM .04 .10
25 Team CL .04 .10

1997-98 UK Kingston Hawks Stickers

Produced by the team owner, this 20-sticker set came with a wall chart and the stickers could be bought as a set or singles.

COMPLETE SET (20) 4.80 12.00
1 Keith Milhench CO .10 .25
2 Bobby McEwen ACO .10 .25
3 Malcolm Bell .30 .75
4 Michael Knights .30 .75
5 Paul Simpson .30 .75
6 Kelly Reid .30 .75
7 Dominic Love .30 .75
8 Phil Brook .30 .75
9 Anthony Payne .30 .75
10 Chris Hobson .30 .75
11 Steve Smillie .30 .75
12 Andy Steel .30 .75
13 Ashley Tait .30 .75
14 Slava Koulikov .30 .75
15 Norman Pinnington .30 .75
16 Tony McAleavy .30 .75
17 Pasi Raitinen .30 .75
18 The Kingston Kid .10 .25
19 Ian Defty .30 .75
20 Michael Tasker .30 .75

1999-00 UK London Knights

This postcard sized set features the Knights of the top British league. The set was produced by Armchair Sports and sold by that card shop, as well as by the team at home games.

COMPLETE SET (17) 3.60 9.00
1 Tom Ashe .20 .50
2 Mark Bultje .20 .50
3 John Byce .30 .75
4 Scott Campbell .20 .50
5 Mark Cavallin .30 .75
6 Ryan Duthie .20 .50
7 Jeff Hoad .20 .50
8 Marc Hussey .30 .75
9 Guy Leveque .20 .50
10 Neal Martin .20 .50
11 Chris McSorley CO .20 .50
12 Tim Murray .20 .50
13 Scott Rex CO .10 .25
14 Paul Rushforth .20 .50
15 Claudio Scremin .30 .75
16 Mike Ware .30 .75
17 Todd Wetzel .20 .50

2001-02 UK London Knights

This set was produced by Armchair Sports in England.

COMPLETE SET (28) 5.00 12.00
1 Logo and Checklist .02 .10
2 Doug Serle .20 .50
3 Gerald Adams .20 .50
4 Kim Ahlroos .20 .50
5 Sean Blanchard .20 .50
6 Trevor Roenick .30 .75
7 David Struch .20 .50
8 Dave Clark .20 .50
9 Nathan Leslie .20 .50
10 Maurizio Mansi .20 .50
11 Steve Thornton .20 .50
12 Mark Kolesar .20 .50
14 Mike Barrie .20 .50
15 Greg Burke .20 .50
16 Bob Leslie HCO .02 .10
17 Ian McIntyre .20 .50
18 Ritchie Bronilla .20 .50
19 Vezio Sacratini .20 .50
20 Trevor Robins .20 .50
21 Jason Ellery EQM .02 .10
22 Mike Ware .20 .50
23 Rob Donovan .20 .50
24 David Trofimenkoff .20 .50
25 Dominic Amodeo .30 .75
26 Scott Bailey .30 .75
27 Paul Rushforth .20 .50
28 Mighty Knight MASCOT .02 .10

2002-03 UK London Knights

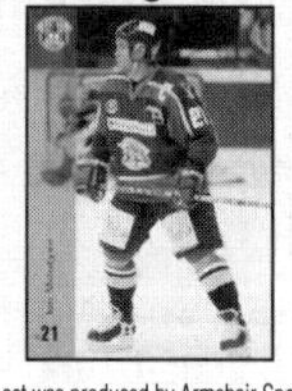

This set was produced by Armchair Sports in England.

COMPLETE SET (24) 5.00 10.00
1 Checklist .01 .01
2 Ake Lilljebjorn .20 .50
3 Gerald Adams .20 .50
4 Kim Ahlroos .20 .50
5 Nathan Leslie .20 .50
6 Moe Mansi .20 .50
7 Mark Kolesar .30 .75
8 A.J. Kelham .20 .50
9 Jeff Hoad .20 .50
10 Chris Slater .20 .50
11 Ian McIntyre .20 .50
12 Greg Burke .20 .50
13 Steve Aronson .20 .50
14 Rich Bronilla .20 .50
15 Vezio Sacratini .20 .50
16 Dave Trofimenkoff .30 .75
17 Paul Rushforth .20 .50
18 Sean Blanchard .30 .75
19 Dennis Maxwell .30 .75
20 Ed Patterson .30 .75
21 Bob Leslie CO .02 .10
22 Mighty Knight .02 .10
23 Jim Brithen CO .02 .10
24 Jason Ellery EQM .02 .10

2003-04 UK London Racers

COMPLETE SET (20) 5.00 10.00
1 Chris Bailey .20 .50
2 Noel Burkitt .20 .50
3 Nick Burton .20 .50
4 Lukas Filip .20 .50
5 Kalle Konsti .20 .50
6 Zoran Kozic .20 .50
7 Evan Lindsay .30 .75
8 Marc Long .20 .50
9 Mike McKinnon .20 .50
10 Brian McLaughlin .20 .50
11 Sean Murdoch .20 .50
12 Mojmir Musil .20 .50
13 Oscar MASCOT .01 .01
14 Jason Robinson .20 .50
15 Mark Scott .20 .50
16 Jani Touminen .20 .50
17 Warren Tait .20 .50
18 Matt Van der Velden .30 .75
19 Erik Zachrisson .20 .50

2004-05 UK London Racers

According to minor league expert Ralph Slate, there were just 50 copies produced of this set. As a result, you'll no doubt understand why we have no pricing information for this series.

COMPLETE SET (18)
1 Scott Nichol
2 Eric Cairns
3 Jeremy Cornish
4 Dennis Maxwell
5 Denis Ladouceur
6 Joe Watkins
7 Mark Gouett
8 Jim Vickers
9 Ian McIntyre
10 Jason Robinson
11 Steve Moria
12 Joe Ciccarello
13 Mark Thomas
14 Jason Hewitt
15 Adam Dopson
16 Mark Foord
17 Richard Hargreaves
18 J.J. McGrath

2004-05 UK London Racers Playoffs

COMPLETE SET (18) 6.00 15.00
1 Eric Cairns .60 1.50
2 Joe Ciccarello .30 .75
3 Jeremy Cornish .30 .75
4 Adam Dobson .40 1.00
5 Matt Foord .30 .75
6 Mark Gouett .30 .75
7 Richard Hargreaves .30 .75
8 Jason Hewitt .30 .75
9 Denis Ladouceur .30 .75
10 Dennis Maxwell .30 .75
11 J.J. McGrath .30 .75
12 Ian McIntyre .30 .75
13 Steve Moria .30 .75
14 Scott Nichol .60 1.50
15 Jason Robinson .30 .75
16 Mark Thomas .30 .75
17 Jim Vickers .30 .75
18 Joe Watkins .30 .75

2003-04 UK Manchester Phoenix

COMPLETE SET (22) 5.00 10.00
1 Jayme Platt .30 .75
2 Rick Brebant .20 .50
3 Dave Clancy .30 .75
4 Dwight Parrish .20 .50
5 Mike Lankshear .20 .50
6 Mark Thomas .20 .50
7 Carl Greenhous .20 .50
8 Mark Bultje .20 .50
9 David Kozier .20 .50
10 Mike Morin .20 .50
11 Petteri Lotila .20 .50
12 Chad Brandimore .20 .50
13 George Awada .20 .50
14 Marc Lovell .20 .50
15 Jason Hewitt .20 .50
16 Aaron Davies .20 .50
17 Darcy Anderson .20 .50
18 Mika Skytta .20 .50
19 Jeff Sebastian .20 .50
20 Nick Poole .20 .50
21 Manace MASCOT .02 .10
NNO Checklist .01 .01
NNO Checklist .01 .01

2001-02 UK Manchester Storm

Produced by Cardtraders.com, this 24-card set was available at Storm home games. The production run was limited to just 495 sets. Card #13 was not printed for superstitious reasons. Card #24 card was redeemable for a limited edition 12"x12" team card that was individually serial-numbered to 125.

COMPLETE SET (24) 4.80 12.00
1 Paul Ferone .20 .50
2 Dan Preston .20 .50
3 Trevor Gallant .20 .50
4 Mike Morin .20 .50
5 Dwight Parrish .20 .50
6 Mark Bultje .20 .50
7 Joe Busillo .20 .50
8 Ivan Matulik .20 .50
9 Pierre Allard .20 .50
10 Russ Romaniuk .20 .50
11 Joe Cardarelli .20 .50
12 Stevie Lyle .30 .75
14 Mike Torchia .40 1.00
15 Kayle Short .20 .50
16 Justin Hocking .30 .75
17 Kris Miller .20 .50
18 Russ Richardson .20 .50
19 Daryl Lipsey HCO .04 .10
20 Mike Torchia .30 .75
21 Stevie Lyle .30 .75
22 Lightning Jack MASCOT .04 .10
23 Rob Wilson .04 .10
24 Redemption Card .40 1.00
25 Checklist .04 .10

2001-02 UK Manchester Storm Retro

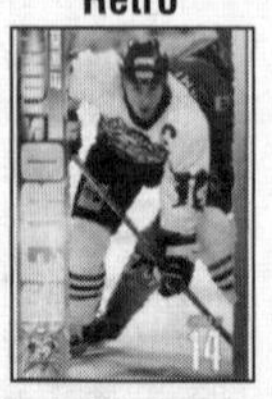

This 21-card set featured some of the most popular players from the history of the Manchster Storm of the British Ice Hockey Superleague. Cards are not numbered and are listed below by jersey number.

COMPLETE SET (21) 5.00 10.00
1 Dale Jago .20 .50
2 Craig Woodcroft .20 .50
3 Trevor Gallant .20 .50
4 Kelly Askew .20 .50
5 Jeff Tomlinson .20 .50
6 Daryl Lipsey .20 .50
7 Mike Morin .20 .50
8 Shawn Byram .20 .50
9 Pierre Allard .20 .50
10 Mark Bernard .20 .50
11 John Finnie .20 .50
12 Blair Scott .20 .50
13 Hilton Ruggles .20 .50
14 David Trofimenkoff .20 .50
15 Jim Hrivnak .30 .75
16 Frank Pietrangelo .30 .75
17 Brad Rubachuk .20 .50
18 Stefan Ketola .20 .50
19 Jeff Jablonski .20 .50
20 Kris Miller .20 .50
21 Logo Card .01 .01

2002-03 UK Manchester Storm

This set was produced by Armchair Sports in England.

COMPLETE SET (21) 5.00 10.00
1 Colin Pepperall .20 .50
2 Dan Preston .20 .50
3 Shawn Maltby .20 .50
4 Geoff Peters .20 .50
5 Mike Perna .20 .50
6 Pasi Nielikainen .20 .50
7 Dwight Parrish .20 .50
8 Mark Bultje .20 .50
9 Rob Wilson .20 .50
10 Ivan Matulik .20 .50
11 Pierre Allard .20 .50
12 David Longstaff .20 .50
13 Ryan Stewart .20 .50
14 Joe Cardarelli .20 .50
15 Stevie Lyle .30 .75
16 Mike Torchia .30 .75
17 Dan Hodge .20 .50
18 Daryl Lipsey HCO .02 .10
19 Mike Torchia .30 .75
20 Stevie Lyle .30 .75
21 Checklist .01 .01

2004-05 UK Milton Keynes Lightning

The Lightning play in the English Premier Ice Hockey League. Reportedly just 200 sets were produced, but some of those were apparently broken by the team in order to sell some cards individually. We have not confirmed any sales of these sets or singles and thus are leaving the set unpriced for now.

COMPLETE SET (20)
1 Checklist
2 Steve Carpenter
3 Michael Wales
4 Phil Wooderson
5 Bari McKenzie
6 Gary Clarke
7 Kurt Irvine
8 Dean Campbell
9 Adam Carr
10 Jamie Randall
11 Chris McEwen
12 Dwayne Newman
13 Mikko Skinnari
14 Allen Sutton
15 Matt Van der Velden
16 Greg Randall
17 Simon Howard
18 Ross Bowers
19 Nick Poole
20 David Coffey
Tom Ledgard

2000-01 UK Nottingham Panthers

This set features the Panthers of Britain's top hockey league. The cards were produced by Cardtraders.com; and available from the team on game nights. Card #13 does not exist due to superstitious reasons.

COMPLETE SET (30) 4.80 12.00
1 Checklist .04 .10
2 Jordan Willis .30 .75
3 Paul Moran .16 .40
4 Duncan Paterson .16 .40
5 Kevin Hoffman .16 .40
6 David Struch .16 .40
7 Randall Weber .16 .40
8 Greg Hadden .16 .40
9 Daryl Lavoie .16 .40
10 P.C. Drouin .20 .50
11 Marc Levers .16 .40
12 Darryl Moxam .20 .50
14 Greg Burke .16 .40
15 Ashley Tait .16 .40
16 Ryan Gillis .16 .40
17 Jim Paek .20 .50
18 Chris Baxter .16 .40
19 Jamie Leach .30 .75
20 Eoin McInerney .30 .75
21 Robert Nordmark .16 .40
22 Graham Garden .16 .40
23 Casson Masters .16 .40
24 Barry Nieckar .20 .50
25 Eric Lavigne .20 .50
27 Peter Woods CO .04 .10
28 Redemption Voucher .01
29 Alex Dampier DOH .04 .10
30 Gary Moran GM .04 .10
31 Team Photo .16 .40
32 Player Awards .16 .40
NA Robert Nordmark .16 .40

2001-02 UK Nottingham Panthers

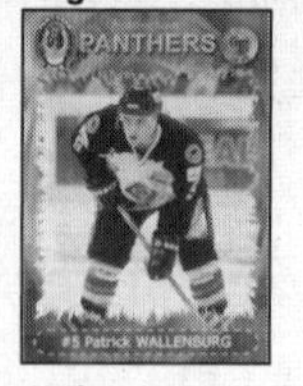

Produced by Cardtraders.com, this 28-card set was available at Panthers home games. The production run was limited to just 495 sets, and each card states that on the card back. Card #13 was not printed for superstitious reasons.

COMPLETE SET (28) 4.80 12.00
1 Team Logo .04 .10
2 Brent Pope .20 .50
3 Clayton Norris .20 .50
4 Patrick Wallenberg .20 .50
5 Randall Weber .20 .50
6 Greg Hadden .20 .50
7 Frank Evans .20 .50
8 Claude Savoie .20 .50
9 P.C. Drouin .30 .75
10 Steve Moira .20 .50
11 Ashley Tait .30 .75
12 Paul Adey CO .04 .10
14 Jimmy Drolet .30 .75
15 Danny Lorenz .30 .75
16 Joel Poirier .30 .75
17 Paul Moran .20 .50
18 Barry Nieckar .30 .75
19 Darren Maloney .20 .50
20 Calle Carlsson .20 .50
21 Pasi Hakkinen .20 .50
22 A.J. Kelham .20 .50
23 Alex Dampier CO .04 .10
24 Lee Jinman .30 .75
25 Gary Moran GM .04 .10
26 Paws MASCOT .04 .10
27 Equipment Managers .04 .10
28 Trainers .04 .10
29 Head Office .04 .10

2002-03 UK Nottingham Panthers

Produced by cardtraders.uk, this 22-card set featured the Nottingham Panthers of the British Ice Hockey Superleague. The cards are unnumbered and are listed below in checklist order.

COMPLETE SET (22) 4.00 10.00
1 Mika Pietila .20 .50
2 Jim Paek .20 .50
3 Marc Hussey .20 .50
4 Eric Charron .20 .50
5 Greg Hadden .20 .50
6 Dody Wood .30 .75
7 Briane Thompson .20 .50
8 Jason Elders .20 .50
9 Kristian Taubert .20 .50
10 Scott Allison .20 .50
11 Mark Cadotte .20 .50
12 Petter Sandstrom .20 .50
13 John Purves .30 .75
14 Paul Moran .20 .50
15 Barry Nieckar .30 .75
16 Jason Clarke .20 .50
17 Lee Jinman .30 .75
18 Paul Adey .20 .50
19 Mascot .02 .10
20 Gary Moran GM .02 .10
21 Checklist .02 .10
22 Front Office .02 .10

2003-04 UK Nottingham Panthers

COMPLETE SET (18) 5.00 10.00
1 Niklas Sundberg .30 .75
2 David Clarke .20 .50
3 Kim Ahlroos .20 .50
4 James Morgan .20 .50
5 David Struch .20 .50
6 Robert Stancok .20 .50
7 Briane Thompson .20 .50
8 Marc Levers .20 .50
9 Kristian Taubert .20 .50
10 Mikko Koivunoro .20 .50
11 Geoff Woolhouse .30 .75
12 Joel Salonen .20 .50
13 Mark Cadotte .30 .75
14 Paul Moran .20 .50
15 Daniel Scott .20 .50
16 Calle Carlsson .20 .50
17 John Craighead .30 .75
18 Paul Addey CO .02 .10

2004-05 UK Nottingham Panthers

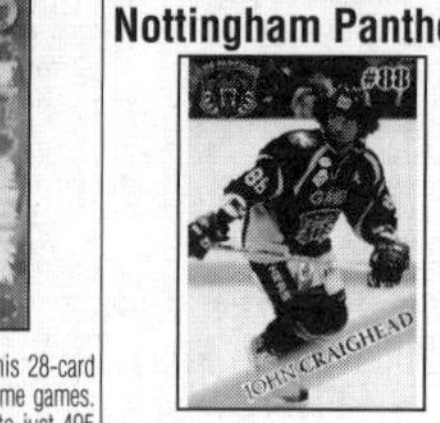

Produced by the team and sold in the club shop.

COMPLETE SET (20) 5.00 10.00
1 Paul Adey CO .02 .10
2 Kim Ahlroos .20 .50
3 Calle Carlsson .20 .50
4 David Clarke .20 .50
5 Mark Codotte .20 .75
6 John Craighead .20 .50
7 Curtis Cruickshank .30 .50
8 Marek Ivan .20 .50
9 Konstantin Kalmikov .20 .50
10 Jan Krulis .20 .50
11 Jan Magdosko .20 .50
12 Steve McKenna .40 1.00
13 Gary Moran GM .02 .10
14 Paul Moran .20 .50
15 Matt Myers .20 .50
16 Scott Ricci .20 .50
17 Daniel Scott .20 .50
18 Roman Tvrdon .20 .50
19 Richard Wojciak .20 .50
20 Geoff Woolhouse .20 .50

2006-07 UK Nottingham Panthers

COMPLETE SET (20) 8.00 15.00
1 Joe Cardarelli .30 .75
2 David Clarke .30 .75
3 James Cooke .30 .75
4 James Ferrara .30 .75
5 Jan Krajicek .30 .75
6 Sean McAslan .30 .75
7 Danny Meyers .30 .75
8 Paul Moran .30 .75
9 Matt Myers .30 .75
10 James Neil .30 .75
11 Corey Neilson .30 .75
12 Matus Petricko .30 .75
13 Mike Rees .30 .75
14 Rastislav Rovnianek .30 .75
15 Ryan Shmyr .30 .75
16 Steve Simoes .30 .75
17 Rod Stevens .30 .75
18 Geoff Woolhouse .60 1.50
19 Mike Ellis CO .02 .10
20 Calle Carlsson ACO .02 .10

2002-03 UK Peterborough Phantoms

This set was produced by Armchair Sports in England.

COMPLETE SET (18) 5.00 10.00
1 Luc Chabot .30 .75
2 James Moore .25 .60
3 David Whitwell .25 .60
4 Craig Britton .25 .60
5 Jon Fone .25 .60
6 Pete Morley .25 .60
7 Jessie Hammill .25 .60
8 Jason Buckman .25 .60
9 Lewis Buckman .25 .60
10 Russell Coleman .25 .60
11 Duncan Cook .25 .60
12 Darren Cotton .25 .60
13 Jon Cotton .25 .60
14 James Ellwood .25 .60
15 Grant Hendry .25 .60
16 Doug McEwen .25 .60
17 Shaun Yardley .25 .60
18 Checklist .01 .01

2004-05 UK Ron Shudra Testimonial

COMPLETE SET (16) 3.00 8.00
1 Ron Shudra 1990-91 .20 .50
2 Ron Shudra 1991-92 .20 .50
3 Ron Shudra 1992-93 .20 .50
4 Ron Shudra 1993-94 .20 .50
5 Ron Shudra 1994-95 .20 .50
6 Ron Shudra 1995-96 .20 .50
7 Ron Shudra 1996-97 .20 .50
8 Ron Shudra 1997-98 .20 .50
9 Ron Shudra 1998-99 .20 .50
10 Ron Shudra 1999-00 .20 .50
11 Ron Shudra 2000-01 .20 .50
12 Ron Shudra 2001-02 .20 .50
13 Ron Shudra 2002-03 .20 .50
14 Ron Shudra 2003-04 .20 .50
15 Ron Shudra 2004-05 .20 .50
16 Ron Shudra CL .20 .50

2000-01 UK Sekonda Superleague

This 206-card set produced by Kudos featured the players of the British Superleague. The cards were unnumbered, and so are listed in team set order below. The last 36 cards of the set were available as an update set to the original 170-card base set. Cards were available at most Superleague venues in 5-card cello packs or as team sets or the complete league set.

COMPLETE SET (170) 20.00 50.00
COMPLETE UPDATE SET (36) 4.00 10.00
1 Ice Hockey Superleague .10 .25
2 Jim Lynch CO .10 .25
3 Paul Heavey ACO .10 .25
4 Philippe DeRouville .40 1.00
5 Colin Ryder .30 .75
6 Trevor Doyle .20 .50
7 Derek Eberle .20 .50
8 Anders Hillstrom .20 .50
9 Jan Mikel .20 .50
10 Johan Silfwerplatz .20 .50
11 Scott Young .20 .50
12 Dainius Bauyba .20 .50
13 Cam Bristow .20 .50
14 Shawn Byram .20 .50
15 Ed Courtenay .30 .75
16 Tony Hand .30 .75
17 Rhett Gordon .20 .50
18 Mike Harding .20 .50
19 Mark Montanari .20 .50
20 Jonathan Weaver .20 .50
21 Teeder Wynne .20 .50
22 David Whistle CO .10 .25
23 Mark Cavallin .20 .50
24 Todd Kelman .20 .50
25 Kevin Riehl .20 .50
26 Paxton Schulte .20 .50
27 Colin Ward .20 .50
28 Jeff Hoad .20 .50
29 Shane Johnson .20 .50
30 Enio Sacilotto CO .10 .25
31 Brian Greer .20 .50
32 Joe Watkins .20 .50
33 Matej Bukna .20 .50
34 Jimmy Drolet .20 .50
35 Jason Mansoff .20 .50
36 Mark Matier .20 .50
37 Steve O'Rourke .20 .50
38 Reid Simonton .20 .50
39 Brent Bobyck .20 .50
40 Chris Brant .20 .50
41 Mark Bultje .20 .50
42 Joe Cardarelli .20 .50
43 Dan Ceman .20 .50
44 Joe Ciccarello .20 .50
45 Darren Hurley .20 .50
46 Blake Knox .20 .50
47 Stephane Roy .20 .50
48 Brad Wingfield .20 .50
49 Doug McCarthy CO .10 .25
50 Troy Walkington CO .10 .25
51 Stevie Lyle .80 2.00
52 Derek Herlofsky .40 1.00
53 Frank Evans .20 .50
54 Kip Noble .20 .50
55 Clayton Norris .10 .25
56 Dwight Parrish .20 .50
57 Alan Schuler .20 .50
58 Rick Strachan .20 .50
59 Denis Chasse .20 .50
60 James Hanlon .20 .50
61 Rick Kowalsky .20 .50
62 Ivan Matulik .20 .50
63 Ian McIntyre .20 .50
64 Steve Moria .20 .50
65 John Parco .20 .50
66 Vezio Sacratini .20 .50
67 Steve Thornton .20 .50
68 Mike Ware .20 .50
69 Chris McSorley CO .20 .50
70 Trevor Robins .20 .50
71 Shawn Silver .20 .50
72 Rich Bronilla .20 .50
73 Neal Martin .20 .50
74 Randy Perry .20 .50
75 Mikael Tjallden .20 .50
76 Nicky Chinn .30 .75
77 Pat Ferschweiler .20 .50
78 Claude Jutras .20 .50
79 Mikko Koivunoro .20 .50
80 Mark Kolesar .20 .50
81 Jay Neal .20 .50
82 Bryan Richardson .20 .50
83 Paul Rushforth .20 .50
84 David Vallieres .20 .50
85 Darby Walker .20 .50
86 Brendan Yarema .20 .50
87 Terry Cristensen CO .10 .25
88 Daryl Lipsey ACO .10 .25
89 Frank Pietrangelo .40 1.00
90 Dave Trofimenkoff .40 1.00
91 Curtis Bowen .20 .50
92 Matt Eldred .20 .50
93 Perry Johnson .20 .50
94 Troy Neumeier .20 .50
95 Rob Robinson .20 .50
96 Blair Scott .20 .50
97 Pierre Allard .20 .50
98 Kevin Brown .20 .50
99 Greg Bullock .20 .50
100 Doug Doull .20 .50
101 Marty Flichel .20 .50
102 Trevor Gallant .10 .25
103 Jason Glover .20 .50

104 Mike Morin .20 .50
105 Corey Spring .20 .50
106 Shayne Stevenson .20 .50
107 Rob Trumbley .20 .50
108 Jukka Jalonen CO .10 .25
109 Jim Hibbert .20 .50
110 Tommi Satosaari .20 .50
111 Craig Binns .20 .50
112 Santeri Immonen .20 .50
113 Arttu Kaykho .20 .50
114 Miroslav Mosnar .20 .50
115 Darren McAusland .20 .50
116 Rob Wilson .20 .50
117 Tero Arkiomaa .20 .50
118 Louis Bedard .20 .50
119 Tomas Kupka .20 .50
120 Matt Oates .20 .50
121 Joel Poirer .20 .50
122 Timo Salonen .20 .50
123 Tommi Sova .20 .50
124 Alex Dampier CO .10 .25
125 Eoin McInerney .40 1.00
126 Jordan Willis .40 1.00
127 Greg Burke .20 .50
128 Ryan Gillis .20 .50
129 Eric Lavigne .20 .50
130 Daryl Lavoie .20 .50
131 Jim Paek .20 .50
132 Duncan Paterson .20 .50
133 P. C. Drouin .20 .50
134 Graham Garden .20 .50
135 Greg Hadden .20 .50
136 Jamie Leach .20 .50
137 Daryl Moxam .20 .50
138 Barry Nieckar .20 .50
139 David Struch .20 .50
140 Ashley Tait .20 .50
141 Randall Weber .20 .50
142 Mike Blaisdell CO .20 .50
143 Mike O'Neill .40 1.00
144 Steve Carpenter .20 .50
145 Shayne McCosh .20 .50
146 Jeff Sebastian .20 .50
147 Kayle Short .20 .50
148 Adam Smith .20 .50
149 Dennis Vial .40 1.00
150 Scott Allison .20 .50
151 Paul Beraldo .20 .50
152 Rick Brebant .20 .50
153 Dale Craigwell .20 .50
154 David Longstaff .20 .50
155 Scott Metcalfe .20 .50
156 Warren Norris .20 .50
157 Steve Roberts .20 .50
158 Kent Simpson .20 .50
159 Jason Weaver .20 .50
160 Brent Bobyck .20 .50
161 Ayr Eagles .10 .25
162 Belfast Giants .10 .25
163 Bracknell Bees .10 .25
164 Cardiff Devils .10 .25
165 London Knights .10 .25
166 Manchester Storm .10 .25
167 Newcastle Jesters .10 .25
168 Nottingham Panthers .10 .25
169 Sheffield Steelers .10 .25
170 Lucky Card .40 1.00
171 Tony Hand .20 .50
172 Jason Bowen .10 .25
173 Paul Ferone .10 .25
174 Todd Goodwin .10 .25
175 Kory Karlander .10 .25
176 Jerry Keefe .10 .25
177 Steve Roberts .10 .25
178 Doug Searle .10 .25
179 Rod Stevens .10 .25
180 Rob Stewart .10 .25
181 Derek Wilkinson .40 1.00
182 Jason Wright .10 .25
183 Bob Maudie .10 .25
184 Jason Heywood .10 .25
185 Frank Defrenza .10 .25
186 J-F Tremblay .10 .25
187 Kim Ahlroos .10 .25
188 Aaron Boh .20 .50
189 Terry Marchant .10 .25
190 Grant Richison .10 .25
191 Mikael Tjallden .10 .25
192 Brendan Yarema .20 .50
193 Brent Bobyck .10 .25
194 Pat Mazzoli .10 .25
195 Barrie Moore .10 .25
196 Eric Fenton .20 .50
197 Daniel Lacroix .20 .50
198 Chris Baxter .10 .25
199 Casson Masters .10 .25
200 Robert Nordmark .10 .25
201 Paul Adey .10 .25
202 Kent Simpson .10 .25
203 Mike Torchia .40 1.00
204 Checklist .04 .10
205 Checklist .04 .10
206 Checklist .04 .10

1993-94 UK Sheffield Steelers

This 19-card set was produced as part of a Drugs Freeze program and originally came with a collector's album.

COMPLETE SET (19) 4.00 10.00
1 Andy Havenhand .20 .50
2 Alan Hague .20 .50
3 Tim Cranston .20 .50
4 Neil Abel .20 .50
5 Scott Neil .20 .50
6 Steve Nemeth .20 .50
7 Tommy Plommer .20 .50
8 Ivan Matulik .20 .50
9 Danny Boome .20 .50
10 Mark Wright .20 .50
11 Chris Kelland .20 .50
12 Les Millie .20 .50
13 Selmar Odeline .20 .50
14 Ron Shudra .20 .50
15 Martin McKay .20 .50
16 Dampier w/Tuyl .20 .50
17 Netminders .30 .75
18 Team Photo .30 .75
19 Sheffield Scimitars .20 .50

1994-95 UK Sheffield Steelers

This set features the Steelers of the British league. The cards are regulation size and were sold by the team at home games as part of a Drugs Freeze program.

COMPLETE SET (25) 4.00 10.00
1 Alex Dampier MGR .10 .25
2 Clyde Tuyl CO .10 .25
3 Paul Jackson .30 .75
4 Scott Neil .20 .50
5 Team Photo .20 .50
6 Ron Handy .20 .50
7 Patrick O'Conner .20 .50
8 Dean Smith .20 .50
9 Mike O'Conner .20 .50
10 Backroom Staff .10 .25
11 Tim Cranston .20 .50
12 Les Millie .20 .50
13 Alan Hague .20 .50
14 Perry Doyle .20 .50
15 Ron Shudra .20 .50
16 Mark Wright .20 .50
17 Tommy Plommer .20 .50
18 Scott Heaton .20 .50
19 Neil Abel .20 .50
20 Steeler Dan .10 .25
21 Rob Wilson .20 .50
22 Chris Kelland .20 .50
23 Andy Havenhand .20 .50
24 Martin McKay .20 .50
25 Steve Nemeth .30 .75

1995-96 UK Sheffield Steelers

This set features the Steelers of the British league. This 24-card set was produced as part of a Drugs Freeze program and originally came with a collector's album.

COMPLETE SET (24) 4.00 10.00
1 Martin McKay .16 .40
2 Ron Shudra .16 .40
3 Ken Priestlay .20 .50
4 Steve Nemeth .20 .50
5 Tommy Plommer .16 .40
6 Nicky Chinn .40 1.00
7 Tony Hand .40 1.00
8 Mike O'Conner .16 .40
9 Mark Wright .16 .40
10 Chris Kelland .16 .40
11 Andre Malo .16 .40
12 Les Millie .16 .40
13 Sheffield Arena .10 .25
14 Team Photo .16 .40
15 Scott Heaton .16 .40
16 Tim Cranston .16 .40
17 Neil Abel .16 .40
18 Scott Neil .16 .40
19 Perry Doyle .16 .40
20 Backroom Staff .10 .25
21 Alex Dampier MGR .10 .25
22 Clyde Tuyl CO .10 .25
23 The Silverware .10 .25
24 Steeler Foggy Dan .10 .25

1997-98 UK Sheffield Steelers

This set features the Steelers of the British Ice Hockey League. This 25-card set was produced as part of a Drugs Freeze program and originally came with a collector's album. The sets were available on game nights.

COMPLETE SET (25) 4.80 12.00
1 James Hibbert .20 .50
2 Tim Cranston .20 .50
3 Rob Wilson .20 .50
4 Ken Priestlay .30 .75
5 Tommy Plommer .20 .50
6 Frank Kovacs .20 .50
7 Nicky Chinn .30 .75
8 David Longstaff .20 .50
9 Tony Hand .30 .75
10 Dion Del Monte .20 .50
11 Scott Allison .20 .50
12 Chris Kelland .20 .50
13 Sheffield Arena .10 .25
14 Team Photo .10 .25
15 Andre Malo .20 .50
16 Jamie Van Der Horst .20 .50
17 Andre Malo .20 .50
18 Mike Ware .20 .50
19 Ron Shudra .20 .50
20 Ed Courtenay .30 .75
21 Piero Greco .20 .50
22 Corey Beaulieu .20 .50
23 Steeler Foggy Dan .10 .25
24 Alex Dampier MGR .10 .25
25 Clyde Tuyl CO .10 .25

1999-00 UK Sheffield Steelers

This postcard size set features the Steelers of the top British league. The cards were produced by Armchair Sports, a British card shop, and sold there and by the team.

COMPLETE SET (22) 4.80 12.00
1 Mike Blaisdell CO .20 .50
2 Dan Ceman .30 .75
3 Greg Clancy .20 .50
4 Ed Courtenay .30 1.00
5 Dale Craigwell .30 1.00
6 Matt Hoffman .20 .50
7 Dale Junkin .20 .50
8 Derek Laxdal .30 .75
9 David Longstaff .20 .50
10 Andre Malo .20 .50
11 Mark Matier .20 .50
12 Shayne McCosh .20 .50
13 Don McKee CO .20 .10
14 Kip Noble .20 .50
15 Thomas Plommer .20 .50
16 Kayle Short .20 .50
17 Shawn Silver .20 .50
18 Grant Sjerven .20 .50
19 Dennis Vial .40 1.00
20 Jason Weaver .20 .50
21 Rob Wilson .20 .50
22 Teeder Wynne .20 .50

2000-01 UK Sheffield Steelers

This set features the Steelers of the British Sekonda league, the top division in the UK. The cards were sold in set form by the team.

COMPLETE SET (27) 4.00 10.00
1 Logo Card .10 .25
2 Champions .14 .35
3 Team Photo .14 .35
4 Paul Adey .14 .35
5 Scott Allison .14 .35
6 Andy & Paul .04 .10
7 Paul Beraldo .20 .50
8 Mike Blaisdell .20 .50
9 Brent Bobyck .14 .35
10 Rick Brebant .14 .35
11 Steve Carpenter .14 .35
12 Dale Craigwell .30 .75
13 Steeler Dan MASCOT .10 .25
14 David Longstaff .14 .35
15 Shayne McCosh .14 .35
16 Scott Metcalfe .20 .50
17 Warren Norris .14 .35
18 Mike O'Neill .30 .75
19 Steve Roberts .14 .35
20 Jeff Sebastian .14 .35
21 Kayle Short .14 .35
22 David Simms CO .10 .25
23 Kent Simpson .14 .35
24 Adam Smith .14 .35
25 Mike Torchia .40 1.00
26 Dennis Vial .20 .50
27 Jason Weaver .14 .35

2000-01 UK Sheffield Steelers Centurions

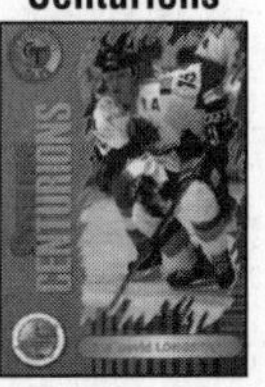

Produced by Cardtraders.com, this 18- card set celebrates the players who have represented Sheffield in more than 100 games. The set was sold on game nights and was also available through Armchair Sports.

COMPLETE SET (18) 4.00 10.00
1 Ed Courtenay .40 1.00
2 Tommy Plommer .20 .50
3 David Longstaff .20 .50
4 Rob Wilson .20 .50
5 Ron Shudra .20 .50
6 Tim Cranston .20 .50
7 Chris Kelland .20 .50
8 Andre Malo .20 .50
9 Ken Priestlay .30 .75
10 Scott Neil .20 .50
11 Tony Hand .40 1.00
12 Kayle Short .20 .50
13 Mike O'Connor .20 .50
14 Scott Allison .20 .50
15 Neil Abel .20 .50
16 Steve Nemeth .20 .50
17 Checklist .04 .10
18 Ron Shudra .20 .50
Player of the Decade

2001-02 UK Sheffield Steelers

COMPLETE SET (19) 5.00 10.00
1 Scott Allison .20 .50
2 Ryan Bach .30 .75
3 Cal Benazic .20 .50
4 Mike Blaisdell CO .20 .50
5 Brent Bobyck .20 .50
6 Chris Brant .20 .50
7 Rick Brebant .20 .50
8 Jeff Brown .20 .50
9 Mark Dutiaume .20 .50
10 Paul Kruse .30 .75
11 Mark Laniel .20 .50
12 Brad Lauer .20 .50
13 Peter Leboutillier .30 .75
14 Chris Lipsett .20 .50
15 Jason Mansoff .20 .50
16 Bob Maudie .20 .50
17 Kevin Miehm .20 .50
18 Jeff Sebastian .20 .50
19 Ron Shudra .20 .50

2002-03 UK Sheffield Steelers

COMPLETE SET (19) 5.00 10.00
1 Mike Blaisdell CO .20 .50
2 Brent Bobyck .20 .50
3 Rick Brebant .20 .50
4 Jeff Brown .20 .50
5 Calle Carlsson .20 .50
6 Dion Darling .20 .50
7 Mark Dutiaume .20 .50
8 Iain Fraser .20 .50
9 Rhett Gordon .20 .50
10 Joel Laing .30 .75
11 Marc Laniel .20 .50
12 Scott Levins .20 .50
13 Mike Morin .20 .50
14 Warren Norris .20 .50
15 Trevor Prior .30 .75
16 Jason Sessa .30 .75
17 Kent Simpson .20 .50
18 Chris Szysky .20 .50
19 Timo Willman .20 .50

2003-04 UK Sheffield Steelers

COMPLETE SET (21) 5.00 10.00
1 Gerald Adams .20 .50
2 Erik Anderson .20 .50
3 Mike Blaisdell CO .20 .50
4 Ben Bliss .20 .50
5 Brent Bobyck .20 .50
6 Kevin Bolibruck .20 .50
7 Christian Bronsard .30 .75
8 Dion Darling .20 .50
9 Kirk DeWaele .20 .50
10 Rob Dopson .30 .75
11 Steve Duncombe .20 .50
12 Mark Dutiaume .20 .50
13 Steve Ellis .20 .50
14 Gavin Farrand .20 .50
15 Joel Irving .20 .50
16 Ryan Lake .20 .50
17 David Lawrence .30 .75
18 Marc Lefebvre .30 .75
19 Mike Peron .20 .50
20 Pasi Raitanan UER .30 .75
21 Ron Shudra .30 .75

2003-04 UK Sheffield Steelers Stickers

COMPLETE SET (18) 7.00
1 Mark Dutiaume .20 .50
2 Gavin Farrand .20 .50
3 Mike Peron .20 .50
4 Ryan Lake .20 .50
5 Dion Darling .20 .50
6 Davey Lawrence .30 .75
7 Rob Dopson .30 .75
8 Steve Ellis .20 .50
9 Ron Shudra .30 .75
10 Brent Bobyck .20 .50
11 Erik Anderson .20 .50
12 Kirk DeWaele .20 .50
13 Joel Irving .20 .50
14 Steve Duncombe .20 .50
15 Dan Hughes .20 .50
16 Marc Lefebvre .30 .75
17 Ben Bliss .20 .50
18 Gerald Adams .20 .50

2004-05 UK Sheffield Steelers

COMPLETE SET (20) 5.00 10.00
1 Jayme Platt .20 .50
2 David Lawrence .20 .50
3 Daryl Andrews .20 .50
4 Gerad Adams .20 .50
5 Steve Duncombe .20 .50
6 Ron Shudra .30 .75
7 Dion Darling .30 .75
8 David Cousineau .30 .75
9 Marc Lefebvre .30 .75
10 Mike Peron .20 .50
11 Mark Dutiaume .20 .50
12 Rob Stewart .20 .50
13 Erik Anderson .20 .50
14 Gavin Ferrand .20 .50
15 Joe Ciccarello .20 .50
16 Ben Bliss .20 .50
17 Paul Sample .20 .50
18 Jeff Christian .20 .50
19 Brent Bobyck .20 .50
20 Checklist .01 .01

1994-95 UK Solihul Barons

This set features the Barons of the British league. Any additional information can be forwarded to hockeymag@beckett.com.

COMPLETE SET (15) 5.00 10.00
1 Jake Armstrong .30 .75
2 Stephen Doyle .30 .75
3 Paul Frankum .30 .75
4 Justin George .30 .75
5 Andy Havenhand .30 .75
6 Nick Henry .30 .75
7 Richard Hillas .30 .75
8 Phil Lee .30 .75
9 Declan McNaughton .30 .75
10 Joel Pickering .30 .75
11 Dan Prachar .30 .75
12 Gareth Roddis .30 .75
13 Jamie Van der Horst .30 .75
14 Dave Wilkie .30 .75
15 Liam Young .30 .75

1995-96 UK Solihull Barons

This set features the Barons of the British league. Little is known about this set beyond the confirmed checklist. Additional information can be forwarded to hockeymag@beckett.com.

COMPLETE SET (13) 2.00 5.00
1 Jamie Van Der Horst .20 .50
2 Nick Henry .20 .50
3 Gareth Roddis .20 .50
4 Jake Armstrong .20 .50
5 Andy Havenhand .20 .50
6 Paul Frankum .20 .50
7 David Wilkie .20 .50
8 Phil Lee .20 .50
9 Dan Pracher .20 .50
10 Alan Hague .20 .50
11 Justin George .20 .50
12 Liam Young .20 .50
13 Stephen Doyle .20 .50

2004-05 UK Steven Carpenter Testimonial

COMPLETE SET (10) 2.00 5.00
1 Steven Carpenter 1996-97 .20 .50
2 Steven Carpenter 1997-98 .20 .50
3 Steven Carpenter 1998-99 .20 .50
4 Steven Carpenter 1999-00 .20 .50
5 Steven Carpenter 2000-01 .20 .50
6 Steven Carpenter 2001-02 .20 .50
7 Steven Carpenter 2002-03 .20 .50
8 Steven Carpenter 2003-04 .20 .50
9 Steven Carpenter 2004-05 .20 .50
10 Steven Carpenter CL .20 .50

2004-05 UK Thommo's Top 10

COMPLETE SET (10) 5.00 10.00
1 Greg Hadden .40 1.00
2 Tony Hand .60 1.50
3 Claudio Scremin .40 1.00
4 Rick Brebant .40 1.00
5 Mike Blaisdell .40 1.00
6 Joel Laing .40 1.00
7 Darryl Olsen .40 1.00
8 Marty Dallman .40 1.00
9 Dennis Vial .60 1.50
10 Patrice Lefebvre .60 1.50

2004-05 UK U-20 Team

COMPLETE SET (23) 5.00 10.00
1 David Lawrence .20 .50
2 Kevin Phillips .20 .50
3 Simon Butterworth .20 .50
4 Shaun Thompson .20 .50
5 Kurt Reynolds .20 .50
6 Shane Moore .20 .50
7 Steven Duncombe .20 .50
8 Leigh Jamieson .20 .50
9 Adam Brittle .20 .50
10 Chad Reekie .20 .50
11 Chace Ferrand .20 .50
12 David Phillips .20 .50
13 Bari McKenzie .20 .50
14 Lee Mitchell .20 .50
15 Tom Carlon .20 .50
16 Mark Richardson .20 .50
17 Adam Walker .20 .50
18 Euan Forsyth .20 .50
19 Andrew Thornton .20 .50
20 Luke Boothroyd .20 .50
21 Lewis Day .20 .50
22 Geoffrey Woolhouse .20 .50
23 Checklist .01 .01

1998-99 Abilene Aviators

This set features the Aviators of the WPHL. The set was issued as a promotional giveaway in set form. The Don Margettie card was issued separately at another promotional event and is not part of the complete set proper. The cards are unnumbered and are listed alphabetically.

COMPLETE SET (21) 8.00 20.00
1 Erik Noack .40 1.00
2 Jeff Triano CO .20 .50
3 Don Margettie .40 1.00
4 Tony Martino .40 1.00
5 Mathieu Raby .60 1.50
6 Derek Booth .40 1.00
7 Mario Dumoulin .40 1.00
8 Charlie Lawson .40 1.00
9 Jean-Francois Gregoire .40 1.00
10 Craig Perrett .40 1.00
11 Eric Naud .60 1.50
12 Stephane Roy .40 1.00
13 Charles Poulin .40 1.00
14 Jayson Brunette .40 1.00
15 Stephen Maltby .40 1.00
16 Terho Koskela .40 1.00
17 Francois Archambault .40 1.00
18 Marty Dallman .40 1.00
19 Mario Cormier .40 1.00
20 Eric Brule .40 1.00
21 Don Margettie PROMO 2.00 5.00

1995-96 Adirondack Red Wings

This 25-card set produced by Split Second features the Adirondack Red Wings of the AHL. The sets were available at games and by mail. The cards feature a glossy action photo along with team and manufacturer logos on the front. The cards are unnumbered and listed below in alphabetical order.

COMPLETE SET (25) 4.80 12.00
1 Jeff Bloemberg .16 .40
2 Curtis Bowen .16 .40
3 Dave Chyzowski .16 .40
4 Sylvain Cloutier .16 .40
5 Ryan Duthie .16 .40
6 Anders Eriksson .30 .50
7 Yan Golubovski .30 .75
8 Ben Hankinson .16 .40
9 Kevin Hodson .40 1.00
10 Scott Hollis .16 .40
11 Mike Knuble .40 1.00
12 Jason MacDonald .20 .50
13 Mark Major .16 .40
14 Norm Maracle .40 1.00
15 Kurt Miller .16 .40
16 Mike Needham .16 .40
17 Troy Neumeier .16 .40
18 Mark Ouimet .16 .40
19 Jamie Pushor .30 .50
20 Stacy Roest .40 1.00
21 Brandon Smith .20 .50
22 Kerry Toporowski .16 .40
23 Wes Walz .40 1.00
24 Aaron Ward .30 .75
25 Hockeye MASCOT .04 .10

1999-00 Adirondack IceHawks

This set features the IceHawks of the UHL. The cards were produced by Blue Line Sports and were sold at home games.

COMPLETE SET (25) 4.00 10.00
1 Header/Checklist .10 .25
2 Stephan Brochu .20 .50
3 Eric Boyte .20 .50
4 David Dartsch .20 .50
5 John Batten .20 .50
6 Larry Empey .20 .50
7 Chris Ross .20 .50
8 Trent Schachle .20 .50
9 Checklist .10 .25
10 Shawn Yakimishyn .20 .50
11 Francois Sasseville .20 .50
12 Guillaume Rodrigue .20 .50
13 Trevor Jobe .20 .50
14 Tony Cimellaro .20 .50
15 Cameron MacDonald .20 .50
16 Bobby Cunningham .20 .50
17 Checklist .10 .25
18 Alexei Deev .20 .50
19 Wade Welte .20 .50
20 Alexei Yegorov .30 .75
21 Chad Ford .20 .50
22 Jack Greig .20 .50
23 Ben Metzger .20 .50
24 Robbie Nichols .20 .50
25 Hawkeye .10 .25

1999-00 AHL All-Stars

This 12-card set showcases the 2000 AHL All-Stars with full-color action photos. The cards were available at the rink the day of the AS Game. The cards are not numbered and are listed below alphabetically.

COMPLETE SET (12) 8.00 20.00
1 Martin Brochu .80 1.50
2 Craig Ferguson .40 1.00
3 Peter Ferraro .40 1.00
4 Michael Gaul .40 1.00
5 Miikka Kiprusoff 2.00 5.00
6 Christian Matte .60 1.50
7 Chris O'Sullivan .40 1.00
8 Martin St. Louis 2.00 5.00
9 Brad Tiley .40 1.00
10 Daniel Trebil .40 1.00
11 Alexandre Volchkov .40 1.00
12 Bob Wren .40 1.00

2004-05 AHL All-Stars

COMPLETE SET (49) 10.00 20.00
1 Keith Ballard .10 .25
2 Nolan Baumgartner .10 .25
3 Sean Bergenheim .10 .25
4 Patrice Bergeron 1.25 3.00
5 Brandon Bochenski .30 .75
6 Rene Bourque .20 .50
7 Jay Bouwmeester .40 1.00
8 Dustin Brown .40 1.00
9 Mike Cammalleri .40 1.00
10 Craig Darby .10 .25
11 Christian Ehrhoff .10 .25
12 Steve Eminger .10 .25
13 Simon Gamache .20 .50
14 Mathieu Garon .30 .75
15 Denis Grebeshkov .10 .25
16 Dan Hamhuis .10 .25
17 Andy Hilbert .10 .25
18 Michael Holmqvist .10 .25
19 Andrew Hutchinson .10 .25
20 Ryan Kesler .10 .25
21 Jason King .10 .25
22 Chuck Kobasew .30 .75
23 Mikko Koivu .40 1.00
24 Niklas Kronwall .30 .75
25 Jason Labarbera .20 .50
26 Kari Lehtonen 1.25 3.00
27 Joey MacDonald .20 .50
28 Ryan Miller .60 1.50
29 Antero Niittymaki .40 1.00
30 Lawrence Nycholat .10 .25
31 Michel Ouellet .10 .25
32 Zach Parise 1.25 3.00
33 Eric Perrin .10 .25
34 Joni Pitkanen .20 .50
35 Tomas Plekanec .20 .50
36 Brian Pothier .10 .25
37 Travis Roche .10 .25
38 Tony Salmelainen .10 .25
39 Patrick Sharp .10 .25
40 Jason Spezza .75 2.00
41 Eric Staal .60 1.50
42 Alexander Svitov .10 .25
43 Brad Tiley .10 .25
44 Anton Volchenkov .10 .25
45 Kyle Wellwood .30 .75
46 Dennis Wideman .10 .25
47 Finland Representatives .20 .50
48 Manchester Monarchs .10 .25
49 Checklist .01 .01

2002-03 AHL Top Prospects

This series was produced by Choice Marketing in conjunction with the PHPA and the AHL. The set was sold online and at rinks around the league. The set features a number of top prospects on their first pro cards.

COMPLETE SET (45) 8.00 20.00
1 Ramzi Abid .10 .25
2 Alex Auld .30 .75
3 Jared Aulin .20 .50
4 Jason Bacashihua .20 .50
5 Kris Beech .10 .25
6 Brad Boyes .30 .75
7 Scott Clemmensen .20 .50
8 Ty Conklin .20 .50
9 Niko Dimitrakos .10 .25
10 Rick DiPietro .60 1.50
11 Micki Dupont .10 .25
12 Ray Emery .40 1.00
13 Shane Endicott .10 .25
14 Garnet Exelby .20 .50
15 Jim Fahey .10 .25
16 Ron Hainsey .20 .50
17 Darren Haydar .20 .50
18 Jonathan Hedstrom .10 .25
19 Jeff Heerema .10 .25
20 Andy Hilbert .10 .25
21 Trent Hunter .20 .50
22 Mike Komisarek .20 .50
23 Tomas Kopecky .20 .50
24 Pascal Leclaire .40 1.00
25 Guillaume Lefebvre .10 .25
26 Michael Leighton .20 .50
27 Roman Lyashenko .10 .25
28 Tomas Malec .10 .25
29 Ryan Miller .75 2.00
30 Shaone Morrisonn .20 .50
31 Filip Novak .10 .25
32 Steve Ott .40 1.00
33 Maxime Ouellet .20 .50
34 Justin Papineau .10 .25
35 John Pohl .10 .25
36 Brandon Reid .10 .25
37 Jani Rita .10 .25
38 Phillippe Sauve .20 .50
39 Jason Spezza 1.25 3.00
40 Charlie Stephens .10 .25
41 Jeff Taffe .10 .25
42 J.P. Vigier .10 .25
43 Kyle Wanvig .10 .25
44 Duvie Westcott .10 .25
45 Tomas Zizka .10 .25

2003-04 AHL Top Prospects

This series was produced by Choice Marketing and sold in complete set form at AHL rinks.

COMPLETE SET (46) 6.00 15.00
1 Anton Babchuk .10 .25
2 Jason Bacashihua .20 .50
3 Ryan Bayda .10 .25
4 Brad Boyes .20 .50
5 Ilja Bryzgalov .20 .50
6 Peter Budaj .20 .50
7 Carlo Colaiacovo .10 .25
8 Ray Emery .40 1.00
9 Kurtis Foster .10 .25
10 Denis Grebeshkov .10 .25
11 Chris Higgins .40 1.00
12 Jiri Hudler .40 1.00
13 Ryan Kesler .20 .50
14 Mike Komisarek .10 .25
15 Lukas Krajicek .10 .25
16 Niklas Kronwall .30 .75
17 Brooks Laich .20 .50
18 Pascal Leclaire .20 .50
19 Kari Lehtonen .75 2.00
20 David LeNeveu .20 .50

21 Ross Lupaschuk .10 .25
22 Justin Mapletoft .10 .25
23 Jay McClement .10 .25
24 Ryan Miller .40 1.00
25 Shaone Morrisonn .10 .25
26 Maxime Ouellet .20 .50
27 Johnny Pohl .10 .25
28 Jason Pominville .40 1.00
29 Mark Popovic .10 .25
30 Jani Rita .10 .25
31 Derek Roy .40 1.00
32 Patrick Sharp .10 .25
33 Charlie Stephens .10 .25
34 Alexander Suglobov .10 .25
35 Tomas Surovy .10 .25
36 Jeff Taffe .10 .25
37 Petr Taticek .10 .25
38 Hannu Toivonen .40 1.00
39 Fedor Tjutin .10 .25
40 Scott Upshall .20 .50
41 Stephane Veilleux .10 .25
42 Kyle Wanvig .10 .25
43 Stephen Weiss .20 .50
44 Kyle Wellwood .40 1.00
45 Jeff Woywitka .10 .25
NNO Checklist .01 .01

2004-05 AHL Top Prospects

COMPLETE SET (61) 10.00 25.00
1 Zach Parise 1.00 2.50
2 Alexander Suglobov .10 .25
3 Jason Spezza .60 1.50
4 Antoine Vermette .20 .50
5 Anton Volchenkov .10 .25
6 Sean Bergenheim .10 .25
7 Kari Lehtonen 1.00 2.50
8 Karl Stewart .10 .25
9 Joffrey Lupul .30 .75
10 Stanislav Chistov .10 .25
11 Marcel Goc .10 .25
12 Brad Winchester .10 .25
13 Doug Lynch .10 .25
14 Niklas Kronwall .30 .75
15 Nathan Robinson .10 .25
16 Tomas Plekanec .20 .50
17 Trevor Daley .10 .25
18 Jozef Balej .10 .25
19 Jason Labarbera .20 .50
20 Peter Budaj .20 .50
21 Pierre-Marc Bouchard .30 .75
22 Brent Burns .20 .50
23 Mikko Koivu .40 1.00
24 Eric Staal .60 1.50
25 Chuck Kobasew .20 .50
26 Brent Krahn .20 .50
27 Yanick Lehoux .10 .25
28 Mike Cammalleri .40 1.00
29 Dustin Brown .20 .50
30 Denis Grebeshkov .10 .25
31 Jason King .10 .25
32 Ryan Kesler .10 .25
33 Timofei Shishkanov .10 .25
34 Scottie Upshall .20 .50
35 Jordin Tootoo .40 1.00
36 Mikhail Yakubov .10 .25
37 Anton Babchuk .10 .25
38 R.J. Umberger .20 .50
39 Joni Pitkanen .20 .50
40 Antero Niittymaki .40 1.00
41 Steve Eminger .10 .25
42 Jakub Klepis .10 .25
43 Patrice Bergeron 1.00 2.50
44 Hannu Toivonen .40 1.00
45 Derek Roy .20 .50
46 Thomas Vanek 1.00 2.50
47 Stephen Weiss .20 .50
48 Jay Bouwmeester .30 .75
49 Nathan Horton .30 .75
50 Adam Henrich .10 .25
51 Kyle Wellwood .30 .75
52 Matthew Stajan .30 .75
53 Carlo Colaiacovo .20 .50
54 Alexander Svitov .10 .25
55 David LeNeveu .20 .50
56 Michel Ouellet .10 .25
57 Ryan Whitney .30 .75
58 Marc-Andre Fleury .60 1.50
59 Mike Glumac .10 .25
60 Peter Sejna .10 .25
NNO Checklist .01 .01

2005-06 AHL All-Stars

COMPLETE SET (45) 10.00 25.00
1 Keith Aucoin .20 .50
2 Sven Butenschon .20 .50
3 Braydon Coburn .20 .50
4 Yann Danis .40 1.00
5 Andy Delmore .20 .50
6 Eric Fehr .20 .50
7 Valtteri Filppula .40 1.00
8 Wade Flaherty .40 1.00
9 Bruno Gervais .20 .50
10 Denis Grebeshkov .20 .50
11 Denis Hamel .20 .50
12 Mark Hartigan .20 .50
13 Eric Healey .20 .50
14 Jiri Hudler .40 1.00
15 Vitaly Kolesnik .40 1.00
16 Kirby Law .20 .50
17 Junior Lessard .40 1.00
18 Corey Locke .20 .50
19 Donald MacLean .20 .50
20 Al Montoya .75 2.00
21 Mike Mottau .20 .50
22 Curtis Murphy .20 .50
23 Filip Novak .20 .50
24 Lawrence Nycholat .20 .50
25 Patrick O'Sullivan .40 1.00
26 Nathan Paetsch .20 .50
27 Libor Pivko .20 .50
28 Thomas Pock .20 .50
29 Johnny Pohl .20 .50
30 Richie Regehr .20 .50
31 Pekka Rinne .40 1.00
32 Pat Rissmiller .20 .50
33 Jimmy Roy .20 .50
34 Dany Sabourin .40 1.00
35 Ryan Shannon .20 .50
36 John Slaney .20 .50
37 Martin St. Pierre .20 .50
38 Alexander Suglobov .20 .50
39 Jeff Tambellini .20 .50
40 Layne Ulmer .20 .50
41 Ryan Vesce .20 .50
42 Noah Welch .20 .50
43 Erik Westrum .40 1.00
44 AHL All-Stars .20 .50
NNO Checklist .01 .01

2005-06 AHL Top Prospects

COMPLETE SET (50) 15.00 25.00
1 Nicklas Bergfors .20 .50
2 Steve Bernier .40 1.00
3 Kevin Bieksa .20 .50
4 Chris Bourque .40 1.00
5 Alexandre Burrows .20 .50
6 Braydon Coburn .20 .50
7 Jeremy Colliton .20 .50
8 Ryan Craig .20 .50
9 Yann Danis .40 1.00
10 Nigel Dawes .20 .50
11 Patrick Eaves .40 1.00
12 Dan Ellis .40 1.00
13 Eric Fehr .20 .50
14 Valtteri Filppula .40 1.00
15 Tomas Fleischmann .20 .50
16 Bruno Gervais .20 .50
17 Mike Glumac .20 .50
18 Josh Harding .40 1.00
19 Jim Howard .40 1.00
20 Jean-Francois Jacques .20 .50
21 Matt Jones .20 .50
22 Vitaly Kolesnik .40 1.00
23 Staffan Kronwall .20 .50
24 Ryan Lannon .20 .50
25 Al Montoya .75 2.00
26 Eric Nystrom .20 .50
27 Patrick O'Sullivan .40 1.00
28 Nathan Paetsch .20 .50
29 Dustin Penner .40 1.00
30 Alexandre Picard .20 .50
31 Libor Pivko .20 .50
32 Geoff Platt .20 .50
33 Konstantin Pushkarev .20 .50
34 Tyler Redenbach .20 .50
35 Pekka Rinne .40 1.00
36 Peter Sejna .20 .50
37 Ryan Shannon .20 .50
38 Brian Sipotz .20 .50
39 Martin St. Pierre .20 .50
40 Yan Stastny .20 .50
41 Barry Tallackson .20 .50
42 Jeff Tambellini .20 .50
43 Chris Thorburn .20 .50
44 Lauri Tukonen .20 .50
45 Ryan Vesce .20 .50
46 Roman Voloshenko .20 .50
47 Ben Walter .20 .50
48 Noah Welch .20 .50
49 Jeremy Williams .40 1.00
50 Checklist .01 .01

2006-07 AHL Top Prospects

1 Kyle Cumiskey .20 .50
2 Justin Peters .20 .50
3 Andrew Ebbett .20 .50
4 Josh Hennessy .30 .75
5 Jeff Tambellini .20 .50
6 Robert Nilsson .20 .50
7 Blake Comeau .20 .50
8 Brett Stirling .30 .75
9 Nathan Oystrick .20 .50
10 Boris Valabik .20 .50
11 Jonathan Ericsson .20 .50
12 Jimmy Howard .40 1.00
13 Jaroslav Halak .75 2.00
14 Ryan Callahan .20 .50
15 Daniel Girardi .30 .75
16 Jeff Schultz .20 .50
17 Benoit Pouliot .40 1.00
18 Joel Lundqvist .40 1.00
19 Vojtech Polak .20 .50
20 Andy Greene .20 .50
21 Matt Moulson .20 .50
22 Peter Harrold .20 .50
23 Colby Genoway .20 .50
24 Alex Edler .30 .75
25 Rich Peverley .20 .50
26 Cal O'Reilly .20 .50
27 Troy Brouwer .30 .75
28 Dustin Byfuglien .20 .50
29 Corey Crawford .30 .75
30 Dustin Boyd .30 .75
31 Curtis McElhinney .20 .50
32 Roman Polak .20 .50
33 Marek Schwarz .40 1.00
34 Stefan Ruzicka .20 .50
35 Ryan Shannon .20 .50
36 David Krejci .30 .75
37 Matt Lashoff .30 .75
38 Clarke MacArthur .20 .50
39 Drew Stafford .75 2.00
40 Bill Thomas .20 .50
41 Blair Jones .20 .50
42 Karri Ramo .30 .75
43 Tomas Popperle .20 .50
44 Colin Murphy .20 .50
45 Justin Pogge .75 2.00
46 Jonathan Filewich .20 .50
47 Rob Schremp .60 1.50
48 Jeff Drouin-Deslauriers .30 .75
49 Joe Pavelski .40 1.00
50 Thomas Greiss .30 .75

1995-96 AHCA

This 10-card set was produced by the American Hockey Coaches Association for the College Hockey Centennial and features black-and-white photos in a tan border. The backs carry information about the events pictured on the front, which all are key in the history of the development of hockey in the United States.

COMPLETE SET (10) 2.00 5.00
1 The Pioneers .20 .50
2 The Inspiration .40 1.00
Hobey Baker
3 The Personalities .20 .50
John Mariucci
4 The Champions .20 .50
Michigan
5 The Colleges .20 .50
Edward Jeremiah
6 The Coaches .20 .50
Ron Mason
7 The Records .20 .50
1970 Cornell squad
8 The Moments .20 .50
Dean Talafous
9 The Traditions .20 .50
1978 Boston University Champions
10 The Future .40 1.00
Cammi Granato

1991-92 Air Canada SJHL

This 250-card standard-size set features players in the Saskatchewan Junior Hockey League. The set included an entry form for a contest sponsored by Air Canada and Old Dutch, which entitled the winner to a trip for two to anywhere in North America. The cards features posed color player photos with team color-coded shadow borders. The pictures are set on thin, white card stock with the team name in a yellow bar at the top. The player's name appears in the white margin at the bottom. The backs are white and carry biographical information and a player profile. The cards are numbered on the back and were issued in five series denoted by the letters A, B, C, D, and E as card number prefixes.

COMPLETE SET (250) 14.00 35.00
A1 Dean Normand .12 .30
A2 Dan Meyers .10 .25
A3 Tyson Balog .08 .20
A4 Tyler McMillan .08 .20
A5 Jason Selkirk .08 .20
A6 Bryce Bohun .08 .20
A7 Blaire Hornung .08 .20
A8 Craig McKechnie .08 .20
A9 Rejean Stringer .08 .20
A10 Corri Moffat .08 .20
A11 Dion Johnson .08 .20
A12 Rod Krushel .08 .20
A13 Mike Langen .08 .20
A14 Jeff Hassman .08 .20
A15 Dean Moore .08 .20
A16 Trevor Wathen .08 .20
A17 Curtis Knight .08 .20
A18 Chris Morgan .08 .20
A19 Trevor Thurstan .08 .20
A20 Wayne Filipenko .08 .20
A21 Jason Feiffer .08 .20
A22 Layne Douglas .08 .20
A23 Dave Gardner .08 .20
A24 Ryan Sandholm .08 .20
A25 Corey McKee .08 .20
A26 Trevor Schmiess .08 .20
A27 Todd Hollinger .20 .50
A28 Jay Dunn .08 .20
A29 Jamie Ling .12 .30
A30 Todd Small .08 .20
A31 Barret Kropf .08 .20
A32 Dean Gerard .08 .20
A33 Christian Dutil .08 .20
A34 Tyler Scheidt .08 .20
Aaron Campbell
A35 Dean Sideroff .08 .20
A36 Dan Dufresne .08 .20
A37 Cam Yager .08 .20
A38 Richard Nagy .10 .25
A39 Aaron Cain .20 .50
A40 Rob Beck .08 .20
A41 Blair Wagar .08 .20
A42 Kim Maier .08 .20
A43 Brent Hoiness .08 .20
A44 Troy Edwards .08 .20
A45 Evan Anderson .08 .20
A46 Carlin Nordstrom .08 .20
A47 Dean Seymour .08 .20
A48 Scott Wotton .12 .30
A49 Curtis Joseph 4.00 10.00
SJHL All Star
B1 Richard Boscher .08 .20
B2 James Schaeffer .08 .20
B3 Wes Rommel .08 .20
B4 Corey Thompson .08 .20
B5 Rob Phillips .12 .30
B6 Jim McLean .08 .20
B7 Trevor Warrener .20 .50
B8 Peter Boake .08 .20
B9 Kevin Riffel .08 .20
B10 Tom Perry .08 .20
B11 Mark Baird .08 .20
B12 Stacy Prevost .08 .20
B13 Taras Lendzyk .08 .20
B14 Shawn Reis .08 .20
B15 Shawn Thompson .08 .20
B16 Curtis Kleisinger .08 .20
B17 Kent Rogers .08 .20
B18 Scott Christion .12 .30
B19 Gerald Tallaire .12 .30
B20 Kelly Hollingshead .12 .30
B21 Mike Savard .08 .20
B22 Darren Maloney .08 .20
B23 Jason Hynd .08 .20
B24 Scott Stewart .08 .20
B25 Scott Beattie .12 .30
SJHL All Star
B26 Dave McAmmond .08 .20
B27 Myles Gibb .08 .20
B28 Ryan Bach .20 .50
B29 Martin Smith .08 .20
B30 Leigh Brookbank .08 .20
B31 Todd Markus .08 .20
B32 The Boys From PA .12 .30
Dean Gerard
Darryn Listwan
Scott Rogers
Brad Federenko
Derek Simonson
Jeff Greenwood
B33 Randy Muise .08 .20
B34 George Gervais .08 .20
B35 Keith Harris .08 .20
B36 Jamie Stelmak .08 .20
B37 Bart Vanstaalduinen .08 .20
B38 Scott Murray .08 .20
B39 Danny Galarneau .08 .20
B40 Keith Murphy .08 .20
B41 Jeff Kungle .12 .30
B42 Michel Cook .08 .20
B43 Daryl Krauss .08 .20
B44 Derek Wynne .08 .20
B45 Derek Crimin .08 .20
B46 Jason Brown .08 .20
B47 Bruce Matatall .08 .20
B48 Chris Hatch .08 .20
B49 Kurtise Souchotte .08 .20
B50 Michael Brennan .08 .20
B51 Orrin Hergott .08 .20
C1 Craig Matatall .08 .20
C2 Brad Prefontaine .08 .20
C3 Mike Evans .08 .20
C4 Jody Reiter .08 .20
C5 Jeremy Mylymok .08 .20
C6 Dave Doucet .12 .30
C7 Randy Kerr .08 .20
C8 Gordon McCann .08 .20
C9 Quinn Fair .08 .20
C10 Kyle Niemegeers .08 .20
C11 Ryan Smith .12 .30
C12 Mike Hillock .08 .20
C13 Vern Anderson .08 .20
C14 Trent Hamm .08 .20
C15 Curtis Folkett ACO .08 .20
C16 Warren Pickford .08 .20
C17 Craig Volstad .08 .20
C18 Sean Tallaire .08 .20
C19 Jason Yaganiski .12 .30
C20 Jim McLarty .08 .20
C21 Jamie Byfuglien .08 .20
C22 Terry Metro .08 .20
C23 Todd Kozak .08 .20
C24 Jeff Huckle .08 .20
C25 Darren McLean .08 .20
C26 Bret Mohninger .08 .20
C27 Tim Slukynsky .08 .20
C28 Roman Mrhalek .08 .20
C29 Joel Martinson .08 .20
C30 Ron Patterson .08 .20
C31 Mark Gorgi .08 .20
C32 Tom Thomson .08 .20
C33 Greg Wahl .08 .20
C34 Craig Perrett .08 .20
C35 Mike Harder .08 .20
C36 Jeff Cole .08 .20
C37 Justin Christoffer .08 .20
C38 Nolan Weir .08 .20
C39 Jeff Knight .08 .20
C40 Lyle Vaughan .08 .20
C41 Scott Bellefontaine .08 .20
C42 Trevor Mathias .08 .20
C43 Chris Schinkel .12 .30
C44 Scott Rogers .08 .20
C45 Shane Holunga .08 .20
C46 Dwayne Rhinehart .08 .20
C47 Eddy Marchant .08 .20
C48 Travis Smith .08 .20
C49 Not Known .08 .20
C50 Mike Hidlebaugh .08 .20
D1 Darcy Herlick .08 .20
D2 Joel Appleton .08 .20
D3 Bobby Standish .08 .20
D4 Kory Karlander .12 .30
D5 Brett Kinaschuk .08 .20
D6 Kevin Messer .08 .20
D7 Jason Martin .08 .20
D8 Devin Zimmer .08 .20
D9 David Foster .08 .20
D10 Bob Schwark .08 .20
D11 Ted Grayling .08 .20
D12 Travis Vantighem .12 .30
D13 Darren Houghton .08 .20
D14 Wade Welte .08 .20
D15 1991 NB All Stars .20 .50
Martin Smith
Ron Gunville
Derek Knorr
Geoff McMaster
Trevor Converse
D16 Kevin Powell .08 .20
D17 Returning Hounds .08 .20
Dave Lovesin
Bernie Adlys
Bart Vanstaalduinen
Scott Christion
Bob MacIntosh
Rice Thompson
Adam Thompson
D18 Dennis Budeau .08 .20
D19 Darren Opp .08 .20
D20 Jeff Greenwood .08 .20
D21 Mark Daniels .20 .50
D22 Todd Murphy .08 .20
D23 Scott Weaver .08 .20
D24 Robby Bear .08 .20
D25 Nigel Werenka .12 .30
D26 Sean Timmins .08 .20
D27 Ken Malenfant .08 .20
D28 Greg Taylor .08 .20
D29 Sheldon Bylsma .08 .20
D30 Clint Hooge .08 .20
D31 Bob McIntosh .12 .30
D32 Dave Lovsin .08 .20
D33 Jeremy Mathies .08 .20
D34 Blaine Fomradas .08 .20
D35 Cory Borys .08 .20
D36 Brad Purdie .08 .20
D37 J. Sotropa .08 .20
D38 Duane Vardale .08 .20
D39 Jim Nellis .08 .20
D40 Brent Sheppard .08 .20
D41 Cam Bristow .08 .20
D42 Steven Brent .08 .20
D43 Mike Matteucci .08 .20
D44 Bryan Cossette .08 .20
D45 Tyler Kuhn .08 .20
D46 Dave Debusschere .08 .20
D47 Darryl Dickson .08 .20
D48 Derek Meikle .08 .20
D49 Parris Duffus .20 .50
Ex SJHLer
D50 Lance Wakefield .12 .30
E1 Brooke Battersby .08 .20
E2 Jay Dobrescu .08 .20
E3 Blair Allison .08 .20
E4 Shane Johnson .08 .20
E5 Carson Cardinal .08 .20
E6 Dean Pooyak .08 .20
E7 Mark Loeppky .08 .20
E8 Travis Cheyne .08 .20
E9 Karl Johnson .08 .20
E10 Jason Ahenakew .08 .20
E11 Darren Schmidt .12 .30
E12 Larry Empey .08 .20
E13 Colin Froese .08 .20
E14 Darryn Listwan .08 .20
E15 Todd MacMillan .08 .20
E16 Ken Ruddock .08 .20
E17 Derek Simonson .08 .20
E18 Lyle Ehrmantraut .08 .20
E19 Jody Weller .08 .20
E20 Danny Dennis .08 .20
E21 Trent Harper .08 .20
E22 Jason Prokopetz .12 .30
E23 Tom Thomson .08 .20
E24 Trent Dumaine .12 .30
E25 Mike Wevers .08 .20
E26 Darren Duncalfe .08 .20
E27 Regan Simpson .08 .20
E28 Jeff Bloski .08 .20
E29 Blake Sutton .12 .30
E30 Darcy Blair .12 .30
E31 Marty Craigdallie .08 .20
E32 Jason Krug .08 .20
E33 Mark Hansen .08 .20
E34 Bernie Adlys .08 .20
E35 Brett Colborne .08 .20
E36 Tony Bergin .12 .30
E37 Ian Adamson .08 .20
E38 Darren MacMillan .08 .20
E39 Rob Neighbour .08 .20
E40 Jeff Lawson .08 .20
E41 Derrick Brucks .08 .20
E42 Todd Schoenroth .08 .20
E43 Jody Forseth .08 .20
E44 Derek Beuselinck .08 .20
E45 Clint Wensley .08 .20
E46 Darren Donald .08 .20
E47 Shane Stangby .08 .20
E48 Jamie Dunn .08 .20
E49 Steve Sabo .08 .20
E50 Anthony Toth .08 .20

1991-92 Air Canada SJHL All-Stars

This 50-card standard-size set features Saskatchewan Junior Hockey League All-Stars. The set included an entry form for a contest sponsored by Air Canada and Old Dutch, which entitled the winner to a trip for two to anywhere in North America. The cards feature posed color player photos with yellow shadow borders. The pictures are set against a white card face accented with an screened pale purple star pattern. The words "All Star" appear in red within a yellow and black striped bar at the top, while the player's name is printed below the photo. The backs carry the player's name, biographical information, and a player profile.

COMPLETE SET (50) 4.80 12.00
1 Jeff Kungle .16 .40
2 Jay Dunn .10 .25
3 Kevin Dickie .10 .25
4 Martin Smith .10 .25
5 Jeff Cole .10 .25
6 Trent Hamm .10 .25
7 Kent Rogers .10 .25
8 Dean Gerard .10 .25
9 Jim McLarty .10 .25
10 Malcolm Kostuchenko .10 .25
11 Mark Scollan .10 .25
12 Brad Federenko .20 .50
13 Rob Beck .10 .25
14 Bryce Bohun .10 .25
15 Kory Karlander .16 .40
16 Scott Christion .16 .40
17 Tyler Kuhn .10 .25
18 Corri Moffatt .10 .25
19 Layne Douglas .10 .25
20 Shane Holunga .10 .25
21 Mike Matteucci .10 .25
22 Bart Vanstaalduinen .10 .25
23 Brad McEwen .10 .25
24 Kim Maier .10 .25
25 Jamie Ling .20 .50
26 Dean Seymour .10 .25
27 Derek Crimin .10 .25
28 Evan Anderson .10 .25
29 Craig Matatall .10 .25
30 Keith Murphy .10 .25
31 Jason Feiffer .10 .25
32 Michel Cook .10 .25
33 Rod Krushel .10 .25
34 Tyler Rice .16 .40
35 Gerald Tallaire .20 .50
36 Richard Nagy .10 .25
37 Taras Lendzyk .10 .25
38 Jeff Knight .10 .25
39 Darren Opp .10 .25
40 Dwayne Rhinehart .10 .25
41 Minot Americans .10 .25
Layne Douglas
Derek Crimin
42 Scott Bellefontaine .10 .25
43 Darren Maloney .10 .25
44 North Division .20 .50
All-Star Team
Team Photo
45 Yorkton Terriers .20 .50
All Stars
Michel Cook
Dean Seymour
Scott Bellefontaine
46 Melville Millionaires .20 .50
All Stars
Team Photo
47 Best 1992 All-Stars .20 .50
Kevin Dickie CO
Mike Matteucci
Kory Karlander
Kim Maier
Darren Opp
Richard Nagy
Mark Scollan
48 Estevan Bruins .20 .50
All Stars
Gerald Tallaire
Kim Maier
Mike Matteucci
Evan Anderson
49 Notre Dame Hounds .20 .50
All Stars
Tyler Rice
Scott Christion
Bart Van Staalduinen
Jamie Ling
Craig Matatall
50 Bob Robson CO .10 .25

2003-04 Alaska Aces

Produced by RBI Sports and sold at the team's rink.

COMPLETE SET (16) 10.00 20.00
1 Jordan Cameron .50 1.25
2 Kimbi Daniels .50 1.25
3 Bret DeCecco .50 1.25
4 Wes Dorey .50 1.25
5 Jonathan Gauthier .50 1.25
6 Malcolm Hutt .50 1.25
7 Mike Jones .50 1.25
8 Charles Linglet .50 1.25
9 Chris Lipsett .50 1.25
10 Lance Mayes .75 2.00
11 Keith McCambridge .50 1.25
12 Ryan Moren .50 1.25
13 Dan Murphy .75 2.00
14 Shane Palahicky .50 1.25
15 Garrett Prosofsky .50 1.25
16 Mark Smitha .50 1.25

1995-96 Alaska Gold Kings

This 19-card set of the Alaska Gold Kings appears to be the first set produced for a club in the West Coast Hockey League. The set was manufactured and distributed by Jessen Associates. The fronts feature action color photos, complemented by the player's name, number and position, the team logo and the league name. The backs contain biographical and statistical data. The set is unnumbered, and listed in alphabetical order.

COMPLETE SET (19) 3.60 9.00
1 Title Card .10 .25
2 Derby Bognar .20 .50
3 Geoff Bumstead .30 .75
4 Chris Cahill .20 .50
5 Warren Carter .20 .50
6 John Haddad .20 .50
7 Todd Henderson .20 .50
8 Wade Klippenstein .20 .50
9 Matt Koleski .20 .50
10 Donald Lester .20 .50
11 Derek Linnell .20 .50
12 Jamie Loewen .20 .50
13 Travis MacMillan .20 .50
14 Kirk Patton .20 .50
15 Guy Prince .20 .50
16 Rob Proffitt .20 .50
17 Ryan Reynard .20 .50
18 Wayne Sawchuk CO .04 .10
19 Shawn Ulrich .20 .50

1996-97 Alaska Gold Kings

This 14-card set of "Alaska's 1st Professional Hockey Team" features the Gold Kings of the West Coast Hockey League. The set was produced by Split Second, using unusually heavy card stock, and features grainy action photos on the front, along with the player's name and jersey number, and the team logo. The backs all include the team logo, as well as those of sponsors Coca-Cola of Fairbanks, Winchell's, Club Golf and Twisted Stitches. No player info is included. The cards are unnumbered, and are listed below alphabetically.

COMPLETE SET (14) 3.20 8.00
1 Mark Costea .30 .75
2 Shane Fisher .30 .75
3 Colin Foley .30 .75
4 Chris French .30 .75
5 Yoshifumi Fujtsawa .30 .75
6 Todd Henderson .30 .75
7 Kelly Hrycun .30 .75
8 Shawn Lofroth .30 .75
9 Brad McCaughey CO .04 .10
10 Billy McGuigan .30 .75
11 Jay Murphy .30 .75
12 Sergei Olympiev .30 .75
13 Orion The Lion .04 .10
Mascot
14 Shawn Ulrich .30 .75

1996-97 Albany River Rats

This set features the River Rats of the AHL. The set was produced by Split Second and sold by the team at the rink for $5.

COMPLETE SET (26) 6.00 15.00
1 Eric Bertrand .20 .50
2 Brad Bombardir .20 .50
3 Steve Brule .20 .50
4 Mike Dunham .40 1.00
5 Patrik Elias .75 2.00
6 Bryan Helmer .20 .50
7 Bobby House .20 .50
8 Geordie Kinnear .20 .50
9 Chris McAlpine .20 .50
10 Krzysztof Oliwa .40 1.00
11 Jay Pandolfo .40 1.00
12 Denis Pederson .30 .75
13 Pascal Rheaume .30 .75
14 Vadim Sharifijanov .20 .50
15 Richard Shulmistra .30 .75
16 Peter Sidorkiewicz .30 .75
17 Zdenek Skorepa .20 .50
18 Sheldon Souray .20 .50
19 Mark Strobel .20 .50
20 Steve Sullivan .40 1.00
21 Sergei Vyshedkevich .20 .50
22 John Cunniff CO .04 .10
23 Dennis Gendron CO .04 .10
24 Rowdy MASCOT .04 .10
25 AHL Web Site .01
26 PHPA Web Site .01

1997-98 Albany River Rats

This set features the River Rats of the AHL. The set was produced by SplitSecond and was sold by the team at home games.

COMPLETE SET (26) 6.00 15.00
1 Eric Bertrand .16 .40
2 Jiri Bicek .40 1.00
3 Steve Brule .16 .40
4 Bryan Helmer .16 .40
5 Bobby House .16 .40
6 Geordie Kinnear .20 .50
7 Sasha Lakovic .20 .50
8 Judd Lambert .20 .50
9 John Madden .80 2.00
10 Brendan Morrison .80 2.00
11 Jay Pandolfo .20 .50
12 Richard Rochefort .16 .40
13 Vadim Sharifijanov .20 .50
14 Peter Sidorkiewicz .20 .50
15 Zdenek Skorepa .16 .40
16 Rob Skrlac .16 .40
17 Ken Sutton .16 .40
18 Paul Traynor .16 .40
19 Sergei Vyshedkevich .20 .50
20 Colin White .30 .75
21 Jeff Williams .16 .40
22 Peter Zezel .30 .75
23 John Cunniff CO .10 .25
24 Dennis Gendron CO .10 .25
25 PHPA Web Site .01
26 AHL Web Site .01

1998-99 Albany River Rats

This set features the River Rats of the AHL. The set was produced by Split Second and was sold by the team at its souvenir stands.

COMPLETE SET (25) 4.80 12.00
1 Eric Bertrand .16 .40
2 Jiri Bicek .30 .75
3 Steve Brule .20 .50
4 Mike Buzak .16 .40
5 David Cunniff .16 .40
6 Pierre Dagenais .30 .75
7 Josh DeWolf .16 .40
8 Sascha Goc .20 .50

9 Frederic Henry .16 .40
10 Geordie Kinnear .20 .50
11 John Madden .80 2.00
12 Rob Pattison .16 .40
13 Henrik Rehnberg .16 .40
14 Richard Rochefort .16 .40
15 Alexander Semak .16 .40
16 Rob Skrlac .16 .40
17 Ken Sutton .16 .40
18 Chris Thompson .16 .40
19 Sergei Vyshedkevich .16 .40
20 Colin White .30 .75
21 Jeff Williams .16 .40
22 Red Gendron CO .04 .10
23 John Cunniff CO .04 .10
24 Rowdy MASCOT .04 .10
25 AHL Web Site .01

1999-00 Albany River Rats

This 26-card set showcases the AHL River Rats, and was sold by the team at its souvenir shop. The cards are not numbered so they are listed alphabetically.

COMPLETE SET (26) 4.80 12.00
1 George Awada .14 .35
2 Jiri Bicek .30 .75
3 Steve Brule .20 .50
4 Bobby Carpenter ACO .20 .50
5 Sylvain Cloutier .14 .35
6 David Cunniff .14 .35
7 John Cunniff CO .14 .35
8 Pierre Dagenais .30 .75
9 Jean-Francois Damphousse .60 1.50
10 Josh DeWolf .20 .50
11 Dennis Gendron ACO .14 .35
12 Sascha Goc .30 .75
13 Stanislav Gron .40 1.00
14 Frederic Henry .30 .75
15 Steve Kelly .20 .50
16 Andre Lakos .14 .35
17 Sasha Lakovic .20 .50
18 Carlyle Lewis .14 .35
19 David Maley .14 .35
20 Willie Mitchell .14 .35
21 Richard Rochefort .14 .35
22 Rob Skrlac .14 .35
23 Ken Sutton .14 .35
24 Rowdy MASCOT .04 .10
25 Colin White .30 .75
26 Jeff Williams .14 .35

2000-01 Albany River Rats

This set features the River Rats of the AHL and was produced by Choice Marketing. The cards were sold in set form by the team at its souvenir stands.

COMPLETE SET (27) 4.00 10.00
1 Daryl Andrews .14 .35
2 Jiri Bicek .30 .75
3 Max Birbraer .20 .50
4 Josef Boumedienne .14 .35
5 Sylvain Cloutier .14 .35
6 Mike Commodore .20 .50
7 Pierre Dagenais .30 .75
8 Chris Ferraro .14 .35
9 Sascha Goc .20 .50
10 Stanislav Gron .40 1.00
11 Mike Jefferson .20 .50
12 Andre Lakos .14 .35
13 Jason Lehoux .14 .35
14 Carlyle Lewis .14 .35
15 Willie Mitchell .20 .50
16 Lucas Nehrling .14 .35
17 Henrik Rehnberg .14 .35
18 Richard Rochefort .14 .35
19 Michael Rupp .40 1.00
20 Rob Skrlac .14 .35
21 Ed Ward .14 .35
22 Jean-Francois Damphousse .30 .75
23 Frederic Henry .20 .50
24 John Cunniff CO .04 .10
25 Bobby Carpenter ACO .10 .25
26 Alex Zinevych .14 .35
27 Team CL .04 .10

2001-02 Albany River Rats

This set features the River Rats of the AHL. The cards were produced by Choice Marketing and sold at home games.

COMPLETE SET (28) 6.00 12.00
1 Checklist .04 .01
2 Sylvain Cloutier .10 .25
3 Jean-Francois Damphousse .20 .50
4 Mike Commodore .10 .25
5 Daryl Andrews .10 .25
6 Andre Lakos .10 .25
7 Mikko Jokela .20 .50
8 Joel Dezainde .10 .25
9 Jiri Bicek .20 .75
10 Stanislav Gron .30 .75
11 Brian Gionta .40 1.00
12 Richard Rochefort .10 .25
13 Michael Rupp .20 .75
14 Ted Drury .10 .25
15 Max Birbraer .20 .50
16 Christian Berglund .10 .25
17 Scott Cameron .10 .25
18 Jason Lehoux .10 .25
19 Brett Clouthier .10 .25
20 Bruce Gardiner .10 .25
21 Stephen Guolla .20 .50
22 Victor Uchevatov .10 .25
23 Joel Bouchard .10 .25
24 Ari Ahonen 2.00 3.00
25 Scott Clemmensen .80 1.00
26 Bob Carpenter CO .04 .10
27 Geordie Kinnear ACO .04 .10
28 Rowdy .10

2002-03 Albany River Rats

This set was produced by Choice Marketing and sold at home games.

COMPLETE SET (28) 5.00 12.00
1 Ari Ahonen .40 1.00
2 Alex Brooks .20 .50
3 Brett Clouthier .20 .50
4 Christian Berglund .20 .50
5 Craig Darby .20 .50
6 Chris Hartsburg .20 .50
7 Daryl Andrews .20 .50
8 David Roche .20 .50
9 Eric Johansson .20 .50
10 Jiri Bicek .20 .50
11 Joe Hulbig .20 .50
12 Jason Lehoux .20 .50
13 Krisjanis Redlihs .20 .50
14 Ken Sutton .20 .50
15 Max Birbraer .40 1.00
16 Mikko Jokela .20 .50
17 Mike Matteucci .20 .50
18 Michael Rupp .40 1.00
19 Ray Giroux .20 .50
20 Rob Skrlac .20 .50
21 Scott Cameron .20 .50
22 Scott Clemmensen .40 1.00
23 Victor Uchevatov .20 .50
24 Greg Crozier .20 .50
25 Dennis Gendron HCO .02 .10
26 Geordie Kinnear ACO .02 .10
27 Gates Orlando ACO .02 .10
NNO Checklist .01 .01

2002-03 Albany River Rats AAP

This set was issued as a promotional giveaway at a late-season game. The card backs all feature an ad for Advance Auto Parts. The cards are unnumbered and so are listed below in alphabetical order.

COMPLETE SET (25) 10.00 20.00
1 Checklist card .01 .01
2 Ari Ahonen .50 1.25
3 Daryl Andrews .40 1.00
4 Max Birbraer .50 1.25
5 Alex Brooks .40 1.00
6 Scott Cameron .40 1.00
7 Scott Clemmensen .50 1.25
8 Brett Clouthier .40 1.00
9 Greg Crozier .40 1.00
10 Craig Darby .40 1.00
11 Ray Giroux .40 1.00
12 Red Gendron CO .02 .10
13 Chris Hartsburg .40 1.00
14 Joe Hulbig .40 1.00
15 Eric Johansson .40 1.00
16 Mikko Jokela .40 1.00
17 Jason Lehoux .40 1.00
18 Mike Matteucci .40 1.00
19 Krisjanis Redlihs .40 1.00
20 Dave Roche .40 1.00
21 Rowdy MASCOT .02 .10
22 Michael Rupp .50 1.25
23 Rob Skrlac .40 1.00
24 Ken Sutton .40 1.00
25 Victor Uchevatov .40 1.00

2003-04 Albany River Rats

This set was produced by Choice Marketing and sold at home games.

COMPLETE SET (30) 5.00 12.00
1 Checklist .01 .01
2 Ari Ahonen .30 .75
3 Maxim Balmochnykh .15 .40
4 Jiri Bicek .15 .40
5 Alex Brooks .15 .40
6 Scott Clemmensen .30 .75
7 Brett Clouthier .15 .40
8 Greg Crozier .15 .40
9 Craig Darby .15 .40
10 Matt DeMarchi .15 .40
11 Adrian Foster .15 .40
12 Ray Giroux .15 .40
13 Tyler Hanchuck .15 .40
14 Chris Hartsburg .15 .40
15 Joe Hulbig .15 .40
16 Eric Johansson .15 .40
17 Steve Kariya .60 1.50
18 Matus Kostur .15 .40
19 Mike Matteucci .15 .40
20 Ryan Murphy .15 .40
21 Ahren Nittel .30 .75
22 Tuomas Pihlman .30 .75
23 Ilkka Pikkarainen .15 .40
24 Krisjanis Redlihs .15 .40
25 Rob Skrlac .15 .40
26 Alexander Suglobov .15 .40
27 Victor Uchevatov .15 .40
28 Dennis Gendron CO .02 .10
29 Gates Orlando ACO .02 .10
30 Geordie Kinnear ACO .02 .10

2003-04 Albany River Rats Kinko's

COMPLETE SET (26) 15.00 30.00
1 Ari Ahonen .60 1.50
2 Maxim Balmochnykh .40 1.00
3 Jiri Bicek .40 1.00
4 Alex Brooks .40 1.00
5 Scott Clemmensen .60 1.50
6 Brett Clouthier .40 1.00
7 Greg Crozier .40 1.00
8 Craig Darby .40 1.00
9 Matt DeMarchi .40 1.00
10 Adrian Foster .40 1.00
11 Ray Giroux .40 1.00
12 Tyler Hanchuck .40 1.00
13 Chris Hartsburg .40 1.00
14 Joe Hulbig .40 1.00
15 Eric Johansson .40 1.00
16 Steve Kariya 1.25 3.00
17 Matus Kostur .40 1.00
18 Mike Matteucci .40 1.00
19 Ryan Murphy .40 1.00
20 Ahren Nittel .75 2.00
21 Tuomas Pihlman .40 1.00
22 Ilkka Pikkarainen .40 1.00
23 Krisjanis Redlihs .40 1.00
24 Rob Skrlac .40 1.00
25 Alexander Suglobov .40 1.00
26 Victor Uchevatov .40 1.00

2004-05 Albany River Rats

COMPLETE SET (25) 6.00 15.00
1 Ari Ahonen .30 .75
2 Bobby Allen .15 .40
3 Alex Brooks .15 .40
4 Scott Clemmensen .30 .75
5 Brett Clouthier .15 .40
6 Matt DeMarchi .15 .40
7 Adrian Foster .15 .40
8 David Hale .40 1.00
9 Cam Janssen .40 1.00
10 Eric Johansson .15 .40
11 Teemu Kesa .15 .40
12 Ivan Khomutov .15 .40
13 Dean McAmmond .15 .40
14 Ryan Murphy .15 .40
15 Ahren Nittel .30 .75
16 Zach Parise 2.00 5.00
17 Tuomas Pihlman .15 .40
18 Ilkka Pikkarainen .15 .40
19 Krisjanis Redlihs .15 .40
20 Pascal Rheaume .15 .40
21 Ray Schultz .15 .40
22 Rob Skrlac .15 .40
23 Aaron Voros .15 .40
24 Aleksander Suglobov .15 .40
25 Robbie Florek CO .02 .10

2005-06 Albany River Rats

COMPLETE SET (28) 6.00 15.00
1 Ari Ahonen .40 1.00
2 Bobby Allen .20 .50
3 Nicklas Bergfors .20 .50
4 Alex Brooks .20 .50
5 Ben Carpentier .20 .50
6 David Clarkson .20 .50
7 Matt DeMarchi .20 .50
8 Frank Doyle .40 1.00
9 Adrian Foster .20 .50
10 David Hale .20 .50
11 Cam Janssen .40 1.00
12 Teemu Kesa .20 .50
13 Ivan Khomutov .20 .50
14 Bryan Miller .20 .50
15 Ryan Murphy .20 .50
16 Ahren Nittel .40 1.00
17 Tuomas Pihlman .20 .50
18 Ilkka Pikkarainen .20 .50
19 Krisjanis Redlihs .20 .50
20 Pascal Rheaume .20 .50
21 Jason Ryznar .20 .50
22 Ray Schultz .20 .50
23 Mike Sgroi .20 .50
24 Aleksander Suglobov .20 .50
25 Barry Tallackson .40 1.00
26 Aaron Voros .20 .50
27 Petr Vrana .20 .50
28 Robbie Florek .02 .10

2006-07 Albany River Rats

COMPLETE SET (27) 5.00 12.00
1 Kevin Estrada .20 .50
2 Keith Aucoin .20 .50
3 Ryan Bayda .20 .50
4 Joe Barnes .20 .50
5 Jesse Boulerice .20 .50
6 Johnny Boychuck .20 .50
7 Tim Conboy .20 .50
8 Kyle Cumiskey .20 .50
9 Dan DaSilva .20 .50
10 Pat Dwyer .20 .50
11 Jeff Finger .20 .50
12 Dave Gove .20 .50
13 Ben Guite .20 .50
14 Scott Kelman .20 .50
15 Mitch Love .20 .50
16 Cody McLeod .20 .50
17 Matt Murley .20 .50
18 Justin Peters .30 .75
19 Jakub Petruzalek .20 .50
20 Peter Tsimikalis .20 .50
21 Tyler Weiman .30 .75
22 Shane Willis .20 .50
23 Brett Carson .20 .50
24 Tom Rowe HC .02 .10
25 Joe Sacco CO .02 .10
NNO Checklist .01 .01
NNO Rowdy MASCOT .02 .10

1999-00 Alexandria Warthogs

This set features the Warthogs of the WPHL. The singles were handed out one per home game throughout the season. The card of Jason Leveille was not widely distributed to the public because of an early season trade. A few copies, however, have made their way onto the secondary market.

COMPLETE SET (23) 20.00 50.00
1 Mark Biesenthal .80 2.00
2 Jeff Blair .80 2.00
3 Jason Desloover .80 2.00
4 Josh Dobbyn .80 2.00
5 Valeri Ermolov .80 2.00
6 Dion Hagan .80 2.00
7 Daniel Korber .80 2.00
8 Chris Low .80 2.00
9 Jay Mazur .80 2.00
10 Jim Mroz .80 2.00
11 Matt Osiecki .80 2.00
12 Chris Peach .80 2.00
13 Marc Pethke .80 2.00
14 Robert Plante .80 2.00
15 Regan Stocco .80 2.00
16 Matt Turek .80 2.00
17 Colby Van Tassel .80 2.00
18 Miles Van Tassel .80 2.00
19 Mike Zruna CO .40 1.00
20 Jason Leveille 4.00 10.00
21 Marcus Adolfsson .80 2.00
22 Bill Weir .80 2.00
23 Chad Wilchynski .80 2.00

1998-99 Amarillo Rattlers

This 21-card set was a promotional giveaway that was handed out over five Rattlers home games.

COMPLETE SET (21) 10.00 25.00
1 Matt Brenner .60 1.50
2 Chris Brooks .60 1.50
3 Stephen Douglas .60 1.50
4 Steve Ferranti .60 1.50
5 Bob Gohde .60 1.50
6 Brad Haelzle .60 1.50
7 Derek Innanen .60 1.50
8 Trevor Janicki .60 1.50
9 Brendan Kenny .60 1.50
10 Todd Laurin .60 1.50
11 Adam Lord .60 1.50
12 Cal McGowan .80 2.00
13 Jim McLean .60 1.50
14 David Rattray .60 1.50
15 Jaynen Rissling .60 1.50
16 Per Schlyter .60 1.50
17 Scott W. Stevens .60 1.50
18 Neil Gondek ACO .10 .25
19 Ken Karpuk CO .10 .25
20 Amarillo Rattlers .10 .25
21 Greg Sieg TR .10 .25

2000-01 Amarillo Rattlers

This set features the Rattlers of the WPHL. It is believed that the set was a promotional giveaway, but that cannot be confirmed.

COMPLETE SET (20) 8.00 20.00
1 Eric Andersen .40 1.00
2 Chris Bell .40 1.00
3 Rodney Bowers .40 1.00
4 Jeff Cheeseman .40 1.00
5 Marc Dupuis .40 1.00
6 Larry Empey .40 1.00
7 Vincent Grant .40 1.00
8 Brad Haelzle .40 1.00
9 Toby Harris .40 1.00
10 Robert Holsinger .75 2.00
11 Todd MacDonald .75 2.00
12 Jeff Mancini .40 1.00
13 Jodi Murphy .75 2.00
14 Billy Newson .40 1.00
15 Jay Pecora .40 1.00
16 Doug Shepherd .40 1.00
17 Tony White .40 1.00
18 Chad Wilchynski .40 1.00
19 Kevin Abrams CO .08 .25
20 Team Card .08 .25

1993-94 Amos Les Forestiers

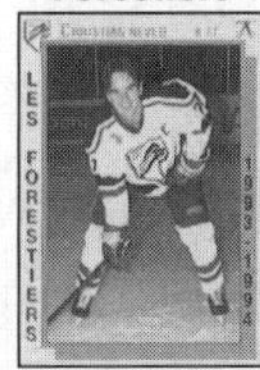

This 26-card standard-size set features Les Forestiers, a Midget AAA team in the province of Quebec. Les Forestiers is one of ten teams in the province from which the junior teams pick their players. The production run was reportedly 505 sets, including 60 autographed sets randomly placed in the lot. On a white card face, the fronts display posed color player photos framed by blue on the left and top and by magenta on the right and bottom. Player identification is printed in the top border, and the team name is printed in the left border. The backs present biographical and trivia information. The set includes 1995 NHL first rounder, Martin Biron.

COMPLETE SET (26) 14.00 35.00
1 Jean-Francois Belley .40 1.00
2 Carl Benoit .40 1.00
3 Martin Biron 6.00 15.00
4 David Bolduc .40 1.00
5 Martin Bradette .40 1.00
6 Dave Fontaine .40 1.00
7 Paul-Sebastien Gagnon .40 1.00
8 Eric Germain .40 1.00
9 Eric Houle .40 1.00
10 Jacques Larrivee ACO .10 .25
11 Yannick Lavoie .40 1.00
12 Mathieu Letourneau .40 1.00
13 Vincent Levasseur .40 1.00
14 Jonathan Levesque .40 1.00
15 Eric Naud .40 1.00
16 Christian Neveu .40 1.00
17 Patrick Pelchat .40 1.00
18 John Pyliotis .40 1.00
19 Luc St-Germain .40 1.00
20 Frederick Servant .40 1.00
21 Philippe Tremblay .40 1.00
22 Serge Trepanier CO .10 .25
23 Dany Villeneuve .40 1.00
24 Les Veterans .40 1.00
Christian Neveu
Mathieu Letourneau
25 Team Photo/CL .40 1.00
26 Title card .10 .25

1992-93 Anaheim Bullfrogs RHI

This set features the Bullfrogs of Roller Hockey International. The set was sold by the team at home games.

COMPLETE SET (20) 4.00 10.00
1 Header Card .04 .10
2 Maury Silver .20 .50
3 Stuart Silver .20 .50
4 Marc Lyons .20 .50
5 Kevin Kerr .20 .50
6 Grant Sonier ACO .10 .25
7 Barry Potomski .30 .75
8 Bob McKillop .20 .50
9 Rob Laurie .30 .75
10 Bill Horn .20 .50
11 Savo Mitrovic .20 .50
12 Chris McSorley CO .20 .50
13 Victor Gervais .30 .75
14 Darren Perkins .20 .50
15 Christian LaLonde .20 .50
16 Joe Cook .20 .50
17 Ken Murchison .20 .50
18 Brad McCaghey .20 .50
19 Devin Edgerton .20 .50
20 Mike Butters .20 .50

1993-94 Anaheim Bullfrogs RHI

This 21-piece set commemorates one of the most successful teams in the brief-lived Roller Hockey International. Along with traditional cards, each set also came with a POG slammer. The cards are unnumbered, and so are listed below alphabetically

COMPLETE SET (21) 3.20 10.00
1 Shayne Arsenault .20 .50
2 Steve Beadle .20 .50
3 Jim Brown .20 .50
4 Joe Cook .20 .50
5 Victor Gervais .20 .50
6 Chris Gordon .20 .50
7 Kevin Kerr .30 .75
8 Yuri Krivokhija .20 .50
9 Christian Lalonde .20 .50
10 Darren Langdon .30 .75
11 Rob Laurie .30 .75
12 Brad McCaughey .20 .50
13 Bobby McKillop .30 .75
14 Savo Mitrovic .20 .50
15 Ken Murchison .20 .50
16 Darren Perkins .20 .50
17 Grant Sonier CO .10 .25
NNO Header .04 .10
NNO Medallion Slammer .20 .50
NNO 1993 RHI World Champions .20 .50
NNO The Mask .30 .75

1994-95 Anaheim Bullfrogs RHI

This set features the Bullfrogs of Roller Hockey Intl. The 20-card set was sold by the team at home games. Because the singles are not numbered, the players appear alphabetically.

COMPLETE SET (20) 3.60 10.00
1 Darren Banks .30 .75
2 Jared Bednar .20 .50
3 Steve Cadieux .20 .50
4 Joe Cook .20 .50
5 Mark Deazeley .20 .50
6 Victor Gervais .30 .75
7 Chris Gordon .20 .50
8 Fredrik Jax .20 .50
9 Rick Judson .20 .50
10 Rob Laurie .30 .75
11 BJ MacPherson .20 .50
12 Brad McCaughey .20 .50
13 Savo Mitrovic .20 .50
14 Marc Ouimet .30 .75
15 Darren Perkins .20 .50
16 Daniel Shank .30 .75
17 Grant Sonier CO .04 .10
18 Brad Tiley .20 .50
19 Todd Wetzel .20 .50
20 Header/Checklist .01 .01

1995-96 Anaheim Bullfrogs RHI

Little is known about this set beyond the confirmed checklist. Any additional information can be forwarded to hockeymag@beckett.com.

COMPLETE SET (20) 2.80 7.00
1 Checklist .04 .10
2 Grant Sonier CO .04 .10
3 Brad McCaughey ACO .04 .10
4 Victor Gervais .16 .40
5 Darren Perkins .16 .40
6 Savo Mitrovic .16 .40
7 Joe Cook .16 .40
8 Todd Wetzel .16 .40
9 Scott Bell .16 .40
10 Rick Judson .16 .40
11 BJ MacPherson .16 .40
12 Rob Laurie .16 .40
13 Darren Banks .20 .50
14 Sean O'Brien .16 .40
15 Jakub Ficenec .16 .40
16 Mark Stitt .16 .40
17 Glenn Stewart .16 .40
18 Mark DeSantis .16 .40
19 Tom Menicci .16 .40
20 Eric Raymond .16 .40

1996-97 Anaheim Bullfrogs RHI

This 21-card set was available late in the season, and could only be purchased at games. The cards are unnumbered, and are listed below in the order they were packaged. They were produced by Star Images Assoc.

COMPLETE SET (21) 3.60 9.00
1 Bullfrogs Logo .04 .10
2 Zeus Mascot .04 .10
3 Rob Laurie .20 .50
4 Victor Gervais .20 .50
5 Doug McCarthy .20 .50
6 Kurt Seher .20 .50
7 Marty Yewchuk .20 .50
8 David Goverde .24 .60
9 BJ MacPherson .04 .10
10 Rick Judson .24 .60
11 Jakub Ficenec .20 .50
12 Tom Menicci .20 .50
13 Glenn Stewart .20 .50
14 Mark Stitt .20 .50
15 Jim Bermingham .20 .50
16 Todd Wetzel .20 .50
17 Joe Cook .20 .50
18 Ray Edwards .20 .50
19 Chris Newans .20 .50
20 Darren Perkins .20 .50
21 Brad McCaughey CO .04 .10

1994-95 Anchorage Aces

This set features the Aces of the WCHL. Little is known about this set beyond the checklist, which was provided by Ralph Slate of www.hockeydb.com. Any additional information can be forwarded to hockeymag@beckett.com.

COMPLETE SET (27) 4.80 12.00
1 Kevin Fitzgerald .20 .50
2 Tony Link .20 .50
3 Zack Westin .20 .50
4 Kory Wright .20 .50
5 Kord Cernich .20 .50
6 Darrin Semeniuk .20 .50
7 Brian Kraft .20 .50
8 Raymond Blackadar .20 .50
9 Jim Tobin .20 .50
10 Tracy Link .20 .50
11 Michael Warde .20 .50
12 Garvin Federenko .20 .50
13 Jim Mayes .20 .50
14 Vern Hickel .20 .50
15 Derek Donald .20 .50
16 Brian Majeske .20 .50
17 Chad Meyhoff .20 .50
18 Doug Spooner .20 .50
19 Maurice Hall .20 .50
20 Pete McEnaney .20 .50
21 Keith Street .20 .50
22 Georg Thiele .20 .50
23 Tim Molle .20 .50
24 Brian Bethard .20 .50
25 Dean Trboyevich .20 .50
26 Logo Card .04 .11
27 Team Photo/Checklist .20 .50

1996-97 Anchorage Aces

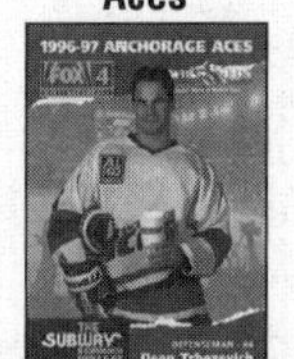

This 16-card set was produced as a promotional giveaway for the Anchorage Aces of the WCHL. The fronts feature posed photos with the players blatantly shilling for the Subway chain; that company's logo is prominently displayed in the lower left corner, along with those of the local FOX TV outlet and KWHL radio. The backs feature sketchy bio information. As the cards are unnumbered, they are listed below in alphabetical order.

COMPLETE SET (16) 3.20 8.00
1 Alaska's Morning Show .04 .10
2 Derek Donald .30 .75
3 Kiddie Fox .04 .10
4 Dean Larson .30 .75
5 Steve MacSwain .30 .75
6 Mark The Hitman .04 .10
7 J.J. Michaels .30 .75
8 Black Mike .04 .10
9 Craig Mittleholt .30 .75
10 Chris Newans .30 .75
11 Frank Ouellette .30 .75
12 Chad Richard .30 .75
13 Sean Rowe .30 .75
14 Keith Street .30 .75
15 Dean Trboyevich .30 .75
16 Free Q-Zar Game Card .01

1997-98 Anchorage Aces

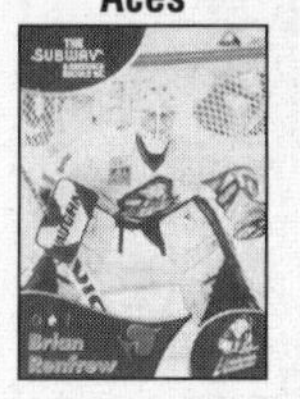

This set features the Aces of the WCHL. The set was produced by the team and sold at home games.

COMPLETE SET (25) 3.60 9.00
1 Title Card .04 .10
2 Walt Poddubny CO .20 .50
3 Kenny Huizenga .20 .50
4 Kord Cernich .20 .50
5 Bobby Cunningham .20 .50
6 Derek Donald .20 .50
7 Dallas Ferguson .20 .50
8 Derek Gauthier .20 .50
9 Jason Gibson .20 .50
10 Marc LaForge .20 .50
11 Dean Larson .20 .50
12 Dave Latta .20 .50
13 Steve MacSwain .20 .50
14 Chris Newans .20 .50
15 Hayden O'Rear .20 .50
16 Brian Renfrew .20 .50
17 Sean Rowe .20 .50
18 Jason Shmyr .20 .50
19 Keith Street .20 .50
20 Sergei Tkachenko .20 .50
21 George Wilcox .20 .50
22 Paul Williams .20 .50
23 Mascot .04 .10
24 Mascot .04 .10
25 Mascot .04 .10

1998-99 Anchorage Aces

This set features the Aces of the WHL. The cards measure 2 1/2 by 3 1/2 and feature a full-bleed color photo on the front. The team logo is blown up in the lower left corner. The backs feature stats over a ghosted player head shot.

COMPLETE SET (26) 4.00 10.00
1 Checklist/Team Photo .20 .50
2 Dean Trboyevich .20 .50
3 Kevin Epp .20 .50
4 Hayden O'Rear .20 .50
5 Richard Peacock .20 .50
6 Sean Rowe .20 .50
7 Boomer Mascot .04 .10
8 George Wilcox .20 .50
9 Sergei Tkachenko .20 .50
10 Frank Jury TR .04 .10
11 Walt Poddubny HCO .20 .50
12 Kent Baumbach .20 .50
13 Wade Brookbank .20 .50
14 Keith Street .20 .50
15 Bob Cunningham .20 .50
16 Kord Cernich .20 .50
17 Paul Williams .20 .50
18 Evgeny Kourilin .20 .50
19 Jason Gibson .20 .50
20 Steve MacSwain .20 .50
21 Dean Larson .20 .50
22 Dallas Ferguson .20 .50
23 Derek Gauthier .20 .50
24 Yvan Corbin .20 .50
25 Sponsor Card .04 .10
26 Fred Rannard BR .04 .10

1999-00 Anchorage Aces

This set features the Aces of the WCHL. The card fronts feature a full-bleed color photo, along with the logos of sponsors Subway and Wideo City. The backs contain a b/w head shot and stats from the previous season.

COMPLETE SET (28) 4.00 10.00
1 Bob Wilkie HCO .10 .25
2 Fred Rannard .20 .50
3 Paul Williams .20 .50
4 Steve MacSwain .20 .50
5 Marc Charbonneau .20 .50
6 Chad Power .20 .50
7 Brian Elder .20 .50
8 Tim Lozinik .20 .50
9 Sponsor Card .01
10 Sponsor Card .01
11 Kord Cernich .20 .50
12 George Wilcox .20 .50
13 Keith Street .20 .50
14 Derek Gauthier .20 .50
15 Ruslan Batyrshin .30 .75
16 Sean Rowe .20 .50
17 Dean Larson .20 .50
18 Team Photo .20 .50
19 Sponsor Card .01
20 Sponsor Card .01
21 Walt Poddubny HCO .20 .50

22 Dallas Ferguson .20 .50
23 Chad Richard .20 .50
24 Denis Pigolitsyn .20 .50
25 Clayton Read .20 .50
26 Marc Delmore .20 .50
27 Lada Hampeis .20 .50
28 Sponsor Card .01

2001-02 Anchorage Aces

This set features the Aces of the WCHL. The set was given away at a home game late in the season.

COMPLETE SET (22) 8.00 20.00
1 Shane Calder .40 1.00
2 Bob Cunningham .40 1.00
3 Kimbi Daniels .40 1.00
4 Simon Duplessis .40 1.00
5 Yuri Krivokhija .40 1.00
6 Brian LaFleur .40 1.00
7 Dean Larson .40 1.00
8 Michael Marostega .40 1.00
9 Jamie McCaig .40 1.50
10 Chris Newans .40 1.00
11 Denis Pigolitsin .40 1.00
12 Tobin Praznik .40 1.00
13 Chad Richard .40 1.50
14 Olie Sundstrom .60 1.50
15 Paul Williams .40 1.00
16 J.J. Wrobel .40 1.00
17 Jami Yoder .40 1.00
18 B.J. Young .40 1.00
19 Walt Poddubny CO .10 .25
20 Boomer MASCOT .04 .10
21 ACS Wireless .01
22 Team Photo .20 .50

1990-91 Arizona Icecats

Produced by the Ninth Inning, this 16-card standard-size set features members of the Arizona Icecats. Production was reportedly limited to 2,150 sets, obtainable either at the Tucson Convention Center Ice Arena on game days or at the Ninth Inning (a card shop). The front features a posed color photo of the player, with thin black border on white card stock. The upper left and lower right hand corners of the picture are cut out, with the year and the team logo inserted in these spaces respectively. The back presents biographical information in a black box. Although the individual cards are unnumbered, they are checklisted below according to the numbering assigned to them on the checklist card.

COMPLETE SET (16) 3.20 8.00
1 Leo Golembiewski CO .30 .75
2 Icecat Leaders .40 1.00
Kevin Sheehan
John Allen
Leo Golembiewski CO
Kelly Walker
John Wegener
3 John Allen .30 .75
4 Don Carlson .20 .50
5 Dan Divjak .30 .75
6 Frank DeMaio .20 .50
7 Jeremy Goltz .30 .75
8 Aaron Joffe .20 .50
9 Dan O'Day .20 .50
10 Dan Olberg .20 .50
11 Cory Oleson .30 .75
12 Kevin Sheehan .30 .75
13 Dean Sives .20 .50
14 Kelly Walker .30 .75
15 John Wegener .30 .75
16 Logo Card/Checklist .20 .50

1991-92 Arizona Icecats

This 20-card standard-size set features members of the Arizona Icecats. The front features a posed color photo of the player, with thin blue border and a blue shadow-border on white card stock. The player's name appears in the bottom shadow- border. The back presents biographical information and statistics in a black shadow-bordered box. Though the individual cards are unnumbered, they are checklisted below according to the numbering assigned to them on the checklist card.

COMPLETE SET (20) 4.00 10.00
1 Leo Golembiewski CO .10 .25
2 Don Carlson .20 .50
3 Kelly Walker .30 .75
4 Cory Oleson .30 .75
5 Drew Sibr .20 .50
6 Dan Divjak .30 .75
7 Jeremy Goltz .20 .50
8 Aaron Joffe .20 .50
9 Tommy Smith .20 .50
10 Dan Anderson .20 .50
11 Dean Sives .20 .50
12 Steve Hutchings .20 .50
13 Shane Fausel .20 .50
14 Greg Mitchell .20 .50
15 Ricky Pope .20 .50
16 Nate Soules .20 .50
17 Flavio Gentile .20 .50
18 Icecats Leaders .20 .50
Leo Golembiewski CO
Kelly Walker
Cory Oleson
Jeremy Goltz
Dan Divjak
19 Glenn Hall 1.00 2.50
Honorary Captain
20 Logo Card/Checklist .10 .25

1992-93 Arizona Icecats

This 16-card standard-size set features the Arizona Icecats hockey team. The fronts display a posed color player photo with multiple blue drop borders. The player's name appears in a royal blue stripe across the bottom of the picture. The backs carry biographical information and statistics in a black shadow-bordered box. Though the individual cards are unnumbered, they are checklisted below according to the numbering assigned to them on the checklist card.

COMPLETE SET (20) 3.20 8.00
1 Leo Golembiewski CO .10 .25
2 Kelly Walker .24 .60
3 Cory Oleson .24 .60
4 Tommy Smith .20 .50
5 John Allen .20 .50
6 Dan Anderson .20 .50
7 Aaron Joffe .20 .50
8 Dan Divjak .24 .60
9 Jeremy Goltz .20 .50
10 Steve Hutchings .20 .50
11 Greg Mitchell .20 .50
12 Ricky Pope .20 .50
13 Nate Soules .20 .50
14 Matt Glines .20 .50
15 Mark Thawley .20 .50
16 Andre Zafrani .20 .50
17 Chris Noga .20 .50
18 Jim Kolbe .10 .25
Honorary Captain
19 Coach and Top Gun Line .30 .75
Cory Oleson
Leo Golembiewski CO
Kelly Walker
Tommy Smith
John Allen
Dan Anderson
20 Logo Card/Checklist .10 .25

1993-94 Arizona Icecats

Yet another set issued by the most hobby-friendly club hockey team in the United States. This year's celebrity captain is that exemplary American, Oliver North. The set was sold by the team to raise money for the program.

COMPLETE SET (20) 3.20 8.00
1 Header Card .10 .25
2 Leo Golembiewski CO .10 .25
3 Greg Mitchell .20 .50
4 Ricky Pope .20 .50
5 Dan Divjak .24 .60
6 Brian Consolino .20 .50
7 Matt Gines .20 .50
8 Steve Hutchings .20 .50
9 Joel Nusbaum .20 .50
10 Sam Battaglia .20 .50
11 Kiva Gippo .20 .50
12 Jeremy Goltz .20 .50
13 Peter Scott .20 .50
14 Kevin Oztekin .20 .50
15 Nate Soules .20 .50
16 Chris Noga .20 .50
17 Dennis Hands .20 .50
18 Mark Thawley .20 .50
19 Leader Card .10 .25
20 Oliver North .30 .75

1994-95 Arizona Icecats

This low-tech set features the Icecats of the NCAA. The fronts offer a posed on-ice photo, taken in front of a bad backdrop. The backs feature 1993-94 stats and a pre-printed autograph.

COMPLETE SET (24) 3.20 25.00
1 Title Card/CL .01
2 Leo Golembiewski CO .04 .10

3 Steve Hutchings .16 1.00
4 Nate Soules .16 1.00
5 Chris Noga .16 1.00
6 Kevin Oztekin .16 1.00
7 Greg Mitchell .16 1.00
8 Ricky Pope .16 1.00
9 Brian Consolino .16 1.00
10 John Muntz .16 1.00
11 Joel Nusbaum .16 1.00
12 Sam Battaglia .16 1.00
13 Kiva Gippo .16 1.00
14 Peter Scott .16 1.00
15 Dennis Hands .20 1.50
16 Mark Thawley .16 1.00
17 Ryan Rockabrand .16 1.00
18 Joe Joyce .16 1.00
19 Jeremy Walters .16 1.00
20 Ethan Kaulas .16 1.00
21 Reg Kerr#)Glen Hall .40 2.00
22 Leo Golembiewski#)Keith Magnuson .04 1.00
23 Stan Mikita#)Glen Hall#)Keith Magnuson#)Al Secord .20 5.00
24 Madhouse on Main Street .01

1995-96 Arizona Icecats

This set features the Icecats of the ACHA. The cards feature a posed photo on the front, framed by a purple border. The sparse backs offer peronsal data and stats.

COMPLETE SET (23) 25.00
1 Title Card/CL .01
2 Leo Golembiewski CO .04 .10
3 Chris Noga .16 1.00
4 John Muntz .16 1.00
5 Kevin Oztekin .16 1.00
6 Mark Thawley .16 1.00
7 Sam Battaglia .16 1.00
8 Peter Scott .16 1.00
9 Joel Nusbaum .16 1.00
10 Ryan Rockabrand .16 1.00
11 Andy Knick .16 1.00
12 Brian Meehan .16 1.00
13 Bob Majka .16 1.00
14 Ben Ruston .16 1.00
15 Jeff Rice .16 1.00
16 Brian Consolino .16 1.00
17 Bryan Fork .16 1.00
18 Joel Hilshey .20 1.25
19 Joe Joyce .16 1.00
20 Jeremy Goltz ACO .04 .10
21 Icecat Leaders .04 .10
22 Scotty Bowman .40 5.00
23 Scotty Bowman Hon Capt. .40 5.00

1996-97 Arizona Icecats

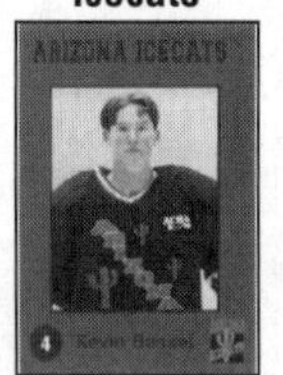

This set features the Icecats of the ACHA. The cards are standard-sized and feature a posed shot framed by a thick red border. The sparse backs list personal data and last season's stats.

COMPLETE SET (25) 4.00 25.00
1 Title Card/CL .01
2 Leo Golembiewski HCO .04 .10
3 Kevin Baskel .16 1.00
4 Sam Battaglia .16 1.00
5 Brian Consolino .16 1.00
6 Josh Flett .16 1.00
7 Eric Holton .16 1.00
8 Paul Juran .16 1.00
9 Andy Knick .16 1.00
10 Eliot Komar .16 1.00
11 Beau Lemire .20 1.25
12 Joe McCaffrey .16 1.00
13 Brian Meehan .16 1.00
14 Joel Nusbaum .16 1.00
15 Ace Pascual .16 1.00
16 Rob Poupard .16 1.00
17 Ben Ruston .16 1.00
18 Peter Scott .16 1.00
19 Mike Tesi .16 1.00
20 Tom Thompson .16 1.00
21 Dave Weiss .16 1.00
22 Bob Majka .16 1.00
23 Leo Golembiewski HCO .04 .10
24 Jeremy Goltz ACO .04 .10
25 Stan Mikita Hon Capt. .80 5.00

1997-98 Arizona Icecats

This set features the Icecats of the ACHA. The cards feature a posed color photo framed by a thick white border. Card numbers are found on the front, lower right. The sparse backs list player personal data.

COMPLETE SET (26) 10.00 25.00
1 Title Card/CL .01
2 Leo Golembiewski HCO .04 .10
3 Benedictine HOF .01
4 Kevin Baskel .16 1.00
5 Jordan Bolton .20 1.50
6 Tyler Brush .16 1.00
7 Ed Carfora .16 1.00
8 Paul Dorn .16 1.00
9 Chad Dyjak .16 1.00
10 Rodney Glassman .16 1.00
11 Mike Graves .16 1.00
12 Marc Harris .16 1.00
13 Joe McCaffrey .16 1.00
14 Charles McCarty .16 1.00
15 Bob Majka .16 1.00
16 Brian Meehan .16 1.00
17 Ace Pascual .16 1.00
18 Joe Peplinski .20 1.50
19 Ben Ruston .16 1.00
20 Mike Tesi .16 1.00
21 Tom Thompson .16 1.00
22 Kory Wagstaff .16 1.00
23 Max Wilkie .16 1.00
24 Jim Wilkey .16 1.00
25 Jeremy Goltz ACO .04 .10
26 Rex Allen, Jr. Hon Capt. .04 1.00

1998-99 Arizona Icecats

COMPLETE SET (27) 10.00 25.00
1 Tyler Brush .40 1.00
2 Ed Carfora .40 1.00
3 Quinn Carter .40 1.00
4 Hunter Cherenack .40 1.00
5 Paul Dorn .40 1.00
6 Andrew Edwards .40 1.00
7 Rodney Glassman .40 1.00
8 Leo Golembiewski CO .02 .10
9 Jeremy Goltz ACO .02 .10
10 Mike Graves .40 1.00
11 Marc Harris .40 1.00
12 Bobby Hull HON CPT 2.00 5.00
13 Pavel Jandura .40 1.00
14 Bob Majka .40 1.00
15 Joe McCaffrey .40 1.00
16 Kyle McNeilance .40 1.00
17 Brian Meehan .40 1.00
18 Kevin Meehan .40 1.00
19 Mark Meister .40 1.00
20 Eugene Mesh .40 1.00
21 Jason Morgan .40 1.00
22 Kyle Neary .40 1.00
23 Jason Royce .40 1.00
24 Mike Tesi .40 1.00
25 Tom Thompson .40 1.00
26 Team Leaders .40 1.00
27 Checklist .02 .10

1999-00 Arizona Icecats

COMPLETE SET (28) 8.00 20.00
1 Tyler Brush .40 1.00
2 Ed Carfora .40 1.00
3 Hunter Cherenack .40 1.00
4 Paul Dorn .40 1.00
5 Andrew Edwards .40 1.00
6 Dave Galardini .40 1.00
7 Leo Golembiewski CO .02 .10
8 Jeremy Goltz ACO .02 .10
9 Mike Graves .40 1.00
10 Marc Harris .40 1.00
11 Chase Hoyt .40 1.00
12 Pavel Jandura .40 1.00
13 Dave Loftus .40 1.00
14 Bob Majka .40 1.00
15 Joe McCaffrey .40 1.00
16 Kyle McNeilance .40 1.00
17 Brian Meehan .40 1.00
18 Kevin Meehan .40 1.00
19 Mark Meister .40 1.00
20 Jason Morgan .40 1.00
21 Kyle Neary .40 1.00
22 Ryan Roth .40 1.00
23 Jason Royce .40 1.00
24 Sgt. Slaughter HON CPT .75 2.00
25 Tom Thompson .40 1.00
26 Team Leaders .40 1.00
27 L.Golembiewski Golf Classic .02 .10
28 Checklist .02 .10

2000-01 Arizona Icecats

COMPLETE SET (30) 8.00 20.00
1 Header/Checklist .02 .10
2 Joe Boysen .40 1.00
3 Tyler Brush .40 1.00
4 Ed Carfora .40 1.00
5 Paul Dorn .40 1.00
6 Andrew Edwards .40 1.00
7 Andrew Fredericks .40 1.00
8 Dave Galardini .40 1.00
9 Mike Graves .40 1.00
10 Marc Harris .40 1.00
11 Pavel Jandura .40 1.00
12 Braden Koprivica .40 1.00
13 Wes Krisay .40 1.00
14 Dave Loftus .40 1.00
15 Kyle McNeilance .40 1.00
16 Kevin Meehan .40 1.00
17 Jason Morgan .40 1.00
18 Kyle Neary .40 1.00
19 Bill Pardue .40 1.00
20 Jason Royce .40 1.00
21 John Saunders .40 1.00
22 Stefan Thomasson .40 1.00
23 Bill Veasey .40 1.00
24 Tom Wood .40 1.00
25 Leo Golembiewski CO .02 .10
26 Brian Meehan ACO .02 .10
27 Bob Leoni ACO .02 .10
28 Team Leaders .20 .50
29 Golf Classic .02 .10
30 Joe Cristiani HON CAPT .02 .10

2001-02 Arizona Icecats

COMPLETE SET (26) 8.00 20.00
1 Bryan Aronchick .40 1.00
2 Shaun Brooks .40 1.00
3 Papa Joe Chevalier HON CPT .20 .50
4 Andrew Fredericks .40 1.00
5 Dave Galardini .40 1.00
6 Leo Golembiewski CO .02 .10
7 Pavel Jandura .40 1.00
8 Matt Johnson .40 1.00
9 Braden Koprivica .40 1.00
10 Wes Krisay .40 1.00
11 Dave Loftus .40 1.00
12 Brian Meehan ACO .02 .10
13 Kevin Meehan .40 1.00
15 Mickey Meehan .40 1.00
16 Matt Naylor .40 1.00
17 Kyle Neary .40 1.00
18 Bill Pardue .40 1.00
19 John Saunders .40 1.00
20 Mike Smith .40 1.00
21 Tom Wolf .40 1.00
22 Tom Wood .40 1.00
23 Nick Woods .40 1.00
24 Jerald Zivic .40 1.00
25 Team Leaders .20 .50
26 Checklist .02 .10

2002-03 Arizona Icecats

COMPLETE SET (32) 10.00 25.00
1 Bryan Aronchick .40 1.00
2 Matt Baumann .40 1.00
3 Shaun Brooks .40 1.00
4 Banks Concepcion .40 1.00
5 Cole Dunlop .40 1.00
6 Andrew Fredericks .40 1.00
7 Justin Guerra .40 1.00
8 Don Holtz .40 1.00
9 Matt Johnson .40 1.00
10 Rick Karasch .40 1.00
11 Braden Koprivica .40 1.00
12 Wes Krisay .40 1.00
13 Dave Loftus .40 1.00
14 Mickey Meehan .40 1.00
15 Keith Mitchell .40 1.00
16 Matt Muller .40 1.00
17 Matt Naylor .40 1.00
18 Eric Ormson .40 1.00
19 Bill Pardue .40 1.00
20 Mike Pelletier .40 1.00
21 Brian Pollock .40 1.00
22 Mike Smith .40 1.00
23 Dan Whitlock .40 1.00
24 Drew Williamson .40 1.00
25 Tim Wochok .40 1.00
26 Nick Woods .40 1.00
27 Leo Golembiewski CO .02 .10
28 Brian Meehan ACO .02 .10
29 Team Leaders .20 .50
30 Dwain Pipe MASCOT .02 .10
31 Don Rickles HON CPT .40 1.00
32 Checklist .02 .10

2003-04 Arizona Icecats

COMPLETE SET (31) 8.00 20.00
1 Bryan Aronchick .40 1.00
2 Shaun Brooks .40 1.00
3 Anthony Capone .40 1.00
4 Banks Concepion .40 1.00
5 Kevin Conners .40 1.00
6 Dave Cwik .40 1.00
7 Cole Dunlop .40 1.00
8 Andrew Fredericks .40 1.00
9 Don Holtz .40 1.00
10 Rick Karasch .40 1.00
11 Jerod Keene .40 1.00
12 Eric Kowalek .40 1.00
13 Casey Leyva .40 1.00
14 Bryan Meagher .40 1.00
15 Mickey Meehan .40 1.00
16 Jeff Merritt .40 1.00
17 Keith Mitchell .40 1.00
18 Josh Parry .40 1.00
19 D.J Pelletier .40 1.00
20 Brian Pollock .40 1.00
21 Mike Smith .40 1.00
22 Dan Whitlock .40 1.00
23 Drew Williamson .40 1.00
24 Tim Wochok .40 1.00
25 Leo Golembiewski CO .02 .10
26 Brian Meehan ACO .02 .10
27 Team Leaders .20 .50
28 Dwain Pipe MASCOT .02 .10
29 Don Rickles .40 1.00
30 John McCain HON CPT .40 1.00
31 Header Card .02 .10

2004-05 Arizona Icecats

COMPLETE SET (34) 6.00 15.00
1 Bryan Aronchick .30 .75
2 Anthony Capone .30 .75
3 Cole Dunlop .30 .75
4 Luke Edwall .30 .75
5 Leo Golembiewski CO .02 .10
6 Don Holtz .30 .75
7 Craig Irwin .30 .75
8 Eric Kowalek .30 .75
9 Dave Lawrence .30 .75
10 Casey Leyva .30 .75
11 Scott Marshall .30 .75
12 Brian Meehan ACO .02 .10
13 Mickey Meehan .30 .75
14 Keith Mitchell .30 .75
15 Josh Parry .30 .75
16 D.J. Pelletier .30 .75
17 Mike Pelletier .30 .75
18 Mark Perzi .30 .75
19 Jay Punsky .30 .75
20 Max Sliwinski .30 .75
21 Mike Smith .30 .75
22 Doug Wilson .30 .75
23 Tim Wochok .30 .75
24 Jerald Zivic .30 .75
25 Team Leaders .20 .50
26 Equipment Managers .02 .10
27 Sgt. Slaughter .40 1.00
28 L. Gombiewski Celebrity Golf .02
.10
29 Dwain Pipe MASCOT .02 .10
30 Sons of the Pioneers .02 .10
31 Team Picture .02 .10
32 Sen. John McCain .40 1.00
33 Willie Nelson HON CPT .40 1.00
34 Header Card .02 .10

2002-03 Arkansas Riverblades

COMPLETE SET (24) 10.00 25.00
1 Jason Bermingham .40 1.00
2 Mike Cirillo .40 1.00
3 Ryan Coole .40 1.00
4 Aaron Davis .40 1.00
5 Scott Fankhouser .75 2.00
6 Ernie Hartlieb .40 1.00
7 Maxim Linnik .40 1.00
8 Eric Long .40 1.00
9 Terry Marchant .40 1.00
10 Matt Pagnutti .40 1.00
11 Samuel Paquet .40 1.00
12 Mike Renzi .40 1.00
13 Jason Saal .75 2.00
14 Mike Sandbeck .40 1.00
15 Mark Scott .40 1.00
16 Bud Smith .40 1.00
17 Jimi St. John .40 1.00
18 Dean Stock .40 1.00
19 Dean Stork .40 1.00
20 Garry Toor .40 1.00
21 Damon Whitton .40 1.00
22 Chris Cichocki HCO .10 .25
23 RiverBabes .40 1.00
24 Rocky Bear-Boa Mascot .02 .10

1999-00 Asheville Smoke

This set was given out in three series at home games. The cards feature jersey numbers on the back, but are listed below in alphabetical order because of duplicate and skipped numbers.

COMPLETE SET (27) 30.00 75.00
1 Checklist .10 .25
2 Francois Bourdeau 1.25 3.00
3 Dan Brenzavich 1.25 3.00
4 Peter Cermak 1.25 3.00
5 Frank DeFrenza 1.25 3.00
6 Paul Giblin 1.25 3.00
7 Brent Gretzky 2.00 5.00
8 Francois Leroux 1.25 3.00
9 Dan McIntyre 1.25 3.00
10 Rob Milliken 1.25 3.00
11 Hayden O'Rear 1.25 3.00
12 Vaclav Pazourek 1.25 3.00
13 Cory Peterson 1.25 3.00
14 Jon Pirrong 2.00 5.00
15 Ken Plaquin 1.25 3.00
16 Ryan Prentice 1.25 3.00
17 Josh Tymchak 1.25 3.00
18 Shawn Ulrich 1.25 3.00
19 Lindsay Vallis 1.25 3.00
20 Richie Walcott 1.25 3.00
21 Bruce Watson 1.25 3.00
22 Cory Peterson 1.25 3.00
(Josh Tymchak
Bruce Watson
23 Keith Gretzky HCO 1.25 3.00
24 Aaron Fackler EM .10 .25
25 Smoky Mascot .10 .25
26 Sponsor Card .01
27 Team Photo .40 1.00

2000-01 Asheville Smoke

This set features the Smoke of the UHL. The set was produced by Roox, and was distributed as a promotional giveaway over the course of three home games.

COMPLETE SET (27) 7.20 18.00
1 Ryan Aikia .30 .75
2 Brent Belecki .30 .75
3 Blue Bennefield .30 .75
4 Derek Crimin .30 .75
5 Alexandre Fomitchev .40 1.00
6 John Hewitt .30 .75
7 Olaf Kjenstad .40 1.00
8 Dominic Maltais .40 1.00
9 Tyler Prosofsky .30 .75
10 Bobby Rapoza .30 .75
11 Bogdan Rudenko .30 .75
12 J.C. Ruid .30 .75
13 Lee Svangstu .30 .75
14 Shawn Ulrich .30 .75
15 Pat Bingham CO .20 .50
16 Smoky MASCOT .04 .10
17 Ingles Zamboni SPONSOR .04 .01
18 Manager TR .04 .10
19 Tom Wilson .30 .75
20 Brett Colborne .30 .75
21 Robert Marshall .30 .75
22 Alex Dumas .30 .75
23 Vitali Andreev .30 .75
24 Evan Lindsay .40 1.00
25 Bruce Watson .40 1.00
26 Asheville Smoke .04 .10
27 He Shoots Team Card .10 .25

2001-02 Asheville Smoke

This set features the Smoke of the UHL. The cards were issued as a promotional giveaway, apparently at three different home games. Any additional information on this set can be forwarded to hockeymag@beckett.com.

COMPLETE SET (24) 8.00 20.00
1 Team Photo .20 .50
2 Kris Mallette .40 1.50
3 Tyler McMillan .40 1.00
4 Mike Payne .40 1.00
5 Chad Wagner .40 1.50
6 Forrest Gore .40 1.00
7 Tom Wilson .40 1.00
8 Todd Bisson .40 1.00
9 Geoff Derouin .40 1.50
10 Bobby Rapoza .40 1.00
11 Kamil Kuriplach .40 1.00
12 Todd MacIsaac .40 1.00
13 Sean Fitzgerald .40 1.00
14 Samuel Paquet .40 1.00
15 Kris Schultz .40 1.00
16 Bob Dalessio EQMG .04 .10
17 Smoky MASCOT .04 .10
18 Curtis Menzul .40 1.00
19 Cory Peterson .40 1.00
20 Jean-Francois Dufour .40 1.00
21 Jeff Petruic .40 1.00
22 J.C. Ruid .40 1.00
23 Blaine Russell .40 1.50
24 Shawn Ulrich CO .04 .10

1992-93 Atlanta Knights

Released by the team, this 24-card set features the 1992-93 Atlanta Knights. Base cards feature full color action photography and white borders. The set's print run was limited to 5000, and they were sold at the Omni Arena during the season for $5. This set is not numbered so it appears in packing order.

COMPLETE SET (24) 4.80 12.00
1 Header Card .04 .10
2 Manon Rheaume 2.00 5.00
3 Jeff Buchanan .10 .25
4 Matt Hervey .10 .25
5 Rick Lanz .10 .25
6 Colin Miller .10 .25
7 Keith Osborne .10 .25
8 Jason Lafreniere .10 .25
9 Jock Callander .40 1.00
10 Brent Gretzky .20 .50
11 Steve Maltais .40 1.00
12 Serguei Ossipov .10 .25
13 Shayne Stevenson .20 .50
14 Scott Boston .10 .25
15 Jean Blouin .10 .25
16 Shawn Rivers .20 .50
17 Dan Vincelette .10 .25
18 Chris Lipuma .10 .25
19 Don Burke .10 .25
20 Christian Campeau .10 .25
21 Tim Bergland .10 .25
22 J.C. Bergeron .20 .50
23 David Littman .20 .50
24 Gene Ubriaco HCO .04 .10

1993-94 Atlanta Knights

Released by the team, this 24-card set features the 1992-93 Atlanta Knights. Base cards feature full color action photography and white borders. Set print run was limited to 5000, and were sold at the Omni Arena during the season for $5.00.

COMPLETE SET (24) 6.00 15.00
1 Mike Greenlay .20 .50
2 Jeff Buchanan .16 .40
3 Eric Charron .16 .40
4 Colin Miller .16 .40
5 Brent Gretzky .20 .75
6 Steve LaRouche .16 .40
7 Marc Tardif .30 .50
8 Jeff Madill .16 .40
9 Devin Edgerton .16 .40
10 Bill McDougall .16 .40
11 Jason Ruff .16 .40
12 Eric Dubois .16 .40
13 Martin Tanguay .16 .40
14 Stan Drulia .30 .75
15 Normand Rochefort .16 .40
16 Shawn Rivers .20 .50
17 Chris Lipuma .16 .40
18 Cory Cross .16 .40
19 Christian Campeau .16 .40
20 Tim Bergland .16 .40
21 J.C. Bergeron .20 .50
22 Manon Rheaume 2.40 6.00
23 Gene Ubriaco HCO .04 .10
CL Header Card .04 .10

1994-95 Atlanta Knights

Released by the team, this 24-card set features the 1992-93 Atlanta Knights. Base cards feature full color action photography and white borders. Set print run was limited to 5000, and were sold at the Omni Arena during the season for $5.00. This set is not numbered so it appears in packing order

COMPLETE SET (27) 3.20 10.00
1 Header Card .04 .10
2 Mike Greenlay .16 .75
3 Chris Nelson .16 .40
4 Derek Mayer .16 .40
5 Drew Bannister .16 .40
6 Allen Pedersen .16 .40
7 Colin Miller .16 .40
8 Brent Gretzky .16 .75
9 Peter Ferraro .16 .40
10 Devin Edgerton .16 .40
11 Chris Ferraro .16 .75
12 Jason Ruff .16 .40
13 Eric Dubois .16 .40
14 Stan Drulia .16 .75
15 Allen Egeland .16 .40
16 Aaron Gavey .16 .40
17 Yves Heroux .16 .40
18 Brian Straub .16 .40
19 Jeff Toms .16 .40
20 Chris Lipuma .16 .40
21 Cory Cross .16 .40
22 Christian Campeau .16 .40
23 Derek Wilkinson .16 .75
24 Brantt Myhres .16 .75
25 John Paris Jr. HCO .04 .10
26 Scott Gordon ACO .04 .10
27 Sir Hat Trick Mascot .04 .10

1995-96 Atlanta Knights

This set features the Knights of the IHL. The set was produced by Edge Ice.

COMPLETE SET (25) 4.80 12.00
1 Drew Bannister .20 .50
2 Doug Barrault .20 .50
3 Corey Beaulieu .20 .50
4 Ryan Brown .20 .50
5 Christian Campeau .20 .50
6 Stan Drulia .30 .75
7 Eric Dubois .20 .50
8 Allan Egeland .20 .50
9 Brantt Myhres .30 .75
10 Mark Greig .20 .50
11 Bob Halkidis .20 .50
12 Alexandre LaPorte .20 .50
13 Chris LiPuma .20 .50
14 Tyler Moss .30 .75
15 Brent Peterson .20 .50
16 Adrien Plavsic .20 .50
17 Jason Ruff .20 .50
18 Reggie Savage .20 .50
19 Corey Spring .20 .50
20 Jeff Toms .20 .50
21 Derek Wilkinson .30 .75
22 John Paris CO .10 .25
23 Scott Gordon CO .10 .25
24 Kurt Harvey TR .04 .10
25 Sir Hat Trick MAS .04 .10

2001-02 Atlantic City Boardwalk Bullies

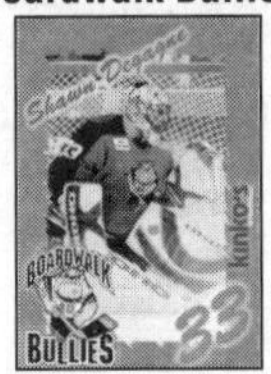

These cards were handed out by the team at home games and player appearances. They appear to be hand cut and, therefore are varying sizes. The checklist may be incomplete.

COMPLETE SET (26) 10.00 20.00
1 Checklist .01 .01
2 Shane Belter .40 1.00
3 John Campbell .40 1.00
4 J.F. Caudron .40 1.00
5 Vratislav Cech .40 1.00
6 Kevin Colley .40 1.00
7 Sasha Cucuz .40 1.00
8 Luke Curtin .40 1.00
9 Shawn Degagne .60 1.50
10 Keith Dupee .40 1.00
11 Kirk Furey .40 1.00
12 Tyler Johnston .40 1.00
13 Jerry Keefe .40 1.00
14 Daniel Lacroix .40 1.00
15 Mark Loeding .40 1.00
16 Scott Matzka .40 1.00
17 Jamie O'Leary .40 1.00
18 Stefan Rivard .60 1.50
19 Rob Stanfield .40 1.00
20 Scott Stirling .60 1.50
21 Ian Walterson .40 1.00
22 Mike Haviland HCO .02 .10
23 Leigh Mendelson ACO .02 .10
24 Rick Bronwell EQM .02 .10
25 Woolly MASCOT .02 .10
26 Damien Hess TR .02 .10

2002-03 Atlantic City Boardwalk Bullies

It is believed these cards were handed out as singles by the team at home games and at public appearances. The checklist below may not be complete. Please forward any additional info to hockeymag@beckett.com.

COMPLETE SET (25) 10.00 20.00
1 Rick Bronwell EQM .02 .10

2 J. F. Caudron .40 1.00
3 Steve Cheredaryk .40 1.00
4 Kevin Colley .60 1.50
5 Luke Curtin .40 1.00
6 Kirk Furey .40 1.00
7 Jade Galbraith .75 2.00
8 Jerry Galway .40 1.00
9 Mike Haviland HCO .02 .10
10 Jimmy Henkel .40 1.00
11 Damien Hess TR .02 .10
12 Mark Loeding .40 1.00
13 Shawn Maltby .60 1.50
14 Scott Matzka .40 1.00
15 Leigh Mendelson ACO .02 .10
16 Ryan Mougenel .40 1.00
17 Steve Munn .40 1.00
18 Mike Nicholishen .40 1.00
19 Stefan Rivard .40 1.00
20 Paul Spadafora .40 1.00
21 Scott Stirling .60 1.50
22 Ian Walterson .40 1.00
23 Matthew Yeats .60 1.50
24 Wooly MASCOT .02 .10
25 Checklist .01 .01

2003-04 Atlantic City Boardwalk Bullies

Little is known about this set, beyond the checklist information provided by the great Ralph Slate.

COMPLETE SET (30) 10.00 25.00
1 Bujar Amidovski .75 2.00
2 Jon Cullen .40 1.00
3 Luke Curtin .40 1.00
4 Chad Dameworth .40 1.00
5 Danny Eberly .40 1.00
6 Brian Fahey .40 1.00
7 Aaron Foster .40 1.00
8 Kirk Furey .40 1.00
9 Jim Henkel .40 1.00
10 Scott Horvath .40 1.00
11 Matt Hubbauer .40 1.00
12 Jim Leger .40 1.00
13 John Longo .40 1.00
14 Preston Mizzi .40 1.00
15 Jake Moreland .40 1.00
16 Steve Munn .40 1.00
17 Sam Paolini .40 1.00
18 Joshua Prudden .40 1.00
19 Dave Reid .40 1.00
20 Stefan Rivard .40 1.00
21 John Sabo .40 1.00
22 Pierre-Luc Sleigher .40 1.00
23 Marc St. Jean .40 1.00
24 Scott Stirling .40 1.00
25 Ian Walterson .40 1.00
26 Kam White .40 1.00
27 Mike Haviland HCO .02 .10
28 Matt Thomas ACO .02 .10
29 Mascot .02 .10
30 Checklist .01 .01

2003-04 Atlantic City Boardwalk Bullies RBI Sports

This team set was sold at home games.

COMPLETE SET (16) 3.00 8.00
17 Jon Cullen .20 .50
18 Luke Curtin .20 .50
19 Danny Eberly .20 .50
20 Brian Fahey .20 .50
21 Aaron Foster .20 .50
22 Scott Horvath .20 .50
23 Jake Moreland .20 .50
24 Steve Munn .20 .50
25 Sam Paolini .20 .50
26 Joshua Prudden .20 .50
27 Dave Reid .20 .50
28 Stefan Rivard .20 .50
29 Pierre-Luc Sleigher .20 .50
30 Scott Stirling .20 .50
31 Ian Walterson .20 .50
32 Kam White .20 .50

2004-05 Atlantic City Boardwalk Bullies

These cards were given away over the course of the season. It's believed the checklist is complete, and the card numbering may be inaccurate. If you know of other cards, please email us at hockeymag@beckett.com.

COMPLETE SET (30) 10.00 25.00
1 Dave Reid .40 1.00
2 Ian Walterson .40 1.00
3 Fraser Clair .40 1.00
4 Brad Both .40 1.00
5 Colin Shields .40 1.00
6 Scott Horvath .40 1.00
7 Kelsey Muench .40 1.00
8 Derek Edwardson .40 1.00
9 Jason Notermann .40 1.00
10 Dustan Heintz .40 1.00
11 Tom Reimann .40 1.00
12 Paul Caponigri .40 1.00
13 Luke Curtin .40 1.00
14 Eric Nelson .40 1.00
15 Trevor Koenig .60 1.50
16 Brian Maddox TR .02 .10
17 Matt Thomas CO .02 .10
18 Mark French ACO .02 .10
19 Chris Burke EQM .02 .10
20 Brian Fahey .40 1.00
21 Vincent Macri .40 1.00
22 Jake Moreland .60 1.50
23 Dan Peters .40 1.00
24 Brett Peterson .40 1.00
25 Peter Bournazakis .40 1.00
26 Shawn Mather .40 1.00
27 Brett Nowak .40 1.00
28 Jean-Francois Plourde .40 1.00
29 Ryan Reid .40 1.00
30 Woolly MASCOT .02 .10

2004-05 Atlantic City Boardwalk Bullies Kinko's

COMPLETE SET (30) 10.00 25.00
1 Kelly Cup CL .02 .10
2 Jake Moreland .40 1.00
3 Bujar Amidovski .75 2.00
4 Steve Munn .40 1.00
5 Brian Fahey .40 1.00
6 Kam Whie .40 1.00
7 Dave Reid .40 1.00
8 Ian Walterson .40 1.00
9 Pierre-Luc Sleigher .40 1.00
10 Danny Eberly .40 1.00
11 Jim Henkel .40 1.00
12 Scott Horvath .40 1.00
13 Sam Paolini .40 1.00
14 John Sabo .40 1.00
15 Josh Prudden .40 1.00
16 John Longo .40 1.00
17 Matt Hubbaer .40 1.00
18 Marc St.Jean .40 1.00
19 Stefan Rivard .40 1.00
20 Chad Dameworth .40 1.00
21 Preston Mizzi .40 1.00
22 Jim Leger .40 1.00
23 Kirk Furey .40 1.00
24 Aaron Foster .40 1.00
25 Luke Curtin .40 1.00
26 Jon Cullan .40 1.00
27 Scott Stirling .40 1.00
28 Mike Haviland .40 1.00
29 Matt Thomas .40 1.00
30 Wooly .02 .10

2001-02 Augusta Lynx

1 Patrick Yetman .80 2.00
2 Scott Morrow .80 2.00
3 Cris Classen .80 2.00
4 Tyler Willis 1.20 3.00
5 Jeff Bes 1.20 3.00
6 Wes Swinson .80 2.00
7 Guy Larose .80 2.00
8 John Whitwell .80 2.00

2002-03 Augusta Lynx

COMPLETE SET (18) 10.00 20.00
61 Ryan Crane .40 1.00
62 Curtis Cruickshank .60 1.50
63 Tom Draper .60 1.50
64 Chris Gustafson .40 1.00
65 Tyson Holly .40 1.00
66 Andrew Ianiero .40 1.00
67 Martin Lapointe .40 1.00
68 Ryan Lauzon .40 1.00
69 Jay Leach .60 1.50
70 Mike Legg .40 1.00
71 Vince Malts .40 1.00
72 Brad Ralph .40 1.00
73 Philippe Roy .40 1.00
74 Josh St. Louis .40 1.00
75 Jim Shepherd .40 1.00
76 Chris Thompson .40 1.00
77 Mark Thompson .40 1.00
78 Andrew Williamson .40 1.00

2003-04 Augusta Lynx

This set was sold by the team at home games. The odd numbering reflects this portion of the entire league run produced by RBI Sports. Production supposedly was limited to 250 sets.

COMPLETE SET (16) 10.00 25.00
33 Todd Bennett .60 1.50
34 Scott Corbett .60 1.50
35 John Cronin .60 1.50
36 Brandon Doria .60 1.50
37 Matt Dzieduszycki .60 1.50
38 Paul Elliott .60 1.50
39 Jonathan Gagnon .60 1.50
40 Louis Goulet .60 1.50
41 Nick Greenough .60 1.50
42 Peter Hamerlik .75 2.00
43 Greg Jacina .60 1.50
44 Scott Kelman .60 1.50
45 Robert Liscak .60 1.50
46 Gregg Naumenko .75 2.00
47 Treavor Peterson .60 1.50
48 Shawn Weiman .60 1.50

2006-07 Augusta Lynx

COMPLETE SET (21) 15.00 30.00
1 Garrett Bembridge .75 2.00
2 Sean Blanchard .60 1.50
3 Mike Erickson .60 1.50
4 Louis Goulet .60 1.50
5 Shane Hynes .60 1.50
6 Jamie Johnson .60 1.50
7 Jason Kostadine .60 1.50
8 Nick Kuiper .60 1.50
9 Ryan Lang .60 1.50
10 Eric Lundberg .60 1.50
11 Roman Marakhovski .60 1.50
12 Nathan Marsters 1.25 3.00
13 David McKee 1.25 3.00
14 Brian Passmore .75 2.00
15 Joe Pereira .60 1.50
16 Jason Platt .60 1.50
17 Nathan Saunders .60 1.50
18 Ken Scuderi .60 1.50
19 Aaron Slattengren .60 1.50
20 Dirk Southern .60 1.50
21 Weston Tardy .60 1.50

1997-98 Austin Ice Bats

This 24-card set featuring the Ice Bats of the WPHL was sold at the final home game and during the playoffs.

COMPLETE SET (24) 5.00 10.00
1 Ryan Anderson .20 .50
2 Chad Erickson .30 .75
3 Tim Findlay .30 .75
4 Todd Harris .20 .50
5 Rob Hartnell .20 .50
6 Chris Haskett .20 .50
7 Kyle Haviland .20 .50
8 Mike Jackson .20 .50
9 Jeff Kungle .20 .50
10 Darrin MacKay .20 .50
11 Dean Mando .20 .50
12 Keith Moran .20 .50
13 Ryan Pawluk .20 .50
14 Derek Riley .20 .50
15 Jason Rose .20 .50
16 Andy Ross .20 .50
17 Brett Seguin .20 .50
18 Christian Soucy .30 .75
19 Jeremy Thompson .20 .50
20 Richard Uniacke .20 .50
21 Joe Van Volsen .20 .50
22 Paul Lawless CO .10 .25
23 Fang Mascot .04 .10
24 Ice Bats Hummer PROMO .04 .10

1999-00 Austin Ice Bats

This set features the Ice Bats of the WPHL. The cards were handed out as promotional giveaways at two home games. The set features two cards (Nos. 29 & 30) that were only given out at Lowe's Home Improvement when a redemption card from the set was turned in.

COMPLETE SET (34) 12.00 30.00
1 Andy Ross .40 1.00
2 Shawn Legault .40 1.00
3 Craig Stahl .40 1.00
4 Ryan Pisiak .40 1.00
5 David Moore .40 1.00
6 David Brosseau .40 1.00
7 Jeff Greenlaw .40 1.00
8 Jeff Kungle .40 1.00
9 Bryan McMullen .40 1.00
10 Dan Price .40 1.00
11 Brent Hughes CO .10 .25
12 Glen Norman .40 1.00
13 Clint Shuman TR .10 .25
14 The IceBatmobile .10 .25
15 Rob Laurie .60 1.50
16 Brent Currie .40 1.00
17 Stu Kulak .40 1.00
18 Kelly Smart .40 1.00
19 Jim Shepherd .40 1.00
20 Ryan Anderson .40 1.00
21 Laird Lidster .40 1.00
22 Matt Sharuga .40 1.00
23 Derek Nicolson .40 1.00
24 Ryan Brindley .40 1.00
25 Tyler Perry .40 1.00
26 Fang MAS .10 .25
27 Ken McRae CO .10 .25
28 Gunner Garrett TR .10 .25
29 Ryan Pisiak 1.20 3.00
30 Ryan Anderson 1.20 3.00
31 Shawn Legault .40 1.00
32 Ryan Anderson .40 1.00
33 David Moore .40 1.00
34 Andy Ross .40 1.00

2000-01 Austin Ice Bats

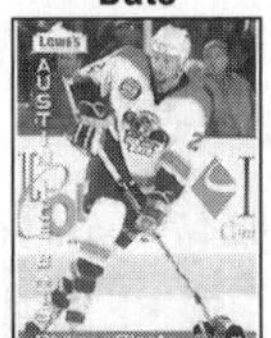

This set features the Ice Bats of the WPHL. The set was released as a promotional giveaway, and was handed out over the course of two home games. Cards # 29 and 30 were redemption cards that could be acquired at a local hardware store.

COMPLETE SET (30) 8.00 30.00
1 Ryan Anderson .30 1.00
2 David Brosseau .30 1.00
3 Bobby Brown .30 1.00
4 Jonathan Forest .30 1.00
5 Mike Gaffney .40 1.50
6 Jeff Greenlaw .30 1.00
7 Daniel Kletke .30 1.00
8 Jeff Kungle .30 1.00
9 Eric Landry .40 1.50
10 Roger Lewis .30 1.00
11 Josh Maser .30 1.00
12 Bryan McMullen .30 1.00
13 Derek Nicolson .30 1.00
14 Erik Noack .30 1.00
15 Keith O'Brien .30 1.00
16 Tyler Perry .30 1.00
17 Philippe Plante .30 1.00
18 Dan Price .30 1.00
19 Brett Seguin .40 1.50
20 Kelly Smart .30 1.00
21 Troy Stonier .30 1.00
22 Daniel Tetrault .30 1.00
23 Brent Hughes CO .20 .50
24 Ken McRae CO .20 .50
25 Clint Shuman TR .10 .50
26 CC Comedy Club .04 .01
27 Hooters Hot Shot .20 .50
28 Fang MASCOT .04 .10
29 Redemption .04 .10
29R Spike & Fang MASCOTS .40 3.00
30 Redemption .04 .10
30R Ice Bats All Stars .80 3.00

2001-02 Austin Ice Bats

This set features the Ice Bats of the WPHL. The set was handed out to fans at a single home game early in 2002.

COMPLETE SET (25) 8.00 20.00
1 Ryan Anderson .40 1.00
2 Bobby Brown .40 1.00
3 Patrick Brownlee .40 1.00
4 Jeff Greenlaw .40 1.00
5 Ian LaRocque .40 1.00
6 Eric Labelle .40 1.00
7 Tab Lardner .40 1.00
8 Darryl McArthur .60 1.50
9 Dan McIntyre .40 1.00
10 Bryan McMullen .40 1.00
11 Dominic Periard .40 1.00
12 Ryan Pisiak .40 1.00
13 Dan Price .40 1.00
14 Brett Seguin .40 1.00
15 Kelly Smart .40 1.00
16 Gerald Tallaire .60 1.50
17 Daniel Tetrault .60 1.50
18 Greg Willers .40 1.00
19 Jeff Worlton .40 1.00
20 Brent Hughes CO .10 .25
21 Ken McRae ACO .10 .25
22 Fang MASCOT .04 .10
23 Glen Norman DB .04 .10
24 Gunner Garrett EQMG .04 .10
24 Clint Shuman TR .04 .10
25 Hootie Celebrates .04 .10

2002-03 Austin Ice Bats

COMPLETE SET (24) 10.00 20.00
1 Matt Barnes .60 1.50
2 Peter Brady .60 1.50
3 Patrick Brownlee .40 1.00
4 Mike Gaffney .40 1.00
5 Jeff Greenlaw .40 1.00
6 Doug Johnson .40 1.00
7 Tab Lardner .40 1.00
8 Shawn Legault .60 1.50
9 Darryl McArthur .40 1.00
10 Scott McCallum .40 1.00
11 Mike Olynyk .40 1.00
12 Randy Ponte .40 1.00
13 Dan Price .40 1.00
14 Mike Rees .40 1.00
15 Brett Seguin .40 1.00
16 Matt Sharuga .40 1.00
17 Kelly Smart .40 1.00
18 Gerald Tallaire .40 1.00
19 Brent Hughes HCO .10 .25
20 Jeff Kungle ACO .10 .25
21 Gunner Garrett EQM .02 .10
22 Fang Mascot .02 .10
23 Fang's Gang .02 .10
24 Clint Shuman TR .02 .10

2003-04 Austin Ice Bats

This set was issued as a promotional giveaway and split over two home games, making it difficult to complete. The cards are unnumbered and listed below in alphabetical order.

COMPLETE SET (24) 15.00 30.00
1 Peter Brady .60 1.50
2 Patrick Brownlee .60 1.50
3 Brandon Carper .60 1.50
4 Shawn Conschafter .60 1.50
5 Jonathan Forest .60 1.50
6 Brent Hughes .60 1.50
7 Tab Lardner .60 1.50
8 Shawn Legault .75 2.00
9 Chris Legg .60 1.50
10 Darryl McArthur .75 2.00
11 Scott McCallum .60 1.50
12 Mike Olynyk .60 1.50
13 Brett Seguin .60 1.50
14 Kelly Smart .60 1.50
15 Josh St. Louis .60 1.50
16 Derek Stone .60 1.50
17 Gerald Tallaire .60 1.50
18 Daniel Tetrault .60 1.50
19 Clint Way .60 1.50
20 Jeff Greenlaw HCO .10 .25
21 Gunner Garrett EQM .02 .10
22 Cheerleaders .10 .25
23 Mascot .02 .10
24 Clint Shuman TR .02 .10

2004-05 Austin Ice Bats

Issued as a stadium giveaway in two parts.

COMPLETE SET (23) 15.00 30.00
1 Peter-Emmanuel Brady .75 2.00
2 Brian Pasko .60 1.50
3 Kelly Smart .60 1.50
4 Ryan Leasa .60 1.50
5 Kris Knoblauch .60 1.50
6 Chris Richards .60 1.50
7 Dallas Anderson 1.25 3.00
8 John McNabb .75 2.00
9 Mike Olynyk .75 2.00
10 Sponsor Card .01 .01
11 Clint Shuman TR .02 .10
12 Fang MASCOT .02 .10
13 Matt Barnes 1.25 2.00
14 Benoit Genesse .60 1.50
15 Jonathan Jolette .60 1.50
16 Jeff Neufeld .60 1.50
17 Jared Dumba .60 1.50
18 Mike Mohr .60 1.50
19 Arturs Kupaks .60 1.50
20 Vinnie Jonasson .60 1.50
21 Greg Gatto CO .02 .10
22 Gunner Garrett EQM .02 .10
23 Bat Girls .20 .50

2006-07 Austin Ice Bats

Set was issued in two, 12-card perforated sheets. The cards are oversized.

1 Miguel Beaudry .60 1.50
2 Adam Holmgren .60 1.50
3 Chad McIver .60 1.50
4 Chris Murphy .60 1.50
5 Chris Ovington .60 1.50
6 Tony Quesada .60 1.50
7 John Ronan .60 1.50
8 Ray Smegal .60 1.50
9 Julian Smith .60 1.50
10 Mike Tucciarone .60 1.50
11 Terry Virtue .60 1.50
12 Logo Card .10 .25
13 Jordan Biachin .75 2.00
14 Kevin Couture .60 1.50
15 Aaron Davis .60 1.50
16 Britt Dougherty .60 1.50
17 Jason Kenyon .60 1.50
18 Henry Kuster .60 1.50
19 John McNabb .60 1.50
20 J.F. Picard .60 1.50
21 Mike Possin .60 1.50
22 Aaron Wilson .60 1.50
23 Fang MASCOT .10 .25
24 Logo Card .10 .25

1999-00 Baie-Comeau Drakkar

This set features the Drakkar of the QMJHL. The set was produced by card store CTM Ste-Foy and was sold at that shop and at home games.

COMPLETE SET (28) 4.00 10.00
1 Daniel Bergeron .16 .40
2 Jerome Bergeron .16 .40
3 Eric Bleau .16 .40
4 Marco Charpentier .16 .40
5 Jean-Philippe Chartier .30 .75
6 Serge Crochetiere .16 .40
7 Sylvain Deschatelets .16 .40
8 Kevin Deslauriers .16 .40
9 Maxime Fortunus .16 .40
10 Jonathan Gautier .16 .40
11 Duilio Grande .16 .40
12 Evgeny Gusakov .16 .40
13 Paul Lavoie .16 .40
14 Robin Leblanc .16 .40
15 Yannick Lehoux .30 .75
16 Charles Linglet .16 .40
17 Andre Mercure .16 .40
18 Chris Page .16 .40
19 Dominic Periard .16 .40
20 Jerome Petit .16 .40
21 Ghyslain Rousseau .30 .75
22 Bruno St. Jacques .30 .75
23 Eric Tremblay .16 .40
24 Guy Turmel .16 .40
25 Patrick Daviault CO .04 .10
26 Richard Martel CO .04 .10
27 Michel Larocque TR .04 .10
28 Brian St.Louis TR .04 .10

2000-01 Baie-Comeau Drakkar

This set features the Drakkar of the QMJHL. The set was produced by CTM-Ste-Foy and was sold through that shop and at home games.

COMPLETE SET (26) 3.60 9.00
1 Jonathan Walsh .14 .35
2 Joel Perrault .14 .35
3 Pierre-Andre Leblanc .14 .35
4 Dominic Periard .14 .35
5 Maxime Fortunus .14 .35
6 Pascal Pelletier .14 .35
7 Robin Leblanc .14 .35
8 Luis Tremblay .14 .35
9 Thierry Douville .14 .35
10 Marco Charpentier .14 .35
11 Premysl Duben .14 .35
12 Yanick Lehoux .40 1.00
13 Duilio Grande .14 .35
14 Kevin Deslauriers .14 .35
15 Matthew Hyde .14 .35
16 Guy Turmel .14 .35
17 Evgeny Gusakov .14 .35
18 Ghyslain Rousseau .20 .50
19 David St. Germain .20 .50
20 Jonathan Jolette .14 .35
21 Martin Mandeville .14 .35
22 Daniel Bergeron .14 .35
23 Charles Linglet .14 .35
24 Jonathan Gautier .14 .35
25 Richard Martel CO CL .04 .10
NNO Snorri MASCOT .04 .10

2000-01 Baie-Comeau Drakkar Signed

This set is exactly the same as the base Drakkar set from this season, save that every card has been hand signed by the player pictured. Each card also is serial numbered out of just 100.

COMPLETE SET (26) 20.00 50.00
1 Jonathan Walsh .80 2.00
2 Joel Perrault .80 2.00
3 Pierre-Andre Leblanc .80 2.00
4 Dominic Periard .80 2.00
5 Maxime Fortunus .80 2.00
6 Pascal Pelletier .80 2.00
7 Robin Leblanc .80 2.00
8 Luis Tremblay .80 2.00
9 Thierry Douville .80 2.00
10 Marco Charpentier .80 2.00
11 Premysl Duben .80 2.00
12 Yanick Lehoux 2.00 5.00
13 Duilio Grande .80 2.00
14 Kevin Deslauriers .80 2.00
15 Matthew Hyde .80 2.00
16 Guy Turmel .80 2.00
17 Evgeny Gusakov .80 2.00
18 Ghyslain Rousseau 2.00 5.00
19 David St. Germain 2.00 5.00
20 Jonathan Jolette .80 2.00
21 Martin Mandeville .80 2.00
22 Daniel Bergeron .80 2.00
23 Charles Linglet .80 2.00
24 Jonathan Gautier .80 2.00
25 Richard Martel CO CL .04 .10
NNO Snorri MASCOT .04 .10

2001-02 Baie-Comeau Drakkar

This set features les Drakkar of the QMJHL. The set was produced by well-known card shop CTM Ste-Foy, and was sold at the team's home games. It was reported that less than 1,000 sets were produced.

COMPLETE SET (25) 4.80 12.00
1 Joel Perrault .20 .50
2 Louis-Philippe Martin .20 .50
3 Jonathan Lachance .20 .50
4 Maxime Fortunus .20 .50
5 Pascal Pelletier .20 .50
6 Robin Leblanc .20 .50
7 Luis Tremblay .20 .50
8 Thierry Douville .20 .50
9 Martin Kuna .20 .50
10 Yanick Lehoux .30 .75
11 Duilio Grande .20 .50
12 Kevin Deslauriers .20 .50
13 Matthew Hyde .20 .50
14 Jean Junior Morin .20 .50
15 Ghyslain Rousseau .30 .75
16 Jonathan Dupras .20 .50
17 Caleb Moffat .20 .50
18 Marc-Andre Roy .20 .50
19 Martin Mandeville .20 .50
20 Daniel Bergeron .30 .75
21 Charles Linglet .20 .50
22 Jean-Francois Savage .20 .50
23 Benoit Mondou .30 .75
24 Jean-Francois Jacques .20 .50
NNO Richard Martel CO/CL .04 .10

2002-03 Baie Comeau Drakkar

COMPLETE SET (26) 5.00 12.00
1 Maxime Belanger .20 .50
2 Joel Perreault .30 .75
3 Alexandre Lamarche .20 .50
4 Jean-Philippe Gauthier .20 .50
5 Louis-Philippe Martin .20 .50
6 Maxime Fortunus .20 .50
7 Pascal Pelletier .20 .50
8 Robin Leblanc .20 .50
9 Luis Tremblay .20 .50
10 Thierry Douville .20 .50
11 Jimmy Arsenault .20 .50
12 Travis Antler .20 .50
13 Kevin Deslauriers .20 .50
14 Patrick Lepage .30 .75
15 Sebastien Leonard .20 .50
16 Philip Lacroix .30 .75
17 Michel Bergevin-Robinson .30 .75
18 Caleb Moffat .20 .50
19 Marc-Andre Roy .20 .50
20 Patrick Thoresen .40 1.00
21 Martin Mandeville .20 .50
22 Charles Linglet .20 .50
23 Benoit Mondou .30 .75
24 Jean-Francois Jacques .20 .50
25 Richard Martel CO/CL .01 .01
26 Snorri MASCOT .01 .01

2003-04 Baie Comeau Drakkar

This set was produced by CTM Sports and sold at home games.

COMPLETE SET (27) 5.00 12.00
1 Ryan-James Hand .20 .50
2 Patrick Simaro .20 .50
3 Ryan Lehr .20 .50
4 Maxime Belanger .20 .50
5 Martin Krayzel .20 .50
6 Alexandre Blais .20 .50
7 Jonathan Duchesneau .20 .50

8 Alexandre Lamarche Froelich .20 .50
9 Maxime Fortunas .20 .50
10 Robin Leblanc .20 .50
11 Luis Tremblay .20 .50
12 Frederic Gariepy .20 .50
13 Vitaly Lanochkin .20 .50
14 Olivier Furlong .20 .50
15 Simon Lepage .20 .50
16 Loic Lacasse .30 .75
17 Patrick Laurin .20 .50
18 Julien Walsh .30 .75
19 Pierre-Luc Leblond-Letourneau .20 .50
20 Martin Mandeville .20 .50
21 Nicolas Robillard .20 .50
22 Petr Preucil .20 .50
23 Philippe Cote .20 .50
24 Jean-Francois Jacques .30 .75
25 Alexandre Dulac Lemelin .20 .50
26 Maxime Fortunas TL .20 .50
27 Jean-Francois Jacques TL .30 .75

2004-05 Baie-Comeau Drakkar

A total of 350 team sets were produced.
COMPLETE SET (24) 10.00
1 Alexandre Blais .50
2 Alexandre Dulac-Lemelin .50
3 Alexandre Picard-Hooper .50
4 Benjamin Breault .50
5 Erick Lajoie .50
6 Francois Bouchard .50
7 Jean-Francois Jacques .50
8 Joakim Jensen .50
9 Jonathan Duchesneau .50
10 Loic Lacasse .75
11 Martin Aubin .50
12 Martin Mandeville .50
13 Mathieu Gravel .50
14 Maxime Belanger .50
15 Michael Dupont .75
16 Nicolas Robillard .50
17 Patrick Simard .50
18 Philippe Cote .50
19 Pierre-Luc Leblond-Letourneau .50
20 Ryan Lehr .50
21 Ryan-James Hand .50
22 Sebastien Blouin .50
23 Tomas Fendek .50
24 Vitaly Lanochkin .50

2005-06 Baie-Comeau Drakkar

COMPLETE SET (22) 5.00 10.00
1 Benjamin Breault .20 .50
2 Charles-Antoine Messier .20 .50
3 Patrick Simard .20 .50
4 Ryan Lehr .20 .50
5 Tomas Fendek .20 .50
6 Alexandre Blais .20 .50
7 Jonathan Duchesneau .20 .50
8 Christian Landry .20 .50
9 Francois Chabot .20 .50
10 Alexandre Picard-Hooper .20 .50
11 Francois Bouchard .20 .50
12 Jean-Sebastien Hogg .20 .50
13 Adam Bourque-Leblanc .20 .50
14 Joakim Jensen .20 .50
15 Alexandre Dulac-Lemelin .20 .50
16 Maxime D. Ouimet .20 .50
17 Oliver Donais .20 .50
18 Samuel Beland .20 .50
19 Francois Filion .20 .50
20 Loic Lacasse .20 .50
21 Michael Dupont .20 .50
22 Martin Aubin .20 .50

1998-99 Bakersfield Condors

This set features the Condors of the WCHL. The cards measure 2 5/8 by 3 5/8 and feature a full-bleed color photo on the front. The backs feature player stats and the logo of sponsor KRAB radio.
COMPLETE SET (24) 4.00 10.00
1 Jamie Adams .40 .75
2 Kevin Barrett .40 .75
3 Brady Blain .40 .75
4 Marc Boxer .40 .75
5 Steve Chelios .60 1.00
6 Jamie Cooke .40 .75
7 Steve Dowhy .40 .75
8 Brad Guzda .40 .75
9 Nick Hriczov .40 .75
10 Kelly Hrycun .40 .75
11 Marcel Kuris .40 .75
12 Dan Marcotte .40 .75
13 Brian McCarthy .40 .75
14 Glen Mears .40 .75
15 Al Murphy .40 .75
16 Jay Neal .40 .75
17 Zbynek Neckar .40 .75
18 Dan Reja .40 .75
19 Stephane St. Amour .60 1.00
20 Briane Thompson .40 .75
21 Peter Zurba .40 .75
22 Bakersfield Centennial Arena .04 .10
23 Kevin MacDonald HCO .04 .10
24 Colonel Claw'd Mascot .04 .10

1999-00 Bakersfield Condors

This set features the Condors of the WCHL. The set was issued as a promotional giveaway at a home game midway through the season. It was later offered for sale at home games and by mail order.
COMPLETE SET (24) 8.00 20.00
1 Cory Banika .40 1.00
2 Philippe Bergeron .40 1.00
3 Kevin Boyd .40 1.00
4 Jamie Cooke .40 1.00
5 Dan Currie .60 1.50
6 Chris Dearden .40 1.00
7 Steve Dowhy .40 1.00
8 Chris Droeske .40 1.00
9 Brad Guzda .40 1.00
10 Paul McInnis .40 1.00
11 Glen Mears .40 1.00
12 Zbynek Neckar .40 1.00
13 Jani Ojala .40 1.00
14 Brad Phillips .40 1.00
15 Clark Polglase .40 1.00
16 Jason Reesor .40 1.00
17 Paul Rosebush .40 1.00
18 Briane Thompson .40 1.00
19 Rhett Trombley .40 1.00
20 Paul Willett .40 1.00
21 Kevin MacDonald CO .10 .25
22 Bakersfield Centennial .10 .25
23 Colonel Claw'd MAS .10 .25
24 Michael Ropchan TR .10 .25

2000-01 Bakersfield Condors

This set features the Condors of the WCHL. The set was issued as a promotional giveaway at a game midway through the season. The cards are unnumbered and are listed below alphabetically.
COMPLETE SET (24) 8.00 20.00
1 Trevor Amundrud .30 .75
2 Cory Banika .30 .75
3 Karel Betik .60 1.50
4 Kevin Boyd .30 .75
5 Jamie Cooke .30 .75
6 Dan Currie .60 1.50
7 Jean-Paul Davis .30 .75
8 Chris Dearden .30 .75
9 Quinn Fair .30 .75
10 Ben Gustavson .30 .75
11 Denis Ivanov .30 .75
12 Bryan Lachance .30 .75
13 Peter MacKellar .30 .75
14 Craig Martin .40 1.00
15 Glen Mears .30 .75
16 Pavel Mikulchik .30 .75
17 Matt Mullin .60 1.50
18 Jason Reesor .30 .75
19 Paul Rosebush .30 .75
20 Paul Willett .60 1.50
21 Paul Willett MVP .60 1.50
22 Kevin MacDonald CO .10 .25
23 Centenial Gardens ARENA .10 .25
24 Coloney/Cal MASCOTS .10 .25

2001-02 Bakersfield Condors

COMPLETE SET (24) 10.00 20.00
1 Ken Baker .40 1.00
2 Peter Brearley .40 1.00
3 Luciano Caravaggio .40 1.00
4 Jamie Cooke .40 1.00
5 Mark Edmundson .40 1.00
6 Todd Esselmont .40 1.00
7 Quinn Fair .40 1.00
8 Chris Felix .40 1.00
9 Jason Firth .40 1.00
10 Jeff Goldie .40 1.00
11 Ryan Hartung .40 1.00
12 Scott Hay .60 1.50
13 Sasha Lakovic .60 1.50
14 Josh Maser .40 1.00
15 Glen Mears .40 1.00
16 David Milek .40 1.00
17 Jason Ralph .40 1.00
18 Paul Rosebush .40 1.00
19 John Vary .40 1.00
20 Paul Willett .40 1.00
21 Paul Kelly HCO .02 .10
22 Condors in the Community .02 .10
23 Baby Cal MASCOT .02 .10
24 Colonel Claw MASCOT .02 .10

2002-03 Bakersfield Condors

COMPLETE SET (24) 10.00 20.00
1 Nate Anderson .40 1.00
2 David Bell .40 1.00
3 Shawn Byram .40 1.00
4 Jamie Cooke .40 1.00
5 Danielle Dube .40 1.00
6 Guy Dupuis .40 1.00
7 Quinn Fair .40 1.00
8 Jeff Goldie .40 1.00
9 Jason Jackman .40 1.00
10 Denis Ladouceur .40 1.00
11 Jonas Lennartsson .40 1.00
12 Christoffer Norgren .40 1.00
13 Jason Ralph .40 1.00
14 Jordan Roach .40 1.00
15 Paul Rosebush .40 1.00
16 Christian Skoryna .40 1.00
17 Jonathan Sorg .40 1.00
18 Kevin St. Pierre .60 1.50
19 Paul Willett .40 1.00
20 J.J. Wrobel .40 1.00
21 Paul Kelly HCO .10 .25
22 Martin Raymond ACO .10 .25
23 Colonel Claw'd/Baby Cal .02 .10

2003-04 Bakersfield Condors

The 25-card main set was issued as a promotional giveaway. No production run was announced.
COMPLETE SET (25) 10.00 25.00
1 Todd Alexander .40 1.00
2 Johan Astrom .40 1.00
3 Jamie Cooke .40 1.00
4 Paul Kelly CO .10 .25
5 Martin Raymond ACO .10 .25
6 Andrew Ianiero .40 1.00
7 Jason Jackman .40 1.00
8 Peter Hirsch .40 1.00
9 Devin Francon .40 1.00
10 Paul Rosebush .40 1.00
11 Kevin Riehl .40 1.00
12 Mascot .02 .10
13 Vince Malts .40 1.00
14 Quinn Fair .40 1.00
15 Jimmy Drolet .40 1.00
16 Glen Mears .40 1.00
17 Jon Mirasty .40 1.00
18 Darren Shakotko .40 1.00
19 Jani Virtanen .40 1.00
20 Joe Watkins .60 1.50
21 Paul Willett .40 1.00
22 Randy Perry .40 1.00
23 Jason Ralph .40 1.00
24 Denis Ladouceur .40 1.00
25 Jonas Lennartsson .40 1.00

2004-05 Bakersfield Condors

COMPLETE SET (24) 15.00 30.00
1 Ryan Coole .40 1.00
2 Guy Dupuis .40 1.00
3 Yutaka Fukufuji 4.00 10.00
4 Ryan Gillis .40 1.00
5 Ty Hennes .40 1.00
6 Mike Hofstrand .40 1.00
7 Connor James .40 1.00
8 David Kudelka .40 1.00
9 Ashlee Langdone .40 1.00
10 Tony Lawrence .40 1.00
11 Brett Lutes .40 1.00
12 Brad Mehalko .40 1.00
13 Dylan Mills .40 1.00
14 Lars Peder Nagel .40 1.00
15 Paul Rosebush .40 1.00
16 Vlad Serov .40 1.00
17 Dennis Shiryaev .40 1.00
18 Kevin St. Jacques .40 1.00
19 Luis Tremblay .40 1.00
20 ChrisTwerdun .40 1.00
21 Jason Wolfe .60 1.50
22 Marty Raymond CO .02 .10
23 Paul Willet ACO .02 .10
24 Mascots .02 .10

2005-06 Bakersfield Condors

COMPLETE SET (23) 8.00 20.00
1 Marty Raymond .40 1.00
2 Kevin Kotyluk .40 1.00
3 Brian Collins .40 1.00
4 Scott Balan .40 1.00
5 Paul Rosebush .40 1.00
6 Reagan Leslie .40 1.00
7 Scott Basiuk .40 1.00
8 Alexandre Bolduc .40 1.00
9 Nick Economakos .40 1.00
10 Oriel McHugh .40 1.00
11 Dennis Shiryaev .40 1.00
12 Kevin St.Jacques .40 1.00
13 Ryan Munce .40 1.00
14 Mike Hofstrand .40 1.00
15 Dave Bonk .40 1.00
16 Scott Borders .40 1.00
17 Andrew Ianiero .40 1.00
18 Eric Neilson .40 1.00
19 Kevin Truelson .40 1.00
20 Sean Venedam .40 1.00
21 Mark Pederson .40 1.00
22 Joel Irving .40 1.00
23 Mathieu Brunelle .40 1.00

2006-07 Bakersfield Condors

1 Sean Venedam .40 1.00
2 Rane Carnegie .60 1.50
3 Steve Rodberg .40 1.00
4 Brett Lutes .40 1.00
5 Coaches .10 .25
6 Kevin Truelson .40 1.00
7 David Kudelka .40 1.00
8 Andrew Oke .40 1.00
9 Andrew Ianiero .40 1.00
10 Alex Kim .40 1.00
11 Danny Taylor .40 1.00
12 Scott Borders .40 1.00
13 Mike Hofstrand .40 1.00
14 Josh Libenow .40 1.00
15 Alexandre Bolduc .40 1.00
16 Alec Rogosheske .40 1.00
17 Tyler Scott .40 1.00
18 Tyler Liebel .40 1.00
19 Jamie Hodson .75 2.00
20 Kevin St. Jacques .40 1.00
21 Scotty Balan .40 1.00
22 Kevin Asselin .40 1.00
23 Todd Griffith .40 1.00
24 Reagan Leslie .40 1.00

1997-98 Bakersfield Fog

Little is known about this set, though it is believed that it was sold by the team throughout the season. Any additional information can be forwarded to hockeymag@beckett.com.
COMPLETE SET (24) 12.00
1 John Devereaux .20 .60
2 Steve Dowhy .20 .60
3 Igor Galkin .20 1.00
4 Jeff Gorman .20 .60
5 Kelly Hrycun .20 .60
6 Jeff Jubenville .20 .60
7 Don Lester .20 .60
8 Brian McCarthy .20 .60
9 Glen Mears .20 .60
10 Rob Milliken .20 1.00
11 Jodi Murphy .20 .60
12 Jay Neal .20 .60
13 Jeff Pierce .20 .60
14 Andrew Plumb .20 .60
15 Iannique Renaud .20 .60
16 Eddy Skazyk .20 1.00
17 Lindsay Vallis .20 .60
18 Wade Welte .20 1.00
19 Jason White .20 .60
20 Keith Gretzky HCO .20 .50
21 Tule Fog Mascot .04 .10
22 Bakersfield Arena .04 .10
23 Sponsor Card .04 .01
24 Dick Earle TR .04 .10

1991-92 Baltimore Skipjacks

This 15-card set was issued as a promotional giveaway in 3-card perforated strips. The set commemorated the team's 10th anniversary and was sponsored by Wendy's and Coca-Cola. The cards are numbered card "xx" of 15.
COMPLETE SET (15) 8.00 20.00
1 Tim Taylor .40 1.00
2 Brent Hughes .30 .75
3 Trevor Halverson .30 .75
4 Bobby Reynolds .30 .75
5 Ken Lovsin .30 .75
6 Olaf Kolzig 4.00 10.00
7 Reggie Savage .30 .75
8 Jim Mathieson .40 1.00
9 Todd Hlushko .40 1.00
10 Mark Ferner .30 .75
11 John Purves .30 .75
12 Steve Seftel .30 .75
13 Craig Duncanson .30 .75
14 Simon Wheeldon .40 1.00
15 Bob Babcock .30 .75

1995-96 Barrie Colts

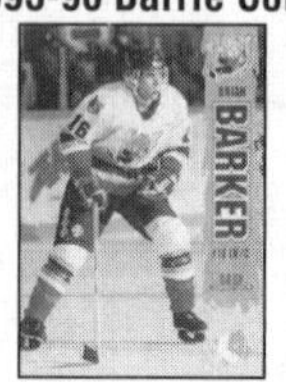

This set features the expansion Colts of the OHL. These attractive cards feature full-bleed photos on the front, along with a dynamic chartreusse design element along the right side. The back's feature a head shot and commentary from coach Bert Templeton. The set was sold by the team at home games and is noteworthy for the inclusion of future NHLers Dan Tkaczuk, Jan Bulis and Jeff Cowan.
COMPLETE SET (28) 4.80 12.00
1 Mauricio Alvarez .20 .50
2 Brian Barker .20 .50
3 Brock Boucher .20 .50
4 Jan Bulis .30 .75
5 Jason Cannon .20 .50
6 Jeff Cowan .30 .75
7 Shane Delaronde .30 .75
8 Robert DuBois .20 .50
9 Shawn Frappier .20 .50
10 Chris George .20 .50
11 In Action .04 .10
12 In Action .04 .10
13 In Action .04 .10
14 In Action .04 .10
15 Gerry Lanigan .20 .50
16 Quade Lightbody .20 .50
17 Jeremy Miculinic .20 .50
18 Andrew Morrison .20 .50
19 Luch Nasato .30 .75
20 Bert Templeton CO .10 .25
21 Jeff Tetzlaff .20 .50
22 Chris Thompson .30 .75
23 Justin Robinson .20 .50
24 Daniel Tkaczuk .30 .75
25 Alexander Volchkov .20 .50
26 Caleb Ward .20 .50
27 Mike White .20 .50
28 Darrell Woodley .20 .50

1996-97 Barrie Colts

This set was produced and sold by the team at home games. It is notable for featuring future NHLers Martin Skoula, Brian Finley and Daniel Tkaczuk. The cards are unnumbered, and so are unnumbered and checklisted below in alphabetical order.
COMPLETE SET (30) 6.00 15.00
1 Brian Barker .20 .50
2 Brock Boucher .20 .50
3 Casey Burnette .20 .50
4 Michael Christian .20 .50
5 Keith Delaney .20 .50
6 Adam Deleeuw .20 .50
7 Chris Feil .20 .50
8 Brian Finley .40 1.00
9 Michael Henrich .30 .75
10 John Hultberg .20 .50
11 Richard Kazda .20 .50
12 Darren Keily TR .04 .10
13 Cody Leibel .20 .50
14 Mihajlo Martinovich .20 .50
15 Kevin McClelland ACO .04 .10
16 Walker McDonald .20 .50
17 Jeff McKercher .20 .50
18 Luch Nasato .24 .60
19 Ryan O'Keefe .20 .50
20 Jason Pinizzotto .20 .50
21 Ryan Shaver .20 .50
22 Martin Skoula .75 1.00
23 Nick Smith .20 .50
24 Brandon Sugden .24 .60
25 Bert Templeton CO .20 .50
26 Jeff Tetzlaff .20 .50
27 Daniel Tkaczuk .30 .75
28 Charlie Horse(Mascot) .04 .10
29 Barrie Colts Team Picture .20 .50
30 Checklist .04 .10

1997-98 Barrie Colts

This attractive set was produced by the team and sold at home games. The set is unnumbered and checklisted below in alphabetical order.
COMPLETE SET (27) 4.80 10.00
1 Brian Barker .16 .40
2 Brock Boucher .16 .40
3 Jan Bulis .30 .75
4 Casey Burnette .16 .40
5 Jason Cannon .16 .40
6 Keith Delaney .16 .40
7 Chris George .16 .40
8 Nick Grady .16 .40
9 Mike Henrich .30 .75
10 John Hultberg .20 .50
11 Marcel Kars .16 .40
12 Darren Keily TR .04 .10
13 Gerry Lanigan .16 .40
14 Kevin McClelland .04 .10
15 Walker McDonald .16 .40
16 Jeff McKercher .16 .40
17 Brad Morgan .16 .40
18 Luch Nasato .30 .75
19 Corey Neilson .16 .40
20 Nick Smith .16 .40
21 Bert Templeton CO .16 .40
22 Jeff Tetzlaff .16 .40
23 Chris Thompson .16 .40
24 Daniel Tkaczuk .30 .75
25 Alexandre Volchkov .20 .50
26 Darrell Woodley .16 .40
27 Charlie Horse MAS .04 .10

1998-99 Barrie Colts

Released by the Colts in conjunction with Coca-Cola, this 25-card set pictures the 1998-99 Barrie Colts. Base cards feature full color action photography, white borders, and a blue nameplate along with the Coca-Cola logo along the bottom of the card.
COMPLETE SET (25) 7.20 15.00
1 Ryan O'Keefe .20 .50
2 Andre Lakos .20 .50
3 Shawn Cation .20 .50
4 Ed Hill .20 .50
5 Joel Dezainde .20 .50
6 Daniel Tkaczuk .30 .75
7 Martin Skoula .75 .75
8 Jerry Connell .20 .50
9 Tim Verbeek .20 .50
10 Rick Hwodeky .20 .50
11 Scott Cameron .40 .75
12 Ryan Barnes .20 .50
13 Sheldon Keefe .40 .75
14 Jeff Tetzlaff .20 .50
15 Chris Feil .20 .50
16 Michael Henrich .30 .75
17 Mike Christian .20 .50
18 Nick Smith .20 .50
19 Mike Jefferson .30 1.00
20 Denis Shvidki .30 .75
21 Brian Finley .40 .75
22 Ben Vanderklok .20 .50
23 Bert Templeton HCO .04 .10
24 Darren Keily TR .04 .10
Gary Scott TR
25 Charlie Horse MASCOT .04 .10

2000-01 Barrie Colts

This set features the Colts of the OHL. The set was sponsored by the Colts and Cops foundation and was distributed by the team's booster club at home games.
COMPLETE SET (24) 4.00 10.00
1 Frantisek Bakrlik .14 .35
2 Tim Branham .20 .50
3 Jordan Brenner .14 .35
4 Dean Byvelds .14 .35
5 David Chant .40 1.00
6 Fraser Clair .14 .35
7 Mike D'Alessandro .30 .75
8 Blaine Down .14 .35
9 Matt Dzieduszycki .14 .35
10 Shayne Fryia .14 .35
11 Matt Grennier .14 .35
12 Bryan Hayes .14 .35
13 Tyler Hanchuck .20 .50
14 Mike Henderson .14 .35
15 Ed Hill .20 .35
16 Charlie Horse Mascot/CL .10 .10
17 Gregg Mizzi .14 .35
18 Stephen Morris .14 .35
19 Jan Platil .14 .35
20 Neil Posillico .14 .35
21 Aaron Power .14 .35
22 Erik Reitz .14 .35
23 Bud Stefanski CO .10 .10
24 Brent Sullivan .14 .35
25 Joey Tenute .14 .35

2001-02 Barrie Colts

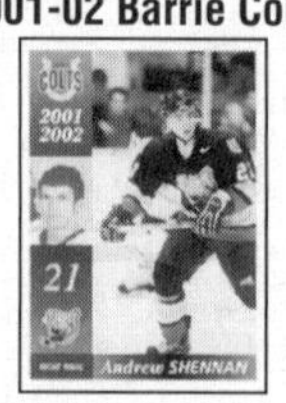

This set is unnumbered and is listed below in the order it appears on the checklist.
COMPLETE SET (23) 5.00 10.00
1 David Chant .40 1.00
2 Ryan Stokes .20 .50
3 Rick Arnaldo .20 .50
4 Eric Reitz .30 .75
5 Aaron Powers .20 .50
6 Steven Morris .20 .50
7 Blaine Down .20 .50
8 Joey Tenute .20 .50
9 Nick Lees .20 .50
10 Tyler Hanchuck .20 .50
11 B.J. Crombeen .20 .50
12 Andrew Shennan .20 .50
13 Jeremy Swanson .20 .50
14 Simon Barq .20 .50
15 Frantisek Bakrlik .20 .50
16 Daniel Girardi .20 .50
17 Kevin Ambroski .20 .50
18 Steve Farquharson .20 .50
19 Jan Platil .20 .50
20 Shayne Fria .20 .50
21 Fraser Clair .20 .50
22 Mascot .02 .10
23 Arena Card .02 .10

2002-03 Barrie Colts

COMPLETE SET (24) 5.00 10.00
1 Evan Brophey .20 .50
2 Justin DaCosta .20 .50
3 Andrew Shennan .20 .50
4 Zach Tranmer .20 .50
5 Michael Tuomi .20 .50
6 Simon Barg .20 .50
7 Ryan Sharp .20 .50
8 Nick Lees .20 .50
9 Hunter Tremblay .20 .50
10 Riley Moher .20 .50
11 Eric Himelfarb .30 .75
12 Mark Langdon .20 .50
13 Luc Chiasson .20 .50
14 Jeremy Swanson .20 .50
15 Kenny Jung .20 .50
16 Tyler Lawson .20 .50
17 Daniel Girardi .20 .50
18 Michael Ouzas .30 .75
19 Paulo Colaiacovo .40 1.00
20 B.J. Crombeen .20 .50
21 Dan Speer .20 .50
22 Jan Platil .20 .50
23 Mascot .02 .10
24 Barrie Molson Centre .02 .10

2003-04 Barrie Colts

Cards are listed according to the order they appear on the checklist card.
COMPLETE SET (24) 6.00 15.00
1 Thomas Lee .30 .75
2 Steve Spade .30 .75
3 Evan Brophey .30 .75
4 Ryan Hamilton .30 .75
5 Andrew Shennan .30 .75
6 Chad Thompson .30 .75
7 Chris Morrison .30 .75
8 Chad Robinson .30 .75
9 Hunter Tremblay .30 .75
10 Bryan Little 1.50 4.00
11 Scott Hotham .40 1.00
12 Mark Langdon .30 .75
13 Jeremy Swanson .30 .75
14 Michael Root .30 .75
15 Travis Fuller .30 .75
16 Paolo Colaiacovo .60 1.50
17 Lukas Bolf .30 .75
18 B.J. Crombeen .30 .75
19 Georgy Ryazantsev .30 .75
20 Dan Speer .30 .75
21 Cory Stillman .30 .75
22 Andrew Dennis .30 .75
23 Mascot/Checklist .02 .10
24 Barrie Molson Centre .02 .10

2004-05 Barrie Colts

Unnumbered cards, listed below in checklist order.
COMPLETE SET (25) 5.00 10.00
1 Jeff Weber .20 .50
2 Nathan Martine .20 .50
3 Michael Lombardi .20 .50
4 Nicholas Plastino .20 .50
5 Ryan Hamilton .20 .50
6 Andrew Shennan .20 .50
7 Dan Speer .20 .50
8 Mike Roelofsen .20 .50
9 Chris Morrison .20 .50
10 Chad Robinson .20 .50
11 Hunter Tremblay .20 .50
12 Bryan Little .40 1.00
13 Scott Hotham .20 .50
14 Aaron Lewicki .20 .50
15 Michael Root .20 .50
16 Travis Fuller .20 .50
17 Michael Birner .20 .50
18 Francois Thuot .20 .50
19 Lukas Bolf .20 .50
20 B.J. Crombeen .30 .75
21 Andrew Marshall .20 .50
22 Jordan Shine .20 .50
23 Andrew Hotham .20 .50
24 Andrew Dennis .20 .50
25 Mascot/Checklist .02 .10

2004-05 Barrie Colts 10th Anniversary

COMPLETE SET (25) 5.00 12.00
1 Daniel Tkaczuk .20 .50
2 Bryan Little .40 1.00
3 Michael Henrich .20 .50
4 Martin Skoula .20 .50
5 Blaine Down .20 .50
6 Jan Bulis .20 .50
7 Erik Reitz .30 .75
8 Jeremy Swanson .20 .50
9 Luch Nasato .20 .50
10 B.J. Crombeen .30 .75
11 Jan Platil .20 .50
12 Denis Shvidki .20 .50
13 Joey Tenute .20 .50
14 Aaron Power .20 .50
15 Alexander Volchkov .20 .50
16 Mark Langdon .20 .50
17 Fraser Clair .20 .50
18 Nick Lees .20 .50
19 Cory Stillman .20 .50
20 Jeff Tetzlaff .20 .50
21 Tim Verbeek .20 .50
22 Matt Dzieduszycki .20 .50
23 Paulo Colaiacovo .30 .75
24 David Chant .30 .75
25 Brian Finley .30 .75

2006-07 Barrie Colts

1 Andrew Perugini .30 .75
2 Michael Hutchinson .20 .50
3 Kyle Van De Bospoort .20 .50
4 Brian Lashoff .20 .50
5 Thomas Marcinko .30 .75
6 Nicolas Plastino .20 .50
7 Shawn Franck .20 .50
8 Alex Hutchings .20 .50
9 Hunter Tremblay .20 .50
10 Bryan Little .60 1.50
11 Stefan Della Rovere .30 .75
12 Richard Clune .20 .50
13 Ryan Bellows .20 .50
14 Mike Webber .20 .50
15 Chris Purves .20 .50
16 Tyson Aitcheson .20 .50
17 Matthew Bragg .20 .50
18 Kris Sparre .20 .50
19 Ryan Gottschalk .20 .50
20 Andrew Marshall .20 .50
21 Cort McGillis .20 .50
22 Vladimir Nikiforov .20 .50
23 George Lovatsis .20 .50
24 Joe Pleckaitis .20 .50
25 Michael Lombardi .20 .50
26 T.J. Battani .20 .50
27 Checklist .02 .10
LE2 Andrew Perugini 2.00 5.00

1951-52 Bas Du Fleuve

This set features top players from the Quebec Senior League. The cards are similar in size to the Parkhurst set that was released this season. The key card in the set pictures Denis Brodeur.
COMPLETE SET (58) 350.00 700.00
1 Gordon Poirier 12.50 25.00
2 Denis Brodeur 25.00 50.00
3 Conrad Poitras 7.50 15.00
4 Clement Tremblay 7.50 15.00
5 Raymond Leduc 7.50 15.00
6 Jacques Armstrong 7.50 15.00
7 Joe Schmidt 7.50 15.00
8 Gilles Laroche 7.50 15.00
9 Frank Pearce 7.50 15.00
10 Wayne Stephenson 7.50 15.00
11 Guy Lapointe 7.50 15.00
12 Guy Delisle 7.50 15.00
13 Ossie Carnegie 10.00 20.00

14 Gilbert Girouard 7.50 15.00
15 Jean-Paul Vandal 7.50 15.00
16 Guy Lalonde 7.50 15.00
17 Roland Bilodeau 7.50 15.00
18 Gaetan Laliberte 7.50 15.00
19 Maurice Benoit 7.50 15.00
20 Thomas McDougall 7.50 15.00
21 Roger Guay 7.50 15.00
22 Bob Brault 7.50 15.00
23 Edouard Theberge 7.50 15.00
24 Paul Lessard 7.50 15.00
25 Lucien Gilbert 7.50 15.00
26 Real Lafreniere 7.50 15.00
27 Ronald Limoges 7.50 15.00
28 Roger Ste. Marie 7.50 15.00
29 Arthur Leyte 7.50 15.00
30 Magella Laforest 7.50 15.00
31 Bill Leblanc 7.50 15.00
32 Pius Gaudet 7.50 15.00
33 Jean-Roch Bellavance 7.50 15.00
34 Gerard Lachance 7.50 15.00
35 Marcel St. Pierre 7.50 15.00
36 Pierre Brillant 7.50 15.00
37 Paul Provost 7.50 15.00
38 Maurice Lamirande 7.50 15.00
39 Roger Hayfield 7.50 15.00
40 Normand Bellavance 7.50 15.00
41 Marcel Houde 7.50 15.00
42 Dan Janelle 7.50 15.00
43 Roland Rossignol 7.50 15.00
44 Roger Gagne 7.50 15.00
45 Jacques Monette 7.50 15.00
46 Bernie Bernaquez 7.50 15.00
47 Paul Gagnon 7.50 15.00
48 Jean-Marie Fillion 7.50 15.00
49 Bert Scullion 7.50 15.00
50 Don Bellringer 7.50 15.00
51 Frank Cote 7.50 15.00
52 Eddy Bolan 7.50 15.00
53 Maurice Parr 7.50 15.00
54 Many McIntyre 7.50 15.00
55 Roger Jodoin 7.50 15.00
56 Mario Senecal 7.50 15.00
57 Denis Fillion 7.50 15.00
58 Marcel Fillion 12.50 25.00

1952-53 Bas Du Fleuve

This set features players from the Quebec Senior League. The cards are similar in size to the 1951-52 Parkhurst set. Noteworthy players include Denis Brodeur (father of Martin and former Canadian Olympic goalie) and Marcel Paille.

COMPLETE SET (65) 400.00 800.00
1 Roger Gagner 12.50 25.00
2 Martial Pruneau 7.50 15.00
3 Fernand Gladu 7.50 15.00
4 Joseph Lacoursiere 7.50 15.00
5 Maurice Lamirande 7.50 15.00
6 Denis Smith 7.50 15.00
7 Real Jacques 7.50 15.00
8 Roland Landry 7.50 15.00
9 Dan Janelle 7.50 15.00
10 Pete Gaudette 7.50 15.00
11 Normand Bellavance 7.50 15.00
12 Roger Hayfield 7.50 15.00
13 Bill LeBlanc 7.50 15.00
14 Victor Corbin 7.50 15.00
15 Gerard Lachance 7.50 15.00
16 Guy Labrie 7.50 15.00
17 Denis Brodeur 15.00 30.00
18 Gerard Paquin 7.50 15.00
19 Irene St. Hilaire 10.00 20.00
20 Guy Gervais 7.50 15.00
21 Marcel Benoit 7.50 15.00
22 Roger Dumas 7.50 15.00
23 Gaston Gervais 7.50 15.00
24 Maurice St. Jean 7.50 15.00
25 Frank Pearce 7.50 15.00
26 Fernand Bernaquez 7.50 15.00
27 Henri-Paul Gagnon 7.50 15.00
28 Jean-Jacques Pichette 7.50 15.00
29 Jim Hayes 7.50 15.00
30 Fernand Rancourt 7.50 15.00
31 Nils Tremblay 7.50 15.00
32 Clement Tremblay 7.50 15.00
33 Jacques Lalancette 7.50 15.00
34 Marcel Fillion 10.00 20.00
35 Jacques Monette 7.50 15.00
36 Frank Cote 7.50 15.00
37 Bernie Lemonde 7.50 15.00
38 Guildor Levesque 7.50 15.00
39 Hector Legris 7.50 15.00
40 Jacques Gagnon 7.50 15.00
41 Donat Deschesnes 7.50 15.00
42 Bertrand LePage 7.50 15.00
43 Paul Lavoie 7.50 15.00
44 Denis Fillion 7.50 15.00
45 Floyd Crawford 12.50 25.00
46 Paul Duchesne 7.50 15.00
47 Rene Pronovost 7.50 15.00
48 Roger Jodoin 7.50 15.00
49 Mario Senecal 7.50 15.00
50 Garry Plamondon 12.50 25.00
51 Marcel Paille 7.50 15.00
52 Rene Pepin 7.50 15.00
53 Gilles Desrosiers 7.50 15.00
54 Edgard Gendron 7.50 15.00
55 Ronald Limoges 7.50 15.00
56 Roland Bilodeau 7.50 15.00
57 Leon Bouchard 7.50 15.00
58 Bob Leger 7.50 15.00
59 Conrad L'Heureux 7.50 15.00
60 Raymond Leduc 7.50 15.00
61 Bob Brault 7.50 15.00
62 Roger Ste. Marie 7.50 15.00
63 Real Lafreniere 7.50 15.00
64 Lucien Gilbert 7.50 15.00
65 Louis Desrosiers 12.50 25.00

1998-99 Baton Rouge Kingfish

This set features the Kingfish of the ECHL. The set was issued in five strips, each containing five cards, as a promotional giveaway at a home game.

COMPLETE SET (25) 8.00 20.00
1 Brett Abrahamson .40 1.00
2 Chris Aldous .40 1.00
3 Cam Brown .40 1.00
4 Jason Byrnes .40 1.00
5 Paul Croteau .40 1.00
6 Luke Curtin .40 1.00
7 Allan Hitchen .40 1.00
8 Scott Humeniuk .40 1.00
9 Trevor Jobe .40 1.00
10 Billy-Jay Johnston .40 1.00
11 Mike Josephson .40 1.00
12 Martin Laroche .40 1.00
13 Michel Massie .40 1.00
14 Eric Montreuil .40 1.00
15 Jon Rempel .40 1.00
16 Bryan Richardson .40 1.00
17 Dan Shermerhorn .40 1.00
18 Bob Westerby .40 1.00
19 Jordan Willis .60 1.50
20 Barry Smith CO .10 .25
21 Ron Hansis GM .04 .10
22 Bob McGill CO .10 .25
23 Huey P. Kingfish MAS .10 .25
24 Pat Loughlin TR .04 .10
25 Chris Kenyon .40 1.00

1998-99 BC Icemen

This set features the BC Icemen of the United Hockey League. Little else is known about this set at this time. Any additional information can be forwarded to hockeymag@beckett.com.

COMPLETE SET (22) 4.80 12.00
1 Mark Dutiaume .30 .75
2 Pete Vandermeer .20 .50
3 Patrice Robitaille .20 .50
4 Ales Dvorak .20 .50
5 Shane Dow .20 .50
6 Scott Ricci .20 .50
7 Doug Johnson .20 .50
8 Justin Kearns .30 .75
9 Justin Plamondon .30 .75
10 Jarno Mensonen .20 .50
11 Jamie Bird .20 .50
12 Greg Pajor .20 .50
13 Derek Knorr .20 .50
14 Chris Kavanagh .20 .50
15 Dallas Mann .20 .50
16 Jon Hillebrandt .30 .75
17 Dieter Kochan .80 2.00
18 Brad Jones HCO .10 .25
19 Brian Waselko TR .10 .25
20 Mike Thornton BR .10 .25
21 Phamtom Mascot .10 .25
22 Bamboni Mascot .10 .25

1998-99 BC Icemen II

This set is numbered out of 25 and features the Iceman of the United Hockey League. It is believed that this set was offered as a promotional giveaway at a late-season home game.

COMPLETE SET (27) 8.00 20.00
1 Ales Dvorak .30 .75
2 Shane Dow .30 .75
3 Scott Ricci .30 .75
4 Pete Vandermeer .30 .75
5 Doug Johnson .30 .75
6 Mark Dutiaume .60 1.50
7 Justin Kearns .30 .75
8 Patrice Robitaille .30 .75
9 Justin Plamondon .40 1.00
10 Chris Greenville .30 .75
11 Jarno Mensonen .30 .75
12 Jamie Bird .30 .75
13 Greg Pajor .30 .75
14 Dmitri Deryabin .30 .75
15 Derek Knorr .30 .75
16 Peter Cermak .30 .75
17 Chris Kavanagh .30 .75
18 Jon Hillebrandt .80 2.00
19 Dieter Kochan 1.60 4.00
20 Brad Jones HCO .20 .50
21 Brian Weslro TR .10 .25
22 Dallas Mann .30 .75
23 Mike Thornton BR .10 .25
24 Phamton Mascot .10 .25
25 Bamboni Mascot .10 .25
NNO UHL Website .04 .10
NNO Checklist .10 .25

2001-02 BC Icemen

This set features the Icemen of the UHL. The set was issued as a promotional giveaway at a last-season home game. The cards are unnumbered and are listed below in alphabetical order.

COMPLETE SET (29) 8.00 20.00
1 Chris Allen .30 .75
2 Eric Andersen .30 .75
3 Alex Andreyev .30 .75
4 Keith Aucoin .30 .75
5 Martin Belanger .30 .75
6 Karel Betik .40 1.00
7 Glendon Cominetti .30 .75
8 Ross Dufresne .30 .75
9 R.J. Gates .30 .75
10 Chris Grenville .30 .75
11 Eric Heffler .30 .75
12 David Jesiolowski .40 1.00
13 Marc Lauzon .30 .75
14 Jim Nagle .30 .75
15 Ryan Pepperall .30 .75
16 Larry Pierce .30 .75
17 Justin Plamondon .30 .75
18 Sean Rowe .60 1.50
19 Erasmo Saltarelli .30 .75
20 Bryan Schoen .40 1.00
21 Trevor Shoaf .30 .75
22 Marc Tropper .30 .75
23 Rob Voltera .30 .75
24 Derek Wood .30 .75
25 Brad Jones CO .10 .25
26 Pedro Trindade MGR .04 .10
27 Bamboni MASCOT .10 .25
28 Phantom MASCOT .10 .25
29 Jason Weinstein PR .04 .10

1983-84 Belleville Bulls

This 30-card police set measures approximately 2 5/8" by 4 1/8" and was sponsored by the Board of Commissioners of Police and other local organizations. The fronts feature posed color player photos with white borders. The player's name and position appear at the bottom. The backs carry P.L.A.Y. (Police, Laws and Youth) Card Tips from The Bulls which consist of a hockey term and relate it to everyday life.

COMPLETE SET (30) 28.00 80.00
1 Belleville Bulls Logo .10 .01
2 Quinte Sports Centre .10 .01
3 Dan Quinn .80 2.00
4 Dave MacLean .20 .50
5 Scott Gardiner .20 .50
6 Mike Knuude .20 .50
7 Brian Martin .20 .50
8 R. Vaughan OWN .10 .25
9 John McDonald .30 .75
10 Brian Small .20 .50
11 Mike Savage .20 .50
12 Dunc MacIntyre .20 .50
13 Charlie Moore .20 .50
14 Jim Andanoff .20 .50
15 Mario Martini .20 .50
16 Rick Adolfi .20 .50
17 Mike Vellucci .20 .50
18 Scott McMichel .20 .50
19 Ali Butorac .20 .50
20 Al Iafrate 2.00 3.00
21 Rob Crocock .20 .50
22 Craig Coxe .60 1.50
23 Grant Robertson .20 .50
24 Craig Billington 1.20 3.00
25 Darren Gani .20 .50
26 Tim Bean .20 .50
27 Wayne Gretzky 24.00 75.00
28 Russ Soule TR .10 .25
29 Larry Mavety CO/GM .10 .25
30 Team Photo .40 .50

1984-85 Belleville Bulls

This 31-card police set measures approximately 2 5/8" by 4 1/8" and was sponsored by the City of Belleville Police Force and other local organizations. The fronts feature posed color player photos with white borders. The player's name, position, and the season (1984-85) appear at the bottom. The backs carry P.L.A.Y. (Police, Laws and Youth) Card Tips from The Bulls which explain a hockey term and relate it to everyday life.

COMPLETE SET (31) 6.00 15.00
1 Team photo .40 .50
2 R. Vaughan OWN .10 .10
3 Larry Mavety CO/MG .10 .10
4 Dunc MacIntyre .20 .50
5 Belleville Bulls Logo .20 .10
6 Mike Knuude .20 .50
7 John Purves .40 1.00
8 Charlie Moore .20 .50
9 Stan Drulia .40 1.00
10 Craig Billington .80 2.00
11 Dave MacLean .20 .50
12 Darren Moxam .20 .50
13 Shane Doyle .20 .50
14 Larry VanHerzele .20 .50
15 Tim Bean .20 .50
16 Kent Brimmer .20 .50
17 Angelo Catenaro .20 .50
18 Steve Linesman .20 .50
19 Grant Robertson .20 .50
20 John Reid .20 .50
21 Dean Whyte .20 .50
22 Darren Gani .20 .50
23 Roger Robertson .20 .50
24 Gary Callaghan .20 .50
25 John Tamer .20 .50
26 Todd Hawkins .20 .50
27 Jim Andanoff .20 .50
28 Chris Rutledge TR .10 .10
29 Matt Taylor .20 .50
30 Mike Hartman .40 1.00
NNO Title Card .10 .01

2000-01 Belleville Bulls

This set features the Bulls of the OHL. The cards were produced by the team and sold at home games. The cards are instantly recognizable by virture of having three colour headshots on the back.

COMPLETE SET (29) 4.80 15.00
1 Team Photo .10 .25
2 Paulo Colaiacovo .40 1.00
3 Nick Policelli .20 .50
4 Matt Coughlin .20 .50

5 Mike Jacobsen .20 .50
6 Malcolm Hutt .20 .50
7 Cody McCormick .20 .50
8 Mike Renzi .20 .50
9 Andrew Brown .20 .50
10 Andre Deveaux .20 .50
11 Matt Stajan .20 1.50
12 Alex White .20 .50
13 David Silverstone .20 .50
14 Randy Rowe .20 .50
15 Brad Efthimiou .20 .50
16 Dan Growden .20 .50
17 Adam Paiement .20 .50
18 Jan Chovan .30 .75
19 Branko Radivojevic .40 1.50
20 David Cornacchia .20 .50
21 Rob Dmytruk .20 .50
22 Nate Robinson .20 .50
23 Kyle Wellwood 1.00 2.50
24 In Action .08 .20
25 In Action .08 .20
26 In Action .08 .20
27 Jim Hulton CO .04 .10
28 Fan Pictures .01
29 Directory .01

2001-02 Belleville Bulls

This set features the Bulls of the OHL. The cards are slightly oversized, and were issued by the team. As they are unnumbered, they are listed below in alphabetical order.

COMPLETE SET (29) 4.80 12.00
1 Title card .04 .11
2 James Boyd ACO .04 .11
3 Andrew Brown .20 .50
4 Rane Carnegie .20 .50
5 Jan Chovan .31 .78
6 Paulo Colaiacovo .31 .78
7 Matt Coughlin .20 .50
8 Andre Deveaux .20 .50
9 Jake Gilmour .20 .50
10 Dan Growden .20 .50
11 Jim Hulton CO .20 .50
12 Malcolm Hutt .20 .50
13 Michael Knight .20 .50
14 Neill MacInnis .20 .50
15 Oliver Maron .20 .50
16 Cody McCormick .20 .50
17 Adam Paiement .20 .50
18 Marc Rancourt .20 .50
19 Michael Renzi .20 .50
20 Nathan Robinson .40 1.00
21 David Silverstone .20 .50
22 Matt Stajan .20 .50
23 Adam Sturgeon .20 .50
24 Kyle Wellwood .75 2.00
25 Alex White .20 .50
26 Celebration card .04 .11
27 Celebration card .04 .11
28 Michael Renzi .40 1.00
Matt Coughlin
Cody McCormick
Kyle Wellwood
29 Bullie Mascot .04 .11

2001-02 Belleville Bulls Update

This set features the Bulls of the OHL. The set was created late in the season simply to take advantage of the presence of hobby favorite Jason Spezza, who was traded to the Bulls from Windsor halfway through the season. The design is the same as that used for the main set issued earlier that season, but these cards are regulation sized. It is believed that as few as 500 of these sets were produced. The cards are unnumbered, so are listed below in alphabetical order.

COMPLETE SET (9) 4.00 10.00
1 David Clarkson .10 .25
2 Steve Cooke .10 .25
3 Michael Mole .40 1.00
4 Neil Smith .10 .25
5 Jason Spezza 1.20 3.00
6 Jason Spezza 1.20 3.00
7 Jason Spezza 1.20 3.00
8 Glenn Ridler .10 .25
9 Lubos Velebny .10 .25

2002-03 Belleville Bulls

COMPLETE SET (30) 6.00 15.00
1 Blake Allan .20 .50
2 Andrew Brown .20 .50
3 Rane Carnegie .20 .50
4 Steve Cooke .20 .50
5 Andre Deveaux .20 .50
6 Jake Gilmour .20 .50
7 Todd Griffith .20 .50
8 Malcolm Hutt .20 .50
9 Mike Knight .20 .50
10 Josh Manning .20 .50
11 Oliver Maron .20 .50
12 Cody McCormick .30 .75
13 Michael Mole .30 .75
14 Adam Paiment .20 .50
15 Marc Rancourt .20 .50
16 Neil Smith .20 .50
17 Matt Stajan .60 1.50
18 Ivan Svarny .20 .50
19 Cody Thornton .20 .50
20 Eric Tobia .30 .75
21 Darcy Tuplin .20 .50
22 Patrick Turcotte .20 .50
23 Jordon Watson .20 .50
24 Coaches .02 .10
25 Michael Mole .30 .75
Eric Tobia
26 Matt Stajan .60 1.50
27 Andre Deveaux .20 .50
28 Rookies .20 .50
29 Defencemen .02 .10
30 Team Captains .02 .10

2003-04 Belleville Bulls

Created by Extreme Sportscards, this 22-card set was sold a home games and by Cartes Timbres Ste-Foy. Cards are unnumbered and are listed below by jersey number.

COMPLETE SET (22) 5.00 10.00
1 Rane Carnegie .20 .50
2 Cody Thornton .20 .50
3 Matt Kelly .20 .50
4 Dan Rogers .20 .50
5 Marc Rancourt .20 .50
6 Eric Tobia .30 .75
7 Ryan Berard .20 .50
8 Josh Francis .20 .50
9 Andrew Brown .20 .50
10 Michael Knight .20 .50
11 Aaron Lewicki .20 .50
12 Geoff Patton .20 .50
13 Jake Gilmour .20 .50
14 Ivan Svarny .20 .50
15 Todd Griffith .20 .50
16 David Edgeworth .20 .50
17 Josh Manning .20 .50
18 Milan Hluchy .20 .50
19 Mike Roelofsen .20 .50
20 Shaun Clinton .20 .50
21 Andrew Brown TL .20 .50
22 Rane Carnegie TL .20 .50

2004-05 Belleville Bulls

A total of 400 team sets were produced.

COMPLETE SET (24) 5.00 12.00
1 Andrew Maksym .20 .50
2 Bobby Davey .20 .50
3 Cody Thornton .20 .50
4 Connor Cameron .20 .50
5 Jeff Leavitt .20 .50
6 Eric Tobia .20 .50
7 Evan Brophey .20 .50
8 Geoff Killing .20 .50
9 John Hughes .20 .50
10 Kevin Lalande .20 .50
11 Kyle Sonnenberg .20 .50
12 Lubomir Stach .20 .50
13 Mark Rancourt .20 .50
14 Marc Johnson .20 .50
15 Martin Novak .20 .50
16 Matt Beleskey .20 .50
17 Matt Kelly .20 .50
18 Pat Sutton .20 .50
19 Ryan Berard .20 .50
20 Ryan Rorabeck .20 .50
21 Scott Baker .20 .50
22 Shawn Matthias .40 1.00
23 Steve Spade .20 .50
NNO Marc Rancourt CAP .75 2.00

2005-06 Belleville Bulls

COMPLETE SET (24) 8.00 15.00
1 Matt Beleskey .30 .75
2 Ryan Rorabeck .30 .75
3 Sebastian Dahm .30 .75
4 Kyle Jukosky .30 .75
5 Matt Smyth .30 .75
6 P.K. Subban .60 1.50
7 Michael Neal .30 .75
8 Scott Baker .30 .75
9 Bryan Cameron .30 .75
10 Bobby Davey .30 .75
11 Bud Kelly .30 .75
12 Geoff Killing .30 .75
13 Nicholas Pageau .30 .75
14 John Hughes .30 .75
15 Bryan Cameron .30 .75
16 Steve Spade .30 .75
17 Kevin Lalande .30 .75
18 Ryan Berard .30 .75
19 Andrew Maksym .30 .75
20 Jeff Leavitt .30 .75
21 Shawn Matthias .40 1.00
22 Cory Tanaka .30 .75
23 Andrew Gibbons .30 .75
24 Andrew Self .30 .75

2006-07 Belleville Bulls

COMPLETE SET (23) 5.00 12.00
1 Matt Pelech .20 .50
2 Bryan Cameron .20 .50
3 Matt Beleskey .20 .50
4 Stephen Blunden .30 .75
5 Erik Caladi .20 .50
6 Tyler Donati .20 .50
7 Andrew Gibbons .20 .50
8 Jeff Leavitt .20 .50
9 Shawn Matthias .30 .75
10 Michael Neal .20 .50
11 Aaron Snow .20 .50
12 Cory Tanaka .20 .50
13 Eric Tangradi .20 .50
14 Matthew Tipoff .20 .50
15 Paul Cianfrini .20 .50
16 Geoff Killing .20 .50
17 Shawn Lalonde .20 .50
18 Nicholas Pageau .20 .50
19 P.K. Subban .75 2.00
20 Steven Whitely .20 .50
21 Kevin Lalande .20 .50
22 Mike Murphy .20 .50
LE2 Shawn Matthias 1.00 2.50

1981-82 Billings Bighorns

We've confirmed one single from this early WHL set to date and it is believed that many others exist as well, possibly including former first overall pick Gord Kluzak. Any additional information can be forwarded to hockeymag@beckett.com.

NNO Harry Mahood 4.00 10.00

1992-93 Binghamton Rangers

Issued by the team, these cards are printed on thin card stock. The cards themselves are not numbered, but numbers are assigned to each on the checklist card. The front is a full bleed photo with the player name appearing only on the back.

COMPLETE SET (24) 4.00 10.00
1 Team Card .16 .40
2 Mike Hurlbut .16 .40
3 Michael Stewart .16 .40
4 Craig Duncanson .16 .40
5 Rick Bennett .16 .40
6 Dave Thomlinson .16 .40
7 Mike Stevens .16 .40
8 Rob Kenny .16 .40
9 Chris Cichocki .16 .40
10 Sergei Zubov .40 1.00
11 Don Biggs .16 .40
12 Joby Messier .16 .40
13 Steven King .16 .40
14 Dave Archibald .16 .40
15 Brian McReynolds .16 .40
16 Dave Marcinyshyn .16 .40
17 Jean-Yves Roy .16 .40
18 Peter Fiorentino .16 .40
19 Daniel Lacroix .16 .40
20 Per Djoos .16 .40
21 Boris Rousson .40 .75
22 Corey Hirsch .30 .75
23 Rockey Ranger Mascot .10 .25
24 Ranger Victory .16 .40

1994-95 Binghamton Rangers

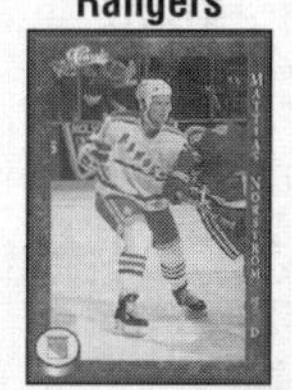

This 22-card standard-size set was manufactured and distributed by Jessen Associates, Inc. for Classic. The fronts display color action player photos with a dark blue marbleized inner border and a black outer border. The player's name, jersey number, and position appear in the teal border on the right edge. Inside a black border on a marbleized background, the backs present biography, statistics, and sponsor logos. The cards are unnumbered and checklisted below in alphabetical order.

COMPLETE SET (22) 4.00 10.00
1 Eric Cairns .30 .75
2 Craig Duncanson .16 .40
3 Peter Fiorentino .16 .40
4 Ken Gernander .16 .40
5 Jim Hiller .16 .40
6 Corey Hirsch .30 .75
7 Rob Kenny .16 .40
8 Andrei Kudinov .16 .40
9 Darren Langdon .30 .75
10 Scott Malone .16 .40
11 Shawn McCosh .16 .40
12 Mike McLaughlin .16 .40
13 Joby Messier .16 .40
14 Jeff Nielsen .16 .40
15 Mattias Norstrom .30 .75
16 Jamie Ram .30 .75
17 Barry Richter .20 .50
18 Jean-Yves Roy .16 .40
19 Brad Rubachuk .16 .40
20 Dave Smith .16 .40
21 Dmitri Starostenko .16 .40
22 Michael Stewart .16 .40
23 Darcy Werenka .16 .40

1995-96 Binghamton Rangers

This 25-card set of the AHL Binghamton Rangers was manufactured and distributed by SplitSecond. The fronts feature color action player photos, while the backs carry player information. The cards are unnumbered and checklisted below in alphabetical order.

COMPLETE SET (25) 4.00 10.00
1 Sylvain Blouin .20 .50
2 George Burnett CO .04 .10
3 Mike Busniuk ACO .04 .10
4 Eric Cairns .30 .75
5 Chris Ferraro .30 .75
6 Peter Ferraro .40 1.00
7 Maxim Galanov .20 .50
8 Ken Gernander .20 .50
9 Brad Jones .16 .40
10 Pavel Komarov .16 .40
11 Andrei Kudinov .16 .40
12 Daniel Lacroix .20 .50
13 Steve Larouche .16 .40
14 Jon Hillebrandt .20 .50
15 Scott Malone .16 .40
16 Cal McGowan .16 .40
17 Jeff Nielsen .16 .40
18 Jamie Ram .20 .50
19 Shawn Reid .16 .40
20 Barry Richter .20 .50
21 Andy Silverman .16 .40
22 Lee Sorochan .20 .50
23 Dmitri Starostenko .16 .40
24 Ryan Vandenbussche .30 .75
25 Rick Willis .16 .40

1996-97 Binghamton Rangers

This 24-card set features the Binghamton Rangers of the AHL. The cards were produced by SplitSecond and distributed by the team. The cards feature an action photo on the front, along with player name, number and team logo. The backs feature limited stats. The unnumbered cards are listed below alphabetically.

COMPLETE SET (24) 4.00 10.00
1 Micah Aivazoff .20 .50
2 Sylvain Blouin .16 .40
3 George Burnett CO .04 .10
4 Mike Busniuk ACO .04 .10
5 Ed Campbell .16 .40
6 Dan Cloutier .60 2.50
7 Chris Ferraro .20 .50
8 Peter Ferraro .20 .50
9 Peter Fiorentino .16 .40
10 Eric Flinton .16 .40
11 Maxim Golanov .16 .40
12 Ken Gernander .16 .40
13 Mike Martin .16 .40
14 Bob Maudie .16 .40
15 Jeff Nielsen .16 .40
16 Rocky Raccoon .04 .10
17 Ken Shepard .16 .40
18 Andy Silverman .16 .40
19 Adam Smith .16 .40
20 Lee Sorochan .20 .50
21 Ryan VandenBussche .30 .75
22 Vladimir Vorobiev .16 .40

23 Rick Willis .16 .40
24 AHL Hockey Card .01

2003-04 Binghamton Senators

This set was sold by the team at home games.

COMPLETE SET (24) 6.00 15.00
1 Steve Bancroft .20 .50
2 Dennis Bonvie .40 1.00
3 Daniel Corso .20 .50
4 Ray Emery .40 1.00
5 Alexandre Giroux .20 .50
6 Denis Hamel .40 1.00
7 Andy Hedlund .20 .50
8 Jody Hull .20 .50
9 David Hymovitz .20 .50
10 Chris Kelly .40 1.00
11 Brooks Laich .20 .50
12 Josh Langfeld .20 .50
13 Chris Leinweber .20 .50
14 Brian McGrattan .40 1.00
15 Serge Payer .20 .50
16 Jan Platil .20 .50
17 Christoph Schubert .20 .50
18 Peter Smrek .20 .50
19 Billy Thompson .40 1.00
20 Tony Tuzzolino .20 .50
21 Julien Vauclair .20 .50
22 Antoine Vermette .40 1.00
23 Greg Watson .20 .50
24 Mascot .02 .10

2003-04 Binghamton Senators Postcards

According to minor league expert Ralph Slate, these cards were issued as a promotional giveaway. A single card was given out each week that a fan bought a newspaper at a Quickway gas station. The cards are numbered on the front, card x of 12, and a bonus 13th card exists of the mascot.

COMPLETE SET (13) 15.00 30.00
1 Chris Kelly 1.25 3.00
2 Josh Langfeld .75 2.00
3 Julien Vauclair .75 2.00
4 Daniel Corso .75 2.00
5 Dennis Bonvie 1.25 3.00
6 David Hymovitz .75 2.00
7 Brooks Laich .75 2.00
8 Brian McGrattan 1.25 3.00
9 Alexandre Giroux .75 2.00
10 Denis Hamel 1.25 3.00
11 Antoine Vermette 1.25 3.00
12 Ray Emery 1.50 4.00
NNO Mascot .75 2.00

2004-05 Binghamton Senators

COMPLETE SET (26) 6.00 15.00
1 Brandon Bochenski .30 .75
2 Danny Bois .20 .50
3 Ray Emery .40 1.00
4 Jesse Fibiger .20 .50
5 Denis Hamel .40 1.00
6 Andy Hedlund .20 .50
7 Pat Kavanagh .20 .50
8 Chris Kelly .30 .75
9 Neil Komadoski .20 .50
10 Josh Langfeld .20 .50
11 Brian McGrattan .40 1.00
12 Arpad Mihaly .20 .50
13 Jan Platil .20 .50
14 Brian Pothier .20 .50
15 Grant Potulny .20 .50
16 Christoph Schubert .20 .50
17 Jason Spezza .50 2.00
18 Charlie Stephens .20 .50
19 Billy Thompson .30 .75
20 Antoine Vermette .30 .75
21 Anton Volchenkov .20 .50
22 Greg Watson .20 .50
23 David Cameron CO .02 .10
24 John Paddock CO .02 .10
25 Mike Busniuk ACO .02 .10
26 Max MASCOT .02 .10

2004-05 Binghamton Senators Hess

Given away one at a time at local gas stations with the purchase of a newspaper. They measure approximately 3 7/8 by 4 7/8.

COMPLETE SET (14) 20.00 35.00
1 Chris Kelly 1.25 3.00
2 Denis Hamel 1.50 4.00
3 Brian Pothier .75 2.00
4 Christoph Schubert .75 2.00
5 Pat Kavanagh .75 2.00
6 Antoine Vermette 1.25 3.00
7 Brandon Bochenski 1.25 3.00
8 Andy Hedlund .75 2.00
9 Brian McGrattan 1.25 3.00
10 Josh Langfeld .75 2.00
11 Anton Volchenkov .75 2.00
12 Jason Spezza 5.00 10.00
13 Ray Emery 1.50 4.00
NNO Cover card .10 .25

2005-06 Binghamton Senators Quickway

COMPLETE SET (22) 10.00 25.00
1 Denis Hamel .40 1.00
2 Danny Bois .40 1.00
3 Jeff Heerema .40 1.00
4 Joe Cullen .40 1.00
5 Jan Platil .40 1.00
6 Charlie Stephens .40 1.00
7 Steve Martins .40 1.00
8 Brad Norton .40 1.00
9 Filip Novak .40 1.00
10 Billy Thompson .75 2.00
11 Grant Potulny .40 1.00
12 Patrick Eaves 1.25 3.00
13 Brett Clouthier .40 1.00
14 Tomas Malec .40 1.00
15 Kelly Guard .75 2.00
16 Neil Petruic .40 1.00
17 Brandon Bochenski .75 2.00
18 Brennan Evans .40 1.00
19 Gregg Johnson .40 1.00
20 Jeff Glass .75 2.00
21 Lance Ward .40 1.00

2006-07 Binghamton Senators

1 Jamie Allison .30 .75
2 Michal Barinka .30 .75
3 Danny Bois .30 .75
4 Charlie Cook .30 .75
5 Andrew Ebbett .30 .75
6 Chanse Fitzpatrick .30 .75
7 Jeff Glass .60 1.50
8 Kelly Guard .60 1.50
9 Andy Hedlund .30 .75
10 Jeff Heerema .30 .75
11 Josh Hennessy .60 1.50
12 Neil Komadoski .30 .75
13 Arttu Luttinen .30 .75
14 Tomas Malec .30 .75
15 Brian Maloney .30 .75
16 Serge Payer .30 .75
17 Cory Pecker .30 .75
18 Neil Petruic .30 .75
19 Grant Potulny .30 .75
20 Bobby Robins .30 .75
21 Ryan Vesce .30 .75
22 Mike Busniuk .30 .75
23 Dave Cameron CO .10 .25
24 Dom Nicoletta TR .02 .10
25 Tom Severance EQ .02 .10
26 Grady Whittenburg ANN .02 .10
27 Maximus MASCOT .02 .10

2006-07 Binghamton Senators 5th Anniversary

COMPLETE SET (35) 10.00 25.00
1 Steve Bancroft .30 .75
2 Cody Bass .30 .75
3 Brandon Bochenski .60 1.50
4 Danny Bois .30 .75
5 Dennis Bonvie .60 1.50
6 Patrick Eaves .60 1.50
7 Ray Emery .60 1.50
8 Alexandre Giroux .30 .75
9 Jeff Glass .40 1.00
10 Kelly Guard .40 1.00
11 Denis Hamel .40 1.00
12 Andy Hedlund .30 .75
13 Jeff Heerema .30 .75
14 David Hymovitz .30 .75
15 Chris Kelly .30 .75
16 Josh Langfeld .30 .75
17 Steve Martins .30 .75
18 Brian McGrattan .60 1.50
19 Joe Murphy .30 .75
20 Filip Novak .30 .75
21 Serge Payer .30 .75
22 Cory Pecker .30 .75
23 Jan Platil .30 .75
24 Brian Pothier .30 .75
25 Grant Potulny .30 .75
26 Bobby Robins .30 .75
27 Christoph Schubert .30 .75
28 Brad Smyth .30 .75
29 Jason Spezza .75 2.00
30 Charlie Stephens .30 .75
31 Billy Thompson .30 .75
32 Julien Vauclair .30 .75
33 Antoine Vermette .40 1.00
34 Anton Volchenkov .40 1.00
35 Max MASCOT .02 .10

1992-93 Birmingham Bulls

The cards are larger than the standard size, and are numbered on the back. The set is sponsored by Fox-21, Coca-Cola and radio station WJOX-FM.

COMPLETE SET (23) 3.20 8.00
1 Logo Card .04 .10
2 Jim Larkin .16 .40
3 Brett Barnett .16 .40
4 Joe Flanagan .16 .40
5 Butch Kaebel .16 .40
6 Scott Matusovich .16 .40
7 Chuck Hughes .16 .40
8 Dave Craievich .16 .40
9 Alexander Khavanov .16 .40
10 Paul Marshall .16 .40
11 Jim Peters .16 .40
12 Chris Marshall .16 .40
13 Jerome Bechard .16 .40
14 Jean-Alain Schneider .16 .40
15 Kevin Kerr .16 .40
16 Rob Krauss .16 .40
17 Greg Burke .16 .40
18 Mark Romaine .16 .40
19 Bruce Garber CO .04 .10
20 Phil Roberto ACO .10 .25
21 Dave Cavaliere TR .04 .10
22 Tim Woodburn ANN .04 .10
NNO Team Logo/ CL .04 .10

1993-94 Birmingham Bulls

Sponsored by Coca-Cola, Fox 21 TV and WJOX AM 690, this 23-card set measures approximately 2 5/8" by 3 5/8" and features the 1993-94 Birmingham Bulls of the East Coast Hockey League. On a white card face, the fronts have posed color player photos. The team name and logo are printed above the photo, while the player's name, his position and sponsor logos appear below the picture. The horizontal backs carry player biography, profile and sponsor logos.

COMPLETE SET (23) 4.00 10.00
1 Logo Card .04 .10
2 Jim Larkin .20 .50
3 Brett Barnett .20 .50
4 Joe Flanagan .20 .50
5 Butch Kaebel .20 .50
6 Scott Matusovich .20 .50
7 Chuck E. Hughes .20 .50
8 Dave Craievich .20 .50
9 Alexander Khavanov .80 2.00
10 Paul Marshall .20 .50
11 Jim Peters .20 .50
12 Chris Marshall .20 .50
13 Jerome Bechard .20 .50
14 Jean-Alain Schneider .20 .50
15 Kevin Kerr .20 .50
16 Rob Krauss .20 .50
17 Greg Burke .20 .50
18 Mark Romaine .20 .50
19 Bruce Garber CO .04 .10
20 Phil Roberto ACO .20 .50
21 Dave Cavaliere TR .04 .10
22 Tim Woodburn ANN .04 .10
NNO Title Card CL .04 .10

1993-94 Birmingham Bulls Birmingham News

This set features the Bulls of the ECHL. It is believed that these were offered as a promotional giveaway. Unlike the other issue available this season, the cards feature an image of the Birmingham News on the front and back.

COMPLETE SET (27) 4.80 12.00
1 Phil Roberto CO .08 .20
2 Phil Roberto CO .08 .20
3 Jerome Bechard .20 .50
4 Marc Beran .20 .50
5 Dave Craievich .20 .50
6 Murray Duval .20 .50
7 Dan Fournel .30 .75
8 Jon Duval .20 .50
9 Joe Flanagan .20 .50
10 Todd Harris .20 .50
11 Bill Kovacs .20 .50
12 Jim Larkin .20 .50
13 Paul Marshall .20 .50
14 Jim Mill .30 .75
15 Brad Mullahy .20 .50
16 Tom Neziol .20 .50
17 Darcy Norton .20 .50
18 Jay Schiavo .20 .50
19 J.A. Schneider .20 .50
20 Brad Smyth .30 .75
21 Rick Girhiny .20 .50
22 Sandy Galuppo .20 .50
23 Jamie Linden .30 .75
24 Ed Krayer ACO .04 .10
25 Joel Stern ANN .04 .10
26 Mark Mills EQM .04 .10
27 Header Card/CL .04 .10

1994-95 Birmingham Bulls

Sponsored by Chevron, WBMG 45, and The New Mix 94.5 FM, this 22-card set measures approximately 2 3/4" by 3 3/4" and features the 1994-95 Birmingham Bulls of the ECHL. On a white card face, the fronts have posed color player photos. The cards are unnumbered and checklisted below in alphabetical order.

COMPLETE SET (22) 3.20 8.00
1 Greg Bailey .16 .40
2 Norm Bazin .16 .40
3 Jerome Bechard .16 .40
4 Dave Boyd .16 .40
5 David Craievich .16 .40
6 Rob Donovan .16 .40
7 Jon Duval .16 .40
8 Sandy Galuppo .20 .50
9 Todd Harris .16 .40
10 Ian Hebert .16 .40
11 Craig Johnson .16 .40
12 John Joyce .16 .40
13 Chris Kerber ANN .04 .10
14 Olaf Kjenstad .20 .50
15 Mike Krassner EQMG .04 .10
16 Jim Larkin .16 .40
17 Craig Lutes .16 .40
18 Mark Michaud .16 .40
19 Jean-Marc Plante .16 .40
20 Phil Roberto CO .16 .40
21 Brad Smyth .16 .40
22 Title Card CL .04 .10

1995-96 Birmingham Bulls

This odd-sized (2 3/4" by 3 3/4") 29-card set features the Birmingham Bulls of the ECHL. The cards feature an action shot along with the team logo and player name on the front. The unnumbered backs contain player stats and sponsor logos. The set also contains a 6-card subset of WJOX DJs. The set was available through the team; apparently, no mail order was available.

COMPLETE SET (29) 4.00 10.00
1 Toro the Bull .04 .10
2 Phil Roberto CO .10 .25
3 Lance Brady .20 .50
4 Jeff Wells .20 .50
5 Brad Prefontaine .20 .50
6 Mark Raiter .20 .50
7 Rob Donovan .20 .50
8 Chris Grenville .20 .50
9 Colin Gregor .20 .50
10 Mike Latendresse .30 .75
11 John Morabito .20 .50
12 Brendan Creagh .20 .50
13 Chris Bergeron .20 .50
14 Jerome Bechard .20 .50
15 Craig Lutes .20 .50
16 Ian Hebert .20 .50
17 John Joyce .20 .50
18 Jeff Callinan .20 .50
19 Jason Dexter .20 .50
20 Olaf Kjenstad .20 .50
21 Chad Erickson .30 .75
22 Ray Pack EQMG .04 .10
23 Chris Kerber ANN .04 .10
24 M.Coulter/S.Griffi DJs .04 .10
25 Doug Laxton DJ .04 .10
26 Randy Armstrong DJ .04 .10
27 Lee Davis DJ .04 .10
28 Herb Winches DJ .04 .10
29 Ben Cook DJ .04 .10

1982-83 Birmingham South Stars

This set is believed to have been issued in the form of perforated program pull-outs. It is not known if this checklist is complete.

COMPLETE SET (16) 24.00 60.00
1 Frank Beaton 1.20 3.00
2 Bob Bergloff 1.20 3.00
3 Bob Boileau 1.20 3.00
4 Rollie Boutin 1.20 3.00
5 Murray Brumwell 1.20 3.00
6 Steve Carlson 8.00 20.00
7 Dave Debol .80 2.00
8 Jim Dobson .80 2.00
9 Dave Richter 1.20 3.00
10 Keith Hanson .80 2.00
11 Peter Hayek .80 2.00
12 Glenn Hicks .80 2.00
13 Craig Homola .80 2.00
14 Wes Jarvis 1.20 3.00
15 Warren Young 2.00 5.00
16 Markus Mattsson 1.20 3.00

2006-07 Bloomington PrairieThunder

COMPLETE SET (24) 8.00 15.00
1 Mike Adamek .30 .75
2 Trevor Baker .30 .75
3 Jon Booras .30 .75
4 Jarad Bourassa .30 .75
5 Steffan Braunlich .30 .75
6 John Spoltore .30 .75
7 Mike Zbriger .30 .75
8 B.J. Gaustad .30 .75
9 Ryan Gillis .30 .75
10 Alex Goupil .30 .75
11 Dion Hyman .30 .75
12 Andrew Lackner .30 .75
13 Andre Niec .30 .75
14 Jason Payne .30 .75
15 Mark Phenow .30 .75
16 Tyler Rennette .30 .75
17 Jeff Reynaert .30 .75
18 Shawn Roed .30 .75
19 Tim Schneider .30 .75
20 Chip MASCOT .02 .10
21 Brad Thompson .30 .75
22 Derek Booth CO .10 .25
23 Clay Roffer EQ MGR .02 .10
24 Chris Walter TR .02 .10

2001-02 Bossier-Shreveport Mudbugs

This set features the Mudbugs of the WPHL. The set was sold by the team at home games. The cards are unnumbered, so they are listed in alphabetical order.

COMPLETE SET (24) 4.00 10.00
1 Tony Bergin .20 .50
2 Trevor Buchanan .20 .50
3 Jason Campbell .20 .50
4 Bob Case TR .04 .11
5 Greg Foster .20 .50
6 Tim Hill .20 .50
7 Mike Johnson .20 .50
8 Derek Kups .20 .50
9 Bill Lang .20 .50
10 Chad Lang .31 .78
11 Dave Lemay .20 .50
12 Forbes MacPherson .20 .50
13 David Mills .20 .50
14 Scott Muscutt CO .04 .11
15 Pat Powers .20 .50
16 Ryan Rintoul .20 .50
17 Mark Rupnow .20 .50
18 Corey Smith .20 .50
19 Jim Sprott .20 .50
20 Brandon Walker BR .04 .11
21 Billy Welker EQMG .04 .11
22 Dan Wildfong .20 .50
23 Clawed MASCOT .04 .11
24 Team Photo .10 .25

2002-03 Bossier-Shreveport Mudbugs

COMPLETE SET (24) 6.00 15.00
1 Jason Basile .30 .75
2 Tony Bergin .30 .75
3 Chris Brassard .30 .75
4 Trevor Buchanan .30 .75
5 Dru Burgess .30 .75
6 Jason Campbell .30 .75
7 Ken Carroll .30 .75
8 Chris Chelios .30 .75
9 Jonathan Forest .30 .75
10 Jeff Glowa .30 .75
11 Willie Hubloo .30 .75
12 Forbes MacPherson .30 .75
13 Craig Minard .30 .75
14 David Oliver .30 .75
15 Mark Rupnow .30 .75
16 Jim Sprott .30 .75
17 Chad Spurr .30 .75
18 Luc Theoret .30 .75
19 Dan Wildfong .30 .75
20 Scott Muscutt CO .02 .10
21 Billy Welker EQM .02 .10
21 George Bullock Jr. TR .02 .10
23 Team Photo .20 .50
24 Steve Mears ANN .02 .10

2003-04 Bossier-Shreveport Mudbugs

COMPLETE SET (25) 6.00 15.00
1 Jason Basile .30 1.00
2 Travis Bell .30 .75
3 Jeff Blair .30 .75
4 Wes Blevins .30 .75
5 Chris Brassard .30 .75
6 Trevor Buchanan .30 .75
7 Jason Campbell .30 .75
8 Ken Carroll .30 .75
9 Colin Kendall .30 .75
10 Quade Lightbody .40 1.00
11 Forbes MacPherson .30 .75
12 Ryan Manitowich .30 .75
13 Craig Minard .40 1.00
14 David Oliver .30 .75
15 Craig Soke .30 .75
16 Jim Sprott .30 .75
17 Chad Spurr .30 .75
18 Dan Wildfong .30 .75
19 Scott Muscutt CO .02 .10
20 John Madden OWN .02 .10
21 George Bullock Jr. TR .02 .10
22 Billy Welker EQM .02 .10
23 Mascot .02 .10
24 Team photo .20 .50
25 Steve Mears ANN .02 .10

2005-06 Bossier-Shreveport Mudbugs

COMPLETE SET (26) 6.00 15.00
1 Jason Basile .30 .75
2 Chris Brassard .30 .75
3 David Cacciola .30 .75
4 Jason Campbell .30 .75
5 Ken Carroll .30 .75
6 Jeremy Downs .30 .75
7 Chad Kemp .30 .75
8 Quade Lightbody .40 1.00
9 Dale Lupul .30 .75
10 Ryan Manitowich .30 .75
11 Blair Manning .30 .75
12 Craig Minard .30 .75
13 Shane Palahicky .30 .75
14 Chris Shaw .30 .75
15 Scott Sheppard .30 .75
16 Brett Smith .30 .75
17 Chad Spurr .30 .75
18 Martin Stuchlik .30 .75
19 Milan Vodrazka .30 .75
20 Dan Wildfong .30 .75
21 Scott Muscutt HC .02 .10
22 Trevor Buchanan AC .02 .10
23 Billy Welker EM .02 .10
24 Clawed & Lil' Bugger MASCOTS .02 .10
25 George Bullock Jr. TR .02 .10
26 Steve Mears ANNCR .02 .10

2003-04 Boston College Eagles

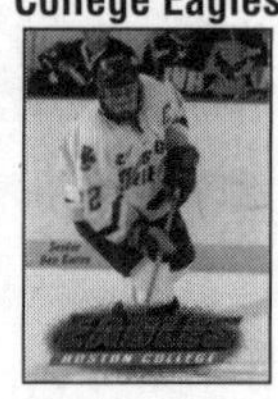

This set was issued as a promotional giveaway at a home game. It comes in a perforated strip and features the Eagles' six graduating seniors and a team photo.

COMPLETE SET (7) 5.00 10.00
1 Ben Eaves .75 2.00
2 Tony Voce .75 2.00
3 Brett Peterson .75 2.00
4 Ty Hennes .75 2.00
5 J.D. Forrest .75 2.00
6 Justin Dziama .75 2.00
7 Team Photo .40 1.00

2003-04 Boston University Terriers

This set was issued as a promotional giveaway at a late-season home game.

COMPLETE SET (27) 25.00
1 Mark Mullen 1.00
2 Stephen Siwiec 1.00
3 Gregg Johnson 1.00
4 John Laliberte 1.00
5 Thomas Morrow 1.00
6 Jack Parker HCO 1.00
7 Stephen Greeley 1.00
8 Brian McConnell 1.00
9 E.J. Solimine 1.00
10 Sean Fields 1.00
11 Bryan Miller 1.00
12 Jakabs Redlihs 1.00
13 Kevin Schaeffer 1.00
14 Brad Zancanaro 1.00
15 Sean Sullivan 1.00
16 Ryan Whitney 3.00
17 David Van Der Gulik 1.00
18 Eric Thomassian 1.00
19 Ken Roche 1.00
20 David Klema 1.00
21 Dan Spang 1.00
22 Ken Magowan 1.00
23 Matt Radoslovich 1.00
24 Harry Agganis Arena .10
25 John Curry 1.00
26 Frantisek Skladany 1.50
27 Mascot .10

2003-04 Bowling Green Falcons

This 18-card set was issued in two series of 9 cards each. Cards in each series were issued on perforated sheets and feature current and former players. Series 1 9cards 1-9) were limited to 2000 sheets while Series 2 was limited to 1000. Both sets were sponsored by the Sentinel Tribune.

COMPLETE SET (18) 35.00
1 Brian Holzinger 2.00
2 Brian Escobedo 1.00
3 Alex Rogosheske 1.00
4 George McPhee 1.00
5 Garry Galley 2.00
6 D'Arcy McConvey 1.00
7 Rob Blake 5.00
8 Mark Wires 1.00
9 Jordan Sigalet 10.00
10 Steve Brudzewski 2.00
11 Erik Eaton 2.00
12 Dan Kane 2.00
13 Gary Kruzich 2.00
14 Dave Ellet 2.00
15 Kevin Bieksa 2.00
16 Ryan Minnabarriet 2.00
17 Gino Cavallini 2.00
18 John Samanski 2.00

1999-00 Brampton Battalion

This set pictures the second-year Brampton Battalions of the Ontario Hockey League. The set was available at the team's rink, and through the mail from sponsor Frozen Pond, a Toronto-based memorabilia dealer. The set is highlighted by 2000 NHL Entry Draft first rounders Raffi Torres and Rostislav Klesla. It also includes a card of 2001 second overall pick Jason Spezza, who played with the team during its inaugural season of 1998-99.

COMPLETE SET (27) 10.00 25.00
1 Header Card .04 .10
2 Team Photo .14 .25
3 David Chant .60 1.50
4 Scott Della Vedova .10 .25
5 Tyler Hanchuck .10 .25
6 Jason Maleyko .10 .25
7 Paul Flache .10 .25
8 Cam McLaughlin .10 .25
9 Rostislav Klesla 1.20 1.50
10 Brad Woods .10 .25
11 Raffi Torres .75 2.00
12 Matt Reynolds .10 .25
13 Chris Rowan .10 .25
14 Lukas Havel .10 .25
15 Mike Rice .10 .25
16 Tyler Dukelow .10 .25
17 Jay McClement .20 .50
18 Matt Grennier .10 .25
19 Kurt MacSweyn .10 .25
21 Aaron Van Leusen .10 .25
21 Chris Cook .10 .25
22 Jay Harrison .40 1.00
23 Richard Kearns .10 .25
24 Jeff Bateman .20 .50
25 Scott Thompson .10 .25
26 Blair McLaughlin .10 .25
27 Jason Spezza 4.00 10.00
28 Stan Butler CO .10 .25
29 Bobby Jones .10 .25
30 Raffi Torres .75 2.00
31 Jason Maleyko .10 .25
32 Inaugural Season .04 .10

2000-01 Brampton Battalion

COMPLETE SET (32) 6.00 15.00
1 Logo .02 .10
2 Team Picture .02 .10
3 2001 WJC Banner .02 .10
4 Brian Finley .30 .75
5Â Travis Parent .20 .50
6 Jason Maleyko .20 .50
7 Paul Flache .20 .50
8 Corey LeClair .20 .50
9 Rostislav Klesla .60 1.50
10 Adam Henrich .20 .50
11 Raffi Torres .60 1.50
12 Chris Clayton .20 .50
13 Chris Rowan .20 .50
14 Lukas Havel .20 .50
15 Jonah Leroux .20 .50
16 Jay McClement .20 .50
17 Kurt MacSweyn .20 .50
18 Aaron Van Leusen .20 .50
19 Jay Harrison .30 .75
20 Ryan Bowness .20 .50
21 Jeff Bateman .20 .50
22 Scott Thompson .20 .50
23 Alex MacDonell .20 .50
24 Anthony Marshall .20 .50
25 Brad Topping .20 .50
26 Stan Butler HCO .02 .10
27 Derrick Smith ACO .02 .10
28 Rostislav Klesla All-Star .60 1.50
29 Raffi Torres All-Star .60 1.50
30 Jay Harrison 1998 First Round .30 .75
31 Jay McClement 1999 First Round .20 .50
32 Adam Henrich 2000 First Round .20 .50

2003-04 Brampton Batallion

The Kreps card was randomly inserted among the team sets.

COMPLETE SET (24) 12.00
1 Ryan Bowness .50
2 Chris Clayton .50
3 Kevin Couture .75
4 Nick Duff .50
5 Jamie Fraser .50
6 Tyler Harrison .50
7 Robert Heickert .50
8 Adam Henrich .50
9 Kamil Kreps 1.50
10 Aaron Lobb .50
11 Martin Lojek .50
12 Howie Martin .50
13 Eliott McCormick .50
14 Brock McPherson .50
15 Geordie Michie .50
16 Phil Oreskovic .50
17 Ryan Oulahen .50
18 Erik Schwanz .50
19 John Seymour .50
20 Stuart Simmons .50
21 Rob Smith .50
22 Patrick Sweeney .50
23 Brad Topping .75
24 Wojtek Wolski 1.50
NNO Kamil Kreps LTD

2004-05 Brampton Battalion

A total of 300 team sets were produced.

COMPLETE SET (25) 12.00
1 Wojtek Wolski 1.50
2 Daren Machesney .50
3 Kevin Couture .50

4 Michael Vernace .50
5 Stuart Simmons .50
6 Phil Oreskovic .75
7 Nick Duff .50
8 Martin Lojek .50
9 Tomas Stryncl .50
10 Dan McDonald .50
11 Aaron Snow .50
12 Brock McPherson .50
13 John de Gray .50
14 Howie Martin .50
15 Luke Lynes .50
16 Graham McNabb .50
17 Luch Aquino .50
18 John Seymour .50
19 Patrick Sweeney .50
20 Tyler Harrison .50
21 J.F. Houle .50
22 Scott Boomsma .50
23 Jason Cassidy .50
24 Ryan Oulahen .50
25 Kyle Sonnenberg .50

2005-06 Brampton Battalion

COMPLETE SET (25) 5.00 12.00
1 Wojtek Wolski .60 1.50
2 Phil Oreskovic .20 .50
3 Nick Duff .20 .50
4 John de Gray .20 .50
5 Daren Machesney .20 .50
6 Bryan Pitton .20 .50
7 Michael Vernace .20 .50
8 Tomas Strycnl .20 .50
9 Stephane Chabot .20 .50
10 Aaron Snow .20 .50
11 Matt Smyth .20 .50
12 Howie Martin .20 .50
13 Luke Lynes .20 .50
14 Graham McNabb .20 .50
15 Justin Levac .20 .50
16 Luch Aquino .20 .50
17 John Seymour .20 .50
18 Nolan Waker .20 .50
19 Taylor Raszka .20 .50
20 Cody Smith .20 .50
21 Jason Cassidy .20 .50
22 Michal Kljna .20 .50
23 Kyle Sonnenburg .20 .50
24 Corey George .20 .50
25 Brock McPherson .20 .50

2006-07 Brampton Battalion

1 Sarge's Checklist .02 .10
2 Patrick Killeen .30 .75
3 Bryan Pitton .30 .75
4 Ken Peroff .30 .75
5 Dalyn Flatt .30 .75
6 Brad Albert .30 .75
7 Tomas Strycnl .30 .75
8 Stephane Chabot .30 .75
9 John De Gray .30 .75
10 Kyle Sonnenburg .30 .75
11 Conor O'Donnell .30 .75
12 Matt Smyth .30 .75
13 Thomas Stajan .30 .75
14 Luke Lynes .30 .75
15 Graham McNabb .30 .75
16 Jason Dale .30 .75
17 Justin Levac .30 .75
18 Cody Hodgson .30 .75
19 John Seymour .30 .75
20 Mike Lomas .30 .75
21 John Hughes .30 .75
22 Kyle Decoste .30 .75
23 Michal Klejna .30 .75

1982-83 Brandon Wheat Kings

This 24-card set measures approximately 2 1/4" by 4" and features posed color player photos with thin yellow borders on a white card face. The player's name appears on the picture at the bottom. The backs carry P.L.A.Y. (Police, Laws and Youth) Tips From The Kings, which consist of a hockey term and relates it to a real life situation. Sponsor logos appear on the lower portion of the back.

COMPLETE SET (24) 12.00 30.00
1 Wheat Kings Logo .20 .50
2 Kevin Pylypow .30 .75
3 Dean Kennedy .40 1.00
4 Sonny Sodke .30 .75
5 Darren Schmidt .30 .75
6 Cam Plante .30 .75
7 Sid Cranston .30 .75
8 Bruce Thomson .30 .75
9 Dave McDowall CO .20 .50
10 Bill Vince .30 .75
11 Kelly Glowa .30 .75
12 Tom McMurchy .30 .75
13 Ed Palichuk .30 .75
14 Roy Caswell .30 .75
15 Allan Tarasuk .30 .75
16 Brent Jessiman .30 .75
17 Randy Slawson .30 .75
18 Gord Smith .30 .75
19 Mike Sturgeon .30 .75
20 Larry Bumstead .30 .75
21 Kirk Blomquist .30 .75
22 Ron Loustel .30 .75
23 Ron Hextall 6.00 15.00
24 Brandon Police Logo .10 .25

1983-84 Brandon Wheat Kings

This 24-card set measures approximately 2 1/4" by 4" and features color posed action player photos with thin yellow borders on a white card face. The player's name is printed on the picture at the bottom. The backs carry P.L.A.Y. (Police, Laws and Youth) Tips From The Kings. Sponsor logos appear in the lower portion of the card.

COMPLETE SET (24) 10.00 25.00
1 Bryan Wells .20 .50
2 Jim Agnew .40 1.00
3 Gord Paddock .20 .50
4 John Dzikowski .20 .50
5 Kelly Kozack .20 .50
6 Byron Lomow .20 .50
7 Pat Loyer .20 .50
8 Rob Ordman .20 .50
9 Brad Wells .20 .50
10 Dave Thomlinson .30 .75
11 Cam Plante .20 .50
12 Jay Palmer .30 .75
13 Boyd Lomow .20 .50
14 Brent Jessiman .20 .50
15 Paul More .20 .50
16 Stacy Pratt .20 .50
17 Brandon City Police .10 .25
18 Jack Sangster CO .20 .50
19 Derek Laxdal .30 .75
20 Ray Ferraro 2.00 5.00
21 Allan Tarasuk .20 .50
22 Randy Cameron .20 .50
23 Dave Curry .20 .50
24 Ron Hextall 4.00 10.00

1984-85 Brandon Wheat Kings

This 24-card set measures approximately 2 1/4" by 4" and features color posed action player photos with thin yellow borders on a white card face. The player's name is printed on the picture at the bottom. The backs carry P.L.A.Y. (Police, Laws and Youth) Tips From The Kings. Sponsor logos appear on the lower portion of the card.

COMPLETE SET (24) 4.80 12.00
1 Garnet Kazuik .20 .50
2 Brent Mireau .20 .50
3 Byron Lomow .20 .50
4 Dean Shaw .20 .50
5 Dean Sexsmith .20 .50
6 Brad Mueller .20 .50
7 John Dzikowski .20 .50
8 Artie Feher .20 .50
9 Pat Loyer .20 .50
10 Murray Rice .20 .50
11 Derek Laxdal .30 .75
12 Perry Fafard .20 .50
13 Lee Trim .20 .50
14 Dan Hart .20 .50
15 Trent Ciprick .20 .50
16 Jeff Waver .20 .50
17 Brandon City Police .20 .50
18 Jack Sangster CO .10 .25
19 Darwin McPherson .20 .50
20 Pokey Reddick .80 2.00
21 Boyd Lomow .20 .50
22 Dave Thomlinson .30 .75
23 Paul More .20 .50
24 Brent Severyn .40 1.00

1985-86 Brandon Wheat Kings

This 24-card set measures approximately 2 1/4" by 4" and features color posed action player photos with thin yellow borders on a white card face. The player's name is printed on the picture at the bottom. The backs carry P.L.A.Y. (Police, Laws and Youth) Tips From The Kings. Sponsor logos appear in the lower portion of the card.

COMPLETE SET (24) 4.80 12.00
1 Kelly Hitchins .20 .50
2 Brent Mireau .20 .50
3 Byron Lomow .20 .50
4 Bob Heeney .20 .50
5 Dean Sexsmith .20 .50
6 Dave Curry .20 .50
7 John Dzikowski .20 .50
8 Artie Feher .20 .50
9 Kevin Mayo .20 .50
10 Murray Rice .20 .50
11 Derek Laxdal .40 1.00
12 Al Cherniwchan .20 .50
13 Lee Trim .20 .50
14 Terry Yake .40 1.00
15 Trent Ciprick .20 .50
16 Jeff Waver .20 .50
17 Team Photo .20 .50
18 Jack Sangster CO .20 .50
19 Mike Morin .20 .50
20 Jason Phillips .20 .50
21 Rod Williams .20 .50
22 Dave Thomlinson .40 1.00
23 Shane Eirickson .20 .50
24 Randy Hoffart .20 .50

1988-89 Brandon Wheat Kings

This 24-card set measures approximately 2 1/4" by 4" and features posed, color player photos with a thin yellow border stripe against a white card face. The backs carry P.L.A.Y. (Police, Laws and Youth) Tips from the Kings and sponsor logos.

COMPLETE SET (24) 6.00 15.00
1 Kevin Cheveldayoff .20 .50
2 Bob Woods .20 .50
3 Dwayne Newman .20 .50
4 Mike Vandenberghe .20 .50
5 Brad Woods .20 .50
6 Gary Audette .20 .50
7 Mark Bassen .20 .50
8 Troy Frederick .20 .50
9 Troy Kennedy .20 .50
10 Barry Dreger .20 .50
11 Bill Whistle .20 .50
12 Jeff Odgers .40 1.00
13 Sheldon Kowalchuk .20 .50
14 Chris Robertson .20 .50
15 Don Laurin .20 .50
16 Curtis Folkett .20 .50
17 Team Photo .20 .50
18 Kelly McCrimmon ACO .20 .50
19 Doug Sauter CO .20 .50
20 Kelly Hitchins .20 .50
21 Trevor Kidd 1.20 3.00
22 Pryce Wood .20 .50
23 Cam Brown .20 .50
24 Greg Hutchings .20 .50

1989-90 Brandon Wheat Kings

This 24-card P.L.A.Y. (Police, Laws and Youth) set measures approximately 2 1/4" by 4". The fronts display color posed action photos inside of yellowish-orange borders. The player's name is printed in black across the bottom of the picture. In addition to sponsor logos, the backs carry "P.L.A.Y. Tips from the Kings" in the form of safety messages.

COMPLETE SET (24) 4.80 12.00
1 Trevor Kidd 1.20 3.00
2 Troy Frederick .20 .50
3 Kelly Thiessen .30 .75
4 Pryce Wood .20 .50
5 Mike Vandenberghe .20 .50
6 Chris Constant .20 .50
7 Hardy Sauter .20 .50
8 Cam Brown .20 .50
9 Bart Cote .20 .50
10 Jeff Hoad .20 .50
11 Kevin Robertson .20 .50
12 Dwayne Newman .20 .50
13 Calvin Flint .20 .50
14 Glen Webster .20 .50
15 Greg Hutchings .30 .75
16 Rob Puchniak .20 .50
17 Gary Audette .20 .50
18 Kevin Schmalz .20 .50
19 Dwayne Gylywoychuk .20 .50
20 Jeff Odgers .30 .75
21 Brian Purdy .20 .50
22 Merv Priest .20 .50
23 Doug Sauter CO .10 .25
24 Team Photo .20 .50

1990-91 Brandon Wheat Kings

This 24-card set measures approximately 2 1/4" by 4". The fronts feature posed color player photos with thin orange borders. The player's name appears on the picture at the bottom, while his uniform number and position are printed in the upper corners. On a white background, the backs carry P.L.A.Y. (Police, Laws and Youth) "Tips From The Kings". Sponsor logos and room for an autograph appear on the lower portion.

COMPLETE SET (24) 5.60 14.00
1 Jeff Hoad .20 .50
2 Merv Priest .20 .50
3 Mike Vandenberghe .20 .50
4 Bart Cote .20 .50
5 Hardy Sauter .20 .50
6 Mark Johnston ACO .10 .25
7 Kelly McCrimmon CO .10 .25
8 Team Photo .20 .50
9 Kevin Robertson .20 .50
10 Glen Webster .20 .50
11 Greg Hutchings .20 .50
12 Dan Kopec .20 .50
13 Dwayne Gylywoychuk .20 .50
14 Brian Purdy .20 .50
15 Trevor Kidd 1.20 3.00
16 Johan Skillgard .20 .50
17 Stu Scantlebury .20 .50
18 Byron Penstock .20 .50
19 Rob Puchniak .20 .50
20 Gary Audette .20 .50
21 Calvin Flint .20 .50
22 Jason White .20 .50
23 Chris Constant .20 .50
24 Glen Gulutzan .20 .50

1992-93 Brandon Wheat Kings

These 24 standard-size cards feature color player action shots on their fronts. Each picture is trimmed in white and has its corners blacked out, giving the impression of a mounted photograph. The cards are unnumbered and checklisted below in alphabetical order.

COMPLETE SET (24) 4.00 10.00
1 Aris Brimanis .16 .40
2 Colin Cloutier .20 .50
3 Chris Dingman .30 .75
4 Mike Dubinsky .20 .50
5 Todd Dutiaume .16 .40
6 Mark Franks .16 .40
7 Craig Geekie .16 .40
8 Dwayne Gylywoychuk .16 .40
9 Scott Hlady .16 .40
10 Jeff Hoad .16 .40
11 Bobby House .16 .40
12 Chris Johnston .16 .40
13 Mark Kolesar .20 .50
14 Scott Laluk .16 .40
15 Mike Maneluk .16 .40
16 Sean McFatridge .16 .40
17 Marty Murray .30 .75
18 Byron Penstock .20 .50
19 Darren Ritchie .16 .40
20 Trevor Robins .20 .50
21 Ryan Smith .16 .40
22 Jeff Staples .16 .40
23 Darcy Werenka .20 .50
24 Willie MASCOT .04 .10

1993-94 Brandon Wheat Kings

This set features the Wheat Kings of the WHL. The cards feature an action photo on the front, framed by black and gold borders. The cards were sold at home games.

COMPLETE SET (24) 6.00 15.00
1 Byron Penstock .30 .75
2 Craig Hordal .30 .75
3 Jeff Staples .20 .50
4 Scott Laluk .20 .50
5 Wade Redden .80 2.00
6 Justin Kurtz .30 .75
7 Sven Butenschon .20 .50
8 Adam Magarrell .20 .50
9 Dwayne Gylywoychuk .20 .50
10 Scott Hlady .20 .50
11 Joel Korenko .20 .50
12 Chris Johnston .20 .50
13 Bobby Brown .20 .50
14 Mark Kolesar .20 .50
15 Chris Low .20 .50
16 Dean Kletzel .20 .50
17 Darren Ritchie .20 .50
18 Mark Dutiaume .20 .50
19 Mike Dubinsky .20 .50
20 Chris Dingman .30 .75
21 Mike Maneluk .30 .75
22 Colin Cloutier .20 .50
23 Paul Bailley .20 .50
24 Marty Murray .30 .75

1994-95 Brandon Wheat Kings

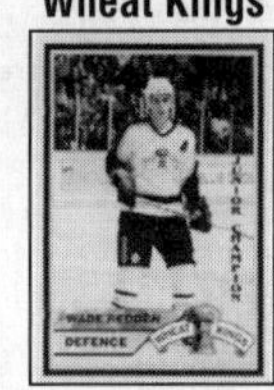

This set features the Wheat Kings of the WHL and was sponsored by 7-Eleven and CKX Radio and was printed by Leech Printing. The set is not numbered and so is listed alphabetically.

COMPLETE SET (24) 6.00 15.00
1 Bobby Brown .20 .50
2 Sven Butenschon .20 .50
3 Colin Cloutier .20 .50
4 Chris Dingman .30 .75
5 Mike Dubinsky .20 .50
6 Mark Dutiaume .20 .50
7 Brian Elder .20 .50
8 Dean Kletzel .20 .50
9 Joel Korenko .20 .50
10 Justin Kurtz .30 .75
11 Scott Laluk .20 .50
12 Chris Low .20 .50
13 Adam Magarrell .20 .50
14 Marty Murray .30 .50
15 Byron Penstock .20 .50
16 Kevin Pozzo .20 .50
17 Wade Redden .80 2.00
18 Darren Ritchie .20 .50
19 Peter Schaefer .60 .75
20 Kelly Smart .20 .50
21 Jeff Staples .20 .50
22 Oleg Tverdovsky .80 1.00
23 Darren Van Oene .20 .50
24 Ian Walterson .20 .50

1995-96 Brandon Wheat Kings

This set was sponsored by 7-11 and was printed by Leech Printing. It is believed that it was sold in set-form by the team. The set is not numbered so the checklist appears below in alphabetical order.

COMPLETE SET (24) 6.00 15.00
1 Bobby Brown .20 .50
2 Sven Butenschon .20 .50
3 Stefan Cherneski .30 .50
4 Cory Cyrenne .30 .75
5 David Draguzas .20 .50
6 Chris Dingman .30 .75
7 Mark Dutiaume .20 .50
8 Brian Elder .20 .50
9 Burke Henry .20 .50
10 Vincent Jonasson .20 .50
11 Dean Kletzel .20 .50
12 Justin Kurtz .30 .75
13 Mike LeClerc .40 1.00
14 Andrei Lupandin .20 .50
15 Wade Redden .80 2.00
16 Ryan Robson .20 .50
17 Peter Schaefer .60 .75
18 Jason Skilnick .20 .50
19 Kelly Smart .20 .50
20 Daryl Stockham .20 .50
21 Jeff Temple .20 .50
22 Daniel Tetrault .20 .50
23 Gerhard Unterluggauer .20 .50
24 Darren Van Oene .30 .75

1996-97 Brandon Wheat Kings

COMPLETE SET (24) 7.00 12.00
1 Les Borsheim .20 .50
2 Daniel Tetrault .20 .50
3 Burke Henry .40 1.00
4 Darryl Stockham .20 .50
5 Gerhard Unterluggauer .20 .50
6 Josh Woitas .20 .50
7 Mark Dutiaume .20 .50
8 Johnathan Aitken .30 .75
9 Dorian Anneck .20 .50
10 Brian Elder .20 .50
11 Andrei Lupandin .20 .50
12 Brad Twordik .20 .50
13 Jeff Katcher .20 .50
14 Kelly Smart .20 .50
15 Peter Schaefer .40 1.00
16 Ryan Robson .20 .50
17 Cory Cyrenne .40 1.00
18 Jason Boyd .20 .50
19 Darren Van Oene .20 .50
20 Stefan Cherneski .20 .50
21 Aaron Goldade .20 .50
22 Justin Kurtz .20 .50
23 David Haun .20 .50
24 Bobby Leavins .20 .50

1997-98 Brandon Wheat Kings

This set features the Wheat Kings of the WHL. The set is sponsored by McDonald's

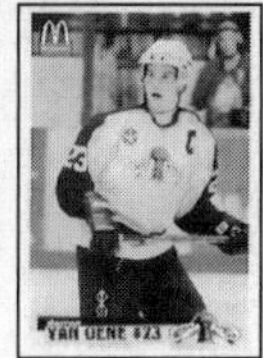

and P.L.A.Y. The cards are unnumbered, so are listed in alphabetical order.

COMPLETE SET (26) 6.00 15.00
1 Alex Argyriou .20 .50
2 Johnathan Aitken .20 .50
3 Les Borsheim .20 .50
4 Stefan Cherneski .30 .50
5 Jomar Cruz .30 .75
6 Cory Cyrenne .40 .75
7 Brett Girard .20 .50
8 Aaron Goldade .20 .50
9 Bevin Guenther .20 .50
10 David Haun .20 .50
11 Burke Henry .20 .50
12 Jamie Hodson .40 1.00
13 Andrew Kaminsky .20 .50
14 Kirby Law .40 1.00
15 Bobby Leavins .20 .50
16 Andrei Lupandin .20 .50
17 Scott McCallum .20 .50
18 Brooks Paisley .20 .50
19 Randy Ponte .20 .50
20 Ryan Robson .20 .50
21 Wade Skolney .20 .50
22 Kelly Smart .20 .50
23 Daniel Tetrault .30 .75
24 Brent Twordik .20 .50
25 Darren Van Oene .30 .50
26 Josh Woitas .20 .50

1998-99 Brandon Wheat Kings

This set features the Wheat Kings of the WHL. The set was sold by the team at home games and was sponsored by McDonald's. The cards are unnumbered, and so are listed below alphabetically.

COMPLETE SET (24) 4.80 12.00
1 Alex Argyriou .20 .50
2 Ryan Craig .20 .50
3 Jomar Cruz .30 .75
4 Jan Fadrny .20 .50
5 Brett Girard .20 .50
6 Aaron Goldade .20 .50
7 Burke Henry .20 .50
8 Jamie Hodson .30 .75
9 Ryan Johnston .20 .50
10 J.D. Kehler .20 .50
11 Petr Kudrna .20 .50
12 Andrew Kaminsky .20 .50
13 Andrei Lupandin .20 .50
14 Scott McCallum .20 .50
15 Richard Mueller .20 .50
16 Randy Ponte .20 .50
17 Ryan Robson .20 .50
18 Wade Skolney .20 .50
19 Daniel Tetrault .20 .50
20 Brett Thurston .20 .50
21 Brad Twordik .20 .50
22 Cory Unser .20 .50
23 Mike Wirll .20 .50
24 Justin Yeoman .20 .50

1999-00 Brandon Wheat Kings

This set features the Wheaties of the WHL. The set was sold by the team at home games. The cards are unnumbered, so are listed below alphabetically.

COMPLETE SET (24) 6.00 25.00
1 Mark Ardelan .20 .50
2 Milan Bartovic .20 .50
3 Les Borsheim .20 .50
4 Ryan Craig .20 .50
5 Brett Dickie .20 .50
6 Ryan Diduck .20 .50
7 Jan Fadrny .20 .50
8 Brett Girard .20 .50
9 Aaron Goldade .20 .50
10 Kevin Harris .20 .50
11 Jamie Hodson .30 .75
12 J.D. Kehler .20 .50
13 Colin McRae .20 .50
14 Robert McVicar .30 .75
15 Richard Mueller .20 .50
16 Randy Ponte .20 .50
17 Bart Rushmer .20 .50
18 Wade Skolney .20 .50
19 Daniel Tetrault .20 .50
20 Brett Thurston .20 .50
21 Jordin Tootoo 6.00 15.00
22 Brad Twordik .20 .50
23 Cory Unser .20 .50
24 Mike Wirll .20 .50

2000-01 Brandon Wheat Kings

COMPLETE SET (24) 10.00 25.00
1 Jordin Tootoo 4.00 10.00
2 Jamie Hodson .30 .75
3 Mark Ardelan .20 .50
4 Reagan Leslie .20 .50
5 Brett Thurston .20 .50
6 Travis Young .20 .50
7 Brett Dickie .20 .50
8 Richard Mueller .20 .50
9 Nolan Yonkman .30 .75
10 Brett Girard .20 .50
11 James Marquis .20 .50
12 Colin McRae .20 .50
13 Aaron Goldade .20 .50
14 Milan Bartovic .20 .50
15 J.D. Kehler .20 .50
16 Lance Monych .40 1.00
17 Tim Konsorada .20 .50
18 Caine Pearpoint .20 .50
19 Ryan Craig 1.25 3.00
20 Randy Ponte .40 1.00
21 Kevin Harris .20 .50
22 Wade Skolney .20 .50
23 Jiri Jakes .20 .50
24 Robert McVicar .30 .75

2001-02 Brandon Wheat Kings

This set features the Wheaties of the WHL. The set was produced by the team and sponsored by McDonald's and was offered for sale at the team's souvenir shop. The cards are black bordered, and so are highly condition sensitive. As they are unnumbered, they are listed below alphabetically.

COMPLETE SET (24) 25.00
1 Andre Blanchette .20 .50
2 Dustin Bru .20 .50
3 Ryan Craig .20 .50
4 Brett Dickie .20 .50
5 Travis Eagles .20 .50
6 Eric Fehr .20 .50
7 Adrian Foster .40 1.00
8 Josh Garbutt .31 .78
9 Kevin Harris .20 .50
10 Jiri Jakes .31 .78
11 Tim Konsorada .20 .50
12 Reagan Leslie .20 .50
13 Geoff McIntosh .20 .50
14 Colin McRae .20 .50
15 Robert McVicar .20 .50
16 Lance Monych .20 .50
17 Caine Pearpoint .20 .50
18 Randy Ponte .40 1.00
19 Wade Skolney .20 .50
20 Ryan Stone .20 .50
21 Brett Thurston .20 .50
22 Jordin Tootoo .80 2.00
23 Willie MASCOT .04 .11
24 Travis Young .20 .50

2002-03 Brandon Wheat Kings

This 23-card set was sold at home games. An early card of Jordin Tootoo highlights this set.

COMPLETE SET (23) 25.00
1 Jonathan Webb .50
2 Reagan Leslie .50
3 Brett Thurston .50
4 Bryan Nathe .50
5 Brett Dickie .50
6 Josh Garbutt .50
7 Andre Blanchette .50
8 Richard Jasovsky .50
9 Tyler Dyck .50
10 Derek Werenka .50
11 Teegan Moore .50
12 Eric Fehr 3.00
13 Ryan Stone .50
14 Lance Monych .50
15 Tim Konsorada .50
16 Rick Kozak .50
17 Jordin Tootoo 10.00
18 Greg Watson 1.00
19 Ryan Craig .50
20 Ole-Kristian Tollefson .50
21 Jeff Topilko .50
22 Geoff McIntosh .75
23 Robert McVicar .75

2003-04 Brandon Wheat Kings

COMPLETE SET (24) 6.00 15.00
1 Josh Harding 1.25 3.00
2 Tyler Boldt .20 .50
3 Stephan Lenoski .20 .50
4 Erik Christensen .40 1.00
5 Lance Monych .40 1.00
6 Mark Derlago .20 .50
7 Corey Courchene .20 .50
8 Richard Jasovsky .20 .50
9 Tim Konsorada .20 .50
10 Codey Burki .20 .50
11 Teegan Moore .20 .50
12 Ryan Stone .40 1.00
13 Reagan Leslie .20 .50
14 Ole-Kristian Tollefsen .40 1.00
15 Steven Later .20 .50
16 Eric Fehr .75 2.00
17 Andre Blanchette .20 .50
18 Jeff Topilko .20 .50
19 Mark Louis .20 .50
20 Mark Shefchyk .20 .50
21 Jonathan Webb .20 .50
22 Tyler Dyck .20 .50
23 Derek LeBlanc .20 .50
24 Mike Nichol .20 .50

2004-05 Brandon Wheat Kings

COMPLETE SET (24) 20.00
1 Mike Nichol .75
2 Jonathan Webb .75
3 Corey Courchene .75
4 Mike Cann .75
5 Theran Yeo .75
6 Steven Later .75
7 Daryl Boyle .75
8 Cole Hunter .75
9 Sami Sandell .75
10 Tyler Strautman .75
11 Eric Fehr 2.00
12 Teegan Moore .75
13 Ryan Stone 1.50
14 Lance Monych 1.00
15 Tim Konsorada 1.00
16 Jakub Sindel .75
17 Riley Day .75
18 Codey Burki .75
19 Derek LeBlanc .75
20 Ryan Reaves .75
21 Jeff Topilko .75
22 Mark Louis .75
23 Stephan Lenoski .75
24 Tyler Plante .75

2005-06 Brandon Wheat Kings

COMPLETE SET (24) 10.00 18.00
1 Keith Aulie .30 .75
2 Daryl Boyle .30 .75
3 Codey Burki .30 .75
4 Andrew Clark .30 .75
5 Corey Courchene .30 .75
6 Riley Day .30 .75
7 Mark Derlago .30 .75
8 Tyler Dittmer .30 .75
9 Chad Erb .30 .75
10 Matt Hallick .30 .75
11 Cole Hunter .30 .75
12 Kurt Jory .30 .75
13 Bryan Kauk .30 .75
14 Dustin Kohn .30 .75
15 Stephan Lenoski .30 .75
16 Mark Louis .30 .75
17 Teegan Moore .30 .75
18 Tyler Plante .30 .75
19 Ryan Reaves .30 .75
20 Sami Sandell .30 .75
21 Tyler Strautman .30 .75
22 Jeff Topilko .30 .75
23 John Wikner .30 .75
24 Theran Yeo .30 .75

1983-84 Brantford Alexanders

This 30-card set measures approximately 2 3/4" by 3 1/2". The fronts feature posed color player photos inside a thin black picture frame and white outer borders. The player's name appears on the picture at the bottom. On a white background, the backs carry the player's name, number, and a short biography in the upper portion; P.L.A.Y. (Police, Laws and Youth) "Tips From The Alexanders And The Brantford and Area Police" in the middle; and sponsor logos in the lower portion.

COMPLETE SET (30) 12.00 30.00
1 Ken Gratton ACO .20 .50
2 Shayne Corson 2.00 5.00
3 Bob Probert 3.20 8.00
4 Bruce Bell .60 1.50
5 Warren Bechard ACO .20 .50
6 Jason Lafreniere .40 1.00
7 Rob Moffat .30 .75
8 Jack Calbeck PR .20 .50
9 Marc West .30 .75
10 Larry Van Herzele .30 .75
11 Doug Stewart .30 .75
12 Brian MacDonald .30 .75
13 Dave Draper CO/GM .20 .50
14 Jeff Jackson .60 1.50
15 Steve Linseman .30 .75
16 Steve Short .30 .75
17 Allan Bester .80 2.00
18 John Weir COP .20 .50
19 Chris Pusey .30 .75
20 Mike Millar .30 .75
21 Chris Glover .30 .75
22 Bob Pierson .30 .75
23 Phil Priddle .30 .75
24 Grant Anderson .30 .75
25 Ken Gagner .30 .75
26 Andy Alway TR .20 .50
27 Todd Francis .30 .75
28 John Meulenbroeks .30 .75
29 Mike Chettleburgh .30 .75
30 Bill Dynes TR .20 .50

1994-95 Brantford Smoke

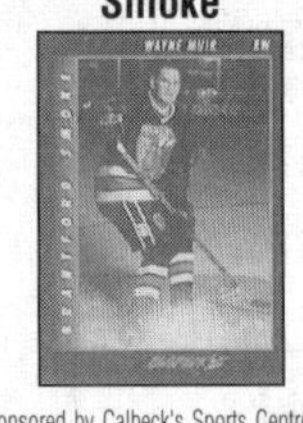

Sponsored by Calbeck's Sports Centre and Davis Fuels, and printed by Slapshot Images Ltd., this 26-card set features the 1994-95 Brantford Smoke of the Colonial Hockey League.

COMPLETE SET (26) 2.80 7.00
1 Checklist .04 .10
2 Bob Delorimiere .16 .40
3 Todd Francis .16 .40
4 Pete Liptrott .16 .40
5 Lorne Knauft .16 .40
6 Paul Polillo .16 .40
7 Rob Arabski .16 .40
8 Derek Gauthier .16 .40
9 Joe Simon .16 .40
10 Brad Barton .16 .40
11 Terry Chitaroni .20 .50
12 Paul Mitton .16 .40
13 Wayne MacPhee .16 .40
14 Brian Blad .20 .50
15 John Laan .16 .40
16 Shane MacEachern .16 .40
17 Wayne Muir .16 .40
18 Ted Miskolczi .16 .40
19 Marc Delorme .16 .40
20 Mike Speer .16 .40
21 Bob Baird TR .04 .10
Ken Crabb TR
22 Ken Gratton CO .04 .10
23 Team Photo .20 .50
24 Craig Newton .04 .10
25 Joe Lowes .04 .10
NNO Ad Card .04 .10

2003-04 Bridgeport Sound Tigers

This set was issued as a promotional giveaway at several home games. The cards were issued in perforated strips, with one strip specific per game. The cards are numbered, but numbers 1-8 are repeated twice.

COMPLETE SET (20) 40.00
1A Wade Dubielewicz 5.00
1B Ryan Kraft 1.50
2A Ben Guite 1.50
2B Kevin Colley 1.50
3A Cole Jarrett 1.50
3B Rob Collins 1.50
4A Alan Letang 1.50
4B Jeff Hamilton 1.50
5A Dieter Kochan 5.00
5B Cail MacLean 1.50
6A Eric Manlow 1.50
6B Justin Mapletoft 3.00
7A Graham Belak 1.50
7B Alain Nasreddine 1.50
8A Martin Kariya 10.00
8B Tomi Pettinen 1.50
9 Brandon Smith 1.50
10 Derek Bekar 1.50
11 Blaine Down 1.50
12 Jody Robinson 1.50

1991-92 British Columbia JHL

This 172-card standard-size set features players of the British Columbia Junior Hockey League The card design features action and posed color player photos. A border design that frames the picture is royal blue at the bottom and fades to pale blue and white at the top. Overlapping this frame at the top is a bar with a blue speckled pattern, which contains the player's name, team name, or card title. The team logo appears within a royal blue circle that is superimposed over the lower right corner of the picture. The backs carry a black-and-white close-up, statistics, and biographical information. Topical subsets featured are Stars of the Future (81, 91, 93, 106, 146-147, 164, 166, 168-169), Coastal All-Stars (151-154, 163), and Interior All-Stars (155-162). The cards are numbered on the back and checklisted below according to teams as follows: Vernon Lakers (1-17, 23-25), Kelowna Spartans (18-22, 26-41), Nanaimo Clippers (42-62, 79-80, 153), Merritt Centennials (63-78, 82, 107), Chilliwack Chiefs (81, 127-145), Surrey Eagles (83, 106, 108-117, 119-126), and Penticton Panthers (85-105, 118, 147).

COMPLETE SET (173) 40.00 100.00
1 Vernon Lakers .10 .25
Team Photo
2 Scott Longstaff .06 .15
3 Rick Crowe .06 .15
4 Sheldon Wolitski .06 .15
5 Kevan Rilcof .06 .15
6 Greg Buchanan .06 .15
7 Vernon Lakers .06 .15
Executives
8 Murray Caton .06 .15
9 Adrian Bubola .06 .15
10 Troy Becker .06 .15
11 Shawn Potyok .06 .15
12 John Morabito .06 .15
13 Peter Zurba .06 .15
14 Chad Schraeder .06 .15
15 Shawn Bourgeois .06 .15
16 Michal Sup .06 .15
17 Rick Eremenko .06 .15
18 David Lemanowicz .06 .15
19 Daniel Blasko .06 .15
20 Gary Audette .06 .50
21 Graham Harder .06 .15
22 Ryan Nessman .06 .15
23 Jason Switzer .06 .15
24 Roland Ramoser .06 .15
25 Dusty McLellan .06 .15
26 Dustin Green .06 .15
27 Steve Roberts .06 .15
28 Jason Lowe .06 .15
29 Brad Knight .06 .15
30 Pavel Suchanek .06 .15
31 Ken Crockett .06 .15
32 Adam Smith .10 .25
33 Glen Pullishy .06 .15
34 Mike Zambon .06 .15
35 Scott Chartier .10 .25
36 Donny Hearn .06 .15
37 Jeff Denham .06 .15
38 Jamie Marriott .06 .15
39 Silverio Mirao .06 .15
40 Darren Tymchyshyn .06 .15
41 Mark Basanta .06 .15
42 Trevor Prest .06 .15
43 Jim Lessard .06 .15
44 Jade Kersey .06 .15
45 Geordie Young .06 .15
46 Darren Holmes .06 .15
47 Wade Dayley .06 .15
48 Dan Murphy .06 .15
49 Paul Taylor .06 .15
50 Sjon Wynia .06 .15
51 Ryan Loxam .06 .15
52 Andy Faulkner .06 .15
53 Scott Kowalski .06 .15
54 Mickey McGuire .06 .15
55 Jason Disiewich .06 .15
56 Jim Ingram .06 .15
57 Ryan Keller .06 .15
58 Brian Schiebel .06 .15
59 Shawn York .06 .15
60 Sean Krause .06 .15
61 Casey Hungle .06 .15
62 Chris Jones .06 .15
63 Doug Stewart .06 .15
64 Jason Sirota .10 .25
65 Dave Dunnigan .06 .15
66 Aaron Hoffman .06 .15
67 Jason Timewell .06 .15
68 Pat Meehan .06 .15
69 Mike Leduc .06 .15
70 Brad Koopmans .06 .15
71 Guy Prince .06 .15
72 Dorel Gecse .06 .15
73 Scott Salmond .06 .15
74 Brian Zakall .06 .15
75 Mike Josephson .06 .15
76 Derek Harper .06 .15
77 John Graham .06 .15
78 Dan Morrissey .10 .25
79 Glenn Calder .06 .15
80 Jason Northard .06 .15
81 Chris Kerr .06 .15
82 Bill Muckalt .80 1.00
83 Greg Hunt .06 .15
84 Paul Kariya 10.00 25.00
1990-91 All-Star Team
85 Dean Rowland .06 .15
86 Paul Kariya 10.00 25.00
(Skating)
87 David Kilduff .06 .15
88 Jeff Tory .06 .15
89 Mike Newman .06 .15
90 Tyler Boucher .06 .15
91 Paul Kariya 10.00 25.00
(Skating with stick)
92 Phil Valk .06 .15
93 Paul Kariya 10.00 25.00
(Passing)
94 Bob Lewis .06 .15
95 Steve Williams .06 .15
96 James Pelzer .06 .15
97 Shawn Carter .06 .15
98 Ryan Erasmas .10 .25
99 John Dehart .06 .15
100 David Green .06 .15
101 Derek Gecse .06 .15
102 Brian Barnes .06 .15
103 Jason Given .06 .15
104 Jason Podollan .20 .50
105 Brian Veale .06 .15
106 Rob Tallas .30 .75
107 Bob McBurnie .06 .15
108 Paul McMillan .06 .15
109 Ryan Donovan .06 .15
110 Kevin Robertson .06 .15
111 Milt Mastad .10 .25
112 Kees Roodbol .06 .15
113 Carey Causey .06 .15
114 Patrick O'Flaherty .06 .15
115 Chad Vestergaard .06 .15
116 Tyler Quiring .10 .25
117 Loui Mellios .06 .15
118 Bob Bell .06 .15
119 Rob Tallas .30 .75
120 Clint MacDonald .06 .15
121 Bart Taylor .06 .15
122 Mark Basanta .06 .15
123 Don McCusker .06 .15
124 Jason Howse .06 .15
125 Mike McKinlay .06 .15
126 Trevor Pennock .06 .15
127 Dean Shmyr .10 .25
128 Chris Kerr .06 .15
129 Erin Thornton .06 .15
130 Dennis Archibald .06 .15
131 Brian McDonald .06 .15
132 Bob Quinnell .06 .15
133 Clint Black .06 .15
134 Jason Peters .06 .15
135 Doug Ast .06 .15
136 Jason Bilous .10 .25
137 Lee Schill .06 .15
138 Jason Sanford .06 .15
139 Jeff Hokanson .06 .15
140 Marc Gagnon .06 .15
141 Gunnar Henrikson .06 .15
142 Jamie Lund .06 .15
143 Jason White .06 .15
144 Jag Bal .06 .15
145 Brad Loring .06 .15
146 Marc Gagnon .06 .15
147 Brian Veale .06 .15
148 Checklist 1 .06 .15
149 Checklist 2 .06 .15
150 The Centennial Cup .10 .25
151 Brian Law .06 .15
152 Al Radke .06 .15
153 Andy Faulkner .10 .25
Jason Disiewich
Darren Holmes
Casey Hungle
Chris Jones
154 1982 Coastal Division .10 .25
Team Photo
155 Dusty McLellan .10 .25
Roland Ramoser
Rick Eremenko
Sheldon Wolitski
Shawn Potyok
Scott Longstaff
156 Hendrikson .10 .25
Anchikoski
Marc Gagnon
Jason White
157 John Graham .10 .25
Dave Dunnigan
158 Scott Chartier .10 .25
Mike Zambon
Paul Taylor
Jason Lowe
159 Jeff Tory .10 .25
Tyler Boucher
David Kilduff
Lee Davidson
John Dehart
Burns
160 Didmon .10 .25
Bentham
Marsh
Walsh
161 Lipsett .10 .25
McNeill
Klyn
Edgington
162 1991 Interior .10 .25
All-Stars Team
Photo
163 Johnson .10 .25
Meek
Welker
Fitzpatrick
Collins
Sofikitas
Hutson
Herman
164 John Dehart .06 .15
165 John Craighead .10 .25
166 Mike Josephson .06 .15
167 Wayne Anchikoski .06 .50
168 Paul Kariya 10.00 25.00
(Stars of the Future
on the front)
169 Jim Lessard .06 .15
170 Tommi Virkgunen .06 .15
NNO Wayne Anchikoski .06 .50
NNO John Craighead .10 .25
NNO Tommi Virkgunen .10 .25

1992-93 British Columbia JHL

This 246-card standard-size set showcases players in the British Columbia Junior Hockey League. The cards feature color, action player photos with white borders. The player's name and position appear at the top. The team name is at the bottom. The backs carry the team logo in orange and black, statistics, and biographical information. The cards are numbered on the back and are in team order as follows: Bellingham Ice Hawks (1-23), Chilliwack Chiefs (24-45), Kelowna Spartans (46-70), Merritt Centennials (71-92), Nanaimo Clippers (93-116, 240), Penticton Panthers (117-140), Powell River Paper Kings (141-163, 245), Surrey Eagles (164-188), Vernon Lakers (189-211), and Victoria Warriors (212-233). The set closes with an Alumni of the BCJHL subset (234-239, 241) and other miscellaneous cards (242-246).

COMPLETE SET (246) 10.00 50.00
1 Tom Wittenberg .10 .25
2 Kendel Kelly .06 .25
3 Gus Rettschlag .06 .25
4 Don Barr .06 .25
5 Dave Kirkpatrick .10 .25
6 Josh Flett .06 .25
7 Paul McKenna .06 .25
8 Brad Wingfield .10 .25
9 Derek Gesce .06 .25
10 Garry Gulash .06 .25
11 Tim Bell .06 .25
12 Dean Stork .06 .25
13 Wes Reusse .10 .25
14 Jason Peipmann .06 .25
15 Tyler Johnston .06 .25
16 Jason Delesoy .06 .25
17 The Ice Man .10 .10
18 Don Barr .06 .25
19 Brad Swain .06 .25
20 Wes Rudy .06 .25
21 Michael Sigouin .06 .25
22 Kevan Rilcof .06 .25
23 Brian Preston .06 .25
24 Doug Ast .06 .25
25 Knut Engqvist .06 .25
26 Zac George .06 .25
27 Clint Black .06 .25
28 Cameron Campbell .06 .25
29 Dan Davies .06 .25
30 Bryce Munro .06 .25
31 Ryan Dayman .06 .25
32 Kevin Kimura .06 .25
33 Paul Nicolls .06 .25
34 Thomas Kraft .06 .25
35 Erin Thornton .06 .25
36 Brad Loring .06 .25
37 Jag Bal .06 .25
38 Jeff Grabinsky .06 .25
39 Johan Ahrgren .06 .25
40 The Lethal Weapon .10 .25
41 Two Unidentified .06 .25
Players
42 Judd Lambert .06 .25
43 Brian Schiebel .06 .25
44 Dennis Archibald .10 .25
45 David Longbroek .06 .25
46 Silverio Mirao .06 .25
47 Jason Haakstad .06 .25
48 Lee Grant .06 .25
49 Ryan Esselmont .06 .25
50 Steve Roberts .06 .25
51 Curtis Fry .06 .25
52 David Dollard .06 .25
53 Diano Zol .06 .25
54 Bob Needham .06 .25
55 Dustin Green .06 .25
56 Darren Tymchyshyn .06 .25
57 Peter Arvanitis .06 .25
58 Don Hearn .06 .25
59 Title Card .10 .01
(Unnumbered)
60 Martin Masa .10 .25
61 Steffon Walby .10 .50
62 Joel Irwin .06 .25
63 Brent Bradford .06 .25
64 Dieter Kochan .06 5.00
65 Brendan Kenny .06 .25
66 Marty Craigdallie .06 .25
67 Graeme Harder .06 .25
68 Pavel Suchanek .06 .25
69 Shane Johnson .06 .25
70 Burt Henderson .06 .25
71 Tyler Willis .10 .25
72 Mike Olaski .06 .25
73 David Green .06 .25
74 Tom Mix .10 .25
75 Walter(Guy) Prince .06 .25
76 Joseph Rybar .06 1.00
77 Bill Muckalt .60 2.00
78 Jason Mansoff .06 .25
79 Duane Puga .06 .25
80 Aaron Hoffman .06 .25
81 Dan Blasko .06 .25
82 Rob Szatmary .06 .25
83 Mike Minnis .06 .25
84 Pat Meehan .06 .25
85 Andre Robichaud .06 .25
86 The Terminator .10 .10
87 Derrek Harper .06 .25
88 Dan Morrissey .06 .25
89 Joey Kennedy .06 .25
90 Derrek Harper .06 .25
91 Lawrence Klyne .06 .25
92 Ryan Beamin .06 .25
93 Sjon Wynia .06 .25
94 Jason Disiewich .06 .25
95 Jason Sanford .06 .25
96 Casey Hungle .06 .25
97 Brent Murcheson .06 .25
98 Glenn Calder .10 .25
99 Jade Kersey .06 .25
100 Shawn York .06 .25
101 Bob Quinnell .06 .25
102 Geordie Dunstan .06 .25
103 Cory Crowther .06 .25
104 Jason Hodson .06 .25
105 Chris Jones .06 .25
106 Cory Green .06 .25
107 Chris Buie .06 .25
108 Shaun Peet .06 .25
109 Jason Wood .06 .25
110 Dan Murphy .06 .25
111 Jason Disiewich .06 .25
112 Cory Dayley .06 .25
113 Brian Veale .06 .25
114 Jason Northard .06 .25
115 Phil Valk .10 .25
116 Wade Dayley .06 .25
117 Brendan Morrison 1.20 10.00
118 Marcel Sakac .06 .25
119 Tyler Boucher .06 .25
120 Ray Guze .06 .25
121 Brian Barnes .10 .25
122 Jason Given .06 .25
123 Michael Dairon .06 .25
124 Mike Newman .06 .25
125 Craig Fletcher .06 .25
126 Ty Davidson .06 .25
127 Miki Antonik .06 .25
128 Rob Pennoyer .06 .25
129 Dave Whitworth .06 .25
130 Steve Williams .06 .25
131 Robbie Trampuh .06 .25
132 Mark Filipenko .06 .25
133 Clint MacDonald .06 .25
134 Colin Ryder .06 .25
135 David Kilduff .10 .25
136 Mickey McGuire .06 .25
137 Randy Polacik .06 .25
138 Jeff Tory .10 .25
139 Chris Buckman .06 .25
140 Bill Moody .06 .25
141 Rick McLarren .06 .25
142 The Phantom .10 .10
143 Jason Zaichkowski .06 .25
144 Tony Hrycuik .06 .25
145 Cameron Knox .06 .25
146 Mike Warriner .06 .25
147 Robb Gordon .10 .25
148 Mike Pawluk .10 .25
149 Tim Harris .06 .25
150 Mike Bzdel .06 .25
151 Chad Wilson .06 .25
152 Andrew Plumb .06 .25
153 Andy MacIntosh .06 .25
154 Stefan Brannare .06 .25
155 Matt Sharrers .06 .25
156 Brent Berry .06 .25
157 Ryan Douglas .06 .25
158 Heath Dennison .06 .25
159 Chad Vizzutti .06 .25
160 Adam Lord .06 .25
161 Brad Klyn .06 .25
162 Andrew Young .06 .25
163 Casey Lemanski .06 .25
164 Mike McKinlay .06 .25
165 Derek Robinson .06 .25
166 Kees Roodbol .06 .25
167 Scott Boucher .06 .25
168 Shawn Gervais .06 .25
169 Ryan Schaffer .06 .25
170 Kevin Robertson .06 .25
171 Ryan Donovan .06 .25
172 Bart Taylor .06 .25
173 Greg Hunt .06 .25
174 Darcy George .06 .25
175 Shane Tidsbury .06 .25
176 Rob Smillie .06 .25
177 Chad Vestergaard .06 .25
178 Al Kinisky .06 .25
179 Patrick O'Flaherty .06 .25
180 Loui Mellios .06 .25
181 Lorin Murdock .10 .25
(Unnumbered)
182 Jason Genik .06 .25
183 Rob Herrington .06 .25
184 Loui Mellios .06 .25
185 Cal Benazic .10 .25
186 Richard Kraus .06 .25
187 Geoff White .06 .25
188 Kirk Buchanan .06 .25
189 Peter Zurba .06 .25
190 John Morabito .06 .25
191 Corey Kruchkowski .06 .25
192 Spencer Ward .06 .25
193 Danny Shermerhorn .06 .25
194 Mark Davies .06 .25
195 Jason Rushton .06 .25
196 Chad Buckle .06 .25
197 Serge Beauchesne .06 .25
198 Todd Kelman .06 .25
199 Jason Switzer .06 .25
200 Eon MacFarlane .06 .25
201 Terry Ryan .10 .50
202 Shawn Bourgeois .06 .25
203 Chad Schraeder .06 .25
204 Dusty McLellan .06 .25
205 The Predator .10 .25
206 Danny Shermerhorn .06 .25
207 Chris Godard .06 .25
208 Jason Chipman .06 .25
209 Christian Twomey .10 .25
210 Ryan Loxam .06 .25
211 Greg Buchanan .06 .25
212 Kees Roodbol .06 .25
213 Ryan Keller .06 .25
214 Kevin Paschal .06 .25
215 David Hebky .06 .25
216 Vince Devlin .06 .25
217 Mike Cole .06 .25
218 Daljit Takhar .06 .25
219 Scott Hall .06 .25
220 Derek Lawrence .06 .25
221 Mark Basanta .06 .25
222 Jan Kloboucek .06 .25
223 Randy Barker .06 .25
224 Kris Gailloux .06 .25
225 Tyson Scheuer .06 .25
226 Brent Wormald .06 .25
227 Vince Devlin .06 .25
228 Gus Miller .06 .25
229 Todd McKave .06 .25
230 Lawrence Oliver .06 .25
231 Scott Garvin .06 .25
232 Rob Milliken .06 .25
233 Roman Kobrc .06 .25
234 Dan Skene .06 .25
235 Blair Marsh .06 .25
236 Maco Balkovec .06 .25
237 Scott Kirton .10 .25
238 Blaine Moore .06 .25
239 Nigel Creightney .06 .25
240 Bill Zapt .06 .25
241 Jason Elders .06 .25
242 BCJHL Officials .06 .10
(Unidentified Referee)
243 Masks of the BCJHL .30 1.00
The Black Panther
244 Masks of the BCJHL .30 1.00
The Puck Pirate
(Unnumbered)
245 Mike Pawluk .10 .25
BCJHL MVP
246 Steffon Walby .10 .50
Captains of the BCJHL

1987-88 Brockville Braves

This 25-card set is printed on thin card stock, measures 2 5/8" by 3 5/8", and features posed color player photos with red studio backgrounds. The pictures are set on a white card face and show the player's name, position, and season in the white margin below the photo.

COMPLETE SET (25) 4.00 10.00
1 Title Card .10 .25
2 Steve Harper TR .10 .25
3 Peter Kelly TR .10 .25
4 Mac MacLean CO/MG .10 .25
5 Mike McCourt .20 .50
6 Paul MacLean .20 .50
7 Mark Michaud .20 .50
8 Alain Marchessault .20 .50
9 Tom Roman .20 .50
10 Darren Burns .20 .50
11 Scott Halpenny .20 .50
12 Ray Gallagher .20 .50
13 Bob Lindsay .20 .50
14 Brett Harkins .40 1.00
15 Dave Hyrsky .20 .50
16 Richard Marchessault .20 .50
17 Scott Boston .20 .50
18 Steve Hogg .30 .75
19 Chris Webster .20 .50
20 Stuart Birnie .20 .50
21 Brett Dunk .20 .50
22 Charles Cusson .20 .50
23 Pat Gooley .20 .50
24 Andy Rodman .20 .50
25 Peter Radlein .20 .50

1988-89 Brockville Braves

This 25-card set is printed on thin card stock, measures 2 5/8" by 3 5/8", and features posed color player photos with pale blue studio backgrounds. The pictures are set on a white card face and show the player's name, position, and season in the white margin below the photo.

COMPLETE SET (25) 4.00 10.00
1 Ray Gallagher .20 .50
2 Peter Kelly TR .10 .25
3 Steve Harper TR .10 .25
4 Winston Jones ACO .10 .25
5 Mac MacLean CO/GM .10 .25
6 Kevin Doherty .20 .50
7 Stuart Birnie .20 .50
8 Charles Cusson .20 .50
9 Paul MacLean .20 .50
10 Bob Lindsay .20 .50
11 Darren Burns .20 .50
12 Rick Pracey .30 .75
13 Mike Malloy .20 .50
14 Dave Hyrsky .20 .50
15 Rob Percival .20 .50
16 Jarrett Eligh .20 .50
17 Pat Gooley .20 .50
18 Michael Bracco .30 .75
19 Ken Crook .20 .50
20 Brad Osborne .20 .50
21 Todd Reynolds .20 .50
22 Mike McCourt .20 .50
23 Chris Webster .20 .50
24 Kevin Lune .20 .50
25 Title Card .20 .50

1951-52 Buffalo Bison

This set features the Bison of the AHL. Little is known about this set, but it is believed to be oversized and distributed in set form by the team.

COMPLETE SET (19) 50.00 100.00
1 Team Photo 5.00 10.00
2 Don Ashbee 5.00 10.00
3 Frankie Christy 2.50 5.00
4 Gerry Couture 4.00 8.00
5 Lou Crowdis 2.50 5.00
6 Harry Dick 2.50 5.00
7 Lloyd Finkbeiner 2.50 5.00
8 Ab Demarco 5.00 10.00
9 Leroy Goldsworthy 2.50 5.00
10 Les Hickey 5.00 10.00
11 Vern Kaiser 2.50 5.00
12 Sam Lavitt 2.50 5.00
13 Stan Long 2.50 5.00
14 Cal Mackay 5.00 10.00
15 Ed Mazur 2.50 5.00
16 Sid McNabney 2.50 5.00
17 George Pargeter 2.50 5.00
18 Gordie Pennell 2.50 5.00
19 Grant Warwick 2.50 5.00

1995 Buffalo Stampedes RHI

This standard size, team issued set, features color borderless fronts with players name and "1994 World Champions" in gold along the left side of the card. Backs are grey and black on a white background and feature biographical information along with 1994 statistics. The set came boxed and was available at home games. Cards are unnumbered and checklisted below by jersey number, each of which is prominently displayed on the card back.

COMPLETE SET (21) 4.00 10.00
14 John Hendry .20 .50
16 Tom Nemeth .30 .75
19 John Vechiarelli .30 .75
19 John Vechiarelli IA .30 .75
20 Len Soccio .20 .50
24 Chris Bergeron .20 .50
32 Mark Major .20 .50
34 Jason Cirone .20 .50
36 Nick Vitucci .30 .75
37 Dave Lemay .20 .50
43 John Blessman .20 .50
44 Jay Neal .20 .50
61 Craig Martin .20 .50
72 Rick Corriveau .20 .50
94 Alex Hicks .30 .75
NNO1 Header Card .04 .10
NNO2 Title Card .04 .10
NNO3 Team Photo .04 .10
NNO4 Terry Buchwald .04 .10
NNO5 Stampede Cheerleaders .20 .50
NNO6 Claude the Trumpeter .10 .25

1998-99 Calgary Hitmen

This 26-card set was sold by the team in set form. It features early cards of several top prospects including Pavel Brendl, Jordan Krestanovich and Kris Beech.

COMPLETE SET (26) 8.00 20.00
1 Matt Kinch .30 .75
2 Ryan Shannon .20 .50
3 Jeff Feniak .20 .50
4 Kenton Smith .30 .75
5 Rod Sarich .20 .50
6 Pavel Brendl .60 1.50
7 Chris Nielsen .30 .75
8 Sean McAslan .20 .50
9 Jordan Krestanovich .60 1.50
10 Michael Bubnick .20 .50
11 Kris Beech .75 2.00
12 Ryan Geremia .20 .50
13 Wade Davis .20 .50
14 Brad Moran .30 .75
15 Lyle Steenbergen .20 .50
16 Curtis Rich .20 .50
17 Ryan Andres .20 .50
18 Brent Dodginghorse .20 .50
19 Jerred Smithson .20 .50
20 Peter Bergman .20 .50
21 Alexandre Fomitchev .30 .75
22 Eric Clark .20 .50
23 Donald Choukalos .30 .75
24 Dean Clark HCO .04 .10
25 Jeff Maher ACO .04 .10
26 Vulk MASCOT .04 .10

1998-99 Calgary Hitmen Autographs

This 26-card set resembles the regular set in every way other than carrying player autographs. Please note that Alexandre Fomitchev did not sign any of his cards though the sets were sold including that card in unsigned form.

COMPLETE SET (26) 40.00 80.00
1 Matt Kinch 1.25 3.00
2 Ryan Shannon 5.00 12.00
3 Jeff Feniak 1.25 3.00
4 Kenton Smith 1.25 3.00
5 Rod Sarich 1.25 3.00
6 Pavel Brendl 4.00 10.00
7 Chris Nielsen 1.25 3.00
8 Sean McAslan 1.25 3.00
9 Jordan Krestanovich 4.00 10.00
10 Michael Bubnick 1.25 3.00
11 Kris Beech 4.00 10.00
12 Ryan Geremia 1.25 3.00
13 Wade Davis 1.25 3.00
14 Brad Moran 1.25 3.00
15 Lyle Steenbergen 1.25 3.00
16 Curtis Rich 1.25 3.00
17 Ryan Andres 1.25 3.00
18 Brent Dodginghorse 1.25 3.00
19 Jerred Smithson 1.25 3.00
20 Peter Bergman 1.25 3.00
21 Alexandre Fomitchev UNSIGNED .20 .50
22 Eric Clark 1.25 3.00
23 Donald Choukalos 1.25 3.00
24 Dean Clark HCO 2.00 5.00
25 Jeff Maher ACO 1.25 3.00
26 Vulk MASCOT .20 .50

1999-00 Calgary Hitmen

This team-issued set features the WHL's Hitmen. It was sold by the team at the rink and through its web site. The set is notable for featuring several first rounders, including Pavel Brendl, Kris Beech and Brent Krahn.

COMPLETE SET (25) 6.00 10.00
1 Kris Beech .40 1.00
2 Pavel Brendl .30 .75
3 Michael Bubnick .10 .25
4 Jared Carli .10 .25
5 Dean Clark CO .04 .10
6 Eric Clark .10 .25
7 Sean Connors .10 .25
8 Wade Davis .10 .25
9 Jeff Feniak .10 .25
10 Owen Fussey .10 .25
11 Robin Gomez .10 .50
12 Matt Kinch .30 .75
13 Brent Krahn .60 1.50
14 Jordan Krestanovich .40 1.00
15 Anders Lovdahl .14 .35
16 Jeff Maher ACO .10 .25
17 Sean McAslan .10 .25
18 Brad Moran .20 .50
19 Chris Nielsen .20 .50
20 Shaun Norrie .10 .25
21 Rod Sarich .10 .25
22 Brandon Segal .10 .25
23 Kenton Smith .14 .35
24 Jerred Smithson .10 .25
25 Vulk Mascot .04 .10
26 Calgary Herald .01
27 Playstation Coupon .01

1999-00 Calgary Hitmen Autographs

This 27-card set features the 1999-00 Calgary Hitmen of the Western Hockey League in an autographed parallel version of the main release. All players except Eric Clark and Jeff Feniak signed their cards, as the two players were dealt before the set was released. These cards are marked below as DNS. Cards are not numbered, so they appear alphabetically.

COMPLETE SET (27) 40.00 100.00
1 Kris Beech 4.00 10.00
2 Pavel Brendl 4.00 7.00
3 Michael Bubnick 1.20 3.00
4 Jared Carli 1.20 3.00
5 Dean Clark CO 1.20 3.00
6 Eric Clark DNS .10 .25
7 Sean Connors 1.20 3.00
8 Wade Davis 1.20 3.00
9 Jeff Feniak DNS .10 .25
10 Owen Fussey 1.20 3.00
11 Robin Gomez 1.20 5.00
12 Matt Kinch 2.80 7.00
13 Brent Krahn 4.00 10.00
14 Jordan Krestanovich 4.00 10.00
15 Anders Lovdahl 2.00 5.00
16 Jeff Maher ACO 1.20 3.00
17 Sean McAslan 1.20 3.00
18 Brad Moran 2.80 7.00
19 Chris Nielsen 2.80 7.00
20 Shaun Norrie 1.20 3.00
21 Rod Sarich 1.20 3.00
22 Brandon Segal 1.20 3.00
23 Kenton Smith 2.00 5.00
24 Jerred Smithson 1.20 3.00
25 Vulk Mascot .40 1.00
26 Calgary Herald .01
27 Playstation Coupon .01

2000-01 Calgary Hitmen

This set features the Hitmen of the WHL. The set was produced by the team, and sold at its souvenir stands at home games.

COMPLETE SET (28) 6.00 15.00
1 Toni Bader .20 .50
2 Kris Beech .40 1.00
3 Brady Block .20 .50
4 John Boychuk .40 1.00
5 Adam Breitkreuz .20 .50
6 Pavel Brendl .60 1.00
7 Michael Bubnick .20 .50
8 Jared Carli .20 .50
9 Dean Clark CO .10 .25
10 Wade Davis .20 .50
11 Mike Egener .20 .50
12 Dan Ehrman .20 .50
13 Owen Fussey .20 .50
14 Robin Gomez .20 .50
15 Matt Kinch .20 .50
16 Brent Krahn .40 1.00
17 Jordan Krestanovich .20 .50
18 Jeff Maher CO .10 .25
19 Sean McAslan .20 .50
20 Shaun Norrie .20 .50
21 Rod Sarich .20 .50
22 Brandon Segal .20 .50
23 Shaun Sutter .20 .50
24 David Vrbata .20 .50
25 The Vulk MASCOT .04 .10
26 Chad Wolkowski .20 .50
27 Calgary Herald .01
28 Toys "R" Us .01

2001-02 Calgary Hitmen

This set features the Hitmen of the WHL. The set was sold by the team at its souvenir stands. The set is noteworthy for including the first card of 2002 first-rounder Fredrik Sjostrom.

COMPLETE SET (26) 4.80 12.00
1 Paul Albers .20 .50

2 Kyle Annesley .20 .50
3 Tyler Beechey .30 .75
4 Johnny Boychuk .40 1.00
5 Adam Breitkreuz .20 .50
6 Michael Bubnick .20 .50
7 Jared Carli .20 .50
8 Wade Davis .20 .50
9 Mike Egener .20 .50
10 Dan Ehrman .20 .50
11 Owen Fussey .20 .75
12 Richard Kromm CO .04 .10
13 Sebastien LaPlante .20 .50
14 Jeff Maher ACO .04 .10
15 Ryan Martin .30 .75
16 Lance Morrison .20 .50
17 Ryan Papaioannou .20 .50
18 Wes Rypien .20 .50
19 Rod Sarich .20 .50
20 Brandon Segal .30 .75
21 Dennis Sergeyev .20 .50
22 Mark Shefchyk .20 .50
23 Fredrik Sjostrom .80 2.00
24 Rob Smith .20 .50
25 The Vulk MASCOT .01
26 Chad Wolkowski .20 .50

2001-02 Calgary Hitmen Autographed

This set features the Hitmen of the WHL. The set was sold in autographed form at team souvenir stands. Unfortunately, the card of team mascot The Vulk is not autographed. The cards are unnumbered, and so are listed below in alphabetical order.

COMPLETE SET (26) 20.00 50.00
1 Paul Albers .80 2.00
2 Kyle Annesley .80 2.00
3 Tyler Beechey 1.20 3.00
4 Johnny Boychuk 1.60 5.00
5 Adam Breitkreuz .80 2.00
6 Michael Bubnick .80 2.00
7 Jared Carli .80 2.00
8 Wade Davis .80 2.00
9 Mike Egener .80 2.00
10 Dan Ehrman .80 2.00
11 Owen Fussey .80 4.00
12 Richard Kromm CO .40 1.00
13 Sebastien LaPlante .80 2.00
14 Jeff Maher ACO .40 1.00
15 Ryan Martin 1.20 3.00
16 Lance Morrison .80 2.00
17 Ryan Papaioannou .80 2.00
18 Wes Rypien .80 2.00
19 Rod Sarich .80 2.00
20 Brandon Segal 1.20 3.00
21 Dennis Sergeyev .80 2.00
22 Mark Shefchyk .80 2.00
23 Fredrik Sjostrom 4.00 10.00
24 Rob Smith .80 2.00
25 The Vulk MASCOT .01
26 Chad Wolkowski .80 2.00

2002-03 Calgary Hitmen

COMPLETE SET (26) 8.00 18.00
1 Lance Morrison .20 .50
2 Michael Bubnick .20 .50
3 Gary Gladue .20 .50
4 Kris Deines .20 .50
5A Kyle Annesley .20 .50
6 Rob Smith .20 .50
7 Mark Shefchyk .20 .50
8 Bruno Campese ACO .02 .10
9 Richard Kromm HCO .02 .10
10 Mascot .02 .10
11 Fredrik Sjostrom .40 1.00
12 Wade Davis .20 .50
13 Paul Albers .20 .50
14 Patrick Wellar .20 .50
15 Marc Lesage .20 .50
16 Aaron Boogaard .20 .50
17 Jiri Cetkovsky .20 .50
18 Brandon Segal .20 .50
19 Owen Fussey .20 .50
20 Tyler Feakes .20 .50
21 Andy Rogers .20 .50
22 Steven Covington .20 .50
23 Johnny Boychuk .40 1.00
24 Michael Egener .40 1.00
25 Brent Krahn .40 1.00
26 Ryan Getzlaf 2.00 5.00

2003-04 Calgary Hitmen

COMPLETE SET (21) 6.00 15.00
1 Scott Bowles .30 .75
2 Brett Carson .20 .50
3 Dmitri Chupilkin .20 .50
4 Steve Covington .20 .50
5 Kris Deines .20 .50
6 Mike Egener .30 .75
7 Gerry Festa .30 .75
8 Paul Gentile .20 .50
9 Ryan Getzlaf 1.00 2.50
10 Dustin Kohn .20 .50
11 Andrew Ladd .75 2.00
12 Shaun Landolt .20 .50
13 Riley Merkley .20 .50
14 Andy Rogers .20 .50
15 Mark Rooneem .20 .50
16 Jeff Schultz .20 .50
17 Brandon Segal .20 .50
18 Tomas Troliga .20 .50
19 Patrick Wellar .20 .50
20 Darryl Yacboski .20 .50
21 Lee Zalasky .20 .50

2004-05 Calgary Hitmen

COMPLETE SET (25) 15.00 25.00
1 Karl Alzner .60 1.50
2 Brett Carlson .30 .75
3 Steven Covington .30 .75
4 Keegan Dansereau .30 .75
5 Brodie Dupont .30 .75
6 Ryan Getzlaf .60 2.00
7 Tyler Harder .30 .75
8 Dustin Kohn .30 .75
9 Andrew Ladd .60 1.50
10 Shaun Landolt .30 .75
11 Tyrel Lucas .30 .75
12 Riley Merkley .30 .75
13 Darryl Moscaluk .30 .75
14 Brett O'Malley .30 .75
15 Justin Pogge 2.00 5.00
16 Konstantin Pushkarev .40 1.00
17 Isaac Reid .30 .75
18 Jeff Schultz .40 1.00
19 Daniel Spence .30 .75
20 Ryan White .30 .75
21 Darryl Yacboski .30 .75
22 Dylan Yeo .30 .75
23 Dean Evason Kelly Kisio CO .02 .10
24 Blaine Forsythe ACO Farley MASCOT .02 .10
25 Ryan Getzlaf/Calgary Herald .60 1.50

2005-06 Calgary Hitmen

COMPLETE SET (28) 8.00 15.00
1 Karl Alzner .40 1.00
2 Brett Carson .30 .75
3 Steve Covington .30 .75
4 Keegan Dansereau .30 .75
5 Kris Deines .30 .75
6 Brodie Dupont .30 .75
7 Curtis Kelner .30 .75
8 Derek LeBlanc .30 .75
9 Ryan Letts .30 .75
10 Craig Lineker .30 .75
11 Carson McMillan .30 .75
12 Riley Merkley .30 .75
13 Shaden Moore .30 .75
14 Fredrik Pettersson .30 .75
15 Alexandre Plante .30 .75
16 Justin Pogge 1.25 3.00
17 Mike Reich .30 .75
18 Jeff Schultz .30 .75
19 Brett Sonne .40 1.00
20 Daniel Spence .30 .75
21 Lukas Vantuch .40 1.00
22 Ryan White .40 1.00
23 Dylan Yeo .30 .75
24 Kelly Kisio CO .10 .25
25 Blaine Forsythe ACO .10 .25
26 Dave Lowry ACO .10 .25
27 Farley the Fox MASCOT .10 .25
28 SPONSORS .01 .01

2003-04 Camrose Kodiaks

Team-issued set from the Tier 2 BCJHL. The cards are not numbered. Checklist courtesy of collector Vinnie Montalbano.

COMPLETE SET (25) 6.00 15.00
1 Dan Bertram .40 1.00
2 Steve Bounds .30 .75
3 MacGregor Sharp .30 .75
4 Jared Veuger .30 .75
5 Jody Pederson .30 .75
6 Matt McKnight .30 .75
7 Travis Friedley .30 .75
8 Kyle Smith .30 .75
9 Rob MacIntyre .30 .75
10 Owen Langis .30 .75
11 Mason Raymond .30 .75
12 Ryan Muspratt .30 .75
13 Ryan Antoniuk .30 .75
14 Chance Olsen .30 .75
15 Logan Gorsalitz .30 .75
16 Ryan Armstrong .30 .75
17 Lee Jubinville .30 .75
18 Justin Taylor .30 .75
19 Chris Wanchulak .30 .75
20 Justin Blacklock .30 .75
21 Todd Steil .30 .75
22 Bob Graham .30 .75
23 David Thompson .30 .75
24 Ryan Muth .30 .75
25 Coaches .02 .10

2004-05 Camrose Kodiaks

The Kodiaks are a Tier 2 Alberta Junior Hockey League squad. This set may not be complete. Additional information can be forwarded to hockeymag@beckett.com.

COMPLETE SET (16?)
1 Jody Pederson 1.00
2 Kirk Irving 1.00
3 Clark Thompson 1.00
4 Ryan Mayko 1.00
5 Logan Gorsalitz 1.00
6 Lee Jubinville 1.00
7 Todd Steil 1.00
8 Derek Wolbeck 1.00
9 Kyle Parkes 1.00
10 MacGregor Sharp 1.00
11 Chance Olsen 1.00
12 David Thompson 1.00
13 Mason Raymond 1.00
14 A.J. Nelson 1.00
15 Jason Roberts 1.00
16 Travis Friedley 1.00

1994-95 Cape Breton Oilers

This 23-card standard-size set was manufactured and distributed by Jessen Associates, Inc. for Classic. The cards are unnumbered and checklisted below in alphabetical order.

COMPLETE SET (23) 4.80 12.00
1 Scott Allison .16 .40
2 Martin Bakula .16 .40
3 Ladislav Benysek .16 .40
4 Dennis Bonvie .30 .75
5 Jozef Cierny .16 .40
6 Duane Dennis .16 .40
7 Greg DeVries .30 .75
8 Joaquin Gage .30 .75
9 Ian Herbers .16 .40
10 Ralph Intranuovo .16 .40
11 Claude Jutras .16 .40
12 Marc LaForge .16 .40
13 Todd Marchant .40 1.00
14 Darcy Martini .16 .40
15 Roman Oksiuta .16 .40
16 David Oliver .30 .75
17 Steve Passmore .40 1.00
18 Nick Stajduhar .16 .40
19 John Van Kessel .16 .40
20 David Vyborny .16 .40
21 Peter White .16 .40
22 Tyler Wright .30 .75
23 Brad Zavisha .16 .40

2001-02 Cape Breton Screaming Eagles

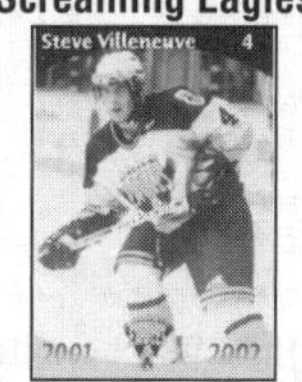

This set features the Screaming Eagles of the QMJHL. The set was produced by CTM Ste-Foy and was sold at Eagles home games. It was reported that less than 1,000 sets were produced.

COMPLETE SET (23) 6.00 15.00
1 Steve Villeneuve .20 .50
2 Maxime Lessard .20 .50
3 Pierre-Luc Laprise .20 .50
4 David Cloutier .20 .50
5 Stuart MacRae .20 .50
6 Dominic Noel .20 .50
7 Jean-Philipe Cote .20 .50
8 Martin Kasik .20 .50
9 Steve Dixon .30 .75
10 Marc-Olivier Vary .20 .50
11 Justin Hawco .20 .50
12 Pierre-Luc Emond .20 .50
13 Guillaume Demers .20 .50
14 Rodrigue Boucher .20 .50
15 George Davis .20 .50
16 Andre Martineau .20 .50
17 Carl McLean .20 .50
18 Pascal Morency .20 .50
19 Mathieu Dumas .20 .50
20 Jean-Francois Dufort .20 .50
21 Marc-Andre Fleury 2.00 5.00
22 Jasen Awalt .20 .50
23 Kevin Asselin .20 .50

2002-03 Cape Breton Screaming Eagles

The cards are not numbered are are listed below in the order they appear on the checklist card.

COMPLETE SET (25) 6.00 15.00
1 Marc-Andre Fleury 1.25 3.00
2 Martin Houle .60 1.50
3 Maxime Lessard .15 .40
4 Nathan Veinot .30 .75
5 Maxime Robert .15 .40
6 Jean-Claude Sawyer .15 .40
7 Vincent Zaore-Vanie .15 .40
8 Stephen Dixon .30 .75
9 Martin Slovak .15 .40
10 Joel Maas .15 .40
11 Pierre-Luc Emond .15 .40
12 Guillaume Demers .15 .40
13 Gregory Hoffe .15 .40
14 Jonathan Labelle .15 .40
15 Kevin Asselin .15 .40
16 Jared Vokey .15 .40
17 Michel Charette .15 .40
18 Samuel Beland .15 .40
19 Jean-Francois Dufort .30 .75
20 Patrick Gilbert .15 .40
21 Martin Trempe .15 .40
22 Steeve Villeneuve .15 .40
23 Stuart McRae .15 .40
24 Jean-Philippe Cote .15 .40
25 George Davis .15 .40
26 Marc-Andre Fleury CL 1.25 3.00

2003-04 Cape Breton Screaming Eagles

COMPLETE SET (24) 6.00 15.00
2 Adam Pardy .20 .50
4 Steve Villeneuve .20 .50
6 Tim Ramholt .20 .50
8 Nathan Veinot .20 .50
11 Francois-Pierre Guenette .20 .50
12 Jean-Claude Sawyer .20 .50
13 Vincent Zaore-Vanie .20 .50
14 Stephen Dixon .30 .75
15 Alexandre Picard .40 1.00
18 Guillaume Demers .20 .50
19 Gregory Hoffe .20 .50
20 Neil Smith .20 .50
21 Michael Tessier .20 .50
22 Kevin Asselin .20 .50
23 Jean-Francois Cyr .20 .50
24 Charles Fontaine .20 .50
26 Samuel Beland .20 .50
27 Philippe Bertrand .20 .50
28 Vincent Lambert .20 .50
29 Marc-Andre Fleury 1.25 3.00
30 Francois Proteau .30 .75
31 Martin Houle .40 1.00
41 Marc-Andre Bernier .40 1.00
84 Nicolas Corbeil .30 .75

2004-05 Cape Breton Screaming Eagles

A total of 750 team sets were produced.

COMPLETE SET (23) 5.00 12.00
1 Martin Houle .40 1.00
2 Kevin Asselin .20 .50
3 Stephen Dixon .30 .75
4 Samuel Beland .20 .50
5 Philippe Bertrand .20 .50
6 Chris Culligan .20 .50
7 Guillaume Demers .20 .50
8 Charles Fontaine .20 .50
9 Luke Gallant .20 .50
10 Vladimir Kubus .20 .50
11 Vincent Lambert .20 .50
12 Brendon MacDonald .20 .50
13 Dean Ouellet .20 .50
14 Adam Pardy .20 .50
15 Leonard Puterman .20 .50
16 Jean-Claude Sawyer .20 .50
17 James Sheppard .60 1.50
18 Neil Smith .20 .50
19 Francois Theriault .20 .50
20 David Victor .20 .50
21 Tyler Whitehead .20 .50
22 Vincent Zaore .20 .50
23 David Davenport .20 .50

2005-06 Cape Breton Screaming Eagles

COMPLETE SET (25) 5.00 12.00
1 James Sheppard .50 1.25
2 Ondrej Pavelec .30 .75
3 Jason Swit .20 .50
4 David Victor .20 .50
5 Darrell Simich .20 .50
6 Chris Culligan .20 .50
7 Robert Slaney .20 .50
8 Dean Ouellet .20 .50
9 Vladimir Kubus .20 .50
10 Brad Gallant .20 .50
11 Jean-Claude Sawyer .20 .50
12 Francois Gauthier .20 .50
13 Philippe Bertrand .20 .50
14 Scott Brannon .20 .50
15 Etienne Breton .20 .50
16 Jeff Grenier .20 .50
17 Brendon MacDonald .20 .50
18 Kevin Asselin .20 .50
19 Francois Theriault .20 .50
20 Charles Fontaine .20 .50
21 Vincent Zaore .20 .50
22 David Davenport .20 .50
23 Paul McIlveen .20 .50
24 Cam Fergus .20 .50
25 Alexandre Blais .20 .50

2006-07 Cape Breton Screaming Eagles

COMPLETE SET (25) 8.00 15.00
1 James Sheppard .60 1.50
2 Ã‰tienne Breton .30 .75
3 Jason Swit .30 .75
4 Daniel Fazzalari .30 .75
5 Chris Culligan .30 .75
6 Robert Sanley .30 .75
7 Dean Ouellet .30 .75
8 Scott Brannon .30 .75
9 Brad Gallant .30 .75
10 Jean-Claude Sawyer .30 .75
11 Cam Fergus .30 .75
12 Jean-Christophe Gauthier .30 .75
13 Oskars Bartulis .30 .75
14 Alexandre Quesnel .30 .75
15 FranÃ§ois Gauthier .30 .75
16 Stephen Ceccanese .30 .75
17 Brendon Macdonald .30 .75
18 Charlie Pens .30 .75
19 Mark Barberio .30 .75
20 Mickey Macdonald .30 .75
21 Nick Macneil .30 .75
22 Paul Mcilveen .30 .75
23 Ondrej Pavelec .40 1.00
24 David Davenport .30 .75
25 Screech MASCOT .02 .10

2003-04 Cape Fear Fire Antz

This set features the fearsome Fire Antz of the SEHL. According to minor league expert Ralph Slate, the cards seem to have been put together by hand, with two matte photo pieces of paper glued together.

COMPLETE SET (17) 15.00 30.00
1 David Bagley .75 2.00
2 Mike Bournazakis .75 2.00
3 Kevin Fines .75 2.00
4 Ryan Kiley .75 2.00
5 Matt Kohanskey .75 2.00
6 Dave Leger .75 2.00
7 Mike Maurice .75 2.00
8 Darren McLean .75 2.00
9 Chris Migliore .75 2.00
10 Marc Milburn .75 2.00
11 Glenn Ridler 1.00 2.50
12 Tim Rink .75 2.00
13 Matt Shannon .75 2.00
14 Aaron Shrieves .75 2.00
15 Rob Vessio .75 2.00
16 Scott Young .75 2.00
17 Scott Rex CO .25

1996-97 Carolina Monarchs

This 30-card set was released by Multi-Ad services and sponsored by Taco Bell, whose logo appears on the front of the card. This set is not numbered so the cards appear alphabetically.

COMPLETE SET (30) 4.80 12.00
1 Checklist .04 .10
2 Chris Armstrong .16 .40
3 Drake Berehowsky .30 .75
4 Ashley Buckberger .16 .40
5 Chad Cabana .16 .40
6 Jon Christiano ACO .16 .40
7 Gilbert Dionne .30 .75
8 Trevor Doyle .16 .40
9 Ivan Droppa .16 .40
10 Craig Ferguson .20 .50
11 Craig Fisher .16 .40
12 Bob Halkidis .16 .40
13 Ryan Johnson .16 .40
14 Richard Kromm HCO .04 .10
15 Filip Kuba .16 .40
16 David Lemanowicz .10 .25
17 Craig Martin .20 .50
18 Eric Montreuil .16 .40
19 David Nemirovsky .16 .40
20 Jason Podollan .16 .40
21 Gaetan Poirier .16 .40
22 Garin Smith .16 .40
23 Geoff Smith .16 .40
24 Herbert Vasiljevs .16 .40
25 Steve Washburn .20 .50
26 Kevin Weekes .40 1.00
27 Dean Ayonce .16 .40
28 Monty MASCOT .04 .10
29 Prospect Card .16 .40
30 PHPA Web Site .01

2006-07 Cedar Rapids RoughRiders

COMPLETE SET (25) 10.00 20.00
1 Richard Bachman .40 1.00
2 Robin Bergman .40 1.00
3 David Boehm .40 1.00
4 Aaron Bogosian .40 1.00
5 Rob Bordson .40 1.00
6 Pat Cannone .40 1.00
7 Jacob Cepis .40 1.00
8 Brett Dickinson .40 1.00
9 Doug Jones .40 1.00
10 Sergei Kolosov .40 1.00
11 Scott Mathis .40 1.00
12 Kent Patterson .40 1.00
13 Mike Seidel .40 1.00
14 Ian Slater .40 1.00
15 Tomi Stahlhammer .40 1.00
16 Evan Stephens .40 1.00

17 Tyler Thompson .40 1.00
18 Matt Tomassoni .40 1.00
19 Kevin Wehrs .40 1.00
20 Casey Wellman .40 1.00
21 Scott Wietecha .40 1.00
22 Tommy Wingels .40 1.00
23 Mark Carlson CO .10 .25
24 Joe Exter ACO .10 .25
25 Ricochet MASCOT .02 .10

1994-95 Central Hockey League

This 127-card standard-size set features the seven teams of the Central Hockey League. Reportedly only 13,000 of each card were produced. The cards were available in pack form only, either at team rinks or from the league for 3.00 by mail. The fronts feature borderless color action player photos except on the left, where a gray bar edges the picture and carries the CHL logo, the player's name and number, and the team logo. On a white background with light gray team logos, the horizontal backs carry a short player biography, profile and stats. The cards are unnumbered, grouped alphabetically within teams and checklisted below alphabetically according to teams as follows: Dallas Freeze (1-18), Ft. Worth Fire (19-36), Memphis Riverkings (37-54), Oklahoma City Blazers (55-72), San Antonio Iguanas (73-90), Tulsa Oilers (91-108), and Wichita Thunder (109-126).

COMPLETE SET (127) 16.00 40.00
1 Jamie Adams .16 .40
2 Wayne Anchikoski .20 .50
3 Jeff Beaudin .16 .40
4 Troy Binnie .20 .50
5 Don Burke .16 .40
6 Derek Crawford .16 .40
7 Ray Desouza .16 .40
8 Ron Flockhart CO .16 .40
9 Jon Gustafson .20 .50
10 Jason Heiland .16 .40
11 James Jensen .16 .40
12 Frank LaScala .16 .40
13 Ryan Leschasin .16 .40
14 Rob Madia .16 .40
15 Rob McCaig .16 .40
16 Jim McGeough .20 .50
17 Doug Roberts .16 .40
18 Jason Taylor .16 .40
19 Scott Allen .16 .40
20 Bruce Bell .20 .50
21 Francois Bourdeau .16 .40
22 Troy Frederick .16 .40
23 Steve Harrison CO .16 .40
24 Alex Kholomeyev .20 .50
25 Dominic Maltais .20 .50
26 Martin Masa .20 .50
27 Jeff Massey .16 .40
28 Mike McCormick .16 .40
29 Pat McGarry .20 .50
30 Dwight Mullins .16 .40
31 Eric Ricard .16 .40
32 Sean Rowe .16 .40
33 Bryan Schoen .16 .40
34 Darren Srochenski .16 .40
35 Andy Stewart .16 .40
36 Stephen Tepper .16 .40
37 Denis Beauchamp .16 .40
38 Herb Boxer CO .16 .40
39 Nicolas Brousseau .16 .40
40 Scott Brower .20 .50
41 Dan Brown .16 .40
42 Brian Cook .16 .40
43 Brent Fleetwood .16 .40
44 Francois Gagon .16 .40
45 Dominic Grand-Maison .16 .40
46 Kyle Haviland .16 .40
47 Jamie Hearn .16 .40
48 Mike Jackson .20 .50
49 Paul Krake .20 .50
50 Layne LeBel .16 .40
51 Steve Magnusson .16 .40
52 Mark McGinn .16 .40
53 Darren Miciak .16 .40
54 Bobby Wallwork .20 .50
55 Ron Aubrey .20 .50
56 Joe Burton .20 .50
57 George Dupont .20 .50
58 Tom Gomes .16 .40
59 Sean Gorman .16 .40
60 Viktor Ignatjev .20 .50
61 Chris Laganas .16 .40
62 Michael McEwen CO .20 .50
63 Chris McMurtry .16 .40
64 Derry Menard .16 .40
65 Sergei Naumov .20 .50
66 Trent Pankewicz .16 .40
67 Alan Perry .30 .75
68 Eric Plante .16 .40
69 Dave Slifka .16 .40
70 Steve Simoni .16 .40
71 Michel St. Jacques .16 .40
72 Tom Thornbury .16 .40
73 Trevor Buchanan .16 .40
74 Link Gaetz .30 .75
75 Sean Goldsworthy .16 .40
76 Fred Goltz .16 .40
77 Sheldon Gorski .16 .40
78 Ross Harris .16 .40
79 Dale Henry .20 .50
80 Paul Jackson .30 .75
81 Scot Kelsey .16 .40
82 John Klaers .16 .40
83 Stu Kulak .20 .50
84 Ken Plaquin .16 .40
85 Brian Shantz .20 .50
86 Dean Shmyr .16 .40
87 Adam Thompson .16 .40
88 John Torchetti .16 .40
89 Ken Venis .16 .40
90 Mike Williams .16 .40
91 Colin Baustad .16 .40
92 Luc Beausoleil .20 .50
93 Mike Berger .16 .40
94 Mark Cavallin .16 .40
95 Shaun Clouston .16 .40
96 Michel Couvrette .16 .40
97 Taylor Hall .16 .40
98 Ryan Harrison .16 .40
99 Sasha Lakovic .30 .75
100 Chuck Loreto .16 .40
101 Tony Martino .20 .50
102 David Moore .16 .40
103 Sylvain Naud .20 .50
104 Dan O'Rourke .16 .40
105 Jody Praznik .16 .40
106 Andy Ross .16 .40
107 Mike Shea .16 .40
108 Garry Unger CO .30 .75
109 Bob Berg .16 .40
110 John DePourcq .20 .50
111 Dave Doucette .20 .50
112 Ron Handy .20 .50
113 Mark Hilton .16 .40
114 Darcy Kaminski .16 .40
115 Mark Karpen .16 .40
116 Jim Latos .16 .40
117 George Maneluk .20 .50
118 Greg Neish .16 .40
119 Brent Sapergia .30 .75
120 Doug Shedden CO .20 .50
121 Greg Smith .16 .40
122 Conrade Thomas .16 .40
123 John Vary .16 .40
124 Rob Weingartner .16 .40
125 Bryan Wells .16 .40
126 Jack Williams .16 .40
127 Title Card CL .16 .40

1995-96 Central Hockey League

This set features the players of the Central Hockey League. The cards feature action photography on the front ensconced in a gray marble border, highlighted by the team logo in the top left corner. The backs contain another photo, and player information. The cards are unnumbered, so they are listed alphabetically by team, and then by name. They were available in packs at CHL games.

COMPLETE SET (90) 14.00 35.00
1 Scott Allen .16 .40
2 Trevor Burgess .16 .40
3 Brian Caruso .16 .40
4 Trevor Converse .16 .40
5 Steve Dykstra .30 .75
6 Troy Frederick .16 .40
7 Phil Groeneveld .16 .40
8 Mark Hilton .20 .50
9 Jeff Massey .16 .40
10 Dennis Miller .16 .40
11 Dwight Mullins .16 .40
12 Steve Plouffe .30 .75
13 Vern Ray .16 .40
14 Kyle Reeves .30 .75
15 Troy Stephens .16 .40
16 Sean Whyte .20 .50
17 Scorch .16 .10
18 Bill McDonald .16 .40
19 Scott Brower .20 .50
20 Dan Brown .16 .40
21 Jamie Cooke .16 .40
22 Kevin Evans .16 .40
23 Brent Fleetwood .16 .40
24 Ron Fogarty .16 .40
25 Trent Gleason .16 .40
26 Derek Grant .16 .40
27 Mike Jackson .30 .75
28 Scot Kelsey .16 .40
29 Steve Magnusson .16 .40
30 Carl Menard .30 .75
31 Chris Morque .20 .50
32 Rick Robus .16 .40
33 Andy Ross .16 .40
34 Stephane Roy .30 .75
35 Doug Stromback .16 .40
36 Herb Boxer .16 .40
37 Kevin Barrett .16 .40
38 Carl Boudreau .30 .75
39 Joe Burton .30 .75
40 George Dupont .20 .50
41 Dominic Fafard .16 .40
42 Jean-Ian Filiatrault .16 .40
43 Tom Gomes .16 .40
44 Todd Harris .16 .40
45 Mervin Kopeck .16 .40
46 Doug Lawrence .30 .75
47 Kevin Lune .16 .40
48 Steve Moore .16 .40
49 Simon Olivier .16 .40
50 Darren Pengelly .16 .40
51 Steve Simoni .16 .40
52 Barkley Swenson .16 .40
53 Serge Tkachenko .20 .50
54 Doug Sauter .16 .40
55 Colin Baustad .16 .40
56 Mike Berger .16 .40
57 Mike Chase .16 .40
58 Trevor Ellerman .16 .40
59 Bryan Forslund .16 .40
60 Taylor Hall .16 .40
61 Craig Hamelin .16 .40
62 Ryan Harrison .16 .40
63 John Laan .16 .40
64 Glen Lang .16 .40
65 Dave Larouche .16 .40
66 Tony Martino .30 .75
67 Sylvain Naud .30 .75
68 Jim Peters .16 .40
69 Cory Peterson .16 .40
70 Chris Robertson .16 .40
71 Kyuin Shim .16 .40
72 Garry Unger .30 .75
73 Clint Black .16 .40
74 Mike Chighisola .16 .40
75 Leonard Devuono .16 .40
76 Ty Eigner .30 .75
77 Anton Fedorov .20 .50
78 Paul Krake .30 .75
79 Antonin Necas .16 .40
80 Ryan Pisiak .16 .40
81 Richard Roesler .16 .40
82 Jason Rushton .16 .40
83 Art Saran .16 .40
84 Stefan Simoes .16 .40
85 Greg Smith .16 .40
86 Dale Thornbull .16 .40
87 Rob Weingartner .16 .40
88 Bryan Wells .16 .40
89 Jack Williams .16 .40
90 Don Jackson .30 .75

1997-98 Central Texas Stampede

Little is known about this set other than the confirmed checklist. Additional information can be forwarded to hockeymag@beckett.com.

COMPLETE SET (20) 3.60 9.00
1 Matt Brenner .20 .50
2 Mike Dick .20 .50
3 Darren Duncalfe .20 .50
4 Larry Dyck .20 .50
5 Dwayne Gylywoychuk .20 .50
6 Ricky Jacob .20 .50
7 Peter Jas .20 .50
8 Dean Kolstad .30 .75
9 Jacques Mailhot .30 .75
10 Don McGrath .20 .50
11 Derek Nicolson .20 .50
12 Jeff Rask .20 .50
13 Layne Roland .20 .50
14 Alex Rummo .20 .50
15 Doug Smith .20 .50
16 Greg Smith .20 .50
17 Joe Tassone .20 .50
18 Jason Taylor .20 .50
19 Peter Zurba .20 .50
20 Wild Thing Mascot .04 .10

1996-97 Charlotte Checkers

This set was only available at the bakery department of a Charlotte Super Shop & Save grocery store, and thus is extremely difficult to find in the secondary market.

COMPLETE SET (20) 14.00 35.00
1 J.F. Aube .80 2.00
2 Eric Boulton .80 5.00
3 David Brosseau .80 2.00
4 Jeff Connolly .80 2.00
5 Kimbi Daniels .80 2.00
6 Mickey Elick .80 2.00
7 Eric Fenton .80 2.00
8 Mick Kempffer .80 2.00
9 Jay Kenney .80 2.00
10 Scott Kirton .80 2.00
11 Darcy Mitani .80 2.00
12 Darryl Norlen .80 2.00
13 Kevin Rappana .80 2.00
14 Matt Robbins .80 2.00
15 Evgeni Ryabchikov .80 2.00
16 Kurt Seher .80 2.00
17 Nick Vitucci 1.20 3.00
18 Shawn Wheeler .80 2.00
19 John Marks HCO .80 2.00
20 Chubby Checker Mascot .20 .10

1997-98 Charlotte Checkers

This 26-card set was given away by both the bakery of a Charlotte Hannaford grocery store and sold by the team. Note: three versions of card #25 exist.

COMPLETE SET (28) 15.00 30.00
1 Matt Alvey .40 1.00
2 Eric Boulton 1.25 3.00
3 David Brosseau .40 1.00
4 Paxton Schafer .60 1.50
5 Kurt Seher .40 1.00
6 Stephane Soulliere .40 1.00
7 Derek Crimin .40 1.00
8 Eric Flinton .40 1.00
9 Justin Gould .40 1.00
10 Jason Kelly .40 1.00
11 Mike Hartman .40 1.00
12 Jeff Heil .40 1.00
13 Jay Kenney .40 1.00
14 Mitt Mastad .40 1.00
15 Dean Moore .40 1.00
16 Darryl Noren .40 1.00
17 Dale Purinton 1.25 3.00
18 Andre Roy 1.25 3.00
19 P.C. Drouin .60 1.50
20 Bill McCauley .40 1.00
21 Shawn Wheeler ACO .04 .10
22 John Marks HCO .04 .10
23 Chubby Checker Mascot .04 .10
24 Checklist .01
25 Eric Flinton CAP .60 1.50
25 Darryl Noren CAP .60 1.50
25 Kurt Seher CAP .60 1.50
26 PHPA Web Site .01

1998-99 Charlotte Checkers

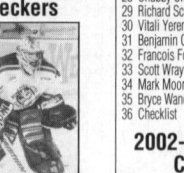

This set was issued as a promotional giveaway through a local grocery store named Hannaford's. As such, it is extremely difficult to find on the secondary market.

COMPLETE SET (24) 10.00 25.00
1 J.F. Aube .60 1.50
2 Shannon Basaraba .40 1.00
3 Doug Battaglia .40 1.00
4 David Brosseau .40 1.00
5 Tom Brown .40 1.00
6 Pat Brownlee .40 1.00
7 Brooke Chateau .40 1.00
8 Jeff Heil .40 1.00
9 Boyd Kane .60 1.50
10 Kevin Kreutzer .40 1.00
11 Darryl Noren .60 1.50
12 Jason Norrie .40 1.00
13 Nikolai Pronin .40 1.00
14 Kurt Seher .60 1.50
15 Bob Sheehan .40 1.00
16 Ryan Sittler .40 1.00
17 Martin Sychra .40 1.00
18 Dean Zayonce .40 1.00
19 Shawn Wheeler CO .10 .25
20 Chubby Checker .10 .25
21 The Captains .40 1.00
22 Doug Battaglia .40 1.00
Pat Brownlee
23 J.F. Aube .60 1.00
Bob Sheehan
24 Checklist .04 .10

1999-00 Charlotte Checkers

This set features the Checkers of the ECHL. The cards were produced by Roox, and handed out as promotional giveaways over the course of several home games.

COMPLETE SET (38) 8.00 20.00
1 Jason Dailey .20 .50
2 Brooke Chateau .20 .50
3 Rocky Welsing .20 .50
4 Kurt Seher .20 .50
5 Kevin Hilton .20 .50
6 Reggie Brezeault .20 .50
7 Lee Hamilton .20 .50
8 Dave Risk .20 .50
9 Taras Lendzyk .20 .50
10 Kurt Mallett .20 .50
11 Tyler Deis .20 .50
12 Mike Rucinski .30 .75
13 Derek Wilkinson .40 1.00
14 Richard Scott .30 1.00
15 David Beauregard .30 .75
16 Mike Jaros .20 .50
17 Darryl Noren .20 .50
18 Marc Tropper .20 .50
19 Scott Bailey .40 1.00
20 Jeff Brown .20 .50
21 Boyd Kane .30 1.00
22 Chubby Checker MASCOT .10 .10
23 The Carolina Cup .10 .10
24 Brooke Chateau .20 .50
24 Marc Tropper .30 .75
25 Mark Burgess TR .10 .10
26 Don MacAdam CO .10 .10
27 Scott Bailey .40 1.00
28 Dean Mando .30 .75
29 Kevin Pozzo .20 .50
30 Martin Cerven .20 .50
31 Marc Tropper AS .30 .75
32 Scott Bailey .40 1.00
33 Mike Rucinski .40 1.00
34 David Beauregard .30 .75
34 Tyler Deis .20 .50
35 Darryl Noren .20 .50
36 Checklist .04 .01

2000-01 Charlotte Checkers

This set features the Checkers of the ECHL. It is believed that it was issued as a promotional giveaway over two home games, then later sold by the team at its souvenir stands.

COMPLETE SET (36) 10.00 25.00
1 Jason Labarbera .60 1.50
2 Scott Bailey .40 1.00
3 Scott King .40 1.00
4 Marc Tropper .30 .75
5 Boyd Kane .30 .75
6 Justin Harney .30 .75
7 Kurt Seher .30 .75
8 Brad Mehalko .30 .75
9 Kevin Hilton .30 .75
10 Mathieu Benoit .30 .75
11 David Oliver .30 .75
12 Lee Hamilton .30 .75
13 Wes Jarvis .30 .75
14 Josh MacNevin .30 .75
15 Kevin Pozzo .30 .75
16 Don MacAdam HCO .08 .25
17 Dave Baseggio CO .08 .25
18 Chubby Checker MASCOT .08 .25
19 Paul Giblin .30 .75
20 Tyler Deis .30 .75
21 Mark Spence .30 .75
22 Bob MacIsaac .30 .75
23 Steve Duke .30 .75
24 Andre Signoretti .30 .75
25 Brandon Dietrich .30 .75
26 Mike Derecola .30 .75
27 Chris Plumhoff .30 .75
28 Chubby Checker MASCOT .08 .25
29 Richard Scott .40 1.00
30 Vitali Yeremeyev .60 1.50
31 Benjamin Carpentier .30 .75
32 Francois Fortier .30 .75
33 Scott Wray .30 .75
34 Mark Moore .30 .75
35 Bryce Wandler .30 .75
36 Checklist .08 .10

2002-03 Charlotte Checkers

COMPLETE SET (18) 20.00
79 Nicholas Bilotto 1.00
80 Kevin Caulfield 1.00
81 Brandon Cullen 1.50
82 Allan Egeland 1.00
83 David Evans 1.00
84 David Inman 1.00
85 Dusty Jamieson 1.00
86 Vince Malts 1.00
87 Walker McDonald 1.00
88 Konrad McKay 1.50
89 Scott Meyer 1.50
90 Eduard Pershin 1.00
91 Kurt Seher 1.00
92 Takahito Suzuki 1.50
94 Craig Weller 1.00
95 Chad Wilchynski 1.00
96 Colin Zulianello 1.00

2003-04 Charlotte Checkers

This set was produced by RBI Sports. The numbering below reflects the entire print run of the RBI ECHL set. It has been reported that just 250 copies of this set were produced.

COMPLETE SET (16) 15.00
65 Nicholas Bilotto 1.00
66 Kevin Caulfield 1.00
67 Doug Christiansen 1.00
68 Ryan Cuthbert 1.00
69 Allan Egeland 1.00
70 Blaz Emersic 1.00
71 Kengo Ito 1.00
72 Steven MacIntyre 1.00
73 Konrad McKay 1.00
74 Scott Meyer 1.50
75 Daisuke Obara 1.00
76 Rory Rawlyk 1.00
77 David St. Germain 1.50
78 Marc St. Jean 1.00
79 Jeff State 1.00
80 Mike Wirll 1.00

2002-03 Chicago Steel

This set features the Steel of the USHL.

COMPLETE SET (24) 20.00
1 Bill Bagron 1.00
2 Jordan Black 1.00
3 Dan Charleston 1.00
4 Adam D'Alba 1.50
5 Jeff Dunne 1.00
6 Josh Elzinga 1.00
7 Rene Gauthier 1.00
8 Ben Geelan 1.00
9 Brady Greco 1.50
10 Michael Grenzy 1.00
11 Eric Helstedt 1.00
12 Mike Kennedy 1.00
13 Vojtech Kloz 1.00
14 Justin Lewandowski 1.00
15 Travis Moran 1.00
16 Joseph Pearce 2.50
17 Topher Scott 1.00
18 Eric Slais 1.00
19 Chad Solberg 1.00
20 Alex Spezia 1.00
21 Lee Sweatt 1.00
22 Blake Williams 1.00
23 A.J. Toews CO .10
24 Rusty Steel MASCOT .10

2003-04 Chicago Steel

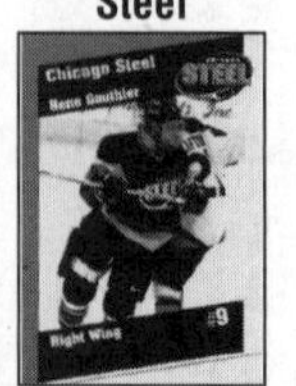

This set features the Steel of the USHL. Little is known about the set beyond the checklist info.

COMPLETE SET (18) 18.00
1 Matt McIlvane 1.50
2 Dan Marziani 1.00
3 Shane Connelly 1.50
4 Mike Van Wagner 1.00
5 Jay Sprague 1.00
6 Matt Clackson 1.00
7 Justin Lewandowski 1.00
8 Kevin Roeder 1.00
9 David Marshall 1.00
10 Chris Walsh 1.00
11 Jeff Dunne 1.00
12 Eric Lampe 1.00
13 Ryan Kim 1.00
14 John Kearns 1.00
15 Ryan Hawkins 1.00
16 T.J. Fox 1.00
17 Alex Spezia 1.00
18 Rene Gauthier
19 Rusty Steel MASCOT .10

2004-05 Chicago Steel

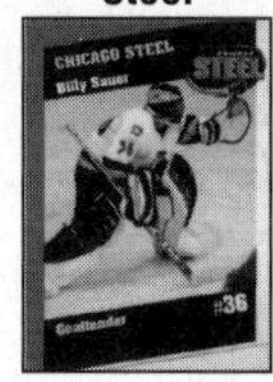

We have confirmed a handful of cards from this USHL set. If you have additional information, please contact us at hockeymag@beckett.com.

COMPLETE SET (?)
1 Nathan Perkovich 1.00
2 T.J. Fox 1.00
3 Kevin Swallow 1.00
4 Eric Slais 1.00
5 Billy Sauer 1.00
6 Shane Connelly 1.00
7 Chris Clackson 1.00
8 Sami Liimainen 1.00
9 Ryan Oldis 1.00
10 Joe Loprieno 1.00

1998-99 Chicago Wolves

This set features the Wolves of the IHL. The set was handed out at a game in March as a promotional item.

COMPLETE SET (25) 8.00 20.00
1 Brent Gretzky .40 1.00
2 Dan Plante .30 .75
3 Tim Bergland .30 .75
4 Steve Maltais .80 2.00
5 Steve Gosselin .40 1.00
6 Scott Pearson .30 .75
7 Niklas Andersson .40 1.00
8 Chris LiPuma .30 .75
9 Pat Jablonski .40 1.00
10 Skates MASCOT .04 .10
11 Tim Breslin .30 .75
12 Chris Marinucci .30 .75
13 Steve Larouche .40 1.00
14 Wendell Young .80 2.00
15 Glen Featherstone .30 .75
16 Bob Nardella .30 .75
17 Guy Larose .30 .75
18 Dennis Vial .40 1.00
19 Kevin Dahl .30 .75
20 Jeremy Mylymok .30 .75
21 Paul Koch .30 .75
22 Tom Tilley .30 .75
23 John Anderson HCO .20 .50
24 Kevin Miller .40 1.00
25 PHPA Web Site .01

1998-99 Chicago Wolves Turner Cup

This 24-card set was handed out at two separate games. It showcases players from the Turner Cup Championship team of 1997-98, although it was released in the 1998-99 season. Note: there at two different versions of card #3.

COMPLETE SET (25) 10.00 25.00
1 Wendell Young .75 2.00
2 John Anderson .20 .50
3 Dave Craievich .20 .50
3 Ray LeBlanc 1.25 3.00
4 Paul Koch .20 .50
5 Kevin Dahl .20 .50
6 Jeremy Mylymok .20 .50
7 Bob Nardella .20 .50
8 Marc Rodgers 1.25 3.00
9 Marc Potvin .75 2.00
10 Steve Larouche .40 1.00
11 Steve Maltais 1.25 3.00
12 Doug Barrault .20 .50
13 Jamie Baker .20 .50
14 Chris Marinucci .20 .50
15 Tim Breslin .20 .50
16 Dennis Vial 1.25 3.00
17 Tom Tilley .20 .50
18 Scott Pearson .20 .50
19 Steve Martins .30 .75
20 Matt Martin .20 .50
21 Tim Bergland .20 .50
22 Alexander Semak .40 1.00
23 Ravil Gusmanov .20 .50
24 Stephane Beauregard .75 2.00

1999-00 Chicago Wolves

This set features the Wolves of the IHL. The set was issued as a promotional giveaway and was limited to 5,000 total sets.

COMPLETE SET (25) 8.00 20.00
1 Header Card/PHPA .01
2 Wendell Young .80 2.00
3 Kevin Dahl .30 .75
4 Dallas Eakins .30 .75
5 Bob Nardella .30 .75
6 Niklas Andersson .30 .75
7 Steve Larouche .80 2.00
8 Steve Maltais .80 2.00
9 Chris Marinucci .30 .75
10 Brian Noonan .40 1.00
11 Guy Larose .30 .75
12 Sean Berens .30 .75
13 Glen Featherstone .30 .75
14 Tom Tilley .30 .75
15 Scott Pearson .30 .75
16 Greg Andrusak .30 .75
17 Dean Malkoc .30 .75
18 David Mackey .30 .75
19 Dan Plante .30 .75
20 Chris LiPuma .30 .75
21 Andrei Trefilov .40 1.00
22 Daniel Lacroix .30 .75
23 John Anderson CO .10 .25
24 Marty Howe CO .20 .50
25 Skates MASCOT .10 .25

2000-01 Chicago Wolves

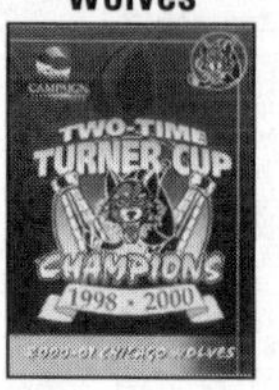

This set features the Wolves of the IHL. The set is noteworthy for the inclusion of Rick DiPietro, the first overall pick of the 2000 NHL Entry Draft. It is oversized, and is believed to have been handed out at a home game in February, 2001.

COMPLETE SET (25) 10.00 25.00
1 John Anderson .20 .50
2 Niklas Andersson .20 .50
3 Jesse Belanger .40 1.00
4 Rob Brown .40 1.00
5 Kevin Dahl .20 .50
6 Rick DiPietro 4.00 10.00
7 Ted Drury .20 .50
8 Dallas Eakins .20 .50
9 Glen Featherstone .20 .50
10 Eric Houde .20 .50
11 Paul Kruse .20 .50
12 Guy Larose .20 .50
13 Steve Larouche .40 1.00
14 Mark Lawrence .30 .75
15 Chris LiPuma .20 .50
16 Steve Maltais .80 2.00
17 Dean Melanson .20 .50
18 Bob Nardella .30 .75
19 Brian Noonan .40 1.00
20 Robert Petrovicky .30 .75
21 Dan Plante .20 .50
22 Tom Tilley .40 1.00
23 Wendell Young .40 1.00
24 Chicago Wolves .20 .25
25 Skates MASCOT .10 .25
NNO Header Card .02 .01

2001-02 Chicago Wolves

This set features the Wolves of the AHL. It was issued as a promotional giveaway at a game in March 2002. The set is slightly oversized. Since the cards are unnumbered, they are listed below in alphabetical order.

COMPLETE SET (25) 9.78 25.00
1 Bryan Adams .30 .75
2 Zdenek Blatny .40 1.00
3 Rob Brown .40 1.00
4 Frederic Cassivi .40 1.00
5 Jeff Dessner .30 .75
6 Dallas Eakins .30 .75
7 Garnet Exelby .40 1.50
8 Kurtis Foster .30 .75
9 Darcy Hordichuk .80 2.00
10 Derek MacKenzie .30 .75
11 Steve Maltais .40 1.00
12 Norm Maracle .40 1.00
13 Bob Nardella .30 .75
14 Pasi Nurminen 1.20 3.00
15 Kamil Piros .60 1.00
16 Dan Plante .30 .75
17 Brian Pothier .40 1.00
18 Luke Sellars .30 .75
19 Ben Simon .30 .75
20 Jarrod Skalde .40 1.00
21 Dan Snyder .40 1.00
22 Brad Tapper .40 1.00
23 J.P. Vigier .40 1.00
24 Mike Weaver .40 1.00
25 Skates MASCOT .10 .25

2002-03 Chicago Wolves

This set was issued as a promotional giveaway at a late-season home game. The cards are unnumbered and are listed below in alphabetical order.

COMPLETE SET (25) 35.00
1 John Anderson CO .25
2 Zdenek Blatny 1.50
3 Rob Brown 1.00
4 Frederic Cassivi 1.50
5 Joey DiPenta 3.00
6 Dallas Eakins 1.00
7 Garnet Exelby 3.00
8 Jeff Farkas 1.00
9 Kurtis Foster 1.00
10 Simon Gamache 3.00
11 Mark Hartigan 1.00
12 Milan Hnilicka 3.00
13 Andreas Karlsson 1.00
14 Francis Lessard 1.00
15 Derek MacKenzie 1.00
16 Steve Maltais 3.00
17 Norm Maracle 3.00
18 Kamil Piros 2.00
19 Kirill Safronov 1.00
20 Luke Sellars 1.00
21 Ben Simon 1.00
22 Skates MASCOT .10

23 Ryan Tobler 1.00
24 Libor Ustrnul 1.00
25 J.P. Vigier 2.00

2003-04 Chicago Wolves

COMPLETE SET (25) 15.00 30.00
1 Stephen Baby .40 1.00
2 Zdenek Blatny .40 1.00
3 Jim Campbell .40 1.00
4 Frederic Cassivi .60 1.50
5 Daniel Corso .40 1.00
6 Joe DiPenta .60 1.50
7 Kurtis Foster .40 1.00
8 Michael Garnett .60 1.50
9 Greg Hawgood .40 1.00
10 Eric Healey .40 1.00
11 Shawn Heins .40 1.00
12 Kari Lehtonen 2.00 5.00
13 Derek MacKenzie .40 1.00
14 Brian Maloney .40 1.00
15 Steve Maltais .60 1.50
16 Kamil Piros .40 1.00
17 Tommi Santala .40 1.00
18 Luke Sellars .40 1.00
19 Karl Stewart .40 1.00
20 Brian Swanson .40 1.00
21 Libor Ustrnul .40 1.00
22 Mike Weaver .40 1.00
23 Brendan Yarema .40 1.00
24 John Anderson HCO .10 .25
25 Mascot .02 .10

2004-05 Chicago Wolves

COMPLETE SET (25) 40.00 75.00
1 Kari Lehtonen 5.00 10.00
2 Brad Larsen 1.00 2.50
3 Travis Roche 1.00 2.50
4 Michael Garnett 1.25 3.00
5 Greg Hawgood 1.00 2.50
6 Joe Corvo 1.00 2.50
7 Libor Ustrnul 1.00 2.50
8 Paul Flache 1.00 2.50
9 Colin Stuart 1.00 2.50
10 Kyle Rossiter 1.00 2.50
11 Brian Maloney 1.00 2.50
12 J.P. Vigier 1.50 4.00
13 Ben Simon 1.00 2.50
14 Brian Sipotz 1.00 2.50
15 Tim Wedderburn 1.00 2.50
16 Lonny Bohonos 1.50 4.00
17 Cory Larose 1.00 2.50
18 Kip Brennan 1.50 4.00
19 Stephen Baby 1.00 2.50
20 Kevin Doell 1.00 2.50
21 Karl Stewart 1.00 2.50
22 Steve Maltais 2.00 5.00
23 Derek MacKenzie 1.00 2.50
24 Tommi Santala 1.00 2.50
25 Skates MASCOT .40 1.00

2005-06 Chicago Wolves

COMPLETE SET (25) 10.00 25.00
1 Ramzi Abid .40 1.00
2 Stephen Baby .40 1.00
3 Scott Barney .40 1.00
4 Braydon Coburn .75 2.00
5 Kevin Doell .40 1.00
6 Pat Dwyer .40 1.00
7 Michael Garnett .75 2.00
8 Tomas Kloucek .40 1.00
9 Francis Lessard .40 1.00
10 Derek MacKenzie .40 1.00
11 Brian Maloney .40 1.00
12 Kip Miller .40 1.00
13 Justin Morrison .40 1.00
14 Nick Naumenko .40 1.00
15 Mark Popovic .40 1.00
16 Travis Roche .40 1.00
17 Jared Ross .40 1.00
18 Brian Sipotz .40 1.00
19 Karl Stewart .40 1.00
20 Colin Stuart .40 1.00
21 Tuomas Tarkki .40 1.00
22 Billy Tibbetts .40 1.00
23 Tim Wedderburn .40 1.00
24 John Anderson HC .02 .10
25 Skates MASCOT .02 .10

1984-85 Chicoutimi Sagueneens

This 24-card set sponsored by Mike's restaurants measures approximately 8 1/2" by 11" and features black-and-white player photos in a white-black-white-red frame. The complete set was issued in a protective folder. This folder is valued at $1. The card backs are blank. The cards are unnumbered and checklisted below in alphabetical order.

COMPLETE SET (24) 16.00 40.00
1 Mario Barbe .40 1.00
2 Mario Bazinet .40 1.00
3 Daniel Bedard .40 1.00
Michel Boivin
Guy Byatt
Jean-Marc Couture
Patrice Gosselin
Jean-Yves Laberge
Germain Munger
Reginald Riverin
4 Daniel Berthiaume 1.20 3.00
5 Francois Breault .60 1.50
6 Gregg Choules .40 1.00
7 Christian Duperron .40 1.00
8 Luc Dufour .40 1.00
9 Luc Duval .40 1.00
10 Patrick Emond .40 1.00
11 Marc Fortier .60 1.50
12 Steven Gauthier .40 1.00
13 Yves Heroux .60 1.50
14 Daniel Jomphe .40 1.00
15 Gilles Laberge .40 1.00
16 Claude Lajoie .40 1.00
17 Serge Lauzon .40 1.00
18 Roch Marinier .60 1.50
19 Pierre Millier .40 1.00
20 Marc Morin .40 1.00
21 Scott Rettew .40 1.00
22 Jean-Marc Richard .40 1.00
23 Stephane Richer 4.80 12.00
24 Pierre Sevigny .40 1.00

2000-01 Chicoutimi Sagueneens

This set features the Sagueneens of the QMJHL. It was produced by CTM-Ste-Foy, and was sold by that company, as well as by the team at home games.

COMPLETE SET (23) 4.80 15.00
1 Olivier Dannel .20 .50
2 Alex Turcotte .20 .50
3 Mathieu Betournay .20 .50
4 Michel Finn .20 .50
5 Eric Betournay .20 .50
6 Jonathan Francoeur .20 .50
7 Sebastien Laprise .20 .50
8 Sylvain Watt .20 .50
9 Sebastien Lucier .20 .50
10 Stanislav Hudec .20 .50
11 Christian Larrivee .20 .50
12 Francois Caron .20 .50
13 Eric Beaudin .20 .50
14 Alain Chenard .20 .50
15 Karl St-Pierre .20 .50
16 Michael Parent .20 .50
17 David Ouellet Beaudry .20 .50
18 Jean-Francois Demers .20 .50
19 Dave Verville .30 .75
20 Guillaume Karrer .20 .50
21 Martin Beauchesne .20 .50
22 Jean-Micheal Martin .20 .50
23 Pierre-Marc Bouchard 2.00 5.00

2000-01 Chicoutimi Sagueneens Signed

This set is exactly the same as the base Sagueneens set from this season, save that every card has been hand signed by the player pictured. Each card also is serial numbered out of just 100.

COMPLETE SET (23) 18.00 50.00
1 Olivier Dannel .80 2.00
2 Alex Turcotte .80 2.00
3 Mathieu Betournay .80 2.00
4 Michel Finn .80 2.00
5 Eric Betournay .80 2.00
6 Jonathan Francoeur .80 2.00
7 Sebastien Laprise .80 2.00
8 Sylvain Watt .80 2.00
9 Sebastien Lucier .80 2.00
10 Stanislav Hudec .80 2.00
11 Christian Larrivee .80 2.00
12 Francois Caron .80 2.00
13 Eric Beaudin .80 2.00
14 Alain Chenard .80 2.00
15 Karl St-Pierre .80 2.00
16 Michael Parent .80 2.00
17 David Ouellet Beaudry .80 2.00
18 Jean-Francois Demers .80 2.00
19 Dave Verville 2.00 5.00
20 Guillaume Karrer .80 2.00
21 Martin Beauchesne .80 2.00
22 Jean-Micheal Martin .80 2.00
23 Pierre-Marc Bouchard 10.00 25.00

2001-02 Chicoutimi Sagueneens

COMPLETE SET (23) 15.00
1 Team Card .01
2 Sebastien Lucier .50
3 Eric Betournay .50
4 Pierre-Alexandre Parenteau .75
5 Stanislav Hudec .50
6 Christian Larrivee .50
7 Patrick Tessier .50
8 Pierre-Luc Briere .50
9 Yvan Busque .50
10 Alexandre Blackburn .50
11 Jean-Francois Demers .50
12 Eric Tetrault .50
13 Jeff Drouin Deslauriers 1.50
14 Eric Borbeau .50
15 Michael Lanthier .50
16 Nicolas Marcotte .50
17 Hugues Verpaelst .50
18 Francis Lemieux .50
19 Jean-Vincent Lachance .50
20 Martin Chabot .50
21 Rosario Ruggeri .50
22 Bruno Champagne .50
23 Pierre-Marc Bouchard 3.00

2004-05 Chicoutimi Sagueneens

A total of 1,100 team sets were produced.

COMPLETE SET (24) 12.00
1 Alexandre Lamarche .50
2 Alexandre Vincent .50
3 Bernard Elhokayen .50
4 Brandon Verge .50
5 Brent Macsween .50
6 David Desharnais .50
7 Francis Lemieux .50
8 Francis Verreault .50
9 Gabriel Houde-Brisson .50
10 Guillaume Lepine .50
11 Julien Brouillette .50
12 Louis-Etienne Leblanc .50
13 Marc-Andre Roy .50
14 Marek Zagrapan 1.50
15 Mathieu Bolduc .50
16 Romy Elayoubi .75
17 Stanislav Lascek .50
18 Maxime Boisclair 1.00
19 Nicolas Blanchard .50
20 Nicolas Marcotte .50
21 Ryan Spaulding .50
22 Shane Tremblay .50
23 Travis Coles .50
24 Yan Gaudette .50

2005-06 Chicoutimi Sagueneens

COMPLETE SET (31) 6.00 15.00
1 David Desharnais .20 .50
2 Stanislav Lascek .20 .50
3 Marek Zagrapan .40 1.00
4 Nicolas Blanchard .20 .50
5 Maxime Boisclair .40 1.00
6 Francis Verreault .20 .50
7 Shayne Tremblay .20 .50
8 Sylvain Michaud .20 .50
9 Alexandre Vincent .20 .50
10 Julien Brouillette .20 .50
11 Geoff Oliver .20 .50
12 Gabriel Carle .20 .50
13 Marc Myre .20 .50
14 Pierre-Luc Huot .20 .50
15 Maxime Tanguay .20 .50
16 Mathieu Bolduc .20 .50
17 Louis-Etienne Leblanc .20 .50
18 Jean-Claude Milot .20 .50
19 Brent MacSween .20 .50
20 Guillaume Lepine .20 .50
21 Oliver Lajeunesse .20 .50
22 Bruno-Pierre Gosselin .20 .50
23 Matthew Block .20 .50
24 Ryan Lehr .20 .50
25 Patrick Coulombe .20 .50
26 Jean-Sebastien Adam .20 .50
27 Gabriel Boies .20 .50
28 Nicolas Lafontaine .20 .50
29 Benoit Piche .20 .50
30 Jean-Sebastien Cote .20 .50
31 Sago MASCOT .02 .10

2006-07 Chicoutimi Sagueneens

COMPLETE SET (23) 8.00 15.00
1 David Desharnais .30 .75
2 Luc-Oliver Blain .30 .75
3 Nicolas Blanchard .30 .75
4 Mathieu Bolduc .30 .75
5 Julien Brouillette .30 .75
6 Patrick Campbell .30 .75
7 Francois Chabot .30 .75
8 Joel Champagne .30 .75
9 Derek Famulare .30 .75
10 Christopher Guay .30 .75
11 Alexandre Imbeault .30 .75
12 Dominic Jalbert .30 .75
13 Marc-Andre Julien .30 .75
14 Francois Levesque .30 .75
15 Jurai Mikus .30 .75
16 Bobby Nadeau .40 1.00
17 Olivier Painchaud .30 .75
18 Maxime Provencher .30 .75
19 Antoine Roussel .30 .75
20 Tommy Tremblay .30 .75
21 Kirill Tulupov .30 .75
22 Francois Verreault-Paul .30 .75
23 Joel Rechlicz .30 .75

2006-07 Chilliwack Bruins

COMPLETE SET (25) 15.00 25.00
1 Alex Archibald .60 1.50
2 Matt Esposito .60 1.50
3 Kevin Boutilier .40 1.00
4 Dylan Chapman .40 1.00
5 Cody Hobbs .40 1.00
6 Nick Holden .40 1.00
7 Craig Lineker .40 1.00
8 Scott Maetche .40 1.00
9 Cam Stevens .40 1.00
10 Matt McCue .40 1.00
11 Josh Aspenlind .40 1.00
12 Patrick Bhungal .40 1.00
13 Donnie Glennie .40 1.00
14 Colton Graf .40 1.00
15 Aki Kangasmaki .40 1.00
16 Colby Kulhanek .40 1.00
17 Matt Meropoulis .40 1.00
18 Dillon Johnstone .40 1.00
19 Oscar Moller .75 2.00
20 Special Edition Oscar Moller .75 2.00
21 Ken Petkau .40 1.00
22 Mark Santorelli .40 1.00
23 Cody Smuk .40 1.00
24 Mike Proudley .40 1.00
25 Bruiser MASCOT CL .02 .10

1990-91 Cincinnati Cyclones

This 23-card set of the Cincinnati Cyclones of the ECHL was produced by 7th Inning Sketch. for distribution by the team. The cards are numbered 19-41 presumably because the company produced card sets for many ECHL teams this year.

COMPLETE SET (23) 3.20 8.00
19 Steve McGrinder .16 .40
20 Steve Shaunessy .16 .40
21 Jay Rose .16 .40
22 Don Gagne .16 .40
23 Mike Williams .16 .40
24 Mike Chighisola .16 .40
25 Daryl Harpe .16 .40
26 Steve Cadieux .16 .40
27 Jeff Salzbrunn .16 .40
28 Rob Gador .16 .40
29 Chris Marshall .16 .40
30 Doug Melnyk .16 .40
31 Mark Turner .16 .40
32 Kevin Kerr .16 .40
33 Rob Krauss .16 .40
34 Mark Marentette .16 .40
35 Jamie Kompon .16 .40
36 Tom Neziol .16 .40
37 John Fletcher .16 .40
38 Dennis Desrosiers CO .10 .25
39 Todd Harrison TR .10 .25
40 Terry Ficorelli .16 .40
41 Craig Daly .16 .40

1991-92 Cincinnati Cyclones

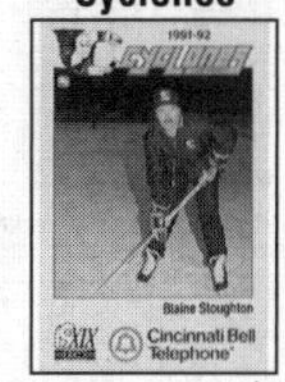

The 1991-92 Cincinnati Cyclones of the East Coast Hockey League are represented in this 25-card set, which was sponsored by Cincinnati Bell Telephone and 19 XIX Fox. The cards measure 2 3/8" by 3 1/2" and feature posed color action shots enclosed by a white border. The team logo and year appear across the top of the card face, with the team name in silver outlined in red. The white front bottom portion of the card carries player information, the 19XIX Fox logo, and the Cincinnati Bell Telephone logo. Horizontally oriented backs carry biography and statistics in a white box surrounded by a gray border. The cards are unnumbered and checklisted below in alphabetical order.

COMPLETE SET (25) 3.20 8.00
1 Dan Beaudette .20 .50
2 Steve Benoit TR .04 .10
3 Steve Cadieux .16 .40
4 Craig Charron .16 .40
5 David Craievich .16 .40
6 Doug Dadswell .20 .50
7 Dennis Desrosiers CO .04 .10
8 Terry Ficorelli ANN .04 .10
9 Jeff Hogden .16 .40
10 Kevin Kerr .16 .40
11 Jaan Luik .16 .40
12 Scott Luik .16 .40
13 Chris Marshall .16 .40
14 Daryn McBride .16 .40
15 Doug Melnyk .16 .40
16 David Moore .16 .40
17 Tom Neziol .16 .40
18 Mark Romaine .16 .40
19 Jay Rose .16 .40
20 Martin St. Amour .20 .50
21 Kevin Scott .16 .40
22 Peter Schure .16 .40
23 Steve Shaunessy .16 .40
24 Blaine Stoughton CO .20 .50
25 Bobby Wallwork .16 .40

1992-93 Cincinnati Cyclones

These standard-sized cards were released in set form and sold by the team. The set includes the logo of sponsor, Bell.

COMPLETE SET (30) 3.20 8.00
1 Bill Armstrong .12 .30
2 Ralph Barahona .16 .40
3 Mike Bodnarchuk .16 .40
4 Craig Charron .16 .40
5 Todd Copeland .16 .40
6 Doug Dadswell .30 .75
7 Mike Dagenais .16 .40
8 Kevin Dean .16 .40
9 Chad Erickson .30 .75
10 Todd Flichel .16 .40
11 Alan Hepple .12 .30
12 Dennis Holland .16 .40
13 Sergei Kharin .16 .40
14 David Latta .16 .40
15 Jeff Madill .16 .40
16 Jon Morris .16 .40
17 Dean Morton .16 .40
18 Chris Nelson .16 .40
19 Darcy Norton .16 .40
20 Howie Rosenblatt .20 .50
21 Scott Shaunessy .16 .40
22 Mario Thyer .16 .40
23 Al Tuer .12 .30
24 Dennis Desrosiers HCO .04 .10
25 Blaine Stoughton ACO .20 .50
26 Alex Ochoa TR .12 .30
27 Mr. Cyclone Mascot .04 .10
28 Steve Benoit EM .04 .10
29 Terry Ficorelli ANN .16 .40
30 Wildman Walker ANN .10 .25

1993-94 Cincinnati Cyclones

Little is known about this set beyond the confirmed checklist. Anyone with additional information should write hockeymag@beckett.com.

COMPLETE SET (32) 4.00 10.00
1 Doug Barrault .16 .40
2 Len Barrie .30 .75
3 Don Biggs .16 .40
4 Chris Cichocki .12 .30
5 Jason Cirone .16 .40
6 Dallas Eakins .20 .50
7 Daniel Gauthier .16 .40
8 Jeff Greenlaw .16 .40
9 Rick Hayward .16 .40
10 Gord Hynes .16 .40
11 Ian Kidd .16 .40
12 Marc LaBelle .16 .40
13 Paul Lawless .16 .40
14 Jamie Leach .16 .40
15 Patrick Lebeau .20 .50
16 Ray LeBlanc .30 .75
17 Jamie Linden .16 .40
18 Jaroslav Nedved .16 .40
19 Darcy Norton .16 .40
20 Pokey Reddick .30 .75
21 Stephane Richer .16 .40
22 Jeff Serowik .16 .40
23 Scott Shaunessy .16 .40
24 Brad Smyth .12 .30
25 Dennis Desrosiers HCO .04 .10
26 Richard Kromm ACO .04 .10
27 Wildman Walker ANN .04 .10
28 Mr. Cyclone Mascot .04 .10
29 Mike Spilman TR .04 .10
30 Steve Benoit EQM .04 .10
31 Terry Ficorelli ANN .04 .10
NNO Header/Checklist .04 .10

1995-96 Cincinnati Cyclones

The set features the Cyclones of the IHL. The set was produced by Edge Ice and was sold by the team at its souvenir stands.

COMPLETE SET (25) 4.00 10.00
1 Don Biggs .20 .50
2 Frederic Chabot .40 1.00
3 Chris Cichocki .20 .50
4 Chris Dahlquist .20 .50
5 Dale DeGray .20 .50
6 Brian Dobbin .20 .50
7 Len Esau .20 .50
8 Jeff Greenlaw .20 .50
9 Todd Hawkins .20 .50
10 Duane Joyce .20 .50
11 Chris Kontos .30 .75
12 Marc LaBelle .20 .50
13 Paul Lawless .30 .75
14 Danny Lorenz .30 .75
15 Doug MacDonald .20 .50
16 Dave Marcinyshyn .20 .50
17 Scott Thomas .20 .50
18 Dave Tomlinson .20 .50
19 Jeff Wells .20 .50
20 Bob Wilkie .20 .50
21 Nick Kenney TR .04 .10
22 Mark Mills TR .04 .10
23 Al Hill CO .04 .10
24 Ron Smith CO .04 .10
25 Snowbird MAS .04 .10

1996-97 Cincinnati Cyclones

This 25-card set was produced by Split Second and was sponsored by WGRR radio and WCPD TV. The unnumbered cards feature an action photo on the front, and stats package on the back. They are numbered below according to their sweater numbers, which are prominently featured on the backs.

COMPLETE SET (25) 4.00 10.00
1 Todd MacDonald .30 .75
3 Duane Joyce .20 .50
4 Ted Crowley .20 .50
5 Jeff Wells .20 .50
6 Myles O'Connor .20 .50
12 Todd Hawkins .20 .50
13 Paul Lawless .20 .50
17 Mike Casselman .20 .50
19 Scott Thomas .30 .75
22 Don Biggs .20 .50
24 Tony Horacek .20 .50
26 Marc Laniel .20 .50
27 Dave Marcinyshyn .20 .50
28 Scott Morrow .20 .50
29 Jeff Greenlaw .20 .50
31 Geoff Sarjeant .30 .75
33 Chris Cichocki .20 .50
37 Eric Dandenault .20 .50
44 Doug MacDonald .20 .50
51 Dale DeGray .20 .50
NNO Mark Mills EQMG .04 .10
NNO Snowbird (Mascot) .04 .10
NNO Al Hill ACO .04 .10
NNO Ron Smith CO .04 .10
NNO Nick Kenney TR .04 .10

1997-98 Cincinnati Cyclones

This set features the Cyclones of the IHL. The cards were sponsored by Cincinnati Bell, and were issued as promotional giveaways.

COMPLETE SET (24) 4.80 12.00
1 Don Biggs .30 .75
2 Paul Broten .20 .50
3 Mike Casselman .20 .50
4 Eric Dandenault .20 .50
5 Gilbert Dionne .30 .75
6 Jeff Greenlaw .20 .50
7 Todd Hawkins .20 .50
8 Burt Henderson .20 .50
9 Steven King .20 .50
10 Marc LaBelle .20 .50
11 Doug MacDonald .20 .50
12 Todd MacDonald .20 .50
13 Pat MacLeod .20 .50
14 Scott Morrow .20 .50
15 Geoff Sarjeant .30 .75
16 Todd Simon .30 .75
17 Jeff Sirkka .20 .50
18 Jeff Wells .20 .50
19 David Williams .20 .50
20 Ron Smith CO .10 .25
21 Chris Cichocki CO .10 .25
22 Snowbird MAS .04 .10
23 Nick Kenney TR .04 .10
24 Mark Mills TR .04 .10

1998-99 Cincinnati Cyclones

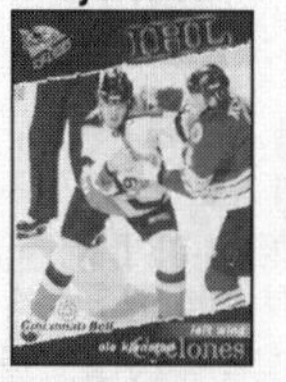

Card fronts feature full color photos along with team name and position. Backs feature 1997-98 statistics and biographical information. Cards are unnumbered and checklisted below in alphabetical order.

COMPLETE SET (30) 6.00 10.00
1 Kaspars Astashenko .20 .50
2 Frederic Cassivi .30 .75
3 Phil Crowe .16 .40
4 Eric Dandenault .16 .40
5 Gilbert Dionne .30 .75
6 Todd Hawkins .16 .40
7 Jani Hurme 2.00 2.00
8 Burt Henderson .16 .40
9 Chris Joseph .16 .40
10 Ole Kjenstad .16 .40
11 Fred Knipscheer .16 .40
12 Doug Macdonald .16 .40
13 Pat Macleod .16 .40
14 Scott Morrow .16 .40
15 Tom Nemeth .16 .40
16 Kirk Nielsen .16 .40
17 Ed Patterson .16 .40
18 Rastislav Pavlikovsky .16 .40
19 Jeff Shevalier .16 .40
20 Todd Simon .16 .40
21 Geoff Smith .16 .40
22 Jeff Wells .16 .40
23 Snowbird Mascot .04 .10
24 Nick Kenney TR .04 .10
25 Mark Mills EQ .04 .10
26 Scott Macpherson ACO .04 .10
27 Chris Cichocki ACO .04 .10
28 Ron Smith CO .04 .10
29 Team Card .04 .10
30 Logo Card .04 .01

1998-99 Cincinnati Cyclones 2

This set features the Cyclones of the IHL. The set was issued as a promotional giveaway and was sponsored by Bell Telephone.

COMPLETE SET (30) 10.00 25.00
1 Todd Hawkins .40 1.00
2 Kirk Nielsen .40 1.00
3 Ed Patterson .40 1.00
4 Fred Knipscheer .40 1.00
5 Doug Macdonald .40 1.00
6 Todd Simon .40 1.00
7 Phil Crowe .40 1.00
8 Gilbert Dionne .40 1.00
9 Scott Morrow .40 1.00
10 Rastislav Pavlikovsky .40 1.00
11 Jeff Shevalier .40 1.00
12 Kaspars Astashenko .40 1.00
13 Eric Dandenault .40 1.00
14 Burt Henderson .40 1.00
15 Chris Joseph .40 1.00
16 Pat MacLeod .40 1.00
17 Geoff Smith .40 1.00
18 Jeff Wells .40 1.00
19 Frederic Cassivi .75 2.00
20 Jani Hurme .75 2.00
21 Tom Nemeth .40 1.00
22 Olaf Kjenstad .40 1.00
23 Team Photo Card .20 .50
24 Ron Smith CO .20 .50
25 Chris Cichocki CO .20 .50
26 Scott MacPherson CO .20 .50
27 Mark Mills EM .20 .50
28 Nick Kenney TR .02 .10
29 Snowbird MASCOT .02 .10
30 PHPA Card .01 .05

1999-00 Cincinnati Cyclones

This team set of the Cincinnati Cyclones of the IHL was sponsored by Cincinnati Bell. The cards show a color action photo of each player on front and individual stats on the card backs. The cards are not numbered and are listed below alphabetically.

COMPLETE SET (27) 4.80 10.00
1 Team Logo .10 .25
2 Craig Adams .20 .50
3 Steve Bancroft .20 .50
4 Eric Dandenault .20 .50
5 Gilbert Dionne .30 .75
6 Gilbert Dionne MVP .30 .75
7 Mark Fitzpatrick .30 .75
8 Len Esau .30 .75
9 Todd Hawkins .20 .50
10 David Karpa .20 .50
11 Greg Koehler .20 .50
12 Greg Kuznik .20 .50
13 Craig McDonald .30 .75
14 Pat McLeod .20 .50
15 Ian McNeil .20 .50
16 Randy Petruk .30 .75
17 Mike Rucinski .20 .50
18 Todd Simon .30 .75
19 Nikos Tselios .30 .75
20 Stefan Ustorf .30 .75
21 Shane Willis .60 1.00
22 Chris Cichocki CO .10 .25
23 Nick Kenney TR .04 .10
24 Mark Mills EM .04 .10
25 Ron Smith HCO .04 .10
26 Snowbird MASCOT .04 .10
27 PHPA Logo .01

2000-01 Cincinnati Cyclones

This set features the Cyclones of the IHL. The cards were produced by Multi-Ad Sports, and were issued as a promotional giveaway.

COMPLETE SET (30) 10.00 20.00
1 Nikos Tselios .40 .75
2 Jeremiah McCarthy .30 .50
3 Greg Kuznik .30 .50
4 Byron Ritchie .40 1.00
5 Craig MacDonald .30 .75
6 Greg Koehler .20 .50
7 Stefan Ustorf .30 .50
8 Jeff Heerema .40 1.00
9 Mike Rucinski .40 1.00
10 Ian MacNeil .20 .50
11 Gilbert Dionne .40 1.00
12 Erik Cole 3.20 3.00
13 Reggie Berg .30 .50
14 Jon Rohloff .20 .50
15 Len Esau .20 .50
16 Brian Felsner .30 .75
17 Brad DeFauw .20 .50
18 Harlan Pratt .20 .50
19 Jaroslav Svoboda .75 1.00
20 Jean-Marc Pelletier .40 1.00
21 Corey Hirsch .30 .75
22 Marc Magliarditi .30 .75
23 Ron Smith CO .10 .25
24 Mark Mills EM .04 .10
25 Nick Kenney TR .04 .10
26 Snowbird MASCOT .04 .10
27 GMC Zamboni SPONSOR .01
28 Team Photo .20 .25
29 The Firstar Center .01
30 PHPA Web Site .01

1998-99 Cincinnati Mighty Ducks

This 29-card set was handed out at a game in February. It is not thought that it was available through any other channels, and therefore is quite difficult to acquire.

COMPLETE SET (29) 8.00 20.00
1 Buster MASCOT .10 .25
2 Marc Andreozzi TR .04 .10
3 Gary Linquist EM .04 .10
4 John Walton .30 .75
5 Ed Johnstone ACO .10 .25
6 Moe Mantha HCO .10 .25
7 Frank Banham .40 1.00
8 Mike LeClerc 1.20 3.00
9 Byron Briske .30 .75
10 Eric Lecompte .30 .75
11 Terran Sandwith .30 .75
12 Jamie Ram .40 1.00
13 Craig Reichert .30 .75
14 Joel Kwiatkowski .30 .75
15 Mike Crowley .40 1.00
16 Matt Leon .30 .75
17 Jeremy Stevenson .30 .75
18 Dan Trebil .30 .75
19 Bob Wren .30 .75
20 Lloyd Shaw .30 .75
21 Igor Nikulin .30 .75
22 Jeff Winter .30 .75
23 Tony Mohagen .30 .75
24 Tony Tuzzolino .30 .75
25 Peter LeBoutillier .30 .75
26 Tom Askey .60 1.50
27 Marc Chouinard .40 1.00
28 Scott Ferguson .30 .75
29 PHPA Web Site .04 .01

1999-00 Cincinnati Mighty Ducks

This set features the Mighty Ducks of the AHL. The set was issued as a promotional giveaway at a home game during March of 2000.

COMPLETE SET (32) 12.00 30.00
1 Parent Clubs .10 .25

2 Moe Mantha CO .10 .25
3 Jason Payne .30 .75
4 Jeff Nielsen ALUM .30 .75
5 Antti Aalto ALUM .40 1.00
6 Ruslan Salei ALUM .30 .75
7 Joel Kwiatkowski .30 .75
8 Aren Miller .40 1.00
9 Dan Trebil .30 .75
10 Rastislav Pavlikovsky .30 .75
11 Frank Banham .40 1.00
12 Scott Ferguson .30 .75
13 Maxim Balmochnykh .60 1.50
14 Darryl Laplante .60 1.50
15 Johan Davidsson .60 1.50
16 Peter Leboutillier .30 .75
17 Jesse Wallin .40 1.00
18 Alexandre Jacques .30 .75
19 B.J. Young .30 .75
20 Ed Johnstone CO .10 .25
21 Ryan Hoople .30 .75
22 Matt Cullen ALUM .80 2.00
22 Pavel Trnka ALUM .30 .75
22 Mike LeClerc .80 2.00
23 Buster MASCOT .10 .25
24 Jeremy Stevenson .30 .75
25 Jay Legault .30 .75
26 Marc Chouinard .40 1.00
27 Torrey DiRoberto .40 1.00
28 Maxim Kuznetsov .40 1.00
29 Shane Hnidy .30 .75
30 Vitali Vishnevsky .40 1.00
31 Bob Wren .30 .75
32 Gregg Naumenko .60 1.50

2001-02 Cincinnati Mighty Ducks

This set features the Mighty Ducks of the AHL. The cards were issued as a promotional giveaway at a home game late in the season. As the cards are unnumbered, they are listed below in alphabetical order.

COMPLETE SET (28) 9.78 25.00
1 Sean Avery .80 2.00
2 Maxim Balmochnykh .40 1.00
3 Drew Bannister .31 .75
4 Ryan Barnes .31 .75
5 Travis Brigley .31 .75
6 Aris Brimanis .31 .75
7 Steve Brule .31 .75
8 Ilja Bryzgalov 2.00 3.00
9 Garrett Burnett .31 1.00
10 Yuri Butsayev .80 .75
11 Josh DeWolf .31 .75
12 Jason Elliott .40 2.00
13 Ryan Gaucher .31 .75
14 Andy McDonald .40 3.00
15 Antti-Jussi Niemi .40 1.00
16 Timo Parssinen .62 1.00
17 Peter Podhradsky .31 .75
18 Bruce Richardson .31 .75
19 Bert Robertsson .31 .75
20 David Roche .31 .75
21 Jonas Ronnqvist .40 1.00
22 Jarrett Smith .31 .75
23 Brian White .31 .75
24 Jason Williams .40 1.00
25 Dwayne Zinger .31 .75
26 Mike Babcock CO .10 1.00
27 Kevin Kaminski ACO .31 .25
28 Buster the Duck MASCOT .10 .10

2002-03 Cincinnati Mighty Ducks

This set was given away over the course of two home games, Dec. 14, 2002 and March 23, 2003. The cards are unnumbered and listed below by series in alphabetical order.

COMPLETE SET (28) 15.00 30.00
A-1 Mike Commodore 1.25 3.00
A-2 Samuel Pahlsson .75 2.00
A-3 Jean-Francois Damphousse .75 2.00
A-4 Todd Reirden .40 1.00
A-5 Jonathan Hedstrom .75 2.00
A-6 Chris O'Sullivan .40 1.00
A-7 Jarrett Smith .40 1.00
A-8 Travis Brigley .40 1.00
A-9 Brian Gornick .40 1.00
A-10 Tony Martensson .40 1.00
A-11 Cory Pecker .75 2.00
A-12 Nick Smith .40 1.00
A-13 Cam Severson 1.25 3.00
A-14 Pete Podrasky .40 1.00
B-1 Ilja Bryzgalov 1.25 3.00
B-2 Darryl Williams ACO .20 .50
B-3 Brad Shaw CO .20 .50
B-4 Buster MASCOT .02 .10
B-5 Puck Boy .02 .10
B-6 Jan Tabacek .40 1.00
B-7 Mark Popovic .75 2.00
B-8 Rob Valicevic .40 1.00
B-9 Ben Guite .75 2.00
B-10 Francis Belanger .40 1.00
B-11 Team Photo .40 1.00
B-12 Josh DeWolf .40 1.00
B-13 Jason Krog .75 2.00
B-14 Alexei Smirnov .40 1.00

2003-04 Cincinnati Mighty Ducks

It's thought that these were issued as promotional giveaways at two Ducks home games. Anyone with additional information, please contact us at hockeymag@beckett.com.

COMPLETE SET (28) 10.00 25.00
A1 Keith Aucoin .40 1.00
A2 Eddie Ferhi .40 1.00
A3 Mike Mottau .40 1.00
A4 Pierre-Alexander Parenteau .40 1.00
A5 Cory Pecker .40 1.00
A6 Mark Popovic .40 1.00
A7 Todd Reirden .40 1.00
A8 Andy Reierson .40 1.00
A9 Cam Severson .40 1.00
A10 Alexei Smirnov .40 1.00
A11 Nick Smith .40 1.00
A12 Joel Stepp .40 1.00
A13 Darryl Williams ACO .10 .25
A14 Puck Boy .10 .25
B1 Juha Alen .40 1.00
B2 Chris Armstrong .40 1.00
B3 Sheldon Brookbank .40 1.00
B4 Ilja Bryzgalov .75 2.00
B5 Brian Gornick .40 1.00
B6 Casey Hankinson .40 1.00
B7 Mikael Holmqvist .40 1.00
B8 Chris Kunitz 1.00 2.50
B9 Tony Martensson .40 1.00
B10 Shane O'Brien .75 2.00
B11 Joel Perreault .40 1.00
B12 Igor Pohanka .40 1.00
B13 Brad Shaw CO .10 .25
B14 Mascot .02 .10

2004-05 Cincinnati Mighty Ducks

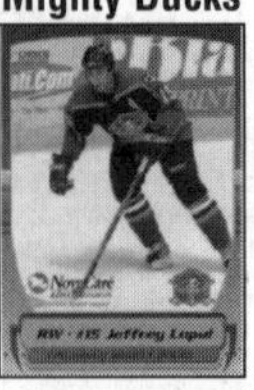

This set was produced by Choice Marketing and given away in two parts at different Mighty Ducks home games.

COMPLETE SET (30) 15.00 30.00
1 Brad Shaw CO .20 .50
2 Dan Bylsma ACO .20 .50
3 Aaron Rome .75 2.00
4 Juha Alen .40 1.00
5 Kurtis Foster .40 1.00
6 Shane O'Brien .75 2.00
7 Mark Popovic .40 1.00
8 Tim Brent .40 1.00
9 Buster MASCOT .02 .10
10 Joel Perrault .40 1.00
11 Zenon Konopka .40 1.00
12 Igor Pohanka .40 1.00
13 Sean O'Connor .40 1.00
14 Chris Kunitz .75 2.00
15 Jeffrey Lupul 1.50 4.00
16 Joel Stepp .40 1.00
17 Sheldon Brookbank .40 1.00
18 Michael Holmqvist .40 1.00
19 Cory Pecker .40 1.00
20 Curtis Glencross .40 1.00
21 Sponsor card .02 .10
22 Alexei Smirnov .40 1.00
23 Stanislav Chistov .75 2.00
24 Dustin Penner 1.50 4.00
25 Pierre Parenteau .40 1.00
26 Checklist .02 .10
27 Tomas Malec .40 1.00
28 Eddie Ferhi .40 1.00
29 Ilja Bryzgalov .75 2.00
30 Frederic Cassivi .75 2.00

1992-93 Clarkson Knights

Issued in 1993 at the end of the hockey season, this 24-card standard-size set features the Clarkson Knights of the ECAC (Eastern Collegiate Athletic Conference). The cards feature on-ice player action and posed photos on the fronts. The pictures are on a white card face with the Clarkson hockey logo and name at the top and the player's name and position at the bottom. The horizontal backs carry biography, statistics for the 1991-92 and 1992-93 seasons, and career summary. The Clarkson hockey logo appears in the lower right. The cards are unnumbered and checklisted below in alphabetical order.

COMPLETE SET (24) 4.80 12.00
1 Josh Bartell .16 .40
2 Hugo Belanger .20 .50
3 Craig Conroy .60 1.50
4 Jason Currie .16 .40
5 Steve Dubinsky .20 .50
6 Shawn Fotheringham .16 .40
7 Dave Green .16 .40
8 Ed Henrich .16 .40
9 Chris Lipsett .16 .40
10 Todd Marchant .80 2.00
11 Brian Mueller .20 .50
12 Kevin Murphy .16 .40
13 Martin d'Orsonnens .16 .40
14 Steve Palmer .16 .40
15 Patrice Robitaille .16 .40
16 Chris Rogles .20 .50
17 Jerry Rosenheck .16 .40
18 Chris de Ruiter .16 .40
19 Guy Sanderson .16 .40
20 David Seitz .16 .40
21 Mikko Tavi .16 .40
22 Patrick Theriault .16 .40
23 Marko Tuomainen .20 .50
24 Men's Hockey 1992-93 .16 .40
Martin d'Orsonnens
Steve Dubinsky

1951-52 Cleveland Barons

This set was issued as a photo pack. The cards are printed on thin card stock, and measure 9 X 6 inches. The last card, Joe Lund, may be from the previous year's set, as he did not play for Cleveland in 1951-52.

COMPLETE SET (20) 75.00 150.00
1 Bun Cook CO 5.00 10.00
2 Fred Shero 10.00 20.00
3 Ed Reigle 3.00 6.00
4 Ike Hildebrand 3.00 6.00
5 Eddie Olson 3.00 6.00
6 Jerry Reid 3.00 6.00
7 Fred Thurier 3.00 6.00
8 Steve Wochy 3.00 6.00
9 Joe Carveth 4.00 8.00
10 Tom Williams 5.00 10.00
11 Johnny Bower 25.00 50.00
12 Jack Gordon 4.00 8.00
13 Ken Schultz 3.00 6.00
14 Fern Perreault 3.00 6.00
15 Ray Ceresino 3.00 6.00
16 Bob Bailey 3.00 6.00
17 Bob Chrystal 4.00 8.00
18 Phil Samis 3.00 6.00
19 Paul Gladu 3.00 6.00
20 Joe Lund 3.00 6.00

1960-61 Cleveland Barons

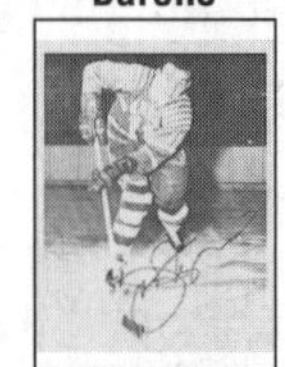

This 19-card set of oversized cards measures approximately 6 3/4" by 5 3/8". The set commemorates the Cleveland Barons 1959-60 season which ended with the team in fourth place after elimination in the Calder Cup Playoffs. The white-bordered fronts display action, black-and-white player photos. A facsimile autograph is printed near the bottom of the photo on all the cards except the team photo card. The backs are blank. Since the cards are unnumbered, they are checklisted below alphabetically.

COMPLETE SET (19) 60.00 120.00
1 Ron Attwell 3.00 6.00
2 Les Binkley 5.00 10.00
3 Bill Dineen 4.00 8.00
4 John Ferguson 10.00 20.00
5 Cal Gardner 4.00 8.00
6 Fred Glover 4.00 8.00
7 Jack Gordon 4.00 8.00
8 Aldo Guidolin 4.00 8.00
9 Greg Hicks 3.00 6.00
10 Wayne Larkin 3.00 6.00
11 Moe Mantha 4.00 8.00
12 Gil Mayer 3.00 6.00
13 Eddie Mazur 3.00 6.00
14 Jim Mikol 3.00 6.00
15 Bill Needham 3.00 6.00
16 Cal Stearns 3.00 6.00
17 Bill Sutherland 4.00 8.00
18 Tom Williams 4.00 8.00
19 Team Photo 5.00 10.00

1992-93 Cleveland Lumberjacks

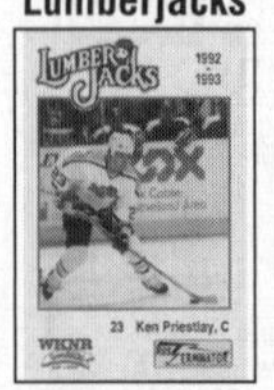

Issued to commemorate the Lumberjacks' first season in Cleveland, these 25 cards feature on their fronts red-trimmed and white-bordered color player action shots and measure 2 3/8" by 3 1/2". The player's name, uniform number and position appear beneath the photo in the lower white margin. The team logo and season are displayed in the margin above the photo. The logos for the two sponsors, WKNR radio and Rusterminator, rest at the bottom. The horizontal backs display the player's name, uniform number, position, biography and stats within the central white rectangle. In the wide gray border, the logos for the team and the sponsors round out the card.

COMPLETE SET (25) 4.00 10.00
1 Title Card .04 .10
2 Larry Gordon GM .04 .10
3 Paul Laus .30 .75
4 Travis Thiessen .20 .50
5 Phil Russell CO .20 .50
6 Gilbert Delorme ACO .20 .50
7 Jamie Heward .20 .50
8 Greg Andrusak .20 .50
9 David Quinn .20 .50
10 Perry Ganchar .20 .50
11 George Zajankala UER .20 .50
(Birthplace misspelled Revelstroke on back)
12 Todd Nelson .20 .50
13 Dave Michayluk .20 .50
14 Bruce Racine .24 .60
15 Rob Dopson .24 .60
16 Bert Godin TR .04 .10
17 Ed Patterson .24 .60
18 Justin Duberman .20 .50
19 Sandy Smith .20 .50
20 Jason Smart .20 .50
21 Ken Priestlay .20 .50
22 Daniel Gauthier .20 .50
23 Robert Melanson .20 .50
24 Mark Major .20 .50
25 Paul Dyck .20 .50

1993-94 Cleveland Lumberjacks

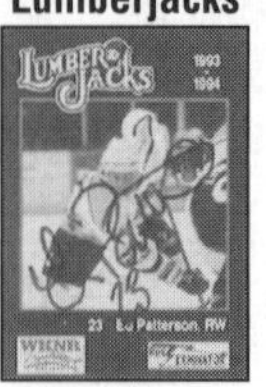

These 24 black-bordered cards feature the 1993-94 Cleveland Lumberjacks of the IHL (International Hockey League). The cards measure approximately 2 3/8" by 3 1/2" and display on their fronts color player action shots framed by red lines. The player's name, uniform number, and position are shown in white lettering in the black margin below the photo. The logos for sponsors WKNR SportsRadio and RusTerminator Electronic Rust Control rest at the bottom. The gray and white horizontal back carries the player's uniform number, name, position, biography, and statistics.

COMPLETE SET (24) 4.00 10.00
1 Title Card .10 .25
2 Rick Paterson CO .10 .25
3 Gilbert Delorme ACO .10 .25
4 Paul Dyck .30 .75
5 Travis Thiessen .20 .50
6 Mike Dagenais .20 .50
7 Chris Tamer .20 .50
8 Greg Andrusak .20 .50
9 Todd Hawkins .20 .50
10 Jamie Black .20 .50
11 Justin Duberman .20 .50
12 Paul Dyck .20 .50
13 Jock Callander UER .30 .75
(Misspelled Jack on front)
14 Leonid Toropchenko .20 .50
15 Victor Gervais .20 .50
16 Perry Ganchar .20 .50
17 Ed Patterson .20 .50
18 Ladislav Karabin .20 .50
19 Dave Michayluk .20 .50
20 Jamie Heward .20 .50
21 Pat Neaton .20 .50
22 Rob Dopson .30 .75
23 Steve Bancroft .20 .50
24 Ollie Sundstrom .20 .50
25 Grant Block .20 .50

1993-94 Cleveland Lumberjacks Postcards

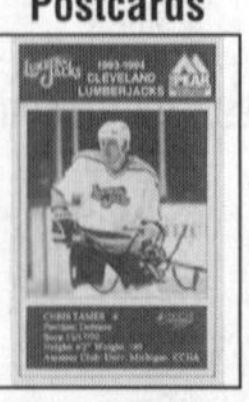

These 21 black-bordered cards feature the 1993-94 Cleveland Lumberjacks of the IHL (International Hockey League). The white-bordered postcards measure approximately 3 1/2" by 5 1/2" and display on their fronts color player action shots. The player's name, uniform number, position, and biography are shown in yellow lettering within a black rectangle beneath the picture. Sponsor logos for WMMS Radio and The Peak (a sports medicine and injury rehab facility) also appear on the front. The white horizontal back carries a tip on how to treat a minor muscle sprain. The cards are unnumbered and checklisted below in alphabetical order.

COMPLETE SET (22) 4.00 10.00
1 Greg Andrusak .20 .50
2 Steve Bancroft .20 .50
3 Jamie Black .20 .50
4 Grant Block .20 .50
5 Jock Callander .30 .75
6 Mike Dagenais .20 .50
7 Gilbert Delorme ACO .10 .25
8 Rob Dopson .30 .75
9 Justin Duberman .20 .50
10 Paul Dyck .30 .75
11 Perry Ganchar .20 .50
12 Todd Hawkins .20 .50
13 Jamie Heward .20 .50
14 Ladislav Karabin .20 .50
15 Dave Michayluk .20 .50
16 Pat Neaton .20 .50
17 Rick Paterson CO .10 .25
18 Ed Patterson .20 .50
19 Olie Sundstrom .20 .50
20 Chris Tamer .20 .50
21 Travis Thiessen .20 .50
22 Leonid Toropchenko .20 .50

1994-95 Cleveland Lumberjacks

This set was a game-night giveaway and features many cards that are identical in appearance to those in the 1993-94 issue. The set is unnumbered.

COMPLETE SET (25) 4.80 12.00
1 Rick Paterson HCO .10 .25
2 Philippe DeRouville .30 .75
3 Paul Dyck .24 .60
4 Rick Hayward .20 .50
5 Mike Dagenais .20 .50
6 Chris Tamer .30 .75
7 Len Barrie .30 .75
8 Eric Murano .20 .50
9 Brad Lauer .20 .50
10 Ian Moran .20 .50
11 Brian Farrell .20 .50
12 Jock Callander .30 .75
13 Jeff Christian .20 .50
14 Larry DePalma .20 .50
15 Joe Dziedzic .20 .50
16 Victor Gervais .20 .50
17 Dominic Pittis .20 .50
18 Perry Ganchar .20 .50
19 Ed Patterson .30 .75
20 Ladislav Karabin .20 .50
21 Dave Michayluk ACO .20 .50
22 Michal Straka .20 .50
23 Corey Beaulieu .20 .50
24 Olie Sundstrom .24 .60
25 Dale DeGray .20 .50

1995-96 Cleveland Lumberjacks

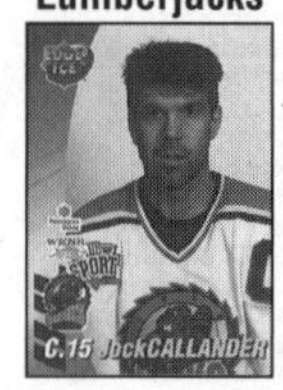

This 24-card set of the Cleveland Lumberjacks was produced by SplitSecond for Collector's Edge. The set is sponsored by Huntington Banks and WKNR Radio. It features color player portraits on the fronts with player information and statistics on the backs. The cards are unnumbered and checklisted below in alphabetical order.

COMPLETE SET (24) 4.80 12.00
1 Peter Allen .16 .40
2 Bill Armstrong .16 .40
3 Len Barrie .30 .75
4 Dave Baseggio .16 .40
5 Oleg Belov .16 .40
6 Drake Berehowsky .16 .40
7 Stefan Bergkvist .16 .40
8 Jock Callander .30 .75
9 Jeff Christian .16 .40
10 Philippe DeRouville .30 .75
11 Rusty Fitzgerald .16 .40
12 Corey Foster .16 .40
13 Perry Ganchar ACO .04 .10
14 Victor Gervais .16 .40
15 Rick Hayward .16 .40
16 Patrick Lalime 1.20 3.00
17 Brad Lauer .16 .40
18 Dave McLlwain .20 .50
19 Dave Michayluk .16 .40
20 Mark Osborne .16 .40
21 Rick Paterson CO .04 .10
22 Dominic Pittis .16 .40
23 Ryan Savoia .16 .40
24 Mike Stevens .16 .40
25 Title Card .04 .10

1996-97 Cleveland Lumberjacks

This postcard set was sponsored by the Peak at Marymount, and was a game-night giveaway. Cards are checklisted below in alphabetical order.

COMPLETE SET (25) 10.00 20.00
1 Peter Allen .30 .75
2 Bill Armstrong .30 .75
3 Serge Aubin .60 1.00
4 Brian Bonin .40 1.00
5 Sven Butenschon .30 .75
6 Buzz MASCOT .10 .25
7 Jock Callendar .80 2.00
8 Jeff Christian .30 .75
9 Rusty Fitzgerald .30 .75
10 Corey Foster .30 .75
11 Rick Hayward .30 .75
12 Jan Hrdina 1.25 1.00
13 Petr Klima .40 1.00
14 Lane Lambert .30 .75
15 Brad Lauer .30 .75
16 Dave McLlwain .40 1.00
17 Dave Michayluk .40 1.00
18 Ian Moran .40 1.00
19 Mark Osborne .30 .75
20 Jim Paek .30 .75
21 Richard Park .30 .75
22 Rick Paterson CO .10 .25
23 Ed Patterson .30 .75
24 Mike Tamburro .30 .75
25 Derek Wilkinson .30 .75

1996-97 Cleveland Lumberjacks Multi-Ad

This set features the Lumberjacks of the IHL. The set was sponsored by Mult-Ad Services and was sold by the team at it souvenir stands.

COMPLETE SET (30) 6.00 15.00
1 Checklist .04 .10
2 Peter Allen .16 .40
3 Bill Armstrong .16 .40
4 Serge Aubin .40 1.00
5 Stefan Bergkvist .16 .40
6 Brian Bonin .20 .50
7 Sven Butenschon .16 .40
8 Jock Callander .30 .75
9 Jeff Christian .16 .40
10 Rusty Fitzgerald .16 .40
11 Corey Foster .16 .40
12 Perry Ganchar CO .04 .10
13 Rick Hayward .16 .40
14 Jan Hrdina 1.20 1.00
15 Patrick Lalime 1.20 3.00
16 Lane Lambert .16 .40
17 Brad Lauer .16 .40
18 Dave McLlwain .30 .75
19 Dave Michayluk .30 .75
20 Ian Moran .20 .50
21 Mark Osborne .16 .40
22 Jim Paek .16 .40
23 Richard Park .16 .40
24 Rick Paterson CO .04 .10
25 Ed Patterson .16 .40
26 Mike Tamburro .16 .40
27 Derek Wilkinson .20 .50
28 Buzz MAS .04 .10
29 Heritage Night .04 .10
30 Logo Card .04 .10

1997-98 Cleveland Lumberjacks

This standard-sized set was distributed by the team and sold at home games.

COMPLETE SET (30) 4.00 20.00
1 Team Photo .04 .10
2 Perry Ganchar HCO .04 .10
3 Mark Osborne ACO .04 .10
4 Dave Baseggio .12 .30
5 Stefan Bergkvist .12 .30
6 Jock Callander .30 1.00
7 Mark Cornforth .12 .30
8 John Craighead .12 .30
9 Joe Dziedzic .12 .30
10 Vadim Epantchinsev .12 .30
11 Rusty Fitzgerald .12 .30
12 Brett Harkins .12 .30
13 Rick Hayward .20 .50
14 Pat Jablonski .30 1.00
15 Alexei Krivchenkov .12 .30
16 Lane Lambert .12 .30
17 Brad Lauer .12 .30
18 Chris Longo .12 .30
19 Jason McBain .12 .30
20 Ryan Mougenel .12 .30
21 Jim Paek .12 .30
22 Rob Pearson .12 .30
23 Eric Perrin .12 2.00
24 Martin St. Louis .75 5.00
25 Mike Tamburro .12 .30
26 Darren Wetherill .12 .30
27 Derek Wilkinson .20 1.00
28 Martin St. Louis .40 5.00
Eric Perrin
29 Buzz Mascot .04 .10
30 PHPA Web site .04 .01

1997-98 Cleveland Lumberjacks Postcards

This set features the Lumberjacks of the AHL. The postcard-sized set was given away as a promotional item at a home game.

COMPLETE SET (25) 7.20 30.00
1 Perry Ganchar HCO .10 .25
2 Mark Osborne ACO .10 .25
3 Darren Wetherill .30 .75
4 Rick Hayward .30 .75
5 Jim Paek .30 .75
6 Dave Baseggio .30 .75
7 Martin St. Louis .75 10.00
8 John Craighead .30 .75
9 Eric Perrin .30 4.00
10 Rusty Fitzgerald .30 .75
11 Chris Longo .30 .75
12 Jock Callander .60 2.00
13 Joe Dziedzic .30 .75
14 Lane Lambert .30 .75
15 Mark Cornforth .30 .75
16 Vadim Epantchisev .30 .75
17 Rob Pearson .30 .75
18 Jason McBain .30 .75
19 Alexei Krivchenkov .30 .75
20 Derek Wilkinson .40 1.00
21 Brad Lauer .30 .75
22 Stefan Bergkvist .30 .75
23 Brett Harkins .30 .75
24 Mike Tamburro .30 .75
25 Buzz Mascot .10 .25

1998-99 Cleveland Lumberjacks

This set was sponsored by The Peak at Marymount, and was initially a game-night giveaway. It later was sold through the team's concession stands.

COMPLETE SET (24) 4.80 12.00
1 Header Card .04 .01
2 Perry Ganchar HCO .04 .10
3 Dave Baseggio .20 .50
4 Jesse Belanger .20 .50
5 Karel Betik .20 .50
6 Zac Bierk .30 2.00
7 Jason Bonsignore .20 .50
8 Jock Callander .40 1.00
9 John Cullen .40 1.00
10 Xavier Delisle .20 .50
11 Brett Harkins .20 .50
12 Lane Lambert .20 .50
13 Mario Larocque .20 .50
14 Eric Lavigne .16 .40
15 Chris Longo .20 .50
16 Jim Paek .20 .50
17 Eduard Pershin .16 .40
18 Brent Peterson .20 .50
19 Jason Ruff .20 .50
20 Corey Schwab .30 .75
21 Andrei Skopintsev .20 .50
22 Corey Spring .16 .40
23 Derek Wilkinson .20 .75
24 Buzz MASCOT .04 .10

1999-00 Cleveland Lumberjacks

This 24-card set pictures the 1999-00 Cleveland Lumberjacks. Cards feature full-color player photos on a non-glossy card stock. Since no number appears, cards are listed alphabetically. It is thought that this set might have been a promotional giveaway.

COMPLETE SET (24) 4.80 12.00
1 Radim Bicanek .10 .25
2 Buzz Mascot .04 .10
3 Kyle Calder .75 2.00
4 Jock Callander .40 1.00
5 Jeff Christian .10 .25
6 Ted Crowley .10 .25
7 Casey Hankinson .10 .25
8 Brett Harkins .20 .50
9 Chris Herperger .10 .25
10 Ty Jones .20 .50
11 Marc Lamothe .20 .50
12 Eric Lavigne .10 .25
13 Chris Longo .10 .25
14 Evgeni Nabokov 2.00 5.00
15 Jim Paek .10 .25
16 Jeff Paul .10 .25
17 Nathan Perrott .30 .75
18 Geoff Peters .10 .25
19 Todd Rohloff .10 .25
20 Remi Royer .20 .50
21 Reid Simpson .20 .50
22 Dmitri Tolkunov .20 .50
23 Todd White .20 .50
24 Header Card .01

2000-01 Cleveland Lumberjacks

This set features the Lumberjacks of the IHL. It is believed that the set was issued as a promotional giveaway in January of 2001.

COMPLETE SET (25) 8.00 20.00
1 Christian Matte .40 1.00
2 Brian Bonin .40 1.00
3 Mike Matteucci .40 1.00
4 Eric Charron .30 .75
5 Nick Naumenko .30 .75
6 Brett McLean .30 .75
7 Pavel Patera .40 .75
8 Chris Longo .30 .75
9 Ian Herbers .40 1.00
10 Pascal Dupuis .30 .75
11 Kai Nurminen .40 1.00
12 David Brumby .30 .75
13 Zac Bierk .60 2.00
14 Jonathon Shockey .30 .75
15 Darryl Laplante .40 1.00
16 J.J. Daigneault .30 .75
17 Garrett Burnett .30 .75
18 Chris Armstrong .30 .75
19 Richard Park .40 1.00
20 Todd McLellan CO .20 .50
21 Jock Callander CO .40 1.00
22 Ray Schultz .30 .75
23 Steve Aronson .40 1.00
24 Derek Gustafson .60 1.50
25 Buzz MASCOT .10 .25

2001-02 Cleveland Barons

This set features the Barons of the AHL. The set was issued as a promotional giveaway, half at a time at two different home games. The cards are unnumbered and are listed in alphabetical order.

COMPLETE SET (24) 9.78 25.00
1 Steve Bancroft .40 .75
2 Matt Carkner .31 .75
3 Jonathan Cheechoo 1.20 5.00
4 Adam Colagiacomo .40 1.00
5 Mike Craig .31 .75
6 Rob Davison .31 .75
7 Jesse Fibiger .31 .75

8 Hannes Hyvonen .40 .75
9 Jeff Jillson .80 2.00
10 Seamus Kotyk .62 2.00
11 Ryan Kraft .31 .75
12 Eric Laplante .31 .75
13 Lynn Loyns .31 1.00
14 Andy Lundbohm .31 .75
15 Graig Mischler .31 .75
16 Robert Mulick .31 .75
17 Adam Nittel .80 1.00
18 Joel Prpic .31 .75
19 Brandon Smith .40 .75
20 Vesa Toskala 1.20 3.00
21 Chad Wiseman .31 .75
22 Miroslav Zalesak .31 .75
23 Roy Sommer CO .10 .25
24 Nick Fotiu ACO .10 .25

2002-03 Cleveland Barons

The cards are unnumbered and listed below in alphabetical order.

COMPLETE SET (24) 10.00 25.00
1 Matt Carkner .40 1.00
2 David Cloutier .40 1.00
3 David Cunniff ACO .02 .10
4 Rob Davison .40 1.00
5 Niko Dimitrakos .60 1.50
6 Jesse Fibiger .40 1.00
7 Tavis Hansen .40 1.00
8 John Jakopin .40 1.00
9 Seamus Kotyk .60 1.50
10 Ryan Kraft .40 1.00
11 Eric Laplante .40 1.00
12 Willie Levesque .40 1.00
13 Lynn Loyns .40 1.00
14 Keith McCambridge .40 1.00
15 Graig Mischler .40 1.00
16 Yuri Moscevsky .40 1.00
17 Robert Mulick .40 1.00
18 Jeff Nelson .40 1.00
19 Pat Rissmiller .40 1.00
20 Roy Sommer CO .02 .10
21 Scott Thomas .40 1.00
22 Vesa Toskala 1.25 3.00
23 Chad Wiseman .40 1.00
24 Miroslav Zalesak .40 1.00

2003-04 Cleveland Barons

COMPLETE SET (25) 5.00 12.00
1 Brad Boyes .40 1.00
2 Matt Carkner .20 .50
3 David Cloutier .20 .50
4 Ryan Clowe .20 .50
5 Jon DiSalvatore .20 .50
6 Niko Dimitrakos .30 .75
7 Christian Ehrhoff .30 .75
8 Jesse Fibiger .20 .50
9 Marcel Goc .40 1.00
10 Tavis Hansen .20 .50
11 Todd Harvey .30 .75
12 Seamus Kotyk .30 .75
13 Lynn Loyns .20 .50
14 Yuri Moscevsky .20 .50
15 Robert Mulick .20 .50
16 Doug Murray .20 .50
17 Dmitri Patzold .40 1.00
18 Tomas Plihal .20 .50
19 Pat Rissmiller .20 .50
20 Grant Stevenson .20 .50
21 Craig Valette .20 .50
22 Miroslav Zalesak .20 .50
23 Roy Sommer HCO .02 .10
24 David Cunniff ACO .02 .10
25 Mascot .02 .10

2004-05 Cleveland Barons

COMPLETE SET (27) 6.00 15.00
1 Riley Armstrong .20 .50
2 Nick Bootland .30 .75
3 Matt Carkner .30 .75
4 Ryan Clowe .40 1.00
5 Tim Conboy .20 .50
6 Scott Dobben .20 .50
7 Christian Ehrhoff .30 .75
8 Jim Fahey .20 .50
9 Aaron Gill .20 .50
10 Marcel Goc .40 1.00
11 Josh Gorges .30 .75
12 Mike Hoffman .20 .50
13 Shane Joseph .20 .50
14 Greg Labenski .20 .50
15 Doug Murray .20 .50
16 Glenn Olson .20 .50
17 Dmitri Patzold .30 .75
18 Tomas Plihal .20 .50
19 Josh Prudden .20 .50
20 Patrick Rissmiller .20 .50
21 Nolan Schaefer .30 .75
22 Garrett Stafford .20 .50
23 Grant Stevenson .20 .50
24 Craig Valette .20 .50
25 Roy Sommer CO .02 .10
26 David Cunniff ACO .02 .10
27 Slapshark MASCOT .02 .10

2005-06 Cleveland Barons

COMPLETE SET (28) 8.00 15.00
1 Riley Armstrong .20 .50
2 Steve Bernier .75 2.00
3 Matt Carkner .20 .50
4 Tom Cavanagh .20 .50
5 Ryan Clowe .30 .75
6 Tim Conboy .20 .50
7 Ray DiLauro .20 .50
8 Josh Gorges .20 .50
9 Josh Hennessy .20 .50
10 Jamie Holden .20 .50
11 Mike Iggulden .20 .50
12 Shane Joseph .20 .50
13 Lukas Kaspar .20 .50
14 Doug Murray .30 .75
15 Glenn Olson .20 .50
16 Dmitri Patzold .40 1.00
17 Tomas Plihal .20 .50
18 Joshua Prudden .20 .50
19 Pat Rissmiller .20 .50
20 Nolan Schaefer .40 1.00
21 Garrett Stafford .20 .50
22 Brad Staubitz .20 .50
23 Grant Stevenson .20 .50
24 Jonathan Tremblay .20 .50
25 Craig Valette .20 .50
26 Roy Sommer HC .02 .10
27 David Cunniff AC .02 .10
28 Jock Callander .02 .10

1998-99 Colorado Gold Kings

This set was handed out at a home game. Sets that weren't given away were later sold by the team at its souvenir shop.

COMPLETE SET (24) 10.00
1 Nicholas Chabot .20 .50
2 Trevor Converse .20 .50
3 R.J. Enga .20 .50
4 Anton Federov .20 .50
5 Wade Fennig .20 .50
6 Mark Fox .20 .50
7 Jeff Grabinsky .20 .50
8 Shawn Harris .20 .50
9 Don Lester .20 .50
10 Kirk Llano .20 .50
11 Craig Lyons .20 .50
12 Rob McCaig .20 .50
13 Rusty McKie .20 .50
14 Kevin McKinnon .20 .50
15 Bryan McMullen .20 .50
16 Chad Penney .20 .50
17 Tom Perry .20 .50
18 Bob Revermann .20 .50
19 Bogdan Rudenko .20 .50
20 Jason Simon .20 .50
21 Jeff Sirkka .20 .50
22 Brad Toporowski .20 .50
23 Kirk Tomlinson CO .20 .25
24 King Midas Mascot .10 .10

1998-99 Colorado Gold Kings Postcards

This 5x7 set was issued with blank backs and is not numbered. It is believed they were used at player signings and were never issued in team set form, making a complete set quite difficult to compile.

COMPLETE SET (22) 25.00
1 Jason Simon .60 1.50
2 Brad Toporowski .60 1.50
3 Tom Perry .60 1.50
4 Jeff Sirkka .60 1.50
5 Chad Penney .60 1.50
6 Bryan McMullen .60 1.50
7 Bogdan Rudenko .60 1.50
8 Kevin McKinnon .60 1.50
9 Bob Revermann .60 1.50
10 Craig Lyons .60 1.50
11 Kirk Tomlinson HCO .60 1.50
12 Trevor Converse .60 1.50
13 Jeff Grabinsky .60 1.50
14 R.J. Enga .60 1.50
15 Shawn Harris .60 1.50
16 Anton Fedorov .60 1.50
17 Hakan Jansson .60 1.50
18 Wade Fennig .60 1.50
19 Don Lester .60 1.50
20 Mark Fox .60 1.50
21 Kirk Llano .60 1.50
22 McDonald's Coupon .01

1999-00 Colorado Gold Kings Taco Bell

This set features the Gold Kings of the WCHL. The set was sponsored by Taco Bell and sold by the team at home games.

COMPLETE SET (26) 4.80 12.00
1 Travis Thiessen .20 .50
2 R.J. Enga .20 .50
3 Tom Perry .20 .50
4 Corey Lyons .20 .50
5 Bogdan Rudenko .20 .50
6 Don Lester CO .10 .25
7 Stephane Madore .20 .50
8 Steve Dowhy .20 .50
9 Greg Eisler .20 .50
10 Jean-Francois Picard .20 .50
11 King Midas MAS .10 .25
12 Steve Vezina .30 .75
13 Kevin McKinnon .20 .50
14 Craig Lyons .20 .50
15 Aaron Schweitzer .20 .50
16 Carl LeBlanc .20 .50
17 Daniel Olers .20 .50
18 Dean Ewen .20 .50
19 Frederik Beaubien .30 .75
20 Kirk Tomlinson .20 .50
21 Wade Fennig .20 .50
22 Kristoffer Eriksson .20 .50
23 Rob McCaig .20 .50
24 Greg Gatto .20 .50
25 Colorado Gold Kings .10 .25
26 Taco Bell Logo .01

1999-00 Colorado Gold Kings Wendy's

This set features the Gold Kings of the WCHL. The set features postcard-sized photos and a Wendy's ad on the back of each. The set was sold by the team at home games.

COMPLETE SET (22) 4.00 10.00
1 Jean-Francois Picard .20 .50
2 Corey Lyons .20 .50
3 Eric Long .20 .50
4 Wade Fennig .20 .50
5 R.J. Enga .20 .50
6 Travis Thiessen .20 .50
7 Daniel Olers .20 .50
8 Carl LeBlanc .20 .50
9 Greg Eisler .20 .50
10 Kevin McKinnon .20 .50
11 Dean Ewen .20 .50
12 Stephane Madore .20 .50
13 Darcy Anderson .20 .50
14 Tom Perry .20 .50
15 Rob McCaig .20 .50
16 Bogdan Rudenko .20 .50
17 Steve Vezina .30 .75
18 Aaron Schweitzer .20 .50
19 Craig Lyons .20 .50
20 Kirk Tomlinson CO .20 .50
21 Don Lester CO .10 .25
22 King Midas MAS .10 .25

2001-02 Colorado Gold Kings

COMPLETE SET (22) 10.00
1 Dwayne Blais .50
2 Aaron Boh .50
3 Zac Boyer .50
4 Chad Cabana .50
5 Colin Chaulk .50
6 Kirk Daubenspeck .75
7 R.J. Enga .50
8 Mike Garrow .50
9 Mark Gowan .50
10 Brent Henley .50
11 Darcy Johnson .50
12 Jason Knox .50
13 Cam Kryway .50
14 Craig Lyons .50
15 Mike Nicholishen .50
16 Tom Perry .50
17 Greg Schmidt .50
18 Juraj Slovak .50
19 Travis Thiessen .50
20 Allen Pedersen HCO .10
21 Kevin McKinnon ACO .10
22 Mascot .10

2003-04 Colorado Eagles

COMPLETE SET (25) 8.00 20.00
1 Lee Arnold .40 1.00
2 Ryan Bach .40 1.00
3 Gian Baldrica .40 1.00
4 Daniel Bohac .40 1.00
5 Igor Bonderev .40 1.00
6 Jesse Cook .40 1.00
7 Phil Crowe .60 1.50
8 Fraser Filipic .40 1.00
9 Aaron Grosul .40 1.00
10 Cam Kuzyk .40 1.00
11 Mike McGhan .40 1.00
12 Riley Nelson .40 1.00
13 Greg Pankewicz .40 1.00
14 Brad Patterson .40 1.00
15 Lee Ruff .40 1.00
16 Scott Swanson .40 1.00
17 Brent Thompson .60 1.50
18 Ryan Tobler .60 1.50
19 Brad Williamson .40 1.00
20 Karlis Zirnis .40 1.00
21 Chris Stewart CO .02 .10
22 Ralph Backstrom GM .02 .10
23 Mascot .02 .10
24 Team Photo .02 .10
25 Staff .02 .10

2004-05 Colorado Eagles

COMPLETE SET (24) 15.00
1 Team Card .10
2 Ralph Backstrom .10
3 Paulo Colaiacovo 1.00
4 Jesse Cook .75
5 Matt Desrosiers .75
6 Fraser Filipic .75
7 Aaron Grosul .75
8 Chris Hartsburg .75
9 Mike Lephart .75
10 Kris Mallette .75
11 Kevin Marsh .75
12 Kevin McDonald .75
13 Riley Nelson .75
14 Greg Pankewicz .75
15 Sean Robertson .75
16 Lee Ruff .75
17 Chris Stewart CO .75
18 David Svagrovsky .75
19 Ryan Tobler .75
20 Tyler Weiman .75
21 Brad Williamson .75
22 Karlis Zirnis .75
23 Slapshot MASCOT .10
24 Team Staff .10

2005-06 Colorado Eagles

COMPLETE SET (26) 8.00 20.00
1 Erik Adams .40 1.00
2 Lee Arnold .40 1.00
3 Jeff Blair .40 1.00
4 Les Borsheim .40 1.00
5 Paulo Colaiacovo .60 1.50
6 Matt Desrosiers .40 1.00
7 Fraser Filipic .40 1.00
8 Aaron Grosul .40 1.00
9 Chris Hartsburg .40 1.00
10 Garrett Larson .40 1.00
11 Jason Lundmark .40 1.00
12 Ed McGrane .40 1.00
13 Riley Nelson .40 1.00
14 Greg Pankewicz .40 1.00
15 Nick Parillo .40 1.00
16 Scott Polaski .40 1.00
17 Sean Robertson .40 1.00
18 Ryan Tobler .40 1.00
19 Brad Williamson .40 1.00
20 Chris Stewart CO .02 .10
21 Phil Crowe AC .02 .10
22 Ralph Backstrom PRES/GM .10 .25
23 Team Staff .02 .10
24 Eagles Chicks DANCERS .40 1.00
25 Slapshot MASCOT .02 .10
26 Colorado Eagles .20 .50

2006-07 Colorado Eagles

COMPLETE SET (31) 8.00 15.00
1 Team Card .10 .25
2 Erik Adams .30 .75
3 Lee Arnold .30 .75
4 Jay Birnie .30 .75
5 Tim Boron .30 .75
6 Les Borsheim .30 .75
7 Paulo Colaiacovo .40 1.00
8 Marco Emond .30 .75
9 Fraser Filipic .30 .75
10 Steve Haddon .30 .75
11 Chris Hartsburg .30 .75
12 Brent Hughes .30 .75
13 Seth Leonard .30 .75
14 Ed McGrane .30 .75
15 Riley Nelson .30 .75
16 Greg Pankewicz .30 .75
17 Scott Polaski .30 .75
18 Sean Robertson .30 .75
19 Aaron Schneekloth .30 .75
20 Craig Strain .30 .75
21 Ryan Tobler .30 .75
22 Brad Williamson .30 .75
23 Slapshot MASCOT .10
24 Chris Stewart CO .10 .25
25 Phil Crowe ACO .10 .25
26 Ryan Bach ACO .10 .25
27 Ralph Backstrom PRES .10 .25
28 Tony Deynzer EQ MGR .10
29 Chris Porowski TR .10
30 Tori Holt ANN .02 .10
31 Eagles Chicks DANCERS .20 .50

2002-03 Columbia Inferno

COMPLETE SET (18) 25.00
97 Josh Blackburn 2.00
98 Paul Cabana 1.25
99 Robin Carruthers 1.25
100 Trevor Demmans 1.25
101 Regan Darby 1.25
102 Corey Hessler 1.25
103 Eric Labelle 2.00
104 Denis Martynyuk 1.25
105 Barrie Moore 1.25
106 Justin Morrison 1.25
107 Sean Owens 1.25
108 Chris Pittman 1.25
109 Tim Smith 1.25
110 Chris St. Croix 1.25
111 Rejean Stringer 1.25
112 Matt Ulwelling 1.25
113 Dennis Vial 3.00
114 Shawn Wansborough 1.25

2003-04 Columbia Inferno

This set was sold by the team at home games. The numbering reflects this set as part of the entire run of RBI Sports series this year. The production run was reported to be 250 sets.

COMPLETE SET (16) 25.00
97 Greg Amadio 1.50
98 Josh Blackburn 2.00
99 Alexandre Burrows 1.50
100 Paul Cabana 1.50
101 Robin Carruthers 1.50
102 Derek Eastman 1.50
103 Terry Harrison 1.50
104 Corey Hessler 1.50
105 Eric Labelle 1.50
106 Robert McVicar 2.00
107 Barrie Moore 1.50
108 Brandon Nolan 1.50
109 Chris Pittman 1.50
110 Tim Smith 2.00
111 Chris St. Croix 1.50
112 Dennis Vial 2.00

2003-04 Columbia Inferno Update

Produced by RBI Sports as a late season update, this was limited to 250 sets.

COMPLETE SET (6) 5.00
50 Mike Hanson 1.00
51 Sean Owens 1.00
52 Mike Roemensky 1.00
53 Marc-Andre Roy 1.00
54 Jesse Schultz 1.00
55 Matt Ulwelling 1.00

1966-67 Columbus Checkers

This 16-card set measures 4 x 7 1/4" and features a black and white photo on the front along with players name at the bottom. Backs are blank. Cards are unnumbered and checklisted below alphabetically.

COMPLETE SET (16) 35.00 70.00
1 John Bailey 2.50 5.00
2 Moe Bartoli 2.50 5.00
3 Kerry Bond 2.50 5.00
4 Andre Daoust 2.50 5.00
5 Bert Fizzell 2.50 5.00
6 Marcel Goudreau 2.50 5.00
7 Jim Graham 2.50 5.00
8 Paul Jackson 2.50 5.00
9 Ken Laidlaw 2.50 5.00
10 Noel Lirette 2.50 5.00
11 Gary Longman 2.50 5.00
12 Garry Macmillan 2.50 5.00
13 Gary Mork 2.50 5.00
14 Matt Thorpe 2.50 5.00
15 Jack Turner 2.50 5.00
16 Alton White 2.50 5.00

1967-68 Columbus Checkers

Little is known about this early team-issued photo set from the Checkers of the IHL. It is believed they were issued as a promotional item in response to mailed-in requests from fans. Any further information can be forwarded to hockeymag@beckett.com.

COMPLETE SET (16) 37.50 75.00
1 Team Photo 2.50 5.00
2 Moe Bartoli 2.50 10.00
3 Bill Bond 2.50 5.00
4 Serge Boudreault 2.50 5.00
5 Gord Dibley 2.50 10.00
6 Bert Fizzell 2.50 5.00
7 Chuck Kelly 2.50 5.00
8 Ken Saunders 2.50 5.00
9 Nelson Leclair 2.50 5.00
10 Real Paquette 2.50 5.00
11 Dick Proceviat 2.50 5.00
12 Hartley Estabrooks 2.50 5.00
13 Ken Sutyla 2.50 5.00
14 Nelson Tremblay 2.50 5.00
15 Jack Turner 2.50 5.00
16 Al White 2.50 5.00

1997-98 Columbus Cottonmouths

This 24-card set was handed out over the span of five games, and thus is extremely difficult to find in complete form.

COMPLETE SET (24) 8.00 20.00
1 Jerome Bechard .40 1.00
2 Chris Bergeron .40 1.00
3 Claude Fillion .40 1.00
4 Eric Germain .40 1.00
5 Brian Idalski .40 1.00
6 Mick Kempffer .40 1.00
7 Olaf Kjenstadt .40 1.00
8 Doug Mann .40 1.00
9 Grady Manson .40 1.00
10 Derek Marchand .40 1.00
11 Bobby Marshall .40 1.00
12 Randy Murphy .40 1.00
13 Frankie Ouellette .60 1.50
14 Kevin Plager .40 1.00
15 Brad Prefontaine .40 1.00
16 Marcel Richard .40 1.00
17 John Sincinski .40 1.00
18 Greg Taylor .40 1.00
19 David Wainwright .40 1.00
20 Tom Wilson .40 1.00
21 Phil Roberto GM .10 .25
22 Bruce Garber HCO .10 .25
23 Charles B. Morrow .10 .25
24 Pete Carson .40 1.00

1998-99 Columbus Cottonmouths

This 24-card set was handed out at a home game in March of that season, and was later sold for at the team's souvenir stands for $5 per set.

COMPLETE SET (24) 3.60 9.00
1 Jerome Bechard .20 .50
2 Dan Brown .20 .50
3 Derek Crimin .20 .50
4 Claude Fillion .20 .50
5 Brian Idalski .20 .50
6 Mick Kempffer .20 .50
7 Grady Manson .20 .50
8 Roman Markhovski .20 .50
9 Mike Martens .20 .50
10 David Neilson .20 .50
11 Frankie Ouellette .20 .50
12 Kevin Plager .20 .50
13 Brad Prefontaine .20 .50
14 Marcel Richard .20 .50
15 Corwin Saurdiff .20 .50
16 Jean-Alain Schneider .20 .50
17 Robbie Sinclair .20 .50
18 Thomas Stewart .20 .50
19 Tom Wilson .20 .50
20 Derek Marchand ACO .04 .10
21 Phil Roberto GM .04 .10
22 Bruce Garber HCO .04 .10
23 Pete Carson HTR .04 .10
24 Martha Morrow .20 .50

1999-00 Columbus Cottonmouths

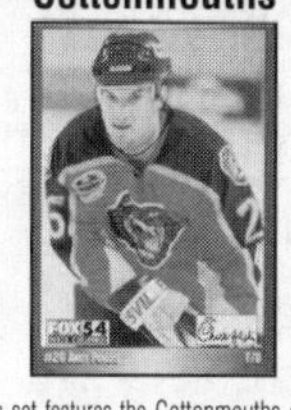

This set features the Cottonmouths of the CHL. The set was handed out as a promotional giveaway at home games, with one five-card strip being issued at each game. The complete set was later sold by the team for $5.

COMPLETE SET (28) 4.80 12.00
1 Aaron Vickar .20 .50
2 Kamil Kuriplach .20 .50
3 Mick Kempffer .20 .50
4 Kevin Plager .20 .50
5 Martha Morrow OWN .10 .25
6 Derek Crimin .20 .50
7 Jason Given .20 .50
8 Marcel Richard .20 .50
9 Ryan Aikia .20 .50
10 Phil Roberto GM .10 .25
11 Jerome Bechard .20 .50
12 Doug Mann .20 .50
13 Mark Martins .20 .50
14 Tommi Santala .30 .75
15 Bruce Garber HCO .10 .25
16 Mark Scott .20 .50
17 Kelly Van Hiltgen .20 .50
18 Frankie Ouellette .30 .75
19 Jaroslav Kerestes .20 .50
20 Brian Idalski ACO .10 .25
21 Per Fernhall .20 .50
22 Jackson Hegland .20 .50
23 Robert Frid .20 .50
24 Olaf Kjenstad .30 .75
25 Randy Scrimshire EQM .10 .25
26 Brodie Coffin .20 .50
27 Andy Powers .20 .50
28 Tonda Jackson AGM .10 .25

2000-01 Columbus Cottonmouths

This set features the Cottonmouths of the CHL. The cards were issued as giveaways over the course of five home dates, in the form of five-card perforated strips.

COMPLETE SET (25) 8.00 20.00
1 Jerome Bechard .40 1.00
2 Ryan Brown .40 1.00
3 Kris Cantu .40 1.00
4 Mick Kempffer .40 1.00
5 Jaroslav Kerestes .40 1.00
6 Doug Mann .40 1.00
7 Bobby Marshall .40 1.00
8 Mike Martens .40 1.00
9 Martin Menard .40 1.00
10 Riley Nelson .40 1.00
11 Frankie Ouellette .40 1.00
12 Daniel Payette .40 1.00
13 Andy Powers .40 1.00
14 Greg Quebec .40 1.00
15 Blaine Russell .40 1.00
16 Drew Schoneck .40 1.00
17 Kris Schultz .40 1.00
18 Rob Schweyer .40 1.00
19 Blake Sheane .40 1.00
20 Craig Stahl .40 1.00
21 Bruce Garber CO .10 .25
22 Phil Roberto GM .10 .25
23 Randy Scrimpshire EM .10 .25
24 Boomer MASCOT .10 .25
25 Teri LaSalle TR .10 .25

2002-03 Columbus Cottonmouths

COMPLETE SET (24) 20.00
1 Jerome Bechard 1.00
2 Phil Cole 1.00
3 Randy Copley 1.50
4 Brent Cullaton 1.00
5 Mitch Fritz 1.00
6 Chad Hamilton 1.00
7 J.J.Hunter 1.00
8 Matus Kostur 1.50
9 Mike Lee 1.50
10 Carlyle Lewis 1.50
11 Andrew Long 1.00
12 Sean McAslan 1.00
13 Darren McAusland 1.00
14 John Morlang 1.00
15 Mike Morrison 1.50
16 Ryan Risidore 1.00
17 Bart Rushmer 1.00
18 Darren Tiemstra 1.00
19 Jeff Zehr 1.50
20 Phil Roberto GM/CO .25
21 Larry Kish ACO .25
22 Randy Scrimpshire EQM .25
23 Boomer Mascot .10
24 Owners .01

2003-04 Columbus Cottonmouths

This set was issued as a promotional giveaway over two home games. The cards were issued in perforated sheet form.

COMPLETE SET (30) 15.00 30.00
1 Salvador Diaz-Verson OWN .02 .10
2 Shelby Amos OWN .02 .10
3 Brian Curran CO .02 .10
4 Jerome Bechard ACO .02 .10
5 Heath Kaufman EQM .02 .10
6 Jason Stevens TR .02 .10
7 Rumun Ndur .75 2.00
8 Jason Tapp .75 2.00
9 Mitch Fritz .75 2.00
10 Marc-Andre Thinel .75 2.00
11 Ryan Davis .40 1.00
12 Joel Martin .75 2.00
13 Olivier Michaud .60 1.50
14 Tomas Micka .40 1.00
15 Mascot .02 .10
16 Brad Voth .40 1.00
17 Colin Pepperall .40 1.00
18 Dan Tudin .40 1.00
19 Matt Shasby .40 1.00
20 Mathieu Roy .75 2.00
21 Carlyle Lewis .40 1.00
22 John Morlang .40 1.00
23 Kenton Smith .40 1.00
24 Peter Hogan .40 1.00
25 Ryan Risidore .40 1.00
26 Christian Larrivee .75 2.00
27 Dan Tessier .75 2.00
28 Jean-Francois Plourde .40 1.00
29 Ray DiLauro .40 1.00
30 Matus Kostur .75 2.00

2004-05 Columbus Cottonmouths

Very little is known about this set featuring the Cottonmouths of the SPHL and no pricing is available. Please forward any additional info to hockeymag@beckett.com.

COMPLETE SET (?)
1 Terry Friesen
2 Mick Kempffer
3 Joel Pullman
4 Chris Rook
5 Chad Rycroft
6 Brent Toews
7 Orrin Hergott
8 Tylor Keller
9 Ryan Haggerty
10 Tom McMonagle
11 Colby Will
12 Lorne Misita
13 Matt Mathias
14 Ryan Rutz
15 Craig Stahl
16 Ryan Aikia
17 Brock Johnson
18 Tim Green
19 Daryl Moor
20 Doug Mann
21 Jim Underwood
22 Jerome Bechard CO
23 Michael Slayton EQM
24 Jason Stevens TR

2003-04 Columbus Stars

This set features the Stars of the UHL. The set is labeled as a "youth season pass" on the front. The names of the players are not listed, but they can be identified by their jersey numbers. The back of each card lists the Stars schedule. Since the team folded midway through the season, only a handful of these cards were given out. Due to lack of market activity, we are unable to price these cards.

COMPLETE SET (5)
1 Tom Nemeth
2 Eric Naud
3 Greg Hewitt
4 Scott Levins
5 Chris Taliercio

2000-01 Connecticut Huskies

This set features the Huskies of the NCAA. It is believed that it was issued as a promotional giveaway as are all NCAA issues, but that has not been confirmed. The cards are printed on heavier card stock than usual and feature a swirling blue design along the bottom front.

COMPLETE SET (18) 15.00 30.00
1 Mike Anderson .75 2.00
2 Bret Bostock .75 2.00
3 Mike Boylan .75 2.00
4 Scott Brown .75 2.00
5 Ron D'Angelo .75 2.00
6 Eric Goclowski .75 2.00
7 Michael Goldkind .75 2.00
8 Matt Herhal .75 2.00
9 Anders Johnson .75 2.00

10 Kurt Kamienski	.75	2.00
11 Trent Landry	.75	2.00
12 Ciro Longobardi	.75	2.00
13 Charles Ridolf	.75	2.00
14 Evan Schwarz	.75	2.00
15 Travis Wood	.75	2.00
16 Bruce Marshall CO	.20	.50
17 UCONN Huskies	.20	.50
18 UCONN SCHEDULE	.04	.10

1992-93 Cornell Big Red

This set features Cornell of the NCAA and is believed to be a promotional giveaway. The cards measure an oversized 2 3/4 by 3 3/4. They feature a posed color photo on the front with a white border and the words Cornell Hockey 92 93 on the front.The cards are listed below in alphabetical order.

COMPLETE SET (30)	6.00	15.00
1 Andrew Bandurski	.20	1.00
2 Etienne Belzile	.20	.50
3 Geoff Bumstead	.30	.75
4 Brad Chartrand	.20	.50
5 Rick Davis	.20	.50
6 John DeHart	.20	.50
7 Andre Doll	.20	.50
8 P.C. Drouin	.30	1.00
9 Dan Dufresne	.20	.50
10 Blair Ettles	.20	.50
11 Christian Felli	.20	.50
12 Russ Hammond	.20	.50
13 Shaun Hannah	.20	.50
14 Steve Hayden	.20	.50
15 Bill Holowatiuk	.20	.50
16 Ryan Hughes	.20	.50
17 Jake Karam	.20	.50
18 Jiri Kloboucek	.20	.50
19 Geoff Lopatka	.20	.50
20 Joel McArter	.20	.50
21 Tyler McManus	.20	.50
22 Devon Nielsen	.20	.50
23 Geoff Raynak	.20	.50
24 Mike Sancimino	.20	.50
25 Mark Scollan	.20	.50
26 Tim Shean	.20	.50
27 Greg Swenson	.20	.50
28 Alex Vershinin	.20	.50
29 Jason Vogel	.20	.50
30 Mark Taylor ACO	.04	.10

1993-94 Cornell Big Red

As typically is the case with NCAA sets, this series was issued as a promotional giveaway. The cards are unnumbered, so the set is checklisted below in alphabetical order.

COMPLETE SET (30)	4.80	12.00
1 Vincent Auger	.16	.40
2 Andrew Bandurski	.16	.40
3 Geoff Bumstead	.16	.40
4 Brad Chartrand	.16	.40
5 Matt Cooney	.16	.40
6 John DeHart	.16	.40
7 Andre Doll	.16	.40
8 Dan Dufresne	.16	.40
9 Blair Ettles	.16	.40
10 Christian Felli	.16	.40
11 Tony Fergin	.16	.40
12 Shaun Hannah	.16	.40
13 Bill Holowatiuk	.16	.40
14 Jake Karam	.16	.40
15 Jason Kendall	.16	.40
16 Jiri Kloboucek	.16	.40
17 Geoff Lopatka	.16	.40
18 Joel McArter	.16	.40
19 Tyler McManus	.16	.40
20 Jamie Papp	.16	.40
21 Mike Sancimino	.16	.40
22 Mark Scollan	.16	.40
23 Tim Shean	.16	.40
24 Eddy Skazyk	.16	.40
25 Alex Vershinin	.16	.40
26 Jason Weber	.16	.40
27 Steve Wilson	.16	.40
28 Chad Wilson	.16	.40
29 Jason Zubkus	.16	.40
30 Mark Taylor ACO	.04	.10

1991-92 Cornwall Royals

This 28-card set measures approximately 2 5/8" by 3 3/4". The fronts feature borderless posed color player photos. The player's name appears in the left upper corner, while the team logo is in the right upper corner. The Religious Hospitallers Of St. Joseph Health Centre Of Cornwall logo is printed in a white bar under the photo. On a white background, the backs carry "Royals Against Illegal Drug Tips from Cornwall Police Service" in the upper portion and sponsor logos below.

COMPLETE SET (28)	4.00	10.00
1 Jason Meloche	.16	.40
2 Mark Desantis	.16	.40
3 Richard Raymond	.16	.40
4 Gord Pell	.16	.40
5 Dave Lemay	.16	.40
6 John Lovell CO	.04	.10
7 Ryan Vandenbussche	.20	1.00
8 David Babcock	.16	.40
9 Sam Oliveira	.16	.40
10 Jeremy Stevenson	.20	.50
11 Todd Walker	.16	.40
12 Jean-Alain Schneider	.16	.40
13 Ilpo Kauhanen	.20	.50
14 Guy Leveque	.20	.50
15 Shayne Gaffar	.16	.40
16 Rival Fullum	.16	.40
17 Mike Prokopec	.20	.50
18 Nathan LaFayette	.20	.50
19 Larry Courville	.20	.50
20 Chris Clancy	.16	.40
21 Tom Nemeth	.20	.50
22 Jeff Reid	.16	.40
23 Paul Andrea	.16	.40
24 John Slaney	.30	1.00
25 Alan Letang	.16	.40
26 Rob Dykeman	.20	.50
27 Paul Fixter CO Brian O'Leary CO	.04	.10
28 Chief of Police	.04	.10

1999-00 Cornwall Colts

This set features the Colts of the COHL, a tier 2 junior league. The listing below is NOT complete. Any additional information can be forwarded to hockeymag@beckett.com.

COMPLETE SET (?)
1 Travis Albers
2 Joel Bergeron
3 Matt Collins
4 Jeff Legue
5 Kacey McDonell
6 Luc Paquin

2003-04 Cornwall Colts

The Colts play in the Central Junior Hockey League in Ontario, a Tier 2 circuit. Only two cards are confirmed to exist for this set so far. Information on others can be sent to hockeymag@beckett.com.

COMPLETE SET (?)		
1 Aaron Bogosian		1.00
2 Sean Flanagan		1.00

1999-00 Corpus Christi IceRays

This set features the IceRays of the WPHL. The set was produced by Grandstand and issued in two series. The second series was issued during the playoffs, so these contain complete 1999-2000 stats. The cards are unnumbered, and so are listed in alphabetical order.

COMPLETE SET (46)	8.00	20.00
1 Tyler Boucher	.20	.50
2 Geoff Bumstead	.30	.75
3 Paul Doherty	.20	.50
4 Pat Dunn	.20	.50
5 Jason Genik	.20	.50
6 Regan Harper	.20	.50
7 Brent Hoiness	.20	.50
8 Trevor Janicki	.20	.50
9 Cory Johnson	.20	.50
10 Alex Kholomeyev	.30	.75
11 Roger Lewis	.20	.50
12 Dustin McArthur	.20	.50
13 Darryl Olsen	.20	.50
14 Jody Praznik	.20	.50
15 Tobin Praznik	.20	.50
16 Bob Quinnell	.20	.50
17 Chris Robertson	.20	.50
18 Layne Roland	.20	.50
19 Andy Ross	.20	.50
20 Dennis Shiryaev	.20	.50
21 Eddy Skazyk	.20	.50
22 Mike Tomlinson	.20	.50
23 Phil Valk	.20	.50
24 Quinten Van Horlick	.20	.50
25 Mike Vandenberghe	.20	.50
26 Kurt Wickenheiser	.20	.50
27 Brad Wingfield	.20	.50
28 Taylor Hall CO	.20	.50
29 Jody Praznik	.20	.50
30 Scott Brower	.20	.50
31 Geoff Bumstead AS	.30	.75
32 Tobin Praznik	.20	.50
32 Jody Praznik	.20	.50
33 Geoff Bumstead	.30	.75
33 Brad Wingfield	.10	.25
34 Kurt Wickenheiser	.20	.50
34 Geoff Bumstead	.30	.75
34 Tobin Praznik	.10	.25
35 Radio Celebrities	.04	.01
36 Home Opener	.10	.10
37 Corpus Christi Icegirls	.30	.75
38 Party Patrol	.10	.10
39 SugarRay MASCOT	.10	.25
40 Corpus Christi IceRays	.20	.50
41 Best Fans in the WPHL	.10	.10
42 ValueBank Texas	.04	.01

1992-93 Dallas Freeze

This 20-card standard-size set features the Dallas Freeze of the Central Hockey League. White-bordered color player photos adorn the fronts of these cards. The Freeze logo appears on both sides of the card. In the border beneath the photo are the player's name and position. The cards are unnumbered and checklisted below in alphabetical order.

COMPLETE SET (20)	3.20	8.00
1 Wayne Anchikoski	.20	.50
2 Gary Audette	.20	.50
3 Jeff Beaudin	.20	.50
4 Troy Binnie	.20	.50
5 Brian Bruininks	.20	.50
6 Derek Crawford	.20	.50
7 Dave Doucette	.20	.50
8 Don Dwyer	.20	.50
9 Joe Eagan	.20	.50
10 Ron Flockhart CO	.30	.75
11 Frank Lascala	.20	.50
12 Robert Lewis	.20	.50
13 Joey Mittelsteadt	.20	.50
14 Rico Rossi	.20	.50
15 Dean Shmyr	.20	.50
16 Doug Sinclair	.20	.50
17 Greg Smith	.20	.50
18 Jason Taylor	.20	.50
19 Mike Zanier	.30	.75
20 Team Photo	.20	.50

1993-94 Dallas Freeze

These oddly shaped round cards are approximately the size of a hockey puck. They came in a plastic container with the team logo on the front and were available from the team's booster club at home games.

COMPLETE SET (18)	2.40	6.00
1 Wayne Anchikoski	.20	.50
2 Jeff Beaudin	.16	.40
3 Troy Binnie	.20	.50
4 Brian Bruininks	.16	.40
5 Derek Crawford	.16	.40
6 Dave Doucette	.20	.50
7 Don Dwyer	.16	.40
8 Mark Holick	.16	.40
9 Randy Jaycock	.16	.40
10 Frank LaScala	.16	.40
11 Robert Lewis	.16	.40
12 Joey McTamney	.16	.40
13 Joey Mittelsteadt	.16	.40
14 Dean Shmyr	.16	.40
15 Greg Smith	.16	.40
16 Jason Taylor	.16	.40
17 Jason White	.16	.40
18 Ron Flockhart CO	.20	.50

2005-06 Danbury Trashers

COMPLETE SET	5.00	12.00
1 Alex Goupil	.20	.50
2 Donny Glover	.20	.50
3 Eric Lind	.20	.50
4 Drew Omicioli	.20	.50
5 Danny Stewart	.20	.50
6 Sergei Durden	.20	.50
7 David Beauregard	.20	.50
8 Frederic Belanger	.20	.50
9 Jayme Platt	.20	.50
10 Regan Kelly	.20	.50
11 Sylvain Daigle	.20	.50
12 Dave MacIsaac	.20	.50
13 Mike Omicioli	.20	.50
14 Luke Sellers	.20	.50
15 Troy Smith	.20	.50
16 Mario Larocque	.20	.50
17 2005-06 UHL All-Stars	.20	.50
18 Ryan Barnes	.20	.50
19 Ed Campbell	.20	.50
20 Jamie Thompson	.20	.50
21 Jean-Michel Daoust	.20	.50
22 Brad Wingfield	.20	.50
23 Shawn Collymore	.20	.50
24 Jeff Daw	.20	.50
25 David Hymovitz	.20	.50
26 Paul Gillis CO	.02	.10
27 Paul Sacco	.02	.10
28 A.J. Galante OWN	.02	.10
29 Scrappy MASCOT	.02	.10

1992-93 Dayton Bombers

This set features the Bombers of the ECHL. Just 2,500 sets were produced, with 2,300 given away as a game-night promotion and the remaining 200 sold for $5. The cards are unnumbered and checklisted below in alphabetical order.

COMPLETE SET (24)	4.00	10.00
1 John Beaulieu DJ	.04	.10
2 Steve Bogoyevac	.20	.50
3 Christopher DJ	.04	.10
4 Darren Colbourne	.20	.50
5 Derek Crawford	.20	.50
6 Dan-O DJ	.04	.10
7 Derek Donald	.20	.50
8 Ray Edwards	.20	.50
9 Doug Evans	.20	.50
10 Sandy Galuppo	.30	.75
11 Shayne Green	.20	.50
12 Rod Houk	.20	.50
13 Peter Kasowski	.20	.50
14 Steve Kerrigan	.20	.50
15 Frank Kovacs	.20	.50
16 Darren Langdon	.30	.75
17 Denis Larocque	.20	.50
18 Darwin McPherson	.20	.50
19 Tom Nemeth	.20	.50
20 Claude Noel CO	.04	.10
21 Tony Peters	.20	.50
22 Marshall Phillips	.20	.50
23 Mike Reier	.20	.50
24 Steve Wilson	.20	.50

1993-94 Dayton Bombers

This set features the Bombers of the ECHL. 2,500 sets were produced and given away as a game-night promotion. Cards 19-28 feature radio disc jockeys.

COMPLETE SET (28)	2.80	7.00
1 Title Card CL	.04	.10
2 Jeff Levy	.16	.40
3 Steve Wilson	.16	.40
4 Jason Downey	.16	.40
5 Jim Peters	.16	.40
6 Ondrej Kriz	.16	.40
7 Steve Bogoyevac	.16	.40
8 Jason Disiewich	.16	.40
9 Marc Savard	.16	.40
10 Dan O'Shea	.16	.40
11 Tom Nemeth	.16	.40
12 Guy Prince	.16	.40
13 Ray Edwards	.16	.40
14 Sergei Kharin	.16	.40
15 Derek Donald	.16	.40
16 Darwin McPherson	.16	.40
17 Jeff Stolp	.16	.40
18 Adam Bomber (Mascot)	.04	.10
19 Kim	.04	.10
20 Robby	.04	.10
21 Lisa	.04	.10
22 Marshall Phillips	.04	.10
23 Dan-O	.04	.10
24 John(B-Man) Beaulieu	.04	.10
25 Christopher	.04	.10
26 Steve Kerrigan	.16	.40
27 Tony Peters	.16	.40
28 Shaun Higgins Major Dick Hale	.04	.10

1994-95 Dayton Bombers

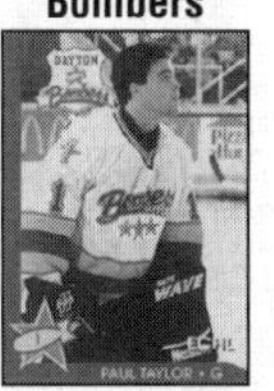

This set features the Bombers of the ECHL. 5,000 sets were produced, 1,500 of which were given away as a game night promotion.

COMPLETE SET (24)	3.20	8.00
1 Title Card CL	.04	.10
2 Paul Taylor	.16	.40
3 Steve Wilson	.16	.40
4 Jason Downey	.16	.40
5 Craig Charron	.16	.40
6 Jim Lessard	.16	.40
7 Karson Kaebel	.16	.40
8 Jamie Steer	.16	.40
9 Rob Hartnell	.16	.40
10 Mike Doers	.16	.40
11 Sean Gagnon	.20	.50
12 Kevin Brown	.16	.40
13 John Brill	.16	.40
14 Dean Fedorchuk	.16	.40
15 Tony Gruba	.16	.40
16 Steve Lingren	.16	.40
17 Brandon Smith	.16	.40
18 Jeff Stolp	.20	.50
19 Mike Vandenberghe	.16	.40
20 Jim Playfair	.16	.40
21 Goal Celebration	.16	.40
22 Jamie Steer AS	.16	.40
23 Steve Wilson AW	.16	.40
24 Jeff Stolp AW	.20	.50

1995-96 Dayton Bombers

This set features the Bombers of the ECHL. The cards are oversized (5 by 7 inches). The cards were limited in production to 500 copies each. One card was given away during each of 32 home games (3 games did not feature a card) inside the official game program. Purchase of a program was required to obtain a card.

COMPLETE SET (32)	10.00	25.00
1 Jim Playfair CO	.30	.75
2 Sean Ortiz	.30	.75
3 Derek Herlofsky	.60	1.50
4 Paul Andrea	.30	.75
5 Nick Poole	.30	.75
6 Steve Lingren	.40	1.00
7 Kevin Brown	.30	.75
8 Jason Downey	.30	.75
9 Sergei Kharin	.40	1.00
10 Matt McElwee	.30	.75
11 Mike Naylor	.30	.75
12 Ted Russell	.30	.75
13 Colin Miller	.40	1.00
14 Brent Brekke	.30	.75
15 John Brill	.30	.75
16 Mike Murray	.30	.75
17 Sean Gagnon	.60	1.50
18 Brian Renfrew	.40	1.00
19 Rob Peters	.30	.75
20 Jeff Petruic	.30	.75
21 Steve Roberts	.30	.75
22 George Zajankala	.30	.75
23 Adam Bomber MASCOT	.20	.50
24 Steve Lingren AS	.30	.75
25 Jim Playfair CO AS	.30	.75
26 Jerry Buckley	.40	1.00
27 Jeremy Stasiuk	.30	.75
28 Greg Burke	.30	.75
29 Chris Johnston	.30	.75
30 Dwayne Gylywoychuk	.30	.75
P1 Sean Gagnon	.80	2.00
P2 Sergei Kharin	.80	2.00

1996-97 Dayton Bombers

This set features the Bombers of the ECHL. The cards were issued as a promotional item within copies of the official game program. They were issued in 2-card strips, with the cards separated by a thin ad for sponsor WTUE radio. One strip was inserted during each of 12 home games over the course of the season. Purchase of the program was required to obtain the cards. The cards themselves were printed on thin stock, with color photos surrounded by a red border. Production was limited to 500 copies of each strip.

COMPLETE SET (24)	10.00	25.00
1 Steve Roberts	.40	1.00
2 Chris Sullivan	.40	1.00
3 Steve Lingren	.40	1.00
4 Jordan Shields	.40	1.00
5 Ildar Yubin	.40	1.00
6 Dwight Parrish	.40	1.00
7 Brian Ridolfi	.40	1.00
8 Jordan Willis	.80	2.00
9 Dale Hooper	.40	1.00
10 Will Clarke	.40	1.00
11 Tavis Morrison	.40	1.00
12 Trent Schachle	.40	1.00
13 John Emmons	.60	1.50
14 Sam McKenney	.40	1.00
15 Bryan Richardson	.40	1.00
16 Ryan Gillis	.40	1.00
17 Marty Flichel	.60	1.50
18 Jason Downey	.40	1.00
19 Troy Christensen	.40	1.00
20 Derek Herlofsky	.80	2.00
21 Sal Manganaro	.40	1.00
22 Tom Nemeth	.60	1.50
23 Evgeny Ryabchikov	.80	2.00
24 Colin Miller	.40	1.00

1998-99 Dayton Bombers

This set was handed out at a game late in the season, making it very difficult to acquire on the secondary market. Any additional information about the set can be forwarded to hockeymag@beckett.com.

COMPLETE SET (25)	4.80	12.00
1 Frederic Bouchard	.30	.75
2 Bobby Brown	.20	.50
3 Norman Dezainde	.30	.75
4 Travis Dillabough	.20	.50
5 Ryan Furness	.20	.50
6 Dan Hendrickson	.20	.50
7 Trevor Koenig	.20	.50
8 Justin Krall	.20	.50
9 Aaron Kriss	.20	.50
10 Jamie Ling	.40	1.00
11 Jim Logan	.20	.50
12 Colin Miller	.20	.50
13 Tom Nemeth	.30	.75
14 Brian Regan	.20	.50
15 Brian Ridolfi	.20	.50
16 Brian Secord	.20	.50
17 Chris Wismer	.20	.50
18 John Beaulieu ANN	.04	.10
19 Dale Coulthard EQM	.04	.10
20 Greg Ireland HCO	.04	.10
21 Buddy Mascot	.04	.10
22 Kerrigan & Christopher	.04	.10
23 Team Photo	.20	.50
24 Larry Thornton TR	.04	.10
25 Lee Stieg	.20	.50

1998-99 Dayton Bombers EBK

This 21-card set was different than the giveaway set from the same year, and was sold at games late in the season.

COMPLETE SET (21)	2.80	7.00
1 Frederic Bouchard	.20	.50
2 Aaron Kriss	.16	.40
3 Brian Secord	.16	.40
4 Colin Miller	.16	.40
5 Jamie Ling	.30	.75
6 Bobby Brown	.16	.40
7 Tom Nemeth	.20	.50
8 Brian Ridolfi	.16	.40
9 Travis Dillabough	.16	.40
10 Justin Krall	.16	.40
11 Dan Hendrickson	.16	.40
12 Ed Gingher ACO	.04	.10
13 Brian Regan	.16	.40
14 Trevor Koenig	.16	.40
15 Greg Ireland HCO	.04	.10
16 Colin Miller Tom Nemeth ACO	.04	.10
17 Bucky Mascot	.04	.10
18 Brandon Sugden	.20	.50
19 Norman Dezainde	.20	.50
20 Kiley Hill	.16	.40
NNO Checklist	.04	.10

1996-97 Dayton Ice Bandits

This set features the Ice Bandits of the ECHL. The set was initially given away as a promotional item, with remaining copies sold by the team at last-season home games.

COMPLETE SET (29)	4.00	10.00
1 Checklist	.04	.10
2 Jesse Austin	.20	.50
3 Mike Bajurny	.20	.50
4 Dan Belisle HCO	.04	.10
5 Dan Carter	.20	.50
6 Cosmo Clarke	.20	.50
7 Bob Clouston	.20	.50
8 Tom Colasanto	.20	.50
9 Brad Cook	.20	.50
10 Richard Fatrola	.20	.50
11 Jack Greig	.20	.50
12 Kelly Melton	.20	.50
13 Andrew Plumb	.20	.50
14 Brian Renfrew	.20	.50
15 Bobby Rapoza	.20	.50
16 Jacque Rodrigue	.20	.50
17 Fred Scott	.20	.50
18 Troy Stevens	.20	.50
19 Larry Thornton TR	.04	.10
20 Mike Thornton	.20	.50
21 Scott Vettraino	.20	.50
22 Marty Wells	.20	.50
23 Kevin Young	.20	.50
24 The Phantom Mascot	.04	.10
25 The Famous Chicken	.04	.10
26 WTUE Employees	.04	.10
27 WTUE Employees	.04	.10
28 WTUE Employees	.04	.10
29 WTUE Employees	.04	.10

1996-97 Denver University Pioneers

This 10-card set features color action photos on the front and a team schedule on the back. It was issued as a game-night giveaway.

COMPLETE SET (10)	3.20	8.00
1 Travis Smith	.40	1.00
2 Jim Mullin	.30	.75
3 Mike Corbett	.30	.75
4 Petri Gunther	.30	.75
5 Garrett Buzan	.30	.75
6 Antti Laaksonen	.40	1.00
7 Charlie Host	.30	.75
8 Erik Andersson	.30	.75
9 Warren Smith	.30	.75
10 Anders Bjork	.30	.75

1999-00 Des Moines Buccaneers

This set features the Buccaneers of the USHL. The set was produced by Roox and sold by the team at home games.

COMPLETE SET (24)	4.00	12.00
1 Dominic Torretti	.20	.50
2 Felipe Larranaga	.20	.50
3 Paul Baumgartner	.20	.50
4 Nathan Berry	.20	.50
5 Matt Weber	.20	.50
6 Troy Riddle	.20	.50
7 Nick Dimella	.20	.50
8 Jesse Lane	.20	.50
9 Peter Sejna	.40	2.00
10 Landon Bathe	.20	.50
11 Travis Doan	.20	.50
12 Mark Murphy	.20	.50
13 Rob Novak	.20	.50
14 Alex Kim	.20	.50
15 Wade Chiodo	.20	.50
16 Jerrid Reinholz	.20	.50
17 Miroslav Durak	.20	.50
18 Ryan Kirchhoff	.20	.50
19 Mark Mullen	.20	.50
20 Ryan Bennett	.20	.50
21 Jeff Ronkoske	.20	.50
22 Mike Mantua	.20	.50
23 Paul Morrissey	.20	.50
24 Winger MASCOT	.04	.10

1993-94 Detroit Jr. Red Wings

Sponsored by Compuware and printed by Slapshot Images Ltd., this standard size 26-card set features the 1993-94 Detroit Jr. Red Wings. On a geometrical red and white background, the fronts feature color action player photos with thin black borders.

COMPLETE SET (26)	4.00	10.00
1 Todd Harvey	.40	1.00
2 Jason Saal	.20	.50
3 Aaron Ellis	.16	.40
4 Chris Mailloux	.16	.40
5 Robin Lacour	.16	.40
6 Mike Rucinski	.16	.40
7 Eric Cairns	.20	.50
8 Matt Ball	.16	.40
9 Dale Junkin	.16	.40
10 Bill McCauley	.16	.40
11 Jeremy Meehan	.16	.40
12 Mike Harding	.16	.40
13 Brad Cook	.16	.40
14 Jeff Mitchell	.16	.40
15 Jamie Allison	.16	.40
16 Dan Pawlaczyk	.16	.40
17 Kevin Brown	.16	.40
18 Duane Harmer	.16	.40
19 Gerry Skrypec	.16	.40
20 Shayne McCosh	.16	.40
21 Sean Haggerty	.16	.40
22 Nic Beaudoin	.16	.40
23 Paul Maurice CO	.20	.50
24 Pete DeBoer ACO	.20	.50
25 Bob Wren	.16	.40
NNO Slapshot Ad Card		.01

1994-95 Detroit Jr. Red Wings

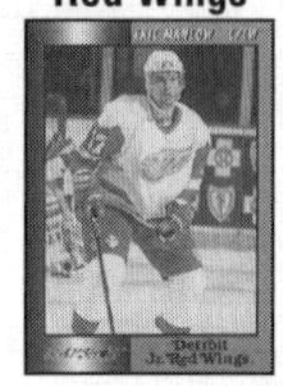

Sponsored by Compuware and printed by Slapshot Images Ltd., this 25-card set features the 1994-95 Detroit Jr. Red Wings. On a red and gray background, the fronts feature color action player photos with thin black borders.

COMPLETE SET (25)	4.00	10.00
1 Team Photo CL	.16	.40
2 Darryl Foster	.16	.40
3 Quade Lightbody	.16	.40
4 Ryan MacDonald	.16	.40
5 Mike Rucinski	.16	.40
6 Murray Sheehan	.16	.40
7 Matt Ball	.16	.40
8 Gerry Lanigan	.16	.40
9 Mike Morrone	.16	.40
10 Tom Buckley	.16	.40
11 Eric Manlow	.30	.75
12 Bill McCauley	.16	.40
13 Andrew Taylor	.16	.40
14 Scott Blair	.16	.40
15 Jeff Mitchell	.16	.40
16 Jason Saal	.24	.60
17 Jamie Allison	.20	.50
18 Bryan Berard	.40	1.00
19 Dan Pawlaczyk	.16	.40
20 Milan Kostolny	.16	.40
21 Duane Harmer	.16	.40
22 Shayne McCosh	.16	.40
23 Sean Haggerty	.16	.40
24 Nic Beaudoin	.16	.40
25 Paul Maurice CO/GM	.16	.40

1994-95 Detroit Vipers Pogs

This set was handed out at a Vipers game. It was released in the form of a 6-inch circular disk which contains 5 player Pogs and one team logo Pog.

COMPLETE SET (6)	.80	2.00
1 John Craighead	.20	.50
2 Peter Ciavaglia	.20	.50
3 Brad Tiley	.20	.50
4 Al Conroy	.20	.50
5 Daniel Shank	.20	.50
6 Logo Pog	.20	.50

1996-97 Detroit Vipers

This odd-sized set commemorates the Detroit Vipers of the IHL. The set was produced by the club as a game-night premium. The cards were issued one per night at twenty different home games, beginning January 3, 1997 and ending April 13. The giveaway dates for each card can be found on the backs of the cards, along with a mugs hot, player nickname and biographical data. The fronts feature an action photo, a reproduction of the player's autograph, and the logo of sponsor Ameritech. The unnumbered cards are listed below alphabetically. The set is noteworthy for the inclusion of 1997 draft pick Sergei Samsonov.

COMPLETE SET (20) 30.00 75.00
1 Darren Banks .80 2.00
2 Peter Ciavaglia .80 2.00
3 Yvon Corriveau .80 2.00
4 Phil Crowe .60 1.50
5 Mike Donnelly .80 2.00
6 Stan Drulia 1.20 3.00
7 Len Esau .80 2.00
8 Ian Herbers .60 1.50
9 Bobby Jay .60 1.50
10 Dan Kesa .60 1.50
11 Rich Parent 1.20 3.00
12 Jeff Parrott .60 1.50
13 Wayne Presley .60 1.50
14 Jeff Reese 1.20 3.00
15 Sergei Samsonov 16.00 40.00
16 Brad Shaw 1.20 3.00
17 Todd Simon .80 2.00
18 Patrice Tardif .80 2.00
19 Phil Von Steffenelli .60 1.50
20 Steve Walker .60 1.50

1997-98 Detroit Vipers

The cards in this oversized set was handed out by the team over the course of twenty different games and is nearly impossible in complete set form.

COMPLETE SET (20) 16.00 30.00
1 Peter Ciavaglia .80 2.00
2 Phil Crowe .40 1.00
3 Dan Kesa .40 1.00
4 Stan Drulia .80 2.00
5 Bob Jay .40 1.00
6 Ian Herbers .40 1.00
7 Brad Shaw .80 2.00
8 Steve Walker .80 2.00
9 Trent McCleary .40 1.00
10 Scott Thomas .80 2.00
11 Johan Hedberg 2.00 5.00
12 Jimmy Carson .80 2.00
13 Clayton Beddoes .40 1.00
14 Tim Murray .40 1.00
15 John Gruden .40 1.00
16 Jeff Reese .80 2.00
17 Keith Aldridge .40 1.00
18 Brent Fedyk .40 1.00
19 Darren Banks .80 2.00
20 Vipe-Bear Mascot .40 1.00

1998-99 Detroit Vipers

This set was produced by EBK Sports and was sold through its Web site, as well as at Vipers home games. Cards were numbered "XX of 27" on the card backs.

COMPLETE SET (26) 6.00 15.00
1 Keith Aldridge .20 .50
2 Brad Shaw .40 1.00
3 Tim Murray .16 .40
4 Brian Felsner .16 .40
5 Peter Ciavaglia .30 .75
6 Andy Bezeau .16 .40
7 Mike Gaffney .16 .40
8 Phil Crowe .16 .40
9 John Emmons .16 .40
10 Kory Karlander .16 .40
11 Mike Prokopec .16 .40
12 Stan Drulia .40 1.00
13 Bob Jay .20 .50
14 Darren Banks .20 .50
15 Jeff Whittle .16 .40
16 Steve Walker .16 .40
17 Ian Herbers .16 .40
18 Jani Hurme 1.60 4.00
19 John Gruden .16 .40
20 Kevin Weekes .80 2.00
21 Vipe-Bear Mascot .04 .10
22 Steve Ludzik HCO .04 .10
23 John Blum ACO .04 .10
24 Dave Boyer TR .04 .10
25 Mike Astalos EQM .04 .10
26 Checklist .04 .10
27 IHL/PHPA

1998-99 Detroit Vipers Freschetta

This set was issued as a giveaway late in the season in four different four-card strips. Each strip featured a different color background, and the four colors used are green (cards 1-4), yellow (cards 5-8), red (cards 9-12), and purple (cards 13-16). The cards were unnumbered.

COMPLETE SET (16) 12.00 30.00
1 Kevin Weekes 1.60 4.00
2 Peter Ciavaglia .80 2.00
3 Bob Jay .60 1.50
4 Keith Aldridge .60 1.50
5 Andy Bezeau .60 1.50
6 Stan Drulia 1.20 3.00
7 Ian Herbers .60 1.50
8 John Emmons .60 1.50
9 Mike Prokopec .60 1.50
10 Tim Murray .60 1.50
11 Brad Shaw 1.20 3.00
12 Steve Walker .60 1.50
13 John Gruden .60 1.50
14 Darren Banks .80 2.00
15 Brian Felsner .60 1.50
16 Geoff Sarjeant .80 2.00

1999-00 Detroit Vipers

Given out by the team over the span of 15 home games, this 15-card set features the 1999-2000 Detroit Vipers. The set is listed in the order that the players were given away. The dates are as follows: Jan. 15, Jan. 21, Jan. 22, Jan. 25, Jan. 27, Feb. 1, Feb. 6, Feb. 8, Feb. 15, Feb. 22, Feb. 24, Feb. 27, Mar. 12, Mar. 16, and Mar. 28.

COMPLETE SET (15) 14.00 35.00
1 Andy Bezeau 1.20 3.00
2 Nils Ekman 1.20 3.00
3 Mario Larocque 1.20 3.00
4 Steve Walker .80 2.00
5 Matt Elich 1.20 3.00
6 Jeff Shevalier .80 2.00
7 Peter Ciavaglia 1.20 3.00
8 Alek Stojanov .80 2.00
9 Dave Baseggio .80 2.00
10 Zac Bierk 1.50 4.00
11 Kyle Kos .80 2.00
12 Tim Thomas 1.50 4.00
13 Dale Rominski .80 2.00
14 Kyle Freadrich .80 2.00
15 Samuel St. Pierre .80 2.00

1999-00 Detroit Vipers Kid's Club

This 9-card set was given out free to members of the Detroit Vipers Kids Club. The set was issued as one three-by-three, 9-card panel, with perforations to allow the cards to be torn off. The set was sponsored by Keebler and Meijer. The cards are unnumbered and are standard-size. The fronts are full color with green borders. The backs are white with dark purple printing, containing player statistics. The final card in the set was intended to be a "membership card" for the Detroit Vipers Kids Club, containing a blank "name" spot on the card's front.

COMPLETE SET (9) 10.00 25.00
1 Team Logo Card .40 1.00
2 Peter Ciavaglia 2.00 5.00
3 Andy Bezeau 2.00 5.00
4 Stan Drulia 2.00 5.00
5 Steve Walker 2.00 5.00
6 Ian Herbers 2.00 5.00
7 Paulin Bordeleau HCO 2.00 5.00
8 Vipe-Bear Mascot .40 1.00
9 Kid's Club Membership Card .40 1.00

1996-97 Detroit Whalers

This 25-card set was produced by the team and available for sale at games and by mail order for $5. The standard-size cards feature a color action photo with a sea foam green border. The backs contain a headshot, bio and stats.

COMPLETE SET (25) 4.00 10.00
1 Jessie Boulerice .30 .75
2 Mark Cadotte .20 .50
3 Chad Cavanagh .16 .40
4 Harold Druken .40 1.00
5 Steve Dumonski .20 .50
6 Robert Esche .80 2.00
7 Sergei Fedotov .20 .50
8 Randy Fitzgerald .20 .50
9 Eric Gooldy .16 .40
10 Kevin Holdridge .16 .40
11 John Paul Luciuk .16 .40
12 Mike Morrone .16 .40
13 Pat Parthenais .20 .50
14 Julian Smith .16 .40
15 Troy Smith .16 .40
16 Andrew Taylor .16 .40
17 Anthony Terzo .16 .40
18 Jan Vodrazka .16 .40
19 Steve Wasylko .20 .50
20 Nathan West .16 .40
21 Peter DeBoer CO .10 .25
22 Luc Rioux .16 .40
23 Slapshot MASCOT .01
24 Checklist .01
25 Discount Card .01

1993-94 Drummondville Voltigeurs

This set features the Voltigeurs of the QMJHL. The set was printed by Slapshot Images and was sold at home games.

COMPLETE SET (28) 3.20 8.00
1 Title Card .04 .10
Checklist
2 Stephane Routhier .16 .40
3 Yannick Gagnon .16 .40
4 Sebastien Bety .16 .40
5 Martin Latulippe .16 .40
6 Nicolas Savage .16 .40
7 Sylvain Ducharme .16 .40
8 Yan St. Pierre .16 .40
9 Emmanuel Labranche .16 .40
10 Ian Laperriere .30 .75
11 Louis Bernard .16 .40
12 Stephane St. Amour .16 .40
13 Vincent Tremblay .16 .40
14 Denis Gauthier Jr. .30 .75
15 Eric Plante .16 .40
16 Christian Marcoux .16 .40
17 Patrice Charbonneau .16 .40
18 Raymond Delarosbil .16 .40
19 Patrick Livernoche .16 .40
20 Luc Decelles .16 .40
21 Francois Sasseville .16 .40
22 Steve Tardif .16 .40
23 Mathieu Sunderland .16 .40
24 Alexandre Duchesne .16 .40
25 Jean Hamel CO GM .04 .10
26 Mario Carrier ACO .04 .10
27 Me Andre Lepage TR .04 .10
28 Slapshot Ad Card .04 .10

2001-02 Drummondville Voltigeurs

This set features the Voltigeurs of the QMJHL. The set was produced by CTM Ste-Foy, and was sold at that shop as well as at home games. The production run is believed to be fewer than 1,000 sets.

COMPLETE SET (23) 4.00 10.00
1 Jean-Francois Racine .31 .78
2 Patrick Turbide .20 .50
3 Evgueni Nourislamov .20 .50
4 Jean-Philippe Glaude .20 .50
5 Thierry Kaszap .20 .50
6 Eric Jean .20 .50
7 Louis-Philippe Lessard .20 .50
8 Andre Vincent .20 .50
9 Steve Proulx .20 .50
10 Oliver Proulx .20 .50
11 Martin Autotte .20 .50
12 Yanick Riendeau .20 .50
13 Michael Stacey .20 .50
14 Frederic Faucher .20 .50
15 Benoit Paris .20 .50
16 Vincent Tougas .20 .50
17 Kirill Alexeev .20 .50
18 Jean-Francois Cyr .20 .50
19 Carl Zacharie .20 .50
20 Kevin Rainville .20 .50
21 Sylvain Michaud .20 .50
22 Maxime Bouchard .20 .50
NNO Title Card/CL .04 .11

2002-03 Drummondville Voltigeurs

COMPLETE SET (25) 12.00
1 Francis Breault CO .10
2 Evgueni Nourislamov .50
3 Todd Paul .50
4 Andre Joaniss .50
5 Jules Melanson .50
6 Andre Vincent .50
7 Dominic Fiset .50
8 Kevin Lacombe .50
9 Alexandre Demers .50
10 Laurent Lanoie .50
11 Yannick Riendeau .50
12 Patrick Levesque .50
13 Sebastien Laprise .50
14 Benoit Duhamel .50
15 Jonathan Dick .50
16 Kevin Mailhiot .50
17 Jason D'Ascanio .50
18 Thomas Bellemare .50
19 Samuel Villeneuve .50
20 Kevin Duchaine .50
21 Eric Dagenais .50
22 Sylvain Michaud 1.00
23 Pierre Olivier Girouard .75
24 Pier Olivier Begin .75
25 Checklist/Logo .01

2003-04 Drummondville Voltigeurs

COMPLETE SET (22) 6.00 15.00
1 Thomas Bellemare .20 .50
2 David Bouchard .20 .50
3 Maxim Chamberland .20 .50

4 Michel Charrette .20 .50
5 Alexandre Demers .20 .50
6 Keven Gagne .20 .50
7 Samuel Gibbons .20 .50
8 Gabriel Houde-Brisson .20 .50
9 Andre Joanisse .20 .50
10 Kevin Lacombe .20 .50
11 Guillaume Latendresse 2.00 5.00
12 Kevin Mailhiot .20 .50
13 Louis-Philippe Martin .20 .50
14 Jamie McCabe .20 .50
15 Jules Melanson .20 .50
16 Sylvain Michaud .30 .75
17 Pierre Morvan .20 .50
18 Ervins Mustukovs .30 .75
19 Jean-Francois Parent .20 .50
20 Yannick Riendeau .20 .50
21 Frederic St. Denis .20 .50
22 Andre Vincent .20 .50

2004-05 Drummondville Voltigeurs

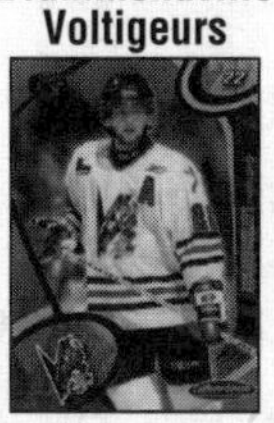

A total of 330 sets were produced. The NNO cards do not appear in every sealed team bag.

COMPLETE SET (30) 6.00 20.00
1 Guillaume Latendresse .75 2.00
2 Philippe Roberge .20 .50
3 Pier-Olivier Pelletier .60 1.50
4 Derick Brassard 1.25 3.00
5 Chaz Johnson .20 .50
6 Henrick Lavoie .20 .50
7 Mathieu Ste-Marie .20 .50
8 Alexandre Demers .20 .50
9 Keven Gagne .20 .50
10 Andre Vincent .20 .50
11 Frederic St-Denis .20 .50
12 Andre Joanisse .20 .50
13 Louis-Philippe Martin .20 .50
14 Dave Bouchard .20 .50
15 Jules Melanson .20 .50
16 Steve Cacciotti .20 .50
19 Romy Elayoubi .20 .50
20 Cedric Archambault .20 .50
21 Maxime Frechette .20 .50
22 Julien Beaulieu .20 .50
23 Maxime Aubut .20 .50
24 Jean-Philippe Cote .20 .50
25 Maxim Chamberland .20 .50
26 Kevin Mailhiot .20 .50
27 Gaby Roch .20 .50
28 Simon Archambault .20 .50
29 Sylvain Michaud .40 1.00
30 Jesse Arko .20 .50
NNO Derick Brassard 2.00 5.00
NNO Pier-Olivier Pelletier 2.00 5.00

2005-06 Drummondville Voltigeurs

COMPLETE SET (33) 6.00 15.00
1 Guillaume Latendresse .60 1.50
2 Derick Brassard .60 1.50
3 Pier-Olivier Pelletier .30 .75
4 Pierre-Alexandre Marion .15 .40
5 Jules Melanson .15 .40
6 Kevin Mailhiot .15 .40
7 Maxim Mallette .15 .40
8 Joey Pell .15 .40
9 Andre Joanisse .15 .40
10 Maxime Frechette .15 .40
11 Tomas Zohorna .15 .40
12 Dave Bouchard .15 .40
13 Nicolas Sigouin .15 .40
14 Steven Cacciotti .15 .40
15 Tomas Svoboda .15 .40
16 Gaby Roch .15 .40
17 Alexandre Demers .15 .40
18 Frederic St-Denis .15 .40
19 Vincent Beaulieu .15 .40
20 Keven Gagne .15 .40
21 Maxime Aubut .15 .40
22 Paul Yovanic .15 .40
23 Olivier Fortier .15 .40
24 Tirobut .02 .10
25 Bryan Wilson .15 .40
26 Olivier Legault .15 .40
27 Yanick Charron .15 .40
28 Nicolas D'Aoust .15 .40
29 Simon Bouchard .15 .40
30 Olivier Donovan .15 .40
31 Loic Lacasse .30 .75
32 Francis Charette .15 .40
33 Jean-Michel Bolduc .15 .40

2006-07 Drummondville Voltigeurs

COMPLETE SET (26) 8.00 15.00
1 Derick Brassard .75 2.00
2 Bryan Wilson .20 .50
3 Mackenzie Micks .20 .50
4 Drew Paris .20 .50
5 Simon Bouchard .20 .50
6 Benoit Levesque .20 .50
7 Jonathan Duchesneau .20 .50
8 Tomas Zohorna .20 .50
9 Eric Campeau-Charron .20 .50
10 Steven Cacciotti .20 .50
11 Olivier Jannard .20 .50
12 Corey Garland .20 .50
13 Tomas Svoboda .20 .50
14 Gaby Roch .20 .50
15 Alexandre Demers .20 .50
16 Frederic St. Denis .20 .50
17 Stephen Valente .20 .50
18 Sebastien Bernier .20 .50
19 Etienne Bellavance-Martin .20 .50
20 Marc-Olivier Vachon .20 .50
21 Scott Howes .20 .50
22 Maxime Frechette .20 .50
23 Francis Charette .20 .50
24 Pier-Olivier Pelletier .30 .75
25 Maxime Gougeon .30 .75
26 Pierre-Alexandre Marion .20 .50

1994-95 Dubuque Fighting Saints

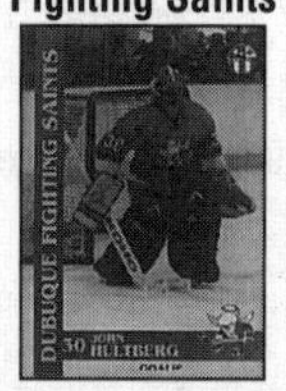

This 29-card set measures the standard size. The fronts feature color action player photos with the player's name, jersey number, and team logo at the bottom. The team name runs down the left side of the front. The backs carry a black-and-white player portrait, the player's name, jersey number, biographical information, statistics, career summary, and team logo. The cards are unnumbered and checklisted below in alphabetical order.

COMPLETE SET (29) 4.00 10.00
1 Title Card .04 .10
Season schedule
2 Chris Addesa .20 .50
3 Matt Addesa .20 .50
4 Mark Allegrezza .16 .40
5 Todd Barclay .16 .40
6 Jay Boxer ACO .04 .10
7 Geoff Collard .16 .40
8 John Dwyer .16 .40
9 Jayme Filipowicz .20 .50
10 Zach Ham .16 .40
11 Mike Herrera .16 .40
12 Roger Holeczy .16 .40
13 Steve Holeczy .16 .40
14 John Hultberg .30 .75
15 Ryan Karasek .16 .40
16 Mike Kramer TR .04 .10
17 Chris Masters .16 .40
18 A.J. Melanson .16 .40
19 Mike Minichiello .16 .40
20 Berk Nelson .16 .40
21 Nik Patronas .16 .40
22 Andy Powers .16 .40
23 Matt Romaniski .16 .40
24 Tom Ryles .16 .40
25 John Sadowski .16 .40
26 Chris Showalter .16 .40
27 Dan Stepanek .16 .40
28 Trevor Tallackson .16 .40
29 Troy Ward GM/CO .04 .10

1997-98 Dubuque Fighting Saints

This set features the Fighting Saints of the USHL. The set was produced by the team and sold at home games. Card No. 30 was recently confirmed to be Josh Blackburn. Thanks to collector Joseph Bonnett for this information.

COMPLETE SET (30) 4.00 10.00
1 Dubuque Fighting Saints .16 .40
2 Justin Aufmann .16 .40
3 Travis Rotariu .16 .40
4 Marty Rychley .16 .40
5 Mario LeBlanc .16 .40
6 David Patch .16 .40
7 Evan Stensrud .16 .40
8 Josh Kern .16 .40
9 Christian Fletcher .16 .40
10 Scott Deopere .16 .40
11 Jeff Tarala .16 .40
12 Phil Lewandowski .16 .40
13 Joe Dudek .16 .40
14 Trent Landry .16 .40
15 Tom Rouleau .16 .40
16 Kris Harris .16 .40
17 Anders Johnson .16 .40
18 Matt Herhal .16 .40
19 Josh Myers .16 .40
20 David Brien .16 .40
21 Carl Hanson .16 .40
22 Scott Brown .16 .40
23 Adam Pobiak .16 .40
24 Todd Sanden CO .04 .10
25 Tom Hasenzahl CO .04 .10
26 Corey Courtney TR .04 .10
27 Sebastian St. Bernard MAS .04 .10
28 USHL Team Directory .04 .10
29 Schedule .04 .10
30 Josh Blackburn .30 .75

1998-99 ECHL All-Star Northern Conference

Released by EBK Sports, this 21-card set was available for sale at the 1999 ECHL All-Star Game. It was later available for purchase through the PHPA web site.

COMPLETE SET (21) 15.00 40.00
1 Tom O'Connor .75 2.00
2 Duane Harmer 1.25 3.00
3 Jamie Ling 1.25 3.00
4 Darren Maloney .75 2.00
5 Bret Meyers .75 2.00
6 Jim Bermingham 1.25 3.00
7 Jamie Thompson .75 2.00
8 Andrew Williamson .75 2.00
9 Marc Tropper .75 2.00
10 Bobby Brown .75 2.00
11 Jakub Ficenec 1.25 3.00
12 Arturs Kupaks 1.25 3.00
13 Dru Burgess .75 2.00
14 Dan Ceman .75 2.00
15 Ryan Kraft 1.25 3.00
16 Joe Blaznek .75 2.00
17 Casey Kesselring .75 2.00
18 Matt Mullen 1.25 3.00
19 Maxime Gingras 1.50 4.00
20 Karl Infanger .75 2.00
21 Checklist .04 .10

1998-99 ECHL All-Star Southern Conference

Released by EBK Sports, this 21-card set was available for purchase at the All-Star Game, then later through the PHPA web site.

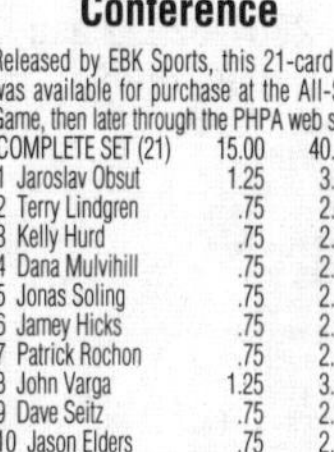

COMPLETE SET (21) 15.00 40.00
1 Jaroslav Obsut 1.25 3.00
2 Terry Lindgren .75 2.00
3 Kelly Hurd .75 2.00
4 Dana Mulvihill .75 2.00
5 Jonas Soling .75 2.00
6 Jamey Hicks .75 2.00
7 Patrick Rochon .75 2.00
8 John Varga 1.25 3.00
9 Dave Seitz .75 2.00
10 Jason Elders .75 2.00
11 Cail MacLean .75 2.00
12 Allan Sirois .75 2.00
13 Shane Calder .75 2.00
14 Chris Valicevic 1.25 3.00
15 J.F. Lube .75 2.00
16 Luke Curtin .75 2.00
17 Jan Kobezda .75 2.00
18 Bujar Amidovski 1.50 4.00
19 Chris Hynnes .75 2.00
20 Chris Wickenheiser 1.50 4.00
21 Checklist .04 .10

1999-00 ECHL All-Star Northern Conference

Released by EBK Sports, this 22-card set was available for purchase through the PHPA web site and at the rink during the 2000 ECHL All-Star Game.

COMPLETE SET (22) 8.00 20.00
1 Alexei Krovopuskov .30 .75
2 Andrew Williamson .30 .75
3 Blaine Fitzpatrick .30 .75
4 Bujar Amidovski .75 2.00
5 Calvin Elfring .30 .75
6 Chad Ackerman .30 .75
7 Chris Gignac .30 .75
8 Curtis Wilgosh .30 .75
9 Derek Walser .30 .75
10 Duane Harmer .30 .75
11 Jamie Ling .30 .75
12 Jan Lasak 1.00 2.50
13 Jason Lawmaster .30 .75
14 Jeff Mitchell .30 .75
15 Joel Irving .30 .75
16 Marc Tropper .30 .75
17 Mark Murphy .30 .75
18 Mike Perna .30 .75
19 Peter Vandermeer .75 2.00
20 Ryan Kraft .75 2.00
21 Sean Matile .30 .75
22 EBK Sports .01

1999-00 ECHL All-Star Southern Conference

Released by EBK Sports, this 22-card set was available for purchase through the PHPA web site and at the rink during the 2000 ECHL All-Star Game.

COMPLETE SET (22) 8.00 20.00
1 Bobby Stewart .30 .75
2 Brad Dexter .30 .75
3 Buddy Smith .30 .75
4 Chris Valicevic .75 2.00
5 Dany Bousquet .40 1.00
6 David Brumby .30 .75
7 Eric Naud .30 .75
8 Greg Schmidt .30 .75
9 Jeff Lazaro .30 .75
10 Jeff Maund .75 2.00
11 John McNabb .30 .75
12 John Spoltore .75 2.00
13 Kelly Perrault .30 .75
14 Luke Curtin .30 .75
15 Marc Magliarditi .75 2.00
16 Neil Fewster .30 .75
17 Sean Venedam .60 1.50
18 Steve O'Brien .30 .75
19 Wes Mason .30 .75
20 Ryan Gaucher .30 .75
21 Olivier Morin .30 .75
22 EBK Sports .01

2002-03 ECHL All-Star Northern

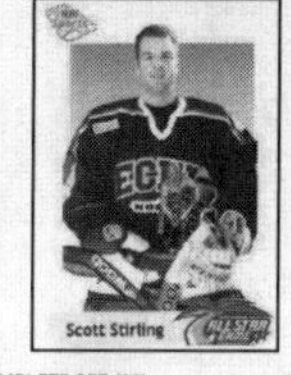

COMPLETE SET (20) 20.00
19 Kevin Colley 1.00
20 Pierre-Luc Courchesne 1.00
21 Ryan Gaucher 1.00
22 Jim Henkel 1.00
23 Jamie Herrington 1.00
24 Andrew Ianiero 1.00
25 Jason Jaffray 1.00
26 Zenon Konopka 1.50
27 Dan Lombard 1.00
28 Brian McCullough 1.00
29 Chris McNamara 1.00
30 Nick Parillo 1.00
31 Geno Parrish 1.00
32 Tyler Rennette 1.00
33 Brad Rooney 1.00
34 Mike Smith 1.00
35 Scott Stirling 1.00
36 Takahito Suzuki 1.50
37 Simon Tremblay 1.00
39 Jonathan Zion 1.00
39 Dustin Wood 1.00

2002-03 ECHL All-Star Southern

COMPLETE SET (21) 20.00
40 Jim Baxter 1.00
41 Kent Davyduke 1.00
42 Mike Glumac 1.00
43 Joe Guenther 1.00
44 Adam Hauser 2.00
45 Corey Hessler 1.00
46 J.J. Hunter 1.00
47 Marty Johnston 1.00
48 Judd Medak 1.00
49 Laurent Meunier 1.00
50 Justin Morrison 1.00
51 Ryan O'Keefe 1.00
52 Rod Sarich 1.00
53 Aaron Schneekloth 1.00
54 Bud Smith 1.00
55 Rejean Stringer 1.00
56 Matt Underhill 1.50
57 Steffon Walby 1.00
58 Brad Williamson 1.00
59 Patrick Yetman 1.00
60 Rob Zepp 2.00

2002-03 ECHL Update

COMPLETE SET (27) 20.00
U-1 Rick Adduono HCO .25
U-2 Derrick Byfuglien 1.00
U-3 Sebastien Centomo 3.00
U-4 Jason Christie HCO .25
U-5 Pierre-Luc Courchesne 1.00
U-6 Kent Davyduke 1.00
U-7 Gord Dineen HCO .25
U-8 Gerry Fleming HCO .25
U-9 Joe Guenther 1.00
U-10 Adam Hauser 1.50
U-11 Jamie Hodson 1.50
U-12 Zenon Konopka 1.50
U-13 David-Lohrei HCO .25
U-14 Don MacAdam HCO .25
U-15 Chris McNamara 1.00
U-16 John Marks HCO .25
U-17 Ryan O'Keefe 1.00
U-18 Mike Oliveira 1.00
U-19 Davis Payne HCO .50
U-20 Bryan Richardson 1.00
U-21 Rod Sarich 1.00
U-22 Bud Smith 1.00
U-23 Niklas Sundberg 1.00
U-24 Mark Turner 1.00
U-25 Scott White HCO .25
U-26 Dustin Wood 1.00
U-27 Patrick Yetman 1.00

2003-04 ECHL All-Stars

This was actually issued as two separate team-bagged sets, one for the East and one for the West, but it is combined here. The numbering reflects that this as part of the full season's run of ECHL products released by RBI Sports.

COMPLETE SET (42) 50.00 100.00
241 Morten Ask 3.00
242 Alexandre Burrows 3.00
243 Cory Campbell 3.00
244 Brian Fahey 3.00
245 Chris Houle 2.00
246 Jason Jaffray 2.00
247 Dusty Jamieson 2.00
248 Nate Kiser 2.00
249 Shawn Limpright 2.00
250 Chris Lynch 2.00

251 Jason Maleyko 3.00
252 David Masse 2.00
253 Brian McCullough 2.00
254 Mark McRae 2.00
255 Jason Notermann 2.00
256 Sam Paolini 2.00
257 Tom Reimann 2.00
258 Randy Rowe 2.00
259 Kevin Spiewak 2.00
260 Scott Stirling 2.00
261 Jonathan Zion 2.00
262 Greg Barber 2.00
263 Greg Chambers 2.00
264 Frederic Cloutier 3.00
265 David Cornacchia 2.00
266 David Cousineau 2.00
267 Dan Ellis 5.00
268 Nick Ganga 2.00
269 Michael Garnett 4.00
270 Brent Gauvreau 2.00
271 Andrew Ianiero 2.00
272 Greg Jacina 3.00
273 Justin Kelly 2.00
274 Charles Linglet 2.00
275 Troy Milam 2.00
276 Corey Neilson 2.00
277 Jean-Francois Plourde 2.00
278 John Snowden 2.00
279 Ben Storey 2.00
280 Joe Talbot 2.00
281 Kevin Truelson 2.00
282 Steffon Walby 3.00

2003-04 ECHL Update RBI Sports

It's believed these cards were issued late in the season and limited to just 250 copies each, in three sets (A, B and C). Little else is known about their distribution.

COMPLETE SET (48) 60.00
49 Joe Talbot 1.00
56 Todd Alexander 1.00
57 Shane Bendera 2.00
58 Jon Mirasty 1.00
59 Joe Watkins 2.00
60 Lucas Lawson 1.00
61 Brett Clouthier 2.00
62 Phil Cole 1.00
63 Tyler Masters 1.00
64 Doug Teskey 1.00
113 Kristian Antila 1.00
114 Matus Kostur 2.00
115 Christian Larrivee 1.00
116 Olivier Michaud 4.00
117 Tomas Micka 1.00
118 Matt Shasby 1.00
119 Marc-Andre Thinel 2.00
120 Sean Connolly 1.00
121 Riley Cote 1.00
122 Jason Crain 1.00
123 Miguel Delisle 1.00
124 Janne Jokila 1.00
125 Andrew Penner 2.00
126 Olivier Proulx 1.00
127 Nicolas Corbeil 1.00
128 Daniel Boisclair 2.00
129 Mark Concannon 1.00
130 Brian Passmore 1.00
131 Michel Robinson 1.00
132 Russell Spence 1.00
133 Anthony Aquino 2.00
134 Wes Fox 1.00
135 Phil Lewandowski 1.00
136 Trevor Prior 2.00
137 Dan Ellis 4.00
138 Armands Berzins 1.00
139 Maxime Fortunus 1.00
140 Derek Gustafson 2.00
141 Jamie Johnson 1.00
142 Ed McGrane 1.00
143 Jean-Francois Soucy 2.00
144 Jeremy Van Hoof 1.00
283 Dustin Johner 1.00
284 Paul Ballantyne 1.00
285 Scott Kabotoff 1.00
286 Joe Exter 4.00
287 Tyler MacKay 1.00
288 Patrick Couture 2.00

1997-98 El Paso Buzzards

Little is known about this set beyond the confirmed checklist. Additional information can be forwarded to hockeymag@beckett.com.

COMPLETE SET (32) 4.00 10.00
1 Jamie Thompson .20 .50
2 Brent Scott .20 .50
3 Mark Sakala .20 .50
4 Jason Rose .20 .50
5 Corri Moffat .20 .50
6 Chris MacKenzie .20 .50
7 Trent Eigner .20 .50
8 Rusty McKie .30 .75
9 Jason Welch .20 .50
10 Martin Balleux .20 .50
11 Corey Heon .20 .50
12 Derek Riley .30 .75
13 Chris Gordon .20 .50
14 Bill Trew .20 .50
15 Jason Carey .20 .50
16 Sandy Lamarre .20 .50
17 Dan Carter .20 .50
18 Robert Haddock .20 .50
19 Mark Hilton .20 .50
20 Todd Brost CO .04 .10
21 Swoop Mascot .04 .10
22 Teresa Fernandez RG .04 .10
23 Greg Sieg TR .04 .10
24 KLAQ Morning Show .04 .10
25 KISS Morning Show .04 .10
26 KROD Morning Show .04 .10
27 Paul Strelzin ANNC .04 .10
28 DJ Card .04 .10
29 TV-7 Anchors .04 .10
30 TV-7 Sports Team .04 .10
31 DJ Card .04 .10
32 TV-7 Reporters .04 .10

1998-99 El Paso Buzzards

This set features the Buzzards of the WPHL. It was produced by the team and was sold at home games. The cards are not numbered, but are ordered by the listing on the checklist card.

COMPLETE SET (28) 20.00 40.00
1 Trent Eigner 1.25 3.00
2 Chris Gordon .75 2.00
3 Robert Haddock .75 2.00
4 Corey Heon .75 2.00
5 Alex Herbison .75 2.00
6 Bill Trew .75 2.00
7 Jeremy Vanin .75 2.00
8 Jason Welch .75 2.00
9 Deuce Wynes .75 2.00
10 Todd Brost CO .40 1.00
11 Steve Pottie .75 2.00
12 Mike Rees .75 2.00
13 Iannique Renaud .75 2.00
14 Jason Rushton .75 2.00
15 Blake Sheane .75 2.00
16 Mark Costea .75 2.00
17 Sandy Lamarre .75 2.00
18 Marc Labelle .75 2.00
19 Corri Moffat .75 2.00
20 Eric Peterson .75 2.00
21 McArthur/Palka .75 2.00
22 Warner/Casas .75 2.00
23 The Mike & Grace Show .04 .10
24 Cruz/Adams/Keith/Steele .04 .10
25 Garcia/Medina/Kaplowitz .04 .10
26 Dodson/Romano .04 .10
27 Paul Strelzin ANN .04 .10
28 Checklist .04 .10

2001-02 El Paso Buzzards

COMPLETE SET (20) 20.00
1 Trent Eigner 1.00
2 Van Burgess 1.00
3 Clint Collins 1.00
4 Rhett Dudley 1.00
5 Kelly Riou 1.00
6 Chris Zaleski 1.00
7 Jeremy Vanin 1.00
8 Derrell Upton 1.00
9 Mike Rees 1.00
10 Justin Van Parys 1.00
11 Trevor Hammer 1.00
12 Jason Tessier 1.00
13 Dory Tisdale 1.00
14 Rob Laurie 1.50
15 Troy Linna 1.00
16 Jeff Levy 1.00
17 Aaron Phillips 1.00
18 Kory Baker 1.00
19 Corey Waring 1.00
20 John Hanson 1.00

2002-03 El Paso Buzzards

This checklist is NOT complete. If you have any information about this set or the cards in it, please email hockeymag@beckett.com.

COMPLETE SET (???)
1 Jeff Levy
2 Rhett Dudley
3 Chris Zaleski
4 John Hanson
5 Aaron Phillips
6 Rob Laurie
7 Kory Baker

2003-04 Elmira Jackals

COMPLETE SET (25) 12.00
1 Peter Aubry .75
2 Cal Benazic .50
3 J.F. Boutin .50
4 Trevor Burgess .50
5 Tom Clayton .50
6 Carl Drakensjo .50
7 Nathan Gillies .50
8 Dean Jackson .50
9 Greg Koehler .50
Mike Thompson
10 Ed Lowe .50
11 Kris Mallette .75
12 Ryan McIntosh .75
13 Randy Murphy .50
14 Geoff O'Leary .50
15 Matt Osborne .50
16 Neil Posillico .50
17 Michael Prochazka .50
18 Trevor Segstro .50
19 James Sheehan .50
20 Don Smith .50
21 Jamie Thompson .50
23 Todd Brost HCO .20
24 Spud Hamilton EQM .10
25 Brandon Dionne TR .10
26 Team Photo .50

2003-04 Erie Otters

COMPLETE SET (24) 6.00 15.00
1 Derrick Bagshaw .20 .50
2 Michael Blunden .40 1.00
3 Brad Bonello .20 .50
4 Chris Campoli .30 .75
5 Sean Courtney .20 .50
6 Josh Disher .30 .75
7 Tomas Galasek .20 .50
8 Bryan Hamm .20 .50
9 Jacob Heller .20 .50
10 David Herring .20 .50
11 Rob Hisey .20 .50
12 Alex Karaulchuk .20 .50
13 Brian Lee .20 .50
14 Chad Loikets .20 .50
15 Matthew Lynn .20 .50
16 Mike Melinko .20 .50
17 Derek Merlini .20 .50
18 Sean O'Connor .20 .50
19 Ryan O'Marra .40 1.00
20 Josh Patterson .20 .50
21 Geoff Platt .40 1.00
22 Vince Scott .20 .50
23 Jhase Sniderman .30 .75
24 Jason Speight .20 .50

2004-05 Erie Otters

A total of 700 team sets were produced. The NNO cards are randomly inserted.

COMPLETE SET (25) 5.00 12.00
1 Michael Blunden .30 .75
2 Tomas Galasek .20 .50
3 Derek Merlini .20 .50
4 Brett MacLean .20 .50
5 Jhase Sniderman .30 .75
6 Geoff Platt .30 .75
7 Chris Greene .20 .50
8 Sean O'Connor .20 .50
9 Vince Scott .20 .50
10 Jake Heller .20 .50
11 Derrick Bagshaw .20 .50
12 Andrew Hotham .20 .50
13 Brian Lee .20 .50
14 Chad Loikets .20 .50
15 Peter Sergeant .20 .50
16 Josh Kidd .20 .50
17 Ryan O'Marra .40 1.00
18 Eric Regan .20 .50
19 Andrew Shennan .20 .50
20 Jason Speight .20 .50
21 Josh Disher .30 .75
22 David Herring .20 .50
23 Dave MacQueen CO .20 .10
24 Peter Sidorkiewicz ACO .20 .25
25 Shooter MASCOT .20 .10
NNO Geoff Platt LTD 1.50 4.00
NNO Ryan O'Marra LTD 2.00 5.00

2005-06 Erie Otters

COMPLETE SET (23) 5.00 12.00
1 Ryan O'Marra .40 1.00
2 Derrick Bagshaw .20 .50
3 Michael Blunden .40 1.00
4 Chris Greene .20 .50
5 Justin Hodgman .20 .50
6 Patrick Lee .20 .50
7 Jordan Nolan .20 .50
8 Sean O'Connor .20 .50
9 Vince Scott .20 .50
10 Christian Seest Olsen .20 .50
11 Nick Palmieri .20 .50
12 Anthony Peluso .20 .50
13 Josh Vatri .20 .50
14 Jake Heller .20 .50
15 Andrew Hotham .20 .50
16 Josh Kidd .20 .50
17 Chad Loikets .20 .50
18 Josh Disher .20 .50
19 Ryan Ludzik .20 .50
20 Adam Berti .20 .50
21 Bret Nasby .20 .50
22 Jonathan Hull .20 .50
23 Tyler McKinley .20 .50

2006-07 Erie Otters

COMPLETE SET (24) 8.00 15.00
1 Nick Palmieri .20 .50
2 Sean O'Connor .20 .50
3 Patrick Lee .20 .50
4 Derrick Bagshaw .20 .50
5 Mitchell Forbes .20 .50
6 Stanislav Polodna .20 .50
7 Luke Gazdic .20 .50
8 Justin Hodgman .20 .50
9 Josh Vatri .20 .50
10 Shayne Taylor .20 .50
11 Kelly Geoffrey .20 .50
12 Kyle Ramsay .20 .50
13 Zack Torquato .60 1.50
14 Ronny Rogers .20 .50
15 Josh Kidd .20 .50
16 Mitch Gaulton .20 .50
17 Andrew Hotham .20 .50
18 Anthony Peluso .20 .50
19 Brian Shaw .20 .50
20 Michael Liambas .20 .50
21 Ryan Henry .20 .50
22 Jonathan Laniel .40 1.00
23 Justin Garay .40 1.00
24 Ryan Ludzik .40 1.00

1994-95 Erie Panthers

Produced by CJ Sports, this 20-card standard-size set features the Erie Panthers of the East Coast Hockey League. The fronts display color action player photos with gray borders. The player's name, position, and sponsor's name are below. The team name and logo appear at the top. The backs are white, grey, and black with player biography and statistics.

COMPLETE SET (20) 3.20 8.00
1 Title Card .04 .10
2 Ron Hansis CO .04 .10
3 Barry Smith ACO .04 .10
4 Patrick Laughlin TR .04 .10
5 Larry Empey .20 .50
6 Vassili Demin .20 .50
7 Sergei Stas .20 .50
8 Brad Harrison .20 .50
9 Cam Brown .20 .50
10 Kevin McKinnon .20 .50
11 Andrei Kozlov .20 .50
12 Chris Tschupp .20 .50
13 Jason Smith .20 .50
14 Justin Peca .20 .50
15 Francis Ouellette .20 .50
16 Vern Guetens .30 .75
17 Scott Burfoot .30 .75
18 Vyacheslav Polikarkin .20 .50
19 Stephane Charbonneau .20 .50
20 Ian Decorby .20 .50

2003-04 Everett Silvertips

COMPLETE SET (28) 5.00 12.00
1 Checklist .01 .01
2 Bryan Nathe .20 .50
3 Marc Desloges .20 .50
4 Jovan Matic .20 .50
5 Mike Wall .30 .75
6 Michael Wuchterl .20 .50
7 Mark Kress .20 .50
8 Devin Wilson .20 .50
9 Martin Ruzicka .20 .50
10 Curtis Billsten .20 .50
11 Barry Horman .20 .50
12 Shaun Heshka .20 .50
13 Jeff Schmidt .20 .50
14 Cody Thoring .20 .50
15 Ryan Blatchford .20 .50
16 Torrie Wheat .20 .50
17 Mitch Love .20 .50
18 Devin Welsh .20 .50
19 Riley Armstrong .20 .50
20 Tyler Dietrich .20 .50
21 John Dahl .20 .50
22 Jeff Harvey .30 .75
23 Ivan Baranka .20 .50
24 Chad Bassen .20 .50
25 Doug Soetaert GM .02 .10
26 Kevin Constantine CO .02 .10
27 John Becanic ACO .02 .10
28 Jay Varady ACO .02 .10

2004-05 Everett Silvertips

COMPLETE SET (?) 10.00 20.00
1 Header Card .02 .10
2 Tyler Dietrich .20 .50
3 Alex Leavitt .20 .50
4 Mitch Love .20 .50
5 Doug Soetaert .02 .10
6 Mike Wuchterl .20 .50
7 Cody Thoring .20 .50
8 Karel Hromas .20 .50
9 Ryan Blatchford .20 .50
10 Zach Sim .20 .50
11 Mark Kress .20 .50
12 Brennan Zasitko .20 .50
13 Torrie Wheat .20 .50
14 Michael Wall .40 1.00
15 Graham Potuer .20 .50
16 Matt Sawa .20 .50
17 Randy King .20 .50
18 Leland Irving 1.25 3.00
19 Shaun Heshka .20 .50
20 Jonathan Harty .20 .50
21 Zach Hamill 1.25 3.00
22 Taylor Ellington .20 .50
23 Jeremy Creurer .20 .50
24 Brady Calla .30 .75
25 Curtis Billsten .20 .50
26 Ivan Baranka .20 .50
27 Kyle Annesley .20 .50
28 Jay Varady .20 .50
29 John Becanic .20 .50
30 Kevin Constantine .02 .10

2005-06 Everett Silvertips

COMPLETE SET (30) 10.00 20.00
1 Damir Alic .30 .75
2 Brady Calla .30 .75
3 Zack Dailey .30 .75
4 Eric Doyle .30 .75
5 Taylor Ellington .30 .75
6 Matt Esposito .30 .75
7 Ondrej Fiala .40 1.00
8 Jason Fransoo .30 .75
9 Zach Hamill .75 2.00
10 Shane Harper .30 .75
11 Jonathon Harty .30 .75
12 Shaun Heshka .30 .75
13 Karel Hromas .30 .75
14 Leland Irving .75 2.00
15 Mark Kress .30 .75
16 John Lammers .30 .75
17 Jonathan Milhouse .30 .75
18 Peter Mueller .75 2.00
19 Graham Potuer .30 .75
20 Ryan Sawka .30 .75
21 Zach Sim .30 .75
22 Jesse Smyke .30 .75
23 Brennan Sonne .30 .75
24 Cody Thoring .30 .75
25 Torrie Wheat .30 .75
26 Kevin Constantine HC .02 .10
27 John Becanic AC .02 .10
28 Jay Varady AC .02 .10
29 Scott Scoville DPP .02 .10
30 Zoran Rajcic DO .02 .10

2005 Extreme Top Prospects Signature Edition

This 30-card set was sold only in set form and was limited to just 400 sets. Each card carried a certified player autograph. The Sidney Crosby stick/auto card was inserted in one out of 4 sets and was limited to 150 copies though only 100 copies were used in the sets. The other 50 cards were given to Crosby. Please note that there are two cards numbered S7 and that card S26 does not exist.

S1 Sidney Crosby/300 150.00 250.00
S2 Alex Bourret 6.00 15.00
S3 Guillaume Latendresse 12.00 30.00
S4 Marc-Antoine Pouliot 10.00 25.00
S5 Jean-Francois Jacques 6.00 15.00
S6 David Krejci 6.00 15.00
S7 Corey Perry 12.50 30.00
S7 Daren Machesney 6.00 15.00
S8 Rob Schremp 10.00 25.00
S9 Danny Syrvet 8.00 20.00
S10 Petr Vrana 10.00 25.00
S11 Derick Brassard 10.00 25.00
S12 Stephen Dixon 6.00 15.00
S13 James Sheppard 8.00 20.00
S14 Marc Staal 8.00 20.00
S15 Benoit Pouliot 8.00 20.00
S16 Anthony Stewart 6.00 15.00
S17 Michael Ouzas 6.00 15.00
S18 Patrick O'Sullivan 10.00 25.00
S19 Lukas Kaspar 6.00 15.00
S20 Bobby Ryan 10.00 25.00
S21 Stanislav Lascek 6.00 15.00
S22 Marek Zagrapan 6.00 15.00
S23 Josh Hennessy 6.00 15.00
S24 Alexander Radulov 10.00 25.00
S25 Julien Ellis-Plante 8.00 20.00
S27 Wojtek Wolski 10.00 25.00
S28 Michael Richards 10.00 25.00
S29 Boris Valabik 6.00 15.00
S30 Ryan O'Marra 6.00 15.00
SS1 Sidney Crosby Stick AU/100 200.00 400.00

1998-99 Fayetteville Force

Little is known about this Central Hockey League team set beyond the confirmed checklist. Any additional information can be forwarded to hockeymag@beckett.com.

COMPLETE SET (18) 3.60 9.00
1 David Lohrei HCO .20 .50
2 Darren McLean .20 .50
3 Rod Butler .20 .50
4 Steven Toll .20 .50
5 Justin Tomberlin .20 .50
6 Alexsandr Chunchukov .20 .50
7 Casey Hungle .20 .50
8 Jason Wright .20 .50
9 Roddy MacCormick .20 .50
10 Lon Hovland .20 .50
11 Chris Bernard .20 .50
12 Dan Dennis .20 .50
13 Chris Ford .20 .50
14 Ryan Guzior .20 .50
15 Chad Remackel .20 .50
16 Colin Muldoon .20 .50
17 Stephen Sangermano .20 .50
18 Tim Hill .20 .50

2006-07 Fayetteville FireAntz

COMPLETE SET (21) 20.00 40.00
1 Mike Clarke .75 2.00
2 Chad CollinsÂ 1.25 3.00
3 Bryan Dobek .75 2.00
4 Chris Furguson .75 2.00
5 Gavin Hodgson .75 2.00
6 Garrett KindredÂ 1.25 3.00
7 Nick Kormanyos .75 2.00
8 John MarksÂ HC .20 .50
9 Rob ManchoffÂ CO .20 .50
10 Adam Meyer .75 2.00
11 Marc Norrington .75 2.00
12 Josh Piro .75 2.00
13 Jarrett Robertson .75 2.00
14 Dylan Row .75 2.00
15 Pekka Saittakari .75 2.00
16 Rob Sich .75 2.00
17 B.J. Stephens .75 2.00
18 Josh Tataryn .75 2.00
19 Tim Velemirovich .75 2.00
20 Josh Welter .75 2.00
21 Chad Wilcox .75 2.00

1991-92 Ferris State Bulldogs

This 30-card standard-size set features the 1991-92 Ferris State Bulldogs. The cards were available in the Ferris State University Pro Shop at the arena. The cards are unnumbered and checklisted below in alphabetical order.

COMPLETE SET (30) 4.00 10.00
1 Aaron Asp .20 .50
2 Seth Appert .20 .50
3 J.J. Bamberger .20 .50
4 Kevin Beals ACO .04 .10
5 Scot Bell .20 .50
6 Brad Burnham .20 .50
7 Dan Chaput .20 .50
8 Tim Christian .20 .50
9 Bob Daniels .20 .50
10 Colin Dodunski .20 .50
11 Mick Dolan .20 .50
12 John Duff .20 .50
13 Daryl Filipek .20 .50
14 John Gruden .20 .50
15 Luke Harvey .20 .50
16 Jeff Jestadt .20 .50
17 Dave Karpa .30 .75
18 Gary Kitching .20 .50
19 Mike Kolenda .20 .50
20 Craig Lisko .20 .50
21 Mike May .20 .50
22 Pat Mazzoli .20 .50
23 Robb McIntyre .20 .50
24 Kevin Moore .20 .50
25 Greg Paine .20 .50
26 Dwight Parrish .20 .50
27 Val Passarelli .20 .50
28 Keith Sergott .20 .50
29 Doug Smith .20 .50
30 The Bulldog MASCOT .04 .10

1992-93 Ferris State Bulldogs

This set features the Bulldogs of the NCAA. The cards were issued as a giveaway and are unnumbered, so are listed below in alphabetical order.

COMPLETE SET (30) 8.00 20.00
1 Seth Appert .30 .75
2 Aaron Asp .30 .75
3 J.J. Bamberger .30 .75
4 Kevin Beals .30 .75
5 Scot Bell .30 .75
6 Brad Burnham .30 .75
7 Daniel Chaput .30 .75
8 Tim Christian .30 .75
9 Bob Daniels CO .10 .25
10 Colin Dodunski .30 .75
11 Mick Dolan .30 .75
12 John Duff .30 .75
13 Daryl Filipek .30 .75
14 John Gruden .40 1.00
15 Luke Harvey .30 .75
16 Jeff Jestadt .30 .75
17 Dave Karpa .40 1.00
18 Gary Kitching .30 .75
19 Mike Kolenda .30 .75
20 Craig Lisko .30 .75
21 Mike May .30 .75
22 Pat Mazzoli .30 .75
23 Robb McIntyre .30 .75
24 Kevin Moore .30 .75
25 Greg Paine .30 .75
26 Dwight Parrish .30 .75
27 Val Passarelli .40 1.00
28 Keith Sergott .30 .75
29 Doug Smith .30 .75
30 The Bulldog MASCOT .04 .10

1993-94 Flint Generals

This set of 20 cards features the Flint Generals of the Colonial Hockey League. It was produced for team distribution by Rising Star Sport Promotions. The fronts feature a posed photo, along with league logo and player information. The backs contain a smattering of biographical data and career numbers. The set is unnumbered.

COMPLETE SET (20) 40.00 75.00
1 Header Card .40 1.00
2 Brent Stickney 1.50 4.00
3 Brett Strot 1.50 4.00
4 Brian Sakic 2.00 5.00
5 Chris O'Rourke 1.50 4.00
6 Dan Elsener 1.50 4.00
7 Darcy Austin 1.50 4.00
8 Dominic Niro 1.50 4.00
9 Jim Duhart 1.50 4.00
10 John Heasty 1.50 4.00
11 Keith Whitmore 1.50 4.00
12 Ken Spangler 1.50 4.00
13 Kevin Kerr 1.50 4.00
14 Larry Bernard 1.50 4.00
15 Lorne Knauft 1.50 4.00
16 Marc Vachon 1.50 4.00
17 Mark Gowens 2.00 5.00
18 Peter Horachek 1.50 4.00
19 Stephane Brochu 1.50 4.00
20 Todd Humphrey 2.00 5.00

1994-95 Flint Generals

This 24-card set of the Flint Generals of the Colonial Hockey League was produced by and distributed through the team. The set's familiar look comes from its homage to the lamentable 1991-92 Pro Set issue. The card backs also ape the design, although they are in black and white, containing another photo and player stats.

COMPLETE SET (24) 20.00 50.00
1 Kevin Barrett .75 2.00
2 Larry Bernard .75 2.00
3 Ken Blum .75 2.00
4 Stephane Brochu .75 2.00
5 Keith Carney .75 2.00
6 Ryan Douglas .75 2.00
7 Jim Duhart .75 2.00
8 Ray Gallagher .75 2.00
9 Mark Gowens .75 2.00
10 Peter Horachek .75 2.00
11 Todd Humphrey .75 2.00
12 Fredrik Jax 1.00 2.50
13 Doug Jones .75 2.00
14 Kevin Kerr 1.00 2.50
15 Petr Leska .75 2.00
16 Stan Matwijiw 1.25 3.00
17 Glen Mears .75 2.00
18 Kyle Reeves 1.00 2.50
19 Brian Sakic 1.00 2.50
20 Stefan Simoes .75 2.00
21 Ken Spangler .75 2.00
22 Keith Whitmore .75 2.00
23 Jeff Whittle .75 2.00
24 Team Photo .75 2.00

1995-96 Flint Generals

This 25-card set features the Flint Generals of the CHL. The set was produced by, and available only through, the team's booster club. The fronts feature an action photo and team and booster club logos. The back includes another photo, player stats and a brief bio.

COMPLETE SET (25) 4.80 12.00
1 Erin Whitten 1.00 2.50
2 Kevin Kerr .30 .75
3 Sverre Sears .16 .40
4 Scott Burfoot .20 .50
5 John Batten .16 .40
6 Chad Grills .16 .40
7 Lady Generals .30 .75
8 General Rally MASCOT .04 .10
9 Rob Nichols GM/CO .04 .10
10 Mikhail Nemirovsky .16 .40
11 Robin Bouchard .16 .40
12 Dominic Grandmaison .16 .40
13 Andrei Mezin .30 .75
14 Steve Beadle .16 .40
15 Darryl Lafrance .16 .40
16 Chris Gotziaman .16 .40
17 Gerry St. Cyr .30 .75
18 Derek Knorr .16 .40
19 Chris Gordon .20 .50
20 Brett MacDonald .16 .40
21 Brian Sakic .20 .50
22 Jamie Hearn .16 .40
23 Jeff Whittle .16 .40
24 Stephane Brochu .16 .40
25 Jim Duhart .16 .40

1996-97 Flint Generals

This 28-card set was issued as a promotional giveaway over the span of several games. This set is not numbered so the cards appear in alphabetical order.

COMPLETE SET (28) 10.00 25.00
1 Steve Beadle .40 1.00
2 Pascal Belanger .40 1.00
3 Robin Bouchard .40 1.00
4 Stephane Brochu .40 1.00
5 Neil Eisenhut .40 1.00
6 Nick Forbes .40 1.00
7 Igor Galkin .40 1.00
8 Jason Glover .40 1.00
9 Chad Grills .40 1.00
10 John Heasty .40 1.00
11 Kevin Kerr .40 1.00
12 Lorne Knauft .40 1.00
13 Brett MacDonald .40 1.00
14 Andrei Mezin .60 1.50
15 Jason Payne .40 1.00
16 Jason Ralph .40 1.00
17 Dmitri Rodine .40 1.00
18 Zdenek Sikl .40 1.00
19 Ken Spangler .40 1.00
20 Matt Weder .40 1.00
21 Jeff Whittle .40 1.00
22 Ross Wilson .40 1.00
23 Rob Nichols HCO .20 .50
24 Karl Lawson .40 1.00
25 General Rally Mascot .20 .50
26 1996 Colonial Cup Champs .40 1.00
27 1996 Tarry Cup Champs .40 1.00
28 Checklist .20 .50

1997-98 Flint Generals

This set features the Generals of the UHL. The cards were issued as promotional giveaways in 10-card packs at three different games.

COMPLETE SET (30) 12.00 30.00
1 Steve Beadle .40 1.00
2 Stephane Brochu .60 1.50
3 Ian Crockford .40 1.00
4 Nick Forbes .40 1.00
5 Mark Giannetti .40 1.00
6 Jason Glover .40 1.00
7 Chad Grills .40 1.00
8 John Heasty .40 1.00
9 Raitis Ivanans .40 1.00
10 Kevin Kerr .60 1.50
11 Lorne Knauft .40 1.00
12 Ray LeBlanc .40 2.00
13 Brett MacDonald .40 1.00
14 Bryan McMullen .40 1.00
15 Andrei Mezin .80 2.00
16 Matt Mullin .60 1.50
17 Dmitri Rodine .40 1.00
18 Brian Sakic .60 1.50
19 Jeremy Sladovnik .40 1.00
20 Ken Spangler .40 1.00
21 Kahlil Thomas .40 1.00
22 Jeff Whittle .40 1.00
23 Ross Wilson .40 1.00
24 Rob Nichols CO .10 .25
25 General Rally MASCOT .10 .25
26 Mike Zanzarella TR .10 .25
27 Robert Roe STAFF .10 .25
28 Pam The Prize Lady .20 .50
29 Lady Generals .40 1.00
30 Flint Generals .40 1.00

1997-98 Flint Generals EBK

This set features the Generals of the UHL. The set was produced by ebk Sports and was sold by the team at home playoff games.

COMPLETE SET (23) 4.00 10.00
1 Checklist .04 .10
2 Kahlil Thomas .20 .50
3 Ken Spangler .30 .75
4 Stephane Brochu .30 .75
5 Lorne Knauft .20 .50
6 Janis Tomans .20 .50
7 Nick Forbes .20 .50
8 Trevor Jobe .20 .50
9 John Heasty .20 .50
10 Brian Sakic .30 .75
11 Kevin Kerr .30 .75
12 Chad Grills .20 .50
13 UHL All-Stars .20 .50
14 Jeremy Sladovnik .20 .50
15 Jeff Whittle .20 .50
16 Jason Glover .20 .50
17 Steve Beadle .20 .50
18 Bryan McMullen .20 .50
19 Emmanuel Labranche .20 .50
20 Brett MacDonald .20 .50
21 John Batten .20 .50
22 Ross Wilson .20 .50
23 Rob Nichols CO .10 .25

1998-99 Flint Generals

This set features the Generals of the UHL. The cards were issued in packs as a promotional giveaway at one home game. Reports conflict as to whether the packs contained four, six or eight cards. Anyone with additional information can forward it to hockeymag@beckett.com.

COMPLETE SET (22) 8.00 20.00
1 Logo Card .04 .10
2 Chad Grills .40 1.00
3 Jason Payne .40 1.00
4 Jeremy Sladovnik .40 1.00
5 Stephane Brochu .40 1.00
6 Jeff Whittle .40 1.00
7 Rob Nichols CO .10 .25
8 Brian Sakic .60 1.50
9 Checklist .04 .10
10 Nick Forbes .40 1.00
11 Mike Bondy .40 1.00
12 Peter Ambroziak .40 1.00
13 Luch Nasato .60 1.50
14 Mikhail Nemirovsky .40 1.00
15 Bobby Reynolds .40 1.00
16 Generals Staff .04 .10
17 Lorne Knauft .40 1.00
18 Rob Laurie .60 1.50
19 Ross Wilson .40 1.00
20 Jason Glover .40 1.00
21 Brett MacDonald .40 1.00
22 Kahlil Thomas .40 1.00

2001-02 Flint Generals

COMPLETE SET (24) 20.00
1 Joey Bastien 1.00
2 Sylvain Dufresne 1.00
3 Jim Duhart 1.00
4 Stu Dunn 1.50
5 Tim Findlay 1.00
6 Dale Greenwood 1.00
8 Lee Jelenic 1.00
9 Lorne Knauft 1.00
10 Corey Laniuk 1.00
11 Tom McKinnon 1.50
12 Frankie Nault 1.00
13 Eric Perricone 1.00
14 Jean-Francois Picard 1.00
15 Bobby Reynolds 1.00
16 Gary Roach 1.00
17 Mike Rutter 1.00
18 Jordan Trew 1.00
19 Mike Varhaug 1.50
20 Martin Woods 1.00
21 Vaclav Zavoral 1.00
22 Kirk Tomlinson HCO .50
23 General Rally MASCOT .10
24 The Lady Generals .10

1987-88 Flint Spirits

This 20-card standard-size set features white-bordered posed color player photos. The team name and the player's name edge the picture on the left and lower edges respectively. Team logos in the bottom border round out the front. The horizontal backs carry biography, player profile, and statistics.

COMPLETE SET (20) 4.80 12.00
1 Mario Chitaroni .20 .50
2 John Cullen .40 1.00
3 Bob Fleming .20 .50
4 Keith Gretzky .40 1.00
5 Todd Hawkins .20 .50
6 Mike Hoffman .20 .50
7 Curtis Hunt .20 .50
8 Dwaine Hutton .20 .50
9 Trent Kaese .20 .50
10 Tom Karalis .20 .50
11 Ray LeBlanc .40 1.00
12 Darren Lowe .20 .50
13 Brett MacDonald .20 .50
14 Chris McSorley .40 1.00
15 Mike Mersch .20 .50
16 Victor Posa .20 .50
17 Kevin Schamehorn .20 .50
18 Ron Stern .40 1.00
19 Don Waddell .20 .50
20 Dan Woodley .20 .50

1988-89 Flint Spirits

This 22-card standard-size features posed color player photos. The pictures are set at an angle on the card with green borders on the top and bottom. The player's name appears in the lower green border, while the team appears above. A thin blue line borders the front. The horizontal backs carry the player's name, biographical information, statistics, and career highlights. The cards are unnumbered and checklisted below in alphabetical order.

COMPLETE SET (22) 4.00 10.00
1 Dean Anderson .20 .50
2 Rob Bryden .20 .50
3 John Devereaux .20 .50
4 Stephane Giguere .20 .50
5 Steve Harrison .20 .50
6 Yves Heroux .30 .75
7 Mike Hoffman .20 .50
8 Peter Horachek .20 .50
9 Guy Jacob .20 .50
10 Bob Kennedy .20 .50
11 Gary Kruzich .20 .50
12 Lonnie Loach .40 1.00
13 Brett MacDonald .20 .50
14 Mike MacWilliam .20 .50
15 Moe Mansi .20 .50
16 Mike Mersch .20 .50
17 Michel Mongeau .40 1.00
18 Ken Spangler .20 .50
19 Three Amigos .30 .75
Steve Harrison
Mike Mersch
Mike Hoffman
20 Mark Vichorek .20 .50
21 Troy Vollhoffer .20 .50
22 Don Waddell GM .20 .50

2003-04 Florence Pride

COMPLETE SET (16) 15.00
145 Jack Baker 1.00
146 Craig Brunel 1.00
147 Adam Elzinga 1.00
148 Ryan Gaucher 1.00
149 Wes Goldie 1.00
150 Vladimir Gusev 1.00
151 Kyle Kidney 1.00
152 Dan Lombard 1.00
153 Mark McRae 1.00
154 Matt Reid 1.00
155 Bobby Russell 1.00
156 Allan Sirois 1.00
157 Jeff Szwez 1.00
158 Shaun Sutter 1.00
159 Mike Torney 1.00
160 Matt Underhill 1.50

1998-99 Florida Everblades

Little is known about this East Coast League team set beyond the confirmed checklist. Any additional information can be forwarded to hockeymag@beckett.com.

COMPLETE SET (27) 7.20 50.00
1 Brett Bruininks .30 2.00
2 Matt Brush .30 2.00
3 Nick Checco .30 2.00
4 Matt Demarski .30 2.00
5 Sergei Fedotov .30 2.00
6 Tim Ferguson .30 2.00
7 Bob Ferguson CO .04 .10
8 Hugh Hamilton .30 2.00
9 Mike Jickling .30 2.00
10 Gary Koehler .30 2.00
11 Greg Kuznik .30 2.00
12 Dane Litke .30 2.00
13 Marc Magliarditi .60 5.00
14 Kevin McDonald .30 2.00
15 Pat Mikesch .30 2.00
16 P.K. O'Handley ACO .04 .10
17 Josh Penn EQ .04 .10
18 Randy Petruk .60 5.00
19 Jason Prokopetz .30 2.00
20 Dan Keimann .30 2.00
21 Eric Ricard .30 2.00
22 Eric Rud .30 2.00
23 Steve Tardif .30 2.00
24 Andrew Taylor .30 2.00
25 Todd Wisocki .30 2.00
26 Mascot .04 .10
27 Title Card .04 .10

1999-00 Florida Everblades

This set features the Everblades of the ECHL. The set was produced by Roox and handed out as a promotional giveaway at a late-season home game.

COMPLETE SET (26) 8.00 20.00
1 Jeff Maund .60 1.50
2 Hugh Hamilton .30 .75
3 Greg Kuznik .30 .75
4 Dane Litke .30 .75
5 Peter Kasper .30 .75
6 Tim Ferguson .30 .75
7 Brent Cullaton .30 .75
8 Reggie Berg .40 1.00
9 Steve Moffatt .30 .75
10 Tom Buckley .30 .75
11 Eric Rud .30 .75
12 Jason Prokopetz .30 .75
13 Terry Lindgren .40 1.00
14 Matt Demarski .30 .75
15 Marc Magliarditi .60 1.50
16 Ty Jones .40 1.00
17 Harlan Pratt .30 .75
18 John Varga .40 1.00
19 Joe Cardarelli .30 .75
20 Steve Tardif .30 .75
21 Andy MacIntyre .30 .75
22 Jason Morgan .30 .75
23 Bob Ferguson CO .10 .25
24 P.K. O'Handley CO .10 .25
25 Swampy MAS .10 .25
26 Celluar One .04 .10

2000-01 Florida Everblades

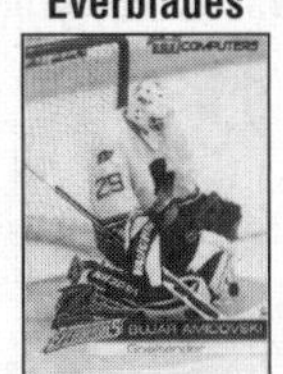

This set features the Everblades of the ECHL. The set was produced by Roox as a promotional giveaway.

COMPLETE SET (26) 8.00 20.00
1 Bujar Amidovski .80 2.00
2 Reggie Berg .40 1.00
3 Sean Blanchard .40 1.00
4 Tom Buckley .40 1.00
5 Sandy Cohen .40 1.00
6 Randy Copley .40 1.00
7 Matt Demarski .30 .75
8 Bob Ferguson CO .20 .50
9 Hugh Hamilton .30 .75
10 Devin Hartnell .30 .75
11 Darrell Hay .40 1.00
12 Pete Hogan .30 .75
13 John Jennings EM .10 .25
14 Mike Jickling .30 .75
15 Terry Lindgren .40 1.00
16 Andy MacIntyre .30 .75
17 Marc Magliarditi .60 1.50
18 Brent McDonald .30 .75
19 Jason Metcalfe .30 .75
20 Jason Morgan .30 .75
21 P.K. O'Handley CO .20 .50
22 Brent Pope .30 .75
23 Swampee MASCOT .20 .50
24 David Vallieres .30 .75
25 Todd Wisocki TR .10 .25
26 TTI Computers .01

2001-02 Florida Everblades

This set features the Everblades of the ECHL. The cards were produced by Choice Marketing and were issued as a giveaway. A total of 2,000 sets were produced. Each set also includes the ultimate whip, a card promoting a Pikachu cartoon.

COMPLETE SET (21) 8.00 20.00
1 Checklist .20 .50
2 Gerry Fleming CO .20 .50
3 P.K. O'Handley ACO .20 .50
4 Vince Williams .40 1.00
5 Terry Lindgren .62 1.56
6 Duane Harmer .40 1.00
7 Andrew Long .40 1.00
8 Reggie Berg .40 1.00
9 Brent McDonald .40 1.00
10 Tom Buckley .40 1.00
11 Briane Thompson .40 1.00
12 Mike Cirillo .40 1.00
13 Don Smith .40 1.00
14 Joe Blaznek .40 1.00
15 Peter Reynolds .40 1.00
16 Paul Spadafora .62 1.56
17 Keith Anderson .40 1.00
18 Shaun Fisher .40 1.00
19 Randy Petruk .62 1.56
20 Ryan Murphy .40 1.00
21 Swampee .20 .50

2002-03 Florida Everblades

This set was produced by Choice Marketing and given away at a home game.

COMPLETE SET (26) 25.00
1 Keith Anderson 1.00
2 George Awada 1.00
3 Anthony Battaglia 1.00
4 Joe Blaznek 1.00
5 Kevin Brown 1.00
6 Tom Buckley 1.00
7 Sean Curry 1.00
8 Brian Goudie 1.00
9 Duane Harmer 1.00
10 Ed Hill 1.00
11 Marty Johnston 1.00
12 Cam McCormick 1.50
13 Laurent Meunier 1.00
14 Ryan Murphy 1.00
15 Tom Nelson 1.00
16 Peter Reynolds 1.00
17 Lee Ruff 1.00
18 Don Smith 1.00
19 Ryan Stewart 1.00
20 Jimmy Verdule 2.00
21 Jon Insana 1.00
22 Rob Zepp 2.00
23 Gerry Fleming CO .50
24 Terry Lindgren ACO .10
25 Swampee MASCOT .10
26 Checklist .10

2002-03 Florida Everblades RBI

COMPLETE SET (18) 20.00
115 Keith Anderson 1.00
116 George Awada 1.00
117 Anthony Battaglia 1.00
118 Joe Blaznek 1.00
119 Tom Buckley 1.00
120 Brian Goudie 1.00
121 Duane Harmer 1.00
122 Marty Johnston 1.00
123 Cam McCormick 1.50
124 Brent McDonald 1.00
125 Laurent Meunier 1.00
126 Ryan Murphy 1.00
127 Tom Nelson 1.00
128 Jared Newman 1.00
129 Peter Reynolds 1.00
130 Don Smith 1.00
131 Jimmy Verdule 2.00
132 Rob Zepp 2.00

2003-04 Florida Everblades

This set was issued by Choice Marketing and given away at one home game.

COMPLETE SET (25) 8.00 20.00
1 Keith Anderson .40 1.00
2 Reggie Berg .40 1.00
3 Jim Brown .40 1.00
4 Brandon Coalter .40 1.00
5 Paul Esdale .40 1.00
6 Gerry Fleming CO .07 .20
7 Ian Forbes .40 1.00
8 Chris Heisten .40 1.00
9 Tom Buckley .40 1.00
10 Jon Insana .40 1.00
11 Chad Larose .40 1.00
12 Jay Legault .40 1.00
13 Terry Lindgren ACO .07 .20
14 Tim O'Connell .40 1.00
15 Jeff Maund .60 1.50
16 Brian McCullough .40 1.00
17 Brent McDonald .40 1.00
18 Jared Newman .40 1.00
19 Matt Pagnutti .40 1.00
20 Paul Vincent .40 1.00
21 Gray Shaneberger .40 1.00
22 Mascot .07 .20
23 Chris Thompson .40 1.00
24 Ryan Van Buskirk .40 1.00
25 Rob Zepp .75 2.00

2003-04 Florida Everblades RBI Sports

This set was issued by RBI Sports, and is limited to just 250 copies. The numbering sequence continues across all RBI Sports sets issued this season.

COMPLETE SET (16) 18.00
161 Reggie Berg 1.00
162 Brandon Coalter 1.00
163 Paul Esdale 1.00
164 Kevin Holdridge 1.00
165 Jon Insana 1.00
166 Chad Larose 1.00
167 Carl Mallette 1.25
168 Jeff Maund 1.50
169 Brian McCullough 1.00
170 Jared Newman 1.00
171 Stuart Pietersma 1.00
172 Peter Reynolds 1.00
173 Gray Shaneberger 1.25
174 Damian Surma 1.00
175 Ryan Van Buskirk 1.00
176 Rob Zepp 2.00

2004-05 Florida Everblades

COMPLETE SET (30) 20.00
1 Tyler MacKay .75
2 Jared Newman .75
3 Matt Pagnutti .75
4 Shane Hnidy .75
5 Simon Tremblay .75
6 Reggie Berg .75
7 Brent MacDonald .75
8 Steve Saviano .75
9 Ryan Brindley .75
10 Tim Branham .75
11 Brandon Coalter .75
12 Matt Hendricks .75
13 David Lundbohm .75
14 Tim O'Connell .75
15 Bryce Charpentier .75
16 Kris Vernarsky 1.00
17 Brad Church 1.00
18 Greg Hornby .75
19 Keith Anderson .75
20 Damian Surma .75
21 Rob Zepp 1.00
22 Craig Kowalski .75
23 Chris Lee .75
24 Jason Nobili .75
25 Gerry Fleming .10
26 Todd Wisocki .10
27 John Jennings .10
28 Swampee MASCOT .10
29 Sponsor card .01
30 Checklist .01

2005-06 Florida Everblades

COMPLETE SET (25) 6.00 15.00
1 Jonathan Lehun .30 .75
2 Martin Tuma .30 .75
3 Paul Cabana .30 .75
4 Reggie Berg .30 .75
5 Swampee MASCOT .02 .10
6 Phil Aucoin .30 .75
7 Brandon Coalter .30 .75
8 Ernie Hartlieb .30 .75
9 Phil Osaer .30 1.00
10 Steve Saviano .30 .75
11 Ryan Brindley .30 .75
12 Bryce Charpentier .30 .75
13 Craig Kowalski .30 .75
14 Daniel Sisca .30 .75
15 Anders Strome .30 .75
16 Sean Stefanski .30 .75
17 Corey Neilson .30 .75
18 Grant McNeill .30 .75
19 Chris Lee .30 .75
20 Kevin Bergin .30 .75
21 John Adams .30 .75
22 Vince Bellissimo .30 .75
23 John Ronan .30 .75
24 Jeremy Swanson .30 .75
25 Gerry Fleming HC .02 .10

1990-91 Fort Saskatchewan Traders

This sheet contains 24 standard-size cards. Each card contains a color action player photo with his jersey number and name at the top on a white background. Above this are listed the player's position with the team name and years. At the lower right are the words "Next Generation Sport Cards." Each photo is framed by a thin red line and white border. The cards are unnumbered and checklisted below in alphabetical order.

COMPLETE SET (24) 2.40 6.00
1 Michael Buzak .16 .40
2 Wade Fennig .16 .40
3 Mark Goodkey .16 .40
4 Richard Groten .16 .40
5 Brett Gullion .16 .40
6 Keith Hill .16 .40
7 Justin Hocking .30 .75
8 Ian Kallay .16 .40
9 Scott Lindsay .16 .40
10 Faron Luchkow .16 .40
11 Wayne MacDonald .16 .40
12 Ted Oloriz .16 .40
13 Jason Plandowski .16 .40
14 Dory Reich .16 .40
15 Shawn Reich .16 .40
16 Darren Smith .16 .40
17 Mark Souch .16 .40
18 Bryan Stewart .16 .40
19 Paul Strand .16 .40
20 Tim Wiwchar .16 .40
21 Paul Wozney .16 .40
22 Allen Young .16 .40
23 Jason Yuzda .16 .40
24 Team Photo .20 .50

1993-94 Fort Wayne Komets

Cards are unnumbered and are listed below in alphabetical order.

COMPLETE SET (27) 6.00 15.00
1 Ian Boyce .30 .75
2 Colin Chin .30 .75
3 Lee Davidson .30 .75
4 Guy Dupuis .30 .75
5 Steve Fletcher .75 2.00
6 Sean Gauthier .30 .75
7 Darryl Gilmour .40 1.00
8 Kelly Hurd .30 .75
9 Carey Lucyk .30 .75
10 Kevin MacDonald .30 .75
11 Igor Malykhin .30 .75
12 Brian McKee .30 .75
13 Mitch Messier .40 1.00
14 Max Middendorf .40 1.00
15 John Purves .40 1.00
16 Grant Richison .30 .75
17 Darin Smith .30 .75
18 Dave Smith .30 .75
19 Shayne Stevenson .30 .75
20 David Tretowicz .30 .75
21 Vladimir Tsyplakov .30 .75
22 Doug Wickenheiser .40 1.00
23 Bruce Boudreau CO .20 .50
24 Derek Ray ACO .20 .50
25 Joe Franke TR .20 .50
26 Galen Head EQM .20 .50
27 Team Photo .20 .50

1995-96 Fort Wayne Komets

This set features the Komets of the IHL. The set was produced by Edge Ice and sold at the team's souvenir stands.

COMPLETE SET (25) 4.80 12.00
1 Andy Bezeau .20 .50
2 Colin Chin .20 .50
3 Shawn Cronin .20 .50
4 Guy Dupuis .20 .50
5 Pat Elynuik .20 .50
6 Bob Essensa .30 .75
7 Shawn Evans .20 .50
8 Steven Fletcher .20 .50
9 Peter Ing .20 .50
10 Andrew McBain .20 .50
11 Mitch Messier .20 .50
12 Rob Murphy .20 .50
13 Alex Nikolic .20 .50
14 Grant Richison .20 .50
15 Jeff Rohlicek .20 .50
16 Konstantin Shafronov .20 .50
17 Darin Smith .20 .50
18 Sergei Stas .20 .50
19 Brian Straub .20 .50
20 Chris Tok .20 .50
21 Paul Willett .20 .50
22 Kevin Wortman .20 .50
23 Oleg Yashin .20 .50
24 Derek Ray CO .10 .25
25 Icy MAS .04 .10

1997-98 Fort Wayne Komets

Little is known about this set beyond the confirmed checklist. Additional information can be forwarded to hockeymag@beckett.com.

COMPLETE SET (21) 4.00 10.00
1 Guy Dupuis .20 .50
2 Ian Boyce .20 .50
3 Lee Davidson .20 .50
4 Bruce Racine .30 .75
5 Dan Currie .20 .50
6 Robin Bawa .20 .50
7 Tom Nemeth .20 .50
8 Ed Campbell .20 .50
9 Vyacheslav Butsayev .20 .50
10 Steffon Walby .20 .50
11 Derek Eberle .20 .50
12 Chris Armstrong .20 .50
13 Norm Batherson .20 .50
14 Konstantin Shafronov .20 .50
15 Tom Pederson .20 .50
16 Andrei Bashkirov .20 .50
17 Carlin Nordstrom .20 .50
18 Trevor Doyle .20 .50
19 Eric Boguniecki .30 .75
20 Kevin Weekes .60 1.50
21 Icy D. Eagle Mascot .04 .10

1998-99 Fort Wayne Komets

Little is known about this team set beyond the confirmed checklist. Any additional information can be forwarded to hockeymag@beckett.com.

COMPLETE SET (29) 4.00 10.00
1 Ed Campbell .16 .40
2 Vyacheslav Butsayev .20 .50
3 Ian Boyce .16 .40
4 Eric Boguniecki .20 .50
5 Robin Bawa .16 .40
6 Gerard Gallant ACO .16 .40
7 Icy D. Eagle Mascot .04 .10
8 Guy Dupuis .16 .40
9 Dion Darling .16 .40
10 Bob Chase .16 .40
11 Brad Purdie .16 .40
12 Andrei Petrakov .16 .40
13 David Nemirovsky .20 .50
14 Mike Martin .16 .40
15 Tero Lehtera .20 .50
16 Oleg Shargorodsky .16 .40
17 Shawn Selmser .20 .50
18 Andre Roy .20 .50
19 Eldon Reddick .20 .50
20 Bruce Racine .20 .50
21 Memorial Coliseum .04 .10
22 Derek Wood .16 .40
23 Lee Sorochan .20 .50
24 Grant Sonier HCO .04 .10
25 Checklist .04 .10
26 Shawn Penn .16 .40
27 PHPA Web Site .01
28 IHL Web Site .01
29 Andrei Bashkirov .16 .40

1999-00 Fort Wayne Komets Points Leaders

This set was produced by the Komets of the UHL to honor their all-time leading scorers. However, since this was their first season in the league, the players pictured performed for the team during its IHL days. The cards are believed to have been issued as a promotional giveaway, but this has not been confirmed.

COMPLETE SET (16) 6.00 15.00
1 Header Card .04 .10
2 Len Thornson .40 1.00
3 Eddie Long .40 1.00
4 Terry McDougall .40 1.00
5 Colin Chin .40 1.00
6 John Goodwin .40 1.00
7 Reg Primeau .40 1.00
8 Merv Dubchek .40 1.00
9 Barry Scully .40 1.00
10 Rob Laird .40 1.00
11 Jim Burton .60 1.50
12 Lionel Repka .40 1.00
13 Norman Waslowski .40 1.00
14 Ron Leef .40 1.00
15 Bobby Rivard .40 1.00
16 Dale Baldwin .40 1.00

1999-00 Fort Wayne Komets Penalty Leaders

This set was produced by the Komets of the UHL to honor their all-time leading pugilists. However, since this was their first season in the league, the players pictured performed for the team during its IHL days. The cards are believed to have been issued as a promotional giveaway, but this has not been confirmed.

COMPLETE SET (16) 8.00 35.00
1 Header Card .04 .10
2 Steven Fletcher .80 3.00
3 Dale Baldwin .60 2.00
4 Cal Purinton .80 3.00
5 Rob Laird .60 2.00
6 Dave Norris .60 2.00
7 Robin Bawa .60 3.00
8 Terry Pembroke .60 2.00
9 Andy Bezeau .80 3.00
10 Eddie Long .60 2.00
11 Craig Channell .60 2.00
12 Steve Salvucci .60 2.00
13 Carey Lucyk .60 2.00
14 Lionel Repka .60 2.00
15 Scott Gruhl .80 3.00
16 Guy Dupuis .60 2.00

2000-01 Fort Wayne Komets

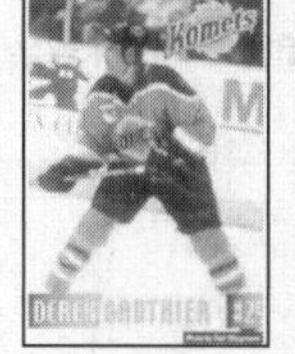

This set was produced by the team and sold at home games throughout the season. The cards are unnumbered, and are listed below in alphabetical order.

COMPLETE SET (24) 4.80 12.00
1 Frederic Bouchard .20 .50
2 Dave Butler .20 .50
3 Keli Corpse .30 .75
4 Derek Gauthier .30 .75
5 Jason Goulet .20 .50
6 Brent Gretzky .30 .75
7 Kelly Hurd .20 .50
8 Rick Judson .20 .50
9 Dave Lemay .20 .50
10 Jim Logan .20 .50
11 Igor Malykhin .20 .50
12 Darren Martens .20 .50
13 Mike McKay .20 .50
14 Geno Parrish .20 .50
15 Kevin Popp .20 .50
16 Sergei Radchenko .20 .50
17 Gary Ricciardi .20 .50
18 Dan Ronan .20 .50
19 Konstantin Simchuk .20 .50
20 Fred Slukynsky .20 .50
21 Doug Teskey .20 .50
22 Brad Twordik .20 .50
23 Greg Puhalski CO .10 .25
24 Ice Eagle MASCOT .04 .10

2000-01 Fort Wayne Komets Shoe Carnival

This set features the Komets of the UHL. The set was a promotional giveaway, sponsored by a local shoe store. The cards were released in five-card strips, featuring four players and a store coupon.

COMPLETE SET (16) 6.00 15.00
1 Rhett Trombley .40 1.00
2 Gary Ricciardi .40 1.00
3 Jason Goulet .40 1.00
4 Rick Judson .40 1.00
5 Igor Malykhin .40 1.00
6 Doug Teskey .40 1.00
7 Kelly Hurd .40 1.00
8 Mike McKay .40 1.00
9 Brent Gretzky .80 2.00
10 Geno Parrish .40 1.00
11 Dave Lemay .40 1.00
12 Jim Logan .40 1.00
13 Frederic Bouchard .40 1.00
14 Brad Twordik .40 1.00
15 Dan Ronan .40 1.00
16 Derek Gauthier .40 1.00

2001-02 Fort Wayne Komets

This set features the Komets of the UHL. It was produced by Choice Marketing and was sold by the team at its souvenir shop. The production was announced at 1,000 sets.

COMPLETE SET (22) 4.00 10.00
1 Doug Teskey .20 .50
2 Igor Bondarev .20 .50
3 Frederic Bouchard .31 .78
4 Christian Bragnalo .20 .50
5 Derek Gauthier .31 .78
6 Dustin Virag .20 .50
7 Chad Grills .20 .50
8 Kevin Holliday .20 .50
9 Icy D. Eagle Mascot .04 .11

10 Erik Landman .20 .50
11 Jim Logan .20 .50
12 Michael Massie .20 .50
13 David Mayes .20 .50
14 Mike McKay .20 .50
15 Kelly Miller .31 .78
16 Martin Fillion .20 .50
17 Kevin Schmidt .20 .50
18 Ryan Severson .20 .50
19 Matt Swain .20 .50
20 Kevin Bertram .20 .50
21 Steven Desjardins .20 .50
22 Brent Gretzky CO .31 .78

2001-02 Fort Wayne Komets Shoe Carnival

The set of the UHL's Fort Wayne franchise features players from both the current Komets team and former greats. The set was issued as a promotional giveaway, with four cards handed out per night at four different games.

COMPLETE SET (16) 6.00 15.00
1 Dustin Virag .40 1.00
2 Reg Primeau .40 1.00
3 Kevin Holliday .40 1.00
4 Steven Fletcher .80 2.00
5 Brent Gretzky .40 1.00
6 Len Thornson .40 1.00
7 Derek Gauthier .40 1.00
8 Robin Bawa .40 1.00
9 Frederic Bouchard .40 1.00
10 Lionel Repka .40 1.00
11 Michel Masse .40 1.00
12 Eddie Long .40 1.00
13 Doug Teskey .40 1.00
14 Chuck Adamson .40 1.00
15 Jim Logan .40 1.00
16 Ian Boyce .40 1.00

2002-03 Fort Wayne Komets

COMPLETE SET (25) 10.00
1 Marc Barlow .50
2 David Beauregard .50
3 Kevin Bertram .50
4 Ken Boone .50
5 Colin Chaulk .50
6 Parris Duffus .75
7 Joe Franke .50
8 Kevin Kotyluk .75
9 Tom Lawson .75
10 Adam Lewis .50
11 Michel Massie .50
12 Troy Neumeier .50
13 Jake Ortmeyer .50
14 Kelly Perrault .50
15 Eldon Reddick .75
16 Kevin Schmidt .50
17 Jason Selleke .50
18 Ryan Severson .50
19 Bart Stevens .50
20 Bobby Stewart .50
21 Sean Venedam .50
22 Dustin Virag .50
23 Icy D. Eagle MASCOT .01
24 Greg Puhalski HCO .10
NNO Checklist .01

2002-03 Fort Wayne Komets Shoe Carnival

COMPLETE SET (16) 30.00
1 Kelly Perrault 2.00
2 David Beauregard 2.00
3 Jake Ortmeyer 2.00
4 Michel Massie 2.00
5 Tom Lawson 2.00
6 Bobby Stewart 2.00
7 Ryan Severson 2.00
8 Eldon Reddick 3.00
9 Sean Venedam 2.00
10 Kevin Bertram 2.00
11 Marc Barlow 2.00
12 Dustin Virag 2.00
13 Icy D. Eagle MASCOT .10
14 Kevin Schmidt 2.00
15 Colin Chaulk 2.00
16 Adam Lewis 2.00

2003-04 Fort Wayne Komets

This series was produced by Choice Marketing and sold at home games.

COMPLETE SET (23) 10.00
1 Bobby Stewart .50
2 Colin Chaulk .50
3 David Beauregard .50
4 Sean Venedam .50
5 Dan Stewart .50
6 Ryan Severson .50
7 Michel Massie .50
8 Dustin Virag .50
9 Kevin Kotyluk .75
10 Adam Lewis .50
11 Dan Price .50
12 Mascot .10
13 Andy Townsend .50
14 Kevin Schmidt .50
15 Mark Cole .50
16 Mike Perna .50
17 Kelly Perrault .50
18 Kevin Bertram .50
19 Troy Neumeier .50
20 Kelly Shields .75
21 Kevin St. Pierre .75
22 Ryan Coole .50
23 Steve Rodberg .50

2003-04 Fort Wayne Komets 2003 Champions

COMPLETE SET (21) 8.00
1 Colin Chaulk .50
2 Kelly Perrault .50
3 Dustin Virag .50
4 Sean Venedam .50
5 Tom Lawson .50
6 Colin Chaulk .50
7 Tom Lawson .50
8 Parading the Cup .20
9 Dustin Virag .50
10 Kevin Bertram .50
11 Greg Puhalski HCO .20
12 Kelly Perrault .50
13 Dustin Virag .50
14 Michel Massie .50
15 Marc Barlow .50
16 Tom Lawson .50
17 Team Photo .50
17 Komets Fans .10
18 Kelly Perrault .50
19 Kevin Kotyluk .75
20 Sponsor .01

2003-04 Fort Wayne Komets Shoe Carnival

These were issued as a promotional giveaway over the course of four home games. The cards came in four-card perforated strips.

COMPLETE SET (16) 15.00
1 Kelly Perrault 1.00
2 Kevin Schmidt 1.00
3 Kevin Bertram 1.00
4 Adam Lewis 1.00
5 Troy Neumeier 1.00
6 Colin Chaulk 1.00
7 Kevin Kotyluk 1.50
8 Bobby Stewart 1.00
9 Kevin St. Pierre 1.50
10 David Beauregard 1.00
11 Michel Massie 1.00
12 Sean Venedam 1.00
13 Dan Price 1.00
14 Dan Stewart 1.00
15 Ryan Severson 1.00
16 Dustin Virag 1.00

2004-05 Fort Wayne Komets

This set was produced by Choice Marketing and sold at the pro shop.

COMPLETE SET (22) 10.00
1 Colin Chaulk 1.00
2 P.C. Drouin .75
3 Jonathan Goodwin .50
4 Chris Grenville .50
5 Rob Guinn .50
6 David Hukalo .50
7 Jason Kean .50
8 Shane Kenny .50
9 Tyler Masters .75
10 Tom Nelson .50
11 Tom Nemeth .50
12 Troy Neumeier .50
13 Steve Rodberg .50
14 Kevin St. Pierre .75
15 Danny Stewart .50
16 Andy Townsend .50
17 Sean Venedam .50
18 Dustin Virag .50
19 Jeff Worlton .50
20 Team Checklist .01
21 Mascot .10
22 Sponsor Card .01

2004-05 Fort Wayne Komets Shoe Carnival

This set was issued as a promotional giveaway at a home game.

COMPLETE SET (16) 25.00
1 Colin Chaulk 3.00
2 P.C. Drouin 2.00
3 Jonathan Goodwin 1.50
4 Chris Grenville 1.50
5 Rob Guinn 1.50
6 Jason Kean 1.50
7 Shane Kenny 1.50
8 Tim Krueckl 1.50
9 Corey Lucas 1.50
10 Tyler Masters 2.00
11 Troy Neumeier 1.50
12 Kevin St. Pierre 2.00
13 Dan Stewart 1.50
14 Sean Venedam 2.00
15 Dustin Virag 1.50
16 Jeff Worlton 1.50

2005-06 Fort Wayne Komets Choice

COMPLETE SET (25) 10.00
1 Kevin St. Pierre .20 .50
2 Jeff Worlton .20 .50
3 Jonathan Goodwin .20 .50
4 David Hukalo .20 .50
5 David Frawley .20 .50
6 David Carpentier .20 .50
7 Andrew Luciuk .20 .50
8 Brent Rumble .20 .50
9 Matt Hunter .20 .50
10 Kelly Miller .20 .50
11 Garrett Summerfield .20 .50
12 P.C. Drouin .20 .50
13 Unknown
14 Lance Galbraith .20 .50
15 Mark Smith .20 .50
16 Kevin Kurk .20 .50
17 Guy Dupuis .20 .50
18 Jason Kean .20 .50
19 John Jarram .20 .50
20 A.J. Bozoian .20 .50
21 Rob Guinn .20 .50
22 Mark Lindsay .20 .50
23 Troy Neumeier .20 .50
24 Ryan Jorde .20 .50
25 Icy D. Eagle MASCOT .02 .10

2005-06 Fort Wayne Komets Sprint

COMPLETE SET (16) 20.00
1 A.J. Bozoian .60 1.50
2 David Carpentier .60 1.50
3 Colin Chaulk .60 1.50
4 P.C. Drouin .60 1.50
5 Guy Dupuis .60 1.50
6 Lance Galbraith .60 1.50
7 Lance Galbraith .60 1.50
8 Jonathan Goodwin .60 1.50
9 Rob Guinn .60 1.50
10 David Hukalo .60 1.50
11 John Jarram .60 1.50
12 Ryan Jorde .60 1.50
13 Mark Lindsay .60 1.50
14 Troy Neumeier .60 1.50
15 Brent Rumble .60 1.50
16 Kevin St. Pierre .60 1.50

2006-07 Fort Wayne Komets

COMPLETE SET (24) 10.00 20.00
1 A.J. Bozoian .40 1.00
2 Mike Dombkiewicz .40 1.00
3 Guy Dupuis .40 1.00
4 Martin Gascon .40 1.00
5 Daniel Goneau .40 1.00
6 Jonathan Goodwin .40 1.00
7 Kevin Hansen .40 1.00
8 Jani Honkanen .40 1.00
9 David Hukalo .40 1.00
10 Arthur Kiyaga .40 1.00
11 Jean-Francois Labarre .40 1.00
12 Mario Larocque .75 2.00
13 Dan McWhinney .60 1.50
14 Pascal Morency .40 1.00
15 Bruce Richardson .40 1.00
16 Bogdan Rudenko .40 1.00
17 J.C. Ruid .40 1.00
18 Kevin St. Pierre .60 1.50
19 Matt Syroczynski .40 1.00
20 Brent Henley .40 1.00
21 K.J. Voorhees .40 1.00
22 Pat Bingham .40 1.00
23 Icy D. Eagle MASCOT .02 .10
24 Nesquik SPONSOR .01 .01

1997-98 Fort Worth Brahmas

This 21-card set was sold at home games for $4. The cards do not bear numbers, so they are listed alphabetically.

COMPLETE SET (21) 4.00 10.00
1 Chris Albert .20 .50
2 Steve Carter .20 .50
3 Brian Caruso .20 .50
4 Cosmo DuPaul .20 .50
5 David Graff .20 .50
6 Craig Hayden .20 .50
7 Murray Hogg .20 .50
8 Alex Kholomeyev .30 .75
9 Stephane Larocque .30 .75
10 Rob Laurie .30 .75
11 Mike McCormick .20 .50
12 Nolan McDonald .20 .50
13 Terry Menard .30 .75
14 Max Middendorf .20 .50
15 Mark O'Donnell .20 .50
16 Adam Robbins .20 .50
17 Todd St. Louis .20 .50
18 Mark Strohack .20 .50
19 Gatis Tseplis .20 .50
20 Dwight Mullins ACO .04 .10
21 Bill McDonald CO .04 .10

1998-99 Fort Worth Brahmas

This 20-card set was handed out at a home game and is extremely scarce on the secondary market.

COMPLETE SET (20) 8.00 20.00
1 Terry Menard CO .20 .50
2 Steve Plouffe .60 1.50
3 Tim Green .40 1.00
4 Scott Shaunessy .40 1.00
5 Jim Dinneen .40 1.00
6 Martin Machacek .40 1.00
7 Francois Albert .40 1.00
8 Sean Brady .40 1.00
9 Murray Hogg .40 1.00
10 Ryan Black .40 1.00
11 Mark Strohack .40 1.00
12 Richie Walcott .40 1.00
13 Stephane Larocque .60 1.50
14 Barry Cummins .40 1.00
15 Phil Miaskowski .40 1.00
16 Martin Lamarche .40 1.00
17 Cosmo Dupaul .40 1.00
18 Jon Olofson .60 1.50
19 Craig Hayden .60 1.50
20 Steve Carter .40 1.00

1999-00 Fort Worth Brahmas

This 20-card set features the 1999-00 Fort Worth Brahmas on extra glossy card stock. In the upper left hand corner of each card appears "The Hockey Store" logo from a shop in Arlington, Texas. Cards are not numbered so they appear alphabetically. It is believed that they were issued as a promotional giveaway.

COMPLETE SET (20) 4.00 40.00
1 Louis Bernard .20 2.00
2 Bruiser MASCOT .20 .10
3 Jason Disher .20 2.00
4 Cosmo Dupaul .20 2.00
5 Cory Evans .20 2.00
6 Ross Harris .20 2.00
7 Murray Hogg .20 2.00
8 Alex Kholomeyev .30 2.00
9 Derek Kups .20 2.00
10 Martin Lamarche .20 2.00
11 Stephane Larocque .20 2.00
12 Terry Menard CO .20 2.00
13 Jon Olofson .40 3.00
14 Steve Plouffe .40 5.00
15 Bobby Pochyly .20 2.00
16 Al Rooney .20 2.00
17 Mike Sanderson .30 2.00
18 Dennis Shiryaev .20 2.00
19 Mike Tilson .20 2.00
20 Gatis Tseplis .20 2.00

2000-01 Fort Worth Brahmas

This set features the Brahmas of the WPHL. The set was issued as a promotional giveaway in the form of a pair of unperforated nine-card sheets. The cards are not numbered so they appear below in alphabetical order.

COMPLETE SET (18) 4.80 12.00
1 Clint Cabana .30 .75
2 Justin Cardwell .30 .75
3 Jason Carey .30 .75
4 Steve Dowhy .30 .75
5 Ben Gorewich .30 .75
6 Jake Harney .30 .75
7 Ross Harris .30 1.00
8 Casey Hungle .30 .75
9 Craig Johnson .30 .75
10 Todd Lalonde CO .08 .25
11 Rob Laurie .30 1.00
12 Jason Pain .30 .75
13 Mike Rusk .30 .75
14 Ryan Shannon .30 .75
15 Mike Tilson .30 .75
16 Daniel Villeneuve .30 .75
17 Chad Woollard .30 .75
18 Mark Zacharias .30 .75

2001-02 Fort Worth Brahmas

This set features the Brahmas of the WPHL. The set was handed out at a game early in the season. Because the cards are unnumbered, they are listed below in alphabetical order.

COMPLETE SET (20) 8.00 20.00
1 Brady Austin .40 1.00
2 Jeff Bateman .62 1.56
3 Dave Bourque .40 1.00
4 Justin Cardwell .40 1.00
5 Jason Clarke .40 1.00
6 Kory Cooper .40 1.00
7 Dave Csumrik .40 1.00
8 Adam Davis .40 1.00
9 Sean Hughes .40 1.00
10 Craig Johnson .40 1.00
11 Chris Johnston .40 1.00
12 Cody Leibel .40 1.00
13 Todd Lalonde CO .20 .50
14 Cam MacDonald .40 1.00
15 Mike Tilson .62 1.56
16 Joe Van Volsen .62 1.56
17 Daniel Villeneuve .40 1.00
18 Chad Woollard .40 1.00
19 Scott Wray .40 1.00
20 Bruiser MASCOT .04 .11

2002-03 Fort Worth Brahmas

This set was issued as a promotional giveaway in two 10-card subsets at home games. The cards were printed on thin paper stock and are listed below in alphabetical order. Thanks to Ralph Slate for this checklist.

COMPLETE SET (20) 20.00
1 Adam Davis 1.00
2 Jason Fricker 1.50
3 David Fry 1.00
4 Rob Giffin 1.00
5 Chad Grills 1.00
6 Sean Hughes 1.00
7 Lee Jacobson 1.50
8 Lloyd Marks 1.00
9 Mike McKinnon 1.00
10 Jim Midgley 1.00
11 John Murphy 2.00
12 Jason Reesor 1.00
13 Mike Rusk 1.00
14 Joe Van Volsen 1.00
15 T.J. Warkus 1.00
16 Jeff Washbrook 1.00
17 Justin Williams 1.00
18 Chad Woollard 1.00
19 Bill Inglis CO .10
20 Bruiser MASCOT .10

2003-04 Fort Worth Brahmas

This set was issued as a promotional giveaway over the course of two home games.

COMPLETE SET (20) 20.00
1 Gary Baronick 1.00
2 Joey Bastien 1.00
3 Aaron Davis 1.00
4 Adam Davis 1.00
5 Scott English 1.50
6 Taras Foremsky 1.00
7 Chad Grills 1.00
8 Jan Jas 1.00
9 Jay McGee 1.00
10 Tyler Nilsson 1.50
11 Jason Reesor 1.00
12 Erasmo Saltarelli 1.50
13 Jeff Scharf 1.00
14 Peter Trumbley 1.00
15 Derrell Upton 1.00
16 Jeremy Vanin 1.00
17 Justin Williams 1.00
18 Chad Woollard 1.00
19 Al Sims HCO .20
20 Mascot .10

2004-05 Fort Worth Brahmas

Set was issued as a giveaway at two home games, 10 cards at a time.

COMPLETE SET (20) 30.00
1 Jay Banach 1.50
2 Brian Basner 2.50
3 Brandon Carper 1.50
4 Dave Csumrik 1.50
5 Aaron Davis 1.50
6 Adam Davis 1.50
7A Mark Hynes ERR 1.50
(Adam Davis back
7B Mark Hynes COR 1.50
8A Jan Jas ERR 1.50
(Mark Hynes back
8B Jan Jas COR 1.50
9 Brad Lukowich 2.00
10 Bryan Lundbohm 1.50
11 Dan Murphy 2.00
12 Sheldon Nedjelski 1.50
13 Martin Paquet 1.50
14 Larry Sterling 2.00
15 Nick Udovicic 1.50
16 Derrell Upton 1.50
17 Jorin Welsh 1.50
18 Chad Woollard 1.50
19 Al Sims CO .50
20 Bruiser MASCOT .10

1992-93 Fort Worth Fire

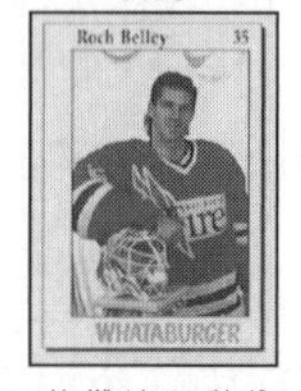

Sponsored by Whataburger, this 18-card set was issued as a cut set and also as a sheet. The sheet was rimmed on the left and right sides by a row of coupons redeemable at Whataburger. Card strips featuring three player cards sandwiched between two coupons were also produced. The cards measure the standard size and feature posed, color player photos with either a peach or a white studio background on white card stock. The picture is set off-center on a white area framed by a thin black line and shadow-bordered. The player's name and uniform number are printed above the photo, while "Whataburger" is printed in burnt orange below. The backs carry biographical information and career highlights. The cards are unnumbered and checklisted below in alphabetical order.

COMPLETE SET (18) 4.00 10.00
1 Ron Aubrey .20 .50
2 Roch Belley .40 1.00
3 Jason Brousseau .20 .50
4 Eric Brule .20 .50
5 Todd Drevitch .20 .50
6 Trevor Duhaime .20 .50
7 Steve Harrison ACO .10 .25
8 Ernest Hornak .20 .50
9 Alex Kholomeyev .30 .75
10 Curt Krolak .20 .50
11 Ryan Leschasin .20 .50
12 Peter Mahovlich CO .80 2.00
13 Mike McCormick .20 .50
14 Mike O'Hara .20 .50
15 Pat Penner .20 .50
16 Paolo Racicot .20 .50
17 Dan Rolfe .20 .50
18 Mike Sanderson .20 .50

1993-94 Fort Worth Fire

This 18-card set is similar in design to the Dallas Freeze issue of this year. The round cards are approximately the size of a hockey puck and came packaged in a plastic container with the team logo on the front. The sets were sold by the team's booster club at home games, and may have been made available through the mail.

COMPLETE SET (18) 2.40 75.00
1 Ron Aubrey 2.00 5.00
2 Derby Bognar 2.00 5.00
3 Reggie Brezeault 2.00 5.00
4 Jason Brousseau 2.00 5.00
5 Ty Eigner 2.00 5.00
6 Todd Huyber 2.00 5.00
7 Chris Jensen 2.00 5.00
8 Chad Johnson 2.00 5.00
9 Ryan Leschasin 2.00 5.00
10 Dominic Maltais 2.00 5.00
11 Mike McCormick 2.00 5.00
12 Patrick McGarry 2.00 5.00
13 Mike O'Hara 2.00 5.00
14 Sean Rowe 2.00 5.00
15 Mike Sanderson 2.00 6.00
16 Rob Striar 2.00 5.00
17 Scott Zygulski 2.00 5.00
18 Steve Harrison CO 2.00 5.00

1995-96 Fort Worth Fire

This 18-card team set features the Fort Worth Fire of the Central Hockey League. The set apparently was distributed by the booster club. In an unusual twist, the cards

were not sold in team sets; instead, a 9-card assortment could be had for $3. Usually, it took three packs to assemble a complete set. The cards feature an action photo on the front, along with player bio and 1994-95 stats on the back.

COMPLETE SET (18) 4.00 10.00
1 Team Photo .30 .75
2 Bill McDonald CO .10 .25
3 Phil Groeneveld .20 .50
4 Vern Ray .20 .50
5 Steve Dykstra .30 .75
6 Trevor Burgess .20 .50
7 Scott Allen .20 .50
8 Sean Whyte .20 .50
9 Troy Frederick .20 .50
10 Troy Stephens .20 .50
11 Jeff Massey .20 .50
12 Dwight Mullins .20 .50
13 Kyle Reeves .40 1.00
14 Mike Gruttaduria .20 .50
15 Mark Hilton .20 .50
16 Brian Caruso .20 .50
17 Dennis Miller .20 .50
18 Steve Plouffe .30 .75

1996-97 Fort Worth Fire

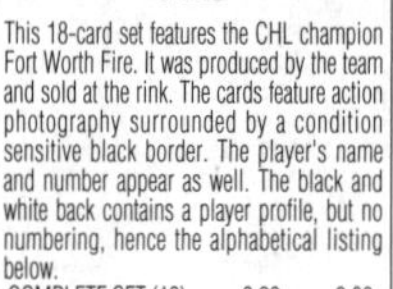

This 18-card set features the CHL champion Fort Worth Fire. It was produced by the team and sold at the rink. The cards feature action photography surrounded by a condition sensitive black border. The player's name and number appear as well. The black and white back contains a player profile, but no numbering, hence the alphabetical listing below.

COMPLETE SET (18) 3.20 8.00
1 Malcolm Cameron .20 .50
2 Steve Carter .20 .50
3 Mike Sanderson .20 .50
4 Stephane Larocque .20 .50
5 Murray Hogg .20 .50
6 Bob Delorimiere .30 .75
7 Steve Plouffe .40 1.00
8 Glenn Painter .20 .50
9 Mark Strohack .20 .50
10 Brian Caruso .20 .50
11 Dwight Mullins .20 .50
12 Terry Menard .20 .50
13 Vern Ray .20 .50
14 Adam Robbins .20 .50
15 Mark O'Donnell .20 .50
16 Mike McCourt .20 .50
17 Ryan Black .20 .50
18 Bill McDonald CO .04 .10

1981-82 Fredericton Express

This 26-card set was issued by the team and endorsed by the Fredericton City Police, R.C.M.P., New Brunswick Highway Patrol, and New Brunswick Police Commission. The cards measure approximately 2"1/2" by 3 3/4" with a white border on the front. The fronts also carry a posed color player photo with the player's name printed below. The cards are numbered on the back.

COMPLETE SET (26) 8.00 20.00
1 Team Photo .20 .50
2 B.J. MacDonald .30 .75
3 Sylvain Cote .20 .50
4 Michel Bolduc .20 .50
5 Gary Lupul .20 .50
6 Clint Malarchuk .80 2.00
7 Tony Currie .20 .50
8 Tim Tookey .20 .50
9 Anders Eldebrink .40 1.00
10 Basil McRae .80 2.00
11 Kelly Elcombe .20 .50
12 Jacques Demers 1.20 3.00
13 Frank Caprice .40 1.00
14 Terry Johnson .20 .50
15 Grant Martin .20 .50
16 Andre Chartrain .20 .50
17 Marc Crawford 1.20 3.00
18 Gaston Therrien .20 .50
19 Andy Schliebener .20 .50
20 Christian Tanguay .20 .50
21 Art Rutland .20 .50
22 Jean MarcGaulin .20 .50
23 Neil Belland .20 .50
24 Andre Cote .20 .50
25 Jim MacRae .20 .50
26 Scott Beckingham .10 .25
Marty Flynn

1982-83 Fredericton Express

Sponsored by CFNB and Pepsi, this 26-card set measures approximately 2 1/2" by 3 3/4"

and features posed, color player photos with white borders. The player's name and sponsor logos appear in the lower white margin.

COMPLETE SET (26) 8.00 20.00
1 Team Photo .40 1.00
2 B.J. MacDonald .30 .75
3 Sylvain Cote .30 .75
4 Michel Bolduc .20 .50
5 Gary Lupul .20 .50
6 Clint Malarchuk .80 2.00
7 Tony Currie .20 .50
8 Tim Tookey .20 .50
9 Anders Eldebrink .20 .50
10 Basil McRae 1.20 3.00
11 Kelly Elcombe .20 .50
12 Jacques Demers .80 2.00
13 Frank Caprice .60 1.50
14 Terry Johnson .20 .50
15 Grant Martin .20 .50
16 Andre Chartrain .20 .50
17 Marc Crawford .80 2.00
18 Gaston Therrien .20 .50
19 Andy Schliebener .20 .50
20 Christian Tanguay .20 .50
21 Art Rutland .20 .50
22 Jean-Marc Gaulin .20 .50
23 Neil Belland .20 .50
24 Andre Cote .20 .50
25 Jim MacRae .20 .50
26 Scott Beckingham TR .10 .25
and Marty Flynn TR

1983-84 Fredericton Express

This 27-card set measures 2 1/2" by 3 3/4" and features posed action color player photos with white borders. The player's name, position, and NHL affiliation appear below the picture in the white margin. The horizontal backs are white and carry Police and Express Tips in French and English.

COMPLETE SET (27) 6.00 15.00
1 Team Photo .40 1.00
2 Frank Caprice .60 1.50
3 Michel Dufour .30 .75
4 Brian Ford .30 .75
5 Jean-Marc Lanthier .20 .50
6 Jim Dobson .20 .50
7 Mike Hough .40 1.00
8 Rick Lapointe .30 .75
9 Michel Bolduc .20 .50
10 Christian Tanguay .20 .50
11 Tony Currie .20 .50
12 Moe Lemay .40 1.00
13 Bruce Holloway .20 .50
14 Neil Belland .20 .50
15 Richard Turmel .20 .50
16 Claude Julien .30 .75
17 Andre Chartrain .20 .50
18 Grant Martin .20 .50
19 Rejean Vignola .20 .50
20 Andre Cote .20 .50
21 Jean-Marc Gaulin .20 .50
22 Andy Schliebener .20 .50
23 Stu Kulak .30 .75
24 Mike Eagles .60 1.50
25 Earl Jessiman CO/GM .10 .25
26 Marty Flynn TR .10 .25
Scott Beckingham TR
NNO Checklist .20 .50

1984-85 Fredericton Express

This 28-card set measures approximately 2 1/2" by 3 3/4" and features posed color player photos against a white card face. The player's name, biography, position, and NHL affiliation appear in black print below the picture. Sponsor logos are in the lower corners. The horizontal backs are white and carry Police and Express Tips in French and English.

COMPLETE SET (28) 6.00 15.00
1 Dave Morrison .20 .50
2 Dave Shaw .40 1.00
3 Bruce Holloway .20 .50
4 Roger Haegglund .20 .50
5 Neil Belland .20 .50
6 Gord Donnelly .40 1.00

7 David Bruce .20 .50
8 Claude Julien .20 .50
9 Dan Wood .20 .50
10 Clint Malarchuk .80 2.00
11 Jere Gillis .20 .50
12 Mike Hough .40 1.00
13 Michel Bolduc .20 .50
14 Peter Loob .20 .50
15 Steve Driscoll .20 .50
16 Newell Brown .20 .50
17 Jim Dobson .20 .50
18 Wendell Young .80 2.00
19 Mark Kumpel .30 .75
20 Mike Eagles .40 1.00
21 Tom Thornbury .20 .50
22 Grant Martin .20 .50
23 Marc Crawford .40 1.00
24 Andy Schliebener .20 .50
25 Earl Jessiman CO/GM .10 .25
26 Yvon Vautour .20 .50
27 Craig Coxe .40 1.00
28 Blake Wesley .20 .50

1985-86 Fredericton Express

This 28-card set measures 2 1/2" by 3 3/4" and features posed color player photos against a white card face. The player's name, biography, position, and NHL affiliation appear in black print below the picture. Sponsor logos are in the lower corners. The horizontal backs are white and carry Police and Express Tips in French and English.

COMPLETE SET (28) 4.80 12.00
1 Scott Tottle .20 .50
2 David Bruce .20 .50
3 Team Photo .30 .75
4 Marc Crawford .40 1.00
5 Mike Stevens .20 .50
6 Gary Lupul .20 .50
7 Alain Lemieux .30 .75
8 Mike Hough .40 1.00
9 Tony Currie .20 .50
10 Dunc MacIntyre .20 .50
11 Jere Gillis .20 .50
12 Wendell Young .60 1.50
13 Jean-Marc Lanthier .20 .50
14 Ken Quinney .30 .75
15 Claude Julien .20 .50
16 Michel Petit .40 1.00
17 Luc Guenette .20 .50
18 Andy Schliebener .20 .50
19 Mark Kirton .20 .50
20 Gord Donnelly .30 .75
21 Tom Karalis .20 .50
22 Daniel Poudrier .20 .50
23 Neil Belland .20 .50
24 Dale Dunbar .20 .50
25 Marty Flynn TR .10 .25
Scott Beckingham TR
26 Jean-Marc Gaulin .20 .50
27 Al MacAdam .30 .75
28 Andre Savard CO/GM .20 .50

1986-87 Fredericton Express

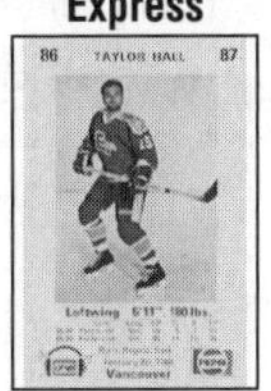

This 26-card set measures 2 1/2" by 3 3/4" and features posed color player photos against a white card face. The player's name, biography, position, statistics, and NHL affiliation appear in black print below the picture. Sponsor logos are in the lower corners. The horizontal backs are white and carry public service messages in French and English. The cards are unnumbered and checklisted below in alphabetical order.

COMPLETE SET (26) 4.00 10.00
1 Jim Agnew .20 .50
2 Brian Bertuzzi .20 .50
3 David Bruce .20 .50
4 Frank Caprice .30 .75
5 Marc Crawford .30 .75
6 Steven Finn .30 .75
7 Marty Flynn TR .10 .25
Scott Beckingham TR
8 Jean-Marc Gaulin .20 .50
9 Scott Gordon .30 .75
10 Taylor Hall .20 .50
11 Yves Heroux .20 .50
12 Mike Hough .30 .75
13 Tom Karalis .20 .50
14 Mark Kirton .20 .50
15 Jean-Marc Lanthier .20 .50
16 Jean LeBlanc .20 .50
17 Brett MacDonald .20 .50
18 Duncan MacIntyre .20 .50
19 Greg Malone .20 .50
20 Terry Perkins .20 .50
21 Daniel Poudrier .20 .50
22 Jeff Rohlicek .20 .50
23 Andre Savard CO .20 .50
24 Mike Stevens .20 .50
25 Trevor Stienburg .20 .50
26 Team Photo .30 .75

1992-93 Fredericton Canadiens

Printed on thin card stock, these 28 standard-size cards feature borderless color player action photos on the fronts. Each has the player's name and uniform number printed near the bottom and carries the Professional Hockey Player's Association logo. The white horizontal back displays a black-and-white posed player head shot in the upper left. The player's name, uniform number, and biography appear in a rectangle in the upper right, along with the Canadiens and Stay in School logos. A stat table is placed beneath, and the Pepsi, Village, and Ben's logos at the bottom round out the card. The cards are unnumbered and checklisted below in alphabetical order.

COMPLETE SET (28) 4.80 12.00
1 Jesse Belanger .30 .75
2 Paulin Bordeleau CO .20 .50
3 Donald Brashear .30 .75
4 Patrik Carnback .20 .50
5 Eric Charron .20 .50
6 Frederic Chabot .40 1.00
7 Alain Cote .20 .50
8 Paul DiPietro .30 .75
9 Craig Ferguson .20 .50
10 Gerry Fleming .20 .50
11 Luc Gauthier .20 .50
12 Robert Guillet .20 .50
13 Patric Kjellberg .30 .75
14 Les Kuntar .30 .75
15 Ryan Kuwabara .20 .50
16 Patrick Langlois TR .04 .10
17 Steve Larouche .20 .50
18 Jacques Parent TR .04 .10
19 Charles Poulin .20 .50
20 Oleg Petrov .20 .50
21 Yves Sarault .20 .50
22 Pierre Sevigny .20 .50
23 Darcy Simon .20 .50
24 Turner Stevenson .30 .75
25 Tricolo (Mascot) .04 .10
26 Lindsay Vallis .20 .50
27 Steve Veilleux .20 .50
28 Title card .10 .25

1993-94 Fredericton Canadiens

Printed on thin card stock, this 29-card standard-size features 1993-94 Fredericton Canadiens of the AHL. The fronts display color action player photos framed by red borders. The player's name and number are printed in the border beneath the picture. The horizontal backs carry a black-and-white close-up photo, biography, statistics, and sponsor logos (Ben's Bakery, Village, and Pepsi). The cards are unnumbered and checklisted below in alphabetical order.

COMPLETE SET (29) 4.80 12.00
1 Brent Bilodeau .20 .50
2 Paulin Bordeleau CO .10 .25
3 Donald Brashear .30 .75
4 Martin Brochu .40 1.00
5 Craig Darby .20 .50
6 Kevin Darby .20 .50
7 Mario Doyon .20 .50
8 Craig Ferguson .20 .50
9 Craig Fiander .20 .50
10 Gerry Fleming .20 .50
11 Luc Gauthier ACO .04 .10
12 Robert Guillet .20 .50
13 Les Kuntar .24 .60
14 Ryan Kuwabara .20 .50
15 Patrick Langlois .20 .50
16 Marc Laniel .20 .50
17 Christian Lariviere .20 .50
18 Kevin O'Sullivan .20 .50
19 Denis Ouellete .20 .50
20 Jacques Parent THER .04 .10
21 Oleg Petrov .30 .75
22 Charles Poulin .20 .50
23 Christian Proulx .20 .50
24 Tony Prpic .20 .50
25 Yves Sarault .20 .50
26 Turner Stevenson .30 .75
27 Tricolo (Mascot) .04 .10
28 Lindsay Vallis .20 .50
29 Title Card .04 .10

1994-95 Fredericton Canadiens

Printed on thin card stock, this 30-card standard-size set features the 1994-95 Fredericton Canadiens of the AHL. The fronts display borderless color action photos. The player's number and position,

as well as his name, are printed vertically down the left and right sides respectively. The cards are unnumbered and checklisted below in alphabetical order.

COMPLETE SET (30) 4.80 12.00
1 Louis Bernard .16 .40
2 Brent Bilodeau .20 .50
3 Paulin Bordeleau CO .16 .40
4 Donald Brashear .40 1.00
5 Martin Brochu .40 1.00
6 Valeri Bure .60 1.50
7 Jim Campbell .20 .50
8 Paul Chagnon .16 .40
9 Craig Conroy .30 .75
10 Craig Darby .20 .50
11 Dion Darling .16 .40
12 Craig Ferguson .16 .40
13 Scott Fraser .16 .40
14 Luc Gauthier ACO .04 .10
15 Patrick Labrecque .20 .50
16 Marc Lamothe .30 .75
17 Patrick Langlois .16 .40
18 Brad Layzelle .16 .40
19 Derek Maguire .16 .40
20 Chris Murray .20 .50
21 Kevin O'Sullivan .16 .40
22 Jacques Parent THER .04 .10
23 Christian Proulx .16 .40
24 Craig Rivet .20 .50
25 Yves Sarault .16 .40
26 Turner Stevenson .20 .50
27 Martin Sychra .16 .40
28 Tim Tisdale .16 .40
29 Tricolo (Mascot) .04 .10
30 David Wilkie .16 .40

1995-96 Fredericton Canadiens

This 29-card set features color action player photos of the Fredericton Canadiens of the AHL. The backs carry biographical information and player statistics. The cards are unnumbered and checklisted below in alphabetical order.

COMPLETE SET (29) 4.80 12.00
1 Louis Bernard .16 .40
2 Paulin Bordeleau CO .10 .25
3 Sebastien Bordeleau .20 .50
4 Martin Brochu .40 1.00
5 Jim Campbell .20 .50
6 Paul Chagnon .16 .40
7 Craig Conroy .30 .75
8 Keli Corpse .16 .40
9 Dion Darling .16 .40
10 Rory Fitzpatrick .16 .40
11 Scott Fraser .16 .40
12 Gaston Gingras .20 .50
13 David Grenier .16 .40
14 Harold Hersh .20 .50
15 Patrick Labrecque .30 .75
16 Marc Lamothe .30 .75
17 Patrick Langlois .16 .40
18 Alan Letang .20 .50
19 Alexei Lojkin .16 .40
20 Xavier Majic .16 .40
21 Chris Murray .20 .50
22 Jacques Parent .16 .40
23 Craig Rivet .20 .50
24 Mario Roberge .16 .40
25 Pierre Sevigny .20 .50
26 Tricolo (Mascot) .04 .10
27 Darcy Tucker .40 1.00
28 Adam Wiesel .16 .40
29 Luc Gauthier ACO .04 .10

1996-97 Fredericton Canadiens

This set features the Canadiens of the AHL. The set was produced by the team and sold at home games, and is notable for containing one of the earliest and toughest issues of Jose Theodore.

COMPLETE SET (30) 40.00 80.00
1 Sebastien Bordeleau .14 .35
2 Brad Brown .40 1.00
3 Earl Cronan .14 .35
4 Dion Darling .14 .35
5 Jimmy Drolet .14 .35
6 Gerry Fleming .40 1.00
7 Scott Fraser .14 .35
8 Francois Groleau .14 .35
9 Miloslav Guren .14 .35
10 Harold Hersh .40 1.00
11 Eric Houde .14 .35
12 Alan Letang .14 .35
13 David Ling .20 .50
14 Alexei Lojkin .14 .35
15 Boyd Olson .14 .35
16 Tony Prpic .14 .35
17 Jesse Rezansoff .14 .35
18 Craig Rivet .40 1.00
19 Pierre Sevigny .20 .50
20 Todd Sparks .14 .35
21 Jose Theodore 20.00 50.00
22 Tomas Vokoun 8.00 20.00
23 Adam Wiesel .14 .35
24 Paulin Bordeleau CO .04 .10
25 Luc Gauthier CO .04 .10
26 Patrick Langlois TR .04 .10
27 Paul Chagnon TR .04 .10
28 Jacques Parent TR .04 .10
29 Tricolo MAS .04 .10
30 Jolly Rancher .01

2000-01 Fresno Falcons

This set features the Falcons of the WCHL. It is believed that the set was a promotional giveaway sponsored by Carl's Jr. restaurants, but that has not been confirmed. The cards are unnumbered, however, and are listed below in alphabetical order.

COMPLETE SET (30) 8.00 20.00
1 Chris Albert .30 .75
2 Matt Alvey .40 1.00
3 Brad Both .30 .75
4 Brodie Coffin .30 .75
5 Kirk DeWaele .30 .75
6 Sheldon Flaman .40 1.00
7 Terry Friesen .40 1.00
8 Glen Gulutzan .30 .75
9 Don Malko .30 .75
10 Mike Mathers .30 .75
11 Mike McCourt .30 .75
12 David Mitchell .30 .75
13 Kory Mullin .40 1.00
14 Cory Murphy .30 .75
15 Kris Porter .30 .75
16 Chris Skoryna .30 .75
17 Adrian Smith .40 1.00
18 Greg Spenrath .30 .75
19 Rejean Stringer .30 .75
20 Darren Wetherill .30 .75
21 Terry Friesen SO .40 1.00
22 Blaine Moore CO .10 .25
23 Freddie Falcon MASCOT .04 .10
24 Mike Carey TR .04 .10
25 Fresno Falcons Celebration .20 .50
26 TV-47 ANCHORS .04 .01
27 Star-101 DJ's SPONSOR .04 .01
28 Mark Kuntz EM .04 .10
29 Brian Clark .30 .75
30 Team Photo .30 .50

2001-02 Fresno Falcons

This set features the Falcons of the WCHL. It was issued as a promotional giveaway at one home game in March, 2002.

COMPLETE SET (30) 8.00 20.00
1 Brad Both .40 1.00
2 Brodie Coffin .40 1.00
3 Kirk DeWaele .40 1.00
4 Joe Frederick .40 1.00
5 Terry Friesen .62 1.56
6 Glen Gulutzan .40 1.00
7 Dale Junkin .40 1.00
8 Dan Kerluke .40 1.00
9 Mike Mathers .40 1.00
10 Mike McCourt .40 1.00
11 David Mitchell .40 1.00
12 Kory Mullin .40 1.00
13 Cory Murphy .40 1.00
14 Kris Porter .40 1.00
15 Chris Skoryna .40 1.00
16 Adrian Smith .20 .50
17 Greg Spenrath .40 1.00
18 Ryan Tocher .40 1.00
19 Alex Todd .40 1.00
20 Jason Weaver .40 1.00
21 Darren Wetherill .40 1.00
22 Blaine Moore CO .10 .25
23 Game Winner Action Photo .10 .25
24 Mike Carey TR .10
25 Mark Kuntz EQMG .10
26 Freddie Falcon MASCOT .10
27 Team Photo .20 .50
28 Carls Jr. .01 .01
29 Fresno Bee .01 .01
30 KRZR 103.7 .01 .01

2002-03 Fresno Falcons

COMPLETE SET (25) 20.00
1 Checklist .01
2 Kevin Haupt 1.00
3 Chris Kenady 1.00
4 Cory Murphy 1.00
5 Mike Mathers 1.00
6 Alex Todd 1.00
7 Brad Both 1.50
8 Steve Lowe 1.00
9 Scott Borders 1.00
10 Jordan Landry 1.00
11 Colin Embley 1.00
12 Glen Gulutzan 1.00
13 Kirk DeWaele 1.00
14 Jason Weaver 1.00
15 Drew Schoneck 1.00
16 Mark Gowan 1.50
17 Terry Friesen 1.50
18 Joe Frederick 1.00
19 Kayle Short 1.00
20 Jason McBain 1.00
21 Kris Porter 1.00
22 Blaine Moore HCO .10
23 Greg Spenrath ACO .10
24 Happy Star .01
25 KRZR-103.7 .01

2003-04 Fresno Falcons

This set was produced by Choice Marketing and sold at home games.

COMPLETE SET (25) 10.00
1 Scott Borders .50
2 Mike Brusseau .75
3 Blair Clarance .50
4 Terry Friesen .75
5 Nathan Horne .50
6 Mark Jackson .50
7 Michael Kiesman .50
8 Jordan Landry .50
9 Mike Mathers .50
10 Blaine Moore CO .50
11 Kory Mullin .50
12 Dominic Periard .50
13 Kris Porter .50
14 Boris Protsenko .50
15 Riku Rahikainen .50
16 Tapio Sammalkangas .50
17 Mike Sandbeck .50
18 Nolan Schaefer .75
19 Drew Schoneck .50
20 Greg Spenrath CO .50
21 Adam Stefishen .50
22 Kevin Truelson .50
23 Jason Weaver .50
24 John Wroblewski .50
25 Mascot .10
NNO Checklist .01

2004-05 Fresno Falcons

COMPLETE SET (TBD) 25.00
1 David Brisson 1.00
2 Clint Cabana 1.00
3 John Dahl 1.00
4 Thierry Douville 1.00
5 Lanny Gare 1.00
6 Shawn Heaphy 1.00
7 Brett Jaegar 2.00
8 Tomas Jasko 1.00
9 Mike Kiesman 1.00
10 Derek Krestanovich 1.00
11 Simon Lajeunesse 2.00
12 Jim Lorentz 1.00
13 Matt O'Dette 1.00
14 Wes Rypien 1.00
15 Curtis Sheptak 1.00
16 Charles Simard 1.00
17 Greg Spenrath 1.00
18 Shaun Sutter 1.00
19 Dan Tessier 1.00
20 Kevin Truelson 1.00
21 Dustin Van Ballegooie 1.00
22 Jason Weaver 1.00
23 John Wroblewski 1.00

2005-06 Fresno Falcons

COMPLETE SET (25) 20.00

2003-04 Gatineau Olympiques

COMPLETE SET (27) 12.00
1 Gabriel Bouthillette .75
2 Scott Brophy .50
3 Bruno Champagne .50
4 Yanick Charron .50
5 Dominic D'Amour .50
6 Jean-Michel Daoust .50
7 Philippe Dupuis .50
8 Vincent Duriau .50
9 Guillaume Fournier .50
10 Martin Frechette .50
11 Nick Fugere .50
12 Derrick Kent .50
13 Olivier Labelle .50
14 Guillaume Labrecque .50
15 Christian Laroche .50
16 Doug O'Brien .50
17 Keven Petit .50
18 Petr Pohl .50
19 Nicolas Ranger .50
20 Maxime Robert .50
21 Sam Roberts .50
22 Maxime Rousseau .50
23 Maxime Talbot .50
24 David Tremblay .75
25 Martin Vagner .75
26 Francis Wathier .50
27 Lance Woodman .50

2004-05 Gatineau Olympiques

A total of 300 team sets were produced.

COMPLETE SET (24) 12.00
1 David Tremblay .75
2 Martin Frechette .50
3 Sam Roberts .50
4 Scott Brophy .50
5 Olivier Laliberte .75
6 Francis Wathier .50
7 Nicolas Ranger .50
8 Keven Petit .50
9 Jonathan Carrier .50
10 Nick Fugere .50
11 Olivier Labelle .50
12 Maxime Rousseau .50
13 Pierre-Luc Lessard .50
14 Brett Morrison .50
15 David Krejci 1.00
16 Petr Pohl .50
17 Ryan Graham .50
18 Guillaume Labrecque .50
19 Cam Fergus .50
20 Dave Starenky .50
21 Bryan Wilson .50
22 Geoffrey Walker .50
23 Francis Gagnon .50
24 Luke Pelham .50

2005-06 Gatineau Olympiques

COMPLETE SET (28) 5.00 12.00
1 David Tremblay .20 .50
2 Olivier Laliberte .20 .50
3 Guillaume Labrecque .20 .50
4 Nick Fugere .20 .50
5 Keven Petit .20 .50
6 Maxime Rousseau .20 .50
7 Claude Giroux .20 .50
8 David Krejci .40 1.00
9 Bryan Wilson .20 .50
10 Martin Frechette .20 .50
11 Jonathan Carrier .20 .50
12 Pierre-Luc Lessard .20 .50
13 Brad Tesink .20 .50
14 Michael Stinziani .20 .50
15 Colin Escott .20 .50
16 Benoit Gervais .20 .50
17 Maxime Malette .20 .50
18 Michel Champagne .20 .50
19 Maxime Langelier-Parent .20 .50
20 Brett Morrison .20 .50
21 Mathieu Curadeau .20 .50
22 Alexandre Boivin .20 .50
23 Bryan Main .20 .50
24 Darryl Smith .20 .50
25 Antonin Manavian .20 .50
26 Matthew Pistilli .20 .50
27 Philippi Cote .20 .50
28 Mascot .02 .10

2006-07 Gatineau Olympiques

COMPLETE SET (28) 8.00 15.00
1 Martin Frechette .20 .50
2 Olivier Laliberte .30 .75
3 Maxime Mallette .20 .50
4 Jonathan Carrier .20 .50
5 Viatcheslav Trukhno .20 .50
6 Steven Delisle .20 .50
7 Daniel Sauve .20 .50
8 Brad Tesink .20 .50
9 Keven Petit .20 .50
10 Brett Morrison .20 .50
11 Jean-Philipp Chabot .20 .50
12 Alexandre Boivin .20 .50
13 Claude Giroux .40 1.00
14 Bryan Main .20 .50
15 Paul Byron .20 .50
16 Benoit Gervais .20 .50
17 Matthew Pistilli .20 .50
18 Darryl Smith .20 .50
19 Travis Stacey .20 .50
20 Michael Stinziani .20 .50
21 Pierre-Marc Guilbeault .20 .50
22 Alexandre Touchette .20 .50
23 Ken Dufresne .20 .50
24 Dave Bertrand-Duclos .20 .50
25 Chad Loikets .20 .50
26 David Kveton .20 .50
27 Ryan Mior .30 .75
28 Tyler Pugh .20 .50

1977-78 Granby Vics

This odd-sized (3 1/2 X7") black and white set features the Granby Vics of the LMJHQ. The card fronts are in a horizontal format, with the left half of the card containing a player photo, and the right featuring a player bio and an ad from a local business. The backs are blank and the cards are unnumbered. They are presented below alphabetically.

COMPLETE SET (20) 17.50 35.00
1 Mario Beauregard 1.00 2.00
2 Luc Breton 1.00 2.00
3 Daniel Caron 1.50 3.00
4 Mario Casavant 1.00 2.00
5 Marc Courtemanche 1.00 2.00
6 Yves Courtemanche 1.00 2.00
7 Sylvain d'Amour 1.00 2.00
8 Rene Delorme 1.00 2.00
9 Denis Dumas Jr. 1.00 2.00
10 Pierre Grondin 1.00 2.00
11 Andre Hebert 1.00 2.00
12 Marcel Lachance 1.00 2.00
13 Andre Lemieux 1.00 2.00
14 Pierre Lepage 1.00 2.00
15 Daniel Menard 1.00 2.00
16 Jacques Pomerleau 1.00 2.00
17 Mario Roy 1.00 2.00
18 Alain Tetrault 1.00 2.00
19 Paul Thibert 1.00 2.00
20 Luc Turgeon 1.00 2.00

1996-97 Grand Rapids Griffins

This odd-sized set (2 3/4" by 4") was produced by Meijer Exhibit Graphic Design and sponsored by Kodak and Jim Hill Photography. The set was released in five series of five cards each (plus one title card per series) over the course of the club's inaugural season. As the cards are unnumbered, they are listed below in alphabetical order.

COMPLETE SET (30) 20.00 50.00
1 Kevyn Adams .60 3.00
2 Dave Allison CO .10 1.00
3 Danton Cole .40 2.00
4 Keli Corpse .40 2.00
5 Pavol Demitra 2.00 10.00
6 Griff .10 .50
Mascot
7 Ben Hankinson .40 2.00
8 Stanislav Jasecko .40 2.00
10 Sean McCann .40 2.00
11 Cory Johnson .40 2.00
12 Jamie Linden .40 2.00
13 Don McSween .40 2.00
14 Tyler Moss .80 4.00
15 Jeff Nelson .40 2.00
16 Todd Nelson .40 2.00
17 Michel Picard .40 2.00
18 Bruce Ramsay .40 2.00
19 Pokey Reddick .80 4.00
20 Chad Remackel .40 2.00
21 Travis Richards .40 2.00
22 Matt Ruchty .40 2.00
23 Darcy Simon .40 2.00
24 1996 Inaugural Face-Off .10 .50
25 1996/97 Inaugural Team .40 2.00
26 Van Andel Arena .10 .50
NNO Title card 1 .04 .20
NNO Title card 2 .04 .20
NNO Title card 3 .04 .20
NNO Title card 4 .04 .20
NNO Title card 5 .04 .20

1997-98 Grand Rapids Griffins

Little is known about this set beyond the confirmed checklist. Additional information can be forwarded to hockeymag@beckett.com.

COMPLETE SET (24) 4.00 10.00
1 Michel Picard .30 .75
2 Tom Ashe .20 .50
3 Greg Clancy .20 .50
4 Danton Cole .20 .50
5 Ian Gordon .20 .50
6 Mark Greig .20 .50
7 Shane Hnidy .30 .75
8 Kerry Huffman .20 .50
9 Glen Metropolit .40 1.00
10 Todd Nelson .20 .50
11 Ed Patterson .20 .50
12 Bruce Ramsay .20 .50
13 Eldon Reddick .30 .75
14 Travis Richards .20 .50
15 Matt Ruchty .20 .50
16 Darcy Simon .20 .50
17 Brian Sullivan .20 .50
18 Sean Tallaire .20 .50
19 Dean Trboyevich .20 .50
20 Jason Weaver .20 .50
21 Dave Allison HCO .04 .10
22 Curtis Hunt ACO .04 .10
23 Griff Mascot .04 .10
24 PHPA Web Site .01

1998-99 Grand Rapids Griffins

Little is known about this IHL team set other than the confirmed checklist. It is believed, however, to be an oversized issue. Any additional information can be forwarded to hockeymag@beckett.com

COMPLETE SET (25) 4.80 12.00
1 Tom Ashe .20 .50
2 Jared Bednar .20 .50
3 Radim Bicanek .30 .75
4 Anders Bjork .20 .50
5 Aris Brimanis .20 .50
6 Danton Cole .20 .50
7 Jed Fiebelkorn .20 .50
8 Ian Gordon .20 .50
9 Todd Hlushko .20 .50
10 Kerry Huffman .20 .50
11 Neil Little .80 2.00
12 Glen Metropolit .40 1.00
13 Vaclav Nedomansky .20 .50
14 Robert Petrovicky .30 .75
15 Bruce Ramsay .20 .50
16 Travis Richards .20 .50
17 Gaetan Royer .20 .50
18 Darren Rumble .20 .50
19 Maxim Spiridonov .20 .50
20 Andrei Vasilyev .20 .50
21 Curtis Hunt ACO .04 .10
22 Guy Charron HCO .04 .10
23 Griff Mascot .04 .10
24 The Zone .01
25 PHPA Web Site .01

1999-00 Grand Rapids Griffins

This set features the Griffins of the IHL. The cards were produced by SplitSecond and were sold by the team at its souvenir stands.

COMPLETE SET (25) 6.00 15.00
1 Viacheslav Butsayev .20 .50
2 Guy Charron CO .10 .25
3 Ivan Ciernik .20 .50
4 Danton Cole CO .10 .25
5 John Emmons .20 .50
6 Mike Fountain .30 .75
7 Rick Goldman .20 .50
8 Konstantin Gorovikov .20 .50
9 John Gruden .20 .50
10 Curtis Hunt CO .10 .25
11 Jani Hurme 1.20 3.00
12 Derek King .20 .50
13 Kevin Miller .20 .50
14 Chris Neil .40 1.00
15 Todd Nelson .20 .50
16 Ed Patterson .20 .50
17 Michel Picard .20 .50
18 Phillippe Plante .20 .50
19 Karel Rachunek .30 .75
20 Travis Richards .20 .50
21 Yves Sarault .20 .50
22 Petr Schastlivy .60 1.50
23 Andrei Sryubko .20 .50
24 Chris Szysky .20 .50
25 Dave Van Drunen .20 .50

2000-01 Grand Rapids Griffins

This set features the Griffins of the IHL. The cards were produced by SplitSecond and were sold by the team at home games.

COMPLETE SET (25) 4.00 10.00
1 Keith Aldridge .14 .35
2 Sean Berens .14 .35
3 Vyacheslav Butsayev .14 .35
4 Mathieu Chouinard .40 1.00
5 Ivan Ciernik .14 .35
6 Ilja Demidov .14 .35
7 Mike Fountain .20 .50
8 Sean Gagnon .14 .35
9 Konstantin Gorovikov .14 .35
10 John Gruden .14 .35
11 Derek King .20 .50
12 Joel Kwiatkowski .14 .35
13 Marty McSorley .40 1.00
14 Kip Miller .20 .50
15 Chris Neil .40 1.00
16 David Oliver .14 .35
17 Ed Patterson .14 .35
18 Travis Richards .14 .35
19 David Roberts .14 .35
20 Petr Schastlivy .40 1.00
21 Chris Szysky .14 .35
22 Todd White .20 .50
23 Bruce Cassidy CO .10 .25
24 Danton Cole CO .10 .25
25 Griff MASCOT .04 .10

2001-02 Grand Rapids Griffins

This set features the Griffins of the AHL. The cards were created by Choice Marketing and were issued both as a promotional giveaway, and later were sold at the team's store. A total of 5,000 sets were produced.

COMPLETE SET (24) 4.80 12.00
1 Julien Vauclair .20 .50
2 John Gruden .20 .50
3 Wade Brookbank .20 .50
4 Kip Miller .20 .50
5 Alexandre Giroux .20 .50
6 Hugo Boisvert .20 .50
7 James Black .20 .50
8 Steve Martins .20 .50
9 David Hymovitz .20 .50
10 Chris Szysky .20 .50
11 Petr Schastlivy .40 1.00
12 Jeff Ulmer .20 .50
13 Josh Langfeld .20 .50
14 Chris Kelly .20 .50
15 Joe Murphy .20 .50
16 Travis Richards .20 .50
17 Martin Prusek .62 1.56
18 Chris Bala .20 .50
19 Dave Van Drunen .20 .50
20 Jason Doig .20 .50
21 Joel Kwiatkowski .20 .50
22 Mathieu Chouinard .62 1.56
23 Toni Dahlman .20 .50
24 Bruce Cassidy CO .04 .11
25 Gene Reilly ACO .04 .11
26 Griff MASCOT .04 .11

2002-03 Grand Rapids Griffins

This series was produced by Choice Marketing and, reportedly, was subject to a very odd distribution in which part of this set was given away as a game night promotion and the remaining cards were sold at the team's pro shop. The full set was never sold as a single unit. If anyone knows exactly how these were broken up, please write us at hockeymag@beckett.com.

COMPLETE SET (27)
1 Bryan Adams
2 Sean Avery
3 Paul Ballantyne
4 Ryan Barnes
5 Gregor Baumgartner
6 Patrick Boileau
7 Hugo Boisvert
8 Sheldon Brookbank
9 Ed Campbell
10 Danton Cole CO
11 Rob Collins
12 Nick Greenough
13 Griff MASCOT
14 Danny Groulx
15 Derek King
16 Tomas Kopecky
17 Marc Lamothe
18 Joey MacDonald
19 Mark Mowers
20 Todd Nelson
21 Michel Picard
22 Travis Richards
23 Nathan Robinson
24 Stacy Roest
25 Tim Skarperud
26 Dave Van Drunen
27 Shoe Carnival Ad

2003-04 Grand Rapids Griffins

This set was issued as a promotional giveaway over the course of several home games. As a result, it is very difficult to find in complete set form. We've recently confirmed five additional cards in the checklist. Thanks to collector Dale Spengler.

COMPLETE SET (29) 20.00 30.40
1 Ryan Barnes .60 1.50
2 Hugo Boisvert .60 1.50
3 Darryl Bootland .75 2.00
4 David Brisson .60 1.50
5 Matt Ellis .60 1.50
6 Danny Groulx .60 1.50
7 Jiri Hudler 2.00 5.00
8 Derek King .60 1.50
9 Tomas Kopecky 1.25 3.00
10 Niklas Kronwall 2.00 5.00
11 Marc Lamothe .75 2.00
12 Joey MacDonald 1.25 3.00
13 Kevin Miller .75 2.00
14 Mark Mowers .75 2.00
15 Anders Myrvold .60 1.50
16 Michel Picard .60 1.50
17 Travis Richards .60 1.50
18 Nathan Robinson .75 2.00
19 Aaron Schneekloth .60 1.50
20 Tim Skarperud .60 1.50
21 David Van Drunen .60 1.50
22 Danton Cole CO .10 .25
23 Greg Ireland ACO .02 .10
24 Brad Thompson EQM .02 .10
25 Jiri Hudler 2.00 5.00
26 Kory Karlander .60 1.50
27 Jeff Nelson .60 1.50
28 Rob Snitzer TR .02 .10
29 Shoe Carnival Ad .02 .10

2004-05 Green Bay Gamblers

This set of the USHL Gamblers is noteworthy for including the first card of the fifth overall pick from 2003, Blake Wheeler.

COMPLETE SET (28) 25.00
1 Jeff Carlson 1.00
2 Corey Couturier 1.00
3 Derek Danowski 1.00
4 Jeremy Dehner 1.00
5 Spencer Dillon 1.00
6 Justin Johnson 1.00
7 Carl Lackey ACO .10
8 Tyler Lehrke 1.00
9 Joe Long 1.00
10 Mark Magnowski 1.00
11 Mark Mazzoleni CO .10
12 Andrew Meyer 1.00
13 Brad Miller 1.00
14 Ryan Peterson 1.00
15 Garren Reisweber 1.00
16 Daniel Rosen 1.00
17 Billy Smith 1.00
18 Chris Stansik 1.00
19 Mark Stockdale 1.00
20 Luke Strand ACO .10
21 Dan Sturges 1.00
22 Garrett Suter 1.00
23 Blake Wheeler 3.00
24 Michael Zacharias 1.00
25 Suter/Dehner/Sturges 1.00
26 Missconducts 1.00
27 Mask Card 1.00
28 Mini Plan .01

1991-92 Greensboro Monarchs

This set features the Monarchs of the ECHL. The cards feature borderless, posed and action color player photos. The player's name and position appear on a mustard-colored hockey stick design at the bottom. The backs are subdivided by a red stripe and carry a close-up picture with biographical information above the stripe, and statistics and career highlights below it. The cards are unnumbered and checklisted below in alphabetical order.

COMPLETE SET (19) 3.20 8.00
1 Rob Bateman .24 .60
2 Phil Berger .20 .50
3 Mike Butters .20 .50
4 John Devereaux .20 .50
5 Eric Dubois .20 .50
6 Todd Gordon .20 .50
7 Chris Laganas .20 .50
8 Eric LeMarque .20 .50
9 Timo Makela .20 .50
10 Greg Menges .20 .50
11 Daryl Noren .20 .50
12 Peter Sentner .20 .50
13 Boyd Sutton .20 .50
14 Nick Vitucci .24 .60
15 Shawn Wheeler .20 .50
16 Scott White .20 .50
17 Chris Wolanin .20 .50
18 Dean Zayonce .20 .50
19 Team Photo .20 .50
(Photo of Jeff Brubaker CO on back)

1992-93 Greensboro Monarchs

Sponsored by RBI Sports Cards Inc., this 19-card standard-size set features full-bleed, color, action player photos. The player's name and position appear in a blue and red stripe near the bottom. The backs display a close-up picture alongside biographical information. A red stripe below the photo divides the card in half and serves as a heading for statistics. A player profile appears below the statistics.

COMPLETE SET (19) 3.20 8.00
1 Team Photo .30 .75
2 Chris Wolanin .20 .50
3 Bill Horn .20 .50
4 Brock Woods .20 .50
5 Phil Berger .20 .50
6 Dan Bylsma .20 .50
7 Davis Payne .30 .75
8 Wayne Muir .20 .50
9 Andrei Iakovenko .20 .50
10 Roger Larche .20 .50
11 Jamie Nicolls .20 .50
12 Darryl Noren .20 .50
13 Todd Gordon .20 .50
14 Claude Maillet .20 .50
15 Dave Burke .20 .50
16 Jamie Steer .24 .60
17 Greg Capson .20 .50
18 Chris Lappin .20 .50
19 Greg Menges .20 .50

1993-94 Greensboro Monarchs

This 16-card set of the Greensboro Monarchs of the ECHL was produced by RBI Sportscards. It is similar in design to the Raleigh Icecaps issue from the same year. The cards feature an action photo on the front, while the backs include career stats.

COMPLETE SET (16) 2.00 5.00
1 Phil Berger .20 .50
2 Trevor Burgess .16 .40
3 Dan Bylsma .20 .50
4 Greg Capson .16 .40
5 Brendan Creagh .16 .40
6 Dan Gravelle .16 .40
7 Sebastien LaPlante .16 .40
8 Savo Mitrovic .16 .40
9 Tom Newman .16 .40
10 Jamie Nicolls .16 .40
11 Davis Payne .20 .50
12 Stig Salomonsson .16 .40
13 Sverre Sears .16 .40
14 Chris Valicevic .16 .40
15 John Young .16 .40
16 Dean Zayonce .16 .40

1994-95 Greensboro Monarchs

This 20-card set of the Greensboro Monarchs of the ECHL was again produced by RBI Sportscards. This year's set mimics the design used by Pinnacle in 1993-94, although the photography lacks somewhat in the area of clarity. The backs are numbered, and contain stats for 1993-94. The sets apparently were not sold by the team; speculation suggests the booster club was in charge of distribution.

COMPLETE SET (20) 4.00 10.00
1 Dean Zayonce .20 .50
2 Jeremy Stevenson .20 .50
3 Glenn Stewart .20 .50
4 Peter Skudra .40 1.00
5 Chad Seibel .20 .50
6 Sverre Sears .20 .50
7 Howie Rosenblatt .40 1.00
8 Hugo Proulx .20 .50
9 Davis Payne .20 .50
10 Ron Pasco .20 .50
11 Monte MASCOT .04 .10
12 Scott McKay .20 .50
13 Arturs Kupaks .20 .50
14 Bill Horn .20 .50
15 Dwayne Gylywoychuk .20 .50
16 Jeff Gabriel .20 .50
17 Doug Evans .20 .50
18 Mark DeSantis .20 .50
19 Brendan Creagh .20 .50
20 Phil Berger .20 .50

1999-00 Greensboro Generals

This set features the Generals of the ECHL. The cards were produced by the team and sold at the souvenir stands.

COMPLETE SET (26) 4.00 10.00
1 Ian Walterson .16 .40
2 Clay Awe .16 .40
3 Sal Manganaro .16 .40
4 Oleg Timchenko .16 .40
5 David Whitworth .16 .40
6 T.J. Tanberg .16 .40
7 Keith O'Connell .16 .40
8 Tracy Egeland .16 .40
9 Igor Boiko .16 .40
10 Martin Galik .16 .40
11 Dean Shmyr .16 .40
12 Juraj Slovak .16 .40
13 Aniket Dhadphale .16 .40
14 Dean Zayonce .16 .40
15 Alexei Krovopuskov .16 .40
16 Van Burgess .16 .40
17 Matt Eisler .16 .40
18 Justin Cardwell .16 .40
19 Joel Irwin .16 .40
20 Wes Swinson .16 .40
21 Francis Larivee .30 .75
22 40th Anniversary Puck Drop .16 .40
23 Group Celebrates .16 .40
24 Settling Differences .80 2.00
25 Bill Flynn .16 .40
26 Greensboro Generals CL .10 .25

2001-02 Greensboro Generals

This set features the Generals of the ECHL. The sets were only available to members of the Generals' Kids Club. Reportedly, just 250 sets were made, making it one of the toughest minor league sets ever issued.

COMPLETE SET (20) 16.00 40.00
1 Daniel Passero .80 2.00
2 Rob Sandrock 1.20 3.00
3 Sal Manganaro .80 2.00
4 Vladislav Serov .80 2.00
5 Jarrett Thompson .80 2.00
6 Ryan Kummu .80 2.00
7 David Whitworth .80 2.00
8 Brian Loney .80 2.00
9 Chris Bell .80 2.00
10 Casey Kesselring .80 2.00
11 Shaun Peet .80 2.00
12 Jason Metcalfe .80 2.00
13 Chris Brassard .80 2.00
14 Dion Lassu .80 2.00
15 Jason Robinson .80 2.00
16 Jonathan Forest .80 2.00
17 Craig Stahl .80 2.00
18 Bujar Amidovski 1.20 3.00
19 Graeme Townshend CO .40 1.00
20 Sarge MASCOT .40 1.00

2002-03 Greensboro Generals RBI

COMPLETE SET (18) 15.00
1 Rod Aldoff 1.00
2 Chris Allen 1.00
3 Alex Andreyev 1.00
4 Chris Bell 1.00
5 Daniel Berthiaume 1.50
6 Shane Campbell 1.00
7 Matt Chandler 1.00
8 Kurt Drummond 1.00
9 Sam Fiorek 1.00
10 Pete Gardiner 1.00
11 Kevin Grimes 1.00
12 Olaf Kjenstad 1.00
13 Roman Marakhovski 1.00
14 Jay Murphy 1.00
15 Geno Parrish 1.00
16 Juraj Slovak 1.00
17 Matt Turek 1.00
18 David Whitworth 1.00

2003-04 Greensboro Generals

COMPLETE SET (16) 15.00
177 Alex Andreyev 1.00
178 Mike Bayrack 1.00
179 Daniel Berthiaume 1.50
180 Matt Chandler 1.00
181 Kurt Drummond 1.00
182 Matt Elich 1.00
183 Eric Fortier 1.00
184 Pete Gardiner 1.00
185 Joe Gerbe 1.00
186 Kevin Grimes 1.00
187 Jamie Hodson 1.50
188 Geno Parrish 1.00
189 Tom Reimann 1.00
190 Dean Shmyr 1.00
191 Matt Turek 1.00
192 Mark Turner 1.00

2001-02 Greenville Grrrowl

This set features the terribly named Grrrowl of the ECHL. The set was handed out as a promotional giveaway at a game in February, 2002. The cards are unnumbered, but they are numbered on a checklist card. The listing below mirrors that checklist.

COMPLETE SET (24) 9.78 24.44
1 John Marks CO .20 .50
2 Nick Vitucci ACO .20 .50
3 Eric Lind .40 1.00
4 Judd Stauss .40 1.00
5 Eric Van Acker .40 1.00
6 Roger Trudeau .40 1.00
7 Jason Windle .40 1.00
8 Sean Venedam .80 2.00
9 Jay Langager .40 1.00
10 Steve Rymsha .40 1.00
11 Jonathan Roy .80 2.00
12 Colin Pepperall .40 1.00
13 Kevin Bergin .40 1.00
14 David Bell .40 1.00
15 Damon Whitten .40 1.00
16 Ryan Stewart .40 1.00
17 Martin Masa .40 1.00
18 David Kaczowka .40 1.00
19 Simon Gamache .80 2.00
20 Tyrone Garner .80 2.00
21 Jayme Platt .40 1.00
22 Chad Nelson .40 1.00
23 Grrruff MASCOT .10 .25
24 Greenville Grrrowl CL .10 .25

2002-03 Greenville Grrrowl

COMPLETE SET (23) 20.00
1 Michael Garnett 2.00
2 Paul Flache 1.00
3 Rico Fatticci 1.00
4 Matt Demarski 1.00
5 Tyler Deis 1.00
6 Alexandre Burrows 1.00
7 Josh Legge 1.00
8 David Kaczowka 1.00
9 Mike Henderson 1.00
10 Grrruff MASCOT .10
11 Mark Gouett 1.00
12 Jonathan Gauthier 1.00
13 Judd Medak 1.00
14 Dan McIntyre 1.00
15 Martin Masa 1.00
16 John Marks HCO .10
17 Chris Lynch 1.00
18 Eric Lind 1.00
19 Krzysztof Wieckowski 1.00
20 Nick Vitucci ACO .10
21 Eric Van Acker 1.00
22 John Nail 1.00
23 Checklist .01

2003-04 Greenville Grrrowl

We've recently confirmed the existence of a 24th card in the set of John Nail. Thanks to collector Dale Spengler.

COMPLETE SET (24) 25.00
1 Stacey Bauman 1.00
2 Daniel Boisclair 3.00
3 Steve Burgess 1.00
4 Michael Chin 1.00
5 Bob Cunningham 1.00
6 Randy Dagenais 1.00
7 Robin Delacoure 1.00
8 Matt Demarski 1.00
9 Mike Henderson 1.00
10 Troy Ilijow 1.00
11 Han-Sung Kim 2.00
12 Scott Kirton 1.00
13 Jeremy Kyte 1.00
14 Bryan Lachapelle 1.00
15 David Lizotte 1.00
16 Jason Metcalfe 1.00
17 Mike Nelson 1.00
18 Michel Robinson 2.00
19 Russell Spence 1.00
20 Ryan Stewart 1.00
21 Jonathan Zion 1.50
22 John Marks CO .10
23 Team Photo .10
24 John Nail

1993-94 Guelph Storm

Sponsored by Domino's Pizza and printed by Slapshot Images Ltd., this standard size 31-card set features the 1993-94 Guelph Storm. On a geometrical blue and grey background, the fronts feature color action player photos with thin black borders. The player's name, position and team name, as well as the producer's logo, appear on the front.

COMPLETE SET (31) 4.80 12.00

1 Title Card .14 .35
2 Jeff O'Neill .80 1.50
3 Mark McArthur .20 .50
4 Kayle Short .14 .35
5 Ryan Risidore .14 .35
6 Mike Rusk .14 .35
7 Regan Stocco .14 .35
8 Duane Harmer .14 .35
9 Sylvain Cloutier .14 .35
10 Eric Landry .14 .35
11 Jamie Wright .20 .50
12 Todd Norman .14 .35
13 Mike Pittman .14 .35
14 Ken Belanger .30 .75
15 Viktor Reuta .14 .35
16 Mike Prokopec .14 .35
17 Jeff Williams .20 .50
18 Chris Skoryna .14 .35
19 Stephane Lefebvre .14 .35
20 Jeff Cowan .20 .50
21 Murray Hogg .14 .35
22 Andy Adams .14 .35
23 Todd Bertuzzi 1.50 3.00
24 Grant Pritchett .14 .35
25 Rumun Ndur .20 .50
26 Jeff O'Neill .80 1.50
27 Paul Brydges ACO .04 .10
28 John Lovell CO .04 .10
29 Team Photo/CL .14 .35
30 Domino's Pizza .04 .10
NNO Slapshot Ad Card .04 .10

1994-95 Guelph Storm

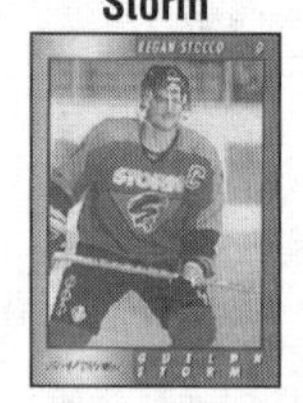

Sponsored by Domino's Pizza and Burger King, and printed by Slapshot Images Inc., this 31-card standard-size set features the Storm of the OHL. The cards were sold in set form at the team's rink.

COMPLETE SET (31) 5.60 10.00
1 Team Photo/CL .14 .35
2 Mark McArthur .20 .50
3 Andy Adams .14 .35
4 Bryan McKinney .14 .35
5 Ryan Risidore .20 .50
6 Joel Cort .14 .35
7 Chris Hajt .20 .50
8 Regan Stocco .14 .35
9 Dwayne Hay .20 .50
10 Andrew Clark .14 .35
11 Neil Fewster .14 .35
12 Jamie Wright .20 .50
13 Jason Jackman .14 .35
14 Pat Barton .14 .35
15 Tom Johnson .14 .35
16 Brian Wesenberg .20 .50
17 Mike Pittman .14 .35
18 Jeff Williams .14 .35
19 Todd Norman .20 .50
20 Mike Rusk .14 .35
21 David Lylyk .14 .35
22 Todd Bertuzzi 1.20 2.00
23 Jeff Cowan .20 .50
24 Rumun Ndur .20 .50
25 Jeff O'Neill .80 1.00
26 Andrew Long .14 .35
27 Craig Hartsburg CO .20 .50
28 Paul Brydges ACO .04 .10
29 Sponsor Card .01
30 Sponsor Card .01
NNO Ad Card .01

1995-96 Guelph Storm

This extremely attractive set was produced by Axiom Communications for distribution by the Storm at the club's pro shop. The set commemorates the team's fifth anniversary, and features strong action photography along with a dazzling design element along the right border. The back features a color mug shot, personal information and logos of sponsors.

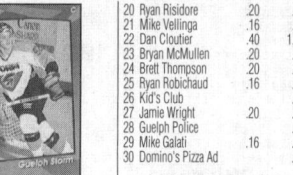

COMPLETE SET (30) 4.00 10.00
1 Checklist .16 .40
2 Andrew Clark .16 .40
3 Dwayne Hay .20 .50
4 Jason Jackman .16 .40
5 Burger King Ad .01
6 Nick Bootland .16 .40
7 Andrew Long .16 .40
8 Todd Norman .20 .50
9 Michael Pittman .16 .40
10 Herbert Vasilijevs .20 .50
11 Jeff Williams .16 .40
12 Joel Cort .20 .50
13 Chris Hajt .20 .50
14 Brian Willsie .20 .50
15 Brian Wesenberg .20 .50
16 Mike Lankshear .16 .40
17 Darryl McArthur .20 .50
18 Bryan McKinney .16 .40
19 Regan Stocco .16 .40
20 Ryan Risidore .20 .50
21 Mike Vellinga .16 .40
22 Dan Cloutier .40 1.00
23 Bryan McMullen .20 .50
24 Brett Thompson .20 .50
25 Ryan Robichaud .16 .40
26 Kid's Club .01
27 Jamie Wright .20 .50
28 Guelph Police .01
29 Mike Galati .16 .40
30 Domino's Pizza Ad .01

1996-97 Guelph Storm

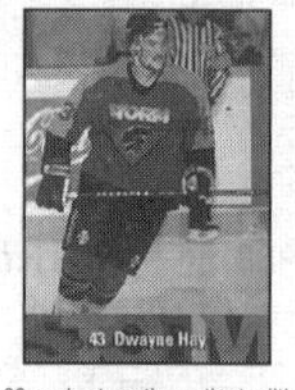

This 36-card set continues the tradition of high-quality sets from the Storm. The heavy-stock cards feature action photography on the front, along with player name and number and team logo. The backs include a mug shot and personal information and a safety tip, but no playing stats. The set is noteworthy for the inclusion of Manny Malhotra, expected to be a high pick in 1998.

COMPLETE SET (36) 4.80 12.00
1 Checklist .04 .10
2 Brett Thompson .16 .40
3 David MacDonald .16 .40
4 John Zubyck .16 .40
5 Denis Ivanov .16 .40
6 Joel Cort .16 .40
7 Chris Hajt .20 .50
8 Manny Malhotra .40 .75
9 Mike Dombkiewicz .16 .40
10 Ryan Robichaud .16 .40
11 Kent McDonell .20 .50
12 Joe Gerbe .16 .40
13 Mike Christian .16 .40
14 Brian Wesenberg .16 .40
15 Todd Norman .20 .50
16 Darryl McArthur .16 .40
17 Richard Irwin .16 .40
18 Brian Willsie .16 .40
19 Mike Vellinga .16 .40
20 Jason Jackman .16 .40
21 Chris Madden .30 .75
22 Dwayne Hay .20 .50
23 Joey Bartley .16 .40
24 Mike Lankshear .20 .50
25 Andrew Long .16 .40
26 Matt Bell .16 .40
27 Nick Bootland .20 .50
28 E.J. McGuire .04 .10
29 Rick Allain .04 .10
30 Burger King Ad .01
31 Burger King Kid's Club .01
32 Guelph Police .40
with Malhotra and Norman
33 Domino's Pizza Ad .01
34 Domino's Pizza Ad .01
35 Chris Hajt/Dwayne Hay .16 .40
36 96-97 Team Picture .16 .40

1996-97 Guelph Storm Premier Collection

This odd-sized (4" X 6") collection was issued by the club along with game programs. The set is noteworthy for its outstanding photography and imaginative posing of the subjects; most appear out of hockey garb and in more expressive outfits and poses.

COMPLETE SET (12) 4.80 10.00
1 Todd Norman .40 1.00
2 Brian Wesenberg .40 1.00
3 Mike Vellinga .40 1.00
4 Brett Thompson .40 1.00
5 Joel Cort .40 1.00
6 Jason Jackman .40 1.00
7 Brian Willsie .40 1.00
8 Mike Lankshear .40 1.00
9 Dwayne Hay .40 1.00
10 Manny Malhotra 1.20 2.00
11 Chris Hajt .40 1.00
12 Nick Bootland .40 1.00

1997-98 Guelph Storm

Card fronts feature a black and white action photo, with players name and number on the bottom. Card backs feature biographical information and are numbered xx/34. Backs also feature sponsor logos and safety tips.

COMPLETE SET (34) 4.80 12.00
1 Header Card .04 .10
2 Chris Thompson .16 .40
3 Daniel Jacques .16 .40
4 Chris Madden .30 .75
5 Kevin Mitchell .16 .40
6 Joey Bartley .16 .40
7 Chris Hajt .20 .50
8 Manny Malhotra .40 .75
9 Mike Dombkiewicz .16 .40
10 Ian Forbes .16 .40
11 Joe Gerbe .16 .40
12 Mike Vellinga .16 .40
13 Lindsay Plunkett .16 .40
14 Kent McDonell .16 .40
15 Matt Lahey .16 .40
16 Bohuslav Subr .16 .40
17 Bob Crummer .16 .40
18 Andrew Long .16 .40
19 Brian McGrattan .16 .40
20 Darryl McArthur .30 .75
21 Brian Willsie .20 .50
22 John Zubyck .16 .40
23 Dusty Jamieson .30 .75
24 Eric Beaudoin .16 .40
25 Jason Jackman .16 .40
26 Nick Bootland .16 .40
27 George Burnett CO .16 .40
28 Rick Allain ACO .04 .10
29 Spyke .04 .10
30 Guelph Police .04 .10
31 Burger King .01
32 Burger King .01
33 Domino's .01
34 Domino's .01

1998-99 Guelph Storm

This set features the Storm of the OHL. The cards feature an action shot on the front, along with a full-color back. The cards were produced by the team and sold at home games.

COMPLETE SET (36) 4.80 12.00
1 Title Card/CL .02 .01
2 Mike D'Alessandro .30 .75
3 Chris Madden .40 1.00
4 Kevin Mitchell .20 .50
5 Jean Sebastien Larocque .20 .50
6 Kevin Dallman .30 .75
7 Matt Rock .20 .50
8 Ian Forbes .20 .50
9 Joe Gerbe .20 .50
10 Bo Subr .30 .75
11 Lindsay Plunkett .20 .50
12 Kent McDonell .20 .50
13 Garrett McAiney .20 .50
14 Nathan Herrington .20 .50
15 Bob Crummer .20 .50
16 Charlie Stephens .30 .75
17 Darryl Knight .20 .50
18 Darryl McArthur .20 .75
19 Ryan Davis .20 .50
20 Joey Bartley .20 .50
21 Frank Jolette .20 .50
22 Eric Beaudoin .20 .50
23 Lucas Nehrling .20 .50
24 Geoff Ward ACO .04 .10
25 Bart Crashley ACO .04 .10
26 Shane Mabey TR .04 .10
27 Russ Hammond ATR .04 .10
28 Spyke MASCOT .04 .10
29 Guelph Police .01
30 1997-98 OHL Champs .04 .10
31 Robertson Cup .04 .10
32 Memorial Cup AS .10 .25
33 Burge King Ad .01
34 Burger King Ad .01
35 Domino's Ad .01
36 Domino's Ad .01

1999-00 Guelph Storm

Released in conjunction with Burger King and Domino's, this 36-card set features the 1999-00 Guelph Storm. Cards are black bordered and contain full color action photography. The last four cards of the set are coupons for Burger King and Domino's.

COMPLETE SET (36) 4.00 10.00
1 Header Card/CL .04 .10
2 Craig Andersson .14 1.50
3 Chris Madden .40 1.00
4 Kevin Mitchell .14 .35
5 Kevin Dallman .14 .35
6 Matt Rock .14 .35
7 Jon Hedberg .14 .35
8 Radek Matalik .14 .35
9 Joe Gerbe .14 .35
10 Bo Suba .14 .35
11 Lindsay Plunkett .14 .35
12 Kent McDonell .30 .75
13 Peter Flache .14 .35
14 Charlie Stephens .30 .75
15 Colt King .30 .75
16 Nick Jones .14 .35
17 Brent Kelly .14 .35
18 Jon Peters .14 .35
19 Derek Hennessey .14 .35
20 Andrew Brown .14 .35
21 Aran Myers .14 .35
22 Matt House .14 .35
23 Eric Beaudoin .14 .35
24 Ian Forbes .14 .35
25 Morgan McCormick .14 .35
26 Paul Gillis .14 .35
27 Bart Crashley .14 .35
28 Shane Mabey .14 .35
29 Russ Hammond .14 .35
30 Spyke Mascot .04 .10
31 Team Photo .14 .35
32 Guelph Police .04 .10
33 Burger King Coupon .01
34 Burger King Coupon .01
35 Domino's Coupon .01
36 Domino's Coupon .01

2000-01 Guelph Storm

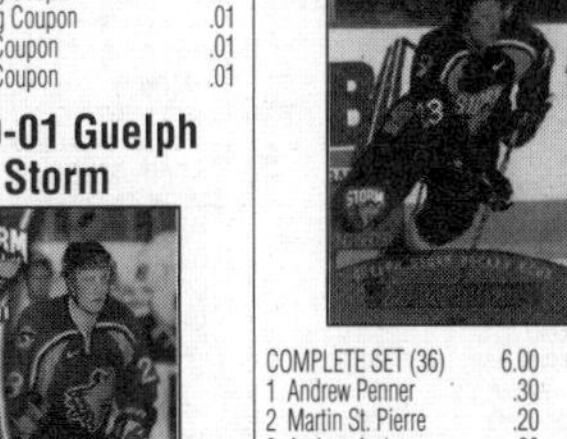

We have confirmed this handful of cards to exist, thanks to collector Vinnie Montalbano. If you know of others, please contact us via hockeymag@beckett.com.

COMPLETE SET (?)
1 Craig Anderson
2 Andrew Archer
3 Dustin Brown
4 Kevin Dallman

2001-02 Guelph Storm

COMPLETE SET (35) 20.00
1 Fedor Tyutin .40 1.00
2 Frank Burgio .20 .50
3 Kevin Dallman .30 .75
4 Leonid Zvachkin .20 .50
5 Tim Branham .20 .50
6 George Bradley .20 .50
7 Martin St. Pierre .20 .50
8 Malcolm MacMillan .20 .50
9 Michael Krelove .20 .50
10 Colin Power .20 .50
11 Aaron Lobb .20 .50
12 Daniel Paille .75 2.00
13 Alex Butkus .20 .50
14 Ryan Thompson .20 .50
15 Luc Chiasson .20 .50
16 Derek Hennessey .20 .50
17 Evan Kotsopoulos .20 .50
18 Matt Puntureri .20 .50
19 Andrew Archer .20 .50
20 Morgan McCormick .20 .50
21 Chris Beckford-Tseu 1.25 3.00
22 Andrew Penner .30 .75
23 Dustin Brown 1.50 4.00
24 Dwight LaBrosse .20 .50
25 Jeff Jackson CO .08 .20
26 Shawn Camp ACO .20 .50
27 Spyke MASCOT .02 .10
28 Shane Mabey TR .20 .50
29 Russ Hammond ATR .20 .50
30 Police Services .02 .10
31 Dominos .02 .10
32 Guelph Dominators .02 .10
33 Guelph Dominators .02 .10
34 M&T Printing Group .02 .10
35 Checklist .02 .10

2001-02 Guelph Storm Memorial Cup

Very similar to other Guelph set of this season, save for the addition of the Memorial Cup logo and a few other small changes in content.

COMPLETE SET (35) 8.00 20.00
1 Fedor Tjutin .60 1.50
2 Kevin Dallman .60 1.50
3 Leonid Zvachkin .30 .75
4 Tim Branham .30 .75
5 Eric Larochelle .30 .75
6 George Bradley .30 .75
7 Martin St. Pierre .30 .75
8 Malcolm MacMillan .30 .75
9 Michael Krelove .30 .75
10 Colin Power .30 .75
11 Aaron Lobb .30 .75
12 Daniel Paille 1.00 2.50
13 Alex Butkus .30 .75
14 Ryan Thompson .30 .75
15 Luc Chiasson .30 .75
16 Derek Hennessey .30 .75
17 Lou Dickenson .30 .75
18 Matt Puntureri .30 .75
19 Scott Rozendal .30 .75
20 Andrew Archer .30 .75
21 Morgan McCormick .30 .75
22 Andrew Penner .40 1.00
23 Dustin Brown 1.50 4.00
24 Dwight LaBrosse .30 .75
25 Jeff Jackson CO .02 .10
26 Shawn Camp ACO .02 .10
27 Spyke MASCOT .02 .10
28 Shane Mabey TR .02 .10
29 Russ Hammond ATR .02 .10
30 Sponsor .02 .10
31 Memorial Cup Card .02 .10
32 Team Photo .02 .10
33 Community .02 .10
34 Community .02 .10
35 Checklist .02 .10

2002-03 Guelph Storm

COMPLETE SET (36) 6.00 15.00
1 Andrew Penner .30 .75
2 Martin St. Pierre .20 .50
3 Andrew Archer .20 .50
4 Ryan Thompson .20 .50
5 Daniel Paille .60 1.50
6 Adam Dennis .30 .75
7 Dustin Brown .60 1.50
8 Eric Larochelle .20 .50
9 George Bradley .20 .50
10 Corey LeClair .20 .50
11 Geoff Patton .20 .50
12 Lou Dickenson .20 .50
13 Matt Ryan .20 .50
14 Colin Power .20 .50
15 Ryan Garlock .40 1.00
16 Steve Zmudczynski .20 .50
17 Leonid Zvachkin .20 .50
18 Brett Trudell .20 .50
19 Michael Okrzesik .20 .50
20 Ryan Callahan .40 1.00
21 Emil Bucic .20 .50
22 Aaron Lobb .20 .50
23 Tyler Haskins .20 .50
24 Malcolm MacMillan .20 .50
25 Matt Puntureri .20 .50
26 Jeff Jackson CO .02 .10
27 Shawn Camp ACO .02 .10
28 Jason Brooks ACO .02 .10
29 Shawn Mabey AT .02 .10
30 Russ Hammond ATR .02 .10
31 Spyke MASCOT .02 .10
32 Ad card .01 .01
33 Junior Storm .01 .01
34 Home Ice .01 .01
35 Guelph Police .01 .01
36 Team Photo/CL .02 .10

2003-04 Guelph Storm

COMPLETE SET (30) 6.00 15.00
1 Header Card .02 .10
2 Danny Taylor .20 .50
3 Mick Okrzesik .20 .50
4 Dan Girardi .40 1.00
5 Kevin Klein .40 1.00
6 Ryan Parent .75 2.00
7 George Bradley .20 .50
8 Marty St. Pierre .20 .50
9 Niko Tuomi .20 .50
10 Mark Lytwyn .20 .50
11 Nathan Spaling .20 .50
12 Steve Zmudczynski .20 .50
13 Dan Paille .40 1.00
14 Brett Trudell .20 .50
15 Shane Hart .20 .50
16 Ryan Garlock .40 1.00
17 Ryan Card .20 .50
18 Matt Ryan .20 .50
19 Ryan Callahan .30 .75
20 Kyle Spurr .20 .50
21 Adam Dennis .40 1.00
22 Jakub Koreis .40 1.00
23 Dustin Brown .40 1.00
24 Shawn Camp CO .02 .10
25 Jason Brooks ACO .02 .10
26 Paul Brydges ACO .02 .10
27 Sponsor Card .02 .10
28 Sponsor Card .02 .10
29 Guelph Police .02 .10
30 Team Photo/CL .02 .10

2004-05 Guelph Storm

COMPLETE SET (31) 8.00 20.00
1 Danny Taylor .30 .75
2 Michael Caruso .30 .75
3 Shawn Haviland .30 .75
4 Michael Okrzesik .30 .75
5 Daniel Girardi .40 1.00
6 Josh Godfrey .30 .75
7 Ryan Parent .40 1.00
8 Brent Mackie .30 .75
9 Andy Hyvarinen .30 .75
10 Jaromir Florian .30 .75
11 Mark Versteeg-Lytwyn .40 1.00
12 Mark O'Leary .30 .75
13 Steve Zmudczynski .30 .75
14 Scot Zimmerman .30 .75
15 Ryan Kitchen .30 .75
16 Mike McLean .30 .75
17 Kyle Paige .30 .75
18 Matt Lyall .30 .75
19 Matt D'Agostini .30 .75
20 Ryan Card .30 .75
21 Darryl Smith .30 .75
22 Ryan Callahan .40 1.00
23 Kyle Spurr .30 .75
24 Tyler Doig .30 .75
25 Adam Dennis .40 1.00
26 Dave Barr CO .02 .10
27 Jason Brooks ACO .02 .10
28 Trent Cull ACO .02 .10
29 Spyke MASCOT .02 .10
30 Team Photo/CL .02 .10
31 Guelph Police .01 .01

2005-06 Guelph Storm

COMPLETE SET (32) 10.00 25.00
A-01 Josh Godfrey .40 1.00
A-02 Jamie Arniel .40 1.00
A-03 Mark O'Leary .40 1.00
A-04 Tyler Doig .40 1.00
A-05 Ryan MacDonald .40 1.00
A-06 Jason Brooks ACO .02 .10
A-07 Guelph Police .01 .01
A-08 Guelph Storm CL1 .02 .10
B-01 Ryan Pottruff .40 1.00
B-02 Ryan Parent 1.00 2.50
B-03 Andy Hyvarinen .40 1.00
B-04 Kelsey Wilson .40 1.00
B-05 Matt D'Agostini .40 1.00
B-06 Domino's Pizza SPONSOR .01 .01
B-07 Dave Barr CO .02 .10
B-08 Guelph Storm CL2 .02 .10
C-01 Michael Caruso .40 1.00
C-02 Drew Doughty 1.50 4.00
C-03 Brandon Biggers .40 1.00
C-04 Leigh Salters .40 1.00
C-05 Rafael Rotter .40 1.00
C-06 M&T Printing SPONSOR .01 .01
C-07 Trent Cull ACO .02 .10
C-08 Guelph Storm CL3 .02 .10
D-01 Shawn Haviland .40 1.00
D-02 Kyle Wharton .40 1.00
D-03 Jason Pitton .40 1.00
D-04 Mike McLean .40 1.00
D-05 Harry Young .40 1.00
D-06 Ryan Callahan .75 2.00
D-07 Jason Guy .40 1.00
D-08 Guelph Storm CL4 .02 .10

2006-07 Guelph Storm

COMPLETE SET (25) 8.00 15.00
1 Thomas McCollum .40 1.00
2 Ryan Pottruff .20 .50
3 Joe Underwood .20 .50
4 Brandon Buck .20 .50
5 Drew Doughty 1.25 3.00
6 Matt Kennedy .20 .50
7 Leigh Salters .20 .50
8 Anthony Nigro .20 .50
9 Jeff Hayes .20 .50
10 Tyler Melancon .20 .50
11 Tyler Doig .20 .50
12 Mike McLean .20 .50
13 Patrick Moran .20 .50
14 Anton Hedman .20 .50
15 Luke Pither .20 .50
16 Grant McGee .20 .50
17 Rafael Rotter .20 .50
18 Tim Priamo .20 .50
19 Jamie Arniel .20 .50
20 Ryan Parent .60 1.50
21 Corey Syvret .20 .50
22 Michael Caruso .20 .50
23 Cody St Jacques .20 .50
24 Dave Barr CO .10 .25
25 Rusty Hammond TR .02 .10

2003-04 Gwinnett Gladiators

This set was sponsored by the Gwinnett Daily Post and was issued as a promotional giveaway at a home game. The oversized cards were issued on a perforated sheet.

COMPLETE SET (36) 30.00
1 Checklist .10
2 Kevin Doell 1.00
3 Brad Peddle 1.00
4 Brandon Dietrich 1.00
5 Chris Durno 1.00
6 Rick Emmett 1.00
7 Anthony Aquino 1.50
8 Steve Slonina 1.00
9 Cam Brown 1.00
10 Wes Fox 1.00
11 Mike Buckley 1.50
12 Paul Flache 1.00
13 Joe Bourne 1.00
14 Blue Bennefield 1.50
15 Michael Garnett 1.50
16 Evan Nielsen 1.00
17 Jim Jackson 1.00
18 Troy Milam 1.00
19 Adam Munro 1.50
20 Kris Goodjohn 1.00
21 Mike Vigilante 1.00
22 Phil Lewandowski 1.00
23 J.P. O'Connor 1.00
24 Jeff Pyle CO .25
25 Megan Guthrie TR .25
26 Patrick Houlihan EQM .25
27 Steve Chapman GM .25
28 Dustin Bixby ANN .25
29 Celebration Photo .50
30 Mascot .25
31 Gladiators first ever goal .50
32 Gladiators win first game .50
33 Opening Night .50
34 Scramble in the crease .50
35 Team Photo .50
36 The Zamboni .25

2003-04 Gwinnett Gladiators RBI Sports

This set was produced by RBI Sports, with a print run of 250 sets. The numbering sequence reflects the entire print run of RBI sets this season.

COMPLETE SET (16) 15.00
193 Blue Bennefield 1.50
194 Joe Bourne 1.00
195 Cam Brown 1.00
196 Brandon Dietrich 1.00
197 Kevin Doell 1.00
198 Chris Durno 1.00
199 Rick Emmett 1.00
200 Paul Flache 1.00
201 Michael Garnett 1.50
202 Kris Goodjohn 1.00
203 Jim Jackson 1.00
204 Troy Milam 1.00
205 Adam Munro 1.50
206 Evan Nielsen 1.00
207 Steve Slonina 1.00
208 Mike Vigilante 1.00

2004-05 Gwinnett Gladiators

COMPLETE SET (30) 8.00 20.00
1 T.J. Aceti .60 1.50
2 Adam Berkhoel .75 2.00
3 Dustin Bixby .30 .75
4 Joe Bourne .30 .75
5 Cam Brown .30 .75
6 Jeff Campbell .30 .75
7 Steve Chapman GM .02 .10
8 Chris Durno .30 .75
9 Rick Emmett .30 .75
10 Brett Engelhardt .30 .75
11 Sean Fields .30 .75
12 Peter Flache .30 .75
13 Kris Goodjohn .30 .75
14 Megan Guthrie TR .02 .10
15 Patrick Houlihan EQMG .02 .10
16 Jim Jackson .30 .75
17 Lane Manson .30 .75
18 Dave McCullough .30 .75
19 Dr. Brian Morgan .02 .10
20 Chris Peterson .30 .75
21 Jeff Pyle CO .02 .10
22 Brad Schell .30 .75
23 Adam Smyth .30 .75
24 Mike Stathopoulos .30 .75
25 Kevin Truelson .30 .75
26 Ryan Van Buskirk .30 .75
27 Mike Vigilante .30 .75
28 Maximus MASCOT .02 .10
29 Team Picture .02 .10
30 Checklist .02 .10

1989-90 Halifax Citadels

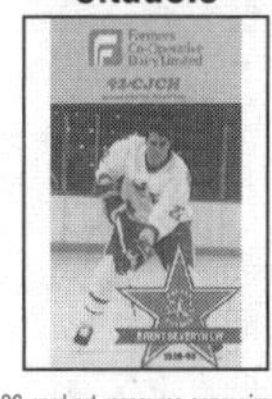

This 26-card set measures approximately 2" by 4 1/4". The fronts feature full-bleed posed action color photos, except at the top where a gray stripe displays the logos of the Farmers Co-Operative Dairy Limited and 92/CJCH. The team logo in the form of a red star appears in the lower right corner, with the player's name in a blue bar that is printed over the team logo. The cards are unnumbered and checklisted below in alphabetical order.

COMPLETE SET (26) 4.80 12.00
1 Joel Baillargeon .20 .50
2 Jamie Baker .24 .60
3 Mario Brunetta .30 .75
4 Gerald Bzdel .20 .50
5 David Espe .20 .50
6 Bryan Fogarty .30 .75
7 Robbie Florek GM .20 .50
8 Scott Gordon .30 .75
9 Dean Hopkins .20 .50
10 Miroslav Ihnacak .20 .50
11 Claude Julien .20 .50
12 Kevin Kaminski .30 .75
13 Claude Lapointe .30 .75
14 Chris McQuaid EQ/MG .10 .25
Brent Smith TR
15 Max Middendorf .20 .50
16 Stephane Morin .20 .50
17 Dave Pichette .20 .50
18 Ken Quinney .20 .50
19 Jean-Marc Richard .20 .50
20 Jean Marc Routhier .20 .50
21 Jaroslav Sevcik .20 .50
22 Brent Severyn .30 .75
23 Greg Smyth .20 .50
24 Trevor Steinburg .20 .50
25 Mark Vermette .20 .50
26 Ladislav Tresl .20 .50

1990-91 Halifax Citadels

This 28-card set measures approximately 2 3/4" by 4 1/4" and features color, posed-action player photos with white borders. The Farmers Co-Operative Dairy Limited and the 92/CJCH logo appear in the top border. The cards are unnumbered and checklisted below in alphabetical order.

COMPLETE SET (28) 4.80 12.00
1 Jamie Baker .20 .50
2 Mike Bishop .16 .40
3 Gerald Bzdel .16 .40
4 Daniel Dore .16 .40
5 Mario Doyon .16 .40
6 Dave Espe .16 .40
7 Stephane Fiset 1.20 3.00
8 Scott Gordon .30 .75
9 Stephane Guerard .16 .40
10 Dean Hopkins ACO .10 .25
11 Miroslav Ihnacak .20 .50
12 Jeff Jackson .20 .50
13 Clement Jodoin CO/MG .10 .25
14 Claude Lapointe .20 .50
15 Dave Latta .16 .40
16 Chris McQuaid EQ MG .10 .25
17 Kip Miller .20 .50
18 Stephane Morin .20 .50
19 Ken Quinney .16 .40
20 Jean-Marc Richard .16 .40
21 Serge Roberge .16 .40
22 Jaroslav Sevcik .16 .40
23 Brent Severyn .30 .75
24 Mike Shuman TR .10 .25
25 Greg Smyth .16 .40
26 Jim Sprott .16 .40
27 Trevor Stienburg .16 .40
28 Mark Vermette .16 .40

1995-96 Halifax Mooseheads

This set features the Mooseheads of the QMJHL. The set was produced by the team, and sold at its souvenir stands.

COMPLETE SET (25) 8.00 25.00
1 Harlin Hayes .20 .50
2 J-S Giguere 4.00 10.00
3 Patrick Lafleur .20 .50
4 Jamie Brown .20 .50
5 Elias Abrahamsson .20 .50
6 Didier Tremblay .20 .50
7 Chris Halverson .20 .50
8 Chris Peyton .20 .50
9 Frederic Belanger .20 .50
10 Joel Theriault .20 .50
11 Mark Lynk .20 .50
12 Derrick Pyke .20 .50
13 Steve Mongrain .20 .50
14 David Carson .20 .50
15 Jody Shelley 2.00 5.00
16 Daniel Payette .20 .50
17 Brian Surette .20 .50
18 Etienne Drapeau .30 .75
19 Billy Manley .20 .50
20 Jan Melichercik .20 .50
21 Nicolas Maheux .20 .50
22 Eric Houde .30 .75
23 Shawn MacKenzie CO .10 .25
24 Clement Jodoin CO .10 .25
25 Chris McQuaid TR .04 .10

1996-97 Halifax Mooseheads I

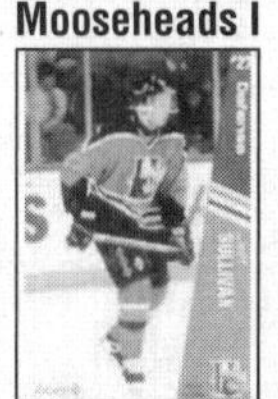

Series one pictures the team in their home uniforms. It was sold in team-set form early in the season.

COMPLETE SET (27) 12.00 30.00
1 Elias Abrahamsson .30 .75
2 Frederic Belanger .20 .50
3 Martin Bilodeau .20 .50
4 Jamie Brown .20 .50
5 Marc Chouinard .40 1.00
6 Benoit Dusablon .80 1.50
7 J-S Giguere 1.20 6.00
8 Andrew Gilby .20 .50
9 Alex Johnstone .20 .50
10 Eric Laplante .30 .75
11 Jean-Simon Lemay .20 .50
12 Mark Lynk .20 .50
13 Billy Manley .20 .50
14 Alexander Mathieu .20 .50
15 Todd Row .20 .50
16 Ryan Rowell .20 .50
17 Francois Sasseville .20 .50
18 Jody Shelley 2.00 4.00
19 Jeffrey Sullivan .20 .50
20 Alex Tanguay 4.00 10.00
21 Didier Tremblay .30 .75
22 Jason Troini .20 .50
23 Clark Udle .20 .50
24 Clement Jodoin HCO .04 .10
25 Shawn MacKenzie ACO .04 .10
26 Chris McQuaid TR .04 .10
27 Team Photo .20 .50

1996-97 Halifax Mooseheads II

Series 2 features the team in their away uniforms. According to various reports, it was issued later in the season and is considered slightly tougher to acquire.

COMPLETE SET (27) 14.22 35.56
1 Elias Abrahamsson .40 1.00
2 Frederic Belanger .30 .75
3 Martin Bilodeau .30 .75
4 Jamie Brown .30 .75
5 Marc Chouinard .50 1.25
6 Benoit Dusablon .80 2.00
7 J-S Giguere 1.60 10.00
8 Andrew Gilby .30 .75
9 Alex Johnstone .30 .75
10 Eric Laplante .40 1.00
11 Jean-Simon Lemay .30 .75
12 Mark Lynk .30 .75
13 Billy Manley .30 .75
14 Alexander Mathieu .30 .75
15 Todd Row .30 .75
16 Ryan Rowell .30 .75
17 Francois Sasseville .30 .75
18 Jody Shelley 2.00 5.00
19 Jeffrey Sullivan .30 .75
20 Alex Tanguay 4.80 12.00
21 Didier Tremblay .40 1.00
22 Jason Troini .30 .75
23 Clark Udle .30 .75
24 Clement Jodoin HCO .04 .10
25 Shawn MacKenzie ACO .04 .10
26 Chris McQuaid TR .04 .10
27 Team Photo .20 .50

1997-98 Halifax Mooseheads I

As with the previous year's set, Series 1 features the team in their home uniforms. The series was sold by the team at home games.

COMPLETE SET (27) 8.00 20.00
1 Frederic Belanger .20 .50
2 Martin Bilodeau .20 .50
3 Marc-Andre Binette .20 .50
4 Alexandre Couture .20 .50
5 Andrew Gilby .20 .50
6 Alex Johnstone .20 .50
7 Eric Laplante .30 .75
8 P.J. Lynch .20 .50
9 Mark Lynk .20 .50
10 Joey MacDonald .30 .75
11 Ali MacEachern .20 .50
12 Billy Manley .20 .50
13 Alexander Mathieu .20 .50
14 Steve Mongrain .20 .50
15 Ryan Power .20 .50
16 Brandon Reid .80 3.00
17 Todd Row .20 .50
18 Dean Stock .20 .50
19 Jeffrey Sullivan .20 .50
20 Alex Tanguay 3.20 8.00
21 Didier Tremblay .30 .75
22 Jason Troini .20 .50
23 Dwight Wolfe .20 .50
24 Danny Grant HCO .04 .10
25 Shawn MacKenzie ACO .04 .10
26 Chris McQuaid TR .04 .10
27 Team Photo .20 .50

1997-98 Halifax Mooseheads II

Series 2 is unnumbered and listed alphabetically. The set features several players who were acquired by the team after the release of Series 1. It also was printed in lesser quantities than the first series.

COMPLETE SET (27) 30.00
1 Checklist .04 .10
2 Frederic Belanger .30 .75
3 Martin Bilodeau .30 .75
4 Marc-Andre Binette .30 .75
5 Alexandre Couture .30 .75
6 Mauro DiPaolo .30 .75
7 Alex Johnstone .30 .75
8 P.J. Lynch .30 .75
9 Joey MacDonald .40 1.00
10 Ali MacEachern .30 .75
11 Boris Majesky .30 .75
12 Billy Manley .30 .75
13 Alexander Mathieu .30 .75
14 Ryan Power .30 .75
15 Stephen Quirk .30 .75
16 Brandon Reid 1.20 4.00
17 A.J.Rivers .30 .75
18 Dean Stock .30 .75
19 Jeffrey Sullivan .30 .75
20 Alex Tanguay 4.00 10.00
21 Jason Troini .30 .75
22 Andrew Warr .30 .75
23 Dwight Wolfe .30 .75

24 Shawn MacKenzie ACO .04 .10
25 Danny Grant HCO .30 .75
26 Hal Mascot .04 .10
27 Alex Tanguay CAN 4.00 10.00
28 Chris McQuad TR .04 .10

1998-99 Halifax Mooseheads

COMPLETE SET (23) 12.00 20.00
1 Alexei Volkov .30 .75
2 Pascal Leclaire .75 2.00
3 Mathieu Paul .20 .50
4 Samuel Seguin .20 .50
5 Billy Manley .20 .50
6 Ladislav Nagy 1.25 3.00
7 Alex Tanguay 1.25 3.00
8 Mike Bray .20 .50
9 Carlyle Lewis .20 .50
10 Frederic Belanger .20 .50
11 David McCutcheon .20 .50
12 Jeff Sullivan .20 .50
13 Alexandre Mathieu .20 .50
14 Jason Troini .20 .50
15 Alex Johnstone .20 .50
16 Ali MacEachern .20 .50
17 Brandon Benedict .20 .50
18 Tyler Reid .20 .50
19 Jasmin Gelinas .20 .50
20 P.J. Lynch .20 .50
21 Mauro DiPaolo .20 .50
22 Brandon Reid .60 1.50
23 Marc-Andre Binette .20 .50
24 Jeff Towriss .20 .50
25 Rocco Anoia .20 .50
26 Daniel Villeneuve .20 .50
27 Alex Tanguay CL .75 2.00

1998-99 Halifax Mooseheads Second Edition

COMPLETE SET (27) 8.00 20.00
1 Tyler Reid .20 .50
2 Jasmin Gelinas .20 .50
3 Hal MASCOT .02 .10
4 Brandon Reid .40 1.00
5 Jeff Sullivan .20 .50
6 Alex Johnstone .20 .50
7 P.J. Lynch .20 .50
8 Mauro Dipaolo .20 .50
9 Marc-andre Binette .20 .50
10 Carlyle Lewis .20 .50
11 David McCutcheon .20 .50
12 Mike Bray .20 .50
13 Samuel Seguin .20 .50
14 Brandon Benedict .20 .50
15 Jason Troini .20 .50
16 Ali MacEachern .20 .50
17 Mathieu Paul .20 .50
18 Alexei Volkov .30 .75
19 Billy Manley .20 .50
20 Frederic Belanger .20 .50
21 Alex Tanguay 1.25 3.00
22 Pascal Leclaire .75 2.00
23 Ladislav Nagy 1.25 3.00
24 Alexandre Mathieu .30 .75
25 World Junior .40 1.00
26 Halifax Radio Team .02 .10
27 Team Card .02 .10

1999-00 Halifax Mooseheads

This 29-card set features the 1999-00 Halifax Mooseheads. Card fronts have white borders, and along the left side, a green status bar containing the player's name fades into a full color action photo. These cards are not numbered, therefore appear in order by the included checklist card.

COMPLETE SET (29) 7.20 18.00
1 Alexei Volkov .40 1.00
2 Pascal Leclaire 2.00 5.00
3 Carlos Sayde .10 .25
4 Joey Dipenta 1.25 3.00
5 Joe Groleau .10 .25
6 Jonathan Boone .10 .25
7 Nick Greenough .10 .25
8 Jason King .10 .25
9 Shawn Lewis .10 .25
10 Ramzi Abid .80 1.00
11 Jonathan St. Louis .10 .25
12 Darrell Jarrett .10 .25
13 Ryan Flinn .60 1.50
14 Robbie Sutherland .10 .25
15 Ali MacEachern .10 .25
16 Brandon Benedict .10 .25
17 Jules-Edy Laraque .40 1.00
18 Jasmin Gelinas .10 .25
19 Hugo Lehoux .10 .25
20 Gary Zinck .10 .25
21 Brandon Reid .80 2.00
22 Benoit Dusablon .40 1.00
23 Hal MASCOT .04 .10
24 Team Photo .10 .25
25 Cover Card 1 .04 .10
26 Cover Card 2 .04 .10
27 Cover Card 3 .04 .10
28 Cover Card 4 .04 .10
29 Cover Card 5 .04 .10

2000-01 Halifax Mooseheads

This attractive set features the Mooseheads of the QMJHL. The set was produced and sold by the team at its souvenir stands. The cards were sponsored by Sobey's and are unnumbered, therefore they are listed below in alphabetical order.

COMPLETE SET (26) 4.80 12.00
1 Brandon Benedict .16 .40
2 Jonathan Boone .16 .40
3 Michael Couch .16 .40
4 Dany Dallaire .30 .75
5 Bruce Gillis .16 .40
6 Nick Greenough .16 .40
7 Milan Jurcina .30 .75
8 Derrick Kent .16 .40
9 Jason King .16 .40
10 Sergei Klyazmin .30 .75
11 Sebastien Laprise .16 .40
12 Jules-Edy Laraque .30 .75
13 Pascal Leclaire 1.25 3.00
14 Hugo Lehoux .16 .40
15 Ali MacEachern .16 .40
16 A.J. Maclean .16 .40
17 Ryan MacPherson .16 .40
18 Louis Mandeville .16 .40
19 Conor McGuire .16 .40
20 Jules Saulnier .16 .40
21 Giulio Scandella .16 .40
22 Robbie Sutherland .16 .40
23 Randy Upshall .16 .40
24 Ryan White .16 .40
25 Gary Zinck .16 .40
26 Team CL .16 .01

2001-02 Halifax Mooseheads

COMPLETE SET (26) 18.00
1 Dany Dallaire 1.00
2 Jonathan Boutin .75
3 Milan Jurcina 1.00
4 Bobby Clarke .75
5 Sergei Klyazmin .75
6 Francois-Pierre Guenette .75
7 A.J. MacLean .75
8 Bruce Gillis .75
9 Jason King 1.25
10 Derrick Kent .75
11 Giulio Scandella .75
12 Jean-Francois Cyr .75
13 Michael Couch .75
14 Robbie Sutherland .75
15 Ryan White .75
16 Randy Upshall .75
17 Patrick Gilbert .75
18 Brandon Benedict .75
19 Marc-Andre Bernier 1.00
20 Louis-Philippe Lessard .75
21 Alexandre Picard .75
22 Louis Mandeville .75
23 Action Shot 1 .25
24 Action Shot 2 .25
25 Action Shot 3 .25
26 Checklist .01

2002-03 Halifax Mooseheads

This set was issued by the Halifax Mooseheads of the QMJHL. The set is unnumbered and listed below in checklist order.

COMPLETE SET (22) 5.00 10.00
1 Checklist .01
2 Guillaume Lavallee .50
3 Jonathan Boutin .50
4 Milan Jurcina 1.00
5 Stuart McRae .50
6 Francois-Pierre Guenette .50
7 A.J. MacLean .50
8 Kyle Doucet .50
9 Thatcher Bell .50
10 Derrick Kent .50
11 Petr Vrana 1.50
12 Frederik Cabana .50
13 Jean-Francois Cyr .50
14 Jordie Preston .50
15 George Davis .50
16 Randy Upshall .50
17 Brandon Benedict .50
18 Marc-Andre Bernier 1.00
19 Colby MacIntyre .50
20 Jimmy Sharrow .50
21 Alexandre Picard 2.00
22 Steve Villeneuve .50

2003-04 Halifax Mooseheads

COMPLETE SET (26) 15.00
1 Jimmy Sharrow .75
2 Bobby Clarke .50
3 James Pouliot .50
4 Justin Munden .50
5 Evan Jones .50
6 Daniel Sparre .50
7 Petr Vrana 1.00
8 George Davis .50
9 Frederik Cabana .50
10 Jared Vokey .50
11 Jan Steber .50
12 Justin Saulnier .50
13 Jason Churchill .75
14 Ryan Moore .50
15 Randy Upshall .50
16 Sebastien Nolet .75
17 Federick Sonier .50
18 Jean-Francois Brault .50
19 Colby MacIntyre .50
20 Franklin MacDonald .50
21 David Brine .50
22 Pierre-Olivier Beaulieu .50
23 Luciano Lomanno .50
24 Kenzie Sheppard .50
NNO Petr Vrana TL 1.00
NNO Jimmy Sharrow TL .75

2004-05 Halifax Mooseheads

A total of 900 team sets were produced. There is a variation of card #4. The first version featured David Brine with a full cage and a different sweater number. The card was pulled and replaced with an updated photo. A few of the original version made their way into packs, although these all are found with a large black X over the image.

COMPLETE SET (26) 15.00
1 Alexandre Picard 1.00
2 Bryce Swan .50
3 Daniel Sparre .50
4A David Brine 20.00
full cage, X
4B David Brine .50
common version
5 Francois-Pierre Guenette .50
6 Franklin MacDonald .50
7 Frederik Cabana .50
8 James Pouliot .50
9 Jan Steber .50
10 Jason Churchill 1.00
11 Jean-Francois Brault .50
12 Jeff MacAuley .50
13 Jimmy Sharrow .50
14 Ryan Moore .50
15 Justin Saulnier .50
16 Kenzie Sheppard .50
17 Kevin Cormier .50
18 Luciano Lomanno .50
19 Marc-Andre Bernier 1.00
20 Petr Vrana 1.00
21 Pierre-Olivier Beaulieu .50
22 Rane Carnegie .75
23 Roger Kennedy 1.00
24 Ryan Hillier .50
25 Austin Corredato .50
26 Jeremy Duchesne 1.00

2005-06 Halifax Mooseheads

COMPLETE SET (25) 8.00 20.00
1 Jeremy Duchesne .30 .75
2 Roger Kennedy .30 .75
3 Andrew Bodnarchuk .60 1.50
4 Jiri Suchy .30 .75
5 Luciano Lomanno .30 .75
6 Rane Carnegie .30 .75
7 James Pouliot .30 .75
8 Garrett Peters .30 .75
9 Kirk Forrest .30 .75
10 Bryce Swan .30 .75
11 Ryan Hillier .30 .75
12 Justin Saulnier .30 .75
13 Philippe Poirier .30 .75
14 Logan MacMillan .30 .75
15 Daniel Smith .30 .75
16 Ben Macaskill .30 .75
17 Kevin Cormier .30 .75
18 Brent Lynch .30 .75
19 Justin Pender .30 .75
20 Jean-Francois Brault .30 .75
21 Mikhail Aseev .30 .75
22 Franklin MacDonald .30 .75
23 David Brine .30 .75
24 Yuri Cheremetiev .30 .75
25 Frederik Cabana .30 .75

2006-07 Halifax Mooseheads

COMPLETE SET (21) 10.00 18.00
1 Jeremy Duchesne .40 1.00
2 Andrew Bodnarchuk .40 1.00
3 Roger Kennedy .40 1.00
4 Jiri Suchy .30 .75
5 Luciano Lomanno .30 .75
6 Ryan Seymour .30 .75
7 James Pouliot .30 .75
8 Garrett Peters .30 .75
9 Logan Macmillan .30 .75
10 Benjamin Chaisson .30 .75
11 Daniel Smith .30 .75
12 Bryce Swan .30 .75
13 Ryan Hillier .30 .75
14 Jakub Voracek 1.25 3.00
15 Andrew White .30 .75
16 Justin Pender .30 .75
17 Ben Macaskill .30 .75
18 Gabriel O'Connor .30 .75
19 Colby Pridham .30 .75
20 Yuri Cheremetiev .30 .75
21 Eric Louis-Seize .30 .75

1975-76 Hamilton Fincups

This 18-card standard-size set features sepia-tone player portraits. The player's name and position are printed in the lower border, which is also sepia-tone. The team name is superimposed over the picture at the bottom center. The backs are blank and grayish in color. The cards are unnumbered and checklisted below in alphabetical order.

COMPLETE SET (18) 15.00 30.00
1 Jack Anderson .75 1.50
2 Mike Clarke .75 1.50
3 Greg Clause .75 1.50
4 Joe Contini .75 1.50
5 Mike Fedorko .75 1.50
6 Paul Foley .75 1.50
7 Greg Hickey .75 1.50
8 Tony Horvath .75 1.50
9 Mike Keating .75 1.50
10 Archie King .75 1.50
11 Ted Long .75 1.50
12 Dale McCourt 2.50 5.00
13 Dave Norris .75 1.50
14 Greg Redquest .75 1.50
15 Glen Richardson .75 1.50
16 Ron Roscoe .75 1.50
17 Ric Seiling 1.25 2.50
18 Danny Shearer .75 1.50

1999-00 Hamilton Bulldogs

This set features the Bulldogs of the AHL. The cards were produced by SplitSecond and were sold at home games and by mail order.

COMPLETE SET (25) 4.00 10.00
1 Mike Minard .30 .75
2 Chris Hajt .16 .40
3 Brad Norton .16 .40
4 Walt Kyle CO .10 .25
5 Eric Houde .16 .40
6 Kevin Bolibruck .16 .40
7 Daniel Cleary .20 .50
8 Vladimir Vorobiev .20 .50
9 Dan LaCouture .20 .50
10 Brian Swanson .20 .50
11 Martin Laitre .16 .40
12 Peter Sarno .20 1.00
13 Alex Zhurik .16 .40
14 Chad Hinz .16 .40
15 Kevin Brown .16 .40
16 Matthieu Descoteaux .16 .40
17 Jason Chimera .40 1.00
18 Alex Henry .30 .75
19 Sean Selmser .20 .50
20 Ryan Risidore .16 .40
21 Michel Riesen .40 .75
22 Sergei Yerkovich .16 .40
23 Elias Abrahamsson .16 .40
24 Eric Heffler .16 .40
25 Bruiser MASCOT .10 .25

2000-01 Hamilton Bulldogs

This set features the Bulldogs of the AHL. The set was produced by the team and sold at its souvenir stands late in the season.

COMPLETE SET (28) 4.80 12.00
1 Chris Madden .30 .75
2 Terran Sandwith .16 .40
3 Ryan Risidore .16 .40
4 Kurt Drummond .16 .40
5 Chris Hajt .16 .40
6 Brad Norton .16 .40
7 Maxim Spiridonov .16 .40
8 Patrick Cote .30 .75
9 Alex Henry .30 .75
10 Paul Healey .16 .40
11 Jason Chimera .40 1.00
12 Peter Sarno .30 .75
13 Brian Urick .16 .40
14 Michael Henrich .16 .40
15 Brian Swanson .20 .50
16 Martin Laitre .16 .40
17 Chris Albert .16 .40
18 Fernando Pisani .16 1.00
19 Lloyd Shaw .16 .40
20 Scott Ferguson .16 .40
21 Michel Riesen .40 1.00
22 Alain Nasreddine .16 .40
23 Chad Hinz .16 .40
24 Joaquin Gage .30 .75
25 Claude Julien CO .10 .25
26 Morey Gare CO .10 .25
27 Bruiser MASCOT .04 .10
28 Team CL .10 .01

2001-02 Hamilton Bulldogs

This set features the Bulldogs of the AHL. It was created by the well-known card shop CTM Ste-Foy, and was sold at that store, as well as by the team. Less than 1,000 sets were reportedly produced.

COMPLETE SET (26) 4.80 12.00
1 Ales Pisa .20 .50
2 Chris Hajt .20 .50
3 Alex Henry .31 .78
4 Jan Horacek .20 .50
5 Kevin Brown .20 .50
6 Jason Chimera .40 1.00
7 Peter Sarno .20 .50
8 Craig Reichert .20 .50
9 Greg Leeb .20 .50
10 Marc-Andre Bergeron .20 .50
11 Brian Swanson .20 .50
12 Jani Rita .40 1.00
13 Fernando Pisani .20 .50
14 Michael Henrich .20 .50
15 Sean Selmser .20 .50
16 Ty Conklin .40 1.00
17 Alain Nasreddine .20 .50
18 Alexei Semenov .31 .78
19 Adam Dewan .20 .50
20 Marc Lamothe .31 .78
21 Sven Butenschon .20 .50
22 Chad Hinz .20 .50
23 Claude Julien CO .04 .11
24 Geoff Ward ACO .04 .11
25 Bruiser Mascot .04 .11
NNO Title Card/CL .04 .11

2002-03 Hamilton Bulldogs

COMPLETE SET (28) 8.00 20.00
1 Bobby Allen .20 .50
2 Ben Carpentier .20 .50
3 Ron Hainsey .40 1.00
4 Tony Salmelainen .20 .50
5 Chad Hinz .20 .50
6 Nate DiCasmirro .20 .50
7 Tomas Plekanec .40 1.00
8 Jason Ward .30 .75
9 Jarret Stoll .40 1.00
10 Matt O'Dette .20 .50
11 Marc-Andre Bergeron .20 .50
12 Jani Rita .30 .75
13 Francois Beauchemin .40 1.00
14 Fernando Pisani .30 .75
15 Michael Ryder 1.25 3.00
16 Michael Henrich .20 .50
17 Ty Conklin .30 .75
18 Eric Fichaud .30 .75
19 Alexei Semenov .20 .50
20 Adam Dewan .20 .50
21 Mathieu Garon .40 1.00
22 Benoit Gratton .20 .50
23 Francois Bouillon .30 .75
24 Mike Komisarek .30 .75
25 Jozef Balej .40 1.00
26 Marcel Hossa .40 1.00
27 Bruiser MASCOT .02 .10
28 Checklist .01 .01

2004-05 Hamilton Bulldogs

COMPLETE SET (30) 20.00
1 Andrew Archer .50
2 Ben Carpentier .50
3 JP Cote .50
4 Trevor Daley .50
5 Yann Danis 1.50
6 Benoit Dusablon .50
7 Dan Ellis 1.50
8 Jonathan Ferland .50
9 Dan Focht .50
10 Ron Hainsey 1.00
11 Chris Higgins 1.00
12 Raitis Ivanans .50
13 Dan Jancevski .50
14 Doug Jarvis CO .10
15 Andrei Kostitsyn 2.50
16 Michael Lambert .50
17 Christian Larrivee .50
18 Corey Locke .50
19 Antti Miettinen 1.00
20 Duncan Milroy .50
21 Gavin Morgan .50
22 Steve Ott 1.50
23 Tomas Plekanec 1.00
24 Philippe Plante .50
25 James Sanford .50
26 Matt Shasby .50
27 Marc-Andre Thinel .75
28 Jason Ward .75
29 Ron Wilson ACO .10
30 Bruiser MASCOT .10

2005-06 Hamilton Bulldogs

COMPLETE SET 6.00 15.00
1 Jonathan Aitken .20 .50
2 Andrew Archer .20 .50
3 Ryan Barnes .20 .50
4 Andre Benoit .20 .50
5 Jean-Philippe Cote .20 .50
6 Yann Danis .40 1.00
7 Jeff Drouin-Deslauriers .40 1.00
8 Jonathan Ferland .20 .50
9 Ron Hainsey .20 .50
10 Raitis Ivanans .40 1.00
11 Jean-Francois Jacques .20 .50
12 Andrei Kostitsyn .40 1.00
13 Michael Lambert .20 .50
14 Maxim Lapierre .20 .50
15 Francis Lemieux .20 .50
16 Corey Locke .20 .50
17 Olivier Michaud .40 1.00
18 Duncan Milroy .20 .50
19 Garth Murray .20 .50
20 Jeff Paul .20 .50
21 Marc-Antoine Pouliot .40 1.00
22 Mathieu Roy .75 2.00
23 James Sanford .20 .50
24 Dan Smith .20 .50
25 Danny Syvret .20 .50
26 Peter Vandermeer .40 1.00
27 Brad Winchester .20 .50
28 Don Lever .02 .10
29 Ron Wilson .02 .10
30 Bruiser .02 .10

2006-07 Hamilton Bulldogs

COMPLETE SET (26) 8.00 15.00
1 Andrew Archer .20 .50
2 Mathieu Aubin .20 .50
3 Ajay Baines .20 .50
4 Andre Benoit .20 .50
5 Kyle Chipchura .30 .75
6 Jean-Philippe Cote .20 .50
7 Matt D'Agostini .20 .50
8 Yann Danis .30 .75
9 Eric Manlow .20 .50
10 Jonathan Ferland .20 .50
11 Jon Gleed .20 .50
12 Mikhail Grabovsky .20 .50
13 Danny Groulx .20 .50
14 Jaroslav Halak .75 2.00
15 Dan Jancevski .20 .50
16 Andrei Kostitsyn .40 1.00
17 Michael Lambert .20 .50
18 Maxim Lapierre .30 .75
19 Francis Lemieux .20 .50
20 Corey Locke .20 .50
21 Duncan Milroy .20 .50
22 Ryan O'Byrne .20 .50
23 Mathieu Roy .40 1.00
24 Zach Stortini .40 1.00
25 Patrick Traverse .20 .50
26 Cory Urquhart .20 .50

1992-93 Hamilton Canucks

Created by Diamond Memories Sportscards to commemorate the Canucks' inaugural season, these 30 standard-size cards feature black-bordered color player action photos on the fronts. The cards are unnumbered and checklisted below in alphabetical order.

COMPLETE SET (30) 4.00 10.00
1 Shawn Antoski .30 .75
2 Robin Bawa .14 .35
3 Jamie Carlson TR .04 .10
4 Jassen Cullimore .20 .50
5 Alain Deeks .14 .35
6 Neil Eisenhut .14 .35
7 Mike Fountain .30 .75
8 Troy Gamble .30 .75
9 Jason Herter .14 .35
10 Pat Hickey PR .04 .10
11 Dane Jackson .14 .35
12 Dan Kesa .14 .35
13 Jeff Lumby ANN .04 .10
14 Mario Marois UER .20 .50
(Last name misspelled Marios on front)
15 Bob Mason .30 .75
16 Mike Maurice .14 .35
17 Jay Mazur .14 .35
18 Jack McIlhargey CO .04 .10
19 Sandy Moger .30 .75
20 Stephane Morin .14 .35
21 Eric Murano .14 .35
22 Troy Neumeier .14 .35
23 Matt Newsom GM .04 .10
24 Libor Polasek .14 .35
25 Phil von Stefenelli .14 .35
26 Doug Torrel .14 .35
27 Doug Tretiak TR .04 .10
28 Rick Vaive CO .14 .35
29 Opening Night .14 .35
Puck-Drop
Mario Marois
Pat Hickey PR
AHL President
30 Team Photo .20 .50
(Checklist)

1961-62 Hamilton Red Wings

This oversized set features members of the top farm team of the Red Wings. They were sold as a set by the team.

COMPLETE SET (21) 37.50 75.00
1 Bud Blom 1.50 3.00
2 Eddie Bush 2.00 4.00
3 Bob Dean 1.50 3.00
4 John Gofton 1.50 3.00
5 Bob Hamilton 1.50 3.00
6 Bob Hamilton 1.50 3.00
7 Ron Harris 2.00 4.00
8 Earl Heiskala 2.00 4.00
9 Paul Henderson 7.50 15.00
10 Roger Lafreniere 1.50 3.00
11 Lowell Macdonald 4.00 8.00
12 Pit Martin 5.00 10.00
13 Jim Mclellan 1.50 3.00
14 Harvey Meisenheimer 1.50 3.00
15 Howie Menard 1.50 3.00
16 Wayne Rivers 4.00 8.00
17 Jim Peters 2.00 4.00
18 Bob Wall 1.50 3.00
19 Jack Wildfong 1.50 3.00
20 Terry Urkewicz 1.50 3.00
21 Larry Zilliotto 1.50 3.00

1989-90 Hampton Roads Admirals

This 21-card set of the Hampton Roads Admirals of the ECHL features color photos on the front. The cards are unnumbered, and are listed below in alphabetical order. We've recently learned that 19 of the 21 cards have variations, ie, one version showing a head shot, the other an action shot. We've listed them with letter suffixes detailing action (A) or head shot (H). A complete set includes only one version or the other. We cannot say which (if either) is more scarce, so we are showing no price difference between the two versions for the time being. The set, which last year was valued at $10, was the subject of fierce bidding wars each time it appeared on eBay in 2005 and earned one of the greatest value jumps in recent memory.

COMPLETE SET (21) 4.00 400.00
1A Mike Black .20 20.00
1H Mike Black
2 John Brophy CO .20 25.00
3A David Buckley .20 20.00
3H David Buckley
4A Pat Cavanagh .20 20.00
4H Pat Cavanagh
5A Mike Flanagan .20 20.00
5H Mike Flanagan
6A Frank Furlan .20 20.00
6H Frank Furlan
7A Don Gagne .20 20.00
7H Don Gagne
8A Steve Greenberg .20 20.00
8H Steve Greenberg
9A Murray Hood .20 20.00
9H Murray Hood
10A Trevor Jobe .20 20.00
10H Trevor Jobe
11A Trevor Kruger .20 20.00
11H Trevor Kruger
12A Chris Lukey .20 20.00
12H Chris Lukey
13A Brian Martin .20 20.00
13H Brian Martin
14A Dennis McEwen .20 20.00
14H Dennis McEwen
15A Bobby McGrath .20 20.00
15H Bobby McGrath
16A Darren Miciak .20 20.00
16H Darren Miciak
17A Al Murphy .20 20.00
17H Al Murphy
18A Jody Praznik .20 20.00
18H Jody Praznik
19A Alain Raymond .20 20.00
19H Alain Raymond
20A Wayne Stripp .20 20.00
20H Wayne Stripp
21 Scott Taylor .20 20.00

1990-91 Hampton Roads Admirals

This 20-card set was issued by the Hampton Roads Admirals of the ECHL. They feature color action photography on the front, along with another photo and statistical information on the back. The numbering of the set is a mystery, as it clearly carries on from another issue. Interestingly, the previous year's Admirals set is unnumbered. The set, therefore, may be numbered consecutively with other ECHL issues from the same season.

COMPLETE SET (20) 3.20 8.00
41 Scott King .20 .50
42 Greg Bignell .16 .40
43 David Buckley .16 .40
44 Jody Praznik .16 .40
45 John East .16 .40
46 Steve Greenberg .16 .40
47 Darcy Kaminski .16 .40
48 Glen Kehrer .16 .40
49 Murray Hood .16 .40
50 Dennis McEwen .16 .40
51 Billy Nolan .16 .40
52 Bill Thomas .16 .40

53 Pat Cavanagh .16 .40
54 Cory Banika .20 .50
55 Al Murphy .16 .40
56 Harry Mews .16 .40
57 Mark Bernard .16 .40
58 Brian Martin .16 .40
59 Curt Brackenbury ACO .10 .25
60 John Brophy CO .16 .40

1991-92 Hampton Roads Admirals

This 20-card set was produced by the team and available at the rink. The cards feature action photos on the front, with stats and bio on the back. This set, which features an early pro card of Olaf Kolzig, is unnumbered, and listed below alphabetically.

COMPLETE SET (20) 4.00 50.00
1 Mark Bernard .16 3.00
2 Mike Chighisola .16 2.00
3 John East .16 2.00
4 Victor Gervais .16 2.00
5 Murray Hood .16 2.00
6 Scott Johnson .16 2.00
7 Olaf Kolzig 1.60 15.00
8 Paul Krepelka .16 2.00
9 Al MacIsaac .16 2.00
10 Brian Martin .16 2.00
11 Dennis McEwen .16 2.00
12 Dave Morissette .16 2.00
13 Billy Nolan .16 2.00
14 Randy Pearce .16 2.00
15 Steve Poapst .20 3.00
16 Pete Siciliano .16 2.00
17 Shawn Snesar .16 2.00
18 Keith Whitmore .16 2.00
19 John Brophy CO .16 1.00
20 Darcy Kaminski ACO .04 .10

1992-93 Hampton Roads Admirals

This set is unnumbered and was sponsored by Ward's Corner Sporting Goods, Ogden Services, and radio station WCMS. The set is listed by the order of the player's jersey number, which is listed on the back.

COMPLETE SET (20) 3.20 8.00
1 Shawn Snesar .20 .50
2 Paul Krepelka .20 .50
3 Claude Barthe .20 .50
4 Steve Poapst .30 .75
5 Kelly Sorenson .20 .50
6 Trevor Duhaime .20 .50
7 Steve Mirabile .20 .50
8 Kurt Kabat .20 .50
9 Victor Gervais .24 .60
10 Jason Rathbone .20 .50
11 Rod Taylor .20 .50
12 Al MacIsaac CO .10 .25
13 Brian Martin .20 .50
14 Dave Morissette .20 .50
15 Harry Mews .20 .50
16 Mark Bernard .20 .50
17 Nick Vitucci .30 .75
18 Steve Martell .20 .50
19 Chris Scarlata TR .04 .10
20 John Brophy CO .20 .50

1993-94 Hampton Roads Admirals

This set features the Admirals of the ECHL. The set was sponsored by Ward's Corner Sporting Goods, Ogden Services and radio station WCMS. The set is nearly identical in design to the previous year's set. The cards are unnumbered, and so they are listed alphabetically.

COMPLETE SET (20) 3.20 8.00
1 John Brophy CO .20 .50
2 Rick Burrill TR .04 .10
3 Daniel Chaput .20 .50
4 Brendan Curley .20 .50
5 Victor Gervais .20 .50
6 Brian Goudie .20 .50
7 Shamus Gregga .20 .50
8 Jason MacIntyre .20 .50
9 Al MacIsaac ACO .04 .10
10 Kevin Malgunas .20 .50
11 Dennis McEwen .20 .50
12 Mark Michaud .20 .50
13 Ron Pascucci .20 .50
14 Darren Perkins .20 .50
15 Steven Perkovic .20 .50
16 Shawn Snesar .20 .50
17 Kelly Sorenson .20 .50
18 Rod Taylor .20 .50
19 Richie Walcott .20 .50
20 Shawn Wheeler .20 .50

1994-95 Hampton Roads Admirals

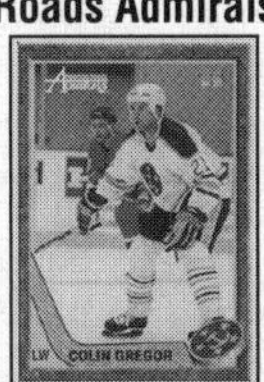

This 23-card set measures the standard size. On a white card face, the fronts feature color action player photos with a simulated blue marble frame and a thin yellow, inner border. The player's name appears inside a hockey stick on the bottom of the photo, with the team logo next to it.

COMPLETE SET (23) 4.80 12.00
1 John Brophy CO .20 .50
2 Al MacIsaac ACO .04 .10
3 Patrick Lalime 2.00 5.00
4 Colin Gregor .16 .40
5 Ron Pascucci .16 .40
6 John Porco .16 .40
7 Trevor Halverson .20 .50
8 Rod Taylor .16 .40
9 Brian Goudie .16 .40
10 Chris Phelps .16 .40
11 Tom Menicci .16 .40
12 Anthony MacAulay .16 .40
13 Rick Kowalsky .16 .40
14 Dennis McEwen .16 .40
15 Kelly Sorenson .16 .40
16 Brendan Curley .16 .40
17 Jason MacIntyre .16 .40
18 Jim Brown .16 .40
19 Matt Mallgrave .16 .40
20 Ron Majic .16 .40
21 Corwin Saurdiff .16 .40
22 Rick Burrill TR .04 .10
23 Team Photo CL .16 .40
NNO Logo Card .04 .10

1995-96 Hampton Roads Admirals

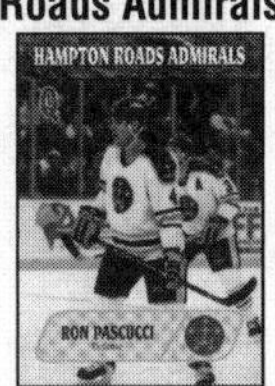

This 25-card set showcases the Hampton Roads Admirals of the ECHL. The set was produced by Q-Cards, and distributed by Ward's Corner Sporting Goods; it may also have been sold through the team at games. The set features action photography on the front and an expanded player information section on the numbered back.

COMPLETE SET (25) 4.00 10.00
1 Team Photo .16 .40
2 John Brophy CO .16 .40
3 Al MacIsaac ACO .04 .10
4 Darryl Paquette .20 .50
5 Mark Bernard .16 .40
6 Ron Pascucci .16 .40
7 Dominic Maltais .16 .40
8 Jason MacIntyre .16 .40
9 Serge Aubin .40 1.00
10 Rick Kowalsky .10 .25
11 Claude Fillion .20 .50
12 Rod Taylor .16 .40
13 Alexei Krivchenkov .16 .40
14 David St. Pierre .16 .40
15 Steve Richards .16 .40
16 Trevor Halverson .30 .75
17 Chris Phelps .16 .40
18 Jeff Kostuch .16 .40
19 Sean Selmser .30 .75
20 Aaron Downey .40 1.00
21 Bob Woods .16 .40
22 Sergei Voronov .16 .40
23 Corwin Saurdiff .20 .50
24 Rick Burrell TR .04 .10
25 Gary Mansfield EQMG .04 .10

1997-98 Hampton Roads Admirals

This 24-card set was produced by a former player with the Ads and was handed out as a promotional giveaway at a home game.

COMPLETE SET (24) 7.20 18.00
1 Chad Ackerman .30 .75
2 Alexander Alexeev .30 .75
3 Rob Bonneau .30 .75
4 Dan Carney .30 .75
5 Dan Ceman .40 1.00
6 Sebastien Charpentier .40 1.00
7 Marty Clapton .30 .75
8 Victor Gervais .30 .75
9 Alexander Kharlamov .40 1.00
10 Rick Kowalsky .30 .75
11 Mike Larkin .30 .75
12 Bill Lincoln .30 .75
13 Ron Majic .30 .75
14 Jason Mansoff .30 .75
15 Chris Phelps .30 .75
16 Joel Poirier .30 .75
17 Jason Saal .60 1.50
18 Kayle Short .30 .75
19 Rod Taylor .30 .75
20 Joel Theriault .30 .75
21 Yuri Yuresko .30 .75
22 John Brophy HCO .20 .50
23 Al MacIsaac ACO .04 .10
24 Trainers .04 .10

1996-97 Hampton Roads Admirals

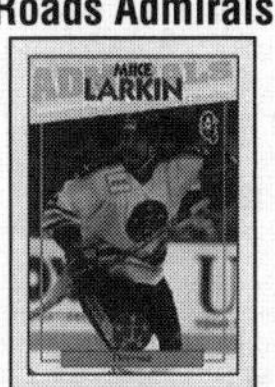

This 25-card set of the Hampton Roads Admirals of the ECHL was produced by Blueline Communications, and sponsored by Kline Chevrolet and The Score, 1310 AM. The cards feature action photos on the front, along with the player name. The backs include statistical and biographical data.

COMPLETE SET (25) 4.00 10.00
HRA1 Darryl Paquette .20 .50
HRA2 Mike Larkin .16 .40
HRA3 Chris Phelps .16 .40
HRA4 Alex Alexeev .16 .40
HRA5 Joel Theriault .16 .40
HRA6 Neal Martin .16 .40
HRA7 Ryan Mulhern .16 .40
HRA8 Darryl Shedden .16 .40
HRA9 Victor Gervais .16 .40
HRA10 Rod Taylor .16 .40
HRA11 Andy Weidenbach .16 .40
HRA12 Alain Savage .16 .40
HRA13 Randy Pearce .16 .40
HRA14 Chad Ackerman .16 .40
HRA15 Alexei Krivchenkov .16 .40
HRA16 Rick Kowalsky .16 .40
HRA17 Dominic Maltais .16 .40
HRA18 Joel Poirier .20 .50
HRA19 Marc Seliger .30 .75
HRA20 Aaron Downey .30 .75
HRA21 John Brophy CO .20 .50
HRA22 Al MacIsaac ACO .04 .10
HRA23 G.Mansfield EQMG .04 .10
K.Bender TR
HRA24 Salty (Mascot) .04 .10
NNO Team Photo .16 .40

1998-99 Hampton Roads Admirals

This 26-card set was handed out as a promotional giveaway at an Admirals game. Little else is known about the set, other than a confirmation that two versions of card #25 were released.

COMPLETE SET (26) 6.00 15.00
1 Mascot/Checklist .10 .25
2 John Brophy .20 .50
3 Al MacIsaac ACO .10 .25
4 Chris Phelps .20 .50
5 Trevor Johnson .20 .50
6 Jami Yoder .20 .50
7 Joel Poirier .30 .75
8 Alexander Kharlamov .30 .75
9 Bobby Russell .20 .50
10 Trever Fraser .20 .50
11 Jason Deleurme .20 .50
12 Henry Higdon .20 .50
13 Rod Taylor .20 .50
14 Jeff Corbett .20 .50
15 Derek Ernest .20 .50
16 Charlie Retter .20 .50
17 Chad Ackerman .20 .50
18 Boris Zelenko .20 .50
19 Dan Ceman .30 .75
20 Marty Clapton .20 .50
21 Milt Mastad .20 .50
22 Dominic Maltais .30 .75
23 Stephen Valiquette .80 2.00
24 Jason Saal .40 1.00
25 Scott Boggs EM .10 .25
25 Stu Bender TR .10 .25

1998-99 Hampton Roads Admirals 10th Anniversary

This 30-card set was handed out at a game in December, and features alumni of the Admirals, including several prominent NHLers. Because of the unique distribution method, the cards are quite scarce.

COMPLETE SET (30) 10.00 25.00
1 John Brophy HCO .20 .50
2 Rod Taylor .20 .50
3 Victor Gervais .20 .50
4 Brian Martin .20 .50
5 Dennis McEwen .20 .50
6 Chris Phelps .20 .50
7 Randy Pearce .20 .50
8 Murray Hood .20 .50
9 Olaf Kolzig 2.00 5.00
10 Kelly Sorenson .20 .50
11 Mark Bernard .20 .50
12 Andrew Brunette .40 1.00
13 Trevor Halverson .20 .50
14 Rick Kowalsky .20 .50
15 Aaron Downey .80 2.00
16 Patrick Lalime 1.60 4.00
17 Steve Poapst .30 .75
18 Alexander Alexeev .20 .50
19 Harry Mews .20 .50
20 Al MacIsaac .20 .50
21 John Parco .20 .50
22 Kent Hawley .20 .50
23 Dave Flanagan .20 .50
24 Billy Nolan .20 .50
25 Brendan Curley .20 .50
26 Ron Pascucci .20 .50
27 Mark Michaud .20 .50
28 Shawn Snesar .20 .50
29 Byron Dafoe 1.60 3.00
30 Sebastien Charpentier .40 1.00

1999-00 Hampton Roads Admirals

This set features the Admirals of the ECHL. The set was produced by Q-Cards and issued as a promotional giveaway at a home game, and later at Ragazzi's, a local restaurant.

COMPLETE SET (25) 8.00 20.00
1 Chad Ackerman .30 .75
2 Gerad Adams .30 .75
3 Louis Bedard .40 1.00
4 Brad Church .40 1.00
5 Marty Clapton .30 .75
6 Curtis Cruickshank .40 1.00
7 Derek Ernest .30 .75
8 Ryan Gillis .30 .75
9 Trevor Johnson .30 .75
10 Rick Kowalsky .30 .75
11 Jan Lasak 1.20 3.00
12 Dominic Maltais .40 1.00
13 Mike Omicioli .30 .75
14 John Parco .30 .75
15 Dwight Parrish .30 .75
16 Colin Pepperall .30 .75
17 Richard Pitirri .30 .75
18 Bobby Russell .30 .75
19 Mike Siklenka .30 .75
20 Dean Stork .30 .75
21 Rod Taylor .30 .75
22 John Brophy CO .10 .25
23 Al MacIsaac CO .10 .25
24 Stu Bender/Scott Boggs TR .10 .25
NNO Checklist .10 .25

1997-98 Hartford Wolf Pack

This set features the Wolf Pack of the AHL. The singles are postcard-sized, and were issued only to members of the team's Kid's Club.

COMPLETE SET (29) 12.00 35.00
1 Derek Armstrong .30 1.00
2 Sylvain Blouin .40 1.50
3 Eric Cairns .40 1.50
4 Dan Cloutier 1.20 4.00
5 Christian Dube .30 1.00
6 Peter Ferraro .40 1.50
7 Maxim Galanov .30 1.00
8 Ken Gernander .30 1.00
9 Daniel Goneau .30 1.00
10 Todd Hall .30 1.00
11 Johan Lindbom .30 1.00
12 Mike Martin .30 1.00
13 Jason Muzzatti .40 1.50
14 Dale Purinton .80 2.00
15 Marc Savard .60 2.00
16 Pierre Sevigny .30 1.00
17 Adam Smith .30 1.00
18 Geoff Smith .30 1.00
19 Brad Smyth .30 1.00
20 Lee Sorochan .30 1.00
21 Robb Stauber .40 1.50
22 P.J. Stock 1.20 4.00
23 Ronnie Sundin .30 1.00
24 Tim Sweeney .30 1.00
25 Brent Thompson .30 1.00
26 Ryan VandenBussche .80 2.00
27 Vladimir Vorobiev .30 1.00
28 Chris Winnes .30 1.00
29 Sonar MASCOT .10 .25

1998-99 Hartford Wolf Pack

This set features the Wolf Pack of the AHL. The set was given only to members of the team's Kid's Club. The cards bear the logos of Brigham's Ice Cream.

COMPLETE SET (28) 14.00 35.00
1 Derek Armstrong .40 1.00
2 Jeff Brown .40 1.00
3 Ed Campbell .40 1.00
4 Ben Carpentier .40 1.00
5 Christian Dube .40 1.00
6 Bob Errey .40 1.00
7 Jeff Finley .40 1.00
8 Ken Gernander .40 1.00
9 Daniel Goneau .40 1.00
10 Todd Hall .40 1.00
11 Boyd Kane .80 2.00
12 Jean-Francois Labbe .80 2.00
13 Mike Martin .40 1.00
14 Dale Purinton .60 1.50
15 Ryan Risidore .40 1.00
16 Marc Savard .80 2.00
17 Adam Smith .40 1.00
18 Lee Sorochan .60 1.50
19 P.J. Stock 2.00 8.00
20 Brent Thompson .40 1.00
21 Alexei Vasiliev .40 1.00
22 Vladimir Vorobiev .40 1.00
23 Kay Whitmore .60 1.50
24 Chris Winnes .40 1.00
25 Johan Witehall .40 1.00
26 Sonar MASCOT .10 .25
27 Rich Brennan .40 1.00
28 Stefan Cherneski .40 1.00

1999-00 Hartford Wolf Pack

This set features the Wolf Pack of the AHL. These cards were handed out to members of the team's Kid's Club at a special practice. The cards are blank-backed and unnumbered, and therefore are listed in alphabetical order.

COMPLETE SET (23) 12.00 30.00
1 Derek Armstrong .40 1.00
2 Drew Bannister .40 1.00
3 Ben Carpentier .40 1.00
4 Stefan Cherneski .40 1.00
5 Jason Doig .60 1.50
6 Francois Fortier .40 1.00
7 Ken Gernander .40 1.00
8 Daniel Goneau .40 1.00
9 Todd Hall .40 1.00
10 Mike Harder .40 1.00
11 Burke Henry .40 1.00
12 Milan Hnilicka 1.60 4.00
13 Chris Kenady .40 1.00
14 Tomas Kloucek .80 2.00
15 Alexander Korobolin .40 1.00
16 Jean-Francois Labbe .80 2.00
17 Dale Purinton .80 2.00
18 Brad Smyth .60 1.50
19 P.J. Stock 1.20 3.00
20 Tony Tuzzolino .60 1.50
21 Alexei Vasiliev .40 1.00
22 Terry Virtue .60 1.50
23 Johan Witehall .60 1.50

2000-01 Hartford Wolf Pack

This set features the Wolf Pack of the AHL. The set was a very tough giveaway item, available only to members of the team's youth fan club. The cards are unnumbered and blank-backed. Three of the cards (Grosek, Labarbera and Mehalko) do not feature names on the front.

COMPLETE SET (29) 10.00 25.00
1 Derek Armstrong .30 .75
2 Drew Bannister .30 .75
3 Ryan Bast .30 .75
4 Ben Carpentier .30 .75
5 Jason Dawe .30 .75
6 Brandon Dietrich .30 .75
7 Jason Doig .30 .75
8 Dave Duerden .30 .75
9 Ken Gernander .30 .75
10 Michal Grosek .30 1.00
11 Todd Hall .30 .75
12 Burke Henry .30 .75
13 Johan Holmqvist .80 2.00
14 Boyd Kane .40 1.00
15 Chris Kenady .30 .75
16 Tomas Kloucek .80 2.00
17 Jason Labarbera .80 2.00
18 Manny Malhotra .60 1.00
19 Brad Mehalko .30 .75
20 Mike Mottau .60 1.50
21 Dale Purinton .40 1.00
22 Bert Robertsson .30 .75
23 Richard Scott .40 1.00
24 Brad Smyth .30 .75
25 Tony Tuzzolino .30 .75
26 Jeff Ulmer .30 .75
27 Terry Virtue .40 1.00
28 Vitali Yeremeyev .60 1.50
29 Sonar MASCOT .10 .25

2001-02 Hartford Wolf Pack

This set features the Wolf Pack of the AHL. These very scarce cards were available only to members of the Wolf Pack Kids Club. The cards are blank backed and unnumbered, so they are listed below in alphabetical order. Minor league expert Ralph Slate reports that Igor Ulanov's card was most likely a late addition, as it is printed on thinner card stock than the rest of the set.

COMPLETE SET (26) 19.56 48.89
1 Benoit Dusablon .80 2.00
2 Jason Dawe .80 2.00
3 Rico Fata .80 2.00
4 Sean Gagnon .80 2.00
5 Ken Gernander .40 1.00
6 Christian Gosselin .40 1.00
7 Michal Grosek .40 1.00
8 Barrett Heisten .80 2.00
9 Johan Holmqvist .80 2.00
10 Wes Jarvis .40 1.00
11 Boyd Kane .80 2.00
12 Matt Kinch .40 1.00
13 Jason Labarbera .80 2.00
14 Jamie Lundmark 4.00 10.00
15 Dave MacIsaac .40 1.00
16 Brad Mehalko .40 1.00
17 Scott Meyer .40 1.00
18 Mike Mottau 1.20 3.00
19 Cam Severson .40 1.00
20 Peter Smrek .80 2.00
21 Brad Smyth .40 1.00
22 Chris St. Croix .40 1.00
23 John Tripp .40 1.00
24 Igor Ulanov 4.00 10.00
25 Terry Virtue .80 2.00
26 Sonar MASCOT .20 .50

2002-03 Hartford Wolf Pack

COMPLETE SET (30) 12.00 30.00
1 Bobby Andrews .40 1.00
2 Dean Arsene .40 1.00
3 Patrick Aufiero .40 1.00
4 Ryan Bast .40 1.00
5 Garrett Burnett .40 1.00
6 Ted Donato .40 1.00
7 Benoit Dusablon .75 2.00
8 Nils Ekman .40 1.00
9 Ken Gernander .40 1.00
10 Johan Holmqvist .75 2.00
11 Dave Karpa .40 1.00
12 Matt Kinch .40 1.00
13 Jason Labarbera .75 2.00
14 Bryce Lampman .40 1.00
15 Cory Larose .40 1.00
16 Janne Laukkanen .40 1.00
17 Roman Lyashenko .40 1.00
18 Garth Murray .40 1.00
19 Chris Pittman .40 1.00
20 Richard Scott .40 1.00
21 Billy Tibbetts 1.25 3.00
22 John Tripp .40 1.00
23 Layne Ulmer .40 1.00
24 Dixon Ward .40 1.00
25 Mike Wilson .40 1.00
26 Patrick Yetman .40 1.00
27 Damon Scott ANN .02 .10
28 Nick Fotiu ACO .20 .50
29 Ryan McGill HCO .20 .50
30 Sonar Mascot .02 .10

2003-04 Hartford Wolf Pack

This set was made available to members of the Wolf Pack Kids Club, according to minor league maven Ralph Slate. The cards are oversized, unnumbered, and are listed below in alphabetical order. The card of Jamie Pushor was most likely a late addition, since it is printed on larger card stock than the rest of the set. It was not included in every set distributed by the team and therefore is considered a short print.

COMPLETE SET (27) 50.00
1 Bobby Andrews 1.00
2 Brandon Cullen 1.00
3 Ryan Cuthbert 1.00
4 Benoit Dusablon 2.00
5 Jayme Filipowicz 1.00
6 Ken Gernander 1.00
7 Paul Healey 1.00
8 Jeff Heerema 2.00
9 John Jakopin 1.00
10 Matt Kinch 1.00
11 Jason Labarbera 3.00
12 Bryce Lampman 1.00
13 Cory Larose 1.00
14 Lucas Lawson 1.00
15 Jason MacDonald 1.00
16 Dominic Moore SP 10.00
17 Garth Murray 1.50
18 Lawrence Nycholat 1.00
19 Phil Osaer 1.00
20 Jamie Pushor SP 10.00
21 Richard Scott 2.00
22 Juris Stals 1.00
23 Jeff State 1.00
24 Fedor Tjutin 3.00
25 Layne Ulmer 1.50
26 Craig Weller 1.00
27 Chad Wiseman 1.00

2004-05 Hartford Wolf Pack

Available only to member's of the team's Kid's Club.

COMPLETE SET (26) 60.00
1 Jozef Balej 3.00
2 Blair Betts 2.00
3 Ken Gernander 2.00
4 Trevor Gillies 3.00
5 Alexandre Giroux 3.00
6 Martin Grenier 2.00
7 Jeff Hamilton 2.00
8 Dwight Helminen 2.00
9 Ryan Hollweg 3.00
10 Jason Labarbera 3.00
11 Bryce Lampman 2.00
12 Lucas Lofton 2.00
13 Dave Liffiton 2.00
14 Jamie Lundmark 3.00
15 Steven MacIntyre 2.00
16 Jeff MacMillan 2.00
17 Dominic Moore 2.00
18 Garth Murray 2.00
19 Lawrence Nycholat 2.00
20 Jed Ortmeyer 3.00
21 Thomas Pock 3.00
22 Jake Taylor 2.00
23 Layne Ulmer 2.00
24 Stephen Valiquette 3.00
25 Craig Weller 2.00
26 Chad Wiseman 2.00

2005-06 Hartford Wolf Pack

COMPLETE SET (28) 15.00 30.00
1 Ivan Baranka .40 1.00
2 Nigel Dawes .75 2.00
3 Lee Falardeau .40 1.00
4 Fedor Fedorov .40 1.00
5 Colby Genoway .40 1.00
6 Robert Gherson .40 1.00
7 Daniel Girardi .75 2.00
8 Alexandre Giroux .40 1.00
9 Bruce Graham .40 1.00
10 Martin Grenier .40 1.00
11 Dwight Helminen .40 1.00
12 Jarkko Immonen .40 1.00
13 Hugh Jessiman .40 1.00
14 Bryce Lampman .40 1.00
15 Dave Liffiton .40 1.00
16 Al Montoya .50 4.00
17 Thomas Pock .40 1.00
18 Dale Purinton .75 2.00
19 Joe Rullier .40 1.00
20 Martin Sonnenberg .40 1.00
21 Daniel Sparre .40 1.00
22 Jake Taylor .40 1.00
23 Craig Weller .40 1.00
24 Chad Wiseman .40 1.00
25 Jim Schoenfeld HC .02 .10
26 Ken Gernander AC .02 .10
27 Ulf Samuelsson AC .02 .10
28 Sonar & Torpedo MASCOTS .01 .01

2006-07 Hartford Wolf Pack

COMPLETE SET (28) 25.00 50.00
1 Ryan Constant .60 1.50
2 Hugh Jessiman .60 1.50
3 Mark Lee .60 1.50
4 Bryce Lampman .60 1.50
5 Corey Potter .60 1.50
6 Bruce Graham .60 1.50
7 Zdenek Bahensky .60 1.50
8 Lee Falardeau .60 1.50
9 Daniel Girardi 1.25 3.00
10 Darius Kasparaitis .60 1.50
11 Steve Valiquette .75 2.00
12 Brad Isbister .60 1.50
13 Jarkko Immonen 1.25 3.00
14 Marvin Degon .60 1.50
15 Lauri Korpikoski 1.25 3.00
16 Jake Taylor .60 1.50
17 Nigel Dawes 1.25 3.00
18 Dale Purinton .60 1.50
19 Dane Byers 1.25 3.00
20 Dwight Helminen .60 1.50
21 Greg Moore .60 1.50
22 Martin Richter .60 1.50
23 Craig Weller .60 1.50
24 Ryan Callahan 1.25 3.00
25 Dave Liffiton .60 1.50
26 Al Montoya 1.25 3.00
27 Francis Lessard .60 1.50
28 Brandon Dubinsky .60 1.50

1992-93 Harvard Crimson

As with most NCAA sets, this product is believed to be a promotional giveaway of some kind. The cards are unnumbered and checklisted below in alphabetical order.

COMPLETE SET (31) 8.00 20.00
1 Brian Adams .30 .75
2 Chris Baird .30 .75
3 Lou Body .30 .75
4 Michel Breistroff .30 .75
5 Perry Cohagen .30 .75
6 Ben Coughlin .30 .75
7 Ted Drury .40 1.00
8 Brian Farell .30 .75
9 Steven Flomenhoft .30 .75
10 Eric Grahling .30 .75
11 Cory Gustafson .30 .75
12 Kevin Hampe ACO .04 .10
13 Steve Hermsdorf .30 .75
14 Tom Holmes .30 .75
15 Aaron Israel .30 .75
16 Jason Karmanos .30 .75
17 Ian Kennish .30 .75
18 Brad Konik .30 .75
19 Bryan Lonsinger .30 .75
20 Derek Maguire .40 1.00
21 Matt Mallgrave .30 .75
22 Geb Marett .30 .75
23 Steve Martins .40 1.00
24 Sean McCann .30 .75
25 Peter McLaughlin .30 .75
26 Keith McLean .30 .75
27 Kirk Nielsen .40 1.00
28 Jerry Pawloski ACO .04 .10
29 Ronn Tomassoni CO .04 .10
30 Tripp Tracy .60 1.50
31 Header Card .04 .10

1994-95 Hershey Bears

This 24-card set was handed out at the Bears charity carnival. The cards are blank-backed so they are listed in alphabetical order.

COMPLETE SET (24) 8.00 20.00
1 Vladislav Boulin .40 1.00
2 Aris Brimanis .40 1.00
3 Bruce Coles .40 1.00
4 Yanick Dupre .40 1.00
5 Tracy Egeland .40 1.00
6 Andre Faust .40 1.00
7 Jeff Finley .40 1.00
8 Milos Holan .40 1.00
9 Paul Jerrard .40 1.00
10 Dan Kordic .40 1.00
11 Les Kuntar .60 1.50
12 Mitch Lamoureux .60 1.50
13 Neil Little 1.20 3.00
14 Mike McHugh .40 1.00
15 Clayton Norris .40 1.00
16 Vaclav Prospal .40 2.00
17 Terran Sandwith .40 1.00
18 Ryan Sittler .40 1.00
19 Bob Wilkie .40 1.00
20 Chris Winnes .40 1.00
21 Mike Stothers ACO .04 .10
22 Brad Dibeler ATR .04 .10
23 Jay Leach HCO .04 .10

1998-99 Hershey Bears

This 40-card set was sponsored by the Lebanon Daily News and features players from the 1998-99 Hershey Bears as well as several cards of past players and teams from this AHL franchise. The team photos carry player checklists on the back of each card.

COMPLETE SET (40) 12.00 30.00
1 Evgeny Lazarev .30 .75
(Mitch Lamoureux
2 Marc Denis 1.20 4.00
3 Jeff Buchanan .16 .40
4 Ted Crowley .16 .40
5 Yuri Babenko .16 .40
6 Evgeny Lazarev .30 .75
7 Scott Parker 1.20 3.00
8 Mike Foligno CO .20 .50
9 Rob Shearer .20 .50
10 Brad Larsen .16 .40
11 1946-47 Team Photo .20 .50
12 Rick Berry .20 .50
13 Troy Crowder .16 .40
14 Dan Hinote .60 1.00
15 Serge Aubin .40 1.00
16 1957-58 Team Photo .20 .50
17 1958-89 Team Photo .20 .50
18 1968-69 Team Photo .20 .50
19 David Aebischer 2.00 5.00
20 Mitch Lamoureux .30 .75
21 Christian Matte .20 .50
22 Dan Smith .16 .40
23 Jay Wells CO .16 .40
24 1973-74 Team Photo .16 .40
25 Ville Nieminen 1.60 2.00
26 Nick Bootland .16 .40
27 1979-80 Team Photo .20 .50
28 Bruce Richardson .16 .40
29 Brian Willsie .16 .40
30 Hershey Park Arena .10 .25
31 Brian White .16 .40
32 1980-81 Team Photo .20 .50
33 1987-88 Team Photo .20 .50
34 Dan Stuck TR .10 .25
35 1996-97 Team Photo .20 .50
36 Frank Mathers .20 .50
37 Arnie Kullman .16 .40
38 Mike Nykoluk .16 .40
39 Tim Tookey .30 .75
40 Team Logo .10 .25

2000-01 Hershey Bears

This set features the Bears of the AHL. This set was produced as a giveaway with the purchase of a local newspaper. Collectors

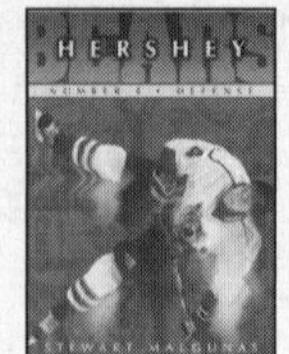

buying a paper at the game would get one card, making a complete set very difficult to piece together.

COMPLETE SET (20) 5.00 25.00
1 Yuri Babenko .20 1.00
2 Rick Berry .20 1.50
3 Nick Bootland .20 1.00
4 Frederic Cassivi .30 2.00
5 Mike Craig .20 1.00
6 Kelly Fairchild .20 1.00
7 Brad Larsen .20 1.00
8 Yevgeny Lazarev .20 1.50
9 Stewart Malgunas .20 1.00
10 Ville Nieminen .60 3.00
11 Joel Prpic .20 1.00
12 Alex Ryazantsev .30 1.50
13 Philippe Sauve .40 4.00
14 Matthew Scorsune .20 1.00
15 Rob Shearer .20 1.50
16 Dan Smith .20 1.00
17 Ben Storey .20 1.00
18 K.C. Timmons .20 1.00
19 Steffon Walby .20 1.00
20 Brian White .20 1.00

2001-02 Hershey Bears

This set features the Bears of the AHL. The cards were issued singly as a promotional giveaway with the purchase of a Hershey Patriot News newspaper at each home game. The last eight cards were apparently issued as an update set. The series is very difficult to complete due to this distribution. Although the player's jersey number appears on the front and back, the cards are considered unnumbered, and thus are listed in alphabetical order.

COMPLETE SET (28) 25.00 50.00
1 Yuri Babenko .60 1.00
2 Frederic Cassivi .60 1.50
3 Mike Cirillo .40 1.00
4 Coco MASCOT .10 .25
5 Larry Courville .40 1.00
6 Jeff Daw .40 1.00
7 Kelly Fairchild .40 1.00
8 Paul Fixter ACO .10 .25
9 Mike Foligno CO .10 .25
10 Riku Hahl 1.20 2.00
11 Matt Herr .60 1.50
12 Jordan Krestanovich .80 1.50
13 Mikhail Kuleshov .60 1.00
14 Yevgeny Lazarev .60 1.00
15 Dave MacIsaac .40 1.00
16 Steve Moore .60 1.00
17 Bryan Muir .60 1.50
18 Vaclav Nedorost 4.00 1.50
19 Brad Norton .40 1.00
20 Jaroslav Obsut .40 1.00
21 Jeff Paul .40 1.00
22 Alex Riazantsev .60 1.50
23 Phil Sauve .80 5.00
24 Matt Scorsune .40 1.00
25 Brent Thompson .40 1.00
26 Rocky Thompson .40 1.00
27 K.C. Timmons .40 1.00
28 Radim Vrbata 4.00 5.00

2002-03 Hershey Bears

COMPLETE SET (30) 30.00
1 Eric Bertrand 1.00
2 Nick Bootland 1.00
3 Steve Brule 1.00
4 Peter Budaj 2.00
5 Marc Busenburg 1.00
6 Brett Clark 1.00
7 Dale Clarke 1.00
8 Pierre-Luc Emond 1.00
9 Mark Freer 1.00
10 Riku Hahl 2.00
11 Jordan Krestanovich 1.00
12 Mikhail Kuleshov 1.00
13 Cail MacLean 1.00
14 Steve Moore 1.00
15 Bryan Muir 1.00
16 Jeff Paul 1.00
17 Alexander Ryazantsev 1.00
18 Philippe Sauve 3.00
19 Agris Saviels 1.00
20 Charlie Stephens 1.00
21 Marek Svatos 3.00
22 Brent Thompson 1.00
23 K.C.Timmons 1.00
24 Rob Voltera 1.00
25 Tim Wedderburn 1.00
26 Brian Willsie 1.00
27 Mike Foligno HCO .25
28 Paul Fixter ACO .25
29 Coco Mascot .10
30 Giant Center Arena .10

2003-04 Hershey Bears

This set was produced by Choice Marketing and sold as a set at home games.

COMPLETE SET (24) 10.00
1 Peter Budaj .75
2 Jeff Finger .50
3 D.J. Smith .50
4 Brett Clark .50
5 Tomas Slovak .50
6 Pascal Trepanier .50
7 Jordan Krestanovich .50
8 Gavin Morgan .50
9 Eric Perrin 1.00
10 Ryan Craig .50
11 Mikhail Kuleshov .50
12 Shane Willis .50
13 Rob Voltera .50
14 Steve Brule .50
15 Bruce Richardson .50
16 Sheldon Keefe .50
17 Agris Saviels .50
18 Charlie Stephens .50
19 Marc Busenburg .50
20 Mark Jerant .50
21 Evgeny Artyukhin .50
22 Tom Lawson .50
23 Paul Fixter HCO .10
24 Paul Jerrard ACO .10

2003-04 Hershey Bears Patriot News

Singles from this set could be acquired only with the purchase of a Patriot News newspaper at select home games, making these cards, and this set, one of the season's toughest to acquire.

COMPLETE SET (30) 40.00
1 Evgeny Artyukhin 1.50
2 Dennis Bonvie 2.00
3 Steve Brule 1.50
4 Peter Budaj 2.00
5 Marc Busenburg 1.50
6 Brett Clark 1.50
7 Ryan Craig 1.50
8 Jeff Finger 1.50
9 Mark Jerant 1.50
10 Sheldon Keefe 1.50
11 Jordan Krestanovich 1.50
12 Mikhail Kuleshov 1.50
13 Brad Larsen 1.50
14 Tom Lawson 2.00
15 Steve Moore 1.50
16 Gavin Morgan 1.50
17 Eric Perrin 3.00
18 Bruce Richardson 1.50
19 Darren Rumble 1.50
20 Agris Saviels 1.50
21 Tomas Slovak 1.50
22 D.J. Smith 1.50
23 Charlie Stephens 1.50
24 Pascal Trepanier 1.50
25 Mikko Viitanen 1.50
26 Rob Voltera 1.50
27 Shane Willis 1.50
28 Paul Fixter HCO .25
29 Paul Jerrard ACO .25
30 Mascot .25

2004-05 Hershey Bears Patriot News

Cards were available individually with the purchase of a Patriot News newspaper.

COMPLETE SET (31) 40.00
1 Dean Arsene 1.00
2 Chris Bala 1.00
3 Greg Barber 1.00
4 Dennis Bonvie 4.00
5 Johnny Boychuk 1.00
6 Peter Budaj 2.00
7 Brett Clark 1.00
8 Carl Corrazzini 2.00
9 Mathieu Darche 2.00
10 Jeff Finger 1.00
11 Paul Fixter CO .50
12 Martin Hlinka 1.00
13 Paul Jerrard ACO .50
14 Sergei Klyazmin 1.00
15 Tom Lawson 2.00
16 David Masse 1.00
17 Frank Mathers 2.00
18 Frank Mathers 2.00
19 Cody McCormick 2.00
20 Cail MacLean 1.00
21 Eric Perrin 3.00
22 Tom Lawson 1.00
23 Agris Saviels 1.00
24 Frantisek Skladany 1.00
25 Mike Souza 1.00
26 Ryan Steeves 1.00
27 Marek Svatos 3.00
28 Jeff Ulmer 1.00
29 Mikko Viitanen 2.00
30 Martin Wilde 2.00
31 Coco MASCOT .10

2005-06 Hershey Bears

COMPLETE SET (28) 8.00 20.00
1 Dean Arsene .30 .75
2 Jared Aulin .30 .75
3 Chris Bourque .60 1.50
4 Frederic Cassivi .60 1.50
5 Jakub Cutta .30 .75
6 Eric Fehr .30 .75
7 Tomas Fleischmann .30 .75
8 Owen Fussey .30 .75
9 Mike Green .30 .75
10 Jonas Johansson .30 .75
11 Boyd Kane .30 .75
12 Jakub Klepis .30 .75
13 Graham Mink .60 1.50
14 Lawrence Nycholat .30 .75
15 Dave Steckel .30 .75
16 Joey Tenute .30 .75
17 Martin Wilde .30 .75
18 Bruce Boudreau HC .02 .10
19 Bob Woods AC .02 .10
20 Coco the Bear MASCOT .02 .10
21 Kirk Daubenspeck .40 1.00
22 Deryk Engelland .30 .75
23 Colin Forbes .30 .75
24 J.F. Fortin .30 .75
25 Brooks Laich .30 .75
26 Louis Robitaille .75 2.00
27 Mark Wotton .30 .75
28 Dwayne Zinger .30 .75

1995-96 Houston Aeros

This set features the Aeros of the IHL. The cards were produced by Edge Ice and sold at the team's souvenir stands.

COMPLETE SET (25) 4.80 12.00
1 Scott Arniel .30 .75
2 Al Conroy .20 .50
3 Paul DiPietro .20 .50
4 Gord Donnelly .20 .50
5 Rob Dopson .30 .75
6 Mark Freer .20 .50
7 Troy Gamble .30 .75
8 Kevin Grant .20 .50
9 Curtis Hunt .20 .50
10 Steve Jaques .20 .50
11 Gord Kruppke .20 .50
12 Mark Lamb .30 .75
13 Marc Laniel .30 .75
14 Kevin Malgunas .20 .50
15 Mike Maurice .20 .50
16 Scott McCrory .20 .50
17 Myles O'Connor .20 .50
18 Jim Paek .20 .50
19 Vadim Slivchenko .20 .50
20 Graeme Townshend .20 .50
21 Sylvain Turgeon .20 .50
22 Carl Valimont .20 .50
23 Mike Yeo .20 .50
24 Dave Tippett .20 .50
25 Terry Ruskowski CO .20 .50

1999-00 Houston Aeros

Created by ebk Sports, this standard size set was created specifically for the 2000 IHL All-Star Game, which featured the defending Turner Cup champion Aeros against the best players from the rest of the league. The set was sold at the Aeros home rink, although production problems delayed its release. The set features color action photos on a plastic-type stock. The cards are prone to poor centering and cutting.

COMPLETE SET (29) 10.00 25.00
1 Paul Dyck .40 1.00
2 Marty Wilford .40 1.00
3 Matt Swanson .40 1.00
4 Mark Lamb .60 1.50
5 Jeff Daw .40 1.00
6 Brian Wiseman .60 1.50
7 Lane Lambert .60 1.50
8 Brian Felsner .40 1.00
9 Terry Marchant .40 1.00
10 Lee Jinman .40 1.00
11 Rudy Poeschek .60 1.50
12 David Oliver .40 1.00
13 Brad Williamson .40 1.00
14 Mark Major .40 1.00
15 David Wilkie .40 1.00
16 Maxime Gingras .80 2.00
17 Greg Pankewicz .40 1.00
18 Gregg Walters .40 1.00
19 Sandy Moger .60 1.50
20 Frederic Chabot 1.20 3.00
21 Ron Low CO .40 1.00
22 Dave Barr ACO .20 .50
25 Mascot .10 .25
NNO Steve Sumner EQ .04 .10
NNO Header Card .04 .10
NNO Jerry Meins TR .04 .10
NNO Checklist .10 .25

2003-04 Houston Aeros

COMPLETE SET (20) 10.00
1 Chris Bala .50
2 Jason Beckett .50
3 Dan Cavanaugh .50
4 Marc Cavosie .50
5 Mark Cullen .50
6 Josh DeWolf .50
7 Chris Dyment .50
8 Matthew Foy .50
9 Mika Hannula .50
10 Chris Heid .50
11 Jeff Hoggan .50
12 Johan Holmqvist .75
13 Jason Marshall .50
14 Zbynek Michalek .50
15 Kevin Mitchell .50
16 Bill Muckalt .50
17 Eric Reitz .50
18 Stephane Veilleux .50
19 Rickard Wallin .50
20 Kyle Wanvig .50

2004-05 Houston Aeros

This set was handed out in 10-card increments at two different Aeros home games. The cards are unnumbered and are listed below in alphabetical order.

COMPLETE SET (20) 30.00
1 Derek Boogaard 2.00
2 Pierre-Marc Bouchard 3.00
3 Brent Burns 3.00
4 Dan Cavanaugh 1.00
5 Mark Cullen 1.00
6 John Erskine 1.50
7 Matt Foy 1.00
8 Ray Giroux 1.00
9 Josh Harding 3.00
10 Mikko Koivu 3.00
11 Kirby Law 1.00
12 Junior Lessard 2.00
13 Zbynek Michalek 1.00
14 Todd Reirden 1.00
15 Eric Reitz 1.00
16 Mike Smith 2.00
17 Patrick Traverse 2.00
18 Stephane Veilleux 1.00
19 Rickard Wallin 1.00
20 Kyle Wanvig 1.00

2006-07 Houston Aeros RetroÂ

COMPLETE SET (10) 5.00 10.00
1 Frederic Chabot .75 2.00
2 Mark Freer A .30 .75
3 Cam Stewart .30 .75
4 Brian Wiseman A .30 .75
5 Derek Boogaard A 1.25 3.00
6 Jeff Christian A .30 .75
7 Manny Fernandez A .40 1.00
8 Curtis MurphyA .30 .75
9 Todd McLellan A .30 .75
10 Dave Tippett CO .30 .75

1987-88 Hull Olympiques

This set features a rare card of Wayne Gretzky, who was pictured as a result of buying the team.

COMPLETE SET (24) 80.00
1 Header Card .25
2 Joe Aloi 1.00
3 Joel Blain 1.00
4 Christian Breton 1.00
5 Benoit Brunet 2.00
6 Guy Dupuis 1.00
7 Martin Gelinas 3.00
8 Jason Glickman 2.00
9 Wayne Gretzky OWN 60.00
10 Herbert Hohenberger 2.00
11 Ken MacDermid 1.00
12 Craig Martin 2.00
13 Mark McLane 1.00
14 Stephane Matteau 2.00
15 Kelly Nester 1.00
16 Marc Saumier 1.00
17 Claude-Charles Sauriol 1.50
18 Daniel Shank 3.00
19 Joe Suk 1.00
20 Alain Vigneault 1.00
21 George Wilcox 1.00
22 Team Card .50
23 Team Card .50
24 Team Card .50

1999-00 Hull Olympiques

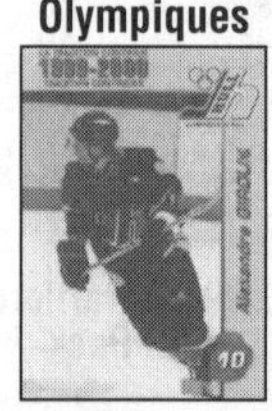

Released by Hull Olympiques in conjunction with the Banque Nationale, this 24-card set features the 1999-00 team. Base cards have gray borders, feature full-color photos, and have both the team logo and the Banque Nationale logo on the card front.

COMPLETE SET (24) 4.80 12.00
1 Erich Paroshy .15 .40
2 Andrew Carver .15 .40
3 Bobby Clarke .15 .40
4 Donald Johnstone .15 .40
5 Bruno Lemire .15 .40
6 Derrick Martin .15 .40
7 Alexandre Giroux .30 .75
8 Dustin Russell .15 .40
9 Daniel Hudgin .15 .40
10 Roberto Bissonnette .15 .40
11 Daniel Clermont .15 .40
12 Radim Vrbata .80 1.00
13 Mario Joly .15 .40
14 Jason Lehoux .15 .40
15 Brock Boucher .15 .40
16 Philippe Lacasse .15 .40
17 Paul Spadafora .15 .40
18 Ryan Lauzon .15 .40
19 Michael Ryder 1.25 3.00
20 Adam Rivet .15 .40
21 Patrick Lafreniere .15 .40
22 Eric Lafrance .20 .50
23 Philippe Sauve .75 1.00
24 Team Photo/CL .15 .40
NNO Luc Robitaille .60 1.50

1999-00 Hull Olympiques Signed

This 24-card set parallels the base Hull Olympiques set in an autographed version. The cards are signed on the front in a ghosted area of the photo, while the backs are serial numbered out of 100. The Luc Robitaille card in the set is limited to 100 copies, but it is not signed.

COMPLETE SET (24) 32.00 80.00
1 Erich Paroshy .80 2.00
2 Andrew Carver .80 2.00
3 Bobby Clarke .80 2.00
4 Donald Johnstone .80 2.00
5 Bruno Lemire .80 2.00
6 Derrick Martin .80 2.00
7 Alexandre Giroux 2.00 5.00
8 Dustin Russell .80 2.00
9 Daniel Hudgin .80 2.00
10 Roberto Bissonnette .80 2.00
11 Daniel Clermont .80 2.00
12 Radim Vrbata 6.00 15.00
13 Mario Joly .80 2.00
14 Jason Lehoux .80 2.00
15 Brock Boucher .80 2.00
16 Philippe Lacasse .80 2.00
17 Paul Spadafora .80 2.00
18 Ryan Lauzon .80 2.00
19 Michael Ryder 15.00 30.00
20 Adam Rivet .80 2.00
21 Patrick Lafreniere .80 2.00
22 Eric Lafrance 1.20 3.00
23 Philippe Sauve 6.00 15.00
24 Team Photo/CL .10 .25
NNO Luc Robitaille 6.00 15.00

2000-01 Hull Olympiques

This set features the Olympiques of the QMJHL. The set was produced by CTM-Ste-Foy and was sold by that card shop, as well as by the team at home games.

COMPLETE SET (24) 6.00 20.00
1 Chris Moher .20 .50
2 Andrew Carver .20 .50
3 Bobby Clarke .20 .50
4 Doug O'Brien .20 .50
5 Bruno Lemire .20 .50
6 John Cilladi .20 .50
7 Derrick Martin .20 .50
8 Roberto Bissonnette .20 .50
9 Ales Hemsky 2.00 10.00
10 Phillippe Chainlere .20 .50
11 Jonathan Labelle .20 .50
12 Mario Joly .20 .50
13 Jason Kostadine .20 .50
14 Carl Rochon .20 .50
15 Philippe Lacasse .20 .50
16 Maxime Talbot .20 .50
17 Jean-Michel Daoust .20 .50
18 Brent G. Roach .20 .50
19 Dale Sullivan .20 .50
20 Adam Rivet .30 .75
21 Eric Lafrance .20 .50
22 Olivier Dannel .30 .75
23 Ian Courville .20 .50
NNO Team CL .10 .01

2000-01 Hull Olympiques Signed

This set is exactly the same as the base Olympiques set from this season, save that every card has been hand signed by the player pictured. Each card also is serial numbered out of just 100. The team CL is not signed.

COMPLETE SET (24) 24.00 60.00
1 Chris Moher .80 2.00
2 Andrew Carver .80 2.00
3 Bobby Clarke .80 2.00
4 Doug O'Brien .80 2.00
5 Bruno Lemire .80 2.00
6 John Cilladi .80 2.00
7 Derrick Martin 1.20 3.00
8 Roberto Bissonnette .80 2.00
9 Ales Hemsky 6.00 30.00
10 Phillippe Chainlere .80 2.00
11 Jonathan Labelle .80 2.00
12 Mario Joly .80 2.00
13 Jason Kostadine .80 2.00
14 Carle Rochon .80 2.00
15 Philippe Lacasse .80 2.00
16 Maxime Talbot .80 2.00
17 Jean-Michel Daoust .80 2.00
18 Brent G. Roach .80 2.00
19 Dale Sullivan .80 2.00
20 Adam Rivet 2.00 5.00
21 Eric Lafrance .80 2.00
22 Olivier Dannel 2.00 5.00
23 Ian Courville .80 2.00
NNO Team CL .10 .25

2001-02 Hull Olympiques

This set features the Olympiques of the QMJHL. The set was produced by CTM Ste-Foy and was sold at Olympiques home games. There were 1,000 copies produced of this set.

COMPLETE SET (23) 4.80 12.00
1 Chris Moher .20 .50
2 Bryan Riddell .20 .50
3 Charles Fontaine .20 .50
4 Dominic D'Amour .20 .50
5 Doug O'Brien .20 .50
6 Francis Wathier .20 .50
7 Derrick Martin .20 .50
8 Philippe Dupuis .20 .50
9 Scott Gibson .20 .50
10 Ales Hemsky .80 5.00
11 Nick Fugere .20 .50
12 Jonathan Labelle .20 .50
13 Martin Vagner .40 1.00
14 Jason Kostadine .20 .50
15 Jesse Lane .31 .75
16 Philippe Lacasse .20 .50
17 Brent Roach .20 .50
18 Maxime Talbot .20 .50
19 Jean-Michel Daoust .20 .50
20 Dale Sullivan .20 .50
21 Eric Lafrance .31 .75
22 Michael DiIorenzo .31 .75
23 Jean-Junior Morin .20 .50

2002-03 Hull Olympiques

COMPLETE SET (24) 12.00
1 Christopher Pottie .50
2 Jeff Smith .50
3 Charles Fontaine .50
4 Dominic D'Amour .50
5 Doug O'Brien .50
6 Sam Roberts .50
7 Francis Wathier .50
8 Jonathan Bellemare .50
9 Phillipe Dupuis .50
10 Guillaume Labrecque .50
11 Nick Fugere .50
12 Olivier Labelle .50
13 Martin Vagner .75
14 Renaud des Alliers .50
15 Andrew Hayes .50
16 Brent Roach .50
17 Maxime Talbot .50
18 Jean Michel Daoust .50
19 Dale Sullivan .50
20 Mathieu Brunelle .50
21 Eric Lafrance .75
22 David Tremblay .50
23 Tyler Reid .50
24 Checklist/Logo .10

2003 Hull Olympiques Memorial Cup

COMPLETE SET (20) 15.00
1 Jonathan Bellemare .75
2 Mathieu Brunelle .75
3 Dominic D'Amour .75
4 Jean-Michel D'Aoust .75
5 Renaud DesAlliers .75
6 Philippe Dupuis .75
7 Nick Fugere .75
8 Olivier Labelle .75
9 Guillaume Labrecque .75
10 Eric Lafrance 1.00
11 Doug O'Brien .75
12 Tyler Reid .75
13 Sam Roberts .75
14 Brent Roach .75
15 Jeff Smith .75
16 Dale Sullivan .75
17 Maxime Talbot .75
18 David Tremblay 1.00
19 Martin Vagner 1.00
20 Francis Wathier .75

1993-94 Huntington Blizzard

Sponsored by WCHS-TV8, this 27-card standard-size set commemorates the 1993-94 inaugural season of the Huntington Blizzard (ECHL). Just 2,500 sets were produced and each was hand-numbered "X of 2,500" on the title card. One thousand sets were given away on trading card night, with the rest being sold at the souvenir shops in the arena. The fronts feature borderless color action and posed player photos. The player's name and the team logo appear on the front. The cards are unnumbered and checklisted below in alphabetical order.

COMPLETE SET (27) 2.80 7.00
1 Ray Alcindor .16 .40
2 Shayne Antoski .16 .40
3 Greg Bailey .16 .40
4 Jared Bednar .16 .40
5 Andy Borggaard .16 .40
6 Malcolm Cameron .16 .40
7 Dave Dimitri .16 .40
8 Mark Franks .16 .40
9 Ray Gallagher .16 .40
10 Murray Garbutt .16 .40
11 Brad Harrison .16 .40
12 Henry's Blizzard Babes .20 .50
13 Todd Huyber .16 .40
14 Klondike MASCOT .04 .10
15 Ron Majic .16 .40
16 Bob May .16 .40
17 Jim Mill .16 .40
18 Jim Mirabello ANN .04 .10
19 Dan Persigehl ANN .04 .10
20 Paul Pickard CO .04 .10
21 Scott Roberts TV .04 .10
22 Greg Scott .16 .40
23 Geoff Simpson .16 .40
24 Doug Stromback .16 .40
25 Dave Weekley TV .04 .10
26 Misty Zambito .20 .50
27 Title Card .04 .01

1994-95 Huntington Blizzard

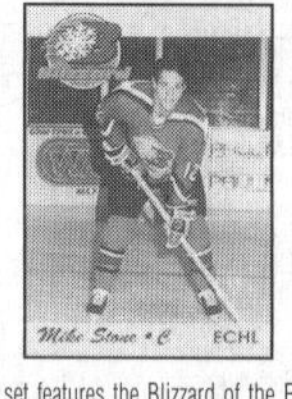

This set features the Blizzard of the ECHL. Approximately 3,000 sets were produced; 1,000 were given away on trading card night, while the others were sold at the souvenir shops in the arena.

COMPLETE SET (32) 4.00 10.00
1 Title Card CL .04 .10
2 Steve Barnes .20 .50
3 Jared Bednar .20 .50
4 Jim Bermingham .20 .50
5 Todd Brost .30 .75
6 Alan Brown .20 .50
7 Ray Edwards .20 .50
8 Trent Eigner .20 .50
9 Dan Fournel .20 .50
10 Mark Franks .20 .50
11 Gord Frantti .20 .50
12 Chris Gordon .20 .50
13 Kelly Harper .20 .50
14 J.C. Ihrig TR/EQMG .04 .10
15 Mitch Kean .20 .50
16 Jeff Levy .20 .50
17 Chris Morque .20 .50
18 Derek Schooley .20 .50
19 Jim Solly .20 .50
20 Mike Stone .20 .50
21 Jason Weinrich .20 .50
22 Mark Woolf .20 .50
23 Paul Pickard CO .04 .10
24 Klondike MASCOT .04 .10
25 Blizzard Babes .30 .75
26 Jim Mirabello ANN .04 .10
27 Dan Persigehl ANN .04 .10
28 Spare DJs .04 .10
29 Spare DJs .04 .10
30 Spare DJs .04 .10
31 TV Anchors .04 .10
32 Title Card .04 .01

1998-99 Huntington Blizzard

Little is known about this ECHL team set beyond the confirmed checklist. Any additional information can be forwarded to hockeymag@beckett.com.

COMPLETE SET (27) 3.20 50.00
1 Bill Baaki .16 2.00
2 Mike Perna .16 2.00
3 Chad Lang .16 4.00
4 Jamie Sokolsky .16 2.00
5 D.J. Harding .16 2.00
6 Jan Slavik .16 2.00
7 Karson Kaebel .16 4.00
8 Jason Bermingham .16 2.00
9 Kelly Harper .16 2.00
10 Derek Smith .16 2.00
11 Jim Bermingham .16 4.00
12 Tracy Egeland .16 2.00
13 Brodie Coffin .16 4.00
14 Rob Stanfield .16 2.00
15 Kevin Paden .16 2.00
16 Mike Schultz .16 2.00
17 Rich Bronilla .16 2.00
18 Jake Deadmarsh .16 4.00
19 Butch Kaebel .16 2.00
20 Blaine Russell .16 2.00
21 Ray Edwards HCO .04 .10
22 Chris Plumhoff EM .04 .10
23 Dave Allen .04 .10
24 Klondike Mascot .04 .10
25 Checklist .04 .10
26 Blizzard Pro Shop .04 .01
27 PHPA/ECHL .04 .01

1999-00 Huntington Blizzard

This set features the Blizzard of the ECHL. The set was produced by Roox and sold by the team at home games.

COMPLETE SET (24) 3.20 50.00
1 Anthony Cappelletti .20 3.00
2 Mike Perna .20 3.00
3 Jamie Pegg .20 3.00
4 Jamie Sokolsky .20 3.00
5 Andrew Pearsall .20 3.00
6 Jason Bermingham .20 3.00
7 Peter Brearley .20 3.00
8 Jim Bermingham .20 3.00
9 Jim Moss .20 3.00
10 Bill Baaki .20 3.00
11 Anthony Terzo .20 3.00
12 David Oliver .20 3.00

13 Keith Cassidy .20 3.00
14 Mark Spence .20 3.00
15 Ryan Hoople .30 4.00
16 Butch Kaebel .20 3.00
17 Blaine Russell .30 4.00
18 WRVC AM390 .04 .10
19 Huntington Blizzard .16 .40
20 Klondike MAS .04 .10
21 Ray Edwards CO .04 .10
22 Dave Allen .04 .10
23 Kelly Harper .04 .10
24 Curtis Bois .04 .10

1998-99 Huntsville Channel Cats

This 22-card set was given out an early season game. The set contains a message card from the president of the Channel Cats that is dated December 25, 1998.

COMPLETE SET (22) 6.00 15.00
1 Chris Stewart HCO .04 .10
2 John Gibson .40 1.00
3 Igor Bonderev .40 1.00
4 Jonathan Dubois .40 1.00
5 Phil Daigle .40 1.00
6 Pat Bingham ACO .04 .10
7 Mike Degurse .40 1.00
8 Ryan Wood .40 1.00
9 Tyler Quiring .40 1.00
10 Greg Lakovic .40 1.00
11 Wade Gibson .40 1.00
12 Josh Erdman .40 1.00
13 Ken Richardson .40 1.00
14 Todd Dougherty .40 1.00
15 Finnley Mascot .04 .10
16 Clint Collins .40 1.00
17 Mike Gamble .40 1.00
18 Marc Vachon .40 1.00
19 Chris George .40 1.00
20 Derek Puppa .40 1.00
21 Schedule Card .04 .10
22 Message Card .04 .10

2003-04 Huntsville Channel Cats

COMPLETE SET (18) 12.00
1 Claude Amstutz .75
2 Joel Bresciani .75
3 Dan Buccella .75
4 Dave Cadarette .75
5 Matt Carmichael 1.00
6 Allan Carr .75
7 Jason Deguehery .75
8 Mike Degurse 1.00
9 Scott Graham 1.00
10 Daniel Kletke .75
11 Shawn Martin .75
12 Jessi Otis .75
13 James Patterson .75
14 Luke Phillips 1.00
15 Greg Snitowsky .75
16 Joe Urbanik .75
17 John Gibson CO .25
18 Finnley MASCOT .10

2004-05 Huntsville Havoc

Features the Havoc of the SPHL. Was issued as a giveaway at the last home game of the season.

COMPLETE SET (27) 20.00
1 Chaos MASCOT .10
2 John Gibson CO .10
3 Adam MacLean 1.50
4 Steve Howard 1.00
5 Jason Deguehery 1.50
6 Tim Plett 1.00
7 Aaron Lewis 1.00
8 Jeremy Law 1.00
9 Jeff Dams 1.00
10 Brandon Doria 1.00
11 James Patterson 1.00
12 Josh Liebenow 1.00
13 Brad McDonald 1.00
14 Mark Cole 1.00
15 Jason Simon 1.00
16 Doug Merrill 1.00
17 Matt Carmichael 2.00
18 Mike Degurse 1.00
19 Derek McKinlay 1.00
20 Luke Phillips 1.00
21 Dan Bucella 1.00
22 DeWayne Manning TR .10
23 Chad Daniels TR .10
24 John Markushewski DR .10
25 Brian Carter DR .10
26 John Greco DR .10
27 Stanton Davis DR .10

1997-98 Idaho Steelheads

Little is known about this set. It is believed that it was issued as a promotional giveaway at one home game, which would explain its scarcity on the secondary market.

COMPLETE SET (22) 30.00
1 Rob Dumas .60 1.50
2 Frederik Beaubien .80 2.00
3 Patrick Moreau .60 1.50
4 Bill McGuigan .60 1.50
5 Alain Savage .60 1.50
6 Mario Therrien .60 1.50
7 Kevin Deschambeault .60 1.50
8 Sean Farmer .60 1.50
9 Scott Davis .60 1.50
10 Lee Svangstu .60 1.50
11 Troy Edwards .60 1.50
12 Andreas Sjolund .60 1.50
13 Pat O'Connell .60 1.50
14 Patrick Gallagher .60 1.50
15 Sam Fields .60 1.50
16 Marco Pietroniro .60 1.50
17 Dmitri Leonov .80 2.00
18 Jamie Cooke .60 1.50
19 Todd Dougherty .60 1.50
20 Carl Menard .60 1.50
21 Bart Hull .80 2.00
22 Dave Langevin HCO .60 1.50

1998-99 Idaho Steelheads

This set features the Steelheads of the WCHL. It was issued as a promotional giveaway at a late-season home game.

COMPLETE SET (23) 10.00 25.00
1 Alex Alepin .40 1.00
2 Frederik Beaubien .60 1.50
3 Francois Bourdeau .40 1.00
4 Scott Davis .40 1.00
5 Rob Dumas .40 1.00
6 Troy Edwards .40 1.00
7 Christian Friberg .40 1.00
8 Marc Genest .40 1.00
9 Cal Ingraham .80 2.00
10 Jason Lammers .40 1.00
11 Dmitri Leonov .60 1.50
12 Sebastian Parent .40 1.00
13 Marco Pietroniro .40 1.00
14 Tony Prpic .40 1.00
15 Bryan Randall .40 1.00
16 Alain Savage .40 1.00
17 Jonathon Shockey .40 1.00
18 Andreas Sjolund .40 1.00
19 Mario Thierren .40 1.00
20 Jeff Trigg .40 1.00
21 All-Star Trio .60 1.50
22 Clint Malarchuk HCO .60 1.50
23 Bonk Mascot .10 .25

1999-00 Idaho Steelheads

This set features the Steelheads of the WCHL. The cards were first issued as a promotional giveaway. Later, remaining copies were sold by the team.

COMPLETE SET (22) 4.00 10.00
1 Cal Ingraham .30 .75
2 Nicolas Chabot .30 .75
3 Troy Edwards .20 .50
4 Todd Robinson .20 .50
5 Dan Marcotte .20 .50
6 Bryan Randall .20 .50
7 Tom Menicci .20 .50
8 Roy Mitchell .20 .50
9 Scott Davis .20 .50
10 Andrei Lupandin .20 .50
11 Gavin Morgan .20 .50
12 Jeff Petruic .20 .50
13 Clint Malarchuk CO .20 .50
14 Marc Genest .20 .50
15 Darcy Loewen .20 .50
16 Rob Dumas .20 .50
17 Rob Hartnell .20 .50
18 Ryan Johnston .20 .50
19 Matt Garver .20 .50
20 Andreas Sjolund .30 .75
21 Kory Cooper .30 .75
22 Bonk MAS .10 .25

2000-01 Idaho Steelheads

This set features the Steelheads of the WCHL. The cards were produced by Grandstand and issued in five-card strips at five separate home games. The strips are not perforated, making it difficult to acquire cards in single form.

COMPLETE SET (25) 6.00 20.00
1 Chad Alban .40 1.00
2 Colin Anderson .24 .75
3 Adam Borzecki .24 .75
4 Scott Burt .24 .75
5 Rob Concannon .24 .75
6 Thom Cullen .24 .75
7 Bobby Hayes .24 .75
8 Cal Ingraham .40 1.50
9 Kevin Knopp .24 .75
10 Arturs Kupaks .24 .75
11 Mike Legg .24 .75
12 Darcy Loewen .24 .75
13 Matt Martin .24 .75
14 Roy Mitchell .24 .75
15 Jeremy Mylymok .40 1.00
16 Vladimir Nemec .24 .75
17 Barry Potomski .40 1.50
18 Eric Rud .24 .75
19 Dan Shermerhorn .24 .75
20 Kendall Sidoruk .24 .75
21 Shawn Wansborough .24 .75
22 Cal Ingraham AS .40 1.00
23 Jeremy Mylymok AS .40 1.00
24 Todd Hine TR .04 .10
25 Khris Bestel EQM .04 .10

2001-02 Idaho Steelheads

COMPLETE SET (24) 25.00
1 Blair Allison 1.50
2 Scott Burt 1.00
3 Adam Copeland 1.00
4 Jason Cugnet 1.50
5 Thom Cullen 1.00
6 Wes Dorey 1.00
7 Cal Ingraham 1.50
8 Dan Kerluke 1.00
9 Jeremy Mylymok 1.00
10 Matt Oates 1.00
11 Zdenek Ondrej 1.00
12 Derek Paget 1.00
13 Eric Rud 1.00
14 Terry Ryan 1.00
15 Dan Shermerhorn 1.00
16 Jeff Shevalier 1.00
17 Kevin Smyth 1.00
18 Bobby Shaver 1.00
19 Petr Suchanek 1.00
20 Scott Swanson 1.00
21 Garry Toor 1.00
22 Jeremy Yablonski 1.50
23 Edgars Zaltkovskis 1.00
24 John Oliver HCO .25

2004-05 Idaho Steelheads

This ECHL set was originally offered as a game-night giveaway, but the team later sold the few remaining sets for $5 at its pro shop.

COMPLETE SET (27) 15.00
1 Mascot .10
2 John Oliver CO .10
3 Blair Allison ACO 1.00
4 Frank Doyle 1.00
5 Jeremy Mylymok .50
6 Petr Suchanek .50
7 Billy Tibbetts .50
8 Ben Keup .50
9 Scott Burt .50
10 Darren McLachlan 1.00
11 Jim Leger .50
12 Dan Vandermeer .50
13 David Morrisett 1.00
14 Frank Lukes .50
15 Jonathan Zion .50
16 Bobby Russell .50
17 Peter Metcalf .50
18 Warren Peters .50
19 Matt Elich .50
20 Landon Bathe .50
21 Colin Zulianello 1.00
22 Tim Verbeek .50
23 Brett Draney .50
24 David Cornacchia .50
25 Darrell Hay .50
26 Marty Flichel .50
27 Lance Galbraith 1.00

2005-06 Idaho Steelheads

COMPLETE SET (26) 10.00 25.00
1 David Bararuk .60 1.50
2 Garrett Bembridge .60 1.50
3 Jarad Bourassa .40 1.00
4 Scott Burt .40 1.00
5 Justin Cox .40 1.00
6 Brian Fahey .40 1.00
7 Marty Flichel .40 1.00
8 Blake Forsyth .40 1.00
9 Mike Gabinet .40 1.00
10 Kevin Gardner .40 1.00
11 Dan Hacker .40 1.00
12 Jim Hakewill .40 1.00
13 Greg Hornby .40 1.00
14 Kurt MacSweyn .40 1.00
15 D'Arcy McConvey .40 1.00
16 Tyrell Moulton .40 1.00
17 Jeremy Mylymok .60 1.50
18 Matt Reid .40 1.00
19 Steve Silverthorn .40 1.00
20 Mike Stutzel .40 1.00
21 Brad Thompson .40 1.00
22 Janos Vas .40 1.00
23 Matthew Yeats .40 1.00
24 Jonathan Zion .40 1.00
25 Derek Laxdal HC .02 .10
26 Bonk MASCOT .02 .10

2006-07 Idaho Steelheads

COMPLETE SET (27) 10.00 20.00
1 Idaho Steelheads .02 .10
2 Kyle Bruce .40 1.00
3 Scott Burt .40 1.00
4 Taggart Desmet .40 1.00
5 Marty Flichel .40 1.00
6 Lance Galbraith .75 2.00
7 Charlie Johnson .40 1.00
8 D'Arcy McConvey .40 1.00
9 Tuomas Mikkonen .40 1.00
10 Derek Nesbitt .40 1.00
11 Greg Rallo .40 1.00
12 Francis Wathier .40 1.00
13 Jeremy Yablonski .75 2.00
14 Cody Blanshan .40 1.00
15 Blake Forsyth .40 1.00
16 Mike Gabinet .40 1.00
17 Darrell Hay .40 1.00
18 Jared Nightingale .40 1.00
19 Colin Peters .40 1.00
20 Kory Scoran .40 1.00
21 Travis Wight .40 1.00
22 John Daigneau .60 1.50
23 Steve Silverthorn .40 1.00
24 Derek Laxdal CO .10 .25
25 Khris Bestel EQ MGR .02 .10
26 Dennis Brogna TR .02 .10
27 Blue MASCOT .02 .10

1998-99 IHL All-Star Eastern Conference

Released by EBK Sports, this 25-card set was available for purchase at the 1999 IHL All-Star Game, then later through the PHPA web site.

COMPLETE SET (25) 14.00 35.00
1 Guy Dupuis .20 .50
2 Viacheslav Butsayev .20 .50
3 Zac Bierk .40 1.00
4 Brian Noonan .20 .50
5 Dave Hymovitz .20 .50
6 Marty Turco 8.00 20.00
7 Jon Sim .60 1.50
8 Brad Shaw .80 2.00
9 Pat Neaton .20 .50
10 Peter Ciavaglia .40 1.00
11 Mike Prokopec .20 .50
12 Stan Drulia .40 1.00
13 Steve Walker .80 2.00
14 Todd Richards .20 .50
15 Maxim Spiridonov .20 .50
16 Robert Petrovicky .20 .50
17 Curtis Murphy .20 .50
18 Mark Beaufait .40 1.00
19 Gilbert Dionne .40 1.00
20 Brad Lukowich .40 1.00
21 Bruce Cassidy ACO .10 .25
22 Steve Ludzik HCO .20 .50
23 Keith Aldridge .30 .75
24 IHL Logo .04 .10
25 Checklist .04 .10

1998-99 IHL All-Star Western Conference

Released by EBK Sports, this 24-card set was available for purchase at the 1999 IHL All-Star Game, then later through the PHPA web site.

COMPLETE SET (24) 8.00 20.00
1 Richard Shulmistra .40 1.00
2 Brett Hauer .20 .50
3 Bill Bowler .60 1.50
4 Pat Jablonski .60 1.50
5 Niklas Andersson .20 .50
6 Steve Maltais .80 2.00
7 Tom Tilley .20 .50
8 Dan Ratushny .20 .50
9 Andy Roach .20 .50
10 Rob Valicevic .80 2.00
11 Jeff Tory .20 .50
12 Patrik Augusta .20 .50
13 Kimmo Timonen .80 2.00
14 Mark Mowers .60 1.50
15 Patrice Lefebvre .60 1.50
16 Cam Stewart .20 .50
17 Brian Wiseman .40 1.00
18 Greg Hawgood .40 1.00
19 John Purves .80 2.00
20 Scott Thomas .80 2.00
21 Randy Carlyle ACO .10 .25
22 Dave Tippett HCO .10 .25
23 IHL Logo .04 .10
24 Checklist .04 .10

1999-00 IHL All-Stars

The set was created by ebk Sports to commemorate the members of the 2000 IHL All-Star team. In an unusual scenario, the game pitted the league champion Houston Aeros against the best players from the rest of the IHL. The set was sold only at the Compaq Center in Houston. Production problems led to many cards being off-centered or poorly cut.

COMPLETE SET (24) 16.00 50.00
1 Mike Crowley .80 2.00
2 Nils Ekman .60 1.50
3 Rich Parent .80 2.00
4 Shane Willis 1.20 3.00
5 John Purves .80 2.00
6 Kevin Miller .80 2.00
7 Mike Prokopec .40 1.00
8 Petr Schastlivy 1.20 3.00
9 Marty Turco 10.00 25.00
10 Stewart Malgunas .40 1.00
11 Curtis Murphy .40 1.00
12 Todd White .60 1.50
13 Brett Hauer .40 1.00
14 David Gosselin .40 1.00
15 David Ling .60 1.50
16 Gilbert Dionne .80 2.00
17 Jeff Sharples .40 1.00
18 John Gruden .40 1.00
19 Jarrod Skalde .80 2.00
20 Steve Maltais .80 2.00
21 Bob Bourne ACO .40 1.00
22 Al Sims CO .40 1.00
NNO Header Card .10 .25
NNO Checklist Card .10 .25

1981-82 Indianapolis Checkers

Sponsored by Pizza Hut, this 20-card standard-size set features the Indianapolis Checkers of the CHL. The cards were available singly at Pizza Hut restaurants and Checkers games on alternate weeks. On a blue background, the fronts have color action player photos with thin white borders. The team name appears above the photo in an orange border that extends down the right side. The player's name, position, and number are printed above the photo. The cards are unnumbered and checklisted below in alphabetical order.

COMPLETE SET (20) 12.00 30.00
1 Bruce Andres .40 1.00
2 Frank Beaton .40 1.00
3 Kelly Davis .40 1.00
4 Kevin Devine .40 1.00
5 Glen Duncan .40 1.00
6 Mats Hallin .60 1.50
7 Neil Hawryliw .40 1.00
8 Bob Holland .40 1.00
9 Mike Hordy .40 1.00
10 Kelly Hrudey 4.00 10.00
11 Randy Johnston .40 1.00
12 Red Laurence .40 1.00
13 Tim Lockridge .40 1.00
14 Garth MacGuigan .40 1.00
15 John Marks .60 1.50
16 Darcey Regier .80 2.00
17 Charlie Skjodt .40 1.00
18 Lorne Stamler .40 1.00
19 Steve Stoyanovich .40 1.00
20 Monty Trottier .40 1.00

1982-83 Indianapolis Checkers

Sponsored by Pizza Hut, this 21-card standard-size set features the Indianapolis Checkers of the CHL. The cards were available singly at Pizza Hut restaurants and Checkers games on alternate weeks. On a red-orange background, the fronts have color action player photos with thin white borders. The team name appears above the photo in an orange border that extends down the right side. The player's name, position, and number are printed above the photo. The cards are unnumbered and checklisted below in alphabetical order.

COMPLETE SET (21) 16.00 40.00
1 Kelly Davis .40 1.00
2 Kevin Devine .40 1.00
3 Gord Dineen .60 1.50
4 Glen Duncan .40 1.00
5 Greg Gilbert .80 2.00
6 Mike Gredder .40 1.00
7 Mats Hallin .80 2.00
8 Dave Hanson 4.00 10.00
9 Rob Holland .40 1.00
10 Scott Howson .40 1.00
11 Kelly Hrudey 3.20 8.00
12 Randy Johnston .40 1.00
13 Red Laurence .40 1.00
14 Tim Lockridge .40 1.00
15 Garth MacGuigan .40 1.00
16 Darcey Regier .60 1.50
17 Dan Revell .40 1.00
18 Dave Simpson .40 1.00
19 Lorne Stamler .40 1.00
20 Steve Stoyanovich .40 1.00
21 Monty Trottier .40 1.00

1992-93 Indianapolis Ice

This 26-card set measures the standard size. On a light blue background, the fronts feature posed, color action photos with a thin red border. The team logo appears on the bottom left side, while the player's number, name and position appear in black letters on the right side. The cards are unnumbered and checklisted below in alphabetical order.

COMPLETE SET (26) 4.00 10.00
1 Alexandr Andrievski .16 .40
2 Steve Bancroft .16 .40
3 Zac Boyer .16 .40
4 Rod Buskas .20 .50
5 Shawn Byram .16 .40
6 Joe Cleary .16 .40
7 Rob Conn .16 .40
8 Joe Crowley .16 .40
9 Trevor Dam .16 .40
10 Ivan Droppa .16 .40
11 Tracy Egeland .16 .40
12 Dave Hakstol .16 .40
13 Kevin Hodson .30 .75
14 Tony Horacek .16 .40
15 Tony Hrkac .30 .75
16 Sergei Krivokrasov .30 .75
17 Brad Lauer .20 .50
18 Ray LeBlanc .30 .75
19 Owen Lessard .16 .40
20 Jim Playfair ACO .04 .10
John Marks CO
21 Kevin St. Jacques .16 .40
22 Michael Speer .16 .40
23 Milan Tichy .16 .40
24 Kerry Toporowski .16 .40
25 Sean Williams .16 .40
26 Craig Woodcroft .16 .40

1993-94 Indianapolis Ice

Set was produced by MJ's Collectibles and features cards that are slightly narrower than standard size. Thanks to Dale Spengler for the complete checklist.

COMPLETE SET (25) 6.00 15.00
1 Hugo Belanger .30 .75
2 Zac Boyer .30 .75
3 Shawn Byram .30 .75
4 Rob Cimetta .30 .75
5 Rob Conn .30 .75
6 Joe Crowley .30 .75
7 Ivan Droppa .30 .75
8 Steve Dubinsky .30 .75
9 Karl Dykhuis .30 .75
10 Dino Grossi .30 .75
11 Dave Hakstol .30 .75
13 Bobby House .30 .75
14 Tony Horacek .30 .75
15 Bob Kellogg .30 .75
16 Jeff Ricciardi .30 .75
17 Sergei Krivokrasov .30 .75
18 Chris Rogles .60 1.50
19 Kevin St. Jacques .30 .75
20 Christian Soucy .60 1.50
21 Michael Speer .30 .75
21 Yves Heroux .30 .75
22 Kerry Toporowski .60 1.50
23 Duane Sutter CO .40 1.00
24 Gene Parlet TR .02 .10
25 Polar Bear MASCOT .02 .10

1994-95 Indianapolis Ice

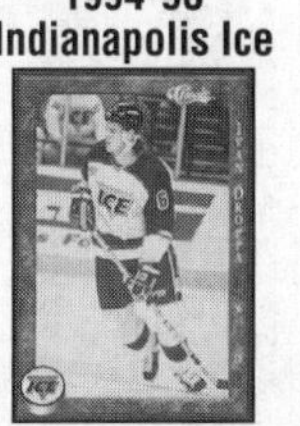

Manufactured and distributed by Jessen Associates, Inc. for Classic, this 26-card standard-size set features the Ice of the IHL. Sets were sold by the team at home games. The cards are unnumbered and checklisted below in alphabetical order.

COMPLETE SET (26) 4.00 10.00
1 Hugo Belanger .16 .40
2 Bruce Cassidy .16 .40
3 Rob Conn .20 .50
4 Ivan Droppa .16 .40
5 Steve Dubinsky .20 .50
6 Karl Dykhuis .20 .50
7 Craig Fisher .16 .40
8 Daniel Gauthier .16 .40
9 Tony Horacek .16 .40
10 Bobby House .16 .40
11 Bob Kellogg .16 .40
12 Sergei Klimovich .16 .40
13 Sergei Krivokrasov .30 .75
14 Andy MacIntyre .16 .40
15 Dean Malkoc .20 .50
16 Matt Oates .16 .40
17 Mike Pomichter .16 .40
18 Mike Prokopec .16 .40
19 Jeff Ricciardi .16 .40
20 Chris Rogles .30 .75
21 Bogdan Savenko .16 .40
22 Jeff Shantz .30 .75
23 Christian Soucy .30 .75
24 Duane Sutter CO .20 .50
25 Travis Thiessen .16 .40
26 Team Photo .16 .40

1995-96 Indianapolis Ice

This 23-card set was produced by SplitSecond for Collector's Edge. The cards featured the standard design element for that season, with the color schemes adapted for that of the team. As they are unnumbered, the cards are listed below alphabetically.

COMPLETE SET (23) 4.00 10.00
1 Bill Armstrong .16 .40
2 James Black .16 .40
3 Jeff Buchanan .16 .40
4 Bruce Cassidy .16 .40
5 Ivan Droppa .16 .40
6 Steve Dubinsky .16 .40
7 Dmitri Filimonov .16 .40
8 Daniel Gauthier .16 .40
9 Ryan Huska .16 .40
10 Sergei Klimovich .16 .40
11 Eric Lecompte .20 .50
12 Andy MacIntyre .16 .40
13 Eric Manlow .16 .40
14 Steve McLaren .16 .40
15 Kip Miller .30 .75
16 Ethan Moreau .30 .75
17 Mike Prokopec .20 .50
18 Andre Racicot .30 .75
19 Jeff Serowik .20 .50
20 Christian Soucy .30 .75
21 Jimmy Waite .30 .75
22 Brad Werenka .20 .50
23 Bob Ferguson .16 .40

1997-98 Indianapolis Ice

Little is known about this set beyond the confirmed checklist. Additional information can be forwarded to hockeymag@beckett.com.

COMPLETE SET (30) 6.00 15.00
1 Bob Ferguson HCO .04 .10
2 Chris Mizer HTR .04 .10
3 Jim Stuckey EM .04 .10
4 Kory Cooper .16 .50
5 Kirk Daubenspeck .30 .75
6 Glen Featherstone .20 .50
7 Brian Felsner .16 .50
8 Martin Gendron .20 .50
9 Jani Hurme 1.60 3.00
10 Ryan Huska .16 .50
11 Marc Hussey .16 .50
12 David Hymovitz .16 .50
13 Marc Lamothe .40 1.00
14 Eric Lecompte .20 .50
15 Eric Manlow .16 .50
16 Steve McLaren .16 .50
17 Kevin Miller .16 .50
18 Craig Mills .20 .50
19 Frank Musil .16 .50
20 Dmitri Nabokov .20 .50
21 Alain Nasreddine .16 .50
22 Ryan Risidore .16 .50
23 Michal Sykora .16 .50
24 Steve Tardif .16 .50
25 Alfie Turcotte .16 .50
26 Petri Varis .20 .50
27 Todd White .20 .50
28 Marty Wilford .16 .50
29 M.J.'s Collectibles .04 .10
30 PHPA Web Site .04 .10

1998-99 Indianapolis Ice

Little is known about this set beyond the confirmed checklist. Any additional information can be forwarded to hockeymag@beckett.com.

COMPLETE SET (29) 4.00 10.00
1 Brian Noonan .20 .50
2 Matt Cooney .16 .40
3 Ryan VandenBussche .30 .75
4 Marty Wilford .16 .40
5 Nathan Perrott .40 1.00
6 Mike Vukonich .16 .40
7 Remi Royer .20 .50
8 Marc Dupuis .16 .40
9 Mike Hall .16 .40
10 Sylvain Cloutier .16 .40
11 Andrei Trefilov .20 .50
12 Andrei Kozyrev .16 .40
13 Chris Herperger .16 .40
14 Marc Lamothe .30 .75
15 Erik Andersson .16 .40
16 Bryan Fogarty .16 .40
17 Slapshot MASCOT .04 .10
18 Bob Lachance .16 .40
19 Kirk Daubenspeck .30 .75
20 Barrie Moore .16 .40
21 Bruce Cassidy HCO .04 .10
22 David Hymovitz .16 .40
23 Justin Hocking .16 .40
24 King Team .01
25 Dale DeGray .16 .40
26 Jeff Paul .16 .40
27 IHL Web Site .01
28 MJ Collectibles .01
29 PHPA Web Site .01

1999-00 Indianapolis Ice

This set features the Ice of the CHL. The set was produced by Roox and sold by the team at home games.

COMPLETE SET (21) 90.00 150.00
1 Mike Berger 3.00 7.00
2 Ken Boone 4.00 10.00
3 Jason Carriere 3.00 7.00
4 Yvan Corbin 3.00 7.00
5 Dan Cousineau 3.00 7.00
6 Robert Davidson 3.00 7.00
7 Jay Hern 3.00 7.00
8 Peter Jas 3.00 7.00
9 Bernie John 3.00 7.00
10 Lubos Krajcovic 3.00 7.00
11 Eric Landry 3.00 7.00
12 Chris MacKenzie 3.00 7.00
13 Jason Mansoff 3.00 7.00
14 Jamie Morris 4.00 10.00
15 Sebastian Pajerski 3.00 7.00
16 Tom Stewart 3.00 7.00
17 Benoit Thibert 4.00 10.00
18 Steven Toll 3.00 7.00
19 M.J. Collectibles .40 1.00
20 Rod Davidson CO 2.00 5.00
21 Joe Trotta CO 2.00 5.00
22 Slapshot MAS 2.00 5.00

2000-01 Indianapolis Ice

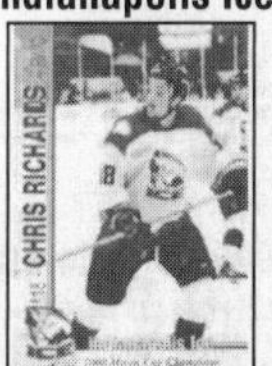

This set features the Ice of the CHL. The cards were sold in team set form at the rink and at a shop called MJ's Collectibles. The latter version actually included an extra card, which featured a swatch of Yvan Corbin's jersey.

COMPLETE SET (23) 4.00 10.00

COMPLETE MJ SET (24) 8.00 20.00
1 Ryan Aho .20 .50
2 Dan Back .20 .50
3 Ken Boone .20 .50
4 Brandon Christian .20 .50
5 Yvan Corbin .20 .50
5GJ Yvan Corbin 4.00 10.00
6 Dan Cousineau .20 .50
7 Robert Davidson .20 .50
8 Casey Harris .20 .50
9 Jan Jas .20 .50
10 Peter Jas .20 .50
11 David Jesiolowski .20 .50
12 Bernie John .20 .50
13 Lubos Krajcovic .20 .50
14 Marc Laforge .20 .50
15 Chris MacKenzie .20 .50
16 Aigars Mironovics .20 .50
17 Jamie Morris .20 .50
18 Chris Richards .20 .50
19 Kevin Schmidt .20 .50
20 Jason Selleke .20 .50
21 Rod Davidson CO .10 .25
22 Slapshot MASCOT .04 .10
23 MJ's Collectibles .04 .10

2001-02 Indianapolis Ice

This set features the Ice of the UHL. The set was sold at home games as a 22-card version, at and MJ's Collectibles, which sold a 23-card version featuring a game jersey card of Bernie John. The latter set is priced below. The cards are unnumbered and are listed in alphabetical order.

COMPLETE SET (23) 8.00 20.00
1 Ryan Aikia .20 .50
2 Mike Berger ACO .04 .11
3 Peter Bournazakis .20 .50
4 Dan Cousineau .20 .50
5 Robert Davidson .20 .50
6 Rod Davidson CO .04 .11
7 Charlie Elezi .20 .50
8 Chris George .20 .50
9 Casey Harris .20 .50
10 Jay Hern .20 .50
11 Bernie John .20 .50
12 Bernie John GJ 4.00 10.00
13 Justin Kearns .31 .78
14 Chris MacKenzie .20 .50
15 Don Malko .20 .50
16 Jamie Morris .20 .50
17 Kevin Popp .20 .50
18 Jason Selleke .20 .50
19 Jonathan Sorg .20 .50
20 Dylan Taylor .20 .50
21 J.C. Wells .20 .50
22 Slapshot MASCOT .10 .25
23 MJs Collectibles .01 .02

2002-03 Indianapolis Ice

COMPLETE SET (23) 10.00
1 Ryan Aikia .50
2 Jason Baird .50
3 Ryan Carter .50
4 Bryce Classen .50
5 Jared Dumba .50
6 Nate Elliott .50
7 Randy Holmes .50
8 Bernie John .50
9 Justin Kearns .75
10 Scott Lewis .50
11 Etienne Morin .50
12 Jamie Morris .50
13 Greg Olsen .50
14 Byron Pool .50
15 Kevin Popp .50
16 Shawn Silver .75
17 Kevin St. Jacques .50
18 Kevin St. Jacques .50
19 Andrew Taylor .50
20 Ken McRae CO .10
21 Darrin Flinchem EQM .10
22 Mascot .10
23 Todd Champlin TR .10

2003-04 Indianapolis Ice

COMPLETE SET (24) 10.00
1 Ryan Aikia .50
2 Jason Baird .50
3 Ken Boone .50
4 Ryan Carter .50
5 Philippe Choiniere .50
6 Mario Doyon .50
7 Jared Dumba .50
8 Nate Elliott .50
9 Dave Gilmore .50
10 Joe Guenther .50
11 Russ Guzior .50
12 Bernie John .50
13 Steve Lecuyer .50
14 Chad McIver .50
15 Adam Redmond .50
16 Remi Royer .50
17 Jeff Sanger .75
18 Jason Selleke .50
19 Mike Zeibaq .50
20 Brent Zelenewich .75
21 Ken McRae CO .25
22 Darren Flinchem EQM .10
23 Mascot .10
24 Marc Schlichtenmyer TR .10

2006-07 Iowa Stars

COMPLETE SET (27) 8.00 15.00
1 Greg Amadio .20 .50
2 Mark Ardelan .20 .50
3 Krys Barch .30 .75
4 Chris Conner .40 1.00
5 Dan Ellis .30 .75
6 Loui Eriksson .60 1.50
7 Mark Fistric .30 .75
8 Mike Green .20 .50
9 Nicklas Grossman .20 .50
10 Dan Hacker .20 .50
11 Yared Hagos .20 .50
12 Marius Holtet .20 .50
13 John Lammers .20 .50
14 Junior Lessard .40 1.00
15 Joel Lundqvist .40 1.00
16 Matt Nickerson .40 1.00
17 Toby Petersen .20 .50
18 Vojtech Polak .20 .50
19 Mario Scalzo .20 .50
20 Marty Sertich .40 1.00
21 Tobias Stephan .40 1.00
22 Janos Vas .20 .50
23 Francis Wathier .20 .50
24 Marty Wilford .20 .50
25 Dave Allison CO .02 .10
26 Paul Jerrard ACO .02 .10
27 Shooter MASCOT .02 .10

2000-01 Jackson Bandits

This set features the Bandits of the ECHL. The set was sold at home games late in the 2000-01 season. The singles are over-sized and numbered on the back.

COMPLETE SET (25) 4.80 12.00
1 Mike Tamburro .20 .50
2 Jeff Helperl .20 .50
3 Derek Gustafson .30 .75
4 Randy Fitzgerald .20 .50
5 Milt Mastad .20 .50
6 Jonathon Shockey .20 .50
7 Chris Wismer .20 .50
8 J.P. O'Connor .20 .50
9 Bobby Russell .20 .50
10 Cory Larose .20 .50
11 Brendan Walsh .20 .50
12 Ryan Mougenel .20 .50
13 Chris Peyton .20 .50
14 Brian Callahan .20 .50
15 Jim Bermingham .20 .50
16 Dan Carney .20 .50
17 Dave Stewart .20 .50
18 Brad Peddle .20 .50
19 Denny Felsner .30 .75
20 Steve Wilson .20 .50
21 Quintin Laing .20 .50
22 J.P. Tessier .20 .50
23 Lee Jinman .30 .75
24 Derek Clancey .20 .50
25 Tim Green .20 .50

2000-01 Jackson Bandits Promos

This set features the Bandits of the ECHL. The cards were issued prior to the main set (which is listed below) as a test of the popularity of trading cards as a promotional item. Apparently, the test went well. Any further info on this set can be forwarded to hockeymag@beckett.com.

COMPLETE SET (8) 3.20 8.00
1 David Brumby .40 1.00
2 Derek Gustafson .60 1.50
3 Denny Felsner .60 1.50
4 Brian Callahan .40 1.00
5 Bobby Russell .40 1.00
6 Dave Stewart .40 1.00
7 Mike Tamburro .40 1.00
8 Brendan Walsh .40 1.50

1999-00 Jacksonville Lizard Kings

This set features the Lizard Kings of the ECHL. This set was handed out as a promotional giveaway at a home game early in the season. It is believed that an update set was issued later in the year. Any information on this set can be forwarded to hockeymag@beckett.com.

COMPLETE SET (15) 4.80 12.00
1 Jean-Philippe Soucy .40 1.00
2 Alex Podalinski .30 .75
3 Rich Bronilla .30 .75
4 Brad Federenko .30 .75
5 Dan Reja .40 1.00
6 Ray LeBlanc .60 1.50
7 Mark Giannetti .30 .75
8 Patrick Gingras .30 .75
9 Derek Eberle .40 1.00
10 Eric Naud .40 1.00
11 Bryan Forslund .30 .75
12 Ryan Cirillo .30 .75
13 Lenny the Lizard MAS .20 .50
14 Alain Lemieux CO .20 .50
15 Jacksonville Lizard Kings .20 .50

1989-90 Johnstown Chiefs

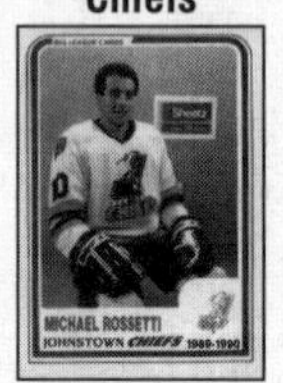

This 18-card set of the Johnstown Chiefs of the ECHL was produced by Big League Cards. The set is believed to have been issued by the team, but that is not a certainty. The set's numbering begins with 19, leading to speculation that a 1988-89 set exists as well. The fronts feature a posed photo, with the player seated beside a prominent logo of sponsor Sheetz convenience store.

COMPLETE SET (18) 6.00 50.00
19 Rick Burchill .20 3.00
20 Bob Goulet .20 2.00
21 John Messuri .20 2.00
22 Darren Servatius .20 2.00
23 Rick Boyd .20 2.00
24 Bob Kennedy .20 2.00
25 Mike Rossetti .20 2.00
26 Dan Williams .20 2.00
27 Mark Bogoslowski .20 2.00
28 Dean Hall .20 2.00
29 Mitch Molloy .20 2.00
30 Darren Schwartz .20 3.00
31 Doug Weiss .20 2.00
32 Marc Vachon .20 2.00
33 Mike Jeffrey .20 3.00
34 Frank Dell ANN .10 .25
35 Sean Finn .20 2.00
36 Steve Carlson CO 2.80 15.00

1991-92 Johnstown Chiefs

This 20-card set features the Johnstown Chiefs of the ECHL. The set was sponsored by Ponderosa Steakhouse and KB Card Company and likely was sold by the team at home games. The fronts feature a posed photo along with team and sponsor logos.

COMPLETE SET (20) 4.00 10.00
1 Steve Carlson CO .80 2.00
2 Dana Heinze TR .04 .10
3 John Fletcher .20 .50
4 Mark Krys .20 .50
5 Doug Sinclair .20 .50
6 Bruce Coles .20 .50
7 Doug Weiss .20 .50
8 Dave MacIntyre .20 .50
9 Bob Woods .20 .50
10 Mike Roberts .20 .50
11 Jeff Beaudin .20 .50
12 Brian Ferreira .20 .50
13 Christian Lariviere .20 .50
14 Ted Miskolczi .20 .50
15 Rob Hrytsak .20 .50
16 Mark Green .20 .50
17 Matt Glennon .20 .50
18 Mike Rossetti .30 .75
19 Stan Reddick .30 .75
20 Perry Florio .20 .50

1993-94 Johnstown Chiefs

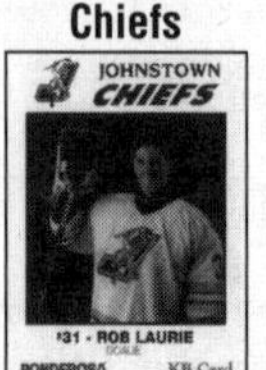

This 22-card set features the Johnstown Chiefs of the ECHL. The set was sponsored by Ponderosa Steakhouse and KB Card Company and likely was sold by the team at home games. The fronts feature a posed photo along with team and sponsor logos.

COMPLETE SET (22) 3.20 8.00
1 John Bradley .16 .40
2 Campbell Blair .16 .40
3 Francois Bourdeau .16 .40
4 Bob Woods .16 .40
5 Ted Dent .16 .40
6 Matt Hoffman .16 .40
7 Gord Christian .16 .40
8 Tim Hanus .16 .40
9 Phil Soukoroff .16 .40
10 Jason Jennings .16 .40
11 Dusty McLellan .16 .40
12 Dennis Purdie .20 .50
13 Chuck Wiegand .16 .40
14 Jamie Adams .16 .40
15 Jan Beran .16 .40
16 Rob Laurie .20 .50
17 Cory Banika .16 .40
18 Perry Florio .16 .40
19 Rob Leask .16 .40
20 Ed Johnstone CO .10 .25
21 John Daley GM .04 .10
22 Matt Koeck TR .04 .10
NNO Header Card .04 .10

1994-95 Johnstown Chiefs

This 24-card set features the Johnstown Chiefs of the ECHL. The set was likely sold by the team at home games. The fronts feature a posed photo along with team and sponsor logos.

COMPLETE SET (24) 3.20 8.00
1 Cover Card CL .04 .10
2 Jason Brousseau .16 .40
3 Brandon Christian .16 .40
4 Gord Christian .16 .40
5 Bruce Coles .16 .40
6 Ted Dent .16 .40
7 Martin D'Orsonnens .16 .40
8 Perry Florio .16 .40
9 Rod Hinks .16 .40
10 Matt Hoffman .16 .40
11 Aaron Israel .16 .40
12 Jason Jennings .16 .40
13 Rob Laurie .16 .40
14 Rob Leask .16 .40
15 Dennis Purdie .40 1.00
16 Kevin Quinn .16 .40
17 Jason Richard .16 .40
18 Dan Sawyer .16 .40
19 Ben Wyzansky .16 .40
20 Matt Yingst .16 .40
21 Training Staff .04 .10
22 Ed Johnstone CO .04 .10
23 WMTZ-FM Personalities .04 .10
24 WMTZ-FM Personalities .04 .10

1996-97 Johnstown Chiefs

This set was produced by Big League Sports and sponsored by Burger King. The set could only be acquired through the team's Kids Club. Note: There are two versions of card #26, both of which are short printed.

COMPLETE SET (31) 10.00 40.00
1 Greg Callahan .40 2.00
2 Brandon Christian .40 2.00
3 Alexsandr Chunchukov .40 2.00
4 Trevor Converse .40 2.00
5 Chad Dameworth .40 2.00
6 Carl Fleury .40 3.00
7 Dan Harrison .40 2.00
8 Jim Krayer .40 2.00
9 Denis Lamoureux .40 2.00
10 Kelly Leroux .40 2.00
11 Martin Masa .40 2.00
12 Klemen Mohoric .40 2.00
13 Sean Perry .40 2.00
14 Ryan Petz .40 2.00
15 Dan Reimann .40 2.00
16 Beau Riedel .40 2.00
17 Ted Russell .40 2.00
18 Ryan Savoia .40 2.00
19 Marc Siegel .40 2.00
20 Lukas Smital .40 2.00
21 Olie Sundstrom .40 2.00
22 Kam White .40 2.00
23 Martin Woods .40 2.00
24 Nick Fotiu HCO .40 1.00
25 Scott Allen ACO .04 .10
26 Mic Midderhoff EM .10 .25
26 Dana Heinze TR .10 .25
27 Chief's Office Staff .10 .25
28 The Iron Dog Mascot .10 .25
29 Home Schedule .10 .25
30 Logo Card .04 .10

1997-98 Johnstown Chiefs

This set features the Chiefs of the ECHL. The cards were issued primarily to members of the team's kid's club. It is believed that local police officers may also have given singles away to local children through other venues. Anyone with additional information may forward it to hockeymag@beckett.com.

COMPLETE SET (29) 6.00 75.00
1 Schedule Card .04 .10
2 Logo Card .04 .10
3 10th Anniversary Logo Card .04 .10
4 The Iron Dog Mascot .04 .10
5 Staff .04 .10
6 Scott Allen ACO .04 .10
7 Nick Fotiu HCO .40 2.00
8 Martin Masa .30 4.00
9 Harold Hersh .30 4.00
10 Lukas Smital .20 4.00
11 Steve Plouffe .60 10.00
12 Jonathan Sorg .20 2.50
13 Dan Harrison .20 2.50
14 Carl Fleury .60 10.00
15 Martin Woods .20 2.50
16 Mark Yannetti .20 2.50
17 Garrett Burnett .20 2.50
18 Greg Callahan .20 2.50
19 Ivo Jan .20 2.50
20 Kelly Leroux .20 2.50
21 Brian Scott .20 2.50
22 Scott Stephens .20 2.50
23 Marcus Draxler .20 2.50
24 Brian Callahan .20 2.50
25 Francois Archambault .20 2.50
26 Dan Dennis .20 2.50
27 Reg Cardinal .20 2.50
28 Ian Smith .20 2.50
29 Yuri Krivokhija .20 2.50

1998-99 Johnstown Chiefs

This set was produced by Big League Sports and, like other Johnstown sets, could only be acquired through the Chiefs' Kid's Club.

COMPLETE SET (23) 8.00 20.00
1 Schedule Card .04 .10
2 Logo Card .04 .10
3 Iron Dog Mascot .04 .10
4 Scott Allen HCO .04 .10
5 Galen Head ACO .04 .10
6 Training Staff .04 .10
7 Office Staff .04 .10
8 Etienne Drapeau .40 1.00
9 Jody Shelley 2.00 5.00
10 Jeremy Thompson .40 1.00
11 Carl Fleury .60 1.50
12 Lukas Smital .40 1.00
13 Jonathan Sorg .40 1.00
14 Matt Eisler .40 1.00
15 Martin Masa .40 1.00
16 Shawn Frappier .40 1.00
17 E.J. Bradley .40 1.00
18 Joel Irving .40 1.00
19 Pavel Nestak .40 1.00
20 Kent Simpson .40 1.00
21 Steve Duke .40 1.00
22 Brad Englehart .40 1.00
23 Eric Normandin .40 1.00

1999-00 Johnstown Chiefs

This set features the Chiefs of the ECHL. The cards were issued as promotional giveaways. Police officers attended each game and handed out cards to children, one per night, making the set very difficult to complete.

COMPLETE SET (28) 10.00 25.00
1 Johnstown Chiefs Schedule .10 .25
2 Johnstown Chiefs .40 1.00
3 Iron Dog MASCOT .10 .25
4 Staff Card .10 .25
5 Scott Allen HCO .10 .25
6 Jason Spence .40 1.00
7 Ryan Chaytors .40 1.00
8 Jeffrey Sullivan .40 1.00
9 Andrew Dale .40 1.00
10 Derrick Walser .40 1.00
11 Dmitri Tarabrin .40 1.00
12 Carl Fleury .60 1.50
13 Joel Irving .40 1.00
14 Shawn Frappier .40 1.00
15 John Tripp .40 1.00
16 Chuck Mindel .40 1.00
17 Andrew Clark .40 1.00
18 Jody Shelley 2.00 5.00
19 Brent Bilodeau .40 1.00
20 Mike Vellinga .40 1.00
21 E.J. Bradley .40 1.00
22 Bryan McKinney .40 1.00
23 Mike Thompson .40 1.00
24 Frederic Deschenes .60 1.50
25 Kevin Kellett .40 1.00
26 Tyrone Garner .60 1.50
27 Training Staff .10 .25
28 Frank Cislo DRVR .10 .25

2000-01 Johnstown Chiefs

This set features the Chiefs of the ECHL The singles were handed out a designated games, one card at a time, to members of the kid's club, making the complete set very difficult to acquire.

COMPLETE SET (28) 12.00 30.00
1 Schedule Card .04 .10
2 Johnstown Chiefs .40 1.00
3 Scott Allen HCO .10 .25
4 Galen Head ACO .10 .25
5 Toby O'Brien .60 1.50
6 Training Staff .04 .10
7 Radio Guys .04 .10
8 Frank Cislo DRVR .04 .10
9 Front Office Staff .04 .10
10 Iron Dog MASCOT .04 .10
11 Frederic Deschenes .80 2.00
12 Dorian Anneck .60 1.50
13 Maxim Potapov .60 1.50
14 Eric Schneider .60 1.50
15 Jason Spence .60 1.50
16 Michael Kiesman .60 1.50
17 Mikko Kuparinen .80 2.00
18 Brent Bilodeau .80 2.00
19 Mike Vellinga .60 1.50
20 Jeffrey Sullivan .60 1.50
21 Andrew Clark .60 1.50
22 Jan Sulc .60 1.50
23 Dany Sabourin .80 2.00
24 Ryan Tocher .60 1.50
25 Dmitri Tarabrin .60 1.50
26 Mike Rodrigues .60 1.50
27 Mark Thompson .60 1.50
28 Andrew Dale .60 1.50

2001-02 Johnstown Chiefs

This set features the Chiefs of the ECHL. The cards were given away to members of the Chiefs' Kids Club at a rate of one card per game over the course of the season. According to minor league expert Ralph Slate, the card fronts can be misleading. Cards No. 1-10 have no season listed, cards No. 11-15 mistakenly read 2000-01, while cards No. 16-29 read 2001-02. Because of the nature of the distribution, this set is extremely difficult to compile.

COMPLETE SET (29) 19.56 50.00
1 Header Card
2 Home Schedule .20 .50
3 Toby & James PRES/GM .20 .50
4 Brent Bilodeau 1.20 3.00
5 Jeffrey Sullivan .80 2.00
6 Kevin Baker .80 2.00
7 Dan Carlson .80 2.00
8 Kevin Clauson .80 2.00
9 Frank Cislo DR .20 .50
10 Staff .20 .50
11 Jim Leger .80 2.00
12 Dany Sabourin 1.20 3.00
13 Lukas Smital .80 2.00
14 J.F. Boutin .80 2.00
15 David Gove 1.20 3.00
16 Frederic Deschenes 1.20 3.00
17 Jason Spence .80 2.00
18 Andrew Clark 1.20 3.00
19 Blair Stayzer 1.20 3.00
20 Mike Rodrigues .80 2.00
21 Philippe Roy .80 2.00
22 Eric Schneider .80 2.00
23 Jim Shepherd .80 2.00
24 Ryan Townsend .80 2.00
25 Chad Onufrechuk .80 2.00
26 Vladimir Nemec .80 2.00
27 Mark White .80 2.00
28 Training Staff .20 .50
29 Mascots .20 .50

2002-03 Johnstown Chiefs

Listed below in alphabetical order.

COMPLETE SET (23) 20.00 40.00
1 Peter Aubry .75 2.00
2 Brent Bilodeau 1.00 2.50
3 J.F. Boutin .75 2.00
4 Pierre-Luc Courchesne .75 2.00
5 Andy Doktorchik .75 2.00
6 Dominic Forget .75 2.00
7 Steve Hildenbrand .75 2.00
8 Jay Langager .75 2.00
9 Jim Leger .75 2.00
10 Vladimir Nemec .75 2.00
11 Toby O'Brien .75 2.00
12 Mike Rodrigues .75 2.00
13 Philippe Roy .75 2.00
14 Mark Scally .75 2.00
15 Lukas Smital .75 2.00
16 Jason Spence .75 2.00
17 Sam St. Pierre .75 2.00
18 Jeff Sullivan .75 2.00
19 Dmitri Tarabrin .75 2.00
20 Ryan Townsend .75 2.00
21 Anniversary Logo .02 .10
22 Mascots .10 .25
23 Training Staff .02 .10

2003-04 Johnstown Chiefs

This set was produced by Big League Cards to be given away to members of the team's kids club. Because they were issued one card per game over the course of the season, it is an incredibly difficult set to complete. It's possible the checklist below is not complete. Please forward additional information to hockeymag@beckett.com. As we have no market information, the cards cannot be priced.

COMPLETE SET (19)
1 Brent Bilodeau
2 Jeffrey Sullivan
3 Dmitri Tarabrin
4 Dominic Forget
5 Ian Manzano
6 Steve Hildenbrand
7 Jay Langager
8 Shawn Mather
9 Josh Piro
10 Cory Campbell
11 Dan Growden
12 Mike James
13 Pierre-Luc Courchesne
14 David Currie
15 Jason Notermann
16 Chad Cavanagh
17 Richard Paul
18 Larry Courville
19 Brent Kelly

2003-04 Johnstown Chiefs RBI Sports

This set was produced by RBI Sports and was limited to 250 copies. The numbering sequence reflects the entire run of RBI series that season.

COMPLETE SET (16) 15.00
209 Brent Bilodeau 1.00
210 Chad Cavanagh 1.00
211 Pierre-Luc Courchesne 1.00
212 Larry Courville 1.00
213 David Currie 1.50
214 Dominic Forget 1.00
215 Steve Hildenbrand 1.00
216 Mike James 1.00
217 Brent Kelly 1.00
218 Jay Langager 1.00
219 Chris Leinweber 1.00
220 Ian Manzano 1.00
221 Shawn Mather 1.00
222 Jason Notermann 1.00
223 Dmitri Patzold 1.50
224 Dmitri Tarabrin 1.00

2004-05 Johnstown Chiefs

An album to store these cards was also produced.

COMPLETE SET (21) 15.00
1 Brent Bilodeau 1.00
2 David Bowman .75
3 David Cann 1.00
4 Chad Cavanagh .75
5 P.L. Courchesne .75
6 David Currie 1.00
7 Jean Desrochers .75
8 Steve Hildenbrand .75
9 Mike James 1.50
10 Brent Kelly .75
11 Chris Leinweber .75
12 Ian Manzano .75
13 Shawn Mather .75
14 Dennis Packard .75
15 Matt J. Reid .75
16 Jeff Sullivan .75
17 Joe Tallari .75
18 Dmitri Tarabrin .75
19 Johnathan Tremblay .75
20 Jeremy Van Hoof .75
21 Toby O'Brien CO .10

2005-06 Johnstown Chiefs

COMPLETE SET (20) 6.00 15.00
1 Doug Andress .30 .75
2 J.B. Bittner .30 .75
3 Jonathan Boutin .30 .75
4 Morgan Cey .30 .75
5 Steve Cygan .30 .75
6 Jean Desrochers .30 .75
7 Gerard Dicaire .30 .75
8 Mike Egener .30 .75
9 Brandon Elliott .30 .75
10 Brady Greco .30 .75
11 Adam Henrich .30 .75
12 Justin Kelly .30 .75
13 Ian Manzano .30 .75
14 Brett Peterson .30 .75
15 Randy Rowe .30 .75
16 Jason Spence .30 .75
17 Joe Tallari .30 .75
18 Dmitri Tarabrin .30 .75
19 John Toffey .30 .75
20 Ben Wallace .30 .75

1971-72 Johnstown Jets Acme

This set features the Jets of the EHL. The oversized cards measure 3.5" x 5 " and feature black and white photos. The cards are blank backed and unnumbered, and so are listed below in alphabetical order.

COMPLETE SET (16) 40.00 80.00
1 Dave Birch 2.00 5.00
2 Vern Campigatto 2.00 5.00
3 Len Cunning 2.00 5.00
4 Guy Delparte 2.00 5.00
5 Wynne Dempster 2.00 5.00
6 Ron Docken 2.00 5.00
7 Galen Head 2.00 5.00
8 Eddie Kachur 2.00 5.00
9 Reg Kent(Taschuk) 2.00 5.00
10 Jerry MacDonald 2.00 5.00
11 Gene Peacosh 2.50 6.00
12 Dick Roberge 2.00 5.00
13 Jim Trewin 2.00 5.00
14 Brian Vescio 2.00 5.00
15 Bob Vroman 2.50 6.00
16 Gary Wood 2.00 5.00

1972-73 Johnstown Jets

This set features the Jets of the EHL. The cards reportedly were included as a premium in game day programs and measure an oversized 3 1/2 by 5 inches. The photos on the front are black and white, while the backs are blank.

COMPLETE SET (18) 50.00 100.00
1 Ron Docken 2.50 6.00
2 Brian Coughlin 2.00 5.00
3 Tony McCarthy 2.00 5.00
4 Tom Steeves 2.00 5.00
5 Kevin Collins 2.00 5.00
6 Jerry MacDonald 2.00 5.00
7 Wynne Dempster 2.00 5.00
8 Ted Lanyon 2.00 5.00
9 Brian Vescio 2.00 5.00
10 Denis Erickson 2.50 6.00
11 Vern Campigatto 2.00 5.00
12 Gary Wood 2.00 5.00
13 Dave Birch 2.00 5.00
14 Galen Head 2.50 6.00
15 Reg Kent(Taschuk) 2.00 5.00
16 Tom McVie 2.50 6.00
17 Bill McEwan 2.00 5.00
18 Doug Anderson 2.00 5.00

1952-53 Juniors Blue Tint

The 1952-53 Junior set contains 182 cards measuring approximately 2" by 3". The cards have a blue tint and are numbered on the back. It is not known at this time who sponsored this set. Key cards in this set are "Pre-Rookie Cards" of Al Arbour, Don Cherry, Charlie Hodge, John Muckler, Henri Richard, and Harry Sinden.

COMPLETE SET (182) 1250.00 2500.00
1 Dennis Riggin 7.50 15.00
2 Joe Zorica 5.00 10.00

3 Larry Hillman 10.00 20.00
4 Edward(Ted) Reid 5.00 10.00
5 Al Arbour 37.50 75.00
6 Marlin McAlendin 5.00 10.00
7 Ross Graham 5.00 10.00
8 Cumming Burton 5.00 10.00
9 Ed Palamar 5.00 10.00
10 Elmer Skov 6.00 12.00
11 Eddie Louttit 5.00 10.00
12 Gerry Price 5.00 10.00
13 Lou Dietrich 5.00 10.00
14 Gaston Marcotte 5.00 10.00
15 Bob Brown 5.00 10.00
16 Archie Burton 5.00 10.00
17 Marv Edwards 17.50 35.00
18 Norman Defelice 6.00 12.00
19 Pete Kamula 5.00 10.00
20 Charles Marshall 5.00 10.00
21 Alex Leslie 5.00 10.00
22 Minpy Roberts 5.00 10.00
23 Danny Poliziani 5.00 10.00
24 Allen Kellogg 5.00 10.00
25 Brian Cullen 17.50 35.00
26 Ken Schinkel 6.00 12.00
27 W. Hass 5.00 10.00
28 Don Nash 5.00 10.00
29 Robert Maxwell 5.00 10.00
30 Eddie Mateka 5.00 10.00
31 Joe Kastelic 5.00 10.00
32 Hank Ciesla 6.00 12.00
33 Hugh Barlow 5.00 10.00
34 Claude Roy 5.00 10.00
35 Jean-Guy Gamache 5.00 10.00
36 Leon Michelin 5.00 10.00
37 Gerard Bergeron 5.00 10.00
38 Herve Lalonde 5.00 10.00
39 J.M. Cossette 5.00 10.00
40 Jean-Guy Gendron 10.00 20.00
41 Gamill Bedard 5.00 10.00
42 Alfred Soucy 5.00 10.00
43 Jean Leclerc 5.00 10.00
44 Raymond St.Cyr 6.00 12.00
45 Lester Lahaye 5.00 10.00
46 Yvan Houle 5.00 10.00
47 Louis Desrosiers 5.00 10.00
48 Douglas Lessor 5.00 10.00
49 Irvin Scott 5.00 10.00
50 Danny Blair 5.00 10.00
51 Jim Connelly 6.00 12.00
52 William Chalmers 5.00 10.00
53 Frank Bettiol 5.00 10.00
54 James Holmes 5.00 10.00
55 Birley Dimme 5.00 10.00
56 Donald Beattie 5.00 10.00
57 Terrance Chattington 5.00 10.00
58 Bruce Wallace 5.00 10.00
59 William McCreary 6.00 12.00
60 Fred Brady 5.00 10.00
61 Ronald Murphy 6.00 12.00
62 Lavi Purola 5.00 10.00
63 George Whyte 5.00 10.00
64 Marcel Paille 25.00 50.00
65 Maurice Collins 5.00 10.00
66 Gerard(Butch) Houle 6.00 12.00
67 Gilles Laperriere 5.00 10.00
68 Robert Chevalier 5.00 10.00
69 Bertrand Lepage 5.00 10.00
70 Michel Labadie 5.00 10.00
71 Gabriel Alain 5.00 10.00
72 Jean-Jacques Pichette 6.00 12.00
73A Camille Henry (Citadelles) 12.50 25.00
73B Camille Henry (New York) 100.00 200.00
74 Jean-Guy Gignac 5.00 10.00
75 Leo Amadio 6.00 12.00
76 Gilles Thibault 6.00 12.00
77 Gaston Pelletier 6.00 12.00
78 Adolph Kukulowicz 6.00 12.00
79 Roland Leclerc 5.00 10.00
80 Phil Watson CO 20.00 40.00
81 Raymond Cyr 6.00 12.00
82 Jacques Marcotte 5.00 10.00
83 Floyd (Bud) Hillman 6.00 12.00
84 Bob Attersley 5.00 10.00
85 Harry Sinden 37.50 75.00
86 Stan Parker 5.00 10.00
87 Bob Mader 5.00 10.00
88 Roger Maisonneuve 5.00 10.00
89 Phil Chapman 5.00 10.00
90 Don McIntosh 5.00 10.00
91 Jack Armstrong 5.00 10.00
92 Carlo Montemurro 5.00 10.00
93 Ken Courtney 5.00 10.00
94 Bill Stewart 6.00 12.00
95 Gerald Casey 5.00 10.00
96 Fred Etcher 5.00 10.00
97 Orrin Carver 5.00 10.00
98 Ralph Willis 5.00 10.00
99 Kenneth Robertson 5.00 10.00
100 Don Cherry 175.00 350.00
101 Fred Pletsch 5.00 10.00
102 Larry Thibault 5.00 10.00
103 James Robertson 5.00 10.00
104 Orval Tessier 10.00 20.00
105 Jack Higgins 5.00 10.00
106 Robert White 5.00 10.00
107 Doug Mohns 17.50 35.00
108 William Sexton 5.00 10.00
109 John Martan 5.00 10.00
110 Tony Poeta 6.00 12.00
111 Don McKenney 10.00 20.00
112 Bill Harrington 5.00 10.00
113 Allen (Skip) Peal 5.00 10.00
114 John Ford 5.00 10.00
115 Kenneth Collins 6.00 12.00
116 Marc Boileau 6.00 12.00
117 Doug Vaughan 5.00 10.00
118 Gilles Boisvert 5.00 10.00
119 Buddy Horne 5.00 10.00
120 Graham Joyce 5.00 10.00
121 Gary Collins 5.00 10.00
122 Roy Greenan 5.00 10.00
123 Beryl Klynck 5.00 10.00
124 Grieg Hicks 5.00 10.00
125 Jack (Red) Novak 5.00 10.00
126 Ken Tennant 5.00 10.00
127 Glen Cressman 5.00 10.00
128 Curly Davies 5.00 10.00
129 Charlie Hodge 37.50 75.00
130 Bob McCord 6.00 12.00
131 Gordie Hollinworth 5.00 10.00
132 Ronald Pilon 5.00 10.00
133 Brian Mackay 5.00 10.00
134 Yvon Chasle 5.00 10.00
135 Denis Boucher 6.00 12.00
136 Claude Boileau 5.00 10.00
137 Claude Vinet 5.00 10.00
138 Claude Provost 20.00 40.00
139 Henri Richard 137.50 275.00
140 Les Lilley 5.00 10.00
141 Phil Goyette 17.50 35.00
142 Guy Rousseau 5.00 10.00
143 Paul Knox 5.00 10.00
144 Bill Lee 5.00 10.00
145 Ted Topazzini 6.00 12.00
146 Marc Reaume 6.00 12.00
147 Bill Dineen 17.50 35.00
148 Ed Plata 5.00 10.00
149 Noel Price 6.00 12.00
150 Mike Ratchford 5.00 10.00
151 Jim Logan 5.00 10.00
152 Art Clune 5.00 10.00
153 Jerry MacNamara 5.00 10.00
154 Jack Caffery 6.00 12.00
155 Les Duff 5.00 10.00
156 Murray Costello 6.00 12.00
157 Ed Chadwick 40.00 80.00
158 Mike Desilets 5.00 10.00
159 Ross Watson 5.00 10.00
160 Roger Landry 5.00 10.00
161 Terry O'Connor 5.00 10.00
162 Ovila Gagnon 5.00 10.00
163 Dave Broadbelt 5.00 10.00
164 Sandy Monrisson 5.00 10.00
165 John MacGillvray 5.00 10.00
166 Claude Beaupre 5.00 10.00
167 Eddie Eustache 5.00 10.00
168 Stan Rodek 5.00 10.00
169 Maurice Mantha 6.00 12.00
170 Hector Lalande 6.00 12.00
171 Bob Wilson 5.00 10.00
172 Frank Bonello 5.00 10.00
173 Peter Kowalchuch 5.00 10.00
174 Les Binkley 25.00 50.00
175 John Muckler 20.00 40.00
176 Ken Wharram 17.50 35.00
177 John Sleaver 5.00 10.00
178 Ralph Markarian 5.00 10.00
179 Ken McMeekin 5.00 10.00
180 Ron Boomer 5.00 10.00
181 Kenneth (Red) Crawford 5.00 10.00
182 Jim McBurney 7.50 15.00

2001-02 Kalamazoo K-Wings

This set features the K-Wings of the UHL. It was produced by Choice Marketing and sold at the team's souvenir stands.

COMPLETE SET (24) 4.00 10.00
1 Andrew Huggett .20 .50
2 Michael Goldkind .20 .50
3 Sergei Deshevyy .20 .50
4 Randy Holmes .20 .50
5 Michael Ford .20 .50
6 Jeff Scharf .20 .50
7 Mathieu Paul .20 .50
8 Jim Brown .20 .50
9 Darcy Anderson .20 .50
10 Harry Schwefel .20 .50
11 Greg Dupre .20 .50
12 Benoit Beausoleil .20 .50
13 Craig Paterson .20 .50
14 Jeff Foster .20 .50
15 Mark Lawrence .31 .78
16 Steve Moore .20 .50
17 Tim Knudsen .31 .78
18 Scott Langkow .31 .78
19 Brad Cook .20 .50
20 Sandy Lamarre .20 .50
21 Ted Laviolette .20 .50
22 Dennis Desrosiers CO .04 .11
23 Scott Allison TR .04 .11
24 Slappy MASCOT .04 .11
NNO Team CL .04 .11

1977-78 Kalamazoo Wings

These standard size cards, sponsored by ISB bank, feature black and white photos with a white border. Backs feature players name, position, and card number.

COMPLETE (15) 15.00 30.00
1 George Klsons 1.00 2.00
2 Ron Wilson 1.00 2.00
3 Bob Lemieux 1.00 2.00
4 Len Ircandia 1.00 2.00
5 Ron Kennedy 1.00 2.00
6 Daniel Poulin 1.00 2.00
7 Terry Evans 1.00 2.00
8 Yvon Douris 1.00 2.00
9 Tom Milani 1.00 2.00
10 Mike Wanchuk 1.00 2.00
11 Steve Lee 1.00 2.00
12 Yves Guilmette 1.00 2.00
13 Al Genovy 1.00 2.00
15 Jim Baxter 1.00 2.00
18 Alvin White 1.00 2.00

2002-03 Kalamazoo Wings

COMPLETE SET (29) 20.00
1 Checklist .10
2 Kirill Alexeev 1.00
3 Tyson Turgeon 1.00
4 Eric Lawson 1.00
5 Quade Lightbody 1.00
6 Herman Hultgren 1.00
7 Bryan Farquhar 1.00
8 Mike Ford 1.00
9 Peter Roed 1.00
10 Joe Pecoraro 1.00
11 Jordan Trew 1.00
12 Glendon Cominetti 1.00
13 Pete Pierman 1.00
14 Kurt Miller 1.00
15 Mark Phenow 1.00
16 Craig Bilick 1.00
17 Mark Lawrence 1.00
18 Justin Cardwell 1.00
19 Richard Keyes 1.00
20 Chad Dameworth 1.00
21 Chad Alban 1.50
22 Brian Rogers 1.00
23 Jeff Reynaert 1.00
24 Mark Kaufman CO .10
25 Mike Modugno ANN .10
26 Scott Allison TR .10
27 Slappy Mascot .10
28 Shoe Carnival .01
29 Burger King .01

2003-04 Kalamazoo Wings

COMPLETE SET (32) 4.00 10.00
1 Checklist .01 .05
2 Mark Reeds CO .02 .10
3 Mark Vilneff .15 .40
4 Guy Dupuis .15 .40
5 Tyson Turgeon .15 .40
6 Jim Dube .15 .40
7 Kevin Caudill .15 .40
8 Daniel Carriere .15 .40
9 Steve Doherty .15 .40
10 Tyler Willis .30 .75
11 Jeff Turner .15 .40
12 Kurt Miller .15 .40
13 Marty Flichel .15 .40
14 Tim Turner .15 .40
15 David Hukalo .15 .40
16 Yannick Carpentier .15 .40
17 Pat O'Leary .15 .40
18 Josh Akright .15 .40
19 Andrew Luciuk .15 .40
20 Dan Watson .15 .40
21 Chad Alban .30 .75
22 Brock McGillis .30 .75
23 Brent Rumble .15 .40
24 Nick Bootland .30 .75
25 Joe Ritson .15 .40
26 Team Staff .02 .10
27 Mike Modugno ANN .02 .10
28 Mascot .02 .10
29 Ad Card .01 .05
30 Ad Card .01 .05
31 Ad Card .01 .05
32 Ad Card .01 .05

2004-05 Kalamazoo Wings

COMPLETE SET (30) 5.00 12.00
1 Checklist .02 .10
2 Mark Reeds CO .02 .10
3 Josh Elzinga .20 .50
4 Mark Vilneff .20 .50
5 Kevin Holdridge .20 .50
6 Tyson Turgeon .20 .50
7 Shaun Fisher .20 .50
8 Daniel Carriere .20 .50
9 Greg Labenski .20 .50
10 Tyler Willis .20 .50
11 Tom Ditzer .20 .50
12 Steve Doherty .20 .50
13 Tim Turner .20 .50
14 Matt Noga .20 .50
15 Tim Krueckl .20 .50
16 Yannick Carpentier .20 .50
17 Ryan Crane .20 .50
18 Gray Shaneberger .20 .50
19 Andrew Luciuk .20 .50
20 Sean Starke .20 .50
21 Kevin Kotyluk .20 .50
22 Chad Alban .40 1.00
23 Joel Martin .20 .50
24 Mike Manley .20 .50
25 Daniel Carriere AS .20 .50
Greg Labenski AS
26 Trainers .02 .10
27 Slappy MASCOT .02 .10
28 Announcer .02 .10
29 Rocker Morning Show .02 .10
30 WKFR Morning Show .02 .10

2005-06 Kalamazoo Wings

COMPLETE SET (30) 8.00 20.00
1 Kalamazoo Wings CL .02 .10
2 Mark Reeds HC .02 .10
3 Josh Elzinga .40 1.00
4 Mark Vilneff .40 1.00
5 Mike Dombkiewicz .40 1.00
6 Jason Deitsch .40 1.00
7 Daniel Carriere .40 1.00
8 Tyler Willis .40 1.00
9 Damian Surma .40 1.00
10 Tim Turner .40 1.00
11 Lucas Drake .40 1.00
12 Tyler Rennette .40 1.00
13 Dustin Virag .40 1.00
14 Adam Elzinga .40 1.00
15 Lee Ruff .40 1.00
16 Brad Church .40 1.00
17 Greg Labenski .40 1.00
18 Kory Karlander .40 1.00
19 Jeff Reynaert .40 1.00
20 Mike Manley .40 1.00
21 Joel Martin .40 1.00
22 Nick Bootland .40 1.00
23 K-Wings Alumni .40 1.00
24 Mike Plandowski TR .02 .10
25 Eric Bechtol EQM .02 .10
26 Slappy MASCOT .02 .10
27 Mike Modugno ANN .02 .10
28 The Rocker Morning Show .02 .10
29 The KFR Morning Show .02 .10
30 Scoopie MASCOT .02 .10

1984-85 Kamloops Blazers

This set features color action photos on the front along with team name, position, and number. Backs feature safety tips and sponsor logos. Cards are unnumbered and checklisted below in alphabetical order.

COMPLETE SET (24) 8.00 20.00
1 Will Anderson .30 .75
2 Brian Benning .30 .75
3 Brian Bertuzzi .30 .75
4 Rob Brown .60 1.50
5 Todd Carnelley .30 .75
6 Dean Clark .40 1.00
7 Rob Dimaio .80 2.00
8 Greg Evtushevski .30 .75
9 Mark Ferner .30 .75
10 Greg Hawgood .60 1.50
11 Ken Hitchcock CO .80 2.00
12 Mark Kachowski .30 .75
13 Bob Labrier ACO .10 .25
14 Pat Mangold .30 .75
15 Gord Mark .30 .75
16 Len Mark .30 .75
17 Rob McKinley .40 1.00
18 Mike Nottingham .30 .75
19 Neil Pilon .30 .75
20 Rudy Poeschek .80 2.00
21 Daryl Reaugh .80 2.00
22 Ryan Stewart .30 .75
23 Mark Thietke .30 .75
24 Gord Walker .30 .75

1985-86 Kamloops Blazers

This standard size set features full color fronts along with sponsor logs and hockey tips on the backs. Cards are unnumbered and checklisted below in alphabetical order.

COMPLETE SET (26) 8.00 40.00
1 Robin Bawa .30 2.00
2 Craig Berube .40 5.00
3 Pat Bingham .30 1.00
4 Rob Brown .40 2.00
5 Todd Carnelly .30 1.00
6 Randy Hansch .40 2.00
7 Greg Hawgood .40 2.00
8 Ken Hitchcock CO .80 5.00
9 Mark Kachowski .30 1.00
10 Troy Kennedy .30 1.00
11 R.T. Labrier ACO .08 .20
12 Dave Marcinyshyn .30 1.00
13 Len Mark .30 1.00
14 Rob McKinley .30 1.00
15 Ken Morrison .30 1.00
16 Pat Nogier .30 1.00
17 Mike Nottingham .30 1.00
18 Doug Pickell .30 1.00
19 Rudy Poeschek .60 5.00
20 Mike Ragot .30 1.00
21 Don Schmidt .30 1.00
22 Ron Shudra .30 1.00
23 Peter Soberlak .30 1.00
24 Lonnie Spink .30 1.00
25 Chris Tarnowski .30 1.00
26 Greg Wallace TR .08 .20

1986-87 Kamloops Blazers

This 24-card set was issued in nine four-card sheets. Six of the panels feature two cards and an advertisement, while the other three panels feature four cards per panel. The sheets are perforated vertically but not horizontally, which produces two-card stripes. If cut, the cards would measure the standard size. On a white card face, the fronts display posed action photos inside a bright blue border. The cards are unnumbered and checklisted below in alphabetical order.

COMPLETE SET (24) 12.00 30.00
1 Warren Babe .20 .50
2 Robin Bawa .20 .50
3 Rob Brown .60 1.50
4 Dean Cook .40 1.00
5 Scott Daniels .20 .50
6 Mario Desjardines .20 .50
7 Bill Harrington .20 .50
8 Greg Hawgood .40 1.00
9 Serge Lajoie .20 .50
10 Dave Marcinyshyn .20 .50
11 Len Mark .20 .50
12 Rob McKinley .40 1.00
13 Casey McMillan .20 .50
14 Darcy Norton .20 .50
15 Kelly Para .20 .50
16 Doug Pickell .20 .50
17 Rudy Poeschek .60 1.50
18 Mark Recchi 6.00 15.00
19 Don Schmidt .20 .50
20 Ron Shudra .20 .50
21 Chris Tarnowski .20 .50
22 Steve Wienke .20 .50
23 Rich Wiest .20 .50
24 Team Photo .20 .50

1987-88 Kamloops Blazers

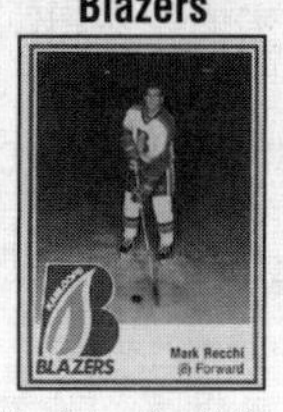

This 24-card set was issued in three-card perforated strips each consisting of two player cards and one advertisement or coupon card. (As listed below, two of these advertisement cards display team logos on the front). The strips measure 7 1/2" by 3 1/2", and if cut, the individual cards would measure the standard size. The front features a color posed-action player photo with thin blue borders on a white card face. The cards are unnumbered and checklisted below in alphabetical order.

COMPLETE SET (24) 12.00 30.00
1 Warren Babe .30 .75
2 Paul Checknita .30 .75
3 Dave Chyzowski .40 1.00
4 Dean Cook .40 1.00
5 Greg Davies .30 .75
6 Kim Deck .30 .75
7 Todd Decker .30 .75
8 Bill Harrington .30 .75
9 Phil Huber .30 .75
10 Steve Kloepzig .30 .75
11 Willie MacDonald .40 1.00
12 Pat MacLeod .30 .75
13 Glenn Mulvenna .40 1.00
14 Mike Needham .30 .75
15 Darcy Norton .30 .75
16 Devon Oleniuk .30 .75
17 Doug Pickell .30 .75
18 Garth Premak .30 .75
19 Mark Recchi 6.00 15.00
20 Don Schmidt .30 .75
21 Alec Sheflo .30 .75
22 Team Photo .20 .50
23 Logo Card .10 .25
24 Logo Card .10 .25

1988-89 Kamloops Blazers

This 36-card set was issued in three-card perforated strips that measure approximately 7 1/2" by 3 1/2". After perforation, the individual cards measure approximately 2 1/2" by 3 1/2". One of the cards on each three-card strip has the Kamloops logo in blue and orange on the front and the back contains a coupon. The regular player cards have white borders with an inner royal blue line surrounding a posed player photo. The cards are unnumbered and are checklisted below in alphabetical order.

COMPLETE SET (36) 7.20 18.00
COMMON AD CARD (25-36) .04 .10
1 Cory Anderson .20 .50
2 Pat Bingham .20 .50
3 Ed Bertuzzi .20 .50
4 Zac Boyer .20 .50
5 Trevor Buchanan .20 .50
6 Dave Chyzowski .20 .50
7 Dean Cook .30 .75
8 Cory Crichton .20 .50
9 Kim Deck .20 .50
10 Ryan Harrison .20 .50
11 Brad Heschuk .20 .50
12 Corey Hirsch 1.20 3.00
13 Phil Huber .20 .50
14 Len Jorgenson .20 .50
15 Paul Kruse .30 .75
16 Dave Linford .20 .50
17 Pat MacLeod .20 .50
18 Darwin McClelland .20 .50
19 Cal McGowan .20 .50
20 Mike Needham .20 .50
21 Don Schmidt .20 .50
22 Brian Shantz .20 .50
23 Darryl Sydor 1.20 3.00
24 Steve Yule .20 .50
25 Hasty Market Ad .01
26 McDonalds Ad .01
27 Mr. Mike's Ad .01
28 Yellow Submarine Ad .01
29 Blazers Logo .04 .10
30 Blazers Logo .04 .10
31 Blazers Logo .04 .10
32 Blazers Logo .04 .10
33 Blazers Logo .04 .10
34 Blazers Logo .04 .10
35 Blazers Logo .04 .10
36 Blazers Logo .04 .10

1989-90 Kamloops Blazers

This 24-card set is believed to have been released in three-card panel form, as were previous Blazers issues. It is noteworthy for featuring the first card of All-Star defender Scott Niedermayer.

COMPLETE SET (24) 6.00 15.00
1 Len Barrie .20 .50

2 Craig Bonner .20 .50
3 Jarrett Bousquet .20 .50
4 Zac Boyer .24 .60
5 Murray Duval .20 .50
6 Shea Esselmont .20 .50
7 Todd Esselmont .20 .50
8 Todd Harris .20 .50
9 Corey Hirsch .60 1.50
10 Phil Huber .20 .50
11 Lance Johnson .20 .50
12 Paul Kruse .24 .60
13 Dean Malkoc .20 .50
14 Dale Mason .20 .50
15 Cal McGowan .20 .50
16 Joey Mittelsteadt .20 .50
17 Mike Needham .24 .60
18 Scott Niedermayer 1.60 4.00
19 Brian Shantz .20 .50
20 Trevor Sim .20 .50
21 Darryl Sydor .80 2.00
22 Jeff Waatchorn .20 .50
23 Clayton Young .20 .50
24 Steve Yule .20 .50

1993-94 Kamloops Blazers

This 24-card set was issued on three-card perforated strips each consisting of two player cards and one advertisement or coupon card. The strips measure 7 1/2" by 3 1/2", and if cut, the individual cards would measure the standard size. The fronts feature a color posed-action player photo with thin blue borders on a white background. The cards are unnumbered and checklisted below in alphabetical order.

COMPLETE SET (24) 12.00 35.00
1 Nolan Baumgartner .30 .75
2 Rod Branch .20 .50
3 Jarrett Deuling .20 .50
4 Shane Doan 2.00 5.00
5 Hnat Domenichelli .30 .75
6 Scott Ferguson .20 .50
7 Greg Hart .20 .50
8 Jason Holland .20 .50
9 Ryan Huska .20 .50
10 Jarome Iginla 4.00 15.00
11 Mike Josephson .20 .50
12 Aaron Keller .20 .50
13 Mike Krooshoop .20 .50
14 Scott Loucks .20 .50
15 Brad Lukowich .40 1.00
16 Bob Maudie .20 .50
17 Chris Murray .20 .50
18 Tyson Nash 1.50 3.00
19 Steve Passmore .60 1.50
20 Rod Stevens .20 .50
21 Jason Strudwick .30 .75
22 Darcy Tucker 1.50 4.00
23 Bob Westerby .20 .50
24 David Wilkie .20 .50

1994-95 Kamloops Blazers

This set features the Blazers of the WHL. It is believed that it was issued as a promotional giveaway.

COMPLETE SET (24) 12.00 30.00
1 Darcy Tucker .80 2.00
2 Jarome Iginla 4.00 10.00
3 Nolan Baumgartner .40 1.00
4 Jeff Oldenborger .20 .50
5 Ivan Vologjaninov .20 .50
6 Shawn McNeil .20 .50
7 Donnie Kinney .20 .50
8 Bob Maudie .20 .50
9 Jason Holland .20 .50
10 Greg Hart .20 .50
11 Shane Doan 1.20 3.00
12 Brad Lukowich .40 1.00
13 Randy Petruk .40 1.00
14 Jason Strudwick .40 1.00
15 Jeff Ainsworth .20 .50
16 Aaron Keller .20 .50
17 Rod Branch .20 .50
18 Bob Westerby .20 .50
19 Tyson Nash 1.20 3.00
20 Hnat Domenichelli .40 1.00
21 Ryan Huska .20 .50
22 Jeff Henkelman .20 .50
23 Cam Severson .20 .50
24 Kamloops Arena .04 .11

1995-96 Kamloops Blazers

This set features the Blazers of the WHL. Although the checklist is confirmed, little else is known about the distribution of this set. Additional information can be forwarded to hockeymag@beckett.com.

COMPLETE SET (31) 8.00 20.00
1 Jarome Iginla 2.00 5.00
2 Nolan Baumgartner .20 .50
3 Jake Deadmarsh .20 .50
4 Scott Reid .20 .50
5 Randy Petruk .30 .75
6 Brad Lukowich .40 1.00
7 Shawn McNeil .30 .75
8 Ed Dempsey CO .10 .25
9 Peter Bergman .20 .50
10 Greg Hart .20 .50
11 Hnat Domenichelli .40 1.00
12 Al Glendenning CO .10 .25
13 Digger MAS .04 .10
14 Rob Skrlac .20 .50
15 Donnie Kinney .20 .50
16 Chris St. Croix .20 .50
17 Jeff Oldenborger .20 .50
18 Steve Albrecht .20 .50
19 Bob Maudie .20 .50
20 Blair Rota .20 .50
21 Brian Henderson CO .10 .25
22 Aaron Keller .20 .50
23 Ryan Rishaug .20 .50
24 Steve Gainey .40 1.00
25 Jeff Ainsworth .20 .50
26 Ajay Baines .20 .50
27 Jordan Landry .20 .50
28 Jason Holland .20 .50
29 Kamloops Arena .10 .25
30 Cadrin Smart .20 .50
31 Konrad Brand .20 .50

1996-97 Kamloops Blazers

This 28-card set was distributed in 3-panel strips, each of which contained two player cards and one ad card for a local business. When separated the cards are standard size and feature color photos with player name, number and position at the top, while the bottom left corner is dominated by a flame-like element and an icon identifying the set as the '96-97 Limited Edition. The cards are unnumbered and are listed below in alphabetical order.

COMPLETE SET (28) 8.00 20.00
1 Jeff Ainsworth .30 .75
2 Steve Albrecht .30 .75
3 Nils Antons .30 .75
4 Ajay Baines .30 .75
5 Konrad Brand .30 .75
6 Wade Burt .30 .75
7 Jake Deadmarsh .30 .75
8 Ed Dempsey CO .10 .25
9 Digger MAS .04 .10
10 Micki DuPont .30 1.00
11 Steve Gainey .60 1.00
12 Jonathan Hobson .30 .75
13 Drew Kehler .30 .75
14 Donnie Kinney .30 .75
15 Alan Manness .30 .75
16 Shawn McNeil .30 .75
17 Randy Petruk .40 1.00
18 Clayton Pool .40 1.00
19 Gennady Razin .30 .75
20 Robyn Regehr .60 1.50
21 Blair Rota .30 .75
22 Thomas Scantlebury .30 .75
23 Steve Shrum .30 .75
24 Rob Skrlac .30 .75
25 Darcy Smith .30 .75
26 Chris St. Croix .30 .75
27 Spike Wallace .10 .25
28 Darren Wright .30 .75

1998-99 Kamloops Blazers

These cards are unnumbered and so are listed below in alphabetical order.

COMPLETE SET (24) 12.00 20.00
1 Jared Aulin .40 1.00
2 Ajay Baines .40 1.00
3 Anton Borodkin .30 .75
4 Mike Brown .30 .75
5 Paul Deniset .30 .75
6 Adam Dombrowski .30 .75
7 Brett Draney .30 .75
8 Micki Dupont .40 1.00
9 Kenric Exner .40 1.00
10 Jordon Flodell .30 .75
11 Steve Gainey .40 1.00
12 Aaron Gionet .30 .75
13 Gable Gross .30 .75
14 Jonathan Hobson .30 .75
15 Donnie Kinney .30 .75
16 David Klatt .30 .75
17 Kevin MacKie .30 .75
18 Alan Manness .30 .75
19 Konstantin Panov .30 .75
20 Robyn Regehr .75 2.00
21 Steve Shrum .30 .75
22 Chris St. Croix .30 .75
23 Chad Starling .30 .75
24 Ryan Thorpe .30 .75

1999-00 Kamloops Blazers

This set features the Blazers of the WHL. The set was produced by the team and sold at its souvenir stands. The cards are unnumbered, so are listed below alphabetically.

COMPLETE SET (24) 6.00 15.00
1 Jared Aulin .80 2.00
2 Jason Bone .30 .75

3 Anton Borodkin .20 .50
4 Erik Christensen .20 .50
5 Paul Deniset .20 .50
6 Blaine Depper .20 .50
7 Brett Draney .20 .50
8 Micki DuPont .40 1.00
9 Aaron Gionet .30 .75
10 Gable Gross .20 .50
11 Jonathan Hobson .20 .50
12 Kyle Ladobruk .20 .50
13 Kevin Mackie .20 .50
14 Grant McCune .30 .75
15 Shaone Morrisonn .60 1.50
16 Mike Munro .20 .50
17 Konstantin Panov .30 .75
18 Davis Parley .30 .75
19 Mark Rooneem .20 .50
20 Chad Schockenmaier .20 .50
21 Steve Shrum .20 .50
22 Chad Starling .20 .50
23 Jordan Walker .20 .50
24 Digger MASCOT .10 .25

2000-01 Kamloops Blazers

COMPLETE SET (24) 6.00 15.00
1 Jared Aulin .20 .50
2 Steve Belanger .40 1.00
3 Tyler Boldt .20 .50
4 Josh Bonar .20 .50
5 Pat Brandreth .20 .50
6 Erik Christensen .40 1.00
7 Paul Elliott .20 .50
8 Aaron Gionet .40 1.00
9 Gable Gross .20 .50
10 Jonathan Hobson .20 .50
11 Nikita Korovkin .20 .50
12 Derek Krestanovich .20 .50
13 Kyle Ladobruk .20 .50
14 Jarret Lukin .20 .50
15 Shaone Morrisonn .40 1.00
16 Colton Orr 1.25 3.00
17 Konstantin Panov .20 .50
18 Davis Parley .40 1.00
19 Mark Rooneem .20 .50
20 Chad Shockenmaier .20 .50
21 Conlan Seder .20 .50
22 Tyler Sloan .20 .50
23 Scottie Upshall .75 2.00
24 Digger MASCOT .02 .10

2002-03 Kamloops Blazers

Based on previous Kamloops issues, it's possible this checklist is NOT complete. If you know of other cards in the series, please contact us at hockeymag@beckett.com.

COMPLETE SET (19?)
1 The Coaches .02 .10
2 Mascot .02 .10
3 Devan Dubnyk 1.25 3.00
4 Paul Brown .30 .75
5 Wade Davis .30 .75
6 Reid Jorgensen .30 .75
7 Jason Lloyd .30 .75
8 Moises Gutierrez .30 .75
9 Cam Cunning .30 .75
10 Grant Jacobsen .30 .75
11 Josh Morrow .30 .75
12 Davis Parley .60 1.50
13 Jonas Johansson .60 1.50
14 Nikita Korovkin .30 .75
15 Tyler Boldt .30 .75
16 Scottie Upshall .60 1.50
17 Erik Christensen .60 1.50
18 Aaron Gionet .30 .75
19 Kris Hogg .30 .75

2003-04 Kamloops Blazers

COMPLETE SET (24) 8.00 20.00
1 Geoff McIntosh .30 .75
2 Roman Tesliuk .30 .75
3 Kalvin Sagert .30 .75
4 Max Gordichuk .30 .75
5 Josh Garbutt .30 .75
6 Grant Jacobsen .30 .75
7 Jonas Johansson .60 1.50
8 Nathan Grochmal .30 .75
9 Cam Cunning .30 .75
10 Kris Hogg .30 .75
11 Kyle Sheen .30 .75
12 Brock Nixon .30 .75
13 Rick Kozak .30 .75
14 Paul Brown .40 1.00
15 Conlan Seder .30 .75
16 Codey Becker .30 .75
17 Ryan Bender .30 .75
18 Ray Macias .30 .75
19 Moises Gutierrez .30 .75
20 Devan Dubnyk 1.00 2.50
21 Jarret Lukin .30 .75
22 Reid Jorgensen .30 .75
23 Derek Werenka .30 .75
24 Checklist .02 .10

2004-05 Kamloops Blazers

We have confirmed only a handful of cards from this set. It was issued in 12 strips of three, and contains 36 cards. If you have additional information, please contact us at hockeymag@beckett.com.

COMPLETE SET (36)
1 Checklist
2 Bryan Kauk
3 Reid Jorgensen
4 Devan Dubnyk
5 Ray Macias
6 Adam Chorneyko

2005-06 Kamloops Blazers

COMPLETE SET (25) 6.00 15.00
1 Checklist .02 .10
2 Michael Maniago .30 .75
3 Roman Tesliuk .30 .75
4 Garrett Thiessen .30 .75
5 Keaton Ellerby .30 .75
6 Ryan White .40 1.00
7 Victor Bartley .30 .75
8 Ashton Rome .40 1.00
9 Janick Steinmann .30 .75
10 C.J. Stretch .30 .75
11 Travis Dunstall .30 .75
12 Scott Skrudland .30 .75
13 T.J. Mulock .30 .75
14 Brady Mason .30 .75
15 Brock Nixon .30 .75
16 Matt Kassian .30 .75
17 Kevin Hayman .30 .75
18 Terrance Delaronde .30 .75
19 Ryan Bender .30 .75
20 Ray Macias .30 .75
21 Moises Gutierrez .30 .75
22 Devan Dubnyk .60 1.50
23 Joel Eisenkirch .30 .75
24 Reid Jorgensen .30 .75
25 911 Digger MASCOT .02 .10

2006-07 Kamloops Blazers

COMPLETE SET (25) 10.00 18.00
1 Victor Bartley .30 .75
2 Ryan Bender .30 .75
3 Dustin Butler .40 1.00
4 Terrance Delaronde .30 .75
5 Brenden Dowd .30 .75
6 Travis Dunstall .30 .75
7 Keaton Ellerby .30 1.25
8 Dalyn Flette .40 1.00
9 Sasha Golin .30 .75
10 Mark Hall .30 .75
11 Reid Jorgensen .30 .75
12 Matt Kassian .30 .75
13 Kevin Kraus .30 .75
14 Raymond Macias .30 .75
15 Brady Mason .30 .75
16 Brock Nixon .30 .75
17 Juuso Puustinen .30 .75
18 Alex Rodgers .30 .75
19 Ivan Rohac .30 .75
20 Jordan Rowley .30 .75
21 Tyler Shattock .30 .75
22 C.J. Stretch .30 .75
23 Ryan White .30 .75
24 Kamloops Blazers CL .01 .05
25 Digger MASCOT .02 .10

1990-91 Kansas City Blades

This 20-card standard-size set features posed, color player photos on a black card face. The pictures are bordered on three sides by a red design similar to a shadow border. Player information appears below the photo in the red border. The year and team name are printed at the upper left corner.

COMPLETE SET (20) 4.00 10.00
1 Claudio Scremin .20 .50
2 Jeff Odgers .30 .75
3 Wade Flaherty .30 .75
4 Rick Barkovich .20 .50
5 Ron Handy .20 .50
6 Kevin Sullivan .20 .50
7 Randy Exelby .30 .75
8 Darin Smith .20 .50
9 Stu Kulak .20 .50
10 Andrew Akervik .20 .50
11 Scott White .20 .50
12 Claude Julien .20 .50
13 Mike Hiltner .20 .50
14 Michael Colman .20 .50
15 Kurt Semandel .20 .50
16 Mike Kelfer .20 .50
17 Mark Karpen .20 .50
18 Lee Giffin .20 .50
19 Cam Plante .20 .50
20 Jim Latos .30 .75

1991-92 Kansas City Blades

This set features the Blades of the IHL. It is believed the set was sold by the team at its souvenir stands. The set is noteworthy as Kansas City won the Turner Cup that year. It also features an early card goaltender Arturs Irbe, who in 1991-92 was an IHL First Team All-Star. The checklist was provided by collector Jeff Barak.

COMPLETE SET (20) 4.80 12.00
1 Pat McLeod .20 .50
2 Rick Lessard .20 .50
3 Duane Joyce .20 .50
4 David Williams .20 .50
5 Arturs Irbe 1.20 3.00
6 Murray Garbutt .20 .50
7 Gary Emmons .20 .50
8 Jeff Madill .20 .50
9 Ron Handy .20 .50
10 Peter Lappin .20 .50
11 Mike Colman .20 .50
12 Ed Courtenay .20 .50
13 Mikhail Kravets .20 .50
14 Claudio Scremin .20 .50
15 Dale Craigwell .20 .50
16 Wade Flaherty .30 .75
17 Kevin Evans .20 .50
18 Larry DePalma .20 .50
19 Dean Kolstad .20 .50
20 Gord Frantti .20 .50

1992-93 Kansas City Blades

Little is known about this set beyond confirmation of the checklist and some recent sales. Any additional information should be forwarded to hockeymag@beckett.com.

COMPLETE SET (20) 4.00 10.00
1 Wade Flaherty .30 .75
2 David Williams .20 .50
3 Duane Joyce .20 .50
4 Jeff Sharples .20 .50
5 Victor Ignatjev .20 .50
6 Jeff McLean .20 .50
7 Brian Lawton .20 .50
8 Troy Frederick .20 .50
9 Jaroslav Otevrel .20 .50
10 Gary Emmons .20 .50
11 Dody Wood .20 .50
12 Ed Courtenay .20 .50
13 Mark Beaufait .20 .50
14 J.F. Quintin .20 .50
15 Dale Craigwell .20 .50
16 Mikhail Kravets .20 .50
17 John Weisbrod .20 .50
18 Mike Colman .20 .50
19 Claudio Scremin .20 .50
20 Dean Kolstad .20 .50

1993-94 Kansas City Blades

Little is known about this set beyond the confirmed checklist. Any additional information should be forwarded to hockeymag@beckett.com.

COMPLETE SET (20) 4.00 10.00
1 Duane Joyce .20 .50
2 Sean Gorman .20 .50
3 Victor Ignatjev .20 .50
4 Jeff McLean .20 .50
5 Kip Miller .30 .75
6 Jaroslav Otevrel .20 .50
7 David Bruce .20 .50
8 Gary Emmons .20 .50
9 Dody Wood .20 .50
10 Lee Leslie .20 .50
11 Alexander Cherbayev .20 .50
12 J.F. Quintin .20 .50
13 Ed Courtenay .20 .50
14 Andrei Nazarov .30 .75
15 Mikhail Kravets .20 .50
16 Mike Colman .20 .50
17 Vlastimil Kroupa .20 .50
18 Andrei Buschan .20 .50
19 Trevor Robins .20 .50
20 Wade Flaherty .30 .75

1994-95 Kansas City Blades

This set features the Blades of the IHL. Beyond the confirmed checklist, we don't have too many details to offer. Anyone up on this set is encouraged to contact us.

COMPLETE SET (20) 4.00 10.00
1 Duane Joyce .20 .50
2 Ken Hammond .20 .50
3 Michal Sykora .20 .50
4 Kevin Wortman .20 .50
5 Andrei Buschan .20 .50
6 Chris Tancill .20 .50
7 Ken Hodge .20 .50
8 David Bruce .20 .50
9 Jan Caloun .30 .75
10 Gary Emmons .20 .50
11 Dody Wood .20 .50
12 Lee Leslie .20 .50
13 Alexander Cherbayev .20 .50
14 J.F. Quintin .20 .50
15 Claudio Scremin .20 .50
16 Dean Grillo .20 .50
17 Andrei Nazarov .30 .75
18 Todd Holt .20 .50
19 Vlastimil Kroupa .20 .50
20 Trevor Robins .20 .50

1995-96 Kansas City Blades

Little is known about this set beyond the confirmed checklist. Additional information should be forwarded to hockeymag@beckett.com.

COMPLETE SET (25) 4.00 10.00
1 Larry Dyck .16 .40
2 Paul Dyck .16 .40
3 Jeff Batters .16 .40
4 David Bruce .16 .40
5 Jan Caloun .30 .75
6 Alexander Cherbayev .20 .50
7 Gary Emmons .16 .40
8 Dean Ewens .16 .40
9 Pat Ferschweiler .16 .40
10 Dean Grillo .16 .40
11 Ken Hammond .16 .40
12 Alexander Osadchy .16 .40
13 Jeff McLean .16 .40
14 Fredrik Nilsson .20 .50
15 Fredrik Oduya .16 .40
16 J.F. Quintin .16 .40
17 Geoff Sarjeant .20 .50
18 Claudio Scremin .16 .40
19 Chris Tancill .20 .50
20 Alexi Yegorov .20 .50
21 Viktor Kozlov .40 1.00
22 Sergei Bautin .16 .40
23 Vasily Tikhonov HCO .04 .10
24 Drew Remenda ACO .04 .10
25 Chilly MASCOT .04 .10

1996-97 Kansas City Blades

Little is known about this set beyond confirmation of the checklist. Additional information can be forwarded to hockeymag@beckett.com.

COMPLETE SET (25) 4.80 12.00
1 Ian Boyce .20 .50
2 David Bruce .30 .75
3 Jason Cirone .20 .50
4 Dale Craigwell .30 .75
5 Brent Cullaton .20 .50
6 Philippe DeRouville .40 .75
7 Larry Dyck .20 .50
8 Paul Dyck .20 .50
9 Gary Emmons .20 .50
10 Dean Ewen .20 .50
11 Bryan Fogarty .20 .50
12 Jason Herter .20 .50
13 Jim Kyte .20 .50
14 Jeff Madill .20 .50
15 Jeff McLean .20 .50
16 John Purves .30 .75
17 J.F. Quintin .20 .50
18 Normand Rochefort .20 .50
19 Claudio Scremin .20 .50
20 Brian Stacey .20 .50
21 Dean Sylvester .30 .75
22 Don Jackson HCO .04 .10
23 Lucien DeBlois ACO .20 .50
24 KC Blades .04 .10
25 PHPA Web Site .04 .10

1997-98 Kansas City Blades Magnets

These magnets were released as promotional giveaways over a series of five games.

COMPLETE SET (5) 4.00 10.00
1 Claudio Scremin .80 2.00
2 Gary Emmons .80 2.00
3 David Bruce .80 2.00
4 Jan Caloun .80 2.00
5 Dean Grillo .80 2.00

1998-99 Kansas City Blades

Little is known about this set beyond the checklist. Any additional information can be forwarded to hockeymag@beckett.com.

COMPLETE SET (30) 6.00 15.00
1 Title Card .04 .10
2 Brian Leitza .20 .50
3 Dan Ratushny .20 .50
4 Trevor Sherban .20 .50
5 Eric Rud .20 .50
6 Tuomas Gronman .20 .50
7 Eric Perrin .20 .50
8 Brendan Yarema .20 .50
9 Brian Bonin .20 .50
10 Pat Ferschweiler .20 .50
11 Dody Wood .40 1.00
12 David Ling .40 1.00
13 Rocky Weising .20 .50
14 Jean-Guy Trudel .30 .75
15 Vlastimil Kroupa .20 .50
16 Steven Low .20 .50
17 Ryan Mulhern .20 .50
18 Brent Bilodeau .20 .50
19 Grant Richison .20 .50
20 Dave Chyzowski .20 .50
21 David Vallieres .20 .50
22 Patrick Lalime .80 2.00
23 Jean Sebastien Aubin .80 2.00
24 Jason Cirone .20 .50
25 Paul MacLean CO .04 .10
26 Gary Emmons ACO .04 .10
27 John Doolan EQ .04 .10
28 Jeff Kreuser TR .04 .10
29 Scrapper Mascot .04 .10
30 Logo Card .04 .10

1999-00 Kansas City Blades

These two oversized cards are likely part of a larger set offered to fans at autograph signing sessions. Information on others can be forwarded to hockeymag@beckett.com.

COMPLETE SET (2) .80 2.00
1 Gary Emmons .40 1.00
2 Wade Flaherty .40 1.00

1999-00 Kansas City Blades Supercuts

This 29-card set was sponsored by Supercuts and featured an action photo of each player with a small bio on back of each card. The cards are not numbered and are listed below in alphabetical order. It is believed that the cards were offered as a promotional giveaway.

COMPLETE SET 6.00 15.00
1 Tom Askey .40 1.00
2 Joe Blaznek .20 .50
3 Aris Brimanis .20 .50
4 Dave Chyzowski .20 .50
5 Jason Cirone .20 .50
6 Pat Ferschweiler .20 .50
7 Forrest Gore .20 .50
8 Sean Haggerty .20 .50
9 David Ling .40 1.00
10 Steve Lingren .20 .50
11 Tyler Moss .40 1.00
12 Nick Naumenko .20 .50
13 Eric Perrin .20 .50
14 Michal Pivonka .40 1.00
15 Bruce Racine .40 1.00
16 Grant Richison .20 .50
17 Jon Rohloff .20 .50
18 Ray Schultz .20 .50
19 David Valliers .20 .50
20 Jan Vodrazka .20 .50
21 Dody Wood .40 1.00
22 Brendan Yarema .20 .50
23 Scrapper MASCOT .10 .25
24 Jeff Kreuser TR .10 .25
25 John Doolan MGR .10 .25
26 Gary Emmons CO .10 .25
27 Paul MacLean HCO .10 .25
28 PHPA Logo .01
29 Supercuts Coupon .01

2000-01 Kansas City Blades

This set features the Blades of the IHL. The set was issued as a promotional giveaway early in the season and was sponsored by Dick's Sporting Goods.

COMPLETE SET (27) 6.00 15.00
1 Ryan Bonni .30 .75
2 Jan Vodrazka .20 .50
3 Bryan Allen .30 .75
4 Zenith Komarniski .20 .50
5 Sean Tallaire .20 .50
6 Ryan Ready .20 .50
7 Regan Darby .20 .50
8 Dody Wood .30 .75
9 Harold Druken .40 1.00
10 Darrell Hay .20 .50
11 Vadim Sharifijanov .30 .75
12 Steve Lingren .20 .50
13 Josh Holden .40 1.00
14 Mike Brown .30 .75
15 Jeff Scissons .20 .50
16 Jarkko Ruutu .30 .75
17 Pat Kavanagh .20 .50
18 Brad Leeb .20 .50
19 Bryan Helmer .20 .50
20 Artem Chubarov .30 .75
21 Corey Schwab .30 .75
22 Alfie Michaud .30 .75
23 Stan Smyl CO .20 .50
24 Barry Smith CO .10 .25
25 Ryno SPONSOR .01
26 Dick's SPONSOR .01
27 PHPA SPONSOR .01

1998-99 Kelowna Rockets

This 28-card set features the Kelowna Rockets of the Western Hockey League. Among the players featured are 2001 first-round pick Kiel McLeod and San Jose Sharks defender Scott Hannan.

COMPLETE SET (28) 6.00 15.00
1 Ryan Cuthbert .20 .50
2 Jan Dusanek .20 .50
3 B.J. Fehr .20 .50
4 Vernon Fiddler .30 .75
5 Mitch Fritz .20 .50
6 Carsen Germyn .20 .50
7 Scott Hannan .40 1.00
8 Bruce Harrison .20 .50
9 Trevor Hitchings .20 .50
10 J.J. Hunter .20 .50
11 Justin Jack .20 .50
12 Clint Keichinger .20 .50
13 Kevin Korol .20 .50
14 Corey Koski .20 .50
15 Quintin Laing .20 .50
16 Lindsey Materi .20 .50
17 Rory McDade .20 .50
18 Brett McLean .30 .75
19 Gavin McLeod .20 .50
20 Kiel Mcleod .40 1.00
21 Lubomir Pistek .20 .50
22 Robby Sandrock .20 .50
23 David Selthun .20 .50
24 Joe Suderman .20 .50
25 Kevin Swanson .20 .50
26 Ryan Wade .20 .50
27 Nolan Yonkman .30 .75
28 Rocky Racoon MASCOT .04 .10

2000-01 Kelowna Rockets

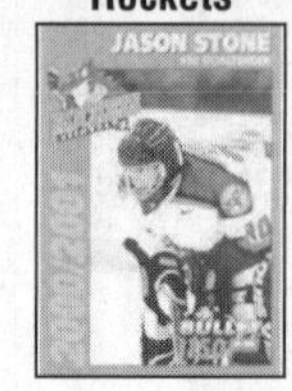

This set features the Rockets of the WHL. It was originally issued in the form of two-card perforated strips as a promotional giveaway. The cards are unnumbered, and so are listed alphabetically.

COMPLETE SET (22) 6.00 15.00
1 Kiel McLeod .40 1.00
2 Rory McDade .30 .75
3 Tomas Oravec .30 .75
4 Carsen Germyn .40 1.00
5 Chris Di Ubaldo .30 .75
6 Ryan Cuthbert .30 .75
7 Randall Gelech .30 .75
8 Blaine Depper .30 .75
9 Gavin McLeod .30 .75
10 Bart Rushmer .30 .75
11 Tyler Mosienko .30 .75
12 Josh Gorges .30 .75
13 Jason Stone .30 .75
14 Brett Palin .30 .75
15 Richie Regehr .40 1.00
16 David Selthun .30 .75
17 Seth Leonard .30 .75
18 Jan Fadrny .30 .75
19 Joe Suderman .30 .75
20 Kevin Swanson .30 .75
21 Rocky Raccoon MASCOT .02 .10
22 Marc Habscheid CO .10 .25
23 Paul Hurd .20 .50
24 Cam Paddock .20 .50
25 Richard Kelly .20 .50
26 Travis Moen .40 1.00

2001-02 Kelowna Rockets

The cards were issued as a promotional giveaway. As they are unnumbered, they are listed in alphabetical order.

COMPLETE SET (28) 20.00
1 Shane Bendera 1.00
2 Jeff Coulter .75
3 Ryan Cuthbert .75
4 Jesse Ferguson .75
5 Randall Gelech .75
6 Josh Gorges 1.00
7 Richard Kelly .75
8 Chuck Kobasew 3.00
9 Seth Leonard .75
10 Josh Lepp .75
11 Nick Marach .75
12 Ryan Mayko .75
13 Kiel McLeod 1.00
14 Travis Moen 1.00
15 Tyler Mosienko .75
16 Tomas Oravec .75
17 Cam Paddock .75
18 Brett Palin .75
19 Bart Rushmer .75
20 Tomas Slovak .75
21 Stephen Sunderman .75
22 Kevin Young .75
23 Marc Habscheid HCO .20
24 Larry Keating ACO .10
25 Jeff Truitt ACO .10
26 Scott Hoyer TR .10
27 Regan Bartel PA .10
28 Mascot .10

2002-03 Kelowna Rockets

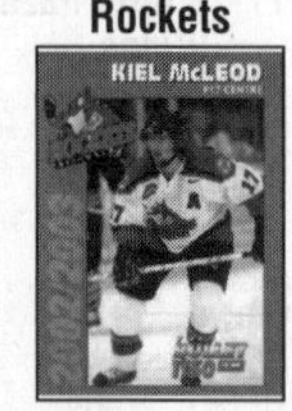

COMPLETE SET (28) 15.00
1 Josh Lepp .75
2 Cam Paddock .50
3 Kiel McLeod 1.00
4 Joel Henituik .50
5 Brett Palin .50
6 Richard Kelly .50
7 Stephen Sunderman .50
8 Tyler Spurgeon .50
9 Joni Lindolf .50
10 Darren Deschamps .50
11 Shea Weber 2.00
12 Randall Gelech .50
13 David Jacobson .50
14 Jesse Schultz .50
15 Blake Comeau .50
16 Ryan Mayko .50
17 Mike Card .50
18 Josh Gorges 1.00
19 Tomas Slovak .75
20 Kelly Guard 1.00
21 Troy Bodie .50
22 Ryan Cuthbert .50
23 Tyler Mosienko .50
24 Mark Olafson .50
25 Nick Tarnasky .50
26 Marc Habscheid HCO .50
27 Jeff Truitt ACO .10
28 Mascot .10

2003 Kelowna Rockets Memorial Cup

Cards are unnumbered and listed below in alphabetical order.

COMPLETE SET (20) 15.00
1 Troy Brodie .75
2 Mike Card .75
3 Blake Comeau .75
4 Ryan Cuthbert .75
5 Simon Ferguson .75
6 Randall Gelech .75
7 Josh Gorges 1.00
8 Kelly Guard 1.50
9 Duncan Keith .75
10 Josh Lepp 1.00
11 Joni Lindolf .75
12 Kiel McLeod 1.00
13 Tyler Mosienko .75
14 Mark Olafson .75
15 Cam Paddock .75
16 Brett Palin .75
17 Jesse Schultz 1.00
18 Tomas Slovak 1.00
19 Tyler Spurgeon .75
20 Shea Weber .75

2003-04 Kelowna Rockets

COMPLETE SET (28) 10.00 25.00
1 Michael Blanar .40 1.00
2 Troy Bodie .40 1.00
3 Mike Card .40 1.00
4 Blake Comeau .75 2.00
5 Kyle Cumiskey .40 1.00
6 Darren Deschamps .40 1.00
7 Simon Ferguson .40 1.00
8 Randall Gelech .40 1.00
9 Josh Gorges .75 2.00
10 Kelly Guard .75 2.00
11 Brent Howarth .40 1.00
12 Justin Keller .40 1.00
13 Joni Lindlof .40 1.00
14 Tyler Mosienko .40 1.00
15 Mark Olafson .40 1.00
16 Cam Paddock .40 1.00
17 Brett Palin .40 1.00
18 Chris Ray .40 1.00
19 Kevin Reinholt .40 1.00
20 Tyler Spurgeon .40 1.00
21 Nolan Waker .40 1.00
22 Shea Weber 1.25 3.00
23 Derek Yeomans .40 1.00
24 Marc Habscheid CO .02 .10
25 Jeff Truitt ACO .02 .10
26 Regan Bartel ANN .02 .10
27 Scott Hoyer TR .02 .10
28 Rocky Raccoon MASCOT .02 .10

2004-05 Kelowna Rockets

COMPLETE SET (28) 8.00 20.00
1 Troy Bodie .30 .75
2 Shea Weber 1.25 3.00
3 Justin Keller .30 .75
4 Craig Cuthbert .30 .75
5 Darren Deschamps .30 .75
6 Kristofer Westblom .30 .75
7 Brett Palin .30 .75
8 Kyle Cumiskey .30 .75
9 Chris Ray .30 .75
10 Lauris Darzins .30 .75
11 Rockey Raccoon .02 .10
12 Jeff Truitt .30 .75
13 Colin Joe .30 .75
14 Tyler Mosienko .30 .75
15 Blake Comeau .50 1.25
16 Tyler Spurgeon .30 .75
17 Derek Yeomans .30 .75
18 Ryan Huska .30 .75
19 Scott Hoyer .30 .75
20 Regan Bartel .30 .75
21 Gary Sylvester .30 .75
22 Troy Otukany .30 .75
23 Kirt Hill .30 .75
24 Brent Howarth .30 .75
25 Clayton Bauer .30 .75
26 Michal Blanar .30 .75
27 Mike Card .30 .75
28 Kevin Reinholt .30 .75

2005-06 Kelowna Rockets

COMPLETE SET (28) 8.00 20.00
1 Cody Almond .30 .75
2 Josiah Anderson .30 .75
3 Clayton Bauer .30 .75
4 Troy Bodie .30 .75
5 Mike Card .30 .75
6 Blake Comeau .60 1.50

7 Liam Couture .30 .75
8 Kyle Cumiskey .30 .75
9 Craig Cuthbert .30 .75
10 Lauris Darzins .30 .75
11 Tysen Dowzak .30 .75
12 Alexander Edler .30 .75
13 Kirt Hill .30 .75
14 Brent Howarth .30 .75
15 Colin Joe .30 .75
16 Justin Keller .30 .75
17 Colin Long .30 .75
18 Myles MacRae .30 .75
19 Troy Ofukany .30 .75
20 Chris Ray .30 .75
21 Kevin Reinholt .30 .75
22 Rob Roteliuk .30 .75
23 Luke Schenn .30 .75
24 Tyler Spurgeon .30 .75
25 Kristofer Westblom .30 .75
26 Derek Yeomans .30 .75
27 Jeff Truitt HC .02 .10
28 Rocky Raccoon MASCOT .02 .10

1984-85 Kelowna Wings

This 56-card safety standard-size set was sponsored by A and W, Pizza Patio, CKIQ (a radio station), and the Kelowna Wings. The cards feature black-and-white posed and action player photos. The words "Kelowna Wings 1984-85" are at the top of card numbers 2-22, while the words "Junior Hockey Grads" appear at the top of card numbers 1 and 23-56. The player's name, position, and the card number are at the bottom. The cards are numbered on the front in the lower right corner.

COMPLETE SET (56) 32.00 80.00
1 Checklist .20 .50
2 Darcy Wakaluk .60 1.50
3 Stacey Nickel .20 .50
4 Jeff Sharples .30 .75
5 Greg Zuk .20 .50
6 Daryn Sivertson .20 .50
7 Randy Cameron .20 .50
8 Mark Fioretti .20 .50
9 Ron Viglasi .20 .50
10 Ian Herbers .20 .50
11 Mike Wegleitner .20 .50
12 Terry Zaporzan .20 .50
13 Dwaine Hutton .20 .50
14 Rod Williams .20 .50
15 Jeff Rohlicek .20 .50
16 Brent Gilchrist .60 1.50
17 Rocky Dundas .20 .50
18 Grant Delcourt .20 .50
19 Cam Laroruk .20 .50
20 Tony Horacek .20 .50
21 Mark Wingerter .20 .50
22 Mick Vukota .30 .75
23 Danny Gare .60 1.50
24 Rich Sutter .40 1.00
25 Alfie Turcotte .20 .50
26 Bryan Trottier 4.00 10.00
27 Bill Derlago .40 1.00
28 Stan Smyl .80 2.00
29 Brent Sutter .80 2.00
30 Mel Bridgman .40 1.00
31 Paul Cyr .30 .75
32 Gary Lupul .20 .50
33 Ray Neufeld .30 .75
34 Brian Propp .80 2.00
35 Bob Nystrom .80 2.00
36 Ryan Walter .40 1.00
37 Russ Courtnall .80 2.00
38 Larry Playfair .20 .50
39 Ron Delorme .20 .50
40 Ron Sutter .40 1.00
41 Bobby Clarke 4.00 10.00
42 Bob Bourne .40 1.00
43 Cam Neely 12.00 40.00
44 Murray Craven .40 1.00
45 Clark Gillies 1.20 3.00
46 Ron Flockhart .40 1.00
47 Harold Snepsts 1.20 3.00
48 Duane Sutter .40 1.00
49 Garth Butcher .40 1.00
50 Bill Hajt .20 .50
51 Jim Benning .20 .50
52 Ray Allison .20 .50
53 Ken Wregget .80 2.00
54 Phil Russell .30 .75
55 Brad McCrimmon .60 1.50
56 Dan Hodgson .20 .50

1996-97 Kentucky Thoroughblades

This set was sold at the Kentucky team store, and featured an SRP of $3.00. Set features color action photos on the front, with statistics and biographical information on the back.

COMPLETE SET (26) 4.80 12.00
1 Ken Belanger .30 .75
2 Alexandre Boikov .20 .50
3 Jan Caloun .30 .75
4 Denis Chervyakov .20 .50
5 Jarrett Deuling .20 .50
6 Iain Fraser .20 .50
7 Dean Grillo .20 .50
8 Steve Guolla .30 .75
9 Sean Haggerty .20 .50
10 Jason Holland .20 .50
11 Lance Leslie .20 .50
12 Chris Lipuma .20 .50
13 Pat Mikesch .20 .50
14 Fredrik Oduya .20 .50
15 Jamie Ram .30 .75
16 Chris Tancill .30 .75
17 Jason Strudwick .30 .75
18 Steve Webb .30 .75
19 Jason Widmer .20 .50
20 Jim Wiley .20 .50
21 Alexei Yegorov .30 .75
NNO Ad Card-In Your Face .01
NNO Ad Card-PHPA .01
NNO Lucky the Mascot .04 .10
NNO Rupp Arena .04 .10
NNO Team Photo .10 .25

1997-98 Kentucky Thoroughblades

Little is known about this set beyond the confirmed checklist. Additional information can be forwarded to hockeymag@beckett.com.

COMPLETE SET (25) 8.00 20.00
1 Team Photo .04 .10
2 Peter Allen .20 .50
3 Niklas Andersson .20 .50
4 Alexandre Boikov .20 .50
5 Zdeno Chara .40 3.00
6 Steve Guolla .24 .60
7 Sean Haggerty .20 .50
8 Jason Holland .20 .50
9 Alexander Korolyuk .30 .75
10 Evgeni Nabokov 4.00 10.00
11 Fredrik Oduya .20 .50
12 Chad Penney .20 .50
13 Jamie Ram .30 .75
14 Peter Roed .20 .50
15 Jason Strudwick .20 .50
16 Tony Tuzzolino .30 .75
17 Steve Webb .30 .75
18 Jason Widmer .20 .50
19 Brendan Yarema .20 .50
20 Alexei Yegorov .24 .60
21 Andrei Zyuzin .30 .75
22 Jim Wiley HCO .04 .10
23 Lucky Mascot .04 .10
24 PHPA Web Site .01
25 AHL Web Site .01

1998-99 Kentucky Thoroughblades

This 25-card set was released after the regular season had ended. It was produced by Split Second. All cards are unnumbered, and are listed in alphabetical order.

COMPLETE SET (25) 8.00 20.00
1 Peter Allen .16 .40
2 Eric Boulton .75 2.00
3 Dan Boyle .30 .75
4 Matt Bradley .20 .50
5 Mike Craig .16 .40
6 Jarrett Deuling .16 .40
7 Curtis Doell .16 .40
8 Dave Duerden .16 .40
9 Sean Gauthier .16 .40
10 Christian Gosselin .16 .40
11 Steve Guolla .20 .50
12 Harold Hersh .20 .50
13 Alexander Korolyuk .20 .50
14 Filip Kuba .20 .50
15 Steve Lingren .20 .50
16 Andy MacIntyre .12 .30
17 Evgeni Nabokov 4.00 10.00
Nickname "John" on card front
18 Jarrod Skalde .30 .75
19 Mark Smith .60 1.50
20 Herbert Vasilijevs .16 .40
21 Eric Veilleux .16 .40
22 Andrei Zyuzin .30 .75
23 Roy Sommer HCO .04 .10
24 Lucky Mascot .04 .10
25 AHL Web Site .01

1999-00 Kentucky Thoroughblades

This set features the Thoroughblades of the AHL. The slightly oversized set was produced by the team and sold at home games.

COMPLETE SET (25) 8.00 20.00
1 Kentucky Thoroughblades .10 .25
2 Coaching Staff .10 .25
3 Chris Armstrong .20 .50
4 Matt Bradley .20 .50
5 Garrett Burnett .20 .50
6 Adam Colagiacomo .30 .75
7 Jon Coleman .20 .50
8 Larry Courville .20 .50
9 Mike Craig .20 .50
10 Jarrett Deuling .20 .50
11 Doug Friedman .20 .50
12 Christian Gosselin .20 .50
13 Scott Hannan .30 .75
14 Johan Hedberg 2.00 5.00
15 Shawn Heins .30 .75
16 Robert Jindrich .30 .75
17 Miikka Kiprusoff 1.20 5.00
18 Eric Landry .20 .50
19 Chris Lipsett .20 .50
20 Andy Lundbohm .20 .50
21 Robert Mulick .20 .50
22 Adam Nittel .40 1.00
23 Peter Roed .20 .50
24 Mark Smith .30 .75
25 Lucky MASCOT .10 .25

2000-01 Kentucky Thoroughblades

This set features the Thoroughblades of the AHL. It is believed that the set was sold by the team, but this is not confirmed. It's also believed that the final five cards were available as redemptions at an area business, which accounts for their scarcity. Any additional information can be forwarded to hockeymag@beckett.com.

COMPLETE SET (30) 30.00 80.00
1 Greg Andrusak .14 .35
2 Steve Bancroft .14 .35
3 Zoltan Batovsky .14 .35
4 Matt Bradley .14 .35
5 Jonathan Cheechoo 4.00 10.00
6 Adam Colagiacomo .20 .50
7 Larry Courville .20 .50
8 Rob Davison .20 .50
9 Jarrett Deuling .14 .35
10 Christian Gosselin .14 .35
11 Robert Jindrich .20 .50
12 Miikka Kiprusoff 4.00 10.00
13 Ryan Kraft .14 .50
14 Eric Laplante .14 .35
15 Chris Lipsett .14 .35
16 Andy Lundbohm .14 .35
17 Dave MacIsaac .14 .35
18 Jim Montgomery .20 .50
19 Robert Mulick .14 .35
20 Adam Nittel .40 1.00
21 Mikael Samuelsson .20 .50
22 Mark Smith .30 .75
23 Vesa Toskala 2.00 5.00
24 Miroslav Zalesak .10 .25
25 Roy Sommer CO .10 .25
Nick Fotiu CO
L1 Kentucky Thoroughblades .40 1.00
P1 Adam Nittel 1.00 2.50
P2 Jonathan Cheechoo 10.00 25.00
SP1 Ryan Kraft .60 2.00
SP2 Evgeni Nabokov 10.00 25.00

1981-82 Kingston Canadians

This 25-card set measures approximately 2 5/8" by 4" and features posed, color player photos on thin white card stock. The player's name, position, and the team logo are printed in black below the picture.

COMPLETE SET (25) 12.00 30.00
1 Canadians Logo .20 .50
2 Scott MacLellan .20 .50
3 Dave Courtemanche .20 .50
4 Mark Reade .20 .50
5 Shawn Babcock .20 .50
6 Phil Bourque .40 1.00
7 Ian MacInnis .20 .50
8 Neil Trineer .20 .50
9 Syl Grandmaitre .20 .50
10 Carmine Vani .30 .75
11 Chuck Brimmer .20 .50
12 Mike Linseman .20 .50
13 Steve Seguin .20 .50
14 Dan Wood .20 .50
15 Kirk Muller 6.00 15.00
16 Jim Aldred .20 .50
17 Rick Wilson .60 1.50
18 Mike Siltala .20 .50
19 Howie Scruton .20 .50
20 Mike Stothers .40 1.00
21 Dennis Smith .20 .50
22 Steve Richey .20 .50
23 Mike Moffat .80 2.00
24 Jim Morrison CO/MG .20 .50
25 Randy Plumb .20 .50

1982-83 Kingston Canadians

This 27-card set measures approximately 2 5/8" by 4 1/8" and features posed action, color player photos with white borders on thin card stock. The player's name, position, and year of issue appear below the picture between the team logo and the Kingston Police Force insignia.

COMPLETE SET (27) 6.00 15.00
1 Jim Morrison MG .10 .25
2 Dennis Smith .30 .75
3 Curtis Collin .30 .75
4 Joel Brown .30 .75
5 Ron Handy .30 .75
6 Carmine Vani .30 .75
7 Al Andrews .40 1.00
8 Mike Siltala .30 .75
9 Syl Grandmaitre .30 .75
10 Steve Seguin .30 .75
11 Brian Dobbin .40 1.00
12 Mark Reade .30 .75
13 John Kemp .40 1.00
14 Dan Mahon .30 .75
15 Keith Knight .30 .75
16 Ron Sanko .30 .75
17 John Landry .30 .75
18 Chris Brant .30 .75
19 Dave Simurda .30 .75
20 Mike Lafoy .30 .75
21 Scott MacLellan .30 .75
22 Brad Walcot .30 .75
23 Steve Richey .30 .75
24 Rod Graham CO .10 .25
25 Ben Levesque .30 .75
26 Canadians Logo .10 .25
27 International Hockey .20 .50
Hall of Fame

1983-84 Kingston Canadians

This 30-card set measures slightly larger than standard at 2 5/8" by 3 5/8" and features posed color player photos with white borders on thin card stock. The player's name, position, and year appears below the picture between the Canadians logo and the Kingston Police Force insignia.

COMPLETE SET (30) 6.00 15.00
1 Checklist .10 .25
2 Dennis Smith .20 .50
3 Ben Levesque .20 .50
4 Const. Arie Moraal .10 .25
5 Tom Allen .20 .50
6 Mike Plesh .20 .50
7 Roger Belanger .20 .50
8 Jeff Chychrun .40 1.00
9 Mike King .20 .50
10 Scott Metcalfe .30 .75
11 David Lundmark .20 .50
12 Tim Salmon .20 .50
13 Ted Linesman .20 .50
14 Chris Clifford .30 .75
15 Todd Elik .40 1.00
16 Kevin Conway .20 .50
17 Barry Burkholder .20 .50
18 Joel Brown .20 .50
19 Steve King .20 .50
20 Craig Kales .20 .50
21 John Humphries TR .10 .25
22 David James .20 .50
23 Dave Simurda .20 .50
24 Allen Bishop .20 .50
25 Jeff Hogg .30 .75
26 Rick Cornacchia CO .30 .75
27 Ken Slater DPP .10 .25
28 Const. Bill Dextater .10 .25
29 Canadians Crest .10 .25
30 IHHOF logo .10 .25

1984-85 Kingston Canadians

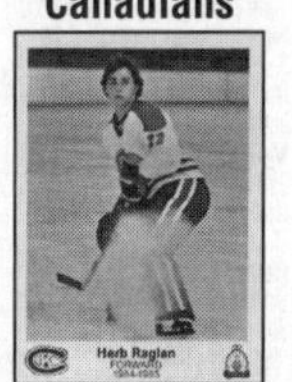

This 30-card features the Canadians of the OHL. It measures 2 5/8" by 3 5/8" and features color, posed action player photos with white borders. The player's name, position, and year appear at the bottom.

COMPLETE SET (30) 6.00 15.00
1 Kingston Police Crest .10 .25
2 Rick Cornacchia CO .20 .50
3 Const. Arie Moraal .10 .25
4 Ken Slater DPP .10 .25
5 Kingston Crest .10 .25
6 Scott Metcalfe .30 .75
7 Chris Clifford .30 .75
8 Todd Elik .30 .75
9 Len Spratt .30 .75
10 Mike Plesh .20 .50
11 Marc Lyons .20 .50
12 Barry Burkholder .20 .50
13 Rick Fera .20 .50
14 David Hoover .20 .50
15 Andy Rivers .20 .50
16 Marc Laforge .30 .75
17 Peter Viscovich .20 .50
18 Jeff Chychrun .30 .75
19 Wayne Erskine .20 .50
20 Todd Clarke .20 .50
21 Darren Wright .20 .50
22 Tony Rocca .20 .50
23 Brian Verbeek .20 .50
24 Herb Raglan .30 .75
25 Daril Holmes .20 .50
26 Len Coyle TR .10 .25
27 Ted Linesman .20 .50
28 IHHOF logo .10 .25
29 Troy MacNevin .20 .50
30 Peter Campbell TR .10 .25

1985-86 Kingston Canadians

This 30-card set measures approximately 2 5/8" by 3 5/8" and features color, posed action player photos with white borders. The player's name and position appear at the bottom.

COMPLETE SET (30) 4.80 12.00
1 Kingston Police Crest .10 .25
2 Dale Sandles ACO .10 .25
3 Const. Arie Moraal .10 .25
4 Fred O'Donnell GM/CO .10 .25
5 Kingston Crest .10 .25
6 Scott Metcalfe .20 .50
7 Chris Clifford .30 .75
8 Steve Seftel .20 .50
9 Andy Pearson .20 .50
10 Jeff Cornelius .20 .50
11 Marc Lyons .20 .50
12 Barry Burkholder .20 .50
13 Bryan Fogarty .30 .75
14 Jeff Sirkka .20 .50
15 Scott Pearson .30 .75
16 Marc Laforge .20 .50
17 Peter Viscovich .20 .50
18 Jeff Chychrun UER .30 .75
(Name misspelled Chycren)
19 Wayne Erskine .20 .50
20 Todd Clarke .20 .50
21 Darren Wright .20 .50
22 Mike Maurice .20 .50
23 Brian Verbeek .20 .50
24 Mike Fiset .20 .50
25 Daril Holmes .20 .50
26 Len Coyle TR .10 .25
27 Ted Linesman .20 .50
28 IHHOF logo .10 .25
29 Troy MacNevin .20 .50
30 Peter Campbell TR .10 .25

1986-87 Kingston Canadians

This 30-card set measures approximately 2 5/8" by 3 5/8" and features color, posed player portraits with blue studio backgrounds set on a white card face. The player's name, position, and year appear at the bottom.

COMPLETE SET (30) 4.00 10.00
1 Kingston Crest .10 .25
2 Fred O'Donnell GM/CO .04 .10
3 Arie Moraal COP .04 .10
4 Dale Sandles CO .04 .10
5 Kingston Police Crest .04 .10
6 Brian Tessier .30 .75
7 Franco Giammarco .30 .75
8 Peter Liptrott .20 .50
9 Chris Clifford .30 .75
10 Scott Metcalfe .20 .50
11 Scott Pearson .30 .75
12 Bryan Fogarty .30 .75
13 Daril Holmes .20 .50
14 Andy Rivers .20 .50
15 Troy MacNevin .20 .50
16 Marc Laforge .20 .50
17 Wayne Erskine .20 .50
18 Peter Viskovich .20 .50
19 Mike Maurice .20 .50
20 Steve Seftel .20 .50
21 Chad Badaway .20 .50
22 Marc Lyons .20 .50
23 Jeff Sirkka .20 .50
24 Mike Fiset .20 .50
25 John Battice .20 .50
26 Len Coyle TR .04 .10
27 Sloan Torti .20 .50
28 Alain Laforge .20 .50
29 Ted Linesman .20 .50
30 Peter Campbell TR .04 .10

1987-88 Kingston Canadians

This 30-card P.L.A.Y. (Police, Laws and Youth) set measures approximately 2 3/4" by 3 5/8" and features color player portraits with blue studio backgrounds. The fronts are accented by white borders.

COMPLETE SET (30) 4.80 12.00
1 Arie Moraal COP .04 .10
2 Gord Wood GM .04 .10
3 Kingston Police Crest .10 .25
4 Jacques Tremblay CO .10 .25
5 Rhonda Sheridan PR .04 .10
6 Jeff Wilson .30 .75
7 Franco Giammarco .30 .75
8 Peter Liptrott .20 .50
9 David Weiss .30 .75
10 Joel Morin .20 .50
11 Mark Turner .20 .50
12 Jeff Sirkka .20 .50
13 James Henckle .20 .50
14 Mike Bodnarchuk .20 .50
15 Mike Cavanaugh .20 .50
16 Darcy Cahill .20 .50
17 Kevin Falesy .20 .50
18 Dean Pella .20 .50
19 Brad Gratton .20 .50
20 Steve Seftel .20 .50
21 Bryan Fogarty .20 .50
22 Scott Pearson .20 .50
23 Tyler Pella .20 .50
24 Mike Fiset .20 .50
25 John Battice .20 .50
26 Len Coyle TR .04 .10
27 Geoff Schneider .20 .50
28 Chris Lukey .20 .50
29 Trevor Smith .20 .50
30 Peter Campbell TR .04 .10

1993-94 Kingston Frontenacs

Printed by Slapshot Images Ltd., this standard size 25-card set features the 1993-94 Kingston Frontenacs. On a team color-coded background with black stripes, the fronts feature color action player photos with thin black borders. The team name is printed diagonally in the upper left corner of the photo, while the player's name and number appear in a yellow bar in the bottom edge of the photo.

COMPLETE SET (25) 4.00 10.00
1 Greg Lovell .16 .40
2 Marc Lamothe .16 .40
3 Tyler Moss .20 .50
4 Marc Moro .16 .40
5 Trevor Doyle .16 .40
6 Jeff Dacosta .16 .40
7 Gord Walsh .16 .40
8 Brian Scott .16 .40
9 Jason Disher .16 .40
10 Alexander Zhurik .16 .40
11 Ken Boone .16 .40
12 Cail MacLean .16 .40
13 Bill Maranduik .16 .40
14 Martin Sychra .16 .40
15 Duncan Fader .16 .40
16 David Ling .20 .75
17 Chad Kilger .30 .75
18 Greg Kraemer .16 .40
19 Trent Cull .16 .40
20 Steve Parson .16 .40
21 Craig Rivet .16 .40
22 Keli Corpse .16 .40
23 Brett Lindros .30 .75
24 David Allison CO .04 .10
Michael Allison ACO
NNO Slapshot Ad Card .04 .10

1998-99 Kingston Frontenacs

The set features the Frontenacs of the OHL. Sponsored by the Community Sport and Activity News, this team-issued set features color action photos on the front of each card with a headshot and stats of each player on the back. The cards are unnumbered, so they are listed alphabetically.

COMPLETE SET (25) 4.80 12.00
1 Eric Braff .20 .50
2 Brett Clouthier .20 .50
3 Curtis Cruickshank .20 .50
4 Matt Elich .30 .75
5 Aaron Fransen .20 .50
6 Sean Griffin .20 .50
7 Kevin Grimes .20 .50
8 Andrew Ianiero .20 .50
9 Chad Lynch .20 .50
10 D.J. Maracle .20 .50
11 Larry Mavety HCO .10 .25
12 Morgan McCormick .20 .50
13 Walker McDonald .20 .50
14 Matt Price .20 .50
15 Mike Oliveira .20 .50
16 Brett Ormond .20 .50
17 Ryan Rivard .20 .50
18 Jonathan Schill .20 .50
19 Colin Scotland .20 .50
20 Nathan Tennant .20 .50
21 Darryl Thomson .20 .50
22 Ian Turner .20 .50
23 Jamie Young .20 .50
24 Mike Zigomanis .40 1.00
25 Checklist .04 .10

1999-00 Kingston Frontenacs

This set features the Frontenacs of the OHL. The slightly oversized cards were produced by the team and sold at home games. The set is noteworthy for an early appearance of goalie Andrew Raycroft and forwards Cory Stillman and Mike Zigomanis.

COMPLETE SET (23) 6.00 15.00
1 Checklist .04 .10
2 Sean Avery .60 1.50
3 Eric Braff .20 .50
4 Brett Clouthier .30 .75
5 Chris Cook .20 .50
6 Sean Griffin .20 .50
7 Brad Horan .20 .50
8 Andrew Ianiero .20 .50
9 Matt Junkins .20 .50
10 Darryl Knight .20 .50
11 Travis Lisabeth .20 .50
12 Doug MacIver .20 .50
13 Shaun Peet .20 .50
14 Jason Polera .20 .50
15 Andrew Raycroft 1.00 2.50
16 Johnathan Schill .20 .50
17 J-F Seguin .20 .50
18 Tomas Skvaridlo .20 .50
19 Mike Smith .20 .50
20 Cory Stillman .40 1.00
21 Nathan Tennant .30 .75
22 Darryl Thomson .20 .50
23 Michael Zigomanis .40 1.00

2000-01 Kingston Frontenacs

This set features the Frontenacs of the OHL. The set was produced by the team and sold at its souvenir stands. The cards are unnumbered, and so are listed below in alphabetical order.

COMPLETE SET (23) 4.80 10.00
1 Eric Braff .20 .40
2 Derek Campbell .20 .40
3 Brett Clouthier .30 .75
4 Chris Cook .20 .40
5 Count Frontenac MASCOT .04 .10
6 Peter Hamerlik .40 1.00
7 Brad Horan .20 .40
8 Andrew Ianiero .20 .40
9 Travis Lisabeth .20 .40
10 Doug MacIver .20 .40
11 The Coaches .10 .10
12 Justin McCutcheon .20 .40
13 Sean McMorrow .20 .50
14 Shane O'Brien .20 .40
15 Glenn Ridler .30 .75
16 Corey Sabourin .20 .40
17 J.F. Seguin .20 .40
18 Tomas Skvaridlo .20 .40
19 Cory Stillman .40 1.00
20 Nathan Tennant .20 .40
21 Darryl Thomson .20 .40
22 Brody Todd .20 .40
23 Mike Zigomanis .40 1.00
NNO Coca Cola .04 .01
NNO Title Card .04 .01

2001-02 Kingston Frontenacs

This set features the Frontenacs of the OHL. The cards were sold by the team at its souvenir stands.

COMPLETE SET (25) 4.80 14.00
1 Header Card .04 .10
2 Chris Cook .20 .50
3 Lou Dickenson .30 .75
4 Josh Gratton .20 .50
5 Peter Hamerlik .40 1.00
6 Chris Hardill .20 .50
7 Brad Horan .20 .50
8 Andrew Ianiero .30 .75
9 Drew Kivell .20 .50
10 Sean Langdon .20 .50
11 Doug MacIver .20 .50
12 Brandon McBride .20 .50
13 Justin McCutcheon .20 .50
14 Kyle Neufeld .20 .50
15 Shane O'Brien .20 .50
16 Scott Sheppard .20 .50
17 Mike Smith .20 .50
18 Sean Stefanski .20 .50
19 Anthony Stewart .20 3.00
20 Cory Stillman .30 .75
21 Justin Suda .20 .50
22 Nathan Tennant .30 .75
23 Ed Van Herpt .20 .50
24 Nick Van Herpt .20 .50
25 Coca-Cola Ad .01

2002-03 Kingston Frontenacs

COMPLETE SET (25) 12.00
1 Header Card .01
2 Chris Cook .50
3 Austin Corredato .50
4 Miguel Delisle .50
5 Drew Fata .50

6 Peter Hamerlik	.75
7 Brad Horan	.50
8 Bill Kinkel	.50
9 Drew Kivell	.50
10 Dwight LaBrosse	.50
11 Scott Maher	.50
12 Brandon McBride	.50
13 Justin McCutcheon	.50
14 Danny McDonald	.50
15 Clay McFadden	.50
16 Richard Power	.50
17 Bryan Rodney	.50
18 Ryan Stephenson	.50
19 Anthony Stewart	2.00
20 Cory Stillman	.50
21 Justin Suda	.50
22 Dan Turple	.50
23 Nick Van Herpt	.50
24 The Count MASCOT	.10
25 Ad card	.01

2004-05 Kingston Frontenacs

A total of 500 team sets were produced.

COMPLETE SET (24)	12.00
1 Evan Kotsopoulos	.50
2 Anthony Stewart	1.00
3 Bobby Bolt	.50
4 Chris Stewart	.50
5 Dayne Davis	.50
6 David Edgeworth	.50
7 Cory Emmerton	.50
8 Shawn Futers	.50
9 Todd Griffith	.50
10 Bobby Hughes	.50
11 Michael Kolarz	.50
12 Derek Lyons	.50
13 Phil Mangan	.50
14 Adam Nemeth	.50
15 Chris Petrow	.50
16 Blake Pronk	.50
17 Dany Revelle	.50
18 Ben Shutron	.50
19 Radek Smolenak	.50
20 Justin Suda	.50
21 Justin Wallingford	.50
22 Tony Rizzi	.50
23 Greg Williams	.50
24 Brady Morrison	.50

2005-06 Kingston Frontenacs

COMPLETE SET (23)	8.00	20.00
1 Cory Emmerton	.60	1.50
2 Chris Stewart	.60	1.50
3 Ben Shutron	.30	.75
4 Shawn Connors	.30	.75
5 Adam Nemeth	.30	.75
6 Matt Reis	.30	.75
7 Blake Pronk	.30	.75
8 Radek Smolenak	.30	.75
9 Luke Pither	.30	.75
10 Andrew Kizito	.30	.75
11 Tony Rizzi	.30	.75
12 Andrew Wilson	.30	.75
13 Bobby Hughes	.30	.75
14 Justin Wallingford	.30	.75
15 Todd Griffith	.30	.75
16 Michael Kolarz	.30	.75
17 Bobby Bolt	.30	.75
18 Connor Cameron	.30	.75
19 Mike Looby	.30	.75
20 Peder Skinner	.30	.75
21 J.F. Houle	.30	.75
22 Danny Taylor	.40	1.00
23 Daryl Borden	.40	1.00

2006-07 Kingston Frontenacs

COMPLETE SET (23)	8.00	15.00
1 Chris Stewart	.40	1.00
2 Kyle Bochek	.30	.75
3 Bobby Mignardi	.30	.75
4 Nathan Moon	.30	.75
5 Peder Skinner	.30	.75
6 Matt Auffrey	.30	.75
7 Matthew Kang	.30	.75
8 Bobby Nyholm	.30	.75
9 Jesse Biduke	.30	.75
10 Bobby Hughes	.30	.75
11 Josh Brittain	.30	.75
12 Bobby Bolt	.30	.75
13 Cory Emmerton	.40	1.00
14 Peter Stevens	.30	.75
15 Michael Kolarz	.30	.75
16 Ben Shutron	.40	1.00
17 Kevin Mole	.40	1.00
18 Adam Nemeth	.30	.75
19 Jonathan Sciacca	.30	.75
20 Andrew Kizito	.30	.75
21 Justin Wallingford	.30	.75
22 Daryl Borden	.30	.75
23 Jason Guy	.30	.75

1982-83 Kitchener Rangers

This 30-card set measures approximately 2 3/4" by 3 1/2" and features posed action color player photos with black inner borders and white outer borders.

COMPLETE SET (30)	16.00	40.00
1 Waterloo Regional Police Crest	.10	.25
2 Harold Basse Chief of Police	.10	.25
3 Sponsors' Card	.10	.25
4 Joe Crozier GM/CO	.20	.50
5 Checklist	.10	.25
6 Kerry Kerch	.30	.75
7 Tom St. James	.20	.50
8 Wendell Young	.80	2.00
9 David Shaw	.60	1.50
10 Darryl Boudreau	.30	.75
11 David Bruce	.40	1.00
12 Wayne Presley	.60	1.50
13 Garnet McKechney	.20	.50
14 Kevin Petendra	.20	.50
15 Brian Wilks	.20	.50
16 Jim Quinn	.20	.50
17 Al MacInnis	8.00	20.00
18 Dave Nicholls	.20	.50
19 Mike Eagles	.60	1.50
20 Mike Hough	.60	1.50
21 Greg Puhalski	.20	.50
22 Darren Wright	.20	.50
23 Todd Steffen	.20	.50
24 John Tucker	.60	1.50
25 Kent Paynter	.20	.50
26 Andy O'Brien	.20	.50
27 Les Bradley TR	.10	.25
28 Scott Biggs	.20	.50
29 Chris Martin TR	.10	.25
30 Dave Webster	.20	.50

1983-84 Kitchener Rangers

The Kitchener Rangers of the OHL are featured in this 30-card P.L.A.Y. (Police, Law and Youth) set, which was sponsored by the Waterloo Regional Police in conjunction with several company sponsors. The cards measure approximately 2 3/4" by 3 1/2" and are printed on thin card stock. The fronts feature color photos with the players posed in action stances. The photos are framed by black and white borders, and a facsimile autograph is inscribed across the bottom of the picture.

COMPLETE SET (30)	6.00	15.00
1 Joe Mantione	.40	1.00
2 Jim Quinn	.20	.50
3 Kitchener Rangers logo Checklist	.10	.25
4 Rob MacInnis	.20	.50
5 Louie Berardicurti	.20	.50
6 Neil Sandilands	.20	.50
7 Darren Wright	.20	.50
8 Tom Barrett CO/GM	.10	.25
9 Brian Wilks	.20	.50
10 Garnet McKechney	.20	.50
11 David Bruce	.40	1.00
12 Kent Paynter	.20	.50
13 Sponsor's card P.L.A.Y. Rules	.10	.25
14 Scott Kerr	.20	.50
15 Greg Puhalski	.20	.50
16 Wayne Presley	.40	1.00
17 Carmine Vani	.20	.50
18 Shawn Burr	.80	2.00
19 Dave Latta	.30	.75
20 John Tucker	.60	1.50
21 Mike Stevens	.20	.50
22 Harold Basse Chief of Police	.10	.25
23 Waterloo Regional Police	.10	.25
24 Peter Bakovic	.20	.50
25 Brian Ross	.20	.50
26 Brad Balshin	.20	.50
27 David Shaw	.40	1.00
28 Chris Trainer TR	.10	.25
29 Les Bradley TR	.10	.25
30 Ray LeBlanc	.80	2.00

1984-85 Kitchener Rangers

The Kitchener Rangers of the OHL are featured in this 30-card P.L.A.Y. (Police, Law and Youth) set, which was sponsored by the Waterloo Regional Police in conjunction with several company sponsors. The cards measure approximately 2 3/4" by 3 1/2" and are printed on thin card stock. The fronts feature color photos with the players posed in action stances. The photos are framed by black and white borders, and a facsimile autograph is inscribed across the bottom of the picture.

COMPLETE SET (30)	4.80	12.00
1 Waterloo Regional Police Crest	.10	.25
2 Harold Basse Chief of Police	.10	.25
3 Garnet McKechney	.20	.50
4 Tom Barrett GM/CO	.10	.25
5 Kitchener Rangers logo Checklist	.10	.25
6 Mike Bishop	.30	.75
7 Craig Wolanin	.40	1.00
8 Steve Marcolini	.20	.50
9 Peter Langlois	.20	.50
10 Dave Weiss	.30	.75
11 Ken Alexander	.20	.50
12 Ian Pound	.20	.50
13 Doug Stromback	.20	.50
14 Joel Brown	.20	.50
15 Brian Wilks	.20	.50
16 Robin Rubic	.20	.50
17 Kent Paynter	.20	.50
18 Jon Helinski	.20	.50
19 Greg Puhalski	.20	.50
20 Wayne Presley	.40	1.00
21 Dave McLlwain	.40	1.00
22 Shawn Burr	.40	1.00
23 Dave Latta	.24	.60
24 John Keller	.20	.50
25 Mike Stevens	.20	.50
26 Sponsors' Card	.10	.25
27 Richard Adolfi	.20	.50
28 Grant Sanders	.20	.50
29 Les Bradley TR	.10	.25
30 Sponsors' Card	.10	.25

1985-86 Kitchener Rangers

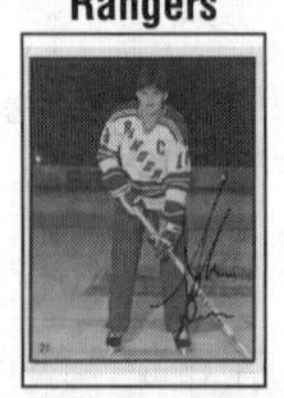

This 30-card set measures approximately 2 3/4" by 3 1/2" and is printed on thin card stock. The fronts feature posed, color player photos with thin black borders on a white card face. A facsimile autograph is inscribed across the picture. The cards are numbered on the front and back.

COMPLETE SET (30)	4.80	12.00
1 Waterloo Regional Police Crest	.10	.25
2 Harold Basse Chief of Police	.10	.25
3 Sponsors' Card	.10	.25
4 Tom Barrett GM/CO	.10	.25
5 Kitchener Rangers logo Checklist	.20	.50
6 Dave Weiss	.30	.75
7 Steve Marcolini	.20	.50
8 Kevin Gant	.20	.50
9 Ken Alexander	.20	.50
10 Mike Volpe	.30	.75
11 Ian Pound	.20	.50
12 Brett MacDonald	.20	.50
13 Scott Taylor	.20	.50
14 Greg Hankkio	.20	.50
15 Mike Morrison	.20	.50
16 Mike Wolak	.20	.50
17 Craig Booker	.20	.50
18 Jeff Noble	.20	.50
19 Shawn Tyers	.20	.50
20 Peter Lisy	.20	.50
21 Shawn Burr	.40	1.00
22 David Latta	.20	.50
23 Ron Sanko	.20	.50
24 Doug Jones	.20	.50
25 Paul Penelton	.20	.50
26 Blair MacPherson	.20	.50
27 Richard Hawkins	.20	.50
28 Brad Sparkes	.20	.50
29 Ron Goodall	.20	.50
30 Kevin Duguay TR	.10	.25

1986-87 Kitchener Rangers

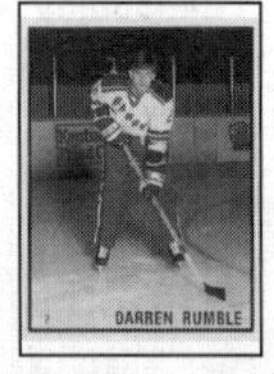

The Kitchener Rangers of the OHL are featured in this 30-card P.L.A.Y. (Police, Law and Youth) set, which was sponsored by the Waterloo Regional Police in conjunction with several corporate sponsors. The cards measure approximately 2 3/4" by 3 1/2" and are printed on thin card stock. The fronts feature color photos with the players posed in action stances. The photos are framed by black and white borders. The player's name appears in the lower right corner. The cards are numbered on both sides.

COMPLETE SET (30)	4.00	10.00
1 Waterloo Police Crest	.04	.10
2 Harold Basse COP	.04	.10
3 Sponsor's Card	.04	.10
4 Tom Barrett GM/CO	.04	.10
5 Checklist	.10	.25
6 Dave Weiss	.30	.75
7 Darren Rumble	.20	.50
8 Kevin Grant	.20	.50
9 Len Fawcett	.20	.50
10 Darren Beals	.30	.75
11 Ed Kister	.20	.50
12 Scott Taylor	.20	.50
13 Darren Moxam	.20	.50
14 Paul Epoch	.20	.50
15 Richard Borgo	.20	.50
16 Allan Lake	.20	.50
17 Jeff Noble	.20	.50
18 Mark Montanari	.20	.50
19 Jim Hulton	.20	.50
20 Kelly Cain	.20	.50
21 Craig Booker	.20	.50
22 David Latta	.20	.50
23 Doug Jones	.20	.50
24 Gary Callahan	.20	.50
25 Bruno Lapensee	.20	.50
26 Scott Montgomery TR	.04	.10
27 Ron Goodall	.20	.50
28 Discount Card	.04	.10
29 Steve Ewing	.20	.50
30 Joe McDonnell ACO	.10	.25

1987-88 Kitchener Rangers

This 30-card set measures approximately 2 3/4" by 3 1/2" and was sponsored by Waterloo Region Optimist Clubs. The cards, which are printed on thin card stock, feature color posed action player photos with white borders. The card number, the player's name, and the season year appear in black print across the bottom of the photo The cards are numbered on both sides.

COMPLETE SET (30)	4.00	10.00
1 Waterloo Regional Police Crest	.04	.10
2 Harold Basse Chief of Police	.04	.10
3 Children's Bonus Card	.04	.10
4 Joe McDonnell GM/CO	.04	.10
5 Kitchener Ranger logo Checklist	.10	.25
6 Gus Morschauser	.30	.75
7 Rick Allain	.20	.50
8 Kevin Grant	.20	.50
9 Rob Thiel	.20	.50
10 Darren Beals	.30	.75
11 Cory Keenan	.20	.50
12 Rival Fullum	.20	.50
13 Tony Crisp	.20	.50
14 Tyler Ertel	.20	.50
15 Richard Borgo	.20	.50
16 Steven Rice	.20	.50
17 Rob Sangster	.20	.50
18 Jeff Noble	.20	.50
19 Mark Montanari	.20	.50
20 Jim Hulton	.20	.50
21 Craig Booker	.20	.50
22 Doug Jones	.20	.50
23 Randy Pearce	.20	.50
24 Darren Rumble	.20	.50
25 Joe Ranger	.20	.50
26 Optimist's Sponsor Card (A-K)	.04	.10
27 Ron Goodall	.20	.50
28 Allan Lake	.20	.50
29 Scott Montgomery TR	.04	.10
30 Optimist's Sponsor Card (L-W)	.04	.10

1988-89 Kitchener Rangers

The Kitchener Rangers of the OHL are featured in this 30-card P.L.A.Y. (Police, Law and Youth) set, which was sponsored by the Waterloo Regional Police in conjunction with several area Optimist Clubs. The cards measure approximately 2 3/4" by 3 1/2" and are printed on thin card stock. The fronts feature color photos with the players posed in action stances. The photos are framed by black and white borders. The cards are numbered on both sides.

COMPLETE SET (30)	4.00	10.00
1 Waterloo Regional Police Crest	.04	.10
2 Harold Basse Chief of Police	.04	.10
3 Children's Bonus Card	.04	.10
4 Joe McDonnell GM/CO	.04	.10
5 Kitchener Rangers logo Checklist	.20	.50
6 Mike Torchia	.30	.75
7 Rick Allain	.20	.50
8 John Uniac	.20	.50
9 Rob Thiel	.20	.50
10 Gus Morschauser	.30	.75
11 Cory Keenan	.20	.50
12 Rival Fullum	.20	.50
13 Jason Firth	.20	.50
14 Joey St. Aubin	.20	.50
15 Richard Borgo	.20	.50
16 Steven Rice	.20	.50
17 Rob Sangster	.20	.50
18 Gilbert Dionne	.30	.75
19 Mark Montanari	.20	.50
20 Shayne Stevenson	.30	.75
21 Pierre Gagnon	.20	.50
22 Kirk Tomlinson	.20	.50
23 Randy Pearce	.20	.50
24 Brad Barton	.20	.50
25 Chris LiPuma	.20	.50
26 Optimist's Sponsor's Card (A-K)	.04	.10
27 Steve Herniman	.20	.50
28 Darren Rumble	.20	.50
29 Rick Chambers TR	.04	.10
30 Optimist's Sponsor's Card (L-W)	.04	.10

1989-90 Kitchener Rangers

The Kitchener Rangers of the OHL are featured in this 30-card P.L.A.Y. (Police, Law and Youth) set, which was sponsored by the Waterloo Regional Police in conjunction with several area Optimist Clubs. The cards measure approximately 2 3/4" by 3 1/2" and are printed on thin card stock. The fronts feature posed color player photos inside a black picture frame and white outer borders. Most cards are numbered on both sides.

COMPLETE SET (30)	4.80	12.00
1 Waterloo Police Crest	.04	.10
2 Harold Basse COP	.04	.10
3 Children's Bonus Card	.04	.10
4 Joe McDonnell GM/CO	.04	.10
5 Logo/Checklist	.10	.25
6 Mike Torchia	.30	.75
7 Rick Allain	.20	.50
8 John Uniac	.20	.50
9 Jack Williams	.20	.50
10 Dave Schill	.30	.75
11 John Copley	.20	.50
12 Cory Keenan	.20	.50
13 Rival Fullum	.20	.50
14 Jason Firth	.20	.50
15 Joey St. Aubin	.20	.50
16 Richard Borgo	.20	.50
17 Steven Rice	.20	.50
18 Rob Sangster	.20	.50
19 Gilbert Dionne	.30	.75
20 Jamie Israel	.20	.50
21 Shayne Stevenson	.30	.75
22 Gib Tucker	.20	.50
23 Randy Pearce	.20	.50
24 Brad Barton	.20	.50
25 Chris Li Puma	.20	.50
26 Optimist's Sponsors' Card (A-L)	.04	.10
27 Kevin Falesy	.20	.50
28 Steve Smith	.20	.50
29 Rick Chambers TR	.04	.10
30 Optimist's Sponsors' Card (M-W)	.04	.10

1990-91 Kitchener Rangers

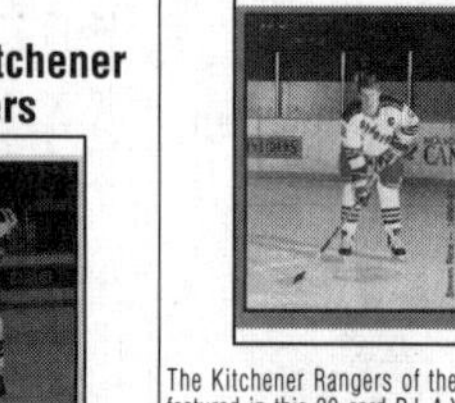

The Kitchener Rangers of the OHL are featured in this 30-card P.L.A.Y. (Police, Law and Youth) set, which was sponsored by the Waterloo Regional Police in conjunction with several area Optimist Clubs. The cards measure approximately 2 3/4" by 3 1/2" and are printed on thin card stock. The fronts feature color photos with the players posed in action stances. The photos are framed by black and red borders The cards are numbered on both sides.

COMPLETE SET (30)	3.20	8.00
1 Waterloo Regional Police Crest	.04	.10
2 Harold Basse Chief of Police	.04	.10
3 Joe McDonnell GM/CO	.04	.10
4 Rick Chambers TR	.04	.10
5 Kitchener Rangers logo Checklist	.10	.25
6 Mike Torchia	.20	.50
7 Len DeVuono	.12	.30
8 John Uniac	.12	.30
9 Steve Smith	.12	.30
10 Rob Stopar	.12	.30
11 Tony McCabe	.12	.30
12 Jason Firth	.12	.30
13 Joey St. Aubin	.12	.30
14 Richard Borgo	.12	.30
15 Norm Dezainde	.12	.30
16 Jeff Szeryk	.12	.30
17 Derek Gauthier	.12	.30
18 Jamie Israel	.12	.30
19 Shayne McCosh	.12	.30
20 Gib Tucker	.12	.30
21 Paul McCallion	.12	.30
22 Mike Allen	.12	.30
23 Brad Barton	.12	.30
24 Chris LiPuma	.16	.40
25 Justin Cullen	.12	.30
26 Optimist's Sponsor's Card (A-K)	.04	.10
27 Rod Saarinen	.12	.30
28 Jack Williams	.12	.30
29 Steven Rice	.20	.50
30 Optimist's Sponsor's Card (K-W)	.04	.10

1993-94 Kitchener Rangers

Sponsored by Domino's Pizza and printed by Slapshot Images Ltd., this standard size 31-card set features the Kitchener Rangers of the OHL. On a geometrical blue and red background, the fronts feature color action player photos with thin grey borders. The player's name, position and team name, as well as the producer's logo, appear on the front.

COMPLETE SET (31)	3.60	9.00
1 Eric Manlow Jason Gladney Tim Spitig Checklist	.16	.40
2 David Belitski	.20	.50
3 Darryl Whyte	.20	.50
4 Greg McLean	.16	.40
5 Jason Hughes	.16	.40
6 Gord Dickie	.16	.40
7 Travis Riggin	.16	.40
8 Norm Dezainde	.16	.40
9 Tim Spitzig	.16	.40
10 Trevor Gallant	.16	.40
11 Chris Pittman	.16	.40
12 Ryan Pawluk UER (Name misspelled Pawluck on back)	.16	.40
13 Jason Morgan	.16	.40
14 James Boyd	.16	.40
15 Todd Warriner	.30	.75
16 Mark Donahue	.16	.40
17 Peter Brearley	.16	.40
18 Andrew Taylor	.16	.40
19 Jason Gladney	.16	.40
20 Wes Swinson	.16	.40
21 Matt O'Dette	.16	.40
22 Darren Schmidt	.16	.40
23 Jason Johnson	.16	.40
24 Eric Manlow	.16	.40
25 Jeff Lillie	.16	.40
26 Sergei Olympiev	.16	.40
27 Joe McDonnell CO	.04	.10
28 Rick Chambers TR	.04	.10
29 Andrew Taylor Travis Riggin David Belitski Top Prospects	.16	.40
30 Sponsor Card Domino's Pizza	.04	.01
NNO Slapshot Ad Card	.04	.01

1994-95 Kitchener Rangers

Sponsored by Domino's Pizza and printed by Slapshot Images Ltd., this 31-card set features the Rangers of the OHL. The sets were sold by the team at home games.

COMPLETE SET (31)	3.20	8.00
1 Checklist	.04	.10
2 David Belitski	.20	.50
3 Darryl Whyte	.20	.50
4 Daniel Godbout	.16	.40
5 Greg McLean	.16	.40
6 Jason Hughes	.16	.40
7 Jason Byrnes	.16	.40
8 Paul Traynor	.16	.40
9 Travis Riggin	.16	.40
10 Tim Spitzig	.16	.40
11 Trevor Gallant	.16	.40
12 Chris Pittman	.20	.50
13 Rick Emmett	.16	.40
14 Jason Morgan	.16	.40
15 Luch Nasato	.30	.75
16 Ryan Pepperall	.20	.50
17 Keith Welsh	.16	.40
18 Bill McGuigen	.16	.40
19 Chris Brassard	.16	.40
20 Andrew Taylor	.16	.40
21 Rob Deciantis	.16	.40
22 Wes Swinson	.20	.50
23 Lucas Miller	.16	.40
24 Sergei Olympiev	.16	.40
25 Rob Maric	.16	.40
26 Eric Manlow	.20	.50
27 Geoff Ward CO	.04	.10
28 Bob Ertel GM	.04	.10
29 Rick Chambers TR Dave Nicholls TR	.04	.10
30 Sponsor Card Domino's Pizza	.04	.01
NNO Ad Card	.04	.01

1994-95 Kitchener Rangers Update

This update set has the same design as the 1994-95 Kitchener Rangers set and features players that were traded to the Rangers during the 1994-95 season. It was sold separately and also included a Slapshot ad card with a 1995 calendar on the back. The numbering is a continuation of the regular set.

COMPLETE SET (7)	.80	2.00
31 Brian Scott	.20	.50
32 Robin LaCour	.16	.40
33 Jim Ensom	.20	.50
34 Dylan Seca	.16	.40
35 Garrett Burnett	.16	.40
NNO Craig Bignell ACO Mike Wright ACO	.16	.40
NNO Ad Card		.01

1996-97 Kitchener Rangers

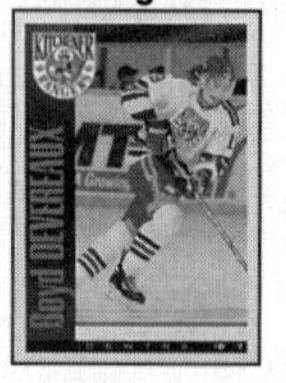

This set was sold by the team at home games. The cards are unnumbered and so are listed in alphabetical order.

COMPLETE SET (30)	4.00	15.00
1 Jeff Ambrosio	.16	.50
2 David Belitski	.20	1.00
3 Jason Byrnes	.16	.50
4 Peter Bureaux	.16	.50
5 Vratislav Cech	.20	.50
6 Rob DeCiantis	.16	.50
7 Shawn Degagne	.16	.50
8 Boyd Devereaux	.30	1.50
9 Boyd Devereaux	.30	1.50
10 Bryan Duce	.16	.50
11 Michal Dvorak	.16	.50
12 Darcy Harris	.16	.50
13 Bryan Hayton ACO	.04	.10
14 Wes Jarvis	.16	.50
15 Dan Lebold TR	.04	.10
16 Adam Lewis	.16	.50
17 Rob Marc	.16	.50
18 Mark McMahon	.16	.50
19 Ryan Milanovic	.20	.75
20 Ryan Mougenel	.16	.50
21 Serge Payer	.16	.50
22 Ryan Pepperall	.16	.50
23 Alan Rourke	.16	.50
24 Rob Stanfield	.16	.50
25 Paul Traynor	.16	.50
26 Tim Verbeek	.16	.50
27 Geoff Ward CO	.04	.10
28 Keith Welsh	.16	.50
29 Header Card	.04	.10
30 Checklist	.04	.10

1999-00 Kitchener Rangers

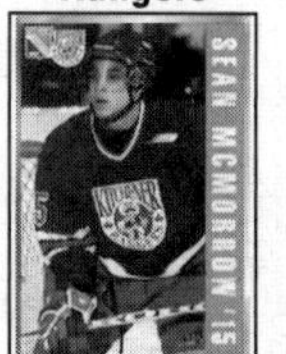

This 30-card set features the 1999-00 Kitchener Rangers. Base cards have white and gray borders with a red nameplate along the right side of the card. The set was sold by the team at its souvenir stands.

COMPLETE SET (30)	4.00	10.00
1 John Eminger	.14	.35
2 Matt Armstrong	.14	.35
3 Serge Payer	.20	.50
4 Steve Eminger	.60	1.50
5 Andrew Peters	.14	1.00
6 Mike Amodeo	.14	.35
7 Bill Browne	.14	.35
8 Maxim Sharifijanov	.20	.50
9 Tex Mascot	.04	.10
10 Dan Lebold	.14	.35
11 Michael Wehrstedt	.14	.35
12 Jeff Snyder	.14	.35
13 Ryan Held	.20	.50
14 John Dunphy	.14	.35
15 Rusian Akhmadulin	.14	.35
16 Bobby Naylor	.14	.35
17 Jimmy Gagnon	.14	.35
18 Brandon Merli	.14	.35
19 Chris Brannen	.14	.35
20 Alan Rourke	.14	.35
21 Sean McMorrow	.20	.75
22 Mike Mazzuca	.14	.35
23 Reg Bourcier	.20	.50
24 Scott Dickie	.20	.50

25 Kevin Bloch .14 .35
26 Jeff McGee .14 .35
27 Derek Roy .60 2.00
28 Header Card/CL .01
29 Kinsmen Club .01
30 Kinsmen Club .01

2000-01 Kitchener Rangers

This set features the Rangers of the OHL. The set was produced by the team and sold at its souvenir stands during home games. The cards are unnumbered, so are listed in alphabetical order.

COMPLETE SET (30) 4.80 10.00
1 Team CL .16 .01
2 Matt Armstrong .16 .40
3 Josh Bennett .16 .40
4 Andre Benoit .16 .40
5 Vasily Bizyayev .16 .40
6 Kevin Bloch CO .04 .10
7 Chris Brannen .16 .40
8 Chris Cava .20 .50
9 Travis Chapman .16 .40
10 Scott Dickie .30 .75
11 John Dunphy .16 .40
12 Steve Eminger .60 1.00
13 Jimmy Gagnon .16 .40
14 Mike Hough .20 .50
15 Jeff Johnston .30 .75
16 Brad Larter .16 .40
17 Dan Lebold TR .04 .10
18 Jamie Minchella .16 .40
19 Steve Richards .16 .40
20 Matt Rock .16 .40
21 Derek Roy .40 1.50
22 Derrick Shultz .30 .75
23 Scott Sheppard .16 .40
24 Sam Skwarchuk .16 .40
25 Marcus Smith .16 .40
26 Jeff Snyder CO .04 .10
27 Tex MASCOT .04 .10
28 Brock Yates .16 .40
29 Kinsmen Club .01
30 Kinsmen Club 2 .01

2001-02 Kitchener Rangers

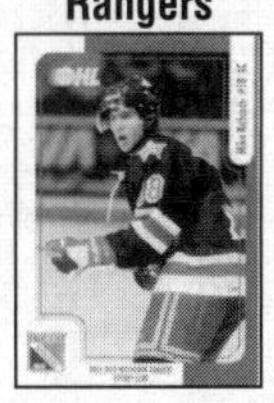

COMPLETE SET (22) 12.00
1 Scott Dickie .75
2 Nick Policelli .50
3 Thomas Harrison .50
4 Ryan Ramsay .50
5 Steve Eminger .75
6 Peter Kanko 1.00
7 Mike Amodeo .50
8 Matt Grennier .50
9 Derek Roy .75
10 Andre Benoit .50
11 Mike Richards 1.50
12 Petr Hemsky .50
13 John Osborne .50
14 Rafal Martynowski .50
15 Marcus Smith .50
16 T.J. Eason .50
17 Adam Keefe .50
18 Matt Harpwood .50
19 Bill Kinkel .50
20 Jeff Szwez .50
21 Chad McCaffrey .50
22 Checklist .01

2002-03 Kitchener Rangers

COMPLETE SET(19) 12.00
1 Andre Benoit .50
2 Jesse Boucher .50
3 Greg Campbell 1.00
4 David Clarkson .50
5 Carlo DiRienzo .50
6 Scott Dickie .75
7 T.J. Eason .50
8 Steve Eminger 1.00
9 Matt Grennier .50
10 George Halkidis .50
11 Peter Kanko 1.00
12 Adam Keefe .50
13 Rafal Martynowski .50
14 Chad McCaffrey .50
15 Evan McGrath .50
16 Nathan O'Nabigon .50
17 Mike Richards 1.50
18 Derek Roy 1.00
19 Marcus Smith .50

2002-03 Kitchener Rangers Postcards

These five singles were recently confirmed. If you have any additional information about this set, please contact us at hockeymag@beckett.com.

COMPLETE SET (?)
1 Steve Eminger
2 Petr Kanko
3 Michael Richards
4 Derek Roy
5 Evan McGrath

2003-04 Kitchener Rangers

COMPLETE SET (24) 12.00
1 Andre Benoit .50
2 Jesse Boucher .50
3 Mike Chmielewski .50
4 David Clarkson .50
5 Patrick Davis .50
6 Carlo DiRienzo .50
7 Nick Duff .50
8 Cam Fergus .50
9 Peter Franchin .50
10 Chris Gravelding .50
11 Thomas Harrison .50
12 Devereaux Heshmatpour .50
13 Petr Kanko .75
14 Adam Keefe .50
15 Tyson Kellerman .75
16 Matt Lashoff .50
17 Rafal Martynowski .50
18 Paul McFarland .50
19 Evan McGrath .50
20 Nathan O'Nabigon .50
21 Anthony Pototschnik .50
22 Mike Richards 1.00
23 Marcus Smith .50
24 Boris Valabik .75

2003 Kitchener Rangers Memorial Cup

Cards are unnumbered and are listed below in alphabetical order.

COMPLETE SET (19) 18.00
1 Andre Benoit .75
2 Jesse Boucher .75
3 Gregory Campbell 1.50
4 David Clarkson .75
5 Scott Dickie 1.00
6 Carlo Dirienzo 1.00
7 T.J. Eason .75
8 Steve Eminger 1.50
9 Matt Grennier .75
10 George Halkidis .75
11 Petr Kanko 1.50
12 Adam Keefe .75
13 Rafal Martynowski .75
14 Chad McCaffrey .75
15 Evan McGrath .75
16 Nathan O'Nabigon .75
17 Michael Richards 2.00
18 Derek Roy 1.00
19 Marcus Smith .75

2004-05 Kitchener Rangers

A total of 600 team sets were produced.

COMPLETE SET (24) 15.00
1 Michael Richards 1.50
2 Andre Benoit .50
3 Boris Valabik .75
4 Mark Packwood .50
5 Craig Voakes .50
6 Dan Turple .50
7 Dan Cyenes .50
8 David Clarkson .50
9 Eric Pfligler .50
10 Evan McGrath 1.00
11 Jack Combs .50
12 Jakub Kindl .75
13 Joe McCann .50
14 Justin Azevedo .50
15 Justin Piquette .50
16 Kevin Henderson .50
17 Mark Fraser .50
18 Matt Lashoff 1.00
19 Matt Pepe .50
20 Adam Keefe .50
21 Michael Duco .50
22 Myles Applebaum .50
23 Patrick Davis .50
24 Paul McFarland .50

2005-06 Kitchener Rangers

COMPLETE SET (27) 8.00 15.00
1 Dan Turple 1.00
2 Julien Machabee .75
3 Mark Packwood 1.00
4 Matt Lashoff 1.00
5 Patrick Davis .75
6 Justin Azevedo .75
7 Evan McGrath 1.00
8 Sean Smyth .75
9 Dan Gyenes .75
10 Boris Valabik 1.00
11 Kevin Henderson .75
12 Matt Thomson .75
13 Mark Fraser .75
14 Jakub Kindl .75
15 Nick Spaling .75
16 Mike Duco .75
17 Yves Bastien .75
18 Matt Pepe .75
19 Craig Voakes .75
20 Michael Pelech .75
21 Jean-Michel Rizk .75
22 Ryan Donally .75
23 Myles Applebaum .75
24 Matt Auffrey .75
25 Cory Konecny .75
26 David Lomas .75
27 Victor Oreskovich .75

2006-07 Kitchener Rangers

COMPLETE SET (25) 8.00 15.00
1 Jakub Kindl .30 .75
2 Steve Tarasuk .30 .75
3 Nick Spaling .30 .75
4 Scott Timmins .30 .75
5 Mike Duco .30 .75
6 Justin Azevedo .30 .75
7 Yves Bastien .30 .75
8 Mike Mascioli .30 .75
9 Matt Halischuk .30 .75
10 Nazem Kadri .30 .75
11 Matt Pepe .30 .75
12 Robert Bortuzzo .30 .75
13 Dan Gyenes .30 .75
14 Denver Manderson .30 .75
15 Mark Packwood .40 1.00
16 John Murray .40 1.00
17 Jean-Michel Rizk .30 .75
18 Adam Zamec .30 .75
19 Kevin Henderson .30 .75
20 Victor Oreskovich .30 .75
21 Yannick Weber .30 .75
22 Brian Soso .30 .75
23 Phil Varone .30 .75
24 Dan Kelly .30 .75
LE1 Justin Azevedo 1.25 3.00

1990-91 Knoxville Cherokees

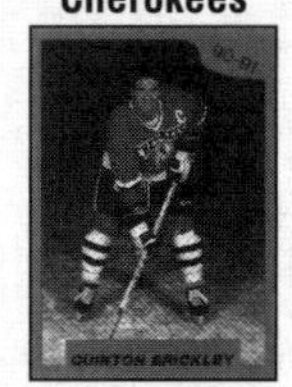

This 19-card set of the Knoxville Cherokees of the ECHL was produced by 7th Inning Sketch, and offered for sale by the team at home games. Interestingly, the set is numbered 101-119, suggesting it is the continuation of a larger (all ECHL?) set. The fronts feature a posed shot, while the backs offer limited player information and logos for the club and the Knoxville News-Sentinel.

COMPLETE SET (19) 3.60 9.00
101 David Williams .24 .60
102 Paul Laus .40 1.00
103 Don Jackson CO .10 .25
104 Steve Ryding .20 .50
105 Jeff Lindsay .20 .50
106 Daniel Gauthier .20 .50
107 Stan Drulia .24 .60
108 Mike Murray .20 .50
109 Tom Sasso .20 .50
110 Butch Kaebel .20 .50
111 Don McClennan .20 .50
112 Jamie Hanlon .20 .50
113 Troy Mick .20 .50
114 Brett Strot .20 .50
115 Dean Anderson .20 .50
116 Quinton Brickley .20 .50
117 Greg Batters .20 .50
118 Alex Daviault .20 .50
119 Mike Greenlay .30 .75

1991-92 Knoxville Cherokees

This 20-card set of the ECHL's Knoxville Cherokees was sponsored by the News-Sentinel, and offered for sale by the team at home games. The cards feature posed shots on the front; the unnumbered backs include vital statistics and a brief career history.

COMPLETE SET (20) 3.60 9.00
1 Bill Nyrop CO .20 .50
2 Galen Head TR .04 .10
3 Mike Greenlay .30 .75
4 Karl Clauss .30 .75
5 Steve Ryding .20 .50
6 Mike Gober .20 .50
7 Chad Thompson .20 .50
8 Trevor Forsythe .20 .50
9 Greg Pankewicz .20 .50
10 David Shute .20 .50
11 Jamie Dabanovich .20 .50
12 Shawn Lillie .20 .50
13 Joel Gardner .20 .50
14 Roman Hubalek .20 .50
15 Bruno Villeneuve .20 .50
16 Troy Mick .20 .50
17 Dean McDonald .20 .50
18 Brett Lawrence .20 .50
19 Dean Anderson .20 .50
20 Robert Melanson .20 .50

1993-94 Knoxville Cherokees

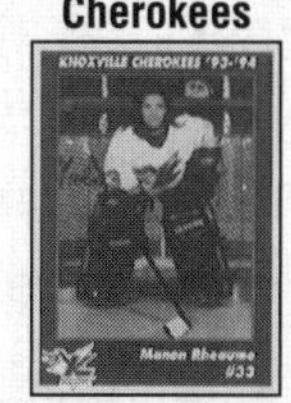

This 20-card standard-size set features the Knoxville Cherokees. On a black background with white borders, the fronts have color action and posed player photos with thin teal borders. The team name appears above the photo, while the player's name, position, and the team logo are under the photo. The cards are unnumbered and checklisted below in alphabetical order.

COMPLETE SET (20) 6.00 15.00
1 Scott Boston .16 .40
2 Cory Cadden .16 .40
3 Tim Chase .16 .40
4 Steven Flomenhoft .16 .40
5 Scott Gordon .20 .50
6 Jon Larson .16 .40
7 Carl LeBlanc .16 .40
8 Kim Maier .16 .40
9 Wes McCauley .16 .40
10 Scott Metcalfe .16 .40
11 Mike Murray .16 .40
12 Hayden O'Rear .16 .40
13 Jeff Reid .16 .40
14 Manon Rheaume 3.20 8.00
15 Marc Rodgers .16 .40
16 Doug Searle .16 .40
17 Barry Smith CO .10 .25
18 Martin Tanguay .16 .40
19 Nicholas Vachon .20 .50
20 Bruno Villeneuve .16 .40

1994-95 Knoxville Cherokees

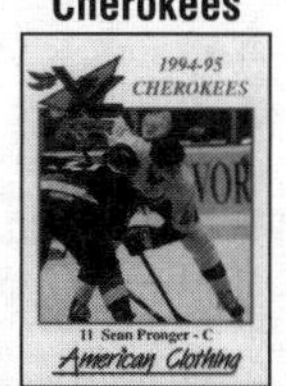

This 24-card set of the Knoxville Cherokees of the ECHL was issued by the team and available at home games.

COMPLETE SET (24) 3.20 8.00
1 Checklist .04 .10
2 Barry Smith CO .10 .25
3 Aaron Fackler TR .04 .10
4 Andy Davis ANN .04 .10
5 Stephane Menard .16 .40
6 Doug Searle .16 .40
7 Hayden O'Rear .16 .40
8 Sean Brown .16 .40
9 Mike Murray .16 .40
10 Jon Jenkins .16 .40
11 Sean Pronger .30 .75
12 Steven Flomenhoft .16 .40
13 David Neilson .16 .40
14 Jack Callahan .16 .40
15 Carl LeBlanc .16 .40
16 Alain Deeks .20 .50
17 George Zajankala .16 .40
18 Chris Fess .16 .40
19 Michel Gaul .16 .40
20 Pat Murray .16 .40
21 Robb McIntyre .16 .40
22 Vaclav Nedomansky, Jr .16 .40
23 Cory Cadden .16 .40
24 Michael Burman .16 .40

1996-97 Knoxville Cherokees

The 22-card base set was sold in team set form at home games. Cards numbered P1 and P2 were available one night-only giveaways at two Cherokee home games. The designs are the same as those of the base set. Because of the unique distribution of these two cards, they are not considered part of the complete set.

COMPLETE SET (20) 4.00 10.00
1 Knoxville Cherokees .20 .50
2 Barry Smith HCO .20 .50
3 Sean Halifax .20 .50
4 Daniel Chaput .20 .50
5 Jamie Bird .20 .50
6 Matt Turek .20 .50
7 Chris Fees .20 .50
8 Kelly Hollingshead .20 .50
9 Darren Johnson .20 .50
10 Vaclav Nedomansky .20 .50
11 Kent Fearns .20 .50
12 Martin Tanguay .20 .50
13 Wayne Anchikoski .20 .50
14 Jim Brown .20 .50
15 Garrett Burnett .20 1.00
16 Stephane Soulliere .20 .50
17 Dean Moore .20 .50
18 David Neilson .20 .50
19 Mike Vandenberghe .20 .50
20 Brad Guzda .20 1.00
21 Olaf Kjenstad .20 .50
22 PHPA Web Site .04 .10
P1 Brad Guzda LL 2.00 5.00
P2 Jim Brown LL 2.00 5.00

2004-05 Knoxville Ice Bears

Little is known about this set beyond the checklist, therefore it is not priced. Additional info can be forwarded to hockeymag@beckett.com.

COMPLETE SET (24)
1 K.C. Caudill
2 Chris Bodnar
3 Kevin Swider
4 Todd MacIsaac
5 Marcus Forsberg
6 Civic Colisseum
7 Chilly MASCOT
8 TCS card
9 Doug Serle
10 Craig Desjarlais
11 Mike Cragen
12 Darren Caine
13 Curtis Menzul
14 Terry Dunbar
15 Free Kid's Ticket
16 David Bagley
17 Matt Moore
18 Jeff Hansen
19 James Ronayne
20 Miss Icebear
21 Liam McCarthy
22 Jim Bermingham
23 Rob Miller
24 K.J. Voorhees

2005-06 Knoxville Ice Bears

COMPLETE SET (24) 6.00 15.00
1 Jason Bermingham .30 .75
2 Patrick Carriere .30 .75
3 Kevin Caudill .30 .75
4 Mike Craigen .30 .75
5 Nathan Daly .30 .75
6 Marcus Forsberg .30 .75
7 Aaron Lewis .30 .75
8 Ben Manny .30 .75
9 Liam McCarthy .30 .75
10 Curtis Menzul .30 .75
11 Rob Miller .30 .75
12 Matt Moore .30 .75
13 Ryan Person .30 .75
14 Bob Rangus .30 .75
15 Jamie Ronayne .30 .75
16 Doug Searle .30 .75
17 Kevin Swider .30 .75
18 K.J. Voorhees .30 .75
19 Jim Bermingham HC .02 .10
20 Dance Team .02 .10
21 Drew Kitts EM .02 .10
22 Chilly MASCOT .02 .10
23 Tim Douglas TP .02 .10
24 Knoxville Ice Bears .20 .50

1999-00 Knoxville Speed

This set features the Speed of the UHL. The cards were issued as a promotional giveaway, with the first 15 cards going on one night, followed by a second set of 15 (a sponsor card was doubled up).

COMPLETE SET (29) 6.00 15.00
1 Sponsor Card .01
2 Sponsor Card .01
3 Bradley Denis .30 .75
4 Hockey History .01
5 UHL History .01
6 Trevor Jobe .40 1.00
7 Cam Law .30 .75
8 Rusty McKie .40 1.00
9 Eric Mohntreuil .30 .75
10 Mike Murray .30 .75
11 Dan Myre .30 .75
12 Sergei Radchenko .30 .75
13 Bill Russell .30 .75
14 Eric Schneider .30 .75
15 Mike Schultz .30 .75
16 Doug Searle .30 .75
17 Jordan Shaw .30 .75
18 Konstantin Simchuk .30 1.00
19 Jeff Suggitt .30 .75
20 Jeremy Thompson .30 .75
21 Andrew Tortorella .30 .75
22 Dmitry Ustyuzhanin .30 .75
23 Team on the Bench .20 .50
24 Mike Wilhelm EM .04 .10
25 Terry Ruskowski CO .20 .50
26 Tim Douglas TR .04 .10
27 Hersheys/Pilot .01
28 Hersheys/Pilot .01
29 Eyewitness Sports .01

2000-01 Knoxville Speed

This set features the Speed of the UHL. The set was released as a promotional giveaway, with a different mixture of cards being given away at various home games to allow collectors to trade amongst themselves to complete sets.

COMPLETE SET (29) 10.00 30.00
1 Alex Alepin .30 1.00
2 Bradley Denis .60 1.50
3 Craig Desjarlais .60 1.50
4 Brad Guzda .40 1.50
5 Tom Lawson .30 1.00
6 David Mayes .30 1.00
7 Alain Savage .30 1.00
8 Mike Schultz .30 1.00
9 Dean Shmyr .40 1.50
10 Mike Vandenberghe .30 1.00
11 Mike Wilhelm EM .04 .10
12 Nick Paranjape (Fox 43) .04 .10
13 Brad Domonsky .80 2.00
14 Dmitry Ustyuzhanin .30 1.00
15 Yannick Latour .30 1.00
16 Sergei Petrov .60 1.50
17 Iannique Renaud .30 1.00
18 Mikko Sivonen .40 1.50
19 Mike Henderson .80 2.00
20 Geno Parrish .30 1.00
21 Andrew Tortorella .60 1.50
22 Mark Karpen .30 1.00
23 Dan Myre .30 1.00
24 Mike Murray .30 1.00
25 Mike Green .30 1.00
26 Oleg Kuzmin .30 1.00
27 Terry Ruskowski CO .20 .50
28 Tim Douglas TR .04 .10
29 JBG SPONSOR .04 .10

1998-99 Kootenay Ice

This set features the Ice of the WHL. Each card measures approximately 3" x 6" and is unnumbered. The cards were sold by the team at home games.

COMPLETE SET (24) 18.00
1 Clayton Pool .20 .50
2 Scott Roles .20 .50
3 Dean Arsene .20 .50
4 Jesse Ferguson .20 .50
5 Dion Lassu .20 .50
6 Mark Thompson .20 .50
7 Steve McCarthy .80 2.00
8 Rod Leroux .20 .50
9 Mike Green .20 .50
10 Wade Burt .20 .50
11 Nick Marach .20 .50
12 Jaroslav Svoboda .80 1.00
13 Trevor Wasyluk .40 1.00
14 Jarret Stoll 1.20 3.00
15 Jason Jaffray .20 .50
16 Trevor Johnson .20 .50
17 Kyle Wanvig .80 2.00
18 Tyler Beechey .20 .50
19 Stanislav Gron .80 1.00
20 Colin Sinclair .20 .50
21 Jeremy Yablonski .20 .50
22 Graham Belak .20 .50
23 B.J. Boxma .20 .50
24 Brad Tutschek .20 .50

2000-01 Kootenay Ice

This set features the Ice of the WHL. The cards are oversized by about 1/2 inch in height and width, and were sold by the team at home games. The cards are unnumbered, so are listed below in alphabetical order.

COMPLETE SET (24) 8.00 20.00
1 Dean Arsene .20 .50
2 Tyler Beechey .20 .50
3 Dan Blackburn .75 2.00
4 Zdenek Blatny .80 1.00
5 Eric Bowen .20 .50
6 Bret DeCecco .40 1.00
7 Brennan Evans .20 .50
8 Cole Fischer .20 .50
9 Richard Hamula .20 .50
10 Jeff Harvey .20 .50
11 Pat Iannone .20 .50
12 Jason Jaffray .20 .50
13 Trevor Johnson .20 .50
14 Mike Lee .20 .50
15 Steve Makway .20 .50
16 Lance Morrison .20 .50
17 Aaron Rome .20 .50
18 Mascot Shivers .04 .10
19 Colin Sinclair .20 .50
20 Jarret Stoll 1.25 3.00
21 Marek Svatos 2.00 5.00
22 Adam Taylor .20 .50
23 Andy Thompson .20 .50
24 Craig Weller .20 .50

2002-03 Kootenay Ice

We have confirmed a handful of singles from this set, thanks to collector Vinnie Montalbano. If you have any other information about this set, please email us at hockeymag@beckett.com.

COMPLETE SET (?)
1 Gerard Dicaire
2 Duncan Milroy
3 Tomas Plihal
4 Adam Taylor

2003-04 Kootenay Ice

COMPLETE SET (25) 8.00 20.00
1 Taylor Dakers .30 .75
2 Jeff Glass 2.00 5.00
3 Derek Price .30 .75
4 Donny Lloyd .30 .75
5 James Cherewyk .30 .75
6 Brad Zanon .30 .75
7 Brad Cole .30 .75
8 Travis Featherstone .30 .75
9 Nigel Dawes .75 2.00
10 Mike Boxma .30 .75
11 Glenn Olson .30 .75
12 Josh Morrow .30 .75
13 Adam Taylor .30 .75
14 Igor Agarunov .30 .75
15 Adam Cracknell .30 .75
16 Jeremy Schenderling .30 .75
17 Dale Mahovsky .30 .75
18 Ryan Russell .30 .75
19 Aaron Bader .30 .75
20 Sean Affleck .30 .75
21 Martin Sagat .30 .75
22 Brett Sutter .60 1.50
23 Checklist .02 .10
24 Shivers MASCOT .02 .10
25 Sponsor .02 .10

2004-05 Kootenay Ice

COMPLETE SET (25) 20.00
1 Laine Allen .75
2 Andy Bossence .75
3 Michael Busto .75
4 James Cherewyk .75
5 Brad Cole .75
6 Adam Cracknell .75
7 Steven DaSilva .75
8 Taylor Dakers .75
9 Nigel Dawes 1.50
10 Joshua Fauth .75
11 Jeff Glass 3.00
12 Chad Greenan .75
13 Casey Lee .75
14 Dale Mahovsky .75
15 Ben Maxwell .75
16 Roman Polak .75
17 Derek Price .75
18 Ryan Russell .75
19 Martin Sagat .75
20 Josh Saywell .75
21 Brett Sutter 1.00
22 Adam Taylor .75
23 Devin Welsh .75
24 Commitment .10
25 Sponsor Card .01

2005-06 Kootenay Ice

COMPLETE SET (25) 15.00
1 Andrew Bailey .30 .75
2 Curtis Billsten .30 .75
3 Lukas Bohunicky .30 .75
4 Michael Busto .30 .75
5 Adam Cracknell .30 .75
6 Steven DaSilva .30 .75
7 Taylor Dakers .30 .75
8 Dalyn Flatt .30 .75
9 Trent Fussi .30 .75
10 Chad Greenan .30 .75
11 Paul Kurceba .30 .75
12 Kris Lazaruk .30 .75
13 Casey Lee .30 .75
14 Paul MacDonald .30 .75
15 Dale Mahovsky .30 .75
16 Ben Maxwell .30 .75
17 John Negrin .30 .75
18 Michal Psurny .30 .75
19 Ryan Russell .30 .75

20 Dustin Sylvester .30 .75
21 Devin Welsh .30 .75
22 Luke Wiens .30 .75
23 Shivers MASCOT .02 .10
24 Concord Pacific SPONSOR .01 .01
25 Kootenay Ice

1991-92 Lake Superior State Lakers

This set features the Lakers of the NCAA. The cards are unnumbered and so are listed in alphabetical order.

COMPLETE SET (28) 20.00
1 1991 CCHA Champs .10 .25
2 Dan Angelelli .30 .75
3 Mark Astley .30 .75
4 Mike Bachusz .30 .75
5 Steve Barnes .30 .75
6 Clayton Beddoes .30 .75
7 Paul Constantin .30 .75
8 Vincent Faucher .30 .75
9 David Gartshore .30 .75
10 Tim Hanley .30 .75
11 John Hendry .30 .75
12 Dean Hulett .30 .75
13 Jeff Jackson CO .20 .50
14 Blaine Lacher .40 1.00
15 Darrin Madeley .40 1.00
16 Kurt Miller .30 .75
17 Sandy Moger .40 1.00
18 Mike Morin .30 .75
19 Jay Ness .30 .75
20 Jim Peters .30 .75
21 Brian Rolston .80 2.00
22 Michael Smith .30 .75
23 Wayne Strachan .30 .75
24 Jason Trzcinski .30 .75
25 Rob Valicevic .60 1.50
26 Darren Wetherill .30 .75
27 Brad Willner .30 .75
28 Jason Welch .30 .75

1992-93 Lake Superior State Lakers

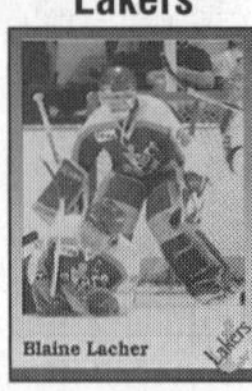

This 33-card standard-size set features the 1992 NCAA Champion Lake Superior State Lakers. The cards feature color, action player photos with gradated blue borders. The player's name and the Lakers logo appears below the picture. The backs carry black-and-white close-up photos along with biographical information, quick facts, and statistics. The cards are unnumbered and checklisted below in alphabetical order.

COMPLETE SET (33) 6.00 15.00
1 Team Photo .20 .50
1992 NCAA Champions
2 Team Photo .16 .50
1992 CCHA Champions
3 Keith Aldridge .20 .50
4 Dan Angelelli .16 .40
5 Mark Astley .20 .50
6 Mike Bachusz .16 .40
7 Steven Barnes .16 .40
8 Clayton Beddoes .16 .40
9 David Gartshore .16 .40
10 Tim Hanley .16 .40
11 Matt Hansen .16 .40
12 John Hendry .16 .40
13 Dean Hulett .16 .40
14 Jeff Jackson .20 .50
15 Blaine Lacher .40 1.00
16 Darrin Madeley .20 .50
17 Mike Matteucci .16 .40
18 Scott McCabe .16 .40
19 Kurt Miller .16 .40
20 Mike Morin .16 .40
21 Jay Ness .16 .40
22 Gino Pulente .16 .40
23 Brian Rolston .80 2.00
24 Paul Sass .16 .40
25 Michael Smith .16 .40
26 Wayne Strachan .16 .40
27 Sean Tallaire .16 .40
28 Adam Thompson .16 .40
29 Jason Trzcinski .16 .40
30 Rob Valicevic .60 1.50
31 Jason Welch .16 .40
32 Darren Wetherill .16 .40
33 Brad Willner .16 .40

2004-05 Lakehead University Thunderwolves

These cards, featuring the CIAU Thunderwolves, were available individually from Quality Markets, making the sets extremely difficult to piece together. The set features Drew Kivell, who appeared in the TV show Making The Cut.

COMPLETE SET (27) 20.00
1 Joel Scherban .75
2 Chris Shaffer .75
3 Jeff Richards .75
4 Erik Lodge .75
5 Murray Magill .75
6 Jason Lange .75
7 Robert Hillier .75
8 Francis Walker .75
9 Andrew Brown .75
10 Kris Callaway .75
11 Jouni Kuokkanen .75
12 Leon Cooper .75
13 Hugo Lehoux .75
14 Michael Wehrstedt .75
15 Mike Self .75
16 Austin Wycisk .75
17 Steve Rawski .75
18 Grant McCune .75
19 Sean Stefanski .75
20 Drew Kivell .75
21 Jesse Baraniuk .75
22 Dene Poulin .75
23 Tobias Whelan .75
24 Chris Whitley .75
25 Peter Cava 1.00
26 Mark Robinson .75
27 Brad Priestlay .75

1993-94 Lakeland Ice Warriors

This set consists of player photos with photocopied biographies glued to the backs. There are variations of several players in this set.

COMPLETE SET (25) 25.00
1 Lakeland Ice Warriors .80 2.00
2 Chief Mascot .40 1.00
3 Chris Babkirk .40 1.00
4 Chris Baxter .40 1.00
5 Pat Bingham .40 1.00
6 Ian Collins .40 1.00
7 Ian Collins .40 1.00
8 Eric Daoust .40 1.00
9 Eric Daoust .40 1.00
10 Derek Edgerly .40 1.00
11 Andrew Ernst .40 1.00
12 John Finnie .40 1.00
13 John Finnie .40 1.00
14 Sean Gabriele .40 1.00
15 John Grand .40 1.00
16 Manny Hawkins .40 1.00
17 Jules Jardine .40 1.00
18 John Labenski .40 1.00
19 Francois Michaud .40 1.00
20 Bob Nicholls .40 1.00
21 Ed Sabo .40 1.00
22 Brent Selman .40 1.00
23 Gary Thomas .40 1.00
24 Dean Turgeon .40 1.00
25 Dave Wright .40 1.00

2004-05 Langley Hornets

This set features the Hornets of the BCJHL. The cards feature an Upper Deck logo as they were produced by the company's personalized card division.

COMPLETE SET (22) 25.00
1 Matt Allen 1.00
2 Aaron Berman 1.00
3 Justin Binab 1.00
4 Tyler Boice 1.00
5 Marcel Bruinsma 1.00
6 Gary Butler 1.00
7 Tyson Chernask 1.00
8 Steve Christie 2.00
9 Tyson Daniels 1.50
10 Gord Edmondson 1.00
11 Brian Harris 1.00
12 Steve Matic 1.00
13 Taylor Moore 2.00
14 Robert Pritchard 1.00
15 Graham Sheppard 1.00
16 Luke Shier 2.00
17 Justin Taylor 1.00
18 Chris Vassos 1.00
19 Nathan Westover 1.00
20 Mike Wilson 1.00
21 Jason Wright 1.00
22 Robert Pritchard#}Brian Harris AS
1.00

2003-04 Laredo Bucks

According to minor league afficionado Ralph Slate, this set was released by the team's booster club, which limited production to just 200 sets and charged a whopping $50 a set to raise funds.

COMPLETE SET (23) 60.00
1 Mike Amodeo 4.00
2 Jeff Bes 3.00
3 Max Birbraer 4.00
4 Brent Cullaton 3.00
5 Jean-Francois David 3.00
6 Serge Dube 3.00
7 Marco Emond 4.00
8 Chris Grenville 3.00
9 David Guerrera 4.00
10 James Hiebert 3.00
11 Dion Hyman 3.00
12 Mark Matier 3.00
13 Bobby-Chad Mitchell 3.00
14 Patrik Nilson 3.00
15 Adam Paiement 3.00
16 Gabriel Proulx 3.00
17 Steve Simoes 3.00
18 Jason Spence 3.00
19 Mike Vellinga 3.00
20 Steve Weidlich 3.00
21 Terry Ruskowski CO 1.00
22 Derek Craft EQM .50
23 Bobby Moore TR .50

1998-99 Las Vegas Coyotes RHI

This 20-card set was handed out as a promotional giveaway at a home game in late July of that season. The cards are not numbered, so they are listed in alphabetical order.

COMPLETE SET (20) 3.20 8.00
1 Konstantin Simchuk .20 .50
2 Jay Neal .20 .50
3 Mike Ciolli .20 .50
4 Jakub Ficenec .20 .50
5 Blake Knox .20 .50
6 Darren Meek .20 .50
7 Mike Jorgensen .20 .50
8 Kirk Llano .20 .50
9 Jamie Cooke .20 .50
10 Tom Perry .20 .50
11 Don Parsons .20 .50
12 Rich Bronilla .20 .50
13 Gerry St. Cyr .30 .75
14 Brad Guzda .20 .50
15 Rob Pallin .20 .50
16 Dan Reja .20 .50
17 Chris McSorley CO .20 .50
18 Howl N. Coyote Mascot .04 .10
19 KOMP Morning Crew .04 .10
20 1999 Las Vegas Coyotes .04 .10

1993-94 Las Vegas Thunder

Sponsored by Saturn, bc and More, and KVBC (Channel 3), this 32-card standard-size set features the 1993-94 Las Vegas Thunder of the IHL. On a black card face, the fronts have posed color player photos with thin white borders. The player's name and number appear under the picture. The team and sponsor logos are printed in the four corners. The cards are unnumbered and checklisted below in alphabetical order. This set may also have been issued as a perforated sheet.

COMPLETE SET (32) 3.20 8.00
1 Brent Ashton .16 .40
2 Boom Boom (Mascot) .04 .10
3 Bob Bourne CO .16 .40
4 Rod Buskas .10 .25
5 Lyndon Byers .30 .75
6 Rich Campbell TR .04 .10
7 Colin Cowherd ANN .04 .10
8 Butch Goring CO .16 .40
9 Steve Gotaas .10 .25
10 Marc Habscheid .10 .25
11 Brett Hauer .10 .25
12 Shawn Heaphy .10 .25
13 Scott Hollis .10 .25
14 Peter Ing .20 .50
15 Steve Jaques .10 .25
16 Bob Joyce .10 .25
17 Jim Kyte .10 .25
18 Patrice Lefebvre .30 .75
19 Clint Malarchuk .20 .50
20 Ken Quinney .10 .25
21 Jean-Marc Richard .10 .25
22 Todd Richards .10 .25
23 Marc Rodgers .10 .25
24 Jeff Sharples .10 .25
25 Randy Smith .10 .25
26 Greg Spenrath .10 .25
27 Bob Strumm GM .04 .10
28 Kirk Tomlinson .10 .25
29 Kerry Toporowski .16 .40
30 Mark Vermette .10 .25
31 Steve Wissman EQMG .04 .10
32 Title Card .04 .10

1994-95 Las Vegas Thunder

This 29-card standard-size set was manufactured and distributed by Jessen Associates, Inc. for Classic. The fronts display color action player photos with a teal marbleized inner border and a black outer border. The player's name, jersey number, and position appear in the teal border on the right edge. The cards are unnumbered and checklisted below in alphabetical order.

COMPLETE SET (29) 4.80 12.00
1 James Black .10 .25
2 Radek Bonk .40 1.00
3 Boom Boom MASCOT .04 .10
4 Rich Campbell TR .04 .10
5 Frank Evans .10 .25
6 Marc Habscheid .20 .50
7 Alex Hicks .20 .50
8 Bob Joyce .20 .50
9 Jim Kyte .10 .25
10 Lark and Craig, DJs .04 .10
11 Patrice Lefebvre .40 1.00
12 Darcy Loewen .20 .50
13 Sal Lombardi EQMG .04 .10
14 Clint Malarchuk .20 .50
15 Andrew McBain .20 .50
16 Chris McSorley CO .20 .50
17 David Neilson .10 .25
18 Jerry Olenyn .10 .25
19 Ken Quinney .20 .50
20 Pokey Reddick .20 .50
21 Jeff Reid .10 .25
22 Manon Rheaume 2.00 5.00
23 Jean-Marc Richard .20 .50
24 Todd Richards .10 .25
25 Marc Rodgers .10 .25
26 Jeff Sharples .10 .25
27 Jarrod Skalde .20 .50
28 Bob Strumm GM/CO .04 .10
29 Kerry Toporowski .20 .50

1995-96 Las Vegas Thunder

This 26-card set of the Las Vegas Thunder of the IHL was produced by Split Second for Collector's Edge Ice. The set was available through the team at home games and by mail. The cards are unnumbered, so are listed alphabetically. The set is notable for containing 1996 Anaheim first rounder Ruslan Salei, as well as bright NHL prospect Bill Bowler.

COMPLETE SET (26) 4.80 12.00
1 Bill Bowler .30 .75
2 Peter Fiorentino .16 .40
3 Greg Hawgood .30 .75
4 Sasha Lakovic .16 .40
5 Patrice Lefebvre .40 1.00
6 Darcy Loewen .16 .40
7 Gord Marx .16 .40
8 Blaine Moore .16 .40
9 Vaclav Nedomansky, Jr .16 .40
10 Pokey Reddick .30 .75
11 Jeff Ricciardi .16 .40
12 Jean-Marc Richard .16 .40
13 Marc Rodgers .40 1.00
14 Chris Rogles .30 .75
15 Ken Quinney .20 .50
16 Ruslan Salei .20 .50
17 Jeff Sharples .20 .50
18 Daniel Shank .20 .50
19 Todd Simon .20 .50
20 Rhett Trombley .16 .40
21 Vladimir Tsyplakov .20 .50
22 Sergei Zholtok .30 .75
23 Chris McSorley CO .10 .25
24 Clint Malarchuk AGM .20 .50
25 Bob Strumm GM .04 .10
26 BoomBoom .04 .10

1996-97 Las Vegas Thunder

This 24-card set of the Las Vegas Thunder of the IHL was produced by Multi-Ad Services and sponsored by Heineken and U.S. Home, among others. The cards were sold by the team at the rink or through the mail. The cards are unnumbered, and are listed below alphabetically.

COMPLETE SET (24) 4.80 12.00
1 Egor Bashkatov .20 .50
2 Boom Boom (Mascot) .04 .10
3 Kevin Dahl .20 .50
4 Chris Dahlquist .20 .50
5 Pavol Demitra .60 1.50
6 Parris Duffus .30 .75
7 Martin Gendron .20 .50
8 Brent Gretzky .20 .50
9 Kerry Huffman .20 .50
10 Igor Karpenko .30 .75
11 Don Larner .20 .50
12 Patrice Lefebvre .40 1.00
13 Darcy Loewen .20 .50
14 Clint Malarchuk AGM .20 .50
15 Chris McSorley CO .04 .10
16 Blaine Moore .20 .50
17 Ken Quinney .30 .75
18 Jeff Serowik .20 .50
19 Jason Simon .20 .50
20 Bob Strumm GM .04 .10
21 Rhett Trombley .20 .50
22 Sergei Yerkovich .20 .50
23 Sergei Zholtok .30 .75
24 Logo Card .04 .10

1997-98 Las Vegas Thunder

This set features the Thunder of the IHL and was sold by the team at home games. The cards are standard-sized and are numbered on the back.

COMPLETE SET (28) 4.80 12.00
1 Ken Quinney .30 .75
2 Manny Legace .60 1.50
3 Jesse Belanger .20 .50
4 Joe Day .20 .50
5 Darcy Loewen .20 .50
6 Trevor Roenick .20 .50
7 Steve Bancroft .20 .50
8 Thom Cullen .20 .50
9 John Slaney .20 .50
10 Sergei Yerkovich .20 .50
11 Bob Strumm GM .04 .10
12 Chris McSorley HCO .10 .25
13 Doug Tretiak EQM .04 .10
14 KKLZ .04 .10
15 Patrice Lefebvre .40 1.00
16 Tim Cheveldae .40 1.00
17 Jeff Christian .20 .50
18 Sergei Klimovich .20 .50
19 Rob Pattison .20 .50
20 Dan Shermerhorn .20 .50
21 Ilya Byakin .20 .50
22 Justin Kurtz .20 .50
23 Radoslav Suchy .20 .50
24 Boom Boom MASCOT .04 .10
25 Clint Malarchuk AGM .20 .50
26 Van Parfet TR .04 .10
27 Dave McCann TV .04 .10
28 PHPA Web Site .04 .01

1998-99 Las Vegas Thunder

Little is known about this set beyond the confirmed checklist. Any additional information can be forwarded to hockeymag@beckett.com.

COMPLETE SET (30) 4.00 10.00
1 Drew Bannister .16 .40
2 Sean Berens .16 .40
3 Dampy Brar .16 .40
4 Dean Ewen .16 .40
5 Petr Franek .16 .40
6 Brad Guzda .16 .40
7 Sami Helenius .30 .75
8 Bryan Helmer .20 .50
9 Scott Hollis .16 .40
10 Kevin Kaminski .30 .75
11 Patrice Lefebvre .30 .75
12 Jason McBain .16 .40
13 Taj Melson .16 .40
14 Brad Miller .16 .40
15 Nick Naumenko .20 .50
16 Petr Nedved .30 .75
17 Trevor Roenick .20 .50
18 Russ Romaniuk .20 .50
19 Konstantin Simchuk .16 .40
20 Andrei Sryubko .16 .40
21 Stefan Ustorf .20 .50
22 Shawn Wansborough .16 .40
23 Mike Wilson .16 .40
24 Bob Strumm GM .04 .10
25 Bob Bourne CO .04 .10
26 Rod Buskas ACO .04 .10
27 Van Parfet TR .04 .10
28 Bubba Kennedy .04 .10
Richard Krouse EQ
29 BoomBoom Mascot .04 .10
30 Logo Card .04 .10

2003-04 Las Vegas Wranglers

COMPLETE SET (24) 10.00
1 Jeff Attard .50
2 Blaine Bablitz .50
3 Cam Bristow .50
4 Ryan Christie .50
5 David Cousineau .50
6 Greg Day .50
7 Deryk Engelland .50
8 Justin Kelly .50
9 Chris Kenady .50
10 Brent Krahn 1.00
11 Marc Magliarditi .75
12 Jason McBain .50
13 Mike McBain .50
14 Tom Nelson .50
15 Kevin O'Flaherty .50
16 Eric Schneider .50
17 Jonathon Shockey .50
18 Kayle Short .50
19 Riku Varjamo .50
20 Chris Wheaton .50
21 Doug Wright .50
22 Glen Gulutzan GM/CO .10
23 Mascot .10
24 Checklist .01

2003-04 Las Vegas Wranglers RBI

This set was produced by RBI Sports and was limited to 250 copies. The set numbering reflects the entire run of RBI sets that season.

COMPLETE SET (16) 15.00
225 Jeff Attard 1.00
226 Cam Bristow 1.00
227 Ryan Christie 1.00
228 David Cousineau 1.00
229 Greg Day 1.00
230 Deryk Engelland 1.00
231 Chris Kenady 1.00
232 Brent Krahn 2.00
233 Marc Magliarditi 1.50
234 Jason McBain 1.00
235 Mike McBain 1.00
236 Tom Nelson 1.00
237 Kevin O'Flaherty 1.00
238 Eric Schneider 1.00
239 Jonathon Shockey 1.00
240 Doug Wright 1.00

2004-05 Las Vegas Wranglers

COMPLETE SET (24) 20.00
1 Mike McBain 1.00
2 Jon Krall 1.00
3 Deryk Engelland 1.00
4 Jason McBain 1.00
5 Dustin Johner 1.00
6 Christian Chartier 1.00
7 Chris Stanley 1.00
8 Adam Huxley 1.00
9 Dana Lattery 1.00
10 Dan Tudin 1.00
11 Jeff Attard 1.00
12 Marc Magliarditi 1.50
13 Regan Darby 1.00
14 Shawn Limpright 1.00
15 Darren Lynch 1.00
16 Doug Wright 1.00
17 Jason Spence 1.00
18 Sebastien Centomo 2.00
19 Ryan Gaucher 1.00
20 Glen Gulutzan CO .10
21 Drew Schoneck ACO .10
22 Joe Frederick ACO .10
23 Jeff Sharples ACO .10
24 The Duke MASCOT .10

2005-06 Las Vegas Wranglers

COMPLETE SET (25) 15.00
1 Todd Alexander .30 .75
2 Nick Anderson .30 .75
3 Thomas Bellemare .30 .75
4 Christian Chartier .30 .75
5 Steven Crampton .30 .75
6 Matt Dzieduszycki .30 .75
7 Derek Edwardson .30 .75
8 Lee Green .30 .75
9 Tim Hambly .30 .75
10 Shawn Limpright .30 .75
11 Darren Lynch .30 .75
12 Marc Magliarditi .40 1.00
13 Mike McBain .30 .75
14 Mike McKenna .30 .75
15 Chris Neiszner .30 .75
16 Sean O'Connor .30 .75
17 Adam Pardy .30 .75
18 Marco Peluso .30 .75
19 Scott Schoneck .30 .75
20 Tyler Sloan .30 .75
21 Chris Stanley .30 .75
22 Dan Tudin .30 .75
23 Glen Gulutzan CO .02 .10
24 Brent Bilodeau ACO .02 .10
25 The Duke MASCOT .02 .10

2006-07 Las Vegas Wranglers

COMPLETE SET (25) 10.00 20.00
1 Nick Anderson .30 .75
2 Ryan Bonni .30 .75
3 Adam Cracknell .30 .75
4 Steve Crampton .60 1.50
5 Kelly Czuy .30 .75
6 Ryan Donally .30 .75
7 Derek Edwardson .30 .75
8 Jason Jozsa .30 .75
9 Jason Krischuk .30 .75
10 Shawn Limpright .30 .75
11 Marc Magliarditi .60 1.50
12 Mike McBain .30 .75
13 Mike McKenna .30 .75
14 Arpad Mihaly .30 .75
15 Tyler Mosienko .30 .75
16 Kevin Nastiuk .60 1.50
17 Chris Neiszner .30 .75
18 Marco Peluso .30 .75
19 Aaron Power .30 .75
20 Scott Schoneck .30 .75
21 Aki Seitsonen .30 .75
22 Joe Tallari .30 .75
23 Bryce Thoma .30 .75
24 Brent Bilodeau ACO .10 .25
25 Glen Gulutzan CO .10 .25

1951-52 Laval Dairy Lac St. Jean

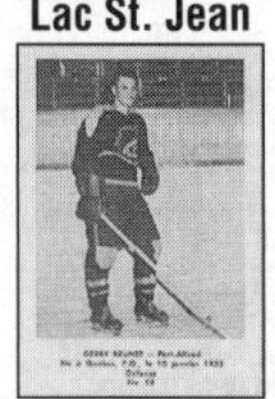

The 1951-52 Laval Dairy Lac St. Jean set includes 59 green-and-white tinted cards measuring approximately 1 3/4" by 2 1/2". The backs are blank. The cards are numbered on the front.

COMPLETE SET (59) 750.00 1500.00
1 Eddy Daoust 25.00 50.00
2 Guy Gareau 20.00 40.00
3 Gilles Desrosiers 20.00 40.00
4 Robert Desbiens 20.00 40.00
5 James Hayes 20.00 40.00
6 Paul Gagnon 20.00 40.00
7 Gerry Perreault 20.00 40.00
8 Marcel Dufour 20.00 40.00
9 Armand Bourdon 20.00 40.00
10 Jean-Marc Pichette 25.00 50.00
11 Gerry Gagnon 20.00 40.00
12 Jules Racette 20.00 40.00
13 Real Marcotte 20.00 40.00
14 Gerry Theberge 20.00 40.00
15 Rene Harvey 20.00 40.00
16 Joseph Lacoursiere 20.00 40.00
17 Fernand Benaquez 20.00 40.00
18 Andre Boisvert 20.00 40.00
19 Claude Chretien 20.00 40.00
20 Norbert Clark 20.00 40.00
21 Sylvio Lambert 20.00 40.00
22 Lucien Roy 20.00 40.00
23 Gerard Audet 20.00 40.00
24 Jacques Lalancette 20.00 40.00
25 Maurice St.Jean 20.00 40.00
26 Camille Lupien 20.00 40.00
27 Rodrigue Pelchat 20.00 40.00
28 Conrad L'Heureux 20.00 40.00
29 Paul Tremblay 20.00 40.00
30 Robert Vincent 20.00 40.00
31 Charles Lamirande 20.00 40.00
32 Leon Gaudreault 20.00 40.00
33 Maurice Thiffault 20.00 40.00
34 Marc-Aurele Tremblay 20.00 40.00
35 Rene Pronovost 20.00 40.00
36 Victor Corbin 20.00 40.00
37 Tiny Tamminen 25.00 50.00
38 Guildor Levesque 20.00 40.00
39 Gaston Lamirande 20.00 40.00
40 Guy Gervais 20.00 40.00
41 Rayner Makila 25.00 50.00
42 Jules Tremblay 20.00 40.00
43 Roland Girard 20.00 40.00
44 Germain Bergeron 20.00 40.00
45 Paul Duchesne 20.00 40.00
46 Roger Beaudoin 20.00 40.00
47 Georges Archibal 20.00 40.00
48 Claude Basque 20.00 40.00
49 Roger Sarda 20.00 40.00
50 Edgard Gendron 20.00 40.00
51 Gaston Labossiere 20.00 40.00
52 Roland Clantara 20.00 40.00
53 Florian Gravel 20.00 40.00
54 Jean-Guy Thompson 20.00 40.00
55 Yvan Forton 20.00 40.00
56 Yves Laporte 20.00 40.00
57 Claude Germain 20.00 40.00
58 Gerry Brunet 20.00 40.00
59 Maurice Courteau 25.00 50.00

1951-52 Laval Dairy QSHL

The 1951-52 Laval Dairy QSHL set include 109 black and white blank-back card measuring approximately 1 3/4" by 2 1/2 These cards were issued in the province Quebec and the Ottawa region. The cards a numbered and dated on the front. Key card in this set are "Pre-Rookie Cards" of Jea Beliveau and Jacques Plante. The car numbering is organized by team as follow Aces de Quebec (1-18 and 37), Chicoutin (19-36), Sherbrooke (38-51), Shawiniga Falls (52-67), Valleyfield (68-84), Royals d Montreal (85-100), and Ottawa (101-109).

COMPLETE SET (109) 1000.00 2000.00
1 Jean Beliveau 375.00 750.00
2 Jean Marois 5.00 10.00
3 Joe Crozier 12.50 25.00
4 Jack Gelineau 5.00 10.00
5 Murdo McKay 6.00 12.00
6 Arthur Leyte 5.00 10.00
7 W.(Bill) Leblanc 5.00 10.00
8 Robert Hayes 5.00 10.00
9 Yogi Kraiger 6.00 12.00
10 Frank King 5.00 10.00
11 Ludger Tremblay 6.00 12.00
12 Jackie Leclair 20.00 40.00
13 Martial Pruneau 5.00 10.00
14 Armand Gaudreault 5.00 10.00
15 Marcel Bonin 20.00 40.00
16 Herbie Carnegie 37.50 75.00
17 Claude Robert 5.00 10.00
18 Phil Renaud 5.00 10.00
19 Roland Hebert 5.00 10.00
20 Donat Duschene 5.00 10.00
21 Jacques Gagnon 5.00 10.00
22 Normand Dussault 6.00 12.00
23 Stan Smrke 10.00 20.00
24 Louis Smrke 6.00 12.00
25 Floyd Crawford 5.00 10.00
26 Germain Leger 5.00 10.00
27 Delphis Franche 5.00 10.00
28 Dick Wray 5.00 10.00
29 Guildor Levesque 7.50 15.00
30 Georges Roy 5.00 10.00
31 J.P. Lamirande 5.00 10.00
32 Gerard Glaude 5.00 10.00
33 Marcel Pelletier 10.00 20.00
34 Pete Tkachuck 5.00 10.00
35 Sherman White 5.00 10.00
36 Jimmy Moore 5.00 10.00
37 Punch Imlach 50.00 100.00
38 Alex Sandalax 5.00 10.00
39 William Kyle 5.00 10.00
40 Kenneth Biggs 5.00 10.00
41 Peter Wright 5.00 10.00
42 Rene Pepin 5.00 10.00
43 Tod Campeau 6.00 12.00
44 John Smith 5.00 10.00
45 Thomas McDougall 5.00 10.00
46 Jos. Lepine 5.00 10.00
47 Guy Labrie 5.00 10.00
48 Roger Bessette 5.00 10.00
49 Yvan Dugre 6.00 12.00
50 James Planche 5.00 10.00
51 Nils Tremblay 5.00 10.00
52 Bill MacDonagh 5.00 10.00
53 Georges Ouellet 5.00 10.00
54 Billy Arcand 5.00 10.00
55 Johnny Mahaffy 6.00 12.00
56 Bucky Buchanan 10.00 20.00
57 Al Miller 5.00 10.00
58 Don Penniston 5.00 10.00
59 Spike Laliberte 5.00 10.00
60 Ernie Oakley 5.00 10.00

61 Jack Bownass 5.00 10.00
62 Ted Hodgson 5.00 10.00
63 Lyall Wiseman 5.00 10.00
64 Erwin Grosse 5.00 10.00
65 Mel Read 5.00 10.00
66 Lloyd Henchberger 5.00 10.00
67 Jack Taylor 5.00 10.00
68 Marcel Bessette 5.00 10.00
69 Jack Schmidt 5.00 10.00
70 Paul Saindon 5.00 10.00
71 J.P. Bisaillon 5.00 10.00
72 Eddie Redmond 5.00 10.00
73 Larry Kwong 10.00 20.00
74 Andre Corriveau 5.00 10.00
75 Kitoute Joanette 5.00 10.00
76 Toe Blake 75.00 150.00
77 Georges Bougie 5.00 10.00
78 Jack Irvine 5.00 10.00
79 Paul Larivee 5.00 10.00
80 Paul Leclerc 5.00 10.00
81 Bertrand Bourassa 5.00 10.00
82 Jacques Deslauriers 5.00 10.00
83 Bingo Ernst 5.00 10.00
84 Gaston Gervais 5.00 10.00
85 Gerry Plamondon 6.00 12.00
86 Glen Harmon 5.00 10.00
87 Bob Friday 5.00 10.00
88 Rolland Rousseau 5.00 10.00
89 Billy Goold 5.00 10.00
90 Lloyd Finkbeiner 5.00 10.00
91 Cliff Malone 5.00 10.00
92 Jacques Plante 375.00 750.00
93 Gerard Desaulniers 6.00 12.00
94 Arthur Rose 5.00 10.00
95 Jacques Locas 5.00 10.00
96 Walter Clune 5.00 10.00
97 Louis Denis 5.00 10.00
98 Fernand Perreault 5.00 10.00
99 Douglas McNeil 6.00 12.00
100 Les Douglas 5.00 10.00
101 Howard Riopelle 10.00 20.00
102 Vic Grigg 5.00 10.00
103 Bobby Roberts 5.00 10.00
104 Legs Fraser 5.00 10.00
105 Butch Stahan 5.00 10.00
106 Fritz Frazer 5.00 10.00
107 Bill Robinson 5.00 10.00
108 Eddie Emberg 5.00 10.00
109 Leo Gravelle 12.50 25.00

1951-52 Laval Dairy Subset

The 1951-52 Laval Dairy Subset includes 66 skip-numbered black and white blank-back cards measuring approximately 1 3/4" by 2 1/2". Apparently, this set was intended to update the QSHL set and was issued after the QSHL set perhaps even as late as the 1952-53 season. The card numbering is organized by team as follows: Aces de Quebec (7-15 and 117), Chicoutimi (25-38), Sherbrooke (39-57), Shawinigan Falls (59-67, 89-90, 94-95, 115, 118, and 120), Valleyfield (68-84 and 116), Royals de Montreal (85-86, 92-93, and 96-97), and Ottawa (98-114, 119, and 121).

COMPLETE SET (66) 750.00 1500.00
4 Jack Gelineau SP 25.00 50.00
7 Al Miller 10.00 20.00
8 Walter Pawlyshyn 10.00 20.00
9 Yogi Kraiger SP 25.00 50.00
10 Al Baccari 10.00 20.00
12 Denis Smith 10.00 20.00
13 Pierre Brillant 10.00 20.00
14 Frank Mario 10.00 20.00
15 Danny Nixon 10.00 20.00
25 Leon Bouchard 10.00 20.00
26 Pete Taillefer 10.00 20.00
29 Bucky Buchanan 12.50 25.00
36 Marius Groleau 10.00 20.00
38 Fernand Perreault 10.00 20.00
39 Robert Drainville 10.00 20.00
40 Ronnie Matthews 10.00 20.00
44 Roger Roberge 10.00 20.00
46 Pete Wywrot 10.00 20.00
50 Gilles Dube 10.00 20.00
51 Nils Tremblay SP 25.00 50.00
52 Bob Pepin 10.00 20.00
53 Dewar Thompson 10.00 20.00
55 Irene St.Hilaire 10.00 20.00
56 Martial Pruneau 10.00 20.00
57 Jacques Locas 10.00 20.00
59 Nelson Podolsky 10.00 20.00
60 Bert Giesebrecht 10.00 20.00
61 Steve Brklaicich 10.00 20.00
65 Jack Hamilton 10.00 20.00
66 Dave Gatherum 10.00 20.00
67 Jean-Marie Plante 10.00 20.00
68 Gordie Haworth 12.50 25.00
69 Jack Schmidt SP 25.00 50.00
70 Bruce Cline 12.50 25.00
72 Phil Vitale 10.00 20.00
81 Carl Smelle 10.00 20.00
84 Tom Smelle 10.00 20.00
85 Gerry Plamondon 12.50 25.00
86 Glen Harmon 10.00 20.00
89 Frank Bathgate 10.00 20.00
90 Bernie Lemonde 10.00 20.00
92 Jacques Plante 375.00 750.00
93 Gerard Desaulniers 10.00 20.00
94 J.C. Lebrun 10.00 20.00
95 Bob Leger 10.00 20.00
96 Walter Clune 10.00 20.00
97 Louis Denis 10.00 20.00
98 Jackie Leclair 15.00 30.00
99 John Arundel 10.00 20.00
100 Leslie(Les) Douglas 10.00 20.00
103 Bobby Robertson 10.00 20.00
104 Ray Fredericks 10.00 20.00
106 Emile Dagenais 10.00 20.00
108 Al Kuntz 10.00 20.00
110 Red Johnson 10.00 20.00
111 John O'Flaherty 10.00 20.00
112 Jack Giesebrecht 12.50 25.00
113 Bill Richardson 10.00 20.00
114 Bep Guidolin 20.00 40.00
115 Roger Bedard 10.00 20.00
116 Renald Lacroix 10.00 20.00
117 Gordie Hudson 10.00 20.00
118 Dick Wray 10.00 20.00
119 Ronnie Hurst 10.00 20.00
120 Eddie Joss 10.00 20.00
121 Lyall Wiseman 10.00 20.00

1988-89 Lethbridge Hurricanes

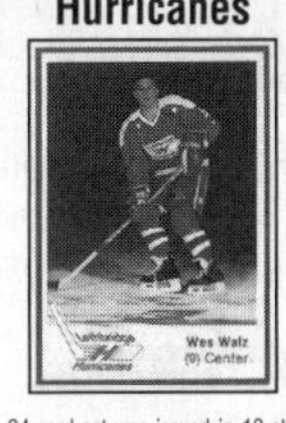

This 24-card set was issued in 12 strips of three perforated cards with the third card on each strip being an ad or coupon card. The strips measure approximately 7 1/2" by 3 1/2". The fronts feature color posed player photos with a heavy black line framing the edge of the card leaving white space between the line and the picture. The team name, player's name, jersey number, and position appear in the white margin at the bottom. The cards are unnumbered and checklisted below in alphabetical order.

COMPLETE SET (24) 4.80 12.00
1 Mark Bassen .20 .50
2 Pete Berthelsen .20 .50
3 Bryan Bosch .20 .50
4 Paul Checknita .20 .50
5 Kelly Ens .20 .50
6 Jeff Ferguson .30 .75
7 Scott Fukami .20 .50
8 Colin Gregor .20 .50
9 Mark Greig .30 .75
10 Rob Hale .20 .50
11 Ted Hutchings .20 .50
12 Dusty Imoo .30 .75
13 Ivan Jessey .20 .50
14 Mark Kuntz .20 .50
15 Corey Lyons .20 .50
16 Shane Mazutinec .20 .50
17 Casey McMillan .20 .50
18 Pat Pylypuik .20 .50
19 Brad Rubachuk .20 .50
20 Jason Ruff .20 .50
21 Chad Seibel .20 .50
22 Wes Walz .60 1.50
23 Jim Wheatcroft .20 .50
24 Team Picture .20 .50

1989-90 Lethbridge Hurricanes

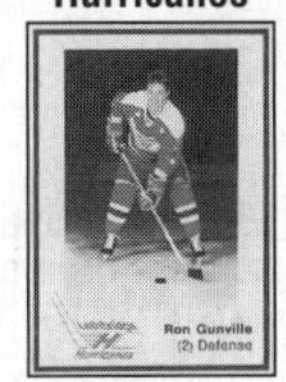

Showing signs of perforation, this 24-card set was issued in strips of several cards each. The cards measure the standard size when separated and feature posed, color player photos. The photos are set on a white card face with a heavy black line framing the edge of the card, leaving white space between the line and the picture. The player's name, jersey number, and position appear in the white margin at the bottom. The backs carry "Tips from the Hurricanes," which are hockey tips and public service messages. The cards are unnumbered and checklisted below in alphabetical order.

COMPLETE SET (24) 8.00 20.00
1 Doug Barrault .30 .75
2 Peter Berthelsen .30 .75
3 Bryan Bosch .30 .75
4 Kelly Ens .30 .75
5 Mark Greig .30 .75
6 Ron Gunville .30 .75
7 Rob Hale .30 .75
8 Neil Hawryluk .30 .75
9 David Holzer .30 .75
10 Dusty Imoo .60 1.50
11 Darcy Kaminski ACO .10 .25
12 Bob Loucks CO .10 .25
13 Corey Lyons .30 .75
14 Duane Maruschak .30 .75
15 Jamie McLennan 1.20 3.00
16 Shane Peacock .30 .75
17 Pat Pylypuik .30 .75
18 Gary Reilly .30 .75
19 Brad Rubachuk .30 .75
20 Jason Ruff .30 .75
21 Kevin St. Jacques .30 .75
22 Wes Walz .60 1.50
23 Darcy Werenka .40 1.00
24 Brad Zimmer .30 .75

1993-94 Lethbridge Hurricanes

This 24-card set was issued on three-card perforated strips each consisting of two player cards and one advertisement or coupon card. The strips measure 7 1/2" by 3 1/2", and if cut, the individual cards would measure the standard size. The fronts of each card feature a color posed player photo with thin red borders on a white background. The cards are unnumbered and checklisted below in alphabetical order.

COMPLETE SET (24) 4.80 12.00
1 Rob Daum CO .10 .25
2 Kirk DeWaele .20 .50
3 Derek Diener .20 .50
4 Scott Grieco .20 .50
5 David Jesiolowski .20 .50
6 Todd MacIsaac .20 .50
7 Stan Matwijiw .40 1.00
8 Larry McMorran .20 .50
9 Brad Mehalko .20 .50
10 Shane Peacock .20 .50
11 Randy Perry .20 .50
12 Domenic Pittis .30 .75
12 Byron Ritchie .24 .60
14 Bryce Salvador .40 1.00
15 Ryan Smith .20 .50
16 Lee Sorochan .30 .75
17 Mark Szoke .20 .50
18 Scott Townsend .20 .50
19 David Trofimenkoff .20 .50
20 Twister (Mascot) .04 .10
21 Ivan Vologjaninov .20 .50
22 Jason Widmer .20 .50
23 Derek Wood .20 .50
24 Aaron Zarowny .20 .50

1995-96 Lethbridge Hurricanes

This 25-card set was issued on three-card perforated strips measuring approximately 7 1/2" by 3 1/2". Each strip consists of two player cards and one advertisement card. The cards include player jersey numbers on the front, but are checklisted below alphabetically.

COMPLETE SET (25) 8.00 20.00
1 Mike Bayrack .40 1.00
2 John Bradley .40 1.00
3 Travis Brigley .40 1.00
4 David Brumby .40 1.00
5 Derek Diener .40 1.00
6 Scott Grieco .40 1.00
7 Lee Hamilton .40 1.00
8 Trevor Hanas .40 1.00
9 Ryan Hoople .40 1.00
10 Mike Josephson .40 1.00
11 Kirby Law .40 1.00
12 Bryan Maxwell CO .04 .10
13 Doyle McMorris .40 1.00
14 Brad Mehalko .40 1.00
15 Dennis Mullen .40 1.00
16 Jiri Novotny .40 1.00
17 Mike O'Grady .40 1.00
18 Randy Perry .40 1.00
19 Byron Ritchie .40 1.00
20 Bryce Salvador .60 1.50
21 Darren Shakotko .40 1.00
22 Mark Smith .40 1.00
23 Dave Taylor .40 1.00
24 Luc Theoret .40 1.00
25 Windy MASCOT .04 .10

1996-97 Lethbridge Hurricanes

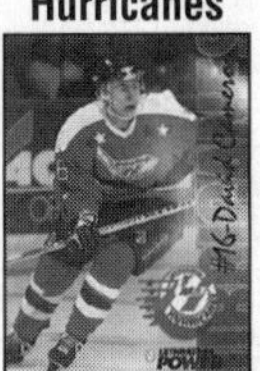

This 24-card set features color player photos with the club's nickname serving as a design element along the right border. The player's name and number, along with the team's anniversary logo also are featured. The unnumbered cards are checklisted below alphabetically.

COMPLETE SET (24) 4.80 12.00
1 Travis Brigley .20 .50
2 David Cameron .20 .50
3 Matt Demarski .20 .50
4 Paul Elliott .20 .50
5 Jason Hegberg .20 .50
6 Martin Hohenberger .20 .50
7 Ryan Hoople .20 .50
8 Mark Ivan .20 .50
9 Mike Josephson .20 .50
10 Kirby Law .20 .75
11 Mike O'Grady .20 .50
12 Dale Purinton .20 2.00
13 Byron Ritchie .30 .75
14 Bryce Salvador .30 .75
15 Richard Seeley .20 .50
16 Cam Severson .20 .50
17 Darren Shakotko .20 .50
18 Wes Schneider .20 .50
19 Parry Shockey CO .10 .25
Bryan Maxwell GM
20 Mark Smith .20 .50
21 Dave Taylor .20 .50
22 Luc Theoret .20 .50
23 Evgeni Tsybouk .24 .60
24 Shane Yellowhorn .20 .50

1997-98 Lethbridge Hurricanes

This set features the Hurricanes of the WHL. Little else is known about this set beyond the confirmed checklist. Additional information can be forwarded to hockeymag@beckett.com.

COMPLETE SET (25) 4.80 12.00
1 Derrick Atkinson .20 .50
2 Brady Block .20 .50
3 Scott Borders .20 .50
4 Jeff Church .20 .50
5 Jason Hegberg .20 .50
6 Derek Holland .20 .50
7 Curtis Huppe .20 .50
8 Dustin Kazak .20 .50
9 Chad Kletzel .20 .50
10 Vladislav Klochkov .20 .50
11 Charlie Mattersdorfer .20 .50
12 Jason McLean .20 .50
13 Sean Robertson .20 .50
14 Bart Rushmer .20 .50
15 Thomas Scantlebury .20 .50
16 Darren Shakotko .20 .50
17 Mark Smith .40 1.00
18 Shaun Sutter .40 1.00
19 Luc Theoret .20 .50
20 Kaleb Toth .20 .50
21 Evgeni Tsybouk .30 .75
22 Mike Varhaug .20 .50
23 Trevor Wasyluk .20 .50
24 Shane Willis .40 1.00
25 Lethbridge Power .04 .10

1999-00 Lethbridge Hurricanes

This set features the Hurricanes of the WHL. The set was produced by the team and sold at home games. The cards are unnumbered, and thus are listed alphabetically.

COMPLETE SET (25) 4.80 12.00
1 Derek Atkinson .20 .50
2 Brian Ballman .20 .50
3 Nathan Barrett .20 .50
4 Brady Block .30 .75
5 Scott Borders .20 .50
6 Phil Cole .20 .50
7 Radek Duda .30 .75
8 Simon Ferguson .20 .50
9 Jordon Flodell .20 .50
10 Eric Godard .30 .75
11 Jason Hegberg .20 .50
12 Brandon Janes .20 .50
13 Ryan Jorde .20 .50
14 Dustin Kazak .20 .50
15 Angel Krstev .20 .50
16 Petr Kudrna .20 .50
17 Darren Lynch .20 .50
18 Warren McCutheon .20 .50
19 Justin Ossachuk .20 .50
20 Derek Parker .20 .50
21 Brian Patterson .20 .50
22 Derrick Ruck .20 .50
23 Thomas Scantlebury .20 .50
24 Eric Sonnenberg .20 .50
25 Chad Yaremko .20 .50

2000-01 Lethbridge Hurricanes

This set features the Hurricanes of the WHL. The set was produced by the team and sold at home games.

COMPLETE SET (25) 4.80 40.00
1 Brian Ballman .20 1.50
2 Nathan Barrett .40 5.00
3 Scott Borders .20 1.50
4 Phil Cole .20 1.50
5 Simon Ferguson .20 1.50
6 Matt Fetzner .20 1.50
7 Mark Forth .20 1.50
8 Tim Green .20 1.50
9 Matt Jacques .20 1.50
10 Adam Johnson .20 1.50
11 Andrew Jungwirth .20 1.50
12 Tomas Kopecky .30 5.00
13 Ryley Layden .20 1.50
14 Darren Lynch .20 1.50
15 Joel Martin .30 2.00
16 Warren McCutcheon .20 1.50
17 Brett O'Malley .20 1.50
18 Brian Patterson .20 1.50
19 Martin Podlesak .30 2.00
20 Derek Ruck .20 1.50
21 Thomas Scantlebury .20 1.50
22 Blake Ward .30 2.00
23 Twister MASCOT .04 .10
24 Header Card .04 .01
25 Sponsor Card .01

2001-02 Lethbridge Hurricanes

COMPLETE SET (23) 12.00
1 Matthew Berger .50
2 Simon Ferguson .50
3 Stewart Thiessen .50

4 Tim Green .50
5 Braden Appleby .50
6 Tomas Kopecky .75
7 Paul McBrien .50
8 Nathan Barrett .75
9 Martin Podlesak .50
10 Kris Callaway .50
11 Brian Patterson .50
12 Ryley Layden .50
13 D.J. King .50
14 Logan Koopmans .75
15 Brett O'Malley .50
16 Scott Borders .50
17 David Selthun .50
18 Clay Plume .50
19 Blake Ward .75
20 Brent Seabrook .50
21 Jeremy Jackson .50
22 Nick Chibi .50
23 Tyrell Moulton .50

2003-04 Lethbridge Hurricanes

We have confirmed a handful of singles from this set, thanks to collector Vinnie Montalbano. If you have any other information about this set, please email us at hockeymag@beckett.com.

COMPLETE SET (?)
1 Joel Andresen
2 John Lammers
3 Jake Riddle
4 Brent Seabrook
5 Nick Tarnasky
6 Kris Versteeg

2004-05 Lethbridge Hurricanes

Cards are not numbered.

COMPLETE SET (24) 25.00
1 Mark Ashton 1.00
2 Shawn Mezei 1.00
3 Brennan Chapman 1.00
4 Brent Seabrook 1.00
5 Tyler Redenbach 1.00
6 Kris Versteeg 1.50
7 Mark Olafson 1.00
8 John Lammers 1.00
9 Martin Ruzicka 1.00
10 Colton Yellow Horn 1.50
11 Kyle Pess 1.00
12 Michael Kaye 1.00
13 Kenny Petkau 1.00
14 Jonathan Filewich 1.00
15 Chase Hentuik 1.00
16 Neil Kodman 1.00
17 Rob Klinkhammer 1.00
18 Michal Gulasi 1.00
19 Mike Ulrich 1.00
20 Lenny Thunderchild 1.00
21 Jesse Dudas 1.00
22 Aaron Sorochan 1.50
23 Scott Bolland 1.50
24 MASCOT .10

2005-06 Lethbridge Hurricanes

COMPLETE SET (24) 8.00 20.00
1 Mark Ashton .40 1.00
2 Andrew Bentz .40 1.00
3 Zach Boychuk .40 1.00
4 Ryan Bryce .40 1.00
5 Mike Cann .40 1.00
6 Jacob Dietrich .40 1.00
7 Mitch Fadden .40 1.00
8 Yashar Farmanara .40 1.00
9 Kris Hogg .40 1.00
10 Michael Kaye .40 1.00
11 Ryan Kerr .40 1.00
12 Dwight King .40 1.00
13 Randy King .40 1.00
14 Tomas Kudelka .40 1.00
15 Justin Leclerc .40 1.00
16 Gavin McHale .40 1.00
17 Mark Olafson .40 1.00
18 Isaac Reid .40 1.00
19 Brad Riege .40 1.00
20 Roman Wick .40 1.00
21 Ben Wright .40 1.00

22 Michael Wuchterl .40 1.00
23 Colton Yellowhorn .75 2.00
24 Twister MASCOT .02 .10

2003-04 Lewiston Maineiacs

COMPLETE SET (28) 12.00 20.00
1 Mathieu Aubin .30 .75
2 Gabriel Balasescu .30 .75
3 Vladislav Balaz .30 .75
4 Alex Bourret .60 1.50
5 Marc-Andre ClichÃ© .60 1.50
6 Nicolas Cowan .30 .75
7 Matthew Davis .30 .75
8 Chad Denny .30 .75
9 Pierre-Luc Faubert .30 .75
10 Karl Fournier .30 .75
11 Bobby Gates .30 .75
12 Olivier Legault .30 .75
13 Travis Mealey .30 .75
14 Ryan Murphy .30 .75
15 Jonathan Paiement .30 .75
16 Alexandre Picard .75 2.00
17 Brandon Roach .30 .75
18 Maxime Robert .30 .75
19 Richard Stehlik .30 .75
20 Francis Trudel .30 .75
21 Kevin Turgeon .30 .75
22 Brandon Verge .30 .75
23 Sheldon Wenzel .30 .75
24 Mario Durocher CO .02 .10
25 Jeff Guay ACO .02 .10
26 Ed Harding ACO .02 .10
27 Lewy MASCOT .02 .10
28 Team Photo/CL .10 .25

2002-03 Lexington Men O'War

COMPLETE SET (26) 20.00
1 Team Photo .50
2 Jim Wiley .75
3 Justin Van Parys .75
4 Mike Smith .75
5 Marc-Andre Thinel .75
6 Jared Smyth .75
7 Jesse Cook .75
8 Ben Storey .75
9 Mark Smith 1.50
10 Dan Murphy 1.50
11 Daryl Moor .75
12 Alexander Mathieu .75
13 Dominic Periard .75
14 Chris Dirkes .75
15 Van Burgess .75
16 Fraser Clair .75
17 Terry Craven .75
18 Brett Draney .75
19 Joe Vandermeer .75
20 Aaron Miskovich .75
21 Jay Banach .75
22 Ryan Fultz .75
23 Mike Sgroi .75
24 Josh Mizerek .75
25 Kevin Knopp .75
26 Mow MASCOT .10

2000-01 Lincoln Stars

This set featured the Lincoln Stars of the USHL. Cards are numbered XX of 28 on the card backs.

COMPLETE SET (28)
1 Nick Fouts .75
2 Ken Scruderi .40
3 Tom Watkins .40
4 Andy Schneider .40
5 Matt Wavra .40
6 Chris Fournier .40
7 Mike Fournier .40
8 John Snowden .40
9 Nick Fuher .40
10 Preston Callander .40
11 Bobby John Byfuglien .40
12 Josh Magnuson .40
13 Brandon Polich .40
14 Chad Hontvet .40
15 Billy Hengen .40
16 Ryan Young .40
17 Matthew Trojovsky .40
18 Lee Marvin .40
19 Brandon Bochenski .40
20 Trevor Frischmon .40
21 Marco Peluso .40
22 Jake Brandt .75
23 Justin Johnson .75
24 Beau Fritz .75
25 Steve Johnson HCO .10
26 Steve Ross ACO .10
27 Corey Courtney TR .10
28 Mascot .10

2001-02 Lincoln Stars

This 28-card set features the Lincoln Stars of the USHL.

COMPLETE SET (28) 12.00
1 Ben Assenmacher .50
2 David Backes .50
3 Josh Budish .50
4 Jamie Dowhatko .50
4 Mike Eickman .50
6 Luke Erickson .50
7 Matt Erickson .50
8 Mike Fournier .50
9 Trevor Frischmon .50
10 Beau Fritz .75
11 Ethan Graham .50
12 Billy Hengen .50
13 Chad Hontvet .50
14 Dan Irmen .50
15 Patrick Knutson .50
16 Philippe Lamoureux .75
17 Lee Marvin .50
18 T.J. McElroy .50
19 Ryan Potulny .50
20 John Snowden .50
21 Dirk Southern .50
22 Ryan Swanson .50
23 Matt Wavra .50
24 Nate Ziegelmann .75
25 Steve Johnson HCO .10
26 Mark Pivetz ACO .10
27 Corey Courtney TR .10
28 Mascot .10

2002-03 Lincoln Stars

This series was issued in two parts. Cards 31-48 were issued as a supplemental set.

COMPLETE SET (48) 20.00
1 Philippe Lamoureux .50
2 Ethan Graham .50
3 David Backes .50
4 Mike Eickman .50
5 Chris Porter .50
6 Ryan Potulny .50
7 Danny Irmen .50
8 Mike Fournier .50
9 Tyler Magura .50
10 John Snowden .50
11 Ben Gordon .50
12 Jamison Orr .50
13 Mick Berge .50
14 Mike Nesdill .50
15 Brent Borgen .50
16 Matt Hayek .50
17 David Carlisle .50
18 Luke Erickson .50
19 Jesse Lindenberg .50
20 Keith Rodger .50
21 Robbie Bina .50
22 Joel Gasper .50
23 Ross Cherry .50
24 Nate Ziegelmann .50
25 Steve Johnson .50
26 Mark Pivetz .50
27 Rob Facca .50
28 Corey Courtney .50
29 Starzan MASCOT .10
30 Checklist .01
31 Mark Schwamberger .50
32 Jeff McFarland .50
33 Per Mars .50
34 David Backes AS .50
35 Chris Porter AS .50
36 Ryan Potulny AS .50
37 Dan Irmen AS .50
38 John Snowden AS .50
39 Nate Ziegelmann AS .50
40 Philippe Lamoureux .50
41 Ethan Graham .50
42 David Backes .50
43 Mike Eickman .50
44 Ryan Potulny .50
45 Dan Irmen .50
46 John Snowden .50
47 Nate Ziegelmann .50
48 Update Checklist .10

2003-04 Lincoln Stars

COMPLETE SET (29) 12.00
1 Philippe Lamoureux .50
2 Morgan Simonson .50
3 Kaj Kallarsson .50
4 Jared Boll .50
5 Evan Rankin .50
6 Nick Tuzzolino .50
7 Garrett Raboin .50
8 Tyler Magura .50
9 Ben Gordon .50
10 Mick Berge .50
11 Michael Nesdill .50
12 Brent Borgen .50
13 Alexcei McAvoy .50
14 Matt Hayek .50
15 David Carlisle .50
16 Andrew Guyer .50
17 Jesse Lindenberg .50
18 Chris Tarkir .50
19 Keith Rodger .50
20 Adam Bartholomay .50
21 Michael Waidlich .50
22 Dan Comrie .50
23 Aaron Walski .50
24 Aaron McCloy .50
25 Steve Johnson CO .10
26 Rob Facca ACO .10
27 Corey Courtney TR .01
28 Mascot .10
29 Checklist .01

2003-04 Lincoln Stars Update

COMPLETE SET (18) 3.00 8.00
30 Checklist .02 .10
31 John Vadnais .20 .50

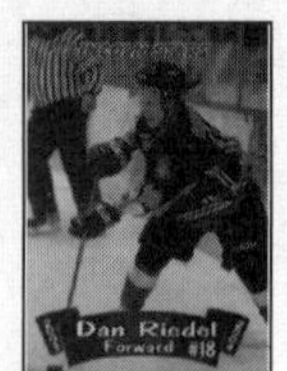

32 Dan Riedel .20 .50
33 Derek Whitmore .20 .50
34 Jered Bye .20 .50
35 Chris Robinson .20 .50
36 John Swanson .20 .50
37 Matt Weir .20 .50
38 Checklist .02 .10
39 Philippe Lamoureux/Tyler Magura .20 .50
40 Ben Gordon/Mick Berge .20 .50
41 Mike Nesdill/Brent Borgen .20 .50
42 Matt Hayek/David Carlisle .20 .50
43 Philippe Lamoureux RB .20 .50
44 Philippe Lamoureux AS .20 .50
45 Evan Rankin AS .20 .50
46 Nick Tuzzolino AS .20 .50
47 David Carlisle AS .20 .50

2004-05 Lincoln Stars

This USHL set was sold at home games. Reportedly, there were certified autographs included in some sets. We have yet to confirm their existence. If you can help, write us at hockeymag@beckett.com.

COMPLETE SET (30) 12.00
1 Jordan Pearce 1.00
2 Brian Bina .50
3 John Vadnais .50
4 Jared Boll 1.00
5 Dillon Duncan .50
6 Dan Riedel .50
7 Garrett Raboin .50
8 Erik Condra .50
9 Eli Vlaisavljevich .50
10 J.J. Koehler .50
11 Ryan Hohl .50
12 Shawn Gawrys .50
13 Chris Nugent .50
14 David Carlisle .50
15 Mike Kramer .50
16 Mick Berge .50
17 Tom Sawatske .50
18 Brock Trotter .50
19 Chris Robinson .50
20 John Swanson .50
21 Steve Jakiel .50
22 Patrik Valcak .50
23 Linus Klasen .50
24 Steve Johnson CO .10
25 Ryan Bencurik ACO .10
26 Derek Reynolds ACO .10
27 Corey Courtney TR .10
28 Starzan MASCOT .10
29 Checklist .01
30 contest card

2004-05 Lincoln Stars Update

Issued on Feb. 21, 2005 as an update to the team set issued earlier in the season. It has been reported that just 350 copies of the Update series were produced. The set is noteworthy for the inclusion of Brian Lee, the ninth overall pick in 2005.

COMPLETE SET (18) 12.00
31 Brian Lee 4.00
32 Kyle Hardwick .50
33 Chris Vande Velde 1.00
34 Russ Sinkewich .50
35 Ryan Salvis .50
36 Chris Murphy .50
37 Ryan Kelly .50
38 Taylor Raszka .50
39 Jared Boll 1.00
40 Dan Riedel .50
41 Garrett Raboin .50
42 David Carlisle .50
43 Mick Berge .50
44 Chris Robinson .50
45 Jordan Pearce AS 1.00
46 Jared Boll AS 1.00
47 Dan Riedel AS .50
48 Tom Sawatske AS .50

2006-07 Lincoln Stars

COMPLETE SET (29) 10.00 18.00
1 Lincoln Stars .10 .25
2 David Brack .30 .75
3 Chad Langlais .30 .75
4 Rick Carden .30 .75
5 Eric Lake .30 .75
6 Chris Stansik .30 .75
7 Jared Brown .30 .75
8 Matt Bartkowski .30 .75
9 Stephen Schultz .30 .75
10 Ryan Ruikka .30 .75
11 Jason Gregoire .40 1.00
12 Brandon Bollig .30 .75
13 Danny Baco .30 .75
14 Ross Henry .30 .75
15 Mike Kramer .30 .75
16 Ryan Lowery .30 .75
17 Colby Cohen .30 .75
18 Kyle O'Kane .30 .75
19 Pat McAuley .30 .75
20 Jon Morrow .40 1.00
21 Kyle Follmer .30 .75
22 Bryan Hogan .40 1.00
23 Anthony Principato .30 .75
24 Carter Camper .30 .75
25 Steve Johnson CO .10 .25
26 Ryan Bencurik ACO .02 .10
27 Jim McGroarty ACO .02 .10
28 Corey Courtney TR .02 .10
29 Starzan MASCOT .02 .10

2006-07 Lincoln Stars Traded

COMPLETE SET (18) 5.00 12.00
1T Checklist .02 .10
2T Patrick Johnson .30 .75
3T Joey Miller .30 .75
4T J.J Crew .30 .75
5T Mike Hull .30 .75
6T Dan Lawson .30 .75
7T Bryce Christianson .30 .75
8T Chad Langlais .30 .75
9T Chris Stansik .30 .75
10T Jared Brown .30 .75
11T Brandon Bollig .30 .75
12T Danny Baco .30 .75
13T Mike Kramer .30 .75
14T Bryan Hogan .30 .75
15T Chad Langlais .30 .75
16T Stephen Schultz .30 .75
17T Colby Cohen .30 .75
18T Carter Camper .40 1.00

2006-07 Lincoln Stars Upper Deck Signature Series

Each card is signed and serial numbered out of 9, except for the cards of O'Kane and McAuley, who were traded prior to the cards being issued.

1 Danny Baco 20.00 50.00
2 Matt Bartowski 20.00 50.00
3 Brandon Bollig 25.00 60.00
4 David Brack 20.00 50.00
5 Jared Brown 20.00 50.00
6 Carter Camper 20.00 50.00
7 Rick Carden 20.00 50.00
8 Bryce Christianson 20.00 50.00
9 Colby Cohen 20.00 50.00
10 J.J. Crew 20.00 50.00
11 Kyle Follmer 20.00 50.00
12 Jason Gregoire 25.00 60.00
13 Ross Henry 20.00 50.00
14 Bryan Hogan 25.00 60.00
15 Mike Hull 20.00 50.00
16 Patrick Johnson 20.00 50.00
17 Mike Kramer 20.00 50.00
18 Eric Lake 20.00 50.00
19 Chad Langlais 20.00 50.00
20 Dan Lawson 20.00 50.00
21 Pat McAuley 4.00 10.00
22 Joey Miller 20.00 50.00
23 Kyle O'Kane 4.00 10.00
24 Stephen Schultz 20.00 50.00
25 Chris Stansik 20.00 50.00

1985-86 London Knights

The London Knights of the OHL are featured in this 30-card P.L.A.Y. (Police, Law and Youth) set, which was sponsored by the London Crime Prevention Committee in conjunction with area businesses. The cards measure approximately 2 3/4" by 3 1/2" and are printed on thin card stock. The fronts feature color photos with the players posed in action stances. A facsimile autograph is inscribed at the bottom of the picture.

COMPLETE SET (30) 20.00 50.00
1 LaVerne Shipley CoP .10 .25
2 Joe Ranger .20 .50
3 Kellogg's Ad CL .10 .25
4 Don Boyd GM/CO .10 .25
5 Harry E. Sparling COP .10 .25
6 Murray Nystrom .20 .50
7 Bob Halkidis .30 .75
8 Morgan Watts .20 .50
9 Brendan Shanahan 16.00 40.00
10 Brian Dobbin .30 .75
11 Ed Kister .20 .50
12 Darin Smith .20 .50
13 Greg Puhalski .20 .50
14 Dave Haas .20 .50
15 Pete McLeod .20 .50
16 Frank Tremblay .20 .50
17 Matthew Smyth .20 .50
18 Glen Leslie .20 .50
19 Mike Zombo .20 .50
20 Jamie Groke .20 .50
21 Brad Schlegel .30 .75
22 Kelly Cain .20 .50
23 Tom Allen .20 .50
24 Rod Gerow .20 .50
25 Pat Vachon .20 .50
26 Paul Cook ACO .10 .25
27 Jeff Reese .60 1.50
28 Fred Kean PR .10 .25
29 Scott Cumming .30 .75
30 John Williams ACO .10 .25

1986-87 London Knights

The London Knights of the OHL are featured in this 30-card P.L.A.Y. (Police, Law and Youth) set, which was sponsored by the London Crime Prevention Committee in conjunction with area businesses. The cards measure approximately 2 3/4" by 3 1/2" and are printed on thin card stock. The fronts feature color photos with the players posed in action stances. The set is noteworthy for featuring a card of Brendan Shanahan issued prior to his RC.

COMPLETE SET (30) 14.00 35.00
1 LaVerne Shipley CoP .10 .25
2 Tom Gosnell Mayor .10 .25
3 Kellogg's Ad CL .10 .25
4 Wayne Maxner CO/GM .20 .50
5 Harry E. Sparling COP .10 .25
6 Brendan Shanahan 10.00 25.00
7 Pat Vachon .20 .50
8 Brad Schlegel .20 .50
9 Barry Earhart .20 .50
10 Jean Marc MacKenzie .20 .50
11 Jason Simon .20 .50
12 Jim Sprott .20 .50
13 Bill Long VP .10 .25
14 Murray Nystrom .20 .50
15 Shayne Stevenson .30 .75
16 Don Martin .20 .50
17 Ian Pound .20 .50
18 Peter Lisy .20 .50
19 Steve Marcolini .20 .50
20 Craig Majaury .20 .50
21 Trevor Dam .20 .50
22 Dave Akey .20 .50
23 Dennis McEwen .20 .50
24 Shane Whelan .20 .50
25 Greg Hankkio .20 .50
26 Pat Kelly TR .10 .25
27 Stephen Titus .30 .75
28 Fred Kean PR .10 .25
29 Chris Somers .30 .75
30 Gord Clark MD .10 .25

1993-94 London Knights

This standard size set was issued at home games during the 1993-94 season. Card fronts feature posed, color photos. Card backs feature statistics and biographical information. Cards are unnumbered and checklisted below alphabetically.

COMPLETE SET (29) 4.80 12.00
1 Jason Allison 2.00 5.00
2 Ryan Appel .16 .40
3 Tim Bacik .10 .25
4 Ryan Black .10 .25
5 Chris Brassard .10 .25
6 Ryan Burgoyne .10 .25
7 Brodie Coffin .10 .25
8 Rob Frid .10 .25
9 David Gilmore .10 .25
10 Roy Gray .10 .25
11 John Guirestante .10 .25
12 Brent Holdsworth .10 .25
13 Don Margettie .10 .25
14 Dan Reja .10 .25
15 Daryl Rivers .10 .25
16 Gord Ross .10 .25
17 Kevin Slota .10 .25
18 Brian Stacey .10 .25
19 Nick Stajduhar .10 .25
20 Bill Tibbetts .40 1.00
21 Ben Walker .10 .25
22 Jordan Willis .16 .40
23 Chris Zanutto .10 .25
24 Knights Top Picks .10 .25
Ryan Appel
Ben Walker
Den Reja
Roy Gray
25 Knights Future Stars .40 1.00
Nick Stajduhar
Jason Allison
John Guirestante
Ryan Black
Jordan Willis
26 Gary Agnew CO .04 .10
27 Steve Stoyanovich ACO .04 .10
Tom Hedican CO
28 Murray Nystrom ACO .04 .10
29 Title Card .04 .10

2000-01 London Knights

This series features a 27-card main set and an eight-card "update." The series also features the first junior cards of Rick Nash.

COMPLETE SET (35) 25.00 50.00
1 Mark Hunter/Dale Hunter .20 .50
2 Bobby Turner .20 .50
3 Matt Cooper .20 .50
4 Aaron Lobb .20 .50
5 Lou Dickenson .20 .50
6 Lindsay Hofford ACO .02 .10
7 Kyle Neufeld .20 .50
8 Petr Hemsky .20 .50
9 Rick Nash 8.00 20.00
10 Brent Varty .20 .50
11 Danny Bois .30 .75
12 Joel Scherban .20 .50
13 Brian Dobbin .20 .50
14 Aaron Molnar .30 .75
15 Mike Clarke .20 .50
16 Ian Turner .20 .50
17 John Eminger .20 .50
18 Dan Jancevski .40 1.00
19 Jason Davies .20 .50
20 Logan Hunter .40 1.00
21 Checklist card .01 .01
22 Don Brankley TR .01 .01
23 Josh Chambers .20 .50
24 Chris Kelly .20 .50
25 Matt Albiani .20 .50
26 Matt Junkins .20 .50
27 Mike Stathopoulos .20 .50
U1 Chris Kelly .40 1.00
U2 Mark Hunter ACO .10 .25
U3 Dan Jancevski .40 1.00
U4 Logan Hunter .40 1.00
U5 Dale Hunter CO .20 .50
U6 Danny Bois .40 1.00
U7 Scorch MASCOT .02 .10
U8 Rick Nash 10.00 25.00

2001-02 London Knights

This set features the Knights of the OHL. The set was produced by the team and was sold at its souvenir stands. It's believed that 1,000 total sets were produced. The set is noteworthy for the inclusion of a card of Rick Nash, the first-overall pick in 2002, and Dale Hunter, owner of the Knights.

COMPLETE SET (30) 12.00 25.00
1 Title Card/CL .04 .10
2 Sean Dixon .20 .50
3 Dennis Wideman .30 .75
4 Patrick Barbieri .20 .50
5 Bryan Thompson .20 .50
6 Chris Bain .20 .50
7 Mike Stathopoulos .20 .50
8 Danny Bois .20 .50
9 Matt Iannetta .20 .50
10 Charlie Stephens .20 .75
11 Dylan Hunter .20 .50
12 Logan Hunter .20 .50
13 Sean McMorrow .20 .75
14 Chad Thompson .20 .50
15 Rick Steadman .20 .50
16 Matt Junkins .20 .50
17 Dan Buccella .20 .50
18 Rick Nash 6.00 15.00
19 Robbie Colangelo .20 .50
20 Matt Iorianni .20 .50
21 Ian Turner .20 .50
22 Corey Perry 1.50 4.00
23 Jan Chovan .30 .75
24 Matt Weir .20 .50
25 Alex White .20 .50
26 Jacques Beaulieu ACO .04 .10
27 Lindsay Hofford ACO .04 .10
28 Dale Hunter CO .20 .50
29 Don Brankley TR .04 .01
NNO Mission Hockey AD .01

2002-03 London Knights

COMPLETE CHECKLIST 8.00 20.00
1 Team Picture/CL .02 .10
2 Dennis Wideman .30 .75
3 Logan Hunter .30 .75
4 Corey Perry .75 2.00
5 Mike Stathopoulos .20 .50
6 Danny Bois .30 .75
7 Ryan Hare .20 .50
8 Dylan Hunter .40 1.00
9 Rick Steadman .20 .50
10 Matt Weir .20 .50
11 David Bolland .75 2.00
12 Kyle Piwowarczyk .20 .50
13 Brandon Prust .30 .75
14 Chris Bain .20 .50
15 Adam Nemeth .20 .50
16 Zach Trammer .20 .50
17 Danny Syrvet .30 .75
18 Jimmy Ball .20 .50
19 Kyle Quincey .40 1.00
20 Marc Methot .30 .75
21 Gerald Coleman .40 1.00
22 Chris Houle .20 .50
23 Jayme Helmer .20 .50
24 Robbie Drummond .20 .50
25 Tomas Linhart .20 .50
26 Matt Iorianni .20 .50
27 Dale Hunter CO .20 .50
28 Don Brankley TR .01 .01
29 Jacques Beaulieu ACO .02 .10
30 Opening Night .02 .10

2003-04 London Knights

This 26-card set was sponsored by Remax and created by Extreme Sports cards. The set was sold at home games. The Perry team

leader card at the end of the checklist is not considered part of the set and the set is complete without it.

COMPLETE SET (26) 10.00 20.00
1 Rob Schremp 1.25 3.00
2 Corey Perry .60 1.50
3 Adam Nemeth .30 .75
4 Danny Syvret .30 .75
5 Ivan Khomutov .20 .50
6 Jacques Beaulieu ACO .02 .10
7 Don Brankley TR .01 .01
8 Trevor Kell .20 .50
9 Dennis Wideman .30 .75
10 Marc Methot .20 .50
11 Vadim Karaga .20 .50
12 Scott Sheppard .20 .50
13 Dale Hunter CO .20 .50
14 Logan Hunter .30 .75
15 Rick Steadman .20 .50
16 Ryan MacDonald .40 1.00
17 Danny Bois .20 .50
18 David Bolland .40 1.00
19 Tommy Mannino .20 .50
20 Gerald Coleman .40 1.00
21 Dylan Hunter .40 1.00
22 Josh Beaulieu .20 .50
23 Robbie Drummond .20 .50
24 Ryan Pottruff .20 .50
25 Brandon Prust .30 .75
26 Danny Richmond .40 1.00
27 Corey Perry TL 2.50 6.00

2004-05 London Knights

Note: there is no card #24. Two cards bear the #25. A total of 2,600 team sets were produced.

COMPLETE SET (26) 15.00
1 Ryan MacDonald .75
2 Rick Steadman .50
3 Steve Ferry .50
4 Rob Schremp 1.00
5 Trevor Kell .50
6 Robbie Drummond .50
7 Bryan Rodney .50
8 Brandon Prust .50
9 Corey Perry 2.00
10 Frank Rediker .50
11 Danny Syvret .75
12 Gerald Coleman .75
13 David Bolland 1.00
14 Josh Beaulieu .50
15 Dylan Hunter 1.00
16 Drew Larman .50
17 Jordan Foreman .50
18 Ryan Pottruff .50
19 Kelly Thomson .50
20 Shawn Futers .50
21 Marc Methot .75
22 Jeff Whitfield .50
23 Dale Hunter CO .50
25 Jacques Beaulieu ACO .10
25 Don Brankley TR .01
NNO Re/Max Sponsor Card .01

2005-06 London Knights

COMPLETE SET (26) 5.00 12.00
1 Rob Schremp .60 1.50
2 Dylan Hunter .40 1.00
3 Trevor Kell .20 .50
4 Kris Belan .20 .50
5 Matt Clarke .20 .50
6 Jamie Vanderveeken .20 .50
7 Sergei Kostitsyn .40 1.00
8 Jordan Foreman .20 .50
9 Adam Perry .20 .50
10 David Bolland .40 1.00
11 Frank Rediker .20 .50
12 Matt McCready .20 .50
13 Scott Aarssen .20 .50
14 Steve Ferry .20 .50
15 Robbie Drummond .20 .50
16 Andrew Wilkins .20 .50
17 Ryan Martinelli .20 .50
18 Corey Syvret .20 .50
19 Josh Beaulieu .20 .50
20 Adam Dennis .40 1.00
21 Steve Mason .20 .50
22 Dale Hunter CO .02 .10
23 Jaques Beaulieu ACO .02 .10
24 Jeff Perry ACO .02 .10
25 Don Brankley WATERBOY .01 .01
26 Chris Maton .02 .10

2006-07 London Knights

COMPLETE SET (26) 12.00 20.00
1 Sam Gagner 1.25 4.00
2 Patrick Kane 3.00 8.00
3 Steve Mason .30 .75
4 Todd Perry .30 .75
5 Kevin Bodker .20 .50
6 Scott Aarssen .20 .50
7 David Jarram .20 .50
8 Josh Beaulieu .20 .50
9 Matt Clarke .20 .50
10 Philip Mcrae .20 .50
11 Robbie Drummond .20 .50
12 Tony Dehart .20 .50
13 Sergei Kostitsyn .40 1.00
14 Andrew Wilkins .20 .50
15 Ryan Martinelli .20 .50
16 Jordan Shine .20 .50
17 Adam Hasani .20 .50
18 Stephane Cesar .20 .50
19 Luke Vanmoerkerke .20 .50
20 David Meckler .20 .50
21 Jordan Foreman .20 .50
22 Corey Syvret .20 .50
23 Adam Perry .20 .50
24 Dale Hunter .20 .50
25 Dave Gagner .20 .50
26 Todd Bidner .10 .25

1997-98 Long Beach Ice Dogs

Little is known about this set beyond the confirmed checklist. Additional information can be forwarded to hockeymag@beckett.com.

COMPLETE SET (20) 4.00 10.00
1 Doug Ast .20 .50
2 Patrik Augusta .20 .50
3 Collin Bauer .20 .50
4 Mike Buzak .20 .50
5 John Byce .20 .50
6 Brian Chapman .20 .50
7 Mark Ferner .20 .50
8 Victor Ignatjev .20 .50
9 Rob Kenny .20 .50
10 Dan Lambert .40 1.00
11 Mike Matteucci .20 .50
12 Joby Messier .20 .50
13 Stephane Morin .20 .50
14 Shawn Penn .20 .50
15 Russ Romaniuk .20 .50
16 Nicholas Vachon .20 .50
17 Andrei Vasilyev .20 .50
18 Kay Whitmore .40 1.00
19 Darryl Williams .20 .50
20 Spike MASCOT .04 .10

1998-99 Long Beach Ice Dogs

Little is known about this set beyond the confirmed checklist. Any additional information can be forwarded to hockeymag@beckett.com.

COMPLETE SET (20) 6.00 15.00
1 Doug Ast .20 .50
2 Patrik Augusta .20 .50
3 John Byce .20 .50
4 Dan Bylsma .20 .50
5 Mark Ferner .20 .50
6 Mike Jickling .20 .50
7 Frederick Jobin .20 .50
8 Claude Jutras .20 .50
9 Dan Lambert .30 .75
10 Manny Legace .60 1.50
11 Jocelyn Lemieux .20 .50
12 Mike Matteucci .20 .50
13 Sacha Molin .20 .50
14 Jan Nemecek .20 .50
15 Andy Roach .20 .50
16 Pavel Rosa .20 .50
17 Patrik Stefan 2.00 5.00
18 Darryl Williams .20 .50
19 John Van Boxmeer HCO .10 .25
20 Spike MASCOT .04 .10

1998-99 Long Beach Ice Dogs Promo

This single card of 1999 first-overall pick Patrik Stefan was given out to fans who attended a Long Beach Ice Dogs game during the 1998-99 season. The card was sponsored by Ice Breakers gum and was licensed by the Ice Dogs and the IHL.

NNO Patrik Stefan 2.00 5.00

1999-00 Long Beach Ice Dogs

This 10-card set was given away one card per home game during the 1999-2000 season. As such, complete sets are nearly impossible to find.

COMPLETE SET (10) 6.00 15.00
1 Rene Chapdelaine .80 2.00
2 Pavel Rosa .80 2.00
3 Mike Crowley .80 2.00
4 Mike O'Neill .80 2.00
5 Len Barrie .80 2.00
6 Mike Matteucci .40 1.00
7 Scott Thomas .80 2.00
8 Doug Ast .40 1.00
9 Spike Mascot .40 1.00
10 John Van Boxmeer HCO .40 1.00

1994-95 Los Angeles Blades RHI

This set features the Blades of Roller Hockey International. The cards were sold in set form by the team at home games.

COMPLETE SET (20) 3.20 8.00
1 Checklist .04 .10
2 Chris Nelson .20 .50
3 Mike Burman .20 .50
4 Steve Wilson .20 .50
5 Vaclav Nedomansky, Jr. .20 .50
6 Rob Hartnell .20 .50
7 Kraig Nienhuis .30 .75
8 Eric LeMarque .20 .50
9 Peter Kasowski .20 .50
10 Brett Kurtz .20 .50
11 Terran Sandwith .20 .50
12 Brad Sholl .20 .50
13 Mike Doers .20 .50
14 Steve Bogoyevac .20 .50
15 Sean Gauthier .20 .50
16 Eric Lavigne .20 .50
17 Mike Callahan .20 .50
18 Bobby Hull Jr. CO .20 .50
19 Jeanie Buss .04 .10
20 Los Angeles Blades Logo .04 .10

1995-96 Louisiana Ice Gators

This 21-card set of the Louisiana Ice Gators of the ECHL features borderless color player photos with the player's name, position, and jersey number printed in a green bar across the bottom. The backs carry player information. The cards are unnumbered and checklisted below in alphabetical order. This is the first of two sets released by the Ice Gators in 1995-96, their inaugural season.

COMPLETE SET (21) 4.80 12.00
1 Bob Berg .20 .50
2 John Depourcq .20 .50
3 Wade Fournier .20 .50
4 Fred Goltz .20 .50
5 Ron Handy .20 .50
6 Mike Heany .20 .50
7 Dean Hulett .20 .50
8 Jim Latos .20 .50
9 George Maneluk .30 .75
10 Rob McCaig .20 .50
11 Jason McQuat .20 .50
12 Rod Pasma .30 .75
13 Sean Rowe .20 .50
14 Bryan Schoen .30 .75
15 Darryl Shedden .20 .50
16 Doug Shedden CO .20 .50
17 Fred Spoltore .20 .50
18 Chris Valicevic .20 .50
19 Rob Valicevic .80 2.00
20 John Vary .20 .50
21 Marty Yewchuk .20 .50

1995-96 Louisiana Ice Gators Playoffs

This 21-card set features borderless color player photos with the player's name and jersey number printed in a black bar across the bottom. The backs carry player information. A note on the card back reveals no more than 2,500 sets were produced. The cards are unnumbered and checklisted below in alphabetical order.

COMPLETE SET (21) 4.00 10.00
1 Bob Berg .20 .50
2 Aaron Boh .20 .50
3 Eric Cloutier .20 .50
4 John DePourcq .20 .50
5 Wade Fournier .20 .50
6 Ron Handy .24 .60
7 Mike Heaney .20 .50
8 Dean Hulett .20 .50
9 Jim Latos .20 .50
10 George Maneluk .24 .60
11 Rob McCaig .20 .50
12 Jason McQuat .20 .50
13 Chad Nelson .20 .50
14 Dan O'Rourke .20 .50
15 Rod Pasma .30 .75
16 Darryl Shedden .20 .50
17 Doug Shedden CO .24 .60
18 John Spoltore .24 .60
19 Chuck Thuss .24 .60
20 Rob Valicevic .40 1.00
Chris Valicevic
21 John Vary .20 .50

1995 Louisiana Ice Gators Glossy

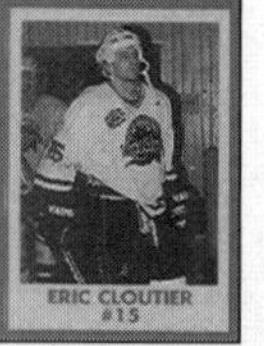

We have confirmed the existence of five cards in what might be a larger series of Ice Gators cards. These singles have a laminated finish, unlike the larger base set of Ice Gators cards this season. The cards are unnumbered and listed below in alphabetical order. If you have additional information, please contact us at hockeymag@beckett.com

COMPLETE SET (?)
1 Aaron Boh 10.00
2 Eric Cloutier 10.00
3 Chad Nelson 10.00
4 Dan O'Rourke 10.00
5 Chuck Thuss 12.00

1996-97 Louisiana Ice Gators

This set features the Ice Gators of the ECHL. It is believed that this set was issued by the team early in the season. Any additional information can be forwarded to hockeymag@beckett.com.

COMPLETE SET (23) 4.80 12.00
1 Bujar Amidovski .40 1.00
2 Doug Bonner .30 .75
3 Eric Cloutier .20 .50
4 Mark DeSantis .20 .50
5 Louis Dumont .20 .50
6 Blair Manning .20 .50
7 Roger Maxwell .20 .50
8 Jason McQuat .20 .50
9 Stan Melanson .20 .50
10 Jay Murphy .20 .50
11 Michael Murray .20 .50
12 Matt Pagnutti .20 .50
13 Don Parsons .20 .50
14 Team Photo .20 .50
15 Gary Roach .20 .50
16 Ryan Shanahan .20 .50
17 John Spoltore .30 .75
18 Chris Valicevic .30 .75
19 John Varga .30 .75
20 Rob Weingartner .20 .50
21 Billy Thurlow/Bruce Livin .20 .50
22 Doug Shedden HCO .10 .25
23 Alphonse MAS .04 .10

1996-97 Louisiana Ice Gators II

This set was issued by the team later in the season (or during the playoffs) and includes players acquired through the course of the season.

COMPLETE SET (22) 4.00 10.00
1 Aaron Boh .20 .50
2 John DePourcq .20 .50
3 Mark Delmore .20 .50
4 Louis Dumont .20 .50
5 Ron Handy .20 .50
6 Mikhail Kravets .20 .50
7 James Latos .20 .50
8 Rob McCaig .20 .50
9 Jason McQuat .20 .50
10 Stan Melanson .20 .50
11 Joey Mittelsteadt .30 .75
12 Chad Nelson .20 .50
13 Dan O'Rourke .20 .50
14 Ken Ruddick .20 .50
15 Dean Seymour .20 .50
16 Ryan Shanahan .20 .50
17 Darryl Shedden .20 .50
18 Sergei Tkachenko .20 .50
19 Chris Valicevic .30 .75
20 Rob Weingartner .20 .50
21 Jack Williams .20 .50
22 Doug Shedden HCO .10 .25

1997-98 Louisiana Ice Gators

This set features the Ice Gators of the ECHL. Little is known about this set beyond the confirmed checklist. Additional information can be forwarded to hockeymag@beckett.com.

COMPLETE SET (22) 4.00 10.00
1 Louis Dumont .20 .50
2 Jason McQuat .20 .50
3 Alphonse MAS .04 .10
4 Matt Pagnutti .20 .50
5 Richard Smit .20 .50
6 John Varga .30 .75
7 Jay Murphy .20 .50
8 Darrel Woodley .20 .50
9 Scott McKay .20 .50
10 Jack Williams .20 .50
11 Stan Melanson .20 .50
12 Brad Toporowski .20 .50
13 John Jennings EM .04 .10
14 Eric Cloutier .20 .50
15 Ryan Pisiak .20 .50
16 John Spoltore .30 .75
17 Mikhail Kravets .20 .50
18 Paul Rushforth .20 .50
19 Doug Bonner .30 .75
20 Chad Nelson .20 .50
21 Doug Shedden HCO .10 .25
22 Don Parsons .20 .50

1998-99 Louisiana Ice Gators

This set features the Ice Gators of the ECHL. The set was produced by Starz Cards and was sold by the team at home games.

COMPLETE SET (26) 4.00 10.00
1 Mascot .16 .40
2 Bujar Amidovski .16 .75
3 Doug Bonner .16 .75
4 Eric Cloutier .16 .40
5 Mark Desantis .16 .40
6 Louis Dumont .16 .40
7 Blair Manning .16 .40
8 Roger Maxwell .16 .40
9 Jason McQuat .16 .40
10 Stan Melanson .16 .40
11 Jay Murphy .30 .75
12 Mike P. Murray .20 .50
13 Matthew Pagnutti .16 .40
14 Don Parsons .16 .40
15 Gary Roach .16 .40
16 Ryan Shanahan .30 .75
17 Doug Shedden CO .16 .40
18 John Spoltore .04 .10
19 Billy Thurlow .30 .75
Bruce Livin CO
20 Chris Valicevic .16 .75
21 John Varga .20 .50
22 Rob Weingartner .16 .40
23 Team Card .04 .10

1999-00 Louisiana Ice Gators

This set features the Ice Gators of the ECHL. This set was produced by Roox, and sold by the team at home games. The numbering system of the set is less than ideal, as there are two versions of both card No. 1 and 2. It is believed that cards No 21-23 also exist, but they have not yet been confirmed. Anyone with additional information should contact hockeymag@beckett.com.

COMPLETE SET (25) 4.80 12.00
1 Sean Gauthier .20 .50
1 Vaclav Nedomansky .20 .50
2 Mike Oliveira .20 .50
2 Michael Murray .20 .50
3 Matt Pagnutti .20 .50
4 Jesse Rezansoff .20 .50
5 Mike Kucsulain .20 .50
6 Stan Melanson .20 .50
7 Shawn McNeil .20 .50
8 Ryan Shanahan .20 .50
9 John DePourcq .30 .75
10 Hugo Marchand .20 .50
11 Corey Neilson .20 .50
12 Chris Bogas .20 .50
13 Jason McQuat .30 .75
14 John Spoltore .30 .75
15 Dave Arsenault .20 .50
16 Chris Valicevic .30 .75
17 Jason Sessa .20 .50
18 Mark Cadotte .20 .50
19 Jay Murphy .20 .50
20 John Jennings TR .04 .10
24 Dennis Holland CO .04 .10
25 Don Murdoch CO .04 .10
26 Claw'd MAS .10 .25

2000-01 Louisiana Ice Gators

This set features the Ice Gators of the ECHL. The set was sponsored by the Tamahka Trails Golf Club and was sold by the team at its souvenir stands.

COMPLETE SET (25) 4.00 10.00
1 Stan Melanson .16 .40
2 Jay Murphy .16 .40
3 Nathan Borega .16 .40
4 Shawn McNeil .16 .40
5 Ryan Shanahan .16 .40
6 Roman Marakhovski .16 .40
7 Mike Kucsulain .16 .40
8 Dalen Hrooshkin .16 .40
9 Kevin Karlander .16 .40
10 Corey Neilson .16 .40
11 Bruce Richardson .16 .40
12 Jason Saal .30 .75
13 Michael Murray .16 .40
14 Jason McQuat .16 .40
15 John Spoltore .30 .75
16 Mike Valley .16 .40
17 Magnus Nilsson .30 .75
18 Dan Tessier .30 .75
19 Matt Pagnutti .16 .40
20 Roger Maxwell .16 .40
21 Dave Farrish HCO .10 .25
22 John DePourcq ACO .10 .25
23 Johnny Gomez TR .04 .10
24 Greg Sieg EM .04 .10
25 Andy Davis DOB .04 .10

2001-02 Louisiana Ice Gators

This set features the Ice Gators of the ECHL. The set was produced by Starz Sports and was sold by the team at home games.

COMPLETE SET (26) 4.00 10.00
1 Header Card .04 .10
2 Steve Aronson .20 .50
3 Frederic Cloutier .20 .50
4 Cory Cyrenne .30 .75
5 Andy Davis DBR .04 .10
6 John DePourcq ACO .04 .10
7 Dave Farrish CO .10 .25
8 Dominic Forget .30 .75
9 Russell Hewson .20 .50
10 Konstantin Kalmikov .30 .75
11 Branislav Kvetan .20 .50
12 Greg Labenski .20 .50
13 Marc Magliarditi .30 .75
14 Ryan Marsh .20 .50
15 Shawn McNeil .20 .50
16 Kevin Mitchell .20 .50
17 Jay Murphy .20 .50
18 Corey Neilson .20 .50
19 Dennis Shiryaev .20 .50
20 Randy Perry .20 .50
21 Nathan Rempel .20 .50
22 Ryan Shanahan .20 .50
23 Ricky Casataneda TR .04 .10
Greg Sieg EQMG
24 Chris Valicevic .30 .75
25 Alphonse MASCOT .04 .10

2002-03 Louisiana Ice Gators

COMPLETE SET (25) 12.00
1 Header Card .10
2 Semir Ben-Amor .50
3 Cal Benazic .50
4 Bobby Brown .50
5 Frederic Cloutier .75
6 Kenny Corupe .50
7 John DePourcq .50
8 Daniel Goneau .75
9 Kyle Kettles .50
10 Branislav Kvetan .50
11 Louis Mass .50
12 Shawn McNeil .50
13 Kevin Mitchell .50
14 J.P. Morin .50
15 Nathan Rempel .50
16 Bruce Richardson .50
17 Rod Sarich .50
18 Dennis Shiryaev .50
19 Shawn Skiehar .50
20 Chris Taliercio .50
21 Tony Tuzzolino .50
22 Jeff Worlton .50
23 Dave Farrish HCO .10
24 Andy Davis ANN .10
25 Greg Sieg EQM .10

2003-04 Louisiana Ice Gators

COMPLETE SET (25) 12.00
1 Armands Berzins .50
2 Bobby Brown .50
3 Frederic Cloutier .75
4 Kenny Corupe .50
5 Maxime Fortunus .50
6 Derek Gustafson .75
7 Jason Hamilton .75
8 Brian Herbert .50
9 Jamie Johnson .50
10 Konstantin Kalmikov .50
11 Ben Kilgour .50
12 Martin Masa .50
13 Milt Mastad .50
14 Alex Materukhin .50
15 Ed McGrane .50
16 Kevin Mitchell .50
17 Josh Mizerek .50
18 Rod Sarich .50
19 Dennis Shiryaev .75
20 Ben Storey .50
21 Jim Vickers .50
22 Dave Farrish CO .10
23 Team Photo .50
24 Checklist .01
25 Mascot .01

2004-05 Louisiana Ice Gators

COMPLETE SET (26) 15.00
1 David Bararuk 2.00
2 Josh Barker 1.00
3 Ricky Castaneda TR .10
4 Randy Dagenais .75
5 John Evangelista .75
6 Maxime Fortunus 1.00
7 Jody Green EQMG .10
8 Todd Gordon CO .10
9 Kyle Kettles .75
10 Roger Leonard .75
11 Doug Maciver .75
12 Nathan Marsters .75
13 Wes Mason .75
14 Alex Materukhin .75
15 Mike Omicioli .75
16 Jake Ortmeyer 1.00
17 Pascal Pelletier .75
18 Bryan Perez .75
19 Mark Rooneem .75
20 Shawn Skiehar .75
21 Troy Smith .75
22 Chris Thompson .75
23 Gator Girls .25
24 Gator Girls .25
25 Mascots .01
26 Announcers .01

1999-00 Louisville Panthers

This set features the Panthers of the AHL. The cards were produced by Roox and issued as a promotional giveaway at a late-season home game.

COMPLETE SET (33) 8.00 20.00
1 Craig Ferguson .30 .75
2 Brent Thompson .30 .75
3 Craig Reichert .30 .75
4 Eric Boguniecki .60 1.50
5 Dan Boyle .40 1.00
6 Ivan Novoseltsev .40 1.00
7 Dave Duerden .30 .75
8 Curtis Doell .30 .75
9 Sean Gauthier .40 1.00
10 Peter Ratchuk .30 .75
11 John Jakopin .30 .75
12 Marcus Nilson .40 1.00
13 Paws MASCOT .10 .25
14 Chris Wells .30 .75
15 Kirby Law .40 1.00
16 Chris Allen .30 .75
17 Chad Cabana .30 .75
18 Richard Shulmistra .40 1.00
19 Dwayne Hay .30 .75
20 Joey Tetarenko .60 1.50
21 Paul Brousseau .30 .75
22 Nick Smith .40 1.00
23 Brad Ference .40 1.00
24 Lance Ward .30 .75
25 Jeff Ware .30 .75
26 Paul Harvey .10 .25
27 Andrew Long .30 .75
28 Joe Paterson CO .10 .25
29 Gerard Gallant CO .10 .25
30 Tamer Afr PRES .10 .25
31 Chuck Fletcher GM .10 .25
32 UPS Zamboni .10 .25
33 Indiana Casino Zamboni .10 .25

2000-01 Louisville Panthers

This set features the Panthers of the AHL. The cards were issued as promotional giveaways at two separate games, in two sets of 12-cards apiece.

COMPLETE SET (24) 7.20 18.00
1 Team CL .10 .01
2 Brent Thompson .40 1.00
3 Paul Brousseau .30 .75
4 David Emma .30 .75
5 Joey Tetarenko .40 1.00
6 Peter Ratchuk .40 .75
7 Dave Duerden .30 .75
8 Sean Gauthier .30 .75
9 Kyle Rossiter .30 .75
10 Rocky Thompson .30 .75
11 Denis Shvidki .60 1.00
12 Brad Ference .40 1.00
13 Joe Paterson CO .20 .50
14 Gord Dineen ACO .20 .50
15 Travis Brigley .40 1.00
16 Ryan Bach .40 1.00
17 Andrei Podkonicky .40 .75
18 Mike Harder .40 1.00
19 Evgeny Korolev .30 .75
20 Eric Godard .30 .75
21 Mike Cirillo .30 .75
22 Eric Beaudoin .30 .75
23 Paul Harvey .30 .75
24 Paws Mascot .10 .25

1996-97 Louisville Riverfrogs

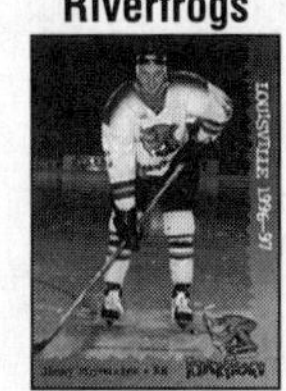

This 30-card set of the Louisville Riverfrogs of the ECHL was sponsored by Winn-Dixie, Surge and Fox 41. The cards feature action photography on the front, with '95-96 stats on the back. The cards were sold by the club at the rink and through the mail.

COMPLETE SET (30) 4.00 20.00
1 Checklist .04 .10
2 Sandy Allan .30 1.50
3 Gino Santerre .16 .75
4 Pete Liptrott .16 .75
5 Jason Hanchuk .16 .75
6 Adam Young .16 .75
7 Dan Reja .16 .75
8 Terry Lindgren .16 .75
9 Sheldon Gorski .16 .75
10 Jeff Kostuch .16 .75
11 Randy Stevens .16 .75
12 Chris Rowland .16 .75
13 Chris DeProfio .16 .75
14 Mike Sancimino .16 .75
15 Dean Seymour .16 .75
16 Stephane Madore .16 .75
17 Chet Cullic .16 .75
18 Tim Chase .16 .75
19 Jack Kowal .16 .75
20 Tom MacDonald .16 .75
21 Jimmy Provencher .16 .75
22 Lance Leslie .16 .75
23 Warren Young CO .10 .25
24 R.J. Romero TR .04 .10
25 Mark Shepherd EQMG .04 .10
26 David Wilson ANN .04 .10
27 Rowdy the Riverfrog .04 .10
28 Sandy Allan AS .30 1.50
29 Warren Young CO .10 .25
Brett Young
30 Team Photo .16 .75

1997-98 Louisville Riverfrogs

Little is known about this set beyond the confirmed checklist. Additional information can be forwarded to hockeymag@beckett.com.

COMPLETE SET (29) 4.00 10.00
1 Title Card .04 .10
2 Craig Nelson .16 .40
3 P.J. Lepler .16 .40
4 Jason Pain .16 .40
5 Terry Lindgren .16 .40
6 Michael Flynn .16 .40
7 Sheldon Gorski .16 .40
8 Jeff Kostuch .16 .40
9 Steve Ferranti .16 .40
10 Bob Gohde .16 .40
11 Marko Makinen .16 .40
12 Mike Sancimino .16 .40
13 Tobias Ablad .16 .40
14 Jeff Kikesch .16 .40
15 Stephane Madore .16 .40
16 Chris DeProfio .16 .40
17 Danny Reja .16 .40
18 Jack Kowal .16 .40
19 Dan Reimann .16 .40
20 Rob Frid .16 .40
21 Deiter Kochan .60 1.50
22 Lance Leslie .16 .40
23 Warren Young CO .16 .40
24 R.J. Romeiro TR .04 .10
25 Mark Miller EQ .04 .10
26 Matt Gorsky BR .04 .10
27 Rowdy Mascot .04 .10
28 Sheldon Gorski .16 .40
29 Team Photo .16 .40

1999-00 Lowell Lock Monsters

This set features the Lock Monsters of the AHL. This set was issued in the form of a perforated album, with four pages of cards. The album/set was issued as a promotional giveaway at a game in Feb. 2000.

COMPLETE SET (27) 6.00 15.00
1 Ray Giroux .30 .75
2 Dave MacIsaac .20 .50
3 Richard Seeley .20 .50
4 Nathan LaFayette .20 .50
5 Rich Brennan .30 .75
6 Petr Mika .20 .50
7 Donald MacLean .20 .50
8 Cody Bowtell .20 .50
9 Vladimir Chebaturkin .20 .50
10 David Hymovitz .20 .50
11 Sean Blanchard .20 .50
12 Eric Belanger .20 .50
13 Dmitri Nabokov .20 .50
14 Vladimir Orszagh .20 1.00
15 Greg Phillips .20 .50
16 Jason Krog .40 1.00
17 Eric Brewer .80 2.00
18 Travis Scott .30 1.00
19 Evgeny Korolev .20 .50
20 Stephen Valiquette .60 1.50
21 Jason Podollan .20 .50
22 Jack Baldwin .20 .50
23 Lowell Lock Monsters .10 .25
24 Louie MASCOT .10 .10
25 Bruce Boudreau CO .10 .25
26 Steve Stirling CO .10 .25
27 Tom Rowe GM .10 .25

2000-01 Lowell Lock Monsters

This set features the Lock Monsters of the AHL. The cards were issued as a promotional giveaway in the form of an album with perforatable images. They were distributed at a game in December, 2000.

COMPLETE SET (30) 7.20 20.00
1 Joe Corvo .30 .75
2 Andreas Lilja .30 .75
3 Joe Rullier .30 .75
4 Jeff Daw .20 .50
5 Petr Mika .30 .75
6 Rich Brennan .20 .50
7 Brad Chartrand .20 .50
8 Marko Tuomainen .30 .75
9 Eric Veilleux .20 .50
10 Eric Belanger .40 1.00
11 Peter Leboutillier .20 .50
12 David Hymovitz .20 .50
13 Juraj Kolnik .40 1.00
14 Chris Schmidt .20 .50
15 Kevin Baker .20 .50
16 Steve Passmore .40 1.00
17 Richard Seeley .20 .50
18 Jason Krog .30 1.00
19 Travis Scott .30 1.00
20 Marcel Cousineau .30 1.00
21 Nate Miller .20 .50
22 Branislav Mezei .40 1.00
23 Mathieu Biron .30 .75
24 Kip Brennan .40 1.00
25 Greg Phillips .20 .50
26 Louie MAS .04 .10
27 Mike Pudlick .20 .50
28 Bruce Boudreau CO .10 .25
29 Steve Stirling CO .10 .25
30 Tom Rowe GM .04 .10

2002-03 Lowell Lock Monsters

COMPLETE SET (25) 20.00
1 Igor Knyazev 1.00
2 Nikos Tselios 1.00
3 Sean Curry 1.00
4 Ed Hill 1.00
5 Mike Zigomanis 1.00
6 Ryan Bayda 1.00
7 Craig MacDonald 1.00
8 Jeff Daw 1.00
9 Steve Halko 1.00
10 Jeff Heerema 1.00
11 Brent McDonald 1.00
12 Mike Watt 1.00
13 Tomas Kurka 1.00
14 Damian Surma 1.00
15 Kaspars Astashenko 1.00
16 Greg Kuznik 1.00
17 Tommy Westlund 1.00
18 Randy Petruk 1.50
19 Brett Lysak 1.00
20 Ryan Bast 1.00
21 Jean-Marc Pelletier 1.50
22 Brad DeFauw 1.00
23 Tomas Malec 1.00
24 Lowell Lock Monsters AU .10
25 Lowell Lock Monsters AU .10

2003-04 Lowell Lock Monsters

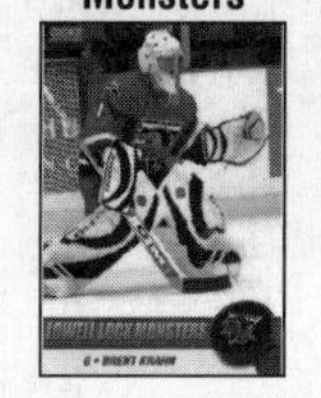

This set was produced by Choice Marketing and sold at home games.

COMPLETE SET (25) 10.00
1 Alan Rourke .40
2 Brad DeFauw .40
3 Brad Fast .40
4 Brennan Evans .40
5 Brent Krahn .75
6 Brett Lysak .40
7 Damian Surma .40
8 Dany Sabourin .75
9 Dan Sullivan .40
10 Jason Morgan .40
11 Jesse Wallin .40
12 Joey Tetarenko .40
13 Josh Green .40
14 Martin Sonnenberg .40
15 Matt Davidson .40
16 Mike Commodore .40
17 Mike Zigomanis .40
18 Patrick DesRochers .75
19 Pavel Brendl .40
20 Robert Dome .40
21 Ryan Bayda .40
22 Sean Curry .40
23 Tomas Kurka .40
24 Tomas Malec .40
25 Checklist .01

2003-04 Lowell Lock Monsters Photo Album

This was issued as a promotional item in Nov. 2003. The cards came in a perforated album format.

COMPLETE SET (25) 20.00
1 Mike Commodore .75
2 Jesse Wallin .75
3 Sean Curry .75
4 Ryan Bayda .75
5 Jason Morgan .75
6 Mike Zigomanis .75
7 Tomas Kurka .75
8 Damian Surma .75
9 Brad Fast .75
10 Martin Sonnenberg .75
11 Allan Rourke .75
12 Josh Green .75
13 Autograph Card .01
14 Dan Sullivan .75
15 Brett Lysak .75
16 Joey Tetarenko 1.00
17 Robert Dome .75
18 Brad DeFauw .75
19 Pavel Brendl .75
20 Matt Davidson .75
21 Brennan Evans .75
22 Tomas Malec .75
23 Autograph Card .01
24 Dany Sabourin 1.50
25 Patrick DesRochers 1.50

2004-05 Lowell Lock Monsters

COMPLETE SET (24) 15.00
1 Ryan Bayda .50
2 Mike Commodore .50
3 Sean Curry .50
4 Gordie Dwyer 1.00
5 Brennan Evans .50
6 Brad Fast .75
7 Colin Forbes .50
8 Carsen Germyn .50
9 Mark Giordano .50
10 Jim Henkel .50
11 Chuck Kobasew 1.00
12 Brent Krahn 1.00
13 Chad Larose .50
14 Lynn Loyns .50
15 Craig MacDonald .50
16 Brantt Myhres 1.50
17 Richie Regehr .50
18 Danny Richmond .50
19 Allan Rourke .50
20 Eric Staal 2.00
21 Bruno St. Jacques 1.00
22 Justin Taylor .50
23 Cam Ward .40 1.00
24 Mike Zigomanis .50

2004-05 Lowell Lock Monsters Photo Album

This set was issued as a game night giveaway in January of 2005. The cards were distributed in an album format with perforations.

COMPLETE SET (25) 30.00
1 Ryan Bayda 1.00
2 Mike Commodore 1.00
3 Sean Curry 1.00
4 Gordie Dwyer 2.00
5 Brennan Evans 1.00
6 Brad Fast 1.50
7 Colin Forbes 1.00
8 Carsen Germyn 1.00
9 Mark Giordano 1.00
10 Jim Henkel 1.00
11 Chuck Kobasew 2.00
12 Brent Krahn 2.00
13 Chad Larose 1.00
14 Lynn Loyns 1.00
15 Craig MacDonald 1.00
16 Brantt Myhres 3.00
17 Richie Regehr 1.00
18 Danny Richmond 1.00
19 Allan Rourke 1.00
20 Bruno St. Jacques 2.00
21 Eric Staal 4.00
22 Justin Taylor 1.00
23 Cam Ward 2.00
24 Mike Zigomanis 1.00
25 Logo Card .01

2000-01 Lubbock Cotton Kings

This set features the Cotton Kings of the WPHL. It was produced by the team and sold at its souvenir stands.

COMPLETE SET (20) 4.00 10.00
1 Kyle Reeves .30 .75
2 Tracy Egeland .20 .50
3 Jan Melichercik .20 .50
4 Peter Cava .20 .50
5 Dave MacIntyre .20 .50
6 Patrick Brownlee .20 .50
7 Chris Rowland .20 .50
8 Bill McDonald HCO .10 .25
9 Neil Savary .30 .75
10 Lance Leslie .20 .50
11 Mike Hiebert .20 .50
12 Ryan Shmyr .20 .50
13 Brandon Carper .20 .50
14 Trevor Burgess .20 .50
15 Tom Menicci .20 .50
16 Derek Holland .20 .50
17 Walker McDonald .20 .50
18 Cosmo DuPaul .30 .75
19 Adam Robbins .20 .50
20 Lubbock Cotton Kings .20 .25

2003-04 Lubbock Cotton Kings

This set was produced by Choice Marketing and sold at home games.

COMPLETE SET (20) 8.00
1 Checklist .01
2 Craig Binns .50
3 Steve Birch .50
4 Joe Blaznek .50
5 Mike Brusseau .75
6 Jeff Dewar .50
7 Chris Duggan .50
8 Kevin Fines .75
9 Paul Fioroni .50
10 Derek Holland .50
11 Jean-Francois Labarre .50
12 Dave MacIntyre .50
13 Jan Melichercik .50
14 Mathieu Paul .50
15 Sebastien Roy .50
16 Jim Shepherd .50
17 Jeremy Symington .75
18 Rob Vessio .50
19 Kirk Tomlinson HCO .10
20 Mascot .10
NNO Sponsor .01
NNO Sponsor .01

2002-03 Macon Trax

This set features the Trax of the Atlantic Coast league. It was sponsored by Applebees and sold at home games.

COMPLETE SET (20) 8.00
1 Corey Smith .50
2 Dan Welch .50
3 David Deeves .50
4 Landon Bathe .50
5 Tom Stewart .50
6 Corey Lucas .50
7 Rick Emmett .50
8 Jeremy Kyte .50
9 Brad Rice .50
10 Nolan Weir .50
11 Brad Bourhis .50
12 Stephane Desjardins .50
13 Luke Murphy .50
14 Steve Howard .50
15 Geoff Faulkner .50
16 Dennis Brogna TR .10
17 Brian Curran HCO .10
18 Dave Monteiro ACO .10
19 Todd MacGowan EM .10
20 Mascot .10
NNO Checklist .10

1997-98 Macon Whoopee

This 18-card set was produced and sold by the Macon Whoopee Booster Club at home games for $10 each. This set was also available in an autographed version and in uncut sheets.

COMPLETE SET (18) 3.60 9.00
1 Steve Vezina .30 .75
2 Martin Belanger .20 .50
3 John Paris HCO .04 .10
4 Sebastien Parent .20 .50
5 Gary Golczewski .20 .50
6 Jocelyn Langlois .20 .50
7 Joe Letendre .20 .50
8 Martin LaChaine .20 .50
9 Todd MacIsaac .20 .50
10 Patrice Charbonneau .30 .75
11 Marc Genest .20 .50
12 Claude Fillion .20 .50
13 Craig Willard .20 .50
14 Raymond Delarosbil .20 .50
15 Francois Leroux .20 .50
16 Trent Cavicchi .20 .50
17 Alexei Deev .30 .75
18 Alain Cote .20 .50

1997-98 Macon Whoopee Autographs

This 18-card set is the same as the base 1997-98 Macon Whoopee set, but with each card autographed. Autographed uncut sheets were available also. This set was originally sold at the arena for $20.

COMPLETE SET (18) 14.00 35.00
1 Steve Vezina 1.60 4.00
2 Martin Belanger .80 2.00
3 John Paris HCO .80 2.00
4 Sebastien Parent 1.60 4.00
5 Gary Golczewski .80 2.00
6 Jocelyn Langlois .80 2.00
7 Joe Letendre .80 2.00
8 Martin LaChaine .80 2.00
9 Todd MacIsaac .80 2.00
10 Patrice Charbonneau 1.20 3.00
11 Marc Genest .80 2.00
12 Claude Fillion .80 2.00
13 Craig Willard .80 2.00
14 Raymond Delarosbil .80 2.00
15 Francois Leroux .80 2.00
16 Trent Cavicchi .80 2.00
17 Alexei Deev 1.20 3.00
18 Alain Cote .80 2.00

2001-02 Macon Whoopee

This set features the Whoopee of the CHL. The set was produced by Choice Marketing and was issued by the team as a promotional giveaway. The production was limited to 1,000 copies.

COMPLETE SET (21) 8.00 20.00
1 Checklist .40 1.00
2 Andrew Allen .80 2.00
3 Krikor Arman .40 1.00
4 Nic Beaudoin .40 1.00
5 David Brosseau .40 1.00
6 Travis Dillabough .40 1.00
7 Gord Dineen CO .40 1.00
8 Rick Emmett .40 1.00
9 Paul Giblin .40 1.00
10 Mike Green .40 1.00
11 Mike Josefowicz .40 1.00
12 Chris Madden .80 2.00
13 Milt Mastad .40 1.00
14 Luke Murphy .40 1.00
15 Johan Olsson .40 1.00
16 Michel Periard .40 1.00
17 Doug Schueller .40 1.00
18 Kris Waltze .60 1.50
19 Alex Zinevych .40 1.00
20 Casey Kesselring .40 1.00
21 Header Card/CL .04 .10

1995-96 Madison Monsters

This 24-card set features the Madison Monsters of the Colonial Hockey League and was sponsored by Z-104 and Electrolarm. The cards, which apparently were a game night giveaway, feature a color shot on the front, along with the player name and team logo. The backs feature one of the most comprehensive player information packages ever seen on cardboard, including career stats and personal biography. The cards are unnumbered.

COMPLETE SET (24) 8.00 25.00
1 Duane Derksen .75 2.00
2 Brian Downey .40 1.00
3 Dmitri Alekhin .40 1.00
4 Monster MASCOT .04 .10
5 Sean Wilmert .40 1.00
6 Corey Grassel .40 1.00
7 Dan Ruoho .40 1.00
8 Billy Brown TR .04 .10
9 Kent Hawley .40 1.00
10 Dan Laughlin .40 1.00
11 Vyacheslav Polikarkin .40 1.00
12 Todd Dvorak .40 1.00
13 Brian Idalski .40 1.00
14 Gunnar Kroseberg .40 1.00
15 Brett Larson .40 1.00
16 Paul Clatney .40 1.00
17 Matt Loen .40 1.00
18 Stanislav Tkach .60 1.50
19 Glenn Painter .40 1.00
20 Joe Bonvie .60 1.50
21 Mark Johnson CO .60 1.50
22 Justin Morrison .60 1.50
23 Marcel Richard .60 1.50
24 Sponsor card .01 .05

1996-97 Madison Monsters

This 24-card set was given away over the course of four card nights, and was sold later in the season. The cards are not numbered and so they are listed in the order in which they were distributed.

COMPLETE SET (24) 8.00 20.00
1 Electroalarm Services .04 .10
2 Dave Schultz HCO .60 1.50
3 Kent Hawley .40 1.00
4 Alexander Galchenyuk .40 1.00
5 Jeremie Legault .40 1.00
6 Randy Holmes .40 1.00
7 Fran Reed .40 1.00
8 Chris Markstrom .40 1.00
9 Team Photo .40 1.00
10 Duane Derksen .60 1.50
11 Brian Downey .40 1.00
12 Matt Loen .40 1.00
13 Justin Morrison .40 1.00
14 Dave Rowe .40 1.00
15 Colby Van Tassel .40 1.00
16 Dan Ruoho .40 1.00
17 ElectroAlarm Security Sys .04 .10
18 Brian Idalski .40 1.00
19 Brian LaVack .40 1.00
20 Todd Passini .40 1.00
21 Stas Tkatch .40 1.00
22 Joakin Wiberg .40 1.00
23 Jeff Winter .40 1.00
24 Jose Ortiz TR .20 .50

1998-99 Madison Monsters

This set features the Monsters of the UHL. The cards were produced by Roox, and intended as a season-long promotional giveaway. Apparently there was a problem at some point and the promotion was cancelled after the distribution of just 16 cards. If anyone knows of any other cards in this set, please write hockeymag@beckett.com.

COMPLETE SET (16) 8.00 20.00
1 Kent Hawley CO .10 .25
2 Andrew Wilhelm OWN .10 .25
3 Dana Doll TR .10 .25
4 Jason Disher .60 1.50
5 Kelly Stephens .60 1.50
6 Derek Beuselinck .60 1.50
7 Cory Holland .60 1.50
8 Mike Maurice .60 1.50
9 Luke Strand .60 1.50
10 Brian Downey .60 1.50
11 David Fletcher .60 1.50
12 Andy Faulkner .60 1.50
13 Jim Duhart .60 1.50
14 Jay Wilson .60 1.50
15 Ed Corwin .60 1.50
16 Monster Madness .40 1.00

1992-93 Maine Black Bears

This set features the Black Bears of the NCAA. The set was issued as two series (1-16 and 17-36). This set includes one of the first cards of NHL superstar Paul Kariya.

COMPLETE SET (36) 20.00 50.00
1 Title Card .10 .01
2 Mike Dunham 1.20 3.00
3 Andy Silverman .20 .50
4 Matt Martin .20 .50
5 Chris Imes .20 .50
6 Jason Weinrich .20 .50
7 Scott Pellerin .30 .75
8 Dan Murphy .20 .50
9 Dave LaCouture .20 .50
10 Patrice Tardif .20 1.00
11 Eric Fenton .20 .50
12 Jim Montgomery .20 1.00
13 Kent Salfi .20 .50
14 Jean-Yves Roy .20 1.00
15 Garth Snow .40 1.00
16 Cal Ingraham .20 1.00
17 Title Card .10 .01
18 Mike Dunham 1.20 3.00
19 Chris Imes .20 .50
20 Paul Kariya 14.00 35.00
21 Mike Latendresse .20 .50
22 Dan Murphy .20 .50
23 Dave MacIsaac .20 .50
24 Dave LaCouture .20 .50
25 Chris Ferraro .40 1.00
26 Peter Ferraro .40 1.00
27 Jim Montgomery .20 1.00
28 Brad Purdie .20 .50
29 Lee Saunders .20 .50
30 Justin Tomberlin .20 .50
31 Chuck Texeira .20 .50
32 Martin Mercier .20 .50
33 Garth Snow .40 1.00
34 Cal Ingraham .20 1.00
35 Greg Hirsch .20 .50
36 Jamie Thompson .20 .50

1993-94 Maine Black Bears

Measuring the standard size, this 26-card set features the Maine Black Bears. The fronts feature color action player photos with light blue, dark blue, and white borders. A black stripe near the bottom carries the player's name and position in white print.

The team logo is superimposed on the picture. The backs carry biographical information, career highlights, and statistics along with a small black-and-white player headshot. The numbering continues where the previous year's numbering left off.

COMPLETE SET (25) 24.00 60.00
37 Paul Kariya 4.00 10.00
Leo Wlasow
Title Card
38 Andy Silverman .20 .50
39 Jason Weinrich .20 .50
40 Jason Mansoff .20 .50
41 Paul Kariya 8.00 20.00
42 Mike Latendresse .20 .50
43 Barry Clukey .20 .50
44 Wayne Conlan .20 .50
45 Dave MacIsaac .20 .50
46 Patrice Tardif .30 .75
47 Brad Purdie .20 .50
48 Dan Shermerhorn .20 .50
49 Lee Saunders .20 .50
50 Justin Tomberlin .20 .50
51 Chuck Texeira .20 .50
52 Tim Lovell .20 .50
53 Cal Ingraham .20 .50
54 Leo Wlasow .20 .50
55 Blair Allison .20 .50
56 Blair Marsh .20 .50
57 Marcel Pineau .20 .50
58 Trevor Roenick .20 .50
59 Reg Cardinal .20 .50
60 Paul Kariya 8.00 20.00
61 Jim Montgomery 4.00 10.00
Paul Kariya
Division I Champions

2004-05 Maine Black Bears

Issued as a promotional giveaway.

COMPLETE SET (32) 50.00
1 Mike Lundin 2.00
2 Tom Zabkowicz 2.00
3 Steve Mullin 2.00
4 Travis Wight 2.00
5 Troy Barnes 2.00
6 Matt Deschamps 2.00
7 John Ronan 2.00
8 Michel Leveille 2.00
9 Keith Johnson 2.00
10 Keenan Hopson 2.00
11 Billy Ryan 2.00
12 Greg Moore 2.00
13 Robert Bellamy 2.00
14 Ben Murphy 2.00
15 Josh Soares 2.00
16 Tim Maxwell 2.00
17 Mike Hamilton 2.00
18 Jon Jankus 2.00
19 Wes Clark 2.00
20 Travis Ramsey 2.00
21 Derek Damon 2.00
22 Brent Shepheard 2.00
23 Matt Lundin 2.00
24 Jimmy Howard 3.00
25 Matt Greyeyes 2.00
26 Ryan Shelley 2.00
27 Bret Tyler 2.00
28 Jeff Mushaluk 2.00
29 Staff .10
30 Erik Soltys ACO .10
31 Tim Whitehead CO .10
32 Team Picture .50

2005-06 Maine Black Bears

COMPLETE SET (32) 10.00 25.00
1 Rob Bellamy .75
2 Ben Bishop 2.00
3 Wes Clark .75
4 Derek Damon .75
5 Simon Danis-Pepin 2.00
6 Matt Duffy .75
7 Chris Hahn .75
8 Mike Hamilton .75
9 John Hopson .75
10 Keenan Hopson .75
11 Jon Jankus .75
12 Keith Johnson .75
13 Vince Laise .75
14 Michel Leveille .75
15 Matt Lundin 1.50
16 Mike Lundin .75
17 Jeff Marshall .75
18 Greg Moore .75
19 Steve Mullin .75
20 Brian Plasszcz .75
21 Travis Ramsey .75
22 Billy Ryan .75
23 Ryan Shelley .75
24 Brent Shepheard .75
25 Josh Soares .75
26 Bret Tyler .75
27 Travis Wight .75
28 Tim Whitehead HC .25
29 Campbell Blair AC .25
30 Dan Kerluke AC .25
31 Grant Standbrook AC .25
32 Maine Black Bears .50

2001-02 Manchester Monarchs

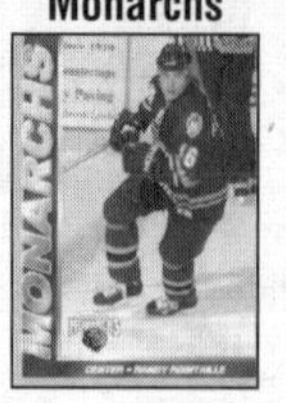

This set features the Monarchs of the AHL. The set was released in two series of 15 cards each and was sold at the team's souvenir stands. Each series was limited to 1,000 copies. As the cards from both series are numbered 1-15, we have added an A and B suffix to differentiate between them.

COMPLETE SET (30) 8.00 20.00
1A Randy Robitaille .24 .60
1B Dane Jackson .24 .60
2A Derek Bekar .24 .60
2B Travis Scott .30 .75
3A Brad Chartrand .24 .60
3B Ted Donato .24 .60
4A Nate Miller .24 .60
4B Joe Rullier .24 .60
5A Andre Payette .24 .60
5B Rich Brennan .24 .60
6A Brett Hauer .24 .60
6B Eric Healey .24 .60
7A Chris Schmidt .24 .60
7B Jason Holland .24 .60
8A Mike Pudlick .24 .60
8B Richard Seeley .24 .60
9A Kip Brennan .30 .75
9B Jaroslav Bednar .40 1.00
10A Tomas Zizka .24 .60
10B Ryan Flinn .60 1.50
11A Jerred Smithson .24 .60
11B Rob Valicevic .60 1.50
12A Joe Corvo .24 .60
12B Steve Kelly .24 .60
13A Stephane Fiset .60 1.50
13B Dan Riva .24 .60
14A Marcel Cousineau .30 .75
14B Scott Thomas .24 .60
15A Bruce Boudreau CO .04 .10
15B Maximillian MASCOT .04 .10

2002-03 Manchester Monarchs

COMPLETE SET (30) 18.00
1 Chris Aldous .50
2 Scott Barney .50
3 Bruce Boudreau HCO .10
4 Kip Brennan .75
5 Mike Cammalleri 2.00
6 Joe Corvo .50
7 Eric Healey .50
8 Steve Heinze .50
9 Dane Jackson .50
10 Steve Kelly .75
11 Yanick Lehoux .75
12 Mike Pudlick .50
13 Joe Rullier .50
14 Travis Scott .75
15 Richard Seeley .50
16 Derek Armstrong .50
17 Jared Aulin 1.50
18 Derek Bekar .50
19 Chris Bogas .50
20 Ryan Flinn 1.00
21 Jeff Giuliano .50
22 Jason Holland .50
23 Cristobal Huet 2.00
24 Maximillian MASCOT .10
25 Dan Riva .50
26 Pavel Rosa .50
27 Chris Schmidt .50
28 Jerred Smithson .50
29 Mat Snesrud .50
30 Tomas Zizka .75

2003-04 Manchester Monarchs

This set was produced by Choice Marketing and sold at home games.

COMPLETE SET (25) 10.00
1 Scott Barney .50
2 Noah Clarke .75
3 Ryan Flinn .75
4 Jeff Giuliano .50
5 Denis Grebeshkov .50
6 Adam Hauser .75
7 Leon Hayward .50
8 Steve Kelly .50
9 Yanick Lehoux .50
10 Bryan Muir .50
11 Doug Nolan .50
12 George Parros .50
13 Pavel Rosa .50
14 Joe Rullier .50
15 Chris Schmidt .50
16 Richard Seeley .50
17 Jerred Smithson .50
18 John Tripp .50
19 Dan Welch .50
20 Tomas Zizka .50
21 Mascot .10
22 Bruce Boudreau HCO .10
23 Jim Hughes ACO .10
24 Verizon Wireless Arena .01
25 Checklist .01

2003-04 Manchester Monarchs Team Issue

This set was given away at a game in Jan. 2004. The set was sponsored by the New Hampshire Tobacco Prevention/Control program. The cards are unnumbered and so are listed below in alphabetical order.

COMPLETE SET (20) 20.00
1 Scott Barney 1.00
2 Mathieu Chouinard 1.50
3 Noah Clarke 1.50
4 Ryan Flinn 1.50
5 Jeff Giuliano 1.00
6 Denis Grebeshkov 1.00
7 Milan Hnilicka 1.50
8 Steve Kelly 1.00
9 Yanick Lehoux 1.00
10 Bryan Muir 1.00
11 Doug Nolan 1.00
12 George Parros 1.00
13 Pavel Rosa 1.00
14 Joe Rullier 1.00
15 Chris Schmidt 1.00
16 Richard Seeley 1.00
17 Jerred Smithson 1.00
18 John Tripp 1.00
19 Dan Welch 1.00
20 Tomas Zizka 1.00

2004-05 Manchester Monarchs

Produced by Choice Marketing.

COMPLETE SET (26) 15.00
1 Adam Hauser 1.00
2 Brad Smyth 1.00
3 Chris Schmidt .40
4 Dan Welch .40
5 Dave Steckel .75
6 Denis Grebeshkov .40
7 Doug Nolan .40
8 Dustin Brown 1.00
9 George Parros .40
10 Greg Hogeboom .40
11 Jeff Giuliano .40
12 Joe Rullier .75
13 Mathieu Garon 1.50
14 Matt Ryan .40
15 Michael Cammalleri 1.00
16 Mike Weaver .40
17 Noah Clarke 1.00
18 Petr Kanko 1.00
19 Ryan Flinn 1.00
20 Scott Barney .40
21 Tim Gleason .75
22 Tom Kostopoulos .75
23 Troy Milam .40
24 Yanick Lehoux .75
25 Maximillian MASCOT .01
NNO Checklist .10

2004-05 Manchester Monarchs Tobacco

These cards were issued as a promotional giveaway.

COMPLETE SET (25) 30.00
1 Mathieu Garon 3.00
2 Adam Hauser 2.00
3 Brad Smyth 2.00
4 Chris Schmidt .75
5 Dan Welch .75
6 Dave Steckel 1.50
7 Denis Grebeshkov .75
8 Doug Nolan .75
9 Dustin Brown 2.00
10 George Parros .75
11 Greg Hogeboom .75
12 Jeff Guiliano .75
13 Joe Rullier 1.50
14 Matt Ryan .75
15 Mike Cammalleri 2.00
16 Mike Weaver .75
17 Noah Clarke 2.00
18 Petr Kanko 2.00
19 Ryan Flinn 2.00
20 Scott Barney .75
21 Tim Gleason 1.50
22 Tom Kostopoulos 1.50
23 Troy Milam .75
24 Yanick Lehoux 1.50
25 Mascot .10

2005-06 Manchester Monarchs

This set was issued in two series. The fist series included (1-24), while series 2 had (25-48).

COMPLETE SET (48) 30.00
COMPLETE SER. 1 (24) 15.00
COMPLETE SER. 2 (24)
1 Barry Brust .40 1.00
2 Noah Clarke .25 .60
3 Brad Fast .25 .60
4 Ryan Flinn .40 1.00
5 Jeff Giuliano .25 .60
6 Denis Grebeshkov .25 .60
7 Adam Hauser .40 1.00
8 Connor James .25 .60
9 Petr Kanko .25 .60
10 Joey Mormina .25 .60
11 Ryan Murphy .25 .60
12 Doug Nolan .25 .60
13 Richard Petiot .25 .60
14 Konstantin Pushkarev .25 .60
15 Dany Roussin .25 .60
16 Matt Ryan .25 .60
17 Richard Seeley .25 .60
18 Brad Smyth .25 .60
19 Jeff Tambellini .40 1.00
20 Lauri Tukonen .60 1.50
21 Marty Wilford .40 1.00
22 Derek Clancey AC .02 .10
23 Jim Hughes HC .02 .10
24 Maximillian MASCOT .25 .10
25 Brendan Bernakevitch .25 .60
26 Dustin Brown .40 1.00
27 Michael Cammalleri .40 1.00
28 Noah Clarke .25 .60
29 Ryan Flinn .40 1.00
30 Yutaka Fukufuji .75 2.00
31 Mathieu Garon .40 1.00
32 Jeff Giuliano .25 .60
33 Tim Gleason .25 .60
34 Denis Grebeshkov .25 .60
35 Adam Hauser .40 1.00
36 Greg Hogeboom .25 .60
37 Connor James .25 .60
38 Petr Kanko .25 .60
39 Tom Kostopoulos .25 .60
40 Yanick Lehoux .25 .60
41 George Parros .60 1.50
42 Richard Petiot .25 .60
43 Reagan Rome .25 .60
44 Dany Roussin .25 .60
45 Matt Ryan .25 .60
46 Jeff Tambellini .40 1.00
47 Mike Weaver .25 .60
48 Eric Werner .25 .60

2006-07 Manchester Monarchs

COMPLETE SET (24) 7.00 12.00
1 Barry Brust .30 .75
2 Brendan Buckley .20 .50
3 Bryan Schmidt .20 .50
4 Dany Roussin .30 .75
5 Doug Nolan .20 .50
6 Eric Werner .20 .50
7 Jason Labarbera .30 .75
8 Jeff Giuliano .30 .75
9 Joey Mormina .20 .50
10 John Zeiler .20 .50
11 Konstantin Pushkarev .20 .50
12 Lauri Tukonen .40 1.00
13 Matt Moulson .20 .50
14 Matt Ryan .20 .50
15 Ned Lukacevic .20 .50
16 Noah Clarke .20 .50
17 Peter Harrold .20 .50
18 Petr Kanko .20 .50
19 Ryan Murphy .20 .50
20 Shay Stephenson .20 .50
21 Tim Jackman .20 .50
22 Mark Morris CO .02 .10
23 Scott Pellerin ACO .02 .10
24 Max MASCOT .02 .10

1992-93 Manitoba Junior League

We have confirmed the existence of one card in this series. If you have any information about the rest of the checklist, please email us at hockeymag@beckett.com.

COMPLETE SET (?)
181 Dane Litke

1997-98 Manitoba Moose

These oversized cards were inserted in game programs in two series. Cards 7 and 8 in each series were only available at Grapes Leon's Centre with any kid's menu purchase.

COMPLETE SET (16) 40.00
A1 Ralph Intranuovo .80 2.00
A2 Russ Romaniuk .80 2.00
A3 Randy Gilhen .80 2.00
A4 Dave Thomlinson .80 2.00
A5 Fred Brathwaite 2.00 5.00
A6 Mick E. Moose Mascot .40 1.00
A7 Scott Arniel 2.00 5.00
A8 Randy Carlyle HCO 2.00 5.00
B1 Brian Chapman .80 2.00
B2 Radim Bicanek .80 2.00
B3 Michael Stewart .80 2.00
B4 Jason Christie .80 2.00
B5 Greg Pankewicz .80 2.00
B6 Brad Purdie .80 2.00
B7 Kent Fearns 2.00 5.00
B8 Mike Ruark 2.00 5.00

1998-99 Manitoba Moose

This oversized set was issued in two series, with each card inserted into various game programs. The series are numbered C and D which continues the numbering from the previous season. Cards 7 and 8 in each series are much tougher as they were only available at Grapes Leon's Centre with a food purchase.

COMPLETE SET (16) 16.00 40.00
C1 Scott Arniel 1.20 3.00
C2 Bill Bowler 1.20 3.00
C3 Kent Fearns .80 2.00
C4 Brett Hauer .80 2.00
C5 Ralph Intranuovo .80 2.00
C6 Mike Ruark .80 2.00
C7 Michael Stewart 2.00 5.00
C8 Scott Thomas 2.00 5.00
D1 Jason MacDonald 1.20 3.00
D2 Christian Bronsard 1.20 3.00
D3 Jeff Parrott .80 2.00
D4 Brian Chapman .80 2.00
D5 Richard Shulmistra 1.20 3.00
D6 Jimmy Roy .80 2.00
D7 Rhett Gordon 2.00 5.00
D8 Patrice Tardif 2.00 5.00

1999-00 Manitoba Moose

Released in conjunction with Grapes, Husky, and Mohawk, this 22-card set pictures the 1999-00 Manitoba Moose. Each card measures 6.25x9.5" and comes complete with two perforated coupons on the bottom.

COMPLETE SET (22) 10.00 25.00
1 Manny Legace 1.20 3.00
2 Michael Stewart .40 1.00
3 Vladislav Serov .40 1.00
4 Lonny Bohonos .80 2.00
5 Mike Prokopec .80 2.00
6 Jeff Parrott .40 1.00
7 Bill Bowler .80 2.00
8 Mike Ruark .40 1.00
9 Eric Veilleux .40 1.00
10 Brett Hauer .40 1.00
11 Jason Elliott .80 2.00
12 Cory Cyrenne .60 1.50
13 Justin Kurtz .40 1.00
14 Patrice Tardif .80 2.00
15 Jimmy Roy .40 1.00
16 Jason MacDonald .40 1.00
17 Larry Shapley .40 1.00
18 Brian Chapman .40 1.00
19 Marc Rodgers .80 2.00
20 Jim Montgomery .40 1.00
21 M2K Header Card .20 .50
22 Checklist .20 .50

2000-01 Manitoba Moose

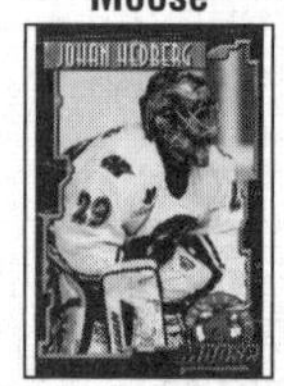

This set features the Moose of the IHL. The set was oversized and was sold by the team at home games and through its Web site. The set is noteworthy for the card of Johan Hedberg, who became a huge hobby star after being acquired by the Penguins during this season.

COMPLETE SET 6.00 12.00
1 Mel Angelstad .30 .75
2 Doug Ast .20 .50
3 Cal Benazic .20 .50
4 Philippe Boucher .20 .50
5 Steve Brule .20 .50
6 Brian Chapman .20 .50
7 Dion Darling .20 .50
8 Bobby Dollas .20 .50
9 Rusty Fitzgerald .20 .50
10 Daniel Goneau .20 .50
11 Brett Hauer .20 .50
12 Johan Hedberg 2.00 3.00
13 Dan Kesa .20 .50
14 Justin Kurtz .20 .75
15 Dmitri Leonov .20 .50
16 John MacLean .30 .75
17 Sean Pronger .20 .50
18 Bruce Richardson .20 .50
19 Jimmy Roy .20 .75
20 Mike Ruark .20 .50
21 Scott Thomas .20 .50
22 Ken Wregget .30 .75
23 Mick E. Moose MASCOT .02 .10

2001-02 Manitoba Moose

This set features the Moose of the AHL. The set was sold by the team at its souvenir stand for $15. The cards are slightly oversized. Since they are unnumbered, the cards are listed alphabetically.

COMPLETE SET (23) 6.00 15.00
1 Header Card .04 .10
2 Bryan Allen .30 .75
3 Ryan Bonni .30 .75
4 Brian Chapman .30 .75
5 Artem Chubarov .30 .75
6 Jason Cipolla .30 .75
7 Regan Darby .30 .75
8 Fedor Fedorov .30 .75
9 Darrell Hay .30 .75
10 Bryan Helmer .30 .75
11 Josh Holden .75
12 Steve Kariya .40 1.00
13 Pat Kavanagh .30 .75
14 Zenith Komarniski .30 .75
15 Justin Kurtz .30 .75
16 Brad Leeb .30 .75
17 Alfie Michaud .40 1.00

18 Justin Morrison .30 .75
19 Ryan Ready .30 .75
20 Brandon Reid .40 1.00
21 Jimmy Roy .30 .75
22 Andre Savage .30 .75
23 Mick E. Moose MASCOT .10 .25

2002-03 Manitoba Moose

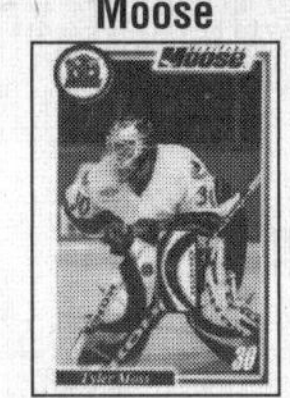

COMPLETE SET (26) 15.00
1 Header Card .10
2 Mick E. Moose Mascot .10
3 Zenith Komarniski .50
4 Bryan Helmer .50
5 Ryan Ready .50
6 Steve Kariya 1.50
7 Nolan Baumgartner .50
8 Regan Darby .50
9 Jimmy Roy .50
10 Fedor Fedorov 1.00
11 Jaroslav Obsut .50
12 Jason King .50
13 Darrell Hay .50
14 Tyler Moss .75
15 Herbert Vasiljevs .50
16 Nathan Smith .50
17 Alex Auld 1.00
18 Bryan Allen .50
19 Brandon Reid 1.50
20 Jason Goulet .50
21 Justin Kurtz .50
22 Brian Chapman .50
23 Pat Kavanagh .50
24 Rene Vydareny .50
25 Tyler Bouck .50
26 Jason Shmyr .50

2003-04 Manitoba Moose

This set was sold by the team at home games.

COMPLETE SET (24) 15.00
1 Checklist .01
2 Autograph Card .01
3 Mascot .10
4 Tomas Mojzis .60
5 Mikko Jokela .60
6 Nolan Baumgartner .60
7 Chris Nielsen .60
8 Tyler Bouck .60
9 Nathan Smith .60
10 Ryan Ready .60
11 Pat Kavanagh .60
12 Ryan Kesler 2.00
13 Sean Pronger .60
14 Rene Vydareny .60
15 Jimmy Roy .60
16 Justin Morrison .60
17 Martin Grenier .60
18 Tyler Moss 1.00
19 Alex Auld 1.00
20 Dallas Eakins .60
21 Jaroslav Obsut .60
22 Kirill Koltsov .60
23 Brandon Reid 1.00
24 Fedor Fedorov 1.00

2004-05 Manitoba Moose

COMPLETE SET (24) 20.00
1 Kevin Bieksa 1.00
2 Tomas Mojzis 1.00
3 Joey DiPenta 1.50
4 Kent Huskins 1.00
5 Nolan Baumgartner 1.00
6 Justin Morrison 1.00
7 Jeff Heerema 1.00
8 Ryan Kesler 1.50
9 Peter Sarno 1.00
10 Nathan Smith 1.00
11 Jimmy Roy 1.00
12 Jesse Schultz 1.00
13 Brandon Nolan 1.00
14 Jason King 1.50
15 Wade Flaherty 1.50
16 Alex Auld 1.50
17 Josh Green 1.00
18 Lee Goren 1.50
19 Wade Brookbank 1.00
20 Johnathan Aitken 1.00
21 Autograph Card .01
22 MTS Centre 1st Goal .10
23 Inaugural Season .10
24 Mick E. Moose MASCOT .10

2005-06 Manitoba Moose

COMPLETE SET (27) 12.00
1 Jozef Balej .20 .50
2 Ryan Bayda .20 .50
3 Kevin Bieksa .20 .50
4 Mike Brown .20 .50
5 Alexandre Burrows .30 .75
6 Sven Butenschon .20 .50
7 Craig Darby .20 .50
8 Wade Flaherty .40 1.00
9 Maxime Fortunus .20 .50
10 Josh Green .20 .50
11 Jason Jaffray .20 .50
12 Mike Keane .20 .50
13 Nathan McIver .20 .50
14 Tomas Mojzis .20 .50
15 Yuri Moscevsky .20 .50
16 Maxime Ouellet .40 1.00
17 Jimmy Roy .20 .50
18 Prestin Ryan .20 .50
19 Rick Rypien .20 .50
20 Jesse Schultz .40 1.00
21 Brett Skinner .20 .50
22 Nathan Smith .20 .50
23 AHL All-Star Classic .02 .10
24 Autograph Card .02 .10
25 The Home of Hockey .02 .10
26 Manitoba Moose CL .02 .10
27 Mick E. Moose MASCOT .02 .10

2006-07 Manitoba Moose

COMPLETE SET (27) 12.00 20.00
1 Mick E. Moose MASCOT .10 .25
2 Drew McIntyre .40 1.00
3 Alexander Edler .30 .75
4 Prestin Ryan .30 .75
5 Joe Rullier .30 .75
6 Nathan McIver .30 .75
7 Brandon Reid .40 1.00
8 Mike Keane .30 .75
9 Mike Brown .30 .75
10 Jason Jaffray .30 .75
11 Jannik Hansen .60 1.50
12 J.J. Hunter .30 .75
13 Nathan Smith .30 .75
14 Brad Moran .30 .75
15 Jesse Schultz .30 .75
16 Dustin Wood .30 .75
17 Adam Keefe .30 .75
18 Maxime Fortunus .30 .75
19 Marc-Andre Bernier .30 .75
20 Tyler Bouck .30 .75
21 Wade Flaherty .40 1.00
22 Julien Ellis .40 1.00
23 Lee Goren .40 1.00
24 Yannick Tremblay .30 .75
25 Patrick Coulombe .30 .75
26 Shaun Heshka .30 .75
27 Alexandre Bolduc .30 .75

1982-83 Medicine Hat Tigers

These 21 blank-backed cards measure approximately 3" by 4" and feature white-bordered, black-and-white posed studio head shots of the WHL Tigers on the left halves of the cards. The player's name, jersey number and biography, along with a space for an autograph, appear on the right half. The cards are unnumbered and checklisted below in alphabetical order.

COMPLETE SET (21) 8.00 20.00
1 Al Conroy .60 1.50
2 Murray Craven .80 2.00
3 Mark Frank .40 1.00
4 Kevan Guy .40 1.00
5 Jim Hougen .40 1.00
6 Ken Jorgenson .40 1.00
7 Matt Kabayama .40 1.00
8 Brent Kisilivich .40 1.00
9 Mark Lamb 1.20 3.00
10 Mike Lay .40 1.00
11 Dean McArthur .40 1.00
12 Brent Meckling .40 1.00
13 Shawn Nagurny .40 1.00
14 Kodie Nelson .40 1.00
15 Al Pedersen .60 1.50
16 Todd Pederson .40 1.00
17 Jay Reid .40 1.00
18 Gord Shmyrko .40 1.00
19 Brent Steblyk .40 1.00
20 Rocky Trottier .40 1.00
21 Dan Turner .40 1.00

1983-84 Medicine Hat Tigers

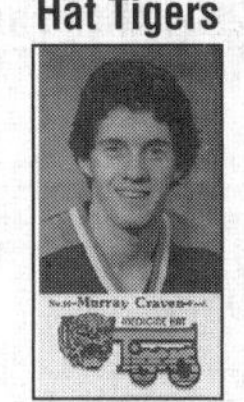

This 23-card P.L.A.Y. (Police, Laws and Youth) set measures approximately 2 3/4" by 5" and features color player portraits with a wide white bottom border. The border contains the player's jersey number and name. The team logo is also printed in this area. The backs carry sponsor logos and public service "Tips From The Tigers."

COMPLETE SET (23) 12.00 40.00
1 Murray Craven .80 2.00
2 Shane Churla 2.00 5.00
3 Don Herczeg .40 1.50
4 Gary Johnson .40 1.50
5 Brent Kisilivich .40 1.50
6 Blair MacGregor .40 1.50
7 Terry Knight .40 1.50
8 Mark Lamb 1.20 3.00
9 Al Pedersen .60 2.00
10 Trevor Semeniuk .40 1.50
11 Dan Turner .40 1.50
12 Brent Steblyk .40 1.50
13 Rocky Trottier .40 2.00
14 Kevan Guy .40 2.00
15 Bobby Bassen .80 2.00
16 Brent Meckling .40 1.50
17 Matt Kabayama .40 1.50
18 Gord Hynes .60 2.00
19 Daryl Henry .40 1.50
20 Jim Kambeitz .40 1.50
21 Mike Lay .60 2.00
22 Gord Shmyrko .40 1.50
23 Al Conroy .60 2.00

1985-86 Medicine Hat Tigers

This 24-card set measures approximately 2 1/4" by 4" and features posed, color player photos on white card stock. The player's name and the team logo are printed in the larger white margin at the bottom. The player's jersey number and position are printed on the picture in the upper corners. A thin red line encloses the picture, player's name, and logo. The backs display P.L.A.Y. (Police, Laws, and Youth) tips and sponsor logos.

COMPLETE SET (24) 8.00 20.00
1 Mike Claringbull .30 .75
2 Doug Houda .40 1.00
3 Mark Kuntz .30 .75
4 Guy Phillips .30 .75
5 Rob DiMaio .80 2.00
6 Al Conroy .40 1.00
7 Craig Berube .80 2.00
8 Doug Sauter CO .20 .50
9 Dean Chynoweth .40 1.00
10 Scott McCrady .30 .75
11 Neil Brady .30 .75
12 Dale Kushner .30 .75
13 Jeff Wenaas .30 .75
14 Wayne Hynes .30 .75
15 Troy Gamble .80 2.00
16 Bryan Maxwell ACO .20 .50
17 Gord Hynes .30 .75
18 Wayne McBean .40 1.00
19 Mark Pederson .40 1.00
20 Darren Cota .30 .75
21 Randy Siska .30 .75
22 Dave Mackey .30 .75
23 Mark Fitzpatrick 1.20 3.00
24 Doug Ball TR .10 .25

1995-96 Medicine Hat Tigers

This 21-card set features color player photos of the Medicine Hat Tigers of the WHL and was sponsored by Pizza Hut. The black front border is highly susceptible to dings, and thus the set is considered condition sensitive. Although the cards feature player jersey numbers on the fronts, they are unnumbered, and thus the set is checklisted below in alphabetical order.

COMPLETE SET (21) 6.00 15.00
1 Johnathan Aitken .30 .75
2 Brady Austin .30 .75
3 Cal Benazic .30 .75
4 Scott Buhler .30 .75
5 Clint Cabana .30 .75
6 Mike Eley .30 .75
7 Josh Green .40 1.00
8 Curtis Huppe .30 .75
9 Henry Kuster .30 .75
10 Aaron Millar .30 .75
11 Mark Polak .30 .75
12 Bryan Randall .30 .75
13 Chad Reich .30 .75
14 Kyle Ronan .30 .75
15 Rroary MASCOT .04 .10
16 Blair St. Martin .30 .75
17 Paxton Schafer .30 .75
18 Derek Senkow .30 .75
19 Darcy Smith .30 .75
20 Rocky Thompson .40 1.00
21 Trevor Wasyluk .40 1.00

1996-97 Medicine Hat Tigers

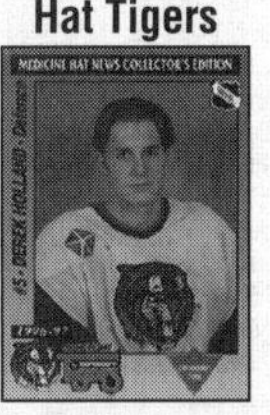

This 25-card set features posed color player photos surrounded by an orange/yellow border. The player's name, number and position are listed along the left border, while the logos of the team and Canadian Tire can be found along the bottom. The top reads "Medicine Hat News Collector's Edition", leading to speculation that the set was issued as a premium either through the paper, or at a game night sponsored by the paper. The backs contain a large Canadian Tire logo, along with biographical info for the player. The cards are unnumbered, and are checklisted below in alphabetical order.

COMPLETE SET (25) 6.00 15.00
1 Berkeley Buchko .30 .75
2 Scott Buhler .30 .75
3 Jason Chimera .80 1.50
4 Michael Dyck ACO .04 .10
5 Mike Eley .30 .75
6 Josh Green .40 .75
7 Derek Holland .30 .75
8 Curtis Huppe .30 .75
9 Henry Kuster .40 .75
10 Kurt Lackten CO .04 .10
11 Kevin McDonald .30 .75
12 Aaron Millar .30 .75
13 Doug Mosher GM .04 .10
14 Jaroslav Obsut .40 .75
15 Colin O'Hara .30 .75
16 Mark Polak .30 .75
17 Rroary MASCOT .04 .10
18 Blair St. Martin .30 .75
19 Rob Sandrock .30 .75
20 Dustin Schwartz .30 .75
21 Lee Svangstu .30 .75
22 Jeff Temple .30 .75
23 Rocky Thompson .40 .75
24 Trevor Wasyluk .30 .75
25 Chad Wilchynski .30 .75

1997-98 Medicine Hat Tigers

This set features the Tigers of the WHL. The set was sponsored by the Medicine Hat News and was sold at home games. The cards are unnumbered, and so are listed below in alphabetical order.

COMPLETE SET (25) 4.80 12.00
1 Steve Albrecht .20 .50
2 James Boyd .20 .50
3 Konrad Brand .20 .50
4 Berkeley Buchko .20 .50
5 Scott Buhler .31 .78
6 Rick Carriere CO .04 .11
7 Jason Chimera .80 2.00
8 Randall Dyck .20 .50
9 Shaun Hill .20 .50
10 Derek Holland .20 .50
11 Henry Kuster .20 .50
12 Kevin McDonald .20 .50
13 Aaron Millar .20 .50
14 Derek Rupprecht .20 .50
15 Rob Sandrock .20 .50
16 Brett Scheffelmaier .30 .75
17 Justin Schwartz .30 .75
18 Blair Simpson .20 .50
19 Blair St. Martin .20 .50
20 Jeff Temple .20 .50
21 Brad Voth .20 .50
22 Trevor Wasyluk .20 .50
23 Travis Willie .20 .50
24 Randy Wong ACO .04 .10
25 Rroary MASCOT .04 .10

1998-99 Medicine Hat Tigers

This set features the Tigers of the WHL. The set was sponsored by the Medicine Hat News and was sold at home games. The cards are unnumbered, and so are listed below in alphabetical order.

COMPLETE SET (25) 4.80 12.00
1 Brady Austin .20 .50
2 James Boyd .20 .50
3 Konrad Brand .20 .50
4 Berkeley Buchko .20 .50
5 Scott Buhler .30 .75
6 Rick Carriere CO .04 .10
7 Jason Chimera .60 1.50
8 Martin Cibak .40 1.00
9 Frazer Donahue .20 .50
10 Paul Elliott .20 .50
11 Kris Graf .20 .50
12 Shaun Hill .20 .50
13 Denny Johnston .20 .50
14 Tyson Kentel .20 .50
15 Cody Lyseng .20 .50
16 Aaron Millar .20 .50
17 Derek Rupprecht .20 .50
18 Brett Scheffelmaier .30 .75
19 Justin Schwartz .30 .75
20 Blair Simpson .20 .50
21 Ben Thompson .20 .50
22 Brad Voth .20 .50
23 Kevin Young .20 .50
24 Randy Wong ACO .04 .10
25 Rroary MASCOT .04 .10

1999-00 Medicine Hat Tigers

This set was produced on very thin card stock and is highly susceptible to damage. The cards were sold by the team at its souvenir stands. The set is noteworthy for featuring the first card of 2002 first-rounder Jay Bouwmeester.

COMPLETE SET (25) 10.00 25.00
1 Header Card .04 .10
2 Chris Ferguson .20 .50
3 Jay Bouwmeester 6.00 15.00
4 Josh Morrow .20 .50
5 Paul Elliott .20 .50
6 Tyson Mulock .20 .50
7 Kevin Labbe .20 .50
8 Ryan Hollweg .30 .75
9 Berkeley Buchko .20 .50
10 Chris St. Jacques .20 .50
11 Cody Jensen .20 .50
12 Ben Thompson .20 .50
13 Brad Voth .20 .50
14 Martin Cibak .20 .50
15 Denny Johnston .20 .50
16 Konrad Brand .20 .50
17 Shaun Sutter .30 .75
18 Ken Davis .20 .50
19 Ryan Kinasewich .20 .50
20 Brett Scheffelmaier .30 .75
21 Justin Taylor .20 .50
22 Vladimir Sicak .20 .50
23 Ben McMullin .30 .75
24 Kyle Kettles .30 .75
25 Josh Maser .20 .50
27 Brett Scheffelmaier .20 .50
28 Justin Taylor .20 .50
29 Vladimir Sicak .20 .50
30 Ben McMullin .20 .50
31 Kyle Kettles .20 .50
32 Jash Maser .20 .50

2000-01 Medicine Hat Tigers

This set features the Tigers of the WHL. The set was sold by the team at its souvenir stands. The cards are unnumbered and is listed below alphabetically. The set features an early card of top prospect Jay Bouwmeester.

COMPLETE SET (26) 8.00 25.00
1 Jay Bouwmeester 4.00 8.00
2 Ryan Chieduch .16 .40
3 Petr Chivojka .16 .40
4 Ken Davis .16 .40
5 Brett Draney .16 .40
6 Bryan Ellerman ACO .04 .10
7 B.J. Fehr .16 .40
8 Vernon Fiddler .16 .40
9 Jeremy Goetzinger .16 .40
10 Ryan Hollweg .30 .75
11 Denny Johnston .16 .40
12 Kyle Kettles .16 .40
13 Ryan Kinasewich .16 .40
14 Bob Loucks HCO .04 .10
15 Joffrey Lupul 2.00 10.00
16 Ben McMullin .20 .50
17 Josh Morrow .16 .40
18 Tyson Mulock .16 .40
19 Ryan Olynyk .16 .40
20 Brett Scheffelmaier .30 .75
21 Chris St. Jacques .16 .40
22 Ben Thompson .16 .40
23 David Ullmann .16 .40
24 Brad Voth .16 .40
25 Mascot .04 .10
26 Randy Wong ACO .04 .10

2002-03 Medicine Hat Tigers

These cards are unnumbered and are listed below in alphabetical order.

COMPLETE SET (25) 8.00 20.00
1 Curtis Austring .20 .50
2 Cam Barker .60 1.50
3 Chad Bassen .20 .50
4 Kieran Block .20 .50
5 Brenden Cuthbert .20 .50
6 Riley Day .20 .50
7 Tyler Dietrich .20 .50
8 Nick Harsulla .20 .50
9 Ryan Hollweg .30 .75
10 Daniel Idema .20 .50
11 Martin Kubaliak .20 .50
12 Joffrey Lupul 2.00 5.00
13 Steve Marr .20 .50
14 Tommy Maxwell .20 .50
15 Stefan Meyer .20 .50
16 Clarke MacArthur .40 1.00
17 Kevin Nastiuk .60 1.50
18 Kyle Pess .20 .50
19 Adam Redmond .20 .50
20 Steven Regier .20 .50
21 Darren Reid .20 .50
22 Mark Vodden .20 .50
23 Chris St. Jacques .20 .50
24 Ryan Stempfle .20 .50
25 Ben Thomson .20 .50

2003-04 Medicine Hat Tigers

This checklist is incomplete, but the cards below have been confirmed to exist. If you can help complete this listing, please email hockeymag@beckett.com.

COMPLETE SET (?)
1 Cam Barker
2 Riley Day
3 Ryan Hollweg
4 Clarke MacArthur
5 Stefan Meyer
6 Kevin Nastiuk

7 Darren Reid
8 Yannick Seidenberg

2004-05 Medicine Hat Tigers

COMPLETE SET (25) 20.00
1 Gord Baldwin .75
2 Cam Barker 1.50
3 Jordan Bendfeld .75
4 Cody Blanshan .75
5 Kieran Block .75
6 Derek Dorsett .75
7 Nathan Exner .75
8 Trevor Glass .75
9 Darren Helm .75
10 Matt Keetley .75
11 Jarret Lukin .75
12 Clarke MacArthur 1.00
13 Steve Marr .75
14 Tommy Maxwell .75
15 Stefan Meyer .75
16 Kevin Nastiuk 1.50
17 Roman Psurny .75
18 Brett Robertson .75
19 Kris Russell .75
20 David Schlemko .75
21 Daine Todd .75
22 Devyn Tremblay .75
23 Kevin Undershute .75
24 Willie Desjardins CO .10
25 Shaun Clouston ACO .10

2005-06 Medicine Hat Tigers

COMPLETE SET (25) 8.00 20.00
1 Gord Baldwin .30 .75
2 Cam Barker .60 1.50
3 Jason Battershill .30 .75
4 Jordan Bendfeld .30 .75
5 Kieran Block .30 .75
6 Brennan Bosch .30 .75
7 Shayne Brown .30 .75
8 Marek Curilla .30 .75
9 Derek Dorsett .30 .75
10 Tyler Ennis .30 .75
11 Trevor Glass .30 .75
12 Darren Helm .30 .75
13 Matt Keetley .30 .75
14 Tommy Maxwell .30 .75
15 Blaine Neufeld .30 .75
16 Roman Psurny .30 .75
17 Brett Robertson .30 .75
18 Kris Russell .30 .75
19 Jerrid Sauer .30 .75
20 David Schlemko .30 .75
21 Matt Sokol .30 .75
22 Chris Stevens .30 .75
23 Daine Todd .30 .75
24 Kevin Undershute .30 .75
25 Scott Wasden .30 .75

2006-07 Medicine Hat Tigers

COMPLETE SET (25) 12.00 20.00
1 Gord Baldwin .30 .75
2 Jordan Bendfeld .30 .75
3 Brennan Bosch .30 .75
4 Shayne Brown .30 .75
5 Derek Dorsett .30 .75
6 Tyler Ennis .30 .75
7 Trevor Glass .30 .75
8 Colton Grant .30 .75
9 Darren Helm .30 .75
10 Jordan Hickmott .30 .75
11 Ryan Holfeld .40 1.00
12 Mark Isherwood .30 .75
13 Matt Keetley .40 1.00
14 Matt Lowry .30 .75
15 Jakub Rumpel .30 .75
16 Kris Russell .75 2.00
17 Jerrid Sauer .30 .75
18 Michael Sauer .30 .75
19 David Schlemko .30 .75
20 Chris Stevens .30 .75
21 Tyler Swystun .30 .75
22 Daine Todd .30 .75
23 Kevin Undershute .30 .75
24 Scott Wasden .30 .75
25 Willie Desjardins CO .10 .25

1993-94 Memphis RiverKings

Like most of the CHL sets issued that season, these round cards are approximately the size of a hockey puck. They were sold in a plastic container with the team logo on the front, and were sold by the booster club for $5..

COMPLETE SET (18) 3.60 9.00
1 Rocco Amonte .20 .50
2 Peter D'Amario .20 .50
3 Roydon Gunn .20 .50
4 Kyle Haviland .20 .50
5 Mike Jackson .20 .50
6 Scot Johnston .20 .50
7 Robert Kelley .20 .50
8 Mark McGinn .20 .50
9 Antoine Mindjimba .20 .50
10 David Moore .20 .50
11 Glenn Painter .20 .50
12 Scott Phillips .20 .50
13 Mike Roberts .20 .50
14 Andy Ross .20 .50
15 Steve Shaunessy .20 .50
16 Ken Venis .20 .50
17 Bobby Wallwork .20 .50
18 Randy Boyd CO .10 .25

1994-95 Memphis RiverKings

Available in 14-card CHL packs that contained an assortment of teams, this 18-card set featured players of the RiverKings.

COMPLETE SET (18) 3.20 8.00
1 Denis Beauchamp .20 .50
2 Nicolas Brousseau .20 .50
3 Scott Bower .30 .75
4 Dan Brown .20 .50
5 Brian Cook .20 .50
6 Brent Fleetwood .20 .50
7 Francois Gagnon .20 .50
8 Dominic Grand'maison .20 .50
9 Kyle Haviland .20 .50
10 Jamie Hearn .20 .50
11 Mike Jackson .30 .75
12 Paul Krake .30 .75
13 Layne LeBel .20 .50
14 Steve Magnusson .20 .50
15 Darren Miciak .20 .50
16 Mark McGinn .20 .50
17 Bobby Wallwork .20 .50
18 Herb Boxer CO .10 .25

1999-00 Memphis RiverKings All-Time

This set features the RiverKings of the CHL. Rather than commemorate the current roster, it features the best players ever to don the River Kings sweater. The set was originally issued as a promotional giveaway, but later was sold by the team as well.

COMPLETE SET (20) 4.00 10.00
1 Tom Mutch .20 .50
2 Doug Stromback .20 .50
3 Mike Jackson .30 .75
4 Mark McGinn .20 .50
5 Antoine Mindjimba .30 .75
6 Andrew Miller .20 .50
7 Dan Brown .20 .50
8 Hugo Hamelin .20 .50
9 Derek Grant .20 .50
10 Steve Thorpe .20 .50
11 Bobby Wallwork .20 .50
12 Peter D'Amario .20 .50
13 John Batten .20 .50
14 Andy Ross .20 .50
15 Kyle Haviland .20 .50
16 Scot Kelsey .20 .50
17 Scott Brower .20 .50
18 Jamie Cooke .30 .75
19 Craig Lindsay .30 .75
20 Riverthing MAS .10 .25

2001-02 Memphis RiverKings

This set features the RiverKings of the CHL. The set was sold by the team at home games late in the season, after goalie Sebastien Centomo had moved on to the AHL and later, the NHL. The cards are unnumbered, although they are listed on a checklist. The set is listed in the order it appears on the checklist.

COMPLETE SET (21) 6.00 15.00
1 Team CL Centomo .30 .75
2 Kahlil Thomas .20 .50
3 Brad Mueller .20 .50
4 Kevin Fricke .20 .50
5 Anthony DiPalma .30 .75
6 Michal Stastny .30 .75
7 Jean-Francois Picard .20 .50
8 Jay Neal .20 .50
9 Jacques Lariviere .30 .75
10 Rob Palahnuk .20 .50
11 Kevin Ryan .20 .50
12 Sebastien Centomo 2.00 5.00
13 Don Parsons .20 .50
14 Luch Nasato .30 .75
15 Mark Richards .20 .50
16 Brian Tucker .20 .50
17 Don Martin .20 .50
18 Ben Gorewich .20 .50
19 A.J. Aitken .20 .50
20 Jonathan Gagnon .20 .50
21 Doug Shedden CO .20 .50

2003-04 Memphis RiverKings

COMPLETE SET 6.00 15.00
1 Jeremy Cornish .40 1.00
2 Trent Dickson .30 .75
3 Juraj Durco .30 .75
4 Jonathan Gagnon .30 .75
5 Jasmin Gelinas .30 .75
6 Jerry Gernander .30 .75
7 Jeremy Goetzinger .30 .75
8 Chad Grills .30 .75
9 Derek Landmesser .40 1.00
10 Stephen Margeson .30 .75
11 Alexandre Mathieu .40 1.00
12 Mike Minard .40 1.00
13 Brad Mueller .30 .75
14 Jay Neal .30 .75
15 Brent Ozarowski .30 .75
16 Don Parsons .40 1.00
17 Jean-Francois Racine .60 1.50
18 Mark Richards .30 .75
19 Tim Schneider .30 .75
20 Brian Tucker .30 .75
21 David Turon .30 .75

2004-05 Memphis RiverKings

COMPLETE SET (22) 15.00
1 Header Card .10
2 Aaron Lewis .50
3 Allan Carr .50
4 Brad Mueller .50

5 David Lemanowicz 1.50
6 Derek Landmesser .50
7 Don Parsons .75
8 J.F. Racine 1.50
9 Jeremy Goetzinger .50
10 Jeremy Wray .50
11 Ken Goetz 1.50
12 Mark Richards .50
13 Peter Robertson .50
14 Phil Aucoin .50
15 Ryan Rome .50
16 Scott English 2.00
17 Stephen Margeson .50
18 Ted Crowley .50
19 Tim Plett .50
20 Travis Banga .50
21 Tyson Gajda .50
22 Wayne Hall .50

1991-92 Michigan Falcons

This set features the Falcons of the UHL. According to minor league expert Ralph Slate, the set wasn't widely distributed until 1994-95, but based on the players involved and the fact that the manufacturer -- 7th Inning Sketch -- actually went out of business in 1992, this set must have been intended for distribution during that season.

COMPLETE SET (21) 8.00 20.00
1 Christian LaLonde .40 1.00
2 Victor Posa .40 1.00
3 Al Murphy .40 1.00
4 Bill Horn .40 1.00
5 Rich Sewell .40 1.00
6 Dan Fowler .40 1.00
7 Kip Noble .40 1.00
8 Ange Guzzo .40 1.00
9 Dean Morton .40 1.00
10 Jeff Lindsay .40 1.00
11 Mike Vellucci .60 1.50
12 Brett Strot .40 1.00
13 Rick Berens .40 1.00
14 Kevin Clayton .40 1.00
15 Todd Humphrey .40 1.00
16 Ray De Grendel ACO .10 .25
16 Tom Viggiano ACO .10 .25
16 Terry Christensen CO .10 .25
17 Bill Gutenberg .40 1.00
18 Jamie Stewart .40 1.00
19 Bob McKillop .40 1.00
20 Clayton Young .40 1.00
21 Steve Beadle .40 1.00

1996-97 Michigan K-Wings

This set features the K-Wings of the IHL. The set was sponsored by BJ Sports, and sold by the team at home games.

COMPLETE SET (27) 4.80 10.00
1 Dan Keczmer .16 .40
2 Dennis Smith .16 .40
3 Brad Berry .16 .40
4 Shane Peacock .16 .40
5 Jason Lafreniere .16 .40
6 Collin Bauer .16 .40
7 Sergei Gusev .16 .40
8 Igor Korolev .16 .40
Misspelled "Horolev" on front
9 Brent Fedyk .16 .40
10 Pat Elynuik .16 .40
11 Jamie Wright .16 .40
12 Lee Jinman .16 .40
13 Jeff Mitchell .16 .40
14 Brad Lukowich .20 .50
15 Derrick Smith .16 .40
16 Petr Buzek .16 .40
17 Patrick Cote .30 .75
18 Mark Lawrence .16 .40
19 Jim Storm .16 .40
20 Roman Turek .80 1.00
21 Neil Brady .16 .40
22 Manny Fernandez .80 2.00
23 Claude Noel CO .04 .10
24 Jim Playfair CO .04 .10
25 Checklist .01
26 PHPA Web Site .01
27 BJ Sports .01

1998-99 Michigan K-Wings

This 21-card set features the K-Wings of the IHL on an extra glossy card stock. The cards are not numbered so they appear in the order that was released on the checklist card.

COMPLETE SET (21) 8.00 25.00
1 Mel Angelstad .40 1.00
2 Jason Botterill .16 .40
3 Ryan Christie .40 .40
4 Doug Doull .30 2.00
5 Kelly Fairchild .16 .40
6 Marty Flichel .16 .40
7 Aaron Gavey .30 .75
8 Greg Leeb .16 .40
9 Jeff Mitchell .16 .40
10 Dave Roberts .16 .40
11 Jon Sim .30 .75
12 Brad Berry .16 .40
13 Petr Buzek .30 .75
14 Richard Jackman .30 .75
15 Brad Lukowich .30 .75
16 Matt Martin .16 .40
17 Evgueni Tsybouk .16 .40
18 Mike Bales .30 .75
19 Marty Turco 4.00 15.00
20 IHL Logo card .01
21 Header/Checklist .04 .01

1999-00 Michigan K-Wings

This set features the K-Wings of the IHL. The set was produced by EBK Sports and was sold by the team at its souvenir stands. Each card also is serial numbered out of 1,000.

COMPLETE SET (21) 14.00 40.00
1 Jamie Wright .30 .75
2 Keith Aldridge .30 .75
3 Steve Gainey .40 .75
4 Jonathan Sim .40 1.00
5 Mike Martin .20 .50
6 Gaetan Royer .20 .50
7 Jeff MacMillan .20 .50
8 Aaron Gavey .20 .50
9 Evgeny Tsybouk .20 .50
10 Marty Turco 8.00 20.00
11 Matt Martin .20 .50
12 Ryan Christie .60 .50
13 Greg Leeb .20 .50
14 Mark Wotton .20 .50
15 Kelly Fairchild .20 .50
16 Gregor Baumgartner .20 .50
17 Brenden Morrow 4.00 10.00
18 Mel Angelstad .80 2.00
19 Mike Bales .30 .75
20 Richard Jackman .30 .75
21 Roman Lyashenko .40 1.00

1992-93 Michigan State Spartans

This set features the Spartans of the NCAA. The cards are unnumbered and so are listed below in alphabetical order. The cards were issued as a promotional giveaway.

COMPLETE SET (30) 15.00 40.00
1 Team Photo .60 1.50
2 Ron Mason HCO .60 1.50
3 Matt Albers .60 1.50
4 Michael Burkett .60 1.50
5 Mike Buzak .60 1.50
6 Anson Carter 2.50 6.00
7 Brian Clifford .60 1.50
8 Scott Dean .60 1.50
9 Ryan Fleming .60 1.50
10 Ryan Folkening .60 1.50
11 Steve Guolla 1.25 3.00
12 Kelly Harper .60 1.50
13 Eric Kruse .60 1.50
14 James Lambros .60 1.50
15 Mike Mattis .60 1.50
16 Wes McCauley .60 1.50
17 Rem Murray 1.25 3.00
18 Steve Norton .60 1.50
19 Nicolas Perreault .60 1.50
20 Bill Shalawylo .60 1.50
21 Chris Smith .60 1.50
22 Bryan Smolinski 1.25 3.00
23 Steve Suk .60 1.50
24 Chris Sullivan .60 1.50
25 Bart Turner .60 1.50
26 Bart Vanstaalduinen .60 1.50
27 Mike Ware .60 1.50
28 John Weidenbach .60 1.50
29 Rob Woodward .60 1.50
30 Scott Worden .60 1.50

1993-94 Michigan State Spartans

This set features the Spartans of the NCAA. The cards were produced by Phipps Sports Marketing, Inc and were issued as a promotional giveaway. The cards are unnumbered and checklisted below in alphabetical order.

COMPLETE SET (32) 15.00 40.00
1 Matt Albers .40 1.00
2 Michael Burkett .40 1.00
3 Mike Buzak .40 1.00
4 Anson Carter 2.00 5.00
5 Brian Clifford .75 2.00
6 Brian Crane .40 1.00
7 Steve Ferranti .40 1.00
8 Ryan Fleming .40 1.00
9 Steve Guolla .75 2.00
10 Kelly Harper .40 1.00
11 Eric Kruse .40 1.00
12 Ron Mason CO .40 1.00
13 Mike Mattis .40 1.00
14 Rem Murray .75 2.00
15 Steve Norton .40 1.00
16 Nicolas Perreault .40 1.00
17 Tom Ross .75 2.00
Spartan Great
18 Chris Slater .40 1.00
19 Chris Smith .40 1.00
20 Bryan Smolinski 1.25 3.00
21 Sparty (Mascot) .04 .10
22 Chris Sullivan .40 1.00
23 Steve Suk .40 1.00
24 Bart Turner .40 1.00
25 Tony Tuzzolino 1.25 3.00
26 Bart Vanstaalduinen .40 1.00
27 Mike Ware .40 1.00
28 John Weidenbach .40 1.00
29 Josh Wiegand .40 1.00
30 Scott Worden .40 1.00
31 Munn Arena .04 .10
32 Title Card .04 .10

2000-01 Michigan State Spartans

This set features the Spartans of the NCAA. It was handed out as a promotional giveaway at a pair of home games in 2000. The set is noteworthy for including an early card of hot prospect Ryan Miller.

COMPLETE SET (21) 10.00 35.00
1 Joe Blackburn .80 2.00
2 Andrew Bogle .40 1.00
3 Steve Clark .40 1.00
4 Rustyn Dolyny .40 1.00
5 Brad Fast .40 1.00
6 Troy Ferguson .40 1.00
7 Joe Goodenow .40 1.00
8 Adam Hall .40 5.00
9 Andrew Hutchinson .40 2.00
10 Jon Insana .40 1.00
11 Steve Jackson .40 1.00
12 Kris Koski .40 1.00
13 John-Michael Liles .40 5.00
14 Brian Maloney .40 1.00
15 Ryan Miller 6.00 15.00
16 John Nail .40 1.00
17 Sean Patchell .40 1.00
18 Damon Whitten .40 1.00
19 Ron Mason CO .40 1.00
20 White Out Game 3/2/01 .10 .25
21 Chevy Fans.Com .04 .01

1990-91 Michigan Tech Huskies

This 31-card standard-size set was sponsored by The Daily Mining Gazette and showcases the Michigan Tech Huskies of the WCHA. Reportedly only 500 sets were produced. The cards are printed on thin cardboard stock. Borderless high gloss player photos grace the fronts, with the jersey number, team name, player name, and position given in a black stripe at the bottom of the card face. On a black and pale yellow background, each back has a black and white head shot, biography, statistics, and career summary. A "Huskies Hockey Quick Fact" completes the card back. The cards are unnumbered and checklisted below in alphabetical order.

COMPLETE SET (31) 6.00 15.00
1 Jim Bonner .20 .50
2 Newell Brown CO .10 .25
3 Dwight DeGiacomo .20 .50
4 Rod Ewacha .20 .50
5 Peter Grant .20 .50
6 Tim Hartnett .20 .50
7 Mike Hauswirth .20 .50
8 Kelly Hurd .20 .50
9 Kelly Hurd .20 .50
Red Wings
10 Layne Lebel .20 .50
Jeff Hill
11 Randy Lewis .20 .50
12 Jay Luknowsky .20 .50
13 Ken Martel CO .10 .25
Mark Leach CO
14 Darcy Martini .20 .50
15 Reid McDonald .20 .50
16 Hugh McEwen .30 .75
Jim Storm
Kevin Manninen
17 Don Osborne .20 .50
18 Greg Parnell .20 .50
19 Davis Payne .20 .50
20 Kirby Perrault .20 .50
Darren Brkic
21 Ken Plaquin .20 .50
22 Damian Rhodes .80 2.00
23 Geoff Sarjeant .30 .75
24 Jamie Steer .20 .50
25 Rob Tustian .20 .50
26 Scott Vettraino .30 .75
Jamie Ram
27 Tim Watters .20 .50
(black and white)
28 John Young .20 .50
29 John Young .20 .50
Kelly Hurd
30 1991 MacInnes Cup .20 .50
31 1975 NCAA Champions .20 .50

1991-92 Michigan Tech Huskies

This 36-card standard-size set features the 1992-93 Michigan Tech Huskies. Reportedly approximately 2,000 sets were produced. The fronts features full-bleed color action player photos. A gray and yellow stripe at the bottom contains the player's name. The Huskies logo overlaps the picture and the stripe. Some players have two cards, the second of which is distinguished by a subtitle. The cards are unnumbered and checklisted below in alphabetical order.

COMPLETE SET (36) 6.00 15.00
1 Jim Bonner .20 .50
2 Darren Brkic .20 .50
3 Rod Ewacha .20 .50
4 Tim Hartnett .20 .50
5 Mike Hauswirth .20 .50
6 Jeff Hill .20 .50
7 Layne LeBel .20 .50
8 Randy Lewis .20 .50
9 Randy Lewis .20 .50
Hit Squad
10 John MacInnes CO .04 .10
11 Darcy Martini .20 .50
12 Darcy Martini .20 .50
Rink Blaster
13 Reid McDonald .20 .50
14 Hugh McEwen .20 .50
15 Bob Olson ANN .04 .10
16 Don Osborne .20 .50
17 Greg Parnell .20 .50
18 Davis Payne .20 .50
19 Kirby Perrault .20 .50
20 Ken Plaquin .20 .50
21 Jamie Ram .30 .75
22 Geoff Sarjeant .30 .75
23 Geoff Sarjeant .30 .75
WCHA Student-Athlete
24 Jamie Steer .20 .50
25 Jamie Steer .20 .50
Blade Runner
26 Jim Storm .20 .50
27 Scott Vettraino .20 .50
28 John Young .20 .50
29 Credits (Team .20 .50
huddling on ice)
30 Freshman .20 .50
Justin Peca
Liam Garvey
Randy Stevens
Brent Peterson
Travis Seale
31 Great Lakes .04 .10
Invitational
32 Home Ice .04 .10
MacInnes Student Ice Arena
33 Team Photo .20 .50
34 NHL Draft .20 .50
Darcy Martini
Davis Payne
Geoff Sarjeant
Ken Plaquin
Jim Storm
Jamie Ram
Jamie Steer
Jim Bonner
35 Pep Band .04 .10
36 Michigan Tech Univ. .04 .10

1993-94 Michigan Tech Huskies

The set features the Huskies of the NCAA. As is the case with most collegiate sets, this is believed to have been issued as a promotional giveaway. Any additional information can be forwarded to hockeymag@beckett.com.

COMPLETE SET (25) 4.80 12.00
1 Pat Mikesch .20 .50
2 Eric Jensen .20 .50
3 Kyle Peterson .20 .50
4 Jay Storm .20 .50
5 Jason Hanchuk .20 .50
6 Mike Figliomeni .20 .50
7 Randy Stevens .20 .50
8 Brent Peterson .20 .50
9 Kirby Perrault .20 .50
10 Brian Hunter .20 .50
11 Travis Seale .20 .50
12 Jamie Ram .30 .75
13 Jeff Hill .20 .50
14 Justin Peca .20 .50
15 Layne LeBel .20 .50
16 Jeff Mikesch .20 .50
17 John Kisil .20 .50
18 Liam Garvey .20 .50
19 Kyle Ferguson .20 .50
20 Jason Wright .20 .50
21 Luciano Caravaggio .20 .50
22 Mitch Lane .20 .50
23 Randy Wakeham .20 .50
24 Martin Machacek .20 .50
25 Winter Carnival .04 .10

2001-02 Michigan Tech Huskies

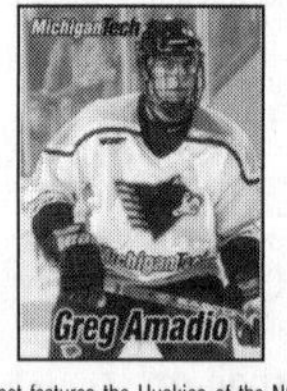

This set features the Huskies of the NCAA. The set was issued as a promotional giveaway. As the cards are unnumbered, they are listed below in alphabetical order.

COMPLETE SET (33) 8.00 20.00
1 Greg Amadio .30 .75
2 Justin Brown .30 .75
3 Paul Cabana .30 .75
4 Tony DeLorenzo .30 .75
5 Jaron Doetzel .30 .75
6 Chris Durno .30 .75
7 Cam Ellsworth .40 1.00
8 Brett Engelhardt .30 .75
9 Chuck Fabry .30 .75
10 Brady Greco .30 .75
11 John Hartman .30 .75
12 Blizzard T. Husky .04 .10
13 Tom Kaiman .30 .75
14 Bryan Konkel .30 .75
15 Tim Laurila .40 1.00
16 Ryan Lenton .30 .75
17 MacInnes Arena .04 .10
18 Ryan Markham .30 .75
19 Pep Band .04 .10
20 Colin Murphy .30 .75
21 Bob Olson ANN .04 .10
22 Brad Patterson .30 .75
23 Bryan Perez .30 .75
24 Phil Pietila .30 .75
25 Jon Pittis .30 .75
26 Bob Rangus .30 .75
27 Rob Rankin .30 .75
28 Brian Rogers .40 1.00
29 Mike Sertich CO .10 .25
30 Josh Singer .30 .75
31 Brad Sullivan .30 .75
32 Frank Werner .30 .75
33 Clay Wilson .30 .75

1991-92 Michigan Wolverines

Little is known about this set beyond confirmation of the checklist. These cards are unnumbered and checklisted below in alphabetical order. Additional info can be forwarded to hockeymag@beckett.com

COMPLETE SET (25) 6.00 15.00
1 Doug Evans .20 .50
2 Denny Felsner .20 .50
3 Anton Fedorov .20 .50
4 Chris Gordon .20 .50
5 David Harlock .20 .50
6 Mike Helber .20 .50
7 Tim Hogan .20 .50
8 Mike Knuble .30 .75
9 Ted Kramer .20 .50
10 Pat Neaton .20 .50
11 David Oliver .30 .75
12 David Roberts .20 .50
13 Marc Ouimet .20 .50
14 Ron Sacka .20 .50
15 Mark Sakala .20 .50
16 Steve Shields 1.20 3.00
17 Alan Sinclair .20 .50
18 Cam Stewart .30 .75
19 Dan Stiver .20 .50
20 Mike Stone .20 .50
21 Chris Tamer .24 .60
22 Aaron Ward .30 .75
23 Rick Willis .20 .50
24 Brian Wiseman .20 .50
25 Team Card .04 .10

1993-94 Michigan Wolverines

This set features the Wolverines of the NCAA. As is the case with most collegiate sets, this is believed to be a promotional giveaway. The cards are unnumbered and checklisted below in alphabetical order.

COMPLETE SET (28) 8.00 20.00
1 John Arnold .20 .50
2 Jason Botterill .30 .75
3 Peter Bourke .20 .50
4 Drew Denzin .20 .50
5 Anton Fedorov .20 .50
6 Chris Frescoln .20 .50
7 Chris Gordon .20 .50
8 Steve Halko .20 .50
9 Kevin Hilton .20 .50
10 Tim Hogan .20 .50
11 Mike Knuble .30 .75
12 Mike Legg .20 .50
13 Al Loges .20 .50
14 Warren Luhning .20 .50
15 John Madden 1.60 4.00
16 Brendan Morrison .80 2.00
17 David Oliver .20 .50
18 Ron Sacka .20 .50
19 Mark Sakala .20 .50
20 Harold Schock .20 .50
21 Steve Shields .60 1.50
22 Alan Sinclair .20 .50
23 Ryan Sittler .20 .50
24 Blake Sloan .40 1.00
25 Mike Stone .20 .50
26 Rick Willis .20 .50
27 Brian Wiseman .20 .50
28 Team Photo .20 .50

2002-03 Michigan Wolverines

COMPLETE SET (30) 35.00
1 Billy Powers ACO .10
2 Danny Richmond 2.00
3 Mike Roemensky 1.00
4 David Wyzgowski 1.00
5 Charlie Henderson 1.00
6 Jed Ortmeyer 2.00
7 Jeff Tambellini 3.00
8 David Moss 1.00
9 Gordon Berenson HCO 1.00
10 NCAA Frozen Four .25
11 Eric Nystrom 3.00
12 John Shouneyia 1.00
13 Andrew Ebbett 1.00
14 Michael Woodford 1.00
15 Mel Pearson ACO .25
16 Brandon Rogers 1.00
17 Joe Kautz 1.00
18 Mark Mink 1.00
19 Nick Martens 1.00
20 2002 CCHA Champions .25
21 Jason Ryznar 1.00
22 Andy Burnes 1.00
23 Dwight Helminen 1.00
24 Milan Gajic 1.00
25 Yost Arena .10
26 2002 CCHA Tournament Champs .25
27 J.J. Swistak 1.00
28 Al Montoya 10.00
29 Brandon Kaleniecki 1.00
30 Eric Werner 1.00

2003-04 Michigan Wolverines

This set was issued as a promotional giveaway.

COMPLETE SET (30) 20.00 40.00
1 Jeff Tambellini 1.25 3.00
2 Mike Mayhew .40 1.00
3 David Moss .75 2.00
4 Red Berenson CO .40 1.00
5 Endowed Scholarships .02 .10
6 Jason Ryznar .40 1.00
7 Andy Burnes .40 1.00
8 Dwight Helminen .40 1.00
9 Milan Gajic .40 1.00
10 Reilly Olson .40 1.00
11 Brandon Rogers .40 1.00
12 Joe Kautz .40 1.00
13 Tim Cook .40 1.00
14 Nick Martens .40 1.00
15 T.J. Hensick .75 2.00
16 Eric Werner .40 1.00
17 Brandon Kaleniecki .40 1.00
18 Al Montoya 3.00 8.00
19 Mike Brown .40 1.00
20 Noah Ruden .40 1.00
21 David Rohlfs .40 1.00
22 Eric Nystrom 1.25 3.00
23 Andrew Ebbett .40 1.00
24 Michael Woodford .40 1.00
25 Mel Pearson ACO .02 .10
26 Charlie Henderson .40 1.00
27 David Wyzgowski .40 1.00
28 Jason Dest .40 1.00
29 Matt Hunwick .75 2.00
30 Billy Powers ACO .02 .10

2004-05 Michigan Wolverines

This set was given out at home games in five strips of five cards.

COMPLETE SET (25) 30.00
1 David Rohlfs 1.00
2 Andrew Ebbett 1.00
3 Brandon Kaleniecki 1.00
4 Al Montoya 5.00
5 Gameday .10
6 Chad Kolarik 1.00
7 Kevin Porter 1.00
8 Mike Brown 1.00
9 Tim Cook 1.00
10 Yost Arena .10
11 Jason Dest 1.00
12 Matt Hunwick 1.50
13 T.J. Hensick 2.00
14 Mike Mayhew 1.00
15 Endowed Scholarships .10
16 Nick Martens 1.00
17 David Moss 1.00
18 Eric Nystrom 3.00
19 Reilly Olson 1.00
20 Mel Pearson ACO .10
21 Noah Ruden 1.00
22 Jeff Tambellini 3.00
23 Milan Gajic 1.00
24 Charlie Henderson 1.00
25 Billy Powers 1.00

2004 Michigan Wolverines TK Legacy

This multi-sport series features sporting greats from the University of Michigan. Only those cards depicting hockey players are included in this listing, which includes base cards and autographs.

COMPLETE HOCKEY SET (6) 3.00
1950A John Matchefts AU 10.00
1950B Willard Ikola AU 10.00
1966C Red Berenson 15.00
1996A Marty Turco AU 25.00
1996B Brendan Morrison 20.00
H1 Red Berenson .75
H2 John Matchefts .50
H3 Willard Ikola .50
H4 Brendan Morrison 1.00
H5 Marty Turco 1.50
H6 Dave Debol .50
HL1 Marty Turco 50.00
Red Berenson AU
HL9 Willard Ikola 20.00
John Matchefts AU
VH1 John Matchefts AU 10.00
VH2 Willard Ikola AU 10.00
VH3 Marty Turco AU 25.00
VH4 Red Berenson AU 15.00
VH5 Brendan Morrison AU 20.00
VH6 Dave Debol AU 10.00

1981-82 Milwaukee Admirals

This 15-card standard-size set was produced by TCMA and features the members of the Milwaukee Admirals. The cards are made of thick card stock. On the front, a black-and-white player photo with thin black borders is framed in bright yellow. The team name appears in the yellow border above the photo, while the player's name, jersey number, and position appear below. The horizontal backs carry biography and statistics.

COMPLETE SET (15) 6.00 15.00
1 Pat Rabbitt .40 1.00
2 Real Paiement .40 1.00
3 Fred Berry .40 1.00
4 Blaine Peerless .40 1.00
5 John Flesch .40 1.00
6 Yves Preston .40 1.00
7 Bruce McKay .40 1.00
8 Dale Yakiwchuk .40 1.00
9 Lorne Bokshowan .40 1.00
10 Danny Lecours .40 1.00
11 Sheldon Currie .40 1.00
12 Doug Robb .40 1.00
13 Rob Polman Tuin .60 1.50
14 Bob Collyard .40 1.00
15 Tim Ringler TR .20 .50

1994-95 Milwaukee Admirals

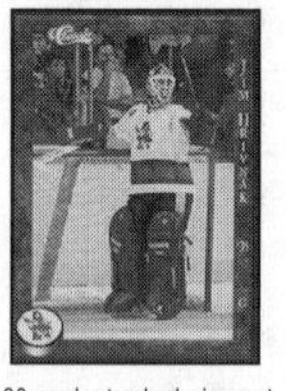

This 28-card standard-size set was manufactured and distributed by Jessen Associates, Inc. for Classic. The fronts display color action player photos with a dark blue marbleized inner border and a black outer border. The player's name, jersey number, and position appear in the teal border on the right edge. The cards are unnumbered and checklisted below in alphabetical order.

COMPLETE SET (28) 3.20 8.00
1 Doug Agnew TR .04 .10
2 Peter Bakovic ACO .04 .10
3 Matt Block .10 .25
4 Gino Cavallini .16 .40
5 Sylvain Couturier .16 .40
6 Brian Dobbin .16 .40
7 Shawn Evans .10 .25
8 Fabulous Fritz .04 .10
9 Chris Govedaris .20 .50
10 Jim Hrivnak .30 .75
11 Tony Hrkac .20 .50
12 Fabian Joseph .20 .50
13 Mark Laforest .20 .50
14 Don MacAdam ACO .04 .10
15 Dave Mackey .10 .25
16 Pat MacLeod .16 .40
17 Dave Marcinyshyn .10 .25
18 Bob Mason .30 .75
19 Mike McNeill .20 .50
20 Kent Paynter .10 .25
21 Ken Sabourin .10 .25
22 Trevor Sim .10 .25
23 Martin Simard .10 .25
24 Mike Tomlak .10 .25
25 Steve Tuttle .10 .25
26 Randy Velischek .16 .40
27 Brad Werenka .16 .40
28 Phil Wittliff CO .04 .10

1995-96 Milwaukee Admirals

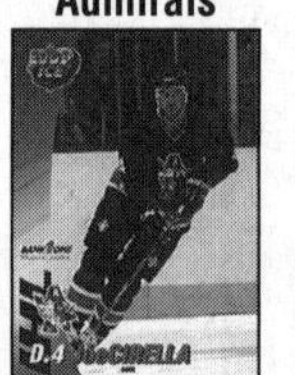

This high-quality 25-card set was produced for the team by Collector's Edge and sponsored by Bank One. The card fronts feature color action photography, along with the logos of the club, the bank and the manufacturer. The last card in the set, entitled Dream Ride, features on the back the lyrics to the song of the same name, which apparently is near and dear to the hearts of Admirals fans everywhere. This marks what could be the first ever appropriation of song lyrics for the edification of card collectors. As they cards are unnumbered, they are listed below alphabetically.

COMPLETE SET (25) 4.00 10.00
1 Shawn Anderson .20 .50
2 Jergus Baca .20 .50
3 Gino Cavallini .30 .75
4 Joe Cirella .20 .50
5 Sylvain Couturier .20 .50
6 Tom Draper .30 .75
7 Robert Guillet .20 .50
8 Tony Hrkac .30 .75
9 Fabian Joseph .20 .50
10 Mark LaForest .30 .75
11 Dave MacIsaac .20 .50
12 Mike McNeill .20 .50
13 Dave Mackey .20 .50
14 Kent Paynter .20 .50
15 Ken Sabourin .20 .50

16 Andrew Shier .20 .50
17 Tom Tilley .20 .50
18 Mike Tomlak .20 .50
19 Steve Tuttle .20 .50
20 Terry Yake .30 .75
21 Phil Wittliff CO .04 .10
22 Peter Bakovic ACO .04 .10
23 Rob Irsch ACO .04 .10
24 Doug Agnew TR .04 .10
25 Dream Ride .04 .10

1995-96 Milwaukee Admirals Postcards

Postcard series measures 3 1/2" x 5 1/2" and was sponsored by Sports Medicine Institute.

COMPLETE SET (21) 10.00 25.00
1 Dave MacIsaac .40 1.00
2 Kent Paynter .40 1.00
3 Garry Gulash .40 1.00
4 Jergus Baca .40 1.00
5 Fabian Joseph .40 1.00
6 Sylvain Couturier .40 1.00
7 Mike McNeill .40 1.00
8 Terry Yake .40 1.00
9 David Mackey .40 1.00
10 Bruce Ramsay .40 1.00
11 Tony Hrkac .75 2.00
12 Robert Guillet .40 1.00
13 Shawn Anderson .40 1.00
14 Andrew Shier .40 1.00
15 Steve Tuttle .40 1.00
16 Mike Tomlak .40 1.00
17 Tom Draper .75 2.00
18 Mark Laforest .75 2.00
19 Mikhail Kravets .40 1.00
20 Gino Cavallini .75 2.00
21 Ken Sabourin .40 1.00

1996-97 Milwaukee Admirals

This odd-sized (2 1/2" X 4") 27-card set features the Milwaukee Admirals of the IHL. The cards were produced by the club and sponsored by Bank One as a promotional item. The cards feature action photography on the front surrounded by a thin white border. The logos of Bank One and the PHPA are in the top corners, while the player's name, position and uniform number are listed along the bottom. The cards are unnumbered, and are listed in alphabetical order.

COMPLETE SET (27) 4.00 10.00
1 Doug Agnew TR .04 .10
2 Peter Bakovic ACO .04 .10
3 Sylvain Couturier .16 .40
4 Larry DePalma .16 .40
5 Peter Douris .16 .40
6 Denny Felsner .16 .40
7 Eric Fenton .16 .40
8 Shannon Finn .16 .40
9 Tony Hrkac .30 .75
10 Fabian Joseph ACO .16 .40
11 Jacques Joubert .16 .40
12 Rick Knickle .30 .75
13 Brad Layzell .16 .40
14 Danny Lorenz .30 .75
15 Chris Luongo .16 .40
16 Dave Mackey .16 .40
17 Mike McNeill .16 .40
18 Michel Mongeau .30 .75
19 Kent Paynter .16 .40
20 Christian Proulx .16 .40
21 Patrice Robitaille .16 .40
22 Ken Sabourin .16 .40
23 Steve Strunk .16 .40
24 Tom Tilley .16 .40
25 Mike Tomlak .16 .40
26 Steve Tuttle .16 .40
27 Phil Wittliff CO .04 .10

1997-98 Milwaukee Admirals

Little is known about this set beyond the confirmed checklist. Additional information can be forwarded to hockeymag@beckett.com.

COMPLETE SET (25) 3.60 9.00
1 Jason Cipolla .16 .40
2 Kerry Clark .16 .40
3 Jarrett Deuling .16 .40
4 Kelly Fairchild .20 .50
5 Eric Fenton .16 .40
6 Shannon Finn .16 .40
7 Martin Gendron .30 .75
8 Mike Harder .16 .40
9 Marc Hussey .16 .40
10 Danny Lorenz .30 .75
11 Dave MacIntyre .16 .40
12 Mike McNeill .16 .40
13 Don McSween .16 .40
14 Jeff Nelson .16 .40
15 Brent Peterson .16 .40
16 Christian Proulx .16 .40
17 Ken Sabourin .16 .40
18 Mike Tomlak .16 .40
19 Mike Torchia .30 .75
20 Steve Tuttle .16 .40
21 Mark Visheau .16 .40
22 Al Sims HCO .04 .10
23 Peter Bakovic ACO .04 .10
24 Fabian Joseph ACO .04 .10
25 Doug Agnew TR .04 .10

1998-99 Milwaukee Admirals

Little is known about this set beyond the confirmed checklist. Additional information can be forwarded to hockeymag@beckett.com.

COMPLETE SET (24) 4.00 10.00
1 Al Sims CO .04 .10
2 Jeff Daniels .16 .40
3 Sergei Klimentiev .16 .40
4 Chris Mason .20 .50
5 Eric Fenton .16 .40
6 Shannon Finn .16 .40
7 Jason Cipolla .16 .40
8 Jeff Kealty .16 .40
9 Bobby Russell .16 .40
10 David Gosselin .30 .75
11 Richard Lintner .30 .75
12 Jeff Nelson .20 .50
13 Kay Whitmore .24 .60
14 Claude Noel ACO .04 .10
15 Karlis Skrastins .20 .50
16 Mark Mowers .20 .50
17 Craig Darby .20 .50
18 Roscoe MASCOT .04 .10
19 Doug Friedman .16 .40
20 Matt Henderson .16 .40
21 Marc Moro .30 .75
22 Petr Sykora .30 .75
23 Jeff Staples .16 .40
24 Marian Cisar .40 1.00

1998-99 Milwaukee Admirals Postcards

This set features the Admirals of the IHL. These postcard-sized issues were given out at autograph sessions and other promotional ventures. Anyone knowing of additional cards in the set are encouraged to write hockeymag@beckett.com.

COMPLETE SET (11)
1 Doug Friedman .20 .50
2 Brad Smyth .20 .50
3 Jeff Staples .20 .50
4 Matt Henderson .20 .50
5 Petr Sykora .40 .50
6 Jeff Kealty .20 .50
7 Jason Cipolla .20 .50
8 Richard Lintner .40 1.00
9 Kimmo Timonen .40 1.00
10 Vitali Yachmenev .30 .75
11 Tomas Vokoun .80 3.00

1999-00 Milwaukee Admirals Keebler

This set was issued in sheet form as a promotional giveaway.

COMPLETE SET (20)
1 Corey Hirsch
2 Marian Cisar
3 Chris Mason
4 Jayme Filipowicz
5 Bubba Berenzweig
6 Mark Mowers
7 Brent Peterson
8 Phil Crowe
9 Dan Keczmer
10 Jason Dawe
11 Eric Fenton
12 Matt Eldred
13 Alexandre Boikov
14 Marc Moro
15 Paul Healey
16 Daniel Riva
17 Ryan Tobler
18 David Gosselin
19 Al Sims CO
20 Claude Noel ACO

2000-01 Milwaukee Admirals Keebler

This 20-card set features players from the 2000-01 Milwaukee Admirals of the IHL. The cards were issued in perforated sheets of five which consisted of 4 player cards and one coupon for Keebler products. The card fronts carry an action photo with a Keebler logo in the top left corner, the backs carry biographical information, career stats and accomplishments. The cards are not numbered and are listed below in alphabetical order.

COMMON CARD (20) 8.00 20.00
1 Jonas Andersson .60 1.50
2 Denis Arkhipov .60 2.00
3 Bubba Berenzweig .30 .75
4 Greg Classen .30 1.00
5 Mark Eaton .30 .75
6 Jayme Filipowicz .30 .75
7 Sean Haggerty .30 .75
8 Jan Lasak .40 2.00
9 Chris Mason .40 1.00
10 Marc Moro .40 1.00
11 Mark Mowers .30 1.00
12 John Namestnikov .30 .75
13 Ville Peltonen .40 1.00
14 Daniel Riva .30 .75
15 Petr Sachl .30 .75
16 Pavel Skrbek .30 1.00
17 Jeremy Stevenson .30 1.00
18 Ryan Tobler .30 .75
19 Alexei Vasiliev .30 .75
20 Mike Watt .30 .75

2000-01 Milwaukee Admirals Postcards

This set features the Admirals of the IHL. These postcard-like issues were handed out a various games in conjunction with player autograph sessions. They are not numbered and are listed below in alphabetical order.

COMPLETE SET (18) 6.00 15.00
1 Jonas Andersson .60 1.50
2 Andrew Berenzweig .30 .75
3 Alexandre Boikov .30 .75
4 Jayme Filipowicz .30 .75
5 David Gosselin .60 1.50
6 Jason Goulet .30 .75
7 Sean Haggerty .30 .75
8 Jan Lasak .80 2.00
9 Chris Mason .40 1.00
10 Mark Mowers .40 1.00
11 Ville Peltonen .40 1.00
12 Dan Riva .30 .75
13 Petr Sachl .30 .75
14 Pavel Skrbek .40 1.00
15 Ryan Tobler .30 .75
16 Alexei Vasiliev .30 .75
17 Mike Watt .30 .75
18 Alex Westlund .30 .75

2001-02 Milwaukee Admirals

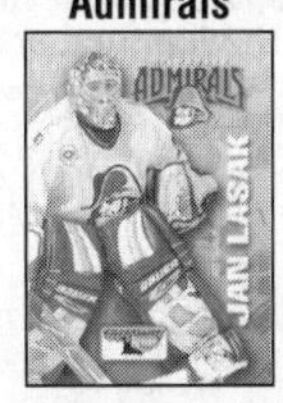

This set features the Admirals of the AHL. The set was issued as a promotional giveaway in the form of five six-card strips. Each strip contains five player cards and one coupon for a product of Keebler, the sponsor of the set. The cards are unnumbered, so they are listed in alphabetical order.

COMPLETE SET (25) 8.00 20.00
1 Erik Anderson .30 .75
2 Jonas Andersson .30 .75
3 Martin Bartek .30 .75
4 Bubba Berenzweig .30 .75
5 Alexandre Boikov .30 .75
6 Frederic Bouchard .30 .75
7 Marian Cisar .40 1.00
8 Kevin Dean .30 .75
9 Steve Dubinsky .30 .75
10 David Gosselin .40 1.00
11 Jason Goulet .30 .75
12 Chris Mason .40 1.00
13 Brett Hauer .30 .75
14 Timo Helbling .30 .75
15 Jan Lasak .80 2.00
16 Jay Legault .30 .75
17 Bryan Lundbohm .30 .75
18 Marc Moro .60 1.50
19 Mark Mowers .40 1.00
20 Konstantin Panov .30 .75
21 Nathan Perrott .60 1.50
22 Petr Sachl .30 .75
23 Yves Sarault .30 .75
24 Robert Schnabel .30 .75
25 Jeremy Stevenson .30 .75

2001-02 Milwaukee Admirals Postcards

This set features the Admirals of the AHL. These cards were given out individually at player autograph sessions, making set building difficult. This checklist is not believed to be complete. If you have information on other singles, please forward it to hockeymag@beckett.com..

COMPLETE SET (11) 2.00 5.00
1 Robert Schnabel .20 .50
2 Bryan Lundbohm .20 .50
3 Yves Sarault .20 .50
4 Timo Helbling .20 .50
5 Martin Bartek .20 .50
6 Kevin Dean .20 .50
7 David Gosselin .30 .75
8 Marc Moro .40 1.00
9 Jason Goulet .20 .50
10 Jonas Andersson .20 .50
11 Roscoe MASCOT .10 .25

2002-03 Milwaukee Admirals

These cards were issued as promotional giveaways in five-card strips over the course of five home games. They were sponsored by Keebler.

COMPLETE SET (25) 35.00
1 Tomas Kloucek 3.00
2 Chris Madden 3.00
3 Wyatt Smith 1.00
4 Brian Finley 3.00
5 Dan Hamhuis 3.00
6 Andrew Hutchinson 2.00
7 Robert Schnabel 1.00
8 Bob Wren 1.00
9 Reid Simpson 1.00
10 Jan Lasak 3.00
11 Cameron Mann 2.00
12 Domenic Pittis 2.00
13 Martin Erat 2.00
14 Jonas Andersson 1.00
15 Greg Koehler 1.00
16 Bubba Berenzweig 1.00
17 Konstantin Panov 1.00
18 Peter Smrek 1.00
19 Vernon Fiddler 1.00
20 Jason Beckett 1.00
21 Greg Classen 1.00
22 Timo Helbling 1.00
23 Darren Haydar 2.00
24 Pascal Trepanier 1.00
25 Bryan Lundbohm 1.00

2002-03 Milwaukee Admirals Postcards

These postcards were issued as singles at player signing sessions. It's likely the checklist is incomplete. Please forward any additional information to hockeymag@beckett.com

COMPLETE SET (15) 15.00
1 Jonas Andersson .75
2 Jason Beckett .75
3 Bubba Berenzweig .75
4 Greg Classen .75
5 Martin Erat 1.50
6 Vern Fiddler .75
7 Dan Hamhuis 2.00
8 Darren Haydar 1.00
9 Tomas Kloucek 2.00
10 Jan Lasak 2.00
11 Chris Madden 2.00
12 Cameron Mann 1.00
13 Konstantin Panov .50
14 Robert Schnabel .50
15 Pascal Trepanier .50

2003-04 Milwaukee Admirals

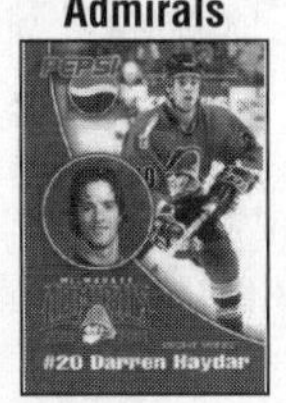

COMPLETE SET (30) 15.00
1 Kirill Safronov .50
2 Jay Henderson .50
3 Brian Finley .75
4 Timo Helbling .50
5 Cheerleaders .10
6 Darren Haydar .75
7 Curtis Murphy .50
8 Tony Hrkac .50
9 Andrew Hutchinson .75
10 Mascot .10
11 Brad Tiley .50
12 Timofei Shishkanov .50
13 Vernon Fiddler .50
14 Scott Upshall 2.00
15 Claude Noel CO .10
16 Raitis Ivanans .50
17 Mathieu Darche .50
18 Wade Flaherty .75
19 Brandon Segal .50
20 Arena .01
21 Greg Zanon .50
22 Simon Gamache 1.00
23 Greg Classen .50
24 Wyatt Smith .50
25 Team Photo .25
26 Ray Schultz .50
27 Mike Farrell .50
28 Bryan Lundbohm .50
29 Libor Pivko .50
30 Todd Richards ACO .10

2003-04 Milwaukee Admirals Postcards

These oversized cards were issued at team events in singles form.

COMPLETE SET (23) 20.00
1 Greg Classen .75
2 Mathieu Darche .75
3 Mike Farrell .75
4 Vernon Fiddler .75
5 Brian Finley 1.00
6 Wade Flaherty 1.00
7 Simon Gamache 1.50
8 Darren Haydar 1.00
9 Timo Helbling .75
10 Jay Henderson .75
11 Tony Hrkac .75
12 Andrew Hutchinson 1.00
13 Raitis Ivanans .75
14 Bryan Lundbohm .75
15 Curtis Murphy .75
16 Libor Pivko .75
17 Kirill Safronov .75
18 Ray Schultz .75
19 Timofei Shishkanov .75
20 Wyatt Smith .75
21 Brad Tiley .75
22 Scott Upshall 2.50
23 Greg Zanon .75

2004-05 Milwaukee Admirals

These cards were issued as promotional giveaways on various nights throughout the season in five-card strips.

COMPLETE SET (30) 50.00
1 Brian Finley 3.00
2 Jeremy Yablonski 1.00
3 Brad Tiley 1.00
4 Cam Severson 2.00
5 Roscoe MASCOT .10
6 Seamus Kotyk 2.00
7 Paul Brown 1.00
8 Burke Henry 1.00
9 Libor Pivko 1.00
10 Brendan Yarema 1.00
11 Jerred Smithson 1.00
12 Bryan Lundbohm 2.00
13 Ryan Suter 3.00
14 Brandon Segal 1.00
15 Calder Cup Winners 1.00
16 Jordin Tootoo 10.00
17 Scottie Upshall 3.00
18 Dan Hamhuis 2.00
19 Andrew Hutchinson 2.00
20 Admirals Ice Angels 1.00
21 Greg Zanon 1.00
22 Simon Gamache 2.00
23 Kevin Klein 1.00
24 Wyatt Smith 1.00
25 Todd Richards 1.00
26 Darren Haydar 1.00
27 Timofei Shishkanov 1.00
28 Vernon Fiddler 1.00
29 Tony Hrkac 1.00
30 Claude Noel 1.00

2005-06 Milwaukee Admirals Choice

COMPLETE SET (19) 10.00
1 Kris Beech .20 .50
2 Sheldon Brookbank .20 .50
3 Paul Brown .20 .50
4 Greg Classen .20 .50
5 Vern Fiddler .20 .50
6 Brian Finley .30 .75
7 Darren Haydar .20 .50
8 Kevin Klein .20 .50
9 Libor Pivko .20 .50
10 T.J. Reynolds .20 .50
11 Pekka Rinne .40 1.00
12 Marco Rosa .20 .50
13 Brandon Segal .20 .50
14 Timofei Shishkanov .20 .50
15 Jordin Tootoo .75 2.00
16 Shea Weber .20 .50
17 Jeremy Yablonski .20 .50
18 Greg Zanon .20 .50
19 Claude Noel HC .02 .10

2005-06 Milwaukee Admirals Pepsi

COMPLETE SET (26) 25.00
1 Kris Beech .40 1.00
2 Rick Berry .40 1.00
3 Sheldon Brookbank .40 1.00
4 Paul Brown .40 1.00
5 Greg Classen .40 1.00
6 Chris Durno .40 1.00
7 Brian Finley .60 1.50
8 Simon Gamache .40 1.00
9 Darren Haydar .40 1.00
10 Kevin Klein .40 1.00
11 Nathan Lutz .40 1.00
12 Scott May .40 1.00
13 Rich Peverley .40 1.00
14 Libor Pivko .40 1.00
15 T.J. Reynolds .40 1.00
16 Pekka Rinne .75 2.00
17 Brandon Segal .40 1.00
18 Zach Stortini .40 1.00
19 Jordin Tootoo 1.25 3.00
20 Scottie Upshall .75 2.00
21 Shea Weber .40 1.00
22 Jeremy Yablonski .40 1.00
23 Greg Zanon .40 1.00
24 Claude Noel HC .02 .10
25 Todd Richards AC .02 .10
26 Roscoe MASCOT .02 .10

2006-07 Milwaukee Admirals

COMPLETE SET (24) 10.00 18.00
1 Ramzi Abid .30 .75
2 Sheldon Brookbank .40 1.00
3 Chris Durno .30 .75
4 Karl GoehringÂ .40 1.00
5 Jason Guerriero .30 .75
6 Alex Henry .30 .75
7 Bracken Kearns .30 .75
8 Kevin Klein .30 .75
9 Ville Koistinen .30 .75
10 John Laliberte .30 .75
11 Patrick Leahy .30 .75
12 Cal O'Reilly .30 .75
13 Rich Peverley .30 .75
14 T.J. Reynolds .30 .75
15 Pekka RinneÂ .40 1.00
16 Brandon Segal .30 .75
17 Kim Staal .30 .75
18 Victor Uchevatov .30 .75
19 John Vigilante .30 .75
20 Kelsey Wilson .60 1.50
21 Nolan Yonkman .30 .75
22 Claude NoelÂ CO .10 .25
23 Lane LambertÂ ACO .10 .25
24 Roscoe MASCOT .02 .10

1984-85 Minnesota-Duluth Bulldogs

This set features the Bulldogs of the NCAA and was confirmed to exist in 2002 by Ralph Slate of hockeydb.com reknown. The set was produced by Tim and Larry's Sportscards and features the first card of Brett Hull. It is believed that as few as 250 sets were produced.

COMPLETE SET (33) 100.00
1 Ben Duffey .40 1.00
2 Brett Hull 30.00 75.00
3 Danny May .40 1.00
4 Dave Morrow .40 1.00
5 Joe Delisle .40 1.00
6 Brian Nelson .40 1.00
7 Jon Downing .40 1.00
8 Brian Nelson .40 1.00
9 Sean Toomey .40 1.00
10 Brian Durand .40 1.00
11 Jim Plankers .40 1.00
12 Mark Odnokon .40 1.00
13 Jim Sprenger .40 1.00
14 Tom Lorentz .40 1.00
15 Darin Illikainen .40 1.00
16 Rick Kosti .40 1.00
17 Norm Maciver .80 2.00
18 Guy Gosselin .40 1.00
19 Matt Christensen .40 1.00
20 Jim Johnson .80 2.00
21 Mark Baron .40 1.00
22 Bill Watson .40 1.00
23 Bruce Fishback .40 1.00
24 Dave Cowan .40 1.00
25 Mike Cortes .40 1.00
26 Jim Toninato .40 1.00
27 Skeeter Moore .40 1.00
28 Mike DeAngelis .40 1.00
29 Tom Herzig .40 1.00
30 Mike Sertich CO .10 .25
31 Bulldog Cheerleaders .40 1.00
32 Bulldogs Assistants .10 .25
33 Team Photo .10 .25

1985-86 Minnesota-Duluth Bulldogs

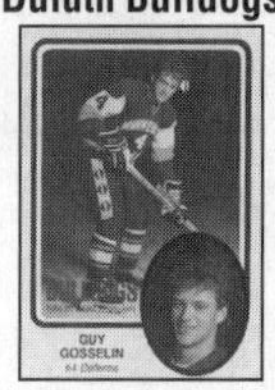

This 36-card standard-size set features color action player photos with rounded corners and black borders against a white card face. An oval inset at the lower right shows a head shot. The player's name is printed in black at the bottom. The cards are numbered on the back. It has been reported that this set may have been reprinted to take advantage of the popularity of Brett Hull.

COMPLETE SET (36) 12.00 30.00
1 Skeeter Moore .30 .75
2 Terry Shold .20 .50
3 Mike DeAngelis .20 .50
4 Rob Pallin .20 .50
5 Norm Maciver .30 .75
6 Wayne Smith .20 .50
7 Dave Cowan .20 .50
8 Darin Illikainen .20 .50
9 Rick Hayko .20 .50
10 Guy Gosselin .30 .75
11 Paul Roff .20 .50
12 Jim Toninato .20 .50
13 Tom Hanson .20 .50
14 Mike Cortes .20 .50
15 Matt Christensen .20 .50
16 Bruce Fishback .20 .50
17 Mark Odnokon .20 .50
18 Brian Johnson .20 .50
19 Bob Alexander .20 .50
20 Tom Lorentz .20 .50
21 Roman Sindelar .20 .50
22 Jim Sprenger .20 .50
23 Dan Tousignant .20 .50
24 Sean Toomey .20 .50
25 Brian Durand .20 .50
26 John Hyduke .20 .50
27 Brian Nelson .20 .50
28 Brett Hull 8.00 20.00
29 Joe DeLisle .20 .50
30 Pat Janostin .20 .50
31 Ben Duffy .20 .50
32 Sean Krakiwsky .20 .50
33 Mike Sertich .20 .50
34 Coaching Staff .10 .25
Jim Knapp ACO
Glenn Kulyk ACO
Tim McDonald ACO
Mike Valesano ACO
Rick Menz EQUIP
Dale Hoganson EQUIP
Betty Fleissner TR
35 Cheerleaders .40 1.00
36 Jay Jackson (Mascot) .10 .25
The Maroon Loon

1993-94 Minnesota-Duluth Bulldogs

These 30 standard-size cards feature on their fronts white-bordered color player action shots. The player's name and position, along with the Minnesota Bulldog logo, appear within the brown stripe across the bottom of the photo. The back carries the player's name, position, biography, and statistics on the left. His career highlights appear on the right. The set was produced by Collect-A-Sport and features a card of Chris Marinucci, 1993-94 Hobey Baker winner. The cards are unnumbered and checklisted below in alphabetical order.

COMPLETE SET (30) 4.00 10.00
1 Rod Aldoff .16 .40
2 Niklas Axelson .16 .40
3 David Buck .16 .40
4 Jerome Butler .16 .40
5 Brian Caruso .20 .50
6 Matt Christian .20 .50
Chet Culic
7 Marc Christian .16 .40
8 Joe Ciccarello .16 .40
9 Kyle Erickson .16 .40
Adam Roy
10 Brad Federenko .20 .50
11 Rusty Fitzgerald .20 .50
12 Jason Garatti .16 .40
13 Greg Hanson .20 .50
14 Don Jablonic .16 .40
15 Kraig Karakas .16 .40
16 Brett Larson .20 .50
17 Taras Lendzyk .16 .40
18 Derek Locker .16 .40
19 Chris Marinucci .20 .50
20 Todd Mickolajak .20 .50
Chris Snell
21 Rod Miller .16 .40
22 Rick Mrozik .20 .50
23 Aaron Novak .16 .40
24 Corey Osmak .16 .40
25 Sergei Petrov .16 .40
26 Jeff Romfo .16 .40
27 Mike Sertich CO .04 .10
28 Chris Sittlow .16 .40
29 Joe Tamminen .16 .40
30 Title Card .10 .25
Roster

1993-94 Minnesota-Duluth Commemorative

These four standard-size cards feature black-and-white fronts with color photos on the backs. The set was produced by Collect-A-Sport to commemorate the 1992-93 WCHA champs.

COMPLETE SET (4) 1.60 4.00
1 Chris Marinucci .40 1.00
2 Derek Plante .80 2.00
3 Brett Hauer .40 1.00
4 Jon Rohloff .40 1.00

2004-05 Minnesota-Duluth Bulldogs

The cards came in three packs of seven cards and two packs of six cards and were handed out over five different home games.

COMPLETE SET (33) 30.00
1 Nick Anderson 1.00
2 Tyler Brosz 1.00
3 T. J. Caig 1.00
4 Dan Carlson 1.00
5 Mike Curry 1.00
6 Steve Czech 1.00
7 Travis Gawryletz 1.00
8 Ryan Garis 1.00
9 Tim Hambly 1.00
10 Brett Hammond 1.00
11 Josh Johnson 1.50
12 Blair Lefebvre 1.00
13 Jeff McFarland 1.00
14 Bryan McGregor 1.00
15 Matt McKnight 1.50
16 Josh Miskovich 1.00
17 Marco Peluso 1.00
18 Neil Petruic 1.00
19 Isaac Reichmuth 1.50
20 Jay Rosehill 1.00
21 Evan Schwabe 1.50
22 Todd Smith 1.00
23 Tim Stapleton 1.00
24 Luke Stauffacher 1.00
25 Ryan Swanson 1.00
26 Justin Williams 1.00
27 Lee Davidson ACO#}Scott Sandelin CO#}Steve Rohlik ACO .10
28 Tom Kurvers' 1.00
29 Junior Lessard 2.00
30 Chris Marinucci 2.00
31 Bill Watson 1.00
32 Mascots .10
33 Sponsor .01

1991-92 Minnesota Golden Gophers

Sponsored by MCI, this 26-card standard-size set features the 1991-92 Minnesota Golden Gophers. On a maroon background, the horizontal and vertical fronts have color action player photos along with the player's name and the name of the high school he attended. The white backs carry the player's name, number, biography, and profile. The cards are unnumbered and checklisted below in alphabetical order.

COMPLETE SET (26) 6.00 15.00
1 Scott Bell .20 .50
2 Tony Bianchi .20 .50
3 John Brill .20 .50
4 Jeff Callinan .20 .50
5 Joe Dziedzic .30 .75
6 Sean Fabian .20 .50
7 Jed Fiebelkorn .20 .50
8 Nick Gerebi .20 .50
9 Darby Hendrickson .30 .75
10 Craig Johnson .30 .75
11 Trent Klatt .40 1.00
12 Cory Laylin .20 .50
13 Steve Magnusson .30 .75

14 Chris McAlpine .30 .75
15 Justin McHugh .20 .50
16 Eric Means .20 .50
17 Mike Muller .20 .50
18 Tom Newman .20 .50
19 Jeff Nielsen .20 .50
20 John O'Connell .20 .50
21 Larry Olimb .20 .50
22 Travis Richards .20 .50
23 Brandon Steege .20 .50
24 Jeff Stolp .20 .50
25 Todd Westlund .20 .50
26 Doug Zmolek .30 .75

1992-93 Minnesota Golden Gophers

Featuring the 1992-93 Minnesota Golden Gophers hockey team (WCHA), this 25-card set measures the standard-size. The fronts feature full-bleed, posed, color player photos. A gray bar at the top (or right edge) displays the school name, while the player's name is printed in maroon lettering in a yellow bar at the bottom. The cards are unnumbered and checklisted below in alphabetical order.

COMPLETE SET (25) 4.00 10.00
1 Scott Bell .16 .40
2 Jesse Bertogliat .40 1.00
Brian Bonin
3 Tony Bianchi .16 .40
4 John Brill .16 .40
5 Jeff Callinan .16 .40
6 Bobby Dustin .16 .40
Dave Larson
7 Joe Dziedzic .20 .50
8 Jed Fiebelkorn .16 .40
9 Darby Hendrickson .20 .50
10 Craig Johnson .16 .40
11 Steve Magnusson .20 .50
12 Chris McAlpine .20 .50
13 Justin McHugh .16 .40
14 Eric Means .16 .40
15 Jeff Moen .16 .40
16 Tom Newman .16 .40
17 Jeff Nielsen .20 .50
18 Travis Richards .16 .40
19 Brandon Steege .16 .40
20 Matt Stelljes .16 .40
Ryan Alstead
21 Dan Trebil .04 .10
Greg Zwakman
22 Charlie Wasley .16 .40
Mike McAlpine
23 Todd Westlund .16 .40
24 Dan Woog .10 .25
Jim Hillman
25 Doug Woog CO .10 .25

1993-94 Minnesota Golden Gophers

This set features the Golden Gophers of the NCAA. The cards were printed by the team and issued as a promotional giveaway. On a maroon background, the fronts feature posed, color action player photos and portraits with a thin yellow border. The player's name is printed in yellow letters with a maroon outline on the bottom of the photo. The cards are unnumbered and checklisted below in alphabetical order.

COMPLETE SET (30) 6.00 100.00
1 Brett Abrahamson .20 3.50
2 Jesse Bertogliat .20 3.50
3 Tony Bianchi .20 3.50
4 Brian Bonin .30 5.00
5 Andy Brink .20 3.50
6 Jeff Callinan .20 3.50
7 Nick Checco .20 3.50
8 Bobby Dustin .20 3.50
9 Joe Dziedzic .30 5.00
10 Jed Fiebelkorn .20 3.50
11 Brent Godbout .20 3.50
12 Dan Hendrickson .20 3.50
13 Jim Hillman .20 3.50
14 John Hillman .20 3.50
15 Brian LaFleur .20 3.50
16 Dave Larson .20 3.50
17 Steve Magnusson .20 3.50
18 Chris McAlpine .30 5.00
19 Mike McAlpine .20 3.50
20 Justin McHugh .20 3.50
21 Eric Means .20 3.50
22 Jeff Moen .20 3.50
23 Jeff Nielsen .30 5.00
24 Brandon Steege .20 3.50
25 Dan Trebil .20 3.50
26 Charlie Wasley .20 3.50
27 Dan Woog ACO .04 1.00
28 Doug Woog CO .20 2.00
29 Greg Zwakman .20 3.50
30 Title Card .04 .10

1994-95 Minnesota Golden Gophers

This set features the Golden Gophers of the NCAA. The cards were sponsored by SuperAmerica and EverReady and issued as a promotional giveaway. On a white card face with team color-coded stripes in the background, the fronts display action shots or water color portraits by artist M.L. Sahlberg. The cards are unnumbered and checklisted below in alphabetical order.

COMPLETE SET (31) 10.00 25.00
1 Will Anderson .30 .75
2 Scott Bell .30 .75
3 Jesse Bertogliat .30 .75
4 Brian Bonin .40 1.00
5 Andy Brink .30 .75
6 Aaron Broten .80 2.00
Neal Broten
Paul Broten
7 Jeff Callinan .30 .75
8 Nick Checco .30 .75
9 Mike Crowley .80 2.00
10 Steve DeBus .30 .75
11 Bobby Dustin .30 .75
12 Jed Fiebelkorn .30 .75
13 Brent Godbout .30 .75
14 Jason Godbout .30 .75
15 Casey Hankinson .30 .75
16 Dan Hendrickson .30 .75
17 Ryan Kraft .30 .75
18 Brian LaFleur .30 .75
19 Dave Larson .30 .75
20 Justin McHugh .30 .75
21 Jeff Moen .30 .75
22 Jay Moser .30 .75
23 Lou Nanne .40 1.00
24 Joe Pankratz .30 .75
25 Jason Seils .30 .75
26 Brandon Steege .30 .75
27 Dan Trebil .40 1.00
28 Charlie Wasley .30 .75
29 Dan Woog .10 .25
30 Doug Woog CO .10 .25
31 Greg Zwakman .30 .75

1995-96 Minnesota Golden Gophers

This set was issued by the team as a promotional giveaway. The cards are unnumbered so the set is checklisted in alphabetical order.

COMPLETE SET (30) 100.00 175.00
1 Checklist .50 1.00
2 Doug Woog CO 1.00 2.00
3 Brett Abrahamson 3.00 6.00
4 Mike Anderson 3.00 6.00
5 Reggie Berg 3.00 6.00
6 Jesse Bertogliat 3.00 6.00
7 Brian Bonin 5.00 10.00
8 Andy Brink 3.00 6.00
9 Nick Checco 3.00 6.00
10 Nick Crowley 3.00 6.00
11 Steve Debus 3.00 6.00
12 Bobby Dustin 3.00 6.00
13 Jason Godbout 3.00 6.00
14 Casey Hankinson 3.00 6.00
15 Dan Hendrickson 3.00 6.00
16 Clint Johnson 3.00 6.00
17 Bill Kohn 3.00 6.00
18 Ryan Kraft 3.00 6.00
19 Brian LaFleur 3.00 6.00
20 Dave Larson 3.00 6.00
21 Jeff Moen 3.00 6.00
22 Jay Moser 3.00 6.00
23 Tom Nevers 3.00 6.00
24 Erik Rasmussen 5.00 10.00
25 Jason Seils 3.00 6.00
26 Wyatt Smith 3.00 6.00
27 Dan Trebil 3.00 6.00
28 Charlie Wasley 3.00 6.00
29 Dan Woog ACO 1.00 2.00
30 Greg Zwakman 3.00 6.00

1996-97 Minnesota Golden Gophers

Little is known about this set beyond the confirmed checklist and the fact that it was issued as a promotional giveaway. Any additional information can be forwarded to hockeymag@beckett.com.

COMPLETE SET (27) 25.00 50.00
1 Checklist .02 .10
2 Doug Woog CO .02 .10
3 Brett Abrahamson .60 1.50
4 Mike Anderson .60 1.50
5 Reggie Berg 1.25 3.00
6 Nick Checco 1.25 3.00
7 Ben Clymer 1.25 3.00
8 Mike Crowley 1.25 3.00
9 Eric Day .60 1.50
10 Steve DeBus .60 1.50
11 Brent Godbout .60 1.50
12 Jason Godbout .60 1.50
13 Casey Hankinson 1.25 3.00
14 Dan Hendrickson 1.25 3.00
15 Bill Kohn .60 1.50
16 Ryan Kraft 1.25 3.00
17 Brian LaFleur .60 1.50
18 Mike Lyons .60 1.50
19 Willy Marvin .60 1.50
20 Cory Miller .60 1.50
21 Nate Miller .60 1.50
22 Rico Pagel .60 1.50
23 Erik Rasmussen 1.25 3.00
24 Wyatt Smith 1.25 3.00
25 Dave Spehar .60 1.50
26 Ryan Trebil .60 1.50
27 Dan Woog .02 .10

1997-98 Minnesota Golden Gophers

This set was handed out as a promotional giveaway at one home game, making it quite scarce on the secondary market.

COMPLETE SET (26) 15.00 30.00
1 Checklist .10 .25
2 Doug Woog HCO .20 .50
3 Mike Anderson .40 1.00
4 Stev Debus .40 1.00
5 Ryan Kraft .60 1.50
6 Nate Miller .40 1.00
7 Brett Abrahamson .40 1.00
8 Erik Day .40 1.00
9 Bill Kohn .40 1.00
10 Cory Miller .40 1.00
11 Ben Clymer .75 2.00
12 Casey Hankinson .40 1.00
13 Willy Marvin .40 1.00
14 Reggie Berg .40 1.00
15 Jason Godbout .40 1.00
16 Mike Lyons .40 1.00
17 Ryan Trebil .40 1.00
18 Dylan Mills .40 1.00
19 Dave Spehar .40 1.00
20 Erik Westrum .75 2.00
21 Wyatt Smith .60 1.50
22 Aaron Miskovich .40 1.00
23 Rico Pagel .40 1.00
24 Matt Leimbeck .40 1.00
25 Stuart Senden .40 1.00
26 Goldy Gopher Mascot .20 .50

1998-99 Minnesota Golden Gophers

This set features the Golden Gophers of the NCAA. Like most NCAA issues, this set was handed out as a promotional giveaway at a single home game.

COMPLETE SET (30) 20.00 35.00
1 Header Card .02 .10
2 Doug Woog HCO .20 .50
3 Mark Nenovich .40 1.00
4 Erik Wendell .75 2.00
5 Dylan Mills .40 1.00
6 Nate Miller .40 1.00
7 Rob LaRue .40 1.00
8 Reggie Berg .40 1.00
9 Bill Kohn .40 1.00
10 Mike Lyons .40 1.00
11 Cory Miller .40 1.00
12 Mike Anderson .40 1.00
13 Jordon Leopold 1.50 4.00
14 Ryan Westrum .40 1.00
15 Doug Meyer .40 1.00
16 Rico Pagel .40 1.00
17 Stuart Senden .40 1.00
18 Nick Angell .40 1.00
19 Dave Spehar .40 1.00
20 Pat O'Leary .40 1.00
21 Ryan Trebil .40 1.00
22 Adam Hauser .75 2.00
23 Wyatt Smith .75 2.00
24 Brad Timmons .40 1.00
25 Matt Leimbeck .40 1.00
26 Aaron Miskovich .40 1.00
27 Erik Daly .40 1.00
28 Erik Westrum .75 2.00
29 John Pohl .75 2.00
30 Goldy Gopher Mascot .10 .25

1998-99 Minnesota Golden Gophers Women

Issued as a giveaway at a late-season home game.

COMPLETE SET (25) 10.00 25.00
1 Angela Borek .40 1.00
2 Winny Brodt .40 1.00
3 Emily Buchholz .40 1.00
4 Tracy Donaghue .40 1.00
5 Tracy Engstrom .40 1.00
6 Lacey Franzmeier .40 1.00
7 Laura Halldorson CO .10 .25
8 Amber Hegland .40 1.00
9 David Horn ACO .10 .25
10 Courtney Kennedy .40 1.00
11 Shannon Kennedy .40 1.00
12 Erica Killewald .40 1.00
13 Betsey Kukowski .40 1.00
14 Megan Milbert .40 1.00
15 Nadine Muzerall .40 1.00
16 Crystal Nicholas .40 1.00
17 Kelly Olson .40 1.00
18 Sarma Pone .40 1.00
19 Brittny Ralph .40 1.00
20 Jenny Schmidgall 1.25 3.00
21 Kris Scholz .40 1.00
22 Laura Slominski .40 1.00
23 Ambria Thomas .40 1.00
24 Tai Thorsheim .40 1.00
25 Libby Witchger ACO .10 .25

1999-00 Minnesota Golden Gophers

This set features the Golden Gophers of the NCAA. The cards were issued as a promotional giveaway at a late-season game. The cards are unnumbered, and so are listed in alphabetical order.

COMPLETE SET (30) 8.00 20.00
1 Nick Angell .20 .50
2 Nick Anthony .20 .50
3 Matt DeMarchi .20 .50
4 Goldy Gopher MAS .10 .25
6 Ben Hamilton .20 .50
7 Adam Hauser .40 2.00
8 Matt Leimbeck .20 .50
9 Jordan Leopold 1.20 3.00
10 Don Lucia CO .10 .25
11 Mike Lyons .20 .50
12 Doug Meyer .20 .50
13 Nate Miller .20 .50
14 Dylan Mills .20 .50
15 Aaron Miskovich .20 .50
16 Mark Nenovich .20 .50
17 Pat O'Leary .20 .50
18 Rico Pagel .20 .50
19 John Pohl .30 3.00
20 Chad Roberge .20 .50
21 Pete Samargia .20 .50
22 Stuart Senden .20 .50
23 Dave Spehar .20 .50
24 Jeff Taffe 2.00 5.00
25 Ben Tharp .20 .50
26 Ryan Trebil .20 .50
27 University of Minnesota .10 .25
28 Dan Welch .20 .50
29 Erik Wendell .30 .75
30 Erik Westrum .40 1.00

2000-01 Minnesota Golden Gophers

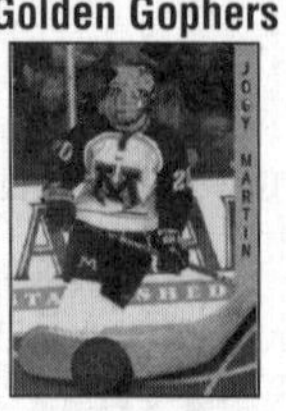

This set features the Golden Gophers of the NCAA. The cards were issued as a promotional giveaway late in the season. The cards are unnumbered, so are listed below in alphabetical order.

COMPLETE SET (28) 15.00 25.00
1 Header Card .04 .01
2 Nick Angell .30 .75
3 Nick Anthony .30 .75
4 Matt DeMarchi .30 .75
5 Goldy Gopher MASCOT .04 .10
6 Adam Hauser .75 2.00
7 Rod Johnson FOOTBALL .30 .75
8 Matt Koalska .30 .75
9 Matt Leimbeck .30 .75
10 Jordan Leopold 1.25 3.00
11 Don Lucia CO .10 .25
12 Joey Martin .30 .75
13 Paul Martin .30 .75
14 Dylan Mills .30 .75
15 Aaron Miskovich .30 .75
16 Mark Nenovich .30 .75
17 Pat O'Leary .30 .75
18 John Pohl .75 2.00
19 Grant Potulny .40 1.00
20 Troy Riddle .30 .75
21 Chad Roberge .30 .75
22 Pete Samargia .30 .75
23 Stuart Senden .30 .75
24 Jeff Taffe 1.25 3.00
25 Ben Tharp .30 .75
26 Jon Waibel .30 .75
27 Erik Wendell .30 .75
28 Erik Westrum .75 2.00

2001-02 Minnesota Golden Gophers

This set features the Golden Gophers of the NCAA in their championship season. The set was issued as a promotional giveaway at a game in January, 2002.

COMPLETE SET (29) 12.00 30.00
1 Header Card .10 .25
2 Don Lucia CO .10 .25
3 Goldy Gopher MASCOT .04 .10
4 Nick Anthony .40 1.00
5 Mike Erickson .40 1.00
6 Chad Roberg .60 1.50
7 Keith Ballard .60 1.50
8 Erik Wendell .60 1.50
9 Paul Martin .40 1.00
10 John Pohl .60 1.50
11 Judd Stevens .40 1.00
12 Jon Waibel .40 1.00
13 Jordan Leopold 1.20 3.00
14 Mark Nenovich .40 1.00
15 Adam Hauser .40 1.00
16 Garrett Smaagaard .40 1.00
17 Grant Potulny .40 1.00
18 Matt DeMarchi .40 1.00
19 Joey Martin .40 1.00
20 Troy Riddle .40 1.00
21 Jeff Taffe 1.20 3.00
22 Matt Koalska .40 1.00
23 Pat O'Leary .40 1.00
24 Nick Angell .40 1.00
25 Barry Tallackson .40 1.00
26 Brett MacKinnon .40 1.00
27 Jake Fleming .40 1.00
28 Travis Weber .40 1.00
29 Justin Johnson .40 1.00

2002-03 Minnesota Golden Gophers

COMPLETE SET (31) 20.00 40.00
1 Nick Anthony .40 1.00
2 P.J. Atherton .40 1.00
3 Keith Ballard 1.00 2.50
4 Matt DeMarchi .40 1.00
5 Mike Erickson .40 1.00
6 Jake Fleming .40 1.00
7 Gino Guyer .60 1.50
8 Chris Harrington .40 1.00
9 Tyler Hirsch .40 1.00
10 Justin Johnson .40 1.00
11 Peter Kennedy .40 1.00
12 Matt Koalska .40 1.00
13 Brett MacKinnon .40 1.00
14 Joey Martin .40 1.00
15 Paul Martin .75 2.00
16 Grant Potulny .60 1.50
17 Jerrid Reinholz .40 1.00
18 Troy Riddle .40 1.00
19 Chad Roberg .40 1.00
20 Andrew Sertich .40 1.00
21 Garrett Smaagaard .40 1.00
22 Dustin Smieja .40 1.00
23 Judd Stevens .40 1.00
24 Barry Tallackson .75 2.00
25 Thomas Vanek 6.00 15.00
26 Jon Waibel .40 1.00
27 Travis Weber .40 1.00
28 Dan Welch .40 1.00
29 Don Lucia HCO .10 .25
30 Goldy Gopher Mascot .02 .10
31 NCAA Champs .20 .50

2003-04 Minnesota Golden Gophers

This set was issued as a promotional giveaway over the course of four home games in the form of four seven-card strips.

COMPLETE SET (28) 20.00 40.00
1 Barry Tallackson .75 2.00
2 Jake Taylor .50 1.25
3 Thomas Vanek 3.00 8.00
4 Mike Vannelli .50 1.25
5 Jon Waibel .50 1.25
6 Dustin Smieja .50 1.25
7 Championship Team Photo .10 .25
8 Don Lucia CO .02 .10
9 P.J. Atherton .50 1.25
10 Keith Ballard 1.00 2.50
11 Kellen Briggs .75 2.00
12 Jake Fleming .50 1.25
13 Gino Guyer 1.00 2.50
14 Chris Harrington .50 1.25
15 Tyler Hirsch .50 1.25
16 Dan Irmen .75 2.00
17 Justin Johnson .75 2.00
18 Peter Kennedy .50 1.25
19 Matt Koalska .60 1.50
20 Brett MacKinnon .50 1.25
21 Joey Martin .50 1.25
22 Grant Potulny .50 1.25
23 Ryan Potulny 1.25 3.00
24 Jerrid Reinholz .50 1.25
25 Troy Riddle .50 1.25
26 Andy Sertich .60 1.50
27 Garrett Smaagaard .50 1.25
28 Judd Stevens .50 1.25

2004-05 Minnesota Golden Gophers

COMPLETE SET (27) 25.00
1 PJ Atherton 1.00
2 Brent Borgen 1.00
3 Kellen Briggs 1.50
4 Kris Chucko 2.00
5 Jake Fleming 1.00
6 Alex Goligoski 1.25 3.00
7 Ben Gordon 1.00
8 Gino Guyer 1.00
9 Nate Hagemo 1.00
10 Chris Harrington 1.00
11 Tyler Hirsch 1.00
12 Mike Howe 1.00
13 Danny Irmen 1.00
14 Justin Johnson 1.00
15 Evan Kaufman 1.00
16 Peter Kennedy 1.00
17 Don Lucia 1.00
18 Derek Peltier 1.00
19 Tom Pohl 1.00
20 Ryan Potulny 2.00
21 Jerrid Reinholz 1.00
22 Andy Sertich 2.00
23 Garrett Smaagaard 1.00
24 Brent Solei 1.00
25 Judd Stevens 1.00
26 Barry Tallackson 2.00
27 Mike Vannelli 1.00

2004-05 Minnesota Golden Gophers Women

COMPLETE SET (14) 15.00
1 Natalie Darwitz 2.50
2 Krissy Wendell 2.50
3 Anya Miller 1.00
4 Erica McKenzie 1.00
5 Natalie Lamme 1.00
6 Krista Johnson 1.00
7 Jody Horak 1.00
8 Stacy Troumbly 1.00
9 Becky Wacker 1.00
10 Lyndsay Wall 1.00
11 Whitney Graft 1.00
12 Chelsey Brodt 1.00
13 Ashley Albrecht 1.00
14 Laura Halldorson CO .10

2005-06 Minnesota Golden Gophers

COMPLETE SET (27) 15.00 30.00
1 R.J. Anderson .30 .75
2 P.J. Atherton .30 .75
3 Brent Borgen .30 .75
4 Justin Bostrom .30 .75
5 Kellen Briggs .30 .75
6 Kris Chucko .60 1.50
7 Jeff Frazee 1.25 3.00
8 Alex Goligoski .75 2.00
9 Ben Gordon .30 .75
10 Gino Guyer .40 1.00
11 Nate Hagemo .40 1.00
12 Chris Harrington .30 .75
13 Mike Howe .30 .75
14 Danny Irmen .40 1.00
15 Evan Kaufmann .30 .75
16 Peter Kennedy .30 .75
17 Phil Kessel 10.00
18 Derek Peltier .30 .75
19 Tom Pohl .30 .75
20 Ryan Potulny 1.25 3.00
21 Andy Sertich .30 .75
22 Brent Solei .30 .75
23 Ryan Stoa .60 1.50
24 Mike Vannelli .30 .75
25 Blake Wheeler .75 2.00
26 Don Lucia HC .02 .10
27 Goldy Gopher MASCOT .02 .10

2006-07 Minnesota Golden Gophers

COMPLETE SET (25) 25.00 35.00
1 R.J. Anderson .40 1.00
2 Jay Barriball .60 1.50
3 Justin Bostrom .40 1.00
4 Kellen Briggs .40 1.00
5 Mike Carman .40 1.00
6 David Fischer .40 1.00
7 Ryan Flynn .40 1.00
8 Jeff Frazee .75 2.00
9 Alex Goligoski .75 2.00
10 Ben Gordon .40 1.00
11 Mike Howe .40 1.00
12 Erik Johnson 2.00 5.00
13 Evan Kaufmann .40 1.00
14 Tony Lucia .40 1.00
15 Jim O'Brien .75 2.00
16 Kyle Okposo 2.00 5.00
17 Derek Peltier .40 1.00
18 Tom Pohl .40 1.00
19 Brian Schack .40 1.00
20 Brent Solei .40 1.00
21 Ryan Stoa .75 2.00
22 Mike Vannelli .40 1.00
23 Blake Wheeler .75 2.00
24 Don Lucia CO .10 .25
25 Goldy Gopher MASCOT .10 .25

1994-95 Minnesota Moose

This set features the Moose of the IHL. The set was issued as a promotional giveaway in the form of four, four-card perforated strips. It is believed that all were issued on the same night, but that is not yet verified.

COMPLETE SET (16) 8.00 20.00
1 Dave Christian .60 1.50
2 Kris Miller .60 1.50
3 John Young .60 1.50
4 Tom Draper .80 2.00
5 Daniel Shank .60 1.50
6 Dean Kolstad .60 1.50
7 Yvon Corriveau .60 1.50
8 Frank Serratore CO .20 .50
9 Dave Snuggerud .60 1.50
10 Mark Osiecki .60 1.50
11 Brad Miller .60 1.50
12 Frank Pietrangelo .80 2.00
13 Stephane Morin .60 1.50
14 Sean Williams .60 1.50
15 Dave Hakstol .60 1.50
16 Mick E. Moose MAS .20 .50

1995-96 Minnesota Moose

This set features the Moose of the IHL. It is believed to have been issued as a promotional giveaway, but that has not been confirmed. Any additional information can be forwarded to hockeymag@beckett.com.

COMPLETE SET (16) 6.00 15.00
1 Dave Christian .40 1.00
2 Chris Jensen .40 1.00
3 Sandy Smith .60 1.50
4 Stephane Morin .60 1.50
5 Dave Gagnon .60 1.50
6 Sean Williams .40 1.00
7 Yvon Corriveau .40 1.00
8 Chris Govedaris .40 1.00
9 Mike Hurlbut .40 1.00
10 Dave Hakstol .40 1.00
11 Bryan Fogarty .40 1.00
12 Dave Morissette .40 1.00
13 Brad Miller .40 1.00
14 Kris Miller .40 1.00
15 Frank Serratore CO .20 .50
16 Mick E. Moose MASCOT .20 .50

2003-04 Minnesota State Mavericks

This set was issued as a promotional giveaway. The cards are unnumbered and so are listed below in alphabetical order.

COMPLETE SET (20) 20.00
1 Cole Bassett 1.00
2 Brock Becker 1.00
3 Jake Brenk 1.00
4 Chad Clower 1.00
5 Jon Dubel 1.00
6 Aaron Forsythe 1.00
7 Adam Gerlach 1.00
8 Jon Hart 1.00
9 Steven Johns 1.00
10 Shane Joseph 1.00
11 Rick Kisskeys 1.00
12 Jeff Marler 1.00
13 Ryan McKelvie 1.00
14 Nate Metcalf 1.00
15 Kyle Nixon 1.50
16 Matt Paluczak 1.00
17 Dana Sorensen 1.00
18 Brad Thompson 1.00
19 Christian Toll 1.00
20 Jon Volp 1.50

2000-01 Mississauga Ice Dogs

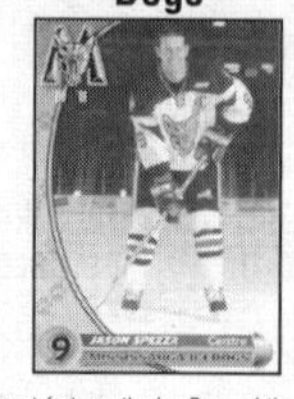

This set features the Ice Dogs of the OHL. The set was produced by the team and sold at its souvenir shop. The cards are unnumbered, so the set is listed in alphabetical order. It is noteworthy for including an early card of top prospect Jason Spezza.

COMPLETE SET (28) 8.00 20.00
1 Team CL .04 .01
2 Brett Angel .20 .50
3 Blue and Baby Blue MASCOT .16 .25
4 Grant Buckley .16 .40
5 Don Cherry OWN .80 2.00
6 Steve Cherry CO .04 .10
7 Fraser Clair .16 .40
8 Mark Cranley .16 .40
9 David Dalliday .16 .40
10 Andrew Davis .16 .40
11 Justin Dumont .16 .40
12 Omar Ennaffati .16 .40
13 John Jarram .16 .40
14 Patrick Jarrett .80 1.00
15 Brent Labre .16 .40
16 Brian McGrattan .16 .40
17 Sean McMorrow .16 1.00
18 Michael Mole .20 1.00
19 Chris Osborne .16 .40
20 Jeff Paisley .16 .40
21 Brandon Robinson .16 .40
22 Adam Solnik .16 .40
23 Jason Spezza 4.00 10.00
24 Dan Sullivan .16 .40
25 Chris Thaler .16 .40
26 Rick Vaive CO .16 .25
27 Mike Wehrstedt .16 .40
28 Chad Wiseman .16 .40

2001-02 Mississauga Ice Dogs

COMPLETE SET (26) 12.00
1 Team card .10
2 Matt Tanel .40
3 T.J. Reynolds .40
4 Travis Parent .40
5 Nathan O'Nabigon .40
6 Patrick O'Sullivan 1.50
7 Chris Churran .40
8 Dan Rudisuela .40
9 Mike Wehrstedt .40
10 Tyler Eady .40
11 John Kozoriz .40
12 Adam Sturgeon .40
13 Chris Hawley .40
14 Alexander Skorohod .40
15 Miguel Beaudry .40
16 Andrew Smale .40
17 Bob Turner .40
18 John Eminger .40
19 Igor Radulov 2.00
20 Greg Jacina .40
21 Mike Barrett .40
22 Daniel Sisca .40
23 Don Cherry OWN 2.00
24 Steve Cherry GM .10
25 Joel Washkurak ACO .10
26 Blue MASCOT .10

2002-03 Mississauga Ice Dogs

COMPLETE SET (23) 15.00
1 Checklist .01
2 Travis Parent .50
3 Ian Maracle .50
4 Scott Hotham .50
5 Derek Lyons .50
6 Chris Curran .50
7 Dan Rudisuela .50
8 Tyler Eady .50
9 Tomas Linhart .75
10 Chris Hawley .50
11 Pavel Voroshin .75
12 Wes Rypien .50
13 Miguel Beaudry .75
14 Matt Harpwood .75
15 Daniel Buccella .50
16 Rob Schremp 3.00
17 Salvatore Malandrino .50
18 Greg Jacina .50
19 Ryan Stokes .50
20 Patrick O'Sullivan 1.50
21 Dany Revelle .50
22 Blair Jarrett .50
23 Daniel Sisca .50

2003-04 Mississauga Ice Dogs

COMPLETE SET (24) 12.00
1 Adam Abraham .50
2 Chris Bain .75
3 Cody Bass .50
4 Anthony Butera .50
5 Rick Caughell .50
6 Chris Chimienti .50
7 Chris Curran .50
8 Brad Efthimiou .50
9 Brandon Elliott .50
10 Lukas Grauwiler .50
11 Doug Groenestege .75
12 Blair Jarrett .50
13 Daryl Knowles .50
14 Mark O'Leary .50
15 Patrick O'Sullivan .75
16 Chad Painchaud .50
17 Kyle Quincey .50
18 Dany Revelle .50
19 Dan Rudisuela .50
20 David Shantz 1.50
21 Ryan Stokes .50
22 Nick Van Herpt .50
23 Tom Zanoski .50
24 Scott Zimmerman .50

2004-05 Mississauga Ice Dogs

A total of 300 team sets were produced.
COMPLETE SET (24) 15.00
1 Anthony Butera .75
2 Bradley Snetsinger .50
3 Adam Abraham .50
4 Cody Bass .50
5 David Shantz 1.50
6 Dustin Jeffrey .50
7 Kyle Quincey .75
8 Michael Swift .50
9 Gianluc Caputi .50
10 Craig Cescon .50
11 Tom Zanoski .50
12 Vladimir Svacina .50
13 Patrick O'Sullivan 1.50
14 Daniel Carcillo .50
15 John Hecimovic .50
16 Paul Merchese .50
17 Michael Ouzas .50
18 David Pszenyczny .50
19 Frankie Santini .50
20 Justin DaCosta 1.00
21 Stefan Legein .50
22 Nathan Hooper .50
23 Jordan Owens .50
24 Aaron Barton .50

2005-06 Mississauga Ice Dogs

COMPLETE SET (24) 6.00 15.00
1 Cody Bass .75
2 Vladimir Svacina .75
3 Jordan Owens .75
4 Drew Schiestel .75
5 Michael Smift .75
6 Keith Wynn .75
7 Lucas Lobsinger 1.00
8 Luca Caputi .75
9 Kyle Lamb .75
10 Justin Gvora .75
11 Jordan Skellett .75
12 Andrew Marcoux .75
13 Andrew Merrett .75
14 Oskar Osala .75
15 Brett Oliphante .75
16 Justin Dacosta .75
17 Kyle Knechtel .75
18 Joshua Day .75
19 Franck Santini .75
20 Nathan Martine .75
21 Drew McAvoy .75
22 Stefan Legein .75
23 Jadran Beljo .75
24 Chris Lawrence .75

2006-07 Mississauga Ice Dogs

COMPLETE SET (23) 8.00 15.00
1 Cody Bass .25 .60
2 Alex Pietrangelo .25 .60
3 Stephan Legein .25 .60
4 Jadran Beljo .25 .60
5 Chris Lawrence .25 .60
6 Jordan Owens .25 .60
7 Brett Oliphant .25 .60
8 Michael Swift .25 .60
9 Luca Caputi .25 .60
10 Barry Sanderson .25 .60
11 Jordan Skellett .25 .60
12 Andrew Merrett .25 .60
13 Travis Fuller .25 .60
14 Oskar Osala .25 .60
15 Steven Manojlovic .25 .60
16 Josh Day .25 .60
17 Franck Santini .25 .60
18 Nathan Martine .25 .60
19 Drew Mcavoy .25 .60
20 Drew Schiestel .25 .60
21 Kyle Lamb .25 .60
22 Lucas Lobsinger .40 1.00
23 Andrew Loverrock .40 1.00

1996-97 Mississippi Sea Wolves

This set was sold by the team at home games and was sponsored by Play It Again Sports.
COMPLETE SET (22) 4.00 10.00
1 Frederik Beaubien .30 .75
2 Alexei Budayev .20 .50
3 Sylvain Daigle .20 .50
4 Kevin Evans .20 .50
5 Quinn Fair .20 .50
6 Shawn Frappier .20 .50
7 Kevin Hilton .20 .50
8 Kelly Hurd .20 .50
9 Derek Innanen .20 .50
10 Yanick Jean .20 .50
11 John Kosobud .20 .50
12 Troy Mann .20 .50
13 Roger Maxwell .20 .50
14 Mike Muller .30 .75
15 Simon Oliver .20 .50
16 Patrick Rochon .20 .50
17 Jeff Rohlicek .30 .75
18 Mark Rupnow .20 .50
19 Joaikin Wassberger .20 .50
20 Steven Yule .20 .50
21 Bruce Boudreau HCO .10 .25
22 Hook Mascot .04 .10

1997-98 Mississippi Sea Wolves

Little is known about this set beyond the confirmed checklist. Additional information can be forwarded to hockeymag@beckett.com.
COMPLETE SET (22) 4.00 10.00
1 Sinuhe Wallinheimo .20 .50
2 Neal Martin .20 .50
3 Don Chase .20 .50
4 John Kosobud .20 .50
5 Jeff Rohlicek .20 .50
6 Kelly Hurd .20 .50
7 Chad Dameworth .20 .50
8 Bruce Boudreau HCO .04 .10
9 Teemu Numminen .20 .50
10 Dan Back .20 .50
11 Dean Hulett .20 .50
12 Mark Rupnow .20 .50
13 Hook Mascot .04 .10
14 Patrick Rochon .20 .50
15 Troy Mann .20 .50
16 Quinn Fair .20 .50
17 Shawn Frappier .20 .50
18 Brian Farrell .20 .50
19 Steve Yule .20 .50
20 Kevin Evans .20 .50
21 Brad Guzda .20 .50
22 Forbes MacPherson .20 .50

1999-00 Mississippi Sea Wolves

This set features the Sea Wolves of the ECHL. The set was produced by Roox and was sold by the team at home games.
COMPLETE SET (25) 20.00 50.00
1 Rob Flahiff EQM .04 .10
2 Marc Potvin HCO .75 2.00
3 Hook MAS .04 .10
4 Team Photo .75 2.00
5 Cynthia Dedeaux TR .04 .10
6 Trevor Gillies .75 2.00
7 Steve Duke .75 2.00
8 Sean Gillam .75 2.00
9 Bob Woods .75 2.00
10 Cody Bowtell .75 2.00
11 Patrick Rochon .75 2.00
12 Jonathan Weaver .75 2.00
13 John Kosobud .75 2.00
14 Brad Essex 1.25 3.00
15 Scott King .75 2.00
16 Ryan Gaucher .75 2.00
17 Brad Goulet .75 2.00
18 Mike Martone .75 2.00
19 J.F. Aube .75 2.00
20 Dave Paradise .75 2.00
21 John Evangelista .75 2.00
22 Mikhail Kravets .75 2.00
23 Chuck Thuss 1.25 3.00
24 Sylvain Daigle 1.25 3.00
25 Mark Rupnow .75 2.00

1999-00 Mississippi Sea Wolves Kelly Cup

This set features the Sea Wolves of the ECHL. The set was produced by the team and features players from the previous season to honor their league championship win. The set was sold by the team at home games for $10.
COMPLETE SET (25) 4.00 10.00
1 Bruce Boudreau CO .20 .50
2 Hook MAS .04 .10
3 James Carey TR .04 .10
4 Cynthia Dedeaux TR .04 .10
5 Karl Infanger .20 .50
6 Sean Blanchard .20 .50
7 Bob Woods .20 .50
8 Cody Bowtell .20 .50
9 Vaclav Nedomansky .20 .50
10 Patrick Rochon .20 .50
11 John Kosobud .20 .50
12 Brad Essex .30 .75
13 Andrew Dale .20 .50
14 Dean Mando .20 .50
15 Kevin Hilton .20 .50
16 Quinn Fair .20 .50
17 Chris Schmidt .20 .50
18 Mike Martone .20 .50
19 Kelly Hurd .20 .50
20 Mikhail Kravets .20 .50
21 Travis Scott .30 .75
22 Mark Rupnow .20 .50
23 Troy Mann .20 .50
24 Chuck Thuss .30 .75
25 Mississippi Sea Wolves .20 .50

2003-04 Mississippi Sea Wolves

These cards were given away as promotional items at several home games. It's believed that other cards exist in this series. If you have additional info, please forward it to hockeymag@beckett.com. Because we could not gather enough confirmed sales data, the cards are not priced.
COMPLETE SET (17)
1 Anthony Battaglia
2 Brent Gauvreau
3 Louis Dumont
4 Greg Gardner
5 Jeff Hutchins
6 Andrei Lupandin
7 Austin Miller
8 Steve O'Rourke
9 John Evangelista
10 Travis Lisabeth
11 Sean Matile
12 Roger Maxwell
13 Patrick Rochon
14 Kerry Ellis-Toddingto
15 Steffon Walby
16 Mascot
17 Checklist

1999-00 Missouri River Otters

This set features the River Otters of the UHL. The cards were printed by Roox and sold by the team. They are not numbered, so they are listed below in alphabetical order.
COMPLETE SET (28) 4.00 10.00
1 Team Photo .20 .50
2 Tomas Baluch .16 .40
3 Chris Bernard .16 .40
4 Charles Blyth .16 .40
5 Colin Chaulk .16 .40
6 Randy Gallatin .16 .40
7 Forrest Gore .16 .40
8 Ben Gorewich .16 .40
9 Jay Hebert .16 .40
10 Kiley Hill .16 .40
11 Jan Kobezda .16 .40
12 Lonnie Loach .30 .75
13 Jeremiah McCarthy .20 .50
14 Jeremy Rebek .16 .40
15 Brian Regan .16 .40
16 Allan Roulette .16 .40
17 Alain St. Hilaire .16 .40
18 Curtis Sayler .16 .40
19 Trevor Sherban .16 .40
20 Marty Standish .16 .40
21 Michal Stastny .30 .75
22 Chris Tok .16 .40
23 Dan Tompkins .16 .40
24 Mark Reeds HCO .16 .40
25 Scott Bell CO .16 .40
26 Oscar MASCOT .10 .25
27 Otter Mobile .10 .25
28 Checklist .10 .25

2000-01 Missouri River Otters

This set features the River Otters of the UHL. The cards were issued as promotional giveaways, apparently on three separate occasions, and in subsets of nine cards. Collectors needed to attend all three games to compile the entire set.
COMPLETE SET (27) 7.20 18.00
1 Team CL #1 .04 .10
2 Lonnie Loach .40 1.00
3 Chris Tok .30 .75
4 Colin Chaulk .40 1.00
5 Kiley Hill .40 1.00
6 Jeremy Rebek .30 .75
7 Trevor Sherban .30 .75
8 Jay Hebert .30 .75
9 Randy Gallatin .30 .75
10 Team CL #2 .04 .10
11 Darin Kimble .40 1.00
12 Troy Michalski .30 .75
13 Benoit Thibert .30 .75
14 Eric Murano .40 1.00
15 Lee Cole .30 .75
16 Robert Starke .30 .75
17 Ryan Johnston .30 .75
18 Mark Reeds CO .10 .25
19 Team CL #3 .04 .10
20 Kevin Plager .30 .75
21 Mike Bayrack .30 .75
22 Jay Woodcroft .30 .75
23 Jared Reigstad .30 .75
24 Anthony Cappelletti .30 .75
25 Kiley Hill AS .30 .75
26 Colin Chaulk AS .30 .75
27 Jim Jeans EM .04 .10
27 John Sheehan TR .04 .10

1999-00 Missouri River Otters Sheet

This set features the River Otters of the UHL. The cards were issued as a promotional giveaway in the form of a three-panel perforated sheet. The set was sponsored by a local pub and by Disney.
COMPLETE SET (25) 7.20 18.00
1 Tomas Baluch .30 .75
2 Charlie Blythe .30 .75
3 Colin Chaulk .30 .75
4 Randy Gallatin .30 .75
5 Yuri Gerasimov .30 .75
6 Ben Gorewich .30 .75
7 Jay Hebert .30 .75
8 Kiley Hill .30 .75
9 Jan Kobezda .30 .75
10 Lonnie Loach .40 1.00
11 Jeremiah McCarthy .30 .75
12 Jeremy Rebek .30 .75
13 Brian Regan .30 .75
14 Alan Roulette .30 .75
15 Alain St. Hilaire .30 .75
16 Curtis Sayler .30 .75
17 Trevor Sherban .30 .75
18 Marty Standish .30 .75
19 Michal Stastny .40 1.00
20 Jason Stewart .30 .75
21 Chris Tok .30 .75
22 Dan Tompkins .30 .75
23 Mark Reeds CO .10 .25
24 Scott Bell .30 .75
25 Oscar the Otter MASCOT .04 .10

2001-02 Missouri River Otters

This set features the River Otters of the UHL. The set was issued as a promotional giveaway in two 15-card series, and then was later sold by the team as a complete 30-card issue.
COMPLETE SET (30) 8.00 20.00
1 Missouri River Otters Logo .04 .10
2 Aaron Vickar .30 .75
3 Lonnie Loach .40 1.00
4 Dustin Whitecotton .30 .75
5 Troy Mann .30 .75
6 Anthony Cappelletti .30 .75
7 Casey VanSchagen .30 .75
8 Ben White .30 .75
9 Curtis Voth .40 1.00
10 Charlie Blyth .30 .75
11 Scott Perry .30 .75
12 Kelvin Solari .30 .75
13 Mark Reeds CO .30 .75
14 Oscar the River Otter MASCOT .04 .10
15 Checklist 1 .04 .10
16 Missouri River Otters .30 .75
17 Brian Regan .30 .75
18 Darin Kimble .60 1.50
19 Eric Murano .40 1.00
20 Jason Gudmundson .30 .75
21 Mike Jaros .30 .75
22 Joe Ritson .30 .75
23 Tony White .30 .75
24 Simon Poirier .30 .75
25 Vaclav Pazourek .30 .75
26 Joe Pecoraro .30 .75
27 Kevin Chabbert .30 .75
28 John Sheehan TR .04 .10
29 Team Photo .30 .75
30 Checklist 2 .04 .10

2003-04 Missouri River Otters

This set was issued in two series as a promotional giveaway.
COMPLETE SET (24) 20.00
1 Checklist .01
2 Anthony Cappelletti 1.00
3 Charlie Blyth 1.00
4 Jesse Heerema 1.00
5 Jeff Cameron 1.00
6 Jeff Petruic 1.00
7 Colin Embley 1.00
8 Bobby Rapoza 1.00
9 Troy Mann 1.00
10 Tony White 1.00
11 Chad Moore 1.00
12 Team Photo .25
13 Checklist .01
14 Ben White 1.00
15 Kevin Chabbert 1.00
16 Forrest Gore 1.00
17 Joe Ritson 1.00
18 Brian Regan 1.50
19 Dave Cantrall 1.50
20 River Otters Kids Club .10
21 Ryan Gillis 1.00
22 Tim Knudsen 1.50
23 Rob Davidson 1.00
24 Lonnie Loach HCO .25

2004-05 Missouri River Otters

This set was issued in two parts by the River Otters of the UHL. Each 16-card series was sold for $4 at the team's merchandise shop.
COMPLETE SET (32) 12.00
1 Header .01
2 Charlie Blyth .50
3 Jason Tapp .50
4 B.J. Heckendorn .50
5 Barrie Moore .50
6 Mike Dombkiewicz .50
7 Cole Bassett .50
8 Ryan Johnson .75
9 Riku Varjamo .50
10 Mat Snesrud .50
11 Quinten Van Horlick .75
12 Jim Montgomery .75
13 Kevin Kaminski CO .50
14 Ice Zone .01
15 Prize Card .01
16 Checklist Series 1 .01
17 Header .01
18 Bob Rapoza .50
19 Josh Legge .50
20 Kevin Reiter .50
21 Lars Pettersen .50
22 Mark Odut .50
23 George Cantrall .50
24 Justin Quenneville .50
25 Glen Detulleo .50
26 Rod Sundquist .50
27 Brad MacMillan .50
28 Barret Jackman 1.50
29 Team Photo .50
30 Sponsor Card .01
31 Prize Card .01
32 Checklist Series 2 .01

2005-06 Missouri River Otters

COMPLETE SET (24) 20.00
1 Missouri River Otters .10
2 Kevin Kaminski HC .10
3 Richard Paul 1.00
4 Dave Stewart 1.00
5 Martin Vasut 1.00
6 Jim Murphy 1.00
7 J.P. Beilsten 1.00
8 Lars Pettersen 1.00
9 B.J. Heckendorn 1.00
10 Tyler Butler 1.00
11 Mark Lindsay 1.00
12 Brenden Cuthbert 1.00
13 Missouri River Otters .10
14 Brad Church 1.00
15 Tim O'Connell 1.00
16 Jimmy Callahan 1.00
17 Frank Littlejohn 1.00
18 Mark Odut 1.00
19 Brad MacMillan 1.00
20 Kevin Reiter 1.00
21 Damian Surma 1.00
22 Oscar [Mascot] .10
23 Matt Suderman 1.00
24 Scott Horvath 1.00

1997-98 Mobile Mysticks

This set features the Mysticks of the ECHL. The cards were produced by Starzsports, and were sold by the team at home games.
COMPLETE SET (21) 4.00 10.00
1 Chuck Thuss .20 .50
2 Mike Mayhew .20 .50
3 Matt Shaw CO .10 .25
4 Dave Craievich .20 .50
5 Jim Jensen .20 .50
6 Anton Fedorov .20 .50
7 Russell Monteith .20 .50
8 Yanick Jean .20 .50
9 Dave Larson .20 .50
10 Chris Brooks .20 .50
11 Brandon Carper .20 .50
12 Phil Valk .20 .50
13 Patrice Paquin .20 .50
14 Kevin Hilton .20 .50
15 Fredrick Nasvall .20 .50
16 Andrew Will .20 .50
17 Steve Suk .20 .50
18 Mike Lenarduzzi .30 .75
19 Neil Donovan .20 .50
20 Hugues Gervais .20 .50
21 Chad Remackel .20 .50

1997-98 Mobile Mysticks Kellogg's

This set features the Mysticks of the ECHL. These cards were issued as a promotional giveaway in four-card strips at seven different home games. Each strip contained three player cards and one Kellogg's ad card. The players on cards No. 2 and 4 are not known at this time. Identification should be sent to hockeymag@beckett.com.
COMPLETE SET (21) 6.00 15.00
1 Andrew Will .40 1.00
2 unknown
3 Neil Donovan .40 1.00
4 unknown
5 Dave Larson .40 1.00
6 Jim Jensen .40 1.00
7 Mike Mayhew .40 1.00
8 Matt Shaw HCO .14 .35
9 Yanick Jean .40 1.00
10 Steve Suk .40 1.00
11 Chad Remackel .40 1.00
12 Tom Neziol ACO .10 .25
13 Dave Craievich .40 1.00
14 Chris Brooks .40 1.00
15 Fredrick Nasvall .40 1.00
16 Puck MAS .10 .25
17 Anton Fedorov .40 1.00
18 Hugues Gervais .40 1.00
19 Phil Valk .40 1.00
20 Mike Lenarduzzi .60 1.50
21 Russell Monteith .40 1.00

1998-99 Mobile Mysticks

This 22-card set was handed out as a promotional giveaway at five different home games, making it an extremely difficult set to acquire. The cards were distributed in perforated strips.
COMPLETE SET (22) 6.00 15.00
1 Russell Monteith .40 1.00
2 Slapshot Mascot .04 .10
3 Tom Neziol ACO .04 .10
4 Kevin Kerr .40 1.00
5 Steve Debus .40 1.00
6 Steve Chapman GM .04 .10
7 Puck Mascot .04 .10
8 Yanick Jean .40 1.00
9 Dave Craievich .40 1.00
10 Jason Elders .40 1.00
11 Alain Savage .40 1.00
12 Joel Theriault .40 1.00
13 Chad Alban .60 1.50
14 John McCabe .40 1.00
15 Simmons/Jeffreys/Young .20 .50
16 Hughes Gervais .40 1.00
17 Brandon Carper .40 1.00
18 Craig Binns .40 1.00
19 Jeff Pyle HCO .10 .25
20 Jim Shepherd .40 1.00
21 Andrew Will .40 1.00
22 Francois Page .40 1.00

1999-00 Mobile Mysticks

This set features the Mysticks of the ECHL. The set was issued as a promotional giveaway at an early-season game.
COMPLETE SET (23) 6.00 50.00
1 Dave Craievich .30 2.50
2 David Van Drunen .30 2.50
3 Mitch Vig .30 2.50
4 Benoit Cotnoir .30 2.50
5 Bobby Stewart .30 2.50
6 John McCabe .30 2.50
7 Hugues Gervais .30 2.50
8 Tom Nolan .30 2.50
9 Chad Onufrechuk .30 2.50
10 Jason Elders .30 2.50
11 B.J. Kilbourne .30 2.50
12 Mark Turner .30 2.50
13 Jeff Kozakowski .30 2.50
14 Josh Harrold .30 2.50
15 Russ Guzior .30 2.50
16 Anders Sorensen .30 2.50
17 Jason Clarke .30 2.50
18 Chad Alban .40 5.00
19 Steve Debus .30 5.00
20 Scott Cherrey .30 2.50
21 Jeff Pyle CO .10 2.50
22 Tom Neziol CO .10 .25
23 Southern Ford Dealers .01

1983-84 Moncton Alpines

The Moncton Alpines are featured in this 28-card P.L.A.Y. (Police, Law and Youth) set, which was sponsored by the Moncton Police in conjunction with several company sponsors. The cards measure approximately 2 1/2" by 3 3/4" and are printed on thin card stock. The fronts feature color photos with the players posed in action stances. The photos are framed by white borders. The player's name and position are printed below the picture between Coke and Hostess logos. The backs have biography, statistics, and safety tips in English and French.
COMPLETE SET (28) 6.00 15.00
1 Doug Messier CO .20 .50
2 Chris Smith .20 .50
3 Marco Baron .40 1.00
4 Mike Zanier .40 1.00
5 Dwayne Boettger .20 .50
6 Lowell Loveday .20 .50
7 Joe McDonnell .20 .50
8 Peter Dineen .20 .50
9 John Blum .30 .75
10 Steve Smith .80 2.00
11 Reg Kerr .30 .75
12 Tom Rowe .20 .50
13 Ross Lambert .20 .50
14 Pat Conacher .40 1.00
15 Paul Miller .20 .50
16 Bert Yachimel .20 .50
17 Tom Gorence .30 .75
18 Jeff Crawford .20 .50
19 Serge Boisvert .30 .75
20 Todd Strueby .30 .75
21 Todd Bidner .20 .50
22 Dean Dachyshyn .20 .50
23 Ray Cote .20 .50
24 Shawn Babcock .20 .50
25 Shawn Dineen .20 .50
26 Marc Habscheid .40 1.00
27 Charlie Lavalee TR .10 .25
Kevin Ferris TR
NNO Checklist Card .20 .50

1984-85 Moncton Golden Flames

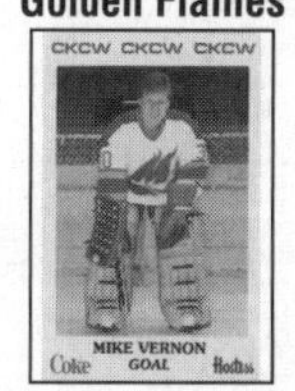

The Moncton Golden Flames are featured in this 26-card P.L.A.Y. (Police, Law and Youth) set, which was sponsored by the Moncton Police in conjunction with several company sponsors. The cards measure approximately 2 1/2" by 3 3/4" and are printed on thin card stock. The fronts feature color photos with the players posed in action stances.
COMPLETE SET (26) 10.00 25.00
1 Brian Patafie TR .10 .25
2 Mike Blanni TR .10 .25
3 Pierre Page CO .20 .50
4 Neil Sheehy .40 1.00
5 George White .20 .50
6 Mark Lamb .40 1.00
7 Dan Kane .20 .50
8 Dan Bolduc .40 1.00
9 Lou Kiriakou .20 .50
10 Joel Otto .80 2.00
11 Dale Degray .40 1.00
12 Mike Clayton .20 .50
13 Mickey Volcan .20 .50
14 Ted Pearson .20 .50
15 Mario Simioni .20 .50
16 Keith Hanson .20 .50
17 Yves Courteau .20 .50
18 Dan Cormier .20 .50
19 Todd Hooey .20 .50
20 Mike Vernon 4.00 10.00
21 Dave Meszaros .20 .50
22 Bruce Eakin .20 .50
23 Ed Kastelic .40 1.00
24 Tony Stiles .20 .50
25 Pierre Rioux .20 .50
26 Gino Cavallini .40 1.00

1985-86 Moncton Golden Flames

The Moncton Golden Flames are featured in this 28-card P.L.A.Y. (Police, Law and Youth) set, which was sponsored by the Moncton Police in conjunction with several company sponsors. The cards measure approximately 2 1/2" by 3 3/4" and are printed on thin card stock. The fronts feature color photos with the players posed in action stances. The photos are framed by white borders. The player's name and position are printed below the picture between Coke and Hostess logos. The backs have biography, statistics, and safety tips in English and French.
COMPLETE SET (28) 8.00 20.00
1 Terry Crisp GM/CO .40 1.00
2 Dan Bolduc ACO .10 .25
3 Terry Crisp GM/CO .40 1.00
Dan Bolduc ACO
4 Al Pedersen .30 .75
5 Dave Meszaros .20 .50
6 George White .20 .50
7 Mark Lamb .60 1.50
8 Doug Kostynski .20 .50
9 Brian Bradley .80 2.00
10 Rob Kivell .20 .50
11 Geoff Courtnall 1.20 3.00
12 Tony Stiles .20 .50
13 Jim Buettgen .20 .50
14 Cleon Daskalakis .40 1.00
15 Rick Kosti .20 .50
16 Kevan Guy .20 .50
17 John Blum .20 .50
18 Brian Patafie TR .10 .25
Mike Baiani
Jamie Druet
19 Greg Johnston .30 .75
20 Dale Degray .20 .50
21 John Meulenbroeks .20 .50
22 Dave Reid .40 1.00
23 Jay Miller 1.20 3.00
24 Yves Courteau .20 .50
25 Robin Bartel .20 .50
26 Benoit Doucet .20 .50
27 Pete Bakovic .20 .50
28 Team Photo .40 1.00

1986-87 Moncton Golden Flames

The Moncton Golden Flames are featured in this 28-card P.L.A.Y. (Police, Law and Youth) set, which was sponsored by the Moncton Police in conjunction with several company sponsors. The cards measure approximately 2 1/2" by 3 3/4" and are printed on thin card stock. The fronts feature color photos with the players posed in action stances. This set includes first pro cards of Brett Hull, Gary Roberts, Bill Ranford, and Lyndon Byers.
COMPLETE SET (28) 30.00 75.00
1 Terry Crisp CO/GM .40 1.00
2 Danny Bolduc ACO .10 .25
3 Doug Dadswell .40 1.00
4 Doug Kostynski .20 .50
5 Bill Ranford 6.00 15.00
6 Brian Patafie TR .10 .25
7 Dave Pasin .30 .75
8 Darwin McCutcheon .20 .50
9 Team Photo .40 1.00
10 Kevan Guy .30 .75
11 Kraig Nienhuis .30 .75
12 Gary Roberts 2.00 5.00
13 Ken Sabourin .30 .75
14 Marc D'Amour .40 1.00
15 Don Mercier .20 .50
16 Wade Campbell .20 .50
17 Mark Paterson .20 .50
18 Cleon Daskalakis .40 1.00
19 Lyndon Byers 2.00 5.00
20 Brett Hull 16.00 40.00
21 Bob Sweeney .40 1.00
22 Gord Hynes .20 .50
23 Peter Bakovic .20 .50
24 Dave Reid .40 1.00
25 Mike Rucinski .20 .50
26 Ray Podloski .20 .50
27 Bob Bodak .20 .50
28 John Carter .30 .75

1987-88 Moncton Hawks

Sponsored by Coke, Shoppers Drug Mart, and CKCW, this 25-card set measures approximately 2 1/2" by 3 3/4" and features posed, color player photos with white studio backgrounds. The fronts have white borders with sponsor names printed in red above and below the picture. The player's name and position are printed in black just below the photo. The cards are unnumbered and checklisted below in alphabetical order.

COMPLETE SET (25) 4.80 12.00
1 Joel Baillargeon .20 .50
2 Rick Bowness CO .20 .50
3 Rick Carrano TR .10 .25
Wayne Flemming EQMG
4 Bobby Dollas .30 .75
5 Peter Douris .30 .75
6 Iain Duncan .20 .50
7 Bob Essensa .80 2.00
8 Todd Flichel .20 .50
9 Rob Fowler .20 .50
10 Randy Gilhen .30 .75
11 Matt Hervey .20 .50
12 Brent Hughes .30 .75
13 Jamie Husgen .20 .50
14 Mike Jeffrey .20 .50
15 Guy Larose .20 .50
16 Chris Levasseur .20 .50
17 Len Nielson .20 .50
18 Roger Ohman .20 .50
19 Dave Quigley .20 .50
20 Ron Pesetti .20 .50
21 Steve Penney .40 1.00
22 Scott Schneider .20 .50
23 Ryan Stewart .20 .50
24 Gord Whitaker .20 .50
25 Team Photo .40 1.00

1990-91 Moncton Hawks

These 25 cards measure approximately 2 7/16" by 3 5/8" and feature on their fronts white-bordered posed-on-ice color shots of the '90-91 Moncton Hawks. The player's name and position appear at the lower left. The logos for the set's sponsors, Hostess, Frito Lay, and CKCW Radio, also appear on the front. The cards are unnumbered and checklisted below in alphabetical order.

COMPLETE SET (25) 4.00 10.00
1 Larry Bernard .16 .40
2 Lee Davidson .16 .40
3 Iain Duncan .16 .40
4 Craig Duncanson .16 .40
5 Dallas Eakins .20 .50
6 Dave Farrish CO/GM .04 .10
7 Wayne Flemming EQMG .04 .10
8 Todd Flichel .16 .40
9 Peter Hankinson .16 .40
10 Matt Hervey .16 .40
11 Brent Hughes .20 .50
12 Anthony Joseph .16 .40
13 Sergei Kharin .16 .40
14 Denis Larocque .16 .40
15 Guy Larose .20 .50
16 Scott Levins .20 .50
17 Bryan Marchment .40 1.00
18 Chris Norton .16 .40
19 Mike O'Neill .30 .75
20 Grant Richison .16 .40
21 Scott Schneider .16 .40
22 Rob Snitzer TR .04 .10
23 Rick Tabaracci .40 1.00
24 Simon Wheeldon .20 .50
25 Team Card .20 .50

1991-92 Moncton Hawks

This 28-card set measures approximately 2 1/2" by 3 5/8" and was sponsored by the Moncton Police Force, the Sackville Police Force, and the Hostess/Frito Lay company. The fronts feature color photos with the players posed in action stances. The photos are framed by white borders. The player's name and position appear in the lower left corner, while the Hostess/Frito Lay logo is in the lower right corner.The cards are unnumbered and checklisted below in alphabetical order.

COMPLETE SET (28) 4.00 10.00
1 Luciano Borsato .16 .40
2 Jason Cirone .16 .40
3 Rob Cowie .16 .40
4 Lee Davidson .16 .40
5 Kris Draper .40 1.00
6 Dallas Eakins .20 .50
7 Dave Farrish GM/CO .04 .10
8 Wayne Flemming EQMG .04 .10
9 Sean Gauthier .20 .50
10 Ken Gernander .20 .50
11 Tod Hartje .16 .40
12 Bob Joyce .20 .50
13 Claude Julien .16 .40
14 Chris Kiene .16 .40
15 Mark Kumpel P/ACO .16 .40
16 Derek Langille .16 .40
17 Tyler Larter .16 .40
18 John LeBlanc .16 .40
19 Scott Levins .16 .40
20 Rob Murray .16 .40
21 Kent Paynter .16 .40
22 Rudy Poeschek .20 .50
23 Dave Prior CO .04 .10
24 Warren Rychel .20 .50
25 Rob Snitzer TR .04 .10
26 Rick Tabaracci .40 1.00
27 The Hawk (Mascot) .04 .10
28 Darren Veitch .20 .50

2001-02 Moncton Wildcats

This set features the Wildcats of the QMJHL. The cards were produced by CTM Ste-Foy and were sold at that shop, as well as at the team's home games. It was reported that less than 1,000 sets were produced.

COMPLETE SET (26) 6.00 15.00
1 Bill Ruggiero .30 .75
2 Andrew Carver .20 .50
3 James Sanford .20 .50
4 Kyle Murnaghan .20 .50
5 Daniel Hudgin .20 .50
6 Mathieu Betournay .20 .50
7 Karl Gagne .20 .50
8 Ian Seguin .20 .50
9 Michel Dube .20 .50
10 Francois Caron .20 .50
11 Nathan Saunders .20 .50
12 Brad Larter .20 .50
13 Teddy Kyres .20 .50
14 Kevin Glode .20 .50
15 David Philpott .20 .50
16 Ryan Salvis .20 .50
17 Collin Circelli .20 .50
18 Corey Crawford .30 .75
19 Matt Davis .30 .75
20 Patrick Thoreson .80 2.00
21 Maxime Desruisseaux .20 .50
22 Julien Lavoie .20 .50
23 Scott English .20 .50
24 Luke Pelham .20 .50
25 Steve Bernier 1.00 2.50
NNO Title Card/CL .04 .10

2002-03 Moncton Wildcats

COMPLETE SET (26) 8.00 15.00
1 Nathan Saunders .20 .50
2 Matt Davis .20 .50
3 Francois Caron .20 .50
4 Evgeni Artukhin .30 .75
5Â Evgeni Artukhin WJC .30 .75
6 Corey Crawford .40 1.00
7 Bruce Graham .30 .75
8 James Sanford .30 .75
9 Patrick Sampson .20 .50
10 Mathieu Betournay .20 .50
11 Ryan Salvis .20 .50
12 Kevin Glode .20 .50
13 Luke Pelham .20 .50
14 Maxime Desruisseaux .20 .50
15 Kevin Hamel .20 .50
16 Josh Hepditch .20 .50
17 Jonathan Favreau .20 .50
18 Kyle Murnaghan .20 .50
19 Daniel Hudgin .20 .50
20 Michel Dube .20 .50
21 Sebastien Strozynski .20 .50
22 Yannick Searles .20 .50
23 Carl McLean .20 .50
24 Karl Gagne .20 .50
25 Steve Bernier 1.25 3.00
26 Team Picture .10 .25

2003-04 Moncton Wildcats

COMPLETE SET (25) 12.00
1 James Sanford .40
2 Yan Ouimet .40
3 Bruce Graham 1.00
4 Mathieu Betournay .40
5 Karl Gagne .40
6 Christian Gaudet .40
7 Martin Karsums 1.00
8 Francois Caron .40
9 Kevin Hamel .40
10 Nathan Saunders .40
11 Kevin Glode .40
12 Thierry Douville .40
13 Cody Doucette .40
14 Joshua Hepditch .40
15 Mathieu Wathier .40
16 Ryan Salvis .40
17 Bobby Mazerolle .40
18 Konstantin Zakharov .40
19 Corey Crawford .75
20 Ryan Papaioannou .75
21 Luke Pelham .40
22 Maxime Desruisseaux .40
23 Steve Bernier 1.00
NNO James Sanford TL .40
NNO Steve Bernier TL 1.00

2004-05 Moncton Wildcats

A total of `1,050 team sets were produced.

COMPLETE SET (25) 12.00
1 Wesley Welcher .50
2 Oskars Barulis .50
3 Corey Crawford 1.00
4 Charles Bergeron .50
5 Kevin Glode .50
6 Brad Marchand 2.00
7 Adam Blanchette .50
8 Charles Tanguay .50
9 Luke Pelham .50
10 Christian Gaudet .50
11 Jean-Sebastien Adam .50
12 Stephane Goulet .50
13 Jason Demers .50
14 Ryan Salvis .50
15 Adam Pineault .50
16 Yan Ouimet .50
17 Jean-Christophe Blanchard 1.00
18 Stanson Donovan .50
19 Martins Karsums 1.00
20 Bruce Graham .75
21 Steve Bernier 1.00
22 Jerome Samson .50
23 Josh Hepditch .50
24 Guillaume Veilleux .50
25 Nathan Saunders .50

2005-06 Moncton Wildcats

COMPLETE SET (30) 8.00 15.00
1 Adam Pineault 1.00
2 Stephane Goulet .75
3 Jean Christophe Blanchard .75
4 Matt Eagles .75
5 Brad Marchand 1.00
6 Christian Gaudet .75
7 Guillaume Blouin .75
8 Oskars Bartulis .75
9 Keith Yandle .75
10 Josh Hepditch .75
11 Maxime Belanger .75
12 Tim Spencer .75
13 Martins Karsums 1.50
14 Jerome Samson .75
15 Jean Sebastien Adam .75
16 Andrew MacDonald .75
17 Philippe Dupuis .75
18 Nathan Welton .75
19 Nick Emanuele .75
20 Jason Demers .75
21 Ian-Mathieu Girard .75
22 Jean-Philip Chabot .75
23 Matt Marquardt .75
24 Chris Morehouse .75
25 Brad Ouskun .75
26 Brad Smith .75
27 Jhase Sniderman .75
28 Josh Tordjman 1.00
29 Luc Bourdon 1.50
30 David MacDonald .75

2006-07 Moncton Wildcats

COMPLETE SET (24) 8.00 15.00
1 Nicola Riopel .40 1.00
2 Andrew Macdonald .25 .60
3 Roopertti Martikainen .25 .60
4 Matthew Brenton .25 .60
5 Randy Cameron .25 .60
6 Jason Lepage .25 .60
7 Jerome Samson .25 .60
8 Pierre-Marc Lessard .25 .60
9 Matt Marquardt .25 .60
10 Matt Eagles .25 .60
11 Nathan Welton .25 .60
12 Murdock Maclellan .25 .60
13 Jhase Sniderman .40 1.00
14 Nick Emanuele .25 .60
15 Alexi Pianosi .25 .60
16 Brad Smith .25 .60
17 Marc-Andre Labelle .25 .60
18 Chris Morehouse .25 .60
19 Brad Ouskun .25 .60
20 Patrick Campbell .25 .60
21 Igor Voroshilov .25 .60
22 Matt Boyle .25 .60
23 Kelan Herr .25 .60
24 Christian Gaudet .25 .60

1997-98 Moose Jaw Warriors

COMPLETE SET (19) 12.00
1 Jay Ewasiuk 1.00
2 Jordon Flodell .75
3 Justin Hansen .75
4 Cory Hintz .75
5 Chad Hinz .75
6 Brent Hobday .75
7 Marek Ivan .75
8 Trevor Johnson .75
9 Tim McEachen .75
10 Donavan Nunweiler 1.00
11 Dustin Paul .75
12 Nathan Read .75
13 Scott Schoneck .75
14 Shawn Skolney .75
15 Dave Taylor .75
16 Chris Twerdun .75
17 Dreu Volk .75
18 Jason Weitzel .75
19 Dayle Wilcox .75

2001-02 Moose Jaw Warriors

This set features the Warriors of the WHL. The set was produced by CTM Ste-Foy and was sold at Warriors home games. The production run for the set was 1,000 copies.

COMPLETE SET (22) 4.80 12.00
1 Ryan Jorde .20 .50
2 Jarad Bourassa .20 .50
3 Deryk Engelland .20 .50
4 Nathan Paetsch .40 1.00
5 Bobby-Chad Mitchell .20 .50
6 Kyle Brodziak .20 .50
7 Derek Krestanovich .40 1.00
8 Steve Crampton .20 .50
9 Sean O'Connor .20 .50
10 Brian Sutherby .60 1.50
11 Tim Plett .20 .50
12 Shawn Limpright .20 .50
13 Lee Zalasky .20 .50
14 Harlan Anderson .20 .50
15 Tyler Johnson .20 .50
16 David Bararuk .20 .50
17 Mark Kitts .20 .50
18 Craig Olynick .30 .75
19 Lane Manson .20 .50
20 Shaun Landolt .20 .50
21 Kyle Kettles .20 .50
22 Blake Grenier .20 .50

2002-03 Moose Jaw Warriors

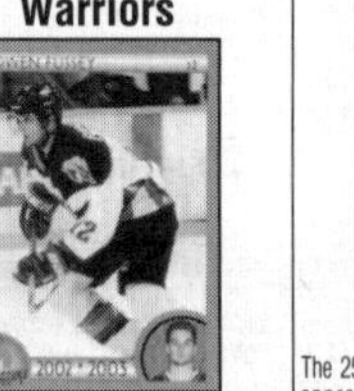

COMPLETE SET (22) 12.00
1 John Boychuk 1.00
2 Jarad Bourassa .50
3 Deryk Engelland .50
4 Nathan Paetsch 1.00
5 Michael Busto .50
6 Kyle Brodziak .50
7 Tomas Fleischmann 2.00
8 Derek Krestanovich .75
9 Owen Fussey .75
10 Petr Jelinek .50
11 Jon Kress .50
12 Harlan Anderson .50
13 Tyler Johnson .50
14 David Bararuk .50
15 Troy Brouwer .50
16 Ashton Rome .50
17 Lane Manson .50
18 Dustin Boyd .50
19 Cam Lilley .50
20 Blake Grenier .75
21 Steve Belanger .75
22 Checklist/Logo .01

2004-05 Moose Jaw Warriors

COMPLETE SET (24) 20.00
1 Greg Park .75
2 Jordan Henry .75
3 Cole Simpson .75
4 Cole Butterfield .75
5 Dan Ehrman .75
6 Dylan Chapman .75
7 Jacob Dietrich .75
8 Justin Scott .75
9 Kenndal McArdle 3.00
10 Blair Jones .75
11 Garrett Robinson .75
12 Dustin Boyd .75
13 Andre Hermanson .75
14 Brennen Wray .75
15 Masi Marjamaki 1.00
16 Stuart Kerr .75
17 Riley Holzapfel .75
18 Troy Brouwer .75
19 Steven Gillen .75
20 Ian McKenzie .75
21 Carter Smith .75
22 Joey Perricone .75
23 Josh Lepp 1.00
24 Checklist .10

2005-06 Moose Jaw Warriors

COMPLETE SET (25) 15.00
1 Jason Bast .60
2 Dustin Boyd 1.50
3 Troy Brouwer .60
4 Dylan Chapman .60
5 Travis Ehrhardt .60
6 Kyle Fecho .60
7 Steven Gillen .60
8 Martin Grundling .60
9 Matthew Hansen .60
10 Andre Herman .60
11 Riley Holzapfel .60
12 Blair Jones .60
13 Andrew Leslie .50
14 Kendall McArdle 1.50
15 Ian McKenzie .60
16 Joey Perricone 1.00
17 Garrett Robinson .60
18 Cole Simpson .60
19 Carter Smith .60
20 Bjorn Svensson .60
21 Brennen Wray .60
22 Jesse Zetariuk .60
23 Old Dutch Foods SPONSOR .01
24 Boston Pizza SPONSOR .01
25 Air Waves SPONSOR .01

2006-07 Moose Jaw Warriors

COMPLETE SET (24) 10.00 18.00
1 Jock Sutter .30 .75
2 Travis Hamonic .30 .75
3 Ryan Stanton .30 .75
4 Chad Suer .30 .75
5 Travis Ehrhardt .30 .75
6 Martin Grundling .30 .75
7 Keith Voytechek .30 .75
8 Neal Prokop .30 .75
9 Brady Calla .30 .75
10 Matt Isbister .30 .75
11 Garrett Robinson .30 .75
12 Brad Riege .30 .75
13 Ryley Grantham .30 .75
14 Jordan Knackstedt .30 .75
15 Jason Bast .30 .75
16 Riley Holzaphel .40 1.00
17 Michael Hengen .30 .75
18 Steven Gillen .30 .75
19 Jason Reese .30 .75
20 Cody Thoring .30 .75
21 Jason Grecica .30 .75
22 Joey Perricone .40 1.00
23 Kurt Jory .40 1.00
24 Giffen Nyren .30 .75

1990-91 Montreal-Bourassa AAA

The 25 cards in this oversized set measure approximately 3" by 3 3/4" and feature players from the AAA Midget squad based in Bourassa, a suburb of Montreal. The cards feature a posed color photo on the front, with an anti-drug inscription written in French along the bottom. The crudely designed backs have biographical data, along with the logo celebrating the 15th anniversary of the club.

COMPLETE SET (25) 2.00 5.00
1 Team Card .04 .10
2 Police Card .04 .10
3 Coach Card .04 .10
4 Coach Card .04 .10
5 Coach Card .04 .10
6 Peter Arvanitis .10 .25
7 Luc Bilodeau .10 .25
8 Luc Corriveau .10 .25
9 David Desnoyers .10 .25
10 Alexandre Duchesne .10 .25
11 Dominic Gagne .10 .25
12 Benoit Goyer .10 .25
13 Serge Kiopini .10 .25
14 Ted Laviolette .10 .25
15 Ian McIntyre .10 .25
16 Nathan Morin .10 .25
17 Valentino Passarelli .10 .25
18 Jean-Sebastien Perras .10 .25
19 Sylvain Pinel .10 .25
20 Sebastien Plouffe .16 .40
21 Simon Roy .10 .25
22 Erasmo Saltarelli .16 .40
23 Alain Savage .10 .25
24 Christian Sbrocca .10 .25
25 Patrick Traverse .30 .75

1979-80 Montreal Juniors

This oversized set (approximately 4X6) features black and white images. Little is known about the set outside of the checklist below, provided by collector Steve Coran. As we have no confirmed sales info, the cards are listed below without pricing.

COMPLETE SET (29)
1 Jeff Barratt
2 Andre Begin
3 Dennis Champagne
4 Denis Cyr
5 Ghyslain Cyr
6 Roland Diotte
7 Pierre Dubois
8 Sylvain Gagne
9 Guy Jacob
10 Mike Krushelnyski
11 Ron Lapointe
12 Richard Lavallee
13 Daniel Laxton
14 Francois Laxton
15 Francois Lecompte
16 Eikke Leime
17 Pierre Martin
18 Bill Mulcahey
19 Gates Orlando
20 Patrice Pare
21 Mario Patry
22 Fabian Pavlin
23 Roger Poitras
24 Constant Prindolo
25 Denis Savard
26 Eric Taylor
27 Denis Tremblay
28 J.J. Vezina
29 Taras Zytynsky

1955-56 Montreal Royals

This set features the Royals, Montreal's top farm team. Cards measure 5 1/4" x 4 1/2" and were issued by Hygrade Franks. Card fronts are black and white and card backs feature an ad for Hygrade Franks that encourages purchasers to collect all six cards.

COMPLETE SET (6) 50.00 350.00
1 Walter Cline 6.00 50.00
2 Andre Corriveau 6.00 50.00
3 Jacques Deslauriers 6.00 50.00
4 Cec Hoekstra 10.00 60.00
5 Gerry McNeil 20.00 100.00
6 Guy Rousseau 10.00 60.00

1993-94 Muskegon Fury

This 20-card set of the Muskegon Fury of the Colonial Hockey League was produced by Rising Star Sports Promotions. The cards feature action photography on the front inside a teal border, along with league logo and player name, number and position. the backs have complete stats but are unnumbered.

COMPLETE SET (20) 10.00 25.00
1 Header Card .10 .25
2 Steve Ludzik CO .50 1.25
3 Bob Jones .50 1.25
4 Darrel Newman .50 1.25
5 Brett Seguin .50 1.25
6 Dan Woodley .75 2.00
7 Jodi Murphy .50 1.25
8 Mark Karpen .50 1.25
9 Robert Melanson .50 1.25
10 Paul Kelly .50 1.25
11 Joey Simon .50 1.25
12 Scott Feasby .50 1.25
13 Scott Campbell .50 1.25
14 Joe Hawley .50 1.25
15 Justin Morrison .50 1.25
16 Roch Belley 1.25 3.00
17 Todd Charlesworth .75 2.00
18 Kevin Barrett .50 1.25
19 Mark Turner .50 1.25
20 Steve Herniman .50 1.25

1994-95 Muskegon Fury

This 18-card set of the Muskegon Fury of the CHL was produced by Rising Star Sports Promotions and sponsored by McDonald's. The cards feature and action photo inside a teal border. The logos of Rising Star and the CHL are prominently displayed alongside the player's name and position. Card backs contain complete career and personal stats, but are unnumbered. These cards are very similar in design to other Muskegon sets; check the stats on the back to determine the year of your set.

COMPLETE SET (18) 3.20 8.00
1 Header Card .04 .10
2 Rich Parent .40 1.00
3 Grant Block .20 .50
4 Justin Morrison .20 .50
5 Scott Feasby .20 .50
6 Scott Campbell .20 .50
7 Mark Vilneff .20 .50
8 Brett Seguin .20 .50
9 Todd Charlesworth .20 .50
10 Marc Saumier .20 .50
11 Norm Krumpschmid .20 .50
12 Darryl Gilmour .30 .75
13 Paul Kelly .20 .50
14 Steve Walker .20 .50
15 Wes McCauley .20 .50
16 Steve Herniman .20 .50
17 Andy Bezeau .20 .50
18 Jamie Black .20 .50

1995-96 Muskegon Fury

This 20-card set produced by Rising Star Promotions and sponsored by McDonald's features the Muskegon Fury of the Colonial Hockey League. The card fronts have a color action photo within a teal border. The league logo is in the lower left, with player name, number and position along the bottom. The back contains career information for each player. The cards are unnumbered. The design for this set is eerily similar to the previous two years: collectors should check the stats on the back to ascertain which year their set is from.

COMPLETE SET (20) 4.00 10.00
1 Team Photo .20 .50
2 Mark Vilneff .20 .50
3 Kyle Haviland .20 .50
4 Brett Seguin .20 .50
5 Rick Girhiny .20 .50
6 Cory Johnson .20 .50
7 Paul Kelly .20 .50
8 Mark Turner .20 .50
9 Scott Feasby .20 .50
10 Stephen Webb .30 .75
11 Bobby Wallwork .20 .50
12 Richard Fatrola .20 .50
13 Steve Walker .20 .50
14 Robert Melanson .20 .50
15 Rich Parent .60 1.50
16 Jamie Hearn .20 .50
17 Brian Greer .20 .50
18 Steve Herniman .20 .50
19 Terry Ficorelli ANN .04 .10
20 McDonald's Sponsor .04 .10

1998-99 Muskegon Fury

This set features the Fury of the UHL. The cards were issued as promotional giveaways over the course of several home games, making the set difficult to complete.

COMPLETE SET (30) 12.00 30.00
1 Terry Ficorelli ANN .04 .10
2 Jason Pain .60 1.50
3 Furious Fred MAS .04 .10
4 Lubos Krajcovic .60 1.50
5 Chris Maillet .60 1.50
6 Robin Bouchard .60 1.50
7 Randy Cantu TR .04 .10
8 Francis Nault .60 1.50
9 Checklist .04 .10
10 Richard Kromm CO .04 .10
11 Joe Dimaline .60 1.50
12 Richard Kromm CO .04 .10
13 David Bouskill .60 1.50
14 Cory Banika .80 2.00
15 Rob Melanson .60 1.50
16 John Vary .60 1.50
17 Ginman Tire AD .01
18 Andy Bezeau .80 2.00
18 Steve Webb .80 2.00
19 Paul Willett .60 1.50
20 Mike Feasby .60 1.50
21 Sergei Kharin .80 2.00
22 Denis Khlopotnov .80 2.00
23 David Beauregard .80 2.00
24 Dmitri Emilyantsev .60 1.50
25 Mark Vilneff .60 1.50
26 Scott Feasby .60 1.50
27 Andrei Petrunin .80 2.00
28 Vadim Podrezov .60 1.50
29 Grant Richison .60 1.50
30 Tony Lisman GM .04 .10

1999-00 Muskegon Fury

This set features the Fury of the UHL. The set was produced by Roox and issued as a promotional giveaway over the course of several games throughout the season.

COMPLETE SET (36) 8.00 20.00
1 Sergei Kharin .30 .75
2 Vadim Podrezov .30 .75
3 Andrei Petrunin .40 1.00
4 Scott Feasby .30 .75
5 Joe Dimaline .40 1.00

6 Rob Melanson .30 .75
7 Robin Bouchard .30 .75
8 Muskegon Fury .30 .75
9 Quinn Hancock .30 .75
10 Francis Nault .30 .75
11 Alex Vasilevski .30 .75
12 Mark Vilneff .30 .75
13 Andrew Luciuk .30 .75
14 Bob Janosz .40 1.00
15 Chris Maillet .30 .75
16 Tomas Kapusta .30 .75
17 Mike McCourt .30 .75
18 Brian Tucker .30 .75
19 Aaron Porter .30 .75
20 Jason Rose .30 .75
21 Alain LaPlante .30 .75
22 Mike Feasby .10 .25
23 Terry Ficorelli .10 .25
24 Furious Fred MAS .10 .25
25 Richard Kromm CO .10 .25
26 Phil Kopinski TR .10 .25
27 Mikhail Nemirovsky .30 .75
28 Don McSween .30 .75
29 Dalen Hrooshkin .30 .75
30 Lucas Nehrling .30 .75
31 1999-00 Fury AS .30 .75
32 Tony Lisman GM .10 .25
33 Checklist .10 .25
34 Rob Hutson .30 .75
35 Joel Gardner .30 .75
36 Muskegon Fury .20 .50

2000-01 Muskegon Fury

This set features the Fury of the UHL. The cards were handed out as promotional giveaways over the course of several games, and were sponsored by a local tire store.

COMPLETE SET (30) 15.00 30.00
1 Robin Bouchard .40 1.00
2 Philippe Roy .60 1.50
3 Alain O'Driscoll .40 1.00
4 Todd Robinson .60 1.50
5 J.F. Tremblay .40 1.00
6 Ed Kowalski .40 1.00
7 Dean Mayrand .40 1.00
8 Glenn Crawford .60 1.50
9 Sergei Kharin .40 1.00
10 Andrew Luciuk .40 1.00
11 Sylvain Daigle .60 1.50
12 Maxim Linnik .60 1.50
13 Andrew Merrick .40 1.00
14 Mark Vilneff .40 1.00
15 Rob Melanson .40 1.00
16 Scott Feasby .60 1.50
17 Quinn Hancock .40 1.00
18 Francis Nault .40 1.00
19 Krikor Arman .40 1.00
20 Richard Kromm CO .40 1.00
21 Joe Dimaline .40 1.00
22 Justin Martin .40 1.00
23 Alexei Krovopuskov .40 1.00
24 Rob Hutson .40 1.00
25 Furious Fred MAS .04 .10
26 Scott Hlady .40 1.00
27 Phil Kopinski TR .04 .10
28 Rick Emmett .40 1.00
29 Scott Myers .40 1.00
30 Terry Ficorelli ANN .04 .10

2002-03 Muskegon Fury

COMPLETE SET (27) 10.00
1 Brant Blackned .50
2 Robin Bouchard .50
3 Josh Burk .50
4 Mike Busniuk HCO .10
5 Sylvain Daigle .75
6 Rustyn Dolyny .50
7 Terry Ficorelli ANN .10
8 John Glavota .50
9 Shane Glover .50
10 Scott Hollis .50
11 Rob Kennedy EQM .10
12 Jeff Kozakowski .50
13 Tony Lisman OWNER .10
14 Andrew Luciuk .50
15 Jeff Lukasak .50
16 Mike Feasby ACO .10
17 Steven MacIntyre .50
18 Philippe Plante .50
19 Chris Porowski TR .10
20 Billy Pugliese .50
21 Gary Ricciardi .50
22 Todd Robinson .50
23 Scott Feasby .50
24 Brandon Snee .50
25 Travis Thiessen .50
26 Furious Fred Mascot .10
NNO Checklist .01

2003-04 Muskegon Fury

COMPLETE SET (23) 10.00
1 David Ambler .50
2 Brant Blackned .50
3 Robin Bouchard .50
4 Sylvain Daigle .75
5 Rustyn Dolyny .50
6 Scott Feasby .50
7 B.J. Gaustad .50
8 Brian Haaland .75
9 Scott Hollis .50
10 Jason Jaworski .50
11 Trevor Johnson .50
12 Jason Lawmaster .75
13 Jeff Nelson .50
14 Dave Noel-Bernier .50
15 Tyler Palmer .50
16 Michal Pinc .50
17 Billy Pugliese .50
18 Todd Robinson .50
19 Petr Suchanek .50
20 Garry Toor .50
21 Todd Nelson CO .10
22 Chris Davidson-Adams EQM .10
23 Brad Chavis TR .10

2005-06 Muskegon Fury

COMPLETE SET (24) 15.00
1 Brett Angel 1.00
2 Robin Bouchard .75
3 Bill Collins .75
4 Rustyn Dolyny .75
5 Ken Fels 1.00
6 Nigel Hawryliw .75
7 Jon Insana .75
8 Trevor Johnson .75
9 Ryan Keller .75
10 Kevin LaPointe 1.00
11 Jason Lawmaster 1.00
12 Jeff Nelson .75
13 Steve O'Rourke .75
14 Jeff Petruic .75
15 Joe Pomaranski .75
16 Clayton Pool 1.00
17 Todd Robinson .75
18 David Van Drunen .75
19 Clay Wilson .75
20 David Wrigley .75
21 Bill Zalba .75
22 Todd Nelson CO .10
23 Furious Fred MASCOT .01
24 Terry Ficorelli VPC .01

1984-85 Nanaimo Clippers

Thi set features the Clippers of the BCJHL. The cards are oversized (3 X 5) and feature posed shots on the ice. The set was sponsored by the RCMP and local businesses. The cards are unnumbered and so are listed in alphabetical order. Checklist provided by the good folks at Ab. D Cards.

COMPLETE SET (22) 8.00 20.00
1 Team Picture .20 .50
2 Jay Barner .40 1.00
3 Dale Brisco .40 1.00
4 Chris Calverley .40 1.00
5 Jamie Cayford .40 1.00
6 Carey Coroy .40 1.00
7 Brian Deleeuw .40 1.00
8 Frank Furlan .60 1.50
9 Bill Hardy .40 1.00
10 Rick Hunt .40 1.00
11 Rob Jack .60 1.50
12 Al Johnson .40 1.00
13 Gery Keremidschieff .40 1.00
14 Wade Michalenko .40 1.00
15 Mitch Poulin .40 1.00
16 Kevin Rabbitt .40 1.00
17 Rob Schmidt .40 1.00
18 Ron Sparks .40 1.00
19 Joe Stanley .40 1.00
20 Rod Summers .40 1.00
21 Kevin Thorlakson .40 1.00
22 Darren Wourns .60 1.50

1991-92 Nanaimo Clippers

This oversized set features the Nanaimo Clippers of the British Columbia JHL. The cards measure approximately 3 1/2 x 5 and are full color. They were produced by DEC.

COMPLETE SET (22) 3.20 8.00
1 Glenn Calder .16 .40
2 Wade Dayley .16 .40
3 Jason Disiewich .16 .40
4 Andy Faulkner .16 .40
5 Darren Holme .16 .40
6 Casey Hungle .16 .40
7 Jim Ingram .16 .40
8 Chris Jones .16 .40
9 Ryan Keller .16 .40
10 Jade Kersey .16 .40
11 Scott Kowalski .16 .40
12 Sean Krause .16 .40
13 Jim Lessard .16 .40
14 Ryan Loxam .16 .40
15 Mickey McGuire .16 .40
16 Dan Murphy .16 .40
17 Jason Northand .16 .40
18 Trevor Post .16 .40
19 Brian Schiebel .16 .40
20 Sjon Wynia .16 .40
21 Shawn York .16 .40
22 Geordie Young .16 .40

1989-90 Nashville Knights

This 23-card standard-size set was sponsored by Lee's Famous Recipe Country Chicken (a restaurant chain). The fronts feature color photos with the players in a variety of action and still poses. White borders enhance the front, and the player's name appears in the border below the picture. The cards are unnumbered and checklisted below in alphabetical order.

COMPLETE SET (23) 3.20 8.00
1 Pat Bingham .16 .40
2 Andre Brassard .16 .40
3 Mike Bukta .16 .40
4 Chris Cambio .16 .40
5 Chick-E-Lee (Mascot) .10 .25
6 Glen Engevik .16 .40
7 Matt Gallagher .10 .25
Dir. Player Development
Scott Greer AGM
8 Archie Henderson CO .20 .50
9 Billy Huard .30 .75
10 Craig Jenkins ANN .10 .25
Dave Cavaliere TR
11 Todd Jenkins .16 .40
12 Brock Kelly .16 .40
13 Paul Krayer .16 .40
14 Garth Lamb .16 .40
15 Bob Levasseur .16 .40
16 Dan O'Brien .16 .40
17 Bob Polk OWN .10 .25
Ron Fuller OWN
18 John Reid (In action) .16 .40
19 John Reid (Portrait) .16 .40
20 Jeff Salzbrunn .16 .40
21 Mike Schwalb .20 .50
22 Ron Servatius .16 .40
23 Jason Simon .20 .50

1991-92 Nashville Knights

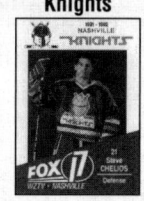

This 24-card set of the Nashville Knights of the East Coast Hockey League was issued as a game premium. The set is unnumbered; the cards are listed by order of the player's jersey number, which is listed on the front of the card. It was sponsored by TV station WZTV, whose logo is garishly emblazoned across the card fronts.

COMPLETE SET (25) 2.80 50.00
1 Header Card .04 .10
2 San Jose Sharks .20 1.00
3 Chris Harvey .16 3.00
4 Chris Grassie .16 2.00
5 Daryll Mitchell .20 2.00
6 Ron Majic .16 2.00
7 Daniel Rolfe .16 2.00
8 Mark Hilton .16 2.00
9 Angelo Russo .16 2.00
10 Jeff Jablonski .16 2.00
11 Rob Dumas .16 2.00
12 Chuck Wiegand .16 2.00
13 Steve Chelios .16 2.00
14 Kevin Sullivan .16 2.00
15 Mike Hiltner .16 2.00
16 Brock Kelly .16 3.00
17 Paul Cohen .16 3.00
18 Scott Taylor .16 2.00
19 Mike DeCarle .16 2.00
20 Jim Ritchie .16 2.00
21 Michael Seaton .16 2.00
22 Frank Anzalone CO .10 .25
23 Dave Cavaliere TR .04 .10
24 Mike Eruzione OWNER .30 5.00
25 Sean Tomalty 2.00

1992-93 Nashville Knights

This 25-card set of the Nashville Knights of the ECHL was sponsored by WZTV and issued as a game premium. The cards feature posed photos on the front and cursory stats on the back, along with card number.

COMPLETE SET (25) 3.20 8.00
1 Header Card .10 .25
2 Nick Fotiu CO .20 .50
3 George Kozak ACO .04 .10
4 Tom Cole .16 .40
5 Scott Matusovich .16 .40
6 Chris Grassie .16 .40
7 Bob Creamer .16 .40
8 Ray DeSouza .20 .50
9 Stanislav Tkach .16 .40
10 Don Parsons .16 .40
11 Steve Sullivan .16 .40
12 Brian Ferreira .16 .40
13 Rob Dumas .16 .40
14 Michael Seaton .16 .40
15 Mike DeCarle .16 .40
16 Trevor Jobe .16 .40
17 Brian Horan .16 .40
18 Andrey Dylevsky .16 .40
19 Rob Pallante .16 .40
20 Bryan Krygier .16 .40
21 Troy Mick .20 .50
22 Darcy Kaminski .16 .40
23 Olie Sundstrom .20 .50
24 Dale King TR .04 .10
25 Kevin Krueger MED .04 .10

1995-96 Neepewa Natives

This blank backed set features color photos of each player along with their name and the team logo.

COMPLETE SET (24) 10.00
1 Ryan Anderson .20 .50
2 Ryan Brunel .20 .50
3 Jeff Hudson .20 .50
4 Darren Kirk .20 .50
5 Dwayne Ripley .20 .50
6 Trevor Angus .20 .50
7 Mike Baranyk .20 .50
8 Duane Hoey .20 .50
9 Spencer Platt .20 .50
10 Jeremy Robinson .20 .50
11 Ryan Ogilvie .20 .50
12 Angelo Kokanas .20 .50
13 Craig Anderson .20 .50
14 Dale Isfeld .20 .50
15 Derek Henkelman .20 .50
16 Darcy Pengelly .20 .50
17 Kori Pearson .20 .50
18 Brett Hagberg .20 .50
19 Keith Carson .20 .50
20 Todd Barth .20 .50
21 Craig Martin .20 .50
22 Jason Glover .20 .50
23 Danny Senff .20 .50
24 Billy Joe Stasiuk HCO .10 .25

1996-97 New Hampshire Wildcats

This set was handed out in conjunction with the local DARE program. The cards below are the only ones known to exist, but the numbering suggests that others were released at some point.

COMPLETE SET (10) 9.78 25.00
21 Derek Bekar .80 2.00
22 Eric Boguniecki 2.00 5.00
23 Christian Bragnalo .80 2.00
24 Eric Fitzgerald .80 2.00
25 Jason Krog 1.60 4.00
26 Mark Mowers 1.60 4.00
27 Eric Nickulas 1.60 4.00
28 Tim Murray .80 2.00
29 Tom Nolan .80 2.00
30 Steve O'Brien .80 2.00

1997-98 New Hampshire Wildcats

This set features the Wildcats of the NCAA. The cards were produced by the team and handed out to kids by members of the local police force. The odd numbering suggests other cards might exist in this series. Information on additional singles can be forwarded to hockeymag@beckett.com.

COMPLETE SET (12)
13 Steve O'Brien .40 1.00
14 Dan Enders .40 1.00
15 Jason Krog 1.20 3.00
16 Dylan Dellezay .40 1.00
17 Sean Matile .60 1.50
18 Chad Onufrechuk .40 1.00
19 Tim Walsh .40 1.00
20 Tom Nolan .40 1.00
21 Derek Bekar .60 1.50
22 Erik Johnson .40 1.00
23 Ryan Harris .40 1.00
24 Christian Bragnalo .40 1.00

1998-99 New Hampshire Wildcats

This set features the Wildcats of the NCAA. The singles were handed out to kids by local police officers. The set is noteworthy for including members of the school's men's and women's teams.

COMPLETE SET (18) 10.00 25.00
1 John Sadowski .40 1.00
2 Chad Onufrechuk .40 1.00
3 Dan Enders .40 1.00
4 Jason Krog .60 3.00
5 Sean Matile .60 1.50
6 Michelle Thornton .80 2.00
7 Kim Knox .80 2.00
8 Tina Carrabba .80 2.00
9 Megan Hales .80 2.00
10 Allicia Roberts .80 2.00
11 Samantha Holmes .80 2.00
12 Steve O'Brien .40 1.00
13 Ryan Harris .40 1.00
14 Jay Shipulski .40 1.00
15 Tim Walsh .40 1.00
16 Jayme Filipowicz .80 2.00
17 Mike Souza .40 1.00
18 Christian Bragnalo .40 1.00

1998-99 New Haven Beast

This set features the Beast of the AHL. The cards were produced by the team and sold at its souvenir stands.

COMPLETE SET(24) 4.80 10.00
1 Craig Ferguson .16 .40
2 Ian MacNeil .16 .40
3 Marek Malik .16 .40
4 Craig MacDonald .16 .40
5 Byron Ritchie .16 .40
6 Steve Halko .16 .40
7 Shane Willis .40 1.00
8 Todd MacDonald .16 .40
9 Scott Levins .16 .40
10 Dwayne Hay .16 .40
11 Chad Cabana .16 .40
12 Tom Buckley .16 .40
13 Ryan Johnson .16 .40
14 Mike Fountain .30 .75
15 Ashlin Halfnight .16 .40
16 John Jakopin .16 .40
17 Peter Ratchuk .16 .40
17 Chris Allen .16 .40
18 Lance Ward .16 .40
18 Joey Tetarenko .40 1.00
19 Greg Koehler .16 .40
19 Andrew Long .16 .40
20 Marcus Nilsson .30 .75
20 Tommy Westlund .16 .40

1989-90 New Haven Nighthawks

This black-and-white set was issued on the 20th anniversary of the Nighthawks of the ECHL. It commemorates the best players of the team's past. The set was sponsored by Casio. It is unnumbered and is listed alphabetically by player name.

COMPLETE SET (15) 4.80 12.00
1 Ken Baumgartner .80 2.00
2 John Bednarski .20 .50
3 Tom Colley .20 .50
4 Daryl Evans .30 .75
5 Ed Johnstone .30 .75
6 Alain Langlais .20 .50
7 Mark Lofthouse .30 .75
8 Hubie McDonough .60 1.50
9 Bill Plager .80 2.00
10 Ron Scott .30 .75
11 Bobby Sheehan .40 1.00
12 Doug Soetaert .60 1.50
13 Jim Wiemer .30 .75
14 Rick Dudley CO .40 1.00
15 Parker McDonald GM/CO .30 .75

1997-98 New Mexico Scorpions

Little is known about this set beyond the confirmed checklist. It is believed that this set was sold by this WPHL team early in the season. Additional information can be forwarded to hockeymag@beckett.com.

COMPLETE SET (30) 4.80 12.00
1 Team Photo .16 .40
2 Regan Harper .16 .40
3 Eric Ricard .16 .40
4 Darren Wright .16 .40
5 Derek Crawford .16 .40
6 Sylvain Naud .30 .75
7 Mike Sanderson .16 .40
8 Brian Barnes .16 .40
9 Craig Hamelin .16 .40
10 Darcy Pengelly .16 .40
11 Todd Marcellus .16 .40
12 George Dupont .16 .40
13 Jordan Shields .16 .40
14 Francois Chaput .16 .40
15 Nick Hriczov .16 .40
16 Frederik Beaubien .30 .75
17 David Lessard .16 .40
18 Hugh Bertrand .16 .40
19 Kelly Morel .16 .40
20 Derek Shybunka .16 .40
21 Tony Martino .20 .50
22 Marc Sigel .16 .40
23 Brad Wingfield .16 .40
24 Tyler Boucher .16 .40
25 Carl Paradis .16 .40
26 Aldo Iaquinta .16 .40
27 Garry Unger CO .20 .50
28 Spencer MAS .04 .10
29 Team shot .16 .40
30 New Year's Celebration .04 .10

1997-98 New Mexico Scorpions II

This 12-card set was a late-season release, and contains multiple photos of a few of the team's key players.

COMPLETE SET (12) 2.40 6.00
1 Center Ice .10 .25
2 Eric Ricard .20 .50
3 Sylvain Naud .30 .75
4 Sylvain Naud .30 .75
5 Tony Martino .30 .75
6 Tony Martino .30 .75
7 Tyler Boucher .20 .50
8 Tyler Boucher .20 .50
9 Tyler Boucher .20 .50
10 George Dupont .20 .50
11 Aldo Iaquinta .20 .50
12 Spencer the Scorpion .10 .25

2001-02 New Mexico Scorpions

This set features the Scorpions of the WPHL. The set was produced by Choice Marketing and was issued as a promotional giveaway in March, 2002. A total of 2,000 sets were produced.

COMPLETE SET (23) 40.00 80.00
1 Sergei Radchenko .80 4.00
2 Trevor Hammer .60 4.00
3 Jay Banach .60 4.00
4 Shaun Fairweather .60 4.00
5 Mike O'Malley .60 4.00
6 Peter Ambroziak .80 5.00
7 Chris Richards .60 4.00
8 Yann Joseph .60 4.00
9 Jonathan St. Louis .60 4.00
10 Tyler Baines .60 4.00
11 Alek Stojanov .80 5.00
12 Jonathan Delisle .60 4.00
13 Scott Myers .60 4.00
14 Travis Van Tighem .60 4.00
15 Arturs Kupaks .80 4.00
16 David Cornacchia .60 4.00
17 Donald Choukalos .80 5.00
18 Steve Zoryk .60 4.00
19 Gatis Tseplis .60 1.50
20 Tony Martino CO .10 .50
21 Robert Haddock ACO .10 .50
22 The Scorpion MASCOT .10 .50
NNO Header Card .04 .10

2002-03 New Mexico Scorpions

COMPLETE SET (23) 20.00
1 Peter Ambroziak 1.00
2 Tyler Baines 1.00
3 Peter Brearley 1.00
4 Luciano Caravaggio 1.50
5 Leigh Dean 1.00
6 Mario Dumoulin 1.00
7 Arturs Kupaks 1.00
8 Stephen Margeson 1.00
9 Nate Mauer 1.00
10 Scott Myers 1.50
11 Mike O'Malley 1.00
12 Shaun Peet 1.00
13 Neil Breen 1.00
14 Tobin Praznik 1.00
15 Chris Richards 1.00
16 Craig Stahl 1.00
17 Dave Bourque 1.00
18 Bill McDonald HCO .10
19 Mike Payne 1.00
21 Travis Van Tighem ACO .10
22 Stanley the Scorpion Mascot
.10
NNO Checklist .01

2003-04 New Mexico Scorpions

This set was produced by Choice Marketing and sold at home games.

COMPLETE SET (22) 10.00
1 Checklist .01
2 Erik Adams .50
3 Jeff Alcombrack .50
4 Ben Gorewich .50
5 Brian Barker .50
6 Chris Richards .50
7 Clint Wensley .50
8 Danny Lorenz .75
9 Vladimir Hartinger .50
10 Jaroslav Kerestes .50
11 Kevin Edgar .50
12 Arturs Kupaks .50
13 Matt Mathias .50
14 Miguel Beaudry .75
15 Mike Oliveira .50
16 Mike Possin .50
17 Shaun Peet .50
18 Peter Ambroziak .50
19 Craig Stahl .50
20 Walker McDonald .50
21 Bill McDonald HCO .10
22 Mascot .10

2004-05 New Mexico Scorpions

These cards were issued in strips of five as stadium giveaways at several home games.

COMPLETE SET (25) 30.00
1 Peter Ambroziak 1.00
2 Miguel Beaudry 2.00
3 Jordan Bianchin 1.00
4 Vladimir Hartinger 1.00
5 Mike Possin 1.00
6 Ladislav Kouba 1.00
7 Alexandre Piche 1.00
8 Aaron Schneekloth 1.00
9 Guy St. Vincent 1.00
10 Matt Weber 1.00
11 Erik Adams 1.00
12 Trevor Hammer 1.00
13 Andrew Katzburg 2.00
14 Konrad McKay 1.00
15 Ivan Svarny 1.00
16 Shawn Legault 2.50
17 Daryl Moor 1.00
18 Randy Murphy 1.00
19 Mike Oliveira 1.00
20 Daniel Tetrault 1.00
21 Ladislav Kouba 1.00
22 Alexandre Piche 1.00
23 Aaron Schneekloth 1.00
24 Guy St. Vincent 2.00
25 Matt Weber 1.00

2006-07 New Mexico Scorpions

COMPLETE SET (21) 20.00 35.00
1 Ray Edwards CO .10 .25
2 Randy Murphy ACO .10 .25
3 Stanley The Scorpion MASCOT .02 .10
4 Chris Robertson .60 1.50
5 Mike Falk .60 1.50
6 Scott Reid .75 2.00
7 Dave Cacciola .75 2.00
8 Andrew Smale .60 1.50
9 Ryan McLeod .60 1.50
10 Rob Guinn .60 1.50
11 Konrad Reeder .60 1.50
12 Mike Prpich .75 2.00
13 Kevin Harvey .60 1.50
14 Craig MacDonald .60 1.50
15 Jamie Herrington .60 1.50
16 Lance Heraut .60 1.50
17 Josh Garbutt .60 1.50
18 Matt Frick .60 1.50
19 Peter Kennedy .60 1.50
20 Aaron MacInnis .60 1.50
21 Vladimir Hartinger .60 1.50

1997-98 New Orleans Brass

Little is known about this set beyond the confirmed checklist. Additional information can be forwarded to hockeymag@beckett.com.

COMPLETE SET (21) 4.00 10.00
1 Jeff Lazaro .30 .75
2 Darryl LaFrance .20 .50
3 Eric Montreuil .20 .50
4 Steve Cheredaryk .30 .75
5 Brad Symes .20 .50
6 Bill McKay .20 .50
7 Martin Villeneuve .20 .50
8 Martin Woods .20 .50
9 Joe Seroski .20 .50
10 Russ Guzior .20 .50
11 Scratch Mo Mascot .04 .10
12 Kevin Pozzo .20 .50
13 Pierre Gendron .20 .50
14 Mike Minard .30 .75
15 Scott Allegrino TR .04 .10
16 Mikhail Nemirovsky .20 .50
17 Kyle Peterson .20 .50
18 Ted Sator HCO .04 .10
19 Scott King .30 .75
20 Jason Downey .20 .50
21 Eric Brule .30 .75

1990-91 Newmarket Saints

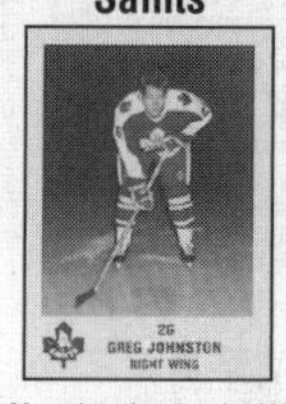

This 26-card set features the 1990-91 Newmarket Saints of the AHL (American Hockey League). Measuring approximately 2 1/2" by 3 3/4", the fronts feature on-ice color posed action shots framed by white borders. The cards are unnumbered and checklisted below in alphabetical order.

COMPLETE SET (26) 4.00 10.00
1 Frank Anzalone CO .10 .25
2 Tim Bean .16 .40
3 Brian Blad .16 .40
4 Bryan Cousineau COP .04 .10
5 Alan Hepple .16 .40
6 Donald Hillock COP .04 .10
7 Robert Horyna .16 .40
8 Kent Hulst .16 .40
9 Mike Jackson .16 .40
10 Greg Johnston .20 .50
11 Eldred King MAYOR .04 .10
12 Frank Kovacs COP .04 .10
13 Derek Langille .16 .40
14 Lanny the dog .04 .10
15 Mike Millar .16 .40
16 Mike Moes .16 .40
17 Bill Purcell ACO .04 .10
18 Bobby Reynolds .16 .40
19 Damian Rhodes .60 1.50
20 Bill Root .20 .50
21 Joe Sacco .30 .75
22 Darryl Shannon .30 .75
23 Doug Shedden .30 .75
24 Mike Stevens .20 .50
25 Darren Veitch .20 .50
26 Greg Walters .16 .40

1988-89 Niagara Falls Thunder

This 25-card set measures approximately 2 5/8" by 4 1/8" and was sponsored by the Niagara Falls Fire Department and area businesses. The cards are printed on thin card stock. The fronts have a white card face and feature color action player photos with two thin black lines forming a border.

COMPLETE SET (25) 8.00 20.00
1 Title Card .10 .25
2 Brad May .80 2.00
3 Paul Wolanski .20 .50
4 Keith Primeau 3.20 8.00
5 Mark Lawrence .20 .50
6 Mike Rosati .40 1.00
7 Dennis Vial .30 .75
8 Shawn McCosh .20 .50
9 Jason Soules .20 .50
10 Rob Fournier .20 .50
11 Scott Pearson .20 .50
12 Jamie Leach .20 .50
13 Colin Miller .20 .50
14 Bryan Fogarty .20 .50
15 Keith Osborne .20 .50
16 Stan Drulia .40 1.00
17 Paul Laus .40 1.00
18 Adrian Van Der Sloot .20 .50
19 Greg Allen .20 .50
20 Don Pancoe .20 .50
21 Alain LaForge .20 .50
22 Bill LaForge GM/CO .10 .25
23 Steve Locke .20 .50
24 Benny Rogano ACO .10 .25
25 Heavy Evason ACO .10 .25

1989-90 Niagara Falls Thunder

Sponsored by local Arby's and Pizza Pizza stores, these 25 cards measure approximately 2 5/8" by 4 1/8" and feature on their fronts white-bordered posed-on-ice color shots of the 1989-90 Niagara Falls Thunder. The player's name appears in red lettering within the white bottom margin. The cards are unnumbered and checklisted below in alphabetical order.

COMPLETE SET (25) 6.00 15.00
1 Greg Allen .20 .50
2 Roch Belley .30 .75
3 David Benn .20 .50
4 Andy Bezeau .20 .50

5 George Burnett CO .20 .50
6 Todd Coopman .20 .50
7 Randy Hall ACO .10 .25
8 John Johnson .20 .50
9 Paul Laus .40 1.00
10 Mark Lawrence .20 .50
11 Brad May .40 1.00
12 Don McConnell .20 .50
13 Brian Mueggler .20 .50
14 Don Pancoe .20 .50
15 Keith Primeau 2.00 5.00
16 Geoff Rawson .20 .50
17 Ken Ruddick .20 .50
18 Greg Suchan .20 .50
19 Trainers .10 .25
Paul Bruneau
Dennis Scott
20 Steve Udvari .30 .75
21 Jeff Walker .20 .50
22 Jason Winch .20 .50
23 Paul Wolanski .20 .50
24 Title Card .10 .25
25 Checklist Card .20 .50

1993-94 Niagara Falls Thunder

Printed by Slapshot Images Ltd., this 29-card set features the 1993-94 Niagara Falls Thunder. The cards measure standard size (2 1/2" by 3 1/2"). On a geometrical purple and green background, the fronts feature color action player photos with thin grey borders.

COMPLETE SET (29) 4.00 10.00
1 Title Card/Checklist .04 .10
2 Jimmy Hibbert .16 .40
3 Darryl Foster .16 .40
4 Gerry Skrypec .16 .40
5 Greg de Vries .30 .75
6 Tim Thompson .16 .40
7 Joel Yates .16 .40
8 Yianni Ioannou .16 .40
9 Steve Nimigon .16 .40
10 Jeff Johnstone .16 .40
11 Brandon Convery .16 .40
12 Dale Junkin .16 .40
13 Ethan Moreau .30 .75
14 Derek Grant .16 .40
15 Neil Fewster .16 .40
16 Jason Reesor .16 .40
17 Tom Moores .16 .40
18 Matthew Mayo .16 .40
19 Bogdan Savenko .16 .40
20 Corey Bricknell .16 .40
21 Derek Sylvester .16 .40
22 Anatoli Filatov .16 .40
23 Jason Bonsignore .16 .40
24 Mike Perna .16 .40
25 Manny Legace .40 1.00
26 Randy Hall CO GM .04 .10
27 Chris Johnstone CO .04 .10
28 Jason Bonsignore .20 .50
Ethan Moreau
Brandon Convery
Towering Prospects
NNO Slapshot Ad Card .01

2001-02 Norfolk Admirals

This set features the Admirals of the AHL. It is believed that this set was produced by the team and sold at home games.

COMPLETE SET (27) 4.80 12.00
1 Ajay Baines .20 .50
2 Bill Bowler .30 .75
3 Bobby Russell .14 .35
4 Casey Hankinson .30 .75
5 Chris McAlpine .14 .35
6 Craig Andersson .60 1.50
7 Dmitri Tolkunov .14 .35
8 Jean-Yves Leroux .14 .35
9 Jeff Helperl .14 .35
10 Jim Campbell .14 .35
11 Kent Huskins .14 .35
12 Matt Henderson .14 .35
13 Michael Leighton .80 2.00
14 Mike Peluso .30 .75
15 Mike Souza .14 .35
16 Nolan Baumgartner .14 .35
17 Peter White .14 .35
18 Quintin Laing .14 .35
19 Rumun Ndur .14 .35
20 Shawn Thornton .14 .35
21 Steve McCarthy .20 .50
22 Ty Jones .20 .50
23 Tyler Arnason .30 .75
24 Valeri Zelepukin .14 .35
25 Vladimir Chebaturkin .14 .35
26 Trent Yawney CO .04 .10
NNO Team CL .04 .10

2002-03 Norfolk Admirals

COMPLETE SET (26) 15.00
1 Johnathan Aitken .50
2 Craig Andersson 1.00
3 Ajay Baines .50
4 Scotty Balan .50
5 Cam Bristow .50
6 Brandin Cote .50
7 Louie DeBrusk .50
8 Casey Hankinson .50
9 Jeff Helperl .50
10 Matt Henderson .50
11 Burke Henry .50
12 Kent Huskins .50
13 Quintin Laing .50
14 Mike Leighton 1.50
15 Steve McCarthy .75
16 Brett McLean .50
17 Travis Moen .50
18 Mike Peluso .50
19 Igor Radulov 2.00
20 Shawn Thornton 1.00
21 Dmitri Tolkunov .50
22 Yorick Treille .50
23 Marty Wilford .50
24 Mikhail Yakubov 1.00
25 Trent Yawney CO .10
NNO Checklist .01

2003-04 Norfolk Admirals

COMPLETE SET (24) 5.00 12.00
1 Johnathan Aitken .30 .75
2 Craig Andersson .40 1.00
3 Anton Babchuk .20 .50
4 Ajay Baines .20 .50
5 Michal Barinka .20 .50
6 Blake Bellefeuille .30 .75
7 Brandin Cote .20 .50
8 Matt Ellison .20 .50
9 Carsen Germyn .30 .75
10 Burke Henry .20 .50
11 Duncan Keith .30 .75
12 Matt Keith .20 .50
13 Lasse Kukkonen .20 .50
14 Quintin Laing .40 1.00
15 Adam Munro .40 1.00
16 Steve Passmore .40 1.00
17 Bobby Russell .20 .50
18 Shawn Thornton .20 .50
19 Yorick Treille .20 .50
20 Pavel Vorobiev .20 .50
21 Marty Wilford .20 .50
22 Mikhail Yakubov .20 .50
23 Trent Yawney CO .02 .10
24 Checklist .02 .10

2004-05 Norfolk Admirals

COMPLETE SET (26) 15.00
1 Craig Anderson 1.00
2 Anton Babchuk .50
3 Ajay Baines .50
4 Michal Barinka .50
5 Rene Bourque 1.00
6 Mike Brown .50
7 Brandin Cote .50
8 Matt Ellison .50
9 Duncan Keith .50
10 Matt Keith .50
11 Nick Kuiper .50
12 Quintin Laing .75
13 Michael Leighton 1.00
14 Travis Moen .50
15 Jason Morgan .50
16 Eric Nickulas .75
17 Igor Radulov .50
18 Shawn Thornton 1.00
19 Jim Vandermeer 1.00
20 Pavel Vorobiev .50
21 Marty Wilford .75
22 James Wisniewski .50
23 Mikhail Yakubov .50
24 Trent Yawney CO .10
25 Training Staff .10
NNO Checklist .01

2005-06 Norfolk Admirals

COMPLETE SET (30) 12.00
1 Norfolk Admirals .10
2 Steve Munn .50
3 Michal Barinka .50
4 Brian Lee .50
5 Carl Corazzini .50
6 Anton Babchuk .50
7 Martin St. Pierre .50
8 Milan Bartovic .50
9 Mark Cullen .50
10 Colin Fraser .75
11 Dustin Byfuglien .50
12 Jason Morgan .50
13 Nathan Barrett .50
14 James Wisniewski .50
15 Mike Brown .50
16 Matt Keith .50
17 Nick Kuiper .50
18 Eric Meloche .50
19 Quintin Laing .50
20 Corey Crawford 1.00
21 Ajay Baines .50
22 Adam Munro 1.00
23 Mikhail Yakubov .50
24 Shawn Thornton 1.00
25 Mike Haviland HC .10
26 Rick Kowalsky AC .10
27 McClung/Bender TR .10
28 Cinq-Mars/Holden EQM .10
29 Al MacIsaac GM .10
30 Pascal Bedard .50

2006-07 Norfolk Admirals

COMPLETE SET (28) 8.00 15.00
1 Patrick Lalime .30 .75
2 David Koci .20 .50
3 Brandon Rogers .20 .50
4 Cam Barker .20 .50
5 Jordan Hendry .20 .50
6 Bruno St. Jacques .20 .50
7 Craig MacDonald .20 .50
8 Troy Brouwer .30 .75
9 David Bolland .40 1.00
10 Bryan Bickell .20 .50
11 Adam Burish .20 .50
12 Jonas Nordqvist .20 .50
13 Michael Blunden .30 .75
14 Pierre Parenteau .20 .50
15 Reed Low .30 .75
16 Adam Berti .20 .50
17 Brandon Bochenski .20 .50
18 Danny Richmond .20 .50
19 Steve Munn .20 .50
20 Carl Corazzini .20 .50
21 Martin St. Pierre .20 .50
22 Colin Fraser .20 .50
23 Dustin Byfuglien .20 .50
24 Corey Crawford .30 .75
25 Mike Haviland CO .10 .25
26 Al MacIsaac GM .02 .10
27 Ted Dent ACO .02 .10
28 Trainers .02 .10

1982-83 North Bay Centennials

This 24-card set was printed on thick card stock. The fronts feature a mix of action poses and portraits bordered in white. The backs carry biographical information and sponsor logos, Aunt May's City Bakery (Northern) Limited and CFCH-600 Radio. The cards are unnumbered and checklisted below in alphabetical order.

COMPLETE SET (24) 8.00 20.00
1 Allen Bishop .30 .75
2 John Capel .30 .75
3 Rob Degagne .30 .75
4 Phil Drouillard .30 .75
5 Jeff Eatough .30 .75
6 Tony Gilliard .30 .75
7 Paul Gillis .60 1.50
8 Pete Handley .30 .75
9 Mark Hatcher .30 .75
10 Tim Helmer .30 .75
11 Craig Kales .30 .75
12 Bob LaForest .30 .75
13 Mark LaForest .80 2.00
14 Bill Maguire .30 .75
15 Andrew McBain .60 1.50
16 Ron Meighan .30 .75
17 Rick Morocco .30 .75
18 Alain Raymond .30 .75
19 Joe Reekie .80 2.00
20 Joel Smith .40 1.00
21 Bert Templeton CO .30 .75
22 Kevin Vescio .30 .75
23 Peter Woodgate .30 .75
24 Don Young .30 .75

1983-84 North Bay Centennials

This 25-card set measures approximately 2 1/2" by 4" and is printed on thin card stock. The fronts carry color, posed action player photos with white borders. The player's name appears in a butterscotch-colored plaque that is superimposed over the picture.The cards are unnumbered and checklisted below in alphabetical order.

COMPLETE SET (25) 8.00 20.00
1 Sponsor's Card .10 .25
2 Peter Abric .30 .75
3 Richard Benoit .30 .75
4 Scott Birnie .30 .75
5 John Capel .30 .75
6 Curtis Collin .30 .75
7 Rob Degagne .30 .75
8 Kevin Hatcher 1.20 3.00
9 Mark Hatcher .30 .75
10 Tim Helmer .30 .75
11 Jim Hunter .30 .75
12 Kevin Kerr .30 .75
13 Nick Kypreos .60 1.50
14 Mike Larouche .30 .75
15 Greg Larsen .30 .75
16 Mark Lavarre .30 .75
17 Brett MacDonald .30 .75
18 Wayne Macphee .30 .75
19 Peter McGrath .30 .75
20 Rob Nichols .30 .75
21 Ron Sanko .30 .75
22 Kevin Vescio .30 .75
23 Mike Webber .30 .75
24 Peter Woodgate .30 .75
25 Bert Templeton CO/GM .30 .75

1993-94 North Bay Centennials

Co-sponsored by MCTV and Collectors Corner and printed by Slapshot Images Ltd., this standard size 26-card set features the 1993-94 North Bay Centennials. On a geometrical yellow and black background, the fronts feature color action player photos with thin grey borders. The player's name, position and team name, as well as the producer's logo, appear on the front.

COMPLETE SET (26) 4.00 10.00
1 Brad Brown .20 .50
2 Sandy Allan .20 .50
3 Rob Lave .16 .40
4 Steve McLaren .16 .40
5 Andy Delmore .40 1.00
6 Corey Neilson .16 .40
7 Jason Campeau .16 .40
8 Jim Ensom .16 .40
9 Bill Lang .16 .40
10 Ryan Gillis .16 .40
11 Michael Burman .16 .40
12 Stefan Rivard .16 .40
13 B.J. MacPherson .16 .40
14 Lee Jinman .16 .40
15 Scott Cherrey .16 .40
16 Damien Bloye .16 .40
17 Denis Gaudet .16 .40
18 Bob Thornton .16 .40
19 John Guirestante .16 .40
20 Jeff Shevalier .16 .40
21 Scott Roche .20 .50
22 Vitali Yachmenev .30 .75
23 Bert Templeton CO .16 .40
24 Rob Kirsch ACO .04 .10
25 Brad Brown .16 .40
Vitali Yachmenev
Top Prospects
NNO Slapshot Ad Card .01

1994-95 North Bay Centennials

Sponsored by MCTV, Guardian and Wingate Lottery, and printed by Slapshot Images Ltd., this 26-card set features the 1994-95 North Bay Centennials. On a yellow and black background, the fronts feature color action player photos with thin gray borders. The player's name, position and team name, as well as the producer's logo, appear on the front.

COMPLETE SET (26) 4.00 10.00
1 Joel Gagnon .16 .40
2 Scott Roche .20 .50
3 Derek Lahnalampi .16 .40
4 Brad Brown .20 .50
5 Steve McLaren .16 .40
6 Kam White .16 .40
7 Corey Neilson .16 .40
8 Jason Campeau .16 .40
9 Stephen Carpenter .16 .40
10 Trevor Gallant .16 .40
11 Alex Matvichuk .16 .40
12 Ryan Gillis .16 .40
13 Kris Cantu .16 .40
14 Stefan Rivard .16 .40
15 Brian Whitley .16 .40
16 Dustin Virag .16 .40
17 Lee Jinman .20 .50
18 Scott Cherrey .16 .40
19 Damien Bloye .16 .40
20 Justin Robinson .16 .40
21 Kody Grigg .16 .40
22 John Guirestante .16 .40
23 Gary Roach .16 .40
24 Vitali Yachmenev .30 .75
25 Shane Parker CO/GM .04 .10
Tom Hedican ACO
NNO Ad Card .01

1992-93 North Dakota Fighting Sioux

This scarce promotional giveaway set features North Dakota of the NCAA. The cards are unnumbered and checklisted below alphabetically. Thirteen additional cards in this series (28-40) were recently confirmed by collector Dale Sprenger. Cards #28-32, including a key issue of Ed Belfour, were apparently included with the base set. The remaining eight cards feature ND alumni and a design similar to the Belfour and Casey base set cards. These final eight cards were available only with a purchase at local Subway sandwich shops. We have no pricing info on these cards.

COMPLETE SET (32) 8.00 20.00
1 Akil Adams .30 .75
2 Darren Bear .30 .75
3 Sean Beswick .30 .75
4 Brad Bombardir .40 1.00
5 Joby Bond .30 .75
6 Troy Davis .30 .75
7 Chris Gotziaman .30 .75
8 Dean Grillo .30 .75
9 Corey Howe .30 .75
10 Brett Hryniuk .30 .75
11 Greg Johnson .80 2.00
12 Chad Johnson .30 .75
13 Corey Johnson .30 .75
14 Todd Jones .30 .75
15 Scott Kirton .30 .75
16 Page Klostreich .30 .75
17 Jon Larson .30 .75
18 Jeff Lembke .30 .75
19 John McCoy .30 .75
20 Kevin McKinnon .30 .75
21 Darcy Mitani .30 .75
22 Keith Murphy .30 .75
23 Nick Naumenko .40 1.00
24 Jarrod Olson .30 .75
25 Lars Oxholm .30 .75
26 Kevin Powell .30 .75
27 Kevin Rappana .30 .75
28 Don Riendeau
29 Marty Schriner
30 Teeder Wynne
31 Ed Belfour ALUM
32 Jon Casey ALUM
33 Dave Christian ALUM
34 Tony Hrkac ALUM
35 Bob Joyce ALUM
36 Troy Murray ALUM
37 James Patrick ALUM
38 Russ Romaniuk ALUM
39 Gary Valk ALUM
40 Dixon Ward ALUM

2003-04 North Dakota Fighting Sioux

These cards were issued over the course of six home games. A five-card pack was given to the first 1,000 attendees who asked for them at each game. Thanks to collector Dale Sprenger for the info.

COMPLETE SET (30) 20.00 50.00
1 Brandon Bochenski 1.25 3.00
2 Nate Ziegelmann .40 1.00
3 James Massen .40 1.00
4 Quinn Fylling .40 1.00
5 Mike Prpich .40 1.00
6 Ryan Hale .40 1.00
7 Tyler Palmiscno .40 1.00
8 Matt Jones .75 2.00
9 Brad Berry ACO .20 .50
10 Chris Porter .40 1.00
11 Zach Parise 8.00 20.00
12 Drew Stafford 2.00 5.00
13 Colby Genoway .75 2.00
14 Lee Marvin .40 1.00
15 Team Logo .02 .10
16 Andy Schneider .40 1.00
17 Brady Murray 1.25 3.00
18 Engelstad Arena .02 .10
19 Rory McMahon .40 1.00
20 Matt Smaby 1.25 3.00
21 Jordan Parise 1.25 3.00
22 Brian Canady .40 1.00
23 Robbie Bina .40 1.00
24 Jake Brandt .40 1.00
25 Dean Blais CO .20 .50
26 Matt Greene 1.25 3.00
27 Erik Fabian .40 1.00
28 David Lundholm .40 1.00
29 Dave Hakstol .75 2.00
30 Nick Fuher .40 1.00

2004-05 North Dakota Fighting Sioux

These were issued as a stadium giveaway. They were handed out in five-card perforated strips only on Friday night games and only at certain doors. It was stated on the UND website that only the first 1,000 people would receive the cards so there is a potential of just 1,000 sets.

COMPLETE SET (30) 40.00
1 Header Card .10
2 Robbie Bina 1.00
3 Jake Brandt 2.00
4 Brian Canady 1.00
5 Erik Fabian 1.00
6 Scott Foyt 1.00
7 Nick Fuher 1.00
8 Quinn Fylling 1.00
9 Colby Genoway 1.00
10 Matt Greene 1.00
11 Matt Jones 2.00
12 Rylan Kaip 1.00
13 Philippe Lamoureux 2.00
14 Lee Marvin 1.00
15 James Massen 1.00
16 Rory McMahon 1.00
17 Brady Murray 2.00
18 Jordan Parise 3.00
19 Chris Porter 1.00
20 Mike Prpich 1.00
21 Kyle Radke 1.00
22 Andy Schneider 1.00
23 Matt Smaby 2.00
24 Rastislav Smirko 2.00
25 Drew Stafford 3.00
26 Travis Zajac 3.00
27 Brad Berry ACO .50
28 Carey Eades ACO .50
29 Dave Hakstol CO .50
30 Team Photo .50

1995-96 North Iowa Huskies

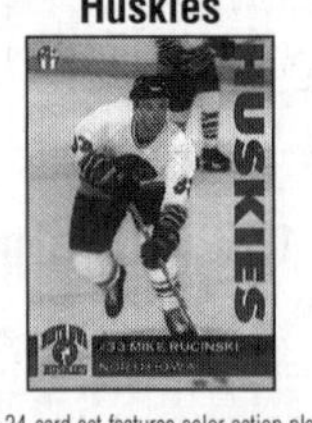

This 34-card set features color action player photos on the fronts with player information on the backs. The set contains a 1995-96 season schedule of games listed below as card number 33. The cards are unnumbered and so are checklisted below in alphabetical order.

COMPLETE SET (34) 20.00 50.00
1 Dave Boehm .75 2.00
2 Mike Cerniglia .75 2.00
3 Lionel Crump .75 2.00
4 Peter Cullen .75 2.00
5 Nate Dicasmirro .75 2.00
6 D.J. Drayna .75 2.00
7 Andy Fermoyle .75 2.00
8 Matt Fetterman .75 2.00
9 Mike Fryar 1.25 3.00
10 Shane Fukushima .75 2.00
11 Bucky Gruber .75 2.00
12 Jason Helgeson TR .04 .10
13 Mark Hicks ACO .04 .10
14 Huskies CL .04 .10
15 Furlin Husky (Mascot) .04 .10
16 Ryan James .75 2.00
17 Tom Lund .75 2.00
18 Kevin Mackey .75 2.00
19 Erik Macy .75 2.00
20 Josh Mizerek .75 2.00
21 Joe Mussey ACO .04 .10
22 Gregg Naumenko 2.00 5.00
23 Matt Noga .75 2.00
24 P.K. O'Handley CO .04 .10
25 Mark Pannitto 1.25 3.00
26 Matt Romaniski .75 2.00
27 Mike Romano .75 2.00
28 Mike Rucinski 1.25 3.00
29 R.J. Schriefer .75 2.00
30 Mike Skogland .75 2.00
31 Matt Snesrud .75 2.00
32 Team Media .04 .10
33 Season Schedule .04 .10
34 Title Card .04 .10

1992-93 Northern Michigan Wildcats

Little is known about this set beyond the confirmed checklist. Any additional information can be forwarded to hockeymag@beckett.com.

COMPLETE SET (32) 4.80 12.00
1 Brian Barker .20 .50
2 Steve Carpenter .20 .50
3 Chad Dameworth .20 .50
4 Dustin Fahl .20 .50
5 Joe Frederick .20 .50
6 Bryan Ganz .20 .50
7 Scott Green .20 .50
8 Greg Hadden .20 .50
9 Steve Hamilton .20 .50
10 Mike Harding .20 .50
11 Jason Hehr .20 .50
12 Dave Huettl .20 .50
13 Troy Johnson .20 .50
14 Karson Kaebel .20 .50
15 Kory Karlander .20 .50
16 Rob Kruhlak .20 .50
17 Garett MacDonald .20 .50
18 Bill MacGillivray .20 .50
19 Don McCusker .20 .50
20 Brent Riplinger .20 .50
21 Dan Ruoho .20 .50
22 Corwin Saurdiff .20 .50
23 Kyuin Shim .20 .50
24 Geoff Simpson .20 .50
25 Scott Smith .20 .50
26 Paul Taylor .20 .50
27 Steve Woog .20 .50
28 Rick Comley CO .04 .10
29 Pat Ford ACO .04 .10
30 Morey Gare ACO .04 .10
31 Dave Shyiak .20 .50
32 Wildcat Willy .04 .10

1993-94 Northern Michigan Wildcats

This 32-card set was issued at one home game as a promotional giveaway. Any additional information can be forwarded to hockeymag@beckett.com.

COMPLETE SET (32) 6.00 15.00
1 Brian Barker .20 .50
2 Keith Bartholomaus .20 .50
3 Steve Carpenter .20 .50
4 Darcy Dallas .20 .50
5 Chad Dameworth .20 .50
6 Bryan Ganz .20 .50
7 Justin George .20 .50
8 Scott Green .20 .50
9 Greg Hadden .20 .50
10 Steve Hamilton .20 .50
11 Patrick Hansson .20 .50
12 Mike Harding .20 .50
13 Jason Hehr .20 .50
14 Mike Hillock .20 .50
15 Trevor Janicki .20 .50
16 Karson Kaebel .20 .50
17 Kory Karlander .20 .50
18 Dieter Kochan .40 1.00
19 Roger Lewis .20 .50
20 Garett MacDonald .20 .50
21 Bill MacGillivray .20 .50
22 Don McCusker .20 .50
23 Brent Riplinger .20 .50
24 Dean Seymour .20 .50
25 Scott Smith .20 .50
26 Paul Taylor .20 .50
27 Shayne Tomlinson .20 .50
28 Jason Welch .20 .50
29 Steve Woog .20 .50
30 Pat Ford ACO .04 .10
31 Morey Gare ACO .04 .10
32 Rick Comley CO .04 .10

2004-05 Northern Michigan Wildcats

This set was given away over the course of several NMU home games.

COMPLETE SET (27) 30.00
1 Pat Bateman 1.00
2 Matt Ciancio 1.00
3 Dusty Collins 1.00
4 Andrew Contois 1.00
5 Blake Cosgrove 1.00
6 Kevin Gardner 1.00
7 Tim Hartung 1.00
8 Josh Hatinger 1.00
9 Bob Helminen 1.00
10 Clayton Lainsbury 1.00
11 Rob Lehtinen 1.00
12 Matt Maunu 1.00
13 Jamie Milam 1.00
14 John Miller 1.00
15 Patrick Murphy 1.00
16 Dan Olver 2.00
17 Nathan Oystrick 1.00
18 Mike Santorelli 1.00
19 Andrew Sarauer 1.00
20 Bobby Selden 1.00
21 Matt Siddall 1.00
22 Dirk Southern 1.00
23 Alan Swanson 1.00
24 Zach Tarkir 1.00
25 Tuomas Tarkki 2.00
26 Geoff Waugh 1.00
27 Bill Zaniboni 2.00

2001-02 Notre Dame Fighting Irish

This set features the Fighting Irish of the NCAA. Little is known about this set, its distribution or if this is a full checklist. If you have any additional information, please forward it to hockeymag@beckett.com. Thanks to Vinnie Montalbano for updating this information.

COMPLETE SET (?) 15.00 30.00
1 Jeremiah Kimento .75 2.00
2 David Inman .75 2.00
3 Jon Maruk .75 2.00
4 Sam Cornelius .75 2.00
5 Rob Globke 1.25 3.00
6 Neil Komadoski .75 2.00
7 Brett Lebda .75 2.00
8 Connor Dunlop 1.25 3.00
9 Evan Neilsen .75 2.00
10 T.J. Mathieson .75 2.00
11 Brad Wanchulak .75 2.00
12 Ryan Mundt .75 2.00
13 Paul Harris .75 2.00
14 Aaron Gill .75 2.00
15 John Wroblewski .75 2.00
16 Derek Smith .75 2.00
17 Cory McLean .75 2.00
18 Michael Chin .75 2.00

2002-03 Notre Dame Fighting Irish

COMPLETE SET (16) 12.00 20.00
1 Jake Wiegand .60 1.50
2 Connor Dunlop .75 2.00
3 Michael Chin .60 1.50
4 Tony Zasowski .60 1.50
5 John Wroblewski .60 1.50
6 Ad card .01 .01
7 Evan Nielsen .60 1.50
8 team card .02 .10
9 Ad card .01 .01
10 Kyle Dolder .60 1.50
11 Tom Galvin .60 1.50
12 Neil Komadoski .60 1.50
13 Brett Lebda 1.25 3.00
14 Rob Globke .75 2.00
15 Aaron Gill .60 1.50
16 T.J. Mathieson .75 2.00

2003-04 Notre Dame Fighting Irish

These cards were issued as a promotional giveaway. It's believed there could be more cards in this series. Please forward any information to hockeymag@beckett.com.

1 Joe Zurenko 1.00
2 Derek Smith 1.00
3 Cory McLean 1.00
4 Brad Wanchulak 1.00
5 Morgan Cey 1.50
6 T.J. Mathieson 1.00
7 Brett Lebda 1.00

8 Rob Globke	3.00
9 Neil Komadoski	1.00
10 Tom Galvin	1.00
11 Aaron Gill	1.50

2004-05 Notre Dame Fighting Irish

This set was issued as a promotional giveaway. It's possible the checklist is not complete. Please forward additional info to hockeymag@beckett.com.

COMPLETE SET (25)	25.00
1 Wes O'Neill	2.00
2 David Brown	2.00
3 Bryan D'Arcy	1.00
4 Mark Van Guilder	1.00
5 Victor Oreskovich	1.00
6 Evan Rankin	1.00
7 Brock Sheahan	1.00
8 Andrew Eggert	1.00
9 Luke Lucyk	1.00
10 Dave Venard	1.00
11 Michael Bartlett	1.00
12 T.J. Jindra	1.00
13 Matt Williams-Kovacs	1.00
14 Josh Sciba	1.00
15 Noah Babin	1.00
16 Jason Paige	1.00
17 Rory Walsh	2.00
18 Tim Wallace	1.00
19 Tony Gill	1.00
20 Mike Walsh	1.00
21 Matt Amado	1.00
22 Chris Trick	1.00
23 Joe Zurenko	1.00
24 Cory McLean	1.00
25 Morgan Cey	2.00

2005-06 Notre Dame Freshmen

COMPLETE SET (5)	5.00
1 Eric Condra	1.00
2 Justin White	1.00
3 Garrett Regan	1.00
4 Jordan Pierce	1.00
5 Christian Hanson	1.00

1984-85 Nova Scotia Oilers

This 26-card police set features the Nova Scotia Oilers of the American Hockey League. The cards measure approximately 2 1/2" by 3 3/4" and were sponsored by Q104 (an FM radio station), Coca-Cola, Hostess, and the Bedford Town Police, and the Halifax City Police. The cards display posed color player photos on a white card face. The player's name and position appear at the bottom.

COMPLETE SET (26)	6.00	15.00
1 Mark Holden	.30	.75
2 Dave Allison	.20	.50
3 Dwayne Boettger	.20	.50
4 Lowell Loveday	.20	.50
5 Rejean Cloutier	.20	.50
6 Ray Cote	.20	.50
7 Pat Conacher	.40	1.00
8 Ken Berry	.40	1.00
9 Steve Graves	.20	.50
10 Todd Strueby	.40	1.00
11 Steve Smith	.80	2.00
12 Archie Henderson	.30	.75
13 Dean Dachyshyn	.20	.50
14 Marc Habscheid	.40	1.00
15 Larry Melnyk	.30	.75
16 Raimo Summanen	.40	1.00
17 Jim Playfair	.20	.50
18 Mike Zanier	.40	1.00
19 Ian Wood	.20	.50
20 Dean Hopkins	.20	.50
21 Norm Aubin	.20	.50
22 Tony Currie	.20	.50
23 Ross Lambert	.20	.50
24 Terry Martin	.20	.50
25 Ed Chadwick CO	.40	1.00
Larry Kish CO		
Bob Boucher CO		
26 Lou Christian TR	.10	.25
Kevin Farris TR		

1985-86 Nova Scotia Oilers

This 28-card police set features the Nova Scotia Oilers. The cards measure approximately 2 1/2" by 3 3/4" and were sponsored by Coca-Cola, Hostess, Q104 (an FM radio station), IGA food stores, and the Halifax City Police. The fronts display color action photos on a white card face. The sponsor logos appear across the top and in

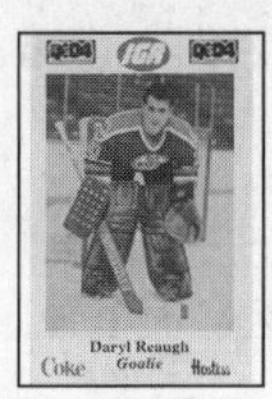

the lower corners. The player's name and position is below the picture.

COMPLETE SET (28)	6.00	15.00
1 Dean Hopkins	.20	.50
2 Jeff Larmer	.20	.50
3 Mike Moller	.20	.50
4 Dean Dachyshyn	.20	.50
5 Bruce Boudreau	.30	.75
6 Ken Solheim	.20	.50
7 Jeff Beukeboom	.30	.75
8 Mark Lavarre	.20	.50
9 John Ollson	.20	.50
10 Lou Crawford	.20	.50
11 Warren Skorodenski	.40	1.00
12 Dwayne Boettger	.20	.50
13 Daryl Reaugh	1.20	3.00
14 John Miner	.20	.50
15 Jim Ralph	1.20	3.00
16 Wayne Presley	.30	.75
17 Steve Graves	.20	.50
18 Tom McMurchy	.20	.50
19 Darin Sceviour	.20	.50
20 Kent Paynter	.20	.50
21 Larry Kish GM/CO	.10	.25
22 Jim Playfair	.20	.50
23 Kevin Farris TR	.10	.25
Ralph Mosher TR		
24 Mickey Volcan	.20	.50
25 Ron Low ACO	.40	1.00
26 Don Biggs	.20	.50
27 Bruce Eakin	.20	.50
28 Team Photo	.30	.75

1976-77 Nova Scotia Voyageurs

Set was sponsored by Farmers Twin Cities Co-op Dairy Ltd. Cards measure 4"x 6". Cards are listed below in alphabetical order. It is not known whether this list is complete and we have no pricing data; additional info can be forwarded to hockeymag@beckett.com. Thanks to collector Dale Sprenger for providing the info below.

COMPLETE SET (?)
1 Bruce Baker
2 Mike Busniuk
3 Jim Cahoon
4 Cliff Cox
5 Dave Elenbaas
6 Brian Engblom
7 Don Howse
8 Pat Hughes
9 Peter Lee
10 Chuck Luksa
11 Gilles Lupien
12 Al McNeil CO
13 Gord McTavish
14 Pierre Mondou
15 Hal Phillipoff
16 Mike Polich
17 Rod Schutt
18 Ed Walsh
19 Ron Wilson
20 Paul Woods

1977-78 Nova Scotia Voyageurs

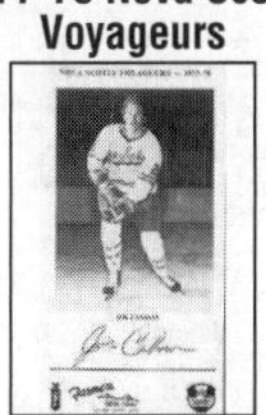

Sponsored by the Farmers Twin Cities Co-op Dairy Ltd., this 24-card set measures approximately 3 1/4" by 6" and features the Nova Scotia Voyageurs of the American Hockey League. The fronts feature posed action player photos bordered in white. In the top border appears "Nova Scotia Voyageurs 1977-78," while the player's name, facsimile autograph, sponsor name and logo, and team logo are printed below the picture. The backs are blank. The cards are unnumbered and checklisted below in alphabetical order.

COMPLETE SET (24)	15.00	30.00
1 Bruce Baker	.50	1.00
2 Maurice Barrette	.50	1.00
3 Barry Borrett	.50	1.00
4 Tim Burke	.50	1.00
5 Jim Cahoon	.50	1.00
6 Norm Dupont	.75	1.50
7 Greg Fox	.75	1.50
8 Mike Hobin	.50	1.00
9 Bob Holland	.50	1.00
10 Don Howse	.50	1.00
11 Pat Hughes	1.00	2.00
12 Chuck Luksa	.50	1.00
13 Dave Lumley	1.00	2.00
14 Al MacNeil CO	.75	1.50
15 Gord McTavish	.50	1.00
16 Rick Meagher	1.50	3.00
17 Mike Polich	.50	1.00
18 Moe Robinson	.50	1.00
19 Gaeton Rochette	.50	1.00
20 Pierre Roy	.50	1.00
21 Frank St.Marseille	1.00	2.00
22 Derrick St.Marseille TR	.25	.50
23 Rod Schutt	.50	1.00
24 Ron Wilson	1.00	2.00

1983-84 Nova Scotia Voyageurs

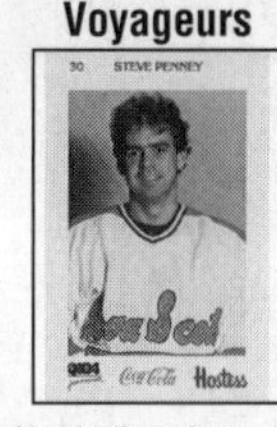

This 24-card police set features the Nova Scotia Oilers of the American Hockey League. The cards measure approximately 2 1/2" by 3 3/4" and were sponsored by Q104 (an FM radio station), Coca-Cola, and Hostess. The cards display posed color player photos on a white card face. The player's name and jersey number appear at the top. The three sponsors' logos are in the bottom white border.

COMPLETE SET (24)	6.00	15.00
1 Mark Holden	.40	1.00
2 Bill Kitchen	.20	.50
3 Dave Allison	.20	.50
4 Stephane Lefebvre	.20	.50
5 Stan Hennigar	.20	.50
6 Steve Marengere	.20	.50
7 John Goodwin	.20	.50
8 John Newberry	.20	.50
9 Bill Riley	.30	.75
10 Norman Baron	.30	.75
11 Brian Skrudland	.80	2.00
12 Mike Lalor	.40	1.00
13 Blair Barnes	.20	.50
14 Remi Gagne	.20	.50
15 Steve Penney	.80	2.00
16 Michel Therrien	.30	.75
17 Dave Stoyanovich	.20	.50
18 Brian Patafie TR	.10	.25
Lou Christian TR		
19 Mike McPhee	.80	2.00
20 Wayne Thompson	.20	.50
21 Ted Fauss	.20	.50
22 Jeff Teal	.20	.50
23 Larry Landon	.20	.50
24 Greg Moffett	.20	.50

1996-97 OCN Blizzard

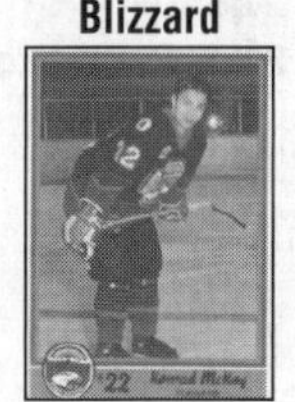

COMPLETE SET (25)	10.00
1 Rick Gregory	.50
2 Reynold Monias	.50
3 Dave Patenaude	.50
4 Clint Miller	.50
5 Alec Durocher	.50
6 Peter Bird	.50
7 Steve Ford	.50
8 Devin Salisbury	.50
9 John Brass	.50
10 Barrett Labossiere	.50
11 Cliff Duchesne	.50
12 Mike Stevenson	.50
13 Wally Wuttunee	.50
14 Don Boyer	.50
15 Jay Seymour	.50
16 Darren Kirk	.50
17 Tobias Hall	.50
18 John O'Toole	.50
19 Chad Ramsay	.50
20 Clayton Debray	.50
21 Konrad Mckay	.50
22 Ryan Belbas	.50
23 John McCusker	.50
24 Ryan Person	.50
25 Patrick Herman	.50

1997-98 OCN Blizzard

COMPLETE SET (24)	20.00
1 Team Picture	.50
2 Tucker Madder	.50
3 Kevin Wilson	.50
4 Larry Willerton	.50
5 Terence Tootoo	10.00
6 Clayton Quinn	.50
7 Shaun Rose	.50
8 Brad Hicks	.50
9 Barrett Labossiere	.50
10 Curtis Baldwin	.50
11 Jimmie Ronnback	.50
12 Wally Wuttunee	.50
13 Don Boyer	.50
14 Aaron Porter	.50
15 Alec Durocher	.50
16 Cliff Duchesne	.50
17 Devin Salisbury	.50
18 Cory Dittmer	.50
19 Derek Ernest	.50
20 Konrad Mckay	.50
21 Ryan Belbas	.50
22 John McCusker	.50
23 Ryan Person	.50
24 Tyler Love	.50

1998-99 OCN Blizzard

This set features the first card of the extremely popular Inuit star, Jordin Tootoo.

COMPLETE SET (24)	40.00
1 Team Picture	1.00
2 Terence Tootoo	10.00
3 Kevin Wilson	.50
4 Larry Willerton	.50
5 Morris Elderkin	.50
6 Darcy Johnson	.50
7 Shaun Rose	.50
8 Brad Hicks	.50
9 Barrett Labossiere	.50
10 Kevin Stoneman	.50
11 Jamie Vossen	.50
12 Jordin Tootoo	25.00
13 Aaron Porter	.50
14 Chad Ryan	.50
15 Cliff Duchesne	.50
16 Devin Salisbury	.50
17 Jimmie Ronnback	.50
18 Tom Herman	.50
19 Konrad Mckay	.50
20 Ryan Belbas	.50
21 John McCusker	.50
22 Ryan Person	.50
23 Preston McKay	.50
24 Brian Tucker	.50

1999-00 OCN Blizzard

COMPLETE SET (24)	
1 Team Picture	.50
2 Rob Hrabec	.50
3 Justin Relland	.50
4 Cory Sawatzky	.50
5 Justin Seaborg	.50
6 Gary Lafreniere	.50
7 Darcy Johnson	.50
8 Darryl Crumb	.50
9 Kirk Ziefflie	.50
10 Jamie Muswagon	.50
11 Michael Young	.50
12 Ryan Braun	.50
13 Mike Glover	.50
14 Dustin Rogers	.50
15 Phillip Albert	.50
16 Justin Williams	.50
17 Dave Splawinski	.50
18 Steve Reid	.50
19 Clifford Scatch	.50
20 Tom Herman	.50
21 Terence Tootoo	10.00
22 Dwayne Twerdin	.50
23 Jeff Grandfield	.50
24 Preston McKay	.50

2000-01 OCN Blizzard

COMPLETE SET (25)	20.00
1 Team Picture	.25
2 Marc-Andre Leclerc	.50
3 Garrett Hildebrandt	.50
4 Matko Malbasa	.50
5 Jared Lang	.50
6 Darcy Johnson	.50
7 Alton Jackson	.50
8 Kirk Ziefflie	.50
9 Jamie Muswagon	.50
10 Michael Young	.50
11 Ryan Braun	.50
12 Shayne Emmons	.50
13 Derek Sharp	.50
14 Phillip Albert	.50
15 Justin Williams	.50
16 Curtis Campbell	.50
17 Clifford Scatch	.50
18 Trevor Len	.50
19 Terence Tootoo	10.00
20 Justin Tetrault	.50
21 Jeff Grandfield	.50
22 Dan Joyal	.50
23 Steve Macintyre	.50
24 Tim Haun	.50
25 Dave Splawinski	.50

2001-02 OCN Blizzard

COMPLETE SET (27)	12.00
1 Header Card	.01
2 Team Picture	.25
3 Louis Chabot	.50
4 Mike Gooch	.50
5 Garrett Hildebrandt	.50
6 Jeff Froese	.50
7 Cody Reynolds	.50
8 Andy Coates	.50
9 Aaron Starr	.50
10 Alton Jackson	.50
11 Kirk Ziefflie	.50
12 Jamie Muswagon	.50
13 Michael Young	.50
14 Ryan Braun	.50
15 Russell Spence	.50
16 Phillip Albert	.50
17 Justin Williams	.50
18 Justin Seaborg	.50
19 Leighton Alexson	.50
20 Trevor Len	.50
21 Mark Wallmann	.50
22 Justin Tetrault	.50
23 Mike Ouellet	.50
24 Everett Bear	.50
25 Dylan Rochon	.50
26 Marc-Andre Leclerc	.50
27 Dave Splawinski	.50

2002-03 OCN Blizzard

COMPLETE SET (27)	12.00
1 Team Picture	.25
2 Andrew Gallant	.50
3 Mike Gooch	.50
4 Garrett Hildebrandt	.50
5 Dallas Jackson	.50
6 Paul Wallmann	.50
7 Andy Coates	.50
8 Aaron Starr	.50
9 Alton Jackson	.50
10 Jared Lang	.50
11 Michael Young	.50
12 Ryan Braun	.50
13 Kiel Wilgosh	.50
14 Daniel Mayer	.50
15 Jason Kowalski	.50
16 Mike Kaluzny	.50
17 Ryan Weistche	.50
18 Trevor Len	.50
19 Tyler Rhyorchuk	.50
20 Jason Marin	.50
21 Everett Bear	.50
22 Chop Melnyk	.50
23 Dylan Rochon	.50
24 Ryan Constant	.50
25 Jonathon Meyer	.50
26 Mark Wallmann	.50
27 League Champs	.10

2003-04 OCN Blizzard

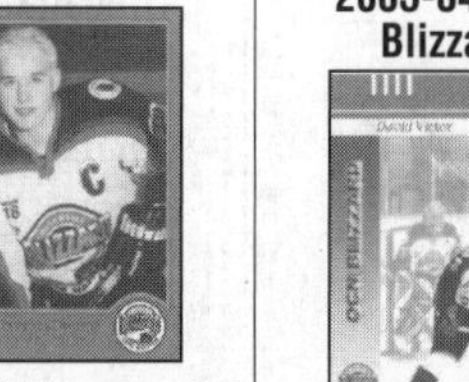

COMPLETE SET (27)	10.00
1 Header Card	.01
2 Everett Bear	.50
3 Jason Butler	.50
4 Ryan Constant	.50
5 Pierre-Olivier Girouard	.50
6 Mike Gooch	.50
7 Tim Hammell	.50
8 Cole Hunter	.50
9 Dallas Jackson	.50
10 Travis Kotyk	.50
11 Jared Lang	.50
12 Daniel Mayer	.50
13 Lyle McKay	.50
14 Don Melnyk	.50
15 Jonathon Meyer	.50
16 Brett Needham	.50
17 Lem Randell	.50
18 Jonathon Romic	.50
19 Aaron Starr	.50
20 Matt Summers	.50
21 Stephen Sunderman	.50
22 David Victor	.50
23 Mark Wallmann	.50
24 Paul Wallmann	.50
25 Kiel Wilgosh	.50
26 Michael Young	.50
27 Team Photo	.10

1998-99 Odessa Jackalopes

This 22-card set of the WPHL Jackalopes was handed out as a promotional giveaway at a home game in November, 1998.

COMPLETE SET (22)	10.00	25.00
1 Jacque Rodrigue	.40	1.00
2 Rob Lukacs	.80	2.00
3 Ryan Equale	.40	1.00
4 Rick Girhiny	.80	2.00
5 Terry Flynn	.40	1.00
6 Paul Fioroni	.40	1.00
7 Mike Ross	.60	1.50
8 Johan Hagman	.40	1.00
9 Sami Laine	.60	1.50
10 Anders Lindberg	.80	2.00
11 Dan Lavergne	.40	1.00
12 Bo Anderson	.40	1.00
13 Shayne LeBreton	.40	1.00
14 Michael Tornquist	.60	1.50
15 Christian Wibner	.80	2.00
16 Chris Morque	.40	1.00
17 Bill Pye	.80	2.00
18 Martin Ohestedt	.80	2.00
19 Joe Clark CO	.04	.10
20 Pat Kerin EM	.04	.10
21 Greg Andis TR	.04	.10
22 Golden Corral	.04	.10

1999-00 Odessa Jackalopes

This set featuring the Jackalopes of the WPHL was issued as a promotional giveaway at a home game in December of 1999.

COMPLETE SET (21)	5.60	20.00
1 Michael Tornquist	.30	1.00
2 Paul Vincent	.30	1.00
3 Chris Morque	.30	1.00
4 Fredrick Lindh	.30	1.00
5 Bill Pye	.40	2.00
6 Sami Laine	.40	2.00
7 Jason Pellerin	.30	1.00
8 Eric Perricone	.30	1.00
9 Karson Kaebel	.30	1.00
10 Roy Gray	.30	1.00
11 Rick Girhiny	.30	1.00
12 Mark Smith	.30	1.00
13 John Bossio	.30	1.00
14 Mike Vandenberghe	.30	1.00
15 Gary Coupal	.40	2.00
16 Jacque Rodrigue	.30	1.00
17 Savo Mitrovic	.30	1.00
18 George Umunna	.30	1.00
19 Greg Andis TR	.04	.10
20 Joe Harrell EQM	.04	.10
21 Kentucky Fried Chicken	.04	.01

2001-02 Odessa Jackalopes

This set features the Jackalopes of the WPHL. The set was issued as a promotional giveaway at a home game. The cards are unnumbered, so they are listed in alphabetical order.

COMPLETE SET (21)	12.00	30.00
1 Trevor Allman	.60	1.50
2 Jeffrey Ambrosio	.80	2.00
3 John Bossio	.60	1.50
4 Kenny Corupe	.80	2.00
5 Matt Cressman	.60	1.50
6 Adam Doyle	.60	1.50
7 Robert Frid	.60	1.50
8 Mike Gorman	.60	1.50
9 Joe Harris	.60	1.50
10 Jeff Haydar	.60	1.50
11 Scott Hillman	.60	1.50
12 Doug Johnson	.60	1.50
13 Derek Laxdal ACO	.10	.25
14 Alexander Lyubimov	.60	1.50
15 Don Margettie	.60	1.50
16 Don McKee CO	.10	.25
17 Jacque Rodrigue	.60	1.50
18 Mike Sanderson	.80	2.00
19 Mark Smith	.60	1.50
20 Tim Stay	.60	1.50
21 Team Photo	.20	.50

2002-03 Odessa Jackalopes

COMPLETE SET (24)	20.00
1 John Bossio	1.00
2 Matt Carney	1.50
3 Matt Cressman	1.00
4 Jerry Cunningham	1.00
5 Denis Desmarais	1.00
6 Adam Doyle	1.00
7 Ryan Edwards	1.00
8 David Francis	1.00
9 Robert Frid	1.00
10 Greg Gatto	1.00
11 Mike Gorman	1.50
12 Scott Green	1.00
13 Kevin Hansen	1.00
14 Scott Hillman	1.00
15 Don Margettie	1.00
16 Mike Rutter	1.00
17 Sebastien Thinel	1.00
18 Greg Willers	1.00
19 Jami Yoder	1.00
20 Don McKee HCO	.25
21 Derek Laxdal ACO	.25
22 Joe Harrell EQM	.10
23 Greg Andis TR	.10
24 Sonic Ad	.01

2003-04 Odessa Jackalopes

Produced by Grandstand Cards, this set was sold by the team at home games. The cards are unnumbered and are listed in alphabetical order.

COMPLETE SET (22)	10.00
1 Header Card	.01
2 John Bossio	.50
3 Mark Cairns	.75
4 Matt Cressman	.50
5 Adam Doyle	.50
6 Shaun Fairweather	.50
7 Jeff Goldie	.50
8 Mike Gorman	.75
9 Scott Green	.50
10 Wayne Hall	.50
11 Scott Hillman	.50
12 Jaroslav Kerestes	.50
13 Sal Lettieri	.50
14 Joel Martin	.75
15 Matt Price	.50
16 Mike Rutter	.50
17 Pat Stachniak	.75
18 Sebastien Thinel	.75
19 Danny Williams	.50
20 Jami Yoder	.50
21 Don McKee HCO	.10
22 Greg Gatto ACO	.10

2004-05 Odessa Jackalopes

This team set was issued as a stadium giveaway at a late-season home game.

COMPLETE SET (21)	20.00
1 B.J. Adams	1.00
2 Pascal Bedard	1.00
3 Matt Cressman	1.00
4 Paul Davies	1.00
5 Derek Dolson	2.00
6 Adam Doyle	1.50
7 Mike Gorman	2.00
8 Mike Hanson	1.00
9 Scott Hillman	1.00
10 Joel Irving	1.00
11 Tom Kotsopolous	2.00
12 John Kozoriz	1.00
13 R.C. Lyke	1.00
14 Don Margettie	1.00
15 Chris Paradise	1.00
16 Mike Rutter	2.00
17 Sebastien Thinel	2.00
18 Ben Wallace	1.00
19 Don McKee CO	.50
20 Slappy MASCOT	.10
21 Midland Memorial Hospital	.01

2005-06 Odessa Jackalopes

COMPLETE SET (19)	15.00
1 Pascal Bedard	.75
2 Chris Brannen	.75
3 Mike Carter	.75
4 Matt Cressman	.75
5 Paul Davies	.75
6 Andrew Davis	.75
7 Derek Dolson	1.50
8 Jeff Ewasko	.75
9 Mike Gorman	1.50
10 Scott Hillman	.75
11 John Kozoriz	.75
12 Josh Legge	.75
13 Dominic Leveille	.75
14 Adam Loncan	1.50
15 Jamie Lovell	.75
16 Don Margettie	.75
17 Mike Rutter	.75
18 Sebastien Thinel	.75
19 Don McKee HC	.25

2006-07 Odessa Jackalopes

COMPLETE SET (21)	15.00	30.00
1 Blaine Bablitz	.60	1.50
2 Pascal Bedard	.60	1.50
3 Chris Brannen	.60	1.50
4 Matt Cressman	.60	1.50
5 Andrew Davis	.60	1.50
6 Derek Dolson	1.00	2.50
7 Alex Dunn	.60	1.50
8 Jeff Ewasko	1.25	3.00
9 Mike Gorman	1.00	2.50
10 Scott Hillman	.60	1.50
11 John Kozoriz	.60	1.50
12 Jay Latulippe	.60	1.50
13 Josh Legge	.60	1.50
14 Don Margettie	.60	1.50
15 Mike Ramsay	.60	1.50
16 Mike Rutter	.60	1.50
17 Steve Shrum	.60	1.50
18 Brian Swiniarski	.60	1.50
19 Nathan Ward	.60	1.50
20 Don McKee CO	.20	.50
21 Doug Johnson ACO	.20	.50

1999-00 Ohio State Buckeyes

This set features the Buckeyes of the NCAA. The set was issued as a promotional giveaway at a home game.

COMPLETE SET (20)	6.00	20.00
1 Ray Aho	.40	1.50
2 Peter Broccoli	.30	1.00
3 Louie Colsant	.30	1.00
4 Jason Crain	.30	1.00
5 Yan DesGagne	.30	1.00
6 Jean-Francois Dufour	.30	1.00
7 Jaisen Freeman	.30	1.00
8 Nick Ganga	.30	1.00
9 Ryan Jestadt	.30	1.00
10 Miguel LaFleche	.30	1.00
11 Mike McCormick	.30	1.00

12 Eric Meloche .30 1.00
13 Luke Pavlas .40 1.50
14 Jason Selleke .30 1.00
15 Andre Signoretti .30 1.00
16 Ryan Skaleski .30 1.00
17 Ryan Smith .30 1.00
18 Scott Titus .30 1.00
19 Benji Wolke .30 1.00
20 Brutus Buckeye MASCOT .10 .25

2000-01 Ohio State Buckeyes

This set features the Buckeyes of the NCAA. The set was issued as a promotional giveaway in Jan. 2001. The set is noteworthy for featuring the first cards of 2001 first-rounders Dave Steckel and R. J Umberger.

COMPLETE SET (20) 8.00 20.00
1 Andre Signoretti .30 .75
2 Jean-Francois Dufour .30 .75
3 Jaisen Freeman .30 .75
4 Jason Crain .30 .75
5 Mike McCormick .30 .75
6 Scott Titus .30 .75
7 Nick Ganga .30 .75
8 Yan DesGagne .30 .75
9 Miguel LaFleche .30 .75
10 Ryan Smith .30 .75
11 Peter Broccoli .30 .75
12 Luke Pavlas .40 1.00
13 Peter Wishloff .30 .75
14 Mike Betz .30 .75
15 R.J. Umberger 2.00 5.00
16 Dave Steckel 1.20 3.00
17 Scott May .30 .75
18 Doug Andress .30 .75
19 Brutus Buckeye MASCOT .10 .25
20 John Markell CO .10 .25

2001-02 Ohio State Buckeyes

This set features the Buckeyes of the NCAA. It was issued as a promotional giveaway at a last-season home game. The cards, which are slightly smaller than standard size, are unnumbered, and thus are listed in alphabetical order.

COMPLETE SET (20) 12.00 30.00
1 Doug Andress .60 1.50
2 Daymen Bencharski .60 1.50
3 Mike Betz .60 1.50
4 Peter Broccoli .60 1.50
5 Paul Caponigri .60 1.50
6 Jason Crain .60 1.50
7 Yan DesGagne .60 1.50
8 Miguel LaFleche .60 1.50
9 T.J. Latorre .60 1.50
10 Scott May .60 1.50
11 Mike McCormick .60 1.50
12 Chris Olsgard .60 1.50
13 Luke Pavlas .80 2.00
14 Eric Skaug .60 1.50
15 Ryan Smith .60 1.50
16 Dave Steckel 1.20 3.00
17 Scott Titus .60 1.50
18 R.J. Umberger 1.20 3.00
19 Reed Whiting .60 1.50
20 Brutus Buckeye MASCOT .10 .25

2002-03 Ohio State Buckeyes

COMPLETE SET (20) 20.00
1 Doug Andress 1.00
2 Daymen Bencharski 1.00
3 Mike Betz 1.50
4 J.B. Bittner 1.00
5 Peter Broccoli 1.00
6 Paul Caponigri 1.00
7 Miguel LaFleche 1.00
8 Scott May 1.00
9 Chris Olsgard 1.00
10 Luke Pavlas 1.00
11 Eric Skaug 1.00
12 Lee Spector 1.00
13 Dave Steckel 1.50
14 Scott Titus 1.00
15 R.J. Umberger 2.50
16 Thomas Welsh 1.00
17 Reed Whiting 1.00
18 John Markell HCO .25
19 Brutus Buckeye .10
20 Nathan Guenin .50
Ryan Kesler
Dan Knapp(#Rod Pelley
Dave Caruso

2003-04 Ohio State Buckeyes

This set was given away to the first 5,000 fans at the Jan. 17, 2004 home game. The cards are smaller than standard size. They are unnumbered and so are listed below in alphabetical order.

COMPLETE SET (20) 8.00 20.00
1 Doug Andress .40 1.00
2 Daymen Bencharski .40 1.00
3 Mike Betz .60 1.50
4 J.B. Bittner .40 1.00
5 Paul Caponigri .40 1.00
6 Dave Caruso .60 1.50
7 Nathan Guenin .40 1.00
8 Kelly Holowaty .40 1.00
9 Dan Knapp .40 1.00
10 Scott May .40 1.00
11 Chris Olsgard .40 1.00
12 Rod Pelley .40 1.00
13 Lee Spector .40 1.00
14 Dave Steckel .75 2.00
15 Thomas Welsh .40 1.00
16 Reed Whiting .40 1.00
17 Sean Collins .40 1.00
Andrew Schembri
18 Matt Beaudoin .40 1.00
Kenny Bernard
Matt Waddell
19 Bryce Anderson(#Tyson Strachan .40 1.00
Dave Barton
20 Mascot .10 .25

2004-05 Ohio State Buckeyes

COMPLETE SET (20) 10.00 25.00
1 Bryce Anderson .40 1.00
2 Dave Barton .40 1.00
3 Matt Beaudoin .40 1.00
4 Kenny Bernard .40 1.00
5 J.B. Bittner .40 1.00
6 Dave Carusa .75 2.00
7 Sean Collins .40 1.00
8 Nate Guenin .75 2.00
9 Dan Knapp .40 1.00
10 Rod Pelley .40 1.00
11 Andrew Schembri .40 1.00
12 Lee Spector .40 1.00
13 Tyson Strachan .40 1.00
14 Matt Waddell .40 1.00
15 Thomas Welsh .40 1.00
16 Ian Keserich .75 2.00
Johan Krull
17 Matt McIlvane .40 1.00
Domenic Maiani
18 Tom Fritsche .75 2.00
Kyle Hood
19 John Dingle .40 1.00
Jason DeSantis
20 Sam Campbell .40 1.00
Phil Lauderdale
Zach Pelletier

2004-05 Ohio State Buckeyes Women

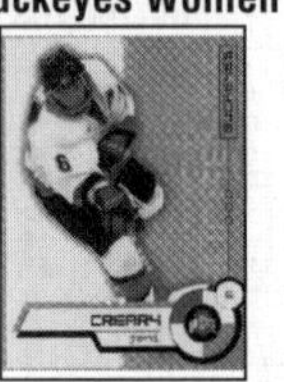

This set was issued as a promotional giveaway. The design mirrors that of the men's set from the same season.

COMPLETE SET (20) 8.00 20.00
1 Melissa Glasser .75 2.00
2 Jennifer Desson .40 1.00
3 Jeni Creary .40 1.00
4 Jaclyn Haines .40 1.00
5 Meaghan Mulvaney .40 1.00
6 Jana Harrigan .40 1.00
7 Crystal Sayther .40 1.00
8 Katie Sershen .40 1.00
9 Tessa Bonhomme .40 1.00
10 Amber Bowman .40 1.00
11 Katie Maroney .40 1.00
12 Lacey Schultz .40 1.00
13 Krysta Skarda .40 1.00
14 Erika Vanderweer .75 2.00
15 Shelby Aldous .75 2.00
Lisa Chesson
16 Jody Heywood .40 1.00
Erin Keyes
17 Jill Mauch .75 2.00
Pamela Patterson
18 Mallory Peckels .40 1.00
Rachel Vanscoy
19 Jackie Barto CO .02 .10
20 Buckeye MASCOT .02 .10

2005-06 Ohio State Buckeyes

COMPLETE SET (25) 8.00 20.00
1 Bryce Anderson .30 .75
2 Dave Barton .30 .75
3 Matt Beaudoin .30 .75
4 Kenny Bernard .30 .75
5 Dave Caruso .60 1.50
6 Sean Collins .30 .75
7 Tom Fritsche .60 1.50
8 Nate Guenin .30 .75
9 Kyle Hood .30 .75
10 Dan Knapp .30 .75
11 Domenic Maiani .30 .75
12 Rod Pelley .60 1.50
13 Andrew Schembri .30 .75
14 Tyson Strachan .30 .75
15 Matt Waddell .30 .75
16 Ian Keserich SO .60 1.50
17 Zach Pelletier SO .30 .75
18 Jason DeSantis SO .30 .75
19 Phil Lauderdale SO .30 .75
20 Johann Kroll SO .30 .75
21 Sam Campbell SO .30 .75
22 Matt McIlvane SO .30 .75
23 John Dingle SO .30 .75
24 Corey Elkins FR .30 .75
25 Nick Biondo FR .30 .75

2006-07 Ohio State Buckeyes

COMPLETE SET (25) 15.00 25.00
1 Bryce Anderson .40 1.00
2 Dave Barton .40 1.00
3 Matt Beaudoin .40 1.00
4 Kenny Bernard .40 1.00
5 Sean Collins .40 1.00
6 Jason DeSantis .40 1.00
7 John Dingle .40 1.00
8 Tommy Goebel .40 1.00
9 Johann Kroll .40 1.00
10 Domenic Maiani .40 1.00
11 Matt McIlvane .40 1.00
12 Andrew Schembri .40 1.00
13 Tyson Strachan .40 1.00
14 Matt Waddell .40 1.00
15 Phil Lauderdale .40 1.00
16 Nick Filion .60 1.50
17 Corey Elkins .40 1.00
18 Nick Biondo .40 1.00
19 Tom Fritsche .60 1.50
20 Zach Pelletier .40 1.00
21 Kyle Hood .40 1.00
22 Sam Campbell .40 1.00
23 Joe Palmer .60 1.50
24 Mathieu Picard .40 1.00
25 Brutus Buckeye MASCOT .10 .25

2006-07 Ohio State Buckeyes Women

COMPLETE SET (20) 15.00 25.00
1 Mallory Peckels .50 1.25
2 Katie Maroney .50 1.25
3 Jody Heywood .50 1.25
4 Tessa Bonhomme .50 1.25
5 Erika Vanderveer .50 1.25
6 Whitney Miller .50 1.25
7 Hayley Klassen .50 1.25
8 Lisa Chesson .50 1.25
9 Liana Bonanno .50 1.25
10 Krysta Skarda .50 1.25
11 Jill Mauch .50 1.25
12 Erin Keys .50 1.25
13 Kelly Cahill .50 1.25
14 Olivia Antognoli .50 1.25
15 Lacey Schultz .50 1.25
16 Morgan Marziali .50 1.25
17 Megan Hostasek .50 1.25
18 Amber Bowman .50 1.25
19 Shelby Aldous .50 1.25
20 The Freshmen .50 1.25

2005-06 OHL Bell All-Star Classic

COMPLETE SET (38) 8.00 20.00
1 Kevin Lalande .20 .50
2 David Bolland .20 .50
3 Wojtek Wolski .40 1.00
4 Bobby Ryan .40 1.00
5 Matt Lashoff .20 .50
6 John Vigilante .20 .50
7 Cory Emmerton .20 .50
8 Derek Joslin .20 .50
9 Andrej Sekera .20 .50
10 Marc Staal .20 .50
11 Chris Stewart .20 .50
12 Jonathan D'Aversa .20 .50
13 Ryan Parent .20 .50
14 Peter Aston .20 .50
15 Benoit Pouliot .40 1.00
16 Dan Lacosta .20 .50
17 Jordan Owens .40 1.00
18 Patrick McNeill .20 .50
19 Peter Tsimikalis .20 .50
20 Andrew Marshall .20 .50
21 Bobby Sanguinetti .20 .50
22 Michael Blunden .40 1.00
23 Ryan Callahan .20 .50
24 Adam Dennis .40 1.00
25 Justin Donati .20 .50
26 Steve Downie .75 2.00
27 Tyler Haskins .20 .50
28 Dylan Hunter .20 .50
29 Tyler Kennedy .20 .50
30 Scott Lehman .20 .50
31 Bryan Little .40 1.00
32 Ryan MacDonald .20 .50
33 Evan McGrath .40 1.00
34 Ryan O'Marra .40 1.00
35 Chad Painchaud .20 .50
36 Tommy Pyatt .20 .50
37 Robbie Schremp .40 1.00
38 Jordan Staal 1.25 3.00
39 Matt Kelly .20 .50
40 Jamie Tardif .20 .50

1992-93 Oklahoma City Blazers

This 18-card standard-size set was sponsored by TD's Sports Cards (a Tulsa baseball card store) and Planters Nuts and Snacks. Ten thousand sets were produced. Randomly inserted throughout the sets were 350 autographed cards of each player. The cards feature color action player photos with white borders. The player's name is superimposed on the photo at the bottom. The cards are unnumbered and checklisted

below in alphabetical order.

COMPLETE SET (18) 3.20 8.00
1 Title Card .10 .25
2 Carl Boudreau .20 .50
3 Joe Burton .20 .50
4 Sylvain Fleury .20 .50
5 Brendan Garvey .20 .50
6 Guy Girouard .20 .50
7 Sean Gorman .20 .50
8 Jamie Hearn .20 .50
9 Craig Johnson .20 .50
10 Paul Krake .30 .75
11 Chris Laganas .20 .50
12 Daniel Larin .20 .50
13 Mark McGinn .20 .50
14 Alan Perry .30 .75
15 Steve Simoni .20 .50
16 Jim Solly .20 .50
17 Boyd Sutton .20 .50
18 Team Photo .20 .50

1993-94 Oklahoma City Blazers

Like each of the CHL sets issued that year, these are round cards approximately the size of a hockey puck. They come in a plastic container with the team logo on the front, and were sold at home games by the booster club for about $5.

COMPLETE SET (18) 3.20 8.00
1 Kent Anderson .20 .50
2 Carl Boudreau .20 .50
3 Joe Burton .20 .50
4 Mike Ciolli .20 .50
5 Guy Girouard .20 .50
6 Jules Jardine .20 .50
7 Craig Johnson .20 .50
8 Chris Laganas .20 .50
9 Jeff Massey .20 .50
10 Derry Menard .20 .50
11 Trent Pankewicz .20 .50
12 Alan Perry .30 .75
13 James Richmond .20 .50
14 Bruce Shoebottom .20 .50
15 Steve Simoni .20 .50
16 Jim Solly .20 .50
17 Mike Williams .20 .50
18 Mike McEwen CO .08 .20

1998-99 Oklahoma City Blazers

This 23-card set of the CHL Blazers was sold by the team late in the season at its souvenir stands.

COMPLETE SET (23) 4.00 10.00
1 Peter Arvanitis .20 .50
2 Dan Fournel .20 .50
3 Dominic Fafard .20 .50
4 Craig Willard .20 .50
5 Simon Olivier .20 .50
6 Joe Burton .30 .75
7 Craig Johnson .20 .50
8 Tom Gomes .20 .50
9 Steve Moore .20 .50
10 Jim Jensen .20 .50
11 Brad Preston .20 .50
12 Rod Butler .20 .50
13 Michael Pozzo .20 .50
14 Chris Johnston .20 .50
15 Hardy Sauter .20 .50
16 Jean-Ian Filiatrault .30 .75
17 Mike Williams .20 .50
18 Doug Sauter HCO .04 .10
19 Corey MacIntyre .20 .50
20 Daniel Larin .20 .50
21 Brandon Rose TR .04 .10
22 Team Photo .20 .50
23 Checklist .04 .10

2003-04 Oklahoma City Blazers

This set was sold at home games. The cards are unnumbered and listed in alphabetical order.

COMPLETE SET (24) 4.00 10.00
1 Header Card .01 .01
2 Peter Arvanitis .20 .50
3 Boyd Ballard .30 .75
4 Les Borsheim .20 .50
5 Ryan Campbell .20 .50
6 Sean Connors .30 .75
7 Qamil "Charlie" Elezi .30 .75
8 Tyler Fleck .20 .50
9 Bryan Forslund .20 .50
10 Brad Herauf .20 .50
11 Stefan Katalina .20 .50
12 Justin Kot .20 .50
13 Tim Laurila .20 .50
14 Mike Lucci .20 .50
15 Blair Manning .20 .50
16 Peter Robertson .20 .50
17 Jesse Saltmarsh .20 .50
18 Hardy Sauter .20 .50
19 Doug Sheppard .20 .50
20 Marty Standish .30 .75
21 Ryan Watson .20 .50
22 Doug Sauter HCO .02 .10
23 Sponsor .01 .01
24 Sponsor .01 .01

2004-05 Oklahoma City Blazers

COMPLETE SET (24) 10.00 25.00
1 B.J. Ballas .40 1.00
2 Jarad Bourassa .40 1.00
3 Michel Beausoleil .60 1.50
4 Brenden Morrow 4.00 10.00
5 Hardy Sauter .60 1.50
6 Pat Hallett .40 1.00
7 Tyler Fleck .40 1.00
8 Brad Herauf .40 1.00
9 Scott Selig .40 1.00
10 Cody Loughlean .40 1.00
11 Bryan Forslund .40 1.00
12 Garrett Prosofsky .60 1.50
13 Boyd Ballard .60 1.50
14 Jason Goulet .60 1.50
15 Sean Connors .60 1.50
16 Kevin Harris .40 1.00
17 Kahlil Thomas .40 1.00
18 Shawn Weiman .40 1.00
19 Doug Sauter CO .02 .10
20 Team Photo .02 .10
21 Clyde S. Dale MASCOT .01 .01
22 Crash Test Dummies .01 .01
23 Sponsor .01 .01
NNO Header Card .01 .01

1995-96 Oklahoma Coyotes RHI

This set features the Coyotes of Roller Hockey Intl. Only 500 of these 18 card sets were printed. They were available through the Coyotes Booster Club over a several game span at the end of the season. The cards are not numbered, and therefore are listed alphabetically.

COMPLETE SET (18) 6.00 15.00
1 Kevin Barrett .30 .75
2 Joe Burton .40 1.00
3 Scott Drevitch .30 .75
4 George Dupont .30 .75
5 Jason Elders .30 .75
6 Jean-Ian Filiatrault .40 1.00
7 Johan Finnstrom .30 .75
8 Tom Gomes .30 .75
9 Radek Hamr .30 .75
10 Ross Harris .40 1.00
11 Jason Knox .30 .75
12 Perry Neufeld .30 .75
13 Darcy Pengelly .30 .75
14 Trevor Sherban .30 .75
15 Peter Skudra .80 2.00
16 Darren Stolk .30 .75
17 Rob Weingartner .30 .75
18 Guy Gadowsky CO .10 .25

2006-07 Okotoks Oilers

COMPLETE SET (24) 12.00 20.00
1 Nathan Brummit .40 1.00
2 Jesse Budkins .40 1.00
3 Derrick Burnett .40 1.00
4 David Civitarese .40 1.00
5 Dan Conacher .40 1.00
6 Justin Daigle .40 1.00
7 Bradley Eidsness .40 1.00
8 Mark Jensen .40 1.00
9 Curtis Leinweber .40 1.00
10 Zack MacKinnon .40 1.00
11 Spencer Mcelhinney .40 1.00
12 Carter Madsen .40 1.00
13 Jeff Matheson .40 1.00
14 Andrew Owsiak .40 1.00
15 Jesse Perrin .40 1.00
16 Jeff Sapisha .40 1.00
17 Brian Schmautz .40 1.00
18 Kyle Schussler .40 1.00
19 Elliott Sheen .40 1.00
20 Everett Sheen .40 1.00
21 Devin Welsh .40 1.00
22 Garry VanhereweghеÂ COÂ .10 .25
23 Trevor McFarlaneÂ ACOÂ .10 .25
24 Jeff TotzÂ ACOÂ .10 .25

1993-94 Omaha Lancers

This set features the Lancers of the USHL. The set was available at hobby shops in the Omaha area and at AK-SAR-BEN arena where the Lancers play. The fronts feature posed action shots inside borders. The team name and player information appears in two stripes immediately below the picture. The cards are unnumbered and checklisted below in alphabetical order.

COMPLETE SET (28) 4.00 10.00
1 Ryan Bencurik .16 .40
2 Jeff Borders .16 .40
3 Sean Bowman .16 .40
4 Doc Del Castillo ACO .04 .10
5 Jeff Edwards .16 .40
6 Tony Gasparini .16 .40
7 Mike Guentzel CO .04 .10
8 Scott Haig .16 .40
9 Ken Hemenway .16 .40
10 Bill Hubbard .16 .40
11 Klage Kaebel .16 .40
12 Rob Klasnick .16 .40
13 Tony Kolozsy .16 .40
14 Tom Kowal .16 .40
15 Charlie Lentz .16 .40
16 Justin Lyle .16 .40
17 Chris Marvel .16 .40
18 Mike Peluso .16 .40
19 Scott Pionk ACO .04 .10
20 Dan Riva .16 .40
21 Nathan Rocheleau .16 .40
22 Eric Runyan .16 .40
23 Joe Russo .16 .40
24 Brian Swanson .40 1.00
25 Scott Swanson .16 .40
26 Justin Theel .16 .40
27 Jamie Thompson .16 .40
28 Brendan Walsh .16 .40

2001-02 Omaha Lancers

We have confirmed the existence of one card in this series. If you have any additional info, please email hockeymag@beckett.com.

COMPLETE SET (?)
1 Yale Lewis

2002-03 Orlando Seals

It's possible this checklist is incomplete. If you have additions, please contact us at hockeymag@beckett.com.

COMPLETE SET (???) 15.00
1 B.J. Stephens 1.00
2 Mike Correia 1.00
3 Stan Drulia HCO 1.00
4 Mascot .10
5 Todd Bennett 1.00
6 Chris LiPuma 1.00
7 Louis Goulet 1.00
8 Zac Boyer 1.00
9 David Goverde 1.50
10 Mark White 1.00
11 Jad Ramsay 1.00
12 Joe Spencer 1.00
13 Sponsor Card .01
14 Ethan Burnes 1.00
15 Ryan Anderson 1.00
16 Mascot .10
17 Chris Cerrella 1.00
18 Todd Nowicki 1.00
19 Joe Seroski 1.00

1998-99 Orlando Solar Bears

This set features the Solar Bears of the IHL. This issue was sold in team set form at home games and is much easier to find than the giveaway cards issued later that season.

COMPLETE SET (19) 4.00 10.00
1 Checklist/Logo card .04 .10
2 Patrick Neaton .20 .50
3 Sean McCann .20 .50
4 Clayton Norris .20 .50
5 Hubie McDonough .30 .75
6 Shawn Carter .20 .50
7 Grigori Panteleyev .30 .75
8 Todd Richards .30 .75
9 Shawn Wansborough .20 .50
10 Mark Beaufait .40 1.00
11 Scott Hollis .20 .50
12 David Mackey .20 .50
13 David Littman .30 .75
14 Grigori Panteleyev AS .30 .75
15 Mark Beaufait AS .40 1.00
16 Curt Fraser CO .20 .50
17 Peter Horachek ACO .20 .50
18 Orlando Arena .20 .50
19 Shades MASCOT .20 .50

1998-99 Orlando Solar Bears II

This set was given away at two different home games. The cards were issued in perforated sheets and are unnumbered. They are extremely difficult to find in complete set form.

COMPLETE SET (22) 25.00
1 David Littman .60 1.50
2 Mark Beaufait .80 2.00
3 Shawn Carter .40 1.00
4 David Mackey .40 1.00
5 Sean McCann .40 1.00
6 Hubie McDonough .60 1.50
7 Patrick Neaton .40 1.00
8 Clayton Norris .40 1.00
9 Grigori Panteleyev .60 1.50
10 Todd Richards .60 1.50
11 Curt Fraser HCO .60 1.50
12 Scott Bailey .60 1.50
13 Rob Bonneau .40 1.00
14 Allan Egeland .40 1.00
15 Todd Krygier .40 1.00
16 Kirby Law .40 1.00
17 Curtis Murphy .40 1.00
18 Mike Nicholishen .40 1.00
19 Frederik Oduya .40 1.00
20 Ken Sabourin .40 1.00
21 Pierre Sevigny .40 1.00
22 Peter Horachek ACO .40 1.00

1980-81 Oshawa Generals

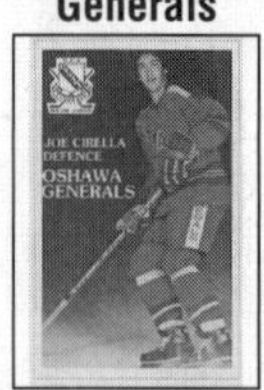

This 25-card P.L.A.Y. (Police, Laws and Youth) set measures approximately 2 5/8" by 4 1/8" and features color posed action player photos and is bordered by white borders accented by a thin red line. The player's name, position, and team are superimposed in white letters on the picture.

COMPLETE SET (25) 62.50 125.00
1 Generals Logo .50 1.00
2 Ray Flaherty .50 1.00
3 Craig Kitchener .50 1.00
4 Dan Revell .50 1.00
5 Bob Kucheran .50 1.00
6 Pat Poulin .50 1.00
7 Dave Andreychuk 7.50 15.00
8 Barry Tabobondung .50 1.00
9 Steve Konroyd 1.50 3.00
10 Paul Edwards .50 1.00
11 Dale Degray 1.50 3.00
12 Joe Cirella 1.50 3.00
13 Norm Schmidt .50 1.00
14 Markus Lehto .75 1.50
15 Mitch Lamoureux .75 1.50
16 Tony Tanti 2.00 4.00
17 Bill Laforge .50 1.00
18 Greg Gravel .50 1.00
19 Mike Lekun .50 1.00
20 Chris Smith .50 1.00
21 Peter Sidorkiewicz 2.00 4.00
22 Greg Stefan 2.00 4.00
23 Tom McCarthy 2.00 4.00
24 Rick Lanz 2.00 4.00
25 Bobby Orr 40.00 80.00

1981-82 Oshawa Generals

This 25-card P.L.A.Y. (Police, Laws and Youth) set measures approximately 2 5/8" by 4 1/8" and features color posed action player photos. The backs carry "Tips from the Generals" that include a hockey tip and its application to a life situation.

COMPLETE SET (25) 24.00 60.00
1 Generals Logo .40 1.00
2 Chris Smith .60 1.50
3 Peter Sidorkiewicz 1.60 4.00
4 Ali Butorac .60 1.50
5 Dan Revell .60 1.50
6 Mitch Lamoureux .80 2.00
7 Norm Schmidt .60 1.50
8 Paul Edwards .60 1.50
9 Dan Nicholson .60 1.50
10 John Hutchings .60 1.50
11 Dave Gans .60 1.50
12 Dave Andreychuk 6.00 15.00
13 Mike Stern .60 1.50
14 Dale Degray .80 2.00
15 Mike Lekun .60 1.50
16 Greg Gravel .60 1.50
17 Dave MacLean .60 1.50
18 Tony Tanti 1.20 3.00
19 John MacLean 6.00 15.00
20 Jim Uens .60 1.50
21 Guy Jacob .60 1.50
22 Jeff Steffan .60 1.50
23 Paul Theriault .60 1.50
24 Sherry Bassin .60 1.50
25 Durham Regional .20 .50
Police Logo

1982-83 Oshawa Generals

This 25-card set measures approximately 2 5/8" by 4 1/8" and features color, posed action player photos framed by thin red border lines that rest on a white card face. The player's name, position, and the team logo are superimposed across the top of the picture in white lettering.

COMPLETE SET (25) 14.00 35.00
1 Generals Logo .20 .50
2 Jeff Hogg .60 1.50
3 Peter Sidorkiewicz 1.20 3.00
4 Dale Degray .60 1.50
5 Joe Cirella .60 1.50
6 Todd Smith .40 1.00
7 Scott Brydges .40 1.00
8 Jeff Steffen .40 1.00
9 Don Biggs .40 1.00
10 Todd Hooey .40 1.00
11 Tony Tanti .80 2.00
12 Danny Gratton .40 1.00
13 Steve King .40 1.00
14 Dan Defazio .40 1.00
15 John MacLean 3.20 8.00
16 Tim Burgess .40 1.00
17 Mike Stern .40 1.00
18 Dan Nicholson .40 1.00
19 David Gans .40 1.00
20 John Hutchings .40 1.00
21 Norm Schmidt .40 1.00
22 Todd Charlesworth .40 1.00
23 Paul Theriault CO .30 .75
24 Sherry Bassin GM .40 1.00
25 Durham Regional .20 .50
Police Logo

1983-84 Oshawa Generals

This 30-card P.L.A.Y. (Police, Laws and Youth) set measures approximately 2 5/8" by 4 1/8" and features color posed action player photos. The backs carry "Tips from the Generals" that include a hockey tip and its application to a life situation.

COMPLETE SET (30) 12.00 30.00
1 Peter Sidorkiewicz .80 2.00
2 Kirk McLean 4.00 10.00
3 Todd Charlesworth .40 1.00
4 Ian Ferguson .30 .75
5 John Hutchings .30 .75
6 Generals Logo .10 .25
7 Mark Haarmann .30 .75
8 Joel Curtis .30 .75
9 Dan Gratton .30 .75
10 Steve Hedington .30 .75
11 Scott Brydges .30 .75
12 CKAR Radio .10 .25
13 Brad Walcot .30 .75
14 Paul Theriault CO .30 .75
15 Jon Jenkins Chief of Police .10 .25
16 Sherry Bassin GM .40 1.00
17 Craig Morrison .30 .75
18 Bolahood's .10 .25
19 Bruce Melanson .30 .75
20 Mike Stern .30 .75
21 Gary McColgan .30 .75
22 Lee Giffin .40 1.00
23 Brent Maki .30 .75
24 Ronald McDonald .20 .50
25 Jeff Steffen .30 .75
26 John Stevens .30 .75
27 David Gans .30 .75
28 Don Biggs .40 1.00
29 Chip Crandall .30 .75
30 Durham Police Logo .10 .25

1989-90 Oshawa Generals

These over-sized cards (approximately 2 5/8 X 4 1/8 inches) feature color action photos on the front and sponsor logos on the back. Cards were printed by Whitby Business Forms. The Lindros single has been widely counterfeited. Collectors should be wary when purchasing that card in single form. Your best bet is to purchase the complete set if you want a legitimate copy.

COMPLETE SET (35) 14.00 35.00
1 Corey Banika .20 .50
2 David Craievich .20 .50
3 Scott Hollis .20 .50
4 Mike Decoff .20 .50
5 Joe Busillo .20 .50
6 Matt Hoffman .20 .50
7 Craig Donaldson .20 .50
8 Jason Denomme .20 .50
9 Brian Grieve .20 .50
10 Wade Simpson .20 .50
11 Dale Craigwell .40 1.00
12 Mike Lenarduzzi .20 .50
13 Rick Cornacchia CO .04 .10
14 Dave Edwards .20 .50
15 Kevin Butt .40 1.00
16 Team Photo .08 .20
17 Clair Cornish .20 .50
18 Jarrod Skalde .40 1.00
19 Mark Deazeley .20 .50
20 Jean Paul Davis .20 .50
21 Todd Coopman .04 .10
22 Trevor McIvor .20 .50
23 Mike Craig .40 1.00
24 Paul O'Hagan .20 .50
25 Iain Fraser .20 .50
26 Brent Grieve .20 .50
27 Lions International .04 .10
28 National Sports Centre .04 .10
29 Durham Regional Police .04 .10
30 Oshawa Generals .04 .10
31 Eric Lindros 8.00 20.00
32 Bill Armstrong .20 .50
33 Chris Vanclief .20 .50
34 Scott Luik .20 .50
35 Fred Brathwaite 1.20 3.00

1989-90 Oshawa Generals 7th Inning Sketch

This set of the 1989-90 Oshawa Generals of the OHL was released by 7th Inning Sketch in advance of its full 1989-90 OHL issue. The cards, numbered 1-23, are the same as those found in the larger set. Card #1, featuring Eric Lindros, has been widely counterfeited. Collectors should exercise caution when purchasing this card as a single. Your best precaution is to use a jeweler's loupe to carefully study the print pattern on the front of the card.

COMPLETE SET (23) 4.80 12.00
1 Eric Lindros 2.00 5.00
2 Jarrod Skalde .30 .75
3 Joe Busillo .20 .50
4 Dale Craigwell .30 .75
5 Clair Cornish .20 .50
6 Jean-Paul Davis .20 .50
7 Craig Donaldson .20 .50
8 Wade Simpson .20 .50
9 Mike Craig .20 .50
10 Mark Deazeley .20 .50
11 Scott Hollis .20 .50
12 Brian Grieve .20 .50
13 Dave Craievich .20 .50
14 Paul O'Hagan .20 .50
15 Matt Hoffman .20 .50
16 Trevor McIvor .20 .50
17 Cory Banika .20 .50
18 Kevin Butt .30 .75
19 Iain Fraser .20 .50
20 Bill Armstrong .20 .50
21 Scott Luik .20 .50
22 Brent Grieve .20 .50
23 Fred Brathwaite .60 1.50

1991-92 Oshawa Generals

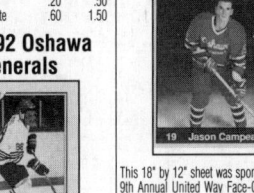

This 32-card standard-size set was sponsored by Coca-Cola and Domino's Pizza. The cards feature color action player photos framed by a royal blue double line. A white circle at the lower right corner carries the player's jersey number or the season year '91-'92.

COMPLETE SET (32) 8.00 20.00
1 Mike Fountain .30 .75
2 Brian Grieve .16 .40
3 Trevor Burgess .16 .40
4 Wade Simpson .16 .40
5 Ken Shepard .16 .40
6 Stephane Yelle .30 .75
7 Matt Hoffman .16 .40
8 Neil Iserhoff .16 .40
9 Rob Leask .16 .40
10 Kevin Spero .16 .40
11 Scott Hollis .16 .40
12 Sean Brown .20 .50
13 Todd Bradley .16 .40
14 Darryl LaFrance .16 .40
15 Markus Brunner .20 .50
16 B.J. MacPherson .16 .40
17 Jason Campeau .16 .40
18 Jason Weaver .16 .40
19 Jan Benda .20 .50
20 Jason Arnott 1.60 4.00
21 Eric Lindros 3.20 8.00
22 Wayne Daniels Dir. of Operations .04 .10
23 Joe Cook .16 .40
24 Can't Beat the Real Thing (Coke Ad) .04 .10
25 Experience the Domino's Effect (Pizza Ad) .04 .10
26 Mark Deazeley .16 .40
27 Jean-Paul Davis .16 .40
28 Brian Grieve .16 .40
29 Oshawa Generals Team Photo .40 1.00
30 Ian Young CO Larry Marson CO5 Rick Cornacchia CO .04 .10
31 Sponsor Ads Checklist .04 .10
32 Prosport's Action .04 .10

1991-92 Oshawa Generals Sheet

This 18" by 12" sheet was sponsored by the 8th Annual United Way Face-Off Breakfast. The front features posed, color player cards with the players' names printed in a black stripe that appears below each picture. The center of the sheet carries the words "8th Annual United Way Face-Off Breakfast" in sky blue print. The team name also appears in the center, along with the year, the individual sheet number, and the production run (5,000). The players are checklisted below as they appear from left to right. Although these typically are found in sheet form, we are listing values for singles below as well as the complete sheet price.

COMPLETE SHEET (26) 8.00 20.00
1 Scott Hollis .16 .40
2 Jan Benda .20 .50
3 Joe Cook .16 .40
4 Wade Simpson .16 .40
5 B.J. MacPherson .16 .40
6 David Anderson .16 .40
7 Stephane Yelle .30 .75
8 Troy Sweet .16 .40
9 Matt Hoffman .16 .40
10 Trevor Burgess .16 .40
11 Jason Weaver .16 .40
12 Craig Lutes .16 .40
13 Darryl LaFrance .16 .40
14 Jason Arnott 1.60 4.00
15 Eric Lindros 3.20 8.00
16 Brian Grieve .16 .40
17 Mark Deazeley .16 .40
18 Mike Cote .16 .40
19 Markus Brunner .20 .50
20 Kevin Spero .16 .40
21 Todd Bradley .16 .40
22 Mike Fountain .30 .75
23 Fred Brathwaite .30 .75
24 Jean-Paul Davis .16 .40
25 Jason Campeau .16 .40
26 Neil Iserhoff .16 .40

1992-93 Oshawa Generals Sheet

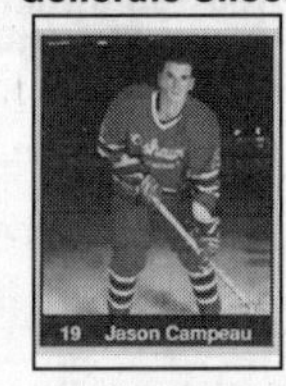

This 18" by 12" sheet was sponsored by the 9th Annual United Way Face-Off Breakfast. The front features posed, color player cards with the players' names printed in a black stripe that appears below each picture. The center of the sheet carries the words "9th Annual United Way Face-Off Breakfast" in black print. The team name also appears in the center, along with the year, the individual sheet number, and the production run (5,000). Although these typically are found in sheet form, we are listing values for singles below as well as the complete sheet price.

COMPLETE SHEET (26) 6.00 15.00
1 Wade Simpson .20 .50
2 Jamie Kress .20 .50
3 Sean Brown .24 .60
4 Jason Arnott 1.20 3.00
5 Mark Brooks .20 .50
6 Rob McQuat .20 .50
7 Joe Cook .20 .50
8 Chris Hall .20 .50
9 Jason McQuat .20 .50
10 Jason Julian .20 .50
11 Kevin Spero .20 .50
12 Steve Haight .20 .50
13 B.J. MacPherson .20 .50
14 Billy-Jay Johnston .20 .50
15 Stephane Soulliere .20 .50
16 Todd Bradley .20 .50
17 Darryl Lafrance .20 .50
18 Aaron Albright .20 .50
19 Trevor Burgess .20 .50
20 Scott Hollis .20 .50
21 Serge Dunphy .20 .50
22 Joel Gagnon .30 .75
23 Brian Kent .30 .75
24 Stephane Yelle .40 1.00
25 Jason Campeau .20 .50
26 Neil Iserhoff .20 .50

1993-94 Oshawa Generals

Printed by Slapshot Images Ltd., this standard size 27-card set features the 1993-94 Oshawa Generals. Reportedly only 3,000 of these sets were produced; the title card also serves as a Certificate of Authenticity and has the number 3,000 printed in the lower right corner. On a geometrical team color-coded background, the fronts feature color action player photos with thin black borders. The player's name, position and team name, as well as the producer's logo, appear on the front.

COMPLETE SET (27) 4.00 10.00
1 Title Card Checklist .04 .10
2 Joel Gagnon .20 .50
3 Ken Shepard .20 .50
4 Jan Snopek .20 .50
5 David Froh .16 .40
6 Brandon Gray .16 .40
7 Damon Hardy .16 .40
8 Sean Brown .24 .60
9 Jeff Andrews .16 .40
10 Stephane Yelle .30 .75
11 Stephane Soulliere .16 .40
12 Andrew Power .16 .40
13 Todd Bradley .16 .40
14 Darryl Lafrance .20 .50
15 Darryl Moxam .16 .40
16 Robert Dubois .16 .40
17 Kevin Vaughan .16 .40
18 Rob McQuat .20 .50
19 B.J. Johnston .16 .40
20 Paul Doherty .16 .40
21 Eric Boulton .20 1.00
22 Marc Savard .40 1.00
23 Chris Hall .16 .40
24 Jason McQuat .16 .40
25 Ryan Lindsay .16 .40
26 Rick Cornacchia CO Wayne Daniels DIR Brian Drumm ACO .04 .10
NNO Slapshot Ad Card .04 .10

2001-02 Oshawa Generals

We have confirmed the existence of one card in this series. Please forward any additional information you might have to hockeymag@beckett.com.

COMPLETE SET (?)
1 Nathan Horton

2003-04 Oshawa Generals

COMPLETE SET (26) 5.00 12.00
1 Dan Turple .30 .75
3 John Neal .20 .50
4 Chris Petrow .20 .50
6 Bret Nasby .20 .50
7 Clay McFadden .20 .50
8 Fred Hatziioannou .20 .50
10 Tyler Donati .20 .50
11 Andrew Gibbons .20 .50
12 Justin Donati .20 .50
14 Andy Reiss .20 .50
15 Aaron Lobb .20 .50
16 Mike McLean .20 .50
17 Chris Hulit .20 .50
19 Jordan Beirnes .20 .50
20 Justin Wallingford .20 .50
21 Adam Berti .20 .50
22 Mike Kavanagh .20 .50
23 Brandon McBride .20 .50
24 Ryan Kitchen .20 .50
25 Ben Eager .40 1.00
26 Paul Ranger .20 .50
27 Gary Friesen .20 .50
28 Tobias Whelan .20 .50
31 Ryan Gibb .30 .75
NNO Paul Ranger TL .75 2.00
NNO Ben Eager TL .75 2.00

2004-05 Oshawa Generals

COMPLETE SET (22) 5.00 12.00
1 Carlo Di Rienzo .40 1.00
2 Ryan Gibb .40 1.00
3 John Neal .60 1.50
4 Trevor Waddell .20 .50
5 Bret Nasby .20 .50
6 Brett Trudell .20 .50
7 Justin Allen .20 .50
8 Peter Tsimikalis .20 .50
9 Tom Jefferson .20 .50
10 Cal Clutterbuck .40 1.00
11 Matt Piva .20 .50
12 Matt Puntureri .20 .50
13 Jesse Biduke .20 .50
14 Devereaux Heshmatpour .30 .75
15 Adam Berti .40 1.00
16 Mike Kavanaugh .20 .50
17 Brandon McBride .20 .50
18 Chad Thompson .20 .50
19 James DeLory .20 .50
20 David Halasz .20 .50
21 Gary Friesen .20 .50
22 Checklist .01 .01

2004-05 Oshawa Generals Autographs

One autographed player card was inserted into every 2004-05 Oshawa Generals team set. It is believed that every member of the Generals signed for inclusion in this insert. If anyone has information to the contrary, please contact us at hockeymag@beckett.com.

COMPLETE SET (21) 60.00

2006-07 Oshawa Generals

COMPLETE SET (24) 12.00 20.00
1 John Tavares 3.00 8.00
2 Dale Mitchell .40 1.00
3 Tyler Taylor .20 .50
4 Igor Gongalsky .20 .50
5 Cal Clutterbuck .20 .50
6 Dean Howard .20 .50
7 Kory Nagy .20 .50
8 Brett Maclean .40 1.00
9 Corey Cowick .20 .50
10 Kyle Paige .20 .50
11 Kody Musselman .20 .50
12 Shea Kewin .20 .50
13 Brett Parnham .20 .50
14 Ziga Pance .20 .50
15 Trevor Koverko .20 .50
16 Michael Del Zotto .60 1.50
17 Matt Seegmiller .20 .50
18 Peter Aston .20 .50
19 Eric Regan .20 .50
20 Billy Siekris .20 .50
21 James Delory .20 .50
22 Loic Lacasse .30 .75
23 Mark Packwood .30 .75
24 Oshawa Generals .10 .25

1981-82 Ottawa 67's

The cards measure approximately 5 1/2" by 8 1/2" and feature black-and-white player portraits in white borders. A facsimile autograph and player's jersey number are printed in the wide bottom margin. The backs are blank. The cards are unnumbered and checklisted below in alphabetical order. Thanks to collector Stan Mendes for providing additional checklist information.

COMPLETE SET (25) 12.00 30.00
1 James Allison .30 .75
2 John Boland .30 .75
3 Randy Boyd .30 .75
4 Adam Creighton 1.20 3.00
5 Bill Dowd .30 .75
6 Dwayne Davison .30 .75
7 Alan Hepple .30 .75
8 Mike James .30 .75
9 Brian Kilrea CO .80 2.00
10 Moe Lemay .60 1.50
11 Benny Longe .30 .75
12 Doug Stewart .30 .75
12 Paul Louttit .30 .75
13 Don McLaren .30 .75
13 Fraser Wood .30 .75
14 John Ollson .30 .75
15 Brian Patafie TR .20 .50
16 Mark Paterson .40 1.00
17 Phil Patterson .30 .75
18 Larry Power .30 .75
19 Jim Ralph 2.00 5.00
20 Darcy Roy .40 1.00
21 Brad Shaw 1.20 3.00
22 Brian Small .30 .75
23 Doug Stewart .30 .75
24 Jeff Vaive .30 .75
25 Fraser Wood .30 .75

1982-83 Ottawa 67's

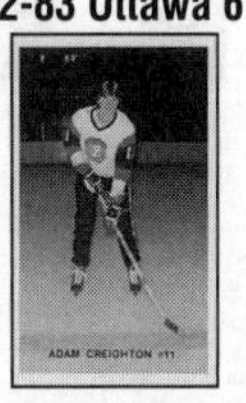

Sponsored by Coke and Channel 12, this 25-card set measures approximately 2 5/8" by 4 1/8" and features posed, color player photos with white borders. The player's name and jersey number are printed in black across the bottom of the picture. The cards are unnumbered and checklisted below in alphabetical order.

COMPLETE SET (25) 12.00 30.00
1 Bruce Cassidy .30 .75
2 Greg Coram .30 .75
3 Adam Creighton .80 2.00
4 Bill Dowd .30 .75
5 Gord Hamilton ACO .20 .50
6 Scott Hammond .30 .75
7 Alan Hepple .30 .75
8 Alan Hepple .30 .75
9 Jim Jackson TR .20 .50
10 Mike James .30 .75
11 Brian Kilrea CO .80 2.00
12 Paul Louttit .30 .75
13 Brian McKinnon .30 .75
14 Don McLaren .30 .75
15 John Ollson .30 .75
16 Darren Pang 2.00 5.00
17 Mark Paterson .30 .75
18 Phil Patterson .30 .75
19 Larry Power .30 .75
20 Gary Roberts 3.20 8.00
21 Brian Rome .30 .75
22 Darcy T. Roy .30 .75
23 Brad Shaw 1.00 2.50
24 Doug Stewart .30 .75
25 Jeff Vaive .30 .75
26 Larry MacAndrew .30 .75
27 Gord Hamilton Jr. .30 .75

1983-84 Ottawa 67's

Sponsored by Coke and Channel 12, this 27-card set measures approximately 2 5/8" by 4 1/8". The fronts feature posed, color player photos with white borders. The player's name and jersey number are printed in black across the bottom of the picture. The cards are unnumbered and checklisted below in alphabetical order.

COMPLETE SET (27) 10.00 25.00
1 Richard Adolfi .20 .50
2 Bill Bennett .20 .50
3 Bruce Cassidy .30 .75
4 Todd Clarke .20 .50
5 Greg Coram .30 .75
6 Adam Creighton .80 2.00
7 Bob Giffin .20 .50
8 Gord Hamilton ACO .10 .25
9 Gord Hamilton Jr. TR .10 .25
10 Scott Hammond .20 .50
11 John Hanna .20 .50
12 Tim Helmer .20 .50
13 Steve Hrynewich .20 .50
14 Jim Jackson TR .10 .25
15 Mike James .20 .50
16 Brian Kilrea CO/MG .40 1.00
17 Larry MacAndrew TR .10 .25
18 Brian McKinnon .20 .50
19 Don McLaren .30 .75
20 Roy Myllari .20 .50
21 Darren Pang 1.60 4.00
22 Mark Paterson .30 .75
23 Phil Patterson .20 .50
24 Gary Roberts 2.00 5.00
25 Darcy Roy .20 .50
26 Brad Shaw .80 2.00
27 Steve Simoni .20 .50

1984-85 Ottawa 67's

This 28-card set was sponsored by Coca-Cola and Focus Photographic Services Commercial Photography. The cards measure approximately 2 5/8" by 4 1/8" and feature color, full-length, posed player photos with white borders. The player's name and jersey number are superimposed on the bottom of the picture. The cards are unnumbered and checklisted below in alphabetical order.

COMPLETE SET (28) 8.00 20.00
1 Tom Allen .30 .75
2 Graydon Almstedt .30 .75
3 Bill Bennett .30 .75
4 Bruce Cassidy .30 .75
5 Greg Coram .40 1.00
6 Bob Ellett CO .10 .25
7 Tony Geesink .30 .75
8 Bob Giffin .30 .75
9 John Hanna .30 .75
10 Tim Helmer .30 .75
11 Andy Helmuth .30 .75
12 Steve Hrynewich .30 .75
13 Rob Hudson .30 .75
14 Jim Jackson TR .10 .25
15 Steve Kayser .30 .75
16 Bill Kuchma .30 .75
17 Mike Larouche .30 .75
18 Tom Lawson MG .10 .25
19 Richard Lessard .30 .75
20 Gary Roberts 1.60 4.00
21 Jerry Scott .30 .75
22 John Shepherd PR .10 .25
23 Steve Simoni .30 .75
24 Greg Sliz .30 .75
25 Gord Thomas TR .10 .25
26 Chris Vickers .30 .75
27 Bert Weir .30 .75
28 Dennis Wigle .30 .75

1992-93 Ottawa 67's

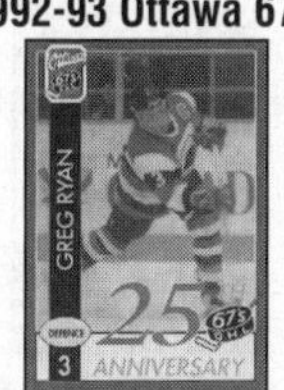

Celebrating the 25th anniversary of the Ottawa 67's, this 24-card standard-size set features color posed and action player photos with purple borders. The player's name, position, and jersey number appear in a black vertical stripe on the left side of the card. The phrase "25th Anniversary" is printed at the bottom in large red and blue letters. The cards are unnumbered and checklisted below in alphabetical order.

COMPLETE SET (24) 4.80 12.00
1 Ken Belanger .30 .75
2 Curt Bowen .20 .50
3 Rich Bronilla .20 .50
4 Mathew Burnett .20 .50
5 Shawn Caplice .20 .50
6 Mike Carr .20 .50
7 Chris Coveny .20 .50
8 Howard Darwin (Founder) .10 .25
9 Shean Donovan .40 1.00
10 Mark Edmundson .20 .50
11 Billy Hall .20 .50
12 Mike Johnson .20 .50
13 Brian Kilrea GM/CO .20 .50
14 Grayson Lafoley .20 .50
15 Grant Marshall .40 1.00
16 Cory Murphy .20 .50
17 Mike Peca 1.20 3.00
18 Greg Ryan .20 .50
19 Jeff Salajko .20 .50
20 Gerry Skrypec .20 .50
21 Sean Spencer .20 .50
22 Steven Washburn .24 .60
23 Mark Yakabuski .20 .50
24 Title Card .10 .25

1999-00 Ottawa 67's

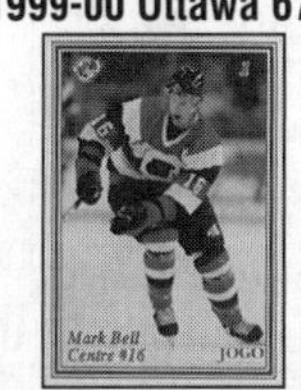

Released in 1999 by JOGO Incorporated, this full-color set features the Ottawa 67's of the OHL. Card backs contain black and white portraits and a short blurb about each player highlighting his career. The checklist card features a shot of the Memorial Cup winning 1998-99 Ottawa 67's.

COMPLETE SET (30) 4.80 12.00
1 Mark Bell .60 1.50
2 Matt Zultek .20 .50
3 Adam Chapman .10 .25
4 Miguel Delisle .30 .75
5 Randy Davidson .10 .25
6 Lance Galbraith .20 .50
7 Ian Jacobs .10 .25
8 Mike James .10 .25
9 Zenon Konopka .20 .50
10 Marc Lefebvre .10 .25
11 Joe Talbot .10 .25
12 Josh Tataryn .10 .25
13 Dan Tessier .20 .50
14 Vincent Grant .20 .50
15 Brendan Bell .10 .25
16 Chris Cava .10 .25
17 Kevin Malcolm .10 .25
18 Mike Gresdal .10 .25
19 Russ Moyer .10 .25
20 Luke Sellars .20 .50
21 Jeremy Van Hoof .20 .50
22 Jon Zion .30 .75
23 Seamus Kotyk .40 1.00
24 Lavente Szuper .40 1.00
25 Jeff Hunt .10 .25
26 Brian Kilrea HCO .20 .50
27 Bert O'Brien ACO .04 .10
28 Vince Mallette ACO .04 .10
29 Jeff Keech TR .04 .10
30 Checklist .04 .10

2000-01 Ottawa 67's

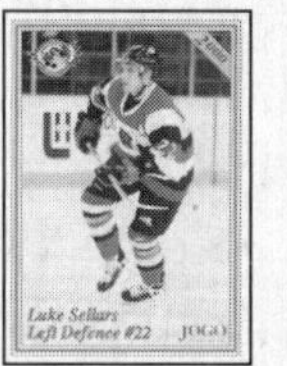

This thick-stock set was produced by Jogo, and sold by the team at its gift shop for $5. Production was limited to 3,000 copies. There are at least two spelling errors on the checklist card, neither of which were corrected.

COMPLETE SET (30) 4.80 12.00
1 Joe Talbot .20 .50
2 Lance Galbraith .20 .50
3 Jeremy Van Hoof .20 .50
4 Jon Zion .20 .50
5 Russ Moyer .16 .40
6 Pierre Mitsou .16 .40
7 Brendan Bell .20 .50
8 Adam Smyth .16 .40
9 Marc Lefebvre .16 .40
10 Sean Scully .16 .40
11 Brett McGrath .16 .40
12 Zenon Konopka .20 .50
13 Rodney Bauman .16 .40
14 Luke Sellars .20 .50
15 Miguel Delisle .20 .50
16 Vadim Sozinov .20 .50
17 Adam Chapman .16 .40
18 Bryan Rodney .16 .40
19 Sebastien Savage .16 .40
20 Seamus Kotyk .30 .75
21 John Ceci .16 .40
22 Vince Mallette CO .10 .25
23 Bert O'Brien CO .10 .25
24 Brian Kilrea CO .20 .50
25 Jeff Hunt OWN .04 .10
26 Riley & Killer Puck MASCOT .04
.10
27 Brian Kilrea 900 .20 .50
28 Doug Wilson .20 .50
29 Team Photo .20 .25
30 Team CL .10 .01

2001-02 Ottawa 67's

This set features the 67's of the OHL. The set was produced by Jogo and sold at the team's souvenir stand.

COMPLETE SET (30) 4.80 12.00
1 J.F. Perras .30 .75
2 Jon Ceci .20 .50
3 Karol Sloboda .20 .50
4 Carter Trevisani .20 .50
5 Jon Zion .30 .75
6 Russ Moyer .20 .50
7 Pierre Mitsou .20 .50
8 Adam Smyth .20 .50
9 Brendan Bell .30 .75
10 Matthew Albiani .20 .50
11 Lane Moodie .20 .50
12 Sean Scully .20 .50
13 Brett McGrath .20 .50
14 Zenon Konopka .30 .75
15 Rodney Bauman .20 .50
16 Miguel Delisle .20 .50
17 Jeremy Akeson .20 .50
18 Mark Mancari .20 .50
19 Adam Chapman .20 .50
20 Bryan Rodney .20 .50
21 Corey Locke .20 .50
22 Vince Malette ACO .04 .10

23 Bert O'Brien ACO .04 .10
24 Brian Kilrea CO .20 .50
25 Jeff Hunt OWN .04 .10
26 Banner Ceremony .04 .10
27 Brad Marsh .20 .50
28 Riley and Riley Jr. .04 .10
29 Killer Puck .04 .10
30 Dance Team/ CL .20 .50

2002-03 Ottawa 67's

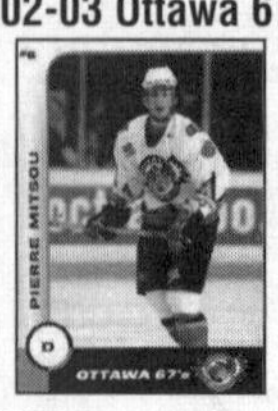

COMPLETE SET 5.00 12.00
1 Chris Hardill .30 .75
2 Karol Sloboda .20 .50
3 Carter Trevisani .20 .50
4 Will Colbert .20 .50
5 Russ Moyer .20 .50
6 Pierre Mitsou .20 .50
7 Adam Smyth .20 .50
8 Brendan Bell .30 .75
9 Matthew Albiani .20 .50
10 Lou Dickenson .20 .50
11 Scott Sheppard .20 .50
12 Bryan Bickell .20 .50
13 Sean Scully .20 .50
14 Peter Tsimikalis .20 .50
15 Rodney Bauman .20 .50
16 Kyle Wharton .20 .50
17 Jeremy Akeson .20 .50
18 Mark Mancari .20 .50
19 Julian Talbot .20 .50
20 Lukas Mensator .40 1.00
21 Matthew Foy .30 .75
22 Corey Locke .60 1.50
23 Jeff Hunt Owner .02 .10
24 Brian Kilrea HCO .10 .25
25 Bert O'Brien ACO .02 .10
26 Vince Malette ACO .02 .10
27 Mascot .02 .10
28 XFM Girls .10 .25
29 Mike Peca .20 .50
Brian Kilrea
30 Girl Guides of Canada .01 .01

2003-04 Ottawa 67's

COMPLETE SET (25) 6.00 15.00
1 Tyson Aitcheson .20 .50
2 Jeremy Akeson .20 .50
3 Matthew Albiani .20 .50
4 Danny Battochio .30 .75
5 Rodney Bauman .20 .50
6 Brodie Beard .20 .50
7 Bryan Bickell .20 .50
8 Will Colbert .20 .50
9 Greg Goodnough .20 .50
10 David Halasz .20 .50
11 Brad Hartley .20 .50
12 Robbie Lawrance .20 .50
13 Corey Locke .40 1.00
14 Mark Mancari .20 .50
15 Phil Mangan .20 .50
16 Lukas Mensator .40 1.00
17 Pierre Mitsou .20 .50
18 Elgin Reid .20 .50
19 Julian Talbot .20 .50
20 Brody Todd .20 .50
21 Peter Tsimikalis .20 .50
22 Kyle Wharton .20 .50
NNO Corey Locke TL .75 2.00
NNO Brian Kilrea CO .02 .10
NNO Lukas Mensator TL .75 2.00

2004-05 Ottawa 67's

A total of 1,000 team sets were produced.
COMPLETE (23) 12.00
1 Lukas Kaspar .50
2 Anthony Guadagnolo 1.00
3 Bryan Bickell .50
4 Brodie Beard .50
5 Pat Ouellette .50
6 Robbie Lawrance .50
7 Jeremy Akeson .50
8 Mark Mancari .50
9 Julian Talbot .50
10 Brad Bonello .50
11 Nick Van Herpt .50
12 Danny Battochio 1.50
13 Will Colbert .50
14 David Jarram .50
15 Brad Staubitz 1.00
16 Jamie Vanderveeken .50
17 Arron Alphonso .50
18 Derek Joslin .50
19 Elgin Reid .50
20 Jamie McGinn .50
21 Chris Hulit 1.00
22 Jakub Petruzalek .50
23 Matt Lahey .50

2005-06 Ottawa 67's

COMPLETE SET (25) 8.00 15.00
1 Julian Talbot .20 .50
2 Brodie Beard .20 .50
3 Bryan Bickell .20 .50
4 Pat Campbell .20 .50
5 Shea Kewin .20 .50
6 Thomas Kiriakou .20 .50
7 Robbie Lawrence .20 .50
8 Pat Ouellette .20 .50
9 Sean Ryan .20 .50
10 Jakub Vojta .20 .50
11 Brent Mackie .20 .50
12 Danny Battochio .40 1.00
13 Arron Alphonso .20 .50
14 Logan Couture 1.00 2.50
15 Pat Daley .20 .50
16 Chris Hulit .20 .50
17 Brady Morrison .40 1.00
18 Derek Joslin .20 .50
19 Matt Lahey .20 .50
20 Jamie McGinn .30 .75
21 Joe Pleckaitis .20 .50
22 Tibor Radulay .20 .50
23 Elgin Reid .20 .50
24 Joe Grimaldi .20 .50
25 Brett Liscomb .20 .50

2006-07 Ottawa 67s

COMPLETE SET (22) 8.00 15.00
1 Logan Couture .60 1.50
2 Scott Cowie .25 .60
3 Thomas Kiriakou .25 .60
4 Matt Lahey .25 .60
5 Cody Lindsay .25 .60
6 Brett Liscomb .40 1.00
7 Jamie Mcginn .40 1.00
8 Matthieu Methot .25 .60
9 Thomas Nesbitt .25 .60
10 Matt Ribeiro .25 .60
11 Brodie Beard .25 .60
12 Tyler Cuma .25 .60
13 Julien Demers .25 .60
14 Joe Grimaldi .25 .60
15 Derek Joslin .25 .60
16 Sean Ryan .25 .60
17 Jakub Vojta .25 .60
18 Arron Alphonso .25 .60
19 Jason Bailey .25 .60
20 Julian Cimadamore .25 .60
21 Lukas Flueler .40 1.00
22 Brady Morrison .40 1.00

2000-01 Owen Sound Attack

This set features the Attack of the OHL. The cards were produced by the team and sold at its souvenir stands. The cards are unnumbered and so are listed below in alphabetical order.

COMPLETE SET (26) 4.80 12.00
1 Michael Barrett .20 .50
2 Trevor Blanchard .20 .50
3 Luc Chiasson .20 .50
4 Richard Colwill .20 .50
5 Justin Day .30 .75
6 Kris Fraser .20 .50
7 Justin Hodgins .20 .50
8 Greg Jacina .20 .50
9 Bryan Kazarian .30 .75
10 Josh Legge .20 .50
11 Paul MacDermid CO .10 .25
12 Jason Nobili CO .10 .25
13 Brian O'Leary CO .10 .25
14 Dene Poulin .20 .50
15 Richard Power .20 .50
16 Corey Roberts .30 .75
17 Agris Saviels .30 .75
18 Ryan Sharp .20 .50
19 Daniel Sisca .20 .50
20 Shawn Snider .20 .50
21 Dan Sullivan .20 .50
22 Brandon Verner .20 .50
23 Nick Vukovic .20 .75
24 Joel Ward .20 .50
25 Bill Zalba .20 .50
26 Team Photo .20 .25

2001-02 Owen Sound Attack

This set features the Attack of the OHL. The cards were produced by the team and sold at its souvenir shop. The cards are unnumbered, and are listed below in alphabetical order.

COMPLETE SET (24) 4.80 12.00
1 Robert Chapman .20 .50
2 Richard Colwill .20 .50
3 Ryan Courtney .20 .50
4 David Dalliday .20 .50
5 Justin Day .30 .75
6 Jesse Gimblett .20 .50
7 Fred Hatziioannou .20 .50
8 Greg Jacina .30 .75
9 Michael Jacobsen .20 .50
10 Ladislav Kolda .20 .50
11 Jeff MacDermid .20 .50
12 Kyle McAllister .30 .75
13 Richard Power .20 .50
14 Justin Renner .30 .75
15 Brad Richardson .20 .50
16 Cory Roberts .30 .75
17 Dan Rogers .20 .50
18 Agris Saviels .30 .75
19 Ryan Sharp .20 .50
20 Daniel Sisca .20 .50
21 Sean Stefanski .20 .50
22 Dan Sullivan .20 .50
23 John Wheaton .20 .50
24 Tom Zanoski .20 .50

2002-03 Owen Sound Attack

COMPLETE SET (26) 5.00 12.00
1 Mascot .02 .10
2 Brett Howden .20 .50
3 Pat Sutton .20 .50
4 Jiri Paska .20 .50
5 Mark Giordano .20 .50
6 Patrick Jarrett .40 1.00
7 Dan Rogers .20 .50
8 Matt Passfield .20 .50
9 Tom Zanoski .20 .50
10 Jesse Gimblett .20 .50
11 Michael Gough .20 .50
12 Brad Richardson .20 .50
13 Andrew Maksym .20 .50
14 Steve Henwood .20 .50
15 Brett McGrath .20 .50
16 Justin Renner .20 .50
17 Ladislav Kolda .20 .50
18 John Weathon .20 .50
19 Fred Hatziioannou .20 .50
20 Jeff McDermid .20 .50
21 Miguel Delisle .20 .50
22 David Edgeworth .20 .50
23 Mike Angelidis .20 .50
24 Dan LaCosta .30 .75
25 Marty Magers .30 .75
26 Checklist .02 .10

2003-04 Owen Sound Attack

COMPLETE SET (25) 6.00 15.00
1 The Bear Cubby .01 .05
2 Matt Smyth .20 .50
3 Wes Cunningham .20 .50
4 Pat Sutton .20 .50
5 Justin Dacosta .20 .50
6 Mark Giordano .20 .50
7 Patrick Jarrett .30 .75
8 Bobby Ryan 1.50 4.00
9 Andrew Maksym .20 .50
10 Richard Hornseth .20 .50
11 Brad Richardson .20 .50
12 Kevin Baker .20 .50
13 Kevin Harvey .20 .50
14 Jonathan Lehun .20 .50
15 Pavel Voroshnin .30 .75
16 Andre Deveaux .20 .50
17 Jim Kehoe .20 .50
18 Stefan Ruzicka .40 1.00
19 Jeff MacDermid .20 .50
20 John Wires .20 .50
21 Adam Smyth .20 .50
22 Mike Angelidis .20 .50
23 Dan LaCosta .30 .75
24 Robert Gherson .30 .75
25 Checklist .01 .05

2004-05 Owen Sound Attack

A total of 500 team sets were produced.
COMPLETE SET (24) 6.00 15.00
1 Mike Angelidis .20 .50
2 Neil Conway .40 1.00
3 Igor Gongalsky .20 .50
4 Derek Brochu .20 .50
5 Brad Richardson .20 .50
6 Kevin Baker .20 .50
7 Matthew Kang .20 .50
8 Colin Hanley .20 .50
9 Jonathan Lehun .20 .50
10 Matt Smyth .20 .50
11 Bob Sanguinetti .40 1.00
12 Stefan Ruzicka .40 1.00
13 Theo Peckham .20 .50
14 Payton Liske .20 .50
15 Robin Big Snake .60 1.50
16 Andrej Sekera .20 .50
17 Dan Lacosta .20 .50
18 Wes Cunningham .20 .50
19 Trevor Koverko .40 1.00
20 Justin Dacosta .20 .50
21 Scott Giles .20 .50
22 Patrick Jarrett .30 .75
23 Bobby Ryan 1.50 4.00
24 Cubby MASCOT .02 .10

2005-06 Owen Sound Attack

COMPLETE SET (24) 8.00 15.00
1 Bobby Ryan .75 2.00
2 Neil Conway .40 1.00
3 Andrej Sekera .20 .50
4 Kyle Lamb .20 .50
5 Trevor Koverko .20 .50
6 Jeff Moor .20 .50
7 Scott Giles .20 .50
8 Igor Gongalsky .20 .50
9 Derek Brochu .20 .50
10 Scott Tregunna .20 .50
11 Josh Catto .20 .50
12 Jeff Kyrzakos .20 .50
13 Matthew Kang .20 .50
14 Zach McCullough .20 .50
15 Joshua Bailey .20 .50
16 Marcus Carroll .20 .50
17 Bob Sanguinetti .40 1.00
18 Theo Peckham .40 1.00
19 Marek Bartanus .20 .50
20 Payton Liske .20 .50
21 Mike Angelidis .20 .50
22 Miles Cope .20 .50
23 Justin Allen .20 .50
24 Kyle Knechtel .40 1.00

2006-07 Owen Sound Attack

COMPLETE SET (22) 8.00 15.00
1 Theo Peckham .20 .50
2 Michael D'orazio .20 .50
3 Neil Conway .40 1.00
4 Dalyn Flatt .20 .50
5 Andrew Shorkey .20 .50
6 David Kolomatis .20 .50
7 Guy Carteciano .20 .50
8 Bobby Ryan .75 2.00
9 Derek Brochu .20 .50
10 Scott Tregunna .20 .50
11 Lane Macdermid .20 .50
12 Thomas Stajan .20 .50
13 Wayne Simmonds .20 .50
14 Zach Mccullough .20 .50
15 Josh Bailey .20 .50
16 Michael Farrell .20 .50
17 Marcus Carroll .20 .50
18 Bobby Sanguinetti .40 1.00
19 Marek Bartanus .20 .50
20 Anton Hedman .20 .50
21 Trevor Lewis .60 1.50
22 Scott Bowles .40 1.00

1993-94 Owen Sound Platers

Sponsored by Domino's Pizza, The Eastwood Network, and The Sport Stop, this 36-card set measures the standard size. The fronts feature posed and action color player photos with white borders. The player's name and number appears in a black bar under the picture. The cards are unnumbered and checklisted below in alphabetical order.

COMPLETE SET (36) 8.00 20.00
1 Craig Binns .16 .40
2 Jim Brown .16 .40
3 Andrew Brunette .60 1.50
4 Luigi Calce .16 .40
5 Jason Campbell .16 .40
6 Draft Veterans .16 .40
Rod Hinks
Jason MacDonald
Kevin Weekes
Marian Kacir
7 Paddy Flynn ACO .04 .10
8 Kirk Furey .16 .40
9 Jerry Harrigan CO .04 .10
10 Joe Harris .16 .40
11 Rod Hinks .16 .40
12 Marian Kacir .16 .40
13 Shane Kenny .16 .40
14 Jeff Kostuch .16 .40
15 Dave Lemay .16 .40
16 Jason MacDonald .20 .50
17 Rick Mancini TR .04 .10
18 Kirk Maltby .40 1.00
19 Brian Medeiros .16 .40
20 Mike Morrone .16 .40
21 Ryan Mougenel .16 .40
22 Scott Penton .16 .40
23 Wayne Primeau .40 1.00
24 Jeremy Rebek .16 .40
25 Rob Schweyer .16 .40
26 Willie Skilliter .16 .40
27 Jamie Storr .60 1.50
28 Jamie Storr .60 1.50
Pure Gold
29 Jamie Storr's Mask .60 1.50
30 Jamie Storr .60 1.50
Wayne Primeau
Sure Picks
31 Scott Walker .40 1.00
32 Kevin Weekes .60 1.50
33 Kevin Weekes' Mask .40 1.00
34 Shayne Wright .16 .40
35 Title Card .04 .10
Domino's Ad Card
36 Title Card .04 .10
Eastwood Ad Card

1994-95 Owen Sound Platers

This set features the Platers of the OHL and was sponsored by Domino's Pizza. Frankly, that's about all we know on this one. Have any additional info? Send it to hockeymag@beckett.com.

COMPLETE SET (36) 6.00 15.00
1 Shawn Silver .20 .50
2 Shane Kenny .16 .40
3 Kevin Young .16 .40
4 Kirk Furey .16 .40
5 Peter MacKellar .16 .40
6 Willie Skilliter .16 .40
7 Joe Harris .16 .40
8 Brian Medeiros .16 .40
9 David Zunic .16 .40
10 Jeff Kostuch .16 .40
11 Jason Campbell .16 .40
12 Scott Smith .16 .40
13 Rob Schweyer .16 .40
14 Shayne Wright .16 .40
15 Scott Seiling .16 .40
16 Jeremy Rebek .16 .40
17 Rob Fitzgerald .16 .40
18 Ryan Mougenel .16 .40
19 John Argiropoulos .16 .40
20 Wayne Primeau .20 .50
21 Chris Wismer .16 .40
22 Matt Osborne .16 .40
23 Murray Hogg .16 .40
24 Brent Johnson 2.00 5.00
25 Jamie Storr (Jersey #31) .31 .78
26 Jamie Storr (Jersey #92 .31 .78
27 Jamie Storr (King Tut Mask) .31 .78
28 Jamie Storr Draft .31 .78
28 Shayne Wright Draft .16 .40
28 Wayne Primeau Draft .20 .50
29 Wayne Primeau Prime Time .20 .50
30 Coaching Staff .04 .11
31 Larry Gibson SB .04 .11
32 Joel Traplin TR .04 .11
33 Broadcast Team .04 .11
34 Ed Schambers Bus Dr. .04 .11
35 Domino's Pizza .01 .02
36 Jim Gardhouse Motors .01 .02

1995-96 Owen Sound Platers

This set features the Platers of the OHL. The set was produced by the team and sold at its souvenir stands.

COMPLETE SET (36) 4.80 12.00
1 Team Photo Card .16 .40
2 Ric Seiling CO .04 .10
3 Gus Eyers CO .04 .10
4 Brian Warrilow CO .04 .10
5 Rick Mancini TR .04 .10
6 Wayne Primeau .20 .50
7 Shawn Gallant .16 .40
8 Shane Kenny .16 .40
9 Chris Biagini .16 .40
10 Marek Babic .16 .40
11 Oleg Tsirkounov .16 .40
12 Peter MacKellar .16 .40
13 Ryan Davis .16 .40
14 John Argiropoulos .16 .40
15 Jason Campbell .16 .40
16 Dan Snyder .16 1.00
17 Steve Gallace .16 .40
18 Scott Seiling .16 .40
19 Jeremy Rebek .16 .40
20 Adam Mair .20 .50
21 Ryan Christie .20 .50
22 Larry Paleczny .20 .50
23 Wayne Primeau .20 .50
24 Chris Wismer .16 .40
25 Matt Osborne .16 .40
26 Mike Loach .16 .40
27 Brent Johnson .80 2.00
28 Jim Ensom .16 .40
29 Brent Johnson .80 2.00
30 Mike Loach .16 .40
31 Jim Ensom .16 .40
32 Wayne Primeau .20 .50
33 Shane Kenny .16 .40
34 Sun Times News .01
35 Jim Gardhouse Motors .01
36 Domino's Pizza .01

1996-97 Owen Sound Platers

This set features the Platers of the OHL. The set was produced by the team and sold at its souvenir stands.

COMPLETE SET (27) 15.00
1 John Lovell CO .04 .10
2 Brian O'Leary CO .04 .10
3 Curtis Sanford .30 1.50
4 Shawn Gallant .16 .40
5 Brent Johnson .80 2.00
6 Joel Dezainde .16 .40
7 Kyle Dafoe .16 .40
8 Kyle Flaxey .16 .40
9 Matt Osborne .16 .40
10 Jamie Sokolsky .16 .40
11 Kurt Walsh .16 .40
12 Andrew Williamson .16 .40
13 Ryan Davis .16 .40
14 Sean Avery .80 2.00
15 Pascal Daze .16 .40
16 Dan Snyder .16 1.00
17 Steve Gallace .16 .40
18 Scott Wray .16 .40
19 Adam Mair .30 .75
20 Larry Paleczny .20 .50
21 Ryan Christie .30 .40
22 Chris Wismer .16 .40
23 Todd Miller .16 .40
24 Adam Campbell .16 .40
25 Jason Doyle .30 .75
26 Wes Goldie .16 .40
27 Owen Sound Platers .16 .40

1997-98 Owen Sound Platers

This set features the Platers of the OHL. The set was produced by the team and sold at home games.

COMPLETE SET (26) 4.80 12.00
1 Owen Sound Platers .20 .50
2 Curtis Sanford .30 .75
3 Adam Campbell .20 .50
4 Kyle Dafoe .20 .50
5 Kyle Flaxey .20 .50
6 Chris Hopiavuori .20 .50
7 Jamie Sokolsky .20 .50
8 Colin Beardsmore .20 .50
9 Dave Stephenson .20 .50
10 Ryan Davis .20 .50
11 Ryan Rivard .20 .50
12 Sean Avery .80 2.00
13 Dan Snyder .20 1.00
14 Wes Goldie .20 .50
15 Adam Mair .30 .75
16 Larry Paleczny .20 .50
17 Ryan Christie .30 .50
18 Randy Davidson .20 .50
19 Joel Ward .20 .50
20 Chris Wismer .20 .50
21 Jason Doyle .30 .75
22 Brendan Brooks .20 .50
23 Adam Collins .20 .50
24 Eoin McInerney .40 1.00
25 Brian O'Leary CO .10 .25
26 Kirk Maltby .30 .75

1998-99 Owen Sound Platers

This set features the Platers of the OHL. It is believed that the set was produced by the team and sold at its souvenir stands.

COMPLETE SET (28) 4.80 12.00
1 Owen Sound Platers .10 .25
2 Curtis Sanford .30 1.00
3 Mike Barrett .16 .40
4 Kyle Flaxey .16 .40
5 Chris Hopiavuori .20 .50
6 Mike Dombkiewicz .16 .40
7 Jeff Kaufman .16 .40
8 Dave Stephenson .16 .40
9 Chris Minard .30 .75
10 Stephane Savage .16 .40
11 Sean Avery .60 1.00
12 Peter Campbell .16 .40
13 Dan Snyder .16 1.00
14 Jan Sulc .16 .40
15 Wes Goldie .30 .75
16 Adam Mair .30 .75
17 Chad Woollard .20 .50
18 Stephen Lafleur .20 .50
19 Randy Davidson .20 .50
20 Joel Ward .20 .50
21 Juri Golicic .20 .50
22 Bryan Kazarian .20 .50
23 Nick Vukovic .30 .75
24 Brent Sullivan .16 .40
25 Adam Campbell .16 .40
26 Corey Roberts .16 .40
27 Adam Mair .30 .75
28 Coaches .04 .10

1999-00 Owen Sound Platers

This 31-card set features the OHL's Platers. Cards feature full color action shots and a black border along the bottom that contains the player's name, position, number, and team logo. These cards are not numbered, therefore they appear in the order they came out of the sealed set.

COMPLETE SET (31) 4.00 10.00
1 Brian O'Leary ACO .04 .10
2 Dave Siciliano HCO .04 .10
3 Michael Barrett .14 .35
4 Kenny Corupe .20 .50
5 Tim Hamel .14 .35
6 Curtis Sanford .40 1.00
7 Agris Saviels .20 .50
8 Joel Ward .14 .35
9 Bill Zalba .14 .35
10 Matt Rock .14 .35
11 Mike Lymer .14 .35
12 Adam Campbell .14 .35
13 Chris Hopiavuori .14 .35
14 Mike Dombkiewicz .14 .35
15 Cory Roberts .20 .50
16 Greg Jacina .14 .35
17 Wes Goldie .20 .50
18 Dave Stephenson .14 .35
19 Daniel Sisca .14 .35
20 Bryan Kazarian .30 .75
21 Kyle McAllister .30 .75
22 Shawn Snider .14 .35
23 Trevor Blanchard .14 .35
24 Derek Campbell .14 .35
25 Jason Kowalski .14 .35
26 Brent Sullivan .14 .35
27 Alexei Salaschenko .14 .35
28 Nick Vukovic .14 .35
29 Kris Fraser .14 .35
30 Chris Minard .14 .35
31 Team Photo .04 .10

2003-04 Pacific AHL Prospects

COMPLETE SET 15.00 40.00
1 Ari Ahonen 1.25 3.00
2 Adrian Foster .25 .60
3 Tuomas Pihlman .40 1.00
4 Aleksander Suglobov .40 1.00
5 Ray Emery 1.25 3.00
6 Alexandre Giroux .25 .60
7 Chris Kelly .25 .60

8 Julien Vauclair .40 1.00
9 Wade Dubielewicz 1.25 3.00
10 Jeff Hamilton .25 .60
11 Justin Mapletoft .25 .60
12 Mattias Weinhandl .40 1.00
13 Kari Lehtonen 3.00 8.00
14 Tommi Santala .25 .60
15 Karl Stewart .25 .60
16 Ilja Bryzgalov 1.25 3.00
17 Chris Kunitz .40 1.00
18 Tony Martensson .25 .60
19 Brad Boyes .40 1.00
20 Marcel Goc .40 1.00
21 Seamus Kotyk 1.25 3.00
22 Garrett Stafford .25 .60
23 Miroslav Zalesak .40 1.00
24 Jiri Hudler 2.00 3.00
25 Niklas Kronwall .40 1.00
26 Marc Lamothe 1.25 3.00
27 Nathan Robinson .25 .60
28 Benoit Gratton .25 .60
29 Alexander Perezhogin .40 1.00
30 Tomas Plekanec .40 1.00
31 Eero Somervuori .25 .60
32 Jozef Balej .40 1.00
33 Jason LaBarbera 1.25 3.00
34 Dominic Moore .40 1.00
35 Fedor Tyutin .40 1.00
36 Layne Ulmer .25 .60
37 Chad Wiseman .25 .60
38 Peter Budaj 1.25 3.00
39 Eric Perrin .40 1.00
40 Dan Cavanaugh .25 .60
41 Kyle Wanvig 1.25 3.00
42 Patrick DesRochers .40 1.00
43 Dany Sabourin 1.25 3.00
44 Mike Zigomanis .40 1.00
45 Scott Barney .25 .60
46 Mathieu Chouinard 1.25 3.00
47 Noah Clarke .25 .60
48 Denis Grebeshkov .40 1.00
49 Adam Hauser 1.25 3.00
50 Steve Kelly .25 .60
51 Yanick Lehoux .25 .60
52 Pavel Rosa .25 .60
53 Fedor Fedorov .40 1.00
54 Kirill Koltsov .40 1.00
55 Brandon Reid .40 1.00
56 Simon Gamache .40 1.00
57 Darren Haydar .40 1.00
58 Andrew Hutchinson .25 .60
59 Timofei Shishkanov .40 1.00
60 Scottie Upshall EXISTS?
61 Anton Babchuk .40 1.00
62 Matt Ellison .25 .60
63 Kirby Law .25 .60
64 Antero Niittymaki 2.00 2.00
65 Graham Mink .40 1.00
66 Maxime Ouellet 1.25 3.00
67 Pat Leahy .40 1.00
68 Colton Orr .40 1.00
69 Hannu Toivonen 2.50 6.00
70 Ryan Miller 1.25 3.00
71 Jason Pominville .40 1.00
72 Eric Beaudoin .40 1.00
73 Mike Green .25 .60
74 Lukas Krajicek .40 1.00
75 Denis Shvidki .40 1.00
76 Petr Taticek .40 1.00
77 David LeNeveu 1.25 3.00
78 Fredrik Sjostrom .40 1.00
79 Jeff Taffe .40 1.00
80 Brendan Bell .25 .60
81 Sebastien Centomo 1.25 3.00
82 Mikael Tellqvist 1.25 3.00
83 Kyle Wellwood .40 1.00
84 Tim Jackman .40 1.00
85 Aaron Johnson .40 1.00
86 Pascal Leclaire 1.25 3.00
87 Brad Moran .25 .60
88 Doug Lynch .25 .60
89 Mike Morrison 1.25 3.00
90 Jani Rita .40 1.00
91 Steve Valiquette 1.25 3.00
92 Jason Bacashihua 1.25 3.00
93 Dan Jancevski .25 .60
94 Colby Armstrong .40 1.00
95 Andy Chiodo 2.00 2.00
96 Michel Ouellet 1.25 3.00
97 Michal Sivek .40 1.00
98 Jay McClement .40 1.00
99 Johnny Pohl .40 1.00
100 Peter Sejna .40 1.00

2003-04 Pacific AHL Prospects Gold

*GOLD: 2X TO 5X BASE HI
PRINT RUN 925 SER.#'d SETS

2003-04 Pacific AHL Prospects Autographs

COMMON CARD (1-6)
PRINT RUN 500 SER.#'d SETS
1 Kari Lehtonen 15.00 40.00
2 Ryan Miller 12.50 30.00
3 Wade Dubielewicz 12.50 30.00
4 David LeNeveu 12.50 30.00
5 Ari Ahonen 15.00 40.00
6 Pascal Leclaire 12.50 30.00

2003-04 Pacific AHL Prospects Crease Lightning

STATED ODDS 1:10
1 Ari Ahonen 1.50 4.00
2 Kari Lehtonen 3.00 8.00
3 Phil Sauve 1.50 4.00
4 Alex Auld 1.50 4.00
5 Rastislav Stana 2.50 6.00
6 Andrew Raycroft 3.00 8.00
7 Ryan Miller 2.50 6.00
8 Pascal Leclaire 2.00 5.00

2003-04 Pacific AHL Prospects Destined for Greatness

COMMON CARD (1-10) 1.25 3.00
STATED ODDS 1:5
1 Jason Spezza 3.00 8.00
2 Antoine Vermette 1.25 3.00
3 Rick DiPietro 1.25 3.00
4 Trent Hunter 2.50 6.00
5 Jonathan Cheechoo 3.00 8.00
6 Jiri Hudler 1.50 4.00
7 Michael Ryder 2.00 5.00
8 Jason King 1.25 3.00
9 Carlo Colaiacovo 1.25 3.00
10 Peter Sejna 1.25 3.00

2003-04 Pacific AHL Prospects Jerseys

STATED ODDS ONE PER HOBBY BOX
1 Wade Dubielewicz 10.00 25.00
2 Jeff Hamilton 6.00 15.00
3 Tomas Plekanec 5.00 12.00
4 Denis Shvidki 5.00 12.00
5 David LeNeveu 8.00 20.00
6 Matt Murley 8.00 20.00

1995-96 PEI Senators

This set features the Senators of the AHL. These postcard-sized (5X7) collectibles are blank backed and are believed to have been issued as a promotional giveaway.
COMPLETE SET (24) 6.00 15.00
1 Scott Allison .20 .50
2 Radim Bicanek .20 .50
3 Patrick Charbonneau .20 .50
4 Pavol Demitra 1.20 3.00
5 Cosmo Dupaul .20 .50
6 Daniel Guerard .20 .50
7 Steve Guolla .30 .75
8 Shawn Heaphy .20 .50
9 Justin Hocking .20 .50
10 Martin Lamarche .20 .50
11 Eric Lavigne .20 .50
12 Kaj Linna .30 .75
13 Darrin Madeley .30 .75
14 Chad Penney .20 .50
15 Michel Picard .20 .50
16 Lance Pitlick .30 .75
17 Jean-Yves Roy .30 .75
18 Claude Savoie .20 .50
19 Darcy Simon .20 .50
20 Steve Strunk .20 .50
21 Patrick Traverse .20 .50
22 Jason Zent .20 .50
23 Coaching Staff .10 .25
24 Brutus MAS .04 .10

2003-04 P.E.I. Rocket

COMPLETE SET (24) 5.00 12.00
1 Julien Beaulieu .20 .50
2 Jimmy Bonneru .20 .50
3 Jonathan Boutin .30 .75
4 Pierre-Andre Bureau .20 .50
5 Yanick Charron .20 .50
6 Marc-Andre Gragnani .20 .50
7 Tyler Hawes .20 .50
8 Milan Hruska .20 .50
9 David Laliberte .20 .50
10 Michael Lambert .20 .50
11 Mark Lee .20 .50
12 Fabien Laniel .20 .50
13 Maxim Lapierre .20 .50
14 Jeff Macauley .20 .50
15 Tyler Noye .20 .50
16 Brent Maclellan .20 .50
17 Ryan Mior .30 .75
18 Sebastien Nolet .30 .75
19 Steve Pelletier .20 .50
20 Jonathan Persson .20 .50
21 Jean-Francois Roux .20 .50
22 Dominic Soucy .20 .50
23 Steve Tilley .20 .50
24 Cory Urquhart .20 .50

2004-05 P.E.I. Rocket

A total of 400 team sets were produced. Card #23 does not exist.
COMPLETE SET (30) 5.00 12.00
1 Alexandre Boivin .15 .40
2 Anthony Pototschnik .15 .40
3 Billy Bezeau .15 .40
4 Connor MacDonald .15 .40
5 David Laliberte .15 .40
6 David MacDonald .15 .40
7 Dominic Soucy .15 .40
8 Greg O'Brien .15 .40
9 Jimmy Bonneau .15 .40
10 Jonathan Boutin .40 1.00
11 Julien Beaulieu .15 .40
12 Kris MacDonald .15 .40
13 Marc-Andre Gragnani .15 .40
14 Maxim Lapierre .15 .40
15 Michael Dubuc .15 .40
16 Michel Charette .15 .40
17 Pierre-Andre Bureau .15 .40
18 Riku Korpinen .15 .40
19 Ryan Mior .40 1.00
20 Tyler Hawes .15 .40
21 Viatcheslav Trukhno .30 .75
22 Yanick Charron .15 .40
24 Kevin Hamel .15 .40
25 Alexander Ennaffati .15 .40
26 Pierre Bergeron .15 .40
27 Jean-Francois Boucher .15 .40
28 Jean-Francois Bernard .40 1.00
29 Fabien Laniel .15 .40
30 Louis-Phillippe Lachance .15 .40
31 Alain Vigneault CO .15 .40

2005-06 PEI Rocket

COMPLETE SET (29) 6.00 15.00
1 Ryan Mior .40 1.00
2 Stephen Lund .20 .50
3 Louis-Phillippe LaChance .20 .50
4 Travis Mealy .20 .50
5 Nathan Snowie .20 .50
6 Alexandre Boivin .20 .50
7 Geoff Walker .20 .50
8 Slava Trukhno .40 1.00
9 Greg O'Brien .20 .50
10 Stanson Donovan .20 .50
11 David Laliberte .20 .50
12 Devan Praught .20 .50
13 Olivier Gauthier .20 .50
14 Tyler Hawes .20 .50
15 Anton Skorykh .20 .50
16 Lucasz Steciuk .20 .50
17 Nicolas Leduc .20 .50
18 Jean-Claude Milot .20 .50
19 Joseph Haddad .20 .50
20 Michael Dubuc .20 .50
21 Chad Locke .20 .50
22 Steve Natywary .20 .50
23 Matthew LaChaine .20 .50
24 Antoine Lafleur .40 1.00
25 Simon Bolduc .20 .50
26 David MacDonald .20 .50
27 Pascal Lebel .20 .50
28 Marc-Andre Gragnani .20 .50
29 Danny Stewart .20 .50

2006-07 PEI Rocket

COMPLETE SET (23) 8.00 15.00
1 David Laliberte .25 .60
2 Geoff Walker .25 .60
3 Ryan Mior .30 .75
4 Antoine Lafleur .50 1.25
5 Stephen Lund .25 .60
6 Pierre-Marc Guilbault .25 .60
7 Jordon Southorn .25 .60
8 Pierre-Luc Lessard .25 .60
9 Marc-Andre Gragnani .40 1.00
10 Pascal Boutin .25 .60
11 Chris Doyle .25 .60
12 Martin Latal .25 .60
13 Guillaume Doucet .25 .60
14 Lucas Mckinley .25 .60
15 Devan Praught .25 .60
16 Benoit Levesque .25 .60
17 Tyles Hawes .25 .60
18 Peter Cmorej .25 .60
19 Matthew Lachaine .25 .60
20 Maxim ClichÃ© .25 .60
21 Joey Haddad .25 .60
22 Chad Locke .25 .60
23 Gregory Paynter .25 .60

2002-03 Pee Dee Pride RBI

COMPLETE SET (18) 8.00 20.00
133 B.J. Adams .40 1.00
134 Daniel Carriere .40 1.00
135 Aaron Gates .40 1.00
136 Mike Glumac .60 1.50

137 Wes Goldie .40 1.00
138 Derek Halldorson .40 1.00
139 Kyle Kidney .40 1.00
140 Gregor Krajnc .40 1.00
141 Ryan Knox .40 1.00
142 Eric Naud .40 1.00
143 Jason Metcalfe .40 1.00
144 Matt Reid .40 1.00
145 Jason Robinson .40 1.00
146 Greg Schmidt .40 1.00
147 Allan Sirois .40 1.00
148 Mike Torney .40 1.00
149 Matt Underhill .40 1.00
150 Ron Vogel .75 2.00

1996-97 Pensacola Ice Pilots

This set features the Ice Pilots of the ECHL. The standard-sized cards were produced by DLUX printing and sold by the team at home games.
COMPLETE SET (24) 4.00 10.00
1 Craig Brown .16 .40
2 Stephane Julien .16 .40
3 David Borrozino .16 .40
4 Jeremy Mylymok .16 .40
5 Patrik Alvin .16 .40
6 Rostislav Saglo .16 .40
7 Glen Metropolit .40 1.00
8 Chad Quenneville .16 .40
9 Trevor Buchanan .16 .40
10 Brandon Gray .16 .40
11 Jon Pirrong .30 .75
12 Brent Gretzky .30 .75
13 Martin LaChaine .16 .40
14 Brian Secord .16 .40
15 Hugo Belanger .16 .40
16 Christian Sbrocca .16 .40
17 Tony Prpic .16 .40
18 Shane Calder .16 .40
19 Nick Stajduhar .16 .40
20 Brendan Concannon .16 .40
21 Sean Gauthier .20 .50
22 Al Pederson CO .16 .40
23 George Kozak .16 .40
NNO Header Card .04 .10

1997-98 Pensacola Ice Pilots

This 25-card set features the Ice Pilots of the ECHL. The set apparently was handed out at as a promotional item at several late-season games.
COMPLETE SET (25) 4.80 12.00
1 Team Photo .20 .50
2 J.F. Aube .30 .75
3 Craig Brown .20 .50
4 Michael Burkett .20 .50
5 Shane Calder .20 .50
6 Martin Chouinard .20 .50
7 Brendan Concannon .20 .50
8 Jon Dunmar .20 .50
9 Sean Gauthier .20 .50
10 Christian Gosselin .20 .50
11 Brian LaFleur .20 .50
12 Steven Low .20 .50
13 Scott Malone .20 .50
14 Mike Mayhew .20 .50
15 Keith O'Connell .20 .50
16 Val Passarelli .30 .75
17 Mark Polak .20 .50
18 Chad Quenneville .20 .50
19 Andrew Rodgers .20 .50
20 Nick Stajduhar .20 .50
21 Mike Sullivan .20 .50
22 Kelly Hultgren .20 .50
23 George Kozak ACO .04 .10
24 Allen Pedersen HCO .04 .10
25 D-Lux Printing .04 .10

1998-99 Pensacola Ice Pilots

This set features the Ice Pilots of the ECHL. According to various sources, the sets were intended to be issued as a promotional giveaway, but legal or financial issues forced cancellation of those plans. Several players and team officials were given sets, however, and some have made their way into the secondary market. Because of the nature of this distribution, there is not enough market activity to accurately price these cards. They are checklisted below without values.
COMPLETE SET(27)
1 Shane Calder
2 Nick Stajduhar
3 Etienne Beaudry
4 Bob Wilkie
5 Don Chase
6 Stephen Naughton
7 Chad Quenneville
8 Keith O'Connell
9 Brendan Concannon
10 Keli Corpse
11 Andrew Rodgers
12 Dave Ivaska
13 Rob Phillips
14 Mark Polak
15 Craig Brown
16 Tom Noble
17 Eon MacFarlane
18 Allen Pedersen CO
19 George Kosak CO
20 Iceman MAS
21 Pensacola Ice Pilots
22 The Hangar
23 Pensacola Ice Pilots
24 Kelly Hultgren
25 Mike Sullivan
26 Pensacola Ice Pilots CL
27 PHPA Web Site

2003-04 Pensacola Ice Pilots

This set was produced by RBI Sports with a production run limited to 250 copies. The numbering sequence reflects the entire run of RBI sets that season.
COMPLETE SET (16) 8.00 20.00
337 Tyler Beechey .40 1.00
338 Greg Chambers .40 1.00
339 Brian Collins .40 1.00
340 Brad Cruikshank .40 1.00
341 Brian Eklund .75 2.00
342 Brandon Fleenor .40 1.00
343 Brett Gibson .40 1.00
344 Jade Galbraith .40 1.00
345 Aaron Gionet .40 1.00
346 Dwayne Hay .40 1.00
347 Andreas Holmqvist .40 1.00
348 Evgeny Konstantinov .75 2.00
349 Wes Mason .40 1.00
350 Corey Neilson .75 2.00
351 Aaron Phillips .40 1.00
352 Kent Sauer .40 1.00

2004-05 Penticton Vees

The Vees play in the BC Tier 2 Junior League.
COMPLETE SET (25) 15.00
1 History Card .01 .05
2 Checklist .01 .05
3 Josh Brown .30 .75
4 Aaron Agnew .30 .75
5 Ben Robinson .30 .75
6 Brian Lebler .30 .75
7 Shaun MacDonald .30 .75
8 Ryan Coghlan .60 1.50
9 Jon Cara .30 .75
10 Colin Williams .30 .75
11 Mike Towns .30 .75
12 Jason Harding .30 .75
13 Kevin Borba .60 1.50
14 Cody Collins .30 .75
15 Alex MacLeod .30 .75
16 Chris Rengert .30 .75
17 Peter Farrell .30 .75
18 Justin Coutu .30 .75
19 John Kopp .30 .75
20 Adrian Jack .30 .75
21 Brad Thiessen .30 .75
22 Corey Milan .60 1.50
23 Bruno Campese CO .02 .10
24 Ken Law ACO .02 .10
25 Dan Marshall ANN .02 .10

2005-06 Penticton Vees

COMPLETE SET (24) 10.00 20.00
1 Brennan Barker .40 1.00
2 Jordan Cheveldave .40 1.00
3 Ryan Costanzo .40 1.00
4 Deron Cousens .40 1.00
5 Peter Farrell .40 1.00
6 Tanner House .40 1.00
7 John Kopp .40 1.00
8 Justin Krueger .40 1.00
9 Brian Lebler .40 1.00
10 Alex MacLeod .40 1.00
11 Corey Milan .40 1.00
12 T.J. Miller .40 1.00
13 Ivo Musa .40 1.00
14 Lee Pagee .40 1.00
15 Ben Robinson .40 1.00
16 Robert Skinner .40 1.00
17 Gary Sylvester .40 1.00
18 Mike Towns .40 1.00
19 Evan Trupp .40 1.00
20 Ryan Wagner .40 1.00
21 Mark Walters .40 1.00
22 Jordan White .40 1.00
23 Bruno Campese CO .10 .25
24 1986 Penticton Knights .10 .25

2006-07 Penticton Vees

COMPLETE SET (25) 12.00 20.00
1 Jeremy Beller .30 .75
2 Travis Briard .30 .75
3 Steve Cameron .30 .75
4 Deron Cousens .30 .75
5 Brad Davis .30 .75
6 Dustin Donaghy .30 .75
7 Nigel Dube .30 .75
8 Joel Eisenkirch .30 .75
9 Jordan Funk .30 .75
10 Elias Grossmann .30 .75
11 Michael Guzzo .30 .75
12 Brett Hextall .30 .75
13 Tanner House .30 .75
14 Alex MacLeod .30 .75
15 Kyle McMurphy .30 .75
16 Corey Milan .30 .75
17 Bryant Molle .40 1.00
18 Robert Skinner .30 .75
19 Evan Smith .30 .75
20 Gary Sylvester .30 .75
21 Mike Towns .30 .75
22 Evan Trupp .30 .75
23 Ryan Wagner .30 .75
24 Bruno Campese HC .30 .75
25 72-73 Penticton Broncos Team Photo .30 .75

1992-93 Peoria Rivermen

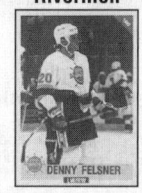

Sponsored by Coca-Cola and Kroger, this 30-card set measures the standard size. The fronts feature color player photos with a white border. The team logo, the player's name, and position appear in a gray bar under the photo, while "1992" is printed in white letters on a blue triangle in the top right corner of the photo. The cards are unnumbered and checklisted below in alphabetical order.
COMPLETE SET (30) 4.00 10.00
1 Jeff Batters .16 .40
2 Parris Duffus .20 .50
3 Greg Eberle TR .04 .10
4 John Faginkrantz MG .04 .10
5 Denny Felsner .16 .40
6 Derek Frenette .16 .40
7 Ron Handy .16 .40
8 Joe Hawley .16 .40
9 Terry Hollinger .16 .40
10 Ron Hoover .16 .40
11 Daniel Laperriere .20 .50
12 Lee J. Leslie .16 .40
13 Dave Mackey .16 .40
14 Jason Marshall .20 .50
15 Brian McKee .16 .40
16 Rick Meagher CO .16 .40
17 Kevin Miehm .16 .40
18 Brian Pellerin ACO .04 .10
19 Mark Reeds .16 .40
20 Kyle Reeves .16 .40
21 Rob Robinson .16 .40
22 Jason Ruff .16 .40
23 Geoff Sarjeant .30 .75
24 Richard Pion .16 .40
25 Darren Veitch .16 .40
26 Doug Wickenheiser .16 .40
27 Shawn Wheeler .16 .40
28 Checklist .04 .10
29 Coca Cola Coupon .04 .10
30 Title Card .04 .10

1993-94 Peoria Rivermen

Produced by 1993 Hat Tricks, Inc., this 31-card D.A.R.E. (Drug Abuse Resistance Education) set measures approximately 2 3/8" by 3 1/4" and celebrates the tenth anniversary of the Peoria Rivermen (International Hockey League). The fronts feature full-bleed color action photos, except at the bottom where an orange stripe separates a thicker blue stripe carrying player information. The 10th anniversary logo in the lower right corner completes the front. The cards are unnumbered and checklisted below in alphabetical order.
COMPLETE SET (31) 4.00 10.00
1 Mark Bassen .16 .40
2 Jeff Batters .16 .40
3 Rene Chapdelaine .16 .40
4 Doug Crossman .20 .50
5 Parris Duffus .30 .75
6 Greg Eberle TR .04 .10
7 Doug Evans .16 .40
8 Kevin Evans .16 .40
9 John Faginkrantz EQMG .04 .10
10 Denny Felsner .16 .40
11 Derek Frenette .16 .40
12 Terry Hollinger .16 .40
13 Ron Hoover .16 .40
14 Butch Kaebel .16 .40
15 Nathan Lafayette .16 .40
16 Dan Laperriere .20 .50
17 Dave Mackey .16 .40
18 Paul MacLean CO .16 .40
19 Michel Mongeau .20 .50
20 Brian Pellerin .16 .40
21 Rick Pion .16 .40
22 Vitali Prokhorov .16 .40
23 Mark Reeds ACO .04 .10
24 John Roderick .16 .40
25 Geoff Sarjeant .20 .75
26 Steve Staios .20 .50
27 Darren Veitch .16 .40
28 Nick Vitucci .20 .75
29 Title card .04 .10
30 Checklist .04 .10
31 Alcohol Awareness .04 .10

1995-96 Peoria Rivermen

This standard-sized, 24-card set was produced by the Rivermen and offered for sale through the club at games and by mail. The cards are unnumbered and listed below in alphabetical order.
COMPLETE SET (24) 4.00 10.00
1 Jon Casey .30 .75
2 Rene Chapdelaine .20 .50
3 Doug Evans .20 .50
4 Eric Fenton .20 .50
5 Shannon Finn .16 .40
6 Martin Hamrlik .16 .40
7 Ron Hoover .16 .40
8 Jacques Joubert .16 .40
9 Lee J. Leslie .20 .50
10 Dave MacIntyre .20 .50
11 Jason Miller .16 .40
12 Michel Mongeau .30 .75
13 Glenn Mulvenna .20 .50
14 Eric Murano .16 .40
15 Keith Osborne .16 .40
16 Greg Paslawski .20 .50
17 Jon Pratt .16 .40
18 Dan Ratushny .20 .50
19 Patrice Robitaille .20 .50
20 Paul Taylor .16 .40
21 Travis Thiessen .16 .40
22 Steve Thornton .16 .40
23 Kirk Tomlinson .20 .50
24 Steve Wilson .16 .40

1996-97 Peoria Rivermen

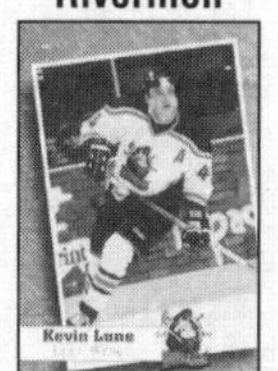

This 25-card set marks the debut of the Rivermen as a member club of the ECHL, but continues the tradition of fine sets. The cards feature action photos on the front, and full stats and bio on the reverse. The unnumbered cards are listed below in alphabetical order.
COMPLETE SET (25) 4.00 10.00
1 Mike Barrie .20 .50
2 Doug Bonner .30 .75
3 Greg Eberle/John Krouse .04 .10
4 Brad Essex .16 .40
5 Doug Evans ASST CO .04 .10
6 Liam Garvey .16 .40
7 Trevor Hanas .16 .40
8 Jon Hillebrandt .30 .75
9 Dan Hodge .20 .50
10 Butch Kaebel .16 .40
11 Karson Kaebel .16 .40
12 Justin Krall .16 .40
13 Jeff Kungle .16 .40
14 Kevin Lune .16 .40
15 Darren Maloney .16 .40
16 Dustin McArthur .16 .40
17 Jon Pratt .16 .40
18 Brad Purdie .16 .40
19 Mark Reeds CO .04 .10
20 Jason Saal .30 .75
21 Jan Slavik .16 .40
22 Marc Terris .16 .40
23 Jean-Guy Trudel .20 .50
24 Paul Vincent .20 .50
25 Title Card .04 .10

1996-97 Peoria Rivermen Photo Album

This 24-card set was released in perforated album form as a game night promotional giveaway. The cards are unnumbered and therefore are listed below in alphabetical order.
COMPLETE SET (24) 8.00 20.00
1 Mike Barrie .30 .75
2 Doug Bonner .60 1.50
3 Greg Eberle TR .20 .50
4 Brad Essex .30 .75
5 Doug Evans ASST CO .20 .50
6 Liam Garvey .30 .75
7 Trevor Hanas .30 .75
8 Jon Hillebrandt .60 1.50
9 Dan Hodge .30 .75
10 Butch Kaebel .30 .75
11 Karson Kaebel .30 .75
12 Justin Krall .30 .75
13 John Krouse EQUIP .20 .50
14 Jeff Kungle .30 .75
15 Kevin Lune .30 .75
16 Darren Maloney .30 .75
17 Dustin McArthur .30 .75
18 Jon Pratt .30 .75
19 Brad Purdie .30 .75
20 Jason Saal .60 1.50
21 Jan Slavik .30 .75
22 Marc Terris .30 .75
23 Jean-Guy Trudel .40 1.00
24 Paul Vincent .30 .75

1997-98 Peoria Rivermen

Little is known about this set beyond the confirmed checklist. Additional information can be forwarded to hockeymag@beckett.com.
COMPLETE SET (29) 4.00 10.00
1 Garry Gruber .16 .40
2 Derek Diener .16 .40
3 Samy Nasreddine .20 .50
4 Doug Evans .16 .40
5 Darren Maloney .16 .40
6 Joe Craigen .20 .50
7 Rob Phillips .16 .40
8 Brian Clifford .16 .40
9 Darcy Smith .16 .40
10 Butch Kaebel .20 .50
11 Jean Guy Trudel .20 .50
12 Brad Essex .16 .40
13 Justin Krall .16 .40
14 John Dance .16 .40
15 Marc Terris .16 .40
16 Trevor Hanas .16 .40
17 Dave Paradise .16 .40
18 David Vallieres .16 .40
19 Scott Roche .30 .75
20 Marcel Kuris .16 .40
21 Jon Pratt .16 .40
22 Rob Giffin .20 .50
23 Mark Reeds .20 .50
24 Greg Eberle .16 .40
25 John Krouse EQ .04 .10
26 Mascot .04 .10
27 Title Card .04 .10
28 Header Card .04 .10

1998-99 Peoria Rivermen

This set features the Rivermen of the ECHL. The set was produced by ebk Sports and was sold by the team at home games.
COMPLETE SET (27) 4.80 12.00
1 Darren Maloney .16 .40
2 Dan Hodge .16 .40
3 Doug Evans .16 .40
4 Dan Carney .16 .40
5 Chris Coveny .16 .40
6 Alexandre Couture .16 .40
7 Jamie Thompson .16 .40
8 Jay Kenney .16 .40
9 J.F. Boutin .16 .40
10 Joe Craigen .30 .75
11 Darcy Smith .16 .40
12 Dan Murphy .16 .40
13 Quinn Hancock .16 .40
14 Mark Reeds CO .04 .10
15 Marek Ivan .16 .40
16 Kory Karlander .16 .40
17 Ken Boone .16 .40
18 Jeff Trembecky .16 .40
19 Steve MacKinnon .16 .40
20 Joe Rybar .30 .75
21 Peoria Rivermen .16 .40
22 Scott Roche .30 .75
23 Chad Lang .30 .75
24 Kevin Paden .20 .50
25 Blaine Fitzpatrick .16 .40
26 Mike Schultz .16 .40
27 Darren Maloney AS .04 .10
28 Jamie Thompson AS .16 .40

1999-00 Peoria Rivermen

This set features the Rivermen of the ECHL. The set was produced by Roox and was issued as a promotional giveaway at a home game.
COMPLETE SET (36) 6.00 100.00
1 Rocky MAS .10 .25
2 Don Granato CO .04 1.00
3 Greg Eberle TR .04 .10
4 Jamie Healy TR .04 .10
5 Trevor Baker .20 4.00
6 Duane Derksen .40 8.00
7 Darren Clark .20 4.00
8 Jason Christie .20 4.00
9 Blaine Fitzpatrick .20 4.00
10 John Gurskis .20 4.00
11 Alexandre Couture .20 4.00
12 Darren Maloney .20 4.00
13 Blaz Emersic .20 4.00
14 Cody Rudkowsky .30 8.00
15 J.F. Boutin .20 4.00
16 Joe Rybar .40 5.00
17 Matt Smith .20 4.00
18 Tomaz Razinger .20 4.00
19 Craig Anderson .20 4.00
20 Jason Lawmaster .20 4.00
21 Bret Meyers .20 4.00
22 Sean Farmer .20 4.00
23 Darin Kimble .40 8.00
24 Dan Hodge .20 4.00
25 Luke Gruden .20 4.00
26 Tyler McMillan .20 4.00
27 Kenzie Homer .20 4.00
28 James Desmarais .20 4.00
29 John Butler PRES .04 .10
30 Mike Nelson VP .04 .10
31 Bart Rogers GM .04 .10
32 Michael Sauers GM .04 .10
33 Jim Small GM .04 .10
34 Norm Ulrich DOB .04 .10
35 Manda Girard SALES .04 .10
36 B.J. Stone SALES .04 .10

2001-02 Peoria Rivermen

This set features the Rivermen of the UHL. We have no additional information besides the checklist. If you can shed some light on this issue, please write to hockeymag@beckett.com.
COMPLETE SET (24) 8.00 20.00

1 Checklist .04 .10
2 Jason Christie CO .04 .10
3 Curtis Sanford .40 2.00
4 Bob Gassoff Jr. .40 1.00
5 Chad Starling .40 1.00
6 Blake Evans .40 1.00
7 Kevin Tucker .40 1.00
8 Trevor Baker .40 1.00
9 Jonathan Fauteux .40 1.00
10 Randy Rowe .40 1.00
11 Dustin Kuk .40 1.00
12 Bret Meyers .40 1.00
13 Kevin Granato .40 1.00
14 Dan Hodge .40 1.00
15 Tyler Rennette .40 1.00
16 Ryan Finnerty .40 1.00
17 Brad Voth .40 1.00
18 Joe Rybar .60 1.50
19 Darren Clark .40 1.00
20 Matt Golden .40 1.00
21 Phil Osaer .40 1.00
22 Jason Lawmaster .40 1.00
23 Arvid Rekis .40 1.00
24 Kevin Cloutier .40 1.00

2000-01 Peoria Rivermen

This set features the Rivermen of the ECHL. The set was produced by Roox and sold by the team at its souvenir stands.

COMPLETE SET (21) 4.00 10.00
1 Curtis Sanford .30 2.00
2 Didier Tremblay .20 .50
3 Luke Gruden .20 .50
4 J.F. Boutin .20 .50
5 Lauri Kinos .20 .50
6 Darren Maloney .20 .50
7 Trevor Baker .20 .50
8 Tyler Willis .20 .50
9 Bret Meyers .20 .50
10 Dustin Kuk .20 .50
11 Dan Hodge .20 .50
12 Joe Rybar .20 .50
13 Blaine Fitzpatrick .20 .50
14 Darren Clark .20 .50
15 Matt Golden .20 .50
16 Kenric Exner .40 1.00
17 Jason Lawmaster .20 .50
18 Arvid Rekis .20 .50
19 Tomaz Razinger .20 .50
20 Joe Trotta ACO .10 .25
21 Jason Christie HCO .10 .25

2002-03 Peoria Rivermen

COMPLETE SET (25) 5.00 12.00
1 Jason Christie HCO .10 .25
2 Simon Lajeunesse .40 1.00
3 Trevor Gillies .20 .50
4 Lauri Kinos .20 .50
5 Darren Clark .20 .50
6 Trevor Baker .20 .50
7 Greg Day .20 .50
8 Brett DeCecco .20 .50
9 Randy Rowe .20 .50
10 Randy Copley .20 .50
11 Duane Derksen .40 1.00
12 Kevin Granato .20 .50
13 Tyler Rennette .20 .50
14 Ryan Finnerty .20 .50
15 Brad Voth .20 .50
16 Brendan Brooks .20 .50
17 Derek Booth .20 .50
18 Scott Crawford .20 .50
19 Jeremy Yablonski .20 .50
20 Jason Lawmaster .20 .50
21 Josh Kern .20 .50
22 Arvid Rekis .20 .50
23 Anthony Belza .20 .50
24 Alfie Michaud .40 1.00
NNO Checklist .02 .10

2002-03 Peoria Rivermen Photo Pack

These oversized (11X14) photos were sold in set form by the team. Each card in the set is autographed in black Sharpie and is serial numbered out of 100. The cards are unnumbered and so are listed below in alphabetical order.

COMPLETE SET (8) 50.00
1 Trevor Baker 6.00
2 Brendan Brooks 6.00
3 Darren Clark 6.00
4 Duane Derksen 10.00
5 Ryan Finnerty 6.00
6 Jason Lawmaster 6.00
7 Alfie Michaud 10.00
8 Tyler Rennette 6.00

2002-03 Peoria Rivermen RBI Sports

COMPLETE SET (18) 8.00 20.00
151 Trevor Baker .40 1.00
152 Anthony Belza .40 1.00
153 Derek Booth .40 1.00
154 Brendan Brooks .40 1.00
155 Darren Clark .40 1.00
156 Randy Copley .40 1.00
157 Scott Crawford .40 1.00
158 Greg Day .40 1.00
159 Duane Derksen .75 2.00
160 Trevor Gillies .40 1.00
161 Josh Kern .40 1.00
162 Jason Lawmaster .75 2.00
163 Alfie Michaud .75 2.00
164 Arvid Rekis .40 1.00
165 Tyler Rennette .40 1.00
166 Randy Rowe .40 1.00
167 Rod Taylor .40 1.00
168 Brad Voth .40 1.00

2003-04 Peoria Rivermen

This set was produced by Choice Marketing and sold at home games.

COMPLETE SET (24) 4.00 10.00
1 Adam Edinger .15 .40
2 Brendan Brooks .15 .40
3 Bret DeCecco .15 .40
4 Brett Scheffelmaier .15 .40
5 Chad Starling .15 .40
6 Colin Hemingway .15 .40
7 Craig Olynick .15 .40
8 Doug MacIver .15 .40
9 George Halkidis .15 .40
10 Greg Black .15 .40
11 Joe Pereira .15 .40
12 Joe Vandermeer .15 .40
13 Ken Goetz .30 .75
14 Levente Szuper .40 1.00
15 Malcolm Hutt .15 .40
16 Malcolm MacMillan .15 .40
17 Marty Johnston .15 .40
18 Mike Valley .30 .75
19 Randy Rowe .15 .40
20 Scott Crawford .15 .40
21 Scott Turner .15 .40
22 Trevor Baker .30 .75
23 Tyler Rennette .15 .40
24 Jason Christie HCO .02 .10
NNO Checklist .01 .05

2004-05 Peoria Rivermen

COMPLETE SET (25) 5.00 12.00
1 Chad Starling .20 .50
2 Warren Toews .20 .50
3 Mark Jarant .20 .50
4 Chris Bogas .20 .50
5 Brian McCullough .20 .50
6 Randy Rowe .20 .50
7 Trevor Baker .20 .50
8 Justin Maiser .20 .50
9 Travis Rycroft .20 .50
10 Scott Turner .20 .50
11 Alfie Michaud .40 1.00
12 Chris Beckford-Tsue .40 1.00
13 Kris Kasper .40 1.00
14 Ed Hill .20 .50
15 Jake Riddle .20 .50
16 James Sanford .20 .50
17 Patrick Wellar .20 .50
18 David Kaczowka .20 .50
19 Tyler Rennette .20 .50
20 Joe Pereira .20 .50
21 Rejean Stringer .02 .10
22 Stringer MASCOT .02 .10
23 Colin Hemingway .20 .50
24 Trevor Byrne .20 .50
25 Jason Christie CO .02 .10

2005-06 Peoria Rivermen

COMPLETE SET (24) 15.00
1 Curtis Sanford .40 1.00
2 Mike Mottau .30 .75
3 Rocky Thompson .20 .50
4 Trevor Byrne .20 .50
5 Brendan Buckley .20 .50
6 Gavin Morgan .20 .50
7 Colin Hemingway .20 .50
8 Jon DiSalvatore .20 .50
9 Mike Stuart .20 .50
10 Blake Evans .20 .50
11 Mike Glumac .20 .50
12 D.J. King .20 .50
13 Aaron MacKenzie .20 .50
14 Troy Riddle .20 .50
15 Trent Whitfield .20 .50
16 Peter Sejna .20 .50
17 Brendan Brookes .20 .50
18 Ryan Ramsay .20 .50
19 Chris Beckford-Tseu .75 2.00
20 Doug Lynch .20 .50
21 Jason Bacashihua .40 1.00
22 Patrick Lalime .40 1.00
23 Jeff Woywitka .20 .50
24 Steve Pleau CO .02 .10

2006-07 Peoria Rivermen

COMPLETE SET (25) 8.00 15.00
1 Chris Beckford-Tseu .60 1.50
2 Michal Birner .20 .50
3 Jon DiSalvatore .20 .50
4 Zack Fitzgerald .20 .50
5 Mike Glumac .30 .75
6 Cam Keith .20 .50
7 D.J. King .20 .50
8 Charles Linglet .20 .50
9 Doug Lynch .20 .50
10 Aaron MacKenzie .20 .50
11 Ryan MacMurchy .20 .50
12 Tomas Mojzis .20 .50
13 Gavin Morgan .20 .50
14 Roman Polak .20 .50
15 Ryan Ramsay .30 .75
16 Marek Schwarz .75 2.00
17 Peter Sejna .20 .50
18 Mike Stuart .20 .50
19 Rocky Thompson .20 .50
20 Trent Whitfield .20 .50
21 Stephen Wood .20 .50
22 Jeff Woywitka .20 .50
23 Konstantin Zakharov .20 .50
24 Dave Baseggio .20 .50
25 Checklist .02 .10

1989-90 Peterborough Petes

This 25-card set paralleled the 7th Inning Sketch OHL league set but featured players of the Peterborough club. The card stock was thicker than the league set and the pictures were sharper.

COMPLETE SET (26) 10.00 25.00
98 Troy Stephens .40 1.00
99 Dan Brown .40 1.00
100 Mike Ricci 1.25 3.00
101 Brent Pope .40 1.00
102 Mike Dagenais .40 1.00
103 Scott Campbell .40 1.00
104 Jamie Pegg .40 1.00
105 Joe Hawley .40 1.00
106 Jason Dawe .40 1.00
107 Paul Mitton .40 1.00
108 Mike Tomlinson .40 1.00
109 Dave Lorentz .40 1.00
110 Dale McTavish .40 1.00
111 Willie McGarvey .40 1.00
112 Don O'Neill .40 1.00
113 Mark Myles .40 1.00
114 Chris Longo .40 1.00
115 Tom Hopkins .40 1.00
116 Jassen Cullimore .40 1.00
117 Geoff Ingram .40 1.00
118 Twohey .40 1.00
Bovair TR
119 Doug Searle .40 1.00
120 Bryan Gendron .40 1.00
121 Andrew Verner .60 1.50
122 Todd Bocjun .60 1.50
123 Dick Todd CO .20 .50

1991-92 Peterborough Petes

This 30-card P.L.A.Y. (Police, Laws and Youth) set measures approximately 2 1/2" by 3 3/4" and features posed, color player photos with bright blue and white borders. The player's name is printed on the picture in white letters in the upper left corner. The team logo appears in the upper right corner.

COMPLETE SET (30) 8.00 20.00
1 Jason Dawe .30 .75
2 Chris Pronger 3.20 8.00
3 Scott Turner .20 .50
4 Chad Grills .20 .50
5 Brent Tully .20 .50
6 Mike Harding .20 .50
7 Chris Longo .20 .50
8 Slapshot MASCOT .04 .10
9 Doug Searle .20 .50
10 Mike Tomlinson .20 .50
11 Bryan Gendron .20 .50
12 Andrew Verner .30 .75
13 Ryan Black .20 .50
14 Don O'Neill .20 .50
15 Jeff Twohey MG/CO .04 .10
16 Dale McTavish .20 .50
17 Jeff Walker .20 .50
18 Matt St. Germain .20 .50
19 Dave Roche .20 .50
20 Colin Wilson .20 .50
21 Jassen Cullimore .20 .50
22 Chad Lang .30 .75
23 Dick Todd MG/CO .20 .50
24 Geordie Kinnear .20 .50
25 Shawn Heins .24 .60
26 John Johnson .20 .50
27 Kelly Vipond .20 .50
NNO Police Crest .04 .10
NNO Kiwanis Sponsor Card .04 .10
NNO Quaker Sponsor Card .04 .10

1993-94 Peterborough Petes

Sponsored by Cardboard Heroes and printed by Slapshot Images Ltd., this standard-size 31-card set features the 1993-94 Peterborough Petes. Only 3,000 of these sets have been produced; the first card also serves as a Certificate of Authenticity and has the individual set number printed in the upper left corner. On a grey background, the fronts feature color action player photos with thin maroon borders. The player's name, position and team name, as well as the producer's logo, appear on the front.

COMPLETE SET (31) 6.00 15.00
1 1992-93 OHL Champions .14 .35
2 Jonathan Murphy .14 .35
3 Dave Roche .14 .35
4 Rob Giffin .14 .35
5 Mike Harding .14 .35
6 Tim Hill .14 .35
7 Darryl Moxam .14 .35
8 Pat Paone .14 .35
9 Brent Tully .14 .35
10 Zac Bierk .30 .75
11 Chad Grills .14 .35
12 Matt St. Germain .14 .35
13 Henrik Eppers .14 .35
14 Rick Emmett .14 .35
15 Chad Lang .20 .50
16 Cameron Mann .40 1.00
17 Steve Hogg .14 .35
18 Mike Williams .14 .35
19 Ryan Nauss .14 .35
20 Jamie Langenbrunner .40 1.00
21 Ryan Douglas .14 .35
22 Matt Johnson .30 .75
23 Kelvin Solari .14 .35
24 Dan Delmonte .14 .35
25 Quayde Lightbody .14 .35
26 Adrian Murray .14 .35
27 Jason Dawe .14 .35
28 Mike Harding .14 .35
29 Chris Pronger 2.00 5.00
30 Sponsor Card .04 .10
Cardboard Heroes
Greg Ball
Kevin Ball
NNO Slapshot Ad Card .04 .10

2001-02 Peterborough Petes

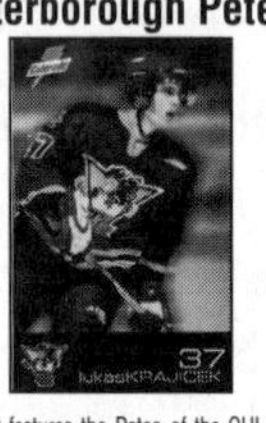

This set features the Petes of the OHL. The cards are an oversized 4X6, and feature blurred colour photos on front, with a Gatorade logo upper left and player name and number along the bottom. The cards are not numbered, but are listed in order of jersey number, as they were released. It is believed they were issued as a promotional giveaway by the team.

COMPLETE SET (20) 8.00 20.00
1 Cody Spicer .60 1.50
2 Dustin Wood .40 1.00
3 Bryan Hamm .40 1.00
4 Mark Flood .40 1.00
5 Trevor Hendrix .40 1.00
6 James Edgar .40 1.00
7 Jason Penner .40 1.00
8 Jon Howse .40 1.00
9 Ryan Card .40 1.00
10 Eric Staal 4.00 10.00
11 Josh Patterson .40 1.00
12 Jim Gagnon .40 1.00
13 Brad Self .40 1.00
14 Matt Herneisen .40 1.00
15 Adam Elzinga .40 1.00
16 Greg Chambers .40 1.00
17 Jamie Tardif .40 1.00
18 Matt Armstrong .40 1.00
19 David Currie .60 1.50
20 Lukas Krajicek .75 2.00

2002-03 Peterborough Petes

COMPLETE SET (24) 6.00 15.00
1 Rick Allain CO .02 .10
2 Steve Smith ACO .02 .10
3 Aaron Dawson .20 .50
4 Mark Flood .20 .50
5 Shawn Futers .20 .50
6 Trevor Hendrix .20 .50
7 Jordan Morrison .20 .50
8 Jon Howse .20 .50
9 Ryan Card .20 .50
10 Eric Staal 2.00 5.00
11 Evgeny Kadatskiy .20 .50
12 Josh Patterson .20 .50
13 Jason Penner .20 .50
14 Greg Williams .20 .50
15 Chad Robinson .20 .50
16 Mike Ramsay .20 .50
17 Patrick Kaleta .20 .50
18 Adam Elzinga .20 .50
19 Greg Chambers .20 .50
20 Jamie Tardif .20 .50
21 Mike McKeown .20 .50
22 Jeff MacDougald .20 .50
23 David Currie .20 .50
24 Lukas Krajicek .40 1.00

2004-05 Peterborough Petes Postcards

This set of 5X7 postcard-sized singles were sold in set form by the team.

COMPLETE SET (25) 25.00
1 Jordan Staal 3.00
2 Liam Reddox 1.00
3 Daniel Ryder 1.00
4 Jamie Tardif 1.00
5 Eero Kilpelainen 2.00
6 Patrick Kaleta 1.00
7 Jordan Morrison 1.00

8 Trevor Henrikx 1.00
9 Mark Flood 1.00
10 Niko Vainio 1.00
11 Justin Carauna 1.00
12 Mike Montgomery 1.00
13 Aaron Barton 1.00
14 Patrick Kaleta 1.00
15 Aaron Dawson 1.00
16 Scott Cowie 1.00
17 Justin Soryal 1.00
18 Darryl Flowers 1.00
19 Ryan Young 1.00
20 Peter Aston 1.00
21 Jadran Baljo 1.00
22 Greg Stewart 1.00
23 Greg Williams 1.00
24 Corey Gault 1.00
25 Jeff MacDougald 1.00

2002-03 Philadelphia Phantoms

COMPLETE SET (26) 6.00 15.00
1 Antero Niittymaki .75 2.00
2 Bruno St. Jacques .20 .50
3 Dan Peters .20 .50
4 Mark Greig .20 .50
5 Kirby Law .30 .75
6 Peter White .30 .75
7 Eric Betournay .20 .50
8 Jack Baker .20 .50
9 Patrick Sharp .30 .75
10 Guillaume Lefebvre .30 .75
11 Pete Vandermeer .30 .75
12 Andre Savage .20 .50
13 Jim Vandermeer .30 .75
14 Mike Siklenka .30 .75
15 Ian MacNeil .20 .50
16 Ben Stafford .20 .50
17 John Slaney .20 .50
18 Mike Lephart .20 .50
19 Brad Tiley .20 .50
20 Wade Skolney .20 .50
21 Neil Little .40 1.00
22 David Harlock .20 .50
23 John Stevens CO .02 .10
24 Phlex Mascot .02 .10
25 Subway Coupon .01 .01
NNO Checklist .02 .10

2003-04 Philadelphia Phantoms

This set was produced by Choice Marketing and sold at home games.

COMPLETE SET (26) 12.00
1 Checklist .01
2 Antero Niittymaki 1.50
3 Ben Stafford .40
4 Boyd Kane .40
5 Craig Berube .40
6 Dennis Seidenberg .40
7 Freddy Meyer .40
8 Ian MacNeil .40
9 Jeff Woywitka .50
10 Joey Hope .40
11 John Slaney .40
12 Kirby Law .75
13 Mark Murphy .40
14 Mike Peluso .40
15 Mike Siklenka .40
16 Neil Little 1.00
17 Nick Deschenes .40
18 P.J. Stock 1.00
19 Patrick Sharp .40
20 Pete Vandermeer .75
21 Peter White .40
22 Randy Jones .40
23 Wade Skolney .40
24 John Stevens .40
25 Mascot .10
26 Sponsor .01

2004-05 Philadelphia Phantoms

COMPLETE SET (25) 6.00 15.00
1 Riley Cote .20 .50
2 Ben Eager .30 .75
3 Todd Fedoruk .40 1.00
4 Josh Gratton .60 1.50
5 Joey Hope .20 .50
6 Randy Jones .20 .50
7 Boyd Kane .30 .75
8 Neil Little .40 1.00
9 Eric Meloche .20 .50
10 Freddy Meyer .30 .75
11 Mark Murphy .20 .50
12 Antero Niittymaki .75 2.00
13 Joni Pitkanen .40 1.00
14 David Printz .20 .50
15 Ryan Ready .20 .50
16 Dennis Seidenberg .20 .50
17 Patrick Sharp .30 .75
18 Jon Sim .30 .75
19 Wade Skolney .20 .50
20 John Slaney .20 .50
21 Jeff Smith .20 .50
22 Ben Stafford .20 .50
23 R.J. Umberger .60 1.50
24 Tony Voce .20 .50
NNO Checklist .01 .01

2005-06 Philadelphia Phantoms

COMPLETE SET (26) 5.00 12.00
1 Philadelphia Phantoms CL .01 .01
2 B.J. Abel .20 .50
3 Rejean Beauchemin .40 1.00
4 Marc Cavosie .20 .50
5 Eric Chouinard .20 .50
6 Charlie Cook .20 .50
7 Riley Cote .20 .50
8 Ben Eager .20 .50
9 Triston Grant .20 .50
10 Josh Gratton .40 1.00
11 Joey Hope .20 .50
12 Randy Jones .20 .50
13 Pat Kavanagh .20 .50
14 Eric Meloche .20 .50
15 Freddy Meyer .20 .50
16 Alexandre Picard .20 .50
17 David Printz .20 .50
18 Ryan Ready .20 .50
19 Stefan Ruzicka .20 .50
20 Wade Skolney .20 .50
21 John Slaney .20 .50
22 Jamie Storr .30 .75
23 R.J. Umberger .40 1.00
24 Tony Voce .20 .50
25 John Stevens HC .02 .10
26 Phlex MASCOT .02 .10

2005-06 Philadelphia Phantoms All-Decade Team

COMPLETE SET (12) 8.00 15.00
1 Patrick Sharp .40 1.00
2 Frank Bialowas .75 2.00
3 Mark Greig .40 1.00
4 John Slaney .40 1.00
5 John Stevens .40 1.00
6 Neil Little .75 2.00
7 Peter White .40 1.00
8 Mike Maneluk .40 1.00
9 Kirby Law .40 1.00
10 Freddy Meyer .40 1.00
11 Dennis Seidenberg .40 1.00
12 Antero Niittymaki .75 2.00

2006-07 Philadelphia Phantoms

COMPLETE SET (30) 10.00 18.00
1 Joe Mullen ACO .10 .25
2 Kjell Samuelsson CO .10 .25
3 Ryan Potulny .60 1.50
4 Niko Dimitrakos .30 .75
5 Lars Jonsson .20 .50
6 Denis Tolpeko .20 .50
7 Eric Meloche .20 .50
8 John Slaney .20 .50
9 Martin Houle .40 1.00
10 Rejean Beauchemin .40 1.00
11 Scott Munroe .20 .50
12 Tony Voce .20 .50
13 Triston Grant .40 1.00
14 David Printz .30 .75
15 Nate Guenin .30 .75
16 Ben Eager .30 .75
17 Martin Grenier .20 .50
18 Riley Cote .20 .50
19 Matt Ellison .20 .50
20 Alexandre Picard .20 .50
21 Nolan Baumgartner .20 .50
22 Stefan Ruzicka .30 .75
23 Mark Cullen .20 .50
24 Matt Davis .20 .50
25 Don Morrison .20 .50
26 Jussi Timonen .20 .50
27 Darren Reid .20 .50
28 Frederik Cabana .20 .50
29 Peter Zingoni .20 .50
30 Gino Pisellini .20 .50

1993-94 Phoenix Cobras RHI

This set features the Cobras of Roller Hockey Intl. The set was produced by the team and sold at home games.

COMPLETE SET (20) 3.20 8.00
1 Header Card .04 .10
2 Lee Kasper .20 .50
3 Stuart Silver .20 .50
4 Lou Franceschetti HCO .04 .10
5 Aaron Boh .20 .50
6 Todd Brost .30 .75
7 Michel Couvrette .20 .50
8 Wade Gibson .20 .50
9 Rickard Gronborg .20 .50
10 Hugo Hamelin .20 .50
11 Daniel Larin .20 .50
12 Mike O'Hara .20 .50
13 Sergei Olympiev .20 .50
14 John Redinger .20 .50
15 Brent Sapergia .30 .75
16 Daniel Shank .30 .75
17 Troy Stephens .20 .50
18 Boyd Sutton .20 .50
19 Mike Vukonich .20 .50
20 Alex Zhurik .20 .50

1992-93 Phoenix Roadrunners

Sponsored by Safeway, this 28-card standard-size set features color action photos on the front edged by a blue border on the top and left margins, with full bleed on the bottom and right. The IHL logo is in the top right corner. The player's name and jersey number are printed in red at the bottom while the team name is printed in white immediately above. The team logo is in the lower right and the player's position is printed in red inside a hockey puck in the lower left. The cards are unnumbered and checklisted below in alphabetical order.

COMPLETE SET (28) 4.00 10.00
1 Tim Bothwell CO .16 .40
2 Frank Breault .16 .40
3 Tim Breslin .16 .40
4 Rene Chapdelaine .16 .40
5 Sylvain Couturier .20 .50
6 Phil Crowe .20 .50
7 Darryl Gilmour .20 .50
8 David Goverde .20 .50
9 Ed Kastelic .16 .40
10 Rick Kozuback ACO .04 .10
11 Ted Kramer .16 .40
12 Robert Lang .30 .75
13 Guy Leveque .16 .40
14 Jim Maher .16 .40
15 Brad McCaughey .16 .40
16 Shawn McCosh .16 .40
17 John Mokosak .16 .40
18 Keith Redmond .16 .40
19 Mike Ruark .16 .40
20 Brandy Semchuk .16 .40
21 Dave Stewart .16 .40
22 Brad Tiley .16 .40
23 Dave Tretowicz .16 .40
24 Mike Vukonich .16 .40
25 Tim Watters .20 .50
26 Sean Whyte .16 .40
27 Darryl Williams .16 .40
28 Rocky Roadrunner .04 .10
(Mascot)

1993-94 Phoenix Roadrunners

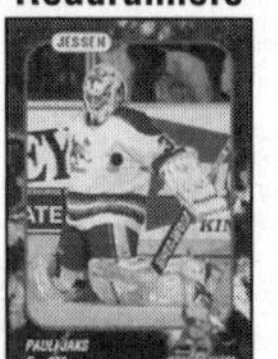

This 25-card set measures the standard size. On a black and white marbleized background, the fronts feature color action player photos with rounded corners and a thin blue border. The player's name, position, and number appear under the photo, along with the team logo. The cards are unnumbered and checklisted below in alphabetical order.

COMPLETE SET (25) 4.00 10.00
1 Tim Breslin .16 .40
2 Brian Chapman .16 .40
3 Stephane Charbonneau .16 .40
4 Dan Currie .20 .50
5 Rick Dudley CO .20 .50
6 Marc Fortier .20 .50
7 David Goverde .20 .50
8 Kevin Grant .16 .40
9 Mark Hardy P/CO .16 .40
10 Dean Hulett .16 .40
11 Pauli Jaks .20 .50
12 Bob Jay .16 .40
13 Rick Knickle .30 .75

14 Guy Leveque .20 .50
15 Eric Lavigne .20 .50
16 Dominic Lavoie .16 .40
17 Jim Maher .16 .40
18 Brian McReynolds .16 .40
19 Rob Murphy .16 .40
20 Keith Redmond .16 .40
21 Dave Stewart .16 .40
22 Dave Thomlinson .16 .40
23 Brad Tiley .16 .40
24 Jim Vesey .16 .40
25 Darryl Williams .16 .40

1995-96 Phoenix Roadrunners

This 24-card set was produced by Jessen Associates for Collector's Edge. The full colour cards were available as a free promotional item at a game; they also were sold through the team's pro shop for $6. Approximately 8,000 sets were made. The cards are unnumbered and are checklisted below in alphabetical order.

COMPLETE SET (24) 4.80 12.00
1 Ruslan Batyrshin .16 .40
2 Frederik Beaubien .30 .75
3 John Blue .30 .75
4 Mike Boback .16 .40
5 Kevin Brown .20 .50
6 Jim Burton .16 .40
7 Dan Bylsma .20 .50
8 Brian Chapman .16 .40
9 Rob Cowie .16 .40
10 Devin Edgerton .16 .40
11 Ken McRae .16 .40
12 Barry Potomski .30 .75
13 Daniel Rydmark .16 .40
14 Jeff Shevalier .20 .50
15 Gary Shuchuk .20 .50
16 Chris Snell .20 .50
17 Jamie Storr .80 2.00
18 Dave Thomlinson .16 .40
19 Nicholas Vachon .16 .40
20 Jan Vopat .20 .50
21 Steve Wilson .16 .40
22 Training staff .04 .10
23 Rob Laird CO .04 .10
24 Rocky Roadrunner .04 .10

1998-99 Phoenix Mustangs

This oversized set was issued in perforated strip form. It was handed out at a home game as a promotional giveaway, and most of the singles were sponsored by local doctors.

COMPLETE SET (25) 150.00
1 Hugo Belanger .40 8.00
2 David Goverde .60 8.00
3 Dana G. Seltzer MD .10 .25
4 Iannique Renaud .30 6.00
5 Mark Spence .30 6.00
6 Daniel Shank 1.00 20.00
7 Stu Kulak .40 8.00
8 Rusty McKie .30 6.00
9 Gene Bono .30 6.00
10 Jamie Allan .30 6.00
11 Michel Couvrette .30 6.00
12 Sebastien Fortier .30 6.00
13 Corey Laniuk .30 6.00
14 Doug McCarthy .30 6.00
15 Tom Menicci .30 6.00
16 Savo Mitrovic .30 6.00
17 Matt Oliver .30 6.00
18 Teemu Numminen .40 8.00
19 Bobby Rapoza .30 6.00
20 Jason Rose .30 6.00
21 Darren Veitch .30 6.00
22 Sean Whyte .30 6.00
23 Brad McCaughey HCO .10 .25
24 Dick Earle TR .10 .25
25 Rusty the Wrangler Mascot .10 .25

1983-84 Pinebridge Bucks

These card are unnumbered and measure 4 1/8" by 2 3/8". There are reports that there may be as many as 20 cards in this set, this checklist represents the 12 that are confirmed.

COMPLETE SET (12) 15.00
1 Dave Burke .60 1.50
2 Dan Burrows .60 1.50
3 Kim Collins .60 1.50
4 Bob Fleming .60 1.50
5 Rick Harris .60 1.50
6 Steve Heittola .60 1.50
7 Ken Latta .60 1.50
8 Tom Madsen .60 1.50
9 Larry Mollard .60 1.50
10 Kelly Rissling .60 1.50
11 Frank Perkins CO .20 .50
12 Frank Juror TR .20 .50

2001-02 Plymouth Whalers

COMPLETE SET (32) 15.00 30.00
1 Libor Ustrnul .30 .75
2 Jared Newman .30 .75
3 Stephen Weiss 1.25 3.00
4 Nathan Tennant .30 .75
5 Damian Surma .30 .75
6 Chad LaRose .60 1.50

7 Jeff Phillips .30 .75
8 Kyle Neufeld .30 .75
9 Brad Yeo .30 .75
10 Paul Drew .30 .75
11 Cole Jarrett .30 .75
12 Nate Kiser .30 .75
13 Karl Stewart .60 1.50
14 John Mitchell .30 .75
15 Greg Campbell .60 1.50
16 George Nistas .30 .75
17 Tim Sestito .30 .75
18 Kris Vernarsky .30 .75
19 James Wisniewski .30 .75
20 Danny McDonald .30 .75
21 Jason Bacashihua 1.25 3.00
22 Jonas Fiedler .30 .75
23 David Liffiton .60 1.50
24 Roberts ACO .02 .10
25 Mike Vellucci CO .02 .10
26 Dan Reed .30 .75
27 Bryan Thompson .30 .75
28 Stephen Weiss AS 1.25 3.00
29 Jason Bacashihua AS 1.25 3.00
30 Chad LaRose AS .60 1.50
31 Greg Campbell TP .40 1.00
32 James Wisniewski TP .30 .75

2002-03 Plymouth Whalers

COMPLETE SET (30) 5.00 12.00
1 Cole Jarrett .15 .40
2 Nate Kiser .15 .40
3 Karl Stewart .30 .75
4 John Mitchell .15 .40
5 Jimmy Gagnon .15 .40
6 Sean Thompson .15 .40
7 Chad LaRose .40 1.00
8 John Vigilante .15 .40
9 Taylor Raszka .15 .40
10 Ryan Ramsay .15 .40
11 Mike Letizia .15 .40
12 Steve Phillips .15 .40
13 Paul Drew .30 .75
14 Jonas Fielder .15 .40
15 Brent Mahon .15 .40
16 Cole Jarrett AS .15 .40
17 Tim Sestito .15 .40
18 Martin Cizek .15 .40
19 Chad LaRose AS .40 1.00
20 Chris Thorburn .30 .75
21 James Wisniewski .30 .75
22 Mike Nelson .15 .40
23 Nick Vernelli .15 .40
24 Jeff Weber .30 .75
25 Erik Lundmark .15 .40
26 David Liffiton .30 .75
27 David Liffiton .30 .75
Top Prospect
28 Mascot .02 .10
29 Pat Peake RET .10 .25
30 Team Photo .10 .25

2003-04 Plymouth Whalers

COMPLETE SET (28) 6.00 15.00
1 Rane Carnegie .30 .75
2 Dan Collins .20 .50
3 Jonas Fiedler .20 .50
4 Jordan Grant .20 .50
5 Brent Mahon .20 .50
6 Mike Martinelli .20 .50
7 Vaclav Meidl .20 .50
8 John Mitchell .20 .50
9 Gino Pisellini .20 .50
10 Ryan Ramsay .20 .50
11 Tim Sestito .20 .50
12 Sean Thompson .20 .50
13 Nick Vernelli .20 .50
14 John Vigilante .20 .50
15 Craig Cescon .20 .50
16 Mike Knight .20 .50
17 David Liffiton .30 .75
18 Erik Lundmark .20 .50
19 Ryan McGinnis .20 .50
20 Richard Power .20 .50
21 James Wisniewski .30 .75
22 Paul Drew .20 .50
23 Dan Miller .20 .50
24 Ryan Nie .20 .50
25 Michael Vellucci CO .02 .10
26 Coaching Staff .02 .10
27 Alex Roberts .20 .50
28 Mascot .02 .10

2005-06 Plymouth Whalers

COMPLETE SET (29) 8.00 15.00
A-01 John Vigilante .20 .50
A-02 John Armstrong .20 .50
A-03 Jared Boll .30 .75
A-04 Steve Ward .20 .50
A-05 Cory Tanaka .20 .50
A-06 Tom Sestito .20 .50
A-07 Gino Pisellini .30 .75
A-08 Ryan Nie .20 .50
A-09 James Neal .30 .75
A-10 Vaclav Meidl .30 .75
A-11 Ryan McGinnis .20 .50
A-12 Mike Letizia .20 .50
A-13 Andrew Fournier .20 .50
A-14 Dan Collins .20 .50
B-01 Justin Peters .30 .75
B-02 Justin Garay .20 .50
B-03 Jeremy Smith .20 .50
B-04 Ondrej Otcenas .20 .50
B-05 Wes Cunningham .20 .50
B-06 Derek Merlini .20 .50
B-07 Zack Shepley .20 .50
B-08 Joe McCann .20 .50
B-09 Brett Bellemore .20 .50
B-10 Leo Jenner .20 .50
B-11 Chris Terry .20 .50
B-12 Joe Gaynor .20 .50
B-13 Ryan Stephenson .20 .50
B-14 Evan Brophey .20 .50
B-15 Plymouth Whalers CL .01 .01

2006-07 Plymouth Whalers

COMPLETE SET (29) 12.00 20.00
1 John Armstrong .20 .50
2 Brett Bellemore .20 .50
3 Jared Boll .20 .50
4 Evan Brophey .20 .50
5 Dan Collins .20 .50
6 Vern Cooper .30 .75
7 Wes Cunningham .20 .50
8 Andrew Fournier .20 .50
9 Joe Gaynor .20 .50
10 Kaine Geldart .20 .50
11 A.J. Jenks .20 .50
12 Leo Jenner .20 .50
13 Joe McCann .20 .50
14 Ryan McGinnis .20 .50
15 James Neal .60 1.50
16 Michal Neuvirth .60 1.50
17 Sean O'Connor .20 .50
18 Dan Ryder .40 1.00
19 Tom Sestito .40 1.00
20 Zack Shepley .20 .50
21 Jozef Sladok .20 .50
22 Jeremy Smith .60 1.50
23 Chris Terry .40 1.00
24 Brett Valliquette .20 .50
25 Steve Ward .20 .50
26 Steven Whitely .20 .50
27 James Neal .60 1.50
28 Plymouth Whalers .10 .25
29 Shooter MASCOT .02 .10

2003-04 Port Huron Beacons

This set was issued as a promotional giveaway at several Beacons home games. The cards were issued in perforated strip form.

COMPLETE SET (23) 25.00
1 Michel Beausoleil 1.00
2 David Bell 1.00
3 Aaron Brand 1.00
4 Kory Cooper 1.50
5 Mike Corneau 1.00
6 Adam Dewan 1.00
7 Stu Dunn 1.50
8 Ken Fels 1.00
9 Jason Firth 1.50
10 Benoit Genesse 1.00
11 Matt Goody 1.00
12 Brent Gretzky 1.00
13 Casey Harris 1.00
14 Ian Jacobs 1.00
15 Trevor Karasiewicz 1.00
16 Barry McKinlay 1.00
17 Sam Miller 1.00
18 Simon Poirier 1.00
19 Michael Prochazka 1.00
20 Joey Sewell 1.00
21 Josh Tataryn 1.00
22 John Vary 1.00
23 Wade Winkler 1.00

1998-99 Port Huron Border Cats

This set features the Border Cats of the UHL. The set was produced by ebk Sports, and sold by the team at its souvenir stands.

COMPLETE SET (26) 4.80 12.00
1 Wayne Muir .30 .75
2 Mike O'Grady .20 .50
3 Adam Robbins .20 .50
4 Curtis Sayler .20 .50
5 Olie Sundstrom .20 .50
6 Bob McKillop .20 .50
7 Chris Bergeron .20 .50
8 Lee Cole .20 .50
9 Chad Dameworth .20 .50
10 Mike Zanzarella TR .04 .10
11 Bernie John .20 .50
12 Matt Carmichael .20 .50
13 Kevin Brown .20 .50
14 Kevin Boyd .20 .50
15 Jeff Blum .20 .50
16 Bruce Watson .20 .50
17 Andrei Sryubko .20 .50
18 Paul Polillo .20 .50
19 Kraig Nienhuis .30 .75
20 Brock Myles EM .04 .10
21 Nikolai Syrtsov .20 .50
22 Greg Puhalski CO .10 .25
23 Bridges MASCOT .04 .10
24 Fedor Fedorov .80 2.00
25 Konstantin Simchuk .30 .75
26 Team CL .04 .10

2006-07 Port Huron Flags

COMPLETE SET (25) 12.00 20.00
1 Team Photo .10 .25
2 Craig Mahon .30 .75
3 Pat Sutton .30 .75
4 Mike Olynyk .30 .75
5 Bobby Kukulka .30 .75
6 Kris Vernarsky .30 .75
7 Robert Snowball .75 2.00
8 Jeremy Tucker .30 .75
9 Mike James .30 .75
10 B.J. Adams .30 .75
11 Mark Cadotte .30 .75
12 Ben Gustovson .30 .75
13 Greg Bullock .30 .75
14 Ryan Markham .30 .75
15 Scott Wray .30 .75
16 Trevor Edwards .30 .75
17 John Doherty .30 .75
18 Dustin Traylen .40 1.00
19 Noah Ruden .40 1.00
20 Shayne Tomlinson .30 .75
21 Steve Hildebrand .30 .75
22 Chris Bogas .30 .75
23 Colt King .75 2.00
24 Garett Cameron .30 .75
25 Slapshot MASCOT .02 .10

1993-94 Portland Pirates

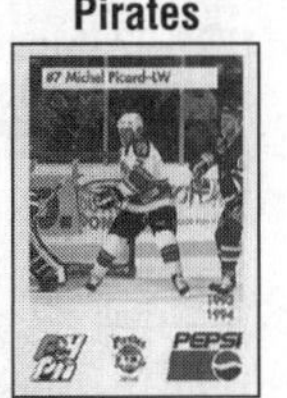

This 24-card set of the Portland Pirates of the American Hockey League was sponsored by Pepsi. The glossy cards were available at home games and through the mail. The glossy cards are numbered on the back.

COMPLETE SET (24) 4.80 12.00
1 Randy Pearce .16 .40
2 Crackers MASCOT .04 .10
3 Barry Trotz CO .10 .25
4 Paul Gardner ACO .04 .10
5 Chris Jensen .10 .25
6 Ken Klee .20 .50
7 Steve Poapst .16 .40
8 Jason Woolley .20 .50
9 Jim Mathieson .16 .40
10 Michel Picard .16 .40
11 Jeff Nelson .16 .40
12 Kent Hulst .16 .40
13 Eric Fenton .16 .40
14 Martin Jiranek .16 .40
15 Mike Boback .16 .40
16 Darren McAusland .16 .40
17 Chris Longo .16 .40
18 Kerry Clark .16 .40
19 Jeff Sirkka .16 .40
20 John Slaney .20 .50
21 Kevin Kaminski .20 .50
22 Byron Dafoe 1.20 2.00
23 Olaf Kolzig 1.20 3.00
24 Todd Nelson .16 .40
NNO Header Card .04 .10

1994-95 Portland Pirates

This 23-card standard-size set was manufactured and distributed by Jessen Associates, Inc. for Classic. The fronts display color action player photos with a red marbleized inner border and a black outer border. The player's name, jersey number, and position appear in the teal border on the right edge.The cards are unnumbered and checklisted below in alphabetical order.

COMPLETE SET (23) 4.00 10.00
1 Norm Batherson .16 .40
2 Mike Boback .16 .40
3 Andrew Brunette .40 1.00
4 Jim Carey .30 .75
5 Jason Christie .16 .40
6 Kerry Clark .16 .40
7 Brian Curran .16 .40
8 Martin Gendron .30 .75
9 Sergei Gonchar .40 1.00
10 Kent Hulst .16 .40
11 Chris Jensen .16 .40
12 Kevin Kaminski .20 .50
13 Ken Klee .16 .40
14 Chris Longo .16 .40
15 Jim Mathieson .16 .40
16 Darren McAusland .16 .40
17 Jeff Nelson .20 .50
18 Todd Nelson .16 .40
19 Mike Parson .20 .50
20 Steve Poapst .16 .40
21 Andre Racicot .20 .50
22 Sergei Tertyshny .16 .40
23 Stefan Ustorf .20 .50

1995-96 Portland Pirates

This 24-card set of the Portland Pirates was sponsored by Dunkin' Donuts and features color action player photos framed in red and shades of gray. The backs carry a small black-and-white player head photo with biographical information and player statistics. The cards are unnumbered and checklisted below in alphabetical order.

COMPLETE SET (24) 6.00 15.00
1 Alexander Alexeev .16 .40
2 Jason Allison 1.20 2.00
3 Norm Batherson .16 .40
4 Frank Bialowas .40 1.00
5 Patrick Boileau .16 .40
6 Andrew Brunette .60 1.50
7 Stephane Charbonneau .16 .40
8 Jason Christie .16 .40
9 Crackers MASCOT .04 .10
10 Brian Curran .10 .25
11 Martin Gendron .20 .50
12 Kent Hulst .16 .40
13 Alexander Kharlamov .16 .40
14 Jim Mathieson .20 .50
15 Darren McAusland .16 .40
16 Jeff Nelson .16 .40
17 Darryl Paquette .20 .50
18 Rob Pearson .20 .50
19 Steve Poapst .16 .40
20 Joel Poirier .16 .40
21 Sergei Tertyshny .16 .40
22 Barry Trotz CO .10 .25
23 Ron Tugnutt .80 1.50
24 Stefan Ustorf .20 .50

1996-97 Portland Pirates

This 25-card set was produced by Split Second. The set features action photos on the front and a statistical package on the reverse. The unnumbered cards feature the player's sweater number prominently on the back, and are numbered thusly below.

COMPLETE SET (25) 4.80 12.00
1 Robb Stauber .30 .75
3 Steve Poapst .20 .50
4 Stewart Malgunas .20 .50
5 Nolan Baumgartner .20 .50
6 Ron Pascucci .20 .50
7 Norm Batherson .20 .50
9 Marc Potvin .30 .75
10 Kent Hulst .20 .50
12 Brad Church .20 .50
14 Richard Zednik .40 1.00
15 Jaroslav Svejkovsky .30 .75
16 Darren McAusland .20 .50
19 Andrew Brunette .40 1.00
20 Miika Elomo .20 .50
21 Jason Christie .20 .50
22 Alexander Kharlamov .20 .50
24 Daniel Laperriere .20 .50
25 Benoit Gratton .20 .50
27 Patrick Boileau .20 .50
28 Trevor Halverson .20 .50
30 Martin Brochu .40 1.00
33 Anson Carter .60 1.50
NNO Paul Gardner ACO .04 .10
NNO Barry Trotz CO .10 .25
NNO AHL Ad Card .01

1996-97 Portland Pirates Shop N' Save

This set features the Pirates of the AHL. The cards were issued as promotional giveaways at a local grocery store.

COMPLETE SET (10) 4.00 10.00
1 Robb Stauber .50 1.25
2 Steve Poapst .40 1.00
3 Nolan Baumgartner .40 1.00
4 Norm Batherson .40 1.00
5 Kent Hulst .40 1.00
6 Jaroslav Svejkovsky .40 1.00
7 Andrew Brunette .80 2.00
8 Miika Elomo .80 2.00
9 Jason Christie .40 1.00
10 Benoit Gratton .40 1.00

1997-98 Portland Pirates

Little is known about this set beyond the confirmed checklist, but it is believed that the cards were sold in team set form at home games. Additional information can be forwarded to hockeymag@beckett.com.

COMPLETE SET (26) 4.80 12.00
1 Nolan Baumgartner .20 .50
2 Jan Benda .16 .40
3 Patrick Boileau .16 .40
4 Martin Brochu .40 1.00
5 Andrew Brunette .40 1.00
6 Sebastien Charpentier .30 .75
7 Jason Christie .16 .40
8 Brad Church .16 .40
9 Miika Elomo .16 .40
10 Benoit Gratton .30 .75
11 David Harlock .20 .50
12 Dwayne Hay .20 .50
13 Kent Hulst .16 .40
14 Kevin Kaminski .30 .75
15 Mark Major .16 .40
16 Stewart Malgunas .16 .40
17 Rick Mrozik .16 .40
18 Ryan Mulhern .16 .40
19 Mike O'Neill .30 .75
20 Steve Poapst .20 .50
21 Kayle Short .16 .40
22 Alexandre Volchkov .20 .50
23 Jay Wells ACO .04 .10
24 Bryan Trottier HCO .40 1.00
25 PHPA Web Site .01
26 AHL Web Site .01

1998-99 Portland Pirates

This set features the Pirates of the AHL. The set was produced and sold by the team. Research has determined that two versions exist of card #19.

COMPLETE SET (26) 4.80 12.00
1 J-P Dumont .80 2.00
2 Patrick Boileau .16 .40
3 Martin Brochu .30 .75
4 Trevor Halverson .16 .40
5 Matt Herr .20 .50
6 Benoit Gratton .20 .50
7 Nolan Baumgartner .16 .40
8 Casey Hankinson .16 .40
9 Kent Hulst .16 .40
10 Rick Kowalsky .16 .40
11 Daniel Cleary .30 .75
12 Todd Rohloff .16 .40
13 Jeff Toms .16 .40
14 Steve Poapst .16 .40
15 Mike Peluso .30 .75
16 Young/Soutuyo .16 .40
17 Mike Rosati .30 .75
18 Trent Whitfield .30 .75
19 Mark Kumpel HCO .04 .10
19 Neil Belland ACO .04 .10
20 Craig Mills .20 .50
21 Stewart Malgunas .16 .40
22 Rick Mrozik .16 .40
23 Dwight Parrish .16 .40
24 Mark Major .16 .40
25 AHL Web Site .01

1999-00 Portland Pirates

This 25-card set features the Pirates of the AHL. The series was produced by Split Second and sold by the team at home games. Since the cards are not numbered, they are listed below in alphabetical order.

COMPLETE SET (25) 4.00 10.00
1 Nolan Baumgartner .20 .50
2 Alexei Tezikov .30 .75
3 Patrick Boileau .14 .35
4 Martin Brochu .40 1.00
5 Sebastien Charpentier .40 1.00
6 Miika Elomo .20 .50
7 Jakub Ficenec .14 .35
8 J.F. Fortin .20 .50
9 Matt Herr .14 .35
10 Kent Hulst .14 .35
11 Jamie Huscroft .14 .35
12 Martin Kumpel .14 .35
Glen Hanlon
13 Mascot .04 .10
14 Glen Metropolit .30 .75
15 Barrie Moore .14 .35
16 Ryan Mulhern .14 .35
17 Jeff Nelson .14 .35
18 Mike Peluso .20 .50
19 Steve Poapst .14 .35
20 Steve Shirreffs .14 .35
21 Jason Shmyr .20 .50
22 Trainer Card .04 .10
23 Alexandre Volchkov .14 .35
24 Trent Whitfield .30 .75
25 Rob Zettler .14 .35

2000-01 Portland Pirates

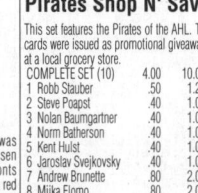

This set features the Pirates of the AHL. The set was produced by Choice Marketing and issued initially as a kid's club giveaway. Later, it was available with purchase at a local sub shop.

COMPLETE SET (20) 4.80 12.00
1 Kent Hulst .20 .50
2 Jeff Nelson .20 .50
3 Krys Barch .30 .75
4 Mark Murphy .20 .50
5 Patrick Boileau .20 .50
6 Todd Rohloff .20 .50
7 Jean-Francois Fortin .20 .50
8 Sebastien Charpentier .40 1.00
9 Glen Metropolit .30 .75
10 Remi Royer .20 .75
11 Derek Bekar .20 .50
12 Martin Hlinka .20 .50
13 Corey Hirsch .40 1.00
14 Alexei Tezikov .40 1.00
15 Rob Zettler .20 .50
16 Mike Farrell .20 .50
17 Jakub Ficenec .20 .50
18 Matt Pettinger .40 1.00
19 Jason Shmyr .20 .50
20 Brad Church .30 .75

2004-05 Portland Pirates

Set was given out in 12-card segments at two home games.

COMPLETE SET (12) 12.00
1 Steve Eminger .50
2 Brian Sutherby .75
3 Boyd Gordon .50
4 Owen Fussey .50
5 Jason Ulmer .50
6 Justin Eddy .50
7 Jeff Paul .50
8 Jared Aulin .75
9 Michel Periard .50
10 Graham Mink 1.00
11 Chris Hajt .50
Mike Amodeo
12 Cam McCaffrey .50
Jonas Johansson
13 Jakub Cutta .50
14 Brooks Laich .75
15 Carlyle Lewis .50
16 Shaone Morrisonn .50
17 Maxime Ouellet 1.00
18 Louis Robitaille .50
19 Garrett Stroshein 1.00
20 Darcy Verot 1.00
21 Trent Whitfield 1.00
22 Nolan Yonkman .50
23 Dwayne Zinger .50
24 Jakub Klepis 1.00
Tomas Fleischmann

2005-06 Portland Pirates

COMPLETE SET (24) 8.00 15.00
1 Geoff Peters .20 .50
2 Aaron Rome .40 1.00
3 Shane O'Brien .20 .50
4 Tim Brent .20 .50
5 Aaron Gavey .20 .50
6 Pierre Parenteau .20 .50
7 Corey Perry .60 1.50
8 Curtis Glencross .20 .50
9 Jordan Smith .20 .50
10 Kenny Smith .20 .50
11 Dieter Kochan .60 1.50
12 Ryan Shannon .20 .50
13 Joel Perrault .20 .50
14 Nathan Saunders .20 .50
15 Ryan Getzlaf .60 1.50
16 Ladislav Smid .40 1.00
17 Igor Pohanka .20 .50
18 Kent Huskins .20 .50
19 Bruno St. Jaques .20 .50
20 Dustin Penner .40 1.00
21 Simon Ferguson .20 .50
22 Nathan Marsters .40 1.00
23 Shane Hynes .20 .50
24 Trevor Gillies .60 1.50

2006-07 Portland Pirates

COMPLETE SET (24) 10.00 18.00
1 Bruce Crowder ACO .10 .25
2 Eric Weinrich ACO .10 .25
3 Zenon Konopka .30 .75
4 Aaron Rome .30 .75
5 Nathan Marsters .30 .75
6 Tim Brent .30 .75
7 Clay Wilson .30 .75
8 Brian Salcido .30 .75
9 Curtis Glencross .30 .75
10 Chris Durno .30 .75
11 Colby Genoway .30 .75
12 Simon Ferguson .30 .75
13 Geoff Peters .30 .75
14 Brett Skinner .30 .75
15 Drew Miller .60 1.50
16 Matt Keith .30 .75
17 Shawn Thornton .40 1.00
18 Petteri Wirtanen .30 .75
19 Bjorn Melin .30 .75
20 Trevor Gillies .40 1.00
21 Ryan Carter .40 1.00
22 Kent Huskins .30 .75
23 Mike Wall .40 1.00
24 Kevin Dineen CO .10 .25

1986-87 Portland Winter Hawks

Sponsored by AM-PM Mini-Market, this 24-card set measures the standard size. The white-bordered fronts feature posed-on-ice color player photos. The player's name, number, and position appear in black lettering within the white margin beneath the picture, while the team name is printed vertically along the left border. The sponsor's logo appears at the upper right.

The cards are unnumbered and checklisted below in alphabetical order.

COMPLETE SET (24) 15.00 40.00
1 Dave Archibald 1.00 2.50
2 Bruce Basken .60 1.50
3 Thomas Bjuhr .60 1.50
4 Shaun Clouston .60 1.50
5 Jeff Finley .60 1.50
6 Bob Foglietta .60 1.50
7 Brian Gerrits .60 1.50
8 Darryl Gilmour 1.00 2.50
9 Dennis Holland .60 1.50
10 Steve Kloepzig .60 1.50
11 Jim Latos .60 1.50
12 Dave McLay .60 1.50
13 Scott Melnyk .60 1.50
14 Troy Mick .60 1.50
15 Roy Mitchell .60 1.50
16 Jamie Nicolls .60 1.50
17 Trevor Pohl .60 1.50
18 Troy Pohl .60 1.50
19 Glen Seymour 1.00 2.50
20 Jeff Sharples .60 1.50
21 Jay Stark .60 1.50
22 Jim Swan .60 1.50
23 Glen Wesley 2.00 5.00
24 Dan Woodley .60 1.50

1987-88 Portland Winter Hawks

Sponsored by Fred Meyer and Pepsi, this 21-card standard-size set features the 1987-88 Portland Winter Hawks of the Western Hockey League. Inside white borders, the fronts feature color player photos shot on the ice at the stadium. The wider left border carries the team name, while the upper right corner of the picture has been cut off to allow space for the sponsor logo. The cards are unnumbered and checklisted below in alphabetical order.

COMPLETE SET (21) 4.80 12.00
1 Wayne Anchikoski .20 .50
2 Eric Badzgon .30 .75
3 Chad Biafore .20 .50
4 James(Hamish) Black .20 .50
5 Terry Black .20 .50
6 Shaun Clouston .20 .50
7 Byron Dafoe 1.20 3.00
8 Brent Fleetwood .20 .50
9 Rob Flintoft .20 .50
10 Bryan Gourlie .20 .50
11 Mark Greyeyes .20 .50
12 Dennis Holland .20 .50
13 Kevin Jorgenson .20 .50
14 Greg Leahy .20 .50
15 Troy Mick .20 .50
16 Roy Mitchell .20 .50
17 Joey Mittelsteadt .20 .50
18 Mike Moore .20 .50
19 Scott Mydan .20 .50
20 Calvin Thudiun .20 .50
21 Pepsi Ad Card .04 .10

1988-89 Portland Winter Hawks

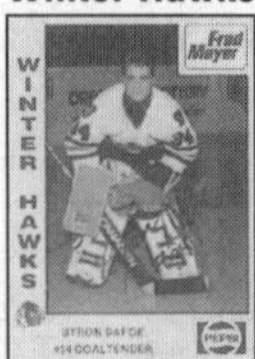

Sponsored by Pepsi and Fred Meyer, this 21-card set measures the standard size. On a white background, the fronts feature posed color player photos with a facsimile autograph in the bottom part of the picture. The player's name, number, and position appear under the picture, while the team name is printed alongside the left border. The cards are unnumbered and checklisted below in alphabetical order.

COMPLETE SET (21) 4.80 12.00
1 Wayne Anchikoski .20 .50
2 Eric Badzgon .30 .75
3 Chad Biafore .20 .50
4 James(Hamish) Black .20 .50
5 Terry Black .20 .50
6 Shaun Clouston .20 .50
7 Byron Dafoe 1.20 3.00
8 Brent Fleetwood .20 .50
9 Rob Flintoft .20 .50
10 Bryan Gourlie .20 .50
11 Mark Greyeyes .20 .50
12 Dennis Holland .20 .50
13 Kevin Jorgenson .20 .50
14 Greg Leahy .20 .50
15 Troy Mick .20 .50
16 Roy Mitchell .20 .50
17 Joey Mittelsteadt .20 .50
18 Mike Moore .20 .50
19 Scott Mydan .20 .50
20 Calvin Thudiun .20 .50
21 Pepsi Coupon .04 .10

1989-90 Portland Winter Hawks

Sponsored by Pepsi and Fred Meyer, this 21-card set measures the standard size. The fronts feature posed color player photos inside a black picture frame and white outer borders. A facsimile autograph is inscribed across the picture. The player's name, number, and position appear under the photo, while the team name is printed alongside the left border. The cards are unnumbered and checklisted below in alphabetical order.

COMPLETE SET (21) 4.80 12.00
1 Jamie Black .20 .50
2 Vince Cocciolo .20 .50
3 Byron Dafoe 1.20 2.00
4 Cam Danyluk .20 .50
5 Kim Deck .20 .50
6 Dean Dorchak .20 .50
7 Brent Fleetwood .20 .50
8 Rick Fry .20 .50
9 Bryan Gourlie .20 .50
10 Brad Harrison .20 .50
11 Judson Innes .20 .50
12 Dean Intwert .30 .75
13 Kevin Jorgenson .20 .50
14 Todd Kinniburgh .20 .50
15 Greg Leahy .20 .50
16 Jamie Linden .20 .50
17 Scott Mydan .20 .50
18 Mike Ruark .20 .50
19 Jeff Sebastian .20 .50
20 Brandon Smith .24 .60
21 Steve Young .20 .50

1993-94 Portland Winter Hawks

This is a tough team-issued set from the Winter Hawks of the WHL. The cards are unnumbered and are checklisted below in alphabetical order.

COMPLETE SET (27) 8.00 15.00
1 Mike Arbulic .12 .30
2 Lonny Bohonos .20 .50
3 Shannon Briske .12 .30
4 Dave Cammock .12 .30
5 Shawn Collins .12 .30
6 Matt Davidson .12 .30
7 Adam Deadmarsh 1.60 3.00
8 Adam Deadmarsh GM 1.60 3.00
9 Jake Deadmarsh .12 .30
10 Brett Fedorak .12 .30
11 Colin Foley .12 .30
12 Brad Isbister 1.60 1.50
13 Scott Langkow .40 1.00
14 Mike Little .12 .30
15 Dmitri Markovsky .12 .30
16 Jason McBain .12 .30
17 Scott Nichol .12 .30
18 Brent Peterson .12 .30
19 Nolan Pratt .20 .50
20 Scott Rideout .12 .30
21 Layne Roland .12 .30
22 Dave Scatchard .30 .75
23 Brandon Smith .12 .30
24 Brad Swanson .12 .30
25 Brad Symes .12 .30
26 Jason Wiemer .80 2.00
27 Mike Williamson .12 .30

1997-98 Portland Winter Hawks

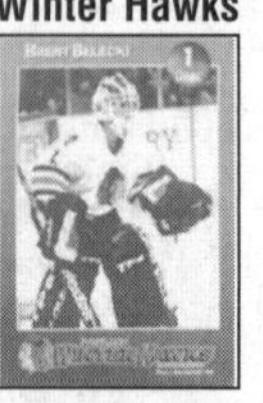

This set of standard-sized cards was sold in set form by the team. It features early cards of hobby heroes Marian Hossa and Brenden Morrow.

COMPLETE SET (27) 16.00 40.00
1 Checklist .04 .10
2 Brent Belecki .16 .40
3 Mike Muzechka .16 .40
4 Marian Hossa 6.00 15.00
5 Ken Davis .16 .40
6 Jerad Smith .16 .40
7 Josh Green .80 1.00
8 Bobby Russell .16 .40
9 Kyle Chant .16 .40
10 Brenden Morrow 4.00 10.00
11 Derek MacLean .40 1.00
12 Todd Hornung .16 .40
13 Andrej Podkonicky .30 .75
14 Bobby Duncan .16 .40
15 Todd Robinson .16 .40
16 Chris Jacobson .16 .40
17 Shon Jones-Parry .16 .40
18 Kevin Haupt .16 .40
19 Ryan Thrussell .16 .40
20 Marty Standish .16 .40
21 Jason Labarbera .80 2.00
22 Matt Walker .16 .40
23 Andrew Ference .40 1.00
24 Joey Tetarenko .80 3.00
25 Brent Peterson HCO .10 .25
26 Mike Williamson ACO .04 .10
27 Julius Supler ACO .04 .10

2003-04 Portland Winter Hawks

This set was sold by the team at home games.

COMPLETE SET (29) 12.00
1 Dustin Butler .75
2 Tomas Fojtik .40
3 Taylor Sutherlin .40
4 Michael Funk .40
5 Richie Regehr .75
6 Brendan Mikkelson .40
7 Cody McLeod .40
8 Aaron Roberge .40
9 Brian Woolger .40
10 C.J. Jackson .40
11 Chad Wolkowski .40
12 Shane Halifax .40
13 Robin Big Snake .75
14 Alex Aldred .40
15 Brandon Dubinsky .40
16 Ivan Dornic .40
17 Dan Da Silva .40
18 Braydon Coburn .40
19 Frazer McLaren .40
20 Derek Poplawski .40
21 Kyle Bailey .40
22 Kevin Opsahl .75
23 Krister Toews .75
24 Ivan Dornic Draft .40
25 Braydon Coburn Draft 1.50
26 Mike Williamson HCO .10
27 Blake Wesley ACO .10
28 Mascot .10
29 Checklist .01

2004-05 Portland Winter Hawks

We've confirmed the existence of a handful of cards from this set. If you know of others, please contact us at hockeymag@beckett.com. The three unnumbered bonus cards were available outside of the team set. The Coburn was available only at the Mock Crest Tavern, whose ad is on the back. The other two were available only at the booster club's table.

COMPLETE SET (25)
1 Dustin Butler
2 Cameron Cepek
3 Braydon Coburn
4 Dan DaSilva
5 Brandon Dubinsky
6 Michael Funk
7 Frazer McLaren
8 Mike Sauer
9 Brian Woolger
10 Paul Gaustad
11 Richie Regehr
12 Cody McLeod
13 Robin Big Snake
NNO Braydon Coburn MCT
NNO C. McLeod/R. Big Snake
NNO R. Regehr/P. Gaustad

1984-85 Prince Albert Raiders Stickers

This set of 22 stickers was sponsored by Autotec Oil and Saskatchewan Ronald McDonald House. Each sticker measures 2" by 1 3/4" and could be pasted on a 17" by 11" poster printed in thin glossy paper. The stickers display a black-and-white head shot; the uniform number is also printed on the front. The stickers are unnumbered and checklisted below in alphabetical order.

COMPLETE SET (22) 10.00 25.00
1 Ken Baumgartner 1.20 3.00
2 Brad Bennett .40 1.00
3 Dean Braham .40 1.00
4 Rod Dallman .40 1.00
5 Neil Davey .40 1.00
6 Pat Elynuik .60 1.50
7 Collin Feser .40 1.00
8 Dave Goertz .40 1.00
9 Steve Gotaas .40 1.00
10 Tony Grenier .40 1.00
11 Roydon Gunn .40 1.00
12 Doug Hobson .40 1.00
13 Dan Hodgson .60 1.50
14 Curtis Hunt .40 1.00
15 Kim Issel .40 1.00
16 Ward Komonosky .40 1.00
17 David Manson .40 1.00
18 Dale McFee .40 1.00
19 Ken Morrison .40 1.00
20 Dave Pasin .60 1.50
21 Don Schmidt .40 1.00
22 Emanuel Viveiros .40 1.00

1990-91 Prince Albert Raiders

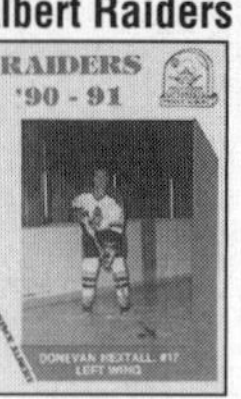

Sponsored by the High Noon Optimist Club, these 25 standard-size cards of the WHL's Prince Albert Raiders are printed on thin card stock and feature on their fronts color posed-on-ice player photos with white outer borders and yellow and green inner borders. The player's name, jersey number, and position appear in white lettering within the green inner border beneath the picture. The cards are unnumbered and checklisted below in alphabetical order.

COMPLETE SET (25) 4.00 10.00
1 Scott Allison .16 .40
2 Laurie Billeck .16 .40
3 Jeff Gorman .16 .40
4 Donevan Hextall .20 .50
5 Troy Hjertaas .16 .40
6 Dan Kesa .20 .50
7 Jason Kwiatkowski .16 .40
8 Travis Laycock .16 .40
9 Lee J. Leslie .20 .50
10 Jamie Linden .16 .40
11 Dean McAmmond .30 .75
12 Dave Neilson .16 .40
13 Jeff Nelson .20 .50
14 Troy Neumeier .16 .40
15 Pat Odnokon .16 .40
16 Brian Pellerin .16 .40
17 Darren Perkins .16 .40
18 Curt Regnier .20 .50
19 Chad Seibel .16 .40
20 Mark Stowe .16 .40
21 Darren Van Impe .30 .75
22 Shane Zulyniak .16 .40
23 Title Card .04 .10
24 Info Card (Strangers) .04 .10
25 Info Card (Vandalism) .04 .10

1991-92 Prince Albert Raiders

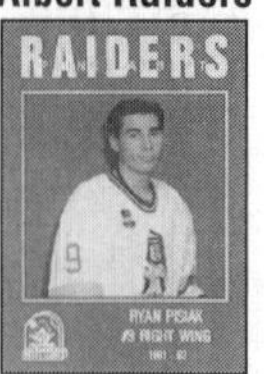

Sponsored by the High Noon Optimist Club, these 24 standard-size cards of the WHL's Prince Albert Raiders are printed on thin card stock and feature on their fronts color posed-on-ice player photos enclosed by green borders. The player's name, jersey number, and position appear in white lettering within the green border near the bottom. The cards are unnumbered and checklisted below in alphabetical order.

COMPLETE SET (24) 3.20 8.00
1 Mike Fedorko CO .04 .10
2 Jeff Gorman .16 .40
3 Merv Haney .16 .40
4 Donevan Hextall .20 .50
5 Troy Hjertaas .16 .40
6 Dan Kesa .20 .50
7 Jason Klassen .16 .40
8 Jason Kwiatkowski .16 .40
9 Jeff Lank .16 .40
10 Travis Laycock .16 .40
11 Lee J. Leslie .16 .40
12 Stan Matwijiw .20 .50
13 Dean McAmmond .20 .50
14 David Neilson .16 .40
15 Jeff Nelson .20 .50
16 Mark Odnokon ACO .04 .10
17 Darren Perkins .16 .40
18 Ryan Pisiak .16 .40
19 Nick Polychronopoulos .16 .40
20 Curt Regnier .20 .50
21 Jason Renard .16 .40
22 Barkley Swenson .16 .40
23 Darren Van Impe .20 .50
24 Shane Zulyniak .16 .40

1993-94 Prince Albert Raiders

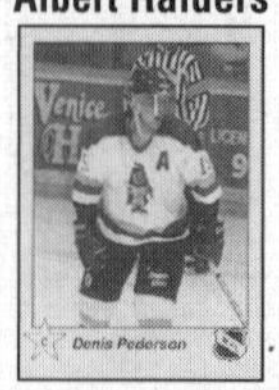

This 22-card standard-size set was sponsored by High Noon Prince Albert Optimists and "Stay in School Canada." On a white card face, the fronts feature color action player photos inside a black picture frame. The player's name appears in a yellow bar under the picture. The cards are unnumbered and checklisted below in alphabetical order.

COMPLETE SET (22) 4.00 10.00
1 Ryan Bast .16 .40
2 Rodney Bowers .16 .40
3 Van Burgess .16 .40
4 Brad Church .30 .75
5 Joaquin Gage .30 .75
6 Jeff Gorman .16 .40
7 Merv Haney .16 .40
8 Greg Harvey .16 .40
9 Paul Healey .16 .40
10 Shane Hnidy .30 .75
11 Russell Hogue .16 .40
12 Jason Issel .16 .40
13 Steve Kelly .30 .75
14 Jeff Lank .16 .40
15 Mike McGhan .16 .40
16 Denis Pederson .30 .75
17 Mitch Shawara .16 .40
18 Shayne Toporowski .16 .40
19 David Van Drunen .16 .40
20 Dean Whitney .16 .40
21 Darren Wright .16 .40
22 Shane Zulyniak .16 .40

1994-95 Prince Albert Raiders

This 23-card set of the Prince Albert Raiders of the WHL was sponsored by the Prince Albert Optimists and "Stay in School Canada." The design mirrors that of the 1993-94 set. The set is noteworthy for the inclusion of several NHL first rounders, including Brad Church, Steve Kelly and Dennis Pederson. The cards are unnumbered, and are checklisted below alphabetically.

COMPLETE SET (23) 4.80 12.00
1 Sandy Allan .20 .50
2 Ryan Bast .20 .50
3 Brad Church .30 .75
4 Kris Fizzell .16 .40
5 Paul Healey .16 .40
6 Rob Hegberg .16 .40
7 Shane Hnidy .30 .75
8 Russell Hogue .16 .40
9 Craig Hordal .20 .50
10 Jason Issel .16 .40
11 Neil Johnston .16 .40
12 Steve Kelly .30 .75
13 Jeff Lank .16 .40
14 Mike McGhan .16 .40
15 Denis Pederson .60 1.50
16 Sean Robertson .16 .40
17 Mitch Shawara .16 .40
18 Shayne Toporowski .20 .50
19 Kaleb Toth .16 .40
20 Dave Van Drunen .20 .50
21 Shane Willis .60 1.50
22 Darren Wright .16 .40
23 Shane Zulyniak .16 .40

1995-96 Prince Albert Raiders

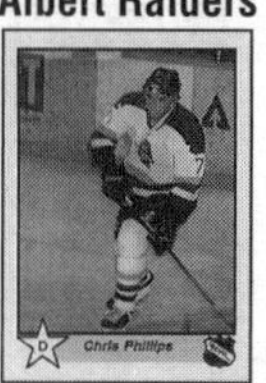

This 22-card set of the Prince Albert Raiders of the WHL was sponsored by the Prince Albert Optimists and features color action player photos in a thin back border on a white background. The player's name is printed in a yellow bar with his position in a white star below the picture. This set includes several first round selections, including 1996 first overall selection Chris Phillips. The cards are unnumbered and checklisted below in alphabetical order.

COMPLETE SET (22) 4.80 25.00
1 Rod Branch .20 1.00
2 Curtis Brown .40 2.00
3 Brad Church .20 1.00
4 Kris Fizzell .16 1.00
5 Dallas Flaman .16 1.00
6 Don Halverson .16 1.00
7 Shane Hnidy .20 1.00
8 Russell Hogue .16 1.00
9 Jason Issel .16 1.00
10 Garnet Jacobson .16 1.00
11 Kevin Kellett .16 1.00
12 Steve Kelly .30 1.50
13 Dylan Kemp .16 1.00
14 Michael McGhan .16 1.00
15 Marian Menhart .20 1.00
16 Chris Phillips .60 2.00
17 Blaine Russell .16 1.00
18 Mitch Shawara .16 1.00
19 Dave Van Drunen .20 1.00
20 Roman Vopat .20 1.00
21 Shane Willis .80 1.50
22 Darren Wright .16 1.00

1996-97 Prince Albert Raiders

Sponsored by the Prince Albert Optimists Clubs, this 23-card set features color player photos and jersey numbers on the front, and is checklisted below alphabetically.

COMPLETE SET (23) 4.80 12.00
1 Trevor Baker .20 .50
2 Scott Botterill .20 .50
3 Craig Brunel .20 .50
4 Marco Cefalo .20 .50
5 Dallas Flaman .20 .50
6 Jeremy Goetzinger .20 .50
7 Don Halverson .20 .50
8 Russell Hogue .20 .50
9 Jason Issel .20 .50
10 Garnet Jacobson .20 .50
11 Kevin Kellett .20 .50
12 Dylan Kemp .20 .50
13 Evan Lindsay .30 .75
14 Marian Menhart .20 .50
15 Cory Morgan .20 .50
16 Derek Paget .20 .50
17 Chris Phillips .60 1.50
18 Harlan Pratt .20 .50
19 Blaine Russell .16 .40
20 Adam Stewart .20 .50
21 Dave Van Drunen .30 .75
22 Steve Wilejto .20 .50
23 Shane Willis .80 1.00

1997-98 Prince Albert Raiders

This set features the Raiders of the WHL. The set was sponsored by the Prince Albert Optimists Club and was sold at home games. The cards are unnumbered, and so are listed below in alphabetical order.

COMPLETE SET (21) 4.00 10.00
1 Scott Botterill .20 .50
2 Derek Brandon .20 .50
3 Craig Brunel .20 .50
4 David Cameron .20 .50
5 Clayton Chartrand .20 .50
6 Dallas Flaman .20 .50
7 Jeremy Goetzinger .20 .50
8 Don Halverson .20 .50
9 Trevor Hitchings .20 .50
10 Kevin Kellett .20 .50
11 Evan Lindsay .30 .75
12 Ross Lupaschuk .40 1.00
13 Brady Magneson .20 .50
14 Grant McCune .30 .75
15 Cory Morgan .20 .50
16 Derek Paget .20 .50
17 Harlan Pratt .30 .75
18 Richard Seeley .20 .50
19 Cam Severson .20 .50
20 Brad Swanson .20 .50
21 Steve Wilejto .20 .50

1998-99 Prince Albert Raiders

This 22-card set was produced by Action Printing LTD and is not numbered. The set is listed in alphabetical order

COMPLETE SET (22) 12.00 20.00
1 Derek Brandon .20 .50
2 Marc Brown .20 .50
3 Craig Brunel .20 .50
4 Clayton Chartrand .20 .50
5 Riley Cote .20 .50
6 Todd Fedoruk .80 2.00
7 Dallas Flaman .20 .50
8 Jeremy Goetzinger .20 .50
9 Scott Hartnell 2.00 5.00
10 Shaun Hill .20 .50
11 Cody Jensen .20 .50
12 Kevin Kellet .20 .50
13 Milan Kraft 2.00 2.00
14 Evan Lindsay .30 .75
15 Ross Lupachuk .60 1.00
16 Grant McCune .20 .50
17 Cory Morgan .20 .50
18 Kerry Nice .20 .50
19 Derek Paget .20 .50
20 Garrett Prosofsky .20 .50
21 Nick Schultz .80 2.00
22 Richard Seeley .20 .50

2000-01 Prince Albert Raiders

This set features the Raiders of the WHL. The cards were sold by the team at home games. Because they are unnumbered, they are listed below alphabetically.

COMPLETE SET (25) 4.80 12.00
1 Jay Batchelor .20 .50
2 Anton Borodkin .20 .50
3 Kyle Bruce .20 .50
4 Jordan Clarke .20 .50
5 Riley Cote .20 .50
6 Cary Grant TR .04 .11
7 Ryan Haggarty .20 .50
8 J.J. Hunter .20 .50
9 Dustin Kazak .20 .50
10 Jon Kress .20 .50
11 Landon Lillejord .20 .50
12 Connor Lowe .20 .50
13 Grant McCune .31 .78
14 Grant McNeill .20 .50
15 Scott McQueen .20 .50
16 Jon Mirasty .20 .50
17 Chris Harper .20 .50
18 Igor Pohanka .20 .50
19 Garett Prosofsky .31 .78
20 Riley MASCOT .04 .11
21 Jeff Schmidt .20 .50
22 Nick Schultz .80 2.00
23 Aaron Sorochan .31 .78
24 Blain Stowards .20 .50
25 Greg Watson .31 .78

2001-02 Prince Albert Raiders

This set features the Raiders of the WHL. The cards are slightly taller than standard-size and feature a pair of photos on the front, accentuated by a red and yellow border. The black and white backs feature stats. It's

believed the cards were sold by the team at home games.

COMPLETE SET (24) 6.00 15.00
1 Jay Batchelor .30 .75
2 Kyle Bruce .30 .75
3 Jeremy Colliton .30 1.50
4 Riley Cote .30 .75
5 Justin Cruse .30 .75
6 James Demone .30 .75
7 Paul Deniset .30 .75
8 Perry Faul .30 .75
9 Luke Fritshaw .30 .75
10 Jon Kress .30 .75
11 Wade Klippenstein CO .10 .25
12 Landon Lillejord .30 .75
13 Rastislav Lipka .30 .75
14 Grant McNeill .30 .75
15 Brett Novak .30 .75
16 Igor Pohanka .30 .75
17 Jeff Schmidt .30 .75
18 Drew Schoneck ACO .10 .25
19 Jesse Schultz .30 .75
20 Aaron Sorochan .40 1.00
21 Joe Suderman .30 .75
22 Thomas Vicars .40 1.00
23 Greg Watson .40 1.00
24 Mike Wirll .30 .75

2002-03 Prince Albert Raiders

COMPLETE SET (23) 8.00 20.00
1 Rejean Beauchemin 1.25 3.00
2 Kyle Bruce .30 .75
3 Dane Byers .60 1.50
4 Kyle Chipchura .75 2.00
5 Jeremy Colliton .75 2.00
6 Mark Cress .30 .75
7 Justin Cruse .30 .75
8 Chris Di Ubaldo .30 .75
9 Perry Faul .30 .75
10 Luke Fritshaw .30 .75
11 Kevin Harris .30 .75
12 Jon Kress .30 .75
13 Colin Lafreniere .30 .75
14 Seth Leonard .30 .75
15 Rastislav Lipka .30 .75
16 Grant McNeill .30 .75
17 Brett Novak .30 .75
18 Igor Pohanka .30 .75
19 Rory Rawlyk .30 .75
20 Evan Schafer .30 .75
21 Aaron Sorochan .30 .75
22 Greg Watson .30 .75
23 Andy Zulyniak .30 .75

2003-04 Prince Albert Raiders

This checklist may be incomplete. Please forward additional info to hockeymag@beckett.com.

COMPLETE SET (25) 6.00 15.00
1 Aki Seitsonen .30 .75
2 Brandon Peet .20 .50
3 Brant Hilton .20 .50
4 Brett Novak .20 .50
5 Caine Pearpoint .20 .50
6 Colin Lafreniere .20 .50
7 Dane Byers .60 1.50
8 Dave Manson .20 .50
9 Evan Schafer .20 .50
10 Garth Collins .20 .50
11 Jeff May .20 .50
12 Jeremy Colliton .60 1.50
13 Jordan Morgan .20 .50
14 Justin Cruse .20 .50
15 Kyle Chipchura .60 1.50
16 Luke Fritshaw .20 .50
17 Mark Ardelan .20 .50
18 Michal Polak .20 .50
19 Mike Gauthier .20 .50
20 Mike Hellyer .20 .50
21 Perry Faul .20 .50
22 Peter Anholt .20 .50
23 Rejean Beauchemin .60 1.50
24 Seth Leonard .20 .50
25 Travis Young .20 .50

2004-05 Prince Albert Raiders

COMPLETE SET (24) 8.00 20.00
1 Alex Archibald .30 .75
2 Mike Gauthier .30 .75
3 Jeff May .30 .75
4 Evan Schafer .30 .75
5 Luke Fritshaw .40 1.00
6 Landon Jones .30 .75
7 Scott Doucet .30 .75
8 Mike Hellyer .30 .75
9 Brandon Peet .30 .75
10 Brad Erickson .30 .75
11 Brett Ottmann .30 .75
12 Nolan Waker .30 .75
13 Kyle Chipchura .60 1.50
14 Aki Seitsonen .40 1.00
15 Ryan Depape .30 .75
16 Brett Novak .30 .75
17 Jeremy Colliton .60 1.50
18 Josh Elder .30 .75
19 Caine Pearpoint .30 .75
20 Chris Schlenker .30 .75
21 Dane Byers .60 1.50
22 Garth Collins .30 .75
23 Rejean Beauchemin .75 2.00
24 Peter Anholt CO .02 .10

2005-06 Prince Albert Raiders

COMPLETE SET (26) 8.00 20.00
1 Alex Archibald .40 1.00
2 Dane Byers .60 1.50
3 Kyle Chipchura .60 1.50
4 Peter Cmorej .30 .75
5 Ryan DePape .30 .75
6 Jesse Deckert .40 1.00
7 Scott Doucet .30 .75
8 Jarrid Dowhay .30 .75
9 Josh Elder .30 .75
10 Brad Erickson .30 .75
11 Mike Gauthier .30 .75
12 Mike Hellyer .30 .75
13 Ashton Hewson .30 .75
14 Kyle Howarth .30 .75
15 Jeff May .30 .75
16 Brett Novak .30 .75
17 Brent Ottmann .30 .75
18 Justin Palazzo .30 .75
19 Evan Schafer .30 .75
20 Aki Seitsonen .40 1.00
21 A.J. Thelen .60 1.50
22 Kevin Tipper .30 .75
23 Peter Anholt CO .02 .10
24 Dave Manson ACO .20 .50
25 Mark Odnokon ACO .02 .10
26 Duane Bartley AT .02 .10

2006-07 Prince Albert Raiders

COMPLETE SET (26) 12.00 20.00
1 David Aime .40 1.00
2 Jesse Deckert .40 1.00
3 Mike Gauthier .40 1.00
4 Jeff May .30 .75
5 A.J. Thelen .60 1.50
6 Blaine Tendler .30 .75
7 Cody Vann .30 .75
8 Scott Doucet .30 .75
9 Mike Hellyer .30 .75
10 Jarrid Dowhay .30 .75
11 Matthew Robertson .30 .75
12 Brent Ottmann .30 .75
13 Milan Jurik .30 .75
14 Lukas Zeliska .30 .75
15 Jordan Trach .30 .75
16 Ryan DePape .30 .75
17 Cody Gross .30 .75
18 Andy Smith .40 1.00
19 Josh Elder .30 .75
20 Ashton Hewson .30 .75
21 Justin Palazzo .30 .75
22 Bryce Lamb .30 .75
23 Shane Malone .30 .75
24 Peter Anholt CO .10 .25
25 Dave Manson ACO .20 .50
26 Kris Knoblauch ACO .10 .25

1998-99 Prince George Cougars

This set features the Cougars of the WHL. The set was sponsored by Sight and Sound Music and was sold at home games. The cards are unnumbered and so are listed below in alphabetical order.

COMPLETE SET (27) 15.00 40.00
1 Header card .01
2 Mike Bayrack .20 1.00
3 Blair Betts .30 2.00
4 Tyler Bouck .30 2.00
5 Eric Brewer 2.00 5.00
6 Tyler Brough .20 1.00
7 Justin Cox .20 1.00
8 Travis Eagles .20 1.00
9 Dan Hamhuis 4.00 10.00
10 Trent Hunter 2.00 5.00
11 Michael Kiesman .20 1.00
12 Petr Kubos .20 1.00
13 Adam Loncan .20 1.00
14 Jozef Mrena .20 1.00
15 Scott Myers .30 2.00
16 Mike Olynyk .20 1.00
17 Jonathan Parker .20 1.00
18 Owen Richey .20 1.00
19 Jarrett Smith .40 2.00
20 Kevin Swanson .30 2.00
21 Curtis Tipler .30 2.00
22 Gary Toor .20 1.00
23 Jordan Walker .20 1.00
24 Ian Walterson .20 1.00
25 Tim Wedderburn .20 1.00
26 Jeff Zorn .20 1.00
27 Cougar Coaches .04 .10

1999-00 Prince George Cougars

This set features the Cougars of the WHL. It is believed that the cards were produced by the team and sold at its souvenir stands. The set includes the first card of 2001 first-rounder Dan Hamhuis.

COMPLETE SET (25) 6.00 15.00
1 Scott Meyers .20 .50
2 Tim Wedderburn .20 .50
3 Ryan Chieduch .20 .50
4 Jeff Zorn .20 .50
5 Dan Hamhuis 1.20 2.00
6 Kevin Seibel .20 .50
7 Gary Toor .20 .50
8 Devin Wilson .20 .50
9 Jozef Mrena .20 .50
10 Aaron Foster .20 .50
11 Tyler Bouck .40 .75
12 Jonathan Parker .20 .50
13 Shon Jones-Parry .20 .50
14 Roman Takac .20 .50
15 Chris Falloon .20 .50
16 Justin Hansen .20 .50
17 Trent Hunter .20 2.00
18 Blair Betts .40 1.00
19 Travis Eagles .20 .50
20 Ed Dempsey CO .04 .10
21 Dallas Thompson CO .04 .10
22 Paul Valaitis .20 .50
23 Billy Thompson .20 .50
24 Justin Cox .30 .75
25 Dan Baum .20 .50

2000-01 Prince George Cougars

This set features the Cougars of the WHL. It is believed that the cards were sponsored by Dairy Queen and sold by the team, but that has not been confirmed. The set is noteworthy for including an early card of 2001 first rounder Dan Hamhuis.

COMPLETE SET (25) 4.80 12.00
1 Team Card .10 .25
2 Billy Thompson .16 .75
3 Tim Wedderburn .16 .40
4 David Koci .16 .40
5 Dan Hamhuis 1.20 2.00
6 Gary Gladue .16 .40
7 Joey Hope .16 .40
8 Devin Wilson .16 .40
9 Chris Falloon .16 .40
10 Nathan Brice .16 .40
11 Christian Chartier .30 .75
12 Berkeley Buchko .30 .75
13 Scott Lynch .16 .40
14 Aaron Foster .16 .40
15 John Filewich .16 .40
16 Tomas Tesarek .16 .40
17 Dan Baum .16 .40
18 Adam Stefishen .16 .40
19 Mark Kitts .16 .40
20 Willy Glover .16 .40
21 Brett Allan .16 .40
22 Travis Eagles .16 .40
23 Justin Cox .16 .40
24 Duane Perillat .16 .40
25 Derek Boogaard .16 .50

2001-02 Prince George Cougars

We have confirmed the existence of two cards in this series. If you know of others, please contact us at hockeymag@beckett.com.

COMPLETE SET (?)
1 Jonathan Filewich
2 Dan Hamhuis

2003-04 Prince George Cougars

COMPLETE SET (25) 8.00 20.00
1 Header Card .02 .10
2 Justin Pogge 4.00 10.00
3 Devin Featherstone .20 .50
4 Curtis Cooper .20 .50
5 Dustin Byfuglien .40 1.00
6 Brett Dickie .20 .50
7 Mike Fogolin .20 .50
8 Dennis Rehak .20 .50
9 Chris Falloon .20 .50
10 Nicholas Drazenovic .20 .50
11 Stanislav Bolshakov .20 .50
12 Dylan Yeo .30 .75
13 Brad Priestlay .20 .50
14 Jonathan Filewich .20 .50
15 Joshua Aspenlind .20 .50
16 Eric Hunter .20 .50
17 Greg Gardiner .20 .50
18 Danny Lapointe .20 .50
19 Myles Zimmer .30 .75
20 Steven Later .20 .50
21 Colin Patterson .20 .50
22 Tyrell Moulton .30 .75
23 Brett Parker .20 .50
24 Todd Ford .20 .50
25 Team Photo .20 .50

1988-89 ProCards AHL

This set of 348 cards features the 14 teams of the American Hockey League. The cards measure the standard size, 2 1/2" by 3 1/2". The fronts feature color player photos accented by a beige-colored hockey stick superimposed on the right and lower sides of the picture. The AHL logo appears in the lower left corner, and the photo is bordered on all sides by red. The cards are unnumbered and checklisted below alphabetically according to teams as follows (teams in alphabetical order and players listed alphabetically within each team): Adirondack Red Wings (1-25), Baltimore Skipjacks (26-48), Binghamton Whalers (49-72), Cape Breton Oilers (73-96), Halifax Citadels (97-119), Hershey Bears (120-147), Maine Mariners (148-169), Moncton Hawks (170-190), New Haven Nighthawks (191-222), Newmarket Saints (223-244), Rochester Americans (245-268), Sherbrooke Canadiens (269-299), Springfield Indians (300-324), and Utica Devils (325-348). Although the team sets were originally packaged individually, they are listed below as one giant set.

COMPLETE SET (348) 32.00 80.00
1 Rob Nichols .08 .20
2 Bill Dineen CO .10 .25
3 Tim Paris Asst.TR .02 .05
4 Glenn Merkosky .06 .15
5 Mike Gober .08 .20
6 Dave Casey TR .02 .05
7 Sam St.Laurent .30 .75
8 Mark Reimer .10 .25
9 Dennis Smith .08 .20
10 Lou Crawford .08 .20
11 John Mokosak .08 .20
12 Murray Eaves .08 .20
13 Dave Korol .08 .20
14 Miroslav Ihnacak .20 .50
15 Dale Krentz .08 .20
16 Brent Fedyk .20 .50
17 Dean Morton .08 .20
18 Jeff Brubaker .16 .40
19 Tim Cheveldae .60 1.50
20 Randy McKay .40 1.00
21 Peter Dineen .08 .20
22 Rob Doyle .08 .20
23 Daniel Shank .40 1.00
24 Joe Ferras .08 .20
25 John Blum .10 .25
26 Tim Bergland .08 .20
27 Robin Bawa .08 .20
28 Shawn Simpson .08 .20
29 Chris Felix .10 .25
30 Jeff Greenlaw .08 .20
31 Frank Dimuzio .08 .20
32 Tyler Larter .08 .20
33 Rob Whistle .08 .20
34 Dallas Eakins .08 .20
35 Mark Hatcher .08 .20
36 Dave Farrish .10 .25
37 Bill Houlder .20 .50
38 Doug Keans .30 .75
39 Lou Franceschetti .10 .25
40 Rob Murray .06 .15
41 Terry Murray GM/CO .20 .50
42 Steve Seftel .08 .20
43 J.P. Mattingly TR .02 .05
44 Mike Richard .08 .20
45 Shawn Cronin .20 .50
46 Scott McCrory .08 .20
47 Mike Millar .08 .20
48 Dave Sherrid TR .02 .05
49 Marc Laforge .08 .20
50 David O'Brien .08 .20
51 Dave Rowbotham .08 .20
52 Kay Whitmore .40 1.00
53 Richard Brodeur .20 .50
54 Mike Vellucci .08 .20
55 Terry Yake .20 .50
56 Roger Kortko .08 .20
57 Jon Smith TR .02 .05
58 Lindsay Carson UER .08 .20
(Misspelled Lindsy on card front)
59 Chris Brant .08 .20
60 Claude Larose CO .10 .25
61 Dallas Gaume .08 .20
62 Charlie Bourgeois .08 .20
63 Todd Krygier .20 .50
64 Gary Callahan .08 .20
65 Mark Reeds .08 .20
66 Al Tuer .08 .20
67 Brian Chapman .08 .20
68 Mark Lavarre .08 .20
69 Mark Dumas .08 .20
70 Jim Culhane .08 .20
71 Larry Trader .08 .20
72 Tom Mitchell GM .02 .05
73 Rob MacInnis .08 .20
74 John B. Hanna .08 .20
75 Dan Currie .20 .50
76 Dave Roach .08 .20
77 Jamie Nicolls .08 .20
78 Alan May .10 .25
79 David Haas .08 .20
80 Daryl Reaugh .60 1.50
81 Mike Ware .08 .20
82 Mike Glover .08 .20
83 Nick Beaulieu .08 .20
84 Mario Barbe .08 .20
85 Darren Beals .08 .20
86 Kim Issel .08 .20
87 Shaun Van Allen .20 .50
88 Jim Ennis .08 .20
89 Mark Lamb .40 1.00
90 Larry Floyd .08 .20
91 Ron Shudra .08 .20
92 Fabian Joseph .10 .25
93 Selmar Odelein .10 .25
94 Don Martin .08 .20
95 Jim Wiemer .10 .25
96 Brad MacGregor .08 .20
97 Gerald Bzdel .08 .20
98 Mike Hough .20 .50
99 Ken McRae .10 .25
100 Bobby Dollas .10 .25
101 Joel Baillargeon .08 .20
102 Ladislav Tresl .06 .15
103 Jacques Mailhot .20 .50
104 Dean Hopkins .08 .20
105 Claude Julien .08 .20
106 Brent Severyn .30 .75
107 Keith Miller .08 .20
108 Scott Shaunessy .08 .20
109 Jaroslav Sevcik .08 .20
110 Darin Kimble .20 .50
111 Jean-Marc Routhier .08 .20
112 Ken Quinney .08 .20
113 Max Middendorf .08 .20
114 Marc Fortier .16 .40
115 Jean-Marc Richard .08 .20
116 Mike Natyshak .08 .20
117 Ron Tugnutt 1.60 4.00
118 Scott Gordon .20 .50
119 Doug Carpenter CO/GM .04 .10
120 Jeff Harding .08 .20
121 Jocelyn Perrault .08 .20
122 Darryl Gilmour .20 .50
123 John Stevens .08 .20
124 Warren Harper .08 .20
125 Chris Jensen .08 .20
126 Mark Freer .10 .25
127 Gordon Paddock .08 .20
128 Bruce Randall .08 .20
129 Glen Seabrooke .08 .20
130 Mike Stothers .08 .20
131 Dave Fenyves .10 .25
132 Mark Lofthouse .08 .20
133 Marc D'Amour .20 .50
134 Shaun Sabol .08 .20
135 Craig Kitteringham .08 .20
136 J.J. Daigneault .20 .50
137 Don Biggs .10 .25
138 Kent Hawley .08 .20
139 Tony Horacek .08 .20
140 Al Hill .10 .25
141 Don Nachbaur .08 .20
142 John Paddock CO .08 .20
143 Kevin McCarthy CO .08 .20
144 Dan Stuck TR .02 .05
145 Doug Yingst .08 .20
146 Frank Mathers PR/GM .08 .20
147 Brian Bucciarelli TR .02 .05
148 Terry Taillefer .08 .20
149 Paul Beraldo .08 .20
150 Jeff Lamb .08 .20
151 Mitch Molloy .08 .20
152 Darren Lowe .08 .20
153 Stephane Quintal .40 1.00
154 Norm Foster .10 .25
155 Jean-Marc Lanthier .08 .20
156 Carl Mokosak .08 .20
157 Mike Neill .08 .20
158 Mike Jeffrey .08 .20
159 Steve Tsujiura .08 .20
160 Scott Drevitch .08 .20
161 Paul Guay .10 .25
162 Scott Wykoff ANN .02 .05
163 John Carter .10 .25
164 Phil Degaetano .08 .20
165 Doug Foerster PB/TKTS .02 .05
166 Bruce Shoebottom .10 .25
167 Ray Podloski .08 .20
168 Greg Hawgood .20 .50
169 Joe Flaherty .08 .20
170 Todd Flichel .08 .20
171 Steven Fletcher .10 .25
172 Len Nielson .08 .20
173 Neil Meadmore .08 .20
174 Gilles Hamel .10 .25
175 Ron Wilson .20 .50
176 Stu Kulak .10 .25
177 Scott Schneider .08 .20
178 Mike Warus .08 .20
179 Jamie Husgen .08 .20
180 Tom Draper .20 .50
181 Guy Gosselin .08 .20
182 Guy Larose .10 .25
183 Stephane Beauregard .30 .75
184 Brent Hughes .16 .40
185 Sean Clement .08 .20
186 Matt Hervey .06 .15
187 Chris Norton .08 .20
188 Rob Snitzer THER .02 .05
189 Rick Bowness CO .20 .50
190 Wayne Flemming MG .02 .05
191 Tim Tookey .10 .25
192 Ken Baumgartner .40 1.00
193 John English .08 .20
194 Darryl Williams .08 .20
195 Hubie McDonough .20 .50
196 Brad Hyatt .08 .20
197 Phil Sykes .06 .15
198 Mario Chitaroni .08 .20
199 Tom Pratt .08 .20
200 Sal Lombardi TR .02 .05
201 Rick Dudley CO .10 .25
202 John Tortorella CO .02 .05
203 Chris Panek .08 .20
204 Scott Green TR .02 .05
205 Eric Germain .08 .20
206 Bob Kudelski .20 .50
207 Joe Paterson .08 .20
208 Al Loring .08 .20
209 Mark Fitzpatrick 1.20 3.00
210 Dan Gratton .08 .20
211 Sylvain Couturier .08 .20
212 Pat Hickey DIR .02 .05
213 Petr Prajsler .06 .15
214 Lyle Phair .08 .20
215 Bob Logan .08 .20
216 Francois Breault .08 .20
217 Paul Kelly .08 .20
218 Steve Richmond .08 .20
219 Denis Larocque .08 .20
220 Brian Wilks .08 .20
221 Dave Pasin .10 .25
222 Gordie Walker .08 .20
223 Marty Dallman .08 .20
224 Jim Ralph .80 2.00
225 Mike Blaisdell .20 .50
226 Sean McKenna .08 .20
227 Mark Kirton .10 .25
228 Greg Hotham .08 .20
229 Bill Root .10 .25
230 Wes Jarvis .08 .20
231 Daryl Evans .08 .20
232 Jack Capuano .08 .20
233 Tim Armstrong .08 .20
234 Alan Hepple .08 .20
235 Brian Blad .08 .20
236 Ken Yaremchuk .10 .25
237 Paul Gagne .16 .40
238 Doug Shedden .20 .50
239 Brian Hoard .08 .20
240 Greg Terrion .16 .40
241 Trevor Jobe .02 .05
242 Jeff Reese .40 1.00
243 Darryl Shannon .20 .50
244 Tim Bernhardt .30 .75
245 The Moose Mascot .04 .10
246 Paul Brydges .08 .20
247 Ken Priestlay .10 .25
248 Jacques Cloutier .20 .50
249 Steve Smith .08 .20
250 Jim Jackson .10 .25
251 Grant Tkachuk .08 .20
252 Kevin Kerr .08 .20
253 Mark Ferner .10 .25
254 Jeff Parker .08 .20
255 Don McSween .10 .25
256 Jim Hofford .08 .20
257 Darcy Wakaluk .60 1.50
258 Scott Metcalfe .08 .20
259 Richie Dunn .08 .20
260 Wayne Van Dorp .16 .40
261 Shawn Anderson .10 .25
262 Jeff Capello .08 .20
263 Mike Donnelly .20 .50
264 Mikael Anderson .20 .50
265 Robert Ray 1.60 4.00
266 Jody Gage .30 .75
267 Francois Guay .06 .15
268 John Van Boxmeer CO .10 .25
269 Jim Nesich .08 .20
271 J.J. Daigneault .20 .50
272 Randy Exelby .10 .25
273 Jyrki Lumme .60 1.50
275 Francois Gravel .08 .20
276 Jacques Parent THER .02 .05
277 Bobby Boulanger MG .02 .05
278 Benoit Brunet .40 1.00
279 Martin Nicoletti .08 .20
280 Mark Pederson .10 .25
281 Stephan Lebeau .40 1.00
282 Claude Larose CO .10 .25
283 Steve Bisson .08 .20
284 Scott Sandelin .08 .20
285 Rocky Dundas .08 .20
286 Serge Roberge .08 .20
287 Rob Bryden .08 .20
288 Marc Saumier .08 .20
289 Jean Hamel CO .08 .20
290 Mario Roberge .10 .25
291 Jocelyn Lemieux .20 .50
292 Ron Chyzowski .08 .20
293 Martin Desjardins .08 .20
294 Steven Martinson .08 .20
295 Jose Charbonneau .10 .25
296 Stephane J.G. Richer .06 .15
297 Sylvain Lefebvre .30 .75
298 Donald Dufresne .10 .25
299 Luc Gauthier .08 .20
300 Shawn Evans .06 .15
301 Mike Stevens .08 .20
302 Bruce Boudreau .20 .50
303 Todd McLellan .08 .20
304 Jeff Hackett 1.60 4.00
305 Bill Berg .20 .50
306 Stu Burnie .08 .20
307 Duncan McPherson .08 .20
308 Jeff Finley .10 .25
309 Ralph Calvanese MG .02 .05
310 Rob DiMaio .40 1.00
311 Chris Pryor .08 .20
312 Jim Roberts CO .08 .20
313 Vern Smith .08 .20
314 Mike Walsh .08 .20
315 Ed Tyburski TR .02 .05
316 Rod Dallman .08 .20
317 George Maneluk .10 .25
318 Richard Kromm .10 .25
319 Kerry Clark .08 .20
320 Hank Lammens .10 .25
321 Tom Fitzgerald .20 .50
322 Dale Henry .08 .20
323 Shawn Byram .08 .20
324 Doug Weiss .08 .20
325 John Walker .08 .20
326 Paul Ysebaert .30 .75
327 Chris Cichocki .08 .20
328 Marc Laniel .08 .20
329 Kevin Todd .20 .50
330 Dan Delianedls .08 .20
331 Robert Bill TR .02 .05
332 Jeff Croop TR .02 .05
333 Craig Billington .80 2.00
334 Alan Stewart .08 .20
335 Jeff Madill .10 .25
336 Scott Moon TR .02 .05
337 Neil Brady .10 .25
338 Murray Brumwell .08 .20
339 Anders Carlsson .08 .20
340 Dan Dorion .08 .20
341 Tom McVie CO .10 .25
342 David Marcinyshyn .08 .20
343 John Blessman .08 .20
344 Chris Terreri .80 2.00
345 Eric Weinrich .30 .75
346 Janne Ojanen .20 .50
347 Tim Lenardon .08 .20
348 Jamie Huscroft .20 .50

1988-89 ProCards IHL

This set of 119 cards features players from the teams of the International Hockey League. The cards measure the standard size 2 1/2" by 3 1/2". The fronts feature color player photos accented by a beige-colored hockey stick superimposed on the right and lower sides of the picture. The cards are unnumbered and checklisted below alphabetically according to teams as follows: Indianapolis Ice (1-22), Kalamazoo Wings (23-42), Muskegon Lumberjacks (43-65), Peoria Rivermen (66-94), and Saginaw Hawks (95-119). Although the team sets were originally sold with a suggested retail price of 3.00 per team set and packaged individually, they are listed below as one giant set. In many cases that was the way they were advertised and sold, i.e., as a complete set of all the teams in the IHL.

COMPLETE SET (119) 20.00 50.00
1 Bob Lakso .08 .20
2 Rick Boyd .08 .20
3 Alan Perry .20 .50
4 Mark Teevens .08 .20
5 Gary Stewart .08 .20
6 Randy Taylor .08 .20
7 Scott Clements .08 .20
8 Chris McSorley .20 .50
9 Dave Allison .08 .20
10 Shane Doyle .08 .20
11 Darwin McCutcheon .08 .20
12 Geoff Benic .08 .20
13 Rich Oberlin TR .02 .05
14 Glen Johannesen .08 .20
15 Graeme Bonar .08 .20
16 Ron Handy .08 .20
17 Archie Henderson .10 .25
18 Brent Sapergia .08 .20
19 Brad Beck .08 .20
20 Paul Houck .08 .20
21 Jimmy Mann .20 .50
22 Rick Barkovich' .08 .20
23 Scott McCrady .08 .20
24 Andy Akervik .08 .20
25 Rob Zettler .20 .50
26 Jarmo Myllys .40 1.00
27 D'Arcy Norton .08 .20
28 Ken Hodge Jr. .20 .50
29 Emanuel Viveiros .08 .20
30 Scott Bjugstad .08 .20
31 Mike Berger .08 .20
32 Joe Lockwood .08 .20
33 Stephane Roy .10 .25
34 Randy Smith .10 .25
35 Mike McHugh .08 .20
36 Warren Babe .08 .20
37 Gary McColgan .08 .20
38 Darin Baker .08 .20
39 Neil Wilkinson .20 .50
40 Kirk Tomlinson .08 .20
41 Larry Dyck .16 .40
42 Dave Schofield .08 .20
43 Brad Aitken .08 .20
44 Jock Callander .40 1.00
45 Todd Charlesworth .08 .20
46 Jeff Cooper .08 .20
47 Jeff Daniels .20 .50
48 Greg Davies .08 .20
49 Lee Giffin .08 .20
50 Dave Goertz .08 .20
51 Steve Gotaas .08 .20
52 Scott Gruhl .40 1.00
53 Doug Hobson .08 .20
54 Kevin MacDonald .08 .20
55 Pat Mayer .08 .20
56 Dave McLlwain .20 .50
57 Dave Michayluk .08 .20
58 Glenn Mulvenna .08 .20
59 Jim Paek .20 .50
60 Frank Pietrangelo .30 .75
61 Bruce Racine .20 .50
62 Mark Recchi 3.20 8.00
63 Troy Vollhoffer .08 .20
64 Jeff Waver .08 .20
65 Mitch Wilson .08 .20
66 Mitch Messier .10 .25
67 Dave Lowry .20 .50
68 Tim Bothwell .10 .25
69 Sheryl Reeves ADM .02 .05
70 Shane MacEachern .10 .25
71 Glen Featherstone .20 .50
72 Charlie Thompson MGR .02 .05
73 Wayne Thomas CO .10 .25
74 Dominic Lavoie .10 .25
75 Team Photo .20 .50
Peoria Rivermen
76 Scott Paluch .08 .20
77 Wayne Gagne .08 .20
78 Dave Thomlinson .20 .50
79 Tony Twist 2.00 5.00
80 Brad McCaughey .08 .20
81 Kelly Chase 1.20 3.00
82 Scott Harlow .08 .20
83 Peter Douris .20 .50
84 Cliff Ronning 1.00 2.50
85 Lyle Odelein .40 1.00
86 Terry MacLean .08 .20
87 Darin Smith .08 .20
88 Skip Probst .08 .20
89 Ed McMurray MGR .02 .05
90 Greg Eberle TR .02 .05
91 Jim Vesey .08 .20
92 Toby Ducolon .08 .20
93 Pat Jablonski .60 1.50
94 Darrell May .08 .20
95 Ed Belfour 10.00 25.00
96 Bruce Cassidy .10 .25
97 Chris Clifford .20 .50
98 Mario Doyon .08 .20
99 Bill Gardner .08 .20
100 Mark Kurzawski .08 .20
101 Lonnie Loach .20 .50
102 Steve Ludzik .10 .25
103 David Mackey .08 .20
104 Dale Marquette .08 .20
105 Gary Moscaluk .08 .20
106 Marty Nanne .08 .20
107 Brian Noonan .40 1.00
108 Mark Paterson .08 .20
109 Kent Paynter .08 .20
110 Guy Phillips .08 .20
111 John Reid .08 .20
112 Mike Rucinski .08 .20
113 Warren Rychel .30 .75
114 Everett Sanipass .20 .50
115 Mike Stapleton .10 .25
116 Darryl Sutter .40 1.00
117 Jari Torkki .08 .20
118 Bill Watson .10 .25
119 Sean Williams .10 .25

1989-90 ProCards AHL

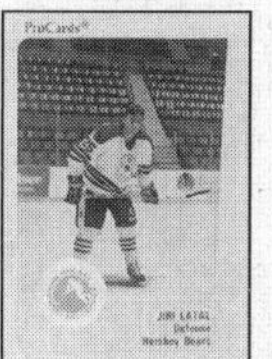

This set of 360 standard-size cards features the 14 teams of the American Hockey League. Although the team sets were originally sold with a suggested retail price of 3.00 per team set and packaged individually, they are listed below as one giant set. In many cases that was the way they were advertised and sold, i.e., as a complete set of all the teams in the AHL. The set is constructed in team order.

COMPLETE SET (360) 36.00 90.00
1 New Haven Checklist .02 .05
2 Francois Breault .10 .25
3 Paul Kelly .10 .25
4 Phil Sykes .16 .40
5 Ron Scott .16 .40
6 Micah Aivazoff .16 .40
7 Sylvain Couturier .10 .25
8 Carl Repp .10 .25
9 Murray Brumwell .10 .25
10 Todd Elik .20 .50
11 Darwin Bozek .10 .25
12 Eric Germain .10 .25
13 Scott Young 1.20 1.00
14 Chris Kontos .20 .50
15 Scott Bjugstad .16 .40
16 Eric Ricard .10 .25
17 Ross Wilson .10 .25
18 Graham Stanley .10 .25
19 Chris Panek .10 .25
20 Nick Fotiu .30 1.00
21 Rene Chapdelaine .10 .25
22 Gordie Walker .10 .25
23 Tim Bothwell .16 .40
24 Kevin MacDonald .10 .25
25 Darryl Williams .10 .25
26 John Van Kessel .10 .25
27 Paul Brydges .10 .25
28 Moncton Checklist .02 .05
29 Guy Larose .16 .40
30 Danton Cole .16 .40
31 Brent Hughes .16 .40
32 Larry Bernard .10 .25
33 Stu Kulak .10 .25
34 Bob Essensa .80 2.00
35 Luciano Borsato .16 .40
36 Guy Gosselin .10 .25
37 Todd Flichel .10 .25
38 Brian Hunt .10 .25
39 Neil Meadmore .10 .25
40 Matt Hervey .10 .25
41 Dallas Eakins .10 .25
42 Brad Jones .10 .25
43 Chris Norton .10 .25
44 Bryan Marchment .40 1.00
45 Rick Tabaracci .60 1.50
46 Grant Richison .10 .25
47 Brian McReynolds .10 .25
48 Tony Joseph .10 .25
49 Dave Farrish .16 .40
50 Rob Snitzer .02 .05
51 Ron Wilson .16 .40
52 Scott Schneider .10 .25
53 Maine Checklist .02 .05
54 Dave Buda .10 .25
55 Paul Beraldo .10 .25
56 Lou Crawford .10 .25
57 Mark Montanari .10 .25
58 Don Sweeney .40 1.00
59 Jeff Sirkka .10 .25
60 Norm Foster .20 .50
61 Greg Poss .10 .25
62 Gord Cruickshank .10 .25
63 Bruce Shoebottom .10 .25
64 Mark Ziliotto .10 .25
65 Ron Hoover .10 .25
66 Scott Harlow .10 .25
67 Mike Millar .10 .25
68 Bob Beers .20 .50
69 Ray Neufeld .16 .40
70 Graeme Townshend .20 .50
71 Billy O'Dwyer .10 .25
72 Frank Caprice .20 .50
73 John Blum .10 .25
74 Jerry Foster .10 .25
75 Bill Sutherland and .10 .25

Rick Bowness
76 Scott Drevitch .10 .25
77 Baltimore Checklist .02 .05
78 John Purves .10 .25
79 Jeff Greenlaw .10 .25
80 Jim Taylor .10 .25
81 Alfie Turcotte .10 .25
82 Dan Redmond .02 .05
83 Chris Felix .10 .25
84 Bobby Babcock .10 .25
85 Steve Maltais .10 .25
86 Mike Richard .10 .25
87 Team Picture .10 .25
88 Bob Mason .30 .75
89 Mark Ferner .16 .40
90 Steve Seftel .10 .25
91 Brian Tutt .10 .25
92 Terry Murray .16 .40
93 Jim Hrivnak .20 .50
94 Tyler Larter .10 .25
95 Tim Bergland .10 .25
96 Dennis Smith .10 .25
97 Steve Hollett .10 .25
98 Shawn Simpson .10 .25
99 Robin Bawa .10 .25
100 John Druce .20 .50
101 Kent Paynter .10 .25
102 Alain Cote .16 .40
103 J.P. Mattingly .02 .05
104 Newmarket Checklist .02 .05
105 Dean Anderson .10 .25
106 Wes Jarvis .10 .25
107 Brian Blad .10 .25
108 Derek Laxdal .10 .25
109 Kent Hulst .10 .25
110 Tim Bernhardt .20 .50
111 Brian Hoard .10 .25
112 Bill Root .16 .40
113 Paul Gardner .10 .25
114 Tim Armstrong .10 .25
115 Sean McKenna .10 .25
116 Tim Bean .10 .25
117 Alan Hepple .10 .25
118 Greg Hotham .10 .25
119 Scott Pearson .20 .50
120 Peter Ihnacak .16 .40
121 John McIntyre .10 .25
122 Paul Gagne .10 .25
123 Darren Veitch .16 .40
124 Mark LaForest .16 .40
125 Doug Shedden .16 .40
126 Bobby Reynolds .10 .25
127 Tie Domi 3.20 8.00
128 Ken Hammond .16 .40
129 Cape Breton Checklist .02 .05
130 Wade Campbell .10 .25
131 Chris Joseph .16 .40
132 Mario Barbe .10 .25
133 Mike Greenlay .20 .50
134 Peter Soberlak .10 .25
135 Bruce Bell .16 .40
136 Dan Currie .10 .25
137 Fabian Joseph .16 .40
138 Stan Drulia .30 .75
139 Todd Charlesworth .10 .25
140 Norm Maciver .20 .50
141 David Haas .10 .25
142 Tim Tisdale .10 .25
143 Eldon Reddick .20 .50
144 Alexander Tyznych .10 .25
145 Kim Issel .10 .25
146 Corey Foster .10 .25
147 Tomas Kapusta .10 .25
148 Brian Wilks .10 .25
149 John LeBlanc .10 .25
150 Ivan Matulik .10 .25
151 Shaun Van Allen .30 .75
152 Halifax Checklist .02 .05
153 Scott Gordon .20 .50
154 Trevor Steinburg .10 .25
155 Miroslav Ihnacak .16 .40
156 Jamie Baker .16 .40
157 Robbie Ftorek .20 .50
158 C. McQuaid and B.Smith .02 .05
159 Mario Brunetta .20 .50
160 Jean-Marc Routhier .10 .25
161 David Espe .10 .25
162 Ken Quinney .10 .25
163 Mark Vermette .10 .25
164 Dean Hopkins .10 .25
165 Claude Julien .10 .25
166 Claude Lapointe .20 .50
167 Stephane Morin .20 .50
168 Bryan Fogarty .20 .50
169 Dave Pichette .10 .25
170 Kevin Kaminski .16 .40
171 Brent Severyn .20 1.00
172 Max Middendorf .10 .25
173 Jean-Marc Richard .10 .25
174 Gerald Bzdel .10 .25
175 Ladislav Tresl .10 .25
176 Jaroslav Sevcik .10 .25
177 Greg Smyth .16 .40
178 Joel Baillargeon .10 .25
179 Sherbrooke Checklist .02 .05
180 Andre Racicot .20 .50
181 Jean-Claude Bergeron .20 .50
182 Jim Nesich .10 .25
183 Todd Richards .10 .25
184 Francois Gravel .10 .25
185 Lyle Odelein .40 1.00
186 Benoit Brunet .30 .75
187 Mario Roberge .16 .40
188 Marc Saumier .10 .25
189 Norman Desjardins .10 .25
190 Dan Woodley .10 .25
191 Andrew Cassels .30 .75
192 Roy Mitchell .10 .25
193 Guy Darveau .10 .25
194 Ed Cristofoli .10 .25
195 Stephane J.G. Richer .10 .25
196 Jacques Parent .02 .05
197 Luc Gauthier .10 .25
198 John Ferguson .10 .25
199 Mathieu Schneider .40 1.00
200 Serge Roberge .10 .25
201 Jean Hamel .10 .25
202 Utica Checklist .02 .05
203 Jason Simon .10 .25
204 Jeff Madill .10 .25
205 Kevin Todd .20 .50
206 Myles O'Connor .10 .25
207 Jon Morris .16 .40
208 Bob Hoffmeyer .10 .25
209 Paul Ysebaert .30 .75
210 Steve Rooney .16 .40
211 Claude Vilgrain .20 .50
212 Paul Guay .10 .25
213 Roland Melanson .30 .75
214 Tom McVie .16 .40
215 David Marcinyshyn .10 .25
216 Perry Anderson .10 .25
217 Jamie Huscroft .20 .50
218 Bob Woods .10 .25
219 Pat Conacher .20 .50
220 Jean-Marc Lanthier .10 .25
221 Chris Kiene .10 .25
222 Eric Weinrich .20 .50
223 Brian Fitzgerald .02 .05
224 Craig Billington .60 1.50
225 Jim Thomson .16 .40
226 Tim Budy .10 .25
227 Marc Laniel .10 .25
228 Robert Bill .02 .05
229 Springfield Checklist .02 .05
230 Mike Walsh .10 .25
231 Dale Henry .10 .25
232 Bill Berg .20 .50
233 Hank Lammens .10 .25
234 Rob DiMaio .40 1.00
235 Shawn Byram .10 .25
236 Jeff Hackett 1.20 2.00
237 Wayne McBean .16 .40
238 Tim Hanley .10 .25
239 Tom Fitzgerald .16 .40
240 Mike Stevens .10 .25
241 George Maneluk .10 .25
242 Dean Ewen .10 .25
243 Dale Kushner .10 .25
244 Shawn Evans .10 .25
245 Rod Dallman .10 .25
246 Mike Kelfer .10 .25
247 Sean LeBrun .10 .25
248 Kerry Clark .10 .25
249 Ed Tyburski .02 .05
250 Derek King .40 1.00
251 Marc Bergevin .20 .50
252 Jeff Finley .16 .40
253 Jim Roberts .10 .25
254 Chris Pryor .10 .25
255 Rochester Checklist .02 .05
256 Robert Ray 1.20 5.00
257 Ken Priestlay .16 .40
258 Darcy Wakaluk .30 .75
259 Richie Dunn .10 .25
260 Ken Sutton .20 .50
261 Terry Martin .10 .25
262 Scott Metcalfe .10 .25
263 Joel Savage .10 .25
264 Brad Miller .10 .25
265 Donald Audette .80 2.00
266 John Van Boxmeer .10 .25
267 The Moose .02 .05
268 Brian Ford .10 .25
269 Darcy Loewen .10 .25
270 Bob Halkidis .16 .40
271 Steve Ludzik .16 .40
272 Steve Smith .10 .25
273 Francois Guay .10 .25
274 Mike Donnelly .20 .50
275 Darrin Shannon .30 .75
276 Jody Gage .40 1.00
277 Dave Baseggio .10 .25
278 Bob Corkum .30 .75
279 Jim Jackson .10 .25
280 Don McSween .10 .25
281 Jim Hofford .10 .25
282 Scott McCrory .10 .25
283 Binghamton Checklist .02 .05
284 Raymond Saumier .10 .25
285 Mike Berger .10 .25
286 Corey Beaulieu .10 .25
287 Doug McKay .20 .50
288 Blair Atcheynum .10 .25
289 Al Tuer .10 .25
290 Chris Lindberg .16 .40
291 Daryl Reaugh .80 2.00
292 James Black .10 .25
293 Vern Smith .10 .25
294 Todd Krygier .20 .50
295 Bob Bodak .10 .25
296 Jon Smith .02 .05
297 Michel Picard .16 .40
298 Jim Culhane .10 .25
299 Brian Chapman .10 .25
300 Jim Ennis .10 .25
301 Jacques Caron .10 .25
302 Jim McKenzie .16 .40
303 Kay Whitmore .40 1.00
304 Terry Yake .16 .40
305 Mike Moller .10 .25
306 Adirondack Checklist .02 .05
307 Bob Wilkie .10 .25
308 Chris McRae .10 .25
309 Chris Kotsopoulos .16 .40
310 Steve Sumner .02 .05
311 Timothy Abbott .02 .05
312 Gord Kruppke .10 .25
313 Mike Gober .10 .25
314 Al Conroy .10 .25
315 Sam St.Laurent .16 .40
316 Dave Casey .02 .05
317 Yves Racine .20 .50
318 Randy McKay .20 .50
319 Dale Krentz .10 .25
320 Sheldon Kennedy .30 .75
321 Barry Melrose 1.20 3.00
322 Dennis Holland .10 .25
323 Glenn Merkosky .10 .25
324 Murray Eaves .10 .25
325 Mark Reimer .10 .25
326 Tim Cheveldae .40 1.00
327 Peter Dineen .10 .25
328 Dean Morton .10 .25
329 Derek Mayer .16 .40
330 Hershey Checklist .02 .05
331 Don Biggs .10 .25
332 Scott Sandelin .10 .25
333 Shaun Sabol .10 .25
334 Murray Baron .16 .40
335 Dave Fenyves .10 .25
336 Glen Seabrooke .10 .25
337 Mark Freer .16 .40
338 Ray Allison .10 .25
339 Chris Jensen .10 .25
340 Ross Fitzpatrick .10 .25
341 Brian Dobbin .10 .25
342 Darren Rumble .10 .25
343 Mike Stothers .10 .25
344 Jiri Latal .10 .25
345 Don Nachbaur .10 .25
346 John Stevens .10 .25
347 Steven Fletcher .10 .25
348 Kent Hawley .10 .25
349 Bill Armstrong .10 .25
350 Bruce Hoffort .16 .40
351 Gordon Paddock .10 .25
352 Marc D'Amour .20 .50
353 Tim Tookey .10 .25
354 Reid Simpson .10 .25
355 Mark Bassen .10 .25
356 Rocky Trottier .10 .25
357 Harry Bricker .02 .05
358 Dan Stuck .02 .05
359 Al Hill .10 .25
360 Kevin McCarthy .10 .25

1989-90 ProCards IHL

This set of 208 standard-size cards features the nine teams of the International Hockey League. Although the team sets were originally sold with a suggested retail price of 3.00 per team set and packaged individually, they are listed below as one giant set. In many cases that was the way they were advertised and sold, i.e., as a complete set of all the teams in the IHL.

COMPLETE SET (208) 28.00 70.00
1 Peoria Checklist .02 .05
2 Darwin McPherson .10 .25
3 Pat Jablonski .30 .75
4 Scott Paluch .10 .25
5 Guy Hebert 2.80 5.00
6 Rich Pilon .16 .40
7 Curtis Joseph 10.00 20.00
8 Robert Dirk .20 .50
9 Darin Smith .10 .25
10 Terry McLean .10 .25
11 Kevin Miehm .16 .40
12 Toby Ducolon .10 .25
13 Mike Wolak .10 .25
14 Adrien Plavsic .20 .50
15 Dave Thomlinson .16 .40
16 Jim Vesey .10 .25
17 Michel Mongeau .20 .50
18 Tom Nash .02 .05
19 David O'Brien .10 .25
20 Dominic Lavoie .20 .50
21 Keith Osborne .10 .25
22 Rob Robinson .10 .25
23 Wayne Thomas .16 .40
24 Flint Checklist .02 .05
25 Jason Lafreniere .16 .40
26 Rick Knickle .30 .75
27 Jerry Tarrant .10 .25
28 Paul Broten .20 .50
29 Kevin Miller .40 1.00
30 Jim Latos .10 .25
31 Daniel Lacroix .16 .40
32 Dennis Vial .16 1.00
33 Denis Larocque .10 .25
34 Mike Golden .10 .25
35 Mike Hurlbut .10 .25
36 Scott Brower .10 .25
37 Lee Giffin .10 .25
38 Jeff Bloemberg .10 .25
39 Simon Wheeldon .20 .50
40 Rob Zamuner .40 1.00
41 Joe Paterson .10 .25
42 Barry Chyzowski .10 .25
43 Peter Laviolette .10 .25
44 Corey Millen .20 .50
45 Darren Lowe .10 .25
46 Peter Fiorentino .10 .25
47 Soren True .10 .25
48 Mike Richter 4.80 10.00
49 Ice Checklist .02 .05
50 Sean Williams .10 .25
51 Bruce Cassidy .10 .25
52 Mark Kurawski .10 .25
53 Bob Bassen .20 .50
54 Marty Nanne .10 .25
55 Jari Torkki .10 .25
56 Ryan McGill .16 .40
57 Mike Peluso .80 2.00
58 Darryl Sutter .30 1.00
59 Dan Vincelette .10 .25
60 Lonnie Loach .16 .40
61 Mike Rucinski .10 .25
62 Jim Playfair .10 .25
63 Everett Sanipass .10 .25
64 Dale Marquette .10 .25
65 Gary Moscaluk .10 .25
66 Mario Doyon .10 .25
67 Ray LeBlanc .40 1.00
68 Mike Eagles .16 .40
69 Warren Rychel .20 .50
70 Jim Johannson .16 .40
71 Cam Russell .20 .50
72 Mike McNeil .10 .25
73 Jimmy Waite .30 .75
74 Kalamazoo Checklist .02 .05
75 Kevin Schamehorn .10 .25
76 Kevin Evans .10 .25
77 D'Arcy Norton .10 .25
78 Scott Robinson .10 .25
79 Larry DePalma .10 .25
80 Ed Courtenay .16 .40
81 Rob Zettler .20 .50
82 Dusan Pasek .10 .25
83 Gary Emmons .10 .25
84 Peter Lappin .10 .25
85 Mario Thyer .10 .25
86 Mike McHugh .10 .25
87 Randy Smith .16 .40
88 Link Gaetz .20 1.00
89 Ken Hodge Jr. .16 .40
90 Pat MacLeod .20 .50
91 Neil Wilkinson .20 .50
92 Brett Barnett .10 .25
93 Larry Dyck .16 .40
94 Dean Kolstad .10 .25
95 Jarmo Myllys .40 1.00
96 Paul Jerrard .10 .25
97 Jean-Francois Quintin .16 .40
98 Mitch Messier .10 .25
99 Phoenix Checklist UER .02 .05
(110 Jeff Lamb not listed)
100 Bryant Perrier .10 .25
101 Keith Gretzky .40 1.00
102 Don Martin .10 .25
103 David Littman .16 .40
104 Mike DeCarle .10 .25
105 Grant Tkachuk .10 .25
106 Richard Novak .10 .25
107 Chris Luongo .10 .25
108 Bruce Boudreau .16 .40
109 Nick Beaulieu .10 .25
110 Jeff Lamb .10 .25
111 Rob Nichols .10 .25
112 Garry Unger .20 .50
113 Larry Floyd .10 .25
114 Brent Sapergia .10 .25
115 Randy Exelby .16 .50
116 Jim McGeough .10 .25
117 Tom Karalis .10 .25
118 Ken Spangler .10 .25
119 Jacques Mailhot .10 .25
120 Shawn Dineen .10 .25
121 Dave Korol .10 .25
122 Fort Wayne Checklist .02 .05
123 Colin Chin .10 .25
124 Scott Shaunessy .10 .25
125 Bob Lakso .10 .25
126 Duane Joyce .10 .25
127 Joe Stephan .10 .25
128 Ron Shudra .10 .25
129 Bob Fowler .10 .25
130 Steve Bisson .10 .25
131 Craig Endean .10 .25
132 Carl Mokosak .10 .25
133 Carey Lucyk .10 .25
134 Craig Channell .10 .25
135 Frederic Chabot .40 2.00
136 Brian Hannon .10 .25
137 Keith Miller .10 .25
138 Al Sims .20 .50
139 Stephane Beauregard .30 .75
140 Ron Handy .10 .25
141 Byron Lomow .10 .25
142 Muskegon Checklist .02 .05
143 Jamie Leach .10 .25
144 Chris Clifford .10 .25
145 Dave Capuano .16 .40
146 Jeff Daniels .10 .25
147 Dave Goertz .10 .25
148 Perry Ganchar .10 .25
149 Mitch Wilson .10 .25
150 Scott Gruhl .40 1.00
151 Randy Taylor .10 .25
152 Bruce Racine .20 .50
153 Dave Michayluk .16 .40
154 Richard Zemlak .16 .40
155 Brad Aitken .10 .25
156 Paul Stanton .16 .40
157 Darren Stolk .10 .25
158 Jim Paek .16 .40
159 Mark Kachowski .10 .25
160 Dan Frawley .10 .25
161 Mike Mersch .10 .25
162 Glenn Mulvenna .10 .25
163 Phil Russell .16 .40
164 Blair McDonald .10 .25
165 Milwaukee Checklist .02 .05
166 Shaun Clouston .10 .25
167 Steve Veilleux .10 .25
168 Peter Bakovic .10 .25
169 Peter DeBoer .20 .50
170 Ernie Vargas .10 .25
171 Keith Street .10 .25
172 Rob Murphy .16 .40
173 David Bruce .20 .50
174 Shannon Travis .10 .25
175 Jeff Rohlicek .10 .25
176 Jay Mazur .10 .25
177 Kevan Guy .10 .25
178 Troy Gamble .40 1.00
179 Ronnie Stern .20 .50
180 Jim Revenberg .10 .25
181 Jose Charbonneau .10 .25
182 Ian Kidd .10 .25
183 Todd Hawkins .10 .25
184 Carl Valimont .10 .25
185 Jim Agnew .10 .25
186 Curtis Hunt .10 .25
187 Dean Cook .10 .25
188 Ron Wilson .16 .40
189 Ron Lapointe .10 .25
190 Salt Lake City Checklist .02 .05
191 Brian Glynn .16 .40
192 Stephane Matteau .30 .75
193 Rick Barkovich .10 .25
194 Jeff Wenaas .10 .25
195 Darryl Olsen .10 .25
196 Rick Lessard .10 .25
197 Kevin Grant .10 .25
198 Rich Chernomaz .10 .25
199 Stu Grimson .80 3.00
200 Jamie Hislop and Bob Francis .10 .25
201 Doug Pickell .10 .25
202 Chris Biotti .10 .25
203 Tim Sweeney .20 .50
204 Ken Sabourin .16 .40
205 Randy Bucyk .10 .25
206 Wayne Cowley .16 .40
207 Rick Hayward .10 .25
208 Marc Bureau .20 .50

1990-91 ProCards AHL/IHL

This 629-card standard-size set features players who started or were expected to start the 1990-91 season in the minors. Players from the American Hockey League and the International Hockey League are included in this set. This set features red borders with a yellow hockey stick on the left side of the card diagonally framing a full-color picture of the player while the backs of the cards feature the basic factual information about the player as well as a complete statistical history. There are two number 99's: and the set is arranged by teams: Binghamton Rangers (1-25), Hershey Bears (26-53), Fredericton Canadiens (54-75), Peoria Rivermen (76-99) Kalamazoo Wings (99-122), Maine Mariners (123-145), Newmarket Saints (146-170), Springfield Indians (171-194), Baltimore Skipjacks (195-219), Cape Breton Oilers (220-242), Moncton Hawks (243-264, 343-344), Rochester Americans (265-295), San Diego Gulls (296-321), Milwaukee Admirals (322-342), Phoenix Roadrunner (345-369), Muskegon Lumberjacks (370-392), Indianapolis Ice (393-414), New Haven Nighthawks (415-441), Halifax Citadels (442-468), Adirondack Red Wings (469-493), Capital District Islanders (494-514), Albany Choppers (515-535), Fort Wayne Komets (536-556), Utica Devils (557-581), Kansas City Blades (582-602), and Salt Lake City Golden Eagles (603-628). Each team has its own team checklist (TC) card as the last card in the team's numbering sequence. Although the team sets were originally sold with a suggested retail price of 4.00 per team set and packaged individually, they are listed below as one giant set.

COMPLETE SET (629) 40.00 100.00
1 Rob Zamuner .30 .75
2 Todd Charlesworth .06 .15
3 Bob Bodak .06 .15
4 Len Hachborn .10 .25
5 Peter Fiorentino .06 .15
6 Kord Cernich .06 .15
7 Daniel Lacroix .20 .50
8 Joe Paterson .06 .15
9 Sam St.Laurent .20 .50
10 Jeff Bloemberg .06 .15
11 Mike Golden .06 .15
12 Mike Hurlbut .10 .25
13 Mark LaForest .20 .50
14 Chris Cichocki .06 .15
15 John Paddock .10 .25
16 Peter Laviolette .20 .50
17 Martin Bergeron .06 .15
18 Rudy Poeschek .30 1.00
19 Eric Germain .06 .15
20 Al Hill ACO .06 .15
21 Rick Bennett .10 .25
22 Tie Domi 2.00 5.00
23 Ross Fitzpatrick .06 .15
24 Brian McReynolds .10 .25
25 Binghampton Rangers TC .02 .05
26 Mike Eaves CO .06 .15
27 Lance Pitlick .16 .40
28 Dale Kushner .06 .15
29 Reid Simpson .06 .15
30 Craig Fisher .10 .25
31 Dominic Roussel .30 .75
32 Dave Fenyves .06 .15
33 Brian Dobbin .06 .15
34 Darren Rumble .16 .40
35 Murray Baron .16 .40
36 Bruce Hoffort .10 .25
37 Steve Beadle .06 .15
38 Chris Jensen .06 .15
39 Mike Stothers .06 .15
40 Kent Hawley .06 .15
41 Scott Sandelin .06 .15
42 Guy Phillips .06 .15
43 Mark Bassen .06 .15
44 Steve Scheifele .06 .15
45 Bill Armstrong .06 .15
46 Shaun Sabol .06 .15
47 Mark Freer .06 .15
48 Claude Boivin .10 .25
49 Len Barrie .10 .25
50 Bill Armstrong .06 .15
51 Tim Tookey .10 .25
52 Harry Bricker ACO .02 .05
53 Hershey Bears TC .02 .05
54 Alain Cote .10 .25
55 Luc Gauthier .06 .15
56 Eric Charron .06 .15
57 Mario Roberge .06 .15
58 Tom Sagissor .06 .15
59 Brent Bobyck .06 .15
60 John Ferguson .06 .15
61 Jim Nesich .06 .15
62 Gilbert Dionne .16 .40
63 Herbert Hohenberger .06 .15
64 Dan Woodley .06 .15
65 Roy Mitchell .06 .15
66 Frederic Chabot .40 2.00
67 Andre Racicot .20 .50
68 Paul DiPietro .20 .50
69 Norman Desjardins .06 .15
70 Martin St.Amour .06 .15
71 Jesse Belanger .20 .50
72 Ed Cristofoli .06 .15
73 Patrick Lebeau .10 .25
74 Paulin Bordeleau CO .06 .15
75 Fredericton Canadiens TC .02 .05
76 Keith Osborne .06 .15
77 Rich Pilon .16 .40
78 Alain Raymond .06 .15
79 Rob Robinson .06 .15
80 Andy Rymsha .06 .15
81 Randy Skarda .10 .25
82 Dave Thomlinson .10 .25
83 Tom Tilley .16 .40
84 Steve Tuttle .06 .15
85 Tony Twist 1.20 4.00
86 David Bruce .10 .25
87 Kelly Chase .20 1.00
88 Nelson Emerson .80 2.00
89 Guy Hebert 1.60 3.00
90 Tony Hejna .06 .15
91 Michel Mongeau .16 .40
92 David O'Brien .06 .15
93 Kevin Miehm .10 .25
94 Darwin McPherson .06 .15
95 Dominic Lavoie .06 .15
96 Yves Heroux .06 .15
97 Pat Jablonski .30 .75
98 Bob Plager CO .20 .50
99A Peoria Rivermen TC .02 .05
99B Jayson More .10 .25
100 Kevin Evans .06 .15
101 Warren Babe .06 .15
102 Mitch Messier .06 .15
103 John Blue .20 .50
104 Larry Dyck .10 .25
105 Duane Joyce .06 .15
106 Kari Takko .16 .40
107 Brett Barnett .06 .15
108 Pat MacLeod .10 .25
109 Peter Lappin .06 .15
110 Link Gaetz .16 1.00
111 Larry DePalma .06 .15
112 Steve Gotaas .06 .15
113 Mike McHugh .06 .15
114 Dan Keczmer .10 .25
115 Jackson Penney .06 .15
116 Ed Courtenay .16 .40
117 Jean-Francois Quintin .06 .15
118 Scott Robinson .06 .15
119 Mario Thyer .06 .15
120 Enrico Ciccone .30 .75
121 Kevin Constantine and John Marks .16 .40
122 Kalamazoo Wings TC .02 .05
123 Shayne Stevenson .20 .50
124 Jeff Lazaro .10 .25
125 Matt DelGuidice .20 .50
126 Ron Hoover .06 .15
127 John Mokosak .06 .15
128 John Blum .06 .15
129 Mike Parson .20 .50
130 Bruce Shoebottom .06 .15
131 Dave Donnelly .06 .15
132 Ralph Barahona .06 .15
133 Graeme Townshend .10 1.00
134 Ken Hodge Jr. .16 .40
135 Norm Foster .20 .50
136 Greg Poss .06 .15
137 Brad James .06 .15
138 Lou Crawford .06 .15
139 Rick Allain .06 .15
140 Bob Beers .16 .40
141 Ken Hammond .10 .25
142 Mark Montanari .06 .15
143 Rick Bowness CO .10 .25
144 Bob Gould P/CO .06 .15
145 Maine Mariners TC .02 .05
146 Mike Stevens .06 .15
147 Greg Walters .06 .15
148 Mike Moes .06 .15
149 Kent Hulst .06 .15
150 Len Esau .06 .15
151 Darryl Shannon .16 .40
152 Bobby Reynolds .06 .15
153 Derek Langille .06 .15
154 Jeff Serowik .10 .25
155 Darren Veitch .16 .40
156 Joe Sacco .16 .40
157 Alan Hepple .06 .15
158 Doug Shedden .16 .40
159 Steve Bancroft .06 .15
160 Greg Johnston .16 .40
161 Trevor Jobe .06 .15
162 Bill Root .16 .40
163 Tim Bean .06 .15
164 Brian Blad .06 .15
165 Robert Hornya .06 .15
166 Dean Anderson .06 .15
167 Damian Rhodes .80 2.00
168 Mike Millar .06 .15
169 Mike Jackson .06 .15
170 Newmarket Saints TC .02 .05
171 Cal Brown .06 .15
172 Michel Picard .16 .40
173 Cam Brauer .06 .15
174 Jim Burke .06 .15
175 Jim McKenzie .16 .40
176 Mike Tomlak .06 .15
177 Ross McKay .06 .15
178 Blair Atcheynum .20 .50
179 Chris Tancill .10 .25
180 Mark Greig .10 .25
181 Joe Day .06 .15
182 Jim Roberts CO .06 .15
183 Emanuel Viveiros .06 .15
184 Daryl Reaugh .40 2.00
185 Tommie Eriksen .06 .15
186 Terry Yake .16 .40
187 Chris Govedaris .06 .15
188 Chris Bright .06 .15
189 John Stevens .06 .15
190 Brian Chapman .06 .15
191 James Black .10 .25
192 Scott Daniels .06 .15
193 Kelly Ens .06 .15
194 Springfield Indians TC .02 .05
195 Ken Lovsin .06 .15
196 Kent Paynter .06 .15
197 Jim Mathieson .20 .50
198 Bob Mendel .06 .15
199 Reggie Savage .10 .25
200 Alfie Turcotte .06 .15
201 Victor Gervais .06 .15
202 Todd Hlushko .20 .50
203 Steve Seftel .06 .15
204 Thomas Sjogren .06 .15
205 Steve Maltais .10 .25
206 Bob Joyce .16 .40
207 Tyler Larter .06 .15
208 Mark Ferner .10 .25
209 Bobby Babcock .06 .15
210 Jeff Greenlaw .06 .15
211 Tim Taylor .30 .75
212 John Purves .06 .15
213 Chris Felix .16 .40
214 Jiri Vykoukal .06 .15
215 Shawn Simpson .06 .15
216 Jim Hrivnak .20 .50
217 Rob Laird CO/GM .02 .05
218 Barry Trotz Asst.CO .20 .50
219 Baltimore Skipjacks TC .02 .05
220 David Haas .06 .15
221 Wade Campbell .06 .15
222 Dan Currie .06 .15
223 Shaun Van Allen .16 .40
224 Norm Maciver .20 .50
225 Mike Greenlay .20 .50
226 Peter Soberlak .06 .15
227 Tim Tisdale .06 .15
228 Mario Barbe .06 .15
229 Shjon Podein .40 1.00
230 Trevor Sim .06 .15
231 Corey Foster .10 .25
232 Mike Ware .06 .15
233 Marc Laforge .06 .15
234 Bruce Bell .10 .25
235 Tomas Kapusta .06 .15
236 Alexander Tyjynch .06 .15
237 Tomas Srsen .06 .15
238 Collin Bauer .06 .15
239 Francois Leroux .20 .50
240 Don MacAdam CO .02 .05
241 Norm Ferguson ACO .02 .05
242 Cape Breton Oilers TC .02 .05
243 Tony Joseph .06 .15
244 Brent Hughes .16 .40
245 Larry Bernard .06 .15
246 Simon Wheeldon .06 .15
247 Todd Flichel .06 .15
248 Craig Duncanson .06 .15
249 Iain Duncan .06 .15
250 Bryan Marchment .20 .50
251 Matt Hervey .06 .15
252 Chris Norton .06 .15
253 Dallas Eakins .06 .15
254 Peter Hankinson .06 .15
255 Grant Richison .06 .15
256 Lee Davidson .06 .15
257 Denis Larocque .06 .15
258 Scott Levins .16 .40
259 Guy Larose .10 .25
260 Scott Schneider .06 .15
261 Sergei Kharin .06 .15
262 Hawk .02 .05
263 Dave Farrish CO .06 .15
264 Moncton Hawks TC .02 .05
265 Kevin Haller .20 .50
266 Joel Savage .06 .15
267 Scott Metcalfe .06 .15
268 Ian Boyce .06 .15
269 David Littman .20 .50
270 Dave Baseggio .06 .15
271 Ken Sutton .16 .40
272 Brad Miller .06 .15
273 Bill Houlder .20 .50
274 Dan Frawley .16 .40
275 Scott McCrory .06 .15
276 Steve Ludzik .16 .40
277 Robert Ray .60 4.00
278 Darrin Shannon .20 .50
279 Dale Degray .06 .15
280 Bob Corkum .30 .75
281 Grant Tkachuk .06 .15
282 Kevin Kerr .06 .15
283 Mitch Molloy .06 .15
284 Darcy Loewen .10 .25
285 Jody Gage .20 .50
286 Jiri Sejba .06 .15
287 Steve Smith .06 .15
288 Darcy Wakaluk .20 .50
289 Donald Audette .80 2.00
290 Don McSween .10 .25
291 Francois Guay .06 .15
292 Terry Martin ACO .02 .05
293 Don Lever CO .06 .15
294 The Moose .02 .05
295 Rochester Americans TC .02 .05
296 Mike O'Connell CO .16 .40
297 Paul Marshall .06 .15
298 Darin Bannister .06 .15
299 Rob Nichols .06 .15
300 Charlie Simmer P/CO .20 .50
301 Bob Jones .06 .15
302 Scott Brower .06 .15
303 Taylor Hall .06 .15
304 Carl Mokosak .06 .15
305 Glen Hanlon .20 .50
306 Peter Dineen .06 .15
307 Mike Sullivan .20 .50
308 Steven Martinson .06 .15
309 Dave Korol .06 .15
310 Darren Lowe .06 .15
311 Mark Reimer .10 .25
312 Mike Gober .06 .15
313 Al Tuer .06 .15
314 Dean Morton .06 .15
315 Jim McGeough .06 .15
316 Clark Donatelli .06 .15
317 Steven Dykstra .06 .15
318 Brent Sapergia .06 .15
319 Lloyd Floyd .06 .15
320 D'Arcy Norton .06 .15
321 San Diego Gulls TC .02 .05
322 Garry Valk .20 .50
323 Ian Kidd .06 .15
324 Todd Hawkins .06 .15
325 Carl Valimont .06 .15
326 Peter Bakovic .06 .15
327 Curt Fraser ACO .16 .40
328 David Mackey .06 .15
329 Jim Benning .20 .50
330 Peter DeBoer .10 .25
331 Steve Weeks .20 .50

332 Steve Veilleux .06 .15
333 Shaun Clouston .06 .15
334 Gino Odjick .60 2.00
335 Mike Murphy CO .10 .25
336 Cam Brown .06 .15
337 Patrice LeFebvre .10 .25
338 Eric Murano .06 .15
339 Jim Revenberg .06 .15
340 Don Gibson .06 .15
341 Steve McKichan .06 .15
342 Milwaukee Admirals TC .02 .05
343 Rick Tabaracci .30 .75
344 Mike O'Neill .20 .50
345 Rick Hayward .06 .15
346 Sean Whyte .06 .15
347 Petr Prajsler .06 .15
348 John Van Kessel .06 .15
349 Mario Gosselin .20 .50
350 Kyosti Karjalainen .06 .15
351 Mikael Lindholm .06 .15
352 David Goverde .10 .25
353 Graham Stanley .06 .15
354 Stephane J.G. Richer Defenseman .06 .15
355 Brian Lawton .16 .40
356 Jerome Bechard .06 .15
357 Jeff Rohlicek .06 .15
358 Steve Jacques .06 .15
359 Chris Kontos .20 .50
360 Sylvain Couturier .06 .15
361 Peter Sentner .06 .15
362 Steve Graves .06 .15
363 Daryn McBride .06 .15
364 Steve Rooney .16 .40
365 Mickey Volcan .06 .15
366 Kevin MacDonald .06 .15
367 Ralph Backstrom CO .20 .50
368 Garry Unger ACO .20 .50
369 Phoenix Roadrunners TC .02 .05
370 Rob Dopson .20 .50
371 Jock Callander .40 1.00
372 Chris Clifford .20 .50
373 Sandy Smith .06 .15
374 Jim Kyte .16 .40
375 Mike Needham .16 .40
376 Mitch Wilson .06 .15
377 Dave Goertz .06 .15
378 Mark Kachowski .06 .15
379 Perry Ganchar .06 .15
380 Mark Major .10 .25
381 Joel Gardner .06 .15
382 Scott Gruhl .30 .75
383 Todd Nelson .06 .15
384 Darren Stolk .06 .15
385 Scott Shaunessy .06 .15
386 Mike Mersch .06 .15
387 Glenn Mulvenna .06 .15
388 Brad Aitken .06 .15
389 Dave Michayluk .06 .15
390 Blair MacDonald CO .06 .15
391 Phil Russell ACO .10 .25
392 Muskegon Lumberjacks TC .02 .05
393 Sean Williams .06 .15
394 Ryan McGill .06 .15
395 Mike Eagles .16 .40
396 Jim Johannson .16 .40
397 Marty Nanne .06 .15
398 Jim Playfair .06 .15
399 Warren Rychel .30 .75
400 Cam Russell .20 .50
401 Jimmy Waite .20 .50
402 Mike Stapleton .06 .15
403 Trevor Dam .06 .15
404 Tracy Egeland .06 .15
405 Owen Lessard .06 .15
406 Jeff Sirkka .06 .15
407 Mike Dagenais .06 .15
408 Alex Roberts .06 .15
409 Dominik Hasek 10.00 25.00
410 Martin Desjardins .06 .15
411 Frantisek Kucera .16 .40
412 Carl Mokosak .06 .15
413 Dave McDowell .06 .15
414 Indianapolis Ice TC .02 .05
415 Paul Saundercook .06 .15
416 Darryl Williams .06 .15
417 Micah Aivazoff .06 .15
418 Robb Stauber .20 .50
419 Tom Martin .06 .15
420 Billy O'Dwyer .06 .15
421 Scott Harlow .06 .15
422 Jim Thomson .06 .15
423 Jim Pavese .06 .15
424 Ron Scott .06 .15
425 Dave Pasin .06 .15
426 Serge Roy .06 .15
427 Darryl Gilmour .16 .40
428 Mike Donnelly .20 .50
429 Rene Chapdelaine .06 .15
430 Brandy Semchuk .06 .15
431 Paul Holden .06 .15
432 Bob Berg .06 .15
433 Ladislav Tresl .06 .15
434 Eric Ricard .06 .15
435 Murray Brumwell .06 .15
436 Shawn McCosh .06 .15
437 Ross Wilson .06 .15
438 Scott Young .60 1.00
439 David Moylan .06 .15
440 Marcel Comeau CO .06 .15
441 New Haven Nighthawks TC .02 .05
442 David Espe .06 .15
443 Mario Doyon .06 .15
444 Gerald Bzdel .06 .15
445 Claude Lapointe .20 .50
446 Dean Hopkins .06 .15
447 Clement Jodoin .06 .15
448 Kevin Kaminski .20 1.00
449 Jamie Baker .16 .40
450 Mark Vermette .06 .15
451 Iiro Jarvi .16 .40
452 Kip Miller .40 1.00
453 Greg Smyth .10 .25
454 Serge Roberge .06 .15
455 Stephane Morin .20 .50
456 Brent Severyn .20 1.00
457 Jean-Marc Richard .06 .15
458 Ken Quinney .06 .15
459 Jeff Jackson .16 .40
460 Jaroslav Sevcik .06 .15
461 David Latta .06 .15
462 Trevor Steinburg .06 .15
463 Miroslav Ihnacak .06 .15
464 Jim Sprott .06 .15
465 Mike Bishop .06 .15
466 Stephane Fiset .80 2.00
467 Scott Gordon .20 .50
468 Halifax Citadels TC .02 .05
469 Gord Kruppke .06 .15
470 Glenn Merkosky .16 .40
471 Dennis Holland .06 .15
472 Chris McRae .06 .15
473 Al Conroy .06 .15
474 Yves Racine .20 .50
475 Jim Nill P/CO .06 .15
476 Barry Melrose CO .80 2.00
477 Bob Wilkie .06 .15
478 Guy Dupuis .06 .15
479 Doug Houda .16 .40
480 Tom Bissett .06 .15
481 Bill McDougall .10 .25
482 Glen Goodall .06 .15
483 Kory Kocur .06 .15
484 Chris Luongo .06 .15
485 Serge Anglehart .06 .15
486 Marc Potvin .16 1.00
487 Stewart Malgunas .06 .15
488 John Chabot .20 .50
489 Daniel Shank .20 .50
490 Randy Hansch .20 .50
491 Dave Gagnon .10 .25
492 Scott King .06 .15
493 Adirondack Red Wings TC .02 .05
494 Derek Laxdal .06 .15
495 Sean LeBrun .06 .15
496 Shawn Bryan .06 .15
497 Wayne Doucet .06 .15
498 Rich Kromm .06 .15
499 Chris Pryor P/CO .06 .15
500 George Maneluk .06 .15
501 Brad Lauer .10 .25
502 Wayne McBean .10 .25
503 Jeff Finley .16 .40
504 Jim Culhane .06 .15
505 Paul Cohen .06 .15
506 Brent Grieve .10 .25
507 Kevin Cheveldayoff .06 .15
508 Dennis Vaske .10 .25
509 Dave Chyzowski .06 .15
510 Travis Green .80 2.00
511 Dean Chynoweth .20 .50
512 Rob DiMaio .30 .75
513 Paul Guay .06 .15
514 Capital District Islanders TC .02 .05
515 Rick Knickle .20 .50
516 Curtis Hunt .06 .15
517 Bruce Racine .20 .50
518 Yves Heroux .06 .15
519 Joe Stefan .06 .15
520 Torrie Robertson .20 .50
521 Nick Beaulieu .06 .15
522 Dave Richter .10 .25
523 Jeff Waver .06 .15
524 Gordon Paddock .06 .15
525 Darryl Noren .06 .15
526 Byron Lomow .06 .15
527 Ivan Matulik .06 .15
528 Dan Woodley .06 .15
529 Dale Henry .06 .15
530 Soren True .06 .15
531 Stuart True .06 .15
532 Rob MacInnis .06 .15
533 Vern Smith .06 .15
534 Paul Laus .30 1.00
535 Albany Choppers TC .02 .05
536 Robin Bawa .06 .15
537 Steven Fletcher .06 .15
538 Lonnie Loach .10 .25
539 Al Sims CO .10 .25
540 Colin Chin .06 .15
541 Bruce Boudreau P/CO .06 .15
542 Bob Lakso .06 .15
543 John Anderson .16 .40
544 Kevin Kaminski .20 1.00
545 Bruce Major .06 .15
546 Stephane Brochu .06 .15
547 Peter Hankinson .06 .15
548 Carey Lucyk .06 .15
549 Tom Karalis .06 .15
550 Bob Jay .06 .15
551 Mike Butters .06 .15
552 Brian McKee .06 .15
553 Ray LeBlanc .20 .50
554 Tom Draper .16 .40
555 Steve Laurin .06 .15
556 Fort Wayne Komets TC .02 .05
557 Sergei Starikov .06 .15
558 Claude Vilgrain .16 .40
559 Jeff Sharples .10 .25
560 Bob Woods .06 .15
561 Perry Anderson .10 .25
562 Brennan Maley .06 .15
563 Mike Posma .06 .15
564 Tom McVie GM/CO .06 .15
565 Chris Palmer .06 .15
566 Bill Huard .16 .40
567 Marc Laniel .06 .15
568 Neil Brady .06 .15
569 Jason Simon .10 .25
570 Kevin Todd .20 .50
571 Jeff Madill .10 .25
572 Jeff Christian .06 .15
573 Todd Copeland .06 .15
574 Mike Bodnarchuk .06 .15
575 Chris Kiene .06 .15
576 Myles O'Connor .10 .25
577 Jamie Huscroft .16 .40
578 Mark Romaine .06 .15
579 Rollie Melanson .20 .50
580 Utica Devils Team .10 .25
581 Utica Devils TC .02 .05
582 Ron Handy .06 .15
583 Cam Plante .06 .15
584 Lee Giffin .10 .25
585 Jim Latos .06 .15
586 Stu Kulak .10 .25
587 Claude Julien .06 .15
588 Rick Barkovich .06 .15
589 Randy Exelby .20 .50
590 Mark Vichorek .06 .15
591 Darin Smith .06 .15
592 Mike Kelfer .06 .15
593 Andy Akervik .06 .15
594 Mike Hiltner .06 .15
595 Kevin Sullivan .06 .15
596 Troy Frederick .06 .15
597 Claudio Scremin .06 .15
598 Kurt Semandel .06 .15
599 Mike Colman .06 .15
600 Jeff Odgers .30 1.00
601 Wade Flaherty .20 .50
602 Kansas City Blades TC .02 .05
603 Marc Bureau .20 .50
604 Darryl Olsen .06 .15
605 Rick Lessard .06 .15
606 Kevin Grant .06 .15
607 Rich Chernomaz .06 .15
608 Randy Bucyk .06 .15
609 Wayne Crowley .06 .15
610 Ken Sabourin .06 .15
611 Bob Francis CO .02 .05
612 Jamie Hislop CO .06 .15
613 Kevan Melrose .06 .15
614 Scott McCrady .06 .15
615 Corey Lyons .06 .15
616 Martin Simard .06 .15
617 C.J. Young .10 .25
618 Mark Osiecki .10 .25
619 Bryan Deasley .06 .15
620 Kerry Clark .06 .15
621 Paul Kruse .16 .40
622 Darren Banks .16 1.00
623 Richard Zemlak .10 .25
624 Todd Harkins .06 .15
625 Warren Sharples .06 .15
626 Andrew McKim .16 .40
627 Steve Guenette .10 .25
628 Salt Lake City Golden Eagles TC .02 .05

1991-92 ProCards

This 620-card standard-size set was produced by ProCards and features players from the American, International and Colonial Leagues. Fronts feature a posed color photo enclosed by a white border. The player's name is in black within a gold bar at the top and the team name appears beneath in a yellow bar. The photo appears in a red and black speckled "frame" enclosed by a small blue border. The respective league logo (American Hockey League, Colonial Hockey League, or International Hockey League) appears in the lower right corner. The cards are numbered on the back and checklisted below according to teams as follows: Rochester Americans (1-24), Peoria Rivermen (25-47), Maine Mariners (48-69), Fredericton Canadiens (70-92), Springfield Indians (93-117), Adirondack Red Wings (118-142), Kalamazoo Wings (143-163), Moncton Hawks (164-189), Binghamton Rangers (190-214), Cape Breton Oilers (215-238), Fort Wayne Komets (239-262), Hershey Bears (263-287), Muskegon Lumberjacks (288-310), San Diego Gulls (311-334), St. John's Maple Leafs (335-359), New Haven Nighthawks (360-383), Phoenix Roadrunners (384-407), Utica Devils (408-428), Flint Bulldogs of the Colonial Hockey League (429-451), Capital District Islanders (452-476), Indianapolis Ice (477-504), Kansas City Blades (505-527), Halifax Citadels (528-546), Baltimore Skipjacks (547-573), Salt Lake City Golden Eagles (574-594), and Milwaukee Admirals (595-620). Although the team sets were originally sold with a suggested retail price of 4.00 per team set and packaged individually, they are listed below as one giant set.

COMPLETE SET (620) 40.00 100.00
1 Bill Houlder .16 .40
2 Brian Curran .10 .25
3 Dan Frawley .10 .25
4 Darcy Loewen .10 .25
5 Jiri Sejba .10 .25
6 Lindy Ruff .10 .25
7 Chris Snell .10 .25
8 Bob Corkum .20 .50
9 Dave Baseggio .06 .15
10 Sean O'Donnell .06 .15
11 Brad Rubachuk .06 .15
12 Peter Ciavaglia .10 .25
13 Joel Savage .06 .15
14 Jason Winch .06 .15
15 Steve Ludzik .10 .25
16 Don McSween .10 .25
17 David DaVita .06 .15
18 Greg Brown .10 .25
19 David Littman .20 .50
20 Tom Draper .20 .50
21 Jody Gage .30 1.00
22 Terry Martin .08 .20
23 Don Lever .10 .25
24 Rochester Checklist .02 .05
25 Jason Marshall .10 .25
26 Michel Mongeau .10 .25
27 Derek Frenette .06 .15
28 Kevin Miehm .10 .25
29 Guy Hebert .80 2.00
30 Greg Poss .06 .15
31 Dave Mackey .10 .25
32 Dan Fowler .10 .25
33 Mark Bassen .08 .20
34 Yves Heroux .10 .25
35 Harold Snepsts .40 1.00
36 Bruce Shoebottom .08 .20
37 Jaan Luik .06 .15
38 Alain Raymond .06 .15
39 Kyle Reeves .06 .15
40 Brian McKee .06 .15
41 Steve Tuttle .10 .25
42 Rob Tustian .06 .15
43 Richard Pion .10 .25
44 Joe Hawley .06 .15
45 Brian Pellerin .06 .15
46 Jason Ruff .10 .25
47 Rivermen Checklist .02 .05
48 Wes Walz .30 .75
49 Steve Bancroft .06 .15
50 John Blue .20 .50
51 Rick Allain .06 .15
52 Mike Walsh .10 .25
53 Dave Thomlinson .10 .25
54 Dennis Smith .06 .15
55 Jack Capuano .10 .25
56 Mike Rossetti .06 .15
57 Petr Prajsler .10 .25
58 Matt Glennon .06 .15
59 John Byce .10 .25
60 Howie Rosenblatt .10 .25
61 Brad Tiley .06 .15
62 Lou Crawford .06 .15
63 Matt Hervey .10 .25
64 Peter Douris .10 .25
65 Jeff Lazaro .10 .25
66 David Reid .20 .50
67 E.J. McGuire .06 .15
68 Frank Bathe .08 .20
69 Maine Checklist .02 .05
70 Paul DiPietro .10 .25
71 Darcy Simon .06 .15
72 Patrick Lebeau .20 .50
73 Gilbert Dionne .20 .50
74 John Ferguson .10 .25
75 Norman Desjardins .06 .15
76 Luc Gauthier .08 .20
77 Jean-Claude Bergeron .20 .50
78 Andre Racicot .16 .40
79 Steve Veilleux .06 .15
80 Patrice Brisebois .20 .50
81 Tom Sagissor .06 .15
82 Lindsay Vallis .06 .15
83 Steve Larouche .10 .25
84 Sean Hill .20 .50
85 Jesse Belanger .20 .50
86 Stephane J.G. Richer .06 .15
87 Marc Labelle .06 .15
88 Pierre Sevigny .10 .25
89 Eric Charron .10 .25
90 Ed Ronan .10 .25
91 Paulin Bordeleau .10 .25
92 Fredericton Checklist .02 .05
93 Daryl Reaugh .40 2.00
94 Jergus Baca .10 .25
95 Karl Johnston .06 .15
96 Shawn Evans .06 .15
97 Scott Humeniuk .06 .15
98 Cam Brauer .06 .15
99 Scott Eichstadt .06 .15
100 Paul Cyr .10 .25
101 James Black .10 .25
102 Chris Govedaris .10 .25
103 Joe Day .10 .25
104 Chris Tancill .10 .25
105 Kerry Russell .08 .20
106 Denis Chalifoux .06 .15
107 Blair Atcheynum .10 .25
108 John Stevens .06 .15
109 Brian Chapman .06 .15
110 Chris Bright .06 .15
111 Jim Burke .06 .15
112 Scott Daniels .10 .25
113 Kelly Ens .06 .15
114 Mike Tomlak .10 .25
115 Mario Gosselin .20 .50
116 Jay Leach .06 .15
117 Springfield Checklist .02 .05
118 Allan Bester .20 .50
119 Daniel Shank .20 .50
120 Lonnie Loach .10 .25
121 Mark Reimer .10 .25
122 Kirk Tomlinson .06 .15
123 Stewart Malgunas .10 .25
124 Serge Anglehart .06 .15
125 Chris Luongo .06 .15
126 Keith Primeau 1.20 3.00
127 Ken Quinney .10 .25
128 Dave Flanagan .06 .15
129 Pete Stauber .06 .15
130 Mike Sillinger .20 .50
131 Micah Aivazoff .06 .15
132 Gary Schuchuk .10 .25
133 Bill McDougall .10 .25
134 Sheldon Kennedy .20 .50
135 Derek Mayer .06 .15
136 Darin Bannister .06 .15
137 Guy Dupuis .06 .15
138 Gord Kruppke .20 .50
139 Jason York .20 .50
140 Barry Melrose .40 1.00
141 Glenn Merkosky .10 .25
142 Adirondack Checklist .02 .05
143 Larry Dyck .10 .25
144 Roy Mitchell .06 .15
145 Greg Spenrath .06 .15
146 Steve Herniman .06 .15
147 Brad Berry .10 .25
148 Jim Nesich .06 .15
149 Tim Lenardon .06 .15
150 Steve Guenette .10 .25
151 Paul Jerrard .10 .25
152 Cal McGowan .10 .25
153 Scott Robinson .06 .15
154 Mitch Messier .10 .25
155 Tony Joseph .06 .15
156 Steve Maltais .30 1.00
157 Steve Gotaas .06 .15
158 Doug Barrault .10 .25
159 Dave Moylan .06 .15
160 Mario Thyer .10 .25
161 Bob Hoffmeyer .06 .15
162 Wade Dawson .06 .15
163 Wings Checklist .02 .05
164 Rob Murray .08 .20
165 Chris Kiene .06 .15
166 Lee Davidson .06 .15
167 Rudy Poeschek .20 1.00
168 Kent Paynter .06 .15
169 John LeBlanc .08 .20
170 Dallas Eakins .06 .15
171 Claude Julien .06 .15
172 Bob Joyce .10 .25
173 Derek Langille .06 .15
174 Rob Cowie .10 .25
175 Warren Rychel .20 1.00
176 Tom Karalis .06 .15
177 Kris Draper .40 1.00
178 Ken Gernander .06 .15
179 Tod Hartje .10 .25
180 Sean Gauthier .06 .15
181 Tyler Larter .06 .15
182 Scott Levins .10 .25
183 Jason Cirone .06 .15
184 Mark Kumpel .10 .25
185 Rick Tabaracci .40 1.00
186 Luciano Borsato .10 .25
187 Dave Farrish .10 .25
188 Dave Prior .06 .15
189 Moncton Checklist .02 .05
190 Peter Fiorentino .06 .15
191 Glen Goodall .06 .15
192 John Mokosak .06 .15
193 Sam St.Laurent .20 .50
194 Daniel Lacroix .20 .50
195 Guy Larose .10 .25
196 Mike Hurlbut .10 .25
197 Peter Laviolette .10 .25
198 Eric Bennett .06 .15
199 Steven King .10 .25
200 Boris Rousson .30 1.00
201 Jody Hull .16 .40
202 Shaun Sabol .06 .15
203 Joe Paterson .06 .15
204 Rob Zamuner .30 .75
205 Don Biggs .10 .25
206 Chris Cichocki .08 .20
207 Ross Fitzpatrick .06 .15
208 Mark LaForest .10 .25
209 Brian McReynolds .08 .20
210 Jeff Bloemberg .10 .25
211 Kord Cernich .06 .15
212 Ron Smith .06 .15
213 Al Hill .10 .25
214 Binghamton Checklist .02 .05
215 Francois Leroux .16 .40
216 Marc Laforge .06 .15
217 Max Middendorf .08 .20
218 Shjon Podein .30 .75
219 Jason Soules .06 .15
220 Collin Bauer .06 .15
221 Shaun Van Allen .16 .40
222 Eldon Reddick .20 .50
223 Evgeny Belosheiken .20 .50
224 David Haas .06 .15
225 Norm Foster .20 .50
226 Greg Hawgood .20 .50
227 Steven Rice .16 .40
228 Dan Currie .10 .25
229 Peter Soberlak .06 .15
230 Martin Rucinsky .60 1.00
231 Tomas Kapusta .10 .25
232 Dean Antos .06 .15
233 Craig Fisher .08 .20
234 Tomas Srsen .06 .15
235 Don McAdam .06 .15
236 Norm Ferguson .06 .15
237 Coaching Staff .02 .05
238 Cape Breton Checklist .02 .05
239 Peter Hankinson .06 .15
240 Chris McRae .06 .15
241 Craig Martin .10 .25
242 Carey Lucyk .06 .15
243 Jean-Marc Richard .06 .15
244 Grant Richison .06 .15
245 Mark Turner .06 .15
246 Todd Flichel .06 .15
247 Scott Shaunessy .06 .15
248 Darin Smith .06 .15
249 Ian Boyce .06 .15
250 Colin Chin .08 .20
251 Bob Jones .06 .15
252 Bob Jay .08 .20
253 Kelly Hurd .06 .15
254 Scott Gruhl .30 1.00
255 Kory Kocur .08 .20
256 Steven Fletcher .06 .15
257 Bob Lakso .08 .20
258 Dusty Imoo .20 .50
259 Mike O'Neill .20 .50
260 Bruce Boudreau .20 .50
261 Al Sims .16 .40
262 Komets Checklist .02 .05
263 Ray Letourneau .06 .15
264 Marc D'Amour .20 .50
265 Dominic Roussel .30 .75
266 Bill Armstrong (LW) .08 .20
267 Al Conroy .06 .15
268 Dale Kushner .10 .25
269 Toni Porkka .06 .15
270 Mike Stothers .06 .15
271 Darren Rumble .10 .25
272 Reid Simpson .10 .25
273 Claude Boivin .10 .25
274 Len Barrie .10 .25
275 Chris Jensen .10 .25
276 Pat Murray .10 .25
277 Eric Dandenault .06 .15
278 Rod Dallman .06 .15
279 Mark Freer .10 .25
280 Bill Armstrong (D) .10 .25
281 Tim Tookey .10 .25
282 Jamie Cooke .06 .15
283 Dave Fenyves .10 .25
284 Steve Morrow .06 .15
285 Martin Hostak .10 .25
286 Mike Eaves .10 .25
287 Hershey Checklist .02 .05
288 Dave Michayluk .06 .15
289 Glenn Mulvenna .08 .20
290 Jean Blouin .06 .15
291 Jock Callander .30 1.00
292 Perry Ganchar .06 .15
293 Paul Laus .30 .75
294 Mark Major .06 .15
295 Bruce Racine .20 .50
296 Daniel Gauthier .06 .15
297 Mike Needham .10 .25
298 Jeff Daniels .10 .25
299 Sandy Smith .06 .15
300 Gilbert Delorme .10 .25
301 Rob Dopson .20 .50
302 Eric Brule .06 .15
303 Alain Morissette .06 .15
304 Paul Dyck .06 .15
305 Jason Smart .06 .15
306 Gord Dineen .10 .25
307 Todd Nelson .10 .25
308 Jamie Heward .06 .15
309 Paul Russell .06 .15
310 Lumberjack Checklist .02 .05
311 Soren True .06 .15
312 Murray Duval .06 .15
313 Dmitri Kvartalnov .16 .40
314 Larry Floyd .06 .15
315 Alan Legett .06 .15
316 Alan Hepple .06 .15
317 Ron Duguay .20 .50
318 Len Hachborn .10 .25
319 Steve Martinson .10 .25
320 Rick Knickle .30 .75
321 Darcy Norton .06 .15
322 Keith Gretzky .20 .50
323 Brian Straub .06 .15
324 Denny Lambert .10 .25
325 Jason Prosofsky .10 .25
326 Bruce Hoffort .10 .25
327 Sergei Starikov .08 .20
328 Dave Korol .06 .15
329 Robbie Nichols .06 .15
330 Kord Cernich .06 .15
331 Brent Sapergia .10 .25
332 Don Waddell .06 .15
333 Charlie Simmer .20 .50
334 San Diego Checklist .02 .05
335 Rob Mendel .06 .15
336 Curtis Hunt .06 .15
337 Jeff Serowik .10 .25
338 Bruce Bell .10 .25
339 Yanic Perreault .30 .75
340 Brad Aitken .06 .15
341 Keith Osborne .06 .15
342 Todd Hawkins .06 .15
343 Andrew McKim .10 .25
344 Kevin McClelland .10 .25
345 Mike Stevens .10 .25
346 Dave Tomlinson .10 .25
347 Kevin Maguire .10 .25
348 Mike MacWilliams .06 .15
349 Greg Walters .06 .15
350 Guy Lehoux .06 .15
351 Todd Gillingham .06 .15
352 Len Esau .06 .15
353 Greg Johnston .10 .25
354 Felix Potvin 2.40 5.00
355 Damian Rhodes .40 1.00
356 Joel Quenneville .06 .15
357 Marc Crawford .30 .75
358 Mike Eastwood .10 .25
359 St.Johns Checklist .02 .05
360 Lou Franceschetti .10 .25
361 Bobby Reynolds .06 .15
362 Scott Schneider .06 .15
363 James Bechard .06 .15
364 Mario Doyon .08 .20
365 Jeff Jackson .10 .25
366 John Tanner .10 .25
367 Al Tuer .06 .15
368 Paul Willett .06 .15
369 Darryl Williams .06 .15
370 George Maneluk .10 .25
371 Eric Ricard .06 .15
372 Trevor Stienburg .10 .25
373 Jerry Tarrant .06 .15
374 Michael McEwen .10 .25
375 Brian Dobbin .10 .25
376 David Latta .06 .15
377 Jim Sprott .06 .15
378 Trevor Pochipinski .06 .15
379 Stan Drulia .20 .50
380 Kent Hulst .06 .15
381 Brad Turner .06 .15
382 Doug Carpenter .10 .25
383 New Haven Checklist .02 .05
384 Bob Berg .06 .15
385 Steve Jaques .06 .15
386 Chris Norton .06 .15
387 Vern Smith .06 .15
388 Kevin MacDonald .06 .15
389 Ross Wilson .06 .15
390 Shawn McCosh .06 .15
391 Mike Vukonich .06 .15
392 Marc Saumier .06 .15
393 Mike Ruark .06 .15
394 Kris Miller .06 .15
395 Tim Breslin .06 .15
396 Paul Holden .06 .15
397 Jeff Rohlicek .06 .15
398 Kyosti Karjalainen .10 .25
399 David Goverde .20 .50
400 John Van Kessel .06 .15
401 Sean Whyte .06 .15
402 Brent Thompson .10 .25
403 Darryl Gilmour .20 .50
404 Scott Bjugstad .06 .15
405 Ralph Backstrom .16 .40
406 Rick Kozuback .06 .15
407 Roadrunner Checklist .02 .05
408 Brent Severyn .20 1.00
409 Dean Malkoc .10 .25
410 Matt Ruchty .06 .15
411 Jarrod Skalde .20 .50
412 Brian Sullivan .06 .15
413 Ben Hankinson .10 .25
414 Bill Huard .16 .40
415 Jeff Christian .06 .15
416 Corey Schwab .20 .50
417 Kevin Dean .06 .15
418 Todd Copeland .06 .15
419 Mike Bodnarchuk .06 .15
420 Jason Miller .06 .15
421 Chad Erickson .20 .50
422 David Craievich .06 .15
423 Jim Dowd .20 .50
424 Jamie Huscroft .16 .40
425 Myles O'Connor .10 .25
426 Jon Morris .10 .25
427 Valeri Zelepukin .20 .50
428 Utica Checklist .02 .05
429 Brad Beck .06 .15
430 Brett MacDonald .06 .15
431 Jacques Mailhot .10 .25
432 Francois Ouellette .06 .15
433 Ron Kinghorn .06 .15
434 Dennis Miller .06 .15
435 Darren Miciak .06 .15
436 Tom Sasso .06 .15
437 Peter Corbett .06 .15
438 Brian Horan .06 .15
439 John Messuri .06 .15
440 E.J. Sauer .06 .15
441 Tom Mutch .06 .15
442 Jason Simon .06 .15
443 Steve Sullivan .06 .15
444 Scott Allen .06 .15
445 Stephane Brochu .10 .25
446 Ken Spangler .10 .25
447 Lee Odelein .06 .15
448 Antti Autere .06 .15
449 John Reid .06 .15
450 Skip Probst CO .02 .05
451 Flint Checklist .06 .15
452 Dean Ewen .06 .15
453 Brent Grieve .16 .40
454 Jim Culhane .06 .15
455 Joni Lehto .06 .15
456 Graeme Townshend .10 .25
457 Danny Lorenz .10 .25
458 Phil Huber .06 .15
459 Kevin Cheveldayoff .08 .20
460 Dennis Vaske .16 .40
461 Wayne Doucet .06 .15
462 Greg Parks .08 .20
463 Dean Chynoweth .06 .15
464 Lee Giffin .10 .25
465 Richard Kromm .10 .25
466 Derek Laxdal .10 .25
467 Travis Green .60 1.00
468 Iain Fraser .10 .25
469 Rick Hayward .10 .25
470 Jeff Finley .10 .25
471 Dave Chyzowski .08 .20
472 Mark Fitzpatrick .40 1.00
473 Hubie McDonough .10 .25
474 Sean LeBrun .06 .15
475 Chris Pryor .06 .15
476 Capital District CL .02 .05
477 Jeff Sirkka .06 .15
478 Owen Lessard .06 .15
479 Jim Playfair .06 .15
480 Dan Vincelette .08 .20
481 Tracey Egeland .06 .15
482 Shawn Byram .06 .15
483 Trevor Dam .06 .15
484 Martin Desjardins .06 .15
485 Milan Tichy .10 .25
486 Cam Russell .16 .40
487 Mike Speer .06 .15
488 Sean Williams .06 .15
489 Paul Gillis .10 .25
490 Brad Lauer .10 .25
491 Trent Yawney .16 .40
492 Craig Woodcroft .10 .25
493 Justin LaFayette .06 .15
494 Rob Conn .10 .25
495 Frantisek Kucera .10 .25
496 Mike Peluso .40 1.00
497 Roch Belley .20 .50
498 Ryan McGill .08 .20
499 Kerry Toporowski .10 .25
500 Dominik Hasek 4.00 8.00
501 Adam Bennett .08 .20
502 Ray LeBlanc .20 .50
503 John Marks .08 .20
504 Ice Checklist .02 .05
505 Mikhail Kravets .08 .20
506 Gary Emmons .06 .15
507 Ed Courtenay .10 .25
508 Claudio Scremin .06 .15
509 Jarmo Myllys .40 1.00
510 Mike Colman .06 .15
511 Kevin Evans .10 .25
512 Troy Frederick .06 .15
513 Ron Handy .06 .15
514 Murray Garbutt .06 .15
515 Gordon Frantti .06 .15
516 Dale Craigwell .20 .50
517 Wade Flaherty .30 .75
518 Dean Kolstad .10 .25
519 Rick Lessard .10 .25
520 Craig Coxe .20 1.00
521 Jeff Madill .10 .25
522 Peter Lappin .10 .25
523 Duane Joyce .06 .15
524 Larry DePalma .10 .25
525 Pat MacLeod .10 .25
526 Andy Akervik .06 .15
527 Blades Checklist .02 .05
528 Mike Dagenais .06 .15
529 Gerald Bzdel .06 .15
530 Stephane Fiset .60 1.00
531 David Espe .06 .15
532 Patrick Labrecque .20 .50
533 Niclas Andersson .10 .25
534 Jon Klemm .30 .75
535 Denis Chasse .20 .50
536 Stephane Charbonneau .06 .15
537 Ivan Matulik .06 .15
538 Serge Roberge .06 .15
539 Daniel Dore .06 .15
540 Sergei Kharin .10 .25
541 Jamie Baker .10 .25
542 Ken McRae .10 .25
543 David Marcinyshyn .08 .20
544 Clement Jodoin .06 .15
545 Dean Hopkins .06 .15
546 Checklist .02 .05
547 Jeff Greenlaw .20 .50
548 Byron Dafoe .80 1.00
549 Jim Hrivnak .20 .50
550 Olaf Kolzig 1.20 3.00
551 John Purves .08 .20
552 Bobby Reynolds .06 .15
553 Simon Wheeldon .20 .50
554 Jim Mathieson .20 .50
555 Trevor Halverson .10 .25
556 Steve Seftel .06 .15
557 Ken Lovsin .10 .25

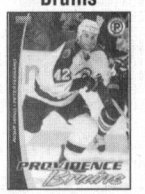

558 Victor Gervais .06 .15
559 Steve Martell .10 .25
560 Chris Clarke .06 .15
561 Brent Hughes .10 .25
562 Jiri Vykoukal .06 .15
563 Tim Taylor .20 .50
564 Richie Walcott .06 .15
565 Harry Mews .06 .15
566 Craig Duncanson .10 .25
567 Todd Hlushko .10 .25
568 Mark Ferner .10 .25
569 Bobby Babcock .08 .20
570 Reggie Savage .10 .25
571 Rob Laird .06 .15
572 Barry Trotz .02 .05
573 Baltimore Checklist .02 .05
574 Kevan Melrose .06 .15
575 Kevin Grant .06 .15
576 Kevan Guy .10 .25
577 Darryl Olsen .06 .15
578 Kevin Worthman .06 .15
579 Darren Stolk .06 .15
580 Bryan Deasley .06 .15
581 Paul Kruse .10 .25
582 Darren Banks .10 1.00
583 Corey Lyons .06 .15
584 Kenny Clark .06 .15
585 Todd Strueby .10 .25
586 Rich Chernomaz .06 .15
587 Tim Harris .06 .15
588 Shawn Heaphy .06 .15
589 Todd Harkins .10 .25
590 Richard Zemlak .10 .25
591 Warren Sharples .10 .25
592 Jason Muzzatti .20 .50
593 Dennis Holland .06 .15
594 Salt Lake City CL .02 .05
595 Shawn Antoski .16 .40
596 Peter Bakovic .06 .15
597 Robin Bawa .08 .20
598 Cam Brown .06 .15
599 Neil Eisenhut .10 .25
600 Jason Herter .08 .20
601 Ian Kidd .06 .15
602 Troy Neumeier .06 .15
603 Carl Valimont .06 .15
604 Phil Von Stefenelli .10 .25
605 Andrew McBain .10 .25
606 Eric Murano .10 .25
607 Rob Murphy .10 .25
608 Brian Blad .06 .15
609 Randy Boyd .06 .15
610 Don Gibson .06 .15
611 Paul Guay .10 .25
612 Jay Mazur .10 .25
613 Jeff Larmer .10 .25
614 Ladislav Tresl .10 .25
615 Dennis Snedden .06 .15
616 Corrie D'Alessio .10 .25
617 Bob Mason .20 .50
618 Jack McIlhargey .10 .25
619 Curt Fraser .10 .25
620 Admirals Checklist .02 .05

1996-97 Providence Bruins

This 25-card set was produced by SplitSecond for sale by the club at the team shop. It was originally offered for sale for $5. The cards feature the standard SplitSecond design. The cards are listed below according to jersey number, which is displayed prominently on the card.

COMPLETE SET (25) 4.00 10.00
2 Mark Cornforth .16 .40
3 Charles Paquette .16 .40
4 John Gruden .16 .40
6 Peter Laviolette .20 .50
8 Jean-Yves Roy .16 .40
9 Justin Gould .16 .40
10 David Emma .16 .40
11 Davis Payne .20 .50
13 Martin Simard .20 .50
14 Kirk Nielsen .16 .40
17 P.C. Drouin .20 .50
18 Jay Moser .16 .40
19 Bill McCauley .16 .40
21 Tim Sweeney LL .16 .40
22 Mitch Lamoureux .20 .50
23 Yevgeny Shaldybin .16 .40
25 Kevin Sawyer .30 .75
27 Brad Konik .16 .40
28 Milt Mastad .16 .40
29 Rob Tallas .30 .75
34 Bob Beers .20 .50
44 Brett Harkins .16 .40
49 Andre Roy .20 .50
NNO AHL Web Site .01
NNO Bob Francis CO .04 .10

1997-98 Providence Bruins

This set features the Bruins of the AHL. The set was produced by the team and sold at home games for $8.

COMPLETE SET (26) 4.80 12.00
1 Rob Tallas .30 .75
2 Elias Abrahamsson .16 .40
3 Bill Armstrong .16 .40
4 Dean Chynoweth .16 .40
5 Aaron Downey .40 1.50
6 Hal Gill .30 .75
7 John Grahame .60 1.50
8 Antti Laaksonen .20 .50
9 Cameron Mann .30 .50
10 Anders Myrvold .20 .50
11 Eric Naud .16 .40
12 Kirk Nielsen .16 .40
13 Charles Paquette .16 .40
14 Joel Prpic .16 .40
15 Barry Richter .20 .50
16 Randy Robitaille .30 .75
17 Jon Rohloff .16 .40
18 Andre Roy .30 .75
19 Jean-Yves Roy .16 .40
20 Yevgeny Shaldybin .16 .40
21 Landon Wilson .30 .50
22 Andrei Yakhanov .16 .40
23 Tom McVie HCO .04 .10
24 Rod Langway ACO .04 .10
25 PHPA Web Site .01
26 AHL Web Site .01

1998-99 Providence Bruins

This set features the Bruins of the AHL. The set was produced by Split Second and sold by the team at its souvenir stands.

COMPLETE SET (25) 4.80 10.00
1 Peter Laviolette CO .20 .50
2 Elias Abrahamsson .16 .40
3 Johnathan Aitken .16 .40
4 Bill Armstrong .16 .40
5 Steve Bancroft .16 .40
6 Shawn Bates .30 .75
7 Jim Carey .30 .75
8 Aaron Downey .60 1.50
9 John Grahame .60 1.50
10 Joe Harney .16 .40
11 Jay Henderson .20 .50
12 Antti Laaksonen .30 .75
13 Cameron Mann .20 .50
14 Marquis Mathieu .20 .50
15 Eric Nickulas .20 .50
16 Peter Nordstrom .16 .40
17 Joel Prpic .16 .40
18 Randy Robitaille .20 .50
19 Andre Savage .30 .75
20 Brandon Smith .20 .50
21 Mattias Timander .16 .40
22 Joel Trottier .16 .40
23 Terry Virtue .20 .50
24 Landon Wilson .40 .50
25 AHL Web Site .01

1999-00 Providence Bruins

This set features the Bruins of the AHL. The set was produced by SplitSecond and was sold by the team at home games.

COMPLETE SET (25) 4.80 12.00
1 Elias Abrahamsson .16 .40
2 Johnathan Aitken .16 .40
3 Shane Belter .16 .40
4 Nick Boynton .40 1.00
5 Jeremy Brown .16 .40
6 Vratislav Cech .16 .40
7 Jassen Cullimore .16 .40
8 Aaron Downey .60 1.50
9 Peter Ferraro .16 .40
10 Maxime Gingras .30 .75
11 John Grahame .60 1.50
12 Jay Henderson .30 .75
13 Joe Hulbig .16 .40
14 Antti Laaksonen .16 .40
15 Tim Lovell .16 .40
16 Cameron Mann .30 .75
17 Marquis Mathieu .20 .50
18 Keith McCambridge .16 .40
19 Eric Nickulas .30 .75
20 Joel Prpic .16 .40
21 Andre Savage .20 .50
22 Brandon Smith .20 .50
23 Denis Timofeev .16 .40
24 Jeff Wells .16 .40
25 Kay Whitmore .20 .50

2000-01 Providence Bruins

This set features the Bruins of the AHL. The set was produced by Choice Marketing and sold by the team at its souvenir stands.

COMPLETE SET (22) 6.00 10.00
1 Kay Whitmore .30 .75
2 Keith McCambridge .20 .50
3 Nick Boynton .40 1.00
4 Eric Manlow .20 .50
5 Zdenek Kutlak .20 .50
6 Cameron Mann .30 .75
7 Eric Nickulas .30 .50
8 Pavel Kolarik .20 .50
9 Jay Henderson .20 .50
10 Lee Goren .40 .75
11 Peter Vandermeer .20 .75
12 Marquis Mathieu .30 .50
13 Ivan Huml .60 1.00
14 Terry Hollinger .20 .50
15 Elias Abrahamsson .20 .50
16 Jeremy Brown .20 .50
17 Brandon Smith .20 .50
18 Mattias Karlin .30 .50
19 Jon Coleman .20 .50
20 Jonathan Girard .40 1.00
21 Peter Ferraro .20 .50
22 Kay Whitmore .30 .75
NNO Team CL .10 .01

2001-02 Providence Bruins

This set features the Bruins of the AHL. The 21-card set was produced by Choice Marketing and sold by the team at its souvenir shop. It is known that 1,000 of these sets were produced.

COMPLETE SET (21) 4.80 12.00
1 Andrew Raycroft .40 1.00
2 Jeff Maund .20 .50
3 Keith McCambridge .14 .35
4 Bobby Allen .14 .35
5 Chris Kelleher .14 .35
6 Eric Manlow .14 .35
7 Zdenek Kutlak .20 .50
8 Tony Tuzzolino .20 .50
9 Pavel Kolarik .14 .35
10 Lee Goren .40 1.00
11 John Emmons .14 .35
12 Andy Hilbert .60 1.50
13 Joe Hulbig .14 .35
14 Carl Corazzini .14 .35
15 Ivan Huml .40 1.00
16 Sean Haggerty .14 .35
17 Dennis Bonvie .20 .50
18 Mattias Karlin .20 .50
19 Martin Wilde .14 .35
20 Greg Crozier .20 .50
21 Jonathan Girard .40 1.00
NNO Title Card/CL .04 .10

2002-03 Providence Bruins

COMPLETE SET (21) 5.00 12.00
1 Andrew Raycroft .75 2.00
2 Kevin Dallman .20 .50
3 Chris Kelleher .20 .50
4 Keith Aucoin .20 .50
5 Rich Brennan .20 .50
6 Zdenek Kutlak .20 .50
7 Matt Herr .20 .50
8 Martin Samuelsson .40 1.00
9 Kris Vernarsky .30 .75
10 Jay Henderson .20 .50
11 Chris Paradise .20 .50
12 Andy Hilbert .30 .75
13 Shaone Morrisonn .40 1.00
14 Darren Van Oene .20 .50
15 Peter Metcalf .20 .50
16 Lee Goren .30 .75
17 Mike Gellard .20 .50
18 Brantt Myhres .20 .50
19 Pat Leahy .30 .75
20 Tim Thomas .75 2.00
NNO Checklist .01 .05

2003-04 Providence Bruins

This set was produced by Choice Marketing and sold at home games.

COMPLETE SET (24) 5.00 12.00
1 Rich Brennan .15 .40
2 Ed Campbell .15 .40
3 Carl Corazzini .15 .40
4 Kevin Dallman .15 .40
5 Mike Gellard .15 .40
6 Matt Herr .15 .40
7 Andy Hilbert .30 .75
8 Ivan Huml .15 .40
9 Milan Jurcina .30 .75
10 Zdenek Kutlak .15 .40
11 Pat Leahy .30 .75
12 Robert Liscak .15 .40
13 Peter Metcalf .15 .40
14 Brett Nowak .15 .40
15 Colton Orr .40 1.00
16 Martin Samuelsson .15 .40
17 Andre Savage .15 .40
18 Tim Thomas .60 1.50
19 Hannu Toivonen 1.25 3.00
20 Darren Van Oene .15 .40
21 Kris Vernarsky .15 .40
22 Brendan Walsh .15 .40
23 Brian White .15 .40
24 Martin Wilde .15 .40
NNO Checklist .01 .05

2004-05 Providence Bruins

This set was sold by the team at home games.

COMPLETE SET (25) 5.00 12.00
1 Pat Aufiero .20 .50
2 Patrice Bergeron .60 1.50
3 Brad Boyes .40 1.00
4 Carl Corazzini .20 .50
5 Kevin Dallman .20 .50
6 Chris Dyment .20 .50
7 Jayme Filipowicz .20 .50
8 David Gove .20 .50
9 Ben Guite .20 .50
10 Jay Henderson .20 .50
11 Andy Hilbert .20 .50
12 Milan Jurcina .20 .50
13 Pat Leahy .20 .50
14 Steve Munn .20 .50
15 Colton Orr .40 1.00
16 Martin Samuelsson .20 .50
17 Brent Thompson .20 .50
18 Yorick Treille .20 .50
19 Kris Vernarsky .20 .50
20 Brendan Walsh .20 .50
21 Peter Hamerlik .30 .75
22 Hannu Toivonen .75 2.00
23 Scott Gordon CO .02 .10
24 Rob Murray ACO .02 .10
25 Checklist .02 .10

2005-06 Providence Bruins

COMPLETE SET (25) 6.00 15.00
1 Zdenek Blatny .20 .50
2 Sean Curry .20 .50
3 Chris Dyment .20 .50
4 Scott Ford .30 .75
5 Ben Guite .20 .50
6 Eric Healey .20 .50
7 Jay Leach .20 .50
8 David Lundbohm .20 .50
9 Jason MacDonald .20 .50
10 Eric Nickulas .20 .50
11 Pascal Pelletier .30 .75
12 Tyler Redenbach .20 .50
13 Jeremy Reich .20 .50
14 Nathan Robinson .40 1.00
15 Michael Schutte .20 .50
16 Jonathan Sigalet .40 1.00
17 Jordan Sigalet .75 2.00
18 Garret Stroshein .40 1.00
19 Mark Stuart .40 1.00
20 Tim Thomas .60 1.50
21 Nate Thompson .20 .50
22 Ben Walter .20 .50
23 Scott Gordon HC .02 .10
24 Rob Murray AC .02 .10
NNO Providence Bruins CL .02 .10

2006-07 Providence Bruins

COMPLETE SET (25) 8.00 15.00
1 Bobby Allen .20 .50
2 Chris Collins .30 .75
3 Sean Curry .20 .50
4 Nathan Dempsey .20 .50
5 Nate DiCasmirro .20 .50
6 Brian Finley .30 .75
7 Petr Kalus .30 .75
8 Martin Karsums .20 .50
9 David Krejci .30 .75
10 Matt Lashoff .30 .75
11 Jay Leach .20 .50
12 Dennis Packard .20 .50
13 Pascal Pelletier .20 .50
14 Wacey Rabbit .60 1.50
15 Jeremy Reich .30 .75
16 Jonathan Sigalet .40 1.00
17 Jordan Sigalet .75 2.00
18 Yan Stastny .20 .50
19 Mark Stuart .40 1.00
20 Philippe Sauve .30 .75
21 Nate Thompson .30 .75
22 T.J. Trevelyan .40 1.00
23 Kris Versteeg .20 .50
24 Ben Walter .20 .50
25 Dwayne Zinger .20 .50

1936-37 Providence Reds

Printed on thin card stock, this 10-card set measures approximately 2 1/4" by 3 1/2". The fronts feature black-and-white player photos bordered in white. The player's name and position are printed beneath the picture, along with the statement "A New 'Reds' Picture Every Amateur Hockey Night". Unlike the other nine cards, the name of the player on card 10 is not printed beneath his picture. From his facsimile autograph on the picture, his first name may be "Jacques," but his last name remains unidentified. The backs are blank. The cards are unnumbered and checklisted below in alphabetical order.

COMPLETE SET (10) 200.00 400.00
1 Bobby Bauer 37.50 75.00
2 Paddy Byrne 12.50 25.00
3 Woody Dumart 37.50 75.00
4 Jackie Keating 12.50 25.00
5 Art Lesieur 12.50 25.00
6 Bert McInenly 12.50 25.00
7 Gus Rivers 12.50 25.00
8 Milt Schmidt 75.00 150.00
9 Jerry Shannon 12.50 25.00
10 Player Unidentified 12.50 25.00

1999 QMJHL All-Star Game Program Inserts

We are attempting to compile this checklist with the help of readers. If you have any cards from this set, please send the name, number and scan (if possible) to hockeymag@beckett.com.

COMPLETE SET (?)
1 Samuel St. Pierre

2000 QMJHL All-Star Program Inserts

These oversized cards were issued as perforated inserts inside the 2000 QMJHL All-Star Game program.

COMPLETE SET (46) 20.00 50.00
1 Guy Chouinard CO .20 .50
2 Maxime Ouellet .60 1.50
3 Sebastien Caron .75 2.00
4 Joe Rullier .40 1.00
5 Marc-Andre Bergeron .75 2.00
6 Chris Lyness .40 1.00
7 Jonathan Gautier .40 1.00
8 Francois Beauchemin 1.25 3.00
9 Michel Periard .40 1.00
10 Mike Ribeiro .75 2.00
11 Wesley Scanzano .40 1.00
12 Jonathan Roy .40 1.00
13 Carl Malette .40 1.00
14 Ramzi Abid .40 1.00
15 Simon Gamache .40 1.00
16 Marco Charpentier .40 1.00
17 Marc-Andre Thinel .40 1.00
18 Jerome Tremblay .40 1.00
19 Brandon Reid .75 2.00
20 Benoit Dusablon .40 1.00
21 Eric Chouinard .40 1.00
22 Claude Julien CO .40 1.00
23 Alexei Volkov .40 1.00
24 Drew MacIntyre .40 1.00
25 Joey DiPenta .75 2.00
26 Kirill Safronov .40 1.00
27 Alexander Riazantsev .40 1.00
28 Daniel MacLeod .40 1.00
29 Roustam Bakhriddinov .40 1.00
30 Adam Rivet .40 1.00
31 Miroslav Zalesak .40 1.00
32 Edo Terglav .40 1.00
33 Maxim Potapov .40 1.00
34 Thatcher Bell .40 1.00
35 Radim Vrbata 1.25 3.00
36 Jan-Philippe Cadieux .40 1.00
37 Dmitri Afanassenkov .40 1.00
38 Michael Ryder 2.00 5.00
39 Artem Rybin .40 1.00
40 Andrei Shefer .40 1.00
41 Brad Richards 4.00 10.00
42 Juraj Kolnik .40 1.00
43 Danny Bowie .40 1.00
44 All-Star Game Logo .02 .10
45 Team World Logo .02 .10
46 Team Quebec Logo .02 .10

1996-97 Quad-City Mallards

This 22-card set is circular in design. It was initially released as a giveaway only promotion with two cards inserted in Whitey's Ice Cream Bars, and other cards handed out at the games. Later in the season the entire set was sold at Whitey's.

COMPLETE SET (22) 8.00 20.00
1 Todd Newton .40 1.00
2 Brad Barton .40 1.00
3 Travis Tucker .40 1.00
4 Stephen Sangermano .40 1.00
5 Dave Larson .40 1.00
6 Jim Ensom .40 1.00
7 Justin McHugh .40 1.00
8 Fredrick Nasvall .40 1.00
9 Hugo Proulx .40 1.00
10 Carl LeBlanc .40 1.00
11 Glenn Stewart .40 1.00
12 Brett Strot .40 1.00
13 Andy Faulkner .40 1.00
14 Mark McFarlane .40 1.00
15 Howie Rosenblatt .60 1.50
16 Rick Emmett .40 1.00
17 Sergei Zvyagin .40 1.00
18 David Fletcher .40 1.00
19 John Batten .40 1.00
20 John Anderson HCO .40 1.00
21 Matt Shaw ACO .40 1.00
22 Mo Mallard Mascot .20 .50

1997-98 Quad-City Mallards

This set features the Mallards of the UHL. The cards were produced by Roox, and sold by the team at its souvenir stands.

COMPLETE SET (23) 4.80 12.00
1 Glenn Stewart .20 .50
2 Rick Emmett .20 .50
3 Sergei Zvyagin .20 .50
4 Howie Rosenblatt .30 .75
5 Brad Barton .20 .50
6 Kirk Llano .20 .50
7 Wayne Muir .30 .75
8 Hugo Proulx .20 .50
9 Mark McFarlane .20 .50
10 Steve Chelios .30 .75
11 Travis Tucker .20 .50
12 Carl LeBlanc .20 .50
13 Stas Tkatch .20 .50
14 Andy Faulkner .20 .50
15 Steve Gibson .20 .50
16 Tom Perry .20 .50
17 Matt Mullin .30 .75
18 Bogdan Rudenko .30 .75
19 Ryan Gelinas .30 .75
20 Jim Brown .20 .50
21 Kerry Toporowski .30 .75
22 Corey Neilson .20 .50
23 Quad City Mallards CL .04 .10

1998-99 Quad-City Mallards

This set features the Mallards of the UHL. The set was produced by Roox and was sold by the team at home games.

COMPLETE SET (24) 4.00 10.00
1 Sergei Zvyagin .20 .50
2 Brendan Brooks .20 .50
3 Scott Burfoot .04 .10
4 Matt Carey .20 .50
5 Rick Emmett .20 .50
6 Martin Fillion .20 .50
7 Rusty Fitzgerald .20 .50
8 Chad Ford .20 .50
9 Robert Frid .20 .50
10 Steve Gibson .20 .50
11 Garry Gulash .20 .50
12 Kevin Kerr .30 .75
13 Brian LaFleur .20 .50
14 Carl LeBlanc .30 .75
15 Mark McFarlane .20 .50
16 Stephanie Madore .20 .50
17 Mike Melas .20 .50
18 Hugo Proulx .20 .50
19 Bruce Richardson .20 .50
20 Howie Rosenblatt .30 .75
21 Scott Thompson .20 .50
22 Bill Weir .20 .50
23 Glenn Stewart .20 .50
24 Team CL .04 .10

1999-00 Quad-City Mallards

This set features the Mallards of the UHL. The set was produced by Roox and sold at home games. There are two number one cards in the set.

COMPLETE SET (24) 4.00 10.00
1 Iannique Renaud .20 .50
1 Moe Mallard MAS .04 .10
2 Yannick Latour .20 .50
3 Steve Gibson .20 .50
4 Garry Gulash .20 .50
5 Mike Melas .20 .50
6 Rick Emmett .20 .50
7 Ryan Lindsay .20 .50
8 Patrick Nadeau .20 .50
9 Hugo Proulx .20 .50
10 Paul Johnson .20 .50
11 Brendan Buckley .20 .50
12 Martin Hlinka .20 .50
13 Brendan Brooks .20 .50
14 Rusty Fitzgerald .20 .50
15 Kelly Hultgren .20 .50
16 Mark McFarlane .20 .50
17 Glenn Stewart .20 .50
18 Martin Villeneuve .30 .75
19 Brian LaFleur .20 .50
20 Robert DeCiantis .20 .50
21 Kevin Kerr .30 .75
22 Scott Buhler .30 .75
24 Quad City Mallards CL .04 .10

2000-01 Quad-City Mallards

This set features the Mallards of the UHL. The cards were produced by Roox and sold by the team at its souvenir stands.

COMPLETE SET (27) 4.00 10.00
1 Team CL .04 .01
2 Andy Fermoyle .16 .40
3 Garry Gulash .16 .40
4 Frederick Jobin .16 .40
5 Vlad Serov .16 .40
6 Dan Bjornlie .16 .40
7 Peter Armbrust .16 .40
8 Patrick Nadeau .16 .40
9 Ryan Lindsay .16 .40
10 Jason Ulmer .16 .40
11 Hugo Proulx .16 .40
12 Mike Sim .16 .40
13 Chad Power .16 .40
14 Paul Johnson .16 .40
15 Kelly Perrault .16 .40
16 Mark McFarlane .16 .40
17 Etienne Drapeau .20 .50
18 Martin Hlinka .16 .40
19 Rick Emmett .20 .50
20 Martin Villeneuve .16 .40
21 Scott Myers .16 .40
22 Cam Severson .16 .75
23 Steve Gibson .16 .40
24 Kerry Toporowski .20 .50
25 Paul MacLean CO .10 .25
26 Mo Mallard MASCOT .04 .10
27 Ima Duck MASCOT .04 .10

2001-02 Quad-City Mallards

This set features the Mallards of the UHL. The set was sold by the team at home games. The cards are unnumbered and so are listed below in alphabetical order.

COMPLETE SET (24) 4.80 12.00
1 Peter Armbrust .20 .50
2 Dan Bjornlie .20 .50
3 Keli Corpse .30 .75
4 Joe Dimaline .20 .50
5 Andy Fermoyle .20 .50
6 Nick Ganga .20 .50
7 Steve Gibson .30 .75
8 Garry Gulash .20 .50
9 Frederick Jobin .20 .50
10 Kyle Kidney .20 .50
11 Sanny Lindstrom .20 .50
12 Brian McCullough .20 .50
13 Mark McFarlane .20 .50
14 Paul MacLean CO .20 .50
15 Dylan Mills .20 .50
16 Aaron Miskovich .30 .75
17 Patrick Nadeau .20 .50
18 Brant Nicklin .20 .50
19 Hugo Proulx .30 .75
20 Jesse Rooney .20 .50
21 Brandon Sampair .20 .50
22 Kerry Toporowski .30 .75
23 Jason Ulmer .30 .75
24 Mo and Ima MASCOTS .04 .10

2005-06 Quad City Mallards

COMPLETE SET (25) 6.00 12.00
1 Anthony Blumer .20 .50
2 Tom Clayton .20 .50
3 Glenn Detulleo .20 .50
4 Terry Friesen .40 1.00
5 Tom Galvin .20 .50
6 Jason Jaworski .20 .50
7 Andrei Lupandin .20 .50
8 Rafal Martynowski .20 .50
9 Patrick Nadeau .20 .50
10 Samy Nasreddine .40 1.00
11 Mike Olynyk .20 .50
12 Joe Pace .20 .50
13 Joel Pullman .20 .50
14 Matt Radoslovich .20 .50
15 Jesse Rycroft .20 .50
16 Jason Tapp .40 1.00
17 Jonathan Tremblay .20 .50
18 Noah Whyte .20 .50
19 Chad Wollard .20 .50
20 J. J. Wrobel .20 .50
21 Jami Yoder .20 .50
22 Brian Curran CO .02 .10
23 Larry Easter TR .02 .10
24 Jason Rivera TR .02 .10
25 Aaron Roof ANN .02 .10

2006-07 Quad City Mallards

COMPLETE SET (20) 12.00 20.00
1 Justin Chwedoruk .40 1.00
2 Brian Curran CO .20 .50
3 Brent Currie .75 2.00
4 Sergei Durdin .40 1.00
5 Travis Granbois .40 1.00
6 Nick Harloff .40 1.00
7 Andrei Lupandin .40 1.00
8 Patrick Nadeau .40 1.00
9 Don Parsons .40 1.00
10 Jeff Petruic .40 1.00
11 Brett Pilkington .40 1.00
12 Matt Radoslovich .40 1.00
13 Zach Sikich .60 1.50
14 Sean Starke .40 1.00
15 Luke Stauffacher .75 2.00
16 Blake Stewart .40 1.00
17 Jason Tapp .75 2.00
18 Mathieu Wathier .40 1.00
19 Chad Woollard .40 1.00
20 Jami Yoder .40 1.00

1956-57 Quebec Aces

The set was also issued on a limited basis as a factory set in a black presentation box. This 15-card set measures approximately 5" by 7" and features black-and-white posed action player photos with a white border. The player's name is inscribed across the lower portion of the photo. On a white background, the backs carry the sponsor (Maurice Pollack Limitee) and team logos. The cards are unnumbered and checklisted below in alphabetical order.

COMPLETE SET (16) 75.00 150.00
1 Gene Achtynichuk 3.00 6.00
2 Bob Beckett 6.00 12.00
3 Marcel Bonin 7.50 15.00
4 Joe Crozier 10.00 20.00
5 Jacque Gagne 3.00 6.00
6 Dick Garnelle 3.00 6.00
7 Floyd Hillman 6.00 12.00
8 Jean Paul Lamonde 3.00 6.00
9 Jean-Marie Loisette 3.00 6.00
10 Brent MacNab 3.00 6.00
11 Al Millar 3.00 6.00
12 Willie O'Ree 15.00 30.00
13 Nick Tabuchie 3.00 6.00
14 Skip Teal 3.00 6.00
15 Orval Tessier 7.50 15.00
16 Ludger Tremblay 5.00 10.00

1962-63 Quebec Aces

This 21-card set features the Quebec Aces of the Quebec Senior Hockey League. The cards measure approximately 3 1/2" by 5 1/2" and have black and white posed action photos with white borders. The player's name is printed in black at the bottom. The backs are blank. The cards are unnumbered and checklisted below in alphabetical order. The existence of a corrected version of the Bill Dineen card recently has been confirmed. The set is considered complete with either version.

COMPLETE SET (21) 50.00 100.00
1 Ronald Attwell 2.00 4.00
2 Serge Aubry 3.00 6.00
3 Guy Black 2.00 4.00
4 Skippy Burchell 2.00 4.00
5 Jean Marie Cossette 2.00 4.00
6 Robert Courcy 2.00 4.00
7A Bill Dineen ERR 6.00 12.00
(Misspelled Dinenn)
7B Bill Dineen COR 7.50 15.00
8 Terry Gray 5.00 10.00
9 Reggie Grigg 2.00 4.00
10 John Hanna 2.00 4.00
11 Michel Harvey 2.00 4.00
12 Charlie Hodge 12.50 25.00
13 Ed Hoekstra 3.00 6.00
14 Michel Labadie 2.00 4.00
15 Claude Labrosse 2.00 4.00
16 Danny Lewicki 4.00 8.00
17 Frank Martin 2.00 4.00
18 Jim Morrison 3.00 6.00
19 Guy Rousseau 2.00 4.00
20 Dollard St. Laurent 5.00 10.00
21 Bill Sutherland 3.00 6.00

1963-64 Quebec Aces

This 23-card set features the Quebec Aces of the Quebec Senior Hockey League. The cards measure approximately 3 1/2" by 5 1/2" and have black and white posed action photos with white borders. The player's name is printed in black at the bottom. The backs are blank. The cards are unnumbered and checklisted below in alphabetical order.

COMPLETE SET (23) 75.00 150.00
1 Gilles Banville 1.50 3.00
2 Don Blackburn 1.50 3.00
3 Skippy Burchell 1.50 3.00
4 Billy Carter 1.50 3.00
5 Floyd Curry CO 5.00 10.00
6 Bill Dineen 5.00 10.00
7 Wayne Freitag 1.50 3.00
8 Jean Gauthier 1.50 3.00
9 Terry Gray 2.50 5.00
10 John Hanna 1.50 3.00
11 Doug Harvey 15.00 30.00
12 Wayne Hicks 1.50 3.00
13 Charlie Hodge 7.50 15.00
(Standing before net)
14 Charlie Hodge 7.50 15.00
(Spread out before net in defensive posture)
15 Ed Hoekstra 2.50 5.00
16 Frank Martin 1.50 3.00
17 Rene LaCasse 1.50 3.00
18 Cleland Mortson 1.50 3.00
19 Gerry O'Drowski 2.50 5.00
20 Rino Robazzo 2.50 5.00
21 Leon Rochefort 1.50 3.00
22 Cliff Pennington 2.50 5.00
23 Lorne Worsley 17.50 35.00

1964-65 Quebec Aces

This 19-card set features the Quebec Aces of the Quebec Senior Hockey League. The cards measure approximately 3 1/2" by 5 1/2". The fronts have posed black-and-white player photos with white borders. The player's name is printed in black at the bottom. The backs are blank. The cards are unnumbered and checklisted below in alphabetical order.

COMPLETE SET (19) 62.50 125.00
1 Gilles Banville 1.50 3.00
2 Red Berenson 5.00 10.00
3 Don Blackburn 1.50 3.00
4 Jean Guy Gendron 4.00 8.00
5 Bernard Geoffrion 15.00 30.00
6 Terry Gray 4.00 8.00
7 John Hanna 1.50 3.00
8 Doug Harvey 12.50 25.00
9 Wayne Hicks 1.50 3.00
10 Edward Hoekstra 2.50 5.00
11 Rene Lacasse 1.50 3.00
12 Raymond Larose 1.50 3.00
13 Jimmy Morrison 2.50 5.00
14 Cleland Mortson 1.50 3.00
15 Leon Rochefort 4.00 8.00
16 Guy Rousseau 1.50 3.00
17 Bill Sutherland 2.00 4.00
18 Brian Watson 2.00 4.00
19 Lorne Worsley 12.50 25.00

1965-66 Quebec Aces

This 19-card set measures 3 1/2" by 5 1/2". The fronts feature white-bordered posed action shots. The player's name is printed in the wider white border at the bottom. The backs are blank. The cards are unnumbered and checklisted below in alphabetical order.

COMPLETE SET (19) 37.50 75.00
1 Gilles Banville 1.50 3.00
2 Gary Bauman 1.50 3.00
3 Don Blackburn 1.50 3.00
4 Jean-Guy Gendron 2.50 5.00
5 Bernard Geoffrion CO 12.50 25.00
6 Terry Gray 2.50 5.00
7 John Hanna 1.50 3.00
8 Wayne Hicks 1.50 3.00
9 Ed Hoekstra 2.50 5.00
10 Don Johns 1.50 3.00
11 Gordon Labossiere 2.50 5.00
12 Yvon Lacoste 1.50 3.00
13 Jimmy Morrison 2.50 5.00
14 Cleland Mortson 1.50 3.00
15 Simon Nolet 4.00 8.00
16 Noel Price 2.50 5.00
17 Rino Robazzo 2.50 5.00
18 Leon Rochefort 2.50 5.00
19 Bill Sutherland 2.00 4.00

1950 Quebec Citadelles

These 20 blank-backed photos of the Quebec Citadelles measure 4" by 6" and feature cream-bordered sepia tones of the suited-up players posed on the ice. The players' facsimile autographs appear near the bottom of the pictures. The photos are unnumbered and checklisted below in alphabetical order. Blue-tinted variations of these cards exist. More difficult to locate, they command a premium of up to two times. This set includes the earliest known card-like element of all-time great, Jean Beliveau.

COMPLETE SET (20) 200.00 400.00
1 Neil Amadio 5.00 10.00
2 Jean Beliveau 125.00 250.00
3 Georges Bergeron CO 4.00 8.00
4 Bruce Cline 6.00 12.00
5 Norm Diviney 4.00 8.00
6 Guy Gervais 4.00 8.00
7 Bernard Guay 4.00 8.00
8 Gord Haworth 5.00 10.00
9 Camille Henry 12.50 25.00
10 Gordie Hudson 4.00 8.00
11 Claude Larochelle 6.00 12.00
12 Bernie Lemonde 4.00 8.00
13 Paul-Emile Legault 4.00 8.00
14 Copper Leyte 4.00 8.00
15 Rainer Makila 5.00 10.00
16 Marcel Paille 12.50 25.00
17 Jean-Marie Plante 4.00 8.00
18 Claude Senechal 4.00 8.00
19 Jean Tremblay 12.50 25.00
20 Alphonses Gagnon CO 4.00 8.00

1999-00 Quebec Citadelles

This set features the Citadelles of the AHL. The set was produced by card shop CTM-Ste-Foy and was sold at that store and home games as well.

COMPLETE SET (26) 4.80 12.00
1 Mike McBain .16 .40
2 Gennady Razin .16 .40
3 Chris Albert .16 .40
4 Xavier Delisle .16 .40
5 Darcy Harris .16 .40
6 Marc Beaucage .16 .40
7 Stephane Robidas .16 .40
8 Jason Ward .30 .75
9 Francois Groleau .16 .40
10 Jonathan Delisle .16 .40
11 Stephane Roy .16 .40
12 Patrice Tardif .30 .75
13 Pierre Sevigny .30 .75
14 Jesse Belanger .16 .40
15 Eric Fichaud .30 .75
16 Andre Bashkirov .16 .40
17 Mathieu Garon .60 1.50
18 Dave Morissette .16 .40
19 Miloslav Guren .16 .40
20 Matthieu Descoteaux .16 .40
21 Jeff Shevalier .16 .40
22 Josh DeWolf .16 .40
23 Boyd Olson .16 .40
24 Matt Higgins .16 .40
25 Arron Asham .20 .50
NNO Quebec Citadelles .10 .25

2000-01 Quebec Citadelles

This set features the Citadelles of the AHL. The cards were produced by CTM-Ste-Foy and sold by that card shop, as well as by the team.

COMPLETE SET (24) 6.00 15.00
1 Gennady Razin .20 .50
2 Eric Chouinard .60 1.00
3 Francois Beauchemin .20 .50
4 Xavier Delisle .20 .50
5 Marc Beaucage .20 .50
6 Jason Ward .30 .75
7 Matt Higgins .20 .50
8 Mike McBain .20 .50
9 Miloslav Guren .20 .50
10 Pierre Sevigny .20 .50
11 Michael Ryder .30 2.00
12 Jonathan Delisle .20 .50
13 Eric Fichaud .30 .75
14 Andrei Bashkirov .30 .75
15 Mathieu Garon .60 1.50
16 Matt O'Dette .20 .50
17 Mathieu Raby .20 .50
18 Barry Richter .20 .50
19 Matthieu Descoteaux .20 .50
20 Josh DeWolf .20 .50
21 Eric Bertrand .20 .50
22 Arron Asham .30 .75
23 Mike Ribeiro .40 1.00
NNO Team CL .10 .01

2000-01 Quebec Citadelles Signed

This set is exactly the same as the base Citadelles set from this season, save that every card has been hand signed by the player pictured. Each card also is serial numbered out of just 100. The team CL is not signed.

COMPLETE SET (24) 30.00 75.00
1 Gennady Razin 1.20 3.00
2 Eric Chouinard 4.00 10.00
3 Francois Beauchemin 1.20 3.00
4 Xavier Delisle 1.20 3.00
5 Marc Beaucage 1.20 3.00
6 Jason Ward 2.00 5.00
7 Matt Higgins 1.20 3.00
8 Mike McBain 1.20 3.00
9 Miloslav Guren 1.20 3.00
10 Pierre Sevigny 1.20 3.00
11 Michael Ryder 2.00 20.00
12 Jonathan Delisle 1.20 3.00
13 Eric Fichaud 1.20 3.00
14 Andrei Bashkirov 1.20 3.00
15 Mathieu Garon 6.00 15.00
16 Matt O'Dette 1.20 3.00
17 Mathieu Raby 1.20 3.00
18 Barry Richter 1.20 3.00
19 Matthieu Descoteaux 1.20 3.00
20 Josh DeWolf 1.20 3.00
21 Eric Bertrand 1.20 3.00
22 Arron Asham 1.20 3.00
23 Mike Ribeiro 4.00 10.00
NNO Team CL .10 .25

2001-02 Quebec Citadelles

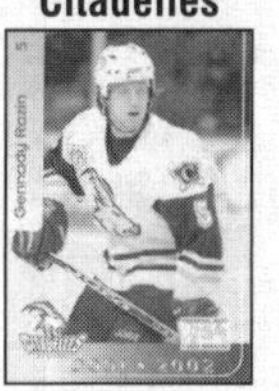

This set features the Citadelles of the AHL. The set was produced by CTM Ste-Foy and was sold at home games. Production of the set was limited to 1,000 copies.

COMPLETE SET (28) 8.00 20.00
1 Gennady Razin .20 .50
2 Eric Chouinard .30 .75
3 Eric Landry .20 .50
4 Ron Hainsey .60 1.50
5 Jason Ward .20 .50
6 Craig Darby .20 .50
7 Marc-Andre Thinel .30 .75
8 Martti Jarventie .30 .75
9 Francois Bouillon .30 .75
10 Francis Belanger .20 .50
11 Francois Beauchemin .20 .50
12 Pierre Sevigny .20 .50
13 Michael Ryder .40 1.00
14 Jonathan Delisle .20 .50
15 Vadim Tarasov .60 1.50
16 Mathieu Garon .40 1.00
17 Matt O'Dette .20 .50
18 Luc Belanger .30 .75
19 Jayme Filipowicz .20 .50
20 Mathieu Descoteaux .20 .50
21 Benoit Gratton .20 .50
22 Timo Vertala .20 .50
23 Arron Asham .20 .50
24 Andrei Markov .20 .50
25 Xavier Delisle .20 .50
26 Mike Ribeiro .30 .75
27 Manuel Hossa 1.60 4.00
28 Title Card/CL .04 .10

1992 Quebec Pee-Wee Tournament

This set features the best 12 and 13-year-old teams in the world that participated in the annual Quebec Pee-Wee Tournament. Though there are more than 1,900 cards in the set, we list only those players that might be familiar to the average collector.

COMPLETE SET (1903) 50.00 125.00
COMMON CARD (1-1903) .02 .05
495 Daniel Tkaczuk .75 2.00
560 J-P Dumont 1.25 3.00
777 J.F. Damphousse .75 2.00
836 Steve Begin .75 2.00
1002 Bobby Allen .75 2.00
1120 Chris Bala .75 2.00
1403 David Aebischer 2.00 5.00
1464 Dainius Zubrus .40 1.00
1576 Mike York 1.25 3.00
17241 Robert Dome .40 1.00
1776 Sergei Samsonov 4.00 10.00

1993 Quebec Pee-Wee Tournament

This 1808-card set measures the standard size (2 1/2" by 3 1/2") and features posed, color player photos of participants at the Quebec International Pee-Wee Tournament. The pictures are framed by a wide stripe that is purple at the top and blends to a pinkish-purple shade toward the bottom. The player's name is printed in white in the purple border above the photo, while the team name is printed below. The player's country is printed on both sides of the photo. The backs have the same purple color scheme and carry a small, close-up photo along with biographical information and the appropriate national flag. The series was available only as one giant set boxes in acrylic, making singles somewhat difficult to acquire. Because of the vast numbers of players never to be heard from again, we only list players of some note in the book. Card numbers 1446, 1499, 1570, 1736, 1738, 1741, 1744, 1746, 1747, 1757, 1780, 1807 are missing. Card 1758 Donald Pierce is listed as 1757 on the checklist card.

COMPLETE SET (1808) 80.00 200.00
COMMON CARD (1-1808) .02 .05
15 Sebastien Caron 1.25 3.00
30 Wesley Scanzano .20 .50
116 Eric Chouinard .75 2.00
227 Eric Lecompte .20 .50
228 Simon Roy .10 .25
272 Simon Lajeunesse 1.25 3.00
301 Frederic Brindamour .40 1.00
342 Simon Gagne 10.00 25.00
346 Carl Menard .10 .25
348 Jean-Francois Damphousse 1.25 3.00
349 Benoit Dusablon .40 1.00
432 Sebastien Caron 1.25 3.00
523 Alex Tanguay 8.00 20.00
538 Sylvain Plamondon .10 .25
554 Jay Legault .40 1.00
562 Daniel Tkaczuk .75 2.00
565 Peter Sarno .40 1.00
597 Paul Mara 1.25 3.00
664 Tim Connolly 1.25 3.00
673 Chris Madden .20 .50
704 Niklos Tselios .30 .75
836 Shawn Sutter .20 .50
877 Brian Gionta 4.00 10.00
903 Jonathan Girard .75 2.00
911 Eric Bertrand .20 .50
1053 Philippe Sauve 1.25 3.00
1080 Jean-Francois Fortin .10 .25
1152 Mike Comrie 2.00 5.00
1227 Jason Labarbera .75 2.00
1327 Nick Chin .20 .50
1339 Marc Ouimet .10 .25
1391 Mike Ribeiro 1.25 3.00
1398 Patrick Desrosiers .40 1.00
1406 Tommy Kotsopoulos .75 2.00
1408 Adam Colagiacomo .40 1.00
1417 Michael Ryder 2.00 5.00
1441 Matt Zultek .40 1.00
1529 Gregor Baumgartner .20 .50
1554 Marian Hossa 12.00 30.00
1560 Robert Dome .40 1.00
1638 Oliver Aeschlimann .20 .50
1704 Ladislav Nagy 2.00 5.00
1717 Jan Lasak 1.25 3.00
1756 Joseph R. Blackburn .40 1.00
1775 Sascha Goc .30 .75
NNO Manon Rheaume 2.00 5.00

1993 Quebec Pee-Wee Tournament Gold

This three-card insert standard-size set features color player photos with metallic-gold borders on white card stock. The player's name is printed in the border at the top, while the card title is printed below the picture. The backs carry a player profile against a metallic-gold background with white borders. Two of the cards are numbered, while one is not. The listing below reflects this numbering.

COMPLETE SET (3) 4.80 12.00
1 Brad Park .80 2.00
2 Manon Rheaume 4.00 10.00
NNO Guy Chouinard .40 1.00

1994 Quebec Pee-Wee Tournament

This set features the best 12 and 13-year-old teams in the world that participated in the annual Quebec Pee-Wee Tournament. Though there are more than 1,800 cards in the set, we list only those players who might be familiar to the average collector.

COMPLETE SET (1853) 60.00 150.00
COMMON CARD (1-1853) .02 .05
11 Vincent Lecavalier 6.00 25.00
246 John-Michael Liles 1.50 4.00
345 Eric Chouinard .40 1.00
418 Ramzi Abid .40 1.00
497 Mathieu Chouinard .40 1.00
512 Phillipe Sauve 1.25 3.00
565 Seamus Kotyk .40 1.00
573 Rico Fata .40 1.00
617 Jonathan Girard .40 1.00
628 Martin Grenier .40 1.00
649 Tim Connolly .75 2.00
806 Justin Papineau .60 1.50
888 David Legwand 1.25 3.00
902 Junior Lessard 1.50 4.00
934 Marcel Rodman .40 1.00
1025 Norm Milley .75 2.00
1077 Simon Gagne 6.00 10.00
1148 Maxime Ouellet 1.25 3.00
1169 Jordan Krestanovich .40 1.00
1182 Brian Eklund .75 2.00
1202 Freddy Meyer .75 2.00
1211 Rick DiPietro 6.00 15.00
1256 Michael Ryan .40 1.00
1607 Dominic Moore .75 2.00
1717 Sheldon Keefe .40 1.00
1752 Mathieu Biron .40 1.00

1995 Quebec Pee-Wee Tournament

This set features the best 12 and 13-year-old teams in the world that participated in the annual Quebec Pee-Wee Tournament. Though there are more than 1,800 cards in the set, we list only those players who might be familiar to the average collector.

COMPLETE SET (1825) 50.00 125.00
COMMON CARD (1-1825) .02 .05
1 Jozef Balej .40 1.00
109 Brandon Reid 1.25 3.00
234 Simon Gamache .75 2.00
278 Antoine Vermette 2.00 5.00
378 Maxime Ouellet .75 2.00
448 Marc-Andre Thinel .75 2.00
516 Tim Connolly .75 2.00
552 Zenon Konopka .40 1.00
607 Dusty Jamieson .40 1.00
608 Michael Leighton 1.25 3.00
617 Jamie Chamberlain .40 1.00
692 Justin Williams 1.50 4.00
762 Andy Hilbert .75 2.00
764 Damian Surma .40 1.00
834 Luke Sellars .40 1.00
1054 Craig Andersson .75 2.00
1153 Alexandre Giroux .40 1.00
1205 Luca Cereda .40 1.00
1243 Ron Hainsey 1.25 3.00
1318 Jason Pominville 2.00 5.00
1438 Jamie Lundmark .75 2.00

1996 Quebec Pee-Wee Tournament

This set features the best 12 and 13-year-old teams in the world that participated in the annual Quebec Pee-Wee Tournament. Though there are more than 1,400 cards in the set, we list only those players who might be familiar to the average collector. It is worth noting, however, that there are a number of female players in this set. Although they are not worth listing individually, we have confirmed sales for some of these cards anywhere from $1 to $5.

COMPLETE SET (1474) 50.00 125.00
COMMON CARD (1-1474) .02 .05
1 Jozef Balej .40 1.00
2 Michal Barinka .40 1.00
16 Daniel Boisclair .75 2.00
23 Bobby Goeppert 1.50 4.00
32 Ryan Shannon .75 2.00
166 Brett Lebda .75 2.00
245 Jared Aulin 1.25 3.00
328 Pascal Leclaire 2.00 5.00
333 Yanick Lehoux .75 2.00
335 Jason Pominville 1.50 4.00
531 Rob Globke 1.00 2.50
560 J-F Racine 1.25 3.00
578 Gregory Campbell 1.25 3.00
668 Tim Gleason 1.50 4.00
678 Jim Slater .75 2.00
680 Kris Vernarsky .75 2.00
720 Jay Bouwmeester 6.00 15.00
899 Michael Komisarek 2.00 5.00
975 Sean McMorrow .75 2.00
992 Alexandre Vermette 1.50 4.00
1174 Michael Cammalleri 2.00 5.00
1227 M-A Pouliot 2.00 5.00
1288 Charline Labonte 2.00 5.00
1406 Scottie Upshall 2.00 5.00

1997 Quebec Pee-Wee Tournament

This set features the best 12 and 13-year-old teams in the world that participated in the annual Quebec Pee-Wee Tournament. Though there are nearly 1,400 cards in the set, we list only those players who might be familiar to the average collector.

COMPLETE SET
COMMON CARD .05
284 Stephen Werner .40 1.00
290 Scottie Upshall 1.50 4.00
820 Eric Nystrom 2.00 5.00
831 Chris Higgins 2.00 5.00
835 Bobby Goeppert 1.00 2.50
1113 Oliver Setzinger .40 1.00
1118 Thomas Vanek 8.00 20.00
1126 Tobias Stephan 1.50 4.00
1165 Ryan Whitney 2.00 5.00
1234 Sean Collins .40 1.00
1384 Marcel Goc 1.25 3.00

1998 Quebec Pee Wee Tournament

This mammoth set features the best 12 and 13-year-old teams in the world. Several players have achieved some notoriety in the intervening years. We list only those players.

COMPLETE SET
157 Ryan Kesler 1.25 3.00
544 Danny Richmond .40 1.00
1032 Igor Mirnov .40 1.00
1225 Christopher Campoli .75 2.00

1999 Quebec Pee Wee Tournament Collection Souvenir

Sponsored by Compuware, this set features color action photos of many current NHL superstars who played in the Quebec Pee Wee Hockey World Championships before they were famous.

COMPLETE SET (30) 16.00 40.00
1 Brad Park .40 1.00
2 Guy Chouinard .10 .25
3 Manon Rheaume 1.25 3.00
4 Patrick Roy 4.00 10.00
5 Joe Juneau .20 .50
6 Sergei Samsonov 1.25 3.00
7 Dainius Zubrus .20 .50
8 Robert Dome .10 .25
9 Daniel Tkaczuk .20 .50
10 Alex Tanguay 1.25 3.00
11 Jean-Marc Pelletier .40 1.00
12 Oleg Kvasha .20 .50
13 Steve Begin .10 .25
14 Daniel Corso .20 .50
15 Sacha Goc .20 .50
16 Marian Hossa 2.00 5.00
17 Paul Mara .40 1.00
18 J-F Damphousse .40 1.00
19 Philippe Sauve .75 2.00
20 Gregor Baumgartner .10 .25
21 Ladislav Nagy .75 2.00
22 Vincent Lecavalier 2.00 5.00
23 David Legwand .75 2.00
24 Rico Fata .40 1.00
25 Mathieu Chouinard .40 1.00
26 Eric Chouinard .40 1.00
27 Mathieu Biron .75 .50
28 Simon Gagne 1.50 4.00
29 Mike Ribeiro .40 1.00
30 Jonathan Girard .40 1.00

2000 Quebec Pee Wee Tournament

COMPLETE SET
1276 Evan McGrath .75 2.00
1347 Robbie Schremp 4.00 10.00

1980-81 Quebec Remparts

This 22-card set measures approximately 2" by 3" and features posed color player photos. The cards were issued as part of a contest. The pictures are full-bleed except for a white bottom border that contains the team logo, player's name, and jersey number. The backs are blank. The collector who obtained the entire set and turned it in became eligible to enter a contest in which the grand prize was a trip to Disney World. The cards are unnumbered and checklisted below in alphabetical order.

COMPLETE SET (22) 10.00 20.00
1 Marc Bertrand .38 .75
2 Jacques Chouinard .38 .75
3 Roger Cote .38 .75
4 Gaston Drapeau CO .25 .50
5 Claude Drouin .38 .75
6 Gaetan Duchesne 1.00 2.00
7 Scott Fraser .50 1.00
8 Jean-Marc Lanthier .50 1.00
9 Jean Paul Lariviere .38 .75
10 Andre Larocque .38 .75
11 Roberto Lavoie .38 .75
12 Marc Lemay .38 .75
13 Stephane Lessard .38 .75
14 Paul Levesque .38 .75
15 Richard Linteau .38 .75
16 Patrice Masse .38 .75
17 David Pretty .38 .75
18 Guy Riel .38 .75
19 Daniel Rioux .38 .75
20 Roberto Romano 1.00 2.00
21 Michel Therrien 1.00 2.00
22 Gilles Tremblay .75 1.50

1998-99 Quebec Remparts

This 25-card set was produced by Cartes Timbres Monnaies in conjunction with the Quebec Remparts of the QMJHL. It features several top prospects, including Eric Chouinard and Maxime Ouellet.

COMPLETE SET (25) 16.00 40.00
1 David Archambault .20 .50
2 David Bernier .20 .50
3 Nicholas Bilotto .20 .50
4 Tommy Bolduc .20 .50
5 Eric Chouinard 1.20 2.00
6 Ray Dalton .20 .50
7 Joey Fetta .20 .50
8 Simon Gagne 6.00 15.00
9 Martin Grenier .80 1.00
10 Eric Laplante .20 .50
11 Jeff Leblanc .20 .50
12 Pierre Loiselle .20 .50
13 Jerome Marois .20 .50
14 Andre Martineau .20 .50
15 Martin Moise .20 .50
16 Alexandre Morel .20 .50
17 Maxime Ouellet 4.00 10.00
18 Sylvain Plamondon .20 .50
19 Wesley Scanzano .20 .50
20 Simon Tremblay .20 .50
21 Dmitri Tolkunov .80 2.00
22 Antoine Vermette 1.20 3.00
23 Jonathan Wilhelmy .20 .50
24 Travis Zachary .20 .50
25 Title Card .04 .10

1998-99 Quebec Remparts Signed

This 25-card set was produced by Cartes Timbres Monnaies in conjunction with the Quebec Remparts. Production was limited to just 100 serial #'d sets and the entire set is signed (except for Joey Fetta who was traded). Set is unnumbered and checklisted below in alphabetical order.

COMPLETE SET (25) 40.00 100.00
1 David Archambault 1.20 3.00
2 David Bernier 1.20 3.00
3 Nicholas Bilotto 1.20 3.00
4 Tommy Bolduc 1.20 3.00
5 Eric Chouinard 4.80 10.00
6 Ray Dalton 1.20 3.00
7 Joey Fetta 1.20 3.00
8 Simon Gagne 16.00 40.00
9 Martin Grenier 2.40 5.00
10 Eric Laplante 1.20 3.00
11 Jeff Leblanc 1.20 3.00
12 Pierre Loiselle 1.20 3.00
13 Jerome Marois 1.20 3.00
14 Andre Martineau 1.20 3.00
15 Martin Moise 1.20 3.00
16 Alexandre Morel 1.20 3.00
17 Maxime Ouellet 10.00 25.00
18 Sylvain Plamondon 1.20 3.00
19 Wesley Scanzano 1.20 3.00
20 Simon Tremblay 1.20 3.00
21 Dmitri Tolkunov 2.40 5.00
22 Antoine Vermette 4.00 10.00
23 Jonathan Wilhelmy 1.20 3.00
24 Travis Zachary 1.20 3.00
25 Title Card .40 .25

1999-00 Quebec Remparts

This 25-card set pictures the Remparts of the QMJHL. Base cards feature full-color action photography and a red border along the right edge and bottom of the card which contains player names and the team logo.

COMPLETE SET (25) 4.80 12.00
1 Jean Mallette .14 .35
2 Patrick Chouinard .14 .35
3 Kirill Safronov .30 .75
4 Eric Chouinard .40 1.00
5 Patrick Grandmaitre .14 .35
6 Eric Laplante .14 .35
7 Wesley Scanzano .14 .35
8 Chris Lyness .14 .35
9 Tommy Bolduc .14 .35
10 Jean-Francois Touchette .14 .35
11 Philippe Paris .14 .35
12 Karl Morin .14 .35
13 Andre Martineau .14 .35
14 Sylvain Plamondon .14 .35
15 Martin Moise .14 .35
16 Martin Grenier .30 .75
17 Andre Hart .14 .35
18 Maxime Ouellet 1.20 3.00
19 Martin Pare .14 .35
20 Eric Cloutier .14 .35
21 Kristian Kudroc .30 .75
22 Casey Leggett .14 .35
23 Shawn Collymore .20 .50
24 Mike Ribeiro .40 1.00
25 Header Card/CL .04 .10

1999-00 Quebec Remparts Signed

This 25-card set parallels the base Quebec Remparts set in an autographed version. The cards are signed on a unique ghosted area on the card front, while the backs are serial numbered out of 100. The header card remains in the set, but it is not signed.

COMPLETE SET (25) 30.00 75.00
1 Jean Mallette .80 2.00
2 Patrick Chouinard .80 2.00
3 Kirill Safronov 2.00 5.00
4 Eric Chouinard 4.00 10.00
5 Patrick Grandmaitre .80 2.00
6 Eric Laplante .80 2.00
7 Wesley Scanzano .80 2.00
8 Chris Lyness .80 2.00
9 Tommy Bolduc .80 2.00
10 Jean-Francois Touchette .80 2.00
11 Philippe Paris .80 2.00
12 Karl Morin .80 2.00
13 Andre Martineau .80 2.00
14 Sylvain Plamondon .80 2.00
15 Martin Moise .80 2.00
16 Martin Grenier 2.00 5.00
17 Andre Hart .80 2.00
18 Maxime Ouellet 8.00 20.00
19 Martin Pare .80 2.00
20 Eric Cloutier .80 2.00
21 Kristian Kudroc 2.00 5.00
22 Casey Leggett .80 2.00
23 Shawn Collymore 1.25 3.00
24 Mike Ribeiro 4.00 10.00
25 Header Card/CL .04 .25

2000-01 Quebec Remparts

This set features the Remparts of the QMJHL. The cards were produced by CTM-Ste-Foy and sold by that shop, as well as by

the team.
COMPLETE SET (24) 4.80 12.00
1 Jean Mallette .20 .50
2 Sebastian Bourgon .20 .50
3 Richard Paul .20 .50
4 David Boilard .20 .50
5 Jeff Hadley .20 .50
6 Remi Bergeron .20 .50
7 Sebastian Morissette .20 .50
8 Philippe Paris .20 .50
9 Justin Stewart .20 .50
10 Yannick Searles .20 .50
11 Mike Bray .20 .50
12 Guillaume Fournier .20 .50
13 Robert Pearce .20 .50
14 Petr Preucil .20 .50
15 Philippe Parent .20 .50
16 Didier Bochatay .20 .50
17 Scott Della Vedova .30 .75
18 Alexandre Reuben .20 .50
19 David Masse .20 .50
20 Shawn Collymore .20 .75
21 Guillaume Berube .20 .50
22 Kevin Lachance .30 .75
23 Cory Urquhart .20 .50
NNO Team CL .04 .01

2000-01 Quebec Remparts Signed

This set is exactly the same as the base Remparts set from this season, save that every card has been hand signed by the player pictured. Each card also is serial numbered out of just 100. The team CL is not signed.

COMPLETE SET (24) 14.00 35.00
2 Sebastian Bourgon .80 2.00
3 Richard Paul .80 2.00
5 Jeff Hadley .80 2.00
6 Remi Bergeron .80 2.00
7 Sebastian Morissette .80 2.00
8 Philippe Paris .80 2.00
9 Justin Stewart .80 2.00
10 Yannick Searles .80 2.00
11 Mike Bray .80 2.00
12 Guillaume Fournier .80 2.00
13 Robert Pearce .80 2.00
14 Petr Preucil .80 2.00
15 Philippe Parent .80 2.00
17 Scott Della Vedova 2.00 5.00
20 Shawn Collymore .80 5.00
21 Guillaume Berube .80 2.00
22 Kevin Lachance 2.00 5.00
NNO Team CL .04 .25

2001-02 Quebec Remparts

This set features the Remparts of the QMJHL. The set was produced by CTM Ste-Foy and was sold at Remparts home games. It is believed that less than 1,000 sets were produced.

COMPLETE SET (24) 4.80 12.00
1 Jean-Michel Bolduc .20 .50
2 Sebastien Bourgon .20 .50
3 Yan Turcotte .20 .50
4 Jeff Hadley .20 .50
5 Josh Hennessy .20 .50
6 Mark Hurtubise .20 .50
7 Mathieu Dery .20 .50
8 Robert Pearce .20 .50
9 Yannick Searles .20 .50
10 Mike Bray .20 .50
11 Tomas Spila .20 .50
12 Samuel Duplain .20 .50
13 Petr Preucil .20 .50
14 Daniel Houle .20 .50
15 Didier Bochatay .20 .50
16 Denis Berube .20 .50
17 Jeff MacAulay .20 .50
18 Mario Joly .20 .50
19 David Masse .20 .50
20 Shawn Collymore .20 .50
21 Guillaume Berube .20 .50
22 Kevin Lachance .20 .50
23 Sebastien Thinel .20 .50
24 Cory Urquhart .20 .50

2002-03 Quebec Remparts

Cards U12-U23 available as an update set.

COMPLETE SET (23) 18.00
1 Jean-Michel Bolduc .75
2 Sebastien Bourgon .50
3 Colin Ledaire .50
4 Josh Hennessy .50
5 Mark Hurtubise .50
6 Vladimir Kutny .50
7 Robert Pearce .50
8 Jordan LaVallee .50
9 Timofei Shishkanov 1.00
10 Jason Kostadine .50
11 Curtis Tidball .50
12 Frederic Faucher .50
13 Karl St. Pierre .50
14 Didier Bochatay .50
15 Ben McMullin .75
16 David Masse .50
17 Shawn Collymore .75
18 Guillaume Berube .50
19 Steve Pelletier .50
20 Kevin Lachance .75
21 Pierre-Olivier Beaulieu .50
22 Chris Montgomery .50
U12 Evan Shaw .50
U14 Jean-Michel Filiatrault 2.00
U15 Alexandre Rouleau .75
U16 Aaron Johnson .50
U17 Pierre Morvan .50
U20 Benoit Beauchemin .50
U21 Remy Tremblay .50
U22 Checklist/Logo .10
U23 Jamie McCabe .50
NNO Checklist .10

2003 Quebec Remparts Memorial Cup

Cards are unnumbered and thus are listed in alphabetical order.

COMPLETE SET (21) 18.00
1 Guillaume Berube .75
2 Jean-Michel Bolduc 1.00
3 Sebastien Bourgon .75
4 Frederic Faucher .75
5 Jean-Michel Filiatrault 2.50
6 Josh Hennessy .75
7 Aaron Johnson .75
8 Jason Kostadine .75
9 Vladimir Kutny .75
10 Kevin Lachance 1.00
11 Jordan Lavallee .75
12 David Masse .75
13 Jamie McCabe .75
14 Chris Montgomery .75
15 Pierre Morvan .75
16 Robert Pearce .75
17 Alexandre Rouleau 1.00
18 Evan Shaw .75
19 Timofei Shishkanov 1.25
20 Karl St.Pierre .75
21 Curtis Tidball .75

2003-04 Quebec Remparts

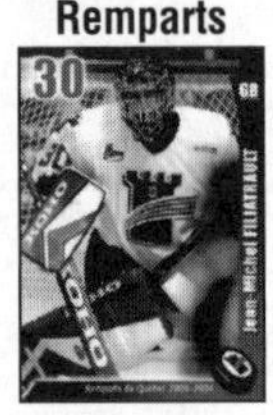

COMPLETE SET (28) 5.00 12.00
1 Andrew Andricopoulos .20 .50
2 Adam Blanchette .20 .50
3 Christian Brideau .20 .50
4 Tyler Chambers .20 .50
5 Jean-Michel Cote .30 .75
6 Kevin Coughlin .20 .50
7 Simon Courcelles .20 .50
8 Jean-Michel Filiatrault .40 1.00
9 Ian Girard .20 .50
10 Stephane Goulet .20 .50
11 Josh Hennessy .30 .75
12 Alexandre Imbeault .20 .50
13 Alexandre Kojevnikov .20 .50
14 Louis-Phillipe Lachance .20 .50
15 Jordan LaVallee .20 .50
16 Justin Laverdiere .20 .50
17 Maxime Lincourt .20 .50
18 Eric L'Italien .20 .50
19 Mathieu Melanson .20 .50
20 Corey Pastershank .20 .50
21 Robert Pearce .20 .50
22 Joey Ryan .20 .50
23 Evan Shaw .20 .50
24 Alexei Shkotov .20 .50
25 Brandon Tidball .20 .50
26 Marc-Edouard Vlasic .60 1.50
27 Nathan Welton .20 .50
28 Checklist/Title Card .01 .05

2004-05 Quebec Remparts

A total of 400 team sets were produced.

COMPLETE SET (25) 6.00 15.00
1 Gennady Churilov .20 .50
2 Jordan LaVallee .20 .50
3 Karl Gagne .20 .50
4 Maxime Lacroix .20 .50
5 Maxime Lincourt .20 .50
6 Simon Courcelles .20 .50
7 Andrew Andricopoulos .20 .50
8 Ian Girard .20 .50
9 Maxime Joyal .20 .50
10 Alexander Radulov 1.50 4.00
11 Brandon Tidball .40 1.00
12 Marc-Edouard Vlasic 1.25 3.00
13 Max Gratchev .20 .50
14 Josh Hennessy .40 1.00
15 Mathieu Melanson .20 .50
16 Drew Paris .20 .50
17 Jonathan Alain-Rochette .20 .50
18 Joey Ryan .20 .50
19 Sebastien Bernier .20 .50
20 Kevin Coughlin .20 .50
21 Jonathan Boutin .30 .75
22 Alexandre Mineault .20 .50
23 Michael Tessier .20 .50
24 Guillaume Veilleux .20 .50
25 Evan Shaw .20 .50

2005-06 Quebec Remparts

COMPLETE SET (25) 10.00 18.00
1 Angelo Esposito 2.00 5.00
2 Alexander Radulov .75 2.00
3 Stephen Valente .20 .50
4 Joey Ryan .20 .50
5 Drew Paris .20 .50
6 Michal Sersen .20 .50
7 Simon Coucelles .20 .50
8 Felix Petit .20 .50
9 Maxime Lacroix .20 .50
10 Alexandre Mineault .20 .50
11 Max Gratchev .20 .50
12 Andrew Andricopoulos .20 .50
13 Jordan Lavallee .20 .50
14 Cedrick Desjardins .30 .75
15 Kevin Desfosses .20 .50
16 Kenzie Sheppard .20 .50
17 Nicolas Robillard .20 .50
18 Pierre Bergeron .20 .50
19 Brent Aubin .20 .50
20 Christophe Poirier .20 .50
21 Guillaume Veilleux .20 .50
22 Marc-Edouard Vlasic .20 .50
23 Todd Chinova .20 .50
24 Yan Ouimet .20 .50
25 Mathieu Melanson .20 .50

2006-07 Quebec Remparts

COMPLETE SET (27) 12.00 20.00
1 Angelo Esposito 2.00 5.00
2 Andrew Andricopoulos .20 .50
3 Joey Ryan .20 .50
4 Pierre Bergeron .20 .50
5 Kelsey Tessier .40 1.00
6 Roman Bashkirov .40 1.00
7 Hubert Genest .20 .50
8 Felix Petit .20 .50
9 Brent Aubin .40 1.00
10 Maxime Sauve .20 .50
11 Loic Lacasse .20 .50
12 Alexandre Mineault .20 .50
13 Ruslan Bashkirov .40 1.00
14 Billy Bezeau .20 .50
15 Kevin Desfosses .40 1.00
16 Boby Fugere .20 .50
17 Maxime Lacroix .20 .50
18 Christophe Poirier .20 .50
19 Philippe Poirier .20 .50
20 Joel Roch .20 .50
21 Benjamin Rubin .20 .50
22 Kenzie Sheppard .20 .50
23 Matthew Smith .40 1.00
24 Marc-Olivier Vallerand .20 .50
25 Guillaume Veilleux .20 .50
26 Mathieu Lavoie .20 .50
EL2 Brent Aubin .20 .50

1992-93 Raleigh Icecaps

This 38-card standard-size set features the Raleigh Icecaps of the ECHL. Inside a blue-and-white border design, the fronts feature on-ice posed color player photos with rounded corners. The player's name and position appear under the photo, while the words "1992-93 Raleigh IceCaps" are printed above the photo. The backs carry biography, stats, and a player profile. The cards were issued in two separate series. The first series cards, produced by Sportsprint (Atlanta, GA), are unnumbered and checklisted below in alphabetical order, whereas the second series cards, produced by RBI Sports Cards Inc. (Greensboro, North Carolina), are numbered on the back.

COMPLETE SET (38) 6.00 15.00
1 Cappy Bear (Mascot) .04 .10
2 Sean Cowan .20 .50
3 Joel Gardner .20 .50
4 Bill Kovacs .20 .50
5 Alan Leggett .20 .50
6 Kirby Lindal .20 .50
7 Derek Linnell .20 .50
8 Jim Mill .20 .50
9 Kris Miller .20 .50
10 Todd Person .20 .50
11 Chic Pojar .20 .50
12 Jim Powers .20 .50
13 Stan(Smokey) Reddick .30 .75
14 Doug Roberts .20 .50
15 Jeff Robison .20 .50
16 Jeff Tomlinson .20 .50
17 Brian Tulik .20 .50
18 Bruno Villeneuve .20 .50
19 Lyle Wildgoose .20 .50
20 Team Photo DP .16 .40
21 Bruno Villeneuve .20 .50
22 Jeff Robison .20 .50
23 Jim Powers .20 .50
24 Derek Linnell .20 .50
25 Chris Marshall .20 .50
26 Kris Miller .20 .50
27 Joel Gardner .20 .50
28 Stan(Smokey) Reddick .30 .75
29 Jim Mill .20 .50
30 Alan Leggett .20 .50
31 Brian Tulik .20 .50
32 Kirby Lindal .20 .50
33 Sean Cowan .20 .50
34 Lyle Wildgoose .20 .50
35 Todd Person .20 .50
36 Chic Pojar .20 .50
37 Mike Lappin .20 .50
38 Doug Bacon .20 .50

1993-94 Raleigh Icecaps

Produced by RBI Sports Cards, this 20-card standard-size set features the Raleigh Icecaps of the ECHL. On a white card face, the fronts feature color action player photos inside purple borders. The player's name appears under the photo.

COMPLETE SET (20) 2.80 7.00
1 Ralph Barahona .16 .40
2 Rick Barkovich .16 .40
3 Matt Delguidice .20 .50
4 Martin D'Orsonnens .16 .40
5 Jamie Erb .16 .40
6 Chad Erickson .20 .50
7 Donevan Hextall .20 .50
8 Shaun Kane .16 .40
9 Al Leggett .16 .40
10 Derek Linnell .16 .40
11 Joe McCarthy .16 .40
12 Chris Nelson .16 .40
13 Barry Nieckar .16 .40
14 Jim Powers .16 .40
15 Stan Reddick .20 .50
16 Kevin Riehl .16 .40
17 Jeff Robison .16 .40
18 David Shute .16 .40
19 Lyle Wildgoose .16 .40
20 Kurt Kleinendorst CO .10 .25

1994-95 Raleigh Icecaps

Produced by RBI Sports Cards, this 19-card standard-size set features the Raleigh Icecaps of the ECHL. Just 1,000 sets were produced. On a black card face, the fronts feature color action and posed player photos inside a white frame. The player's name appears under the photo, while the team name is printed above the photo. There are several production errors in this set. Card number 12 was not produced. Card numbers 9 and 18 were mistakenly duplicated and explains the absence of card numbers 10 and 19.

COMPLETE SET (19) 3.20 8.00
1 John Blessman .20 .50
2 Rick Barkovich CO .10 .25
3 Alexsandr Chunchukov .20 .50
4 Frank Cirone .20 .50
5 Brett Duncan .20 .50
6 Anton Fedorov .20 .50
7 Todd Hunter .20 .50
8 Rodrigo Lavinsh .30 .75
9 Derek Linnell .20 .50
10 Eric Long UER .20 .50
(Card misnumbered 9 on back)
11 Scott MacNair .20 .50
13 Brad Mullahy .20 .50
14 Lenny Pereira .20 .50
15 Jimmy Powers .20 .50
16 Chic Pojar .20 .50
17 Kevin Riehl .20 .50
18 Todd Reirden .30 .75
19 Justin Tomberlin UER .20 .50
(Card misnumbered 18 on back)
20 Lyle Wildgoose .20 .50

1989-90 Rayside-Balfour Jr. Canadians

This 20-card set is printed on thin card stock and measures approximately 2 3/8" by 3 3/8." The cards feature full-bleed, color, posed player photos. The player's name and jersey number are printed in black at the bottom. The team logo and name are printed at the top. The cards are unnumbered and checklisted below in alphabetical order.

COMPLETE SET (20) 3.20 8.00
1 Team Photo .40 1.00
2 Dave Barrett .20 .50
3 Dan Baston .20 .50
4 Rick Chartrand .20 .50
5 Simon Chartrand .20 .50
6 Ron Clark .20 .50
7 Brian Dickinson .20 .50
8 Trevor Duncan .20 .50
9 Don Gauthier .20 .50
10 Shawn Hawkins .20 .50
11 Roy Hildebrandt .20 .50
12 Al Laginski .20 .50
13 Eric Lanteigne .20 .50
14 Mike Leblanc .20 .50
15 Kevin MacDonald .20 .50
16 Mike Mooney .20 .50
17 Rick Potvin .20 .50
18 Rick Poulin .20 .50
19 Steve Prior .20 .50
20 Scott Sutton .20 .50

1990-91 Rayside-Balfour Jr. Canadians

This 23-card set is printed on thin card stock and measures approximately 2 3/8" by 3 1/4." The cards feature full-bleed, color, posed player photos. The player's name and jersey number are printed in black at the bottom. The team logo and name are printed at the top. The cards are unnumbered and checklisted below in alphabetical order.

COMPLETE SET (23) 2.80 7.00
1 Dan Baston .16 .40
2 Jon Boeve .16 .40
3 Jordan Boyle .16 .40
4 Serge Coulombe .16 .40
5 Mike Dore .16 .40
6 Denis Gosselin .16 .40
7 Mike Gratton .16 .40
8 Jason Hall .16 .40
9 Grant Healey .16 .40
10 Marc Lafreniere .16 .40
11 Alain Leclair .16 .40
12 Mike Longo .16 .40
13 Troy Mallette .30 .75
1985-86 rookie photo
14 Matthew Mooney .16 .40
15 Virgil Nose .16 .40
16 Trevor Oystrick .16 .40
17 Steve Proceviat .16 .40
18 Chris Puskas .16 .40
19 Yvon Quenneville .16 .40
20 Michael Sullivan .20 .50
21 Trevor Tremblay .16 .40
22 Sean Van Amburg .16 .40
23 Title Card .04 .10

1991-92 Rayside-Balfour Jr. Canadians

This 23-card set measures approximately 2 3/8" by 3 5/16" and is printed on thin card stock. The fronts feature color, full-bleed, posed action player photos. The player's name and jersey number are printed in black at the bottom. The team logo appears in either red or white at the upper left corner. The cards are unnumbered and checklisted below in alphabetical order.

COMPLETE SET (23) 3.20 8.00
1 Dan Baston .20 .50
2 Don Cucksey .20 .50
3 Dean Cull .20 .50
4 Mike Dore .20 .50
5 Denis Gosselin .20 .50
6 Jason Hall .20 .50
7 Grant Healey .20 .50
8 Marc Lafreniere .20 .50
9 Mike Longo .20 .50
10 Scott Maclellan .20 .50
11 Matt Mooney .20 .50
12 Rob Moxness .20 .50
13 Virgil Nose .20 .50
14 Trent Oystrick .20 .50
15 Jon Stewart .20 .50
16 Jon Stos .20 .50
17 Dave Sutton .20 .50
18 Scott Sutton .20 .50
19 Trevor Tremblay .20 .50
20 Jaak Valiots .20 .50
21 Sean Van Amburg .20 .50
22 Jason Young .04 .10
Stickboy
23 Title Card .04 .10

2002-03 Reading Royals

COMPLETE SET (32) 10.00 25.00
1 Series 1 Header Card .02 .10
2 Francois Drainville .40 1.00
3 David Lohrei CO .20 .50
4 Matt Snesrud .40 1.00
5 Ray DiLauro .40 1.00
6 Chris Bogas .40 1.00
7 Simon Tremblay .40 1.00
8 Jim Dube .40 1.00
9 Series 2 Header Card .02 .10
10 Jonathon Shockey .40 1.00
11 Colin Pepperall .40 1.00
12 Brad Rooney .40 1.00
13 Brandon Dietrich .40 1.00
14 Kris Waltze .40 1.00
15 Hunter Lahache .40 1.00
16 Jeff Giuliano .40 1.00
17 Series 3 Header Card .20 .50
18 Sean Gauthier .40 1.00
19 Steve Rymsha .40 1.00
20 Tom Rouleau .40 1.00
21 Geoff Peters .40 1.00
22 Duilio Grande .40 1.00
23 Keegan McAvoy .40 1.00
24 Brian McCullough .40 1.00
25 Series 4 Header Card .02 .10
26 Steve Shirreffs .40 1.00
27 Ryan Flinn .60 1.50
28 Scott Fankhouser .60 1.50
29 Jeff Sanger .40 1.00
30 Antoine Bergeron .40 1.00
31 Alex Kim .40 1.00
32 Dan Riva .40 1.00

2002-03 Reading Royals RBI Sports

COMPLETE SET (18) 8.00 20.00
169 Antoine Bergeron .40 1.00
170 Craig Brunel .40 1.00
171 Brandon Dietrich .40 1.00
172 Ray DiLauro .40 1.00
173 Jim Dube .40 1.00
174 Jeff Giuliano .40 1.00
175 Duilio Grande .40 1.00
176 Alex Kim .40 1.00
177 Brian McCullough .40 1.00
178 Colin Pepperall .40 1.00
179 Dan Riva .40 1.00
180 Brad Rooney .40 1.00
181 Remi Royer .75 2.00
182 Tom Rouleau .40 1.00
183 Steve Rymsha .40 1.00
184 Jeff Sanger .75 2.00
185 Mat Snesrud .40 1.00
186 Simon Tremblay .40 1.00

2003-04 Reading Royals

This set was issued in four mini-sets as a promotional giveaway over the course of the 2003-04 season.

COMPLETE SET (30) 12.00 30.00
1 Header Card Series One .01 .05
2 Derek Clancey .40 1.00
3 Adam Hauser 1.25 3.00
4 Mat Snesrud .40 1.00
5 Jason Maleyko .40 1.00
6 Tomas Slovak .40 1.00
7 Jonathan Zion .40 1.00
8 Leon Hayward .40 1.00
9 Header Card Series Two .01 .05
10 Judd Medak .40 1.00
11 David Masse .40 1.00
12 Nick Lent .40 1.00
13 Jeff Finger .40 1.00
14 Francis Nault .40 1.00
15 Graig Mischler .40 1.00
16 Header Card Series Three .01 .05
17 Peter Hay .40 1.00
18 Ian Turner .40 1.00
19 Kent Davyduke .40 1.00
20 Dean Arsene .40 1.00
21 Darryl Laplante .40 1.00
22 Dave Stewart .75 2.00
23 Header Card Series Four .01 .05
24 Mascot .02 .10
25 Reading Royals .02 .10
26 Brad Church .40 1.00
27 Cody Rudkowsky .75 2.00
28 Terry Denike .75 2.00
29 Matt Passfield .40 1.00
30 Doug Nolan .40 1.00

2003-04 Reading Royals RBI Sports

This set was produced by RBI Sports and limited to just 250 copies. The numbering sequence reflects the entire run of RBI sets over the course of the season.

COMPLETE SET (18) 15.00
289 Brad Church 1.00
290 Kent Davyduke 1.00
291 Peter Hay 1.00
292 Leon Hayward 1.00
293 Nick Lent 1.00
294 Jason Maleyko 1.00
295 Judd Medak 1.00
296 Graig Mischler 1.00
297 Francis Nault 1.00
298 Doug Nolan 1.00
299 Matt Passfield 1.00
300 Cody Rudkowsky 1.50
301 Tomas Slovak 1.00
302 Scooter Smith 1.00
303 Mat Snesrud 1.00
304 Ian Turner 1.00
305 David Belitski 1.50
306 Josh Barker 1.00

2004-05 Reading Royals

These cards were given away at four separate home games. We do not have a checklist for the first series of six cards. If you know of them, please forward the info to hockeymag@beckett.com.

COMPLETE SET (28
1 unknown
2 unknown
3 unknown
4 unknown
5 unknown
6 unknown
7 David Masse
8 Tom Galvin
9 Cail MacLean
10 Aaron Smith
11 Graig Mischler
12 Barry Brust
13 Ryan Kinasewich
14 Ian Turner
15 Mike Souza
16 Preston Mizzi
17 Dan Welch
18 Larry Courville
19 Slapshot MASCOT
20 Nick Greenough
21 Jeff Miles
22 Martin Wilde
23 Mikko Viitanen
24 Adam Borzecki
NNO Header Card
NNO Header Card
NNO Header Card
NNO Header Card

2005-06 Reading Royals

COMPLETE SET (19) 8.00 15.00
1 Chris Bala .30 .75
2 Doug Christiansen .30 .75
3 Larry Courville .30 .75
4 Jon Francisco .30 .75
5 Yutaka Fukufuji .75 2.00
6 Tyler Hanchuck .30 .75
7 T.J. Kemp .30 .75
8 Mike Kompon .30 .75
9 Malcolm MacMillan .30 .75
10 John Morlang .30 .75
11 Reagan Rome .30 .75
12 Dany Roussin .60 1.50
13 Cody Rudkowsky .60 1.50
14 Jeff State .30 .75
15 Shay Stephenson .30 .75
16 Eric Werner .30 .75
17 Karl Taylor HC .02 .10
18 Slapshot MASCOT .02 .10
19 Reading Royals .02 .10

2006-07 Reading Royals

COMPLETE SET (18) 15.00 30.00
1 Rob Lalonde .75 2.00
2 Shawn German .60 1.50
3 Taylor Christie .60 1.50
4 Reagan Rome .60 1.50
5 Jason Becker .60 1.50
6 Malcolm Macmillan 1.00 2.50
7 Shawn Collymore .60 1.50
8 Joe Zappala .60 1.50
9 John Snowden .60 1.50
10 Jon Francisco .60 1.50
11 Dany Roussin .60 1.50
12 Ned Lukacevic .60 1.50
13 Kevin Saurette .60 1.50
14 Greg Hogeboom .60 1.50
15 Chris Bala .60 1.50
16 Jeff Pietrasiak .75 2.00
17 Yutaka Fukufuji 2.00 5.00
18 Karl Taylor CO .20 .50

1993-94 Red Deer Rebels

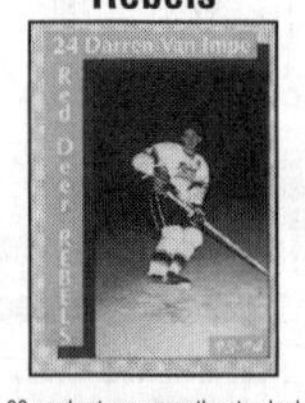

This 30-card set measures the standard size. The fronts feature posed action on-ice player photos with hatched borders. The player's name and number are printed in white letters inside a silver bar above the picture, while the team name appears alongside the left side. The cards are unnumbered and checklisted below in alphabetical order.

COMPLETE SET (30) 4.00 10.00
1 Peter Anholt CO .04 .10
2 Byron Briske .16 .40
3 Curtis Cardinal .16 .40
4 Jason Clague .16 .40
5 Dale Donaldson .16 .40
6 Dave Greenway .16 .40
7 Scott Grimwood TR .04 .10
8 Sean Halifax .16 .40
9 Chris Kibermanis .16 .40
10 Pete LeBoutillier .16 .40
11 Pete LeBoutillier .16 .40
In Action
12 Terry Lindgren .16 .40
13 Chris Maillet .16 .40
14 Eddy Marchant .16 .40
15 Mike McBain .16 .40
16 Mike Moller ACO .04 .10
17 Andy Nowicki ACO .04 .10
18 Berkley Pennock .16 .40
19 Tyler Quiring .16 .40

20 Craig Reichert .16 .40
21 Ken Richardson .16 .40
22 Sean Selmser .16 .40
23 Vaclav Slansky .16 .40
24 Mark Toljanich .16 .40
25 Darren Van Impe .20 .50
26 Pete Vandermeer .16 .75
27 Chris Wickenheiser .20 .50
28 Brad Zimmer .16 .40
29 Jonathan Zukiwsky .16 .40
30 The Centrum .04 .10

1995-96 Red Deer Rebels

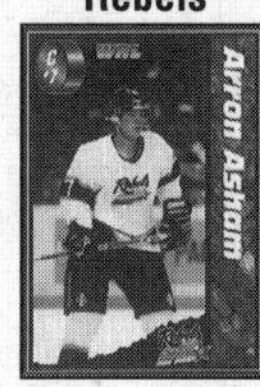

This 24-card set of the Red Deer Rebels of the WHL features extremely blurry color player photos in gray and black borders. The backs carry a player profile. The cards are unnumbered and checklisted below in alphabetical order.

COMPLETE SET (24) 4.00 10.00
1 Arron Asham .16 .40
2 Bryan Boorman .16 .40
3 Aleksei Boudaev .16 .40
4 Mike Broda .16 .40
5 Mike Brown .20 .50
6 Jay Henderson .30 .75
7 David Hruska .16 .40
8 Chris Kibermanis .16 .40
9 Brad Leeb .30 .75
10 Terry Lindgren .16 .40
11 Mike McBain .20 .50
12 Brent McDonald .16 .40
13 Ken McKay .16 .40
14 Harlan Pratt .16 .40
15 Greg Schmidt .16 .40
16 Pete Vandermeer .16 .75
17 Jesse Wallin .20 .50
18 Lance Ward .20 .50
19 Mike Whitney .16 .40
20 Chris Wickenheiser .30 .75
21 B.J. Young .16 .40
22 Jonathan Zukiwsky .20 .50
23 Drug Awareness Team .04 .10
24 Team Picture .16 .40

1996-97 Red Deer Rebels

Sold by the team at home games. Sponsored by RCMP and Parkland Colour Press.

COMPLETE SET (29) 6.00 15.00
1 Collector Series Card .01 .05
2 Team Photo .10 .25
3 Mike McBain .20 .50
4 Jesse Wallin .20 .50
5 Arron Asham .40 1.00
6 Kyle Kos .20 .50
7 Jonathan Zukiwsky .20 .50
8 Stephen Peat .75 2.00
9 Brent McDonald .20 .50
10 Greg Schmidt .20 .50
11 Chris Ovington .20 .50
12 Martin Tomasek .20 .50
13 Brad Rohrig .20 .50
14 Devin Francon .20 .50
15 B.J. Young .20 .50
16 Mike Broda .20 .50
17 Matt Van Horlick .20 .50
18 Mike Brown .20 .50
19 Lance Ward .20 .50
20 Kris Knoblauch .20 .50
21 Brad Leeb .20 .50
22 Garnet Stevenson .20 .50
23 Lloyd Shaw .20 .50
24 Mike Whitney .20 .50
25 Jesse Wallin .20 .50
26 Lance Ward .20 .50
27 The Centrum .02 .10
28 Drug Awareness .02 .10
29 Rowdy MASCOT .02 .10

1997-98 Red Deer Rebels

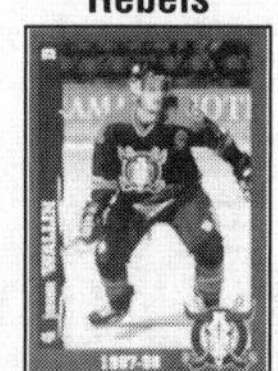

This set features the Rebels of the WHL. The set was produced by the team and sold at home games. The cards are unnumbered, and so are listed alphabetically.

COMPLETE SET (25) 4.80 12.00
1 Team photo .16 .40
2 Arron Asham .20 .75
3 Andrew Bergen .16 .40
4 Joel Boschman .16 .40
5 Chris Cederstrand .16 .40
6 Devin Francon .16 .40
7 John Kachur .16 .40
8 Kyle Kos .16 .40
9 Brad Leeb .16 .40
10 Justin Mapletoft .60 1.50
11 Brent McDonald .16 .40
12 Shawn McNeil .16 .40
13 Scott McQueen .16 .40
14 Frank Mrazek .20 .50
15 Cam Ondrik .16 .40
16 Chris Ovington .16 .40
17 Stephen Peat .40 1.50
18 Brad Rohrig .16 .40
19 Robert Schnabel .20 .50
20 Jesse Wallin .40 .75
21 Lance Ward .30 .75
22 Mike Whitney .16 .40
23 Jon Zukiwsky .20 .50
24 Woolly Bully MASCOT .04 .10
25 Drug Awareness .01

1998-99 Red Deer Rebels

This set features the Rebels of the WHL. The cards were sold by the team at home games. They are unnumbered, so they are listed below in alphabetical order.

COMPLETE SET (24) 4.80 12.00
1 Jay Batchelor .20 .50
2 Lukas Bednarik .20 .50
3 Andrew Bergen .20 .50
4 Michael Clague .30 .75
5 Andrew Coates .20 .50
6 Devin Francon .20 .50
7 Kyle Kos .20 .50
8 Brad Leeb .20 .50
9 Justin Mapletoft .60 1.50
10 Kevin Marsh .20 .50
11 Brett McDonald .20 .50
12 Shawn McNeil .20 .50
13 Scott McQueen .20 .50
14 Frank Mrazek .20 .50
15 Rhett Nevill .20 .50
16 Chris Ovington .20 .50
17 Stephen Peat .60 1.50
18 Dustin Schwartz .30 .75
19 Jeff Smith .20 .50
20 Jim Vandermeer .20 .50
21 Justin Wallin .20 .50
22 Jordan Watt .30 .75
23 Wooly Bully MASCOT .04 .10
24 Drug Awareness Card .01

2000-01 Red Deer Rebels

This set features the Rebels of the WHL. The set is noteworthy for capturing the team during its Memorial Cup-winning season. The cards were sold by the team and are unnumbered, so they are listed below in alphabetical order.

COMPLETE SET (24) 4.80 15.00
1 Checklist .04 .10
2 Colby Armstrong .40 1.50
3 Shane Bendera .40 1.00
4 Andrew Bergen .16 .40
5 Devin Francon .16 .40
6 Michael Garnett .16 .40
7 Boyd Gordon .16 .40
8 Shane Grypiuk .16 .40
9 Diarmuid Kelly .16 .40
10 Ladislav Kouba .16 .40
11 Ross Lupaschuk .30 .75
12 Doug Lynch .30 .75
13 Justin Mapletoft .60 1.50
14 Derek Meech .16 .40
15 Donovan Rattray .16 .40
16 Jeff Smith .16 .40
17 Shay Stephenson .16 .40
18 Joel Stepp .16 .40
19 Bryce Thoma .16 .40
20 Jim Vandermeer .16 .75
21 Martin Vymazal .16 .40
22 Justin Wallin .16 .40
23 Kyle Wanvig .60 1.50
24 Jeff Woywitka .40 1.50

2000-01 Red Deer Rebels Signed

This set is exactly the same as the base Rebels set from this season, save that every card has been hand signed by the player pictured. Amazingly, this set was originally made available by the team for the bargain price of $10.

COMPLETE SET (24) 24.00 60.00
1 Checklist .04 .10
2 Colby Armstrong 2.00 7.50
3 Shane Bendera 2.00 5.00
4 Andrew Bergen .80 2.00
5 Devin Francon .80 2.00
6 Michael Garnett .80 2.00
7 Boyd Gordon .80 2.00
8 Shane Grypiuk .80 2.00
9 Diarmuid Kelly .80 2.00
10 Ladislav Kouba .80 2.00
11 Ross Lupaschuk 2.00 5.00
12 Doug Lynch 2.00 5.00
13 Justin Mapletoft 3.00 7.50
14 Derek Meech .80 2.00
15 Donovan Rattray .80 2.00
16 Jeff Smith .80 2.00
17 Shay Stephenson .80 2.00
18 Joel Stepp .80 2.00
19 Bryce Thoma .80 2.00
20 Jim Vandermeer .80 3.00
21 Martin Vymazal .80 2.00
22 Justin Wallin .80 2.00
23 Kyle Wanvig 3.00 7.50
24 Jeff Woywitka 2.00 7.50

2001-02 Red Deer Rebels

COMPLETE SET (21) 6.00 15.00
1 Cover Card .01 .05
2 Colby Armstrong .40 1.00
3 Shane Bendera .40 1.00
4 Andrew Bergen .20 .50
5 Derek Endicott .20 .50
6 Jason Ertl .20 .50
7 Colin Fraser .20 .50
8 Boyd Gordon .40 1.00
9 Diarmuid Kelly .20 .50
10 Ladislav Kouba .20 .50
11 Doug Lynch .30 .75
12 Derek Meech .30 .75
13 Chris Neiszner .20 .50
14 Joel Rupprecht .20 .50
15 Jeff Smith .20 .50
16 Shay Stephenson .20 .50
17 Joel Stepp .20 .50
18 Bryce Thoma .20 .50
19 Cam Ward 4.00 10.00
20 Mikhail Yakubov .40 1.00
21 Woolly Bully MAS .02 .10

2002-03 Red Deer Rebels

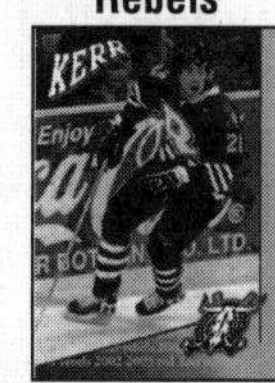

This set features the Rebels of the WHL. The cards are listed in the order they appear on the checklist card.

COMPLETE SET (26) 15.00 40.00
1 Cam Ward/CL 2.00 5.00
2 Derek Meech .40 1.00
3 Dion Phaneuf 6.00 15.00
4 Bryce Thoma .20 .50
5 Jeff Woywitka .40 1.00
6 Cody Holzapfel .20 .50
7 Masi Marjamaki .40 1.00
8 Matt Ellison .20 .50
9 Joel Stepp .20 .50
10 Colin Fraser .30 .75
11 Blair Jones .20 .50
12 Jason Ertl .20 .50
13 Jared Walker .20 .50
14 Derek Endicott .20 .50
15 Carsen Germyn .20 .50
16 Boyd Gordon .40 1.00
17 Stuart Kerr .20 .50
18 Ladislav Kouba .20 .50
19 Matt Keith .20 .50
20 Diarmuid Kelly .20 .50
21 Shay Stephenson .20 .50
22 Nathan Brice .20 .50
23 Jesse Zetariuk .20 .50
24 Chris Neiszner .20 .50
25 Cam Ward 2.00 5.00
26 Adam Jennings .30 .75

2003-04 Red Deer Rebels

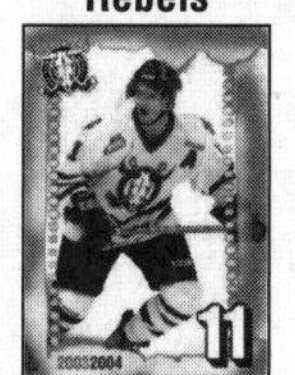

COMPLETE SET (24) 10.00 25.00
1 Derek Meech .30 .75
2 Dion Phaneuf 6.00 15.00
3 Paul Kurceba .20 .50
4 Dan Mercer .20 .50
5 Mikko Kuukka .20 .50
6 Andre Herman .20 .50
7 Colin Fraser .30 .75
8 Kyle Ross .20 .50
9 Jason Ertl .20 .50
10 Jared Walker .20 .50
11 Derek Endicott .20 .50
12 Justin Taylor .20 .50
13 Ted Vandermeer .20 .50
14 Stuart Kerr .30 .75
15 Blair Jones .20 .50
16 Shay Stephenson .20 .50
17 Nathan Brice .20 .50
18 Jesse Zetariuk .20 .50
19 Chris Neiszner .20 .50
20 Cam Ward 1.50 4.00
21 Trevor Peeters .30 .75
22 Woolly Bully MASCOT .02 .10
23 Brent Sutter CO .20 .50
24 Team Photo .20 .50

2005-06 Red Deer Rebels

COMPLETE SET (25) 8.00 15.00
1 Brennan Chapman .20 .50
2 Matthew Cline .20 .50
3 Luke Egener .20 .50
4 Eric Frere .20 .50
5 Tanner Gillies .20 .50
6 Matthew Hansen .20 .50
7 Garrett Klotz .20 .50
8 Jordan Knackstedt .20 .50
9 Pierre-Paul Lamoureux .20 .50
10 Devon LeBlanc .20 .50
11 Andrew Leslie .40 1.00
12 Vladimir Mihalik .20 .50
13 Karey Pieper .20 .50
14 Alex Poulter .20 .50
15 James Reimer .20 .50
16 Justin Scott .20 .50
17 Jonathon Smith .20 .50
18 Brandon Sutter .75 2.00
19 Brett Sutter .40 1.00
20 Ted Vandermeer .20 .50
21 Kris Versteeg .40 1.00
22 Roman Wick .20 .50
23 Mike Berube .20 .50
24 Josh Bray .20 .50
25 Red Deer Rebels CL .01 .01

1981-82 Regina Pats

No. 5 - Garth Butcher - D

This 25-card set measures approximately 2 5/8" by 4 1/8" and is printed on thin card stock. The fronts feature color, posed action player photos with white borders accented by a thin red line. The player's jersey number, name, and position appear in black print across the bottom of the picture. The cards are unnumbered and checklisted below in alphabetical order.

COMPLETE SET (25) 12.00 30.00
1 Pats Logo .20 .50
2 Garth Butcher .80 2.00
3 Lyndon Byers 2.00 5.00
4 Jock Callander 1.60 4.00
5 Marc Centrone .40 1.00
6 Dave Goertz .40 1.00
7 Evans Dobni .40 1.00
8 Dale Derkatch .40 1.00
9 Jeff Crawford .40 1.00
10 Jim Clarke .40 1.00
11 Jayson Meyer .40 1.00
12 Gary Leeman .80 2.00
13 Bruce Holloway .40 1.00
14 Ken Heppner .40 1.00
15 Taylor Hall .40 1.00
16 Wally Schreiber .60 1.50
17 Kevin Pylypow .40 1.00
18 Ray Plamondon .40 1.00
19 Brent Pascal .40 1.00
20 Dave Michayluk .60 1.50
21 Barry Trotz .40 1.00
22 Al Tuer .60 1.50
23 Tony Vogel .40 1.00
24 Martin Wood .40 1.00
25 Regina Police Logo .20 .50

1982-83 Regina Pats

No. 12 - Gary Leeman - Def.

This 25-card set measures approximately 2 5/8" by 4 1/8" and features color, posed action player photos on white card stock. The pictures are framed by a thin red line. The player's name, jersey number, and position are printed in black on the photo.

COMPLETE SET (25) 10.00 25.00
1 Regina Pats and Police Logo .10 .25
2 Todd Lumbard .40 1.00
3 Jamie Reeve .40 1.00
4 Dave Goertz .30 .75
5 John Miner .30 .75
6 Doug Trapp .30 .75
7 R.J. Dundas .30 .75
8 Stu Grimson 1.60 4.00
9 Al Tuer .30 .75
10 Rick Herbert .30 .75
11 Tony Vogel .30 .75
12 John Bekkers .30 .75
13 Dale Derkatch .60 1.50
14 Gary Leeman .80 2.00
15 Nevin Markwart .40 1.00
16 Kurt Wickenheiser .30 .75
17 Jeff Frank .30 .75
18 Marc Centrone .30 .75
19 Taylor Hall .30 .75
20 Lyndon Byers 1.60 4.00
21 Jayson Meyer .30 .75
22 Jeff Crawford .30 .75
23 Don Boyd CO .20 .50
24 Barry Trapp ACO .20 .50
25 K-9 Big Blue (Mascot) .10 .25

1983-84 Regina Pats

No. 21 - Jeff Frank - Fwd.

This 25-card set measures approximately 2 5/8" by 4 1/8" and features color, posed action player photos with white borders accented by a thin red line. The player's name is superimposed at the bottom of the picture.

COMPLETE SET (25) 8.00 20.00
1 Title Card .10 .25
2 Todd Lumbard .40 1.00
3 Jamie Reeve .40 1.00
4 Dave Goertz .30 .75
5 John Miner .30 .75
6 Doug Trapp .30 .75
7 R.J. Dundas .30 .75
8 Stu Grimson 1.20 3.00
9 Al Tuer .30 .75
10 Rick Herbert .30 .75
11 Tony Vogel .30 .75
12 John Bekkers .30 .75
13 Dale Derkatch .40 1.00
14 Gary Leeman .60 1.50
15 Nevin Markwart .40 1.00
16 Kurt Wickenheiser .30 .75
17 Jeff Frank .30 .75
18 Marc Centrone .30 .75
19 Taylor Hall .30 .75
20 Lyndon Byers 1.20 3.00
21 Jayson Meyer .30 .75
22 Jeff Crawford .30 .75
23 Don Boyd CO .20 .50
24 Barry Trapp ACO .20 .50
25 K-9 Big Blue (Mascot) .10 .25

1986-87 Regina Pats

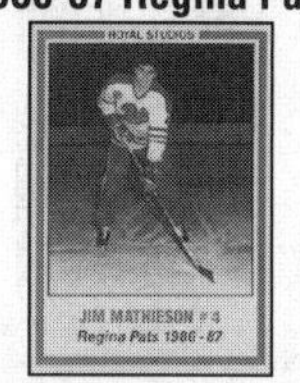

JIM MATHIESON # 4
Regina Pats 1986 - 87

Produced by Royal Studios, this 30-card set measures the standard size. The fronts feature color posed action player photos with red and white borders. The player's name and number are printed in red in the bottom white margin along with the team name and year, which are printed in black. The cards are unnumbered and checklisted below in alphabetical order.

COMPLETE SET (30) 6.00 15.00
1 Troy Bakogeorge .20 .50
2 Grant Chorney .20 .50
3 Gary Dickie .20 .50
4 Milan Dragicevic .20 .50
5 Mike Dyck .20 .50
6 Craig Endean .20 .50
7 Mike Gibson .20 .50
8 Erin Ginnell .20 .50
9 Brad Hornung .20 .50
10 Mark Janssens .30 .75
11 K-9 (Mascot) .10 .25
12 Trent Kachur .20 .50
13 Craig Kalawsky .20 .50
14 Dan Logan .20 .50
15 Jim Mathieson .20 .50
16 Darin McInnes .20 .50
17 Darrin McKechnie .20 .50
18 Rob McKinley .30 .75
19 Brad Miller .20 .50
20 Stacy Nickel .20 .50
21 Cregg Nicol .20 .50
22 Len Nielsen .20 .50
23 Darren Parsons .20 .50
24 Doug Sauter .20 .50
25 Ray Savard .20 .50
26 Dennis Sobchuk .30 .75
27 Chris Tarnowski .20 .50
28 Mike Van Slooten .20 .50
29 Brian Wilkie .20 .50
30 Rod Williams .20 .50

1987-88 Regina Pats

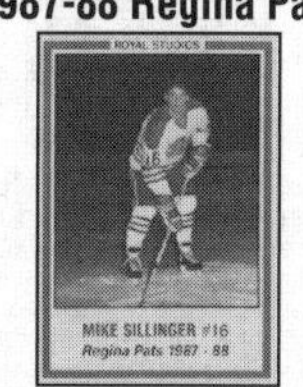

MIKE SILLINGER #16
Regina Pats 1987 - 88

Produced by Royal Studios, this 28-card standard-size set features color, posed action player photos with red and white borders. The player's name is printed in red in the bottom white margin along with the team name and year, which are printed in black. The cards are unnumbered and checklisted below in alphabetical order.

COMPLETE SET (28) 4.80 12.00
1 Kevin Clemens .20 .50
2 Gary Dickie .20 .50
3 Milan Dragicevic .20 .50
4 Mike Dyck .20 .50
5 Craig Endean .20 .50
6 Kevin Gallant PR .10 .25
7 Jamie Heward .20 .50
8 Rod Houk .20 .50
9 Mark Janssens .30 .75
10 Trent Kachur .20 .50
11 Craig Kalawsky .20 .50
12 K-9 (Mascot) .10 .25
13 Frank Kovacs .20 .50
14 Darren Kwiatkowski .20 .50
15 Brian Leibel .20 .50
16 Tim Logan .20 .50
17 Jim Mathieson .20 .50
18 Darrin McKechnie .20 .50
19 Rob McKinley .20 .50
20 Brad Miller .20 .50
21 Cregg Nicol .20 .50
22 Doug Sauter CO .10 .25
23 Dan Sexton .20 .50
24 Mike Sillinger .40 1.00
25 Dennis Sobchuk .30 .75
26 Stanley Szumlak TR .10 .25
27 Mike Van Slooten .20 .50
28 Team Photo .20 .50

1988-89 Regina Pats

MIKE SILLINGER/16
Regina Pats 1988-89

This 25-card standard-size set features color, posed action player photos with red and white borders. The player's name is printed in red in the bottom white margin along with the team name and year, which are printed in black. The cards are unnumbered and checklisted below in alphabetical order.

COMPLETE SET (24) 4.80 12.00
1 Shane Bogden .20 .50
2 Cam Brauer .20 .50
3 Scott Daniels .24 .60
4 Gary Dickie .20 .50
5 Mike Dyck .20 .50
6 Dave Gerse .20 .50
7 Kevin Haller .24 .60
8 Jamie Heward .20 .50
9 Terry Hollinger .20 .50
10 Rod Houk .20 .50
11 Frank Kovacs .20 .50
12 Brian Leibel .20 .50
13 Bernie Lynch CO .20 .50
14 Kelly Markwart .20 .50
15 Jim Mathieson .30 .75
16 Brad Mcginnis .20 .50
17 Brad Miller .20 .50
18 Dwayne Montieth TR .10 .25
19 Curtis Nykyforuk .20 .50
20 Darren Parsons .20 .50
21 Cory Paterson .20 .50
22 Jeff Sebastian .20 .50
23 Mike Sillinger .30 .75
24 Chad Silver .20 .50
25 Jamie Splett .20 .50

1989-90 Regina Pats

Sponsored by Mr. Lube, this 22-card set measures approximately 4" by 6" and is printed on thin card stock. The fronts feature black-and-white posed action photos with royal blue borders. The player's jersey number and name are printed in white in the bottom margin along with the team and sponsor logo.The cards are unnumbered and checklisted below in alphabetical order.

COMPLETE SET (21) 4.00 10.00
1 Kelly Chotowetz .20 .50
2 Hal Christiansen .20 .50
3 Scott Daniels .24 .60
4 Wade Fennig .20 .50
5 Jason Glickman .20 .50
6 Kevin Haller .75
7 Jamie Heward .30 .75
8 Terry Hollinger .20 .50
9 Frank Kovacs .20 .50
10 Mike Kirby .50
11 Kelly Markwart .20 .50
12 Jim Mathieson .30 .75
13 Cam McLellan .20 .50
14 Troy Mick .20 .50
15 Greg Pankewicz .20 .50
16 Cory Paterson .20 .50
17 Garry Pearce .20 .50
18 Mike Risdale .20 .50
19 Colin Ruck .20 .50
20 Mike Sillinger .30 .75
21 Jamie Splett .20 .50
22 Heath Weenk .20 .50

1996-97 Regina Pats

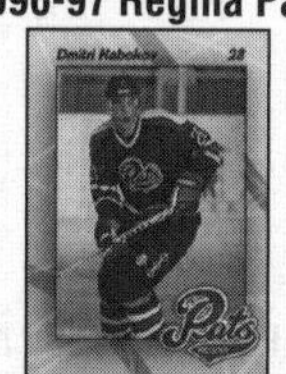

This 25-card set features the Regina Pats of the WHL. The cards were produced by the team and offered for sale for $7 at the team shop. The fronts feature a color action photo superimposed over a cutaway rink shot. The player's name and number appear at the top, with the team logo in the bottom right. The set includes several prominent prospects, including NHL first rounders Josh Holden, Dmitri Nabokov, Derek Morris, Kyle Calder and Brad Stuart.

COMPLETE SET (25) 7.20 15.00
1 Josh Holden .40 .75
2 Curtis Tipler .16 .40
3 Shane Lanigan .16 .40
4 Brad Stuart 1.60 3.00
5 David Maruca .16 .40
6 Perry Johnson .16 .40
7 Chad Mercier .16 .40
8 Kyle Calder .80 1.00
9 Josh Dobbyn .16 .40
10 Aaron Mori .16 .40
11 Gerald Adams .16 .40
12 Boyd Kane .20 .50
13 Lars Pattersen .16 .40
14 Dean Arsene .16 .40
15 Andy Adams .16 .40
16 Derek Morris 1.20 2.00
17 Kyle Freadrich .20 .50
18 Bryan Randall .16 .40
19 Clint Orr .16 .40
20 Brett Lysak .30 .75
21 Joey Bouvier .16 .40
22 Cody Jensen .16 .40
23 Rich Preston CO .10 .25
24 Team Photo .16 .40
25 Dmitri Nabokov .16 .40

1997-98 Regina Pats

This set features the Pats of the WHL. The set was sponsored by local police, and was handed out by officers to kids.

COMPLETE SET (25) 7.20 20.00
1 Gerad Adams .20 .50
2 Kyle Calder .80 2.00
3 Boyd Kane .30 .75
4 Brett Lysak .30 .75
5 Kevin Saurette .20 .50
6 Travis Churchman .20 .50
7 Dean Arsene .20 .50
8 Barret Jackman .40 5.00
9 Scott Roles .20 .50
10 John Cirjak .20 .50
11 Ronald Petrovicky .30 .75
12 Kyle Freadrich .30 .75
13 David Maruca .20 .50
14 Drew Kehler .20 .50
15 Bryan Randall .20 .50
16 Joey Bouvier .20 .50
17 Cody Jensen .20 .50
18 Shane Lanigan .20 .50
19 Mark Thompson .20 .50
20 Dennis Bassett .20 .50
21 Chris Kwas .20 .50
22 Derek Morris .80 2.00
23 Aaron Mori .20 .50
24 Brad Stuart 1.20 3.00
25 Josh Holden .40 1.00

2001-02 Regina Pats

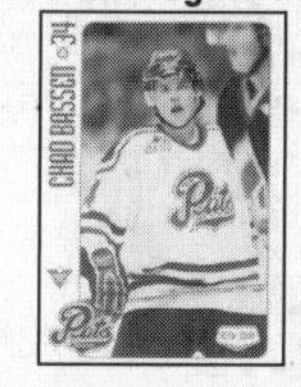

This set was produced by the Pats of the WHL. It's uncertain how they were distributed, but it's believed they were issued as a promotional giveaway, based on the wealth of sponsor logos. The set we obtained was signed by every player, save for Bassen and Yacboski. It's not known whether they were widely issued signed, or if this was a limited edition that was made available. Any additional information can be forwarded to hockeymag@beckett.com. The cards are unnumbered, and so are listed in alphabetical order.

COMPLETE SET (24) 10.00 25.00
1 Curtis Austring .40 1.00
2 Chad Bassen .40 1.00
3 Corey Becker .40 1.00
4 Dean Beuker .40 1.00
5 Drew Callender ACO .04 .10
6 Brennan Chapman .40 1.00
7 Chad Davidson .80 2.00
8 Jeff Feniak .40 1.00
9 Josh Harding .80 2.00
10 Grant Jacobsen .40 1.00
11 Kevin Korol .40 1.00
12 Kyle Ladobruk .40 1.00
13 Bob Lowes CO .10 .25
14 David McDonald .40 1.00
15 Chad Mercier ACO .04 .10
16 Tyson Moulton .40 1.00
17 Garth Murray .80 2.00
18 Filip Novak .80 2.00
19 Zach Roe .40 1.00
20 Chris Schlenker .40 1.00
21 Eric Sonnenberg .40 1.00
22 Matej Trojovsky .40 1.00
23 Daniel Waschuk .40 1.00
24 Darryl Yacboski .40 1.00

2002-03 Regina Pats

COMPLETE SET (23) 8.00 20.00
1 Grant Jacobsen .30 .75
2 Matt Trojovsky .30 .75
3 Petr Dvorak .30 .75
4 Matt Hubbauer .30 .75
5A Darryl Yacboski .30 .75
6 Jesse Deckert .30 .75
7 Todd Davison .30 .75
8 Rick Rypien .40 1.00
9 David Graden .30 .75
10 Wade Davis .30 .75
11 Britt Dougherty .30 .75
12 Curtis Austring .30 .75
13 Kyle Ladobruk .30 .75
14 Codey Becker .30 .75
15 Chris Schlenker .30 .75
16 Tyson Mulock .30 .75
17 Daniel Waschuk .30 .75
18 David McDonald .30 .75

19 Jordan McGillivary .30 .75
20 Brennan Chapman .30 .75
21 Tyson Moulton .40 1.00
22 Kyle Fecho .30 .75
23 Josh Harding 1.25 3.00

2003-04 Regina Pats

COMPLETE SET (24) 5.00 12.00
1 Paul Albers .20 .50
2 Craig Lineker .20 .50
3 Kyle Deck .20 .50
4 Derek Reinhart .20 .50
5 Landon Jones .20 .50
6 Tanner Stockwell .20 .50
7 Lance Morrison .20 .50
8 Rick Rypien .30 .75
9 David McDonald .20 .50
10 Kyle Lamb .20 .50
11 Dan Waschuk .20 .50
12 Ivo Kratena .20 .50
13 Kamil Vavra .20 .50
14 Kyle Nason .20 .50
15 Chris Schlenker .20 .50
16 Codey Becker .20 .50
17 Jonathan Bubnick .20 .50
18 Mike O'Dwyer .20 .50
19 Jordan McGillivray .20 .50
20 Andrew DeSousa .20 .50
21 Nick Olynyk .20 .50
22 Jesse Deckert .20 .50
23 Josh Harding .75 2.00
24 Britt Dougherty .20 .50

2004-05 Regina Pats

COMPLETE SET (24) 5.00 12.00
1 Regina Pats CL .01 .05
2 Paul Albers .20 .50
3 Craig Lineker .20 .50
4 Kyle Deck .20 .50
5 Derek Reinhart .20 .50
6 Logan Pyett .20 .50
7 Rick Rypien .30 .75
8 Kyle Ross .20 .50
9 Justin Bernhardt .20 .50
10 Braden Appleby .20 .50
11 Dan Waschuk .20 .50
12 Ryan McDonald .20 .50
13 Ian Duval .20 .50
14 Kyle Nason .20 .50
15 Terrance Delaronde .20 .50
16 Brent Hill .20 .50
17 Jonathan Bubnick .20 .50
18 Jordan McGillivray .20 .50
19 Jan Zapletal .20 .50
20 David Reekie .20 .50
21 Jordan Fuder .20 .50
22 Dustin Slade .20 .50
23 Craig Schira .20 .50
24 Preston Mosewich .20 .50

2005-06 Regina Pats

COMPLETE SET (28) 8.00 15.00
1 Justin Bernhardt .20 .50
2 Kyle Deck .20 .50
3 Ian Duval .20 .50
4 Garrett Festerling .20 .50
5 Spencer Fraipont .20 .50
6 Jordan Fuder .20 .50
7 Shane Halifax .20 .50
8 Petr Kalus .60 1.50
9 Brett Leffler .20 .50
10 Levi Lind .20 .50
11 Jason MacDonald .20 .50
12 Jordan McGillivray .20 .50
13 Curtis Patterson .20 .50
14 Logan Pyett .20 .50
15 David Reekie .40 1.00
16 Derek Reinhart .20 .50
17 Matt Robinson .20 .50
18 Kyle Ross .20 .50
19 Nick Ross .20 .50
20 Linden Rowatt .40 1.00
21 Andy Schenn .20 .50
22 Craig Schira .20 .50
23 Michael Senseman .20 .50
24 Tyson Sievert .20 .50
25 Denis Tolpeko .20 .50
26 Ryan McDonald .20 .50
27 Matt MacDermott .20 .50
28 Joshua Fauth .20 .50

2006-07 Regina Pats

COMPLETE SET (23) 12.00 20.00
1 Justin Bernhardt .40 1.00
2 Scott Brownlee .40 1.00
3 Kyle Deck .40 1.00
4 Matt Delahey .40 1.00
5 Ian Duval .40 1.00
6 Jordan Eberle .60 1.50
7 Garrett Festerling .40 1.00
8 Derek Hulak .40 1.00
9 Jared Jagow .40 1.00
10 Brett Leffler .40 1.00
11 Levi Lind .40 1.00
12 Jason MacDonald .40 1.00
13 Ryan McDonald .40 1.00
14 Logan Pyett .40 1.00
15 Derek Reinhart .40 1.00
16 Kyle Ross .40 1.00
17 Nick Ross .40 1.00
18 Linden Rowatt .60 1.50
19 Craig Schira .40 1.00
20 Justin Scott .40 1.00
21 Niko Snellman .40 1.00
22 Colten Teubert .40 1.00
23 Regina Pats .10 .25

1996 RHI Inaugural Edition

This nineteen-card Roller Hockey International set features the logos of all the teams from the hip, new game on the front, with franchise information on the back.

COMPLETE SET (19) 1.20 3.00
1 Los Angeles Blades .10 .25
2 Long Island Jaws .10 .25
3 Empire State Cobras .10 .25

4 Denver DareDevils .10 .25
5 Anaheim Bullfrogs .10 .25
6 Orlando Jackals .10 .25
7 Ottawa Loggers .10 .25
8 Oklahoma Coyotes .10 .25
9 Oakland Skates .10 .25
10 New Jersey Rockin Rollers .10 .25
11 Montreal Roadrunners .10 .25
12 Minnesota Arctic Blast .10 .25
13 Vancouver VooDoo .10 .25
14 St. Louis Vipers .10 .25
15 San Jose Rhinos .10 .25
16 San Diego Barracudas .10 .25
17 Sacramento River Rats .10 .25
18 Philadelphia Bulldogs .10 .25
NNO Checklist .04 .10

1984-85 Richelieu Riverains

This 19-card set of the Richelieu Riverains of the Quebec Midget AAA league measures approximately 4" by 5 1/2". The fronts feature black-and-white posed player portraits with a facsimile autograph and jersey number on the left. The backs are blank. The cards are unnumbered and checklisted below in alphabetical order.

COMPLETE SET (19) 4.80 12.00
1 Miguel Baldris .30 .75
2 Nicolas Beaulieu .30 .75
3 Martin Cote .30 .75
4 Sylvain Coutourier .40 1.00
5 Dominic Edmond .30 .75
6 Yues Gaucher .30 .75
7 Eric Gobel .30 .75
8 Carl Lemieux .30 .75
9 Michel Levesque .30 .75
10 Brad Loi .30 .75
11 Eric Primeau .30 .75
12 Stephane Quintal .60 1.50
13 Jean-Michel Ray .30 .75
14 Serge Richard .30 .75
15 Stephane Robinson .30 .75
16 Danny Rochefort .30 .75
17 Martin Savaria .30 .75
18 Sylvain Senecal .30 .75
19 Eric Sharron .30 .75

1988-89 Richelieu Riverains

Cards measure approximately 3" x 4" with card fronts featuring color posed photos. Card backs have players name and number along with safety tips in French.

COMPLETE SET (30) 4.80 12.00
1 Header Card .08 .20
2 Marc Beaurivage .20 .50
3 Denis Benoit .20 .50
4 Jonathan Black .20 .50
5 Richard Boisvert .20 .50
6 Hugues Bouchard .20 .50
7 Francois Bourdeau .20 .50
8 Guy Caplette .20 .50
9 Bertrand Cournoyer .20 .50
10 Yves Cournoyer .20 .50
11 Michel Deguise .20 .50
12 Patrick Grise .20 .50
13 Robert Guillet .20 .50
14 Jimmy Lachance .20 .50
15 Roger Laporte .20 .50
16 Frederic Lefebvre .20 .50
17 Frederic Maltais .20 .50
18 Andre Kid Millette .20 .50
19 Joseph Napolitano .20 .50
20 Remy Patoine .20 .50
21 Jean Plamondon .20 .50
22 Steve Plasse .20 .50
23 Jean Francois Poirier .20 .50
24 Jacques Provencal .20 .50
25 Alain Rancourt .20 .50
26 Francois St.Germain .20 .50
27 Frederic Savard .20 .50
28 Martin Tanguay .20 .50
29 Richard Valois .20 .50
30 Stephane Valois .20 .50

1990-91 Richmond Renegades

Produced by 7th Inning Sketch and sponsored by Richmond Comix and Cardz Inc., this 18-card standard-size set features posed color player photos with red borders. The player's name appears at the bottom.

COMPLETE SET (18) 3.20 8.00
1 Brad Turner .20 .50
2 Victor Posa .20 .50
3 Antti Autere .20 .50
4 Phil Huber .20 .50
5 Steve Spott .20 .50
6 Kelly Mills .20 .50
7 Paul Cain .20 .50
8 Shawn Lillie .20 .50
9 Kirby Lindal .20 .50
10 Dave Aiken .20 .50
11 Terry McCutcheon .20 .50
12 Jordan Fois .20 .50
13 Brad Beck .20 .50
14 Doug Pickell .20 .50
15 Frank Lascala .20 .50
16 John Haley .20 .50
17 Peter Harris .20 .50
18 Chris McSorley CO .30 .75

1991-92 Richmond Renegades

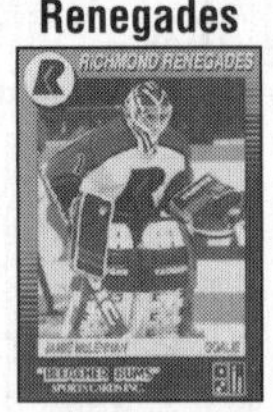

Sponsored by "Bleacher Bums" Sports Cards Inc. and Domino's Pizza, this 20-card set was issued as a trifold sheet, one 12 1/2" by 7" team photo and two sheets with ten standard-size player cards per sheet. The fronts feature color action player photos accented by a border design that shades from orange at the top to black at the bottom. The player's name and position appear below the picture, as do sponsor names.

COMPLETE SET (20) 3.60 9.00
1 Rob Vanderydt .20 .50
2 Larry Rooney .16 .40
3 Brendan Flynn .16 .40
4 Scott Drevitch .16 .40
5 Joni Lehto .16 .40
6 Todd Drevitch .16 .40
7 Paul Rutherford .16 .40
8 Dave Aiken .16 .40
9 Pat Bingham .16 .40
10 Trevor Jobe .16 .40
11 Bob Berg .16 .40
12 Mark Kuntz .16 .40
13 Joe Cappirini .16 .40
14 Trevor Converse .16 .40
15 Steve Scheifele .16 .40
16 Jon Gustafson .20 .50
17 Marco Fuster .16 .40
18 Guy Gadowsky .16 .40
19 Dave Allison CO .10 .25
20 Jamie McLennan .40 1.00
NNO Large Team Photo .80 2.00

1992-93 Richmond Renegades

Sponsored by "Bleacher Bums" Sports Cards Inc. and Kellogg's, this 20-card set was issued as a trifold sheet, one 12 1/2" by 7" team photo and two sheets with ten standard-size player cards per sheet. The fronts feature color action player photos accented by a black and orange border design. The picture itself is rimmed by an orange and white frame. Outside the frame is an orange design with varying sizes of stripes against a black background. The player's name and position appear below the picture as do sponsor names. The cards are unnumbered and checklisted below in alphabetical order.

COMPLETE SET (20) 3.20 8.00
1 Will Averill .16 .40
2 Frank Bialowas .20 .50
3 Scott Drevitch .16 .40
4 Brendan Flynn .16 .40
5 Guy Gadowsky ACO .04 .10
6 Jon Gustafson .20 .50
7 Phil Huber .16 .40
8 Mike James .16 .40
9 Jeffery Kampersal .16 .40
10 Mark Kuntz .16 .40
11 Sean LeBrun .16 .40
12 Kevin Malgunas .16 .40
13 Jim McGeough .20 .50
14 Ed Sabo .16 .40
15 Jeff Saterdalen .16 .40
16 Alan Schuler .16 .40
17 Martin Smith .16 .40
18 Roy Sommer CO .04 .10
19 Jeff Torrey .16 .40
20 Ben Wyzansky .16 .40
NNO Large Team Photo 1.00 2.50

1993-94 Richmond Renegades

Sponsored by "Bleacher Bum" Collectibles, Inc., radio station XL102, and Kellogg's, this 20-card set features the 1993-94 Richmond Renegades. The standard-size cards are printed on thin card stock. On a team color-coded background, the fronts feature color action player photos with purple borders, along with the player's name, position and team name.

COMPLETE SET (20) 3.20 8.00
1 Ken Weiss .16 .40
2 Guy Phillips .16 .40
3 Alexander Zhdan .16 .40
4 Alan Schuler .16 .40
5 John Craighead .16 .40
6 Colin Gregor .16 .40
7 Rob MacInnis .16 .40
8 Devin Derksen .20 .50
9 Jason Renard .16 .40
10 Peter Allen .16 .40
11 Roy Sommer CO .10 .25
12 Milan Hnilicka .60 1.50
13 Oleg Santurian .16 .40
14 Brendan Flynn .16 .40
15 Ken Blum .16 .40
16 Steve Bogoyevac .16 .40
17 Eric Germain .16 .40
18 Chris Foy .16 .40
19 Darren Colbourne .16 .40
20 Jon Gustafson .20 .50

1994-95 Richmond Renegades

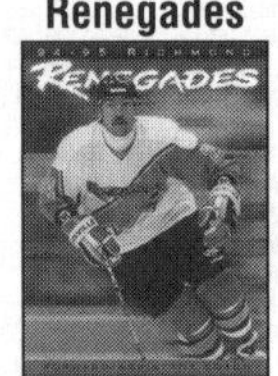

This 20-card set produced by Bleacher Bums and sponsored by Q-94 features the Richmond Renegades of the ECHL. The sets were available through the team. The fronts feature dynamic action shots over a blurred background, while the backs include player stats. The cards are unnumbered and are listed below as they came out of the team bag. Reportedly, production was significantly shorter for this set than the previous two Richmond issues.

COMPLETE SET (20) 4.00 10.00
1 Andrew Shier .20 .50
2 Shane Henry .20 .50
3 Shawn Snesar .20 .50
4 Steve Bogoyevac .20 .50
5 Chris Foy .20 .50
6 Scott Gruhl .30 .75
7 Blaine Moore .20 .50
8 Don Lester .20 .50
9 Kurt Mallett .20 .50
10 Garett MacDonald .20 .50
11 Jay Murphy .20 .50
12 Darren Wetherill .20 .50
13 Grant Sjerven .20 .50
14 Jan Benda .30 .75
15 Lou Body .20 .50
16 Mike Taylor .20 .50
17 Sean O'Brien .20 .50
18 Chris Tucker .20 .50
19 Jason Currie .20 .50
20 Roy Sommer CO .10 .25

1995-96 Richmond Renegades

This 25-card set of the Richmond Renegades of the ECHL was produced by Bleacher Bum and was supported by a wealth of sponsors. The cards were originally issued in a strip, thus single cards will have perforated edges. The cards feature a dynamic front design including an action photo and the Riley Cup Championship logo in the bottom right. The cards are unnumbered, and are ordered as they appeared on the strips.

COMPLETE SET (25) 3.60 9.00
1 Greg Hadden .16 .40
2 Mike Taylor .16 .40
3 Jay Murphy .16 .40
4 Todd Sparks .16 .40
5 Lou Body .16 .40
6 Sandy Allan .30 .75
7 Darren Wetherill .16 .40
8 Brian Goudie .16 .40
9 Brendan Flynn .16 .40
10 Kurt Mallett .16 .40
11 Dmitri Pankov .16 .40
12 Steve Carpenter .16 .40
13 Jason Mallon .16 .40
14 Scott Gruhl .40 1.00
15 Trevor Senn .16 .40
16 Garett MacDonald .16 .40
17 Martin Roy .16 .40
18 Michael Burman .16 .40
19 Grant Sjerven .16 .40
20 Mike Morin .16 .40
21 Andy Davis ANN .04 .10
22 The Gade -- Mascot .04 .10
23 Rob Jones TR .04 .10
24 Roy Sommer CO .04 .10
25 C.Laughlin GM .04 .10
H.Feuerstein CEO

1996-97 Richmond Renegades

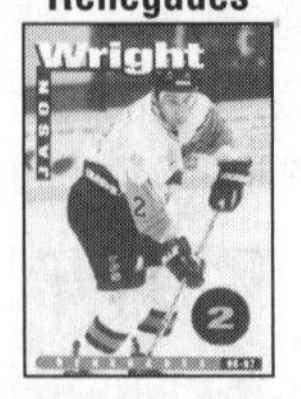

These cards feature full-color fronts with statistical information and a profile photo on the back. Cards are unnumbered and checklisted below in alphabetical order.

COMPLETE SET (25) 3.20 8.00
1 Scott Burfoot .20 .50
2 Taylor Clarke .16 .40
3 David Dartsch .16 .40
4 Freezer .04 .10
5 Gade .04 .10
6 Matt Garzone .16 .40
7 Brian Goudie .16 .40
8 Scott Gruhl CO .20 .50
9 Garry Gulash .16 .40
10 Mike Harding .16 .40
11 Tommy Holmes .16 .40
12 Rod Langway ACO .20 .50
13 Paul Lepler .16 .40
14 Jay McNeill .16 .40
15 Craig Paterson .16 .40
16 Chris Pittman .16 .40
17 Mike Rucinski .16 .40
18 Brian Secord .16 .40
19 Trevor Senn .16 .40
20 Grant Sjerven .16 .40
21 Andrew Shier .16 .40
22 Mike Taylor .16 .40
23 Tripp Tracy .30 .75
24 Jason Wright .16 .40
25 Title Card .04 .10

2000-01 Richmond Renegades

This set features the Renegades of the ECHL. The set was produced as a promotional giveaway and was handed out after the All-Star break. The cards are slightly oversized and are printed on very thin cardstock. The cards are unnumbered, and so are listed below in alphabetical order.

COMPLETE SET (19) 8.00 20.00
1 Gerad Adams .40 1.00
2 Brian Goudie .40 1.00
3 Nathan Forster .40 1.00
4 Joe Blaznek .40 1.00
5 Bob Thornton .40 1.00
6 Forrest Gore .40 1.00
7 Dan Vandermeer .40 1.00
8 Joe Vandermeer .40 1.00
9 Rod Taylor .40 1.00
10 Richard Pitirri .40 1.00
11 George Awada .40 1.00
12 Ryan Skaleski .40 1.00
13 Derek Schutz .40 1.00
14 Frank Novock .40 1.00
15 Matt Noga .40 1.00
16 Mike Siklenka .40 1.00
17 Sean Matile .60 1.50
18 Rastislav Stana .80 2.00
19 Brian McCullough .40 1.00

2006-07 Richmond Renegades

COMPLETE SET (20) 8.00 15.00
1 Jay Chrapala .40 1.00
2 Scott Corbett .30 .75
3 Brett Cross .30 .75
4 Andre Gill .30 .75
5 Mat Goody .75 2.00
6 Brian Goudie .30 .75
7 Doug Groenestege .40 1.00
8 Dean Jackson .30 .75
9 Don Melnyk .30 .75
10 David Mitchell .30 .75
11 Mike Owens .30 .75
12 Joe Pace .30 .75
13 Richard Reichenbach .30 .75
14 Tyler Schremp .30 .75
15 Danny White .30 .75
16 Duane Whitehead .30 .75
17 J.J. Wrobel .30 .75
18 Phil Youngclaus .30 .75
19 John Brophy CO .30 .75
20 Graffiti Ink Gallery SPONSOR .01 .01

2004-05 Richmond Riverdogs

This set features the Riverdogs of the UHL.

COMPLETE SET (28) 5.00 12.00
1 Checklist .01 .05
2 Donny Martin CO .02 .10
3 Glenn Morelli OWN .02 .10
4 Jim Duhart .40 1.00
5 Simo Pulkki .20 .50
6 Brian Goudie .20 .50
7 Ivan Curic .40 1.00
8 Francis Belanger .40 1.00
9 Ryan Prentice .20 .50
10 David Hymovitz .40 1.00
11 Mark Turner .20 .50
12 Mark Langdon .20 .50
13 David Brosseau .20 .50
14 Luch Nasato .20 .50
15 Trevor Senn .20 .50
16 Brian Herbert .20 .50
17 J.J. Wrobel .20 .50
18 Dennis Vial .40 1.00
19 Derek Shutz .20 .50
20 Brett Cross .20 .50
21 Anthony Dipalma .20 .50
22 Brent Belecki .20 .50
23 Dan McIntyre .20 .50
24 Semir Ben-Amor .20 .50
25 Razz MASCOT .02 .10
26 Team Photo .02 .10
27 Zamboni .02 .10
28 Richmond Coliseum .02 .10

1996-97 Rimouski Oceanic

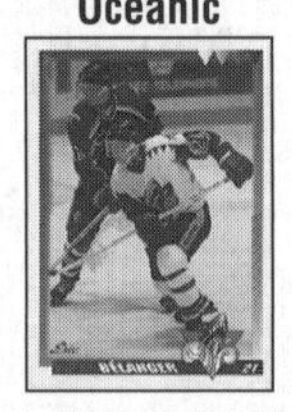

This 28-card set was the first of two this season to feature the Oceanic of the QMJHL. The cards featured a color action photo and jersey number on the front, with a head shot and statistical data on the back. It was sold through the team and at convenience stores in the region. The set is unnumbered, and listed in alphabetical order. The most noteworthy player in the set is Vincent Lecavalier, a forward looked upon as an early favorite for the top pick in the 1998 NHL Entry Draft. Less than 3,000 of these sets were produced.

COMPLETE SET (28) 12.00 25.00
1 Jonathan Beaulieu .16 .40
2 Martin Bedard .16 .40
3 Eric Belzile .16 .40
4 Denis Boily .16 .40
5 Dave Bolduc .16 .40
6 Yan Bouchard .20 .50
7 Nicolas Chabot .20 .50
8 Eryc Collin .16 .40
9 Eric Drouin .16 .40
10 Yannick Dupont .16 .40
11 Frederic Girard .16 .40
12 Jimmy Grondin .16 .40
13 Bobby Lebel CO .10 .25
14 Vincent Lecavalier 8.00 15.00
15 Frederic Levac .16 .40
16 Francois Levesque .16 .40
17 Philippe Lord .16 .40
18 Dave Malenfant .16 .40
19 Eric Normandin .20 .50
20 Mathieu Normandin .16 .40
21 Philippe Plante .16 .40
22 Martin Poitras .20 .50
23 Saison 1996-1997 .10 .25
24 Philippe Sauve .60 3.00
25 Sebastien Simard .16 .40
26 David St-Onge .16 .40
27 Mathieu Sunderland .20 .50
28 Gaston Therrien CO .10 .25

1996-97 Rimouski Oceanic Quebec Provincial Police

Card fronts feature color photos, along with players jersey number and the Rimouski logo. Card backs feature statistical information and all text is in French. Each card also bears a serial number. Cards are unnumbered and checklisted below alphabetically.

COMPLETE SET (26) 16.00 40.00
1 Jonathan Beaulieu .20 .50
2 Martin Bedard .20 .50
3 Eric Belzile .20 .50
4 Maxime Blouin .20 .50
5 Denis Boily .20 .50
6 Yan Bouchard .20 .50
7 Nicolas Chabot .20 .50
8 Eryc Collin .20 .50
9 Eric Drouin .20 .50
10 Yannick Dupont .20 .50
11 Frederic Girard .20 .50
12 Jimmy Grondin .20 .50
13 Vincent Lecavalier 12.00 25.00
14 Frederic Levac .20 .50
15 Francois Levesque .20 .50
16 Philipe Lord .20 .50
17 Dave Malenfant .20 .50
18 Eric Normandin .20 .50
19 Mathieu Normandin .20 .50
20 Philippe Plante .20 .50
21 Martin Poitras .20 .50
22 Philippe Sauve 1.20 5.00
23 Nicola Spaccucci .20 .50
24 David St-Onge .20 .50
25 Sebastien Tremblay .20 .50
26 Title Card .04 .10

1996-97 Rimouski Oceanic Update

This 10-card set was produced as a companion set to the basic Rimouski series issued earlier in the season. The design for both series is identical. The players featured in the update were late arrivals due to trades. Less than 1200 of these sets were produced. The cards are unnumbered and thus are listed in alphabetical order.

COMPLETE SET (10) 2.40 6.00
1 Eric Belanger (LW) .20 .50
2 Eric Belanger (C) .60 1.50
3 Philippe Grondin .20 .50
4 Jasson Lehoux .20 .50
5 Jonathan Levesque .20 .50
6 Louki MASCOT .10 .25
7 Guillaume Rodrigue .20 .50
8 Joe Rullier .40 1.00
9 Russell Smith .20 .50
10 Derrick Walser .30 .75

1997-98 Rimouski Oceanic

This set was produced by the team and sold at home games. It is noteworthy for including early cards of Vincent Lecavalier and Brad Richards.

COMPLETE SET (25) 10.00 25.00
4 Vincent Lecavalier 4.00 10.00
7 Joe Rullier .30 .75
9 Jonathan Beaulieu .16 .40
10 David Bilodeau .16 .40
11 Jimmy Grondin .16 .40
14 Dave Malenfant .16 .40
17 Kevin Bolduc .16 .40
19 Eric Normandin .16 .40
20 Francois Drainville .16 .40
21 Eric Belanger .30 .75
22 Eric Drouin .16 .40
24 Julien Desrosiers .16 .40
25 David St-Onge .16 .40
27 Phillippe Grondin .16 .40
33 Phillippe Sauve .40 3.00
35 Jean-Marc Pelletier .60 1.50
36 Jonathan St-Louis .16 .40
39 Brad Richards 2.80 12.00
44 Guillaume Couture .16 .40
45 Chad Gagnon .16 .40
55 Casey Leggett .16 .40
79 Denis Boily .16 .40
91 Derrick Walser .30 .75
98 Adam Borzecki .16 .40
NNO Team Card .16 .40

1999-00 Rimouski Oceanic

This 24-card set features the QMJHL's Oceanic, the Memorial Cup winners for that season. Base cards contain full color action photography and have purple borders along the top and the right hand side which feature the player's name and team logo.

COMPLETE SET (24) 6.00 15.00
1 Nicolas Pilote .14 .35
2 Joe Rullier .30 .75
3 Jonathan Beaulieu .14 .35
4 Nicolas Poirier .14 .35
5 Thatcher Bell .40 .50
6 Brent Maclellan .14 .35
7 Alexandre Tremblay .14 .35
8 Jean-Francois Babin .14 .35
9 Benoit Martin .14 .35
10 Jan Philippe Cadieux .14 .35
11 Jean-Philippe Briere .14 .35
12 Alexis Castonguay .14 .35
13 Rene Vydareny .14 .35
14 Ronnie Decontie .14 .35
15 Shawn Scanzano .14 .35
16 Michel Ouellet .14 .35
17 Jacques Lariviere .14 .35
18 Eric Salvail .14 .35
19 Sebastien Caron .60 1.00
20 Brad Richards 2.00 5.00
21 Aaron Johnson .14 .35
22 Juraj Kolnik .60 1.50
23 Michel Periard .30 .75
24 Header Card/CL .04 .10

1999-00 Rimouski Oceanic Signed

This set of 23 cards parallels the base Rimouski Oceanic Set. The main differences are that the cards are signed on a specially imprinted area on the front of the card, while the backs are serial numbered out of 100.

COMPLETE SET (24) 30.00 75.00
1 Nicolas Pilote .80 2.00
2 Joe Rullier 1.60 4.00
3 Jonathan Beaulieu .80 2.00
4 Nicolas Poirier .80 2.00
5 Thatcher Bell 2.40 4.00
6 Brent Maclellan .80 2.00
7 Alexandre Tremblay .80 2.00
8 Jean-Francois Babin .80 2.00
9 Benoit Martin .80 2.00
10 Jan Philippe Cadieux .80 2.00

11 Jean-Philippe Briere .80 2.00
12 Alexis Castonguay .80 2.00
13 Rene Vydareny .80 2.00
14 Ronnie Decontie .80 2.00
15 Shawn Scanzano .80 2.00
16 Michel Ouellet .80 2.00
17 Jacques Lariviere .80 2.00
18 Eric Salvail .80 2.00
19 Sebastien Caron 3.20 5.00
20 Brad Richards 10.00 25.00
21 Aaron Johnson .80 2.00
22 Juraj Kolnik 3.20 8.00
23 Michel Periard 1.60 4.00
24 Header Card/CL .10 .25

2000-01 Rimouski Oceanic

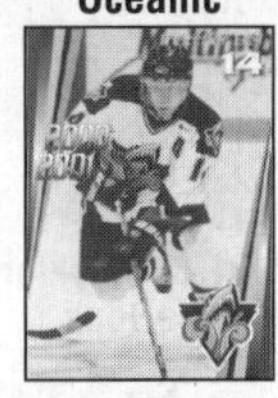

This set features the Oceanic of the QMJHL. The set was produced by CTM-Ste-Foy, and was sold both by that card shop, as well as by the team.

COMPLETE SET (26) 4.80 12.00
1 Phillippe Lauze .20 .75
2 Tim Sinasac .20 .50
3 Jonathan Beaulieu .20 .50
4 Nichola Pilote .20 .50
5 Nicolas Poirier .20 .50
6 Thatcher Bell .30 .50
7 Tomas Malec .20 .50
8 Brent MacLellan .20 .50
9 Jean-Francois Plourde .20 .50
10 Jean-Francois Babin .20 .50
11 Benoit Martin .20 .50
12 Daniel Petiquay .20 .75
13 Jean-Philippe Briere .20 .50
14 Ryan Clowe .40 1.00
15 Mathieu Fournier .20 .50
16 Gabriel Balasescu .20 .50
17 Mathieu Simard .20 .50
18 Samuel Gibbons .20 .50
19 Michel Ouellet .20 .50
20 Jonathan Pelletier .30 .75
21 Eric Salvail .30 .75
22 Aaron Johnson .20 .50
23 Sebastien Bolduc .20 .75
24 Louky MASCOT .04 .10
25 Doris Labonte CO .04 .10
NNO Team CL .04 .01

2000-01 Rimouski Oceanic Signed

This set is exactly the same as the base Oceanic set from this season, save that every card has been hand signed by the player pictured. Each card also is serial numbered out of just 100.

COMPLETE SET (26) 16.00 40.00
1 Phillippe Lauze .80 4.00
2 Tim Sinasac .80 2.00
3 Jonathan Beaulieu .80 2.00
4 Nichola Pilote .80 2.00
5 Nicolas Poirier .80 2.00
6 Thatcher Bell 1.20 3.00
7 Tomas Malec .80 2.00
8 Brent MacLellan .80 2.00
9 Jean-Francois Plourde .80 2.00
10 Jean-Francois Babin .80 2.00
11 Benoit Martin .80 2.00
12 Daniel Petiquay .80 4.00
13 Jean-Philippe Briere .80 2.00
14 Ryan Clowe 2.00 5.00
15 Mathieu Fournier .80 2.00
16 Gabriel Balasescu .80 2.00
17 Mathieu Simard .80 2.00
18 Samuel Gibbons .80 2.00
19 Michel Ouellet .80 2.00
20 Jonathan Pelletier 1.20 4.00
21 Eric Salvail 1.20 4.00
22 Aaron Johnson .80 2.00
23 Sebastien Bolduc .80 4.00
24 Louky MASCOT .04 .10
25 Doris Labonte CO .04 .10
NNO Team CL .04 .10

2001-02 Rimouski Oceanic

This set features the Oceanic of the QMJHL. The set was produced by CTM Ste-Foy and was sold at Oceanic home games. It was reported that less than 1,000 sets were produced.

COMPLETE SET (23) 4.80 12.00
1 Chaz Johnson .20 .50
2 Philippe Lauze .20 .50
3 Dany Stewart .20 .50
4 Michael Gavalier .20 .50
5 Nicolas Poirier .40 1.00
6 Thatcher Bell .30 .75
7 Thomas Malec .30 .75
8 Brent Maclellan .20 .50
9 Jean-Francois Plourde .20 .50
10 Benoit Martin .20 .50
11 Daniel Petiquay .20 .50
12 Jean-Philippe Briere .20 .50
13 Ryan Clowe .30 .75
14 Mathieu Fournier .20 .50
15 Gabriel Balasescu .20 .50
16 Samuel Gibbons .20 .50
17 Michel Ouellet .20 .50
18 Eric Neilson .20 .50
19 Patrick Lepage .40 1.00
20 Eric Salvail .40 1.00
21 Aaron Johnson .40 1.00
22 Sebastien Bolduc .40 1.00
23 Marc-Antoine Pouliot 1.25 3.00

2002-03 Rimouski Oceanic

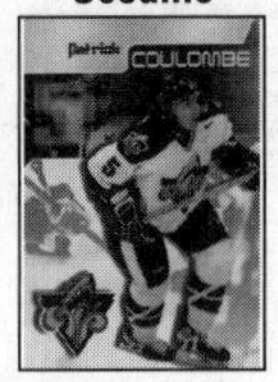

COMPLETE SET (22) 5.00 12.00
1 Guillaume Chicoine .20 .50
2 Patrick Coulombe .20 .50
3 Jason D'Ascanio .20 .50
4 Francois Gauthier .20 .50
5 Michel Gavalier .20 .50
6 Zbynek Hrdel .20 .50
7 Danick Jasmin-Riel .20 .50
8 Philippe Lauze .20 .50
9 Mattews Lemaire .20 .50
10 Eric Neilson .20 .50
11 Sebastien Nolet .20 .50
12 Daniel Petiquay .20 .50
13 Marc-Antoine Pouliot .75 2.00
14 Jonathan Robert .20 .50
15 Dany Roussin .40 1.00
16 Eric Salvail .20 .50
17 Christopher Sorensen .20 .50
18 Dany Stewart .20 .50
19 Mark Tobin .20 .50
20 Erick Tremblay .20 .50
21 Jeremy Turgeon .20 .50
22 Alexander Vachon .40 1.00

2003-04 Rimouski Oceanic

This regulation-sized set was produced by CTM Ste-Foy and Extreme Cards and features the first two licensed cards of Sidney Crosby. Not every set includes the NNO cards, so the set is considered complete without them.

COMPLETE SET (25) 15.00 30.00
1 Benoit Arsenault .20 .50
2 Charles Bergeron .20 .50
3 Francois Bolduc .20 .50
4 Jean-Michael Bolduc .20 .50
5 Jean-Sebastien Cote .20 .50
6 Patrick Coulombe .20 .50
7 Sidney Crosby 8.00 20.00
8 Cedrick Desjardins .40 1.00
9 Olivier Didier .20 .50
10 Zbynek Hrdel .20 .50
11 Danick Jasmin-Riel .20 .50
12 Philippe Lauze .20 .75
13 Guillaume Lavallee .20 .50
14 Mattews Lemaire .20 .50
15 Eric Neilson .20 .50
16 Marc-Antoine Pouliot .40 1.00
17 Michal Sersen .20 .50
18 Danny Stewart .20 .50
19 Mark Tobin .20 .50
20 Erick Tremblay .20 .50
21 Alexandre Vachon .20 .50
22 Guillaume Veilleux .20 .50
23 Hubert Veilleux .20 .50
NNO Sidney Crosby TL 12.00 30.00
NNO Marc-Antoine Pouliot TL .75 2.00

2003-04 Rimouski Oceanic Sheets

This team issued set of 5 sheets featured players of the Oceanic from the 2003-04 season. Sheets measured approximately 17" x 6".

COMPLETE SET (5) 20.00 40.00
1 Mattews Lemaire 2.00 5.00
Charles Bergeron
Eric Nelson
Olivier Didier
Danick Jasmin Riel
2 Erick Tremblay 2.00 5.00
Dany Roussin
Philippe Lauze
Jean-Sebastien Cote
Michal Sersen
3 Mark Tobin 2.00 5.00
Patrick Coulombe
Marc-Antoine Pouliot
Francois Bolduc
Cedrick Desjardins
4 Guillame Veilleux 10.00 25.00
Sidney Crosby
Guillame Lavallee
Alexandre Vachon
5 Jean-Michal Bolduc 2.00 5.00
Hubert Veilleux
Zbynek Hrdel
Dany Stewart
Benoit Arsenault

2004-05 Rimouski Oceanic

A total of 5,000 team sets were produced, with additional cards being available in wax form. The Limited Edition cards of Crosby and Pouliot were available in random team sets.

COMPLETE SET (23) 10.00 25.00
1 Sidney Crosby 4.00 10.00
2 Alexandre Vachon .40 1.00
3 Dany Roussin .40 1.00
4 Graham Bona .20 .50
5 Sebastien Aspirot .20 .50
6 Nicolas Bachand .20 .50
7 Jamie Blom .20 .50
8 Francois Bolduc .20 .50
9 Francis Charette .20 .50
10 Jean-Sebastien Cote .20 .50
11 Patrick Coulombe .20 .50
12 Cedrik Desjardins .40 1.00
13 Maxime Desruisseaux .20 .50
14 Zbynek Hrdel .20 .50
15 Sebastien Laferriere .20 .50
16 Eric Neilson .40 1.00
17 Marc-Antoine Pouliot .40 1.00
18 Michal Sersen .20 .50
19 Danny Stewart .20 .50
20 Mark Tobin .20 .50
21 Erick Tremblay .20 .50
22 Jean-Michel Filiatrault .75 2.00
23 Jean-Michel Bolduc .20 .50
LE1 Sidney Crosby LTD/300 15.00 40.00
LE2 Marc-Antoine Pouliot LTD/300 4.00 10.00

2004-05 Rimouski Oceanic Season Ticket

This set of six cards was available only to purchasers of season tickets to the 2004-05 Oceanic. The cards are printed on clear plastic, are horizontally oriented, and have a serial number on the back. They are unnumbered, and so are listed below in alphabetical order.

COMPLETE SET (6) 20.00 50.00
1 Jonathan Beaulieu .75 2.00
2 Sebastien Caron 1.50 4.00
3 Sidney Crosby 15.00 40.00
4 Vincent Lecavalier 4.00 10.00
5 Brad Richards 4.00 10.00
6 Allan Sirois .75 2.00

2005-06 Rimouski Oceanic

COMPLETE SET (30) 6.00 15.00
1 Patrick Coulombe .20 .50
2 Erick Tremblay .20 .50
3 Jean-Michel Bolduc .20 .50
4 Jamie Blom .20 .50
5 Mark Tobin .20 .50
6 Sebastien Aspirot .20 .50
7 Francois Bolduc .20 .50
8 Jean-Sebastien Cote .20 .50
9 Sebastien Laferriere .20 .50
10 Graham Bona .20 .50
11 Francis Charette .20 .50
12 Maxime Lincourt .20 .50
13 Philippe Roberge .40 1.00
14 David Skokan .40 1.00
15 Pierre-Alexandre Joncas .20 .50
16 Maxime Macenauer .20 .50
17 David Bouchard .40 1.00
18 Jason Caron .20 .50
19 Nicholas Goyens .20 .50
20 Guillaume Mailloux .20 .50
21 Dave Plante .20 .50
22 Michael Chiasson .20 .50
23 Marc-Andre Laroche .20 .50
24 Guillaume Letourneau .20 .50
25 Olivier Fortier .20 .50
26 Philippe Garnier .20 .50
27 Drew Paris .20 .50
28 Max Gratchev .20 .50
29 Maxime Tanguay .20 .50
30 Tommy Legault .20 .50

2006-07 Rimouski Oceanic

COMPLETE SET (24) 8.00 15.00
1 Olivier Fortier .25 .60
2 Maxime Tanguay .40 1.00
3 Philippe Garnier .25 .60
4 Maxime Gratchev .40 1.00
5 FranÃ§ois Bolduc .25 .60
6 Graham Bona .25 .60
7 David Skokan .25 .60
8 Pierre-Alexandre Joncas .25 .60
9 David Bouchard .25 .60
10 Nicholas Goyens .25 .60
11 Dave Plante .25 .60
12 Marc-AndrÃ© Laroche .25 .60
13 Philippe Cornet .25 .60
14 Patrice Cormier .25 .60
15 Alexandre NÃ©ron .25 .60
16 Jordan Caron .25 .60
17 Alexandre Brunet .25 .60
18 Louis-Philippe Lachance .25 .60
19 Christopher Stevens .25 .60
20 FrÃ©dÃ©ric Desrochers .25 .60
21 Michal Frolik .60 1.50
22 Kevin Cormier .25 .60
23 Tommy Legault .40 1.00
24 Michael Chiasson .40 1.00

1993-94 Roanoke Express

Sponsored by Advance Auto Parts, First Virginia Bank, radio station J93.5 FM and WJPR TV 27, this 25-card standard-size set commemorates the inaugural season of the Roanoke Express. The fronts feature borderless color action player photos. The team logo appears on the bottom left with the player's name, position and number in two red bars next to it. The cards are unnumbered and checklisted below in alphabetical order.

COMPLETE SET (25) 2.80 7.00
1 Frank Anzalone CO .10 .25
2 Will Averill .16 .40
3 Claude Barthe .16 .40
4 Lev Berdichevsky .16 .40
5 Hughes Bouchard .16 .40
6 Reggie Brezeault .16 .40
7 Ilja Dubkov .16 .40
8 Pat Ferschweiler .16 .40
9 Kyle Galloway .16 .40
10 Jeff Jestadt .16 .40
11 Roger Larche .16 .40
12 Dana McGuane TR .04 .10
13 Jim Mill .16 .40
14 Dave Morissette .16 .40
15 Chris Potter .16 .40
16 Dan Ryder .16 .40
17 Gairin Smith .16 .40
18 Michael Smith .16 .40
19 Tony Szabo .16 .40
20 Stephen Tepper .16 .40
21 Oleg Yashin .16 .40
22 Team Photo .16 .40
23 Dave Morissette .04 .10
First Franchise Goal
24 Sponsor Card .04 .10
Advance Auto Parts
25 Sponsor Card .04 .10
First Virginia Bank

1994-95 Roanoke Express

This 24-card set features the Roanoke Express of the ECHL. The cards -- which were printed on extremely thin paper -- were available through the team, and possibly offered as a game night promotion. The fronts feature a blurry action photo, with team logo and player name and position. The unnumbered backs include stats and the logos of several sponsors.

COMPLETE SET (24) 4.00 10.00
1 Team Photo .20 .50
2 Dave Gagnon .30 .75
3 Chris Potter .30 .75
4 Dave Stewart .20 .50
5 Michael Smith .20 .50
6 Jon Larson .20 .50
7 Carl Fleury .20 .50
8 Jeff Jestadt .20 .50
9 Marty Schriner .20 .50
10 Rouslan Toujikov .20 .50
11 Jason Clarke .20 .50
12 Stephane Desjardins .20 .50
13 Robin Bouchard .20 .50
14 Oleg Yashin .20 .50
15 Ilja Dubkov .20 .50
16 Derek Laxdal .30 .75
17 Mark Luger .20 .50
18 Pat Ferschweiler .20 .50
19 Dan Ryder .20 .50
20 Frank Anzalone CO .10 .25
21 Dana McGuane TR .04 .10
22 Loco Mascot .04 .10
23 Board of Directors .04 .10
24 Fan Card .01

1995-96 Roanoke Express

This 25-card set of the Roanoke Express of the ECHL was a team-produced issue, and available only through the club. The fronts feature sharp, pseudo-action shots with the player's name in a red border along the left, and position and number in a green border along the top. A gold foil Express logo graces the lower right corner.

COMPLETE SET (25) 4.00 10.00
1 Jeff Jestadt .16 .40
2 Dave Stewart .16 .40
3 Matt DelGuidice .30 .75
4 Dave Holum .16 .40
5 Mike Stacchi .16 .40
6 Paul Croteau .16 .40
7 Marty Schriner .16 .40
8 L.P. Charbonneau .16 .40
9 Michael Smith .16 .40
10 Ilja Dubkov .20 .50
11 Tim Christian .16 .40
12 Brian Gallentine .16 .40
13 Jeff Jablonski .16 .40
14 Daniel Berthiaume .40 1.00
15 Duane Harmer .16 .40
16 Jason Clarke .16 .40
17 Tim Hanley .16 .40
18 Jon Larson .16 .40
19 Nick Jones .16 .40
20 Chris Potter .16 .40
21 Craig Herr .16 .40
22 Frank Anzalone CO .10 .25
23 Chris Pollack TR .04 .10
24 Loco MASCOT .04 .10
25 Team Photo .04 .10

1996-97 Roanoke Express

This 24-card set of the Roanoke Express of the ECHL was team issued. The cards feature action photography on the front, along with a comprehensive stats package on the reverse. The cards prominently feature the player's jersey number on the back, and are listed below thusly.

COMPLETE SET (24) 3.20 8.00
1 Dave Gagnon .20 .50
2 Dave Stewart .16 .40
3 Eric Landry .16 .40
5 Michael Smith .16 .40
7 Jeff Loder .16 .40
8 Duane Harmer .16 .40
10 Bobby Brown .16 .40
11 J.F. Tremblay .16 .40
12 Ryan Equale .16 .40
14 Doug Searle .16 .40
15 Jeff Jablonski .16 .40
17 Jeff Cowan .20 .50
18 Sean Brown .20 .50
21 Ilya Dubkov .16 .40
22 Matt O'Dette .16 .40
23 Chris Lipsett .16 .40
24 Tim Christian .16 .40
35 Larry Moberg .20 .50
NNO Elmer the Engine .04 .10
NNO Mike Holden TR .04 .10
NNO Checklist .04 .10
NNO Team Photo .16 .40
NNO Frank Anzalone CO .04 .10
NNO Loco the Railyard Dog .04 .10

1998-99 Roanoke Express

These card were handed out at Express home games. They are numbered on the back on the lower left hand corner in small print. Card #7 is unconfirmed to date, but is believed to exist. Anyone with additional information is urged to forward it to the publisher.

COMPLETE SET (26) 25.00
1 Tony Mancuso GM .20 .50
2 Scott Gordon HCO .20 .50
3 Perry Florio ACO .20 .50
4 Darren Abbott DOB .20 .50
5 Dave Gagnon .60 1.50
6 Daniel Berthiaume .80 2.00
7 Unknown .40 1.00
8 Doug Searle .40 1.00
9 Jason Dailey .40 1.00
10 Duane Harmer .40 1.00
11 Mike Peron .40 1.00
12 Kris Cantu .40 1.00
13 Travis Smith .40 1.00
14 J.C. Ruid .40 1.00
15 Ben Schust .40 1.00
16 Jeremy Schaefer .40 1.00
17 J.F. Tremblay .40 1.00
18 Mike Mader .40 1.00
19 Nicholas Windsor .40 1.00
20 Peter Brearley .40 1.00
21 Nic Beaudoin .40 1.00
22 Chris Lipsett .40 1.00
23 Tim Christian .40 1.00
24 Dru Burgess .40 1.00
25 Chris Wismer .40 1.00
26 Loco Mascot .20 .50

2000-01 Roanoke Express

This set features the Express of the ECHL. The set was issued as a promotional giveaway. Local police officers attended several games, handing out a different card to children at each one. That makes accumulating a complete set a difficult task, indeed.

COMPLETE SET (22) 8.00 20.00
1 Roanoke Express .40 .50
2 Mike Peron .40 1.00
3 Joe Dusbabek .40 1.00
4 Troy Lake .40 1.00
5 Jeff Burgoyne .40 1.00
6 Ben Schust .40 1.00
7 Dave Gagnon .60 1.50
8 Calvin Elfring .40 1.00
9 Colin Anderson .40 1.00
10 Todd Compeau .40 1.00
11 Daniel Berthiaume .60 1.50
12 Loco MASCOT .10 .25
13 Aaron Gates .40 1.00
14 Travis Smith .40 1.00
15 John Sadowski .40 1.00
16 Perry Florio CO .10 .25
17 Nate Handrahan .40 1.00
18 Jeff Sproat .40 1.00
19 Jay Shipulski .40 1.00
20 Doug Sheppard .40 1.00
21 George McMillan SHERIFF .04 .01
22 Adam Dewan .40 1.00

2001-02 Roanoke Express

This set features the Express of the ECHL. The cards were handed out to children, one card at a time, from police officers at Express games. Because of this, complete sets are nearly impossible to compile.

COMPLETE SET (24) 20.00 50.00
1 Daniel Berthiaume 1.20 3.00
2 Chris Cava .80 2.00
3 Steve Chabbert .80 2.00
4 Duncan Dalmao .80 2.00
5 Brett DeCecco 1.20 3.00
6 Joe Dusbabek .80 2.00
7 Brad Essex .80 2.00
8 Vernon Fiddler .80 2.00
9 Pete Gardiner .80 2.00
10 Jeff Helperl .80 2.00
11 Marty Hughes .80 2.00
12 Rick Kowalsky .80 2.00
13 Troy Lake .80 2.00
14 Frank Novock .80 2.00
15 Mike Omicioli 1.20 3.00
16 Mike Peron .80 2.00
17 Gary Ricciardi 1.20 3.00
18 Travis Smith .80 2.00
19 Jeff Sproat .80 2.00
20 Terence Tootoo 2.00 5.00
21 Jordan Willis 1.60 4.00
22 Perry Florio CO .20 .50
23 Mark Bernard ACO .20 .50
24 George McMillan .80 2.00

2002-03 Roanoke Express

COMPLETE SET (25) 15.00 40.00
1 Sebastien Laplante .75 2.00
2 Sheriff McMillan .10 .25
3 Dan Sullivan .75 2.00
4 Loco Mascot .10 .25
5 Cole Fischer .75 2.00
6 Perry Florio HCO .10 .25
7 Tony MacAulay ACO .10 .25
8 Scotty Balan .75 2.00
9 Josh Barker .75 2.00
10 Dan Carlson .75 2.00
11 Adam Colagiacomo .75 2.00
12 Duncan Dalmao .75 2.00
13 Joe Dusbabek .75 2.00
14 Brad Essex .75 2.00
15 Dylan Gyori 1.25 3.00
16 Jason Jaffray .75 2.00
17 Rick Kowalsky .75 2.00
18 Shawn Limpright .75 2.00
19 Evan Lindsay .75 2.00
20 Chad Mazurak .75 2.00
21 Frank Novock .75 2.00
22 Mike Peron .75 2.00
23 Doug Schueller .75 2.00
24 David Silverstone .75 2.00
25 Tim O'Connell .75 2.00

2002-03 Roanoke Express RBI Sports

COMPLETE SET (18) 10.00 18.00
187 Josh Barker .40 1.00
188 Scotty Balan .40 1.00
189 Cam Bristow .40 1.00
190 Dan Carlson .40 1.00
191 Duncan Dalmao .40 1.00
192 Joe Dusbabek .40 1.00
193 Brad Essex .40 1.00
194 Cole Fisher .40 1.00
195 Dylan Gyori .60 1.50
196 Jason Jaffray .40 1.00
197 Rick Kowalsky .40 1.00
198 Sebastien Laplante .60 1.50
199 Chad Mazurak .40 1.00
200 Frank Novock .40 1.00
201 Tim O'Connell .40 1.00
202 Mike Peron .40 1.00
203 Doug Schueller .40 1.00
204 David Silverstone .40 1.00

2003-04 Roanoke Express

COMPLETE SET (16) 6.00 15.00
305 Josh Barker .40 1.00
306 David Belitski .60 1.50
307 Kevin Bergin .40 1.00
308 Dan Carlson .40 1.00
309 Dan Carney .40 1.00
310 Duncan Dalmao .40 1.00
311 Joe Dusbabek .40 1.00
312 Rick Kowalsky .40 1.00
313 Shawn Limpright .40 1.00
314 Andrew McPherson .40 1.00
315 Andrew Oke .40 1.00
316 Bryan Perez .40 1.00
317 Doug Scatchard .40 1.00
318 Robert Snowball .40 1.00
319 Blair Stayzer .40 1.00
320 Jason Wolfe .60 1.50

2005-06 Roanoke Valley Vipers

We have no pricing information on this set.

1 David Beauregard
2 Jonathan Charette
3 Shawn Conschafter
4 Michael Krelove
5 Gray Shaneberger
6 Matt Miller
7 Rico Fatticci
8 Jan Jas
9 Branislav Kvetan
10 Mark Scott
11 Travis Smith

1963-64 Rochester Americans

Printed on thin paper stock, this set of twenty photos, was issued in two series and measures approximately 4" by 6". This set features borderless black-and-white posed or action shots of the AHL (American Hockey League) Amerks. The white back carries the player's name, age, height, weight, and statistics from previous years in the minors. The cards are unnumbered and checklisted below in alphabetical order.

COMPLETE SET (20) 100.00 200.00
1 Lou Angotti 4.00 8.00
2 Al Arbour 10.00 20.00
3 Norm Armstrong 2.50 5.00
4 Ed Babiuk 2.50 5.00
5 Wally Boyer 4.00 8.00
6 Arnie Brown 4.00 8.00
7 Gerry Cheevers UER 25.00 50.00
(Misspelled Jerry on card back)
8 Don Cherry 30.00 60.00
9 Mike Corbett 2.50 5.00
10 Joe Crozier CO 2.50 5.00
11 Jack Curran TR 2.50 5.00
12 Les Duff 2.50 5.00
13 Gerry Ehman 2.50 5.00
14 Dick Gamble 4.00 8.00
15 Larry Hillman 2.50 5.00
16 Bronco Horvath 7.50 15.00
17 Eddie Lawson 2.50 5.00
18 Jim Pappin 4.00 8.00
19 Darryl Sly 2.50 5.00
20 Stan Smrke 3.00 6.00

1971-72 Rochester Americans

Cards measure 5" x 7" and feature black and white glossy photos on the front, along with a facsimile autograph. Backs are blank. Cards are unnumbered and checklisted below alphabetically.

COMPLETE SET (18) 37.50 75.00
1 Red Armstrong 2.50 5.00
2 Guy Burrowes 2.50 5.00
3 Gaye Cooley 2.50 5.00
4 Bob Craig 2.50 5.00
5 Bob Ellett 2.50 5.00
6 Ron Fogal 2.50 5.00
7 Rod Graham 2.50 5.00
8 Dave Hrechkosy 3.50 7.00
9 Herman Karp 2.50 5.00
10 Bob Kelly 5.00 10.00
11 Larry McKillop 2.50 5.00
12 Bob Malcolm 2.50 5.00
13 Barry Merrell 2.50 5.00
14 Wayne Morusyk 2.50 5.00
15 Rick Pagnutti 2.50 5.00
16 Gerry Sillers 2.50 5.00
17 Gene Sobchuk 2.50 5.00
18 Lynn Zimmerman 2.50 5.00

1977-78 Rochester Americans

These cards feature black and white front photos with a facsimile autograph. Front also features players name, position, biographical information, and statistics. Cards are unnumbered and checklisted below in alphabetical order.

COMPLETE SET (24) 12.50 25.00
1 Team Photo .50 1.00
2 Duane Rupp .75 1.50
3 Nate Angelo TR .25 .50
4 Earl Anderson .75 1.50
5 Bill Bennett .50 1.00
6 Daryl Drader .50 1.00
7 Rene Drolet .50 1.00
8 Rene Drolet .50 1.00
9 Darryl Edestrand .75 1.50
10 Ron Garwasiuk .50 1.00
11 Rod Graham .50 1.00
12 Rod Graham .50 1.00
13 Doug Halward .75 1.50
14 Bjorn Johansson .50 1.00
15 Steve Langdon .50 1.00
16 Ray Maluta .50 1.00
17 Brian McGregor .50 1.00
18 Clayton Pachal .50 1.00
19 Dave Parro .75 1.50
20 Jim Pettie .50 1.00
21 Sean Shanahan .50 1.00
22 Al Sims 1.00 2.00
23 Barry Smith .75 1.50

1979-80 Rochester Americans

These cards are oversized, measuring 8-by-10.5 inches. They are blank backed and unnumbered. The set was sponsored by Wendy's.

1 Mike Boland 2.00 5.00
2 Mike Breen 2.00 5.00
3 Paul Crowley 2.00 5.00
4 Daryl Drader 2.00 5.00
5 Ron Garwasiuk 2.00 5.00
6 Chris Halyk 2.00 5.00
7 Bill InglisÂ Â CO 1.50 4.00
8 Randy Ireland 2.00 5.00
9 Joe Kowal 2.00 5.00
10 Normand Lefebvre 2.00 5.00
11 Bob Mongrain 2.00 5.00
12 Wayne Ramsey 2.00 5.00
13 Jacques Richard 3.00 8.00
14 Geordie Robertson 2.00 5.00
15 Andre Savard 3.00 10.00
16 Ron Schock 3.00 8.00
17 Dave Schultz 12.00 30.00
18 Barry Smith 2.00 5.00
19 Bill Stewart 2.00 5.00
20 Richard Suwek 2.00 5.00
21 Mark Toffolo 2.00 5.00
22 Jim Turkiewicz 2.00 5.00
23 Ed Walsh 2.00 5.00
24 Jim Walsh 2.00 5.00

1991-92 Rochester Americans Dunkin' Donuts

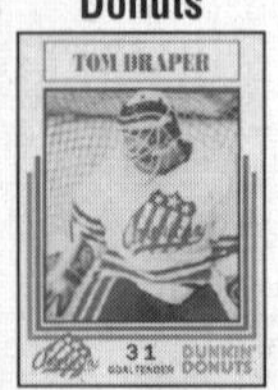

Sponsored by Dunkin' Donuts, this 20-card set measures the standard size. It was issued in four perforated strips, each consisting of four player cards and a Dunkin' Donuts coupon. On white card stock, the fronts feature color action player photos. Blue and red border stripes edge the picture on the bottom and half way on each side. The player's name is printed in a red-lined box above the picture, while logos and additional player information appear beneath it. In black print on a white background, the backs carry biography, statistics, and sponsor logo. The cards are unnumbered and checklisted below in alphabetical order.

COMPLETE SET (20) 4.00 10.00
1 Greg Brown .20 .50
2 Peter Ciavaglia .30 .75
3 Bob Corkum .30 .75
4 Brian Curran .20 .50
5 David DiVita .20 .50
6 Tom Draper .30 .75
7 Jody Gage .40 1.00
8 Dan Frawley .20 .50
9 Dave Littman .30 .75
10 Darcy Loewen .20 .50
11 Don McSween .30 .75
12 Brad Rubachuk .20 .50
13 Lindy Ruff .40 1.00
14 Joel Savage .20 .50
15 Jiri Sejba .20 .50
16 Chris Snell .20 .50
17 Coupon Dunkin' Donuts .02 .05
18 Coupon Dunkin' Donuts .02 .05
19 Coupon Dunkin' Donuts .02 .05
20 Coupon Dunkin' Donuts .02 .05

1991-92 Rochester Americans Kodak

The 1991-92 Rochester American Team Photo and Trading Card Set was co-sponsored by Kodak and Wegmons Photo Center. It consists of three 11 1/4" by 9 1/2" sheets joined together and tri-folded. The first sheet displays a team photo of the

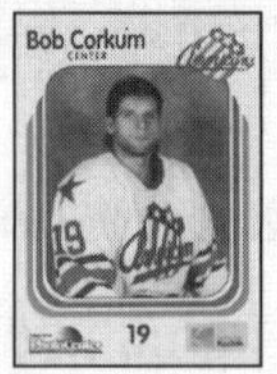

players dressed in street clothes. The second and third sheets consist of 15 cards each arranged in three rows of five cards. The last four slots of the third sheet display sponsor coupons. After perforation, the cards would measure approximately 2 1/4" by 3 1/8". The player photos on the fronts have rounded corners and are poses shot from the waist up against a studio background. Team color-coded (red and blue) stripes edge the pictures on the bottom and each side. The player's name, position, and the team logo are above the picture, while sponsor logos and the uniform number are below it. In red and blue print, the backs carry biography and statistics. The cards are checklisted below as they are arranged in the album, with coaches presented first and then the players in alphabetical order.

COMPLETE SET (26) 4.80 12.00
1 Don Lever CO .10 .25
2 Terry Martin ACO .10 .25
3 Ian Boyce .20 .50
4 John Bradley .20 .50
5 Greg Brown .20 .50
6 Keith Carney .20 .50
7 Peter Ciavaglia .20 .50
8 Bob Corkum .30 .75
9 Brian Curran .20 .50
10 David DiVita .20 .50
11 Lou Franceschetti .30 .75
12 Dan Frawley .20 .50
13 Jody Gage .40 1.00
14 Kevin Haller .30 .75
15 Dave Littman .24 .60
16 Darcy Loewen .20 .50
17 Steve Ludzik .20 .50
18 Don McSween .20 .50
19 Brad Miller .20 .50
20 Sean O'Donnell .30 .75
21 Brad Rubachuk .20 .50
22 Lindy Ruff .40 1.00
23 Joel Savage .20 .50
24 Jiri Sejba .20 .50
25 Chris Snell .20 .50
26 Jason Winch .20 .50

1991-92 Rochester Americans Postcards

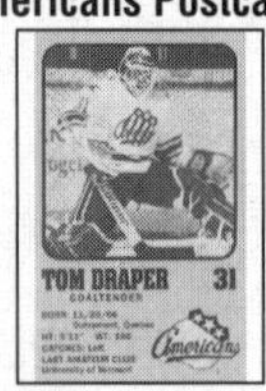

Sponsored by Genny Light, this 21-card set measures approximately 3 1/2" by 5 1/2" and features the 1991-92 Rochester Americans of the American Hockey League. The fronts have black-and-white action player photos with rounded corners and black borders. The player's name, uniform number, position, biography and last amateur club appear beneath the photo, along with the team logo. The backs are in postcard format and carry the sponsor's logo along with the words "STOP DWI. Don't Drink and Drive". The cards are unnumbered and checklisted below in alphabetical order.

COMPLETE SET (21) 4.00 10.00
1 Dave Baseggio .20 .50
2 John Bradley .20 .50
3 Greg Brown .20 .50
4 Keith Carney .20 .50
5 Peter Ciavaglia .20 .50
6 Bob Corkum .30 .75
7 David DiVita .20 .50
8 Tom Draper .30 .75
9 Lou Franceschetti .30 .75
10 Dan Frawley .20 .50
11 Bill Houlder .30 .75
12 Don Lever CO .10 .25
13 David Littman .30 .75
14 Terry Martin ACO .10 .25
15 Don McSween .20 .50
16 Sean O'Donnell .30 .75
17 Lindy Ruff .30 .75
18 Joel Savage .20 .50
19 Jiri Sejba .20 .50
20 Chris Snell .20 .50
21 Ed Zawatsky .20 .50

1992-93 Rochester Americans Dunkin' Donuts

Sponsored by Dunkin' Donuts, this 20-card set measures the standard size. It was issued in four perforated strips, each consisting of five player cards. On white card stock, the fronts feature color action player photos framed by team color-coded (red and blue) border stripes. Logos, jersey number, and position are printed above the picture, while the player's name is printed on the wider blue stripe beneath the picture. In black print on a white background, the backs carry biography, statistics, and sponsor logo. The cards are unnumbered and checklisted below in alphabetical order.

COMPLETE SET (20) 6.00 15.00
1 Peter Ambroziak .20 .50
2 Greg Brown .20 .50
3 Peter Ciavaglia .24 .60
4 Jozef Cierny .20 .50
5 David DiVita .20 .50
6 Dan Frawley .20 .50
7 Jody Gage .30 .75
8 Andrei Jakovenko .20 .50
9 Olaf Kolzig 2.00 5.00
10 Doug Macdonald .20 .50
11 Mike McLaughlin .20 .50
12 Sean O'Donnell .30 .75
13 Bill Pye .30 .75
14 Brad Rubachuk .20 .50
15 Bruce Shoebottom .20 .50
16 Todd Simon .20 .50
17 Jeff Sirkka .20 .50
18 Chris Snell .20 .50
19 Scott Thomas .30 .75
20 Jason Young .20 .50

1992-93 Rochester Americans Kodak

The 1992-93 Rochester American Team Photo and Trading Card Set was co-sponsored by Kodak and Wegmons Photo Center. It consists of three 11 1/4" by 9 1/2" sheets joined together and tri-folded. The first sheet displays a team photo of the players in uniform. The second and third sheets consist of 15 cards each arranged in three rows of five cards. (The last four slots of the third sheet display sponsor coupons.) After perforation, the cards would measure approximately 2 1/4" by 3 1/8". The player photos on the fronts have rounded corners and are poses shot from the waist up against a studio background. The player's name, position, and the team logo are above the picture, while sponsor logos and the uniform number are below it. In red and blue print, the backs carry biography and statistics. The cards are checklisted below as they are arranged in the album, with coaches presented first and then the players in alphabetical order.

COMPLETE SET (26) 15.00 40.00
1 John Van Boxmeer CO .40 1.00
2 Terry Martin ACO .10 .25
3 Peter Ambroziak .40 1.00
4 Greg Brown .40 1.00
5 Peter Ciavaglia .40 1.00
6 Jozef Cierny .40 1.00
7 David DiVita .40 1.00
8 Dan Frawley .40 1.00
9 Jody Gage 1.00 2.50
10 The Moose (mascot) .10 .25
11 Tony Iob .40 1.00
12 Olaf Kolzig 4.00 10.00
13 Doug MacDonald .40 1.00
14 Mike McLaughlin .40 1.00
15 Sean O'Donnell 1.00 2.50
16 Brad Pascall 1.00 2.50
17 Bill Pye 1.00 2.50
18 Brad Rubachuk .40 1.00
19 Joel Savage .40 1.00
20 Bruce Shoebottom .75 2.00
21 Todd Simon .40 1.00
22 Jeff Sirkka .40 1.00
23 Chris Snell .40 1.00
24 Scott Thomas 1.00 2.50
25 Jason Winch .40 1.00
26 Jason Young .40 1.00

1993-94 Rochester Americans Kodak

This 25-card set of the Rochester Americans of the AHL was sponsored by Kodak and distributed by the team's booster club. The set was issued in sheet form, with each card measuring 2 1/2" by 3 1/4". The card fronts carry a posed photo, player name and position and logos of the club and sponsors. The backs are unnumbered, but carry comprehensive stats.

COMPLETE SET (25) 4.80 12.00
1 John Van Boxmeer CO .20 .50
2 Terry Martin ACO .10 .25
3 Peter Ambroziak .24 .60
4 Mike Bavis .24 .60
5 James Black .24 .60
6 Derek Booth .24 .60
7 Philippe Boucher .24 .60
8 David Cooper .24 .60
9 Todd Flichel .24 .60
10 Jody Gage .40 1.00
11 Viktor Gordiouk .24 .60
12 Bill Horn .24 .60
13 Markus Ketterer .30 .75
14 Mark Krys .24 .60
15 Doug MacDonald .24 .60
16 Dean Melanson .24 .60
17 Moose -- Mascot .10 .25
18 Sean O'Donnell .30 .75
19 Brad Pascall .24 .60
20 Sergei Petrenko .24 .60
21 Brad Rubachuk .24 .60
22 Todd Simon .24 .60
23 Scott Thomas .30 .75
24 Mikhail Volkov .24 .60
25 Jason Young .24 .60

1995-96 Rochester Americans

This 25-card set of the Rochester Americans of the AHL was produced for the team by Split Second. The sets were available at games and by mail through the club. The set features a blurry action photo on the front and complete stats on the back. As they are unnumbered, the cards are presented in alphabetical order.

COMPLETE SET (25) 6.00 15.00
1 Craig Charron .20 .50
2 David Cooper .20 .50
3 Dan Frawley .20 .50
4 Jody Gage .40 1.00
5 Terry Hollinger .24 .60
6 Dane Jackson .20 .50
7 Ladislav Karabin .20 .50
8 Sergei Klimentiev .20 .50
9 Jamie Leach .20 .50
10 Jay Mazur .20 .50
11 Dean Melanson .20 .50
12 Scott Metcalfe .20 .50
13 Barrie Moore .20 .50
14 Scott Nichol .20 .50
15 Rumun Ndur .24 .60
16 Scott Pearson .20 .50
17 Serge Roberge .20 .50
18 Steve Shields .80 2.00
19 Robb Stauber .30 .75
20 Mikhail Volkov .20 .50
21 Dixon Ward .30 .75
22 Bob Westerby .20 .50
23 Mike Wilson .20 .50
24 Shayne Wright .20 .50
25 John Tortorella CO .10 .25

1996-97 Rochester Americans

This set features the Americans of the AHL. The set was produced by SplitSecond and was sold at home games for $5.

COMPLETE SET (26) 4.00 10.00
1 Rochester Americans .16 .40
2 Sergei Klimentiev .16 .40
3 Craig Charron .16 .40
4 Craig Millar .16 .40
5 Scott Metcalfe .16 .40
6 Ed Ronan .16 .40
7 Terry Hollinger .16 .40
8 Shayne Wright .16 .40
9 Barrie Moore .16 .40
10 Scott Nichol .16 .40
11 Charlie Huddy .16 .40
12 Vaclav Varada .20 .50
13 Wayne Primeau .30 .75
14 Terry Yake .16 .40
15 Dan Frawley .16 .40
16 Frederic Deschenes .16 .40
17 Steve Shields .40 1.00
18 Paul Rushforth .16 .40
19 Dane Jackson .16 .40
20 Rumun Ndur .20 .50
21 Greg Walters .16 .40
22 Eric Lavigne .16 .40
23 John Tortorella CO .04 .10
24 Moose MAS .04 .10
25 AHL Web Site .01
26 PHPA Web Site .01

1997-98 Rochester Americans

This set features the Amerks of the AHL. The cards were sponsored by Pepsi and issued as a promotional giveaway. The cards came in five-card sheets, and were given out at five different games.

COMPLETE SET (25) 8.00 20.00
1-1 Dane Jackson .30 .75
1-2 Scott Metcalfe .30 .75
1-3 Denis Hamel .30 .75
1-4 Mark Dutiaume .30 .75
1-5 Daniel Bienvenue .30 .75
2-1 Craig Charron .30 .75
2-2 Scott Nichol .30 .75
2-3 Martin Menard .30 .75
2-4 Erik Rasmussen .40 1.00
2-5 Mike Zanutto .30 .75
3-1 Vaclav Varada .40 1.00
3-2 Dan Frawley .30 .75
3-3 Patrice Tardif .40 1.00
3-4 Greg Walters .30 .75
3-5 Matt Davidson .30 .75
4-1 Mike Hurlbut .30 .75
4-2 Shayne Wright .30 .75
4-3 Mike McKee .30 .75
4-4 Dean Melanson .30 .75
4-5 Eric Lavigne .30 .75
5-1 Martin Biron 2.00 5.00
5-2 Sergei Klimentiev .30 .75
5-3 Mike Bales .40 1.00
5-4 Rumun Ndur .30 .75
5-5 Jean-Luc Grand-Pierre .30 .75

1998-99 Rochester Americans

This set features the Amerks of the AHL. The set was issued in five-card strips at five home games late in the season.

COMPLETE SET (25) 6.00 15.00
1 Craig Fisher .20 .50
2 Greg Walters .20 .50
3 Matt Davidson .20 .50
4 Randy Cunneyworth .20 .50
5 Martin Biron 1.20 3.00
6 Mike Hurlbut .20 .50
7 Tom Draper .30 .75
8 Mike Harder .20 .50
9 Denis Hamel .20 .50
10 Jean-Luc Grand-Pierre .20 .50
11 Scott Nichol .20 .50
12 Francois Methot .20 .50
13 Dean Melanson .20 .50
14 Jason Mansoff .20 .50
15 Jason Holland .20 .50
16 Darren Van Oene .20 .50
17 Dean Sylvester .30 .75
18 Cory Sarich .20 .50
19 Erik Rasmussen .30 .75
20 Dominic Pittis .20 .50
21 The Moose MAS .04 .10
22 Darwin McCutcheon CO .04 .10
23 Jody Gage .30 .75
24 Shane Kenny .20 .50
25 Steffon Walby .20 .50

2000-01 Rochester Americans

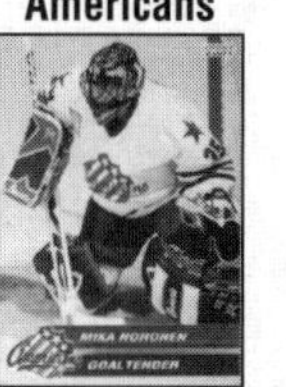

This set features the Americans of the AHL. The set was produced by Choice Marketing, and sold by the team at its souvenir stands.

COMPLETE SET (29) 4.80 12.00
1 Jeremy Adduono .14 .35
2 Tom Askey .20 .50
3 Martin Biron .80 2.00
4 Kevin Bolibruck .14 .35
5 Craig Brunel .14 .35
6 Brian Campbell .14 .35
7 Craig Charron .14 .35
8 Jason Cipolla .14 .35
9 Jason Holland .14 .35
10 Doug Houda .14 .35
11 Mike Hurlbut .14 .35
12 Dane Jackson .14 .35
13 Jaroslav Kristek .30 .75
14 Mike Mader .14 .35
15 Francois Methot .14 .35
16 Norm Milley .30 .75
17 Joe Murphy .14 .35
18 Todd Nelson .14 .35
19 Mika Noronen .80 1.50
20 Andrew Peters .14 1.00
21 Chris Taylor .14 .35
22 Paul Traynor .14 .35
23 Darren Van Oene .14 .35
24 Randy Cunneyworth CO .10 .25
25 Jon Christiano CO .04 .10
26 Dave A. Williams EM .04 .10
27 Kent Weisbeck TR .04 .10
28 The Moose MASCOT .04 .10
NNO Team CL .04 .01

2002-03 Rochester Americans

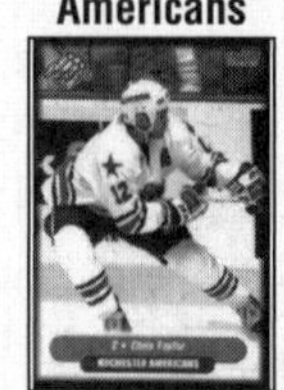

COMPLETE SET (26) 8.00 20.00
1 Tom Askey .30 .75
2 Milan Bartovic .20 .50
3 Jason Botterill .20 .50
4 Rory Fitzpatrick .20 .50
5 Paul Gaustad .20 .50
6 Denis Hamel .30 .75
7 Radoslav Hecl .20 .50
8 Doug Houda .20 .50
9 Doug Janik .20 .50
10 Ryan Jorde .20 .50
11 Jaroslav Kristek .30 .75
12 Sean McMorrow .30 .75
13 Francois Methot .20 .50
14 Ryan Miller 2.00 5.00
15 Norm Milley .20 .50
16 Karel Mosovsky .20 .50
17 Jiri Novotny .30 .75
18 Andrew Peters .60 1.50
19 Jason Pominville .60 1.50
20 Peter Ratchuk .20 .50
21 Chris Taylor .20 .50
22 Ryan Miller 2.00 5.00
23 Randy Cunneyworth HCO .02 .10
24 Jon Christiano ACO .02 .10
25 The Moose Mascot .02 .10
NNO Checklist .01 .05

2003-04 Rochester Americans

This set was produced by Choice Marketing and sold at home games.

COMPLETE SET (29) 6.00 15.00
1 Doug Houda ACO .02 .10
2 Tom Askey .30 .75
3 Milan Bartovic .12 .30
4 Jason Botterill .12 .30
5 Brian Chapman .12 .30
6 David Cullen .12 .30
7 Randy Cunneyworth .12 .30
8 Pete Gardiner .12 .30
9 Paul Gaustad .20 .50
10 Doug Janik .12 .30
11 Ryan Jorde .12 .30
12 Steve Lingren .12 .30
13 Sean McMorrow .30 .75
14 Ryan Miller 1.25 3.00
15 Jason Dawe .12 .30
16 Norm Milley .30 .75
17 Karel Mosovsky .12 .30
18 Rick Mrozik .12 .30
19 Jiri Novotny .30 .75
20 Nathan Paetsch .30 .75
21 Geoff Peters .30 .75
22 Domenic Pittis .20 .50
23 Jason Pominville .75 2.00
24 Scott Ricci .12 .30
25 Derek Roy .75 2.00
26 Derek Roy .75 2.00
27 Michael Ryan .20 .50
28 Mascot .02 .10
29 Chris Thorburn .12 .30
NNO Checklist .01 .05

2004-05 Rochester Americans

COMPLETE SET (30) 8.00 20.00
1 Checklist .01 .05
2 Tom Askey .30 .75
3 Milan Bartovic .20 .50
4 Jason Botterill .20 .50
5 David Cullen .20 .50
6 Paul Gaustad .20 .50
7 Doug Janik .20 .50
8 Jeff Jillson .20 .50
9 Ryan Jorde .20 .50
10 Steve Lingren .20 .50
11 Sean McMorrow .30 .75
12 Ryan Miller .75 2.00
13 Norm Milley .20 .50
14 Jiri Novotny .20 .50
15 Nathan Paetsch .20 .50
16 Daniel Paille .40 1.00
17 Geoff Peters .60 1.50
18 Jason Pominville .40 1.00
19 Todd Rohloff .20 .50
20 Derek Roy .40 1.00
21 Michael Ryan .20 .50
22 Brandon Smith .20 .50
23 Chris Taylor .20 .50
24 Chris Thorburn .20 .50
25 Thomas Vanek .75 2.00
26 The Moose MASCOT .02 .10
27 Ryan Miller .75 2.00
28 Derek Roy .40 1.00
29 Thomas Vanek .75 2.00
30 Randy Cunneyworth CO .02 .10
Doug Houda CO

1999-00 Rockford IceHogs

This set features the IceHogs of the UHL. The set was produced by Roox and was sold by the team at home games. Because of the obtuse numbering system on the card backs, they have been listed below in alphabetical order.

COMPLETE SET (26) 4.00 50.00
1 Brant Blackned .16 2.00
2 Peter Cava .20 3.00
3 Patrice Charbonneau .16 2.00
4 Mike Correia .16 2.00
5 Dan Davies .16 2.00
6 Raymond Delarosbil .16 2.00
7 Mike Figliomeni .20 3.00
8 Jason Firth .20 3.00
9 Sheldon Gorski .20 3.00
10 Jeff Kostuch .16 2.00
11 Evgeny Krivomaz .16 2.00
12 Derek Landmesser .16 2.00
13 Alexandre Makombo .20 3.00
14 Barry McKinley .16 2.00
15 Normand Paquet .16 2.00
16 Jean-Francois Rivard .16 2.00
17 Shawn Smith .16 2.00
18 Carlos Soke .16 2.00
19 Wayne Strachan .16 2.00
20 Curtis Tipler .16 2.00
21 Jesse Welling .16 2.00
22 Scott Burfoot CO .10 .25
23 Dale DeGray CO .10 .25
24 Hamilton E. Hog MASCOT .04 .10
25 Mike Figliomeni AS .20 3.00
26 Jason Firth AS .20 3.00

2000-01 Rockford IceHogs

This set features the IceHogs of the UHL. The set was produced by the team and sold at its souvenir stands. The cards are unnumbered and are listed below alphabetically.

COMPLETE SET (25) 4.00 10.00
1 Curtis Bois .20 .50
2 Patrice Charbonneau .20 .50
3 Nick Checco .20 .50
4 Curtis Cruickshank .30 .75
5 Jeff DaCosta .20 .50
6 Dan Davies .20 .50
7 Steve Dumonski .20 .50
8 Chris Fattey .20 .50
9 Mike Figliomeni .20 .50
10 Justin Kearns .30 .75
11 Evgeny Krivomaz .20 .50
12 Jocelyn Langlois .20 .50
13 Michel Periard .20 .50
14 Jean-Francois Rivard .20 .50
15 David Runge .20 .50
16 Francois Sasseville .20 .50
17 Shawn Smith .20 .50
18 Mike Tobin .20 .50
19 Yan Turgeon .20 .50
20 Eduard Zankovets .20 .50
21 Dale DeGray CO .10 .25
22 Scott Burfoot CO .10 .25
23 Hamilton E. Hog MASCOT .10 .25
24 Logo Card .04 .01
25 Header Card .04 .01

2001-02 Rockford IceHogs

COMPLETE SET (25) 8.00 20.00
1 Ben Christopherson .40 1.00
2 Clint Wensley .40 1.00
3 Dan Davies .40 1.00
4 Darwin Murray .40 1.00
5 David Hoogsteen .40 1.00
6 Ernie Thorp .40 1.00
7 Forrest Gore .40 1.00
8 Hamilton E. Hog .40 1.00
9 Harold Hersh .10 .25
10 J.F. Rivard .40 1.00
11 Jared Reigstad .40 1.00
12 Jeff Antonovich .40 1.00
13 Jeff Dacosta .40 1.00
14 Jeremy Vokes .40 1.00
15 Joe Statkus .40 1.00
16 Mike Sgroi .40 1.00
17 Nick Checco .40 1.00
18 Oak Hewer .40 1.00
19 Quinten Van Horlick .40 1.00
20 Scott Bell CO .10 .25
21 Sergei Petrov .40 1.00
22 Steve Debus .40 1.00
23 T.J. Guidarelli .40 1.00
24 Wes Blevins .40 1.00
NNO Team CL .40 1.00

2002-03 Rockford Ice Hogs

COMPLETE SET (25) 8.00 20.00
1 Scott Bell CO .02 .10
2 Darwin Murray .40 1.00
3 Raitis Ivanans .40 1.00
4 Kenzie Homer .40 1.00
5 Alexander Alexeev .40 1.00
6 Oak Hewer .40 1.00
7 Erik Wendell .40 1.00
8 Jeff Antonovich .40 1.00
9 Matt Loen .40 1.00
10 Jeremy Rebek .40 1.00
11 Steve Cygan .40 1.00
12 Clint Wensley .40 1.00
13 Quinten Van Horlick .40 1.00
14 Steve Dumonski .40 1.00
15 Nick Angell .40 1.00
16 Joe Statkus .40 1.00
17 Jay Hebert .40 1.00
18 Dan Davies .40 1.00
19 Brad Olsen .40 1.00
20 Jeff Dacosta .40 1.00
21 Brant Nicklin .40 1.00
22 Ryan McIntosh .40 1.00
23 Mascot .02 .10
24 Mascot .02 .10
25 Team card/CL .02 .10

2003-04 Rockford Ice Hogs

This set was produced by Choice Marketing and sold at home games. Minor league collector Ralph Slate reports just 300 sets were produced.

COMPLETE SET (20) 6.00 15.00
1 B.J. Adams .30 .75
2 Justin Cardwell .30 .75
3 Steve Cygan .30 .75
4 Dan Davies .30 .75
5 Jeff Ewasko .40 1.00
6 John Glavota .30 .75
7 Kenzie Homer .30 .75
8 Dale Junkin .30 .75
9 Nathan Lutz .30 .75
10 Don Margettie .40 1.00
11 Kelly Miller .30 .75
12 Bob Nardella .30 .75
13 Dave Paradise .30 .75
14 Gary Ricciardi .30 .75
15 Paul Schonfelder .40 1.00
16 Adam Solnik .30 .75
17 Ron Vogel .40 1.00
18 Owen Walter .30 .75
19 Maris Ziedins .30 .75
20 Mark Bernard HCO .10 .25

2005-06 Rockford Ice Hogs

COMPLETE SET (27) 8.00 15.00
1 Greg Barber .20 .50
2 Robin Big Snake .75 2.00
3 Dan Boeser .20 .50
4 Ryan Carrigan .20 .50
5 Matt Gens .20 .50
6 Corey Hessler .20 .50
7 Chaz Johnson .40 1.00
8 Nathan Lutz .20 .50
9 Preston Mizzi .20 .50
10 Bob Nardella .20 .50
11 Jason Notermann .40 1.00
12 Steve Pelletier .20 .50
13 Olivier Proulx .20 .50
14 Jason Ralph .40 1.00
15 Billy Tibbetts .40 1.00
16 Yannick Tifu .20 .50
17 Rob Voltera .20 .50
18 Bruce Watson .40 1.00
19 Steve Yetman .20 .50
20 Tom Zabkowicz .20 .50
21 Josh Mizerek .20 .50
22 Ron Vogel .40 1.00
23 Michel Robinson .20 .50
24 Steve Martinson .20 .50
25 Hammer Hog MASCOT .02 .10
26 Hamilton E. Hog MASCOT .02 .10
NNO Rockford Ice Hogs CL .02 .10

2006-07 Rockford IceHogs

COMPLETE SET (27) 12.00 20.00
1 Jesse Bennefield .30 .75
2 Kaleb Betts .40 1.00
3 Robin Big Snake .75 2.00
4 Dan Boeser .30 .75
5 Paul Brown .30 .75
6 Frederic CloutierÂ .60 1.50
7 Bryce Cockburn .30 .75
8 Nicolas Corbeil .30 .75
9 Mike Doyle .30 .75
10 Luke Fritshaw .30 .75
11 Matt Gens .30 .75
12 Corey Hessler .30 .75
13 Chaz Johnson .30 .75
14 Mike Letizia .30 .75
15 Erik Lizon .30 .75
16 Nathan Lutz .30 .75
17 Preston Mizzi .40 1.00
18 Jake Moreland .40 1.00
19 Jason Notermann .30 .75
20 Jason Ralph .30 .75
21 Kevin Ulanski .30 .75
22 Bruce Watson .30 .75
23 Tim Wedderburn .30 .75
24 Steve MartinsonÂ CO .20 .50
25 Hammer Hog MASCOT .02 .10
26 Hamilton E. Hog MASCOT .02 .10
27 Team Card .10 .25

1995-96 Roller Hockey Magazine RHI

This 6-card set was inserted as a promotional enticement into the September 1996 issue of Roller Hockey Magazine.

COMPLETE SET (6) 2.00 5.00
1 Oleg Yashin .40 1.00
2 Frankie Ouellette .40 1.00
3 Nick Vitucci .60 1.50
4 Mike Martens .40 1.00
5 Alain Morissette .40 1.00
6 Simon Roy .40 1.00

1999-00 Rouyn-Noranda Huskies

This set features the Huskies of the QMJHL. The set was produced by card shop CTM-Ste-Foy and was sold at the store and at home games.

COMPLETE SET (26) 4.80 12.00
1 Kyrill Alexeev .16 .40
2 Marc-Andre Binette .16 .40
3 Maxime Bouchard .16 .40
4 Bruno Cadieux .16 .40
5 Sebastien Centomo .60 1.50
6 Kevin Cloutier .16 .40
7 Jonathan Gauthier .16 .40
8 Patrick Gilbert .16 .40
9 Andre Hart .16 .40
10 Robert Horak .16 .40
11 Eric L'Italien .16 .40
12 Mathieu Leclerc .16 .40
13 Jason Lehoux .16 .40
14 Jonathan Pelletier .16 .40
15 Bertrand-Pierre Plouffe .16 .40
16 Matthew Quinn .16 .40
17 Mike Ribeiro .60 1.50
18 Shawn Scanzano .16 .40
19 Jason Tessier .16 .40
20 Jerome Tremblay .16 .40
21 Alain Turcotte .16 .40
22 Steve Vandal .16 .40
23 Guy Boucher CO .04 .10
24 Andre Parke CO .04 .10
25 Jean Pronovost CO .16 .40
26 Michel Maroux TR .04 .10

2000-01 Rouyn-Noranda Huskies

This set features the Huskies of the QMJHL. The cards were produced by CTM-Ste-Foy, and were sold both by that card shop and by the team.

COMPLETE SET (27) 6.00 15.00
1 Dominic D'Amour .20 .50
2 Jonathan Gauthier .20 .50
3 Matthew Quinn .20 .50
4 Kirill Alexeev .20 .50
5 Sebastian Strozynski .20 .50
6 Bertrand Pierre Plouffe .20 .50
7 Maxime Talbot .20 .50
8 Guillaume Lefebvre .40 1.00
9 Alexandre Morel .20 .50
10 Michal Pinc .20 .50
12 Mathieu Leclerc .20 .50
13 Jerome Marois .20 .50
14 Patrice Theriault .20 .50
15 Patrick Gilbert .20 .50
16 Maxime Ouellet .80 2.00
17 Louis Mandeville .20 .50
18 Wesley Scanzano .30 .75
19 Sebastien Centomo 1.20 1.00
20 Maxime Bouchard .20 .50
21 Bruno Cadieux .20 .50
22 Jean-Philippe Hamel .20 .50
23 Shawn Scanzano .20 .50
24 Jonathan Gagnon .20 .50
25 Marc-Andre Binette .20 .50
26 Jean Pronovost CO .20 .25
NNO Lappy MASCOT .04 .10

2000-01 Rouyn-Noranda Huskies Signed

This set is exactly the same as the base Huskies set from this season, save that every card has been hand signed by the player pictured. Each card also is serial numbered out of just 100.

COMPLETE SET (27) 24.00 60.00
1 Dominic D'Amour .80 2.00
2 Jonathan Gauthier .80 2.00
3 Matthew Quinn .80 2.00
4 Kirill Alexeev .80 2.00
5 Sebastian Strozynski .80 2.00
6 Bertrand Pierre Plouffe .80 2.00
7 Maxime Talbot .80 2.00
8 Guillaume Lefebvre 2.00 5.00
9 Alexandre Morel .80 2.00
10 Michal Pinc .80 2.00
12 Mathieu Leclerc .80 2.00
13 Jerome Marois .80 2.00
14 Patrice Theriault .80 2.00
15 Patrick Gilbert .80 2.00
16 Maxime Ouellet 4.00 10.00
17 Louis Mandeville .80 2.00
18 Wesley Scanzano 1.20 3.00
19 Sebastien Centomo 6.00 7.50
20 Maxime Bouchard .80 2.00
21 Bruno Cadieux .80 2.00
22 Jean-Philippe Hamel .80 2.00
23 Shawn Scanzano .80 2.00
24 Jonathan Gagnon .80 2.00
25 Marc-Andre Binette .80 2.00
26 Jean Pronovost CO .80 2.00
NNO Lappy MASCOT .04 .10

1993-94 RPI Engineers

This 31-card set of the RPI Engineers was produced by Collect-A-Sport. Reportedly, production was limited to 2,000 sets, all of which were offered for sale at the arena on game nights.

COMPLETE SET (31) 4.00 10.00
1 Kelly Askew .16 .40
2 Adam Bartell .16 .40
3 Kobie Boykins .16 .40
4 Jeff Brick .16 .40
5 Tim Carvel .16 .40
6 Wayne Clarke .16 .40
7 Cam Cuthbert .16 .40
8 Steve Duncan ACO .04 .10
9 Dan Fridgen ACO .04 .10
10 Jeff Gabriel .16 .40
11 Craig Hamelin .16 .40
12 Chris Kiley .16 .40
13 Ken Kwasniewski .16 .40
14 Brad Layzell .16 .40
15 Neil Little .30 .75
16 Xavier Majic .20 .50
17 Jeff Matthews .16 .40
18 Chris Maye .16 .40
19 Jeff O'Connor .16 .40
20 Ron Pasco .16 .40
21 Eric Perardi .16 .40
22 Jon Pirrong .16 .40
23 Buddy Powers CO .04 .10
24 Tim Regan .16 .40
25 Bryan Richardson .16 .40
26 Patrick Rochon .16 .40
27 Mike Rolanti .16 .40
28 Tim Spadafore .16 .40
29 Mike Tamburro .16 .40
30 1993-94 Team .16 .40
31 Checklist .04 .10

1976-77 Saginaw Gears

This set features black and white player photos on slightly oversized stock. It's possible that the checklist is not complete. If you have additional information, please forward it to hockeymag@beckett.com.

COMPLETE SET (13) 17.50 35.00
1 Rick Chinnink 1.50 3.00
2 Marcel Comeau 1.50 3.00
3 Michel DeGuise 1.50 3.00
4 Marc Gaudreault 1.50 3.00
5 Greg Hotham 1.50 3.00
6 Stu Irving 1.50 3.00
7 Kevin Kemp 1.50 3.00
8 Mario Lessard 1.50 3.00
9 Gord Malinoski 1.50 3.00
10 Mike Ruest 1.50 3.00
11 D'Arcy Ryan 1.50 3.00
12 Dave Westner 1.50 3.00
13 Wayne Zuk 1.50 3.00

1978-79 Saginaw Gears

This 20-card set features black-and-white posed player photos. The team name and year appear in the top white border with the player's name printed in the bottom border. The player's position is listed on a puck at the bottom left of the photo. The backs are blank. The cards are unnumbered and checklisted below in alphabetical order. This set was the subject of a number of fierce bidding wars over the past two years, leading to a tremendous value increase in this edition.

COMPLETE SET (20) 12.50 300.00
1 Wren Blair .75 15.00
2 Marcel Comeau .75 15.00
3 Dennis Desrosiers .50 15.00
4 Jon Fontas .50 15.00
5 Bob Froese 2.00 25.00
6 Gunnar Garrett TR .25 1.00
7 Bob Gladney .50 15.00
8 Warren Holmes .50 15.00
9 Stu Irving .50 15.00
10 Larry Hopkins .50 15.00
11 Scott Jessee .50 15.00
12 Lynn Jorgenson .50 15.00
13 Doug Keans 1.50 25.00
14 Claude Larochelle .50 15.00
15 Paul McIntosh .50 15.00
16 Don Perry .50 15.00
17 Greg Steel .50 15.00
18 Mark Suzor .50 15.00
19 Mark Toffolo .50 15.00
20 Dave Westner .50 15.00

1999-00 Saginaw Gears

This set features the Gears of the UHL. Little is known about this set, other than that is was produced by Roox as part of a series of promotional giveaways. The Loder issue is actually a magnet, while the others are traditional cards. Any additional information can be forwarded to hockeymag@beckett.com.

COMPLETE SET (4) 2.00 5.00
1 Brian Mueller .40 1.00
2 Derek Pinfold .40 1.00
3 Jeff Loder .80 2.00
4 Keith Osborne .40 1.00

2002-03 Saginaw Spirit

We have confirmed the existence of one card in this series. If you have information about others, please contact us at hockeymag@beckett.com.

COMPLETE SET (?)
1 Colt King
2 Chris Thorburn

2003-04 Saginaw Spirit

COMPLETE SET (28) 5.00 12.00
1 Patrick Asselin .20 .50
2 Paul Bissonnette .20 .50
3 Daniel Borges .20 .50
4 Mike Brown .30 .75
5 Chase Crowder .20 .50
6 Steve Dix .20 .50
7 Adam Gibson .20 .50
8 Jesse Gimblett .20 .50
9 Jesse Jenish .20 .50
10 Phil Kozak .20 .50
11 Nick Lees .20 .50
12 Justin McCutcheon .20 .50
13 Patrick McNeill .20 .50
14 Georgi Misharin .20 .50
15 Mike Pain .20 .50
16 Eric Pfligler .20 .50
17 Geoff Platt .20 .50
18 Tom Pyatt .30 .75
19 Taylor Raszka .20 .50
20 Jean-Michel Rizk .30 .75
21 Marc-Andre Rizk .20 .50
22 Adam Sturgeon .20 .50
23 Mike Suggs .20 .50
24 Stephen Sunderman .20 .50
25 Team Card .02 .10
26 Rizk Brothers .20 .50
27 Moe Mantha CO .02 .10
28 Bryan and Jose .02 .10

2004-05 Saginaw Spirit

COMPLETE SET (24) 5.00 12.00
1 Patrick McNeill .20 .50
2 Marek Kvapil .20 .50
3 Jean-Michel Rizk .20 .50
4 Paul Bissonnette .20 .50
5 Patrick Asselin .20 .50
6 Peter Franchin .20 .50
7 Rick Caughell .20 .50
8 Kevin Tuckey .20 .50
9 Gary Klapkowski .20 .50
10 Scott Fletcher .20 .50
11 Daniel Borges .20 .50
12 Jamie Klie .20 .50
13 Chris Ferguson .20 .50
14 Taylor Raszka .20 .50
15 Dan Idema .20 .50
16 Chase Crowder .20 .50
17 Tom Pyatt .30 .75
18 Thomas Harrison .20 .50
19 Sean Courtney .20 .50
20 Aaron Rock .20 .50
21 Jesse Gimblett .20 .50
22 Matt Corrente .40 1.00
23 Mike Brown .30 .75
24 Mascot .02 .10

2005-06 Saginaw Spirit

COMPLETE SET (24) 6.00 12.00
1 Patrick Asselin .20 .50
2 Michal Birner .20 .50
3 Chris Chappell .20 .50
4 Jack Combs .20 .50
5 Matt Corrente .40 1.00
6 Tom Craig .20 .50
7 Ryan Daniels .20 .50
8 Chris Ferguson .20 .50
9 Scott Fletcher .20 .50
10 Jesse Gimblett .20 .50
11 Tyson Gimblett .20 .50
12 Jamie Klie .20 .50
13 Erik Lundmark .20 .50
14 Tom Mannino .20 .50
15 Joe McCann .20 .50
16 Ryan McDonough .20 .50
17 Patrick McNeill .20 .50
18 Tim Priamo .20 .50
19 Tom Pyatt .40 1.00
20 Garrett Sinfield .20 .50
21 Anthony Soboczynski .20 .50
22 Francois Thuot .40 1.00
23 Zack Torquato .20 .50
24 Steven Whitely .20 .50

2006-07 Saginaw Spirit

COMPLETE SET (25) 8.00 15.00
1 Tom Pyatt .40 1.00
2 Patrick Mcneill .30 .75
3 Garrett Sinfield .20 .50
4 Curtis Cooper .20 .50
5 Nick Crawford .20 .50
6 Tommy Mannino .20 .50
7 Christopher Breen .20 .50
8 Tomas Zaborsky .20 .50
9 Jan Mursak .20 .50
10 Matt Corrente .30 .75
11 Tyler Haskins .20 .50
12 Andrew Cloutier .20 .50
13 Tom Craig .20 .50
14 Chris Chappell .20 .50
15 Ryan Daniels .40 1.00
16 Jack Combs .20 .50
17 Zack Torquato .40 1.00
18 Patrick Asselin .20 .50
19 Jovica Zelenbaba .20 .50
20 T.J. Brodie .20 .50
21 Ryan Berard .20 .50
22 Ryan Mcdonouh .20 .50
23 Sammy Spirit MASCOT .10 .25
24 Steagle Colbeagle MASCOT .40 1.00
LE1 Patrick Mcneill .75 2.00

1994-95 Saint John Flames

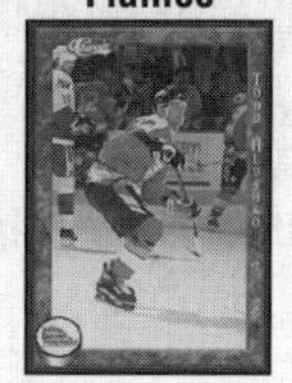

This 26-card standard-size set was manufactured and distributed by Jessen Associates, Inc. for Classic. The fronts display color action player photos with a red marbleized inner border and a black outer border. The player's name, jersey number, and position appear in the teal border on the right edge. The cards are unnumbered and checklisted below in alphabetical order.

COMPLETE SET (26) 3.20 8.00
1 Joel Bouchard .20 .50
2 Rick Carriere ACO .04 .10
3 Ryan Duthie .10 .25
4 Neil Eisenhut .10 .25
5 Leonard Esau .10 .25
6 Bob Francis CO .04 .10
7 Mark Greig .10 .25
8 Francois Groleau .10 .25
9 Sami Helenius .30 .75
10 Todd Hlushko .20 .50
11 Dale Kushner .10 .25
12 Bobby Marshall .10 .25
13 Scott Morrow .10 .25
14 Michael Murray .10 .25
15 Jason Muzzatti .30 .75
16 Barry Nieckar .10 .25
17 Nicolas Perreault .10 .25
18 Jeff Perry .10 .25
19 Dwayne Roloson .30 .75
20 Todd Simpson .10 .25
21 Harbour Station .04 .10
22 Cory Stillman .30 .75
23 David Struch .10 .25
24 Niklas Sundblad .10 .25
25 Andrei Trefilov .20 .50
26 Vesa Viitakoski .10 .25

1996-97 Saint John Flames

This set features the Flames of the AHL. The cards were produced by SplitSecond and sold at home games. The cards are unnumbered, and so are listed below alphabetically.

COMPLETE SET (26) 4.00 10.00
1 Jamie Allison .16 .40
2 Chris Dingman .20 .50
3 Scott Fraser .16 .40
4 Denis Gauthier .16 .40
5 Ian Gordon .16 .40
6 Patrik Haltia .20 .50
7 Sami Helenius .20 .75
8 Marc Hussey .16 .40
9 Marko Jantunen .20 .50
10 Ladislav Kohn .16 .40
11 Martin Lamarche .16 .40
12 Jesper Mattsson .20 .50
13 Keith McCambridge .16 .40
14 Dale McTavish .16 .40
15 Burke Murphy .16 .40
16 Marty Murray .30 .75
17 Paxton Schulte .16 .40
18 Jarrod Skalde .30 .75
19 Jason Smith .30 .75
20 Clarke Wilm .20 .50
21 Ravil Yakubov .16 .40
22 Paul Baxter CO .10 .25
23 Jeff Perry CO .10 .25
24 Fleaburn MAS .04 .10
25 AHL Web Site .01
26 PHPA Web Site .01

1995-96 Saint John Flames

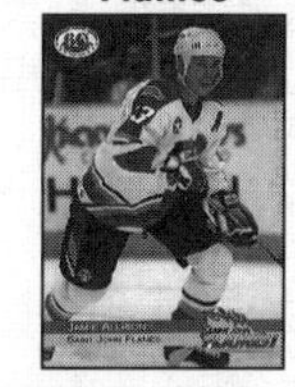

This 25-card set features borderless color action player photos of the Saint John Flames of the AHL. The backs carry player information and statistics. The cards are unnumbered and checklisted below in alphabetical order.

COMPLETE SET (25) 4.00 50.00
1 Jamie Allison .16 1.50
2 Paul Baxter CO .04 .10
3 Joel Bouchard .20 1.50
4 Tom Coolen CO .04 .10
5 Brett Duncan .16 1.50
6 Ian Gordon .16 1.50
7 Sami Helenius .20 3.00
8 Todd Hlushko .16 1.50
9 Marc Hussey .16 1.50
10 Ladislav Kohn .20 1.50
11 Frank Kovacs .16 1.50
12 David Ling .20 2.00
13 Jesper Mattsson .20 1.50
14 Keith McCambridge .16 1.50
15 Marty Murray .20 2.00
16 Michael Murray .16 1.50
17 David Neilson .16 1.50
18 Jeff Perry .16 1.50
19 Darren Ritchie .16 1.50
20 Dwayne Roloson .20 15.00
21 Todd Simpson .16 1.50
22 Jarrod Skalde .30 2.00
23 David Struch .16 1.50
24 Niklas Sundblad .20 2.00
25 Vesa Viitakoski .20 1.50

1997-98 Saint John Flames

This set features the Flames of the AHL. The cards were produced by the team and sold at home games and via mail.

COMPLETE SET (25) 8.00 15.00
1 Jamie Allison .15 .40
2 Erik Andersson .15 .40
3 Ryan Bast .15 .40
4 Travis Brigley .15 .40
5 Eric Charron .15 .40
6 Jeff Cowan .30 .75
7 Hnat Domenichelli .20 .50
8 Jim Dowd .20 .50
9 Denis Gauthier .30 .75
10 J-S Giguere 2.00 5.00
11 Sami Helenius .30 .75
12 Ladislav Kohn .15 .40
13 Eric Landry .15 .40
14 Jesper Mattsson .15 .40
15 Keith McCambridge .15 .40
16 Tyler Moss .20 .50
17 Burke Murphy .15 .40
18 Marty Murray .20 .50
19 Chris O'Sullivan .15 .40
20 Paxton Schulte .20 .50
21 Rocky Thompson .15 .40
22 John Tripp .20 .50
23 Clarke Wilm .15 .40
24 Bill Stewart HCO .10 .25
25 Jeff Perry CO .10 .25

2005-06 Saint John's Sea Dogs

COMPLETE SET (24) 6.00 12.00
1 Jason Churchill .40 1.00
2 Alex Grant .20 .50
3 Alexandre Monahan .20 .50
4 Alexandre Labonte .20 .50
5 Brett Gallant .20 .50
6 Cedric Archambault .20 .50
7 Charles Bergeron .40 1.00
8 Felix Schutz .40 1.00
9 Jean-Philippe Cote .20 .50
10 Jeff Caron .20 .50
11 Jevin Maclellan .20 .50
12 Jonathan Laberge .20 .50
13 Kevin Coughlin .20 .50
14 Martin Bartos .20 .50
15 Maxime Dubuc .20 .50
16 Mike Neil .20 .50
17 Patrick Leask .20 .50
18 Riley Whitlock .40 1.00
19 Ryan Moore .20 .50
20 Ryan Sparling .20 .50
21 Sebastien Rioux .20 .50
22 Vincent Lambert .20 .50
23 Matthew Block .20 .50
24 Luc Melanson .20 .50

2006-07 Saint Johns Sea Dogs

COMPLETE SET (25) 8.00 15.00
1 Alex Grant .40 1.00
2 Mike Noyers .25 .60
3 Ryan Sparling .25 .60
4 Felix Schutz .40 1.00
5 David Macdonald .25 .60
6 Dave Bouchard .25 .60
7 Bruce Crawford .25 .60
8 Sebastien Rioux .25 .60
9 Jonathan Laberge .25 .60
10 Mike Thomas .25 .60
11 Charles Bergeron .25 .60
12 Shayne Tremblay .25 .60
13 Maxime Dubuc .25 .60
14 Alexandre Labonte .25 .60
15 Olivier Painchaud .25 .60
16 David Stich .25 .60
17 Chris Didomenico .25 .60
18 Alexandre Monohan .25 .60
19 Anthony Bergin .25 .60
20 Maxime Joyal .40 1.00
21 Aaron Barton .40 1.00
22 Pascal Amyot .25 .60
23 Brett Gallant .25 .60
24 Yann Sauve .25 .60
LE1 Alex Grant .75 2.00

2003-04 Salmon Arm Silverbacks

The set features the Silverbacks of the BCJHL, including two 2004 first rounders in Chucko and Zajac. The set is unnumbered and listed in alphabetical order.

COMPLETE SET (25) 8.00 20.00
1 Evan Barlow .20 .50
2 Jay Birnie .40 1.00
3 Steve Christie .40 1.00
4 Kris Chucko 1.25 3.00
5 Rick Cleaver .20 .50
6 Spencer Dillon .20 .50
7 Bryn Gagnon .20 .50
8 Trevor Geiger .20 .50
9 Blaine Jarvis .20 .50
10 Jaye Judd .20 .50
11 Patrick Lepage .40 1.00
12 Julian Marcuzzi .20 .50
13 Tyrell Mason .20 .50
14 Ryan McLeod .20 .50
15 Jason Miller .20 .50
16 Travis Ramsey .20 .50
17 Chris Shudo .20 .50
18 Kiel Sonne .40 1.00
19 Ben Street .20 .50
20 Craig Switzer .20 .50
21 Travis Zajac 2.00 5.00
22 Header Card .01 .05
23 Award Winners .40 1.00
24 Header Card .01 .05
25 Team Photo .20 .50

2004-05 Salmon Arm Silverbacks

COMPLETE SET (24) 5.00 12.00
1 Jamie Silverson .30 .75
2 Brendon Nash .30 .75
3 Dustin Degagne .30 .75
4 Robbie Rodgers .30 .75
5 Mark Santorelli .30 .75
6 Brodie Sheahan .30 .75
7 Ben Street .30 .75
8 Tyrell Mason .30 .75
9 Darcy Zajac .40 1.00
10 Bryn Gagnon .30 .75
11 Trevor Geiger .30 .75
12 Luke Cain .30 .75
13 Ryan Duncan .30 .75
14 Ernie Stewart .30 .75
15 Kiel Sonne .30 .75
16 Jesse Deckert .30 .75
17 Brad Atkinson .30 .75
18 Evan Barlow .30 .75
19 Julian Marcuzzi .30 .75
20 Jesse Griffith .30 .75
21 Kong MASCOT .02 .10
22 Team Card .02 .10
23 Logo Card .02 .10
24 Logo Card .30 .75

2005-06 Salmon Arm Silverbacks

COMPLETE SET (25) 10.00 20.00
1 Logo .01 .01
2 Logo .01 .01
3 August Aiken .40 1.00
4 Billy Blase .40 1.00
5 Luke Cain .40 1.00
6 Dustin Degagne .40 1.00
7 Matt Dyck .40 1.00
8 Jesse Griffith .40 1.00
9 Travis Holloway .40 1.00
10 Damon Kipp .40 1.00
11 Josh Lund .40 1.00
12 Cam Macintyre .40 1.00
13 Brendon Nash .40 1.00
14 Evan Pighin .40 1.00
15 Chris Rawlings .40 1.00
16 Rob Rodgers .40 1.00
17 Brodie Sheahan .40 1.00
18 Erik Spady .40 1.00
19 Ernie Stewart .40 1.00
20 Justin Taylor .40 1.00
21 Ben Winnet .40 1.00
22 Shaun Witschen .40 1.00
23 Darcy Zajac .40 1.00
24 KongÂ MASCOT .01 .01
25 AdÂ Card .01 .01

1988-89 Salt Lake Golden Eagles

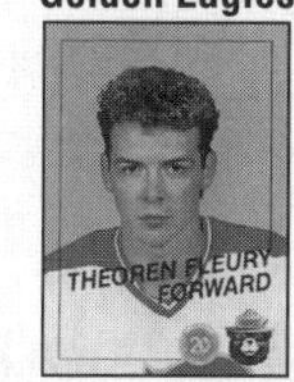

Commemorating the 20th anniversary of the Salt Lake Golden Eagles, this 24-card standard-size set features color close-up shots against a light blue background. The player's name and position are printed diagonally in black across the front. The set was sponsored by the USDA Forest Service and Utah State Lands and Forestry agency. Card number 10 was never issued.

COMPLETE SET (24) 12.00 30.00
1 Rick Barkovich .20 .50
2 Michael Dark .20 .50
3 Terry Perkins .20 .50
4 Peter Lappin .20 .50
5 Wayne Cowley .20 .50
6 Rich Chernomaz .20 .50
7 Steve Smith .40 1.00
8 Theo Fleury 8.00 20.00
9 Dave Reierson .20 .50
10 Not Issued .20 .50
11 Martin Simard .20 .50
12 Stu Grimson .80 3.00
13 Darwin McCutcheon .20 .50
14 Doug Clarke .20 .50
15 Doug Pickell .20 .50
16 Randy Bucyk .20 .50
17 Jim Johannson .20 .50
18 Rick Lessard .20 .50
19 Ken Sabourin .20 .50
20 Chris Biotti .20 .50
21 Jeff Wenaas .20 .50
22 Mark Holmes .20 .50
23 Bob Bodak .20 .50
24 Marc Bureau .40 1.00
NNO Smokey the Bear .20 .50

1992-93 Salt Lake Golden Eagles

Little is known about this set beyond the confirmed checklist. Any additional information should be forwarded to hockeymag@beckett.com.

COMPLETE SET (26) 4.00 10.00
1 Todd Brost .16 .40
2 Rod Buskas .16 .40
3 Rich Chernomaz .16 .40
4 Kerry Clark .16 .40
5 Tomas Forslund .16 .40
6 Todd Gillingham .16 .40
7 Todd Harkins .16 .40
8 Tim Harris .16 .40
9 Shawn Heaphy .16 .40
10 Paul Holden .16 .40
11 Trevor Kidd .40 1.00
12 Paul Kruse .20 .50
13 Patrick Lebeau .20 .50
14 Sandy McCarthy .30 .75
15 Kris Miller .16 .40
16 Jason Muzzatti .20 .50
17 Alex Nikolic .16 .40
18 Ken Sabourin .16 .40
19 David St. Pierre .16 .40
20 Darren Stolk .16 .40
21 David Sturch .16 .40
22 Andrei Trefilov .20 .50
23 Kevin Wortman .16 .40
24 Bob Francis CO .10 .25
25 Brian Patafie TR .04 .10
26 Team card .16 .40

1998-99 San Angelo Outlaws

This 27-card set was handed out early in the season over the span of several home games.

COMPLETE SET (27) 7.20 18.00
1 Jason Abel .30 .75
2 Jean Blouin .30 .75
3 Carl Boudreau .40 1.00
4 Daniel Chaput .30 .75
5 Ryan Connolly .30 .75
6 Brad Cook .30 .75
7 Marty Diamond .30 .75
8 Chad Erickson .40 1.00
9 Sandis Girvitch .30 .75
10 Ross Harris .40 1.00
11 Kevin McKinnon .30 .75
12 Aigars Mironovics .30 .75
13 Skeeter Moore .30 .75
14 Carl Paradis .40 1.00
15 Ryan Reid .30 .75
16 Al Rooney .30 .75
17 Shayne Stevenson .40 1.00
18 Mike Vandenberghe .30 .75
19 Kris Waltze .30 .75
20 Tom Nurre .30 .75
21 Rich Van Patten EM .10 .25
22 Shaun Clouston CO .10 .25
23 Ransom Mascot .10 .25
24 Rusty Mascot .10 .25
25 Jay Willman ANNC .10 .25
26 Jonathan Luce .30 .75
27 Joe Briley TR .10 .25

1999-00 San Angelo Outlaws

This 31-card set was sold by the team a the rink and through the mail. The set is numbered on the back up to 35, however, card numbers 16,20,25,and 30 do not exist.

COMPLETE SET (31) 30.00 75.00
1 Mike Bajurny .30 4.00
2 Scott Chartier .20 3.00
3 Jamie Garrick .20 3.00
4 Sandis Girvitch .20 3.00
5 Corey Isen .20 3.00
6 Ed Kowalski .20 3.00
7 Kevin Kreutzer .30 4.00
8 Adam Lord .30 4.00
9 Dave Lylyk .20 3.00
10 Kevin McKinnon .20 3.00
11 Skeeter Moore .20 3.00
12 Erik Noack .20 3.00
13 Carl Paradis .30 4.00
14 Pavel Evstigneev .20 3.00
15 Robby Sandrock .20 3.00
17 Kris Waltze .30 4.00
18 Dion Wandler .20 3.00
19 Darren Wright .20 3.00
21 San Angelo Coliseum .04 1.00
22 Frank Froio EQM .04 1.00
23 Jeff Smith .20 3.00
24 Harvard/Henry .04 1.00
26 Mike Collins CO .04 1.00
27 Off-Ice Officials .04 1.00
28 Ransom Mascot .04 1.00
29 Rusty Mascot .04 1.00
31 Inflatable Rusty .04 1.00
32 Side Rink Action .04 1.00
33 Team Photo .04 1.00
34 Jay Willman .20 3.00
35 Booster Club .04 1.00

1998-99 San Antonio Iguanas

This 21-card set was sold by the team at games and via mail order. The Jason MacIntyre card may have been pulled from some of the sets due to his lifetime ban from the WCHL that was issued during this season.

COMPLETE SET (21) 4.80 12.00
1 Ken Shepard .20 .50
2 John Hultberg .40 1.00
3 Brian Shantz .40 1.00
4 Paul Jackson .40 1.00
5 Iggy Mascot .04 .10
6 Jason MacIntyre .80 2.00
7 Pat Caron .20 .50
8 Mike Tobin .20 .50
9 Dave Doucette .20 .50
10 Marc Laforge .20 .50
11 Kevin Lune .20 .50
12 Jay Pylypuik .20 .50
13 Johnny Brdarovic .20 .50
14 Roy Gray .20 .50
15 Ricky Jacob .20 .50
16 Blair Rota .20 .50
17 Cheyne Lazar .20 .50
18 Trevor Matschke .20 .50
19 Fred Goltz .20 .50
20 Todd Gordon HCO .04 .10
21 Iguanas Cheerleaders .40 1.00

1999-00 San Antonio Iguanas

This set features the Iguanas of the CHL. The set was produced and sold by the team at home games.

COMPLETE SET (25) 4.00 10.00
1 San Antonio Iguanas .20 .50
2 Church's Chicken .01
3 Jason MacIntyre .20 .50
4 Trevor Matschke .20 .50
5 Johnny Brdarovich .20 .50
6 Scott Green .20 .50
7 Brian Shantz .30 .75
8 Henry Kuster .30 .75
9 Bob Westerby .30 .75
10 Blair Rota .20 .50
11 Garnet Jacobson .20 .50
12 Ricky Jacob .20 .50
13 Jeff Boettger .20 .50
14 Wade Gibson .20 .50
15 Sam Fields .20 .50
16 Marc Laforge .30 .75
17 Trevor Anderson .20 .50
18 Corwin Saurdiff .30 .75
19 Mitch Shawara .20 .50
20 Chris Stewart CO .10 .25
21 Craig Coxe CO .30 .75
22 Manny Sanchez TR .04 .10
23 Chad Daniels TR .04 .10
24 Iggy MAS .04 .10
25 San Antonio Iguanas CL .04 .10

2003-04 San Antonio Rampage

COMPLETE SET (24) 5.00 12.00
1 Scott Allen HCO .02 .10
2 Ian Herbers ACO .02 .10
3 Lukas Krajicek .30 .75
4 Daryl Andrews .30 .75
5 Mascot .02 .10
6 Kent Huskins .20 .50
7 Paul Elliott .20 .50
8 Grant McNeill .20 .50
9 Vaclav Nedorost .20 .50
10 Greg Campbell .30 .75
11 Sean O'Connor .20 .50
12 Ryan Jardine .20 .50
13 Brent Cullaton .20 .50
14 Denis Shvidki .20 .50
15 Josh Olson .20 .50
16 Eric Beaudoin .20 .50
17 Matt Dzieduszycki .20 .50
18 Petr Taticek .40 1.00
19 Michel Periard .20 .50
20 Simon Lajeunesse .40 1.00
21 Kristian Kudroc .20 .50
22 Lee Goren .30 .75
23 Travis Scott .30 .75
24 Sponsor .01 .05

2004-05 San Antonio Rampage

These cards are not numbered. Issued as a stadium giveaway.

COMPLETE SET (22) 10.00 25.00
1 Mascot .02 .10
2 Lukas Krajicek .40 1.00
3 T.J. Reynolds .40 1.00
4 Jay Bouwmeester .75 2.00
5 Filip Novak .40 1.00
6 Joel Kwiatkowski .40 1.00
7 Serge Payer .40 1.00
8 Stephen Weiss .75 2.00
9 Chris Nielsen .40 1.00
10 Gregory Campbell .75 2.00
11 Joe Cullen .40 1.00
12 Ryan Jardine .40 1.00
13 Rob Globke .75 2.00
14 Nathan Horton .75 2.00
15 Juraj Kolnik .40 1.00
16 Jeff Brown .40 1.00
17 Petr Taticek .40 1.00
18 Kamil Kreps .40 1.00
19 Patrick DesRochers 2.00
20 Victor Uchevatov .40 1.00
21 Travis Scott .40 1.00
22 Greg Jacina .40 1.00

1995-96 San Diego Barracudas RHI

This 14-card set is blank-backed, and features card fronts with varying border colours. Any additional information can be forwarded to hockeymag@beckett.com.

COMPLETE SET (14) 2.00 5.00
1 Dan Elsener .20 .50
2 Sandy Gasseau .20 .50
3 Brad Belland .20 .50
4 Stephen Grogg .20 .50
5 Frankie Ouellette .30 .75
6 Alan Leggett .20 .50
7 Soren True .20 .50
8 John Spoltore .30 .75
9 Ralph Barahona .20 .50
10 Oleg Yashin .20 .50
11 Stephane St. Amour .20 .50
12 Max Middendorf .30 .75
13 Clark Polgase .20 .50
14 Steve Martinson HCO .10 .25

1992-93 San Diego Gulls

This 24-card standard-size set features full-bleed, color player photos. The player's name is superimposed on the picture in red lettering. The player's position appears in a black circle in the lower left corner. The cards are unnumbered and checklisted below in alphabetical order.

COMPLETE SET (24) 4.00 10.00
1 John Anderson .20 .50
2 Perry Anderson .16 .40
3 Scott Arniel .20 .50
4 Michael Brewer .16 .40
5 Dale DeGray .16 .40
6 Gord Dineen .16 .40
7 Rick Dudley CO .16 .40
8 Larry Floyd .16 .40
9 Keith Gretzky .20 .50
10 Peter Hankinson .16 .40
11 Bill Houlder .20 .50
12 Andrei Iakovenko .16 .40
13 Rick Knickle .30 .75
14 Denny Lambert .20 .50
15 Mitch Lamoureux .20 .50
16 Clint Malarchuk .30 .75
17 Steve Martinson .16 .40
18 Hubie McDonough .20 .50
19 Don McSween .16 .40
20 Mitch Molloy .16 .40
21 Robbie Nichols .16 .40
22 Lindy Ruff .20 .50
23 Daniel Shank .30 .75
24 Sergei Starikov .16 .40

1999-00 San Diego Gulls

This set features the Gulls of the WCHL. The unnumbered cards were handed out in two different packs of 10 at a single home game late in the season.

COMPLETE SET (20) 6.00 15.00
1 Rod Aldoff .20 .50
2 Brad Belland .20 .50
3 Jamie Black .30 .75
4 Frederick Jobin .20 .50
5 Olaf Kjenstadt .30 .75
6 Brett Larson .20 .50
7 Steven Low .20 .50
8 B.J. MacPherson .20 .50
9 Petr Marek .20 .50
10 Taj Melson .20 .50
11 Sergei Naumov .60 1.50
12 Barry Potomski .60 1.50
13 Dennis Purdie .60 1.50
14 Martin St. Amour .30 .75
15 Stephane St. Amour .30 .75
16 Mark Woolf .30 .75
17 Steve Martinson HCO .30 .75
18 Gulls Win .20 .50
19 Goal Celebration .20 .50
20 Gulls Girls Cheerleaders .40 1.00

2000-01 San Diego Gulls

This set features the Gulls of the WCHL. The set was produced by Grandstand Cards and was sold by the team at its souvenir stands.

COMPLETE SET (22) 3.60 10.00
1 Jamie Black .16 .40
2 Cris Classen .16 .75
3 Serge Crochetiere .16 .40
4 Dan Gravelle .16 .40
5 Trevor Koenig .16 .75
6 Ashley Langdone .16 1.00
7 Brett Larson .16 .40
8 Cory Laylin .16 .40
9 B.J. MacPherson .16 .40
10 Kevin Mackie .16 .40
11 Petr Marek .16 .40
12 Taj Melson .16 .40
13 Brian Morrison .16 .40
14 Samy Nasreddine .16 .40
15 Jeff Petruic .16 .40
16 Dennis Purdie .30 .75
17 Mark Stitt .16 .40
18 Mike Taylor .16 .40
19 Chad Wagner .16 .40
20 Mark Woolf .16 .40
21 Gulls Score! .10 .25
22 San Diego Gulls Bench .16 .40

2001-02 San Diego Gulls

This set features the Gulls of the WCHL. These cards were handed out at a game on December 28, 2001. The set is unnumbered and is listed in alphabetical order.

COMPLETE SET (24) 10.00 25.00
1 Boyd Ballard .40 1.00
2 Jamie Black .40 1.00
3 Clint Cabana .40 1.00
4 Serge Crochetiere .40 1.00
5 Jaisen Freeman .40 1.00
6 Dan Gravelle .40 1.00
7 Trevor Koenig .40 1.00
8 Ashley Langdone .40 1.00
9 Shawn Mansoff .40 1.00
10 Petr Marek .40 1.00
11 Taj Melson .40 1.00
12 Brian Morrison .40 1.00
13 Samy Nasreddine .60 1.50
14 Billy Pugliese .40 1.00
15 Dennis Purdie .80 2.00
16 Trevor Sherban .40 1.00
17 John Spoltore .80 2.00
18 Mark Stitt .40 1.00
19 Mark Woolf .80 2.00
20 B.J. MacPherson .60 1.50
21 Gulls Girls .80 2.00
22 Sandy MASCOT .04 .10
23 Gulls Bench .04 .10
24 Gulls Score! .20 .50

1994-95 San Jose Rhinos RHI

This set features the Rhinos of Roller Hockey Intl. The cards were sold in set form by the team at home games.

COMPLETE SET (16) 3.20 8.00
1 Rocky Mascot .10 .25
2 Ken Blum .20 .50
3 Steve Carpenter .20 .50
4 Will Clarke .20 .50
5 Darren Colbourne .20 .50
6 Bart Cote .20 .50
7 Brian Goudie .20 .50
8 Jon Gustafson .30 .75
9 Greg Hadden .20 .50
10 Blaine Moore .20 .50
11 Jay Murphy .20 .50
12 Dennis Purdie .40 1.00
13 Roy Sommer CO .10 .25
14 Mike Taylor .20 .50
15 Darren Wetherill .20 .50
16 Mark Woolf .30 .75

1994-95 Sarnia Sting

Sponsored by Big V Drug Stores and Pizza Hut and printed by Slapshot Images Ltd., this 31-card set commemorates the Sting's inaugural year. On a black and silver background, the fronts feature color action player photos with thin grey borders. The player's name, position and team name, as well as the producer's logo, also appear on the front.

COMPLETE SET (31) 4.00 10.00
1 Checklist .04 .10
2 Ken Carroll .10 .30
3 Scott Hay .10 .30
4 Kam White .10 .30
5 Joe Doyle .10 .30
6 Tom Brown .10 .30
7 Jeremy Miculinic .10 .30
8 Darren Mortier .10 .30
9 Aaron Brand .14 .50
10 Chris George .10 .30
11 Stephane Soulliere .10 .30
12 Paul McInnes .10 .30
13 Trevor Letowski 1.20 1.00
14 Dustin McArthur .10 .30
15 Rob Massa .10 .30
16 Brendan Yarema .10 .30
17 Dan DelMonte .10 .30
18 B.J. Johnston .10 .30
19 Wes Mason .10 .30
20 Rob Guinn .10 .30
21 Jeff Brown .10 .30
22 Dennis Maxwell .10 .30
23 Damon Hardy .10 .30
24 Alan Letang .16 .50
25 Matt Hogan .10 .30
26 Sasha Cucuz .10 .30
27 Rich Brown CO .04 .10
28 Gord Hamilton TR .04 .10
29 Dino Ciccarelli .20 .50
Shawn Burr
30 Buzz MASCOT .04 .10
NNO Ad Card .04 .01

1995-96 Sarnia Sting

COMPLETE SET (25) 5.00 12.00
1 Jeff Salajko .20 .50
2 Patrick DesRochers .30 .75
3 Gerald Moriarity .20 .50
4 Allan Carr .20 .50
5 Tom Brown .20 .50
6 Andy Delmore .30 .75
7 Darren Mortier .20 .50
8 Aaron Brand .20, .50
9 Eric Boulton .60 1.50
10 Jonathan Sim .30 .75
11 Trevor Letowski .30 .75
12 Mike Hanson .20 .50
13 Todd Miller .20 .50
14 Brendan Yarema .20 .50
15 Brad Simms .20 .50
16 David Nemirovsky .20 .50
17 Jeff Brown .20 .50
18 Andrew Proskurnicki .20 .50
19 Wes Mason .20 .50
20 Scott Corbett .20 .50
21 Dave Bourque .20 .50
22 Sean Brown .20 .50
23 Marcin Snita .20 .50
24 Rich Brown ACO .02 .10
25 Mark Hunter HCO .10 .25

1996-97 Sarnia Sting

This attractive 31-card set was produced by Haines Printing for the Sting and was distributed by the club at the rink. The cards feature action photography on the front, with the player's name and number, and the insignia of the sponsor, Bayview Chrysler, along the bottom. The set is noteworthy for the inclusion of a special card of captain Trevor Letowski as a member of the Canadian National Junior team.

COMPLETE SET (31) 6.00 10.00
1 Bill Abercrombie ACO .04 .10
2 Louie Blackbird .16 .40
3 Bryan Blair .16 .40
4 Dave Bourque .16 .40
5 Joe Canale CO .10 .25
6 Scott Corbett .16 .40
7 Andy Delmore .40 .75
8 Patrick DesRochers .30 .75
9 Michael Hanson .16 .40
10 Abe Herbst .20 .50
11 Shane Kenny .16 .40
12 Darryl Knight .16 .40
13 Trevor Letowski .80 1.00
14 Trevor Letowski .80 1.00
Team Canada
15 Wes Mason .20 .50
16 Darren Mortier .16 .40
17 Kevin Mota .16 .40
18 Eoin McInerney .30 .75
19 Lucas Nehrling .16 .40
20 Dan Pawlaczyk .16 .40
21 Andrew Proskurnicki .16 .40
22 Richard Rochefort .16 .40
23 Bogdan Rudenko .16 .40
24 Jon Sim .40 1.00
25 Brad Simms .16 .40
26 Marcin Snita .16 .40
27 Casey Wolak .16 .40
28 Season Line-Up .01
29 Title Card .01
30 Team Logo .04 .10
31 Calendar Card .01

2000-01 Sarnia Sting

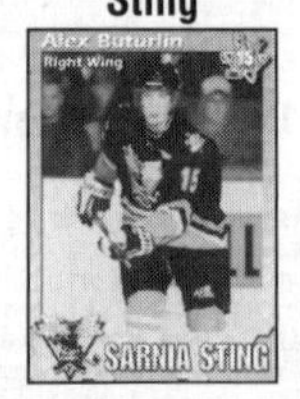

This set features the Sting of the OHL. The set was produced by the team and sold at home games. The cards are unnumbered, and are listed below alphabetically.

COMPLETE SET (24) 4.80 12.00
1 Header Card .04 .01
2 Larry Bernard CO .10 .25
3 Chris Berti .20 .50
4 Cory Brekelmans .20 .50
5 Rick Brown CO .10 .25
6 Alex Buturlin .30 .50
7 Adam Campbell .20 .50
8 Tyler Coleman .20 .50
9 Ryan Fraser .20 .50
10 Robert Gherson .30 1.00
11 Julius Halfkenny .20 .50
12 Ryan Hare .20 .50
13 John Hecimovic .20 .50
14 Scott Heffernan .20 .50
15 Eric Himelfarb .30 1.00
16 Dusty Jamieson .30 .75
17 Jeff Luckovitch .20 .50
18 Preston Mizzi .20 .50
19 Kris Newbury .30 .75
20 Robb Palahnuk .20 .50
21 Jason Penner .30 .75
22 Tom Rogerson .20 .50
23 Maxim Rybin .30 .75
24 Reg Thomas .20 .50

2003-04 Sarnia Sting

COMPLETE SET (23) 5.00 12.00
1 Charles Amodeo .20 .50
2 John Barrow .30 .75
3 Marco Caprara .30 .75
4 Daniel Carcillo .20 .50
5 Marek Chvatal .20 .50
6 Richard Clune .20 .50
7 Craig Foster .20 .50
8 Dan Fritsche .75 2.00
9 Micheal Haley .20 .50
10 John Hecimovic .20 .50
11 Anton Kadeykin .20 .50
12 Colt King .30 .75
13 Drew Larman .20 .50
14 Matt Manias .20 .50
15 Ryan Munce .60 1.50
16 Matt Pelech .20 .50
17 David Pszenyczny .20 .50
18 Daniel Sisca .20 .50
19 Trevor Solomon .20 .50
20 Joey Tenute .30 .75
21 Steve Ward .20 .50
22 Jeff Whitfield .20 .50
23 Kelsey Wilson .20 .50

2006-07 Sarnia Sting

COMPLETE SET (22) 12.00 20.00
1 Steven Stamkos 1.50 4.00
2 Trevor Kell .30 .75
3 Tomas Pospisil .30 .75
4 Steven Reese .30 .75
5 Steve Ferry .30 .75
6 Sebastian Dahm .40 1.00
7 Ryan Wilson .30 .75
8 Parker Van Buskirk .40 1.00
9 Mike Roelofsen .30 .75
10 Matt Martin .30 .75
11 Mark Katic .50 1.25
12 Kyle Tront .30 .75
13 Justin Dibenedetto .30 .75
14 Jared Gomes .30 .75
15 Harrison Reed .30 .75
16 Danny Anger .30 .75
17 Daniel Lombardi .30 .75
18 Dalton Prout .30 .75
19 Christian Steingraber .30 .75
20 Chris Mifflen .30 .75
21 Brandon Mashinter .30 .75
22 Bobby Davey .30 .75

1992-93 Saskatchewan JHL

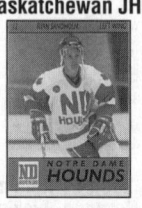

This 168-card set features players in the Saskatchewan Junior Hockey League. The cards are slightly larger than standard size, measuring 2 9/16" by 3 9/16." The fronts feature color action player photos with team color-coded borders at the top and bottom. The player's name and position appear in the top border. The team name and logo appear in the wider bottom border.

COMPLETE SET (168) 8.00 20.00
1 Troy Edwards .06 .15
2 Simon Oliver .06 .15
3 Gerald Tallaire .06 .15
4 Blair Allison .06 .15
5 Mads True .06 .15
6 Steve Brent .06 .15
7 Jay Dobrescu .06 .15
8 Dave Debusschere .06 .15
9 Bryan Cossette .06 .15
10 Brooke Battersby .06 .15
11 Kyle Niemegeers .06 .15
12 Darren McLean .06 .15
13 Carson Cardinal .06 .15
14 Bill McKay .06 .15
15 Chris Hatch .06 .15
16 Nolan Weir .06 .15
17 Karl Johnson .06 .15
18 Jason Brown .06 .15
19 Tyler Kuhn .06 .15
20 Daniel Dennis .06 .15
21 Wally Spence .06 .15
22 Rob Beck .06 .15
23 Aaron Cain .20 .50
24 Darryl Dickson .06 .15
25 Travis Cheyne .06 .15
26 Mark Leoppky .06 .15
27 Jason Ahenakew .06 .15
28 Kyle Paul .06 .15
29 Dean Normand .06 .15
30 Brett Kinaschuk .06 .15
31 Darren Schmidt .06 .15
32 Chris Schinkel .06 .15
33 David Foster .06 .15
34 Jason Zimmerman .06 .15
35 Tom Perry .06 .15
36 Kent Kinaschuk .06 .15
37 Colin Froese .06 .15
38 Shawn Zimmerman .06 .15
39 Larry Empey .06 .15
40 Curtis Knight .06 .15
41 Blake Shipley .06 .15
42 Cory Heon .06 .15
43 Steve Pashulka .06 .15
44 Rob Kinch .06 .15
45 Dean Gerard .06 .15
46 Matt Desmarais .06 .15
47 Chad Rusnak .06 .15
48 Brad Bagu .06 .15
49 Cam Bristow .06 .15
50 Derek Simonson .06 .15
51 Ken Ruddock .06 .15
52 Tyler Deis .06 .15
53 Steve Tansowny .06 .15
54 Bill Stait .06 .15
55 Garfield Henderson .06 .15
56 Lonny Deobald .06 .15
57 Lyle Ehrmantraut .06 .15
58 Layne Humenny .06 .15
59 Darren Balcombe .06 .15
60 Jeff McCutheon .06 .15
61 Trevor Wathen .06 .15
62 Derek Wynne .06 .15
63 Matt Russo .06 .15
64 Bruce Matatall .06 .15
65 Derek Crimin .06 .15
66 Chad Crumley .06 .15
67 Mike Hillock .06 .15
68 Art Houghton .06 .15
69 Lee Materi .06 .15
70 Nick Dyhr .06 .15
71 Darren Maloney .06 .15
72 Kurtise Souchotte .06 .15
73 Noel Kamel .06 .15
74 Trent Harper .06 .15
75 Ted Grayling .06 .15
76 Keith Harris .06 .15
77 Corri Moffat .06 .15
78 Travis Vantighem .06 .15
79 Darren Houghton .06 .15
80 Wade Welte .06 .15
81 Dave Doucet .06 .15
82 Jason Prokopetz .06 .15
83 Gordon McCann .06 .15
84 Clint Hooge .06 .15
85 Glen McGillvary .06 .15
86 Regan Simpson .06 .15
87 Mike Masse .06 .15
88 Jeremy Procyshyn .06 .15
89 Jim Nellis .06 .15
90 Todd Kozak .06 .15
91 Brent Hoiness .06 .15
92 Josh Welter .06 .15
Jason Welter
93 Eldon Barker .06 .15
94 Duane Vandale .06 .15
95 Brad McEwen .06 .15
96 Trent Tibbatts .06 .15
97 Jody Reiter .06 .15
98 Greg Moore .06 .15
99 Jon Rowe .06 .15
100 Mike Evans .06 .15
101 Jason Krug .06 .15
102 Jon Bracco .06 .15
103 Ryan Sandholm .06 .15
104 Darryl Sangster .06 .15
105 Brett Colborne .06 .15
106 Dean Moore .06 .15
107 Chris Dechaine .06 .15
108 Steve McKenna .06 .15
109 Tony Bergin .06 .15
110 Tim Murray .06 .15
111 Casey Kesselring .06 .15
112 Todd Barth .06 .15
113 Ryan McConnell .06 .15
114 Ian Adamson .06 .15
115 Warren Pickford .06 .15
116 Todd Murphy .06 .15
117 Rob Phillips .06 .15
118 Trevor Demmans .06 .15
119 Jeff Greenwood .06 .15
120 Kevin Messer .06 .15
121 Dion Johnson .06 .15
122 Rejean Stringer .06 .15
123 Scott Mead .06 .15
124 Jeff Lawson .06 .15
125 Scot Newberry .06 .15
126 Bill Reid .06 .15
127 Chris Winkler .06 .15
128 Kyle Girgan .06 .15
129 Trevor Warrener .06 .15
130 Richard Boscher .06 .15
131 Tom Thomson .06 .15
132 Mike Wevers .06 .15
133 Barton Holt .06 .15
134 Kent Rogers .06 .15
135 Richard Gibbs .06 .15
136 Jared Witt .06 .15
137 Jamie Stelmak .06 .15
138 Greg Wahl .06 .15
139 J. Sotropa .06 .15
140 Mark Pivetz .06 .15
141 Travis Kirby .06 .15
142 Jason Scanzano .06 .15
143 Tyson Balog .06 .15
144 Daryl Krauss .06 .15
145 Mike Harder .06 .15
146 Tyler McMillan .06 .15
147 Darcy Herlick .06 .15
148 Dave Zwyer .06 .15
149 Craig McKechnie .06 .15
150 Cam Cook .06 .15
151 Derek Bruselinck .06 .15
152 Travis Smith .06 .15
153 Daryl Jones .06 .15
154 Mike Savard .06 .15
155 Jeremy Matthies .06 .15
156 Michel Cook .06 .15
157 Leigh Brookbank .06 .15
158 Christian Dutil .06 .15
159 Scott Heshka .06 .15
160 Danny Galarneau .06 .15
161 Jamie Dunn .06 .15
162 Nigel Werenka .06 .15
163 Steve Sabo .06 .15
164 Tony Toth .06 .15
165 Sebastien Moreau .06 .15
166 Tim Slukynsky .06 .15
167 Sheldon Bylsma .06 .15
168 Stacy Prevost .12 .30

1981-82 Saskatoon Blades

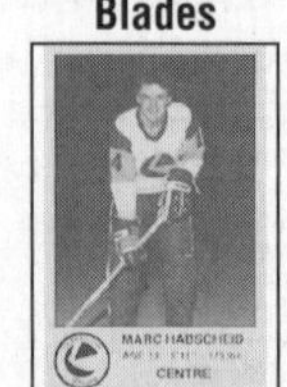

This 25-card P.L.A.Y. (Police, Laws and Youth) set was sponsored by the Saskatoon Police Department and area businesses. The cards measure approximately 2 1/2" by 3 3/4" and are printed on thin card stock. The fronts feature white-bordered color photos with the player's posed in action stances. The player's name, biographical information, and position appear in the bottom white margin. The team logo appears in the lower left corner.

COMPLETE SET (25) 10.00 25.00
1 Blades Team Photo .80 2.00
2 Daryl Stanley .30 .75
3 Leroy Gorski .30 .75
4 Donn Clark .30 .75

5 Brad Duggan .30 .75
6 Dave Chartier .30 .75
7 Dave Brown 1.20 3.00
8 Adam Thompson .30 .75
9 Bruce Eakin .30 .75
10 Brian Skrudland 1.20 3.00
11 Roger Kortko .30 .75
12 Ron Dreger .30 .75
13 Daryl Lubiniecki .30 .75
14 Marc Habscheid .80 2.00
15 Saskatoon Police Logo .20 .50
16 Todd Strueby .40 1.00
17 Craig Hurley .30 .75
18 Bill Hlynsky .30 .75
19 Lane Lambert .80 2.00
20 Mike Bloski .30 .75
21 Bruce Gordon .30 .75
22 Perry Ganchar .40 1.00
23 Ron Loustel .30 .75
24 Blades Logo .20 .50
25 Checklist Card .20 .50

1983-84 Saskatoon Blades

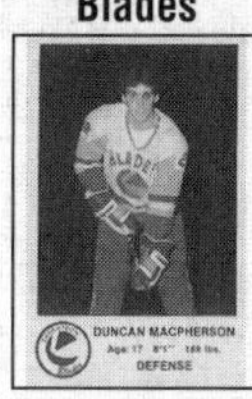

This set contains 24 P.L.A.Y. (Police, Law and Youth) cards and features the Saskatoon Blades of the Western Hockey League. The cards measure approximately 2 7/16" by 3 3/4". The fronts feature a color posed action shot with white borders. The team logo appears in the lower left corner, with player information to the right in black lettering.

COMPLETE SET (24) 12.00 30.00
1 Team Photo .40 1.00
2 Trent Yawney .40 1.00
3 Grant Jennings .40 1.00
4 Duncan MacPherson .20 .50
5 Greg Holtby .20 .50
6 Dan Leier .20 .50
7 Dwaine Hutton .20 .50
8 Wendel Clark 6.00 15.00
9 Kerry Laviolette .20 .50
10 Dave Chartier .20 .50
11 Dale Henry .20 .50
12 Randy Smith .20 .50
13 Kevin Kowalchuk .20 .50
14 Todd McLellan .20 .50
15 Title Card .10 .25
Saskatoon Police
16 Larry Korchinkski .20 .50
17 Curtis Chamberlain .20 .50
18 Greg Lebsack .20 .50
19 Ron Dreger .20 .50
20 Doug Kyle .20 .50
21 Rick Smith .20 .50
22 Joey Kocur 2.00 5.00
23 Allan Larochelle .20 .50
24 Mark Thietke .20 .50

1984-85 Saskatoon Blades Stickers

This set of 20 stickers was sponsored by Autotec Oil and Saskatchewan Ronald McDonald House. Each sticker measures approximately 2" by 1 3/4" and could be pasted on a 17" by 11" poster printed in thin glossy paper. The stickers display a black-and-white head shot; the uniform number is also printed on the front. The stickers are unnumbered and checklisted below in alphabetical order.

COMPLETE SET (20) 10.00 25.00
1 Jack Bowkus .30 .75
2 Curtis Chamberlain .30 .75
3 Wendel Clark 6.00 15.00
4 Ron Dreger .30 .75
5 Randy Hoffart .30 .75
6 Mark Holick .30 .75
7 Greg Holtby .30 .75
8 Grant Jennings .40 1.00
9 Kevin Kowalchuk .30 .75
10 Bryan Larkin .30 .75
11 James Latos .30 .75
12 Duncan MacPherson .30 .75
13 Rod Matechuk .30 .75
14 Todd McLellan .30 .75
15 Darren Moren .30 .75
16 Mike Morin .30 .75
17 Devon Oleniuk .30 .75
18 Grant Tkachuk .30 .75
19 Troy Vollhoffer .30 .75
20 Trent Yawney .40 1.00

1986-87 Saskatoon Blades Photos

This set is comprised of 25 photos of members of the WHL's Saskatoon Blades. The photos measure a large 8 X 11.5 inches, and bear the mark of sponsor Shell Oil.

COMPLETE SET (24) 14.00 35.00
1 Blair Atcheynum .80 2.00
2 Colin Bayer .40 1.00
3 Jack Bowkus .40 1.00
4 Mike Butkas .40 1.00
5 Kelly Chase 2.00 5.00
6 Tim Cheveldae .80 2.00
7 Blaine Chrest .40 1.00
8 Kerry Clark .40 1.00
9 Brian Glynn .40 1.00
10 Mark Holick .40 1.00
11 Kevin Kaminski .80 2.00
12 Tracey Katelnikoff .40 1.00
13 Kory Kocur .40 1.00
14 Bryan Larkin .40 1.00
15 Curtis Leschyshyn .80 2.00
16 Dan Logan .40 1.00
17 Todd MacLellan .40 1.00
18 Devon Oleniuk .40 1.00
19 Marty Prazma .40 1.00
20 Marty Weimer .40 1.00
21 Walter Shutter .40 1.00
22 Grant Tkachuk .40 1.00
23 Tony Twist 2.00 5.00
24 Shaun Van Allen .80 2.00

1988-89 Saskatoon Blades

This standard size set features posed color photos on the front, and safety tips and logos on the back. Cards are numbered as seen below.

COMPLETE SET (25) 4.00 10.00
1 Joe Penkala .20 .50
2 Saskatoon Police Emblem .08 .20
3 Marcel Comeau .20 .50
4 Dean Kuntz .20 .50
5 Mike Greenlay .20 .50
6 Jody Praznik .20 .50
7 Ken Sutton .20 .50
8 Sawn Snesar .20 .50
9 Shane Langager .20 .50
10 Dean Holdien .20 .50
11 Rob Lelacheur .20 .50
12 David Struch .20 .50
13 Collin Bauer .20 .50
14 Kevin Yellowaga .20 .50
15 Drew Sawtell .20 .50
16 Brian Gerrits .20 .50
17 Kirk Roworth .20 .50
18 Tracey Katelnikoff .20 .50
19 Scott Scissons .20 .50
20 Jason Smart .20 .50
21 Jason Christie .20 .50
22 Daren Bader .20 .50
23 Kevin Kaminski .20 .50
24 Kory Kocur .20 .50
25 Darwin McPherson .20 .50

1989-90 Saskatoon Blades

These standard-sized cards feature the Blades of the Western Hockey League. It is believed that they were issued individually by members of the local police, rather than issued in team set form.

COMPLETE SET (25) 6.00 15.00
1 Terry Ruskowski .30 .75
2 Cam Moon .20 .50
3 Damon Kustra .20 .50
4 Trevor Robins .20 .50
5 Mark Raiter .20 .50
6 Mark Wotton .30 .75
7 Shawn Snesar .20 .50
8 Trevor Sherban .20 .50
9 Shane Langager .20 .50
10 Dean Holdien .20 .50
11 Rob Lelacheur .20 .50
12 David Struch .20 .50
13 Derek Tibbatts .20 .50
14 Drew Sawtell .20 .50
15 Richard Matvichuk .60 1.50
16 Trent Coghill .20 .50
17 Jeff Buchanan .20 .50
18 Grant Chorney .20 .50
19 Shawn Yakimishyn .20 .50
20 Scott Scissons .20 .50
21 Jason Smart .20 .50
22 Jason Christie .20 .50
23 Darin Bader .20 .50
24 Dean Rambo .20 .50
25 Collin Bauer .20 .50

1990-91 Saskatoon Blades

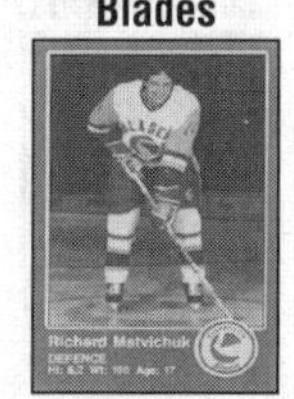

This 27-card P.L.A.Y. (Police, Laws and Youth) set was sponsored by the Saskatoon Police Department and area businesses. The cards measure approximately 2 1/2" by 3 3/4" and are printed on thin card stock. On a blue card face, the fronts feature white-bordered posed action color photos. The player's name, position, and biographical information appear in the bottom blue margin. The yellow and blue team logo appears in the lower right corner.

COMPLETE SET (27) 4.80 12.00
1 Terry Ruskowski CO .24 .60
2 Trevor Robins .20 .50
3 Cam Moon .20 .50
4 Jeff Buchanan .20 .50
5 Mark Raiter .20 .50
6 Trevor Sherban .20 .50
7 Jason Knox .20 .50
8 Dean Rambo .20 .50
9 Rob LeLacheur .20 .50
10 David Struch .20 .50
11 Greg Leahy .20 .50
12 Derek Tibbatts .20 .50
13 Shane Calder .20 .50
14 Richard Matvichuk .40 1.00
15 Trent Coghill .20 .50
16 Mark Wotton .24 .60
17 Kelly Markwart .20 .50
18 Mark Franks .20 .50
19 Scott Scissons .20 .50
20 Tim Cox .20 .50
21 Gaetan Blouin .20 .50
22 Darin Bader .20 .50
23 Shawn Yakimishyn .20 .50
24 Ryan Strain .20 .50
25 Jason Peters .20 .50
26 Team Card .20 .50
27 Title Card .20 .50

1991-92 Saskatoon Blades

This 25-card P.L.A.Y. (Police, Laws and Youth) set was issued as a sheet measuring approximately 12 1/2" by 17 1/2", with five rows of five cards each. If cut, the individual cards would measure the standard size. On a black card face, the fronts feature posed color player photos with thin white borders. The player's name and biography along with the team's 25th anniversary logo appear below the picture.

COMPLETE SET (25) 4.80 12.00
1 Lorne Molleken CO .10 .25
2 Trevor Robins .20 .50
3 Norm Maracle .40 1.00
4 Jeff Buchanan .20 .50
5 Mark Raiter .20 .50
6 Bryce Goebel .20 .50
7 Rhett Trombley .30 .75
8 Chad Rusnak .20 .50
9 Jason Knight .20 .50
10 David Struch .20 .50
11 Shane Calder .20 .50
12 Derek Tibbatts .20 .50
13 Glen Gulutzan .20 .50
14 Richard Matvichuk .60 1.50
15 Chad Michalchuk .20 .50
16 Mark Wotton .30 .75
17 Mark Franks .20 .50
18 Andy MacIntyre .20 .50
19 Ryan Fujita .20 .50
20 Sean McFatridge .20 .50
21 Jason Becker .20 .50
22 Shawn Yakimishyn .20 .50
23 James Startup .20 .50
24 Paul Buczkowski .20 .50
NNO McGruff .04 .10

1993-94 Saskatoon Blades

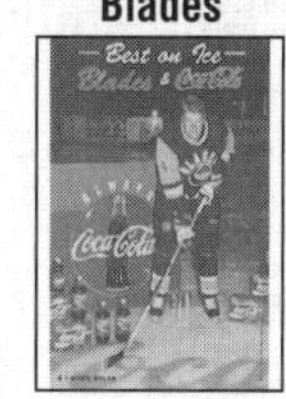

Sponsored by Coca-Cola, this is an oversized 24-card set measuring approximately 8 1/2" by 5 1/2". The borderless fronts feature posed color player photos on the ice surrounded by a Coca-Cola advertising display. The player's name and number in black letters appear in the lower left corner. The words "Best on Ice - Blades and Coca-Cola" are printed over the top of the photo in red, white, and blue. The backs are blank. The cards are unnumbered and checklisted below in alphabetical order.

COMPLETE SET (24) 4.80 12.00
1 Chad Allan .20 .50
2 Frank Banham .24 .60
3 Frank Banham .24 .60
Mark Deyell
Ivan Salon
4 Wade Belak .20 .50
5 Paul Buczkowski .20 .50
6 Shane Calder .24 .60
7 Mark Deyell .30 .75
8 Jason Duda .20 .50
9 Trevor Ethier .20 .50
10 Mike Gray .20 .50
11 Trevor Hanas .20 .50
12 Devon Hanson .20 .50
13 Andrew Kemper .20 .50
14 Kirby Law .20 .50
15 Andy Macintyre .20 .50
16 Norm Maracle .40 1.00
17 Ivan Salon .20 .50
18 Todd Simpson .20 .50
19 Derek Tibbatts .20 .50
20 Derek Tibbatts .20 .50
Clarke Wilm
Andy Macintyre
21 Rhett Warrener .30 .75
22 Clarke Wilm .30 .75
23 Mark Wotton .24 .60
24 Team Photo .20 .50

1995-96 Saskatoon Blades

The 27 oversized (2 1/2" by 4 1/2") cards set feature the Saskatoon Blades of the WHL. Apparently, the cards were issued as a promotional giveaway at PW Pharmacies in Saskatoon. The front displays a color action photo, along with the player's name and number and the Blades logo. A Carlton cards logo appears in the upper right. The backs contain biographical information as well as the logos of all participating sponsors. Complete cards also included a coupon for savings on various products at PW. The cards are worth 50 percent of the value below without the coupon. The cards are unnumbered and thus are checklisted below in alphabetical order.

COMPLETE SET (27) 4.80 12.00
1 Chad Allan .20 .50
2 Frank Banham .30 .75
3 Dennis Bassett .20 .50
4 Wade Belak .30 .75
5 Ryan Bonni .30 .75
6 Paul Buczkowski .20 .50
7 Don Clark CO .20 .50
8 Mattieu Cusson .20 .50
9 Mark Deyell .30 .75
10 Pavel Kriz .20 .50
11 Jeromie Kufflick .20 .50
12 Laird Laluk .20 .50
13 Erik Leefe .20 .50
14 Richard Peacock .20 .50
15 Greg Phillips .20 .50
16 Garrett Prosofsky .30 .75
17 Nathan Rempel .20 .50
18 Cory Sarich .40 1.00
19 Jeremy Schaefer .20 .50
20 Mark Smith .20 .50
21 Martin Sonnenberg .20 .50
22 Randy Weinberger .20 .50
23 Clark Wilm .30 .75
24 Team Logo CL .04 .10
25 Crime Stoppers Logo .04 .10
26 Celebration 30 Years .04 .10
27 Assistant Coaches .04 .10
Chartier
Engele
Federke

1996-97 Saskatoon Blades

This set of the Saskatoon Blades features 28 oversized (2 1/2" X 4 1/2") cards. The fronts display color photos, with the player's name, jersey number and Blades logo inscribed along the bottom. The backs feature biographical data, a safety tip, and the locations of every PW Pharmacy in Saskatoon. PW sponsored the set as a promotional giveaway at local stores. Interestingly, the backs exhort fans to collect all 27 cards, but the set contains 28. The cards come attached to money-saving coupons from PW; if the coupon is removed, the value is 50 percent that listed below. The unnumbered cards are checklisted below alphabetically.

COMPLETE SET (28) 4.80 12.00
1 Stewart Bacharuk .20 .50
2 Jon Barkman .20 .50
3 Justin Bekkering .20 .50
4 Derek Bjornson .20 .50
5 Ryan Bonni .20 .50
6 Christian Chartier .30 .75
7 Matt Cockell .20 .50
8 Mathieu Cusson .20 .50
9 Jared Dumba .20 .50
10 Ryan Gaucher .20 .50
11 Ryan Henderson .20 .50
12 Ryan Johnston .20 .50
13 Vladislav Klochkov .20 .50
14 Laird Laluk .20 .50
15 Tyler Love .20 .50
16 Sheldon Nedielski .20 .50
17 Greg Phillips .20 .50
18 Garrett Prosofsky .20 .50
19 Nathan Rempel .20 .50
20 Cory Sarich .20 .50
21 Brian Skrudland .20 .50
22 Martin Sonnenberg .20 .50
23 Lyle Steenbergen .20 .50
24 Rhett Warrener .30 .75
25 Kyle Werner .20 .50
26 Team Logo CL .10 .25
27 Action/Goal .10 .25
28 Team(Reebok) .10 .25

1997-98 Saskatoon Blades

Released by the Blades in conjunction with Coca-Cola, this 25-card set features oversized cards with full color action photography and blank backs. The fronts also feature a ghosted area to facilitate autographing. One card remains unidentified in this set. If you have information on their identities, please forward them to hockeymag@beckett.com. The set is not numbered, therefore it appears in alphabetical order.

COMPLETE SET (25) 4.80 12.00
1 Jon Barkman .20 .50
2 Derek Bjornson .20 .50
3 Ryan Bonni .30 .75
4 Christian Chartier .30 .75
5 Matt Cockell .20 .50
6 Mathieu Cusson .20 .50
7 Chad Elmy .20 .50
8 Ryan Gaucher .20 .50
9 Derek Halldorson .20 .50
10 Ryan Johnston .20 .50
11 Dylan Kemp .20 .50
12 Tyler Mackay .20 .50
13 Kevin McKay .30 .75
14 Matt Miller .20 .50
15 Dennis Mullen .20 .50
16 Greg Phillips .20 .50
17 Petja Pietilainen .20 .50
18 Garrett Prosofsky .30 .75
19 Nathan Rempel .20 .50
20 Darcy Robinson .20 .50
21 Cory Sarich .30 .75
22 Martin Sonnenberg .30 .75
23 Mascot .10 .25
24 Header Card .10 .25
25 unknown .20 .50

2000-01 Saskatoon Blades

This set features the Blades of the WHL. The cards were sold at the team's home games.

COMPLETE SET (32) 4.80 12.00
1 Logo Card .04 .11
2 Team Photo .16 .40
3 Kevin Dickie CO .10 .25
4 Bruno Baseotto ACO .10 .25
5 Tim Cheveldae ACO .16 .40
6 Jason Goulet .16 .40
7 Matt Suderman .16 .40
8 Scotty Balan .16 .40
9 Ryan Stempfle .16 .40
10 Kane Ludwar .16 .40
11 Adrian Foster .40 1.00
12 Martin Erat .40 1.00
13 Garrett Bembridge .16 .40
14 Davin Heintz .16 .40
15 Justin Wallin .16 .40
16 Trent Adamus .16 .40
17 Jeff Coulter .16 .40
18 Chris Manchakowski .16 .40
19 Justin Kanigan .16 .40
20 David Cameron .16 .40
21 Derek Halldorson .16 .40
22 Aaron Starr .16 .40
23 Ryan Kehrig .16 .40
24 Rob Woods .16 .40
25 Warren Peters .16 .40
26 Petr Prochazka .16 .40
27 Justin Kelly .16 .40
28 Michael Garnett .16 .40
29 Tony Kolewaski .16 .40
30 Martin Vymazal .16 .40
31 Helmutt MASCOT .04 .11
32 Jay Richards DJ .04 .11

2001-02 Saskatoon Blades

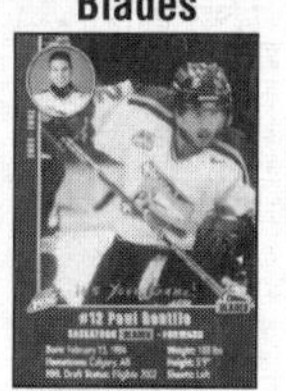

This set features the Blades of the WHL. Little has been confirmed to date regarding this set, but it is believed that they were sold at home games.

COMPLETE SET (32) 6.00 15.00
1 Header .04 .10
2 Derek Couture .20 .50
3 Paul Gentile .20 .50
4 Willy Glover .20 .50
5 Kyle Harris .20 .50
6 Davin Heintz .20 .50
7 Adam Huxley .20 .50
8 Justin Keller .20 .50
9 Ryan Keller 1.00 2.00
10 Justin Kelly .20 .50
11 Richard Mueller .20 .50
12 Warren Peters .20 .50
13 Tim Preston .20 .50
14 Daniel Volrab .20 .50
15 Trent Adamus .20 .50
16 Tiger Williams/Kelly Hrudey .40 1.00
17 Scotty Balan .20 .50
18 Mike Green .20 .50
19 Kane Ludwar .20 .50
20 Stephen Mann .20 .50
21 Sean Moir .20 .50
22 Ryan Stempfle .20 .50
23 Matt Suderman .20 .50
24 Rob Woods .20 .50
25 Michael Garnett .50 1.00
26 Ryan Senft .20 .50
27 Helmutt .04 .10
28 Steve Hildebrand TR .04 .10
29 Kevin Dickie CO .04 .10
30 Bruno Baseotto .04 .10
31 Wendel Clark Night .40 1.00
32 Team Photo .20 .50

2002-03 Saskatoon Blades

COMPLETE SET (30)
1 Evan Haw .50
2 Sean Moir .50
3 Matt Suderman .50
4 Matt Bergen .50
5 Steven Later .50
6 Denny Johnston .50
7 Trent Adamus .50
8 Michael Bubnick .50
9 Marcus Paulsson .50
10 Adam Houle .50
11 Daniel Volrab .50
12 Wacey Rabbit .50
13 Derek Couture .50
14 Joe Barnes .50
15 Rob Woods .50
16 Warren Peters .50
17 Adam Huxley .75
18 Mike Green .50
19 John Dahl .50
20 Stephen Mann .50
21 Adam Ward .75
22 Brett Jaeger .75
23 Ryan Keller .50
24 Tanner Shultz .50
25 Jack Brodsky PRES .10
26 Brent McEwan GM .10
27 Kevin Dickie CO .10
28 Bruno Baseotto ACO .10
29 Stev Hildebrand TR .10
30 Team Photo/CL .10

2003-04 Saskatoon Blades

COMPLETE SET (23) 6.00 15.00
1 Mascot .02 .10
2 Team Photo .02 .10
3 Boris Lekovic .30 .75
4 Adam Ward .30 .75
5 Joel Eisenkirch .30 .75
6 Dane Crowley .30 .75
7 Evan Haw .30 .75
8 Nicolaus Knudsen .30 .75
9 Ben Van Lare .30 .75
10 Richard Kelly .30 .75
11 Rob Woods .30 .75
12 Matt Fetzner .30 .75
13 Mike Green .40 1.00
14 Bjorn Svensson .30 .75
15 Ryan Cyr .30 .75
16 Dayln Flatt .30 .75
17 Joe Barnes .30 .75
18 Trent Adamus .30 .75
19 Derek Couture .30 .75
20 Tanner Shultz .30 .75
21 Wacey Rabbit .75 2.00
22 Devin Setoguchi .75 2.00
23 Ryan Keller .30 .75

2004-05 Saskatoon Blades

This set was issued in two parts: a 12-card first series and a 10-card second series.

COMPLETE SET (22) 8.00 20.00
1 Nicolaus Knudsen .30 .75
2 Joel Eisenkirch .30 .75
3 Justin McCrae .30 .75
4 Russell Monette .30 .75
5 Tyson Sievert .30 .75
6 Aaron Bader .30 .75
7 Daniel Waschuk .30 .75
8 Chris Cloud .30 .75
9 Ben Van Lare .30 .75
10 Tyler Boldt .30 .75
11 Mike Green .40 1.00
12 Zdenek Bahensky .40 1.00
13 Ryan Cyr .30 .75
14 Ryan Keller .30 .75
15 Devin Setoguchi .75 2.00
16 Joe Barnes .30 .75
17 Dayln Flatt .40 1.00
18 Dane Crowley .30 .75
19 Evan Haw .30 .75
20 Wacey Rabbit .75 2.00
21 Ryan Menei .30 .75
22 Bjorn Svensson .30 .75

2005-06 Saskatoon Blades

COMPLETE SET (24) 10.00 20.00
1 Aaron Bader .30 .75
2 Zdenek Bahensky .30 .75
3 Joe Barnes .30 .75
4 Chris Cloud .30 .75
5 Brad Cole .30 .75
6 Ryan Funk .30 .75
7 Adam Geric .30 .75
8 Colton Gillies .30 .75
9 Michael Hengen .30 .75
10 Anton Khudobin .40 1.00
11 Chad Klassen .30 .75
12 Joe Logan .30 .75
13 Michael MacAngus .30 .75
14 Blair MacAulay .30 .75
15 Justin McCrae .30 .75
16 Ryan Menei .30 .75
17 Todd Panchyson .30 .75
18 Derek Price .30 .75
19 Wacey Rabbit .60 1.50
20 David Schulz .30 .75
21 Devin Setoguchi .60 1.50
22 Brett Ward .30 .75
23 Jim Watt .40 1.00
24 Brennan Zasitko .30 .75

2006-07 Saskatoon Blades

COMPLETE SET (24) 8.00 15.00
1 Dustin Cameron .25 .60
2 Chris Cloud .25 .60
3 Brad Cole .25 .60
4 Troy Crowley .25 .60
5 Craig Cuthbert .25 .60
6 Kenton Dulle .25 .60
7 Ryan Funk .25 .60
8 Adam Geric .25 .60
9 Colton Gillies .25 2.00
10 Braden Holtby .25 .60
11 Derek Hulak .25 .60
12 Sam Klassen .25 .60
13 Garrett Klotz .25 .60
14 Rastislav Konecny .25 .60
15 Joe Logan .25 .60
16 Blair MacAulay .25 .60
17 Justin McCrae .25 .60
18 Ryan Menei .25 .60
19 Gaelan Patterson .25 .60
20 Bohdan Visnak .25 .60
21 Brett Ward .25 .60
22 Walker Wintoneak .25 .60
23 Teigan Zahn .25 .60
24 Garrett Zemlak .25 .60

1980-81 Sault Ste. Marie Greyhounds

Sponsored by Blue Bird Bakery Limited and Coke, this 25-card set captures the 1980-81 Soo Greyhounds of the OHL. The cards measure approximately 2 1/2" by 4" and feature posed, color player photos. Of interest to collectors are the first cards of current NHL stars John Vanbiesbrouck and Ron Francis.

COMPLETE SET (25) 37.50 75.00
1 Ken Porteous .38 .75
2 Brian Petterle .38 .75
3 Gord Dineen .50 1.00
4 Tony Cella .38 .75
5 Doug Shedden .75 1.50
6 Terry Tait .38 .75
7 Greyhounds Logo .25 .50
8 Steve Smith .38 .75
9 Huey Larkin .38 .75
10 Steve Gatzos .38 .75
11 Tim Zwijack .38 .75
12 Vic Morin .38 .75
13 John Vanbiesbrouck 12.50 25.00
14 Ron Francis 12.50 25.00
15 Tony Butorac .38 .75
16 John Goodwin .38 .75
17 Ron Handy .38 .75
18 Jim Pavese .50 1.00
19 Sault Ste. Marie .25 .50
Police Logo
20 Rick Morocco .38 .75
21 Ken Latta .38 .75
22 Kirk Rueter .38 .75
23 OMJHL Logo .25 .50
24 Terry Crisp 1.25 2.50
25 Marc D'Amour 1.00 2.00

1981-82 Sault Ste. Marie Greyhounds

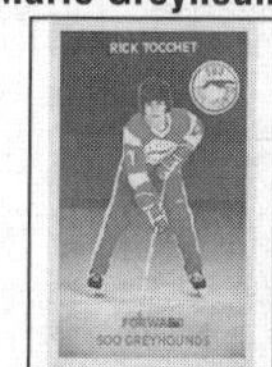

Sponsored by Blue Bird Bakery Limited, Coke, 920 CKCY radio, and Canadian Tire, this 28-card set measures approximately 2 1/8" by 4 1/8" and features posed, color player photos with white borders. The player's name is printed in white on the picture, above the player's head. His position and the team name are printed in fuchsia at the bottom. The cards are unnumbered and checklisted below in alphabetical order. This set contains early cards of Rick Tocchet, John Vanbiesbrouck and Ron Francis.

COMPLETE SET (28) 32.00 80.00
1 Jim Aldreda .30 .75
2 Dave Andreoli .30 .75
3 Richard Beaulne .30 .75
4 Bruce Bell .30 .75
5 Chuck Brimmer .30 .75
6 Tony Cella .30 .75
7 Kevin Conway .30 .75
8 Terry Crisp CO .80 2.00
9 Marc D'Amour .60 1.50
10 Gord Dineen .40 1.00
11 Chris Felix .40 1.00
12 Ron Francis 10.00 25.00
13 Steve Graves .30 .75
14 Wayne Groulx .30 .75
15 Huey Larkin .30 .75

16 Ken Latta .30 .75
17 Mike Lococo .30 .75
18 Jim Pavese .40 1.00
19 Dirk Rueter .30 .75
20 Steve Smith .30 .75
21 Terry Tait .30 .75
22 Rick Tocchet 8.00 20.00
23 John Vanbiesbrouck 10.00 25.00
24 Harry Wolfe ANN .20 .50
25 J.D. Yari .04 .10
26 Bluebird Bakery .04 .10
Limited Logo
27 Canadian Tire Logo .04 .10
28 Coca-Cola Ad .04 .10

1982-83 Sault Ste. Marie Greyhounds

Sponsored by Blue Bird Bakery Limited and 920 CKCY radio station, this 25-card set measures approximately 2 1/2" by 4" and feature color, posed player photos with white borders. The player's name is superimposed on the photo in white lettering. His position is in black at the bottom. The cards are unnumbered and checklisted below in alphabetical order.

COMPLETE SET (25) 16.00 40.00
1 Jim Aldred .30 .75
2 John Armelin .30 .75
3 Richard Beaulne .30 .75
4 Jeff Beukeboom .60 1.50
5 Tony Cella .30 .75
6 Kevin Conway .30 .75
7 Terry Crisp .60 1.50
8 Chris Felix .40 1.00
9 Steve Graves .30 .75
10 Gus Greco .30 .75
11 Wayne Groulx .30 .75
12 Sam Haidy .30 .75
13 Tim Hoover .30 .75
14 Pat Lahey .30 .75
15 Huey Larkin .30 .75
16 Mike Lococo .30 .75
17 Mike Neill .30 .75
18 Ken Sabourin .30 .75
19 Steve Smith .30 .75
20 Terry Tait .30 .75
21 Rick Tocchet 4.00 10.00
22 John Vanbiesbrouck 6.00 15.00
23 Harry Wolfe ANN .20 .50
24 Station Mall Sponsor .04 .10
25 Bluebird Bakery Ltd. .04 .10

1983-84 Sault Ste. Marie Greyhounds

Sponsored by 920 CKCY radio, Coke, and IGA, the cards in this 25-card set measure approximately 2 1/2" by 4" and feature color, posed player photos with white borders. The player's name appears in an orange bar at the bottom of the picture. The cards are unnumbered and checklisted below in alphabetical order.

COMPLETE SET (25) 8.00 20.00
1 Jeff Beukeboom .40 1.00
2 Graeme Bonar .20 .50
3 Chris Brant .20 .50
4 John English .20 .50
5 Chris Felix .40 1.00
6 Rick Fera .20 .50
7 Marc Tournier .20 .50
8 Steve Graves .20 .50
9 Gus Greco .20 .50
11 Wayne Groulx .20 .50
11 Sam Haidy .20 .50
12 Tim Hoover .20 .50
13 Jerry Iuliano .20 .50
14 Pat Lahey .20 .50
15 Mike Lococo .20 .50
16 Jean-Marc MacKenzie .20 .50
17 Mike Oliverio .20 .50
18 Brit Peer .20 .50
19 Joey Rampton .20 .50
20 Ken Sabourin .40 1.00
21 Jim Samec .20 .50
22 Rick Tocchet 3.20 8.00
23 Harry Wolfe ANN .20 .50
24 IGA Sponsor Card .04 .10
25 Coke Sponsor Card .04 .10

1984-85 Sault Ste. Marie Greyhounds

Sponsored by 920 CKCY radio, Coke, and IGA, this 25-card set measures approximately 2 1/2" by 4" and features white-bordered, posed, color photos of the players on ice with a blue studio background. The player's name appears on a bright red plaque near the bottom. The cards are unnumbered and checklisted below in alphabetical order.

COMPLETE SET (25) 8.00 20.00

1 Marty Abrams .20 .50
2 Jeff Beukeboom .30 .75
3 Graeme Bonar .20 .50
4 Chris Brant .20 .50
5 Terry Crisp CO .40 1.00
6 Chris Felix .40 1.00
7 Scott Green .20 .50
8 Wayne Groulx .20 .50
9 Steve Hollett .20 .50
10 Tim Hoover .20 .50
11 Derek King .60 1.50
12 Tyler Larter .20 .50
13 Jean-Marc MacKenzie .20 .50
14 Scott Mosey .20 .50
15 Mike Oliverio .20 .50
16 Brit Peer .20 .50
17 Wayne Presley .40 1.00
18 Bob Probert 2.40 6.00
19 Brian Rome .20 .50
20 Ken Sabourin .30 .75
21 Rob Veccia .20 .50
22 Harry Wolfe ANN .10 .25
23 Rob Zettler .40 1.00
24 IGA Ad .10 .25
25 Coca-Cola Ad .10 .25

1987-88 Sault Ste. Marie Greyhounds

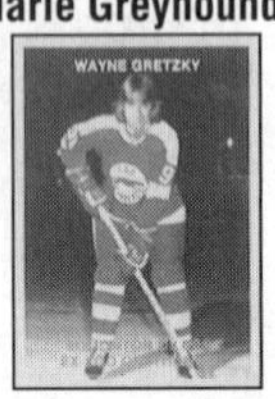

Printed on thin card stock, this 35-card set features players from the 1987-88 season of the Sault Ste. Marie Greyhounds and also past Greyhounds players who have gone on to NHL fame, such as Wayne Gretzky. The fronts feature white-bordered posed-on-ice color player photos. The player's name appears in white lettering near the top; his position and the team name appear in blue lettering near the bottom.

COMPLETE SET (35) 50.00 125.00
1 Barry King .10 .25
Chief of Police
2 Dan Currie .20 .50
3 Mike Glover .20 .50
4 Tyler Larter .20 .50
5 Bob Jones .20 .50
6 Lyndon Slewidge .10 .25
National Anthem Singer
7 Brad Jones .20 .50
8 Ron Francis 2.80 7.00
9 Dale Turnbull .20 .50
10 Don McConnell .20 .50
11 Chris Felix .30 .75
12 Steve Udvari .20 .50
13 Shawn Simpson .20 .50
14 Rob Zettler .40 1.00
15 Phil Esposito 6.00 15.00
Co-owner
16 John Vanbiesbrouck 6.00 15.00
17 Mike Oliverio .20 .50
18 Colin Ford .20 .50
19 Steve Herniman .20 .50
20 Troy Mallette .40 1.00
21 Craig Hartsburg .40 1.00
22 Don Boyd CO/GM .10 .25
23 Peter Fiorentino .20 .50
24 Jeff Columbus .20 .50
25 Brad Stepan .20 .50
26 Rick Tocchet 2.00 5.00
27 Shane Sargant .20 .50
28 Wayne Muir .20 .50
29 Wayne Gretzky 40.00 100.00
30 Gary Luther .20 .50
31 Harry Wolfe ANN .10 .25
32 Rod Thacker .20 .50
33 Coaches Card .10 .25
Terry Tait
Ted Nolan
Mark Pavoni
34 Brian Hoard .20 .50
35 Glen Johnston .20 .50

1989-90 Sault Ste. Marie Greyhounds

This 30-card P.L.A.Y. (Police, Law and Youth) set measures 2 3/4" by 3 1/2". The fronts feature posed on-ice player photos with black and white borders. The player's name and number appear on the bottom. The backs carry sponsor logos at the bottom and "Tips from the Hounds."

COMPLETE SET (30) 8.00 20.00
1 Barry King CL .10 .25
Chief of Police
2 Sault Ste. Marie .10 .25
Police Logo
3 Ted Nolan CO .30 .75
4 Team Logo .20 .50
5 Sherry Bassin GM .20 .50
6 Jim Ritchie .20 .50
7 Bob Boughner .30 .75
8 Denny Lambert .40 1.00
9 Doug Minor .20 .50
10 Rick Pracey .20 .50
11 Colin Miller .20 .50
12 Kevin King .20 .50
13 Ron Francis 2.00 5.00
14 Rick Kowalsky .20 .50
15 Adam Foote .80 2.00
16 Wade Whitten .20 .50
17 Dale Turnbull .20 .50
18 Bob Jones .20 .50
19 David Carrie .20 .50
20 Brad Tiley .20 .50
21 Wayne Muir .20 .50
22 Dave Babcock .20 .50
23 David Matsos .20 .50
24 Dan Ferguson .20 .50
25 Jeff Szeryk .20 .50
26 Mike Zuke ACO .10 .25
27 Dave Doucette .20 .50
28 John Campbell .10 .25
Constable
29 Graeme Harvey .20 .50
30 John Fuselli ACO .10 .25

1993-94 Sault Ste. Marie Greyhounds

Sponsored by Pino's Food Trunk Road and Sault Ste. Marie Public Utilities Commission, and printed by Slapshot Images Ltd., this standard-size 30-card set features the 1993-94 Sault Ste. Marie Greyhounds. On a geometrical team color-coded background, the fronts feature color action player photos with thin black borders. The player's name, position and team name, as well as the producer's logo, also appear on the front.

COMPLETE SET (30) 4.80 10.00
1 Andrea Carpano .16 .40
2 Ryan Douglas .16 .40
3 Dan Cloutier .60 2.00
4 Oliver Pastinsky .16 .40
5 Scott King .24 .60
6 Drew Bannister .24 .60
7 Sean Gagnon .16 .40
8 Andre Payette .16 .40
9 Peter MacKellar .16 .40
UER Name spelled
Mackellar on front
10 Richard Uniacke .16 .40
11 Steve Zoryk .16 .40
12 Brad Baber .16 .40
13 Gary Roach .16 .40
14 Jeff Gies .16 .40
15 Tom MacDonald .16 .40
16 Rhett Trombley .16 .40
17 Joe Van Volsen .16 .40
18 Andrew Clark .16 .40
19 Briane Thompson .16 .40
20 Aaron Gavey .24 .60
21 Wade Gibson .16 .40
22 Chad Grills .16 .40
23 Jeff Toms .16 .40
24 Steve Sullivan .60 1.50
25 Jeremy Stevenson .16 .40
26 Corey Moylan .16 .40
27 Steve Spina .16 .40
28 Dave Mayville GM .04 .10
29 Ted Nolan CO .30 .75
30 Dan Flynn ACO .04 .10
Mike Zuke ACO

1993-94 Sault Ste. Marie Greyhounds Memorial Cup

This 32-card standard-size set was printed by Precision Litho. The fronts feature color action player photos with rounded corners and gray-and-red team color-coded borders. The team name and logo are printed above the photos, while the player's name and number appear below. The backs present biography, 1992-93 statistics, an anti-drug or alcohol slogan, and sponsor logos.

COMPLETE SET (32) 6.00 15.00
1 Memorial Cup .40 1.00
2 Dan Tanevski .16 .40
3 Mark Matier .16 .40
4 Oliver Pastinsky .16 .40
5 Peter MacKellar .16 .40
6 Drew Bannister .20 .50
7 Sean Gagnon .20 .50
8 Joe Clarke .16 .40
9 Chad Penney .16 .40
10 Neal Martin .16 .40
11 Perry Pappas .16 .40
12 David Matsos .16 .40
13 Rick Kowalsky .16 .40
14 Gary Roach .16 .40
15 Jarret Reid .16 .40
16 Steve Sullivan .60 1.50
17 Tom MacDonald .16 .40
18 Jodie Murphy .16 .40
19 Ralph Intranuovo .16 .40
20 Brad Baber .16 .40
21 Briane Thompson .16 .40
22 Aaron Gavey .20 .50
23 Wade Gibson .16 .40
24 Kiley Hill .16 .40
25 Jeff Toms .16 .40
26 Joe Van Volsen .16 .40
27 Dan Cloutier .60 2.00
28 Kevin Hodson .60 1.50
29 David Mayville DIR .04 .10
Sherry Bassin GM
30 Ted Nolan CO .20 .50
Danny Flynn ACO
31 Executive Staff .04 .10
32 Mike Zuke ACO .04 .10
Forrest Varcoe TR
John Mayne TR
Maurice Sicard TR

1995-96 Sault Ste. Marie Greyhounds

This 30-card set was produced by the Greyhounds for distribution at the rink, by mail, and through the team's web page. The cards feature action photography on the front, with player name, number and bio superimposed over a Hounds logo on the back. The cards are unnumbered, and are listed below alphabetically. The set is noteworthy for including the first cards ever of several outstanding prospects, including Joe Thornton, Rico Fata and Richard Jackman.

COMPLETE SET (30) 10.00 25.00
1 Peter Cava .16 .40
2 Scott Cherrey .16 .40
3 Dan Cloutier 1.20 1.50
4 Lee Cole .16 .40
5 Jason Doyle .20 .50
6 Rico Fata .30 .75
7 Blaine Fitzpatrick .16 .40
8 Jeff Gies .16 .40
9 Richard Jackman .30 .75
10 Steve Lowe .16 .40
11 Dave Mayville GM .04 .10
12 Robert Mulick .16 .40
13 Kevin Murnaghan .16 .40
14 Cory Murphy .16 .40
15 Joe Paterson CO .04 .10
16 Andre Payette .16 .40
17 Michal Podolka .30 .75
18 Ben Schust .16 .40
19 Brian Stacey .16 .40
20 Brian Stewart .16 .40
21 Joe Thornton 6.00 15.00
22 Trevor Tokarczyk .16 .40
23 Richard Uniacke .20 .50
24 Joe Van Volsen .16 .40
25 Jamie Wentzell .16 .40
26 M.Zuke/B.Jones ACO .04 .10
27 Greyhounds Staff .04 .10
28 Toronto Bank and Trust .04 .10
29 School of Business .04 .10
30 Team Photo .04 .10

1996-97 Sault Ste. Marie Greyhounds

This 30-card set may stand as the top junior issue of the year. The cards feature color action photography, along with the player's name and number. The backs feature comprehensive stats, but are unnumbered, hence the alphabetical listing below. The set is noteworthy for the inclusion of two cards of Joe Thornton, the top pick in the '97 NHL draft. The second card features him as a member of the Canadian National Junior Team.

COMPLETE SET (30) 10.00 25.00
1 Wes Booker .20 .40
2 Bill Browne .20 .40
3 Peter Cava .20 .40
4 Justin Davis .20 .40
5 J.J. Dickie .20 .40
6 Oak Hewer .20 .40
7 Richard Jackman .20 .50
8 Richard Jackman .20 .50
Team Canada 1997
9 Matt Lahey .20 .40
10 David Mayville .04 .10
Director of Operations
11 Jake McCracken .30 .75
12 Marc Moro .30 .75
13 Robert Mulick .20 .40
14 Joe Paterson CO .04 .10
15 Daniel Passero .20 .40
16 Nathan Perrott .30 .75
17 Michael Podolka .30 .75
18 Nick Robinson .20 .40
19 Ben Schust .20 .40
20 Joe Seroski .20 .40
21 Chad Spurr .20 .40
22 Brian Stewart .20 .40
23 Joe Thornton 2.80 10.00
24 Joe Thornton 2.80 10.00
Team Canada 1997
25 Trevor Tokarczyk .20 .40
26 Richard Uniacke .20 .40
27 David Wight .20 .40
28 Chad Woollard .20 .40
29 Mike Zuke ACO .04 .10
B.Jones ACO
30 Team Photo .20 .10

1996-97 Sault Ste. Marie Greyhounds Autographed

Along with the regular version of the team set, the Hounds also offered a completely signed version for $15. This set includes two signed cards from 1997 top pick Joe Thornton. The cards do not bear any authenticating marks, so it is possible that an autographed set could be compiled individually.

COMPLETE SET (24) 40.00 100.00
1 Wes Booker .80 2.00
2 Bill Browne .80 2.00
3 Peter Cava .80 2.00
4 Justin Davis .80 2.00
5 J.J. Dickie .80 2.00
6 Oak Hewer .80 2.00
7 Richard Jackman 1.20 3.00
8 Richard Jackman 1.20 3.00
Team Canada 1997
9 Matt Lahey .80 2.00
11 Jake McCracken 1.60 4.00
12 Marc Moro 2.00 5.00
13 Robert Mulick .80 2.00
14 Joe Paterson CO .80 2.00
15 Daniel Passero .80 2.00
16 Nathan Perrott 2.00 5.00
17 Michael Podolka 1.60 4.00
18 Nick Robinson .80 2.00
19 Ben Schust .80 2.00
20 Joe Seroski 1.20 3.00
21 Chad Spurr .80 2.00
22 Brian Stewart .80 2.00
23 Joe Thornton 14.00 35.00
24 Joe Thornton 14.00 35.00
Team Canada 1997
25 Trevor Tokarczyk .80 2.00
26 Richard Uniacke 1.20 3.00
27 David Wight .80 2.00
28 Chad Woollard .80 2.00
29 Mike Zuke ACO .80 2.00
B.Jones ACO

2002-03 Sault Ste. Marie Greyhounds

COMPLETE SET (23) 8.00 20.00
1 Adam Munro .40 1.00
2 Joey Biasucci .30 .75
3 Trevor Daley .40 1.00
4 Jeff Carter 3.00 8.00
5 Michael Krelove .20 .50
6 Matt Herneisen .20 .50
7 Jeff Doyle .20 .50
8 Mike Moher .20 .50
9 Tyler Kennedy .20 .50
10 Tyler Dutchyshen .20 .50
11 Brian Rempel .20 .50
12 Petr Taticek .40 1.00
13 Jeff Larsh .20 .50
14 Sean Stefanski .20 .50
15 Jordan Smith .20 .50
16 Mike Amodeo .20 .50
17 Jiri Ortina .20 .50
18 Niko Tuomi .20 .50
19 Ryan Kitchen .20 .50
20 Scott Dobben .20 .50
21 Brad Staubitz .20 .50
22 Jordan Kennedy .20 .50
23 Ryan McKay .20 .50

2003-04 Sault Ste. Marie Greyhounds

COMPLETE SET (32) 6.00 15.00
1 Jakub Cechs .30 .75
2 Travis Chapman .20 .50
3 Brett Connolly .20 .50
4 Andrew Desjardins .20 .50
5 Scott Dobben .20 .50
6 Jeffrey Doyle .20 .50
7 Kevin Druce .30 .75
8 Brad Good .20 .50
9 Jeff Carter 1.50 4.00
10 David Jarram .20 .50
11 Tyler Kennedy .20 .50
12 Jacob King .20 .50
13 Jeff Larsh .20 .50
14 Chris Lawrence .20 .50
15 Matt Leszczynski .20 .50
16 Aaron Lewicki .20 .50
17 Mike Looby .20 .50
18 Jason Pitton .20 .50
19 Matt Puntureri .20 .50
20 Jordan Smith .20 .50
21 Brad Staubitz .20 .50
22 Reg Thomas .20 .50
23 Martin Tuma .20 .50
24 Marty Abrams CO .02 .10
25 Denny Lambert ACO .02 .10
26 Terry Barbeau ACO .02 .10
27 Andy Martin EQM .02 .10
28 Dave Torrie GM .02 .10
29 Rod Bogart TR .02 .10
30 Header Card .01 .05
31 Header Card .01 .05
32 Checklist .01 .05

2004-05 Sault Ste. Marie Greyhounds

COMPLETE SET (25) 6.00 15.00
1 Jakub Cech .20 .50
2 Kyle Gajewski .20 .50
3 Brad Good .20 .50
4 David Jarram .20 .50
5 Joshua Day .20 .50
6 Jeff Carter 1.25 3.00
7 Tyler Cuthbert .20 .50
8 Chris Lawrence .20 .50
9 Ryan McInerny .20 .50
10 Brandon MacLean .20 .50
11 Tyler Kennedy .20 .50
12 Tyler McKinley .20 .50
13 Jason Pitton .20 .50
14 Jeff Larsh .20 .50
15 Jordan Smith .20 .50
16 Jacob King .20 .50
17 Andrew Desjardins .20 .50
18 Matt Puntureri .30 .75
19 Matthew Leszczynski .20 .50
20 Blair Jarrett .20 .50
21 Brad Staubitz .20 .50
22 Martin Tuma .20 .50
23 Jacob Lalonde .20 .50
24 Reg Thomas .20 .50
25 Checklist .01 .05

1993-94 Seattle Thunderbirds

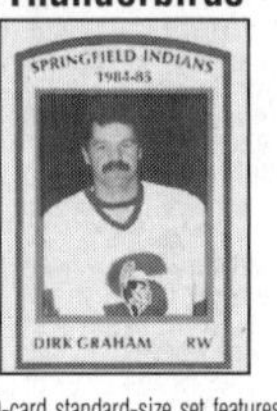

This 30-card standard-size set features the 1993-94 Seattle Thunderbirds of the Western Hockey League (WHL). On a white card face, the fronts display posed color player photos. The pictures are edged by a row of blue stars on the left and by "Thunderbirds" in green print on the right. At the top left corner appears the team logo, while the player's name and position are printed in black beneath the photo.

COMPLETE SET (30) 4.80 12.00
1 Mike Barrie .20 .50
2 Doug Bonner .20 .50
3 Davie Carson .20 .50
4 Jeff Dewar .20 .50
5 Brett Duncan .20 .50
6 Shawn Gervais .20 .50
7 Chris Herperger .30 .75
8 Troy Hyatt .20 .50
9 Curt Kamp TR .04 .10
10 Olaf Kjenstadt .20 .50
11 Walt Kyle CO .04 .10
12 Milt Mastad .20 .50
13 Larry McMorran .20 .50
14 Jim McTaggart ACO .04 .10
15 Regan Mueller .20 .50
16 Kevin Mylander .20 .50
17 Drew Palmer .20 .50
18 Jeff Peddigrew .20 .50
19 Darryl Plandowski ACO .04 .10
20 Deron Quint .30 .75
21 Darrell Sandback .20 .50
22 Chris Schmidt .20 .50
23 Lloyd Shaw .20 .50
24 Alexandre Matvichuk .20 .50
25 Darcy Smith .20 .50
26 Rob Tallas .30 .75
27 Paul Vincent .20 .50
28 Chris Wells .20 .50
29 Brendan Witt .30 .75
30 Team photo .20 .50

1995-96 Seattle Thunderbirds

This 32-card set was produced and sold by the club. The fronts feature action photography, while the backs include a headshot, stats and bio. The set is noteworthy for including the first appearance of Patrick Marleau, the second player selected in the 1997 Entry Draft. The cards are unnumbered and are listed below in alphabetical order.

COMPLETE SET (32) 10.00 30.00
1 Perry Andrusiak ACO .04 .10
2 Shane Belter .20 .50
3 Rick Berry .30 .75
4 Jeff Blair .20 .50
5 Doug Bonner .30 .75
6 Kevin Borris .16 .40
7 Torrey DiRoberto .16 .40
8 Michal Divisek .16 .40
9 Paul Ferone .16 .40
10 Shawn Gervais .16 .40
11 Jan Hrdina 1.60 2.00
12 Curt Kamp TR .04 .10
13 Greg Kuznik .16 .40
14 Blair Manning .16 .40
15 Patrick Marleau 6.00 20.00
16 Jim McTaggart ACO .04 .10
17 Tony Mohagen .16 .40
18 Don Nachbaur CO .04 .10
19 Jason Norrie .16 .40
20 Drew Palmer .16 .40
21 Tyler Perry .16 .40
22 Jame Pollock .16 .40
23 Kevin Popp .16 .40
24 Jeremy Reich .20 .50
25 Cody Rudkowsky .30 1.00
26 Chris Schmidt .16 .40
27 Lloyd Shaw .16 .40
28 Chris Thompson .16 .40
29 Dan Tompkins .16 .40
30 Cool Bird MASCOT .04 .10
32 Seattle Key Arena .04 .01
NNO Title Card .04 .01

1996-97 Seattle Thunderbirds

This 28-card set was produced by S&H Ltd. The cards were available through the team at the rink or through the mail. The cards feature action photos on the front, and statistical analysis on the backs. The player's sweater number is displayed in the lower right hand corner. As the cards themselves are unnumbered, they are listed below according to the sweater number. The set is noteworthy for the inclusion of Patrick Marleau, the second overall pick in the 1997 NHL Entry Draft.

COMPLETE SET (28) 8.00 20.00
1 Jeff Blair .20 .50
3 Rod LeRoux .20 .50
4 Nathan Forster .20 .50
5 Brad Swanson .20 .50
6 Rick Berry .30 .75
7 Paul Ferone .20 .50
8 Jame Pollock .20 .50
9 Tyler Willis .20 .50
11 Chris Thompson .20 .50
12 Patrick Marleau 2.80 7.00
13 Jouni Kuokkanen .20 .50
14 Martin Cerven .20 .50
15 Jeremy Reich .30 .75
16 Bret DeCecco .40 1.00
17 Tony Mohagen .20 .50
18 Torrey DiRoberto .20 .50
19 Nick Szadkowski .20 .50
21 Brian Ballman .20 .50
22 Greg Kuznik .20 .50
23 Randy Perry .20 .50
24 Shawn Skolney .20 .50
30 Cody Rudkowsky .40 1.00
31 Kris Cantu .20 .50
32 Shane Belter .20 .50
NNO Don Nachbaur CO .04 .10
NNO Cool Bird MASCOT .04 .10
NNO Thunderbirds .04 .10
Through the Years
NNO Rob Sumner ACO .04 .10

1997-98 Seattle Thunderbirds

This set features the Thunderbirds of the WHL. It was sold in set form by the team. It features early cards of NHL young star Mark Parrish.

COMPLETE SET (1-27) 7.20 15.00
1 Header Card .04 .10
2 Cool Bird Mascot .04 .10
3 Rod Leroux .20 .50
4 Nathan Forster .20 .50
5 Jason Beckett .20 .50
6 Rick Berry .40 .75
7 Chris Thompson .20 .50
8 Jame Pollock .20 .50
9 David Morisset .30 .75
10 Jeff Blair .20 .50
11 Jouni Kuokkanen .20 .50
12 Scott Kelman .40 .75
13 Jeremy Reich .30 .75
14 Brett DeCecco .30 .75
15 Tim Preston .20 .50
16 Torrey DiRoberto .30 .75
17 Petr Vala .20 .50
18 Ryan Tresk .20 .50
19 Greg Kuznik .20 .50
20 Matt Demarski .20 .50
21 Mark Parrish 1.60 2.00
22 Stanislav Gron .80 1.50
23 Cody Rudkowsky .20 1.00
24 A.J. Van Bruggen .20 .50
25 Don Nachbaur HCO .10 .25
26 Rob Sumner ACO .04 .10
27 Curt Kamp TR .04 .10

1969-70 Seattle Totems

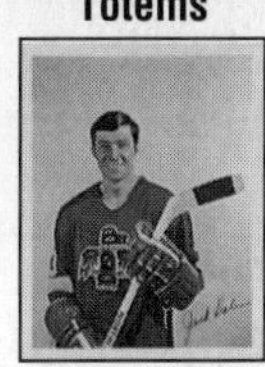

This set features the Totems of the old WHL. A White Front Stores exclusive at stores in Aurora, Tacoma, Burien, and Bellevue, this set of 20 team photos measures approximately 8" by 10". Printed on thin paper, the front features a posed color player photo with a studio background. The pictures have white borders, and the player's signature is inscribed in the lower right corner. In black print on white, the backs present biography and statistics from the past season.

COMPLETE SET (20) 60.00 150.00
1 Don Head 8.00 20.00
2 Chuck Holmes 3.00 8.00
3 Bob Courcy 3.00 8.00
4 Marc Boileau 3.00 8.00
5 Gerry Leonard 3.00 8.00
6 Art Stratton 3.00 8.00
7 Gary Kilpatrick 3.00 8.00
8 Don Ward 3.00 8.00
9 Jack Michie 3.00 8.00
10 Ronald Ingram 3.00 8.00
11 John Hanna 3.00 8.00
12 Ray Larose 3.00 8.00
13 Jack Dale 3.00 8.00
14 Tom McVie 3.00 8.00
15 Gerry Meehan 6.00 15.00
16 Chris Worthy 3.00 8.00
17 Bobby Schmautz 8.00 20.00
18 Dwight Carruthers 3.00 8.00
19 Patrick Dunn TR .75 2.00
20 Bill MacFarland CO .75 2.00

1989-90 7th Inn. Sketch OHL

This 200-card standard-size set was issued by 7th Inning Sketch featuring members of the Ontario Hockey League. The fronts of the cards have yellow borders which surround the player's photo and on the bottom of the front is the player's name. In the upper right hand corner, the team's name is featured. The set has been popular with collectors since it features early cards of Eric Lindros. The set was also issued on a limited basis (a numbered edition of 3000) as a factory set; however, the factory set only included 167 cards as 33 cards were dropped for unspecified reasons.

COMPLETE SET (200) 12.00 30.00
COMPLETE FACT.SET (167) 12.00 30.00
1 Eric Lindros 1.60 4.00
(Beware counterfeits)
2 Jarrod Skalde .20 .50
3 Joe Busillo .04 .10
4 Dale Craigwell .10 .25
5 Clair Cornish .04 .10
6 Jean-Paul Davis .04 .10
7 Craig Donaldson .04 .10
8 Wade Simpson .04 .10
9 Mike Craig .10 .25
10 Mark Deazeley .04 .10
11 Scott Hollis .04 .10
12 Brian Grieve .04 .10
13 Dave Craievich .04 .10
14 Paul O'Hagan .04 .10
15 Matt Hoffman .04 .10
16 Trevor McIvor .04 .10
17 Cory Banika .04 .10
18 Kevin Butt .08 .20
19 Iain Fraser .04 .10
20 Bill Armstrong .08 .20
21 Scott Luik .04 .10
22 Brent Grieve .04 .10
23 Fred Brathwaite .40 1.00
24 Paul Holden .04 .10
25 Trevor Dam .04 .10
26 Chris Taylor .04 .10
27 Mark Guy .04 .10
28 Louie DeBrusk .10 .75
29 John Battice .04 .10
30 Chris Crombie .04 .10
31 Sean Basilio .08 .20
32 Aaron Nagy .04 .10
33 Greg Ryan .04 .10
34 Steve Martell .04 .10
35 Scott MacKay .04 .10
36 Dennis Purdie .10 .75
37 Steve Boyd .04 .10
38 John Tanner .10 .25
39 David Anderson .04 .10
40 Rick Corriveau .04 .10
41 Todd Hlushko .10 .25
42 Doug Synish .04 .10
43 Dan LeBlanc .08 .20
44 Dave Noseworthy .04 .10
45 Karl Taylor .04 .10
46 Jeff Hodgen .04 .10
47 Mike Kelly .02 .05
Gary Agnew
48 Wayne Maxner .04 .10
49 Brett Seguin .04 .10
50 Greg Walters .04 .10
51 Chris Snell .04 .10
52 Troy Binnie .04 .10
53 Joni Lehto .04 .10
54 Steve Kluczkowski .04 .10
55 Ryan Kuwabara .08 .20
56 Chris Simon .40 1.00
57 Jerrett DeFazio .08 .20
58 Rob Sangster .04 .10
59 Greg Clancy .04 .10
60 Peter Ambroziak .04 .10
61 Jeff Ricciardi .04 .10
62 John East .04 .10
63 Joey McTamney .04 .10
64 Dan Poirier .04 .10
65 Gairin Smith .04 .10
66 Wade Gibson .04 .10
67 Checklist Card .02 .05
68 Andrew Brodie .04 .10
69 Craig Wilson .04 .10
70 Peter McGlynn .04 .10
71 George Dourian .04 .10
72 Bob Berg .08 .20
73 Richard Fatrola .04 .10
74 Craig Fraser .04 .10
75 Brent Gretzky .20 .50
76 Jake Grimes .04 .10
77 Darren McCarty 1.20 2.00
78 Ted Miskolczi .04 .10
79 Rob Pearson .10 .25
80 Gordon Pell .04 .10
81 John Porco .04 .10
82 Ken Rowbotham .04 .10
83 Scott Thornton .20 .50
84 Shawn Way .04 .10
85 Steve Bancroft .04 .10
86 Greg Bignell .04 .10
87 Scott Boston .04 .10
88 Scott Feasby .04 .10
89 Derek Morin .08 .20
90 Sean O'Reilly .08 .20
91 Jason Skelet .04 .10
92 Greg Dreveny .04 .10
93 Jeff Fife .04 .10
94 Rob Stopar .04 .10
95 Joe Desrosiers .02 .05
96 Danny Flynn .04 .10
97 Dr. R.L. Vaughan .02 .05
98 Troy Stephens .04 .10
99 Dan Brown .04 .10
100 Mike Ricci .40 1.00
101 Brent Pope .04 .10
102 Mike Dagenais .08 .20
103 Scott Campbell .04 .10
104 Jamie Pegg .04 .10
105 Joe Hawley .04 .10
106 Jason Dawe .10 .25
107 Paul Mitton .04 .10
108 Mike Tomlinson .04 .10
109 Dave Lorentz .04 .10
110 Dale McTavish .04 .10
111 Willie McGarvey .04 .10
112 Don O'Neill .04 .10
113 Mark Myles .04 .10
114 Chris Longo .08 .20
115 Tom Hopkins .04 .10
116 Jassen Cullimore .04 .10
117 Geoff Ingram .04 .10
118 Twohey .02 .05
Bovair TR
119 Doug Searle .04 .10
120 Bryan Gendron .04 .10
121 Andrew Verner .10 .25
122 Todd Bocjun .08 .20
123 Dick Todd .04 .10
124 George Burnett .04 .10
125 Brad May .30 .75
126 David Benn .04 .10
127 Brian Mueggler .04 .10
128 Todd Coopman .04 .10
129 Geoff Rawson .04 .10
130 Keith Primeau .80 2.00
131 Mark Lawrence .08 .20
132 Randy Hall .04 .10
133 Greg Suchan .04 .10
134 Ken Ruddick .04 .10
135 Jason Winch .08 .20
136 Paul Wolanski .04 .10
137 Dennis Scott .02 .05
138 Steve Udvari .04 .10
139 Roch Belley .08 .20
140 Don Pancoe .04 .10
141 Paul Bruneau .02 .05
142 Paul Laus .20 .50
143 Mike St. John .04 .10
144 John Johnson .04 .10
145 Greg Allen .04 .10
146 Don McConnell .04 .10
147 Andy Bezeau .04 .10
148 Jeff Walker .04 .10
149 John Spoltore .04 .10
150 Derek Switzer .08 .20
151 Tyler Ertel .04 .10
152 Shawn Antoski .10 .25
153 Jason Corrigan .04 .10
154 Derian Hatcher .30 .75
155 John Vary .04 .10
156 Jamie Caruso .04 .10
157 Trevor Halverson .04 .10
158 Robert Deschamps .04 .10
159 Jeff Gardiner .08 .20
160 Gary Miller .04 .10
161 Shayne Antoski .10 .25
162 John Van Kessel .04 .10
163 Colin Austin .04 .10
164 Tom Purcell .04 .10
165 Joel Morin .04 .10
166 Tim Favot .04 .10
167 Checklist Card .02 .05
168 Jason Beaton .04 .10
169 Chris Ottmann .04 .10
170 Mike Matuszek .04 .10
171 Rob Fournier .04 .10
172 Ron Bertrand .08 .20
173 Bert Templeton .04 .10
174 Casey Jones .02 .05
175 Robert Frayn .04 .10
176 Claude Noel .04 .10
177 Sean Basilio Award .04 .10
178 Chris Longo Rookie .04 .10
179 Cory Keenan AS .04 .10
180 Owen Nolan Award .60 1.00
181 Steven Rice AS .10 .25
182 Shayne Stevenson .10 .25
Scorer
183 Mike Ricci Award .20 .50
184 Jason Firth Award .04 .10
185 John Slaney Award .04 .10
186 Iain Fraser Award .04 .10
187 Steven Rice Star .10 .25
188 Eric Lindros Scorer 1.20 3.00
189 Keith Primeau Scorer .40 1.00
190 Mike Ricci Award .20 .50
191 Mike Torchia AS .10 .25
192 Mike Torchia Star .08 .20
193 Jarrod Skalde Champs .10 .25
194 Paul O'Hagan Award .04 .10
195 Eric Lindros 1.20 3.00
(Where in 1991)
196 Eric Lindros AS 1.20 3.00
197 Jeff Fife Award .04 .10
198 Iain Fraser MVP .04 .10
199 Bill Armstrong Winner .04 .10
200 Checklist Card .02 .05

1990-91 7th Inn. Sketch OHL

The 7th Inning Sketch OHL Hockey set contains 400 standard-size cards. The front features a full color photo, enframed by different color borders. The player's position appears in a star at the lower left hand corner, with his name and "OHL" in the bar below the picture. The back has another color photo, with biographical information and career summary in a box running the length of the card. This set features a regular card (1) as well as a promo card of hockey star Eric Lindros. The promo version has the same front as Lindros' card number 1 but has an asterisk in the card number position on the card back. Players from the following teams are represented in this set: Oshawa Generals (1, 325-339, 341-345, 347-350), Belleville Bulls (2-10, 12-21, 23, 340, 346), Kingston Frontenacs (11, 51-75), Cornwall Royals (22, 24-50), Ottawa 67's (76-100, 230), Detroit Compuware Ambassadors (101-121, 123-125), North Bay Centennials (122, 301-324), London Knights (126-149), Sault Ste. Marie Greyhounds (150-173, 175-176), Windsor Spitfires (174, 177-200), Dukes of Hamilton (201-225), Kitchener Rangers (226-229, 231-250, 370), Niagara Falls Thunder (251-275), Owen Sound Platers (276-299), Peterborough Petes (351-369, 371-376), and Sudbury Wolves (377-400). First round picks (1991 NHL Draft) in this set include Eric Lindros (1), Alex Stojanov (7), Pat Peake (14), Glen Murray (18), and Trevor Halverson (21). First round picks (1992 NHL Draft rank indicated in parenthesis) in this set include Todd Warriner (4), Cory Stillman (6), Brandon Convery (8), Curtis Bowen (22), and Grant Marshall (23). A factory set, a numbered edition of 9000 sets, was produced and marketed separately.

COMPLETE SET (400) 8.00 20.00
COMPLETE FACT.SET (400) 10.00 25.00
1 Eric Lindros 1.60 4.00
2 Greg Dreveny .04 .10
3 Belleville Checklist UER .02 .05
4 Richard Fatrola .04 .10
5 Craig Fraser .04 .10
6 Robert Frayn .04 .10
7 Brent Gretzky .14 .35
8 Jake Grimes .04 .10
9 Darren Hurley .04 .10
10 Rick Marshall .04 .10
11 Checklist UER .02 .05
12 Darren McCarty .80 2.00
13 Derek Morin .04 .10
14 Sean O'Reilly .04 .10
15 Rob Pearson UER .10 .25
(Listed on Oshawa CL
but reverse says
Belleville Bulls)
16 John Porco .04 .10
17 Ken Rowbotham .04 .10
18 Ken Ruddick .04 .10
19 Jim Sonmez .04 .10
20 Brad Teichmann .04 .10
21 Chris Varga .04 .10
22 Checklist Card .02 .05
23 Larry Mavety CO .02 .05
24 Rival Fullum .04 .10
25 Nathan Lafayette .04 .10
26 Darren Bell .04 .10
27 Craig Brocklehurst .04 .10
28 Shawn Caplice .04 .10
29 Mike Cavanaugh .04 .10
30 Jason Cirone .04 .10
31 Chris Clancy .04 .10
32 Mark DeSantis .04 .10
33 Rob Dykeman .04 .10
34 Shayne Gaffar .04 .10
35 Ilpo Kauhanen .04 .10
36 Rob Kinghan .04 .10
37 Dave Lemay .04 .10
38 Guy Leveque .04 .10
39 Matt McGuffin .04 .10
40 Marcus Middleton .04 .10
41 Thomas Nemeth .04 .10
42 Rod Pasma .04 .10
43 Richard Raymond .04 .10
44 Jeff Reid .04 .10
45 Jerry Ribble .04 .10
46 Jean-Alain Schneider .04 .10
47 John Slaney .04 .10
48 Jeremy Stevenson .04 .10
49 Ryan VandenBussche .30 1.00
50 Marc Crawford CO .20 .50
51 Tony Bella .04 .10
52 Drake Berehowsky .20 .50
53 Jason Chipman .04 .10
54 Tony Cimellaro .04 .10
55 Keli Corpse .04 .10
56 Mike Dawson .04 .10
57 Sean Gauthier UER .04 .10
58 Fred Goltz .04 .10
59 Gord Harris .04 .10
60 Tony Iob .04 .10
61 John Bernie .04 .10
62 Dale Junkin .04 .10
63 Nathan Lafayette .04 .10
64 Blake Martin .04 .10
65 Mark McCague .04 .10
66 Bob McKillop .04 .10
67 Justin Morrison .04 .10
68 Bill Robinson .04 .10
69 Joel Sandie .04 .10
70 Kevin King .04 .10
71 Dave Stewart .04 .10
72 Joel Washkurak .04 .10
73 Brock Woods .04 .10
74 Randy Hall CO .04 .10
75 John Vary .04 .10
76 Peter Ambroziak .04 .10
77 Troy Binnie .04 .10
78 Curt Bowen .04 .10
79 Andrew Brodie .04 .10
80 Ottawa Checklist .04 .10
81 Greg Clancy .04 .10
82 Jerrett DeFazio .04 .10
83 Kris Draper .40 1.00
84 Wade Gibson .04 .10
85 Ryan Kuwabara .04 .10
86 Joni Lehto .04 .10
87 Donald MacPherson .04 .10
88 Grant Marshall .20 .50
89 Peter McGlynn .04 .10
90 Maurice O'Brien .04 .10
91 Jeff Ricciardi .04 .10
92 Brett Seguin .04 .10
93 Len DeVuono .04 .10
94 Gerry Skrypec .04 .10
95 Chris Snell .04 .10
96 Jason Snow .04 .10
97 Sean Spencer .04 .10
98 Brad Spry .04 .10
99 Matt Stone .04 .10
100 Brian Kilrea CO .04 .10
101 Kevin Butt .10 .25
102 Glen Craig .04 .10
103 Paul Doherty .04 .10
104 Mark Donahue .04 .10
105 Jeff Gardiner .04 .10
106 Trent Gleason .04 .10
107 Troy Gleason .04 .10
108 Mark Lawrence .10 .25
109 Trevor McIvor .04 .10
110 Paul Mitton .04 .10
111 David Myles .04 .10
112 Jeffery Nolan .04 .10
113 Rob Papineau .04 .10
114 Pat Peake .04 .10
115 Chris Phelps .04 .10
116 John Pinches .04 .10
117 James Shea .04 .10
118 James Sheehan .04 .10
119 John Stos .04 .10
120 Tom Sullivan .04 .10
121 John Wynne .04 .10
122 Robert Thorpe .04 .10
123 David Benn .04 .10
124 Andy Weidenbach CO UER .02 .05
125 Detroit Checklist .02 .05
126 David Anderson .02 .05
127 Sean Basilio .10 .25
128 Brent Brownlee .04 .10
129 Rick Corriveau .04 .10
130 Derrick Crane .04 .10
131 Chris Crombie .04 .10
132 Louie DeBrusk .10 1.00
133 Mark Guy .04 .10
134 Brett Marrietti .04 .10
135 Steve Martell .04 .10
136 Scott McKay .04 .10
137 Aaron Nagy .04 .10
138 Brett Nicol .04 .10
139 Barry Potomski .20 1.00
140 Dennis Purdie .10 1.00
141 Kelly Reed .04 .10
142 Gregory Ryan .04 .10
143 Brad Smyth .04 .10
144 Nick Stajduhar .04 .10
145 John Tanner .10 .25
146 Chris Taylor .04 .10
147 Mark Visheau .04 .10
148 Gary Agnew CO .04 .10
149 London Checklist .10 .25
150 Sault Ste. Marie .04 .10
Checklist
151 David Babcock .04 .10
152 Drew Bannister .04 .10
153 Bob Boughner .30 .75
154 Joe Busillo .04 .10
155 Mike DeCoff .04 .10
156 Jason Denomme .04 .10
157 Adam Foote .80 2.00
158 Kevin Hodson .30 .75
159 Shaun Imber .04 .10
160 Ralph Intranuovo .04 .10
161 Kevin King .04 .10
162 Rick Kowalsky .04 .10
163 Chris Kraemer .04 .10
164 Dan Lambert .10 .25
165 Mike Lenarduzzi .10 .25
166 Tom MacDonald .04 .10
167 Mark Matier .04 .10
168 David Matsos .04 .10
169 Colin Miller .04 .10
170 Perry Pappas .04 .10
171 Jarrett Reid .04 .10
172 Kevin Reid .04 .10
173 Brad Tiley UER .04 .10
174 Windsor Checklist .02 .05
175 Wade Whitten .04 .10
176 Ted Nolan CO .20 .50
177 Sean Burns .04 .10
178 Jason Cirone .04 .10
179 John Copley .04 .10
180 Tyler Ertel .04 .10
181 Brian Forestell .04 .10
182 Rival Fullum .20 .50
183 Steve Gibson .04 .10
184 Leonard MacDonald .04 .10
185 Mike Speer .04 .10
186 Kevin MacKay .04 .10
187 Ryan Merritt .04 .10
188 Doug Minor .04 .10
189 Rick Morton .04 .10
190 Sean O'Hagan .10 .25
191 Mike Polano .04 .10
192 Cory Stillman .20 .50
193 Jason Stos .04 .10
194 Trevor Walsh .04 .10
195 Todd Warriner .20 .50
196 Jeff Wilson .04 .10
197 Jason York .20 .50
198 Jason Zohil .04 .10
199 Steve Smith .04 .10
200 Brad Smith CO .04 .10
201 Jeff Bes .04 .10
202 Mike Blum .04 .10
203 Sean Brown .04 .10
204 Darcy Cahill .04 .10
205 Dale Chokan .04 .10
206 Chris Code .04 .10
207 George Dourion .04 .10
208 Todd Gleason .04 .10
209 Hamilton Checklist UER .02 .05
210 Michael Hartwick .04 .10
211 Scott Jenkins .04 .10
212 Rob Leask .04 .10
213 Gordon Pell .04 .10
214 Michael Reier .04 .10
215 Kayle Short .04 .10
216 Jason Skellett .04 .10
217 Gairin Smith .04 .10
218 Jeff Smith .04 .10
219 Jason Soules .04 .10
220 Alex Stojanov .04 .10
221 Dan Tanevski .04 .10
222 Gary Taylor .04 .10
223 Brent Watson .04 .10
224 Steve Woods .04 .10
225 Jay Johnston CO UER .02 .05
226 Mike Allen .04 .10
227 Brad Barton .04 .10
228 Richard Borgo .04 .10
229 Justin Cullen .04 .10
230 Lenny DeVuono .04 .10
231 Norman Dezainde .04 .10
232 Jason Firth .04 .10
233 Derek Gauthier .04 .10
234 Jamie Israel .04 .10
235 Chris LiPuma .04 .10
236 Tony McCabe .04 .10
237 Paul McCallion .04 .10
238 Shayne McCosh .04 .10
239 Rod Saarinen .04 .10
240 Steve Smith .04 .10
241 Joey St.Aubin .04 .10
242 Rob Stopar .04 .10
243 Jason Zohil UER .04 .10
244 Mike Torchia .10 .25
245 Gib Tucker .04 .10
246 John Uniac .04 .10
247 Jack Williams .04 .10
248 Joe McDonnell CO .04 .10
249 Steven Rice .04 .10
250 Mike Polano .04 .10
251 Greg Allen .04 .10
252 Roch Belley .10 .25
253 Andy Bezeau .04 .10
254 Derek Booth .04 .10
255 Kevin Brown .04 .10
256 Mark Cardiff .04 .10
257 Jason Coles .10 .25
258 Todd Coopman .04 .10
259 Richard Girhiny .04 .10
260 Brian Holk .04 .10
261 John Johnson .04 .10
262 Dan Krisko .10 1.00
263 Manny Legace .80 2.00
264 Brad May .30 .75
265 Don McConnell .04 .10
266 Niagara Falls .02 .05
Checklist UER
(Nigara& sic)
267 Aaron Morrison .04 .10
268 Cory Pageau .04 .10
269 Geoff Rawson .04 .10
270 Todd Simon .04 .10
271 Steve Staios .10 .25
272 Jeff Walker .04 .10
273 Todd Wetzel .04 .10
274 Jason Winch .04 .10
275 Paul Wolanski .04 .10
276 Owen Sound Checklist .02 .05
277 Andrew Brunette .40 1.00
278 Wyatt Buckland .04 .10
279 Jason Buetow .04 .10
280 Jason Castellan .04 .10
281 Trent Cull .04 .10
282 Robert Deschamps .04 .10
283 Chris Driscoll .04 .10
284 Bryan Drury .04 .10
285 Todd Hunter .04 .10
286 Troy Hutchinson .04 .10
287 Kirk Maltby .30 .75
288 Geordie Maynard .04 .10
289 Kevin McDougall .04 .10
290 Ted Miskolczi .04 .10
291 Steve Parson .04 .10
292 Jeff Perry .04 .10
293 Grayden Reid .04 .10
294 Mike Speer .04 .10
295 Mark Strohack .04 .10
296 Mark Vilneff .04 .10
297 Keith Whitmore .04 .10
298 Jim Brown .04 .10
299 Len McNamara CO .02 .05
300 David Branch COMM .04 .10
301 Shayne Antoski .04 .10
302 Jason Beaton .04 .10
303 Ron Bertrand .04 .10
304 Michael Burman .04 .10
305 Jamie Caruso .04 .10
306 Allan Cox .04 .10
307 Tim Favot .04 .10
308 Trevor Halverson .04 .10
309 Derian Hatcher .40 1.00
310 Bill Lang .04 .10
311 Jason MacDonald .04 .10
312 Gary Miller .04 .10
313 Chris Ottmann .04 .10
314 Chad Penney .04 .10
315 Rick Pollard .04 .10
316 Bradley Shepard .04 .10
317 John Spoltore .10 .25
318 Derek Switzer .04 .10
319 Karl Taylor .04 .10
320 John Vary .04 .10
321 Kevin White .04 .10
322 Billy Wright .04 .10
323 Bert Templeton CO .04 .10
324 North Bay Checklist .02 .05
325 Oshawa Checklist UER .02 .05
326 Jan Benda .04 .10
327 Fred Brathwaite .40 1.00
328 Markus Brunner .04 .10
329 Trevor Burgess .04 .10
330 Clair Cornish .04 .10
331 Mike Cote .04 .10
332 Dave Craievich .04 .10
333 Dale Craigwell .20 .50
334 Jean-Paul Davis .04 .10
335 Mark Deazeley .04 .10
336 Mike Fountain .10 .25
337 Brian Grieve .04 .10
338 Matt Hoffman .04 .10
339 Scott Hollis .04 .10
340 Scott Boston .04 .10
341 Scott Luik .04 .10
342 Craig Lutes .04 .10
343 William MacPherson .04 .10
344 Paul O'Hagan .04 .10
345 Wade Simpson .04 .10
346 Jarrod Skalde UER .20 .50
(Listed on Belleville CL
but reverse says
Oshawa Generals)
347 Troy Sweet .04 .10
348 Jason Weaver .04 .10
349 Rick Cornacchia CO .04 .10
350 The Trophy .04 .10
351 Greg Bailey .04 .10
352 Ryan Black .04 .10
353 Todd Bocjun UER .10 .25
(Reversed negative
on card front)
354 Toby Burkitt .04 .10
355 Scott Campbell .04 .10
356 Jassen Cullimore .04 .10
357 Jason Dawe .10 .25
358 Dan Ferguson .04 .10
359 Bryan Gendron .04 .10
360 Michael Harding .04 .10
361 Joe Hawley .04 .10
362 Peterborough Checklist .02 .05
UER
363 Geordie Kinnear .04 .10
364 Chris Longo UER .04 .10
365 Dale McTavish .04 .10
366 Mark Myles .04 .10
367 Don O'Neill .04 .10
368 Jamie Pegg .04 .10
369 Brent Pope .04 .10
370 Kitchener Checklist .02 .05
UER
371 Doug Searle .04 .10
372 Troy Stephens .04 .10
373 Mike Tomlinson .04 .10
374 Brent Tully .04 .10
375 Andrew Verner .10 .25
376 Dick Todd CO .04 .10
377 John Tanner .10 .25
378 Adam Bennett .04 .10
379 Kyle Blacklock .04 .10
380 Terry Chitaroni .04 .10
381 Brandon Convery .04 .10
382 J.D. Eaton .04 .10
383 Derek Etches .04 .10
384 Rod Hinks .04 .10
385 Bill Kovacs .04 .10
386 Alain Laforge .04 .10
387 Jamie Matthews .04 .10
388 Glen Murray .80 2.00
389 Dean Cull .04 .10
390 Sean O'Donnell .20 .50
391 Sudbury Checklist UER .02 .05
392 Mike Peca .80 2.00
393 Shawn Rivers .04 .10
394 Dan Ryder .04 .10
395 Alastair Still .04 .10
396 Michael Yeo .04 .10
397 Barry Young .04 .10
398 Jason Young .04 .10
399 Ken MacKenzie CO .04 .10
400 Bob Berg UER .04 .10
(Missing draft eligi-
bility information)
NNO Eric Lindros promo 2.00 5.00

1990-91 7th Inn. Sketch QMJHL

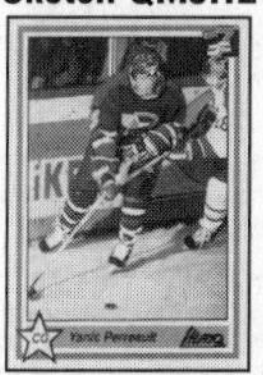

This 268-card standard-size set was produced by 7th Inning Sketch featuring players from the Quebec Major Junior Hockey League. First round picks (1991 NHL Draft) in this set include Patrick Poulin (9), Martin Lapointe (10), and Philippe Boucher (13). The best known players in the set, however, are 1990 second-rounder Felix Potvin and 1991 first-rounder Martin Brodeur. A factory set, a numbered edition of 4,800, was produced and marketed separately.

COMPLETE SET (268) 8.00 20.00
COMPLETE FACT.SET (268) 10.00 25.00
1 Patrick Poulin .10 .25
2 Steve Lupien .10 .25
3 Pierre Gagnon .10 .25
4 Eric Plante .04 .10
5 Stephane Desjardins .04 .10
6 Peter Valenta .04 .10
7 Alexander Legault .04 .10
8 Patrice Brisebois .20 .50
9 Martin Charrois .04 .10
10 Eric Dandenault .04 .10
11 Claude Jutras Jr. .04 .10
12 David Pekarek .04 .10
13 Denis Chasse .10 .25
14 Ian Laperriere .10 .25
15 Roger Larche .04 .10
16 Dave Paquet .04 .10
17 Pascal Lebrasseur .04 .10
18 Eric Meloche .04 .10
19 The Face Off .02 .05
20 Sylvain Rodrigue .10 .25
21 Dary Giarard .04 .10
22 Eric Rochette .04 .10
23 Steve Gosselin .04 .10
24 Martin Lavalle .04 .10
25 Martin Lapointe .80 2.00
26 Eric Brule .04 .10
27 Richard Boivin .04 .10
28 Patrice Martineau .04 .10
29 Dave Tremblay .04 .10
30 Steve Larouche .04 .10
31 Danny Beauregard .04 .10
32 Francois Belanger .04 .10
33 Michel St.Jacques .04 .10
34 Patric Sissillan .04 .10
35 Felix Potvin 1.60 4.00
36 Sebastien Parent .04 .10
37 Eric Duchesne .04 .10
38 Gilles Bouchard .04 .10
39 Martin Gagne .04 .10
40 Stephane Charbonneau .04 .10
41 Martin Beaupre .04 .10
42 Daniel Paradis .04 .10
43 Joe Canale .04 .10
44 Georges Vezina Arena .04 .10
45 Francois Leblanc .10 .25
46 Martin Chaput .04 .10
47 Marc Beaucage .04 .10
48 Carl Mantha .04 .10
49 Jim Bermingham .04 .10
50 Philippe Boucher .10 .25
51 Denis Chalifoux .04 .10
52 Sylvain Naud .04 .10
53 Jean Roberge .04 .10
54 Sandy McCarthy .30 1.00
55 Eric Dubois .04 .10
56 Jean Blouin .04 .10
57 Jason Brousseau .04 .10
58 Pierre Sandke .04 .10
59 Benoit Larose .04 .10
60 Yanick Frechette .04 .10
61 Pierre Calder .04 .10
62 Patric Grise .04 .10
63 Martin Balfeux .04 .10
64 Boris Rousson .20 1.00
65 Martin Trudeli .04 .10
66 Carl Leblanc .04 .10
67 Martin Brochu .20 1.00
68 Benoit Terrien .04 .10
69 QMJHL Action .04 .10
70 Pascal Vincent .04 .10
71 Christian Tardi .04 .10
72 Christian Campeau .04 .10
73 Eric Raymond .10 .25
74 John Kovacs .04 .10
75 Steve Areas .04 .10
76 Pascal Dufalt .04 .10
77 Greg MacEachern .04 .10
78 Remi Belliveau .04 .10
79 Jocelyn Langlois .04 .10
80 Carl Menard .04 .10
81 Sebastein Foneir .04 .10
82 Jean-Franco Gregoire .04 .10
83 Normand Demers .04 .10
84 Nicolas Lefebvre .04 .10
85 Dominic Maltais .04 .10
86 Mario Therrien .04 .10
87 Daniel Thibault .04 .10
88 Jean-Francois Labbe .10 1.00
89 Alain Cote .04 .10
90 Eric Prillo .04 .10
91 Patrick Nadeau .04 .10
92 Claude Poner .04 .10
93 Stephane Julier .04 .10
94 Patrice Rene .04 .10
95 Francis Coutineir .04 .10
96 Guy Lefebvre .04 .10
97 Carl Boudreau .04 .10
98 Jacques Parent .04 .10
99 Stephane Bouquet .04 .10
100 Yanic Perreault .20 .50
101 Yvan Bergeron .04 .10
102 Jean-Francois Rivard .10 .25
103 Daniel Laflamme .04 .10
104 Francois Bourdeau .04 .10
105 Yvan Charrois .04 .10
106 Patric Genest .04 .10
107 Herve Lapointe .04 .10
108 Jean-Francois Jomphe .10 .25
109 Marc Tardif .04 .10
110 Eric Cardinal .04 .10
111 Denis Cloutier .04 .10
112 QMJHL Action .04 .10
113 Alain Samscartier .02 .05
114 Marquis Mathieu .10 .25
115 Stephan Tartari .04 .10
116 QMJHL Action .04 .10
117 QMJHL Action .04 .10
118 Martin Ray .04 .10
119 David Boudreault .04 .10
120 Mario Durroulin .04 .10
121 Jean-Francis Dieard .04 .10
122 QMJHL Action .04 .10
123 QMJHL Action .04 .10
124 Mausime Gagne .04 .10

125 Stephane Guellet .04 .10
126 Steven Paiement .04 .10
127 Francois Olympique .04 .10
128 Eric Coci .04 .10
129 Simon Toupin .04 .10
130 Shane Doirrin .04 .10
131 Todd Sparks .04 .10
132 Bruno Lajeunesse .04 .10
133 Marcel Cousineau .20 .50
134 Claude-Charl Sauirol .04 .10
135 Eric Bellerose .04 .10
136 QMJHL Action .04 .10
137 QMJHL Action .04 .10
138 Martin Lepage .04 .10
139 Michael Langauer .04 .10
140 Fredric Boivin .04 .10
141 Steven Dion .04 .10
142 QMJHL Action .04 .10
143 QMJHL Action .04 .10
144 Dan Paolucci .04 .10
145 Bruno Villeneuve .04 .10
146 Checklist Card .10 .25
(Yanic Perreault)
147 Checklist Card .02 .05
148 Stefan Simoes .04 .10
149 Joel Blain .04 .10
150 Eric Lavigne .04 .10
151 Checklist Card .02 .05
152 Checklist Card .04 .10
(Patrick Poulin)
153 Robert Melanson .04 .10
154 Brian Rogger .04 .10
155 Checklist Card .02 .05
156 Checklist Card .02 .05
157 Francois Ouellette .10 .25
158 QMJHL Action .04 .10
159 Checklist Card .80 2.00
(Felix Potvin)
160 Checklist Card .02 .05
161 Checklist Card .02 .05
162 Checklist Card .02 .05
163 QMJHL Action .04 .10
164 QMJHL Action .04 .10
165 Checklist Card .02 .05
166 Checklist Card .02 .05
167 QMJHL Action .04 .10
168 QMJHL Action .04 .10
169 Pierre Fillon .04 .10
170 Yanick Degrace .10 .25
171 Paul Daigneault .04 .10
172 Stacy Dallaire .04 .10
173 Steve Searles .04 .10
174 Todd Gillingham .04 .10
175 Yves Sarault .04 .10
176 Jason Downey .04 .10
177 Paul Brousseau .04 .10
178 Raymond Delarosbi .04 .10
179 Yvan Corbin .04 .10
180 Gaston Drapeau .04 .10
181 Celebration .04 .10
182 Reginald Brezeault .04 .10
183 Eric Lafrance .04 .10
184 Martin Lavalle .10 .25
185 Sebastein Lavallere .04 .10
186 Martin Lefebvre .04 .10
187 Richard Hamelin .04 .10
188 Eric Beauvois .04 .10
189 Hughes Mongeon .04 .10
190 Alaine Cole .04 .10
191 Eric Desrochers .10 .25
192 Eric Joyal .04 .10
193 Steve Dortigny .04 .10
194 Fredrick Lefebvre .04 .10
195 Patrick Hebert .04 .10
196 Johnny Lorenzo .10 .25
197 Sylvain Cornier .04 .10
198 QMJHL Action .04 .10
199 Dave Morissette .04 .10
200 Yanick Dupre .04 .10
201 Eric Marcoux .04 .10
202 Bruno Ducharme .04 .10
203 Martin Caron .04 .10
204 Yves Meunier .04 .10
205 Eric Bissonette .04 .10
206 Jason Underhill .04 .10
207 Dave Belliveau .04 .10
208 Steve Lapointe .04 .10
209 Dean Melanson .04 .10
210 Trevor Dehaime .04 .10
211 Jacques Leblanc .04 .10
212 Normand Pacquet .04 .10
213 Huges Laliberte .04 .10
214 Craig Prior .04 .10
215 Patrick Labrecque .10 .25
216 Patrick Cloutier .04 .10
217 Michael Bazinet .04 .10
218 Christian Proulx .04 .10
219 QMJHL Action .04 .10
220 Charles Poulin .04 .10
221 Christian Larivierre .04 .10
222 Martin Brodeur 2.80 8.00
223 Yanick Lemay .04 .10
224 Dennis Leblanc .04 .10
225 Francois Groleau .04 .10
226 Pierre Sevigny .04 .10
227 Pierre Allard .04 .10
228 Craig Martin .04 .10
229 Karl Dykhuis .10 .25
230 Etienne Lavoie .04 .10
231 Stan Melanson .04 .10
232 Dominic Rheaume .04 .10
233 Mario Nobili .04 .10
234 Martin Gendron .10 .25
235 Stephane Menard .04 .10
236 David St.Pierre .04 .10
237 Yan Arsenault .04 .10
238 Norman Flynn .02 .05
239 QMJHL Action .04 .10
240 David Chouinard .04 .10
241 Robert Guilliet .04 .10
242 Martin Lajeunesse .04 .10
243 Nichol Cloutier .04 .10
244 Joel Brouchard .10 .25
245 Donald Brashear .30 1.00
246 Sebastein Tremblay .04 .10
247 Dominique Grandmaison .04 .10
248 Nicolas Lefebvre .04 .10
249 Joseph Napolitano .04 .10
250 Marc Savard .04 .10
251 Alain Gauthier .04 .10
252 Patrick Cole .04 .10
253 Richard Aimonette .04 .10
254 Martin Laitre .04 .10
255 Carl Lamonthe .04 .10
256 QMJHL Action .04 .10
257 Andre Durocher .04 .10
258 Jocelyn Martel .04 .10
259 Jeanot Ferlard .04 .10
260 Claude Savoie .04 .10
262 Denis Beauchamp .04 .10
263 Jean-Francois Gagnon .04 .10
264 Andre Boulaine .04 .10
265 Paul-Emile Exantus .04 .10
266 Danny Nolet .04 .10
267 Jean Lebreau .04 .10
268 Claude Barthe .04 .10

1990-91 7th Inn. Sketch WHL

The 7th Inning Sketch WHL Hockey set contains 347 standard-size cards. The front features a full color photo, framed by different color borders, with the player's name and "WHL" in the bar below the picture. The set includes noteworthy cards of Scott Niedermayer and, Chris Osgood. A factory set, (a numbered edition of 6,000), was produced and marketed separately. Card number 120 was never issued.

COMPLETE SET (347) 7.20 18.00
COMPLETE FACT.SET (347) 8.00 20.00
1 Brent Bilodeau .10 .25
2 Craig Chapman .04 .10
3 Jeff Jubenville .04 .10
4 Al Kinisky .04 .10
5 Kevin Malgunas .04 .10
6 Andy MacIntyre .04 .10
7 Darren McAusland .04 .10
8 Mike Seaton .04 .10
9 Turner Stevenson .20 .50
10 Lindsay Valis .04 .10
11 Dave Wilkie .10 .25
12 Jesse Wilson .04 .10
13 Dody Wood .04 .10
14 Bradley Zavisha .04 .10
15 Vince Boe .04 .10
16 Scott Davis .04 .10
17 Troy Hyatt .04 .10
18 Trevor Pennock .04 .10
19 Corey Schwab .20 .50
20 Scott Bellefontaine .10 .25
21 Travis Kelln .04 .10
22 Peter Anholt CO/GM .02 .05
23 Sonny Mignacca UER .10 .25
24 Chris Osgood 1.20 2.00
25 Murray Garbutt .04 .10
26 Kalvin Knibbs .04 .10
27 Jason Krywulak .04 .10
28 Jason Miller .04 .10
29 Rob Niedermayer .30 .75
30 Clayton Norris .04 .10
31 Jason Prosofsky .04 .10
32 Dana Rieder .04 .10
33 Kevin Riehl .04 .10
34 Tyler Romanchuk .04 .10
35 Dave Shute .04 .10
36 Lorne Toews .04 .10
37 Scott Townsend .04 .10
38 David Cooper .04 .10
39 Jon Duval .04 .10
40 Dan Kordic .10 .25
41 Mike Rathje .20 .50
42 Tim Bothwell CO .04 .10
43 Brent Thompson .10 .25
44 Jeff Knight .04 .10
45 Van Burgess .04 .10
46 Kimbi Daniels .10 .25
47 Curtis Friesen .04 .10
48 Todd Holt .04 .10
49 Blake Knox .04 .10
50 Trent McCleary .04 .10
51 Mark McFarlane .04 .10
52 Eddie Patterson .04 .10
53 Lloyd Pellitier .04 .10
54 Geoff Sanderson .30 .75
55 Andrew Schneider .04 .10
56 Tyler Wright .10 .25
57 Joel Dyck .04 .10
58 Len MacAusland .04 .10
59 Evan Marble .04 .10
60 David Podlubny .04 .10
61 Kurt Seher .04 .10
62 Jason Smith .04 .10
63 Justin Burke .10 .25
64 Kelly Thiessen .10 .25
65 Todd Esselmont .04 .10
66 Graham James CO/GM .01
67 Chris Herperger .04 .10
68 Mark McCoy .04 .10
69 Dean Malkoc .10 .25
70 Dennis Sproxton .10 .25
71 Centennial Civic .04 .10
Center
72 Kimbi Daniels .10 .25
73 Shane Calder .04 .10
74 Mark Franks .04 .10
75 Greg Leahy .04 .10
76 Dean Rambo .04 .10
77 Scott Scissons .04 .10
78 David Struch .04 .10
79 Derek Tibbatts .04 .10
80 Shawn Yakimishyn .04 .10
81 Trent Coghill .04 .10
82 Robert Lelacheur .04 .10
83 Richard Matvichuk .30 .75
84 Mark Raiter .04 .10
85 Trevor Sherban .04 .10
86 Mark Wotton .10 .25
87 Cam Moon .10 .25
88 Trevor Robins .10 .25
89 Jeff Buchanan .04 .10
90 Ryan Strain .04 .10
91 Tim Cox .04 .10
92 Terry Ruskowski CO .04 .10
93 Saskatchewan Place .04 .10
94 Darin Bader .04 .10
95 Gaetan Blouin .04 .10
96 Rick Kozuback CO/GM .02 .05
97 Jason Bowen .04 .10
98 Fran Deferenza .04 .10
99 Terry Degner .04 .10
100 Devin Derksen .04 .10
101 Martin Svetlik .04 .10
102 Jeremy Warring .10 .25
103 Corey Jones .10 .25
104 Dan Tiltgen UER .04 .10
105 Ryan Fujita .04 .10
106 Jeff Fancy .04 .10
107 Terry Virtue .20 .50
108 Dennis Pinfold .04 .10
109 Kyle Reeves .04 .10
110 Steve McNutt UER .04 .10
111 Todd Klassen .04 .10
112 Darren Hastman .04 .10
113 Bill Lindsay .20 .50
114A Brian Sakic ERR .04 .10
(Misspelled Buan
on card front)
114B Brian Sakic COR .04 .10
115 Dan Sherstenka .04 .10
116 Don Blishen .10 .25
117 Jason Marshall .04 .10
118 Dean Zayonce .04 .10
119 Brad Loring .04 .10
121 Darcy Austin UER .10 .25
122 Darcy Werenka .04 .10
123 Shane Peacock .04 .10
124 Rob Hartnell UER .04 .10
125 Brad Zimmer .04 .10
126 Allan Egeland .04 .10
127 Brad Rubachuk .04 .10
128 Jamie Pushor .20 .50
129 Jamie McLennan UER .30 .75
130 Lance Burns .04 .10
131 Ryan Smith .04 .10
132 Jason McBain .04 .10
133 Duane Maruschak UER .04 .10
134 Kevin St.Jacques .04 .10
135 Jason Sorochan .04 .10
136 Jason Widmer .04 .10
137 Bob Loucks CO .04 .10
138 Jason Ruff .04 .10
139 Pat Pylypuik .04 .10
140 Scott Adair .04 .10
141 Radek Sip .04 .10
142 Russ West .04 .10
143 Scott Thomas .04 .10
144 Kent Staniforth .04 .10
145 Travis Thiessen .04 .10
146 Mark Hussey .04 .10
147 Kevin Masters .04 .10
148 Todd Johnson .04 .10
149 Bob Loucks .04 .10
150A Rob Reimer ERR .04 .10
(Numbered 149 on back)
150B Rob Reimer COR .04 .10
151 Jeff Petruic .04 .10
152 Chris Schmidt .04 .10
153 Scott Barnstable .04 .10
154 Ian Layton .04 .10
155 Kevin Smyth .04 .10
156 Kim Deck .04 .10
157 Jason White .04 .10
158 Peter Cox .04 .10
159 Jeff Calvert UER .10 .25
160 Paul Dyck UER .04 .10
161 Derek Kletzel .04 .10
162 Jason Fitzsimmons UER .10 .25
163 Darcy Jerome .04 .10
164 Hal Christiansen .04 .10
165 Terry Hollinger .04 .10
166 Mike Risdale .10 .25
167 Jamie Heward .04 .10
168 Louis Dumont .04 .10
169 Cory Dosdall .04 .10
170 Terry Bendera .04 .10
171 Jamie Hayden .04 .10
172 Kelly Chotowetz .04 .10
173 Brad Scott .04 .10
174 Jeff Shantz .30 .75
175 Kelly Markwart .04 .10
176 Gary Pearce .04 .10
177 Kerry Biette .04 .10
178 Jamie Splett .04 .10
179 Frank Kovacs .04 .10
180 Greg Pankewicz .04 .10
181 Colin Ruck .04 .10
182 Brad Tippett CO .04 .10
183 Dusty Imoo .10 .25
184 Derek Eberle .04 .10
185 Heath Weenk .04 .10
186 Mike Sillinger .20 .50
187 Erin Thornton .04 .10
188 Mike Chrun .04 .10
189 Pat Falloon .20 .50
190 Bobby House UER .04 .10
191 Mike Jickling .04 .10
192 Trevor Tovall UER .04 .10
193 Steve Junker .04 .10
194 Shane Maitland .04 .10
195 Chris Lafreniere .04 .10
196 Frank Evans .04 .10
197 Jon Klemm .30 .75
198 Shawn Dietrich UER .10 .25
199 Dennis Saharchuk UER .04 .10
200 Mark Woolf .04 .10
201 Ray Whitney .20 .50
202 Scott Bailey .10 .25
203 Mark Ruark .04 .10
204 Brent Thurston .04 .10
205 Dan Faassen .04 .10
206 Kerry Toporowski .04 .10
207 Des Christopher .10 .25
208 Geoff Grandberg .04 .10
209 Bryan Maxwell CO .04 .10
210 Cam Danyluk .04 .10
211 Bram Vanderkracht .04 .10
212 Calvin Thudium .04 .10
213 Mark Szoke UER .04 .10
214 Kelly McCrimmon CO/GM .04 .10
215 Kevin Robertson UER .04 .10
216A Brian Purdy ERR .04 .10
(Misspelled Puroy
on card front)
216B Brian Purdy COR .04 .10
217 Hardy Sauter .04 .10
218 Dwayne Gylywoychuk .04 .10
219 Bart Cote .04 .10
220 Merv Priest .04 .10
221 Jeff Hoad .04 .10
222 Glen Gulutzan .04 .10
223 Johan Skillgard .04 .10
224 Byron Penstock .10 .25
225A Mike Vadenberghe ERR .04 .10
(Misspelled Vandenberghe
on card front)
225B Mike Vadenberghe COR .04 .10
226 Trevor Kidd .40 1.00
227 Dan Kopec .04 .10
228 Greg Hutchings .04 .10
229 Chris Constant .04 .10
230 Glen Webster .04 .10
231 Rob Puchniak .04 .10
232 Calvin Flint .04 .10
233 Stuart Scantlebury .04 .10
234 Jason White .04 .10
235 Gary Audette .04 .10
236 Kevin Schmalz .04 .10
237 Dwayne Newman .04 .10
238 Chris Catellier .04 .10
239 Todd Harris .04 .10
240 Mike Shemko .04 .10
241 John Badduke .04 .10
242 Mark Cipriano .04 .10
243 Brad Bagu .04 .10
244 Ross Harris .04 .10
245 Dino Caputo .04 .10
246 Cam Bristow .04 .10
247 Jarret Zukiwsky UER .04 .10
248 Jason Knox .04 .10
249 Gerry St.Cyr .04 .10
250 Larry Woo .04 .10
251 Jason Peters .04 .10
252 Shane Stangby .04 .10
253 Dave McMillen .04 .10
254 Colin Gregor UER .04 .10
255 Steve Passmore .40 1.00
256 Shayne Green UER .04 .10
257 Kevin Koopman .10 .25
258 Larry Watkins UER .04 .10
259 Scott Fukami UER .04 .10
260 Rick Hopper CO .02 .05
261 Laurie Billeck .04 .10
262 Rob Daum CO/GM UER .02 .05
263 Mark Stowe .04 .10
264 Curtis Regnier .04 .10
265 David Neilson .04 .10
266 Brian Pellerin .04 .10
267 Dean McAmmond .20 .50
268 Darren Van Impe .16 .40
269 Troy Neumeier .04 .10
270 Mike Langen .10 .25
271 Dan Kesa .04 .10
272 Travis Laycock .10 .25
273 Scott Allison .04 .10
274 Jeff Gorman .04 .10
275 Lee J. Leslie .04 .10
276 Jason Kwiatkowski .04 .10
277 Donevan Hextall UER .04 .10
278 Shane Zulyniak .04 .10
279 Darren Perkins .04 .10
280 Chad Seibel .04 .10
281 Jeff Nelson .04 .10
282 Troy Hjertas .04 .10
283 Jamie Linden .04 .10
284 Zac Boyer .04 .10
285 Jarret Bousquet .04 .10
286 Steven Yule .04 .10
287 Tommy Renney CO UER .10 .25
(Renny on back)
288 Lance Johnson .04 .10
289 Scott Niedermayer .60 2.00
290 Ryan Harrison .04 .10
291 Ed Patterson .10 .25
292 Jeff Watchorn .04 .10
293 Cal McGowan .04 .10
294 Dale Masson .10 .25
295 Joey Mittelsteadt UER .04 .10
296 Scott Loucks .04 .10
297 Shea Esselmont .04 .10
298 Craig Bonner .04 .10
299 Mike Mathers .04 .10
300 Fred Hettle .04 .10
301 Craig Lyons .04 .10
302 Murray Duval .04 .10
303 Jamie Barnes .04 .10
304 Bryan Gourlie .04 .10
305 Chad Berezniuk .04 .10
306 Corey Hirsch .20 .50
307 Darryl Sydor .30 .75
308 Jarrett Deuling .04 .10
309 Cory Stock .04 .10
310 Chris Rowland .04 .10
311 Mike Ruark .04 .10
312 Steve Konowalchuk .30 .75
313 Jeff Sebastian .04 .10
314 Brandon Smith .10 .25
315 Greg Gatto .04 .10
316 Brad Harrison .04 .10
317 Brantt Myhres .10 1.00
318 Jamie Black .04 .10
319 Colin Foley .04 .10
320 Cam Danyluk .04 .10
321 Dean Dorchak .04 .10
322 Ryan Slemko .04 .10
323 Kim Deck .04 .10
324 Kelly Harris .04 .10
325 Murray Bokenfohr .04 .10
326 Dean Intwert .10 .25
327 Dennis Saharchuk UER .04 .10
328 Shane Seiker UER .04 .10
329 Terry Virtue .04 .10
330 Josh Erdman .04 .10
331 Layne Roland .04 .10
332 Michel Michon .04 .10
333 Scott Mydan UER .04 .10
334 Brandon Wheat Kings .02 .05
335 Moose Jaw Warriors .02 .05
336 Swift Current Broncos .02 .05
337 Regina Pats UER .02 .05
338 Saskatoon Blades .02 .05
339 Medicine Hat Tigers .02 .05
340 The Goalmouth .02 .05
341 Portland Winter Hawks .02 .05
342 Kamloops Blazers UER .02 .05
343 Victoria Cougars .02 .05
344 Tri City Americans .02 .05
345 Spokane Chiefs .02 .05
346 Seattle Thunderbirds .02 .05
347 Lethbridge Hurricanes .02 .05
348 Prince Albert Raiders .02 .05

1990 7th Inn. Sketch Memorial Cup

The 7th Inn. Sketch Memorial Cup Hockey set consists of 100 standard-size cards. The front features a borderless color posed photo of the player against an aqua blue background. The upper right corner of the picture is cut off and various hockey league logos are placed there. The set features players from the four semi-final teams in the 1990 Memorial Cup playoffs, Kamloops Blazers (1-25), Kitchener Rangers (26-49), Laval Titans (50-74), and Oshawa Generals (75-100). These cards were only issued as factory sets, with a numbered edition of 3,000 sets. The set features cards of future NHL players Corey Hirsch, Eric Lindros, Martin Lapointe, Scott Niedermayer, and Darryl Sydor.

COMPLETE SET (100) 30.00 50.00
1 Len Barrie .20 .50
2 Zac Boyer .20 .50
3 Dave Chyzowski .20 .50
4 Shea Esselmont .20 .50
5 Todd Esselmont .20 .50
6 Phil Huber .20 .50
7 Lance Johnson .20 .50
8 Paul Kruse .20 .50
9 Cal McGowan .20 .50
10 Mike Needham .20 .50
11 Brian Shantz .20 .50
12 Darryl Sydor .80 2.00
13 Jeff Watchorn .20 .50
14 Jarrett Bousquet .20 .50
15 Todd Harris .20 .50
16 Deen Malkoc .20 .50
17 Joey Mittelstadt .20 .50
18 Scott Niedermayer 1.60 3.00
19 Clayton Young .20 .50
20 Trevor Sim .20 .50
21 Murray Duval .20 .50
22 Steve Yule .20 .50
23 Craig Bonner .20 .50
24 Dale Masson .20 .50
25 Corey Hirsch .40 1.00
26 Joe McDonnell .20 .50
27 Rick Chambers .10 .50
28 John Finnie .20 .50
29 Randy Pearce .20 .50
30 Mark Montanari .20 .50
31 Mike Torchia .20 .50
32 Jason York .40 .75
33 Jason Firth .20 .50
34 Jamie Israel .20 .50
35 Richard Borgo .20 .50
36 John Uniac .20 .50
37 Steve Smith .20 .50
38 Steven Rice .20 .50
39 Gilbert Dionne .30 .75
40 Cory Keenan .20 .50
41 Rick Allain .20 .50
42 John Copley .20 .50
43 Gib Tucker .20 .50
44 Chris LiPuma .20 .50
45 Brad Barton .20 .50
46 Rival Fullum .20 .50
47 Joey St.Aubin .20 .50
48 Jack Williams .20 .50
49 Shayne Stevenson .30 .50
50 Pierre Creamer .20 .50
51 Carl Mantha .20 .50
52 Julian Cameron .20 .50
53 Sandy McCarthy .80 2.00
54 Gino Odjick .40 1.00
55 Eric Raymond .20 .50
56 Carl Boudreau .20 .50
57 Greg MacEachern .20 .50
58 Allen Kerr .20 .50
59 Patrice Brisebois .40 .75
60 Eric Bissonette .20 .50
61 Martin Lapointe 1.60 3.00
62 Michel Gingras .20 .50
63 Sylvain Naud .20 .50
64 Pat Caron .20 .50
65 Regis Tremblay .20 .50
66 Francois Pelletier .20 .50
67 Jason Brousseau .20 .50
68 Eric Dubois .20 .50
69 Claude Boivin .20 .50
70 Denis Chalifoux .20 .50
71 Jim Bermingham .20 .50
72 Daniel Arsenault .20 .50
73 Normand Demers .20 .50
74 Serge Anglehart .20 .50
75 Rick Cornacchia .20 .50
76 Kevin Butt .20 .50
77 Fred Brathwaite 1.60 3.00
78 Paul O'Hagan .20 .50
79 Craig Donaldson .20 .50
80 Jean-Paul Davis .20 .50
81 Brian Grieve .20 .50
82 Bill Armstrong .20 .50
83 Wade Simpson .20 .50
84 Dave Craievich .20 .50
85 Dale Craigwell .30 .75
86 Joe Busillo .20 .50
87 Cory Banika .20 .50
88 Eric Lindros 12.00 20.00
89 Iain Fraser .20 .50
90 Mike Craig .20 .50
91 Jarrod Skalde .30 .75
92 Brent Grieve .20 .50
93 Scott Luik .20 .50
94 Matt Hoffman .20 .50
95 Trevor McIvor .20 .50
96 Scott Hollis .20 .50
97 Mark Deazeley .20 .50
98 Clair Cornish .20 .50
99 Oshawa Wins 4.00 5.00
(Eric Lindros holding
up Memorial Cup)
100 Checklist Card .10 .10

1991-92 7th Inn. Sketch OHL

This 384-card standard-size set was issued by 7th Inning Sketch and features players of the Ontario Hockey League. The production run was limited to 9,000 factory sets, with each set individually numbered "X of 9,000." On a white card face, the fronts feature color action player photos enclosed by different color frames. The player's name, the year and league, and the team name appear below the picture. The cards are numbered on the back and checklisted below according to teams. Cards numbered 98, 147, 293 and 360 were never produced.

COMPLETE SET (384) 8.00 20.00
1 John Slaney .08 .20
2 Jason Meloche .04 .10
3 Mark DeSantis .04 .10
4 Richard Raymond .04 .10
5 Dave Lemay .04 .10
6 Matt McGuffin .04 .10
7 Sam Oliveira .04 .10
8 Jeremy Stevenson .06 .15
9 Todd Walker .04 .10
10 Jean-Alain Schneider .04 .10
11 Guy Leveque .06 .15
12 Shayne Gaffar .04 .10
13 Mike Prokopec .06 .15
14 Nathan LaFayette .08 .20
15 Larry Courville .10 .25
16 Chris Clancy .04 .10
17 Tom Nemeth .06 .15
18 Jeff Reid .04 .10
19 Ilpo Kauhanen .10 .25
20 Rob Dykeman .10 .25
21 Rival Fullum .06 .15
22 Ryan VandenBussche .10 .25
23 Gordon Pell .06 .15
24 Paul Andrea UER .04 .10
Team affiliation says
Generals; should
say Royals
25 John Lovell CO UER .02 .05
Team affiliation says
Generals; should
say Royals
26 Alan Letang .04 .10
27 Chris Phelps .04 .10
28 John Wynne .04 .10
29 Rob Kinghan .04 .10
30 Glen Craig .04 .10
31 Eric Cairns .10 1.00
32 John Pinches .04 .10
33 Todd Harvey .20 .50
34 Craig Fraser .04 .10
35 Pat Peake .10 .25
36 Chris Skoryna .04 .10
37 Bob Wren .06 .15
38 Chris Varga .04 .10
39 David Benn .04 .10
40 Mark Lawrence .06 .15
41 Jeff Kostuch .04 .10
42 J.D. Eaton .04 .10
43 Derek Etches .04 .10
44 Jeff Gardiner .04 .10
45 James Shea .10 .25
46 Brad Teichmann .10 .25
47 Jim Rutherford CO .06 .15
48 Derek Wilkinson .06 .15
49 OHL Action .04 .10
50 OHL Action .04 .10
51 Sandy Allan .10 .25
52 Ron Bertrand .10 .25
53 Brad Brown .10 .25
54 Dennis Bonvie .06 1.00
55 Bradley Shepard .04 .10
56 Allan Cox .04 .10
57 Jack Williams .06 .15
58 Chad Penney .04 .10
59 Jason Firth .04 .10
60 Bill Lang .04 .10
61 Ryan Merritt .04 .10
62 Michael Burman .04 .10
63 Billy Wright .04 .10
64 Dave Szabo .04 .10
65 James Sheehan .04 .10
66 John Spoltore .04 .10
67 Paul Rushforth .04 .10
68 Jeff Shevalier .08 .20
69 Robert Thorpe .04 .10
70 Drake Berehowsky .10 .25
71 Patrick Barton .04 .10
72 Bert Templeton CO .06 .15
73 Wade Gibson .04 .10
74 C.J. Denomme UER .10 .25
Name spelled C. Jay
on back
75 Mike Torchia .10 .25
76 Mike Polano .04 .10
77 Tony McCabe .04 .10
78 Chris Kraemer .04 .10
79 Tim Spitzig .04 .10
80 Trevor Gallant .04 .10
81 Yvan Corbin .04 .10
82 Norman Dezainde .06 .15
83 Marc Robillard .04 .10
84 Derek Gauthier .04 .10
85 Gib Tucker .04 .10
86 Paul McCallion .04 .10
87 Eric Manlow .06 .15
88 Jamie Caruso .06 .15
89 Gary Miller .04 .10
90 Jason Stevenson .04 .10
91 Shayne McCosh .04 .10
92 Jason Gladney .04 .10
93 Brad Barton .04 .10
94 Chris LiPuma .08 .20
95 Justin Cullen .04 .10
96 Bill Smith SCOUT .02 .05
97 Joe McDonnell CO .02 .05
99 Brent Gretzky .10 .25
100 Gairin Smith .04 .10
101 Blair Scott .04 .10
102 Daniel Godbout .04 .10
103 Dan Preston .04 .10
104 Ian Keiller .04 .10
105 Rick Marshall .04 .10
106 Aaron Morrison .04 .10
107 Dominic Belanger .04 .10
108 Kevin Brown .06 .15
109 Tony Cimellaro .04 .10
110 Larry Mavety CO .02 .05
111 Jake Grimes .06 .15
112 Greg Dreveny .10 .25
113 Darren McCarty .80 2.00
114 Doug Doull .04 .10
115 Scott Boston .06 .15
116 Dale Chokan .04 .10
117 Darren Hurley .04 .10
118 Brian Mielko UER .04 .10
Card misnumbered 61
119 Richard Gallace UER .04 .10
Card misnumbered 65
120 Shayne Antoski .10 .25
121 Greg Bailey .04 .10
122 Keith Redmond .04 .10
123 Dick Todd CO .06 .15
124 Scott Turner .04 .10
125 Colin Wilson .04 .10
126 Mike Tomlinson .04 .10
127 Dale McTavish .04 .10
128 Chris Longo .04 .10
129 Chad Lang .10 .25
130 Brent Tully .06 .15
131 Shawn Heins .06 .15
132 Geordie Kinnear .06 .15
133 Jeff Walker .04 .10
134 Chris Pronger 1.20 3.00
135 Chad Grills .04 .10
136 Michael Harding .04 .10
137 Matt St.Germain .04 .10
138 Don O'Neill .04 .10
139 Dave Roche .10 .25
140 Doug Searle .04 .10
141 Bryan Gendron .04 .10
142 Kelly Vipond .06 .15
143 Andrew Verner .10 .25
144 Ryan Black .04 .10
145 Jason Dawe .10 .25
146 Jassen Cullimore .10 .25
148 Jason Arnott 1.20 1.00
149 Jan Benda .06 .15
150 Todd Bradley .04 .10
151 Markus Brunner .06 .15
152 Jason Campeau .04 .10
153 Mark Deazeley .04 .10
154 Matt Hoffman .04 .10
155 Scott Hollis .04 .10
156 Neil Iserhoff .04 .10
157 Darryl Lafrance .04 .10
158 B.J. MacPherson .06 .15
159 Troy Sweet .04 .10
160 Jason Weaver .04 .10
161 Stephane Yelle .20 .50
162 Trevor Burgess .04 .10
163 Joe Cook .04 .10
164 Jean-Paul Davis .04 .10
165 Brian Grieve .04 .10
166 Rob Leask .08 .20
167 Wade Simpson .04 .10
168 Kevin Spero .04 .10
169 Fred Brathwaite .40 1.00
170 Mike Fountain .10 .25
171 Rick Cornacchia .06 .15
172 Checklist 1-98 .02 .05
173 Todd Warriner .10 .25
174 Reuben Castella .04 .10
175 Cory Stillman .20 .50
176 Steve Gibson .04 .10
177 Trent Cull .04 .10
178 John Copley .04 .10
179 Craig Binns .04 .10
180 Ryan O'Neill .04 .10
181 Matthew Mullin .10 .25
182 Todd Hunter .04 .10
183 Jason Stos .04 .10
184 Robert Frayn .04 .10
185 Leonard MacDonald .04 .10
186 Tom Sullivan .04 .10
187 Steve Smith .04 .10
188 Bill Bowler .10 .25
189 James Allison .04 .10
190 Kevin MacKay .04 .10
191 David Myles .04 .10
192 Wayne Maxner GM CO .04 .10
193 Dave Prpich CO UER .02 .05
Windsor on front;
should say Spitfires
194 Brady Blain .04 .10
195 Eric Stamp UER .04 .10
Windsor on front;
should say Spitfires
196 OHL Action .04 .10
197 David Babcock .04 .10
198 Brad Love .04 .10
199 Dale Junkin .04 .10
200 Rick Corriveau .04 .10
201 Scott Campbell .04 .10
202 Jason Clarke .04 .10

203 George Burnett .04 .10
204 Ryan Tocher .04 .10
205 Dennis Maxwell .10 .25
206 Greg Scott .04 .10
207 Mark Tardiff .04 .10
208 Neil Fewster .04 .10
209 Jason Coles .04 .10
210 Randy Hall CO .02 .05
211 Todd Simon .06 .15
212 Ethan Moreau .30 .75
213 Todd Wetzel .04 .10
214 Tom Moores .04 .10
215 Geoff Rawson .04 .10
216 Dan Krisko .04 .10
217 Manny Legace .40 1.00
218 Kevin Brown .06 .15
219 Steve Staios .08 .20
220 Checklist 99-196 .02 .05
221 Checklist 197-290 .02 .05
222 Tony Bella .04 .10
223 Shawn Caplice .04 .10
224 Keli Corpse .06 .15
225 Chris Gratton .40 1.00
226 Gord Harris .04 .10
227 Cory Johnson .04 .10
228 Kevin King .04 .10
229 Justin Morrison .06 .15
230 Alastair Still .04 .10
231 Chris Scharf .04 .10
232 Brian Stagg .04 .10
233 Mike Dawson .04 .10
234 Rod Pasma .04 .10
235 Craig Rivet .10 .25
236 Dave Stewart .04 .10
237 John Vary .04 .10
238 Jason Wadel .04 .10
239 Joel Yates .04 .10
240 Marc Lamothe .10 .25
241 Pete McGlynn .10 .25
242 OHL Action .04 .10
243 Checklist 291-383 .02 .05
244 Joel Sandie .04 .10
245 Glen Murray .20 1.00
246 Derek Armstrong .04 .10
247 Michael Peca .60 1.00
248 Barry Young .04 .10
249 Bernie John .04 .10
250 Terry Chitaroni .06 .15
251 Jason Young .04 .10
252 Rod Hinks .04 .10
253 Michael Yeo .04 .10
254 Kyle Blacklock .04 .10
255 Dan Ryder .10 .25
256 Doug Mason CO .02 .05
257 Jamie Rivers .10 .25
258 Brandon Convery .08 .20
259 Barrie Moore .04 .10
260 Shawn Rivers .06 .15
261 Jamie Matthews .08 .20
262 Tim Favot .04 .10
263 Bob MacIsaac .04 .10
264 Sean Gagnon .04 .10
265 Ken MacKenzie GM CO .02 .05
266 George Dourion .04 .10
267 Brian MacKenzie .04 .10
268 Jason Zohil .04 .10
269 Rick Tarasuk .04 .10
270 Jamie Storr .30 .75
271 Sean Basilio .10 .25
272 Rick Morton .04 .10
273 Jason Hughes .04 .10
274 Scott Walker .20 1.00
275 Willie Skilliter .04 .10
276 Shawn Krueger .04 .10
277 Jason MacDonald .04 .10
278 Kirk Maltby .20 .50
279 Brock Woods .04 .10
280 Troy Hutchinson .04 .10
281 Geordie Maynard .04 .10
282 Luigi Calce .04 .10
283 Steven Parson .04 .10
284 Andrew Brunette .20 .50
285 Robert MacKenzie .04 .10
286 Jason Buetow .04 .10
287 Wyatt Buckland .04 .10
288 Jim Brown .04 .10
289 Gord Dickie .04 .10
290 Jeff Smith .04 .10
291 Peter Ambroziak .06 .15
292 Mark O'Donnell UER .04 .10
Name spelled
O'donnell on back
294 Grayden Reid .06 .15
295 Sean Spencer .10 .25
296 Gerry Skrypec .04 .10
297 Billy Hall .04 .10
298 Sean Gawley .04 .10
299 Grant Marshall .10 .25
300 Michael Johnson .04 .10
301 Brett Seguin .04 .10
302 Chris Coveny .04 .10
303 Ryan Kuwabara .06 .15
304 Jeff Ricciardi .04 .10
305 Curt Bowen .06 .15
306 Zbynek Kukacka .04 .10
307 Chris Gignac .04 .10
308 Steve Washburn .10 .25
309 Brian Kilrea CO .06 .15
310 Mike Lenarduzzi .10 .25
311 Matt Stone .04 .10
312 Ken Belanger .04 .10
313 Chris Simon .20 .50
314 Kiley Hill .04 .10
315 Chris Grenville .04 .10
316 Aaron Gavey .10 .25
317 Briane Thompson .04 .10
318 Ted Nolan CO .10 .25
319 Perry Pappas .04 .10
320 Kevin Hodson .20 .50
321 Colin Miller .04 .10
322 Tom MacDonald .04 .10
323 Shaun Imber .04 .10
324 Jarret Reid .04 .10
325 Tony Iob .04 .10
326 Mark Matier .04 .10
327 Drew Bannister .08 .20
328 Jason Denomme .04 .10
329 David Matsos .04 .10
330 Rick Kowalsky .04 .10
331 Tim Bacik .10 .25
332 Ralph Intranuovo .08 .20
333 Jonas Rudberg .04 .10
334 Jeff Toms .04 .10
335 Jason Julian .04 .10
336 Brian Goudie .04 .10
337 Gary Roach .04 .10
338 Brad Baber .04 .10
339 Todd Gleason UER .06 .15
Team affiliation says
Greyhounds; should
say Storm
340 Chris McMurtry .04 .10
341 Matt Turek .04 .10
342 Shane Johnson .04 .10
343 Grant Pritchett .04 .10
344 Mike Cote .04 .10
345 Duane Harmer .04 .10
346 Jeff Bes .06 .15
347A Wade Whitten .04 .10
347B Dan Tanevski UER .04 .10
(Should be number 360)
348 Bill Kovacs .06 .15
349 Kayle Short .04 .10
350 Sylvain Cloutier .08 .20
351 Brent Watson .04 .10
352 Brent Pope .04 .10
353 Craig Lutes .04 .10
354 Michael Hartwick .04 .10
355 Kevin Reid .04 .10
356 Toby Burkitt .04 .10
357 Todd Bertuzzi .40 2.00
358 Angelo Amore .10 .25
359 Jeff Pawluk .04 .10
361 Gordon Ross .04 .10
362 Dennis Purdie .06 .75
363 Dave Gilmore .04 .10
364 Brent Brownlee .10 .25
365 Aaron Nagy .04 .10
366 Barry Potomski .10 1.00
367 Steve Smillie .04 .10
368 Kelly Reed .04 .10
369 Gary Agnew CO .02 .05
370 Chris Taylor .06 .15
371 Brett Marietti .04 .10
372 Cory Evans .04 .10
373 Brian Stacey .04 .10
374 Chris Crombie .04 .10
375 Derrick Crane .04 .10
376 Scott McKay .06 .15
377 Gregory Ryan .04 .10
378 Mark Visheau .04 .10
379 Gerry Arcella .04 .10
380 Nick Stajduhar .06 .15
381 Jason Allison 1.20 2.00
382 Sean O'Reilly .04 .10
383 Paul Wolanski .04 .10
XXX Chris Schushack .06 .15
numbered 000

1991-92 7th Inn. Sketch QMJHL

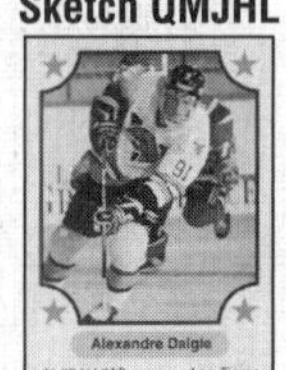

This 298-card standard-size set was issued by 7th Inning Sketch and features players of the Quebec Major Junior Hockey League. The production run was limited to 4,000 factory sets, with each set individually numbered "X of 4,000." On a white card face, the fronts feature color action player photos enclosed by different color frames. The corners of the picture are cut out to permit space for gold stars. The player's name, the year and league, and the team name appear below the picture. In a horizontal format, the backs have biography, statistics, and player profile in French and English. The cards are numbered on the back and checklisted below according to teams as follows: St. Hyacinthe Laser (1-28), Granby Bisons (29-52), Shawinigan Cataractes (53-77), Chicoutimi Sagueneens (78-101), Trois Rivieres Draveurs (102-125), Verdun College Francais (126-150), St. Jean Lynx (151-172), Beauport Harfangs (173-198), Hull Olympiques (199-223), Laval Titan (224-248), Victoriaville Tigres (249-273), and Drummondville Voltigeurs (274-298). Card number 256 was never produced.

COMPLETE SET (297) 6.00 15.00
1 Martin Brodeur 1.60 4.00
2 Normand Paquet .04 .10
3 David Desnoyers .04 .10
4 Carlo Colombi .04 .10
5 Stephane Menard .10 .25
6 Sebastien Berube .04 .10
7 Marc Desgagne .04 .10
8 Mil Sukovic .04 .10
9 Patrick Belisle .04 .10
10 Patrick Poulin .10 .25
11 Martin Trudel .04 .10
12 Charles Poulin .06 .15
13 Etienne Thibault .04 .10
14 Pierre Allard .04 .10
15 Francois Gagnon .04 .10
16 Stephane Huard .04 .10
17 Yannik Lemay .04 .10
18 Dany Fortin .04 .10
19 Carl Menard .04 .10
20 Serge Labelle .04 .10
21 Dean Melanson .04 .10
22 Yves Meunier .04 .10
23 Pierre Petroni CO .02 .05
24 Mario Pouliot CO UER .02 .05
(Team affiliation says
Bisons; should say Laser)
25 Alain Cote UER .06 .15
(Team affiliation on
front says Bisons;
should say Lasers;
Back erroneously says
Kingston Frontenancs)
26 Hugues Laliberte .04 .10
27 Martin Gendron .10 .25
28 Stan Melanson .04 .10
29 Carl Leblanc .04 .10
30 Patrick Grise .04 .10
31 Yves Charron .04 .10
32 Hughes Mongeon .04 .10
33 Christian Tardif .04 .10
34 Patrick Tessier .04 .10
35 Christian Campeau .04 .10
36 Mario Therrien .04 .10
37 Martin Balleux .04 .10
38 Joel Brassard .04 .10
39 Sebastien Fortier .04 .10
40 Jocelyn Langlois .04 .10
41 Giuseppe Argentos .04 .10
42 Sylvain Brisson .04 .10
43 Philippe Boucher .10 .25
44 Martin Brochu .20 1.00
45 Marc Rodgers .04 .10
46 Pascal Gagnon .04 .10
47 Benoit Therrien .04 .10
48 Robin Bouchard .04 .10
49 Michel Savoie .04 .10
50 Jean-Sebastien Boiteau .04 .10
51 Patrick Lamoureux .04 .10
52 Stephane Giard .10 .25
53 Maxime Jean .04 .10
54 Alain Cote .06 .15
55 Francois Groleau .06 .15
56 Richard Hamelin .06 .15
57 Eric Beauvis UER .06 .15
(Name misspelled
Beavis on back)
58 Steve Laplante .04 .10
59 Yves Meunier .04 .10
60 Steve Dontigny .04 .10
61 Simon Roy .04 .10
62 Jean-Francois Laroche .04 .10
63 Patrick Traverse .10 .25
64 Eric Joyal .04 .10
65 Jean-Francois .04 .10
Gregoire UER
(Name misspelled
Jean-Fracois on front)
66 Jocelyn Charbonneau .06 .15
67 Jean Imbeau .06 .15
68 Francois Bourdeau .04 .10
69 Alain Savage Jr. .04 .10
70 Johnny Lorenzo .10 .25
71 Patrick Lalime 1.20 2.00
72 Patrick Melfi .04 .10
73 Marc Tardif .04 .10
74 Marc Savard .04 .10
75 Alain Sanscartier CO .02 .05
76 Pascal Lebrasseur .06 .15
77 Checklist 1-101 .02 .05
78 Dany Girard .04 .10
79 Eddy Gervais .04 .10
80 Dave Tremblay .04 .10
81 Dany Larochelle .04 .10
82 Michel St.Jacques .04 .10
83 Rodney Petawabano .04 .10
84 Eric Duchesne .04 .10
85 Patrick Clement .04 .10
86 Steve Gosselin .04 .10
87 Patrick Lacombe .04 .10
88 Patrice Martineau .04 .10
89 Danny Beauregard .04 .10
90 Martin Lamarche .04 .10
91 Sebastien Parent .04 .10
92 Christian Caron .04 .10
93 Sylvain Careau .10 .25
94 Martin Beaupre .04 .10
95 Daniel Paradis .04 .10
96 Sylvain Rodrigue .10 .25
97 Joe Canale CO .02 .05
98 Patrick Lampron .04 .10
99 Carl Blondin .04 .10
100 Carl Wiseman .04 .10
101 Hugo Hamelin .10 .25
102 Claude Poirier .04 .10
103 Charles Paquette .04 .10
104 Carl Fleury UER .06 .15
(Name spelled FLeury
on front)
105 Paolo Racicot .04 .10
106 Sebastien Moreau .04 .10
107 Pascal Trepanier .04 .10
108 Dominic Maltais .06 .15
109 Steve Ares .04 .10
110 Daniel Thibault .04 .10
111 Eric Messier .20 .50
112 Stephane Julien .04 .10
113 Dave Paquet .04 .10
114 Nicolas Turmel .04 .10
115 Pascal Rheaume .20 .50
116 Carl Boudreau .04 .10
117 Dave Boudreault .04 .10
118 Eric Bellerose .06 .15
119 Steve Searles .04 .10
120 Patrick Nadeau .06 .15
121 Stephan Viens .04 .10
122 Jean-Francois Labbe .20 1.00
123 Jocelyn Thibault 1.20 3.00
124 Gaston Drapeau CO .02 .05
125 Checklist 102-198 .02 .05
126 Martin Lajeunesse .04 .10
127 Etienne Lavoie .04 .10
128 Dominic Rheaume .04 .10
129 Robert Guillet .04 .10
130 Francois Rivard .04 .10
131 Phillippe DeRouville .16 .40
132 Andrej Dobrota .04 .10
133 Pierre Gendron .04 .10
134 Dave Chouinard .04 .10
135 Martin Tanguay .06 .15
136 Jacques Blouin .04 .10
137 Martin Larochelle .04 .10
138 Jean-Martin Morin .04 .10
139 Donald Brashear .10 1.00
140 Stephane Paradis .04 .10
141 Jan Simcik .04 .10
142 Yan Arsenault .04 .10
143 Joel Bouchard .10 .25
144 Jean-Sebastien .04 .10
Lefebvre
145 David St. Pierre UER .06 .15
(Name misspelled
St-Pierre on front)
146 Mario Nobili .04 .10
147 Stacy Dallaire .04 .10
148 Carl Lamothe .06 .15
149 Andre Bouliane .10 .25
150 Simon Arial .04 .10
151 Stephane Madore .04 .10
152 Hughes Bouchard .04 .10
153 Steve Decaen .04 .10
154 Jason Downey .04 .10
155 Raymond Delarosbil .04 .10
156 Lino Salvo .04 .10
157 Reginald Brezeault .04 .10
158 Nathan Morin .04 .10
159 Samuel Groleau .06 .15
160 Patrick Carignan .04 .10
161 Stephane St-Amour .04 .10
162 Marquis Mathieu .06 .15
163 Yves Sarault .06 .15
164 Dave Belliveau .04 .10
165 Trevor Duhaime .04 .10
166 Eric O'Connor .04 .10
167 Christian Proulx .06 .15
168 Martin Lavallee .10 .25
169 Jean-Francois Gagnon .10 .25
170 Eric Lafrance .04 .10
171 Enrico Scardocchio .04 .10
172 David Bergeron .04 .10
173 Guillaume Morin .10 .25
174 Charlie Boucher .04 .10
175 Martin Rozon .04 .10
176 Brandon Piccarreto .04 .10
177 Simon Toupin .06 .15
178 Jamie Bird .04 .10
179 Herve Lapointe .04 .10
180 Ian MacIntyre .04 .10
181 Jean-Francois Rivard .10 .25
182 Alain Chainey CO .04 .10
183 Daniel Laflamme .04 .10
184 Patrice Paquin .04 .10
185 Patrick Deraspe .04 .10
186 Martin Roy .04 .10
187 Jeannot Ferland .04 .10
188 Patrick Genest .04 .10
189 Matthew Barnaby .30 1.00
190 Jean-Guy Trudel .04 .10
191 Eric Moreau .04 .10
192 Eric Cool .06 .15
193 Alexandre Legault .04 .10
194 Gregg Pineo .04 .10
195 LHJMQ Action .04 .10
196 Radoslav Balaz .04 .10
197 Stefan Simoes .04 .10
198 LHJMQ Action .04 .10
199 Francois Paquette .04 .10
200 Paul Macdonald .04 .10
201 Shane Doiron .04 .10
202 Michal Longauer .04 .10
203 Joe Crowley .04 .10
204 Joey Deliva .04 .10
205 Pierre-Francois .04 .10
Lalonde
206 Paul Brousseau .06 .15
207 Martin Lepage .04 .10
208 Yanick DeGrace .10 .25
209 Jim Campbell .10 .25
210 Sebastien Bordeleau .04 .10
211 Marc Legault .10 .25
212 Joel Blain .04 .10
213 Claude Jutras .04 .10
214 Eric Lavigne .06 .15
215 Todd Sparks .04 .10
216 Sylvain Lapointe .04 .10
217 Eric Lecompte .10 .25
218 Thierry Mayer .04 .10
219A Harold Hersh ERR .10 .25
(Jim Campbell photo
on back)
219B Harold Hersh COR .04 .10
220 Frederic Boivin .04 .10
221 Steven Dion .04 .10
222 Alain Vigneault .16 .40
223 Checklist 199-298 .02 .05
224 Petr Valenta .04 .10
225 LHJMQ Action .04 .10
226 Jim Bermingham .04 .10
227 Yanick Dube .10 .25
228 Sandy McCarthy .20 1.00
229 Dany Michaud .04 .10
230 Jason Brousseau .04 .10
231 Marc Beaucage .04 .10
232 Eric Cardinal .04 .10
233 Martin Chaput .04 .10
234 Jean Roberge .04 .10
235 Philip Gathercole .04 .10
236 Michael Gaul .04 .10
237 Yannick Frechette .04 .10
238 Sylvain Blouin .04 .10
239 David Pekarek .04 .10
240 John Kovacs .04 .10
241 Eric Raymond .10 .25
242 Emmanuel Fernandez 1.20 3.00
243 Yan St. Pierre .04 .10
244 Brant Blackned .04 .10
245 Eric Veilleux .04 .10
246 Pascal Vincent .04 .10
247 Benoit Larose .04 .10
248 Olivier Guillaume .04 .10
249 Alain Gauthier .10 .25
250 Bruno Ducharme .10 .25
251 Patrick Charbonneau .10 .25
252 Daniel Germain .04 .10
253 Pascal Chiasson .04 .10
254 Marc Thibeault .04 .10
255 Martin Woods .04 .10
257 Dominic Grand'maison .04 .10
258 Carl Poirer .04 .10
259 Stephane Larocque .04 .10
260 Mario Dumoulin .04 .10
261 Yan Laterreur .04 .10
262 Claude Savoie .06 .15
263 Denis Beauchamp .04 .10
264 Patrick Bisaillon .04 .10
265 Pascal Bernier .04 .10
266 Nicolas Lefebvre .04 .10
267 LHJMQ Action .04 .10
268 Joseph Napolitano .04 .10
269 Sebastien Tremblay .04 .10
270 Alexandre Daigle .20 .50
271 Pierre Pillion .04 .10
272 Yves Lambert .04 .10
273 Pierre Aubry CO .02 .05
274 Yves Loubier .10 .25
275 Pierre Sandke UER .04 .10
(First name Peter
on back)
276 Louis Bernard .04 .10
277 Alain Nasreddine .06 .15
278 Sylvain Ducharme .04 .10
279 Jeremy Caissie .04 .10
280 Eric Meloche .04 .10
281 Ian Laperriere .20 .50
282 Hugo Proulx .08 .20
283 Dave Whittom .04 .10
284 Yanick Dupre .06 .15
285 Eric Plante .04 .10
286 Stephane Desjardins .04 .10
287 Rene Corbet .20 .50
288 David Lessard .04 .10
289 Eric Marcoux .04 .10
290 Alexandre Duchesne .04 .10
291 Maxime Petitclerc UER .04 .10
(Name misspelled
Peticlerc on front)
292 Pierre Gagnon .10 .25
293 Roger Larche UER .04 .10
(Name misspelled
Larache on front)
294 Jean Hamel .04 .10
295 Alexandre Gaumond .04 .10
296 Paul-Emile Exentus .04 .10
297 LHJMQ Action .04 .10
298 LHJMQ Action .04 .10

1991-92 7th Inn. Sketch WHL

This 361-card standard-size set was issued by 7th Inning Sketch and features players of the Western Hockey League. The production run was limited to 7,000 factory sets, with each set individually numbered "X of 7,000." On a white card face, the fronts feature color action player photos enclosed by different color frames. The corners of the picture are cut out to permit space for gold stars. The player's name, the year and league, and the team name appear below the picture. The cards are numbered on the back and checklisted below according to team order.

COMPLETE SET (361) 6.00 15.00
1 Valeri Bure .30 .75
2 Hardy Sauter .04 .10
3 Bryan Maxwell CO .04 .10
4 Scott Bailey .10 .25
5 Mike Gray .04 .10
6 Mark Szoke .04 .10
7 Mike Jickling .04 .10
8 Frank Evans .04 .10
9 Steve Junker .08 .20
10 Greg Gatto .04 .10
11 Jared Bednar .04 .10
12 Justin Hocking .08 .20
13 Paxton Schulte .08 .20
14 Brad Toporowski .04 .10
15 Shane Maitland .04 .10
16 Aaron Boh .04 .10
17 Ryan Duthie .06 .15
18 Craig Reichert .06 .15
19 Danny Faassen .04 .10
20 Randy Toye .04 .10
21 Geoff Grandberg .04 .10
22 Jeremy Warring .10 .25
23 Tyler Romanchuck .04 .10
24 Jamie Linden .06 .15
25 1990-91 Champs .04 .10
26 Corey Jones .10 .25
27 Brandon Smith .04 .10
28 Mike Williamson .04 .10
29 Adam Murray .04 .10
30 Steve Konowalchuk .20 .50
31 Shawn Stone .04 .10
32 Adam Deadmarsh .80 1.00
33 Rick Mearns .04 .10
34 Chris Rowland .04 .10
35 Brandon Coates .04 .10
36 Dave Cammock .04 .10
37 Colin Foley .04 .10
38 Dennis Saharchuk .04 .10
39 Jiri Beranek .04 .10
40 Chad Seibel .04 .10
41 Kelly Harris .04 .10
42 Layne Roland .04 .10
43 Cale Hulse .06 .15
44 Ken Hodge CO .04 .10
45 Peter Cox .04 .10
46 Joaquin Gage .20 .50
47 Brent Peterson CO .04 .10
48 Jason McBain .04 .10
49 John Badduke .04 .10
50 Rick Hopper .02 .05
51 Dave Hamilton .10 .25
52 Dwayne Newman .04 .10
53 Chris Catellier .04 .10
54 Fran Defrenza .04 .10
55 Randy Chadney .04 .10
56 David Hebky .04 .10
57 Craig Fletcher .04 .10
58 Kane Chaloner .04 .10
59 Ross Harris .04 .10
60 Mike Barrie .04 .10
61 Steve Lingren .04 .10
62 Shea Esselmont .04 .10
63 Matt Smith .04 .10
64 Gerry St.Cyr .06 .15
65 Andrew Laming .04 .10
66 Jeff Fancy .04 .10
67 Ryan Pellaers .04 .10
68 Steve Passmore .40 1.00
69 Scott Fukami .04 .10
70 Darcy Mattersdorfer .04 .10
71 Chris Hawes .04 .10
72 The Goalies I .06 .15
73 Checklist 1-97 .02 .05
74 Riverside Coliseum .04 .10
75 Tom Renney .08 .20
76 Corey Hirsch .20 .50
77 Scott Ferguson .04 .10
78 Steve Yule .04 .10
79 Todd Johnson .04 .10
80 Jarrett Bousquet .04 .10
81 Mike Mathers .04 .10
82 Rod Stevens .04 .10
83 Lance Johnson .04 .10
84 Zac Boyer .04 .10
85 Craig Lyons .06 .15
86 Dale Masson .10 .25
87 Scott Loucks .06 .15
88 Darcy Tucker .20 .50
89 Shayne Green .06 .15
90 Michal Sup .04 .10
91 Craig Bonner .04 .10
92 Jeff Watchorn .04 .10
93 Jarrett Dueling .06 .15
94 Ed Patterson .08 .20
95 David Wilkie .10 .25
96 The Goalies III .06 .15
97 A Goal .04 .10
98 Andy MacIntyre .04 .10
99 Rhett Trombley .08 .20
100 Lorne Molleken CO .02 .05
101 Trevor Robins .10 .25
102 Jeff Buchanan .04 .10
103 Mark Raiter .04 .10
104 Bryce Goebel .04 .10
105 Paul Buczkowski .04 .10
106 James Startup .04 .10
107 Chad Rusnak .04 .10
108 Sean McFatridge .04 .10
109 Shane Calder .06 .15
110 Ryan Fujita .04 .10
111 Derek Tibbatts .04 .10
112 Glen Gulutzan .04 .10
113 Richard Matvichuk .20 .50
114 Chad Michalchuk .04 .10
115 Mark Wotton .08 .20
116 Mark Franks .04 .10
117 Norm Maracle .20 .50
118 Jason Becker .04 .10
119 Shawn Yakimishyn .04 .10
120 Ed Chynoweth PRES .06 .15
121 Checklist 98-195 .02 .05
122 Craig Chapman .04 .10
123 Jeff Jubenville .04 .10
124 George Zajankala .04 .10
125 Turner Stevenson .20 .50
126 Rob Tallas .20 .50
127 Ryan Brown .04 .10
128 Andrew Kemper .04 .10
129 Brendan Witt .20 .50
130 Troy Hyatt .04 .10
131 Mike Kennedy .10 .25
132 Jesse Wilson .04 .10
133 Kurt Seher .06 .15
134 Dody Wood .06 .15
135 Darren McAusland .04 .10
136 Jeff Sebastian .04 .10
137 Eric Bouchard .04 .10
138 Joel Dyck .04 .10
139 Blake Knox .04 .10
140 Peter Anholt CO .02 .05
141 Chris Wells .10 .25
142 Andrew Reimer .08 .20
143 Along the Boards .04 .10
144 Which Way Is Up .02 .05
145 Checklist 196-287 .02 .05
146 Tacoma Dome .04 .10
147 Opening Ceremonies .04 .10
148 Marcel Comeau CO .04 .10
149 Donn Clark CO .02 .05
150 John Varga .06 .15
151 Joey Young .04 .10
152 Laurie Billeck .04 .10
153 Jeff Calvert .10 .25
154 Tuomas Gronman .10 .25
155 Jason Knox .04 .10
156 Kevin Malgunas .04 .10
157 Dave McMillen .04 .10
158 Darryl Onofrychuk .10 .25
159 Mike Piersol .04 .10
160 Lasse Pirjeta .04 .10
161 Drew Schoneck .04 .10
162 Corey Stock .04 .10
163 Ryan Strain .04 .10
164 Michal Sykora .06 .15
165 Scott Thomas .06 .15
166 Toby Weishaar .04 .10
167 Jeff Whittle .06 .15
168 The Rockettes .04 .10
169 Allan Egeland .06 .15
170 Van Burgess .04 .10
171 Trever Fraser .04 .10
172 Jamie Black .06 .15
173 WHL Action .04 .10
174 Andy Schneider .06 .15
175 John McMulkin .04 .10
176 Rick Girard .06 .15
177 Shane Hnidy .04 .10
178 Jason Krywulak .06 .15
179 Jeremy Riehl .06 .15
180 Brent Bilodeau .10 .25
181 Mark McCoy .04 .10
182 Matt Young .04 .10
183 Dan Sherstenka .04 .10
184 Jarrod Daniel .10 .25
185 Lennie MacAusland .04 .10
186 Keith McCambridge .04 .10
187 Jason Horvath .04 .10
188 Kevin Koopman .10 .25
189 Chris Herperger .06 .15
190 Trent McCleary .10 .25
191 Tyler Wright .10 .25
192 Todd Holt .06 .15
193 Ashley Buckberger .06 .15
194 Bram Vanderkracht .04 .10
195 Ken Zilka .04 .10
196 Chris Osgood 1.20 2.00
197 Rob Puchniak .04 .10
198 Todd Dutiaume .04 .10
199 Mike Maneluk .08 .20
200 Shawn Dietrich .10 .25
201 Chris Johnston .04 .10
202 Brian Purdy .06 .15
203 Mike Chrun .04 .10
204 Dan Kopec .04 .10
205 Ryan Smith .06 .15
206 Marty Murray .10 .25
207 Merv Priest .04 .10
208 Bobby House .06 .15
209 Chris Constant .04 .10
210 Dwayne Gylywoychuk .04 .10
211 Stu Scantlebury .04 .10
212 Mark Kolesar .08 .20
213 Craig Geekie .04 .10
214 Terran Sandwith .04 .10
215 Jeff Hoad .04 .10
216 Kelly McCrimmon .04 .10
217 Carlos Bye .04 .10
218 Trevor Hanas .04 .10
219 Jeff Shantz .20 .50
220 Heath Weenk .04 .10
221 Nathan Dempsey .04 .10
222 Louis Dumont .04 .10
223 Garry Pearce .04 .10
224 Terry Bendera .04 .10
225 Hal Christiansen .04 .10
226 Jason Smith .20 .50
227 Kerry Biette .04 .10
228 Barry Becker .10 .25
229 Derek Eberle .04 .10
230 Ken Richardson .04 .10
231 Niklas Barklund .04 .10
232 Frank Kovacs .04 .10
233 Not Issued .02 .05
234 Not Issued .02 .05
235 Lloyd Pelletier .10 .25
236 Dale Vossen .02 .05
237 A.J. Kelham .04 .10
238 Mike Risdale .10 .25
239 Brad Bagu .04 .10
240 Niko Ovaska .04 .10
241 Brad Tippett CO .02 .05
242 The Goalies II .06 .15
243 Lee J. Leslie .06 .15
244 Darren Perkins .04 .10
245 Jason Kwiatkowski .06 .15
246 Jason Renard .04 .10
247 Dan Kesa .08 .20
248 Jason Klassen .04 .10
249 Nick Polychronopoulus .04 .10
250 David Neilson .04 .10
251 Merv Haney .04 .10
252 Troy Hjertaas .04 .10
253 Curt Regnier .08 .20
254 Dean McAmmond .20 .50
255 Travis Laycock .10 .25
256 Jeff Lank .04 .10
257 Barkley Swenson .04 .10
258 Darren Van Impe .10 .25
259 Ryan Pisiak .04 .10
260 Jeff Gorman .04 .10
261 Stan Matwijiw .10 .25
262 Mike Fedorko .04 .10
263 Mark Odnokon .02 .05
264 Shane Zulyniak .04 .10
265 Jeff Nelson .08 .20
266 Donevan Hextall .08 .20
267 Kevin Masters .04 .10
268 Chris Schmidt .04 .10
269 Jeff Budai .04 .10
270 Bill Hooson .04 .10
271 Fred Hettle .04 .10
272 Kent Staniforth .04 .10
273 Travis Stevenson .04 .10
274 David Jesiolowksi .04 .10
275 Mike Babcock CO .02 .05
276 Scott Allison .04 .10
277 Travis Thiessen .04 .10
278 Marc Hussey .04 .10
279 Kevin Smyth .06 .15
280 Jason Fitzsimmons .10 .25
281 Jeff Petruic .04 .10
282 Russ West .04 .10
283 Derek Kletzel .06 .15
284 Jarret Zukiwsky .04 .10
285 Jason Carey .04 .10
286 Close Checking .04 .10
287 Checklist 288-360 .02 .05
288 Jason Bowen .06 .15
289 Dean Tiltgen .06 .15
290 Terry Degner .08 .20
291 Jodie Murphy .04 .10
292 Brian Sakic .06 .15
293 Jamie Barnes .04 .10
294 Darren Hastman .04 .10
295 Todd Klassen .06 .15
296 Mirsad Mujcin .04 .10
297 Trevor Sherban .04 .10
298 Chadden Cabana .04 .10
299 Adam Rettschlag .04 .10
300 Mark Toljanich .04 .10
301 Kory Mullin .04 .10
302 Byron Penstock .10 .25
303 Vladimir Vujtek .08 .20
304 Bill Lindsay .10 .25
305 Jeff Cej .04 .10
306 Mike Busniak CO .04 .10
307 Todd Harris .04 .10
308 Cory Dosdall .04 .10
309 Jason Smith .20 .50
310 Mark Dawkins .10 .25
311 Dan O'Rourke .04 .10
312 Darby Walker .04 .10
313 Olaf Kjenstadt .06 .15
314 Sonny Mignacca .10 .25
315 Jon Duval .04 .10
316 Lorne Toews .04 .10
317 Dana Rieder .04 .10
318 Clayton Norris .06 .15
319 David Cooper .08 .20
320 Larry Watkins .04 .10
321 Evan Marble .04 .10
322 Scott Lindsay .06 .15
323 Ryan Petz .04 .10
324 Jeramie Heistad .04 .10
325 Scott Townsend .04 .10
326 Stacy Roest .20 .50
327 Rob Niedermayer .30 .75
328 Tim Bothwell CO .06 .15
329 Kevin Riehl .08 .20
330 Mike Rathje .10 .25

331 Bryan McCabe .20 .50
332 MHT Tiger MASCOT .04 .10
333 Dean Intwert .10 .25
334 Mike Vandenberghe .04 .10
335 Cam Danyluk .04 .10
336 Darcy Austin .10 .25
337 Jason Knight .04 .10
338 Lee Sorochan .10 .25
339 Al Kinisky .04 .10
340 Rob Hartnell .04 .10
341 Radek Sip .04 .10
342 Jamie Pushor .10 .25
343 Shane Peacock .04 .10
344 Cadrin Smart .04 .10
345 Maurice Meagher .04 .10
346 Lance Burns .04 .10
347 Dominic Pittis .06 .50
348 Todd MacIsaac .04 .10
349 Brad Zimmer .04 .10
350 Jason Sorochan .04 .10
351 Darcy Werenka .08 .20
352 Kevin St.Jacques .06 .15
353 David Trofimenkoff .04 .10
354 Terry Hollinger .06 .15
355 Travis Munday .04 .10
356 Slade Stephenson .04 .10
357 Jason Widmer .08 .20
358 Brad Zavisha .06 .15
359 Bob Loucks CO .02 .05
360 Brantt Myhres .08 1.00
0 Garfield Henderson .06 .15
Numbered 000

1991 7th Inn. Sketch CHL Award Winners

This 30-card boxed standard-size set features Canadian Hockey League Award Winners. Each box has on its back a checklist and the set serial number. The cards feature action color player photos with gray borders against a black card face. The player's specific achievement is printed in gray in the black margin at the top. His name and team appear in white at the bottom.

COMPLETE SET (30) 4.00 10.00
1 Eric Lindros 1.00 2.00
2 Dale Craigwell .10 .25
3 Nathan Lafayette .08 .20
4 Chris Snell .10 .25
5 Cory Stillman .20 .50
6 Mike Torchia .10 .50
7 George Burnett .08 .20
8 Eric Lindros 1.00 2.00
9 Sherwood Bassin .08 .20
10 Eric Lindros 1.00 2.00
11 Scott Niedermayer .20 .50
12 Pat Falloon .10 .25
13 Scott Niedermayer .20 .50
14 Darryl Sydor .20 .50
15 Donevan Hextall .08 .20
16 Jamie McLennan .16 .40
17 Tom Renney .10 .25
18 Frank Evans .08 .20
19 Bob Brown .08 .20
20 Ray Whitney .16 .50
21 Philippe Boucher .08 .20
22 Yanic Perreault .16 .40
23 Benoit Larose .08 .20
24 Patrice Brisebois .10 .25
25 Philippe Boucher .08 .20
26 Felix Potvin .40 1.00
27 Joe Canale .08 .20
28 Christian Lariviere .08 .20
29 Roland Janelle .08 .20
30 Yanic Perreault .16 .40

1991 7th Inn. Sketch Memorial Cup

The 1991 7th Inn. Sketch Memorial Cup Hockey set captures the four teams that participated in the Canadian junior hockey championship, with one team each from the OHL and WHL, and two from the QMJHL (the host league). The cards measure the standard size and feature on the fronts color action player photos enclosed by silver borders. The upper right and lower left corners are cut off to permit space for the CHL and '91 Memorial Cup logos, respectively. The player's name in the bottom silver border rounds out the card face. The set is skip-numbered due to the fact that several cards were withdrawn from the set after only a few sets had been released. These 17 card numbers are 21, 36 (Rob Dykeman), 96 (Eric Lindros), 106 (Pat Peake), 107 (Steve Staios), 110 (Alex Stojanov), 111 (Glen Murray), 113 (Jason Dawe), 114 (Nathan Lafayette), 116 (Guy Leveque), 118 (Shayne Antoski), 119 (Eric Lindros), 120 (Dennis Purdie), 121 (Terry Chitaroni), and 124 (Jamie Matthews).

COMPLETE SET (130) 50.00 100.00
COMPLETE SHORT SET (113) 6.00 15.00
1 Mike Lenarduzzi .10 .25
2 Kevin Hodson .20 .50
3 OHL Action .06 .15
Sault Ste. Marie vs. Oshawa
4 Bob Boughner .20 .50
5 Adam Foote .30 .75
6 Brad Tiley .06 .15
7 Brian Goudie .06 .15
8 Wade Whitten .06 .15
9 Jason Denomme .06 .15
10 David Matsos .06 .15
11 Rick Kowalsky .06 .15
12 Jarret Reid .06 .15
13 Perry Pappas .06 .15
14 Tom MacDonald .06 .15
15 Mike DeCoff .06 .15
16 Joe Busillo .06 .15
17 Denny Lambert .10 .25
18 Mark Matier .06 .15
19 Shaun Imber .06 .15
20 Ralph Intranuovo .10 .25
21 Chris Snell SP 1.00 2.00
22 Tony Iob .06 .15
23 Colin Miller .06 .15
24 Ted Nolan .10 .50
25 Sylvain Rodrigue .06 .15
26 Felix Potvin 1.60 4.00
27 Martin Lavallee .06 .15
28 Eric Brule .06 .15
29 Steve Larouche .06 .15
30 Michel St-Jacques .06 .15
31 Patrick Clement .06 .15
32 Patrick Bisaillon .06 .15
33A Checklist 62-131 SP 1.00 2.00
33B Checklist 62-131 .10 .25
(Withdrawn numbers omitted)
34 Gilles Bouchard .06 .15
35 Eric Rochette .06 .15
36 Rob Dykeman SP 1.00 2.00
37A Checklist 1-61 SP 1.00 2.00
37B Checklist 1-61 .10 .25
(Withdrawn numbers omitted)
38 Patrice Martineau .06 .15
39 Danny Beauregard .06 .15
40 Francois Belanger .06 .15
41 Sebastien Parent .10 .25
42 Martin Gagne .06 .15
43 Stephane Charbonneau .06 .15
44 Martin Beaupre .06 .15
45 Daniel Paradis .06 .15
46 Joe Canale .06 .15
47 OHL Action .06 .15
Sault Ste. Marie vs. Oshawa
48 Jubilation .06 .15
49 Steve Lupien .06 .15
50 Pierre Gagnon .06 .15
51 Alexandre Legault .06 .15
52 Martin Charrois .06 .15
53 Eric Dandenault .06 .15
54 Denis Chasse .10 .25
55 Guy Lehoux .06 .15
56 Ian Laperriere .20 .50
57 Hugo Proulx .06 .15
58 Dave Whittom .06 .15
59 Yanick Dupre UER .10 .25
60 Eric Plante .06 .15
61 Stephane Desjardins .10 .25
62 Patrice Brisebois .10 .25
63 Rene Corbet .20 .50
64 Marc Savard .06 .15
65 Claude Jutras Jr. .06 .15
66 David Pekarek .06 .15
67 Roger Larche UER .06 .15
(Name misspelled Larohe on front)
68 Dave Paquet .10 .25
69 Eric Meloche .06 .15
70 CHL Action .06 .15
Spokane vs. Lethbridge
71 Celebration .16 .40
Ed Chynoweth PRES
Jon Klemm
72 Felix Potvin MVP 1.60 4.00
73 Scott Bailey .20 .50
74 Trevor Kidd .30 .75
75 Chris Lafreniere .06 .15
76 Frank Evans .06 .15
77 Jon Klemm .20 .50
78 Brent Thurston .06 .15
79 Jamie McLennan .20 .50
80 Steve Junker .06 .15
81 Mark Szoke .06 .15
82 Ray Whitney .20 1.00
83 Geoff Grandberg .06 .15
84 Cam Danyluk .06 .15
85 Kerry Toporowski .06 .15
86 Trevor Tovell .06 .15
87 Pat Falloon .20 .50
88 Bram Vanderkracht .06 .15
89 Mike Jickling .06 .15
90 Murray Garbutt .06 .15
91 Calvin Thudium .06 .15
92 Mark Woolf .06 .15
93 Shane Maitland .06 .15
94 Bart Cote .06 .15
95 Bryan Maxwell .06 .15
96 Eric Lindros SP 16.00 30.00
97 Scott Niedermayer .40 1.00
98 Patrick Poulin .10 .25
99 Brent Bilodeau .10 .25
100 Pat Falloon .20 .50
101 Darcy Werenka .10 .25
102 Martin Lapointe .60 1.50
103 Philippe Boucher .10 .25
104 Jeff Nelson .10 .25
105 Rene Corbet .20 .50
106 Pat Peake SP 1.20 2.00
107 Steve Staios SP 1.00 2.00
108 Richard Matvichuk .20 .50
109 Dean McAmmond .20 .50
110 Alex Stojanov SP 1.00 2.00
111 Glen Murray SP 1.60 4.00
112 Tyler Wright .10 .25
113 Jason Dawe SP 1.20 3.00
114 Nathan Lafayette SP 1.00 2.00
115 Yanic Perreault .20 .50
116 Guy Leveque SP 1.00 2.00
117 Darren Van Impe .10 .25
118 Shawn Antoski SP 1.00 2.00
119 Eric Lindros SP 16.00 30.00
120 Dennis Purdie SP 1.00 2.00
121 Terry Chitaroni SP 1.00 2.00
122 Jamie Pushor .10 .25
123 Chris Osgood 1.60 4.00
124 Jamie Matthews SP 1.00 2.00
125 Yves Sarault .06 .15
126 Yanic Dupre UER .10 .25
127 Brad Zimmer .06 .15
128 Copps Coliseum .06 .15
129 Jason Widmer .10 .25
130 Marc Savard .06 .15
131 Mike Torchia
132 Andrew Verner

1999-00 Shawinigan Cataractes

This 24-card set features the QMJHL Cataractes. Base cards feature full-color action photography and have green borders along the right side and the bottom of the card where the team logo is also pictured.

COMPLETE SET (24) 4.00 10.00
1 Jonathan Lessard .14 .35
2 Philippe Gelinas .14 .35
3 Jonathan Bellemare .14 .35
4 Anthony Quessy .20 .50
5 Alexandre Blackburn .14 .35
6 Pascal Dupuis .14 .35
7 Marc-Andre Bergeron .14 .50
8 Francis Desauriers .14 .35
9 Jean-Sebastien Trudelle .14 .35
10 Jean-Philippe Pare .20 .50
11 Jean-Francois David .14 .35
12 Philippe Deblois .14 .35
13 Dave Verville .14 .35
14 Mathieu Chouinard .60 1.50
15 Gilbert Lefrancois .14 .35
16 Denis Desmarais .14 .35
17 Yannick Noiseux .14 .35
18 Dominic Forget .14 .35
19 Conor McGuire .14 .35
20 Jean-Francois Dufort .14 .35
21 Andre Landry .14 .35
22 David Chicoine .14 .35
23 Jason Pominville .40 1.50
24 Header Card/CL .04 .10

1999-00 Shawinigan Cataractes Signed

This 24-card set parallels the base Shawinigan Cataractes set in an autographed version. The fronts feature autographs on a ghosted-out portion of the photo, while the backs are serial numbered out of 100.

COMPLETE SET (24) 20.00 50.00
1 Jonathan Lessard .80 2.00
2 Philippe Gelinas .80 2.00
3 Jonathan Bellemare .80 2.00
4 Anthony Quessy .80 2.00
5 Alexandre Blackburn .80 2.00
6 Pascal Dupuis .80 2.00
7 Marc-Andre Bergeron .80 4.00
8 Francis Desauriers .80 2.00
9 Jean-Sebastien Trudelle .80 2.00
10 Jean-Philippe Pare 1.60 4.00
11 Jean-Francois David .80 2.00
12 Philippe Deblois .80 2.00
13 Dave Verville .80 2.00
14 Mathieu Chouinard 4.00 10.00
15 Gilbert Lefrancois .80 2.00
16 Denis Desmarais .80 2.00
17 Yannick Noiseux .80 2.00
18 Dominic Forget .80 2.00
19 Conor McGuire .80 2.00
20 Jean-Francois Dufort .80 2.00
21 Andre Landry .80 2.00
22 David Chicoine .80 2.00
23 Jason Pominville .80 10.00
24 Header Card/CL .20 .50

2000-01 Shawinigan Cataractes

This set features the Cataractes of the QMJHL. The set was produced by CTM Ste-Foy and was sold both by that card shop and by the team.

COMPLETE SET (24) 6.00 15.00
1 Denis Desmarais .16 .40
2 Zbynek Michalek .16 .40
3 Jonathan Beaulieu .16 .40
4 Jonathan Lessard .16 .40
5 Jonathan Bellemare .16 .40
6 Patrick Bolduc .16 .40
7 Anthony Quessy .16 .40
8 David Chicoine .16 .40
9 Gilbert Lefrancois .16 .40
10 Radim Vrbata .60 1.00
11 Yannick Noiseux .16 .40
12 Marc-Andre Bergeron .16 .50
13 Jimmy Cuddihy .20 1.00
14 Kevin Bergin .16 .40
15 Francois Gagnon .16 .40
16 Olivier Michaud 2.00 3.00
17 Frederic Cloutier .16 1.00
18 Jean-Francois David .16 .40
19 Alexandre Menard Burrows .16 .40
20 Jason Pominville .40 1.50
21 Dominic Forget .16 .40
22 Trevor Ettinger .16 .40
23 Jean-Francois Dufort .16 .40
NNO Coaches .10 .25

2000-01 Shawinigan Cataractes Signed

This set is exactly the same as the base Cataractes set from this season, save that every card has been hand signed by the player pictured. Each card also is serial numbered out of just 100.

COMPLETE SET (24) 24.00 60.00
1 Denis Desmarais .80 2.00
2 Michalek Zbynek .80 2.00
3 Jonathan Beaulieu .80 2.00
4 Jonathan Lessard .80 2.00
5 Jonathan Bellemare .80 2.00
6 Patrick Bolduc .80 2.00
7 Anthony Quessy .80 2.00
8 David Chicoine .80 2.00
9 Gilbert Lefrancois .80 2.00
10 Radim Vrbata 3.20 8.00
11 Yannick Noiseux .80 2.00
12 Marc-Andre Bergeron .80 4.00
13 Jimmy Cuddihy 1.20 5.00
14 Kevin Bergin .80 2.00
15 Francois Gagnon .80 2.00
16 Olivier Michaud 6.00 15.00
17 Frederic Cloutier .80 5.00
18 Jean-Francois David .80 2.00
19 Alexandre Menard Burrows .80 2.00
20 Jason Pominville 2.00 10.00
21 Dominic Forget .80 2.00
22 Trevor Ettinger .80 2.00
23 Jean-Francois Dufort .80 2.00
NNO Coaches .10 .25

2001-02 Shawinigan Cataractes

This set features les Cataractes of the QMJHL. The set was produced by well-known card store CTM Ste-Foy, and was sold by that shop and at the team's souvenir stand. Production was limited to no more than 1,000 sets.

COMPLETE SET (24) 6.00 15.00
1 Denis Desmarais .20 .50
2 Zbynek Michalek .20 .50
3 Paul-Andre Bourgoin .20 .50
4 Jimmy Fillion .30 .75
5 Jonathan Lessard .20 .50
6 Jonathan Bellemore .20 .50
7 Mathieu Gravel .20 .50
8 Jonathan Villeneuve .20 .50
9 David Chicoine .20 .50
10 Armands Berzins .20 .50
11 Philippe Bastarache .20 .50
12 Jimmy Cuddihy .40 1.00
13 Chris Hodgson .20 .50
14 Thiery Poudrier .20 .50
15 Olivier Michaud 2.00 5.00
16 Guillaume Lavallee .20 .50
17 David Leroux .20 .50
18 Jean-Francois David .20 .50
19 Jonathan Boutin .20 .50
20 Alexandre Burrows .20 .50
21 Mathieu Payette .20 .50
22 Jason Pominville .30 .75
23 Jean-Francois Dufort .20 .50
NNO Title Card/CL .04 .10

2002-03 Shawinigan Cataractes

COMPLETE SET (25) 5.00 12.00
1 Julien Ellis .30 .75
2 Dave Grenier .20 .50
3 Paul-Andre Bourgouin .20 .50
4 Frederic Gariepy .20 .50
5 Mathieu Gravel .20 .50
6 Karl Morin .20 .50
7 Armands Berzins .20 .50
8 Danick Bouchard .20 .50
9 Jimmy Cuddihy .30 .75
10 Mathieu Fournier .20 .50
11 Kevin Deslauriers .20 .50
12 Thiery Poudrier .20 .50
13 David Leroux .20 .50
14 Sebastien Gauthier .20 .50
15 Jonathan Villeneuve .20 .50
16 Michel Bergevin-Robinson .30 .75
17 Jonathan Boutin .20 .50
18 Justin Vienneau .20 .50
19 Marek Hascak .20 .50
20 Simon-Pierre Sauve .20 .50
21 Dominic Plante .20 .50
22 Benoit Mondou .30 .75
23 Nicolas Desilets .20 .50
24 Charles Gauthier .20 .50
25 Checklist .02 .10

2003-04 Shawinigan Cataractes

COMPLETE SET (23) 5.00 12.00
1 Eric Begin .20 .50
2 Steve Bellefleur .20 .50
3 Danick Bouchard .20 .50
4 Jonathan Boutin .20 .50
5 Ben Chaisson .20 .50
6 Jimmy Cuddihy .30 .75
7 Marty Doyle .30 .75
8 Nicolas Desilets .20 .50
9 Julien Ellis .30 .75
10 Charles Gauthier .20 .50
11 Sebastien Gauthier .20 .50
12 Michal Gavalier .20 .50
13 Marc-Olivier Gignac .30 .75
14 Mathieu Gravel .20 .50
15 Pierre-Marc Guilbault .20 .50
16 Marek Hascak .20 .50
17 Jonathan Jolette .20 .50
18 Benoit Mondou .30 .75
19 Jean-Philippe Paquet .20 .50
20 Pascal Pelletier .30 .75
21 Thiery Poudrier .20 .50
22 Simon-Pierre Sauve .20 .50
23 Justin Vienneau .20 .50

2005-06 Shawinigan Cataractes

COMPLETE SET (23) 6.00 12.00
1 Julien Ellis .30 .75
2 Ben MacFarlane .20 .50
3 Alex Bourret .40 1.00
4 Benoit Mondou .30 .75
5 Jean-Philippe Paquet .20 .50
6 Justin Vienneau .20 .50
7 Patrick Begin .20 .50
8 Steve Bellefleur .20 .50
9 Patrick Bernier .20 .50
10 Danick Bouchard .20 .50
11 Nicolas Desilets .20 .50
12 Guillaume Durand .20 .50
13 Pierre-Marc Guilbault .20 .50
14 Kyell Henegan .20 .50
15 Cedric Lalonde-McNicoll .20 .50
16 Triston Manson .20 .50
17 Francis Pare .20 .50
18 Mathieu Petrin .20 .50
19 Egor Egorov .20 .50
20 Charles Milette .20 .50
21 Guillaume Labreque .20 .50
22 Jan Danecek .04 .10
23 Sean Smyth .20 .50

1986-87 Sherbrooke Canadiens

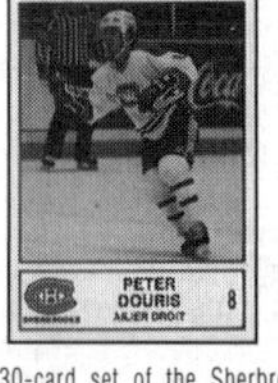

This 30-card set of the Sherbrooke Canadiens of the AHL was produced by Graphique Estrie, Inc. The cards feature action photos on the front, surrounded by a white border. The team logo, player name and sweater name appear along the bottom, along with the position in French. These unnumbered cards are listed below in alphabetical order.

COMPLETE SET (30) 4.00 10.00
1 Entraineurs 1986-87 .04 .10
2 Soigneurs 1986-87 .04 .10
3 Coupe Stanley 1986 .20 .50
4 Joel Baillargeon .16 .40
5 Daniel Berthiaume .30 .75
6 Serge Boisvert .16 .40
7 Graeme Bonar .16 .40
8 Randy Bucyk .16 .40
9 Bill Campbell .16 .40
10 Jose Charbonneau .16 .40
11 Rejean Cloutier .16 .40
12 Bobby Dollas .16 .40
13 Peter Douris .16 .40
14 Steven Fletcher .16 .40
15 Perry Ganchar .16 .40
16 Luc Gauthier .16 .40
17 Randy Gilhen .16 .40
18 Scott Harlow .16 .40
19 Rick Hayward .16 .40
20 Kevin Houle .16 .40
21 Rick Knickle .30 .75
22 Vincent Riendeau .30 .75
23 Guy Rouleau .16 .40
24 Scott Sandelin .16 .40
25 Karel Svoboda .16 .40
26 Peter Taglianetti .16 .40
27 Gilles Thibaudeau .16 .40
28 Ernie Vargas .16 .40
29 Andre Villeneuve .16 .40
30 Brian Williams .16 .40

2000-01 Sherbrooke Castors

This set features the Castors of the QMJHL and was produced by CTM- Ste-Foy. They were made available through that card shop, as well as at the team's home games. Although the set is numbered to 23, it apparently contains just 19 cards. It's not known whether certain cards were pulled, or never produced.

COMPLETE SET (19) 3.60 10.00
1 Drew MacIntyre .20 .75
2 Sebastien Courcelles .20 .50
3 Simon Tremblay .20 .50
4 Eric Lavigne .20 .50
5 Patrick Gosselin .20 .50
6 Steve Morency .20 .50
7 Francis Trudel .20 .50
9 Jonathan Robert .20 .50
11 Eric Dagenais .20 .50
12 Louis-Philip Lemay .20 .75
13 Artem Trmavski .20 .50
14 Joey Neale .20 .50
15 Benoit Genesse .20 .50
16 Pierre-Luc Courchesne .20 .50
17 Mathieu Thibodeau .20 .50
18 Nicolas Corbeil .40 1.00
21 Francois Belanger .20 .50
22 Cajou MAS .04 .10
23 Jos Canale CO .20 .50

2000-01 Sherbrooke Castors Signed

This set is exactly the same as the base Castors set from this season, save that every card has been hand signed by the player pictured. Each card also is serial numbered out of just 100.

COMPLETE SET (19) 16.00 40.00
1 Drew MacIntyre 1.00 5.00
2 Sebastien Courcelles 1.00 2.50
3 Simon Tremblay 1.00 2.50
4 Eric Lavigne 1.00 2.50
5 Patrick Gosselin 1.00 2.50
6 Steve Morency 1.00 2.50
7 Francis Trudel 1.00 2.50
9 Jonathan Robert 1.00 2.50
11 Eric Dagenais 1.00 2.50
12 Louis-Philip Lemay 1.00 5.00
13 Artem Trmavski 1.00 2.50
14 Joey Neale 1.00 2.50
15 Benoit Genesse 1.00 2.50
16 Pierre-Luc Courchesne 1.00 2.50
17 Mathieu Thibodeau 1.00 2.50
18 Nicolas Corbeil 2.00 5.00
21 Francois Belanger 1.00 2.50
22 Cajou MAS .04 .10
23 Jos Canale CO 1.00 2.50

2001-02 Sherbrooke Castors

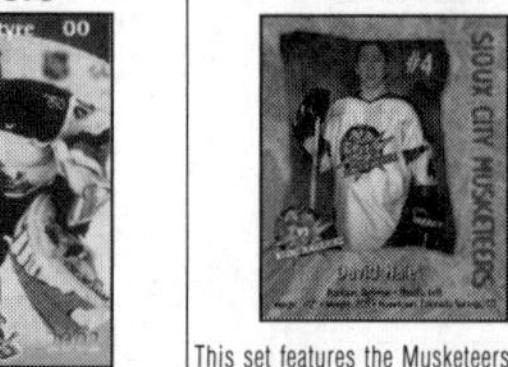

This set features the Castors of the QMJHL. The set was produced by CTM Ste-Foy and was sold at Castors home games. It was reported that less than 1,000 sets were produced.

COMPLETE SET (21) 4.80 12.00
1 Drew MacIntyre .30 .75
2 Eric Dagenais .20 .50
3 Dany Roussin .20 .50
4 Juha-Pekka Ketola .20 .50
5 Patrik Levesque .20 .50
6 David Chicoine .20 .50
7 Jonathan Paiement .20 .50
8 Cedrick Duhamel .20 .50
9 Yan Gaudette .20 .50
10 Francis Trudel .20 .50
11 Maxime Boisclair .30 .75
12 Jonathan Robert .20 .50
13 Mathieu Wathier .20 .50
14 Louis-Philip Lemay .30 .75
15 Bertrand-Pierre Plouffe .30 .75
16 Sebastien Courcelles .20 .50
17 Patrick Mbaraga .20 .50
18 Pierre-Luc Courchesne .20 .50
19 Nicolas Corbeil .40 1.00
20 Bruno D'Amico .20 .50
21 Francois Belanger .20 .50

1993-94 Sherbrooke Faucons

Recently confirmed set features unnumbered cards. They are listed below by jersey number.

COMPLETE SET 6.00 15.00
1 Jocelyn Thibault 2.00 5.00
2 Mathieu Dandenault .40 1.00
3 Christian Dube .20 .50
4 Luc Belanger .20 .50
5 Dany Larochelle .20 .50
6 Charles Paquette .20 .50
7 Daniel Villeneuve .20 .50
8 Etienne Beaudry .20 .50
9 Jean-Francois Boutin .20 .50
10 Lachlan Coombe .20 .50
11 Pascal Trepanier .30 .75
12 Dave Douville .20 .50
13 Stephane Larocque .20 .50
14 Eric Messier .30 .75
15 Francois Archambault .20 .50
16 Stephane Julien .20 .50
17 Dave Belliveau .20 .50
18 Hugo Turcotte .20 .50
19 Rocco Anoia .20 .50
20 Carl Fleury .30 .75
21 Mirko Langlois .20 .50
22 Hugo Hamelin .20 .50
23 Steven Low .20 .50
24 Aloucou MASCOT .02 .10
25 Guy Chouinard HCO .10 .25
26 Mario Durocher ACO .02 .10

1974-75 Sioux City Musketeers

This 20-card set is printed on yellow stock. According to the producer, the cards were intended to be standard size but actually came out a little larger. The fronts feature bordered, posed player photos that have a dark green tint to them. In dark green lettering, the team name is printed above the picture while the player's name is printed below it. The cards are unnumbered and checklisted below in alphabetical order. Reportedly only 250 sets were made and they were originally sold at home games for $2.50.

COMPLETE SET (20) 50.00 100.00
1 Steve Boyle 2.50 5.00
2 Dave Davies 2.50 5.00
3 Steve Desloges 2.50 5.00
4 Greg Gilbert 2.50 5.00
5 Barry Head 2.50 5.00
6 Steve Heathwood 2.50 5.00
7 Dave Kartio 2.50 5.00
8 Ralph Kloiber 2.50 5.00
9 Pete Maxwell 2.50 5.00
10 Randy McDonald 2.50 5.00
11 Terry Mulroy 2.50 5.00
12 Sam Nelligan 2.50 5.00
13 Julian Nixon 2.50 5.00
14 Mike Noel 2.50 5.00
15 Jim Peck 2.50 5.00
16 Bogdan Podwysocki 2.50 5.00
17 John Saville P/CO 2.50 5.00
18 Alex Shibicky Jr. 5.00 10.00
19 Bob Thomerson 2.50 5.00
20 Jim White 5.00 10.00

1998-99 Sioux City Musketeers

This set features the Musketeers of the USHL. The oversized (5X6) cards feature an action photo and bio info on the front, along with a blank back. They were issued by the team and sold at the rink. The set is noteworthy for featuring top prospects Rostislav Klesla, David Hale and Ruslan Fedotenko. The set is unnumbered and listed below alphabetically.

COMPLETE SET (25) 8.00 15.00
1 Lee Arnold .16 .50
2 Michael Betz .16 .50
3 Mark Bry .16 .50
4 Chad Dahlen .16 .50
5 Ruslan Fedotenko .80 2.00
6 Cullen Flaherty .16 .50
7 David Hale .40 1.00
8 Tim Judy .16 .50
9 Rostislav Klesla 4.00 5.00
10 Nathan Kotewa .16 .50
11 A.J. Kratofil .16 .50
12 Jordan Lashmett .16 .50
13 Brendan McCartin .16 .50
14 Jake Moreland .16 .50
15 Trent Mozak .16 .50
16 Chad Nordhagen .16 .50
17 Pat O'Leary .16 .50
18 Chris Olsgard .16 .50
19 Tyler Palmiscno .16 .50
20 Luke Pavlas .30 .75
21 Morgan Roach .16 .50
22 Tim Skarperud .16 .50
23 Jeff Van Dyke .16 .50
24 Adam Wallace .16 .50
25 B.J. Willis .16 .50

1999-00 Sioux City Musketeers

This set features the Musketeers of the USHL. It is believed the set was produced by the team and sold at its souvenir stands. The set is noteworthy for including the first card of David Hale, a 2000 first-round choice of the New Jersey Devils.

COMPLETE SET (21) 4.00 10.00
1 Mike Betz .20 .50
2 Max Bull .20 .50
3 Matt Ciancio .20 .50
4 Chad Dahlen .20 .50
5 Henry Dryden .20 .50
6 Lukas Fiala .20 .50
7 David Hale .40 1.00
8 Eric Helstedt .20 .50
9 Justin Hillier .20 .50
10 Steve Jones .20 .50
11 Tim Judy .20 .50
12 A.J. Kratofil .20 .50
13 Brendan McCartin .20 .50
14 John Miller .20 .50
15 Trent Mozak .20 .50
16 Chad Nordhagen .20 .50
17 Chris Olsgard .20 .50
18 Tyler Palmiscno .20 .50
19 Scott Palaski .20 .50

20 Brandon Schmitt .20 .50
21 Jeff Van Dyke .20 .50

2000-01 Sioux City Musketeers

This set features the Musketeers of the USHL. Little is known about the set beyond the confirmed checklist. Additional information can be forwarded to hockeymag@beckett.com.

COMPLETE SET (30) 8.00 20.00
1 Cover Card .04 .10
2 Casey Beauvais .30 .75
3 Matt Ciancio .30 .75
4 Dan Cohen .30 .75
5 Jeff Van Dyke .30 .75
6 Dan Fallon .30 .75
7 Arthur Femenella .30 .75
8 Matt Fetzer .30 .75
9 Justin Fletcher .30 .75
10 Ryan Geris .30 .75
11 Brent Halverson .30 .75
12 Fred Harbinson CO .10 .25
13 Tim Judy .30 .75
14 Erik Johnson .30 .75
15 Brian Kerr .30 .75
16 Zechariah Klann .30 .75
17 Patrick Knutson .30 .75
18 Jack Kowal CO .10 .25
19 Brendan McCartin .30 .75
20 Trent Mozak .30 .75
21 Brian Panik .30 .75
22 Scott Polaski .30 .75
23 Brandon Schmitt .30 .75
24 Brandon Schwartz .30 .75
25 Dave Siciliano CO .10 .25
26 Bryan Smith .30 .75
27 Mitch Thortsen .30 .75
28 Aaron Venasky .30 .75
29 David Vychodil .30 .75
30 John Zeiler .30 .75

2004-05 Sioux City Musketeers

COMPLETE SET (30) 8.00 20.00
1 Brian Bales .30 .75
2 Justin Bostrom .30 .75
3 Kent Bostrom .30 .75
4 Chris Butler .30 .75
5 John Cartera .30 .75
6 Joe Charlebois .30 .75
7 Adam Davis .30 .75
8 Phil DeSimone .30 .75
9 Corey Elkins .30 .75
10 Steve Kampfer .30 .75
11 Nick Kemp .30 .75
12 Tim Kennedy .30 .75
13 Peter Lenes .30 .75
14 Louis Liotti .30 .75
15 Blake Martin .30 .75
16 Dennis McCauley .60 1.50
17 Josh Meyers .30 .75
18 Christian Minella UER .30 .75
19 Jon Ralph .30 .75
20 Chris Spicer .30 .75
21 Jimmy Spratt .60 1.50
22 Travis Turnbull .30 .75
23 Jeff Zatkoff .60 1.50
24 Team Picture .30 .75
25 Schedule .02 .10
26 Mascot .02 .10
27 Dave Siciliano CO .02 .10
28 Marty Quarters ACO .02 .10
29 Chris Brandenberger TR .02 .10
30 Bill Danderand EQM .02 .10

2000-01 Sioux Falls Stampede

Set was produced by the team and sponsored by Wells Fargo Bank. The cards are oversized (5" X 6"). The cards are unnumbered and are listed alphabetically. The checklist may be incomplete. If you know of other cards, please contact us at hockeymag@beckett.com.

COMPLETE SET (21) 10.00 25.00
1 Robbie Barker .30 .75
2 J.B. Bittner .30 .75
3 Jon Booras .30 .75
4 Kellen Briggs .30 .75
5 Jeff Corey .30 .75
6 Donny DeMars .30 .75
7 Mike Doyle .30 .75
8 Jon Dubel .30 .75
9 John Funk .30 .75
10 Dave Iannazzo .30 .75
11 Joe Jensen .30 .75
12 Josh Grahn .30 .75
13 Dustan Lick .30 .75
14 James Massen .30 .75
15 Jamie Mattie .30 .75
16 Zach Sikich .30 .75
17 Dinos Stamoulis .30 .75
18 Thomas Vanek 4.00 10.00
19 Eric Werner .30 .75
20 Tom Zaleski .30 .75
21 Stomp MASCOT .02 .10

2001-02 Sioux Falls Stampede

These cards are unnumbered. They measure 5 X 6. The set features the first card of Marty Sertich, the 2005 Hobey Baker winner.

COMPLETE SET (19) 10.00 25.00
1 Cody Blanshan .30 .75
2 Kellen Briggs .75 2.00
3 Mike Forconi .30 .75
4 Alex Foster .30 .75
5 Quinn Fylling .60 1.50
6 Joe Jensen .30 .75
7 Jacob Micflikier .30 .75
8 Jason Moul .30 .75
9 Eric Przepiorka .30 .75
10 Layne Sedevie .40 1.00
11 Marty Sertich 1.50 4.00
12 Jeremy Smith .30 .75
13 Jesse Stokke .30 .75
14 Kelly Sullivan .30 .75
15 Thomas Vanek 3.00 8.00
16 Mike Vannelli .30 .75
17 Merit Waldrop .30 .75
18 Jake Wilkens .30 .75
19 Chris Wothe .30 .75

2004-05 Sioux Falls Stampede

Set features the Stampede of the USHL. They measure 3"x 4" and are unnumbered. They were issued on four six-card perforated sheets. Set includes 2005 first-rounder T. J. Oshie and Patrick Mullen, son of HOFer Joe Mullen. Thanks to collector Dale Spengler for the list.

COMPLETE SET (24) 15.00 30.00
1-1 Andrew Carroll .40 1.00
1-2 Tom Gorowsky .40 1.00
1-3 Nate Prosser .40 1.00
1-4 Greg Barrett .75 2.00
1-5 Ryan Thang .40 1.00
1-6 T.J. Oshie 2.00 5.00
2-1 Chris Peluso .40 1.00
2-2 Stewart Carlin .40 1.00
2-3 Aleksanders Jerofejevs .40 1.00
2-4 Joe Vitale .40 1.00
2-5 Justin White .40 1.00
2-6 Andreas Nodl .40 1.00
3-1 Evan Stephens .40 1.00
3-2 Warren Byrne .40 1.00
3-3 Joe Finley .75 2.00
3-4 John Murray .75 2.00
3-5 Ben Holmstrom .40 1.00
3-6 Blake Friesen .40 1.00
4-1 Justin Milo .40 1.00
4-2 Jacob Hipp .40 1.00
4-3 Jon Globke .40 1.00
4-4 Patrick Mullen .75 2.00
4-5 Buffalo Wild Wings ad .02 .10
4-6 Brandon Harrington .40 1.00

2006-07 Sioux Falls Stampede

COMPLETE SET (24) 12.00 20.00
1 Brad Malone .40 1.00
2 Patrick Tiesling .40 1.00
3 Drew Fisher .40 1.00
4 Ryan Guentzel .40 1.00
5 David Grun .40 1.00
6 Matt Lundin .75 2.00
7 Joey Miller .40 1.00
8 David Solway .40 1.00
9 Eric Peterson .40 1.00
10 Robbie Vrolyk .40 1.00
11 Doug SchuellerÂ ACO .10 .25
12 Nick Dineen .40 1.00
13 Stu Bickel .40 1.00
14 Jake Bauer .40 1.00
15 Sam Zabkowicz .40 1.00
16 Zach Redmond .40 1.00
17 Chris Huxley .40 1.00
18 Zach Hansen .40 1.00
19 Dan Sexton .40 1.00
20 Stomp Mascot .02 .10
21 Alexi Dostoinov .40 1.00
22 Jake Drewiske .40 1.00
23 Kevin HartzellÂ CO .10 .25
24 Corey Tropp .75 2.00

2001-02 Sorel Royaux

This set features the Royaux of the Quebec Senior League. The cards are standard sized and, because they are unnumbered, are listed below alphabetically. Note: the Patrick Roy listed below is not the famous NHL goaltender.

COMPLETE SET (28) 4.80 12.00
1 Daniel Archambault .20 .50
2 Francois Bourdeau .20 .50
3 Michel Caron .20 .50
4 L.P. Charbonneau .20 .50
5 Georges-Etienne Cote .20 .50
6 Dany Couette .20 .50
7 Christian Deschenes .20 .50
8 Stephane Groleau .20 .50
9 Eric Joyal .20 .50
10 Patrick Labrecque .40 1.00
11 Martin Lacroix .20 .50
12 Stephane Larocque .20 .50
13 Jamie Leinhos .20 .50
14 Justin Leinhos .20 .50
15 Yanick Levesque GM .04 .10
16 Dominic Maltais .40 1.00
17 Francois Paquette .20 .50
18 Guillaume Rodrigue .20 .50
19 Patrick Roy .20 .50
20 Carl St. Germain .20 .50
21 Yannick Theriault .20 .50
22 Dan Tice .20 .50
23 Steve Vincent .20 .50
24 Sponsor Card .04 .10
25 Coaching Staff .04 .10
26 Rink Staff .04 .10
27 Team Photo .20 .50
28 History Card .20 .50

1995-96 South Carolina Stingrays

This 24-card set of the South Carolina Stingrays of the ECHL was produced for the team by Multi-Ad Services. The set was distributed through the team as well. The fronts feature a blurry action photo, along with team and player name. The numbered backs include a portrait and stats.

COMPLETE SET (24) 3.60 9.00
1 Rick Vaive CO .20 .50
2 Dan Wiebe ACO .04 .10
3 Joseph Cramp TR .04 .10
4 Aaron Fackler EQMG .04 .10
5 Mikhail Volkov .16 .40
6 Jason Cipolla .16 .40
7 Mike Ross .16 .40
8 Rob Concannon .16 .40
9 Dan Fournel .16 .40
10 Mark Bavis .16 .40
11 Darren Ritchie .16 .40
12 Mike Barrie .16 .40
13 Marc Tardif .16 .40
14 Chris Foy .16 .40
15 Scott Boston .20 .50
16 Carl LeBlanc .16 .40
17 Brett Marietti .16 .40
18 Jared Bednar .16 .40
19 Paul Rushforth .16 .40
20 Kevin Knopp .16 .40
21 Todd Sullivan .20 .50
22 Justin Duberman .16 .40
23 Sean Gauthier .20 .50
24 Mark Rupnow .16 .40
NNO Header Card .04 .10

1996-97 South Carolina Stingrays

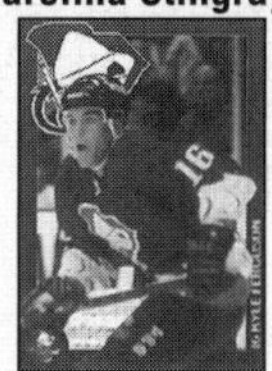

This 27-card set features the South Carolina Stingrays of the ECHL, and was produced by the team, in conjunction with Marvin Foy Marketing, Inc. The cards feature action photography on the front, complemented by a pair of Stingrays logos on the left side, and the player's name along the lower right border. The back contains two more photos, as well as statistical and biographical data. The set is noteworthy for the rare inclusion of a card depicting a fight in progress (Dan Fournel). The cards boldly feature the player's sweater number on the back of the card, precipitating their numbering thusly below.

COMPLETE SET (28) 4.00 10.00
9 Mike Ross .16 .40
10 Marc Genest .16 .40
11 Dan Fournel .40 1.00
12 David Mayes .16 .40
14 David Seitz .16 .40
15 Jeff Romfo .16 .40
16 Kyle Ferguson .16 .40
17 Marc Tardif .16 .40
18 Steve Parson .16 .40
19 Doug Wood .16 .40
20 Scott Boston .30 .75
21 Rob Concannon .16 .40
22 Rob Butler .16 .40
24 Brett Marietti .16 .40
25 Jared Bednar .16 .40
27 Ed Courtenay .20 .50
28 Kevin Knopp .16 .40
29 Jay Moser .16 .40
30 Corey Cadden .16 .40
31 Jason Fitzsimmons .16 .40
33 Chris Hynnes .16 .40
35 Taras Lendzyk .16 .40
NNO Header card
NNO Rick Adduono ACO .04 .10
NNO Randy Page ANN .04 .10
NNO Aaron Fackler EQMG .04 .10
NNO Kenny Snider TR .04 .10
NNO Rick Vaive CO .20 .50

2001-02 South Carolina Stingrays

This set features the Stingrays of the ECHL. The set was handed out over the course of several games during the season. The cards are unnumbered and are listed below in alphabetical order.

COMPLETE SET (20) 12.00 30.00
1 Rick Adduono CO .20 .50
2 Jared Bednar .80 2.00
3 Ryan Brindley .60 1.50
4 Adam Calder .60 1.50
5 Marty Clapton .60 1.50
6 Jason Fitzsimmons ACO .20 .50
7 Alan Fyfe .60 1.50
8 Zach Ham .60 1.50
9 Jamie Hodson .80 2.00
10 Joel Irving .60 1.50
11 Trevor Johnson .60 1.50
12 Jody Lehman .60 1.50
13 Hugo Marchand .60 1.50
14 Brett Marietti .60 1.50
15 David Seitz .60 1.50
16 Jason Sessa .80 2.00
17 Paul Traynor .80 2.00
18 Buddy Wallace .60 1.50
19 Chris Wheaton .60 1.50
20 Brad Williamson .60 1.50

2002-03 South Carolina Stingrays

This set was sponsored by Mills Printing and was issued as a promotional giveaway at a Stingrays home game.

COMPLETE SET (24) 8.00 20.00
1 Peter Armbrust .40 1.00
2 Jeff Boulanger .40 1.00
3 Ryan Brindley .40 1.00
4 Adam Calder .40 1.00
5 Marty Clapton .40 1.00
6 Kirk Daubenspeck .60 1.50
7 Matt Desrosiers .40 1.00
8 Robin Gomez .60 1.50
9 Brent Henley .60 1.50
10 Curtis Huppe .40 1.00
11 Joel Irving .40 1.00
12 Mike Jickling .40 1.00
13 Trevor Johnson .40 1.00
14 Brett Marietti .40 1.00
15 Andy Powers .40 1.00
16 Aaron Schneekloth .40 1.00
17 David Seitz .40 1.00
18 Rod Taylor .40 1.00
19 Dean Weasler .40 1.00
20 Brad Williamson .40 1.00
21 Jason Fitzsimmons CO .10 .25
22 Jared Bednar ACO .10 .25
23 DJ Church TR .01 .05
24 Jocko Cayer EQM .10 .25

2002-03 South Carolina Stingrays RBI

COMPLETE SET (18) 8.00 20.00
205 Ryan Brinkley .40 1.00
206 David Brumby .60 1.50
207 Adam Calder .40 1.00
208 Marty Clapton .40 1.00
209 Matt Desrosiers .40 1.00
210 Kirk Daubenspeck .60 1.50
211 Robin Gomez .60 1.50
212 Brent Henley .60 1.50
213 Curtis Huppe .40 1.00
214 Joel Irving .40 1.00
215 Mike Jickling .40 1.00
216 Trevor Johnson .40 1.00
217 Brett Marietti .40 1.00
218 Andy Powers .40 1.00
219 Aaron Schneekloth .40 1.00
220 David Seitz .40 1.00
221 Rod Taylor .40 1.00
222 Brad Williamson .40 1.00

2003-04 South Carolina Stingrays

COMPLETE SET (16) 6.00 15.00
321 Chris Allen .40 1.00
322 Jeff Boulanger .40 1.00
323 David Brumby .60 1.50
324 Ed Courtenay .40 1.00
325 Kirk Daubenspeck .60 1.50
326 Robin Gomez .60 1.50
327 Curtis Huppe .40 1.00
328 Mike Jickling .40 1.00
329 Colin Johnson .40 1.00
330 Trevor Johnson .60 1.50
331 Jim Lorentz .40 1.00
332 Aaron Power .40 1.00
333 David Seitz .40 1.00
334 Shawn Skiehar .40 1.00
335 Steven Spencer .40 1.00
336 Kevin Spiewak .40 1.00

2005-06 South Carolina Stingrays

COMPLETE SET (16) 10.00 20.00
1 Matt Reid .75 2.00
2 Jeff Legue .75 2.00
3 Chick-Fil-A Cow .01 .01
4 Ticket Voucher Card .01 .01
5 Trevor Johnson .75 2.00
6 Robin Gomez .75 2.00
7 Maxime Daigneault 1.50 4.00
8 Ticket Voucher Card .01 .01
9 Cail McLean .75 2.00
10 Marty Clapton .75 2.00
11 Steve Spencer .75 2.00
12 Ticket Voucher Card .01 .01
13 Brad Parsons .75 2.00
14 Nate Kiser .75 2.00
15 Aaron Power .75 2.00
16 Ticket Voucher Card .01 .01

1989-90 Spokane Chiefs

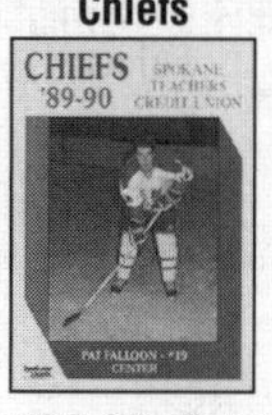

Sponsored by the Spokane Teachers Credit Union, this 20-card standard-size set of the 1989-90 Spokane Chiefs features color posed-on-ice player photos on its fronts. The photos are bordered in team colors (red, white, and blue). The player's name, uniform number, and position appear within the blue border below the picture. The cards are unnumbered and checklisted below in alphabetical order. Reportedly only 3,600 sets were made.

COMPLETE SET (20) 6.00 15.00
1 Mike Chrun .20 .50
2 John Colvin .20 .50
3 Shawn Dietrich .20 .50
4 Milan Dragicevic .20 .50
5 Frank Evans .20 .50
6 Pat Falloon .40 1.00
7 Scott Farrell .20 .50
8 Jeff Ferguson .20 .50
9 Travis Green 1.20 3.00
10 Mike Hawes .20 .50
11 Bobby House .20 .50
12 Mike Jickling .20 .50
13 Steve Junker .20 .50
14 Jon Klemm .40 1.00
15 Chris Rowland .20 .50
16 Dennis Saharchuk .20 .50
17 Kerry Toporowski .20 .50
18 Trevor Tovell .20 .50
19 Bram Vanderkracht .20 .50
20 Ray Whitney 1.20 3.00

1993-94 Spokane Chiefs

This set features the Chiefs of the WHL. The set was produced by the team and sold at home games for $5. The cards are unnumbered and so are listed below in alphabetical order.

COMPLETE SET (30) 6.00 15.00
1 Barry Becker .30 .75
2 Maxim Bets .20 .50
3 Valeri Bure .80 2.00
4 Shaun Byrne .20 .50
5 Joe Cardarelli .20 .50
6 John Cirjak .20 .50
7 Dion Darling .20 .50
8 Derek Descoteau .20 .50
9 Ryan Duthie .20 .50
10 Randy Favaro .20 .50
11 Craig Geekie .20 .50
12 Sean Gillam .20 .50
13 Hugh Hamilton .20 .50
14 David Jesiolowski .20 .50
15 Dmitri Leonov .20 .50
16 Bryan Maxwell CO .04 .10
17 Bryan McCabe .40 1.00
18 Memorial Cup Champs .20 .50
19 Rick More TR .04 .10
20 Jason Podollan .20 .50
21 Kevin Popp .20 .50
22 Kevin Sawyer .80 2.00
23 Trevor Shoaf .20 .50
24 Darren Sinclair .20 .50
25 Darren Smadis .30 .75
26 Jeremy Stasiuk .20 .50
27 Scott Townsend .20 .50
28 Spokane Coliseum .04 .10
29 Checklist .04 .10
30 Clover Club Cheerleaders .20 .50

1994-95 Spokane Chiefs

This set features the Chiefs of the WHL. The cards are standard-sized and were sold at home games. Any additional information can be forwarded to hockeymag@beckett.com.

COMPLETE SET (32) 6.00 15.00
1 Randy Favaro .20 .50
2 Jarrod Daniel .20 .50
3 Jason Podollan .31 .78
4 Trent Whitfield .31 .78
5 Greg Leeb .20 .50
6 Jay Bertsch .20 .50
7 Joe Cardarelli .20 .50
8 Robby Sandrock .20 .50
9 Kevin Sawyer .40 1.00
10 Sean Gillam .20 .50
11 Ryan Berry .20 .50
12 Mike Haley .20 .50
13 John Cirjak .20 .50
14 Jared Hope .20 .50
15 Joel Boschman .20 .50
16 Derek Descoteau .20 .50
17 Jeremy Stasiuk .20 .50
18 Tomas Pisa .20 .50
19 Darren Sinclair .20 .50
20 Paul Bailley .20 .50
21 Dmitri Leonov .20 .50
22 Bryan McCabe .40 1.00
23 Hugh Hamilton .20 .50
24 Scott Fletcher .20 .50
25 David Lemanowicz .31 .78
26 Mike Babcock CO .04 .11
27 Parry Schockey CO .04 .11
28 T.D. Forbes EQMG .04 .11
29 Ted Schott EQMG .04 .11
30 Veterans Memorial .04 .11
31 Veterans Memorial .04 .11
32 Veterans Memorial .04 .11

1995-96 Spokane Chiefs

This 30-card set features color player photos in a thin red border on a silver background. The backs carry player information.

COMPLETE SET (30) 4.80 12.00
1 David Lemanowicz .30 .75
2 Scott Fletcher .20 .50
3 Hugh Hamilton .20 .50
4 Chris Lane .20 .50
5 Dmitri Leonov .20 .50
6 Darren Sinclair .20 .50
7 Ty Jones .30 .75
8 Kris Graf .20 .50
9 Trent Whitfield .30 .75
10 Martin Cerven .30 .75
11 Randy Favaro .20 .50
12 Jason Podollan .30 .75
13 Joel Boschman .20 .50
14 Jared Hope .20 .50
15 Greg Leeb .20 .50
16 John Cirjak .20 .50
17 Mike Haley .20 .50
18 Ryan Berry .20 .50
19 Sean Gillam .20 .50
20 Derek Schutz .20 .50
21 Joe Cardarelli .20 .50
22 Adam Magarrell .20 .50
23 Jay Bertsch .20 .50
24 John Shockey .20 .50
25 Mike Babcock CO .16 .40
26 Parry Shockey ACO .04 .10
27 T.D. Forss EQMG .04 .10
28 Ted Schott AEQMG .04 .10
29 Dan Mitchell .04 .10
30 Aren Miller .30 .75

1996-97 Spokane Chiefs

This set features the Chiefs of the WHL. It is believed to have been produced and distributed by the team. Any additional information pertinent to this set can be forwarded to hockeymag@beckett.com.

COMPLETE SET (30) 6.00 15.00
1 Aren Miller .30 .75
2 Brad Ference .40 1.00
3 Hugh Hamilton .20 .50
4 Chris Lane .20 .50
5 Yegor Mikhailov .20 .50
6 Ty Jones .30 .75
7 Kris Graf .20 .50
8 Trent Whitfield .30 .75
9 Blake Evans .20 .50
10 Jared Smyth .20 .50
11 Joel Boschman .20 .50
12 Greg Leeb .30 .75
13 John Cirjak .20 .50
14 Mike Haley .20 .50
15 Kyle Rossiter .30 .75
16 Derek Schutz .40 1.00
17 Marian Cisar .80 1.00
18 Joe Cardarelli .20 .50
19 Adam Magarrell .20 .50
20 Jay Bertsch .20 .50
21 Curtis Suter .20 .50
22 Marc Brown .20 .50
23 Marc Magliarditi .30 .75
24 Boomer Mascot .04 .10
25 Mike Babcock HCO .04 .10
26 Brett Cox ACO .04 .10
27 T.D. Forss TR .04 .10
28 Ted Schott EM .04 .10
29 Dan Mitchell DRM .04 .10
30 Spokane All-Star Game .04 .10

1997-98 Spokane Chiefs

This set features the Chiefs of the WHL. It is believed to have been produced and distributed by the team. Any additional information pertinent to this set can be forwarded to hockeymag@beckett.com.

COMPLETE SET (30) 15.00
1 Aren Miller .30 .75
2 Brad Ference .30 1.00
3 Perry Johnson .20 .50
4 Mark Forth .20 .50
5 Zenith Komarniski .30 .75
6 Justin Ossachuk .20 .50
7 Cole Fischer .20 .50
8 Brandin Cote .20 .50
9 Ty Jones .30 .75
10 Kris Graf .20 .50
11 Trent Whitfield .30 .75
12 Jared Smyth .20 .50
13 Marc Brown .20 .50
14 Greg Leeb .30 .75
15 Justin Kelly .20 .50
16 Ben Johnson .20 .50
17 Kyle Rossiter .30 .75
18 Derek Schutz .30 .75
19 Marian Cisar .60 1.00
20 Lynn Loyns .20 1.00
21 Kris Waltze .20 .50
22 Curtis Suter .20 .50
23 Josh Maser .20 .50
24 Ron Grimard .20 .50
25 Dan Vandermeer .20 .50
26 Shaun Fleming .20 .50
27 Mike Babcock HCO .04 .10
28 Mike Pelino ACO .04 .10
29 T.D. Forss TR .04 .10
30 Dan Mitchell DRM .04 .10

1998-99 Spokane Chiefs

COMPLETE SET (28) 6.00 15.00
1 Mike Babcock CO .20 .50
2 Daniel Bohac .20 .50
3 Kris Callaway .20 .50
4 Brandin Cote .20 .50
5 Jeremy Farr .20 .50
6 Brad Ference .30 .75
7 Cole Fischer .20 .50
8 Mark Forth .20 .50
9 David Hajek .20 .50
10 Chris Harper .20 .50
11 David Haun .20 .50
12 Simon Jones .20 .50
13 Ty Jones .30 .75
14 Tim Krymusa .20 .50
15 Bobby Leavins .20 .50
16 Mike Lencucha .20 .50
17 Lynn Loyns .30 .75
18 Josh Maser .20 .50
19 Mike Pelino .20 .50
20 Kyle Rossiter .20 .50
21 Derek Schutz .20 .50
22 Cam Severson .40 1.00
23 Tim Smith .20 .50
24 Jared Smyth .20 .50
25 Curtis Suter .20 .50
26 Shawn Thompson .20 .50
27 Dan Vandermeer .20 .50
28 Mason Wallin .20 .50

1999-00 Spokane Chiefs

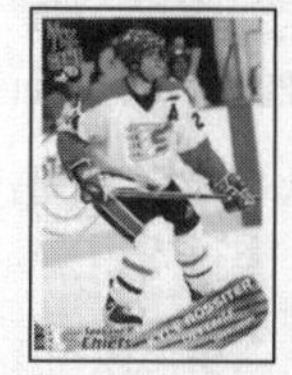

This set features the Chiefs of the WHL. It is believed that the cards were sold in set form by the team. The cards are unnumbered, and are listed below in alphabetical order.

COMPLETE SET (28) 12.00
1 Mike Babcock CO .10 .25
2 Chris Barr .20 .50
3 Daniel Bohac .20 .50
4 Boomer MASCOT .04 .10
5 David Boychuk .20 .50
6 Kris Callaway .20 .50
7 Brandin Cote .20 .50
8 Jeremy Farr .20 .50
9 T.D. Forss EQMG .04 .10
10 Chris Heid .20 .50
11 Matt Keith .20 .50
12 Tim Krymusa .20 .50
13 Mike Lencucha .30 .75
14 Lynn Loyns .30 .75
15 Jeff Lucky .20 .50
16 Tyler MacKay .20 .50
17 Dan Mitchell STAFF .04 .10
18 Bill Peters ACO .04 .10
19 Scott Roles .20 .50
20 Kyle Rossiter .40 1.00
21 Kurt Sauer .30 .75
22 Beau Schott EQMG .04 .10
23 Derek Schutz .20 .50
24 Tim Smith .20 .50
25 Shawn Thompson .20 .50
26 Ryan Thorpe .20 .50
27 Roman Tvrdon .20 .50
28 Mason Wallin .20 .50
29 Spokane Arena .04 .10

2000-01 Spokane Chiefs

This set features the Chiefs of the WHL. It is believed that the cards were sold in set form by the team. The cards are unnumbered and so are listed below in alphabetical order.

COMPLETE SET (30) 4.80 12.00
1 Chris Barr .20 .50
2 David Boychuk .20 .50
3 Barry Brust .30 .75
4 Brandin Cote .20 .50
5 Jevon Desautels .20 .50
6 T.D. Forss EQMG .04 .10
7 Perry Ganchar CO .04 .10
8 Chris Heid .20 .50
9 Barry Horman .20 .50
10 Joff Kehler .20 .50
11 Matt Keith .20 .50
12 Justin Keller .20 .50
13 Tim Krymusa .20 .50
14 Ratislav Lipka .20 .50
15 Lynn Loyns .20 1.00
16 Jeff Lucky .20 .50
17 Tyler MacKay .30 .75
18 Stephen Mann .20 .50
19 Dan Mitchell STAFF .04 .10
20 Chris Ovington .20 .50
21 Craig Perry .20 .50
22 Bill Peters ACO .04 .10
23 Kurt Sauer .30 .75
24 Brad Schell .20 .50
25 Tim Smith .20 .50

26 Shawn Thompson .20 .50
27 Ryan Thorpe .20 .50
28 Roman Tvrdon .20 .50
29 Mason Wallin .20 .50
30 Boomer MASCOT .04 .10

2001-02 Spokane Chiefs

COMPLETE SET (28) 5.00 12.00
1 Header Card .02 .10
2 Chris Barr .20 .50
3 David Boychuk .20 .50
4 Barry Brust .40 1.00
5 Jordan Clarke .20 .50
6 Brandin Cote .20 .50
7 Curtis Darling .40 1.00
8 Jevon Desautels .20 .50
9 Ivan Garcia .20 .50
10 Chris Heid .20 .50
11 Barry Horman .20 .50
12 Joff Kehler .20 .50
13 Matt Keith .30 .75
14 Stuart Kerr .20 .50
15 Chad Klassen .20 .50
16 Tim Krymusa .20 .50
17 Jeff Lucky .20 .50
18 Jeff Lynch .20 .50
19 Kurt Sauer .30 .75
20 Brad Schell .20 .50
21 Scott Scherger .20 .50
22 Mason Wallin .20 .50
23 Perry Ganchar CO .02 .10
24 Bill Peters ACO .02 .10
25 Dan Mitchell TR .02 .10
26 Darcy Bishop TR .02 .10
27 Boomer MASCOT .02 .10
28 Overagers .20 .50

2002-03 Spokane Chiefs

COMPLETE SET (30) 5.00 12.00
1 Chris Barr .20 .50
2 Ryan Blatchford .20 .50
3 Barry Brust .40 1.00
4 Liam Couture .20 .50
5 Andrew DeSousa .20 .50
6 Jevon Desautels .20 .50
7 Chris Heid .20 .50
8 Barry Horman .20 .50
9 Joff Kehler .20 .50
10 Chad Klassen .20 .50
11 Tim Krymusa .20 .50
12 Jakub Langhammer .20 .50
13 Darren Lefebvre .20 .50
14 Jeff Lucky .20 .50
15 Ned Lukacevic .20 .50
16 Doug Lynch .30 .75
17 Jeff Lynch .20 .50
18 Joel Rupprecht .20 .50
19 Brad Schell .20 .50
20 Andy Schenn .20 .50
21 Scott Scherger .20 .50
22 Miroslav Stolc .20 .50
23 Mason Wallin .20 .50
24 Jim Watt .20 .50
25 Colby Zavisha .20 .50
26 Al Conroy CO .02 .10
27 Jamie Huscroft ACO .02 .10
28 Dan Mitchell TR .02 .10
29 Boomer MASCOT .02 .10
30 Darcy Bishop TR .02 .10

2004-05 Spokane Chiefs Magnets

These cards have magnetic backs and were handed out one per night at Wednesday home games.
1 Gary Gladue .75 2.00
2 Jevon Desautels .75 2.00
3 Scott Lynch .75 2.00
4 Chad Klassen .75 2.00
5 Jim Watt .75 2.00
6 Ned Lukacevic .75 2.00
7 Gustav Engman .75 2.00
8 Jeff Lynch .75 2.00

1996-97 Springfield Falcons

This 21-card set was produced by Split Second. These unnumbered cards feature an action photo on the front with a stats package on the reverse. The cards were available through the club at the rink or by mail order.
COMPLETE SET (21) 4.00 10.00
3 Brent Thompson .30 .75
4 Deron Quint .30 .75
5 Steve Cheredaryk .16 .40
10 Kent Manderville .16 .40
11 Hnat Domenichelli .30 .75
12 Steve Martins .30 .75
14 Tom Buckley .16 .40
15 Juha Ylonen .30 .75
16 Chris Longo .16 .40
17 Rhett Gordon .16 .40
19 Tavis Hansen .16 .40
20 Steve Halko .16 .40
22 Scott Levins .16 .40
23 Rob Murray .16 .40
25 Jason McBain .16 .40
27 Jeff Daniels .16 .40
28 Ryan Risidore .20 .50
30 Manny Legace .60 1.50
33 Reggie Savage .16 .40
34 Nolan Pratt .20 .50
35 Scott Langkow .30 .75
44 Kevin Brown .16 .40
NNO AHL Ad Card .01

1997-98 Springfield Falcons

This set features the Falcons of the AHL. The set was produced by SplitSecond and was sold by the team at home games.
COMPLETE SET (26) 4.00 12.00
1 Daniel Briere .75 2.00
2 Ruslan Batyrshin .16 .40
3 Ted Crowley .16 .40
4 Sylvain Daigle .16 .40
5 Andrew Dale .16 .40
6 Shane Doan .40 2.00
7 Jason Doig .20 .50
8 Dan Focht .16 .40
9 Sean Gagnon .16 .40
10 Rhett Gordon .16 .40
11 Tavis Hansen .16 .40
12 Chad Kilger .30 .75
13 Scott Langkow .30 .75
14 Trevor Letowski .40 1.00
15 Scott Levins .20 .50
16 Richard Lintner .20 .50
17 Jason Morgan .16 .40
18 Rob Murray .16 .40
19 Mike Pomichter .16 .40
20 Jeff Shevalier .16 .40
21 Martin Simard .16 .40
22 Brad Tiley .16 .40
23 Dave Farrish CO .10 .25
24 Ron Wilson CO .10 .25
25 PHPA Web Site .01
26 AHL Web Site .01

2002-03 Springfield Falcons

COMPLETE SET (24) 6.00 15.00
1 Ramzi Abid .30 .75
2 Dmitry Afanasenkov .30 .75
3 Nikita Alexeev .40 1.00
4 Frank Banham .20 .50
5 Goran Bezina .20 .50
6 Zac Bierk .40 1.00
7 Jason Bonsignore .20 .50
8 Martin Cibak .20 .50
9 Dan Focht .20 .50
10 Corey Foster .20 .50
11 Martin Grenier .30 .75
12 Jason Jaspers .20 .50
13 Boyd Kane .40 1.00
14 Evgeny Konstantinov .30 .75
15 Kristian Kudroc .20 .50
16 Norm Maciver ACO .02 .10
17 Marty McSorley HCO .20 .50
18 Rob Murray .20 .50
19 Darren Rumble .20 .50
20 Michael Schutte .20 .50
21 Dan Smith .20 .50
22 Jeff Taffe .40 1.00
23 Erik Westrum .40 1.00
24 Shane Willis .20 .50

2003-04 Springfield Falcons Postcards

These singles were recently confirmed. If you have any additional information about this set, please contact us at hockeymag@beckett.com.
COMPLETE SET (28) 15.00 30.00
1 Goran Bezina .40 1.00
2 Trevor Gillies .40 1.00
3 Kiel McLeod .40 1.00
4 Erik Westrum .75 2.00
5 Dustin Wood .40 1.00
6 Igor Knyazev .40 1.00
7 Nikos Tselios .40 1.00
8 Martin Podlesak .40 1.00
9 Darren McLachlin .40 1.00
10 Frederik Sjostrom .40 1.00
11 Jason Jaspers .40 1.00
12 Bryan Helmer .40 1.00
13 Mike Stutzel .40 1.00
14 Peter Ferraro .40 1.00
15 Gary Shuchuk .40 1.00
16 Frank Lukes .40 1.00
17 Chris Ferraro .40 1.00
18 Chris Dyment .40 1.00
19 Frank Banham .75 2.00
20 Jean-Marc Pelletier .75 2.00
21 Mike Wilson .40 1.00
22 Ladislav Kouba .40 1.00
23 Jeremiah McCarthy .40 1.00
24 David LeNeveu .75 2.00
25 Michael Schutte .40 1.00
26 Marty McSorley CO .40 1.00
27 Gord Dineen ACO .20 .50
28 MASCOT .02 .10

2004-05 Springfield Falcons

COMPLETE SET (27) 6.00 15.00
1 Adam Henrich .20 .50
2 Andre Deveaux .20 .50
3 Andreas Holmqvist .20 .50
4 Brian Chapman .20 .50
5 Brian Eklund .30 .75
6 Craig Darby .20 .50
7 Darren Reid .20 .50
8 Dennis Packard .20 .50
9 Derek Bekar .20 .50
10 Doug O'Brien .20 .50
11 Evgeny Artukhin .20 .50
12 Gerard DiCaire .20 .50
13 Harlan Pratt .20 .50
14 Jamie Storr .30 .75
15 Jason Jaspers .20 .50
16 Marc Busenburg .20 .50
17 Mike Egener .20 .50
18 Mitch Fritz .40 1.00
19 Nick Tarnasky .40 1.00
20 Nikita Alexeev .20 .50
21 Nikos Tselios .20 .50
22 Paul Ranger .20 .50
23 Ryan Craig .75 2.00
24 Shane Willis .20 .50
25 Steve McLaren .20 .50
26 Phil Russell ACO .02 .10
27 Dirk Graham CO .02 .10

2005-06 Springfield Falcons

COMPLETE SET (27) 8.00 15.00
1 Adam Henrich .20 .50
2 Andre Deveaux .20 .50
3 Brad Tiley .20 .50
4 Brian Eklund .30 .75
5 Darren Reid .20 .50
6 Dennis Packard .20 .50
7 Doug O'Brien .20 .50
8 Evgeny Artyukhin .20 .50
9 Gerald Coleman .40 1.00
10 Gerard Dicaire .20 .50
11 Harlan Pratt .20 .50
12 Jason Jaspers .20 .50
13 Jim Campbell .20 .50
14 Marek Kvapil .20 .50
15 Mike Egener .40 1.00
16 Mitch Fritz .40 1.00
17 Nick Tarnasky .30 .75
18 Norm Milley .20 .50
19 Paul Ranger .20 .50
20 Steve McLaren .20 .50
21 Ryan Craig .40 1.00
22 Ryan Vesce .20 .50
23 Timo Helbling .20 .50
24 Todd Rohloff .20 .50
25 Dirk Graham CO .02 .10
26 Phil Russell ACO .02 .10
27 Darren Rumble ACO .02 .10

1983-84 Springfield Indians

Produced by Card Collectors Closet (Springfield, MA), this 25-card standard-size set features black-and-white player portraits on a white card face. The team name and year are printed in black at the top. The player's name and position appear at the bottom.
COMPLETE SET (25) 7.20 18.00
1 Gil Hudon .30 .75
2 Jim Ralph 1.20 3.00
3 Todd Bergen .30 .75
4 Len Hachborn .40 1.00
5 John Ollson .20 .50
6 Steve Tsujiura .40 1.00
7 Gordie Williams .20 .50
8 Dave Brown 1.20 3.00
9 Dan Frawley .20 .50
10 Tom McMurchy .20 .50
11 Dave Michayluk .30 .75
12 Bob Mormina .20 .50
13 Perry Pelensky .20 .50
14 Andy Brickley .40 1.00
15 Ross Fitzpatrick .20 .50
16 Florent Robidoux .20 .50
17 Jeff Smith .20 .50
18 Rod Willard .20 .50
19 Darrell Anholt .20 .50
20 Steve Blyth .20 .50
21 Don Dietrich .20 .50
22 Steve Smith .20 .50
23 Daryl Stanley .40 1.00
24 Taras Zytynsky .20 .50
25 Doug Sauter CO .20 .50

1984-85 Springfield Indians

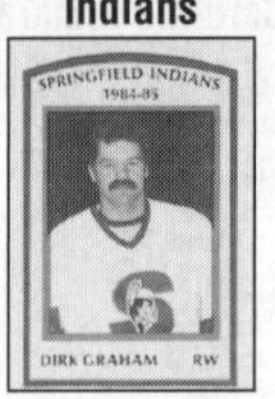

Produced by Card Collectors Closet (Springfield, MA), this 25-card standard-size set features black-and-white player portraits on a white card face. The team name and year are printed in black at the top. The player's name and position appear at the bottom. The pictures are framed by a royal blue border while a red border encloses the photo and the text.
COMPLETE SET (25) 6.00 15.00
1 Mike Sands .40 1.00
2 Lorne Molleken .20 .50
3 Todd Lumbard .20 .50
4 Randy Velischek .30 .75
5 David Jensen .30 .75
6 Ken Leiter .20 .50
7 Vern Smith .20 .50
8 Alan Kerr .30 .75
9 Scott Howson .20 .50
10 Tim Coulis .20 .50
11 Terry Tait .20 .50
12 Tim Trimper .20 .50
13 Rob Flockhart .30 .75
14 Ron Handy .20 .50
15 Jiri Poner .20 .50
16 Chris Pryor .20 .50
17 Dale Henry .20 .50
18 Mark Hamway .20 .50
19 Monty Trottier .20 .50
20 Miroslav Maly .20 .50
21 Dirk Graham 1.20 3.00
22 Roger Kortko .20 .50
23 Bob Bodak .20 .50
24 Lorne Henning CO .30 .75
25 Checklist Card .20 .50

2003-04 St. Georges de Beauce Garaga

This set was produced by Extreme Sports Cards. The Shantz card is incorrectly identified as Daniel Shank.
COMPLETE SET (20) 4.00 10.00
1 Philippe Audet .20 .50
2 Kevin Cloutier .20 .50
3 Philippe Deblois .20 .50
4 Raymond Delarosbil .20 .50
5 Jonathan Delisle .20 .50
6 Carl Fleury .20 .50
7 Francois Garand .20 .50
8 Steve Gosselin .20 .50
9 Jason Groleau .20 .50
10 Jean-Francois Labbe .20 .50
11 Daniel Laflamme .20 .50
12 Jean-Yves Leroux .20 .50
13 Dannick Lessard .20 .50
14 Claude Morin .20 .50
15 Normand Rochefort .20 .50
16 Paul Shantz UER .20 .50
17 Steve Tardif .20 .50
18 Hugo Turcotte .20 .50
19 Mathieu Vachon .20 .50
20 Frederic Vermette .20 .50

2004-05 St Georges de Beauce Garaga

COMPLETE SET (24) 6.00 15.00
1 Steve Tardif .30 .75
2 Jonathan Forest .30 .75
3 Paul Shantz .30 .75
4 Nicolas Poirier .30 .75
5 Claude Morin .30 .75
6 Raymond Delarosbil .30 .75
7 Martin Fillion .30 .75
8 Eric Bertrand .30 .75
9 David Lessard .30 .75
10 Jonathan Delisle .30 .75
11 Mathieu Vachon .30 .75
12 Tommy Bolduc .30 .75
13 Daniel Laflamme .30 .75
14 Kevin Cloutier .30 .75
15 Jean-Philippe Soucy .40 1.00
16 Mike Bajurny .60 1.50
17 Carl Paradis .30 .75
18 John Murphy .30 .75
19 Hugo Levesque .30 .75
20 Jason Rushton .30 .75
21 Didier Tremblay .30 .75
22 Rejean Dufour .30 .75
23 Brandon Christian .30 .75
24 Randy Copley .30 .75

1957-58 St. Catherine's Tee Pees

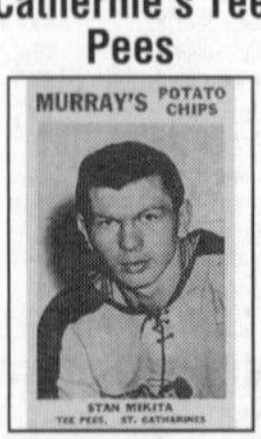

This set features the Tee Pees of the old OHA. The set features players who were in the Chicago Blackhawks farm system. The set is also known as the Murray's Potato Chips set, due to that name appearing on top of these undersized, black and white issues. The cards apparently were distributed in conjunction with the purchase of a bag of chips. The checklist is known to be incomplete, so no set price is listed. Any additional information can be forwarded to hockeymag@beckett.com. While the cards are numbered, we were able to confirm the numbering on just four of the eight singles. Until the rest of the numbering is confirmed, the remaining cards will be listed as NNOs.
1 Roy Edwards 20.00 40.00
16 Chico Maki 20.00 40.00
17 Don Grosso 10.00 20.00
18 Bob Corupe 10.00 20.00
NNO Matt Ravlich 15.00 30.00
NNO John McKenzie 30.00 60.00
NNO Stan Mikita 100.00 200.00
NNO Ed Hoekstra 15.00 30.00

1993-94 St. Cloud State Huskies

This set features the Huskies of the NCAA. The set was issued as a promotional giveaway at a single home game in the form of a large perforated sheet. The cards have traded hands in both complete and singles form, so both values are listed.
COMPLETE SHEET (30) 15.00
1 Randy Best .20 .50
2 Chad Brennan .20 .50
3 Neil Cooper .20 .50
4 Chris Dopp .20 .50
5 Marc Gagnon .20 .50
6 Sandy Gasseau .20 .50
7 Jay Geisbaur .20 .50
8 Tony Gruba .20 .50
9 Dave Holum .20 .50
10 Kelly Hultgren .20 .50
11 Jason Jiskra .20 .50
12 Eric Johnson .20 .50
13 P.J. Lepler .20 .50
14 Brett Lievers .20 .50
15 Billy Lund .20 .50
16 Mike Maristuen .20 .50
17 Chris Markstrom .20 .50
18 Taj Melson .20 .50
19 Brad Nelson .20 .50
20 Mike O'Connell .20 .50
21 Dave Paradise .20 .50
22 Dan Reimann .20 .50
23 Kelly Rieder .20 .50
24 Adam Rodak .20 .50
25 Gino Santerre .20 .50
26 Jeff Schmidt .20 .50
27 Grant Sjerven .20 .50
28 Coaching Staff .20 .50
29 Marc Gagnon IA .20 .50
30 Kelly Rieder IA .20 .50

2003-04 St. Cloud State Huskies

These cards were issued as a promotional giveaway at a late-season home game.
COMPLETE SET (31) 8.00 20.00
1 Casey Borer .30 .75
2 Tim Boron .40 1.00
3 Grant Clafton .30 .75
4 Tim Conboy .30 .75
5 Adam Coole .40 1.00
6 Mike Doyle .30 .75
7 Justin Fletcher .30 .75
8 Matt Gens .30 .75
9 Matt Hendricks .30 .75
10 Billy Hengen .30 .75
11 Brock Hooton .30 .75
12 Gary Houseman .30 .75
13 Dave Iannazzo .30 .75
14 Joe Jensen .30 .75
15 Ryan LaMere .30 .75
16 Garrett Larson .30 .75
17 Bille Luger .30 .75
18 Andy Lundbohm .30 .75
19 Brian McCormack .30 .75
20 T.J. McElroy .30 .75
21 Jason Montgomery .40 1.00
22 Colin Peters .30 .75
23 Nate Raduns .30 .75
24 Konrad Reeder .30 .75
25 Peter Szabo .30 .75
26 Nate Wright .30 .75
27 Craig Dahl CO .02 .10
28 Brad Willner ACO .02 .10
29 Fred Harbinson ACO .02 .10
30 Mascot .02 .10
31 Team Photo .10 .25

2004-05 St. Cloud State Huskies

Issued as a promotional giveaway. Cards are unnumbered so are listed below in alphabetical order.
COMPLETE SET (32) 10.00 25.00
1 Chris Anderson .40 1.00
2 Casey Borer .40 1.00
3 Tim Boron .40 1.00
4 Aaron Brocklehurst .40 1.00
5 Grant Clafton .40 1.00
6 Nate Dey .40 1.00
7 Mike Doyle .40 1.00
8 Justin Fletcher .40 1.00
9 Matt Francis .40 1.00
10 Sean Garrity .40 1.00
11 Matt Gens .40 1.00
12 Andrew Gordon .40 1.00
13 Matt Hartman .40 1.00
14 Billy Hengen .40 1.00
15 Brock Hooton .40 1.00
16 Gary Houseman .40 1.00
17 Dave Iannazzo .40 1.00
18 Joe Jensen .40 1.00
19 Ethan Lyerly .40 1.00
20 T.J. McElroy .40 1.00
21 Marty Mjelleli .40 1.00
22 Jason Montgomery .40 1.00
23 Nate Raduns .40 1.00
24 Konrad Reeder .40 1.00
25 Josh Singer .40 1.00
26 Matt Stephenson .40 1.00
27 Peter Szabo .40 1.00
28 Craig Dahl CO .10 .25
29 Fred Harbinson ACO .10 .25
30 Brad Willner ACO .10 .25
31 Sean Donley TR .10 .25
32 Jeremiah Minkel EQM .10 .25

2005-06 St. Cloud State Huskies

COMPLETE SET (33) 10.00 20.00
1 Chris Anderson .30 .75
2 Casey Borer .30 .75
3 Tim Boron .30 .75
4 Aaron Brocklehurst .30 .75
5 David Carlisle .30 .75
6 Grant Clafton .30 .75
7 Nate Dey .30 .75
8 Justin Fletcher .30 .75
9 Matt Francis .30 .75
10 Sean Garrity .30 .75
11 Bobby Goepfert .60 1.50
12 Andrew Gordon .30 .75
13 Matt Hartman .30 .75
14 Billy Hengen .30 .75
15 Brock Hooton .30 .75
16 Gary Houseman .30 .75
17 Joe Jensen .30 .75
18 Dan Kronick .30 .75
19 T.J. McElroy .30 .75
20 Marty Mjelleli .30 .75
21 Jason Montgomery .30 .75
22 Michael Olson .30 .75
23 Nate Raduns .30 .75
24 Konrad Reeder .30 .75
25 Josh Singer .30 .75
26 Matt Stephenson .30 .75
27 John Swanson .30 .75
28 Bob Motzko CO .02 .10
29 Fred Harbinson ACO .02 .10
30 Eric Rud ACO .02 .10
31 Bryan Demaine TR .02 .10
32 Jeremiah Minkel EQM .02 .10
33 Blizzard MASCOT .02 .10

2003-04 St. Francis Xavier X-Men

St. Francis plays in the CIS.
COMPLETE SET (30) 5.00 12.00
1 Ryan White .20 .50
2 Ryan Armstrong .20 .50
3 Stuart MacRae .20 .50
4 Wes Jarvis .20 .50
5 Mike Martone .20 .50
6 Bobby Reed .20 .50
7 Blake Robson .20 .50
8 Ben Berthiaume .20 .50
9 Troy Smith .20 .50
10 Mike Smith .20 .50
11 Danny White .20 .50
12 Graham Power .20 .50
13 Patrick Grandmaitre .20 .50
14 Dustin Russell .20 .50
15 Darren MacMillan .20 .50
16 Alan Dwyer .20 .50
17 Colin Circelli .20 .50
18 Dwayne Bateman .20 .50
19 Ryan Walsh .20 .50
20 Omar Ennaffati .20 .50
21 Eric Braff .20 .50
22 Mike Mole .40 1.00
23 Shawn Snider .20 .50
24 Chris Brannen .20 .50
25 Dallas Flaman .20 .50
26 Todd Norman .20 .50
27 Danny Flynn CO .02 .10
28 Greg MacDonald ACO .02 .10
29 John Kibyuk ACO .02 .10
30 Kyle MacIsaac ACO .02 .10

2004-05 St. Francis Xavier X-Men

COMPLETE SET (24) 5.00 12.00
1 Ryan Armstrong .20 .50
2 Eric Braff .20 .50
3 Collin Circelli .20 .50
4 Alan Dwyer .20 .50
5 Tyler Dyck .20 .50
6 Omar Ennaffati .20 .50
7 Patrick Grandmaitre .20 .50
8 Wes Jarvis .30 .75
9 Jim Kehoe .20 .50
10 Tyson Kellerman .20 .50
11 Matthew Lynn .20 .50
12 Ryan MacKay .20 .50
13 Stuart MacRae .20 .50
14 Darren McMillan .20 .50
15 Michael Mole .40 1.00
16 Graham Power .20 .50
17 Bobby Reed .20 .50
18 Blake Robson .20 .50
19 Mike Smith .20 .50
20 Shawn Snider .20 .50
21 Niko Tuomi .20 .50
22 Ryan Walsh .20 .50
23 Danny White .20 .50
24 Ryan White .20 .50

2003-04 St. Jean Mission

The Mission played in the LNAH, the Quebec semi-pro circuit. The cards were sold at home games.
COMPLETE SET (28) 6.00 15.00
1 Luc Bilodeau .20 .50
2 Murray Cobb .20 .50
3 Alain Cote .20 .50
4 Greg Davis .20 .50
5 Mario DeBenedictis .20 .50
6 Martin Dicaire .20 .50
7 Bobby Dollas .20 .50
8 Corey Foster .20 .50
9 Link Gaetz .75 2.00
10 Pierre Gendron .20 .50
11 Victor Gervais .20 .50
12 Daniel Guerard .20 .50
13 Hugo Hamelin .20 .50
14 Eric Lachapelle .20 .50
15 Steven Low .20 .50
16 Dominique Maltais .20 .50
17 Eric McIntyre .20 .50
18 Rob Murphy .20 .50
19 Charles Paquette .30 .75
20 Pierre Pelletier .20 .50
21 Jean-Francois Piche .20 .50
22 Guillaume Richard .20 .50
23 Sebastien Roger .20 .50
24 Christian Sbrocca .20 .50
25 Dan Tice .20 .50
26 Ronny Valenti .20 .50
27 Steve Vezina .30 .75
28 Dan Zimmerman .20 .50

1992-93 St. John's Maple Leafs

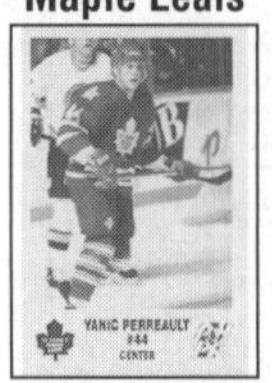

Measuring approximately 2 1/2" by 3 3/4", this 25-card set features the St. John's Maple Leafs of the American Hockey League. The fronts display color action player photos framed by white borders. In the wider bottom border, the player's name, uniform number, position, and logos are printed in black. The cards are unnumbered and checklisted below in alphabetical order.
COMPLETE SET (25) 4.00 10.00
1 Patrik Augusta .14 .35
2 Drake Berehowsky .20 .50
3 Robert Cimetta .14 .35
4 Marc Crawford CO .20 .50
5 Ted Crowley .14 .35
6 Mike Eastwood .30 .75
7 Todd Hawkins .14 .35
8 Curtis Hunt .14 .35
9 Eric Lacroix .20 .50
10 Guy Lehoux .14 .35
11 Kent Manderville .20 .50
12 Kevin McClelland .14 .35
13 Ken McRae .14 .35
14 Brad Miller .14 .35
15 Yanic Perreault .40 1.00
16 Rudy Poeschek .30 .75
17 Joel Quenneville ACO .10 .25
18 Damian Rhodes .40 1.00
19 Joe Sacco .14 .35
20 Jeff Serowik .14 .35
21 Scott Sharples .14 .35
22 Dave Tomlinson .14 .35
23 Nick Wohlers .14 .35
24 Team Photo .14 .35
25 Buddy (Mascot) .04 .10

1993-94 St. John's Maple Leafs

This 25-card standard-size set features the St. John's Maple Leafs of the American Hockey League. The fronts feature color action player photos with white borders and a gray shadow border. The team name "Leafs" in blue lettering edges the left side of the picture. The cards are unnumbered and checklisted below in alphabetical order.
COMPLETE SET (25) 4.00 10.00
1 Patrik Augusta .14 .35
2 Frank Bialowas .20 .50
3 Buddy (Mascot) .04 .10
4 Rich Chernomaz .14 .35
5 Terry Chitaroni .14 .35
6 Marcel Cousineau .20 .50
7 Marc Crawford CO .20 .50
8 Todd Gillingham .14 .35
9 Chris Govedaris .14 .35
10 Paul Holden .14 .35
11 Curtis Hunt .14 .35
12 Alexei Kudashov .14 .35
13 Eric Lacroix .40 1.00
14 Guy Lehoux .14 .35
15 Matt Mallgrave .14 .35
16 Grant Marshall .20 .50
17 Ken McRae .14 .35
18 Yanic Perreault .30 .75
19 Bruce Racine .20 .50
20 Damian Rhodes .40 1.00
21 Chris Snell .14 .35
22 Dan Stiver .14 .35
23 Andy Sullivan .14 .35
24 Ryan Vandenbussche .20 .50
25 Steffon Walby .14 .35

1994-95 St. John's Maple Leafs

This 24-card standard-size set was manufactured and distributed by Jessen Associates, Inc. for Classic. The fronts display color action player photos with a dark blue marbleized inner border and a black outer border. The player's name, jersey

number, and position appear in the teal border on the right edge. The cards are unnumbered and checklisted below in alphabetical order.

COMPLETE SET (24)	3.60	9.00
1 Patrik Augusta	.10	.25
2 Ken Belanger	.20	.50
3 Frank Bialowis	.40	1.00
4 Rich Chernomaz	.10	.25
5 Brandon Convery	.10	.25
6 Marcel Cousineau	.20	.50
7 Trent Cull	.10	.25
8 Nathan Dempsey	.20	.50
9 Kelly Fairchild	.20	.50
10 Janne Gronvall	.10	.25
11 David Harlock	.10	.25
12 Darby Hendrickson	.10	.25
13 Marc Hussey	.10	.25
14 Kenny Jonsson	.40	1.00
15 Mark Kolesar	.10	.25
16 Alexei Kudashov	.10	.25
17 Guy Lehoux	.10	.25
18 Guy Leveque	.10	.25
19 Matt Martin	.10	.25
20 Robb McIntyre	.10	.25
21 Bruce Racine	.20	.50
22 Ryan Vandenbussche	.30	.75
23 Steffon Walby	.10	.25
24 Todd Warriner	.20	.50

1995-96 St. John's Maple Leafs

This 25-card set of the St. John's Maple Leafs of the AHL was produced by Split Second for distribution by the team at home games and via mail order.

COMPLETE SET (25)	4.00	10.00
1 Team Photo	.16	.40
2 Ken Belanger	.30	.75
3 Rob Butz	.16	.40
4 Brandon Convery	.20	.50
5 Marcel Cousineau	.20	.50
6 Trent Cull	.16	.40
7 Nathan Dempsey	.16	.40
8 Kelly Fairchild	.16	.40
9 Brent Gretzky	.20	.50
10 Janne Gronvall	.16	.40
11 David Harlock	.20	.50
12 Jamie Heward	.20	.50
13 Mark Kolesar	.16	.40
14 Guy Lehoux	.16	.40
15 Kent Manderville	.30	.75
16 Kory Mullin	.16	.40
17 Jason Saal	.20	.50
18 Shayne Toporowski	.16	.40
19 Paul Vincent	.16	.40
20 Steffon Walby	.16	.40
21 Mike Ware	.16	.40
22 Todd Warriner	.30	.75
23 Tom Watt CO	.04	.10
24 Mike Foligno CO	.10	.25
25 Buddy -- Mascot	.04	.10

1996-97 St. John's Maple Leafs

This standard size set features color action photos on the front and backs are loaded with biographical information. The players name and position are featured in a triangle in the lower right corner of the card front. Cards are unnumbered and checklisted below in alphabetical order. This set was sponsored in part by the Royal Canadian Mounted Police.

COMPLETE SET (25)	4.00	10.00
1 Don Beaupre	.30	.75
2 Jared Bednar	.16	.40
3 Aaron Brand	.20	.50
4 Rich Brown CO	.16	.40
5 Buddy MAS	.04	.10
6 Greg Bullock	.16	.40
7 Rob Butz	.16	.40
8 Shawn Carter	.16	.40
9 Jason Cipolla	.16	.40
10 Brandon Convery	.20	.50
11 David Cooper	.16	.40
12 John Craighead	.16	.75
13 Trent Cull	.16	.40
14 Nathan Dempsey	.20	.50
15 Mark Deyell	.20	.50
16 Jamie Heward	.16	.40
17 Mark Hunter CO	.16	.40
18 Mark Kolesar	.20	.50
19 Guy Lehoux	.20	.50
20 Sgt. Randy Mercer	.16	.40
21 Jason Saal	.30	.75
22 Greg Smyth	.16	.40
23 Shayne Toporowski	.16	.40
24 Yannick Tremblay	.20	.50
25 Brian Wiseman	.16	.40

1997-98 St. John's Maple Leafs

This set features the Leafs of the AHL. It was produced by the team and sold at home games.

COMPLETE SET (25)	4.00	10.00
1 Kevyn Adams	.30	.75
2 Lonny Bohonos	.20	.50
3 Aaron Brand	.16	.40
4 Rich Brown ACO	.04	.10
5 Buddy	.04	.10
6 Shawn Carter	.16	.40
7 David Cooper	.16	.40
8 Marcel Cousineau	.30	.75
9 Nathan Dempsey	.16	.40
10 Mark Deyell	.20	.50
11 Todd Gillingham	.16	.40
12 Per Gustafsson	.16	.40
13 Mike Kennedy	.16	.40
14 Francis Larivee	.30	.75
15 Al MacAdam CO	.04	.10
16 Daniil Markov	.30	.75
17 Zdenek Markov	.16	.40
18 Clayton Norris	.16	.40
19 Warren Norris	.16	.40
20 Ryan Pepperall	.16	.40
21 Jason Podollan	.16	.40
22 D.J. Smith	.20	.50
23 Greg Smyth	.16	.40
24 Shawn Thornton	.16	.40
25 Jeff Ware	.16	.40

1999-00 St. John's Maple Leafs

This 25-card set features players of the St. John's Maple Leafs of the AHL. The front of the card features an action photo with the left edge colored purple and carrying the players last name and the team logo.

COMPLETE SET (25)	4.00	10.00
1 Kevyn Adams	.30	.75
2 Vladimir Antipov	.14	.35
3 Syl Apps	.14	.35
4 Jason Bonsignore	.20	.50
5 Aaron Brand	.14	.35
6 Craig Charron	.14	.35
7 Nathan Dempsey	.30	.75
8 Tyler Harlton	.14	.35
9 Justin Hocking	.14	.35
10 Bobby House	.14	.35
11 Konstantin Kalmikov	.20	.50
12 Alan MacAdam CO	.10	.25
13 Dennis Maxwell	.14	.35
14 David Nemirovsky	.20	.50
15 Adam Mair	.20	.50
16 Ryan Pepperall	.14	.35
17 Marek Posmyk	.20	.50
18 Marc Robitaille	.14	.35
19 Terry Ryan	.20	.50
20 Terran Sandwith	.14	.35
21 Darrin Shannon	.14	.35
22 D.J. Smith	.20	.50
23 Shawn Thornton	.14	.35
24 Jimmy Waite	.30	.75
25 Dimitri Yakushin	.14	.35

2000-01 St. John's Maple Leafs

This set features the Maple Leafs of the AHL. The set was produced by the team and sold at home games. The set also features five former AHL All-Stars who once toiled on the Rock.

COMPLETE SET (30)	4.80	12.00
1 Chad Allan	.14	.35
2 Syl Apps	.14	.35
3 Patrik Augusta	.20	.50
4 Buddy The Puffin MASCOT	.04	.10
5 Rich Chernomaz	.20	.50
6 David Cooper	.14	.35
7 Lou Crawford CO	.10	.25
8 Nathan Dempsey	.30	.75
9 Jeff Farkas	.30	.75
10 Mikael Hakanson	.14	.35
11 Tyler Harlton	.14	.35
12 Bobby House	.14	.35
13 Konstantin Kalmikov	.30	.75
14 Jacques Lariviere	.14	.35
15 Don MacLean	.20	.50
16 Adam Mair	.20	.50
17 Kevin McClelland CO	.10	.25
18 Mike Minard	.14	.35
19 Frank Mrazek	.14	.35
20 Yanic Perreault	.30	.75
21 Alexei Ponikarovsky	.30	.75
22 Felix Potvin	.40	1.00
23 Alan Rourke	.14	.35
24 D.J. Smith	.20	.75
25 Chris Snell	.14	.35
26 Shawn Thornton	.14	.75
27 Michal Travnicek	.14	.35
28 Jimmy Waite	.20	.75
29 Morgan Warren	.14	.35
30 Dmitri Yakushin	.14	.35

2001-02 St. John's Maple Leafs

This set features the Leafs of the AHL. The set was sold by the team at its souvenir stands. The set included a contest card that would allow winners to enjoy a special weekend at the AHL All-Star Game, held that season in St. John's. The cards are unnumbered, and are listed alphabetically.

COMPLETE SET (30)	7.20	18.00
1 Russ Adam ACO	.04	.10
2 Nikolai Antropov	.40	1.00
3 Francois Bouchard	.20	.50
4 Luca Cereda	.40	1.00
5 Christian Chartier	.20	.50
6 Lou Crawford CO	.10	.25
7 Nathan Dempsey	.30	.75
8 Doug Doull	.20	.50
9 Jeff Farkas	.40	1.00
10 Paul Healey	.20	.50
11 Bobby House	.20	.50
12 Jacques Lariviere	.20	.50
13 Donald MacLean	.20	.50
14 Kevin McClelland ACO	.10	.25
15 Craig Mills	.20	.50
16 Mike Minard	.30	.75
17 Frank Mrazek	.20	.50
18 Karel Pilar	.40	1.00
19 Alexei Ponikarovsky	.40	1.00
20 Alan Rourke	.20	.50
21 D.J. Smith	.40	1.00
22 Petr Svoboda	.20	.50
23 Mikael Tellqvist	1.20	3.00
24 Michal Travnicek	.30	.75
25 Morgan Warren	.20	.50
26 Marty Wilford	.30	.75
27 Bob Wren	.30	.75
28 Mile One Stadium	.04	.10
29 Buddy the Puffin MASCOT	.04	.10
30 All-Star Game PROMO	.04	.10

2001-02 St. John's Maple Leafs Police

Each card features a player and a local police officer. Banner across the top reads 'Clarenville Area Citizens' Crime Prevention'. These cards were given out one at a time at a sick childrens hospital about 175 miles from St.John's. Reportedly, just 100 of each card were produced.

COMPLETE SET (16)	15.00	30.00
1 Luca Cereda	.75	2.00
2 Christian Chartier	.75	2.00
3 Nathan Dempsey	1.25	3.00
4 Doug Doull	2.00	5.00
5 Jeff Farkas	.75	2.00
6 Paul Healey	.75	2.00
7 Bobby House	.75	2.00
8 Donald MacLean	.75	2.00
9 Craig Mills	.75	2.00
10 Mike Minard	.75	2.00
11 Alexei Ponikarovsky	1.25	3.00
12 Allan Rourke	.75	2.00
13 D.J.Smith	1.25	3.00
14 Petr Svoboda	.75	2.00
15 Morgan Warren	.75	2.00
16 Marty Wilford	.75	2.00

2002-03 St. John's Maple Leafs Aliant

The cards in this oversized set appear similar to a bookmark. The checklist is possibly incomplete. If you have additional info, please forward to hockeymag@beckett.com.

COMPLETE SET (6)	10.00
1 Doug Doull	2.00
2 Aaron Gavey	1.00
3 Mikael Tellqvist UER (Misspelled Mikeal	5.00
4 Brad Boyes	2.00
5 Josh Holden	1.00
6 Craig Mills	1.00

1996-97 St. Louis Vipers RHI

This 16-card set was originally supposed to be a 3-series issue, but printer problems forced the third series to be cancelled. The set (except for checklists and headers) is serial numbered out of 500.

COMPLETE SET (16)	75.00	125.00
1 Frank LaScala	.30	10.00
2 Russ Parent	.30	10.00
3 Jeff Beaudin	.30	10.00
4 Perry Turnbull HCO	.20	5.00
5 Chris Skoryna	.30	10.00
6 Chris Rogles	.40	15.00
7- Kevin Plager	.30	10.00
8 Wayne Anchikoski	.30	15.00
9 Vipers Record Holders	.20	10.00
10 Frank Cirone	.30	10.00
11 C.J. Yoder	.30	10.00
12 Victor Viper Mascot	.08	5.00
13 Series 1 Checklist	.08	5.00
14 Series 2 Checklist	.08	5.00
15 Series 1 Header	.08	5.00
16 Series 2 Header	.08	5.00

1952-53 St. Lawrence Sales

This 108-card black and white set put out by St. Lawrence Sales Agency featured members of the QSHL. The card backs are written in French. The cards measure approximately 1 15/16" by 2 15/16" and are numbered on the back. The key cards in the set are those of future (at that time) NHL greats Jean Beliveau and Jacques Plante. The complete set price includes both versions of card number 17.

COMPLETE SET (108)	700.00	1400.00
1 Jacques Plante	175.00	350.00
2 Glen Harmon	5.00	10.00
3 Jimmy Moore	5.00	10.00
4 Gerard Desaulniers	5.00	10.00
5 Les Douglas	5.00	10.00
6 Fred Burchell	6.00	12.00
7 Ed Litzenberger	7.50	15.00
8 Rollie Rousseau	5.00	10.00
9 Roger Leger	5.00	10.00
10 Phil Samis	5.00	10.00
11 Paul Masnick	6.00	12.00
12 Walter Clune	5.00	10.00
13 Louis Denis	5.00	10.00
14 Gerry Plamondon	6.00	12.00
15 Cliff Malone	5.00	10.00
16 Pete Morin	6.00	12.00
17A Jack Schmidt	6.00	12.00
17B Aldo Guidolin	10.00	20.00
18 Paul Leclerc	5.00	10.00
19 Larry Kwong	6.00	12.00
20 Rosario Joanette	5.00	10.00
21 Tom Smelle	5.00	10.00
22 Gordie Haworth	6.00	12.00
23 Bruce Cline	6.00	12.00
24 Andre Corriveau	5.00	10.00
25 Jacques Deslauriers	5.00	10.00
26 Bingo Ernst	5.00	10.00
27 Jacques Chartrand	5.00	10.00
28 Phil Vitale	5.00	10.00
29 Renald Lacroix	5.00	10.00
30 J.P. Bisaillon	5.00	10.00
31 Jack Irvine	5.00	10.00
32 Georges Bougie	5.00	10.00
33 Paul Larivee	5.00	10.00
34 Carl Smelle	5.00	10.00
35 Walter Pawlyschyn	5.00	10.00
36 Jean Marois	5.00	10.00
37 Jack Gelineau	5.00	10.00
38 Danny Nixon	5.00	10.00
39 Jean Beliveau	200.00	400.00
40 Phil Renaud	5.00	10.00
41 Leon Bouchard	5.00	10.00
42 Dennis Smith	5.00	10.00
43 Joe Crozier	7.50	15.00
44 Al Bacari	5.00	10.00
45 Murdo MacKay	6.00	12.00
46 Gordie Hudson	5.00	10.00
47 Claude Robert	5.00	10.00
48 Yogi Kraiger	6.00	12.00
49 Ludger Tremblay	6.00	12.00
50 Pierre Brillant	5.00	10.00
51 Frank Mario	5.00	10.00
52 Copper Leyth	5.00	10.00
53 Herbie Carnegie	20.00	50.00
54 Punch Imlach	20.00	40.00
55 Howard Riopelle	5.00	10.00
56 Ken Laufman	5.00	10.00
57 Jackie Leclair	7.50	15.00
58 Bill Robinson	5.00	10.00
59 George Ford	5.00	10.00
60 Bill Johnson	5.00	10.00
61 Leo Gravelle	5.00	10.00
62 Jack Giesebrecht	5.00	10.00
63 John Arundel	5.00	10.00
64 Vic Gregg	5.00	10.00
65 Bep Guidolin	7.50	15.00
66 Al Kuntz	5.00	10.00
67 Emile Dagenais	5.00	10.00
68 Bill Richardson	5.00	10.00
69 Bob Robertson	5.00	10.00
70 Ray Fredericks	5.00	10.00
71 James O'Flaherty	5.00	10.00
72 Butch Stahan	5.00	10.00
73 Roger Roberge	5.00	10.00
74 Guy Labrie	5.00	10.00
75 Gilles Dube	5.00	10.00
76 Pete Wywrot	5.00	10.00
77 Tod Campeau	6.00	12.00
78 Roger Bessette	5.00	10.00
79 Martial Pruneau	5.00	10.00
80 Nils Tremblay	5.00	10.00
81 Jacques Locas	5.00	10.00
82 Rene Pepin	5.00	10.00
83 Bob Pepin	5.00	10.00
84 Tom McDougall	5.00	10.00
85 Peter Wright	5.00	10.00
86 Ronnie Matthews	5.00	10.00
87 Irene St-Hilaire	5.00	10.00
88 Dewar Thompson	5.00	10.00
89 Bob Dainville	5.00	10.00
90 Marcel Pelletier	5.00	10.00
91 Delphis Franche	5.00	10.00
92 Georges Roy	5.00	10.00
93 Andy McCallum	5.00	10.00
94 Lou Smrke	5.00	10.00
95 J.P. Lamirande	5.00	10.00
96 Normand Dussault	5.00	10.00
97 Stan Smrke	6.00	12.00
98 Jack Bownass	5.00	10.00
99 Billy Arcand	5.00	10.00
100 Lyall Wiseman	5.00	10.00
101 Jack Hamilton	5.00	10.00
102 Bob Leger	5.00	10.00
103 Larry Regan	6.00	12.00
104 Erwin Grosse	5.00	10.00
105 Roger Bedard	5.00	10.00
106 Ted Hodgson	5.00	10.00
107 Dave Gatherum	7.50	15.00

2000-01 St. Michaels Majors

This set features the Majors of the OHL. The set was produced by the team and sold at its souvenir stands. The cards are unnumbered, so are listed in alphabetical order.

COMPLETE SET (27)	4.80	12.00
1 Team CL	.04	.10
2 Team Photo	.16	.40
3 Majors Review	.10	.25
4 Matt Bacon	.16	.40
5 Matt Bannan	.16	.40
6 Darryl Bootland	.16	.75
7 Chris Boucher	.16	.40
8 Tim Brent	.30	.75
9 Peter Budaj	.60	1.50
10 Dave Cameron CO	.10	.25
11 Andy Chiodo	.40	2.00
12 Tyler Cook	.16	.40
13 Adam Deleeuw	.30	.75
14 Matt Ellis	.16	.40
15 Steve Farquharson	.16	.40
16 Drew Fata	.30	.75
17 Michael Gough	.16	.40
18 Bob Jones CO	.04	.10
19 Kevin Klein	.16	1.00
20 Frantisek Lukes	.16	.40
21 Lorne Misita	.16	.40
22 Lindsay Plunkett	.16	.40
23 Mark Popovic	.40	1.00
24 T.J. Reynolds	.16	.40
25 Ryan Robert	.16	.40
26 Mike Sellan	.16	.40
27 Ryan Walsh	.16	.40

2001-02 St. Michaels Majors

Set was produced and sold by the team. The cards are unnumbered, and so are listed in order of jersey number.

COMPLETE SET (28)	6.00	15.00
1 Logo Checklist	.01	.05
2 Team Photo	.02	.10
3 Geoff Patton	.20	.50
4 Scott Heffernan	.20	.50
5 Tyson Gimblett	.20	.50
6 Steven Rawski	.20	.50
7 Kevin Klein	.30	.75
8 Mark Popovic	.30	.75
9 Tim Brent	.40	1.00
10 Drew Fata	.20	.50
11 Jordan Freeland	.20	.50
12 Jerrod Smith	.20	.50
13 Michael Gouch	.20	.50
14 Kyle Spurr	.20	.50
15 Ryan Rorabeck	.20	.50
16 Matt Bacon	.20	.50
17 Frantisek Lukes	.20	.50
18 Matt Ellis	.20	.50
19 Darryl Boyce	.20	.50
20 Daryl Knowles	.20	.50
21 Matt Seymour	.20	.50
22 Joe Guenther	.30	.75
23 Darryl Bootland	.30	.75
24 Peter Budaj	.60	1.50
25 Andy Chiodo	.75	2.00
26 Dave Cameron	.20	.50
27 Bob Jones	.20	.50
28 Mascot	.02	.10

2002-03 St. Michaels Majors

COMPLETE SET (28)	5.00	12.00
1 Justin Peters	.30	.75
2 Ted Perry	.15	.40
3 Martin Karafiat	.15	.40
4 Tyson Gimblett	.15	.40
5 Steven Rawski	.15	.40
6 Kevin Klein	.40	1.00
7 Nathan McIver	.15	.40
8 Tim Brent	.40	1.00
9 Drew Fata	.40	1.00
10 Scott Lehman	.15	.40
11 Scott Horvath	.15	.40
12 Chris Rebernik	.15	.40
13 Kyle Spurr	.15	.40
14 Ryan Rorabeck	.15	.40
15 Matt Bacon	.15	.40
16 Frantisek Lukes	.15	.40
17 Connor Cameron	.15	.40
18 Darryl Boyce	.15	.40
19 Alan Nolan	.15	.40
20 Matt Seymour	.15	.40
21 Cory Vitarelli	.15	.40
22 Darryl Knowles	.15	.40
23 Sal Peralta	.15	.40
24 Andy Chiodo	.75	2.00
25 Dave Cameron CO	.02	.10
26 Bob Jones CO	.02	.10
27 Mascot	.02	.10
28 Logo/CL	.01	.05

2003-04 St. Michael's Majors

Cards are unnumbered, so they're listed below in the order they appear on the checklist card.

COMPLETE SET (27)	5.00	12.00
1 Justin Peters	.30	.75
2 Ted Perry	.20	.50
3 Jamie Vanderveeken	.20	.50
4 Ryan Wilson	.20	.50
5 Nathan McIver	.20	.50
6 Tim Brent	.30	.75
7 Ryan Rorabeck	.20	.50
8 Chris Cunningham	.20	.50
9 Scott Lehman	.20	.50
10 Cal Clutterbuck	.40	1.00
11 Colin Power	.30	.75
12 Tyler Haskins	.20	.50
13 Brent Small	.20	.50
14 Ian Maracle	.20	.50
15 Conner Cameron	.20	.50
16 Richard Kelly	.20	.50
17 Thomas Waugh	.20	.50
18 Darryl Boyce	.20	.50
19 Joe Rand	.20	.50
20 Cory Vitarelli	.20	.50
21 Dustin Vanballegooie	.20	.50
22 Sal Peralta	.20	.50
23 Michael Ouzas	.30	.75
24 Dave Cameron CO	.02	.10
25 Bob Jones ACO	.02	.10
26 Mikey MASCOT	.02	.10
27 Checklist	.01	.05

2004-05 St. Michael's Majors

Cards are unnumbered and so are listed below in checklist order.

COMPLETE SET (24)	5.00	12.00
1 Justin Peters	.30	.75
2 Steve Whitely	.20	.50
3 Jamie Vanderveeken	.20	.50
4 Ryan Wilson	.20	.50
5 Dale Good	.20	.50
6 Nathan McIver	.20	.50
7 Matt Halischuk	.20	.50
8 John Adamsa	.20	.50
9 Chris Cunningham	.20	.50
10 Scott Lehman	.20	.50
11 Cal Clutterbuck	.30	.75
12 Colin Power	.20	.50
13 Tyler Haskins	.20	.50
14 Cassidy Preston	.20	.50
15 Justin DiBenedetto	.20	.50
16 Alexei Ivanov	.20	.50
17 Scott Levigne	.20	.50
18 Travis Elder	.20	.50
19 Darryl Boyce	.20	.50
20 Joe Rand	.20	.50
21 Cory Vitarelli	.20	.50
22 Jaroslav Mrazek	.20	.50
23 Wayne Savage	.20	.50
24 Checklist	.01	.05

2005-06 Stockton Thunder

COMPLETE SET (25)	6.00	15.00
1 Likit Andersson	.30	.75
2 Casey Bartzen	.30	.75
3 Landon Bathe	.30	.75
4 Derek Campbell	.30	.75
5 Aaron Foster	.30	.75
6 Nick Greenough	.30	.75
7 Joel Irwin	.30	.75
8 Tony Johnson	.30	.75
9 Jason Kostadine	.30	.75
10 Mike Lalonde	.30	.75
11 Aaron MacInnis	.30	.75
12 Nathan Martz	.30	.75
13 Dave McCulloch	.30	.75
14 Jason Metcalfe	.30	.75
15 Jake Moreland	.30	.75
16 Geno Parrish	.30	.75
17 Steve Slonina	.30	.75
18 Dean Stork	.30	.75
19 Jeff Weber	.30	.75
20 Maris Ziedins	.30	.75
21 Opening Night		.10
22 Chris Cichocki HC	.02	.10
23 Stockton Arena	.02	.10
24 Thor MASCOT	.02	.10
NNO Stockton Thunder CL	.02	.10

2006-07 Stockton Thunder

COMPLETE SET (25)	15.00	30.00
1 Jason Beckett	.75	2.00
2 Devan DubnykÂ	.75	2.00
3 Stephane Goulet	.40	1.00
4 Jeff Lang	.40	1.00
5 Fans Tribute Card	.02	.10
6 Beau Geisler	.40	1.00
7 Mike Lalonde	.40	1.00
8 Tim Sestito	.40	1.00
9 Tyler Spurgeon	.40	1.00
10 Thor MASCOT	.02	.10
16 Tim Verbeek	.75	2.00
17 Eric Main	.40	1.00
18 Bryan Young	.40	1.00
19 Jim Dahl	.40	1.00
20 Adam Huxley	.40	1.00
11a Troy Bodie	.40	1.00
11b Stephen Slonina	.40	1.00
12a Cam EllsworthÂ	.40	1.00
12b Liam Reddox	.40	1.00
13a Brendon Hodge	.40	1.00
13b Mark Adamek	.40	1.00
14a Nathan Martz	.40	1.00
14b Frank Rediker	.40	1.00
15a Chris Cichocki CO	.40	1.00
15b Tim O'Connell	.02	.10

1961-62 Sudbury Wolves

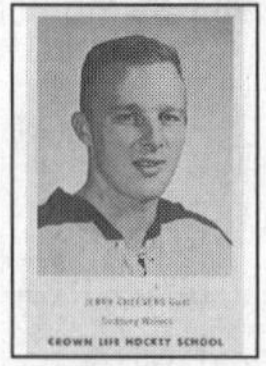

This 18-card set measures approximately 4" by 6 1/8" and features black-and-white player portraits with white borders. The player's name and position, the team name and the words "Crown Life Hockey School" appear under the photo. The backs are blank. The cards are unnumbered and checklisted below in alphabetical order.

COMPLETE SET (18)	62.50	125.00
1 Norm Armstrong	2.50	5.00
2 Ed Babiuk	2.50	5.00
3 Vern Buffey	2.50	5.00
4 Murph Chamberlain CO	2.50	5.00
5 Gerry Cheevers UER (misspelled Jerry)	25.00	50.00
6 Wally Chevrier	2.50	5.00
7 Marc Dufour	2.50	5.00
8 Edgar Ehrenverth	2.50	5.00
9 Bill Friday	3.50	7.00
10 Jim Johnson	2.50	5.00
11 Chico Kozuruk	2.50	5.00
12 Gord LaBossiere	3.50	7.00
13 Dunc McCallum	4.00	8.00
14 Dave McComb	2.50	5.00
15 Mike McMahon	2.50	5.00
16 Joe Spence	2.50	5.00
17 Ted Taylor	2.50	5.00
18 Bob Woytowich	3.50	7.00

1962-63 Sudbury Wolves

These 22 blank-backed cards measure approximately 4" by 6" and feature white-bordered, posed black-and-white studio head shots of Wolves players (Eastern Professional Hockey League). The player's name and position appear above the team name within the broad white bottom border. The imprint, "Crown Life Hockey School," rounds out the card at the bottom. The cards are unnumbered and checklisted below in alphabetical order.

COMPLETE SET (22)	37.50	75.00
1 Paul Andrea	2.50	5.00
2 Norm Armstrong	1.50	3.00
3 Ed Babiuk	1.50	3.00
4 Hub Beaudry ANN	.75	1.50
5 Vern Buffey REF	1.50	3.00
6 Murph Chamberlain CO	1.50	3.00
7 Gerry Cheevers UER (Misspelled Jerry on card front)	15.00	30.00
8 Wally Chevrier	1.50	3.00
9 Marc Dufour	2.00	4.00
10 Edgar Ehrenverth	1.50	3.00
11 Bill Friday REF	2.50	5.00
12 Jim Johnson	1.50	3.00
13 Chico Kozuruk TR	.75	1.50
14 Gord Labossiere	2.00	4.00
15 Dunc McCallum	4.00	8.00
16 Dave McComb	1.50	3.00
17 Hugh McLean REF	1.50	3.00
18 Mike McMahon	1.50	3.00
19 Dave Richardson	1.50	3.00
20 Joe Spence ANN	.75	1.50
21 Ted Taylor	1.50	3.00
22 Bob Woytowich	4.00	8.00

1984-85 Sudbury Wolves

This 16-card set measures approximately 3 1/2" by 6" and features color, action player photos accented by a hockey stick graphic design in white, green, gray, and red. The player's name and sponsor logos are printed on the design. A discount coupon for 2.50

off any children's admission to a game is attached at the bottom and can be torn along perforations. The card measures approximately 5 1/4" tall when the coupon is removed. The backs carry biographical information and sponsor logos. The cards are numbered on the front near the right edge.

COMPLETE SET (16)	6.00	15.00
1 Andy Spruce CO	.20	.50
2 Sean Evoy	.60	1.50
3 Mario Martini	.40	1.00
4 Brent Daugherty	.40	1.00
5 Mario Chitaroni	.40	1.00
6 Dan Chiasson	.40	1.00
7 Jeff Brown	.80	2.00
8 Todd Sepkowski	.40	1.00
9 Brad Belland	.40	1.00
10 Glenn Greenough	.40	1.00
11 John Landry	.40	1.00
12 Max Middendorf	.40	1.00
13 David Moylan	.40	1.00
14 Jamie Nadjiwan	.40	1.00
15 Warren Rychel	.80	2.00
16 Ed Smith	.40	1.00

1985-86 Sudbury Wolves

This 26-card set measures approximately 2 3/4" by 4" and features color, posed player photos with white borders. A facsimile autograph is inscribed across the bottom of the picture.

COMPLETE SET (26)	4.80	12.00
1 Sudbury Police Crest	.10	.01
2 Sponsor Card	.10	.01
3 Logo Checklist	.20	.50
4 Chief of Police	.10	.10
5 Wayne Maxner CO	.20	.50
6 Sean Evoy	.20	.50
7 Todd Lalonde	.20	.50
8 Costa Papista	.20	.50
9 Robin Rubic	.20	.50
10 Dave Moylan	.20	.50
11 Brent Daugherty	.20	.50
12 Glenn Greenough	.20	.50
13 Mario Chitaroni	.30	.75
14 Ken McRae	.30	.75
15 Mike Hudson	.40	1.00
16 Andy Paquette	.20	.50
17 Ed Lemaire	.20	.50
18 Mark Turner	.20	.50
19 Craig Duncanson	.20	.50
20 Jeff Brown	.40	1.00
21 Team Photo	.40	1.00
22 Max Middendorf	.20	.50
23 Keith Van Rooyen	.20	.50
24 Brad Walcot	.20	.50
25 Rob Wilson	.20	.50
26 Bill White	.20	.50

1986-87 Sudbury Wolves

Cards measure approximately 3" x 4" and feature color action photos and a facsimile autograph on the front. The card backs feature biographical information along with P.L.A.Y. public service messages.

COMPLETE SET (33)	4.80	12.00
1 Ted Mielczarek	.30	.75
2 Todd Lalonde	.20	.50
3 Costa Papista	.20	.50
4 Justin Corbeil	.20	.50
5 Dave Moylan	.20	.50
6 Brent Daugherty	.20	.50
8 Mario Chitaroni	.30	.75
9 Jim Way	.20	.50
10 Dean Jalbert	.20	.50
11 Joe Dragon	.20	.50
12 Ken McRae	.20	.50
14 Steve Hedington	.20	.50
15 Mike Hudson	.30	.75
16 Pierre Gagnon	.20	.50
17 Peter Hughes	.20	.50
18 Mark Turner	.20	.50
19 Sudbury Police Logo	.10	.25
20 Wayne Doucet	.20	.50
21 Paul Dipietro	.24	.60
22 Max Middendorf	.30	.75
23 Phil Paquette	.20	.50
25 Rob Wilson	.20	.50
26 Checklist	.10	.25
27 Chief of Police	.10	.25
28 Claude D'Amour	.20	.50
29 Guy Blanchard	.20	.50
30 Joe Desrosiers	.20	.50
31 Jake Disschops	.20	.50
33 Bill White	.30	.75
34 Anders Hogberg	.20	.50

1987-88 Sudbury Wolves

This 26-card set measures approximately 3" by 4 1/8" and features color, posed action player photos with white borders. The player's name, jersey number, and position are superimposed on the photo at the bottom.

COMPLETE SET (26)	4.00	10.00
1 Checklist Card	.10	.25
2 Ted Mielczarek	.30	.75
3 Dan Gatenby	.20	.50
4 Todd Lalonde	.20	.50
5 Justin Corbeil	.20	.50
6 Jordan Fois	.20	.50
7 Rodney Lapointe	.20	.50
8 Dave Akey	.20	.50
9 Jim Smith	.20	.50
10 Fred Pennell	.20	.50
11 Joey Simon	.20	.50
12 Luciano Fagioli	.20	.50
13 Robb Graham	.20	.50
14 John Uniac	.20	.50
15 Dave Carrie	.20	.50
16 Pierre Gagnon	.20	.50
17 Peter Hughes	.20	.50
18 Scott McCullough	.20	.50
19 Dean Guitard	.20	.50
20 Pat Holley	.20	.50
21 Chad Badaway	.20	.50
22 Paul DiPietro	.20	.50
23 Derek Thompson	.20	.50
24 Scott Luce	.20	.50
25 Rob Wilson	.20	.50
26 R. Zanibbi Chief of Police	.04	.10

1988-89 Sudbury Wolves

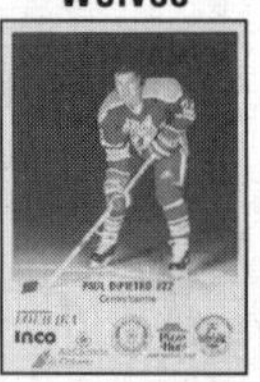

This 26-card set measures approximately 3" by 4 1/8" and features color, posed action player photos with white borders. The player's name, jersey number, and position are superimposed on the photo at the bottom.

COMPLETE SET (26)	4.00	10.00
1 Checklist	.10	.25
2 David Goverde	.30	.75
3 Ted Mielczarek	.30	.75
4 Adam Bennett	.20	.50
5 Kevin Grant	.20	.50
6 Jordan Fois	.20	.50
7 Sean O'Donnell	.30	.75
8 Kevin Meisner	.20	.50
9 Jim Smith	.20	.50
10 Red Pennell	.20	.50
11 Tyler Pella	.20	.50
12 Dean Pella	.20	.50
13 Darren Bell	.20	.50
14 Derek Thompson	.20	.50
15 Terry Chitaroni	.20	.50
16 Sean Stansfield	.20	.50
17 Alastair Still	.20	.50
18 Jim Sonmez	.20	.50
19 Shannon Bolton	.20	.50
20 Andy Paquette	.20	.50
21 Mark Turner	.20	.50
22 Paul DiPietro	.20	.50
23 Robert Knesaurek	.20	.50
24 Todd Lalonde	.20	.50
25 Scott Herniman	.20	.50
26 R. Zanibbi Chief of Police	.10	.25

1989-90 Sudbury Wolves

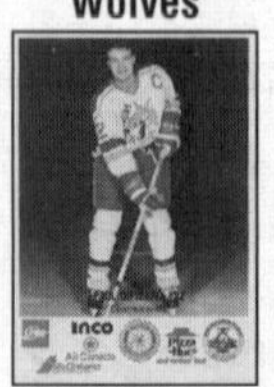

This 25-card set measures approximately 3" by 4 1/8" and features color, posed action player photos with white borders. The player's name, jersey number, and position are superimposed on the photo at the bottom.

COMPLETE SET (25)	4.80	12.00
1 Checklist NNO	.10	.25
2 Alastair Still	.20	.50
3 Bill Kovacs	.20	.50
4 Darren Bell	.20	.50
5 Scott Mahoney	.20	.50
6 Glen Murray	.80	2.00
7 Alain Laforge	.20	.50
8 Jamie Matthews	.20	.50
9 Jon Boeve	.30	.75
10 Adam Bennett	.20	.50
11 Derek Etches	.20	.50
12 Marcus Middleton	.20	.50
13 Jim Sonmez	.20	.50
14 Leonard MacDonald	.20	.50
15 Paul DiPietro	.30	.75
16 Neil Ethier	.20	.50
17 Sean O'Donnell	.20	.50
18 Andy MacVicar	.20	.50
19 David Goverde	.30	.75
20 Jason Young	.20	.50
21 Wade Bartley	.20	.50
22 Barry Young	.20	.50
23 R. Zanibbi Chief of Police	.10	.25
24 Terry Chitaroni	.20	.50
25 Rob Knesaurek	.20	.50

1990-91 Sudbury Wolves

This 25-card P.L.A.Y. (Police, Law and Youth) set measures approximately 3" by 4 1/8" and features color posed action player photos with white borders. The player's name and position is superimposed on the picture at the bottom. For the most part, the cards are numbered on both sides after the player's jersey number (except for card number 7 and 18).

COMPLETE SET (25)	4.80	12.00
1 Darryl Paquette	.24	.60
2 Adam Bennett	.20	.50
3 Barry Young	.20	.50
4 Jon Boeve	.20	.50
5 Kyle Blacklock	.20	.50
6 Sean O'Donnell	.24	.60
7 Dan Ryder	.24	.60
8 Wade Bartley	.20	.50
9 Jamie Matthews	.20	.50
10 Rod Hinks	.20	.50
11 Derek Etches	.20	.50
12 Brandon Convery	.20	.50
13 Glen Murray	.80	2.00
14 Bill Kovacs	.20	.50
15 Terry Chitaroni	.20	.50
16 Jason Young	.20	.50
17 Alastair Still	.20	.50
18 Shawn Rivers	.20	.50
19 Alain Laforge	.20	.50
20 J.D. Eaton	.20	.50
21 Mike Peca	.80	2.00
22 Howler (Mascot)	.04	.10
23 Mike Yeo	.20	.50
24 L'il Rookie Checklist	.04	.10
25 R. Zanibbi Chief of Police	.04	.10

1991-92 Sudbury Wolves

This 25-card set measures approximately 3" by 4 1/8" and features color, posed action player photos with white borders. The player's name, jersey number, and position are superimposed on the photo at the bottom.

COMPLETE SET (25)	4.80	12.00
1 R. Zanibbi Chief of Police	.04	.10
2 Howler (Mascot)	.04	.10
3 Team Photo	.20	.50
4 Kyle Blacklock	.16	.40
5 Sean Gagnon	.20	.50
6 Bernie John	.16	.40
7 Bob MacIsaac	.16	.40
8 Jamie Rivers	.20	.50
9 Shawn Rivers	.16	.40
10 Joel Sandie	.16	.40
11 Barry Young	.16	.40
12 George Dourian	.16	.40
13 Dan Ryder	.30	.75
14 Derek Armstrong	.16	.40
15 Terry Chitaroni	.16	.40
16 Brandon Convery	.20	.50
17 Tim Favot	.16	.40
18 Rod Hinks	.16	.40
19 Jamie Matthews	.20	.50
20 Barrie Moore	.20	.50
21 Glen Murray	.40	1.00
22 Michael Peca	.80	2.00
23 Michael Yeo	.16	.40
24 Jason Young	.16	.40
25 Jason Zohil	.16	.40

1992-93 Sudbury Wolves

These 27 oversized bilingual cards measure approximately 3" by 4 3/16" and feature on their fronts white-bordered color posed-on-

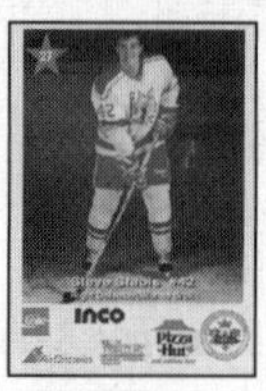

ice player photos. The player's name, jersey number, and position are displayed on each card in white lettering at the bottom of the photo.

COMPLETE SET (27)	4.80	12.00
1 Howler and Lil Rookie	.04	.10
2 Sudbury Regional Police	.04	.10
3 Bob MacIsaac	.20	.50
4 Joel Sandie	.20	.50
5 Rory Fitzpatrick	.20	.50
6 Mike Wilson	.20	.50
7 Shawn Frappier	.20	.50
8 Bernie John	.20	.50
9 Jamie Rivers	.30	.75
10 Jamie Matthews	.20	.50
11 Zdenek Nedved	.20	.50
12 Ryan Shanahan	.20	.50
13 Corey Crane	.20	.50
14 Matt Kiereck	.20	.50
15 Rick Bodkin	.20	.50
16 Derek Armstrong	.20	.50
17 Barrie Moore	.20	.50
18 Rod Hinks	.20	.50
19 Kayle Short	.20	.50
20 Michael Yeo	.20	.50
21 Gary Coupal	.20	.50
22 Dennis Maxwell	.20	.50
23 Steve Potvin	.20	.50
24 Joel Poirier	.20	.50
25 Greg Dreveny	.20	.50
26 Mark Gowan	.30	.75
27 Steve Staios	.24	.60

1993-94 Sudbury Wolves

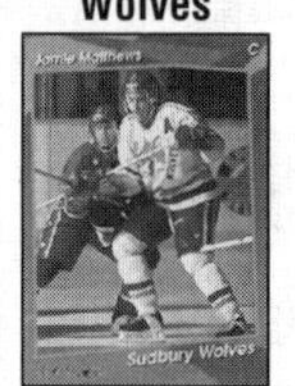

Sponsored by The Sudbury Star, CoverStory, and Sudbury Sports North, and printed by Slapshot Images Ltd., this standard-size 25-card set features the 1993-94 Sudbury Wolves. On a geometrical team color-coded background, the fronts feature color action player photos with thin grey borders. The player's name, position and team name, as well as the producer's logo, also appear on the front.

COMPLETE SET (25)	4.00	10.00
1 Shawn Silver	.20	.50
2 Jeff Melnechuk	.16	.40
3 Jay McKee	.30	.75
4 Chris McMurtry	.16	.40
5 Rory Fitzpatrick	.20	.50
6 Mike Wilson	.20	.50
7 Shawn Frappier	.16	.40
8 Jamie Rivers	.30	.75
9 Zdenek Nedved	.20	.50
10 Ryan Shanahan	.20	.50
11 Sean Venedam	.20	.50
12 Andrew Dale	.16	.40
13 Mark Giannetti	.16	.40
14 Rick Bodkin	.20	.50
15 Barrie Moore	.20	.50
16 Jamie Matthews	.20	.50
17 Gary Coupal	.16	.40
18 Ilya Lysenko	.16	.40
19 Simon Sherry	.16	.40
20 Steve Potvin	.16	.40
21 Joel Poirier	.20	.50
22 Mike Yeo	.16	.40
23 Bob MacIsaac	.16	.40
24 Paul DiPietro	.20	.50
NNO Slapshot Ad Card	.04	.10

1993-94 Sudbury Wolves Police

This traditional over-sized issue was released in conjunction with the Sudbury Police. It features color photos on the front, with safety tips and player info on the back.

COMPLETE SET (26)	4.00	10.00
1 Chief of Police	.08	.20
2 The Howler	.08	.20
3 Jay McKee	.30	.75
4 Chris McMurtry	.16	.40
5 Rory Fitzpatrick	.20	.50
6 Mike Wilson	.20	.50
7 Shawn Frappier	.16	.40
8 Jamie Rivers	.30	.75
9 Jamie Matthews	.20	.50
10 Zdenek Nedved	.20	.50
11 Ryan Shanahan	.20	.50
12 Andrew Dale	.16	.40
13 Mark Giannetti	.16	.40
14 Rick Bodkin	.20	.50
15 Barrie Moore	.20	.50
16 Gary Coupal	.16	.40
17 Ilya Lysenko	.16	.40
18 Simon Sherry	.16	.40
19 Steve Potvin	.16	.40
20 Joel Poirier	.20	.50
21 Shawn Silver	.20	.50
22 Micheal Yeo	.16	.40
23 Jeff Melnechuk	.16	.40
24 Sean Venedam	.20	.50
25 Bob Macisaac	.16	.40
26 Sudbury Police	.08	.20

1994-95 Sudbury Wolves

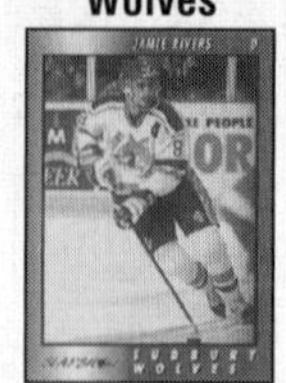

Sponsored by The Sudbury Star CoverStory, Sudbury Sports North and Nick's Sports Cards, and printed by Slapshot Images Ltd., this 26-card set features the 1994-95 Sudbury Wolves. On a silver and blue background, the fronts feature color action player photos with thin black borders. The player's name, position and team name, as well as the producer's logo, also appear on the front.

COMPLETE SET (26)	4.00	10.00
1 Checklist	.04	.10
2 Dave MacDonald	.16	.40
3 Rory Fitzpatrick	.16	.40
4 Mike Wilson	.16	.40
5 Neal Martin	.16	.40
6 Shawn Frappier	.16	.40
7 Jamie Rivers	.20	.50
8 Zdenek Nedved	.16	.40
9 Ryan Shanahan	.16	.40
10 Sean Venedam	.20	.50
11 Andrew Dale	.16	.40
12 Rick Bodkin	.16	.40
13 Luc Gagne	.16	.40
14 Barrie Moore	.16	.40
15 Richard Rochefort	.16	.40
16 Krystof Secemski	.16	.40
17 Jason Bonsignore	.16	.40
18 Liam MacEachern	.16	.40
19 Simon Sherry	.16	.40
20 Ethan Moreau	.30	.75
21 Matt Mullin	.20	.50
22 Aaron Starnyski	.16	.40
23 Ron Newhook	.30	.75
24 Glenn Merkosky CO/GM Todd Lalonde ACO/MG	.04	.10
25 Dan Lebold TR Jason Allen ATR	.04	.10
NNO Ad Card	.04	.10

1994-95 Sudbury Wolves Police

Card fronts feature a posed color photo surrounded by a white border. The card number is located in a star in the upper left corner. Card backs contain hockey and safety tips in French and English.

COMPLETE SET (27)	4.80	12.00
1 Chief of Police	.04	.10
2 The Howler	.04	.10
3 Rick Bodkin	.16	.40
4 Gary Coupal	.16	.40
5 Andrew Dale	.16	.40
6 Luc Gagne	.16	.40
7 Chester Gallant	.04	.10
8 Kiley Hill	.16	.40
9 Liam MacEachern	.16	.40
10 Barrie Moore	.16	.40
11 Zdenek Nedved	.20	.50
12 Ron Newhook	.40	1.00
13 Richard Rochefort	.16	.40
14 Krysztof Secemski	.16	.40
15 Ryan Shanahan	.16	.40
16 Simon Sherry	.16	.40
17 Sean Venedam	.40	1.00
18 Rory Fitzpatrick	.16	.40
19 Shawn Frappier	.16	.40
20 Gregg Lalonde	.16	.40
21 Neal Martin	.16	.40
22 Jay McKee	.40	1.00
23 Jamie Rivers	.20	.50
24 Mike Wilson	.20	.50
25 Dave Macdonald	.16	.40
26 Matt Mullin	.30	.75
27 Steve Valiquette	.40	1.00

1995-96 Sudbury Wolves

This 25-card set was one of two produced to commemorate the '95-96 Wolves. This one was released by the team, in conjunction with sponsors Four Star Sports and Belanger's. The set is standard size with an action photo on the front, while the backs contain a player bio.

COMPLETE SET (25)	4.00	10.00
1 Sean Venedam	.20	.50
2 Brad Domonsky	.20	.50
3 Joe Lombardo	.16	.40
4 Tyson Flinn	.16	.40
5 Luc Gagne	.16	.40
6 Ryan Shanahan	.16	.40
7 Simon Sherry	.16	.40
8 Kevin Hansen	.16	.40
9 Gregg Lalonde	.16	.40
10 Liam MacEachern	.16	.40
11 Jeremy Adduono	.20	.50
12 Ron Newhook	.30	.75
13 Noel Burkitt	.16	.40
14 Neal Martin	.16	.40
15 Tim Swartz	.16	.40
16 Rob Butler	.16	.40
17 Darryl Moxam	.16	.40
18 Steve Valiquette	.30	.75
19 Ryan Sly	.16	.40
20 Dave MacDonald	.20	.50
21 Andrew Dale	.16	.40
22 Belanger's All-Star Team	.04	.10
23 Four Star Sports	.04	.10
24 Richard Rochefort	.16	.40
25 Title Card	.04	.10

1995-96 Sudbury Wolves Police

This 24-card P.L.A.Y. set measures approximately 3" by 4 1/8" and features color posed player photos augmented by a white border. The player's name and position is superimposed on the photo along the bottom.

COMPLETE SET (24)	4.00	10.00
1 Chief Alex McCauley	.04	.10
2 The Howler Mascot	.04	.10
3 Jeremy Adduono	.20	.50
4 Noel Burkitt	.16	.40
5 Rob Butler	.16	.40
6 Andrew Dale	.16	.40
7 Brad Domonsky	.20	.50
8 Tyson Flinn	.16	.40
9 Luc Gagne	.16	.40
10 Kevin Hansen	.16	.40
11 Gregg Lalonde	.16	.40
12 Joe Lombardo	.16	.40
13 Dave MacDonald	.20	.50
14 Liam MacEachern	.16	.40
15 Neal Martin	.16	.40
16 Darryl Moxam	.16	.40
17 Ron Newhook	.30	.75
18 Richard Rochefort	.16	.40
19 Ryan Shanahan	.16	.40
20 Simon Sherry	.16	.40
21 Ryan Sly	.16	.40
22 Shawn Sobush	.16	.40
23 Steve Valiquette	.30	.75
24 Sean Venedam	.20	.50

1996-97 Sudbury Wolves

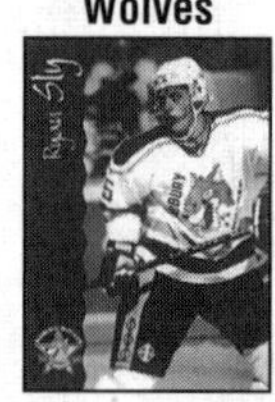

One of two sets issued to commemorate the Wolves' 25th anniversary season, this 27-card standard sized issue was produced by the team and sponsored by Play It Again Sports, The Great Canadian Card. Co. and the Sudbury Star. The cards were produced by the team and sold through arena concessions. The cards feature action photography on the front complemented by a black border containing the player's name and the team logo on the left.

COMPLETE SET (27)	4.80	12.00
1 Title card	.10	.25
2 Jeremy Adduono	.20	.50
3 Louie Blackbird	.16	.40
4 Tom Brown	.20	.50
5 Peter Campbell	.16	.40
6 Brad Domonsky	.16	.40
7 Jason Gaggi	.20	.50
8 Luc Gagne	.16	.40
9 Kevin Hansen	.16	.40
10 Jason Hurlbut	.16	.40
11 Konstantin Kalmikov	.20	.50
12 Robin LaCour	.16	.40
13 Paul Mara	.40	1.00
14 Norm Milley	.60	1.50
15 Gerald Moriarty	.16	.40
16 Scott Page	.16	.40
17 Steve Reid	.16	.40
18 Richard Rochefort	.16	.40
19 Brian Scott	.16	.40
20 Chris Shanahan	.16	.40
21 Ryan Sly	.16	.40
22 Jonas Soling	.16	.40
23 Steve Valiquette	.60	1.50
24 Sean Venedam	.20	.50
25 Great Canadian Card Co.		.01
26 LaSalle Court Plaza		.01
27 Derek Chartrand	.10	.25

1996-97 Sudbury Wolves Police

This oversized (3" by 4 3/16"), 26-card set was issued in conjunction with the Sudbury Police Department. The card fronts feature a posed color photo surrounded by a white border. The player's name, number and position are along the bottom, with the card number is displayed in a star in the upper left corner.

COMPLETE SET (26)	4.80	12.00
1 Chief Alex McCauley	.04	.10
2 The Howler MASCOT	.04	.10
3 Sudbury Wolves 25th	.04	.10
4 Jeremy Adduono	.20	.50
5 Louie Blackbird	.16	.40
6 Tom Brown	.20	.50
7 Peter Campbell	.16	.40
8 Brad Domonsky	.16	.40
9 Tyson Flinn	.16	.40
10 Jason Gaggi	.16	.40
11 Luc Gagne	.16	.40
12 Kevin Hansen	.16	.40
13 Konstantin Kalmikov	.20	.50
14 Robin Lacour	.16	.40
15 Joe Lombardo	.16	.40
16 Paul Mara	.40	1.00
17 Norm Milley	.60	1.50
18 Scott Page	.16	.40
19 Richard Rochefort	.16	.40
20 Brian Scott	.16	.40
21 Chris Shanahan	.16	.40
22 Ryan Sly	.16	.40
23 Jonas Soling	.16	.40
24 Tim Swartz	.16	.40
25 Steve Valiquette	.60	1.50
26 Sean Venedam	.16	.40

1997-98 Sudbury Wolves Police

Card fronts feature a posed color photo surrounded by a white border. The card number is located in a star in the upper left corner. Card backs contain hockey and safety tips in French and English.

COMPLETE SET (25)	8.00	20.00
1 Chief of Police	.04	.10
2 Jeremy Adduono	.16	.40
3 Ryan Barnes	.16	.40
4 Peter Campbell	.16	.40
5 Konstantin Kalmikov	.20	.50
6 Tom Watt	.16	.40
7 Norm Milley	.60	1.50
8 Scott Page	.16	.40
9 Jonas Soling	.16	.40
10 Mike Fisher	.80	2.00
11 Taylor Pyatt	1.20	1.00
12 Derek MacKenzie	.60	1.00
13 Nevin Patterson	.16	.40
14 Jasón Sands	.16	.40
15 Colin Scotland	.16	.40
16 Paul Mara	.40	1.00
17 David Cornacchia	.16	.40
18 Ryan McKie	.16	.40
19 Michael Tilson	.16	.40
20 Brad Morgan	.16	.40
21 Matthew Hodges	.16	.40
22 Brad Simms	.16	.40
23 Steve Valiquette	.60	1.50
24 Andrew Raycroft	1.20	4.00
25 The Howler	.04	.10

1998-99 Sudbury Wolves

This set features the Wolves of the OHL. The slightly oversized cards were handed out by local police officers.

COMPLETE SET (25)	7.20	18.00
1 Alex McCauley POLICE	.04	.10
2 Ken MacKenzie CO	.04	.10
3 Alexei Salashchenko	.20	.50
4 Kevin Beaumont	.20	.50
5 Norm Milley	.40	1.00
6 Derek MacKenzie	.40	1.00
7 Reg Higgs CO	.04	.10
8 Matt Barnhardt	.20	.50
9 Mike Fisher	.80	1.50
10 Tom Kotsopoulos	.40	1.00
11 Marc Long	.20	.50
12 Kyle Dafoe	.20	.50
13 Jason Jaspers	.40	1.00
14 Glenn Crawford	.20	.50
15 Ryan McKie	.20	.50
16 Corey Sabourin	.20	.50
17 Kip Brennan	.80	2.00
18 Serge Dube	.20	.50
19 Brad Morgan	.20	.50
20 Brian McGrattan	.20	.50
21 Taylor Pyatt	.80	1.00
22 Abe Herbst	.20	.50
23 Kevin Mota	.20	.50
24 Mark Aggio	.20	.50
25 Andrew Raycroft	1.25	3.00

1999-00 Sudbury Wolves

This slightly oversized set features the Wolves of the OHL. The set was sold by the team at the rink, and features 1999 first-rounders Taylor Pyatt and Mike Fisher.

COMPLETE SET (26)	4.80	12.00
1 Chief Alex McCauley	.04	.10
2 Bert Templeton CO	.10	.25
3 Darren Keily ACO	.04	.10
4 Corey Sabourin	.14	.35
5 Kyle Dafoe	.14	.35
6 Abe Herbst	.14	.35
7 Dennis Wideman	.14	.35
8 Kevin Mota	.14	.35
9 Norm Milley	.40	1.00
10 Taylor Pyatt	.60	1.00
11 Mike Fisher	.60	1.50
12 Alexei Semenov	.40	1.00

13 Alexei Salashcenko .14 .35
14 Derek MacKenzie .40 1.00
15 Steve Ellis .14 .35
16 Warren Hefford .14 .35
17 Jason Jaspers .40 1.00
18 Brian Mcgrattan .14 .35
19 Drew Kivell .14 .35
19B Tom Kotsopoulos .40 1.00
21 Brad Morgan .14 .35
22 Scott Smith .14 .35
23 R.A. Mobile .04 .10
24 Mike Vaillancourt .14 .35
25 Mike Gorman .14 .35
26 Miguel Beaudry .14 .35

2000-01 Sudbury Wolves

This set features the Wolves of the OHL. The cards are slightly oversized and were produced as part of the P.L.A.Y. series. They were apparently distributed primarily by police officers to school-aged children.

COMPLETE SET (26) 8.00 20.00
1 Chief Alex McCauley .04 .01
2 Bert Templeton CO .20 .50
3 Darren Keily CO .10 .25
4 T.J. Warkus .30 .75
5 Dave Csumrik .30 .75
6 Jason Hicks .30 .75
7 Wally Prawdzik .30 .75
8 Dennis Wideman .30 .75
9 Mike Vaillancourt .30 .75
10 Troy Duncan .30 .75
11 Ladislav Reznicek .30 .75
12 Alexei Semenov .60 1.50
13 Chad Starling .30 .75
14 Nathan Harrington .30 .75
15 Derek MacKenzie .40 1.00
16 Jerry Connell .30 .75
17 Steve Ellis .30 .75
18 Adam Keefe .30 .75
19 Jason Jaspers .60 1.00
20 Jason Bone .30 .75
21 Drew Kivell .30 .75
22 Tom Kotsopoulos .60 1.00
23 Fedor Fedorov .40 1.50
24 Mike Smith .30 .75
25 Miguel Beaudry .30 .75
26 Howler MASCOT .04 .10

2001-02 Sudbury Wolves

This set features the Wolves of the OHL. It measures the standard size and was sold by the team at home games. It is believed that less than 1,000 sets were produced.

COMPLETE SET (30) 6.00 15.00
1 Shandor Alphonso .24 .60
2 Trevor Blanchard .24 .60
3 Travis Chapman .24 .60
4 Bob Chaumont .24 .60
5 Jerry Connell .24 .60
6 Ryan Hastings .24 .60
7 Jim Kehoe .24 .60
8 Darren Keily ACO .04 .10
9 Josh Legge .24 .60
10 Tyler Leggo .24 .60
11 Andrei Mikhnov .60 1.50
12 Dene Poulin .24 .60
13 Jean-Francois Seguin .24 .60
14 Jeff Shaw .24 .60
15 Rob Shilton .24 .60
16 Sam Skwarchuk .24 .60
17 Mike Smith .40 1.00
18 Shawn Snider .24 .60
19 Dan Speer .24 .60
20 Zach Stortini .24 .60
21 Bert Templeton CO .20 .50
22 Brody Todd .24 .60
23 Joel Whitmarsh .40 1.00
24 John Winstanley .24 .60
25 Sudbury Wolves Card .10 .25
26 Wolves Season Line-Up .10 .25
27 Randy Carlyle No. Retired .20 .50
28 Sudbury Carpetland .01
29 Sudbury City Centre .04 .10
30 Sudbury King Sportswear .01

2001-02 Sudbury Wolves Police

This set features the Wolves of the OHL. The cards are slightly oversized, and were issued as promotional giveaways by the team and the Sudbury Police. It is believed that less than 1,000 sets exist.

COMPLETE SET (26) 6.00 15.00
1 Chief Alex McCauley .01
2 Bert Templeton CO .04 .10
3 Darren Keily ACO .04 .10
4 Brody Todd .30 .75
5 Travis Chapman .30 .75
6 Jim Kehoe .30 .75
7 Josh Legge .30 .75
8 J.F. Seguin .30 .75
9 Andrei Mikhnov .60 1.00
10 John Winstanley .30 .75
11 Shawn Snider .30 .75
12 Jeff Shaw .30 .75
13 Bobby Chaumont .30 .75
14 Rob Shilton .30 .75
15 Tyler Leggo .30 .75
16 Shandor Alphonso .30 .75
17 Jerry Connell .30 .75
18 Zack Stortini .30 .75
19 Dan Speer .30 .75
20 Trevor Blanchard .30 .75
21 Sam Skwarchuk .30 .75
22 Dene Poulin .30 .75
23 Ryan Hastings .30 .75
24 Mike Smith .40 1.00
25 Joel Whitmarsh .40 1.00
26 Howler MASCOT .04 .10

2003-04 Sudbury Wolves

COMPLETE SET (25) 6.00 15.00
1 Header Card .01 .05
2 Shandor Alphonso .25 .60
3 Kevin Beech .40 1.00
4 Stefan Blaho .25 .60
5 Bobby Chaumont .25 .60
6 Jonathan D'Aversa .25 .60
7 Luke Dubbin .25 .60
8 Alexander Eaton .30 .75
9 Patrick Ehelechner .60 1.50
10 Chanse Fitzpatrick .25 .60
11 Ryan Hastings .25 .60
12 Kyle Lamb .25 .60
13 Sean Langdon .25 .60
14 Eric Larochelle .25 .60
15 Matt Maccarone .25 .60
16 Rafal Martynowski .25 .60
17 Adam McQuaid .25 .60
18 Mike Mills .25 .60
19 Dene Poulin .25 .60
20 Jordan Prevost .25 .60
21 Chris Robertson .25 .60
22 Marc Staal .75 2.00
23 Sean Stefanski .25 .60
24 Zach Stortini .25 .60
25 Mike Foligno HCO .10 .25

2004-05 Sudbury Wolves

A total of 1,000 team sets were produced.

COMPLETE SET (26) 8.00 20.00
1 Luke Dubbin .30 .75
2 Bobby Chaumont .40 1.00
3 Tomas Sample .30 .75
4 Marc Staal .75 2.00
5 Nicholas Foligno .75 2.00
6 Kevin Beech .30 .75
7 Zach Stortini .30 .75
8 Stefan Blaho .30 .75
9 Devin Didiomete .30 .75
10 Kyle Musselman .30 .75
11 Patrick Ehelechner .60 1.50
12 Alexander Eaton .30 .75
13 Stephen Miller .30 .75
14 Ryan Hastings .30 .75
15 Adam McQuaid .30 .75
16 Ryan McDonough .30 .75
17 Benoit Pouliot 1.25 3.00
18 Mike Mills .30 .75
19 Jonathan D'Aversa .30 .75
20 Rafal Martynowski .30 .75
21 Troy Murray .30 .75
22 Kevin Baker .30 .75
23 Mike Foligno CO .02 .10
24 Bob Jones ACO .02 .10
25 Bryan Verrault ACO .02 .10
26 Howler MASCOT .02 .10

2005-06 Sudbury Wolves

COMPLETE SET (26) 8.00 15.00
1 Marc Staal .60 1.50
2 Kevin Beech .20 .50
3 Chris Abbey .20 .50
4 Ryan Hastings .20 .50
5 Adam McQuaid .20 .50
6 Troy Murray .20 .50
7 Jonathan D'Aversa .20 .50
8 Ryan Crouch .20 .50
9 Kevin Baker .20 .50
10 Matt Dias .20 .50
11 Nicholas Foligno .60 1.50
12 Devin Didiomete .20 .50
13 Anton Hedman .20 .50
14 Akim Aliu .20 .50
15 Mike Mills .20 .50
16 Mark Versteeg-Lytwyn .20 .50
17 Gary Friesen .20 .50
18 Ryan Donally .20 .50
19 Nicholas Tuzzolino .20 .50
20 Justin Allen .20 .50
21 Gerome Giudice .20 .50
22 Mike Foligno .10 .25
23 Bob Jones .20 .50
24 Bryan Verreault .20 .50
25 Howler .02 .10
26 Benoit Pouliot .60 1.50

2006-07 Sudbury Wolves

COMPLETE SET (27) 8.00 20.00
1 Marc Staal .60 1.50
2 Andrew Self .20 .50
3 J.K. Gill .20 .50
4 Matt Dias .20 .50
5 Nick Foligno .60 1.50
6 Gerome Giudice .20 .50
7 Kyle Tarini .20 .50
8 Gary Friesen .20 .50
9 Geoff Guimond .20 .50
10 Devin Didiomete .20 .50
11 Jared Staal 2.00 5.00
12 Patrik Lusnak .20 .50
13 Justin Larson .20 .50
14 Akim Aliu .60 1.50
15 Justin Donati .20 .50
16 Kevin Baker .20 .50
17 Ryan Crouch .20 .50
18 Stephen Miller .20 .50
19 Zach Mccullough .20 .50
20 Adam Mcquaid .40 1.00
21 Tyler Arps .20 .50
22 Jonathan D'Aversa .20 .50
23 Sebastien Dahm .40 1.00
24 Michael Swick .40 1.00
25 Mike Foligno CO .20 .50
26 Bob Jones .10 .25
27 Bryan Verreault .10 .25

1996-97 Surrey Eagles

We have confirmed just this one card from this set that appears to feature the BCJHL Eagles. If you have any additional information, please contact us at hockeymag@beckett.com.

COMPLETE SET (?)
NNO Scott Gomez

2004-05 Surrey Eagles

Features the Eagles of the BCJHL. Set was produced by Upper Deck through its personalized card set division.

COMPLETE SET (23) 6.00 15.00
1 Tyson Angus .30 .75
2 Tim Crowder .30 .75
3 Korey Diehl .30 .75
4 Chris Difrancescantonio .30 .75
5 Tyler Eckford .30 .75
6 Matt Girling .30 .75
7 Rick Hillier CO .02 .10
8 Dan Idema .30 .75
9 Andrew Kozek .30 .75
10 Kyle Kuehner .30 .75
11 Aaron McKenzie .40 1.00
12 Brock Meadows .30 .75
13 TJ. Miller .30 .75
14 David Moncour .30 .75
15 Tyson Moulton .40 1.00
16 T.J. Mulock .40 1.00
17 Kyle Nason .30 .75
18 Blake Reilly .30 .75
19 David Rutherford .30 .75
20 Corey Rymut .30 .75
21 Dustin Slade .40 1.00
22 Stewart Thiessen .30 .75
23 Matt Wiest .30 .75

1995-96 Swift Current Broncos

This 20-card set features color player photos on a blue-and-green background. The backs carry player information. The cards are unnumbered and so are checklisted below in alphabetical order.

COMPLETE SET (20) 3.20 8.00
1 Derek Arbez .16 .40
2 Chad Beagle .16 .40
3 Kurt Drummond .16 .40
4 Terry Friesen .30 .75
5 Ryan Geremia .16 .40
6 Jeff Henkelman .16 .40
7 Jeff Kirwan .16 .40
8 Brad Larsen .30 .75
9 Aaron MacDonald .20 .50
10 Craig Millar .16 .40
11 Jaroslav Obsut .20 .50
12 Colin O'Hara .16 .40
13 Jeff Schaeffer .16 .40
14 Brent Sopel .30 .75
15 Josh St. Louis .16 .40
16 Chris Szysky .16 .40
17 Jesse Rezansoff .16 .40
18 Jeremy Rondeau .16 .40
19 Sergei Varlamov .30 .75
20 Tyler Willis .16 .40

1996-97 Swift Current Broncos

This 24-card set was produced by the club for distribution at the rink and by mail. The cards feature an action photograph surrounded by a blue, white and green borders. The black and white backs feature a mug shot, team logo, personal stats and bio and an anti-drug tip.

COMPLETE SET (24) 4.00 10.00
1 Terry Friesen .30 .75
2 Lindsey Materi .20 .50
3 Kevin Mackie .16 .40
4 Jeff Henkelman .16 .40
5 Michal Rozsival .30 .75
6 Brent Sopel .30 .75
7 Lawrence Nycholat .16 .40
8 Chad Beagle .16 .40
9 Jeff Schaeffer .16 .40
10 Tyler Shybunka .16 .40
11 Josh St. Louis .16 .40
12 Chris Szysky .20 .50
13 Tyler Perry .16 .40
14 Dreu Volk .16 .40
15 Nathan Strueby .16 .40
16 Kurt Drummond .16 .40
17 Brad Larsen .30 .75
18 Ryan Tobler .30 .75
19 Jeremy Rondeau .16 .40
20 Jeff Kirwan .16 .40
21 Brett Allan .16 .40
22 Andrew Milne .16 .40
23 Sergei Varlamov .30 .75
24 Derek Arbez .20 .50

1997-98 Swift Current Broncos

This set features the Broncos of the WHL. It is believed to have been produced and distributed by the team. Any additional information pertinent to this set can be forwarded to hockeymag@beckett.com.

COMPLETE SET (22) 4.80 12.00
1 Terry Friesen .40 .75
2 Lindsey Materi .20 .50
3 Tyson Motz .20 .50
4 Jeffrey Beatch .20 .50
5 Jeff Henkelman .20 .50
6 Michal Rozsival .30 .75
7 Dan Hulak .20 .50
8 Lawrence Nycholat .20 .50
9 Toni Bader .20 .50
10 Chad Beagle .20 .50
11 Jeff Schaeffer .20 .50
12 Tyler Shybunka .20 .50
13 Tyler Murray .20 .50
14 Tony Mohagen .20 .50
15 Layne Ulmer .30 .75
16 Dean Serdachny .20 .50
17 Brent Twordik .20 .50
18 Quinn Sherdahl .20 .50
19 Jeff Kirwan .20 .50
21 Brett Allan .20 .50
22 Sergei Varlamov .40 .75

1998-99 Swift Current Broncos

This set features the Chiefs of the WHL. It is believed to have been produced and distributed by the team. Because of the players featured, it is though to have been sold late in the season. Any additional information pertinent to this set can be forwarded to hockeymag@beckett.com.

COMPLETE SET (24) 4.80 12.00
1 Chad Beagle .20 .50
2 Brett Allan .20 .50
3 Quinn Sherdahl .20 .50
4 Bryce Wandler .20 .50
5 Dean Serdachny .20 .50
6 Danis Zaripov .20 .50
7 Kurt Drummond .20 .50
8 Tyler Murray .20 .50
9 Toni Bader .20 .50
10 Brent Twordik .20 .50
11 Nathan Smith .20 .50
12 Jakub Cutta .40 1.00
13 Lawrence Nycholat .20 .50
14 Ben Ondrus .20 .50
15 Tyson Motz .20 .50
16 Jay Langager .20 .50
17 Brad Rohrig .20 .50
18 Jeremy Reich .30 .75
19 Layne Ulmer .40 1.00
20 Chris Sotiropolous .20 .50
21 Josh Maser .20 .50
22 Dan Hulak .20 .50
23 Dustan Heintz .20 .50
24 Jeremy Rondeau .20 .50

1999-00 Swift Current Broncos

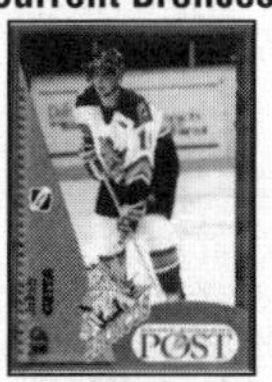

This set features the Broncos of the WHL. The set features standard-sized cards with a purple border. The cards are unnumbered, and so are listed below in alphabetical order.

COMPLETE SET (25) 6.00 15.00
1 Brett Allan .20 .50
2 Jay Batchelor .20 .50
3 Jakub Cutta .30 .75
4 Houston Hair .20 .50
5 Scott Henkelman .20 .50
6 James Hiebert .20 .50
7 Todd Hornung .20 .50
8 Dan Hulak .20 .50
9 Jay Langager .20 .50
10 Duncan Milroy .40 1.00
11 Tyson Motz .40 1.00
12 Lawrence Nycholat .20 .50
13 Ben Ondrus .20 .50
14 Colton Orr .40 1.00
15 Craig Priestlay .20 .50
16 Jeremy Reich .20 .50
17 Dean Serdachny .20 .50
18 Nathan Smith .30 .75
19 Matt Sommerfeld .20 .50
20 Clay Thoring .20 .50
21 Brent Twordik .20 .50
22 Layne Ulmer .40 1.00
23 Igor Valeev .20 .50
24 Brendan Vanthuyne .20 .50
25 Bryce Wandler .30 .75

2000-01 Swift Current Broncos

This set features the Broncos of the WHL. The cards were issued by the team and sold at home games. As they are unnumbered, they are listed below in alphabetical order.

COMPLETE SET (24) 4.80 15.00
1 B.J. Boxma .40 1.00
2 Ales Cerny .20 .50
3 Jakub Cutta .40 1.00
4 John Dahl .20 .50
5 Paul Deniset .20 .50
6 Adam Dumbrowski .20 .50
7 Todd Ford .40 1.00
8 Dustin Friesen .30 .75
9 Scott Henkelman .20 .50
10 James Hiebert .20 .50
11 Jay Langager .20 .50
12 Duncan Milroy .60 1.50
13 Tyson Motz .40 1.00
14 Ben Ondrus .20 .50
15 Craig Priestlay .20 .50
16 Kevin Seibel .20 .50
17 Dean Serdachny .20 .50
18 Nathan Smith .30 .75
19 Matt Sommerfeld .20 .50
20 Clay Thoring .20 .50
21 Ian White .20 2.00
22 Header Card .04 .10
23 Checklist .04 .10
24 Charlie MASCOT .04 .10

2001-02 Swift Current Broncos

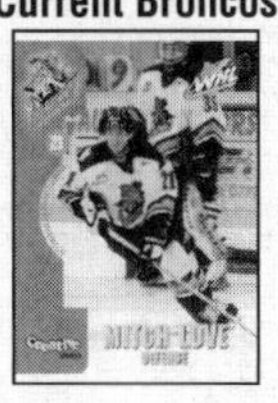

COMPLETE SET (24) 5.00 12.00
1 Steven Spencer .20 .50
2 Ales Cerny .20 .50
3 Kevin Seibel .20 .50
4 Travis Friedley .20 .50
5 Ian White .40 1.00
6 Aaron Richards .20 .50
7 James Hiebert .20 .50
8 Nathan Smith .20 .50
9 Tim Smith .20 .50
10 Dustin Friesen .20 .50
11 Jason Roberts .20 .50
12 Ben Ondrus .40 1.00
13 John Dahl .20 .50
14 Luke Hunter .20 .50
15 Mitch Love .20 .50
16 Brent Twordik .20 .50
17 Torrie Wheat .20 .50
18 Colin Slobodian .20 .50
19 Ivan Usenko .20 .50
20 Duncan Milroy .40 1.00
21 Matt Sommerfeld .20 .50
22 Todd Ford .20 .50
23 B.J. Boxma .20 .50
24 Mascot .02 .10

2002-03 Swift Current Broncos

COMPLETE SET (24) 5.00 12.00
1 John Dahl .20 .50
2 Todd Ford .20 .50
3 Travis Friedlay .20 .50
4 Dustin Friesen .20 .50
5 Jeff Harvey .20 .50
6 Marian Havel .20 .50
7 James Hiebert .20 .50
8 Luke Hunter .20 .50
9 Alex Lentowich .20 .50
10 Mitch Love .20 .50
11 Darryl Moscaluk .20 .50
12 Ben Ondrus .20 .50
13 Derek Poplawski .20 .50
14 Aaron Richards .20 .50
15 Jason Roberts .20 .50
16 Aaron Rome .40 1.00
17 David Schulz .20 .50
18 Dennis Sergeyev .20 .50
19 Steven Spencer .20 .50
20 Colin Stone .20 .50
21 Torrie Wheat .20 .50
22 Ian White .40 1.00
23 Jeremy Williams .40 1.00
24 Charlie Horse MASCOT .02 .10

2003-04 Swift Current Broncos

COMPLETE SET (24) 6.00 15.00
1 Bryn Brucks .20 .50
2 Jason Fransoo .20 .50
3 Dustin Friesen .20 .50
4 Davin Heintz .20 .50
5 Michael Hengen .20 .50
6 Luke Hunter .20 .50
7 Alex Leavitt .20 .50
8 Alex Lentowich .20 .50
9 Kyle Moir .30 .75
10 Ty Morris .20 .50
11 Darryl Moscaluk .20 .50
12 Tyler Redenbach .30 .75
13 Aaron Richards .20 .50
14 Aaron Rome .30 .75
15 Myles Rumsey .20 .50
16 Jerrid Sauer .20 .50
17 David Schulz .20 .50
18 Colin Stone .20 .50
19 Michael Szczachor .20 .50
20 Matej Trojovsky .30 .75
21 Brent Walker .30 .75
22 Ian White .40 1.00
23 Bobby Williams .20 .50
24 Jeremy Williams .40 1.00

2004-05 Swift Current Broncos

COMPLETE SET (24) 8.00 15.00
1 Travis Brisebois .30 .75
2 Marc Defoe .30 .75
3 Marc Desloges .30 .75
4 Tyler Feakes .30 .75
5 Jason Fransoo .30 .75
6 Michael Hengen .30 .75
7 Barry Horman .30 .75
8 Luke Hughson .30 .75
9 Luke Hunter .30 .75
10 Marek Knebl .30 .75
11 Brady Leavold .30 .75
12 Andrew Leslie .30 .75
13 Don Lloyd .30 .75
14 Kyle Moir .40 1.00
15 Tyler Redenbach .40 1.00
16 Myles Rumsey .30 .75
17 Jerrid Sauer .30 .75
18 Jeremy Schenderling .30 .75
19 David Schulz .30 .75
20 Blair Stengler .30 .75
21 Colin Stone .30 .75
22 Michael Szczachor .30 .75
23 Matej Trojovsky .40 1.00
24 Andrew Wasmuth .30 .75

2005-06 Swift Current Broncos

COMPLETE SET (24) 8.00 15.00
1 Karl Benke .30 .75
2 Michael Hengen .30 .75
3 Derek Price .30 .75
4 Thomas Raffl .30 .75
5 Andrew Wasmuth .30 .75
6 Daniel Rakos .30 .75
7 R.J. Larochelle .30 .75
8 Travis Yonkman .30 .75
9 Kyle Bortis .30 .75
10 Kyle Moir .30 .75
11 Luke Hunter .30 .75
12 Spencer McAvoy .30 .75
13 Donny Lloyd .30 .75
14 Josh Aspenlind .30 .75
15 Levi Nelson .40 1.00
16 Grant Toulmin .30 .75
17 Dale Weise .30 .75
18 Charlie Horse .02 .10
19 Paul Postma .30 .75
20 Jeremy Schenderling .30 .75
21 Myles Rumsey .30 .75
22 Ned Lukacevic .30 .75
23 Marc Desloges .30 .75
24 Zack Smith .30 .75

2006-07 Swift Current Broncos

COMPLETE SET (24) 12.00 20.00
1 Travis Yonkman .60 1.50
2 Kyle Moir .60 1.50
3 David Stieler .30 .75
4 Grant Toulmin .30 .75
5 R.J Larochelle .30 .75
6 Ryan Molle .30 .75
7 Levi Nelson .60 1.50
8 Geordie Wudrick .30 .75
9 Dale Weise .30 .75
10 Kyle Bortis .30 .75
11 Phil Gervais .30 .75
12 Michael Wilson .30 .75
13 Daniel Rakos .30 .75
14 Brady Leavold .30 .75
15 Spencer Mcavoy .30 .75
16 Matt Tassone .30 .75
17 Paul Postma .30 .75
18 Derek Claffey .30 .75
19 Zack Smith .30 .75
20 Myles Rumsey .30 .75
21 Dane Crowley .30 .75
22 Jeremy Schenderling .30 .75
23 Levi Nelson .60 1.50
Dane Crowley
24 Charlie Horse .10 .25

1996-97 Syracuse Crunch

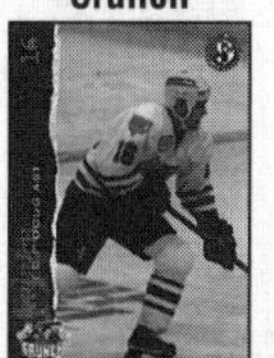

This 25-card set was produced by Split Second and sponsored by Y94 radio and Healthsource. The set features action photos on the front, and statistical information on the back. The cards were sold by the club at the rink or through the mail. The unnumbered cards are listed below according to their sweater numbers, which are displayed prominently in the upper left hand corner of each card back.

COMPLETE SET (25) 4.80 12.00
1 Mike Fountain .30 .75
4 Mark Wotton .16 .40
5 Mark Krys .16 .40
9 Robb Gordon .30 .75
10 Darren Sinclair .16 .40
11 Ian McIntyre .16 .40
14 John Badduke .16 .40
16 Doug Ast .16 .40
17 Brian Loney .16 .40
18 Tyson Nash .60 1.50
19 Lonny Bohonos .20 .50
21 Dave Scatchard .30 .75
23 Chad Allan .16 .40
25 Bogdan Savenko .16 .40
26 John Namestnikov .16 .40
27 Bert Robertsson .20 .50
28 Chris McAllister .20 .50
30 Frederic Cassivi .30 .75
35 Larry Courville .20 .50
37 Rick Girard .16 .40
38 Rod Stevens .16 .40
44 Brent Tully .16 .40
NNO Jack McIlhargey CO .04 .10
NNO Crunchman (Mascot) .04 .10
NNO AHL Ad Card .01

1999-00 Syracuse Crunch

This set features the Crunch of the AHL. The set was released as a promotional giveaway. Sixteen of the cards were given out in sets of eight at two Crunch home games. The remaining cards were available at Tully's Restaurant.

COMPLETE SET (25) 10.00 25.00
1 Harold Druken .40 1.00
2 Matt Cooke .80 2.00
3 Brian Bonin .40 1.00
4 Zenith Komarniski .40 1.00
5 Chad Allan .40 1.00
6 Crunchman MASCOT .10 .25
7 Ryan Ready .40 1.00
8 Brad Leeb .40 1.00
9 Reggie Savage .40 1.00
10 Trent Klatt .40 1.00
11 Martin Gendron .40 1.00
12 Lubomir Vaic .40 1.00
13 Ryan Bonni .40 1.00
14 Brent Sopel .60 1.50
15 Christian Bronsard .60 1.50
16 Barry Smith CO .20 .50
17 Stan Smyl CO .40 1.00
18 Alfie Michaud .60 1.50
19 Trevor Doyle .40 1.00
20 Jarkko Ruutu .40 1.00
21 Chris O'Sullivan .40 1.00
22 Ryan Shannon .40 1.00
23 Pat Kavanagh .40 1.00
24 Mike Brown .40 1.00
25 Tully's Restaurant .04 .10

2000-01 Syracuse Crunch

This set features the Crunch of the AHL. The set was produced by Choice Marketing and apparently was distributed in two 12-card subsets at a pair of home games.

COMPLETE SET (24) 10.00 25.00
1 Marc Lamothe .80 1.50
2 Jean-Francois Labbe .60 1.50
3 Andrei Sryubko .40 1.00
4 Jonas Junkka-Andersson .40 1.00
5 Mike Gaul .40 1.00
6 Dan Watson .40 1.00
7 Bill Bowler .60 1.50
8 Chris Nielsen .40 1.00
9 Jody Shelley 2.00 5.00
10 Mathieu Darche .80 1.50
11 Blake Bellefeuille .60 1.50
12 Jeremy Reich .40 1.00
13 Jeff Williams .40 1.00
14 Martin Spanhel .60 1.50
15 Brad Moran .40 1.00
16 Scott Hollis 1.00
17 Jeff Ware .40 1.00
18 Matt Davidson .40 1.00
19 Sean Selmser .40 1.00
20 Radim Bicanek .40 1.00
21 Reggie Savage .40 1.00
22 Gary Agnew CO .10 .25
23 Ross Yates CO .10 .25
24 Al MASCOT .04 .10

2001-02 Syracuse Crunch

This set features the Crunch of the AHL. The cards were produced by Choice Marketing and were sold at home games.

COMPLETE SET (25) 6.00 15.00

1 Jean-Francois Labbe .30 .75
2 Andrei Sryubko .20 .50
3 Dan Watson .20 .50
4 Paul Manning .20 .50
5 Matt Davidson .30 .75
6 Duvie Westcott .30 .75
7 Jody Shelley .60 3.00
8 Mathieu Darche .30 .75
9 Blake Bellefeuille .30 .75
10 Jeremy Reich .20 .50
11 Martin Spanhel .30 .75
12 David Ling .30 .75
13 Sean Pronger .20 .50
14 Brad Moran .30 .75
15 Derrick Walser .30 .75
16 Jeff Ware .20 .50
17 Martin Paroulek .20 .50
18 Darrel Scoville .20 .50
19 Kent McDonell .20 .50
20 Adam Borzecki .20 .50
21 Andrej Nedorost .30 .75
22 Brett Harkins .20 .50
23 Jonathan Schill .20 .50
24 Tully's Ad Card .01
25 Al MASCOT .04 .10

2002-03 Syracuse Crunch

COMPLETE SET (25) 12.00
1 Karl Goehring .75
2 Pascal Leclaire 1.50
3 Tyler Sloan .50
4 Dan Watson .50
5 Paul Manning .50
6 Matt Davidson .50
7 Mathieu Darche .75
8 Blake Bellefeuille .50
9 Jeremy Reich .50
10 Tim Jackman .50
11 David Ling .50
12 Jonathan Schill .50
13 Brad Moran .50
14 Pauli Levokari .50
15 Darrel Scoville .50
16 Kent McDonell .50
17 Adam Borzecki .50
18 Andrej Nedorost .50
19 Radim Bicanek .50
20 Trevor Ettinger .50
21 Matt Dzieduszycki .50
22 Mike Pandolfo .50
23 Trent Cull .50
24 Al the Gorilla Mascot .10
NNO Quickway Ad .01

2002-03 Syracuse Crunch Sheets

These sheets measure 8/5 X 11 and likely were issued as program inserts. The checklist is incomplete. If you know of others, please write us at hockeymag@beckett.com. Thanks to collector Dale Spengler for this list.
COMPLETE SET (20)
1 Unknown
2 Unknown
3 Kent McDonnell
4 David Ling
5 Unknown
6 Jeremy Reich
7 Duvie Westcott
8 Brad Moran
9 Trent Cull
10 Darrel Scoville
11 Chris Neilson
12 Blake Bellefeuille
13 Mathieu Darche
14 Adam Borzecki
15 Pascal Leclaire
16 Dan Watson
17 Tim Jackman
18 Karl Goehring
19 Andrej Nedorost
20 Mike Pandolfo

2003-04 Syracuse Crunch

This set was produced by Choice Marketing and sold at home games.
COMPLETE SET (24) 4.00 10.00
1 Karl Goehring .30 .75
2 Jamie Pushor .15 .40
3 Mark Hartigan .20 .50
4 Darrel Scoville .15 .40
5 Zenith Komarniski .15 .40
6 Ben Knopp .15 .40
7 Todd Rohloff .15 .40
8 Paul Traynor .15 .40
9 Donald MacLean .15 .40
10 Jeremy Reich .20 .50
11 Tim Jackman .15 .40
12 Joe Motzko .15 .40
13 Brad Moran .15 .40
14 Derrick Walser .15 .40
15 Pauli Levokari .15 .40
16 Aaron Johnson .15 .40
17 Kent McDonell .15 .40
18 Tyler Sloan .15 .40
19 Brandon Sugden .30 .75
20 Pascal Leclaire .40 1.00
21 Anders Eriksson .15 .40
22 Mike Pandolfo .15 .40
23 Trent Cull .15 .40
24 Mascot .01 .05

2004-05 Syracuse Crunch

Produced by Choice Marketing and sold at home games.
COMPLETE SET (25) 5.00 12.00
1 Header/Checklist .01 .05
2 Karl Goehring .30 .75
3 Jamie Pushor .20 .50
4 Mark Hartigan .20 .50
5 Zenith Komarniski .20 .50
6 Ole-Kristian Tollefsen .20 .50
7 Prestin Ryan .20 .50
8 Matthias Trattnig .20 .50
9 Jeremy Reich .20 .50
10 Tim Jackman .20 .50
11 Steven Goertzen .20 .50
12 Alexander Svitov .20 .50
13 Joe Motzko .20 .50
14 Brad Moran .20 .50
15 Andre Lakos .20 .50
16 Aaron Johnson .20 .50
17 Francois Beauchemin .30 .75
18 Brandon Sugden .40 1.00
19 Raffaele Sannitz .20 .50
20 Pascal Leclaire .40 1.00
21 Greg Mauldin .20 .50
22 Jeff Panzer .20 .50
23 Mike Pandolfo .20 .50
24 Al MASCOT .01 .05
25 Sponsor card .01 .05

2005-06 Syracuse Crunch

COMPLETE SET (26) 8.00 15.00
1 Mike Ayers .20 .50
2 Marc Methot .30 .75
3 Mark Hartigan .20 .50
4 Darcy Verot .20 .50
5 Ben Simon .20 .50
6 Geoff Platt .30 .75
7 Andrew Murray .20 .50
8 Tyler Kolarik .20 .50
9 Steven Goertzen .20 .50
10 Peter Sarno .30 .75
11 Joe Motzko .20 .50
12 Brett Nowak .20 .50
13 Alexandre Picard .60 1.50
14 Jeff MacMillan .20 .50
15 Jamie Pushor .20 .50
16 Andy Canzanello .20 .50
17 Ole-Kristian Tollefsen .20 .50
18 Brandon Sugden .40 1.00
19 Martin Prusek .30 .75
20 Tim Konsorada .20 .50
21 Andrew Penner .40 1.00
22 Joakim Lindstrom .30 .75
23 Greg Mauldin .20 .50
24 Aaron Johnson .20 .50
25 Andy Delmore .20 .50
26 Al MASCOT .02 .10

2006-07 Syracuse Crunch

COMPLETE SET (26) 8.00 15.00
1 Tomas Popperle .30 .75
2 Marc Methot .20 .50
3 Mark Hartigan .20 .50
4 Filip Novak .20 .50
5 Darcy Verot .30 .75
6 Ben Simon .20 .50
7 Geoff Platt .30 .75
8 Andrew Murray .20 .50
9 Adam Pineault .30 .75
10 Philippe Dupuis .20 .50
11 Steven Goertzen .20 .50
12 Janne Hauhtonen .20 .50
13 Joe Motzko .20 .50
14 Alexandre Picard .30 .75
15 Tomas Kloucek .20 .50
16 Jeff Szwez .20 .50
17 Ryan Caldwell .20 .50
18 Jamie Pushor .20 .50
19 Andy Canzanello .20 .50
20 Derrick Walser .20 .50
21 Dan LaCosta .20 .50
22 Jekabs Redlihs .20 .50
23 Ty Conklin .30 .75
24 Joakim Lindstrom .30 .75
25 Olivier Labelle .20 .50
26 Al MASCOT .02 .10

1992-93 Tacoma Rockets

This 30-card standard-size set features hatch-bordered, posed-on-ice color player photos. In a white field under the photo are the player's name, and in the right corner, the team logo of crossed red rockets. The team name appears in a diagonal across the top left corner of the photo and the player's position is in blue letters across the top. The cards are unnumbered and checklisted below in alphabetical order.
COMPLETE SET (30) 4.00 10.00
1 Alexander Alexeev .16 .40
2 Jamie Black .20 .50
3 Jamie Butt .20 .50
4 Jeff Calvert .16 .40
5 Don Clark ACO .04 .10
6 Marcel Comeau CO .16 .40
7 Duane Crouse TR .04 .10
8 Allan Egeland .20 .50
9 Marty Flichel .16 .40
10 Trever Fraser .16 .40
11 Jason Kwiatkowski .16 .40
12 Todd MacDonald .16 .40
13 Dave McMillen .16 .40
14 Tony Pechthalt TR .04 .10
15 Ryan Phillips .16 .40
16 Mike Piersol .16 .40
17 Dennis Pinfold .16 .40
18 Kevin Powell .16 .40
19 Tyler Prosofsky .16 .40
20 Stu Scantlebury .16 .40
21 Drew Schoneck .16 .40
22 Adam Smith .16 .40
23 Corey Stock .16 .40
24 Barkley Swenson .16 .40
25 Michal Sykora .20 .50
26 Dallas Thompson .16 .40
27 John Varga .16 .40
28 Toby Weishaar .16 .40
29 Michal Sykora IA .20 .50
30 Cover Card (Team Logo) .10 .25

1993-94 Tacoma Rockets

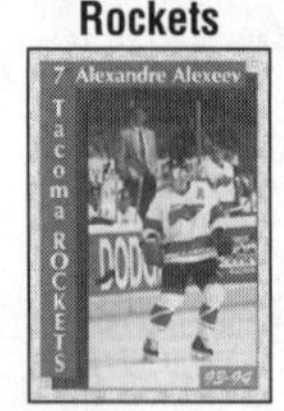

This 30-card standard-size set features the 1993-94 Tacoma Rockets. The set is printed on thin card stock. The fronts have hatch-bordered color action player photos, with the player's name and position printed in white letters in a dark turquoise shadowed border above the photo. The team name also appears in a dark turquoise shadowed bar to the left of the photo. The cards are unnumbered and checklisted below in alphabetical order.
COMPLETE SET (30) 4.80 12.00
1 Alexander Alexeev .20 .50
2 Jamie Butt .20 .50
3 Trevor Cairns .16 .40
4 Jeff Calvert .16 .40
5 Marcel Comeau CO .16 .40
6 Jason Deleurme .16 .40
7 Allan Egeland .20 .50
8 Marty Flichel .16 .40
9 Trever Fraser .16 .40
10 Michal Grosek .40 1.00
11 Lada Hampeis .16 .40
12 Tavis Hansen .20 .50
13 Burt Henderson .16 .40
14 Jeff Jubenville .16 .40
15 Todd MacDonald .20 .50
16 Kyle McLaren .60 1.50
17 Kory Mullin .16 .40
18 Steve Oviatt TR .04 .10
19 Ryan Phillips .16 .40
20 Mike Piersol .16 .40
21 Dennis Pinfold .16 .40
22 Tyler Prosofsky .20 .50
23 Jamie Reeve ACO .04 .10
24 Adam Smith .16 .40
25 Corey Stock .16 .40
26 Dallas Thompson .16 .40
27 John Varga .20 .50
28 Team Photo .20 .50
29 The Tacoma Dome .04 .10
30 The Tacoma Rockets .16 .40
In Action
Marty Flichel

1998-99 Tacoma Sabercats

This set of the WCHL Sabercats was handed out as a promotional giveaway at one home game, making it extremely difficult to find on the secondary market.
COMPLETE SET (25) 8.00 20.00
1 Blair Allison .30 .75
2 Jergis Bertins .30 .75
3 Scott Boston .60 1.50
4 Dampy Brar .30 .75
5 Jamie Butt .60 1.50
6 Scott Drevitch .60 1.50
7 Brett Duncan .30 .75
8 Jim Gattolliat .30 .75
9 Scott Green .30 .75
10 Casey Hungle .30 .75
11 Tim Lovell .60 1.50
12 Kim Maier .30 .75
13 Trevor Matter .30 .75
14 Brad Mehalko .40 1.00
15 Alex Mukhanov .40 1.00
16 Chris Nelson .30 .75
17 Alex Podalinski .30 .75
18 Chad Richard .30 .75
19 Kevin Smyth .30 .75
20 Paul Taylor .30 .75
21 Edgar Zaltkovskis .30 .75
22 John Olver HCO .20 .50
23 Sponsor Card .04 .10
24 Mike Carey TR .10 .25
25 Sponsor Card .04 .10

1999-00 Tacoma Sabercats

This set features the Sabercats of the WCHL. The set was produced by Grandstand and issued as a promotional giveaway at one home game.
COMPLETE SET (25) 6.00 15.00
1 Scott Boston .40 1.00
2 Alexander Alexeev .40 1.00
3 Pavel Mikulchik .30 .75
4 Trever Fraser .30 .75
5 Chad Richard .30 .75
6 Cory Morgan .30 .75
7 Brian Leitza .30 .75
8 Alexander Kharlamov .40 1.00
9 Craig Chapman .30 .75
10 Ashley Buckberger .30 .75
11 Trevor Roenick .30 .75
12 Scott Drevitch .40 1.00
13 Jim Gattolliat .30 .75
14 Dampy Brar .30 .75
15 Blair Allison .30 .75
16 Brandon Fleenor .30 .75
17 Kim Maier .30 .75
18 Edgars Zaltkovskis .30 .75
19 Shayne Green .30 .75
20 Brett Duncan .30 .75
21 Local Electician .01
22 Local Electician .01
23 Local Electician .01
24 John Olver CO .10 .25
25 Mike Carey TR .10 .25

2000-01 Tacoma Sabercats

This set features the Sabercats of the WCHL. The set was produced by Grandstand and was used as a promotional giveaway at a late-season game.
COMPLETE SET (24) 8.00 20.00
1 Cory Morgan .40 1.00
2 Scott Boston .50 1.25
3 Trever Fraser .40 1.00
4 Jarrett Whidden .40 1.00
5 Charlie Blyth .40 1.00
6 Rob Dumas .40 1.00
7 Alexei Deev .40 1.00
8 Danny Lorenz .50 1.25
9 Alexander Alexeev .40 1.00
10 Ashley Buckberger .50 1.25
11 Brandon Fleenor .40 1.00
12 Luke Curtin .40 1.00
13 Gavin Hodgson .40 1.00
14 Dampy Brar .40 1.00
15 Steve Lowe .40 1.00
16 Dennis Pinfold .40 1.00
17 Scott Drevitch .40 1.00
18 Curtis Menzul .40 1.00
19 Phil Husak .40 1.00
20 Robert Dirk CO .10 .25
21 Jason Kirkman TR .04 .10
22 Sponsor .01
23 Sponsor .01
24 Sponsor .04 .10

2001-02 Tacoma Sabercats

This set features the Sabercats of the WCHL. It was handed out at a game in late February, 2002 and is very difficult to find on the secondary market.
COMPLETE SET (24) 8.00 20.00
1 Alexander Alexeev .40 1.00
2 Eric Bowen .40 1.00
3 Dampy Brar .60 1.50
4 Mike Brusseau .40 1.00
5 Etienne Drapeau .40 1.00
6 Scott Drevitch .60 1.50
7 Marty Flichel .60 1.50
8 Trever Fraser .40 1.00
9 David Goverde .60 1.50
10 Nathan Horne .40 1.00
11 Yannick Latour .40 1.00
12 Matt Loen .40 1.00
13 Casson Masters .40 1.00
14 Dennis Pinfold .40 1.00
15 Clayton Read .40 1.00
16 Francois Sasseville .40 1.00
17 Brian Stacey .40 1.00
18 Jarrett Whidden .40 1.00
19 Jeff Winter .40 1.00
20 Dampy Brar .60 1.50
21 Scott Drevitch .60 1.50
22 Robert Dirk CO .10 .25
23 Fang MASCOT .10 .25
24 Saberkitty MASCOT .10 .25

1995-96 Tallahassee Tiger Sharks

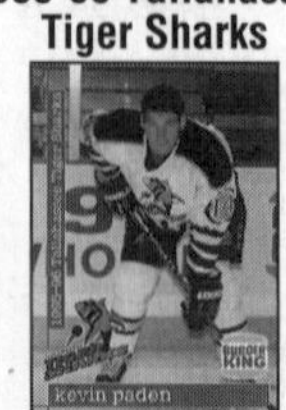

This 27-card set of the Tallahassee Tiger Sharks of the ECHL was sponsored by Burger King and features color action player photos. The backs carry player information.
COMPLETE SET (27) 3.20 8.00
1 Rodrigo Lavinsh .16 .40
2 Jon Engfer .16 .40
3 Rod Aldoff .16 .40
4 Aaron Kriss .16 .40
5 Ron Pasco .16 .40
6 Mark Deazley .20 .50
7 Sean O'Brien .20 .50
8 Kevin Paden .16 .40
9 Darren Schwartz .16 .40
10 Jim Paradise .16 .40
11 John Uniac .16 .40
12 Cal Ingraham .16 .40
13 Matt Osiecki .16 .40
14 Greg Geldart .16 .40
15 Alexander Savchenkov .16 .40
16 Casey Hungle .16 .40
17 Mark Richards .20 .50
18 Bob Bell .16 .40
19 Frenzy (Mascot) .04 .10
20 Jim Mirabello ANN .04 .10
21 Mark Richards .20 .50
Bob Bell
22 Terry Christensen CO .04 .10
23 Jack Capuano ACO .04 .10
24 Jerry Hilker TR .04 .10
25 Walter Edwards VP/GM .04 .10
26 Tony Mancuso AGM .04 .10
27 John Summers ANN .04 .10

1999-00 Tallahassee Tiger Sharks

This set features the Tiger Sharks of the ECHL. The set was produced by the team and issued as a promotional giveaway.
COMPLETE SET (26) 6.00 15.00
1 Kevin Kellett .24 .60
2 Derek Paget .24 .60
3 Jason Reid .24 .60
4 Darren McAusland .24 .60
5 Adam Copeland .24 .60
6 David Thibeault .24 .60
7 Matt Oates .24 .60
8 Paul Buczkowski .24 .60
9 Alexandre LaPorte .24 .60
10 Mike Thompson .24 .60
11 Kimbi Daniels .24 .60
12 Ian Perkins .24 .60
13 Chris Wickenheiser .40 1.00
14 Larry Shapley .24 .60
15 Chad Hinz .30 .75
16 Brent Cullaton .24 .60
17 Jean-Francois Houle .24 .60
18 Jason Weinrich .24 .60
19 Maxim Spiridonov .30 .75
20 Pavel Smirnov .24 .60
21 Marc-Andre Gaudet .24 .60
22 Terry Christensen CO .10 .25
23 Jim Paradise CO .10 .25
24 Cory Paterson .24 .60
24 Kyle Schultz .24 .60
25 Frenzy MAS .10 .25

1994 Tampa Bay Tritons RHI

This set features the Tritons of Roller Hockey Intl. The cards were sold in an oversized package featuring team information. The set is noteworthy for featuring what is one of the scarcest cards of Mark Messier, who was part-owner of the club.
COMPLETE SET (21) 7.20 25.00
1 Paul Messier HCO .10 .25
2 Mark Messier 4.00 15.00
3 Mike Jickling .16 .40
4 John Spoltore .30 1.00
5 Todd Goodwin .16 .40
6 Craig Streu .16 .40
7 Dennis Sproxton .16 .40
8 Norman Dezainde .16 1.00
9 Peter Esdale ACO .10 .25
10 Trevor Sherban .16 .40
11 Duane Dennis .16 .40
12 Jarret Zukiwsky .16 .40
13 Dion Darling .20 1.00
14 Sean Basilio .20 1.00
15 Jeff MacLeod .16 .40
16 Cheerleaders .20 .50
17 Sean Rowe .20 .50
18 George Dupont .16 .40
19 Team Photo .16 .40
20 Doug Messier ACO .10 .25
21 Brad Woods .16 .40

2006-07 Texas Tornados

COMPLETE SET (25) 15.00 25.00
1 Thomas Murphy .40 1.00
2 Lyon Messier 2.00 5.00
3 Troy Puente .40 1.00
4 Jake Newton .40 1.00
5 Nielsson Arcibal .40 1.00
6 Dylan Cooper .40 1.00
7 Justin King .40 1.00
8 Julian Mikola .40 1.00
9 Ryan Fuller .40 1.00
10 Colin Long .40 1.00
11 Tom Brooks .40 1.00
12 Sean Roadhouse .40 1.00
13 Adam Flink .40 1.00
14 John Bullis .40 1.00
15 Brendan Brickley .40 1.00
16 Ben Miller .40 1.00
17 Rob Blanchette .40 1.00
18 Brian Reagan .40 1.00
19 Stephane Da Costa .40 1.00
20 Paul Yovanic .40 1.00
21 Mike Cifelli .40 1.00
22 Corson Cramer .40 1.00
23 Thomas Tragust .60 1.50
24 Tony Curtale CO .02 .10
25 Tom Murphy ACO .02 .10

1998-99 Thetford Mines Coyotes

This set features players from the Thetford Mines Coyotes of the Quebec Semi-Professional Hockey League, one of the most entertaining leagues in all of hockey.
COMPLETE SET (23) 4.00 10.00
1 Steven Paiement .20 .50
2 Marco Sevigny .20 .50
3 Stephane Nepveu .20 .50
4 Jean-Pierre Tardif .20 .50
5 Eric Roy .20 .50
6 Eric Deblois .20 .50
7 Nick Perreault .20 .50
8 Sebastian Vallee .20 .50
9 Yohan Bedard .20 .50
10 Francois Allaire .20 .50
11 Bernard Bouffard .20 .50
12 Philippe Morin .20 .50
13 Pierre Perron .20 .50
14 Michel Dodier .20 .50
15 Frederic Barbeau .20 .50
16 Yves Loubier .20 .50
17 Michel Bisson .20 .50
18 David Desnoyers .20 .50
19 Dominic Cote .20 .50
20 Jean Roberge .20 .50
21 Pierre Marcoux .20 .50
22 Nathan Morin .20 .50
23 Marc Rodrigue .20 .50

2001-02 Thetford Mines Coyotes

This set features the Coyotes of the Quebec Senior League. The set sold by the team at home games. The set we received did not include card #14, but the checklist indicates this card pictures Daniel Payette. If anyone has a set and can verify this, please contact us at hockeymag@beckett.com
COMPLETE SET (25) 10.00 25.00
1 Sebastien Bety .60 1.50
2 Louis Bernard .40 1.00
3 Terry Bartlett .40 1.00
4 Stephane Thivierge .40 1.00
5 Mathieu Gagne .40 1.00
6 Frederic Barbeau .40 1.00
7 Jean-Francois Brunelle .40 1.00
8 Martin Fillion .40 1.00
9 Pierre Perron .40 1.00
10 Eric Roy .40 1.00
11 Francois Page .40 1.00
12 Eric Drouin .40 1.00
13 Jean Roberge .40 1.00
14 Daniel Payette 1.00
15 Marc-Andre Gaudet .40 1.00
16 Denis Desbiens .40 1.00
17 Yves Loubier .40 1.00
18 Daniel Poudrier .40 1.00
19 Pierre Marcoux .40 1.00
20 Hugo Poulin .40 1.00
21 Patrice Tardif .80 2.00
22 Bryan Faucher .40 1.00
23 David Thibeault .40 1.00
24 Martin Lamarche .40 1.00
NNO Checklist .10 .25

2002-03 Thetford Mines Coyotes

COMPLETE SET (23) 5.00 12.00
1 Benoit Beausoleil .20 .50
2 Louis Bernard .20 .50
3 Sebastien Bety .30 .75
4 Jean-Francois Brunelle .20 .50
5 Christian Caron .20 .50
6 Denis Desbiens .20 .50
7 Frederic Deschenes .20 .50
8 Jason Disher .20 .50
9 Eric Drouin .20 .50
10 Martin Fillion .20 .50
11 Marc-Andre Gaudet .20 .50
12 Guy Loranger .20 .50
13 Pierre Marcoux .20 .50
14 Andre Martineau .20 .50
15 Francois Page .20 .50
16 Daniel Payette .20 .50
17 Daniel Poudrier .20 .50
18 Hugo Poulin .20 .50
19 Jean Roberge .20 .50
20 Eric Roy .20 .50
21 Claude Savoie .20 .50
22 Patrice Tardif .30 .75
23 David Thibeault .20 .50

2003-04 Thetford Mines Prolab

COMPLETE SET (24) 4.00 10.00
1 Benoit Beausoleil .20 .50
2 Louis Bernard .20 .50
3 Eric Betournay .20 .50
4 Sebastien Bety .20 .50
5 Patrick Bolduc .20 .50
6 Denis Desbiens .20 .50
7 Frederic Deschenes .20 .50
8 Martin Fillion .20 .50
9 Marc-Andre Gaudet .20 .50
10 Eric Lavigne .20 .50
11 David Lessard .20 .50
12 Pierre Marcoux .20 .50
13 Andre Martineau .20 .50
14 Simon Olivier .20 .50
15 Francois Page .20 .50
16 Daniel Poudrier .20 .50
17 Hugo Poulin .20 .50
18 Christian Proulx .20 .50
19 Jean Roberge .20 .50
20 Eric Roy .20 .50
21 Claude Savoie .20 .50
22 Pierre Sevigny .20 .50
23 Patrice Tardif .20 .50
24 David Thibeault .20 .50

2004-05 Thetford Mines Prolab

COMPLETE SET (24) 6.00 15.00
1 David Thibeault .20 .50
2 Benoit Deschamps .20 .50
3 Marc-Andre Gaudet .20 .50
4 Dany Lavoie .20 .50
5 Patrice Tardif .20 .50
6 Michel Picard .30 .75
7 Frederic Deschenes .30 .75
8 Andre Martineau .20 .50
9 Serge Poudrier .20 .50
10 Marquis Mathieu .40 1.00
11 Francois Page .20 .50
12 Eric Lavigne .20 .50
13 Samuel Groleau .20 .50
14 Yves Racine .20 .50
15 Hugo Poulin .20 .50
16 Glen Kjernisted .20 .50
17 Frederic Henry .20 .50
18 Jean-Francois Beliveau .20 .50
19 Samuel Gagnon .20 .50
20 Simon Olivier .20 .50
21 Mathieu Biron .20 .50
22 Matt Holmes .20 .50
23 Dennis Leblanc .20 .50
24 Benoit Beausoleil .20 .50
25 Ryan Pisiak .20 .50
26 Link Gaetz .75 2.00
27 Gaetan Royer .20 .50
28 Frederic Deschenes .30 .75

2004-05 Thetford Mines Prolab Autographs

It is thought that these cards were issued as inserts with the purchase of a base Thetford Mines set. We have confirmed the existence only of the cards listed below. If you know of others, please contact us at hockeymag@beckett.com.
COMPLETE SET (?)
7 Frederic Deschenes

1993-94 Thunder Bay Senators

This 19-card set of the Thunder Bay Senators of the Colonial Hockey League was produced for the team by Rising Star Sports Promotions. The set was available through the club, and may have been offered as a game night premium.
COMPLETE SET (19) 4.00 10.00
1 Jean-Francois Labbe .40 1.00
2 Jamie Hayden .20 .50
3 Llew NcWana .20 .50
4 Chris Hynnes .20 .50
5 Trent McCleary .40 1.00
6 Richard Borgo .20 .50
7 Bryan Wells .20 .50
8 Don Osborne .20 .50
9 Todd Howarth .20 .50
10 Bruce Ramsay .20 .50
11 Brian Downey .20 .50
12 Barry McKinley .20 .50
13 Ron Talakowki .20 .50
14 Tom Warden .20 .50
15 Mel Angelstad .30 .75
16 Tommi Hietala .20 .50
17 Vern Ray .20 .50
18 Gerry St. Cyr .20 .50
19 Terry Menard .20 .50

1994-95 Thunder Bay Senators

This 20-card set of the Thunder Bay Senators of the CHL was produced for the team by Rising Star Sports Promotions. The cards were available through the team and may have been issued as a game night giveaway.
COMPLETE SET (20) 3.20 8.00
1 Todd Howarth .16 .40
2 Darren Perkins .16 .40
3 Derek Scanlan .16 .40
4 Pat Szturm .20 .50
5 Barry McKinley .16 .40
6 Jake Grimes .16 .40
7 Alain Cote .16 .40
8 Rival Fullum .16 .40
9 Terry Menard .20 .50
10 Mike McCourt .16 .40
11 Mel Angelstad .40 1.00
12 Jason Firth .16 .40
13 Llew NcWana .16 .40
14 Lance Leslie .16 .40
15 Neal Purdon .16 .40
16 Steve Parson .16 .40
17 Chris Rowland .16 .40
18 Bruce Ramsay .16 .40
19 Don Osborne .16 .40
20 Jean Blouin .16 .40

1995-96 Thunder Bay Senators

This 20-card set of the Thunder Bay Senators of the Colonial Hockey League was produced by Rising Star Sports Promotions. The cards were only available through Shoppers Drug Mart stores in Thunder Bay, making hobby acquisition difficult. The cards feature a blurry action photo on the front, an complete stats on the back, along with the Shoppers logos. The cards are unnumbered and so are listed below alphabetically.

COMPLETE SET (20) 6.00 15.00
1 Team Photo .30 .75
2 Mel Angelstad .40 1.00
3 Omer Belisle .30 .75
4 Frederic Cassivi .60 1.50
5 Brandon Christian .30 .75
6 Jason Disher .30 .75
7 Jason Firth .30 .75
8 Rival Fullum .30 .75
9 Todd Howarth .30 .75
10 Chris Hynnes .30 .75
11 Barry McKinley .30 .75
12 Terry Menard .30 .75
13 Derek Nicolson .30 .75
14 Llew NcWana .30 .75
15 Steve Parson .30 .75
16 Darren Perkins .30 .75
17 Dan Poirier .30 .75
18 Neal Purdon .30 .75
19 Bruce Ramsay .30 .75
20 Pat Szturm .40 1.00

1998-99 Thunder Bay Thunder Cats

This set features the Thunder Cats of the UHL. The singles were given away with issues of the local paper. There also have been reports that the complete set could be purchased directly through the paper at the end of the season.

COMPLETE SET (21) 4.00 10.00
1 Jason Lehman .20 .50
2 Barry McKinlay .20 .50
3 David Mayes .20 .50
4 Darrin Szczygiel .20 .50
5 Allan Roulette .20 .50
6 Normand Paquet .20 .50
7 Wayne Strachan .20 .50
8 Kevin Holliday .20 .50
9 Dan Brenzavich .20 .50
10 Mike Henderson .20 .50
11 Neal Purdon .20 .50
12 Nikolai Pronin .20 .50
13 Dan Myre .20 .50
14 Derek Landmesser .30 .75
15 Jason Firth .30 .75
16 Shawn Smith .20 .50
17 Jean-Francois Rivard .20 .50
18 Brant Blackned .20 .50
19 Darrell Clarke TR .04 .10
20 Tom Warden CO .04 .10
21 Sean McEachran .20 .50

1992-93 Thunder Bay Thunder Hawks

This set features the Thunder Hawks of the UHL. The cards were sold by the team at its souvenir stands, and are notable for being slightly smaller than typical cards.

COMPLETE SET (30) 15.00
1 Checklist .04 .10
2 Bill McDonald CO .04 .10
3 Larry Wintoneak ACO .04 .10
4 Mark Michaud .20 .50
5 Marc Lyons .20 .50
6 Jamie Hayden .20 .50
7 Llew Ncwana .20 .50
8 Marc LaBelle .20 .50
9 Gary Callaghan .20 .50
10 Jason Firth .30 .75
11 Mike Martens .30 .75
12 Gerry St. Cyr .30 .75
13 Everton Blackwin .20 .50
14 Bryan Wells .20 .50
15 Brian Downey .20 .50
16 Todd Howarth .20 .50
17 Bruce Rendall .20 .50
18 Vern Ray .20 .50
19 Bruce Ramsay .20 .50
20 Chris Rowland .20 .50
21 Barry McKinlay .20 .50
22 Vincent Faucher .20 .50
23 Tom Warden .20 .50
24 Brock Shyiak .20 .50
25 Mel Angelstad .40 1.00
26 Harijs Vitolinsh .20 .50
27 Steve Hogg .30 .75
28 Terry Menard .30 .75
29 Mark Woolf .30 .75
30 Darrell Clarke TR .04 .10

1992-93 Toledo Storm

This 25-card set features the Toledo Storm of the ECHL. The set features action photography -- which often suffers from the poor quality -- on the front, with stats and bio on the back. The cards were offered for sale by the club at the rink on game nights.

COMPLETE SET (25) 2.80 7.00
1 Checklist .04 .10
2 Chris McSorley CO .20 .50
3 Scott Luhrmann EQMG .04 .10
4 Barry Soskin GM .04 .10
5 Tim Mouser PR .04 .10
6 Jeff Gibbons PR .04 .10
7 Claude Scott .04 .10
The Happy Trumpeter
8 Scott King .20 .50
9 Andy Suhy .16 .40
10 Pat Pylypuik .16 .40
11 Alex Roberts .16 .40
12 Mark Deazley .16 .40
13 John Johnson .16 .40
14 Jeff Rohlicek .16 .40
15 Dan Wiebe .16 .40
16 Jeff Jablonski .16 .40
17 Greg Puhalski .16 .40
18 Bruce MacDonald .16 .40
19 Iain Duncan .16 .40
20 Rick Judson .16 .40
21 Alex Hicks .20 .50
22 Barry Potomski .20 .50
23 Derek Booth .16 .40
24 Rick Corriveau .16 .40
25 Mark Richards .16 .40

1992-93 Toledo Storm Team Issue

Little is known about this set beyond the confirmed checklist. Any additional information can be forwarded to hockeymag@beckett.com.

COMPLETE SET (30) 3.20 8.00
1 Logo Card .04 .10
2 Chris McSorley CO .20 .50
3 Scott Luhrmann EQMG .04 .10
4 Barry Soskin GM .20 .50
5 Tim Mouser PR .04 .10
6 Jeff Gibbons PR .16 .40
7 Mike Williams .16 .40
8 Scott King .20 .50
9 Alex Hicks .20 .50
10 Rick Judson .16 .40
11 Brent Sapergia .10 .25
12 Iain Duncan .16 .40
13 Mark Deazeley .16 .40
14 Jeff Jablonski .16 .40
15 Bruce MacDonald .16 .40
16 Rick Corriveau .16 .40
17 Pat Pylypuik .16 .40
18 Alex Roberts .16 .40
19 Derek Booth .16 .40
20 Andy Suhy .16 .40
21 Jason Stos .16 .40
22 Greg Puhalski .16 .40
23 Wade Bartley .10 .25
24 Distillery Crew .04 .10
25 The Dawnbusters .04 .10
26 Becky Shock .04 .10
27 Don Davis .04 .10
28 Beth Daniels .04 .10
29 Dennis O'Brien .04 .10
30 Will Worster .04 .10

1993-94 Toledo Storm

This 29-card standard-size set features the 1992-93 Riley Cup Champions Toledo Storm of the ECHL (East Coast Hockey League). Inside a white and a thin red border, the fronts feature color action player photos with the player's name and position in a red border at the bottom of the card. The team logo also appears at the bottom.

COMPLETE SET (29) 4.00 10.00
1 Checklist Card .04 .10
2 Chris McSorley CO .20 .50
3 Barry Soskin PRES .04 .10
4 Tim Mouser MG .04 .10
5 Jeff Gibbons ANN .04 .10
6 Scott Luhrmann TR .04 .10
7 Nick Vitucci .20 .50
8 Andy Suhy .10 .25
9 Pat Pylypuik .10 .25
10 Chris Belanger .10 .25
11 Mike Markovich .10 .25
12 Darren Perkins .10 .25
13 Dennis Snedden .10 .25
14 Mark Deazeley .20 .50
15 Mark McCreary .10 .25
16 Jeff Rohlicek .10 .25
17 Chris Bergeron .10 .25
18 John Hendry .10 .25
19 Greg Puhalski .10 .25
20 Bruce MacDonald .10 .25
21 Marc Lyons .10 .25
22 Rick Judson .10 .25
23 Alex Hicks .20 .50
24 Barry Potomski .30 .75
25 Rick Corriveau .20 .50
26 Kyle Reeves .20 .50
27 Erin Whitten 1.20 3.00
28 Brian Schoen .10 .25
29 Riley Cup Champions .10 .25

1994-95 Toledo Storm

This 24-card standard-size set features the 1993-94 Riley Cup Champion Storm of the ECHL. The borderless fronts have color action player photos with the player's name, number and position across the bottom. The words "Toledo Hockey" are printed vertically down the right edge, while the team logo appears in the upper left corner. The cards are unnumbered and checklisted below in alphabetical order.

COMPLETE SET (24) 2.80 7.00
1 Dave Bankoske .16 .40
2 Wyatt Buckland .16 .40
3 Rick Corriveau .16 .40
4 Norm Dezainde .20 .50
5 Iain Duncan .16 .40
6 Jeff Gibbons .16 .40
7 Alain Harvey .20 .50
8 John Hendry .16 .40
9 Ed Henrich .16 .40
10 Rick Judson .16 .40
11 Mike Latendresse .16 .40
12 Scott Luhrmann TR .04 .10
13 B.J. MacPherson .16 .40
14 Jim Maher .16 .40
15 Jay Neal .16 .40
16 Marquis Mathieu .16 .40
17 Shawn Penn .16 .40
18 Darren Perkins .16 .40
19 Greg Puhalski CO .04 .10
20 Barry Soskin PR/GM .04 .10
21 Gerry St. Cyr .16 .40
22 Rhett Trombley .20 .50
23 Nick Vitucci .20 .50
24 1993-94 Riley Cup Champions .20 .50

1995-96 Toledo Storm

This 26-card set of the Toledo Storm of the ECHL was sponsored by Frito-Lay and available through the team and its booster club. The fronts feature an action photo along with team, league and sponsor logos. The unnumbered backs contain player analysis and stats.

COMPLETE SET (26) 3.20 8.00
1 Rob Laurie .16 .40
2 Nicolas Perreault .20 .50
3 Brandon Carper .16 .40
4 Paul Koch .16 .40
5 Glen Mears .16 .40
6 Dan Carter .16 .40
7 Patrick Gladu .16 .40
8 Todd Wetzel .16 .40
9 B.J. MacPherson .16 .40
10 Mark Stitt .16 .40
11 Dennis Purdie .20 .50
12 Rick Judson .16 .40
13 Mike Whitton .16 .40
14 Norm Dezainde .16 .40
15 Jason Gladney .16 .40
16 Wade Bartley .16 .40
17 Jason Smart .16 .40
18 Mike Kolenda .16 .40
19 Shawn Penn .16 .40
20 David Goverde .20 .50
21 Barry Soskin OWN .04 .10
22 Greg Puhalski CO .04 .10
23 Chuck Imburgia DIR .04 .10
24 Scott Luhrmann EQMG .04 .10
25 Mark Kelly ANN .04 .10
26 Sponsor Card .04 .10

1996-97 Toledo Storm

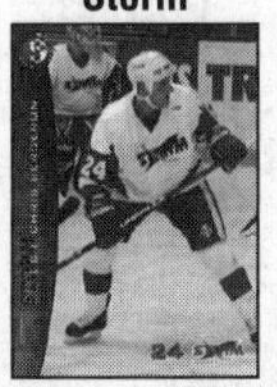

This 23-card set was produced by Split Second. The unnumbered cards feature an action photo on the front, with a brief statistical package on the back. The club offered them for sale at games and through the mail.

COMPLETE SET (23) 3.20 8.00
1 Ryan Bach .30 .75
5 Paul Koch .16 .40
6 Ryan Bast .16 .40
11 Brian Clifford .16 .40
14 Mike Sullivan .16 .40
17 Alex Matvichuk .16 .40
18 Arturs Kupaks .16 .40
19 Dennis Purdie .20 .50
20 Rick Judson .16 .40
22 Norm Dezainde .16 .40
23 Jason Gladney .16 .40
24 Chris Bergeron .16 .40
25 Mike Whitton .16 .40
27 Mike Kolenda .16 .40
28 Dan Pawlaczyk .16 .40
29 Jeremy Mylymok .16 .40
30 Don Larner .16 .40
33 Rob Thorpe .16 .40
35 David Goverde .30 .75
NNO Scott Luhrmann TR .04 .10
NNO Greg Puhalski CO .04 .10
NNO Mark Kelly ANN .04 .10
NNO Barry Soskin PRES .04 .10

1997-98 Toledo Storm

This set was made by Grandstand and were sold by the team at home games. The cards are unnumbered, and are listed below in the order they were inserted in the pack.

COMPLETE SET (30) 3.20 8.00
1 Louis Bernard .12 .30
2 Robert Thorpe .12 .30
3 Greg Lakovic .12 .30
4 Alexandre Jacques .12 .30
5 Gordy Hunt .12 .30
6 Andrei Sryubko .12 .30
7 Sean Venedam .12 .30
8 Jeremy Rebek .12 .30
9 Sean Ortiz .12 .30
10 Tony Prpic .12 .30
11 Brian Blad .12 .30
12 Ron Newhook .20 .50
13 Nick Vitucci .20 .50
14 Dennis Holland .12 .30
15 Mark Deazeley .12 .30
16 Rick Judson .12 .30
17 Lee Cole .12 .30
18 Mike Kolenda .12 .30
19 Dave Arsenault .12 .30
20 Jason Gladney .12 .30
21 Bruce MacDonald .12 .30
22 Kevin Brown .12 .30
23 Andrew Williamson .12 .30
24 Shawn Maltby .12 .30
25 Mike Loach .12 .30
26 Greg Puhalski HCO .04 .10
27 Barry Soskin PR .04 .10
28 Team Staff .04 .10
29 Mark Kelly .04 .10
30 Matt Bresnan EM .04 .10

2003-04 Toledo Storm

These cards were issued as promotional giveaways throughout the 2003-04 season. The cards came in four-card perforated strips. It's believed this checklist is incomplete. If you have further info, please email us at hockeymag@beckett.com.

COMPLETE SET (12) 4.00 10.00
1 Toledo Storm .02 .10
2 Doug Teskey .60 1.50
3 Mike Nelson .40 1.00
4 Josh Legge .40 1.00
5 Morten Ask .40 1.00
6 Nick Parillo .40 1.00
7 Tom Nemeth .40 1.00
8 Alexandre Jacques .40 1.00
9 Rick Judson .40 1.00
10 Landon Bathe .40 1.00
11 Kris Waltze .40 1.00
12 Jim Abbott .40 1.00

2006-07 Toledo Storm

COMPLETE SET (26) 8.00 15.00
1 Andrew Martin .30 .75
2 Jamie Tardif .30 .75
3 Jason Maleyko .30 .75
4 Tim Songin .30 .75
5 P.J. Martin .30 .75
6 Paul Crosty .40 1.00
7 Jon Sitko .30 .75
8 Jason Schweinsberg EQ MGR .02 .10
9 Mike Brodeur .40 1.00
10 Dominic Vicari .40 1.00
11 Scooter Smith .30 .75
12 Chris Blight .30 .75
13 Logan Koopmans .40 1.00
14 Mike James .30 .75
15 Taylor Raszka .30 .75
16 Ken Magowan .30 .75
17 Nick Parillo .30 .75
18 Jeff Attard .30 .75
19 Gerry Burke .30 .75
20 Dan Watson .30 .75
21 Mike Walsh .30 .75
22 Matt Zultek .30 .75
23 Nick Vitucci CO .10 .25
24 Rick Judson CO .02 .10
25 Barry Soskin PRES .02 .10
26 Dukes MASCOT .02 .10

1998-99 Topeka Scarecrows

This 23-card set of the WPHL Scarecrows was sold at home games. Note: there are two versions of card #21. It is not known whether either version is scarcer than the other.

COMPLETE SET (23) 4.00 10.00
1 Topeka Scarecrows CL .04 .10
2 Michal Podolka .30 .75
3 Shawn Randall .20 .50
4 Mike Rusk .20 .50
5 Brett Seguin .20 .50
6 Tom Stewart .20 .50
7 Andy Adams .20 .50
8 Chad Antonishyn .20 .50
9 Chris Bowen .20 .50
10 Joe Coombs .20 .50
11 Scott Dickson .20 .50
12 Troy Frederick .20 .50
13 Dave Gregory .20 .50
14 Trevor Hanas .20 .50
15 Kyle Haviland .20 .50
16 Haywire Mascot .04 .10
17 Kevin Lune .20 .50
18 Sergei Olympiev .20 .50
19 Ryan Phillips .20 .50
20 Paul Kelly HCO .04 .10
21 Michael Podolka NM .40 1.00
21 Andy Adams NM .40 1.00
22 Team Photo .20 .50

1999-00 Topeka Scarecrows

This set features the Scarecrows of the CHL. The set was produced by Roox and was sold by the team at home games.

COMPLETE SET (21) 4.00 10.00
1 Topeka Scarecrows .20 .50
2 John Vary .20 .50
3 Oleg Tsirkounov .20 .50
4 Bill Monkman .20 .50
5 Sergei Deschevvy .20 .50
6 Randy Best .20 .50
7 Blair Manning .20 .50
8 Steve Moore .20 .50
9 Kirk Llano .20 .50
10 Joey Beaudry .20 .50
11 Trevor Hanas .20 .50
12 David Bouskill .20 .50
13 Rod Branch .20 .50
14 Joe Coombs .20 .50
15 Mike Rusk .20 .50
16 Scot Bell .20 .50
17 Michal Podolka .30 .75
18 Brett Seguin .30 .75
19 Haywire MAS .10 .25
20 Paul Kelly CO .10 .25
21 Topeka Scarecrows .20 .50

2002-03 Topeka Scarecrows

COMPLETE SET (30) 10.00 25.00
1 Layne Sedevie .40 1.00
2 Slavomir Tomko .40 1.00
3 Tony Gliniany .40 1.00
4 Phil Angell .40 1.00
5 Jeff Balvin .40 1.00
6 Ryan Peterson .40 1.00
7 Nick Pernula .40 1.00
8 J.P. Platisha .40 1.00
9 Justin White .40 1.00
10 Luke Erickson .40 1.00
11 Wade Harstad .40 1.00
12 James Unger .40 1.00
13 Steve Eastman .40 1.00
14 Ryan Miller .40 1.00
15 Erik Fabian .40 1.00
16 Eric Vesely .40 1.00
17 Brent Cummings .40 1.00
18 Nick Miller .40 1.00
19 Rob Rankin .40 1.00
20 Mark Buchholz .40 1.00
21 Adam Bartholomay .40 1.00
22 Michael Zacharias .40 1.00
23 Mascots .02 .10
24 Zambeauty-Taumi .20 .50
25 Zambeauty-Janea .20 .50
26 Zambeauty-Audrey .20 .50
27 Zambeauty-Tara .20 .50
28 Zambeauty-Melissa .20 .50
29 Zambeauty-Amanda .20 .50
30 Scarecrows logo .02 .10

2006-07 Toronto Marlies

COMPLETE SET (34) 12.00 20.00
1 J.S. Aubin .30 .75
2 Bates Battaglia .20 .50
3 Brendan Bell .20 .50
4 Brad Brown .20 .50
5 Carlo Colaiacovo .20 .50
6 Jeff Corey .20 .50
7 Dominic D'Amour .20 .50
8 Duke The Dog MASCOT .02 .10
9 Robbie Earl .40 1.00
10 Brett Engelhardt .20 .50
11 Alex Foster .20 .50
12 Owen Fussey .20 .50
13 Greg Gilbert CO .02 .10
14 Jay Harrison .20 .50
15 Staffan Kronwall .20 .50
16 Brad Leeb .20 .50
17 John Mitchell .20 .50
18 Marc Moro .30 .75
19 Colin Murphy .20 .50
20 Kris Newbury .20 .50
21 Ben Ondrus .20 .50
22 Justin Pogge .75 2.00
23 John Pohl .30 .75
24 J.F. Racine .30 .75
25 Martin Sagat .20 .50
26 Justin Sawyer .20 .50
27 Jamie Sifers .20 .50
28 Chris St. Jacques .20 .50
29 Alexander Suglobov .20 .50
30 Jiri Tlusty .40 1.00
31 Erik Westrum .40 1.00
32 Ian White .20 .50
33 Jeremy Williams .20 .50
34 Andy Wozniewski .20 .50

2003-04 Toronto Star

Available through select retailers in late October 2003, fans could purchase packs consisting of four random cards from the 100-card base set plus the special foil insert card for that day. The cost of each pack was $3.49 (Canadian funds) plus taxes. A coupon was inserted into each daily issue of the Toronto Star offering one dollar off on a pack of cards. Each coupon was specific to the day's special pack. The promotion ran for 30 days. The cards were produced by In the Game,Inc for the paper.

COMPLETE SET (100) 10.00 25.00
1 J-S Giguere .20 .50
2 Petr Sykora .08 .20
3 Stanislav Chistov .08 .20
4 Dany Heatley .30 .75
5 Ilya Kovalchuk .40 1.00
6 Glen Murray .08 .20
7 Joe Thornton .40 1.00
8 Sergei Samsonov .20 .50
9 Martin Biron .20 .50
10 Miroslav Satan .08 .20
11 Ryan Miller .40 1.00
12 Rod Brind'Amour .08 .20
13 Jeff O'Neill .08 .20
14 Ron Francis .08 .20
15 Rick Nash .40 1.00
16 Rostislav Klesla .08 .20
17 Jarome Iginla .40 1.00
18 Eric Daze .08 .20
19 Jocelyn Thibault .20 .50
20 Alex Tanguay .20 .50
21 Joe Sakic .50 1.25
22 Milan Hejduk .20 .50
23 Patrick Roy 1.50 4.00
24 Peter Forsberg .75 1.50
25 Rob Blake .08 .20
26 Bill Guerin .08 .20
27 Marty Turco .20 .50
28 Mike Modano .25 .60
29 Brendan Shanahan .25 .60
30 Brett Hull .30 .75
31 Chris Chelios .20 .50
32 Dominik Hasek .40 1.00
33 Henrik Zetterberg .20 .50
34 Nicklas Lidstrom .20 .50
35 Pavel Datsyuk .20 .50
36 Steve Yzerman 1.25 3.00
37 Mike Comrie .08 .20
38 Ryan Smyth .20 .50
39 Jay Bouwmeester .08 .20
40 Kristian Huselius .08 .20
41 Roberto Luongo .25 .60
42 Olli Jokinen .08 .20
43 Alexander Frolov .08 .20
44 Jason Allison .08 .20
45 Zigmund Palffy .08 .20
46 Marian Gaborik .40 1.00
47 Manny Fernandez .20 .50
48 Jose Theodore .25 .60
49 Saku Koivu .20 .50
50 Jeff Friesen .08 .20
51 Martin Brodeur 1.00 2.50
52 Patrik Elias .08 .20
53 Scott Niedermayer .08 .20
54 Scott Stevens .08 .20
55 Jamie Langenbrunner .08 .20
56 Alexei Yashin .08 .20
57 Rick DiPietro .20 .50
58 Alexei Kovalev .08 .20
59 Anson Carter .08 .20
60 Eric Lindros .25 .60
61 Mark Messier .25 .60
62 Mike Dunham .20 .50
63 Pavel Bure .25 .60
64 Daniel Alfredsson .08 .20
65 Jason Spezza .25 .60
66 Marian Hossa .20 .50
67 Martin Havlat .20 .50
68 Patrick Lalime .20 .50
69 Jeremy Roenick .25 .60
70 John LeClair .08 .20
71 Simon Gagne .08 .20
72 Tony Amonte .08 .20
73 Sean Burke .20 .50
74 Mario Lemieux 1.50 4.00
75 Evgeni Nabokov .25 .60
76 Pavol Demitra .08 .20
77 Al MacInnis .08 .20
78 Barret Jackman .08 .20
79 Chris Pronger .08 .20
80 Doug Weight .08 .20
81 Keith Tkachuk .20 .50
82 Brad Richards .25 .60
83 Nikolai Khabibulin .25 .60
84 Vincent Lecavalier .25 .60
85 Martin St.Louis .25 .60
86 Owen Nolan .08 .20
87 Alexander Mogilny .08 .20
88 Carlo Colaiacovo .08 .20
89 Nikolai Antropov .08 .20
90 Ed Belfour .25 .60
91 Gary Roberts .08 .20
92 Mats Sundin .25 .60
93 Tie Domi .08 .20
94 Tomas Kaberle .08 .20
95 Ed Jovanovski .08 .20
96 Markus Naslund .08 .20
97 Todd Bertuzzi .08 .20
98 Jaromir Jagr .40 1.00
99 Olaf Kolzig .20 .50
100 Peter Bondra .08 .20

2003-04 Toronto Star Foil

These foil cards were inserted one per pack and the available card changed each day of the promotion.

ONE PER PACK
1 Mario Lemieux 2.00 5.00
2 Steve Yzerman 1.50 4.00
3 Peter Forsberg 1.25 3.00
4 Marian Gaborik .75 2.00
5 Dominik Hasek .75 2.00
6 Joe Thornton .75 2.00
7 Henrik Zetterberg .40 1.00
8 Mike Modano .75 2.00
9 Ed Belfour .40 1.00
10 Marian Hossa .40 1.00
11 Owen Nolan .40 1.00
12 Pavel Bure .75 2.00
13 Jose Theodore .75 2.00
14 Mike Comrie .40 1.00
15 Tie Domi .40 1.00
16 Roberto Luongo .75 2.00
17 Saku Koivu .40 1.00
18 Jarome Iginla .75 2.00
19 Brett Hull .75 2.00
20 Markus Naslund .40 1.00
21 Jaromir Jagr 1.25 3.00
22 Jason Spezza .75 2.00
23 Rick Nash 1.25 3.00
24 J-S Giguere .40 1.00
25 Mats Sundin .75 2.00
26 Ilya Kovalchuk 1.25 3.00
27 Dany Heatley .75 2.00
28 Joe Sakic 1.25 3.00
29 Martin Brodeur 1.50 4.00
30 Patrick Roy 2.00 5.00

2000-01 Trenton Titans

This set features the Titans of the ECHL. The cards were actually distributed in the form of two 12-card sets at different points of the season. Each set had a retail price of $15.

COMPLETE SET (24) 12.00 30.00
1 Scott Bertoli .60 1.50
2 Sandy Cohen .80 2.00
3 Aniket Dhadphale .60 1.50
4 Mike Hall .60 1.50
5 Cail MacLean .60 1.50
6 Steve O'Brien .60 1.50
7 Alain St. Hilaire .60 1.50
8 Scott Stirling .60 1.50
9 Jed Whitchurch .60 1.50
10 Vince Williams .60 1.50
11 Mike Haviland ACO .10 .25
12 Troy Ward HCO .10 .25
13 Dennis Bassett .60 1.50
14 Shane Belter .60 1.50
15 Sasha Cucuz .60 1.50
16 Ian Forbes .60 1.50
17 Butch Kaebel .60 1.50
18 Sean Molina .60 1.50
19 Benoit Morin .60 1.50
20 Jeff Potter .60 1.50
21 Paul Spadafora .60 1.50
22 Kam White .60 1.50
23 David Whitworth .60 1.50
24 Clash MASCOT .10 .25

2001-02 Trenton Titans

This set features the Titans of the ECHL. The set was sold by the team at home games in two 12-card series. The first was released in Jan. 2002, the second in March. Both series retailed for $15 each. The cards are unnumbered and so they are listed alphabetically by 12-card series.

COMPLETE SET (24) 12.00 30.00
1-1 Syl Apps .80 2.00
1-2 Marco Charpentier .60 1.50
1-3 Aniket Dhadphale .60 1.50
1-4 Kirk Lamb .60 1.50
1-5 Matt Libby .60 1.50
1-6 Cail MacLean .60 1.50
1-7 John Nail .60 1.50
1-8 Geoff Peters .60 1.50
1-9 Scott Ricci .60 1.50
1-10 David St. Germain .60 1.50
1-11 Chuck Weber ACO .10 .25
1-12 Matt Zultek .80 2.00
2-1 Graham Belak .80 2.00
2-2 Scott Bertoli .60 1.50
2-3 Ian Forbes .60 1.50
2-4 Peter Horachek CO .20 .50
2-5 Pat Leahy .60 1.50
2-6 Andreas Moborg .60 1.50
2-7 Dan Murphy .60 1.50
2-8 Steve O'Brien .60 1.50
2-9 Alain St. Hilaire .80 2.00
2-10 Ben Stafford .60 1.50
2-11 Kam White .60 1.50
2-12 Rivet MASCOT .10 .25

2002-03 Trenton Titans

COMPLETE SET (24) 20.00
A-1 Scott Bertoli 1.00
A-2 Adam Edinger 1.00
A-3 Andy Hedlund 1.00
A-4 Yann Joseph 1.00
A-5 B.J. Kilbourne 1.00
A-6 John Nail 1.00
A-7 Cody Rudkowsky 3.00
A-8 Kam White 1.00
A-9 Dustin Wood 1.00
A-10 Matt Zultek 1.50
A-11 Bill Armstrong CO .10
A-12 Rivet MASCOT .10
B-1 Syl Apps 1.00
B-2 Tyler Beechey 1.00
B-3 Sean Connolly 1.00
B-4 Shaun Fisher 1.00
B-5 Ian Forbes 1.00
B-6 Mike Hurley 1.00
B-7 Steve O'Brien 1.00
B-8 David St. Germain 1.00
B-9 Jeff Smith 1.00
B-10 Daniel Tetrault 1.00
B-11 Vince Williams 1.00
B-12 Clash MASCOT .10

2003-04 Trenton Titans

This set was produced by RBI Sports and reportedly limited to just 250 copies. The number sequencing includes all sets produced by RBI that season.

COMPLETE SET (16) 6.00 15.00

353 B.J. Abel .40 1.00
354 Andrew Allen .50 1.25
355 Scott Bertoli .40 1.00
356 Mathieu Brunelle .40 1.00
357 Bill Cass .40 1.00
358 Bryce Cockburn .40 1.00
359 Nick Deschenes .40 1.00
360 Peter Fregoe .40 1.00
361 Jay Leach .40 1.00
362 P.J. Martin .40 1.00
363 Devin Rask .40 1.00
364 Dan Riva .40 1.00
365 Jeff Smith .50 1.25
366 Pete Summerfelt .40 1.00
367 Vince Williams .40 1.00
368 Matt Zultek .60 1.50

1994-95 Tri-City Americans

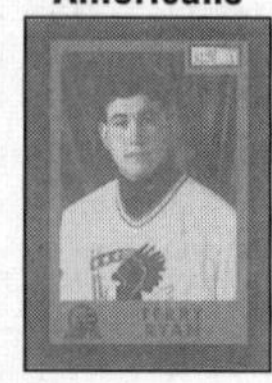

This unusual series was produced by Summit. Four of the cards (#4-7) are standard size, while the other four are slightly oversized, suggesting that they may have been released at different times, or in two separate series. The larger four cards also have a slightly darker blue border around the posed studio shot. All of the cards appear to be laminated, or made strictly from a plastic-type material. The checklist below may be incomplete. Additional information from the readership would be appreciated.

COMPLETE SET (8) 10.00 25.00
1 Dorian Anneck .40 1.00
2 Brent Ascroft .20 .50
3 Brian Boucher 6.00 15.00
4 Rob Butz .20 .50
5 Chad Cabana .30 .75
6 Daymond Langkow 2.00 5.00
7 Ryan Marsh .20 .50
8 Terry Ryan .80 2.00

1995-96 Tri-City Americans

This 31-card set was produced by S&H Ltd. The cards feature action photos on the front, with a mug shot and bio on the back. Unnumbered, the cards are listed below in alphabetical order. The set is noteworthy for the inclusion of three first round selections from the 1995 Entry Draft: Daymond Langkow (TB), Terry Ryan (MTL) and Brian Boucher (PHI).

COMPLETE SET (31) 8.00 20.00
1 Chris Anderson .16 .40
2 Dorian Anneck .20 .50
3 Brent Ascroft .16 .40
4 Aaron Baker .20 .50
5 Alexandre Boikov .16 .40
6 Brian Boucher 2.00 5.00
7 Byron Briske .20 .50
8 Bob Brown GM .04 .10
9 Jerry Fredericksen TR .04 .10
10 Dan Focht .20 .50
11 Dylan Gyori .30 .75
12 Mark Hurley .16 .40
13 Mike Hurley .16 .40
14 Zenith Komarniski .20 .50
15 Daymond Langkow .80 2.00
16 Jody Lapeyre .16 .40
17 Bob Loucks CO .04 .10
18 Scott McCallum .16 .40
19 Boyd Olson .16 .40
20 Warren Renden ACO .04 .10
21 Terry Ryan .30 .75
22 Eric Schneider .16 .40
23 Dan Smith .16 .40
24 Craig Stahl .16 .40
25 Jaroslav Svejkovsky .30 .75
26 Jeremy Thompson .16 .40
27 Gary Toor .16 .40
28 Tom Zavediuk .16 .40
29 Eddie the Eagle (Mascot) .04 .10
30 Brian Boucher 1.20 3.00
(Daymond Langkow
Terry Ryan)
31 Logo Card .04 .10

1998-99 Tri-City Americans

This set of the WHL Americans was issued by the team and sold at its souvenir stands. It features several promising NHLers including Josef Melichar, Jaroslav Kristek and 1999 Rookie of the Year Scott Gomez.

COMPLETE SET (28) 8.00 20.00
1 Jeff Blair .20 .50
2 Josef Melichar .40 1.00
3 Andrew DeSousa .30 .75
4 Darrell Hay .40 1.00
5 Jeff Katcher .20 .50
6 Toni Bader .20 .50
7 Jaroslav Kristek .40 1.00
8 Ken McKay .20 .50
9 Eric Johansson .20 .50
10 Scott Gomez 1.20 3.00
11 Ryley Layden .20 .50
12 Tim Green .20 .50
13 Blake Evans .20 .50
14 K.C. Timmons .20 .50
15 Jordan Landry .20 .50
16 Dylan Gyori .40 1.00
17 Brad Ference .60 1.50
18 Mike Muzechka .20 .50
19 Stephen Peat .60 1.50
20 Curtis Huppe .30 .75
21 Mike Lee .20 .50
22 Jody Lapeyre .20 .50
23 Andrew Guindon .20 .50
24 Blake Ward .30 .75
25 Terry Bangen ACO/AGM .04 .10
26 Training Staff .04 .10
27 Don Hay HCO/GM .20 .50
28 Craig West BR .04 .10

2002-03 Tri-City Stormfront

COMPLETE SET (25) 20.00 40.00
1 Cover Card .10 .25
2 Stormy MASCOT .10 .25
3 Brian Kilburg .75 2.00
4 Nick Klaren .75 2.00
5 Luke Lucyk. 1.25 3.00
6 Mark Agnew .75 2.00
7 Tim Madsen .75 2.00
8 Geoff Paukovich .75 2.00
9 Chris Nathe .75 2.00
10 Ryan Dingle .75 2.00
11 Josh Leddy .75 2.00
12 Matt Scherer .75 2.00
13 Bill Thomas .75 2.00
14 Scott Parse .75 2.00
15 Steve Wagner .75 2.00
16 Tom Pohl .75 2.00
17 David Boguslawski .75 2.00
18 James Martin .75 2.00
19 Chad Anderson .75 2.00
20 Mark Van Guilder .75 2.00
21 T.J. Dahl .75 2.00
22 Casey Mapes .75 2.00
23 Eric Aarnio .75 2.00
24 Tom Kowal .75 2.00
25 Regg Simon .75 2.00

1997-98 Tucson Gila Monsters

This set features the Gila Monsters of the WCHL. These postcard-sized singles are blank backed, and were issued by the team as a promotional giveaway.

COMPLETE SET (10) 4.00 10.00
1 Jon Rowe .40 1.00
2 Dan Marcotte .40 1.00
3 David Piirto .40 1.00
4 Peter Romeo .40 1.00
5 Patrick Bisaillon .40 1.00
6 Jason Crane .40 1.00
7 Chris Everett .40 1.00
8 Sam Fields .40 1.00
9 Pierre Gagnon .40 1.00
10 Aigars Mironovics .40 1.00

1966-67 Tulsa Oilers

Little is known about this set featuring the Oilers of the old CHL beyond the confirmed checklist. The cards were oversized black and white images and likely were issued in photo-pack form. Any additional information can be forwarded to hockeymag@beckett.com.

COMPLETE SET (12) 25.00 50.00
1 Ken Campbell 1.50 3.00
2 Andrew Champagne 1.50 3.00
3 Doug Dunville 1.50 3.00
4 Bill Flett 5.00 10.00
5 Nick Harbaruk 1.50 3.00
6 Lowell MacDonald 5.00 10.00
7 Jim McKenny 2.50 5.00
8 Al Millar 1.50 3.00
9 Marc Reaume 2.00 4.00
10 Harry Shaw 1.50 3.00
11 Gary Venneruzzo 2.50 5.00
12 Ron Ward 2.00 4.00

1972-73 Tulsa Oilers Milk Panels

This recently discovered collectible is a 3 1/2" X 6" card cut from the side of a milk carton. The words "Carnation Introduces Your Tulsa Oilers - Meet The Oilers" are prominently displayed, along with player information. Based on Lundrigan's data and the info on the card, we've placed the season of issue at 1972-73. It seems very likely that other panels exist in this series. Any information on them can be sent to hockeymag@beckett.com.

COMPLETE SET (?)
1 Joe Lundrigan

1992-93 Tulsa Oilers

This 18-card standard-size set was sponsored by Crown Auto World. Ten thousand were sets were reportedly produced. Randomly inserted throughout the sets were 350 autographed cards of each player. The cards feature color photos of players in action and still poses. The pictures have white borders, and the player's name is printed in black on the photo at the bottom. The cards are unnumbered and checklisted below in alphabetical order.

COMPLETE SET (18) 3.20 8.00
1 Mike Berger .20 .50
2 Pat Cavanagh .20 .50
3 Shaun Clouston .20 .50
4 Brian Fiatt .20 .50
Tony Martino
5 Tony Fiore .20 .50
6 Taylor Hall .30 .75
7 Tom Karalis .20 .50
8 Greg MacEachern .20 .50
9 Terry MacLean .20 .50
10 Al Murphy .20 .50
11 Sylvain Naud .30 .75
12 Mario Nobili .20 .50
13 Jody Praznik .20 .50
14 E.J. Sauer .20 .50
15 Craig Shepherd .20 .50
16 Garry Unger .40 1.00
17 Team Photo .20 .50
18 Title Card .20 .50

1993-94 Tulsa Oilers

As with the other teams sets issued throughout the Central Hockey League this season, these are round cards approximately the size of a hockey puck. They come in a plastic container with the team logo on the front, and were sold by the booster club at home games for $5 per set.

COMPLETE SET (18) 3.20 8.00
1 Luc Beausoleil .30 .75
2 Mike Berger .20 .50
3 Shaun Clouston .20 .50
4 Craig Coxe .30 .75
5 Brian Flatt .20 .50
6 Taylor Hall .20 .50
7 Tom Karalis .20 .50
8 Doug Lawrence .30 .75
9 Jamie Loewen .20 .50
10 Mike MacWilliam .20 .50
11 Al Murphy .20 .50
12 Sylvain Naud .30 .75
13 Jody Praznik .20 .50
14 Chad Seibel .20 .50
15 Brian Shantz .20 .50
16 Sean Whyte .20 .50
17 Garry Unger CO .30 .75
18 Crown Auto World Sponsor .04 .10

2003-04 Tulsa Oilers

These cards are unnumbered and thus are listed below in alphabetical order.

COMPLETE SET (24) 4.00 10.00
1 Header Card .01 .05
2 Jason Bermingham .20 .50
3 Rod Branch .30 .75
4 Anthony D'Arpino .20 .50
5 Jordon Flodell .20 .50
6 Dan Gravelle .20 .50
7 Regan Harper .20 .50
8 Tim Kelleher .30 .75
9 Cam Kuzyk .20 .50
10 Branislav Kvetan .20 .50
11 Todd Marcellus .20 .50
12 Rob Meanchoff .20 .50
13 Aaron Millar .20 .50
14 Chris Page .20 .50
15 Derek Reynolds .20 .50
16 Jordan Roach .20 .50
17 Shawn Scanzano .20 .50
18 Wes Scanzano .20 .50
19 Lukas Sedlacek .20 .50
20 Butch Kaebel CO .02 .10
21 Steve Enlow EQM .02 .10
22 Ad card .01 .05
23 Ad card .01 .05
24 Stuart Nichols TR .02 .10

2004-05 Tulsa Oilers

Cards are listed below in alphabetical order. Set is noteworthy for inclusion of Angela Ruggiero, the member of the American women's team who played briefly with the Oilers. The print run was reported to be 2,500 copies.

COMPLETE SET (24) 6.00 15.00
1 Cover Card .01 .05
2 Jason Birmingham .30 .75
3 Cameron Breitkreuz .30 .75
4 Mike Brusseau .30 .75
5 Jeff Cameron .30 .75
6 Jaroslav Cesky .30 .75
7 Lucas Dora .30 .75
8 Steve Enlow .30 .75
9 John Glavota .30 .75
10 Dan Gravelle .30 .75
11 Malcolm Hutt .30 .75
12 Mario Joly .30 .75
13 Butch Kaebel CO .02 .10
14 Klage Kaebel .30 .75
15 Justin Laird .30 .75
16 Todd Marcellus .30 .75
17 Justin Ossachuk .30 .75
18 Todd Paul .30 .75
19 Chris Pelletier .30 .75
20 Doug Pirnak .30 .75
21 Angela Ruggiero 1.25 3.00
22 Bill Ruggiero .40 1.00
23 Dallas Steward .30 .75
24 Oklahoma Trooper .01 .05

1999-00 Tupelo T-Rex

This set features the T-Rex of the WPHL. The cards were produced by SuperCard and were sold by the team at $2 each or a complete set for $30. The cards are very low quality, with a computer-generated bio glued to the back.

COMPLETE SET (19) 12.00 30.00
1 Brent Scott 1.20 3.00
2 Trevor Amundrud 1.20 3.00
3 Bob Brandon 1.20 3.00
4 Jay Pecora .80 2.00
5 Marc Vachon .80 2.00
6 Dave Szabo .80 2.00
7 Joe Van Volsen .80 2.00
8 Regan Harper .80 2.00
9 Jeff Mercer .80 2.00
10 Dave Wilejto .80 2.00
11 Clint Black .80 2.00
12 Pat Powers .80 2.00
13 Roby Gropp 1.20 3.00
14 Casey Hungle .80 2.00
15 Mike Mayhew .80 2.00
16 Jason Dexter .80 2.00
17 Kevin Evans .80 2.00
18 Martin Belanger .80 2.00
19 Ryan Rintoul .80 2.00

1998-99 UHL All-Stars

This set features players who earned a spot in the 1999 UHL All-Star Game. The cards were produced by ebk Sports and were supposed to be sold at the rink the day of the game. Apparently, that was not the case, but a few sets have leaked out onto the secondary market.

COMPLETE SET (22) 16.00 40.00
1 Ross Wilson .80 2.00
2 Stephane Brochu .80 2.00
3 Brian Downey .80 2.00
4 Mark Bultje .80 2.00
5 David Beauregard .80 2.00
6 Joe Dimaline .80 2.00
7 John Vary .80 2.00
8 Paul Willett .80 2.00
9 Vadim Podrezov .80 2.00
10 Wayne Muir .80 2.00
11 Brian Mueller .80 2.00
12 Alexei Deev .80 2.00
13 Lindsay Vallis .80 2.00
14 Patrice Robitaille .80 2.00
15 Jean-Francois Rivard .80 2.00
16 Jason Firth .80 2.00
17 Wayne Strachan .80 2.00
18 Brian LaFleur .80 2.00
19 Kevin Kerr .80 2.00
20 Garry Gulash .80 2.00
21 Mike Melas .80 2.00
22 Glenn Stewart .80 2.00

1999-00 UHL All-Stars East

This set, produced by ebk Sports, was sold at the rink during the 2000 UHL All-Star Game. Due to various production problems, #6T was also released as #2T, #15T released as #6T and #18T released as #1T. It is not known whether any variation is printed in shorter quantities than the others.

COMPLETE SET (22) 4.80 12.00
1T Yevgeny Shaldybin .20 .50
2T Stephan Brochu .20 .50
3T Nick Stajduhar .20 .50
4T Sam Myre .20 .50
5T Mike Maurice .20 .50
6T Chris Palmer .20 .50
7T Chris Grenville .20 .50
8T Gary Roach .20 .50
9T David Mayes .20 .50
10T John Vecchiarelli .40 1.00
11T Nic Beaudoin .20 .50
12T Peter Cermak .20 .50
13T Jay Neal .20 .50
14T Alexei Deev .20 .50
15T Chad Grills .20 .50
16T Dieter Kochan .80 2.00
17T Mark Richards .20 .50
18T Lindsay Vallis .20 .50
19T Ross Wilson .20 .50
20T Doug Searle .20 .50
21T Brent Gretzky .40 1.00
22T Header/Checklist .10 .25

1999-00 UHL All-Stars West

This set was produced by ebk Sports and was offered for sale during the 2000 UHL All-Star Game.

COMPLETE SET (22) 4.80 12.00
1T Kelly Hurd .20 .50
2T Frederic Bouchard .20 .50
3T Jim Durhart .20 .50
4T Jeff Winter .20 .50
5T Lonnie Loach .40 1.00
6T Brian Regan .30 .75
7T Ryan Lindsay .20 .50
8T Jeremy Rebek .20 .50
9T Colin Chaulk .20 .50
10T Scott Feasby .20 .50
11T Joe Dimaline .20 .50
12T Quinn Hancock .20 .50
13T Mike McCourt .20 .50
14T Keith Osborne .30 .75
15T Jeff Loder .20 .50
16T Garry Gulash .20 .50
17T Hugo Proulx .20 .50
18T Glenn Stewart .20 .50
19T Kevin Kerr .40 1.00
20T Jason Firth .30 .75
21T Mike Figliomeni .20 .50
22T Header/Checklist .10 .25

1990 UMD Hull Collection

This 12-card standard-size set (The Brett Hull Collection), was issued by University Minnesota-Duluth in conjunction with World Class Marketing and Collect-A-Sport. The cards have maroon and gold borders on the top and the bottom and are borderless on the side. Cards numbered 10 and 11 are in black and white while the rest of the set was issued with color photos. The set was issued in a special white box with a photo of Brett Hull on the front as well. The sets are numbered (out of 5,000) on the backs of the number 1 card.

COMPLETE SET (12) 6.00 15.00
COMMON CARD (1-12) .60 1.50
1 Hull Portrait 1.20 3.00

1999-00 Utah Grizzlies

This set features the Grizzlies of the IHL. The set was produced by the team and handed out as a promotional giveaway in the form of seven cards at five different home games.

COMPLETE SET (36) 8.00 20.00
1 Volkswagon Golf .01
2 Rich Parent .80 2.00
3 Richard Park .30 .75
4 John Purves .80 2.00
5 Jarrod Skalde .80 2.00
6 Bob Bourne CO .20 .50
7 Checklist .04 .10
8 Volkswagon Jetta .01
9 Gord Dineen .10 .25
10 Sean Tallaire .30 .75
11 Micah Aivazoff .80 2.00
12 Shawn Penn .30 .75
13 Larry Ness TR .10 .25
14 Utah Grizzlies .08 .25
15 Volkswagon New Beetle .01
16 Joe Frederick .30 .75
17 Stewart Malgunas .30 .75
18 Mick Vukota .30 .75
19 Patrick Neaton .30 .75
20 Dean Chynoweth .30 .75
21 Gord Dineen .10 .25
21 Micah Aivazoff .80 2.00
22 Volkswagon Passat .01
23 Rob Bonneau .30 .75
24 Ian Gordon .30 .75
25 Brad Lauer .30 .75
26 Neil Brady .30 .75
27 Grizbee MAS .10 .25
28 Mick Vukota .30 .75
29 Volkswagon GTI .01
30 Brad Miller .30 .75
31 Jeff Sharples .30 .75
32 Darcy Werenka .30 .75
33 Zarley Zalapski .30 .75
34 Greg Payette TR .10 .25
35 Utah Freezz Indoor Soccer .04 .10

2000-01 Utah Grizzlies

This set features the Grizzlies of the IHL. The set was issued as a promotional giveaway at three home games. The cards were issued in perforated strips.

COMPLETE SET (37) 10.00 25.00
1 Volkswagon GTI SPONSOR .01
2 Mike Bales .40 1.50
3 Steve Gainey .80 1.50
4 Brad Lauer .30 1.00
5 Jeff MacMillan .30 1.00
6 Bob Bourne CO .20 .50
7 Utah Grizzlies CL .10 .10
8 Passat SPONSOR .01
9 Patrick Neaton .30 1.00
10 John Erskine .80 2.00
11 John Purves .40 1.50
12 Greg Leeb .40 1.00
13 Jason Taylor CO .10 .25
14 Team Photo .30 1.00
15 New Beetle SPONSOR .01
16 Rick Tabaracci .40 1.50
17 Chris Wells .30 1.00
18 Ryan Christie .60 1.00
19 Alan Letang .30 1.00
20 Craig Ludwig CO .30 1.00
21 1997-98 Team Photo .10 .25
22 Jetta SPONSOR .01
23 Evgeny Tsybouk .40 1.00
24 Eric Houde .40 1.00
25 David Ling .40 1.50
26 Gavin Morgan .30 1.00
27 Payette/Ness/Lund STAFF .04 .10
28 1996-97 Team Photo .10 .25
29 Golf SPONSOR .01
30 Richard Jackman .40 1.00
31 Gregor Baumgartner .40 1.00
32 Jamie Wright .40 1.00
33 Mark Wotton .30 1.00
34 Grizzbee MASCOT .04 .10
35 1995-96 Team Photo .10 .25
36 1998-99 Team Photo
37 1999-00 Team Photo

2001-02 Utah Grizzlies

This set features the Grizzlies of the AHL. The cards were handed out over the course of the season in 6-card strips, one strip at

different games. Each strip featured five player cards and one ad card featuring a Volkswagen car. The series features several former Grizzlies, as well as current players.

COMPLETE SET (35) 14.22 35.56
1 Paul Elliott .40 1.00
2 John Erskine .80 2.00
3 Gregor Baumgartner .40 1.00
4 Jon Sim .62 1.56
5 Tommy Salo 1.20 3.00
6 Mascot .04 .11
7 The New Beetle .01 .02
8 Greg Hawgood .40 1.00
9 John Purves .80 2.00
10 Steve Gainey .80 2.00
11 Serge Payer .40 1.00
12 Zigmund Palffy 1.20 3.00
13 Equipment Assistants .04 .11
14 The Cabrino GL .01 .02
15 Mark Wotton .40 1.00
16 Marc Kristoffersson .62 1.56
17 Eric Beaudoin .40 1.00
18 Roman Lyashenko .62 1.56
19 Vladimir Orszagh .40 1.00
20 Bob Bassen ACO .04 .11
21 The GTI .01 .02
22 Jeff MacMillan .40 1.00
23 Cameron Mann .62 1.56
24 Ryan Jardine .62 1.56
25 Jim Montgomery .62 1.56
26 Chad Alban .80 2.00
27 EQMG and TR .04 .11
28 The New Passat .01 .02
29 Dan Jancevski .62 1.56
30 Justin Cox .40 1.00
31 Kyle Rossiter .62 1.56
32 Gavin Morgan .40 1.00
33 Wade Flaherty .62 1.56
34 Don Hay CO .04 .11
35 The Jetta Wagon .01 .02

2002-03 Utah Grizzlies

COMPLETE SET (30) 15.00 40.00
1 Jonathan Sim .60 1.50
2 Steve Ott 3.00 8.00
3 Dan Jancevski .40 1.00
4 Eric Chouinard .40 1.00
5 Justin Cox .40 1.00
6 Checklist .02 .10
7 John Erskine 4.00 1.00
8 Corey Hirsch .60 1.50
9 Barrett Heisten .60 1.50
10 David Gosselin .40 1.00
11 Jim Montgomery .40 1.00
12 Don Hay HCO .02 .10
13 Steve Gainey .40 1.00
14 Marc-Andre Thinel .40 1.00
15 Jeff Bateman .40 1.00
16 Greg Hawgood .40 1.00
17 David Oliver .40 1.00
18 Bob Bassen ACO .02 .10
19 Jason Bacashihua 2.00 5.00
20 Marc Kristoffersson .60 1.50
21 Jeff MacMillan .40 1.00
22 Alexei Komarov .40 1.00
23 Matthieu Descoteaux .40 1.00
24 Richard Krouse EM .02 .10
25 Gavin Morgan .40 1.00
26 Mark Wotton .40 1.00
27 Mike Smith .40 1.00
28 Eric Landry .40 1.00
29 Mascot .02 .10
30 Greg Payette .40 1.00

1998-99 Val d'Or Foreurs

Card measure 8 1/2 x 11 and feature color action photos on the front and stats and biographical information on the back. Back also features a white box to obtain autographs. Card #S3 features a complete checklist with the dates the cards were made available at Val d'Or Foreurs games.

COMPLETE SET (29) 16.00 40.00
1 Christian Daigle .40 1.00
2 Benoit Dusablon 1.20 3.00
3 Guillaume Lamoureux .40 1.00
4 Danny Groulx .40 1.00
5 Alain Charbonneau .40 1.00
6 Jonathan Fauteux .40 1.00
7 Didier Tremblay .40 1.00
8 Dynamit MASCOT .40 1.00
9 Roberto Luongo 6.00 15.00
10 Nick Greenough .40 1.00
11 Lucio DeMartinis .40 1.00
12 Gaston Therien .40 1.00
13 Francois Hardy .40 1.00
14 David St. Germain .40 1.00
15 Sebastien Laprise .40 1.00
16 Luc Girard .40 1.00
17 Simon Gamache 1.60 4.00
18 Steve Morency .40 1.00
19 Seneque Hyacinthe .40 1.00
20 Dave Verville .40 1.00
21 Alexandre Page .40 1.00
22 Denis Boily .40 1.00
23 Dwight Wolfe .40 1.00
24 Jerome Petit .40 1.00
25 Eric Dubois .40 1.00
26 Jonathan Charron .40 1.00
S1 Anthony Quessy .40 1.00
S2 Mathieau Lendick .40 1.00
S3 Philippe Ouellette .40 1.00

2000-01 Val d'Or Foreurs

This set features les Foreurs of the QMJHL. The set was produced by CTM-Ste-Foy, and was sold by that card shop, as well as by the team.

COMPLETE SET (25) 6.00 15.00
1 Mathieu Roy .16 .40
2 Yan Hallee .16 .40
3 Chris Lyness .16 .40
4 Hugo Levesque .16 .40
5 Luc Girard .16 .40
6 David Cloutier .16 .40
7 Tomas Psenka .16 .40
8 Nicolas Pelletier .30 .75
9 Kory Baker .16 .40
10 Steve Pelletier .16 .40
11 Alex Turcotte .16 .40
12 Simon Gamache .80 3.00
13 Simon Lajeunesse .80 2.00
14 Alexandre Rouleau .16 .40
15 Samuel Duplain .16 .40
16 Pierre Morvan .16 .40
17 Brandon Reid .40 3.00
18 Mathieu Bastien .16 .40
19 Maxime Daigneault 1.20 2.00
20 Jerome Bergeron .16 .40
21 Frederic Bedard .16 .40
22 Eric Fortier .16 .40
23 Stephane Veilleux .16 .40
24 Seneque Hyacinthe .16 .40
NNO Team CL .04 .01

2000-01 Val d'Or Foreurs Signed

This set is exactly the same as the base Foreurs set from this season, save that every card has been hand signed by the player pictured. Each card also is serial numbered out of just 100.

COMPLETE SET (25) 30.00 75.00
1 Mathieu Roy .80 2.00
2 Yan Hallee .80 2.00
3 Chris Lyness .80 2.00
4 Hugo Levesque .80 2.00
5 Luc Girard .80 2.00
6 David Cloutier .80 2.00
7 Tomas Psenka .80 2.00
8 Nicolas Pelletier 1.60 4.00
9 Kory Baker .80 2.00
10 Steve Pelletier .80 2.00
11 Alex Turcotte .80 2.00
12 Simon Gamache 4.00 15.00
13 Simon Lajeunesse 4.00 10.00
14 Alexandre Rouleau .80 2.00
15 Samuel Duplain .80 2.00
16 Pierre Morvan .80 2.00
17 Brandon Reid 4.00 15.00
18 Mathieu Bastien .80 2.00
19 Maxime Daigneault 6.00 10.00
20 Jerome Bergeron .80 2.00
21 Frederic Bedard .80 2.00
22 Eric Fortier .80 2.00
23 Stephane Veilleux .80 2.00
24 Seneque Hyacinthe .80 2.00
NNO Team CL .04 .25

2001-02 Val d'Or Foreurs

This set features the Foreurs of the QMHJL. The set was produced by CTM Ste-Foy and was sold at Foreurs home games. There were 1,000 copies produced of this set.

COMPLETE SET (24) 4.80 12.00
1 Philippe Seguin .20 .50
2 Hugo Levesque .20 .50
3 Chaz Johnson .20 .50
4 Remy Tremblay .20 .50
5 Steve Richards .20 .50
6 Jonathan Gautier .20 .50
7 Vincent Duriau .20 .50
8 Jeff Cotton .20 .50
9 Patrice Bilodeau .20 .50
10 Frederic Bedard .20 .50
11 Nicolas Pelletier .20 .50
12 Francois Gagnon .20 .50
13 Alexandre Rouleau .20 .50
14 Pierre Morvan .20 .50
15 Mathieu Roy .20 .50
16 Samuel Gibbons .20 .50

17 Jonathan Charette .20 .50
18 Kyle Schutte .20 .50
19 Steve Pelletier .20 .50
20 Maxime Daigneault .40 1.00
21 Eric Fortier .30 .75
22 Mathieu Simard .20 .50
23 Adam Morneau .20 .50
24 David Rodman .20 .50

2002-03 Val d'Or Foreurs

COMPLETE SET (24) 5.00 12.00
1 Eric Glaude .20 .50
2 Pierre-Luc Laprise .20 .50
3 Patrice Bilodeau .20 .50
4 Vincent Duriau .20 .50
5 Mark Hurtubise .20 .50
6 Frederic Bedard .20 .50
7 Artem Kozitsyn .20 .50
8 Mathieu Curadeau .20 .50
9 Francois Gagnon .20 .50
10 Erik Lajoie .20 .50
11 Mathieu Dumas .20 .50
12 Denis Berube .30 .75
13 Olivier Latendresse .30 .75
14 Mathieu Roy .60 1.50
15 Benoit Genesse .20 .50
16 Jonathan Charette .20 .50
17 Shawn Collymore .30 .75
18 Didier Bochatay .20 .50
19 Maxime Daigneault .30 .75
20 Jeff Cotton .20 .50
21 Dominic Lachaine .20 .50
22 David Rodman .20 .50
23 Chaz Johnson .20 .50
24 Checklist .01 .05

2003-04 Val d'Or Foreurs

Created by Extreme Sportscards, this 23-card set was sold a home games and by Cartes Timbres Ste-Foy. Cards are unnumbered and are listed below iby jersey number.

COMPLETE SET (23) 5.00 12.00
1 Benoit Lessard .20 .50
2 Etienne Grandmont .20 .50
3 Dominic Lachaine .20 .50
4 Patrice Bilodeau .20 .50
5 Mark Hurtubise .20 .50
6 Luc Bourdon .75 2.00
7 Vladimir Kutny .20 .50
8 Artem Kozitsyn .20 .50
9 Jonathan Charette .20 .50
10 Francois Gagnon .20 .50
11 Erik Lajoie .20 .50
12 Mathieu Dumas .20 .50
13 Francois Thuot .30 .75
14 Olivier Latendresse .20 .50
15 Benoit Piche .20 .50
16 Shawn Collymore .20 .50
17 Guillaume Chicoine .20 .50
18 Maxime Daigneault .40 1.00
19 Jeff Cotton .20 .50
20 Patrick Bordeleau .20 .50
21 Mathieu Curadeau .20 .50
22 Sebastien Bisaillon .20 .50
23 Chaz Johnson .20 .50

2001-02 Vancouver Giants

This set features the expansion Giants of the WHL. The cards were produced by the team and sold at souvenir stands for $10 per set. The cards came in a sealed wrapper with an image that emulates the title card. The cards themselves feature an action photo on the front, and black and white player data on the back. Although jersey numbers appear on the front, the cards are unnumbered and thus are listed below alphabetically.

COMPLETE SET (25) 4.80 12.00
1 Title Card .10 .25
2 Mark Ardelan .20 .50
3 Mark Ashton .20 .50
4 Chad Bassen .20 .50
5 Jeff Beatch .20 .50
6 Robin Big Snake .20 1.00
7 Josh Bonar .20 .50
8 Pat Brandreth .20 .50
9 Jeff Coulter .20 .50
10 Don Choukalos .30 .75
11 Andrew Davidson .20 .50
12 Andrew DeSousa .20 .50
13 Marian Havel .30 .75
14 Jeremy Jackson .20 .50
15 Brett Jaeger .20 .50
16 Robin Kovar .20 .50
17 Darren Lynch .30 .75
18 Nick Marach .20 .50
19 Tyson Marsh .20 .50
20 T.J. Mulock .20 .50
21 Jack Redlick .20 .50
22 Dave Selthun .20 .50
23 Chris Stubel .20 .50
24 Ryan Thomas .20 .50
25 Clay Thoring .20 .50

2003-04 Vancouver Giants

COMPLETE SET (25) 10.00 25.00
1 Title Card .01 .05
2 Jordan McLaughlin .20 .50
3 Aaron Sorochan .20 .50
4 Ryan Mayko .20 .50
5 Chad Scharff .20 .50
6 Mark Fistric .30 .75
7 Brennan Chapman .20 .50
8 Joe Logan .20 .50
9 Marcin Kolusz .20 .50
10 Adam Courchaine .20 .50
11 Triston Grant .20 .50
12 Kyle Bruce .20 .50
13 Darrell May .20 .50
14 Gilbert Brule 6.00 15.00
15 Kevin Hayman .20 .50
16 Mitch Bartley .20 .50
17 Braden Appleby .20 .50
18 Matt Kassian .20 .50
19 Tyson Marsh .30 .75
20 Darren Lynch .20 .50
21 Tim Kraus .20 .50
22 Ty Morris .20 .50
23 Lukas Pulpan .20 .50
24 Dean Evason HCO .02 .10
25 Team Photo .20 .50

2004-05 Vancouver Giants

COMPLETE SET 8.00 20.00
1 Luke Egener .20 .50
2 Mark Fistric .30 .75
3 Cody Franson .20 .50
4 Stewart Thiessen .20 .50
5 Jason Reese .20 .50
6 Matt Robinson .20 .50
7 J.D. Watt .20 .50
8 Adam Courchaine .20 .50
9 Triston Grant .20 .50
10 Keith Voytechek .20 .50
11 Shaun Vey .20 .50
12 Andrej Meszaros .40 1.00
13 Gilbert Brule 2.00 5.00
14 Mitch Bartley .20 .50
15 Matt Kassian .20 .50
16 Max Gordichuk .20 .50
17 Garet Hunt .20 .50
18 Paul Albers .20 .50
19 Kyle Lamb .20 .50
20 Tim Kraus .20 .50
21 Chad Scharff .20 .50
22 Marek Schwarz .75 2.00
23 Conlan Seder .20 .50
24 Adam Jennings .20 .50

2005-06 Vancouver Giants

COMPLETE SET (25) 20.00
1 Paul Albers .75
2 Mitchell Bartley .75
3 Mario Bliznak .75
4 Jonathan Blum .75
5 Gilbert Brule 5.00
6 Mitch Czibere .75
7 Brett Festerling .75
8 Mark Fistric 1.00
9 John Flatters .75
10 Cody Franson .75
11 Garet Hunt .75
12 Tim Kraus .75
13 Kyle Lamb .75
14 Milan Lucic 2.00
15 Spencer Machacek .75
16 Brendan Mikkelson 1.00
17 Jason Reese .75
18 Michal Repik .75
19 David Rutherford .75
20 Chad Scharff .75
21 Tyson Sexsmith .75
22 Dustin Slade .75
23 Tommy Tartaglione .75
24 J.D. Watt .75
25 Vancouver Giants .10

1995 Vancouver VooDoo RHI

This 25-card set from Slapshot Images features the Vancouver VooDoo of Roller Hockey International. The cards feature color player photos in a thin gray frame on a black background with a purple zigzag stripe down the left. The backs carry player information.

COMPLETE SET (25) 3.20 8.00
1 Title Card CL .04 .10
2 Dave "Tiger" Williams .40 1.00
3 James Jenson .20 .50
4 Laurie Billeck .16 .40
5 Doug McCarthy .16 .40
6 Jason Knox .16 .40
7 Brent Thurston .16 .40
8 Dave Cairns CO .04 .10
9 Jason Jennings .16 .40
10 Shayne Green .16 .40
11 Rob Dumas .16 .40
12 Ivan Matulik .16 .40
13 Rob Stewart .16 .40
14 Doug Ast .20 .50
15 Chris Morrison .16 .40
16 Kevin Hoffman .16 .40
17 Ryan Harrison .16 .40
18 Ken Kinney .20 .50
19 Merv Priest .16 .40
20 Steve Brown .16 .40
21 Ryan Harrison .16 .40
1994 All Star Card
22 VooDoo Dolls .16 .40
23 1995 Season Schedules .04 .10
24 VooDoo Merchandise Card .04 .10
25 Titan (Mascot) .04 .10

2003-04 Vernon Vipers

This set features the Vipers of the BCJHL.

COMPLETE SET (22) 4.00 10.00
1 Checklist .01 .05
2 Steve Belanger .20 .50
3 David Boudreau .20 .50
4 Cole Byers .20 .50
5 Dustin Claffey .20 .50
6 Dallas Costanzo .20 .50
7 Scott Dafoe .20 .50
8 Ryan Kindret .20 .50
9 Reed Kipp .20 .50
10 Andrew Lord .20 .50
11 Mark Nelson .20 .50
12 Luke Pierce .20 .50
13 Les Reaney .20 .50
14 Mike Santorelli .20 .50
15 Mark Sibbald .20 .50
16 Aaron Volpatti .20 .50
17 Jake Wilkens .20 .50
18 Mark Wilson .20 .50
19 Andy Zulyniak .20 .50
20 Mike Vandekamp CO .02 .10
21 Bob Dever ACO .02 .10
22 Shawn Bourgeois ACO .02 .10

2004-05 Vernon Vipers

This set features the Vipers from the BCJHL.

COMPLETE SET (25) 6.00 15.00
1 Checklist Card .01 .05
2 Mark Nelson .30 .75
3 Mark Sibbald .30 .75
4 Dean Strong .30 .75
5 Matt Watkins .30 .75
6 History Card .01 .05
7 Sssniper MASCOT .01 .05
8 Andy Zulyniak .30 .75
9 Ryan Whitfield .30 .75
10 Scott Wallace .30 .75
11 Aaron Volpatti .30 .75
12 Mike Ullrich .30 .75
13 Rob Turville .30 .75
14 Lyle Tassone .30 .75
15 Matt Swerhone .30 .75
16 Aaron Schepers .30 .75
17 Mick McCrimmon .30 .75
18 Reed Kipp .30 .75
19 Corey Gannon .30 .75
20 Jeff Fedyk .30 .75
21 Wade Davison .30 .75
22 Dallas Costanzo .30 .75
23 Kurtis Colling .30 .75
24 Troy Cherwinski .30 .75
25 Matt Bourdreau .30 .75

2005-06 Vernon Vipers

COMPLETE SET (25) 6.00 15.00
1 Vernon Vipers CL .02 .10
2 David Arduin .30 .75
3 Hunter Bishop .30 .75
4 Travis Brisebois .30 .75
5 Patrick Cey .30 .75
6 Troy Cherwinski .30 .75
7 Andrew Coburn .30 .75
8 Chris Crowell .30 .75
9 Wade Davison .30 .75
10 Korey Gannon .30 .75
11 Chay Genoway .30 .75
12 Jerry Holden .30 .75
13 Kevyn Kirbyson .30 .75
14 Mickey McCrimmon .30 .75
15 Cody McMullin .30 .75
16 Mike Nichol .30 .75
17 Jon Olthuis .30 .75
18 Shawn Overton .30 .75
19 Matt Swerhone .30 .75
20 Mike Ullrich .30 .75
21 Aaron Volpatti .30 .75
22 Chad Wren .30 .75
23 Andy Zulyniak .30 .75
24 Viper History .02 .10
25 Sniper MASCOT .02 .10

1981-82 Victoria Cougars

This 16-card set was sponsored by the West Coast Savings Credit Union and Saanich Police Department Community Services. The cards measure approximately 3" by 5" and feature posed, color player photos with white borders. The player's name, position, and biographical information appear at the bottom. The cards are unnumbered and checklisted below in alphabetical order.

COMPLETE SET (16) 8.00 20.00
1 Bob Bales .40 1.00
2 Greg Barber .40 1.00
3 Ray Benik .40 1.00
4 Rich Chernomaz .60 1.50
5 Daryl Coldwell .40 1.00
6 Geoff Courtnall 2.80 7.00
7 Paul Cyr .80 2.00
8 Wade Jenson .40 1.00
9 Stu Kulak .60 1.50
10 Peter Martin .40 1.00
11 John Mokosak .40 1.00
12 Mark Morrison .40 1.00
13 Bryant Seaton .40 1.00
14 Jack Shupe .40 1.00
15 Eric Thurston .40 1.00
16 Randy Wickware .40 1.00

1982-83 Victoria Cougars

Featuring current and past players, this 24-card set features the Cougars of the WHL. The cards measure approximately 3" by 5" and feature color player portraits with red and blue borders on a white card face. Past player cards have the words "Graduation Series" stamped in the lower right corner of the picture (card numbers 7, 8, 13, 20-21). The cards are unnumbered and checklisted below in alphabetical order. The Doug Hannesson card has recently been confirmed. It apparently was pulled from the set before release and most copies destroyed. Because we have not yet confirmed one of these cards ever actually appearing in a team set, we no longer recognize it as part of the complete set.

COMPLETE SET (23) 20.00 40.00
1 Steve Bayliss .20 .50
2 Ray Benik .20 .50
3 Rich Chernomaz .40 1.00
4 Geoff Courtnall 1.20 3.00
5 Russ Courtnall 2.00 5.00
6 Paul Cyr .40 1.00
7 Curt Fraser .60 1.50
8 Grant Fuhr 10.00 25.00
9 Shawn Green .20 .50
10 Fabian Joseph .40 1.00
11 Stu Kulak .40 1.00
12 Brenn Leach .20 .50
13 Gary Lupul .20 .50
14 Jack MacKeigan .20 .50
15 Dave Mackey .40 1.00
16 Mark McLeary .20 .50
17 Dan Moberg .20 .50
18 John Mokosak .20 .50
19 Mark Morrison .20 .50
20 Brad Palmer .40 1.00
21 Barry Pederson .80 2.00
22 Eric Thurston .20 .50
23 Ron Viglasi .20 .50
24 Doug Hannesson 10.00 25.00

1983-84 Victoria Cougars

Featuring current and past players, this 24-card set was sponsored by the West Coast Savings Credit Union, CFAX 1070 Radio, and the Greater Victoria Police Departments. The cards measure approximately 3" by 5" and feature color player portraits with red and blue borders on a white card face. The player's name, position, and biographical information appear at the bottom. Past player cards have the words "Graduation Series" stamped in the lower right corner of the picture (card number 2 and 20). The cards are unnumbered and checklisted below in alphabetical order.

COMPLETE SET (24) 8.00 20.00
1 Misko Antisin .40 1.00
2 Murray Bannerman .80 2.00
3 Steve Baylis .20 .50
4 Paul Bifano .20 .50
5 Russ Courtnall 2.00 5.00
6 Greg Davies .20 .50
7 Dean Drozdiak .20 .50
8 Jim Gunn .20 .50
9 Richard Hajdu .20 .50
10 Randy Hansch .40 1.00
11 Matt Hervey .20 .50
12 Fabian Joseph .40 1.00
13 Rob Kivell .20 .50
14 Brenn Leach .20 .50
15 Jack Mackeigan .20 .50
16 Dave Mackey .20 .50
17 Tom Martin .20 .50
18 Darren Moren .30 .75
19 Adam Morrison .20 .50
20 Gord Roberts .20 .50
21 Dan Sexton .20 .50
22 Randy Siska .20 .50
23 Eric Thurston .20 .50
24 Simon Wheeldon .40 1.00

1984-85 Victoria Cougars

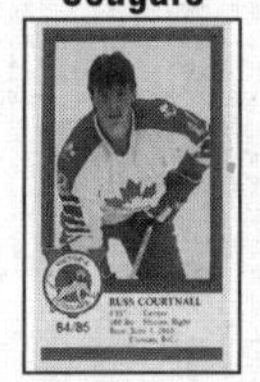

Featuring current and past players, this 24-card set was sponsored by the West Coast Savings Credit Union, CFAX 1070 Radio, and the Greater Victoria Police Departments. The cards measure approximately 3" by 5" and feature color player portraits with red and blue borders on a white card face. The player's name, position, and biographical information appear at the bottom. Past player cards have the words "Graduation Series" stamped in the lower right corner of the picture (card numbers 6 and 20). The cards are unnumbered and checklisted below in alphabetical order.

COMPLETE SET (24) 6.00 15.00
1 Misko Antisin .30 .75
2 Greg Batters .20 .50
3 Mel Bridgman .60 1.50
4 Chris Calverley .20 .50
5 Darin Choquette .20 .50
6 Geoff Courtnall .80 2.00
7 Russ Courtnall 1.20 3.00
8 Rick Davidson .20 .50
9 Bill Gregoire .20 .50
10 Richard Hajdu .30 .75
11 Randy Hansch .30 .75
12 Rob Kivell .20 .50
13 Brad Melin .20 .50
14 Jim Mentis .20 .50
15 Adam Morrison .20 .50
16 Mark Morrison .20 .50
17 Kodie Nelson .20 .50
18 Ken Priestlay .30 .75
19 Bruce Pritchard .20 .50
20 Torrie Robertson .40 1.00
21 Trevor Semeniuk .20 .50
22 Dan Sexton .20 .50
23 Randy Siska .20 .50
24 Chris Tarnowski .20 .50

1989-90 Victoria Cougars

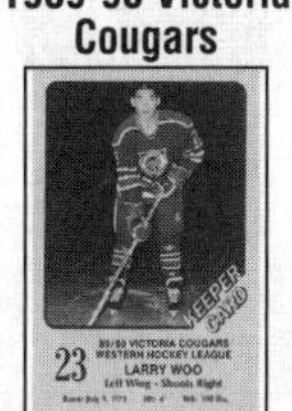

Sponsored by Safeway and Romeo's, this 21-card set measures approximately 2 3/4" by 4" and was sponsored by Flynn Printing and other area businesses. The cards feature color, posed action player photos with rounded corners on a yellow card face. The lower right corner of the picture is cut off and the words "Keeper Card" are written diagonally. The cards are unnumbered and checklisted below in alphabetical order.

COMPLETE SET (21) 4.00 10.00
1 John Badduke .20 .50
2 Terry Bendera .20 .50
3 Trevor Buchanan .20 .50
4 Jaret Burgoyne .30 .75
5 Dino Caputo .20 .50
6 Chris Catellier .20 .50
7 Mark Cipriano .20 .50
8 Milan Drag .20 .50
9 Dean Dyer .20 .50
10 Shayne Green .20 .50
11 Ryan Harrison .20 .50
12 Corey Jones .30 .75
13 Terry Klapstein .20 .50
14 Jason Knox .20 .50
15 Curtis Nykyforuk .20 .50
16 Jason Peters .20 .50
17 Blair Scott .20 .50
18 Mike Seaton .20 .50
19 Rob Sumner .20 .50
20 Larry Woo .20 .50
21 Jarret Zukiwsky .20 .50

2000-01 Victoriaville Tigres

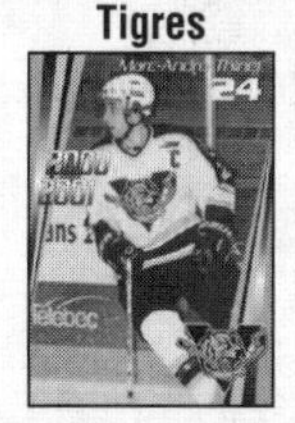

This set features les Tigres of the QMJHL. The set was produced by CTM-Ste-Foy and was sold by that card shop, as well as by the team.

COMPLETE SET (24) 4.80 12.00
1 James Sanford .20 .50
2 Carl Mallette .30 .75
3 Matthew Lombardi .20 .50
4 Teddy Kyres .20 .50
5 Martin Autotte .20 .50
6 Simon St-Pierre .20 .50
7 Pierre-Luc Daneau .20 .50
8 Antoine Vermette .40 1.00
9 Marc-Andre Thinel .40 1.00
10 Mathieu Wathier .20 .50
11 Pierre-Luc Sleigher .20 .50
12 Sandro Sbrocca .20 .50
13 Jonathan Fauteux .20 .50
14 Sergei Kaltygen .20 .50
15 Adam Wojcik .20 .50
16 Jean-Francois Nogues .30 .75
17 Richard Paul .20 .50
18 David Masse .20 .50
19 Luc Levesque .20 .50
20 Mathieu Brunelle .20 .50
21 Sebastien Morissette .20 .50
22 Sebastien Thinel .20 .50
23 Danny Groulx .20 .50
24 Mario Durocher CO .10 .25

2000-01 Victoriaville Tigres Signed

This set is exactly the same as the base Tigres set from this season, save that every card has been hand signed by the player pictured. Each card also is serial numbered out of just 100.

COMPLETE SET (24) 20.00 50.00
1 James Sanford .80 2.00
2 Carl Mallette 1.20 3.00
3 Matthew Lombardi .80 2.00
4 Teddy Kyres .80 2.00
5 Martin Autotte .80 2.00
6 Simon St-Pierre .80 2.00
7 Pierre-Luc Daneau .80 2.00
8 Antoine Vermette 2.00 5.00
9 Marc-Andre Thinel 2.00 5.00
10 Mathieu Wathier .80 2.00
11 Pierre-Luc Sleigher .80 2.00
12 Sandro Sbrocca .80 2.00
13 Jonathan Fauteux .80 2.00
14 Sergei Kaltygen .80 2.00
15 Adam Wojcik .80 2.00
16 Jean-Francois Nogues 1.20 3.00
17 Richard Paul .80 2.00
18 David Masse .80 2.00
19 Luc Levesque .80 2.00
20 Mathieu Brunelle .80 2.00
21 Sebastien Morissette .80 2.00
22 Sebastien Thinel .80 2.00
23 Danny Groulx .80 2.00
24 Mario Durocher CO .80 2.00

2003-04 Victoriaville Tigers

COMPLETE SET (29) 6.00 15.00
1 Matthew Augustine .20 .50
2 Justin Belanger .20 .50
3 Gabriel Boies .20 .50
4 Francis Charland .20 .50
5 Renaud Des Alliers .20 .50
6 Benoit Doucet .20 .50
7 Kyle Doucet .20 .50
8 Jeremy Duchesne .30 .75
9 Cole Fetzner .20 .50
10 Benoit Fournier .20 .50
11 Guillaume Fournier .20 .50
12 Scott Gibson .20 .50
13 Ryan Jenner .20 .50
14 Martin Kasik .20 .50
15 Arthur Kiyaga .20 .50
16 Tommy Lafontaine .20 .50
17 Christian Laroche .20 .50
18 Daniel Manzato .30 .75
19 Olivier Plouffe .20 .50
20 Michael Ramsay .20 .50
21 Robin Richards .20 .50
22 Jonathan Ryan .20 .50
23 Mario Scalzo .40 1.00
24 Daniel Sparre .20 .50
25 Simon St-Pierre .20 .50
26 Josh Tordjman .40 1.00
27 Guillaume Trudel .20 .50
NNO Mario Scalzo TL .20 .50
NNO Francis Charland TL .20 .50

2004-05 Victoriaville Tigres

A total of 350 team sets were produced.

COMPLETE SET (30) 6.00 15.00
1 Maxim Noreau .20 .50
2 Jeremy Duchesne .20 .50
3 Justin Belanger .20 .50
4 Jan Danecek .20 .50
5 Gabriel Boies .20 .50
6 Pierre-Olivier Dupere .20 .50
7 Danny Hollet .20 .50
8 Alexandre Imbeault .20 .50
9 Josh Tordjman .40 1.00
10 Jason Legault .20 .50
11 Tommy Lafontaine .20 .50
12 Bruce Noivo .20 .50
13 Mike Ramsay .20 .50
14 Arthur Kiyaga .20 .50
15 Matt Nickerson .40 1.00
16 Renaud Des Alliers .20 .50
17 Mario Scalzo Jr .40 1.00
18 Samuel Hounsell .20 .50
19 Benoit Doucet .20 .50
20 Francis Guerette-Charland .20 .50
21 Kyle Doucet .20 .50
22 Trevor Mock .20 .50
23 Erick Lizon .20 .50
24 Ryan Jenner .20 .50
25 Maxime Desruisseaux .20 .50
26 Brant Miller .20 .50
27 Nicolas Laplante .20 .50
28 Gabriel Houde-Brisson .20 .50
29 Toby Lafrance .20 .50
30 Alexandre Vachon .20 .50

2005-06 Victoriaville Tigres

COMPLETE SET (22) 6.00 15.00
1 Keven Guerette-Charland .30 .75
2 Jason Legault .30 .75
3 Ryan Jenner .30 .75
4 Benoit Doucet .30 .75
5 Josh Tordjman .60 1.50
6 Benoit Massicotte .30 .75
7 Toby Lafrance .30 .75
8 Gabriel Boies .30 .75
9 Jan Danecek .30 .75
10 Renaud Des Alliers .30 .75
11 Philippe Brisebois .30 .75
12 Alexandre Imbeault .30 .75
13 Maxim Noreau .30 .75
14 Brant Miller .60 1.50
15 Carl Chamberland .30 .75
16 Pierre-Olivier Duperre .30 .75
17 Matthew David .30 .75
18 Erick Lizon .30 .75
19 Trevor Mock .30 .75
20 Francis Guerette-Charland .30 .75
21 Adam Ross .30 .75
22 Stephan Lebeau .30 .75

2006-07 Victoriaville Tigres

COMPLETE SET (24) 5.00 12.00
1 Morten Madsen .40 1.00
2 Keven Veilleux .40 1.00
3 Jean-Christophe Blanchard .20 .50
4 Kevin Poulin .20 .50
5 Maxim Noreau .20 .50
6 Carl Chamberland .20 .50
7 Erick Tremblay .20 .50
8 Jan Kolarik .20 .50
9 Sansdrick Lavoie .20 .50
10 Dave Nolin .20 .50
11 Maxime Robichaud .20 .50
12 Jason Demers .20 .50
13 Jason Legault .20 .50
14 David Foucher .20 .50
15 Keven Guerette-Charland .20 .50
16 Dany Roch .20 .50
17 Adam Ross .20 .50
18 Vincent Zaore-Vanie .20 .50
19 Philippe-Michael Devos .20 .50
20 Kyle Kelly .20 .50
21 Kyle Mcneil .20 .50
22 Benoit Doucet .20 .50
23 Francis Guerette-Charland .20 .50
24 Toby Lafrance .20 .50

1993-94 Waterloo Black Hawks

This 27-card standard-size set features the Waterloo Black Hawks of the USHL. The fronts feature color action player photos, with the team name and logo in a red border above the photo, and the player's name, number, and position beneath it. The cards are unnumbered and checklisted below in alphabetical order.

COMPLETE SET (27) 3.60 9.00
1 Brent Bessey .16 .40
2 Jason Blake .30 .75
3 Scott Brand GM .04 .10
4 Eric Brown .16 .40
5 Rod Butler .16 .40
6 Chris Coakley .16 .40
7 Austin Crawford .16 .40
8 Doug Dietz ACO .04 .10
9 Jon Garver .16 .40
10 Brian Folden .16 .40
11 Bobby Hayes .16 .40
12 Jake Jacoby .16 .40
13 Terry Jarkowsky .16 .40
14 Jeff Kozakowski UER .16 .40
(Misspelled Kozakowski on front)
15 Josh Lampman .16 .40
16 Marty Laurila .16 .40
17 Steve McCall ANN .04 .10
18 Bill McNelis .16 .40
19 Rich Metro .16 .40
20 Scott Mikesch CO .04 .10
21 Barry Soskin PR .04 .10
22 Ben Stadey .16 .40
23 Ed Stanek .16 .40
24 Todd Steinmetz .16 .40
25 Scott Swanjord .20 .50
26 Miles Van Tassel .16 .40
27 Supporting Staff .04 .10
Dave Christians
Mike Christians
Bill Eggers

1995-96 Waterloo Blackhawks

Thanks to collector Dale Sprenger for providing this checklist and the information for many other unusual minor and junior sets.

COMPLETE SET (26) 25.00 50.00
1 Jayme Adduono 1.00 2.50
2 Chris Cerrella 1.00 2.50
3 Mark Eaton 1.25 3.00
4 Jason Furness 1.00 2.50
5 Joe Gray UER .10 .25
6 Zach Ham 1.00 2.50
7 Trevor Hanger 1.00 2.50
8 Kris Harris 1.00 2.50
9 Steve Holecy 1.00 2.50
10 Lubos Krajcovic 1.00 2.50
11 Jeff Melnechuk 1.00 2.50
12 Jimmy Mroz 1.00 2.50
13 Bobby Owen 1.00 2.50
14 Anthony Perardi 1.00 2.50
15 Chad Poliquin 1.00 2.50
16 Dan Ragusett 1.00 2.50
17 Ryan Rentz 1.00 2.50
18 Ryan Sarazin 1.00 2.50
19 Doug Schmidt 1.00 2.50
20 Andrew Tortorella 1.00 2.50
21 Roger Trudeau 1.00 2.50
22 Mark Wilkinson 1.00 2.50
23 Scott MikeschÂ COÂ .10 .25
24 Barry Soskin Owner .10 .25
25 Scott Brand GM .10 .25
26 Jason Shaver PR .10 .25

2003-04 Waterloo Blackhawks

Team-issued set features the Blackhawks of the USHL. The checklist below may not be complete. The cards are unnumbered. Checklist courtesy of collector Vinnie Montalbano.

COMPLETE SET (21) 8.00 20.00
1 Joel Hanson .40 1.00
2 Joe Pavelski .40 1.00
3 Matt Fornataro .40 1.00
4 Kevin Regan .75 2.00
5 Garrett Regan .40 1.00
6 Zach Bearson .40 1.00
7 Dan Sturges .40 1.00
8 Tim Filangieri .40 1.00
9 Mike Radja .40 1.00
10 Michael Annett .40 1.00
11 Andrew Thomas .40 1.00
12 Aaron Johnson .75 2.00
13 John Vadnais .40 1.00
14 Jesse Vesel .40 1.00
15 Jake Schwan .40 1.00
16 Josh Duncan .40 1.00
17 Jon-Paul Testwuide .40 1.00
18 Mike Dagenais .40 1.00
19 Dustin Molle .40 1.00
20 David Meckler .40 1.00
21 Peter MacArthur .40 1.00

2004-05 Waterloo Blackhawks

This unnumbered set was issued as a game-night giveaway over the course of several nights. It's likely that the checklist is incomplete. Additional information can be forwarded to hockeymag@beckett.com.

COMPLETE SET (15?)

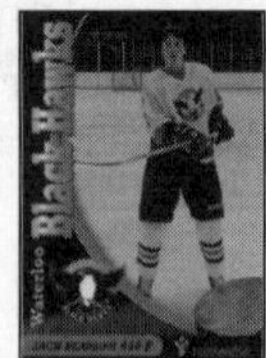

1 Drew Dobson
2 Tomas Petruska
3 Michael Annett
4 Nathan Lawrence
5 Zach Bearson
6 Matt Arhontas
7 Dustin Molle
8 Joe Grossman
9 Mike Testwuide
10 Jesse Vesel
11 Thomas Fortney
12 Garrett Regan
13 Drew O'Connell
14 Chris Tok ACO
15 Zac Headrick ACO

2005-06 Waterloo Blackhawks

COMPLETE SET (30) 6.00 15.00
1 Ricky Akkerman .20 .50
2 Matt Arhontas .20 .50
3 Zach Bearson .20 .50
4 Eric Bennett .20 .50
5 Andy Bohmbach .20 .50
6 Mike Borisnok .20 .50
7 Cody Chupp .20 .50
8 Kurt Davis .20 .50
9 Drew Dobson .20 .50
10 Tim Gilbert .20 .50
11 Joe Grossman .20 .50
12 Brad Hoelzer .20 .50
13 Christian Jensen .20 .50
14 Vincent LeVerde .20 .50
15 James Marcou .20 .50
16 Clark Oliver .20 .50
17 Kyle Reeds .20 .50
18 mitch Ryan .40 1.00
19 Pasko Skarica .20 .50
20 Joe Sova .20 .50
21 Jeremy Tejchma .20 .50
22 Mike Testwuide .20 .50
23 Isak Tranvik .20 .50
24 Kenny Wochele .40 1.00
25 P K O'HandleyÂ CO .20 .50
26 Chris TokÂ ACO .20 .50
27 Zac Headrick ACO .20 .50
28 Derrick Johnson ACO .20 .50
29 Dave Graham EQM .20 .50
30 Todd Klein TR .20 .50

1992-93 Western Michigan Broncos

These 30 standard-size cards feature color player photos on their fronts, some are action shots, others are posed. These photos are borderless on the sides. The player's name and position appear in a brown bar upon a yellow stripe across the bottom. His uniform number appears within a brown stripe across the top. The cards are unnumbered and checklisted below in alphabetical order.

COMPLETE SET (30) 4.80 12.00
1 Chris Belanger .20 .50
2 Joe Bonnett .16 .40
3 Brent Brekke .20 .50
4 Chris Brooks .16 .40
5 Craig Brown .16 .40
6 Jeremy Brown .16 .40
7 Tom Carriere .16 .40
8 Scott Chartier .20 .50
9 Ryan D'Arcy .16 .40
10 Pat Ferschweiler .16 .40
11 Brian Gallentine .16 .40
12 Jim Holman .16 .40
13 Derek Innanen .16 .40
14 Jason Jennings .20 .50
15 Mikhail Lapin .20 .50
16 Francois Leroux .20 .50
17 Jamal Mayers .60 1.50
18 Kevin McCaffrey ACO .04 .10
19 Dave Mitchell .16 .40
20 Brian Renfrew .16 .40
21 Mike Schafer ACO .04 .10
22 Derek Schooley .16 .40
23 Neil Smith .20 .50
WMU Hall of Fame
24 Colin Ward .16 .40
25 Dave Weaver .16 .40
26 Mike Whitton .16 .40
27 Bill Wilkinson CO .04 .10
28 Peter Wilkinson .16 .40
29 Byron Witkowski .16 .40
30 Lawson Arena .04 .10

1993-94 Western Michigan Broncos

These 30 standard-size cards feature color player photos on their fronts, some are action shots, others are posed. These photos are borderless on three sides. The player's

name and uniform number appear vertically in the brown left margin. The cards are unnumbered and checklisted below in alphabetical order.

COMPLETE SET (30) 6.00 15.00
1 David Agnew .20 .50
2 Brent Brekke .30 .75
3 Chris Brooks .20 .50
4 Craig Brown .20 .50
5 Jeremy Brown .20 .50
6 Justin Cardwell .20 .50
7 Tom Carriere .20 .50
8 Tony Code .20 .50
9 Matt Cressman .20 .50
10 Jim Culhane ACO .04 .10
11 Ryan D'Arcy .20 .50
12 Brian Gallentine .20 .50
13 Matt Greene .20 .50
14 Rob Hodge .20 .50
WMU Hall of Fame
15 Jim Holman .20 .50
16 Derek Innanen .20 .50
17 Mark Jodoin .20 .50
18 Brendan Kenny .20 .50
19 Misha Lapin .20 .50
20 Darren Maloney .20 .50
21 Jamal Mayers .80 2.00
22 Dave Mitchell .20 .50
23 Brian Renfrew .20 .50
24 Mike Schafer ACO .04 .10
25 Derek Schooley .20 .50
26 Colin Ward .20 .50
27 Mike Whitton .20 .50
28 Bill Wilkinson CO .04 .10
29 Peter Wilkinson .20 .50
30 Shawn Zimmerman .20 .50

2001-02 Western Michigan Broncos

This set features the Broncos of the NCAA. Little is known about the set and its distribution, or even if the checklist is complete. If you have any additional information, please forward it to hockeymag@beckett.com.

COMPLETE SET (10) 4.00 10.00
1 Anthony Battaglia .40 1.00
2 Mike Bishai .40 1.00
3 Ryan Crane .40 1.00
4 Bryan Farquhar .40 1.00
5 Chad Kline .40 1.00
6 Austin Miller .40 1.00
7 Jeff Reynaert .40 1.00
8 Wayne Gagne ATG .40 1.00
9 Harry Lawson CO .40 1.00
10 Team Photo .40 1.00

2006-07 Westside Warriors

COMPLETE SET (21) 6.00 15.00
1 The General MASCOT .02 .10
2 Mark Howell CO .02 .10
3 Stephen Caple .30 .75
4 Eric Fraser .30 .75
5 Brock Meadows .30 .75
6 Joel Woznikoski .30 .75
7 Chris Santiago .30 .75
8 Denis Semenov .30 .75
9 Craig Eisenhut .30 .75
10 Kevin Walrod .30 .75
11 Tommy Grant .30 .75
12 Micah Anderson .30 .75
13 Chris Vassos .30 .75
14 Ron Kelly .30 .75
15 Brad Plumton .30 .75
16 Trevor Bailey .30 .75
17 Brendan Ellis .30 .75
18 August Aiken .30 .75
19 Konrad Becker .30 .75
20 Bryce Kakoske .30 .75
21 Sam Huston .30 .75
22 Milrod Kos .30 .75
23 Marcel Bruinsma .30 .75
24 Mark Howell CO .02 .10

1996-97 Wheeling Nailers

This 23-card set of the Wheeling Nailers of the ECHL was produced by Split Second. The cards feature action photography on the front, along with the player's name and number and the team logo. The backs have a brief stats package, along with a larger interpretation of the player's number. As these cards are unnumbered otherwise, they are listed alphabetically below.

COMPLETE SET (23) 3.20 8.00
1 Scotty Allegrino TR .04 .10
2 John Badduke .20 .50
3 Frederic Barbeau .16 .40
4 John Blessman .16 .40
5 Francois Bouillon .16 .40
6 Greg Callahan .16 .40
7 Don Chase .16 .40
8 Jason Clark .16 .40
9 Keli Corpse .16 .40
10 Chad Dameworth .16 .40
11 Ryan Haggerty .20 .50
12 Martin LePage .16 .40
13 Ian McIntyre .16 .40
14 Greg McLean .16 .40
15 Mike Minard .20 .50
16 Perry Pappas .16 .40
17 Eric Royal .16 .40
18 Brad Symes .16 .40
19 John Tanner .20 .50
20 Rob Trumbley .16 .40
21 John Varga .30 .75
22 Tom McVie CO .16 .40
23 Spike Mascot .04 .10

1997-98 Wheeling Nailers

This 25-card set was given out at games as a sheet of perforated cards in a photo pack. The cards measure 2x3". The set was sponsored by TV-WTOV, Nickles, and Undo's. The cards are listed in the order they appear on the sheet.

COMPLETE SET (25) 3.20 8.00
1 J.F. Boutin .16 .40
2 Chris Jensen .16 .40
3 Dan Jablonic .16 .40
4 Dmitri Tarabrin .16 .40
5 Matt Garzone .16 .40
6 Jeremy Brown .16 .40
7 Joe Harney .16 .40
8 Scott Kirton .16 .40
9 Patrick Charbonneau .16 .40
10 Matt Van Horlick .16 .40
11 Mike Latendresse .20 .50
12 Karl Infanger .16 .40
13 Olie Sundstrom .20 .50
14 Stefan Brannare .16 .40
15 Fredrik Svensson .16 .40
16 Marquis Mathieu .30 .75
17 Sergei Radchenko .20 .50
18 Alex Matvichuk .16 .40
19 Kurt Brown .16 .40
20 Quinten Van Horlick .16 .40
21 Nailers Logo .04 .10
22 Swaze Armstrong TR .04 .10
23 Vinny Ferraiuolo EM .04 .10
24 Spike Mascot .04 .10
25 Peter Laviolette HCO .20 .50

1997-98 Wheeling Nailers Photo Pack

This 25-card set measures 2 1/8" X 3 1/8". It was a game-night giveaway sponsored by Nickles Bread. The set is attached as a single sheet. The set is not numbered so the cards appear in sheet order.

COMPLETE SET (25) 4.80 12.00
1 J.F. Boutin .20 .50
2 Chris Jensen .20 .50
3 Dan Jablonic .20 .50
4 Dmitri Tarabrin .30 .75
5 Matt Garzone .20 .50
6 Jeremy Brown .20 .50
7 Joe Harney .20 .50
8 Scott Kirton .20 .50
9 Patrick Charbonneau .20 .50
10 Matt Van Horlick .20 .50
11 Mike Latendresse .30 .75
12 Karl Infanger .20 .50
13 Olie Sundstrom .30 .75
14 Stefane Brannare .20 .50
15 Fredrik Svensson .20 .50
16 Marquis Mathieu .40 1.00
17 Sergei Radchenko .30 .75
18 Alex Matvichuk .20 .50
19 Kurt Brown .20 .50
20 Quinten Van Horlick .20 .50
21 Nailers History Card .04 .10
22 Swaze Armstrong TR .04 .10
23 Vinny Ferraiuolo MGR .04 .10
24 Spike Mascot .04 .10
25 Peter Laviolette HCO .20 .50

2003-04 Wheeling Nailers

COMPLETE SET (16) 20.00
81 Nick Boucher 2.00
82 Steven Crampton 1.25
83 Jean-Francois Dufour 1.25
84 Drew Fata 1.50
85 Brendon Hodge 1.25
86 Jason Jaffray 1.25
87 Mark Kosick 1.25
88 Kamil Kuriplach 1.25
89 Mario Larocque 1.25
90 Brad Mehalko 1.25
91 Jake Ortmeyer 1.25
92 Eduard Pershin 1.25
93 T.J. Reynolds 2.00
94 Alexandre Rouleau 1.25
95 Bogdan Rudenko 1.25
96 J.C. Ruid 1.25

2004-05 Wheeling Nailers Riesbeck's

This set was available with a minimum food purchase at Riesbeck's Food Market in Wheeling.

COMPLETE SET (20) 8.00 20.00
1 Team Card .20 .50
2 Alexandre Rouleau .40 1.00
3 Amands Berzins .40 1.00
4 Team Staff .20 .50
5 Cam Paddock .40 1.00
6 Cliff Loya .40 1.00
7 Curtiss Patrick .40 1.00
8 Dany Sabourin 1.25 3.00
9 Ed McGrane .40 1.00
10 Evgeny Lazarev .40 1.00
11 Brendon Hodge .40 1.00
12 James Laux .40 1.00
13 Joe Exter .40 1.00
14 Kenny Corupe .75 2.00
15 Pascal Morency .40 1.00
16 Randy Perry .40 1.00
17 Ray DiLauro .40 1.00
18 Steve Crampton .40 1.00
19 Kraft Sponsor .02 .10
20 FritoLay Sponsor .02 .10

2004-05 Wheeling Nailers SGA

These cards were given away at home games. We have confirmed the cards given away at two such games on Nov. 14 and March 15. It's likely that others exist. Please contact us at hockeymag@beckett.com if you have further information.

COMPLETE SET(?)
1 Mark Kosick
2 Ben Blais
3 Brendon Hodge
4 Pat Bingham CO
5 AAP Sponsor
6 KoSports Sponsor
7 Joe Exter
8 Randy Perry
9 Pascal Morency
10 McDonald's Sponsor
11 Newspaper Sponsor

1992-93 Wheeling Thunderbirds

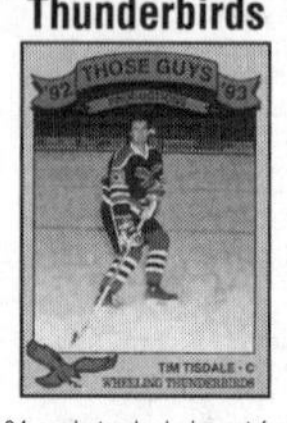

This 24-card standard-size set features color, posed action player photos. The pictures are set on a gray card face with a red banner above the photo that contains the year and the manufacturer name (Those Guys Productions). The player's name, position, and team name are printed below the picture.

COMPLETE SET (24) 2.80 7.00
1 Title Card .04 .10
2 Claude Barthe .16 .40
3 Joel Blain .16 .40
4 Derek DeCosty .16 .40
5 Marc Deschamps .16 .40
6 Tom Dion .16 .40
7 Devin Edgerton .16 .40
8 Pete Heine .16 .40
9 Kim Maier .16 .40
10 Mike Millham .20 .50
11 Cory Paterson .16 .40
12 Trevor Pochipinski .16 .40
13 Tim Roberts .16 .40
14 Mark Rodgers .16 .40
15 Darren Schwartz .16 .40
16 Trevor Senn .16 .40
17 Tim Tisdale .16 .40
18 John Uniac .20 .50
19 Denny Magruder MG .04 .10
20 Chuck Greenwood .04 .10
Jim Smith (Producers)
21 Larry Kish VP/MG .04 .10
22 Doug Sauter CO .04 .10
23 T-Bird (Mascot) .04 .10
24 Doug Bacon .16 .40

1993-94 Wheeling Thunderbirds

Minor league expert Ralph Slate reports that these cards were distributed in three different manners: Cards 1-21 were the standard team set, available all season long at home games. Cards PC1-PC4 were handed out as premiums at games. Cards UD1-UD10 comprise a late-season update set which was sold separately. The three are combined here for cataloguing purposes, but may be found on the market as separate entities.

COMPLETE SET (21) 10.00 25.00
1 Header Card CL .04 .10
2 Darren Schwartz .16 .40
3 Cory Paterson .16 .40
4 Derek DeCosty .16 .40
5 Jim Bermingham .16 .40
6 Brock Woods .16 .40
7 Tim Roberts .16 .40
8 Eric Raymond .16 .40
9 Brett Abel .16 .40
10 Sebastien Fortier .16 .40
11 John Johnson .16 .40
12 Brent Pope .16 .40
13 Marquis Mathieu .30 .75
14 Terry Virtue .20 .50
15 Vadim Slivchenko .20 .50
16 Clayton Gainer .16 .40
17 Sylvain LaPointe .16 .40
18 Doug Sauter CO .04 .10
19 Larry Kish VP GM .04 .10
20 Denny Magruder GM .04 .10
21 Bill Cordery ASST TR .04 .10
PC1 Wheeling Thunderbirds 2.00 5.00
PC2 Darren Schwartz 2.00 5.00
PC3 Tim Tisdale 2.00 5.00
PC4 Cory Paterson 2.00 5.00
UD1 Update Checklist .04 .10
UD2 Tim Tisdale .40 1.00
UD3 John Van Kessel .40 1.00
UD4 Rival Fullum .40 1.00
UD5 Steve Gibson .40 1.00
UD6 Dave Goucher .04 .10
Director of Communication
UD7 Gary Zearott .04 .10
Photographer
UD8 Darren Schwartz .04 .10
T-Bird Leader
UD9 Vadim Slivchenko .40 1.00
T-Bird Leader
UD10 Brock Woods .40 1.00
T-Bird Leader

1994-95 Wheeling Thunderbirds

This 25-card set of the Wheeling Thunderbirds of the ECHL was produced by Those Guys for the team. The set was available through the club at games. The stylish fronts featured a player photo, name, number and position, along with team logo.

COMPLETE SET (25) 2.00 5.00
1 Checklist .10 .25
2 Tim Tisdale .20 .50
3 Brock Woods .20 .50
4 Vadim Slivchenko .20 .50
5 Tim Roberts .20 .50
6 Derek DeCosty .20 .50
7 Steve Gibson .20 .50
8 Xavier Majic .24 .60
9 Peter Marek .20 .50
10 Greg Louder .20 .50
11 Gairin Smith .20 .50
12 Darren McAusland .20 .50
13 Brent Pope .10 .25
14 Dominic Fafard .10 .25
15 Pat Barton .10 .25
16 Patrick Labrecque .10 .25
17 Lorne Toews .10 .25
18 Scott Matusovich .10 .25
19 Louis Bernard .10 .25
20 Doug Sutter .10 .25
21 Scott Allegrino TR .10 .25
22 Bill Cordery .10 .25
23 Mark Landini .10 .25
PC1 Xavier Majic .30 .75
PC2 Vadim Slivchenko .30 .75

1995-96 Wheeling Thunderbirds

Sponsored by Nickles Bread, this 24-card set was produced by Zee Productions. The cards measure 2 1/8" X 3 1/8" and were released as part of a perforated sheet, with a large team photo at the top of the set.

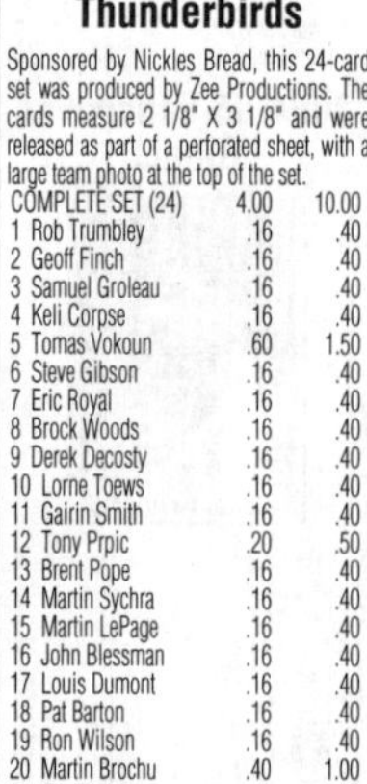

COMPLETE SET (24) 4.00 10.00
1 Rob Trumbley .16 .40
2 Geoff Finch .16 .40
3 Samuel Groleau .16 .40
4 Keli Corpse .16 .40
5 Tomas Vokoun .60 1.50
6 Steve Gibson .16 .40
7 Eric Royal .16 .40
8 Brock Woods .16 .40
9 Derek Decosty .16 .40
10 Lorne Toews .16 .40
11 Gairin Smith .16 .40
12 Tony Prpic .20 .50
13 Brent Pope .16 .40
14 Martin Sychra .16 .40
15 Martin LePage .16 .40
16 John Blessman .16 .40
17 Louis Dumont .16 .40
18 Pat Barton .16 .40
19 Ron Wilson .16 .40
20 Martin Brochu .40 1.00
21 Tim Tisdale .16 .40
22 Larry Kish HCO .04 .10
23 Scott Allegrino TR .04 .10
24 T Bird Mascot .04 .10

1995-96 Wheeling Thunderbirds Series II

Sponsored by Nickles Bread, this 20-card set was produced by Zee Productions. The cards measure 2 1/8" X 3 1/8" and came attached with large photos of the two goalies Geoff Finch and Tomas Vokoun.

COMPLETE SET (20) 3.20 8.00
1 John Badduke .20 .50
2 Pat Barton .16 .40
3 John Blessman .16 .40
4 Keli Corpse .16 .40
5 Louis Dumont .16 .40
6 Geoff Finch .30 .75
7 Steve Gibson .16 .40
8 Samuel Groleau .16 .40
9 Martin LePage .16 .40
10 Kevin Lune .16 .40
11 Brent Pope .16 .40
12 Tim Roberts .16 .40
13 Eric Royal .16 .40
14 Gairin Smith .16 .40
15 Lorne Toews .16 .40
16 Tim Tisdale .16 .40
17 Rob Trumbley .16 .40
18 Tomas Vokoun .60 1.50
19 Ron Wilson .16 .40
20 Brock Woods .16 .40

1993-94 Wichita Thunder

As with all CHL sets issued this season, these are round cards approximately the size of a hockey puck. They come in a plastic container with the team logo on the front, and were sold by the team's booster club for about $5 per set.

COMPLETE SET (18) 3.20 8.00
1 Bob Berg .20 .50
2 Mark Bourgeois .20 .50
3 Steve Chelios .20 .50
4 Robert Desjardins .20 .50
5 Paul Dukovac .20 .50
6 Yannick Gosselin .20 .50
7 Ron Handy .20 .50
8 Jamie Hearn .20 .50
9 Roger Hunt .20 .50
10 Paul Jackson .20 .50
11 James Latos .20 .50
12 Greg Neish .20 .50
13 Brent Sapergia .20 .50
14 Darren Srochenski .20 .50
15 Stephane Venne .20 .50
16 Rob Weingartner .20 .50
17 Jack Williams .20 .50
18 Doug Shedden CO .08 .20

1998-99 Wichita Thunder

This 25-card set was given out at a game late in the season and then was sold at the merchandise stand.

COMPLETE SET (25) 4.80 12.00
1 Checklist .04 .10
2 Vernon Beardy .20 .50
3 Travis Clayton .20 .50
4 Chris Dashney .20 .50
5 Mike Donaghue .20 .50
6 Jason Duda .20 .50
7 Rhett Dudley .20 .50
8 Trevor Folk .20 .50
9 Todd Howarth .20 .50
10 John Kachur .20 .50
11 Mark Karpen .20 .50
12 Lance Leslie .30 .75
13 Brad Link .20 .50
14 Mark Macera .30 .75
15 Walker McDonald .20 .50
16 John McGeough .20 .50
17 Thomas Migdal .20 .50
18 Aaron Novak .20 .50
19 Sean O'Reilly .30 .75
20 Kevin Powell .20 .50
21 Greg Smith .30 .75
22 Travis Tipler .20 .50
23 Troy Yarosh .20 .50
24 Bryan Wells HCO .04 .10
25 Goodwrench Dealer Logo .01

1999-00 Wichita Thunder

This set features the Thunder of the CHL. The cards feature full color fronts with name and position on the lower front of the card. Backs feature statistical and biographical information. The cards are unnumbered and checklisted below in alphabetical order.

COMPLETE SET (25) 4.00 10.00
1 Vern Beardy .16 .40
2 Travis Clayton .30 .75
3 Chris Dashney .16 .40
4 Mike Donaghue .16 .40
5 Jason Duda .16 .40
6 Rhett Dudley .16 .40
7 Trevor Folk .16 .40
8 Todd Howarth .16 .40
9 John Kachur .16 .40
10 Mark Karpen .16 .40
11 Lance Leslie .30 .75
12 Brad Link .16 .40
13 Mark Macera .16 .40
14 Walker McDonald .16 .40
15 Jim McGeough .16 .40
16 Thomas Migdal .16 .40
17 Aaron Novak .16 .40
18 Sean O'Reilly .16 .40
19 Kevin Powell .16 .40
20 Greg Smith .30 .75
21 Travis Tipler .16 .40
22 Troy Yarosh .16 .40
23 Bryan Wells .16 .40
24 Title Card .04 .10
25 Dealer Logo Card .04 .10

2000-01 Wichita Thunder

This set features the Thunder of the CHL. Little is known about the set beyond the confirmed checklist. Any additional information can be forwarded to hockeymag@beckett.com.

COMPLETE SET (22) 6.00 15.00
1 Jerod Bina .30 .75
2 Troy Caley .30 .75
3 Travis Clayton .30 .75
4 Trevor Converse .30 .75
5 Mike Donaghue .30 .75
6 Jason Duda .30 .75

7 Rhett Dudley .30 .75
8 Rocky Florio .30 .75
9 Trevor Folk .30 .75
10 Dwayne Gylywoychuk .30 .75
11 Derrek Harper .30 .75
12 Mike Hiebert .30 .75
13 Mark Karpen .30 .75
14 Lance Leslie .30 .75
15 Jim McGeough .30 .75
16 Aaron Novak .30 .75
17 Sean O'Reilly .30 .75
18 Kevin Powell .30 .75
19 Kris Schultz .30 .75
20 Greg Smith .30 .75
21 Mark Strohack .30 .75
22 Checklist .02 .10

2000-01 Wilkes-Barre Scranton Penguins

This set features the Penguins of the AHL. The set was produced by Choice Marketing and handed out as a game night promotion late in the season.

COMPLETE SET (28) 5.00 20.00
1 Dennis Bonvie .20 1.50
2 Brendan Buckley .20 .75
3 Sven Butenschon .20 .75
4 Sebastien Caron .40 1.50
5 Greg Crozier .20 1.00
6 Trent Cull .20 .75
7 Andrew Ference .30 1.00
8 Dylan Gyori .20 1.00
9 Chris Kelleher .20 .75
10 Tom Kostopoulos .20 1.00
11 Joel Laing .20 .75
12 Jim Leger .20 .75
13 Jason MacDonald .20 .75
14 Alexandre Mathieu .20 .75
15 Josef Melichar .20 .75
16 Eric Meloche .20 .75
17 Rich Parent .30 1.00
18 Glenn Patrick HCO .08 .25
19 Toby Petersen .20 1.00
20 John Slaney .20 .75
21 Martin Sonnenberg .20 .75
22 Jean-Philippe Soucy .30 1.00
23 Billy Tibbetts .40 1.50
24 Darcy Verot .20 .75
25 Mike Yeo ACO .20 .10
26 Alexander Zevakhin .20 .75
27 Tux MASCOT .20 .10
28 Checklist .20 .01

2001-02 Wilkes-Barre Scranton Penguins

This set features the Penguins of the AHL. The set was produced by Choice Marketing and was sold at home games.

COMPLETE SET (26) 4.80 12.00
1 Robbie Tallas .30 .75
2 Robert Scuderi .20 .50
3 David Koci .20 .50
4 Brooks Orpik .30 .75
5 Darcy Robinson .20 .50
6 Mike Wilson .20 .50
7 Darcy Verot .20 .50
8 Ross Lupaschuk .20 .50
9 Martin Sonnenberg .20 .50
10 Jan Fadrny .20 .50
11 Alexander Zevakhin .20 .50
12 Shane Endicott .40 1.00
13 Brendan Buckley .20 .50
14 Jason MacDonald .20 .50
15 Tomas Surovy .20 .50
16 Tom Kostopoulos .20 .50
17 Alexandre Mathieu .20 .50
18 Peter Ratchuk .20 .50
19 Sebastien Caron .30 .75
20 Steve Parsons .30 .75
21 Robert Dome .20 .50
22 Eric Meloche .30 .75
23 Glenn Patrick CO .04 .10
24 Mike Yeo ACO .04 .10
25 Tux MASCOT .04 .10
NNO Checklist .01

2002-03 Wilkes-Barre Scranton Penguins

COMPLETE SET (27) 12.00
1 Rob Scuderi .50
2 Brooks Orpik .75
3 Darcy Robinson .50
4 Mike Wilson .50
5 Michel Ouellet .50
6 Ross Lupaschuk .50
7 Matt Hussey .50
8 Milan Kraft .75
9 Alexander Zevakhin .50
10 Kris Beech .75
11 Shane Endicott .75
12 Toby Petersen .50
13 Colby Armstrong .75
14 Michal Sivek .75
15 Matt Murley .50
16 Brendan Buckley .50
17 Jason MacDonald .50
18 Tomas Surovy .75
19 Francois Leroux .50
20 Konstantin Koltsov .75
21 Tom Kostopoulos .50
22 Rob Tallas .75
23 Sebastien Caron .75
24 Eric Meloche .50
25 Glen Patrick HCO .10
26 Mike Yeo ACO .10
NNO Checklist .01

2003-04 Wilkes-Barre Scranton Penguins

This set was produced by Choice Marketing and sold at home games.

COMPLETE SET (30) 10.00
1 Checklist .01
2 Colby Armstrong .75
3 Jean-Sebastien Aubin .75
4 Kris Beech .75
5 Patrick Boileau .40
6 Martin Brochu .75
7 Brendan Buckley .40
8 Andy Chiodo 1.50
9 Shane Endicott .40
10 Drew Fata .40
11 Matt Hussey .40
12 David Koci .40
13 Tom Kostopoulos .40
14 Guillaume Lefebvre .40
15 Ross Lupaschuk .40
16 Marquis Mathieu .40
17 Eric Meloche .40
18 Matt Murley .40
19 Michel Ouellet .40
20 Toby Petersen .40
21 Darcy Robinson .40
22 Alexandre Rouleau .40
23 Rob Scuderi .40
24 Reid Simpson .40
25 Michal Sivek .40
26 Tomas Surovy .40
27 Steve Webb .40
28 Michel Therrien CO .10
29 Mike Yeo ACO .10
30 Mascot .10

2004-05 Wilkes-Barre Scranton Penguins

COMPLETE SET (30) 6.00 15.00
1 Checklist .01 .05
2 Rob Scuderi .20 .50
3 David Koci .20 .50
4 Chris Kelleher .20 .50
5 Darcy Robinson .20 .50
6 Ryan Whitney .30 .75
7 Michel Ouellet .20 .50
8 Ross Lupaschuk .20 .50
9 Colby Armstrong .30 .75
10 Kris Beech .20 .50
11 Ben Eaves .30 .75
12 Shane Endicott .20 .50
13 Cam Paddock .20 .50
14 Erik Christensen .30 .75
15 Guillaume Lefebvre .20 .50
16 Ramzi Abid .20 .50
17 Mike Sgroi .20 .50
18 Maxime Talbot .20 .50
19 Matt Murley .20 .50
20 Tomas Surovy .20 .50
21 Drew Fata .20 .50
22 Matt Hussey .20 .50
23 Marc-Andre Fleury 1.00 2.50
24 Alain Nasredine .20 .50
25 Dany Sabourin .40 1.00
26 Andy Chiodo .40 1.00
27 Tux MASCOT .02 .10
28 Michel Therrien CO .02 .10
29 Mike Yeo ACO .02 .10
30 Wachovia Arena .01 .05

2005-06 WBS Penguins

COMPLETE SET (29) 6.00 15.00
1 Colby Armstrong .40 1.00
2 Dennis Bonvie .40 1.00
3 Daniel Carcillo .20 .50
4 Sebastien Caron .40 1.00
5 Erik Christensen .40 1.00
6 Kenny Corupe .20 .50
7 Stephen Dixon .20 .50
8 Ben Eaves .20 .50
9 Rico Fata .20 .50
10 Daniel Fernholm .20 .50
11 Jonathan Filewich .20 .50
12 Marc-Andre Fleury .75 2.00
13 Matt Hussey .20 .50
14 Chris Kelleher .20 .50
15 David Koci .20 .50
16 Konstantin Koltsov .20 .50
17 Ryan Lannon .20 .50
18 Guillaume Lefebvre .30 .75
19 Arpad Mihaly .20 .50
20 Alain Nasredinne .20 .50
21 Michel Ouellet .40 1.00
22 Dany Sabourin .40 1.00
23 Andy Schneider .20 .50
24 Ryan Stone .20 .50
25 Tomas Surovy .20 .50
26 Noah Welch .30 .75
27 Ryan Whitney .40 1.00
28 Joe Mullen ACO .20 .50
29 Al Sims CO .07 .20

2006-07 Wilkes-Barre Scranton Penguins

COMPLETE SET (25) 5.00 12.00
1 Alain Nasreddine .30 .75
2 Alexei Mikhnov .20 .50
3 Andrew Penner .30 .75
4 Connor James .20 .50
5 Daniel Carcillo .30 .75
6 Dennis Bonvie .40 1.00
7 Erik Christensen .30 .75
8 Jeff Deslauriers .30 .75
9 Jonathan Filewich .30 .75
10 Kyle Brodziak .20 .50
11 Marc-Antoine Pouliot .30 .75
12 Matt Carkner .20 .50
13 Maxime Talbot .20 .50
14 Micki DuPont .20 .50
15 Noah Welch .20 .50
16 Rob Schremp .40 1.00
17 Ryan Lannon .30 .75
18 Ryan Stone .40 1.00
19 Stephen Dixon .20 .50
20 Tom Gilbert .20 .50
21 Tyler Kennedy .20 .50
22 Wade Skolney .20 .50
23 Dan Bylsma ACO .02 .10
24 Todd Richards CO .02 .10
NNO Checklist .01 .01

2006-07 Wilkes-Barre Scranton Penguins Jerseys

COMPLETE SET (22) 125.00 300.00
1 Jeff Deslauriers 8.00 20.00
2 Andrew Penner 8.00 20.00
3 Micki DuPont 6.00 15.00
4 Kyle Brodziak 6.00 15.00
5 Jonathan Filewich 6.00 15.00
6 Ryan Lannon 6.00 15.00
7 Connor James 6.00 15.00
8 Noah Welch 6.00 15.00
9 Tom Gilbert 6.00 15.00
10 Stephen Dixon 6.00 15.00
11 Tyler Kennedy 6.00 15.00
12 Daniel Carcillo 8.00 20.00
13 Dennis Bonvie 10.00 25.00
14 Tim Sesito 6.00 15.00
15 Erik Christensen 10.00 25.00
16 Maxime Talbot 10.00 25.00
17 Matt Carkner 6.00 15.00
18 Ryan Stone 10.00 25.00
19 Marc Antoine Pouliot 10.00 25.00
20 Wade Skolney 6.00 15.00
21 Alain Nasreddine 6.00 15.00
22 Rob Schremp 10.00 25.00

2004-05 Williams Lake Timberwolves

Set from the BCJHL is noteworthy for the inclusion of the first card of Fabio Luongo, younger brother of NHL All-Star Roberto Luongo.

COMPLETE SET (28) 8.00 20.00
1 Andrew Braithwaite .40 1.00
2 Cody Brookwell .30 .75
3 Matt Crowell .30 .75
4 Bryce Dale .30 .75
5 Mark Ehl .30 .75
6 Kevin Galan .30 .75
7 Zach Gieszler .30 .75
8 Alex Greenlay .30 .75
9 Dustin Honing .30 .75
10 Dave Krisky .30 .75
11 Mike Leidl .30 .75
12 Fabio Luongo 1.25 3.00
13 Trent Manchur .30 .75
14 Tyler Mazzei .30 .75
15 Josh Murray .30 .75
16 Brad Reaney .30 .75
17 Les Reaney .40 1.00
18 Trever Turner .30 .75
19 Steve Van Oosten .30 .75
20 Duane Whitehead .30 .75
21 Shaun Witschen .30 .75
22 Josh Murray .30 .75
23 Dave Krisky .30 .75
24 Rick Pitta CO .02 .10
25 Peter Martin ACO .02 .10
26 Zamboni .02 .10
27 Action photo .02 .10
28 T.H. Wolf MASCOT .02 .10

1989-90 Windsor Spitfires

This 22-card standard-size set features members of the 1989-90 Windsor Spitfires of the Ontario Hockey league (OHL). The fronts feature posed shots of the players in front of their lockers. The cards are unnumbered and checklisted below in alphabetical order.

COMPLETE SET (22) 4.00 10.00
1 Sean Burns .20 .50
2 Glen Craig .20 .50
3 Brian Forestell .20 .50
4 Chris Fraser .20 .50
5 Trent Gleason .20 .50
6 Jon Hartley .20 .50
7 Ron Jones .20 .50
8 Bob Leeming .20 .50
9 Kevin MacKay .20 .50
10 Kevin McDougall .20 .50
11 Ryan Merritt .20 .50
12 David Myles .20 .50
13 Sean O'Hagan .30 .75
14 Mike Polano .20 .50
15 Jason Snow .20 .50
16 Brad Smith CO .30 .75
17 Jason Stos .20 .50
18 Jon Stos .20 .50
19 Jamie Vargo .20 .50
20 Trevor Walsh .20 .50
21 K.J. White .20 .50
22 Jason Zohl .20 .50

1992-93 Windsor Spitfires

Sponsored by the Devonshire Mall, these 31 cards measure approximately 2 5/8" by 3 5/8" and feature on their fronts posed-on-ice color shots of the 1992-93 Windsor Spitfires bordered in red, white, and blue. The player's name and the Spitfires logo appear in the white area above the photo.

COMPLETE SET (31) 4.80 12.00
1 Team Card/Checklist .10 .25
2 Mike Martin .14 .35
3 Luke Clowes .14 .35
4 Jason Haelzle .14 .35
5 Adam Graves 1.20 3.00
6 Craig Lutes .14 .35
7 David Pluck .14 .35
8 Colin Wilson .14 .35
9 Bill Bowler .30 .75
10 Ryan O'Neill .14 .35
11 Adam Young .14 .35
12 Gerrard Masse .14 .35
13 Daryl Lavoie .14 .35
14 Peter Allison .14 .35
15 Ernie Godden RET .14 .35
16 Brady Blain .14 .35
17 Todd Warriner .30 .75
18 Rick Marshall .14 .35
19 Craig Johnson .14 .35
20 Kelly Vipond .14 .35
21 Devy Bear MASCOT .04 .10
22 Stephen Webb .14 .35
23 Scott Miller RET .14 .35
24 Dennis Purdie .20 .50
25 Steve Gibson .14 .35
26 Mike Hartwick .14 .35
27 Shawn Heins .30 .75
28 David Benn .14 .35
29 Matt Mullin .20 .50
30 David Mitchell .14 .35
31 The Dynamic Duo .20 .50
Todd Warriner
Cory Stillman

1993-94 Windsor Spitfires

Co-sponsored by Pizza Hut and radio station CKLW AM 800, and printed by Slapshot Images Ltd., this 27-card standard-size set features the 1993-94 Windsor Spitfires. On a geometrical team color-coded background, the fronts feature color action player photos with thin grey borders. The player's name, position and team name, as well as the producer's logo, also appear on the front.

COMPLETE SET (27) 4.80 12.00
1 Ed Jovanovski .80 2.00
2 Shawn Silver .20 .50
3 Travis Scott .20 .50
4 Mike Martin .20 .50
5 Daryl Lavoie .16 .40
6 Craig Lutes .16 .40
7 David Pluck .16 .40
8 Bill Bowler .20 .50
9 David Green .16 .40
10 Adam Young .16 .40
11 Mike Loach .16 .40
12 Brady Blain .16 .40
13 Shayne McCosh .16 .40
14 Rob Shearer .20 .50
15 Joel Poirier .16 .40
16 Cory Evans .16 .40
17 Vladimir Kretchine .16 .40
18 Dave Roche .20 .50
19 Ryan Stewart .16 .40
20 Dave Geris .16 .40
21 Dan West .16 .40
22 Luke Clowes .16 .40
23 John Cooper .16 .40
24 Akil Adams .16 .40
25 Sponsor Card .04 .10
Pizza Hut
26 Sponsor Card .04 .10
Steve Bell
Radio station AM 800
NNO Slapshot Ad Card .04 .10

1994-95 Windsor Spitfires

Sponsored by Pizza Hut, Mr. Lube, CKLW AM 800, and printed by Slapshot Images Ltd., this 29-card set features the 1994-95 Windsor Spitfires. On a red and blue background, the fronts feature color player action photos with thin black borders. The player's name, position and team name, as well as the producer's logo, also appear on the front.

COMPLETE SET (29) 5.60 14.00
1 Checklist .01
2 Jamie Storr .30 .75
3 Travis Scott .20 .50
4 Paul Beazley .16 .40
5 Mike Martin .16 .40
6 Chris Van Dyk .16 .40
7 Denis Smith .20 .50
8 Glenn Crawford .16 .40
9 David Pluck .16 .40
10 Bill Bowler .30 .75
11 David Green .16 .40
12 Adam Young .16 .40
13 Wes Ward .16 .40
14 Ed Jovanovski 1.20 3.00
15 Kevin Paden .16 .40
16 Rob Shearer .20 .50
17 Joel Poirier .16 .40
18 Cory Evans .16 .40
19 Vladimir Kretchine .16 .40
20 David Roche .20 .50
21 Rick Emmett .16 .40
22 David Geris .16 .40
23 Caleb Ward .16 .40
24 Luke Clowes .16 .40
25 John Cooper .16 .40
26 Tim Findlay .20 .50
27 Pizza Hut .01
28 Radio station AM 800 .01
NNO Ad Card .01

1998-99 Windsor Spitfires

This set features the Spitfires of the OHL. It is believed that they were issued as part of a fire safety program, and may only have been available to school children. Additional information can be forwarded to us at hockeymag@beckett.com.

COMPLETE SET (9) 3.20 8.00
1 Fire Chief .04 .11
2 Coaches .04 .11
3 Duke MASCOT .04 .11
4 Michael Hanson .40 1.00
5 Jeff Kapitanchuk .40 1.00
6 Michael Leighton 1.20 3.00
7 Jason Polera .40 1.00
8 Blair Stayzer .80 2.00
9 Curtis Watson .40 1.00

2002-03 Windsor Spitfires

This oversized set was sold at Spitfires home games. The cards are unnumbered, but are listed in the order they were issued in (roughly by jersey number, with non-team members interspersed throughout.)

COMPLETE SET (30) 4.80 20.00
1 Title Card/Checklist .01
2 Ryan Aschaber .30 1.00
3 Frank Rediker .30 1.00
4 David Lomas .16 .40
5 Iain McPhee .16 .40
6 Mitchell Maunu .30 1.50
7 Tim Gleason .40 2.00
8 Mike James .16 .40
9 David Bowman .16 .40
10 Chief of Police .01
11 Jason Dixon .16 .40
12 Rob Hennigar .20 .75
13 Craig Kennedy .20 .75
14 Elmer Mascot .04 .10
15 Ahren Nittel .20 .50
17 Phil Gibson .16 .40
18 Ryan Donnally .16 .75
19 Paul Giallonardo .16 .40
20 Josh Gratton .16 .40
21 Alexander Shevchenko .16 .40
22 Darryl Lloyd .16 .40
23 Jeff Leavitt .16 .40
24 Duke Mascot .04 .10
25 Ryan Dickie .16 .40
26 Matt Anthony .16 .40
27 John-Scott Dickson .16 .40
28 Denis Khudyakov .20 1.00
29 Mike Self .16 .40
30 Kyle Wellwood .60 4.00
116 Cam Janssen .30 2.00

2003-04 Wisconsin Badgers

Two cards from this set were handed out at Badger home games over the course of the 2003-04 season. The cards are unnumbered and thus are listed below in alphabetical order.

COMPLETE SET (30) 20.00 40.00
1 Dan Boeser .30 .75
2 Rene Bourque 1.50 4.00
3 Andy Brandt .75 2.00
4 Bernd Bruckler .60 1.50
5 Adam Burish .75 2.00
6 A.J. Degenhardt .30 .75
7 Jake Dowell .30 .75
8 Robbie Earl 1.25 3.00
9 John Eichelberger .30 .75
10 Brian Elliott .60 1.50
11 John Funk .30 .75
12 Brent Gibson .30 .75
13 Tom Gilbert 1.25 3.00
14 Mark Heatley .75 2.00
15 Andrew Joudrey .30 .75
16 Chris Julka .30 .75
17 Luke Kohtala .60 1.50
18 Jon Krall .30 .75
19 Nick Licari .30 .75
20 Jeff Likens .30 .75
21 Ryan MacMurchy .30 .75
22 Joey McElroy .30 .75
23 Matt Olinger .30 .75
24 Ken Rowe .30 .75
25 Tom Sawatske .30 .75
26 Ryan Suter 1.50 4.00
27 Pete Talafous .30 .75
28 Andy Wozniewski .60 1.50
29 Mike Eaves HCO .20 .50
30 Mascot .02 .10

2004-05 Wisconsin Badgers

Set was issued as a promotional giveaway at a home game. The cards are not numbered.

COMPLETE SET (28) 15.00 30.00
1 Brian Elliott .40 1.00
2 Matt Olinger .40 1.00
3 Matt Auffrey .40 1.00
4 Robbie Earl 1.25 3.00
5 Pete Talafous .40 1.00
6 Matt Ford .75 2.00
7 Davis Drewiske .40 1.00
8 Bernd Bruckler .75 2.00
9 Ken Rowe .40 1.00
10 Jeff Likens .40 1.00
11 John Funk .40 1.00
12 Andy Brandt .40 1.00
13 Jake Dowell .40 1.00
14 Kyle Klubertanz .40 1.00
15 Joe Pavelski .40 1.00
16 Mike Eaves CO .20 .50
17 Joe Piskula .40 1.00
18 Ryan MacMurchy .40 1.00
19 Ross Carlson .40 1.00
20 A.J. Degenhardt .40 1.00
21 Josh Engel .40 1.00
22 Tom Gilbert 1.25 3.00
23 Andrew Joudrey .40 1.00
24 Nick Licari .40 1.00
25 Jeff Slinde .40 1.00
26 Luke Kohtala .75 2.00
27 Mark Heatley .75 2.00
28 Adam Burish .75 2.00

2004-05 Wisconsin Badgers Women

Issued as a promotional giveaway.

COMPLETE SET (24) 10.00 25.00
1 Sara Bauer .40 1.00
2 Nikki Burish .40 1.00
3 Sharon Cole .40 1.00
4 Vicki Davis .40 1.00
5 Christine Dufour .40 1.00
6 Molly Engstrom .40 1.00
7 Jackie Friesen .40 1.00
8 Meghan Horras .40 1.00
9 Grace Hutchins .40 1.00
10 Mark Johnson CO .40 1.00
11 Cyndy Kenyon .40 1.00
12 Heidi Kletzien .40 1.00
13 Carla MacLeod .75 2.00
14 Lindsay Macy .40 1.00
15 Meaghan Mikkelson .40 1.00
16 Phoebe Monteleone .40 1.00
17 Emily Morris .40 1.00
18 Mikka Nordby .40 1.00
19 Bobbi-Jo Slusar .40 1.00
20 Nicole Uliasz .40 1.00
21 Amy Vermeulen .40 1.00
22 Jesse Vetter .40 1.00
23 Kristen Witting .40 1.00
24 Jinelle Zaugg .40 1.00

2005-06 Wisconsin Badgers

COMPLETE SET (27) 15.00 30.00
1 Andy Brandt .40 1.00
2 Adam Burish .40 1.00
3 Ross Carlson .40 1.00
4 Shane Connelly .75 2.00
5 A.J. Degenhardt .40 1.00
6 Jake Dowell .40 1.00
7 Davis Drewiske .40 1.00
8 Robbie Earl .75 2.00
9 Brian Elliott .75 2.00
10 Josh Engel .40 1.00
11 Matthew Ford .40 1.00
12 Tom Gilbert .40 1.00
13 Tom Gorowsky .40 1.00
14 Ryan Jeffery .40 1.00
15 Andrew Joudrey .40 1.00
16 Kyle Klubertanz .40 1.00
17 Nick Licari .40 1.00
18 Jeff Likens .40 1.00
19 Ryan MacMurchy .40 1.00
20 Matt Olinger .40 1.00
21 Joe Pavelski .40 1.00
22 Joe Piskula .40 1.00
23 Jack Skille 2.00 5.00
24 Jeff Slinde .40 1.00
25 Ben Street .40 1.00
26 Mike Eaves HC .20 .50
27 Bucky Badger MASCOT .02 .10

2000-01 Worcester Icecats

This set features the IceCats of the AHL. The set was produced by Choice Marketing and was handed out over the course of two games as a promotional giveaway.

COMPLETE SET (30) 8.00 20.00
1 Ed Campbell .20 .50
2 Daniel Corso .40 1.00
3 Justin Papineau .40 1.00
4 Jaroslav Obsut .20 .50
5 Ladislav Nagy .80 2.00
6 Marc Brown .20 .50
7 Pascal Rheaume .20 .50
8 Mike Van Ryn .40 1.00
9 Cody Rudkowsky .40 1.50
10 Andrei Troschinsky .20 .50
11 Mark Rycroft .40 1.00
12 Matt Walker .20 .50
13 Jamie Thompson .20 .50
14 Darren Rumble .30 .75
15 Scratch MASCOT .04 .10
16 Team CL .04 .01
17 Dwayne Roloson .40 2.00
18 Jame Pollock .20 .50
19 Eric Boguniecki .40 1.50
20 Chris Murray .40 1.00
21 Tyler Rennette .20 .50
22 Marty Reasoner .40 1.00
23 Dale Clarke .30 .75
24 Tyler Willis .30 .75
25 Jan Horacek .30 .75
26 Peter Smrek .30 .75
27 Mike Peluso .30 .75
28 Doug Friedman .20 .50
29 Shawn Mamane .20 .50
30 Don Granato CO .10 .25

2001-02 Worcester Icecats

This set features the Icecats of the AHL and actually features two separately released series of cards. The sets -- one issued early in the season, another late -- weres produced by Choice Marketing and was sold by the team at its souvenir shop. Each series was limited to 2,000 copies.

COMPLETE SET (15) 10.00 25.00
1 Darren Rumble .30 .75
2 Marc Brown .30 .75
3 Ed Campbell .30 .75
4 Jeff Panzer .30 .75
5 Cody Rudkowsky .40 1.00
6 Igor Valeev .30 .75
7 Dale Clarke .40 .75
8 Mike Van Ryn .40 1.00
9 Barret Jackman .40 2.00
10 Jame Pollock .30 .75
11 Daniel Tkaczuk .30 .75
12 Greg Davis .30 .75
13 Jamie Thompson .30 .75
14 Tyson Nash .60 1.50
15 Scratch MASCOT .10 .10
16 Team Photo/CL .10 .25
17 Reinhard Divis .40 1.50
18 Andrei Troschinsky .30 .75
19 Steve Halko .30 .75
20 Matt Walker .30 .75
21 Eric Boguniecki .40 1.00
22 Justin Papineau .40 1.00
23 Christian Laflamme .30 .75
24 Brad Voth .40 .75
25 Mark Rycroft .40 .75
26 Steve McLaren .30 .75
27 Eric Nickulas .30 .75
28 Justin Papineau .30 .75
Jeff Panzer
Eric Boguniecki AS
29 Brent Johnson .80 2.00
30 Don Granato CO .10 .25

2002-03 Worcester IceCats

COMPLET SET (28) 6.00 15.00
1 Checklist .01 .05
2 Terry Virtue .20 .50
3 Steve Bancroft .20 .50

4 Aris Brimanis .20 .50
5 John Pohl .75 2.00
6 Jame Pollock .20 .50
7 Eric Nickulas .20 .50
8 Jason Dawe .20 .50
9 Blake Evans .20 .50
10 Greg Davis .20 .50
11 Marc Brown .20 .50
12 Steve Dubinsky .20 .50
13 Steve McLaren .20 .50
14 Brett Scheffelmaier .20 .50
15 Mark Rycroft .20 .50
16 Christian Laflamme .20 .50
17 Justin Papineau .20 .50
18 Igor Valeev .20 .50
19 Matt Walker .20 .50
20 Jeff Panzer .20 .50
21 Sergei Varlamov .20 .50
22 Christian Backman .20 .50
23 Curtis Sanford .60 1.50
24 Phil Osaer .20 .50
25 Reinhard Divis .40 1.00
26 Eric Boguniecki MVP .20 .50
27 Don Granato HCO .02 .10
28 Scratch Mascot .02 .10

2003-04 Worcester Ice Cats

This set was produced by Choice Marketing and sold at home games.

COMPLETE SET (28) 4.00 10.00
1 Checklist .01 .05
2 Curtis Sanford .40 1.00
3 Joe Vandermeer .15 .40
4 Terry Virtue .15 .40
5 Jon Coleman .15 .40
6 Trevor Byrne .15 .40
7 Aris Brimanis .15 .40
8 Johnny Pohl .40 1.00
9 Tom Koivisto .15 .40
10 Jame Pollock .15 .40
11 Greg Black .15 .40
12 Mike Stuart .15 .40
13 Blake Evans .15 .40
14 Mike Glumac .15 .40
15 Chris Corrinet .15 .40
16 Marc Brown .15 .40
17 Jay McClement .15 .40
18 Steve McLaren .30 .75
19 Aaron MacKenzie .15 .40
20 Colin Hemingway .15 .40
21 Ernie Hartlieb .15 .40
22 Steve Martins .15 .40
23 Brett Scheffelmaier .15 .40
24 Jeff Panzer .15 .40
25 Sergei Varlamov .15 .40
26 Reinhard Divis .30 .75
27 Don Granato CO .02 .10
28 Steve Pleau ACO .02 .10

2003-04 Worcester Ice Cats 10th Anniversary

This special set was produced by Choice Marketing to commemorate the team's anniversary and was sold at home games.

COMPLETE SET (20) 4.00 10.00
1 Checklist .01 .05
2 Dwayne Roloson .40 1.00
3 Brent Johnson .40 1.00
4 Barret Jackman .30 .75
5 Bryce Salvador .15 .40
6 Terry Virtue .30 .75
7 Matt Walker .15 .40
8 Ed Campbell .15 .40
9 Rory Fitzpatrick .15 .40
10 Ricard Persson .15 .40
11 Eric Boguniecki .15 .40
12 Justin Papineau .15 .40
13 Marty Reasoner .15 .40
14 Ladislav Nagy .30 .75
15 Jeff Panzer .15 .40
16 Stephane Roy .15 .40
17 Jochen Hecht .15 .40
18 Johnny Pohl .30 .75
19 Michal Handzus .15 .40
20 Reed Low .15 .40

2004-05 Worcester IceCats

COMPLETE SET (26) 5.00 12.00
1 Curtis Sanford .40 1.00
2 Mike Mottau .20 .50
3 Trevor Byrne .20 .50
4 Aris Brimanis .20 .50
5 Brendan Buckley .20 .50
6 Johnny Pohl .40 1.00
7 Jon DiSalvatore .20 .50
8 Mike Stuart .20 .50
9 Blake Evans .20 .50
10 Mike Glumac .20 .50
11 Erkki Rajamaki .20 .50
12 Jay McClement .20 .50
13 D.J. King .20 .50
14 Aaron MacKenzie .20 .50
15 Alexei Shkotov .20 .50
16 Peter Sejna .20 .50
17 Dennis Wideman .20 .50
18 Brendan Brooks .20 .50
19 Jason Bacashihua .60 1.50
20 Jeff Hoggan .40 1.00
21 Ryan Ramsay .20 .50
22 Robin Gomez .20 .50
23 Don Granato CO .02 .10
24 Steve Pleau ACO .02 .10
25 Mascots .02 .10
NNO Checklist .01 .05

2003-04 Yarmouth Mariners

COMPLETE SET (31) 4.00 10.00
1 Checklist .01 .05
2 Travis Antler .20 .50
3 Todd Ballah .20 .50
4 Jamie Barbour .20 .50
5 Brent Boardman .20 .50
6 Jarrett Bottomley .20 .50
7 Tim Clayton .20 .50
8 Georges d'Entremont .20 .50
9 Justin d'Entremont .20 .50
10 Jason Hedges .20 .50
11 Steve Holland .20 .50
12 Grant Kenny .20 .50
13 Brad Larter .20 .50
14 Jordan McMullen .20 .50
15 Jody Mosher .20 .50
16 Matt Oxtoby .20 .50
17 David Philpott .20 .50
18 Mark Plenzich .20 .50
19 Jason Robichaud .20 .50
20 Curtis Thorne .20 .50
21 Michael DiIorenzo .20 .50
22 Josh Vanderbreggen .20 .50
23 Sean Wadden .20 .50
24 Steve Yetman .20 .50
25 Paul Currie CO .02 .10
26 Laurie Barron ACO .02 .10
27 Mark Muise EQM .02 .10
28 Mark Wheeler TR .02 .10
29 One Team One Goal .02 .10
30 Mariner Pressure .02 .10
31 Hard to the Net .02 .10

1991 Arena Draft Picks

The 1991 Arena Draft Picks boxed set consists of 33 standard-size cards. The set was produced in English as well as French versions, with both versions currently carrying the same values. One thousand cards (numbered out of 667 for the English version, 333 for the French) signed by each player were randomly inserted throughout the sets with one autograph per approximately ten sets or two per case. Moreover, a Pat Falloon hologram was produced in conjunction with this set, although its release came much later. The Falloon hologram is not included in the complete set price below. The production run was reported to be 198,000 English and 99,000 French sets, and each set was issued with a numbered certificate of authenticity. The full-bleed fronts have a white background and show the hockey player in an action pose wearing a tuxedo.

COMPLETE SET (33) 1.20 3.00
1 Pat Falloon .04 .10
2 Scott Niedermayer .10 .25
3 Scott Lachance .02 .05
4 Peter Forsberg UER .40 1.00
5 Alek Stojanov .02 .05
6 Richard Matvichuk .04 .10
7 Patrick Poulin .02 .05
8 Martin Lapointe .02 .05
9 Tyler Wright .02 .05
10 Philippe Boucher .02 .05
11 Pat Peake .02 .05
12 Markus Naslund UER .20 .50
13 Brent Bilodeau .02 .05
14 Glen Murray .20 .50
15 Niklas Sundblad .02 .05
16 Trevor Halverson .02 .05
17 Dean McAmmond .04 .10
18 Rene Corbet .02 .05
19 Eric Lavigne .02 .05
20 Steve Staios .02 .05
21 Jim Campbell .04 .10
22 Jassen Cullimore .02 .05
23 Jamie Pushor .04 .10
24 Donevan Hextall .02 .05
25 Andrew Verner .04 .10
26 Jason Dawe .02 .05
27 Jeff Nelson .02 .05
28 Darcy Werenka .02 .05
29 Francois Groleau .02 .05
30 Guy Leveque .02 .05
31 Yanic Perreault .06 .15
32 Pat Falloon and Scott Lachance .04 .10
NNO Checklist Card .02 .01
HOLO Pat Falloon Hologram .10 .25

1991 Arena Draft Picks Autographs

The 1991 Arena Draft Picks autographs consists of 33 standard-size cards. One thousand cards (numbered out of 667 for the English version, 333 for the French) signed by each player were randomly inserted throughout the sets with one autograph per approximately ten sets or two per case. The full-bleed fronts have a white background and show the hockey player in an action pose wearing a tuxedo.

COMPLETE SET (33) 75.00 125.00
1 Pat Falloon 2.00 5.00
2 Scott Niedermayer 6.00 15.00
3 Scott Lachance 1.20 3.00
4 Peter Forsberg UER 30.00 75.00
5 Alek Stojanov 1.20 3.00
6 Richard Matvichuk 2.00 5.00
7 Patrick Poulin 1.20 3.00
8 Martin Lapointe 6.00 15.00
9 Tyler Wright 1.20 3.00
10 Philippe Boucher 1.20 3.00
11 Pat Peake 1.20 3.00
12 Markus Naslund UER 6.00 15.00
13 Brent Bilodeau 1.20 3.00
14 Glen Murray 6.00 15.00
15 Niklas Sundblad 1.20 3.00
16 Trevor Halverson 1.20 3.00
17 Dean McAmmond 2.00 5.00
18 Rene Corbet 2.00 5.00
19 Eric Lavigne 1.20 3.00
20 Steve Staios 1.20 3.00
21 Jim Campbell 1.20 3.00
22 Jassen Cullimore 1.20 3.00
23 Jamie Pushor 1.20 3.00
24 Donevan Hextall 1.20 3.00
25 Andrew Verner 2.00 5.00
26 Jason Dawe 1.20 3.00
27 Jeff Nelson 1.20 3.00
28 Darcy Werenka 1.20 3.00
29 Francois Groleau 1.20 3.00
30 Guy Leveque 1.20 3.00
31 Yanic Perreault 2.00 5.00

1997 Bowman CHL

The 1997-98 Bowman CHL set was issued in one series totaling 165 cards and was distributed in eight-card packs with a suggested retail price of $1.89. It marks Topps first venture into minor league hockey. The set features color photos of established CHL stars as well as 40 NHL 1997 Draft Prospects. The 40 Draft Prospects each autographed cards that were distributed at the rate of one in 24 to form the Bowman CHL Prospects Autographs insert set. Each of these cards is authenticated by the Topps Certified Autograph Issue stamp.

COMPLETE SET (160) 10.00 25.00
1 Jan Bulis .15 .40
2 Daniel Cleary .15 .40
3 Dave Duerden .08 .20
4 Cameron Mann .08 .20
5 Alyn McCauley .15 .40
6 Tyler Rennette .08 .20
7 Marc Savard .20 .50
8 Daniel Tkaczuk .15 .40
9 John Tripp .08 .20
10 Joel Trottier .08 .20
11 Sean Yenedam .08 .20
12 Alexander Volchkov .08 .20
13 Sean Blanchard .08 .20
14 Kevin Bolibruck .08 .20
15 Nick Boynton .20 .50
16 Paul Mara .15 .40
17 Marc Moro .08 .20
18 Marty Wilford .08 .20
19 Zac Bierk .20 .50
20 Kory Cooper .08 .20
21 Richard Rochefort .08 .20
22 Matt Cooke .20 .50
23 Boyd Devereaux .20 .50
24 Rico Fata .15 .40
25 Dwayne Hay .08 .20
26 Trevor Letowski .08 .20
27 Ryan Mougenel .08 .20
28 Todd Norman .08 .20
29 Larry Paleczny .08 .20
30 Colin Pepperall .08 .20
31 Jonathan Sim .08 .20
32 Joe Thornton 1.50 4.00
33 Brian Wesenberg .08 .20
34 Andy Delmore .08 .20
35 Chris Hajt .08 .20
36 Richard Jackman .08 .20
37 Denis Smith .08 .20
38 Jamie Sokolsky .08 .20
39 Paul Traynor .08 .20
40 Patrick DesRochers .15 .40
41 Robert Esche .30 1.00
42 Roberto Luongo 1.50 4.00
43 Frederic Henry .08 .20
44 Marc Oliver Roy .08 .20
45 Samy Nasreddine .08 .20
46 Jean-Francois Fortin .08 .20
47 Martin Ethier .08 .20
48 Jason Doig .08 .20
49 Dominic Perna .08 .20
50 Daniel Briere .30 .75
51 Pavel Rosa .08 .20
52 Philippe Audet .08 .20
53 Gordie Dwyer .08 .20
54 Martin Menard .08 .20
55 Jonathan Delisle .08 .20
56 Peter Worrell .20 .50
57 Francois Methot .08 .20
58 Steve Begin .08 .20
59 Karol Bartanus .08 .20
60 J-P Dumont .40 1.00
61 Marc Denis .40 1.00
62 J-S Giguere 1.25 2.00
63 Jason Gorleau .08 .20
64 Radoslav Suchy .08 .20
65 Stephane Robidas .08 .20
66 Marc-Andre Gaudet .08 .20
67 Eric Drouin .08 .20
68 Derrick Walser .08 .20
69 Vincent Lecavalier 1.25 3.00
70 Denis Hamel .08 .20
71 Daniel Corso .08 .20
72 Martin Moise .08 .20
73 Eric Belanger .08 .20
74 Olivier Morin .08 .20
75 Jerome Tremblay .08 .20
76 Jody Shelley .20 .75
77 Eric Normandin .08 .20
78 David Thibeault .08 .20
79 Christian Daigle .15 .40
80 Alexandre Jacques .08 .20
81 Brian Boucher .75 1.00
82 Randy Petruk .15 .40
83 Hugh Hamilton .08 .20
84 Joel Kwiatkowski .08 .20
85 Zenith Komarniski .08 .20
86 Joey Tetarenko .20 .50
87 Tyler Willis .08 .20
88 Patrick Marleau .75 2.00
89 Trent Whitfield .08 .20
90 Martin Cerven .08 .20
91 Donnie Kinney .08 .20
92 Brad Isbister .15 .40
93 Todd Robinson .08 .20
94 Greg Leeb .08 .20
95 John Cirjak .08 .20
96 Randy Perry .08 .20
97 Derek Schutz .08 .20
98 Brenden Morrow .40 1.00
99 Shawn McNeil .08 .20
100 Brad Ference .08 .20
101 Ryan Hoople .08 .20
102 Brian Elder .08 .20
103 Mike McBain .08 .20
104 Jesse Wallin .08 .20
105 Chris Phillips .20 .50
106 Kelly Smart .08 .20
107 Arron Asham .08 .20
108 Byron Ritchie .08 .20
109 Derek Morris .20 .50
110 Travis Brigley .08 .20
111 Justin Kurtz .08 .20
112 B.J. Young .08 .20
113 Shane Willis .08 .20
114 Josh Holden .08 .20
115 Cory Sarich .08 .20
116 Brad Larsen .08 .20
117 Stefan Cherneski .08 .20
118 Peter Schaefer .08 .20
119 Dmitri Nabokov .08 .20
120 Sergei Varlamov .20 .50
121 Daniel Cleary TP .08 .20
122 Jarrett Smith TP .08 .20
123 Alexandre Mathieu TP .08 .20
124 Matt Elich TP .08 .20
125 Joe Thornton TP .75 2.00
126 Mike Brown TP .08 .20
127 Derek Schutz TP .08 .20
128 Benoit Cote TP .08 .20
129 Jason Ward TP .08 .20
130 Karol Bartanus TP .08 .20
131 Tyler Rennette TP .08 .20
132 Matt Zultek TP .15 .40
133 Brad Ference TP .15 .40
134 Daniel Tetrault TP .08 .20
135 Ray Bonni TP .08 .20
136 Kevin Grimes TP .08 .20
137 Paul Mara TP .15 .40
138 Nikos Tselios TP .08 .20
139 Curtis Cruickshank TP .08 .20
140 Pierre-Luc Therrien TP .08 .20
141 Patrick Marleau TP .40 1.00
142 Ty Jones TP .08 .20
143 Jeremy Reich TP .08 .20
144 Adam Mair TP .15 .40
145 Adam Colagiacomo TP .08 .20
146 Harold Druken TP .15 .40
147 Brenden Morrow TP .30 .75
148 Jay Legault TP .08 .20
149 Jeff Zehr TP .08 .20
150 Scott Barney TP .08 .20
151 Gregor Baumgartner TP .08 .20
152 Daniel Tkaczuk TP .20 .50
153 Eric Brewer TP .20 .50
154 Nick Boynton TP .20 .50
155 Vratislav Cech TP .08 .20
156 Kyle Kos TP .08 .20
157 Jean-Francois Fortin TP .08 .20
158 Wes Jarvis TP .08 .20
159 Roberto Luongo TP .75 2.00
160 J-F Damphousse TP .08 .20
NNO B.B.Redempt. .40 1.00
NNO Ref.Redempt. .40 1.00
NNO Ato.Ref.Redempt. .40 1.00
NNO Auto.Redempt. .40 1.00

1997 Bowman CHL OPC

Randomly inserted in packs at the rate of 1:6, this 160 card set is an O-Pee-Chee parallel version of the basic Bowman CHL issue.

COMPLETE SET (160) 300.00 600.00
*STARS: 4X TO 10X BASIC CARDS

1997 Bowman CHL Autographs

Randomly inserted at the rate of 1:46, this 37-card set features cards signed by the top NHL draft picks. Each of these cards is authenticated by the Topps Certified Autograph Issue stamp.

COMPLETE SET (40) 150.00 200.00
2 Jarrett Smith 2.00 5.00
3 Alexandre Mathieu 2.00 5.00
4 Matt Elich 2.00 5.00
10 Karol Bartanus 2.00 5.00
11 Tyler Rennette 2.00 5.00
13 Brad Ference 2.00 5.00
14 Daniel Tetrault 2.00 5.00
15 Ray Bonni 2.00 5.00
16 Kevin Grimes 2.00 5.00
18 Nikos Tselios 2.00 5.00
19 Curtis Cruickshank 2.00 5.00
20 Pierre-Luc Therrien 2.00 5.00
22 Ty Jones 2.00 5.00
23 Jeremy Reich 2.00 5.00
24 Adam Mair 2.00 5.00
25 Adam Colagiacomo 2.00 5.00
26 Harold Druken 2.00 5.00
28 Jay Legault 2.00 5.00
29 Jeff Zehr 4.00 10.00
30 Scott Barney 2.00 5.00
31 Gregor Baumgartner 2.00 5.00
33 Eric Brewer 5.00 12.00
34 Nick Boynton 5.00 12.00
35 Vratislav Cech 2.00 5.00
36 Kyle Kos 2.00 5.00
37 Jean Francois Fortin 2.00 5.00
38 Wes Jarvis 2.00 5.00
39 Roberto Luongo 5.00 20.00
121 Daniel Cleary 2.00 5.00
125 Joe Thornton 20.00 40.00
126 Mike Brown 2.00 5.00
127 Derek Schutz 2.00 5.00
128 Benoit Cote 2.00 5.00
129 Jason Ward 4.00 10.00
132 Matt Zultek 2.00 5.00
147 Brenden Morrow 12.50 20.00
160 Jean-Francois Damphousse 5.00 12.00

1997 Bowman CHL Bowman's Best

This 20-card set was randomly inserted in packs at the rate of one in 12 and features color player photos printed on laser-cut cards using chromium technology. Refractor and atomic refractor parallels were also created and randomly inserted. Refractors were inserted at a rate of 1:24 and atomic refractors at 1:48.

COMPLETE SET (20) 25.00 35.00
*REF.STARS: 1.5X TO 3X BASIC BOWMAN'S BEST
*ATOMIC REF: 2.5X TO 5X BASIC BOWMAN'S BEST
1 Joe Thornton 4.00 10.00
2 Patrick Marleau 2.50 4.00
3 Paul Mara .60 1.50
4 Daniel Tkaczuk .60 1.50
5 Jason Ward .60 1.50
6 Nick Boynton .75 2.00
7 Daniel Cleary .60 1.50
8 Eric Brewer .75 2.00
9 Brad Ference .60 1.50
10 Stefan Cherneski .60 1.50
11 Ryan Bonni .60 1.50
12 Adam Colagiacomo .60 1.50
13 Mike Brown .60 1.50
14 Scott Barney .60 1.50
15 Jarrett Smith .60 1.50
16 Brenden Morrow 2.50 3.00
17 Jean-Francois Fortin .60 1.50
18 Roberto Luongo 6.00 10.00
19 Curtis Cruickshank .60 1.50
20 Pierre-Luc Therrien .60 1.50

1998 Bowman CHL

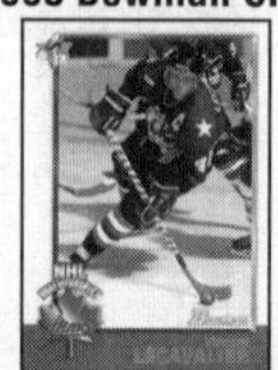

The 1998 Bowman CHL set was issued in one series totaling 165 cards and was distributed in eight-card packs with a suggested retail price of $1.89. The set features action color photos of established CHL stars as well as 40 NHL 1998 Draft Prospects. The backs carry player information and statistics.

COMPLETE SET (165) 20.00 50.00
1 Robert Esche .20 .50
2 Chris Hajt .08 .20
3 Mark McMahon .08 .20
4 Jeff Brown .08 .20
5 Richard Jackman .08 .20
6 Greg Labenski .08 .20
7 Marek Posmyk .08 .20
8 Brian Willsie .08 .20
9 Jason Ward .08 .20
10 Manny Malhotra .08 .20
11 Matt Cooke .40 1.00
12 Mike Gorman .08 .20
13 Rodney Richard .08 .20
14 David Legwand .40 1.00
15 Jon Sim .08 .20
16 Peter Sarno .08 .20
17 Andrew Long .08 .20
18 Peter Cava .08 .20
19 Colin Pepperall .08 .20
20 Jay Legault .08 .20
21 Brian Finley .20 .50
22 Martin Skoula .08 .20
23 Brian Campbell .08 .20
24 Sean Blanchard .08 .20
25 Bryan Allen .08 .20
26 Peter Hogan .08 .20
27 Nick Boynton .40 1.00
28 Matt Bradley .08 .20
29 Jeremy Adduono .08 .20
30 Mike Henrich .08 .20
31 Justin Papineau .20 .50
32 Bujar Amidovski .40 1.00
33 Robert Mailloux .08 .20
34 Daniel Tkaczuk .08 .20
35 Sean Avery .40 1.00
36 Mark Bell .20 .50
37 Kevin Colley .08 .20
38 Norm Milley .40 1.00
39 Scott Barney .08 .20
40 Joel Trottier .08 .20
41 Brent Belecki .08 .20
42 Randy Petruk .20 .50
43 Brad Ference .08 .20
44 Perry Johnson .08 .20
45 Joel Kwiatkowski .08 .20
46 Zenith Komarniski .08 .20
47 Greg Kuznik .08 .20
48 Andrew Ference .08 .20
49 Jason Deleurme .08 .20
50 Trent Whitfield .08 .20
51 Dylan Gyori .08 .20
52 Todd Robinson .08 .20
53 Marian Hossa .40 1.00
54 Mike Hurley .08 .20
55 Greg Leeb .08 .20
56 Andrej Podkonicky .20 .50
57 Quinn Hancock .08 .20
58 Marian Cisar .08 .20
59 Bret DeCecco .08 .20
60 Brenden Morrow .20 .50
61 Evan Lindsay .20 .50
62 Terry Friesen .20 .50
63 Ryan Shannon .08 .20
64 Michal Rozsival .08 .20
65 Luc Theoret .08 .20
66 Brad Stuart .40 1.00
67 Burke Henry .08 .20
68 Cory Sarich .08 .20
69 Martin Sonnenberg .08 .20
70 Mark Smith .20 .50
71 Shawn McNeil .08 .20
72 Brad Moran .08 .20
73 Josh Holden .08 .20
74 Cory Cyrenne .08 .20
75 Shane Willis .08 .20
76 Stefan Cherneski .08 .20
77 Jay Henderson .08 .20
78 Ronald Petrovicky .08 .20
79 Sergei Varlamov .08 .20
80 Chad Hinz .08 .20
81 Mathieu Garon .20 .50
82 Mathieu Chouinard .20 .50
83 Dominic Perna .08 .20
84 Didier Tremblay .08 .20
85 Mike Ribeiro .20 .50
86 Marty Johnston .08 .20
87 Remi Royer .08 .20
88 Patrick Pelchat .08 .20
89 Daniel Corso .08 .20
90 Francois Fortier .08 .20
91 Marc-Andre Gaudet .08 .20
92 Francois Beauchemin .08 .20
93 Michel Tremblay .08 .20
94 Jean-Philippe Pare .08 .20
95 Francois Methot .08 .20
96 David Thibeault .08 .20
97 Jonathan Girard Jr. .20 .50
98 Karol Bartanus .08 .20
99 Peter Ratchuk .08 .20
100 Pierre Dagenais .20 .50
101 Philippe Sauve .40 1.00
102 Remi Bergeron .08 .20
103 Vincent Lecavalier .20 .50
104 Eric Chouinard .40 1.00
105 Oleg Timchenko .08 .20
106 Sebastien Roger .08 .20
107 Simon Gagne .40 1.00
108 Alex Tanguay .40 1.00
109 David Gosselin .08 .20
110 Ramzi Abid .20 .50
111 Eric Drouin .08 .20
112 Dominic Auger .08 .20
113 Martin Moise .08 .20
114 Randy Copley .08 .20
115 Alexandre Mathieu .08 .20
116 Brad Richards .20 .50
117 Dmitri Tolkunov .08 .20
118 Alexei Tezikov .08 .20
119 Derrick Walser .08 .20
120 Adam Borzecki .08 .20
121 Ramzi Abid .20 .50
122 Brett Allan .08 .20
123 Mark Bell .20 .50
124 Blair Betts .08 .20
125 Randy Copley .08 .20
126 Simon Gagne .40 1.00
127 Mike Henrich .08 .20
128 Vincent Lecavalier .20 .50
129 Norman Milley .40 1.00
130 Chris Neilsen .08 .20
131 Rico Fata .20 .50
132 Mike Ribeiro .08 .50
133 Bryan Allen .08 .20
134 John Erskine .20 .50
135 Jonathan Girard Jr. .20 .50
136 Stephen Peat .40 1.00
137 Robyn Regehr .40 .75
138 Brad Stuart .40 1.00
139 Patrick Desrochers .20 .50
140 Jason Labarbera .20 .50
141 David Cameron .08 .20
142 Jonathan Cheechoo .20 1.00
143 Eric Chouinard .40 1.00
144 Brent Gauvreau .08 .20
145 Scott Gomez .20 .50
146 Jeff Heerema .08 .20
147 David Legwand .40 1.00
148 Manny Malhotra .20 .50
149 Justin Papineau .08 .20
150 Andrew Peters .08 .20
151 Michael Rupp .40 1.00
152 Alex Tanguay .40 1.00
153 Francois Beauchemin .08 .20
154 Mathieu Biron .08 .20
155 Jiri Fischer .40 1.00
156 Alex Henry .20 .50
157 Kyle Rossiter .08 .20
158 Martin Skoula .08 .20
159 Mathieu Chouinard .20 .50
160 Philippe Sauve .40 1.00
161 Brian Finley .20 .50
162 Brent Belecki .08 .20
163 Dominic Perna .08 .20
164 Jonathan Cheechoo .20 1.00
165 Checklist .08 .20

1998 Bowman CHL Golden Anniversary

Randomly inserted in packs at the rate of 1:57, this 165-card set is a gold-foil parallel version of the base set and is sequentially numbered to 50 in honor of the 50 years of Bowman cards.

*STARS: 12.5X TO 30X BASIC CARDS

1998 Bowman CHL OPC International

Inserted one in every pack, this 165-card set is parallel to the base set and features color player photos with a national indication in the background by way of a map printed on 16 pt. mirror board. Each back is written in the language of that player's native country.

*STARS: .75X TO 2X BASIC CARDS

1998 Bowman CHL Autographs Blue

Randomly inserted in packs at the rate of 1:39, this 40-card set features cards signed by the top 40 NHL draft prospects and authenticated by a blue foil "Topps Certified Issue" stamp. Silver and blue variations were also created and inserted randomly. Silver autos were inserted at a rate of 1:157 and gold at 1:470.

*SILVER AU's: .75X TO 2X BASIC AU
*GOLD AU's: 2X TO 5X BASIC AU
A1 Justin Papineau 2.50 6.00
A2 Jason Labarbera 4.00 10.00
A3 Michael Rupp 4.00 10.00
A4 Stephen Peat 5.00 12.00
A5 Manny Malhotra 2.50 6.00
A6 Michael Henrich 2.50 6.00
A7 Kyle Rossiter 2.50 6.00
A8 Mark Bell 5.00 12.00
A9 Mathieu Chouinard 5.00 12.00
A10 Vincent Lecavalier 8.00 20.00
A11 David Legwand 5.00 12.00
A12 Bryan Allen 2.50 6.00
A13 Francois Beauchemin 2.50 6.00
A14 Robyn Regehr 5.00 12.00
A15 Eric Chouinard 4.00 10.00
A16 Norman Milley 4.00 10.00
A17 Alex Henry 2.50 6.00
A18 Ramzi Abid 2.50 6.00
A19 Jiri Fischer 5.00 12.00
A20 Patrick Desrochers 4.00 10.00
A21 Mathieu Biron 2.50 6.00
A22 Brad Stuart 5.00 12.00
A23 Philippe Sauve 8.00 20.00
A24 John Erskine 4.00 10.00
A25 Jonathan Cheechoo 6.00 20.00
A26 Brett Allan 2.50 6.00
A27 Scott Gomez 3.00 15.00
A28 Chris Neilsen 2.50 6.00
A29 David Cameron 2.50 6.00
A30 Jonathan Girard Jr. 5.00 12.00

A31 Jeff Heerema 2.50 6.00
A32 Blair Betts 2.50 6.00
A33 Andrew Peters 2.50 6.00
A34 Randy Copley 4.00 10.00
A35 Alex Tanguay 5.00 15.00
A36 Simon Gagne 5.00 15.00
A37 Brent Gauvreau 2.50 6.00
A38 Mike Ribeiro 5.00 12.00
A39 Martin Skoula 2.50 6.00
A40 Rico Fata 4.00 10.00

1998 Bowman CHL Scout's Choice

Randomly inserted in packs at the rate of 1:12, this 21-card set features color photos of players picked by Bowman Hockey Scouts and printed on borderless, double-etched foil cards.

COMPLETE SET (21) 30.00 60.00
SC1 Bryan Allen .40 1.00
SC2 Manny Malhotra .40 1.00
SC3 Daniel Tkaczuk .40 1.00
SC4 Bujar Amidovski .40 1.00
SC5 Patrick Desrochers .40 1.00
SC6 Brad Ference .40 1.00
SC7 Marian Hossa .60 1.50
SC8 Brad Stuart .40 1.00
SC9 Sergei Varlamov .40 1.00
SC10 Randy Petruk .40 1.00
SC11 Karol Bartanus .40 1.00
SC12 Vincent Lecavalier .50 1.25
SC13 Jonathan Girard .40 1.00
SC14 Peter Ratchuk .40 1.00
SC15 Alex Tanguay .60 1.50
SC16 Rico Fata .40 1.00
SC17 Brian Finley .50 1.25
SC18 Jonathan Cheechoo .40 1.00
SC19 Scott Gomez .40 1.00
SC20 Michal Rozsival .40 1.00
SC21 Mathieu Garon .40 1.00

1998 Bowman Chrome CHL

The 1998-99 Bowman Chrome CHL hobby-only set was issued in one series totaling 165 cards. The 4-card packs retail for $3.00 each. The fronts feature color action photography on chromium technology. The Bowman Rookie Card stamp appears on all cards for players making their first appearance in the set. The scheduled release date was September, 1998.

COMPLETE SET (165) 30.00 60.00
1 Robert Esche .60 1.50
2 Chris Hajt .15 .40
3 Mark McMahon .15 .40
4 Jeff Brown .15 .40
5 Richard Jackman .15 .40
6 Greg Labenski .15 .40
7 Marek Posmyk .15 .40
8 Brian Willsie .15 .40
9 Jason Ward .15 .40
10 Manny Malhotra .15 .40
11 Matt Cooke .75 2.00
12 Mike Gorman .15 .40
13 Rodney Richard .15 .40
14 David Legwand .75 2.00
15 Jon Sim .15 .40
16 Peter Sarno .60 1.50
17 Andrew Long .15 .40
18 Peter Cava .15 .40
19 Colin Pepperall .15 .40
20 Jay Legault .15 .40
21 Brian Finley .60 1.50
22 Martin Skoula .15 .40
23 Brian Campbell .15 .40
24 Sean Blanchard .15 .40
25 Bryan Allen .15 .40
26 Peter Hogan .15 .40
27 Nick Boynton .75 2.00
28 Matt Bradley .15 .40
29 Jeremy Adduono .15 .40
30 Mike Henrich .15 .40
31 Justin Papineau .15 .40
32 Bujar Amidovski .60 1.50
33 Robert Mailloux .15 .40
34 Daniel Tkaczuk .15 .40
35 Sean Avery .75 2.00
36 Mark Bell .75 2.00
37 Kevin Colley .15 .40
38 Norman Milley .60 1.50
39 Scott Barney .15 .40
40 Joel Trottier .15 .40
41 Brent Belecki .15 .40
42 Randy Petruk .60 1.50
43 Brad Ference .15 .40
44 Perry Johnson .15 .40
45 Joel Kwiatkowski .15 .40
46 Zenith Komarniski .15 .40
47 Greg Kuznik .15 .40
48 Andrew Ference .60 1.50
49 Jason Deleurme .15 .40
50 Trent Whitfield .15 .40
51 Dylan Gyori .15 .40
52 Todd Robinson .15 .40
53 Marian Hossa .75 2.00
54 Mike Hurley .15 .40
55 Greg Leeb .15 .40
56 Andrej Podkonicky .15 .40
57 Quinn Hancock .15 .40
58 Marian Cisar .15 .40
59 Bret DeCecco .15 .40
60 Brenden Morrow .60 1.50
61 Evan Lindsay .60 1.50
62 Terry Friesen .60 1.50
63 Ryan Shannon .15 .40
64 Michal Rozsival .15 .40
65 Luc Theoret .15 .40
66 Brad Stuart .75 2.00
67 Burke Henry .15 .40
68 Cory Sarich .15 .40
69 Martin Sonnenberg .15 .40
70 Mark Smith .60 1.50
71 Shawn McNeil .15 .40
72 Brad Moran .15 .40
73 Josh Holden .15 .40
74 Cory Cyrenne .15 .40
75 Shane Willis .15 .40
76 Stefan Cherneski .15 .40
77 Jay Henderson .15 .40
78 Ronald Petrovicky .15 .40
79 Sergei Varlamov .15 .40
80 Chad Hinz .15 .40
81 Mathieu Garon .15 1.00
82 Mathieu Chouinard .60 1.50
83 Dominic Perna .15 .40
84 Didier Tremblay .15 .40
85 Mike Ribeiro .15 1.00
86 Marty Johnston .15 .40
87 Remi Royer .15 .40
88 Patrick Pelchat .15 .40
89 Daniel Corso .15 .40
90 Francois Fortier .15 .40
91 Marc-Andre Gaudet .15 .40
92 Francois Beauchemin .15 .40
93 Michel Tremblay .15 .40
94 Jean-Philippe Pare .15 .40
95 Francois Methot .15 .40
96 David Thibeault .15 .40
97 Jonathan Girard Jr. .60 1.50
98 Karol Bartanus .15 .40
99 Peter Ratchuk .15 .40
100 Pierre Dagenais .60 1.50
101 Philippe Sauve .75 2.00
102 Remi Bergeron .15 .40
103 Vincent Lecavalier .60 1.50
104 Eric Chouinard .60 1.50
105 Oleg Timchenko .15 .40
106 Sebastien Roger .15 .40
107 Simon Gagne .75 2.00
108 Alex Tanguay .60 2.00
109 David Gosselin .15 .40
110 Ramzi Abid .15 .40
111 Eric Drouin .15 .40
112 Dominic Auger .15 .40
113 Martin Moise .15 .40
114 Randy Copley .15 .40
115 Alexandre Mathieu .15 .40
116 Brad Richards .60 1.50
117 Dmitri Tolkunov .15 .40
118 Alexei Tezikov .15 .40
119 Derrick Walser .15 .40
120 Adam Borzecki .15 .40
121 Ramzi Abid .15 .40
122 Brett Allan .15 .40
123 Mark Bell .15 1.00
124 Blair Betts .15 .40
125 Randy Copley .60 1.50
126 Simon Gagne .75 2.00
127 Mike Henrich .15 .40
128 Vincent Lecavalier .60 1.50
129 Norman Milley .60 1.50
130 Chris Nielsen .15 .40
131 Rico Fata .60 1.50
132 Mike Ribeiro .15 1.00
133 Bryan Allen .15 .40
134 John Erskine .60 1.50
135 Jonathan Girard Jr. .60 1.50
136 Stephen Peat .75 2.00
137 Robyn Regehr .15 1.50
138 Brad Stuart .75 2.00
139 Patrick Desrochers .60 1.50
140 Jason Labarbera .60 1.50
141 David Cameron .15 .40
142 Jonathan Cheechoo 1.25 3.00
143 Eric Chouinard .60 1.50
144 Brent Gauvreau .15 .40
145 Scott Gomez .15 1.00
146 Jeff Heerema .15 .40
147 David Legwand .75 2.00
148 Manny Malhotra .15 .40
149 Justin Papineau .15 .40
150 Andrew Peters .15 .40
151 Michael Rupp .60 1.50
152 Alex Tanguay .60 2.00
153 Francois Beauchemin .15 .40
154 Mathieu Biron .15 .40
155 Jiri Fischer .75 2.00
156 Alex Henry .15 .40
157 Kyle Rossiter .15 .40
158 Martin Skoula .15 .40
159 Mathieu Chouinard .60 1.50
160 Philippe Sauve .75 2.00
161 Brian Finley .60 1.50
162 Brent Belecki .15 .40
163 Dominic Perna .15 .40
164 Jonathan Cheechoo .15 2.00
165 Checklist .15 .40
NNO Puck Redemption .15 .40

1998 Bowman Chrome CHL Golden Anniversary

Randomly inserted in packs at a rate of 1:39, this 165-card parallel offers the same players as in the Bowman Chrome CHL base set. The set is sequentially numbered to 50. Cards are randomly inserted into packs. A refractor variation was also created and inserted randomly. Refractors were serial numbered to just 5 and are not priced due to scarcity.

*STARS: 10X TO 25X BASIC CARDS

1998 Bowman Chrome CHL OPC International

Randomly inserted in packs at a rate of 1:8, this 165-card parallel features the same players as in the Bowman Chrome CHL base set. The set also offers background map designs of the player's homeland and vital statistics written in that player's native language. A refractor variation was also created and inserted at a rate of 1:48.

*STARS: 2.5X TO 5X BASIC CARD
*REF.STARS: 8X TO 20X BASIC CARDS

1998 Bowman Chrome CHL Refractors

Randomly inserted in packs at a rate of 1:12, this 165-card parallel offers a refractive version of the same players as in the Bowman Chrome CHL base set.

REF.STARS: 4X TO 10X BASIC CARD

1999 Bowman CHL

Released as a 165-card set, 1999 Bowman CHL set features 122 CHL superstars, 40 NHL draft prospects, two dual player cards of stars from the WHL, OHL, QMJHL and Prospects All-Star Game, and one checklist.

COMPLETE SET (165) 20.00 50.00
1 Alex Auld .30 .75
2 Maxime Ouellet .30 .75
3 Nolan Yonkman .08 .20
4 Jeff Beatch .08 .20
5 Pavel Brendl .20 .50
6 Jamie Chamberlain .08 .20
7 Kyle Wanvig .08 .20
8 Chris Kelly .08 .20
9 Scott Kelman .08 .20
10 Derek MacKenzie .08 .20
11 Tim Connolly .20 .50
12 Alexandre Giroux .08 .20
13 Oleg Saprykin .20 .50
14 Sheldon Keefe .20 .50
15 Branislav Mezei .20 .50
16 Brett Lysak .08 .20
17 Peter Reynolds .08 .20
18 Ross Lupaschuk .08 .20
19 Mirko Murovic .08 .20
20 Steve McCarthy .08 .20
21 Radim Vrbata .20 .50
22 Dusty Jamieson .08 .20
23 Matt Carkner .08 .20
24 Denis Shvidki .20 .50
25 Jonathan Fauteux .08 .20
26 Martin Grenier .08 .20
27 Marc-Andre Thinel .20 .50
28 Luke Sellars .08 .20
29 Brad Ralph .08 .20
30 Scott Cameron .08 .20
31 Charlie Stephens .08 .20
32 Jamie Lundmark .20 .50
33 Justin Mapletoft .20 .50
34 Kristopher Beech .20 .50
35 Taylor Pyatt .20 .50
36 Michael Zigomanis .20 .50
37 Edward Hill .08 .20
38 Barret Jackman .30 1.00
39 Simon LaJeunesse .30 .75
40 Brian Finley .30 .75
41 Maxime Ouellet .30 .75
42 Alexei Volkov .30 .75
43 Roberto Luongo .30 1.00
44 Chris Lyness .08 .20
45 Simon Tremblay .08 .20
46 Eric Tremblay .08 .20
47 Jonathan Girard .20 .50
48 Dimitri Tolkunov .08 .20
49 Philippe Plante .08 .20
50 Eric Chouinard .20 .50
51 Wesley Scanzano .08 .20
52 Vincent Dionne .08 .20
53 Sebastien Roger .08 .20
54 Ladislav Nagy .20 1.00
55 Alex Tanguay .40 1.00
56 Martin Moise .08 .20
57 Brad Richards .40 1.00
58 Juraj Kolnik .20 .50
59 Simon Gagne .40 1.00
60 Gregor Baumgartner .08 .20
61 Mathieu Benoit .08 .20
62 Pierre-Luc Therrien .08 .20
63 Danny LaVoie .08 .20
64 Mathieu Chouinard .08 .20
65 Andrew Carver .08 .20
66 Jiri Fischer .20 .50
67 Alexander Ryazantsev .08 .20
68 Didier Tremblay .08 .20
69 Mathieu Biron .08 .20
70 Michel Periard .08 .20
71 Mike Ribeiro .30 .75
72 Francois Fortier .08 .20
73 Benoit Dusablon .08 .20
74 Jerome Tremblay .08 .20
75 Samuel St.Pierre .08 .20
76 Marc-Andre Thinel .20 .50
77 Alexandre Tremblay .08 .20
78 Patrick Grandmaitre .08 .20
79 Christian Daigle .08 .20
80 David Thibeault .08 .20
81 Dominic Forget .08 .20
82 James Desmarais .08 .20
83 Pavel Brendl .20 .50
84 Kyle Calder .20 .50
85 Jason Chimera .20 .50
86 Chad Hinz .08 .20
87 Curtis Huppe .08 .20
88 Milan Kraft .20 .50
89 Brad Leeb .08 .20
90 Jamie Lundmark .20 .50
91 Brett Lysak .08 .20
92 Brad Moran .20 .50
93 Frantisek Mrazek .08 .20
94 Brad Twordik .08 .20
95 Kurt Drummond .08 .20
96 Burke Henry .08 .20
97 Steve McCarthy .20 .50
98 Richard Seeley .08 .20
99 Brad Stuart .30 .75
100 Luc Theoret .08 .20
101 Alexandre Fomitchev .08 .20
102 Brady Block .08 .20
103 Ajay Baines .08 .20
104 Blair Betts .20 .50
105 Tyler Bouck .20 .50
106 Mike Brown .08 .20
107 Bret DeCecco .08 .20
108 Scott Gomez .30 .75
109 Dylan Gyori .08 .20
110 Donnie Kinney .08 .20
111 Ken McKay .08 .20
112 Brett McLean .08 .20
113 Brenden Morrow .30 .75
114 Marty Standish .08 .20
115 Andrew Ference .20 .50
116 Brad Ference .08 .20
117 Scott Hannan .30 .75
118 Darrell Hay .08 .20
119 Robyn Regehr .30 .75
120 Chris St. Croix .08 .20
121 Kenric Exner .30 .75
122 Cody Rudkowsky .30 .75
123 Scott Barney .08 .20
124 Kevin Colley .08 .20
125 Sheldon Keefe .20 .50
126 Norman Milley .20 .50
127 Scott Page .08 .20
128 Justin Papineau .20 .50
129 Ryan Ready .08 .20
130 Denis Shvidki .20 .50
131 Chris Stanley .08 .20
132 Dan Tessier .08 .20
133 Daniel Tkaczuk .08 .20
134 Michael Zigomanis .20 .50
135 Jim Baxter .08 .20
136 Branislav Mezei .20 .50
137 Brian Campbell .08 .20
138 Greg Labenski .08 .20
139 Jeff McKercher .08 .20
140 Martin Skoula .20 .50
141 Brian Finley .30 .75
142 Seamus Kotyk .30 .75
143 Adam Colagiacomo .08 .20
144 Tim Connolly .20 .50
145 Harold Druken .20 .50
146 Rico Fata .20 .50
147 David Legwand .30 .75
148 Adam Mair .08 .20
149 Kent McDonell .08 .20
150 Ivan Novoseltsev .20 .50
151 Peter Sarno .20 .50
152 Dan Snyder .20 1.00
153 Jason Spezza 1.25 3.00
154 Jason Ward .08 .20
155 Alex Henry .08 .20
156 Wes Jarvis .08 .20
157 Paul Mara .20 .50
158 Kevin Mitchell .08 .20
159 Dan Passero .08 .20
160 Dan Watson .08 .20
161 Gene Chiarello .08 .20
162 Chris Madden .30 .75
163 M.Ouellet/B.DeCecco .30 .75
164 S.Barney/M.Thinel .08 .20
165 Checklist .08 .20

1999 Bowman CHL Gold

Randomly inserted in packs, this 165-card set parallels the base Bowman CHL set on cards enhanced with a "Bowman Gold" stamp on the card front. Each card is randomly inserted at a rate of one in eight packs and sequentially numbered to 99.

*STARS: 6X TO 15X BASIC CARDS

1999 Bowman CHL OPC International

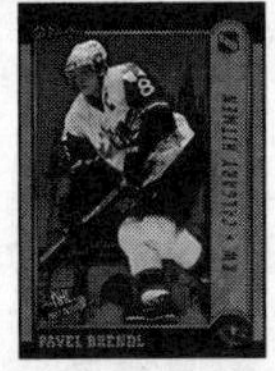

Randomly seeded in packs, this 165-card set parallels the base Bowman CHL set on cards with enhanced backgrounds featuring a monument from the player's home province or country. Card backs contain relevant stats written in the featured player's native language.

COMPLETE SET (165) 50.00 100.00
*STARS: .75X TO 2X BASIC CARDS

1999 Bowman CHL Autographs

Randomly inserted in packs at the rate of 1:16, this 40-card set features authentic autographs coupled with action photography. Each card contains the gold foil "Bowman Certified Autograph" stamp in the upper right hand corner. Silver and gold variations were also created and inserted randomly, Silver autos were inserted at a rate of 1:43 and gold at 1:128. Note: Card #BA19, long thought not to exist, has been confirmed. We do not have any pricing information, however.

*SILVER: 1X TO 2X BASIC CARDS
*GOLD: 2.5X TO 5X BASIC CARDS
BA1 Brian Finley 4.00 10.00
BA2 Simon Lajeunesse 4.00 10.00
BA3 Barret Jackman 5.00 12.00
BA4 Edward Hill 2.00 5.00
BA5 Michael Zigomanis 4.00 10.00
BA6 Taylor Pyatt 4.00 10.00
BA7 Kristopher Beech 4.00 10.00
BA8 Justin Mapletoft 4.00 10.00
BA9 Jamie Lundmark 4.00 10.00
BA10 Charlie Stephens 2.00 5.00
BA11 Scott Cameron 2.00 5.00
BA12 Brad Ralph 2.00 5.00
BA13 Luke Sellars 2.00 5.00
BA14 Marc-Andre Thinel 4.00 10.00
BA15 Martin Grenier 4.00 10.00
BA16 Jonathan Fauteux 2.00 5.00
BA17 Denis Shvidki 2.00 5.00
BA18 Matt Carkner 2.00 5.00
BA19 Dusty Jamieson
BA20 Radim Vrbata 5.00 12.00
BA21 Alex Auld 6.00 15.00
BA22 Maxime Ouellet 4.00 10.00
BA23 Nolan Yonkman 2.00 5.00
BA24 Jeff Beatch 2.00 5.00
BA25 Pavel Brendl 4.00 10.00
BA26 Jamie Chamberlain 2.00 5.00
BA27 Kyle Wanvig 4.00 10.00
BA28 Chris Kelly 2.00 5.00
BA29 Scott Kelman 2.00 5.00
BA30 Derek MacKenzie 2.00 5.00
BA31 Tim Connolly 4.00 10.00
BA32 Alexandre Giroux 2.00 5.00
BA33 Oleg Saprykin 4.00 10.00
BA34 Sheldon Keefe 2.00 5.00
BA35 Branislav Mezei 2.00 5.00
BA36 Brett Lysak 4.00 10.00
BA37 Peter Reynolds 4.00 10.00
BA38 Ross Lupaschuk 2.00 5.00
BA39 Mirko Murovic 2.00 5.00
BA40 Steve McCarthy 2.00 5.00

1999 Bowman CHL Scout's Choice

Randomly inserted in packs at the rate of 1:16, this 21-card set double-etched foil and identifies top ranked CHL players. Card backs carry an "SC" prefix.

SC1 Tim Connolly 1.25 3.00
SC2 Scott Kelman .75 2.00
SC3 Pavel Brendl .75 2.00
SC4 Maxime Ouellet 1.25 3.00
SC5 Brian Finley 1.25 3.00
SC6 Denis Shvidki .75 2.00
SC7 Michael Zigomanis .75 2.00
SC8 Taylor Pyatt .75 2.00
SC9 Kris Beech .75 2.00
SC10 Jamie Lundmark .75 2.00
SC11 Jason Spezza 2.00 5.00
SC12 Rico Fata .75 2.00
SC13 David Legwand 1.25 3.00
SC14 Daniel Tkaczuk .75 2.00
SC15 Brad Stuart .75 2.00
SC16 Jiri Fischer .75 2.00
SC17 Simon Gagne 1.50 4.00
SC18 Alex Tanguay 1.25 3.00
SC19 Scott Gomez .75 2.00
SC20 Ladislav Nagy .75 2.00
SC21 Roberto Luongo 1.50 4.00

1991 Classic

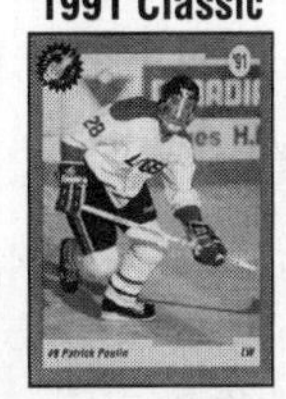

The set features 50 of the top 60 NHL draft picks. The set was issued in a run of 360,000 factory sets and included an individually numbered certificate of authenticity. The cards were issued in both English and French and carry the same value.

COMPLETE SET (50) 2.00 3.00
*FRENCH: SAME VALUE
1 Eric Lindros 1.00 1.50
2 Pat Falloon .01 .10
3 Scott Niedermayer
4 Scott Lachance .01 .10
5 Peter Forsberg .75 2.00
6 Alek Stojanov .01 .10
7 Richard Matvichuk .01 .10
8 Patrick Poulin .01 .10
9 Martin Lapointe .08 .25
10 Tyler Wright .01 .10
11 Philippe Boucher .01 .10
12 Pat Peake .01 .10
13 Markus Naslund
14 Brent Bilodeau .01 .10
15 Glen Murray
16 Niklas Sundblad .01 .10
17 Martin Rucinsky .08 .25
18 Trevor Halverson .01 .10
19 Dean McAmmond .01 .10
20 Ray Whitney .08 .25
21 Rene Corbet .01 .10
22 Eric Lavigne .01 .10
23 Zigmund Palffy .30 .40
24 Steve Staios .01 .10
25 Jim Campbell .01 .10
26 Jassen Cullimore .01 .10
27 Martin Hamrlik .01 .10
28 Jamie Pushor .01 .10
29 Donevan Hextall .01 .10
30 Andrew Verner .01 .10
31 Jason Dawe .01 .10
32 Jeff Nelson .01 .10
33 Darcy Werenka .01 .10
34 Jozef Stumpel .08 .25
35 Francois Groleau .01 .10
36 Guy Leveque .01 .10
37 Jamie Matthews .01 .10
38 Dody Wood .01 .10
39 Yanic Perreault .08 .25
40 Jamie McLennan .08 .25
41 Yanic Dupre UER .01 .10
42 Sandy McCarthy .08 .25
43 Chris Osgood .30 .50
44 Fredrik Lindquist .01 .10
45 Jason Young .01 .10
46 Steve Konowalchuk .08 .25
47 Michael Nylander UER .08 .25
48 Shane Peacock .01 .10
49 Yves Sarault .01 .10
50 Marcel Cousineau .08 .25
NNO Rocket Ismail .08 .25
NNO Patrick Poulin AU/1100 .40 2.00

1991 Classic Promos

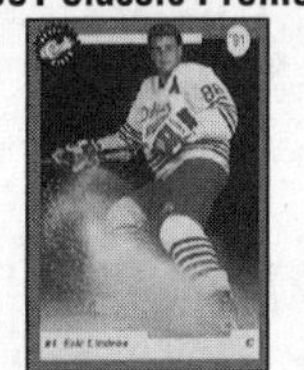

The two standard size promo cards were issued by Classic to show collectors and dealers the style of their new hockey draft picks set.

COMPLETE SET (2) 1.20 3.00
1 Eric Lindros 1.20 3.00
2 Pat Falloon .10 .25

1992 Classic

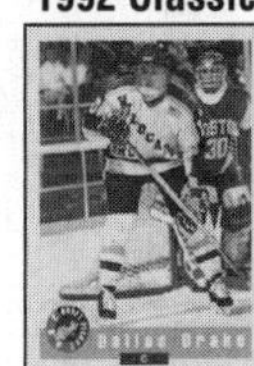

The 1992 Classic Hockey Draft Picks set consists of 120 standard-size cards. The production run for the regular issue cards was reportedly 9,966 ten-box cases. Classic also issued the 1992 Draft Pick set in a Gold version. The Gold factory sets were packaged in a walnut display case. The Gold sets also included an individually numbered card signed by Valeri and Pavel Bure. The set included the first card of female goaltender Manon Rheaume.

COMPLETE SET (120) 5.00 10.00
1 Roman Hamrlik .02 .10
2 Alexei Yashin .02 .10
3 Mike Rathje .02 .10
4 Darius Kasparaitis .02 .10
5 Cory Stillman .02 .10
6 Robert Petrovicky .02 .10
7 Andrei Nazarov .02 .10
8 Cory Stillman CL .02 .10
9 Jason Bowen .02 .10
10 Jason Smith .02 .10
11 David Wilkie .02 .10
12 Curtis Bowen .02 .10
13 Grant Marshall .02 .10
14 Valeri Bure .10 .30
15 Jeff Shantz .02 .10
16 Justin Hocking .02 .10
17 Mike Peca .20 .50
18 Marc Hussey .02 .10
19 Sandy Allan .10 .30
20 Kirk Maltby .10 .30
21 Cale Hulse .02 .10
22 Sylvain Cloutier .10 .30
23 Martin Gendron .02 .10
24 Kevin Smyth .02 .10
25 Jason McBain .02 .10
26 Lee J. Leslie .02 .10
27 Ralph Intranuovo .02 .10
28 Martin Reichel .02 .10
29 Stefan Ustorf .02 .10
30 Jarkko Varvio .02 .10
31 Jere Lehtinen .15 .40
32 Janne Gronvall .02 .10
33 Martin Straka .15 .40
34 Libor Polasek .02 .10
35 Jozef Cierny .02 .10
36 Jan Vopat .02 .10
37 Ondrej Steiner .02 .10
38 Jan Caloun .02 .10
39 Petr Hrbek .02 .10
40 Richard Smehlik .02 .10
41 Sergei Gonchar CL .02 .10
42 Sergei Krivokrasov .02 .10
43 Sergei Gonchar .10 .30
44 Boris Mironov .02 .10
45 Denis Metlyuk .02 .10
46 Sergei Klimovich .02 .10
47 Sergei Brylin .02 .10
48 Andrei Nikolishin .02 .10
49 Alexander Cherbayev .02 .10
50 Sergei Zholtok .02 .10
51 Vitali Prokhorov .02 .10
52 Nikolai Borschevsky .02 .10
53 Vitali Tomilin .02 .10
54 Alexander Alexeyev .02 .10
55 Roman Zolotov .02 .10
56 Konstantin Korotkov .02 .10
57 Laperriere Family .02 .10
58 Lacroix Family .02 .10
59 Manon Rheaume 2.00 4.00
60 Hamrlik/Yashin/Rathje CL .02 .10
61 Viktor Kozlov CL .02 .10
62 Viktor Kozlov .10 .30
63 Denny Felsner CL .02 .10
64 Denny Felsner .02 .10
65 Darrin Madeley .02 .10
66 Mario Lemieux FLB .60 1.50
67 Sandy Moger .02 .10
68 Dave Karpa .02 .10
69 Martin Jiranek .02 .10
70 Dwayne Norris .02 .10
71 Michael Stewart .02 .10
72 Joby Messier .02 .10
73 Mike Bales .10 .30
74 Scott Thomas .02 .10
75 Dan Laperriere .02 .10
76 Mike Lappin .02 .10
77 Eric Lacroix .02 .10
78 Martin Lacroix .02 .10
79 Scott LaGrand .02 .10
80 Jean-Yves Roy .02 .10
81 Scott Pellerin .02 .10
82 Rob Gaudreau .02 .10
83 Mike Boback .02 .10
84 Dixon Ward .02 .10
85 Jeff McLean .02 .10
86 Dallas Drake .02 .10
87 Bret Hedican .02 .10
88 Doug Zmolek .02 .10
89 Trent Klatt .02 .10
90 Larry Olimb .02 .10
91 Duane Derksen .10 .30
92 Doug MacDonald .02 .10
93 Dmitri Kvartalnov CL .02 .10
94 Jim Cummins .02 .10
95 Lonnie Loach .02 .10
96 Keith Jones .02 .10
97 Jason Woolley .02 .10
98 Rob Zamuner .10 .30
99 Brad Werenka .02 .10
100 Brent Grieve .02 .10
101 Sean Hill .10 .30
102 Keith Carney .02 .10
103 Peter Ciavaglia .02 .10
104 David Littman .10 .30
105 Bill Guerin .25 .60
106 Mikhail Kravets .02 .10
107 J.F. Quintin .02 .10
108 Mike Needham .02 .10
109 Jason Ruff .02 .10
110 Mike Vukonich .02 .10
111 Shawn McCosh .02 .10
112 Dave Tretowicz .02 .10
113 Todd Harkins .02 .10
114 Jason Muzzatti .02 .10
115 Paul Kruse .02 .10
116 Kevin Wortman .02 .10
117 Sean Burke .10 .30
118 Keith Gretzky .02 .10
119 Ray Whitney .10 .30
120 Dmitri Kvartalnov .02 .10
SP Mario Lemieux FLB 4.00 5.00
AU1 M.Lemieux AU/2000 40.00 80.00
AU2 Bure Brothers AU/6000 10.00 20.00

1992 Classic Gold

Classic also issued the 1992 Draft Picks set in a Gold version. The singles sell for between three and eight times the corresponding regular cards. Reportedly only 6,000 sets and 7,500 uncut sheets were produced. The sets were packaged in a walnut display case. The Gold factory sets also included an individually numbered card signed by Valeri and Pavel Bure.

*GOLD STARS: 1.5X TO 4X BASIC CARDS

1992 Classic Autographs

We've recently confirmed the existence of this single, which mirrors the front of the basic Classic #85 McLean single but features a back with a certification of the autograph's authenticity. If you know of any others, please contact us at hockeymag@beckett.com.

COMPLETE SET (?)
NNO Jeff McLean

1992 Classic Gold Promo

The front features a black-and-white action player photo bordered in white. The player's name is printed in a gold foil stripe beneath the picture, with the position given on a short black bar. On a gold background, the back has draft information, statistics, player profile, and a second black-and-white photo that is horizontally oriented. The card is unnumbered and has the disclaimer "For Promotional Purposes Only" printed on the back.

NNO Mario Lemieux 3.00 7.50

1992 Classic LPs

This ten-card standard-size set features hockey draft picks. The cards are numbered on the back with an "LP" prefix. The cards were random inserts in packs of 1992 Classic Hockey Draft Picks.

COMPLETE SET (10) 2.50 6.00
LP1 Roman Hamrlik .20 .50
LP2 Alexei Yashin .20 .50
LP3 Mike Rathje .20 .50
LP4 Darius Kasparaitis .20 .50
LP5 Cory Stillman .20 .50
LP6 Dmitri Kvartalnov .20 .50
LP7 David Wilkie .20 .50
LP8 Curtis Bowen .20 .50
LP9 Valeri Bure .40 1.00
LP10 Joby Messier .20 .50

1992 Classic Promos

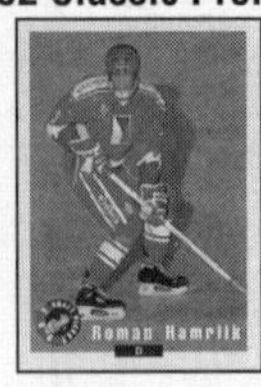

These three cards measure the standard size and feature color action player photos with white borders, except for the Lemieux card, which has a black and white picture with the words "Flash Back 92" printed at the top. The player's name is printed in a gold stripe at the bottom, which intersects the Classic logo at the lower left corner. The gold backs have horizontally oriented player photos, again the Lemieux being black and white and the others color. The text on the back is vertically oriented, except for the biography, and includes draft information, career highlights, and the words "For Promotional Purposes Only". The cards are unnumbered and checklisted below in alphabetical order.

COMPLETE SET (3) 3.20 8.00
1 Roman Hamrlik 1.20 3.00
2 Mario Lemieux 2.00 5.00
(Flash Back 92)
3 Ray Whitney .40 1.00

1992-93 Classic Manon Rheaume C3 Presidential

This standard-size card pictures Rheaume holding a hockey stick and carrying an equipment bag over her shoulder. The picture is bordered in white, and her name and position are printed on the wider right border. The Classic "C3 Presidential" logo is gold foil stamped across the top of the picture. The back has a color close-up photo and a player quote. Reportedly only 5,000 of these cards were produced.

1 Manon Rheaume 4.00 10.00

1992-93 Classic Manon Rheaume Promo

Manon Rheaume, professional hockey's first female player, signed her trading card for fans before the Atlanta Braves playoff game Wednesday, October 7, 1992. Sponsored by Power 99, a local radio station, this promotion was advertised by "Pennies from Heaven," an urban renewal movement championed by former President Jimmy Carter and Atlanta Braves third baseman Terry Pendleton. Fans who brought a jar of pennies or a 10.00 donation were given the autographed Rheaume promotional card; close to 1,000 cards were signed and about 2,500 promo bags were given away. The front of this standard size card features a posed color player photo with white borders. Her name appears in a gold stripe across the bottom of the picture. The words "A Classic First" are printed in gold at the upper right corner of the picture. The center back shows the yellow and green Classic logo. The disclaimer "For Promotional Purposes Only" is printed in black at the top and bottom and in gray over the rest of the card back.

NNO Manon Rheaume 4.00 10.00

1993 Classic

The 1993 Classic Hockey Draft set consists of 150 standard-size cards. Production was reported to be 14,500 sequentially-numbered ten-box cases. More than 15,000 autographed cards from Manon Rheaume, Doug Gilmour, Mark Recchi, Mike Bossy, Jeff O'Neill and other hockey stars were randomly inserted throughout the packs. Subsets featuring foil-stamped cards are Top 10, The Class of '94, The Daigle File, Flashbacks, College Champions, Manon Rheaume, and Hockey Art.

COMPLETE SET (150) 4.00 10.00
1 Alexandre Daigle .02 .10
2 Chris Pronger .20 .50
3 Chris Gratton .10 .25
4 Paul Kariya .40 1.00
5 Rob Niedermayer .02 .10
6 Viktor Kozlov .10 .25
7 Jason Arnott .20 .50
8 Niklas Sundstrom .02 .10
9 Todd Harvey .02 .10
10 Jocelyn Thibault .20 .50
11 Checklist 1 .02 .10
Top Draft Picks
12 Pat Peake .02 .10
1993 CHL POY
13 Jason Allison .25 .60
14 Todd Bertuzzi .20 .50
15 Maxim Bets .02 .10
16 Curtis Bowen .02 .10
17 Kevin Brown .02 .10
18 Valeri Bure .10 .25
19 Jason Dawe .02 .10
20 Adam Deadmarsh .02 .10
21 Aaron Gavey .02 .10
22 Nathan Lafayette .02 .10
23 Eric Lecompte .02 .10
24 Manny Legace .20 .50
25 Mike Peca .20 .50
26 Denis Pederson .02 .10
27 Jeff Shantz .02 .10
28 Nick Stadjuhar .02 .10
29 Cory Stillman .02 .10
30 Michal Sykora .02 .10
31 Brent Tully .02 .10
32 Mike Wilson .02 .10
33 Junior Production Line .02 .10
Kevin Brown
Pat Peake
Bob Wren
34 Checklist 2 .02 .10
Dynamic Duo
Alexandre Daigle
Alexei Yashin
35 Antti Aalto .02 .10
36 Radim Bicanek .02 .10
37 Vladimir Chebaturkin .02 .10
38 Alexander Cherbayev .02 .10
39 Markus Ketterer .02 .10
40 Saku Koivu .20 .50
41 Vladimir Kretchine .02 .10
42 Alexei Kudashov .02 .10
43 Janne Laukkanen .02 .10
44 Janne Niinimaa .02 .10
45 Juha Riihijarvi .02 .10
46 Nikolai Tsulygin .02 .10
47 Vesa Viitakoski .02 .10
48 David Vyborny .02 .10
49 Nikolai Zavarukhin .02 .10
50 Alexandre Daigle .02 .10
1991 QMJHL Draft
51 Alexandre Daigle .02 .10
1991-92 QMJHL Rookie
52 Alexandre Daigle .02 .10
1992 CHL ROY
53 Alexandre Daigle .02 .10
Emerging Superstar
1992-93
54 Alexandre Daigle .02 .10
First Draft Pick
55 Jim Montgomery .02 .10
56 Mike Dunham .02 .10
57 Matt Martin .02 .10
58 Garth Snow .10 .25
59 Shawn Walsh .02 .10
60 Mark Bavis .02 .10
Mike Davis
61 Scott Chartier .02 .10
62 Craig Darby .02 .10
63 Ted Drury .02 .10
64 Steve Dubinsky .02 .10
65 Joe Frederick .02 .10
66 Cammi Granato .20 .50
67 Brett Hauer .02 .10
68 Jon Hillebrandt .02 .10
69 Ryan Hughes .02 .10
70 Dean Hulett .02 .10
71 Kevin O'Sullivan .02 .10
72 Dan Plante .02 .10
73 Derek Plante .02 .10
74 Travis Richards .02 .10
75 Barry Richter .02 .10
76 David Roberts .02 .10
77 Chris Rogles .02 .10
78 Jon Rohloff .02 .10
79 Brian Rolston .02 .10
80 David Sacco .02 .10
81 Brian Savage .10 .25
82 Mike Smith .02 .10
83 Chris Tamer .02 .10
84 Chris Therien .02 .10
85 Aaron Ward .02 .10
86 Russian Celebration .02 .10
87 Vyacheslav Butsayev .02 .10
88 Jan Kaminsky .02 .10
89 Alexander Karpovtsev .02 .10
90 Valeri Karpov .02 .10
91 Sergei Petrenko .02 .10
92 Andrei Sapozhnikov .02 .10
93 Sergei Sorokin .02 .10
94 German Titov .02 .10
95 Andrei Trefilov .02 .10
96 Alexei Yashin .20 .50
97 Dimitri Yushkevich .02 .10
98 Radek Bonk .02 .10
99 Jason Bonsignore .02 .10
100 Brad Brown .02 .10
101 Chris Drury .40 1.00
102 Jeff Friesen .02 .10
103 Sean Haggerty .02 .10
104 Jeff Kealty .02 .10
105 Alexander Kharlamov .02 .10
106 Stanislav Neckar .02 .10
107 Tom O'Connor .02 .10
108 Jeff O'Neill .20 .50
109 Deron Quint .02 .10
110 Vadim Sharifianov .02 .10
111 Oleg Tverdovsky .10 .25
112 Manon Rheaume COMIC .30 .75
113 Paul Kariya COMIC .20 .50
114 Alexandre Daigle COMIC .02 .10
115 Jeff O'Neill COMIC .02 .10
116 Mike Bossy .20 .50
117 Pavel Bure .20 .50
118 Chris Chelios .20 .50
119 Doug Gilmour .10 .25
120 Roman Hamrlik .10 .25
121 Jari Kurri .20 .50
122 Alexander Mogilny .10 .25
123 Felix Potvin .20 .50
124 Teemu Selanne .40 1.00
125 Tommy Soderstrom .10 .25
126 Mike Bales .02 .10
127 Jozef Cierny .02 .10
128 Ivan Droppa .02 .10
129 Anders Eriksson .02 .10
130 Anatoli Fedotov .02 .10
131 Martin Gendron .02 .10
132 Daniel Guerard .02 .10
133 Corey Hirsch .02 .10
134 Milos Holan .02 .10
135 Kenny Jonsson .02 .10
136 Steven King .02 .10
137 Alexei Kovalev .20 .50
138 Sergei Krivokrasov .02 .10
139 Mats Lindgren .02 .10
140 Grant Marshall .02 .10
141 Jesper Mattsson .02 .10
142 Sandy McCarthy .02 .10
143 Dean Melanson .02 .10
144 Robert Petrovicky .02 .10
145 Mike Rathje .02 .10
146 Manon Rheaume .40 1.00
147 Claude Savoie .02 .10
148 Mikhail Shtalenkov .10 .25
149 Manon Rheaume .40 1.00
A Season To Remember
150 Manon Rheaume .40 1.00
Up Close And Personal
MR1 Manon Rheaume Acetate 10.00 25.00

1993 Classic Autographs

AU1 Mike Bossy AU/975 12.50 30.00
AU2 Pavel Bure AU/900 20.00 50.00
AU3 Chris Chelios AU/1800 15.00 40.00
AU4 Doug Gilmour AU/1850 15.00 40.00
AU5 Alexander Mogilny/950 12.50 30.00
AU6 Jim Montgomery AU/1800 2.00 5.00
AU7 Rob Niedermayer AU/2500 12.50 30.00
AU8 Jeff O'Neill AU/2225 8.00 20.00
AU9 Pat Peake AU/790 2.00 5.00
AU10 Mark Recchi AU/1725 12.00 30.00
AU11 Manon Rheaume AU/1500 20.00 50.00
AU12 Geoff Sanderson AU/875 2.00 5.00

1993 Classic Class of '94

These standard size cards were randomly inserted throughout the foil packs. The cards are acetates and the player's last name is in capital letters in the clear potion. The fronts also have a color action photo of the player. The backs have player statistics. The cards are numbered on the back with a "CL" prefix.

COMPLETE SET (7) 3.00 8.00
CL1 Jeff O'Neill .60 1.50
CL2 Jason Bonsignore .40 1.00
CL3 Jeff Friesen .40 1.00
CL4 Radek Bonk .40 1.00
CL5 Deron Quint .40 1.00
CL6 Vadim Sharifianov .40 1.00
CL7 Tom O'Connor .40 1.00

1993 Classic Crash Numbered

This 10-card standard-size set was randomly inserted throughout the foil packs and 15,000 individually numbered copies were made of each. The fronts have a color action photo with the player's name at the bottom in the icy border. The backs have a color photo on the right-side and player information and statistics on the left. The cards are numbered on the back with a "N" prefix.

COMPLETE SET (10) 30.00 80.00
N1 Alexandre Daigle 2.00 5.00
N2 Paul Kariya 6.00 15.00
N3 Jeff O'Neill 1.25 3.00
N4 Jason Bonsignore 2.00 5.00
N5 Teemu Selanne 6.00 15.00
N6 Pavel Bure 2.00 5.00
N7 Alexander Mogilny 2.00 5.00
N8 Manon Rheaume 5.00 12.00
N9 Felix Potvin 2.00 5.00
N10 Radek Bonk 1.25 3.00

1993 Classic Manon Rheaume Promo

This standard-size promo card features then-Atlanta Knights goaltender, Manon Rheaume. Inside a light gray border, the fronts features Rheaume in a sleeveless white blouse. The horizontal back has player information on the left and a second picture on the right with Rheaume dressed in black. The disclaimer "For Promotional Purposes Only" appears on the left beneath the text. The card is unnumbered.

NNO Manon Rheaume 2.00 5.00
Up Close and Personal

1993 Classic Previews

These five standard-size cards were inserted on an average of three per case of 1993 Classic Basketball Draft Picks. The fronts have a color action photo with the player's name at the bottom in the icy border. The backs say "preview" and tells that it is one of 17,500 preview cards of that player. The cards are unnumbered.

COMPLETE SET (5) 4.00 5.00
HK1 Alexandre Daigle .40 .50
HK2 Manon Rheaume 1.50 4.00
HK3 Barry Richter .40 .50
HK4 Teemu Selanne 2.50 2.00
HK5 Alexei Yashin .40 .50

1993 Classic Promos

These four standard-size promo cards feature gray-bordered glossy color player action shots on the fronts. The player's name and position appears in blue lettering within the bottom border. The back carries another color player action shot, but bordered in white. The player's biography and draft status are printed in black lettering within the broad lower border. The unnumbered Paul Kariya card was distributed at the San Francisco Labor Day Sports Collectors Convention, held in September 1993. The cards are numbered on the back with a "PR" prefix.

COMPLETE SET (4) 8.00 20.00
1 Alexandre Daigle 2.00 5.00
2 Jeff O'Neill 2.00 5.00
Jason Bonsignore
Jeff Friesen
The Class of '94
3 Pavel Bure 2.00 5.00
NNO Paul Kariya 2.00 5.00

1993 Classic Team Canada

This seven-card standard size set was randomly inserted throughout the foil packs. These acetate cards have a color action photo on the left clear portion with player name at the bottom. The right-side has a letter so the complete set spells Canada. The backs have the player's name and statistics. The cards are numbered on the back with a "TC" prefix.

COMPLETE SET (7) 7.50 15.00
TC1 Greg Johnson .75 2.00
TC2 Paul Kariya 2.00 5.00
TC3 Brian Savage .75 2.00
TC4 Bill Ranford .75 2.00
TC5 Mark Recchi .75 2.00
TC6 Geoff Sanderson .75 2.00
TC7 Adam Graves .75 2.00

1993 Classic Top Ten

Measuring the standard-size, these ten acetate cards were randomly inserted throughout the foil packs. The cards have a color action photo, visible on both sides. the backs also have player statistics. The cards are numbered on the back with a "DP" prefix.

COMPLETE SET (10) 10.00 20.00
DP1 Alexandre Daigle .40 1.00
DP2 Chris Pronger 1.00 2.50
DP3 Chris Gratton .40 1.00
DP4 Paul Kariya 2.00 5.00
DP5 Rob Niedermayer .40 1.00
DP6 Viktor Kozlov .40 1.00
DP7 Jason Arnott .40 1.00
DP8 Niklas Sundstrom .40 1.00
DP9 Todd Harvey .40 1.00
DP10 Jocelyn Thibault 1.00 2.50

1994 Classic

The 1994 Classic Hockey set consists of 120 standard-size cards. Production was reported at 6,000 U.S. and 2,000 Canadian 10-box foil cases. The Jason Arnott Canada World Champs card (numbered TC1) was randomly inserted into Canadian packs. Classic also offered a redemption program in which a collector sending in wrappers received various prizes. For each 216 wrappers redeemed a collector received either a Cam Neely or a Doug Gilmour autographed card. For each 360 wrappers redeemed, a Manon Rheaume autograph card was sent by Classic.

COMPLETE SET (120) 4.00 10.00
1 Ed Jovanovski .02 .10
2 Oleg Tverdovsky .01 .05
3 Radek Bonk .01 .05
4 Jason Bonsignore .01 .05
5 Jeff O'Neill .01 .05
6 Ryan Smyth .08 .25
7 Jamie Storr .02 .10
8 Jason Wiemer .01 .05
9 Nolan Baumgartner .01 .05
10 Jeff Friesen .01 .05
11 Wade Belak .01 .05
12 Ethan Moreau .02 .10
13 Alexander Kharlamov .01 .05
14 Eric Fichaud .02 .10
15 Wayne Primeau .01 .05
16 Brad Brown .01 .05
17 Chris Dingman .01 .05
18 Evgeni Ryabchikov .01 .05
19 Yan Golubovsky .01 .05
20 Chris Wells .01 .05
21 Vadim Sharifianov .01 .05
22 Dan Cloutier .08 .25
23 Checklist .01 .05
24 Jamie Langenbrunner .01 .05
25 Kenny Jonsson .01 .05
26 Curtis Bowen .01 .05
27 Sergei Gonchar .02 .10
28 Stefan Bergqvist .01 .05
29 Vaclav Prospal .01 .05
30 Valeri Bure .01 .05
31 Richard Shulmistra .01 .05
32 Chris Armstrong .01 .05
33 Brian Farrell .01 .05
34 Brian Savage .02 .10
35 Blaine Lacher .01 .05
36 Kevin Brown .01 .05
37 Joe Dziedzic .01 .05
38 Peter Ferraro .01 .05
39 Chris Ferraro .01 .05
40 Todd Harvey .02 .10
41 Eric Lecompte .01 .05
42 Dean Grillo .01 .05
43 Valeri Karpov .01 .05
44 Andrew Shier .01 .05
45 Vesa Viitakoski .01 .05
46 Xavier Majic .01 .05
47 Kevin Smyth .01 .05
48 Jeff Nelson .01 .05
49 Cory Stillman .01 .05
50 Clayton Beddoes .01 .05
51 Craig Conroy .01 .05
52 Dean Fedorchuk .01 .05
53 John Gruden .01 .05
54 Chris McAlpine .01 .05
55 Sean McCann .01 .05
56 Derek Maguire .01 .05
57 David Oliver .01 .05
58 Mike Pomichter .01 .05
59 Jamie Ram .01 .05
60 Shawn Reid .01 .05
61 Dwayne Roloson .01 .05
62 Steve Shields .08 .25
63 Brian Wiseman .01 .05
64 Drew Bannister .01 .05
65 Matt Johnson .01 .05
66 Scott Malone .01 .05
67 Sergei Berezin .01 .05
68 Chad Penney .01 .05
69 Ian Laperriere .01 .05
70 Andrei Nikolishin .01 .05
71 Kelly Fairchild .01 .05
72 Jere Lehtinen .08 .25
73 Ravil Gusmanov .01 .05
74 Checklist .01 .05
75 Neil Little .01 .05
76 Brian Rolston .02 .10
77 David Vyborny .01 .05
78 Nikolai Tsulygin .01 .05
79 Niklas Sundstrom .01 .05
80 Patrik Juhlin .01 .05
81 Dan Plante .01 .05
82 Brandon Convery .01 .05
83 Nick Stajduhar .01 .05
84 Garth Snow .02 .10
85 Corey Hirsch .02 .10
86 Craig Darby .01 .05
87 Andrei Nazarov .01 .05
88 Todd Marchant .01 .05
89 Jeff Neilson .01 .05
90 Brendan Witt .01 .05
91 Denis Metlyuk .01 .05
92 Maxim Bets .01 .05
93 Sean Pronger .01 .05
94 Chris Tamer .01 .05
95 Saku Koivu .08 .25
96 Mattias Norstrom .02 .10
97 Ville Peltonen .02 .10
98 Rene Corbet .01 .05
99 Brent Gretzky .01 .05
100 Chris Marinucci .01 .05
101 Ian Moran .01 .05
102 Janne Laukkanen .01 .05
103 Todd Bertuzzi .08 .25
104 Darby Hendrickson .01 .05
105 Janne Niinimaa .01 .05
106 David Roberts .01 .05
107 Pat Neaton .01 .05
108 Mats Lindgren .01 .05
109 Todd Warriner .01 .05
110 Jason Allison .08 .25
111 Radim Bicanek .01 .05
112 Denis Pederson .02 .10
113 Viktor Kozlov .02 .10
114 Mike Murray .01 .05
115 Aaron Gavey .01 .05
116 Mike Peca .08 .25
117 Jason Zent .01 .05
118 Jason MacDonald .01 .05
119 Aaron Israel .01 .05
120 Manon Rheaume .60 1.50
TC1 Jason Arnott CWC .75 2.00
AU1 Doug Gilmour AU 8.00 20.00
AU2 Cam Neely AU 12.50 30.00
AU3 Manon Rheaume AU 12.50 30.00

1994 Classic Gold

Each of the 120 regular issue cards was issued as a parallel set with a gold-foil stamp and inserted at a rate of one gold card per pack. The card design is identical to the regular issue, except that the city name is printed in gold-foil stamped letters. In addition, collectors could acquire gold cards by mail. If Classic received either 36 or 54 wrappers in their redemption program from any collector, the collector received 10 gold cards. If a collector mailed in 108 wrappers, there were 25 gold cards sent from Classic. Also, a complete gold factory set was available to collectors who redeemed the Field card from the "Rookie of the Year?" insert set/contest.

*STARS: 1.25X TO 3X BASIC CARDS

1994 Classic All-Americans

Found only in U.S. cases and inserted at a rate of one card per box, this ten-card standard-size set spotlights first team NCAA All-Americans. The cards are serially numbered out of 6,000 on the back.

COMPLETE SET (10) 3.00 8.00
AA1 Craig Conroy .50 1.00
AA2 John Gruden .50 1.00
AA3 Chris Marinucci .50 1.00
AA4 Chris McAlpine .50 1.00
AA5 Sean McCann .50 1.00
AA6 David Oliver .50 1.00
AA7 Mike Pomichter .50 1.00
AA8 Jamie Ram .50 1.00
AA9 Shawn Reid .50 1.00
AA10 Dwayne Roloson .75 2.00

1994 Classic All-Rookie Team

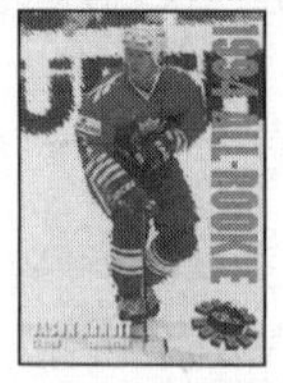

Inserted in both U.S. and Canadian cases at a rate of one card per box. Each card is serially numbered out of 13,500.

COMPLETE SET (6) 4.00 10.00
AR1 Martin Brodeur 4.00 10.00
AR2 Jason Arnott .20 .50
AR3 Alexei Yashin .20 .50
AR4 Oleg Petrov .08 .25
AR5 Chris Pronger .75 2.00
AR6 Alexander Karpovtsev .08 .25

1994 Classic Autographs

Inserted at a rate of one card per box, this 36-card set measures the standard size. The backs carry a congratulatory message which serves to authenticate the signature. The autograph cards that correspond to the regular draft cards are listed in numerical order while those autograph cards not in the regular set are listed in alphabetical order. In addition to the insertion of one per box, these cards were redeemable on a random basis in exchange for sending 72 wrappers to Classic.

3 Radek Bonk/4940 1.50 4.00
4 Jason Bonsignore/4300 .75 2.00
5 Jeff O'Neill/5380 1.50 4.00
10 Jeff Friesen/6145 4.00 10.00
34 Brian Savage/4930 1.50 4.00
38 Peter Ferraro/4875 .75 2.00
39 Chris Ferraro/4770 .75 2.00
76 Brian Rolston/2400 1.50 4.00
86 Craig Darby/1915 .75 2.00
94 Chris Tamer/1900 .75 2.00
106 David Roberts/1970 .75 2.00
NNO Scott Chartier/1930 .75 2.00
NNO Rob Niedermayer/950 8.00 20.00
NNO Ted Drury/1920 .75 2.00
NNO Brett Harkins/1885 .75 2.00
NNO Mike Bavis/1955 4.00 10.00
NNO Aaron Ward/1965 .75 2.00
NNO Brett Hauer/1930 .75 2.00
NNO David Sacco/1975 .75 2.00
NNO Barry Richter/1935 .75 2.00
NNO Dan Plante .75 2.00
NNO Chris Gratton/2000 6.00 15.00
NNO Doug Gilmour/1950 15.00 30.00
NNO Dallas Drake/960 .75 2.00
NNO Chris Rogles/1920 .75 2.00
NNO Jon Hillebrandt/1570 .75 2.00
NNO Mike Dunham/1955 4.00 10.00
NNO Fred Knipscheer/1945 .75 2.00
NNO Eric Fenton/1845 .75 2.00
NNO Ryan Hughes/1940 .75 2.00
NNO Manon Rheaume/2400 15.00 40.00
NNO Dean Hulett/1955 .75 2.00
NNO John Lilley/2460 .75 2.00
NNO Cam Stewart/970 .75 2.00
NNO Travis Richards/1950 .75 2.00
NNO Derek Plante/1970 1.50 4.00
NNO Jon Rohloff/2010 .75 2.00
NNO Chris Marinucci .75 2.00
NNO Jim Storm/1950 .75 2.00
NNO Stanislav Neckar/4645 .75 2.00

1994 Classic CHL All-Stars

This 10-card standard-size set was randomly inserted in Canadian foil packs only. The fronts have a color action photo with the player's name at the top along with the CHL emblem. The backs have a full-color action photo with player information and the number printed out of 2,000. The cards are numbered on the back with a "C" prefix.

COMPLETE SET (10)	7.50	20.00
C1 Jason Allison	1.25	3.00
C2 Yanick Dube	.40	1.00
C3 Eric Fichaud	.75	2.00
C4 Jeff Friesen	.40	1.00
C5 Aaron Gavey	.40	1.00
C6 Ed Jovanovski	.75	2.00
C7 Jeff O'Neill	1.25	3.00
C8 Ryan Smyth	1.25	3.00
C9 Jamie Storr	.75	2.00
C10 Brendan Witt	.40	1.00

1994 Classic CHL Previews

Randomly inserted in Canadian foil packs only, this six-card standard-size set was created to preview Classic's 1995 CHL set. Unfortunately, the company was unable to complete negotiations with the league, and the full set was never created.

COMPLETE SET (6)	15.00	25.00
CP1 Wayne Primeau	1.50	3.00
CP2 Eric Fichaud	2.50	6.00
CP3 Wade Redden	2.50	5.00
CP4 Jason Doig	1.50	3.00
CP5 Vitali Yachmenev	1.50	3.00
CP6 Nolan Baumgartner	1.50	3.00

1994 Classic Draft Day

Issued in a ten-card cello pack, these cards were issued on the occasion of the NHL draft, which took place on June 28-29, 1994. The cards measure the standard size, and were available through a wrapper redemption offer. The fronts feature borderless color action player photos; the player's name is printed in a bar at the bottom that intersects the Classic logo at the lower left corner. The city (or state) of the teams that were likely to draft the player is printed vertically in block lettering along the right edge. The backs carry the "Draft Day 94" logo superimposed over a color painting of a hockey player. A tagline at the bottom rounds out the back and gives the production figures "1 of 10,000". The cards are unnumbered and checklisted below in alphabetical order.

COMPLETE SET (10)	12.50	30.00
1 Radek Bonk	1.50	4.00
Anaheim Mighty Ducks		
2 Radek Bonk	1.50	4.00
Florida Panthers		
3 Radek Bonk	1.50	4.00
Ottawa Senators		
4 Jason Bonsignore	1.50	4.00
Edmonton Oilers		
5 Ed Jovanovski	1.50	4.00
Anaheim Mighty Ducks		
6 Ed Jovanovski	1.50	4.00
Florida Panthers		
7 Ed Jovanovski	1.50	4.00
Ottawa Senators		
8 Jeff O'Neill	1.50	4.00
Anaheim Mighty Ducks		
9 Jeff O'Neill	1.50	4.00
Florida Panthers		
10 Jeff O'Neill	1.50	4.00
Ottawa Senators		

1994 Classic Draft Prospects

Found only in U.S. cases and inserted at a rate of one card per box, this ten-card standard-size set features players expected to be selected early in the 1995 NHL entry draft. The fronts feature the player's name in capital letters on the top with a small notation underneath that he is a 1995 Draft Prospect. The majority of the card is devoted to the player's photo. The reverse of the card features the player's photo on the left side of the cards with a biography on the right side. The cards are numbered in the top left corner. Each card is serially numbered out of 6,000 on the bottom.

COMPLETE SET (10)	5.00	12.00
DP1 Bubba Berenzweig	.40	1.00
DP2 Aki Berg	.40	1.00
DP3 Chad Kilger	.40	1.00
DP4 Daymond Langkow	.75	2.00
DP5 Alyn McCauley	.75	2.00
DP6 Igor Melyakov	.40	1.00
DP7 Erik Rasmussen	.40	1.00
DP8 Marty Reasoner	.75	2.00
DP9 Scott Roche	.75	2.00
DP10 Petr Sykora	2.00	5.00

1994 Classic Enforcers

Featured in both U.S. and Canadian cases and inserted on average of three cards per box, this ten-card standard-size set captures the toughest players in the minor leagues. The horizontal fronts feature color action player photos with the player's name in a black bar at the bottom. The set name also appears at the bottom. On a background consisting of a crude drawing of the front photo, the back carries a player profile.

COMPLETE SET (10)	7.50	15.00
E1 Donald Brashear	1.25	3.00
E2 Daniel Lacroix	.60	1.50
E3 Dale Henry	.60	1.50
E4 John Badduke	.60	1.50
E5 Corey Schwab	1.25	3.00
E6 Craig Martin	.60	1.50
E7 Kerry Clark	.60	1.50
E8 Kevin Kaminski	.60	1.50
E9 Jim Kyte	.60	1.50
E10 Mark DeSantis	.60	1.50

1994 Classic Enforcers Promo

This standard-size card was issued to promote the 1994 Classic hockey series. The horizontal front features Richard Zemlak preparing to fight another player. On a background consisting of a crude drawing of the front photo, the back presents an advertisement for Classic hockey cards. The card is numbered on the back in the upper right corner.

PR1 Richard Zemlak	.40	1.00

1994 Classic Picks

This five-card standard-size set was randomly inserted in packs. The fronts feature color action photos with the player's name and the Classic logo at the bottom. The backs carry the player's name in the upper left, card number in the upper right, career and biographical information, logos, and a small color player photo.

COMPLETE SET (5)	6.00	15.00
CP11 Ed Jovanovski	2.00	5.00
CP12 Oleg Tverdovsky	.75	2.00
CP13 Radek Bonk	.75	2.00
CP14 Jason Allison	2.00	5.00
CP15 Manon Rheaume	2.00	5.00

1994 Classic Previews

Randomly inserted in 1994 Classic basketball packs, this 5-card set measures the standard-size. The fronts feature full-bleed color action photos, except at the bottom where a color stripe carries the player's name. The word "PREVIEW" is printed vertically in large block letters running down the right edge. On a purple-tinted action photo, the backs display the Classic logo and a short congratulatory message. The cards are unnumbered and checklisted below in alphabetical order.

COMPLETE SET (5)	10.00	20.00
HK1 Jason Allison	1.50	4.00
HK2 Radek Bonk	2.00	2.00
HK3 Xavier Majic	.75	2.00
HK4 Manon Rheaume	7.50	15.00
HK5 Oleg Tverdovsky	2.00	4.00

1994 Classic ROY Sweepstakes

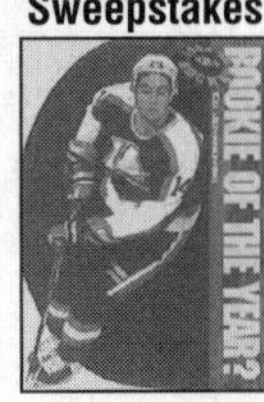

This 20-card standard-size set was featured in U.S. and Canadian cases and inserted on average of five cards per case. Holders of the winning Field Card could redeem it for a complete set of 1994 Classic Hockey Gold cards. The fronts feature a color action player cutout superimposed over a large hockey puck. The words "Rookie of the Year?" and the player's name appear along the right. The backs carry the checklist, along with information on how to claim the prize. The deadline for redeeming cards was September 1, 1995.

COMPLETE SET (20)	4.00	10.00
R1 Jason Allison	.60	1.50
R2 Radek Bonk	.20	.50
R3 Jason Bonsignore	.08	.25
R4 Valeri Bure	.20	.50
R5 Jeff Friesen	.20	.50
R6 Aaron Gavey	.08	.25
R7 Todd Harvey	.20	.50
R8 Kenny Jonsson	.20	.50
R9 Ed Jovanovski	.60	1.50
R10 Patrik Juhlin	.08	.25
R11 Valeri Karpov	.08	.25
R12 Viktor Kozlov	.20	.50
R13 Blaine Lacher	.20	.50
R14 Andrei Nikolishin	.08	.25
R15 Jeff O'Neill	.40	1.00
R16 David Oliver	.08	.25
R17 Garth Snow	.20	.50
R18 Jamie Storr	.20	.50
R19 Oleg Tverdovsky	.20	.50
R20 Field Card WIN G	.08	.25

1994 Classic Tri-Cards

Featured in both U.S. and Canadian cases and inserted at a rate of two cards per box, this 26-card standard-size set showcases the top three prospects from each NHL city. The horizontal fronts feature three borderless color player photos next to each other, with the player's name in a black bar under each photo, and the team name in a purple bar directly below. The backs carry three small color player portraits with a brief player profile. The cards are arranged alphabetically by city name. Each card has three numbers.

COMPLETE SET (26)	30.00	60.00
T1 Valeri Karpov	1.50	3.00
T2) Nikolai Tsulygin		
T3) Oleg Tverdovsky		
T4 Fred Knipscheer	1.50	3.00
T5) Blaine Lacher		
T6) Evgeni Ryabchikov		
T7 David Cooper	.80	2.00
T8) Wayne Primeau		
T9) Steve Shields		
T10 Chris Dingman	.80	2.00
T11) Cory Stillman		
T12) Vesa Viitakoski		
T13 Eric Lecompte	.80	2.00
T14) Ethan Moreau		
T15) Mike Pomichter		
T16 Todd Harvey	1.50	3.00
T17) Jamie Langenbrunner		
T18) Jere Lehtinen		
T19 Curtis Bowen	.80	2.00
T20) Yan Golubovsky		
T21) Kevin Hodson		
T22 Jason Bonsignore	1.50	3.00
T23) Mats Lindgren		
T24) David Oliver		
T25 Chris Armstrong	2.00	4.00
T26) Ed Jovanovski		
T27) Jason Podollan		
T28 Andrei Nikolishin	.80	2.00
T29) Jeff O'Neill		
T30) Kevin Smyth		
T31 Kevin Brown	1.50	3.00
T32) Matt Johnson		
T33) Jamie Storr		
T34 Valeri Bure	3.50	7.00
T35) Saku Koivu		
T36) Brian Savage		
T37 Denis Pederson	.80	2.00
T38) Brian Rolston		
T39) Vadim Sharifijanov		
T40 Todd Bertuzzi	.80	2.00
T41) Chris Marinucci		
T42) Dan Plante		
T43 Corey Hirsch	.80	2.00
T44) Niklas Sundstrom		
T45) Scott Malone		
T46 Radim Bicanek	1.50	3.00
T47) Radek Bonk		
T48) Chad Penney		
T49 Patrik Juhlin	.80	2.00
T50) Denis Metlyuk		
T51) Janne Niinimaa		
T52 Greg Andrusak	.80	2.00
T53) Pat Neaton		
T54) Chris Wells		
T55 Rene Corbet	.80	2.00
T56) Adam Deadmarsh		
T57) Garth Snow		
T58 David Roberts	.80	2.00
T59) Ian Laperriere		
T60) Patrice Tardiff		
T61 Jeff Friesen	1.50	4.00
T62) Viktor Kozlov		
T63) Ville Peltonen		
T64 Aaron Gavey	.80	2.00
T65) Brent Gretzky		
T66) Jason Weimer		
T67 Brandon Convery	2.00	4.00
T68) Eric Fichaud		
T69) Kenny Jonsson		
T70 Mike Fountain	.80	2.00
T71) Rick Girard		
T72) Mike Peca		
T73 Jason Allison	.80	2.00
T74) Alexander Kharlamov		
T75) Brendan Witt		
T76 Mika Alatalo	.80	2.00
T77) Ravil Gusmanov		
T78) Deron Quint		

1994 Classic Women of Hockey

Inserted in both U.S. and Canadian product at a rate of one card per pack, this 40-card standard-size set features female hockey players who represented Canada (1-21) and the U.S.A. (22-40) at the 1994 World Women's Ice Hockey Championships. The fronts have color action player cutouts superimposed over a Canadian or American flag with a metallic sheen. The words "Team Canada Women" or "Team USA Women" appear alongside the right, while the player's name is printed at the bottom. The backs carry a close-up color player photo, along with stats from the tournament (won by Canada) and player profile.

COMPLETE SET (40)	8.00	20.00
W1 Manon Rheaume	1.25	3.00
W2 France St. Louis	.20	.50
W3 Cheryl Pounder	.20	.50
W4 Therese Brisson	.20	.50
W5 Cassie Campbell	.75	2.00
W6 Angela James	.20	.50
W7 Danielle Goyette	.20	1.00
W8 Jane Robinson	.20	.50
W9 Stacy Wilson	.20	.50
W10 Margot Page	.20	.50
W11 Laura Leslie	.20	.50
W12 Judy Diduck	.20	.50
W13 Hayley Wickenheiser	2.00	5.00
W14 Nathalie Picard	.20	.50
W15 Leslie Reddon	.20	.50
W16 Marianne Grnak	.20	.50
W17 Andria Hunter	.20	.50
W18 Nancy Drolet	.20	1.00
W19 Geraldine Heaney	.20	.50
W20 Karen Nystrom	.20	.50
W21 Manon Rheaume CL	.40	1.00
W22 Kelly Dyer	.20	.50
W23 Vicki Movsessian	.20	.50
W24 Lisa Brown	.20	.50
W25 Shawna Davidson	.20	.50
W26 Colleen Coyne	.20	.50
W27 Karyn Bye	.75	2.00
W28 Suzanne Merz	.20	.50
W29 Gretchen Ulion	.20	.50
W30 Sandra Whyte	.20	.50
W31 Cindy Curley	.20	.50
W32 Michele DiFronzo	.20	.50
W33 Stephanie Boyd	.20	.50
W34 Shelley Looney	.20	.50
W35 Jeanine Sobek	.20	.50
W36 Beth Beagan	.20	.50
W37 Cammi Granato	.75	2.00
W38 Christina Bailey	.20	.50
W39 Kelly O'Leary	.20	.50
W40 Erin Whitten	.30	.75

1995 Classic

This 100-card standard-size set marked the conclusion of the fifth (and so far, final) set Classic issued featuring hockey prospects. 3,990 sequentially numbered American cases and 999 Canadian cases were issued with 12 boxes in a case, 36 packs in a box and 10 cards in a pack. There was also a special Manon Rheaume autograph card issued on the average of one per case. One Hot Box, containing nothing but inserts, was inserted one every five cases.

COMPLETE SET (100)	4.00	8.00
1 Bryan Berard	.05	.15
2 Wade Redden	.01	.05
3 Aki Berg	.01	.05
4 Chad Kilger	.01	.05
5 Daymond Langkow	.05	.15
6 Steve Kelly	.01	.05
7 Shane Doan	.08	.25
8 Terry Ryan	.01	.05
9 Mike Martin	.01	.05
10 Radek Dvorak	.08	.25
11 Jarome Iginla	.08	.25
12 Teemu Riihijarvi	.01	.05
13 J-S Giguere	.08	.25
14 Peter Schaefer	.01	.05
15 Jeff Ware	.01	.05
16 Martin Biron	.60	1.50
17 Brad Church	.01	.05
18 Petr Sykora	.08	.25
19 Denis Gauthier	.01	.05
20 Sean Brown	.01	.05
21 Brad Isbister	.20	.50
22 Miikka Elomo	.01	.05
23 Mathieu Sunderland	.01	.05
24 Marc Moro	.01	.05
25 Jan Hlavac	.08	.25
26 Brian Wesenberg	.01	.05
27 Mike McBain	.01	.05
28 Georges Laraque	.08	.25
29 Marc Chouinard	.08	.25
30 Donald MacLean	.01	.05
31 Jason Doig	.01	.05
32 Aaron MacDonald	.01	.05
33 Patrick Cote	.01	.05
34 Christian Dube	.01	.05
35 Chris McAllister	.01	.05
36 Denis Smith	.01	.05
37 Mark Dutiaume	.01	.05
38 Dwayne Hay	.01	.05
39 Nathan Perrott	.01	.05
40 Christian Laflamme	.01	.05
41 Paxton Schafer	.01	.05
42 Shane Kenny	.01	.05
43 Nic Beaudoin	.01	.05
44 Philippe Audet	.01	.05
45 Brad Larsen	.01	.05
46 Ryan Pepperall	.01	.05
47 Mike Leclerc	.05	.15
48 Shane Willis	.12	.30
49 Darryl Laplante	.01	.05
50 Larry Courville	.01	.05
51 Mike O'Grady	.01	.05
52 Petr Buzek	.01	.05
53 Alyn McCauley	.01	.05
54 Scott Roche	.01	.05
55 John Tripp	.01	.05
56 Johnathan Aitken	.01	.05
57 Blake Bellefeuille	.01	.05
58 Daniel Briere	.08	.25
59 Josh DeWolf	.01	.05
60 Josh Green	.01	.05
61 Chris Hajt	.01	.05
62 Josh Holden	.01	.05
63 Henry Kuster	.01	.05
64 Dan Lacouture	.01	.05
65 Oleg Orekhovsky	.01	.05
66 Andrei Petrunin	.01	.05
67 Tom Poti	.01	.05
68 Peter Ratchuk	.01	.05
69 Andrei Zyuzin	.01	.05
70 George Breen	.01	.05
71 Greg Bullock	.01	.05
72 Kent Fearns	.01	.05
73 Eric Flinton	.01	.05
74 Brian Holzinger	.01	.05
75 Chris Kenady	.01	.05
76 Kaj Linna	.01	.05
77 Brian Mueller	.01	.05
78 Brent Peterson	.01	.05
79 Chad Quenneville	.01	.05
80 Randy Stevens	.01	.05
81 Adam Wiesel	.01	.05
82 Barrie Colts	.01	.05
83 Belleville Bulls	.01	.05
84 Detroit Jr. Whalers	.01	.05
85 Guelph Storm	.01	.05
86 Kingston Frontenacs	.01	.05
87 Kitchener Rangers	.01	.05
88 London Knights	.01	.05
89 Niagara Falls Thunder	.01	.05
90 North Bay Centennials	.01	.05
91 Oshawa Generals	.08	.25
92 Ottawa 67's	.01	.05
93 Owen Sound Platers	.01	.05
94 Peterborough Petes	.01	.05
95 S.S. Marie Greyhounds	.50	1.25
96 Sarnia Sting	.01	.05
97 Sudbury Wolves	.01	.05
98 Windsor Spitfires	.01	.05
99 Bryan Berard CL	.01	.05
100 Wade Redden CL	.01	.05

1995 Classic Gold

This 100 card set is a parallel to the regular Classic issue. The cards are inserted one per American pack.

COMPLETE SET (100)	20.00	40.00
*STARS: 1.25X TO 3X BASIC CARDS		

1995 Classic Printer's Proofs

These cards were inserted approximately one per box. The cards are numbered out of 749.

COMPLETE SET (100)	150.00	300.00
*STARS: 8X TO 20X BASIC CARDS		

1995 Classic Printer's Proofs Gold

These 100 cards are a parallel to the Classic Gold set. The cards were inserted one every three boxes and are numbered out of 249.

*STARS:12.5X TO 30X BASIC CARDS

1995 Classic Silver

This 100 card standard-size set is a parallel to the regular Classic issue. The cards were inserted one per Canadian pack.

COMPLETE SET (100)	20.00	40.00
*STARS: .6X TO 1.5X BASIC CARDS		

1995 Classic Autographs

These 24 standard-size cards were inserted on the average of one per box. Classic guaranteed that there would be one autographed card in each box. The front is a picture of the card along with the signature. The back is a congratulatory message that you have received an authentic signed card.

1 George Breen/2400	.75	2.00
2 Greg Bullock/2485	.75	2.00
3 Petr Buzek/3978	1.50	4.00
4 Radek Dvorak/4022	2.00	5.00
5 Kent Fearns/4034	.75	2.00
6 Eric Flinton/2495	.75	2.00
7 Josh Green/4293	.75	2.00
8 Josh Holden/4994	.75	2.00
9 Brian Holzinger/2599	.75	2.00
10 Ed Jovanovski/2584	1.50	4.00
11 Chris Kenady/2480	.75	2.00
12 Henry Kuster/2490	.75	2.00
13 Josef Marha/2584	.75	2.00
14 Brian Mueller/2488	.75	2.00
15 Angel Nikolov/2500	.75	2.00
16 Oleg Orekhovsky/5090	.75	2.00
17 Brent Peterson/2468	.75	2.00
18 Andrei Petrunin/4764	.75	2.00
19 Chad Quenneville/2594	.75	2.00
20 Miroslav Satan/2487	12.50	30.00
21 Randy Stevens/2591	.75	2.00
22 Petr Sykora/792	12.50	30.00
23 Adam Wiesel/2511	.75	2.00
24 Andrei Zyuzin/5076	.75	2.00
NNO Manon Rheaume/6300	12.50	30.00

1995 Classic CHL All-Stars

These cards feature all-stars of the CHL. They were inserted into Canadian packs at a ratio of 1:72. The cards are numbered with a "AS" prefix.

COMPLETE SET (18)	25.00	50.00
AS1 Nolan Baumgartner	.75	2.00
AS2 Wade Redden	1.50	4.00
AS3 Henry Kuster	.75	2.00
AS4 Daymond Langkow	1.50	4.00
AS5 Shane Doan	2.00	5.00
AS6 Steve Kelly	.75	2.00
AS7 Tyler Moss	.75	2.00
AS8 Bryan Berard	1.50	4.00
AS9 Ed Jovanovski	1.50	4.00
AS10 Chad Kilger	.75	2.00
AS11 Daniel Cleary	.75	2.00
AS12 Ethan Moreau	.75	2.00
AS13 J-S Giguere	1.50	4.00
AS14 Denis Gauthier	.75	2.00
AS15 Jason Doig	.75	2.00
AS16 Etienne Drapeau	.75	2.00
AS17 Daniel Briere	1.50	4.00
AS18 Mark Chouinard	.75	2.00

1995 Classic Ice Breakers

These cards were randomly inserted into packs at a ratio of approximately one every other box. The cards are sequentially numbered an less than 2,000 of each card were printed. The cards feature some of the leading prospects which included Bryan Berard, Nolan Baumgartner and Wade Redden. A die-cut version of these cards were issued as well. These cards were sequentially numbered to 495. The cards are numbered with a "BK" prefix.

COMPLETE SET (20)	30.00	60.00
*DIE CUT STARS: 2X TO 4X BASIC CARDS		
BK1 Bryan Berard	2.00	5.00
BK2 Wade Redden	2.00	5.00
BK3 Aki Berg	.75	2.00
BK4 Chad Kilger	.75	2.00
BK5 Daymond Langkow	2.00	5.00
BK6 Steve Kelly	.75	2.00
BK7 Shane Doan	2.50	6.00
BK8 Terry Ryan	.75	2.00
BK9 Radek Dvorak	2.50	6.00
BK10 Miikka Elomo	.75	2.00
BK11 Teemu Riihijarvi	.75	2.00
BK12 J-S Giguere	2.00	5.00
BK13 Martin Biron	5.00	12.00
BK14 Jeff Ware	.75	2.00
BK15 Brad Church	.75	2.00
BK16 Petr Sykora	2.50	6.00
BK17 Jason Bonsignore	.75	2.00
BK18 Brian Holzinger	.75	2.00
BK19 Ed Jovanovski	2.00	5.00
BK20 Nolan Baumgartner	.75	2.00

1993 Classic Pro Prospects

The 1993 Classic Pro Hockey Prospects set features 150 standard-size cards. The production run was 6,500 sequentially numbered cases, and female hockey phenom Manon Rheaume autographed 6,500 cards for random insertion into the foil packs.

COMPLETE SET (150)	4.00	10.00
1 Manon Rheaume	.40	1.00
Draveurs Promote		
Female Goaltender		
2 Manon Rheaume	.40	1.00
Quebec League Welcomes		
Female Netminder		
3 Manon Rheaume	.40	1.00
4 Manon Rheaume	.40	1.00
5 Manon Rheaume	.40	1.00
6 Manon Rheaume	.40	1.00
7 Manon Rheaume	.40	1.00
8 Oleg Petrov	.01	.05
9 Shjon Podein	.01	.05
10 Alexei Kovalev AS	.08	.25
11 Roman Oksiuta	.01	.05
12 Dave Tomlinson	.01	.05
13 Jason Miller	.01	.05
14 Andrew McKim	.01	.05
15 Dallas Drake	.01	.05
16 Rob Gaudreau	.01	.05
17 Darrin Madeley	.01	.05
18 Scott Pellerin	.01	.05
19 Scott Thomas	.01	.05
20 Chris Tancill AS	.01	.05
21 Patrick Kjellberg	.01	.05
22 Jim Dowd	.01	.05
23 Daniel Gauthier	.01	.05
24 Mark Beaufait	.01	.05
25 Milan Tichy AS	.01	.05
26 Chris Osgood	.50	1.25
27 Charles Poulin	.01	.05
28 Patrick Lebeau	.01	.05
29 Chris Govedaris	.01	.05
30 Andrei Trefilov AS	.01	.05
31 Kevin Stevens MLG	.08	.25
32 Dmitri Kvartalnov MLG	.01	.05
33 Patrick Roy MLG	.60	1.50
34 Mark Recchi MLG	.20	.50
35 Adam Oates MLG	.20	.50
36 Patrick Augusta	.01	.05
37 Gerry Fleming	.01	.05
38 Sergei Krivokrasov	.01	.05
39 Mike O'Neill	.01	.05
40 Darrin Madeley AS	.01	.05
41 Lindsay Vallis	.01	.05
42 Todd Nelson	.01	.05
43 Keith Jones	.01	.05
44 Howie Rosenblatt	.01	.05
45 Jason Ruff AS	.01	.05
46 Robert Lang	.01	.05
47 Andre Faust	.01	.05
48 Steve Bancroft	.01	.05
49 Iain Fraser	.01	.05
50 Roman Hamrlik AS	.01	.05
51 Pierre Sevigny	.01	.05
52 Jeff Levy	.01	.05
53 Len Barrie	.01	.05
54 David Goverde	.01	.05
55 Vladimir Malakhov AS	.01	.05
56 Scott White	.01	.05
57 Dmitri Motkov	.01	.05
58 Jason Herter	.01	.05
59 Drake Berehowsky	.01	.05
60 Steve King AS	.01	.05
61 Doug Barrault	.01	.05
62 Martin Hamrlik	.01	.05
63 Kevin Miehm	.01	.05
64 Shaun Van Allen	.01	.05
65 Corey Hirsch AS	.01	.05
66 Dwayne Norris	.01	.05
67 Petr Hrbek	.01	.05
68 Philippe Boucher	.01	.05
69 Denis Chervyakov	.01	.05
70 Sergei Zubov AS	.01	.05
71 Geoff Sarjeant	.01	.05
72 Les Kuntar	.01	.05
73 Byron Dafoe	.20	.50
74 Checklist	.01	.05
Alexei Kovalev		
Sergei Zubov		
Steve King		

Corey Hirsch
75 Alexander Andrievski AS .01 .05
76 Checklist .01 .05
Joby Messier
Mitch Messier
77 Brian Sullivan .01 .05
78 Steve Larouche .01 .05
79 Denis Chasse .01 .05
80 Felix Potvin AS .20 .50
81 Josef Beranek .01 .05
82 Ken Klee .01 .05
83 Jozef Stumpel .08 .25
84 Andrew Verner .01 .05
85 Keith Osborne AS .01 .05
86 Igor Malykhin .01 .05
87 Gilbert Dionne .01 .05
88 Viktor Gordiouk .01 .05
89 Glen Murray .01 .05
90 Scott Pellerin AS .01 .05
91 Tommy Soderstrom .08 .25
92 Terry Chitaroni .01 .05
93 Viktor Kozlov .08 .25
94 Mikhail Shtalenkov .08 .25
95 Leonid Toropchenko .01 .05
96 Alexei Galchenyuk .01 .05
97 Anatoli Fedotov .01 .05
98 Igor Chibirev .01 .05
99 Keith Gretzky .01 .05
100 Manon Rheaume .60 1.50
101 Sean Whyte .01 .05
102 Steve Konowalchuk .08 .25
103 Richard Borgo .01 .05
104 Paul DiPietro .01 .05
105 Patrik Carnback AS .01 .05
106 Mike Fountain .01 .05
107 Jamie Heward .01 .05
108 David St. Pierre .01 .05
109 Sean O'Donnell .01 .05
110 Greg Andrusak AS .01 .05
111 Damian Rhodes .08 .25
112 Ted Crowley .01 .05
113 Chris Taylor .01 .05
114 Terran Sandwith .01 .05
115 Jesse Belanger AS .01 .05
116 Justin Duberman .01 .05
117 Arturs Irbe .20 .50
118 Chris LiPuma .01 .05
119 Mike Torchia .01 .05
120 Niclas Andersson AS .01 .05
121 Rick Knickle .01 .05
122 Scott Gruhl .01 .05
123 Dave Michayluk .01 .05
124 Guy Leveque .01 .05
125 Scott Thomas AS .01 .05
126 Travis Green .01 .05
127 Joby Messier .01 .05
128 Victor Ignatjev .01 .05
129 Brad Tiley .01 .05
130 Grigori Panteleyev AS .01 .05
131 Vyatcheslav Butsayev .01 .05
132 Danny Lorenz .01 .05
133 Marty McInnis .01 .05
134 Ed Ronan .01 .05
135 Slava Kozlov AS .20 .50
136 Kevin St. Jacques .01 .05
137 Pavel Kostichkin .01 .05
138 Mike Hurlbut .01 .05
139 Tomas Forslund .01 .05
140 Rob Gaudreau AS .01 .05
141 Shawn Heaphy .01 .05
142 Radek Hamr .01 .05
143 Jaroslav Otevrel .01 .05
144 Keith Redmond .01 .05
145 Tom Pederson AS .01 .05
146 Jaroslav Modry .01 .05
147 Darren McCarty .01 .05
148 Terry Yake .01 .05
149 Ivan Droppa .01 .05
150 The VCR Line .01 .05
Shaun Van Allen
Dan Currie
Steven Rice
AU1 Dmitri Kvartalnov 2.00 5.00
AU/4000
(Certified Autograph)
AU2 Manon Rheaume 20.00 40.00
AU/6500
(Certified Autograph)

1993 Classic Pro Prospects BCs

One BC card was inserted in each jumbo pack. The cards are numbered on the back with a "BC" prefix.

COMPLETE SET (20) 15.00 30.00
BC1 Alexei Kovalev .40 1.00
BC2 Andrei Trefilov .20 .50
BC3 Roman Hamrlik .20 .50
BC4 Vladimir Malakhov .20 .50
BC5 Corey Hirsch .30 .75
BC6 Sergei Zubov .20 .50
BC7 Felix Potvin .40 1.00
BC8 Tommy Soderstrom .30 .75
BC9 Viktor Kozlov .30 .75
BC10 Manon Rheaume 1.50 4.00
BC11 Jesse Belanger .20 .50
BC12 Rick Knickle .20 .50
BC13 Joby Messier .20 .50
BC14 Vyacheslav Butsayev .20 .50
BC15 Tomas Forslund .20 .50
BC16 Jozef Stumpel .30 .75
BC17 Dmitri Kvartalnov MLG .20 .50
BC18 Adam Oates MLG .40 1.00
BC19 Dallas Drake .20 .50
BC20 Mark Recchi MLG .40 1.00

1993 Classic Pro Prospects LPs

The cards are numbered on the back with an "LP" prefix.

COMPLETE SET (5) 12.50 25.00
LP1 Manon Rheaume 6.00 15.00
LP2 Alexei Kovalev 1.25 3.00
LP3 Rob Gaudreau .75 2.00
LP4 Viktor Kozlov 1.25 3.00
LP5 Dallas Drake .75 2.00

1993 Classic Pro Prospects Prototypes

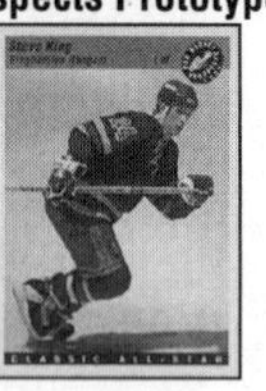

These three standard-size promo cards were issued to show the design of the 1993 Classic Pro Hockey Prospects set. Inside white borders, the fronts display color action player photos. A color bar edges the top of each picture and carries the player's name, team, and position. Also a black bar edges the bottom of each picture. On a gray background, the backs feature a color close-up photo, logos, biographical information, statistics, and career summary. A black bar that accents the top carries the card number and the disclaimer "For Promotional Purposes Only".

COMPLETE SET (3) 3.20 8.00
PR1 Steve King .60 1.50
PR2 Manon Rheaume 2.40 6.00
PR3 Rob Gaudreau .60 1.50

1994 Classic Pro Prospects

This 250-card set includes more than 100 foil-stamped subset cards. Randomly inserted throughout the foil packs were 25 limited print clear acetate cards and over 10,000 randomly inserted autographed cards of Radek Bonk, Alexei Yashin, Chris Pronger, Manon Rheaume, Joe Juneau, and more.

COMPLETE SET (250) 3.00 8.00
1 Radek Bonk .01 .05
2 Radek Bonk .01 .05
3 Radek Bonk .01 .05
4 Vlastimil Kroupa .01 .05
5 Mattias Norstrom .01 .05
6 Jaroslav Nedved .01 .05
7 Steve Dubinsky .01 .05
8 Christian Proulx .01 .05
9 Michal Grosek .01 .05
10 Pat Neaton .01 .05
11 Jason Arnott .01 .05
12 Martin Brodeur .40 1.00
13 Alexandre Daigle .01 .05
14 Ted Drury .01 .05
15 Iain Fraser .01 .05
16 Chris Gratton .08 .25
17 Greg Johnson .01 .05
18 Paul Kariya .40 1.00
19 Alexander Karpovtsev .01 .05
20 Chris Lipuma .01 .05
21 Kirk Maltby .01 .05
22 Sandy McCarthy .01 .05
23 Darren McCarty .01 .05
24 Jaroslav Modry .01 .05
25 Jim Montgomery .01 .05
26 Markus Naslund .20 .50
27 Rob Niedermayer .08 .25
28 Chris Osgood .30 .75
29 Pat Peake .01 .05
30 Derek Plante .01 .05
31 Chris Pronger .20 .50
32 Mike Rathje .01 .05
33 Mikael Renberg .08 .25
34 Damian Rhodes .08 .25
35 Garth Snow .08 .25
36 Cam Stewart .01 .05
37 Jim Storm .01 .05
38 Michal Sykora .01 .05
39 Jocelyn Thibault .20 .50
40 Alexei Yashin .01 .05
41 Checklist 1 .01 .05
42 Vesa Viitakoski .01 .05
43 Jake Grimes .01 .05
44 Jim Dowd .01 .05
45 Craig Ferguson .01 .05
46 Mike Boback .01 .05
47 Francois Groleau .01 .05
48 Juha Riihijarvi .01 .05
49 Mikhail Shtalenkov .08 .25
50 Zigmund Palffy .08 .25
51 Felix Potvin .20 .50
52 Alexei Kovalev .08 .25
53 Larry Robinson .08 .25
54 John LeClair .30 .75
55 Dominic Roussel .08 .25
56 Geoff Sanderson .08 .25
57 Greg Pankewicz .01 .05
58 Brent Bilodeau .01 .05
59 Brandon Convery .01 .05
60 Fred Knipscheer .01 .05
61 Igor Chibirev .01 .05
62 Anatoli Fedotov .01 .05
63 Bob Kellogg .01 .05
64 Mike Maurice .01 .05
65 Chad Penney .01 .05
66 Mike Bavis .01 .05
67 Eric Veilleux .01 .05
68 Parris Duffus .01 .05
69 Daniel Lacroix .01 .05
70 Milos Holan .01 .05
71 Mike Muller .01 .05
72 Micah Aivazoff .01 .05
73 Krzysztof Oliwa .01 .05
74 Ryan Hughes .01 .05
75 Christian Soucy .01 .05
76 Keith Redmond .01 .05
77 Mark De Santis .01 .05
78 Craig Martin .01 .05
79 Mike Kennedy .01 .05
80 Pauli Jaks .01 .05
81 Colin Chin .01 .05
82 Jody Gage .01 .05
83 Don Biggs .01 .05
84 Tim Tookey .01 .05
85 Clint Malarchuk .08 .25
86 Jozef Cierny .01 .05
87 Radek Hamr .01 .05
88 Jason Dawe .01 .05
89 Chris Longo .01 .05
90 Brian Rolston .08 .25
91 Mike McKee .01 .05
92 Vitali Prokhorov .01 .05
93 Chris Snell .01 .05
94 Martin Brochu .08 .25
95 Dan Plante .01 .05
96 Darcy Werenka .01 .05
97 Steffon Walby .01 .05
98 David Emma .01 .05
99 Dan Stiver .01 .05
100 Radek Bonk .01 .05
101 Mark Visheau .01 .05
102 Dean Melanson .01 .05
103 Vladimir Tsyplakov .01 .05
104 Mikhail Volkov .01 .05
105 Aaron Miller .01 .05
106 Alexei Kudashov .01 .05
107 Shawn Rivers .01 .05
108 Ladislav Karabin .01 .05
109 Matt Mallgrave .01 .05
110 Craig Darby .01 .05
111 Marcel Cousineau .01 .05
112 Jamie McLennan .08 .25
113 Yanic Perreault .08 .25
114 Zac Boyer .01 .05
115 Sergei Zubov .01 .05
116 Dan Kesa .01 .05
117 Jim Hiller .01 .05
118 Dmitri Starostenko .01 .05
119 Chris Tamer .01 .05
120 Aaron Ward .01 .05
121 Claude Savoie .01 .05
122 Jamie Black .01 .05
123 Jean-Francois Jomphe .01 .05
124 Paxton Schulte .01 .05
125 Jarkko Varvio .01 .05
126 Jaroslav Otevrel .01 .05
127 Dane Jackson .01 .05
128 Brent Grieve .01 .05
129 Checklist .30 .75
Pascal Rheaume
Manon Rheaume
130 Rene Corbet .01 .05
131 Joe Frederick .01 .05
132 Martin Tanguay .01 .05
133 Fredrik Jax .01 .05
134 Jamie Linden .01 .05
135 Jason Smith .01 .05
136 Rick Kowalsky .01 .05
137 Dino Grossi .01 .05
138 Aris Brimanis .01 .05
139 Jeff McLean .01 .05
140 Tyler Wright .01 .05
141 Roman Gorev .01 .05
142 Dean Hulett .01 .05
143 Niklas Sundblad .01 .05
144 Jeff Bes .01 .05
145 Pascal Rheaume .01 .05
146 Donald Brashear .01 .05
147 Hugo Belanger .01 .05
148 Blair Scott .01 .05
149 Steve Staios .01 .05
150 Matt Martin .01 .05
151 Richard Matvichuk .01 .05
152 Paul Brousseau .01 .05
153 Evgeny Namestnikov .01 .05
154 Mike Peca .20 .50
155 Jeff Nelson .01 .05
156 Greg Andrusak .01 .05
157 Norm Batherson .01 .05
158 Martin Bakula .01 .05
159 Ed Patterson .01 .05
160 Steve Larouche .01 .05
161 Libor Polasek .01 .05
162 Jon Hillebrandt .01 .05
163 Guy Leveque .01 .05
164 Eric Lacroix .01 .05
165 Scott Walker .01 .05
166 Robert Burakovsky .01 .05
167 Markus Ketterer .01 .05
168 Mike Speer .01 .05
169 Martin Jiranek .01 .05
170 Andy Schneider .01 .05
171 Terry Hollinger .01 .05
172 Mark Lawrence .01 .05
173 Martin Lapointe .20 .50
174 Vaclav Prospal .01 .05
175 Mike Fountain .01 .05
176 Alexander Kerch .01 .05
177 Oleg Petrov .01 .05
178 Derek Armstrong .01 .05
179 Matthew Barnaby .01 .05
180 Andrei Nazarov .01 .05
181 Andrei Trefilov .01 .05
182 Jean-Yves Roy .01 .05
183 Boris Rousson .01 .05
184 Dan Laperriere .01 .05
185 Yan Kaminsky .01 .05
186 Ralph Intranuovo .01 .05
187 Sandy Moger .01 .05
188 Grant Marshall .01 .05
189 Denny Felsner .01 .05
190 Coty Stillman .01 .05
191 Eric Lavigne .01 .05
192 Jarrod Skalde .01 .05
193 Steve Junker .01 .05
194 Alexander Cherbayev .01 .05
195 Nathan Lafayette .01 .05
196 Ed Ward .01 .05
197 Harijs Vitolinsh .01 .05
198 Jarmo Kekalainen .01 .05
199 Neil Eisenhut .01 .05
200 Radek Bonk .01 .05
201 Jason Bonsignore .01 .05
202 Jeff Friesen .01 .05
203 Ed Jovanovski .08 .25
204 Brett Lindros .01 .05
205 Jeff O'Neill .20 .50
206 Deron Quint .01 .05
207 Vadim Sharifjanov .01 .05
208 Oleg Tverdovsky .01 .05
209 Checklist .01 .05
Jeff O'Neill
Jeff Friesen
210 David Cooper .01 .05
211 Doug McDonald .01 .05
212 Leonid Toropchenko .01 .05
213 Chris Rogles .01 .05
214 Slava Kozlov .08 .25
215 Denis Metlyuk .01 .05
216 Scott McKay .01 .05
217 Brian Loney .01 .05
218 Kevin Hodson .01 .05
219 Bobby House .01 .05
220 Sergei Krivokrasov .01 .05
221 Brett Harkins .01 .05
222 Cale Hulse .01 .05
223 Marc Tardif .01 .05
224 Jon Rohloff .01 .05
225 Kevin Smyth .01 .05
226 Jason Young .01 .05
227 Sergei Zholtok .01 .05
228 Todd Simon .01 .05
229 Jerome Bechard .01 .05
230 Matt Robbins .01 .05
231 Joe Cook .01 .05
232 John Brill .01 .05
233 Dan Goldie .01 .05
234 Dan Gravelle .01 .05
235 Shawn Wheeler .01 .05
236 Brad Harrison .01 .05
237 Joe Dragon .01 .05
238 Jason Jennings .01 .05
239 Manon Rheaume .75 2.00
240 Jamie Steer .01 .05
241 Scott Rogers .01 .05
242 Lyle Wildgoose .01 .05
243 Darren Colbourne .01 .05
244 Mike Smith .01 .05
245 Chris Bright .01 .05
246 Chris Belanger .01 .05
247 Darren Schwartz .01 .05
248 Cammi Granato .60 1.50
249 Erin Whitten .20 .50
250 Manon Rheaume .75 2.00
NNO Arnott/Yashin ROY .40 1.00

1994 Classic Pro Prospects Autographs

This 9-card set includes over 10,000 randomly inserted autographed cards of Radek Bonk, Alexei Yashin, Chris Pronger, Manon Rheaume, Joe Juneau, and more.

AU1 Radek Bonk/2400 5.00 10.00
AU2 Jason Bonsignore/2450 5.00 10.00
AU3 Jeff Friesen/2450 10.00 25.00
AU4 Joe Juneau/1370 8.00 20.00
AU5 Alexei Kovalev/1900 5.00 10.00
AU6 Chris Pronger/1400 12.50 30.00
AU7 Manon Rheaume/1900 30.00 80.00
AU8 Erin Whitten/1800 12.50 30.00
AU9 Alexei Yashin/1400 6.00 15.00

1994 Classic Pro Prospects Ice Ambassadors

This standard-size set features young players from all over the world. The cards were inserted one per jumbo sheet in a late-season, retail-only repackaging configuration. The fronts feature a player photo with a stripe down the right side carrying the player's name. On the bottom of the card in gold lettering is the identification of the team. The reverse of the card features a player photo on the top half with statistical information on the bottom half.

COMPLETE SET (20) 3.00 8.00
IA1 Adrian Aucoin .08 .25
IA2 Corey Hirsch .15 .40
IA3 Paul Kariya 1.00 2.50
IA4 David Harlock .08 .25
IA5 Manny Legace .30 .75
IA6 Chris Therien .08 .25
IA7 Todd Warriner .08 .25
IA8 Todd Marchant .08 .25
IA9 Matt Martin .08 .25
IA10 Peter Ferraro .08 .25
IA11 Brian Rolston .15 .40
IA12 Jim Campbell .08 .25
IA13 Mike Dunham .30 .75
IA14 Craig Johnson .08 .25
IA15 Saku Koivu 1.00 2.50
IA16 Jere Lehtinen .30 .75
IA17 Viktor Kozlov .15 .40
IA18 Andrei Nikolishin .08 .25
IA19 Sergei Gonchar .15 .40
IA20 Valeri Karpov .08 .25

1994 Classic Pro Prospects International Heroes

Randomly inserted through the foil packs, these 25 clear acetate standard-size cards predominantly feature the U.S. and Canadian National Teams. The cards are numbered on the back with an "LP" prefix. The nationalities of the players are as follows: U.S. (1-10); Canadian (11-20, 24); Czech (21); Russian (22, 25); and Finnish (23).

COMPLETE SET (25) 20.00 40.00
LP1 Jim Campbell .75 2.00
LP2 Ted Drury .75 2.00
LP3 Mike Dunham 1.25 3.00
LP4 Chris Ferraro .75 2.00
LP5 Peter Ferraro .75 2.00
LP6 Darby Hendrickson .75 2.00
LP7 Craig Johnson .75 2.00
LP8 Todd Marchant .75 2.00
LP9 Matt Martin .75 2.00
LP10 Brian Rolston .75 2.00
LP11 Adrian Aucoin .75 2.00
LP12 Martin Gendron .75 2.00
LP13 David Harlock .75 2.00
LP14 Corey Hirsch .75 2.00
LP15 Paul Kariya 3.00 8.00
LP16 Manny Legace 1.25 3.00
LP17 Brett Lindros .75 2.00
LP18 Brian Savage .75 2.00
LP19 Chris Therien .75 2.00
LP20 Todd Warriner .75 2.00
LP21 Radek Bonk .75 2.00
LP22 Pavel Bure 1.25 3.00
LP23 Teemu Selanne 3.00 8.00
LP24 Mark Recchi 1.50 4.00
LP25 Alexei Yashin 1.50 4.00

1994 Classic Pro Prospects Promo

This standard-size promo card was issued to show the design of the 1994 Classic Pro Hockey Prospects set. Inside white borders, the front displays a color action player photo. The player's name, team, and position appear in a black bar at the bottom of the card. Also inside white borders, the back features another color player photo, logos, biographical information, and scoring totals. The disclaimer "For Promotional Purposes Only" is printed on the back.

1 Radek Bonk 1.60 4.00

1994 Classic Pro Prospects Prototype

Given away at the 1994 National Sports Convention in Houston, this prototype card measures the standard size. The front features a borderless color action player photo, with the player's name on the bottom. The word "PROTOTYPE" is written vertically in red block lettering along the right edge. On a screened background, the back carries an advertisement for the convention in gold foil lettering. The card is unnumbered.

NNO Jason Arnott 2.00 5.00

1996 Collector's Edge Future Legends

This set features top performers from the AHL and IHL. The cards were sold in wax pack form and featured thin card stock with stylized metallic etching on the front.

COMPLETE SET (50) 6.00 15.00
1 Brad Bombardir .08 .20
2 Niklas Andersson .08 .20
3 Mike Dunham .20 .50
4 Anders Eriksson .08 .20
5 Kelly Fairchild .08 .20
6 Chris Ferraro .08 .20
7 Peter Ferraro .08 .20
8 Eric Fichaud .15 .40
9 Manny Legace .20 .50
10 David Ling .08 .20
11 Jim Montgomery .08 .20
12 Chris Murray .08 .20
13 Rob Brown .08 .20
14 Rem Murray .08 .20
15 Rob Murray .08 .20
16 Jan Caloun .08 .20
17 Frederic Chabot .15 .40
18 Craig Fisher .08 .20
19 Dwayne Roloson .15 .40
20 Brad Smyth .08 .20
21 Steve Sullivan .20 .50
22 Petr Sykora .08 .20
23 Darcy Tucker .15 .40
24 Landon Wilson .15 .40
25 Greg Hawgood .08 .20
26 Stephane Beauregard .15 .40
27 Aki Berg .08 .20
28 Matt Johnson .08 .20
29 Curtis Joseph .20 .50
30 Dan Lambert .08 .20
31 Eric LeCompte .08 .20
32 Brett Lievers .08 .20
33 Mark McArthur .15 .40
34 Ethan Moreau .15 .40
35 Marty Murray .08 .20
36 Wayne Primeau .08 .20
37 John Purves .08 .20
38 Manon Rheaume 1.00 2.50
39 Barry Richter .08 .20
40 Jamie Rivers .08 .20
41 Tommy Salo .20 .50
42 Jamie Storr .20 .50
43 Tom Tilley .08 .20
44 Derek Wilkinson .15 .40
45 Mike Wilson .08 .20
46 Sandis Ozolinsh .08 .20
47 Andrew Brunette .15 .40
48 James Black .08 .20
49 Terry Yake .08 .20
50 Mike Prokopec .08 .20

1996 Collector's Edge Future Legends Autographed Hot Picks

Randomly inserted at 2 per box, these cards carry full color photos and autographs of the featured player.

COMPLETE SET (4) 10.00 20.00
1 Chris Phillips 2.00 5.00
2 Boyd Devereaux 2.00 5.00
3 Richard Jackman 2.00 5.00
4 Marcus Nilsson 2.00 5.00

1996 Collector's Edge Ice

This 200 card standard-size set features members of the America Hockey League and the International Hockey League. The cards are sequenced in alphabetical order within alphabetical team order. A parallel prismatic version of these cards were issued, they are valued as a multiple of the regular cards.

COMPLETE SET (200) 15.00 30.00
1 Curtis Bowen .02 .10
2 Anders Eriksson .02 .10
3 Kevin Hodson .08 .25
4 Martin Lapointe .20 .50
5 Aaron Ward .02 .10
6 Mike Dunham .20 .50
7 Chris McAlpine .02 .10
8 Brian Rolston .20 .50
9 Corey Schwab .08 .25
10 Steve Sullivan .20 .50
11 Petr Sykora .20 .50
12 Darren Van Impe .02 .10
13 Mike Maneluk .02 .10
14 David Sacco .02 .10
15 Jarrod Skalde .08 .25
16 Nikolai Tsulygin .02 .10
17 Peter Ferraro .02 .10
18 Chris Ferraro .02 .10
19 Corey Hirsch .08 .25
20 Mattias Norstrom .08 .25
21 Jamie Ram .08 .25
22 Chris Armstrong .02 .10
23 Alexei Kudashov .02 .10
24 Todd MacDonald .02 .10
25 Steve Washburn .02 .10
26 Kevin Weekes .20 .50
27 Rene Corbet .02 .10
28 Janne Laukkanen .02 .10
29 Aaron Miller .02 .10
30 Landon Wilson .08 .25
31 Fred Brathwaite .20 .50
32 Ryan Haggerty .02 .10
33 Ralph Intranuovo .02 .10
34 Todd Marchant .20 .50
35 David Oliver .02 .10
36 Marko Tuomainen .02 .10
37 Peter White .02 .10
38 Sebastien Bordeleau .02 .10
39 Martin Brochu .08 .25
40 Valeri Bure .08 .25
41 Craig Conroy .08 .25
42 Darcy Tucker .20 .50
43 David Wilkie .02 .10
44 Paul Healey .02 .10
45 Chris Herperger .02 .10
46 Jim Montgomery .02 .10
47 Chris Therien .02 .10
48 Pavol Demitra .20 .50
49 Michel Picard .02 .10
50 Jason Zent .02 .10
51 Patrick Boileau .02 .10
52 Jim Carey .08 .25
53 Sergei Gonchar .08 .25
54 Jeff Nelson .02 .10
55 Stefan Ustorf .02 .10
56 Alexander Kharlamov .02 .10
57 Ron Tugnutt .20 .50
58 Scott Bailey .08 .25
59 Clayton Beddoes .02 .10
60 Andre Roy .08 .25
61 Evgeny Ryabchikov .08 .25
62 Mark Astley .02 .10
63 Jody Gage .08 .25
64 Sergei Klimentiev .02 .10
65 Barrie Moore .02 .10
66 Mike Wilson .02 .10
67 Shayne Wright .02 .10
68 Michal Grosek .08 .25
69 Tavis Hansen .02 .10
70 Nikolai Khabibulin .30 .75
71 Scott Langkow .08 .25
72 Jason McBain .02 .10
73 Dwayne Roloson .08 .25
74 Cory Stillman .08 .25
75 Jamie Allison .02 .10
76 Jesper Mattson .02 .10
77 David Ling .02 .10
78 Brandon Convery .02 .10
79 Darby Hendrickson .02 .10
80 Janne Gronvall .02 .10
81 Jason Saal .02 .10
82 Brent Gretzky .02 .10
83 Kent Manderville .02 .10
84 Shayne Toporowski .02 .10
85 Paul Vincent .02 .10
86 Mark Kolesar .02 .10
87 Lonny Bohonos .02 .10
88 Larry Courville .02 .10
89 Jassen Cullimore .02 .10
90 Scott Walker .08 .25
91 Mike Buzak .02 .10
92 Craig Darby .02 .10
93 Eric Fichaud .08 .25
94 Andreas Johansson .02 .10
95 Jamie Rivers .02 .10
96 Jason Strudwick .02 .10
97 Patrice Tardif .02 .10
98 Alex Vasilevskii .02 .10
99 Drew Bannister .02 .10
100 Stan Drulia .08 .25
101 Aaron Gavey .02 .10
102 Reggie Savage .02 .10
103 Derek Wilkinson .08 .25
104 Rob Brown .02 .10
105 Dan Currie .02 .10
106 Kevin MacDonald .02 .10
107 Steve Maltais .08 .25
108 Shawn Rivers .02 .10
109 Wendell Young .08 .25
110 Don Biggs .02 .10
111 Dale DeGray .02 .10
112 Paul Lawless .02 .10
113 Danny Lorenz .02 .10
114 Dave Tomlinson .02 .10
115 Jock Callander .08 .25
116 Phillipe DeRouville .02 .10
117 Ryan Savoia .02 .10
118 Mike Stevens .02 .10
119 Chris Tamer .08 .25
120 Peter Bondra .20 .50
121 Peter Ciavaglia .02 .10
122 Rick Knickle .02 .10
123 Lonnie Loach .02 .10
124 Michal Pivonka .02 .10
125 Andy Bezeau .02 .10
126 Bob Essensa .08 .25
127 Andrew McBain .02 .10
128 Kevin Miehm .02 .10
129 Scott Arniel .02 .10
130 Kevin Dineen .08 .25
131 Rob Dopson .08 .25
132 Mark Freer .02 .10
133 Troy Gamble .08 .25
134 Ethan Moreau .08 .25
135 Sergei Klimovich .02 .10
136 Eric Lecompte .02 .10
137 Eric Manlow .02 .10
138 Kip Miller .02 .10
139 Manny Fernandez .20 .50
140 Mike Kennedy .02 .10
141 Jamie Langenbrunner .20 .50
142 Derrick Smith .02 .10
143 Jordan Willis .08 .25
144 Jan Caloun .02 .10
145 Viktor Kozlov .08 .25
146 Andrei Nazarov .02 .10
147 Geoff Sarjeant .02 .10
148 Patrik Augusta .02 .10
149 Viktor Gordiouk .02 .10
150 Dave Littman .08 .25
151 Todd Gillingham .02 .10
152 Greg Hawgood .02 .10
153 Patrice Lefebvre .02 .10
154 Pokey Reddick .08 .25
155 Manon Rheaume .75 2.00
156 Jeff Sharples .02 .10
157 Todd Simon .02 .10
158 Radek Bonk .20 .50
159 Gino Cavallini .02 .10
160 Tom Draper .08 .25
161 Tony Hrkac .02 .10
162 Fabian Joseph .08 .25
163 Mark Laforest .02 .10
164 Dave Christian .02 .10
165 Bryan Fogarty .02 .10
166 Chris Govedaris .02 .10
167 Mike Hurlbut .02 .10
168 Chris Imes .02 .10
169 Stephane Morin .02 .10
170 Allan Bester .08 .25
171 Kerry Clark .02 .10
172 Neil Eisenhut .02 .10
173 Craig Fisher .02 .10
174 Patrick Neaton .02 .10
175 Todd Richards .02 .10
176 Jon Casey .08 .25
177 Doug Evans .02 .10
178 Michel Mongeau .02 .10
179 Greg Paslawski .02 .10
180 Darren Veitch .02 .10

181 Frederick Beaubien .02 .10
182 Kevin Brown .02 .10
183 Rob Cowie .02 .10
184 Yanic Perreault .08 .25
185 Chris Snell .02 .10
186 Jan Vopat .02 .10
187 Robin Bawa .02 .10
188 Stephane Beauregard .08 .25
189 Dale Craigwell .02 .10
190 John Purves .08 .25
191 Jeff Madill .02 .10
192 Gord Dineen .02 .10
193 Chris Marinucci .08 .25
194 Mark McArthur .02 .10
195 Zigmund Palffy .20 .50
196 Tommy Salo .20 .50
197 Checklist .02 .10
198 Checklist .02 .10
199 Checklist .02 .10
200 Checklist .02 .10

1996 Collector's Edge Ice Crucibles

This 25 card standard-size set was randomly inserted into packs. The fronts feature the players photo along with the word "Crucible" on the top and his name on the bottom. The cards are numbered with a "C" prefix. The backs include a player head shot as well as recent stats.

COMPLETE SET (25) 15.00 30.00
C1 David Roberts .40 1.00
C2 Ian Laperriere .40 1.00
C3 Kevin Dineen .40 1.00
C4 Kenny Jonsson .40 1.00
C5 Jim Carey .75 2.00
C6 Todd Marchant .40 1.00
C7 David Oliver .40 1.00
C8 Yanic Perreault .75 2.00
C9 Chris Therien .40 1.00
C10 Viktor Kozlov .75 2.00
C11 Valeri Bure .40 1.00
C12 Nikolai Khabibulin 1.00 2.50
C13 Steven Rice .40 1.00
C14 Mike Kennedy .40 1.00
C15 Peter Bondra .75 2.00
C16 Sergei Zubov .40 1.00
C17 Slava Kozlov .75 2.00
C18 Chris Osgood .75 2.00
C19 Darren McCarty .40 1.00
C20 Jason Dawe .40 1.00
C21 Trevor Kidd 1.00 2.50
C22 Tommy Salo 1.00 2.50
C23 Michal Pivonka .40 1.00
C24 Zigmund Palffy .75 2.00
NNO Checklist .40 1.00

1996 Collector's Edge Ice Livin' Large

This set was randomly inserted into packs. The cards feature top players. The cards are numbered with a "L" prefix.

COMPLETE SET (11) 20.00 40.00
L1 Adam Graves .75 2.00
L2 Marty McSorley .75 2.00
L3 Adam Oates 1.25 3.00
L4 Keith Primeau .75 2.00
L5 Bill Ranford 1.25 3.00
L6 Curtis Joseph 1.50 4.00
L7 Felix Potvin 1.50 4.00
L8 Mike Vernon 1.25 3.00
L9 Theo Fleury .75 2.00
L10 Kevin Stevens .75 2.00
L11 Martin Brodeur 8.00 20.00
NNO Checklist .75 2.00

1996 Collector's Edge Ice Platinum Club

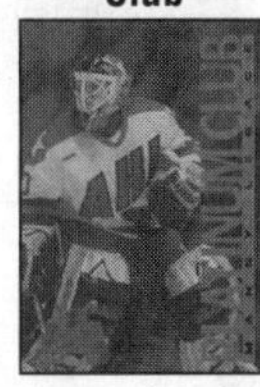

Random inserts in packs of Collectors Edge Ice.

COMPLETE SET (8) 10.00 25.00
1 Mike Dunham 2.00 5.00
2 Eric Fichaud .75 2.00
3 Manny Legace 2.00 5.00
4 Steve Sullivan .75 2.00
5 Darcy Tucker .75 2.00
6 Jamie Langenbrunner .75 2.00
7 Ethan Moreau .75 2.00
8 Jamie Storr .75 2.00

1996 Collector's Edge Ice Prism

This 200-card set was issued as a parallel to the base set. They weren't issued as inserts, however. Instead, they were sold in team set form on a localized basis across the AHL and IHL. These cards are actually quite scarce, and provide a real challenge for player collectors.

*PRISM CARDS: 2X to 5X BASIC CARDS

1996 Collector's Edge Ice Promos

This 7-card set was issued as a promotional device to entice dealers to purchase the upcoming Collector's Edge Ice set of minor league stars. The cards mirror the design of the regular issue cards, save for the numbering, which comes with a PR-prefix.

COMPLETE SET (7) .80 2.00
PR1 Todd Marchant .10 .25
PR2 Tommy Salo .20 .50
PR3 Michael Dunham .20 .50
PR4 Viktor Kozlov .16 .40
PR5 Dwayne Roloson .16 .40
PR6 Tony Hrkac .10 .25
NNO Title Card .20 .50

1996 Collector's Edge Ice QuantumMotion

This 13 card set was randomly inserted into packs. The full-bleed cards feature a player photo over most of it. The words "Quantum Motion" are located in the lower right corner.

COMPLETE SET (13) 15.00 30.00
1 Manny Fernandez 2.00 4.00
2 Pokey Reddick .75 2.00
3 Yanic Perreault .75 2.00
4 Rob Brown .75 2.00
5 Hubie McDonough .75 2.00
6 Stan Drulia .75 2.00
7 Michel Picard .75 2.00
8 Jim Carey 1.25 3.00
9 Martin Lapointe 1.25 3.00
10 Valeri Bure .75 2.00
11 Martin Brochu 1.25 3.00
12 Corey Schwab 1.25 3.00
NNO Checklist .75 2.00

1996 Collector's Edge Ice Signed, Sealed and Delivered

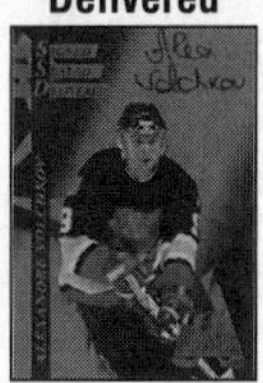

This 8-card set highlights youngsters set to make their power known in the NHL. Cards were randomly inserted in packs at an unknown ratio.

COMPLETE SET (8) 8.00 20.00
1 Alexandre Volchkov 1.25 3.00
2 Chris Allen 1.25 3.00
3 Brian Bonin 1.25 3.00
4 Josh Green 1.25 3.00
5 Chris Hajt 1.25 3.00
6 Josh Holden 1.25 3.00
8 Andrei Zyuzin 1.25 3.00
NNO Alexandre Volchkov 1.25 3.00

1996 Collector's Edge Ice The Wall

This 13 card die-cut set was inserted as a set in each sealed foil box. The cards feature goaltenders and their masks are on the front. The backs are devoted to a player photo. Also on the backs are vital statistics, and a brief biography. The cards are numbered with a "TW" prefix.

COMPLETE SET (12) 6.00 12.00
TW1 Ray LeBlanc .40 1.00
TW2 Manny Fernandez .75 2.00
TW3 Rick Knickle .40 1.00
TW4 Troy Gamble .40 1.00
TW5 Pokey Reddick .40 1.00
TW6 Wendell Young .40 1.00
TW7 Jim Carey .40 1.00
TW8 Dwayne Roloson .40 1.00
TW9 Les Kuntar .40 1.00
TW10 Mike Dunham .75 2.00
TW11 Eric Fichaud .40 1.00
TW12 Kevin Hodson .40 1.00

1995 Images

This 100-card set features top NHL prospects currently playing in the juniors, minors or overseas. The standard-sized cards feature full-bleed color photography over a metallic sheen background. The Classic logo is in the upper left corner, while the Images logo, player name and position rest on a blue and silver bar near the bottom. The backs feature another color photo, stats and the logos of the licensing bodies. One autographed card was found in each box. A total of 1995 individually numbered 12-box cases were produced.

COMPLETE SET (100) 5.00 12.00
1 Bryan Berard .07 .20
2 Jeff Friesen .02 .10
3 Tommy Salo .25 .60
4 Jim Carey .07 .20
5 Wade Redden .07 .20
6 Jocelyn Thibault .15 .40
7 Ian Laperriere .02 .10
8 Todd Marchant .02 .10
9 Blaine Lacher .02 .10
10 Pavel Bure .15 .40
11 Alex Vasilevskii .02 .10
12 Jason Doig .02 .10
13 Eric Fichaud .07 .20
14 Eric Daze .07 .20
15 Ed Jovanovski .07 .20
16 Alexander Selivanov .02 .10
17 Brent Gretzky .02 .10
18 Terry Ryan .02 .10
19 Chris Wells .02 .10
20 Wade Belak .02 .10
21 Kevin Dineen .02 .10
22 Craig Fisher .02 .10
23 Jan Caloun .02 .10
24 Manny Fernandez .15 .40
25 Radek Bonk .02 .10
26 Dave Christian .02 .10
27 Patrice Tardif .02 .10
28 Kevin Brown .02 .10
29 Hubie McDonough .02 .10
30 Yan Golubovsky .02 .10
31 Steve Larouche .02 .10
32 Chris Therien .02 .10
33 Craig Darby .02 .10
34 Dwayne Norris .02 .10
35 Roman Oksiuta .02 .10
36 Steve Washburn .02 .10
37 Todd Bertuzzi .15 .40
38 Cory Stillman .07 .20
39 Steve Kelly .02 .10
40 Nathan LaFayette .02 .10
41 Dwayne Roloson .07 .20
42 Nikolai Khabibulin .15 .40
43 Radim Bicanek .02 .10
44 Jeff O'Neill .02 .10
45 Jason Bonsignore .02 .10
46 Shean Donovan .02 .10
47 Wayne Primeau .02 .10
48 Jamie Langenbrunner .02 .10
49 Dan Cloutier .15 .40
50 Ethan Moreau .07 .20
51 Brad Bombardir .02 .10
52 Jason Muzzatti .02 .10
53 Jassen Cullimore .02 .10
54 Jason Zent .02 .10
55 Sergei Gonchar .07 .20
56 Steve Rucchin .02 .10
57 Rob Cowie .02 .10
58 Miroslav Satan .40 1.00
59 Kenny Jonsson .02 .10
60 Adam Deadmarsh .02 .10
61 Mike Dunham .15 .40
62 Corey Hirsch .02 .10
63 Janne Laukkanen .02 .10
64 Craig Conroy .02 .10
65 Ryan Sittler .02 .10
66 Jeff Nelson .02 .10
67 Michel Picard .02 .10
68 Mark Astley .02 .10
69 Lonny Bohonos .02 .10
70 Evgeny Ryabchikov .02 .10
71 Chris Osgood .07 .20
72 Manon Rheaume 1.00 2.50
73 Mike Kennedy .02 .10
74 Deron Quint .02 .10
75 Jamie Storr .07 .20
76 Aris Brimanis .02 .10
77 Valeri Bure .02 .10
78 Rene Corbet .02 .10
79 David Oliver .02 .10
80 Chris McAlpine .02 .10
81 Petr Sykora .15 .40
82 Brad Church .07 .20
83 Daymond Langkow .15 .40
84 Chad Kilger .02 .10
85 Shane Doan .20 .50
86 Jeff Ware .02 .10
87 Christian Laflamme .02 .10
88 Cory Cross .02 .10
89 Al Secord .02 .10
90 Jason Woolley .02 .10
91 Bryan McCabe .07 .20
92 Travis Richards .02 .10
93 Andrei Nazarov .02 .10
94 Mike Pomichter .02 .10
95 Chris Marinucci .02 .10
96 Jean-Yves Roy .02 .10
97 Brian Rolston .07 .20
98 Aaron Ward .02 .10
99 Jim Carey CL .02 .10
100 Pavel Bure CL .07 .20

1995 Images Gold

These 100 standard-size cards were issued as a one-per-pack parallel to the Images set. The card design is identical to the standard Images card, except for the metallic background being a golden tone rather than the standard silver.

*STARS: 1.25X TO 2.5X BASIC CARDS

1995 Images Autographs

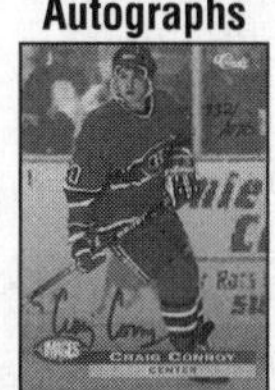

These 22 standard-size cards were random inserts throughout the packs. The card design is identical to the standard Images card except for the facsimile autograph inscribed across the picture. The number of cards signed is indicated in parenthesis.

2A Jeff Friesen/1500 4.00 10.00
6A Jocelyn Thibault/1185 4.00 10.00
9A Blaine Lacher/1500 2.00 5.00
25A Radek Bonk/970 3.00 8.00
30A Yan Golubovsky/1500 .75 2.00
36A Steve Washburn/1500 .75 2.00
41A Dwayne Roloson/1115 .75 2.00
45A Jason Bonsignore/1500 2.00 5.00
46A Shean Donovan/1500 .75 2.00
48A J.Langenbrunner/1500 5.00 12.00
54A Jason Zent/1125 .75 2.00
59A Kenny Jonsson/1180 2.00 5.00
60A Adam Deadmarsh/1500 6.00 15.00
64A Craig Conroy/1170 .75 2.00
74A Deron Quint/1500 .75 2.00
76A Aris Brimanis/1500 .75 2.00
79A David Oliver/1500 .75 2.00
80A Chris McAlpine/1185 .75 2.00
81A Petr Sykora/1500 3.00 8.00
94A Mike Pomichter/1175 .75 2.00
95A Chris Marinucci/1500 .75 2.00
98A Aaron Ward/1190 .75 2.00

1995 Images Clear Excitement

This 20-card standard-size set was randomly inserted only in Hot boxes. Essentially, the odds of finding one of these cards was 1, 152 packs. Each pack in a Hot box has 3 cards from any of the five insert sets. These clear cards feature color player action cutouts on their fronts. The player's name appears in a blue bar on the left. The backs carry the reverse image as a shadow with the player's name in an oval across it. The blue bar on the left contains information about the player and the card number at the top.

COMPLETE SET (20) 75.00 150.00
CE1 Bryan Berard 2.50 6.00
CE2 Jeff Friesen 2.00 5.00
CE3 Tommy Salo 3.00 8.00
CE4 Jim Carey 2.50 6.00
CE5 Wade Redden 2.50 6.00
CE6 Jocelyn Thibault 3.00 8.00
CE7 Ian Laperriere 2.00 5.00
CE8 Todd Marchant 2.00 5.00
CE9 Blaine Lacher 2.00 5.00
CE10 Pavel Bure 3.00 8.00
CE11 Petr Sykora 3.00 8.00
CE12 Daymond Langkow 2.50 6.00
CE13 Radek Bonk 2.00 5.00
CE14 Patrice Tardif 2.00 5.00
CE15 Jeff Nelson 2.00 5.00
CE16 Jeff O'Neill 2.00 5.00
CE17 Ed Jovanovski 2.50 6.00
CE18 Jason Doig 2.00 5.00
CE19 Chris Marinucci 2.00 5.00
CE20 Manon Rheaume 12.50 30.00

1995 Images Platinum Players

The cards in this 10 card standard-size set were randomly inserted at a rate of one per 36 packs. The fronts have a color action photo with a green and silver foil background. The word "Images" is at the top and "Platinum Player" is at the bottom. The backs have a color action photo with a green tint in the background. Player information appears at the bottom and each card is numbered out of 1,995.

COMPLETE SET (10) 10.00 20.00
PL1 Pavel Bure 1.50 4.00
PL2 Tony Granato .40 1.00
PL3 Kevin Dineen .40 1.00
PL4 Ron Hextall 1.25 3.00
PL5 Claude Lemieux .40 1.00
PL6 Mark Recchi 1.50 4.00
PL7 Benoit Hogue .40 1.00
PL8 Tim Cheveldae .40 1.00
PL9 Darcy Wakaluk .40 1.00
PL10 Todd Gill .40 1.00

1995 Images Platinum Premier Draft Choice

One card from this 10 standard-size set was randomly inserted in every 48 packs. The card of Bryan Berard, the no. 1 draft choice, was redeemable for a 25.00 Manon Rheaume autographed phone card. The offer expired 12/31/95. The fronts feature a player action photo on a borderless blue and silver background with the player's name printed vertically down the left side. The backs carry the card number and players name in a marble blue stripe at the top with the redemption directions below. A checklist of the 10 cards is printed at the bottom.

COMPLETE SET (10) 10.00 20.00
PD1 Bryan Berard 1.00 2.50
PD2 Wade Redden 1.00 2.50
PD3 Steve Kelly .40 1.00
PD4 Petr Sykora 3.00 8.00
PD5 Brad Church .40 1.00
PD6 Daymond Langkow 1.50 4.00
PD7 Chad Kilger .40 1.00
PD8 Terry Ryan .40 1.00
PD9 Jason Doig .40 1.00
PD10 Field Card .40 1.00

1995 Images Platinum Prospects

The ten cards in this set (found 1:36 packs) feature some of the top prospects for NHL stardom. The cards feature a color player photo over a diagonally split silver and blue metallic background. The Images logo is in the top left corner, while the Platinum Prospects logo rests in the bottom right, beside the player's name in stylized script. The backs feature another color photo and a blurb assessing the player's chances. Each card is serially numbered out of 1,995 at the bottom left corner.

COMPLETE SET (10) 10.00 20.00
PR1 Jeff Nelson .40 1.00
PR2 Jim Carey 1.25 3.00
PR3 Ian Laperriere .40 1.00
PR4 Chris Osgood 1.25 3.00
PR5 Todd Marchant .40 1.00
PR6 Radek Bonk .40 1.00
PR7 Chris Marinucci .40 1.00
PR8 Tommy Salo 2.50 5.00
PR9 Manny Fernandez 1.50 4.00
PR10 Jan Caloun .40 1.00

2007 ITG Going For Gold World Juniors

COMPLETE SET (30) 10.00 25.00
1 Carey Price .75 2.00
2 Leland Irving .40 1.00
3 Karl Alzner .40 1.00
4 Ryan Parent .20 .50
5 Kristopher Letang .30 .75
6 Luc Bourdon .30 .75
7 Kris Russell .20 .50
8 Marc Staal .40 1.00
9 Cody Franson .20 .50
10 Steve Downie .40 1.00
11 Andrew Cogliano .40 1.00
12 Marc-Andre ClichÃ© .20 .50
13 Kenndal McArdle .30 .75
14 Darren Helm .30 .75
15 Brad Marchand .20 .50
16 James Neal .20 .50
17 Bryan Little .30 .75
18 Daniel Bertram .20 .50
19 Ryan O'Marra .20 .50
20 Tom Pyatt .20 .50
21 Jonathan Toews 2.00 5.00
22 Sam Gagner .75 2.00
23 Eric Lindros .40 1.00
24 Roberto Luongo .60 1.50
25 Jason Spezza .40 1.00
26 Dion Phaneuf .40 1.00
27 Marc-Andre Fleury .60 1.50
28 Joe Thornton .60 1.50
29 Justin Pogge .40 1.00
30 Checklist .02 .10

2007 ITG Going For Gold World Juniors Autographs

1 Carey Price 40.00 80.00
2 Leland Irving 15.00 40.00
3 Karl Alzner 12.00 30.00
4 Ryan Parent 10.00 25.00
5 Kristopher Letang 10.00 25.00
6 Luc Bourdon 10.00 25.00
7 Kris Russell 8.00 20.00
8 Marc Staal 10.00 25.00
9 Cody Franson 6.00 15.00
10 Steve Downie 12.00 30.00
11 Andrew Cogliano 10.00 25.00
12 Marc-Andre ClichÃ© 6.00 15.00
13 Kenndal McArdle 8.00 20.00
14 Darren Helm 8.00 20.00
15 Brad Marchand 6.00 15.00
16 James Neal 6.00 15.00
17 Bryan Little 8.00 20.00
18 Daniel Bertram 6.00 15.00
19 Ryan O'Marra 6.00 15.00
20 Tom Pyatt 6.00 15.00
21 Jonathan Toews 30.00 80.00
22 Sam Gagner 15.00 40.00
23 Eric Lindros 10.00 25.00
24 Roberto Luongo 15.00 40.00
25 Jason Spezza 10.00 25.00
26 Dion Phaneuf 10.00 25.00
27 Marc-Andre Fleury 15.00 40.00
28 Joe Thornton 15.00 40.00
29 Justin Pogge 12.00 30.00

2007 ITG Going For Gold World Juniors Emblems

STATED PRINT RUN 20 SETS
GUE1 Carey Price 30.00 80.00
GUE2 Leland Irving 25.00 60.00
GUE3 Karl Alzner 25.00 60.00
GUE4 Ryan Parent 20.00 50.00
GUE5 Kristopher Letang 20.00 50.00
GUE6 Luc Bourdon 20.00 50.00
GUE7 Kris Russell 25.00 60.00
GUE8 Marc Staal 25.00 60.00
GUE9 Cody Franson 20.00 50.00
GUE10 Steve Downie 25.00 60.00
GUE11 Andrew Cogliano 25.00 60.00
GUE12 Marc-Andre ClichÃ© 20.00 50.00
GUE13 Kenndal McArdle 20.00 50.00
GUE14 Darren Helm 20.00 50.00
GUE15 Brad Marchand 20.00 50.00
GUE16 James Neal 20.00 50.00
GUE17 Bryan Little 20.00 50.00
GUE18 Daniel Bertram 20.00 50.00
GUE19 Ryan O'Marra 20.00 50.00
GUE20 Tom Pyatt 20.00 50.00
GUE21 Jonathan Toews 30.00 80.00
GUE22 Sam Gagner 25.00 60.00
GUE23 Dion Phaneuf
GUE24 Roberto Luongo
GUE25 Jason Spezza
GUE26 Justin Pogge
GUE27 Marc-Andre Fleury
GUE28 Dany Heatley

2007 ITG Going For Gold World Juniors Jerseys

GUJ1 Carey Price 20.00 50.00
GUJ2 Leland Irving 12.00 30.00
GUJ3 Karl Alzner 12.00 30.00
GUJ4 Ryan Parent 10.00 25.00
GUJ5 Kristopher Letang 12.00 30.00
GUJ6 Luc Bourdon 12.00 30.00
GUJ7 Kris Russell 12.00 30.00
GUJ8 Marc Staal 12.00 30.00
GUJ9 Cody Franson 10.00 25.00
GUJ10 Steve Downie 12.00 30.00
GUJ11 Andrew Cogliano 12.00 30.00
GUJ12 Marc-Andre ClichÃ© 10.00 25.00
GUJ13 Kenndal McArdle 10.00 25.00
GUJ14 Darren Helm 10.00 25.00
GUJ15 Brad Marchand 10.00 25.00
GUJ16 James Neal 10.00 25.00
GUJ17 Bryan Little 12.00 30.00
GUJ18 Daniel Bertram 10.00 25.00
GUJ19 Ryan O'Marra 10.00 25.00
GUJ20 Tom Pyatt 10.00 25.00
GUJ21 Jonathan Toews 15.00 40.00
GUJ22 Sam Gagner 12.00 30.00
GUJ23 Dion Phaneuf
GUJ24 Roberto Luongo
GUJ25 Jason Spezza
GUJ26 Justin Pogge
GUJ27 Marc-Andre Fleury
GUJ28 Dany Heatley

2007 ITG Going For Gold World Juniors Numbers

STATED PRINT RUN 20 COPIES
GUN1 Carey Price 30.00 80.00
GUN2 Leland Irving 25.00 60.00
GUN3 Karl Alzner 25.00 60.00
GUN4 Ryan Parent 20.00 50.00
GUN5 Kristopher Letang 20.00 50.00
GUN6 Luc Bourdon 20.00 50.00
GUN7 Kris Russell 25.00 60.00
GUN8 Marc Staal 25.00 60.00
GUN9 Cody Franson 20.00 50.00
GUN10 Steve Downie 25.00 60.00
GUN11 Andrew Cogliano 20.00 50.00
GUN12 Marc-Andre ClichÃ© 20.00 50.00
GUN13 Kenndal McArdle 20.00 50.00
GUN14 Darren Helm 20.00 50.00
GUN15 Brad Marchand 20.00 50.00
GUN16 James Neal 20.00 50.00
GUN17 Bryan Little 20.00 50.00
GUN18 Daniel Bertram 20.00 50.00
GUN19 Ryan O'Marra 20.00 50.00
GUN20 Tom Pyatt 20.00 50.00
GUN21 Jonathan Toews 30.00 80.00
GUN22 Sam Gagner 25.00 60.00

2004-05 ITG Heroes and Prospects

Released in Novemeber 2004 in the wake of the NHL lockout, this 180-card set focused on top minor league prospects, top juniors and retired greats as well as Russian star Alexander Ovechkin. Heroes and Prospects was available as a hobby product that featured 2 autographs and 1 memorabilia card per box (on average) and also as an arena retail version with no memorabilia and tougher odds on autographs.

COMPLETE SET (230) 30.00 80.00
COMP.SET w/o UPDATE(180) 25.00 60.00
COMP. UPDATE SET (50) 10.00 20.00
1 Cory Pecker .20 .50
2 Hannu Toivonen .40 1.00
3 Duncan Keith .20 .50
4 Jiri Novotny .20 .50
5 Carlo Colaiacovo .20 .50
6 Igor Knyazev .20 .50
7 Pascal Leclaire .30 .75
8 Brad Boyes .20 .50
9 Duncan Milroy .20 .50
10 Jeff Woywitka .20 .50
11 Peter Budaj .20 .50
12 Timofei Shishkanov .20 .50
13 Brandon Nolan .20 .50
14 Denis Grebeshkov .20 .50
15 Danny Groulx .20 .50
16 Martin Kariya .40 1.00
17 Greg Watson .20 .50
18 Tomas Kopecky .20 .50
19 Petr Taticek .20 .50
20 Filip Novak .20 .50
21 Matt Foy .20 .50
22 Adam Hauser .20 .50
23 Yanick Lehoux .20 .50
24 Kari Lehtonen .40 1.00
25 Marcel Goc .20 .50
26 Scottie Upshall .20 .50
27 David LeNeveu .30 .75
28 Kiel McLeod .20 .50
29 Jean-Marc Pelletier .20 .50
30 Colby Armstrong .20 .50
31 Adrian Foster .20 .50
32 Victor Uchevatov .20 .50
33 Jay McClement .20 .50
34 Marc-Andre Fleury 1.00 2.50
35 Kirill Koltsov .20 .50
36 Alexandre Giroux .20 .50
37 Rastislav Stana .20 .50
38 Ryan Miller .40 1.00
39 Mike Glumac .20 .50
40 Chris Kunitz .20 .50
41 Martin Podlesak .20 .50
42 Michel Ouellet .20 .50
43 Ryan Kesler .20 .50
44 Garrett Stafford .20 .50
45 Ray Emery .30 .75
46 Fedor Tjutin .20 .50
47 Jozef Balej .30 .75
48 Antero Niittymaki .60 1.50
49 Tom Lawson .20 .50
50 Grant Stevenson .20 .50
51 Adam Berti .20 .50
52 Alexandre Picard .40 1.00
53 Andrew Ladd .40 1.00
54 Anthony Stewart .40 1.00
55 Bobby Ryan .60 1.50
56 Boris Valabik .20 .50
57 Braydon Coburn .30 .75
58 Brent Seabrook .30 .75
59 Bryan Bickell .20 .50
60 Bryan Little .40 1.00
61 Cam Barker .40 1.00
62 Cam Ward .40 1.00
63 Chris Campoli .20 .50
64 Corey Locke .20 .50
65 Corey Perry .75 2.00
66 Andy Rogers .20 .50
67 Dan Paille .30 .75
68 David Bolland .30 .75
69 David Shantz .30 .75
70 Dennis Wideman .20 .50
71 Devan Dubnyk .30 .75
72 Dion Phaneuf 1.00 2.50
73 Doug O'Brien .20 .50
74 Eric Fehr .20 .50
75 Eric Himelfarb .20 .50
76 Gilbert Brule .60 1.50
77 James Wisniewski .20 .50
78 Jeff Carter .75 2.00
79 Jeff Drouin-Deslauriers .30 .75
80 Jeff Glass .40 1.00
81 Jeff Schultz .20 .50
82 Josh Gorges .20 .50
83 Julien Ellis-Plante .40 1.00
84 Justin Peters .20 .50
85 Kelly Guard .40 1.00
86 Kevin Klein .20 .50
87 Kyle Chipchura .40 1.00
88 Liam Reddox .20 .50
89 Marc Staal .40 1.00
90 Marc-Antoine Pouliot .30 .75
91 Martin Houle .30 .75
92 Martin St. Pierre .30 .75
93 Matt Lashoff .30 .75
94 Maxime Daigneault .30 .75
95 Mike Green .20 .50
96 Mike Richards .40 1.00
97 Paulo Colaiacovo .30 .75
98 Patrick O'Sullivan .40 1.00
99 Philippe Roberge .20 .50
100 Robbie Schremp .60 1.50
101 Ryan Garlock .20 .50
102 Ryan Getzlaf .60 1.50
103 Shawn Belle .30 .75
104 Sidney Crosby 8.00 20.00
105 Stefan Ruzicka .30 .75
106 Steve Bernier .40 1.00
107 Tim Brent .20 .50
108 Tomas Fleischmann .20 .50
109 Vaclav Meidl .20 .50
110 Wojtek Wolski .60 1.50
111 Stephen Weiss .30 .75
112 Fredrik Sjostrom .20 .50
113 Alexander Svitov .20 .50
114 Anton Babchuk .20 .50
115 Jason Spezza .40 1.00
116 Alexander Ovechkin 3.00 8.00
117 Alexander Ovechkin 3.00 8.00
118 Alexander Ovechkin 3.00 8.00
119 Alexander Ovechkin 3.00 8.00
120 Marc-Andre Fleury .75 2.00
121 Marc-Andre Fleury .75 2.00
122 Marc-Andre Fleury .75 2.00
123 Tim Horton .40 1.00
124 Frank Mahovlich .40 1.00
125 Gilbert Perreault .30 .75
126 Ed Giacomin .40 1.00
127 Jean Ratelle .20 .50
128 Marcel Dionne .30 .75
129 Milt Schmidt .20 .50
130 Phil Esposito .40 1.00
131 Bernie Parent .40 1.00
132 Serge Savard .30 .75
133 Stan Mikita .30 .75
134 Tony Esposito .40 1.00
135 Vic Hadfield .20 .50
136 Wayne Cashman .20 .50
137 Yvan Cournoyer .40 1.00
138 Johnny Bower .40 1.00
139 Bill Barber .20 .50
140 Bobby Hull .60 1.50
141 Denis Potvin .30 .75
142 Gerry Cheevers .30 .75
143 Guy Lafleur .40 1.00
144 Larry Robinson .30 .75
145 Rogie Vachon .40 1.00
146 Steve Shutt .20 .50
147 Ted Lindsay .40 1.00

148 Red Kelly .40 1.00
149 Wendel Clark .30 .75
150 Ray Bourque .40 1.00
151 Cam Neely .40 1.00
152 Glenn Hall .40 1.00
153 Jean Beliveau .40 1.00
154 Grant Fuhr .40 1.00
155 Andy Bathgate .30 .75
156 Gump Worsley .40 1.00
157 Henri Richard .40 1.00
158 Mike Bossy .30 .75
159 Johnny Bucyk .30 .75
160 Elmer Lach .20 .50
161 Vladislav Tretiak .30 .75
162 Lanny McDonald .30 .75
163 Guy Lapointe .30 .75
164 Jacques Plante .60 1.50
165 Terry Sawchuk .60 1.50
166 Rocket Richard .75 2.00
167 Doug Harvey .30 .75
168 Howie Morenz .30 .75
169 Bill Barilko .30 .75
170 Brad Park .20 .50
171 Bobby Orr 1.00 2.50
172 Mario Lemieux .75 2.00
173 Paul Coffey .40 1.00
174 Patrick Roy .75 2.00
175 Bobby Clarke .40 1.00
176 Georges Vezina .60 1.50
177 Alex Delvecchio .40 1.00
178 Toe Blake .40 1.00
179 Sid Abel .40 1.00
180 Woody Dumart .30 .75
181 Jason King A .20 .50
182 Yann Danis A .30 .75
183 Zach Parise .60 1.50
184 Dan Hamhuis .40 1.00
185 Thomas Vanek .75 2.00
186 Mikko Koivu .40 1.00
187 Ryan Whitney .40 1.00
188 Jakub Klepis .20 .50
189 Ben Eager .20 .50
190 Kyle Wellwood .40 1.00
191 Jiri Hudler .40 1.00
192 Aaron Voros .20 .50
193 Eric Staal .60 1.50
194 Jay Bouwmeester .20 .50
195 Patrice Bergeron .60 1.50
196 Peter Sarno .20 .50
197 Mike Cammalleri .30 .75
198 Derek Roy .40 1.00
199 R.J. Umberger .40 1.00
200 Junior Lessard .20 .50
201 Rene Vydareny .20 .50
202 Alexander Ovechkin 3.00 8.00
203 Dylan Hunter .20 .50
204 Alexandre Vincent .30 .75
205 Kevin Nastiuk .30 .75
206 Evan McGrath .20 .50
207 Alex Bourret .20 .50
208 Andrej Meszaros .20 .50
209 Benoit Pouliot .20 .50
210 Dany Roussin .20 .50
211 Jeremy Colliton .20 .50
212 Danny Syvret .20 .50
213 Jonathan Boutin .30 .75
214 Ryan Stone .40 1.00
215 Jordan Staal 1.00 2.50
216 Marek Zagrapan .20 .50
217 Clarke MacArthur .30 .75
218 John Hughes .20 .50
219 Alexander Radulov .75 2.00
220 Colin Fraser .20 .50
221 Jakub Petruzalek .20 .50
222 Sidney Crosby 8.00 20.00
223 Nigel Dawes .40 1.00
224 Luc Bourdon .40 1.00
225 Devin Setoguchi .30 .75
226 Carey Price 1.50 4.00
227 Daren Machesney .30 .75
228 Corey Crawford .30 .75
229 Marek Schwarz .30 .75
230 Gerald Coleman .30 .75
NNO Roy/Ovechkin/Crosby
Fleury CL 2.00 5.00

2004-05 ITG Heroes and Prospects Aspiring

STATED PRINT RUN 50 SETS
1 M. Lemieux/S.Crosby 100.00 200.00
2 M.Lemieux/A.Ovechkin 75.00 200.00
3 Patrick Roy/Marc-Andre Fleury 40.00 100.00
4 Patrick Roy/Kari Lehtonen 40.00 100.00
5 Ray Bourque/Dion Phaneuf 30.00 80.00
6 Cam Neely/Alexander Ovechkin 50.00 125.00
7 Mike Bossy/Mike Richards 20.00 50.00
8 Frank Mahovlich/Patrick O'Sullivan 20.00 50.00
9 Phil Esposito/Brad Boyes 20.00 50.00
10 Grant Fuhr/Devan Dubnyk 30.00 80.00
11 Bobby Clarke/Jeff Carter 25.00 60.00
12 Jacques Plante/Julien Ellis-Plante 15.00 40.00
13 Gilbert Perreault/Sidney Crosby 75.00 200.00
14 Stan Mikita/Corey Perry 15.00 40.00
15 Jean Beliveau/Corey Locke 15.00 40.00
16 Gerry Cheevers/David LeNeveu 15.00 40.00

2004-05 ITG Heroes and Prospects Autographs

Inserted on an average of 2 per hobby box, this 160-card set featured certified autographs of young prospects and retired greats. Odds for retail arena boxes were not given. Cards with "U" prefix available in

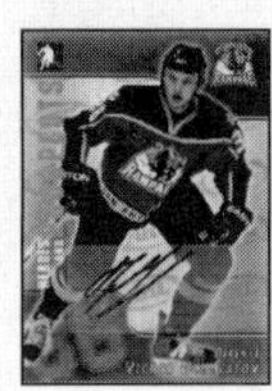

Update sets only, please note that card backs do not carry the "U" prefix, they are for checklisting only.
STATED ODDS 2 PER HOBBY BOX
U PREFIX IN H&P UPDATE SETS ONLY
AB Adam Berti 4.00 10.00
AD Alex Delvecchio 10.00 25.00
AF Adrian Foster 4.00 10.00
AG Alexandre Giroux 4.00 10.00
AH Adam Hauser 4.00 10.00
AL Andrew Ladd 10.00 25.00
AO1 Alexander Ovechkin 100.00 200.00
AO2 Alexander Ovechkin 100.00 200.00
AO3 Alexander Ovechkin 100.00 200.00
AO4 Alexander Ovechkin 100.00 200.00
AP Alexandre Picard 8.00 20.00
AR Andy Rogers 4.00 10.00
AS Anthony Stewart 8.00 20.00
BB Brad Boyes 4.00 10.00
BC Braydon Coburn 8.00 20.00
BH Bobby Hull 25.00 60.00
BL Bryan Little 6.00 15.00
BN Brandon Nolan 4.00 10.00
BO Bobby Orr 75.00 200.00
BP Bernie Parent 12.50 30.00
BR Bobby Ryan 8.00 25.00
BS Brent Seabrook 4.00 10.00
BV Boris Valabik 4.00 10.00
CA Colby Armstrong 8.00 20.00
CB Cam Barker 8.00 20.00
CC Carlo Colaiacovo 4.00 10.00
CK Chris Kunitz 4.00 10.00
CL Corey Locke 4.00 10.00
CN Cam Neely 12.50 30.00
CP Cory Pecker 4.00 10.00
CW Cam Ward 12.50 30.00
DB David Bolland 4.00 10.00
DD Devan Dubnyk 6.00 15.00
DG Denis Grebeshkov 4.00 10.00
DK Duncan Keith 4.00 10.00
DL David LeNeveu 4.00 10.00
DM Duncan Milroy 4.00 10.00
DO Doug O'Brien 4.00 10.00
DP Dan Paille 4.00 10.00
DS David Shantz 4.00 10.00
DW Dennis Wideman 4.00 10.00
EF Eric Fehr 8.00 20.00
EG Ed Giacomin 15.00 40.00
EH Eric Himelfarb 6.00 15.00
EL Elmer Lach 10.00 25.00
FM Frank Mahovlich 8.00 20.00
FN Filip Novak 4.00 10.00
FS Fredrik Sjostrom 4.00 10.00
FT Fedor Tjutin 6.00 15.00
GB Gilbert Brule 15.00 40.00
GC Gerry Cheevers 8.00 20.00
GF Grant Fuhr 10.00 25.00
GH Glenn Hall 10.00 25.00
GL Guy Lafleur 10.00 25.00
GP Gilbert Perreault 10.00 25.00
GS Garrett Stafford 6.00 15.00
GW Greg Watson 4.00 10.00
HR Henri Richard 10.00 25.00
HT Hannu Toivonen 10.00 25.00
JB Jozef Balej 6.00 15.00
JC Jeff Carter 25.00 60.00
JD Jeff Drouin-Deslauriers 6.00 15.00
JE Julien Ellis-Plante 6.00 15.00
JG Jeff Glass 10.00 25.00
JM Jay McClement 4.00 10.00
JN Jiri Novotny 4.00 10.00
JP Jean-Marc Pelletier 4.00 10.00
JR Jean Ratelle 8.00 20.00
JS Jeff Schultz 4.00 10.00
JW Jeff Woywitka 6.00 15.00
KC Kyle Chipchura 8.00 20.00
KG Kelly Guard 4.00 10.00
KM Kiel McLeod 4.00 10.00
LM Lanny McDonald 8.00 20.00
LR Liam Reddox 4.00 10.00
LW Lorne Worsley 10.00 25.00
MC Marcel Goc 8.00 20.00
MF1 Marc-Andre Fleury 12.50 30.00
MF2 Marc-Andre Fleury 12.50 30.00
MF3 Marc-Andre Fleury 12.50 30.00
MF4 Marc-Andre Fleury 12.50 30.00
MH Martin Houle 6.00 15.00
MK Martin Kariya 10.00 25.00
ML Matt Lashoff 4.00 10.00
MO Michel Ouellet 6.00 15.00
MP Martin Podlesak 4.00 10.00
MR Mike Richards 20.00 50.00
MS Marc Staal 12.00 30.00
PB Peter Budaj 4.00 10.00
PC Paulo Colaiacovo 4.00 10.00
PE Phil Esposito 12.50 30.00
PL Pascal Leclaire 4.00 10.00
PO Patrick O'Sullivan 12.50 30.00
PR Philippe Roberge 4.00 10.00
PT Petr Taticek 4.00 10.00
RB Ray Bourque 15.00 40.00
RE Ray Emery 4.00 10.00
RG Ryan Garlock 4.00 10.00
RK Ryan Kesler 4.00 10.00
RM Ryan Miller 10.00 25.00
RV Rogie Vachon 8.00 20.00
SB Shawn Belle 6.00 15.00
SC Sidney Crosby 150.00 350.00
SM Stan Mikita 8.00 20.00
SR Stefan Ruzicka 4.00 10.00
SS Serge Savard 10.00 25.00
SU Scottie Upshall 4.00 10.00
TB Tim Brent 4.00 10.00
TE Tony Esposito 15.00 40.00
TF Tomas Fleischmann 4.00 10.00
TK Tomas Kopecky 4.00 10.00
TL Tom Lawson 4.00 10.00
TS Timofei Shishkanov 4.00 10.00
VH Vic Hadfield 8.00 20.00
VM Vaclav Meidl 4.00 10.00
VT Vladislav Tretiak 15.00 40.00
VU Victor Uchevatov 4.00 10.00
WC Wayne Cashman 6.00 15.00
WW Wojtek Wolski 12.50 30.00
YC Yvan Cournoyer 10.00 25.00
YL Yanick Lehoux 4.00 10.00
ABA Andy Bathgate 8.00 20.00
BBA Bill Barber 6.00 15.00
BBI Bryan Bickell 4.00 10.00
BCL Bobby Clarke 12.50 30.00
BPA Brad Park 6.00 15.00
CCA Chris Campoli 4.00 10.00
CPE Corey Perry 15.00 40.00
DGR Danny Groulx 4.00 10.00
DPH Dion Phaneuf 40.00 100.00
DPO Denis Potvin 10.00 25.00
GLA Guy Lapointe 8.00 20.00
GST Grant Stevenson 4.00 10.00
JBE Jean Beliveau 12.50 30.00
JBO Johnny Bower 8.00 20.00
JBU Johnny Bucyk 6.00 15.00
JGO Josh Gorges 4.00 10.00
JPE Justin Peters 6.00 15.00
JWI James Wisniewski 4.00 10.00
KKL Kevin Klein 4.00 10.00
LRO Larry Robinson 8.00 20.00
MBO Mike Bossy 6.00 15.00
MDI Marcel Dionne 10.00 25.00
MFO Matt Foy 4.00 10.00
MGL Mike Glumac 4.00 10.00
MGR Mike Green 4.00 10.00
MLE Mario Lemieux 40.00 100.00
MPO Marc-Antoine Pouliot 15.00 40.00
MSC Milt Schmidt 8.00 20.00
MSP Martin St. Pierre 4.00 10.00
PCO Paul Coffey 10.00 25.00
PRO Patrick Roy 60.00 125.00
RGE Ryan Getzlaf 25.00 60.00
RKE Red Kelly 6.00 15.00
RSC Robbie Schremp 12.50 30.00
SBE Steve Bernier 8.00 20.00
SSH Steve Shutt 8.00 20.00
TLI Ted Lindsay 8.00 20.00
WCL Wendel Clark 10.00 25.00
U-JBW Jay Bouwmeester 6.00 15.00
U-PSR Peter Sarno 6.00 15.00
U-MCA Mike Cammalleri 4.00 10.00
U-PBE Patrice Bergeron 10.00 25.00
U-MKO Mikko Koivu 6.00 15.00
U-AN Antero Niittymaki 10.00 25.00
U-DH Dan Hamhuis 4.00 10.00
U-DR Derek Roy 6.00 15.00
U-ES Eric Staal 12.50 30.00
U-JH Jiri Hudler 8.00 20.00
U-KW Kyle Wellwood 15.00 40.00
U-MD Maxime Daigneault 4.00 10.00
U-RS Rastislav Stana 6.00 15.00
U-RV Rene Vydareny 4.00 10.00
U-RW Ryan Whitney 4.00 10.00
U-SC2 Sidney Crosby 200.00 400.00
U-SW Stephen Weiss 4.00 10.00
U-TV Thomas Vanek 15.00 40.00
U-ZP Zach Parise 15.00 40.00
ABAB Anton Babchuk 4.00 10.00

2004-05 ITG Heroes and Prospects Combos

Cards 15-18 only available randomly in sets of ITG Heroes and Prospects Update.
CARDS 15-18 AVAIL. H&P UPDATE ONLY
CARDS 1-14 PRINT RUN 50 SETS
1 Marc-Andre Fleury/Kari Lehtonen 30.00 80.00
2 Sidney Crosby/Michel Ouellet 75.00 200.00
3 Devan Dubnyk/Ryan Miller 12.50 30.00
4 R.Getzlaf/B.Boyes 25.00 60.00
5 Brent Seabrook/Garrett Stafford 6.00 15.00
6 Dave Bolland/Kiel McLeod 6.00 15.00
7 Marc-Antoine Pouliot
Tomas Kopecky 8.00 20.00
8 Corey Perry/Scottie Upshall 15.00 40.00
9 Julien Ellis-Plante/Pascal Leclaire 12.50 30.00
10 Jeff Carter/Ray Emery 12.50 30.00
11 Patrick O'Sullivan/Ryan Kesler 12.50 30.00
12 Mike Richards/Mike Green 15.00 40.00
13 Kyle Chipchura/Dion Phaneuf 12.50 30.00
14 Braydon Coburn
Carlo Colaiacovo 15.00 40.00
15 Sidney Crosby 150.00 300.00
Alexander Ovechkin
16 S.Crosby/A.Ovechkin Emblms/20
17 S.Crosby/A.Ovechkin Nmbrs
18 S.Crosby/A.Ovechkin Gloves

2004-05 ITG Heroes and Prospects Complete Emblems

This 30-card memorabilia set featured the entire CHL emblem from the back of player jerseys. Each card was a 1/1.
STATED PRINT RUN 1 SET
NOT PRICED DUE TO SCARCITY
1 Devan Dubnyk
2 Mike Green
3 Corey Perry
4 Corey Locke
5 Kyle Chipchura
6 Mike Richards
7 Brent Seabrook
8 Eric Fehr
9 Anthony Stewart
10 Wojtek Wolski
11 Sidney Crosby
12 Marc-Andre Fleury
13 Colby Armstrong
14 Danny Groulx
15 Michael Garnett
16 Ryan Getzlaf
17 Adrian Foster
18 Eric Healey
19 Tomas Kopecky
20 David LeNeveu
21 Yanick Lehoux
22 Martin Podlesak
23 Matt Foy
24 Kiel McLeod
25 Michel Ouellet
26 Garrett Stafford
27 Grant Stevenson
28 Garth Murray
29 Peter Budaj
30 Brad Boyes

2004-05 ITG Heroes and Prospects Emblems

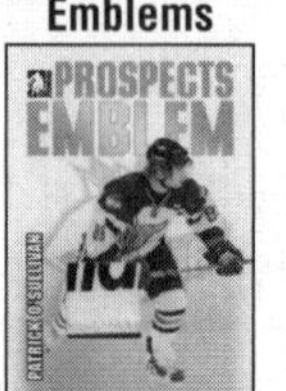

Cards 59-66 were only available randomly in the ITG Heroes and Prospects Update sets.
*EMBLEMS: X TO X BASIC JERSEYS
1-58 PRINT RUN 30 SETS
59-66 PRINT RUN 20 SETS
1-58 GOLD PRINT RUN 10 SETS
59-66 GOLD PRINT RUN 5 SETS
UNDER 25 NOT PRICED DUE TO SCARCITY

2004-05 ITG Heroes and Prospects First Overall

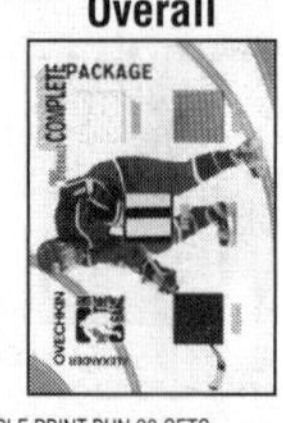

TRIPLE PRINT RUN 20 SETS
COMP.JSY/PKG. PRINT RUN 10 SETS
NOT PRICED DUE TO SCARCITY
1 Alexander Ovechkin/Triple Memorabilia/20
2 Alexander Ovechkin/Complete Jersey/10
3 Alexander Ovechkin/Complete Package/10

2004-05 ITG Heroes and Prospects Gloves

Available only in random sets of ITG Heroes and Prospects Update.
AVAIL. IN UPD.PACKS ONLY
PRINT RUN 50 SETS
GOLD PRINT RUN 10 SETS
GOLD NORT PRICED DUE TO SCARCITY
1 Sidney Crosby 60.00 150.00
SC Sidney Crosby AU

2004-05 ITG Heroes and Prospects He Shoots-He Scores Prizes

STATED PRINT RUN 20 SETS
NOT PRICED DUE TO SCARCITY
1 Marc-Andre Fleury/Kari Lehtonen
2 Sidney Crosby/Alexander Ovechkin
3 Marc-Andre Fleury/Patrick Roy
4 S.Crosby/M. Lemieux
5 Kari Lehtonen/Grant Fuhr
6 Alexander Ovechkin/Marcel Dionne
7 Sidney Crosby/Marc-Andre Fleury
8 Alexander Ovechkin/Eric Fehr
9 Kari Lehtonen/Michael Garnett
10 Ryan Getzlaf/Corey Perry
11 Brad Boyes/Andrew Raycroft
12 Brent Seabrook/David Bolland
13 Wojtek Wolski/Peter Budaj
14 Alexandre Picard/Pascal Leclaire
15 Tomas Kopecky/Danny Groulx
16 Devan Dubnyk/Marc-Antoine Pouliot
17 Anthony Stewart/Stephen Weiss
18 Patrick O'Sullivan/Matt Foy
19 Kyle Chipchura/Corey Locke
20 Scottie Upshall/Timofei Shishkanov
21 Adrian Foster/Ari Ahonen
22 Trent Hunter/Rick DiPietro
23 Fedor Tyutin/Garth Murray
24 Jason Spezza/Ray Emery
25 Jeff Carter/Mike Richards
26 David LeNeveu/Kiel McLeod
27 Grant Stevenson/Garrett Stafford
28 John Pohl/Jason Bacashihua
29 Carlo Colaiacovo/Mikael Tellqvist
30 Brandon Reid/Alex Auld
31 Yanick Lehoux/Denis Grebeshkov
32 Ryan Miller/Mika Noronen
33 Julien Ellis-Plante/Ryan Kesler
34 Maxime Ouellet/Rastislav Stana
35 Colby Armstrong/Michel Ouellet
36 Michael Ryder/Ron Hainsey
37 Jean-Marc Pelletier/Martin Podlesak
38 Ilja Bryzgalov/Mark Popovic
39 Martin Prusek/Julien Vauclair
40 Dion Phaneuf/Braydon Coburn

2004-05 ITG Heroes and Prospects Hero Memorabilia

STATED PRINT RUN 30 SETS
UNLESS OTHERWISE NOTED
1 Tony Esposito 8.00 20.00
2 Stan Mikita 8.00 20.00
3 Gump Worsley/10
4 Ray Bourque 12.50 30.00
5 Phil Esposito 15.00 40.00
6 Patrick Roy 50.00 125.00
7 Mike Bossy 15.00 40.00
8 Marcel Dionne 8.00 20.00
9 Larry Robinson 8.00 20.00
10 Johnny Bower 12.50 30.00
11 Jean Beliveau 25.00 60.00
12 Jacques Plante 25.00 60.00
13 Henri Richard 8.00 20.00
14 Mario Lemieux 40.00 100.00
15 Gilbert Perreault 12.50 30.00
16 Gerry Cheevers 15.00 40.00
17 Ed Giacomin 15.00 40.00
18 Denis Potvin 8.00 20.00
19 Cam Neely 40.00 100.00
20 Frank Mahovlich/10
21 Alex Delvecchio 15.00 40.00
22 Rogie Vachon 15.00 40.00
23 Serge Savard 15.00 40.00
24 Guy Lapointe 12.50 30.00
25 Bill Barber 12.50 30.00
26 Grant Fuhr
27 Ted Lindsay 25.00 60.00
28 Paul Coffey 15.00 40.00
29 Doug Harvey/10
30 Bobby Orr

2004-05 ITG Heroes and Prospects Jersey Autographs

STATED PRINT RUN 5 SETS
NOT PRICED DUE TO SCARCITY
1 Jiri Novotny
2 Marc-Andre Fleury
3 Corey Perry
4 Jeff Carter
5 Kari Lehtonen
6 David LeNeveu
7 Colby Armstrong
8 Adrian Foster
9 Ryan Miller
10 Grant Stevenson
11 Garrett Stafford
12 Michel Ouellet
13 Ray Emery
14 Fedor Tjutin
15 Brad Boyes
16 Marc-Andre Fleury
17 Eric Healey
18 Devan Dubnyk
19 Alexandre Picard
20 Patrick O'Sullivan
21 Corey Locke
22 Kyle Chipchura
23 Jean-Marc Pelletier
24 Mike Richards
25 Michael Ryder
26 Carlo Colaiacovo
37 Denis Grebeshkov
40 Kiel McLeod
41 Chris Kunitz
42 Timofei Shishkanov
43 Peter Budaj
44 Danny Groulx
45 Brent Seabrook
46 Dion Phaneuf
47 Eric Fehr
48 Yanick Lehoux
49 Ryan Getzlaf
50 Matt Foy
51 Marc-Antoine Pouliot
52 Tomas Kopecky
53 David Bolland
54 Wojtek Wolski
55 Sidney Crosby
56 Anthony Stewart
57 Alexander Ovechkin
58 Scottie Upshall

2004-05 ITG Heroes and Prospects Jerseys

Cards 59-66 were only available randomly in the ITG Heroes and Prospects Update sets.
*SINGLE COLOR SWATCH: .25X TO .75X

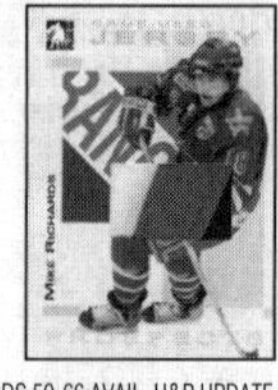

CARDS 59-66 AVAIL. H&P UPDATE ONLY
STATED PRINT RUN 90 SETS
GOLD PRINT RUN 10 SETS
GOLD NOT PRICED DUE TO SCARCITY
1 Jiri Novotny 4.00 10.00
2 Marc-Andre Fleury 15.00 40.00
3 Corey Perry 15.00 40.00
4 Jeff Carter 20.00 50.00
5 Kari Lehtonen 20.00 50.00
6 David LeNeveu 8.00 20.00
7 Colby Armstrong 12.00 30.00
8 Adrian Foster 4.00 10.00
9 Ryan Miller 10.00 25.00
10 Grant Stevenson 4.00 10.00
11 Garrett Stafford 4.00 10.00
12 Michel Ouellet 8.00 20.00
13 Ray Emery 6.00 15.00
14 Fedor Tjutin 4.00 10.00
15 Brad Boyes 6.00 15.00
16 Marc-Andre Fleury 15.00 40.00
17 Eric Healey 8.00 20.00
18 Devan Dubnyk 4.00 10.00
19 Alexandre Picard 10.00 25.00
20 Patrick O'Sullivan 10.00 25.00
21 Corey Locke 6.00 15.00
22 Kyle Chipchura 8.00 20.00
23 Jean-Marc Pelletier 8.00 20.00
24 Mike Richards 15.00 40.00
25 Michael Ryder 12.50 30.00
26 Carlo Colaiacovo 4.00 10.00
27 Garth Murray 4.00 10.00
28 John Pohl 4.00 10.00
29 Mark Popovic 4.00 10.00
30 Trent Hunter 6.00 15.00
31 Ron Hainsey 4.00 10.00
32 Tony Salmelainen 4.00 10.00
33 Jason Spezza 10.00 25.00
34 Fedor Fedorov 8.00 20.00
35 Denis Shvidki 4.00 10.00
36 Andrew Hutchinson 4.00 10.00
37 Denis Grebeshkov 4.00 10.00
38 Julien Vauclair 6.00 15.00
39 Brandon Reid 4.00 10.00
40 Kiel McLeod 4.00 10.00
41 Chris Kunitz 4.00 10.00
42 Timofei Shishkanov 4.00 10.00
43 Peter Budaj 4.00 10.00
44 Danny Groulx 4.00 10.00
45 Brent Seabrook 12.50 30.00
46 Dion Phaneuf 15.00 40.00
47 Eric Fehr 8.00 20.00
48 Yanick Lehoux 4.00 10.00
49 Ryan Getzlaf 15.00 40.00
50 Matt Foy 4.00 10.00
51 Marc-Antoine Pouliot 6.00 15.00
52 Tomas Kopecky 4.00 10.00
53 David Bolland 4.00 10.00
54 Wojtek Wolski 8.00 20.00
55 Sidney Crosby 75.00 150.00
56 Anthony Stewart 8.00 20.00
57 Alexander Ovechkin 40.00 100.00
58 Scottie Upshall 4.00 10.00
59 Alexander Ovechkin 40.00 100.00
61 Patrice Bergeron 8.00 20.00
62 Robbie Schremp 10.00 25.00
63 Ryan Whitney 6.00 15.00
64 Danny Syvret 6.00 15.00
65 Dany Roussin 4.00 10.00
66 Wojtek Wolski 8.00 20.00

2004-05 ITG Heroes and Prospects National Pride

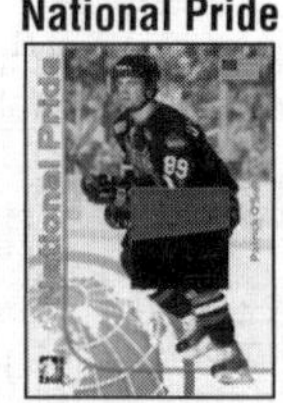

STATED PRINT RUN 50 SETS
1 Sidney Crosby 125.00 200.00
2 Jeff Carter 20.00 50.00
3 Jason Spezza 15.00 40.00
4 Alexander Ovechkin 40.00 100.00
5 Marc-Andre Fleury 25.00 60.00
6 Mike Richards 15.00 40.00
7 Kari Lehtonen 25.00 60.00
8 Patrick O'Sullivan 15.00 40.00

2004-05 ITG Heroes and Prospects Net Prospects

STATED PRINT RUN 60 SETS
GOLD PRINT RUN 20 SETS
GOLD NOT PRICED DUE TO SCARCITY
1 Kari Lehtonen 25.00 50.00
2 Marc-Andre Fleury 25.00 50.00
3 Andrew Raycroft 12.00 30.00
4 Rick DiPietro 6.00 15.00
5 Ilja Bryzgalov 6.00 15.00
6 Antero Niittymaki 12.00 30.00
7 Ryan Miller 12.00 30.00
8 Jason Bacashihua 10.00 25.00
9 Rastislav Stana 6.00 15.00
10 Philippe Sauve 6.00 15.00
11 Ray Emery 10.00 25.00
12 Ari Ahonen 6.00 15.00
13 Alex Auld 10.00 25.00
14 David LeNeveu 10.00 25.00
15 Neil Little 6.00 15.00
16 Tim Thomas 6.00 15.00
17 Devan Dubnyk 10.00 25.00
18 Jean-Marc Pelletier 6.00 15.00
19 Mathieu Garon 10.00 25.00
20 Marc-Andre Fleury 25.00 50.00
21 Michael Garnett 6.00 15.00
22 Sebastien Centomo 6.00 15.00
23 Peter Budaj 6.00 15.00
24 Sebastien Charpentier 6.00 15.00
25 Martin Prusek 6.00 15.00
26 Pascal Leclaire 10.00 25.00
27 Mikael Tellqvist 10.00 25.00
28 Reinhard Divis 6.00 15.00
29 Phil Osaer 6.00 15.00
30 Maxime Ouellet 6.00 15.00
31 Mika Noronen 6.00 15.00
32 Julien Ellis-Plante 10.00 25.00

2004-05 ITG Heroes and Prospects Numbers

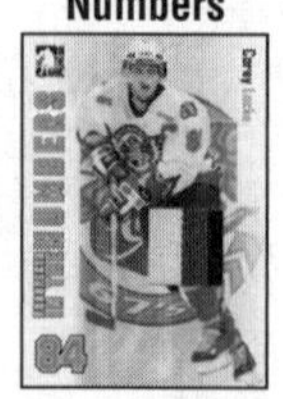

Cards 59-66 were only available randomly in the ITG Heroes and Prospects Update sets.
*NUMBERS: X TO X BASIC JERSEYS
1-58 PRINT RUN 25 SETS
59-66 PRINT RUN 10 SETS
1-58 GOLD PRINT RUN 10 SETS
59-66 GOLD PRINT RUN 5 SETS
UNDER 25 NOT PRICED DUE TO SCARCITY

2004-05 ITG Heroes and Prospects Numbers Gold

STATED PRINT RUN 5 SETS
NOT PRICED DUE TO SCARCITY

2004-05 ITG Heroes and Prospects Top Prospects

1 Wojtek Wolski 1.25 3.00
2 David Shantz .75 2.00
3 Adam Berti .75 2.00
4 Cam Barker 1.25 3.00
5 Dave Bolland .75 2.00
6 Jeff Schultz .75 2.00
7 Alexandre Picard 1.25 3.00
8 Julien Ellis-Plante .75 2.00
9 Vaclav Meidl .75 2.00
10 Eric Fehr .75 2.00
11 Robbie Schremp 1.25 3.00
12 Andrew Ladd 1.25 3.00
13 Devan Dubnyk .75 2.00
14 Boris Valabik .75 2.00
15 Justin Peters .75 2.00
16 Mike Green .75 2.00
17 Bryan Bickell .75 2.00
18 Marc-Andre Fleury 2.00 5.00
19 Anthony Stewart 1.25 3.00
20 Ryan Getzlaf 1.25 3.00

2005-06 ITG Heroes and Prospects

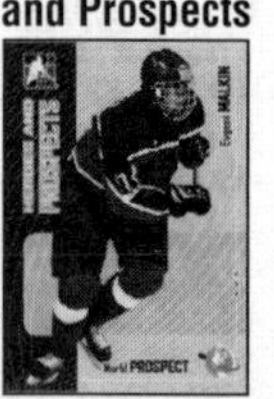

COMPLETE SET (430) 40.00 100.00
COMP.SERIES 1 SET(180) 15.00 40.00
COMP.SERIES 2 SET (200) 15.00 40.00
COMP. UPDATE SET (50) 10.00 20.00
1 Martin Brodeur .60 1.50
2 Bobby Hull .40 1.00
3 Glenn Hall .40 1.00
4 Harry Howell .30 .75

5 Doug Gilmour .30 .75
6 Phil Esposito .40 1.00
7 Red Kelly .40 1.00
8 Cam Neely .40 1.00
9 Jean Beliveau .40 1.00
10 Johnny Bower .40 1.00
11 Milt Schmidt .20 .50
12 Jose Theodore .40 1.00
13 Ray Bourque .40 1.00
14 Dave Keon .40 1.00
15 Henri Richard .30 .75
16 Marcel Dionne .30 .75
17 Paul Henderson .30 .75
18 Wendel Clark .30 .75
19 Steve Yzerman .75 2.00
20 Vladislav Tretiak .30 .75
21 Brett Hull .40 1.00
22 Mike Bossy .30 .75
23 Tony Esposito .40 1.00
24 Bobby Clarke .40 1.00
25 Brian Leetch .40 1.00
26 Guy Lafleur .40 1.00
27 Grant Fuhr .40 1.00
28 Pat LaFontaine .20 .50
29 Jean Ratelle .20 .50
30 Bernie Parent .40 1.00
31 Ed Giacomin .30 .75
32 Darryl Sittler .40 1.00
33 Patrick Roy .75 2.00
34 Dino Ciccarelli .20 .50
35 Frank Mahovlich .40 1.00
36 Stan Mikita .30 .75
37 Neal Broten .20 .50
38 Ted Lindsay .30 .75
39 Derek Sanderson .30 .75
40 Mario Lemieux .75 2.00
41 Cam Ward .40 1.00
42 Brandon Bochenski .20 .50
43 Steve Ott .20 .50
44 Kevin Bieksa .20 .50
45 Ryane Clowe .20 .50
46 Jason Spezza .40 1.00
47 Adam Hauser .30 .75
48 Derek Roy .30 .75
49 R.J. Umberger .30 .75
50 Alex Auld .30 .75
51 Joey MacDonald .30 .75
52 Denis Hamel .20 .50
53 Yann Danis .30 .75
54 Brent Burns .30 .75
55 Josh Harding .30 .75
56 Jason LaBarbera .30 .75
57 Antero Niittymaki .40 1.00
58 Mike Egener .20 .50
59 Thomas Vanek .40 1.00
60 Rene Bourque .30 .75
61 Brad Boyes .30 .75
62 Kari Lehtonen .40 1.00
63 Jeff Carter .60 1.50
64 Ryan Kesler .30 .75
65 Cam Barker .30 .75
66 Ray Emery .30 .75
67 Michel Ouellet .20 .50
68 Andrew Hutchinson .20 .50
69 Mike Richards .40 1.00
70 Yanick Lehoux .20 .50
71 Lawrence Nycholat .20 .50
72 Jay Bouwmeester .20 .50
73 Ryan Whitney .30 .75
74 Zach Parise .40 1.00
75 Jordin Tootoo .40 1.00
76 Joni Pitkanen .30 .75
77 Chris Bourque .30 .75
78 Mikko Koivu .40 1.00
79 Eric Nystrom .20 .50
80 Mathieu Garon .30 .75
81 Patrice Bergeron .40 1.00
82 Eric Staal .60 1.50
83 Dustin Brown .30 .75
84 Marc-Andre Fleury .60 1.50
85 Marek Svatos .30 .75
86 Steve Eminger .20 .50
87 Andy Hilbert .20 .50
88 Chris Campoli .20 .50
89 Pascal Leclaire .30 .75
90 Anton Volchenkov .20 .50
91 Corey Locke .20 .50
92 Ryan Miller .40 1.00
93 Mike Cammalleri .20 .50
94 Simon Gamache .20 .50
95 Chuck Kobasew .30 .75
96 Christian Ehrhoff .20 .50
97 Hannu Toivonen .40 1.00
98 Mike Zigomanis .20 .50
99 Niklas Kronwall .20 .50
100 Patrick Sharp .20 .50
101 Ryan Suter .30 .75
102 Michael Leighton .30 .75
103 Denis Grebeshkov .20 .50
104 Dan Hamhuis .20 .50
105 Sidney Crosby 3.00 8.00
106 Alexander Svitov .20 .50
107 Al Montoya .40 1.00
108 Carlo Colaiacovo .20 .50
109 Alexander Ovechkin 1.50 4.00
110 Evgeni Malkin 2.00 5.00
111 John Tavares 6.00 15.00
112 Bobby Ryan .40 1.00
113 Steve Downie .60 1.50
114 Adam McQuaid .20 .50
115 Robbie Schremp .60 1.50
116 Jordan Staal 1.25 3.00
117 Matt Lashoff .30 .75
118 Ryan O'Marra .40 1.00
119 James Neal .20 .50
120 Bryan Little .30 .75
121 David Bolland .30 .75
122 Evan McGrath .30 .75
123 Kevin Lalande .20 .50
124 Radek Smolenak .20 .50
125 Marc Staal .60 1.50
126 Michael Blunden .20 .50
127 Tom Pyatt .20 .50
128 Daren Machesney .30 .75
129 Evan Brophey .20 .50
130 Jakub Kindl .20 .50
131 Ryan Parent .30 .75
132 Daniel Ryder .20 .50
133 Matt Pelech .20 .50
134 Benoit Pouliot .40 1.00
135 Derick Brassard .60 1.50
136 Brad Marchand .20 .50
137 Alexander Radulov .75 2.00
138 Marc-Andre Cliche .30 .75
139 Luc Bourdon .30 .75
140 David Krejci .20 .50
141 Marek Zagrapan .20 .50
142 Chad Denny .20 .50
143 James Sheppard .30 .75
144 Jean-Philippe Levasseur .30 .75
145 Alex Bourret .20 .50
146 Kristopher Letang .30 .75
147 Pier-Olivier Pelletier .30 .75
148 Jean-Philippe Paquet .20 .50
149 Marc-Edouard Vlasic .40 1.00
150 Nicolas Blanchard .20 .50
151 Guillaume Latendresse .60 1.50
152 Jonathan Bernier .60 1.50
153 Oskars Bartulis .20 .50
154 Corey Perry .40 1.00
155 Alexandre Vincent .20 .50
156 Marc-Andre Gragnani .20 .50
157 Carey Price 1.25 3.00
158 Brett Sutter .20 .50
159 Angelo Esposito 2.00 5.00
160 Devin Setoguchi .30 .75
161 Shea Weber .20 .50
162 Tyler Plante .30 .75
163 Kris Russell .20 .50
164 Gilbert Brule .60 1.50
165 Brendan Mikkelson .20 .50
166 Dustin Kohn .20 .50
167 Chris Durand .20 .50
168 Kristofer Westblom .20 .50
169 Blair Jones .20 .50
170 Raymond Macias .20 .50
171 Michael Sauer .20 .50
172 Brodie Dupont .20 .50
173 Ben Maxwell .20 .50
174 Kenndal McArdle .20 .50
175 Matt Kassian .20 .50
176 J.D. Watt .30 .75
177 Scott Jackson .20 .50
178 Devan Dubnyk .30 .75
179 Tyler Mosienko .30 .75
180 Cody Bass .20 .50
181 Martin Brodeur .60 1.50
182 Ray Bourque .40 1.00
183 Steve Yzerman .50 1.25
184 Dany Heatley .30 .75
185 Herb Carnegie .75 2.00
186 Jim Craig .40 1.00
187 Gilbert Perreault .25 .60
188 Ron Hextall .20 .50
189 Gerry Cheevers .20 .50
190 Yvan Cournoyer .30 .75
191 Larry Robinson .30 .75
192 Borje Salming .30 .75
193 Ted Kennedy .20 .50
194 Rod Gilbert .20 .50
195 Patrick Roy .60 1.50
196 Mario Lemieux .75 2.00
197 Eric Lindros .30 .75
198 Ilya Kovalchuk .30 .75
199 Tod Sloan .20 .50
200 Mark Howe .20 .50
201 Erik Westrum .20 .50
202 Chris Madden .20 .50
203 Alexandre Picard .40 1.00
204 Jeff Tambellini .20 .50
205 Marc-Antoine Pouliot .30 .75
206 Brian Finley .20 .50
207 Sean Bergenheim .30 .75
208 Ryan Shannon .20 .50
209 Clarke MacArthur .20 .50
210 Nicklas Bergfors .30 .75
211 Noah Welch .30 .75
212 Mark Hartigan .20 .50
213 Dan DaSilva .20 .50
214 Eric Fehr .20 .50
215 Shawn Belle .20 .50
216 Joey Tenute .20 .50
217 Maxime Ouellet .20 .50
218 Yan Stastny .20 .50
219 Petr Taticek .20 .50
220 Ladislav Smid .30 .75
221 Curtis Sanford .30 .75
222 Erik Christensen .20 .50
223 Tyler Redenbach .20 .50
224 Roman Voloshenko .20 .50
225 Dustin Penner .40 1.00
226 Rejean Beauchemin .20 .50
227 Martin St. Pierre .20 .50
228 Tim Gleason .20 .50
229 Brent Krahn .20 .50
230 Jason Pominville .30 .75
231 Andrei Kostitsyn .20 .50
232 Steve Gainey .30 .75
233 Pekka Rinne .30 .75
234 Nigel Dawes .20 .50
235 Braydon Coburn .30 .75
236 Corey Crawford .30 .75
237 Ryan Stone .40 1.00
238 Jeremy Colliton .20 .50
239 Ron Hainsey .20 .50
240 Nolan Schaefer .20 .50
241 Jason Bacashihua .30 .75
242 Geoff Platt .20 .50
243 Chad Larose .20 .50
244 Drew MacIntyre .20 .50
245 Peter Sejna .20 .50
246 Ryan Vesce .20 .50
247 Brian Pothier .20 .50
248 Colin Murphy .20 .50
249 Curtis McElhinney .20 .50
250 Mike Glumac .20 .50
251 Lauri Tukonen .20 .50
252 Nathan Marsters .20 .50
253 Matt Ellison .20 .50
254 Kurtis Foster .20 .50
255 Jean-Francois Jacques .20 .50
256 Dmitri Patzold .30 .75
257 John Pohl .20 .50
258 Alexander Perezhogin .20 .50
259 Nathan Paetsch .20 .50
260 Kelly Guard .20 .50
261 Andrew Wozniewski .20 .50
262 Tomi Maki .20 .50
263 Tomas Plekanec .20 .50
264 Noah Clarke .20 .50
265 Steve Bernier .40 1.00
266 Gerald Coleman .30 .75
267 Jiri Hudler .40 1.00
268 Daniel Carcillo .20 .50
269 Bruno Gervais .20 .50
270 Dany Sabourin .20 .50
271 Junior Lessard .20 .50
272 Thomas Pock .20 .50
273 Andy Chiodo .30 .75
274 Vitaly Kolesnik .20 .50
275 Patrick Eaves .20 .50
276 Petr Prucha .40 1.00
277 Henrik Lundqvist .75 2.00
278 Evgeni Malkin 2.00 5.00
279 Alexander Ovechkin 1.50 4.00
280 Nick Foligno .20 .50
281 Chris Stewart .20 .50
282 Ryan MacDonald .20 .50
283 Liam Reddox .20 .50
284 Tyler Kennedy .20 .50
285 Dylan Hunter .20 .50
286 Bob Sanguinetti .20 .50
287 Dan LaCosta .30 .75
288 Derek Joslin .20 .50
289 Ryan Daniels .20 .50
290 Sergei Kostitsyn .20 .50
291 Jonathan D'Aversa .20 .50
292 Cory Emmerton .20 .50
293 Dan Turple .20 .50
294 John de Gray .20 .50
295 Bobby Hughes .20 .50
296 Rafael Rotter .20 .50
297 Justin Garay .20 .50
298 Marek Horsky .20 .50
299 Joe Ryan .20 .50
300 Ondrej Pavelec .20 .50
301 Olivier Latendresse .20 .50
302 Maxime Boisclair .20 .50
303 Mathieu Roy .40 1.00
304 Ryan Hillier .20 .50
305 Stanislav Lascek .20 .50
306 Julien Ellis .40 1.00
307 Mathieu Carle .20 .50
308 Alex Grant .20 .50
309 David Desharnais .20 .50
310 Bryce Swan .20 .50
311 Jeff Schultz .20 .50
312 Zach Hamill .20 .50
313 A.J. Thelen .20 .50
314 Brandon Sutter .20 .50
315 Brady Calla .20 .50
316 Troy Brouwer .20 .50
317 Mark Fistric .20 .50
318 Codey Burki .20 .50
319 Kevin Armstrong .20 .50
320 Michael Funk .20 .50
321 Ty Wishart .20 .50
322 Dustin Boyd .20 .50
323 Peter Mueller .60 1.50
324 Wacey Rabbit .30 .75
325 Andy Rogers .20 .50
326 Leland Irving .60 1.50
327 Logan Stephenson .20 .50
328 Kyle Chipchura .40 1.00
329 Ryan White .30 .75
330 Blake Comeau .20 .50
331 Justin Pogge .75 2.00
332 Corey Perry .40 1.00
333 Ryan Getzlaf .40 1.00
334 Dion Phaneuf .75 2.00
335 Cam Ward .40 1.00
336 Mike Richards .40 1.00
337 Sidney Crosby 3.00 8.00
338 Mario Lemieux .75 2.00
339 Guy Lafleur .20 .50
340 Jeff Carter .40 1.00
341 Eric Lindros .30 .75
342 Jose Theodore .40 1.00
343 Mike Cammalleri .20 .50
344 Jason Spezza .25 .60
345 Patrick Roy .60 1.50
346 Brett Hull .30 .75
347 Ron Hextall .20 .50
348 Kari Lehtonen .25 .60
349 Keith Ballard .20 .50
350 Greg Hogeboom .20 .50
351 Hugh Jessiman .20 .50
352 Chris Beckford-Tseu .40 1.00
353 Mike Brodeur .20 .50
354 Andy Franck .20 .50
355 Brett Jaeger .20 .50
356 D'Arcy McConvey .20 .50
357 Chris Durno .20 .50
358 Rosario Ruggeri .20 .50
359 Garett Bembridge .20 .50
360 Mike Morrison .20 .50
361 Sidney Crosby 3.00 8.00
362 Alexander Ovechkin 1.50 4.00
363 Marek Svatos .20 .50
364 Mike Richards .40 1.00
365 Jeff Carter .50 1.25
366 Eric Nystrom .20 .50
367 Evgeni Malkin 2.00 5.00
368 Ray Emery .20 .50
369 Thomas Vanek .50 1.25
370 Eric Staal .30 .75
371 John Tavares 2.00 5.00
372 Bobby Ryan .40 1.00
373 Angelo Esposito 1.50 4.00
374 Al Montoya .60 1.50
375 Patrick O'Sullivan .30 .75
376 Dion Phaneuf .75 2.00
377 Corey Perry .40 1.00
378 Henrik Lundqvist .75 2.00
379 Andrew Ladd .30 .75
380 Wojtek Wolski .50 1.25
381 Staffan Kronwall .20 .50
382 Ben Walter .30 .75
383 Jamie Holden .20 .50
384 Danny Richmond .20 .50
385 Tomas Fleischmann .20 .50
386 Alexandre Picard .20 .50
387 Jeff Glass .40 1.00
388 Josh Hennessy .20 .50
389 Brad Winchester .30 .75
390 Richie Regehr .20 .50
391 Alexandre Burrows .20 .50
392 Robert Nilsson .30 .75
393 Mark Stuart .30 .75
394 Filip Novak .30 .75
395 Stefan Ruzicka .30 .75
396 Loui Eriksson .30 .75
397 Jay McClement .20 .50
398 Ryan Callahan .20 .50
399 Ben Shutron .20 .50
400 Logan Couture .60 1.50
401 Adam Dennis .20 .50
402 Justin Donati .20 .50
403 Luch Aquino .20 .50
404 John Armstrong .20 .50
405 Matt Beleskey .20 .50
406 Jamie McGinn .20 .50
407 Matthew Corrente .20 .50
408 Theo Peckham .20 .50
409 Mike Weber .20 .50
410 Cal Clutterbuck .30 .75
411 Jean-Christophe Blanchard .20 .50
412 Francois Bouchard .20 .50
413 Claude Giroux .40 1.00
414 Ilya Ejov .20 .50
415 Benjamin Breault .20 .50
416 Keith Yandle .20 .50
417 Ivan Vishnevskiy .20 .50
418 Ondrej Fiala .30 .75
419 Michael Grabner .40 1.00
420 Riley Holzapfel .20 .50
421 Lukas Bohunicky .20 .50
422 Tysen Dowzak .20 .50
423 Colton Yellow Horn .40 1.00
424 Dustin Slade .20 .50
425 Bud Holloway .20 .50
426 David Ruzicka .20 .50
427 Marek Schwarz .30 .75
428 Michael Frolik .60 1.50
429 Cristobal Huet .40 1.00
430 Ray Emery .30 .75

2005-06 ITG Heroes and Prospects AHL Grads

PRINT RUN 70 SETS
GOLD PRINT RUN 10 SETS
GOLD NOT PRICED DUE TO SCARCITY
AG-1 Jason Spezza 6.00 15.00
AG-2 Brett Hull 6.00 15.00
AG-3 Patrick Roy 15.00 40.00
AG-4 Kari Lehtonen 8.00 20.00
AG-5 Keith Ballard 4.00 10.00
AG-6 Jose Theodore 8.00 20.00
AG-7 Ron Hextall 6.00 15.00
AG-8 Mike Cammalleri 4.00 10.00
AG-9 Cam Ward 8.00 20.00

2005-06 ITG Heroes and Prospects Aspiring

PRINT RUN 50 SETS
ASP1 P.Roy/C.Price 40.00 80.00
ASP2 M.Lemieux/E.Malkin 60.00 150.00
ASP3 D.Keon/P.O'Sullivan 15.00 40.00
ASP4 B.Mosienko/T.Mosienko 10.00 25.00
ASP5 P.Coffey/J.Pitkanen 10.00 25.00
ASP6 C.Neely/P.Bergeron 15.00 40.00
ASP7 M.Bossy/R.Schremp 10.00 25.00
ASP8 P.LaFontaine/B.Ryan 10.00 25.00
ASP9 R.Bourque/S.Weber 15.00 40.00
ASP10 B.Parent/A.Niittymaki 15.00 40.00
ASP11 M.Dionne/D.Brown 10.00 25.00
ASP12 B.Clarke/J.Carter 15.00 40.00
ASP13 G.Lafleur/G.Latendresse 15.00 40.00
ASP14 J.Beliveau/F.Bouchard 15.00 40.00
ASP15 D.Sittler/E.Staal 15.00 40.00
ASP16 B.Hull/J.Spezza 20.00 50.00
ASP17 S.Yzerman/B.Pouliot 20.00 50.00
ASP18 M.Brodeur/M.Fleury 25.00 60.00
ASP19 M.Lemieux/S.Crosby 100.00 200.00
ASP20 Mario Lemieux 60.00 150.00
Alexander Ovechkin

2005-06 ITG Heroes and Prospects Autographs

DUAL PRINT RUN 15 SETS
DUALS NOT PRICED DUE TO SCARCITY
A-RSC Robbie Schremp 10.00 25.00
A-AA Alex Auld 6.00 15.00
A-AB Alex Bourret 5.00 12.00
A-AH Adam Hauser 5.00
A-AM Al Montoya 10.00 25.00
A-AN Antero Niittymaki 8.00 20.00
A-AO Alexander Ovechkin 75.00 200.00
A-AR Alexander Radulov 20.00 50.00
A-AS Alexander Svitov 4.00 10.00
A-AV Anton Volchenkov 4.00 10.00
A-BB Brad Boyes 4.00 10.00
A-BD Brodie Dupont 4.00 10.00
A-BJ Blair Jones 4.00 10.00
A-BL Brian Leetch 6.00 15.00
A-BP Benoit Pouliot 6.00 15.00
A-BR Bobby Ryan 12.00 30.00
A-BS Brett Sutter 5.00 12.00
A-CB Cam Barker 6.00 15.00
A-CC Chris Campoli 4.00 10.00
A-CD Chad Denny 4.00 10.00
A-CK Chuck Kobasew 4.00 10.00
A-CL Corey Locke 4.00 10.00
A-CN Cam Neely 12.50 30.00
A-CP Carey Price 20.00 50.00
A-CW Cam Ward 15.00 40.00
A-DB David Bolland 4.00 10.00
A-DC Dino Ciccarelli 4.00 10.00
A-DD Devan Dubnyk 6.00 15.00
A-DG Denis Grebeshkov 4.00 10.00
A-DH Denis Hamel 4.00 10.00
A-DK Dave Keon 25.00 60.00
A-DR Daniel Ryder 4.00 10.00
A-DS Darryl Sittler 8.00 20.00
A-EB Evan Brophey 4.00 10.00
A-EG Ed Giacomin 12.00 30.00
A-EM Evan McGrath 4.00 10.00
A-EN Eric Nystrom 4.00 10.00
A-ES Eric Staal 12.00 30.00
A-FM Frank Mahovlich 8.00 20.00
A-GB Gilbert Brule 12.00 30.00
A-GF Grant Fuhr 8.00 20.00
A-GH Glenn Hall 10.00 25.00
A-GL Guillaume Latendresse 15.00 40.00
A-HH Harry Howell 5.00 12.00
A-HR Henri Richard 10.00 25.00
A-HT Hannu Toivonen 10.00 25.00
A-JB Jean Beliveau 12.50 30.00
A-JC Jeff Carter 12.00 30.00
A-JH Josh Harding 8.00 20.00
A-JK Jakub Kindl 4.00 10.00
A-JM Joey MacDonald 6.00 15.00
A-JN James Neal 5.00 12.00
A-JR Jean Ratelle 8.00 20.00
A-JT John Tavares 150.00 250.00
A-KR Kris Russell 5.00 12.00
A-KW Kristofer Westblom 4.00 10.00
A-LB Luc Bourdon 8.00 20.00
A-LN Lawrence Nycholat 4.00 10.00
A-MB Martin Brodeur 40.00 80.00
A-MC Mike Cammalleri 5.00 12.00
A-MD Marcel Dionne 6.00 15.00
A-ME Mike Egener 4.00 10.00
A-MG Mathieu Garon 6.00 15.00
A-MK Mikko Koivu 8.00 20.00
A-ML Mario Lemieux 40.00 100.00
A-MO Michel Ouellet 6.00 15.00
A-MP Matt Pelech 4.00 10.00
A-MR Mike Richards 10.00 25.00
A-MZ Marek Zagrapan 4.00 10.00
A-NB Neal Broten 6.00 15.00
A-OB Oksars Bartulis 4.00 10.00
A-PE Phil Esposito
A-PH Paul Henderson 6.00 15.00
A-PL Pascal Leclaire 5.00 12.00
A-PR Patrick Roy 40.00 100.00
A-PS Patrick Sharp 5.00 12.00
A-RB Raymond Bourque 15.00 40.00
A-RC Ryane Clowe 5.00 12.00
A-RE Ray Emery 6.00 15.00
A-RK Red Kelly 6.00 15.00
A-RM Raymond Macias 4.00 10.00
A-RO Ryan O'Marra 5.00 12.00
A-RP Ryan Parent 5.00 12.00
A-RS Radek Smolenak 4.00 10.00
A-SC Sidney Crosby 100.00 250.00
A-SD Steve Downie 10.00 25.00
A-SE Steve Eminger 6.00 15.00
A-SG Simon Gamache 4.00 10.00
A-SJ Scott Jackson 4.00 10.00
A-SM Stan Mikita 8.00 20.00
A-SO Steve Ott 5.00 12.00
A-SW Shea Weber 6.00 15.00
A-SY Steve Yzerman 30.00 80.00
A-TE Tony Esposito 8.00 20.00
A-TL Ted Lindsay 6.00 15.00
A-TM Tyler Mosienko 4.00 10.00
A-TP Tom Pyatt 4.00 10.00
A-TV Thomas Vanek 15.00 30.00
A-VT Vladislav Tretiak 15.00 40.00
A-WC Wendel Clark 10.00 25.00
A-YD Yann Danis 6.00 15.00
A-YL Yanick Lehoux 4.00 10.00
A-ZP Zach Parise 8.00 20.00
A-AHI Andy Hilbert 4.00 10.00
A-AHU Andrew Hutchinson 4.00 10.00
A-AMQ Adam McQuaid 4.00 10.00
A-AVI Alexandre Vincent 4.00 10.00
A-BBO Brandon Bochenski 5.00 12.00
A-BBU Brent Burns 5.00 12.00
A-BCL Bobby Clarke 12.50 30.00
A-BLI Bryan Little 8.00 20.00
A-BMA Brad Marchand 5.00 12.00
A-BMI Brendan Mikkelson 4.00 10.00
A-BMX Ben Maxwell 4.00 10.00
A-BOH Bobby Hull 15.00 40.00
A-BPA Bernie Parent 12.50 30.00
A-BRH Brett Hull 15.00 40.00
A-CBA Cody Bass 6.00 15.00
A-CBQ Chris Bourque 8.00 20.00
A-CCO Carlo Colaiacovo 4.00 10.00
A-CDU Chris Durand 4.00 10.00
A-CEO Christian Ehrhoff 4.00 10.00
A-CPE Corey Perry 10.00 25.00
A-DBN Dustin Brown 6.00 15.00
A-DBR Derick Brassard 8.00 20.00
A-DGI Doug Gilmour 6.00 15.00
A-DHA Dan Hamhuis 5.00 12.00
A-DKO Dustin Kohn 5.00 12.00
A-DKR David Krejci 5.00 12.00
A-DMA Daren Machesney 4.00 10.00
A-DRY Derek Roy 6.00 15.00
A-DSA Derek Sanderson 6.00 15.00
A-DSE Devin Setoguchi 6.00 15.00
A-EMA Evgeni Malkin 75.00 175.00
A-GLF Guy Lafleur 8.00 20.00
A-JBE Jonathan Bernier 10.00 25.00
A-JBO Jay Bouwmeester 8.00 20.00
A-JBW Johnny Bower 8.00 20.00
A-JDW J.D. Watt 4.00 10.00
A-JLB Jason LaBarbera 4.00 10.00
A-JPI Joni Pitkanen 4.00 10.00
A-JPL Jean-Philippe Levasseur 4.00 10.00
A-JPP Jean-Philippe Paquet 4.00 10.00
A-JSH James Sheppard 6.00 15.00
A-JST Jordan Staal 40.00 100.00
A-JTH Jose Theodore
A-JTO Jordin Tootoo 8.00 20.00
A-KBI Kevin Bieksa 5.00 12.00
A-KLA Kevin Lalande 4.00 10.00
A-KLT Kristopher Letang 6.00 15.00
A-KMC Kenndal McArdle 5.00 12.00
A-MAC Marc-Andre Cliche 4.00 10.00
A-MAF Marc-Andre Fleury 10.00 25.00
A-MAG Marc-Andre Gragnani 4.00 10.00
A-MBL Michael Blunden 5.00 12.00
A-MBO Mike Bossy 6.00 15.00
A-MEV Marc-Edouard Vlasic 8.00 20.00
A-MKA Matt Kassian 4.00 10.00
A-MLF Matt Lashoff 5.00 12.00
A-MLN Michael Leighton 5.00 12.00
A-MSH Milt Schmidt 6.00 15.00
A-MSR Michael Sauer 4.00 10.00
A-MST Marc Staal 10.00 25.00
A-MSV Marek Svatos 8.00 20.00
A-MZI Mike Zigomanis 4.00 10.00
A-NBL Nicolas Blanchard 4.00 10.00
A-PBR Patrice Bergeron 8.00 20.00
A-PLF Pat LaFontaine 8.00 20.00
A-POP Pier-Olivier Pelletier 4.00 10.00
A-RBQ Rene Bourque 4.00 10.00
A-RJU R.J. Umberger 5.00 12.00
A-RKS Ryan Kesler 5.00 12.00
A-RMI Ryan Miller 12.50 30.00
A-RSU Ryan Suter 8.00 20.00
A-TPL Tyler Plante 4.00 10.00
DA-BB Chris Bourque
Ray Bourque
DA-BC Gilbert Brule
Bobby Clarke
DA-BF Martin Brodeur
Marc-Andre Fleury
DA-BL Jay Bouwmeester
Brian Leetch
DA-BO Patrice Bergeron
Alexander Ovechkin
DA-CR Jeff Carter
Mike Richards
DA-DF Devan Dubnyk
Grant Fuhr
DA-DT Yann Danis
Jose Theodore
DA-HH Brett Hull
Bobby Hull
DA-LL Guillaume Latendresse
Guy Lafleur
DA-ML Evgeni Malkin
Mario Lemieux
DA-MO Evgeni Malkin
Alexander Ovechkin
DA-PM Zach Parise
Frank Mahovlich
DA-PR Carey Price
Patrick Roy
DA-RL Bobby Ryan
Pat LaFontaine
DA-SY Eric Staal
Steve Yzerman

2005-06 ITG Heroes and Prospects Autographs Series II

DUAL SIG PRINT RUN 15 SETS
DUAL NOT PRICED DUE TO SCARCITY
AC Andy Chiodo 6.00 15.00
AF Andy Franck 4.00 10.00
AG Alex Grant 6.00 15.00
AK Andrei Kostitsyn 8.00 20.00
AL Andrew Ladd 6.00 15.00
AP Alexandre Picard 8.00 20.00
AW Andrew Wozniewski 4.00 10.00
BC Braydon Coburn 6.00 15.00
BF Brian Finley 4.00 10.00
BG Bruno Gervais 4.00 10.00
BK Brent Krahn 6.00 15.00
CM Clarke MacArthur 4.00 10.00
CS Chris Stewart 5.00 12.00
DJ Derek Joslin 4.00 10.00
DL Dan LaCosta 4.00 10.00
DP Dion Phaneuf 20.00 50.00
DT Dan Turple 4.00 10.00
EF Eric Fehr 8.00 20.00
EL Eric Lindros 15.00 40.00
EW Erik Westrum 4.00 10.00
GC Gerry Cheevers 10.00 25.00
GP Gilbert Perreault 10.00 25.00
HC Herb Carnegie 30.00 60.00
HJ Hugh Jessiman 4.00 10.00
HL Henrik Lundqvist 20.00 50.00
IK Ilya Kovalchuk 12.00 30.00
JD Bobby Hughes 4.00 10.00
JE Julien Ellis-Plante 6.00 15.00
JG Justin Garay 6.00 15.00
JL Junior Lessard 4.00 10.00
KA Kevin Armstrong 4.00 10.00
KB Keith Ballard 5.00 12.00
KC Kyle Chipchura 6.00 15.00
KF Kurtis Foster 4.00 10.00
KG Kelly Guard 5.00 12.00
LI Leland Irving 8.00 20.00
LR Larry Robinson 6.00 15.00
LS Ladislav Smid 4.00 10.00
LT Lauri Tukonen 4.00 10.00
MH Mark Howe 8.00 20.00
MM Mike Morrison 4.00 10.00
NC Noah Clarke 4.00 10.00
ND Nigel Dawes 5.00 12.00
NF Nick Foligno 5.00 12.00
NM Nathan Marsters 4.00 10.00
NP Nathan Paetsch 4.00 10.00
NS Nolan Schaefer 4.00 10.00
NW Noah Welch 8.00 20.00
OL Olivier Latendresse 6.00 15.00
OP Ondrej Pavelec 4.00 10.00
PM Peter Mueller 10.00 25.00
PP Petr Prucha 15.00 40.00
PT Petr Taticek 4.00 10.00
RD Ryan Daniels 4.00 10.00
RG Ryan Getzlaf 10.00 25.00
RH Ron Hextall 20.00 50.00
RR Rosario Ruggeri 4.00 10.00
RV Roman Voloshenko 6.00 15.00
SB Sean Bergenheim 4.00 10.00
SL Stanislav Lascek 4.00 10.00
TB Troy Brouwer 4.00 10.00
TG Tim Gleason 4.00 10.00
TK Tyler Kennedy 4.00 10.00
TR Tyler Redenbach 4.00 10.00
TS Tod Sloan 4.00 10.00
TW Ty Wishart 4.00 10.00
VK Vitaly Kolesnik 5.00 12.00
WR Wacey Rabbit 6.00 15.00
YC Yvan Cournoyer 8.00 20.00
YS Yan Stastny 4.00 10.00
ZH Zach Hamill 6.00 15.00
AE2 Angelo Esposito 75.00 150.00
AJT A.J. Thelen 4.00 10.00
AM2 Al Montoya 8.00 20.00
AO2 Alexander Ovechkin 75.00 150.00
AO3 Alexander Ovechkin 75.00 150.00
APR Alexander Perezhogin 10.00 25.00
ARG Andy Rogers 4.00 10.00
BCA Brady Calla 4.00 10.00
BCO Blake Comeau 5.00 12.00
BJG Brett Jaeger 4.00 10.00
BJS Borje Salming 10.00 25.00
BPO Brian Pothier 4.00 10.00
BR2 Bobby Ryan 12.00 30.00
BSG Bob Sanguinetti 10.00 25.00
BSU Brandon Sutter 4.00 10.00
BSW Bryce Swan 4.00 10.00
CBK Codey Burki 4.00 10.00
CCR Corey Crawford 5.00 12.00
CDR Chris Durno 4.00 10.00
CEM Cory Emmerton 4.00 10.00
CLR Chad Larose 4.00 10.00
CMD Chris Madden 4.00 10.00
CME Curtis McElhinney 4.00 10.00
CMU Colin Murphy 4.00 10.00
CP2 Corey Perry 8.00 20.00
CP3 Corey Perry 10.00 25.00
CSA Curtis Sanford 8.00 20.00
CW2 Cam Ward 10.00 25.00
DBO Dustin Boyd 6.00 15.00
DCA Daniel Carcillo 4.00 10.00
DDE David Desharnais 4.00 10.00
DDS Dan DaSilva 4.00 10.00
DHE Dany Heatley 10.00 25.00
DHU Dylan Hunter 5.00 12.00
DMC D'Arcy McConvey 4.00 10.00
DMI Drew MacIntyre 4.00 10.00
DP2 Dion Phaneuf 20.00 50.00
DPE Dustin Penner 6.00 15.00
DPZ Dmitri Patzold 5.00 12.00
DSB Dany Sabourin 4.00 10.00
EL2 Eric Lindros 15.00 40.00
EN2 Eric Nystrom 5.00 12.00
ES2 Eric Staal 15.00 40.00
GBE Garrett Bembridge 4.00 10.00
GCL Gerald Coleman 5.00 12.00
GHO Greg Hogeboom 4.00 10.00
GPL Geoff Platt 4.00 10.00
HL2 Henrik Lundqvist 40.00 100.00
JBC Jason Bacashihua 6.00 15.00
JC2 Jeff Carter 12.00 30.00
JC3 Jeff Carter 12.00 30.00
JCO Jeremy Colliton 6.00 15.00
JCR Jim Craig 10.00 25.00
JDA Jonathan D'Aversa 4.00 10.00
JFJ Jean-Francois Jacques 4.00 10.00
JHU Jiri Hudler 6.00 15.00
JOP John Pohl 6.00 15.00
JPG Justin Pogge 30.00 80.00
JPO Jason Pominville 8.00 20.00
JRY Joe Ryan 4.00 10.00
JSC Jeff Schultz 4.00 10.00
JT2 John Tavares 100.00 200.00
JTA Jeff Tambellini 6.00 15.00
JTE Joey Tenute 4.00 10.00
KL2 Kari Lehtonen 12.00 30.00
LRD Liam Reddox 4.00 10.00
LST Logan Stephenson 4.00 10.00
MAP Marc-Antoine Pouliot 8.00 20.00
MB2 Martin Brodeur 40.00 80.00
MBR Mike Brodeur 6.00 15.00
MC2 Mike Cammalleri 5.00 12.00
MCL Mathieu Carle 4.00 10.00
MEL Matt Ellison 4.00 10.00
MFI Mark Fistric 4.00 10.00
MFU Michael Funk 4.00 10.00
MGL Mike Glumac 4.00 10.00
MHA Mark Hartigan 6.00 15.00
MHO Marek Horsky 4.00 10.00
ML2 Mario Lemieux 40.00 100.00
ML3 Mario Lemieux 40.00 100.00
MR2 Mike Richards 10.00 25.00
MR3 Mike Richards 10.00 25.00
MRY Mathieu Roy 6.00 15.00
MSP Martin St. Pierre 4.00 10.00
MXB Maxime Boisclair 6.00 15.00
MXO Maxime Ouellet 6.00 15.00
NBG Nicklas Bergfors 6.00 15.00
POS Patrick O'Sullivan 8.00 20.00
PR2 Patrick Roy 40.00 100.00
PR3 Patrick Roy 40.00 80.00
PRI Pekka Rinne 5.00 12.00
PSJ Peter Sejna 4.00 10.00
RB2 Ray Bourque 25.00 60.00
RBE Rejean Beauchemin 5.00 12.00
RE2 Ray Emery 6.00 15.00
RGI Rod Gilbert 6.00 15.00
RH2 Ron Hextall 10.00 25.00
RHA Ron Hainsey 6.00 15.00
RHI Ryan Hillier 4.00 10.00
RMC Ryan MacDonald 5.00 12.00
RRO Rafael Rotter 4.00 10.00
RSH Ryan Shannon 4.00 10.00
RST Ryan Stone 4.00 10.00
RVE Ryan Vesce 4.00 10.00
RWH Ryan White 4.00 10.00
SBE Shawn Belle 4.00 10.00
SBR Steve Bernier 4.00 10.00
SC2 Sidney Crosby 75.00 150.00
SC3 Sidney Crosby 75.00 150.00
SGA Steve Gainey 4.00 10.00
SKO Sergei Kostitsyn 6.00 15.00
SY2 Steve Yzerman 40.00 80.00
TKE Ted Kennedy 6.00 15.00
TMK Tomi Maki 4.00 10.00
TPC Tomas Plekanec 4.00 10.00
TPK Thomas Pock 4.00 10.00
TV2 Thomas Vanek 12.00 30.00
BRH2 Brett Hull 12.00 30.00
EMA2 Evgeni Malkin 75.00 200.00
EMA3 Evgeni Malkin 75.00 200.00
GLF2 Guy Lafleur 10.00 25.00
JTH2 Jose Theodore 8.00 20.00
MSV2 Marek Svatos 5.00 12.00
BP Martin Brodeur
Justin Pogge
CM2 Jim Craig
Al Montoya
HK Dany Heatley
Ilya Kovalchuk
LN Henrik Lundqvist
Antero Niittymaki
LT2 Eric Lindros
John Tavares
PL Petr Prucha
Henrik Lundqvist
RP Larry Robinson
Dion Phaneuf
RT Patrick Roy
Jose Theodore
YC2 Jim Craig
Vladislav Tretiak

2005-06 ITG Heroes and Prospects Autographs Update

ONE PER UPDATE BOX
A-AE Angelo Esposito SP 75.00 200.00
A-FB Francois Bouchard 3.00 8.00
A-FN Filip Novak 3.00 8.00

A-MF Michael Frolik SP 25.00 60.00
A-OF Ondrej Fiala 3.00 8.00
A-RN Robert Nilsson 4.00 10.00
A-SK Staffan Kronwall 3.00 8.00
A-TD Tysen Dowzak 3.00 8.00
A-TF Tomas Fleischmann 4.00 10.00
A-BSH Ben Shutron 3.00 8.00
A-CBT Chris Beckford-Tseu 15.00 40.00
A-CHT Cristobal Huet SP
A-DRI Danny Richmond 3.00 8.00
A-DRU David Ruzicka SP
A-JGL Jeff Glass 5.00 12.00
A-JHO Jamie Holden 3.00 8.00
A-MCO Matthew Corrente 4.00 10.00
A-MKS Mark Stuart 4.00 10.00
A-MSZ Marek Schwarz SP 15.00 30.00
A-RE3 Ray Emery SP 6.00 15.00
A-RRG Richie Regehr 3.00 8.00
DA-ET John Tavares 125.00 250.00
Angelo Esposito

2005-06 ITG Heroes and Prospects CHL Grads

PRINT RUN 70 SETS
GOLD PRINT RUN 10 SETS
GOLD NOT PRICED DUE TO SCARCITY
CG-1 Marc-Antoine Pouliot 6.00 15.00
CG-2 Gilbert Brule 10.00 25.00
CG-3 Jeff Carter 10.00 25.00
CG-4 Mike Richards 6.00 15.00
CG-5 Mario Lemieux 20.00 50.00
CG-6 Patrick Roy 15.00 40.00
CG-7 Steve Yzerman 15.00 40.00
CG-8 Guy Lafleur 10.00 25.00
CG-9 Dion Phaneuf 15.00 40.00
CG-10 Ryan Getzlaf 10.00 25.00
CG-11 Corey Perry 8.00 20.00
CG-12 Ray Bourque 10.00 25.00
CG-13 Grant Fuhr 10.00 25.00
CG-14 Martin Brodeur 12.00 30.00
CG-15 Eric Fehr 6.00 15.00
CG-16 Sidney Crosby 25.00 60.00

2005-06 ITG Heroes and Prospects Complete Jerseys

PRINT RUN 10 SETS
NOT PRICED DUE TO SCARCITY
UNPRICED GOLD 1/1's EXIST
CJ-1 Al Montoya
CJ-2 Gilbert Brule
CJ-3 David Bolland
CJ-4 Zach Parise
CJ-5 Mike Richards
CJ-6 Jeff Carter
CJ-7 Shawn Belle
CJ-8 Chris Bourque
CJ-9 John Tavares
CJ-10 Carey Price
CJ-11 Robbie Schremp
CJ-12 Bryan Little
CJ-13 Pierre-Marc Bouchard
CJ-14 Alexander Ovechkin
CJ-15 Corey Perry
CJ-16 Antero Niittymaki
CJ-17 Mikko Koivu
CJ-18 Bobby Ryan
CJ-19 Jason Spezza
CJ-20 Cam Ward
CJ-21 Guillaume Latendresse
CJ-22 Marc-Andre Fleury
CJ-23 Patrice Bergeron
CJ-24 Evgeni Malkin
CJ-25 Sidney Crosby
CJ-26 Eric Staal
CJ-27 Thomas Vanek
CJ-28 Brad Boyes
CJ-29 Sean Bergenheim
CJ-30 Alexander Perezhogin
CJ-31 Dion Phaneuf
CJ-32 Jay Bouwmeester
CJ-33 Marc Staal
CJ-34 Benoit Pouliot
CJ-35 Gerald Coleman
CJ-36 Rejean Beauchemin
CJ-37 Justin Pogge
CJ-38 Patrick Eaves
CJ-39 Jeff Tambellini
CJ-40 Chris Campoli

2005-06 ITG Heroes and Prospects Complete Logos

STATED PRINT RUN 1 SET
NOT PRICED DUE TO SCARCITY
AHL-1 Mikko Koivu
AHL-2 Brandon Bochenski
AHL-3 Pavel Vorobiev
AHL-4 Pascal Leclaire
AHL-5 Brian Sutherby
AHL-6 Andy Hilbert
AHL-7 Brent Burns
AHL-8 Boyd Gordon
AHL-9 Jason LaBarbera
AHL-10 Denis Hamel
AHL-11 Ryan Whitney
AHL-12 Lawrence Nycholat
AHL-13 Brad Boyes
AHL-14 Patrick Eaves
AHL-15 Adam Munro
AHL-16 Al Montoya
AHL-17 Brent Krahn
AHL-18 Jeff Tambellini
AHL-19 Dennis Wideman
AHL-20 Yan Stastny
AHL-21 Chris Bourque
AHL-22 Keith Ballard
AHL-23 Matt Ellison
AHL-24 Chris Beckford-Tseu
CHL-1 Bobby Ryan
CHL-2 Guillaume Latendresse
CHL-3 Devin Setoguchi
CHL-4 Chris Durand
CHL-5 Kenndal McArdle
CHL-6 Benoit Pouliot
CHL-7 Carey Price
CHL-8 Shea Weber
CHL-9 Marek Zagrapan
CHL-10 Marc Staal
CHL-11 Eric Staal
CHL-12 Gilbert Brule
CHL-13 Dany Roussin
CHL-14 Alexandre Vincent
CHL-15 David Bolland
CHL-16 John Tavares
CHL-17 Luc Bourdon
CHL-18 Blake Comeau
CHL-19 Kristofer Westblom
CHL-20 Robbie Schremp
CHL-21 Tyler Mosienko
CHL-22 Patrick O'Sullivan
CHL-23 Gerald Coleman
CHL-24 Justin Pogge
CHL-25 Marc-Andre Fleury
ECHL-1 Mike Brodeur

2005-06 ITG Heroes and Prospects Future Teammates

PRINT RUN 30 SETS
FT1 P.Bouchard/M.Koivu 10.00 25.00
FT2 J.Pitkanen/A.Niittymaki 10.00 25.00
FT3 C.Perry/R.Getzlaf 15.00 40.00
FT4 M.Fleury/M.Lemieux 50.00 125.00
FT5 J.Spezza/B.Bochenski 20.00 50.00
FT6 C.Ward/E.Staal 20.00 50.00
FT7 D.Keon/F.Mahovlich 20.00 50.00
FT8 P.Roy/R.Bourque 25.00 60.00
FT9 P.LaFontaine/G.Fuhr 15.00 40.00
FT10 P.Bergeron/B.Boyes 15.00 40.00
FT11 R.Bourque/C.Neely 20.00 50.00
FT12 B.Hull/G.Hall 20.00 50.00
FT13 S.Crosby/E.Malkin 125.00 200.00
FT14 Alexander Ovechkin 50.00 125.00
Eric Fehr

2005-06 ITG Heroes and Prospects He Shoots-He Scores Prizes

PRINT RUN 20 SER.#'d SETS
NOT PRICED DUE TO SCARCITY
1 Sidney Crosby
Mario Lemieux
2 Guillaume Latendresse
Guy Lafleur
3 Kari Lehtonen
Martin Brodeur
4 Dion Phaneuf
Ray Bourque
5 Jose Theodore
Patrick Roy
6 Evgeni Malkin
Alexander Ovechkin
7 Benoit Pouliot
Steve Yzerman
8 Alexander Ovechkin
Mario Lemieux
9 Jay Bouwmeester
Brian Leetch
10 Carey Price
Jose Theodore
11 Evgeni Malkin
Mario Lemieux
12 Tyler Mosienko
Bill Mosienko
13 Eric Staal
Marc Staal
14 Brett Hull
Bobby Hull
15 Danny Syvret
Dan Fritsche
16 Corey Perry
David Bolland
17 Kristofer Westblom
Blake Comeau
18 Bobby Ryan
Ryan Getzlaf
19 Kari Lehtonen
Alexander Ovechkin
20 Patrice Bergeron
Brad Boyes
21 Derek Roy
Ryan Miller
22 Brent Krahn
Dion Phaneuf
23 Cam Ward
Eric Staal
24 Brent Seabrook
Pavel Vorobiev
25 Wojtek Wolski
Marek Svatos
26 Pascal Leclaire
Dan Fritsche
27 Marc-Antoine Pouliot
Rob Schremp
28 Jay Bouwmeester
Anthony Stewart
29 Jason LaBarbera
Mike Cammalleri
30 Mikko Koivu
Patrick O'Sullivan
31 Kyle Chipchura
Guillaume Latendresse
32 Scottie Upshall
Dan Hamhuis
33 Brandon Bochenski
Jason Spezza
34 Antero Niittymaki
Joni Pitkanen
35 Jeff Carter
Mike Richards
36 Sidney Crosby
Evgeni Malkin
37 Marc-Andre Fleury
Ryan Whitney
38 Sidney Crosby
Carlo Colaiacovo
39 Ryan Kesler
Alex Auld
40 Alexander Ovechkin
Eric Fehr
41 Alexander Ovechkin
Alexander Radulov
42 Mario Lemieux
Evgeni Malkin
43 Steve Yzerman
John Tavares
44 Patrick Roy
Angelo Esposito
45 Mark Messier
Steve Downie
46 Frank Mahovlich
Benoit Pouliot
47 Martin Brodeur
Carey Price
48 Jaromir Jagr
Michael Frolik
49 Terry Sawchuk
Leland Irving
50 Maurice Richard
John Tavares
51 Alexander Ovechkin
Dion Phaneuf
52 Mario Lemieux
Jordan Staal
53 Steve Yzerman
Patrick O'Sullivan
54 Patrick Roy
Corey Crawford
55 Mark Messier
Peter Mueller
56 Tim Horton
Marc Staal
57 Martin Brodeur
Marek Schwarz
58 Jaromir Jagr
Jiri Tlusty
59 Brett Hull
Ryan Getzlaf
60 Johnny Bower
Justin Pogge

2005-06 ITG Heroes and Prospects Hero Memorabilia

HM1-HM20 PRINT RUN 50 SETS
HM21-HM41 PRINT RUN 30 SETS
HM42-56 PRINT RUN 60 SETS
HM-1 Mario Lemieux 30.00 80.00
HM-2 Ray Bourque 10.00 25.00
HM-3 Cam Neely 6.00 15.00
HM-4 Doug Gilmour 6.00 15.00
HM-5 Wendel Clark 6.00 15.00
HM-6 Stan Mikita 6.00 15.00
HM-7 Pat LaFontaine 6.00 15.00
HM-8 Patrick Roy 20.00 50.00
HM-9 Dino Ciccarelli 6.00 15.00
HM-10 Ed Giacomin 12.50 30.00
HM-11 Vladislav Tretiak 15.00 40.00
HM-12 Brad Park 6.00 15.00
HM-13 Brett Hull 8.00 20.00
HM-14 Brian Leetch 6.00 15.00
HM-15 Martin Brodeur 25.00 60.00
HM-16 Steve Yzerman 12.50 30.00
HM-17 Jose Theodore 8.00 20.00
HM-18 Bobby Hull 10.00 25.00
HM-19 Jean Beliveau 20.00 50.00
HM-20 Guy Lafleur 10.00 25.00
HM-21 Frank Mahovlich 8.00 20.00
HM-22 Grant Fuhr 12.00 30.00
HM-23 Glenn Hall 6.00 15.00
HM-24 Gerry Cheevers 15.00 40.00
HM-25 Marcel Dionne 6.00 15.00
HM-26 Phil Esposito 12.50 30.00
HM-27 Valeri Kharlamov 20.00 50.00
HM-28 Tony Esposito 8.00 20.00
HM-29 Bobby Clarke 10.00 25.00
HM-30 Eddie Shore 8.00 20.00
HM-31 Bernie Parent 10.00 25.00
HM-32 Mike Bossy 12.50 30.00
HM-33 Jean Ratelle 15.00 40.00
HM-34 Gump Worsley 12.00 30.00
HM-35 Darryl Sittler 8.00 20.00
HM-36 Jacques Plante 35.00 60.00
HM-37 Steve Shutt 8.00 20.00
HM-38 Ted Lindsay 8.00 20.00
HM-39 Red Kelly 8.00 20.00
HM-40 Johnny Bower 12.50 30.00
HM-41 Dave Keon 15.00 40.00
HM-42 Borje Salming 15.00 40.00
HM-43 Lanny McDonald 6.00 15.00
HM-44 Rod Gilbert 6.00 15.00
HM-45 Eric Lindros 6.00 15.00
HM-46 Ilya Kovalchuk 10.00 25.00
HM-47 Dany Heatley 10.00 25.00
HM-48 George Hainsworth 30.00 80.00
HM-49 Bill Barber 6.00 15.00
HM-50 Serge Savard 6.00 15.00
HM-51 Guy Lapointe 6.00 15.00
HM-52 Yvan Cournoyer 6.00 15.00
HM-53 Denis Potvin 10.00 25.00
HM-54 Larry Robinson 6.00 15.00
HM-55 Rogie Vachon 6.00 15.00
HM-56 Mark Howe 6.00 15.00

2005-06 ITG Heroes and Prospects Hero Memorabilia Dual

PRINT RUN 30 SETS
HDM-1 Bill Mosienko 8.00 20.00
HDM-2 Brett Hull 15.00 40.00
HDM-3 Wendel Clark 12.50 30.00
HDM-4 Patrick Roy 25.00 60.00
HDM-5 Ray Bourque 15.00 40.00
HDM-6 Cam Neely 10.00 25.00
HDM-7 Doug Gilmour 8.00 20.00
HDM-8 Steve Yzerman 25.00 60.00
HDM-9 Brian Leetch 10.00 25.00
HDM-10 Grant Fuhr 15.00 40.00
HDM-11 Jose Theodore 10.00 25.00
HDM-12 Guy Lafleur 10.00 25.00
HDM-13 Dave Keon 8.00 20.00
HDM-14 Mario Lemieux 25.00 60.00
HDM-15 Bobby Hull 12.50 30.00
HDM-16 Stan Mikita 8.00 20.00
HDM-17 Ron Hextall 12.50 30.00

2005-06 ITG Heroes and Prospects Jerseys

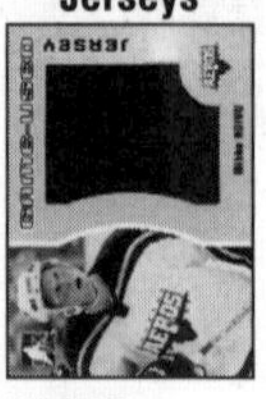

PRINT RUN 100 SETS
GOLD PRINT RUN 10 SETS
GOLD NOT PRICED DUE TO SCARCITY
GUJ-1 Bobby Ryan 10.00 20.00
GUJ-2 Brian Sutherby 4.00 10.00
GUJ-3 Jay Bouwmeester 8.00 20.00
GUJ-4 Denis Hamel 6.00 15.00
GUJ-5 Andy Hilbert 6.00 15.00
GUJ-6 Mike Cammalleri 6.00 15.00
GUJ-7 Mikko Koivu 6.00 15.00
GUJ-8 Boyd Gordon 4.00 10.00
GUJ-9 Brad Boyes 6.00 15.00
GUJ-10 Ryan Kesler 4.00 10.00
GUJ-11 Joni Pitkanen 6.00 15.00
GUJ-12 Pascal Leclaire 4.00 10.00
GUJ-13 Derek Roy 6.00 15.00
GUJ-14 Ryan Whitney 8.00 20.00
GUJ-15 Jason Spezza 8.00 20.00
GUJ-16 Eric Staal 8.00 20.00
GUJ-17 Dustin Brown 4.00 10.00
GUJ-18 Chuck Kobasew 6.00 15.00
GUJ-19 Ray Emery 6.00 15.00
GUJ-20 Jason LaBarbera 4.00 10.00
GUJ-21 Michel Ouellet 8.00 20.00
GUJ-22 Antero Niittymaki 8.00 20.00
GUJ-23 Cam Ward 8.00 20.00
GUJ-24 Marc-Andre Fleury 10.00 25.00
GUJ-25 Devin Setoguchi 6.00 15.00
GUJ-26 Shea Weber 6.00 15.00
GUJ-27 Chris Durand 4.00 10.00
GUJ-28 Guillaume Latendresse 10.0025.00
GUJ-29 Brandon Bochenski 4.00 10.00
GUJ-30 Pavel Vorobiev 4.00 10.00
GUJ-31 P-M Bouchard 4.00 10.00
GUJ-32 Patrice Bergeron 8.00 20.00
GUJ-33 Kenndal McArdle 4.00 10.00
GUJ-34 Patrick O'Sullivan 8.00 20.00
GUJ-35 Marek Zagrapan 6.00 15.00
GUJ-36 Carey Price 6.00 15.00
GUJ-37 Corey Crawford 4.00 10.00
GUJ-38 Rob Schremp 8.00 20.00
GUJ-39 Lee Goren 4.00 10.00
GUJ-40 Tyler Mosienko 4.00 10.00
GUJ-41 Brent Burns 4.00 10.00
GUJ-42 Travis Roche 4.00 10.00
GUJ-43 Kristofer Westblom 4.00 10.00
GUJ-44 Lawrence Nycholat 4.00 10.00
GUJ-45 Wojtek Wolski 8.00 20.00
GUJ-46 Mathieu Garon 4.00 10.00
GUJ-47 Adam Munro 4.00 10.00
GUJ-48 Blake Comeau 4.00 10.00
GUJ-49 Evgeni Malkin 50.00 80.00
GUJ-50 Benoit Pouliot 4.00 10.00
GUJ-51 Gerald Coleman 4.00 10.00
GUJ-52 Marc Staal 8.00 20.00
GUJ-53 Sidney Crosby 50.00 80.00
GUJ-54 Alexander Ovechkin 40.00 60.00
GUJ-55 Al Montoya 8.00 20.00
GUJ-56 Gilbert Brule 8.00 20.00
GUJ-57 David Bolland 8.00 20.00
GUJ-58 Zach Parise 8.00 20.00
GUJ-59 Mike Richards 8.00 20.00
GUJ-60 Jeff Carter 12.00 25.00
GUJ-61 Jeff Tambellini 6.00 15.00
GUJ-62 Chris Campoli 4.00 10.00
GUJ-63 Shawn Belle 4.00 10.00
GUJ-64 Chris Bourque 6.00 15.00
GUJ-65 John Tavares 25.00 50.00
GUJ-66 Tim Thomas 8.00 20.00
GUJ-67 Justin Pogge 25.00 40.00
GUJ-68 Bryan Little 10.00 25.00
GUJ-69 Patrick Eaves 6.00 15.00
GUJ-70 Brett Sutter 4.00 10.00
GUJ-71 Yan Stastny 6.00 15.00
GUJ-72 Gerald Coleman 4.00 10.00
GUJ-73 Rejean Beauchemin 6.00 15.00
GUJ-74 Chris Beckford-Tseu 6.00 15.00
GUJ-75 Luc Bourdon 8.00 20.00
GUJ-76 Matt Ellison 8.00 20.00
GUJ-77 Brian Pothier 4.00 10.00
GUJ-78 Alexandre Vincent 4.00 10.00
GUJ-79 Corey Perry 8.00 20.00
GUJ-80 Anthony Stewart 4.00 10.00
GUJ-81 Ryan Getzlaf 8.00 20.00
GUJ-82 Eric Fehr 6.00 15.00
GUJ-83 Keith Ballard 4.00 10.00
GUJ-84 Marc-Antoine Pouliot 6.00 15.00
GUJ-85 Julien Ellis-Plante 8.00 20.00
GUJ-86 Dany Roussin 4.00 10.00
GUJ-87 Eric Nystrom 8.00 20.00
GUJ-88 Brent Krahn 6.00 15.00
GUJ-89 Evgeni Malkin 50.00 80.00
GUJ-90 Sidney Crosby 50.00 80.00
GUJ-91 Alexander Ovechkin 40.00 60.00
GUJ-92 Maxime Ouellet 8.00 20.00
GUJ-93 Carlo Colaiacovo 4.00 10.00
GUJ-94 Henrik Lundqvist 15.00 30.00
GUJ-95 Alexander Perezhogin 8.00 20.00
GUJ-96 Sean Bergenheim 4.00 10.00
GUJ-97 Kari Lehtonen 8.00 20.00
GUJ-98 Jason Bacashihua 8.00 20.00
GUJ-99 Jordin Tootoo 8.00 20.00
GUJ-100 Marek Svatos 8.00 20.00
GUJ-101 Dennis Wideman 4.00 10.00
GUJ-102 Colby Armstrong 6.00 15.00
GUJ-103 Mike Brodeur 4.00 10.00
GUJ-104 Matt Foy 4.00 10.00
GUJ-105 Grant Stevenson 4.00 10.00
GUJ-106 Ari Ahonen 6.00 15.00
GUJ-107 Andrew Ladd 6.00 15.00
GUJ-108 Adam Hauser 6.00 15.00
GUJ-109 Dion Phaneuf 12.00 30.00
GUJ-110 Jeff Schultz 4.00 10.00
GUJ-111 Petr Prucha 10.00 20.00
GUJ-112 Alexander Mogilny 6.00 15.00
GUJ-113 Devan Dubnyk 10.00 20.00
GUJ-114 Thomas Vanek 10.00 20.00
GUJ-115 Carey Price 8.00 20.00
GUJ-116 Tom Pyatt 4.00 10.00

2005-06 ITG Heroes and Prospects Emblems

*EMBLEMS: .75X TO 2X JSY HI
PRINT RUN 30 SETS
GOLD PRINT RUN 10 SETS
GOLD NOT PRICED DUE TO SCARCITY
GUE-49 Evgeni Malkin 125.00 250.00
GUE-53 Sidney Crosby 150.00 300.00
GUE-54 Alexander Ovechkin 75.00 200.00
GUE-65 John Tavares 75.00 200.00
GUE-89 Evgeni Malkin 125.00 250.00
GUE-90 Sidney Crosby 150.00 300.00
GUE-91 Alexander Ovechkin 75.00200.00

2005-06 ITG Heroes and Prospects Numbers

*NUMBERS: .75X TO 2X JSY HI
PRINT RUN 30 SETS
GOLD PRINT RUN 10 SETS
GOLD NOT PRICED DUE TO SCARCITY
GUN-49 Evgeni Malkin 100.00 250.00
GUN-53 Sidney Crosby 100.00 250.00
GUN-54 Alexander Ovechkin 75.00 200.00
GUN-89 Evgeni Malkin 100.00 250.00
GUN-90 Sidney Crosby 100.00 250.00
GUN-91 Alexander Ovechkin 75.00200.00

2005-06 ITG Heroes and Prospects Making the Bigs

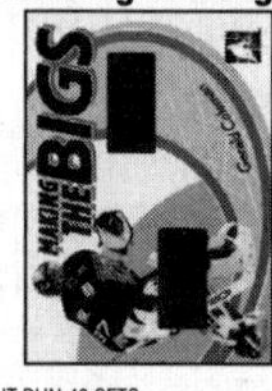

PRINT RUN 40 SETS
MTB-1 Jose Theodore 10.00 25.00
MTB-2 Jason Spezza 10.00 25.00
MTB-3 P-M Bouchard 5.00 12.00
MTB-4 Brian Sutherby 5.00 12.00
MTB-5 Eric Staal 10.00 25.00
MTB-6 Boyd Gordon 5.00 12.00
MTB-7 Alexander Ovechkin 30.00 80.00
MTB-8 Ray Emery 8.00 20.00
MTB-9 Derek Roy 8.00 20.00
MTB-10 Maxime Ouellet 5.00 12.00
MTB-11 Dustin Brown 5.00 12.00
MTB-12 Scottie Upshall 5.00 12.00
MTB-13 Guillaume Latendresse 10.00
25.00
MTB-14 Mike Richards 6.00 15.00
MTB-15 Jeff Carter 10.00 25.00
MTB-16 Gerald Coleman 5.00 12.00

2005-06 ITG Heroes and Prospects Measuring Up

PRINT RUN 60 SETS
GOLD PRINT RUN 10 SETS
GOLD NOT PRICED DUE TO SCARCITY
MU1 Cam Ward 15.00 40.00
Patrick Roy
MU2 Jason LaBarbera 15.00 40.00
Patrick Roy
MU3 Julien Ellis-Plante 15.00 40.00
Patrick Roy
MU4 Jason Bacashihua 15.00 40.00
Patrick Roy
MU5 Alex Auld 15.00 40.00
Patrick Roy
MU6 Scott Clemmensen 15.00 40.00
Patrick Roy
MU7 Maxime Ouellet 15.00 40.00
Patrick Roy
MU8 Brent Krahn 15.00 40.00
Patrick Roy
MU9 Henrik Lundqvist 30.00 80.00
Patrick Roy
MU10 Ryan Miller 30.00 80.00
Patrick Roy
MU11 Antero Niittymaki 20.00 40.00
Patrick Roy
MU12 Marc-Andre Fleury 15.00 40.00
Patrick Roy
MU13 Gerald Coleman 15.00 40.00
Patrick Roy
MU14 Devan Dubnyk 15.00 40.00
Patrick Roy
MU15 Rejean Beauchemin 15.00 40.00
Patrick Roy
MU16 Kelly Guard 15.00 40.00
Patrick Roy
MU17 Carey Price 20.00 50.00
Patrick Roy
MU18 Al Montoya 15.00 40.00
Patrick Roy
MU19 Justin Pogge 20.00 50.00
Patrick Roy
MU20 Kari Lehtonen 20.00 50.00
Patrick Roy

2005-06 ITG Heroes and Prospects Memorial Cup

COMPLETE SET 8.00 20.00
MC-1 Danny Syvret 1.00 2.50
MC-2 Robbie Schremp 2.00 5.00
MC-3 Dylan Hunter 1.00 2.50
MC-4 Corey Perry 2.00 5.00
MC-5 Dan Fritsche 1.25 3.00
MC-6 David Bolland 1.00 2.50
MC-7 Adam Dennis 1.00 2.50
MC-8 Gerald Coleman 1.00 2.50
MC-9 Brandon Prust 1.00 2.50
MC-10 Bryan Rodney 1.00 2.50
MC-11 Drew Larman 1.00 2.50
MC-12 Josh Beaulieu 1.00 2.50
MC-13 Marc Methot 1.00 2.50

2005-06 ITG Heroes and Prospects Nameplates

PRINT RUN 20 SETS
NOT PRICED DUE TO SCARCITY
UNPRICED GOLD 1/1's EXIST

2005-06 ITG Heroes and Prospects National Pride

NPR1-12/22-41 PRINT RUN 60 SETS
NPR13-21 PRIN RUN 20 SETS
NPR12-21 NOT PRICED DUE TO SCARCITY
NPR-1 Kari Lehtonen 6.00 15.00
NPR-2 Marc-Andre Fleury 8.00 20.00
NPR-3 Dany Roussin 4.00 10.00
NPR-4 Jason Spezza 8.00 20.00
NPR-5 Jay Bouwmeester 4.00 10.00
NPR-6 Dion Phaneuf 15.00 40.00
NPR-7 P-M Bouchard 4.00 10.00
NPR-8 Mikko Koivu 4.00 10.00
NPR-9 Mike Cammalleri 4.00 10.00
NPR-10 Evgeni Malkin 30.00 80.00
NPR-11 Sidney Crosby 40.00 100.00
NPR-12 Alexander Ovechkin 30.00 80.00
NPR-13 Tony Esposito
NPR-14 Darryl Sittler
NPR-15 Patrick Roy
NPR-16 Bobby Clarke
NPR-17 Martin Brodeur
NPR-18 Brett Hull
NPR-19 Steve Yzerman
NPR-20 Brian Leetch
NPR-21 Pat LaFontaine
NPR-22 Pelle Lindbergh 15.00 40.00
NPR-23 Phil Esposito 8.00 20.00
NPR-24 Lanny McDonald 4.00 10.00
NPR-25 Dany Heatley 8.00 20.00
NPR-26 Borje Salming 6.00 15.00
NPR-27 Eric Lindros 8.00 20.00
NPR-28 Gilbert Perreault 6.00 15.00
NPR-29 Gerry Cheevers 8.00 20.00
NPR-30 Larry Robinson 6.00 15.00
NPR-31 Ilya Kovalchuk 12.00 30.00
NPR-32 Justin Pogge 20.00 50.00
NPR-33 Alexander Ovechkin 30.00 80.00
NPR-34 Bobby Ryan 8.00 20.00
NPR-35 Evgeni Malkin 30.00 80.00
NPR-36 Sidney Crosby 40.00 100.00
NPR-37 Corey Perry 8.00 20.00
NPR-38 Jeff Carter 8.00 20.00
NPR-39 Mike Richards 6.00 15.00
NPR-40 Al Montoya 6.00 15.00
NPR-41 Anthony Stewart 4.00 10.00

2005-06 ITG Heroes and Prospects Net Prospects

PRINT RUN 80 SETS
GOLD PRINT RUN 10 SETS
GOLD NOT PRICED DUE TO SCARCITY
NP-1 Kari Lehtonen 8.00 20.00
NP-2 Marc-Andre Fleury 8.00 20.00
NP-3 Antero Niittymaki 8.00 20.00
NP-4 Adam Hauser 4.00 10.00
NP-5 Mathieu Garon 4.00 10.00
NP-6 Pascal Leclaire 4.00 10.00
NP-7 Ray Emery 6.00 15.00
NP-8 Adam Munro 4.00 10.00
NP-9 Cam Ward 8.00 20.00
NP-10 Jason LaBarbera 4.00 10.00
NP-11 Ryan Miller 8.00 20.00
NP-12 Brent Krahn 4.00 10.00
NP-13 Alex Auld 6.00 15.00
NP-14 Devan Dubnyk 4.00 10.00
NP-15 Carey Price 6.00 15.00
NP-16 Kyle Moir 4.00 10.00
NP-17 Corey Crawford 4.00 10.00
NP-18 Kevin Nastiuk 4.00 10.00
NP-19 Jonathan Boutin 4.00 10.00
NP-20 Gerald Coleman 6.00 15.00
NP-21 Kristofer Westblom 4.00 10.00

2005-06 ITG Heroes and Prospects Net Prospects Dual

PRINT RUN 80 SETS
GOLD PRINT RUN 10 SETS
GOLD NOT PRICED DUE TO SCARCITY
NPD1 Maxime Ouellet 8.00 20.00
Alex Auld
NPD2 Adam Hauser 8.00 20.00
Jason LaBarbera
NPD3 Antero Niittymaki 8.00 20.00
Rejean Beauchemin
NPD4 Kristofer Westblom 8.00 20.00
Gerald Coleman
NPD5 Al Montoya 15.00 40.00
Pascal Leclaire
NPD6 Brent Krahn 8.00 20.00
Cam Ward
NPD7 Kari Lehtonen 20.00 50.00
Marc-Andre Fleury
NPD8 Devan Dubnyk 15.00 40.00
Justin Pogge
NPD9 Chris Beckford-Tseu 8.00 20.00
Mike Brodeur
NPD10 Carey Price 8.00 20.00
Julien Ellis-Plante

2005-06 ITG Heroes and Prospects Oh Canada

STATED PRINT RUN 50 #'d SETS
OC-1 Liam Reddox 8.00 20.00
OC-2 Julien Ellis-Plante 8.00 20.00
OC-3 Cody Bass 8.00 20.00
OC-4 Derick Brassard 8.00 20.00
OC-5 Ryan O'Marra 8.00 20.00
OC-6 Kristopher Letang 10.00 25.00
OC-7 David Bolland 8.00 20.00
OC-8 Benoit Pouliot 10.00 25.00
OC-9 Blake Comeau 8.00 20.00
OC-10 Ryan Parent 10.00 25.00
OC-11 Dustin Boyd 10.00 25.00
OC-12 Steve Downie 10.00 25.00
OC-13 Kyle Chipchura 8.00 20.00
OC-14 Justin Peters 8.00 20.00
OC-15 Dustin Kohn 8.00 20.00
OC-16 Justin Keller 8.00 20.00
OC-17 Dan LaCosta 8.00 20.00

2005-06 ITG Heroes and Prospects Shooting Stars

COMPLETE SET (12) 8.00 15.00
AS-1 Jason LaBarbera .75 2.00
AS-2 Lawrence Nycholat .40 1.00
AS-3 Dennis Wideman .40 1.00
AS-4 Jason Spezza .75 2.00
AS-5 Mike Cammalleri .75 2.00
AS-6 Michel Ouellet .40 1.00
AS-7 Kari Lehtonen 2.00 5.00
AS-8 Niklas Kronwall .75 2.00
AS-9 Joni Pitkanen .75 2.00
AS-10 Zach Parise .75 2.00
AS-11 Andy Hilbert .40 1.00
AS-12 Dustin Brown 1.00 2.00

2005-06 ITG Heroes and Prospects Team Cherry

TC1 Ty Wishart 2.00 5.00
TC2 Mike Weber 2.00 5.00
TC3 Chris Stewart 2.00 5.00
TC4 Joe Ryan 2.00 5.00
TC5 Theo Peckham 2.00 5.00
TC6 Peter Mueller 3.00 8.00
TC7 Jamie McGinn 2.00 5.00
TC8 Ben Maxwell 2.00 5.00
TC9 Bobby Hughes 2.00 5.00
TC10 Ryan Hillier 2.00 5.00
TC11 Nick Foligno 2.00 5.00
TC12 John de Gray 2.00 5.00
TC13 Cal Clutterbuck 2.00 5.00
TC14 Mathieu Carle 2.00 5.00
TC15 Brady Calla 2.00 5.00
TC16 Derick Brassard 2.50 6.00
TC17 Francois Bouchard 2.00 5.00
TC18 Jonathan Bernier 2.50 6.00
TC19 Matt Beleskey 2.00 5.00
TC20 Kevin Armstrong 2.00 5.00

2005-06 ITG Heroes and Prospects Team Orr

TO1 John Armstrong 2.00 5.00
TO2 Lukas Bohunicky 2.00 5.00
TO3 Benjamin Breault 2.00 5.00
TO4 Codey Burki 2.00 5.00
TO5 Matthew Corrente 2.00 5.00
TO6 Ryan Daniels 2.00 5.00
TO7 Tysen Dowzak 2.00 5.00
TO8 Cory Emmerton 2.00 5.00
TO9 Ondrej Fiala 2.00 5.00
TO10 Claude Giroux 2.50 6.00
TO11 Michael Grabner 2.50 6.00
TO12 Riley Holzapfel 2.50 6.00
TO13 Leland Irving 2.50 6.00
TO14 Bryan Little 3.00 8.00
TO15 Bob Sanguinetti 2.00 5.00
TO16 James Sheppard 2.00 5.00
TO17 Ben Shutron 2.00 5.00
TO18 Jordan Staal 4.00 10.00
TO19 Yvan Vishnevskiy 2.00 5.00
TO20 Ryan White 2.00 5.00

2006-07 ITG Heroes and Prospects

COMPLETE SET (150) 20.00 50.00
COMPLETE UPDATE SET (50) 10.00 20.00
1 Elmer Lach .20 .50
2 Milt Schmidt .20 .50
3 Brian Leetch .30 .75
4 Peter Stastny .20 .50

5 Mark Messier .40 1.00
6 Willie O'Ree .30 .75
7 Bryan Trottier .20 .50
8 Jaromir Jagr .40 1.00
9 Mario Lemieux .75 2.00
10 Luc Robitaille .30 .75
11 Dick Duff .20 .50
12 Ron Francis .20 .50
13 Guy Lafleur .40 1.00
14 Patrick Roy .75 2.00
15 Martin Brodeur .60 1.50
16 Tim Thomas .30 .75
17 Cristobal Huet .40 1.00
18 Jeff Carter .30 .75
19 Marc-Andre Fleury .40 1.00
20 Billy Smith .30 .75
21 Johnny Bower .30 .75
22 Antero Niittymaki .30 .75
23 Brad Boyes .30 .75
24 Sidney Crosby 2.00 5.00
25 Cam Ward .40 1.00
26 Kyle Wellwood .20 .50
27 Jason Spezza .30 .75
28 Wendel Clark .30 .75
29 Denis Potvin .20 .50
30 Bobby Clarke .30 .75
31 Tony Voce .20 .50
32 Martin Houle .30 .75
33 Brendan Bell .20 .50
34 Eric Fehr .20 .50
35 Carsen Germyn .20 .50
36 Yann Danis .30 .75
37 Roman Voloshenko .20 .50
38 Tomas Kopecky .30 .75
39 Ben Ondrus .20 .50
40 Nathan Marsters .20 .50
41 Marc-Antoine Pouliot .30 .75
42 Konstantin Pushkarev .20 .50
43 Ian White .20 .50
44 Jeremy Williams .20 .50
45 Noah Welch .20 .50
46 Rick Rypien .20 .50
47 Lauri Tukonen .20 .50
48 Danny Syvret .20 .50
49 Mark Giordano .20 .50
50 Andrew Penner .20 .50
51 Aleksander Suglobov .20 .50
52 David LeNeveu .30 .75
53 Doug O'Brien .20 .50
54 Martin St. Pierre .20 .50
55 Dan Fritsche .20 .50
56 Connor James .20 .50
57 Dustin Penner .30 .75
58 Ryan Vesce .20 .50
59 Colby Genoway .20 .50
60 Ben Walter .20 .50
61 Richie Regehr .20 .50
62 Trevor Gillies .30 .75
63 Mark Hartigan .20 .50
64 Garett Bembridge .20 .50
65 Ladislav Smid .20 .50
66 Braydon Coburn .30 .75
67 Jeremy Colliton .20 .50
68 Nathan Paetsch .20 .50
69 Pavel Vorobiev .20 .50
70 Matt Jones .20 .50
71 Corey Locke .20 .50
72 Corey Crawford .30 .75
73 Erik Westrum .20 .50
74 Patrick O'Sullivan .30 .75
75 Jeff Tambellini .20 .50
76 Al Montoya .30 .75
77 Matthew Spiller .20 .50
78 Nigel Dawes .20 .50
79 Ryan Shannon .20 .50
80 Steve Stamkos .60 1.50
81 Angelo Esposito 1.00 2.50
82 John Tavares 2.00 5.00
83 Jordan Staal 1.00 2.50
84 Derick Brassard .40 1.00
85 Peter Mueller .40 1.00
86 Bryan Little .30 .75
87 James Sheppard .40 1.00
88 Cory Emmerton .30 .75
89 Bob Sanguinetti .20 .50
90 Ondrej Fiala .20 .50
91 Logan Couture .30 .75
92 Ty Wishart .30 .75
93 Ryan Hillier .20 .50
94 Jared Staal 1.25 3.00
95 Bobby Hughes .20 .50
96 Brady Calla .20 .50
97 Joe Ryan .20 .50
98 Ivan Vishnevskiy .20 .50
99 Gilbert Brule .30 .75
100 Bud Holloway .20 .50
101 Ben Maxwell .20 .50
102 Matt Beleskey .20 .50
103 John Armstrong .20 .50
104 Michael Grabner .30 .75
105 Oskar Osala .20 .50
106 Jamie McGinn .20 .50
107 Luke Lynes .20 .50
108 Drew Doughty .40 1.00
109 Alex Bourret .30 .75
110 Chris Stewart .30 .75
111 Jonathan Bernier .60 1.50
112 Leland Irving .60 1.50
113 Claude Giroux .30 .75
114 Ryan Daniels .20 .50
115 Nick Foligno .30 .75
116 Matthew Corrente .20 .50
117 Francois Bouchard .20 .50
118 Brandon Sutter .20 .50
119 Michael Del Zotto .20 .50
120 Sergei Kostitsyn .30 .75
121 Corey Syvret .20 .50
122 Steve Downie .40 1.00
123 Brett Sutter .20 .50
124 Shawn Matthais .20 .50
125 Alexander Radulov .40 1.00
126 Guillaume Latendresse 1.00 2.50
127 Ryan White .20 .50
128 Luc Bourdon .30 .75
129 Colton Gillies .20 .50
130 Marc Staal .30 .75
131 Anze Kopitar 1.00 2.50
132 Jiri Tlusty .60 1.50
133 Yuri Alexandrov .20 .50
134 Tuukka Rask 1.25 3.00
135 Evgeni Malkin 1.50 4.00
136 Phil Kessel .75 2.00
137 Alexander Vasyunov .20 .50
138 Michael Frolik .40 1.00
139 John Tavares 3.00 8.00
140 Justin Pogge 1.25 3.00
141 Jonathan Bernier .75 2.00
142 Brandon Sutter .40 1.00
143 Luc Bourdon .75 2.00
144 Steve Downie .60 1.50
145 Kristopher Letang .40 1.00
146 Ryan Parent .60 1.50
147 Sidney Crosby 2.00 5.00
148 Marc Staal .60 1.50
149 Guillaume Latendresse 1.00 2.50
150 Tom Pyatt .40 1.00
151 Joe Pavelski .30 .75
152 Chris Harrington .20 .50
153 Bill Thomas .20 .50
154 Loui Eriksson .30 .75
155 Benoit Pouliot .30 .75
156 Eric Nystrom .30 .75
157 Bryan Bickell .20 .50
158 Nicklas Bergfors .20 .50
159 Hugh Jessiman .20 .50
160 Jiri Hudler .20 .50
161 Alexander Radulov .40 1.00
162 Mike Green .20 .50
163 Staffan Kronwell .20 .50
164 Drew Miller .40 1.00
165 Brett Sterling .20 .50
166 Jeff Taffe .20 .50
167 Geoff Platt .20 .50
168 Blake Comeau .20 .50
169 Ryan Carter .20 .50
170 Drew Stafford .60 1.50
171 Petr Kalus .60 1.50
172 Josh Hennessy .30 .75
173 Rob Schremp .30 .75
174 Janis Sprukts .20 .50
175 Patrick Kane 4.00 10.00
176 Bobby Ryan .20 .50
177 Devin Setoguchi .30 .75
178 Michael Frolik .40 1.00
179 Brodie Dupont .20 .50
180 Tom Pyatt .20 .50
181 Kenndal McArdle .20 .50
182 Michael Caruso .20 .50
183 James Neal .30 .75
184 Ben Shutron .20 .50
185 Marc-Andre ClichÃ© .20 .50
186 Felix Schutz .20 .50
187 Cody Bass .20 .50
188 Dustin Kohn .20 .50
189 Marc-Edouard Vlasic .30 .75
190 Dan Ryder .20 .50
191 Mathieu Carle .20 .50
192 Justin Azevedo .20 .50
193 Kristofer Letang .30 .75
194 Kris Russell .30 .75
195 Patrick McNeill .20 .50
196 Marc-Andre Gragnani .20 .50
197 Cody Franson .20 .50
198 Cal Clutterbuck .20 .50
199 Jakub Voracek .40 1.00
200 Sam Gagner .75 2.00

2006-07 ITG Heroes and Prospects AHL All-Star Jerseys

STATED PRINT RUN 80 SETS
GOLD VERSION /10 EXISTS
GOLD NOT PRICED DUE TO SCARCITY
AJ01 Jeff Tambellini 4.00 10.00
AJ02 Martin St. Pierre 4.00 10.00
AJ03 Jiri Hudler 6.00 15.00
AJ04 John Pohl 6.00 15.00
AJ05 Yann Danis 6.00 15.00
AJ06 Patrick O'Sullivan 6.00 15.00
AJ07 Denis Hamel 6.00 15.00
AJ08 Keith Ballard 4.00 10.00
AJ09 Denis Shvidki 4.00 10.00
AJ10 Rick DiPietro 6.00 15.00
AJ11 Phillipe Sauve 6.00 15.00
AJ12 Kyle Wellwood 6.00 15.00

2006-07 ITG Heroes and Prospects AHL All-Star Emblems

*EMBLEMS: 1X TO 2.5X JERSEY HI
STATED PRINT RUN 30 SETS
GOLD VERSION /10 EXISTS
GOLD NOT PRICED DUE TO SCARCITY

2006-07 ITG Heroes and Prospects AHL All-Star Numbers

*NUMBERS: 1X TO 2.5 X JERSEY HI
STATED PRINT RUN 30 SETS
GOLD VERSION /10 EXISTS
GOLD NOT PRICED DUE TO SCARCITY

2006-07 ITG Heroes and Prospects AHL Shooting Stars

COMPLETE SET (12) 6.00 15.00
AS01 Pekka Rinne .75 2.00
AS02 Sven Butenschon .40 1.00
AS03 Noah Welch .75 2.00
AS04 Jiri Hudler .75 2.00
AS05 John Pohl .75 2.00
AS06 Erik Westrum .75 2.00
AS07 Wade Flaherty .75 2.00
AS08 Nathan Paetsch .40 1.00
AS09 John Slaney .40 1.00
AS10 Jimmy Roy .40 1.00
AS11 Kirby Law .40 1.00
AS12 Eric Fehr .75 2.00

2006-07 ITG Heroes and Prospects Autographs

STATED ODDS 1:14
AAB Alex Bourret 5.00 12.00
AAE Angelo Esposito 40.00 80.00
AAK Anze Kopitar 30.00 60.00
AAN Antero Niittymaki 8.00 20.00
AAP Andrew Penner 5.00 12.00
AAR Alexander Radulov 15.00 40.00
AAS Aleksander Suglobov 4.00 10.00
AAV Alexander Vasyunov 5.00 12.00
ABB Brendan Bell 4.00 10.00
ABC Bobby Clarke 10.00 25.00
ABD Brodie Dupont 4.00 10.00
ABH Bobby Hughes 4.00 10.00
ABL Brian Leetch
ABM Ben Maxwell 4.00 10.00
ABO Ben Ondrus 4.00 10.00
ABP Benoit Pouliot 5.00 12.00
ABR Bobby Ryan 4.00 10.00
ABT Bill Thomas 4.00 10.00
ABW Ben Walter 4.00 10.00
ACB Cody Bass 4.00 10.00
ACC Corey Crawford 5.00 12.00
ACE Cory Emmerton 5.00 12.00
ACF Cody Franson 4.00 10.00
ACG Carsen Germyn 4.00 10.00
ACH Cristobal Huet 20.00 50.00
ACJ Connor James 4.00 10.00
ACL Corey Locke 4.00 10.00
ACS Chris Stewart 5.00 12.00
ACW Cam Ward 10.00 25.00
ADB Derick Brassard 10.00 25.00
ADD Dick Duff 8.00 20.00
ADF Dan Fritsche 5.00 12.00
ADK Dustin Kohn 4.00 10.00
ADL David LeNeveu 6.00 15.00
ADM Drew Miller
ADO Doug O'Brien 4.00 10.00
ADP Denis Potvin 6.00 15.00
ADR Dan Ryder 4.00 10.00
ADS Drew Stafford 8.00 20.00
AEF Eric Fehr 6.00 15.00
AEL Elmer Lach 10.00 25.00
AEM Evgeni Malkin 75.00 150.00
AEN Eric Nystrom 4.00 10.00
AEW Erik Westrum 6.00 15.00
AFB Francois Bouchard 4.00 10.00
AFS Felix Schutz 4.00 10.00
AGB Garett Bembridge 4.00 10.00
AGP Geoff Platt 4.00 10.00
AHJ Hugh Jessiman 4.00 10.00
AIV Ivan Vishnevskiy 5.00 12.00
AIW Ian White 5.00 12.00
AJA John Armstrong 4.00 10.00
AJC Jeremy Colliton 4.00 10.00
AJH Jiri Hudler 4.00 10.00
AJJ Jaromir Jagr
AJM Jamie McGinn 4.00 10.00
AJN James Neal 4.00 10.00
AJP Justin Pogge 30.00 60.00
AJR Joe Ryan 5.00 12.00
AJS Jason Spezza 10.00 25.00
AJV Jakub Voracek 30.00 80.00
AJW Jeremy Williams 5.00 12.00
AKL Kristopher Letang 5.00 12.00
AKM Kenndal McArdle 4.00 10.00
AKP Konstantin Pushkarev 4.00 10.00
AKR Kris Russell 5.00 12.00
AKW Kyle Wellwood 8.00 20.00
ALC Logan Couture 8.00 20.00
ALE Loui Eriksson 4.00 10.00
ALI Leland Irving 10.00 25.00
ALL Luke Lynes 4.00 10.00
ALR Luc Robitaille 12.00 30.00
ALS Ladislav Smid 5.00 12.00
ALT Lauri Tukonen 5.00 12.00
AMB Martin Brodeur
AMC Matthew Corrente 4.00 10.00
AMF Michael Frolik 10.00 25.00
AMG Mike Green 4.00 10.00
AMH Martin Houle 6.00 15.00
AMJ Matt Jones 5.00 12.00
AML Mario Lemieux
AMM Mark Messier 50.00 100.00
ANB Nicklas Bergfors 4.00 10.00
AND Nigel Dawes 5.00 12.00
ANF Nick Foligno 5.00 12.00
ANM Nathan Marsters 5.00 12.00
ANP Nathan Paetsch 4.00 10.00
ANW Noah Welch 5.00 12.00
AOF Ondrej Fiala 4.00 10.00
AOO Oskar Osala 4.00 10.00
APK Phil Kessel 12.00 30.00
APM Peter Mueller 6.00 15.00
APR Patrick Roy 60.00 100.00
APS Peter Stastny 8.00 20.00
APV Pavel Vorobiev 4.00 10.00
ARC Ryan Carter 4.00 10.00
ARF Ron Francis
ARH Ryan Hillier 4.00 10.00
ARP Ryan Parent 8.00 20.00
ARR Rick Rypien 4.00 10.00
ARS Ryan Shannon 5.00 12.00
ARV Roman Voloshenko 5.00 12.00
ARW Ryan White 5.00 12.00
ASG Sam Gagner 30.00 60.00
ASK Sergei Kostitsyn 6.00 15.00
ASM Shawn Matthais 4.00 10.00
ASS Steve Stamkos 20.00 50.00
ATG Trevor Gillies 4.00 10.00
ATK Tomas Kopecky 4.00 10.00
ATP Tom Pyatt 6.00 15.00
ATR Tuukka Rask 15.00 40.00
ATT Tim Thomas 8.00 20.00
ATV Tony Voce 4.00 10.00
ATW Ty Wishart 4.00 10.00
AWC Wendel Clark 8.00 20.00
AWO Willie O'Ree 12.00 30.00
AYA Yuri Alexandrov 4.00 10.00
AYD Yann Danis 5.00 12.00
AAMO Al Montoya 8.00 20.00
AAR2 Alexander Radulov 10.00 25.00
ABBI Bryan Bickell 4.00 10.00
ABBO Brad Boyes 6.00 15.00
ABCA Brady Calla 4.00 10.00
ABCM Blake Comeau 4.00 10.00
ABCO Braydon Coburn 6.00 15.00
ABHO Bud Holloway 4.00 10.00
ABLI Bryan Little 6.00 15.00
ABRS Brett Sutter 4.00 10.00
ABS1 Brandon Sutter 6.00 15.00
ABS2 Brandon Sutter 8.00 20.00
ABSA Bob Sanguinetti 4.00 10.00
ABSH Ben Shutron 4.00 10.00
ABSM Billy Smith 8.00 20.00
ABST Brett Sterling 4.00 10.00
ABTR Bryan Trottier 8.00 20.00
ACCL Cal Clutterbuck 4.00 10.00
ACGE Colby Genoway 4.00 10.00
ACGI Colton Gillies 4.00 10.00
ACGR Claude Giroux 5.00 12.00
ACHA Chris Harrington 4.00 10.00
ACSV Corey Syvret 4.00 10.00
ADDO Drew Doughty 5.00 12.00
ADPE Dustin Penner 6.00 15.00
ADSE Devin Setoguchi 4.00 10.00
ADSV Danny Syvret 5.00 12.00
AGBR Gilbert Brule 8.00 20.00
AGLF Guy Lafleur 12.00 30.00
AJAS Jared Staal 15.00 40.00
AJAZ Justin Azevedo 4.00 10.00
AJB1 Jonathan Bernier 10.00 25.00
AJB2 Jonathan Bernier 10.00 25.00
AJBO Johnny Bower 6.00 15.00
AJCA Jeff Carter 6.00 15.00
AJHE Josh Hennessy 4.00 10.00
AJPV Joe Pavelski 8.00 20.00
AJSH James Sheppard 5.00 12.00
AJSP Janis Sprukts 4.00 10.00
AJST Jordan Staal 20.00 50.00
AJT1 John Tavares 75.00 150.00
AJT2 John Tavares 75.00 150.00
AJTA Jeff Tambellini 4.00 10.00
AJTF Jeff Taffe 4.00 10.00
AJTL Jiri Tlusty 12.00 30.00
AKL2 Kristopher Letang 5.00 12.00
ALB1 Luc Bourdon 8.00 20.00
ALB2 Luc Bourdon 8.00 20.00
AMAC Marc-Andre ClichÃ© 4.00 10.00
AMAF Marc-Andre Fleury 10.00 25.00
AMAG Marc-Andre Gragnani 4.00 10.00
AMAP Marc-Antoine Pouliot 6.00 15.00
AMBL Matt Beleskey 4.00 10.00
AMCA Michael Caruso 4.00 10.00
AMCR Mathieu Carle 5.00 12.00
AMDZ Michael Del Zotto 8.00 20.00
AMEV Marc-Edouard Vlasic 5.00 12.00
AMF2 Michael Frolik 4.00 10.00
AMGI Mark Giordano 4.00 10.00
AMGR Michael Grabner 6.00 15.00
AMHA Mark Hartigan 4.00 10.00
AMS1 Marc Staal 10.00 25.00
AMS2 Marc Staal 10.00 25.00
AMSC Milt Schmidt 8.00 20.00
AMSP Matthew Spiller 4.00 10.00
AMST Martin St. Pierre 4.00 10.00
APKA Petr Kalus 4.00 10.00
APKN Patrick Kane 150.00 250.00
APMC Patrick McNeill 4.00 10.00
APOS Patrick O'Sullivan 8.00 20.00
ARDA Ryan Daniels 4.00 10.00
ARRG Richie Regehr 4.00 10.00
ARSC Rob Schremp
ARVE Ryan Vesce 4.00 10.00
ASC1 Sidney Crosby 60.00 100.00
ASC2 Sidney Crosby 60.00 100.00
ASD1 Steve Downie 8.00 20.00
ASD2 Steve Downie 8.00 20.00
ASKR Staffan Kronwall 4.00 10.00
ATP2 Tom Pyatt 4.00 10.00

2006-07 ITG Heroes and Prospects Calder Cup Champions

COMPLETE SET (13) 20.00 50.00
COMMONS 2.00 5.00
CC01 Frederic Cassivi 2.50 6.00
CC02 Tomas Fleischmann 2.00 5.00
CC03 Mike Green 2.00 5.00
CC04 Kris Beech 2.00 5.00
CC05 Brooks Laich 2.00 5.00
CC06 Graham Mink 3.00 8.00
CC07 Boyd Gordon 2.00 5.00
CC08 Dave Steckel 2.00 5.00
CC09 Lawrence Nycholat 2.50 6.00
CC10 Boyd Kane 2.00 5.00
CC11 Joey Tenute 2.50 6.00
CC12 Jeff Schultz 2.00 5.00
CC13 Eric Fehr 2.00 5.00

2006-07 ITG Heroes and Prospects CHL Top Prospects

STATED PRINT RUN 100 SETS
GOLD VERSION /10 EXISTS
GOLD NOT PRICED DUE TO SCARCITY
TP01 Ben Shutron 10.00 25.00
TP02 Claude Giroux 10.00 25.00
TP03 Francois Bouchard 10.00 25.00
TP04 Ivan Visnevskiy 10.00 25.00
TP05 Corey Perry 12.00 30.00
TP06 Mike Richards 12.00 30.00
TP07 Bob Sanguinetti 10.00 25.00
TP08 Derick Brassard 12.00 30.00
TP09 James Sheppard 12.00 30.00
TP10 Jonathan Bernier 12.00 30.00
TP11 Jordan Staal 25.00 60.00
TP12 Matthew Corrente 10.00 25.00
TP13 Ryan Daniels 10.00 25.00
TP14 Tysen Dowzak 10.00 25.00
TP15 Ben Maxwell 10.00 25.00
TP16 Carey Price 12.00 30.00
TP17 Eric Fehr 10.00 25.00
TP18 Julien Ellis 12.00 30.00
TP19 Eric Staal 15.00 40.00

2006-07 ITG Heroes and Prospects Class of 2006

COMPLETE SET (13) 10.00 25.00
STATED ODDS 1:24
CL01 Jordan Staal 2.00 5.00
CL02 Phil Kessel 1.50 4.00
CL03 Derick Brassard 1.25 3.00
CL04 Peter Mueller 1.25 3.00
CL05 James Sheppard 1.25 3.00
CL06 Michael Frolik 1.25 3.00
CL07 Jonathan Bernier 1.25 3.00
CL08 Bryan Little 1.25 3.00
CL09 Michael Grabner .75 2.00
CL10 Ty Wishart .75 2.00
CL11 Chris Stewart .75 2.00
CL12 Bob Sanguinetti .75 2.00
CL13 Claude Giroux .75 2.00

2006-07 ITG Heroes and Prospects Complete AHL Logos

STATED PRINT RUN 1/1
NOT PRICED DUE TO SCARCITY
AHL01 Cam Ward
AHL02 Alexandre Picard
AHL03 Yann Danis
AHL04 Ian White
AHL05 Dustin Penner
AHL06 Jimmy Howard
AHL07 Ryan Miller
AHL08 Jay Bouwmeester
AHL09 Nigel Dawes
AHL10 Martin Houle
AHL11 Jiri Hudler
AHL12 Alexander Radulov
AHL13 Drew Stafford
AHL14 Rob Schremp

2006-07 ITG Heroes and Prospects Complete CHL Logos

STATED PRINT RUN 1/1
NOT PRICED DUE TO SCARCITY
CHL01 Jordan Staal
CHL02 Claude Giroux
CHL03 Angelo Esposito
CHL04 James Sheppard
CHL05 Derick Brassard
CHL06 Peter Mueller
CHL07 Cal Clutterbuck
CHL08 Marc Staal
CHL09 Benoit Pouliot
CHL10 Jonathan Bernier
CHL11 John Tavares
CHL12 Carey Price
CHL13 Angelo Esposito
CHL14 Jakub Voracek
CHL15 Adam Perry
CHL16 Sam Gagner

2006-07 ITG Heroes and Prospects Complete Jerseys

PRINT RUN 10 SER. #'d SETS
NOT PRICED DUE TO SCARCITY
GOLD VERSION /1 EXISTS
GOLD NOT PRICED DUE TO SCARCITY
CJ01 Angelo Esposito
CJ02 John Tavares
CJ03 Leland Irving
CJ04 Marek Schwarz
CJ05 Sidney Crosby
CJ06 Phil Kessel
CJ07 Jordan Staal
CJ08 Michael Frolik
CJ09 Cam Ward
CJ10 Ryan Miller
CJ11 Corey Perry
CJ12 Jiri Tlusty
CJ13 Peter Mueller
CJ14 Marc Staal
CJ15 Alexander Radulov
CJ16 Drew Stafford
CJ17 Justin Pogge
CJ18 Benoit Pouliot

2006-07 ITG Heroes and Prospects Double Memorabilia

STATED PRINT RUN 30 SETS
DM01 Jordan Staal 25.00 50.00
DM02 Mario Lemieux 30.00 60.00
DM03 Sidney Crosby 30.00 80.00
DM04 Martin Brodeur 20.00 50.00
DM05 Patrick Roy 30.00 60.00
DM06 Mark Messier 20.00 40.00
DM07 Joe Sakic 20.00 50.00
DM08 John Tavares 25.00 60.00
DM09 Roberto Luongo 15.00 40.00
DM10 Sam Gagner 15.00 40.00

2006-07 ITG Heroes and Prospects Heroes Memorabilia

HM01 Luc Robitaille 10.00 25.00
HM02 Billy Smith 10.00 25.00
HM03 Steve Yzerman 25.00 60.00
HM04 Ron Francis 10.00 25.00
HM05 Martin Brodeur 20.00 50.00
HM06 Patrick Roy 25.00 60.00
HM07 Jaromir Jagr 12.00 30.00
HM08 Mark Messier 12.00 30.00
HM09 Brian Leetch 10.00 25.00
HM10 Dave Keon 10.00 25.00
HM11 Milt Schmidt 12.00 30.00
HM12 Jacques Plante 20.00 50.00
HM13 Bobby Hull 15.00 40.00
HM14 Frank Mahovlich 12.00 30.00
HM15 Jean Beliveau 20.00 50.00
HM16 Red Kelly 12.00 30.00
HM17 Stan Mikita 15.00 40.00
HM18 Tim Horton 20.00 50.00
HM19 Terry Sawchuk 20.00 50.00
HM20 Johnny Bower 12.00 30.00
HM21 Joe Sakic 15.00 40.00
HM22 Ed Belfour 10.00 25.00
HM23 Joe Thornton 12.00 30.00
HM24 Roberto Luongo 12.00 30.00
HM25 Nicklas Lidstrom 12.00 30.00
HM26 Manny Fernandez 10.00 25.00

2006-07 ITG Heroes and Prospects Jerseys

STATED PRINT RUN 100 SETS
GOLD VERSION /10 EXISTS
GOLD NOT PRICED DUE TO SCARCITY
GUJ01 Marek Schwarz 6.00 15.00
GUJ02 David Ruzicka 4.00 10.00
GUJ03 Jimmy Howard 8.00 20.00
GUJ04 Daniel Girardi 4.00 10.00
GUJ05 Mike Green 4.00 10.00
GUJ06 Nigel Dawes 4.00 10.00
GUJ07 Curtis McElhinney 6.00 15.00
GUJ08 Mike Smith 6.00 15.00
GUJ09 Corey Locke 4.00 10.00
GUJ10 Yann Danis 6.00 15.00
GUJ11 Tomi Maki 4.00 10.00
GUJ12 Erik Christensen 6.00 15.00
GUJ13 Maxime Talbot 6.00 15.00
GUJ14 Tony Voce 4.00 10.00
GUJ15 Josh Harding 6.00 15.00
GUJ16 Ian White 6.00 15.00
GUJ17 Jarkko Immonen 4.00 10.00
GUJ18 Ryan Getzlaf 8.00 20.00
GUJ19 Jeremy Colliton 4.00 10.00
GUJ20 Fernando Pisani 6.00 15.00
GUJ21 Noah Welch 4.00 10.00
GUJ22 Billy Thompson 6.00 15.00
GUJ23 Staffan Kronwall 4.00 10.00
GUJ24 Darryl Bootland 4.00 10.00
GUJ25 Dustin Penner 6.00 15.00
GUJ26 Paul Ranger 4.00 10.00
GUJ27 Alexandre Picard 6.00 15.00
GUJ28 Daniel Paille 4.00 10.00
GUJ29 Andy Rogers 4.00 10.00
GUJ30 Tysen Dowzak 4.00 10.00
GUJ31 Jamie McGinn 4.00 10.00
GUJ32 Ryan Callahan 4.00 10.00
GUJ33 Angelo Esposito 15.00 30.00
GUJ34 John Tavares 25.00 50.00
GUJ35 Tim Thomas 8.00 20.00
GUJ36 Bud Holloway 4.00 10.00
GUJ37 Kevin Lalande 4.00 10.00
GUJ38 Leland Irving 6.00 15.00
GUJ39 Peter Mueller 6.00 15.00
GUJ40 Marc Staal 6.00 15.00
GUJ41 Benoit Pouliot 6.00 15.00
GUJ42 Wojtek Wolski 8.00 20.00
GUJ43 Bryan Little 8.00 20.00
GUJ44 Ben Shutron 4.00 10.00
GUJ45 Ryan O'Marra 4.00 10.00
GUJ46 Adam Perry 4.00 10.00
GUJ47 James Sheppard 6.00 15.00
GUJ48 Nicholas Drazeovic 4.00 10.00
GUJ49 Bobby Ryan 8.00 20.00
GUJ50 Tyler Plante 4.00 10.00
GUJ51 Matt Corrente 4.00 10.00
GUJ52 Ondrej Fiala 6.00 15.00
GUJ53 J-S Aubin 6.00 15.00
GUJ54 Ryan Vesce 4.00 10.00
GUJ55 Petr Taticek 4.00 10.00
GUJ56 Ben Walter 4.00 10.00
GUJ57 Andrew Penner 6.00 15.00
GUJ58 Francois Beauchemin 6.00 15.00
GUJ59 Cristobal Huet 8.00 20.00
GUJ60 Jay Bouwmeester 6.00 15.00
GUJ61 Phil Kessel 10.00 25.00
GUJ62 Petr Kalus 6.00 15.00
GUJ63 Drew Stafford 12.00 30.00
GUJ64 Alexander Radulov 12.00 30.00
GUJ65 Jiri Hudler 6.00 15.00
GUJ66 Cory Emmerton 4.00 10.00
GUJ67 Loui Eriksson 4.00 10.00
GUJ68 Bobby Ryan 6.00 15.00
GUJ69 Jakub Voracek 12.00 30.00
GUJ70 Sam Gagner 12.00 30.00
GUJ71 Michael Grabner 6.00 15.00
GUJ72 Rob Schremp 10.00 25.00
GUJ73 Cal Clutterbuck 4.00 10.00

2006-07 ITG Heroes and Prospects Emblems

*EMBLEMS: 1X TO 2.5X JERSEY HI
STATED PRINT RUN 30 SETS
GOLD VERSION /10 EXISTS
GOLD NOT PRICED DUE TO SCARCITY

2006-07 ITG Heroes and Prospects Numbers

*NUMBERS: 1X TO 2.5X JERSEY HI
STATED PRINT RUN 30 SETS
GOLD VERSION /10 EXISTS
GOLD NOT PRICED DUE TO SCARCITY

2006-07 ITG Heroes and Prospects Making The Bigs

STATED PRINT RUN 70 SETS
GOLD VERSION /10 EXISTS
GOLD NOT PRICED DUE TO SCARCITY
MTB01 Wojtek Wolski 10.00 25.00
MTB02 Tim Gleason 5.00 12.00
MTB03 Cam Ward 12.00 30.00
MTB04 Ryan Miller 10.00 25.00
MTB05 Mike Glumac 5.00 12.00
MTB06 Pascal Leclaire 6.00 15.00
MTB07 Ryan Getzlaf 10.00 25.00
MTB08 Eric Nystrom 5.00 12.00
MTB09 Ray Emery 6.00 15.00
MTB10 Eric Staal 10.00 25.00
MTB11 Marc-Antoine Pouliot 6.00 15.00
MTB12 Alexander Ovechkin 15.00 40.00

2006-07 ITG Heroes and Prospects Memorial Cup Champions

COMPLETE SET (12) 8.00 20.00
MC01 Cedrick Desjardins .75 2.00
MC02 Joe Ryan .60 1.50
MC03 Brent Aubin .60 1.50
MC04 Jordan LaVallee .60 1.50
MC05 Andrew Andricopoulos .60 1.50
MC06 Marc-Edouard Vlasic 1.25 3.00
MC07 Mathieu Melanson .60 1.50
MC08 Michal Sersen .60 1.50
MC09 Angelo Esposito 2.50 6.00
MC10 Maxime Lacroix .60 1.50
MC11 Alexander Radulov 2.00 5.00
MC12 Patrick Roy 3.00 8.00

2006-07 ITG Heroes and Prospects National Pride

STATED PRINT RUN 80 SETS
GOLD VERSION /10 ALSO EXISTS
GOLD NOT PRICED DUE TO SCARCITY
NP01 Logan Stephenson 4.00 10.00
NP02 Sidney Crosby 20.00 50.00
NP03 Frederik Cabana 4.00 10.00
NP04 Alex Bourret 4.00 10.00
NP05 Tom Pyatt 4.00 10.00
NP06 Marc-Andre Gragnani 4.00 10.00
NP07 Olivier Latendresse 4.00 10.00
NP08 Marc Staal 8.00 20.00
NP09 Tyler Kennedy 4.00 10.00
NP10 Stephane Goulet 4.00 10.00
NP11 Devin Setoguchi 8.00 20.00
NP12 Benoit Pouliot 8.00 20.00
NP13 Jeff Schultz 4.00 10.00
NP14 Wacey Rabbit 6.00 15.00
NP15 Patrick McNeill 4.00 10.00
NP16 Steve Downie 10.00 25.00
NP17 Blake Comeau 6.00 15.00
NP18 Dustin Boyd 6.00 15.00
NP19 Kyle Chipchura 6.00 15.00
NP20 Carey Price 15.00 40.00
NP21 Marc Staal 8.00 20.00
NP22 Sam Gagner 10.00 25.00
NP23 Steve Downie 10.00 25.00

2006-07 ITG Heroes and Prospects Net Prospects

STATED PRINT RUN 70 SETS
GOLD VERSION /10 EXISTS
GOLD NOT PRICED DUE TO SCARCITY
NPR01 Leland Irving 8.00 20.00
NPR02 Marek Schwarz 6.00 15.00
NPR03 Jimmy Howard 8.00 20.00
NPR04 Cam Ward 12.00 30.00
NPR05 Cristobal Huet 12.00 30.00
NPR06 Ryan Miller 10.00 25.00
NPR07 Ray Emery 6.00 15.00
NPR08 Justin Pogge 12.00 30.00
NPR09 Carey Price 10.00 25.00
NPR10 Jonathan Bernier 6.00 15.00
NPR11 Hannu Toivonen 8.00 20.00
NPR12 Thomas McCollum 6.00 15.00
NPR13 Justin Pogge 12.00 30.00
NPR14 Mike Smith 6.00 15.00

2006-07 ITG Heroes and Prospects Quad Emblems

STATED PRINT RUN 10 SETS
NOT PRICED DUE TO SCARCITY
GOLD VERSION /1 EXISTS
GOLD NOT PRICED DUE TO SCARCITY
QE01 Bryan Little
Jordan Staal
Chris Stewart
Ben Maxwell
QE02 Sidney Crosby
John Tavares
Angelo Esposito
Brandon Sutter
QE03 Marc Staal
Dion Phaneuf
Luc Bourdon
Shea Weber
QE04 Marc-Andre Fleury
Cam Ward
Kari Lehtonen
Ryan Miller
QE05 Sidney Crosby
Gilbert Brule
Bobby Ryan
Steve Downie
QE06 Alexander Ovechkin
Henrik Lundqvist
Petr Prucha
Evgeni Malkin
QE07 Rob Schremp
Wojtek Wolski
Corey Perry
Benoit Pouliot
QE08 Tyler Plante
Carey Price
Devan Dubnyk
Justin Pogge
QE09 Marek Svatos
Ray Emery
Andrew Ladd
Antero Niittymaki
QE10 Mike Richards
Thomas Vanek
Ryan Getzlaf
Eric Staal
QE11 Stafford
Radulov
Pouliot
Schremp
QE12 Voracek
Esposito
Hamill
Alzner
QE13 Gagner
Kane
Couture
Cann
QE14 Brodeur
Luongo
Belfour

Roy
QE15 Tavares
Price
Esposito
Voracek
QE16 Staal
Kopitar
Brule
Kessel

2006-07 ITG Heroes and Prospects Sticks and Jerseys

STATED PRINT RUN 100 SETS
GOLD VERSION /10 EXISTS
GOLD NOT PRICED DUE TO SCARCITY

Card	Low	High
SJ01 Eric Staal	12.00	30.00
SJ02 John Tavares		
SJ03 Patrice Bergeron	12.00	30.00
SJ04 Alexander Ovechkin	25.00	60.00
SJ05 Peter Mueller	12.00	30.00
SJ06 Brady Calla		20.00
SJ07 Leland Irving	12.00	30.00
SJ08 Ondrej Fiala	8.00	20.00
SJ09 Ryan Miller	15.00	40.00
SJ10 Sidney Crosby		
SJ11 Antero Nittymaki	12.00	30.00
SJ12 Jason Spezza	8.00	20.00
SJ13 Petr Prucha		20.00
SJ14 Henrik Lundqvist	15.00	40.00
SJ15 Al Montoya	12.00	30.00
SJ16 Dion Phaneuf	15.00	40.00
SJ17 Marek Svatos	8.00	20.00
SJ18 Hannu Toivonen	12.00	30.00
SJ19 Ray Emery	8.00	20.00
SJ20 Brad Boyes	8.00	20.00

2006-07 ITG Heroes and Prospects Triple Memorabilia

STATED PRINT RUN 50 SETS
GOLD VERSION /10 EXISTS
GOLD NOT PRICED DUE TO SCARCITY

Card	Low	High
TM01 Mark Messier	40.00	80.00
Grant Fuhr		
Jari Kurri		
TM02 Patrick Roy	60.00	125.00
Martin Brodeur		
Bernie Parent		
TM03 Alexander Ovechkin	60.00	125.00
Evgeni Malkin		
Ilya Kovalchuk		
TM04 Sidney Crosby	100.00	200.00
Evgeni Malkin		
Mario Lemieux		
TM05 Leland Irving	25.00	60.00
Carey Price		
Justin Pogge		
TM06 Guillaume Latendresse	20.00	50.00
Alexander Radulov		
Luc Bourdon		
TM07 Corey Perry	25.00	60.00
Bobby Ryan		
Ryan Getzlaf		
TM08 Eric Staal	25.00	60.00
Marc Staal		
Jordan Staal		
TM09 Radulov	20.00	50.00
Stafford		
Pouliot		
TM10 Sakic	30.00	80.00
Thornton		
Jagr		
TM11 Esposito	15.00	40.00
Gagner		
Alzner		
TM12 Belfour	15.00	40.00
Luongo		
Fernandez		

1995 Signature Rookies

This 70-card standard-size set features a number of NHL draft picks from 1994 as well as several future draft prospects. With a suggested retail price of 5.00, each foil pack contained five regular cards, a mail-in offer or a chase card, and an autographed card. Each player signed 7,750 of their cards. The fronts feature borderless color action player cut-outs on a colorful, computerized background. The player's name in gold-foil appears in a black bar at the bottom, while the production number "1 of 45,000" is printed in a gold-foil bar at the left. The backs carry a small color player photo, along with a short biography and player profile. 1,995 cases were produced; 1,000 cases were supposedly sold out of the country, with the remaining 995 cases available in the U.S. Several error cards exist in the set. Limited numbers of corrected versions exist for four of them, as noted below.

Card	Low	High
COMPLETE SET (70)	5.00	12.00
1 Vaclav Varada	.02	.10
2 Roman Vopat	.02	.10
3 Yannick Dube	.02	.10
4 Colin Cloutier	.02	.10
5 Scott Cherrey	.02	.10
6 Johan Finnstrom	.02	.10
7 Fredrik Modin	.20	.50
8 Stephane Roy	.02	.10
9 Yevgeni Ryabchikov	.02	.10
10 Jose Theodore	.50	1.25
11 Jason Holland	.02	.10
12 Richard Park	.02	.10
13 Jason Podollan	.02	.10
14 Mattias Ohlund	.20	.50
15 Chris Wells	.02	.10
16 Hugh Hamilton	.02	.10
17 Edvin Frylen	.02	.10
18 Wade Belak	.02	.10
19 Sebastien Bety	.02	.10
20 Chris Dingman	.02	.10
21 Peter Nylander	.02	.10
22 Daymond Langkow	.40	1.00
23 Kelly Fairchild	.02	.10
24 Norm Dezainde	.02	.10
25 Nolan Baumgartner	.02	.10
26 Deron Quint	.02	.10
27 Sheldon Souray	.02	.10
28 Stefan Ustorf	.02	.10
29 Juha Vurovirta	.02	.10
30 Mark Seliger	.02	.10
31 Ryan Smyth	.50	1.25
32 Dimitri Tabarin	.02	.10
33 Nikolai Tsulygin	.02	.10
34 Paul Vincent	.02	.10
35 Rhett Warrener	.02	.10
36 Jamie Rivers	.02	.10
37 Rumun Ndur	.02	.10
38 Phil Huber	.02	.10
39 Radek Dvorak	.20	.50
40 Mike Barrie	.02	.10
41 Chris Hynnes	.02	.10
42 Mike Dubinsky	.02	.10
43 Steve Cheredaryk	.02	.10
44 Jim Carey	.08	.25
45A Dorian Anneck ERR	.02	.10
45B Dorian Anneck COR	.02	.10
46 Jorgen Jonsson	.02	.10
47 Alyn McCauley	.02	.10
48 Corey Nielson	.02	.10
49 Daniel Tjarnqvist	.08	.25
50 Vadim Yepanchintsev	.02	.10
51 Sean Haggerty	.02	.10
52A Milan Hejduk	.75	2.50
52B Milan Hejduk COR	.75	2.50
53 Adam Magarrell	.02	.10
54 Dave Scatchard	.08	.25
55 Sebastien Vallee	.02	.10
56 Milos Guren	.02	.10
57 Johan Davidsson	.02	.10
58 Byron Briske	.02	.10
59 Sylvain Blouin	.02	.10
60 Bryan Berard UER (Name misspelled Brian on front)	.60	1.50
61 Tim Findlay	.02	.10
62 Doug Bonner	.02	.10
63 Curtis Brown	.08	.25
64A Brad Symes ERR	.02	.10
64B Brad Symes COR	.02	.10
65 Andrew Taylor	.02	.10
66 Brad Bombardir	.02	.10
67 Joe Dziedzic	.02	.10
68 Valentin Morozov	.02	.10
69A Mark McArthur ERR	.02	.10
69B Mark McArthur COR	.02	.10
70 Checklist	.02	.10
CS1 Martin Brodeur		

1995 Signature Rookies Auto-Phonex

This 41-card set measures standard size. The fronts feature a color action player photo made to look as if breaking out of a blue background. The backs carry a small close-up photo of the player with the team name, position, biographical information and statistics. Each 6-card pack consisted of five regular cards and one hand-signed phone card.

Card	Low	High
COMPLETE SET (41)	2.00	5.00
1 Mika Alatalo	.04	.10
2 Chad Allan UER (Text reads four year veteran of pro hockey; should be junior hockey)	.04	.10
3 Jonas Andersson-Junkka	.04	.10
4 Serge Aubin	.14	.25
5 David Belitski	.06	.15
6 Aki Berg	.10	.10
7 Zac Bierk	.06	.25
8 Lou Body	.04	.10
9 Kevin Bolibruck	.04	.10
10 Brian Boucher	.30	.75
11 Jack Callahan	.04	.10
12 Jake Deadmarsh	.04	.10
13 Andy Delmore	.10	.10
14 Shane Doan	.30	.75
15 Daniel Cleary	.10	.10
16 Ian Gordon	.04	.10
17 Jochen Hecht	.14	.25
18 Martin Hohenberger	.04	.10
19 Thomas Holmstrom	.30	.75
20 Cory Keenan	.04	.10
21 Shane Kenney	.04	.10
22 Pavel Kriz	.04	.10
23 Justin Kurtz	.04	.10
24 Jan Labraaten	.04	.10
25 Brad Larsen	.04	.10
26 Donald MacLean	.04	.10
27 Tavis MacMillan	.04	.10
28 Mike Martin	.04	.10
29 Bryan Berard	.20	.25
30 Dimitri Nabokov	.06	.10
31 Todd Norman	.04	.10
32 Cory Peterson	.04	.10
33 Johan Ramstedt	.04	.10
34 Wade Redden	.20	.25
35 Kevin Riehl	.04	.10
36 David Roberts	.04	.10
37 Terry Ryan	.06	.10
38 Brian Scott	.04	.10
39 Alexander Selivanov	.10	.25
40 Peter Wallin	.04	.10
NNO Checklist	.04	.01

1995 Signature Rookies Auto-Phonex Beyond 2000

Inserted 1:6 packs, this set features five players who were thought to have a great shot at excelling well into the 21st century. The fronts feature the player's photo against a futuristic background. The back has a player portrait along with his position, his '93-94 stats and a quote about that player's abilities. 5,000 sets were produced, and each player signed 200 cards. Signed versions are worth 10X to 20X basic cards.

Card	Low	High
COMPLETE SET (5)	6.00	5.00
B1 Jamie Rivers	.40	.50
B2 Terry Ryan	.40	.50
B3 Ryan Smyth	2.00	2.00
B4 Nolan Baumgartner	.40	.50
B5 Jose Theodore	4.00	3.00

1995 Signature Rookies Auto-Phonex Jaromir Jagr

Inserted 1:6 packs, this 5-card standard-size set showcases Jaromir Jagr. 5,000 sets were produced, and Jagr signed 500 of each card. The front features color photos picturing Jagr in action; the irregular fuchsia borders mimic the effect of water splattering on a surface. The back has a photo of Jagr along with biographical details and personal information located at the upper right corner.

Card	Low	High
COMPLETE SET (5)	8.00	8.00
COMMON JAGR (JJ1-JJ5)	1.60	2.00
JAGR SIGNATURE (JJ1-JJ5)	40.00	100.00

1995 Signature Rookies Auto-Phonex Phone Cards

Inserted one per pack, this 39-phone card set features a number of top NHL prospects. Each phone card bears an authentic signature and is serially numbered on the front. Shane Doan, card 14, did not sign. The backs explain how to use the card. Values below are for unused $3 cards. Scratching the back to reveal the PIN number decreases the value by 50 percent. The higher value NNO phone cards listed at the bottom were random inserts at indeterminate odds.

Card	Low	High
COMPLETE SET (40)	60.00	120.00
1 Mika Alatalo	1.50	4.00
2 Chad Allan	.75	2.00
3 Jonas Andersson-Junkka	.75	2.00
4 Serge Aubin	1.50	4.00
5 David Belitski	.75	2.00
6 Aki Berg	1.25	3.00
7 Zac Bierk	1.25	3.00
8 Lou Body	.75	2.00
9 Kevin Bolibruck	.75	2.00
10 Brian Boucher	8.00	20.00
11 Jack Callahan	.75	2.00
12 Jake Deadmarsh	.75	2.00
13 Andy Delmore	1.25	3.00
14 Shane Doan	2.00	5.00
15 Daniel Cleary	1.25	3.00
16 Ian Gordon	.75	2.00
17 Jochen Hecht	5.00	12.00
18 Martin Hohenberger	.75	2.00
19 Thomas Holmstrom	2.00	5.00
20 Cory Keenan	.75	2.00
21 Shane Kenney	.75	2.00
22 Pavel Kriz	.75	2.00
23 Justin Kurtz	.75	2.00
24 Jan Labraaten	.75	2.00
25 Brad Larsen	.75	2.00
26 Donald MacLean	.75	2.00
27 Tavis MacMillan	.75	2.00
28 Mike Martin	.75	2.00
29 Bryan Berard	1.50	4.00
30 Dimitri Nabokov	.75	2.00
31 Todd Norman	.75	2.00
32 Cory Peterson	.75	2.00
33 Johan Ramstedt	.75	2.00
34 Wade Redden	1.25	3.00
35 Kevin Riehl	.75	2.00
36 David Roberts	.75	2.00
37 Terry Ryan	.75	2.00
38 Brian Scott	.75	2.00
39 Alexander Selivanov	.75	2.00
40 Peter Wallin	.75	2.00
NNO Wade Redden $6 card	1.50	4.00
NNO Nolan Baumgartner $6 card	1.50	4.00
NNO D. Langkow $30 card	1.50	4.00
NNO Terry Ryan $6 card	1.50	4.00

1995 Signature Rookies Auto-Phonex Prodigies

Inserted 1:6 packs, this five-card standard-size set features five young guns. The front features the player showcased in action. The player's name is in red while the word "Prodigies" is printed in big, black bold letters against a yellow background on the bottom. The back features biographical information in the upper left corner. The rest of the reverse features a black-and-white player photo with his '93-94 stars and a quote about the player also placed on the bottom half. 5,000 sets were produced, and each player signed 200 of his cards. Signed versions are worth 5X to 8X basic cards.

Card	Low	High
COMPLETE SET (5)	12.00	5.00
P1 Bryan Berard UER (Name misspelled Brian)	4.00	1.00
P2 Daymond Langkow	2.80	2.00
P3 Daniel Cleary	2.40	1.00
P4 Aki Berg	1.60	1.00
P5 Wade Redden	2.00	2.00

1995 Signature Rookies Club Promos

These five standard-size cards were sent to members of the Signature Rookies Club. The fronts feature the players photo occupying most of the right side of the card. The player's are identified underneath the photos. The cards are autographed just above the player's name while the sequential autograph number is under the player's name. The words Club Promo go vertically down the left side of the card while the Signature Rookies Hockey logo is in the lower left corner. The backs have a smaller duplication of the front photo on the left side while all relevant vital stats and biographical information are on the right side. The Signature Rookies authentic signature sticker is right above their logo on the back. Reports suggest that unsigned versions of these cards exist as well. These cards are marked PROMO, and are numbered One of 2,000. As these are rarely seen, no values have been tracked. It is fair to suggest, however, that they are worth considerably less than the signed versions.

Card	Low	High
COMPLETE SET (5)	20.00	20.00
1 Sergei Luchinkin	4.00	5.00
2 Stefan Ustorf	4.00	5.00
3 Brad Brown	4.00	5.00
4 Yanick Dube	4.00	5.00
5 Vitali Yachmenev	6.00	5.00

1995 Signature Rookies Cool Five

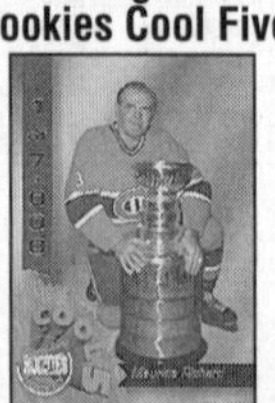

The five cards in this standard-size set were randomly inserted into packs. The left side of the front identifies the card as being 1 of 7,000, with the Cool Five logo in the lower left corner. The remainder is devoted to a full-color player photo which bleeds to the corner. The back has a head-and-shoulders portrait on the left side along with his biography on the right side. Signatures from this 5-card set were randomly inserted throughout the packs.

Card	Low	High
COMPLETE SET (5)	10.00	10.00
CF1 Radek Bonk	2.00	.50
CF2 Brad Park	1.60	2.00
CF3 Brian Leetch	2.00	2.00
CF4 Maurice Richard	4.80	5.00
CF5 Henri Richard	2.00	2.00

1995 Signature Rookies Cool Five Signatures

The five cards in this standard-size set were randomly inserted into packs. The left side of the front identifies the set as 1 of 7,000 and the Cool Five logo is in the lower left corner. The card is autographed over the player's photo and the serial number of the autograph is on the bottom. The remainder of the card is devoted to a full-color player photo that bleeds to the corner. In the middle of the back is the Signature Rookies authentic signature logo. The remainder of the back features a head-and-shoulders player portrait on the left side along with his biography on the right side. The card is numbered in the upper right corner.

Card	Low	High
CF1 Radek Bonk	2.00	5.00
CF2 Brad Park	2.00	15.00
CF3 Brian Leetch	5.00	10.00
CF4 Maurice Richard	40.00	80.00
CF5 Henri Richard	2.00	25.00

1995 Signature Rookies Future Flash

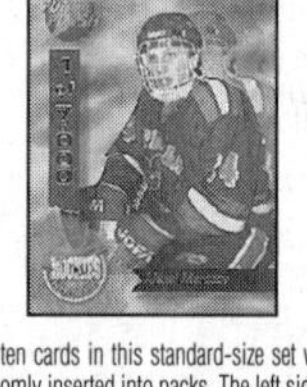

The ten cards in this standard-size set were randomly inserted into packs. The left side of the front identifies the card as being one of 7,000, with the Future Flash logo in the lower left corner. The remainder of the card is devoted to a full-color player photo with a multiple exposure effect that bleeds to the corner. The back has a head-and-shoulders player portrait on the left side along with his biography on the right side. The card is numbered in the upper right corner. Signatures from this 10-card set were randomly inserted throughout the packs.

Card	Low	High
COMPLETE SET (10)	12.00	5.00
FF1 Jeff Ambrosio	1.60	1.00
FF2 Brad Brown	1.60	1.00
FF3 Patrick Juhlin	1.60	1.00
FF4 Sergei Gorbachev	1.60	1.00
FF5 Vasili Kamenev	1.60	4.00
FF6 Oleg Orekhovski	1.60	1.00
FF7 Maxim Kuznetsov	1.60	1.00
FF8 Sergei Luchinkin	1.60	1.00
FF9 Scott Roche	2.40	2.00
FF10 Alexei Morozov	2.40	2.00

1995 Signature Rookies Future Flash Signatures

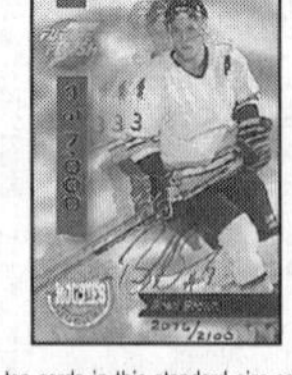

The ten cards in this standard-size set were randomly inserted into packs. The left side of the front identifies the card as being 1 of 2,100, with the Future Flash logo in the lower left corner. The autograph is on the player's photo and is sequentially identified underneath the player's name. The remainder of the card is devoted to a full-color player photo with a multiple exposure effect that bleeds to the corner. The Signature Rookies Authentic Signature Logo is on the right side near the bottom. Other aspects of the back include a head-and-shoulders player portrait on the left side along with his biography on the right side. The cards are numbered in the upper right corner.

Card	Low	High
COMPLETE SET (10)	60.00	120.00
FF1 Jeff Ambrosio	6.00	15.00
FF2 Brad Brown	6.00	15.00
FF3 Patrick Juhlin	6.00	15.00
FF4 Sergei Gorbachev	6.00	15.00
FF5 Vasili Kamenev	6.00	15.00
FF6 Oleg Orekhovski	6.00	15.00
FF7 Maxim Kuznetsov	7.50	20.00
FF8 Sergei Luchinkin	6.00	15.00
FF9 Scott Roche	7.50	20.00
FF10 Alexei Morozov	7.50	20.00

1995 Signature Rookies Miracle on Ice

This 50-card standard-size set features 20 players, two coaches, and special action shots. Just 299 cases were produced, and each six-card pack contained an autograph card. The fronts display color action player photos that are edged on the left and bottom by a red, white and blue American flag design. Also the lower left corner of each card has a small oblique photo of the American team celebrating. The production run ("1 of 24,000"), a special "Miracle On Ice, 1980" emblem, and the player's name are gold foil-stamped on the front. On a ghosted red, white and blue flag design, the backs carry a color close-up photo, biography, and player profile.

Card	Low	High
COMPLETE SET (50)	10.00	20.00
1 Bill Baker	.08	.20
2 Bill Baker	.08	.20
3 Neal Broten	.30	.75
4 Neal Broten	.30	.75
5 Dave Christian	.20	.50
6 Dave Christian	.20	.50
7 Steve Christoff	.08	.20
8 Steve Christoff	.08	.20
9 Jim Craig	.60	1.50
10 Jim Craig	.60	1.50
11 Mike Eruzione	.60	1.50
12 Mike Eruzione	.60	1.50
13 John Harrington	.08	.20
14 John Harrington	.08	.20
15 Steve Janasak	.08	.20
16 Steve Janasak	.08	.20
17 Mark Johnson	.08	.20
18 Mark Johnson	.08	.20
19 Rob McClanahan	.08	.20
20 Rob McClanahan	.08	.20
21 Ken Morrow	.20	.50
22 Ken Morrow	.20	.50
23 Jack O'Callahan	.08	.20
24 Jack O'Callahan	.08	.20
25 Mark Pavelich	.08	.20
26 Mark Pavelich	.08	.20
27 Mike Ramsey	.10	.25
28 Mike Ramsey	.10	.25
29 Buzz Schneider	.08	.20
30 Buzz Schneider	.08	.20
31 Dave Silk	.08	.20
32 Dave Silk	.08	.20
33 Bob Suter	.08	.20
34 Bob Suter	.08	.20
35 Eric Strobel	.08	.20
36 Eric Strobel	.08	.20
37 Phil Verchota	.08	.20
38 Phil Verchota	.08	.20
39 Marc Wells	.08	.20
40 Marc Wells	.08	.20
41 Herb Brooks CO	.60	1.50
42 Herb Brooks CO	.60	1.50
43 Craig Patrick ACO	.20	.50
44 Craig Patrick ACO	.20	.50
45 Clinching The Gold	.20	.50
46 Do You Believe In Miracles	.20	.50
47 Eruzione Decides It	.20	.50
48 Celebration	.20	.50
49 A Dream Becomes Reality	.20	.50
50 Checklist	.08	.20

1995 Signature Rookies Miracle on Ice Signatures

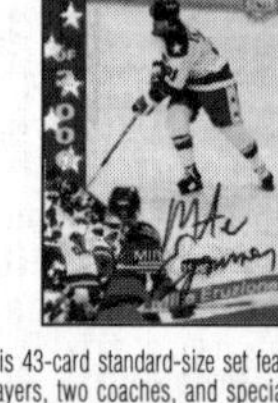

This 43-card standard-size set features 20 players, two coaches, and special action shots. The cards are identical to the regular issue with the addition of authentic signatures inscribed across the fronts. Two thousand of each card were signed. Card numbers 41 and 45-50 were not issued in signed form. Cards are numbered out of 2,000 on front. Both an Eruzione and Brooks celebration promos exist.

Card	Low	High
COMPLETE SET (43)	175.00	350.00
1 Bill Baker	5.00	12.00
2 Bill Baker	5.00	12.00
3 Neal Broten	5.00	12.00
4 Neal Broten	5.00	12.00
5 Dave Christian	5.00	12.00
6 Dave Christian	5.00	12.00
7 Steve Christoff	5.00	12.00
8 Steve Christoff	5.00	12.00
9 Jim Craig	10.00	25.00
10 Jim Craig	10.00	25.00
11 Mike Eruzione	20.00	50.00
12 Mike Eruzione	20.00	50.00
13 John Harrington	5.00	12.00
14 John Harrington	5.00	12.00
15 Steve Janasak	5.00	12.00
16 Steve Janasak	5.00	12.00
17 Mark Johnson	10.00	25.00
18 Mark Johnson	10.00	25.00
19 Rob McClanahan	5.00	12.00
20 Rob McClanahan	5.00	12.00
21 Ken Morrow	4.00	10.00
22 Ken Morrow	4.00	10.00
23 Jack O'Callahan	12.50	30.00
24 Jack O'Callahan	12.50	30.00
25 Mark Pavelich	5.00	12.00
26 Mark Pavelich	5.00	12.00
27 Mike Ramsey	5.00	12.00
28 Mike Ramsey	5.00	12.00
29 Buzz Schneider	10.00	25.00
30 Buzz Schneider	10.00	25.00
31 Dave Silk	4.00	10.00
32 Dave Silk	4.00	10.00
33 Bob Suter	5.00	12.00
34 Bob Suter	5.00	12.00
35 Eric Strobel	10.00	25.00
36 Eric Strobel	10.00	25.00
37 Phil Verchota	5.00	12.00
38 Phil Verchota	5.00	12.00
39 Marc Wells	5.00	12.00
40 Marc Wells	5.00	12.00
42 Herb Brooks CO	20.00	50.00
43 Craig Patrick ACO	4.00	10.00
44 Craig Patrick ACO	4.00	10.00
NNO Celebration Promo Herb Brooks/7500	30.00	80.00
NNO Celebration Promo Mike Eruzione/60		

1995 Signature Rookies Signatures

Inserted one per foil pack, this 69-card issue is a parallel set and features the same design as the regular issue. Each player signed 7,750 of his cards which are hand numbered. The fronts feature borderless color action player cut-outs on a colorful, computerized background. The player's name in gold-foil appears in a black bar at the bottom. The backs carry a small color player photo, along with a short biography and player profile. Because several players could not fulfill their signing commitments in time for packaging, Signature Rookies inserted some redemption cards which specifically identified the player for whom the card could be redeemed. Once the redemption period expires, these cards will have limited market value.

Card	Low	High
COMPLETE SET (69)	50.00	100.00
1 Vaclav Varada	.40	1.00
2 Roman Vopat	.40	1.00
3 Yanick Dube	.40	1.00
4 Colin Cloutier	.40	1.00
5 Scott Cherrey	.40	1.00
6 Johan Finnstrom	.40	1.00
7 Fredrik Modin	2.00	5.00
8 Stephane Roy	.40	1.00
9 Evgeni Ryabchikov	.40	1.00
10 Jose Theodore	2.50	15.00
11 Jason Holland	.40	1.00
12 Richard Park	.40	1.00
13 Jason Podollan	.40	1.00
14 Mattias Ohlund	2.00	5.00
15 Chris Wells	.40	1.00
16 Hugh Hamilton	.40	1.00
17 Edvin Frylen	.40	1.00
18 Wade Belak	.40	1.00
19 Sebastien Bety	.40	1.00
20 Chris Dingman	.40	1.00
21 Peter Nylander	.40	1.00
22 Daymond Langkow	2.00	5.00
23 Kelly Fairchild	.40	1.00
24 Norm Dezainde	.40	1.00
25 Nolan Baumgartner	.40	1.00
26 Deron Quint	.40	1.00
27 Sheldon Souray	.40	1.00
28 Stefan Ustorf	.40	1.00
29 Juha Vuorvirta	.40	1.00
30 Marc Seliger	1.25	3.00
31 Ryan Smyth	2.00	10.00
32 Dimitri Tabarin	.40	1.00
33 Nikolai Tsulygin	.40	1.00
34 Paul Vincent	.40	1.00
35 Rhett Warrener	.40	1.00
36 Jamie Rivers	.40	1.00
37 Rumun Ndur	1.25	3.00
38 Phil Huber	.40	1.00
39 Radek Dvorak	2.00	5.00
40 Mike Barrie	.40	1.00
41 Chris Hynnes	.40	1.00
42 Mike Dubinsky	.40	1.00
43 Steve Cheredaryk	.40	1.00
44 Jim Carey	2.00	5.00
45 Brad Symes	.40	1.00
46 Jorgen Jonsson	.40	1.00
47 Alyn McCauley	.40	1.00
48 Corey Nielson	.40	1.00
49 Daniel Tjarnqvist	1.25	3.00
50 Vadim Epanchintsev	.40	1.00
51 Sean Haggerty	.40	1.00
52 Mark McArthur	.40	1.00
53 Adam Magarrell	.40	1.00
54 Dave Scatchard	1.25	3.00
55 Sebastien Vallee	.40	1.00
56 Milos Guren	.40	1.00
57 Johan Davidsson	.40	1.00
58 Byron Briske	.40	1.00
59 Sylvain Blouin	.40	1.00
60 Bryan Berard UER	1.25	3.00
61 Tim Findlay	.40	1.00
62 Doug Bonner	1.25	3.00
63 Curtis Brown	.40	1.00
64 Dorian Anneck	.40	1.00
65 Andrew Taylor	.40	1.00
66 Brad Bombardir	.40	1.00
67 Joe Dziedzic	.40	1.00
68 Valentin Morozhov	.40	1.00
69 Milan Hejduk	6.00	15.00

1995 Slapshot Memorial Cup

Produced by Slapshot Images Ltd., this 110-card standard-size set commemorates the 1995 Memorial Cup of the Canadian Hockey

League. The set includes the champions of the three member leagues (Detroit/OHL; Hull/LMJHQ; Kamloops/WHL) as well as the host team (Brandon). On a simulated wood background, the fronts feature color action photos inside a jagged black or blue picture frame. The player's name is printed above the photo, while the team name is printed vertically running down the left edge. The backs have biography, a color headshot, and a player profile. The set is arranged according to teams as follows: Kamloops Blazers (1-25), Brandon Wheat Kings (26-50), Hull Olympiques (51-75), and Detroit Jr. Red Wings (76-100).

COMPLETE SET (110) 12.00 30.00
1 Rod Branch .08 .20
2 Jeff Oldenborger .08 .20
3 Jason Holland .08 .20
4 Nolan Baumgartner .14 .35
5 Keith McCambridge .08 .20
6 Ivan Vologjaninov .08 .20
7 Aaron Keller .08 .20
8 Greg Hart .08 .20
9 Jarome Iginla 2.00 5.00
10 Ryan Huska .08 .20
11 Jeff Ainsworth .08 .20
12 Darcy Tucker .40 1.00
13 Hnat Domenichelli .14 .35
14 Tyson Nash .80 2.00
15 Shane Doan 1.20 3.00
16 Jeff Antonovich .08 .20
17 Bonnie Kinney .08 .20
18 Ashley Buckberger .08 .20
19 Brad Lukowich .30 .75
20 Bob Westerby .08 .20
21 Jason Strudwick .14 .35
22 Bob Maudie .08 .20
23 Randy Petruk .20 .50
24 Shawn McNeil .08 .20
25 Don Hay CO .08 .20
26 Bryon Penstock .08 .20
27 Brian Elder .08 .20
28 Jeff Staples .08 .20
29 Scott Laluk .08 .20
30 Kevin Pozzo .08 .20
31 Wade Redden .40 1.00
32 Justin Kurtz .14 .35
33 Sven Butenschon .08 .20
34 Bryan McCabe .20 .50
35 Kelly Smart .08 .20
36 Bobby Brown .08 .20
37 Mike Dubinsky .08 .20
38 Mike LeClerc .30 .75
39 Dean Kletzel .08 .20
40 Darren Ritchie .08 .20
41 Mark Dutiaume .08 .20
42 Ryan Robson .08 .20
43 Chris Dingman .14 .35
44 Darren Van Oene .08 .20
45 Colin Cloutier .08 .20
46 Darryl Stockham .08 .20
47 Peter Schaefer .40 .50
48 Marty Murray .14 .50
49 Alex Vasilevski .08 .20
50 Bob Lowes CO .08 .20
51 Michael Coveny .08 .20
52 Jan Nemecek .14 .35
53 Chris Hall .08 .20
54 Jason Groleau .08 .20
55 Alex Rodrigue .08 .20
56 Jamie Bird .08 .20
57 Harold Hersh .08 .20
58 Carl Prud'Homme .08 .20
59 Sean Farmer .08 .20
60 Carl Beaudoin .08 .20
61 Gordie Dwyer .08 .20
62 Richard Safarik .08 .20
63 Carl Charland .08 .20
64 Jean-Guy Trudel .14 .35
65 Francois Cloutier .08 .20
66 Roddie MacKenzie .08 .20
67 Colin White .30 .75
68 Martin Menard .08 .20
69 Sebastien Bordeleau .08 .20
70 Jonathan Delisle .08 .20
71 Peter Worrell .40 1.00
72 Louis-Philippe Charbonneau .14 .35
73 Jose Theodore 3.20 5.00
74 Neil Savary .14 .35
75 Michael McKay .14 .35
76 Darryl Foster .08 .20
77 Quade Lightbody .08 .20
78 Ryan MacDonald .08 .20
79 Mike Rucinski .08 .20
80 Murray Sheehan .08 .20
81 Matt Ball .08 .20
82 Gerry Lanigan .08 .20
83 Mike Morrone .08 .20
84 Tom Buckley .08 .20
85 Eric Manlow .08 .20
86 Bill McCauley .08 .20
87 Andrew Taylor .08 .20
88 Scott Blair .08 .20
89 Jeff Mitchell .08 .20
90 Jason Saal .14 .35
91 Jamie Allison .14 .35
92 Bryan Berard .30 .50
93 Dan Pawlaczyk .08 .20
94 Milan Kostolny .08 .20
95 Duane Harmer .08 .20
96 Shayne McCosh .08 .20
97 Sean Haggerty .08 .20
98 Nic Beaudoin .08 .20
99 Paul Maurice CO/GM .08 .20
100 Pete Deboer ACO .08 .20
101 Kamloops Checklist .08 .20
102 Brandon Checklist .08 .20
103 Hull Checklist .08 .20
104 Detroit Checklist .08 .20
105 OHL Champions .08 .20
Detroit Jr. Red Wings
106 WHL Champions .08 .20
Kamloops Blazers
107 LMJHQ Champions .08 .20
Hull Olympiques
NNO OHL Playoff Summary .08 .20
NNO LHJMQ Playoff Summary .08 .20
NNO WHL Playoff Summary .08 .20

1991 Star Pics

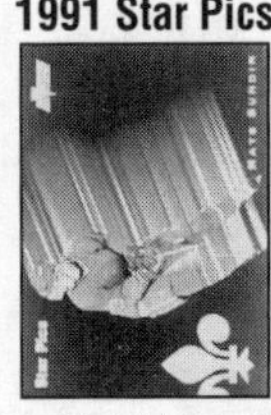

This 72 card standard-size set contained 18 1991 first round draft picks. The cards have glossy action color player photos, with a thin white border on a background picturing a hockey mask. The player's name appears in a white lettering below the picture. The print run was supposed to be 225, 000 individually numbered sets. Autographed cards were randomly inserted into the sets. The autograph cards are valued at 20X to 100X the prices below for Flashback cards and 20X to 50X for the other cards.

SEALED SET (72) 2.00 10.00
1 Al Morganti .01 .10
2 Pat Falloon .01 .10
3 Jamie Pushor .01 .10
4 Jean Beliveau FLB .08 .25
5 Martin Lapointe .02 .50
6 Jamie Matthews .01 .10
7 Rod Gilbert FLB .08 .25
8 Niklas Sundblad .01 .10
9 Steve Konowalchuk .01 .10
10 Alex Delvecchio FLB .08 .25
11 Donevan Hextall .01 .10
12 Dody Wood .01 .10
13 Scott Niedermayer .12 .50
14 Trevor Halverson .01 .10
15 Terry Chitaroni .01 .10
16 Tyler Wright .01 .10
17 Andrei Lomakin UER .01 .10
18 Martin Hamrlik .01 .10
19 Dimitri Filimonov UER .01 .10
20 Ed Belfour FLB .08 .50
21 Andrew Verner .01 .10
22 Yanic Perreault .01 .10
23 Michael Nylander .01 .10
24 Scott Lachance .01 .10
25 Pavel Bure .50 1.50
26 Mike Torchia .01 .10
27 Frank Mahovlich FLB .08 .25
28 Philippe Boucher .01 .10
29 Jiri Slegr .01 .10
30 Sergei Fedorov FLB .25 .75
31 Rene Corbet .01 .10
32 Jamie McLennan .01 .10
33 Shane Peacock .01 .10
34 Mario Nobili .01 .10
35 Peter Forsberg .75 2.00
36 All-Rookie Team .01 .10
Pat Falloon
Tyler Wright
Philippe Boucher
Andrew Verner
Scott Lachance
37 Arturs Irbe .10 .50
38 Alexei Zhitnik .01 .10
39 Pat Peake .01 .10
40 Adam Oates FLB .08 .25
41 Markus Naslund .01 .50
42 Eric Lavigne .01 .10
43 Jeff Nelson .01 .10
44 Yanic Dupre UER .01 .10
45 Justin Morrison .01 .10
46 Alek Stojanov .01 .10
47 Marcel Cousineau .01 .10
48 Alexei Kovalev .02 .25
49 Andrei Trefilov .01 .10
50 Mats Sundin FLB .08 .50
51 Steve Staios .01 .10
52 Glenn Hall FLB .08 .25
53 Brent Bilodeau .01 .10
54 Darcy Werenka .01 .10
55 Chris Osgood .40 1.00
56 Nathan Lafayette .01 .10
57 Richard Matvichuk .01 .10
58 Dimitri Mironov UER .01 .10
59 Jason Dawe .01 .10
60 Mike Ricci FLB .01 .10
61 Gerry Cheevers FLB .10 .25
62 Jim Campbell .01 .10
63 Francois Groleau .01 .10
64 Glen Murray .01 .50
65 Jason Young .01 .10
66 Dean McAmmond .01 .10
67 Guy Leveque .01 .10
68 Patrick Poulin .01 .10
69 Bobby House .01 .10
70 Jaromir Jagr FLB .40 1.00
71 Jassen Cullimore .01 .10
72 Checklist Card .01 .10

2000-01 UD CHL Prospects

This 100-card base set was released in March 2001 with a SRP of $2.49 for a 5-card pack. There was a subset of 10 Draft Prospects included in the base set.

COMPLETE SET (100) 20.00 25.00
1 Jay Harrison .10 .20
2 Jay McClement .10 .20
3 Adam Henrich .10 .20
4 Carlo Colaiacovo .30 .50
5 Nikita Alexeev .30 .50
6 Brad Boyes .40 1.00
7 Peter Hamrlik .30 .50
8 Cory Stillman .10 .20
9 Derek Roy .40 .75
10 Michael Zigomanis .30 .50
11 Jason Spezza 1.50 2.00
12 Chad Wiseman .10 .20
13 Patrick Jarrett .30 .50
14 Chris Thornburn .30 .50
15 John Kozoriz .10 .20
16 Brandon Cullen .10 .20
17 Jonathan Zion .10 .20
18 Miguel Delisle .10 .20
19 Ryan Ramsay .10 .20
20 Marcel Rodman .10 .20
21 Stephen Weiss 1.25 1.50
22 Libor Ustrnul .10 .20
23 Rob Zepp .30 .50
24 Kris Vernarsky .30 .50
25 Jason Penner .10 .20
26 Trevor Daley .30 .50
27 Alexei Semenov .30 .50
28 Mark Popovic .10 .20
29 Tim Gleason .40 .75
30 Craig Kennedy .10 .20
31 Steve Ott .40 .75
32 Brian Finley .30 .50
33 Kyle Wellwood .40 1.00
34 Raffi Torres .30 .50
35 Chris Kelly .10 .20
36 Scott Cameron .10 .20
37 Cole Jarrett .10 .20
38 Maxim Rybin .10 .20
39 Derek MacKenzie .10 .20
40 Ryan Held .10 .20
41 Colt King .10 .20
42 Rick Nash 2.00 5.00
43 Greg Jacina .10 .20
44 Branko Radivojevic .40 .75
45 Jordin Tootoo 1.25 3.00
46 Pavel Brendl .10 .20
47 Ryan Craig .10 .20
48 Owen Fussey .10 .20
49 Brent Krahn .40 .75
50 Erik Christensen .10 .20
51 Jared Aulin .30 .50
52 Kiel McLeod .10 .20
53 Dan Blackburn .40 .75
54 Jeff Woywitka .30 .50
55 Ryan Hollweg .10 .20
56 Jay Bouwmeester 2.00 1.50
57 Ben Knopp .10 .20
58 Marcel Hossa .30 .50
59 Greg Watson .10 .20
60 Justin Mapletoft .30 .50
61 Matt Hubbauer .10 .20
62 Garth Murray .10 .20
63 Matthew Spiller .30 .50
64 Barrett Heisten .40 .75
65 Gerard Dicaire .10 .20
66 Jamie Lundmark .40 .75
67 Duncan Milroy .10 .20
68 Nathan Smith .10 .20
69 Konstantin Panov .10 .20
70 Mike Comrie 1.25 1.00
71 Tomas Kopecky .10 .20
72 Jozef Balej .30 1.00
73 Shane Bendera .30 .50
74 Blake Evans .10 .20
75 Igor Pohanka .10 .20
76 Robin LeBlanc .10 .20
77 Yanick Lehoux .30 .50
78 Jean-Francois Racine .30 .50
79 Pascal LeClaire .40 .75
80 Chris Montgomery .10 .20
81 Brent MacLellan .10 .20
82 Thatcher Bell .10 .20
83 Antoine Vermette .40 .75
84 Carl Mallette .10 .20
85 Nicolas Poirier .10 .20
86 Radim Vrbata .30 .50
87 Maxime Ouellet .40 .75
88 Brandon Reid .40 .75
89 Jason Spezza 1.50 2.00
90 Pascal LeClaire .40 .75
91 Dan Blackburn .40 .75
92 Stephen Weiss 1.25 1.00
93 Tim Gleason .40 .75
94 Duncan Milroy .40 .75
95 Kiel McLeod .30 .50
96 Jay McClement .10 .20
97 Jay Harrison .10 .20
98 Greg Watson .40 .75
99 Jason Spezza 1.50 2.00
100 Jay Bouwmeester 2.00 1.50

2000-01 UD CHL Prospects Autographs

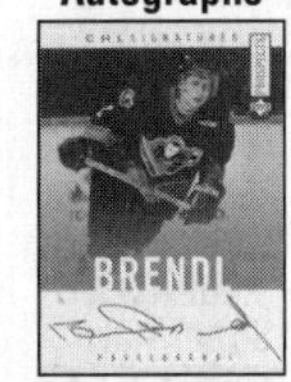

Randomly inserted at a rate of 1:107, this 9-card set features some of the hottest prospects from the CHL in full color photos and player autographs.

A-BK Brent Krahn 15.00
A-BO Bobby Orr 125.00 250.00
A-DB Dan Blackburn 8.00 20.00
A-JB Jay Bouwmeester 10.00 25.00
A-JS Jason Spezza 12.50 30.00
A-PB Pavel Brendl 8.00 10.00
A-PL Pascal LeClaire 15.00
A-RT Raffi Torres 8.00 10.00
A-RZ Rob Zepp 15.00

2000-01 UD CHL Prospects CHL Class

Inserted at a rate of 1:17, this 10-card set featured elite CHL performers on silver foil card stock. The card fronts carry the player's name and jersey number in red foil.

COMPLETE SET (10) 12.50 25.00
CC1 Brian Finley .75 2.00
CC2 Michael Zigomanis .40 1.00
CC3 Jason Spezza 3.00 8.00
CC4 Jay Bouwmeester 2.00 5.00
CC5 Rob Zepp .75 2.00
CC6 Pavel Brendl .40 1.00
CC7 Dan Blackburn 1.25 3.00
CC8 Mike Comrie .75 2.00
CC9 Pascal LeClaire .75 2.00
CC10 Maxime Ouellet .75 2.00

2000-01 UD CHL Prospects Destination the Show

Inserted at a rate of 1:33, this 6-card set features players who are considered locks for the NHL. Each card carries a color action photo and is highlighted by silver and red foil accents.

COMPLETE SET (6) 12.50 15.00
D1 Jason Spezza 4.00 8.00
D2 Dan Blackburn 1.50 3.00
D3 Pavel Brendl 1.25 1.00
D4 Jay Bouwmeester 2.50 5.00
D5 Zdenek Blatny 1.25 1.00
D6 Pascal LeClaire 2.00

2000-01 UD CHL Prospects Future Leaders

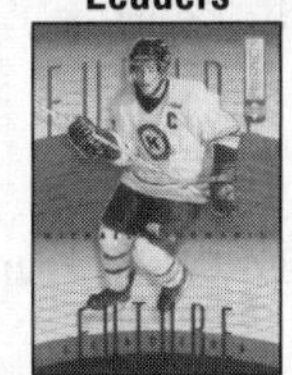

Inserted at 1:17, this 10-card set features player's of the CHL considered to be the future of the NHL. Each card is printed on silver foil card stock with red foil highlights.

COMPLETE SET (10) 12.50 12.00
FL1 Jason Spezza 3.00 5.00
FL2 Raffi Torres .75 2.00
FL3 Brad Boyes .75 2.00
FL4 Stephen Weiss .75 2.00
FL5 Michael Zigomanis .40 1.00
FL6 Jamie Lundmark .40 1.00
FL7 Mike Comrie .75 2.00
FL8 Nathan Smith .40 1.00
FL9 Nathan Vrbata .40 1.00
FL10 Brandon Reid .40 1.00

2000-01 UD CHL Prospects Game Jerseys

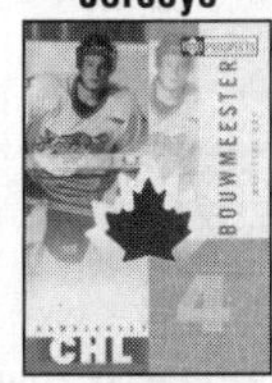

Inserted a rate of 1:18, these cards carry game-worn jersey swatches of some of the biggest names in the CHL. Card fronts carry a color action photo on mostly white stock, the player's name appears vertically on the right side and his jersey number is in grey at the bottom right. The swatch is in the shape of a maple leaf in the center of the card. Autographed parallels were also inserted and numbered to 250 sets.

DBL.JSY STAT.PRINT RUN 250 SER.#'d SETS
BK Brent Krahn 15.00
DB Dan Blackburn 8.00 20.00
JA Jason Spezza 10.00 25.00
Windsor Jersey
JB Jay Bouwmeester 8.00 20.00
JL Jamie Lundmark 5.00 12.00
JS Jason Spezza 10.00 25.00
Mississauga Jersey
NE Nikita Alexeev 5.00 12.00
PB Pavel Brendl 5.00 12.00
RT Raffi Torres 5.00 12.00
RZ Rob Zepp 5.00 12.00
B-B D.Blackburn/B.Krahn 12.50 30.00
B-Z D.Blackburn/R.Zepp 10.00 25.00
L-B J.Lundmark/D.Blackburn 12.50 30.00
L-K J.Lundmark/B.Krahn 8.00 20.00
S-B J.Spezza/J.Bouwmeester 25.00 60.00
S-L J.Spezza/J.Lundmark 20.00 50.00
S-S J.Spezza/J.Spezza 25.00 60.00
S-T J.Spezza/R.Torres 20.00 50.00
S-Z J.Spezza/R.Zepp 12.50 30.00
T-Z R.Torres/R.Zepp 8.00 20.00

2000-01 UD CHL Prospects Great Desire

Inserted at a rate of 1:33, this 6-card set features a small color action photo in the top right hand corner, and a larger photo of the player's eyes in the center surrounded by the words "Great Desire" in red foil. The player's jersey number is in the left bottom corner in silver foil.

COMPLETE SET (6) 12.50 25.00
GD1 Jason Spezza 4.00 8.00
GD2 Jay Bouwmeester 2.50 5.00
GD3 Mike Comrie 3.00
GD4 Raffi Torres 1.25 2.00
GD5 Brandon Reid 1.25 2.00
GD6 Pascal LeClaire 3.00

2000-01 UD CHL Prospects Supremacy

Randomly inserted at 1:17, this 10-card set features elite players of the CHL on silver foil stock. The player's name and jersey number on the card front in red foil. The card back explains why the player was chosen for the set.

COMPLETE SET (10) 12.50 20.00
CS1 Jason Spezza 3.00 8.00
CS2 Brian Finley .75 2.00
CS3 Raffi Torres .40 1.00
CS4 Rob Zepp .75 2.00
CS5 Pavel Brendl .40 1.00
CS6 Justin Mapletoft .40 1.00
CS7 Barrett Heisten .40 1.00
CS8 Mike Comrie .75 2.00
CS9 Jay Bouwmeester 2.00 5.00
CS10 Pascal LeClaire .75 2.00

1999-00 UD Prospects

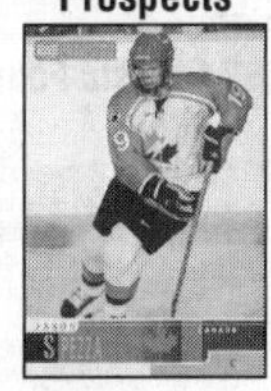

The 1999-00 Upper Deck Prospects set was released as a 90-card set that featured 67 NHL prospects, 22 Canada's Best, and 1 checklist card. Each pack contained 5-cards and carried a suggested retail price of $1.99.

COMPLETE SET (90) 25.00 30.00
1 Wayne Gretzky 1.25 3.00
2 Jason Spezza 3.00 3.00
3 Sheldon Keefe .08 .25
4 Mark Bell .20 .50
5 Justin Papineau .15 .40
6 Denis Shvidki .15 .40
7 Darryl Bootland .20 .50
8 Michael Zigomanis .15 .40
9 Chris Eade .08 .25
10 Brad Boyes .60 1.50
11 Michael Henrich .08 .25
12 Nikita Alexeev .08 .25
13 Libor Ustrnul .08 .25
14 Brian Finley .15 .40
15 Chris Berti .08 .25
16 Agris Saviels .08 .25
17 Kris Newbury .08 .25
18 Jared Newman .08 .25
19 Samu Isosalo .08 .25
20 Mike Van Ryn .15 .40
21 Miguel Delisle .08 .25
22 Rostislav Klesla .20 .50
23 Raffi Torres .20 .50
24 Kurtis Foster .08 .25
25 Lou Dickenson .08 .25
26 Milan Kraft .15 .40
27 Jamie Lundmark .20 .50
28 Scott Hartnell .20 .50
29 Ben Knopp .08 .25
30 Mike Wirll .08 .25
31 Ryan Craig .08 .25
32 Kris Beech .15 .40
33 Pavel Brendl .15 .40
34 Blake Robson .08 .25
35 Jarret Stoll .15 .40
36 Oleg Saprykin .15 .40
37 Eric Johannson .08 .25
38 Warren Peters .08 .25
39 Marcel Hossa .60 .75
40 Shane Endicott .08 .25
41 Craig Olynick .08 .25
42 Brent Krahn .75 .75
43 Matt Pettinger .15 .40
44 Jaroslav Kristek .08 .25
45 Milan Bartovic .08 .25
46 Jared Aulin .15 .40
47 Jakub Cutta .15 .40
48 Blake Ward .08 .25
49 Lynn Lyons .15 .40
50 Jay Bouwmeester 3.00 2.00
51 Nick Schultz .15 .40
52 Filip Novak .08 .25
53 Michael Bubnick .08 .25
54 Charline Labonte 1.00 2.00
55 Thatcher Bell .08 .25
56 Yanick Lehoux .08 .25
57 Antoine Vermette .20 .50
58 Alexei Volkov .15 .40
59 Michal Sivek .15 .40
60 Carl Mallette .08 .25
61 Maxime Ouellet .50 .75
62 Simon Lagace-Daigle .08 .25
63 Andrei Shefer .08 .25
64 Mathieu Chouinard .15 .40
65 Philippe Sauve .20 .50
66 Daniel Sedin .60 .75
67 Henrik Sedin .60 .75
68 Thatcher Bell .08 .25
69 Brad Boyes .60 1.50
70 Jared Aulin .15 .40
71 Dany Heatley 2.00 3.00
72 Ryan Hare .08 .25
73 Scott Hartnell 1.25 .75
74 Jay Bouwmeester 2.00 2.00
75 Kiel McLeod .08 .25
76 Kris Newbury .08 .25
77 Blake Robson .08 .25
78 Jarret Stoll .15 .40
79 Antoine Vermette .20 .50
80 Mike Wirll .08 .25
81 Jason Spezza 3.00 3.00
82 Jay Harrison .08 .25
83 Brandon Janes .08 .25
84 Craig Olynick .08 .25
85 Mark Popovic .08 .25
86 Nick Schultz .15 .40
87 Karl St. Pierre .08 .25
88 Pascal Leclaire .60 .75
89 Blake Ward .08 .25
90 Checklist .08 .25

1999-00 UD Prospects CHL Class

Randomly inserted in packs at 1:4, this 10-card insert set showcases ten of the hottest talents in the CHL. Card backs carry a "C" prefix.

COMPLETE SET (10) 15.00 15.00
C1 Jason Spezza 4.00 5.00
C2 Justin Papineau .60 1.50
C3 Mark Bell .75 2.00
C4 Kris Beech .60 1.50
C5 Jay Bouwmeester 2.00 3.00
C6 Denis Shvidki .60 1.50
C7 Pavel Brendl .60 1.50
C8 Brian Finley .75 2.00
C9 Jamie Lundmark .75 2.00
C10 Thatcher Bell .60 1.50

1999-00 UD Prospects Destination the Show

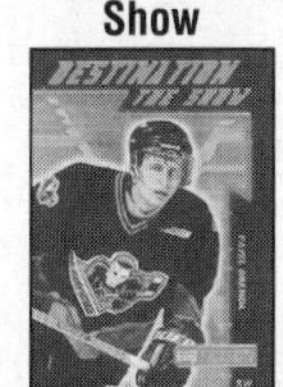

Randomly inserted in packs at 1:17, this 10-card insert set features ten prospects that are preparing for their trip to "The Show". Card backs carry a "DS" prefix.

COMPLETE SET (10) 30.00 35.00
DS1 Jason Spezza 6.00 10.00
DS2 Pavel Brendl 1.25 3.00
DS3 Henrik Sedin 1.50 4.00
DS4 Daniel Sedin 1.50 4.00
DS5 Jamie Lundmark 1.50 4.00
DS6 Taylor Pyatt 1.25 3.00
DS7 Brian Finley 1.50 4.00
DS8 Kris Beech 1.50 4.00
DS9 Denis Shvidki 1.25 3.00
DS10 Jay Bouwmeester 3.00 5.00

1999-00 UD Prospects Game Jerseys

Randomly inserted in packs at 1:215, this 12-card insert features twelve of some of the most collectable phenoms in the game. Card backs are numbered using the players initials.

CL Charline Labonte 40.00 50.00
HS Henrik Sedin 15.00 30.00
JB Jay Bouwmeester 40.00 50.00
JS Jason Spezza 75.00 100.00
KB Kris Beech 15.00 30.00
LD Lou Dickenson 15.00 20.00
PB Pavel Brendl 15.00 20.00
TB Thatcher Bell 15.00 20.00
DSD Daniel Sedin 15.00 30.00

1999-00 UD Prospects International Stars

Randomly inserted in packs at 1:9, this 10-card insert set features the next generation of international superstars. Card backs carry an "IN" prefix.

COMPLETE SET (10) 20.00 40.00
IN1 Daniel Sedin 2.00
IN2 Henrik Sedin 2.00
IN3 Pavel Brendl .60 1.50
IN4 Alexei Volkov 2.00
IN5 Denis Shvidki .60 1.50
IN6 Milan Kraft 2.00
IN7 Nikita Alexeev .60 1.50
IN8 Oleg Saprykin 2.00
IN9 Jaroslav Kristek .60 1.50
IN10 Marcel Hossa 2.00

1999-00 UD Prospects Signatures of Tradition

Randomly inserted in packs at 1:17, this 30-card insert set features autographed cards of future NHL stars. Card backs are numbered using the player's initials.

AV Alexei Volkov 4.00 15.00
BF Brian Finley 4.00 15.00
BM Branislav Mezei 4.00 10.00
CL Charline Labonte 12.50 30.00
DS Daniel Sedin 4.00 15.00
HS Henrik Sedin 4.00 15.00
JB Jay Bouwmeester 12.50 30.00
JL Jamie Lundmark 4.00 15.00
JS Jason Spezza 15.00 40.00
KB Kris Beech 4.00 15.00
MB Mark Bell 4.00 15.00
MC Mathieu Chouinard 4.00 15.00
MO Maxime Ouellet 4.00 15.00
MV Mike Van Ryn 4.00 10.00
PB Pavel Brendl 4.00 10.00
TP Taylor Pyatt 4.00 10.00
WG Wayne Gretzky 250.00 400.00
DSH Denis Shvidki 4.00 10.00

2001-02 UD Prospects

Released in mid-August 2001, this 45-card set focused on young prospects of the CHL.

COMPLETE SET (45) 40.00 30.00
1 Jason Spezza 2.50 3.00
2 Dan Blackburn .75 1.00
3 Daniel Boisclair .40 .75
4 Jeff Woywitka .30 .50
5 Matthew Spiller .30 .50
6 Nathan Paetsch .30 .50
7 Mark Popovic .30 .50
8 Jay McClement .30 .50
9 Garth Murray .30 .50
10 Aaron Lobb .30 .50
11 Derek Roy .75 1.00
12 Jean-Francois Soucy .40 .75
13 Nicolas Corbeil .30 .50
14 Colt King .30 .50
15 Robin Leblanc .30 .50
16 Jay Harrison .30 .50
17 Jiri Jakes .30 .50
18 Lukas Krajicek .40 .75
19 Jason Pominville .40 .75
20 Shawn Collymore .30 .50
21 Michael Garnett .40 .75
22 Adam Munro .40 .75
23 Dan Hamhuis .40 .75
24 Doug Lynch .30 .50
25 Shaone Morrisonn .40 .75

26 Carlo Colaiacovo .40 .75
27 Stephen Weiss .40 .75
28 Joel Stepp .30 .50
29 Jeff Lucky .30 .50
30 Cory Stillman .30 .50
31 Chris Thorburn .30 .50
32 Colby Armstrong .40 .75
33 Brent Maclellan .30 .50
34 Jordin Tootoo 4.00 5.00
35 Greg Watson .30 .50
36 Martin Podlesak .30 .50
37 Duncan Milroy .40 .75
38 Frantisek Bakrlik .30 .50
39 Brendan Bell .30 .50
40 Kiel McLeod .30 .50
41 Jason Spezza 2.50 3.00
42 Jason Spezza 2.50 3.00
43 Jason Spezza 2.50 3.00
44 Jason Spezza 2.50 3.00
45 2001 Top Prospects Summary .30 .50

2001-02 UD Prospects Autographs

Randomly inserted at 1:6 packs, this 23-card set featured authentic player autographs.

A-AM Adam Munro 8.00 20.00
A-BK Brent Krahn 6.00 15.00
A-BO Bobby Orr 75.00 200.00
A-CK Colt King 4.00 10.00
A-CS Cory Stillman 4.00 10.00
A-CT Chris Thorburn 4.00 10.00
A-DB Dan Blackburn 6.00 15.00
A-DH Dan Hamhuis 8.00 20.00
A-DM Duncan Milroy 4.00 10.00
A-GW Greg Watson 4.00 10.00
A-JB Jay Bouwmeester 12.50 25.00
A-JH Jay Harrison 4.00 10.00
A-JL Jamie Lundmark 6.00 15.00
A-JM Jay McClement 4.00 10.00
A-JS Jason Spezza 12.50 30.00
A-KM Kiel McLeod 4.00 10.00
A-MG Michael Garnett 6.00 15.00
A-MP Mark Popovic 4.00 10.00
A-PL Pascal Leclaire 6.00 15.00
A-RK Rostislav Klesla 6.00 15.00
A-RT Raffi Torres 8.00 20.00
A-SW Stephen Weiss 8.00 20.00
A-WG Wayne Gretzky 125.00 300.00

2001-02 UD Prospects Jersey Autographs

Limited to just 30 serial-numbered copies each, this 17-card set featured both game-worn jersey swatches and authentic player autographs.

S-AM Adam Munro 20.00 50.00
S-CK Colt King 15.00 40.00
S-CS Cory Stillman 15.00 40.00
S-CT Chris Thorburn 15.00 40.00
S-DB Dan Blackburn 15.00 40.00
S-DH Dan Hamhuis 30.00 80.00
S-DM Duncan Milroy 15.00 40.00
S-GW Greg Watson 15.00 40.00
S-JH Jay Harrison 15.00 40.00
S-JM Jay McClement 15.00 40.00
S-JS Jason Spezza 60.00 150.00
S-KM Kiel McLeod 15.00 40.00
S-MG Michael Garnett 20.00 50.00
S-MP Mark Popovic 15.00 40.00
S-SW Stephen Weiss 30.00 60.00
S-WA Jason Spezza 60.00 150.00
S-WH Jason Spezza 60.00 150.00

2001-02 UD Prospects Jerseys

Inserted at overall odds of 1 per pack, this 62 card set featured swatches of jerseys worn by the pictured player(s) during the 2001 CHL Top Prospects Game. Dual jersey cards were serial-numbered to 125 copies each. A gold parallel of this set was also created and each card was serial-numbered out of 75.

COMMON CARD 4.00 10.00
J-AL Aaron Lobb 4.00 10.00
J-AM Adam Munro 5.00 12.00
J-BB Brendan Bell 4.00 10.00
J-BM Brent Maclellan 4.00 10.00
J-BO Daniel Boisclair 5.00 12.00
J-CA Colby Armstrong 4.00 10.00
J-CK Colt King 4.00 10.00
J-CS Cory Stillman 4.00 10.00
J-CT Chris Thorburn 4.00 10.00
J-DB Dan Blackburn 6.00 15.00
J-DH Dan Hamhuis 5.00 12.00
J-DL Doug Lynch 4.00 10.00
J-DM Duncan Milroy 4.00 10.00
J-DR Derek Roy 5.00 12.00
J-FB Frantisek Bakrlik 4.00 10.00
J-GM Garth Murray 4.00 10.00
J-GW Greg Watson 4.00 10.00
J-JF Jean-Francois Soucy 5.00 12.00
J-JH Jay Harrison 4.00 10.00
J-JJ Jiri Jakes 4.00 10.00
J-JL Jeff Lucky 4.00 10.00
J-JM Jay McClement 4.00 10.00
J-JP Jason Pominville 5.00 12.00
J-JS Jason Spezza 10.00 25.00
J-JT Jordin Tootoo 15.00 40.00
J-JW Jeff Woywitka 5.00 12.00
J-KM Kiel McLeod 4.00 10.00
J-LK Lukas Krajicek 5.00 12.00
J-MG Michael Garnett 4.00 10.00
J-MP Mark Popovic 4.00 10.00
J-MS Matthew Spiller 4.00 10.00
J-NC Nicolas Corbeil 4.00 10.00
J-NP Nathan Paetsch 4.00 10.00
J-PO Martin Podlesak 4.00 10.00
J-RL Robin Leblanc 4.00 10.00
J-SC Shawn Collymore 4.00 10.00
J-SM Shaone Morrisonn 5.00 12.00
J-ST Joel Stepp 4.00 10.00
J-SW Stephen Weiss 4.00 10.00
J-WA Jason Spezza 10.00 25.00
J-WH Jason Spezza 10.00 25.00
C-BD D. Blackburn/D. Milroy 8.00 20.00
C-BG D. Boisclair/M. Garnett 8.00 20.00
C-BM D. Blackburn/A. Munro 8.00 20.00
C-BS D. Blackburn/J. Spezza 15.00 40.00
C-BW D. Blackburn/S. Weiss 10.00 25.00
C-HM J. Harrison/K. McLeod 8.00 20.00
C-HW D. Hamhuis/S. Weiss 8.00 20.00
C-KP L. Krajicek/M. Podlesak 5.00 12.00
C-KW C. King/G. Watson 8.00 20.00
C-MS J. McClement/C. Stillman 8.00 20.00
C-MT G. Murray/C. Thorburn 8.00 20.00
C-PM M. Popovic/D. Milroy 8.00 20.00
C-RT D. Roy/J. Tootoo 50.00 125.00
C-SA J. Spezza/J. Spezza 15.00 40.00
C-SB J. Spezza/J. Spezza 15.00 40.00
C-SH J. Spezza/D. Hamhuis 12.50 30.00
C-SM J. Spezza/D. Milroy 10.00 25.00
C-SS J. Spezza/J. Spezza 15.00 40.00
C-SW J. Spezza/S. Weiss 15.00 40.00
C-WA J. Woywitka/C. Armstrong 8.00 20.00
C-WM S. Weiss/D. Milroy 10.00 25.00

1991 Ultimate Draft

The 1991 Ultimate/Smokey's Draft Picks hockey set contains 90 standard-size cards. The front design has glossy, color action player photos, bordered in white. The upper left corner of the picture is cut off to allow space for a logo with the words "Sportscards Ultimate Hockey". The player's name, position, and team appear in white lettering in a blue-gray rectangle near the card bottom. Reportedly production quantities were as follows: 6,000 American set cases equaling 120,000 sets, 750 French set cases equaling 15,000 sets, 5,000 American ten-box wax cases, 1,500 French ten-box wax cases, and 500 autographed sets. Currently the French and English cards are valued equally. Autographed versions are worth 30X to 50X basic cards.

COMPLETE SET (90) 3.20 8.00
1 Ultimate/Preview .02 .05
2 Pat Falloon .04 .10
3 Scott Niedermayer .04 .10
4 Scott Lachance .02 .05
5 Peter Forsberg .40 1.00
6 Alek Stojanov .02 .05
7 Richard Matvichuk .04 .10
8 Patrick Poulin .02 .05
9 Martin Lapointe .10 .25
10 Tyler Wright .02 .05
11 Philippe Boucher .02 .05
12 Pat Peake .02 .05
13 Markus Naslund .10 .25
14 Brent Bilodeau .02 .05
15 Glen Murray .10 .25
16 Niklas Sundblad .02 .05
17 Trevor Halverson .02 .05
18 Dean McAmmond UER .02 .05
19 Jim Campbell .02 .05
20 Rene Corbet .02 .05
21 Eric Lavigne .02 .05
22 Steve Staios .02 .05
23 Jassen Cullimore .02 .05
24 Jamie Pushor .02 .05
25 Donevan Hextall .02 .05
26 Andrew Verner .04 .10
27 Jason Dawe .02 .05
28 Jeff Nelson .02 .05
29 Darcy Werenka .02 .05
30 Francois Groleau .02 .05
31 Guy Leveque .02 .05
32 Jamie Matthews .02 .05
33 Dody Wood .04 .10
34 Yanic Perreault .02 .05
35 Jamie McLennan UER .04 .10
36 Yanic Dupre .02 .05
37 1st Round Checklist .02 .05
38 Chris Osgood .40 1.00
39 Fredrik Lindquist .02 .05
40 Jason Young .02 .05
41 Steve Konowalchuk .04 .10
42 Michael Nylander .04 .10
43 Shane Peacock .02 .05
44 Yves Sarault .02 .05
45 Marcel Cousineau .04 .10
46 Nathan Lafayette .02 .05
47 Bobby House .02 .05
48 Kerry Toporowski .02 .05
49 Terry Chitaroni .02 .05
50 Mike Torchia .04 .10
51 Mario Nobili .02 .05
52 Justin Morrison .02 .05
53 Grayden Reid .02 .05
54 Yanic Perreault .02 .05
Underdog
55 2nd Round Checklist .02 .05
56 Niedermayer& Falloon& .04 .10
and Lachance
57 The Goalies .04 .10
58 Pat Falloon FDP .04 .10
59 Scott Niedermayer FDP .04 .10
60 Scott Lachance FDP .02 .05
61 Peter Forsberg FDP .40 1.00
62 Alek Stojanov FDP .02 .05
63 Richard Matvichuk FDP .04 .10
64 Patrick Poulin FDP .02 .05
65 Martin Lapointe FDP .10 .25
66 Tyler Wright FDP .02 .05
67 Philippe Boucher FDP .02 .05
68 Pat Peake FDP .02 .05
69 Markus Naslund FDP .10 .25
70 Brent Bilodeau FDP .02 .05
71 Glen Murray FDP .10 .25
72 Niklas Sundblad FDP .02 .05
73 Trevor Halverson FDP .02 .05
74 Dean McCammond FDP .02 .05
75 Award Winners .02 .05
Philippe Boucher
Jeff Nelson
Scott Niedermayer
76 The Swedes .10 .25
Markus Naslund
Peter Forsberg
77 3rd and 4th Round .02 .05
Checklist
78 Pat Falloon BW .04 .10
79 Scott Niedermayer BW .04 .10
80 Falloon/Niedermayer BW .04 .10
81 Scott Lachance BW .02 .05
82 Philippe Boucher BW .02 .05
83 Markus Naslund BW .10 .25
84 Glen Murray BW .10 .25
85 Niklas Sundblad BW .02 .05
86 Jason Dawe BW .02 .05
87 Yanic Perreault BW .04 .10
88 Offensive Threats .02 .05
Yanic Dupre
Mikael Nylander
89 Group Shot/Overview .02 .05
90 Face the Future/ .02 .05
Ultimate

1991 Ultimate Draft Promos

This three-card standard-size set was given out to dealers and collectors to promote the new Ultimate hockey draft picks cards. The front design is basically the same as the regular issue. The Torchia card displays a different player photo, while the Stojanov card is cropped differently. Also the promos have the team name below the player's name rather than city name as with their regular issue. The backs of the promos differ from those of the regular issue in that the photos on the back are more ghosted and the word "Sample" is stenciled over them. Also the player information on the Stojanov card back is arranged differently on the promo. The cards are unnumbered and checklisted below in alphabetical order.

COMPLETE SET (3) .40 1.00
1 Pat Falloon .20 .50
2 Alex Stojanov .10 .25
3 Mike Torchia .10 .25

1992 Classic Four-Sport *

The 1992 Classic Draft Picks Collection consists of 325 standard-size cards, featuring the top picks from football, basketball, baseball, and hockey drafts. According to Classic, 40,000 12-box foil cases were produced. Randomly inserted in the 12-card packs were over 100,000 autograph cards from over 50 of the top draft picks from basketball, football, baseball, and hockey, including cards autographed by Shaquille O'Neal, Desmond Howard, Roman Hamrlik, and Phil Nevin. Also inserted in the packs were "Instant Win Giveaway Cards" that entitled the collector to the 500,000.00 sports memorabilia giveaway that Classic offered in this contest. There was also a factory set produced with gold parallel cards.

COMPLETE SET (325) 7.50 15.00
151 Roman Hamrlik .01 .05
152 Alexei Yashin
153 Mike Rathje .01 .05
154 Darius Kasparaitis
155 Cory Stillman .01 .05
156 Robert Petrovicky .01 .05
157 Andrei Nazarov .01 .05
158 Jason Bowen .01 .05
159 Jason Smith .01 .05
160 David Wilkie .01 .05
161 Curtis Bowen .01 .05
162 Grant Marshall .01 .05
163 Valeri Bure .01 .05
164 Jeff Shantz .01 .05
165 Justin Hocking .01 .05
166 Mike Peca
167 Marc Hussey .01 .05
168 Sandy Allan .01 .05
169 Kirk Maltby .01 .05
170 Cale Hulse .01 .05
171 Sylvain Cloutier .01 .05
172 Martin Gendron .01 .05
173 Kevin Smyth .01 .05
174 Jason McBain .01 .05
175 Lee J. Leslie .01 .05
176 Ralph Intranuovo .01 .05
177 Martin Reichel .01 .05
178 Stefan Ustorf .01 .05
179 Jarkko Varvio .01 .05
180 Martin Straka
181 Libor Polasek .01 .05
182 Jozef Cierny .01 .05
183 Sergei Krivokrasov
184 Sergei Gonchar
185 Boris Mironov
186 Denis Metlyuk .01 .05
187 Sergei Klimovich .01 .05
188 Sergei Brylin .01 .05
189 Andrei Nikolishin
190 Alexander Cherbayev .01 .05
191 Vitali Tomilin .01 .05
192 Sandy Moger
193 Darrin Madeley .01 .05
194 Denny Felsner .01 .05
195 Dwayne Norris .01 .05
196 Joby Messier .01 .05
197 Michael Stewart .01 .05
198 Scott Thomas .01 .05
199 Daniel Laperriere .01 .05
200 Martin Lacroix
201 Scott LaGrand .01 .05
202 Scott Pellerin .01 .05
203 Jean-Yves Roy .01 .05
204 Rob Gaudreau .01 .05
205 Jeff McLean .01 .05
206 Dallas Drake .01 .05
207 Doug Zmolek .01 .05
208 Duane Derksen .01 .05
209 Jim Cummins .01 .05
210 Lonnie Loach .01 .05
211 Rob Zamuner
212 Brad Werenka
213 Brent Grieve .01 .05
214 Sean Hill .01 .05
215 Peter Ciavaglia .01 .05
216 Jason Ruff .01 .05
217 Shawn McCosh .01 .05
218 Dave Tretowicz .01 .05
219 Mike Vukonich .01 .05
220 Kevin Wortman .01 .05
221 Jason Muzzatti .01 .05
222 Dmitri Kvartalnov .01 .05
223 Ray Whitney
224 Manon Rheaume 2.00 4.00
225 Viktor Kozlov

1992 Classic Four-Sport Autographs *

The 1992 Classic Draft Collection Autograph set consists of 54 standard-size cards. They were randomly inserted throughout the foil packs. Listed after the player's name is how many cards were autographed by that player. An "A" suffix after card number is used here for convenience. Jan Caloun and Jan Vopat were not included in the regular set and hence are unnumbered.

COMPLETE SET (15) 1800.00 2500.00
RANDOM INSERTS IN PACKS
151A Roman Hamrlik/1550
153A Mike Rathje/2075 5.00 10.00
155A Cory Stillman/2125 5.00 10.00
158A Jason Bowen/2075 5.00 10.00
159A Jason Smith/2075 5.00 10.00
165A Justin Hocking/2075 5.00 10.00
170A Cale Hulse/1850 5.00 10.00
181A Libor Polasek/1950 5.00 10.00
185A Boris Mironov/2075
192A Sandy Moger/1075 5.00 10.00
195A Dwayne Norris/1075 5.00 10.00
196A Joby Messier/1075 5.00 10.00
207A Doug Zmolek/1075 5.00 10.00
224A Manon Rheaume/1992 30.00
NNO Jan Vopat/1975 5.00 10.00
NNO Jan Caloun/1975 5.00 10.00

1992 Classic Four-Sport BCs *

Inserted one per jumbo pack, these 20 bonus cards measure the standard size. The fronts feature full-bleed glossy color action player photos. A silver foil strip runs down the card face near the left edge and carries the player's name and position. On a silver panel edged by a dark gray stripe, the backs carry statistics, biography, and career summary; a color player photo running down the right edge rounds out the back. The cards are numbered on the dark gray stripe and arranged according to sport as follows: basketball (1-6), hockey (7-12), football (13-17), and baseball (18-20). A randomly inserted Future Superstars card has a picture of all four players on its front, shot against a horizon with dark clouds and lightning; the back indicates that just 10,000 of these cards were produced.

COMPLETE SET (20) 10.00 20.00
ONE PER JUMBO PACK
FS1 RANDOM INSERT IN JUMBO PACKS
BC7 Roman Hamrlik
BC8 Valeri Bure
BC9 Dallas Drake .08 .25
BC10 Dmitri Kvartalnov .08 .25
BC11 Manon Rheaume 5.00 10.00
BC12 Viktor Kozlov
FS1 Future Superstars 15.00 30.00
Phil Nevin
Shaquille O'Neal
Desmond Howard
Roman Hamrlik

1992 Classic Four-Sport LPs *

Randomly inserted in foil packs, this 25-card standard-size insert set features full-bleed glossy color action player photos on the fronts. A vertical gold foil stripe runs down each card face near the left edge and carries the player's name and position. Parallel to the stripe, "One of 46,080" appears in gold foil characters. The backs carry a brief biography in a silver panel edged on the left by a dark green stripe that contains the player's name and position. A color player photo along the right edge completes the back. The sports represented are football (1-7, 16), basketball (8-14), baseball (17-21), and hockey (22-25). An 8 1/2" by 11" version of Shaquille O'Neal is known to exist.

COMPLETE SET (25) 40.00 70.00
RANDOM INSERTS IN PACKS
LP15 Future Superstars 7.50 15.00
Phil Nevin
Shaquille O'Neal
Roman Hamrlik
Desmond Howard
LP22 Roman Hamrlik
LP23 Mike Rathje .20 .50
LP24 Valeri Bure
LP25 Alexei Yashin

1992 Classic Four-Sport Previews *

These five preview standard-size cards were randomly inserted in baseball and hockey draft picks foil packs. According to the backs, just 10,000 of each card were produced. The fronts display the full-bleed glossy color player photos. At the upper right corner, the word "Preview" surmounts the Classic logo. This logo overlays a black stripe that runs down the left side and features the player's name and position. The gray backs have the word "Preview" in red lettering at the top and are accented by short purple diagonal stripes on each side. Between the stripes are a congratulations and an advertisement. The cards are numbered on the back with a "CC" prefix.

COMPLETE SET (5) 25.00 50.00
CC3 Roman Hamrlik

1993 Fax Pax World of Sport*

Issued in Great Britain, and part of a multi-sport set. Each card was standard size, and was full color. Card backs feature stats and biographical information.

COMPLETE SET (3) 2.00 5.00
25 Wayne Gretzky 1.60 5.00
26 Brett Hull .30 1.00
27 Eric Lindros .60 1.00

1993 FCA 50*

This 50-card standard-size set was sponsored by Fellowship of Christian Athletes. The color player photos on the fronts are accented on three sides by a thin pink stripe; the card face itself shades from blue to white as one moves toward the bottom. The FCA logo, featuring a cross with two olive branches, is superimposed in the upper left corner, while the player's name is printed beneath the picture and his sport in the pink stripe on the left. On a blue background, the backs carry a close-up photo, biography, and the player's testimony.

17 Mike Gartner HK .30 .75

2004 National Trading Card Day *

T7 Rick Nash 1.00
T8 J-S Giguere .75
T12 Jaromir Jagr 1.00
UD10 Patrick Roy 1.50
UD15 Wayne Gretzky 2.00

1997-98 Pinnacle Collector's Club Team Pinnacle *

This 9-card set was part of a much larger multi-sport set available with membership to Pinnacle's Collector's Club. Promo cards carried the player's name across the top of the card not the side like the regular cards.

COMPLETE SET (9) 100.00
H1 Wayne Gretzky 8.00 20.00
H2 Patrick Roy 6.00 15.00
H3 Eric Lindros 3.00 8.00
H4 Paul Kariya 5.00 12.00
H5 Peter Forsberg 5.00 12.00
H6 John Vanbiesbrouck 2.00 5.00
H7 Martin Brodeur 6.00 15.00
H8 Steve Yzerman 6.00 15.00
H9 Jaromir Jagr 4.00 10.00
H10 Mark Messier 3.00 8.00
NNO Wayne Gretzky PROMO 10.00 25.00
NNO Peter Forsberg PROMO 6.00 15.00

2002-03 UD SuperStars *

COMMON CARD (1-250) .15 .40
SEMISTARS/GOALIES .25 .60
UNLISTED STARS .30 .75
6 Paul Kariya .40 1.00
11 Sean Burke .25 .60
22 Ilya Kovalchuk .40 1.00
36 Bobby Orr 1.00 2.50
37 Ray Bourque .40 1.00
41 Jarome Iginla .30 .75
53 Theo Fleury .15 .40
67 Patrick Roy .75 2.00
68 Joe Sakic .40 1.00
69 Peter Forsberg .50 1.25
75 Mike Modano .40 1.00
81 Gordie Howe .75 2.00
82 Steve Yzerman .75 2.00
83 Curtis Joseph .30 .75
84 Wayne Gretzky 1.25 3.00
123 Zigmund Palffy .30 .75
138 Jose Theodore .30 .75
144 Martin Brodeur .40 1.00
165 Pavel Bure .30 .75
166 Michael Peca .15 .40
190 Jeremy Roenick .40 1.00
197 Mario Lemieux 1.00 2.50
216 Teemu Selanne .40 1.00
235 Keith Tkachuk .30 .75
244 Mats Sundin .30 .75
249 Jaromir Jagr .40 1.00
253 T.J. Duckett .40 1.00
I.Kovalchuk
254 S.Chistov .40 1.00
Melvin Ely
255 Dany Heatley .40 1.00
John Ennis
257 Julius Peppers .75 2.00
Erik Cole
261 A.Davis/R.Nash 1.50 4.00
268 H.Zetterberg 1.50 4.00
Kalimba Edwards
269 Jay Bouwmeester 1.00 2.50
Caron Butler
276 Drew Gooden .75 2.00
Scottie Upshall
283 Pierre-Marc Bouchard .20 .50
Igor Rakocevic

2002-03 UD SuperStars Gold *

*GOLD 1-250: 2.5X TO 6X BASIC CARDS
*GOLD 251-300: 2X TO 5X

2002-03 UD SuperStars Benchmarks *

B1 Joe DiMaggio 3.00 8.00
Wayne Gretzky

2002-03 UD SuperStars City All-Stars Dual Jersey *

ABZP Adrian Beltre 4.00 10.00
Zigmund Palffy
BGJS Brian Griese 6.00 15.00
Joe Sakic
CDMS Carlos Delgado 6.00 15.00
Mats Sundin
FPPL Felix Potvin 6.00 15.00
Paul Lo Duca
GAPK Garret Anderson 5.00 12.00
Paul Kariya
JLDS John LeClair 6.00 15.00
Duce Staley
KPBA Keith Primeau 4.00 10.00
Bob Abreu
MLBG M.Lemieux/B.Giles Pants 15.00
40.00
MMAR M.Modano/A.Rodriguez 10.0025.00
MPEL Mike Piazza 10.00 25.00
Eric Lindros
RCPB Roger Clemens 10.00 25.00
Pavel Bure
SSAW Sergei Samsonov 6.00 15.00
Antoine Walker
THRB Todd Helton 6.00 15.00
Rob Blake
WGJG Wayne Gretzky 30.00 60.00
Jason Giambi

2002-03 UD SuperStars City All-Stars Triple Jersey *

DPE Darin Erstad 10.00 25.00
Paul Kariya
Elton Brand
IMD Ivan Rodriguez 15.00 40.00
Mike Modano
Dirk Nowitzki
JKA Jason Kendall 10.00 25.00
Kordell Stewart
Alexei Kovalev
JLP Jason Giambi 10.00 25.00
Latrell Sprewell
Pavel Bure
JMK J.D. Drew 10.00 25.00
Marshall Faulk
Keith Tkachuk
JSB Joey Harrington 40.00 80.00
Steve Yzerman
Ben Wallace
REA Roger Clemens 20.00 50.00
Eric Lindros
Allan Houston
SWK Shawn Green 60.00 120.00
Wayne Gretzky
Kobe Bryant

2002-03 UD SuperStars Keys to the City *

K6 Patrick Roy 1.25 3.00
Todd Helton
K9 Steve Yzerman 1.50 4.00
Joey Harrington

2002-03 UD SuperStars Legendary Leaders Dual Jersey *

SYJH S.Yzerman/J.Harrington 15.00 40.00
ZPSG Zigmund Palffy 6.00 15.00
Shawn Green

2002-03 UD SuperStars Legendary Leaders Triple Jersey *

ADJ Allen Iverson 20.00 50.00
Donovan McNabb
Jeremy Roenick
AEM Alex Rodriguez 30.00 60.00
Emmitt Smith
Mike Modano
CJS Cal Ripken 20.00 50.00
Jaromir Jagr
Stephen Davis
JDM Jason Giambi 15.00 40.00
Drew Bledsoe
Mark Messier
JWL Joe DiMaggio 175.00 300.00
Wayne Gretzky
Larry Bird
LBP Larry Walker 15.00 40.00
Brian Griese
Patrick Roy
MCA Mike Piazza 15.00 40.00
Chad Pennington
Alexei Yashin
MPS McGwire/Manning/Yzerman 40.00
80.00
RJM Clemens/Rice/Lemieux 40.00 80.00
SEB Sammy Sosa 20.00 50.00
Eric Daze
Brian Urlacher
SWK Shawn Green 60.00 120.00
Wayne Gretzky
Kobe Bryant
TEM Gwynn/E.Smith/Lemieux 40.00 80.00

2002-03 UD SuperStars Magic Moments *

STATED ODDS 1:5
MM17 Bobby Orr 1.50 4.00
MM18 Wayne Gretzky 2.00 5.00
MM19 Patrick Roy 1.25 3.00

2002-03 UD SuperStars Rookie Review *

STATED ODDS 1:20
R1 Mark Messier 2.00 5.00
Ozzie Smith

2002-03 UD SuperStars Spokesmen *

*BLACK: 1.25X TO 3X
UD12 Bobby Orr 2.00 5.00
UD13 Gordie Howe 1.50 4.00
UD14 Wayne Gretzky 2.50 6.00
UD27 Bobby Orr 2.00 5.00
UD28 Gordie Howe 1.50 4.00
UD29 Wayne Gretzky 2.50 6.00

2002-03 UD SuperStars Spokesmen Black *

*BLACK: 1.25X TO 3X BASIC CARDS

2002-03 UD SuperStars Spokesmen Gold *

NOT PRICED DUE TO SCARCITY

06Augusta Lynx-19
06Barrie Colts-1
06Barrie Colts-2
06Barrie Colts-3
06Barrie Colts-11
06Barrie Colts-22
06Barrie Colts-LE2
06Cedar Rapids RoughRiders-21
06Ohio State Buckeyes Women-6
06Penticton Vees-11
06ITG Heroes and Prospects-102
Autographs-AMBL

Aab, Vitalij
01German Upper Deck-266
02German DEL City Press-258
All-Stars-AS2
03German DEL-196
03German Nuremberg Ice Tigers Postcards-1
04German Adler Mannheim Eagles Postcards-1
04German DEL-1
05German DEL-161
06German DEL-66

Aaby, Henrik
92Norwegian Elite Series-208
95Swedish World Championships Stickers-255
96Swedish Semic Wien-208
99Norwegian National Team-3

Aalborg, Kent
98Danish Hockey League-43

Aalto, Antti
93Finnish SISU-43
93Finnish SISU-394
93Classic-35
93Classic Four-Sport *-224
Gold-224
94Finest-122
Super Team Winners-122
Refractors-122
94Parkhurst SE-SE227
Gold-SE227
94SP-161
Die Cuts-161
94Upper Deck-511
Electric Ice-511
94Finnish SISU-129
95Finnish SISU-328
95Finnish Semic World Championships-238
96Finnish SISU Redline-147
98Pacific Omega-9
Red-9
Opening Day Issue-9
98UD Choice-9
98UD Choice Preview-9
98UD Choice Prime Choice Reserve-9
98UD Choice Reserve-9
98Upper Deck-1
Exclusives-1
Exclusives 1 of 1-1
Gold Reserve-1
99O-Pee-Chee-225
99O-Pee-Chee Chrome-225
99O-Pee-Chee Chrome Refractors-225
99Topps/OPC-225
99Topps/OPC Chrome-225
Refractors-225
99Upper Deck Gold Reserve-336
99Finnish Cardset Aces High-C-7
99Cincinnati Mighty Ducks-5
00Paramount-1
Copper-1
Gold-1
Holo-Gold-1
Holo-Silver-1
Ice Blue-1
Premiere Date-1
00Upper Deck MVP-1
First Stars-1
Second Stars-1
Third Stars-1
00Finnish Cardset-359
01Finnish Cardset-258
02Finnish Cardset-151
03Finnish Cardset-164
04Finnish Cardset-176
Parallel-176
04Swedish Pure Skills-142
Parallel-142
05Finnish Cardset -157

Aalto, Teemu
99Finnish Cardset-238
00Finnish Cardset-26
01Finnish Cardset-28
02Finnish Cardset-152
03Finnish Cardset-35
04Swedish Elitset-282
Gold-282
04Swedish Pure Skills-91
Parallel-91
05Swedish SHL Elitset-136
Gold-136
06Finnish Cardset-323

Aaltonen, Juhamatti
05Finnish Cardset -277
06Finnish Cardset-280
Playmakers Rookies-2
Playmakers Rookies Gold-2
Playmakers Rookies Silver-2
Signature Sensations-19

Aaltonen, Juhani
70Finnish Jaakiekko-276
71Finnish Suomi Stickers-147
72Finnish Jaakiekko-100
73Finnish Jaakiekko-194

Aaltonen, Lasse
70Finnish Jaakiekko-225

Aaltonen, Petri
93Finnish Jyvas-Hyva Stickers-294
93Finnish SISU-80

Aarnio, Antti
04Finnish Cardset-263
05Swedish SHL Elitset-151
Gold-151
06Finnish Cardset-279

Aarnio, Eric
02Tri-City Stormfront-23

Aarssen, Scott
05London Knights-13
06London Knights-6

Aas, Andre
92Norwegian Elite Series-171

Aayonce, Dean
96Carolina Monarchs-27

Abbass, Keith
93Quebec Pee-Wee Tournament-584

Abbey, Chris
05Sudbury Wolves-3

Abbott, Reggie
48Exhibits Canadian-1

Abbott, Timothy
89ProCards AHL-311

Abel, B.J.
03Trenton Titans-353
05Philadelphia Phantoms-2

Abel, Brett
93Wheeling Thunderbirds-9

Abel, Clarence
33V252 Canadian Gum-1
34Diamond Matchbooks Silver-1

Abel, Gerry
76Old Timers-1
81Red Wings Oldtimers-9

Abel, Jason
98San Angelo Outlaws-1

Abel, Neil
93UK Sheffield Steelers-4
94UK Sheffield Steelers-19
95UK Sheffield Steelers-17
00UK Sheffield Steelers Centurions-15

Abel, Sid
34Beehive Group I Photos-86
39O-Pee-Chee V301-1-68
44Beehive Group II Photos-149
48Exhibits Canadian-43
51Berk Ross-1
51Parkhurst-41
52Royal Desserts-4
60Parkhurst-23
60Shirriff Coins-60
61Shirriff/Salada Coins-61
62Parkhurst-34
64Topps-93
65Topps-41
66Topps-42
76Old Timers-2
83Hall of Fame-2
83Hall of Fame Postcards-A1
85Hall of Fame-2
91Ultimate Original Six-66
French-66
92Hall of Fame Legends-12
94Parkhurst Tall Boys-15
01BAP Ultimate Memorabilia Bloodlines-7
01BAP Ultimate Mem Production Line-2
01BAP Ultimate Mem Production Line-4
01BAP Ultimate Mem Production Line-5
01BAP Ultimate Mem Retired Numbers-1
01BAP Update Passing the Torch-PTT3
01SP Game Used Signs of Tradition-LCSA
01Upper Deck Legendary Cut Signatures-LCSA
01Upper Deck Legends-18
02BAP Ultimate Mem Paper Cuts Autos-29
02BAP Ultimate Mem Retro Teammates-10
02BAP Ultimate Mem Vintage Jerseys-34
02Parkhurst Reprints-160
02Parkhurst Reprints-252
02Parkhurst Reprints-280
02Parkhurst Vintage Teammates-VT6
02SP Authentic Legendary Cuts-LCSA
03BAP Ultimate Memorabilia Emblem Attic-8
03BAP Ultimate Mem Emblem Attic Gold-8
03BAP Ultimate Memorabilia Paper Cuts-35
03BAP Ultimate Mem Raised to the Rafters-7
03BAP Ultimate Mem Retro Teammates-3
03BAP Ultimate Mem Vintage Jerseys-12
03BAP Ultimate Mem Vintage Jerseys Gold-12
03ITG VIP Vintage Memorabilia-7
03Parkhurst Original Six Detroit-41
03Parkhurst Original Six Detroit-67
03Parkhurst Original Six Detroit-77
03Parkhurst Original Six Detroit-81
Inserts-D-4
Inserts-D-6
Memorabilia-DM26
Memorabilia-DM39
Memorabilia-DM53
03Parkhurst Orig Six He Shoots/Scores-30
03Parkhurst Orig Six He Shoots/Scores-30A
03SP Authentic Special Cuts-PROD
04ITG Franchises US West-212
Forever Rivals-WFR2
Forever Rivals Gold-WFR2
Memorabilia-WSM16
Memorabilia Gold-WSM16
Teammates-WTM1
Teammates Gold-WTM1
04ITG Ultimate Memorabilia-133
04ITG Ultimate Memorabilia-138
Gold-133
Gold-138
Autographs-66
Autographs Gold-66
Complete Jerseys-2
Jerseys-16
Jerseys Gold-16
Motown Heroes-7
Original Six-5
Original Six-12
Retro Teammates-6
04ITG Heroes and Prospects-179
04ITG Heroes/Prospects Toronto Expo '05-179
04ITG Heroes/Prospects Expo Heroes/Pros-179
05ITG Ultimate Memorabilia Level 1-86
05ITG Ultimate Memorabilia Level 2-86
05ITG Ultimate Memorabilia Level 3-86
05ITG Ultimate Memorabilia Level 4-86
05ITG Ultimate Memorabilia Level 5-86
05ITG Ultimate Mem Cornerstones Jerseys-4
05ITG Ultimate Mem Cornerst Jerseys Gold-4
05ITG Ultimate Mem Decades Jerseys-2
05ITG Ultimate Mem Decades Jersey Gold-2
05ITG Ultimate Memorabilia Emblem Attic-14
05ITG Ultimate Mem Emblem Attic Gold-14
05ITG Ultimate Mem Motown Heroes Autos-2
05ITG Ultimate Mem Quad Paper Cuts Autos-3
05ITG Ultimate Mem Retro Teammate Jerseys-4
05ITG Ult Mem Retro Teammates Jersey Gold-4
05ITG Ult Mem 3 Star of the Game Jsy-3
05ITG Ult Mem 3 Star of the Game Jsy Gold-3
05The Cup Legendary Cuts-LCSA
06ITG Ultimate Memorabilia-129
Artist Proof-129
Cornerstones-5
Cornerstones Gold-5
Decades-5
Decades Gold-5
Emblem Attic-4
Emblem Attic Gold-4
Lumbergraphs-2
Motown Heroes Autos-2
Retro Teammates-5
Retro Teammates Gold-3
Road to the Cup-1
Road to the Cup Gold-1
06The Cup Legendary Cuts-LCAB

Aberg, Jerry
72Swedish Stickers-203

Aberg, Patric
83Swedish Semic Elitserien-36
84Swedish Semic Elitserien-36
86Swedish Panini Stickers-9
91Swedish Semic Elitserien Stickers-286
92Swedish Semic Elitserien Stickers-302
94Swedish Leaf-181
95Swedish Leaf-7
95Swedish Upper Deck-8

Abid, Ramzi
94Quebec Pee-Wee Tournament-418
98Bowman's Best-141
Refractors-141
Atomic Refractors-141
98OPC Chrome-221
Refractors-221
98Topps-221
O-Pee-Chee-221
98Bowman CHL-110
98Bowman CHL-121
Golden Anniversary-110
Golden Anniversary-121
OPC International-110
OPC International-121
Autographs Blue-A18
Autographs Gold-A18
Autographs Silver-A18
98Bowman Chrome CHL-110
98Bowman Chrome CHL-121
Golden Anniversary-110
Golden Anniversary-121
Golden Anniversary Refractors-110
Golden Anniversary Refractors-121
OPC International-110
OPC International-121
OPC International Refractors-110
OPC International Refractors-121
Refractors-110
Refractors-121
99Halifax Mooseheads-10
00QMJHL All-Star Program Inserts-14
02Coyotes Team Issue-32
02Pacific Calder-88
Silver-88
02Pacific Complete-555
Red-555
02AHL Top Prospects-1
02Springfield Falcons-1
03Pacific-269
Blue-269
Red-269
03Upper Deck-153
Canadian Exclusives-153
HG-153
04Wilkes-Barre Scranton Penguins-16
05Chicago Wolves-1
06Milwaukee Admirals -1

Ablad, Tobias
97Louisville Riverfrogs-13
98Finnish Keräilysarja-143

Abner, Michael
93Quebec Pee-Wee Tournament-1268

Aborn, James
93Quebec Pee-Wee Tournament-633

Abraham, Adam
03Mississauga Ice Dogs-1
04Mississauga Ice Dogs-3

Abraham, Scott
93Quebec Pee-Wee Tournament-863

Abrahamson, Brett
93Minnesota Golden Gophers-1
95Minnesota Golden Gophers-3
96Minnesota Golden Gophers-3
97Minnesota Golden Gophers-7
98Baton Rouge Kingfish-1

Abrahamsson, C.
32Swedish Marabou-4

Abrahamsson, Christer
67Swedish Hockey-1
67Swedish Hockey-95
69Swedish Hockey-110
70Swedish Hockey-66
70Swedish Hockey-275
71Finnish Suomi Stickers-40
71Swedish Hockey-1
71Swedish Hockey-155
72Finnish Jaakiekko-41
72Finnish Panda Toronto-64
72Finnish Semic World Championship-43
72Swedish Stickers-1
72Swedish Stickers-151
72Swedish Semic World Championship-43
73Finnish Jaakiekko-22
73Swedish Stickers-1
73Swedish Stickers-39
74Finnish Jenkki-22
74Finnish Typotor-94
74Swedish Stickers-137
74Swedish Semic World Champ Stickers-1
75O-Pee-Chee WHA-28
76O-Pee-Chee WHA-67
76O-Pee-Chee WHA-110
77Finnish Sportscasters-43-1031
86Swedish Panini Stickers-218
87Swedish Panini Stickers-146
92Swedish Semic Elitserien Stickers-333
93Swedish Semic Elitserien-298
94Swedish Leaf-304

Abrahamsson, Elias
95Halifax Mooseheads-5
96Halifax Mooseheads I-1
96Halifax Mooseheads II-1
97Providence Bruins-2
98Providence Bruins-2
99Hamilton Bulldogs-23
99Providence Bruins-1
00Providence Bruins-15

Abrahamsson, Hans
93Swedish Semic Elitserien-102
94Swedish Leaf-123
95Swedish Leaf-51
95Swedish Upper Deck-78
98German DEL-307

Abrahamsson, Lennart
67Swedish Hockey-246
69Swedish Hockey-202

Abrahamsson, Mats
83Swedish Semic Elitserien-172
84Swedish Semic Elitserien-195
86Swedish Panini Stickers-219

Abrahamsson, Tommy
65Swedish Coralli ISHockey-57
67Swedish Hockey-2
67Swedish Hockey-96
69Swedish Hockey-111
70Finnish Jaakiekko-21
70Swedish Hockey-68
70Swedish Hockey-276
70Swedish Masterserien-155
71Finnish Suomi Stickers-41
71Swedish Hockey-4
71Swedish Hockey-157
72Finnish Jaakiekko-42
72Finnish Hellas-24
72Finnish Panda Toronto-65
72Finnish Semic World Championship-49
72Swedish Stickers-3
72Swedish Stickers-152
72Swedish Semic World Championship-49
73Finnish Jaakiekko-23
73Swedish Stickers-6
73Swedish Stickers-43
74Finnish Typotor-95
74Swedish Stickers-21
74Swedish Stickers-153
74Swedish Semic World Champ Stickers-6
75O-Pee-Chee WHA-127
76O-Pee-Chee WHA-79
77Sportscasters-7104
77Finnish Sportscasters-43-1031

Abramov, Sergei
96Swedish Semic Wien-130

Abrams, Kevin
00Amarillo Rattlers-19

Abrams, Marty
84Sault Ste. Marie Greyhounds-1
03Sault Ste. Marie Greyhounds-24

Abric, Peter
83North Bay Centennials-2

Abstreiter, Peter
99German DEL-320
01German Upper Deck-262
02German DEL City Press-87
04German DEL-143
04German DEL Update-324B
04German Hannover Scorpions Postcards-1
06German DEL-173

Abstreiter, Tobias
92Finnish Semic-190
94German DEL-316
95German DEL-215
96German DEL-358
98German DEL-63
99German DEL-186
99German DEL-386
00German DEL-233
Game Jersey-TA
01German Upper Deck-121
02German DEL City Press-169
Top Stars-GT2
03German DEL-151
04German DEL-183
05German DEL-181

Aceti, T.J.
04Gwinnett Gladiators-1

Achtynichuk, Gene
56Quebec Aces-1

Acker, Gert
02German DEL City Press-170
04German DEL-184
05German DEL-365

Ackerman, Chad
96Hampton Roads Admirals-HRA14
97Hampton Roads Admirals-1
98Hampton Roads Admirals-17
99ECHL All-Star Northern Conference-6
99Hampton Roads Admirals-1

Ackermann, Rene
93Swiss HNL-299
95Swiss HNL-448
96Swiss HNL-458

Ackers, Boris
04German DEL-102
05German DEL-97

Ackestrom, Oscar
90Swedish Semic Elitserien Stickers-36
91Swedish Semic Elitserien Stickers-284
92Swedish Semic Elitserien Stickers-304
93Swedish Semic Elitserien-270
94Swedish Leaf-120
95Swedish Leaf-208
98Finnish Keräilysarja-79
99Finnish Cardset-239
00German DEL-89
01German Upper Deck-91
Skilled Stars-SS5
02Swedish SHL-275
Parallel-275
03Swedish Elite-173
Enforcers-EF2
Silver-173
06Swedish SHL Elitset-207

Acton, Keith
80Canadiens Postcards-1
80Pepsi-Cola Caps-41
81Canadiens Postcards-2
81O-Pee-Chee-181
82Canadiens Postcards-1
82Canadiens Steinberg-1
82O-Pee-Chee-179
82O-Pee-Chee-180
82O-Pee-Chee Stickers-42
82O-Pee-Chee Stickers-43
82Post Cereal-10
82Topps Stickers-42
82Topps Stickers-43
83NHL Key Tags-65
83North Stars Postcards-1
83O-Pee-Chee-184
84North Stars 7-Eleven-6
84North Stars Postcards-1
84O-Pee-Chee-93
85North Stars 7-Eleven-10
85North Stars Postcards-1
85O-Pee-Chee-82
85O-Pee-Chee Stickers-38
85Topps-82
86North Stars Postcards-1
86O-Pee-Chee-172
86Topps-172
87North Stars Postcards-1
87Oilers Team Issue-23
87Panini Stickers-299
88Oilers Tenth Anniversary-77
89Flyers Postcards-1
89O-Pee-Chee-254
89Panini Stickers-301
90Bowman-113
Tiffany-113
90Flyers Postcards-1
90O-Pee-Chee-180
90O-Pee-Chee-355
90Pro Set-497
90Score-301A
Canadian-301A
90Topps-180
90Topps-355
Tiffany-355
90Upper Deck-445
French-445
91Bowman-244
91Flyers J.C. Penney-1
91O-Pee-Chee-77
91Panini Stickers-237
91Score American-133
91Score Canadian Bilingual-133
91Score Canadian English-133
91Stadium Club-247
91Topps-77
92Bowman-184
92Flyers J.C. Penney-1
92Flyers Upper Deck Sheets-4
92Flyers Upper Deck Sheets-25
92Flyers Upper Deck Sheets-35
92O-Pee-Chee-368
92Pinnacle-363
French-363
92Score-341
Canadian-341
92Stadium Club-223
92Topps-199
Gold-199G
92Ultra-368
93Leaf-420
93OPC Premier-407
Gold-407
93Panini Stickers-50
93Score-301
Canadian-301
93Stadium Club-205
Members Only Master Set-205
OPC-205
First Day Issue-205
First Day Issue OPC-205
93Topps/OPC Premier-407
Gold-407
04ITG Franchises US East-435
04ITG Franchises US West-248
Autographs-A-KA

Adair, Jim
73Vancouver Blazers-1

Adair, Scott
907th Inn. Sketch WHL-140
97UK Guildford Flames-7

Adam, Dietrich
94German DEL-21

Adam, Jean-Sebastien
04Moncton Wildcats-11
05Chicoutimi Sagueneens-26
05Moncton Wildcats-15

Adam, Richard
95Czech APS Extraliga-204
98Czech OFS-133
98Czech OFS-306

Adam, Russ
82Maple Leafs Postcards-1
01St. John's Maple Leafs-1

Adamcik, Dusan
95Czech APS Extraliga-240

Adamec, David
06Czech OFS-219

Adamec, Marek
94German First League-478
94German First League-483

Adamec, Vaclav
97Czech APS Extraliga-309
98Czech OFS-62
99Czech Score Blue 2000-44
99Czech Score Red Ice 2000-44

Adamek, Mark
06Stockton Thunder-13

Adamek, Mike
06Bloomington PrairieThunder-1

Adami, Patrick
96Swiss HNL-505

Adamiec, Janusz
89Swedish Semic World Champ Stickers-143
92Finnish Semic-277

Adamik, Peter
73Finnish Jaakiekko-43
74Finnish Jenkki-65

Adams, Akil
92North Dakota Fighting Sioux-1
93Windsor Spitfires-24

Adams, Andy
93Guelph Storm-22
94Guelph Storm-3
95Slapshot-82
95Slapshot-379
96Regina Pats-15
97Topeka Scarecrows-7
98Topeka Scarecrows-21

Adams, B.J.
02Pee Dee Pride RBI-133
03Rockford Ice Hogs-1
04Odessa Jackalopes-1
06Port Huron Flags-10

Adams, Brandon
92Disney Mighty Ducks Movie-1

Adams, Brian
92Harvard Crimson-1

Adams, Bryan
00BAP Memorabilia-81
Emerald-81
Ruby-81
Sapphire-81
Promos-81
00BAP Mem Chicago Sportsfest Copper-81
00BAP Memorabilia Chicago Sportsfest Blue-81
00BAP Memorabilia Chicago Sportsfest Gold-81
00BAP Memorabilia Chicago Sportsfest Ruby-81
00BAP Memorabilia Chicago Sun-Times Ruby-81
00BAP Memorabilia Chicago Sun-Times Gold-81
00BAP Mem Chicago Sun-Times Sapphire-81
00BAP Mem Toronto Fall Expo Copper-81
00BAP Memorabilia Toronto Fall Expo Gold-81
00BAP Memorabilia Toronto Fall Expo Ruby-81
00Pacific-27
Copper-27
Gold-27
Ice Blue-27
Premiere Date-27
00SP Authentic-135
00SPx-175
00Upper Deck Ice-82
01Chicago Wolves-1
02Grand Rapids Griffins-1
03German DEL-137
04German DEL-163
05German DEL-162
06German DEL-130

Adams, Charles F
83Hall of Fame Postcards-D1
85Hall of Fame-47

Adams, Craig
99Cincinnati Cyclones-2
00SP Authentic-140
00Titanium Draft Day Edition-155
00Titanium Draft Day Promos-155
00Upper Deck Ice-84
01BAP Signature Series-33
Autographs-33
Autographs Gold-33
02BAP Sig Series Auto Buybacks 2001-33
03Hurricanes Postcards-1
03ITG Action-187
06Hurricanes Postcards-2
06O-Pee-Chee-93
Rainbow-93

Adams, Erik
03New Mexico Scorpions-2
04New Mexico Scorpions-11
05Colorado Eagles-1
06Colorado EaglesÂ -2

Adams, Gerald
96Regina Pats-11
97Regina Pats-1
99Hampton Roads Admirals-2
00Richmond Renegades-1
01UK London Knights-3
02UK London Knights-3
03UK Sheffield Steelers-1
03UK Sheffield Steelers Stickers-18
04UK Sheffield Steelers-4

Adams, Greg A
82Whalers Junior Hartford Courant-1
85Devils Postcards-1
86Capitals Kodak-1
86Capitals Police-1
86Devils Police-1
86O-Pee-Chee-10
86O-Pee-Chee Box Bottoms-A
86O-Pee-Chee Stickers-196
86Topps-10
86Topps Box Bottoms-A
87Canucks Shell Oil-1
87Capitals Kodak-22
87Capitals Team Issue-1
87O-Pee-Chee-135
87Panini Stickers-84
87Panini Stickers-185
87Topps-135
88Canucks Mohawk-1
88Oilers Tenth Anniversary-85
88O-Pee-Chee-162
88O-Pee-Chee Stickers-66
88Panini Stickers-136
88Topps-162
89Canucks Mohawk-1
89O-Pee-Chee-178
89Panini Stickers-154
89Topps-178
90Bowman-59
Tiffany-59
90Canucks Mohawk-1
90O-Pee-Chee-106
90Panini Stickers-303
90Pro Set-291
90Score-240
Canadian-240
90Topps-106
Tiffany-106
90Upper Deck-342
French-342
91Pro Set Platinum-125
91Bowman-311
91Canucks Panini Team Stickers-1
91Canucks Autograph Cards-1
91Canucks Molson-1
91Canucks Team Issue 8x10-1
91O-Pee-Chee-340
91Panini Stickers-39
91Parkhurst-183
French-183
91Pinnacle-218
French-218
91Pro Set-243
French-243
91Score American-44
91Score Canadian Bilingual-44
91Score Canadian English-44
91Stadium Club-52
91Topps-340
91Upper Deck-426
French-426
92Bowman-333
92Canucks Road Trip Art-1
92O-Pee-Chee-365
92Parkhurst-195
Emerald Ice-195
92Pinnacle-28
French-28
92Score-146
Canadian-146
92Stadium Club-232
92Topps-507
Gold-507G
92Ultra-217
92Upper Deck-192
93Donruss-350
93Leaf-219
93Panini Stickers-173
93Parkhurst-480
Emerald Ice-480
93Pinnacle-247
Canadian-247
93PowerPlay-247
93Score-196
Canadian-196
93Ultra-19
93Upper Deck-77
SP-161
94Canada Games NHL POGS-96
94Canucks Program Inserts-1
94Donruss-101
94Flair-187
94Leaf-222
94OPC Premier-414
Special Effects-414
94Parkhurst SE-SE185
Gold-SE185
94Pinnacle-240
Artist's Proofs-240
Rink Collection-240
94Stadium Club-156
Members Only Master Set-156
First Day Issue-156
Super Team Winner Cards-156
94Topps/OPC Premier-414
Special Effects-414
94Ultra-380
94Upper Deck-211
Electric Ice-211
95Be A Player-22
Signatures-S22
Signatures Die Cuts-S22
95Canada Games NHL POGS-91
95Collector's Choice-286
Player's Club-286
Player's Club Platinum-286
95Donruss-158
95Leaf-112
95Metal-37
95Parkhurst International-327
Emerald Ice-327
95Score-89
Black Ice Artist's Proofs-89
Black Ice-89
95Stars Score Sheet-89
95Ultra-227
95Upper Deck-26
Electric Ice-26
Electric Ice Gold-26
Special Edition-SE113
Special Edition Gold-SE113
96Black Diamond-23
Gold-23
96Donruss-82
Press Proofs-82
96Leaf-103
Press Proofs-103
96Pinnacle-194
Artist's Proofs-194
Foil-194
Premium Stock-194
Rink Collection-194
96Score-39
Artist's Proofs-39
Dealer's Choice Artist's Proofs-39
Special Artist's Proofs-39
Golden Blades-39
96Stars Postcards-1
96Stars Score Sheet-39
96Summit-95
Artist's Proofs-95
Ice-95
Metal-95
Premium Stock-95
96Upper Deck Ice-14
Parallel-14
97Be A Player-164
Autographs-164
Autographs Die-Cuts-164
Autographs Prismatic Die-Cuts-164
97Collector's Choice-71
97Pacific Invincible NHL Regime-59
97Pacific Omega-66
Copper-66
Dark Gray-66
Emerald Green-66
Gold-66
Ice Blue-66
97Upper Deck-265
98Pacific-171
Ice Blue-171
Red-171
98Upper Deck-344
Exclusives-344
Exclusives 1 of 1-344
Gold Reserve-344
99BAP Memorabilia-34
Gold-34
Silver-34
99Pacific-315
Copper-315
Emerald Green-315
Gold-315
Ice Blue-315
Premiere Date-315
Red-315
99Paramount-177
Copper-177
Emerald-177
Gold-177
Holographic Emerald-177
Holographic Gold-177
Holographic Silver-177
Ice Blue-177
Premiere Date-177
Red-177
99Upper Deck MVP-163
Gold Script-163
Silver Script-163
Super Script-163
99Upper Deck Victory-229
00BAP Memorabilia-374
Emerald-374
Ruby-374
Sapphire-374
Promos-374
00BAP Mem Chicago Sportsfest Copper-374
00BAP Memorabilia Chicago Sportsfest Blue-374
00BAP Memorabilia Chicago Sportsfest Gold-374
00BAP Memorabilia Chicago Sportsfest Ruby-374
00BAP Memorabilia Chicago Sun-Times Ruby-374
00BAP Memorabilia Chicago Sun-Times Gold-374
00BAP Mem Chicago Sun-Times Sapphire-374
00BAP Mem Toronto Fall Expo Copper-374
00BAP Memorabilia Toronto Fall Expo Gold-374
00BAP Memorabilia Toronto Fall Expo Ruby-374
00O-Pee-Chee-228
00O-Pee-Chee Parallel-228
00Panthers Team Issue-20
00Topps/OPC-228
Parallel-228

Adams, Greg C.
86O-Pee-Chee-253
87O-Pee-Chee-139
87Topps-139
88O-Pee-Chee-199
90O-Pee-Chee-518
02German DEL City Press-65

Adams, Jack
23V145-1-24
24C144 Champ's Cigarettes-1
24V145-2-53
34Beehive Group I Photos-133
37V356 Worldwide Gum-99
40O-Pee-Chee V301-2-104
83Hall of Fame-182
83Hall of Fame Postcards-J1
85Hall of Fame-182
92Hall of Fame Legends-21
02SP Authentic Legendary Cuts-LCJA
03BAP Ultimate Memorabilia Memorialized-2
03BAP Ultimate Mem Vintage Blade of Steel-14

04ITG Franchises Canadian-84
04ITG Ultimate Memorabilia-186
Gold-186
Paper Cuts Memorabilia-6
05ITG Ultimate Mem Blades of Steel-6
05ITG Ultimate Mem Blades of Steel Gold-6
05ITG Ultimate Memorabilia Lumbergraphs-11
05ITG Ultimate Mem Motown Heroes Autos-4
06ITG Ultimate Memorabilia-70
Artist Proof-70
Blades of Steel-16
Blades of Steel Gold-16

Adams, Jamie
93Johnstown Chiefs-14
94Central Hockey League-1
94Dallas Freeze-2
98Bakersfield Condors-1

Adams, John
74Capitals White Borders-1

Adams, John OHL
04St. Michael's Majors-8
05Florida Everblades-21

Adams, Kevyn
93Donruss Team USA-1
93Pinnacle-488
Canadian-488
93Upper Deck-568
96Grand Rapids Griffins-1
97Pinnacle-22
Artist's Proofs-22
Rink Collection-22
Press Plates Back Black-22
Press Plates Back Cyan-22
Press Plates Back Magenta-22
Press Plates Back Yellow-22
Press Plates Front Black-22
Press Plates Front Cyan-22
Press Plates Front Magenta-22
Press Plates Front Yellow-22
97Score-60
Artist's Proofs-60
Golden Blades-60
97Score Maple Leafs-15
Platinum-15
Premier-15
97St. John's Maple Leafs-1
99BAP Memorabilia-365
Gold-365
Silver-365
99Maple Leafs Pizza Pizza-8
99St. John's Maple Leafs-1
00BAP Memorabilia-352
Emerald-352
Ruby-352
Sapphire-352
Promos-352
00BAP Mem Chicago Sportsfest Copper-352
00BAP Memorabilia Chicago Sportsfest Blue-352
00BAP Memorabilia Chicago Sportsfest Gold-352
00BAP Memorabilia Chicago Sportsfest Ruby-352
00BAP Memorabilia Chicago Sun-Times Ruby-352
00BAP Memorabilia Chicago Sun-Times Gold-352
00BAP Mem Chicago Sun-Times Sapphire-352
00BAP Mem Toronto Fall Expo Copper-352
00BAP Memorabilia Toronto Fall Expo Gold-352
00BAP Memorabilia Toronto Fall Expo Ruby-352
00BAP Signature Series-129
Emerald-129
Ruby-129
Sapphire-129
Autographs-38
Autographs Gold-38
00Paramount-66
Copper-66
Gold-66
Holo-Gold-66
Holo-Silver-66
Ice Blue-66
Premiere Date-66
00Revolution-41
Blue-41
Premiere Date-41
Red-41
00Stadium Club-207
00Topps Chrome-227
OPC Refractors-227
Refractors-227
00Upper Deck-52
Exclusives Tier 1-52
Exclusives Tier 2-52
00Upper Deck Vintage-105
00Upper Deck Vintage-110
01BAP Memorabilia-178
Emerald-178
Ruby-178
Sapphire-178
01Pacific-168
Extreme LTD-168
Hobby LTD-168
Premiere Date-168
Retail LTD-168
01Pacific Arena Exclusives-168
01Parkhurst-169
01Upper Deck-76
Exclusives-76
01Upper Deck MVP-81
01Upper Deck Victory-147
Gold-147
02BAP Sig Series Auto Buybacks 2000-38
02Pacific Complete-187
Red-187
02Upper Deck-277
Exclusives-277
02Upper Deck Beckett UD Promos-277
03Hurricanes Postcards-2
03ITG Action-150
03Pacific Complete-199
Red-199
04German DEL Superstars-SU22
05Be A Player Signatures-KE
05Be A Player Signatures Gold-KE
05Parkhurst-96
Facsimile Auto Parallel-96
06Be A Player-169
Autographs-169
Signatures-KA
06Hurricanes Postcards-3
06O-Pee-Chee-99
Rainbow-99
06Upper Deck-291
Exclusives Parallel-291
High Gloss Parallel-291
Masterpieces-291

Adams, Kyle
93Quebec Pee-Wee Tournament-1463

Adams, Weston W
83Hall of Fame Postcards-I1
85Hall of Fame-122

Adamsky, Martin
02Czech OFS Plus-323
03Czech OFS Plus-196
04Czech HC Plzen Postcards-1
04Czech OFS-137
05Czech HC Plzen-1
06Czech HC Plzen Postcards-9

Adamson, Chuck
01Fort Wayne Komets Shoe Carnival-14

Adamson, Ian
91Air Canada SJHL-E37
92Saskatchewan JHL-114

Adamus, Damian
94German DEL-290
95German DEL-281
96German DEL-90
99German EV Landshut-20

Adamus, Trent
00Saskatoon Blades-16
01Saskatoon Blades-15
02Saskatoon Blades-7
03Saskatoon Blades-18

Addesa, Chris
94Dubuque Fighting Saints-2

Addesa, Matt
94Dubuque Fighting Saints-3

Addington, Oliver
93Quebec Pee-Wee Tournament-166

Adduono, Jayme
95Waterloo Blackhawks -1

Adduono, Jeremy
94Thunder Bay Flyers-1
95Slapshot-391
95Sudbury Wolves-11
95Sudbury Wolves Police-3
96Sudbury Wolves-2
96Sudbury Wolves Police-4
97Sudbury Wolves Police-2
98Bowman CHL-29
Golden Anniversary-29
OPC International-29
98Bowman Chrome CHL-29
Golden Anniversary-29
Golden Anniversary Refractors-29
OPC International-29
OPC International Refractors-29
Refractors-29
00Rochester Americans-1
03German DEL-166
04German Cologne Sharks Postcards-1
04German DEL-204
05German DEL-201
06German DEL-105

Adduono, Rick
01South Carolina Stingrays-1
02ECHL Update-U-1

Adey, Paul
00UK Sekonda Superleague-201
00UK Sheffield Steelers-4
01UK Nottingham Panthers-12
02UK Nottingham Panthers-18
04UK Nottingham Panthers-1

Adlys, Bernie
91Air Canada SJHL-D17
91Air Canada SJHL-E34

Adolfi, Rick
83Belleville Bulls-16
83Ottawa 67's-1
84Kitchener Rangers-27

Adolfsson, Marcus
98German DEL-12
99Alexandria Warthogs-21

Adrian, Birger
56Swedish Alfabilder-71

Adrian, Kjell
57Swedish Alfabilder-123
64Swedish Coralli ISHockey-93
65Swedish Coralli ISHockey-93

Aeberli, Patrick
01Swiss HNL-350
02Swiss HNL-97

Aebersold, Steve
93Swiss HNL-324
95Swiss HNL-169
96Swiss HNL-63
98Swiss Power Play Stickers-304
99Swiss Panini Stickers-311
00Swiss Panini Stickers-63
00Swiss Slapshot Mini-Cards-HCCF8
01Swiss HNL-291
02Swiss HNL-128

Aebi, Lars
95Swiss HNL-449

Aebischer, Beat
93Swiss HNL-238
95Swiss HNL-439
96Swiss HNL-427
98Swiss Power Play Stickers-345
99Swiss Panini Stickers-333
00Swiss Panini Stickers-312
01Swiss HNL-362
02Swiss HNL-414

Aebischer, David
92Quebec Pee-Wee Tournament-1403
95Swiss HNL-58
96Swiss HNL-205
98Swiss Power Play Stickers-79
98Swiss Power Play Stickers-251
98Hershey Bears-19
99Swiss Panini Stickers-253
00BAP Memorabilia-479
Emerald-479
Ruby-479
Sapphire-479
00Black Diamond-114
00Crown Royale-118
21st Century Rookies-7
00Private Stock-111
Gold-111
Premiere Date-111
Retail-111
Silver-111
PS-2001 Rookies-6
00SP Authentic-98
00SP Game Used-65
00SPx-157
00Stadium Club-257
00Titanium-111
Retail-111
00Titanium Draft Day Edition-111
00Titanium Draft Day Promos-111
00Topps Chrome-244
Blue-244
Red-244
OPC Refractors-244
OPC Refractors Blue-244
OPC Refractors Red-244
Refractors-244
Refractors Blue-244
Refractors Red-244
00Topps Gold Label Class 1-103
Gold-103
00Topps Gold Label Class 2-103
00Topps Gold Label Class 2 Gold-103
00Topps Gold Label Class 3-103
00Topps Gold Label Class 3 Gold-103
00Topps Heritage-78
Chrome Parallel-78
00Topps Premier Plus-122
Blue Ice-122
00Topps Stars-117
Blue-117
00UD Heroes-161
00UD Pros and Prospects-99
00UD Reserve-91
00Upper Deck-433
Exclusives Tier 1-433
Exclusives Tier 2-433
00Upper Deck Ice-85
00Vanguard-111
Pacific Proofs-111
00Swiss Panini Stickers National Team-P2
01Avalanche Team Issue-1
01BAP Memorabilia-194
Emerald-194
Ruby-194
Sapphire-194
01BAP Signature Series-180
Autographs-180
Autographs Gold-180
01Between the Pipes-23
01Between the Pipes-164
Jerseys-GJ40
Jersey and Stick Cards-GSJ36
Tandems-GT5
01Crown Royale Calder Collection Gold Ed-8
01Crown Royale Calder Collection AS Ed-C1
01O-Pee-Chee-46
01O-Pee-Chee Heritage Parallel-46
01O-Pee-Chee Heritage Parallel Limited-46
01O-Pee-Chee Premier Parallel-46
01Pacific-95
01Pacific-444
Extreme LTD-95
Hobby LTD-95
Premiere Date-95
Retail LTD-95
01Pacific Adrenaline-44
Blue-44
Premiere Date-44
Red-44
Retail-44
01Pacific Arena Exclusives-95
01Pacific Heads-Up Breaking the Glass-5
01Private Stock PS-2002-16
01Stadium Club New Regime-NR2
01Stadium Club New Regime-NRADA
01Topps-46
Heritage Parallel-46
Heritage Parallel Limited-46
OPC Parallel-46
01Topps Chrome-46
Refractors-46
Black Border Refractors-46
01UD Mask Collection Double Patches-DPDA
01UD Mask Collection Goalie Jerseys-MMDA
01UD Mask Collection Goalie Jerseys-SYDA
01UD Mask Collection Jerseys-J-DA
01UD Mask Collection Jersey and Patch-JPDA
01UD Stanley Cup Champs-34
01Upper Deck Avalanche NHL All-Star Game-HH1
01Upper Deck Avalanche NHL All-Star Game-PP6
01Upper Deck Victory-88
Gold-88
02Avalanche Postcards-4
02BAP First Edition-13
Jerseys-13
02BAP Signature Series-72
Autographs-72
Autograph Buybacks 2001-180
Autographs Gold-72
Golf-GS29
02Between the Pipes-22
Gold-22
Silver-22
Emblems-6
Jerseys-6
Numbers-6
Stick and Jerseys-6
Tandems-2
02Bowman YoungStars-109
Gold-109
Silver-109
Autographs-DA
Jerseys-DA
Patches-DA
Double Stuff-DA
Triple Stuff-DA
Rivals-DARM
Rivals Patches-2
Sticks-DA
02Pacific-86
Blue-86
Red-86
02Pacific Complete-47
Red-47
02SP Game Used Future Fabrics-FFAE
02SP Game Used Future Fabrics Gold-FFAE
02SP Game Used Future Fabrics Rainbow-FFAE
02Topps Total-201
02UD Mask Collection-21
02UD Mask Collection-22
02UD Mask Collection-109
02UD Mask Collection Beckett Promos-21
02UD Mask Collection Beckett Promos-22
02UD Top Shelf Stopper Jerseys-SSDA
02Upper Deck-289
Exclusives-289
02Upper Deck Beckett UD Promos-289
02Upper Deck Classic Portraits Headliners-RA
02Upper Deck Classic Portraits Headliners Limited-RA
02Upper Deck MVP Skate Around Jerseys-SDRA
02Upper Deck Vintage Jerseys-EEDA
02Upper Deck Vintage Jerseys Gold-EE-DA
03Avalanche Team Issue-1
03BAP Memorabilia-115
Emerald-115
Gold-115
Ruby-115
Sapphire-115
Future Wave-FW-3
Masks III-19
Masks III Gold-19
Masks III Silver-19
Masks III Autographs-M-DA
Masks III Memorabilia-19
03BAP Ultimate Memorabilia Autographs-19
Gold-19
03BAP Ultimate Mem Auto Jerseys-19
03BAP Ultimate Mem Complete Package-11
03BAP Ultimate Mem Complete Package Gold-11
03BAP Ultimate Mem Franch Present Future-8
03BAP Ultimate Mem Perennial Power Jersey-8
03BAP Ult Mem Perenn Powerhouse Jsy Stick-8
03BAP Ultimate Mem Perennial Power Emblem-8
03BAP Ultimate Memorabilia Triple Threads-2
03Beehive-52
Gold-52
Silver-52
Signatures-RF7
Sticks Beige Border-BE36
Sticks Red Border-RE17
03Black Diamond-145
Black-145
Green-145
Red-145
Threads-DT-DA
Threads Green-DT-DA
Threads Red-DT-DA
Threads Black-DT-DA
03Bowman-47
Gold-47
Future Fabrics-FF-DA
Future Fabric Patches-DA
Future Rivals-AT
Future Rivals Patches-AT
03Bowman Chrome-47
Refractors-47
Gold Refractors-47
Xfractors-47
03Crown Royale-22
Blue-22
Retail-22
Gauntlet of Glory-6
Global Conquest-9
03ITG Action-184
Jerseys-M91
03ITG Used Signature Series-76
Gold-76
Autographs-DAE
Autographs Gold-DAE
Goalie Gear-21
Goalie Gear Autographs-21
Goalie Gear Gold-21
Triple Memorabilia-30
Triple Memorabilia Gold-30
03O-Pee-Chee-271
03OPC Blue-271
03OPC Gold-271
03OPC Red-271
03Pacific-79
Blue-79
Red-79
03Pacific Complete-490
Red-490
03Pacific Exhibit-35
Blue Backs-35
Yellow Backs-35
03Pacific Heads-Up-23
Hobby LTD-23
Retail LTD-23
Jerseys-7
Stonewallers-3
Stonewallers LTD-3
03Pacific Invincible-20
Blue-20
Red-20
Retail-20
03Pacific Luxury Suite-31A
03Pacific Luxury Suite-31B
03Pacific Quest for the Cup-22
Blue-22
Jerseys-5
03Pacific Supreme Generations-2
03Private Stock Reserve-24
Blue-24
Red-24
Retail-24
Increase Security-5
03SP Authentic-19
Limited-19
Sign of the Times-DA
03SP Game Used-122
Gold-122
Double Threads-DTAR
Signers-SPSDA
03SPx-24
03SPx-175
Radiance-24
Radiance-175
Spectrum-24
Spectrum-175
03Titanium-147
Hobby Jersey Number Parallels-147
Patches-147
Retail-147
Masked Marauders-2
03Topps-271
Blue-271
Gold-271
Red-271
03Topps Pristine-75
Gold Refractor Die Cuts-75
Refractors-75
Mini-PM-DA
Press Plates Black-75
Press Plates Cyan-75
Press Plates Magenta-75
Press Plates Yellow-75
03Topps Traded Future Phenoms-FP-DA
03UD Honor Roll-17
Signature Class-SC1
03UD Premier Collection-13
NHL Shields-SH-DA
Signatures-PS-DA
Signatures Gold-PS-DA
03Upper Deck-51
Canadian Exclusives-51
HG-51
Jersey Autographs-SJ-DA
Patches-SV7
03Upper Deck Classic Portraits-24
03Upper Deck Ice-22
Gold-22
Authentics-IA-DA
Breakers-IB-DA
Breaker Patches-IB-DA
Frozen Fabrics-FF-DA
Frozen Fabric Patches-FF-DA
03Upper Deck MVP-112
Gold Script-112
Silver Script-112
Canadian Exclusives-112
Masked Men-MM9
SportsNut-SN21
03Upper Deck Rookie Update-22
Skills-SKDA
Super Stars-SSDA
03Upper Deck Victory-48
Bronze-48
Gold-48
Silver-48
04Pacific-64
Blue-64
Red-64
In The Crease-3
04SP Authentic-21
Limited-21
Buybacks-37
Buybacks-38
Buybacks-39
Buybacks-40
Buybacks-41
Buybacks-42
Rookie Review-RR-AB
Sign of the Times-ST-AB
Sign of the Times-TS-HTA
Sign of the Times-QS-TAHS
Sign of the Times-FS-GOL
04UD All-World-82
Gold-82
Autographs-82
Triple Autographs-AT-TAR
Quad Autographs-AQ-GOL
Five Autographs-AF-GOL
04Ultimate Collection Dual Logos-UL2-AF
04Upper Deck-48
Canadian Exclusives-48
HG Glossy Gold-48
HG Glossy Silver-48
Jersey Autographs-GJA-DA
05Be A Player Quad Signatures-COLO
05Be A Player Quad Signatures-TLAL
05Be A Player Signatures-AE
05Be A Player Signatures Gold-AE
05Be A Player Triple Signatures-LLA
05Black Diamond-92
Emerald-92
Gold-92
Onyx-92
Ruby-92
05Hot Prospects-51
En Fuego-51
Red Hot-51
White Hot-51
05Panini Stickers-227
05Parkhurst-250
Facsimile Auto Parallel-120
True Colors-TCCOL
True Colors-TCCOL
05SP Authentic-27
Limited-27
05SP Game Used-26
Autographs-26
Gold-26
Authentic Fabrics-AF-AE
Authentic Fabrics Autographs-AAF-AE
Authentic Fabrics Gold-AF-AE
Authentic Fabrics Quad-SATH
Authentic Patches Quad -SATH
Authentic Fabrics Triple-CEA
Authentic Fabrics Triple-RLA
Authentic Patches-AP-AE
Authentic Patches Autographs-AAP-AE
Authentic Patches Triple-CEA
Authentic Patches Triple-RLA
Auto Draft-AD-DA
SIGnificance-DA
SIGnificance Gold-S-DA
SIGnificance Extra-TA
SIGnificance Extra Gold-TA
05SPx-20
Spectrum-20
Winning Combos-WC-AB
Winning Combos Autographs-AWC-AB
Winning Combos Gold-WC-AB
Winning Combos Spectrum-WC-AB
Winning Materials-WM-AE
Winning Materials Autographs-AWM-DA
Winning Materials Gold-WM-AE
Winning Materials Spectrum-WM-AE
05The Cup Honorable Numbers-HNDA
05The Cup Limited Logos-LLDA
05The Cup Noble Numbers-NNLA
05The Cup Scripted Numbers-SNLA
05The Cup Scripted Numbers Dual-DSNGA
05The Cup Signature Patches-SPDA
05The Cup Stanley Cup Titlists-TDA
05UD Artifacts-26
Blue-26
Gold-26
Green-26
Pewter-26
Red-26
Auto Facts-AF-DA
Auto Facts Blue-AF-DA
Auto Facts Copper-AF-DA
Auto Facts Pewter-AF-DA
Auto Facts Silver-AF-DA
Gold Autographed-26
Remarkable Artifacts-RA-DA
Remarkable Artifacts Dual-RA-DA
05UD Powerplay Specialists-TSAB
05UD Powerplay Specialists Patches-SPAB
05UD Toronto Fall Expo Priority Signings-PS-DA
05Ultimate Collection-48
Gold-48
Endorsed Emblems-EEDA
National Heroes Jerseys-NHJDA
National Heroes Patches-NHPDA
05Ultra-54
Gold-54
Ice-54
05Upper Deck-49
Big Playmakers-B-DAE
HG Glossy-49
Jerseys-J-DAE
Notable Numbers-N-AE
Patches-P-DAE
05Upper Deck Ice-25
Rainbow-25
05Upper Deck MVP-103
Gold-103
Platinum-103
ProSign-P-DA
05Upper Deck Rookie Update-51
05Upper Deck Trilogy-22
Honorary Patches-HP-DA
Honorary Patch Scripts-HSP-DA
Honorary Swatches-HS-DA
Honorary Swatch Scripts-HSS-DA
Ice Scripts-IS-DA
Scripts-SFS-DA
05Upper Deck Toronto Fall Expo-49
05Upper Deck Victory-47
Black-47
Gold-47
Silver-47
Stars on Ice-SI15
06Beehive Matted Materials-MMAE
06Beehive Remarkable Matted Materials-MMAE
06Black Diamond Gemography-GDA
06Canadiens Postcards-1
06Flair Showcase Inks-IDA
06Fleer-108
Tiffany-108
Signing Day-SDDA
06Gatorade-37
06Hot Prospects-54
Red Hot-54
White Hot-54
Hot Materials -HMAE
Hot Materials Red Hot-HMAE
Hot Materials White Hot-HMAE
Hotagraphs-HDA
06O-Pee-Chee-258
Rainbow-258
Swatches-S-AE
06SP Authentic Sign of the Times Duals-STHA
06SP Game Used Authentic Fabrics-AFDA
06SP Game Used Authentic Fabrics Parallel-AFDA
06SP Game Used Authentic Fabrics Patches-AFDA
06SP Game Used Authentic Fabrics Dual-AF2AH
06SP Game Used Authentic Fabrics Dual Patches-AF2AH
06SP Game Used Inked Sweaters Dual-IS2HA
06SP Game Used Inked Sweaters Dual Patches-IS2HA
06The Cup Autographed NHL Shields Duals-DASHA
06The Cup Limited Logos-LLDA
06The Cup Signature Patches-SPDA
06UD Artifacts Auto-Facts-AFDA
06UD Artifacts Auto-Facts Gold-AFDA
06Ultra-106
Gold Medallion-106
Ice Medallion-106
06Upper Deck-353
Exclusives Parallel-353
High Gloss Parallel-353
Masterpieces-353
06Upper Deck MVP-156
Gold Script-156
Super Script-156
Autographs-OAGA
Jerseys-OJAR
06Upper Deck Ovation-175
06Upper Deck Sweet Shot Signature Sticks-STDA
06Upper Deck Trilogy Honorary Scripted Patches-HSPDA
06Upper Deck Trilogy Honorary Scripted Swatches-HSSDA
06Upper Deck Trilogy Ice Scripts-ISDA
06Upper Deck Trilogy Scripts-TSDA
06Upper Deck Victory-102
06Upper Deck Victory Black-102
06Upper Deck Victory Gold-102

Aegerter, Bruno
93Swiss HNL-463
95Swiss HNL-287
96Swiss HNL-272
01Swiss HNL-341
02Swiss HNL-388

Aegerter, Daniel
95Swiss HNL-347
96Swiss HNL-320
98Swiss Power Play Stickers-130
99Swiss Panini Stickers-132
00Swiss Panini Stickers-176
00Swiss Slapshot Mini-Cards-LT2
01Swiss HNL-193
02Swiss HNL-323

Aeschbacher, Daniel
93Swiss HNL-374

Aeschlimann, Frank
95Swiss HNL-272

Aeschlimann, Jean-Jacques
93Swiss HNL-95
95Swiss HNL-145
95Swiss HNL-507
95Swiss HNL-509
96Swiss HNL-162
98Swiss Power Play Stickers-163
99Swiss Panini Stickers-162
00Swiss Panini Stickers-206
00Swiss Slapshot Mini-Cards-HCL8
01Swiss HNL-35
02Swiss HNL-26
02Swiss HNL-477

Aeschlimann, Joel
93Swiss HNL-44
95Swiss HNL-81
96Swiss HNL-414

Aeschlimann, Oliver
93Quebec Pee-Wee Tournament-1638

Aeschlimann, Peter
72Finnish Semic World Championship-145
72Swedish Semic World Championship-145

Afanasenkov, Dmitri
00Black Diamond-65
Gold-65
00Upper Deck-200
Exclusives Tier 1-200
Exclusives Tier 2-200
00Upper Deck Ice-45
Immortals-45
Legends-45
Stars-45
00Upper Deck MVP-214
First Stars-214
Second Stars-214
Third Stars-214
00QMJHL All-Star Program Inserts-37
01Upper Deck Victory-388
Gold-388
02Springfield Falcons-2
03BAP Memorabilia-223
03Lightning Team Issue-29
03Pacific Complete-573
Red-573
03Topps Traded-TT60
Blue-TT60
Gold-TT60
Red-TT60
04Russian Back to Russia-6
06Flyers Postcards-14
06Lightning Postcards-2
06O-Pee-Chee-442
Rainbow-442
06Upper Deck-427
Exclusives Parallel-427
High Gloss Parallel-427
Masterpieces-427

Affleck, Bruce
74NHL Action Stamps-55
76O-Pee-Chee NHL-305
77O-Pee-Chee NHL-376
78O-Pee-Chee-279

Affleck, Sean
03Kootenay Ice-20

Afinogenov, Denis
97Czech APS Extraliga-97
98Czech DS Stickers-100
00Russian Hockey League-167
00Russian Hockey League-337
02Russian Transfert-15
02Russian Transfert Promos-4

Afinogenov, Maxim
97Black Diamond-43
Double Diamond-43
Triple Diamond-43
Quadruple Diamond-43
98Black Diamond-108
Double Diamond-108
Triple Diamond-108
Quadruple Diamond-108
98SPx Top Prospects-76
Radiance-76
Spectrum-76
98UD Choice-282
Prime Choice Reserve-282
Reserve-282
99BAP Memorabilia-350
Gold-350
Silver-350
99BAP Millennium Calder Candidates Ruby-C24
99BAP Millennium Calder Candidate Emerald-C24
99BAP Millennium Calder Cand Sapphire-C24
99Crown Royale-16
Limited Series-16
Premiere Date-16
Prospects Parallel-16
99Pacific Omega-24
Copper-24
Gold-24
Ice Blue-24
Premiere Date-24
99Pacific Prism-16
Holographic Blue-16
Holographic Gold-16
Holographic Mirror-16
Holographic Purple-16
Premiere Date-16
99Paramount-253
99SP Authentic-12
Tomorrow's Headliners-TH3
99Stadium Club-168
First Day Issue-168
One of a Kind-168
Printing Plates Black-168
Printing Plates Cyan-168
Printing Plates Magenta-168
Printing Plates Yellow-168
99Topps Arena Giveaways-BUF-MA
99Topps Premier Plus-120
Parallel-120
99Upper Deck Arena Giveaways-BS1
99Russian Stars Postcards-1
99Russian Fetisov Tribute-7
00Aurora-16
Premiere Date-16
00BAP Memorabilia-64
Emerald-64
Ruby-64
Sapphire-64
Promos-64
00BAP Mem Chicago Sportsfest Copper-64
00BAP Memorabilia Chicago Sportsfest Blue-64
00BAP Memorabilia Chicago Sportsfest Gold-64
00BAP Memorabilia Chicago Sportsfest Ruby-64
00BAP Memorabilia Chicago Sun-Times Ruby-64
00BAP Memorabilia Chicago Sun-Times Gold-64
00BAP Mem Chicago Sun-Times Sapphire-64
00BAP Mem Toronto Fall Expo Copper-64
00BAP Memorabilia Toronto Fall Expo Gold-64
00BAP Memorabilia Toronto Fall Expo Ruby-64
00BAP Parkhurst 2000-P12
00BAP Signature Series-83
Emerald-83
Ruby-83
Sapphire-83
Autographs-81
Autographs Gold-81
00Black Diamond-7
Gold-7
00O-Pee-Chee-180
00O-Pee-Chee Parallel-180
00Pacific-46
Copper-46
Gold-46
Ice Blue-46
Premiere Date-46
00Paramount-24
Copper-24
Gold-24
Holo-Gold-24
Holo-Silver-24
Ice Blue-24
Premiere Date-24
00Private Stock-10
Gold-10
Premiere Date-10
Retail-10
Silver-10
Artist's Canvas-4
Artist's Canvas Proofs-4
PS-2001 Action-5
PS-2001 New Wave-3
00Revolution-14
Blue-14
Premiere Date-14
Red-14
00SP Authentic-11
00SP Game Used-7
00Stadium Club-121
00Topps/OPC-180
Parallel-180
Own the Game-OTG28
00Topps Chrome-120
OPC Refractors-120
Refractors-120
00Topps Gold Label Class 1-30
Gold-30
00Topps Gold Label Class 2-30
00Topps Gold Label Class 2 Gold-30
00Topps Gold Label Class 3-30
00Topps Gold Label Class 3 Gold-30
00Topps Heritage-64
Chrome Parallel-64
00Topps Premier Plus Aspirations-PA3
00UD Heroes Player Idols-PI3
00UD Pros and Prospects-12
Now Appearing-NA1
00Upper Deck-23
Exclusives Tier 1-23
Exclusives Tier 2-23
Prospects In Depth-P2
00Upper Deck MVP-25
First Stars-25
Second Stars-25
Third Stars-25
00Upper Deck Victory-32
00Upper Deck Vintage-48
00Vanguard-11
Holographic Gold-11
Holographic Purple-11
Pacific Proofs-11
00Czech Stadion-154
01BAP Memorabilia-9
Emerald-9
Ruby-9
Sapphire-9
01BAP Signature Series-176
Autographs-176
Autographs Gold-176
01O-Pee-Chee-74
01O-Pee-Chee Heritage Parallel-74
01O-Pee-Chee Heritage Parallel Limited-74
01O-Pee-Chee Premier Parallel-74
01Pacific-42
Extreme LTD-42
Hobby LTD-42
Premiere Date-42
Retail LTD-42
01Pacific Arena Exclusives-42
01Parkhurst-64
Gold-64
Silver-64
01SP Game Used Authentic Fabric-AFMA
01SP Game Used Authentic Fabric-DFAB
01SP Game Used Authentic Fabric Gold-AFMA
01SPx-159
Hidden Treasures-DTAD
Hidden Treasures-TTDBA
01Stadium Club-23
Award Winners-23
Master Photos-23
01Topps-74
Heritage Parallel-74
Heritage Parallel Limited-74
OPC Parallel-74
01Topps Chrome-74
Refractors-74
Black Border Refractors-74
01UD Mask Collection Double Patches-DPMA
01UD Mask Collection Jerseys-J-MA
01UD Mask Collection Jersey and Patch-JPMA
01UD Playmakers Combo Jerseys-CJMA
01UD Playmakers Combo Jerseys Gold-CJMA
01UD Playmakers Jerseys-J-MA
01UD Playmakers Jerseys Gold-J-MA
01UD Premier Collection Dual Jerseys-DBA
01UD Premier Collection Dual Jersey Black-DBA
01Upper Deck-22
Exclusives-22
01Upper Deck MVP-17
01Upper Deck Victory-40
Gold-40
01Upper Deck Vintage-28
02BAP First Edition-70
Jerseys-70
02BAP Memorabilia-55
Emerald-55
Ruby-55
Sapphire-55
NHL All-Star Game-55
NHL All-Star Game Blue-55
NHL All-Star Game Green-55
NHL All-Star Game Red-55
02BAP Memorabilia Toronto Fall Expo-55
02BAP Signature Series-50
Autographs-50
Autograph Buybacks 2000-81
Autograph Buybacks 2001-176
Autographs Gold-50
02O-Pee-Chee-177
02O-Pee-Chee Premier Blue Parallel-177
02O-Pee-Chee Premier Red Parallel-177
02O-Pee-Chee Factory Set-177
02Pacific-36
Blue-36
Red-36
02Parkhurst-153
Bronze-153
Gold-153
Silver-153
02SP Authentic-110
Sign of the Times-MA
Sign of the Times-KA
02SP Game Used Future Fabrics-FFMA
02SP Game Used Future Fabrics Gold-FFMA
02SP Game Used Future Fabrics Rainbow-FFMA
02SP Game Used Signature Style-MA
02Stadium Club Passport-15
02Topps-177
OPC Blue Parallel-177
OPC Red Parallel-177
Factory Set-177
02Topps Chrome-103
Black Border Refractors-103
Refractors-103
02Topps Total-230
02UD Artistic Impressions-9
Gold-9
02UD Artistic Impressions Beckett Promos-9
02UD Artistic Impressions Retrospectives-R9
02UD Artistic Impressions Retrospect Gold-R9
02UD Artistic Impress Retrospect Auto-R9
02UD Artistic Impress Retrospect Silver-R9
02UD Artistic Impressions Right Track-RTMA
02UD Artistic Impression Right Track Gold-RTMA
02UD Honor Roll Signature Class-MA
02UD Piece of History Patches-PHMA
02UD Premier Collection Signatures Bronze-SMA
02UD Premier Collection Signatures Gold-SMA
02UD Premier Collection Signatures Silver-SMA
02UD Top Shelf-11
Dual Player Jerseys-RFA
Dual Player Jerseys-STSA
Shooting Stars-SHMA
Sweet Sweaters-SWMA
Triple Jerseys-TSASB
02Upper Deck-20
Exclusives-20
Classic Portraits Hockey Royalty-SCA
Classic Portraits Hockey Royalty Limited-SCA
02Upper Deck MVP-23
Gold-23
Classics-23
Golden Classics-23
02Upper Deck Rookie Update Autographs-MA
02Upper Deck Victory-22
Bronze-22
Gold-22
Silver-22
02Upper Deck Vintage-30
Green Backs-30
Tall Boys-T8
Tall Boys Gold-T8
02Russian Olympic Team-8
02Russian World Championships-8
03Beehive-24
Gold-24
Silver-24
03Black Diamond-115
Black-115

Green-115
Red-115
Signature Gems-SG-1
Threads-DT-MA
Threads Green-DT-MA
Threads Red-DT-MA
Threads Black-DT-MA
03ITG Action-74
03Pacific Complete-252
Red-252
03SPx-11
Radiance-11
Spectrum-11
Fantasy Franchise-FF-DSA
Fantasy Franchise Limited-FF-DSA
VIP-VIP-DA
VIP Limited-VIP-DA
03Topps Pristine Jersey Portions-PPJ-MA
03Topps Pristine Jersey Portion Refractor-PPJ-MA
03Topps Pristine Patches-PP-MA
03Topps Pristine Patch Refractors-PP-MA
03Upper Deck-26
Canadian Exclusives-26
HG-26
Jerseys-GJ-MA
03Upper Deck Classic Portraits-10
Classic Stitches-CS-MA
03Upper Deck MVP-60
Gold Script-60
Silver Script-60
Canadian Exclusives-60
ProSign-PS-MA
Souvenirs-S20
SportsNut-SN13
03Upper Deck Trilogy-10
Limited-10
Scripts-S2MA
Scripts Limited-S2MA
03Upper Deck Victory-23
Bronze-23
Gold-23
Silver-23
04Pacific-28
Blue-28
Red-28
04SP Authentic-13
Limited-13
Buybacks-141
Buybacks-142
Buybacks-143
Buybacks-144
Rookie Review-RR-MA
Sign of the Times-ST-AF
04UD All-World-32
Gold-32
Autographs-32
Dual Autographs-AD-AF
Triple Autographs-AT-ZFA
Quad Autographs-AQ-RUS
Six Autographs-AS-RUS
04Upper Deck-23
Canadian Exclusives-23
HG Glossy Gold-23
HG Glossy Silver-23
World Cup Tribute-PDMAIK
04Russian Back to Russia-15
04Russian Moscow Dynamo-1
04Russian World Championship Team-1
05Black Diamond-9
Emerald-9
Gold-9
Onyx-9
Ruby-9
05Panini Stickers-36
05Parkhurst-51
Facsimile Auto Parallel-51
Signatures-MA
True Colors-TCBUF
True Colors-TCBUF
05SP Game Used-14
Autographs-14
Gold-14
Authentic Fabrics Quad-BADS
Authentic Patches Quad -BADS
Auto Draft-AD-MA
Game Gear-GG-AF
Game Gear Autographs-AG-AF
Signature Sticks-SS-MA
05SPx-10
Spectrum-10
Winning Combos-WC-BA
Winning Combos Autographs-AWC-BA
Winning Combos Gold-WC-BA
Winning Combos Spectrum-WC-BA
05UD Artifacts-13
Blue-13
Gold-13
Green-13
Pewter-13
Red-13
Auto Facts-AF-MA
Auto Facts Blue-AF-MA
Auto Facts Copper-AF-MA
Auto Facts Pewter-AF-MA
Auto Facts Silver-AF-MA
Gold Autographed-13
Remarkable Artifacts-RA-MA
Remarkable Artifacts Dual-RA-MA
05Ultra-27
Gold-27
Ice-27
05Upper Deck-21
Big Playmakers-B-MA
HG Glossy-21
Jerseys-J-MA
Jerseys Series II-J2MA
NHL Generations-TFKA
Notable Numbers-N-MA
Patches-P-MA
05Upper Deck MVP-45
Gold-45
Platinum-45
ProSign-P-MA
05Upper Deck Trilogy-14
Scripts-SFS-MA
05Upper Deck Toronto Fall Expo-21
05Upper Deck Victory-25
Black-25
Gold-25
Silver-25
06Be A Player-168
Autographs-168
Signatures-MX
Signatures 10-186
Signatures 25-186
Signatures Trios-TMAR
06Black Diamond-11
Black-11
Gold-11
Ruby-11
06Flair Showcase Inks-IMA
06Fleer-22
Tiffany-22
06Hot Prospects-14
Red Hot-14
White Hot-14
06O-Pee-Chee-67
Rainbow-67
Swatches-S-MA
06Panini Stickers-30
06SP Game Used Authentic Fabrics Dual-AF2AB
06SP Game Used Authentic Fabrics Dual Patches-AF2AB
06SP Game Used By The Letter-BLAM
06SPx Winning Materials-WMMA
06SPx Winning Materials Spectrum-WMMA
06SPx Winning Materials Autographs-WMMA
06The Cup NHL Shields Duals-DSHDA
06UD Artifacts Tundra Tandems-TTAD
06UD Artifacts Tundra Tandems Black-TTAD
06UD Artifacts Tundra Tandems Blue-TTAD
06UD Artifacts Tundra Tandems Gold-TTAD
06UD Artifacts Tundra Tandems Platinum-TTAD
06UD Artifacts Tundra Tandems Red-TTAD
06UD Artifacts Tundra Tandems Dual Patches Red-TTAD
06UD Powerplay-13
Impact Rainbow-13
06Ultimate Collection Premium Patches-PS-MA
06Ultimate Collection Premium Swatches-PS-MA
06Ultra-23
Gold Medallion-23
Ice Medallion-23
06Upper Deck Arena Giveaways-BUF5
06Upper Deck-277
Exclusives Parallel-277
High Gloss Parallel-277
Masterpieces-277
06Upper Deck MVP-36
Gold Script-36
Super Script-36
Autographs-OADA
Jerseys-OJSA
06Upper Deck Ovation-108
06Upper Deck Sweet Shot-14
Sweet Stitches-SSMA
Sweet Stitches Duals-SSMA
Sweet Stitches Triples-SSMA
06Upper Deck Victory-24
06Upper Deck Victory Black-24
06Upper Deck Victory Gold-24
06Russian Sport Collection Olympic Stars-1
06Russian Torino Olympic Team-12
07Upper Deck Victory-34
Black-34
Gold-34

Afonin, Viktor
74Swedish Stickers-67

Agarkov, Pavel
98Russian Hockey League-85
99Russian Hockey League-195
00Russian Hockey League-264

Agarunov, Igor
03Kootenay Ice-14

Ageev, Alexander
00Russian Hockey League-244

Ageikin, Sergei
87Russian National Team-1
94German First League-367

Aggatts, J. P.
25Dominion Chocolates-68

Aggio, Mark
98Sudbury Wolves-24

Agnel, Benjamin
94Finnish Jaa Kiekko-221
94French National Team-1
95Swedish World Championships Stickers-106

Agnevtshekov, Alexander
00Russian Hockey League-183

Agnew, Aaron
04Penticton Vees-4

Agnew, David
93Western Michigan Broncos-1

Agnew, Gary
907th Inn. Sketch OHL-148
917th Inn. Sketch OHL-369
93London Knights-26
95Slapshot-130
00Syracuse Crunch-22

Agnew, Jim
83Brandon Wheat Kings-2
86Fredericton Express-1
89ProCards IHL-185
90Canucks Mohawk-2
91Canucks Panini Team Stickers-2
92Whalers Dairymart-1

Agnew, Mark
02Tri-City Stormfront-6

Agosta, Meghan
06ITG Going For Gold-9
06ITG Going For Gold Samples-9
06ITG Going For Gold Autographs-AA
06ITG Going For Gold Jerseys-GUJ9

Agren, Ulf
83Swedish Semic Elitserien-179
84Swedish Semic Elitserien-204
85Swedish Panini Stickers-203
86Swedish Panini Stickers-197

Aguilar, Adam
93Quebec Pee-Wee Tournament-695

Agureikin, Yuri
98Danish Hockey League-134

Ahammer, Maximilian
94German First League-186

Ahearn, Kevin
72Finnish Semic World Championship-129
72Swedish Semic World Championship-129

Ahearn, T. Franklin
83Hall of Fame Postcards-E1

Ahearne, JF
83Hall of Fame Postcards-J2
85Hall of Fame-183

Ahenakew, Jason
91Air Canada SJHL-E10
92Saskatchewan JHL-27

Ahern, Fred
76O-Pee-Chee NHL-298
77O-Pee-Chee NHL-280
78O-Pee-Chee-386

Ahl, Boo
91Swedish Semic Elitserien Stickers-105
92Swedish Semic Elitserien Stickers-126
93Swedish Semic Elitserien-99
94Swedish Leaf-186
95Swedish Leaf-49
Spidermen-6
95Swedish Upper Deck-75
96Swedish Semic Wien-41
96Swedish Semic Wien Coca-Cola Dream Team-2
00Swedish Upper Deck-165
Masked Men-M7
SHL Signatures-BA
02Swedish SHL-34
Parallel-34
03Swedish Elite-45
Silver-45
04Swedish Elitset-192
Gold-192

Ahlberg, Jeppe
98Danish Hockey League-79

Ahlberg, Lennart
83Swedish Semic Elitserien-147
92Norwegian Elite Series-36

Ahlberg, Martin
92Norwegian Elite Series-26

Ahlberg, Mats
67Swedish Hockey-114
69Swedish Hockey-127
70Swedish Hockey-82
71Swedish Hockey-174
72Swedish Stickers-160
73Finnish Jaakiekko-42
73Swedish Stickers-16
73Swedish Stickers-48
74Finnish Jenkki-40
74Finnish Typotor-102
74Swedish Stickers-24
74Swedish Stickers-273
74Swedish Semic World Champ Stickers-11
79Panini Stickers-196

Ahlberg, Morten
98Danish Hockey League-75

Ahlberg, Sakari
70Finnish Jaakiekko-118
71Finnish Suomi Stickers-167
72Finnish Jaakiekko-118
72Finnish Panda Toronto-17
73Finnish Jaakiekko-172
74Finnish Jenkki-1
74Swedish Semic World Champ Stickers-96
78Finnish SM-Liiga-53

Ahlberg, Sami
93Finnish SISU-132
94Finnish SISU-117
95Finnish SISU-40
98Finnish Kerailysarja-95
99Finnish Cardset-54
00Finnish Cardset-327

Ahlen, Kjell
71Swedish Hockey-359

Ahlen, Tomas
83Swedish Semic Elitserien-180
84Swedish Semic Elitserien-198
85Swedish Panini Stickers-9
87Swedish Panini Stickers-10
89Swedish Semic Elitserien Stickers-5

Ahlen, Valter
56Swedish Alfabilder-46

Ahlqvist, Aleksis
06Finnish Cardset-195
Between the Pipes-3

Ahlqvist, Timo
65Finnish Hellas-150

Ahlroos, Kim
93Finnish Jyvas-Hyva Stickers-29
93Finnish SISU-94
94Finnish SISU-51
95Finnish SISU-344
00UK Sekonda Superleague-187
01UK Cardiff Devils-4
01UK London Knights-4
02UK Cardiff Devils-4
02UK London Knights-4
03UK Nottingham Panthers-3
04UK Nottingham Panthers-2

Ahlstrand, Christer
70Swedish Hockey-50

Ahlstrom, Bjorn
91Swedish Semic Elitserien Stickers-26
92Swedish Semic Elitserien Stickers-45
94Swedish Leaf-84
95Swedish Leaf-162
95Swedish Upper Deck-16
97Swedish Collector's Choice-16
98Swedish UD Choice-10
99Swedish Upper Deck-10
00Swedish Upper Deck-13
00Swedish Upper Deck-181
Top Draws-T1

Ahlstrom, Erik
84Swedish Semic Elitserien-95
85Swedish Panini Stickers-88

Ahlund, Hakan
90Swedish Semic Elitserien Stickers-140
91Finnish Semic World Champ Stickers-40
91Swedish Semic Elitserien Stickers-190
91Swedish Semic World Champ Stickers-40
92Swedish Semic Elitserien Stickers-218
93Swedish Semic Elitserien-189
94Swedish Leaf-115
95Swedish Leaf-91
95Swedish Upper Deck-148
95Swedish World Championships Stickers-159
98German DEL-276
99German DEL-158

Ahman, Olle
67Swedish Hockey-230
69Swedish Hockey-274
70Swedish Hockey-165
71Swedish Hockey-260
72Swedish Stickers-240
73Swedish Stickers-233
74Swedish Stickers-274

Ahmaoja, Timo
96Finnish SISU Redline-61
97Black Diamond-102
Double Diamond-102
Triple Diamond-102
Quadruple Diamond-102
98UD Choice-280
Prime Choice Reserve-280
Reserve-280
98Finnish Kerailysarja-147
99Finnish Cardset-226
00Finnish Cardset-144
01Finnish Cardset-372

Ahne, Manfred
94German DEL-163

Aho, Harri
00Finnish Cardset-53
01Finnish Cardset-75

Aho, Juha-Pekka
70Finnish Jaakiekko-308
72Finnish Jaakiekko-299

Aho, Kalevi
78Finnish SM-Liiga-217
80Finnish Mallasjuoma-191

Aho, Matti
04Finnish Cardset-310
05Finnish Cardset -163
06Finnish Cardset-166

Aho, Ray
99Ohio State Buckeyes-1
00Indianapolis Ice-1

Ahokainen, Seppo
71Finnish Suomi Stickers-168
72Finnish Jaakiekko-61
72Finnish Jaakiekko-119
72Finnish Hellas-1
73Finnish Jaakiekko-63
73Finnish Jaakiekko-173
74Finnish Jenkki-2
74Finnish Typotor-7
74Finnish Typotor-49
74Swedish Stickers-97
79Panini Stickers-175
80Finnish Mallasjuoma-175
05Finnish Tappara Legendat-24

Ahokas, Pertti
70Finnish Jaakiekko-172
71Finnish Suomi Stickers-96
72Finnish Jaakiekko-137
78Finnish SM-Liiga-204
80Finnish Mallasjuoma-138

Ahola, Peter
91Pro Set Platinum-257
91Parkhurst-65
French-65
91Pinnacle-312
French-312
91Pro Set-540
French-540
91Upper Deck-543
French-543
92Bowman-353
92O-Pee-Chee-268
92Pinnacle-243
French-243
92Pro Set-73
92Score-310
Canadian-310
92Stadium Club-192
92Topps-73
Gold-73G
92Ultra-78
92Ultra-376
92Upper Deck-41
92Upper Deck-526
Euro-Rookie Team-ERT4
Euro-Stars-E5
93Swedish Semic World Champ Stickers-48
94Finnish SISU-270
94Finnish SISU Horoscopes-5
95Finnish SISU-205
Double Trouble-5
95Finnish SISU Limited-57
Leaf Gallery-5
95Finnish SISU Specials-8
96Finnish SISU Redline-3
98Finnish Kerailysarja-235
Leijonat-4
99Finnish Cardset-208
Aces High-C-2
00Finnish Cardset-5
02Finnish Cardset-1
02Swedish SHL-93
Parallel-93
03Swedish Elite-115
Silver-115

Ahonen, Ari
99Finnish Cardset-219
Most Wanted-10
00Finnish Cardset-13
00Finnish Cardset-NNO
00Finnish Cardset Next Generation-5
01Finnish Cardset Haltmeisters-8
01Albany River Rats-24
02BAP Memorabilia-337
02BAP Ultimate Memorabilia-21
02ITG Used-185
02Parkhurst Retro-233
Minis-233
02SP Authentic-210
02SPx-182
02UD Foundations-166
02UD Mask Collection-154
02UD Premier Collection-67A
Gold-67A
Jerseys Bronze-AA
Jerseys Bronze-PA
Jerseys Gold-AA
Jerseys Gold-PA
Jerseys Silver-AA
Jerseys Silver-PA
02Upper Deck Classic Portraits-135
02Upper Deck Rookie Update-119
02Finnish Cardset-153
02Albany River Rats-1
02Albany River Rats AAP-2
03BAP Memorabilia-103
Emerald-103
Gold-103
Ruby-103
Sapphire-103
Deep in the Crease-D4
03ITG Action-305
03O-Pee-Chee-321
03OPC Blue-321
03OPC Gold-321
03OPC Red-321
03SPx Big Futures-BF-AA
03SPx Big Futures Limited-BF-AA
03Topps-321
Blue-321
Gold-321
Red-321
03Albany River Rats-2
03Albany River Rats Kinko's-1
03Pacific AHL Prospects-1
Gold-1
Autographs-5
Crease Lightning-1
04Albany River Rats-1
04ITG Heroes/Prospects He Shoots/Scores-21
04ITG Heroes and Prospects Net Prospects-12
04ITG Heroes and Prosp Net Prospects Gold-12
05Devils Team Issue-9
05Albany River Rats-1
05ITG Heroes and Prospects Jerseys-GUJ-106
05ITG Heroes and Prospects Jerseys Gold-GUJ-106
06Fleer Fabricology-FAA
06Finnish Cardset-182
Between the Pipes-1

Ahonen, Asko
73Finnish Jaakiekko-240

Ahonen, Jukka
72Finnish Jaakiekko-341

Ahonen, Marko
99Finnish Cardset-94

Ahonen, Olli
99Finnish Cardset-19
01Finnish Cardset-273
04Finnish Cardset-10
Parallel-8
05Finnish Cardset -5
06Finnish Cardset-7

Ahonen, Veli-Pekka
94Finnish SISU-351
95Finnish SISU-101
96Finnish SISU Redline-106

Ahrens, Chris
74NHL Action Stamps-143
74O-Pee-Chee NHL-346
75O-Pee-Chee NHL-371

Ahrens, Fabian
96German DEL-214

Ahrgren, Johan
92British Columbia JHL-39

Ahsberg, Roger
83Swedish Semic Elitserien-241

Ahstrom, Goran
69Swedish Hockey-292

Ahvenharju, Matti
70Finnish Jaakiekko-277
71Finnish Suomi Stickers-148

Ahxner, Mathias
98German DEL-280
02Swedish SHL-46
Parallel-46

Aikaa, Sami
92Finnish Jyvas-Hyva Stickers-104

Aikas, Leo
71Finnish Suomi Stickers-166
72Finnish Jaakiekko-117
73Finnish Jaakiekko-215

Aiken, August
05Salmon Arm Silverbacks-3
06Westside Warriors-18

Aiken, Dave
90Richmond Renegades-10
91Richmond Renegades-8
91Richmond Renegades Set 2-11

Aikia, Ryan
99Columbus Cottonmouths-9
00Asheville Smoke-1
01Indianapolis Ice-1
02Indianapolis Ice-1
03Indianapolis Ice-1
04Columbus Cottonmouths-16

Aikula, Jukka
78Finnish SM-Liiga-184

Aima, Ales
99Czech DS-51

Aime, David
06Prince Albert Raiders-1

Aimonette, Richard
907th Inn. Sketch QMJHL-253
94French National Team-2
95Swedish World Championships Stickers-115

Ainsworth, Jeff
94Kamloops Blazers-15
95Kamloops Blazers-25
95Slapshot Memorial Cup-11
96Kamloops Blazers-1

Airaksinen, Erkki
71Finnish Suomi Stickers-276

Airaksinen, Jukka
78Finnish SM-Liiga-44
80Finnish Mallasjuoma-23

Aisbitt, Barrie
95UK Guildford Flames-13
96UK Guildford Flames-20

Aitcheson, Tyson
03Ottawa 67's-1
06Barrie Colts-16

Aitken, A.J.
01Memphis RiverKings-19

Aitken, Brad
88ProCards IHL-43
89ProCards IHL-155
90ProCards AHL/IHL-388
91ProCards-340

Aitken, Johnathan
95Bowman Draft Prospects-P1
95Medicine Hat Tigers-1
95Classic-56
96Brandon Wheat Kings-8
96All-Sport PPF *-75
96All Sport PPF Gold *-75
96Visions Signings *-74
Autographs-74A
Autographs Silver-74A
97Brandon Wheat Kings-2
98Providence Bruins-3
99Providence Bruins-2
00BAP Memorabilia-157
Emerald-157
Ruby-157
Sapphire-157
Promos-157
00BAP Mem Chicago Sportsfest Copper-157
00BAP Memorabilia Chicago Sportsfest Blue-157
00BAP Memorabilia Chicago Sportsfest Gold-157
00BAP Memorabilia Chicago Sportsfest Ruby-157
00BAP Memorabilia Chicago Sun-Times Ruby-157
00BAP Memorabilia Chicago Sun-Times Gold-157
00BAP Mem Chicago Sun-Times Sapphire-157
00BAP Mem Toronto Fall Expo Copper-157
00BAP Memorabilia Toronto Fall Expo Gold-157
00BAP Memorabilia Toronto Fall Expo Ruby-157
00Pacific-45
Copper-45
Gold-45
Ice Blue-45
Premiere Date-45
00SPx-113
Spectrum-113
00Upper Deck-218
Exclusives Tier 1-218
Exclusives Tier 2-218
02Norfolk Admirals-1
03Norfolk Admirals-1
04Manitoba Moose-20
05Hamilton Bulldogs-1

Aitkenhead, Andy
35Diamond Matchbooks Tan 1-1

Aivazoff, Micah
89ProCards AHL-6
90ProCards AHL/IHL-417
91ProCards-131
93Donruss-421
93OPC Premier-345
Gold-345
93Parkhurst-253
Emerald Ice-253
93Stadium Club-263
Members Only Master Set-263
First Day Issue-263
93Topps/OPC Premier-345
Gold-345
93Ultra-303
93Upper Deck-432
94Be A Player Signature Cards-173
94OPC Premier-104
Special Effects-104
94Topps/OPC Premier-104
Special Effects-104
94Classic Pro Prospects-72
96Binghamton Rangers-1
99Utah Grizzlies-11
99Utah Grizzlies-21
01German Upper Deck-226

Akerblom, Bengt
89Swedish Semic Elitserien Stickers-70

Akerblom, Bjorn
83Swedish Semic Elitserien-65
89Swedish Semic Elitserien Stickers-258
90Swedish Semic Elitserien Stickers-168

Akerblom, Markus
90Swedish Semic Elitserien Stickers-216
91Swedish Semic Elitserien Stickers-144
92Swedish Semic Elitserien Stickers-169
93Swedish Semic Elitserien-138
94Swedish Leaf-53
95Swedish Leaf-240
Face to Face-15
95Swedish Upper Deck-108
95Swedish Upper Deck-111
Ticket to North America-NA13
97Swedish Collector's Choice-115
98Swedish UD Choice-131
99Swedish Upper Deck-117
02Swedish SHL-271
Dynamic Duos-8
Parallel-271

Akerlund, Goran
69Swedish Hockey-237
71Swedish Hockey-379

Akerman, Johan
94Swedish Leaf-240
95Swedish Leaf-8
06Swedish SHL Elitset-193

Akerstrom, Roger
86Swedish Panini Stickers-172
87Swedish Panini Stickers-174
89Swedish Semic Elitserien Stickers-153
90Swedish Semic Elitserien Stickers-233
91Swedish Semic Elitserien Stickers-258
92Swedish Semic Elitserien Stickers-284
93Swedish Semic Elitserien-251
93Swedish Semic Elitserien-308
94Swedish Leaf-278
95Swedish Leaf-78
Face to Face-8
95Swedish Upper Deck-120
97Swedish Collector's Choice-122
98Swedish UD Choice-137
99Swedish Upper Deck-139
00Swedish Upper Deck-124
02Swedish SHL-60
Parallel-60
Team Captains-7
03Swedish Elite-228
Silver-228
04Swedish Elitset-216
Gold-216
Signatures Series A-7
04Swedish Pure Skills-50
Parallel-50
06Swedish SHL Elitset-214

Akervik, Andy
88ProCards IHL-24
90Kansas City Blades-10
90ProCards AHL/IHL-593
91ProCards-526

Akeson, Jeremy
01Ottawa 67's-17
02Ottawa 67's-17
03Ottawa 67's-2
04Ottawa 67's-7

Akey, Dave
86London Knights-22
87Sudbury Wolves-8

Akhmadulin, Ruslan
99Kitchener Rangers-15
01Russian Hockey League-61

Akhmetov, Evgeni
00Russian Hockey League-390
01Russian Hockey League-48
02Russian Hockey League-116

Akijev, Alexei
03Russian Hockey League-78

Akkerman, Ricky
05Waterloo Blackhawks-1

Akright, Josh
03Kalamazoo Wings-18

Aksenenko, Alexander
04Russian Under-18 Team-13

Akulinin, Igor
90O-Pee-Chee-491

Alain, Gabriel
52Juniors Blue Tint-71

Alain, Patrick
93Quebec Pee-Wee Tournament-341

Alain-Rochette, Jonathan
04Quebec Remparts-17

Alalauri, Sami
00Finnish Cardset-298

Alander, Karl-Gustaf
70Swedish Hockey-69
71Swedish Hockey-158
86Swedish Panini Stickers-137

Alanen, Johannes
98Finnish Kerailysarja-225
99Finnish Cardset-126
00Finnish Cardset-91
01Finnish Cardset-129
04Finnish Cardset-158
Parallel-117
05Finnish Cardset -246
06Finnish Cardset-75

Alanko, Rami
98Finnish Kerailysarja-103
99Finnish Cardset-57
00Finnish Cardset-42
01Finnish Cardset-51
02Finnish Cardset-154
03Finnish Cardset-5
05Swedish SHL Elitset-182
Gold-182
06Swedish SHL Elitset-41

Alastalo, Juha
05Finnish Cardset -255
06Finnish Cardset-84

Alatalo, Ilkka
78Finnish SM-Liiga-149

Alatalo, Matti
95Swiss HNL-288
01Swiss HNL-380

Alatalo, Mika
92Finnish Jyvas-Hyva Stickers-126
93Finnish Jyvas-Hyva Stickers-234
93Finnish SISU-202
93Finnish SISU Promos-NNO
93Swedish Semic World Champ Stickers-62
94Finnish SISU-165
94Finnish SISU-279
94Finnish SISU Horoscopes-20
94Finnish SISU Specials-1
94Finnish Jaa Kiekko-21
94Classic Tri-Cards-T76
95Finnish SISU-128
Painkillers-2
95Finnish Semic World Championships-15
95Swedish World Championships Stickers-177
95Signature Rookies Auto-Phonex-1
95Signature Rook Auto-Phonex Phone Cards-1
97Swedish Collector's Choice-131
98Finnish Kerailysarja-249
Leijonat-19
99Black Diamond-67
Diamond Cut-67
Final Cut-67
99Pacific Prism-106
Holographic Blue-106
Holographic Gold-106
Holographic Mirror-106
Holographic Purple-106
Premiere Date-106
99Panini Stickers-274
99SP Authentic-113
99Stadium Club-180
First Day Issue-180
One of a Kind-180
Printing Plates Black-180
Printing Plates Cyan-180
Printing Plates Magenta-180
Printing Plates Yellow-180
99Topps Premier Plus-114
Parallel-114
99Wayne Gretzky Hockey-134
99Finnish Cardset Aces High-C-J
99Finnish Cardset Par Avion-1
00BAP Memorabilia-215
Emerald-215
Ruby-215
Sapphire-215
Promos-215
00BAP Mem Chicago Sportsfest Copper-215
00BAP Memorabilia Chicago Sportsfest Blue-215
00BAP Memorabilia Chicago Sportsfest Gold-215
00BAP Memorabilia Chicago Sportsfest Ruby-215
00BAP Memorabilia Chicago Sun-Times Ruby-215
00BAP Memorabilia Chicago Sun-Times Gold-215
00BAP Mem Chicago Sun-Times Sapphire-215
00BAP Mem Toronto Fall Expo Copper-215
00BAP Memorabilia Toronto Fall Expo Gold-215
00BAP Memorabilia Toronto Fall Expo Ruby-215
00BAP Signature Series-188
Emerald-188
Ruby-188
Sapphire-188
Autographs-128
Autographs Gold-128
00Titanium Game Gear-123
00Titanium Game Gear Patches-123
00Titanium Draft Day Edition-74
Patches-74
00Upper Deck-362
Exclusives Tier 1-362
Exclusives Tier 2-362
00Finnish Cardset-360
01Atomic Jerseys-42
01Atomic Patches-42
01Crown Royale Triple Threads-14
01Pacific Jerseys-23
01Pacific Heads-Up Quad Jerseys-16
01Upper Deck Victory-271
Gold-271
01Finnish Cardset-362
02BAP Sig Series Auto Buybacks 2000-128
02Finnish Cardset-2
04Finnish Cardset-181
Parallel-134
05Finnish Cardset -334
06Finnish Cardset-164

Alavaara, Jan-Axel
95Swedish Leaf-278
Rookies-2
97Swedish Collector's Choice-151
98Swedish UD Choice-169
99Swedish Upper Deck-171
00Swedish Upper Deck-153
02Swedish SHL-112
Parallel-112
02Swedish SHL Promos-TCC11
03Swedish Elite-171
Silver-171
04Swedish Elitset-24
Gold-24
05Swedish SHL Elitset-173
Gold-173
06Swedish SHL Elitset-172

Alba, Mats
83Swedish Semic Elitserien-10
84Swedish Semic Elitserien-7
85Swedish Panini Stickers-11

Alban, Chad
98Mobile Mysticks-13
99Mobile Mysticks-18
00Idaho Steelheads-1
01Utah Grizzlies-26
02Kalamazoo Wings-21
03BAP Memorabilia-237
03Kalamazoo Wings-21
04Kalamazoo Wings-22

Albano, Eric
93Quebec Pee-Wee Tournament-810

Albelin, Tommy
83Swedish Semic Elitserien-79
84Swedish Semic Elitserien-79
85Swedish Panini Stickers-76
86Swedish Panini Stickers-59
87Nordiques General Foods-1
87Nordiques Team Issue-23
88Nordiques General Foods-1
88Nordiques Team Issue-1
88O-Pee-Chee-210
88O-Pee-Chee Stickers-184
88Panini Stickers-348
89Devils Caretta-1
89O-Pee-Chee-241
89Panini Stickers-257
89Swedish Semic World Champ Stickers-6
90Devils Team Issue-1
90O-Pee-Chee-323
90Panini Stickers-76
90Pro Set-162
90Score-378
Canadian-378
90Topps-323
Tiffany-323
90Upper Deck-88
French-88
91Score Canadian Bilingual-393
91Score Canadian English-393
93Swedish Semic World Champ Stickers-28
94OPC Premier-251
Special Effects-251
94Pinnacle-508
Artist's Proofs-508
Rink Collection-508
94Topps/OPC Premier-251
Special Effects-251
94Finnish Jaa Kiekko-60
95Parkhurst International-126
Emerald Ice-126
95Swedish Upper Deck-248
95Swedish Globe World Championships-10
96Be A Player-161
Autographs-161
Autographs Silver-161
96Swedish Semic Wien-43
97Pacific Invincible NHL Regime-26
97Panini Stickers-195
97Upper Deck-237
98Panini Stickers-182
99O-Pee-Chee-217
99O-Pee-Chee Chrome-217
99O-Pee-Chee Chrome Refractors-217
99Panini Stickers-187
99Topps/OPC-217
99Topps/OPC Chrome-217
Refractors-217
00Topps Gold Label Class 1-97
Gold-97
00Topps Gold Label Class 2-97
00Topps Gold Label Class 2 Gold-97
00Topps Gold Label Class 3-97
00Topps Gold Label Class 3 Gold-97
01Pacific-56
Extreme LTD-56
Hobby LTD-56
Premiere Date-56
Retail LTD-56
01Pacific Arena Exclusives-56
02Devils Team Issue-4
02Pacific Complete-291
Red-291
03Devils Team Issue-6

Albers, Heinz-Gerd
94German First League-424

Albers, Matt
92Michigan State Spartans-3
93Michigan State Spartans-1

Albers, Paul
01Calgary Hitmen-1
01Calgary Hitmen Autographed-1
02Calgary Hitmen-13
03Regina Pats-1
04Regina Pats-2
04Vancouver Giants-18
05Vancouver Giants-1

Albers, Travis
99Cornwall Colts-1

Albert, Brad
06Brampton Battalion-6

Albert, Chris
95Central Hockey League-91
97Fort Worth Brahmas-1
99Quebec Citadelles-3
00Fresno Falcons-1
00Hamilton Bulldogs-17

Albert, Francois
98Fort Worth Brahmas-7

Albert, Marv
91Pro Set Platinum-291

Albert, Phillip
99OCN Blizzard-15
00OCN Blizzard-14
01OCN Blizzard-16

Alberts, Andrew
04SP Authentic Rookie Redemptions-RR35
05Beehive-143
Beige -143
Blue -143
Gold-143
Red -143
Matte-143
Signature Scrapbook-SSAA
05Black Diamond-148
Emerald-148
Gold-148
Onyx-148
Ruby-148
05Bruins Boston Globe-3
05Hot Prospects-220
En Fuego-220
Hot Materials-HMAA
Red Hot-220
White Hot-220
05Parkhurst-605
Facsimile Auto Parallel-605
Signatures-AL
True Colors-TCBOS
True Colors-TCBOS
05SP Authentic-136
Limited-136
Rarefied Rookies-RRAA
05SP Game Used-141
Autographs-141
Gold-141
Rookie Exclusives-AA
Rookie Exclusives Silver-RE-AA
05SPx-137
Spectrum-137
Xcitement Rookies-XR-AA
Xcitement Rookies Gold-XR-AA
Xcitement Rookies Spectrum-XR-AA
05The Cup-119
Autographed Rookie Patches Gold Rainbow-119
Black Rainbow Rookies-119
Masterpiece Pressplates (Artifacts)-247
Masterpiece Pressplates (Bee Hive)-143
Masterpiece Pressplates (Black Diamond)-148
Masterpiece Pressplates (Ice)-120
Masterpiece Pressplates (MVP)-433
Masterpiece Pressplates (Power Play)-160
Masterpiece Pressplates (Power Play)-160
Masterpiece Pressplates (Rookie Update)-238
Masterpiece Pressplates SPA Autos-136
Masterpiece Pressplates (SP Game Used)-141
Masterpiece Pressplates (SPx)-137
Masterpiece Pressplates (SPx)-137
Masterpiece Pressplates (Trilogy)-177
Masterpiece Pressplates Ult Coll Autos-104

Masterpiece Pressplates (Victory)-258
Masterpiece Pressplates Autographs-119
Platinum Rookies-119
05UD Artifacts-247
05UD PowerPlay-160
05Ultimate Collection-104
Autographed Patches-104
Autographed Shields-104
Ultimate Debut Threads Jerseys-DTJAA
Ultimate Debut Threads Jerseys Autos-DAJAA
Ultimate Debut Threads Patches-DTPAA
Ultimate Debut Threads Patches Autos-DAPAA
05Ultra-204
Gold-204
Ice-204
Rookie Uniformity Jerseys-RU-AA
Rookie Uniformity Jersey Autographs-ARU-AA
Rookie Uniformity Patches-RUP-AA
Rookie Uniformity Patch Autographs-ARP-AA
05Upper Deck-225
HG Glossy-225
Rookie Ink-RIAA
Rookie Threads-RTAA
Rookie Threads Autographs-ARTAA
05Upper Deck Ice-120
Premieres Auto Patches-AIPAA
05Upper Deck MVP-433
Gold-433
Platinum-433
05Upper Deck Rookie Update-238
Inspirations Patch Rookies-238
05Upper Deck Trilogy-177
05Upper Deck Toronto Fall Expo-225
05Upper Deck Victory-258
Black-258
Gold-258
Silver-258
06O-Pee-Chee-46
06O-Pee-Chee-637
Rainbow-46
Rainbow-637
06UD Powerplay Power Marks-PMAA
06Upper Deck-267
Exclusives Parallel-267
High Gloss Parallel-267
Masterpieces-267

Albiani, Matthew
00London Knights-25
01Ottawa 67's-10
02Ottawa 67's-9
03Ottawa 67's-3

Albrecht, Ashley
04Minnesota Golden Gophers Women-13

Albrecht, Markus
94German First League-325

Albrecht, Steve
95Kamloops Blazers-18
96Kamloops Blazers-2
97Medicine Hat Tigers-1

Albrecht, Zdenek
92Norwegian Elite Series-67

Albright, Aaron
92Oshawa Generals Sheet-18

Albright, Clint
44Beehive Group II Photos-295

Alcindor, Ray
93Huntington Blizzard-1

Alcombrack, Jeff
03New Mexico Scorpions-3

Aldcorn, Gary
44Beehive Group II Photos-370
57Parkhurst-T24
58Parkhurst-18
60Parkhurst-33
60Shirriff Coins-53
94Parkhurst Missing Link-122

Aldoff, Rod
93Minnesota-Duluth Bulldogs-1
95Tallahassee Tiger Sharks-3
99San Diego Gulls-1
02Greensboro Generals RBI-1

Aldous, Chris
98Baton Rouge Kingfish-2
02Manchester Monarchs-1

Aldous, Shelby
04Ohio State Buckeyes Women-15
05Ohio State Buckeyes Women-9
06Ohio State Buckeyes Women-19

Aldred, Alex
03Portland Winter Hawks-14

Aldred, Jim
81Kingston Canadians-16
81Sault Ste. Marie Greyhounds-1
82Sault Ste. Marie Greyhounds-1

Aldridge, Keith
92Lake Superior State Lakers-3
97Detroit Vipers-17
98Detroit Vipers-1
98Detroit Vipers Freschetta-4
98IHL All-Star Eastern Conference-23
99Stars Postcards-1
99Michigan K-Wings-2
00SPx-114
Spectrum-114
00Upper Deck-183
Exclusives Tier 1-183
Exclusives Tier 2-183
00Upper Deck MVP-192
First Stars-192
Second Stars-192
Third Stars-192
00Upper Deck Victory-263
00German DEL-87
00Grand Rapids Griffins-1
01German Berlin Polar Bears Postcards-1
01German Upper Deck-31
02German Berlin Polar Bears Postcards-1
02German DEL City Press-2
03German Berlin Polar Bears Postcards-1
03German DEL-61

Aleblad, Hans
65Swedish Coralli ISHockey-200
67Swedish Hockey-263

Alekhin, Dmitri
95Madison Monsters-3

Aleksandrov, Viktor
02Russian SL-46

Alen, Juha
03Cincinnati Mighty Ducks-B1
04Cincinnati Mighty Ducks-4
05Finnish Cardset -215
06Finnish Cardset-43
Playmakers Rookies-9
Playmakers Rookies Gold-9
Playmakers Rookies Silver-9
06Finnish Ilves Team Set-1

Alenius, Antti
66Finnish Jaakiekkosarja-147

Alepin, Alex
98Idaho Steelheads-1
00Knoxville Speed-1

Alexander, Bob
85Minnesota-Duluth Bulldogs-19

Alexander, Brian
93Quebec Pee-Wee Tournament-1459

Alexander, Claire
74Maple Leafs Postcards-1
75Maple Leafs Postcards-1
76Maple Leafs Postcards-1
76O-Pee-Chee NHL-321

Alexander, Ken
84Kitchener Rangers-11
85Kitchener Rangers-9

Alexander, Ricki
94German First League-377

Alexander, Todd
03Bakersfield Condors-1
03ECHL Update RBI Sports-56
05Las Vegas Wranglers-1

Alexandersson, Per-Arne
85Swedish Panini Stickers-213
86Swedish Panini Stickers-205
87Swedish Panini Stickers-204

Alexandrov, Boris
92Future Trends '76 Canada Cup-150

Alexandrov, Igor
92Upper Deck-611
98German DEL-90
99German DEL-240
01German Upper Deck-1
02German DEL City Press-148
04German DEL-164
05German DEL-357

Alexandrov, Viktor
03Russian Hockey League-188

Alexandrov, Yuri
06ITG Heroes and Prospects-133
Autographs-AYA

Alexeenko, Mikhail
73Swedish Stickers-123

Alexeev, Alexander
98Danish Hockey League-36
99Danish Hockey League-213

Alexeev, Kirill
99Rouyn-Noranda Huskies-1
00Rouyn-Noranda Huskies-4
Signed-4
01Drummondville Voltigeurs-17
02Kalamazoo Wings-2

Alexeev, Nikita
99UD Prospects-12
International Stars-IN7
00SPx Rookie Redemption-RR27
00UD CHL Prospects-5
Game Jersey Autographs-S-NE
Game Jerseys-NE
01Atomic-124
Premiere Date-124
Rookie Reaction-10
01Atomic Toronto Fall Expo-124
01BAP Memorabilia-375
Emerald-375
Ruby-375
Sapphire-375
01BAP Signature Series-248
Autographs-248
Autographs Gold-248
01Bowman YoungStars-157
Gold-157
Ice Cubed-157
01Crown Royale-178
Rookie Royalty-20
01O-Pee-Chee-346
01Pacific-462
01Pacific Adrenaline-224
Blue-224
Premiere Date-224
Red-224
Retail-224
Rookie Report-19
01Pacific Heads-Up-119
01Pacific High Voltage-10
01Parkhurst-283
01Parkhurst Beckett Promos-283
01Private Stock-139
Gold-139
Premiere Date-139
Retail-139
Silver-139
01Private Stock Pacific Nights-139
01Private Stock PS-2002-90
01Private Stock Reserve-R10
01SP Authentic-172
Limited-172
Limited Gold-172
01SP Game Used-98
01SPx-128
01Titanium-181
Retail-181
01Titanium Draft Day Edition-167
01Topps-346
01Topps Chrome-164
Refractors-164
Black Border Refractors-164
01Topps Heritage-148
01Topps Reserve-120
01UD Challenge for the Cup-133
01UD Honor Roll-88
01UD Mask Collection-167
Gold-167
01UD Playmakers-142
01UD Premier Collection-107
01UD Top Shelf-75
01Upper Deck-227
Exclusives-227
01Upper Deck Ice-69
01Upper Deck Vintage-297
01Vanguard-129
Blue-129
Red-129
One of Ones-129
Premiere Date-129
Prime Prospects-18
Proofs-129
02BAP First Edition-240
02Lightning Team Issue-1
02O-Pee-Chee-306
02O-Pee-Chee Premier Blue Parallel-306
02O-Pee-Chee Premier Red Parallel-306
02O-Pee-Chee Factory Set-306
02Pacific-345
Blue-345
Red-345
02SP Authentic-133
02Topps-306
OPC Blue Parallel-306
OPC Red Parallel-306
Factory Set-306
02Topps Chrome-148
Black Border Refractors-148
Refractors-148
02Topps Total-372
02Upper Deck-404
Exclusives-404
02Upper Deck Beckett UD Promos-404
02Springfield Falcons-3
03ITG Action-560
03Upper Deck MVP-385
Gold Script-385
Silver Script-385
Canadian Exclusives-385
04Springfield Falcons-20
05Russian Hockey League RHL-9
06Lightning Postcards-3
06O-Pee-Chee-451
Rainbow-451

Alexeyev, Alexander
92Tacoma Rockets-1
92Classic-54
Gold-54
93Tacoma Rockets-1
95Portland Pirates-1
96Hampton Roads Admirals-HRA4
97Hampton Roads Admirals-2
98Hampton Roads Admirals 10th Anniversary-18
99Tacoma Sabercats-2
00Russian Hockey League-188
00Tacoma Sabercats-9
02Rockford Ice Hogs-5

Alexson, Leighton
01OCN Blizzard-19

Alfors, Pekka
65Finnish Hellas-120

Alfredsson, Daniel
92Swedish Semic Elitserien Stickers-319
93Swedish Semic Elitserien-284
94Swedish Leaf-82
NHL Draft-6
95Be A Player-171
Signatures-S171
Signatures Die Cuts-S171
Lethal Lines-LL6
95Bowman-110
All-Foil-110
Bowman's Best-BB16
Bowman's Best Refractors-BB16
95Collector's Choice-406
95Donruss-299
Rated Rookies-14
95Donruss Elite-25
Die Cut Stars-25
Die Cut Uncut-25
Rookies-3
95Finest-116
Refractors-116
95Leaf Limited-25
Rookie Phenoms-2
95Metal-169
95Parkhurst International-257
95Parkhurst International-507
Emerald Ice-257
Emerald Ice-507
Crown Collection Silver Series 2-15
Crown Collection Gold Series 2-15
Parkie's Trophy Picks-PP38
95Select Certified-122
Mirror Gold-122
95Senators Team Issue-1
95SkyBox Impact-214
95SP-100
Holoviews-FX15
Holoviews Special FX-FX15
95Stadium Club-206
Members Only Master Set-206
95Summit-182
Artist's Proofs-182
Ice-182
95Topps-369
OPC Inserts-369
SuperSkills Super Rookies-SR12
95Ultra-329
High Speed-1
95Upper Deck-504
Electric Ice-504
Electric Ice Gold-504
NHL All-Stars-AS12
NHL All-Stars Jumbo-AS12
Predictor Hobby-H23
Predictor Hobby Exchange-H23
95Zenith-149
Rookie Roll Call-10
95Swedish Globe World Championships-47
95Swedish World Championships Stickers-160
96Be A Player Biscuit In The Basket-23
96Black Diamond-141
Gold-141
96Collector's Choice-177
96Collector's Choice-344
MVP-UD39
MVP Gold-UD39
Crash the Game-C13A
Crash the Game-C13B
Crash the Game-C13C
Crash the Game Gold-C13A
Crash the Game Gold-C13B
Crash the Game Gold-C13C
Crash the Game Exchange-CR13
Crash the Game Exchange Gold-CR13
96Collector's Choice Blow-Ups Bi-Way-6
96Donruss Rated Rookies-10
96Donruss Canadian Ice-34
Gold Press Proofs-34
Red Press Proofs-34
96Donruss Elite-100
Die Cut Stars-100
Aspirations-2
96Flair-63
Blue Ice-63
96Fleer-73
96Fleer-136
Rookie Sensations-1
96Fleer Picks-78
Dream Lines-3
Fabulous 50-1
Jagged Edge-1
96Kraft Upper Deck-45
96Leaf-210
Press Proofs-210
Sweaters Away-14
Sweaters Home-14
96Leaf Limited-73
Gold-73
96Leaf Preferred-48
Press Proofs-48
Steel-35
Steel Gold-35
96McDonald's Pinnacle-9
96Metal Universe-103
96NHL Aces Playing Cards-1
96Pinnacle-205
Artist's Proofs-205
Foil-205
Premium Stock-205
Rink Collection-205
By The Numbers-10
By The Numbers Premium-10
Trophies-4
96Pinnacle Mint-10
Bronze-10
Gold-10
Silver-10
Coins Brass-10
Coins Solid Gold-10
Coins Gold Plated-10
Coins Nickel-10
Coins Silver-10
96Playoff One on One-341
96Score-240
Artist's Proofs-240
Dealer's Choice Artist's Proofs-240
Special Artist's Proofs-240
Golden Blades-240
96Select Certified-47
Artist's Proofs-47
Blue-47
Mirror Blue-47
Mirror Gold-47
Mirror Red-47
Red-47
96Senators Pizza Hut-1
96SkyBox Impact-86
96SkyBox Impact-164
NHL on Fox-1
96SP-107
Holoview Collection-HC9
Game Film-GF20
96SPx-32
96SPx-GF1
Gold-32
96Stadium Club Members Only-38
96Summit-167
Artist's Proofs-167
Ice-167
Metal-167
Premium Stock-167
High Voltage-4
High Voltage Mirage-4
96Team Out-42
96Topps Picks Rookie Stars-RS1
96Topps Picks Rookie Stars OPC-RS1
96Ultra-113
Gold Medallion-113
96Upper Deck-113
Generation Next-X6
Superstar Showdown-SS18A
96Upper Deck Ice-95
Parallel-95
96Zenith-103
Artist's Proofs-103
Z-Team-13
96Swedish Semic Wien-72
97SLU Hockey Canadian-1
97SLU Hockey American-1
97Beehive-48
Golden Portraits-48
97Black Diamond-73
Double Diamond-73
Triple Diamond-73
Quadruple Diamond-73
97Collector's Choice-172
Star Quest-SQ51
Stick'Ums-S11
97Crown Royale-89
Emerald Green-89
Ice Blue-89
Silver-89
97Donruss-17
Press Proofs Silver-17
Press Proofs Gold-17
97Donruss Canadian Ice-112
Dominion Series-112
Provincial Series-112
97Donruss Elite-104
Aspirations-104
Status-104
97Donruss Limited-22
97Donruss Limited-186
Exposure-22
Exposure-186
Fabric of the Game-46
97Donruss Preferred-90
Cut to the Chase-90
97Donruss Priority-113
Stamp of Approval-113
Direct Deposit-27
97Esso Olympic Hockey Heroes-44
97Esso Olympic Hockey Heroes French-44
97Gatorade Stickers-1
97Katch-97
Gold-97
Silver-97
97Kenner Starting Lineup Cards-1
97Leaf-145
Fractal Matrix-145
Fractal Matrix Die Cuts-145
97Leaf International-145
Universal Ice-145
97NHL Aces Playing Cards-6
97Pacific-58
Copper-58
Emerald Green-58
Ice Blue-58
Red-58
Silver-58
97Pacific Dynagon-83
Copper-83
Dark Grey-83
Emerald Green-83
Ice Blue-83
Red-83
Silver-83
Tandems-71
97Pacific Invincible-92
Copper-92
Emerald Green-92
Ice Blue-92
Red-92
Silver-92
97Pacific Omega-152
Copper-152
Dark Gray-152
Emerald Green-152
Gold-152
Ice Blue-152
97Panini Stickers-41
97Paramount-122
Copper-122
Dark Grey-122
Emerald Green-122
Ice Blue-122
Red-122
Silver-122
97Pinnacle-155
Press Plates Back Black-155
Press Plates Back Cyan-155
Press Plates Back Magenta-155
Press Plates Back Yellow-155
Press Plates Front Black-155
Press Plates Front Cyan-155
Press Plates Front Magenta-155
Press Plates Front Yellow-155
97Pinnacle Certified-114
Red-114
Mirror Blue-114
Mirror Gold-114
Mirror Red-114
97Pinnacle Inside-26
Coach's Collection-26
Executive Collection-26
97Pinnacle Tot Cert Platinum Blue-114
97Pinnacle Tot Cert Platinum Gold-114
97Pinnacle Totally Certified Platinum Red-114
97Pinnacle Tot Cert Mirror Platinum Gold-114
97Revolution-92
Copper-92
Emerald-92
Ice Blue-92
Silver-92
Team Checklist Laser Cuts-17
97Score-131
Artist's Proofs-131
Golden Blades-131
97SP Authentic-106
Icons-I30
Icons Die-Cuts-I30
Icons Embossed-I30
97SPx-34
Bronze-34
Gold-34
Silver-34
Steel-34
Grand Finale-34
97Studio-94
Press Proofs Silver-94
Press Proofs Gold-94
97Upper Deck-112
Game Dated Moments-112
Sixth Sense Masters-SS27
Sixth Sense Wizards-SS27
Three Star Selects-14A
97Upper Deck Ice-11
Parallel-11
Lethal Lines-L4A
Lethal Lines 2-L4A
Power Shift-11
97Zenith-43
Z-Gold-43
Z-Silver-43
97Zenith 5 x 7-25
Gold Impulse-25
Silver Impulse-25
98Aurora-128
Championship Fever-32
Championship Fever Copper-32
Championship Fever Ice Blue-32
Championship Fever Red-32
Championship Fever Silver-32
Front Line Copper-6
Front Line Ice Blue-6
Front Line Red-6
98Be A Player-98
Press Release-98
98BAP Gold-98
98BAP Autographs-98
98BAP Autographs Gold-98
98BAP Tampa Bay All Star Game-98
98Black Diamond-61
Double Diamond-61
Triple Diamond-61
Quadruple Diamond-61
98Bowman's Best-16
Refractors-16
Atomic Refractors-16
98Crown Royale-92
Limited Series-92
98Finest-13
No Protectors-13
No Protectors Refractors-13
Refractors-13
Centurion-C19
Centurion Refractors-C19
98Katch-97
98OPC Chrome-130
Refractors-130
98Pacific-305
Ice Blue-305
Red-305
98Pacific Dynagon Ice-126
Blue-126
Red-126
98Pacific Omega-163
Red-163
Opening Day Issue-163
98Panini Photocards-1
98Panini Stickers-42
98Paramount-160
Copper-160
Emerald Green-160
Holo-Electric-160
Ice Blue-160
Silver-160
98Revolution-98
Ice Shadow-98
Red-98
98Senators Team Issue-1
98SP Authentic-60
Power Shift-60
Sign of the Times-DA
Sign of the Times Gold-DA
98Topps-130
O-Pee-Chee-130
98Topps Gold Label Class 1-69
Black-69
Black One of One-69
One of One-69
Red-69
Red One of One-69
98Topps Gold Label Class 2-69
98Topps Gold Label Class 2 Black-69
98Topps Gold Label Class 2 Black 1 of 1-69
98Topps Gold Label Class 2 One of One-69
98Topps Gold Label Class 2 Red-69
98Topps Gold Label Class 2 Red One of One-69
98Topps Gold Label Class 3-69
98Topps Gold Label Class 3 Black-69
98Topps Gold Label Class 3 Black 1 of 1-69
98Topps Gold Label Class 3 One of One-69
98Topps Gold Label Class 3 Red-69
98Topps Gold Label Class 3 Red One of One-69
98UD Choice-144
Prime Choice Reserve-144
Reserve-144
98Upper Deck-327
Exclusives-327
Exclusives 1 of 1-327
Gold Reserve-327
98Upper Deck MVP-141
Gold Script-141
Silver Script-141
Super Script-141
99BAP Memorabilia-287
Gold-287
Silver-287
99Crown Royale-94
Limited Series-94
Premiere Date-94
99O-Pee-Chee-157
99O-Pee-Chee Chrome-157
99O-Pee-Chee Chrome Refractors-157
99Pacific-283
Copper-283
Emerald Green-283
Gold-283
Ice Blue-283
Premiere Date-283
Red-283
99Pacific Dynagon Ice-136
Blue-136
Copper-136
Gold-136
Premiere Date-136
99Pacific Omega-156
Copper-156
Gold-156
Ice Blue-156
Premiere Date-156
99Pacific Prism-94
Holographic Blue-94
Holographic Gold-94
Holographic Mirror-94
Holographic Purple-94
Premiere Date-94
99Panini Stickers-112
99Paramount-158
Copper-158
Emerald-158
Gold-158
Holographic Emerald-158
Holographic Gold-158
Holographic Silver-158
Ice Blue-158
Premiere Date-158
Red-158
Silver-158
99Senators Team Issue-1
99SPx-103
Radiance-103
Spectrum-103
99Stadium Club-98
First Day Issue-98
One of a Kind-98
Printing Plates Black-98
Printing Plates Cyan-98
Printing Plates Magenta-98
Printing Plates Yellow-98
Chrome-32
Chrome Refractors-32
99Topps/OPC-157
99Topps/OPC Chrome-157
Refractors-157
99Topps Gold Label Class 1-37
Black-37
Black One of One-37
One of One-37
Red-37
Red One of One-37
99Topps Gold Label Class 2-37
99Topps Gold Label Class 2 Black-37
99Topps Gold Label Class 2 Black 1 of 1-37
99Topps Gold Label Class 2 One of One-37
99Topps Gold Label Class 2 Red-37
99Topps Gold Label Class 2 Red One of One-37
99Topps Gold Label Class 3-37
99Topps Gold Label Class 3 Black-37
99Topps Gold Label Class 3 Black 1 of 1-37
99Topps Gold Label Class 3 One of One-37
99Topps Gold Label Class 3 Red-37
99Topps Gold Label Class 3 Red One of One-37
99Topps Gold Label Quest for the Cup-QC7
99Topps Gold Label Quest for the Cup One of One - QC7
99Topps Gold Label Quest 4 the Cup Black-QC7
99Topps Gold Label Quest for the Cup Black One of One -QC7
99Topps Gold Label Quest for the Cup Red-QC7
99Topps Gold Label Quest for the Cup Red One of One -QC7
99Topps Premier Plus-73
Parallel-73
Calling All Calders-CAC3
99Upper Deck-265
Exclusives-265
Exclusives 1 of 1-265
99Upper Deck Gold Reserve-265
99Upper Deck MVP-140
Gold Script-140
Silver Script-140
Super Script-140
99Upper Deck MVP SC Edition-126
Gold Script-126
Silver Script-126
Super Script-126
99Upper Deck Ovation-40
Standing Ovation-40
99Upper Deck Victory-204
99Wayne Gretzky Hockey-121
00Aurora-99
Premiere Date-99
00BAP Memorabilia-195
Emerald-195
Ruby-195
Sapphire-195
Promos-195
Jersey Cards-J27
Jersey Emblems-E27
Jersey Numbers-N27
Jersey and Stick Cards-JS27
00BAP Mem Chicago Sportsfest Copper-195
00BAP Memorabilia Chicago Sportsfest Blue-195
00BAP Memorabilia Chicago Sportsfest Gold-195
00BAP Memorabilia Chicago Sportsfest Ruby-195
00BAP Memorabilia Chicago Sun-Times Ruby-195
00BAP Memorabilia Chicago Sun-Times Gold-195
00BAP Mem Chicago Sun-Times Sapphire-195
00BAP Mem Toronto Fall Expo Copper-195
00BAP Memorabilia Toronto Fall Expo Gold-195
00BAP Memorabilia Toronto Fall Expo Ruby-195
00BAP Parkhurst 2000-P65
00BAP Signature Series-19
Emerald-19
Ruby-19
Sapphire-19
Autographs-196
Autographs Gold-196
00BAP Ultimate Memorabilia Autographs-14
Gold-14
00Crown Royale-73
Ice Blue-73
Limited Series-73
Premiere Date-73
Red-73
Game-Worn Jersey Redemptions-7
00O-Pee-Chee-105
00O-Pee-Chee Parallel-105
00Pacific-273
00Pacific-443
Copper-273
Copper-443
Gold-273
Gold-443
Ice Blue-273
Ice Blue-443
Premiere Date-273
Premiere Date-443
00Panini Stickers-70
00Paramount-169
Copper-169
Gold-169
Holo-Gold-169
Holo-Silver-169
Ice Blue-169
Premiere Date-169
00Private Stock-68
Gold-68
Premiere Date-68
Retail-68
Silver-68
00Revolution-101
Blue-101
Premiere Date-101
Red-101
00Senators Team Issue-1
00Stadium Club-34
Co-Signers-CO3
Lone Star Signatures-LS4
11 X 14 Autographs-DA
00Titanium Game Gear-41
00Titanium Game Gear-119
00Titanium Game Gear Patches-119
00Titanium Draft Day Edition-70
Patches-70
00Topps/OPC-105
Parallel-105
00Topps Chrome-82
OPC Refractors-82
Refractors-82
00Topps Gold Label Class 1-34
Gold-34
00Topps Gold Label Class 2-34
00Topps Gold Label Class 2 Gold-34
00Topps Gold Label Class 3-34
00Topps Gold Label Class 3 Gold-34
00Topps Heritage-55
Chrome Parallel-55
00Topps Premier Plus-62
Blue Ice-62
00Topps Stars-22
Blue-22
00Upper Deck-121
Exclusives Tier 1-121
Exclusives Tier 2-121
00Upper Deck MVP-122
First Stars-122
Second Stars-122
Third Stars-122
00Upper Deck Victory-163
00Upper Deck Vintage-253
00Vanguard-68
Holographic Gold-68
Holographic Purple-68
Pacific Proofs-68
00Czech Stadion-117
01Atomic-67
Blue-67
Gold-67
Premiere Date-67
Red-67
01BAP Memorabilia-62
Emerald-62
Ruby-62
Sapphire-62
All-Star Jerseys-ASJ49
All-Star Emblems-ASE49
All-Star Numbers-ASN49
Country of Origin-CO30
Stanley Cup Playoffs-SC2
01BAP Signature Series-191
Autographs-191
Autographs Gold-191
Franchise Jerseys-FP-21
He Shoots-He Scores Prizes-34
Jerseys-GJ-78
Emblems-GUE-44
Numbers-ITN-44
Teammates-TM-21
01BAP Ultimate Memorabilia Autographs-3
01BAP Ultimate Mem Autographs Gold-3
01BAP Ultimate Memorabilia Calder Trophy-6
01BAP Ultimate Memorabilia Captain's C-1
01BAP Ultimate Memorabilia Dynamic Duos-15
01Bowman YoungStars-27
Gold-27
Ice Cubed-27
01Crown Royale-99
Blue-99
Premiere Date-99
Red-99
Retail-99
01McDonald's Pacific Jersey Patch Silver-14
01McDonald's Pacific Jersey Patches Gold-14
01O-Pee-Chee-102
01O-Pee-Chee Heritage Parallel-102
01O-Pee-Chee Heritage Parallel Limited-102
01O-Pee-Chee Premier Parallel-102
01Pacific-269
Extreme LTD-269
Hobby LTD-269
Premiere Date-269
Retail LTD-269
01Pacific Adrenaline-131
Blue-131
Premiere Date-131
Red-131
Retail-131
01Pacific Arena Exclusives-269
01Pacific Heads-Up-67
Blue-67
Premiere Date-67
Red-67
Silver-67
Quad Jerseys-19
01Parkhurst-81
Gold-81
Silver-81
Jerseys-PJ10
Sticks-PS10
Teammates-T16
01Private Stock-66
Gold-66
Premiere Date-66
Retail-66
Silver-66
01Private Stock Pacific Nights-66
01Senators Team Issue-1
01SP Authentic-59
Limited-59
Limited Gold-59
01Stadium Club-47
Award Winners-47
Master Photos-47
01Stadium Club Toronto Fall Expo-3
01Titanium-98
Hobby Parallel-98
Premiere Date-98
Retail-98
Retail Parallel-98
Double-Sided Jerseys-30
Double-Sided Jerseys-48
Double-Sided Jerseys-58
Double-Sided Patches-30
Double-Sided Patches-48
Double-Sided Patches-58
Saturday Knights-15
01Titanium Draft Day Edition-64
01Topps-102
Heritage Parallel-102
Heritage Parallel Limited-102
OPC Parallel-102
01Topps Chrome-102
Refractors-102
Black Border Refractors-102
01Topps Heritage-63
Refractors-63
01Topps Reserve-41
01UD Mask Collection-67
Gold-67
01Upper Deck-121
Exclusives-121
Leaders of the Pack-LP10
01Upper Deck Ice-109
01Upper Deck MVP-129
Souvenirs-C-DA
Souvenirs Gold-C-DA
01Upper Deck Victory-245
Gold-245
01Upper Deck Vintage-177
01Upper Deck Vintage-182
01Vanguard-67
Blue-67
Red-67
One of Ones-67
Premiere Date-67
Proofs-67
01Czech Stadion-226
02Atomic-70
Blue-70
Gold-70
Red-70
Cold Fusion-18
Hobby Parallel-70
02BAP All-Star Edition-1
Jerseys-1
Jerseys Gold-1
Jerseys Silver-1
02BAP First Edition-140
Jerseys-140
Scoring Leaders-13
02BAP Memorabilia-22
Emerald-22
Ruby-22
Sapphire-22
All-Star Jerseys-ASJ-1
NHL All-Star Game-22
NHL All-Star Game Blue-22
NHL All-Star Game Green-22
NHL All-Star Game Red-22
Stanley Cup Playoffs-SC-20
02BAP Memorabilia Toronto Fall Expo-22
02BAP Signature Series-12
Autographs-12
Autograph Buybacks 1998-98
Autograph Buybacks 2001-191
Autographs Gold-12
Jerseys-SGJ23
Jersey Autographs-SGJ23
02Bowman YoungStars-85
Gold-85
Silver-85
02Crown Royale-66
Blue-66
Red-66
Retail-66
02eTopps-29
02ITG Used-52
02ITG Used-152
Jerseys-GUJ23
Jersey Autographs-GUJ23
Jersey Gold-GUJ23
Emblems-E23
Jersey and Stick-SJ23
Jersey and Stick Gold-SJ23
02McDonald's Pacific-28
Cup Contenders Die-Cuts-5
Jersey Patches Silver-12
Jersey Patches Gold-12
02NHL Power Play Stickers-103
02O-Pee-Chee-23
02O-Pee-Chee Jumbos-16
02O-Pee-Chee Premier Blue Parallel-23
02O-Pee-Chee Premier Red Parallel-23
02O-Pee-Chee Factory Set-23
02O-Pee-Chee Factory Set Hometown Heroes-HHC10
02Pacific-260
Blue-260
Red-260
Main Attractions-14
02Pacific Calder-13
Silver-13
02Pacific Complete-419
Red-419
02Pacific Exclusive-119
02Pacific Heads-Up-84
Blue-84
Purple-84
Red-84
Inside the Numbers-16
Quad Jerseys-9
Quad Jerseys-31
Quad Jerseys Gold-19
Quad Jerseys Gold-31
02Pacific Quest for the Cup-68
Gold-68
Chasing the Cup-12
Jerseys-12

02Parkhurst-95
Bronze-95
Gold-95
Silver-95
Jerseys-GJ42
Stick and Jerseys-SJ42
Teammates-TT11
02Parkhurst Retro-25
Minis-25
02Private Stock Reserve-70
Blue-70
Red-70
Retail-70
02Senators Team Issue-1
02Senators Team Issue-6
02SP Authentic-62
Beckett Promos-62
02SP Game Used-35
02SPx-54
Spectrum Gold-54
Spectrum Silver-54
02Stadium Club-82
Silver Decoy Cards-82
Proofs-82
Passport-2
World Stage-WS20
02Titanium-71
Blue-71
Red-71
Retail-71
Jerseys-46
Jerseys Retail-46
Patches-46
02Topps-23
OPC Blue Parallel-23
OPC Red Parallel-23
Topps/OPC Hometown Heroes-HHC10
Factory Set-23
02Topps Chrome-23
Black Border Refractors-23
Refractors-23
02Topps Heritage-15
Chrome Parallel-15
Calder Cloth-DA
Calder Cloth Patches-DA
02Topps Total-342
Team Checklists-TTC21
Topps-TT17
02UD Artistic Impressions-63
Gold-63
02UD Artistic Impressions Beckett Promos-63
02UD Artistic Impressions Retrospectives-R63
02UD Artistic Impressions Retrospect Gold-R63
02UD Artistic Impress Retrospect Silver-R63
02UD Honor Roll-51
02UD Honor Roll-91
02UD Piece of History-64
02Upper Deck-123
Exclusives-123
Blow-Ups-C29
02Upper Deck Classic Portraits-70
02Upper Deck MVP-125
Gold-125
Classics-125
Golden Classics-125
02Upper Deck Rookie Update-69
02Upper Deck Victory-148
Bronze-148
Gold-148
Silver-148
National Pride-NP47
02Upper Deck Vintage-181
02Upper Deck Vintage-281
Green Backs-181
Tall Boys-T45
Tall Boys Gold-T45
02Vanguard-69
LTD-69
Jerseys-31
Jerseys Gold-31
03BAP Memorabilia-18
Emerald-18
Gold-18
Ruby-18
Sapphire-18
Stanley Cup Playoffs-SCP-21
03BAP Ultimate Memorabilia Autographs-82
Gold-82
03BAP Ultimate Mem Auto Jerseys-82
03BAP Ultimate Mem Auto Emblems-82
03BAP Ultimate Memorabilia Triple Threads-15
03Beehive-134
Gold-134
Silver-134
03Black Diamond-18
Black-18
Green-18
Red-18
03Bowman-11
Gold-11
Goal to Goal-AY
03Bowman Chrome-11
Refractors-11
Gold Refractors-11
Xfractors-11
03Crown Royale-69
Blue-69
Retail-69
03ITG Action-467
Jerseys-M121
03ITG Used Signature Series-38
Gold-38
Autographs-DA
Autographs Gold-DA
03McDonald's Pacific-35
03O-Pee-Chee-123
03OPC Blue-123
03OPC Gold-123
03OPC Red-123
03Pacific-232
Blue-232
Red-232
Jerseys-27
Jerseys Gold-27
03Pacific Calder-70
03Pacific Calder-152
Silver-70
03Pacific Complete-229
Red-229
03Pacific Exhibit-101
Blue Backs-101
Yellow Backs-101
03Pacific Heads-Up-68
Hobby LTD-68
Retail LTD-68
03Pacific Invincible-68
Blue-68
Red-68
Retail-68
03Pacific Prism-132
Blue-132
Patches-132
Red-132
Retail-132
03Pacific Quest for the Cup-72
Blue-72
03Pacific Supreme-69
Blue-69
Red-69
Retail-69
Generations-6
03Parkhurst Rookie ROYalty-VR-4
03Parkhurst Rookie ROYalty Gold-VR-4
03Private Stock Reserve-185
Blue-185
Patches-185
Red-185
Retail-185
03Senators Postcards-7
03SP Game Used Authentic Fabrics-QSAHL
03SP Game Used Authentic Fabrics Gold-QSAHL
03SP Game Used Top Threads-SAHL
03SPx-68
Radiance-68
Spectrum-68
03Titanium-172
Hobby Jersey Number Parallels-172
Patches-172
Retail-172
03Topps-123
Blue-123
Gold-123
Red-123
Topps/OPC Idols-II4
C55 Relics-TRDA
03Topps Pristine-42
Gold Refractor Die Cuts-42
Refractors-42
Jersey Portions-PPJ-DA
Jersey Portion Refractors-PPJ-DA
Patches-PP-DA
Patch Refractors-PP-DA
Press Plates Black-42
Press Plates Cyan-42
Press Plates Magenta-42
Press Plates Yellow-42
Stick Portions-PPS-DA
Stick Portion Refractors-PPS-DA
03Topps Traded Franchise Fabrics-FF-DA
03UD Honor Roll-58
03Upper Deck-379
Canadian Exclusives-379
HG-379
Team Essentials-TP-DA
UD Exclusives-379
03Upper Deck Classic Portraits-67
03Upper Deck MVP-289
Gold Script-289
Silver Script-289
Canadian Exclusives-289
SportsNut-SN62
03Upper Deck Trilogy-67
Limited-67
03Upper Deck Victory-131
Bronze-131
Gold-131
Silver-131
03Toronto Star-64
04Pacific-181
Blue-181
Red-181
04SP Authentic-60
04SP Authentic-132
Limited-60
Limited-132
Sign of the Times-DS-AH
Sign of the Times-FS-RGT
Sign of the Times-FS-SEN
04UD All-World-57
Gold-57
Autographs-57
04Ultimate Collection Dual Logos-UL2-HA
04Upper Deck-123
Canadian Exclusives-123
HG Glossy Gold-123
HG Glossy Silver-123
World Cup Tribute-PFSUDA
04Swedish Alfabilder Alfa Stars-11
04Swedish Alfabilder Proof Parallels-11
04Swedish Pure Skills-19
Parallel-19
Professional Power-DA
05Be A Player-63
First Period-63
Second Period-63
Third Period-63
Overtime-63
Outtakes-OT35
Signatures-DI
Signatures Gold-DI
World Cup Salute-WCS9
05Beehive-64
Matte-64
Matted Materials-MMDA
Signature Scrapbook-SSDA
05Black Diamond-105
Emerald-105
Gold-105
Onyx-105
Ruby-105
05Hot Prospects-69
En Fuego-69
Red Hot-69
White Hot-69
05McDonalds Upper Deck-32
Top Scorers-TS12
05Panini Stickers-118
05Parkhurst-334
05Parkhurst-518
05Parkhurst-598
Facsimile Auto Parallel-334
Facsimile Auto Parallel-518
Facsimile Auto Parallel-598
True Colors-TCOTT
True Colors-TCOTT
True Colors-TCOTTO
True Colors-TCOTTO
05SP Authentic-71
Limited-71
Prestigious Pairings-PPAH
Sign of the Times Triples-THAS
Sign of the Times Quads-QSHAH
05SP Game Used Authentic Fabrics-AF-DA
05SP Game Used Authentic Fabrics Autos-AAF-DA
05SP Game Used Authentic Fabrics Dual-AH
05SP Game Used Authentic Fabrics Dual-SA
05SP Game Used Authentic Fabric Dual Auto-AH
05SP Game Used Authentic Fabric Dual Auto-SA
05SP Game Used Authentic Fabrics Gold-AF-DA
05SP Game Used Authentic Fabrics Quad-SAHH
05SP Game Used Authentic Patches Quad -SAHH
05SP Game Used Authentic Fabrics Triple-ARS
05SP Game Used Authentic
Fabrics Triple-SHA
05SP Game Used Authentic Patches-AP-DA
05SP Game Used Authentic Patch Autos-AAP-DA
05SP Game Used Authentic Patches Dual-AH
05SP Game Used Authentic Patches Dual-SA
05SP Game Used Authentic Patch Dual Autos-AH
05SP Game Used Authentic Patch Dual Autos-SA
05SP Game Used Authentic Patches Triple-ARS
05SP Game Used Authentic Patches Triple-SHA
05SP Game Used Auto Draft-AD-AL
05SP Game Used Awesome Authentics-AA-DA
05SP Game Used Awesome Authentics Gold-DA-DA
05SP Game Used SIGnificance-AL
05SP Game Used SIGnificance Gold-S-AL
05SP Game Used Significant Numbers-SN-AL
05SP Game Used Statscriptions-ST-DA
05SPx-61
Spectrum-61
Winning Combos-WC-HA
Winning Combos-WC-SA
Winning Combos Autographs-AWC-HA
Winning Combos Autographs-AWC-OT
Winning Combos Gold-WC-HA
Winning Combos Gold-WC-SA
Winning Combos Spectrum-WC-HA
Winning Combos Spectrum-WC-SA
Winning Materials-WM-DA
Winning Materials Gold-WM-DA
Winning Materials Spectrum-WM-DA
Xcitement Superstars-XS-DA
Xcitement Superstars Gold-XS-DA
Xcitement Superstars Spectrum-XS-DA
05The Cup-73
Gold-73
Black Rainbow-73
Dual NHL Shields-DSHA
Dual NHL Shields-DSSA
Masterpiece Pressplates-73
Noble Numbers-NNKA
Patch Variation-P73
05UD Artifacts-68
05UD Artifacts-184
Blue-68
Blue-184
Gold-68
Gold-184
Green-68
Green-184
Pewter-68
Pewter-184
Red-68
Red-184
Gold Autographed-68
Gold Autographed-184
Remarkable Artifacts-RA-AL
Remarkable Artifacts Dual-RA-AL
Treasured Patches-TP-DA
Treasured Patches Autographed-TP-DA
Treasured Patches Dual-TPD-DA
Treasured Patches Dual Autographed-TPD-DA
Treasured Patches Pewter-TP-DA
Treasured Patches Silver-TP-DA
Treasured Swatches-TS-DA
Treasured Swatches Autographed-TS-DA
Treasured Swatches Blue-TS-DA
Treasured Swatches Copper-TS-DA
Treasured Swatches Dual-TSD-DA
Treasured Swatches Dual Autographed-TSD-DA
Treasured Swatches Dual Blue-TSD-DA
Treasured Swatches Dual Copper-TSD-DA
Treasured Swatches Dual Maroon-TSD-DA
Treasured Swatches Dual Pewter-TSD-DA
Treasured Swatches Dual Silver-TSD-DA
Treasured Swatches Maroon-TS-DA
Treasured Swatches Pewter-TS-DA
Treasured Swatches Silver-TS-DA
05UD PowerPlay-60
Rainbow-60
Power Marks-PMDA
Specialists-TSDA
Specialists Patches-SPDA
05Ultimate Collection-64
Gold-64
National Heroes Jerseys-NHJAL
National Heroes Patches-NHPAL
Ultimate Signatures Trios-UTHAS
05Ultra-139
Gold-139
Ice-139
Scoring Kings-SK38
Scoring Kings Jerseys-SKJ-DA
Scoring Kings Jersey Autographs-KAJ-DA
Scoring Kings Patches-SKP-DA
Scoring Kings Patch Autographs-KAP-DA
05Upper Deck-130
05Upper Deck All-Time Greatest-41
05Upper Deck All-Time Greatest-81
05Upper Deck HG Glossy-130
05Upper Deck Hometown Heroes-HH15
05Upper Deck Jerseys Series II-J2DA
05Upper Deck Majestic Materials-MMDA
05Upper Deck Notable Numbers-N-AL
05Upper Deck Patches-P-DAL
05Upper Deck Shooting Stars-S-DA
05Upper Deck Ice-69
Rainbow-69
Frozen Fabrics-FFDA
Frozen Fabrics Autographs-AFFDA
Frozen Fabrics Glass-FFDA
Frozen Fabrics Patches-FFPDA
Frozen Fabrics Patch Autographs-FAPDA
05Upper Deck MVP-273
Gold-273
Platinum-273
ProSign-P-AL
05Upper Deck Rookie Update-67
05Upper Deck Trilogy-60
05Upper Deck Trilogy-146
Crystal-146
Honorary Patches-HP-AL
Honorary Patch Scripts-HSP-AL
Honorary Swatches-HS-AL
Honorary Swatch Scripts-HSS-AL
Ice Scripts-IS-AL
05Upper Deck Toronto Fall Expo-130
05Upper Deck Victory-133
Black-133
Gold-133
Silver-133
Stars on Ice-SI30
05Swedish SHL Elitset-26
Gold-26
Playmakers-4
06Be A Player-167
Autographs-167
Profiles-PP28
Profiles Autographs-PP28
Signatures-AD
Signatures 10-185
Signatures 25-185
Signatures Duals-DSA
Signatures Trios-TSAH
Signatures Foursomes-FFLNA
06Be A Player Portraits-74
06Beehive-34
Blue-34
Matte-34
Red Facsimile Signatures-34
Wood-34
Matted Materials-MMDA
06Black Diamond-116
Black-116
Gold-116
Ruby-116
06Flair Showcase-67
06Flair Showcase-147
06Flair Showcase-252
06Flair Showcase-289
Parallel-67
Parallel-147
Parallel-252
Parallel-289
Stitches-SSDA
06Fleer-135
Tiffany-135
Hockey Headliners-HL9
Total O-017
06Gatorade-49
06Hot Prospects-66
Red Hot-66
White Hot-66
Hot Materials -HMDA
Hot Materials Red Hot-HMDA
Hot Materials White Hot-HMDA
06McDonald's Upper Deck-33
06McDonald's Upper Deck-55
06O-Pee-Chee-346
06O-Pee-Chee-661
06O-Pee-Chee-691
Rainbow-346
Rainbow-661
Rainbow-691
Swatches-S-DA
06Panini Stickers-112
06Senators Postcards-3
06SP Authentic-33
Limited-33
06SP Game Used-70
Gold-70
Rainbow-70
Authentic Fabrics-AFAL
Authentic Fabrics Parallel-AFAL
Authentic Fabrics Patches-AFAL
Authentic Fabrics Triple-AF3OTT
Authentic Fabrics Triple Patches-AF3OTT
Authentic Fabrics Fives-AP5PTS
Authentic Fabrics Fives Patches-AP5PTS
Authentic Fabrics Eights-AF8SWE
Authentic Fabrics Eights Patches-AF8SWE
06SPx-70
Spectrum-70
SPxcitement-X71
SPxcitement Spectrum-X71
Winning Materials-WMDA
Winning Materials Spectrum-WMDA
06The Cup Foundations-CQDA
06The Cup Foundations Patches-CQDA
06The Cup NHL Shields Duals-DSHAS
06The Cup NHL Shields Duals-DSHSA
06UD Artifacts-33
Blue-33
Gold-33
Platinum-33
Radiance-33
Red-33
Frozen Artifacts-FADA
Frozen Artifacts Black-FADA
Frozen Artifacts Blue-FADA
Frozen Artifacts Gold-FADA
Frozen Artifacts Platinum-FADA
Frozen Artifacts Red-FADA
Frozen Artifacts Patches Black-FADA
Frozen Artifacts Patches Blue-FADA
Frozen Artifacts Patches Gold-FADA
Frozen Artifacts Patches Platinum-FADA
Frozen Artifacts Patches Red-FADA
Tundra Tandems-TTDD
Tundra Tandems Black-TTDD
Tundra Tandems Blue-TTDD
Tundra Tandems Gold-TTDD
Tundra Tandems Platinum-TTDD
Tundra Tandems Red-TTDD
Tundra Tandems Dual Patches Red-TTDD
06UD Mini Jersey Collection-71
06UD Powerplay-71
Impact Rainbow-71
06Ultimate Collection Jerseys-UJ-DA
06Ultimate Collection Patches-UJ-DA
06Ultra-137
Gold Medallion-137
Ice Medallion-137
Difference Makers-DM23
Scoring Kings-SK5
06Upper Deck Arena Giveaways-OTT6
06Upper Deck-139
Exclusives Parallel-139
High Gloss Parallel-139
All-Time Greatest-ATG15
Century Marks-CM7
Game Jerseys-JDA
Game Patches-PDA
Masterpieces-139
Walmart Tins Oversize-139
06Upper Deck MVP-205
Gold Script-205
Super Script-205
06Upper Deck Ovation-134
06Upper Deck Sweet Shot-75
Sweet Stitches-SSAL
Sweet Stitches Duals-SSAL
Sweet Stitches Triples-SSAL
06Upper Deck Trilogy-67
06Upper Deck Victory-138
06Upper Deck Victory Black-138
06Upper Deck Victory Gold-138
06Upper Deck Victory GameBreakers-GB34
06Upper Deck Victory Oversize Cards-DA
06Russian Sport Collection Olympic Stars-16
07Upper Deck Ovation-66
07Upper Deck Victory-45
Black-45
Gold-45
GameBreakers-GB5

Alfvendahl, Ake
56Swedish Alfabilder-95

Algotsson, Hakan
89Swedish Semic Elitserien Stickers-264
90Swedish Semic Elitserien Stickers-28
91Swedish Semic Elitserien Stickers-278
92Swedish Semic Elitserien Stickers-300
93Swedish Semic Elitserien-266
93Swedish Semic World Champ Stickers-2
94Finnish Jaa Kiekko-51
94Swedish Leaf-2
Clean Sweepers-10
Gold Cards-7
95Swedish Leaf-137
Spidermen-4
95Swedish Upper Deck-202
95Swedish Globe World Championships-4
99German DEL-243

Alho, Risto
66Finnish Jaakiekkosarja-140

Alic, Damir
05Everett Silvertips-1

Alikoski, Mikko
05Finnish Cardset -274
06Finnish Cardset Signature Sensations-17

Alinc, Jan
94Czech APS Extraliga-224
95Czech APS Extraliga-171
95Czech APS Extraliga-376
95Finnish Semic World Championships-164
97Czech APS Extraliga-364
98Swedish UD Choice-179
99Czech DS-66
99Czech OFS-337
00Czech DS Extraliga-116
00Czech OFS-94
01Czech OFS Update-301
01Czech OFS-5
02Czech OFS Plus-190
03Czech OFS Plus-66
03Czech OFS Plus Insert M-M24
04Czech OFS-42
05Czech HC Karlovy Vary-1
06German DEL-143

Alipov, Eveny
99Czech Score Blue 2000-101
99Czech Score Red Ice 2000-101

Aliu, Akim
05Sudbury Wolves-14
06Sudbury Wolves-14

Alkula, Jukka
66Finnish Jaakiekkosarja-205
71Finnish Suomi Stickers-128
72Finnish Jaakiekko-191
73Finnish Jaakiekko-149
74Finnish Jenkki-3
74Finnish Typotor-25

Alkunen, Kauko
71Finnish Suomi Stickers-277

Allain, Rick
87Kitchener Rangers-7
88Kitchener Rangers-7
89Kitchener Rangers-7
90ProCards AHL/IHL-139
907th Inn. Sketch Memorial Cup-41
91ProCards-51
96Guelph Storm-29
97Guelph Storm-28
02Peterborough Petes-1

Allaire, Benoit
02Coyotes Team Issue-22

Allaire, Francois
86Canadiens Postcards-28
98Thetford Mines Coyotes-10

Allaire, Francois (CO)
86Canadiens Postcards-28

Allaire, Francois CO
87Canadiens Postcards-1
87Canadiens Vachon Stickers-9
88Canadiens Postcards-1
89Canadiens Postcards-1
90Canadiens Postcards-1
91Canadiens Postcards-1

Allaire, Steve
93Quebec Pee-Wee Tournament-99

Allaire, Yannick
93Quebec Pee-Wee Tournament-218

Allan, Andy
94UK Guildford Flames-12
95UK Guildford Flames-3

Allan, Blake
02Belleville Bulls-1

Allan, Brett
96Swift Current Broncos-21
97Swift Current Broncos-21
98Swift Current Broncos-2
98Bowman CHL-122
Golden Anniversary-122
OPC International-122
Autographs Blue-A26
Autographs Gold-A26
Autographs Silver-A26
98Bowman Chrome CHL-122
Golden Anniversary-122
Golden Anniversary Refractors-122
OPC International-122
OPC International Refractors-122
Refractors-122
99Swift Current Broncos-1
00Prince George Cougars-21

Allan, Chad
93Saskatoon Blades-1
94Finest-147
Super Team Winners-147
Refractors-147
94Upper Deck-499
Electric Ice-499
95Donruss Canadian World Junior Team-4
95Donruss Elite World Juniors-3
95Topps Canadian World Juniors-17CJ
95Upper Deck-532
Electric Ice-532
Electric Ice Gold-532
95Saskatoon Blades-1
95Signature Rookies Auto-Phonex-2
95Signature Rook Auto-Phonex Phone Cards-2
96Syracuse Crunch-23
99Syracuse Crunch-5
00St. John's Maple Leafs-1
01UK Belfast Giants-14
02German DEL City Press-127
05German SC Bietigheim-Bissingen Steelers-2

Allan, Jamie
98Phoenix Mustangs-10

Allan, Richard
71Toronto Sun-18

Allan, Sandy
917th Inn. Sketch OHL-51
92Classic-19
Gold-19
92Classic Four-Sport *-168
Gold-168
93North Bay Centennials-2
94Prince Albert Raiders-1
95Richmond Renegades-6
96Louisville Riverfrogs-2
96Louisville Riverfrogs-28

Allan, Sir Montagu
83Hall of Fame Postcards-I2
85Hall of Fame-123

Allard, Jerome
93Quebec Pee-Wee Tournament-319

Allard, Pierre
907th Inn. Sketch QMJHL-227
917th Inn. Sketch QMJHL-14
00UK Sekonda Superleague-97
01UK Manchester Storm-9
01UK Manchester Storm Retro-9
02UK Manchester Storm-11

Allard, Sebasten
93Quebec Pee-Wee Tournament-444

Allegrezza, Mark
94Dubuque Fighting Saints-4

Allegrino, Scott
94Wheeling Thunderbirds-21
94Wheeling Thunderbirds Photo Album-16
95Wheeling Thunderbirds-23
96Wheeling Nailers-1
96Wheeling Nailers Photo Pack-16
97New Orleans Brass-15

Allen, Andrew
01Macon Whoopee-2
03ITG Action-637
03Trenton Titans-354

Allen, Bobby
92Quebec Pee-Wee Tournament-1002
01Providence Bruins-4
02BAP Memorabilia-323
02UD Premier Collection-93
Gold-93
02Hamilton Bulldogs-1
04Albany River Rats-2
05Albany River Rats-2
06Providence Bruins-1

Allen, Bryan
97Upper Deck-401
98Finest Futures Finest-F5
98Finest Futures Finest Refractors-F5
98OPC Chrome-226
Refractors-226
98Topps-226
O-Pee-Chee-226
98Bowman CHL-25
98Bowman CHL-133
Golden Anniversary-25
Golden Anniversary-133
OPC International-25
OPC International-133
Autographs Blue-A12
Autographs Gold-A12
Autographs Silver-A12
Scout's Choice-SC1
98Bowman Chrome CHL-25
98Bowman Chrome CHL-133
Golden Anniversary-25
Golden Anniversary-133
Golden Anniversary Refractors-25
Golden Anniversary Refractors-133
OPC International-25
OPC International-133
OPC International Refractors-25
OPC International Refractors-133
Refractors-25
Refractors-133
00BAP Memorabilia-514
00Kansas City Blades-3
01BAP Memorabilia-299
Emerald-299
Ruby-299
Sapphire-299
01BAP Signature Series-77
Autographs-77
Autographs Gold-77
01O-Pee-Chee-305
01O-Pee-Chee Premier Parallel-305
01Parkhurst-297
01Parkhurst Beckett Promos-297
01Private Stock-110
Gold-110
Premiere Date-110
Retail-110
Silver-110
01Private Stock Pacific Nights-110
01Private Stock PS-2002-91
01Stadium Club-118
Award Winners-118
Master Photos-118
01Topps-305
OPC Parallel-305
01Manitoba Moose-2
02BAP Sig Series Auto Buybacks 2001-77
02NHL Power Play Stickers-150
02O-Pee-Chee-298
02O-Pee-Chee Premier Blue Parallel-298
02O-Pee-Chee Premier Red Parallel-298
02O-Pee-Chee Factory Set-298
02Pacific Complete-391
Red-391
02Topps-298
OPC Blue Parallel-298
OPC Red Parallel-298
Factory Set-298
02Manitoba Moose-18
03Canucks Postcards-1
03Canucks Sav-on-Foods-12
03ITG Action-524
03Upper Deck MVP-420
Gold Script-420
Silver Script-420
Canadian Exclusives-420
05Parkhurst-478
Facsimile Auto Parallel-478
06O-Pee-Chee-222
Rainbow-222

Allen, Chris
95Bowman Draft Prospects-P2
95Slapshot-109
95Slapshot-433
96Collect Edge Ice Sign Sealed Delivered-2
96Visions Signings *-69
Autographs-69A
Autographs Silver-69A
98New Haven Beast-17
99Upper Deck-61
Exclusives-61
Exclusives 1 of 1-61
99Upper Deck Gold Reserve-61
99Upper Deck MVP-91
Gold Script-91
Silver Script-91
Super Script-91
99Louisville Panthers-16
01BC Icemen-1
02Greensboro Generals RBI-2
03South Carolina Stingrays-321

Allen, Dave
98Huntington Blizzard-23
99Huntington Blizzard-22

Allen, George
34Beehive Group I Photos-38
39O-Pee-Chee V301-1-79
43Parade Sportive *-1
45Quaker Oats Photos-61

Allen, Greg
88Niagara Falls Thunder-19
89Niagara Falls Thunder-1
897th Inn. Sketch OHL-145
907th Inn. Sketch OHL-251

Allen, John
90Arizona Icecats-2
90Arizona Icecats-3
92Arizona Icecats-5

Allen, Justin
04Oshawa Generals-7
04Oshawa Generals Autographs-7
05Owen Sound Attack-23
05Sudbury Wolves-20

Allen, Keith
54Parkhurst-47
92Flyers Upper Deck Sheets-44

Allen, Laine
04Kootenay Ice-1

Allen, Marko
92Finnish Jyvas-Hyva Stickers-25
93Finnish Jyvas-Hyva Stickers-55
93Finnish SISU-236
94Finnish SISU-4
95Finnish SISU-20

Allen, Matt
04Langley Hornets-1

Allen, Mike
90Kitchener Rangers-22
907th Inn. Sketch OHL-226
92Quebec Pee-Wee Tournament-737
93Quebec Pee-Wee Tournament-359

Allen, Peter
93Richmond Renegades-10
95Cleveland Lumberjacks-1
95Cleveland Lumberjacks Postcards-1
96Cleveland Lumberjacks-1
96Cleveland Lumberjacks Multi-Ad-2
97Kentucky Thoroughblades-2
98Kentucky Thoroughblades-1
00German DEL-212
01German Upper Deck-227

Allen, Scott
91ProCards-444
94Central Hockey League-19
95Central Hockey League-1
95Fort Worth Fire-7
96Johnstown Chiefs-25
97Johnstown Chiefs-6
98Johnstown Chiefs-4
99Johnstown Chiefs-5
00Johnstown Chiefs-3
03San Antonio Rampage-1

Allen, Tom
83Kingston Canadians-5
84Ottawa 67's-1
85London Knights-23

Allen, Viv
34Beehive Group I Photos-211

Allenspach, Stefan
93Swiss HNL-340

Allford, Ryan
93Quebec Pee-Wee Tournament-1618

Allinger, Jan
64Swedish Coralli ISHockey-75

Allison, Blair
91Air Canada SJHL-E3
92Saskatchewan JHL-4
93Maine Black Bears-55
98Tacoma Sabercats-1
99Tacoma Sabercats-15
01Idaho Steelheads-1
04Idaho Steelheads-3

Allison, David
83Nova Scotia Voyageurs-3
84Nova Scotia Oilers-2
88ProCards IHL-9
91Richmond Renegades-19
93Kingston Frontenacs-24
96Grand Rapids Griffins-2
97Grand Rapids Griffins-21
06Iowa Stars-25

Allison, James
81Ottawa 67's-1

Allison, Jamie
917th Inn. Sketch OHL-189
93Detroit Jr. Red Wings-15
94Upper Deck-464
Electric Ice-464
94Detroit Jr. Red Wings-17
95Saint John Flames-1
95Slapshot Memorial Cup-91
96Saint John Flames-1
96Collector's Edge Ice-75
Prism-75
97Donruss-131
Press Proofs Silver-131
Press Proofs Gold-131
97Pacific-315
Copper-315
Emerald Green-315
Ice Blue-315
Red-315
Silver-315
97Saint John Flames-1
00BAP Memorabilia-10
Emerald-10
Ruby-10
Sapphire-10
Promos-10
00BAP Mem Chicago Sportsfest Copper-10
00BAP Memorabilia Chicago Sportsfest Blue-10
00BAP Memorabilia Chicago Sportsfest Gold-10
00BAP Memorabilia Chicago Sportsfest Ruby-10
00BAP Memorabilia Chicago Sun-Times Ruby-10
00BAP Memorabilia Chicago Sun-Times Gold-10
00BAP Mem Chicago Sun-Times Sapphire-10
00BAP Mem Toronto Fall Expo Copper-10
00BAP Memorabilia Toronto Fall Expo Gold-10
00BAP Memorabilia Toronto Fall Expo Ruby-10
01BAP Memorabilia-464
Emerald-464
Ruby-464
Sapphire-464
01BAP Signature Series-90
Autographs-90
Autographs Gold-90
01SP Authentic Sign of the Times-YA
02BAP Sig Series Auto Buybacks 2001-90
06Binghamton Senators-1

Allison, Jason
917th Inn. Sketch OHL-381
93Donruss Team Canada-1
93Pinnacle-466
Canadian-466
93Upper Deck-537
93London Knights-1
93London Knights-25
93Classic-13
93Classic Four-Sport *-200
Gold-200
94Be A Player-R155
94Finest-55
94Finest-154
Super Team Winners-55
Super Team Winners-154
Refractors-55
Refractors-154
94Flair-195
94Fleer-231
94Leaf-511
Gold Rookies-13
94Leaf Limited-98
94OPC Premier-467
Special Effects-467
94Parkhurst SE-SE194
94Parkhurst SE-SE208
Gold-SE194
Gold-SE208
94Pinnacle-247
94Pinnacle-474
94Pinnacle-530
Artist's Proofs-247
Artist's Proofs-474
Artist's Proofs-530
Rink Collection-247
Rink Collection-474
Rink Collection-530
Rookie Team Pinnacle-7
94Score-206
94Score-231
Gold-206
Gold-231
Platinum-206
Platinum-231
94Select-193
Gold-193
Youth Explosion-YE8
94SP-151
Die Cuts-151
94Stadium Club-118
Members Only Master Set-118
First Day Issue-118
Super Team Winner Cards-118
94Topps/OPC Premier-467
Special Effects-467
94Ultra-386
94Upper Deck-242
94Upper Deck-535
Electric Ice-242
Electric Ice-535
Predictor Canadian-C4
94Upper Deck Predictor Canadian Exch Gold-C4
94Upper Deck Predictor Cdn Exch Silver-C4
94Upper Deck SP Inserts-SP174
94Upper Deck SP Inserts Die Cuts-SP174
94Classic-110
Gold-110
CHL All-Stars-C1
Picks-CP14
Previews-HK1
ROY Sweepstakes-R1
Tri-Cards-T73
94Classic Four-Sport *-160
Gold-160
Printers Proofs-160
95Capitals Team Issue-1
95Donruss-75
Canadian World Junior Team-12
95Emotion-185
95Leaf-103
95Leaf Limited-5
95Parkhurst International-494
Emerald Ice-494
95Playoff One on One-106
95Pro Magnets-31
95Score-128
Black Ice Artist's Proofs-128
Black Ice-128
95Topps Canadian World Juniors-4CJ
95Upper Deck-59
Electric Ice-59
Electric Ice Gold-59
95Portland Pirates-2
95Images Four-Sport *-114
96Be A Player-36
Autographs-36
Autographs Silver-36
96NHL Pro Stamps-31
96SP-168
96Zenith-125
Artist's Proofs-125
97Black Diamond-32
Double Diamond-32
Triple Diamond-32
Quadruple Diamond-32
97Collector's Choice-16
97Crown Royale-6
Emerald Green-6
Ice Blue-6
Silver-6
97Donruss Priority-122
Stamp of Approval-122
97Pacific Dynagon-6
Copper-6
Dark Grey-6
Emerald Green-6
Ice Blue-6
Red-6
Silver-6
Tandems-29
97Pacific Invincible-6
Copper-6
Emerald Green-6
Ice Blue-6
Red-6
Silver-6
97Pacific Omega-10
Copper-10
Dark Gray-10
Emerald Green-10
Gold-10
Ice Blue-10
97Pinnacle-147
Press Plates Back Black-147
Press Plates Back Cyan-147
Press Plates Back Magenta-147
Press Plates Back Yellow-147
Press Plates Front Black-147
Press Plates Front Cyan-147
Press Plates Front Magenta-147
Press Plates Front Yellow-147
97Pinnacle Inside-147
97Revolution-6

Copper-6
Emerald-6
Ice Blue-6
Silver-6
97Score-233
97Score Bruins-7
Platinum-7
Premier-7
97SP Authentic-10
97Upper Deck-8
97Zenith-80
Z-Gold-80
Z-Silver-80
97Zenith 5 x 7-28
Gold Impulse-28
Silver Impulse-28
98Aurora-7
98Be A Player-156
Press Release-156
98BAP Gold-156
98BAP Autographs-156
98BAP Autographs Gold-156
98Black Diamond-6
Double Diamond-6
Triple Diamond-6
Quadruple Diamond-6
98Bowman's Best-51
Refractors-51
Atomic Refractors-51
98Crown Royale-6
Limited Series-6
98Finest-141
No Protectors-141
No Protectors Refractors-141
Refractors-141
Centurion-C8
Centurion Refractors-C8
Red Lighters-R13
Red Lighters Refractors-R13
98Katch-11
98OPC Chrome-125
Refractors-125
Season's Best-SB27
Season's Best Refractors-SB27
98Pacific-41
Ice Blue-41
Red-41
98Pacific Dynagon Ice-7
Blue-7
Red-7
98Pacific Omega-10
Red-10
Opening Day Issue-10
98Panini Photocards-2
98Panini Stickers-14
98Paramount-8
Copper-8
Emerald Green-8
Holo-Electric-8
Ice Blue-8
Silver-8
98Revolution-6
Ice Shadow-6
Red-6
98SP Authentic-6
Power Shift-6
Sign of the Times-JA
Sign of the Times Gold-JA
98SPx Finite-6
Radiance-6
Spectrum-6
98Topps-125
O-Pee-Chee-125
Autographs-A1
Ice Age 2000-I6
Season's Best-SB27
98Topps Gold Label Class 1-50
Black-50
Black One of One-50
One of One-50
Red-50
Red One of One-50
98Topps Gold Label Class 2-50
98Topps Gold Label Class 2 Black-50
98Topps Gold Label Class 2 Black 1 of 1-50
98Topps Gold Label Class 2 One of One-50
98Topps Gold Label Class 2 Red-50
98Topps Gold Label Class 2 Red One of One-50
98Topps Gold Label Class 3-50
98Topps Gold Label Class 3 Black-50
98Topps Gold Label Class 3 Black 1 of 1-50
98Topps Gold Label Class 3 One of One-50
98Topps Gold Label Class 3 Red-50
98Topps Gold Label Class 3 Red One of One-50
98UD Choice-14
Prime Choice Reserve-14
Reserve-14
98Upper Deck-41
Exclusives-41
Exclusives 1 of 1-41
Fantastic Finishers-FF26
Fantastic Finishers Quantum 1-FF26
Fantastic Finishers Quantum 2-FF26
Fantastic Finishers Quantum 3-FF26
Gold Reserve-41
98Upper Deck MVP-13
Gold Script-13
Silver Script-13
Super Script-13
ProSign-JA
99Aurora-9
Premiere Date-9
99BAP Memorabilia-50
Gold-50
Silver-50
99Crown Royale-10
Limited Series-10
Premiere Date-10
99O-Pee-Chee-109
99O-Pee-Chee Chrome-109
99O-Pee-Chee Chrome Refractors-109
99Pacific-17
Copper-17
Emerald Green-17
Gold-17
Ice Blue-17
Premiere Date-17
Red-17
99Pacific Dynagon Ice-20
Blue-20
Copper-20
Gold-20
Premiere Date-20
99Pacific Omega-16
Copper-16
Gold-16
Ice Blue-16
Premiere Date-16
99Pacific Prism-10
Holographic Blue-10
Holographic Gold-10
Holographic Mirror-10
Holographic Purple-10
Premiere Date-10
99Panini Stickers-27
99Panini Stickers-326
99Paramount-16
Copper-16
Emerald-16
Gold-16
Holographic Emerald-16
Holographic Gold-16
Holographic Silver-16
Ice Blue-16
Premiere Date-16
Red-16
Silver-16
99Revolution-10
Premiere Date-10
Red-10
Shadow Series-10
Copper-10
Gold-10
CSC Silver-10
99SPx-12
Radiance-12
Spectrum-12
99Stadium Club-88
First Day Issue-88
One of a Kind-88
Printing Plates Black-88
Printing Plates Cyan-88
Printing Plates Magenta-88
Printing Plates Yellow-88
Eyes of the Game-EG7
Eyes of the Game Refractors-EG7
99Topps/OPC-109
99Topps/OPC Chrome-109
Refractors-109
99Topps Gold Label Class 1-31
Black-31
Black One of One-31
One of One-31
Red-31
Red One of One-31
99Topps Gold Label Class 2-31
99Topps Gold Label Class 2 Black-31
99Topps Gold Label Class 2 Black 1 of 1-31
99Topps Gold Label Class 2 One of One-31
99Topps Gold Label Class 2 Red-31
99Topps Gold Label Class 2 Red One of One-31
99Topps Gold Label Class 3-31
99Topps Gold Label Class 3 Black-31
99Topps Gold Label Class 3 Black 1 of 1-31
99Topps Gold Label Class 3 One of One-31
99Topps Gold Label Class 3 Red-31
99Topps Gold Label Class 3 Red One of One-31
99Topps Premier Plus-30
Parallel-30
99Upper Deck-185
Exclusives-185
Exclusives 1 of 1-185
99Upper Deck Gold Reserve-185
99Upper Deck MVP-15
Gold Script-15
Silver Script-15
Super Script-15
99Upper Deck Victory-27
99Wayne Gretzky Hockey-17
00Aurora-9
Pinstripes-9
Pinstripes Premiere Date-9
Premiere Date-9
00BAP Memorabilia-265
Emerald-265
Ruby-265
Sapphire-265
Promos-265
00BAP Mem Chicago Sportsfest Copper-265
00BAP Memorabilia Chicago Sportsfest Blue-265
00BAP Memorabilia Chicago Sportsfest Gold-265
00BAP Memorabilia Chicago Sportsfest Ruby-265
00BAP Memorabilia Chicago Sun-Times Ruby-265
00BAP Memorabilia Chicago Sun-Times Gold-265
00BAP Mem Chicago Sun-Times Sapphire-265
00BAP Mem Toronto Fall Expo Copper-265
00BAP Memorabilia Toronto Fall Expo Gold-265
00BAP Memorabilia Toronto Fall Expo Ruby-265
00BAP Parkhurst 2000-P191
00BAP Signature Series-102
Emerald-102
Ruby-102
Sapphire-102
Autographs-19
Autographs Gold-19
00BAP Ultimate Mem Game-Used Jerseys-GJ31
00BAP Ultimate Mem Game-Used Emblems-E27
00BAP Ultimate Mem Game-Used Numbers-N27
00BAP Ultimate Mem Game-Used Sticks-GS31
00BAP Ultimate Mem Journey Jerseys-JJ16
00BAP Ultimate Mem Journey Emblems-JE16
00BAP Ultimate Mem Journey Numbers-JI16
00Crown Royale-8
Ice Blue-8
Limited Series-8
Premiere Date-8
Red-8
Jewels of the Crown-4
Now Playing-3
00O-Pee-Chee-193
00O-Pee-Chee Parallel-193
00Pacific-29
Copper-29
Gold-29
Ice Blue-29
Premiere Date-29
00Paramount-16
Copper-16
Gold-16
Holo-Gold-16
Holo-Silver-16
Ice Blue-16
Premiere Date-16
00SP Authentic-8
00SPx-4
Spectrum-4
00Stadium Club-38
00Titanium-4
Blue-4
Gold-4
Premiere Date-4
Red-4
Retail-4
00Topps/OPC-193
Parallel-193
00Topps Chrome-128
OPC Refractors-128
Refractors-128
00Topps Gold Label Class 1-36
Gold-36
00Topps Gold Label Class 2-36
00Topps Gold Label Class 2 Gold-36
00Topps Gold Label Class 3-36
00Topps Gold Label Class 3 Gold-36
00Topps Heritage-44
Chrome Parallel-44
Original Six Relics-OSS-JA
00Topps Premier Plus-33
Blue Ice-33
00Topps Stars-24
Blue-24
Game Gear-GGJA
00UD Heroes-8
00UD Pros and Prospects-8
00UD Reserve-7
00Upper Deck-16
Exclusives Tier 1-16
Exclusives Tier 2-16
00Upper Deck MVP-16
First Stars-16
Game-Used Souvenirs-GSJA
Second Stars-16
Super Game-Used Souvenirs-GSJA
Third Stars-16
00Upper Deck Victory-22
00Upper Deck Vintage-31
00Vanguard-7
High Voltage-4
High Voltage Gold-4
High Voltage Green-4
High Voltage Red-4
High Voltage Silver-4
Holographic Gold-7
Holographic Purple-7
In Focus-3
Pacific Proofs-7
01Atomic-5
Blue-5
Gold-5
Premiere Date-5
Red-5
01BAP Memorabilia-197
01BAP Memorabilia-314
Emerald-197
Emerald-314
Ruby-197
Ruby-314
Sapphire-197
Sapphire-314
01BAP Signature Series Certified 100-C15
01BAP Signature Series Certified 50-C15
01BAP Signature Series Certified 1 of 1's-C15
01BAP Signature Series Autographs-LJAL
01BAP Signature Series Autographs Gold-LJAL
01BAP Update Heritage-H26
01Bowman YoungStars-8
Gold-8
Ice Cubed-8
01Crown Royale-66
Blue-66
Premiere Date-66
Red-66
Retail-66
Jewels of the Crown-15
01O-Pee-Chee-26
01O-Pee-Chee Heritage Parallel-26
01O-Pee-Chee Heritage Parallel Limited-26
01O-Pee-Chee Premier Parallel-26
01Pacific-27
01Pacific-403
01Pacific-426
Extreme LTD-27
Gold-403
Gold-426
Hobby LTD-27
Premiere Date-27
Retail LTD-27
01Pacific Adrenaline-85
Blue-85
Premiere Date-85
Red-85
Retail-85
01Pacific Arena Exclusives-27
01Pacific Arena Exclusives-403
01Pacific Arena Exclusives-426
01Pacific Heads-Up-6
Blue-6
Premiere Date-6
Red-6
Silver-6
01Parkhurst-232
Teammates-T4
01Private Stock-44
Gold-44
Premiere Date-44
Retail-44
Silver-44
01Private Stock Pacific Nights-44
01Private Stock PS-2002-4
01SP Authentic-38
Limited-38
Limited Gold-38
Sign of the Times-JA
01SPx-176
Hidden Treasures-DTJD
01Stadium Club-7
Award Winners-7
Master Photos-7
Souvenirs-JTJASS
01Titanium-63
Hobby Parallel-63
Premiere Date-63
Retail-63
Retail Parallel-63
Double-Sided Jerseys-75
Double-Sided Patches-75
01Titanium Draft Day Edition-41
01Topps-26
Heritage Parallel-26
Heritage Parallel Limited-26
OPC Parallel-26
Captain's Cloth-CC3
Own The Game-OTG4
01Topps Chrome-26
Refractors-26
Black Border Refractors-26
01Topps Heritage-7
Refractors-7
01Topps Reserve-30
Emblems-JAI
Jerseys-JAI
Name Plates-JAI
Numbers-JAI
Patches-JAI
01UD Challenge for the Cup-39
Jerseys-FPJA
Jersey Autographs-FPAL
Jersey Autographs-UCAP
01UD Mask Collection-43
Gold-43
Double Patches-DPJA
Jerseys-J-JA
Jersey and Patch-JPJA
01UD Playmakers-47
01UD Top Shelf-97
Jerseys-JA
Jersey Autographs-JA
01Upper Deck-309
Exclusives-309
01Upper Deck Ice-100
01Upper Deck MVP-11
Souvenirs-S-JA
Souvenirs Gold-S-JA
01Upper Deck Victory-30
Gold-30
01Vanguard-44
Blue-44
Red-44
Memorabilia-48
One of Ones-44
Premiere Date-44
Proofs-44
Quebec Tournament Heroes-12
01Czech Stadion-227
02Kings Team Issue-6
02Atomic-48
Blue-48
Gold-48
Red-48
Hobby Parallel-48
Power Converters-9
Super Colliders-8
02BAP First Edition-216
02BAP First Edition-373
02BAP First Edition-410R
02BAP Memorabilia-102
02BAP Memorabilia-242
Emerald-102
Emerald-242
Ruby-102
Ruby-242
Sapphire-102
Sapphire-242
NHL All-Star Game-102
NHL All-Star Game-242
NHL All-Star Game Blue-102
NHL All-Star Game Blue-242
NHL All-Star Game Green-102
NHL All-Star Game Green-242
NHL All-Star Game Red-102
NHL All-Star Game Red-242
02BAP Memorabilia Toronto Fall Expo-102
02BAP Memorabilia Toronto Fall Expo-242
02BAP Signature Series-107
Autographs-107
Autograph Buybacks 1998-156
Autograph Buybacks 2000-19
Autograph Buybacks 2001-LJAL
Autographs Gold-107
Franchise Players-FJ14
Team Quads-TQ10
02Bowman YoungStars-30
Gold-30
Silver-30
02Crown Royale-44
Blue-44
Red-44
Retail-44
02ITG Used-36
02ITG Used-136
02Kings Game Sheets-23
02Kings Game Sheets-24
02McDonald's Pacific-18
02O-Pee-Chee-240
02O-Pee-Chee Premier Blue Parallel-240
02O-Pee-Chee Premier Red Parallel-240
02O-Pee-Chee Factory Set-240
02Pacific-164
Blue-164
Red-164
Jerseys-21
Jerseys Holo-Silver-21
Main Attractions-9
02Pacific Complete-4
Red-4
02Pacific Exclusive-79
02Pacific Heads-Up-55
Blue-55
Purple-55
Red-55
Bobble Heads-1
Quad Jerseys-1
Quad Jerseys-13
Quad Jerseys Gold-1
Quad Jerseys Gold-13
02Pacific Quest for the Cup-43
Gold-43
02Parkhurst-20
Bronze-20
Gold-20
Silver-20
Teammates-TT6
02Parkhurst Retro-7
Minis-7
Franchise Players-RF14
02Private Stock Reserve-44
Blue-44
Red-44
Retail-44
02SP Authentic-44
Beckett Promos-44
Super Premiums-SPJA
02SP Game Used Authentic Fabrics-AFJA
02SP Game Used Authentic Fabrics Gold-AFJA
02SP Game Used Authentic Fabrics Rainbow-AFJA
02SP Game Used First Rounder Patches-AL
02SP Game Used Piece of History-PHAL
02SP Game Used Piece of History-PHJA
02SP Game Used Piece of History Gold-PHAL
02SP Game Used Piece of History Gold-PHJA
02SP Game Used Piece of History Rainbow-PHAL
02SP Game Used Piece of History Rainbow-PHJA
02SPx Xtreme Talents-JA
02SPx Xtreme Talents Gold-JA
02SPx Xtreme Talents Silver-JA
02Stadium Club-12
Silver Decoy Cards-12
Proofs-12
02Titanium-48
Blue-48
Red-48
Retail-48
02Topps-240
OPC Blue Parallel-240
OPC Red Parallel-240
02Topps Promos-PP2
02Topps Factory Set-240
02Topps Chrome-132
Black Border Refractors-132
Refractors-132
02Topps Heritage-24
02Topps Heritage-110
Chrome Parallel-24
02Topps Total-80
Team Checklists-TTC13
02UD Artistic Impressions-44
Gold-44
02UD Artistic Impressions Beckett Promos-44
02UD Artistic Impressions Retrospectives-R44
02UD Artistic Impressions Retrospect Gold-R44
02UD Artistic Impress Retrospect Silver-R44
02UD Mask Collection Instant Offense-IOJA
02UD Mask Collection Patches-PGJA
02UD Piece of History-43
02UD Top Shelf-40
Dual Player Jerseys-STAB
Shooting Stars-SHJA
Signatures-JA
Sweet Sweaters-SWJA
Triple Jerseys-TSAPP
02Upper Deck-83
Exclusives-83
Difference Makers-JA
02Upper Deck Classic Portraits-47
02Upper Deck MVP-82
Gold-82
Classics-82
Golden Classics-82
Skate Around Jerseys-STDAP
02Upper Deck Victory-97
Bronze-97
Gold-97
Silver-97
02Upper Deck Vintage-118
02Upper Deck Vintage-274
02Upper Deck Vintage-307
Green Backs-118
Tall Boys-T32
Tall Boys Gold-T32
02Vanguard-47
LTD-47
03BAP Memorabilia-35
Emerald-35
Gold-35
Ruby-35
Sapphire-35
03Beehive-90
Gold-90
Silver-90
03Black Diamond-11
Black-11
Green-11
Red-11
03Crown Royale-46
Blue-46
Retail-46
03ITG Action-283
Jerseys-M92
03NHL Sticker Collection-233
03O-Pee-Chee-215
03OPC Blue-215
03OPC Gold-215
03OPC Red-215
03Pacific-151
Blue-151
Red-151
03Pacific Complete-41
Red-41
03Pacific Exhibit-66
03Pacific Exhibit-207
Blue Backs-66
Yellow Backs-66
03Pacific Invincible-44
Blue-44
Red-44
Retail-44
03Pacific Prism-120
Blue-120
Patches-120
Red-120
Retail-120
03Parkhurst Original Six Boston-33
Memorabilia-BM31
03Private Stock Reserve-170
Blue-170
Patches-170
Red-170
Retail-170
03Titanium-159
Hobby Jersey Number Parallels-159
Patches-159
Retail-159
03Topps-215
Blue-215
Gold-215
Red-215
03UD Honor Roll-37
03Upper Deck-332
Canadian Exclusives-332
HG-332
UD Exclusives-332
Classic Portraits Classic Colors-CC-JA
03Upper Deck MVP-194
Gold Script-194
Silver Script-194
Canadian Exclusives-194
Souvenirs-S15
03Upper Deck Victory-85
Bronze-85
Gold-85
Silver-85
03Toronto Star-44
05Beehive-86
Matte-86
05Black Diamond-144
Emerald-144
Gold-144
Onyx-144
Ruby-144
05Parkhurst-450
Facsimile Auto Parallel-450
True Colors-TCTOR
True Colors-TCTOR
True Colors-TCTOMO
True Colors-TCTOMO
05SP Authentic-96
Limited-96
05SP Game Used-94
Gold-94
05SPx-86
Spectrum-86
05Ultimate Collection Jerseys Dual-DJAL
05Ultimate Collection Jerseys Triple-TJSLA
05Ultimate Coll Ultimate Patches Dual-DPAL
05Ultimate Coll Ultimate Patches Triple-TPSLA
05Ultra-187
Gold-187
Ice-187
05Upper Deck-423
Big Playmakers-B-JA
Jerseys Series II-J2JA
Majestic Materials-MMJA
Notable Numbers-N-JAL
05Upper Deck Hockey Showcase-HS12
05Upper Deck Showcase Promos-HS12
05Upper Deck Ice-94
Rainbow-94
05Upper Deck MVP-365
Gold-365
Platinum-365
05Upper Deck Rookie Update-93
05Upper Deck Victory-247
Black-247
Gold-247
Silver-247
06Black Diamond Jerseys-JAL
06Black Diamond Jerseys Black-JAL
06Black Diamond Jerseys Gold-JAL
06Black Diamond Jerseys Ruby-JAL
06UD Artifacts Treasured Patches Black-TSJA
06UD Artifacts Treasured Patches Blue-TSJA
06UD Artifacts Treasured Patches Gold-TSJA
06UD Artifacts Treasured Patches Platinum-TSJA
06UD Artifacts Treasured Patches Red-TSJA
06UD Artifacts Treasured Swatches-TSJA
06UD Artifacts Treasured Swatches Black-TSJA
06UD Artifacts Treasured Swatches Blue-TSJA
06UD Artifacts Treasured Swatches Gold-TSJA
06UD Artifacts Treasured Swatches Platinum-TSJA
06UD Artifacts Treasured Swatches Red-TSJA
06UD Powerplay Specialists-SAL
06UD Powerplay Specialists Patches-PAL
06Upper Deck Game Jerseys-JAL
06Upper Deck Game Patches-PAL
06Upper Deck Victory-189
06Upper Deck Victory Black-189
06Upper Deck Victory Gold-189

Allison, Josh
93Quebec Pee-Wee Tournament-771

Allison, Mike
81O-Pee-Chee-221
81Topps-E94
82Post Cereal-13
86Maple Leafs Postcards-1
87Maple Leafs PLAY-18
88Kings Postcards-13
88Kings Smokey-1
88Panini Stickers-73
89Kings Smokey-4
89O-Pee-Chee-141
89Topps-141
90O-Pee-Chee-417

Allison, Peter
92Windsor Spitfires-14

Allison, Ray
80O-Pee-Chee-126
80Topps-126
83Flyers J.C. Penney-1
83O-Pee-Chee-259
84Kelowna Wings-52
89ProCards AHL-338
93Swiss HNL-375

Allison, Scott
90Score-424
Canadian-424
90Prince Albert Raiders-1
907th Inn. Sketch WHL-273
917th Inn. Sketch WHL-276
94Cape Breton Oilers-1
95PEI Senators-1
97UK Sheffield Steelers-11
99German DEL-157
00UK Sekonda Superleague-150
00UK Sheffield Steelers-5
00UK Sheffield Steelers Centurions-14
01UK Sheffield Steelers-1
01Kalamazoo K-Wings-23
02UK Nottingham Panthers-10
02Kalamazoo Wings-26

Allman, Trevor
01Odessa Jackalopes-1

Allmann, Steve
92Finnish Semic-28
92Norwegian Elite Series-51

Allringer, Johan
98Danish Hockey League-90
99Danish Hockey League-108

Allvin, Patrik
99Swedish Upper Deck-109

Alm, Bengt
71Swedish Hockey-271

Almasy, Peter
92Finnish Semic-239

Almmonen, Jarkko
04Finnish Cardset-206

Almond, Cody
05Kelowna Rockets-1

Almqvist, Anders
72Swedish Stickers-204

Almqvist, Gote
56Swedish Alfabilder-53

Almstedt, Graydon
84Ottawa 67's-2

Almtorp, Jonas
02Swedish SHL-244
Parallel-244
03Swedish MoDo Postcards-1
05Swedish SHL Elitset-152
Gold-152
06Swedish SHL Elitset-7

Aloi, Joe
87Hull Olympiques-2

Alphonso, Arron
04Ottawa 67's-17
05Ottawa 67's-13
06Ottawa 67s-18

Alphonso, Shandor
01Sudbury Wolves-1
01Sudbury Wolves Police-16
03Sudbury Wolves-2

Alserydh, Lars
69Swedish Hockey-76

Alseth, Tor Arne
92Norwegian Elite Series-205

Alstead, Ryan
92Minnesota Golden Gophers-20

Alston, Jan
95Swiss HNL-122
96Swiss HNL-237
96Swiss HNL-571
98German DEL-246
99German Adler Mannheim Eagles Postcards-21
99German DEL-20
00German DEL-14
Profiles-P1
01Swiss HNL-11
02Swiss HNL-16

Altareev, Dmitri
00Russian Hockey League-201

Althoff, Christian
94German DEL-357

Altorfer, Remo
02Swiss HNL-369

Altrichter, Martin
94Czech APS Extraliga-250
95Czech APS Extraliga-125
96Czech APS Extraliga-288
97Czech APS Extraliga-148
97Czech DS Stickers-208
98Czech DS Stickers-188
99Czech Score Blue 2000-132
99Czech Score Red Ice 2000-132
02Czech OFS Plus-103
Trios-T25
Duos-D13
03Czech OFS Plus-141
03Czech OFS Plus Checklists-12
03Czech OFS Plus Insert B-B8
03Czech OFS Plus Insert M-M17
03Czech OFS Plus Insert P-P8
03Czech OFS Plus MS Praha-SE41
04Czech OFS-269
Goals-Against Leaders-12
Goals-Against Leaders-NNO
Save Percentage Leaders-11
Team Cards-13
05Czech HC Hame Zlin-1
06Czech OFS Goalies I-14
06Czech OFS Goalies II-12

Altrichter, Petr
99Czech Score Blue 2000-36
99Czech Score Red Ice 2000-36
04Czech OFS-1

Alvarez, Mauricio
92Quebec Pee-Wee Tournament-1106
95Slapshot-21
95Barrie Colts-1

Alverud, Anders
83Swedish Semic Elitserien-126
84Swedish Semic Elitserien-149

Alvey, Matt
97Charlotte Checkers-1
00Fresno Falcons-2

Alvin, Patrik
96Pensacola Ice Pilots-5

Alzner, Karl
04Calgary Hitmen-1
05Calgary Hitmen-1
06ITG Heroes and Prospects Quad Emblems-QE12
06ITG Heroes and Prospects Triple Memorabilia-TM11
07ITG Going For Gold World Juniors-3
Autographs-3
Emblems-GUE3
Jerseys-GUJ3
Numbers-GUN3

Amadio, Dave
68O-Pee-Chee-157
68Shirriff Coins-59
70O-Pee-Chee-33
70Topps-33

Amadio, Greg
01Michigan Tech Huskies-1
03Columbia Inferno-97
06Iowa Stars-1

Amadio, Leo
52Juniors Blue Tint-75

Amadio, Neil
50Quebec Citadelles-1

Amadio, Oliver
01Swiss HNL-284
02Swiss HNL-125

Amado, Matt
04Notre Dame Fighting Irish-21

Amann, Patrik
00Swiss Panini Stickers-307

Amann, Rick
93Swedish Semic World Champ Stickers-155
94Finnish Jaa Kiekko-273
94German DEL-89
95German DEL-83
95Swedish Globe World Championships-219
98German DEL-NNO
99German DEL-400

Ambler, David
93Quebec Pee-Wee Tournament-588
03Muskegon Fury-1

Ambrosio, Jeffrey
94Parkhurst SE-SE266
Gold-SE266
95Slapshot-143
95Signature Rookies Future Flash-FF1
95Signature Rook Future Flash Sigs-FF1
96Kitchener Rangers-1
01Odessa Jackalopes-2

Ambroski, Kevin
01Barrie Colts-17

Ambroziak, Peter
897th Inn. Sketch OHL-60
907th Inn. Sketch OHL-76
917th Inn. Sketch OHL-291
92Rochester Americans Dunkin' Donuts-1
92Rochester Americans Kodak-3
93Rochester Americans Kodak-3
98Flint Generals-12
01New Mexico Scorpions-6
02New Mexico Scorpions-1
03New Mexico Scorpions-18
04New Mexico Scorpions-1

Ambruz, Martin
98Czech OFS-279
99Czech OFS-457
00Czech DS Extraliga-59
00Czech OFS-364
01Czech OFS-77
02Czech OFS Plus-62
03Czech OFS Plus-24
04Czech OFS-270
04Czech OFS-401

Ambuhl, Andres
01Swiss HNL-109
02Swiss HNL-15
04Swiss Davos Postcards-3

Amidovski, Bujar
95Slapshot-106
96Louisiana Ice Gators-1
98OPC Chrome-239
Refractors-239
98Topps-239
O-Pee-Chee-239
98ECHL All-Star Southern Conference-18
98Louisiana Ice Gators-2
98Bowman CHL-32
Golden Anniversary-32
OPC International-32
Scout's Choice-SC4
98Bowman Chrome CHL-32
Golden Anniversary-32
Golden Anniversary Refractors-32
OPC International-32
OPC International Refractors-32
Refractors-32
99ECHL All-Star Northern Conference-4
00Florida Everblades-1
01Greensboro Generals-18
03Atlantic City Boardwalk Bullies-1
04Atlantic City Boardwalk Bullies Kinko's-3

Amirov, Rustem
99Russian Hockey League-132

Amodeo, Charles
03Sarnia Sting-1

Amodeo, Dominic
92Alberta International Team Canada-1
98Swiss Power Play Stickers-316
99Swiss Panini Stickers-352
01UK London Knights-25

Amodeo, Mike
72O-Pee-Chee-291
78Jets Postcards-1
79Jets Postcards-1
79O-Pee-Chee-268
82Swedish Semic VM Stickers-126
83Swedish Semic VM Stickers-126
99Kitchener Rangers-6
01Kitchener Rangers-7
02Sault Ste. Marie Greyhounds-16
03Laredo Bucks-1
04Portland Pirates-11

Amonte, Rocco
93Memphis RiverKings-1

Amonte, Tony
91Pro Set Platinum-262
91O-Pee-Chee-26
91OPC Premier-11
91Parkhurst-114
91Parkhurst-443
French-114
French-443
91Pinnacle-301
91Pinnacle-390
French-301
French-390
91Pro Set-550
French-550
91Score American-398
91Score Canadian Bilingual-288
91Score Canadian English-288
91Topps-26
91Upper Deck-440
91Upper Deck-450
French-440
French-450
92Bowman-389
92O-Pee-Chee-155
92O-Pee-Chee-255
25th Anniv. Inserts-24
92Panini Stickers-270
92Panini Stickers-T
92Panini Stickers French-270
92Panini Stickers French-T
92Parkhurst-107
92Parkhurst-235
Emerald Ice-107
Emerald Ice-235
92Pinnacle-55
French-55
Team 2000-4
Team 2000 French-4
92Pro Set-118
Rookie Goal Leaders-1
92Score-389
92Score-415
92Score-506
Canadian-389
Canadian-415
Canadian-506
Young Superstars-2
92Seasons Patches-27
92Stadium Club-32
92Stadium Club-250
92Topps-6
92Topps-229
Gold-6G
Gold-229G
92Ultra-133
Rookies-1
92Upper Deck-13
92Upper Deck-138
92Upper Deck-359
92Upper Deck-453
92Upper Deck-635
All-Rookie Team-AR1
All-Rookie Team-AR7
93Donruss-217
93Donruss-411
93Leaf-17
93OPC Premier-70
Gold-70
93Panini Stickers-90
93Parkhurst-129
93Parkhurst-132
93Pinnacle I Samples-1
93Pinnacle-6
Canadian-6
Team 2001-19
Team 2001 Canadian-19
93PowerPlay-156
93Score-215
Canadian-215
93Stadium Club-226
93Stadium Club-458
Members Only Master Set-226
Members Only Master Set-458
OPC-226
First Day Issue-226
First Day Issue-458
First Day Issue OPC-226
93Topps/OPC Premier-70
Gold-70
93Ultra-202
93Upper Deck-64
SP-97
93Upper Deck Locker All-Stars-51
93Swedish Semic World Champ Stickers-188
94Be A Player-R17
Signature Cards-97
94Blackhawks Coke-1
94Canada Games NHL POGS-65
94Donruss-107
94Fleer-37
94Hockey Wit-2
94Leaf-2
94OPC Premier-5
Special Effects-5
94Parkhurst Vintage-V56
94Parkhurst SE-SE36
Gold-SE36
94Pinnacle-16
Artist's Proofs-16
Rink Collection-16
94Post Box Backs-1
94Score-92
Gold-92

Platinum-92
94Select-115
Gold-115
94SP-26
Die Cuts-26
94Topps/OPC Premier-5
Special Effects-5
94Ultra-273
94Upper Deck-4
Electric Ice-4
SP Inserts-SP105
SP Inserts Die Cuts-SP105
94Upper Deck NHLPA/Be A Player-1
95Blackhawks Coke-1
95Canada Games NHL POGS-63
95Collector's Choice-206
Player's Club-206
Player's Club Platinum-206
95Donruss-121
95Leaf-17
95Panini Stickers-160
95Parkhurst International-311
Emerald Ice-311
95Playoff One on One-235
95Score-133
Black Ice Artist's Proofs-133
Black Ice-133
95SP-28
95Stadium Club-117
Members Only Master Set-117
95Summit-165
Artist's Proofs-165
Ice-165
95Topps-79
OPC Inserts-79
Power Lines-4PL
95Ultra-216
95Upper Deck-18
Electric Ice-18
Electric Ice Gold-18
Special Edition-SE18
Special Edition Gold-SE18
95Swedish Globe World Championships-121
96Be A Player-66
Autographs-66
Autographs Silver-66
96Black Diamond-173
Gold-173
96Collector's Choice-49
96Donruss-80
Press Proofs-80
96Flair-14
Blue Ice-14
96Leaf-92
Press Proofs-92
96Metal Universe-24
96Pinnacle-54
Artist's Proofs-54
Foil-54
Premium Stock-54
Rink Collection-54
96Score-169
Artist's Proofs-169
Dealer's Choice Artist's Proofs-169
Special Artist's Proofs-169
Golden Blades-169
96SkyBox Impact-16
96SP-32
Holoview Collection-HC18
96Topps Picks-133
OPC Inserts-133
96Ultra-28
Gold Medallion-28
96Upper Deck-32
96Upper Deck Ice-13
Parallel-13
97Black Diamond-101
Double Diamond-101
Triple Diamond-101
Quadruple Diamond-101
97Blackhawks PowerAde-NNO
97Collector's Choice-44
Blow-Ups-2
Crash the Game-C10A
Crash the Game-C10B
Crash the Game-C10C
Crash the Game Exchange-CR10
Star Quest-SQ65
97Crown Royale-27
Emerald Green-27
Ice Blue-27
Silver-27
97Donruss-102
Press Proofs Silver-102
Press Proofs Gold-102
97Donruss Canadian Ice-34
Dominion Series-34
Provincial Series-34
97Donruss Elite-97
Aspirations-97
Status-97
97Donruss Limited-105
Exposure-105
97Donruss Preferred-64
Cut to the Chase-64
97Donruss Priority-151
Stamp of Approval-151
97Katch-31
Gold-31
Silver-31
97Leaf-139
Fractal Matrix-139
Fractal Matrix Die Cuts-139
97Leaf International-139
Universal Ice-139
97NHL Aces Playing Cards-33
97Pacific-264
Copper-264
Emerald Green-264
Ice Blue-264
Red-264
Silver-264
97Pacific Dynagon-24
Copper-24
Dark Grey-24
Emerald Green-24
Ice Blue-24
Red-24
Silver-24
Tandems-33
97Pacific Invincible-27
Copper-27
Emerald Green-27
Ice Blue-27
Red-27
Silver-27
97Pacific Omega-46
Copper-46
Dark Gray-46
Emerald Green-46
Gold-46
Ice Blue-46
97Panini Stickers-131
97Paramount-40
Copper-40
Dark Grey-40
Emerald Green-40
Ice Blue-40
Red-40
Silver-40
97Pinnacle-148
Press Plates Back Black-148
Press Plates Back Cyan-148
Press Plates Back Magenta-148
Press Plates Back Yellow-148
Press Plates Front Black-148
Press Plates Front Cyan-148
Press Plates Front Magenta-148
Press Plates Front Yellow-148
97Pinnacle Certified-68
Red-68
Mirror Blue-68
Mirror Gold-68
Mirror Red-68
97Pinnacle Inside-53
Coach's Collection-53
Executive Collection-53
97Pinnacle Tot Cert Platinum Blue-68
97Pinnacle Tot Certi Platinum Gold-68
97Pinnacle Totally Certified Platinum Red-68
97Pinnacle Tot Cert Mirror Platinum Gold-68
97Revolution-27
Copper-27
Emerald-27
Ice Blue-27
Silver-27
97Score-114
Artist's Proofs-114
Golden Blades-114
97SP Authentic-29
Icons-I29
Icons Die-Cuts-I29
Icons Embossed-I29
Sign of the Times-TA
97SPx-8
Bronze-8
Gold-8
Silver-8
Steel-8
Grand Finale-8
97Studio-99
Press Proofs Silver-99
Press Proofs Gold-99
97Upper Deck-208
97Upper Deck-245
Game Dated Moments-245
Game Jerseys-GJ6
Sixth Sense Masters-SS18
Sixth Sense Wizards-SS18
Smooth Grooves-SG10
The Specialists-23
The Specialists Level 2 Die Cuts-23
Three Star Selects-9A
97Upper Deck Crash the All-Star Game-1
97Upper Deck Crash the All-Star Game-AR1
97Upper Deck Diamond Vision-19
Signature Moves-19
97Upper Deck Ice-63
Parallel-63
Power Shift-63
97Zenith-78
Z-Gold-78
Z-Silver-78
98SLU Hockey-10
98Aurora-38
98Be A Player-28
Press Release-28
98BAP Gold-28
98BAP Autographs-28
98BAP Autographs Gold-28
98BAP Playoff Game Used Jerseys-G22
98BAP Playoff Practice Used Jerseys-P11
98BAP Tampa Bay All Star Game-28
98Black Diamond-20
Double Diamond-20
Triple Diamond-20
Quadruple Diamond-20
98Bowman's Best-77
Refractors-77
Atomic Refractors-77
98Crown Royale-27
Limited Series-27
98Finest-29
No Protectors-29
No Protectors Refractors-29
Refractors-29
98Katch-31
98Kenner Starting Lineup Cards-1
98OPC Chrome-204
Refractors-204
98Pacific-142
Ice Blue-142
Red-142
98Pacific Dynagon Ice-38
Blue-38
Red-38
98Pacific Omega-48
Red-48
Opening Day Issue-48
98Panini Photocards-3
98Panini Stickers-118
98Paramount-43
Copper-43
Emerald Green-43
Holo-Electric-43
Ice Blue-43
Silver-43
98Revolution-28
Ice Shadow-28
Red-28
All-Star Die Cuts-1
Showstoppers-7
98SP Authentic-17
Power Shift-17
98SPx Finite-18
98SPx Finite-106
Radiance-18
Radiance-106
Spectrum-18
Spectrum-106
98SPx Top Prospects-9
Radiance-9
Spectrum-9
Premier Stars-PS20
98Topps-204
O-Pee-Chee-204
98Topps Gold Label Class 1-33
Black-33
Black One of One-33
One of One-33
Red-33
Red One of One-33
98Topps Gold Label Class 2-33
98Topps Gold Label Class 2 Black-33
98Topps Gold Label Class 2 Black 1 of 1-33
98Topps Gold Label Class 2 One of One-33
98Topps Gold Label Class 2 Red-33
98Topps Gold Label Class 2 Red One of One-33
98Topps Gold Label Class 3-33
98Topps Gold Label Class 3 Black-33
98Topps Gold Label Class 3 Black 1 of 1-33
98Topps Gold Label Class 3 One of One-33
98Topps Gold Label Class 3 Red-33
98Topps Gold Label Class 3 Red One of One-33
98Topps Gold Label Goal Race '99-GR9
98Topps Gold Label Goal Race '99 Black-GR9
98Topps Gold Label Goal '99 Black 1 of 1-GR9
98Topps Gold Label Goal Race 99 1 of 1-GR9
98Topps Gold Label Goal Race '99 Red-GR9
98Topps Gold Label GoalRace 99 Red 1 of 1-GR9
98UD Choice-51
98UD Choice Preview-51
98UD Choice Prime Choice Reserve-51
98UD Choice Reserve-51
98UD Choice StarQuest Blue-SQ26
98UD Choice StarQuest Gold-SQ26
98UD Choice StarQuest Green-SQ26
98UD Choice StarQuest Red-SQ26
98Upper Deck-243
Exclusives-243
Exclusives 1 of 1-243
Fantastic Finishers-FF16
Fantastic Finishers Quantum 1-FF16
Fantastic Finishers Quantum 2-FF16
Fantastic Finishers Quantum 3-FF16
Gold Reserve-243
98Upper Deck MVP-45
Gold Script-45
Silver Script-45
Super Script-45
99Aurora-30
Striped-30
Premiere Date-30
Premiere Date Striped-30
99BAP Memorabilia-94
Gold-94
Silver-94
Jersey Cards-J27
Jersey Emblems-E27
Jersey Numbers-I27
Jersey and Stick Cards-S27
Selects Silver-SL9
Selects Gold-SL9
99BAP Update Teammates Jersey Cards-TM27
99BAP Update Teammates Jersey Cards-TM33
99BAP Millennium-56
Emerald-56
Ruby-56
Sapphire-56
Signatures-56
Signatures Gold-56
Jerseys-J22
Jersey and Stick Cards-JS22
Jersey Emblems-E22
Jersey Numbers-N22
99Black Diamond-22
Diamond Cut-22
Final Cut-22
99Blackhawks Chicago Sun-Times-1
99Blackhawks Lineup Cards-1
99Crown Royale-30
Limited Series-30
Premiere Date-30
Ice Elite-5
Ice Elite Parallel-5
99McDonald's Upper Deck Game Jerseys-GJTA
99McDonald's Upper Deck Signatures-TA
99O-Pee-Chee-187
99O-Pee-Chee Chrome-187
99O-Pee-Chee Chrome Refractors-187
99O-Pee-Chee Chrome Fantastic Finishers-FF3
99OPC Chrome Fantastic Finishers Ref-FF3
99O-Pee-Chee Fantastic Finishers-FF3
99Pacific-84
Copper-84
Emerald Green-84
Gold-84
Ice Blue-84
Premiere Date-84
Red-84
99Pacific Dynagon Ice-46
Blue-46
Copper-46
Gold-46
Premiere Date-46
Checkmates American-4
Checkmates American-19
Checkmates Canadian-19
99Pacific Omega-51
Copper-51
Gold-51
Ice Blue-51
Premiere Date-51
99Pacific Prism-32
Holographic Blue-32
Holographic Gold-32
Holographic Mirror-32
Holographic Purple-32
Premiere Date-32
99Panini Stickers-203
99Panini Stickers-319
99Paramount-52
Copper-52
Emerald-52
Gold-52
Holographic Emerald-52
Holographic Gold-52
Holographic Silver-52
Ice Blue-52
Premiere Date-52
Red-52
Silver-52
Ice Alliance-7
Personal Best-7
99Revolution-32
Premiere Date-32
Red-32
Shadow Series-32
Showstoppers-7
Top of the Line-24
Copper-32
Gold-32
CSC Silver-32
99SP Authentic-19
99SPx-35
Radiance-35
Spectrum-35
99Stadium Club-6
First Day Issue-6
One of a Kind-6
Printing Plates Black-6
Printing Plates Cyan-6
Printing Plates Magenta-6
Printing Plates Yellow-6
Chrome-6
Chrome Refractors-6
99Topps/OPC-187
Fantastic Finishers-FF3
99Topps/OPC Chrome-187
Refractors-187
Fantastic Finishers-FF3
Fantastic Finishers Refractors-FF3
99Topps Gold Label Class 1-8
Black-8
Black One of One-8
One of One-8
Red-8
Red One of One-8
99Topps Gold Label Class 2-8
99Topps Gold Label Class 2 Black-8
99Topps Gold Label Class 2 Black 1 of 1-8
99Topps Gold Label Class 2 One of One-8
99Topps Gold Label Class 2 Red-8
99Topps Gold Label Class 2 Red One of One-8
99Topps Gold Label Class 3-8
99Topps Gold Label Class 3 Black-8
99Topps Gold Label Class 3 Black 1 of 1-8
99Topps Gold Label Class 3 One of One-8
99Topps Gold Label Class 3 Red-8
99Topps Gold Label Class 3 Red One of One-8
99Topps Premier Plus-31
Parallel-31
99Ultimate Victory-19
1/1-19
Parallel-19
Parallel 100-19
99Upper Deck-37
99Upper Deck-168
Exclusives-37
Exclusives-168
Exclusives 1 of 1-37
Exclusives 1 of 1-168
Crunch Time-CT25
Crunch Time Quantum Gold-CT25
Crunch Time Quantum Silver-CT25
Fantastic Finishers-FF12
Fantastic Finishers Quantum Gold-FF12
Fantastic Finishers Quantum Silver-FF12
99Upper Deck Gold Reserve-37
99Upper Deck Gold Reserve-168
99Upper Deck HoloGrFx-12
Ausome-12
99Upper Deck MVP-46
Gold Script-46
Silver Script-46
Super Script-46
99Upper Deck MVP SC Edition-43
Gold Script-43
Silver Script-43
Super Script-43
99Upper Deck Ovation-13
Standing Ovation-13
99Upper Deck Retro-17
Gold-17
Platinum-17
Inkredible-TA
Inkredible Level 2-TA
99Upper Deck Victory-64
99Upper Deck Victory-65
99Upper Deck Victory-327
99Wayne Gretzky Hockey-43
Tools of Greatness-TGTA
00McFarlane Hockey-10
00Aurora-31
Pinstripes-31
Pinstripes Premiere Date-31
Premiere Date-31
00BAP Memorabilia-264
Emerald-264
Ruby-264
Sapphire-264
Promos-264
Jersey Cards-J11
Jersey Emblems-E11
Jersey Numbers-N11
Jersey and Stick Cards-JS11
00BAP Mem Chicago Sportsfest Copper-264
00BAP Memorabilia Chicago Sportsfest Blue-264
00BAP Memorabilia Chicago Sportsfest Gold-264
00BAP Memorabilia Chicago Sportsfest Ruby-264
00BAP Memorabilia Chicago Sun-Times Ruby-264
00BAP Memorabilia Chicago Sun-Times Gold-264
00BAP Mem Chicago Sun-Times Sapphire-264
00BAP Mem Toronto Fall Expo Copper-264
00BAP Memorabilia Toronto Fall Expo Gold-264
00BAP Memorabilia Toronto Fall Expo Ruby-264
00BAP Memorabilia Update Teammates-TM4
00BAP Memorabilia Update Teammates-TM25
00BAP Memorabilia Update Teammates Gold-TM4
00BAP Memorabilia Update Teammates Gold-TM25
00BAP Parkhurst 2000-P2
00BAP Signature Series-220
Emerald-220
Ruby-220
Sapphire-220
Autographs-198
Autographs Gold-198
Franchise Players-F7
He Shoots-He Scores Prizes-34
Jersey Cards-J22
Jersey and Stick Cards-GSJ22
Jersey Cards Autographs-J22
Jersey Emblems-E22
Jersey Numbers-IN22
00BAP Ultimate Memorabilia Autographs-22
Gold-22
00BAP Ultimate Mem Game-Used Jerseys-GJ22
00BAP Ultimate Mem Game-Used Emblems-E20
00BAP Ultimate Mem Game-Used Numbers-N20
00BAP Ultimate Mem Game-Used Sticks-GS22
00BAP Ultimate Memorabilia Teammates-TM18
00Black Diamond-12
Gold-12
00Crown Royale-23
Ice Blue-23
Limited Series-23
Premiere Date-23
Red-23
00Kraft-24
00O-Pee-Chee-17
00O-Pee-Chee Parallel-17
00Pacific-92
Copper-92
Gold-92
Ice Blue-92
Premiere Date-92
Gold Crown Die Cuts-6
00Panini Stickers-126
00Paramount-48
Copper-48
Gold-48
Holo-Gold-48
Holo-Silver-48
Ice Blue-48
Premiere Date-48
Freeze Frame-6
Jersey and Patches-2
00Private Stock-19
Gold-19
Premiere Date-19
Retail-19
Silver-19
Game Gear-15
Game Gear Patches-15
00Revolution-29
Blue-29
Premiere Date-29
Red-29
Game-Worn Jerseys-4
Game-Worn Jersey Patches-4
HD NHL-7
Stat Masters-2
00SP Authentic-20
00SP Game Used-11
Patch Cards-P-TA
Tools of the Game-TA
Tools of the Game Exclusives-TA
00SPx-12
Spectrum-12
SPXcitement-X3
Winning Materials-TO
00Stadium Club-59
Beam Team-BT23
00Titanium-16
Blue-16
Gold-16
Premiere Date-16
Red-16
Retail-16
Game Gear-5
00Titanium Draft Day Edition-16
Patches-16
00Topps/OPC-17
Parallel-17
Autographs-ATA
Combos-TC3
Combos Jumbos-TC3
Own the Game-OTG7
00Topps Chrome-17
OPC Refractors-17
Refractors-17
Combos-TC3
Combos Refractors-TC3
Rocket's Flare-RF7
Rocket's Flare Refractors-RF7
00Topps Gold Label Class 1-74
Gold-74
00Topps Gold Label Class 2-74
00Topps Gold Label Class 2 Gold-74
00Topps Gold Label Class 3-74
00Topps Gold Label Class 3 Gold-74
00Topps Heritage-18
00Topps Heritage-234
Chrome Parallel-18
Arena Relics-OSA-TA
Heroes-HH16
00Topps Premier Plus-27
Blue Ice-27
Masters of the Break-MB4
00Topps Stars-12
Blue-12
Game Gear-GGTA
00UD Heroes-24
00UD Pros and Prospects-21
00UD Reserve-20
On-Ice Success-OS2
00Upper Deck-266
Exclusives Tier 1-266
Exclusives Tier 2-266
Signs of Greatness-STA
UD Flashback-UD2
00Upper Deck Ice-9
Immortals-9
Legends-9
Stars-9
00Upper Deck Legends-29
00Upper Deck Legends-30
Legendary Collection Bronze-29
Legendary Collection Bronze-30
Legendary Collection Gold-29
Legendary Collection Gold-30
Legendary Collection Silver-29
Legendary Collection Silver-30
00Upper Deck MVP-46
First Stars-46
Second Stars-46
Third Stars-46
00Upper Deck Victory-50
00Upper Deck Victory-51
00Upper Deck Victory-290
00Upper Deck Vintage-85
00Upper Deck Vintage-86
National Heroes-NH7
00Vanguard-22
Holographic Gold-22
Holographic Purple-22
Pacific Proofs-22
01McFarlane Hockey Inserts-10
01Atomic-19
Blue-19
Gold-19
Premiere Date-19
Red-19
Jerseys-8
Patches-8
Power Play-7
01BAP Memorabilia-257
Emerald-257
Ruby-257
Sapphire-257
All-Star Jerseys-ASJ20
All-Star Emblems-ASE20
All-Star Numbers-ASN20
All-Star Jersey Doubles-DASJ9
All-Star Teammates-AST8
All-Star Teammates-AST17
All-Star Teammates-AST31
Country of Origin-CO19
He Shoots-He Scores Prizes-35
01BAP Signature Series Certified 100-C45
01BAP Signature Series Certified 50-C45
01BAP Signature Series Certified 1 of 1's-C45
01BAP Signature Series Autographs-LTA
01BAP Signature Series Autographs Gold-LTA
01BAP Signature Series Franchise Jerseys-FP-7
01BAP Sig Series He Shoots/Scores Points-1
01BAP Sig Series He Shoots/Scores Prizes-15
01BAP Sig Series International Medals-IS-2
01BAP Signature Series Jerseys-GJ-12
01BAP Sig Series Jersey and Stick Cards-GSJ-12
01BAP Signature Series Emblems-GUE-12
01BAP Signature Series Numbers-ITN-12
01BAP Signature Series Teammates-TM-7
01BAP Ultimate Memorabilia Autographs-29
01BAP Ultimate Mem Autographs Gold-29
01BAP Ultimate Memorabilia Cornerstones-3
01BAP Ultimate Memorabilia Dynamic Duos-14
01BAP Update Passing the Torch-PTT2
01Bowman YoungStars-13
Gold-13
Ice Cubed-13
01Crown Royale-29
Blue-29
Premiere Date-29
Red-29
Retail-29
01O-Pee-Chee-5
01O-Pee-Chee Heritage Parallel-5
01O-Pee-Chee Heritage Parallel Limited-5
01O-Pee-Chee Premier Parallel-5
01Pacific-82
Extreme LTD-82
Hobby LTD-82
Premiere Date-82
Retail LTD-82
Jerseys-6
01Pacific Adrenaline-38
Blue-38
Premiere Date-38
Red-38
Retail-38
Jerseys-7
01Pacific Arena Exclusives-82
01Pacific Heads-Up-18
Blue-18
Premiere Date-18
Red-18
Silver-18
Quad Jerseys-6
01Parkhurst-76
Gold-76
Silver-76
He Shoots-He Scores Prizes-25
Jerseys-PJ25
Sticks-PS25
Teammates-T9
Waving the Flag-23
01Private Stock-17
Gold-17
Premiere Date-17
Retail-17
Silver-17
Game Gear-20
Game Gear Patches-20
01Private Stock Pacific Nights-17
01SP Authentic-14
Limited-14
Limited Gold-14
Sign of the Times-TA
Sign of the Times-GWA
01SP Game Used-8
Inked Sweaters-DSMA
Patches-PTA
Patches-CPAI
Patches-CPBA
Patches Signed-SPTA
Patches Signed-DSPAB
01SPx-11
Hidden Treasures-DTTD
Hidden Treasures-TTDSA
01Sports Illustrated for Kids III-20
01Stadium Club-13
Award Winners-13
Master Photos-13
Gallery-G32
Gallery Gold-G32
Perennials-P15
01Titanium-28
Hobby Parallel-28
Premiere Date-28
Retail-28
Retail Parallel-28
Double-Sided Jerseys-8
01Titanium Draft Day Edition-20
01Topps-5
Heritage Parallel-5
Heritage Parallel Limited-5
OPC Parallel-5
Captain's Cloth-CC2
Shot Masters-SM8
01Topps Chrome-5
Refractors-5
Black Border Refractors-5
01Topps Heritage-12
Refractors-12
01Topps Reserve-16
Emblems-TA
Jerseys-TA
Name Plates-TA
Numbers-TA
Patches-TA
01UD Challenge for the Cup-14
Jerseys-FPTA
01UD Honor Roll-91
01UD Mask Collection-17
Gold-17
Double Patches-DPTA
Dual Jerseys-PMAD
Jerseys-J-TA
Jersey and Patch-JPTA
01UD Playmakers-22
01UD Premier Collection Dual Jerseys-DAT
01UD Premier Collection Dual Jersey Black-DAT
01UD Premier Collection Jerseys-BTA
01UD Premier Collection Jerseys Black-B-TA
01UD Premier Collection Signatures-TA
01UD Premier Collection Signatures Black-TA
01UD Top Shelf-7
01Upper Deck-38
01Upper Deck-222
Exclusives-38
Exclusives-222
Franchise Cornerstones-FC12
Leaders of the Pack-LP2
Pride of a Nation-PNTA
Pride of a Nation-DPAG
Pride of a Nation-TPAWL
Skilled Stars-SS20
01Upper Deck Ice-7
01Upper Deck MVP-38
Souvenirs-S-TA
Souvenirs Gold-S-TA
01Upper Deck Victory-73
Gold-73
01Upper Deck Vintage-57
01Upper Deck Vintage-61
01Vanguard-18
Blue-18
Red-18
Memorabilia-8
One of Ones-18
Premiere Date-18
Proofs-18
02Atomic-76
Blue-76
Gold-76
Red-76
Hobby Parallel-76
National Pride-U8
02BAP All-Star Edition-2
He Shoots-He Score Prizes-1
Jerseys-2
Jerseys Gold-2
Jerseys Silver-2
02BAP First Edition-101
Jerseys-101
02BAP Memorabilia-144
02BAP Memorabilia-270
02BAP Memorabilia-309
Emerald-144
Emerald-270
Ruby-144
Ruby-270
Sapphire-144
Sapphire-270
All-Star Jerseys-ASJ-2
All-Star Teammmates-AST-19
NHL All-Star Game-144
NHL All-Star Game-270
NHL All-Star Game Blue-144
NHL All-Star Game Blue-270
NHL All-Star Game Green-144
NHL All-Star Game Green-270
NHL All-Star Game Red-144
NHL All-Star Game Red-270
02BAP Memorabilia Toronto Fall Expo-144
02BAP Memorabilia Toronto Fall Expo-270
02BAP Signature Series-115
Autographs-115
Autograph Buybacks 1998-28
Autograph Buybacks 1999-56
Autograph Buybacks 2000-198
Autographs Gold-115
02Bowman YoungStars-3
Gold-3
Silver-3
02Coyotes Team Issue-29
02Crown Royale-73
Blue-73
Red-73
Retail-73
02ITG Used-80
02ITG Used-180
International Experience-IE16
International Experience Gold-IE16
02O-Pee-Chee-9
02O-Pee-Chee-9U
02O-Pee-Chee Premier Blue Parallel-9
02O-Pee-Chee Premier Red Parallel-9
02O-Pee-Chee Factory Set-9
02Pacific-73
Blue-73
Red-73
Jerseys-7
Jerseys Holo-Silver-7
02Pacific Calder-48
Silver-48
02Pacific Complete-207
Red-207
02Pacific Exclusive-130
02Pacific Heads-Up-24
Blue-24
Purple-24
Red-24
Quad Jerseys-7
Quad Jerseys Gold-7
02Pacific Quest for the Cup-73
Gold-73
02Parkhurst-148
Bronze-148
Gold-148
Silver-148
College Ranks-CR10
College Ranks Jerseys-CRM10
02Parkhurst Retro-46
Minis-46
02Private Stock Reserve-76
Blue-76
Red-76
Retail-76
02SP Authentic-70
Beckett Promos-70
02SP Game Used-39
Authentic Fabrics-AFAM
Authentic Fabrics Gold-AFAM
Authentic Fabrics Rainbow-AFAM
Piece of History-PHAM
Piece of History Gold-PHAM
Piece of History Rainbow-PHAM
02SPx-59
Spectrum Gold-59
Spectrum Silver-59
02Stadium Club-110
Silver Decoy Cards-110
Proofs-110
Passport-13
02Titanium-77
Blue-77
Red-77
Retail-77
02Topps-9
02Topps-9U
OPC Blue Parallel-9
OPC Red Parallel-9
Topps/OPC Hometown Heroes-HHU9
Factory Set-9
Factory Set Hometown Heroes-HHU9
02Topps Chrome-9
Black Border Refractors-9
Refractors-9
02Topps Heritage-165
Great Skates-TA
Great Skates Patches-TA
02Topps Total-84
Production-TP10
Team Checklists-TTC23
02UD Artistic Impressions-67
Gold-67
02UD Artistic Impressions Beckett Promos-67
02UD Artistic Impressions Retrospectives-R67
02UD Artistic Impressions Retrospect Gold-R67
02UD Artistic Impress Retrospect Silver-R67
02UD Honor Roll-56
Students of the Game-SG24
02UD Mask Collection-67
02UD Mask Collection Beckett Promos-67
02UD Piece of History-70
02UD Premier Collection-42
02UD Top Shelf All-Stars-ASTA
02UD Top Shelf Goal Oriented-GOTA
02UD Top Shelf Milestones Jerseys-MLNLA
02UD Top Shelf Shooting Stars-SHTA
02UD Top Shelf Triple Jerseys-HTAPS
02UD Top Shelf Triple Jerseys-TSSAT
02Upper Deck-229
Exclusives-136
Exclusives-229
Blow-Ups-C32
Patchwork-PWTA
02Upper Deck Classic Portraits-75
Hockey Royalty-GWA
Hockey Royalty Limited-GWA
02Upper Deck MVP-139
Gold-139
Classics-139
Golden Classics-139
02Upper Deck Rookie Update-74
02Upper Deck Victory National Pride-NP52
02Upper Deck Vintage-199
02Upper Deck Vintage-283
Green Backs-199
Tall Boys-T51
Tall Boys Gold-T51
02Vanguard-76
LTD-76
03BAP Memorabilia-95
Emerald-95
Gold-95
Ruby-95
Sapphire-95
He Shoots-He Scores Prizes-26
Jersey and Stick-SJ-20
03BAP Ultimate Memorabilia Autographs-69
Gold-69
03BAP Ultimate Mem Auto Jerseys-69
03BAP Ultimate Memorabilia Triple Threads-22
03Beehive-144
Variations-144
Gold-144
Silver-144
Jumbo Jerseys-BH16
Jerseys-JT4
03Black Diamond-12
Black-12
Green-12
Red-12
03eTopps-23
03Flyers Program Inserts-3
03Flyers Postcards-1
03ITG Action-408
Jerseys-M122
03ITG Used Signature Series-93
Gold-93
Autographs-TAM
Autographs Gold-TAM
International Experience-30
International Experience Autographs-30
International Experience Emblems Gold-30
International Experience Emblems-30
International Experience Gold-30
Teammates-6
Teammates Gold-6
03NHL Sticker Collection-263
03O-Pee-Chee-180
03OPC Blue-180
03OPC Gold-180
03OPC Red-180
03Pacific-246
Blue-246
Red-246
03Pacific Complete-20
Red-20
03Pacific Exhibit-108
03Pacific Exhibit-211
Blue Backs-108
Yellow Backs-108
03Pacific Heads-Up-72
Hobby LTD-72
Retail LTD-72
03Pacific Invincible-72
Blue-72
Red-72
Retail-72
03Pacific Prism-135
Blue-135
Patches-135
Red-135
Retail-135
03Pacific Quest for the Cup-78
Blue-78
03Pacific Supreme-73
Blue-73
Red-73
Retail-73
Jerseys-19
03Parkhurst Original Six Chicago-44
03Parkhurst Original Six Chicago-76
Memorabilia-CM22
Memorabilia-CM35
Memorabilia-CM53
03Parkhurst Original Six New York-33
03Private Stock Reserve-190
Blue-190
Patches-190
Red-190
Retail-190
03SP Game Used Authentic Fabrics-QARGL
03SP Game Used Authentic Fabrics Gold-QARGL
03SP Game Used Authentic Patches-APTA
03SP Game Used Double Threads-DTRA
03SP Game Used Limited Threads-LTTA
03SP Game Used Limited Threads Gold-LTTA
03SP Game Used Team Threads-TTARL
03SP Game Used Top Threads-ARGL
03SPx-71
03SPx-148
Radiance-71
Radiance-148
Spectrum-71
Spectrum-148
Fantasy Franchise-FF-LRA
Fantasy Franchise Limited-FF-LRA
Winning Materials-WM-TA
Winning Materials Limited-WM-TA
03Titanium-73
Hobby Jersey Number Parallels-73
Retail-73
Retail Jersey Number Parallels-73
03Topps-180
Blue-180
Gold-180
Red-180
Topps/OPC Idols-UI14
03Topps C55-54
Minis-54
Minis American Back-54
Minis American Back Red-54
Minis Bazooka Back-54
Minis Brooklyn Back-54
Minis Hat Trick Back-54
Minis O Canada Back-54
Minis O Canada Back Red-54
Minis Stanley Cup Back-54
03Topps Pristine-91
Gold Refractor Die Cuts-91
Refractors-91

Press Plates Black-91
Press Plates Cyan-91
Press Plates Magenta-91
Press Plates Yellow-91
03UD Premier Collection-42
Teammates-PT-PF1
Teammates Patches-PT-PF1
03Upper Deck-139
Canadian Exclusives-139
HG-139
Highlight Heroes-HH-TA
Highlight Heroes Jerseys-HH-TA
03Upper Deck Classic Portraits-71
Classic Colors-CC-TA
Hockey Royalty-RLA
Starring Cast-SC-TA
03Upper Deck Ice-66
Gold-66
03Upper Deck MVP-307
Gold Script-307
Silver Script-307
Canadian Exclusives-307
Lethal Lineups-LL2
SportsNut-SN67
03Upper Deck Rookie Update Skills-SKTA
03Upper Deck Trilogy-71
Authentic Patches-AP32
Limited-71
03Upper Deck Victory-139
Bronze-139
Gold-139
Silver-139
Freshman Flashback-FF34
Game Breakers-GB39
03Toronto Star-72
04Pacific-190
Blue-190
Red-190
04SP Authentic-136
04Ultimate Collection-83
04Upper Deck-127
Canadian Exclusives-127
HG Glossy Gold-127
HG Glossy Silver-127
World Cup Tribute-CCTA
World Cup Tribute-TASGBG
05Beehive-16
Matte-16
05Black Diamond-107
Emerald-107
Gold-107
Onyx-107
Ruby-107
05Panini Stickers-210
05Parkhurst-70
Facsimile Auto Parallel-70
True Colors-TCCGY
True Colors-TCCGY
05SP Game Used-17
Gold-17
Authentic Fabrics Quad-IAKL
Authentic Patches Quad -IAKL
05SPx-14
Spectrum-14
05The Cup Master Pressplate Rookie Update-200
05UD Powerplay Specialists-TSTA
05UD Powerplay Specialists Patches-SPTA
05Ultra-32
Gold-32
Ice-32
05Upper Deck-272
Big Playmakers-B-TA
Jerseys-J-TA
Jerseys Series II-J2TO
Patches-P-TA
Shooting Stars-S-TA
05Upper Deck Hockey Showcase-HS21
05Upper Deck Showcase Promos-HS21
05Upper Deck Ice-17
Rainbow-17
05Upper Deck MVP-58
Gold-58
Platinum-58
Materials-M-TA
05Upper Deck Rookie Update-200
Inspirations Patch Rookies-200
05Upper Deck Victory-145
05Upper Deck Victory-208
Black-145
Black-208
Gold-145
Gold-208
Silver-145
Silver-208
06Flair Showcase Stitches-SSTA
06Gatorade-11
06O-Pee-Chee-80
Rainbow-80
06Panini Stickers-200
06SP Game Used Authentic Fabrics-AFTA
06SP Game Used Authentic Fabrics Parallel-AFTA
06SP Game Used Authentic Fabrics Patches-AFTA
06Upper Deck MVP-47
Gold Script-47
Super Script-47

Amore, Angelo
917th Inn. Sketch OHL-358

Amoroso, Philip
93Quebec Pee-Wee Tournament-1666

Amstutz, Claude
01Swiss HNL-444
03Huntsville Channel Cats-1

Amundrud, Trevor
99Tupelo T-Rex-2
00Bakersfield Condors-1

Amyot, Pascal
06Saint Johns Sea Dogs-22

Ancay, Pierre-Alain
95Swiss HNL-470
02Swiss HNL-342

Ancheloni, Marc
93Quebec Pee-Wee Tournament-487

Anchikoski, Wayne
87Portland Winter Hawks-1
88Portland Winter Hawks-1
91British Columbia JHL-167
91British Columbia JHL-NNO
92Dallas Freeze-1
93Dallas Freeze-1
94UK Humberside Hawks-9
94Central Hockey League-2
94Dallas Freeze-1
96Knoxville Cherokees-13
96St. Louis Vipers RHI-8

Ancicka, Martin
94Czech APS Extraliga-55
95Czech APS Extraliga-347
99German Bundesliga 2-53
06German DEL-156

Andanoff, Jim
83Belleville Bulls-14
84Belleville Bulls-27

Andelmin, Teuvo
66Finnish Jaakiekkosarja-81

Andenmatten, Florian
95Swiss HNL-471
96Swiss HNL-238
00Swiss Panini Stickers-182
01Swiss HNL-269
02Swiss HNL-88
04Swiss Lausanne HC Postcards-8

Andersen, Bo Nordby
98Danish Hockey League-51
99Danish Hockey League-103

Andersen, Carl Oscar Boe
92Norwegian Elite Series-25
95Swedish World Championships Stickers-240
99Norwegian National Team-11

Andersen, Cato Tom
92Finnish Semic-34
92Norwegian Elite Series-44
92Norwegian Elite Series-46
93Swedish Semic World Champ Stickers-232
94Finnish Jaa Kiekko-253
95Finnish Semic World Championships-181
95Swedish Globe World Championships-192

Andersen, Eric
00Amarillo Rattlers-1
01BC Icemen-2

Andersen, Jesper
98Danish Hockey League-132

Andersen, Lars Hakon
92Norwegian Elite Series-61
99Norwegian National Team-8

Andersen, Martin
92Norwegian Elite Series-42

Andersen, Martin E.
98Danish Hockey League-144
99Danish Hockey League-160

Andersen, Morgan
92Norwegian Elite Series-92

Andersen, Poul B.
98Danish Hockey League-82
99Danish Hockey League-44

Andersen, Vidar
92Norwegian Elite Series-57

Anderson, Bo
98Odessa Jackalopes-12

Anderson, Bryce
03Ohio State Buckeyes-19
04Ohio State Buckeyes-1
05Ohio State Buckeyes-1
06Ohio State Buckeyes-1

Anderson, Chad
02Tri-City Stormfront-19

Anderson, Chris
95Tri-City Americans-1
04St. Cloud State Huskies-1
05St. Cloud State Huskies-1

Anderson, Chris (TCA)
95Tri-City Americans-1

Anderson, Colin
00Idaho Steelheads-2
00Roanoke Express-9

Anderson, Cory
88Kamloops Blazers-1

Anderson, Craig (MIN)
95Neepewa Natives-13
99Peoria Rivermen-19
99Peoria Rivermen-19

Anderson, Dallas
04Austin Ice Bats-7

Anderson, Dan
91Arizona Icecats-10
92Arizona Icecats-6
05Topps Style Fan Favorites Autographs-DA

Anderson, Darcy
99Colorado Gold Kings Wendy's-13
01Kalamazoo K-Wings-9
03UK Manchester Phoenix-17

Anderson, David
897th Inn. Sketch OHL-39
907th Inn. Sketch OHL-126
91Oshawa Generals Sheet-6

Anderson, Dean
88Flint Spirits-1
89ProCards AHL-105
90Knoxville Cherokees-115
90ProCards AHL/IHL-166
91Knoxville Cherokees-19

Anderson, Doug
72Johnstown Jets-18

Anderson, Earl
77O-Pee-Chee NHL-114
77Topps-114
77Rochester Americans-4

Anderson, Erik
01Milwaukee Admirals-1
03UK Sheffield Steelers-2
03UK Sheffield Steelers Stickers-11
04UK Sheffield Steelers-13

Anderson, Ernie
23V128-1 Paulin's Candy-66

Anderson, Evan
91Air Canada SJHL-A45
91Air Canada SJHL All-Stars-28
91Air Canada SJHL All-Stars-48

Anderson, Geoff
93Quebec Pee-Wee Tournament-1464

Anderson, Glenn
80Pepsi-Cola Caps-21
81Oilers Red Rooster-9
81O-Pee-Chee-108
81O-Pee-Chee Stickers-217
81Swedish Semic Hockey VM Stickers-82
82Oilers Red Rooster-9
82O-Pee-Chee-100
82O-Pee-Chee Stickers-99
82O-Pee-Chee Stickers-100
82Post Cereal-6
82Topps Stickers-99
82Topps Stickers-100
83Esso-1
83NHL Key Tags-37
83Oilers McDonald's-24
83O-Pee-Chee-24
83O-Pee-Chee Stickers-92
83O-Pee-Chee Stickers-93
83O-Pee-Chee Stickers-158
83Puffy Stickers-2
83Topps Stickers-92
83Topps Stickers-93
83Topps Stickers-158
83Vachon-21
84Oilers Red Rooster-9
84Oilers Team Issue-1
84O-Pee-Chee-238
84O-Pee-Chee Stickers-247
84O-Pee-Chee Stickers-248
847-Eleven Discs-13
85Oilers Red Rooster-9
85O-Pee-Chee-168
85O-Pee-Chee Stickers-227
86Kraft Drawings-1
86Oilers Red Rooster-9
86Oilers Team Issue-9
86O-Pee-Chee-80
86O-Pee-Chee Stickers-78
86Topps-80
87Oilers Team Issue-9
87O-Pee-Chee-199
87O-Pee-Chee Minis-1
87O-Pee-Chee Stickers-95
87Panini Stickers-265
88Frito-Lay Stickers-26
88Oilers Tenth Anniversary-9
88Oilers Team Issue-1
88O-Pee-Chee-189
88O-Pee-Chee Stickers-229
88Panini Stickers-57
88Topps-189
89Kraft-10
89Oilers Team Issue-1
89O-Pee-Chee-226
89O-Pee-Chee-303
89O-Pee-Chee Stickers-218
89Panini Stickers-77
90Bowman-195
Tiffany-195
90Oilers IGA-1
90O-Pee-Chee-145
90Panini Stickers-227
90Pro Set-81
90Score-114
Canadian-114
90Score Hottest/Rising Stars-54
90Topps-145
Tiffany-145
90Upper Deck-284
French-284
91Bowman-116
91Maple Leafs PLAY-1
91Oilers Panini Team Stickers-1
91O-Pee-Chee-124
91OPC Premier-10
91Panini Stickers-120
91Parkhurst-177
French-177
91Pinnacle-12
French-12
91Pro Set-75
French-75
91Score American-47
91Score Canadian Bilingual-47
91Score Canadian Bilingual-611
91Score Canadian English-47
91Score Canadian English-611
91Score Rookie/Traded-61T
91Stadium Club-116
91Topps-124
91Upper Deck-250
French-250
92Bowman-104
92Maple Leafs Kodak-1
92O-Pee-Chee-134
92Panini Stickers-76
92Panini Stickers French-76
92Parkhurst-178
Emerald Ice-178
92Pinnacle-355
French-355
92Pro Set-185
92Score-241
Canadian-241
92Stadium Club-124
92Topps-162
Gold-162G
92Ultra-207
93Donruss-340
93Donruss-460
93Leaf-41
Maple Leafs Score Black's-3
93OPC Premier-104
Gold-104
93Panini Stickers-225
93Parkhurst-201
Emerald Ice-201
93Pinnacle-398
Canadian-398
93PowerPlay-237
93Score-180
93Score-449
Canadian-180
Canadian-449
93Stadium Club-168
Members Only Master Set-168
OPC-168
First Day Issue-168
First Day Issue OPC-168
93Topps/OPC Premier-104
Gold-104
93Ultra-9
94Donruss-254
94Hockey Wit-50
94Leaf-14
94OPC Premier-270
Special Effects-270
94Topps/OPC Premier-270
Special Effects-270
94Ultra-135
95Collector's Choice-46
Player's Club-46
Player's Club Platinum-46
95German DEL-441
96Pinnacle-171
Artist's Proofs-171
Foil-171
Premium Stock-171
Rink Collection-171
01Greats of the Game-32
Autographs-32
01Upper Deck Legends-21
02UD Foundations-35
02UD Foundations-63
02UD Foundations-90
1000 Point Club-AN
1000 Point Club-AN2
Signs of Greatness-SGGA
04ITG Franchises Canadian-25
Autographs-GA
Complete Jerseys-CJ6
Complete Jerseys Gold-CJ6
Double Memorabilia-DM19
Double Memorabilia Gold-DM19
Memorabilia-SM20
Memorabilia Gold-SM20
Original Sticks-OS16
Original Sticks Gold-OS16
Teammates-TM2
Teammates Gold-TM2
04ITG Ultimate Memorabilia Autographs-50
04ITG Ultimate Mem Autographs Gold-50
04ITG Ultimate Mem Jersey Autos-45
04ITG Ultimate Mem Jersey AutosGold-45
04ITG Ultimate Mem Retro Teammates-8
04UD Legendary Signatures-38
Autographs-GA
Linemates-GAWGJK
04UD Legends Classics-25
Gold-25
Platinum-25
Silver-25
Signature Moments-M32
Signatures-CS32
Signatures-TC11
05SP Game Used Oldtimer's Challenge-OC-GA
05SP Game Used Oldtimer's Challenge Autos-OCA-GA
05SP Game Used Oldtimer's Challenge Patch-OCP-GA
05SP Game Used Oldtime Chall Patch Autoa-OAP-GA
05SPx Xcitement Legends-XL-GA
05SPx Xcitement Legends Gold-XL-GA
05SPx Xcitement Legends Spectrum-XL-GA
05The Cup Signature Patches-SPGA
05The Cup Stanley Cup Titlists-TGA1
05The Cup Stanley Cup Titlists-TGA2
05UD Artifacts-101
Blue-101
Gold-101
Green-101
Pewter-101
Red-101
Gold Autographed-101
05Upper Deck Trilogy Legendary Scripts-LEG-GA
06ITG International Ice-42
06ITG International Ice-87
Gold-42
Gold-87
Autographs-AGA
Autographs-AGA2
06ITG Ultimate Memorabilia Retro Teammates-20
06ITG Ultimate Memorabilia Retro Teammates Gold-20
06ITG Ultimate Memorabilia Road to the Cup-7
06ITG Ultimate Memorabilia Road to the Cup Gold-7
06ITG Ultimate Memorabilia Stick Rack-26
06ITG Ultimate Memorabilia Stick Rack Gold-26
06SP Authentic Sign of the Times Duals-STAS
06SPx Winning Materials-WMAN
06SPx Winning Materials Spectrum-WMAN
06SPx Winning Materials Autographs-WMAN
06The Cup Limited Logos-LLGA
06The Cup Scripted Swatches-SSGA
06The Cup Stanley Cup Signatures-CSGA
06UD Artifacts-101
Blue-101
Gold-101
Platinum-101
Radiance-101
Autographed Radiance Parallel-101
Red-101
Auto-Facts-AFGA
Auto-Facts Gold-AFGA
Frozen Artifacts-FAGA
Frozen Artifacts Black-FAGA
Frozen Artifacts Blue-FAGA
Frozen Artifacts Gold-FAGA
Frozen Artifacts Platinum-FAGA
Frozen Artifacts Red-FAGA
Frozen Artifacts Autographed Black-FAGA
Frozen Artifacts Patches Black-FAGA
Frozen Artifacts Patches Blue-FAGA
Frozen Artifacts Patches Gold-FAGA
Frozen Artifacts Patches Platinum-FAGA
Frozen Artifacts Patches Red-FAGA
Frozen Artifacts Patches Autographed Black Tag Parallel-FAGA
Tundra Tandems-TTAG
Tundra Tandems-TTAK
Tundra Tandems Black-TTAG
Tundra Tandems Black-TTAK
Tundra Tandems Blue-TTAG
Tundra Tandems Blue-TTAK
Tundra Tandems Gold-TTAG
Tundra Tandems Gold-TTAK
Tundra Tandems Platinum-TTAG
Tundra Tandems Platinum-TTAK
Tundra Tandems Red-TTAG
Tundra Tandems Red-TTAK
Tundra Tandems Dual Patches Red-TTAG
Tundra Tandems Dual Patches Red-TTAK
06Upper Deck Trilogy Legendary Scripts-LSGA

Anderson, Grant
83Brantford Alexanders-24

Anderson, Harlan
01Moose Jaw Warriors-14

Anderson, Jack
75Hamilton Fincups-1

Anderson, Jimmy
74Capitals White Borders-2
74O-Pee-Chee NHL-118
74Topps-118

Anderson, John
78Maple Leafs Postcards-1
79Maple Leafs Postcards-1
80Maple Leafs Postcards-1
80O-Pee-Chee-79
80Pepsi-Cola Caps-81
80Topps-79
81Maple Leafs Postcards-1
81O-Pee-Chee-313
81O-Pee-Chee Stickers-107
82Maple Leafs Postcards-2
82O-Pee-Chee-315
82O-Pee-Chee Stickers-73
82O-Pee-Chee Stickers-74
82Post Cereal-18
82Topps Stickers-73
82Topps Stickers-74
83Esso-2
83Maple Leafs Postcards-1
83NHL Key Tags-115
83O-Pee-Chee-325
83O-Pee-Chee Stickers-30
83O-Pee-Chee Stickers-31
83Puffy Stickers-4
83Topps Stickers-30
83Topps Stickers-31
83Vachon-81
84Kellogg's Accordion Discs-5A
84Kellogg's Accordion Discs Singles-1
84Maple Leafs Postcards-1
84O-Pee-Chee-295
84O-Pee-Chee Stickers-18
847-Eleven Discs-44
84Topps-136
85Nordiques General Foods-1
85Nordiques Placemats-6
85Nordiques Provigo-1
85O-Pee-Chee-20
85O-Pee-Chee Stickers-10
85Topps-20
86Nordiques McDonald's-1
86O-Pee-Chee-13
86O-Pee-Chee Stickers-54
86Topps-13
86Whalers Junior Thomas'-1
87O-Pee-Chee-45
87O-Pee-Chee Stickers-204
87Panini Stickers-45
87Topps-45
87Whalers Jr. Burger King/Pepsi-1
88O-Pee-Chee-190
88O-Pee-Chee Stickers-270
88Panini Stickers-239
88Topps-190
88Whalers Junior Ground Round-1
89O-Pee-Chee-124
89Topps-124
90ProCards AHL/IHL-543
92San Diego Gulls-1
93San Diego Gulls-1
96Quad-City Mallards-20
98Chicago Wolves-23
98Chicago Wolves Turner Cup-2
99Chicago Wolves-23
00Chicago Wolves-1
02Maple Leafs Platinum Collection-81
02Chicago Wolves-1
03Chicago Wolves-24
05Chicago Wolves-24
06Parkhurst-2
Autographs-2

Anderson, John Murray
91ProCards-361

Anderson, Josiah
05Kelowna Rockets-2

Anderson, Keith
01Florida Everblades-17
02Florida Everblades-1
02Florida Everblades RBI-115
03Florida Everblades-1
04Florida Everblades-19

Anderson, Micah
06Westside Warriors-12

Anderson, Mike
95Minnesota Golden Gophers-4
96Minnesota Golden Gophers-4
97Minnesota Golden Gophers-3
98Minnesota Golden Gophers-12
00Connecticut Huskies-1

Anderson, Mike (UConn)
00Connecticut Huskies-1

Anderson, Nate
02Bakersfield Condors-1

Anderson, Nick
04Minnesota-Duluth Bulldogs-1
05Las Vegas Wranglers-2
06Las Vegas Wranglers-1

Anderson, Ole
95Slapshot-234

Anderson, Perry
85Devils Postcards-2
86Devils Police-2
88Devils Caretta-1
89ProCards AHL-216
90ProCards AHL/IHL-561
91O-Pee-Chee-501
91Parkhurst-164
French-164
91Pro Set-481
French-481
91Score Canadian Bilingual-649
91Score Canadian English-649
91Score Rookie/Traded-99T
91Sharks Sports Action-1
91Topps-501
92O-Pee-Chee-38
92Stadium Club-89
92Topps-286
Gold-286G
92San Diego Gulls-2

Anderson, Peter
98Swiss Power Play Stickers-155
00Swiss Slapshot Mini-Cards-HCL2

Anderson, R.J.
05Minnesota Golden Gophers-1
06Minnesota Golden Gophers-1

Anderson, Ron
69O-Pee-Chee-14
70Colgate Stamps-48
70Esso Power Players-84
70Sargent Promotions Stamps-18
71O-Pee-Chee-163
71Sabres Postcards-83
71Sargent Promotions Stamps-18
72O-Pee-Chee-298
74Capitals White Borders-3
74NHL Action Stamps-312
74O-Pee-Chee NHL-314

Anderson, Russ
77Penguins Puck Bucks-7
78O-Pee-Chee-156
78Topps-156
79O-Pee-Chee-264
79Topps-264
82Whalers Junior Hartford Courant-2
84Kings Smokey-1

Anderson, Ryan
95Neepewa Natives-1
97Austin Ice Bats-1
99Austin Ice Bats-20
99Austin Ice Bats-30
99Austin Ice Bats-32
00Austin Ice Bats-1
01Austin Ice Bats-1
02Orlando Seals-15

Anderson, Shawn
86Sabres Blue Shield-1
86Sabres Blue Shield Small-1
87Sabres Wonder Bread/Hostess-2
88ProCards AHL-261
89Sabres Campbell's-1
90Nordiques Petro-Canada-29
90Pro Set-513
91Bowman-147
91Stadium Club-358
92Capitals Kodak-1
94Leaf-346
95Milwaukee Admirals-1
95Milwaukee Admirals Postcards-13
00German DEL-111
All-Star Class-A9
01German Upper Deck-196
02German DEL City Press-259
03German DEL All-Stars-AS21

Anderson, Tommy
34Beehive Group I Photos-212
35Diamond Matchbooks Tan 2-1
35Diamond Matchbooks Tan 3-1
39O-Pee-Chee V301-1-61

Anderson, Trevor
99San Antonio Iguanas-17

Anderson, Vern
91Air Canada SJHL-C13

Anderson, Warren
81Swedish Semic Hockey VM Stickers-75

Anderson, Will
84Kamloops Blazers-1
94Minnesota Golden Gophers-1

Andersson, Adam
01Swedish Brynas Tigers-1
02Swedish SHL-5
Next Generation-NG4
Parallel-5
03Swedish Elite-4
Rookies-1
Silver-4
04Swedish Elitset-103
Gold-103
05Swedish SHL Elitset-162
Gold-162
Series Two Signatures-3
06Swedish SHL Elitset-240

Andersson, Ake
83Swedish Semic Elitserien-196

Andersson, Anders
56Swedish Alfabilder-57
64Swedish Coralli ISHockey-11
64Swedish Coralli ISHockey-143
65Swedish Coralli ISHockey-11
65Swedish Coralli ISHockey-143
67Swedish Hockey-80

Andersson, Benny
67Swedish Hockey-133
71Swedish Hockey-144
72Swedish Stickers-131
72Swedish Stickers-132
73Swedish Stickers-186

Andersson, Bertil
57Swedish Alfabilder-130

Andersson, Bosse
67Swedish Hockey-97
72Swedish Stickers-197
83Swedish Semic Elitserien-201

Andersson, Christer
70Swedish Hockey-178
71Swedish Hockey-261
72Finnish Semic World Championship-44
72Swedish Stickers-241
72Swedish Semic World Championship-44
74Swedish Stickers-138
83Swedish Semic Elitserien-63
84Swedish Semic Elitserien-63
85Swedish Panini Stickers-55
86Swedish Panini Stickers-43
87Swedish Panini Stickers-54

Andersson, Dick
89Swedish Semic Elitserien Stickers-193

Andersson, Einar
65Swedish Coralli ISHockey-67

Andersson, Erik
90Swedish Semic Elitserien Stickers-97
91Swedish Semic Elitserien Stickers-25
96Denver University Pioneers-8
97Saint John Flames-2
98Indianapolis Ice-15
99Swedish Upper Deck-17
00Swedish Upper Deck-12
03Swedish Bjorkloven Umea-3
05Swedish SHL Elitset Rookies-4
06Swedish SHL Elitset-60
06Swedish SHL Elitset-197

Andersson, Fred
57Swedish Alfabilder-112

Andersson, Fredrik
86Swedish Panini Stickers-193
87Swedish Panini Stickers-192
89Swedish Semic Elitserien Stickers-169
89Swedish Semic Elitserien Stickers-215
90Swedish Semic Elitserien Stickers-3
91Swedish Semic Elitserien Stickers-201
92Finnish Semic-52
92Swedish Semic Elitserien Stickers-223
93Swedish Semic Elitserien-195
94Swedish Leaf-17
Clean Sweepers-9
95Swedish Leaf-271
02Swedish SHL-100
Parallel-100

Andersson, Gunnar
64Swedish Coralli ISHockey-49
65Swedish Coralli ISHockey-49
67Swedish Hockey-98
69Swedish Hockey-112
70Swedish Hockey-70
71Swedish Hockey-5
71Swedish Hockey-159
72Finnish Semic World Championship-59
72Swedish Stickers-154
72Swedish Semic World Championship-59
73Swedish Stickers-45
74Swedish Stickers-154

Andersson, Hakan
67Swedish Hockey-81
67Swedish Hockey-82
69Swedish Hockey-219
71Swedish Hockey-145
71Swedish Hockey-364
73Swedish Stickers-185

Andersson, Hans
72Swedish Stickers-135
74Swedish Stickers-199

Andersson, Hans-Rickard
87Swedish Panini Stickers-266

Andersson, Hasse
56Swedish Alfabilder-84

Andersson, Henrik
89Swedish Semic Elitserien Stickers-246
90Swedish Semic Elitserien Stickers-156
99Swedish Upper Deck-125
99Swedish Upper Deck-210
02Swedish SHL-51
Parallel-51

Andersson, Jan
71Swedish Hockey-365
74Swedish Stickers-155

Andersson, Jesper
99Swedish Upper Deck-124

Andersson, Johan
05Swedish SHL Elitset-76
Gold-76
06Swedish SHL Elitset-285

Andersson, John
67Swedish Hockey-247
69Swedish Hockey-293
70Swedish Hockey-197
71Swedish Hockey-283

Andersson, Jonas
90Swedish Semic Elitserien Stickers-47
00Black Diamond-67
Gold-67
00Upper Deck-202
Exclusives Tier 1-202
Exclusives Tier 2-202
00Upper Deck Ice-47
Immortals-47
Legends-47
Stars-47
00Upper Deck MVP-216
First Stars-216
Second Stars-216
Third Stars-216
00Milwaukee Admirals Keebler-1
00Milwaukee Admirals Postcards-1
01Milwaukee Admirals-2
01Milwaukee Admirals Postcards-10
02SPx-116
02Upper Deck Vintage-338
02Milwaukee Admirals-14
02Milwaukee Admirals Postcards-1
04Swedish Elitset-274
Gold-274
05Finnish Cardset -217
06Finnish Cardset-221

Andersson, Kenneth
83Swedish Semic Elitserien-69
84Swedish Semic Elitserien-69
85Swedish Panini Stickers-63
86Swedish Panini Stickers-44
90Swedish Semic Elitserien Stickers-196

Andersson, Kent Erik
71Swedish Hockey-146
73Swedish Stickers-182
74Swedish Stickers-200
78North Stars Cloverleaf Dairy-4
78O-Pee-Chee-17
78Topps-17
79Panini Stickers-200
79North Stars Postcards-1
80North Stars Postcards-1
80O-Pee-Chee-383
81North Stars Postcards-1
81O-Pee-Chee-158
81Topps-W102
82O-Pee-Chee-218
82Post Cereal-9
84Swedish Semic Elitserien-109
85Swedish Panini Stickers-109
85Swedish Panini Stickers-129
85Swedish Panini Stickers-130

Andersson, Kjell
57Swedish Alfabilder-109
69Swedish Hockey-328
70Swedish Hockey-250
71Swedish Hockey-308
72Swedish Stickers-292
73Swedish Stickers-146
74Swedish Stickers-201

Andersson, Krister
69Swedish Hockey-275

Andersson, Kurt
55Swedish Alfabilder-31

Andersson, Lars
57Swedish Alfabilder-115
64Swedish Coralli ISHockey-134
65Swedish Coralli ISHockey-134
67Swedish Hockey-99
86Swedish Panini Stickers-45

Andersson, Leif
64Swedish Coralli ISHockey-68
65Swedish Coralli ISHockey-68
67Swedish Hockey-181
69Swedish Hockey-309
70Swedish Hockey-214
72Swedish Stickers-272
74Swedish Stickers-156

Andersson, Lennart
57Swedish Alfabilder-74
71Swedish Hockey-135
72Swedish Stickers-121
73Swedish Stickers-181

Andersson, Likit
05Stockton Thunder-1

Andersson, Magnus
69Swedish Hockey-165

Andersson, Mattias
89Swedish Semic Elitserien Stickers-81
90Swedish Semic Elitserien Stickers-206
91Swedish Semic Elitserien Stickers-134
92Swedish Semic Elitserien Stickers-155

Andersson, Mikael (Swe.)
83Swedish Semic Elitserien-41
84Swedish Semic Elitserien-41
85Swedish Panini Stickers-34
86Swedish Panini Stickers-26
87Swedish Panini Stickers-36
91Swedish Semic Elitserien Stickers-290
93Swedish Semic Elitserien-17

Andersson, NHL
83Swedish Semic Elitserien-234
85Sabres Blue Shield-1
85Sabres Blue Shield Small-1
87Sabres Blue Shield-1
87Sabres Wonder Bread/Hostess-1
88Sabres Blue Shield-1
88Sabres Wonder Bread/Hostess-1
88ProCards AHL-264
89Whalers Junior Milk-1
89Swedish Semic Elitserien Stickers-274
90O-Pee-Chee-35
90Panini Stickers-47
90Pro Set-98
90Topps-35
Tiffany-35
90Whalers Jr. 7-Eleven-1
90Swedish Semic Elitserien Stickers-45
91Pro Set Platinum-180
91Bowman-11
91O-Pee-Chee-197
91Parkhurst-63
French-63
91Pro Set-394
French-394
91Stadium Club-39
91Topps-197
91Upper Deck-238
French-238
91Whalers Jr. 7-Eleven-1
92Bowman-158
92Lightning Sheraton-1
92O-Pee-Chee-214
92OPC Premier-55
92Panini Stickers-258
92Panini Stickers French-258
92Parkhurst-169
Emerald Ice-169
92Pinnacle-384
French-384
92Pro Set-65
92Score-215
Canadian-215
92Stadium Club-348
92Topps-151
Gold-151G
92Ultra-406
92Upper Deck-103
93Donruss-322
93Leaf-285
93Lightning Season in Review-1
93OPC Premier-150
Gold-150
93Panini Stickers-216
93Parkhurst-198
Emerald Ice-198
93Pinnacle-329
Canadian-329
93PowerPlay-440
93Score-427
Canadian-427
93Stadium Club-97
93Stadium Club-427
Members Only Master Set-97
Members Only Master Set-427
OPC-97
First Day Issue-97
First Day Issue-427
First Day Issue OPC-97
93Topps/OPC Premier-150
Gold-150
93Ultra-421
93Swedish Semic World Champ Stickers-37
94Canada Games NHL POGS-220
94Donruss-14
94EA Sports-130
94Leaf-347
94Lightning Photo Album-1
94Lightning Postcards-1
94OPC Premier-287
Special Effects-287
94Parkhurst-226
Gold-226
94Pinnacle-451
Artist's Proofs-451
Rink Collection-451
94Stadium Club-75
Members Only Master Set-75
First Day Issue-75
Super Team Winner Cards-75
94Topps/OPC Premier-287
Special Effects-287
94Ultra-370
94Upper Deck-297
Electric Ice-297
95Collector's Choice-182
Player's Club-182
Player's Club Platinum-182
95Lightning Team Issue-1
95Parkhurst International-196
Emerald Ice-196
95Topps-123
OPC Inserts-123
95Finnish Semic World Championships-72
95Swedish Globe World Championships-42
95Quebec Pee-Wee Tournament-1054
96Be A Player-65
Autographs-65
Autographs Silver-65
96Upper Deck-155
97Pacific Invincible NHL Regime-182
97Panini Stickers-104
98Pacific-395
Ice Blue-395
Red-395
98Panini Stickers-102
99Guelph Storm-2
00BAP Memorabilia-139
Emerald-139
Ruby-139
Sapphire-139
Promos-139
00BAP Mem Chicago Sportsfest Copper-139
00BAP Memorabilia Chicago Sportsfest Blue-139
00BAP Memorabilia Chicago Sportsfest Gold-139
00BAP Memorabilia Chicago Sportsfest Ruby-139
00BAP Memorabilia Chicago Sun-Times Ruby-139
00BAP Memorabilia Chicago Sun-Times Gold-139
00BAP Mem Chicago Sun-Times Sapphire-139
00BAP Mem Toronto Fall Expo Copper-139
00BAP Memorabilia Toronto Fall Expo Gold-139
00BAP Memorabilia Toronto Fall Expo Ruby-139
00Swedish Upper Deck-75
00Swedish Upper Deck-194
SHL Signatures-MA
00Guelph Storm-1
01Norfolk Admirals-6
02BAP Memorabilia-318
02BAP Ultimate Memorabilia-96
02Between the Pipes-90
Gold-90
Silver-90
02Parkhurst-227
Bronze-227
Gold-227
Silver-227
02Parkhurst Retro-236
Minis-236
02SP Authentic-174
02UD Artistic Impressions-132
Gold-132
02UD Honor Roll-114
02UD Mask Collection-146
02UD Premier Collection-65
Gold-65
02Swedish SHL-282
Parallel-282
02Norfolk Admirals-2
03BAP Memorabilia Deep in the Crease-D2
03Blackhawks Postcards-1
03ITG Action-182
03Pacific-68
Blue-68
Red-68
03Pacific Complete-427
Red-427
03Parkhurst Original Six Chicago-20
03Topps Traded-TT35
Blue-TT35
Gold-TT35
Red-TT35
03Norfolk Admirals-2
04Pacific-55
Blue-55
Red-55
04Norfolk Admirals-1
05Parkhurst-107
Facsimile Auto Parallel-107

06Between The Pipes-10
Autographs-ACA
06Rochester Americans-1
Andersson, Niklas
89Swedish Semic Elitserien Stickers-281
90Swedish Semic Elitserien Stickers-39
91Upper Deck-29
French-29
91Swedish Semic Elitserien Stickers-317
91ProCards-533
93Score-460
Canadian-460
93Upper Deck-239
93Swedish Semic World Champ Stickers-44
93Classic Pro Prospects-120
95Bowman-126
All-Foil-126
95Parkhurst International-398
Emerald Ice-398
95Swedish Globe World Championships-51
96Be A Player-98
Autographs-98
Autographs Silver-98
96Collector's Choice-165
96Donruss-214
Press Proofs-214
96Donruss Elite-89
Die Cut Stars-89
96Islander Postcards-1
96Score-248
Artist's Proofs-248
Dealer's Choice Artist's Proofs-248
Special Artist's Proofs-248
Golden Blades-248
96Select Certified-57
Artist's Proofs-57
Blue-57
Mirror Blue-57
Mirror Gold-57
Mirror Red-57
Red-57
96SkyBox Impact-165
96Summit-172
Artist's Proofs-172
Ice-172
Metal-172
Premium Stock-172
96Upper Deck-292
96Collector's Edge Future Legends-2
97Collector's Choice-156
97Pacific-144
Copper-144
Emerald Green-144
Ice Blue-144
Red-144
Silver-144
97Panini Stickers-75
97Kentucky Thoroughblades-3
98Chicago Wolves-7
98IHL All-Star Western Conference-5
99Chicago Wolves-6
00Topps Heritage-202
00Chicago Wolves-2
02Swedish SHL-119
Parallel-119
Signatures-17
03Swedish Elite-31
Silver-31
Stars of the Game-2
04Swedish Elitset-31
04Swedish Elitset-146
Gold-31
Gold-146
Signatures Series A-16
04Swedish Pure Skills-20
Parallel-20
05Swedish SHL Elitset-2
05Swedish SHL Elitset-32
Gold-2
Gold-32
Playmakers-3
Series Two Signatures-5
Star Potential-1
Teammates-4
06Swedish SHL Elitset-37
Performers-3
Playmakers-3
Andersson, Ola
89Swedish Semic Elitserien Stickers-68
90Swedish Semic Elitserien Stickers-66
91Swedish Semic Elitserien Stickers-246
Andersson, Ove
57Swedish Alfabilder-110
64Swedish Coralli ISHockey-25
64Swedish Coralli ISHockey-31
65Swedish Coralli ISHockey-25
67Swedish Hockey-248
Andersson, Paul
89Swedish Semic Elitserien Stickers-283
91Swedish Semic Elitserien Stickers-265
92Swedish Semic Elitserien Stickers-298
93Swedish Semic Elitserien-263
94Swedish Leaf-107
95Swedish Leaf-131
95Swedish Upper Deck-200
Andersson, Pentti
66Finnish Jaakiekkosarja-119
Andersson, Per
83Swedish Semic Elitserien-184
84Swedish Semic Elitserien-207
Andersson, Peter
82Swedish Semic VM Stickers-12
83Swedish Semic Elitserien-105
83Swedish Semic VM Stickers-10
84Swedish Semic Elitserien-105
85Swedish Panini Stickers-94
86Swedish Panini Stickers-14
86Swedish Panini Stickers-88
87Swedish Panini Stickers-32
87Swedish Panini Stickers-92
89Swedish Semic World Champ Stickers-11
90Swedish Semic Elitserien Stickers-128
91Finnish Semic World Champ Stickers-35
91Finnish Semic World Champ Stickers-36
91Swedish Semic Elitserien Stickers-180
91Swedish Semic Elitserien Stickers-343
91Swedish Semic World Champ Stickers-35
91Swedish Semic World Champ Stickers-36
92Upper Deck-481
92Finnish Semic-54
92Finnish Semic-55
92Swedish Semic Elitserien Stickers-345
93Upper Deck-71
93Swedish Semic Elitserien-9
93Swedish Semic World Champ Stickers-27
94OPC Premier-212
Special Effects-212
94Parkhurst-88
Gold-88
94Topps/OPC Premier-212
Special Effects-212
94Swedish Leaf-267
95Finnish Semic World Championships-60
95Swedish Leaf-87
95Swedish Leaf-304
Face to Face-14
95Swedish Upper Deck-138
95Swedish Upper Deck-231
95Swedish Upper Deck-257
95Swedish Globe World Championships-11
96German DEL-276
99Swiss Panini Stickers-155
00Swiss Panini Stickers-200
02Swedish Malmo Red Hawks-20
02Swedish SHL-69
Parallel-69
03Swedish Elite-92
Silver-92
04Swedish Elitset-87
04Swedish Elitset-133
Gold-87
Gold-133
04Swedish Malmo Red Hawks-20
04Swedish Pure Skills-58
Parallel-58
Andersson, Plutten
55Swedish Alfabilder-33
Andersson, Roni
04Finnish Cardset-246
06Finnish Cardset-66
Andersson, Ronny
69Swedish Hockey-329
70Swedish Hockey-244
71Swedish Hockey-301
72Swedish Stickers-286
Andersson, Sivert
83Swedish Semic Elitserien-139
Andersson, Staffan
83Swedish Semic Elitserien-28
87Swedish Panini Stickers-27
Andersson, Stefan
95Swedish Leaf-155
95Swedish Upper Deck-12
Andersson, Steffan
72Swedish Stickers-42
Andersson, Sten
67Swedish Hockey-197
Andersson, Stig
71Swedish Hockey-388
72Swedish Stickers-262
Andersson, Sture
71Swedish Hockey-177
72Swedish Stickers-167
74Swedish Stickers-157
83Swedish Semic Elitserien-151
Andersson, Sven
55Swedish Alfabilder-3
56Swedish Alfabilder-78
Andersson, Tommy
67Swedish Hockey-214
69Swedish Hockey-256
70Swedish Hockey-114
71Swedish Hockey-203
72Swedish Stickers-182
73Swedish Stickers-228
74Swedish Stickers-158
83Swedish Semic Elitserien-195
84Swedish Semic Elitserien-218
Andersson, Torbjorn
83Swedish Semic Elitserien-29
84Swedish Semic Elitserien-28
85Swedish Panini Stickers-27
86Swedish Panini Stickers-5
87Swedish Panini Stickers-28
Andersson, Ulf
84Swedish Semic Elitserien-135
87Swedish Panini Stickers-42
93Swedish Semic Elitserien-18
Andersson-Everberg, Paul
97Swedish Collector's Choice-198
98Swedish UD Choice-193
99Swedish Upper Deck-197
Andersson-Junkka, Jonas
94Parkhurst SE-SE238
Gold-SE238
94Swedish Leaf-184
Rookie Rockets-2
95Swedish Leaf-138
95Signature Rookies Auto-Phonex-3
95Signature Rook Auto-Phonex Phone Cards-3
97Swedish Collector's Choice-154
98Finnish Kerailysarja-11
99Finnish Cardset-32
00Finnish Cardset-23
00Syracuse Crunch-4
02Swedish SHL-57
Parallel-57
02Swedish SHL Promos-TCC6
03Swedish Elite-79
Signatures-11
Silver-79
04Swedish Elitset-71
Gold-71
Andra, Ludwig
94German First League-356
Andrasovsky, Dusan
00Czech OFS-79
01Czech OFS-209
02Czech OFS Plus-254
03Czech OFS Plus-309
03Czech OFS Plus Insert H-H20
04Czech HC Plzen Postcards-2
04Czech OFS-138
Assist Leaders-14
06Czech HC Pardubice Postcards-1
06Czech OFS-110
Andrea, Paul
62Sudbury Wolves-1
68Shirriff Coins-142
70Esso Power Players-87
70O-Pee-Chee-77
70Topps-77
91Cornwall Royals-23
917th Inn. Sketch OHL-24
95Dayton Bombers-4
Andreachuk, Randy
75Roanoke Valley Rebels-14
Andreasen, Andreas
98Danish Hockey League-12
99Danish Hockey League-13
Andreasen, Gert
98Danish Hockey League-65
Andreasson, Bengt-Olov
64Swedish Coralli ISHockey-110
65Swedish Coralli ISHockey-110
67Swedish Hockey-167
Andreev, Vitali
00Asheville Smoke-23
Andren, Anders
69Swedish Hockey-94
71Swedish Hockey-133
Andreoli, Dave
81Sault Ste. Marie Greyhounds-2
Andres, Bruce
81Indianapolis Checkers-1
Andres, Ryan
98Calgary Hitmen-17
98Calgary Hitmen Autographs-17
Andresen, Joel
03Lethbridge Hurricanes-1
Andress, Doug
00Ohio State Buckeyes-18
01Ohio State Buckeyes-1
02Ohio State Buckeyes-1
03Ohio State Buckeyes-1
05Johnstown Chiefs-1
Andrews, Al
82Kingston Canadians-7
Andrews, Bobby
02Hartford Wolf Pack-1
03Hartford Wolf Pack-1
Andrews, Daryl
00Albany River Rats-1
01Albany River Rats-5
02Albany River Rats-7
02Albany River Rats AAP-3
03San Antonio Rampage-4
04UK Sheffield Steelers-3
Andrews, Elliott
94UK Guildford Flames-18
95UK Guildford Flames-14
96UK Guildford Flames-14
Andrews, Jeff
93Oshawa Generals-9
Andrews, Lloyd
23V145-1-21
24C144 Champ's Cigarettes-2
24V145-2-59
Andrey, Thierry
93Swiss HNL-314
95Swiss HNL-238
Andreychuk, Dave
80Oshawa Generals-7
81Oshawa Generals-12
83Canadian National Juniors-1
84O-Pee-Chee-17
84O-Pee-Chee-353
84O-Pee-Chee Stickers-209
84O-Pee-Chee Stickers-210
84Sabres Blue Shield-1
84Topps-13
85O-Pee-Chee-143
85O-Pee-Chee Stickers-187
85Sabres Blue Shield-2
85Sabres Blue Shield Small-2
85Topps-143
86O-Pee-Chee-16
86O-Pee-Chee Stickers-49
86Sabres Blue Shield-2
86Sabres Blue Shield Small-2
86Topps-16
87O-Pee-Chee-3
87O-Pee-Chee Stickers-147
87Panini Stickers-27
87Sabres Blue Shield-2
87Sabres Wonder Bread/Hostess-3
87Topps-3
88O-Pee-Chee-163
88O-Pee-Chee Box Bottoms-M
88O-Pee-Chee Stickers-261
88Panini Stickers-223
88Sabres Blue Shield-2
88Sabres Wonder Bread/Hostess-2
88Topps-163
88Topps Box Bottoms-M
89O-Pee-Chee-106
89O-Pee-Chee-299
89O-Pee-Chee Stickers-258
89Panini Stickers-215
89Sabres Blue Shield-1
89Sabres Campbell's-2
89Topps-106
90Bowman-246
Tiffany-246
90O-Pee-Chee-169
90Panini Stickers-29
90Pro Set-17A
90Pro Set-17B
90Pro Set-363
90Sabres Blue Shield-1
90Sabres Campbell's-1
90Score-189
Canadian-189
90Score Hottest/Rising Stars-87
90Topps-169
Tiffany-169
90Upper Deck-41
French-41
91Pro Set Platinum-8
91Bowman-22
91O-Pee-Chee-38
91Panini Stickers-309
91Parkhurst-17
91Parkhurst-437
French-17
French-437
91Pinnacle-122
French-122
91Pro Set-23
French-23
91Sabres Blue Shield-1
91Sabres Pepsi/Campbell's-1
91Score American-277
91Score Canadian Bilingual-497
91Score Canadian English-497
91Stadium Club-93
91Topps-38
91Upper Deck-124
French-124
92Bowman-44
92Maple Leafs Kodak-2
92Maple Leafs Kodak-3
92O-Pee-Chee-141
92Panini Stickers-249
92Panini Stickers French-249
92Parkhurst-10
92Parkhurst-409
Emerald Ice-10
Emerald Ice-409
92Pinnacle-58
French-58
92Pro Set-15
92Pro Set-17
92Pro Set-249
92Sabres Blue Shield-1
92Sabres Jubilee Foods-1
92Score-204
Canadian-204
92Stadium Club-132
92Topps-164
Gold-164G
92Ultra-12
92Upper Deck-269
92Upper Deck-456
93Donruss-342
93Leaf-63
Gold All-Stars-4
Maple Leafs Score Black's-13
93OPC Premier-235
Gold-235
93Panini Stickers-223
93Parkhurst-200
Emerald Ice-200
93Pinnacle-42
Canadian-42
Nifty Fifty-11
93PowerPlay-238
Slapshot Artists-1
93Score-343
93Score-481
Canadian-343
Canadian-481
Dynamic Duos Canadian-1
93Stadium Club-23
Members Only Master Set-23
OPC-23
First Day Issue-23
First Day Issue OPC-23
93Topps/OPC Premier-235
Gold-235
93Ultra-57
Red Light Specials-1
93Upper Deck-86
NHLPA/Roots-18
SP-155
94Be A Player-R33
Signature Cards-52
94Canada Games NHL POGS-229
94Donruss-323
94EA Sports-136
94Finest-39
Super Team Winners-39
Refractors-39
94Flair-177
94Fleer-212
94Kraft-1
94Leaf-72
94Leaf Limited-34
94Maple Leafs Gangsters-1
94Maple Leafs Kodak-1
94Maple Leafs Pin-up Posters-18
94Maple Leafs Postcards-1
94McDonald's Upper Deck-McD18
94OPC Premier-38
94OPC Premier-510
Special Effects-38
Special Effects-510
94Parkhurst-303
Gold-303
Vintage-V89
94Parkhurst SE-SE182
Gold-SE182
94Pinnacle I Hobby Samples-5
94Pinnacle-5
Artist's Proofs-5
Rink Collection-5
94Score Dream Team-DT11
94Score 90 Plus Club-10
94Select-99
Gold-99
94SP-119
Die Cuts-119
94Stadium Club Members Only-13
94Stadium Club-58
94Stadium Club-140
Members Only Master Set-58
Members Only Master Set-140
First Day Issue-58
First Day Issue-140
Super Teams-23
Super Teams Members Only Master Set-23
Super Team Winner Cards-58
Super Team Winner Cards-140
94Topps/OPC Premier-38
94Topps/OPC Premier-510
Special Effects-38
Special Effects-510
94Topps Finest Inserts-4
94Ultra-211
Power-1
Red Light Specials-1
94Upper Deck-313
Electric Ice-313
Predictor Retail-R6
Predictor Retail-R35
94Upper Deck Predictor Retail Exchange-R6
94Upper Deck Predictor Retail Exchange-R35
94Upper Deck SP Inserts-SP77
94Upper Deck SP Inserts Die Cuts-SP77
95Bashan Super Stickers-119
95Bowman-7
All-Foil-7
95Canada Games NHL POGS-260
95Collector's Choice-20
Player's Club-20
Player's Club Platinum-20
95Donruss-98
95Emotion-168
95Finest-6
Refractors-6
95Hoyle Western Playing Cards-2
95Imperial Stickers-119
95Leaf-270
95Leaf Limited-21
95Metal-141
95Panini Stickers-203
95Parkhurst International-470
Emerald Ice-470
95Pinnacle-31
Artist's Proofs-31
Rink Collection-31
95Playoff One on One-93
95Pro Magnets-76
95Score-109
Black Ice Artist's Proofs-109
Black Ice-109
95Select Certified-28
Mirror Gold-28
95SkyBox Impact-158
95SkyBox Impact-246
95Stadium Club-5
Members Only Master Set-5
95Summit-36
Artist's Proofs-36
Ice-36
95Topps-175
OPC Inserts-175
95Topps SuperSkills-52
Platinum-52
95Ultra-158
Gold Medallion-158
95Upper Deck-367
Electric Ice-367
Electric Ice Gold-367
Special Edition-SE79
Special Edition Gold-SE79
95Zenith-41
96Be A Player-2
Autographs-2
Autographs Silver-2
96Collector's Choice-153
96Devils Team Issue-23
96Donruss-109
Press Proofs-109
96Leaf-24
Press Proofs-24
96Leaf Preferred-51
Press Proofs-51
96Metal Universe-85
96NHL Pro Stamps-76
96Pinnacle-177
Artist's Proofs-177
Foil-177
Premium Stock-177
Rink Collection-177
96Playoff One on One-348
96Score-44
Artist's Proofs-44
Dealer's Choice Artist's Proofs-44
Special Artist's Proofs-44
Golden Blades-44
96SkyBox Impact-67
96Summit-124
Artist's Proofs-124
Ice-124
Metal-124
Premium Stock-124
96Topps Picks-127
OPC Inserts-127
96Ultra-92
Gold Medallion-92
96Upper Deck-89
97Collector's Choice-142
97Devils Team Issue-18
97Donruss-61
Press Proofs Silver-61
Press Proofs Gold-61
97Donruss Canadian Ice-105
97Donruss Canadian Ice-148
Dominion Series-105
Dominion Series-148
Provincial Series-105
Provincial Series-148
97Donruss Limited-22
97Donruss Limited-74
Exposure-22
Exposure-74
97Donruss Preferred-66
Cut to the Chase-66
97Donruss Priority-152
Stamp of Approval-152
97Leaf-116
Fractal Matrix-116
Fractal Matrix Die Cuts-116
97Leaf International-116
Universal Ice-116
97Pacific-84
Copper-84
Emerald Green-84
Ice Blue-84
Red-84
Silver-84
97Pacific Dynagon-67
Copper-67
Dark Grey-67
Emerald Green-67
Ice Blue-67
Red-67
Silver-67
Tandems-37
97Pacific Invincible-75
Copper-75
Emerald Green-75
Ice Blue-75
Red-75
Silver-75
97Panini Stickers-71
97Paramount-100
Copper-100
Dark Grey-100
Emerald Green-100
Ice Blue-100
Red-100
Silver-100
97Pinnacle-131
Press Plates Back Black-131
Press Plates Back Cyan-131
Press Plates Back Magenta-131
Press Plates Back Yellow-131
Press Plates Front Black-131
Press Plates Front Cyan-131
Press Plates Front Magenta-131
Press Plates Front Yellow-131
97Pinnacle Certified-69
Red-69
Mirror Blue-69
Mirror Gold-69
Mirror Red-69
97Pinnacle Inside-118
97Pinnacle Tot Cert Platinum Blue-69
97Pinnacle Tot Certi Platinum Gold-69
97Pinnacle Totally Certified Platinum Red-69
97Pinnacle Tot Cert Mirror Platinum Gold-69
97Score-115
Artist's Proofs-115
Golden Blades-115
97Score Devils-3
Platinum-3
Premier-3
97Upper Deck-96
98Aurora-106
98Be A Player-77
Press Release-77
98BAP Gold-77
98BAP Autographs-77
98BAP Autographs Gold-77
98BAP AS Milestones-M5
98BAP AS Milestones-M21
98BAP Tampa Bay All Star Game-77
98Devils Team Issue-1
98Finest-11
No Protectors-11
No Protectors Refractors-11
Refractors-11
98Pacific-260
Ice Blue-260
Red-260
98Pacific Dynagon Ice-106
Blue-106
Red-106
98Panini Stickers-66
98Paramount-130
Copper-130
Emerald Green-130
Holo-Electric-130
Ice Blue-130
Silver-130
99Pacific Omega-17
Copper-17
Gold-17
Ice Blue-17
Premiere Date-17
99Pacific Prism-11
Holographic Blue-11
Holographic Gold-11
Holographic Mirror-11
Holographic Purple-11
Premiere Date-11
99Panini Stickers-24
99Stadium Club-164
First Day Issue-164
One of a Kind-164
Printing Plates Black-164
Printing Plates Cyan-164
Printing Plates Magenta-164
Printing Plates Yellow-164
99Upper Deck-182
Exclusives-182
Exclusives 1 of 1-182
99Upper Deck Gold Reserve-182
99Upper Deck MVP SC Edition ProSign-DA
00BAP Memorabilia-385
00BAP Memorabilia-418
Emerald-385
Emerald-418
Ruby-385
Ruby-418
Sapphire-385
Sapphire-418
Promos-385
00BAP Mem Chicago Sportsfest Copper-385
00BAP Memorabilia Chicago Sportsfest Blue-385
00BAP Memorabilia Chicago Sportsfest Gold-385
00BAP Memorabilia Chicago Sportsfest Ruby-385
00BAP Memorabilia Chicago Sun-Times Ruby-385
00BAP Memorabilia Chicago Sun-Times Gold-385
00BAP Mem Chicago Sun-Times Sapphire-385
00BAP Mem Toronto Fall Expo Copper-385
00BAP Memorabilia Toronto Fall Expo Gold-385
00BAP Memorabilia Toronto Fall Expo Ruby-385
00O-Pee-Chee-157
00O-Pee-Chee Parallel-157
00Pacific-106
Copper-106
Gold-106
Ice Blue-106
Premiere Date-106
00Stadium Club-215
00Topps/OPC-157
Parallel-157
1000 Point Club-PC9
00Topps Chrome-111
OPC Refractors-111
Refractors-111
1000 Point Club Refractors-9
00Topps Stars-95
Blue-95
00Upper Deck 500 Goal Club-500DA
00Upper Deck 500 Goal Club-500DA
00Upper Deck Vintage-47
01BAP Memorabilia 500 Goal Scorers-GS14
01BAP Signature Series 500 Goal Scorers-13
01BAP Sig Series 500 Goal Scorers Autos-13
01BAP Ultimate Mem 500 Goal Scorers-22
01BAP Ultimate Mem 500 Goal Scorers Autos-4
01BAP Ultimate Mem 500 Goal Jerseys/Stick-22
01BAP Ultimate Mem 500 Goal Emblems-22
01BAP Update Travel Plans-TP15
01Pacific-43
Extreme LTD-43
Hobby LTD-43
Premiere Date-43
Retail LTD-43
01Pacific Arena Exclusives-43
01Parkhurst 500 Goal Scorers-PGS14
01Upper Deck-390
Exclusives-390
02BAP First Edition-222
02BAP Memorabilia-258
Emerald-258
Ruby-258
Sapphire-258
NHL All-Star Game-258
NHL All-Star Game Blue-258
NHL All-Star Game Green-258
NHL All-Star Game Red-258
02BAP Memorabilia Toronto Fall Expo-258
02BAP Signature Series-11
Autographs-11
Autograph Buybacks 1998-77
Autographs Gold-11
02Lightning Team Issue-2
02Maple Leafs Platinum Collection-25
02Pacific-346
Blue-346
Red-346
02Pacific Complete-264
Red-264
02Pacific Exclusive-154
02Private Stock Reserve-90
Blue-90
Red-90
Retail-90
02Topps Total-100
02Upper Deck-406
Exclusives-406
02Upper Deck Beckett UD Promos-406
03Beehive-172
Gold-172
Silver-172
03ITG Action-568
03Lightning Team Issue-25
03NHL Sticker Collection-123
03O-Pee-Chee-211
03OPC Blue-211
03OPC Gold-211
03OPC Red-211
03Pacific-303
Blue-303
Red-303
03Pacific Complete-358
Red-358
03Pacific Exhibit-130
Blue Backs-130
Yellow Backs-130
03Pacific Prism-90
Blue-90
Gold-90
Red-90
03Parkhurst Original Six Toronto-55
03Private Stock Reserve-92
Blue-92
Red-92
Retail-92
03Topps-211
Blue-211
Gold-211
Red-211
03Topps C55-113
Minis-113
Minis American Back-113
Minis American Back Red-113
Minis Bazooka Back-113
Minis Brooklyn Back-113
Minis Hat Trick Back-113
Minis O Canada Back-113
Minis O Canada Back Red-113
Minis Stanley Cup Back-113
03Upper Deck-172
Canadian Exclusives-172
HG-172
03Upper Deck MVP-382
Gold Script-382
Silver Script-382
Canadian Exclusives-382
04Pacific-235
Blue-235
Red-235
04Upper Deck-157
04Upper Deck-190
Canadian Exclusives-157
Canadian Exclusives-190
HG Glossy Gold-157
HG Glossy Gold-190
HG Glossy Silver-157
HG Glossy Silver-190
05Be A Player-83
First Period-83
Second Period-83
Third Period-83
Overtime-83
Dual Signatures-AR
Quad Signatures-SCCH
Signatures-AN
Signatures Gold-AN
05Black Diamond-77
Emerald-77
Gold-77
Onyx-77
Ruby-77
05Panini Stickers-162
05UD PowerPlay-82
05UD PowerPlay-102
05UD PowerPlay-119
Rainbow-82
05Ultra-177
Gold-177
Ice-177
05Upper Deck-419
Notable Numbers-N-DA
Patches-P-DAN
05Upper Deck MVP-347
Gold-347
Platinum-347
Andreyev, Alex
01BC Icemen-3
02Greensboro Generals RBI-3
03Greensboro Generals-177
Andricopoulos, Andrew
03Quebec Remparts-1
04Quebec Remparts-7
05Quebec Remparts-12
05Quebec Remparts Signature Series-12
06Quebec Remparts-2
06ITG Heroes and Prospects Memorial Cup Champions-MC05
Andrijevski, Alexander
91O-Pee-Chee Inserts-31R
92Upper Deck-342
92Indianapolis Ice-1
93Upper Deck-26
93Classic Pro Prospects-75
95Finnish SISU-225
95Finnish SISU-367
96Finnish SISU Redline-20
Mighty Adversaries-3
96Finnish SISU Redline Promos-2
00German DEL-203
01Russian Hockey League-12
Andriyashev, Ivan
99Russian Hockey League-57
Andruff, Ron
76Rockies Coke Cans-1
76Rockies Puck Bucks-1
77O-Pee-Chee NHL-288
77Rockies Coke Cans-1
78O-Pee-Chee-315
Andrusak, Greg
90Alberta International Team Canada-3
92Cleveland Lumberjacks-8
93Cleveland Lumberjacks-8
93Cleveland Lumberjacks Postcards-1
93Classic Pro Prospects-110
94Classic Tri-Cards-T52
94Classic Pro Prospects-156
94Classic Four-Sport *-156
Gold-156
Autographs-156A
Printers Proofs-156
96German DEL-28
98German DEL-174
99Chicago Wolves-16
00SP Authentic-160
00SPx-109
Spectrum-109
00Upper Deck-194
Exclusives Tier 1-194
Exclusives Tier 2-194
00Upper Deck MVP-206
First Stars-206
Second Stars-206
Third Stars-206
00Upper Deck Victory-270
00Kentucky Thoroughblades-1
01German Upper Deck-27
02German DEL City Press-88
Andryiotshenko, Igor
98Russian Hockey League-57
99Russian Hockey League-96
00Russian Hockey League-8
Angel, Brett
00Mississauga Ice Dogs-2
05Muskegon Fury-1
Angelelli, Dan
91Lake Superior State Lakers-2
92Lake Superior State Lakers-4
Angelidis, Mike
02Owen Sound Attack-23
03Owen Sound Attack-22
04Owen Sound Attack-1
05Owen Sound Attack-21
Angell, Nick
98Minnesota Golden Gophers-18
99Minnesota Golden Gophers-1
00Minnesota Golden Gophers-2
01Minnesota Golden Gophers-24
02Rockford Ice Hogs-15
06Swedish SHL Elitset-148
Angell, Phil
02Topeka Scarecrows-4
Angelo, Anthony
93Quebec Pee-Wee Tournament-1419
Angelo, Nate
77Rochester Americans-3
Angelstad, Mel
92Thunder Bay Thunder Hawks-25
93Thunder Bay Senators-15
94Thunder Bay Senators-11
95Thunder Bay Senators-2
98Michigan K-Wings-1
99Michigan K-Wings-18
00Manitoba Moose-1
04SP Authentic-94
04Ultimate Collection-46
Anger, Danny
06Sarnia Sting-16
Anger, Niklas
95Collector's Choice-344
Player's Club-344
Player's Club Platinum-344
95Upper Deck-561
Electric Ice-561
Electric Ice Gold-561
97Swedish Collector's Choice-49
98Swedish UD Choice-15
99Swedish Upper Deck-15
02Swedish SHL-153
Parallel-153
03Swedish Elite-154
Signatures-13
Silver-154
Anglehart, Serge
90ProCards AHL/IHL-485
907th Inn. Sketch Memorial Cup-74
91ProCards-124
Angotti, Lou
63Rochester Americans-1
64Beehive Group III Photos-30
64Beehive Group III Photos-120
64Coca-Cola Caps-86
64Topps-66
66Topps-116
68O-Pee-Chee-103
Puck Stickers-11
68Shirriff Coins-145
68Topps-103
69O-Pee-Chee-134
70Blackhawks Postcards-1
70Colgate Stamps-8
70Dad's Cookies-1
70Esso Power Players-113
70O-Pee-Chee-12
70Sargent Promotions Stamps-40
70Topps-12
71Letraset Action Replays-16
71O-Pee-Chee-212
71Sargent Promotions Stamps-38
71Toronto Sun-63
72O-Pee-Chee-243
72Sargent Promotions Stamps-65
73Blues White Border-1
73O-Pee-Chee-224
74O-Pee-Chee NHL-63
74Topps-63
94Parkhurst Tall Boys-96
95Parkhurst '66-67-28
Coins-28
04ITG Franchises US East Autographs-A-LA
04ITG Franchises US West-173
Angus, Trevor
95Neepewa Natives-6
Angus, Tyson
04South Surrey Eagles-1
04Surrey Eagles-1
04Surrey Eagles-1
Anhelov, Jonas
06Swedish SHL Elitset-176
Anholt, Darrell
83Springfield Indians-19
Anholt, Peter
907th Inn. Sketch WHL-22
917th Inn. Sketch WHL-140
93Red Deer Rebels-1
03Prince Albert Raiders-22
04Prince Albert Raiders-24
05Prince Albert Raiders-23
06Prince Albert Raiders-24
Anikienko, Vitali
03Russian Under-18 Team-6
Anisimov, Andrei
00Russian Hockey League-133
Anisimov, Artem
98Russian Hockey League-120
99Russian Hockey League-55
01Russian Hockey League-46
Anisin, Vyacheslav
72Finnish Jaakiekko-21
72Finnish Hellas-73
73Finnish Jaakiekko-1
73Russian National Team-14
73Swedish Stickers-93
74Finnish Jenkki-42
74Russian National Team-1
74Swedish Stickers-58
91Future Trends Canada '72-90
91Future Trends Canada '72 French-90
99Russian Stars of Hockey-40
Anken, Oliver
93Swiss HNL-188
Ankert, Torsten
05German DEL-351
Anneck, Dorian
94Tri-City Americans-1
95Tri-City Americans-2
95Signature Rookies-45A
95Signature Rookies-45B
Signatures-64
96Brandon Wheat Kings-9
00Johnstown Chiefs-12
Annesley, Kyle
01Calgary Hitmen-2
01Calgary Hitmen Autographed-2
02Calgary Hitmen-5A
04Everett Silvertips-27
Annett, Michael
03Waterloo Blackhawks-10
04Waterloo Blackhawks-3
Annetts, Tom
04UK Guildford Flames-17
05UK Guildford Flames-16
06UK Guildford Flames-16

Anning, Les
49Carrera Ltd Sports Series-44
Anoia, Rocco
93Sherbrooke Faucons-19
98Halifax Mooseheads-25
Anonsen, Hans M.
92Norwegian Elite Series-233
Ansakorpi, Pertti
65Finnish Hellas-157
66Finnish Jaakiekkosarja-157
70Finnish Jaakiekko-208
71Finnish Suomi Stickers-129
72Finnish Jaakiekko-192
73Finnish Jaakiekko-150
Anshakov, Sergei
02Russian Hockey League-106
02Russian Hockey League-186
03Russian Hockey League-216
04Russian World Junior Team-10
Ansoldi, Massimo
94Italian Milano-1
Antal, Dana
04Canadian Womens World Championship Team-1
Anthamatten, Silvan
03Swiss EV Zug Postcards-2
04Swiss EV Zug Postcards-14
Anthony, Keith
93Quebec Pee-Wee Tournament-1287
Anthony, Matt
02Windsor Spitfires-26
Anthony, Nick
99Minnesota Golden Gophers-2
00Minnesota Golden Gophers-3
01Minnesota Golden Gophers-4
02Minnesota Golden Gophers-1
Antila, Kristian
99Finnish Cardset-43
00Finnish Cardset-343
00Finnish Cardset Masquerade-9
01Finnish Cardset-147
02Finnish Cardset-3
03ECHL Update RBI Sports-113
04Swedish Elitset-213
Gold-213
04Swedish Pure Skills-48
Parallel-48
Antipin, Vladimir
96Czech APS Extraliga-249
97Czech DS Stickers-80
98Russian Hockey League-12
99Russian Hockey League-4
99Russian Metallurg Magnetogorsk-49
00Russian Hockey League-124
01Russian Hockey League-50
02Russian Hockey League-89
02Russian Hockey League-246
03Russian Avangard Omsk-25
03Russian Hockey League-88
04Russian RHL-22
Antipov, Anatoli
94German First League-636
99German Bundesliga 2-330
Antipov, Vladimir
99St. John's Maple Leafs-2
01Russian Hockey League-124
02Russian Hockey League-182
02Russian SL-29
02Russian World Championships-6
03Russian World Championship Team 2003-8
04Russian World Championship Team-24
Antisin, Misko
83Victoria Cougars-1
84Victoria Cougars-1
93Swiss HNL-120
95Swedish World Championships Stickers-125
95Swiss HNL-170
96Swiss HNL-532
96Swiss HNL-64
98Swiss Power Play Stickers-164
98Swiss Power Play Stickers-252
99Swiss Panini Stickers-163
00Swiss Panini Stickers-207
00Swiss Slapshot Mini-Cards-HCL9
01Swiss HNL-330
02Swiss HNL-117
Antler, Travis
02Baie Comeau Drakkar-12
03Yarmouth Mariners-2
Antognoli, Olivia
06Ohio State Buckeyes Women-14
Antonen, Juuso
06Finnish Ilves Team Set-2
Antonenko, Oleg
99Czech OFS-441
00Russian Hockey League-85
Antonik, Miki
92British Columbia JHL-127
Antonin, Jiri
95Czech APS Extraliga-322
Antonishyn, Chad
98Topeka Scarecrows-8
Antoniuk, Ryan
03Camrose Kodiaks-13
Antonovich, Jeff
95Slapshot Memorial Cup-16
01Rockford IceHogs-12
02Rockford Ice Hogs-8
Antonovich, Mike
72Minnesota Fighting Saints Postcards WHA-1
74Minnesota Fighting Saints WHA-1
74O-Pee-Chee WHA-37
75O-Pee-Chee WHA-111
76O-Pee-Chee WHA-23
77O-Pee-Chee WHA-34
79O-Pee-Chee-349
83Devils Postcards-1
Antons, Nils
96Kamloops Blazers-3
03German Berlin Polar Bears Postcards-2
04German DEL-122
04German Hamburg Freezers Postcards-1
Antos, Dean
91ProCards-232
Antos, Milan
94Czech APS Extraliga-269
95Czech APS Extraliga-140
96Czech APS Extraliga-330
97Czech APS Extraliga-308
97Czech DS Stickers-167
98Czech DS Stickers-122
98Czech OFS-42
99Czech OFS-117
00Czech DS Extraliga-36
00Czech OFS-73
01Czech OFS-13
02Czech OFS Plus-233
03Czech OFS Plus-171
04Czech HC Slavia Praha Postcards-1
04Czech OFS-158
Antoski, Shawn
897th Inn. Sketch OHL-152
90Score-429
Canadian-429
91O-Pee-Chee-98
91Score American-323
91Score Canadian Bilingual-353
91Score Canadian English-353
91Topps-98
91Upper Deck-351
French-351
917th Inn. Sketch Memorial Cup-118
91ProCards-595
92Canucks Road Trip Art-2
92OPC Premier-10
92Upper Deck-81
92Hamilton Canucks-1
93Donruss-498
93Leaf-368
93OPC Premier-31
Gold-31
93Parkhurst-479
Emerald Ice-479
93Stadium Club-288
Members Only Master Set-288
First Day Issue-288
93Topps/OPC Premier-31
Gold-31
93Ultra-437
93Upper Deck-325
94Canucks Program Inserts-2
94OPC Premier-226
Special Effects-226
94Parkhurst-248
Gold-248
94Topps/OPC Premier-226
Special Effects-226
94Ultra-381
96Be A Player-120
Autographs-120
Autographs Silver-120
96Ducks Team Issue-10
96Upper Deck-318
97Score Mighty Ducks-15
Platinum-15
Premier-15
Antoski, Shayne
897th Inn. Sketch OHL-161
907th Inn. Sketch OHL-301
917th Inn. Sketch OHL-120
93Huntington Blizzard-2
Antropov, Nikolai
98Russian Hockey League-160
99BAP Memorabilia-302
Gold-302
Silver-302
99BAP Millennium-224
Emerald-224
Ruby-224
Sapphire-224
Signatures-224
Signatures Gold-224
Calder Candidates Ruby-C16
Calder Candidates Emerald-C16
Calder Candidates Sapphire-C16
99Black Diamond-83
Diamond Cut-83
Final Cut-83
99Crown Royale-131
Limited Series-131
Premiere Date-131
Prospects Parallel-131
99Maple Leafs Pizza Pizza-13
99O-Pee-Chee Chrome-297
99O-Pee-Chee Chrome Refractors-297
99Pacific-465
99Pacific Dynagon Ice-184
Blue-184
Copper-184
Gold-184
Premiere Date-184
99Pacific Omega-221
Copper-221
Gold-221
Ice Blue-221
Premiere Date-221
99Pacific Prism-134
Holographic Blue-134
Holographic Gold-134
Holographic Mirror-134
Holographic Purple-134
Premiere Date-134
Ice Prospects-8
99SP Authentic-118
99Stadium Club-171
First Day Issue-171
One of a Kind-171
Printing Plates Black-171
Printing Plates Cyan-171
Printing Plates Magenta-171
Printing Plates Yellow-171
99Topps Arena Giveaways-TOR-NA
99Topps/OPC Chrome-297
Refractors-297
99Topps Gold Label Class 1-98
Black-98
Black One of One-98
One of One-98
Red-98
Red One of One-98
99Topps Gold Label Class 2-98
99Topps Gold Label Class 2 Black-98
99Topps Gold Label Class 2 Black 1 of 1-98
99Topps Gold Label Class 2 One of One-98
99Topps Gold Label Class 2 Red-98
99Topps Gold Label Class 2 Red One of One-98
99Topps Gold Label Class 3-98
99Topps Gold Label Class 3 Black-98
99Topps Gold Label Class 3 Black 1 of 1-98
99Topps Gold Label Class 3 One of One-98
99Topps Gold Label Class 3 Red-98
99Topps Gold Label Class 3 Red One of One-98
99Topps Premier Plus-117
Parallel-117
99Ultimate Victory-103
1/1-103
Parallel-103
Parallel 100-103
99Upper Deck Arena Giveaways-TM1
99Upper Deck MVP SC Edition-178
Gold Script-178
Silver Script-178
Super Script-178
00Aurora-136
Pinstripes-136
Pinstripes Premiere Date-136
Premiere Date-136
Autographs-135
00BAP Memorabilia-158
Emerald-158
Ruby-158
Sapphire-158
Promos-158
00BAP Mem Chicago Sportsfest Copper-158
00BAP Memorabilia Chicago Sportsfest Blue-158
00BAP Memorabilia Chicago Sportsfest Gold-158
00BAP Memorabilia Chicago Sportsfest Ruby-158
00BAP Memorabilia Chicago Sun-Times Ruby-158
00BAP Memorabilia Chicago Sun-Times Gold-158
00BAP Mem Chicago Sun-Times Sapphire-158
00BAP Mem Toronto Fall Expo Copper-158
00BAP Memorabilia Toronto Fall Expo Gold-158
00BAP Memorabilia Toronto Fall Expo Ruby-158
00BAP Parkhurst 2000-P32
00BAP Signature Series-176
Emerald-176
Ruby-176
Sapphire-176
Autographs-3
Autographs Gold-3
00McDonald's Pacific-31
Blue-31
00O-Pee-Chee-163
00O-Pee-Chee Parallel-163
00Pacific-384
Copper-384
Gold-384
Ice Blue-384
Premiere Date-384
Autographs-384
00Paramount-226
Copper-226
Gold-226
Holo-Gold-226
Holo-Silver-226
Ice Blue-226
Premiere Date-226
00Private Stock-92
Gold-92
Premiere Date-92
Retail-92
Silver-92
PS-2001 New Wave-24
00Revolution-136
Blue-136
Premiere Date-136
Red-136
HD NHL-33
00SPx-64
Spectrum-64
00Stadium Club-163
Co-Signers-CO3
Lone Star Signatures-LS5
00Topps/OPC-163
Parallel-163
00Topps Chrome-113
OPC Refractors-113
Refractors-113
00Topps Heritage-181
00Topps Stars-65
Blue-65
00Upper Deck MVP-168
First Stars-168
Second Stars-168
Third Stars-168
00Upper Deck Victory-222
00Upper Deck Vintage-336
00Vanguard-91
Holographic Gold-91
Holographic Purple-91
Pacific Proofs-91
01BAP Memorabilia-106
Emerald-106
Ruby-106
Sapphire-106
01O-Pee-Chee-240
01O-Pee-Chee Premier Parallel-240
01Parkhurst-160
01SP Authentic-120
Limited-120
Limited Gold-120
01Topps-240
OPC Parallel-240
01Upper Deck-397
Exclusives-397
Pride of the Leafs-MLNA
01Upper Deck MVP-176
01Upper Deck Victory-333
Gold-333
01Upper Deck Vintage-239
01St. John's Maple Leafs-2
02BAP Sig Series Auto Buybacks 1999-224
02BAP Sig Series Auto Buybacks 2000-3
02BAP Signature Series Golf-GS36
02BAP Signature Series Phenoms-YP11
02Maple Leafs Platinum Collection-21
02Maple Leafs Team Issue-1
02NHL Power Play Stickers-136
02Pacific Complete-363
Red-363
02Parkhurst Retro-196
Minis-196
02SP Authentic-134
02UD Top Shelf Shooting Stars-SHNA
03Black Diamond-71
Black-71
Green-71
Red-71
03Bowman-59
Gold-59
03Bowman Chrome-59
Refractors-59
Gold Refractors-59
Xfractors-59
03Crown Royale Global Conquest-5
03ITG Action-507
Jerseys-M1
03O-Pee-Chee-173
03OPC Blue-173
03OPC Gold-173
03OPC Red-173
03Pacific-314
Blue-314
Red-314
03Pacific Complete-72
Red-72
03Pacific Exhibit-134
Blue Backs-134
Yellow Backs-134
03Pacific Supreme Generations-11
03Parkhurst Original Six Toronto-1
Memorabilia-TM5
03Topps-173
Blue-173
Gold-173
Red-173
03Upper Deck-425
Canadian Exclusives-425
HG-425
UD Exclusives-425
03Upper Deck MVP-394
Gold Script-394
Silver Script-394
Canadian Exclusives-394
03Upper Deck Victory-179
Bronze-179
Gold-179
Silver-179
03Toronto Star-89
04UD All-World-34
Gold-34
04Russian Back to Russia-32
05Beehive Matted Materials-MMNA
05Parkhurst-460
Facsimile Auto Parallel-460
Signatures-NA
True Colors-TCTOR
True Colors-TCTOR
05SP Authentic Sign of the Times Duals-DAS
05SP Game Used-95
Autographs-95
Gold-95
Authentic Fabrics Quad-SNSA
Authentic Patches Quad -SNSA
SIGnificance Extra-SA
SIGnificance Extra Gold-SA
Significant Numbers-SN-NA
Statscriptions-ST-NA
05SPx Winning Combos-WC-NA
05SPx Winning Combos Autographs-AWC-NA
05SPx Winning Combos Autographs-AWC-SA
05SPx Winning Combos Gold-WC-NA
05SPx Winning Combos Spectrum-WC-NA
05SPx Winning Materials-WM-NA
05SPx Winning Materials Gold-WM-NA
05SPx Winning Materials Spectrum-WM-NA
05UD Artifacts-96
Blue-96
Gold-96
Green-96
Pewter-96
Red-96
Auto Facts-AF-NA
Auto Facts Blue-AF-NA
Auto Facts Copper-AF-NA
Auto Facts Pewter-AF-NA
Auto Facts Silver-AF-NA
Gold Autographed-96
05UD Powerplay Specialists-TSNA
05UD Powerplay Specialists Patches-SPNA
05Ultimate Coll National Heroes Jersey-NHJNA
05Ultimate Coll National Heroes Patch-NHPNA
05Ultra-186
Gold-186
Ice-186
05Upper Deck-183
Big Playmakers-B-NA
HG Glossy-183
Jerseys-J-NA
Jerseys Series II-J2NA
Notable Numbers-N-AN
05Upper Deck Ice-91
Rainbow-91
05Upper Deck MVP-360
Gold-360
Platinum-360
ProSign-P-NA
05Upper Deck Trilogy Scripts-SFS-NA
05Upper Deck Toronto Fall Expo-183
06Flair Showcase Inks-INA
06Flair Showcase Stitches-SSNA
06Fleer Fabricology-FNA
06O-Pee-Chee-457
Rainbow-457
06Ultra Fresh Ink-INA
06Ultra Uniformity-UNA
06Ultra Uniformity Patches-UPNA
06Ultra Uniformity Autographed Jerseys-UANA
06Upper Deck-186
Exclusives Parallel-186
High Gloss Parallel-186
Masterpieces-186
06Upper Deck MVP-274
Gold Script-274
Super Script-274
Autographs-OAAT
International Icons-II23
Jerseys-OJSN
06Upper Deck Trilogy Scripts-TSNA
Antti, Petter
84Swedish Semic Elitserien-190
85Swedish Panini Stickers-167
89Swedish Semic Elitserien Stickers-167
Anttila, Kari
70Finnish Jaakiekko-327
Anttila, Marko
05Finnish Cardset -44
06Finnish Cardset-46
06Finnish Ilves Team Set-3
Anttila, Pekka
70Finnish Jaakiekko-365
Anzalone, Frank
90Newmarket Saints-1
91Nashville Knights-22
93Roanoke Express-1
94Roanoke Express-20
95Roanoke Express-22
96Roanoke Express-NNO
Apel, Thorsten
98German DEL-142
Apollo, Per
98Danish Hockey League-102
Appel, David
98Czech OFS-192
99Czech OFS-411
00Czech OFS-232
01Czech OFS Update-307
01Czech OFS-186
02Czech OFS Plus-337
Appel, Frank
99German Bundesliga 2-43
01German Upper Deck-61
02German DEL City Press-171
Appel, Joachim
94German DEL-273
95German DEL-264
96German DEL-158
99German DEL-77
00German DEL-123
Appel, Pascal
02German DEL City Press-66
03German DEL-181
04German Augsburg Panthers Postcards-1
Appel, Ryan
93London Knights-2
93London Knights-24
Appert, Seth
91Ferris State Bulldogs-2
92Ferris State Bulldogs-1
Applebaum, Myles
04Kitchener Rangers-22
05Kitchener Rangers-23
Appleby, Braden
01Lethbridge Hurricanes-5
03Vancouver Giants-17
04Regina Pats-10
Appleton, Joel
91Air Canada SJHL-D2
Apps III, Syl
99St. John's Maple Leafs-3
00St. John's Maple Leafs-2
01Trenton Titans-1-1
02Trenton Titans-B-1
Apps Jr., Syl
70Colgate Stamps-26
70Sargent Promotions Stamps-113
71O-Pee-Chee-77
71Penguins Postcards-1
71Sargent Promotions Stamps-161
71Topps-77
71Toronto Sun-210
72O-Pee-Chee-115
72Sargent Promotions Stamps-169
72Topps-11
73O-Pee-Chee-76
73Topps-160
74Lipton Soup-49
74NHL Action Stamps-222
74O-Pee-Chee NHL-13
74O-Pee-Chee NHL-183
74Penguins Postcards-1
74Topps-13
74Topps-183
75O-Pee-Chee NHL-130
75Topps-130
76O-Pee-Chee NHL-50
76O-Pee-Chee NHL-218
76O-Pee-Chee NHL-392
76Topps-50
76Topps-218
76Topps Glossy Inserts-13
77Coca-Cola-1
77O-Pee-Chee NHL-248
77Penguins Puck Bucks-26
77Topps-248
78O-Pee-Chee-56
78Topps-56
79O-Pee-Chee-366
80O-Pee-Chee-362
04ITG Franchises US West-275
Autographs-A-SA
Apps, Gillian
04Canadian Womens World Championship Team-2
06ITG Going For Gold-10
06ITG Going For Gold Samples-10
06ITG Going For Gold Autographs-AAP
06ITG Going For Gold Jerseys-GUJ10
Apps, Syl
34Beehive Group I Photos-298
36O-Pee-Chee V304D-101
37O-Pee-Chee V304E-141
37V356 Worldwide Gum-23
38Quaker Oats Photos-1
39O-Pee-Chee V301-1-6
40O-Pee-Chee V301-2-118
40O-Pee-Chee V301-2-146
44Beehive Group II Photos-371
45Quaker Oats Photos-1A
45Quaker Oats Photos-1B
45Quaker Oats Photos-1C
55Parkhurst-28
Quaker Oats-28
83Hall of Fame Postcards-O1
85Hall of Fame-212
91Kraft-50
91Kraft-83
94Parkhurst Missing Link Pop-Ups-P5
99Upper Deck Century Legends-33
Century Collection-33
01Upper Deck Legends-56
02BAP Ultimate Mem Paper Cuts Autos-32
02Maple Leafs Platinum Collection-40
03BAP Ultimate Mem Linemates Autos-7
03BAP Ultimate Mem Maple Leafs Forever-2
03BAP Ultimate Memorabilia Paper Cuts-23
03Canada Post-12
03Parkhurst Original Six Toronto-39
03Parkhurst Original Six Toronto-75
03Parkhurst Original Six Toronto-90
Inserts-T4
Inserts-T11
04ITG Franchises Update-494
04ITG Ultimate Memorabilia-41
Gold-41
Maple Leafs Forever-1
05ITG Ultimate Mem Leafs Forever Autos-3
05The Cup Legendary Cuts-LCSY
06ITG Ultimate Memorabilia-133
Artist Proof-133
Aquino, Anthony
96Quebec Pee-Wee Tournament-1179
03ECHL Update RBI Sports-133
03Gwinnett Gladiators-7
05German DEL-358
Aquino, Luch
04Brampton Battalion-17
05ITG Heroes/Prosp Toronto Expo Parallel -403
05Brampton Battalion-16
05ITG Heroes and Prospects-403
Arabski, Rob
94Brantford Smoke-7
Aradsson, Rasmus
98Danish Hockey League-73
99Danish Hockey League-26
Arakaev, Sergei
03Russian Hockey League-160
Aravirta, Hannu
92Finnish Jyvas-Hyva Stickers-69
95Finnish SISU-386
Arbelius, Pekka
71Finnish Suomi Stickers-297
80Finnish Mallasjuoma-110
82Finnish Skopbank-1
82Swedish Semic VM Stickers-46
85Swedish Panini Stickers-218
86Swedish Panini Stickers-206
Arbez, Derek
95Swift Current Broncos-1
96Swift Current Broncos-24
Arbour, Al
44Beehive Group II Photos-75
44Beehive Group II Photos-150
44Beehive Group II Photos-372
52Juniors Blue Tint-5
53Parkhurst-38
57Topps-38
58Topps-64
59Topps-35
60Shirriff Coins-67
60Topps-64
61Shirriff/Salada Coins-60
61York Yellow Backs-33
62Shirriff Coins-20
63Rochester Americans-2
64Beehive Group III Photos-150
68O-Pee-Chee-128
68Shirriff Coins-149
69O-Pee-Chee-178
Four-in-One-13
71Blues Postcards-1
71Toronto Sun-232
74O-Pee-Chee NHL-91
74Topps-91
84Islanders News-29
85Islanders News-29
89Islanders Team Issue-1
90Pro Set-671
92Blues UD Best of the Blues-3
93Kraft-27
94Parkhurst Missing Link-61
01Topps Heritage Autographs-AAA
01Topps Heritage Salute-S2
04ITG Franchises Update Autographs-AA
04ITG Ultimate Memorabilia-165
04ITG Ultimate Memorabilia-187
Gold-165
Gold-187
06Parkhurst-3
06Parkhurst-205
Autographs-3
Autographs-205
Autographs Dual-DAAB
06The Cup-55
Black Rainbow-55
Gold-55
Masterpiece Pressplates-55
Stanley Cup Signatures-CSAA
Stanley Cup Titlists-TAA
Arbour, Amos
23V145-1-20
Arbour, John
68O-Pee-Chee-189
71Blues Postcards-2
71Toronto Sun-233
72Minnesota Fighting Saints Postcards WHA-2
74Minnesota Fighting Saints WHA-2
75O-Pee-Chee WHA-54
Arbour, Ty
23V128-1 Paulin's Candy-44
Arbulic, Mike
93Portland Winter Hawks-1
Arcand, Billy
51Laval Dairy QSHL-54
52St. Lawrence Sales-99
Arcangeloni, Stephane
94Finnish Jaa Kiekko-222
94French National Team-3
95Swedish World Championships Stickers-107
Arcella, Gerry
917th Inn. Sketch OHL-379
Archalous, Jan
99Czech OFS-359
Archambault, Cedric
04Drummondville Voltigeurs-20
05Saint John's Sea Dogs-6
Archambault, Daniel
01Sorel Royaux-1
Archambault, David
98Quebec Remparts-1
Signed-1
Archambault, Francois
93Sherbrooke Faucons-15
97Johnstown Chiefs-25
98Abilene Aviators-17
Archambault, Louis
93Quebec Pee-Wee Tournament-28
Archambault, Michel
72Nordiques Postcards-1
72O-Pee-Chee-320
73Nordiques Team Issue-1
Archambault, Simon
04Drummondville Voltigeurs-30
Archambault, Yves
73Vancouver Blazers-2
Archer, Andrew
00Guelph Storm-2
01Guelph Storm-19
01Guelph Storm Memorial Cup-20
02Guelph Storm-3
04Hamilton Bulldogs-1
05Hamilton Bulldogs-2
06Hamilton Bulldogs-1
Archibal, Georges
51Laval Dairy Lac St. Jean-47
Archibald, Alex
04Prince Albert Raiders-1
05Prince Albert Raiders-1
06Chilliwack Bruins-1
Archibald, Dave
86Portland Winter Hawks-1
87North Stars Postcards-2
88O-Pee-Chee-112
88O-Pee-Chee Stickers-53
88O-Pee-Chee Stickers-184
88Panini Stickers-88
88Topps-112
89O-Pee-Chee-10
89O-Pee-Chee Stickers-201
89Topps-10
90Alberta International Team Canada-9
91Alberta International Team Canada-1
92Score Canadian Olympians-3
92Upper Deck-473
92Binghamton Rangers-14
93Donruss-231
93OPC Premier-458
Gold-458
93PowerPlay-168
93Senators Kraft Sheets-1
93Stadium Club-399
Members Only Master Set-399
First Day Issue-399
93Topps/OPC Premier-458
Gold-458
93Upper Deck-105
94Leaf-432
94Parkhurst SE-SE118
Gold-SE118
94Score-133
Gold-133
Platinum-133
94Senators Team Issue-1
94Upper Deck-383
Electric Ice-383
95Senators Team Issue-2
96German DEL-65
Archibald, Dennis
91British Columbia JHL-130
92British Columbia JHL-44
Arcibal, Nielsson
06Texas Tornados-5
Ardashev, Alexander
00Russian Hockey League-58
Ardelan, Mark
99Brandon Wheat Kings-1
00Brandon Wheat Kings-3
01Vancouver Giants-2
03Prince Albert Raiders-17
06Iowa Stars-2
Arduin, David
05Vernon Vipers-2
Aregger, Matthias
93Swiss HNL-240
Arekaev, Sergei
99Russian Hockey League-194
Arendt, Ronny
99German Bundesliga 2-225
01German Upper Deck-18
02German DEL City Press-1
03German DEL-16
04German Augsburg Panthers Postcards-2
04German DEL-22
05German DEL-241
Ares, Steve
907th Inn. Sketch QMJHL-75
917th Inn. Sketch QMJHL-109
Areshenkoff, Ron
88Oilers Tenth Anniversary-103
Argentos, Giuseppe
917th Inn. Sketch QMJHL-41
Argiropoulos, John
94Owen Sound Platers-19
95Slapshot-291
95Owen Sound Platers-14
Argokov, Artem
99Russian Hockey League-113
00Russian Hockey League-177
Argouin, Jonathan
93Quebec Pee-Wee Tournament-1064
Argyriou, Alex
97Brandon Wheat Kings-1
98Brandon Wheat Kings-1
Arhontas, Matt
04Waterloo Blackhawks-6
05Waterloo Blackhawks-2
Arial, Simon
917th Inn. Sketch QMJHL-150
Arians, Norbert
94German First League-61
Arima, Tony
80Finnish Mallasjuoma-54
94Finnish SISU-281
95Finnish SISU-173
Arkhipov, Denis
98Black Diamond-105
Double Diamond-105
Triple Diamond-105
Quadruple Diamond-105
98SPx Top Prospects-75
Radiance-75
Spectrum-75
98Russian Hockey League-45
99Russian Hockey League-72
99Russian Stars of Hockey-17
00Milwaukee Admirals Keebler-2
01BAP Memorabilia-211
Emerald-211
Ruby-211
Sapphire-211
01BAP Signature Series-42
Autographs-42
Autographs Gold-42
01Upper Deck-101
Exclusives-101
02Atomic-58
Blue-58
Gold-58
Red-58
Hobby Parallel-58
02BAP First Edition-251
02BAP Memorabilia-30
Emerald-30
Ruby-30
Sapphire-30
NHL All-Star Game-30
NHL All-Star Game Blue-30
NHL All-Star Game Green-30
NHL All-Star Game Red-30
02BAP Memorabilia Toronto Fall Expo-30
02BAP Sig Series Auto Buybacks 2001-42
02BAP Signature Series Golf-GS31
02O-Pee-Chee-48
02O-Pee-Chee Premier Blue Parallel-48
02O-Pee-Chee Premier Red Parallel-48
02O-Pee-Chee Factory Set-48
02Pacific-205
Blue-205
Red-205
02Pacific Complete-123
Red-123
02Pacific Exclusive-96
02Pacific Heads-Up-67
Blue-67
Purple-67
Red-67
02Parkhurst-178
Bronze-178
Gold-178
Silver-178
02Private Stock Reserve-56
Blue-56
Red-56
Retail-56
02SP Game Used Future Fabrics-FFDA
02SP Game Used Future Fabrics Gold-FFDA
02SP Game Used Future Fabrics Rainbow-FFDA
02Topps-48
OPC Blue Parallel-48
OPC Red Parallel-48
Factory Set-48
02Topps Heritage-31
Chrome Parallel-31
02Topps Total-137
02UD Top Shelf Goal Oriented-GODA
02Upper Deck-100
Exclusives-100
Bright Futures-DA
Hot Spots-HSDA
02Upper Deck Classic Portraits-54
02Upper Deck MVP-102
Gold-102
Classics-102
Golden Classics-102
02Upper Deck Victory-116
Bronze-116
Gold-116
Silver-116
02Upper Deck Vintage-144
03Black Diamond-112
Black-112
Green-112
Red-112
03ITG Action-325
03NHL Sticker Collection-255
03O-Pee-Chee-145
03OPC Blue-145
03OPC Gold-145
03OPC Red-145
03Pacific-185
Blue-185
Red-185
03Pacific Complete-364
Red-364
03Topps-145
Blue-145
Gold-145
Red-145
03Upper Deck-350
Canadian Exclusives-350
HG-350
UD Exclusives-350
03Upper Deck MVP-238
Gold Script-238
Silver Script-238
Canadian Exclusives-238
03Upper Deck Victory-103
Bronze-103
Gold-103
Silver-103
03Russian World Championship Team 2003-17
03Russian World Championships Preview-4
04Russian Back to Russia-41
05Upper Deck-110
Big Playmakers-B-DAR
HG Glossy-110
Jerseys-J-DAR
05Upper Deck Toronto Fall Expo-110
06Blackhawks Postcards-2
Arkiomaa, Tero
92Finnish Jyvas-Hyva Stickers-136
93Finnish Jyvas-Hyva Stickers-232
93Finnish SISU-198
94Finnish SISU-85
94Finnish SISU-173
94Finnish SISU Fire On Ice-1
94Finnish Jaa Kiekko-23
95Finnish SISU-170
95Finnish SISU-307
95Finnish SISU Limited-33
95Finnish Semic World Championships-31
95Swedish World Championships Stickers-184
96German DEL-13
98Finnish Kerailysarja-269
99Finnish Cardset-155
00UK Sekonda Superleague-117
Arko, Jesse
04Drummondville Voltigeurs-30
Arko, Joey
93Quebec Pee-Wee Tournament-560
Arlbrandt, Par
02Swedish SHL-185
Parallel-185
Arlotta, Jeff
93Quebec Pee-Wee Tournament-808
Arman, Krikor
00Muskegon Fury-19
01Macon Whoopee-3
Armbrust, Peter
00Quad-City Mallards-7
01Quad-City Mallards-1
02South Carolina Stingrays-1
Armelin, John
82Sault Ste. Marie Greyhounds-2
Armitage, Steve
97Pinnacle Hockey Night in Canada-1
Armstrong Sr., Bob
23V128-1 Paulin's Candy-56
Armstrong, Bill
89ProCards AHL-349
90ProCards AHL/IHL-45
91O-Pee-Chee-36
91Topps-36
91ProCards-266
92Cincinnati Cyclones-1
95Indianapolis Ice-1
Armstrong, Bill D.
89Oshawa Generals-32
89Oshawa Generals 7th Inning Sketch-20
897th Inn. Sketch OHL-20
897th Inn. Sketch OHL-199
90ProCards AHL/IHL-50
907th Inn. Sketch Memorial Cup-82
91ProCards-280
95Cleveland Lumberjacks-2
95Cleveland Lumberjacks Postcards-2
96Cleveland Lumberjacks-2
96Cleveland Lumberjacks Multi-Ad-3
97Providence Bruins-3
98Providence Bruins-4
02Trenton Titans-A-11
Armstrong, Bob
44Beehive Group II Photos-1
52Parkhurst-84
54Parkhurst-55
54Topps-7
55Bruins Photos-1
57Bruins Photos-1
57Topps-3
58Bruins Photos-1
58Topps-1
59Topps-39
60Shirriff Coins-118
60Topps-56
61Shirriff/Salada Coins-12
61Topps-13
91Bruins Sports Action Legends-1
91Bruins Sports Action Legends-35
94Parkhurst Missing Link-7
02Parkhurst Reprints-194
Armstrong, Chris
93Donruss Team Canada-2
93Pinnacle-459
Canadian-459
93Upper Deck-546
94Classic-32
Gold-32
96Carolina Monarchs-2
96Collector's Edge Ice-22
Prism-22
97Fort Wayne Komets-12
99Kentucky Thoroughblades-3
00Cleveland Lumberjacks-18
02Swiss EV Zug Postcards-26
02Swiss HNL-65
03Cincinnati Mighty Ducks-B2
04German DEL-82
04German Ingolstadt Panthers-1
05German DEL-141
06German DEL-53

Armstrong, Colby
00Red Deer Rebels-2
Signed-2
01BAP Memorabilia Draft Redemptions-21
01Red Deer Rebels-2
01UD Prospects-32
Jerseys-J-CA
Jerseys-C-WA
Jerseys Gold-J-CA
Jerseys Gold-C-WA
02Wilkes-Barre Scranton Penguins-13
03Pacific AHL Prospects-94
Gold-94
03Wilkes-Barre Scranton Penguins-2
04Wilkes-Barre Scranton Penguins-9
04ITG Heroes and Prospects-30
Autographs-CA
Complete Emblems-13
Emblems-7
Emblems Gold-7
He Shoots-He Scores Prizes-35
Jersey Autographs-7
Jerseys-7
Jerseys Gold-7
Numbers-7
Numbers Gold-7
04ITG Heroes/Prospects Toronto Expo '05-30
04ITG Heroes/Prospects Expo Heroes/Pros-30
05Black Diamond-273
05Hot Prospects-161
En Fuego-161
Red Hot-161
White Hot-161
05Parkhurst-660
Facsimile Auto Parallel-660
05SP Authentic-275
Limited-275
05SP Game Used-230
05SPx-279
05The Cup Masterpiece Pressplate Artifact-316
05The Cup Master Pressplate Black Diamond-273
05The Cup Masterpiece Pressplates (Ice)-249
05The Cup Master Pressplate Rookie Update-168
05The Cup Masterpiece Pressplates SPA-275
05The Cup Masterpiece Pressplates SP GU-230
05The Cup Masterpiece Pressplates (SPx)-279
05The Cup Masterpiece Pressplates Trilogy-294
05The Cup Masterpiece Pressplate Ult Coll-220
05UD Artifacts-316
05Ultimate Collection-220
Gold-220
05Upper Deck Ice-249
05Upper Deck Rookie Update-168
05Upper Deck Trilogy-294
05WBS Penguins-1
05ITG Heroes and Prospects Jerseys-GUJ-102
05ITG Heroes and Prospects Jerseys Gold-GUJ-102
06Be A Player Portraits Signature Portraits-SPCA
06Beehive-22
Matte-22
Signature Scrapbook-SSCA
06Black Diamond-66
Black-66
Gold-66
Ruby-66
06Fleer-156
Tiffany-156
06O-Pee-Chee-399
Rainbow-399
06SP Authentic Sign of the Times-STCA
06SP Authentic Sign of the Times Duals-STSA
06UD Artifacts-23
Blue-23
Gold-23
Platinum-23
Radiance-23
Red-23
06Ultimate Collection Signatures-US-CA
06Ultra-157
Gold Medallion-157
Ice Medallion-157
06Upper Deck Arena Giveaways-PIT2
06Upper Deck-156
Exclusives Parallel-156
High Gloss Parallel-156
Masterpieces-156
06Upper Deck MVP-235
Gold Script-235
Super Script-235
06Upper Deck Ovation-190
06Upper Deck Sweet Shot Signature Shots/Saves-SSCA
06Upper Deck Sweet Shot Signature Shots/Saves Ice Signings-SSICA
06Upper Deck Sweet Shot Signature Shots/Saves Sticks-SSSCA
06Upper Deck Victory-161
06Upper Deck Victory Black-161
06Upper Deck Victory Gold-161

Armstrong, Derek
917th Inn. Sketch OHL-246
91Sudbury Wolves-14
92Sudbury Wolves-16
94Leaf-51
94Classic Tri-Cards-T25
94Classic Pro Prospects-178
96Be A Player-179
Autographs-179
Autographs Silver-179
96Islander Postcards-2
97Pacific-300
Copper-300
Emerald Green-300
Ice Blue-300
Red-300
Silver-300
97Hartford Wolf Pack-1
98Hartford Wolf Pack-1
99Hartford Wolf Pack-1
00Hartford Wolf Pack-1
01Swiss HNL-85
02Kings Game Sheets-39
02Kings Game Sheets-40
02Pacific Complete-430
Red-430
02Manchester Monarchs-16
03ITG Action-223
03Pacific Complete-407
Red-407
04Pacific-118
Blue-118
Red-118
05Kings Team Issue-4
05Parkhurst-223
Facsimile Auto Parallel-223
06O-Pee-Chee-237
Rainbow-237

Armstrong, George
44Beehive Group II Photos-373A
44Beehive Group II Photos-373B
44Beehive Group II Photos-373C
45Quaker Oats Photos-2
52Parkhurst-51
53Parkhurst-11
54Parkhurst-24
55Parkhurst-4
Quaker Oats-4
57Parkhurst-T1
58Parkhurst-7
58Parkhurst-11
58Parkhurst-48
59Parkhurst-7
60Parkhurst-17
60Shirriff Coins-9
60York Photos-1
61Parkhurst-17
61Shirriff/Salada Coins-51
61York Yellow Backs-37
62Parkhurst-13
62Shirriff Coins-10
62York Iron-On Transfers-17
63Chex Photos-1
63Parkhurst-13
63Parkhurst-73
63Toronto Star-1
63York White Backs-16
64Beehive Group III Photos-151
64Topps-69
65Coca-Cola-96
65Maple Leafs White Border-1
65Topps-19
66Maple Leafs Hockey Talks-1
66Topps-84
66Topps USA Test-17
67Post Flip Books-9
67Topps-83
67York Action Octagons-3
67York Action Octagons-4
68Shirriff Coins-159
69Maple Leafs White Border Glossy-1
70O-Pee-Chee-113
70Topps-113
83Hall of Fame-197
83Hall of Fame Postcards-N1
85Hall of Fame-197
92Parkhurst Parkie Reprints-PR17
93Parkhurst Parkie Reprints-PR38
94Parkhurst Missing Link-125
94Parkhurst Tall Boys-122
95Parkhurst '66-67-116
Coins-116
02Maple Leafs Platinum Collection-41
02Parkhurst Reprints-218

Armstrong, Jack
52Juniors Blue Tint-91

Armstrong, Jacques
51Bas Du Fleuve-6

Armstrong, Jake
94UK Solihul Barons-1
95UK Solihull Barons-4
98UK Basingstoke Bison-17

Armstrong, John
05ITG Heroes/Prosp Toronto Expo Parallel -404
05Plymouth Whalers-A-02
05ITG Heroes and Prospects-404
Team Orr-TO1
06Plymouth Whalers-1
06ITG Heroes and Prospects-103
Autographs-AJA

Armstrong, Mark
92Quebec Pee-Wee Tournament-305
94German First League-317

Armstrong, Matt
99Kitchener Rangers-2
00Kitchener Rangers-2
01Peterborough Petes-18

Armstrong, Murray
34Beehive Group I Photos-299
37O-Pee-Chee V304E-146
39O-Pee-Chee V301-1-19

Armstrong, Neil P
91Pro Set HOF Induction-5

Armstrong, Norm
61Sudbury Wolves-1
62Sudbury Wolves-2
63Rochester Americans-3

Armstrong, Red
71Rochester Americans-1

Armstrong, Riley
03Everett Silvertips-19
04Cleveland Barons-1
05Cleveland Barons-1

Armstrong, Ryan
03Camrose Kodiaks-16
03St. Francis Xavier X-Men-2
04St. Francis Xavier X-Men-1

Armstrong, Tim
88ProCards AHL-233
89ProCards AHL-114

Arnaldo, Rick
01Barrie Colts-3

Arnason, Chuck
72Canadiens Postcards-1
72Dimanche/Derniere Heure *-131
74NHL Action Stamps-224
74O-Pee-Chee NHL-385
74Penguins Postcards-2
75O-Pee-Chee NHL-57
75Topps-57
76O-Pee-Chee NHL-92
76Rockies Coke Cans-2
76Rockies Puck Bucks-2
76Topps-92
77O-Pee-Chee NHL-379
78O-Pee-Chee-389

Arnason, Tyler
01BAP Memorabilia-387
Emerald-387
Ruby-387
Sapphire-387
01Parkhurst-309
01Titanium Draft Day Edition-114
01UD Premier Collection-92
01Norfolk Admirals-23
02BAP Ultimate Mem Calder Candidates-7
02Bowman YoungStars-140
Gold-140
Silver-140
Autographs-TA
Jerseys-TA
Patches-TA
Double Stuff-TA
Triple Stuff-TA
Rivals-TABS
Rivals Patches-4
Sticks-TA
02Crown Royale Rookie Royalty-6
02O-Pee-Chee-300
02O-Pee-Chee Premier Blue Parallel-300
02O-Pee-Chee Premier Red Parallel-300
02O-Pee-Chee Factory Set-300
02Pacific Calder-63
Silver-63
Reflections-6
02Pacific Complete-198
Red-198
02Pacific Quest 4 the Cup CalderContender-4
02Parkhurst Retro-65
Minis-65
Hopefuls-CH1
02Private Stock Reserve Class Act-5
02Titanium-21
Blue-21
Red-21
Retail-21
Right on Target-5
02Topps-300
OPC Blue Parallel-300
OPC Red Parallel-300
Factory Set-300
02Topps Total-234
02UD Honor Roll-13
02UD Premier Collection-11
02Upper Deck-200
Exclusives-200
02Upper Deck MVP-198
Gold-198
Classics-198
Golden Classics-198
02Upper Deck Rookie Update-22
02Vanguard-21
LTD-21
Prime Prospects-7
03BAP Ultimate Memorabilia Autographs-55
Gold-55
03Beehive-45
Gold-45
Silver-45
03Black Diamond-141
Black-141
Green-141
Red-141
03Blackhawks Postcards-2
03Bowman-13
Gold-13
Future Fabrics-FF-TA
Future Fabric Patches-TA
Future Rivals-AK
Future Rivals Patches-AK
03Bowman Chrome-13
Refractors-13
Gold Refractors-13
Xfractors-13
03Crown Royale-19
Blue-19
Retail-19
03eTopps-5
03ITG Action-103
Jerseys-M93
03ITG Used Signature Series-78
Gold-78
Autographs-TA
Autographs Gold-TA
Franchise-7
Franchise Autographs-7
Franchise Gold-7
03NHL Sticker Collection-178
03O-Pee-Chee-58
03OPC Blue-58
03OPC Gold-58
03OPC Red-58
03Pacific-69
Blue-69
Red-69
03Pacific Calder Contenders Entry Draft-4
03Pacific Calder-19
Silver-19
03Pacific Complete-43
Red-43
03Pacific Exhibit-30
Blue Backs-30
Yellow Backs-30
03Pacific Invincible New Sensations-8
03Pacific Prism-23
Blue-23
Gold-23
Red-23
Paramount Prodigies-5
Rookie Revolution-4
03Pacific Quest for the Cup-19
Blue-19
03Pacific Supreme-18
Blue-18
Red-18
Retail-18
03Parkhurst Original Six Chicago-1
Memorabilia-CM7
03Parkhurst Orig Six He Shoots/Scores-20
03Parkhurst Orig Six He Shoots/Scores-20A
03SP Authentic-18
Limited-18
03Topps-58
Blue-58
Gold-58
Red-58
Box Toppers-22
Topps/OPC Idols-UI13
Own the Game-OTG7
03Topps C55-25
Minis-25
Minis American Back-25
Minis American Back Red-25
Minis Bazooka Back-25
Minis Brooklyn Back-25
Minis Hat Trick Back-25
Minis O Canada Back-25
Minis O Canada Back Red-25
Minis Stanley Cup Back-25
03Topps Pristine-73
Gold Refractor Die Cuts-73
Refractors-73
Press Plates Black-73
Press Plates Cyan-73
Press Plates Magenta-73
Press Plates Yellow-73
03UD Honor Roll-16
03Upper Deck-42
Canadian Exclusives-42
HG-42
03Upper Deck MVP-94
Gold Script-94
Silver Script-94
Canadian Exclusives-94
04Pacific-56
Blue-56
Red-56
04SP Authentic-19
Limited-19
Sign of the Times-ST-TA
04UD All-World-46
Gold-46
Autographs-46
04Upper Deck-39
Canadian Exclusives-39
HG Glossy Gold-39
HG Glossy Silver-39
05Beehive Signature Scrapbook-SSTA
05Black Diamond-20
Emerald-20
Gold-20
Onyx-20
Ruby-20
05Panini Stickers-215
05Parkhurst-349
Facsimile Auto Parallel-101
05SP Authentic Prestigious Pairings-PPRA
05SP Authentic Scripts to Success-SSTA
05SP Authentic Sign of the Times-TA
05SP Game Used-22
Autographs-22
Gold-22
Auto Draft-AD-TA
SIGnificance-TA
SIGnificance Gold-S-TA
Statscriptions-ST-TA
05UD Artifacts-23
Blue-23
Gold-23
Green-23
Pewter-23
Red-23
Gold Autographed-23
05Ultra-50
Gold-50
Ice-50
05Upper Deck-42
HG Glossy-42
Notable Numbers-N-TA
Ice Glacial Graphs-GGTA
Ice Glacial Graphs Labels-GGTA
05Upper Deck MVP-91
Gold-91
Platinum-91
ProSign-P-TA
05Upper Deck Toronto Fall Expo-42
05Upper Deck Victory-42
Black-42
Gold-42
Silver-42
06Avalanche Team Postcards-1
06O-Pee-Chee-123
Rainbow-123
06Upper Deck-301
Exclusives Parallel-301
High Gloss Parallel-301
Masterpieces-301
Signatures-STA
Signature Sensations-SSTA

Arnesen, Svein Harald
92Norwegian Elite Series-31

Arnholt, P.M.
95German DEL-333

Arniel, Jamie
05Guelph Storm-A-02
06Guelph Storm-19

Arniel, Scott
81Jets Postcards-1
82Jets Postcards-1
82Post Cereal-21
83Jets Postcards-1
83NHL Key Tags-135
83O-Pee-Chee-379
83Puffy Stickers-2
83Vachon-121
84Jets Police-1
84O-Pee-Chee-333
84O-Pee-Chee Stickers-286
847-Eleven Discs-55
85Jets Police-1
86O-Pee-Chee-194
86Sabres Blue Shield-3
86Sabres Blue Shield Small-3
86Topps-194
87O-Pee-Chee-137
87Sabres Blue Shield-3
87Sabres Wonder Bread/Hostess-4
87Topps-137
88O-Pee-Chee-90
88O-Pee-Chee Stickers-258
88Panini Stickers-224
88Sabres Blue Shield-3
88Sabres Wonder Bread/Hostess-3
88Topps-90
89O-Pee-Chee-187
89Panini Stickers-213
89Sabres Blue Shield-2
89Sabres Campbell's-3
89Topps-187
90Bowman-243
Tiffany-243
90Jets IGA-1
90O-Pee-Chee-324
90OPC Premier-1
90Panini Stickers-30
90Pro Set-18A
90Pro Set-18B
90Pro Set-557
90Score-251
Canadian-251
90Score Rookie/Traded-68T
90Topps-324
Tiffany-324
90Upper Deck-397
French-397
91Bowman-206
91Jets Panini Team Stickers-1
91O-Pee-Chee-137
91Panini Stickers-74
91Score Canadian Bilingual-256
91Score Canadian English-256
91Stadium Club-30
91Topps-137
92San Diego Gulls-3
93San Diego Gulls-2
95Houston Aeros-1
96Collector's Edge Ice-129
Prism-129
97Manitoba Moose-A7
98Manitoba Moose-C1

Arnmark, Goran
85Swedish Panini Stickers-200
89Swedish Semic Elitserien Stickers-170
90Swedish Semic Elitserien Stickers-4
91Swedish Semic Elitserien Stickers-202

Arnold, John
93Michigan Wolverines-1

Arnold, Lee
98Sioux City Musketeers-1
03Colorado Eagles-1
05Colorado Eagles-2
06Colorado EaglesA -3

Arnold, Scott
92Quebec Pee-Wee Tournament-285
93Quebec Pee-Wee Tournament-1458

Arnost, Tomas
94Czech APS Extraliga-258
95Czech APS Extraliga-155

Arnott, Jason
91Oshawa Generals-20
91Oshawa Generals Sheet-14
917th Inn. Sketch OHL-148
92Oshawa Generals Sheet-4
93Donruss-120
Rated Rookies-12
Special Print-H
93Kraft-67
93Leaf-382
Freshman Phenoms-7
93Parkhurst-261
Emerald Ice-261
Calder Candidates-C6
Calder Candidates Gold-C6
East/West Stars-W8
93Pinnacle-441
Canadian-441
Super Rookies-7
Super Rookies Canadian-7
93PowerPlay-337
Rookie Standouts-1
93Score-594
Gold-594
Canadian-594
Canadian Gold-594
Dynamic Duos Canadian-7
93Stadium Club-345
Members Only Master Set-345
First Day Issue-345
93Ultra-312
Wave of the Future-1
93Upper Deck-423
Silver Skates-R9
Silver Skates Gold-R9
SP-48
93Classic-7
Top Ten-DP7
93Classic Four-Sport *-191
Gold-191
94Be A Player-R34
94Be A Player-R93
94Be A Player-R134
Signature Cards-110
94Canada Games NHL POGS-97
94Donruss-25
Elite Inserts-1
94Finest-21
Super Team Winners-21
Refractors-21
94Flair-56
Center Spotlight-1
94Fleer-68
Franchise Futures-1
94Kraft-15
94Leaf-133
Gold Rookies-2
Gold Stars-10
Limited Inserts-8
94Leaf Limited-66
94McDonald's Upper Deck-McD37
94OPC Premier-193
94OPC Premier-530
94O-Pee-Chee Finest Inserts-10
94OPC Premier Special Effects-193
94OPC Premier Special Effects-530
94Parkhurst-271
Gold-271
Crash the Game Green-8
Crash the Game Blue-8
Crash the Game Gold-8
Crash the Game Red-8
Vintage-V84
94Parkhurst SE-SE59
Gold-SE59
94Pinnacle-124
94Pinnacle-463
Artist's Proofs-124
Artist's Proofs-463
Rink Collection-124
Rink Collection-463
Northern Lights-NL14
94Post Box Backs-2
94Score Samples-254
94Score-254
Gold-254
Platinum-254
Franchise-TF8
94Select-87
Gold-87
94SP-40
Die Cuts-40
94Stadium Club Members Only-49
94Stadium Club-7
94Stadium Club-115
Members Only Master Set-7
Members Only Master Set-115
First Day Issue-7
First Day Issue-115
Super Team Winner Cards-7
Super Team Winner Cards-115
94Topps/OPC Premier-193
94Topps/OPC Premier-530
Special Effects-193
Special Effects-530
94Ultra-68
All-Rookies-1
All-Rookies Parallel-1
Power-2
Premier Pivots-1
94Upper Deck-305
Electric Ice-305
Ice Gallery-IG2
SP Inserts-SP26
SP Inserts Die Cuts-SP26
94Upper Deck NHLPA/Be A Player-19
94Classic-TC1
All-Rookie Team-AR2
94Classic Pro Prospects-11
94Classic Pro Prospects-NNO
Jumbos-PP1
Prototype-NNO
94Images *-62
94Images *-142
95Bashan Super Stickers-44
Die-Cut-13
95Canada Games NHL POGS-106
95Collector's Choice-41
Player's Club-41
Player's Club Platinum-41
Crash The Game-C19A
Crash The Game-C19B
Crash The Game-C19C
Crash The Game Gold-C19A
Crash The Game Gold-C19B
Crash The Game Gold-C19C
Crash the Game Silver Redeemed-C19
Crash the Game Silver Bonus-C19
Crash the Game Gold Redeemed-C19
Crash the Game Gold Bonus-C19
95Donruss-44
95Donruss Elite-101
Die Cut Stars-101
Die Cut Uncut-101
95Emotion-61
95Finest-139
Refractors-139
95Hoyle Western Playing Cards-3
95Imperial Stickers-44
Die Cut Superstars-13
95Kraft-2
95Leaf-119
95Leaf Limited-22
95McDonald's Pinnacle-MCD-14
95Metal-52
Iron Warriors-1
95NHL Aces Playing Cards-6D
95Panini Stickers-255
95Parkhurst International-73
Emerald Ice-73
95Pinnacle-16
Artist's Proofs-16
Rink Collection-16
Full Contact-8
95Pinnacle FANtasy-22
95Playoff One on One-37
95Post Upper Deck-13
95Pro Magnets-81
95Score Promos-8
95Score-8
Black Ice Artist's Proofs-8
Black Ice-8
Golden Blades-20
95Select Certified-9
Mirror Gold-9
Double Strike-8
Double Strike Gold-8
95SkyBox Impact-59
95SkyBox Impact-237
95SP-51
Holoviews-FX8
Holoviews Special FX-FX8
95Stadium Club Members Only-31
95Stadium Club-171
Members Only Master Set-171
95Stadium Club Master Photo Test-1
95Summit-18
Artist's Proofs-18
Ice-18
Mad Hatters-6
95Topps-17
95Topps-340
OPC Inserts-17
OPC Inserts-340
Canadian Gold-3CG
Marquee Men Power Boosters-17
Young Stars-YS10
95Topps SuperSkills-67
Platinum-67
95Ultra-52
Gold Medallion-52
Crease Crashers-1
High Speed-2
Rising Stars-1
Rising Stars Gold Medallion-1
95Upper Deck-29
Electric Ice-29
Electric Ice Gold-29
Special Edition-SE119
Special Edition Gold-SE119
95Zenith-23
Gifted Grinders-15
95Swedish Globe World Championships-95
95Swedish World Championships Stickers-11
96Be A Player Biscuit In The Basket-21
96Be A Player Link to History-5B
96Be A Player Link to History Autographs-5B
96Be A Player Link to History Auto Silver-5B
96Black Diamond-97
Gold-97
96Collector's Choice-92
96Collector's Choice-317
Crash the Game-C23A
Crash the Game-C23B
Crash the Game-C23C
Crash the Game Gold-C23A
Crash the Game Gold-C23B
Crash the Game Gold-C23C
Crash the Game Exchange-CR23
Crash the Game Exchange Gold-CR23
96Collector's Choice Blow-Ups Bi-Way-3
96Donruss-143
Press Proofs-143
Dominators-5
96Donruss Canadian Ice-68
Gold Press Proofs-68
Red Press Proofs-68
96Donruss Elite-46
96Donruss Elite-150
Die Cut Stars-46
Die Cut Stars-150
96Flair-32
Blue Ice-32
96Fleer-36
96Fleer Picks-58
96Leaf-179
Press Proofs-179
96Leaf Limited-43
Gold-43
96Leaf Preferred-20
Press Proofs-20
Steel-19
Steel Gold-19
96Maggers-1
96Metal Universe-52
96NHL Aces Playing Cards-2
96NHL Pro Stamps-81
96Oilers Postcards-7
96Pinnacle-118
Artist's Proofs-118
Foil-118
Premium Stock-118
Rink Collection-118
96Score-55
Artist's Proofs-55
Dealer's Choice Artist's Proofs-55
Special Artist's Proofs-55
Golden Blades-55
96Select Certified-38
Artist's Proofs-38
Blue-38
Mirror Blue-38
Mirror Gold-38
Mirror Red-38
Red-38
96SkyBox Impact-41
96SP-55
Holoview Collection-HC4
96Summit-103
Artist's Proofs-103
Ice-103
Metal-103
Premium Stock-103
96Team Out-22
96Ultra-57
Gold Medallion-57
96Upper Deck-57
Generation Next-X12
Power Performers-P6
Superstar Showdown-SS19B
96Upper Deck Ice-20
Parallel-20
Stanley Cup Foundation-S9
Stanley Cup Foundation Dynasty-S9
96Zenith-65
Artist's Proofs-65
Assailants-3
96Swedish Semic Wien-97
97SLU Hockey Canadian-2
97SLU Hockey American-2
97Black Diamond-117
Double Diamond-117
Triple Diamond-117
Quadruple Diamond-117
97Collector's Choice-95
Star Quest-SQ7
97Crown Royale-52
Emerald Green-52
Ice Blue-52
Silver-52
97Donruss-145
Press Proofs Silver-145
Press Proofs Gold-145
97Donruss Canadian Ice-117
Dominion Series-117
Provincial Series-117
National Pride-12
97Donruss Elite-95
Aspirations-95
Status-95
97Donruss Limited-27
97Donruss Limited-79
Exposure-27
Exposure-79
97Donruss Preferred-31
Cut to the Chase-31
97Donruss Priority-97
Stamp of Approval-97
Direct Deposit-30
97Katch-55
Gold-55
Silver-55
97Kenner Starting Lineup Cards-2
97Leaf-61
Fractal Matrix-61
Fractal Matrix Die Cuts-61
97Leaf International-61
Universal Ice-61
97NHL Aces Playing Cards-24
97Pacific-79
Copper-79
Emerald Green-79
Ice Blue-79
Red-79
Silver-79
97Pacific Invincible-54
Copper-54
Emerald Green-54
Ice Blue-54
Red-54
Silver-54
97Pacific Omega-125
Copper-125
Dark Gray-125
Emerald Green-125
Gold-125
Ice Blue-125
97Panini Stickers-210
97Paramount-72
Copper-72
Dark Grey-72
Emerald Green-72
Ice Blue-72
Red-72
Silver-72
97Pinnacle-61
Artist's Proofs-61
Rink Collection-61
Press Plates Back Black-61
Press Plates Back Cyan-61
Press Plates Back Magenta-61
Press Plates Back Yellow-61
Press Plates Front Black-61
Press Plates Front Cyan-61
Press Plates Front Magenta-61
Press Plates Front Yellow-61
97Pinnacle Certified-124
Red-124
Mirror Blue-124
Mirror Gold-124
Mirror Red-124
97Pinnacle Inside-55
Coach's Collection-55
Executive Collection-55
97Pinnacle Tot Cert Platinum Blue-124
97Pinnacle Tot Cert Platinum Gold-124
97Pinnacle Totally Certified Platinum Red-124
97Pinnacle Tot Cert Mirror Platinum Gold-124
97Post Pinnacle-6
97Score-136
Artist's Proofs-136
Golden Blades-136
97SP Authentic-59
97SPx-18
Bronze-18
Gold-18
Silver-18
Steel-18
Grand Finale-18
97Studio-35
Press Proofs Silver-35
Press Proofs Gold-35
Portraits-29
97Upper Deck-66
Three Star Selects-17A
98Aurora-107
98Be A Player-78
Press Release-78
98BAP Gold-78
98BAP Autographs-78
98BAP Autographs Gold-78
98BAP Tampa Bay All Star Game-78
98Crown Royale-77
Limited Series-77
98Devils Team Issue-2
98Katch-82
98OPC Chrome-199
Refractors-199
98Pacific-261
Ice Blue-261
Red-261
98Pacific Dynagon Ice-107
Blue-107
Red-107
98Pacific Omega-135
Red-135
Opening Day Issue-135
98Panini Photocards-4
98Paramount-131
Copper-131
Emerald Green-131
Holo-Electric-131
Ice Blue-131
Silver-131
98Revolution-82
Ice Shadow-82
Red-82
98Topps-199
O-Pee-Chee-199
98UD Choice-118
Prime Choice Reserve-118
Reserve-118
98Upper Deck-120
Exclusives-120
Exclusives 1 of 1-120
Gold Reserve-120
98Upper Deck MVP-122
Gold Script-122
Silver Script-122
Super Script-122
ProSign-JAR
99Aurora-83
Premiere Date-83
99BAP Memorabilia-64
Gold-64
Silver-64
99BAP Millennium-148
Emerald-148
Ruby-148
Sapphire-148
Signatures-148
Signatures Gold-148
99Devils Team Issue-18
99O-Pee-Chee-194
99O-Pee-Chee Chrome-194
99O-Pee-Chee Chrome Refractors-194
99Pacific-234
Copper-234
Emerald Green-234
Gold-234
Ice Blue-234
Premiere Date-234
Red-234
99Pacific Dynagon Ice-113
Blue-113
Copper-113
Gold-113
Premiere Date-113
99Pacific Omega-132
Copper-132
Gold-132
Ice Blue-132
Premiere Date-132
99Panini Stickers-84
99Paramount-130
Copper-130
Emerald-130
Gold-130
Holographic Emerald-130
Holographic Gold-130
Holographic Silver-130
Ice Blue-130
Premiere Date-130
Red-130
Silver-130
99Revolution-83
Premiere Date-83
Red-83
Shadow Series-83
Copper-83
Gold-83
CSC Silver-83
99Topps/OPC-194
99Topps/OPC Chrome-194
Refractors-194
99Upper Deck MVP-120
Gold Script-120
Silver Script-120
Super Script-120
99Upper Deck Victory-172
00Aurora-80
Premiere Date-80
00BAP Memorabilia-262
Emerald-262
Ruby-262
Sapphire-262
Promos-262
00BAP Mem Chicago Sportsfest Copper-262
00BAP Memorabilia Chicago Sportsfest Blue-262
00BAP Memorabilia Chicago Sportsfest Gold-262
00BAP Memorabilia Chicago Sportsfest Ruby-262
00BAP Memorabilia Chicago Sun-Times Ruby-262
00BAP Memorabilia Chicago Sun-Times Gold-262
00BAP Mem Chicago Sun-Times Sapphire-262
00BAP Mem Toronto Fall Expo Copper-262
00BAP Memorabilia Toronto Fall Expo Gold-262
00BAP Memorabilia Toronto Fall Expo Ruby-262
00BAP Memorabilia Update Teammates-TM21
00BAP Memorabilia Update Teammates-TM27
00BAP Memorabilia Update Teammates Gold-TM21
00BAP Memorabilia Update Teammates Gold-TM27
00BAP Parkhurst 2000-P39
00BAP Signature Series-232
Emerald-232
Ruby-232
Sapphire-232
Autographs-64
Autographs Gold-64
He Shoots-He Scores Prizes-36
Jersey Cards-J38
Jersey and Stick Cards-GSJ38
Jersey Cards Autographs-J38
Jersey Emblems-E38
Jersey Numbers-IN38
00BAP Ultimate Memorabilia Autographs-46
Gold-46
00BAP Ultimate Mem Game-Used Jerseys-GJ45
00BAP Ultimate Mem Game-Used Emblems-E37
00BAP Ultimate Mem Game-Used Numbers-N37
00BAP Ultimate Mem Game-Used Sticks-GS45
00BAP Ultimate Memorabilia Teammates-TM30
00Black Diamond-101
00Devils Team Issue-1
00O-Pee-Chee-142
00O-Pee-Chee Parallel-142
00Pacific-231
Copper-231
Gold-231
Ice Blue-231

Premiere Date-231
00Paramount-141
Copper-141
Gold-141
Holo-Gold-141
Holo-Silver-141
Ice Blue-141
Premiere Date-141
00Private Stock-56
Gold-56
Premiere Date-56
Retail-56
Silver-56
00Revolution-84
Blue-84
Premiere Date-84
Red-84
00SP Authentic-54
00Stadium Club-99
Beam Team-BT21
00Titanium-53
Blue-53
Gold-53
Premiere Date-53
Red-53
Retail-53
00Topps/OPC-142
Parallel-142
00Topps Chrome-104
00Topps Chrome-165
OPC Refractors-104
OPC Refractors-165
Refractors-104
Refractors-165
00Topps Gold Label Class 1-96
Gold-96
00Topps Gold Label Class 2-96
00Topps Gold Label Class 2 Gold-96
00Topps Gold Label Class 3-96
00Topps Gold Label Class 3 Gold-96
00Topps Gold Label Bullion-B1
00Topps Gold Label Bullion One to One-B1
00Topps Premier Plus-22
Blue Ice-22
00Topps Stars-91
Blue-91
00Upper Deck-106
Exclusives Tier 1-106
Exclusives Tier 2-106
00Upper Deck Victory-140
00Upper Deck Vintage-212
00Vanguard-56
Holographic Gold-56
Holographic Purple-56
Pacific Proofs-56
01Atomic-56
Blue-56
Gold-56
Premiere Date-56
Red-56
Power Play-20
Team Nucleus-8
01BAP Memorabilia-53
01BAP Memorabilia-467
Emerald-53
Emerald-467
Ruby-53
Ruby-467
Sapphire-53
Sapphire-467
He Shoots-He Scores Prizes-10
Stanley Cup Playoffs-SC25
01BAP Signature Series Certified 100-C16
01BAP Signature Series Certified 50-C16
01BAP Signature Series Certified 1 of 1's-C16
01BAP Signature Series Jerseys-GJ-36
01BAP Sig Series Jersey and Stick Cards-GSJ-36
01BAP Signature Series Emblems-GUE-35
01BAP Signature Series Numbers-ITN-35
01BAP Signature Series Teammates-TM-17
01BAP Ultimate Memorabilia Name Plates-36
01Bowman YoungStars-89
Gold-89
Ice Cubed-89
01Crown Royale-84
Blue-84
Premiere Date-84
Red-84
Retail-84
01Devils Team Issue-1
01McDonald's Pacific-23
010-Pee-Chee-31
010-Pee-Chee Heritage Parallel-31
010-Pee-Chee Heritage Parallel Limited-31
010-Pee-Chee Premier Parallel-31
01Pacific-225
Extreme LTD-225
Hobby LTD-225
Premiere Date-225
Retail LTD-225
01Pacific Adrenaline-110
Blue-110
Premiere Date-110
Red-110
Retail-110
01Pacific Arena Exclusives-225
01Pacific Heads-Up-55
Blue-55
Premiere Date-55
Red-55
Silver-55
Stat Masters-10
01Parkhurst-99
01Parkhurst-375
Gold-99
Silver-99
Sticks-PS47
Teammates-T15
01Private Stock-54
Gold-54
Premiere Date-54
Retail-54
Silver-54
01Private Stock Pacific Nights-54
01Private Stock PS-2002-43
01SP Authentic-49
Limited-49
Limited Gold-49
01SPx-39
01Stadium Club-77
Award Winners-77
Master Photos-77
01Titanium-81
Hobby Parallel-81
Premiere Date-81
Retail-81
Retail Parallel-81
Double-Sided Jerseys-68
01Titanium Draft Day Edition-32
01Topps-31
Heritage Parallel-31
Heritage Parallel Limited-31
OPC Parallel-31
Autographs-AJA
Game-Worn Jersey-JJA
Jumbo Jersey Autographs-JJA-JA
01Topps Chrome-31
Refractors-31
Black Border Refractors-31
01Topps Heritage-75
Refractors-75
01Topps Reserve-82
Emblems-JAR
Jerseys-JAR
Name Plates-JAR
Numbers-JAR
Patches-JAR
01UD Mask Collection Dual Jerseys-PMAJ
01UD Playmakers-60
01UD Stanley Cup Champs-72
01Upper Deck-103
Exclusives-103
Tandems-T5
01Upper Deck MVP-115
01Upper Deck Victory-209
Gold-209
01Upper Deck Vintage-151
01Upper Deck Vintage-157
01Vanguard-55
Blue-55
Red-55
One of Ones-55
Premiere Date-55
Proofs-55
02Atomic-31
Blue-31
Gold-31
Red-31
Hobby Parallel-31
Jerseys-3
Jerseys Gold-3
Patches-3
Super Colliders-5
02BAP First Edition-242
02BAP First Edition-409H
02BAP Memorabilia-81
02BAP Memorabilia-247
02BAP Memorabilia-257
Emerald-81
Emerald-247
Emerald-257
Ruby-81
Ruby-247
Ruby-257
Sapphire-81
Sapphire-247
Sapphire-257
NHL All-Star Game-81
NHL All-Star Game-247
NHL All-Star Game-257
NHL All-Star Game Blue-81
NHL All-Star Game Blue-247
NHL All-Star Game Blue-257
NHL All-Star Game Green-81
NHL All-Star Game Green-247
NHL All-Star Game Green-257
NHL All-Star Game Red-81
NHL All-Star Game Red-247
NHL All-Star Game Red-257
02BAP Memorabilia Toronto Fall Expo-81
02BAP Memorabilia Toronto Fall Expo-247
02BAP Memorabilia Toronto Fall Expo-257
02BAP Sig Series Auto Buybacks 1998-78
02BAP Sig Series Auto Buybacks 1999-148
02BAP Sig Series Auto Buybacks 2000-64
02BAP Signature Series Team Quads-TQ16
02Bowman YoungStars-98
Gold-98
Silver-98
020-Pee-Chee-151
020-Pee-Chee Premier Blue Parallel-151
020-Pee-Chee Premier Red Parallel-151
020-Pee-Chee Factory Set-151
02Pacific-110
Blue-110
Red-110
Jerseys-14
Jerseys Holo-Silver-14
02Pacific Calder-17
Silver-17
02Pacific Complete-322
Red-322
02Pacific Exclusive-54
02Pacific Heads-Up-37
Blue-37
Purple-37
Red-37
02Parkhurst-155
Bronze-155
Gold-155
Silver-155
02Parkhurst Retro-103
Minis-103
02Private Stock Reserve-113
Red-113
Retail-113
Patches-113
02SP Game Used First Rounder Patches-JA
02Stars Postcards-24
02Topps-151
OPC Blue Parallel-151
OPC Red Parallel-151
Factory Set-151
02Topps Chrome-92
Black Border Refractors-92
Refractors-92
02Topps Total-338
02UD Piece of History-31
02UD Top Shelf-27
Dual Player Jerseys-STMA
Shooting Stars-SHAR
02Upper Deck-59
Exclusives-59
CHL Graduates-CGJA
CHL Graduates Gold-CGJA
02Upper Deck MVP-62
Gold-62
Classics-62
Golden Classics-62
02Upper Deck Victory-65
Bronze-65
Gold-65
Silver-65
02Upper Deck Vintage-85
Green Backs-85
Tall Boys-T23
Tall Boys Gold-T23
03BAP Ultimate Memorabilia Triple Threads-24
03Crown Royale-31
Blue-31
Retail-31
03ITG Action-167
Jerseys-M2
030-Pee-Chee-65
03OPC Blue-65
03OPC Gold-65
03OPC Red-65
03Pacific-102
Blue-102
Red-102
03Pacific Complete-295
Red-295
03Pacific Exhibit-46
Blue Backs-46
Yellow Backs-46
03Pacific Prism-34
Blue-34
Gold-34
Red-34
03Pacific Supreme-29
Blue-29
Red-29
Retail-29
03Stars Postcards-1
03Titanium-33
Hobby Jersey Number Parallels-33
Retail-33
Retail Jersey Number Parallels-33
03Topps-65
Blue-65
Gold-65
Red-65
03Upper Deck-303
Canadian Exclusives-303
HG-303
UD Exclusives-303
03Upper Deck MVP-131
Gold Script-131
Silver Script-131
Canadian Exclusives-131
03Upper Deck Victory-59
Bronze-59
Gold-59
Silver-59
04Pacific-82
Blue-82
Red-82
04Upper Deck-57
Canadian Exclusives-57
HG Glossy Gold-57
HG Glossy Silver-57
05Be A Player Signatures-JA
05Be A Player Signatures Gold-JA
05Panini Stickers-251
05Parkhurst-161
Facsimile Auto Parallel-161
05SP Authentic Sign of the Times-AT
05SP Authentic Sign of the Times Duals-DMA
05SP Game Used Authentic Fabrics Quad-MTGA
05SP Game Used Authentic Patches Quad -MTGA
05SP Game Used Auto Draft-AD-JA
05SP Game Used SIGnificance-JA
05SP Game Used SIGnificance Gold-S-JA
05SP Game Used Statscriptions-ST-JA
05The Cup Master Pressplate Rookie Update-248
05The Cup Stanley Cup Titlists-TJA
05Upper Deck-63
HG Glossy-63
Jerseys-J-JAR
NHL Generations-DAR
Notable Numbers-N-JAR
Patches-P-JA
05Upper Deck MVP-130
Gold-130
Platinum-130
Materials-M-JA
05Upper Deck Rookie Update-248
05Upper Deck Toronto Fall Expo-63
05Upper Deck Victory-65
Black-65
Gold-65
Silver-65
06Beehive-46
Matte-46
Signature Scrapbook-SSJA
06Black Diamond-46
Black-46
Gold-46
Ruby-46
Jerseys-JJA
Jerseys Black-JJA
Jerseys Gold-JJA
Jerseys Ruby-JJA
06Flair Showcase Stitches-SSJA
06Fleer-113
Tiffany-113
Fabricology-FJA
06NHL POG-35
060-Pee-Chee-286
Rainbow-286
Autographs-A-JA
Swatches-S-JA
06Panini Stickers-305
06SP Authentic Sign of the Times Duals-STVA
06SP Game Used-59
Gold-59
Rainbow-59
Authentic Fabrics Dual-AF2AS
Authentic Fabrics Dual Patches-AF2AS
Authentic Fabrics Triple-AF3NAS
Authentic Fabrics Triple Patches-AF3NAS
Autographs-59
Inked Sweaters-ISJA
Inked Sweaters Patches-ISJA
Inked Sweaters Dual-IS2AS
Inked Sweaters Dual Patches-IS2AS
Letter Marks-LMJA
SIGnificance-SJA
06SPx-58
Spectrum-58
06The Cup Autographed NHL Shields Duals-DASRA
06UD Artifacts Treasured Patches Black-TSAR
06UD Artifacts Treasured Patches Blue-TSAR
06UD Artifacts Treasured Patches Gold-TSAR
06UD Artifacts Treasured Patches Platinum-TSAR
06UD Artifacts Treasured Patches Red-TSAR
06UD Artifacts Treasured Swatches-TSAR
06UD Artifacts Treasured Swatches Black-TSAR
06UD Artifacts Treasured Swatches Blue-TSAR
06UD Artifacts Treasured Swatches Gold-TSAR
06UD Artifacts Treasured Swatches Platinum-TSAR
06UD Artifacts Treasured Swatches Red-TSAR
06UD Artifacts Tundra Tandems-TTKA
06UD Artifacts Tundra Tandems Black-TTKA
06UD Artifacts Tundra Tandems Blue-TTKA
06UD Artifacts Tundra Tandems Gold-TTKA
06UD Artifacts Tundra Tandems Platinum-TTKA
06UD Artifacts Tundra Tandems Red-TTKA
06UD Artifacts Tundra Tandems Dual Patches Red-TTKA
06UD Powerplay Specialists-SJA
06UD Powerplay Specialists Patches-PJA
06Ultimate Collection Jerseys Dual-UJ2-KA
06Ultimate Collection Patches Dual-UJ2-KA
06Ultimate Collection Signatures-US-JA
06Ultra-113
Gold Medallion-113
Ice Medallion-113
Uniformity-UJA
Uniformity Patches-UPJA
Uniformity Autographed Jerseys-UAJA
06Upper Deck Arena Giveaways-NSH5
06Upper Deck-362
Exclusives Parallel-362
High Gloss Parallel-362
Game Jerseys-JJA
Game Patches-PJA
Masterpieces-362
06Upper Deck MVP-163
Gold Script-163
Super Script-163
Jerseys-OJFA
Jerseys-OJWA
06Upper Deck Ovation-15
06Upper Deck Sweet Shot Signature Shots/Saves Sticks-SSSJA
06Upper Deck Trilogy-57
06Upper Deck Victory-67
06Upper Deck Victory-258
06Upper Deck Victory Black-67
06Upper Deck Victory Gold-67
07Upper Deck Ovation-75
07Upper Deck Victory-109
Black-109
Gold-109

Arnoult, Guillaume
93Quebec Pee-Wee Tournament-1646

Aro, Jorma
70Finnish Jaakiekko-119
71Finnish Suomi Stickers-169
72Finnish Jaakiekko-120
72Finnish Panda Toronto-18
73Finnish Jaakiekko-174
74Finnish Jenkki-4
78Finnish SM-Liiga-46
80Finnish Mallasjuoma-25

Aro, Kari
65Finnish Hellas-7

Aro, Seppo
70Finnish Jaakiekko-309
72Finnish Jaakiekko-322

Aromaki, Juhani
66Finnish Jaakiekkosarja-204

Aronchick, Bryan
01Arizona Icecats-1
02Arizona Icecats-1
03Arizona Icecats-1
04Arizona Icecats-1

Aronson, Steve
00Cleveland Lumberjacks-23
01Louisiana Ice Gators-2
02UK London Knights-13

Aronsson, Folke
56Swedish Alfabilder-56

Aronsson, Ivan
56Swedish Alfabilder-61

Arps, Tyler
06Sudbury Wolves-21

Arsenault, Benoit
03Rimouski Oceanic-1
03Rimouski Oceanic Sheets-5

Arsenault, Daniel
907th Inn. Sketch Memorial Cup-72

Arsenault, Dave
97Toledo Storm-19
99Louisiana Ice Gators-15

Arsenault, Jimmy
02Baie Comeau Drakkar-11

Arsenault, Shayne
93Anaheim Bullfrogs RHI-1

Arsenault, Yan
907th Inn. Sketch QMJHL-237
917th Inn. Sketch QMJHL-142

Arsene, Dean
96Regina Pats-14
97Regina Pats-7
98Kootenay Ice-3
00Kootenay Ice-1
02Hartford Wolf Pack-2
03Reading Royals-20
04Hershey Bears Patriot News-1
05Hershey Bears-1

Arseneau, Luis
93Quebec Pee-Wee Tournament-954

Arthur, Fred
820-Pee-Chee-245
82Post Cereal-14

Artursson, Greger
89Swedish Semic Elitserien Stickers-83
90Swedish Semic Elitserien Stickers-256
91Swedish Semic Elitserien Stickers-89
95Swedish Leaf-216
97Swedish Collector's Choice-56
98Swedish UD Choice-86
99Swedish Upper Deck-55
00Swedish Upper Deck-80
SHL Signatures-GA
02Swedish SHL-27
Parallel-27
03Swedish Elite-37
Silver-37
04Swedish Elitset-38
Gold-38

Artursson, Leif
65Swedish Coralli ISHockey-208

Artyukhin, Evgeni
00Russian Hockey League-393
01Russian Hockey League-143
02Russian Hockey League-191
02Moncton Wildcats-4
02Moncton Wildcats-5Å
03Hershey Bears-21
03Hershey Bears Patriot News-1
04SP Authentic Rookie Redemptions-RR27
04Springfield Falcons-11
05Beehive-133
Beige -133
Blue -133
Gold-133
Red -133
Matte-133
05Black Diamond-282
05Hot Prospects-268
En Fuego-268
Hot Materials-HMEA
Red Hot-268
White Hot-268
05Parkhurst-665
Facsimile Auto Parallel-665
Signatures-EA
True Colors-TCTBL
True Colors-TCTBL
05SP Authentic-214
Limited-214
05SP Game Used-173
Gold-173
05SPx-204
Spectrum-204
05The Cup-123
Autographed Rookie Patches Gold Rainbow-123
Black Rainbow Rookies-123
Masterpiece Pressplates (Artifacts)-227
Masterpiece Pressplates (Bee Hive)-133
Masterpiece Pressplates (Black Diamond)-282
Masterpiece Pressplates (Ice)-177
Masterpiece Pressplates (Rookie Update)-234
Masterpiece Pressplates SPA Autos-214
Masterpiece Pressplates (SP Game Used)-173
Masterpiece Pressplates (SPx)-204
Masterpiece Pressplates (Trilogy)-304
Masterpiece Pressplates Ult Coll-174
Masterpiece Pressplates (Victory)-278
Masterpiece Pressplates Autographs-123
Platinum Rookies-123
05UD Artifacts-227
05Ultimate Collection-174
Gold-174
Ultimate Debut Threads Jerseys-DTJEA
Ultimate Debut Threads Patches-DTPEA
05Upper Deck-462
05Upper Deck Rookie Showcase-RS27
05Upper Deck Rookie Showcase Promos-RS27
05Upper Deck Ice-177
05Upper Deck Rookie Update-234
Inspirations Patch Rookies-234
05Upper Deck Trilogy-304
05Upper Deck Victory-278
Black-278
Gold-278
Silver-278
05Springfield Falcons-8
06Black Diamond Jerseys-JEA
06Black Diamond Jerseys Black-JEA
06Black Diamond Jerseys Gold-JEA
06Black Diamond Jerseys Ruby-JEA
06Fleer Signing Day-SDEA
06Ultra-173
Gold Medallion-173
Ice Medallion-173
06Upper Deck Victory-175
06Upper Deck Victory Black-175
06Upper Deck Victory Gold-175
06Upper Deck Victory Next In Line-NL43

Arundel, John
51Laval Dairy Subset-99
52St. Lawrence Sales-63

Arvaja, Mika
92Finnish Jyvas-Hyva Stickers-45
93Finnish Jyvas-Hyva Stickers-144
93Finnish SISU-149
93Finnish SISU-189B
94Finnish SISU-133
95Finnish SISU-244
96Finnish SISU Redline-33
98Finnish Kerailysarja-85
99Finnish Cardset-56
00German DEL-200

Arvaja, Pertti
71Finnish Suomi Stickers-97
72Finnish Jaakiekko-138
73Finnish Jaakiekko-105

Arvanitis, Peter
90Montreal-Bourassa AAA-6
92British Columbia JHL-57
98Oklahoma City Blazers-1
03Oklahoma City Blazers-2

Arvedson, Magnus
93Swedish Semic Elitserien-86
94Swedish Leaf-196
95Swedish Leaf-43
95Swedish Upper Deck-67
97Be A Player-225
Autographs-225
Autographs Die-Cuts-225
Autographs Prismatic Die-Cuts-225
97Pacific Omega-153
Copper-153
Dark Gray-153
Emerald Green-153
Gold-153
Ice Blue-153
97Pinnacle-16
Artist's Proofs-16
Rink Collection-16
Press Plates Back Black-16
Press Plates Back Cyan-16
Press Plates Back Magenta-16
Press Plates Back Yellow-16
Press Plates Front Black-16
Press Plates Front Cyan-16
Press Plates Front Magenta-16
Press Plates Front Yellow-16
97Score-70
Artist's Proofs-70
Golden Blades-70
97Upper Deck-324
97Upper Deck Ice-37
Parallel-37
Power Shift-37
97Zenith Rookie Reign-5
98Pacific-306
Ice Blue-306
Red-306
98Panini Stickers-44
98Paramount-161
Copper-161
Emerald Green-161
Holo-Electric-161
Ice Blue-161
Silver-161
98Senators Team Issue-2
98Upper Deck-138
Exclusives-138
Exclusives 1 of 1-138
Gold Reserve-138
98Upper Deck MVP-142
Gold Script-142
Silver Script-142
Super Script-142
99Aurora-98
Premiere Date-98
99BAP Memorabilia-102
Gold-102
Silver-102
99BAP Millennium-171
Emerald-171
Ruby-171
Sapphire-171
Signatures-171
Signatures Gold-171
990-Pee-Chee-135
990-Pee-Chee Chrome-135
990-Pee-Chee Chrome Refractors-135
990-Pee-Chee Chrome Positive Performers-PP4
99OPC Chrome Pos Performers Ref-PP4
990-Pee-Chee Positive Performers-PP4
99Pacific-284
Copper-284
Emerald Green-284
Gold-284
Ice Blue-284
Premiere Date-284
Red-284
99Pacific Dynagon Ice-137
Blue-137
Copper-137
Gold-137
Premiere Date-137
99Pacific Omega-157
Copper-157
Gold-157
Ice Blue-157
Premiere Date-157
99Panini Stickers-115
99Paramount-159
Copper-159
Emerald-159
Gold-159
Holographic Emerald-159
Holographic Gold-159
Holographic Silver-159
Ice Blue-159
Premiere Date-159
Red-159
Silver-159
99Revolution-101
Premiere Date-101
Red-101
Shadow Series-101
Copper-101
Gold-101
CSC Silver-101
99Senators Team Issue-2
99SPx-105
Radiance-105
Spectrum-105
99Stadium Club-52
First Day Issue-52
One of a Kind-52
Printing Plates Black-52
Printing Plates Cyan-52
Printing Plates Magenta-52
Printing Plates Yellow-52
99Topps/OPC-135
Positive Performers-PP4
99Topps/OPC Chrome-135
Refractors-135
Positive Performers-PP4
Positive Performers Refractors-PP4
99Topps Premier Plus-65
Parallel-65
99Upper Deck MVP-139
Gold Script-139
Silver Script-139
Super Script-139
99Upper Deck Victory-205
00BAP Memorabilia-185
Emerald-185
Ruby-185
Sapphire-185
Promos-185
00BAP Mem Chicago Sportsfest Copper-185
00BAP Memorabilia Chicago Sportsfest Blue-185
00BAP Memorabilia Chicago Sportsfest Gold-185
00BAP Memorabilia Chicago Sportsfest Ruby-185
00BAP Memorabilia Chicago Sun-Times Ruby-185
00BAP Memorabilia Chicago Sun-Times Gold-185
00BAP Mem Chicago Sun-Times Sapphire-185
00BAP Mem Toronto Fall Expo Copper-185
00BAP Memorabilia Toronto Fall Expo Gold-185
00BAP Memorabilia Toronto Fall Expo Ruby-185
00BAP Parkhurst 2000-P206
000-Pee-Chee-264B
000-Pee-Chee Parallel-264B
00Pacific-274
Copper-274
Gold-274
Ice Blue-274
Premiere Date-274
00Panini Stickers-67
00Paramount-170
Copper-170
Gold-170
Holo-Gold-170
Holo-Silver-170
Ice Blue-170
Premiere Date-170
00Senators Team Issue-2
00Topps/OPC-264B
Parallel-264B
00Upper Deck-353
Exclusives Tier 1-353
Exclusives Tier 2-353
00Upper Deck Victory-164
01BAP Signature Series-67
Autographs-67
Autographs Gold-67
01Pacific-270
Extreme LTD-270
Hobby LTD-270
Premiere Date-270
Retail LTD-270
01Pacific Arena Exclusives-270
01Parkhurst-183
01Senators Team Issue-2
01Upper Deck-123
Exclusives-123
01Upper Deck MVP-135
01Upper Deck Victory-249
Gold-249
01Upper Deck Vintage-178
01Upper Deck Vintage-182
02BAP First Edition-161
02BAP Sig Series Auto Buybacks 1999-171
02BAP Sig Series Auto Buybacks 2001-67
02NHL Power Play Stickers-102
02Pacific-261
Blue-261
Red-261
02Pacific Complete-50
Red-50
02Senators Team Issue-2
02Senators Team Issue-13
02Topps Total-176
02Upper Deck-371
Exclusives-371
02Upper Deck Beckett UD Promos-371
02Upper Deck Victory-152
Bronze-152
Gold-152
Silver-152
02Upper Deck Vintage-180
03Beehive-186
Gold-186
Silver-186
03Canucks Postcards-2
03Canucks Sav-on-Foods-11
03ITG Action-460
03NHL Sticker Collection-96
03Pacific-233
Blue-233
Red-233
03Upper Deck-431
Canadian Exclusives-431
HG-431
UD Exclusives-431
03Upper Deck MVP-295
Gold Script-295
Silver Script-295
Canadian Exclusives-295
03Czech Stadion-531

Arvidsson, Berndt
57Swedish Alfabilder-76
64Swedish Coralli ISHockey-45
65Swedish Coralli ISHockey-45

Arvsell, Henrik
93Swedish Semic Elitserien-194
94Swedish Leaf Clean Sweepers-8

Asanger, Peter
94German First League-115

Asberg, Magnus
89Swedish Semic Elitserien Stickers-48

Aschaber, Ryan
02Windsor Spitfires-2

Ascroft, Brent
94Tri-City Americans-2
95Tri-City Americans-3

Aseev, Mikhail
05Halifax Mooseheads-21

Asham, Arron
95Upper Deck-509
Electric Ice-509
Electric Ice Gold-509
95Red Deer Rebels-1
96Red Deer Rebels-5
97Red Deer Rebels-2
97Bowman CHL-107
OPC-107
99BAP Millennium-130
Emerald-130
Ruby-130
Sapphire-130
Signatures-130
Signatures Gold-130
99Upper Deck-70
Exclusives-70
Exclusives 1 of 1-70
99Upper Deck Arena Giveaways-MC2
99Upper Deck Gold Reserve-70
99Upper Deck MVP-105
Gold Script-105
Silver Script-105
Super Script-105
99Upper Deck Victory-144
99Quebec Citadelles-25
00BAP Memorabilia-306
Emerald-306
Ruby-306
Sapphire-306
Promos-306
00BAP Mem Chicago Sportsfest Copper-306
00BAP Memorabilia Chicago Sportsfest Blue-306
00BAP Memorabilia Chicago Sportsfest Gold-306
00BAP Memorabilia Chicago Sportsfest Ruby-306
00BAP Memorabilia Chicago Sun-Times Ruby-306
00BAP Memorabilia Chicago Sun-Times Gold-306
00BAP Mem Chicago Sun-Times Sapphire-306
00BAP Mem Toronto Fall Expo Copper-306
00BAP Memorabilia Toronto Fall Expo Gold-306
00BAP Memorabilia Toronto Fall Expo Ruby-306
00Quebec Citadelles-22
Signed-22
01Quebec Citadelles-23
02BAP Sig Series Auto Buybacks 1999-130
03Black Diamond-93
Black-93
Green-93
Red-93
03ITG Action-319
03Pacific-208
Blue-208
Red-208
03Pacific Complete-304
Red-304
03Upper Deck-369
Canadian Exclusives-369
HG-369
UD Exclusives-369
03Upper Deck MVP-270
Gold Script-270
Silver Script-270
Canadian Exclusives-270
04Upper Deck Jersey Autographs-GJA-AA
05Parkhurst-310
Facsimile Auto Parallel-310
05Upper Deck MVP Materials-M-AA
06Black Diamond Jerseys-JAA
06Black Diamond Jerseys Black-JAA
06Black Diamond Jerseys Gold-JAA
06Black Diamond Jerseys Ruby-JAA
060-Pee-Chee-313
Rainbow-313
Swatches-S-AA
06Upper Deck-373
Exclusives Parallel-373
High Gloss Parallel-373
Game Jerseys-JAA
Game Patches-PAA
Masterpieces-373
Signature Sensations-SSAA

Ashbee, Barry
65Coca-Cola-16
70Esso Power Players-202
70Flyers Postcards-1
71Letraset Action Replays-21
710-Pee-Chee-104
71Toronto Sun-188
720-Pee-Chee-206
73Flyers Linnett-1
04ITG Franchises Update-488

Ashbee, Don
51Buffalo Bison-2

Ashby, Don
75Maple Leafs Postcards-2
75Maple Leafs Postcards-3
76Maple Leafs Postcards-2
770-Pee-Chee NHL-365
780-Pee-Chee-351
88Oilers Tenth Anniversary-112

Ashe, Tom
97Grand Rapids Griffins-2
98Grand Rapids Griffins-1
99UK London Knights-1

Ashley, John G
83Hall of Fame Postcards-02
85Hall of Fame-213

Ashton, Brent
79Canucks Royal Bank-1
80Canucks Silverwood Dairies-1
80Canucks Team Issue-1
80Pepsi-Cola Caps-101
81Rockies Postcards-1
820-Pee-Chee-135
820-Pee-Chee Stickers-227
82Post Cereal-11
82Topps Stickers-227
83NHL Key Tags-75
83North Stars Postcards-2
830-Pee-Chee-225
84Nordiques Postcards-1
85Nordiques General Foods-2
85Nordiques McDonald's-1
85Nordiques Placemats-1
85Nordiques Placemats-6
85Nordiques Provigo-2
85Nordiques Team Issue-1
850-Pee-Chee-170
850-Pee-Chee Stickers-153
86Kraft Drawings-2
86Nordiques General Foods-1
86Nordiques McDonald's-2
860-Pee-Chee-181
860-Pee-Chee Stickers-25
86Topps-181
870-Pee-Chee-100
870-Pee-Chee Stickers-108
87Panini Stickers-244
87Red Wings Little Caesars-1
87Topps-100
88Jets Police-1
88Jets Postcards-1
880-Pee-Chee-128
880-Pee-Chee Stickers-250
88Panini Stickers-40
88Topps-128
89Jets Safeway-1
89Kraft-46
890-Pee-Chee-181
890-Pee-Chee Stickers-138
89Panini Stickers-164
89Topps-181
90Bowman-130
Tiffany-130
90Jets IGA-2
900-Pee-Chee-24
90Panini Stickers-321
90Pro Set-323
90Score-31A
90Score-31B
Canadian-31A
Canadian-31B
90Topps-24
Tiffany-24
90Upper Deck-220
French-220
91Pro Set Platinum-155
91Bowman-211
91Bruins Sports Action-1
91Jets Panini Team Stickers-2
910-Pee-Chee-240
91Panini Stickers-70
91Pinnacle-280
French-280
91Pro Set-272
91Pro Set-352
French-272
French-352
91Score American-78
91Score Canadian Bilingual-78
91Score Canadian English-78
91Score Rookie/Traded-22T
91Stadium Club-90
91Topps-240
91Upper Deck-303
French-303
92Bowman-357
92Parkhurst-258
Emerald Ice-258
92Score-164
Canadian-164
92Stadium Club-146
92Topps-191
Gold-191G
92Ultra-1
93Score-434
Canadian-434
93Stadium Club-51
Members Only Master Set-51
OPC-51
First Day Issue-51
First Day Issue OPC-51
93Las Vegas Thunder-1

Ashton, Mark
01Vancouver Giants-3
04Lethbridge Hurricanes-1
05Lethbridge Hurricanes-1

Asikainen, Mika
95Finnish SISU-255
99Finnish Cardset-98

Ask, Morten
03ECHL All-Stars-241
03Toledo Storm-5
05Finnish Cardset -310
06Swedish SHL Elitset-168

Askarov, Marat
99Russian Hockey League-262

Askew, Kelly
93RPI Engineers-1
01UK Manchester Storm Retro-4

Askey, Tom
98Pacific-67
Ice Blue-67
Red-67
98Upper Deck-36
Exclusives-36
Exclusives 1 of 1-36
Gold Reserve-36
98Cincinnati Mighty Ducks-26
99Kansas City Blades Supercuts-1
00Rochester Americans-2
02Rochester Americans-1
03BAP Memorabilia Deep in the Crease-D13
03Rochester Americans-2
04Rochester Americans-2
05Finnish Cardset -188

Askimov, Sergei
01Russian Hockey League-172
02Russian Hockey League-237

Asland, Glenn
92Norwegian Elite Series-89

Aslin, Peter
83Swedish Semic Elitserien-2
85Swedish Panini Stickers-134
86Swedish Panini Stickers-138

87Swedish Panini Stickers-149
89Swedish Semic Elitserien Stickers-121
90Swedish Semic Elitserien Stickers-100
91Swedish Semic Elitserien Stickers-104
92Swedish Semic Elitserien Stickers-125
93Swedish Semic Elitserien-98
93Swedish Semic World Champ Stickers-1
94Swedish Leaf-54
Clean Sweepers-5

Aslund, Per
06Swedish SHL Elitset-187

Asp, Aaron
91Ferris State Bulldogs-1
92Ferris State Bulldogs-2

Aspenlind, Joshua
03Prince George Cougars-15
05Swift Current Broncos-14
06Chilliwack Bruins-11

Aspirot, Sebastien
04Rimouski Oceanic-5
05Rimouski Oceanic-6

Asplund, Anders
67Swedish Hockey-83

Asplund, Jan
86Swedish Panini Stickers-196

Asplund, Johan
00Swedish Upper Deck-29
01Swedish Brynas Tigers-2
02Swedish SHL-1
Netminders-NM8
Signatures Series II-26
05Swedish SHL Elitset-279
Gold-279
06Swedish SHL Elitset-134

Asselin, Kevin
01Cape Breton Screaming Eagles-23
02Cape Breton Screaming Eagles-15
03Cape Breton Screaming Eagles-22
04Cape Breton Screaming Eagles-2
05Cape Breton Screaming Eagles-18
06Bakersfield Condors-22

Asselin, Patrick
92Quebec Pee-Wee Tournament-1245
03Saginaw Spirit-1
04Saginaw Spirit-5
05Saginaw Spirit-1
06Saginaw Spirit-18

Asselstine, Ron
90Pro Set-681

Asseltine, Jack
23V128-1 Paulin's Candy-25

Assenmacher, Ben
01Lincoln Stars-1

Ast, Doug
91British Columbia JHL-135
92British Columbia JHL-24
95Vancouver VooDoo RHI-14
96Syracuse Crunch-16
97Long Beach Ice Dogs-1
98Long Beach Ice Dogs-1
99Long Beach Ice Dogs-8
00Manitoba Moose-2
01German Upper Deck-106
02German DEL City Press-149
03German DEL-76
All-Stars-AS11
04German DEL-83
04German Ingolstadt Panthers-2
05German DEL-142
06German DEL-92
All-Star Jerseys-AS1

Astafjev, Vladimir
74Swedish Stickers-83

Astashenko, Kaspars
98Cincinnati Cyclones-1
98Cincinnati Cyclones 2-12
00Pacific-382
Copper-382
Gold-382
Ice Blue-382
Premiere Date-382
00SPx-116
Spectrum-116
00Upper Deck-225
Exclusives Tier 1-225
Exclusives Tier 2-225
02Lowell Lock Monsters-15
05Finnish Cardset -205

Astashev, Alexander
03Russian Hockey League-212

Astley, Mark
91Lake Superior State Lakers-3
92Alberta International Team Canada-2
92Lake Superior State Lakers-5
93Donruss-44
93OPC Premier-342
Gold-342
93Parkhurst-295
Emerald Ice-295
93Stadium Club-311
Members Only Master Set-311
93Topps/OPC Premier-342
Gold-342
93Upper Deck-494
93Swiss HNL-138
94Score Team Canada-CT13
95Ultra-209
95Images-68
Gold-68
96Collector's Edge Ice-62
Prism-62
98Swiss Power Play Stickers-156
99Swiss Panini Stickers-156
00Swiss Panini Stickers-201
01Swiss HNL-28
02Swiss HNL-71

Aston, Peter
04Peterborough Petes Postcards-20
05OHL Bell All-Star Classic-14
06Finnish Cardset-346
06Finnish Porin Assat Pelaajakortit-7
06Oshawa Generals-18

Astrahantsev, Konstantin
93Swedish Semic World Champ Stickers-138
94Finnish SISU-339
94Finnish Jaa Kiekko-149
94Swedish Olympics Lillehammer*-280

Astrom, Bo
65Swedish Coralli ISHockey-146
69Swedish Hockey-324
70Swedish Hockey-228
72Swedish Stickers-285

Astrom, Goran
70Swedish Hockey-179
71Swedish Hockey-263

Astrom, Hardy
79Panini Stickers-165
79Rockies Team Issue-1
80O-Pee-Chee-269
83Swedish Semic Elitserien-148
84Swedish Semic Elitserien-219
85Swedish Panini Stickers-222

Astrom, Johan
03Bakersfield Condors-2

Astrom, Lennart
56Swedish Alfabilder-98

Atcheynum, Blair
86Saskatoon Blades Photos-1
89ProCards AHL-288
90ProCards AHL/IHL-178
91ProCards-107
97Be A Player-210
Autographs-210
Autographs Die-Cuts-210
Autographs Prismatic Die-Cuts-210
97Revolution-116
Copper-116
Emerald-116
Ice Blue-116
Silver-116
98Pacific-361
Ice Blue-361
Red-361
98Paramount-120
Copper-120
Emerald Green-120
Holo-Electric-120
Ice Blue-120
Silver-120
98Predators Team Issue-1
98Upper Deck-300
Exclusives-300
Exclusives 1 of 1-300
Gold Reserve-300
99Pacific-351
Copper-351
Emerald Green-351
Gold-351
Ice Blue-351
Premiere Date-351
Red-351
99Upper Deck MVP SC Edition-45
Gold Script-45
Silver Script-45
Super Script-45

Atchinson, A.
12C57-4

Atherton, P.J.
02Minnesota Golden Gophers-2
03Minnesota Golden Gophers-9
04Minnesota Golden Gophers-1
05Minnesota Golden Gophers-2

Atkins, Scott
95Slapshot-209

Atkinson, Brad
04Salmon Arm Silverbacks-17

Atkinson, Derek
97Lethbridge Hurricanes-1
99Lethbridge Hurricanes-1

Atkinson, Steve
70Esso Power Players-86
71O-Pee-Chee-162
71Sabres Postcards-86
72O-Pee-Chee-40
72Sabres Postcards-1
72Sargent Promotions Stamps-40
72Topps-47
73O-Pee-Chee-245
74Capitals White Borders-4
74NHL Action Stamps-311
74O-Pee-Chee NHL-192
74Topps-192

Attard, Jeff
03Las Vegas Wranglers-1
03Las Vegas Wranglers RBI-225
04Las Vegas Wranglers-11
06Toledo Storm-18

Attersley, Bob
52Juniors Blue Tint-84

Attwell, Ron
60Cleveland Barons-1
62Quebec Aces-1

Atyushov, Vitali
02Russian Hockey League-18
02Russian Hockey League-254
03Russian Metallurg Magnitogorsk-1

Aube, J.F.
96Charlotte Checkers-1
97Pensacola Ice Pilots-2
98Charlotte Checkers-1
98Charlotte Checkers-23
98ECHL All-Star Southern Conference-15
99Mississippi Sea Wolves-19

Aubin, Brent
05Quebec Remparts-19
05Quebec Remparts Signature Series-19
06Quebec Remparts-9
06Quebec Remparts-EL2
06ITG Heroes and Prospects Memorial Cup Champions-MC03

Aubin, Jean-Sebastien
98Pacific Omega-192
Red-192
Opening Day Issue-192
98Revolution-115
Ice Shadow-115
Red-115
98SP Authentic-105
Power Shift-105
98Upper Deck-350
Exclusives 1 of 1-350
Gold Reserve-350
98Kansas City Blades-23
99O-Pee-Chee-33
99O-Pee-Chee Chrome-33
99O-Pee-Chee Chrome Refractors-33
99Pacific-350
Copper-350
Emerald Green-350
Gold-350
Ice Blue-350
Premiere Date-350
Red-350
99Pacific Omega-194
Copper-194
Gold-194
Ice Blue-194
Premiere Date-194
99Pacific Prism-112
Holographic Blue-112
Holographic Gold-112
Holographic Mirror-112
Holographic Purple-112
Premiere Date-112
99Topps/OPC-33
99Topps/OPC Chrome-33
Refractors-33
99Upper Deck MVP-172
Gold Script-172
Silver Script-172
Super Script-172
99Upper Deck Victory-240
00Aurora-114
Pinstripes-114
Pinstripes Premiere Date-114
Premiere Date-114
Autographs-115
Styrotechs-9B
00BAP Memorabilia-54
Emerald-54
Ruby-54
Sapphire-54
Promos-54
00BAP Mem Chicago Sportsfest Copper-54
00BAP Memorabilia Chicago Sportsfest Blue-54
00BAP Memorabilia Chicago Sportsfest Gold-54
00BAP Memorabilia Chicago Sportsfest Ruby-54
00BAP Memorabilia Chicago Sun-Times Ruby-54
00BAP Memorabilia Chicago Sun-Times Gold-54
00BAP Mem Chicago Sun-Times Sapphire-54
00BAP Mem Toronto Fall Expo Copper-54
00BAP Memorabilia Toronto Fall Expo Gold-54
00BAP Memorabilia Toronto Fall Expo Ruby-54
00BAP Parkhurst 2000-P142
00BAP Signature Series-170
Emerald-170
Ruby-170
Sapphire-170
Autographs-200
Autographs Gold-200
00BAP Ultimate Memorabilia Goalie Sticks-G24
00Black Diamond Game Gear-LAU
00O-Pee-Chee-238
00O-Pee-Chee Parallel-238
00Pacific-324
Copper-324
Gold-324
Ice Blue-324
Premiere Date-324
00Paramount-195
Copper-195
Gold-195
Holo-Gold-195
Holo-Silver-195
Ice Blue-195
Premiere Date-195
Glove Side Net Fusions-15
Glove Side Net Fusions Platinum-15
00Private Stock-78
Gold-78
Premiere Date-78
Retail-78
Silver-78
PS-2001 New Wave-19
00Revolution-116
Blue-116
Premiere Date-116
Red-116
00SP Authentic Sign of the Times-JA
00SPx-55
Spectrum-55
00Stadium Club-98
00Titanium Game Gear-130
00Titanium Game Gear Patches-130
00Titanium Draft Day Edition-80
Patches-80
00Topps/OPC-238
Parallel-238
00Topps Chrome-148
OPC Refractors-148
Refractors-148
00Topps Gold Label Class 1-84
Gold-84
00Topps Gold Label Class 2-84
00Topps Gold Label Class 2 Gold-84
00Topps Gold Label Class 3-84
00Topps Gold Label Class 3 Gold-84
00Topps Heritage-107
00Topps Premier Plus-32
Blue Ice-32
00UD Heroes-96
00Upper Deck-142
Exclusives Tier 1-142
Exclusives Tier 2-142
00Upper Deck MVP-144
First Stars-144
Second Stars-144
Third Stars-144
00Upper Deck Vintage-285
00Upper Deck Vintage-295
00Upper Deck Vintage-296
Great Gloves-GG14
00Vanguard-78
Holographic Gold-78
Holographic Purple-78
Pacific Proofs-78
01BAP Memorabilia Goalies Jerseys-GJ16
01Between the Pipes-6
01Between the Pipes-96
Goalie Gear-GG27
He Shoots-He Saves Prizes-7
Jerseys-GJ16
Jersey and Stick Cards-GSJ15
Tandems-GT13
01O-Pee-Chee-121
01O-Pee-Chee Premier Parallel-121
01Pacific-310
Extreme LTD-310
Hobby LTD-310
Premiere Date-310
Retail LTD-310
01Pacific Arena Exclusives-310
01Pacific Heads-Up Quad Jerseys-18
01Parkhurst Teammates-T2
01Private Stock Game Gear-75
01Private Stock Game Gear Patches-75
01Topps-121
OPC Parallel-121
01Upper Deck Victory-287
Gold-287
02BAP Signature Series-14
Autographs-14
Autograph Buybacks 2000-200
Autographs Gold-14
02Between the Pipes-30
Gold-30
Silver-30
Double Memorabilia-17
Emblems-10
Jerseys-10
Numbers-10
Pads-11
Stick and Jerseys-10
Tandems-7
02ITG Used Goalie Pad and Jersey-GP7
02ITG Used Goalie Pad and Jersey Gold-GP7
02Pacific-305
Blue-305
Red-305
02Pacific Complete-55
Red-55
02UD Mask Collection-68
02UD Mask Collection-69
02UD Mask Collection Beckett Promos-68
02UD Mask Collection Beckett Promos-69
03BAP Memorabilia Deep in the Crease-D15
03ITG Action-480
03Pacific Complete-470
Red-470
03Wilkes-Barre Scranton Penguins-3
04Pacific-208
Blue-208
Red-208
05Upper Deck MVP-368
Gold-368
Platinum-368
06Between The Pipes Emblems-GUE57
06Between The Pipes Emblems Gold-GUE57
06Between The Pipes Jerseys-GUJ57
06Between The Pipes Jerseys Gold-GUJ57
06Between The Pipes Numbers-GUN57
06Between The Pipes Numbers Gold-GUN57
06Between The Pipes Prospect Trios-PT17
06Between The Pipes Prospect Trios Gold-PT17
06O-Pee-Chee-460
Rainbow-460
06Upper Deck-433
Exclusives Parallel-433
High Gloss Parallel-433
Masterpieces-433
06ITG Heroes and Prospects Jerseys-GUJ53
06ITG Heroes and Prospects Jerseys Gold-GUJ53
06ITG Heroes and Prospects Emblems-GUE53
06ITG Heroes and Prospects Emblems Gold-GUE53
06ITG Heroes and Prospects Numbers-GUN53
06ITG Heroes and Prospects Numbers Gold-GUN53

Aubin, Martin
04Baie-Comeau Drakkar-11
05Baie-Comeau Drakkar-22

Aubin, Mathieu
03Lewiston Maineiacs-1
06Hamilton Bulldogs-2

Aubin, Normand
82Maple Leafs Postcards-3
82O-Pee-Chee-316
82Post Cereal-18
84Nova Scotia Oilers-21

Aubin, Serge
95Hampton Roads Admirals-9
95Signature Rookies Auto-Phonex-4
95Signature Rook Auto-Phonex Phone Cards-4
96Cleveland Lumberjacks-3
96Cleveland Lumberjacks Multi-Ad-4
98Hershey Bears-15
00Crown Royale-119
00O-Pee-Chee-307
00O-Pee-Chee Parallel-307
00Pacific-125
Copper-125
Gold-125
Ice Blue-125
Premiere Date-125
00Paramount-67
Copper-67
Gold-67
Holo-Gold-67
Holo-Silver-67
Ice Blue-67
Premiere Date-67
00Private Stock-112
Gold-112
Premiere Date-112
Retail-112
Silver-112
00SP Authentic-100
Sign of the Times-AU
00SPx-95
Spectrum-95
00Titanium-112
Retail-112
00Titanium Draft Day Edition-112
00Titanium Draft Day Promos-112
00Topps/OPC-307
Parallel-307
00Topps Chrome-202
OPC Refractors-202
Refractors-202
00UD Pros and Prospects-100
00Upper Deck-182
Exclusives Tier 1-182
Exclusives Tier 2-182
00Upper Deck Ice-56
Immortals-56
Legends-56
Stars-56
00Upper Deck MVP-190
First Stars-190
Second Stars-190
Third Stars-190
00Upper Deck Victory-261
00Upper Deck Vintage-377
00Vanguard-112
Pacific Proofs-112
01BAP Memorabilia-130
Emerald-130
Ruby-130
Sapphire-130
01BAP Signature Series-58
Autographs-58
Autographs Gold-58
01Blue Jackets Donatos Pizza-3
01O-Pee-Chee-211
01O-Pee-Chee Premier Parallel-211
01Pacific-109
Extreme LTD-109
Hobby LTD-109
Premiere Date-109
Retail LTD-109
01Pacific Arena Exclusives-109
01Topps-211
OPC Parallel-211
01Upper Deck-52
Exclusives-52
Game Jerseys Series II-GNSA
Ice Jerseys-J-SA
01Upper Deck Victory-98
Gold-98
02BAP Sig Series Auto Buybacks 2001-58
03ITG Action-113
03Thrashers Postcards-1
04Upper Deck-11
Canadian Exclusives-11
HG Glossy Gold-11
HG Glossy Silver-11
05Parkhurst-27
Facsimile Auto Parallel-27
05Upper Deck MVP-18
Gold-18
Platinum-18

Aubrey, Ron
92Fort Worth Fire-1
93Fort Worth Fire-1
94Central Hockey League-55
94Oklahoma City Blazers-1

Aubry, Ludovic
01Swiss HNL-403
02Swiss HNL-402

Aubry, Peter
02Johnstown Chiefs-1
03Elmira Jackals-1

Aubry, Pierre
81Nordiques Postcards-1
82Nordiques Postcards-1
82O-Pee-Chee-277
83NHL Key Tags-107
83Nordiques Postcards-1
83O-Pee-Chee-289
917th Inn. Sketch QMJHL-273

Aubry, Serge
62Quebec Aces-2
72Nordiques Postcards-2
73Nordiques Team Issue-2
75O-Pee-Chee WHA-3
75Stingers Kahn's-1
76Nordiques Postcards-1
88Nordiques General Foods-6
88Nordiques Team Issue-2
89Nordiques Team Issue-1

Aubut, Maxime
04Drummondville Voltigeurs-23
05Drummondville Voltigeurs-21

Aubut, Pascal
93Quebec Pee-Wee Tournament-437

Auclair, Daniel
92Quebec Pee-Wee Tournament-148
93Quebec Pee-Wee Tournament-1101

Aucoin, Adrian
92Alberta International Team Canada-3
92Upper Deck-584
93Alberta International Team Canada-1
93OPC Premier Team Canada-3
93PowerPlay-478
93Ultra-458
93Upper Deck-251
94Score Team Canada-CT14
94Classic Pro Prospects Ice Ambassadors-IA1
94Classic Pro Prospects Intl Heroes-LP11
95Upper Deck-56
Electric Ice-56
Electric Ice Gold-56
96Be A Player-79
Autographs-79
Autographs Silver-79
96Canucks Postcards-6
97Pacific Invincible NHL Regime-198
97Score Canucks-14
Platinum-14
Premier-14
98Bowman's Best-36
Refractors-36
Atomic Refractors-36
98Pacific Omega-234
Red-234
Opening Day Issue-234
99BAP Memorabilia-292
Gold-292
Silver-292
Selects Silver-SL23
Selects Gold-SL23
99BAP Millennium-238
Emerald-238
Ruby-238
Sapphire-238
Signatures-238
Signatures Gold-238
99O-Pee-Chee-180
99O-Pee-Chee Chrome-180
99O-Pee-Chee Chrome Refractors-180
99Pacific-419
Copper-419
Emerald Green-419
Gold-419
Ice Blue-419
Premiere Date-419
Red-419
99Panini Stickers-312
99Panini Stickers-343
99Paramount-232
Copper-232
Emerald-232
Gold-232
Holographic Emerald-232
Holographic Gold-232
Holographic Silver-232
Ice Blue-232
Premiere Date-232
Red-232
Silver-232
99Topps/OPC-180
99Topps/OPC Chrome-180
Refractors-180
99Upper Deck MVP SC Edition-184
Gold Script-184
Silver Script-184
Super Script-184
00BAP Memorabilia-362
Emerald-362
Ruby-362
Sapphire-362
Promos-362
00BAP Mem Chicago Sportsfest Copper-362
00BAP Memorabilia Chicago Sportsfest Blue-362
00BAP Memorabilia Chicago Sportsfest Gold-362
00BAP Memorabilia Chicago Sportsfest Ruby-362
00BAP Memorabilia Chicago Sun-Times Ruby-362
00BAP Memorabilia Chicago Sun-Times Gold-362
00BAP Mem Chicago Sun-Times Sapphire-362
00BAP Mem Toronto Fall Expo Copper-362
00BAP Memorabilia Toronto Fall Expo Gold-362
00BAP Memorabilia Toronto Fall Expo Ruby-362
00O-Pee-Chee-269B
00O-Pee-Chee Parallel-269B
00Pacific-403
Copper-403
Gold-403
Ice Blue-403
Premiere Date-403
00Topps/OPC-269B
Parallel-269B
00Upper Deck-398
Exclusives Tier 1-398
Exclusives Tier 2-398
00Upper Deck Vintage-350
01Parkhurst-355
02BAP First Edition-294
02BAP First Edition-385
02BAP Memorabilia-26
Emerald-26
Ruby-26
Sapphire-26
NHL All-Star Game-26
NHL All-Star Game Blue-26
NHL All-Star Game Green-26
NHL All-Star Game Red-26
02BAP Memorabilia Toronto Fall Expo-26
02BAP Sig Series Auto Buybacks 1999-238
02BAP Signature Series Golf-GS3
02O-Pee-Chee-188
02O-Pee-Chee Premier Blue Parallel-188
02O-Pee-Chee Premier Red Parallel-188
02O-Pee-Chee Factory Set-188
02Pacific-232
Blue-232
Red-232
02Pacific Complete-167
Red-167
02Parkhurst-179
Bronze-179
Gold-179
Silver-179
Hardware-N8
02Topps-188
OPC Blue Parallel-188
OPC Red Parallel-188
Factory Set-188
02Topps Total-120
02Upper Deck MVP-116
Gold-116
Classics-116
Golden Classics-116
03ITG Action-329
03Pacific Complete-259
Red-259
03Upper Deck-121
Canadian Exclusives-121
HG-121
03Upper Deck MVP-269
Gold Script-269
Silver Script-269
Canadian Exclusives-269
04Pacific-163
Blue-163
Red-163
04UD All-World-63
Gold-63
04Upper Deck-111
Canadian Exclusives-111
HG Glossy Gold-111
HG Glossy Silver-111
04Swedish MoDo Postcards-5
04Swedish Pure Skills-64
Parallel-64
05Be A Player Dual Signatures-MA
05Be A Player Signatures-AA
05Be A Player Signatures Gold-AA
05Black Diamond-60
Emerald-60
Gold-60
Onyx-60
Ruby-60
05Panini Stickers-214
05Parkhurst-113
05Parkhurst-507
Facsimile Auto Parallel-113
Facsimile Auto Parallel-507
True Colors-TCCHI
True Colors-TCCHI
05Ultra-51
Gold-51
Ice-51
05Upper Deck-289
Jerseys-J-AA
Notable Numbers-N-AA
05Upper Deck Hockey Showcase-HS15
05Upper Deck Showcase Promos-HS15
05Upper Deck MVP-90
Gold-90
Platinum-90
05Upper Deck Victory-126
Black-126
Gold-126
Silver-126
06Be A Player-166
Autographs-166
Signatures-AA
06Blackhawks Postcards-1
06Fleer Signing Day-SDAA
06O-Pee-Chee-105
Rainbow-105
06Panini Stickers-215
06UD Artifacts Auto-Facts-AFAA
06UD Artifacts Auto-Facts Gold-AFAA
06Upper Deck Arena Giveaways-CHI4
06Upper Deck-294
Exclusives Parallel-294
High Gloss Parallel-294
Masterpieces-294
Trilogy Scripts-TSAA

Aucoin, Keith
01BC Icemen-4
02Providence Bruins-4
03Cincinnati Mighty Ducks-A1
05Hot Prospects-113
En Fuego-113
Red Hot-113
White Hot-113
05The Cup Masterpiece Pressplates (Ice)-258
05The Cup Master Pressplate Rookie Update-115
05Upper Deck Ice-258
05Upper Deck Rookie Update-115
05AHL All-Stars-1
06Albany River Rats-2

Aucoin, Phil
04Memphis RiverKings-14
05Florida Everblades-6

Audet, Alexandre
93Quebec Pee-Wee Tournament-938

Audet, Gerard
51Laval Dairy Lac St. Jean-23

Audet, Jonathan
93Quebec Pee-Wee Tournament-960

Audet, Philippe
95Classic-44
97Bowman CHL-52
OPC-52
02German DEL City Press-2
03German DEL All-Stars-AS10
03St. Georges de Beauce Garaga-1

Audet, Sebastien
92Quebec Pee-Wee Tournament-811
93Quebec Pee-Wee Tournament-965

Audette, Donald
89ProCards AHL-265
90Sabres Blue Shield-2
90Sabres Campbell's-2
90Upper Deck-519
French-519
90ProCards AHL/IHL-289
91Pro Set Platinum-249
91O-Pee-Chee-273
91Parkhurst-11
French-11
91Pinnacle-330
French-330
91Pro Set-524
French-524
91Sabres Blue Shield-2
91Sabres Pepsi/Campbell's-2
91Score American-389
91Score Canadian Bilingual-279
91Score Canadian English-279
91Topps-273
91Upper Deck-585
French-585
92Bowman-288
92O-Pee-Chee-117
92Panini Stickers-U
92Panini Stickers French-U
92Parkhurst-18
92Parkhurst-231
Emerald Ice-18
Emerald Ice-231
92Pinnacle-38
French-38
92Pro Set-18
Rookie Goal Leaders-3
92Sabres Blue Shield-2
92Sabres Jubilee Foods-11
92Score-393
Canadian-393
Sharpshooters-19
Sharpshooters Canadian-19
92Seasons Patches-43
92Stadium Club-112
92Topps-12
92Topps-206
Gold-12G
Gold-206G
92Ultra Rookies-2
92Upper Deck-2
92Upper Deck-306
93Donruss-32
93Leaf-272
93OPC Premier-61
Gold-61
93Panini Stickers-103
93Parkhurst-26
Emerald Ice-26
93Pinnacle-274
Canadian-274
93PowerPlay-295
93Score-77
Canadian-77
93Stadium Club-213
Members Only Master Set-213
OPC-213
First Day Issue-213
First Day Issue OPC-213
93Topps/OPC Premier-61
Gold-61
93Ultra-273
93Upper Deck-5
94Be A Player Signature Cards-31
94Canada Games NHL POGS-48
94Donruss-305
94Flair-15
94Fleer-19
94Leaf-64
94OPC Premier-289
Special Effects-289
94Parkhurst-23
Gold-23
94Pinnacle-244
Artist's Proofs-244
Rink Collection-244
94Score-157
Gold-157
Platinum-157
94Select-26
Gold-26
94Stadium Club-87
Members Only Master Set-87
First Day Issue-87
Super Team Winner Cards-87
94Topps/OPC Premier-289
Special Effects-289
94Ultra-19
94Upper Deck-30
Electric Ice-30
SP Inserts-SP97
SP Inserts Die Cuts-SP97
95Collector's Choice-217
Player's Club-217
Player's Club Platinum-217
95Donruss-141
95Donruss Elite-49
Die Cut Stars-49
Die Cut Uncut-49
95Emotion-14
95Finest-71
Refractors-71
95Leaf-274
95Leaf Limited-12
95Metal-12
95Panini Stickers-19
95Parkhurst International-292
Emerald Ice-292
95Pinnacle-104
Artist's Proofs-104
Rink Collection-104
95Playoff One on One-11
95Pro Magnets-106
95Score-101
Black Ice Artist's Proofs-101
Black Ice-101
95SkyBox Impact-14
95Stadium Club-54
Members Only Master Set-54
95Topps-214
OPC Inserts-214
95Topps SuperSkills-3
Platinum-3
95Ultra-15
Gold Medallion-15
95Upper Deck-2
Electric Ice-2
Electric Ice Gold-2
Special Edition-SE9
Special Edition Gold-SE9
96Be A Player-73
Autographs-73
Autographs Silver-73
96Black Diamond-30
Gold-30
96Metal Universe-12
96NHL Pro Stamps-106
96Pinnacle-59
Artist's Proofs-59
Foil-59
Premium Stock-59
Rink Collection-59
96Score-233
Artist's Proofs-233
Dealer's Choice Artist's Proofs-233
Special Artist's Proofs-233
Golden Blades-233
96Ultra-13
Gold Medallion-13
96Upper Deck-18
97Collector's Choice-28
Crash the Game-C12A
Crash the Game-C12B
Crash the Game-C12C
Crash the Game Exchange-CR12
97Donruss-44
Press Proofs Silver-44
Press Proofs Gold-44
97Donruss Limited-118
Exposure-118
97Donruss Priority-126
Stamp of Approval-126
97Leaf-99
Fractal Matrix-99
Fractal Matrix Die Cuts-99
97Leaf International-99
Universal Ice-99
97Pacific-184
Copper-184
Emerald Green-184
Ice Blue-184
Red-184
Silver-184
97Panini Stickers-16
97Pinnacle-102
Press Plates Back Black-102
Press Plates Back Cyan-102
Press Plates Back Magenta-102
Press Plates Back Yellow-102
Press Plates Front Black-102
Press Plates Front Cyan-102
Press Plates Front Magenta-102
Press Plates Front Yellow-102
97Pinnacle Inside-105
97Score-179
97Score Sabres-4
Platinum-4
Premier-4
97Upper Deck-20
98Katch-17
98Pacific-103
Ice Blue-103
Red-103
98Panini Stickers-17
98UD Choice-28
Prime Choice Reserve-28
Reserve-28
98Upper Deck-227
Exclusives-227
Exclusives 1 of 1-227
Gold Reserve-227
98Upper Deck MVP-96
Gold Script-96
Silver Script-96
Super Script-96
99Aurora-67
Premiere Date-67
99BAP Memorabilia-92
Gold-92
Silver-92
99BAP Millennium-121
Emerald-121
Ruby-121
Sapphire-121
Signatures-121
Signatures Gold-121
99O-Pee-Chee-89
99O-Pee-Chee Chrome-89
99O-Pee-Chee Chrome Refractors-89
99Pacific-186
Copper-186
Emerald Green-186
Gold-186
Ice Blue-186
Premiere Date-186
Red-186
99Paramount-107
Copper-107
Emerald-107
Gold-107
Holographic Emerald-107
Holographic Gold-107
Holographic Silver-107
Ice Blue-107
Premiere Date-107
Red-107
Silver-107
99Revolution-67
Premiere Date-67
Red-67
Shadow Series-67
99Topps/OPC-89
99Topps/OPC Chrome-89
Refractors-89
99Upper Deck-64
Exclusives-64
Exclusives 1 of 1-64
99Upper Deck Gold Reserve-64
99Upper Deck MVP-95
Gold Script-95
Silver Script-95
Super Script-95
ProSign-DA
99Upper Deck Victory-133
00BAP Memorabilia-290
Emerald-290
Ruby-290
Sapphire-290
Promos-290
00BAP Mem Chicago Sportsfest Copper-290
00BAP Memorabilia Chicago Sportsfest Blue-290
00BAP Memorabilia Chicago Sportsfest Gold-290
00BAP Memorabilia Chicago Sportsfest Ruby-290
00BAP Memorabilia Chicago Sun-Times Ruby-290
00BAP Memorabilia Chicago Sun-Times Gold-290
00BAP Mem Chicago Sun-Times Sapphire-290
00BAP Mem Toronto Fall Expo Copper-290
00BAP Memorabilia Toronto Fall Expo Gold-290
00BAP Memorabilia Toronto Fall Expo Ruby-290
00BAP Parkhurst 2000-P171
00Crown Royale-4
Ice Blue-4
Limited Series-4
Premiere Date-4
Red-4
00O-Pee-Chee-148
00O-Pee-Chee Parallel-148
00Pacific-14
Copper-14
Gold-14
Ice Blue-14
Premiere Date-14
00Paramount-9
Copper-9

Gold-9
Holo-Gold-9
Holo-Silver-9
Ice Blue-9
Premiere Date-9
00SP Authentic-5
00Titanium-3
Blue-3
Gold-3
Premiere Date-3
Red-3
Retail-3
00Topps/OPC-148
Parallel-148
00Topps Gold Label Class 1-53
Gold-53
00Topps Gold Label Class 2-53
00Topps Gold Label Class 2 Gold-53
00Topps Gold Label Class 3-53
00Topps Gold Label Class 3 Gold-53
00Topps Heritage-115
00UD Heroes-6
00UD Pros and Prospects-4
00Upper Deck-10
Exclusives Tier 1-10
Exclusives Tier 2-10
00Upper Deck MVP-11
First Stars-11
Second Stars-11
Third Stars-11
00Upper Deck Victory-12
00Upper Deck Vintage-15
01BAP Signature Series Certified 100-C11
01BAP Signature Series Certified 50-C11
01BAP Signature Series Certified 1 of 1's-C11
01BAP Signature Series Autographs-LDA
01BAP Signature Series Autographs Gold-LDA
01Canadiens Postcards-1
01O-Pee-Chee-210
01O-Pee-Chee Premier Parallel-210
01Pacific-44
Extreme LTD-44
Hobby LTD-44
Premiere Date-44
Retail LTD-44
01Pacific Adrenaline-57
Blue-57
Premiere Date-57
Red-57
Retail-57
01Pacific Arena Exclusives-44
01Parkhurst-245
01Parkhurst-381
01SPx-179
01Topps-210
OPC Parallel-210
01Topps Heritage-175
01UD Mask Collection-50
Gold-50
01Upper Deck-60
Exclusives-60
01Upper Deck Ice-102
01Upper Deck Vintage-85
02BAP Memorabilia-32
Emerald-32
Ruby-32
Sapphire-32
NHL All-Star Game-32
NHL All-Star Game Blue-32
NHL All-Star Game Green-32
NHL All-Star Game Red-32
02BAP Memorabilia Toronto Fall Expo-32
02BAP Sig Series Auto Buybacks 1999-121
02BAP Sig Series Auto Buybacks 2001-LDA
02Canadiens Postcards-23
02NHL Power Play Stickers-50
02Pacific-190
Blue-190
Red-190
02Pacific Complete-115
Red-115
02Pacific Heads-Up-62
Blue-62
Purple-62
Red-62
02Topps Total-336
02Upper Deck MVP-98
Gold-98
Classics-98
Golden Classics-98
02Upper Deck Vintage-135
02Upper Deck Vintage-276
03Canadiens Postcards-1
03ITG Action-331
03Pacific-173
Blue-173
Red-173
03Pacific Complete-28
Red-28
03Upper Deck-344
Canadian Exclusives-344
HG-344
UD Exclusives-344

Audette, Gary
88Brandon Wheat Kings-6
89Brandon Wheat Kings-17
90Brandon Wheat Kings-20
907th Inn. Sketch WHL-235
91British Columbia JHL-20
92Dallas Freeze-2

Auer, Thomas
94German First League-361

Auffrey, Matt
04Wisconsin Badgers-3
05Kitchener Rangers-24
06Kingston Frontenacs-6

Aufiero, Patrick
02Hartford Wolf Pack-3
04Providence Bruins-1
05German DEL-1

Aufmann, Justin
97Dubuque Fighting Saints-2

Auge, Les
81Swedish Semic Hockey VM Stickers-97

Auger, Dominic
98Bowman CHL-112
Golden Anniversary-112
OPC International-112
98Bowman Chrome CHL-112
Golden Anniversary-112
Golden Anniversary Refractors-112
OPC International-112
OPC International Refractors-112
Refractors-112

Auger, Patrice
92Quebec Pee-Wee Tournament-673
93Quebec Pee-Wee Tournament-1111

Auger, Vincent
93Cornell Big Red-1

Augris, Maxime
93Quebec Pee-Wee Tournament-1489

Augusta, Josef
69Swedish Hockey-20
74Swedish Stickers-118
92Future Trends '76 Canada Cup-136
94Czech APS Extraliga-276
95Czech APS Extraliga-98
97Czech APS Extraliga-289
98Czech OFS-49
98Czech OFS-443
99Czech OFS-251

Augusta, Patrik
92St. John's Maple Leafs-1
93St. John's Maple Leafs-1
93Classic Pro Prospects-36
94St. John's Maple Leafs-1
96Collector's Edge Ice-148
Prism-148
97Long Beach Ice Dogs-2
98IHL All-Star Western Conference-12
98Long Beach Ice Dogs-2
99German DEL-206
00German DEL-220
00St. John's Maple Leafs-3
01German Upper Deck-151
02German DEL City Press-213
03German DEL-121
04German DEL-144
All-Stars-AS15
04German Hannover Scorpions Postcards-2
05German DEL-121

Augusta, Pavel
94Czech APS Extraliga-231
95Czech APS Extraliga-25
96Czech APS Extraliga-146
97Czech APS Extraliga-251
97Czech DS Extraliga-68
97Czech DS Stickers-247
98Czech DS Stickers-130
98Czech OFS-19
98Czech OFS-292
99German DEL-345
00Czech OFS-332

Augustine, Matthew
03Victoriaville Tigers-1

Augustsson, Bernt
69Swedish Hockey-310
71Swedish Hockey-147
72Swedish Stickers-130

Augustsson, Kjell
69Swedish Hockey-311
71Swedish Hockey-148
72Swedish Stickers-134
86Swedish Panini Stickers-108

Auhuber, Klaus
79Panini Stickers-101

Auld, Alex
99O-Pee-Chee-262
99O-Pee-Chee Chrome-262
99O-Pee-Chee Chrome Refractors-262
99Topps/OPC-262
99Topps/OPC Chrome-262
Refractors-262
99Bowman CHL-1
Gold-1
OPC International-1
Autographs-BA21
Autographs Gold-BA21
Autographs Silver-BA21
01BAP Memorabilia-386
Emerald-386
Ruby-386
Sapphire-386
01Between the Pipes-152
01Parkhurst-376
02BAP First Edition-250
02Between the Pipes-74
Gold-74
Silver-74
Future Wave-11
Tandems-12
02O-Pee-Chee-271
02O-Pee-Chee Premier Blue Parallel-271
02O-Pee-Chee Premier Red Parallel-271
02O-Pee-Chee Factory Set-271
02Pacific Complete-502
Red-502
02Topps-271
OPC Blue Parallel-271
OPC Red Parallel-271
Factory Set-271
02AHL Top Prospects-2
02Manitoba Moose-17
03BAP Memorabilia-101
Emerald-101
Gold-101
Ruby-101
Sapphire-101
Deep in the Crease-D10
Future Wave-FW-9
03BAP Ultimate Mem Franch Present Future-29
03Black Diamond-5
Black-5
Green-5
Red-5
03ITG Action-534
03Pacific Complete-485
Red-485
03Upper Deck-192
Canadian Exclusives-192
HG-192
03Upper Deck Classic Portraits-94
03Upper Deck MVP-422
Gold Script-422
Silver Script-422
Canadian Exclusives-422
SportsNut-SN85
03Upper Deck Trilogy-94
Limited-94
03Upper Deck Victory-185
Bronze-185
Gold-185
Silver-185
03Manitoba Moose-19
03Pacific AHL Prospects Crease Lightning-4
04Manitoba Moose-16
04ITG Heroes/Prospects He Shoots/Scores-30
04ITG Heroes and Prospects Net Prospects-13
04ITG Heroes and Prosp Net Prospects Gold-13
05ITG Heroes/Prosp Toronto Expo Parallel -50
05Hot Prospects-97
En Fuego-97
Red Hot-97
White Hot-97
05Parkhurst-469
Facsimile Auto Parallel-469
True Colors-TCVAN
True Colors-TCVAN
05Upper Deck-190
HG Glossy-190
Jerseys Series II-J2AA
05Upper Deck MVP-382
Gold-382
Platinum-382
05Upper Deck Rookie Update-97
05Upper Deck Toronto Fall Expo-190
05ITG Heroes and Prospects-50
Autographs-A-AA
He Shoots-He Scores Prizes-39
Measuring Up-MU5
Measuring Up Gold-MU5
Net Prospects-NP-13
Net Prospects Dual-NPD1
Net Prospects Dual Gold-NPD1
Net Prospects Gold-NP-13
06Between The Pipes-56
Autographs-AAA
Emblems-GUE68
Emblems Gold-GUE68
Emblems Autographs-GUE68
Jerseys-GUJ68
Jerseys Gold-GUJ68
Jerseys Autographs-GUJ68
Numbers-GUN68
Numbers Gold-GUN68
Numbers Autographs-GUN68
Prospect Trios-PT13
Prospect Trios Gold-PT13
06Flair Showcase Hot Gloves-HG29
06Fleer Fabricology-FAU
06ITG International Ice-109
Gold-109
Autographs-AAA
06O-Pee-Chee-215
Rainbow-215
06Ultra-85
Gold Medallion-85
Ice Medallion-85
06Upper Deck-336
Exclusives Parallel-336
High Gloss Parallel-336
Masterpieces-336
06Upper Deck MVP-125
Gold Script-125
Super Script-125
06Upper Deck Victory-191
06Upper Deck Victory-252
06Upper Deck Victory Black-191
06Upper Deck Victory Gold-191
06Upper Deck Victory Next In Line-NL47

Aulie, Keith
05Brandon Wheat Kings-1

Aulin, Jared
96Quebec Pee-Wee Tournament-245
98Kamloops Blazers-1
99Upper Deck Sobey's Memorial Cup-13
99Kamloops Blazers-1
99UD Prospects-46
99UD Prospects-70
00UD CHL Prospects-51
01Upper Deck-220B
02BAP Memorabilia-393
02BAP Ultimate Memorabilia-75
02Pacific Calder-120
Silver-120
02Pacific Complete-588
Red-588
02Parkhurst-206
Bronze-206
Gold-206
Silver-206
02Parkhurst Retro-207
Minis-207
02SP Authentic-178
02SPx-179
02UD Artistic Impressions-110
Gold-110
Right Track-RTJA
Right Track Gold-RTJA
02UD Honor Roll-136
02UD Mask Collection-148
02UD Premier Collection-103
Gold-103
02Upper Deck Classic Portraits-131
02AHL Top Prospects-3
02Manchester Monarchs-17
03BAP Memorabilia Future of the Game-FG-16
03Beehive Signatures-RF20
03ITG Action-247
Jerseys-M3
03O-Pee-Chee-327
03OPC Blue-327
03OPC Gold-327
03OPC Red-327
03Pacific-152
Blue-152
Red-152
03SP Authentic Sign of the Times-PAF
03Topps-327
Blue-327
Gold-327
Red-327
03Upper Deck-90
Canadian Exclusives-90
HG-90
Jersey Autographs-SJ-JA
Shooting Stars-ST-JA
03Upper Deck MVP-203
Gold Script-203
Silver Script-203
Canadian Exclusives-203
03Upper Deck Trilogy Scripts-S1JA
03Upper Deck Trilogy Scripts Limited-S1JA
04Portland Pirates-8
05Hershey Bears-2
06Springfield Falcons-24

Ault, Eva
03Backcheck: A Hockey Retrospective-19

Aurie, Larry
33O-Pee-Chee V304B-51
33V129-19
33V252 Canadian Gum-2
33V288 Hamilton Gum-44
33V357 Ice Kings-59
34Beehive Group I Photos-87
34Sweet Caporal-36
36O-Pee-Chee V304D-131
05ITG Ultimate Mem Motown Heroes Autos-6

aus den Birken, Danny
03German Mannheim Eagles Postcards-29
04German DEL-2

Austin, Ben
06UK Guildford Flames-18

Austin, Brady
95Medicine Hat Tigers-2
98Medicine Hat Tigers-1
01Fort Worth Brahmas-1

Austin, Colin
897th Inn. Sketch OHL-163

Austin, Darcy
907th Inn. Sketch WHL-121
917th Inn. Sketch WHL-336
93Flint Generals-7

Austin, Jesse
96Dayton Ice Bandits-2

Austman, J.
24Holland Creameries-10

Austring, Curtis
01Regina Pats-1
02Medicine Hat Tigers-1
02Regina Pats-12

Autere, Antti
90Richmond Renegades-3
91ProCards-448

Autotte, Martin
00Victoriaville Tigres-5
Signed-5
01Drummondville Voltigeurs-11

Auvinen, Hannu
70Finnish Jaakiekko-278
71Finnish Suomi Stickers-149

Avanthay, Pascal
95Swiss HNL-463
96Swiss HNL-364
00Swiss Panini Stickers-56
01Swiss HNL-285

Avdejev, Ivan
89Swedish Semic Elitserien Stickers-111

Averchenkov, Igor
99Russian Hockey League-68

Averill, Will
91Richmond Renegades Set 2-14
92Richmond Renegades-1
93Roanoke Express-2

Averkin, Vadim
00Russian Hockey League-91
02Russian Hockey League-53

Avery, Sean
96Owen Sound Platers-14
97Owen Sound Platers-12
98Owen Sound Platers-11
98Bowman CHL-35
Golden Anniversary-35
OPC International-35
98Bowman Chrome CHL-35
Golden Anniversary-35
Golden Anniversary Refractors-35
OPC International-35
OPC International Refractors-35
Refractors-35
99Kingston Frontenacs-2
01BAP Memorabilia-368
Emerald-368
Ruby-368
Sapphire-368
01Parkhurst-334
01SPx-204
01Titanium Draft Day Edition-125
01UD Honor Roll-72
01UD Mask Collection-143
Gold-143
01UD Premier Collection-96
01Cincinnati Mighty Ducks-1
02O-Pee-Chee-310
02O-Pee-Chee Premier Blue Parallel-310
02O-Pee-Chee Premier Red Parallel-310
02O-Pee-Chee Factory Set-310
02Pacific Complete-290
Red-290
02SPx-109
02Topps-310
OPC Blue Parallel-310
OPC Red Parallel-310
Factory Set-310
02Upper Deck-204
Exclusives-204
02Upper Deck MVP-201
Gold-201
Classics-201
Golden Classics-201
02Grand Rapids Griffins-2
03ITG Action-203
05Be A Player Signatures-AV
05Be A Player Signatures Gold-AV
05Parkhurst-226
Facsimile Auto Parallel-226
06Be A Player-165
Autographs-165
Signatures-AS
Signatures Duals-DAS
06O-Pee-Chee-228
06O-Pee-Chee-607
Rainbow-228
Rainbow-607
06Panini Stickers-286
06Upper Deck-343
Exclusives Parallel-343
High Gloss Parallel-343
Masterpieces-343
Statistical Leaders-SL7
06Upper Deck MVP-139
Gold Script-139
Super Script-139
07Upper Deck Victory-25
Black-25
Gold-25

Awada, George
99Albany River Rats-1
00Richmond Renegades-11
02Florida Everblades-2
02Florida Everblades RBI-116
03UK Manchester Phoenix-13

Awalt, Jasen
01Cape Breton Screaming Eagles-22

Awarda, George
04UK EIHL All-Stars-11

Awe, Clay
99Greensboro Generals-2

Awizus, Frank
99German DEL-406

Awrey, Don
65Coca-Cola-17
65Topps-99
67Topps-37
68O-Pee-Chee-3
68O-Pee-Chee-43
68Shirriff Coins-3
68Topps-3
68Topps-43
69O-Pee-Chee-203
70Bruins Postcards-20
70Bruins Team Issue-10
70Dad's Cookies-2
70Esso Power Players-71
70O-Pee-Chee-4
70Sargent Promotions Stamps-2
70Topps-4
71Bruins Postcards-18
71Letraset Action Replays-8
71O-Pee-Chee-3
71Sargent Promotions Stamps-13
71Toronto Sun-2
72O-Pee-Chee-170
Team Canada-1
72Sargent Promotions Stamps-23
73Blues White Border-2
73O-Pee-Chee-240
74NHL Action Stamps-237
74NHL Action Stamps Update-22
74O-Pee-Chee NHL-80
74Topps-80
75Canadiens Postcards-1
75Nabisco Sugar Daddy-22
75O-Pee-Chee NHL-344
76O-Pee-Chee NHL-311
77O-Pee-Chee NHL-137
77Topps-137
78O-Pee-Chee-383
91Future Trends Canada '72-17
91Future Trends Canada '72 French-17
94Parkhurst Tall Boys-19
95Parkhurst '66-67-12
Coins-12
98Bruins Alumni-26
Autographs-26
04ITG Franchises US East-332
Autographs-A-DA
04UD Legendary Signatures-93
Summit Stars-CDN16
Summit Stars Autographs-CDN-DA

Axelson, Niklas
93Minnesota-Duluth Bulldogs-2

Axelsson, Anton
05Swedish SHL Elitset Rookies-2
06Swedish SHL Elitset-180

Axelsson, Magnus
92Swedish Semic Elitserien Stickers-146
93Swedish Semic Elitserien-115

Axelsson, Per-Johan
94Parkhurst SE-SE240
Gold-SE240
94Swedish Leaf-248
95Swedish Leaf-204
97Be A Player-238
Autographs-238
Autographs Die-Cuts-238
Autographs Prismatic Die-Cuts-238
97Katch-7
Gold-7
Silver-7
97Pacific Omega-11
Copper-11
Dark Gray-11
Emerald Green-11
Gold-11
Ice Blue-11
97Upper Deck-220
98Pacific-69
Ice Blue-69
Red-69
98Panini Stickers-9
98Paramount-9
Copper-9
Emerald Green-9
Holo-Electric-9
Ice Blue-9
Silver-9
99Pacific-18
Copper-18
Emerald Green-18
Gold-18
Ice Blue-18
Premiere Date-18
Red-18
99Panini Stickers-28
99Upper Deck MVP SC Edition-15
Gold Script-15
Silver Script-15
Super Script-15
00Pacific-30
Copper-30
Gold-30
Ice Blue-30
Premiere Date-30
00Panini Stickers-12
00Titanium Game Gear-55
00Titanium Game Gear Patches-55
00Titanium Draft Day Edition-3
Patches-3
01Pacific-28
Extreme LTD-28
Hobby LTD-28
Premiere Date-28
Retail LTD-28
01Pacific Arena Exclusives-28
01Pacific Heads-Up Quad Jerseys-3
01Private Stock Game Gear-7
01Private Stock Game Gear Patches-7
01Upper Deck Victory-27
Gold-27
02Pacific Complete-182
Red-182
03Black Diamond-111
Black-111
Green-111
Red-111
03ITG Action-79
03Pacific-23
Blue-23
Red-23
03Pacific Complete-379
Red-379
03Parkhurst Original Six Boston-1
03Upper Deck-16
Canadian Exclusives-16
HG-16
03Upper Deck MVP-37
Gold Script-37
Silver Script-37
Canadian Exclusives-37
04Swedish Alfabilder Alfa Stars-22
04Swedish Alfabilder Autographs-104
04Swedish Alfabilder Limited Autographs-104
04Swedish Alfabilder Proof Parallels-22
04Swedish Elitset-178
Gold-178
04Swedish Pure Skills Signatures-2
05Bruins Boston Globe-24
05Panini Stickers-30
05Parkhurst-42
Facsimile Auto Parallel-42
05Upper Deck-16
HG Glossy-16
05Upper Deck MVP-32
Gold-32
Platinum-32
05Upper Deck Toronto Fall Expo-16
06O-Pee-Chee-34
Rainbow-34
06Panini Stickers-16
06Upper Deck-268
Exclusives Parallel-268
High Gloss Parallel-268
Masterpieces-268

Axelsson, Stefan
89Swedish Semic Elitserien Stickers-269
90Swedish Semic Elitserien Stickers-33
91Swedish Semic Elitserien Stickers-283
92Swedish Semic Elitserien Stickers-306
93Swedish Semic Elitserien-273
94Swedish Leaf-130
95Swedish Leaf-201
95Swedish Upper Deck-206

Ayer, Alain
93Swiss HNL-474
95Swiss HNL-298
96Swiss HNL-282
01Swiss HNL-371

Ayers, Michael
94Quebec Pee-Wee Tournament-1269

Ayres, Vern
33O-Pee-Chee V304B-65
33V357 Ice Kings-51
35Diamond Matchbooks Tan 1-2
35Diamond Matchbooks Tan 2-2
35Diamond Matchbooks Tan 3-2

Azevedo, Justin
04Kitchener Rangers-14
05Kitchener Rangers-6
06Kitchener Rangers-6
06Kitchener Rangers-LE1
06ITG Heroes and Prospects-192
Autographs-AJAZ
Update Autographs-AJAZ

Baaki, Bill
98Huntington Blizzard-1
99Huntington Blizzard-10

Babando, Pete
44Beehive Group II Photos-2
44Beehive Group II Photos-76
44Beehive Group II Photos-151
51Parkhurst-51
52Parkhurst-16

Babchuk, Anton
01Russian Young Lions-6
02BAP Memorabilia Draft Redemptions-21
02Russian Hockey League-21
03BAP Ultimate Memorabilia Autographs-100
Gold-100
03Beehive-225
Gold-225
Silver-225
03Blackhawks Postcards-3
03ITG Action-657
03ITG Toronto Spring Expo Class of 2004-6
03ITG Used Signature Series-189
Gold-189
03ITG VIP Rookie Debut-103
03Pacific Complete-528
Red-528
03Pacific Quest for the Cup-107
03Parkhurst Rookie-175
03Topps Traded-TT164
Blue-TT164
Gold-TT164
Red-TT164
03UD Premier Collection-68
03Upper Deck Rookie Update-141
03AHL Top Prospects-1
03Norfolk Admirals-3
03Pacific AHL Prospects-61
Gold-61
04AHL Top Prospects-37
04Norfolk Admirals-2
04ITG Heroes and Prospects-114
Autographs-ABAB
04ITG Heroes/Prospects Toronto Expo '05-114
04ITG Heroes/Prospects Expo Heroes/Pros-114
05Norfolk Admirals-6
06Hurricanes Postcards-4

Babcock, Bob
89ProCards AHL-84
90ProCards AHL/IHL-209
91Baltimore Skipjacks-15
91ProCards-569
92OPC Premier-56

Babcock, David
89Sault Ste. Marie Greyhounds-22
907th Inn. Sketch OHL-151
91Cornwall Royals-8
917th Inn. Sketch OHL-197

Babcock, Mike
917th Inn. Sketch WHL-275
94Spokane Chiefs-26
95Spokane Chiefs-25
96Spokane Chiefs-25
97Spokane Chiefs-27
98Spokane Chiefs-1
99Spokane Chiefs-1
01Cincinnati Mighty Ducks-26

Babcock, Shawn
81Kingston Canadians-5
83Moncton Alpines-24

Babe, Warren
86Kamloops Blazers-1
87North Stars Postcards-3
87Kamloops Blazers-1
88ProCards IHL-36
90ProCards AHL/IHL-101

Babenko, Nikolai
99Russian Hockey League-178
00Russian Hockey League-369

Babenko, Yuri
98Hershey Bears-5
00Black Diamond-115
00Hershey Bears-1
01Upper Deck Victory-367
Gold-367
01Hershey Bears-1
03Russian Hockey League-53
04Russian Moscow Dynamo-2

Baber, Brad
917th Inn. Sketch OHL-338
93Sault Ste. Marie Greyhounds-12
93Sault Ste. Marie Greyhound Memorial Cup-20

Babic, Marek
95Slapshot-286
95Owen Sound Platers-10

Babin, Jean-Francois
99Rimouski Oceanic-8
Signed-8
00Rimouski Oceanic-10
Signed-10

Babin, Michael
92Finnish Semic-228
93Swedish Semic World Champ Stickers-257
94Finnish Jaa Kiekko-226
94French National Team-4
95Swedish World Championships Stickers-105

Babin, Noah
04Notre Dame Fighting Irish-15

Babinov, Sergei
81Swedish Semic Hockey VM Stickers-41
82Swedish Semic VM Stickers-54
83Swedish Semic VM Stickers-54
84Russian National Team-1

Babiuk, Ed
61Sudbury Wolves-2
62Sudbury Wolves-3
63Rochester Americans-4

Babka, Daniel
02Czech OFS Plus-168
03Czech OFS Plus-256
04Czech OFS Czech/Slovak-23

Babkirk, Chris
93Lakeland Ice Warriors-3

Bablitz, Blaine
03Las Vegas Wranglers-2
06Odessa Jackalopes-1

Baby, John
78O-Pee-Chee-366
79O-Pee-Chee-357

Baby, Stephen
03Chicago Wolves-1
04Chicago Wolves-19
05Chicago Wolves-2

Babych, Dave
80Jets Postcards-1
80Pepsi-Cola Caps-121
81Jets Postcards-2
81O-Pee-Chee-358
81O-Pee-Chee Stickers-137
81Post Standups-26
81Topps-1
82Jets Postcards-2
82O-Pee-Chee-375
82O-Pee-Chee-376
82O-Pee-Chee Stickers-207
82Post Cereal-21
82Topps Stickers-207
83Esso-3
83Jets Postcards-2
83NHL Key Tags-140
83O-Pee-Chee-380
83O-Pee-Chee Stickers-163
83O-Pee-Chee Stickers-285
83O-Pee-Chee Stickers-286
83Puffy Stickers-1
83Topps Stickers-163
83Topps Stickers-285
83Topps Stickers-286
83Vachon-122
84Jets Police-2
84Kellogg's Accordion Discs-4
84Kellogg's Accordion Discs Singles-4
84O-Pee-Chee-334
84O-Pee-Chee Stickers-287
847-Eleven Discs-56
84Topps-150
85O-Pee-Chee-10
85O-Pee-Chee Stickers-249
85Topps-10
86O-Pee-Chee-73
86O-Pee-Chee Stickers-50
86Topps-73
86Whalers Junior Thomas'-2
87O-Pee-Chee-5
87O-Pee-Chee Stickers-208
87Panini Stickers-40
87Topps-5
87Whalers Jr. Burger King/Pepsi-2
88O-Pee-Chee-164
88O-Pee-Chee Stickers-267
88Panini Stickers-236
88Topps-164
88Whalers Junior Ground Round-2
89O-Pee-Chee-46
89O-Pee-Chee Stickers-265
89Panini Stickers-225
89Topps-46
89Whalers Junior Milk-2
90Bowman-256
Tiffany-256
90Kraft-1
90O-Pee-Chee-328
90Panini Stickers-40
90Pro Set-99
90Score-172
Canadian-172
90Topps-328
Tiffany-328
90Upper Deck-194
French-194
90Whalers Jr. 7-Eleven-2
91Canucks Autograph Cards-3
91Canucks Team Issue 8x10-3
91Parkhurst-187
French-187
91Pinnacle-270
French-270
91Pro Set-503
French-503
91Score Canadian Bilingual-584
91Score Canadian English-584
91Score Rookie/Traded-34T
92Bowman-119
92Canucks Road Trip Art-3
92O-Pee-Chee-213
92Panini Stickers-35
92Panini Stickers French-35
92Parkhurst-424
Emerald Ice-424
92Pinnacle-201
French-201
92Pro Set-200
92Score-212
Canadian-212
92Stadium Club-120
92Topps-138
Gold-138G
92Ultra-218
93OPC Premier-428
Gold-428
93Parkhurst-481
Emerald Ice-481
93PowerPlay-456
93Topps/OPC Premier-428
Gold-428
93Upper Deck-376
94Canucks Program Inserts-3
94Leaf-430
94OPC Premier-256
Special Effects-256
94Pinnacle-353
Artist's Proofs-353
Rink Collection-353
94Topps/OPC Premier-256
Special Effects-256
95Be A Player-94
Signatures-S94
Signatures Die Cuts-S94
95Canucks Building the Dream Art-18
95Ultra-315
96Canucks Postcards-44
97Be A Player-49
Autographs-49
Autographs Die-Cuts-49
Autographs Prismatic Die-Cuts-49
97Pacific Invincible NHL Regime-199
97Score Canucks-20
Platinum-20
Premier-20
04ITG Franchises Canadian-148
Autographs-DBB
04ITG Franchises US East-353

Babych, Wayne
78Blues Postcards-1
79O-Pee-Chee-142
79Topps-142
80O-Pee-Chee-281
81O-Pee-Chee-290
81O-Pee-Chee Stickers-130
81Topps-W114
82O-Pee-Chee-299
82O-Pee-Chee Stickers-201
82Post Cereal-17
82Topps Stickers-201
83O-Pee-Chee-310
84O-Pee-Chee-181
85Nordiques Provigo-3
85O-Pee-Chee-108
85O-Pee-Chee Stickers-103
85Topps-108
86O-Pee-Chee-213
86Whalers Junior Thomas'-3
92Blues UD Best of the Blues-10
04ITG Franchises US West-288
Autographs-A-WB
04UD Legendary Signatures-71
Autographs-WB
Linemates-BRBFWB

Baca, Jergus
89Swedish Semic World Champ Stickers-185
90OPC Premier-2
90Score Rookie/Traded-101T
91O-Pee-Chee-131
91Topps-131
91Upper Deck-425
French-425
91ProCards-94
92Topps-64
Gold-64G
92Finnish Semic-130
94Finnish Jaa Kiekko-199
94Swedish Leaf-168
Foreign Affairs-9
95Milwaukee Admirals-2
95Milwaukee Admirals Postcards-4
96Czech APS Extraliga-270
96Swedish Semic Wien-224
97Czech DS Stickers-174
99German DEL-294
00German DEL-211
Game Jersey-JB
01German Upper Deck-212
01Slovakian Kvarteto-1A
02Slovakian Kvarteto-12

Bacashihua, Jason
01BAP Memorabilia Draft Redemptions-26
01Plymouth Whalers-21
01Plymouth Whalers-29
02BAP Memorabilia-399
02BAP Ultimate Memorabilia-65
02Pacific Calder-113
Silver-113
02Pacific Complete-554
Red-554
02Pacific Quest for the Cup-114
Gold-114
02SP Authentic-206
02SPx-188
02Upper Deck Rookie Update-136
02AHL Top Prospects-4
02Utah Grizzlies-19
03BAP Memorabilia-123
Emerald-123
Gold-123
Ruby-123
Sapphire-123
03ITG Action-139
03Pacific Complete-453
Red-453
03SPx Big Futures-BF-JB
03SPx Big Futures Limited-BF-JB
03Upper Deck-64
Canadian Exclusives-64
HG-64
03Upper Deck MVP-138
Gold Script-138
Silver Script-138
Canadian Exclusives-138
03AHL Top Prospects-2
03Pacific AHL Prospects-92
Gold-92
04Worcester IceCats-19
04ITG Heroes/Prospects He Shoots/Scores-28
04ITG Heroes and Prospects Net Prospects-8
04ITG Heroes and Prosp Net Prospects Gold-8
05ITG Heroes/Prosp Toronto Expo Parallel -241
05Peoria Rivermen-21
05ITG Heroes and Prospects-241
Autographs Series II-JBC
Jerseys-GUJ-98
Jerseys Gold-GUJ-98
Measuring Up-MU4
Measuring Up Gold-MU4
Nameplates-N-62
Nameplates Gold-N-62
06Between The Pipes-18
Autographs-AJBA
Emblems-GUE21
Emblems Gold-GUE21
Emblems Autographs-GUE21
Jerseys-GUJ21
Jerseys Gold-GUJ21
Jerseys Autographs-GUJ21
Numbers-GUN21
Numbers Gold-GUN21
Numbers Autographs-GUN21
Prospect Trios-PT16
Prospect Trios Gold-PT16
06Fleer Fabricology-FJB
06Upper Deck Game Jerseys-J2JB
06Upper Deck Game Patches-P2JB

Baccari, Al
51Laval Dairy Subset-10
52St. Lawrence Sales-44

Bach, Lars
98Danish Hockey League-193
99Danish Hockey League-69

Bach, Ryan
91Air Canada SJHL-B28
96Toledo Storm-1
00Louisville Panthers-16
01UK Sheffield Steelers-2
03Colorado Eagles-2
Bachand, Nicolas
04Rimouski Oceanic-6
Bacharuk, Stewart
96Saskatoon Blades-1
Bachler, Matthias
95Swiss HNL-72
96Swiss HNL-16
96Swiss HNL-499
99Swiss Panini Stickers-315
00Swiss Panini Stickers-85
01Swiss HNL-245
Bachman, Richard
06Cedar Rapids RoughRiders-1
Bacho, Pavel
98Czech OFS-76
99Czech OFS-419
Bachofner, Adrian
93Swiss HNL-248
95Swiss HNL-224
96Swiss HNL-137
98Swiss Power Play Stickers-187
Bachschmied, Markus
93Swiss HNL-136
95Swiss HNL-185
96Swiss HNL-340
96Swiss HNL-551
98Swiss Power Play Stickers-328
Bachusz, Jeremy
93Quebec Pee-Wee Tournament-864
Bachusz, Mike
91Lake Superior State Lakers-4
92Lake Superior State Lakers-6
Bacik, Tim
917th Inn. Sketch OHL-331
93London Knights-3
Back, Anders
02Swedish SHL-251
Parallel-251
03Swedish Elite-112
Silver-112
Back, Daniel
97Mississippi Sea Wolves-10
00Indianapolis Ice-2
04Swedish Elitset-105
Gold-105
Back, Jan
64Swedish Coralli ISHockey-38
Back, Rene
01Swiss HNL-237
02Swiss HNL-263
04Swiss EV Zug Postcards-12
Backe, Per
84Swedish Semic Elitserien-18
Backer, Par
02Swedish SHL-175
Dynamic Duos-3
Next Generation-NG2
Parallel-175
03Swedish Elite-41
Signatures II-3
Silver-41
04Swedish Elitset-43
Gold-43
05Swedish SHL Elitset-49
06Swedish SHL Elitset-167
Backes, David
01Lincoln Stars-2
02Lincoln Stars-3
02Lincoln Stars-34
02Lincoln Stars-42
06Hot Prospects-186
06SP Authentic-218
Limited-218
The Cup Masterpiece Pressplates (SP Authentic)-218
06The Cup Masterpiece Pressplates (Ultimate Collection)-93
06Ultimate Collection-93
Backlund, Joakim
89Swedish Semic Elitserien Stickers-144
95Swedish Upper Deck-127
97Swedish Collector's Choice-126
98Swedish UD Choice-190
Backlund, Johan
03Swedish Elite-201
Silver-201
05Swedish SHL Elitset-62
Catchers-6
Catchers Gold-6
Gold-62
06Swedish SHL Elitset-276
Backlund, Patrik
95Swedish Leaf-282
Backman, Bert
71Swedish Hockey-383
72Swedish Stickers-257
Backman, Christian
99Swedish Upper Deck-74
99Swedish Upper Deck-216
00Swedish Upper Deck-62
00Swedish Upper Deck-213
SHL Signatures-CB
02BAP Memorabilia-331
02BAP Ultimate Memorabilia-52
02Upper Deck Rookie Update-175
02Swedish SHL-113
Parallel-113
02Worcester IceCats-22
03Blues Team Set-1
03Pacific Complete-599
Red-599
04Swedish Alfabilder Alfa Stars-8
04Swedish Alfabilder Autographs-122
04Swedish Alfabilder Limited Autographs-122
04Swedish Alfabilder Proof Parallels-8
04Swedish Elitset-172
Gold-172
04Swedish Pure Skills-18
Parallel-18
05Blues Team Set-1
05Parkhurst-423
Facsimile Auto Parallel-423
05SP Authentic Scripts to Success-SSCB
05SP Authentic Sign of the Times-CB
05SP Game Used Statscriptions-ST-CB
05Upper Deck-169
HG Glossy-169
Notable Numbers-N-CB
05Upper Deck MVP-336
Gold-336
Platinum-336
05Upper Deck Toronto Fall Expo-169
06O-Pee-Chee-433
Rainbow-433
Backman, Gunnar
65Swedish Coralli ISHockey-176
65Swedish Coralli ISHockey-209
67Swedish Hockey-116
67Swedish Hockey-265
69Swedish Hockey-128
69Swedish Hockey-183
70Finnish Jaakiekko-22
70Swedish Hockey-83
70Swedish Hockey-274
70Swedish Masterserien-107
71Swedish Hockey-175
71Swedish Hockey-330
72Swedish Stickers-145
Backman, Per
69Swedish Hockey-224
71Swedish Hockey-149
72Swedish Stickers-128
73Swedish Stickers-176
74Swedish Stickers-208
83Swedish Semic Elitserien-25
84Swedish Semic Elitserien-25
85Swedish Panini Stickers-2
87Swedish Panini Stickers-88
Backman, Simon
04Finnish Cardset-302
05Finnish Cardset -329
06Finnish Cardset-158
Backstrom, Anders
83Swedish Semic Elitserien-53
84Swedish Semic Elitserien-53
85Swedish Panini Stickers-49
86Swedish Panini Stickers-36
87Swedish Panini Stickers-52
Backstrom, Nicklas
05Swedish SHL Elitset-154
Star Potential-2
06Swedish SHL Elitset-152
Performers-1
Backstrom, Niklas
98Finnish Keralysarja-29
99Finnish Cardset-218
00Finnish Cardset-200
00Finnish Cardset Masquerade-4
02Finnish Cardset-148
02Finnish Cardset-160
03Finnish Cardset-85
04Finnish Cardset-91
04Finnish Cardset Signatures-21
04Swedish Pure Skills-126
Parallel-126
The Wall-NB
05Finnish Cardset -265
Finnish Cardset Super Snatchers-10
05Swedish SHL Elitset-154
06Black Diamond-164A
Black-164A
Gold-164A
Ruby-164A
06Hot Prospects-164
Red Hot-164
White Hot-164
06O-Pee-Chee-549
Rainbow-549
06SP Authentic-236
Limited-236
06SP Game Used-125
Gold-125
Rainbow-125
06SPx-158
Spectrum-158
06The Cup-137
Autographed Rookie Masterpiece Pressplates-137
Gold Rainbow Autographed Rookie Patches-137
Masterpiece Pressplates (Black Diamond)-164
Masterpiece Pressplates (Marquee Rookies)-549
Masterpiece Pressplates (MVP)-318
Masterpiece Pressplates (SP Authentic)-236
Masterpiece Pressplates (SP Game Used)-125
Masterpiece Pressplates (SPx)-158
Masterpiece Pressplates (Trilogy)-121
Masterpiece Pressplates (Ultimate Collection)-80
Masterpiece Pressplates (Victory)-295
Rookies Black-137
Rookies Platinum-137
06UD Artifacts-245
06Ultimate Collection-80
Ultimate Debut Threads Jerseys-DJ-NB
Ultimate Debut Threads Jerseys Autographs-DJ-NB
Ultimate Debut Threads Patches-DJ-NB
Ultimate Debut Threads Patches Autographs-DJ-NB
06Upper Deck-220
Exclusives Parallel-220
High Gloss Parallel-220
Masterpieces-220
Rookie Materials-RMNB
Rookie Materials Patches-RMNB
06Upper Deck MVP-318
Gold Script-318
Super Script-318
06Upper Deck Sweet Shot-133
Rookie Jerseys Autographs-133
06Upper Deck Trilogy-121
06Upper Deck Victory-295
06Czech Super Six Postcards-1
06Finnish Cardset-92
Superior Snatchers-1
Superior Snatchers Gold-1
Superior Snatchers Silver-1
07Upper Deck Victory-143
Black-143
Gold-143
Backstrom, Ralph
44Beehive Group II Photos-220
58Parkhurst-16
59Parkhurst-29
60NHL Ceramic Tiles-3
60Parkhurst-41
60Parkhurst-56
60Shirriff Coins-31
60York Photos-2
61Parkhurst-39
61Shirriff/Salada Coins-114
61York Yellow Backs-24
62Parkhurst-44
62Shirriff Coins-26
62York Iron-On Transfers-16
63Chex Photos-2
63Parkhurst-24
63Parkhurst-83
63York White Backs-27
64Beehive Group III Photos-97
64Canadiens Postcards-1
64Coca-Cola Caps-59
64Topps-78
65Canadiens Steinberg Glasses-1
65Coca-Cola-59
65Topps-73
66Canadiens IGA-2
66Topps-75
66Topps USA Test-6
67Canadiens IGA-6
67Post Flip Books-11
67Topps-67
67York Action Octagons-14
67York Action Octagons-27
67York Action Octagons-34
68Canadiens IGA-6
68Canadiens Postcards BW-1
68O-Pee-Chee-60
68Post Marbles-1
68Shirriff Coins-82
68Topps-60
69Canadiens Postcards Color-1
69O-Pee-Chee-166
70Canadiens Pins-21
70Colgate Stamps-21
70O-Pee-Chee-54
70Topps-54
71Bazooka-22
71O-Pee-Chee-108
71Topps-108
71Toronto Sun-105
72O-Pee-Chee-131
72Sargent Promotions Stamps-88
72Topps-133
74O-Pee-Chee WHA-47
74Team Canada L'Equipe WHA-1
75O-Pee-Chee WHA-23
76O-Pee-Chee WHA-124
90ProCards AHL/IHL-367
91Ultimate Original Six-7
French-7
91ProCards-405
92Parkhurst Parkie Reprints-PR18
93O-Pee-Chee Canadiens Hockey Fest-33
94Parkhurst Missing Link-77
94Parkhurst Tall Boys-73
95Parkhurst '66-67-64
Coins-64
03Colorado Eagles-22
04ITG Franchises Update Autographs-RBA
04Colorado Eagles-2
05Colorado Eagles-22
06ITG International Ice-153
Gold-153
Autographs-ARBA
06Colorado EaglesÂ -27
Backstrom, Tomas
84Swedish Semic Elitserien-192
Baco, Danny
06Lincoln Stars-13
06Lincoln Stars Traded-12T
06Lincoln Stars Upper DeckÂ Signature Series -1
Bacon, Doug
92Raleigh Icecaps-38
92Wheeling Thunderbirds-24
Bacon, Matt
00St. Michaels Majors-4
01St. Michaels Majors-16
02St. Michaels Majors-15
Bacul, Robin
98Czech OFS-255
99Czech OFS-392
00Czech OFS-101
01Czech OFS-234
02Czech OFS Plus-275
Duos-D18
03Czech OFS Plus-67
Badal, Ales
94Czech APS Extraliga-129
Badaway, Chad
86Kingston Canadians-21
87Sudbury Wolves-21
Badduke, John
89Victoria Cougars-1
907th Inn. Sketch WHL-241
917th Inn. Sketch WHL-49
94Classic Enforcers-E4
95Wheeling Thunderbirds Series II-1
96Syracuse Crunch-14
96Wheeling Nailers-2
96Wheeling Nailers Photo Pack-5
Bader, Aaron
03Kootenay Ice-19
04Saskatoon Blades-6
05Saskatoon Blades-1
Bader, Anton
05German DEL-60
06German DEL-27
Bader, Darin
88Saskatoon Blades-22
89Saskatoon Blades-23
90Saskatoon Blades-22
907th Inn. Sketch WHL-94
Bader, Hansi
94German First League-65
Bader, Mike
94German DEL-431
95German DEL-398
96German DEL-303
99German Bundesliga 2-49
Bader, Toni
97Swift Current Broncos-9
98Swift Current Broncos-9
98Tri-City Americans-6
00Calgary Hitmen-1
Badertscher, Rolf
95Swiss HNL-354
96Swiss HNL-327
99Swiss Panini Stickers-138
00Swiss Panini Stickers-183
00Swiss Slapshot Mini-Cards-LT9
01Swiss HNL-200
02Swiss HNL-444
Badiura, Matej
04Czech OFS-391
Badrutt, Stefan
01Swiss HNL-384
02Swiss HNL-390
Badyukov, Alexei
00Russian Hockey League-225
02Russian Hockey League-22
03Russian National Team-1
Badzgon, Eric
87Portland Winter Hawks-2
88Portland Winter Hawks-2
Baechler, Dave
93Swiss HNL-266
Baechler, Matthias
93Swiss HNL-172
00Swiss Slapshot Mini-Cards-EHCC7
Baev, Denis
01Russian Hockey League-136
Bagley, David
03Cape Fear Fire Antz-1
04Knoxville Ice Bears-16
Bagron, Bill
02Chicago Steel-1
Bagshaw, Derrick
03Erie Otters-1
04Erie Otters-11
05Erie Otters-2
06Erie Otters-4
Bagu, Brad
907th Inn. Sketch WHL-243
917th Inn. Sketch WHL-239
92Saskatchewan JHL-48
Bahensky, Miroslav
00Czech OFS-189
Bahensky, Zdenek
04Saskatoon Blades-12
05Saskatoon Blades-2
06Hartford Wolf Pack-7
Bahnik, Martin
96Swiss HNL-481
Baier, Christian
94German First League-209
Bailey, Ace
32O'Keefe Maple Leafs-6
33Sport Kings R338 *-29
33O-Pee-Chee V304A-13
33Sport Kings R338 *-29
33V129-3
33V252 Canadian Gum-3
33V288 Hamilton Gum-11
33V357 Ice Kings-22
55Parkhurst-30
Quaker Oats-30
83Hall of Fame-198
83Hall of Fame Postcards-N2
85Hall of Fame-198
91Pro Set-335
French-335
92Hall of Fame Legends-32
94Hall of Fame Tickets-5
94Parkhurst Tall Boys Greats-1
01BAP Ultimate Memorabilia Cornerstones-1
01BAP Ultimate Memorabilia Gloves Are Off-24
02BAP Ultimate Memorabilia Gloves Are Off-1
02BAP Ultimate Memorabilia Great Moments-2
02BAP Ultimate Mem Paper Cuts Autos-6
02ITG Used Vintage Memorabilia-VM5
02ITG Used Vintage Memorabilia Gold-VM5
02Maple Leafs Platinum Collection-42
02Parkhurst Vintage Teammates-VT18
02Parkhurst Retro Nicknames-RN13
03BAP Ultimate Mem Maple Leafs Forever-11
03BAP Ultimate Memorabilia Paper Cuts-2
03Parkhurst Original Six Toronto-60
03Parkhurst Original Six Toronto-81
Inserts-T2
Inserts-T9
Memorabilia-TM39
04ITG Franchises Canadian-92
04ITG Ultimate Memorabilia-37
Gold-37
Cornerstones-7
Cornerstones Gold-7
Day In History-38
Day In History Gold-38
Gloves are Off-14
Maple Leafs Forever-9
Nicknames-16
Paper Cuts Memorabilia-18
Retro Teammates-10
05ITG Ultimate Memorabilia Gloves Are Off-14
05ITG Ultimate Mem Gloves Are Off Gold-14
05ITG Ultimate Mem Paper Cut Autos-2
05ITG Ultimate Mem Quad Paper Cuts Autos-6
06ITG Ultimate Memorabilia-1
Artist Proof-1
Lumbergraphs-10
Maple Leafs Forever Autos-1
Bailey, Andrew
05Kootenay Ice-1
Bailey, Bob
44Beehive Group II Photos-374
51Cleveland Barons-16
54Parkhurst-28
57Topps-19
Bailey, Chris
98UK Basingstoke Bison-5
99UK Hull Thunder-20
03UK London Racers-1
Bailey, Christina
94Classic Women of Hockey-W38
Bailey, Garnet
70Bruins Postcards-5
70Bruins Team Issue-1
70Esso Power Players-64
70O-Pee-Chee-10
70Sargent Promotions Stamps-13
70Topps-10
71Bruins Postcards-10
71Toronto Sun-3
72O-Pee-Chee-191
72Sargent Promotions Stamps-28
73Red Wings Team Issue-1
73Red Wings McCarthy Postcards-1
74NHL Action Stamps-251
74O-Pee-Chee NHL-332
75O-Pee-Chee NHL-284
75O-Pee-Chee NHL-330
75Topps-284
75Topps-330
76O-Pee-Chee NHL-304
77O-Pee-Chee NHL-196
77Topps-196
78O-Pee-Chee-276
98Bruins Alumni-18
Autographs-18
Bailey, Greg
907th Inn. Sketch OHL-351
917th Inn. Sketch OHL-121
93Huntington Blizzard-3
94Birmingham Bulls-1
Bailey, Jason
06Ottawa 67s-19
Bailey, John
66Columbus Checkers-1
Bailey, Josh
06Owen Sound Attack-15
Bailey, Joshua
05Owen Sound Attack-15
Bailey, Kyle
03Portland Winter Hawks-21
Bailey, Reid
82Post Cereal-14
Bailey, Ryan
93Quebec Pee-Wee Tournament-655
Bailey, Scott
907th Inn. Sketch WHL-202
917th Inn. Sketch WHL-4
917th Inn. Sketch Memorial Cup-73
95Bowman-158
All-Foil-158
95Parkhurst International-524
Emerald Ice-524
96Pinnacle-215
Artist's Proofs-215
Premium Stock-215
Rink Collection-215
96Zenith-143
Artist's Proofs-143
96Collector's Edge Ice-58
Prism-58
98Orlando Solar Bears II-12
99Charlotte Checkers-19
99Charlotte Checkers-27
99Charlotte Checkers-32
00Charlotte Checkers-2
01UK London Knights-26
Bailey, Trevor
06Westside Warriors-16
Baillargeon, Joel
86Sherbrooke Canadiens-4
87Moncton Hawks-1
88Nordiques General Foods-3
88Nordiques Team Issue-4
88ProCards AHL-101
89Halifax Citadels-1
89ProCards AHL-178
Baillargeon, Jonathan
93Quebec Pee-Wee Tournament-115
Bailley, Paul
93Brandon Wheat Kings-23
94Spokane Chiefs-20
Bain, Chris
01London Knights-6
02London Knights-14
03Mississauga Ice Dogs-2
Bain, Dan
83Hall of Fame Postcards-B1
85Hall of Fame-227
94Hall of Fame Tickets-3
Baines, Ajay
95Kamloops Blazers-26
96Kamloops Blazers-4
98Kamloops Blazers-2
99Bowman CHL-103
Gold-103
OPC International-103
01Norfolk Admirals-1
02Norfolk Admirals-3
03Norfolk Admirals-4
04Norfolk Admirals-3
05Norfolk Admirals-21
06Hamilton Bulldogs-3
Baines, Tyler
01New Mexico Scorpions-10
02New Mexico Scorpions-2
Baird, Chris
92Harvard Crimson-2
Baird, Jason
02Indianapolis Ice-2
03Indianapolis Ice-2
Baird, Joey
98UK Basingstoke Bison-2
99UK Basingstoke Bison-7
Baird, Ken
75O-Pee-Chee WHA-37
77O-Pee-Chee WHA-46
Baird, Mark
91Air Canada SJHL-B11
Baisch, Justin
93Quebec Pee-Wee Tournament-895
Bajurny, Mike
96Dayton Ice Bandits-3
99San Angelo Outlaws-1
04St Georges de Beauce Garaga-16
Bak, Markus
94German First League-425
Baker, Aaron
95Tri-City Americans-4
Baker, Bill
80Canadiens Postcards-2
81Swedish Semic Hockey VM Stickers-95
82Post Cereal-17
83O-Pee-Chee-240
95Signature Rookies Miracle on Ice-1
95Signature Rookies Miracle on Ice-2
95Signature Rook Miracle on Ice Sigs-1
95Signature Rook Miracle on Ice Sigs-2
04UD Legendary Signatures Miracle Men-USA12
04UD Legendary Sigs Miracle Men Autos-USA-BI
Baker, Bruce
76Nova Scotia Voyageurs-1
77Nova Scotia Voyageurs-1
Baker, Darin
88ProCards IHL-38
Baker, Hobey
83Hall of Fame-17
83Hall of Fame Postcards-B2
85Hall of Fame-17
92Hall of Fame Legends-6
95AHCA-2
04ITG Ultimate Memorabilia-182
Gold-182
04Upper Deck-194
Canadian Exclusives-194
HG Glossy Gold-194
HG Glossy Silver-194
06ITG Ultimate Memorabilia-67
Artist Proof-67
Baker, Jack
02Philadelphia Phantoms-8
03Florence Pride-145
Baker, Jamie
89Halifax Citadels-2
89ProCards AHL-156
90Halifax Citadels-1
90ProCards AHL/IHL-449
91Bowman-136
91Pinnacle-348
French-348
91ProCards-541
92Bowman-436
92O-Pee-Chee-41
92Parkhurst-353
Emerald Ice-353
92Senators Team Issue-1
92Stadium Club-136
92Topps-506
Gold-506G
92Ultra-360
92Upper Deck-130
92Upper Deck-464
93Leaf-134
93OPC Premier-22
Gold-22
93Panini Stickers-113
93Parkhurst-459
Emerald Ice-459
93Pinnacle-378
Canadian-378
93Score-57
93Score-546
Gold-546
Canadian-57
Canadian-546
Canadian Gold-546
93Stadium Club-461
Members Only Master Set-461
First Day Issue-461
93Topps Premier Promo Sheet-22
93Topps/OPC Premier-22
Gold-22
93Ultra-6
94EA Sports-93
94Leaf-421
94Pinnacle-502
Artist's Proofs-502
Rink Collection-502
94Stadium Club-249
Members Only Master Set-249
First Day Issue-249
Super Team Winner Cards-249
94Upper Deck-439
Electric Ice-439
95Canada Games NHL POGS-232
95Playoff One on One-301
96Be A Player-17
Autographs-17
Autographs Silver-17
96Playoff One on One-402
96Summit-74
Artist's Proofs-74
Ice-74
Metal-74
Premium Stock-74
97Pacific Invincible NHL Regime-190
97Score Maple Leafs-19
Platinum-19
Premier-19
98Chicago Wolves Turner Cup-13
Baker, Ken
01Bakersfield Condors-1
Baker, Kevin
93Quebec Pee-Wee Tournament-1164
00Lowell Lock Monsters-15
01Johnstown Chiefs-6
03Owen Sound Attack-12
04Owen Sound Attack-6
04Sudbury Wolves-22
05Sudbury Wolves-9
06Sudbury Wolves-16
Baker, Kory
00Val d'Or Foreurs-9
Signed-9
01El Paso Buzzards-18
02El Paso Buzzards-7
Baker, Scott
04Belleville Bulls-21
05Belleville Bulls-8
Baker, Steve
80O-Pee-Chee-346
81O-Pee-Chee-231
Baker, Trevor
96Prince Albert Raiders-1
99Peoria Rivermen-5
00Peoria Rivermen-7
01Peoria Rivermen-8
02Peoria Rivermen-6
02Peoria Rivermen Photo Pack-1
02Peoria Rivermen RBI Sports-151
03Peoria Rivermen-22
04Peoria Rivermen-7
06Bloomington PrairieThunder-2
Bakhmutov, Igor
99Russian Hockey League-98
00Russian Dynamo Moscow-29
00Russian Hockey League-298
Bakhriddinov, Roustam
00QMJHL All-Star Program Inserts-29
Bakogeorge, Troy
86Regina Pats-1
Bakos, Michael
96German DEL-10
98German DEL-282
98German DEL-335
99German DEL-161
02German DEL City Press-235
03German Mannheim Eagles Postcards-28
04German Adler Mannheim Eagles Postcards-3
04German DEL-3
05German DEL-243
06German DEL-93
Bakovic, Peter
83Kitchener Rangers-24
85Moncton Golden Flames-27
86Moncton Golden Flames-23
89ProCards IHL-168
90ProCards AHL/IHL-326
91ProCards-596
94Milwaukee Admirals-2
95Milwaukee Admirals-22
96Milwaukee Admirals-2
97Milwaukee Admirals-23
Bakrlik, Frantisek
00Barrie Colts-1
01Barrie Colts-15
01UD Prospects-38
Jerseys-J-FB
Jerseys Gold-J-FB
Bakula, Martin
94Cape Breton Oilers-2
94Classic Pro Prospects-158
95Czech APS Extraliga-110
96Czech APS Extraliga-102
97Czech APS Extraliga-154
97Czech DS Extraliga-75
97Czech DS Stickers-267
98Czech DS-70
98Czech DS Stickers-192
98Czech OFS-213
99Czech DS-118
99Czech OFS-42
Bakus, Oldrich
99Czech Score Blue 2000-161
99Czech Score Red Ice 2000-161
04Czech OFS-2
Bal, Jag
91British Columbia JHL-144
92British Columbia JHL-37
Bala, Chris
92Quebec Pee-Wee Tournament-1120
01BAP Memorabilia-410
Emerald-410
Ruby-410
Sapphire-410
01Parkhurst-331
01UD Mask Collection-157
Gold-157
01Grand Rapids Griffins-18
02Pacific-262
Blue-262
Red-262
02Upper Deck-216
Exclusives-216
02Upper Deck MVP-212
Gold-212
Classics-212
Golden Classics-212
03Houston Aeros-1
04Hershey Bears Patriot News-2
05Reading Royals-1
06Reading Royals-15
Balan, Scotty
00Saskatoon Blades-8
01Saskatoon Blades-17
02Norfolk Admirals-4
02Roanoke Express-8
02Roanoke Express RBI Sports-188
05Bakersfield Condors-4
06Bakersfield Condors-21
Balan, Stanislav
06Czech OFS-220
Balandin, Andrej
94German First League-48
Balandin, Mikhail
03Russian Hockey League-119
Balasescu, Gabriel
00Rimouski Oceanic-16
Signed-16
01Rimouski Oceanic-15
03Lewiston Maineiacs-2
Balastik, Jaroslav
98Czech OFS-278
99Czech OFS-207
00Czech DS Extraliga-57
00Czech OFS-362
01Czech OFS-95
02Czech DS-37
02Czech OFS Plus-23
02Czech OFS Plus All-Star Game-H1
02Czech National Team Postcards-1
03Czech OFS Plus-130
03Czech OFS Plus MS Praha-SE16
03Czech National Team Postcards-1
04Czech OFS-271
Czech/Slovak-1
Goals Leaders-1
Points Leaders-9
05Black Diamond-230
05Hot Prospects-196
Autographed Patch Variation-196
Autographed Patch Variation Gold-196
Hot Materials-HMJB
Red Hot-196
05Parkhurst-150
Facsimile Auto Parallel-150
True Colors-TCCLB
True Colors-TCCLB
05SP Authentic-152
Limited-152
Sign of the Times-JB
05SP Game Used-121
Autographs-121
Gold-121
Rookie Exclusives-JB
Rookie Exclusives Silver-RE-JB
05SPx-134
Spectrum-134
05The Cup-151
Autographed Rookie Patches Gold Rainbow-151
Black Rainbow Rookies-151
Masterpiece Pressplates (Black Diamond)-230
Masterpiece Pressplates (Ice)-149
Masterpiece Pressplates (Rookie Update)-254
Masterpiece Pressplates SPA Autos-152
Masterpiece Pressplates (SP Game Used)-121
Masterpiece Pressplates (SPx)-134
Masterpiece Pressplates (SPx)-134
Masterpiece Pressplates (Trilogy)-249
Masterpiece Pressplates Ult Coll-142
Masterpiece Pressplates Autographs-151
Platinum Rookies-151
05Ultimate Collection-142
Gold-142
05Ultra-214
Gold-214
Fresh Ink-FI-JA
Fresh Ink Blue-FI-JA
Ice-214
Rookie Uniformity Jerseys-RU-JB
Rookie Uniformity Jersey Autographs-ARU-JB
Rookie Uniformity Patches-RUP-JB
Rookie Uniformity Patch Autographs-ARP-JB
05Upper Deck-239
HG Glossy-239
Rookie Ink-RIJB
Rookie Threads-RTJB
Rookie Threads Autographs-ARTJB
05Upper Deck Ice-149
Premieres Auto Patches-AIPJB
05Upper Deck Rookie Update-254
Inspirations Patch Rookies-254
05Upper Deck Trilogy-249
05Upper Deck Toronto Fall Expo-239
06Hot Prospects Hotagraphs-HJB
06UD Artifacts Auto-Facts-AFJB
06UD Artifacts Auto-Facts Gold-AFJB
06Upper Deck Shootout Artists-SA13
06Czech IIHF World Championship Postcards-1
06Czech LG Hockey Games Postcards-1
Balasz, David
01Czech OFS-197
02Czech OFS Plus-276
06Czech OFS-23
Balaz, Radoslav
917th Inn. Sketch QMJHL-196
Balaz, Vladislav
03Lewiston Maineiacs-3
Balazs, David
94Czech APS Extraliga-227
95Czech APS Extraliga-162
96Czech APS Extraliga-184
97Czech APS Extraliga-94
99Czech OFS-147
03Czech OFS Plus-88
04Czech OFS-89
Balcombe, Darren
92Saskatchewan JHL-59
Balderis, Helmut
74Swedish Stickers-75
77Finnish Sportscasters-47-1113
79Panini Stickers-152
79Russian National Team-20
82Swedish Semic VM Stickers-70
84Russian National Team-2
92Future Trends '76 Canada Cup-130
Baldi, Mattia
95Swiss HNL-197
96Swiss HNL-88
98Swiss Power Play Stickers-14
98Swiss Power Play Stickers-253
99Swiss Panini Stickers-238
99Swiss Panini Stickers-264
00Swiss Panini Stickers-278
00Swiss Panini Stickers National Team-P15
00Swiss Slapshot Mini-Cards-ZSCL7
01Swiss HNL-12
02Swiss HNL-268
Baldrica, Gian
03Colorado Eagles-3
Baldris, Miguel
84Richelieu Riverains-1
Baldwin, Curtis
97OCN Blizzard-10
Baldwin, Dale
99Fort Wayne Komets Points Leaders-16
99Fort Wayne Komets Penalty Leaders-3
Baldwin, Doug
45Quaker Oats Photos-3
Baldwin, Gord
04Medicine Hat Tigers-1
05Medicine Hat Tigers-1
06Medicine Hat Tigers-1
Baldwin, Jack
99Lowell Lock Monsters-22
Balej, Jozef
95Slovakian-Quebec Pee-Wee Tournament-1
95Quebec Pee-Wee Tournament-1
96Slovakian Quebec Pee-Wee Tournament-1
96Quebec Pee-Wee Tournament-1
00UD CHL Prospects-72
02Hamilton Bulldogs-25
03Beehive-226
Gold-226
Silver-226
03ITG Action-660
03ITG Used Signature Series-143
Autographs Gold-143
03ITG VIP Rookie Debut-110
03Pacific Calder-126
Silver-126
03Pacific Complete-583
Red-583
03Parkhurst Rookie-157
03Topps Traded-TT156
Blue-TT156
Gold-TT156
Red-TT156
03Upper Deck Rookie Update-206
03Pacific AHL Prospects-32
Gold-32
04Pacific-291
Blue-291
Red-291
04AHL Top Prospects-18
04Hartford Wolf Pack-1
04ITG Heroes and Prospects-47
Autographs-JB
04ITG Heroes/Prospects Toronto Expo '05-47
04ITG Heroes/Prospects Expo Heroes/Pros-47
05Manitoba Moose-1
Baleno, Mario
93Quebec Pee-Wee Tournament-1430
Bales, Bob
81Victoria Cougars-1
Bales, Brian
04Sioux City Musketeers-1
Bales, Mike
92Classic-73
Gold-73
93Classic-126
93Classic Four-Sport *-230
Gold-230
95Parkhurst International-419
Emerald Ice-419
95Senators Team Issue-3
97Rochester Americans-5-3
98Michigan K-Wings-18
99Michigan K-Wings-19
00Utah Grizzlies-2
01UK Belfast Giants-1
01UK Belfast Giants-33
02German DEL City Press-128
03Swedish Elite-200
Global Impact-GI6
Silver-200
06German DEL-182
Balfeux, Martin
907th Inn. Sketch QMJHL-63
Balfour, Earl
44Beehive Group II Photos-77
44Beehive Group II Photos-375
54Parkhurst-25
58Topps-37
59Topps-50
60Shirriff Coins-68
61Topps-3
61Topps-21
Balfour, Murray
44Beehive Group II Photos-78
59Topps-33
60Shirriff Coins-65
60Topps-12
Stamps-1
61Shirriff/Salada Coins-30
61Topps-33
62Topps-36
63Topps-35
64Beehive Group III Photos-1
64Coca-Cola Caps-9
64Topps-90
94Parkhurst Tall Boys-17
Baljo, Jadran
04Peterborough Petes Postcards-21
Balkovec, Maco
92British Columbia JHL-236
Ball, Jimmy
02London Knights-18
Ball, Matt
93Detroit Jr. Red Wings-8
94Detroit Jr. Red Wings-7
95Slapshot-66
95Slapshot Memorial Cup-81
Ball, Terry
72Minnesota Fighting Saints Postcards WHA-3
78Finnish SM-Liiga-28
Ballah, Todd
03Yarmouth Mariners-3
Ballantyne, Paul
02Grand Rapids Griffins-3
03ECHL Update RBI Sports-284
Ballard, Boyd
03Oklahoma City Blazers-3
04Oklahoma City Blazers-13
Ballard, Harold
78Maple Leafs Postcards-24

79Maple Leafs Postcards-2
80Maple Leafs Postcards-2
81Maple Leafs Postcards-2
81Maple Leafs Postcards-26
83Hall of Fame Postcards-E2
85Hall of Fame-63
85Maple Leafs Postcards-1
86Maple Leafs Postcards-2
87Maple Leafs PLAY-4
88Maple Leafs PLAY-13

Ballard, Keith
01Minnesota Golden Gophers-7
02BAP Memorabilia Draft Redemptions-11
02Minnesota Golden Gophers-3
03Minnesota Golden Gophers-10
04SP Authentic Rookie Redemptions-RR38
04AHL All-Stars-1
05ITG Heroes/Prosp Toronto Expo Parallel -349
05Beehive-132
Beige -132
Blue -132
Gold-132
Red -132
Matte-132
05Black Diamond-160
Emerald-160
Gold-160
Onyx-160
Ruby-160
05Hot Prospects-261
En Fuego-261
Hot Materials-HMKB
Red Hot-261
White Hot-261
05Parkhurst-656
Facsimile Auto Parallel-656
True Colors-TCPHX
True Colors-TCPHX
05SP Authentic-180
Limited-180
Rarefied Rookies-RRKB
Rookie Authentics-RAKB
05SP Game Used-117
Autographs-117
Gold-117
Rookie Exclusives-KB
Rookie Exclusives Silver-RE-KB
05SPx-185
Spectrum-185
Xcitement Rookies-XR-KB
Xcitement Rookies Gold-XR-KB
Xcitement Rookies Spectrum-XR-KB
05The Cup-185
Black Rainbow Rookies-185
Masterpiece Pressplates (Artifacts)-311
Masterpiece Pressplates (Bee Hive)-132
Masterpiece Pressplates (Black Diamond)-160
Masterpiece Pressplates (Ice)-140
Masterpiece Pressplates (MVP)-434
Masterpiece Pressplates (Rookie Update)-226
Masterpiece Pressplates SPA Autos-180
Masterpiece Pressplates (SP Game Used)-117
Masterpiece Pressplates SPx Autos-185
Masterpiece Pressplates (Trilogy)-210
Masterpiece Pressplates Ult Coll Autos-130
Masterpiece Pressplates (Victory)-266
Masterpiece Pressplates Autographs-185
Platinum Rookies-185
05UD Artifacts-311
05UD Rookie Class-12
05Ultimate Collection-130
Autographed Patches-130
Autographed Shields-130
Ultimate Debut Threads Jerseys-DTJKB
Ultimate Debut Threads Jerseys Autos-DAJKB
Ultimate Debut Threads Patches-DTPKB
Ultimate Debut Threads Patches Autos-DAPKB
05Ultra-238
Gold-238
Ice-238
Rookie Uniformity Jerseys-RU-KB
Rookie Uniformity Jersey Autographs-ARU-KB
Rookie Uniformity Patches-RUP-KB
Rookie Uniformity Patch Autographs-ARP-KB
05Upper Deck-232
HG Glossy-232
Rookie Ink-RIKB
Rookie Threads-RTKB
Rookie Threads Autographs-ARTKB
05Upper Deck Ice-140
Glacial Graphs-GGKB
Glacial Graphs Labels-GGKB
Premieres Auto Patches-AIPKB
05Upper Deck MVP-434
Gold-434
Platinum-434
05Upper Deck Rookie Update-226
Inspirations Patch Rookies-226
05Upper Deck Trilogy-210
05Upper Deck Toronto Fall Expo-232
05Upper Deck Victory-266
Black-266
Gold-266
Silver-266
05ITG Heroes and Prospects-349
AHL Grads-AG-5
AHL Grads Gold-AG-5
Autographs Series II-KB
Complete Logos-AHL-22
Jerseys-GUJ-83
Jerseys Gold-GUJ-83
Emblems-GUE-83
Emblems Gold-GUE-83
Numbers-GUN-83
Numbers Gold-GUN-83
06Be A Player-164
Autographs-164
Signatures-KB
Portraits Signature Portraits-SPKB
06Hot Prospects Hotagraphs-HKB
06O-Pee-Chee-382
06O-Pee-Chee-617
Rainbow-382
Rainbow-617
Autographs-A-KB
06SP Game Used SIGnificance-SKB
06Upper Deck-150
Exclusives Parallel-150
High Gloss Parallel-150
Masterpieces-150
Signature Sensations-SSKB
06Upper Deck MVP-227
Gold Script-227
Super Script-227
06Upper Deck Ovation-87
06Upper Deck Victory-156
06Upper Deck Victory Black-156
06Upper Deck Victory Gold-156
06ITG Heroes and Prospects AHL All-Star Jerseys-AJ08
06ITG Heroes and Prospects AHL All-Star Jerseys Gold-AJ08
06ITG Heroes and Prospects AHL All-Star Emblems-AE08
06ITG Heroes and Prospects AHL All-Star Emblems Gold-AE08
06ITG Heroes and Prospects AHL All-Star Numbers-AN08
06ITG Heroes and Prospects AHL All-Star Numbers Gold-AN08

Ballas, B.J.
04Oklahoma City Blazers-1

Balleux, Martin
917th Inn. Sketch QMJHL-37
97El Paso Buzzards-10

Ballman, Brian
96Seattle Thunderbirds-21
99Lethbridge Hurricanes-2
00Lethbridge Hurricanes-1

Balmer, Samuel
91Finnish Semic World Champ Stickers-185
91Swedish Semic World Champ Stickers-185
93Swedish Semic World Champ Stickers-111
93Swiss HNL-87
95Swiss HNL-114
96Swiss HNL-105
96Swiss HNL-528
98Swiss Power Play Stickers-105
99Swiss Panini Stickers-105
00Swiss Panini Stickers-177
00Swiss Slapshot Mini-Cards-LT3
01Swiss HNL-194
02Swiss HNL-324

Balmin, Dmitri
98Russian Hockey League-123
99Russian Hockey League-53
00Russian Hockey League-35
02Russian Hockey League-16

Balmochnyk, Maxim
97Black Diamond-47
Double Diamond-47
Triple Diamond-47
Quadruple Diamond-47
98UD Choice-283
Prime Choice Reserve-283
Reserve-283
99BAP Memorabilia-362
Gold-362
Silver-362
99Russian Stars Postcards-2
99Cincinnati Mighty Ducks-13
00BAP Memorabilia-180
Emerald-180
Ruby-180
Sapphire-180
Promos-180
00BAP Mem Chicago Sportsfest Copper-180
00BAP Memorabilia Chicago Sportsfest Blue-180
00BAP Memorabilia Chicago Sportsfest Gold-180
00BAP Memorabilia Chicago Sportsfest Ruby-180
00BAP Memorabilia Chicago Sun-Times Ruby-180
00BAP Memorabilia Chicago Sun-Times Gold-180
00BAP Mem Chicago Sun-Times Sapphire-180
00BAP Mem Toronto Fall Expo Copper-180
00BAP Memorabilia Toronto Fall Expo Gold-180
00BAP Memorabilia Toronto Fall Expo Ruby-180
00O-Pee-Chee-284
00O-Pee-Chee Parallel-284
00Pacific-1
Copper-1
Gold-1
Ice Blue-1
Premiere Date-1
00Paramount-2
Copper-2
Gold-2
Holo-Gold-2
Holo-Silver-2
Ice Blue-2
Premiere Date-2
00Topps/OPC-284
Parallel-284
00Topps Chrome-179
OPC Refractors-179
Refractors-179
00Topps Premier Plus GameUsed Memorabilia-GPMB
00Topps Premier Plus GameUsed Memorabilia-GPTSMB
00Upper Deck MVP-7
First Stars-7
Second Stars-7
Third Stars-7
00Upper Deck Victory-272
01Cincinnati Mighty Ducks-2
02Russian Hockey League-131
02Russian Hockey League-150
02Russian Hockey League-181
03Albany River Rats-3
03Albany River Rats Kinko's-2

Balog, Tyson
91Air Canada SJHL-A3
92Saskatchewan JHL-143

Balon, Dave
44Beehive Group II Photos-221
44Beehive Group II Photos-296A
44Beehive Group II Photos-296B
60NHL Ceramic Tiles-19
60Shirriff Coins-94
62Topps-56
Hockey Bucks-1
63Chex Photos-3
63Parkhurst-38
63Parkhurst-97
63York White Backs-33
64Beehive Group III Photos-98
64Coca-Cola Caps-69
64Topps-37
64Toronto Star-1
65Topps-72
66Topps-74
68O-Pee-Chee-169
68Shirriff Coins-107
69O-Pee-Chee-191
70Colgate Stamps-33
70Esso Power Players-192
70O-Pee-Chee-61
70Sargent Promotions Stamps-119
70Topps-61
71O-Pee-Chee-229
71Sargent Promotions Stamps-125
71Toronto Sun-168
72Canucks Royal Bank-1
72O-Pee-Chee-162
72Sargent Promotions Stamps-220
72Topps-117
94Parkhurst Tall Boys-68
95Parkhurst '66-67-62
Coins-62

Balshin, Brad
83Kitchener Rangers-26

Baltimore, Bryon
75O-Pee-Chee WHA-9
88Oilers Tenth Anniversary-138

Baluch, Tomas
93Quebec Pee-Wee Tournament-1701
99Missouri River Otters-2
99Missouri River Otters Sheet-1

Balvin, Jeff
02Topeka Scarecrows-5

Balzarek, Urs
93Swiss HNL-341
95Swiss HNL-395
96Swiss HNL-342
98Swiss Power Play Stickers-328

Bamberger, J.J.
91Ferris State Bulldogs-3
92Ferris State Bulldogs-3

Bambuch, Lukas
04Slovakian Poprad Team Set-8

Banach, Jay
01New Mexico Scorpions-3
02Lexington Men O'War-21
04Fort Worth Brahmas-1

Banahan, Frank
98Cincinnati Mighty Ducks-7

Bancroft, Steve
897th Inn. Sketch OHL-85
90ProCards AHL/IHL-159
91ProCards-49
92Indianapolis Ice-2
93Cleveland Lumberjacks-23
93Cleveland Lumberjacks Postcards-2
93Classic Pro Prospects-48
97Las Vegas Thunder-7
98Providence Bruins-5
99Cincinnati Cyclones-3
00Kentucky Thoroughblades-2
01Upper Deck Ice-148
01Cleveland Barons-1
02Worcester IceCats-3
03Binghamton Senators-1
04German Augsburg Panthers Postcards-3
04German DEL-38
06Binghamton Senators 5th Anniversary-1

Bander, Max
94German First League-515

Bandurski, Andrew
92Cornell Big Red-1
93Cornell Big Red-2

Banga, Travis
04Memphis RiverKings-20

Banham, Frank
93Saskatoon Blades-2
93Saskatoon Blades-3
95Saskatoon Blades-2
97Donruss-203
Press Proofs Silver-203
Press Proofs Gold-203
98Pacific-43
Ice Blue-43
Red-43
99Cincinnati Mighty Ducks-11
00Finnish Cardset-130
01Finnish Cardset-263
02Finnish Cardset-4
02Springfield Falcons-4
03Russian Hockey League-272
03Springfield Falcons Postcards-19
04Finnish Cardset-148
04Finnish Cardset Signatures-28

Banika, Cory
89Oshawa Generals-1
89Oshawa Generals 7th Inning Sketch-17
897th Inn. Sketch OHL-17
90Hampton Roads Admirals-54
907th Inn. Sketch Memorial Cup-87
93Johnstown Chiefs-17
98Muskegon Fury-14
99Bakersfield Condors-1
00Bakersfield Condors-2

Bankoske, Dave
94Toledo Storm-1

Banks, Darren
90ProCards AHL/IHL-622
91ProCards-582
92OPC Premier-118
93Parkhurst-286
Emerald Ice-286
94Anaheim Bullfrogs RHI-1
95Anaheim Bullfrogs RHI-13
96Detroit Vipers-1
97Detroit Vipers-19
98Detroit Vipers-14
98Detroit Vipers Freschetta-14

Bannan, Matt
00St. Michaels Majors-5

Bannatyne, Garth
94German First League-651

Bannerman, Murray
80Blackhawks White Border-1
81Blackhawks Borderless Postcards-1
81O-Pee-Chee-68
82Blackhawks Postcards-1
82O-Pee-Chee-61
83Blackhawks Postcards-1
83O-Pee-Chee-97
83O-Pee-Chee Stickers-113
83O-Pee-Chee Stickers-164
83Topps Stickers-113
83Topps Stickers-164
83Victoria Cougars-2
84O-Pee-Chee-32
84O-Pee-Chee Stickers-32
84O-Pee-Chee Stickers-135
84Topps-27
85Blackhawks Team Issue-12
85O-Pee-Chee-27
85O-Pee-Chee Stickers-27
85Topps-27
86Blackhawks Coke-1
86O-Pee-Chee-180
86Topps-180
87Blackhawks Coke-1
87Panini Stickers-221
01Between the Pipes Masks-5
01Between the Pipes Masks Silver-5
01Between the Pipes Masks Gold-5
04ITG Franchises US West-175
Autographs-A-MBN

Bannister, Darin
90ProCards AHL/IHL-298
91ProCards-136

Bannister, Drew
907th Inn. Sketch OHL-152
917th Inn. Sketch OHL-327
93Donruss Team Canada-3
93Pinnacle-460
Canadian-460
93Sault Ste. Marie Greyhounds-6
93Sault Ste. Marie Greyhound Memorial Cup-6
94Atlanta Knights-5
94Classic-64
Gold-64
95Bowman-104
All-Foil-104
95Parkhurst International-467
Emerald Ice-467
95Atlanta Knights-1
96Be A Player-219
96Be A Player-P219
Autographs-219
Autographs Silver-219
96Collector's Edge Ice-99
Prism-99
97Collector's Choice-94
98Las Vegas Thunder-1
99Hartford Wolf Pack-2
00Hartford Wolf Pack-2
01Cincinnati Mighty Ducks-3
02Finnish Cardset-155
04German DEL-244
04German Nuremburg Ice Tigers Postcards-1
05German DEL-182
Defender-DF01

Banville, Gilles
63Quebec Aces-1
64Quebec Aces-1
65Quebec Aces-1

Barabe, David
93Quebec Pee-Wee Tournament-1095

Barada, S.
99Czech OFS-460

Barahona, Ralph
90ProCards AHL/IHL-132
91Upper Deck-496
French-496
92Cincinnati Cyclones-2
93Raleigh Icecaps-1
95San Diego Barracudas RHI-9

Baraniuk, Jesse
04Lakehead University Thunderwolves-21

Baranka, Ivan
03Everett Silvertips-23
04Everett Silvertips-26
05Hartford Wolf Pack-1

Baranka, Michal
96Slovakian Quebec Pee-Wee Tournament-2

Baranov, Alexei
99Russian Hockey League-230

Baranov, Konstantin
02Russian Hockey League-243
03Russian Avangard Omsk-2
03Russian Hockey League-225

Baranov, Roman
98Russian Hockey League-119
99Russian Hockey League-105
01Russian Hockey League-72
02Russian Hockey League-141

Baranyk, Mike
95Neepewa Natives-7

Bararuk, David
01Moose Jaw Warriors-16
04Louisiana Ice Gators-1
05Idaho Steelheads-1
06Finnish Porin Assat Pelaajakortit-31

Barbe, Guillaume
93Quebec Pee-Wee Tournament-905

Barbe, Mario
84Chicoutimi Sagueneens-1
88ProCards AHL-84
89ProCards AHL-132
90ProCards AHL/IHL-228

Barbeau, Frederic
96Wheeling Nailers-3
96Wheeling Nailers Photo Pack-4
98Thetford Mines Coyotes-15
01Thetford Mines Coyotes-6

Barbeau, Terry
03Sault Ste. Marie Greyhounds-26

Barber, Bill
73Flyers Linnett-2
73O-Pee-Chee-81
73Topps-81
74Lipton Soup-31
74NHL Action Stamps-205
74O-Pee-Chee NHL-8
74Topps-8
75Flyers Canada Dry Cans-1
75Heroes Stand-Ups-20
75O-Pee-Chee NHL-226
75Topps-226
76O-Pee-Chee NHL-178
76O-Pee-Chee NHL-215
76O-Pee-Chee NHL-391
76Topps-178
76Topps-215
76Topps Glossy Inserts-12
77O-Pee-Chee NHL-227
77Topps-227
78O-Pee-Chee-69
78O-Pee-Chee-176
78Topps-69
78Topps-176
79O-Pee-Chee-140
79Topps-140
80O-Pee-Chee-200
80Topps-200
81O-Pee-Chee-238
81O-Pee-Chee-247
81O-Pee-Chee-253
81O-Pee-Chee Stickers-155
81O-Pee-Chee Stickers-174
81Topps-2
81Topps-59
81Topps-E123
82McDonald's Stickers-11
82O-Pee-Chee-244
82O-Pee-Chee-246
82O-Pee-Chee-247
82O-Pee-Chee Stickers-110
82O-Pee-Chee Stickers-170
82Post Cereal-14
82Topps Stickers-110
82Topps Stickers-170
83Flyers J.C. Penney-2
83NHL Key Tags-95
83O-Pee-Chee-260
83O-Pee-Chee Stickers-5
83O-Pee-Chee Stickers-194
83Puffy Stickers-9
83Topps Stickers-5
83Topps Stickers-194
84O-Pee-Chee-156
85Flyers Postcards-1
86Flyers Postcards-1
87Flyers Postcards-4
90Score-356
Canadian-356
92Flyers Upper Deck Sheets-44
92Future Trends '76 Canada Cup-169
92Parkhurst-469
Emerald Ice-469
94Hockey Wit-13
01BAP Ultimate Mem Dynasty Jerseys-1
01BAP Ultimate Mem Dynasty Emblems-1
01BAP Ultimate Mem Dynasty Numbers-1
01BAP Ultimate Mem Retired Numbers-2
01BAP Ultimate Mem Retro Teammates-6
01Flyers Postcards-25
01Greats of the Game-38
Autographs-38
01Parkhurst Autographs-PA53
01Upper Deck Legends-55
Jerseys-TTBB
Jerseys Platinum-TTBB
Milestones-MBB
Milestones Platinum-MBB
02BAP Ultimate Mem Vintage Jerseys-5
02Parkhurst Vintage Teammates-VT12
03BAP Ultimate Memorabilia Great Moments-7
03BAP Ultimate Mem Retro Teammates-8
04ITG NHL AS FANtasy AS History Jerseys-SB32
04ITG Franchises He Shoots/Scores Prizes-45
04ITG Franchises US East-417
Autographs-A-BBA
Complete Jerseys-ECJ3
Complete Jerseys Gold-ECJ3
Double Memorabilia-EDM15
Double Memorabilia Autographs-EDM-BB
Double Memorabilia Gold-EDM15
Memorabilia-ESM14
Memorabilia Autographs-ESM-BB
Memorabilia Gold-ESM14
Original Sticks-EOS13
Original Sticks Autographs-EOS-BB
Original Sticks Gold-EOS13
Teammates-ETM3
Teammates Gold-ETM3
04ITG Ultimate Memorabilia-175
Gold-175
Auto Threads-24
Autographs-45
Autographs Gold-45
Broad Street Bullies Jerseys-2
Broad Street Bullies Jersey Autographs-2
Broad Street Bullies Emblems-2
Broad Street Bullies Emblem Autographs-2
Broad Street Bullies Numbers-2
Broad Street Bullies Number Autographs-2
Day In History-11
Day In History Gold-11
Jersey Autographs-4
Jersey Autographs Gold-4
Retro Teammates-11
Stick Autographs-24
Stick Autographs Gold-24
04UD Legendary Signatures-5
Autographs-BB
Linemates-BBBCRL
04UD Legends Classics-4
Gold-4
Platinum-4
Silver-4
Jersey Redemptions-JY27
Signature Moments-M47
Signatures-CS45
Signatures-DC20
Signatures-TC6
04ITG Heroes and Prospects-139
Autographs-BBA
Hero Memorabilia-25
04ITG Heroes/Prospects Toronto Expo '05-139
04ITG Heroes/Prospects Expo Heroes/Pros-139
05ITG Ultimate Memorabilia Stick Autos-28
05ITG Ultimate Mem Stick Autos Gold-28
05ITG Ultimate Memorabilia Triple Autos-2
05ITG Ultimate Mem Triple Autos Gold-2
05SPx Xcitement Legends-XL-BB
05SPx Xcitement Legends Gold-XL-BB
05SPx Xcitement Legends Spectrum-XL-BB
05UD Artifacts-102
Blue-102
Gold-102
Green-102
Pewter-102
Red-102
Gold Autographed-102
05ITG Heroes and Prospects Hero Mem-HM-49
06ITG International Ice-105
Gold-105
Autographs-ABBR
06ITG Ultimate Memorabilia-14
Artist Proof-14
Autos-1
Autos Gold-1
Retro Teammates-13
Retro Teammates Gold-13
Road to the Cup-9
Road to the Cup Gold-9
Stick Rack-15
Stick Rack Gold-15

Barber, Don
90Bowman-179
Tiffany-179
90Jets IGA-3
90O-Pee-Chee-53
90Panini Stickers-259
90Pro Set-558
90Score-284
Canadian-284
90Score Rookie/Traded-14T
90Topps-53
Tiffany-53
90Upper Deck-28
French-28
91Nordiques Petro-Canada-2
91Pro Set-464
French-464

Barber, Greg
81Victoria Cougars-2
03ECHL All-Stars-262
04Hershey Bears Patriot News-3
05Rockford Ice Hogs-1

Barberio, Mark
06Cape Breton Screaming Eagles-19

Barbieri, Patrick
01London Knights-4

Barbour, Jamie
03Yarmouth Mariners-4

Barch, Krys
00Portland Pirates-3
05Iowa Stars-7
06Stars Team Postcards-1
06Iowa Stars-3
07Upper Deck Victory-242
Black-242
Gold-242

Barclay, Todd
94Dubuque Fighting Saints-5

Barczikowski, Thomas
94German First League-380

Bardin, Anatoli
03Russian Avangard Omsk-27

Bardin, Nikolai
01Russian Hockey League-71

Bardzinski, Stefan
94German First League-120

Barefoot, Kevin
93Quebec Pee-Wee Tournament-768

Barek, Martin
99Czech OFS-87
00Czech OFS-33
02Czech OFS Plus-211
03Czech OFS Plus-46
03Czech Pardubice Postcards-1

Barenco, Lorenzo
01Swiss HNL-212

Bares, Petr
99German Bundesliga 2-195
02German DEL City Press-129

Barg, Simon
02Barrie Colts-6

Barica, Dusan
99Czech Score Blue 2000-153
99Czech Score Red Ice 2000-153

Baril, Tony
24Crescent Selkirks-3

Barilko, Bill
44Beehive Group II Photos-376
45Quaker Oats Photos-4A
45Quaker Oats Photos-4B
45Quaker Oats Photos-4C
48Exhibits Canadian-28
51Parkhurst-52
62Wheaties Great Moments in Cdn Sport-1
91Pro Set-340
French-340
93Parkhurst Parkie Reprints-PR35
02BAP Ultimate Mem Blades of Steel-7
02BAP Ultimate Memorabilia Great Moments-6
02BAP Ultimate Mem Paper Cuts Autos-26
02Maple Leafs Platinum Collection-96
03BAP Memorabilia Brush with Greatness-13
03BAP Mem Brush with Greatness Contest C-13
03BAP Ultimate Mem Maple Leafs Forever-17
03BAP Ultimate Memorabilia Paper Cuts-44
03BAP Ultimate Mem Vintage Blade of Steel-1
03ITG VIP Vintage Memorabilia-10
03Parkhurst Original Six Toronto-44
Inserts-T1
Memorabilia-TM26
04ITG Franchises Canadian-113
04ITG Ultimate Memorabilia-4
Gold-4
Blades of Steel-1
Day In History-22
Day In History Gold-22
Maple Leafs Forever-2
Original Six-13
Original Six-20
Paper Cuts-6
Paper Cuts Memorabilia-1
04ITG Heroes and Prospects-169
04ITG Heroes/Prospects Toronto Expo '05-169
04ITG Heroes/Prospects Expo Heroes/Pros-169
05ITG Ultimate Memorabilia Level 1-8
05ITG Ultimate Memorabilia Level 2-8
05ITG Ultimate Memorabilia Level 3-8
05ITG Ultimate Memorabilia Level 4-8
05ITG Ultimate Memorabilia Level 5-8
05ITG Ultimate Mem Blades of Steel-20
05ITG Ultimate Mem Blades of Steel Gold-20
05ITG Ultimate Memorabilia Lumbergraphs-6
05ITG Ultimate Mem Paper Cut Autos-8
05ITG Ultimate Memorabilia Vintage Lumber-28
05ITG Ultimate Mem Vintage Lumber Gold-28
06ITG Ultimate Memorabilia-15
Artist Proof-15
Maple Leafs Forever Autos-5
Stick Rack-28
Stick Rack Gold-28
Vintage Lumber-10
Vintage Lumber Gold-10

Barin, Stephane
92Finnish Semic-229
93Swedish Semic World Champ Stickers-258
94Finnish Jaa Kiekko-228
94Swedish Olympics Lillehammer*-327
96Swedish Semic Wien-191
98German DEL-38
99German DEL-140
00German DEL-235
01German Upper Deck-152
02German DEL City Press-214

Barinev, Alexander
94German First League-348

Barinka, Michal
96Quebec Pee-Wee Tournament-2
02Czech OFS Plus-169
03BAP Memorabilia-233
03ITG Used Signature Series-199
Gold-199
03ITG VIP Rookie Debut-139
03Parkhurst Rookie-79
03UD Premier Collection-97
03Upper Deck Rookie Update-180
03Norfolk Admirals-5
04Norfolk Admirals-4
05Norfolk Admirals-3
06Binghamton Senators-2

Barinka, Peter
03Czech OFS Plus-148
04Czech OFS-272
Goals Leaders-12
05Czech HC Hame Zlin-2

Bark, Sten Ake
72Swedish Stickers-40
72Swedish Stickers-127
73Swedish Stickers-188
74Swedish Stickers-159

Barker, Brennan
05Penticton Vees-1

Barker, Brian
92Northern Michigan Wildcats-1
93Northern Michigan Wildcats-1
95Slapshot-20
95Barrie Colts-2
96Barrie Colts-1
97Barrie Colts-1
03New Mexico Scorpions-5

Barker, Brian (NMU)
92Northern Michigan Wildcats-1
93Northern Michigan Wildcats-1

Barker, Cam
02Medicine Hat Tigers-2
03Medicine Hat Tigers-1
04ITG Top Prospects Spring Expo-4
04Medicine Hat Tigers-2
04ITG Heroes and Prospects-61
Autographs-CB
Top Prospects-4
04ITG Heroes/Prospects Toronto Expo '05-61
04ITG Heroes/Prospects Expo Heroes/Pros-61
05ITG Heroes/Prosp Toronto Expo Parallel -65
05Beehive-174
Matte-174
Signature Scrapbook-SSCB
05Black Diamond-224
05Hot Prospects-115
En Fuego-115
Red Hot-115
White Hot-115
05Parkhurst-617
Facsimile Auto Parallel-617
Signatures-CB
True Colors-TCCHI
True Colors-TCCHI
05SP Authentic-146
Limited-146
Rarefied Rookies-RRCB
Rookie Authentics-RACB
Sign of the Times Duals-DBS
Sign of the Times Triples-TKRB
05SP Game Used-166
Autographs-166
Gold-166
Game Gear-GG-CB
Game Gear Autographs-AG-CB
Rookie Exclusives-CB
Rookie Exclusives Silver-RE-CB
Significant Numbers-SN-CB
05SPx-162
Spectrum-162
Xcitement Rookies-XR-CB
Xcitement Rookies Gold-XR-CB
Xcitement Rookies Spectrum-XR-CB
05The Cup-183
Autographed Rookie Patches Gold Rainbow-183
Black Rainbow Rookies-183
Masterpiece Pressplates (Artifacts)-260
Masterpiece Pressplates (Bee Hive)-174
Masterpiece Pressplates (Black Diamond)-224
Masterpiece Pressplates (Ice)-125
Masterpiece Pressplates (Rookie Update)-204
Masterpiece Pressplates SPA Autos-146
Masterpiece Pressplates (SP Game Used)-166
Masterpiece Pressplates SPx Autos-162
Masterpiece Pressplates (Trilogy)-184
Masterpiece Pressplates Ult Coll Autos-108
Masterpiece Pressplates (Victory)-254
Masterpiece Pressplates Autographs-183
Platinum Rookies-183
05UD Artifacts-260
05Ultimate Collection-108
Autographed Patches-108
Autographed Shields-108
Jerseys Dual-DJSB
Ultimate Debut Threads Jerseys-DTJCB
Ultimate Debut Threads Jerseys Autos-DAJCB
Ultimate Debut Threads Patches-DTPCB
Ultimate Debut Threads Patches Autos-DAPCB
Ultimate Patches Dual-DPSB
05Ultra-212
Gold-212
Fresh Ink-FI-CB
Fresh Ink Blue-FI-CB
Ice-212
Rookie Uniformity Jerseys-RU-CB
Rookie Uniformity Jersey Autographs-ARU-CB
Rookie Uniformity Patches-RUP-CB
Rookie Uniformity Patch Autographs-ARP-CB
05Upper Deck-445
Rookie Ink-RICB
Rookie Threads-RTCB
05Upper Deck Ice-125
Glacial Graphs-GGCB
Glacial Graphs Labels-GGCB
Premieres Auto Patches-AIPCB
05Upper Deck Rookie Update-204
Inspirations Patch Rookies-204
05Upper Deck Trilogy-184
05Upper Deck Victory-254
Black-254
Gold-254
Silver-254
05Medicine Hat Tigers-2
05ITG Heroes and Prospects-65
Autographs-A-CB
06Be A Player Portraits First Exposures-FECB
06Be A Player Portraits Signature Portraits-SPCB
06Black Diamond Gemography-GCB
06SP Game Used SIGnificance-SCB
06Norfolk Admirals-4

Barker, Eldon
92Saskatchewan JHL-93

Barker, Josh
02Roanoke Express-9
02Roanoke Express RBI Sports-187
03Reading Royals RBI Sports-306
03Roanoke Express-305
04Louisiana Ice Gators-2

Barker, Randy
92British Columbia JHL-223

Barker, Robbie
00Sioux Falls Stampede-1

Barkley, Doug
44Beehive Group II Photos-152A
44Beehive Group II Photos-152B
62York Iron-On Transfers-24
63Parkhurst-60
63York White Backs-46
64Beehive Group III Photos-61
64Coca-Cola Caps-41
64Topps-9
65Coca-Cola-41
65Topps-43
76Old Timers-3
94Parkhurst Tall Boys-49

Barklund, Niklas
917th Inn. Sketch WHL-231

Barkman, Jon
96Saskatoon Blades-2
97Saskatoon Blades-1

Barkov, Aleksander
92Russian Stars Red Ace-1
94Finnish SISU-215
95Finnish SISU-117
95Finnish SISU-368
95Finnish SISU Limited-80
96Finnish SISU Redline-132
98Finnish Kerailysarja-219
99Finnish Cardset-125
99Finnish Cardset-174
00Finnish Cardset-335
01Finnish Cardset-126
02Finnish Cardset-156
03Finnish Cardset-148
05Finnish Tappara Legendat-3

Barkovich, Rick
88ProCards IHL-22
88Salt Lake Golden Eagles-1
89ProCards IHL-193
90Kansas City Blades-4
90ProCards AHL/IHL-588
93Raleigh Icecaps-2
94Raleigh Icecaps-2

Barkunov, Alexander
00Russian Hockey League-308

Barlie, Vegar
92Norwegian Elite Series-93
92Norwegian Elite Series-203
94Finnish Jaa Kiekko-267

Barlow, Bob
69O-Pee-Chee-196
70O-Pee-Chee-45
70Sargent Promotions Stamps-93
70Topps-45
74Phoenix Roadrunners WHA Pins-1

Barlow, Evan
03Salmon Arm Silverbacks-1
04Salmon Arm Silverbacks-18

Barlow, Geoff
93Quebec Pee-Wee Tournament-1290

Barlow, Hugh
52Juniors Blue Tint-33

Barlow, Marc
02Fort Wayne Komets-1
02Fort Wayne Komets Shoe Carnival-11
03Fort Wayne Komets 2003 Champions-15

Barnaby, Matthew
917th Inn. Sketch QMJHL-189
92Parkhurst-483
Emerald Ice-483
93Donruss-42
93Leaf-362
93OPC Premier-346
Gold-346
93Parkhurst-296
Emerald Ice-296
93Pinnacle-216
Canadian-216
93Stadium Club-321
Members Only Master Set-321
First Day Issue-321
93Topps/OPC Premier-346
Gold-346
93Ultra-13
93Upper Deck-439
SP-13
94Donruss-289
94Leaf-285
94Classic Pro Prospects-179
95Donruss-383
95Upper Deck-341
Electric Ice-341
Electric Ice Gold-341
96Be A Player-147
Autographs-147
Autographs Silver-147
96Collector's Choice-33
96Donruss-152
Press Proofs-152
96Score-188
Artist's Proofs-188
Dealer's Choice Artist's Proofs-188
Special Artist's Proofs-188
Golden Blades-188
97Collector's Choice-27
97Donruss-170
Press Proofs Silver-170
Press Proofs Gold-170
97Donruss Canadian Ice-84
Dominion Series-84
Provincial Series-84
97Donruss Limited-68
Exposure-68
97Katch-13
Gold-13
Silver-13
97Pacific-210
Copper-210
Emerald Green-210
Ice Blue-210
Red-210
Silver-210
97Paramount-17
Copper-17
Dark Grey-17
Emerald Green-17
Ice Blue-17
Red-17
Silver-17
97Pinnacle-108
Press Plates Back Black-108
Press Plates Back Cyan-108
Press Plates Back Magenta-108
Press Plates Back Yellow-108
Press Plates Front Black-108
Press Plates Front Cyan-108
Press Plates Front Magenta-108
Press Plates Front Yellow-108
97Pinnacle Inside-176
97Revolution-12
Copper-12
Emerald-12
Ice Blue-12
Silver-12
97Score-216
97Score Sabres-5
Platinum-5
Premier-5
97Upper Deck-16
97Upper Deck-393
98Aurora-15
98Be A Player-14
Press Release-14
98BAP Gold-14
98BAP Autographs-14
98BAP Autographs Gold-14
98BAP Tampa Bay All Star Game-14
98Crown Royale-11
Limited Series-11
98Katch-13
98OPC Chrome-213
Refractors-213
98Pacific-36
Ice Blue-36
Red-36
98Pacific Dynagon Ice-16
Blue-16
Red-16
98Pacific Omega-20
Red-20
Opening Day Issue-20
98Paramount-17
Copper-17
Emerald Green-17

Holo-Electric-17
Ice Blue-17
Silver-17
98Revolution-12
Ice Shadow-12
Red-12
Three Pronged Attack-1
Three Pronged Attack Parallel-1
98SP Authentic Sign of the Times-MB
98SP Authentic Sign of the Times Gold-MB
98SPx Finite-11
Radiance-11
Spectrum-11
98Topps-213
O-Pee-Chee-213
98Upper Deck-228
Exclusives-228
Exclusives 1 of 1-228
Gold Reserve-228
98Upper Deck MVP-22
Gold Script-22
Silver Script-22
Super Script-22
99Aurora-114
Premiere Date-114
99BAP Memorabilia-74
Gold-74
Silver-74
99O-Pee-Chee-131
99O-Pee-Chee Chrome-131
99O-Pee-Chee Chrome Refractors-131
99Pacific-333
Copper-333
Emerald Green-333
Gold-333
Ice Blue-333
Premiere Date-333
Red-333
99Pacific Dynagon Ice-157
Blue-157
Copper-157
Gold-157
Premiere Date-157
Checkmates American-13
Checkmates American-28
Checkmates Canadian-13
99Panini Stickers-140
99Paramount-186
Copper-186
Emerald-186
Gold-186
Holographic Emerald-186
Holographic Gold-186
Holographic Silver-186
Ice Blue-186
Premiere Date-186
Red-186
Silver-186
99SPx-125
Radiance-125
Spectrum-125
99Topps/OPC-131
99Topps/OPC Chrome-131
Refractors-131
99Upper Deck-107
Exclusives-107
Exclusives 1 of 1-107
99Upper Deck Gold Reserve-107
99Upper Deck MVP-171
Gold Script-171
Silver Script-171
Super Script-171
99Upper Deck Victory-236
00O-Pee-Chee-39
00O-Pee-Chee Parallel-39
00Pacific-325
Copper-325
Gold-325
Ice Blue-325
Premiere Date-325
00Paramount-196
Copper-196
Gold-196
Holo-Gold-196
Holo-Silver-196
Ice Blue-196
Premiere Date-196
00Titanium Game Gear-143
00Titanium Game Gear Patches-143
00Topps/OPC-39
Parallel-39
00Topps Heritage-167
00Upper Deck-141
Exclusives Tier 1-141
Exclusives Tier 2-141
00Upper Deck MVP-146
First Stars-146
Second Stars-146
Third Stars-146
00Upper Deck Victory-185
01BAP Memorabilia-475
Emerald-475
Ruby-475
Sapphire-475
01BAP Update Tough Customers-TC14
01BAP Update Tough Customers-TC38
01O-Pee-Chee-143
01O-Pee-Chee Premier Parallel-143
01Pacific-349
01Pacific-422
Extreme LTD-349
Gold-422
Hobby LTD-349
Premiere Date-349
Retail LTD-349
01Pacific Arena Exclusives-349
01Pacific Arena Exclusives-422
01Pacific Heads-Up Quad Jerseys-27
01Parkhurst-389
01Topps-143
OPC Parallel-143
01Upper Deck-160
Exclusives-160
01Upper Deck Victory-323
Gold-323
01Upper Deck Vintage-266
02BAP Sig Series Auto Buybacks 1998-14
02Pacific-246
Blue-246
Red-246
02Pacific Complete-293
Red-293
02Rangers Team Issue-1
02Upper Deck-359
Exclusives-359
02Upper Deck Beckett UD Promos-359
02Upper Deck Vintage-169
03ITG Action-388
03Pacific-219
Blue-219
Red-219
03Pacific Complete-154
Red-154
03Parkhurst Original Six New York-1
03Rangers Team Issue-1
03Topps Traded-TT37
Blue-TT37
Gold-TT37
Red-TT37
03Upper Deck-372
Canadian Exclusives-372
HG-372
UD Exclusives-372
03Upper Deck MVP-282
Gold Script-282
Silver Script-282
Canadian Exclusives-282
04Upper Deck-37
Canadian Exclusives-37
HG Glossy Gold-37
HG Glossy Silver-37
05Be A Player Signatures-BA
05Be A Player Signatures Gold-BA
05Beehive Signature Scrapbook-SSBA
05Panini Stickers-217
05Parkhurst-108
Facsimile Auto Parallel-108
05SP Game Used Auto Draft-AD-BY
05SP Game Used Statscriptions-ST-BA
05Upper Deck-41
HG Glossy-41
Notable Numbers-N-MBA
05Upper Deck MVP-89
Gold-89
Platinum-89
05Upper Deck Toronto Fall Expo-41
06Fleer Signing Day-SDBA
06O-Pee-Chee-161
Rainbow-161
06Stars Team Postcards-2

Barner, Jay
84Nanaimo Clippers-2

Barnes, Blair
83Nova Scotia Voyageurs-13

Barnes, Brian
91British Columbia JHL-102
92British Columbia JHL-121
97New Mexico Scorpions-8

Barnes, Jamie
907th Inn. Sketch WHL-303
917th Inn. Sketch WHL-293

Barnes, Joe
02Saskatoon Blades-14
03Saskatoon Blades-17
04Saskatoon Blades-16
05Saskatoon Blades-3
06Albany River Rats-4

Barnes, Matt
02Austin Ice Bats-1
04Austin Ice Bats-13

Barnes, Norm
80O-Pee-Chee-308
81O-Pee-Chee Stickers-67

Barnes, Robert
78Finnish SM-Liiga-72

Barnes, Ryan
97Sudbury Wolves Police-3
98Barrie Colts-12
01Cincinnati Mighty Ducks-4
02Grand Rapids Griffins-4
03ITG Used Signature Series-192
Gold-192
03ITG VIP Rookie Debut-86
03Parkhurst Rookie-94
03Topps Traded-TT148
Blue-TT148
Gold-TT148
Red-TT148
03UD Premier Collection-69
03Upper Deck Rookie Update-105
03Grand Rapids Griffins-1
05Danbury Trashers-18
05Hamilton Bulldogs-3

Barnes, Steven
91Lake Superior State Lakers-5
92Lake Superior State Lakers-7
94Huntington Blizzard-2

Barnes, Stu
89Jets Safeway-2
90Alberta International Team Canada-10
90Score-391
Canadian-391
91Pro Set Platinum-273
91Jets IGA-1
91OPC Premier-109
91Parkhurst-419
French-419
91Pinnacle-319
French-319
91Pro Set-566
French-566
91Score Canadian Bilingual-630
91Score Canadian English-630
91Score Rookie/Traded-80T
91Upper Deck-53
French-53
92Bowman-26
92O-Pee-Chee-39
92Score-319
Canadian-319
92Stadium Club-285
92Topps-210
Gold-210G
92Upper Deck-426
93Donruss-377
93Donruss-432
93Jets Readers Club-1
93Jets Ruffles-1
93Leaf-350
93OPC Premier-351
Gold-351
93Parkhurst-226
Emerald Ice-226
93Pinnacle-426
Canadian-426
93PowerPlay-345
93Score-380
93Score-644
Gold-644
Canadian-380
Canadian-644
Canadian Gold-644
93Topps/OPC Premier-351
Gold-351
93Upper Deck-94
94Canada Games NHL POGS-104
94Donruss-306
94Finest-66
Super Team Winners-66
Refractors-66
94Fleer-76
94Leaf-73
94OPC Premier-458
Special Effects-458
94Panthers Pop-ups-4
94Parkhurst SE-SE66
Gold-SE66
94Pinnacle-47
Artist's Proofs-47
Rink Collection-47
94Score-138
Gold-138
Platinum-138
94SP-43
Die Cuts-43
94Stadium Club-261
Members Only Master Set-261
First Day Issue-261
Super Team Winner Cards-261
94Topps/OPC Premier-458
Special Effects-458
94Ultra-78
94Upper Deck-493
Electric Ice-493
95Bashan Super Stickers-48
95Be A Player-127
Signatures-S127
Signatures Die Cuts-S127
95Canada Games NHL POGS-115
95Collector's Choice-209
Player's Club-209
Player's Club Platinum-209
95Donruss-132
95Emotion-68
95Finest-68
Refractors-68
95Imperial Stickers-48
95Leaf-36
95Metal-58
95Panini Stickers-69
95Parkhurst International-86
Emerald Ice-86
95Pinnacle-40
Artist's Proofs-40
Rink Collection-40
95Playoff One on One-152
95Score-22
Black Ice Artist's Proofs-22
Black Ice-22
95SkyBox Impact-66
95Stadium Club-73
Members Only Master Set-73
95Summit-47
Artist's Proofs-47
Ice-47
95Topps-110
OPC Inserts-110
95Topps SuperSkills-38
Platinum-38
95Ultra-59
Gold Medallion-59
95Upper Deck-345
Electric Ice-345
Electric Ice Gold-345
Special Edition-SE33
Special Edition Gold-SE33
96Collector's Choice-110
96Donruss-68
Press Proofs-68
96Leaf-30
Press Proofs-30
96Pinnacle-135
Artist's Proofs-135
Foil-135
Premium Stock-135
Rink Collection-135
96Score-180
Artist's Proofs-180
Dealer's Choice Artist's Proofs-180
Special Artist's Proofs-180
Golden Blades-180
96Summit-131
Artist's Proofs-131
Ice-131
Metal-131
Premium Stock-131
96Upper Deck-64
97Collector's Choice-212
97Pacific-175
Copper-175
Emerald Green-175
Ice Blue-175
Red-175
Silver-175
97Pacific Omega-181
Copper-181
Dark Gray-181
Emerald Green-181
Gold-181
Ice Blue-181
97Revolution-110
Copper-110
Emerald-110
Ice Blue-110
Silver-110
97Score-237
97Score Penguins-9
Platinum-9
Premier-9
98Aurora-151
98Be A Player-114
Press Release-114
98BAP Gold-114
98BAP Autographs-114
98BAP Autographs Gold-114
98BAP Tampa Bay All Star Game-114
98Finest-131
No Protectors-131
No Protectors Refractors-131
Refractors-131
98Katch-119
98OPC Chrome-98
Refractors-98
98Pacific-348
Ice Blue-348
Red-348
98Pacific Omega-193
Red-193
Opening Day Issue-193
98Panini Photocards-6
98Paramount-189
Copper-189
Emerald Green-189
Holo-Electric-189
Ice Blue-189
Silver-189
98Revolution-116
Ice Shadow-116
Red-116
98SPx Finite-69
Radiance-69
Spectrum-69
98Topps-98
O-Pee-Chee-98
98Topps Gold Label Class 1-52
Black-52
Black One of One-52
One of One-52
Red-52
Red One of One-52
98Topps Gold Label Class 2-52
98Topps Gold Label Class 2 Black-52
98Topps Gold Label Class 2 Black 1 of 1-52
98Topps Gold Label Class 2 One of One-52
98Topps Gold Label Class 2 Red-52
98Topps Gold Label Class 2 Red One of One-52
98Topps Gold Label Class 3-52
98Topps Gold Label Class 3 Black-52
98Topps Gold Label Class 3 Black 1 of 1-52
98Topps Gold Label Class 3 One of One-52
98Topps Gold Label Class 3 Red-52
98Topps Gold Label Class 3 Red One of One-52
98UD Choice-167
98UD Choice Preview-167
98UD Choice Prime Choice Reserve-167
98UD Choice Reserve-167
98Upper Deck-347
Exclusives-347
Exclusives 1 of 1-347
Gold Reserve-347
98Upper Deck MVP-167
Gold Script-167
Silver Script-167
Super Script-167
99BAP Memorabilia-128
Gold-128
Silver-128
99Kraft Face Off Rivals-1
99Pacific-33
Copper-33
Emerald Green-33
Gold-33
Ice Blue-33
Premiere Date-33
Red-33
99Pacific Dynagon Ice-27
Blue-27
Copper-27
Gold-27
Premiere Date-27
99Panini Stickers-40
99Paramount-25
Copper-25
Emerald-25
Gold-25
Holographic Emerald-25
Holographic Gold-25
Holographic Silver-25
Ice Blue-25
Premiere Date-25
Red-25
Silver-25
99Upper Deck MVP Draw Your Own-W25
99Wayne Gretzky Hockey-24
00BAP Memorabilia-393
Emerald-393
Ruby-393
Sapphire-393
Promos-393
00BAP Mem Chicago Sportsfest Copper-393
00BAP Memorabilia Chicago Sportsfest Blue-393
00BAP Memorabilia Chicago Sportsfest Gold-393
00BAP Memorabilia Chicago Sportsfest Ruby-393
00BAP Memorabilia Chicago Sun-Times Ruby-393
00BAP Memorabilia Chicago Sun-Times Gold-393
00BAP Mem Chicago Sun-Times Sapphire-393
00BAP Mem Toronto Fall Expo Copper-393
00BAP Memorabilia Toronto Fall Expo Gold-393
00BAP Memorabilia Toronto Fall Expo Ruby-393
00BAP Parkhurst 2000-P211
00BAP Signature Series-118
Emerald-118
Ruby-118
Sapphire-118
Autographs-182
Autographs Gold-182
00Crown Royale Jersey Redemptions-1
00O-Pee-Chee-122
00O-Pee-Chee Parallel-122
00Pacific-47
Copper-47
Gold-47
Ice Blue-47
Premiere Date-47
00Paramount-25
Copper-25
Gold-25
Holo-Gold-25
Holo-Silver-25
Ice Blue-25
Premiere Date-25
00Titanium Game Gear-58
00Titanium Game Gear Patches-58
00Titanium Draft Day Edition-10
Patches-10
00Topps/OPC-122
Parallel-122
00Upper Deck-249
Exclusives Tier 1-249
Exclusives Tier 2-249
00Upper Deck MVP-22
First Stars-22
Second Stars-22
Third Stars-22
00Upper Deck Vintage-40
01BAP Memorabilia-158
Emerald-158
Ruby-158
Sapphire-158
01Bowman YoungStars-84
Gold-84
Ice Cubed-84
01Crown Royale-14
Blue-14
Premiere Date-14
Red-14
Retail-14
01O-Pee-Chee-153
01O-Pee-Chee Premier Parallel-153
01Pacific-45
Extreme LTD-45
Hobby LTD-45
Premiere Date-45
Retail LTD-45
01Pacific Adrenaline-18
Blue-18
Premiere Date-18
Red-18
Retail-18
01Pacific Arena Exclusives-45
01Pacific Heads-Up Quad Jerseys-4
01Parkhurst-179
01Private Stock Game Gear-9
01Private Stock Game Gear Patches-9
01Private Stock PS-2002-7
01Titanium-12
Hobby Parallel-12
Premiere Date-12
Retail-12
Retail Parallel-12
01Topps-153
OPC Parallel-153
01Topps Chrome-116
Refractors-116
Black Border Refractors-116
01UD Mask Collection-11
Gold-11
01UD Playmakers-12
01Upper Deck-21
Exclusives-21
01Upper Deck MVP-18
01Upper Deck Victory-41
Gold-41
02BAP Memorabilia-119
Emerald-119
Ruby-119
Sapphire-119
NHL All-Star Game-119
NHL All-Star Game Blue-119
NHL All-Star Game Green-119
NHL All-Star Game Red-119
02BAP Memorabilia Toronto Fall Expo-119
02BAP Signature Series-74
Autographs-74
Autograph Buybacks 1998-114
Autographs Gold-74
02Bowman YoungStars-81
Gold-81
Silver-81
02O-Pee-Chee-237
02O-Pee-Chee Premier Blue Parallel-237
02O-Pee-Chee Premier Red Parallel-237
02O-Pee-Chee Factory Set-237
02Pacific-37
Blue-37
Red-37
02Pacific Complete-86
Red-86
02Parkhurst Retro-80
Minis-80
02Sabres Team Issue-1
02Topps-237
OPC Blue Parallel-237
OPC Red Parallel-237
Factory Set-237
02Topps Chrome-130
Black Border Refractors-130
Refractors-130
02Topps Heritage-81
Chrome Parallel-81
02Topps Total-78
02UD Honor Roll-74
02Upper Deck-263
Exclusives-263
02Upper Deck Beckett UD Promos-263
02Upper Deck MVP-19
Gold-19
Classics-19
Golden Classics-19
02Upper Deck Victory-25
Bronze-25
Gold-25
Silver-25
02Upper Deck Vintage-27
02Upper Deck Vintage-264
03Beehive-64
Gold-64
Silver-64
03ITG Action-106
03NHL Sticker Collection-23
03O-Pee-Chee-277
03OPC Blue-277
03OPC Gold-277
03OPC Red-277
03Pacific Complete-275
Red-275
03Stars Postcards-2
03Topps-277
Blue-277
Gold-277
Red-277
03Upper Deck-308
Canadian Exclusives-308
HG-308
UD Exclusives-308
05Panini Stickers-256
05Parkhurst-158
Facsimile Auto Parallel-158
05Upper Deck-65
HG Glossy-65
05Upper Deck MVP-132
Gold-132
Platinum-132
05Upper Deck Toronto Fall Expo-65
06O-Pee-Chee-171
Rainbow-171
06Panini Stickers-251
06Stars Team Postcards-3

Barnes, Troy
04Maine Black Bears-5

Barnet, Sven
94German First League-352

Barnett, Brett
89ProCards IHL-92
90ProCards AHL/IHL-107
92Birmingham Bulls-3
93Birmingham Bulls-3

Barney, Scott
95Slapshot-328
96Black Diamond-14
Gold-14
96Upper Deck-379
97Collector's Choice-310
97Bowman CHL-150
OPC-150
Autographs-30
Bowman's Best-14
Bowman's Best Atomic Refractors-14
Bowman's Best Refractor-14
98Bowman CHL-39
Golden Anniversary-39
OPC International-39
98Bowman Chrome CHL-39
Golden Anniversary-39
Golden Anniversary Refractors-39
OPC International-39
OPC International Refractors-39
Refractors-39
99Bowman CHL-123
99Bowman CHL-164
Gold-123
Gold-164
OPC International-123
OPC International-164
02Manchester Monarchs-2
03Pacific Calder-119
Silver-119
03Pacific Complete-566
Red-566
03Manchester Monarchs-1
03Manchester Monarchs Team Issue-1
03Pacific AHL Prospects-45
Gold-45
04Manchester Monarchs-20
04Manchester Monarchs Tobacco-20
05Chicago Wolves-3

Barnhardt, Mike
98Sudbury Wolves-8

Barnreuther, Horst
94German First League-374

Barnstable, Scott
907th Inn. Sketch WHL-153

Baron, Jan
94German First League-633

Baron, Marco
83Moncton Alpines-3
88Oilers Tenth Anniversary-156
93Swiss HNL-137

Baron, Mark
84Minnesota-Duluth Bulldogs-21

Baron, Murray
89ProCards AHL-334
90Flyers Postcards-2
90Score-399
Canadian-399
90Upper Deck-275
French-275
90ProCards AHL/IHL-35
91Blues Postcards-1
91Bowman-243
91O-Pee-Chee-373
91Pinnacle-204
French-204
91Pro Set-472
French-472
91Score American-183
91Score Canadian Bilingual-183
91Score Canadian Bilingual-616
91Score Canadian English-183
91Score Canadian English-616
91Score Rookie/Traded-66T
91Score Young Superstars-27
91Stadium Club-334
91Topps-373
91Upper Deck-497
French-497
92Bowman-409
92Pinnacle-144
French-144
92Score-176
Canadian-176
92Stadium Club-194
92Topps-354
Gold-354G
93Score-294
Canadian-294
93Ultra-407
94Stadium Club-168
Members Only Master Set-168
First Day Issue-168
Super Team Winner Cards-168
95Be A Player-158
Signatures-S158
Signatures Die Cuts-S158
96Canadiens Postcards-1
96Upper Deck-143
96Upper Deck-198
97Coyotes Face-Off Luncheon -1
97Pacific Dynagon Best Kept Secrets-73
99Stadium Club-68
First Day Issue-68
One of a Kind-68
Printing Plates Black-68
Printing Plates Cyan-68
Printing Plates Magenta-68
Printing Plates Yellow-68
00Upper Deck Vintage-352
01Canucks Postcards-2
01Pacific-376
Extreme LTD-376
Hobby LTD-376
Premiere Date-376
Retail LTD-376
01Pacific Arena Exclusives-376
02Canucks Team Issue-1
02NHL Power Play Stickers-154
03Blues Team Set-2

Baron, Norman
83Nova Scotia Voyageurs-10

Baronick, Gary
03Fort Worth Brahmas-1

Barq, Simon
01Barrie Colts-14

Barr, Chris
99Spokane Chiefs-2
00Spokane Chiefs-1
01Spokane Chiefs-2
02Spokane Chiefs-1

Barr, Dave
86O-Pee-Chee-237
87Red Wings Little Caesars-2
88Red Wings Little Caesars-1
89O-Pee-Chee-13
89O-Pee-Chee Stickers-250
89Panini Stickers-60
89Red Wings Little Caesars-1
89Topps-13
90Bowman-231
Tiffany-231
90O-Pee-Chee-308
90Pro Set-65
90Topps-308
Tiffany-308
90Upper Deck-257
French-257
91Bowman-49
91O-Pee-Chee-147
91OPC Premier-54
91Pro Set-65
French-65
91Score American-187
91Score Canadian Bilingual-187
91Score Canadian Bilingual-597
91Score Canadian English-187
91Score Canadian English-597
91Score Rookie/Traded-47T
91Stadium Club-141
91Topps-147
92Score-315
Canadian-315
92Stadium Club-291
92Topps-197
Gold-197G
93PowerPlay-320
94Stars HockeyKaps-1
99Houston Aeros-22
04Guelph Storm-26
05Guelph Storm-B-07
06Guelph Storm-24

Barr, Don
92British Columbia JHL-4
92British Columbia JHL-18

Barras, Steven
01Swiss HNL-409
02Swiss HNL-407

Barrasso, Tom
84O-Pee-Chee-18
84O-Pee-Chee-212
84O-Pee-Chee-375
84O-Pee-Chee-379
84O-Pee-Chee Stickers-205
84O-Pee-Chee Stickers-206
84O-Pee-Chee Stickers-227
84O-Pee-Chee Stickers-228
84Sabres Blue Shield-2
847-Eleven Discs-3
84Topps-14
84Topps-158
85O-Pee-Chee-105
85O-Pee-Chee-263
85O-Pee-Chee Stickers-55
85O-Pee-Chee Stickers-114
85O-Pee-Chee Stickers-179
85O-Pee-Chee Stickers-189
85Sabres Blue Shield-3
85Sabres Blue Shield Small-3
857-Eleven Credit Cards-2
85Topps-105
85Topps Sticker Inserts-12
86O-Pee-Chee-91
86O-Pee-Chee Stickers-45
86Sabres Blue Shield-4
86Sabres Blue Shield Small-4
86Topps-91
87O-Pee-Chee-78
87O-Pee-Chee Stickers-148
87Panini Stickers-22
87Sabres Blue Shield-4
87Sabres Wonder Bread/Hostess-5
87Topps-78
88Frito-Lay Stickers-19
88O-Pee-Chee-107
88O-Pee-Chee Minis-1
88O-Pee-Chee Stickers-259
88Panini Stickers-219
88Topps-107
89O-Pee-Chee-36
89O-Pee-Chee Stickers-235
89Panini Stickers-312
89Penguins Foodland-15
89Topps-36
89Swedish Semic World Champ Stickers-153
90Bowman-209
Tiffany-209
90O-Pee-Chee-65
90Panini Stickers-134
90Penguins Foodland-5
90Pro Set-227
90Pro Set Player of the Month-P1
90Score-121
Canadian-121
90Topps-65
Tiffany-65
90Upper Deck-121
French-121
91Pro Set Platinum-96
91Bowman-80
91Bowman-419
91Bowman-420
91Bowman-423
91Bowman-424
91O-Pee-Chee-372
91O-Pee-Chee-402
91OPC Premier-103
91Panini Stickers-271
91Parkhurst-139
French-139
91Penguins Foodland-9
91Penguins Foodland Coupon Stickers-4
91Pinnacle-44
French-44
91Pro Set-186
91Pro Set-319
French-186
Platinum PC-PC3
Puck Candy-22
91Score American-225
91Score Canadian Bilingual-225
91Score Canadian English-225
91Stadium Club-155
91Topps-402
91Upper Deck-116
French-116
92Bowman-250
92Kraft-25
92O-Pee-Chee-340
92Panini Stickers-219
92Panini Stickers French-219
92Parkhurst-134
Emerald Ice-134
92Penguins Coke/Clark-1
92Penguins Foodland-5
92Penguins Foodland Coupon Stickers-1
92Pinnacle-298
French-298
92Pro Set-145
92Score-70
92Score-518
Canadian-70
92Seasons Patches-36
92Sports Illustrated for Kids II-9
92Stadium Club-416
92Topps-503
Gold-503G
92Ultra-162
92Upper Deck-243
93Donruss-260
93High Liner Greatest Goalies-6
93Kraft-50
93Leaf-196
Gold All-Stars-5
Painted Warriors-9
93OPC Premier-175
93OPC Premier-204
93OPC Premier-446
93OPC Premier-501
Gold-175
Gold-204
Gold-446
Gold-501
Black Gold-9
93Panini Stickers-88
93Panini Stickers-141
93Parkhurst-157
Emerald Ice-157
93Penguins Foodland-24
93Pinnacle I Samples-2
93Pinnacle-3
Canadian-3
Team Pinnacle-7
Team Canadian-7
93PowerPlay-187
Netminders-1
93Score-225
93Score-483
Canadian-225
Canadian-483
Dream Team-1
93Stadium Club-79
Members Only Master Set-79
OPC-79
First Day Issue-79
First Day Issue OPC-79
Master Photos-12
Master Photos Winners-12
93Topps/OPC Premier-175
93Topps/OPC Premier-204
93Topps/OPC Premier-446
93Topps/OPC Premier-501
Gold-175
Gold-204
Gold-446
Gold-501
93Topps Premier Black Gold-11
93Ultra-26
93Upper Deck-45
SP-120
93Swedish Semic World Champ Stickers-169
94SLU Hockey American-1
94Canada Games NHL POGS-291
94Donruss-208
94EA Sports-108
94Finest Ring Leaders-19
94Flair-133
94Hockey Wit-25
94Kenner Starting Lineup Cards-1
94Kraft-31
94Leaf-103
94OPC Premier-84
94OPC Premier-206
94OPC Premier-311
Special Effects-84
Special Effects-206
Special Effects-311
94Parkhurst-182
Gold-182
94Penguins Foodland-22
94Pinnacle-20
Artist's Proofs-20
Rink Collection-20
Goaltending Greats-GT17
94Score-31
Gold-31
Platinum-31
94Select-88
Gold-88
94Stadium Club Dynasty and Destiny-1
94Stadium Club Dynasty Destiny Members-1
94Topps/OPC Premier-84
94Topps/OPC Premier-206
94Topps/OPC Premier-311
Special Effects-84
Special Effects-206
Special Effects-311
94Ultra-162
94Upper Deck-70
Electric Ice-70
95SLU Hockey Canadian-1
95Be A Player-124
Signatures-S124
Signatures Die Cuts-S124
95Bowman-47
All-Foil-47
95Canada Games NHL POGS-221
95Collector's Choice-53
Player's Club-53
Player's Club Platinum-53
95Donruss-291
95Finest-129
Refractors-129
95Kenner Starting Lineup Cards-1
95Kraft-35
95Metal-115
95Parkhurst International-435
Emerald Ice-435
95Penguins Foodland-10
95Pinnacle-97
Artist's Proofs-97
Rink Collection-97
95Score-152
Black Ice Artist's Proofs-152
Black Ice-152
95Select Certified-95
Mirror Gold-95
95SP-119
95Stadium Club-158
Members Only Master Set-158
Metalists-M6
Metalists Members Only Master Set-M6
95Summit-88
Artist's Proofs-88
Ice-88
95Topps-262
OPC Inserts-262
95Topps SuperSkills-79
Platinum-79
95Ultra-364
95Upper Deck-115
Electric Ice-115
Electric Ice Gold-115
Special Edition-SE68
Special Edition Gold-SE68
95Zenith-90
95Finnish Semic World Championships-215
95Swedish Globe World Championships-102
96SLU Hockey American-1
96Collector's Choice-213
96Donruss-67
Press Proofs-67
96Donruss Canadian Ice-70
Gold Press Proofs-70
Red Press Proofs-70
96Donruss Elite-63
Die Cut Stars-63
96Fleer-84
96Kenner Starting Lineup Cards-1
96Leaf-26
Press Proofs-26
96Leaf Preferred-46
Press Proofs-46
Steel-27
Steel Gold-27
96Maggers-2
96Metal Universe-124
96Penguins Tribune-Review-5
96Pinnacle-95

Artist's Proofs-95
Foil-95
Premium Stock-95
Rink Collection-95
96Score-124
Artist's Proofs-124
Dealer's Choice Artist's Proofs-124
Special Artist's Proofs-124
Golden Blades-124
Net Worth-12
Sudden Death-10
96SkyBox Impact-99
96Summit-93
Artist's Proofs-93
Ice-93
Metal-93
Premium Stock-93
96Ultra-138
Gold Medallion-138
96Upper Deck-132
96Zenith-98
Artist's Proofs-98
97Crown Royale-108
Emerald Green-108
Ice Blue-108
Silver-108
Freeze Out Die-Cuts-16
97Donruss Priority-139
Stamp of Approval-139
Postmaster General-17
Postmaster Generals Promos-17
97Katch-115
Gold-115
Silver-115
97Pacific Invincible NHL Regime-157
97Pacific Omega-182
Copper-182
Dark Gray-182
Emerald Green-182
Gold-182
Ice Blue-182
97Paramount-147
Copper-147
Dark Grey-147
Emerald Green-147
Ice Blue-147
Red-147
Silver-147
Glove Side Laser Cuts-17
97Pinnacle-76
Artist's Proofs-76
Rink Collection-76
Press Plates Back Black-76
Press Plates Back Cyan-76
Press Plates Back Magenta-76
Press Plates Back Yellow-76
Press Plates Front Black-76
Press Plates Front Cyan-76
Press Plates Front Magenta-76
Press Plates Front Yellow-76
Inside Stand Up Guys-1A/B
Inside Stand Up Guys-1C/D
Inside Stand Up Guys Promos-1A/B
Inside Stand Up Guys Promos-1C/D
97Revolution-111
Copper-111
Emerald-111
Ice Blue-111
Silver-111
Return to Sender Die-Cuts-16
97Score-17
Artist's Proofs-17
Golden Blades-17
97Score Penguins-1
Platinum-1
Premier-1
97Zenith-77
Z-Gold-77
Z-Silver-77
98SLU Hockey Classic Doubles-4
98Aurora-152
Championship Fever-39
Championship Fever Copper-39
Championship Fever Ice Blue-39
Championship Fever Red-39
Championship Fever Silver-39
98Bowman's Best-56
Refractors-56
Atomic Refractors-56
98Crown Royale-108
Limited Series-108
98Finest-142
No Protectors-142
No Protectors Refractors-142
Refractors-142
98Katch-115
98NHL Aces Playing Cards-51
98OPC Chrome-209
Refractors-209
Season's Best-SB6
Season's Best Refractors-SB6
98Pacific-35
Ice Blue-35
Red-35
Gold Crown Die-Cuts-28
98Pacific Dynagon Ice-148
Blue-148
Red-148
98Pacific Omega-194
Red-194
Opening Day Issue-194
98Panini Photocards-5
98Panini Stickers-51
98Paramount-190
Copper-190
Emerald Green-190
Holo-Electric-190
Ice Blue-190
Silver-190
Glove Side Laser Cuts-16
98Revolution-117
Ice Shadow-117
Red-117
98SPx Finite-70
Radiance-70
Spectrum-70
98Topps-209
O-Pee-Chee-209
Season's Best-SB6
98Topps Gold Label Class 1-78
Black-78
Black One of One-78
One of One-78
Red-78
Red One of One-78
98Topps Gold Label Class 2-78
98Topps Gold Label Class 2 Black-78
98Topps Gold Label Class 2 Black 1 of 1-78
98Topps Gold Label Class 2 One of One-78
98Topps Gold Label Class 2 Red-78
98Topps Gold Label Class 2 Red One of One-78
98Topps Gold Label Class 3-78
98Topps Gold Label Class 3 Black-78
98Topps Gold Label Class 3 Black 1 of 1-78
98Topps Gold Label Class 3 One of One-78
98Topps Gold Label Class 3 Red-78
98Topps Gold Label Class 3 Red One of One-78
98UD Choice-165
98UD Choice-250
98UD Choice Preview-165
98UD Choice Prime Choice Reserve-165
98UD Choice Prime Choice Reserve-250
98UD Choice Reserve-165
98UD Choice Reserve-250
98Upper Deck-162
Exclusives-162
Exclusives 1 of 1-162
Gold Reserve-162
98Upper Deck MVP-164
Gold Script-164
Silver Script-164
Super Script-164
99Aurora-115
Premiere Date-115
99BAP Memorabilia-77
Gold-77
Silver-77
99Crown Royale-111
Limited Series-111
Premiere Date-111
99Jell-O Partners of Power-2
99O-Pee-Chee-169
99O-Pee-Chee Chrome-169
99O-Pee-Chee Chrome Refractors-169
99Pacific-334
Copper-334
Emerald Green-334
Gold-334
Ice Blue-334
Premiere Date-334
Red-334
In the Cage Net-Fusions-16
99Pacific Dynagon Ice-158
Blue-158
Copper-158
Gold-158
Premiere Date-158
99Panini Stickers-137
99Paramount-187
Copper-187
Emerald-187
Gold-187
Holographic Emerald-187
Holographic Gold-187
Holographic Silver-187
Ice Blue-187
Premiere Date-187
Red-187
Silver-187
Glove Side Net Fusions-17
99Revolution-116
Premiere Date-116
Red-116
Shadow Series-116
Copper-116
Gold-116
CSC Silver-116
99Stadium Club-99
First Day Issue-99
One of a Kind-99
Printing Plates Black-99
Printing Plates Cyan-99
Printing Plates Magenta-99
Printing Plates Yellow-99
Goalie Cam-GC7
99Topps/OPC-169
99Topps/OPC Chrome-169
Refractors-169
99Upper Deck-105
Exclusives-105
Exclusives 1 of 1-105
99Upper Deck Gold Reserve-105
99Upper Deck MVP-168
Gold Script-168
Silver Script-168
Super Script-168
Last Line-LL8
99Upper Deck MVP SC Edition-148
Gold Script-148
Silver Script-148
Super Script-148
99Upper Deck Victory-237
00BAP Memorabilia Georges Vezina-V15
00BAP Ultimate Mem Dynasty Jerseys-D9
00BAP Ultimate Mem Dynasty Emblems-D9
00Black Diamond Game Gear-BTB
00Black Diamond Game Gear-CTB
00O-Pee-Chee-151
00O-Pee-Chee Parallel-151
00Pacific-275
Copper-275
Gold-275
Ice Blue-275
Premiere Date-275
00Topps/OPC-151
Parallel-151
01BAP Memorabilia-493
Emerald-493
Ruby-493
Sapphire-493
01BAP Ultimate Memorabilia Active Eight-2
01BAP Ultimate Memorabilia Calder Trophy-12
01Between the Pipes-78
01Between the Pipes-116
01Between the Pipes-156
01Bowman YoungStars-100
Gold-100
Ice Cubed-100
01Parkhurst-213
01Parkhurst-397
01Titanium-23
Hobby Parallel-23
Premiere Date-23
Retail-23
Retail Parallel-23
Double-Sided Jerseys-44
Double-Sided Jerseys-59
Double-Sided Patches-44
Double-Sided Patches-59
Three-Star Selections-2
01Titanium Draft Day Edition-89
01UD Challenge for the Cup Jerseys-TTB
02Atomic Jerseys-22
02Atomic Jerseys Gold-22
02Atomic Patches-22
02Atomic National Pride-U10
02BAP Ultimate Memorabilia Cup Duels-15
02Between the Pipes-69
Gold-69
Silver-69
Nightmares-GN10
02O-Pee-Chee-66
02O-Pee-Chee Premier Blue Parallel-66
02O-Pee-Chee Premier Red Parallel-66
02O-Pee-Chee Factory Set-66
02Pacific-357
Blue-357
Red-357
02Topps-66
OPC Blue Parallel-66
OPC Red Parallel-66
Factory Set-66
02UD Mask Collection-76
02UD Mask Collection Beckett Promos-76
02UD Top Shelf Milestones Jerseys-MHPBJ
06Between The Pipes-102
Autographs-ATB
Complete Jersey-CJ13
Complete Jersey Gold-CJ13
Double Jerseys-DJ18
Double Jerseys Gold-DJ18
Emblems-GUE16
Emblems Gold-GUE16
Emblems Autographs-GUE16
Jerseys-GUJ16
Jerseys Gold-GUJ16
Jerseys Autographs-GUJ16
Numbers-GUN16
Numbers Gold-GUN16
Numbers Autographs-GUN16
Playing For Your Country-PC05
Playing For Your Country Gold-PC05
Stick and Jersey-SJ40
Stick and Jersey Gold-SJ40
Stick and Jersey Autographs-SJ40
06ITG Ultimate Memorabilia-141
Artist Proof-141
Jerseys Autos-1
Jerseys Autos Gold-1
Road to the Cup-8
Road to the Cup Gold-8

Barratt, Jeff
79Montreal Juniors-1

Barrault, Doug
89Lethbridge Hurricanes-1
91ProCards-158
93PowerPlay-88
93Score-457
Canadian-457
93Cincinnati Cyclones-1
93Classic Pro Prospects-61
94Ultra-294
95Atlanta Knights-2
98Chicago Wolves Turner Cup-12

Barrefjord, Kjell-Olov
64Swedish Coralli ISHockey-156
67Swedish Hockey-249
69Swedish Hockey-294

Barrefjord, Ulf
67Swedish Hockey-250
69Swedish Hockey-295
70Swedish Hockey-203
71Swedish Hockey-290
72Swedish Stickers-77
74Swedish Stickers-202

Barrer, Brett
93Quebec Pee-Wee Tournament-1465

Barrett, Dave
89Rayside-Balfour Jr. Canadians-2

Barrett, Fred
70Esso Power Players-165
71O-Pee-Chee-128
71Toronto Sun-126
73North Stars Postcards-1
73O-Pee-Chee-264
74NHL Action Stamps-135
74O-Pee-Chee NHL-234
74Topps-234
75O-Pee-Chee NHL-124
75Topps-124
76O-Pee-Chee NHL-249
76Topps-249
77O-Pee-Chee NHL-291
78North Stars Cloverleaf Dairy-2
78O-Pee-Chee-185
78Topps-185
79North Stars Postcards-2
80North Stars Postcards-2
80O-Pee-Chee-253
80Topps-253
81North Stars Postcards-2
82North Stars Postcards-1
82Post Cereal-9
83NHL Key Tags-58
04ITG Franchises US West-249
Autographs-A-FB

Barrett, Greg
04Sioux Falls Stampede-1-4

Barrett, Jasmin
93Quebec Pee-Wee Tournament-1224

Barrett, John
82O-Pee-Chee-80
82Post Cereal-5
83O-Pee-Chee-117
84O-Pee-Chee-49
86Capitals Kodak-2
86Capitals Police-2
87Capitals Kodak-6
87Capitals Team Issue-2

Barrett, Kevin
93Muskegon Fury-18
94Flint Generals-1
95Central Hockey League-37
95Oklahoma Coyotes RHI-1
98Bakersfield Condors-2

Barrett, Michael
98Owen Sound Platers-3
99Owen Sound Platers-3
00Owen Sound Attack-1

Barrett, Mike
01Mississauga Ice Dogs-21

Barrett, Nathan
99Lethbridge Hurricanes-3
00Lethbridge Hurricanes-2
01Lethbridge Hurricanes-8
05Norfolk Admirals-13

Barrett, Tom
83Kitchener Rangers-8
84Kitchener Rangers-4
85Kitchener Rangers-4
86Kitchener Rangers-4
95Slapshot-180

Barrette, Maurice
77Nova Scotia Voyageurs-2

Barriball, Jay
06Minnesota Golden Gophers-2

Barrie, Doug
70Esso Power Players-76
71O-Pee-Chee-22
71Sabres Postcards-74
71Sargent Promotions Stamps-28
71Topps-22
71Toronto Sun-23
75O-Pee-Chee WHA-117
76O-Pee-Chee WHA-119

Barrie, Len
89Kamloops Blazers-1
90ProCards AHL/IHL-49
907th Inn. Sketch Memorial Cup-1
91Upper Deck-459
French-459
91ProCards-274
93Parkhurst-351
Emerald Ice-351
93Cincinnati Cyclones-2
93Classic Pro Prospects-53
94Fleer-161
94Leaf-491
94Penguins Foodland-4
94Cleveland Lumberjacks-7
94Cleveland Lumberjacks Postcards-7
95Topps-66
OPC Inserts-66
95Cleveland Lumberjacks-3
95Cleveland Lumberjacks Postcards-3
98German DEL-135
99Long Beach Ice Dogs-5
00BAP Memorabilia-188
Emerald-188
Ruby-188
Sapphire-188
Promos-188
00BAP Mem Chicago Sportsfest Copper-188
00BAP Memorabilia Chicago Sportsfest Blue-188
00BAP Memorabilia Chicago Sportsfest Gold-188
00BAP Memorabilia Chicago Sportsfest Ruby-188
00BAP Memorabilia Chicago Sun-Times Ruby-188
00BAP Memorabilia Chicago Sun-Times Gold-188
00BAP Mem Chicago Sun-Times Sapphire-188
00BAP Mem Toronto Fall Expo Copper-188
00BAP Memorabilia Toronto Fall Expo Gold-188
00BAP Memorabilia Toronto Fall Expo Ruby-188
00Panthers Team Issue-13
00Upper Deck NHLPA-PA37

Barrie, Mike
917th Inn. Sketch WHL-60
93Seattle Thunderbirds-1
95South Carolina Stingrays-12
95Signature Rookies-40
Signatures-40
96Peoria Rivermen-1
96Peoria Rivermen Photo Album-1
01UK London Knights-14

Barrow, John
03Sarnia Sting-2

Barrow, Mark
99UK Basingstoke Bison-15

Barry, Kevin
95Slapshot-168

Barry, Marty
33V129-38
33V357 Ice Kings-27
34Beehive Group I Photos-88
34Beehive Group I Photos-134
34Diamond Matchbooks Silver-2
35O-Pee-Chee V304C-81
36Champion Postcards-1
37V356 Worldwide Gum-4
39O-Pee-Chee V301-1-57
83Hall of Fame-214
83Hall of Fame Postcards-03
85Hall of Fame-214

Barry, Ray
44Beehive Group II Photos-3
51Parkhurst-32

Barski, Phillip
93Quebec Pee-Wee Tournament-1161

Barta, Alexander
01German Berlin Polar Bears Postcards-2
02German Berlin Polar Bears Postcards-2
02German DEL City Press-23
03German Berlin Polar Bears Postcards-3
03German DEL-62
04German Berlin Polar Bears Postcards-1
04German DEL-80
05German DEL-119
05German DEL-294
06German DEL-67
06German DEL-195
German Forwards-GF13

Barta, Bjorn
02German DEL City Press-3
03German DEL-17
04German Augsburg Panthers Postcards-4
04German DEL-23
05German DEL-143
05German DEL-368
06German DEL-94

Barta, Jan
05German DEL-100

Barta, Libor
95Czech APS Extraliga-200
96Czech APS Extraliga-143
97Czech APS Extraliga-244
97Czech DS Extraliga-67
98Czech DS-16
98Czech DS Stickers-127
98Czech OFS-375
99Czech DS-71
Goalies-G6
99Czech OFS-1
99Czech OFS Goalie Die-Cuts-1
00Czech DS Extraliga-85
00Czech OFS-31
00Czech OFS Star Emerald-10
00Czech OFS Star Pink-10
00Czech OFS Star Violet-10
01Czech OFS-207
01Czech OFS H Inserts-H14
02Czech OFS Plus-255
Trios-T10
Duos-D14
03Czech OFS Plus-199
03Czech OFS Plus-397
03Czech OFS Plus Checklists-10
03Czech OFS Plus Insert B-B12
03Czech OFS Plus Insert P-P10
04Czech OFS Save Percentage Leaders-14

Bartanus , Marek
05Owen Sound Attack-19
06Owen Sound Attack-19

Bartanus, Karol
97Bowman CHL-59
97Bowman CHL-130
OPC-59
OPC-130
Autographs-10
98Bowman CHL-98
Golden Anniversary-98
OPC International-98
Scout's Choice-SC11
98Bowman Chrome CHL-98
Golden Anniversary-98
Golden Anniversary Refractors-98
OPC International-98
OPC International Refractors-98
Refractors-98
01Czech OFS-94

Bartecko, Lubos
98Pacific Omega-208
Red-208
Opening Day Issue-208
99Blues Taco Bell-7
99Pacific-352
Copper-352
Emerald Green-352
Gold-352
Ice Blue-352
Premiere Date-352
Red-352
99Upper Deck-115
Exclusives-115
Exclusives 1 of 1-115
99Upper Deck Gold Reserve-115
99Upper Deck MVP-187
Gold Script-187
Silver Script-187
Super Script-187
99Upper Deck Victory-261
00O-Pee-Chee-175
00O-Pee-Chee Parallel-175
00Pacific-339
Copper-339
Gold-339
Ice Blue-339
Premiere Date-339
00Paramount-203
Copper-203
Gold-203
Holo-Gold-203
Holo-Silver-203
Ice Blue-203
Premiere Date-203
00SP Authentic Sign of the Times-LB
00Topps/OPC-175
Parallel-175
00UD Pros and Prospect Game Jsy Auto Excl-S-LB
00UD Pros and Prospects Game Jersey Autos-S-LB
00Upper Deck Victory-202
00Upper Deck Vintage-316
01BAP Signature Series-174
Autographs-174
Autographs Gold-174
01UD Mask Collection-5
Gold-5
01Upper Deck-240
Exclusives-240
02BAP Sig Series Auto Buybacks 2001-174
02O-Pee-Chee-65
02O-Pee-Chee Premier Blue Parallel-65
02O-Pee-Chee Premier Red Parallel-65
02O-Pee-Chee Factory Set-65
02Pacific-12
Blue-12
Red-12
02Pacific Complete-183
Red-183
02Thrashers Postcards-1
02Topps-65
OPC Blue Parallel-65
OPC Red Parallel-65
Factory Set-65
02Topps Total-203
02Upper Deck-6
Exclusives-6
02Upper Deck Victory-12
Bronze-12
Gold-12
Silver-12
02Upper Deck Vintage-11
02Slovakian Kvarteto-20
03ITG Action-53
03Upper Deck MVP-24
Gold Script-24
Silver Script-24
Canadian Exclusives-24
03Czech OFS Plus-337
04Russian Legion-3
04Russian Moscow Dynamo-3
05Swedish Lulea Hockey Postcards-18
05Swedish SHL Elitset-238
Series Two Signatures-20
06Swedish SHL Elitset-93
Playmakers-9

Bartek, Martin
01Milwaukee Admirals-3
01Milwaukee Admirals Postcards-5
04Czech OFS Czech/Slovak-24
04Finnish Cardset-119
06German DEL-28

Bartek, Peter
02Czech OFS Plus-63

Bartel, Regan
04Kelowna Rockets-20

Bartel, Robin
85Moncton Golden Flames-25

Bartell, Adam
93RPI Engineers-2

Bartell, Fred
83Swedish Semic VM Stickers-158

Bartell, Josh
92Clarkson Knights-1

Bartels, Florian
04German Weiden Blue Devils-1

Barth, Todd
92Saskatchewan JHL-112
95Neepewa Natives-20

Barthe, Claude
907th Inn. Sketch QMJHL-268
92Hampton Roads Admirals-3
92Wheeling Thunderbirds-2
93Roanoke Express-3

Barthelemy, Julien
93Quebec Pee-Wee Tournament-1656

Barthelson, Tony
84Swedish Semic Elitserien-10
89Swedish Semic Elitserien Stickers-198
94Swedish Leaf-204
95Swedish Leaf-6
95Swedish Upper Deck-6

Bartholomaus, Keith
93Northern Michigan Wildcats-2

Bartholomay, Adam
02Topeka Scarecrows-21
03Lincoln Stars-20

Bartkowski, Matt
06Lincoln Stars-8
06Lincoln Stars Upper DeckÂ Signature Series -2

Bartlett, Jim
58Topps-26
59Topps-51
60Shirriff Coins-113

Bartlett, Michael
04Notre Dame Fighting Irish-11

Bartlett, Terry
01Thetford Mines Coyotes-3

Bartley, Joey
96Guelph Storm-23
97Guelph Storm-6
98Guelph Storm-20

Bartley, Mitch
03Vancouver Giants-16
04Vancouver Giants-14
05Vancouver Giants-2

Bartley, Victor
05Kamloops Blazers-7
06Kamloops Blazers-1

Bartley, Wade
89Sudbury Wolves-21
90Sudbury Wolves-8
92Toledo Storm Team Issue-23
95Toledo Storm-16

Bartmann, Jamie
95German DEL-316
04German Ingolstadt Panthers-3

Bartoli, Moe
66Columbus Checkers-2
67Columbus Checkers-2

Bartolone, Chris
96German DEL-188
98German DEL-27
99German DEL-139
00German DEL-53
01German Upper Deck-46
02German DEL City Press-150
03German DEL-138

Barton, Aaron
04Mississauga Ice Dogs-24
04Peterborough Petes Postcards-13
06Saint Johns Sea Dogs-21

Barton, Brad
88Kitchener Rangers-24
89Kitchener Rangers-24
90Kitchener Rangers-23
907th Inn. Sketch OHL-227
907th Inn. Sketch Memorial Cup-45
917th Inn. Sketch OHL-93
94Brantford Smoke-10
96Quad-City Mallards-2
97Quad-City Mallards-5

Barton, Dave
03Ohio State Buckeyes-19
04Ohio State Buckeyes-2
05Ohio State Buckeyes-2
06Ohio State Buckeyes-2

Barton, Jakub
02Czech OFS Plus-212

Barton, Jaroslav
06Czech OFS-151

Barton, Pat
94Wheeling Thunderbirds-15
94Wheeling Thunderbirds Photo Album-12
95Wheeling Thunderbirds-18
95Wheeling Thunderbirds Series II-2

Barton, Patrick
917th Inn. Sketch OHL-71
94Guelph Storm-14

Bartos, Martin
05Saint John's Sea Dogs-14

Bartos, Peter
98Czech OFS-208
99Czech DS-37
99Czech OFS-278
99Czech OFS-491
All-Star Game Blue-491
All-Star Game Gold-491
All-Star Game Red-491
All-Star Game Silver-491
00Black Diamond-122
00SP Authentic-111
00UD Reserve-99
01BAP Memorabilia-271
Emerald-271
Ruby-271
Sapphire-271
01Czech OFS-141
02Czech OFS Plus-170
02Czech OFS Plus All-Star Game-H23
02Czech OFS Plus Trios-T1
03Czech OFS Plus-325

Bartosch, Michal
04German Weiden Blue Devils-2

Bartosch, Roman
94German First League-368

Bartovic, Milan
99Brandon Wheat Kings-2
99UD Prospects-45
00Brandon Wheat Kings-14
02Rochester Americans-2
03ITG Action-70
03O-Pee-Chee-310
03OPC Blue-310
03OPC Gold-310
03OPC Red-310
03Pacific-35
Blue-35
Red-35
03Pacific Exhibit-16
Blue Backs-16
Yellow Backs-16
03Pacific Invincible-103
Blue-103
Red-103
Retail-103
03Pacific Prism-13
Blue-13
Gold-13
Red-13
03Pacific Supreme-105
Blue-105
Red-105
Retail-105
03Parkhurst Rookie-61
03Private Stock Reserve-105
Blue-105
Red-105
Retail-105
03SP Game Used-53
Gold-53
03Topps-310
Blue-310
Gold-310
Red-310
03Topps C55-135
Minis-135
Minis American Back-135
Minis American Back Red-135
Minis Bazooka Back-135
Minis Brooklyn Back-135
Minis Hat Trick Back-135
Minis O Canada Back-135
Minis O Canada Back Red-135
Minis Stanley Cup Back-135
03Upper Deck Classic Portraits-162
03Upper Deck MVP-64
Gold Script-64
Silver Script-64
Canadian Exclusives-64
03Upper Deck Victory-22
Bronze-22
Gold-22
Silver-22
03Rochester Americans-3
04SP Authentic Sign of the Times-ST-BA
04Rochester Americans-3
05Black Diamond Gemography-G-BA
05Black Diamond Gemography Emerald-G-BA
05Black Diamond Gemography Gold-G-BA
05Black Diamond Gemography Onyx-G-BA
05Black Diamond Gemography Ruby-G-BA
05Parkhurst-115
Facsimile Auto Parallel-115
Signatures-BA
05SP Game Used Auto Draft-AD-MI
05UD Powerplay Power Marks-PMMB
05Upper Deck Notable Numbers-N-BA
05Norfolk Admirals-8
06Swedish SHL Elitset-232

Bartschi, Deny
02Swiss HNL-38

Bartschi, Patrick
01Swiss HNL-63
02Swiss HNL-296

Bartschi, Peter
93Swiss HNL-70
95Swiss HNL-355
96Swiss HNL-329
98Swiss Power Play Stickers-139

Bartulis, Oskars
05ITG Heroes/Prosp Toronto Expo Parallel -153
05Moncton Wildcats-8
05ITG Heroes and Prospects-153
Autographs-A-OB
06Cape Breton Screaming Eagles-13

Bartzen, Casey
05Stockton Thunder-2

Barulin, Konstantin
02Russian Hockey League-192
04Russian World Junior Team-21

Barulis, Oskars
04Moncton Wildcats-2

Barus, Miroslav
94Czech APS Extraliga-247
95Czech APS Extraliga-12
96Czech APS Extraliga-262
97Czech APS Extraliga-286
97Czech DS Stickers-91
98Czech DS-36
98Czech DS Stickers-81
98Czech OFS-205
99Czech DS-25
99Czech OFS-312
00Czech DS Extraliga-54
00Czech OFS-366
02Czech OFS Plus-104
03Czech OFS Plus-238
04Czech OFS-307

Barz, Benjamin
03German Nuremberg Ice Tigers Postcards-2
04German DEL-245
04German Nuremburg Ice Tigers Postcards-2
05German DEL-261

Basalgin, Andrei
91O-Pee-Chee Inserts-49R

Basanta, Mark
91British Columbia JHL-41
91British Columbia JHL-122
92British Columbia JHL-221

Basaraba, Shannon
98Charlotte Checkers-2

Baseggio, Dave
89ProCards AHL-277
90ProCards AHL/IHL-270
91ProCards-9
91Rochester Americans Postcards-1
95Cleveland Lumberjacks-4
95Cleveland Lumberjacks Postcards-4
97Cleveland Lumberjacks-4
97Cleveland Lumberjacks Postcards-6
98Cleveland Lumberjacks-3
99Detroit Vipers-9
00Charlotte Checkers-17
06Peoria Rivermen-24

Baseotto, Bruno
00Saskatoon Blades-4
01Saskatoon Blades-30
02Saskatoon Blades-28

Bashkatov, Egor
96Las Vegas Thunder-1
99German DEL-224
00German DEL-91
01German Upper Deck-92
03Russian Hockey League-73

Bashkirov, Andrei
97Fort Wayne Komets-16
98Fort Wayne Komets-29
99Quebec Citadelles-16
00Canadiens Postcards-2
00Quebec Citadelles-14
Signed-14
01Swiss HNL-270
02Swiss HNL-299
03Russian National Team-29
04Russian World Championship Team-14

Bashkirov, Roman
06Quebec Remparts-6

Bashkirov, Ruslan
06Quebec Remparts-13

Basile, Jason
92Quebec Pee-Wee Tournament-1857
02Bossier-Shreveport Mudbugs-1
03Bossier-Shreveport Mudbugs-1
05Bossier-Shreveport Mudbugs-1

Basilio, Sean
897th Inn. Sketch OHL-31
897th Inn. Sketch OHL-177
907th Inn. Sketch OHL-127
917th Inn. Sketch OHL-271
94Tampa Bay Tritons RHI-14

Basiuk, Scott
05Bakersfield Condors-7

Baskel, Kevin
96Arizona Icecats-3
97Arizona Icecats-4

Basken, Bruce
86Portland Winter Hawks-2

Basner, Brian
04Fort Worth Brahmas-2

Basque, Claude
51Laval Dairy Lac St. Jean-48

Bass, Cody
04Mississauga Ice Dogs-4
05ITG Heroes/Prosp Toronto Expo Parallel -180
05Mississauga Ice Dogs-1
05ITG Heroes and Prospects-180
Autographs-A-CBA
Oh Canada-OC-3
Oh Canada Gold-OC-3
06Binghamton Senators 5th Anniversary-2
06Mississauga Ice Dogs-1
06ITG Heroes and Prospects-187
Autographs-ACB
Update Autographs-ACB

Basse, Harold
82Kitchener Rangers-2
83Kitchener Rangers-22
84Kitchener Rangers-2
85Kitchener Rangers-2
86Kitchener Rangers-2
87Kitchener Rangers-2
88Kitchener Rangers-2
89Kitchener Rangers-2
90Kitchener Rangers-2

Bassen, Bob
83Medicine Hat Tigers-15
86Islanders Team Issue-5
89Blackhawks Coke-12
89ProCards IHL-53
90Blues Kodak-1
90Pro Set-520
91Blues Postcards-2
91Bowman-379
91O-Pee-Chee-51
91Panini Stickers-29
91Parkhurst-379
French-379
91Pro Set-221
French-221
91Score American-179
91Score Canadian Bilingual-179
91Score Canadian English-179
91Stadium Club-367
91Topps-51
91Upper Deck-319
French-319
92Bowman-378
92O-Pee-Chee-139
92Pinnacle-203
French-203
92Score-132
Canadian-132
92Stadium Club-176
92Topps-454
Gold-454G
92Ultra-182
92Upper Deck-181
93Donruss-476
93Panini Stickers-163
93Parkhurst-445
Emerald Ice-445
93Pinnacle-169
Canadian-169
93Score-279
Canadian-279
93Ultra-408
93Upper Deck-2
94Donruss-257
94Nordiques Burger King-2
94Parkhurst-184
Gold-184
94Pinnacle-327
Artist's Proofs-327
Rink Collection-327
94Upper Deck-481
Electric Ice-481
95Canada Games NHL POGS-83
95Emotion-44
95Playoff One on One-245
95Score-216
Black Ice Artist's Proofs-216
Black Ice-216
95SkyBox Impact-43
96Be A Player-89
96Be A Player-P89
Autographs-89
Autographs Silver-89
96Score-218
Artist's Proofs-218
Dealer's Choice Artist's Proofs-218
Special Artist's Proofs-218
Golden Blades-218
96Stars Postcards-2
96Summit-122
Artist's Proofs-122
Ice-122
Metal-122
Premium Stock-122
99Blues Taco Bell-12
99German DEL-81
00Stadium Club-124
01Utah Grizzlies-20
02Fleer Throwbacks-88
Gold-88
Platinum-88
Scraps-3
Tie Downs-3
02Utah Grizzlies-18

Bassen, Chad
01Regina Pats-2
01Vancouver Giants-4
02Medicine Hat Tigers-3
03Everett Silvertips-24
04German DEL Update-305
05German DEL-98

Bassen, Hank
44Beehive Group II Photos-153
61Shirriff/Salada Coins-80
62Parkhurst-19
64Beehive Group III Photos-62
65Coca-Cola-54
65Topps-106
66Topps-107

Bassen, Mark
88Brandon Wheat Kings-7
88Lethbridge Hurricanes-1
89ProCards AHL-355
90ProCards AHL/IHL-43
91ProCards-33
92Alberta International Team Canada-4
93Peoria Rivermen-1
94German DEL-364
94German DEL-366
95German DEL-239
96German DEL-306
98German DEL-219
99German DEL-96

Bassett, Cole
03Minnesota State Mavericks-1

04Missouri River Otters-7
Bassett, Dennis
95Saskatoon Blades-3
97Regina Pats-20
00Trenton Titans-13
Bassett, Jeff
93Quebec Pee-Wee Tournament-1311
Bassin, Sherry
81Oshawa Generals-24
82Oshawa Generals-24
83Oshawa Generals-16
89Sault Ste. Marie Greyhounds-5
917th Inn. Sketch CHL Award Winners-9
93Sault Ste. Marie Greyhound Memorial Cup-29
Bast, Jason
05Moose Jaw Warriors-1
06Moose Jaw Warriors-15
Bast, Ryan
93Prince Albert Raiders-1
94Prince Albert Raiders-2
96Toledo Storm-6
97Saint John Flames-3
99Upper Deck MVP-153
Gold Script-153
Silver Script-153
Super Script-153
99Upper Deck Victory-217
00Hartford Wolf Pack-3
02Hartford Wolf Pack-4
02Lowell Lock Monsters-20
Bastarache, Philippe
01Shawinigan Cataractes-11
Bastiansen, Anders
06Swedish SHL Elitset-256
Bastiansen, Harald
92Norwegian Elite Series-223
Bastien, Baz
43Parade Sportive *-2
45Quaker Oats Photos-5
Bastien, Joey
93Quebec Pee-Wee Tournament-1150
01Flint Generals-1
03Fort Worth Brahmas-2
Bastien, Mathieu
00Val d'Or Foreurs-18
Signed-18
Bastien, Morris
37V356 Worldwide Gum-131
Bastien, Yves
05Kitchener Rangers-17
06Kitchener Rangers-7
Baston, Dan
89Rayside-Balfour Jr. Canadians-3
90Rayside-Balfour Jr. Canadians-1
91Rayside-Balfour Jr. Canadians-1
Batchelor, Jay
98Red Deer Rebels-1
99Swift Current Broncos-2
00Prince Albert Raiders-1
01Prince Albert Raiders-1
Bateman, Dwayne
03St. Francis Xavier X-Men-18
Bateman, Jeff
99Brampton Battalion-24
00SP Authentic-132
00SP Game Used-87
00SPx-129
Spectrum-129
00UD Pros and Prospects-129
00UD Reserve-118
00Upper Deck-438
Exclusives Tier 1-438
Exclusives Tier 2-438
00Upper Deck Vintage-400
00Brampton Battalion-20
01Fort Worth Brahmas-2
02Utah Grizzlies-13
Bateman, Pat
04Northern Michigan Wildcats-1
Bateman, Rob
91Greensboro Monarchs-1
Bates, Shawn
97Donruss Preferred-156
Cut to the Chase-156
97Pacific Dynagon-NNO
Copper-NNO
Dark Grey-NNO
Emerald Green-NNO
Ice Blue-NNO
Red-NNO
Silver-NNO
97Score Bruins-1
Platinum-1
Premier-1
98Katch-168
98UD Choice-18
Prime Choice Reserve-18
Reserve-18
98Providence Bruins-6
99BAP Memorabilia-246
Gold-246
Silver-246
99O-Pee-Chee-39
99O-Pee-Chee Chrome-39
99O-Pee-Chee Chrome Refractors-39
99Pacific-19
Copper-19
Emerald Green-19
Gold-19
Ice Blue-19
Premiere Date-19
Red-19
99Topps/OPC-39
99Topps/OPC Chrome-39
Refractors-39
99Upper Deck-20
Exclusives-20
Exclusives 1 of 1-20
99Upper Deck Gold Reserve-20
99Upper Deck MVP-18
Gold Script-18
Silver Script-18
Super Script-18
99Upper Deck Victory-24
00Private Stock Game Gear-4
00Private Stock Game Gear Patches-4
00Upper Deck-247
Exclusives Tier 1-247
Exclusives Tier 2-247
01Parkhurst-388
01Private Stock Game Gear-61
01Private Stock Game Gear Patches-61
01Vanguard Memorabilia-18
02BAP Signature Series-87
Autographs-87
Autographs Gold-87
02O-Pee-Chee-243
02O-Pee-Chee Premier Blue Parallel-243
02O-Pee-Chee Premier Red Parallel-243
02O-Pee-Chee Factory Set-243
02Pacific-233
Blue-233
Red-233
02Pacific Complete-146
Red-146
02Parkhurst Retro-178
Minis-178
02Topps-243
OPC Blue Parallel-243
OPC Red Parallel-243
Factory Set-243
02Topps Total-194
02Upper Deck-109
Exclusives-109
02Upper Deck Victory-137
Bronze-137
Gold-137
Silver-137
03ITG Action-382
03NHL Sticker Collection-73
03Pacific-209
Blue-209
Red-209
03Pacific Complete-33
Red-33
05Parkhurst-315
Facsimile Auto Parallel-315
05Upper Deck MVP-253
Gold-253
Platinum-253
06Be A Player-170
Autographs-170
Signatures-BA
06O-Pee-Chee-320
Rainbow-320
06Upper Deck MVP-189
Gold Script-189
Super Script-189
Bathe, Frank
80O-Pee-Chee-389
83Flyers J.C. Penney-3
91ProCards-68
Bathe, Landon
99Des Moines Buccaneers-10
02Macon Trax-4
03Toledo Storm-10
04Idaho Steelheads-20
05Stockton Thunder-3
Batherson, Norm
94Portland Pirates-3
94Classic Pro Prospects-157
95Portland Pirates-3
96Portland Pirates-7
96Portland Pirates Shop N' Save-4
97Fort Wayne Komets-13
98German DEL-5
Bathgate, Andy
44Beehive Group II Photos-297A
44Beehive Group II Photos-297B
44Beehive Group II Photos-377
53Parkhurst-56
54Topps-11
57Topps-60
58Topps-21
59Topps-34
60NHL Ceramic Tiles-32
60Shirriff Coins-89
60Topps-45
Stamps-2
61Shirriff/Salada Coins-88
61Topps-22
61Topps-53
62Shirriff Coins-48
62Topps-52
Hockey Bucks-2
63Topps-52
63Toronto Star-2
64Beehive Group III Photos-63A
64Beehive Group III Photos-63B
64Beehive Group III Photos-152
64Coca-Cola Caps-95
64Coca-Cola Caps-96
64Topps-86
64Toronto Star-2
65Coca-Cola-51
65Topps-48
66Topps-44
68Bauer Ads-1
68O-Pee-Chee-104
68Shirriff Coins-139
68Topps-104
70Esso Power Players-224
70O-Pee-Chee-207
70Sargent Promotions Stamps-173
81TCMA-8
83Hall of Fame-215
83Hall of Fame Postcards-O4
85Hall of Fame-215
91Ultimate Original Six-18
91Ultimate Original Six-74
French-18
French-74
92Parkhurst Parkie Reprints-PR22
93Zeller's Masters of Hockey-1
93Zeller's Masters of Hockey Signed-1
94Hall of Fame Tickets-9
94Parkhurst Missing Link-90
94Parkhurst Missing Link-173
94Parkhurst Tall Boys-124
94Parkhurst Tall Boys-174
95Parkhurst '66-67-44
Coins-44
97Beehive-62
Golden Portraits-62
Golden Originals Autographs-62
99BAP Memorabilia AS American Hobby-AH8
99BAP Memorabilia AS American Hobby Autos-AH8
00Topps Heritage Autographs-HA-AB
00Topps Heritage Autoproofs-11
01Greats of the Game-65
Autographs-65
01Topps Archives-1
02Maple Leafs Platinum Collection-26
02Parkhurst Reprints-182
02Topps Rookie Reprints-4
02Topps Rookie Reprint Autographs-4
03Parkhurst Original Six New York-40
03Parkhurst Original Six New York-78
03Parkhurst Original Six New York-90
Autographs-1
Inserts-N11
04ITG Franchises US East-391
Autographs-A-AB
04ITG Ultimate Memorabilia-45
04ITG Ultimate Memorabilia-188
Gold-45
Gold-188
04UD Legends Classics-2
04UD Legends Classics-89
Gold-2
Gold-89
Platinum-2
Platinum-89
Silver-2
Silver-89
Signature Moments-M6
Signatures-CS6
Signatures-DC21
04ITG Heroes and Prospects-155
Autographs-ABA
04ITG Heroes/Prospects Toronto Expo '05-155
04ITG Heroes/Prospects Expo Heroes/Pros-155
06Parkhurst-9
06Parkhurst-194
Autographs-9
Autographs-194
06The Cup-63
Black Rainbow-63
Gold-63
Hardware Heroes-HHAB
Masterpiece Pressplates-63
06Upper Deck All-Time Greatest-ATG14
06Upper Deck Sweet Shot Signature Shots/Saves
Sticks-SSSAB
Bathgate, Frank
51Laval Dairy Subset-89
Batiani, Alessandro
92Finnish Semic-251
Batkiewicz, Jozef
73Finnish Jaakiekko-85
74Finnish Jenkki-92
79Panini Stickers-126
Batovsky, Zoltan
93Quebec Pee-Wee Tournament-1707
00Kentucky Thoroughblades-3
Battaglia, Anthony
93Quebec Pee-Wee Tournament-1324
01Western Michigan Broncos-1
02Florida Everblades-3
02Florida Everblades RBI-117
03Mississippi Sea Wolves-1
Battaglia, Bates
97Pacific Omega-38
Copper-38
Dark Gray-38
Emerald Green-38
Gold-38
Ice Blue-38
98Bowman's Best Mirror Image Fusion-F1
98Bowmans Best Mirror Im Fusion Ref-F1
98Bowmans Best Mirror Im Fusion Atom Ref-F1
98Hurricanes Team Issue-10
98SP Authentic Sign of the Times-BB
98SP Authentic Sign of the Times Gold-BB
98SPx Finite-17
98SPx Finite-137
Radiance-17
Radiance-137
Spectrum-17
Spectrum-137
98UD Choice-38
Prime Choice Reserve-38
Reserve-38
98UD3-17
98UD3-77
98UD3-137
Die-Cuts-17
Die-Cuts-77
Die-Cuts-137
98Upper Deck-62
Exclusives-62
Exclusives 1 of 1-62
Gold Reserve-62
99Pacific-67
Copper-67
Emerald Green-67
Gold-67
Ice Blue-67
Premiere Date-67
Red-67
99Pacific Prism-27
Holographic Blue-27
Holographic Gold-27
Holographic Mirror-27
Holographic Purple-27
Premiere Date-27
99Panini Stickers-52
99Topps Arena Giveaways-CAR-BB
99Upper Deck-34
Exclusives-34
Exclusives 1 of 1-34
99Upper Deck Gold Reserve-34
99Upper Deck MVP-43
Gold Script-43
Silver Script-43
Super Script-43
99Upper Deck Victory-55
99Wayne Gretzky Hockey-35
00BAP Memorabilia-288
Emerald-288
Ruby-288
Sapphire-288
Promos-288
00BAP Mem Chicago Sportsfest Copper-288
00BAP Memorabilia Chicago Sportsfest Blue-288
00BAP Memorabilia Chicago Sportsfest Gold-288
00BAP Memorabilia Chicago Sportsfest Ruby-288
00BAP Memorabilia Chicago Sun-Times Ruby-288
00BAP Memorabilia Chicago Sun-Times Gold-288
00BAP Mem Chicago Sun-Times Sapphire-288
00BAP Mem Toronto Fall Expo Copper-288
00BAP Memorabilia Toronto Fall Expo Gold-288
00BAP Memorabilia Toronto Fall Expo Ruby-288
00O-Pee-Chee-250
00O-Pee-Chee Parallel-250
00Pacific-78
Copper-78
Gold-78
Ice Blue-78
Premiere Date-78
00Stadium Club-111
00Topps/OPC-250
Parallel-250
00Upper Deck-33
Exclusives Tier 1-33
Exclusives Tier 2-33
00Upper Deck Vintage-62
01BAP Signature Series-178
Autographs-178
Autographs Gold-178
01Pacific-69
Extreme LTD-69
Hobby LTD-69
Premiere Date-69
Retail LTD-69
01Pacific Arena Exclusives-69
01Upper Deck-266
Exclusives-266
01Upper Deck Victory-70
Gold-70
02BAP First Edition-295
02BAP Memorabilia-51
Emerald-51
Ruby-51
Sapphire-51
NHL All-Star Game-51
NHL All-Star Game Blue-51
NHL All-Star Game Green-51
NHL All-Star Game Red-51
02BAP Memorabilia Toronto Fall Expo-51
02BAP Sig Series Auto Buybacks 2001-178
02BAP Signature Series Golf-GS10
02O-Pee-Chee-239
02O-Pee-Chee Premier Blue Parallel-239
02O-Pee-Chee Premier Red Parallel-239
02O-Pee-Chee Factory Set-239
02Pacific-62
Blue-62
Red-62
02Pacific Complete-463
Red-463
02Pacific Exclusive-25
02Parkhurst-10
Bronze-10
Gold-10
Silver-10
02Parkhurst Retro-136
Minis-136
02Topps-239
OPC Blue Parallel-239
OPC Red Parallel-239
Factory Set-239
02Topps Total-353
02Upper Deck-279
Exclusives-279
02Upper Deck Beckett UD Promos-279
02Upper Deck MVP-32
Gold-32
Classics-32
Golden Classics-32
02Upper Deck Victory-41
Bronze-41
Gold-41
Silver-41
03ITG Action-193
Homeboys-HB11
03Pacific-80
Blue-80
Red-80
03Czech Stadion-534
06Toronto Marlies-2
Battaglia, Doug
98Charlotte Checkers-3
98Charlotte Checkers-22
Battaglia, Sam
93Arizona Icecats-10
94Arizona Icecats-12
95Arizona Icecats-7
96Arizona Icecats-4
Battani, T.J.
06Barrie Colts-26
Batten, John
95Flint Generals-5
96Quad-City Mallards-19
97Flint Generals EBK-21
99Adirondack IceHawks-5
99Memphis RiverKings All-Time-13
Batters, Greg
84Victoria Cougars-2
90Knoxville Cherokees-117
Batters, Jeff
92Peoria Rivermen-1
93Peoria Rivermen-2
95Kansas City Blades-3
Battersby, Brooke
91Air Canada SJHL-E1
92Saskatchewan JHL-10
Battershill, Jason
05Medicine Hat Tigers-3
Battice, John
86Kingston Canadians-25
87Kingston Canadians-25
897th Inn. Sketch OHL-29
Battochio, Danny
03Ottawa 67's-4
04Ottawa 67's-12
05Ottawa 67's-12
Batyrshin, Ruslan
95Phoenix Roadrunners-1
97Springfield Falcons-2
99Anchorage Aces-15
00Russian Hockey League-139
03Russian Hockey League-178
Bauba, Dino
04UK Edinburgh Capitals-13
Bauer, Bernard
95Swiss HNL-464
Bauer, Bobby
34Beehive Group I Photos-1
36Providence Reds-1
39O-Pee-Chee V301-1-99
43Parade Sportive *-3
91Bruins Sports Action Legends-36
03BAP Ultimate Mem Linemates Autos-3
04ITG Franchises US East-330
04ITG Ultimate Memorabilia-69
Gold-69
06ITG Ultimate Memorabilia Beantown's Best Autos-7
Bauer, Clayton
04Kelowna Rockets-25
05Kelowna Rockets-3
Bauer, Collin
88Saskatoon Blades-13
89Saskatoon Blades-25
90ProCards AHL/IHL-238
91ProCards-220
96Michigan K-Wings-6
97Long Beach Ice Dogs-3
Bauer, Helmut
94German First League-585
Bauer, Jake
06Sioux Falls Stampede-14
Bauer, Lubomir
96Czech APS Extraliga-73
97Czech APS Extraliga-194
98Czech OFS-395
99Czech OFS-324
Bauer, Reinhold
72Finnish Semic World Championship-113
72Swedish Semic World Championship-113
Bauer, Richard
02Czech OFS Plus-277
03Czech OFS Plus-68
04Czech OFS-215
05Czech HC Vsetin-1
Bauer, Robin
93Swiss HNL-398
96Swiss HNL-14
99Swiss Panini Stickers-239
Bauer, Sara
04Wisconsin Badgers Women-1
Bauer, Stephan
94German DEL-340
95German DEL-296
Bauerle, Reiner
94German First League-242
Baum, Dan
99Prince George Cougars-25
00Prince George Cougars-17
Bauman, Gary
65Quebec Aces-2
68O-Pee-Chee-145
Bauman, Rodney
00Ottawa 67's-13
01Ottawa 67's-15
02Ottawa 67's-15
03Ottawa 67's-5
Bauman, Stacey
03Greenville Grrrowl-1
Baumann, Andre
95Swiss HNL-299
96Swiss HNL-283
98Swiss Power Play Stickers-63
99Swiss Panini Stickers-63
00Swiss Panini Stickers-111
00Swiss Slapshot Mini-Cards-HCD7
01Swiss HNL-86
Baumann, Marco
02Swiss HNL-377
Baumann, Matt
02Arizona Icecats-2
Baumann, Max
93Swiss HNL-437
Baumann, Nicolas
93Swiss HNL-325
Baumbach, Kent
98Anchorage Aces-12
Baume, Thierry
93Swiss HNL-491
Baumgartner, Andrea
95Swiss HNL-320
Baumgartner, Gregor
93Quebec Pee-Wee Tournament-1529
97Bowman CHL-151
OPC-151
Autographs-31
99Michigan K-Wings-16
99Quebec PeeWee Tournament Coll Souv-20
99Bowman CHL-60
Gold-60
OPC International-60
00Utah Grizzlies-31
01Utah Grizzlies-3
02Grand Rapids Griffins-5
Baumgartner, Ken
84Prince Albert Raiders Stickers-1
88Kings Postcards-7
88Kings Smokey-2
88ProCards AHL-192
89New Haven Nighthawks-1
90O-Pee-Chee-414
90Pro Set-178
90Score-265
Canadian-265
90Upper Deck-439
French-439
91O-Pee-Chee-316
91Pinnacle-239
French-239
91Pro Set-432
French-432
91Score American-148
91Score Canadian Bilingual-148
91Score Canadian English-148
91Topps-316
91Upper Deck-402
French-402
92Maple Leafs Kodak-4
92Panini Stickers-85
92Panini Stickers French-85
92Parkhurst-413
Emerald Ice-413
92Score-35
Canadian-35
92Stadium Club-103
92Topps-217
Gold-217G
92Ultra-416
93Maple Leafs Score Black's-17
93Parkhurst-207
Emerald Ice-207
93PowerPlay-448
93Ultra-429
93Upper Deck NHLPA/Roots-29
94Be A Player-R140
94Be A Player-R166
Signature Cards-149
94Donruss-288
94Maple Leafs Gangsters-2
94Maple Leafs Kodak-2
94Maple Leafs Pin-up Posters-19
94Stadium Club-98
Members Only Master Set-98
First Day Issue-98
Super Team Winner Cards-98
94Ultra-212
95Parkhurst International-476
Emerald Ice-476
95Playoff One on One-201
95Playoff One on One-314
96Be A Player-32
Autographs-32
Autographs Silver-32
96Donruss-9
Press Proofs-9
96Ducks Team Issue-12
96Playoff One on One-393
96Score-206
Artist's Proofs-206
Dealer's Choice Artist's Proofs-206
Special Artist's Proofs-206
Golden Blades-206
97Pacific Invincible NHL Regime-1
97Score Bruins-15
Platinum-15
Premier-15
98Be A Player-160
Press Release-160
98BAP Gold-160
98BAP Autographs-160
98BAP Autographs Gold-160
98OPC Chrome-201
Refractors-201
98Pacific-70
Ice Blue-70
Red-70
98Topps-201
O-Pee-Chee-201
02BAP Sig Series Auto Buybacks 1998-160
02Fleer Throwbacks-61
Gold-61
Platinum-61
Autographs-19
Baumgartner, Lukas
02Swiss HNL-34
Baumgartner, Nolan
93Kamloops Blazers-1
94Finest-148
Super Team Winners-148
Refractors-148
94Leaf Limited World Juniors Canada-1
94Pinnacle-525
Artist's Proofs-525
Rink Collection-525
94Upper Deck-505
Electric Ice-505
94Kamloops Blazers-3
94Classic-9
Gold-9
CHL Previews-CP6
94Classic Four-Sport *-124
Gold-124
Autographs-124A
Printers Proofs-124
94Signature Rookies Gold Standard *-76
Signatures-GS4
95Donruss Canadian World Junior Team-3
95Donruss Elite World Juniors-4
95Parkhurst International-491
Emerald Ice-491
95SP-174
95Topps Canadian World Juniors-11CJ
95Upper Deck-353
Electric Ice-353
Electric Ice Gold-353
95Kamloops Blazers-1
95Classic CHL All-Stars-AS1
95Classic Ice Breakers-BK20
95Classic Ice Breakers Die Cuts-BK20
95Images Four-Sport *-102
95Signature Rookies-25
Auto-Phonex Beyond 2000-B4
Signatures-25
95Slapshot Memorial Cup-4
95Classic Five-Sport *-126
Autographs-126
Strive For Five-HK10
95Signature Rookies Tetrad Autobilia *-38
95Signature Rookies Tetrad SR Force *-F1
96Donruss-235
Press Proofs-235
96Fleer-121
96Fleer Picks-168
96Leaf Gold Rookies-6
96Metal Universe-169
96Pinnacle-245
Artist's Proofs-245
Foil-245
Premium Stock-245
Rink Collection-245
96Score-251
Artist's Proofs-251
Dealer's Choice Artist's Proofs-251
Special Artist's Proofs-251
Golden Blades-251
96SkyBox Impact-144
96Summit-173
Artist's Proofs-173
Ice-173
Metal-173
Premium Stock-173
96Portland Pirates-5
96Portland Pirates Shop N' Save-3
96Classic Signings *-73
Blue-73
Die-Cuts-73
Red-73
96Visions *-85
97Portland Pirates-1
98Katch-167
98Upper Deck-387
Exclusives-387
Exclusives 1 of 1-387
Gold Reserve-387
98Portland Pirates-7
99Pacific-450
Copper-450
Emerald Green-450
Gold-450
Ice Blue-450
Premiere Date-450
Red-450
99Upper Deck Victory-313
99Portland Pirates-1
01Norfolk Admirals-16
02Manitoba Moose-7
03Manitoba Moose-6
04AHL All-Stars-2
04Manitoba Moose-5
05Parkhurst-474
Facsimile Auto Parallel-474
06Philadelphia Phantoms-21
Baumgartner, Paul
99Des Moines Buccaneers-3
Baumgartner, Raoul
93Swiss HNL-62
95Swiss HNL-348
96Swiss HNL-321
Baumle, Thomas
02Swiss HNL-452
04Swiss Davos Postcards-4
Baun, Bob
44Beehive Group II Photos-378
57Parkhurst-T20
58Parkhurst-15
59Parkhurst-21
60Parkhurst-11
60Shirriff Coins-7
60York Photos-3
61Parkhurst-11
61Shirriff/Salada Coins-50
61York Yellow Backs-1
62Parkhurst-3
62Shirriff Coins-19
63Chex Photos-4
63Maple Leafs Team Issue-1
63Maple Leafs Team Issue-2
63Parkhurst-18
63Parkhurst-78
63Toronto Star-3
63York White Backs-7
64Beehive Group III Photos-153A
64Beehive Group III Photos-153B
64Coca-Cola Caps-104
64Topps-57
64Toronto Star-3
65Coca-Cola-103
65Maple Leafs White Border-2
65Topps-13
66Topps-83
67Seals Team Issue-1
68O-Pee-Chee-24
68Shirriff Coins-46
68Topps-24
69O-Pee-Chee-57
Four-in-One-1
69Topps-57
70Colgate Stamps-66
70Dad's Cookies-3
70Esso Power Players-32
70O-Pee-Chee-223
70Sargent Promotions Stamps-64
70Topps-24
71Frito-Lay-6
71Letraset Action Replays-9
71Maple Leafs Postcards-1
71O-Pee-Chee-196
71Sargent Promotions Stamps-196
71Toronto Sun-254
72Maple Leafs Postcards-1
72O-Pee-Chee-66
72Sargent Promotions Stamps-199
72Topps-134
91Kraft-28
91Kraft-78
91Ultimate Original Six-30
91Ultimate Original Six-93
French-30
French-93
92Parkhurst Parkie Reprints-PR12
94Parkhurst Missing Link-123
94Parkhurst Tall Boys-120
95Parkhurst '66-67-117
Coins-117
02Maple Leafs Platinum Collection-71
Autographs-71
02Parkhurst Reprints-222
02Parkhurst Reprints-227
02Parkhurst Reprints-239
02Parkhurst Reprints-247
02Parkhurst Reprints-260
02Parkhurst Reprints-272
03Parkhurst Original Six Toronto-45
Autographs-1
04ITG Franchises Canadian-96
Autographs-BB2
04ITG Franchises US West-259
Autographs-A-BB1
04ITG Ultimate Memorabilia-87
Gold-87
04MasterCard Priceless Moments-1
06Parkhurst-10
Autographs-10
06The Cup Stanley Cup Signatures-CSBA
06The Cup Stanley Cup Titlists-TBB
07Maple Leafs 1967 Commemorative-1
Autographs-ABB1
Baustad, Colin
94Central Hockey League-91
95Central Hockey League-55
Bautin, Sergei
92OPC Premier-84
92Parkhurst-435
Emerald Ice-435
92Ultra-440
92Upper Deck-337
92Upper Deck-499
92Russian Stars Red Ace-2
92Russian Stars Red Ace-16
93Donruss-378
93Jets Readers Club-2
93Jets Ruffles-2
93Leaf-242
93OPC Premier-332
Gold-332
93Pinnacle-197
Canadian-197
93PowerPlay-268
93Score-351
Canadian-351
93Topps/OPC Premier-332
Gold-332
93Ultra-10
93Upper Deck-514
95Kansas City Blades-22
97Swedish Collector's Choice-119
98Russian Hockey League-49
99German DEL-38
02Russian Transfert-6
Bauyba, Dainius
00UK Sekonda Superleague-12
Bavaudin, Denis
73Finnish Jaakiekko-304
Bavis, Mark
93Classic-60
95South Carolina Stingrays-10
Bavis, Mike
93Rochester Americans Kodak-4
94Classic Autographs-NNO
94Classic Pro Prospects-66
Bawa, Robin
85Kamloops Blazers-1
86Kamloops Blazers-2
88ProCards AHL-27
89ProCards AHL-99
90ProCards AHL/IHL-536
91ProCards-597
92Hamilton Canucks-2
93Stadium Club-445
Members Only Master Set-445
First Day Issue-445
96Collector's Edge Ice-187
Prism-187
97Fort Wayne Komets-6
98Fort Wayne Komets-5
99Fort Wayne Komets Penalty Leaders-7
01Fort Wayne Komets Shoe Carnival-8
Bawlf, Nick
10C56-18
Baxmann, Jens
03German Berlin Polar Bears Postcards-4
04German Berlin Polar Bears Postcards-2
04German DEL-62
05German DEL-21
Baxter, Chris
93Lakeland Ice Warriors-4
00UK Nottingham Panthers-18
00UK Sekonda Superleague-198
Baxter, Goalie
77Kalamazoo Wings-15
Baxter, Jim
99Bowman CHL-135
Gold-135
OPC International-135
02ECHL All-Star Southern-40
Baxter, Paul
76Nordiques Marie Antoinette-1
76Nordiques Postcards-2
79O-Pee-Chee-372
82O-Pee-Chee-238
82Post Cereal-15
83Penguins Heinz Photos-1
83Vachon-1
85Flames Red Rooster-1
86Flames Red Rooster-1
90Flames IGA/McGavin's-1
91Flames IGA-27
92Blackhawks Coke-12
93Blackhawks Coke-28
95Saint John Flames-2
96Saint John Flames-22
02Fleer Throwbacks-25
Gold-25
Platinum-25
Baxter, Tom
93Quebec Pee-Wee Tournament-506
Bayda, Ryan
02BAP Memorabilia-302
02BAP Ultimate Memorabilia-37
02Pacific Calder-109
Silver-109
02Pacific Complete-514
Red-514
02Pacific Quest for the Cup-110
Gold-110
02SP Authentic-212
02Upper Deck Rookie Update-126
02Lowell Lock Monsters-6
03Hurricanes Postcards-3
03ITG Action-131
03Pacific-58
Blue-58
Red-58
03Upper Deck MVP-84
Gold Script-84
Silver Script-84
Canadian Exclusives-84
03AHL Top Prospects-3
03Lowell Lock Monsters-21
03Lowell Lock Monsters Photo Album-4
04Lowell Lock Monsters-1
04Lowell Lock Monsters Photo Album-1
05Manitoba Moose-2
06Albany River Rats-3
Bayer, Claudio
93Swiss HNL-9
95Swiss HNL-215
96Swiss HNL-128
98Swiss Power Play Stickers-178
99Swiss Panini Stickers-178
00Swiss Panini Stickers-222
00Swiss Slapshot Mini-Cards-RJ1
01Swiss HNL-191
02Swiss HNL-322
Bayer, Colin
86Saskatoon Blades Photos-2
Bayer, Marco
93Swiss HNL-164
95Swedish World Championships Stickers-118
95Swiss HNL-7
95Swiss HNL-531
96Swiss HNL-6
96Swiss HNL-529
98Swiss Power Play Stickers-106
99Swiss Panini Stickers-205
00Swiss Panini Stickers-248
00Swiss Slapshot Mini-Cards-EVZ3
01Swiss HNL-214
Bayes, Rickie
69Swedish Hockey-347
Bayliss, Steve
82Victoria Cougars-1
83Victoria Cougars-1
Bayrack, Mike
95Lethbridge Hurricanes-1
98Prince George Cougars-2
00Missouri River Otters-21
03Greensboro Generals-178
Bazany, Marian
06German DEL-62
06German DEL-40
Bazin, Norm
94Birmingham Bulls-2
Bazinet, Mario
84Chicoutimi Sagueneens-2
Bazinet, Michael
907th Inn. Sketch QMJHL-217
Beach, George
54UK A and BC Chewing Gum-40
Beadle, Steve
90ProCards AHL/IHL-37
91Michigan Falcons-21
93Anaheim Bullfrogs RHI-2
95Flint Generals-8
96Flint Generals-1
97Flint Generals-1
97Flint Generals EBK-17
Beagan, Beth
94Classic Women of Hockey-W36
Beagle, Chad
95Swift Current Broncos-2
96Swift Current Broncos-10
97Swift Current Broncos-10
98Swift Current Broncos-1
Beals, Darren
86Kitchener Rangers-10
87Kitchener Rangers-10
88ProCards AHL-85
Beals, Kevin
91Ferris State Bulldogs-4
92Ferris State Bulldogs-4
Beamin, Ryan
92British Columbia JHL-92
Bean, Jeremy
92Quebec Pee-Wee Tournament-1893
93Quebec Pee-Wee Tournament-1587
Bean, Tim
83Belleville Bulls-26
84Belleville Bulls-15
89ProCards AHL-116
90Newmarket Saints-2
90ProCards AHL/IHL-163
Bear, Darren
92North Dakota Fighting Sioux-2
Bear, Everett
01OCN Blizzard-24
02OCN Blizzard-21
03OCN Blizzard-5
Bear, Robby
91Air Canada SJHL-D24
Beard, Brodie
03Ottawa 67's-6
04Ottawa 67's-6
05Ottawa 67's-2
06Ottawa 67's-11
Beardsmore, Colin

95Slapshot-62
97Owen Sound Platers-8
00German DEL-102
01German Upper Deck-107
02German DEL City Press-151
03German DEL-18
04German Cologne Sharks Postcards-2
04German DEL-205
05German DEL-262
06German DEL-169

Beardy, Vern
98Wichita Thunder-2
99Wichita Thunder-1

Bearson, Zach
03Waterloo Blackhawks-6
04Waterloo Blackhawks-5
05Waterloo Blackhawks-3

Beatch, Jeff
97Swift Current Broncos-4
99Bowman CHL-4
Gold-4
OPC International-4
Autographs-BA24
Autographs Gold-BA24
Autographs Silver-BA24
01Vancouver Giants-5

Beaton, Brian
93Quebec Pee-Wee Tournament-700

Beaton, Frank
81Indianapolis Checkers-2
82Birmingham South Stars-1

Beaton, Jason
897th Inn. Sketch OHL-168
907th Inn. Sketch OHL-302

Beaton, Joe
37British Sporting Personalities-37

Beaton, Kevan
85Swedish Panini Stickers-181

Beatson, David
04UK Edinburgh Capitals-7

Beattie, Donald
52Juniors Blue Tint-56

Beattie, Red
28V128-2 Paulin's Candy-46
33V129-35
33V357 Ice Kings-29
34Beehive Group I Photos-2
34Diamond Matchbooks Silver-3
38Bruins Garden Magazine Supplement-1

Beattie, Scott
91Air Canada SJHL-B25
94Italian Milano-2
96German DEL-201
98Swiss Power Play Stickers-358
99Swiss Panini Stickers-340
00Swiss Panini Stickers-304

Beaubien, Frederick
95Phoenix Roadrunners-2
96Mississippi Sea Wolves-1
96Collector's Edge Ice-181
Prism-181
97Idaho Steelheads-2
97New Mexico Scorpions-16
98Idaho Steelheads-2
99Colorado Gold Kings Taco Bell-19

Beaucage, Marc
907th Inn. Sketch QMJHL-47
917th Inn. Sketch QMJHL-231
99Quebec Citadelles-6
00Quebec Citadelles-5
Signed-5
01German Upper Deck-2
02German DEL City Press-42
03German DEL-182
04German DEL-103
05German DEL-101
06German DEL-68

Beauchamp, Denis
907th Inn. Sketch QMJHL-262
917th Inn. Sketch QMJHL-263
94Central Hockey League-37

Beauchemin, Francois
98Bowman CHL-92
98Bowman CHL-153
Golden Anniversary-92
Golden Anniversary-153
OPC International-92
OPC International-153
Autographs Blue-A13
Autographs Gold-A13
Autographs Silver-A13
98Bowman Chrome CHL-92
98Bowman Chrome CHL-153
Golden Anniversary-92
Golden Anniversary-153
Golden Anniversary Refractors-92
Golden Anniversary Refractors-153
OPC International-92
OPC International-153
OPC International Refractors-92
OPC International Refractors-153
Refractors-92
Refractors-153
00QMJHL All-Star Program Inserts-8
00Quebec Citadelles-3
Signed-3
01Quebec Citadelles-11
02BAP Memorabilia-357
02BAP Ultimate Memorabilia-91
02Upper Deck Rookie Update-132
02Hamilton Bulldogs-13
04Syracuse Crunch-17
05Parkhurst-13
Facsimile Auto Parallel-13
06O-Pee-Chee-11
06O-Pee-Chee-641
Rainbow-11
Rainbow-641
06Upper Deck-6
Exclusives Parallel-6
High Gloss Parallel-6
Masterpieces-6
06Upper Deck MVP-5
Gold Script-5
Super Script-5
06ITG Heroes and Prospects Jerseys-GUJ58
06ITG Heroes and Prospects Jerseys Gold-GUJ58
06ITG Heroes and Prospects Emblems-GUE58
06ITG Heroes and Prospects Emblems Gold-GUE58
06ITG Heroes and Prospects Numbers-GUN58
06ITG Heroes and Prospects Numbers Gold-GUN58

Beauchemin, Rejean
02Prince Albert Raiders-1
03Prince Albert Raiders-23
04Prince Albert Raiders-23
05ITG Heroes/Prosp Toronto Expo Parallel -226
05Philadelphia Phantoms-3
05ITG Heroes and Prospects-226
Autographs Series II-RBE
Complete Jerseys-CJ-36
Complete Jerseys Gold-CJ-36
Jerseys-GUJ-73
Jerseys Gold-GUJ-73
Emblems-GUE-73
Emblems Gold-GUE-73
Numbers-GUN-73
Numbers Gold-GUN-73
Measuring Up-MU15
Measuring Up Gold-MU15
Nameplates-N-67
Nameplates Gold-N-67
Net Prospects Dual-NPD3
Net Prospects Dual Gold-NPD3
06Between The Pipes-44
Autographs-ARB
Emblems-GUE23
Emblems Gold-GUE23
Emblems Autographs-GUE23
Jerseys-GUJ23
Jerseys Gold-GUJ23
Jerseys Autographs-GUJ23
Numbers-GUN23
Numbers Gold-GUN23
Numbers Autographs-GUN23
Prospect Trios-PT04
Prospect Trios Gold-PT04
Shooting Gallery-SG07
Shooting Gallery Gold-SG07
06Philadelphia Phantoms-10

Beauchesne, Francois
93Quebec Pee-Wee Tournament-105

Beauchesne, Martin
93Quebec Pee-Wee Tournament-1591
00Chicoutimi Sagueneens-21
Signed-21

Beauchesne, Serge
92British Columbia JHL-197

Beaudette, Dan
91Cincinnati Cyclones-1

Beaudin, Alexis
93Quebec Pee-Wee Tournament-968

Beaudin, Jeff
91Johnstown Chiefs-11
92Dallas Freeze-3
93Dallas Freeze-2
94Central Hockey League-3
94Dallas Freeze-3
96St. Louis Vipers RHI-3

Beaudin, Norm
70O-Pee-Chee-48
70Topps-48
72O-Pee-Chee-290
72 7-Eleven Slurpee Cups WHA-1
73Quaker Oats WHA-9
74O-Pee-Chee WHA-11

Beaudoin, Alexandre
92Quebec Pee-Wee Tournament-455
93Quebec Pee-Wee Tournament-104

Beaudoin, Carl
95Slapshot Memorial Cup-60

Beaudoin, Eric
97Guelph Storm-24
98Guelph Storm-22
99Guelph Storm-23
00Chicoutimi Sagueneens-13
Signed-13
00Louisville Panthers-22
01BAP Memorabilia-418
Emerald-418
Ruby-418
Sapphire-418
01Utah Grizzlies-17
02Pacific-151
Blue-151
Red-151
02Upper Deck-208
Exclusives-208
02Upper Deck MVP-205
Gold-205
Classics-205
Golden Classics-205
03Pacific AHL Prospects-72
Gold-72
03San Antonio Rampage-16
06Swedish SHL Elitset-259

Beaudoin, Jean-Philippe
93Quebec Pee-Wee Tournament-100

Beaudoin, Matt
03Ohio State Buckeyes-18
04Ohio State Buckeyes-3
05Ohio State Buckeyes-3
06Ohio State Buckeyes-3

Beaudoin, Nic
93Detroit Jr. Red Wings-22
94Detroit Jr. Red Wings-24
95Slapshot-76
95Classic-43
95Slapshot Memorial Cup-98
98Roanoke Express-21
99UHL All-Stars East-11T
01Macon Whoopee-4

Beaudoin, Roger
51Laval Dairy Lac St. Jean-46

Beaudoin, Serge
75Phoenix Roadrunners WHA-1
76Phoenix Roadrunners WHA-1

Beaudry, Etienne
93Sherbrooke Faucons-8
98Pensacola Ice Pilots-3

Beaudry, Joey
99Topeka Scarecrows-10

Beaudry, Miguel
00Sudbury Wolves-25
01Mississauga Ice Dogs-15
02Mississauga Ice Dogs-13
03New Mexico Scorpions-14
04New Mexico Scorpions-2
06Austin Ice Bats-1

Beaufait, Mark
92Kansas City Blades-13
93Pinnacle-206
Canadian-206
93PowerPlay-498
93Stadium Club Team USA-1
93Stadium Club Team USA Members Only-1
93Topps Premier Team USA-6
93Ultra-478
93Classic Pro Prospects-24
95Swedish World Championships Stickers-234
98IHL All-Star Eastern Conference-18
98Orlando Solar Bears-10
98Orlando Solar Bears-15
98Orlando Solar Bears II-2
02German Berlin Polar Bears Postcards-3
02German DEL City Press-24
03German Berlin Polar Bears Postcards-5
03German DEL-63
04German Berlin Polar Bears Postcards-3
04German DEL-63
05German DEL-22
06German DEL-14

Beaule, Alain
94French National Team-5

Beaulieu, Corey
89ProCards AHL-286
94Cleveland Lumberjacks-23
94Cleveland Lumberjacks Postcards-22
95Atlanta Knights-3
97UK Sheffield Steelers-22

Beaulieu, Jacques
01London Knights-26
02London Knights-29
03London Knights-6
04London Knights-25
05London Knights-23

Beaulieu, Jonathan
93Quebec Pee-Wee Tournament-345
96Rimouski Oceanic-1
96Rimouski Oceanic Quebec Police-1
97Rimouski Oceanic-9
99Rimouski Oceanic-3
Signed-3
00Rimouski Oceanic-3
Signed-3
00Shawinigan Cataractes-3
Signed-3
04Rimouski Oceanic Season Ticket-1

Beaulieu, Josh
03London Knights-22
04London Knights-14
05London Knights-19
05ITG Heroes and Prospects Memorial Cup-MC-12
06London Knights-8

Beaulieu, Julien
03P.E.I. Rocket-1
04Drummondville Voltigeurs-22
04P.E.I. Rocket-11

Beaulieu, Nick
84Richelieu Riverains-2
88ProCards AHL-83
89ProCards IHL-109
90ProCards AHL/IHL-521

Beaulieu, Pierre-Olivier
02Quebec Remparts-21
03Halifax Mooseheads-22
04Halifax Mooseheads-21
05Fresno Falcons-1

Beaulieu, Vincent
05Drummondville Voltigeurs-19

Beaulne, Richard
81Sault Ste. Marie Greyhounds-3
82Sault Ste. Marie Greyhounds-3

Beaumont, Kevin
98Sudbury Wolves-4

Beaupre, Claude
52Juniors Blue Tint-166

Beaupre, Don
80North Stars Postcards-3
81North Stars Postcards-3
81O-Pee-Chee-159
81O-Pee-Chee Stickers-89
81O-Pee-Chee Stickers-146
81Topps-W103
82North Stars Postcards-2
82O-Pee-Chee-163
82O-Pee-Chee Stickers-193
82Topps Stickers-193
83NHL Key Tags-63
83North Stars Postcards-3
83O-Pee-Chee-166
83O-Pee-Chee Stickers-122
83Topps Stickers-122
84North Stars Postcards-2
84O-Pee-Chee-94
84Topps-70
85Islanders News Trottier-23
85North Stars 7-Eleven-4
85North Stars Postcards-2
85O-Pee-Chee-142
85Topps-142
86North Stars 7-Eleven-5
86North Stars Postcards-3
86O-Pee-Chee-89
86Topps-89
87North Stars Postcards-4
87O-Pee-Chee-132
87O-Pee-Chee Stickers-51
87Panini Stickers-289
87Topps-132
88O-Pee-Chee-42
88O-Pee-Chee Stickers-196
88Panini Stickers-84
88Topps-42
89Capitals Kodak-33
89Capitals Team Issue-1
90Bowman-72
Tiffany-72
90Capitals Kodak-1
90Capitals Postcards-1
90Capitals Smokey-1
90O-Pee-Chee-253
90O-Pee-Chee Box Bottoms-O
90Panini Stickers-158
90Pro Set-307
90Score-215
Canadian-215
90Topps-253
Tiffany-253
90Topps Box Bottoms-O
90Upper Deck-217
French-217
91Pro Set Platinum-139
91Bowman-304
91Capitals Junior 5x7-1
91Capitals Kodak-1
91O-Pee-Chee-505
91Panini Stickers-201
91Parkhurst-416
French-416
91Pinnacle-148
French-148
91Pro Set-257
91Pro Set-601
French-257
French-601
91Score American-185
91Score Canadian Bilingual-185
91Score Canadian English-185
91Stadium Club-246
91Topps-505
91Upper Deck-197
French-197
92Bowman-222
92Bowman-297
92Capitals Kodak-2
92Kraft-26
92McDonald's Upper Deck-15
92O-Pee-Chee-28
92Panini Stickers-159
92Panini Stickers French-159
92Parkhurst-197
Emerald Ice-197
92Pinnacle-48
92Pinnacle-268
French-48
French-268
92Pro Set-206
92Score-320
Canadian-320
92Seasons Patches-49
92Stadium Club-270
92Topps-195
Gold-195G
92Ultra-229
92Upper Deck-23
92Upper Deck-310
93OPC Premier-304
Gold-304
93Panini Stickers-33
93Parkhurst-225
Emerald Ice-225
93Pinnacle-292
Canadian-292
93PowerPlay-463
93Score-58
Canadian-58
93Stadium Club-71
Members Only Master Set-71
OPC-71
First Day Issue-71
First Day Issue OPC-71
93Topps/OPC Premier-304
Gold-304
93Ultra-28
93Upper Deck-123
94Canada Games NHL POGS-298
94EA Sports-156
94Fleer-141
94Kraft-32
94Pinnacle-355
Artist's Proofs-355
Rink Collection-355
94Select-12
Gold-12
94Senators Team Issue-2
94SP-82
Die Cuts-82
94Ultra-387
94Upper Deck-389
Electric Ice-389
SP Inserts-SP143
SP Inserts Die Cuts-SP143
95Be A Player-96
Signatures-S96
Signatures Die Cuts-S96
95Canada Games NHL POGS-200
95Collector's Choice-11
Player's Club-11
Player's Club Platinum-11
95Donruss-246
95Emotion-121
95Kraft-40
95Leaf-52
95Metal-103
95Panini Stickers-57
95Parkhurst International-152
Emerald Ice-152
95Pinnacle-87
Artist's Proofs-87
Rink Collection-87
95Playoff One on One-177
95Score-246
Black Ice Artist's Proofs-246
Black Ice-246
95Select Certified-104
Mirror Gold-104
95Senators Team Issue-4
95SkyBox Impact-116
95Stadium Club-44
Members Only Master Set-44
95Summit-35
Artist's Proofs-35
Ice-35
95Topps-142
OPC Inserts-142
95Ultra-109
Gold Medallion-109
95Upper Deck-402
Electric Ice-402
Electric Ice Gold-402
Special Edition-SE61
Special Edition Gold-SE61
96Collector's Choice-264
96Playoff One on One-381
96St. John's Maple Leafs-1
97Sudbury Wolves Anniversary-1
01Upper Deck Legends-75
04ITG Franchises Update-485
04ITG Franchises US East-450
Autographs-A-DBR
04ITG Franchises US West-251
06Parkhurst-11
Autographs-11
Autographs Dual-DAMB

Beaupre, Martin
907th Inn. Sketch QMJHL-41
917th Inn. Sketch QMJHL-94
917th Inn. Sketch Memorial Cup-44

Beauregard, Danny
907th Inn. Sketch QMJHL-31
917th Inn. Sketch QMJHL-89
917th Inn. Sketch Memorial Cup-39
93Quebec Pee-Wee 20th Anniversary-10

Beauregard, David
98Muskegon Fury-23
98UHL All-Stars-5
99Charlotte Checkers-15
99Charlotte Checkers-34
02Fort Wayne Komets-2
02Fort Wayne Komets Shoe Carnival-2
03Fort Wayne Komets-3
03Fort Wayne Komets Shoe Carnival-10
05Danbury Trashers-7
05Roanoke Valley Vipers-1

Beauregard, Mario
77Granby Vics-1

Beauregard, Stephane
88ProCards AHL-183
89ProCards IHL-139
90Jets IGA-4
90O-Pee-Chee-223
90Pro Set-648
90Score-282
Canadian-282
90Topps-223
Tiffany-223
90Upper Deck-415
French-415
91Jets Panini Team Stickers-3
91Jets IGA-2
91Parkhurst-426
French-426
91Score Canadian Bilingual-638
91Score Canadian English-638
92Bowman-405
92Flyers J.C. Penney-2
92Flyers Upper Deck Sheets-21
92OPC Premier-88
92Score-402
Canadian-402
92Stadium Club-304
92Topps-62
Gold-62G
92Ultra-369
92Upper Deck-536
93Jets Readers Club-3
93Jets Ruffles-3
93Ultra-451
96Collector's Edge Future Legends-26
96Collector's Edge Ice-188
Prism-188
98Swiss Power Play Stickers-54
98Chicago Wolves Turner Cup-24
99German DEL-212

Beaurivage, Marc
88Richelieu Riverains-2

Beausoleil, Benoit
01Kalamazoo K-Wings-12
02Thetford Mines Coyotes-1
03Thetford Mines Prolab-1
04Thetford Mines Prolab-24

Beausoleil, Luc
94Central Hockey League-92

Beausoleil, Michel
03Port Huron Beacons-1
04Oklahoma City Blazers-3

Beauvais, Casey
00Sioux City Musketeers-2

Beauvais, Ryan
93Quebec Pee-Wee Tournament-813

Beauvis, Eric
907th Inn. Sketch QMJHL-188
917th Inn. Sketch QMJHL-57

Beazley, Paul
94Windsor Spitfires-4

Becanic, John
03Everett Silvertips-27
04Everett Silvertips-29
05Everett Silvertips-27

Beccarelli, Fabio
93Quebec Pee-Wee Tournament-1639
99Swiss Panini Stickers-288
00Swiss Panini Stickers-86
01Swiss HNL-244
02Swiss HNL-370

Beccarelli, Mauro
01Swiss HNL-310
02Swiss HNL-140

Bechard, Jerome
90ProCards AHL/IHL-356
91ProCards-363
92Birmingham Bulls-13
93Birmingham Bulls-13
93Birmingham Bulls Birmingham News-3
94Birmingham Bulls-3
94Classic Pro Prospects-229
95Birmingham Bulls-14
97Columbus Cottonmouths-1
98Columbus Cottonmouths-1
99Columbus Cottonmouths-11
00Columbus Cottonmouths-1
01Columbus Cottonmouths-1
02Columbus Cottonmouths-1
03Columbus Cottonmouths-4
04Columbus Cottonmouths-22

Bechard, Kelly
04Canadian Womens World Championship Team-3

Beck, Barry
77Rockies Coke Cans-2
78O-Pee-Chee-121
78Topps-121
79O-Pee-Chee-35
79Topps-35
80O-Pee-Chee-90
80O-Pee-Chee-170
80Topps-90
80Topps-170
81O-Pee-Chee-220
81O-Pee-Chee-230
81O-Pee-Chee Stickers-168
81Post Standups-14
81Topps-3
81Topps-E124
82McDonald's Stickers-27
82O-Pee-Chee-219
82O-Pee-Chee-220
82O-Pee-Chee Stickers-135
82Post Cereal-13
82Topps Stickers-135
83NHL Key Tags-86
83O-Pee-Chee-241
83O-Pee-Chee Stickers-210
83Puffy Stickers-20
83Topps Stickers-210
84Kellogg's Accordion Discs-5A
84Kellogg's Accordion Discs-5B
84Kellogg's Accordion Discs Singles-3
84O-Pee-Chee-140
84O-Pee-Chee Stickers-100
84 7-Eleven Discs-35
84Topps-105
85O-Pee-Chee-138
85O-Pee-Chee Stickers-82
85 7-Eleven Credit Cards-13
85Topps-138
89Kings Smokey-9
01Greats of the Game-15
Autographs-15
01Upper Deck Legends-73
02Fleer Throwbacks-2
Gold-2
Platinum-2
Squaring Off-5
Squaring Off Memorabilia-5
03Parkhurst Original Six New York-68
03Parkhurst Original Six New York-79
04ITG Franchises US East-388
Autographs-A-BBK1
04ITG Franchises US West-185
Autographs-A-BBK2
06Parkhurst-12
06Parkhurst-197
Autographs-12
Autographs-197
Autographs Dual-DAGB

Beck, Brad
88ProCards IHL-19
90Richmond Renegades-13
91ProCards-429

Beck, Fabian
02Swiss HNL-365

Beck, Rob
91Air Canada SJHL-A40
91Air Canada SJHL All-Stars-13
92Saskatchewan JHL-22

Becker, Alexander
94German First League-356

Becker, Barry
917th Inn. Sketch WHL-228
93Spokane Chiefs-1

Becker, Brock
03Minnesota State Mavericks-2

Becker, Codey
02Regina Pats-14
03Kamloops Blazers-16
03Regina Pats-16

Becker, Corey
01Regina Pats-3

Becker, Jason
91Saskatoon Blades-21
917th Inn. Sketch WHL-118
03UK Cardiff Devils-17
06Reading Royals-5

Becker, Konrad
06Westside Warriors-19

Becker, Troy
91British Columbia JHL-10

Beckett, Bob
56Quebec Aces-2
94Parkhurst Missing Link-13

Beckett, Jason
97Seattle Thunderbirds-5
02Milwaukee Admirals-20
02Milwaukee Admirals Postcards-2
03Houston Aeros-2
06Stockton Thunder-1

Beckford-Tseu, Chris
01Guelph Storm-21
04Peoria Rivermen-12
05ITG Heroes/Prosp Toronto Expo Parallel -352
05Hot Prospects-167
En Fuego-167
Red Hot-167
White Hot-167
05SP Authentic-278
Limited-278
05SPx-283
05The Cup Masterpiece Pressplate Artifact-327
05The Cup Masterpiece Pressplates (Ice)-229
05The Cup Master Pressplate Rookie Update-177
05The Cup Masterpiece Pressplates SPA-278
05The Cup Masterpiece Pressplates (SPx)-283
05The Cup Masterpiece Pressplates Trilogy-301
05UD Artifacts-327
05Upper Deck Ice-229
05Upper Deck Rookie Update-177
05Upper Deck Trilogy-301
05Peoria Rivermen-19
05ITG Heroes and Prospects-352
Autographs Update-A-CBT
Complete Logos-AHL-24
Jerseys-GUJ-74
Jerseys Gold-GUJ-74
Emblems-GUE-74
Emblems Gold-GUE-74
Numbers-GUN-74
Numbers Gold-GUN-74
Nameplates-N-63
Nameplates Gold-N-63
Net Prospects Dual-NPD9
Net Prospects Dual Gold-NPD9
06Between The Pipes-8
Autographs-ACBT
Prospect Trios-PT16
Prospect Trios Gold-PT16
06Peoria Rivermen-1

Beckford-Tsue, Chris
04Peoria Rivermen-12

Bedard, Daniel
84Chicoutimi Sagueneens-3

Bedard, Frederic
00Val d'Or Foreurs-21
Signed-21
01Val d'Or Foreurs-10
02Val d'Or Foreurs-6

Bedard, Gamill
52Juniors Blue Tint-41

Bedard, Jim
44Beehive Group II Photos-79
78O-Pee-Chee-243
78Topps-243
79O-Pee-Chee-62
79Topps-62
80Finnish Mallasjuoma-198

Bedard, Karl
93Quebec Pee-Wee Tournament-302

Bedard, Louis
99Hampton Roads Admirals-3
00UK Sekonda Superleague-118

Bedard, Martin
92Quebec Pee-Wee Tournament-543
96Rimouski Oceanic-2
96Rimouski Oceanic Quebec Police-2

Bedard, Pascal
04Odessa Jackalopes-2
05Odessa Jackalopes-1
06Odessa Jackalopes-2

Bedard, Roger
51Laval Dairy Subset-115
52St. Lawrence Sales-105

Bedard, Sebastien
92Quebec Pee-Wee Tournament-145
93Quebec Pee-Wee Tournament-350

Bedard, Steve
93Quebec Pee-Wee Tournament-1058

Bedard, Yohan
98Thetford Mines Coyotes-9

Beddoes, Clayton
91Lake Superior State Lakers-6
92Lake Superior State Lakers-8
94Classic-50
Gold-50
95Bowman-102
All-Foil-102
95Parkhurst International-286
Emerald Ice-286
96Collector's Edge Ice-59
Prism-59
97Detroit Vipers-13
98German DEL-112
99German Adler Mannheim Eagles Postcards-4
99German DEL-5

Beddow, Warren
93Quebec Pee-Wee Tournament-164

Bednar Jr., Vladimir
98Czech OFS-291

Bednar, Jared
917th Inn. Sketch WHL-11
93Huntington Blizzard-4
94Anaheim Bullfrogs RHI-2
94Huntington Blizzard-3
95South Carolina Stingrays-18
96South Carolina Stingrays-25
96St. John's Maple Leafs-2
98Grand Rapids Griffins-2
01South Carolina Stingrays-2
02South Carolina Stingrays-22

Bednar, Jaroslav
95Czech APS Extraliga-145
96Czech APS Extraliga-22
97Czech APS Extraliga-14
97Czech DS Extraliga-88
97Czech DS Stickers-126
98Czech DS-96
98Czech DS Stickers-217
98Czech OFS-139
99Finnish Cardset-280
00SPx Rookie Redemption-RR14
00Finnish Cardset-140
00Finnish Cardset Master Blasters-4
01Atomic-111
Premiere Date-111
01Atomic Toronto Fall Expo-111
01BAP Memorabilia-363
Emerald-363
Ruby-363
Sapphire-363
01BAP Signature Series-235
Autographs-235
Autographs Gold-235
01Bowman YoungStars-130
Gold-130
Ice Cubed-130
01Crown Royale-163
Rookie Royalty-11
01O-Pee-Chee-358
01Pacific-457
01Pacific Adrenaline-211
Blue-211
Premiere Date-211
Red-211
Retail-211
Rookie Report-10
01Pacific Heads-Up-108
01Parkhurst-255
01Parkhurst Beckett Promos-255
01Private Stock-124
Gold-124
Premiere Date-124
Retail-124
Silver-124
Moments in Time-5
01Private Stock Pacific Nights-124
01Private Stock PS-2002-82
01Private Stock Reserve-R5
01SP Authentic-151
Limited-151
Limited Gold-151
01SP Game Used-80
Authentic Fabric-AFJB
Authentic Fabric Gold-AFJB
01SPx-149
01SPx-149
Rookie Treasures-RTJB
01Titanium-162
Retail-162
01Titanium Draft Day Edition-134
01Topps-358
01Topps Chrome-176
Refractors-176
Black Border Refractors-176
01Topps Heritage-152
01Topps Reserve-106
01UD Challenge for the Cup-109
01UD Honor Roll-93
01UD Premier Collection-64
01Upper Deck-427
Exclusives-427
01Upper Deck Ice-56
01Upper Deck Vintage-282
01Vanguard-115
Blue-115
Red-115
One of Ones-115
Premiere Date-115
Prime Prospects-8
Proofs-115
01Czech DS-24
01Finnish Cardset-25
01Manchester Monarchs-9B
02Pacific Calder Collection AS Fantasy-6
02Pacific Calder Collection All-Star Fantasy Gold-6
02Pacific Calder-71
Silver-71
02Pacific Complete-527
Red-527
02Upper Deck Bright Futures-JB
02Czech DS-44
02Czech DS-58
02Czech National Team Postcards-2
02Finnish Cardset-5
03ITG Action-242
03Pacific-140
Blue-140
Red-140
03Pacific Complete-159
Red-159
03Upper Deck MVP-186
Gold Script-186
Silver Script-186
Canadian Exclusives-186
03Russian Avangard Omsk-21
03Russian Hockey League-224
04Russian Legion-17
05Czech HC Slavia Praha-1
06Czech HC Slavia Praha Postcards-1
06Czech IIHF World Championship Postcards-2
06Czech LG Hockey Games Postcards-2
06Czech OFS-288
Goals Leaders-5
Points Leaders-6
Stars-17

Bednar, Vladimir
69Swedish Hockey-21
70Finnish Jaakiekko-41
70Swedish Hockey-347
70Swedish Masterserien-9
70Swedish Masterserien-76
70Swedish Masterserien-145
70Swedish Masterserien-156
72Finnish Jaakiekko-1
72Finnish Hellas-97
72Finnish Semic World Championship-41
72Swedish Semic World Championship-41
74Finnish Jenkki-66
74Swedish Semic World Champ Stickers-68

Bednarik, Lukas
98Red Deer Rebels-2
99Czech OFS-341
99Czech Score Blue 2000-87
99Czech Score Red Ice 2000-87
00Czech OFS-156
02Czech OFS Plus-125
03Czech OFS Plus-69
04Czech OFS-40
06Czech OFS-128

Bednarski, John
76O-Pee-Chee NHL-231
76Topps-231
88Oilers Tenth Anniversary-125
89New Haven Nighthawks-2

Beech, Kevin
03Sudbury Wolves-3
04Sudbury Wolves-6
05Sudbury Wolves-2

Beech, Kris
98SP Authentic-123
Power Shift-123
Sign of the Times-KB
Sign of the Times Gold-KB
98Upper Deck-400
Exclusives-400
Exclusives 1 of 1-400
Gold Reserve-400
98Calgary Hitmen-11
98Calgary Hitmen Autographs-11
99Black Diamond-93
Diamond Cut-93
Final Cut-93
99O-Pee-Chee-260
99O-Pee-Chee Chrome-260
99O-Pee-Chee Chrome Refractors-260
99SPx-175
Radiance-175
Spectrum-175
99Topps/OPC-260
99Topps/OPC Chrome-260
Refractors-260
99Upper Deck-324
Exclusives-324
Exclusives 1 of 1-324
99Upper Deck Sobey's Memorial Cup-4
99Upper Deck Gold Reserve-324
99Upper Deck MVP SC Edition-214
Gold Script-214
Silver Script-214
Super Script-214
Game-Used Souvenirs-GUKB
Game-Used Souvenirs-SGKB
ProSign-KB
99Upper Deck Ovation-73
Standing Ovation-73
99Calgary Hitmen-1
99Calgary Hitmen Autographs-1
99Bowman CHL-34
Gold-34
OPC International-34
Autographs-BA7
Autographs Gold-BA7
Autographs Silver-BA7
Scout's Choice-SC9
99UD Prospects-32
CHL Class-C4
Destination the Show-DS8
Signatures of Tradition-KB
00BAP Memorabilia-398
Emerald-398
Ruby-398
Sapphire-398
00BAP Parkhurst 2000-P134
00BAP Signature Series-284
Emerald-284
Ruby-284
Sapphire-284
Autographs-246
Autographs Gold-246
00Private Stock-150
Gold-150
Premiere Date-150
Retail-150
Silver-150
00SPx-151
00Stadium Club-230
00Topps Premier Plus-88
Blue Ice-88
Game-Used Memorabilia-GPKB
Game-Used Memorabilia-GPAOKB
00Topps Stars-143
Blue-143
00Calgary Hitmen-2
01Atomic Rookie Reaction-8
01BAP Signature Series-194
Autographs-194
Autographs Gold-194
01Bowman YoungStars-164
Gold-164
Ice Cubed-164
01Crown Royale Rookie Royalty-16
01O-Pee-Chee-273
01O-Pee-Chee Premier Parallel-273
01Pacific Adrenaline Rookie Report-15
01Parkhurst-292
01Parkhurst Beckett Promos-292
01Private Stock-107
Gold-107
Premiere Date-107
Retail-107
Silver-107
01Private Stock Pacific Nights-107
01Private Stock PS-2002-86
01Private Stock Reserve-R9
01SP Authentic-119
Limited-119
Limited Gold-119
01Stadium Club-116
Award Winners-116
Master Photos-116
01Titanium Draft Day Edition-77
01Topps-273
OPC Parallel-273
01Topps Chrome-140
Refractors-140
Black Border Refractors-140
01Topps Heritage-174
01Upper Deck-373
Exclusives-373
01Upper Deck Victory-390
Gold-390
01Vanguard-78
Blue-78
Red-78
One of Ones-78
Premiere Date-78
Proofs-78
02BAP First Edition-237
02BAP Memorabilia-237
Emerald-237
Ruby-237
Sapphire-237

NHL All-Star Game-237
NHL All-Star Game Blue-237
NHL All-Star Game Green-237
NHL All-Star Game Red-237
02BAP Memorabilia Toronto Fall Expo-237
02BAP Sig Series Auto Buybacks 2000-246
02BAP Sig Series Auto Buybacks 2001-194
02O-Pee-Chee-214
02O-Pee-Chee Premier Blue Parallel-214
02O-Pee-Chee Premier Red Parallel-214
02O-Pee-Chee Factory Set-214
02Pacific-306
Blue-306
Red-306
Heads-Up Quad Jerseys-22
Heads-Up Quad Jerseys Gold-22
02Topps-214
OPC Blue Parallel-214
OPC Red Parallel-214
Factory Set-214
02Topps Total-159
02Upper Deck-138
Exclusives-138
02Upper Deck Victory-169
Bronze-169
Gold-169
Silver-169
02AHL Top Prospects-5
02Wilkes-Barre Scranton Penguins-10
03ITG Action-448
03Wilkes-Barre Scranton Penguins-4
04Wilkes-Barre Scranton Penguins-10
05Milwaukee Admirals Choice-1
05Milwaukee Admirals Pepsi-1
06ITG Heroes and Prospects Calder Cup Champions-CC04

Beechey, Tyler
98Kootenay Ice-18
00Kootenay Ice-2
01Calgary Hitmen-3
01Calgary Hitmen Autographed-3
02Trenton Titans-B-2
03Pensacola Ice Pilots-337

Beeck, Markus
94German First League-623

Beer, Marco
93Swiss HNL-349

Beers, Bob
89ProCards AHL-68
90Bowman-34
Tiffany-34
90Bruins Sports Action-1
90O-Pee-Chee-113
90Score-385
Canadian-385
90Topps-113
Tiffany-113
90Upper Deck-125
French-125
90ProCards AHL/IHL-140
91Bruins Sports Action-2
91Pinnacle-326
French-326
91Pro Set-520
French-520
91Upper Deck-490
French-490
92Lightning Sheraton-2
92Parkhurst-401
Emerald Ice-401
92Ultra-407
93Donruss-426
93OPC Premier-44
Gold-44
93Panini Stickers-217
93Pinnacle-186
Canadian-186
93PowerPlay-227
93PowerPlay-338
93Score-369
93Score-575
Gold-575
Canadian-369
Canadian-575
Canadian Gold-575
93Topps/OPC Premier-44
Gold-44
93Ultra-18
94EA Sports-127
94Leaf-43
94Leaf-537
94OPC Premier-41
Special Effects-41
94Pinnacle-419
Artist's Proofs-419
Rink Collection-419
94Score Samples-7
94Score-7
Gold-7
Platinum-7
94Stadium Club Super Teams-8
94Stadium Club Super Team MemberOnly Set-8
94Topps/OPC Premier-41
Special Effects-41
94Ultra-69
95Collector's Choice-107
Player's Club-107
Player's Club Platinum-107
95Swedish World Championships Stickers-220
96Providence Bruins-34
97Pacific Invincible NHL Regime-9
98Bruins Alumni-6
Autographs-6

Beers, Ed
83O-Pee-Chee-76
83O-Pee-Chee Stickers-141
83Topps Stickers-141
83Vachon-2
84O-Pee-Chee-219
84O-Pee-Chee-354
84O-Pee-Chee Stickers-243
84Topps-24
85Flames Red Rooster-2
85O-Pee-Chee-144
85O-Pee-Chee Stickers-214
85Topps-144
86O-Pee-Chee-238

Begg, Gary
69Swedish Hockey-348
70Swedish Masterserien-16
70Swedish Masterserien-191

Begin, Andre
79Montreal Juniors-2

Begin, Eric
05Shawinigan Cataractes-7

Begin, Pier Olivier
02Drummondville Voltigeurs-24

Begin, Steve
92Quebec Pee-Wee Tournament-836
97Paramount-25
Copper-25
Dark Grey-25
Emerald Green-25
Ice Blue-25
Red-25
Silver-25
97Bowman CHL-58
OPC-58
98UD Choice-267
Prime Choice Reserve-267
Reserve-267
98Upper Deck-49
Exclusives-49
Exclusives 1 of 1-49
Gold Reserve-49
99Quebec PeeWee Tournament Coll Souv-13
00O-Pee-Chee-299
00O-Pee-Chee Parallel-299
00Topps/OPC-299
Parallel-299
00Topps Chrome-194
OPC Refractors-194
Refractors-194
01BAP Signature Series-228
Autographs-228
Autographs Gold-228
02NHL Power Play Stickers-22
03Canadiens Postcards-2
03Parkhurst Original Six Montreal-7
05Canadiens Team Issue-1
05Parkhurst-257
Facsimile Auto Parallel-257
05Upper Deck-349
06Canadiens Postcards-3
06O-Pee-Chee-264
Rainbow-264

Behan, Patrik
95Slovakian-Quebec Pee-Wee Tournament-2

Behm, Daniel
91Swedish Semic Elitserien Stickers-162

Behrend, Marc
84Jets Police-3

Behrens, Scott
93Quebec Pee-Wee Tournament-880

Beier, Beat
93Quebec Pee-Wee Tournament-1626

Beilsten, J.P.
05Missouri River Otters-7

Beirnes, Jordan
03Oshawa Generals-19

Bejbom, Hans
69Swedish Hockey-220
71Swedish Hockey-366

Bejegard, Peder
93Swedish Semic Elitserien-22

Bejemark, Peter
71Swedish Hockey-348

Bekar, Derek
96New Hampshire Wildcats-21
97New Hampshire Wildcats-21
00Pacific-355
Copper-355
Gold-355
Ice Blue-355
Premiere Date-355
00Portland Pirates-11
01Manchester Monarchs-2A
02Manchester Monarchs-18
03Bridgeport Sound Tigers-10
04Springfield Falcons-9

Bekbulatov, Vadim
98Czech OFS-13

Bekken, Hans
92Norwegian Elite Series-134

Bekken, Jan
92Norwegian Elite Series-135

Bekkering, Justin
96Saskatoon Blades-3

Bekkers, John
82Regina Pats-12
83Regina Pats-12

Bekkerud, Bjorn Freddy
92Norwegian Elite Series-77

Bela, Michal
95Slovakian-Quebec Pee-Wee Tournament-3

Belak, Graham
98Kootenay Ice-22
01Trenton Titans-2-1
03Bridgeport Sound Tigers-7A
05UK Coventry Blaze-7

Belak, Wade
93Saskatoon Blades-4
94Classic-11
Gold-11
94Classic Four-Sport *-126
Gold-126
Printers Proofs-126
94Signature Rookies Gold Standard *-77
95Saskatoon Blades-4
95Images-20
Gold-20
95Images Four-Sport *-104
95Signature Rookies-18
Signatures-18
97Donruss-222
Press Proofs Silver-222
Press Proofs Gold-222
97Upper Deck-186
98Pacific-156
Ice Blue-156
Red-156
98Pacific Omega-66
Red-66
Opening Day Issue-66
98SPx Finite-25
Radiance-25
Spectrum-25
98Upper Deck-252
Exclusives-252
Exclusives 1 of 1-252
Gold Reserve-252
99Upper Deck MVP-33
Gold Script-33
Silver Script-33
Super Script-33
00BAP Memorabilia Update Tough Materials-T8
00BAP Mem Update Tough Materials Gold-T8
01BAP Signature Series-198
Autographs-198
Autographs Gold-198
01BAP Update Tough Customers-TC15
01BAP Update Tough Customers-TC25
01UD Playmakers-91
02BAP Sig Series Auto Buybacks 2001-198
02Maple Leafs Platinum Collection-1
02NHL Power Play Stickers-127
02Pacific Complete-496
Red-496
03ITG Action-513
03Parkhurst Original Six Toronto-2
03Topps Own the Game-OTG19
03Upper Deck Tough Customers-TC-5
04UK Coventry Blaze-1
04UK Coventry Blaze Champions-3
04UK EIHL All-Stars-2
06O-Pee-Chee-465
Rainbow-465

Belan, Kris
05London Knights-4

Beland, Francois
93Quebec Pee-Wee Tournament-973

Beland, Samuel
02Cape Breton Screaming Eagles-18
03Cape Breton Screaming Eagles-26
04Cape Breton Screaming Eagles-4
05Baie-Comeau Drakkar-18

Belanger, Chris
92Western Michigan Broncos-1
93Toledo Storm-10
94Classic Pro Prospects-246
00Swiss Panini Stickers-292
01Swiss HNL-385
02Swiss HNL-366

Belanger, Dominic
917th Inn. Sketch OHL-107

Belanger, Eric
96Rimouski Oceanic Update-1

Belanger, Eric (NHL)
96Rimouski Oceanic Update-2
97Rimouski Oceanic-21
97Bowman CHL-73
OPC-73
99Lowell Lock Monsters-12
00Private Stock-121
Gold-121
Premiere Date-121
Retail-121
Silver-121
00SP Authentic-107
00SPx-162
00Titanium Draft Day Edition-161
00Titanium Draft Day Promos-161
00Topps Heritage-98
Chrome Parallel-98
00Topps Premier Plus-125
Blue Ice-125
00Topps Stars-121
Blue-121
00UD Pros and Prospects-106
00UD Reserve-96
00Upper Deck-436
Exclusives Tier 1-436
Exclusives Tier 2-436
00Upper Deck Ice-89
00Upper Deck Vintage-380
00Vanguard-123
Pacific Proofs-123
00Lowell Lock Monsters-10
01BAP Signature Series-186
Autographs-186
Autographs Gold-186
01O-Pee-Chee-132
01O-Pee-Chee Premier Parallel-132
01Pacific-179
Extreme LTD-179
Hobby LTD-179
Premiere Date-179
Retail LTD-179
01Pacific Arena Exclusives-179
01SP Authentic-127
Limited-127
Limited Gold-127
01Stadium Club-52
Award Winners-52
Master Photos-52
01Topps-132
OPC Parallel-132
01Topps Heritage-82
Refractors-82
01Upper Deck-80
Exclusives-80
01Upper Deck MVP-89
01Upper Deck Victory-168
Gold-168
01Upper Deck Vintage-118
02BAP Sig Series Auto Buybacks 2001-186
02Kings Game Sheets-9
02Kings Game Sheets-10
02O-Pee-Chee-124
02O-Pee-Chee Premier Blue Parallel-124
02O-Pee-Chee Premier Red Parallel-124
02O-Pee-Chee Factory Set-124
02Pacific Complete-271
Red-271
02SP Game Used Future Fabrics-FFEB
02SP Game Used Future Fabrics Gold-FFEB
02SP Game Used Future Fabrics Rainbow-FFEB
02Titanium-49
Blue-49
Red-49
Retail-49
02Topps-124
OPC Blue Parallel-124
OPC Red Parallel-124
Factory Set-124
02Topps Total-121
02UD Top Shelf Dual Player Jerseys-STAB
02Upper Deck-84
Exclusives-84
Specialists-SEB
02Upper Deck Victory-98
Bronze-98
Gold-98
Silver-98
03ITG Action-225
03O-Pee-Chee-219
03OPC Blue-219
03OPC Gold-219
03OPC Red-219
03Pacific Complete-274
Red-274
03Topps-219
Blue-219
Gold-219
Red-219
03Upper Deck-334
Canadian Exclusives-334
HG-334
UD Exclusives-334
03Upper Deck MVP-192
Gold Script-192
Silver Script-192
Canadian Exclusives-192
05Be A Player Signatures-ER
05Be A Player Signatures Gold-ER
05Kings Team Issue-12
05Panini Stickers-292
05Parkhurst-225
Facsimile Auto Parallel-225
05Upper Deck Victory-90
Black-90
Gold-90
Silver-90
06Hurricanes Postcards-5
06O-Pee-Chee-101
Rainbow-101

Belanger, Francis
01Pacific-202
Extreme LTD-202
Hobby LTD-202
Premiere Date-202
Retail LTD-202
01Pacific Arena Exclusives-202
01Private Stock-127
Gold-127
Premiere Date-127
Retail-127
Silver-127
01Private Stock Pacific Nights-127
01SP Authentic-154
Limited-154
Limited Gold-154
01SPx-108
01UD Top Shelf-57
01UD Top Shelf-57B
01Upper Deck-194
Exclusives-194
01Upper Deck MVP-205
01Upper Deck Victory-377
01Quebec Citadelles-10
02Cincinnati Mighty Ducks-B-10
04Richmond Riverdogs-8

Belanger, Francois
907th Inn. Sketch QMJHL-32
917th Inn. Sketch Memorial Cup-40
00Sherbrooke Castors-21
Signed-21
01Sherbrooke Castors-21

Belanger, Frederic
92Quebec Pee-Wee Tournament-107
92Quebec Pee-Wee Tournament-610
95Halifax Mooseheads-9
96Halifax Mooseheads I-2
96Halifax Mooseheads II-2
97Halifax Mooseheads I-1
97Halifax Mooseheads II-2
98Halifax Mooseheads-10
98Halifax Mooseheads Second Edition-20
05Danbury Trashers-8

Belanger, Hugo
92Clarkson Knights-2
93Indianapolis Ice-1
94Indianapolis Ice-1
94Classic Pro Prospects-147
96Pensacola Ice Pilots-15
98Phoenix Mustangs-1

Belanger, Jesse
90ProCards AHL/IHL-71
91ProCards-85
92Parkhurst-488
Emerald Ice-488
92Fredericton Canadiens-1
93Donruss-123
93Leaf-278
93OPC Premier-451
Gold-451
93Parkhurst-346
Emerald Ice-346
Calder Candidates-C15
Calder Candidates Gold-C15
93PowerPlay-89
Rookie Standouts-2
93Score-454
93Score-585
Gold-585
Canadian-454
Canadian-585
Canadian Gold-585
93Topps/OPC Premier-451
Gold-451
93Ultra-320
93Classic Pro Prospects-115
BCs-BC11
94Canada Games NHL POGS-368
94Donruss-321
94Flair-63
94Fleer-77
94Leaf-145
94Leaf Limited-19
94OPC Premier-197
94OPC Premier-544
94O-Pee-Chee Finest Inserts-12
94OPC Premier Special Effects-197
94OPC Premier Special Effects-545
94Panthers Pop-ups-5
94Parkhurst-86
94Parkhurst-284
Gold-86
Gold-284
Vintage-V31
94Pinnacle-122
Artist's Proofs-122
Rink Collection-122
94Score-257
Gold-257
Platinum-257
94Stadium Club-63
Members Only Master Set-63
First Day Issue-63
Super Team Winner Cards-63
94Topps/OPC Premier-197
94Topps/OPC Premier-544
Special Effects-197
Special Effects-545
94Ultra-79
94Upper Deck-72
Electric Ice-72
SP Inserts-SP119
SP Inserts Die Cuts-SP119
94Classic Pro Prospects Jumbos-PP14
94Images *-32
95Be A Player-143
Signatures-S143
Signatures Die Cuts-S143
95Canada Games NHL POGS-114
95Collector's Choice-66
Player's Club-66
Player's Club Platinum-66
95Donruss-204
95Emotion-69
95Kraft-59
95Leaf-62
95Panini Stickers-70
95Parkhurst International-87
Emerald Ice-87
95Pinnacle-18
Artist's Proofs-18
Rink Collection-18
95Playoff One on One-40
95Playoff One on One-153
95Score-155
Black Ice Artist's Proofs-155
Black Ice-155
95SkyBox Impact-67
95Stadium Club-133
Members Only Master Set-133
95Summit-20
Artist's Proofs-20
Ice-20
95Topps-159
OPC Inserts-159
95Ultra-60
Gold Medallion-60
95Upper Deck-209
Electric Ice-209
Electric Ice Gold-209
96Donruss-70
Press Proofs-70
96Playoff One on One-339
96Score-222
Artist's Proofs-222
Dealer's Choice Artist's Proofs-222
Special Artist's Proofs-222
Golden Blades-222
97Las Vegas Thunder-3
98Cleveland Lumberjacks-4
99Quebec Citadelles-14
00Upper Deck NHLPA-PA55
00Chicago Wolves-3
01Swiss HNL-292
03German DEL-92

Belanger, Justin
03Victoriaville Tigers-2
04Victoriaville Tigers-3

Belanger, Ken
917th Inn. Sketch OHL-312
92Ottawa 67's-1
93Guelph Storm-14
94St. John's Maple Leafs-2
95St. John's Maple Leafs-2
96Kentucky Thoroughblades-1
97Be A Player-145
Autographs-145
Autographs Die-Cuts-145
Autographs Prismatic Die-Cuts-145
97Pacific-351
Copper-351
Emerald Green-351
Ice Blue-351
Red-351
Silver-351
97Upper Deck-190
98Pacific Omega-11
Red-11
Opening Day Issue-11
99BAP Millennium-21
Emerald-21
Ruby-21
Sapphire-21
Signatures-21
Signatures Gold-21
00Topps Heritage-169
00Upper Deck NHLPA-PA7
01BAP Update Tough Customers-TC5
01BAP Update Tough Customers-TC37
01Pacific-403
Gold-403
01Pacific Arena Exclusives-403
02BAP Sig Series Auto Buybacks 1999-21

Belanger, Kevin
93Quebec Pee-Wee Tournament-991

Belanger, Luc
93Sherbrooke Faucons-4
01Quebec Citadelles-18

Belanger, Martin
92Quebec Pee-Wee Tournament-591
97Macon Whoopee-2
97Macon Whoopee Autographs-2
99Tupelo T-Rex-18
01BC Icemen-5

Belanger, Maxime
02Baie Comeau Drakkar-1
03Baie Comeau Drakkar-4
04Baie-Comeau Drakkar-14
05Moncton Wildcats-11

Belanger, Pascal
96Flint Generals-2

Belanger, Roger
83Kingston Canadians-7

Belanger, Steve
00Kamloops Blazers-2
03Vernon Vipers-2

Belanger, Yves
76O-Pee-Chee NHL-168
76Topps-168
77O-Pee-Chee NHL-367
78O-Pee-Chee-44
78Topps-44

Belbas, Ryan
96OCN Blizzard-22
97OCN Blizzard-21
98OCN Blizzard-20

Belecki, Brent
97Portland Winter Hawks-2
98Bowman CHL-41
98Bowman CHL-162
Golden Anniversary-41
Golden Anniversary-162
OPC International-41
OPC International-162
98Bowman Chrome CHL-41
98Bowman Chrome CHL-162
Golden Anniversary-41
Golden Anniversary-162
Golden Anniversary Refractors-41
Golden Anniversary Refractors-162
OPC International-41
OPC International-162
OPC International Refractors-41
OPC International Refractors-162
Refractors-41
Refractors-162
00Asheville Smoke-2
04Richmond Riverdogs-22

Beleskey, Mark
04Belleville Bulls-16
05ITG Heroes and Prospects-405
Team Cherry-TC19

Beleskey, Matt
06Belleville Bulls-3

Belesky, Matt
05Belleville Bulls-1

Belfour, Ed
88Blackhawks Coke-1
88ProCards IHL-95
90Blackhawks Coke-16
90Bowman-7
Tiffany-7
90Pro Set-598
90Score Rookie/Traded-103T
90Upper Deck-55
French-55
91Pro Set Platinum-26
91Blackhawks Coke-1
91Bowman-390
91Gillette-18
91O-Pee-Chee-4
91O-Pee-Chee-20
91O-Pee-Chee-263
91O-Pee-Chee-271
91O-Pee-Chee-288
91O-Pee-Chee-425
91O-Pee-Chee-430
91O-Pee-Chee-518
91O-Pee-Chee-519
91OPC Premier-19
91Panini Stickers-9
91Panini Stickers-337
91Parkhurst-30
91Parkhurst-218
French-30
French-218
91Pinnacle-127
91Pinnacle-388
91Pinnacle-400
French-127
French-388
French-400
91Pro Set-43
91Pro Set-321
91Pro Set-600
French-43
French-321
French-600
Awards Special-AC1
NHL Sponsor Awards-AC19
91Score National-6
91Score Ntnl Candy Wholesalers Convention-6
91Score Fanfest-6
91Score American-290
91Score American-348
91Score American-410
91Score American-411
91Score American-430
91Score American-431
91Score American-433
91Score Canadian Bilingual-300
91Score Canadian Bilingual-301
91Score Canadian Bilingual-320
91Score Canadian Bilingual-321
91Score Canadian Bilingual-323
91Score Canadian Bilingual-378
91Score Canadian Bilingual-510
91Score Canadian English-300
91Score Canadian English-301
91Score Canadian English-320
91Score Canadian English-321
91Score Canadian English-323
91Score Canadian English-378
91Score Canadian English-510
91Score Hot Cards-9
91Score Young Superstars-32
91Stadium Club Charter Member-42
91Stadium Club Charter Member-43
91Stadium Club-333
91Topps-4
91Topps-20
91Topps-263
91Topps-271
91Topps-288
91Topps-425
91Topps-518
91Topps-519
Topps/Bowman Preview Sheet-5
91Upper Deck-39
91Upper Deck-81
91Upper Deck-164
91Upper Deck-625
French-39
French-81
French-164
French-625
Award Winner Holograms-AW2
Award Winner Holograms-AW4
Award Winner Holograms-AW7
91Finnish Semic World Champ Stickers-53
91Swedish Semic World Champ Stickers-53
91Star Pics-20
92Blackhawks Coke-19
92Bowman-90
92Bowman-199
92High-5 Previews-P6
92High-5 Previews-P6
92Kraft-36
92McDonald's Upper Deck-1
92O-Pee-Chee-81
92Panini Stickers-3
92Panini Stickers-284
92Panini Stickers French-3
92Panini Stickers French-284
92Parkhurst-28
92Parkhurst-461
Emerald Ice-28
Emerald Ice-461
92Pinnacle-118
92Pinnacle-265
French-118
French-265
Team Pinnacle-1
Team French-1
92Pro Set-33
92Score-178
Canadian-178
Young Superstars-25
92Seasons Patches-3
92Sports Illustrated for Kids II-33
92Stadium Club-243
92Stadium Club-333
92Topps-22
Gold-22G
92Ultra-32
All-Stars-9
92Upper Deck-203
92Finnish Semic-76
92North Dakota Fighting Sioux-31
93SLU Hockey Canadian-1
93SLU Hockey American-1
93Blackhawks Coke-14
93Donruss-64
93High Liner Greatest Goalies-2
93Kenner Starting Lineup Cards-1
93Kraft-1
93Leaf-62
93Leaf-175
Gold All-Stars-10
Painted Warriors-6
93McDonald's Upper Deck-H6
93OPC Premier-60
93OPC Premier-95
Gold-60
Gold-95
Black Gold-16
93Panini Stickers-140
93Panini Stickers-155
93Parkhurst-44
Emerald Ice-44
93Pinnacle-224
93Pinnacle-227
93Pinnacle-255
Canadian-224
Canadian-227
Canadian-255
All-Stars-42
All-Stars Canadian-42
Team Pinnacle-1
Team Canadian-1
93PowerPlay-46
Netminders-2
93Score-70
93Score-485
Canadian-70
Canadian-485
93Seasons Patches-1
93Stadium Club-99
93Stadium Club-144
93Stadium Club-150
Members Only Master Set-99
Members Only Master Set-144
Members Only Master Set-150
OPC-99
OPC-144
OPC-150
First Day Issue-99
First Day Issue-144
First Day Issue-150
First Day Issue OPC-99
First Day Issue OPC-144
First Day Issue OPC-150
All-Stars-1
All-Stars Members Only-1
All-Stars OPC-1
93Topps/OPC Premier-60
93Topps/OPC Premier-95
Gold-60
Gold-95
93Topps Premier Black Gold-14
93Ultra-22
All-Stars-10
Award Winners-1
93Upper Deck-147
Award Winners-AW3
SP-27
93Upper Deck Locker All-Stars-19
94Blackhawks Coke-2
94Canada Games NHL POGS-276
94Donruss-275
Dominators-7
Ice Masters-1
Masked Marvels-1
94EA Sports-30
94EA Sports-187
94Finest-51
Super Team Winners-51
Refractors-51
Division's Clear Cut-11
94Flair-31
94Fleer-38
Netminders-1
94Hockey Wit-18
94Kraft-33
94Kraft Goalie Masks-1
94Leaf-296
Crease Patrol-2
Gold Stars-7
94Leaf Limited-3
94OPC Premier-285
Special Effects-285
94Parkhurst-41
Gold-41
SE Vintage-14
94Pinnacle-42
Artist's Proofs-42
Rink Collection-42
Goaltending Greats-GT4
94Score-149
Gold-149
Platinum-149
94Select-53
Gold-53
94SP-24
Die Cuts-24
94Stadium Club-155
94Stadium Club-180
Members Only Master Set-155
Members Only Master Set-180
First Day Issue-155
First Day Issue-180
Super Teams-5
Super Teams Members Only Master Set-5
Super Team Winner Cards-155
Super Team Winner Cards-180
94Topps/OPC Premier-285
Special Effects-285
94Ultra-39
94Upper Deck-290
Electric Ice-290
Predictor Hobby-H27
94Upper Deck Predictor Hobby Exch Gold-H27
94Upper Deck SP Inserts-SP15
94Upper Deck SP Inserts Die Cuts-SP15
95Bashan Super Stickers-20
95Bashan Super Stickers-23
95Be A Player-194
Signatures-S194
Signatures Die Cuts-S194
95Blackhawks Coke-2
95Bowman-53
All-Foil-53
95Canada Games NHL POGS-20
95Canada Games NHL POGS-71
95Collector's Choice-109
95Collector's Choice-387
Player's Club-109
Player's Club-387
Player's Club Platinum-109
Player's Club Platinum-387
95Donruss-108
Between The Pipes-10
Dominators-8
95Donruss Elite-20
Die Cut Stars-20
Die Cut Uncut-20
Painted Warriors-4
Painted Warriors-P4
95Emotion-27
95Finest-108
Refractors-108
95Hoyle Western Playing Cards-4
95Imperial Stickers-23
95Kraft-25
95Kraft-52
95Leaf-329
95Leaf Limited-15
Stick Side-8
95McDonald's Pinnacle-MCD-29
95Metal-23
Iron Warriors-2
95NHL Aces Playing Cards-5C
95NHL Cool Trade-14
95NHL Cool Trade-RP14
95Panini Stickers-166
95Parkhurst International-41
Emerald Ice-41
Goal Patrol-6
NHL All-Stars-5
95Pinnacle-153
Artist's Proofs-153
Rink Collection-153
First Strike-7
95Playoff One on One-21
95Pro Magnets-6
95Pro Magnets Iron Curtain Insert-1
95Score-87
95Score-318
Black Ice Artist's Proofs-87
Black Ice Artist's Proofs-318
Black Ice-87
Black Ice-318
95Select Certified-93
Mirror Gold-93
95SkyBox Impact-27
Deflectors-9
95SP-27
95Stadium Club Members Only-35
95Stadium Club-55
Members Only Master Set-55
Metalists-M5
Metalists Members Only Master Set-M5
95Summit-120
Artist's Proofs-120
Ice-120
In The Crease-4
95Topps-130
95Topps-378
OPC Inserts-130
OPC Inserts-378
Home Grown Canada-HGC24
Marquee Men Power Boosters-378
Profiles-PF16
95Topps SuperSkills-90
Platinum-90
95Ultra-30
95Ultra-365
Gold Medallion-30
Premier Pad Men-1
Premier Pad Men Gold Medallion-1
95Upper Deck-216
95Upper Deck-455
Electric Ice-216
Electric Ice-455
Electric Ice Gold-216
Electric Ice Gold-455
NHL All-Stars-AS6
NHL All-Stars Jumbo-AS6
Predictor Hobby-H18
Predictor Hobby Exchange-H18
Special Edition-SE19
Special Edition Gold-SE19
95Zenith-95
95Finnish Semic World Championships-78
95Swedish Globe World Championships-74
96Black Diamond-34
Gold-34
96Collector's Choice-55
96Donruss-62
Press Proofs-62
Between the Pipes-6
96Donruss Canadian Ice-113
Gold Press Proofs-113
Red Press Proofs-113
O Canada-6
96Donruss Elite-91
Die Cut Stars-91
Painted Warriors-7
Painted Warriors Promos-P7
96Flair-83
Blue Ice-83
Hot Gloves-1
96Fleer-15
Vezina-1
Picks Dream Lines-8
96Hockey Greats Coins-1
Gold-1
96Kraft Upper Deck-15
96Leaf-199
Press Proofs-199
Shut Down-4
96Leaf Limited-53
Gold-53
Stubble-6
96Leaf Preferred-30
Press Proofs-30
Masked Marauders-12
Vanity Plates-14
Vanity Plates Gold-14
96Maggers-3
96McDonald's Pinnacle-37
96Metal Universe-25
Armor Plate-1
Armor Plate Super Power-1
96NHL Pro Stamps-6
96Pinnacle-94
Artist's Proofs-94
Foil-94
Premium Stock-94
Rink Collection-94
96Pinnacle Fantasy-FC20
96Playoff One on One-394
96Score-123
Artist's Proofs-123
Dealer's Choice Artist's Proofs-123
Special Artist's Proofs-123
Golden Blades-123
Net Worth-5
Sudden Death-4
96Select Certified-11
Artist's Proofs-11
Blue-11
Mirror Blue-11
Mirror Gold-11
Mirror Red-11
Red-11
Freezers-6
96SkyBox Impact-17
Zero Heroes-1
96SP-28
Game Film-GF11
96Stadium Club Members Only-6
96Summit-97
Artist's Proofs-97
Ice-97
Metal-97

Premium Stock-97
In The Crease-3
In The Crease Premium Stock-3
96Team Out-70
96Topps Picks-179
OPC Inserts-179
96Ultra-29
Gold Medallion-29
96Upper Deck-234
Generation Next-X18
Superstar Showdown-SS22A
96Upper Deck Ice-11
Parallel-11
96Zenith-25
Artist's Proofs-25
96Swedish Semic Wien-75
Super Goalies-SG2
97Be A Player-249
Autographs-249
Autographs Die-Cuts-249
Autographs Prismatic Die-Cuts-249
Stacking the Pads-5
Take A Number-3
97Beehive-10
Golden Portraits-10
97Black Diamond-134
Double Diamond-134
Triple Diamond-134
Quadruple Diamond-134
97Collector's Choice-216
Star Quest-SQ36
Stick'Ums-S20
97Crown Royale-39
Emerald Green-39
Ice Blue-39
Silver-39
Freeze Out Die-Cuts-6
97Donruss-164
Press Proofs Silver-164
Press Proofs Gold-164
97Donruss Canadian Ice-26
Dominion Series-26
Provincial Series-26
National Pride-22
97Donruss Elite-102
Aspirations-102
Status-102
97Donruss Limited-28
97Donruss Limited-164
Exposure-28
Exposure-164
Fabric of the Game-33
97Donruss Preferred-54
Cut to the Chase-54
Color Guard-16
Color Guard Promos-16
97Donruss Priority-71
Stamp of Approval-71
Postmaster General-7
Postmaster Generals Promos-7
97Katch-43
Gold-43
Silver-43
97Leaf-87
Fractal Matrix-87
Fractal Matrix Die Cuts-87
97Leaf International-87
Universal Ice-87
97Pacific-20
Copper-20
Emerald Green-20
Ice Blue-20
Red-20
Silver-20
In The Cage Laser Cuts-19
97Pacific Invincible-123
Copper-123
Emerald Green-123
Ice Blue-123
Red-123
Silver-123
NHL Regime-174
97Pacific Omega-67
Copper-67
Dark Gray-67
Emerald Green-67
Gold-67
Gold-246
Ice Blue-67
No Scoring Zone-3
Team Leaders-6
97Paramount-56
Copper-56
Dark Grey-56
Emerald Green-56
Ice Blue-56
Red-56
Silver-56
Glove Side Laser Cuts-6
97Pinnacle-51
Artist's Proofs-51
Rink Collection-51
Press Plates Back Black-51
Press Plates Back Cyan-51
Press Plates Back Magenta-51
Press Plates Back Yellow-51
Press Plates Front Black-51
Press Plates Front Cyan-51
Press Plates Front Magenta-51
Press Plates Front Yellow-51
97Pinnacle Certified-9
Red-9
Mirror Blue-9
Mirror Gold-9
Mirror Red-9
97Pinnacle Inside-74
Coach's Collection-74
Executive Collection-74
Stoppers-24
97Pinnacle Tot Cert Platinum Blue-9
97Pinnacle Tot Certi Platinum Gold-9
97Pinnacle Totally Certified Platinum Red-9
97Pinnacle Tot Cert Mirror Platinum Gold-9
97Revolution-40
Copper-40
Emerald-40
Ice Blue-40
Silver-40
1998 All-Star Game Die-Cuts-9
Return to Sender Die-Cuts-6
97Score-20
Artist's Proofs-20
Golden Blades-20
Net Worth-18
97SP Authentic-44
Icons-I13
Icons Die-Cuts-I13
Icons Embossed-I13
97Studio-58
Press Proofs Silver-58
Press Proofs Gold-58
97Upper Deck-259
97Zenith-49
Z-Gold-49
Z-Silver-49
97Zenith 5 x 7-10
Gold Impulse-10
Silver Impulse-10
97Zenith Chasing The Cup-10
98SLU Hockey-20
98Aurora-53
Championship Fever-14
Championship Fever Copper-14
Championship Fever Ice Blue-14
Championship Fever Red-14
Championship Fever Silver-14
98Be A Player-190
Press Release-190
98BAP Gold-190
98BAP Autographs-190
98BAP Autographs Gold-190
98BAP AS Game Used Stick Cards-S22
98BAP AS Game Used Jersey Cards-AS24
98BAP Playoff Game Used Jerseys-G19
98BAP Playoff Practice Used Jerseys-P6
98Black Diamond-26
Double Diamond-26
Triple Diamond-26
Quadruple Diamond-26
Winning Formula Gold-WF9
Winning Formula Platinum-WF9
98Bowman's Best-34
Refractors-34
Atomic Refractors-34
98Crown Royale-37
Limited Series-37
Pillars of the Game-9
98Finest-3
No Protectors-3
No Protectors Refractors-3
Refractors-3
98Katch-43
98Kenner Starting Lineup Cards-2
98Kenner Starting Lineup Cards-3
98Lunchables Goalie Greats Rounds-1
98Lunchables Goalie Greats Squares-1
98McDonald's Upper Deck-21
98NHL Aces Playing Cards-11
98OPC Chrome-123
Refractors-123
Season's Best-SB3
Season's Best Refractors-SB3
98Pacific-20
Ice Blue-20
Red-20
Gold Crown Die-Cuts-11
Timelines-6
98Pacific Dynagon Ice-53
Blue-53
Red-53
Watchmen-3
98Pacific Omega-68
Red-68
Opening Day Issue-68
Online-11
Planet Ice-7
Planet Ice Parallel-7
98Panini Photocards-7
98Panini Stickers-6
98Panini Stickers-122
98Paramount-62
Copper-62
Emerald Green-62
Holo-Electric-62
Ice Blue-62
Silver-62
Glove Side Laser Cuts-7
98Revolution-40
Ice Shadow-40
Red-40
All-Star Die Cuts-2
Showstoppers-13
Three Pronged Attack-13
Three Pronged Attack Parallel-13
98SP Authentic-26
Power Shift-26
98SPx Finite-29
Radiance-29
Spectrum-29
98SPx Top Prospects-20
Radiance-20
Spectrum-20
98Topps-123
O-Pee-Chee-123
Season's Best-SB3
98Topps Gold Label Class 1-24
Black-24
Black One of One-24
One of One-24
Red-24
Red One of One-24
98Topps Gold Label Class 2-24
98Topps Gold Label Class 2 Black-24
98Topps Gold Label Class 2 Black 1 of 1-24
98Topps Gold Label Class 2 One of One-24
98Topps Gold Label Class 2 Red-24
98Topps Gold Label Class 2 Red One of One-24
98Topps Gold Label Class 3-24
98Topps Gold Label Class 3 Black-24
98Topps Gold Label Class 3 Black 1 of 1-24
98Topps Gold Label Class 3 One of One-24
98Topps Gold Label Class 3 Red-24
98Topps Gold Label Class 3 Red One of One-24
98UD Choice-63
98UD Choice-249
Mini Bobbing Head-BH26
98UD Choice Preview-63
98UD Choice Prime Choice Reserve-63
98UD Choice Prime Choice Reserve-249
98UD Choice Reserve-63
98UD Choice Reserve-249
98UD Choice StarQuest Blue-SQ17
98UD Choice StarQuest Gold-SQ17
98UD Choice StarQuest Green-SQ17
98UD Choice StarQuest Red-SQ17
98UD3-45
98UD3-105
98UD3-165
Die-Cuts-45
Die-Cuts-105
Die-Cuts-165
98Upper Deck-80
Exclusives-80
Exclusives 1 of 1-80
Frozen In Time-FT26
Frozen In Time Quantum 1-FT26
Frozen In Time Quantum 2-FT26
Frozen In Time Quantum 3-FT26
Game Jerseys-GJ8
Lord Stanley's Heroes-LS23
Lord Stanley's Heroes Quantum 1-LS23
Lord Stanley's Heroes Quantum 2-LS23
Lord Stanley's Heroes Quantum 3-LS23
Gold Reserve-80
98Upper Deck MVP-60
Gold Script-60
Silver Script-60
Super Script-60
99Aurora-43
Striped-43
Premiere Date-43
Premiere Date Striped-43
Championship Fever-10
Championship Fever Copper-10
Championship Fever Ice Blue-10
Championship Fever Silver-10
Glove Unlimited-7
Styrotechs-7
99BAP Memorabilia-174
Gold-174
Silver-174
Jersey Cards-J24
Jersey Emblems-E24
Jersey Numbers-I24
Jersey and Stick Cards-S24
AS Heritage Ruby-H17
AS Heritage Sapphire-H17
AS Heritage Emerald-H17
99BAP Update Double AS Jersey Cards-D8
99BAP Update Teammates Jersey Cards-TM11
99BAP Update Teammates Jersey Cards-TM47
99BAP Update Teammates Jersey Cards-TM48
99BAP Millennium-79
Emerald-79
Ruby-79
Sapphire-79
Signatures-79
Signatures Gold-79
Jerseys-J24
Jersey Autographs-J24
Jersey and Stick Cards-JS24
Jersey Emblems-E24
Jersey Numbers-N24
99Black Diamond-31
Diamond Cut-31
Final Cut-31
A Piece of History-EB
A Piece of History Double-EB
A Piece of History Triple-EB
99Crown Royale-42
Limited Series-42
Premiere Date-42
Ice Elite-9
Ice Elite Parallel-9
99Jell-O Partners of Power-7
99McDonald's Upper Deck-MCD8
99McDonald's Upper Deck-MCD8R
Signatures-EB
99O-Pee-Chee-153
99O-Pee-Chee Chrome-153
99O-Pee-Chee Chrome Ice Masters-IM16
99O-Pee-Chee Chrome Ice Masters Refractor-IM16
99O-Pee-Chee Chrome Refractors-153
99O-Pee-Chee Chrome Postmasters-PM4
99O-Pee-Chee Chrome Postmasters Refractor-PM4
99O-Pee-Chee Ice Masters-IM16
99O-Pee-Chee Post Masters-PM4
99Pacific-117
Copper-117
Emerald Green-117
Gold-117
Ice Blue-117
Premiere Date-117
Red-117
Gold Crown Die-Cuts-13
In the Cage Net-Fusions-6
Past and Present-9
99Pacific Dynagon Ice-63
Blue-63
Copper-63
Gold-63
Premiere Date-63
2000 All-Star Preview-9
99Pacific Omega-70
Copper-70
Gold-70
Ice Blue-70
Premiere Date-70
5 Star Talents-27
5 Star Talents Parallel-27
99Pacific Prism-43
Holographic Blue-43
Holographic Gold-43
Holographic Mirror-43
Holographic Purple-43
Premiere Date-43
Sno-Globe Die-Cuts-8
99Panini Stickers-227
99Paramount-69
Copper-69
Emerald-69
Gold-69
Holographic Emerald-69
Holographic Gold-69
Holographic Silver-69
Ice Blue-69
Premiere Date-69
Red-69
Silver-69
Glove Side Net Fusions-7
Personal Best-12
99Revolution-44
Premiere Date-44
Red-44
Shadow Series-44
Ornaments-8
Showstoppers-12
Copper-44
Gold-44
CSC Silver-44
99SP Authentic-29
99SPx-50
Radiance-50
Spectrum-50
SPXtreme-XT18
99Stadium Club-77
First Day Issue-77
One of a Kind-77
Printing Plates Black-77
Printing Plates Cyan-77
Printing Plates Magenta-77
Printing Plates Yellow-77
Chrome-28
Chrome Refractors-28
Co-Signers-CS10
Co-Signers-CS12
Lone Star Signatures-LS8
Souvenirs-SEB
99Stars Postcards-2
99Topps/OPC-153
Ice Masters-IM16
Postmasters-PM4
99Topps Stanley Cup Heroes-SC19
99Topps Stanley Cup Heroes Refractors-SC19
99Topps/OPC Chrome-153
Refractors-153
Ice Masters-IM16
Ice Masters Refractors-IM16
Postmasters-PM4
Postmasters Refractors-PM4
99Topps Gold Label Class 1-18
Black-18
Black One of One-18
One of One-18
Red-18
Red One of One-18
99Topps Gold Label Class 2-18
99Topps Gold Label Class 2 Black-18
99Topps Gold Label Class 2 Black 1 of 1-18
99Topps Gold Label Class 2 One of One-18
99Topps Gold Label Class 2 Red-18
99Topps Gold Label Class 2 Red One of One-18
99Topps Gold Label Class 3-18
99Topps Gold Label Class 3 Black-18
99Topps Gold Label Class 3 Black 1 of 1-18
99Topps Gold Label Class 3 One of One-18
99Topps Gold Label Class 3 Red-18
99Topps Gold Label Class 3 Red One of One-18
99Topps Premier Plus-48
Parallel-48
Calling All Calders-CAC8
Imperial Guard-IG1
99Ultimate Victory-29
1/1-29
Parallel-29
Parallel 100-29
Net Work-NW4
99Upper Deck-44
Exclusives-44
Exclusives 1 of 1-44
All-Star Class-AS14
All-Star Class Quantum Gold-AS14
All-Star Class Quantum Silver-AS14
Game Jerseys Series II-EB
Game Jerseys Series II-EBS
Game Jersey Patch Series II-EBP
Game Jersey Patch Series II 1 of 1-EB-P1
Ultimate Defense-UD5
Ultimate Defense Quantum Gold-UD5
Ultimate Defense Quantum Silver-UD5
99Upper Deck Gold Reserve-44
99Upper Deck HoloGrFx-20
Ausome-20
99Upper Deck MVP-62
Gold Script-62
Silver Script-62
Super Script-62
Last Line-LL5
99Upper Deck MVP SC Edition-59
Gold Script-59
Silver Script-59
Super Script-59
99Upper Deck Ovation-20
Standing Ovation-20
Lead Performers-LP19
99Upper Deck Retro-26
Gold-26
Platinum-26
99Upper Deck Victory-86
99Upper Deck Victory-347
99Upper Deck Victory-377
99Wayne Gretzky Hockey-55
Tools of Greatness-TGEB
99Slovakian Challengers-25
00SLU Hockey-10
00Aurora-43
Pinstripes-43
Pinstripes Premiere Date-43
Premiere Date-43
Championship Fever-7
Championship Fever Copper-7
Championship Fever Platinum Blue-7
Championship Fever Silver-7
Scouting Reports-8
00BAP Memorabilia-242
Emerald-242
Ruby-242
Sapphire-242
Promos-242
Georges Vezina-V8
Georges Vezina-V10
Goalie Memorabilia-G4
Goalie Memorabilia-G21
Goalie Memorabilia-G22
Jersey Cards-J33
Jersey Emblems-E33
Jersey Numbers-N33
Jersey and Stick Cards-JS33
00BAP Mem Chicago Sportsfest Copper-242
00BAP Memorabilia Chicago Sportsfest Blue-242
00BAP Memorabilia Chicago Sportsfest Gold-242
00BAP Memorabilia Chicago Sportsfest Ruby-242
00BAP Memorabilia Chicago Sun-Times Ruby-242
00BAP Memorabilia Chicago Sun-Times Gold-242
00BAP Mem Chicago Sun-Times Sapphire-242
00BAP Mem Toronto Fall Expo Copper-242
00BAP Memorabilia Toronto Fall Expo Gold-242
00BAP Memorabilia Toronto Fall Expo Ruby-242
00BAP Mem Update Heritage Jersey Cards-H6
00BAP Mem Update Heritage Jersey Gold-H6
00BAP Memorabilia Update Teammates-TM14
00BAP Memorabilia Update Teammates-TM36
00BAP Memorabilia Update Teammates Gold-TM14
00BAP Memorabilia Update Teammates Gold-TM36
00BAP Parkhurst 2000-P118
00BAP Signature Series-158
Emerald-158
Ruby-158
Sapphire-158
Autographs-78
Autographs Gold-78
He Shoots-He Scores Prizes-24
Jersey Cards-J24
Jersey and Stick Cards-GSJ24
Jersey Cards Autographs-J24
Jersey Emblems-E24
Jersey Numbers-IN24
00BAP Ultimate Memorabilia Autographs-24
Gold-24
00BAP Ultimate Memorabilia Active Eight-AE6
00BAP Ultimate Mem Game-Used Jerseys-GJ24
00BAP Ultimate Mem Game-Used Emblems-E22
00BAP Ultimate Mem Game-Used Numbers-N22
00BAP Ultimate Mem Game-Used Sticks-GS24
00BAP Ultimate Mem Goalie Memorabilia-GM5
00BAP Ultimate Mem Goalie Memorabilia-GM11
00BAP Ultimate Mem Goalie Memorabilia-GM13
00BAP Ultimate Memorabilia Goalie Sticks-G10
00BAP Ultimate Mem Plante Jersey Cards-PJ2
00BAP Ultimate Mem Plante Skate Cards-PS2
00BAP Ultimate Mem Journey Jerseys-JJ7
00BAP Ultimate Mem Journey Emblems-JE7
00BAP Ultimate Mem Journey Numbers-JI7
00BAP Ultimate Memorabilia Retro-Active-RA4
00BAP Ultimate Memorabilia Teammates-TM25
00BAP Ultimate Memorabilia Teammates-TM26
00BAP Ultimate Memorabilia Teammates-TM35
00Black Diamond-19
Gold-19
00Crown Royale-34
Ice Blue-34
Limited Series-34
Premiere Date-34
Red-34
Game-Worn Jerseys-7
Game-Worn Jersey Patches-7
Premium-Sized Game-Worn Jerseys-7
00O-Pee-Chee-49
00O-Pee-Chee Parallel-49
00Pacific-126
Copper-126
Gold-126
Ice Blue-126
Premiere Date-126
Autographs-126
00Paramount-73
Copper-73
Gold-73
Holo-Gold-73
Holo-Silver-73
Ice Blue-73
Premiere Date-73
Freeze Frame-11
Game Used Sticks-8
Glove Side Net Fusions-8
Glove Side Net Fusions Platinum-8
00Private Stock-30
Gold-30
Premiere Date-30
Retail-30
Silver-30
Extreme Action-6
Game Gear-34
PS-2001 Action-16
00Revolution-45
Blue-45
Premiere Date-45
Red-45
HD NHL-12
Ice Immortals-7
Stat Masters-14
00SP Authentic-28
Super Stoppers-SS3
00SP Game Used-20
Tools of the Game Combos-C-HB
00SPx-20
Spectrum-20
Winning Materials-WBE
00Stadium Club-7
Beam Team-BT17
Capture the Action-CA4
Capture the Action Game View-4
Glove Save-GS2
00Stars Postcards-1
00Titanium-27
Blue-27
Gold-27
Premiere Date-27
Red-27
Retail-27
Game Gear-81
Game Gear Patches-81
Three-Star Selections-3
00Titanium Draft Day Edition-28
00Topps/OPC-49
Parallel-49
Own the Game-OTG17
00Topps Chrome-40
00Topps Chrome-162
OPC Refractors-40
OPC Refractors-162
Refractors-40
Refractors-162
00Topps Gold Label Class 1-73
Gold-73
00Topps Gold Label Class 2-73
00Topps Gold Label Class 2 Gold-73
00Topps Gold Label Class 3-73
00Topps Gold Label Class 3 Gold-73
00Topps Gold Label Behind the Mask-BTM2
00Topps Gold Label Behind the Mask 1 to 1-BTM2
00Topps Gold Label Bullion-B2
00Topps Gold Label Bullion One to One-B2
00Topps Heritage-23
00Topps Heritage-233
Chrome Parallel-23
Heroes-HH17
00Topps Premier Plus-41
Blue Ice-41
Game-Used Memorabilia-GPEB
Game-Used Memorabilia-GPEBMT
Masters of the Break-MB13
Trophy Tribute-TT6
00Topps Stars-32
Blue-32
Progression-P6
00UD Heroes-38
Second Season Heroes-SS4
00UD Pros and Prospects-29
00UD Reserve-29
00Upper Deck-287
Exclusives Tier 1-287
Exclusives Tier 2-287
Game Jersey Combos-DBH
Skilled Stars-SS7
Triple Threat-TT2
00Upper Deck Legends-38
00Upper Deck Legends-40
Legendary Collection Bronze-38
Legendary Collection Bronze-40
Legendary Collection Gold-38
Legendary Collection Gold-40
Legendary Collection Silver-38
Legendary Collection Silver-40
of the Cage-LC5
00Upper Deck MVP-59
First Stars-59
Masked Men-MM3
Second Stars-59
Third Stars-59
00Upper Deck Victory-71
00Upper Deck Victory-296
00Upper Deck Vintage-118
00Upper Deck Vintage-123
00Upper Deck Vintage-124
Great Gloves-GG7
00Vanguard-33
High Voltage-10
High Voltage Gold-10
High Voltage Green-10
High Voltage Red-10
High Voltage Silver-10
Holographic Gold-33
Holographic Purple-33
Pacific Proofs-33
00Czech Stadion-92
01McFarlane Hockey-10
01McFarlane Hockey-12
01Atomic-31
Blue-31
Gold-31
Premiere Date-31
Red-31
Jerseys-16
Patches-16
Statosphere-2
Team Nucleus-5
01BAP Memorabilia-36
Emerald-36
Ruby-36
Sapphire-36
All-Star Teammates-AST46
Goalies Jerseys-GJ7
He Shoots-He Scores Prizes-6
Stanley Cup Playoffs-SC13
01BAP Signature Series Certified 100-C13
01BAP Signature Series Certified 50-C13
01BAP Signature Series Certified 1 of 1's-C13
01BAP Signature Series Autographs-LEB
01BAP Signature Series Autographs Gold-LEB
01BAP Signature Series Jerseys-GJ-73
01BAP Signature Series Teammates-TM-10
01BAP Ultimate Memorabilia Calder Trophy-11
01BAP Ultimate Mem Journey Jerseys-9
01BAP Ultimate Mem Journey Emblems-9
01BAP Ultimate Mem Legend Terry Sawchuk-7
01BAP Update He Shoots-He Scores Points-9
01BAP Update He Shoots-He Scores Prizes-34
01BAP Update Heritage-H11
01Between the Pipes-10
01Between the Pipes-101
01Between the Pipes-112
01Between the Pipes-168
All-Star Jerseys-ASJ1
He Shoots-He Saves Points-11
He Shoots-He Saves Prizes-30
Jerseys-GJ7
Jersey and Stick Cards-GSJ7
Masks-14
Masks-31
Masks Silver-14
Masks Silver-31
Masks Gold-14
Masks Gold-31
Record Breakers-RB8
Record Breakers-RB12
Tandems-GT7
Trophy Winners-TW22
01Bowman YoungStars-43
Gold-43
Ice Cubed-43
01Crown Royale-46
Blue-46
Premiere Date-46
Red-46
Retail-46
01eTopps-22
01McDonald's Pacific-8
Hometown Pride-6
Jersey Patches Silver-5
Jersey Patches Gold-5
01O-Pee-Chee-90
01O-Pee-Chee Heritage Parallel-90
01O-Pee-Chee Heritage Parallel Limited-90
01O-Pee-Chee Premier Parallel-90
01Pacific-122
Extreme LTD-122
Hobby LTD-122
Premiere Date-122
Retail LTD-122
Impact Zone-8
Steel Curtain-6
01Pacific Adrenaline-58
Blue-58
Premiere Date-58
Red-58
Retail-58
Creased Lightning-5
Jerseys-11
Power Play-12
01Pacific Arena Exclusives-122
01Pacific Heads-Up-29
Blue-29
Premiere Date-29
Red-29
Silver-29
HD NHL-12
Showstoppers-5
01Parkhurst-70
Gold-70
Silver-70
He Shoots-He Scores Prizes-23
Heroes-H11
Jerseys-PJ51
Jersey and Stick-PSJ7
Milestones-M5
Milestones-M40
Teammates-T12
Teammates-T21
01Private Stock-28
Gold-28
Premiere Date-28
Retail-28
Silver-28
Game Gear-34
01Private Stock Pacific Nights-28
01Private Stock PS-2002-23
01Private Stock Reserve-G3
01SP Authentic-24
01SP Authentic-96
Limited-24
Limited-96
Limited Gold-24
Limited Gold-96
Sign of the Times-EB
Sign of the Times-BB
Sign of the Times-JBB
01SP Game Used-15
Authentic Fabric-AFEB
Authentic Fabric-DFMB
Authentic Fabric-TFMNB
Authentic Fabric Gold-AFEB
Inked Sweaters-SEB
Patches-PEB
Patches-TPJBB
Patches Signed-SPEB
Patches Signed-DSPKB
01SPx-20
01Stadium Club-44
Award Winners-44
Master Photos-44
Gallery-G13
Gallery Gold-G13
Perennials-P10
Souvenirs-EBMB
Souvenirs-MTEB
Souvenirs-EBMBPR
01Stars Postcards-1
01Titanium-43
Hobby Parallel-43
Premiere Date-43
Retail-43
Retail Parallel-43
Double-Sided Jerseys-53
Double-Sided Jerseys-65
Double-Sided Patches-53
Double-Sided Patches-65
Saturday Knights-4
01Topps-90
Heritage Parallel-90
Heritage Parallel Limited-90
OPC Parallel-90
Game-Worn Jersey-JEB
Own The Game-OTG29
01Topps Chrome-90
Refractors-90
Black Border Refractors-90
01Topps Heritage-30
Refractors-30
01Topps Reserve-15
Emblems-EB
Jerseys-EB
Name Plates-EB
Numbers-EB
Patches-EB
01UD Challenge for the Cup-24
Jerseys-TEB
Jerseys-UCMB
Jersey Autographs-TBE
Jersey Autographs-TNEB
01UD Honor Roll Jerseys-J-EB
01UD Honor Roll Jerseys Gold-J-EB
01UD Mask Collection-110
01UD Mask Collection-176
Gold-110
Gold-176
Double Patches-DPEB
Dual Jerseys-MBTB
Gloves-GGEB
Goalie Jerseys-SYEB
Goalie Jerseys-VCEB
Jerseys-J-EB
Jersey and Patch-JPEB
01UD Playmakers-31
Practice Jerseys-PJEB
Practice Jerseys Gold-PJEB
01UD Premier Collection-18
Dual Jerseys-DMB
Dual Jerseys Black-DMB
Jerseys-BEB
Jerseys Black-B-EB
01UD Stanley Cup Champs-50
Jerseys-T-EB
Pieces of Glory-G-EB
Sticks-S-EB
01UD Top Shelf-90
Jerseys-EB
Jersey Autographs-EB
01Upper Deck-56
Exclusives-56
Game Jerseys-GJEB
Game Jerseys-MNB
Game Jerseys Series II-FJEB
Game Jerseys Series II-TJNMB
Game Jersey Autographs-SJEB
Goalies in Action-GL2
Last Line of Defense-LL2
Patches-PEB
01Upper Deck Ice-13
01Upper Deck MVP-61
Goalie Sticks-G-EB
Masked Men-MM2
01Upper Deck Victory-108
01Upper Deck Victory-114
01Upper Deck Victory-403
Gold-108
Gold-114
Gold-403
01Upper Deck Vintage-80
01Upper Deck Vintage-87
01Vanguard-31
Blue-31
Red-31
One of Ones-31
Premiere Date-31
Proofs-31
Stonewallers-6
V-Team-3
02McFarlane Hockey Maple Leafs-10
02Atomic-91
Blue-91
Gold-91
Red-91
Denied-20
Hobby Parallel-91
02BAP All-Star Edition-3
He Shoots-He Score Prizes-2
Jerseys-3
Jerseys Gold-3
Jerseys Silver-3
02BAP First Edition-184
Debut Jerseys-5
02BAP Memorabilia-266
02BAP Memorabilia-301
Emerald-266
Ruby-266
Sapphire-266
All-Star Jerseys-ASJ-3
NHL All-Star Game-266
NHL All-Star Game Blue-266
NHL All-Star Game Green-266
NHL All-Star Game Red-266
02BAP Memorabilia Toronto Fall Expo-266
02BAP Sig Series Auto Buybacks 1998-190
02BAP Sig Series Auto Buybacks 1999-79
02BAP Sig Series Auto Buybacks 2000-78
02BAP Signature Series Defensive Wall-DW2
02BAP Signature Series Golf-GS35
02BAP Signature Series Team Quads-TQ2
02BAP Ultimate Memorabilia Active Eight-3
02BAP Ultimate Memorabilia Active Eight-6
02BAP Ultimate Memorabilia Cup Duels-15
02BAP Ultimate Memorabilia Cup Duels-19
02BAP Ultimate Memorabilia Jerseys-9
02BAP Ultimate Mem Journey Jerseys-2
02BAP Ultimate Mem Journey Emblems-2
02BAP Ultimate Mem Lifetime Achievers-4
02BAP Ultimate Memorabilia Nameplates-12
02BAP Ultimate Memorabilia Numerology-23
02BAP Ultimate Memorabilia Retro Trophies-8
02Between the Pipes-33
02Between the Pipes-148
Gold-33
Silver-33
All-Star Stick and Jersey-1
Behind the Mask-19
Inspirations-I6
Jerseys-32
Masks II-28
Masks II Gold-28
Masks II Silver-28
Pads-5
Record Breakers-14
Tandems-14
02Bowman YoungStars-94
Gold-94
Silver-94
02Crown Royale-90
Blue-90
Red-90
Retail-90
Coats of Armor-10
02ITG Used-71
02ITG Used-171
Goalie Pad and Jersey-GP6
Goalie Pad and Jersey Gold-GP6
02Maple Leafs Platinum Collection-2
02Maple Leafs Team Issue-2
02McDonald's Pacific Salt Lake Gold-1
02NHL Power Play Stickers-128
02O-Pee-Chee-245
02O-Pee-Chee-245U
02O-Pee-Chee Premier Blue Parallel-245
02O-Pee-Chee Premier Red Parallel-245
02O-Pee-Chee Factory Set-245
02Pacific-111
Blue-111
Red-111
02Pacific Calder-21
Silver-21
Chasing Glory-9
Hardware Heroes-11
02Pacific Complete-25
Red-25
02Pacific Exclusive-159
Advantage-15
02Pacific Heads-Up-114
Blue-114
Purple-114
Red-114
Quad Jerseys-11
Quad Jerseys Gold-11
02Pacific Quest for the Cup-91
Gold-91
Jerseys-21
02Pacific Toronto Fall Expo-1
Gold-1
02Parkhurst-138
Bronze-138
Gold-138
Silver-138
College Ranks-CR18
College Ranks Jerseys-CRM18
Milestones-MS3
02Parkhurst Retro-150
Minis-150
He Shoots-He Scores Points-9
He Shoots-He Scores Prizes-8
Hopefuls-VH1
Jerseys-RJ8
02Private Stock Reserve-145
Red-145
Retail-145
InCrease Security-20
Patches-145
02SP Authentic-83
Beckett Promos-83
Super Premiums-TPRBB
02SP Game Used-47
Signature Style-EB
Tools of the Game-BE
Tools of the Game-EB
02SPx-71
Spectrum Gold-71
Spectrum Silver-71
02Stadium Club-103
Silver Decoy Cards-103
Proofs-103
02Titanium-92
Blue-92
Red-92
Retail-92
Saturday Knights-8
Masked Marauders-7
02Topps-245
02Topps-245U
OPC Blue Parallel-245
OPC Red Parallel-245
Factory Set-245
02Topps Chrome-134
Black Border Refractors-134
Refractors-134
02Topps Heritage-160
02Topps Total-301
02UD Artistic Impressions-83
Gold-83
02UD Artistic Impressions Beckett Promos-83
02UD Artistic Impressions Retrospectives-R83
02UD Artistic Impressions Retrospect Gold-R83
02UD Artistic Impress Retrospect Silver-R83
02UD Honor Roll-66
02UD Mask Collection-82
02UD Mask Collection-83
02UD Mask Collection-84
02UD Mask Collection-99
02UD Mask Collection Beckett Promos-82
02UD Mask Collection Beckett Promos-83
02UD Mask Collection Beckett Promos-84
02UD Mask Collection Career Wins-CWEB
02UD Mask Collection Great Gloves-GGEB
02UD Mask Collection Mini Masks-EB
02UD Mask Collection Mini Masks Autos-EB
02UD Mask Collection Nation's Best-NOBB
02UD Mask Collection Patches-PWEB
02UD Mask Collection View from the Cage-VEB
02UD Piece of History-84
02UD Premier Collection-51A
Signatures Bronze-SEB
Signatures Gold-SEB
Signatures Silver-SEB
02UD Top Shelf Clutch Performers-CPEB
02UD Top Shelf Dual Player Jerseys-RBD
02UD Top Shelf Hardware Heroes-HBRBD
02UD Top Shelf Hardware Heroes-HHBRK
02UD Top Shelf Stopper Jerseys-SSEB
02UD Top Shelf Triple Jerseys-TSMMB
02Upper Deck-163
Exclusives-163
Blow-Ups-C39
Game Jersey Autographs-EB
Game Jersey Series II-GJEB
Last Line of Defense-LL13
02Upper Deck Classic Portraits-93
02Upper Deck MVP-174
Gold-174
Classics-174
Golden Classics-174
Skate Around Jerseys-SDBP

Skate Around Jerseys-SDTBE
Souvenirs-S-EB
02Upper Deck Rookie Update-94
02Upper Deck Rookie Update-171
02Upper Deck Vintage-240
02Upper Dêck Vintage-288
Green Backs-240
02Vanguard-91
LTD-91
East Meets West-10
Stonewallers-12
V-Team-6
03McFarlane Hockey-200
03McFarlane Hockey-202
03BAP Memorabilia-117
Emerald-117
Gold-117
Ruby-117
Sapphire-117
Brush with Greatness-10
Brush with Greatness Contest Cards-10
Deep in the Crease-D9
He Shoots-He Scores Prizes-21
Jerseys-GJ-25
Tandems-T-10
03BAP Ultimate Memorabilia Active Eight-1
03BAP Ultimate Memorabilia Active Eight-2
03BAP Ultimate Memorabilia Emblems-3
03BAP Ultimate Memorabilia Emblems Gold-3
03BAP Ultimate Memorabilia Heroes-12
03BAP Ultimate Memorabilia Jerseys-20
03BAP Ultimate Memorabilia Jerseys Gold-20
03BAP Ultimate Mem Jersey and Emblems-11
03BAP Ultimate Mem Jersey and Emblem Gold-11
03BAP Ultimate Mem Jersey and Numbers-11
03BAP Ultimate Mem Jersey and Number Gold-11
03BAP Ultimate Mem Journey Jerseys-4
03BAP Ultimate Mem Journey Jerseys Gold-4
03BAP Ultimate Mem Journey Emblems-4
03BAP Ultimate Mem Journey Emblems Gold-4
03BAP Ultimate Memorabilia Numbers-15
03BAP Ultimate Memorabilia Numbers Gold-15
03BAP Ultimate Mem Retro-Active Trophies-16
03BAP Ultimate Memorabilia Triple Threads-4
03Beehive-182
Variations-182
Gold-182
Silver-182
Jumbos-23
Jumbo Variations-23
Jumbo Jerseys-BH14
Jerseys-JT24
Sticks Beige Border-BE26
Sticks Blue Border-BL20
03Black Diamond-102
Black-102
Green-102
Red-102
Signature Gems-SG-36
Threads-DT-EB
Threads Green-DT-EB
Threads Red-DT-EB
Threads Black-DT-EB
03Bowman-46
Gold-46
03Bowman Chrome-46
Refractors-46
Gold Refractors-46
Xfractors-46
03Crown Royale-92
Blue-92
Retail-92
Gauntlet of Glory-19
Jerseys-23
Patches-23
03Duracell-5
03ITG Action-545
Jerseys-M151
Jerseys-M223
Oh Canada-OC12
03ITG Toronto Fall Expo Jerseys-FE21
03ITG Used Signature Series Goalie Gear-34
03ITG Used Sig Series Goalie Gear Autos-34
03ITG Used Sig Series Goalie Gear Gold-34
03ITG Used Sig Series Retrospectives-9A
03ITG Used Sig Series Retrospectives-9B
03ITG Used Sig Series Retrospectives-9C
03ITG Used Sig Series Retrospectives-9D
03ITG Used Sig Series Retrospectives-9E
03ITG Used Sig Series Retrospectives-9F
03ITG Used Sig Series Retrospectives Gold-9A
03ITG Used Sig Series Retrospectives Gold-9B
03ITG Used Sig Series Retrospectives Gold-9C
03ITG Used Sig Series Retrospectives Gold-9D
03ITG Used Sig Series Retrospectives Gold-9E
03ITG Used Sig Series Retrospectives Gold-9F
03ITG Used Signature Series Teammates-15
03ITG Used Sig Series Teammates Gold-15
03ITG VIP Collages-22
03ITG VIP Jerseys-30
03ITG VIP Netminders-3
03Kraft-1
03McDonald's Pacific-46
Patches Silver-22
Patches Gold-22
Patches and Sticks-22
Net Fusions-6
Saturday Night Rivals-5
03NHL Sticker Collection-140
03O-Pee-Chee-55
03OPC Blue-55
03OPC Gold-55
03OPC Red-55
03Pacific-315
Blue-315
Red-315
In the Crease-11
Jerseys-37
Jerseys Gold-37
03Pacific Calder-92
03Pacific Calder-158
Silver-92
03Pacific Complete-449
Red-449
03Pacific Exhibit-194
Blue Backs-194
Standing on Tradition-10
03Pacific Heads-Up-90
Hobby LTD-90
Retail LTD-90
Mini Sweaters-8
Rink Immortals-10
Rink Immortals LTD-10
Stonewallers-11
Stonewallers LTD-11
03Pacific Invincible-89
Blue-89
Red-89
Retail-89
Freeze Frame-22
Jerseys-30
03Pacific Luxury Suite-19A
03Pacific Luxury Suite-19B
03Pacific Luxury Suite-19C
03Pacific Luxury Suite-19D
03Pacific Prism-144
Blue-144
Patches-144
Red-144
Retail-144
Crease Police-8
03Pacific Quest for the Cup-94
Blue-94
Jerseys-18
03Pacific Supreme-90
Blue-90
Red-90
Retail-90
Standing Guard-12
03Pacific Toronto Fall Expo-6
03Parkhurst Original Six Chicago-34
03Parkhurst Original Six Chicago-62
03Parkhurst Original Six Chicago-98
Inserts-C7
Memorabilia-CM20
Memorabilia-CM57
03Parkhurst Orig Six He Shoots/Scores-1
03Parkhurst Orig Six He Shoots/Scores-1A
03Parkhurst Original Six Toronto-3
03Parkhurst Original Six Toronto-100
Memorabilia-TM9
03Parkhurst Rookie-18
Jerseys-GJ-34
Jerseys Gold-GJ-34
Jersey and Sticks-SJ-12
Jersey and Sticks Gold-SJ-12
Retro Rookies-RR-12
Retro Rookies Gold-RR-12
ROYalty-VR-18
ROYalty Gold-VR-18
03Private Stock Reserve-205
Blue-205
Patches-205
Red-205
Retail-205
Increase Security-16
03SP Authentic-81
Limited-81
Breakout Seasons-B27
Breakout Seasons Limited-B27
Foundations-F9
Foundations Limited-F9
Honors-H26
Honors Limited-H26
03SP Game Used-46
Gold-46
Authentic Fabrics-QSNBM
Authentic Fabrics Gold-QSNBM
Authentic Patches-APEB
Double Threads-DTSB
Team Threads-TTSNB
03SPx-92
Radiance-92
Spectrum-92
Origins-O-EB
Style-SPX-BT
Style Limited-SPX-BT
Winning Materials-WM-BE
Winning Materials-WM-EB
Winning Materials Limited-WM-BE
Winning Materials Limited-WM-EB
03Titanium-204
Patches-204
Masked Marauders-10
03Topps-55
Blue-55
Gold-55
Red-55
Box Toppers-8
Topps/OPC Idols-CI6
Lost Rookies-EB
Own the Game-OTG13
03Topps C55-49
Minis-49
Minis American Back-49
Minis American Back Red-49
Minis Bazooka Back-49
Minis Brooklyn Back-49
Minis Hat Trick Back-49
Minis O Canada Back-49
Minis O Canada Back Red-49
Minis Stanley Cup Back-49
Relics-TREB
03Topps Pristine-31
Gold Refractor Die Cuts-31
Refractors-31
Mini-PM-EB
Press Plates Black-31
Press Plates Cyan-31
Press Plates Magenta-31
Press Plates Yellow-31
03UD Honor Roll-81
03UD Honor Roll-131
Grade A Jerseys-TTOR
03UD Premier Collection-53
Teammates-PT-TM2
Teammates Patches-PT-TM2
03Upper Deck-184
All-Star Class-AS-28
Canadian Exclusives-184
HG-184
Patches-SV10
Performers-PS9
03Upper Deck Classic Portraits-93
03Upper Deck Classic Portraits-111
03Upper Deck Classic Portraits-146
Classic Colors-CC-ON
Classic Stitches-CS-EB
Hockey Royalty-BSM
03Upper Deck Ice-80
Gold-80
Breakers-IB-EB
Breaker Patches-IB-EB
Clear Cut Winners-CC-EB
Icons-I-EB
Icons Jerseys-I-EB
03Upper Deck MVP-395
Gold Script-395
Silver Script-395
Canadian Exclusives-395
Masked Men-MM8
SportsNut-SN81
Talent-MT9
Threads-TC6
03Upper Deck Rookie Update-83
Skills-SKEB
Super Stars-SSEB
03Upper Deck Trilogy-93
03Upper Deck Trilogy-114
Authentic Patches-AP29
Crest Variations-114
Limited-93
Limited-114
Limited Threads-LT23
03Upper Deck Victory-183
Bronze-183
Gold-183
Silver-183
Game Breakers-GB15
03Toronto Star-90
Foil-9
04Pacific-244
Blue-244
Red-244
Cramer's Choice-10
In The Crease-10
Milestones-6
04SP Authentic-84
04SP Authentic-146
Limited-84
Limited-146
Buybacks-48
Buybacks-49
Sign of the Times-DS-LB
Sign of the Times-TS-RBT
Sign of the Times-SS-CAN
04Ultimate Collection-40
Dual Logos-UL2-BS
Patches-UP-EB
04Upper Deck-166
Canadian Exclusives-166
HG Glossy Gold-166
HG Glossy Silver-166
NHL's Best-NB-EB
Swatch of Six-SS-EB
05Be A Player Outtakes-OT47
05Beehive-84
05Beehive-217
Beige -84
Blue -84
Gold-84
Red -84
Matte-84
05Black Diamond-143
Emerald-143
Gold-143
Onyx-143
Ruby-143
Jerseys-J-EB
Jerseys Ruby-J-EB
Jersey Duals-DJ-EB
Jersey Triples-TJ-EB
Jersey Quads-QJ-EB
05Hot Prospects-93
En Fuego-93
Red Hot-93
White Hot-93
05McDonalds Upper Deck-39
Goalie Factory-GF13
Goalie Gear-MG10
Jerseys-MJ10
Patches-MP10
05Panini Stickers-164
05Parkhurst-448
05Parkhurst-589
Facsimile Auto Parallel-448
Facsimile Auto Parallel-589
True Colors-TCTOR
True Colors-TCTOR
True Colors-TCOTTO
True Colors-TCOTTO
True Colors-TCTOMO
True Colors-TCTOMO
05SP Authentic-94
Limited-94
Chirography-SPEB
Exquisite Endorsements-EEEB
Marks of Distinction-MDEB
Octographs-OG
Prestigious Pairings-PPBS
Sign of the Times Triples-TBSO
05SP Game Used-92
Autographs-92
Gold-92
Authentic Fabrics-AF-EB
Authentic Fabrics Dual-BM
Authentic Fabrics Gold-AF-EB
Authentic Fabrics Quad-DLBN
Authentic Patches Quad -DLBN
Authentic Fabrics Triple-BBT
Authentic Patches-AP-EB
Authentic Patches Dual-BM
Authentic Patches Triple-BBT
Authentic Patches Triple-BIS
Awesome Authentics-AA-EB
Awesome Authentics Gold-DA-EB
By the Letter-LM-EB
Endorsed Equipment-EE-EB
Significant Numbers-SN-EB
05SPx-85
Spectrum-85
Winning Combos-WC-EM
Winning Combos-WC-TO
Winning Combos Gold-WC-EM
Winning Combos Gold-WC-TO
Winning Combos Spectrum-WC-EM
Winning Combos Spectrum-WC-TO
Winning Materials-WM-EB
Winning Materials Gold-WM-EB
Winning Materials Spectrum-WM-EB
Xcitement Superstars-XS-EB
Xcitement Superstars Gold-XS-EB
Xcitement Superstars Spectrum-XS-EB
05The Cup-92
Gold-92
Black Rainbow-92
Dual NHL Shields-DSSB
Emblems of Endorsement-EEEB
Hardware Heroes-HHEB2
Masterpiece Pressplates-92
Patch Variation-P92
Patch Variation Autographs-AP92
Scripted Numbers-SNBN
Scripted Numbers-SNBR
Scripted Numbers Dual-DSNBB
05UD Artifacts-93
05UD Artifacts-195
Blue-93
Blue-195
Gold-93
Gold-195
Green-93
Green-195
Pewter-93
Pewter-195
Red-93
Red-195
Frozen Artifacts-FA-EB
Frozen Artifacts Autographed-FA-EB
Frozen Artifacts Copper-FA-EB
Frozen Artifacts Dual-FAD-EB
Frozen Artifacts Dual Autographed-FAD-EB
Frozen Artifacts Dual Copper-FAD-EB
Frozen Artifacts Dual Gold-FAD-EB
Frozen Artifacts Dual Maroon-FAD-EB
Frozen Artifacts Dual Pewter-FAD-EB
Frozen Artifacts Dual Silver-FAD-EB
Frozen Artifacts Gold-FA-EB
Frozen Artifacts Maroon-FA-EB
Frozen Artifacts Pewter-FA-EB
Frozen Artifacts Silver-FA-EB
Goalie Gear-FG-EB
Goalie Gear Autographed-FG-EB
Goalie Gear Dual-FGD-EB
Goalie Gear Dual Autographed-FGD-EB
Goalie Gear Pewter-FG-EB
Goalie Gear Silver-FG-EB
Gold Autographed-93
Gold Autographed-195
Remarkable Artifacts-RA-EB1
Remarkable Artifacts-RA-EB2
Remarkable Artifacts Dual-RA-EB1
Remarkable Artifacts Dual-RA-EB2
Treasured Patches-TP-EB
Treasured Patches Autographed-TP-EB
Treasured Patches Dual-TPD-EB
Treasured Patches Dual Autographed-TPD-EB
Treasured Patches Pewter-TP-EB
Treasured Patches Silver-TP-EB
Treasured Swatches-TS-EB
Treasured Swatches Autographed-TS-EB
Treasured Swatches Blue-TS-EB
Treasured Swatches Copper-TS-EB
Treasured Swatches Dual-TSD-EB
Treasured Swatches Dual Autographed-TSD-EB
Treasured Swatches Dual Blue-TSD-EB
Treasured Swatches Dual Copper-TSD-EB
Treasured Swatches Dual Maroon-TSD-EB
Treasured Swatches Dual Pewter-TSD-EB
Treasured Swatches Dual Silver-TSD-EB
Treasured Swatches Maroon-TS-EB
Treasured Swatches Pewter-TS-EB
Treasured Swatches Silver-TS-EB
05UD PowerPlay-84
Rainbow-84
05Ultimate Collection-84
Gold-84
Endorsed Emblems-EEEB
Marquee Attractions-MA46
Marquee Attractions Signatures-SMA46
Ultimate Signatures-USEB
05Ultra-179
Gold-179
Ice-179
05Upper Deck-422
05Upper Deck All-Time Greatest-20
05Upper Deck All-Time Greatest-67
05Upper Deck Big Playmakers-B-EB
05Upper Deck Jerseys-J-EB
05Upper Deck Jerseys Series II-J2EB
05Upper Deck Majestic Materials-MMEB
05Upper Deck Notable Numbers-N-EB
05Upper Deck Patches-P-EB
05Upper Deck Scrapbooks-HS25
05Upper Deck Ice-93
Rainbow-93
Frozen Fabrics-FFEB
Frozen Fabrics Autographs-AFFEB
Frozen Fabrics Glass-FFEB
Frozen Fabrics Patches-FFPEB
Frozen Fabrics Patch Autographs-FAPEB
Signature Swatches-SSEB
05Upper Deck MVP-362
Gold-362
Platinum-362
Rising to the Occasion-RO12
05Upper Deck Rookie Update-92
05Upper Deck Trilogy-84
05Upper Deck Trilogy-128
Crystal-128
Honorary Patches-HP-EB
Honorary Patch Scripts-HSP-EB
Honorary Swatch Scripts-HSS-EB
05Upper Deck Victory-186
Black-186
Gold-186
Silver-186
Blow-Ups-BU38
Stars on Ice-SI41
06Be A Player Portraits-47
06Beehive-57
06Beehive-199
Blue-57
Gold-57
Matte-57
Red Facsimile Signatures-57
Wood-57
5 X 7 Black and White-57
Matted Materials-MMEB
06Between The Pipes-65
06Between The Pipes-125
06Between The Pipes-139
Autographs-AEB
Autographs-AEB2
Emblems-GUE71
Emblems Gold-GUE71
Emblems Autographs-GUE71
Jerseys-GUJ71
Jerseys Gold-GUJ71
Jerseys Autographs-GUJ71
Numbers-GUN71
Numbers Gold-GUN71
Numbers Autographs-GUN71
Pads-GP11
Pads Gold-GP11
The Mask-M24
The Mask Gold-M24
The Mask Silver-M24
06Black Diamond-137
Black-137
Black-165B
Gold-137
Ruby-137
Jerseys-JEB
Jerseys Black-JEB
Jerseys Gold-JEB
Jerseys Ruby-JEB
06Flair Showcase Stitches-SSEB
06Fleer-88
Fabricology-FEB
06Hot Prospects-43
Red Hot-43
White Hot-43
Hot Materials -HMEB
Hot Materials Red Hot-HMEB
Hot Materials White Hot-HMEB
06ITG Ultimate Memorabilia-43
Artist Proof-43
Autos-63
Autos Gold-63
Boys Will Be Boys-28
Boys Will Be Boys Gold-28
Complete Jersey-22
Complete Jersey Gold-22
Cornerstones-9
Cornerstones Gold-9
Decades-2
Decades Gold-2
Double Memorabilia-20
Double Memorabilia Gold-20
Jerseys-15
Jerseys Gold-15
Journey Emblem-11
Journey Emblem Gold-11
Journey Jersey-11
Journey Jersey Gold-11
Passing The Torch-13
Passing The Torch Gold-13
R.O.Y. Autos-13
R.O.Y. Autos Gold-13
R.O.Y. Emblems-13
R.O.Y. Emblems Gold-13
R.O.Y. Jerseys-13
R.O.Y. Jerseys Gold-13
R.O.Y. Numbers-13
R.O.Y. Numbers Gold-13
Sticks Autos-4
Sticks Autos Gold-4
Triple Thread Jerseys-5
Triple Thread Jerseys Gold-5
06O-Pee-Chee-208
06O-Pee-Chee-654
Rainbow-208
Rainbow-654
06Panini Stickers-60
06SP Authentic-58
06SP Authentic-112
Limited-58
Limited-112
06SP Game Used-42
Gold-42
Rainbow-42
Authentic Fabrics-AFEB
Authentic Fabrics Parallel-AFEB
Authentic Fabrics Patches-AFEB
Authentic Fabrics Triple-AF3FLA
Authentic Fabrics Triple Patches-AF3FLA
Authentic Fabrics Quads-AF4BJTW
Authentic Fabrics Quads Patches-AF4BJTW
Authentic Fabrics Sixes-AF6JEN
Authentic Fabrics Sixes-AF6WIN
Authentic Fabrics Sixes Patches-AF6JEN
Authentic Fabrics Sixes Patches-AF6WIN
Authentic Fabrics Sevens-AF7VEZ
Authentic Fabrics Sevens Patches-AF7VEZ
06SPx-44
06SPx-140
Spectrum-44
Spectrum-140
SPxcitement-X46
SPxcitement Spectrum-X46
Winning Materials-WMEB
Winning Materials Spectrum-WMEB
Winning Materials Autographs-WMEB
06The Cup-36
Autographed Foundations-CQEB
Autographed Foundations Patches-CQEB
Autographed NHL Shields Duals-DASBB
Autographed Patches-36
Black Rainbow-36
Foundations-CQEB
Foundations Patches-CQEB
Gold-36
Gold Patches-36
Jerseys-36
Masterpiece Pressplates-36
NHL Shields Duals-DSHEC
NHL Shields Duals-DSHEO
06UD Artifacts-59
06UD Artifacts-186
Blue-59
Blue-186
Gold-59
Gold-186
Platinum-59
Platinum-186
Radiance-59
Radiance-186
Red-59
Red-186
Treasured Patches Black-TSEB
Treasured Patches Blue-TSEB
Treasured Patches Gold-TSEB
Treasured Patches Platinum-TSEB
Treasured Patches Red-TSEB
Treasured Swatches-TSEB
Treasured Swatches Black-TSEB
Treasured Swatches Blue-TSEB
Treasured Swatches Gold-TSEB
Treasured Swatches Platinum-TSEB
Treasured Swatches Red-TSEB
Tundra Tandems-TTEJ
Tundra Tandems Black-TTEJ
Tundra Tandems Blue-TTEJ
Tundra Tandems Gold-TTEJ
Tundra Tandems Platinum-TTEJ
Tundra Tandems Red-TTEJ
Tundra Tandems Dual Patches Red-TTEJ
06UD Mini Jersey Collection-48
06UD Powerplay Specialists-SEB
06UD Powerplay Specialists Patches-PEB
06Ultimate Collection-29
06Ultra Uniformity-UEB
06Ultra Uniformity Patches-UPEB
06Upper Deck Arena Giveaways-FLA5
06Upper Deck-333
Exclusives Parallel-333
High Gloss Parallel-333
Game Jerseys-JEB
Game Patches-PEB
Generations Duals-G2BW
Generations Triples-G3BTW
Generations Patches Dual-G2PBW
Generations Patches Triple-G3PBTW
Masterpieces-333
Oversized Wal-Mart Exclusives-333
Zero Men-ZM7
06Upper Deck MVP-129
Gold Script-129
Super Script-129
Last Line of Defense-LL15
06Upper Deck Sweet Shot-48
Endorsed Equipment-EEEB
06Upper Deck Trilogy-45
Honorary Scripted Patches-HSPEB
Honorary Scripted Swatches-HSSEB
Honorary Swatches-HSEB
06Upper Deck Victory-184
06Upper Deck Victory-251
06Upper Deck Victory Black-184
06Upper Deck Victory Gold-184
06Upper Deck Victory GameBreakers-GB47
06ITG Heroes and Prospects Heroes Memorabilia-HM22
06ITG Heroes and Prospects Quad Emblems-QE14
06ITG Heroes and Prospects Triple Memorabilia-TM12
07Upper Deck Victory-86
Black-86
Gold-86

Belhumeur, Marc
93Quebec Pee-Wee Tournament-89

Belhumeur, Michel
72O-Pee-Chee-273
74Capitals White Borders-5
74O-Pee-Chee NHL-153
74Topps-153
75O-Pee-Chee NHL-232
75Topps-232
76O-Pee-Chee NHL-296

Beliavski, Alexander
93Swedish Semic Elitserien-14
94Swedish Leaf-274
95Swedish Leaf-145
98Swedish UD Choice-25
00Swedish Upper Deck-21
00Swedish Upper Deck-182
SHL Signatures-AB
03Swedish Bjorkloven Umea-7

Belisle, Ian
93Quebec Pee-Wee Tournament-530

Belisle, Omar
95Thunder Bay Senators-3

Belisle, Patrick
917th Inn. Sketch QMJHL-9

Belisle, Teddy
94Thunder Bay Flyers-2

Belitski, David
93Kitchener Rangers-2
93Kitchener Rangers-29
94Slapshot Promos-1
94Parkhurst SE-SE251
Gold-SE251
94Kitchener Rangers-2
95Slapshot-131
95Classic-87
95Signature Rookies Auto-Phonex-5
95Signature Rook Auto-Phonex Phone Cards-5
96Kitchener Rangers-2
99German Bundesliga 2-42
03Reading Royals RBI Sports-305
03Roanoke Express-306

Beliveau, Jean
44Beehive Group II Photos-222
45Quaker Oats Photos-62
48Exhibits Canadian-2
48Exhibits Canadian-3
50Quebec Citadelles-2
51Laval Dairy QSHL-1
52St. Lawrence Sales-39
53Parkhurst-27
54Parkhurst-3
55Parkhurst-44
55Parkhurst-74
55Parkhurst-77
Quaker Oats-44
Quaker Oats-74
Quaker Oats-77
57Parkhurst-M3
58Parkhurst-34
59Parkhurst-6
60NHL Ceramic Tiles-20
60Parkhurst-49
60Parkhurst-59
60Shirriff Coins-30
60York Photos-4
61Parkhurst-45
61Shirriff/Salada Coins-102
61York Yellow Backs-10
62El Producto Discs-1
62Parkhurst-39
62Shirriff Coins-32
62York Iron-On Transfers-8
63Chex Photos-5A
63Chex Photos-5B
63Parkhurst-30
63Parkhurst-89
63Toronto Star-4
63York White Backs-26
64Beehive Group III Photos-99
64Canadiens Postcards-2
64Coca-Cola Caps-58
64Topps-33
64Toronto Star-4
65Canadiens Steinberg Glasses-2
65Coca-Cola-58
65Topps-6
66Topps-73
66Topps-127
66Topps USA Test-31
67Canadiens IGA-4
67General Mills-1
67Post Flip Books-7
67Post Flip Books-8
67Topps-74
67York Action Octagons-3
67York Action Octagons-23
67York Action Octagons-25
67York Action Octagons-28
68Canadiens IGA-4
68Canadiens Postcards BW-2
68O-Pee-Chee-166
Puck Stickers-7
68Post Marbles-2
68Shirriff Coins-80
68Topps-61
69Canadiens Postcards Color-2
69O-Pee-Chee-10
69O-Pee-Chee-220
Four-in-One-5
Stamps-1
69Topps-10
70Canadiens Pins-1
70Dad's Cookies-4
70Esso Power Players-4
70O-Pee-Chee-55
Deckle-21
70Sargent Promotions Stamps-108
70Topps-55
Topps/OPC Sticker Stamps-1
71O-Pee-Chee-263
71Finnish Suomi Stickers-379
71Swedish Hockey-197
72Dimanche/Derniere Heure *-132
72Finnish Semic World Championship-207
72Swedish Semic World Championship-207
73Canadiens Postcards-1
77Sportscasters-1014
77Finnish Sportscasters-33-785
81TCMA-11
83Canadiens Postcards-1
83Hall of Fame-31
83Hall of Fame Postcards-C1
85Hall of Fame-31
88Esso All-Stars-1
91Star Pics-4
92Parkhurst Parkie Reprints-PR30
92Sport-Flash-4
92Sport-Flash Autographs-4
93O-Pee-Chee Canadiens Hockey Fest-14
93O-Pee-Chee Canadiens Hockey Fest-27
93O-Pee-Chee Canadiens Hockey Fest-44
93O-Pee-Chee Canadiens Hockey Fest-59
93O-Pee-Chee Canadiens Panel-1
94Hockey Wit-23
94Parkhurst Missing Link-64
94Parkhurst Missing Link-138
94Parkhurst Missing Link-149
94Parkhurst Missing Link-150
94Parkhurst Missing Link-156
94Parkhurst Missing Link-157
94Parkhurst Missing Link-172
Autographs-5
94Parkhurst Tall Boys-85
94Parkhurst Tall Boys-142
94Parkhurst Tall Boys-146
94Parkhurst Tall Boys-159
94Parkhurst Tall Boys-172
94Zeller's Masters of Hockey-1
94Zeller's Masters of Hockey-NNO
94Zeller's Masters of Hockey Signed-1
95Parkhurst '66-67 Promos-4
95Parkhurst '66-67-73
95Parkhurst '66-67-PR125
Coins-73
96SLU Canadian Timeless Legends-1
96Duracell L'Equipe Beliveau-JB21
96Duracell L'Equipe Beliveau-JB22
97SLU Canadian Timeless Legends-1
99Upper Deck 500 Goal Club-500JB
99Upper Deck 500 Goal Club-500JB
99Upper Deck Century Legends-6
Century Collection-6
Epic Signatures-JEB
Epic Signatures 100-JEB
99Upper Deck Retro-85
Gold-85
Platinum-85
Generation-G5A
Generation Level 2-G5A
Inkredible-JEB
Inkredible Level 2-JEB
00UD Heroes-130
Signs of Greatness-JB
00Upper Deck Legends-64
Legendary Collection Bronze-64
Legendary Collection Gold-64
Legendary Collection Silver-64
Epic Signatures-JBE
01BAP Memorabilia 500 Goal Scorers-GS23
01BAP Memorabilia Rocket's Mates-RM3
01BAP Signature Series 500 Goal Scorers-3
01BAP Sig Series 500 Goal Scorers Autos-3
01BAP Signature Series Vintage Autographs-VA-5
01BAP Signature Series Vintage Autographs-VA-6
01BAP Ultimate Mem All-Star History-7
01BAP Ultimate Memorabilia Autographs-24
01BAP Ultimate Mem Autographs Gold-24
01BAP Ultimate Memorabilia Captain's C-2
01BAP Ultimate Memorabilia Cornerstones-2
01BAP Ultimate Memorabilia Emblem Attic-1
01BAP Ultimate Mem 500 Goal Scorers-7
01BAP Ultimate Mem 500 Goal Scorers Autos-10
01BAP Ultimate Mem 500 Goal Jerseys/Stick-7
01BAP Ultimate Mem 500 Goal Emblems-7
01BAP Ultimate Memorabilia Les Canadiens-11
01BAP Ultimate Mem Prototypical Players-7
01BAP Ultimate Mem Prototypical Players-8
01BAP Ultimate Mem Prototypical Players-9
01BAP Ultimate Mem Retired Numbers-3
01BAP Ultimate Mem Retro Teammates-1
01BAP Ultimate Mem Retro Teammates-10
01BAP Ultimate Mem Stanley Cup Winners-2
01Fleer Legacy-6
01Fleer Legacy-9
Ultimate-6
Ultimate-9
Memorabilia-9
Memorabilia Autographs-1
01Greats of the Game-3
Retro Collection-2
Autographs-3
01Parkhurst Autographs-PA3
01Parkhurst Autographs-PA6
01Parkhurst Autographs-PA27
01Parkhurst 500 Goal Scorers-PGS23
01Parkhurst He Shoots-He Scores Points-1
01Parkhurst He Shoots-He Scores Prizes-40
01Parkhurst Heroes-H1
01Parkhurst Reprints-PR9
01Parkhurst Reprints-PR16
01Parkhurst Reprints-PR33
01Parkhurst Reprints-PR80
01Parkhurst Reprints-PR82
01Parkhurst Reprints-PR107
01Parkhurst Reprints-PR110
01Parkhurst Reprints-PR118
01Parkhurst Reprints-PR130
01Parkhurst Reprints-PR136
01Parkhurst Vintage Memorabilia-PV17
01Parkhurst Vintage Memorabilia-PV18
01Parkhurst Vintage Memorabilia-PV19
01Topps Heritage Arena Relics-RJBE
01Topps Heritage Arena Relics-RJB/JB
01Topps Heritage Arena Relics-ARJBE
01Topps Heritage Arena Relics-ARJB/JB
01Topps Heritage Autographs-AJBE
01Topps Heritage Salute-S7
01UD Stanley Cup Champs-13
01Upper Deck Legends-31
Epic Signatures-JB
Sticks-PHJB
02BAP Memorabilia Mini Stanley Cups-3
02BAP NHL All-Star History-7
02BAP Ultimate Memorabilia All-Star MVP-10
02BAP Ultimate Mem Blades of Steel-3
02BAP Ultimate Memorabilia Conn Smythe-1
02BAP Ultimate Memorabilia Emblem Attic-7
02BAP Ultimate Memorabilia Great Moments-12
02BAP Ultimate Memorabilia Legend-8
02BAP Ultimate Memorabilia Numerology-6
02BAP Ultimate Mem Playoff Scorers-14
02BAP Ultimate Mem Retro Teammates-7
02BAP Ultimate Memorabilia Retro Trophies-7
02BAP Ultimate Mem Scoring Leaders-34
02BAP Ultimate Mem Storied Franchise-22
02BAP Ultimate Mem Vintage Hat Tricks-6
02BAP Ultimate Mem Vintage Jerseys-22
02BAP Ultimate Mem Vintage Jersey Autos-1
02ITG Used Vintage Memorabilia-VM6
02ITG Used Vintage Memorabilia Gold-VM6
02Parkhurst Vintage Memorabilia-VM7
02Parkhurst Vintage Teammates-VT8
02Parkhurst Retro Nicknames-RN20
02UD Foundations 1000 Point Club-BE
02UD Foundations Signs of Greatness-SGJB
03BAP Memorabilia Vintage Memorabilia-VM-18
03BAP Ultimate Memorabilia Autographs-156
Gold-156
03BAP Ultimate Memorabilia Cornerstones-2
03BAP Ultimate Memorabilia Emblem Attic-9
03BAP Ultimate Mem Emblem Attic Gold-9
03BAP Ultimate Mem Jersey and Stick-25
03BAP Ultimate Mem Jersey and Stick Gold-25
03BAP Ultimate Memorabilia Linemates-4
03BAP Ultimate Mem Raised to the Rafters-11
03BAP Ultimate Mem Retro Teammates-7
03BAP Ultimate Mem Retro-Active Trophies-3
03BAP Ultimate Mem Retro-Active Trophies-18
03BAP Ultimate Memorabilia Triple Threads-26
03BAP Ultimate Mem Ultimate Captains-6
03BAP Ultimate Mem Vintage Blade of Steel-20
03BAP Ultimate Mem Vint Complete Jersey-7
03BAP Ultimate Mem Vint Comp Jersey Gold-7
03BAP Ultimate Mem Vintage Jerseys-6
03BAP Ultimate Mem Vintage Jerseys Gold-6
03BAP Ultimate Memorabilia Vintage Lumber-5
03Canada Post-7
Autographs-7
03ITG Used Signature Series-111
Gold-111
Autographs-JB
Autographs Gold-JB
Vintage Memorabilia-7
Vintage Memorabilia Autographs-7
Vintage Memorabilia Gold-7
03ITG VIP Collages-34
03ITG VIP Collage Autographs-34
03ITG VIP MVP-22
03ITG VIP Vintage Memorabilia-18
03Pacific Exhibit-218
03Parkhurst Orig Six He Shoots/Scores-8
03Parkhurst Orig Six He Shoots/Scores-8A
03Parkhurst Original Six Montreal-44
03Parkhurst Original Six Montreal-63
03Parkhurst Original Six Montreal-75
03Parkhurst Original Six Montreal-85
03Parkhurst Original Six Montreal-97
Autographs-1
Inserts-M3
Inserts-M8
Memorabilia-MM24
Memorabilia-MM32
Memorabilia-MM38
Memorabilia-MM55
03SPx-111
Radiance-111
Spectrum-111
03Upper Deck Trilogy-123
Crest Variations-123
Limited-123
Scripts-S3JB
Scripts-CSBU
Scripts-CSBU2
Scripts-CSBU3
Scripts Limited-S3JB
Scripts Red-S3JB
04ITG NHL AS FANtasy AS History Jerseys-SB7
04ITG Franchises Canadian-39
Autographs-JBE
Barn Burners-BB3
Barn Burners Gold-BB3
Complete Jerseys-CJ2
Complete Jerseys Gold-CJ2
Double Memorabilia-DM2
Double Memorabilia Autographs-DM2
Double Memorabilia Gold-DM2
Forever Rivals-FR2
Forever Rivals Gold-FR2
Memorabilia-SM3
Memorabilia Autographs-SM3
Memorabilia Gold-SM3
Original Sticks-OS1
Original Sticks Autographs-OS1
Original Sticks Gold-OS1
Teammates-TM4
Teammates Gold-TM4
Triple Memorabilia-TM7
Triple Memorabilia Autographs-TM7
Triple Memorabilia Gold-TM7
Trophy Winners-TW8
Trophy Winners Gold-TW8
04ITG Franchises He Shoots/Scores Prizes-6
04ITG Franchises Update Linemates-ULI5
04ITG Franchises Update Linemates Gold-ULI5
04ITG Ultimate Memorabilia-153
Gold-153
Art Ross Trophy-2
Auto Threads-16
Autographs-26
Autographs Gold-26
Blades of Steel-12
Complete Jerseys-8
Conn Smythe Trophy-1
Cornerstones-4
Cornerstones Gold-4
Day In History-6
Day In History-37
Day In History Gold-6
Day In History Gold-37
Emblem Attic-2
Emblem Attic Gold-2
Jerseys-9
Jerseys Gold-9
Jersey Autographs-3
Jersey Autographs Gold-3
Jersey and Sticks-7
Jersey and Sticks Gold-7
Nicknames-12
Nickname Autographs-12
Original Six-2
Raised to the Rafters-8
Retro Teammates-15
Stick Autographs-31
Stick Autographs Gold-31
Triple Threads-13
Vintage Lumber-9
04SP Authentic Buybacks-82
04SP Authentic Buybacks-83
04SP Authentic Buybacks-84
04SP Authentic Sign of the Times-QS-BDPB
04SP Authentic Sign of the Times-FS-MON
04UD Legendary Signatures-47
AKA Autographs-AKA-JE
Autographs-JE
04UD Legends Classics-31
04UD Legends Classics-71
04UD Legends Classics-92
Gold-31
Gold-71
Gold-92
Platinum-31
Platinum-71
Platinum-92
Silver-31
Silver-71
Silver-92

Jersey Redemptions-JY2
Signature Moments-M28
Signatures-CS28
Signatures-DC2
Signatures-DC9
Signatures-TC7
Signatures-TC12
04ITG Heroes and Prospects-153
Aspiring-15
Autographs-JBE
Hero Memorabilia-11
04ITG Heroes/Prospects Toronto Expo '05-153
04ITG Heroes/Prospects Expo Heroes/Pros-153
05ITG Heroes/Prosp Toronto Expo Parallel -9
05Beehive-233
05ITG Ultimate Memorabilia Level 1-54
05ITG Ultimate Memorabilia Level 2-54
05ITG Ultimate Memorabilia Level 3-54
05ITG Ultimate Memorabilia Level 4-54
05ITG Ultimate Memorabilia Level 5-54
05ITG Ultimate Mem Blades of Steel-14
05ITG Ultimate Mem Blades of Steel Gold-14
05ITG Ultimate Mem Complete Package-6
05ITG Ultimate Mem Complete Package Gold-6
05ITG Ultimate Mem Cornerstones Jerseys-9
05ITG Ultimate Mem Cornerst Jerseys Gold-9
05ITG Ultimate Mem Decades Jerseys-3
05ITG Ultimate Mem Decades Jerseys Gold-3
05ITG Ultimate Memorabilia Double Autos-8
05ITG Ultimate Mem Double Autos Gold-8
05ITG Ultimate Mem Double Mem Autos-8
05ITG Ultimate Mem Double Mem Autos Gold-8
05ITG Ultimate Memorabilia Emblem Attic-18
05ITG Ultimate Mem Emblem Attic Gold-18
05ITG Ultimate Memorabilia Emblems-8
05ITG Ultimate Memorabilia Emblems Gold-8
05ITG Ultimate Memorabilia In The Numbers-3
05ITG Ultimate Mem In The Numbers Gold-3
05ITG Ultimate Mem Jersey and Emblem-29
05ITG Ultimate Memorabilia Jersey Autos-21
05ITG Ultimate Mem Jersey Autos Gold-21
05ITG Ultimate Mem Jersey Emblems Gold-29
05ITG Ultimate Memorabilia Jerseys-20
05ITG Ultimate Memorabilia Jerseys Gold-20
05ITG Ultimate Mem Pass the Torch Jerseys-13
05ITG Ultimate Mem Passing Torch Jsy Gold-13
05ITG Ultimate Mem Raised to the Rafters-20
05ITG Ultimate Mem Raised Rafters Gold-20
05ITG Ultimate Mem Record Breaker Jerseys-4
05ITG Ultimate Mem RecBreak Jerseys Gold-4
05ITG Ultimate Mem Retro Teammate Jerseys-10
05ITG Ultimate Mem Retro Teammate Jerseys-15
05ITG Ult Mem Retro Teammates Jersey Gold-10
05ITG Ult Mem Retro Teammates Jersey Gold-15
05ITG Ultimate Memorabilia Sextuple Autos-4
05ITG Ultimate Memorabilia Stick Autos-1
05ITG Ultimate Mem Stick Autos Gold-1
05ITG Ultimate Mem Sticks and Jerseys-10
05ITG Ultimate Mem Stick and Jerseys Gold-10
05ITG Ultimate Mem 3 Star of the Game Jsy-8
05ITG Ult Mem 3 Star of the Game Jsy Gold-8
05ITG Ultimate Memorabilia Trifecta Autos-4
05ITG Ultimate Mem Trifecta Autos Gold-4
05ITG Ultimate Memorabilia Triple Autos-8
05ITG Ultimate Memorabilia Triple Autos-17
05ITG Ultimate Mem Triple Autos Gold-8
05ITG Ultimate Mem Triple Autos Gold-17
05ITG Ultimate Memorabilia Ultimate Autos-50
05ITG Ultimate Mem Ultimate Autos Gold-50
05ITG Ultimate Memorabilia Vintage Lumber-15
05ITG Ultimate Mem Vintage Lumber Gold-15
05NHL Legends Medallions-11
05SP Game Used Game Gear-GG-JB
05SP Game Used Signature Sticks-SS-JB
05SPx-129
Spectrum-129
Xcitement Legends-XL-JB
Xcitement Legends Gold-XL-JB
Xcitement Legends Spectrum-XL-JB
05The Cup-54
Gold-54
Black Rainbow-54
Emblems of Endorsement-EEJB
Hardware Heroes-HHJB1
Hardware Heroes-HHJB2
Honorable Numbers-HNJB
Masterpiece Pressplates-54
Noble Numbers-NNBL
Patch Variation-P54
Patch Variation Autographs-AP54
Scripted Numbers-SNJV
Scripted Swatches-SSJB
Stanley Cup Titlists-TJB
05UD Artifacts-103
Blue-103
Gold-103
Green-103
Pewter-103
Red-103
Frozen Artifacts-FA-JB
Frozen Artifacts Autographed-FA-JB
Frozen Artifacts Copper-FA-JB
Frozen Artifacts Dual-FAD-JB
Frozen Artifacts Dual Autographed-FAD-JB
Frozen Artifacts Dual Copper-FAD-JB
Frozen Artifacts Dual Gold-FAD-JB
Frozen Artifacts Dual Maroon-FAD-JB
Frozen Artifacts Dual Pewter-FAD-JB
Frozen Artifacts Dual Silver-FAD-JB
Frozen Artifacts Gold-FA-JB
Frozen Artifacts Maroon-FA-JB
Frozen Artifacts Patches-FP-JB
Frozen Artifacts Patches Autographed-FP-JB
Frozen Artifacts Patches Dual-FPD-JB
Frozen Artifacts Patches Dual Autos-FPD-JB
Frozen Artifacts Patches Pewter-FP-JB
Frozen Artifacts Patches Silver-FP-JB
Frozen Artifacts Pewter-FA-JB
Frozen Artifacts Silver-FA-JB
Gold Autographed-103
05Ultimate Collection Jerseys-JJB
05Ultimate Coll Ultimate Achievements-UAJB
05Ultimate Collection Ultimate Signatures-USJB
05Ultimate Coll Ultimate Sigs Trios-UTLBR
05ITG Heroes and Prospects-9
Aspiring-ASP14
Autographs-A-JB
Hero Memorabilia-HM-19
Spectrum-STM-06
Spectrum Gold-STM-06
06Black Diamond-159B
Gold-159B
Ruby-159B
06ITG Ultimate Memorabilia-75
Artist Proof-75
Autos-2
Autos Gold-2
Blades of Steel-18
Blades of Steel Gold-18
Boys Will Be Boys-5
Boys Will Be Boys Gold-5
Complete Jersey-10
Complete Jersey Gold-10
Cornerstones-2
Cornerstones Gold-2
Decades-3
Decades Gold-3
Double Memorabilia-10
Double Memorabilia Gold-10
Emblem Attic-5
Emblem Attic Gold-5
Jerseys-11
Jerseys Gold-11
Jerseys and Emblems-10
Jerseys and Emblems Gold-10
Jerseys Autos-21
Jerseys Autos Gold-21
Legendary Captains-3
Legendary Captains Gold-3
Passing The Torch-1
Passing The Torch Gold-1
Retro Teammates-6
Retro Teammates Gold-6
Ring Leaders-2
Ring Leaders Gold-2
Road to the Cup-2
Road to the Cup Gold-2
Stick Rack-1
Stick Rack-16
Stick Rack-21
Stick Rack Gold-1
Stick Rack Gold-16
Stick Rack Gold-21
Triple Thread Jerseys-7
Triple Thread Jerseys Gold-7
06Parkhurst-13
06Parkhurst-187
Autographs-13
Autographs-187
Autographs Dual-DABM
06SP Authentic Sign of the Times-STJB
06SP Game Used Legendary Fabrics-LFJB
06SP Game Used Legendary Fabrics Autographs-LFJB
06The Cup-48
Autographed Foundations-CQJB
Black Rainbow-48
Foundations-CQJB
Gold-48
Jerseys-48
Masterpiece Pressplates-48
Stanley Cup Signatures-CSJB
06UD Artifacts-102
Blue-102
Gold-102
Platinum-102
Radiance-102
Autographed Radiance Parallel-102
Red-102
Auto-Facts-AFBE
Auto-Facts Gold-AFBE
Tundra Tandems-TTLB
Tundra Tandems Black-TTLB
Tundra Tandems Blue-TTLB
Tundra Tandems Gold-TTLB
Tundra Tandems Platinum-TTLB
Tundra Tandems Red-TTLB
Tundra Tandems Dual Patches Red-TTLB
06Ultimate Collection Autographed Jerseys-AJ-JB
06Ultimate Collection Autographed Patches-AJ-JB
06Ultimate Collection Jerseys-UJ-JB
06Ultimate Collection Signatures-US-JB
06Ultimate Collection Ultimate Achievements-UA-JB
06Upper Deck Sweet Shot Signature Shots/Saves-SSBE
06Upper Deck Sweet Shot Signature Shots/Saves Sticks-SSSJB
06Upper Deck Sweet Shot Signature Sticks-STJB
06Upper Deck Trilogy Combo Clearcut Autographs-C3BLS
06Upper Deck Trilogy Frozen In Time-FT9
06Upper Deck Trilogy Legendary Scripts-LSJB
06Upper Deck Trilogy Scripts-S1JB
06Upper Deck Trilogy Scripts-S2JB
06ITG Heroes and Prospects Heroes Memorabilia-HM15
06ITG Heroes and Prospects Heroes Memorabilia Gold-HM15

Beliveau, Jean-Francois
04Thetford Mines Prolab-18

Beljo, Jadran
05Mississauga Ice Dogs-23
06Mississauga Ice Dogs-4

Belkin, Oleg
00Russian Hockey League-163
02Russian Hockey League-38
03Russian Hockey League-110

Bell, Bob
91British Columbia JHL-118
95Tallahassee Tiger Sharks-18

Bell, Brendan
99Ottawa 67's-15
00Ottawa 67's-7
01Ottawa 67's-9
01UD Prospects-39
Jerseys-J-BB
Jerseys Gold-J-BB
02Ottawa 67's-8
03Pacific AHL Prospects-80
Gold-80
06Be A Player Portraits-127
06Beehive-155
Matte-155
06Flair Showcase-164
Parallel-164
06Fleer-217
Tiffany-217
06Hot Prospects-136
Red Hot-136
White Hot-136
Hot Materials -HMBE
Hot Materials Red Hot-HMBE
Hot Materials White Hot-HMBE
Hotgraphs-HBB
06O-Pee-Chee-519
Rainbow-519
06SP Authentic-207
Limited-207
06SP Game Used-155
Gold-155
Rainbow-155
Autographs-155
Rookie Exclusives Autographs-REBB
06SPx-169
Spectrum-169
06The Cup-160
Autographed Rookie Masterpiece Pressplates-160
Gold Rainbow Autographed Rookie Patches-160
Masterpiece Pressplates (Artifacts)-216
Masterpiece Pressplates (Be A Player Portraits)-127
Masterpiece Pressplates (Bee Hive)-155
Masterpiece Pressplates (Marquee Rookies)-519
Masterpiece Pressplates (MVP)-326
Masterpiece Pressplates (Power Play)-127
Masterpiece Pressplates (SP Authentic Autographs)-207
Masterpiece Pressplates (SP Game Used)-155
Masterpiece Pressplates (SPx Autographs)-169
Masterpiece Pressplates (Trilogy)-155
Masterpiece Pressplates (Ultimate Collection)-97
Masterpiece Pressplates (Victory)-208
Rookies Black-160
Rookies Platinum-160
06UD Artifacts-216
Blue-216
Gold-216
Platinum-216
Radiance-216
Red-216
06UD Mini Jersey Collection-127
06UD Powerplay-127
Impact Rainbow-127
06Ultimate Collection-97
Ultimate Debut Threads Jerseys-DJ-BB
Ultimate Debut Threads Jerseys Autographs-DJ-BB
Ultimate Debut Threads Patches-DJ-BB
Ultimate Debut Threads Patches Autographs-DJ-BB
06Ultra-227
Gold Medallion-227
Ice Medallion-227
06Upper Deck-245
Exclusives Parallel-245
High Gloss Parallel-245
Masterpieces-245
Rookie Materials-RMBB
Rookie Materials Patches-RMBB
06Upper Deck MVP-326
Gold Script-326
Super Script-326
06Upper Deck Ovation-148
06Upper Deck Trilogy-155
06Upper Deck Victory-208
06Upper Deck Victory Black-208
06Upper Deck Victory Gold-208
06Toronto Marlies-3
06ITG Heroes and Prospects-33
Autographs-ABB
07Upper Deck Rookie Class -39

Bell, Bruce
81Sault Ste. Marie Greyhounds-4
83Brantford Alexanders-4
84Nordiques Postcards-2
85O-Pee-Chee-231
85O-Pee-Chee Stickers-142
87Panini Stickers-308
89ProCards AHL-135
90ProCards AHL/IHL-234
91ProCards-338
94Central Hockey League-20

Bell, Chris
00Amarillo Rattlers-2
01Greensboro Generals-9
02Greensboro Generals RBI-4

Bell, Darren
88Sudbury Wolves-13
89Sudbury Wolves-4
907th Inn. Sketch OHL-26

Bell, David
95Slapshot-259
01Greenville Grrrowl-14
02Bakersfield Condors-2
03Port Huron Beacons-2

Bell, Gordon
45Quaker Oats Photos-6

Bell, Malcolm
94UK Humberside Hawks-2
97UK Kingston Hawks Stickers-3

Bell, Mark
98Bowman's Best-138
Refractors-138
Atomic Refractors-138
98Finest Futures Finest-F7
98Finest Futures Finest Refractors-F7
98OPC Chrome-222
Refractors-222
98Topps-222
O-Pee-Chee-222
98Bowman CHL-36
98Bowman CHL-123
Golden Anniversary-36
Golden Anniversary-123
OPC International-36
OPC International-123
Autographs Blue-A8
Autographs Gold-A8
Autographs Silver-A8
98Bowman Chrome CHL-36
98Bowman Chrome CHL-123
Golden Anniversary-36
Golden Anniversary-123
Golden Anniversary Refractors-36
Golden Anniversary Refractors-123
OPC International-36
OPC International-123
OPC International Refractors-36
OPC International Refractors-123
Refractors-36
Refractors-123
99Black Diamond-106
Diamond Cut-106
Final Cut-106
99Upper Deck-318
Exclusives-318
Exclusives 1 of 1-318
99Upper Deck Sobey's Memorial Cup-5
99Upper Deck Gold Reserve-318
99Upper Deck Ovation-79
Standing Ovation-79
99Ottawa 67's-1
99UD Prospects-4
CHL Class-C3
Signatures of Tradition-MB
00BAP Memorabilia-508
01BAP Memorabilia-252
Emerald-252
Ruby-252
Sapphire-252
01BAP Signature Series-230
Autographs-230
Autographs Gold-230
01Crown Royale-30
Blue-30
Premiere Date-30
Red-30
Retail-30
Crowning Achievement-3
Rookie Royalty-4
01O-Pee-Chee-278
01O-Pee-Chee Premier Parallel-278
01Pacific-83
Extreme LTD-83
Hobby LTD-83
Premiere Date-83
Retail LTD-83
Adrenaline Rookie Report-5
01Pacific Arena Exclusives-83
01Parkhurst-289
01Parkhurst Beckett Promos-289
01Private Stock-102
Gold-102
Premiere Date-102
Retail-102
Silver-102
01Private Stock Pacific Nights-102
01Private Stock PS-2002-79
01SPx-165
01Titanium-29
Hobby Parallel-29
Premiere Date-29
Retail-29
Retail Parallel-29
Double-Sided Jerseys-24
Double-Sided Jerseys-73
Double-Sided Patches-24
Double-Sided Patches-73
Rookie Team-4
Three-Star Selections-24
01Titanium Draft Day Edition-115
01Topps-278
OPC Parallel-278
01Topps Chrome-143
Refractors-143
Black Border Refractors-143
01UD Mask Collection-18
Gold-18
Double Patches-DPBE
Jerseys-J-BE
Jersey and Patch-JPBE
01UD Top Shelf-85
01Upper Deck Victory-366
Gold-366
01Vanguard-19
Blue-19
Red-19
One of Ones-19
Premiere Date-19
Proofs-19
02Atomic-19
Blue-19
Gold-19
Red-19
Hobby Parallel-19
02BAP First Edition-8
02BAP First Edition-419R
Jerseys-8
02BAP Memorabilia-111
Emerald-111
Ruby-111
Sapphire-111
NHL All-Star Game-111
NHL All-Star Game Blue-111
NHL All-Star Game Green-111
NHL All-Star Game Red-111
02BAP Memorabilia Toronto Fall Expo-111
02BAP Signature Series-18
Autographs-18
Autographs Gold-18
02O-Pee-Chee-103
02O-Pee-Chee Premier Blue Parallel-103
02O-Pee-Chee Premier Red Parallel-103
02O-Pee-Chee Factory Set-103
02Pacific-74
Blue-74
Red-74
02Pacific Complete-260
Red-260
02Pacific Entry Draft-3
02Pacific Exclusive-34
02Pacific Heads-Up Quad Jerseys-7
02Pacific Heads-Up Quad Jerseys Gold-7
02Pacific Toronto Spring Expo Rookie Coll-3
02Parkhurst-136
Bronze-136
Gold-136
Silver-136
02Private Stock Reserve-19
Blue-19
Red-19
Retail-19
02SP Game Used Future Fabrics-FFMB
02SP Game Used Future Fabrics Gold-FFMB
02SP Game Used Future Fabrics Rainbow-FFMB
02Titanium Jerseys-13
02Titanium Jerseys Retail-13
02Titanium Patches-13
02Topps-103
OPC Blue Parallel-103
OPC Red Parallel-103
Factory Set-103
02Topps Total-248
02UD Top Shelf Sweet Sweaters-SWBE
02Upper Deck-282
Exclusives-282
02Upper Deck Beckett UD Promos-282
02Upper Deck On the Rise-ORMB
02Upper Deck Vintage-56
03Blackhawks Postcards-4
03ITG Action-155
Jerseys-M4
03Pacific-70
Blue-70
Red-70
03Pacific Calder-20
Silver-20
03Pacific Complete-171
Red-171
03Pacific Heads-Up-20
Hobby LTD-20
Retail LTD-20
03Pacific Quest for the Cup-20
Blue-20
03Parkhurst Original Six Chicago-2
Memorabilia-CM5
03Titanium-24
Hobby Jersey Number Parallels-24
Retail-24
Retail Jersey Number Parallels-24
03Upper Deck MVP-95
Gold Script-95
Silver Script-95
Canadian Exclusives-95
03Upper Deck Rookie Update-18
04Pacific-57
Blue-57
Red-57
05Panini Stickers-220
05Parkhurst-103
Facsimile Auto Parallel-103
05Ultra-53
Gold-53
Ice-53
05Upper Deck-37
HG Glossy-37
Notable Numbers-N-MBL
05Upper Deck MVP-95
Gold-95
Platinum-95
05Upper Deck Toronto Fall Expo-37
05Upper Deck Victory-43
Black-43
Gold-43
Silver-43
06Be A Player-163
Autographs-163
Signatures-MB
Portraits Signature Portraits-SPMB
Portraits Triple Signature Portraits-TSJS
06Black Diamond Jerseys-JMA
06Black Diamond Jerseys Black-JMA
06Black Diamond Jerseys Gold-JMA
06Black Diamond Jerseys Ruby-JMA
06O-Pee-Chee-411
Rainbow-411
06Panini Stickers-332
06UD Artifacts Tundra Tandems-TTPM
06UD Artifacts Tundra Tandems Black-TTPM
06UD Artifacts Tundra Tandems Blue-TTPM
06UD Artifacts Tundra Tandems Gold-TTPM
06UD Artifacts Tundra Tandems Platinum-TTPM
06UD Artifacts Tundra Tandems Red-TTPM
06UD Artifacts Tundra Tandems Dual Patches Red-TTPM
06Ultra-166
Gold Medallion-166
Ice Medallion-166
06Upper Deck-414
Exclusives Parallel-414
High Gloss Parallel-414
Game Jerseys-JBM
Game Patches-PBM
Masterpieces-414
06Upper Deck MVP-242
Gold Script-242
Super Script-242
06Upper Deck Ovation-113
06Upper Deck Victory-45
06Upper Deck Victory-270
06Upper Deck Victory Black-45
06Upper Deck Victory Gold-45

Bell, Matt
96Guelph Storm-26

Bell, Scot
91Ferris State Bulldogs-5

Bell, Scott
91Minnesota Golden Gophers-1
92Ferris State Bulldogs-5
92Minnesota Golden Gophers-1
94Minnesota Golden Gophers-2
95Anaheim Bullfrogs RHI-9
99Missouri River Otters-25
99Missouri River Otters Sheet-24
99Topeka Scarecrows-16
01Rockford IceHogs-20
02Rockford Ice Hogs-11

Bell, Thatcher
99Upper Deck Sobey's Memorial Cup-11
99Rimouski Oceanic-5
Signed-5
99UD Prospects-55
99UD Prospects-68
CHL Class-C10
00QMJHL All-Star Program Inserts-34
00Rimouski Oceanic-6
Signed-6
00UD CHL Prospects-82
01Rimouski Oceanic-6
02Halifax Mooseheads-9

Bell, Tim
92British Columbia JHL-11

Bell, Travis
92Quebec Pee-Wee Tournament-1764
03Bossier-Shreveport Mudbugs-2

Bella, Tony
907th Inn. Sketch OHL-51
917th Inn. Sketch OHL-222

Bellamy, Rob
05Maine Black Bears-1

Bellamy, Robert
04Maine Black Bears-13

Belland, Brad
84Sudbury Wolves-9
94German First League-233
95San Diego Barracudas RHI-3
99San Diego Gulls-2

Belland, Neil
81Fredericton Express-23
82Fredericton Express-23
83Fredericton Express-14
84Canucks Team Issue-1
84Fredericton Express-5
85Fredericton Express-23
98Portland Pirates-19

Bellavance, Jean-Roch
51Bas Du Fleuve-33

Bellavance, Normand
51Bas Du Fleuve-40
52Bas Du Fleuve-11

Bellavance-Martin, Etienne
06Drummondville Voltigeurs-19

Belle, Shawn
04ITG Heroes and Prospects-103
Autographs-SB
04ITG Heroes/Prospects Toronto Expo '05-103
04ITG Heroes/Prospects Expo Heroes/Pros-103
05ITG Heroes/Prosp Toronto Expo Parallel -215
05Iowa Stars-26
05ITG Heroes and Prospects-215
Autographs Series II-SBE
Complete Jerseys-CJ-7
Complete Jerseys Gold-CJ-7
Jerseys-GUJ-63
Jerseys Gold-GUJ-63
Emblems-GUE-63
Emblems Gold-GUE-63
Numbers-GUN-63
Numbers Gold-GUN-63
Nameplates-N-41
Nameplates Gold-N-41
06Be A Player-245
06Hot Prospects-163
Red Hot-163
White Hot-163
06The Cup Masterpiece Pressplates (Ultimate Collection)-79
06Ultimate Collection-79

Bellefeuille, Blake
95Classic-57
00Syracuse Crunch-11
01BAP Memorabilia-362
Emerald-362
Ruby-362
Sapphire-362
01SPx-203
01UD Playmakers-113
01UD Premier Collection-61
01Upper Deck Ice-134
01Syracuse Crunch-9
02Upper Deck Vintage-330
02Syracuse Crunch-8
02Syracuse Crunch Sheets-12
03Norfolk Admirals-6

Bellefeuille, Pete
24Anonymous NHL-61

Bellefleur, Steve
03Shawinigan Cataractes-2
05Shawinigan Cataractes-3

Bellefontaine, Scott
907th Inn. Sketch WHL-20
91Air Canada SJHL-C41
91Air Canada SJHL All-Stars-42
91Air Canada SJHL All-Stars-45

Bellemare, Jonathan
99Shawinigan Cataractes-3
Signed-3
00Shawinigan Cataractes-5
Signed-5
02Hull Olympiques-8
03Hull Olympiques Memorial Cup-1

Bellemare, Thomas
02Drummondville Voltigeurs-18
03Drummondville Voltigeurs-1
05Las Vegas Wranglers-3

Bellemore, Bob
88Devils Caretta-2
89Devils Caretta-2

Bellemore, Brett
05Plymouth Whalers-B-09
06Plymouth Whalers-2

Bellemore, Jonathan
01Shawinigan Cataractes-6

Beller, Jeremy
06Penticton Vees-1

Bellerose, Eric
907th Inn. Sketch QMJHL-135
917th Inn. Sketch QMJHL-118
92Alberta International Team Canada-5

Bellet, Mathieu
93Quebec Pee-Wee Tournament-1481

Belley, Jean-Francois
93Amos Les Forestiers-1

Belley, Roch
89Niagara Falls Thunder-2
897th Inn. Sketch OHL-139
907th Inn. Sketch OHL-252
91ProCards-497
92Fort Worth Fire-2
93Muskegon Fury-16

Bellina, Ryan
93Quebec Pee-Wee Tournament-1742

Bellio, John
82Swedish Semic VM Stickers-127
83Swedish Semic VM Stickers-127

Bellissimo, Vince
05Florida Everblades-22

Belliveau, Dave
907th Inn. Sketch QMJHL-207
917th Inn. Sketch QMJHL-164
93Sherbrooke Faucons-17

Belliveau, Luc
95Slapshot-210

Belliveau, Remi
907th Inn. Sketch QMJHL-78

Bellows, Brian
82North Stars Postcards-3
83NHL Key Tags-61
83North Stars Postcards-4
83O-Pee-Chee-165
83O-Pee-Chee-167
83O-Pee-Chee Stickers-142
83Puffy Stickers-17
83Topps Stickers-142
84North Stars 7-Eleven-4
84North Stars Postcards-3
84O-Pee-Chee-95
84O-Pee-Chee-359
84O-Pee-Chee Stickers-44
84O-Pee-Chee Stickers-45
847-Eleven Discs-26
84Topps-71
85North Stars 7-Eleven-9
85North Stars Postcards-3
85O-Pee-Chee-50
85O-Pee-Chee Box Bottoms-A
85O-Pee-Chee Stickers-41
857-Eleven Credit Cards-9
85Topps-50
85Topps Box Bottoms-A
86North Stars 7-Eleven-12
86North Stars Postcards-4
86O-Pee-Chee-75
86O-Pee-Chee Stickers-167
86Topps-75
87North Stars Postcards-5
87O-Pee-Chee-94
87O-Pee-Chee Stickers-53
87Panini Stickers-296
87Topps-94
88Frito-Lay Stickers-5
88North Stars ADA-1
88O-Pee-Chee-95
88O-Pee-Chee Stickers-203
88Panini Stickers-89
88Topps-95
89O-Pee-Chee-177
89O-Pee-Chee Stickers-200
89Panini Stickers-105
89Topps-177
90Bowman-182
Tiffany-182
90Kraft-2
90O-Pee-Chee-70
90O-Pee-Chee-200
90OPC Premier-3
90Panini Stickers-257
90Pro Set-130A
90Pro Set-130B
90Score-7
90Score-322
Canadian-7
Canadian-322
90Score Hottest/Rising Stars-3
90Topps-70
90Topps-200
Tiffany-70
Tiffany-200
Team Scoring Leaders-15
Team Scoring Leaders Tiffany-15
90Upper Deck-126
90Upper Deck-308
French-126
French-308
91Pro Set Platinum-59
91Pro Set Platinum-143
91Bowman-129
91Kraft-38
91O-Pee-Chee-44
91O-Pee-Chee-110
91Panini Stickers-108
91Parkhurst-79
French-79
91Pinnacle-129
French-129
91Pro Set-109
French-109
Puck Candy-13
91Score American-160
91Score Canadian Bilingual-160
91Score Canadian English-160
91Stadium Club-87
91Topps-110
91Upper Deck-236
French-236
92Bowman-200
92Bowman-260
92Canadiens Postcards-1
92McDonald's Upper Deck-2
92O-Pee-Chee-384
92OPC Premier-75
92Panini Stickers-88
92Panini Stickers French-88
92Parkhurst-87
Emerald Ice-87
92Pinnacle-325
French-325
92Score-335
Canadian-335
92Sports Illustrated for Kids II-20
92Stadium Club-293
92Topps-240
Gold-240G
92Ultra-100
92Ultra-324
92Upper Deck-172
92Upper Deck-471
92Upper Deck-636
Gordie Howe Selects-G1
93Canadiens Molson-1
93Canadiens Postcards-1
93Donruss-170
93Leaf-76
93O-Pee-Chee Canadiens Hockey Fest-60
93OPC Premier-202
Gold-202
93Panini Stickers-15
93Parkhurst-371
Emerald Ice-371
93Pinnacle-22
Canadian-22
93PowerPlay-124
93Score Samples-4
93Score-4
Canadian-4
Dynamic Duos Canadian-6
93Stadium Club-156
Members Only Master Set-156
OPC-156
First Day Issue-156
First Day Issue OPC-156
93Topps/OPC Premier-202
Gold-202
93Ultra-4
93Upper Deck-390
SP-76
94Canada Games NHL POGS-132
94Canadiens Postcards-1
94Donruss-203
94EA Sports-71
94Finest-105
Super Team Winners-105
Refractors-105
94Flair-84
94Fleer-101
94Hockey Wit-11
94Leaf-301
94OPC Premier-219
Special Effects-219
94Parkhurst-112
Gold-112
94Pinnacle-290
Artist's Proofs-290
Rink Collection-290
94Score-73
Gold-73
Platinum-73
94Select-91
Gold-91
94Topps/OPC Premier-219
Special Effects-219
94Ultra-105
94Upper Deck-309
Electric Ice-309
SP Inserts-SP130
SP Inserts Die Cuts-SP130
95Bashan Super Stickers-115
95Be A Player-32
Signatures-S32
Signatures Die Cuts-S32
95Canada Games NHL POGS-253
95Collector's Choice-84
Player's Club-84
Player's Club Platinum-84
95Donruss-341
95Imperial Stickers-115
95Lightning Team Issue-2
95Panini Stickers-128
95Parkhurst International-466
Emerald Ice-466
95Playoff One on One-91
95Score-231
Black Ice Artist's Proofs-231
Black Ice-231
95Summit-11
Artist's Proofs-11
Ice-11
95Topps-253
OPC Inserts-253
95Ultra-307
95Upper Deck-404
Electric Ice-404
Electric Ice Gold-404
96Black Diamond-104
Gold-104
96Donruss-64
Press Proofs-64
96Ducks Team Issue-13
96Leaf-10
Press Proofs-10
96Score-221
Artist's Proofs-221
Dealer's Choice Artist's Proofs-221
Special Artist's Proofs-221
Golden Blades-221
97Pacific-70
Copper-70
Emerald Green-70
Ice Blue-70
Red-70
Silver-70
97Pacific Dynagon-1
Copper-1
Dark Grey-1
Emerald Green-1
Ice Blue-1
Red-1
Silver-1
Tandems-29
97Pacific Invincible-1
Copper-1
Emerald Green-1
Ice Blue-1
Red-1
Silver-1
97Panini Stickers-190
97Pinnacle Inside-140
98Aurora-193
98Be A Player-145
Press Release-145
98BAP Gold-145
98BAP Autographs-145
98BAP Autographs Gold-145
98BAP Tampa Bay All Star Game-145
98OPC Chrome-133
Refractors-133
98Pacific-23
Ice Blue-23
Red-23
98Pacific Omega-243
Red-243
Opening Day Issue-243
98Paramount-241
Copper-241
Emerald Green-241
Holo-Electric-241
Ice Blue-241
Silver-241
98Topps-133
O-Pee-Chee-133
98Upper Deck-204
Exclusives-204
Exclusives 1 of 1-204
Gold Reserve-204
98Upper Deck MVP-213
Gold Script-213
Silver Script-213
Super Script-213
ProSign-BB
99Pacific-435
Copper-435
Emerald Green-435
Gold-435
Ice Blue-435
Premiere Date-435
Red-435
99Paramount-241
Copper-241
Emerald-241
Gold-241
Holographic Emerald-241
Holographic Gold-241
Holographic Silver-241
Ice Blue-241
Premiere Date-241
Red-241
Silver-241
01Greats of the Game-54
Autographs-54
02BAP Sig Series Auto Buybacks 1998-145
02UD Foundations-46
02UD Foundations-49
Signs of Greatness-SGBB
04ITG Franchises US West-250
Autographs-A-BBE
04UD Legendary Signatures-13
Autographs-BE
Linemates-BENBCI
06ITG International Ice-88
Gold-88
Autographs-ABB

Bellows, Ryan
06Barrie Colts-13

Bellringer, Don
51Bas Du Fleuve-50

Belobragin, Mikhail
00Russian Hockey League-97

Belohlav, Radek
94Czech APS Extraliga-110
95Czech APS Extraliga-64
95Czech APS Extraliga-374
96Czech APS Extraliga-255
96Czech APS Extraliga-343
96Swedish Semic Wien-123
97Czech APS Extraliga-43
97Czech DS Extraliga-62
97Czech DS Stickers-8
97Czech DS Stickers-90
98Czech DS-85
98Czech DS Stickers-177
98Czech OFS-108
99Czech OFS-426
99Czech OFS-481
99Czech DS-134
99Czech OFS-256
99Czech OFS-438
00Czech DS Extraliga-81
00Czech OFS-18
01Czech OFS-14
03Czech OFS Plus-257

Belohlavek, Petr
99Czech OFS-72

Belosheikin, Evgeny
87Russian National Team-2
89Swedish Semic World Champ Stickers-78
91ProCards-223

Belousov, Matvei
99Russian Hockey League-133

Belousov, Valeri
98Russian Hockey League-162
03Russian Avangard Omsk-11

Belov, Anton
03Russian Under-18 Team-15
04Russian Hope-4
04Russian Under-18 Team-7

Belov, Oleg
93Upper Deck-274
95Swedish World Championships Stickers-41
95Cleveland Lumberjacks-5
95Cleveland Lumberjacks Postcards-5
99Swedish Upper Deck-92
00Swedish Upper Deck-98
00Swedish Upper Deck-198

SHL Signatures-OB
Top Draws-T6

Belov, Valerij
95Swiss HNL-425
96Czech APS Extraliga-115
97Czech DS Stickers-283
99Russian Hockey League-161

Belsky, Denis
03Russian Hockey League-254

Belter, Shane
95Seattle Thunderbirds-2
96Seattle Thunderbirds-32
99Providence Bruins-3
00Trenton Titans-14
01Atlantic City Boardwalk Bullies-2

Beltrame, Rico
01Swiss HNL-451

Belushi, James
91Pro Set Platinum-300

Belyavski, Igor
98Russian Hockey League-86
99Russian Hockey League-213

Belza, Anthony
02Peoria Rivermen-23
02Peoria Rivermen RBI Sports-152

Belzile, Eric
96Rimouski Oceanic-3
96Rimouski Oceanic Quebec Police-3

Belzile, Etienne
92Cornell Big Red-2

Bembridge, Garrett
00Saskatoon Blades-13
05Idaho Steelheads-2
05ITG Heroes and Prospects-359
Autographs Series II-GBE
06Augusta Lynx-1
06ITG Heroes and Prospects-64
Autographs-AGB

Bemstrom, Jorgen
97Swedish Collector's Choice-174
98Swedish UD Choice-144
99Swedish Upper Deck-146
00Swedish Upper Deck-163
03Swedish Elite-119
Silver-119
04Swedish Elitset-119
Gold-119
05Swedish SHL Elitset-130
Teammates-11

Bemstrom, Stefan
02Swedish SHL-91
Parallel-91
03Swedish Elite-113
Silver-113
04Swedish Elitset-112
Gold-112
05Swedish SHL Elitset-63

Ben-Amor, Semir
00Finnish Cardset-131
01Finnish Cardset-379
02Louisiana Ice Gators-2
04Richmond Riverdogs-24
06Finnish Cardset-190

Benak, Jaroslav
83Swedish Semic VM Stickers-84
94Czech APS Extraliga-168

Benak, Vaclav
98Czech OFS-365
99Czech Score Blue 2000-115
99Czech Score Red Ice 2000-115
00Czech OFS-12
01Czech OFS-202
02Czech OFS Plus-105
03Czech OFS Plus-239
04Czech OFS-292
06Czech HC Plzen Postcards-16
06Czech OFS-269

Benaquez, Fernand
51Laval Dairy Lac St. Jean-17

Benard, Leo
23Crescent Selkirks-2
23V128-1 Paulin's Candy-10
24Crescent Selkirks-11

Benazic, Cal
92British Columbia JHL-185
95Medicine Hat Tigers-3
00Manitoba Moose-3
01UK Sheffield Steelers-3
02Louisiana Ice Gators-3
03Elmira Jackals-2

Bencharski, Daymen
01Ohio State Buckeyes-2
02Ohio State Buckeyes-2
03Ohio State Buckeyes-2

Bencurik, Ryan
93Omaha Lancers-1
04Lincoln Stars-25
05Lincoln Stars-26
06Lincoln Stars-26

Benda, Jan
907th Inn. Sketch OHL-326
91Oshawa Generals-19
91Oshawa Generals Sheet-2
917th Inn. Sketch OHL-149
94Richmond Renegades-14
95Czech APS Extraliga-399
95German DEL-435
95Swedish World Championships Stickers-62
96Czech APS Extraliga-140
97Czech DS Stickers-63
97Portland Pirates-2
98Finnish Kerailysarja-268
99Finnish Cardset-171
99Finnish Cardset-266
Aces High-H-J
99German DEL-365
00Finnish Cardset-44
01Russian Hockey League-158
02Finnish Cardset-6
02Russian Hockey League-27
03Russian Hockey League-20
03Russian World Championship Stars-1
04Russian Legion-35
04Russian Super League All-Stars-24
05Czech HC Hame Zlin-3
05German DEL-300
DEB-Jerseys-TR01
06Czech OFS-129
Goals Leaders-15
Points Leaders-10

Bendelin, Torgny
94Swedish Leaf-295

Bender, Ryan
03Kamloops Blazers-17
05Kamloops Blazers-19
06Kamloops Blazers-2

Bendera, Shane
00Red Deer Rebels-3
Signed-3
00UD CHL Prospects-73
01Kelowna Rockets-1
01Red Deer Rebels-3
03ECHL Update RBI Sports-57

Bendera, Terry
89Victoria Cougars-2
907th Inn. Sketch WHL-170
917th Inn. Sketch WHL-224

Bendfeld, Jordan
04Medicine Hat Tigers-3
05Medicine Hat Tigers-4
06Medicine Hat Tigers-2

Benedict, Brandon
98Halifax Mooseheads-17
98Halifax Mooseheads Second Edition-14
99Halifax Mooseheads-16
00Halifax Mooseheads-1
01Halifax Mooseheads-18
02Halifax Mooseheads-17

Benedict, Clint
12C57-3
12C61 Lacrosse-19
23V145-1-7
24Anonymous NHL-95
24C144 Champ's Cigarettes-3
24V130 Maple Crispette-2
24V145-2-32
28La Presse Photos-1
83Hall of Fame-107
83Hall of Fame Postcards-H1
85Hall of Fame-107
94Hall of Fame Tickets-6
03BAP Ultimate Mem Vintage Blade of Steel-8
04ITG Franchises Canadian-66
04ITG Ultimate Mem Blades of Steel-14
04ITG Ultimate Memorabilia Day In History-19
04ITG Ultimate Memorabilia Day In History-36
04ITG Ultimate Mem Day In History Gold-19
04ITG Ultimate Mem Day In History Gold-36
05ITG Ultimate Mem Blades of Steel-18
05ITG Ultimate Mem Blades of Steel Gold-18
06Between The Pipes Forgotten Franchises-FF07
06ITG Ultimate Memorabilia Blades of Steel-4
06ITG Ultimate Memorabilia Blades of Steel Gold-4

Benes, Stanislav
94Czech APS Extraliga-141
95Czech APS Extraliga-250

Bengtson, Steen
98Danish Hockey League-76
99Danish Hockey League-45

Bengtsson, Anders
69Swedish Hockey-203

Bengtsson, Folke
64Swedish Coralli ISHockey-18
64Swedish Coralli ISHockey-58
65Swedish Coralli ISHockey-18
65Swedish Coralli ISHockey-58
67Swedish Hockey-3
67Swedish Hockey-100
69Swedish Hockey-113
70Swedish Hockey-54
71Swedish Hockey-124

Bengtsson, Kent
71Swedish Hockey-329
74Swedish Stickers-203

Bengtsson, Totte
72Swedish Stickers-109

Benic, Geoff
88ProCards IHL-12

Benik, Ray
81Victoria Cougars-3
82Victoria Cougars-2

Benjaminsen, Henrik
98Danish Hockey League-4
99Danish Hockey League-5

Benjaminsen, Torben
98Danish Hockey League-16
99Danish Hockey League-171

Benke, Karl
05Swift Current Broncos-1

Benn, David
89Niagara Falls Thunder-3
897th Inn. Sketch OHL-126
907th Inn. Sketch OHL-123
917th Inn. Sketch OHL-39
92Windsor Spitfires-28

Bennefield, Blue
00Asheville Smoke-3
03Gwinnett Gladiators-14
03Gwinnett Gladiators RBI Sports-193

Bennefield, Jesse
06Rockford IceHogs -1

Bennett, Adam
88Sudbury Wolves-4
89Sudbury Wolves-10
907th Inn. Sketch OHL-378
90Sudbury Wolves-2
91ProCards-501
92Blackhawks Coke-1
93Parkhurst-334
Emerald Ice-334
93Upper Deck-237
94Leaf-389
94Parkhurst-77
Gold-77
94Upper Deck-202
Electric Ice-202

Bennett, Bill
83Ottawa 67's-2
84Ottawa 67's-3

Bennett, Brad
84Prince Albert Raiders Stickers-2
90Alberta International Team Canada-11

Bennett, Curt
71Blues Postcards-3
72Flames Postcards-1
730-Pee-Chee-149
73Topps-152
74NHL Action Stamps-4
740-Pee-Chee NHL-33
74Topps-33
750-Pee-Chee NHL-8
75Topps-8
760-Pee-Chee NHL-202
760-Pee-Chee NHL-379
76Topps-202
770-Pee-Chee NHL-97
77Topps-97
78Blues Postcards-2
780-Pee-Chee-31
78Topps-31
79Panini Stickers-214
79Flames Postcards-1
79Flames Team Issue-1
790-Pee-Chee-344
04ITG Franchises US East-307
Autographs-A-CBN

Bennett, Eric
91ProCards-198
05Waterloo Blackhawks-4

Bennett, Harvey
770-Pee-Chee NHL-282
78Blues Postcards-3
780-Pee-Chee-163
78Topps-163
79Panini Stickers-219

Bennett, Jim
95UK Guildford Flames-25

Bennett, Josh
00Kitchener Rangers-3

Bennett, LW
77Rochester Americans-5

Bennett, Rick
900-Pee-Chee-252
90Score-400
Canadian-400
90Topps-252
Tiffany-252
90Upper Deck-540
French-540
90ProCards AHL/IHL-21
92Binghamton Rangers-5

Bennett, Ryan
99Des Moines Buccaneers-20

Bennett, Todd
02Orlando Seals-5
03Augusta Lynx-33

Benning, Brian
84Kamloops Blazers-2
87Blues Kodak-1
87Blues Team Issue-1
870-Pee-Chee-122
870-Pee-Chee Minis-2
870-Pee-Chee Stickers-124
87Topps-122
88Blues Kodak-1
88Blues Team Issue-1
880-Pee-Chee-174
880-Pee-Chee Stickers-18
88Panini Stickers-101
88Topps-174
89Kings Smokey-21
890-Pee-Chee-86
890-Pee-Chee Stickers-24
89Panini Stickers-124
89Topps-86
90Kings Smokey-2
900-Pee-Chee-365
90Pro Set-114
90Score-306A
Canadian-306A
90Topps-365
Tiffany-365
91Pro Set Platinum-182
910-Pee-Chee-359
91Pinnacle-402
French-402
91Pro Set-398
French-398
91Score American-186
91Score Canadian Bilingual-186
91Score Canadian English-186
91Topps-359
91Upper Deck-415
French-415
92Bowman-39
92Flyers J.C. Penney-3
92Flyers Upper Deck Sheets-2
920-Pee-Chee-68
92Parkhurst-125
92Parkhurst-284
Emerald Ice-125
Emerald Ice-284
92Pinnacle-45
French-45
92Pro Set-135
92Score-133
Canadian-133
92Stadium Club-91
92Topps-250
Gold-250G
92Ultra-151
92Upper Deck-301
93Donruss-129
93Leaf-328
93Parkhurst-343
Emerald Ice-343
93Pinnacle II Samples-341
93Pinnacle-341
Canadian-341
93PowerPlay-90
93Score-64
93Score-512
Gold-512
Canadian-64
Canadian-512
Canadian Gold-512
93Ultra-3
93Ultra-321
93Upper Deck-496
94Canada Games NHL POGS-111
94Leaf-379
94OPC Premier-389
Special Effects-389
94Parkhurst SE-SE65
Gold-SE65
94Pinnacle-414
Artist's Proofs-414
Rink Collection-414
94Stadium Club-157
Members Only Master Set-157
First Day Issue-157
Super Team Winner Cards-157
94Topps/OPC Premier-389
Special Effects-389
94Upper Deck-217
Electric Ice-217

Benning, Jim
81Maple Leafs Postcards-3
82Maple Leafs Postcards-4
820-Pee-Chee-317
820-Pee-Chee Stickers-64
82Post Cereal-18
82Topps Stickers-64
83Maple Leafs Postcards-2
830-Pee-Chee-326
83Vachon-82
84Maple Leafs Postcards-2
840-Pee-Chee-296
840-Pee-Chee Stickers-21
84Kelowna Wings-51
85Maple Leafs Postcards-2
850-Pee-Chee-250
850-Pee-Chee Stickers-16
87Canucks Shell Oil-2
870-Pee-Chee-260
870-Pee-Chee Stickers-197
88Canucks Mohawk-2
880-Pee-Chee Stickers-58
88Panini Stickers-133
89Canucks Mohawk-2
900-Pee-Chee-455
90Pro Set-292
90ProCards AHL/IHL-329
92Pro Set-181

Benoit, Andre
00Kitchener Rangers-4
01Kitchener Rangers-10
03Kitchener Rangers-1
03Kitchener Rangers Memorial Cup-1
04Kitchener Rangers-2
05Hamilton Bulldogs-4
06Hamilton Bulldogs-4

Benoit, Carl
93Amos Les Forestiers-2

Benoit, Denis
88Richelieu Riverains-3

Benoit, Joe
34Beehive Group I Photos-135
400-Pee-Chee V301-2-121
43Parade Sportive *-4
45Quaker Oats Photos-63

Benoit, Marcel
52Bas Du Fleuve-21

Benoit, Mathieu
99Bowman CHL-61
Gold-61
OPC International-61
00Charlotte Checkers-10

Benoit, Maurice
51Bas Du Fleuve-19

Benoit, Richard
83North Bay Centennials-3

Benoit, Yvan
02Swiss HNL-343

Benson, Bill
34Beehive Group I Photos-215
400-Pee-Chee V301-2-135

Benson, Cory
93Quebec Pee-Wee Tournament-182

Benson, R.J.
23V128-1 Paulin's Candy-65
24Holland Creameries-6

Bentley, Doug
34Beehive Group I Photos-39
43Parade Sportive *-92
44Beehive Group II Photos-80
48Exhibits Canadian-49
51Parkhurst-48
83Hall of Fame-77
83Hall of Fame Postcards-F1
85Hall of Fame-77
94Parkhurst Missing Link Pop-Ups-P11
03BAP Ultimate Mem Linemates Autos-6
04ITG Franchises US West-169
04ITG Ultimate Memorabilia-119
Gold-119
05ITG Ultimate Mem Chi-Town Immortal Auto-4
06ITG Ultimate Memorabilia Chi-Town Immortals Autos-8

Bentley, Max
34Beehive Group I Photos-40
400-Pee-Chee V301-2-131
43Parade Sportive *-92
44Beehive Group II Photos-298
44Beehive Group II Photos-379
45Quaker Oats Photos-7A
45Quaker Oats Photos-7B
45Quaker Oats Photos-7C
48Exhibits Canadian-42
51Parkhurst-81
52Parkhurst-95
53Parkhurst-55
83Hall of Fame-32
83Hall of Fame Postcards-C2
85Hall of Fame-32
99Upper Deck Century Legends-49
Century Collection-49
02BAP Ultimate Mem Paper Cuts Autos-9
02Maple Leafs Platinum Collection-43
02Parkhurst Reprints-181
03BAP Ultimate Mem Linemates Autos-6
03BAP Ultimate Memorabilia Paper Cuts-29
04ITG Franchises US West-170
04ITG Ultimate Memorabilia-46
Gold-46
Chitown Immortals-4
05ITG Ultimate Mem Leafs Forever Autos-4
06ITG Ultimate Memorabilia-102
Artist Proof-102

Benturqui, Malik
01Swiss HNL-261
02Swiss HNL-289

Bentz, Andrew
05Lethbridge Hurricanes-2

Benysek, Ladislav
94Cape Breton Oilers-3
95Czech APS Extraliga-342
96Czech APS Extraliga-271
97Czech APS Extraliga-23
97Czech APS Extraliga-349
97Czech DS Stickers-173
98Czech DS-89
98Czech OFS-132
98Czech OFS-423
98Czech OFS-449
99Czech DS-144
99Czech OFS-257
99Czech OFS-395
99Czech OFS-494
All-Star Game Blue-494
All-Star Game Gold-494
All-Star Game Red-494
All-Star Game Silver-494
00BAP Memorabilia-481
Emerald-481
Ruby-481
Sapphire-481
02Upper Deck-335
Exclusives-335
02Upper Deck Beckett UD Promos-335
03Finnish Cardset-16
06Czech HC Sparta Praha Postcards-1
06Czech OFS-87

Beraldo, Paul
88ProCards AHL-149
89ProCards AHL-55
95German DEL-321
96German DEL-179
00UK Sekonda Superleague-151
00UK Sheffield Steelers-7

Beran, Jan
93Johnstown Chiefs-15

Beran, Karel
95Czech APS Extraliga-203

Beran, Marc
93Birmingham Bulls Birmingham News-4

Beranek, Jiri
917th Inn. Sketch WHL-39
94Czech APS Extraliga-157
95Czech APS Extraliga-87
96Czech APS Extraliga-90
97Czech APS Extraliga-207
97Czech DS Stickers-139
98Czech DS Stickers-238

Beranek, Josef
91Pro Set Platinum-255
91Oilers IGA-1
91Oilers Team Issue-1
91OPC Premier-149
91Parkhurst-47
French-47
91Pinnacle-303
French-303
91Pro Set-534
French-534
91Upper Deck-17
91Upper Deck-595
French-17
French-595
92Bowman-100
92Flyers Upper Deck Sheets-31
92Flyers Upper Deck Sheets-32
92Oilers IGA-2
920-Pee-Chee-178
92Panini Stickers-I
92Panini Stickers French-I
92Parkhurst-360
Emerald Ice-360
92Pinnacle-208
French-208
92Score-105
Canadian-105
92Stadium Club-214
92Topps-177
Gold-177G
92Ultra-56
92Upper Deck-196
Euro-Stars-E11
92Finnish Semic-137
93Donruss-247
93Flyers J.C. Penney-1
93Flyers Lineup Sheets-1
93Leaf-103
93OPC Premier-467
Gold-467
93Parkhurst-153
Emerald Ice-153
93Pinnacle-424
Canadian-424
93PowerPlay-177
93Score-439
Canadian-439
93Stadium Club-69
Members Only Master Set-69
OPC-69
First Day Issue-69
First Day Issue OPC-69
93Topps/OPC Premier-467
Gold-467
93Ultra-17
93Upper Deck-15
SP-113
93Swedish Semic World Champ Stickers-105
93Classic Pro Prospects-81
94Canada Games NHL POGS-356
94Donruss-13
94Fleer-221
94Leaf-31
94OPC Premier-141
Special Effects-141
94Parkhurst-166
Gold-166
94Pinnacle-148
Artist's Proofs-148
Rink Collection-148
94Score-77
Gold-77
Platinum-77
94Topps/OPC Premier-141
Special Effects-141
94Ultra-153
94Upper Deck-117
Electric Ice-117
SP Inserts-SP56
SP Inserts Die Cuts-SP56
94Czech APS Extraliga-243
94Finnish Jaa Kiekko-176
95Collector's Choice-312
Player's Club-312
Player's Club Platinum-312
95Donruss-356
95Emotion-176
95Leaf-232
95Panini Stickers-291
95Parkhurst International-208
Emerald Ice-208
95Pinnacle-140
Artist's Proofs-140
Rink Collection-140
95Score-118
Black Ice Artist's Proofs-118
Black Ice-118
95Topps-149
OPC Inserts-149
95Upper Deck-67
Electric Ice-67
Electric Ice Gold-67
95Czech APS Extraliga-148
95Finnish Semic World Championships-154
95Swedish Globe World Championships-158
95Swedish World Championships Stickers-203
96Czech APS Extraliga-165
96Swedish Semic Wien-127
97Pacific Invincible NHL Regime-158
97Czech APS Extraliga-47
97Czech APS Extraliga-359
97Czech DS Extraliga-3
97Czech DS Stickers-12
97Czech DS Stickers-30
98Be A Player-203
Press Release-203
98BAP Gold-203
98BAP Autographs-203
98BAP Autographs Gold-203
98Pacific Omega-90
Red-90
Opening Day Issue-90
98Czech DS Stickers-183
98Czech OFS-242
98Czech OFS-331
Olympic Winners-18
98Czech Bonaparte-3A
98Czech Pexeso-8
98Czech Spaghetti-3
99BAP Memorabilia-129
99BAP Memorabilia-382
Gold-129
Gold-382
Silver-129
Silver-382
99Pacific-152
Copper-152
Emerald Green-152
Gold-152
Ice Blue-152
Premiere Date-152
Red-152
99Paramount-89
Copper-89
Emerald-89
Gold-89
Holographic Emerald-89
Holographic Gold-89
Holographic Silver-89
Ice Blue-89
Premiere Date-89
Red-89
Silver-89
99Upper Deck MVP-77
Gold Script-77
Silver Script-77
Super Script-77
99Upper Deck Victory-114
99Czech DS National Stars-NS18
99Czech OFS-18
99Czech OFS-381
99Czech OFS Jagr Team Embossed-18
00BAP Memorabilia-356
Emerald-356
Ruby-356
Sapphire-356
Promos-356
00BAP Mem Chicago Sportsfest Copper-356
00BAP Memorabilia Chicago Sportsfest Blue-356
00BAP Memorabilia Chicago Sportsfest Gold-356
00BAP Memorabilia Chicago Sportsfest Ruby-356
00BAP Memorabilia Chicago Sun-Times Ruby-356
00BAP Memorabilia Chicago Sun-Times Gold-356
00BAP Mem Chicago Sun-Times Sapphire-356
00BAP Mem Toronto Fall Expo Copper-356
00BAP Memorabilia Toronto Fall Expo Gold-356
00BAP Memorabilia Toronto Fall Expo Ruby-356
00Upper Deck-370
Exclusives Tier 1-370
Exclusives Tier 2-370
00Upper Deck Vintage-288
00Czech OFS-411
01Pacific Heads-Up Quad Jerseys-28
01Titanium Double-Sided Jerseys-33
01Titanium Double-Sided Patches-33
01Vanguard Memorabilia-23
01Vanguard Patches-23
01Czech DS-38
Ice Heroes-IH4
01Czech National Team Postcards-1
01Czech National Team Postcards-3
01Czech OFS-6
01Czech OFS Red Inserts-RE2D
02BAP Sig Series Auto Buybacks 1998-203
02Czech DS-9
02Czech OFS Plus-234
Trios-T12
Duos-D4
02Czech IQ Sports Blue-2
02Czech IQ Sports Yellow-2
03Czech OFS Plus-172
03Czech OFS Plus Insert C-C8
03Czech OFS Plus Insert M-M5
03Czech OFS Plus MS Praha-SE27
04Czech HC Slavia Praha Postcards-13
04Czech OFS-351
Assist Leaders-1
Points Leaders-1
Stars II-7
04Czech Zuma-4
04Czech Zuma Stars-Z9
04Czech World Championship Postcards-1
05Czech HC Slavia Praha-2
06Czech HC Slavia Praha Postcards-2
06Czech OFS-289
Points Leaders-3

Beranek, Milan
95Czech APS Extraliga-324
02Czech OFS Plus-147

Berard, Bryan
94Finest-114
Super Team Winners-114
Refractors-114
94Leaf Limited World Juniors USA-1
94Parkhurst SE-SE250
Gold-SE250
94Select-149
Gold-149
94SP-174
Die Cuts-174
94Upper Deck-522
Electric Ice-522
94Detroit Jr. Red Wings-18
95Donruss Elite World Juniors-25
95Slapshot-75
95Classic-1
95Classic-84
95Classic-99
CHL All-Stars-AS8
Ice Breakers-BK1
Ice Breakers Die Cuts-BK1
95Images-1
Gold-1
Clear Excitement-CE1
Platinum Premier Draft Choice-PD1
95Signature Rookies-60
Auto-Phonex-29
Auto-Phonex Phone Cards-29
Auto-Phonex Prodigies-P1
Signatures-60
95Slapshot Memorial Cup-92
95Classic Five-Sport *-123
Classic Standouts-CS5
Fast Track-FT5
On Fire-R9
95Signature Rookies Tetrad Autobilia *-39
95Signature Rookies Tetrad SR Force *-F2
96Black Diamond-161
Gold-161
96Collector's Choice-359
96Donruss Canadian Ice-131
Gold Press Proofs-131
Red Press Proofs-131
96Donruss Elite-147
Die Cut Stars-147
Aspirations-23
96Flair-114
Blue Ice-114
96Leaf Limited Rookies-3
96Leaf Limited Rookies Gold-3
96Leaf Preferred-129
Press Proofs-129
96Metal Universe-170
96Select Certified-114
Artist's Proofs-114
Blue-114
Mirror Blue-114
Mirror Gold-114
Mirror Red-114
Red-114
96SP-182
SPx Force-4
96Ultra-98
Gold Medallion-98
Rookies-1
96Upper Deck-294
Generation Next-X23
96Upper Deck Ice-93
Parallel-93
96Zenith-126
Artist's Proofs-126
96All-Sport PPF *-97
96All Sport PPF Gold *-97
96Classic Signings *-70
Blue-70
Die-Cuts-70
Red-70
96Clear Assets *-56
96Visions *-82
96Visions Signings *-77
97Be A Player-18
Autographs-18
Autographs Die-Cuts-18
Autographs Prismatic Die-Cuts-18
Take A Number-9
97Beehive-8
Golden Portraits-8
97Black Diamond-12
Double Diamond-12
Triple Diamond-12
Quadruple Diamond-12
Premium Cut-PC16
Premium Cut Double Diamond-PC16
Premium Cut Quadruple Diamond Horiz-PC16
Premium Cut Triple Diamond-PC16
Premium Cut Quadruple Diamond Verticals-PC16
97Collector's Choice-155
Star Quest-SQ1
97Crown Royale-78
Emerald Green-78
Ice Blue-78
Silver-78
Blades of Steel Die-Cuts-13
97Donruss-163
Press Proofs Silver-163
Press Proofs Gold-163
Line 2 Line-9
Line 2 Line Die Cut-9
97Donruss Canadian Ice-92
Dominion Series-92
Provincial Series-92
97Donruss Elite-29
97Donruss Elite-124
Aspirations-29
Aspirations-124
Status-29
Status-124
Craftsmen-26
Master Craftsmen-26
97Donruss Limited-70
97Donruss Limited-181
97Donruss Limited-182
Exposure-70
Exposure-181
Exposure-182
Fabric of the Game-31
97Donruss Preferred-79
97Donruss Preferred-186
Cut to the Chase-79
Cut to the Chase-186
97Donruss Priority-54
97Donruss Priority-194
Stamp of Approval-54
Stamp of Approval-194
Postcards-25
Postcards Opening Day Issues-20
Stamps-25
Stamps Bronze-25
Stamps Gold-25
Stamps Silver-25
97Katch-85
Gold-85
Silver-85
97Leaf-30
97Leaf-183
Fractal Matrix-30
Fractal Matrix-183
Fractal Matrix Die Cuts-30
Fractal Matrix Die Cuts-183
Banner Season-18
97Leaf International-30
Universal Ice-30
97McDonald's Upper Deck-10
97NHL Aces Playing Cards-40
97Pacific-222
Copper-222
Emerald Green-222
Ice Blue-222
Red-222
Silver-222
97Pacific Dynagon-72
Copper-72
Dark Grey-72
Emerald Green-72
Ice Blue-72
Red-72
Silver-72
Best Kept Secrets-107
Dynamic Duos-9A
Tandems-71
97Pacific Invincible-80
Copper-80
Emerald Green-80
Ice Blue-80
Red-80
Silver-80
Attack Zone-12
97Pacific Omega-136
Copper-136
Dark Gray-136
Emerald Green-136
Gold-136
Ice Blue-136
97Panini Stickers-80
97Panini Stickers-119
97Panini Stickers-247
97Paramount-106
Copper-106
Dark Grey-106
Emerald Green-106
Ice Blue-106
Red-106
Silver-106
97Pinnacle-145
Press Plates Back Black-145
Press Plates Back Cyan-145
Press Plates Back Magenta-145
Press Plates Back Yellow-145
Press Plates Front Black-145
Press Plates Front Cyan-145
Press Plates Front Magenta-145
Press Plates Front Yellow-145
97Pinnacle Certified-40
Red-40
Mirror Blue-40
Mirror Gold-40
Mirror Red-40
97Pinnacle Inside-80
Coach's Collection-80
Executive Collection-80
97Pinnacle Tot Cert Platinum Blue-40
97Pinnacle Tot Certi Platinum Gold-40
97Pinnacle Totally Certified Platinum Red-40
97Pinnacle Tot Cert Mirror Platinum Gold-40
97Revolution-80
Copper-80
Emerald-80
Ice Blue-80
Silver-80
97Score-137
97Score-267
Artist's Proofs-137
Golden Blades-137
Check It-12
97SP Authentic-92
Sign of the Times-BB
Tradition-T4
97SPx-29
Bronze-29
Gold-29
Silver-29
Steel-29
Dimension-SPX8
Grand Finale-29
97Studio-27
Press Proofs Silver-27
Press Proofs Gold-27
Hard Hats-4
Portraits-24
97Upper Deck-98
Blow-Ups 3 x 5-1-3
Game Dated Moments-98
Sixth Sense Masters-SS28
Sixth Sense Wizards-SS28
Smooth Grooves-SG34
The Specialists-29
The Specialists Level 2 Die Cuts-29
Three Star Selects-4A
97Upper Deck Ice-54
Parallel-54
Power Shift-54
97Zenith-53
Z-Gold-53
Z-Silver-53
97Zenith 5 x 7-32
Gold Impulse-32
Silver Impulse-32
98SLU Hockey-30
98Aurora-114
98Be A Player-85
Press Release-85
98BAP Gold-85
98BAP Autographs-85
98BAP Autographs Gold-85
98BAP Tampa Bay All Star Game-85
98Black Diamond Double Diamond-54
98Black Diamond Triple Diamond-54
98Black Diamond Quadruple Diamond-54
98Bowman's Best-80
Refractors-80
Atomic Refractors-80
98Crown Royale-82
Limited Series-82
98Finest-107
No Protectors-107
No Protectors Refractors-107
Refractors-107
Centurion-C2
Centurion Refractors-C2
98Katch-85
98Kenner Starting Lineup Cards-2
98Kenner Starting Lineup Cards-3
98OPC Chrome-198
Refractors-198
98Pacific-275
Ice Blue-275
Red-275
98Pacific Dynagon Ice-113
Blue-113
Red-113
98Pacific Omega-225
Red-225
Opening Day Issue-225
98Panini Photocards-8
98Panini Stickers-78
98Paramount-140
Copper-140
Emerald Green-140
Holo-Electric-140
Ice Blue-140
Silver-140
98SP Authentic-53
Power Shift-53
98SPx Finite-51
Radiance-51
Spectrum-51
98Topps-198
O-Pee-Chee-198
98UD Choice-123
98UD Choice Preview-123
98UD Choice Prime Choice Reserve-123
98UD Choice Reserve-123
98Upper Deck-21
98Upper Deck-127
Exclusives-21
Exclusives-127
Exclusives 1 of 1-21
Exclusives 1 of 1-127
Lord Stanley's Heroes-LS19
Lord Stanley's Heroes Quantum 1-LS19
Lord Stanley's Heroes Quantum 2-LS19
Lord Stanley's Heroes Quantum 3-LS19
Gold Reserve-21
Gold Reserve-127
98Upper Deck MVP-200
Gold Script-200
Silver Script-200
Super Script-200
99BAP Memorabilia-267
Gold-267
Silver-267
99BAP Millennium-229
Emerald-229
Ruby-229
Sapphire-229
Signatures-229

Signatures Gold-229
99Maple Leafs Pizza Pizza-7
99O-Pee-Chee-78
99O-Pee-Chee Chrome-78
99O-Pee-Chee Chrome Refractors-78
99Pacific-401
Copper-401
Emerald Green-401
Gold-401
Ice Blue-401
Premiere Date-401
Red-401
99Panini Stickers-160
99Paramount-221
Copper-221
Emerald-221
Gold-221
Holographic Emerald-221
Holographic Gold-221
Holographic Silver-221
Ice Blue-221
Premiere Date-221
Red-221
Silver-221
99SP Authentic-82
99SPx-146
Radiance-146
Spectrum-146
99Stadium Club-35
First Day Issue-35
One of a Kind-35
Printing Plates Black-35
Printing Plates Cyan-35
Printing Plates Magenta-35
Printing Plates Yellow-35
99Topps/OPC-78
99Topps/OPC Chrome-78
Refractors-78
99Upper Deck-293
Exclusives-293
Exclusives 1 of 1-293
99Upper Deck Gold Reserve-293
99Upper Deck MVP-201
Gold Script-201
Silver Script-201
Super Script-201
99Upper Deck Retro Generation-G1C
99Upper Deck Retro Generation Level 2-G1C
99Upper Deck Victory-282
99Wayne Gretzky Hockey-165
01BAP Ultimate Memorabilia Calder Trophy-5
01Parkhurst-247
02BAP First Edition-54
Jerseys-54
02BAP Memorabilia-259
Emerald-259
Ruby-259
Sapphire-259
NHL All-Star Game-259
NHL All-Star Game Blue-259
NHL All-Star Game Green-259
NHL All-Star Game Red-259
02BAP Memorabilia Toronto Fall Expo-259
02BAP Sig Series Auto Buybacks 1998-85
02BAP Sig Series Auto Buybacks 1999-229
02BAP Ultimate Memorabilia First Overall-2
02Pacific-247
Blue-247
Red-247
02Pacific Calder-11
Silver-11
02Pacific Complete-212
Red-212
02Topps Heritage-170
02Topps Total-106
02Upper Deck-261
Exclusives-261
02Upper Deck Beckett UD Promos-261
03Beehive-39
Gold-39
Silver-39
03ITG Action-16
Jerseys-M5
Jerseys-M225
03O-Pee-Chee-83
03OPC Blue-83
03OPC Gold-83
03OPC Red-83
03Pacific-24
Blue-24
Red-24
03Pacific Complete-398
Red-398
03Pacific Exhibit-12
Blue Backs-12
Yellow Backs-12
03Parkhurst Orig Six Boston Mem -BM12
03Parkhurst Orig Six Boston Mem -BM14
03Parkhurst Original Six Chicago-5
03Parkhurst Orig Six New York Mem-NM28
03Topps-83
Blue-83
Gold-83
Red-83
03Topps Traded-TT6
Blue-TT6
Gold-TT6
Red-TT6
03UD Premier Collection-12
03Upper Deck-15
Canadian Exclusives-15
HG-15
03Upper Deck Ice-16
Gold-16
03Upper Deck MVP-36
Gold Script-36
Silver Script-36
Canadian Exclusives-36
03Upper Deck Rookie Update-17
03Upper Deck Victory-14
Bronze-14
Gold-14
Silver-14
04Pacific-58
Blue-58
Red-58
04Upper Deck Hardware Heroes-AW10
05Be A Player Quad Signatures-HAWK
05Be A Player Signatures-BB
05Be A Player Signatures Gold-BB
05Black Diamond-21
Emerald-21
Gold-21
Onyx-21
Ruby-21
05Panini Stickers-244
05Parkhurst-136
Facsimile Auto Parallel-136
05Ultra-65
Gold-65
Ice-65
05Upper Deck-299
05Upper Deck MVP-120
Gold-120
Platinum-120
05Upper Deck Victory-39
Black-39
Gold-39
Silver-39
06Black Diamond-25
Black-25
Gold-25
Ruby-25
06Fleer-60
Tiffany-60
06SP Game Used Authentic Fabrics Sixes-AF6MAS
06SP Game Used Authentic Fabrics Sixes Patches-AF6MAS
06Ultra-60
Gold Medallion-60
Ice Medallion-60
06Upper Deck-59
Exclusives Parallel-59
High Gloss Parallel-59
Masterpieces-59
06Upper Deck MVP-85
Gold Script-85
Super Script-85

Berard, Ryan
03Belleville Bulls-7
04Belleville Bulls-19
05Belleville Bulls-18
06Saginaw Spirit-21

Berardicurti, Louie
83Kitchener Rangers-5

Berchtold, Armin
93Swiss HNL-367
95Swiss HNL-451

Berclaz, Gregory
01Swiss HNL-422

Berdichevsky, Lev
91O-Pee-Chee Inserts-50R
92Russian Stars Red Ace-32
93Roanoke Express-4
99Russian Dynamo Moscow-21
00Russian Hockey League-65
01Russian Hockey League-141

Berdnikov, Ruslan
02Russian Hockey League-238

Berdnikov, Sergei
98Russian Hockey League-135
99Russian Hockey League-147
00Russian Hockey League-103
01Russian Hockey League-90
02Russian Hockey League-51
03Russian Hockey League-87
03Russian Hockey League-205

Berehowsky, Drake
90Score-434
Canadian-434
90Upper Deck-361
French-361
90 7th Inn. Sketch OHL-52
91Maple Leafs Panini Team Stickers-1
91O-Pee-Chee-70
91Score American-385
91Score Canadian Bilingual-275
91Score Canadian English-275
91Topps-70
91 7th Inn. Sketch OHL-70
92Humpty Dumpty II-1
92Maple Leafs Kodak-5
92OPC Premier-131
92Pinnacle-231
French-231
92Ultra-417
92Upper Deck-415
92St. John's Maple Leafs-2
93Donruss-336
93Maple Leafs Score Black's-14
93OPC Premier-69
Gold-69
93Parkhurst-199
Emerald Ice-199
93PowerPlay-239
93Score-355
Canadian-355
93Stadium Club-331
Members Only Master Set-331
First Day Issue-331
93Topps/OPC Premier-69
Gold-69
93Ultra-90
93Upper Deck-20
93Classic Pro Prospects-59
94Be A Player Signature Cards-55
94Leaf-410
94Maple Leafs Kodak-3
94Parkhurst SE-SE177
Gold-SE177
94Upper Deck-458
Electric Ice-458
95Canada Games NHL POGS-218
95Cleveland Lumberjacks-6
95Cleveland Lumberjacks Postcards-6
96Carolina Monarchs-3
98OPC Chrome-137
Refractors-137
98Predators Team Issue-2
98Topps-137
O-Pee-Chee-137
99Pacific-217
Copper-217
Emerald Green-217
Gold-217
Ice Blue-217
Premiere Date-217
Red-217
99Upper Deck MVP SC Edition-101
Gold Script-101
Silver Script-101
Super Script-101
00O-Pee-Chee-36
00O-Pee-Chee Parallel-36
00Topps/OPC-36
Parallel-36
00Upper Deck-327
Exclusives Tier 1-327
Exclusives Tier 2-327
00Upper Deck MVP-99
First Stars-99
Second Stars-99
Third Stars-99
00Upper Deck Victory-133
00Upper Deck Vintage-200
01Coyotes Team Issue-1
01UD Mask Collection-97
Gold-97
02Coyotes Team Issue-4
03Pacific Complete-283
Red-283
03Upper Deck-399
Canadian Exclusives-399
HG-399
UD Exclusives-399
05German DEL-305

Berek, Miroslav
94German DEL-415
95German DEL-218
96German DEL-68

Berenikin, Sergei
00Russian Hockey League-190

Berens, Rick
91Michigan Falcons-13

Berens, Sean
98Las Vegas Thunder-2
99Chicago Wolves-12
00Grand Rapids Griffins-2
01UK Belfast Giants-9
03UK Belfast Giants-1

Berenson, Red
44Beehive Group II Photos-223A
44Beehive Group II Photos-223B
60NHL Ceramic Tiles-2
62Shirriff Coins-42
63Chex Photos-6
63Parkhurst-26
63Parkhurst-85
63York White Backs-36
64Beehive Group III Photos-100
64Topps-61
64Toronto Star-5
64Quebec Aces-2
65Topps-9
66Topps-92
66Topps USA Test-10
67Topps-24
68O-Pee-Chee-114
68Shirriff Coins-150
68Topps-114
69O-Pee-Chee-20
Four-in-One-16
Stamps-2
69Topps-20
70Colgate Stamps-24
70Dad's Cookies-5
70Esso Power Players-240
70O-Pee-Chee-103
Deckle-25
70Sargent Promotions Stamps-177
70Topps-103
Topps/OPC Sticker Stamps-2
71O-Pee-Chee-91
Posters-10
71Sargent Promotions Stamps-51
71Topps-91
71Toronto Sun-84
72O-Pee-Chee-123
Player Crests-7
Team Canada-2
72Sargent Promotions Stamps-73
72Topps-95
72Finnish Semic World Championship-183
72Swedish Semic World Championship-183
73O-Pee-Chee-10
73Red Wings Team Issue-2
73Topps-174
74Lipton Soup-25
74NHL Action Stamps-104
74NHL Action Stamps Update-30
74O-Pee-Chee NHL-19
74Topps-19
75O-Pee-Chee NHL-22
75Topps-22
76O-Pee-Chee NHL-236
76Topps-236
77O-Pee-Chee NHL-107
77Topps-107
78Blues Postcards-4
78O-Pee-Chee-218
78Topps-218
91Future Trends Canada '72-48
91Future Trends Canada '72 French-48
92Blues UD Best of the Blues-11
94Parkhurst Tall Boys-80
95Parkhurst '66-67-92
Coins-92
02Michigan Wolverines-9
03Michigan Wolverines-4
04ITG Franchises US East-408
04ITG Franchises US West-283
Autographs-A-RBE
04UD Legendary Signatures-67
Autographs-RB
Summit Stars-CDN15
Summit Stars Autographs-CDN-RB
04Michigan Wolverines TK Legacy-1966C
04Michigan Wolverines TK Legacy-H1
04Michigan Wolverines TK Legacy-HL1
04Michigan Wolverines TK Legacy-VH4

Berenzweig, Andrew
94Select-151
Gold-151
94Classic Draft Prospects-DP1
99Milwaukee Admirals Keebler-5
00Upper Deck-187
Exclusives Tier 1-187
Exclusives Tier 2-187
00Milwaukee Admirals Keebler-3
00Milwaukee Admirals Postcards-2
01BAP Memorabilia-262
Emerald-262
Ruby-262
Sapphire-262
01Titanium Draft Day Edition-141
01Milwaukee Admirals-4
02Milwaukee Admirals-16
02Milwaukee Admirals Postcards-3

Berezan, Perry
85Flames Red Rooster-3
86Flames Red Rooster-2
87Flames Red Rooster-1
88Flames Postcards-12
89Panini Stickers-110
90O-Pee-Chee-357
90Pro Set-459
90Score-379
Canadian-379
90Topps-357
Tiffany-357
91O-Pee-Chee-485
91Parkhurst-381
French-381
91Pinnacle-287
French-287
91Pro Set-487
French-487
91Score Canadian Bilingual-527
91Score Canadian English-527
91Score Rookie/Traded-94T
91Sharks Sports Action-2
91Stadium Club-227
91Topps-485
92Bowman-105
92O-Pee-Chee-162
92Pinnacle-148
French-148
92Score-169
Canadian-169
92Stadium Club-441
92Topps-342
Gold-342G
92Upper Deck-451

Berezin, Sergei
94German DEL-221
94Classic-67
Gold-67
95Finnish Semic World Championships-135
95German DEL-217
96Be A Player Link to History-3A
96Be A Player Link to History Autographs-3A
96Be A Player Link to History Auto Silver-3A
96Black Diamond-94
Gold-94
96Collector's Choice-350
96Donruss Canadian Ice-119
Gold Press Proofs-119
Red Press Proofs-119
96Donruss Elite-138
Die Cut Stars-138
Aspirations-17
96Flair-124
Blue Ice-124
96Hockey Greats Coins-21
Gold-21
96Leaf Limited Rookies-7
96Leaf Limited Rookies Gold-7
96Leaf Preferred-123
Press Proofs-123
96Maple Leafs Postcards-4
96Metal Universe-171
96Select Certified-98
Artist's Proofs-98
Blue-98
Mirror Blue-98
Mirror Gold-98
Mirror Red-98
Red-98
96SP-188
SPx Force-4
96Ultra-161
Gold Medallion-161
Rookies-2
96Upper Deck-346
Generation Next-X31
96Upper Deck Ice-103
Parallel-103
96Zenith-127
Artist's Proofs-127
96Swedish Semic Wien-153
All-Stars-AS4
97Collector's Choice-247
Star Quest-SQ48
97Crown Royale-128
Emerald Green-128
Ice Blue-128
Silver-128
97Donruss-165
Press Proofs Silver-165
Press Proofs Gold-165
97Donruss Elite-55
Aspirations-55
Status-55
97Donruss Limited-8
97Donruss Limited-13
97Donruss Limited-154
Exposure-8
Exposure-13
Exposure-154
Fabric of the Game-57
97Donruss Preferred-77
Cut to the Chase-77
97Donruss Priority-28
Stamp of Approval-28
97Leaf-66
Fractal Matrix-66
Fractal Matrix Die Cuts-66
Banner Season-21
97Leaf International-66
Universal Ice-66
97Pacific-36
Copper-36
Emerald Green-36
Ice Blue-36
Red-36
Silver-36
Slap Shots Die-Cuts-10C
97Pacific Dynagon-120
97Pacific Dynagon-144
Copper-120
Copper-144
Dark Grey-120
Dark Grey-144
Emerald Green-120
Emerald Green-144
Ice Blue-120
Ice Blue-144
Red-120
Red-144
Silver-120
Silver-144
Best Kept Secrets-91
Tandems-10
Tandems-27
97Pacific Invincible-135
Copper-135
Emerald Green-135
Ice Blue-135
Red-135
Silver-135
Feature Performers-32
NHL Regime-191
Off The Glass-19
97Pacific Omega-217
Copper-217
Dark Gray-217
Emerald Green-217
Gold-217
Ice Blue-217
97Panini Stickers-180
97Panini Stickers-250
97Paramount-178
Copper-178
Dark Grey-178
Emerald Green-178
Ice Blue-178
Red-178
Silver-178
97Pinnacle-162
Press Plates Back Black-162
Press Plates Back Cyan-162
Press Plates Back Magenta-162
Press Plates Back Yellow-162
Press Plates Front Black-162
Press Plates Front Cyan-162
Press Plates Front Magenta-162
Press Plates Front Yellow-162
97Pinnacle Certified-127
Red-127
Mirror Blue-127
Mirror Gold-127
Mirror Red-127
97Pinnacle Inside-120
97Pinnacle Tot Cert Platinum Blue-127
97Pinnacle Tot Certi Platinum Gold-127
97Pinnacle Totally Certified Platinum Red-127
97Pinnacle Tot Cert Mirror Platinum Gold-127
97Post Pinnacle-15
97Score-145
Artist's Proofs-145
Golden Blades-145
97Score Maple Leafs-6
Platinum-6
Premier-6
97SP Authentic-153
Sign of the Times-SB
97Studio-104
Press Proofs Silver-104
Press Proofs Gold-104
Hard Hats-14
97Upper Deck-161
Smooth Grooves-SG51
Three Star Selects-19A
97Upper Deck Ice-4
Parallel-4
Power Shift-4
98Aurora-179
98Be A Player-285
Press Release-285
98BAP Gold-285
98BAP Autographs-285
98BAP Autographs Gold-285
98Crown Royale-128
Limited Series-128
98OPC Chrome-55
Refractors-55
98Pacific-410
Ice Blue-410
Red-410
98Pacific Dynagon Ice-177
Blue-177
Red-177
98Panini Stickers-166
98Paramount-224
Copper-224
Emerald Green-224
Holo-Electric-224
Ice Blue-224
Silver-224
98Topps-55
O-Pee-Chee-55
98UD Choice-201
98UD Choice Preview-201
98UD Choice Prime Choice Reserve-201
98UD Choice Reserve-201
98Upper Deck-186
Exclusives-186
Exclusives 1 of 1-186
Gold Reserve-186
99Aurora-134
Premiere Date-134
99BAP Memorabilia-273
Gold-273
Silver-273
99BAP Millennium Prototypes-7
99BAP Millennium-232
Emerald-232
Ruby-232
Sapphire-232
Signatures-232
Signatures Gold-232
99Crown Royale-132
Limited Series-132
Premiere Date-132
99Maple Leafs Pizza Pizza-14
99O-Pee-Chee-236
99O-Pee-Chee Chrome-236
99O-Pee-Chee Chrome Refractors-236
99Pacific-402
Copper-402
Emerald Green-402
Gold-402
Ice Blue-402
Premiere Date-402
Red-402
Gold Crown Die-Cuts-33
99Pacific Dynagon Ice-185
Blue-185
Copper-185
Gold-185
Premiere Date-185
99Pacific Omega-222
Copper-222
Gold-222
Ice Blue-222
Premiere Date-222
99Pacific Prism-135
Holographic Blue-135
Holographic Gold-135
Holographic Mirror-135
Holographic Purple-135
Premiere Date-135
99Panini Stickers-161
99Paramount-222
Copper-222
Emerald-222
Gold-222
Holographic Emerald-222
Holographic Gold-222
Holographic Silver-222
Ice Blue-222
Premiere Date-222
Red-222
Silver-222
99Revolution-135
Premiere Date-135
Red-135
Shadow Series-135
Copper-135
Gold-135
CSC Silver-135
99SPx-145
Radiance-145
Spectrum-145
99Stadium Club-53
First Day Issue-53
One of a Kind-53
Printing Plates Black-53
Printing Plates Cyan-53
Printing Plates Magenta-53
Printing Plates Yellow-53
99Topps/OPC-236
99Topps/OPC Chrome-236
Refractors-236
99Topps Gold Label Class 1-62
Black-62
Black One of One-62
One of One-62
Red-62
Red One of One-62
99Topps Gold Label Class 2-62
99Topps Gold Label Class 2 Black-62
99Topps Gold Label Class 2 Black 1 of 1-62
99Topps Gold Label Class 2 One of One-62
99Topps Gold Label Class 2 Red-62
99Topps Gold Label Class 2 Red One of One-62
99Topps Gold Label Class 3-62
99Topps Gold Label Class 3 Black-62
99Topps Gold Label Class 3 Black 1 of 1-62
99Topps Gold Label Class 3 One of One-62
99Topps Gold Label Class 3 Red-62
99Topps Gold Label Class 3 Red One of One-62
99Topps Premier Plus-35
Parallel-35
99Upper Deck-123
Exclusives-123
Exclusives 1 of 1-123
99Upper Deck Gold Reserve-123
99Upper Deck HoloGrFx-56
Ausome-56
99Upper Deck MVP-199
Gold Script-199
Silver Script-199
Super Script-199
99Upper Deck MVP SC Edition-176
Gold Script-176
Silver Script-176
Super Script-176
99Upper Deck Retro-73
Gold-73
Platinum-73
99Upper Deck Victory-283
99Wayne Gretzky Hockey-162
00BAP Memorabilia-205
Emerald-205
Ruby-205
Sapphire-205
Promos-205
00BAP Mem Chicago Sportsfest Copper-205
00BAP Memorabilia Chicago Sportsfest Blue-205
00BAP Memorabilia Chicago Sportsfest Gold-205
00BAP Memorabilia Chicago Sportsfest Ruby-205
00BAP Memorabilia Chicago Sun-Times Ruby-205
00BAP Memorabilia Chicago Sun-Times Gold-205
00BAP Mem Chicago Sun-Times Sapphire-205
00BAP Mem Toronto Fall Expo Copper-205
00BAP Memorabilia Toronto Fall Expo Gold-205
00BAP Memorabilia Toronto Fall Expo Ruby-205
00BAP Parkhurst 2000-P182
00BAP Signature Series-150
Emerald-150
Ruby-150
Sapphire-150
00Crown Royale-99
Ice Blue-99
Limited Series-99
Premiere Date-99
Red-99
00O-Pee-Chee-55
00O-Pee-Chee Parallel-55
00Pacific-385
Copper-385
Gold-385
Ice Blue-385
Premiere Date-385
00Paramount-227
Copper-227
Gold-227
Holo-Gold-227
Holo-Silver-227
Ice Blue-227
Premiere Date-227
00Titanium-90
Blue-90
Gold-90
Premiere Date-90
Red-90
Retail-90
00Topps/OPC-55
Parallel-55
00UD Heroes-110
00UD Reserve-82
00Upper Deck-165
Exclusives Tier 1-165
Exclusives Tier 2-165
00Upper Deck MVP-169
First Stars-169
Second Stars-169
Third Stars-169
00Upper Deck Victory-219
00Upper Deck Vintage-335
01BAP Memorabilia-188
01BAP Memorabilia-488
Emerald-188
Emerald-488
Ruby-188
Ruby-488
Sapphire-188
Sapphire-488
01BAP Signature Series-193
Autographs-193
Autographs Gold-193
01Coyotes Team Issue-2
01O-Pee-Chee-159
01O-Pee-Chee Premier Parallel-159
01Pacific-361
Extreme LTD-361
Hobby LTD-361
Premiere Date-361
Retail LTD-361
01Pacific Adrenaline-145
Blue-145
Premiere Date-145
Red-145
Retail-145
01Pacific Arena Exclusives-361
01Parkhurst-358
01SPx-178
01Titanium Double-Sided Jerseys-72
01Titanium Double-Sided Patches-72
01Titanium Draft Day Edition-48
01Topps-159
OPC Parallel-159
01UD Mask Collection-49
Gold-49
01Upper Deck-363
Exclusives-363
Pride of the Leafs-MLSB
02BAP Sig Series Auto Buybacks 1998-285
02BAP Sig Series Auto Buybacks 1999-232
02BAP Sig Series Auto Buybacks 2001-193
02O-Pee-Chee-157
02O-Pee-Chee Premier Blue Parallel-157
02O-Pee-Chee Premier Red Parallel-157
02O-Pee-Chee Factory Set-157
02Pacific-191
Blue-191
Red-191
Jerseys-25
Jerseys Holo-Silver-25
02Pacific Complete-409
Red-409
02Pacific Heads-Up Quad Jerseys-15
02Pacific Heads-Up Quad Jerseys Gold-15
02Titanium Jerseys-14
02Titanium Jerseys Retail-14
02Titanium Patches-14
02Topps-157
OPC Blue Parallel-157
OPC Red Parallel-157
Factory Set-157
02Topps Total-312
02Upper Deck-281
Exclusives-281
02Upper Deck Beckett UD Promos-281
02Vanguard Jerseys-10
02Vanguard Jerseys Gold-10
03ITG Action-533
03O-Pee-Chee-259
03OPC Blue-259
03OPC Gold-259
03OPC Red-259
03Pacific-339
Blue-339
Red-339
03Pacific Exhibit-146
Blue Backs-146
Yellow Backs-146
03Topps-259
Blue-259
Gold-259
Red-259
03Upper Deck MVP-429
Gold Script-429
Silver Script-429
Canadian Exclusives-429
03Russian Hockey League-218

Berezniuk, Chad
90 7th Inn. Sketch WHL-305

Berg, Aki Petteri
93Finnish SISU-38
94Finnish SISU-335
94Classic Draft Prospects-DP2
95Bowman-146
All-Foil-146
95Collector's Choice-337
95Collector's Choice-410
Player's Club-337
Player's Club Platinum-337
95Donruss-325
95Finest-138
Refractors-138
95Leaf Limited-20
95Metal-170
95Parkhurst International-253
95Parkhurst International-510
Emerald Ice-253
Emerald Ice-510
95Select Certified-127
Mirror Gold-127
95SkyBox Impact-203
95SP-69
95Stadium Club-201
Members Only Master Set-201
95Summit-175
Artist's Proofs-175
Ice-175
95Topps-267
OPC Inserts-267
SuperSkills Super Rookies-SR6
95Ultra-330
95Upper Deck-267
Electric Ice-267
Electric Ice Gold-267
Predictor Hobby-H25
Predictor Hobby Exchange-H25
95Zenith-146
Rookie Roll Call-6
95Finnish SISU Drafted Dozen-1
95Finnish SISU Limited Signed and Sealed-4
95Classic-3
Ice Breakers-BK3
Ice Breakers Die Cuts-BK3
95Signature Rookies Auto-Phonex-6
95Signature Rook Auto-Phonex Phone Cards-6
95Signature Rookies Auto-Phonex Prodigies-P4
95Assets Gold *-4
95Assets Gold Phone Cards $2 *-4
95Classic Five-Sport *-125
Strive For Five-HK12
95Signature Rookies Tetrad Autobilia *-40
95Signature Rookies Tetrad SR Force *-F3
96Collector's Choice-128
96Donruss Elite-108
Die Cut Stars-108
96Metal Universe-72
96Score-264
Artist's Proofs-264
Dealer's Choice Artist's Proofs-264
Special Artist's Proofs-264
Golden Blades-264
96Summit-164
Artist's Proofs-164
Ice-164
Metal-164
Premium Stock-164
96Swedish Semic Wien-30
96Collector's Edge Future Legends-27
96Classic Signings *-72
Blue-72
Die-Cuts-72
Red-72
97Be A Player-155
Autographs-155
Autographs Die-Cuts-155
Autographs Prismatic Die-Cuts-155
97Collector's Choice-121
97Donruss-129
Press Proofs Silver-129
Press Proofs Gold-129
97Donruss Limited-85
Exposure-85
97Donruss Preferred-112
Cut to the Chase-112
97Katch-67
Gold-67
Silver-67
97Pacific Dynagon Best Kept Secrets-44
98Panini Stickers-202
98Finnish Keraliysarja-233
99BAP Memorabilia-221
Gold-221
Silver-221
99SPx-77
Radiance-77
Spectrum-77
99Upper Deck-235
Exclusives-235
Exclusives 1 of 1-235
99Upper Deck Arena Giveaways-LK2
99Upper Deck Gold Reserve-235
99Wayne Gretzky Hockey-83
99Finnish Cardset-181
Aces High-D-5
Most Wanted-1
00BAP Memorabilia-309
Emerald-309
Ruby-309
Sapphire-309
Promos-309
00BAP Mem Chicago Sportsfest Copper-309
00BAP Memorabilia Chicago Sportsfest Blue-309
00BAP Memorabilia Chicago Sportsfest Gold-309
00BAP Memorabilia Chicago Sportsfest Ruby-309
00BAP Memorabilia Chicago Sun-Times Ruby-309
00BAP Memorabilia Chicago Sun-Times Gold-309
00BAP Mem Chicago Sun-Times Sapphire-309
00BAP Mem Toronto Fall Expo Copper-309
00BAP Memorabilia Toronto Fall Expo Gold-309
00BAP Memorabilia Toronto Fall Expo Ruby-309
00Pacific-192
Copper-192
Gold-192
Ice Blue-192
Premiere Date-192
00Finnish Cardset-112
01Upper Deck Victory-335
Gold-335
01Finnish Cardset-165
02Maple Leafs Platinum Collection-3
02NHL Power Play Stickers-132
02Pacific Complete-480
Red-480
02Finnish Cardset-157
03Parkhurst Original Six Toronto-4
03Upper Deck MVP-400
Gold Script-400
Silver Script-400
Canadian Exclusives-400
04Swedish Pure Skills-90
Parallel-90
Professional Power-AB
06Finnish Cardset-334
Enforcers-9

Berg, Bill
88ProCards AHL-305
89ProCards AHL-232
91Bowman-216
91O-Pee-Chee-122
91Pro Set-145
French-145
91Score Canadian Bilingual-541
91Score Canadian English-541
91Stadium Club-385
91Topps-122
92Maple Leafs Kodak-6
93Leaf-287
Maple Leafs Score Black's-15
93Parkhurst-472
Emerald Ice-472
94Be A Player Signature Cards-57
94Maple Leafs Gangsters-3
94Maple Leafs Kodak-4
94Maple Leafs Pin-up Posters-9
94OPC Premier-136
Special Effects-136
94Parkhurst SE-SE181
Gold-SE181
94Pinnacle-57
Artist's Proofs-57
Rink Collection-57
94Topps/OPC Premier-136
Special Effects-136
96Be A Player-84
Autographs-84
Autographs Silver-84
97Score Rangers-9
Platinum-9
Premier-9
98Senators Team Issue-3

Berg, Bob
89 7th Inn. Sketch OHL-72
90ProCards AHL/IHL-432
90 7th Inn. Sketch OHL-400
91ProCards-384
91Richmond Renegades-11
93Wichita Thunder-1
94Central Hockey League-109
95Louisiana Ice Gators-1
95Louisiana Ice Gators Playoffs-1

Berg, Reg
95Donruss Elite World Juniors-32
95Upper Deck-567
Electric Ice-567
Electric Ice Gold-567
95Minnesota Golden Gophers-5
96Minnesota Golden Gophers-5
97Minnesota Golden Gophers-8
98Minnesota Golden Gophers-8
99Florida Everblades-8
00Cincinnati Cyclones-13
00Florida Everblades-2
01Florida Everblades-8
03Florida Everblades-8
03Florida Everblades RBI Sports-161
04Florida Everblades-4
05Florida Everblades-6

Berg, Stale
92Norwegian Elite Series-109

Bergamelli, Thomas
93Quebec Pee-Wee Tournament-1494

Berge, David
96German DEL-248
98German DEL-129
99German DEL-286
99German DEL-390

Berge, Mick
02Lincoln Stars-13
03Lincoln Stars-10
03Lincoln Stars Update-40
04Lincoln Stars-16
04Lincoln Stars Update-43

Bergen, Andrew
97Red Deer Rebels-3
98Red Deer Rebels-3
00Red Deer Rebels-4
Signed-4
01Red Deer Rebels-4

Bergen, Brad
94German DEL-234
95German DEL-81
96German DEL-272
98German DEL-270
98German DEL-330
99German DEL-156

00German DEL-6
01German Upper Deck-166
02German Berlin Polar Bears Postcards-4
02German DEL City Press-25
03German Berlin Polar Bears Postcards-6

Bergen, Matt
02Saskatoon Blades-4

Bergen, Todd
83Springfield Indians-3

Bergenheim, Christer
72Finnish Jaakiekko-139

Bergenheim, Sean
01Finnish Cardset-257
02BAP Memorabilia Draft Redemptions-22
02SPx Rookie Redemption-R206
02Finnish Cardset-158
Bound for Glory-1
02Finnish Cardset Dynamic Duos-10
02Finnish Cardset Signatures-1
03BAP Memorabilia-186
Emerald-186
Gold-186
Ruby-186
Sapphire-186
Super Rookies-SR7
Super Rookies Gold-SR7
Super Rookies Silver-SR7
03BAP Ultimate Mem Rookie Jersey Emblems-30
03BAP Ultimate Mem Rookie Jsy Emblem Gold-30
03BAP Ultimate Mem Rookie Jersey Numbers-30
03BAP Ultimate Mem Rookie Jsy Number Gold-30
03BAP Ultimate Memorabilia Triple Threads-29
03Black Diamond-168
Black-168
Green-168
Red-168
03Bowman-149
Gold-149
Premier Performance-PP-SB
Premier Performance Patches-PP-SB
03Bowman Chrome-149
Refractors-149
Gold Refractors-149
Xfractors-149
03Crown Royale-127
Red-127
Retail-127
03ITG Action-614
03ITG Used Signature Series-154
Gold-154
03ITG VIP Rookie Debut-15
03Pacific Calder-170
03Pacific Complete-559
Red-559
03Pacific Invincible-118
Blue-118
Red-118
Retail-118
03Pacific Luxury Suite-93
Gold-93
03Pacific Supreme-129
Blue-129
Red-129
Retail-129
03Parkhurst Rookie-136
Rookie Emblems-RE-14
Rookie Emblems Gold-RE-14
Rookie Jerseys-RJ-14
Rookie Jerseys Gold-RJ-14
Rookie Numbers-RN-14
Rookie Numbers Gold-RN-14
03Private Stock Reserve-130
Blue-130
Red-130
Retail-130
03SP Authentic-152
Limited-152
Signed Patches-SB
03SP Game Used-72
Gold-72
03SPx-206
Radiance-206
Spectrum-206
03Titanium-128
Hobby Jersey Number Parallels-128
Retail-128
Retail Jersey Number Parallels-128
03Topps C55-146
Minis-146
Minis American Back-146
Minis American Back Red-146
Minis Bazooka Back-146
Minis Brooklyn Back-146
Minis Hat Trick Back-146
Minis O Canada Back-146
Minis O Canada Back Red-146
Minis Stanley Cup Back-146
03Topps Pristine-152
03Topps Pristine-153
03Topps Pristine-154
Gold Refractor Die Cuts-152
Gold Refractor Die Cuts-153
Gold Refractor Die Cuts-154
Refractors-152
Refractors-153
Refractors-154
Press Plates Black-152
Press Plates Black-153
Press Plates Black-154
Press Plates Cyan-152
Press Plates Cyan-153
Press Plates Cyan-154
Press Plates Magenta-152
Press Plates Magenta-153
Press Plates Magenta-154
Press Plates Yellow-152
Press Plates Yellow-153
Press Plates Yellow-154
03Topps Traded-TT125
Blue-TT125
Gold-TT125
Red-TT125
Future Phenoms-FP-SB
03UD Honor Roll-190
03UD Premier Collection-76
03Upper Deck-230
Canadian Exclusives-230
HG-230
03Upper Deck Classic Portraits-181
03Upper Deck MVP-454
03Upper Deck Trilogy-161
Limited-161
03Upper Deck Victory-209
03Finnish Cardset D-Day-DD1
04AHL All-Stars-3
04AHL All-Stars-47
04AHL Top Prospects-6
05ITG Heroes/Prosp Toronto Expo Parallel -207
05Black Diamond Gemography-G-SB
05Black Diamond Gemography Emerald-G-SB
05Black Diamond Gemography Gold-G-SB
05Black Diamond Gemography Onyx-G-SB
05Black Diamond Gemography Ruby-G-SB
05Parkhurst-316
Facsimile Auto Parallel-316
05Upper Deck Trilogy Scripts-SFS-SB
05ITG Heroes and Prospects-207
Autographs Series II-SB
Complete Jerseys-CJ-29
Complete Jerseys Gold-CJ-29
Jerseys-GUJ-96
Jerseys Gold-GUJ-96
Nameplates-N-51
Nameplates Gold-N-51

Bergenstrom, Jens
05Swedish SHL Elitset-65
06Finnish Cardset-317

Berger, Matthew
01Lethbridge Hurricanes-1

Berger, Mike
87North Stars Postcards-6
88ProCards IHL-31
89ProCards AHL-285
92Tulsa Oilers-1
94Central Hockey League-93
95Central Hockey League-56
99Indianapolis Ice-1
01Indianapolis Ice-2

Berger, Phil
91Greensboro Monarchs-2
92Greensboro Monarchs-5
93Greensboro Monarchs-1
94German First League-550
94Greensboro Monarchs-20

Berger, Raphael
92Quebec Pee-Wee Tournament-1391
96Swiss HNL-498
98Swiss Power Play Stickers-204
99Swiss Panini Stickers-206
00Swiss Panini Stickers-128
01Swiss HNL-124
02Swiss HNL-142

Berger, Stanislav
94Czech APS Extraliga-284
95Czech APS Extraliga-268

Berger, Thomas
93Swiss HNL-439
95Swiss HNL-59
96Swiss HNL-104
98Swiss Power Play Stickers-303
99Swiss Panini Stickers-309
00Swiss Panini Stickers-54
00Swiss Slapshot Mini-Cards-HCCF1
01Swiss HNL-146
02Swiss HNL-307
04Swiss Lausanne HC Postcards-6

Bergeron, Antoine
02Reading Royals-30
02Reading Royals RBI Sports-169

Bergeron, Charles
03Rimouski Oceanic-2
03Rimouski Oceanic Sheets-1
04Moncton Wildcats-4
05Saint John's Sea Dogs-7
06Saint Johns Sea Dogs-11

Bergeron, Chris
93Toledo Storm-17
95Birmingham Bulls-13
95Buffalo Stampedes RHI-24
96Toledo Storm-24
97Columbus Cottonmouths-2
98Port Huron Border Cats-7

Bergeron, Daniel
99Baie-Comeau Drakkar-1
00Baie-Comeau Drakkar-22
Signed-22
01Baie-Comeau Drakkar-20

Bergeron, David
917th Inn. Sketch QMJHL-172

Bergeron, Frederic
93Quebec Pee-Wee Tournament-524

Bergeron, Gerard
52Juniors Blue Tint-37

Bergeron, Germain
51Laval Dairy Lac St. Jean-44

Bergeron, J.C.
89ProCards AHL-181
90Canadiens Postcards-2
90OPC Premier-4
90Pro Set-614
90Upper Deck-408
French-408
91Bowman-335
91Canadiens Panini Team Stickers-1
91ProCards-77
92Lightning Sheraton-3
92Atlanta Knights-22
93Panini Stickers-220
93Atlanta Knights-21
94Lightning Photo Album-2
95Donruss-241
95Lightning Team Issue-3
95Parkhurst International-465
Emerald Ice-465
95Topps-174
OPC Inserts-174

Bergeron, Jerome
99Baie-Comeau Drakkar-2
00Val d'Or Foreurs-20
Signed-20

Bergeron, Joel
99Cornwall Colts-2

Bergeron, Marc-Andre
99Shawinigan Cataractes-7
Signed-7
00QMJHL All-Star Program Inserts-5
00Shawinigan Cataractes-12
Signed-12
01Hamilton Bulldogs-10
02BAP Memorabilia-316
02BAP Ultimate Memorabilia-80
02Upper Deck Rookie Update-138
02Hamilton Bulldogs-11
03Oilers Postcards-1
05Parkhurst-194
Facsimile Auto Parallel-194
05Upper Deck-324
06Gatorade-26
06O-Pee-Chee-201
Rainbow-201
06Upper Deck-78
Exclusives Parallel-78
High Gloss Parallel-78
Masterpieces-78
06Upper Deck MVP-122
Gold Script-122
Super Script-122

Bergeron, Martin
90ProCards AHL/IHL-17
94German First League-414
01Swiss HNL-410
02Swiss HNL-201
03Finnish Cardset-182

Bergeron, Mathieu
93Quebec Pee-Wee Tournament-320

Bergeron, Michel
76O-Pee-Chee NHL-71
76O-Pee-Chee NHL-385
76Topps-71
77O-Pee-Chee NHL-159
77Topps-159
78Capitals Team Issue-1
78O-Pee-Chee-273
80Nordiques Postcards-1
81Nordiques Postcards-2
82Nordiques Postcards-2
83Nordiques Postcards-2
84Nordiques Postcards-3
85Nordiques General Foods-3
85Nordiques Provigo-4
85Nordiques Team Issue-2
86Nordiques General Foods-2
89Nordiques Team Issue-2
89Nordiques General Foods-1

Bergeron, Patrice
02SPx Rookie Redemption-R215
03BAP Memorabilia-200
Emerald-200
Gold-200
Ruby-200
Sapphire-200
Super Rookies-SR5
Super Rookies Gold-SR5
Super Rookies Silver-SR5
03BAP Ultimate Memorabilia Autographs-106
Gold-106
03BAP Ultimate Mem Auto Jerseys-106
03BAP Ultimate Mem Auto Emblems-106
03BAP Ultimate Mem Auto Numbers-106
03BAP Ultimate Mem Calder Candidates-7
03BAP Ultimate Mem Calder Candidates Gold-7
03BAP Ultimate Mem Franch Present Future-3
03BAP Ultimate Mem Magnificent Prospects-3
03BAP Ultimate Mem Magnif Prospect Autos-3
03BAP Ultimate Mem Rookie Jersey Emblems-8
03BAP Ultimate Mem Rookie Jsy Emblem Gold-8
03BAP Ultimate Mem Rookie Jersey Numbers-8
03BAP Ultimate Mem Rookie Jsy Number Gold-8
03BAP Ultimate Memorabilia Triple Threads-29
03Beehive-202
Gold-202
Silver-202
03Black Diamond-184
Black-184
Green-184
Red-184
03Bowman-151
Gold-151
03Bowman Chrome-151
Refractors-151
Gold Refractors-151
Xfractors-151
03Crown Royale-103
Red-103
Retail-103
Royal Portraits-2
03eTopps-41
03ITG Action-620
03ITG Toronto Spring Expo Class of 2004-5
03ITG Used Signature Series-127
Autographs Gold-127
03ITG VIP Rookie Debut-6
03O-Pee-Chee-331
03OPC Blue-331
03OPC Gold-331
03OPC Red-331
03Pacific Calder-163
Reflections-2
03Pacific Complete-593
Red-593
03Pacific Exhibit-227
03Pacific Heads-Up-102
Hobby LTD-102
Retail LTD-102
Prime Prospects-2
Prime Prospects LTD-2
03Pacific Invincible-102
Blue-102
Red-102
Retail-102
03Pacific Luxury Suite-82
Gold-82
03Pacific Prism-152
03Pacific Quest for the Cup-102
Calder Contenders-1
03Pacific Supreme-104
Blue-104
Red-104
Retail-104
03Parkhurst Toronto Expo Rookie Preview-PRP-8
03Parkhurst Original Six Boston-18
03Parkhurst Orig Six He Shoots/Scores-18
03Parkhurst Orig Six He Shoots/Scores-18A
03Parkhurst Rookie-184
Calder Candidates-CMC-4
Calder Candidates Gold-CMC-4
Rookie Emblems-RE-1
Rookie Emblem Autographs-RE-PB
Rookie Emblems Gold-RE-1
Rookie Jerseys-RJ-1
Rookie Jersey Autographs-RJ-PB
Rookie Jerseys Gold-RJ-1
Rookie Numbers-RN-1
Rookie Number Autographs-RN-PB
Rookie Numbers Gold-RN-1
Teammates Gold-RT11
Teammates-RT11
03Private Stock Reserve-104
Blue-104
Red-104
Retail-104
03SP Authentic-146
Limited-146
Signed Patches-PB
03SP Game Used-52
Gold-52
Rookie Exclusives-RE1
03SPx-220
Radiance-220
Spectrum-220
03Titanium-207
Patches-207
Right on Target-2
03Topps-331
Blue-331
Gold-331
Red-331
03Topps C55-148
Minis-148
Minis American Back-148
Minis American Back Red-148
Minis Bazooka Back-148
Minis Brooklyn Back-148
Minis Hat Trick Back-148
Minis O Canada Back-148
Minis O Canada Back Red-148
Minis Stanley Cup Back-148
03Topps Pristine-107
03Topps Pristine-108
03Topps Pristine-109
Gold Refractor Die Cuts-107
Gold Refractor Die Cuts-108
Gold Refractor Die Cuts-109
Refractors-107
Refractors-108
Refractors-109
Press Plates Black-107
Press Plates Black-108
Press Plates Black-109
Press Plates Cyan-107
Press Plates Cyan-108
Press Plates Cyan-109
Press Plates Magenta-107
Press Plates Magenta-108
Press Plates Magenta-109
Press Plates Yellow-107
Press Plates Yellow-108
Press Plates Yellow-109
03UD Honor Roll-180
03UD Premier Collection-109
NHL Shields-SH-PB
Signatures-PS-PB
Signatures Gold-PS-PB
Stars-ST-PB
Stars Patches-ST-PB
Teammates-PT-BB2
Teammates Patches-PT-BB2
03Upper Deck-204
Canadian Exclusives-204
HG-204
03Upper Deck Classic Portraits-177
03Upper Deck Ice-122
Glass Parallel-122
03Upper Deck MVP-468
03Upper Deck Rookie Update-151
YoungStars-YS3
YoungStars-YS3A
03Upper Deck Trilogy-143
Limited-143
04Pacific-19
Blue-19
Red-19
04Pacific Montreal International-1
Gold-1
04Pacific Montreal International Gold-1
04Pacific NHL All-Star FANtasy-2
04Pacific NHL All-Star FANtasy Gold-2
04Pacific Toronto Spring Expo-1
Gold-1
04SP Authentic-9
Limited-9
Rookie Review-RR-PB
Sign of the Times-ST-PB
Sign of the Times-DS-PM
Sign of the Times-TS-TRB
Sign of the Times-QS-BBLK
Sign of the Times-QS-NHKS
04Topps NHL All-Star FANtasy-3
04Upper Deck-15
Canadian Exclusives-15
HG Glossy Gold-15
HG Glossy Silver-15
YoungStars-YS-PB
04Upper Deck All-Star Promos-PB
04AHL All-Stars-4
04AHL Top Prospects-43
04Providence Bruins-2
04ITG Heroes and Prospects-195
Autographs-U-PBE
Emblems-61
Emblems Gold-61
Jerseys-61
Jerseys Gold-61
Numbers-61
Numbers Gold-61
04ITG Heroes/Prospects Toronto Expo '05-195
05ITG Heroes/Prosp Toronto Expo Parallel -81
05Be A Player Quad Signatures-BOST
05Be A Player Quad Signatures-RBSS
05Be A Player Signatures-PC
05Be A Player Signatures Gold-PC
05Be A Player Triple Signatures-IBM
05Beehive-7
05Beehive-246
Beige -7
Blue -7
Gold-7
Red -7
Matte-7
Signature Scrapbook-SSPB
05Black Diamond-129
Emerald-129
Gold-129
Onyx-129
Ruby-129
Gemography-G-PB
Gemography Emerald-G-PB
Gemography Gold-G-PB
Gemography Onyx-G-PB
Gemography Ruby-G-PB
05Bruins Boston Globe-13
05Hot Prospects-7
En Fuego-7
Red Hot-7
White Hot-7
05Panini Stickers-22
05Parkhurst-34
05Parkhurst-673
Facsimile Auto Parallel-34
Facsimile Auto Parallel-673
True Colors-TCBOS
True Colors-TCBOS
True Colors-TCMOBO
True Colors-TCMOBO
05SP Authentic-11
Limited-11
Chirography-SPPB
Exquisite Endorsements-EEPB
Marks of Distinction-MDPB
Octographs-OF
Scripts to Success-SSPB
Sign of the Times-PB
Sign of the Times Duals-DBM
Sign of the Times Triples-TRBL
Sign of the Times Quads-QTNBB
05SP Game Used-11
Autographs-11
Gold-11
Authentic Fabrics-AF-PB
Authentic Fabrics Autographs-AAF-PB
Authentic Fabrics Dual-PB
Authentic Fabrics Dual-RB
Authentic Fabrics Dual Autographs-PB
Authentic Fabrics Dual Autographs-RB
Authentic Fabrics Gold-AF-PB
Authentic Fabrics Quad-TRSB
Authentic Patches Quad -TRSB
Authentic Fabrics Triple-TBM
Authentic Patches-AP-PB
Authentic Patches Autographs-AAP-PB
Authentic Patches Dual-PB
Authentic Patches Dual-RB
Authentic Patches Dual Autographs-PB
Authentic Patches Dual Autographs-RB
Authentic Patches Triple-TBM
Auto Draft-AD-PB
Awesome Authentics-AA-PB
Awesome Authentics Gold-DA-PB
By the Letter-LM-PB
Game Gear-GG-BE
Game Gear Autographs-AG-BE
Signature Sticks-SS-PB
SIGnificance-PB
SIGnificance Gold-S-PB
SIGnificance Extra-TB
SIGnificance Extra Gold-TB
Significant Numbers-SN-PB
Statscriptions-ST-PB
05SPx-6
Spectrum-6
Winning Combos-WC-JP
Winning Combos-WC-MP
Winning Combos-WC-RB
Winning Combos-WC-SB
Winning Combos Autographs-AWC-BO
Winning Combos Autographs-AWC-RB
Winning Combos Autographs-AWC-TB
Winning Combos Gold-WC-JP
Winning Combos Gold-WC-MP
Winning Combos Gold-WC-RB
Winning Combos Gold-WC-SB
Winning Combos Spectrum-WC-JP
Winning Combos Spectrum-WC-MP
Winning Combos Spectrum-WC-RB
Winning Combos Spectrum-WC-SB
Winning Materials-WM-PB
Winning Materials Gold-WM-PB
Winning Materials Spectrum-WM-PB
05The Cup-7
Gold-7
Black Rainbow-7
Dual NHL Shields-DSBS
Dual NHL Shields-DSMB
Dual NHL Shields Autographs-ADSMB
Emblems of Endorsement-EEPB
Honorable Numbers-HNPB
Limited Logos-LLPB
Masterpiece Pressplates-7
Masterpiece Pressplates (Rookie Update)-233
Patch Variation-P7
Patch Variation Autographs-AP7
Scripted Numbers-SNBP
Scripted Numbers Dual-DSNBR
Scripted Swatches-SSPB
Signature Patches-SPPB
05UD Artifacts-11
Blue-11
Gold-11
Green-11
Pewter-11
Red-11
Auto Facts-AF-PB
Auto Facts Blue-AF-PB
Auto Facts Copper-AF-PB
Auto Facts Pewter-AF-PB
Auto Facts Silver-AF-PB
Gold Autographed-11
Remarkable Artifacts-RA-PB
Remarkable Artifacts Dual-RA-PB
05UD PowerPlay-38
Rainbow-38
05UD Toronto Fall Expo Priority Signings-PS-BE
05Ultimate Collection-9
Gold-9
Endorsed Emblems-EEPB
Jerseys-JPB
Jerseys Dual-DJBR
Marquee Attractions-MA7
Marquee Attractions Signatures-SMA7
Premium Patches-PPPB
Premium Swatches-PSPB
Ultimate Achievements-UAPB
Ultimate Patches-PPB
Ultimate Patches Dual-DPBR
Ultimate Signatures-USPB
Ultimate Signatures Logos-SLPB
05Ultra-16
Gold-16
Difference Makers-DM8
Difference Makers Jerseys-DMJ-PB
Difference Makers Jersey Autographs-DAJ-PB
Difference Makers Patches-DMP-PB
Difference Makers Patch Autographs-DAP-PB
Fresh Ink-FI-PB
Fresh Ink Blue-FI-PB
Ice-16
05Upper Deck-17
Big Playmakers-B-PB
Goal Rush-GR9
HG Glossy-17
Majestic Materials-MMPB
Notable Numbers-N-PB
Patches-P-PAB
05Upper Deck Ice-9
Rainbow-9
Cool Threads-CTPB
Cool Threads Autographs-ACTPB
Cool Threads Glass-CTPB
Cool Threads Patches-CTPPB
Cool Threads Patch Autographs-CAPPB
Fresh Ice-FIPB
Fresh Ice Glass-FIPB
Fresh Ice Glass Patches-FIPPB
Signature Swatches-SSPB
05Upper Deck MVP-30
Gold-30
Platinum-30
05Upper Deck Rookie Update-9
05Upper Deck Rookie Update-233
Inspirations Patch Rookies-233
05Upper Deck Trilogy-9
05Upper Deck Trilogy-133
Crystal-133
05Upper Deck Toronto Fall Expo-17
05Upper Deck Victory-14
Black-14
Gold-14
Silver-14
Blow-Ups-BU4
05ITG Heroes and Prospects-81
Aspiring-ASP6
Autographs-A-PBR
Autographs-DA-BO
Complete Jerseys-CJ-23
Complete Jerseys Gold-CJ-23
Future Teammates-FT10
He Shoots-He Scores Prizes-20
Jerseys-GUJ-32
Jerseys Gold-GUJ-32
Emblems-GUE-32
Emblems Gold-GUE-32
Numbers-GUN-32
Numbers Gold-GUN-32
Nameplates-N-1
Nameplates Gold-N-01
06Be A Player-162
Autographs-162
Profiles-PP13
Profiles Autographs-PP13
Signatures-BE
Signatures 10-179
Signatures 25-179
Signatures Duals-DBK
Signatures Trios-TBKS
Signatures Foursomes-FIBRC
Up Close and Personal-UC42
Up Close and Personal Autographs-UC42
06Be A Player Portraits-10
Dual Signature Portraits-DSBB
Signature Portraits-SPPB
Timeless Tens-TTCAN
Triple Signature Portraits-TBOS
06Beehive-91
06Beehive-228
Blue-91
Gold-91
Matte-91
Red Facsimile Signatures-91
Wood-91
5 X 7 Black and White-91
Matted Materials-MMPB
PhotoGraphs-PGPB
Remarkable Matted Materials-MMPB
06Black Diamond-128
Black-128
Gold-128
Ruby-128
Gemography-GPB
Jerseys-JBE
Jerseys Black-JBE
Jerseys Gold-JBE
Jerseys Ruby-JBE
Jerseys Black Autographs -JPB
06Flair Showcase-9
06Flair Showcase-173
06Flair Showcase-207
Parallel-9
Parallel-173
Parallel-207
Wave of the Future-WF4
06Fleer-15
Oversized-15
Tiffany-15
Total O-02
06Hot Prospects-7
Red Hot-7
White Hot-7
Hot Materials -HMPB
Hot Materials Red Hot-HMPB
Hot Materials White Hot-HMPB
Hotagraphs-HBE
06ITG International Ice Emblems-GUE17
06ITG International Ice Emblems Gold-GUE17
06ITG International Ice Jerseys-GUJ17
06ITG International Ice Jerseys Gold-GUJ17
06ITG International Ice Numbers-GUN17
06ITG International Ice Numbers Gold-GUN17
06ITG International Ice Triple Memorabilia-TM04
06ITG International Ice Triple Memorabilia Gold-TM04
06McDonald's Upper Deck-3
Autographs-APB
Jerseys-JPB
Patches-PPB
06O-Pee-Chee-36
06O-Pee-Chee-673
Rainbow-36
Rainbow-673
Swatches-S-PB
06Panini Stickers-17
06SP Authentic-92
06SP Authentic-143
Limited-92
Limited-143
Sign of the Times Duals-STKB
Sign of the Times Triples-ST3BBK
06SP Game Used-7
Gold-7
Rainbow-7
Authentic Fabrics-AFPB
Authentic Fabrics Parallel-AFPB
Authentic Fabrics Patches-AFPB
Authentic Fabrics Dual-AF2SB
Authentic Fabrics Dual Patches-AF2SB
Authentic Fabrics Triple-AF3BOS
Authentic Fabrics Triple Patches-AF3BOS
Authentic Fabrics Quads-AF4LMSB
Authentic Fabrics Quads Patches-AF4LMSB
Authentic Fabrics Eights-AF8CEN
Authentic Fabrics Eights Patches-AF8CEN
By The Letter-BLPB
Inked Sweaters Dual-IS2BB
Inked Sweaters Dual Patches-IS2BB
06SPx-7
Spectrum-7
SPxcitement-X8
SPxcitement Spectrum-X8
SPxcitement Autographs-X8
Winning Materials-WMPB
Winning Materials Spectrum-WMPB
Winning Materials Autographs-WMPB
06The Cup-10
Autographed Foundations-CQPB
Autographed Foundations Patches-CQPB
Autographed NHL Shields Duals-DASKB
Autographed NHL Shields Duals-DASPG
Autographed Patches-10
Black Rainbow-10
Foundations-CQPB
Foundations Patches-CQPB
Gold-10
Gold Patches-10
Honorable Numbers-HNPB
Jerseys-10
Limited Logos-LLPB
Masterpiece Pressplates-10
Scripted Swatches-SSPB
Signature Patches-SPPB
06UD Artifacts-92
06UD Artifacts-154
Blue-92
Blue-154
Gold-92
Gold-154
Platinum-92
Platinum-154
Radiance-92
Radiance-154
Red-92
Red-154
Frozen Artifacts-FAPB
Frozen Artifacts Black-FAPB
Frozen Artifacts Blue-FAPB
Frozen Artifacts Gold-FAPB
Frozen Artifacts Platinum-FAPB
Frozen Artifacts Red-FAPB
Frozen Artifacts Patches Black-FAPB
Frozen Artifacts Patches Blue-FAPB
Frozen Artifacts Patches Gold-FAPB
Frozen Artifacts Patches Platinum-FAPB
Frozen Artifacts Patches Red-FAPB
Tundra Tandems-TTBB
Tundra Tandems Black-TTBB
Tundra Tandems Blue-TTBB
Tundra Tandems Gold-TTBB
Tundra Tandems Platinum-TTBB
Tundra Tandems Red-TTBB
Tundra Tandems Dual Patches Red-TTBB
06UD Mini Jersey Collection-7
Jerseys-PB
Jersey Variations-PB
Jersey Autographs-PB
06UD Powerplay-7
Impact Rainbow-7
Specialists-SPB
Specialists Patches-PPB
06Ultimate Collection-4
Jerseys-UJ-PB
Jerseys Dual-UJ2-NB
Patches-UJ-PB
Patches Dual-UJ2-NB
Signatures-US-PB
Ultimate Signatures Logos-SL-PB
06Ultra-14
Gold Medallion-14
Ice Medallion-14
Difference Makers-DM3
Scoring Kings-SK22
06Upper Deck Arena Giveaways-BOS3
06Upper Deck-265
Exclusives Parallel-265
High Gloss Parallel-265
Game Dated Moments-GD42
Game Jerseys-JBE
Game Patches-PBE
Hometown Heroes-HH30
Masterpieces-265
Oversized Wal-Mart Exclusives-265
Signatures-SPB
06Upper Deck MVP-25
Gold Script-25
Super Script-25
Gotta Have Hart-HH22
Jerseys-OJBR
06Upper Deck Ovation-152
06Upper Deck Sweet Shot-7
Signature Shots/Saves-SSPB
Signature Shots/Saves Sticks-SSSPA
Signature Sticks-STPB
Sweet Stitches-SSPB
Sweet Stitches Duals-SSPB
Sweet Stitches Triples-SSPB
06Upper Deck Trilogy-9
Combo Autographed Jerseys-CJNB
Combo Autographed Patches-CJNB
Combo Clearcut Autographs-C2BB
Honorary Scripted Patches-HSPB
Honorary Scripted Swatches-HSSPB
Honorary Swatches-HSPB
Ice Scripts-ISPB
Scripts-S1PB
Scripts-S3PB
06Upper Deck Victory-12
06Upper Deck Victory Black-12
06Upper Deck Victory Gold-12
06Upper Deck Victory GameBreakers-GB4
06Upper Deck Victory Next In Line-NL6
06Upper Deck Victory Oversize Cards-PB
06ITG Heroes and Prospects Sticks and Jerseys-SJ03
06ITG Heroes and Prospects Sticks and Jerseys Gold-SJ03
07Upper Deck Ovation-97
07Upper Deck Victory-67
Black-67
Gold-67
GameBreakers-GB48
Oversize Cards-OS18
Stars on Ice-SI36

Bergeron, Philippe
99Bakersfield Condors-2

Bergeron, Pierre
04P.E.I. Rocket-26
05Quebec Remparts-18
05Quebec Remparts Signature Series-18
06Quebec Remparts-4

Bergeron, Remi
92Quebec Pee-Wee Tournament-595
98Bowman CHL-102
Golden Anniversary-102
OPC International-102
98Bowman Chrome CHL-102
Golden Anniversary-102
Golden Anniversary Refractors-102
OPC International-102
OPC International Refractors-102
Refractors-102
00Quebec Remparts-6
Signed-6

Bergeron, Yvan
907th Inn. Sketch QMJHL-101

Bergeron, Yves
72Nordiques Postcards-3
73Nordiques Team Issue-3

Bergevin, Marc
85Blackhawks Team Issue-10
86Blackhawks Coke-2
87Blackhawks Coke-2
89O-Pee-Chee-249
89ProCards AHL-251
91Pro Set Platinum-176
91Pro Set-397
French-397
91Whalers Jr. 7-Eleven-2
92Durivage Panini-30
92Lightning Sheraton-4
92Pinnacle-385
French-385
92Score-404
Canadian-404
92Stadium Club-174
92Topps-61
Gold-61G
92Ultra-200
93Lightning Season in Review-2
93OPC Premier-373
Gold-373
93Pinnacle-304
Canadian-304
Captains-22
Captains Canadian-22
93Score-363
Canadian-363
93Stadium Club-154
Members Only Master Set-154
OPC-154
First Day Issue-154
First Day Issue OPC-154
93Topps/OPC Premier-373
Gold-373
94Be A Player Signature Cards-10
94Leaf-384
94Lightning Photo Album-3
94OPC Premier-507
Special Effects-507
94Pinnacle-183
Artist's Proofs-183
Rink Collection-183
94Stadium Club-101
Members Only Master Set-101
First Day Issue-101
Super Team Winner Cards-101
94Topps/OPC Premier-507
Special Effects-507
95Swedish World Championships Stickers-9
96Be A Player-85
Autographs-85
Autographs Silver-85
97Pacific Invincible NHL Regime-166
97Score Blues-19
Platinum-19
Premier-19
97Upper Deck-351
99Blues Taco Bell-1
99O-Pee-Chee-242
99O-Pee-Chee Chrome-242
99O-Pee-Chee Chrome Refractors-242
99Panini Stickers-289
99Topps/OPC-242
99Topps/OPC Chrome-242
Refractors-242
00Pacific-340
Copper-340
Gold-340
Ice Blue-340
Premiere Date-340
00Upper Deck NHLPA-PA70
01O-Pee-Chee-253
01O-Pee-Chee Premier Parallel-253
01Topps-253
OPC Parallel-253
03Pacific Complete-347
Red-347

Bergevin-Robinson, Michel
02Baie Comeau Drakkar-17
02Shawinigan Cataractes-16

Bergfors, Nicklas
04Swedish Elitset-273
Gold-273
05Swedish SHL Elitset-127
Star Potential-14
05AHL Top Prospects-1
05Albany River Rats-3
05ITG Heroes and Prospects-210
Autographs Series II-NBG
06ITG Heroes and Prospects-158
Autographs-ANB

Berggren, Bjorn
84Swedish Semic Elitserien-145

Berggren, Bo
69Swedish Hockey-257
70Swedish Hockey-154
71Swedish Hockey-248
72Swedish Stickers-231
74Swedish Stickers-204
74Swedish Semic World Champ Stickers-22

Berggren, Johan
03Swedish Elite-258
Silver-258

Berggren, Pierre
03Swedish Elite-236
Silver-236
04Swedish Elitset-81
Gold-81

Bergin, Kevin
00Shawinigan Cataractes-14
Signed-14
01Greenville Grrrowl-13
03Roanoke Express-307
05Florida Everblades-20

Bergin, Tony
91Air Canada SJHL-E36
92Saskatchewan JHL-109
01Bossier-Shreveport Mudbugs-1
02Bossier-Shreveport Mudbugs-2
06Saint Johns Sea Dogs-19

Bergkvist, Jonas
95Swedish World Championships Stickers-154

Bergkvist, Lars-Arne
67Swedish Hockey-198

Bergkvist, Per Ragnar
95Upper Deck-564
Electric Ice-564
Electric Ice Gold-564
95Swedish Leaf-235

Bergkvist, Stefan
95Cleveland Lumberjacks-7
96Cleveland Lumberjacks Multi-Ad-5
97Cleveland Lumberjacks-5
97Cleveland Lumberjacks Postcards-22
00Swedish Upper Deck-109

Bergland, Tim
88ProCards AHL-26
89Capitals Kodak-11
89ProCards AHL-95
90Capitals Kodak-2
90Capitals Postcards-2
90Capitals Smokey-2
90O-Pee-Chee-507
90Pro Set-550
91Bowman-297
91Capitals Junior 5x7-2
91Capitals Kodak-2
91O-Pee-Chee-34
91Parkhurst-409
French-409
91Pro Set-507
French-507
91Stadium Club-351
91Topps-34
92Lightning Sheraton-5
92Stadium Club-127
92Topps-244
Gold-244G

92Atlanta Knights-21
93Atlanta Knights-20
98Chicago Wolves-3
98Chicago Wolves Turner Cup-21

Bergloff, Bob
82Birmingham South Stars-2

Berglund Sr., Bo
64Swedish Coralli ISHockey-147
65Swedish Coralli ISHockey-147

Berglund, Anders
86Swedish Panini Stickers-94
89Swedish Semic Elitserien Stickers-80
89Swedish Semic Elitserien Stickers-255
90Swedish Semic Elitserien Stickers-6
90Swedish Semic Elitserien Stickers-163
91Swedish Semic Elitserien Stickers-207
91Swedish Semic Elitserien Stickers-268
92Swedish Semic Elitserien Stickers-225
92Swedish Semic Elitserien Stickers-294
93Swedish Semic Elitserien-196
94Swedish Leaf-9
95Swedish Leaf-284
95Swedish Upper Deck-171

Berglund, Art
89Swedish Semic World Champ Stickers-152

Berglund, Bo
81Swedish Semic Hockey VM Stickers-15
83Vachon-61
83Swedish Semic VM Stickers-12
84O-Pee-Chee-276
85North Stars Postcards-4
87Swedish Panini Stickers-17
89Swedish Semic Elitserien Stickers-14
89Swedish Semic World Champ Stickers-14

Berglund, Carl-Axel
69Swedish Hockey-221

Berglund, Challe
04Swedish Alfabilder Alfa Stars-45
04Swedish Alfabilder Alfa Star Golden Ice-7
04Swedish Alfabilder Proof Parallels-45

Berglund, Charles
89Swedish Semic Elitserien Stickers-65
90Swedish Semic Elitserien Stickers-284
91Finnish Semic World Champ Stickers-42
91Swedish Semic Elitserien Stickers-66
91Swedish Semic Elitserien Stickers-351
91Swedish Semic World Champ Stickers-42
92Swedish Semic Elitserien Stickers-86
93Swedish Semic Elitserien-60
94Swedish Leaf-183
Gold Cards-3
95Finnish Semic World Championships-67
95Swedish Globe World Championships-37
95Swedish World Championships Stickers-149
95Swiss HNL-15
96Swiss HNL-15
97Swedish Collector's Choice-41
97Swedish Collector's Choice-210
98Swedish UD Choice-59
99Swedish Upper Deck-44
Lasting Impressions-3
00Swedish Upper Deck-50
04Swedish Alfabilder Autographs-121
04Swedish Alfabilder Limited Autographs-121

Berglund, Christian
99Swedish Upper Deck-68
99Swedish Upper Deck-206
00Swedish Upper Deck-85
00Swedish Upper Deck-190
SHL Excellence-S2
SHL Signatures-CH
01BAP Memorabilia-330
Emerald-330
Ruby-330
Sapphire-330
01Bowman YoungStars-114
Gold-114
Ice Cubed-114
01Parkhurst-327
01SPx-209
01Titanium Draft Day Edition-145
01UD Honor Roll-79
01UD Mask Collection-153
Gold-153
01UD Playmakers-126
01UD Premier Collection-101
01UD Top Shelf-132
01Upper Deck Ice-145
01Upper Deck MVP-227
01Upper Deck Victory-447
01Albany River Rats-16
02Devils Team Issue-13
02O-Pee-Chee-282
02O-Pee-Chee Premier Blue Parallel-282
02O-Pee-Chee Premier Red Parallel-282
02O-Pee-Chee Factory Set-282
02Pacific Calder-78
Silver-78
02Pacific Complete-509
Red-509
02Pacific Exclusive-101
02Private Stock Reserve-60
Blue-60
Red-60
Retail-60
02Topps-282
Factory Set-282
02Topps Total-223
02Albany River Rats-4
03Devils Team Issue-17
03Pacific Complete-92
Red-92
04Swedish Elitset-186
Gold-186
04Swedish Pure Skills-29
Parallel-29

Berglund, Rolf
69Swedish Hockey-75
83Swedish Semic Elitserien-35
84Swedish Semic Elitserien-32
85Swedish Panini Stickers-32
86Swedish Panini Stickers-8
87Swedish Panini Stickers-31

Berglund, Tomas
89Swedish Semic Elitserien Stickers-165
90Swedish Semic Elitserien Stickers-239
91Swedish Semic Elitserien Stickers-169
92Swedish Semic Elitserien Stickers-189
93Swedish Semic Elitserien-161
94Swedish Leaf-78
95Swedish Leaf-81
95Swedish Upper Deck-129
98Swedish UD Choice-141
99Swedish Upper Deck-143
00Swedish Upper Deck-128
02Swedish SHL-139
02Swedish SHL-225
Parallel-139
Parallel-225
03Swedish Elite-85
Enforcers-EF3
Silver-85
04Swedish Elitset-77
04Swedish Elitset-137
Gold-77
Gold-137

Berglund, Ulf
67Swedish Hockey-150

Bergman, Anders
83Swedish Semic Elitserien-149
85Swedish Panini Stickers-199
86Swedish Panini Stickers-192
87Swedish Panini Stickers-191
89Swedish Semic Elitserien Stickers-74
90Swedish Semic Elitserien Stickers-248
91Swedish Semic Elitserien Stickers-79
92Swedish Semic Elitserien Stickers-101
93Swedish Semic Elitserien-74

Bergman, Bo
73Swedish Stickers-231

Bergman, Gary
64Beehive Group III Photos-64
64Coca-Cola Caps-51
64Topps-8
65Coca-Cola-53
65Topps-107
66Topps-47
66Topps USA Test-47
67Topps-47
68Bauer Ads-2
68O-Pee-Chee-25
68Shirriff Coins-34
68Topps-25
69O-Pee-Chee-58
69Topps-58
70Colgate Stamps-73
70Dad's Cookies-6
70Esso Power Players-128
70O-Pee-Chee-154
70Red Wings Marathon-1
70Sargent Promotions Stamps-49
71Letraset Action Replays-19
71O-Pee-Chee-119
71Sargent Promotions Stamps-54
71Topps-119
71Toronto Sun-85
72O-Pee-Chee-164
Player Crests-8
Team Canada-3
72Sargent Promotions Stamps-79
72Topps-49
73Mac's Milk-1
73North Stars Postcards-2
73O-Pee-Chee-65
73Red Wings Team Issue-3
73Topps-65
74NHL Action Stamps-136
74NHL Action Stamps Update-9
75O-Pee-Chee NHL-236A
75O-Pee-Chee NHL-236B
75Topps-236
76Topps-159
81Red Wings Oldtimers-3
91Future Trends Canada '72-87
91Future Trends Canada '72 French-87
91Ultimate Original Six-67
French-67
94Parkhurst Tall Boys-57
95Parkhurst '66-67-41
Coins-41
03Parkhurst Original Six Detroit-59

Bergman, Jan
89Swedish Semic Elitserien Stickers-223
90Swedish Semic Elitserien Stickers-57
91Swedish Semic Elitserien Stickers-230

Bergman, Per
87Swedish Panini Stickers-264

Bergman, Peter
95Kamloops Blazers-9
98Calgary Hitmen-20
98Calgary Hitmen Autographs-20

Bergman, Robin
06Cedar Rapids RoughRiders-2

Bergman, Roger
72Swedish Stickers-287
73Swedish Stickers-154
74Swedish Stickers-160

Bergman, Thommie
69Swedish Hockey-249
70Swedish Hockey-132
71Finnish Suomi Stickers-42
71Swedish Hockey-6
71Swedish Hockey-224
72Finnish Jaakiekko-43
72Finnish Hellas-25
72Finnish Semic World Championship-55
72Swedish Stickers-4
72Swedish Stickers-46
72Swedish Stickers-288
72Swedish Semic World Championship-55
73O-Pee-Chee-204
73Red Wings Team Issue-4
73Red Wings McCarthy Postcards-2
74NHL Action Stamps-108
74O-Pee-Chee NHL-365
74Finnish Jenkki-23
74Swedish Stickers-315
75O-Pee-Chee WHA-29
76O-Pee-Chee WHA-51
79O-Pee-Chee-148
79Red Wings Postcards-1
79Topps-148
87Swedish Panini Stickers-211

Bergmark, Erling
69Swedish Hockey-166

Bergqvist, Fredrik
91Swedish Semic Elitserien Stickers-211
92Swedish Semic Elitserien Stickers-234
93Swedish Semic Elitserien-203
94Swedish Leaf-294
95Swedish Upper Deck 1st Division Stars-DS17
98Swedish UD Choice-21
06Swedish SHL Elitset-128

Bergqvist, Hans
67Swedish Hockey-84

Bergqvist, Jan-Ivar
67Swedish Hockey-231

Bergqvist, Jonas
83Swedish Semic Elitserien-140
84Swedish Semic Elitserien-160
85Swedish Panini Stickers-145
86Swedish Panini Stickers-156
87Swedish Panini Stickers-158
89Swedish Semic World Champ Stickers-17
91Swedish Semic Elitserien Stickers-149
91Swedish Semic Elitserien Stickers-356
92Swedish Semic Elitserien Stickers-167
93Swedish Semic Elitserien-136
94Finnish Jaa Kiekko-73
94Swedish Leaf-250
Gold Cards-9
Studio Signatures-6
95Finnish Semic World Championships-63
95Swedish Leaf-69
Mega-2
95Swedish Upper Deck-105
95Swedish Globe World Championships-34
96Swedish Semic Wien-71
96Swedish Semic Wien Coca-Cola Dream Team-12
97Swedish Collector's Choice-113
97Swedish Collector's Choice-202
97Swedish Collector's Choice-221
Crash the Game Exchange-C10
Crash the Game Redemption-R10
Select-UD10
Stick'Ums-S15
04Swedish Alfabilder Alfa Stars-43
04Swedish Alfabilder Alfa Star Golden Ice-1
04Swedish Alfabilder Autographs-116
04Swedish Alfabilder Limited Autographs-116
04Swedish Alfabilder Proof Parallels-43

Bergqvist, Kenneth
99Swedish Upper Deck-31
99Swedish Upper Deck-202
00Swedish Upper Deck-42
01Swedish Brynas Tigers-3
03Swedish Elite-169
Silver-169
04Swedish Elitset-22
04Swedish Elitset-260
Gold-22
Gold-260
05Swedish SHL Elitset-115
06Swedish SHL Elitset-122

Bergqvist, Stefan
93Swedish Semic Elitserien-125
94Classic-28
Gold-28
95Cleveland Lumberjacks Postcards-7
95Classic-88
96Upper Deck-323
98Swedish UD Choice-122
99Swedish Upper Deck-108
Snapshots-8

Bergseng, Arne
92Norwegian Elite Series-97

Bergseng, Lars
92Norwegian Elite Series-101

Bergstrom, Calle
04Swedish Elitset-255
Gold-255
05Swedish SHL Elitset-106
06German DEL-29
06Swedish SHL Elitset-120

Bergstrom, Erik
92Swedish Semic Elitserien Stickers-276
94Swedish Leaf-169
95Swedish Leaf-127

Bergstrom, Nicklas
05Swedish SHL Elitset-120

Berkery, J.P.
93Quebec Pee-Wee Tournament-684

Berkhoel, Adam
04Gwinnett Gladiators-2
05Beehive-173
Matte-173
05Black Diamond-214
05Hot Prospects-188
Red Hot-188
05Parkhurst Signatures-AB
05SP Authentic-207
05SP Game Used-167
Gold-167
05SPx-202
Spectrum-202
05The Cup-188
Black Rainbow Rookies-188
Masterpiece Pressplates (Artifacts)-246
Masterpiece Pressplates (Bee Hive)-173
Masterpiece Pressplates (Black Diamond)-214
Masterpiece Pressplates (Ice)-144
Masterpiece Pressplates (Rookie Update)-104
Masterpiece Pressplates SPA Autos-207
Masterpiece Pressplates (SP Game Used)-167
Masterpiece Pressplates (SPx)-202
Masterpiece Pressplates (Trilogy)-224
Masterpiece Pressplates Ult Coll-136
Masterpiece Pressplates Autographs-188
Platinum Rookies-188
05UD Artifacts-246
05Ultimate Collection-136
Gold-136
05Ultra-203
Gold-203
Ice-203
05Upper Deck-477
05Upper Deck Ice-144
05Upper Deck Rookie Update-104
05Upper Deck Trilogy-224
06Black Diamond Gemography-GAB

Berks, Greg
93Quebec Pee-Wee Tournament-699

Berlin, Christian
94German First League-482

Berlinquette, Louis
23V128-1 Paulin's Candy-32
24Anonymous NHL-47
24C144 Champ's Cigarettes-4
24V130 Maple Crispette-30
24V145-2-41

Berman, Aaron
04Langley Hornets-2

Bermingham, Jason
98Huntington Blizzard-8
99Huntington Blizzard-6
02Arkansas Riverblades-1
03Tulsa Oilers-2
05Knoxville Ice Bears-1

Bermingham, Jim
907th Inn. Sketch QMJHL-49
907th Inn. Sketch Memorial Cup-71
917th Inn. Sketch QMJHL-226
93Wheeling Thunderbirds-5
94Huntington Blizzard-4
96Anaheim Bullfrogs RHI-15
98ECHL All-Star Northern Conference-6
98Huntington Blizzard-11
99Huntington Blizzard-8
00Jackson Bandits-15
04Knoxville Ice Bears-22
05Knoxville Ice Bears-19

Bernakevitch, Brendan
05Manchester Monarchs-25

Bernaquez, Bernie
51Bas Du Fleuve-46
52Bas Du Fleuve-26

Bernard, Alain
93Swiss HNL-326

Bernard, Chris
98Fayetteville Force-11
99Missouri River Otters-3

Bernard, Jean-Francois
04P.E.I. Rocket-28

Bernard, Kenny
03Ohio State Buckeyes-18
04Ohio State Buckeyes-4
05Ohio State Buckeyes-4
06Ohio State Buckeyes-4

Bernard, Larry
89ProCards AHL-32
90Moncton Hawks-1
90ProCards AHL/IHL-245
93Flint Generals-14
94Flint Generals-2
00Sarnia Sting-2

Bernard, Louis
917th Inn. Sketch QMJHL-276
93Drummondville Voltigeurs-11
94Fredericton Canadiens-1
94Wheeling Thunderbirds-19
95Fredericton Canadiens-1
97Toledo Storm-1
99Fort Worth Brahmas-1
01Thetford Mines Coyotes-2
02Thetford Mines Coyotes-2
03Thetford Mines Prolab-2

Bernard, Mark
90Hampton Roads Admirals-57
91Hampton Roads Admirals-1
92Hampton Roads Admirals-16
95Hampton Roads Admirals-5
98Hampton Roads Admirals 10th Anniversary-11
01UK Manchester Storm Retro-10
01Roanoke Express-23
03Rockford Ice Hogs-20

Bernasconi, Nicolas
01Swiss HNL-286
02Swiss HNL-353

Bernatsky, Sergei
03Russian Hockey League-283

Berndaner, Ignaz
79Panini Stickers-98
83Swedish Semic VM Stickers-104

Berndtsson Sr., Peter
83Swedish Semic Elitserien-117
84Swedish Semic Elitserien-117
87Swedish Panini Stickers-119

Berndtsson, Peter
89Swedish Semic Elitserien Stickers-279
90Swedish Semic Elitserien Stickers-44
91Swedish Semic Elitserien Stickers-295
92Swedish Semic Elitserien Stickers-314
93Swedish Semic Elitserien-281
94Swedish Leaf-70
95Swedish Leaf-143
95Swedish Upper Deck-213
97Swedish Collector's Choice-80
98Swedish UD Choice-77
99Swedish Upper Deck-82

Bernhardt, Justin
04Regina Pats-9
05Regina Pats-1
06Regina Pats-1

Bernhardt, Oliver
99German Bundesliga 2-210
01German Upper Deck-109
02German DEL City Press-152
04German DEL-165
05German SC Bietigheim-Bissingen Steelers-4

Bernhardt, Sascha
94German First League-148

Bernhardt, Tim
85Maple Leafs Postcards-3
85O-Pee-Chee-166
85O-Pee-Chee Stickers-9
86Maple Leafs Postcards-3
88ProCards AHL-244
89ProCards AHL-110

Bernie, John
907th Inn. Sketch OHL-61

Bernier, Art
10C56-25
10Sweet Caporal Postcards-37
11C55-37
12C57-6

Bernier, Danny
93Quebec Pee-Wee Tournament-1116

Bernier, David
92Quebec Pee-Wee Tournament-204
98Quebec Remparts-2
Signed-2

Bernier, Jean
76Nordiques Postcards-3
77O-Pee-Chee WHA-2

Bernier, Jonathan
05ITG Heroes/Prosp Toronto Expo Parallel -152
05ITG Heroes and Prospects-152
Autographs-A-JBE
Team Cherry-TC18
06Between The Pipes-24
Aspiring-AS10
Aspiring Gold-AS10
Autographs-AJBE
Emblems-GUE22
Emblems Gold-GUE22
Emblems Autographs-GUE22
Jerseys-GUJ22
Jerseys Gold-GUJ22
Jerseys Autographs-GUJ22
Numbers-GUN22
Numbers Gold-GUN22
Numbers Autographs-GUN22
Playing For Your Country-PC01
Playing For Your Country Gold-PC01
Prospect Trios-PT06
Prospect Trios-PT12
Prospect Trios-PT14
Prospect Trios Gold-PT06
Prospect Trios Gold-PT12
Prospect Trios Gold-PT14
06ITG International Ice Goaltending Glory-GG09
06ITG International Ice Goaltending Glory Gold-GG09
06ITG Heroes and Prospects-111
06ITG Heroes and Prospects-141
Autographs-AJB1
Autographs-AJB2
CHL Top Prospects-TP10
CHL Top Prospects Gold-TP10
Class of 2006-CL07
Complete CHL Logos-CHL10
Net Prospects-NPR10
Net Prospects Gold-NPR10

Bernier, Marc-Andre
01Halifax Mooseheads-19
02Halifax Mooseheads-18
03Cape Breton Screaming Eagles-41
04Halifax Mooseheads-19
06Manitoba Moose-19

Bernier, Pascal
917th Inn. Sketch QMJHL-265

Bernier, Patrick
05Shawinigan Cataractes-9

Bernier, Sebastien
04Quebec Remparts-19
06Drummondville Voltigeurs-18

Bernier, Serge
70Esso Power Players-214
71Bazooka-24
71O-Pee-Chee-19
71Sargent Promotions Stamps-155
71Topps-19
71Toronto Sun-189
72Flyers Mighty Milk-1
72O-Pee-Chee-152
72Sargent Promotions Stamps-97
72Topps-36
74O-Pee-Chee WHA-5
74Team Canada L'Equipe WHA-2
75O-Pee-Chee WHA-60
75O-Pee-Chee WHA-70
76Nordiques Marie Antoinette-2
76Nordiques Postcards-4
76O-Pee-Chee WHA-109
77O-Pee-Chee WHA-60
79O-Pee-Chee-47
79Topps-47
80Nordiques Postcards-2
80O-Pee-Chee-309
80Pepsi-Cola Caps-61

Bernier, Steve
93Quebec Pee-Wee Tournament-247
01Moncton Wildcats-25
02Moncton Wildcats-23
03BAP Memorabilia Draft Redemptions-16
03Moncton Wildcats-23
03Moncton Wildcats-NNO
04Moncton Wildcats-21
04ITG Heroes and Prospects-106
Autographs-SBE
04ITG Heroes/Prospects Toronto Expo '05-106
04ITG Heroes/Prospects Expo Heroes/Pros-106
05ITG Heroes/Prosp Toronto Expo Parallel -265
05Beehive-150
Beige -150
Blue -150
Gold-150
Red -150
Matte-150
Signature Scrapbook-SSBE
05Black Diamond-274
05Hot Prospects-264
En Fuego-264
Hot Materials-HMSB
05Parkhurst-662
Facsimile Auto Parallel-662
Signatures-SB
True Colors-TCSJS
True Colors-TCSJS
05SP Authentic-194
Limited-194
Rarefied Rookies-RRSB
05SP Game Used-181
Autographs-181
Gold-181
05SPx-240
Spectrum-240
05The Cup-120
Autographed Rookie Patches Gold Rainbow-120
Black Rainbow Rookies-120
Masterpiece Pressplates (Artifacts)-319
Masterpiece Pressplates (Bee Hive)-150
Masterpiece Pressplates (Black Diamond)-274
Masterpiece Pressplates (Ice)-176
Masterpiece Pressplates (Rookie Update)-230
Masterpiece Pressplates SPA Autos-194
Masterpiece Pressplates (SP Game Used)-181
Masterpiece Pressplates SPx Autos-240
Masterpiece Pressplates (Trilogy)-295
Masterpiece Pressplates Ult Coll-187
Masterpiece Pressplates (Victory)-296
Masterpiece Pressplates Autographs-120
Platinum Rookies-120
05UD Artifacts-319
05Ultimate Collection-187
Gold-187
Ultimate Debut Threads Jerseys-DTJSB
Ultimate Debut Threads Jerseys Autos-DAJSB
Ultimate Debut Threads Patches-DTPSB
Ultimate Debut Threads Patches Autos-DAPSB
05Upper Deck-470
05Upper Deck Ice-176
05Upper Deck Rookie Update-230
Inspirations Patch Rookies-230
05Upper Deck Trilogy-295
05Upper Deck Victory-296
Black-296
Gold-296
Silver-296
05AHL Top Prospects-2
05Cleveland Barons-2
05ITG Heroes and Prospects-265
Autographs Series II-SBR
06Be A Player-161
Autographs-161
Signatures-SB
Signatures 10-178
Signatures Duals-DCB
Signatures Trios-TTBM
Portraits Signature Portraits-SPSB
06Beehive Signature Scrapbook-SSSB
06Black Diamond-69
Black-69
Gold-69
Ruby-69
06Flair Showcase Wave of the Future-WF37
06Fleer-165
Tiffany-165
06O-Pee-Chee-407
06O-Pee-Chee-642
Rainbow-407
Rainbow-642
Autographs-A-SB
Swatches-S-SB
06Panini Stickers-334
06SP Authentic Sign of the Times Duals-STCB
06SP Game Used Inked Sweaters-ISSB
06SP Game Used Inked Sweaters Patches-ISSB
06SP Game Used Letter Marks-LMSB
06SP Game Used SIGnificance-SSB
06The Cup Autographed NHL Shields Duals-DASTB
06UD Toronto Fall Expo Priority Signings -PSSB
06Ultimate Collection Signatures-US-SB
06Ultra-165
Gold Medallion-165
Ice Medallion-165
06Upper Deck Arena Giveaways-SJS3
06Upper Deck-165
Exclusives Parallel-165
High Gloss Parallel-165
Game Jerseys-J2SB
Game Patches-J2SB
Masterpieces-165
Signatures-SSB
06Upper Deck MVP-243
Gold Script-243
Super Script-243
Autographs-OABM
06Upper Deck Ovation-194
06Upper Deck Victory-168
06Upper Deck Victory Black-168
06Upper Deck Victory Gold-168

Bernikov, Ruslan
99Russian Hockey League-118
00Russian Hockey League-13
03Russian Hockey League-114

Bernstrom, Jorgen
02Swedish SHL-99
Parallel-99

Beroun, Jiri
03Czech OFS Plus-372
04Czech OFS-402
06Czech OFS-198

Berra, Andre
72Finnish Semic World Championship-142
72Swedish Semic World Championship-142

Berrigan, Pat
92Quebec Pee-Wee Tournament-1611
93Quebec Pee-Wee Tournament-507

Berrington, Paul
01UK Dundee Stars-5
02UK Dundee Stars-5

Berruex, Clement
93Quebec Pee-Wee Tournament-1497

Berry, Bob
70Esso Power Players-158
71O-Pee-Chee-76
71Topps-76
71Toronto Sun-106
72O-Pee-Chee-9
72Sargent Promotions Stamps-98
72Topps-21
73O-Pee-Chee-175
73Topps-172
74NHL Action Stamps-120
74O-Pee-Chee NHL-18
74Topps-18
75O-Pee-Chee NHL-196
75Topps-196
75Topps-320
76O-Pee-Chee NHL-300
77O-Pee-Chee NHL-268
81Canadiens Postcards-3
82Canadiens Postcards-2
83Canadiens Postcards-2
86Penguins Kodak-1
93Kraft-28

Berry, Brad
86Jets Postcards-1
87Jets Postcards-1
89Jets Safeway-3
90Swedish Semic Elitserien Stickers-178
91ProCards-147
92Parkhurst-312
Emerald Ice-312
94Stars HockeyKaps-2
96Michigan K-Wings-3
98Michigan K-Wings-12
03North Dakota Fighting Sioux-9
04North Dakota Fighting Sioux-27

Berry, Brent
92British Columbia JHL-156

Berry, Doug
79Rockies Team Issue-2

Berry, Fred
81Milwaukee Admirals-3

Berry, Ken
81Swedish Semic Hockey VM Stickers-88
84Nova Scotia Oilers-8
88Canucks Mohawk-3
88Oilers Tenth Anniversary-67

Berry, Nathan
99Des Moines Buccaneers-4

Berry, Rick
95Seattle Thunderbirds-3
96Seattle Thunderbirds-6
97Seattle Thunderbirds-6
98Hershey Bears-12
00SPx-156
00Hershey Bears-2
01Avalanche Team Issue-9
01BAP Memorabilia-237
01BAP Memorabilia-485
Emerald-237
Emerald-485
Ruby-237
Ruby-485
Sapphire-237
Sapphire-485
01BAP Signature Series-231
Autographs-231
Autographs Gold-231
01O-Pee-Chee-303
01O-Pee-Chee Premier Parallel-303
01Pacific-96
Extreme LTD-96
Hobby LTD-96
Premiere Date-96
Retail LTD-96
01Pacific Arena Exclusives-96
01Parkhurst-288
01Parkhurst Beckett Promos-288
01Topps-303
OPC Parallel-303
05Milwaukee Admirals Pepsi-2

Berry, Ryan
92Quebec Pee-Wee Tournament-1011
94Spokane Chiefs-11
95Spokane Chiefs-18

Berryman, Nicolas
92Quebec Pee-Wee Tournament-477
93Quebec Pee-Wee Tournament-1382

Bertaggia, Sandro
91Finnish Semic World Champ Stickers-184
91Swedish Semic World Champ Stickers-184
92Finnish Semic-200
93Swedish Semic World Champ Stickers-116
93Swiss HNL-88
95Swedish Globe World Championships-213
95Swedish World Championships Stickers-119
95Swiss HNL-137
95Swiss HNL-507
95Swiss HNL-510
96Swiss HNL-154
96Swiss HNL-530
98Swiss Power Play Stickers-157
99Swiss Panini Stickers-157
00Swiss Panini Stickers-202
00Swiss Slapshot Mini-Cards-HCL4
01Swiss HNL-29
02Swiss HNL-24

Bertell, Kristen
66Finnish Jaakiekkosarja-112

Bertelsen, Jorn Ole
98Danish Hockey League-148

Berthelsen, Peter
88Lethbridge Hurricanes-2
89Lethbridge Hurricanes-2

Berthiaume, Ben
03St. Francis Xavier X-Men-8

Berthiaume, Daniel
84Chicoutimi Sagueneens-4
86Sherbrooke Canadiens-5
87Jets Postcards-2
87O-Pee-Chee-217
87O-Pee-Chee Minis-3
87O-Pee-Chee Stickers-249
87Panini Stickers-356
88Jets Postcards-3
88O-Pee-Chee-142
88O-Pee-Chee Stickers-149
88Panini Stickers-148
88Topps-142
89Jets Safeway-4
89O-Pee-Chee-296
90Kings Smokey-19
90O-Pee-Chee-180
90O-Pee-Chee-247
90OPC Premier-5
90Pro Set-454
90Score Rookie/Traded-73T
90Topps-180
90Topps-247
Tiffany-247
90Upper Deck-381
90Upper Deck-412
French-381
French-412
91Bowman-190
91Bruins Sports Action-3
91O-Pee-Chee-313
91Pinnacle-165
French-165
91Score American-132
91Score Canadian Bilingual-132
91Score Canadian English-132
91Stadium Club-290
91Topps-313
91Upper Deck-150
French-150
91Finnish Semic World Champ Stickers-54
91Swedish Semic World Champ Stickers-54
92Bowman-140
92Parkhurst-359
Emerald Ice-359
92Senators Team Issue-2
92Stadium Club-101
92Topps-505
Gold-505G
92Ultra-361
93Ultra-54
95Roanoke Express-14
98Roanoke Express-6
00Roanoke Express-11
01Roanoke Express-1
02Greensboro Generals RBI-5
03Greensboro Generals-179

Bertholet, Johan
95Swiss HNL-61
96Swiss HNL-260
01Swiss HNL-424

Berti, Adam
03Oshawa Generals-21
04ITG Top Prospects Spring Expo-3
04Oshawa Generals-15
04Oshawa Generals Autographs-15
04ITG Heroes and Prospects-51
Autographs-AB
Top Prospects-3
04ITG Heroes/Prospects Toronto Expo '05-51
04ITG Heroes/Prospects Expo Heroes/Pros-51
05Erie Otters-20
06Norfolk Admirals-16

Berti, Chris
99UD Prospects-15
00Sarnia Sting-3

Bertins, Jergis
98Tacoma Sabercats-2

Bertogliat, Jesse
92Minnesota Golden Gophers-2
93Minnesota Golden Gophers-2
94Minnesota Golden Gophers-3
95Minnesota Golden Gophers-6

Bertoli, Scott
00Trenton Titans-1
01Trenton Titans-2-2
02Trenton Titans-A-1
03Trenton Titans-355

Bertolotti, Reto
95Swiss HNL-NNO

Bertram, Dan
03Camrose Kodiaks-1
07ITG Going For Gold World Juniors-18
Autographs-18
Emblems-GUE18
Jerseys-GUJ18
Numbers-GUN18

Bertram, Kevin
01Fort Wayne Komets-2
02Fort Wayne Komets-3
02Fort Wayne Komets Shoe Carnival-10
03Fort Wayne Komets-18
03Fort Wayne Komets 2003 Champions-10
03Fort Wayne Komets Shoe Carnival-3

Bertram, Preben
98Danish Hockey League-21

Bertrand, Eric
93Quebec Pee-Wee Tournament-911
96Albany River Rats-1
97Albany River Rats-1
98Albany River Rats-1
00Quebec Citadelles-21
Signed-21
02BAP Memorabilia-360
02Parkhurst-237
Bronze-237
Gold-237
Silver-237
02Hershey Bears-1
03German DEL-183
04St Georges de Beauce Garaga-8
05German DEL-183

Bertrand, Hugh
97New Mexico Scorpions-18

Bertrand, Marc
80Quebec Remparts-1

Bertrand, Philippe
03Cape Breton Screaming Eagles-27
04Cape Breton Screaming Eagles-5
05Cape Breton Screaming Eagles-13

Bertrand, Ron
897th Inn. Sketch OHL-172
907th Inn. Sketch OHL-303
917th Inn. Sketch OHL-52

Bertrand-Duclos, Dave
06Gatineau Olympiques-24

Bertsch, Jay
94Spokane Chiefs-6
95Spokane Chiefs-23
96Spokane Chiefs-20

Bertuzzi, Brian
84Kamloops Blazers-3
86Fredericton Express-2

Bertuzzi, Ed
88Kamloops Blazers-3

Bertuzzi, Todd
917th Inn. Sketch OHL-357
93Guelph Storm-23
93Classic-14
93Classic Four-Sport *-204
Gold-204
94Guelph Storm-22
94Classic-103
Gold-103
Tri-Cards-T40
95Be A Player-168
Signatures-S168
Signatures Die Cuts-S168
95Bowman-156
All-Foil-156
Bowman's Best-BB30
Bowman's Best Refractors-BB30
95Donruss-346
Rated Rookies-2
95Donruss Elite-57
Die Cut Stars-57
Die Cut Uncut-57
Rookies-4
95Emotion-103
generatioNext-8
95Finest-146
Refractors-146
95Leaf Limited-19
Rookie Phenoms-10
95Metal-171
95Parkhurst International-264
Emerald Ice-264
Parkie's Trophy Picks-PP44
95Select Certified-123
Mirror Gold-123
95SkyBox Impact-208
95SP-88
95Stadium Club-204
Members Only Master Set-204
95Summit-193
Artist's Proofs-193
Ice-193
95Topps-339
OPC Inserts-339
SuperSkills Super Rookies-SR7
95Ultra-331
High Speed-3
95Upper Deck Special Edition-SE53
95Upper Deck Special Edition Gold-SE53
95Zenith-140
Rookie Roll Call-9
95Classic-85
95Images-37
Gold-37
96Black Diamond-84
Gold-84
96Collector's Choice-164
96Collector's Choice-323
96Collector's Choice-338
96Donruss Rated Rookies-9
96Donruss Canadian Ice-28
Gold Press Proofs-28
Red Press Proofs-28
96Donruss Elite-18
Die Cut Stars-18
Aspirations-4
96Fleer-63
Rookie Sensations-2
96Islander Postcards-3
96Leaf-205
Press Proofs-205
96Leaf Limited-19
Gold-19
Stubble-9
96Leaf Preferred-93
Press Proofs-93
Steel-20
Steel Gold-20
96Metal Universe-91
96Pinnacle-208
Artist's Proofs-208
Foil-208
Premium Stock-208
Rink Collection-208
96Score-244
Artist's Proofs-244
Dealer's Choice Artist's Proofs-244
Special Artist's Proofs-244
Golden Blades-244
96Select Certified-80
Artist's Proofs-80
Blue-80
Mirror Blue-80
Mirror Gold-80
Mirror Red-80
Red-80
96SkyBox Impact-74
96SkyBox Impact-166
NHL on Fox-2
96SP-96
96SPx-30
Gold-30
96Summit-154
Artist's Proofs-154
Ice-154
Metal-154
Premium Stock-154
96Topps Picks-121
OPC Inserts-121
Rookie Stars-RS10
Rookie Stars OPC-RS10
96Ultra-99
Gold Medallion-99
96Upper Deck-291
Generation Next-X14
Power Performers-P7
96Zenith-81
Artist's Proofs-81
Assailants-6
97Be A Player-168
Autographs-168
Autographs Die-Cuts-168
Autographs Prismatic Die-Cuts-168

97Collector's Choice-154
97Donruss-12
Press Proofs Silver-12
Press Proofs Gold-12
97Donruss Limited-30
Exposure-30
97Donruss Priority-155
Stamp of Approval-155
97Leaf-134
Fractal Matrix-134
Fractal Matrix Die Cuts-134
97Leaf International-134
Universal Ice-134
97Pacific Invincible NHL Regime-115
97Paramount-107
Copper-107
Dark Grey-107
Emerald Green-107
Ice Blue-107
Red-107
Silver-107
97SP Authentic-96
97Upper Deck-103
98Aurora-186
98Be A Player-292
Press Release-292
98BAP Gold-292
98BAP Autographs-292
98BAP Autographs Gold-292
98Pacific-424
Ice Blue-424
Red-424
98Pacific Dynagon Ice-185
Blue-185
Red-185
98Paramount-232
Copper-232
Emerald Green-232
Holo-Electric-232
Ice Blue-232
Silver-232
98SPx Finite-85
Radiance-85
Spectrum-85
98UD Choice-212
Prime Choice Reserve-212
Reserve-212
98Upper Deck-194
Exclusives-194
Exclusives 1 of 1-194
Gold Reserve-194
99BAP Memorabilia-23
Gold-23
Silver-23
99O-Pee-Chee-38
99O-Pee-Chee Chrome-38
99O-Pee-Chee Chrome Refractors-38
99Pacific-420
Copper-420
Emerald Green-420
Gold-420
Ice Blue-420
Premiere Date-420
Red-420
99Pacific Omega-231
Copper-231
Gold-231
Ice Blue-231
Premiere Date-231
99Topps/OPC-38
99Topps/OPC Chrome-38
Refractors-38
99Upper Deck Victory-301
00BAP Memorabilia-299
Emerald-299
Ruby-299
Sapphire-299
Promos-299
00BAP Mem Chicago Sportsfest Copper-299
00BAP Memorabilia Chicago Sportsfest Blue-299
00BAP Memorabilia Chicago Sportsfest Gold-299
00BAP Memorabilia Chicago Sportsfest Ruby-299
00BAP Memorabilia Chicago Sun-Times Ruby-299
00BAP Memorabilia Chicago Sun-Times Gold-299
00BAP Mem Chicago Sun-Times Sapphire-299
00BAP Mem Toronto Fall Expo Copper-299
00BAP Memorabilia Toronto Fall Expo Gold-299
00BAP Memorabilia Toronto Fall Expo Ruby-299
00BAP Parkhurst 2000-P20
00BAP Signature Series-81
Emerald-81
Ruby-81
Sapphire-81
Autographs-60
Autographs Gold-60
00O-Pee-Chee-99
00O-Pee-Chee Parallel-99
00Pacific-404
Copper-404
Gold-404
Ice Blue-404
Premiere Date-404
00Panini Stickers-211
00Paramount-236
Copper-236
Gold-236
Holo-Gold-236
Holo-Silver-236
Ice Blue-236
Premiere Date-236
00Revolution-142
Blue-142
Premiere Date-142
Red-142
00Stadium Club-110
00Topps/OPC-99
Parallel-99
00Upper Deck-169
Exclusives Tier 1-169
Exclusives Tier 2-169
00Upper Deck MVP-176
First Stars-176
Second Stars-176
Third Stars-176
00Upper Deck Vintage-349
01BAP Memorabilia-100
Emerald-100
Ruby-100
Sapphire-100
01BAP Signature Series Jerseys-GJ-68
01BAP Signature Series Jersey Autographs-GUTB
01BAP Sig Series Jersey and Stick Cards-GSJ-68
01BAP Update He Shoots-He Scores Points-1
01BAP Update He Shoots-He Scores Prizes-30
01Canucks Postcards-1
01O-Pee-Chee-178
01O-Pee-Chee Premier Parallel-178
01Pacific-377
Extreme LTD-377
Hobby LTD-377
Premiere Date-377
Retail LTD-377
01Pacific Adrenaline-187
Blue-187
Premiere Date-187
Red-187
Retail-187
01Pacific Arena Exclusives-377
01Parkhurst-174
Teammates-T17
01Sports Illustrated for Kids III-280
01Stadium Club-65
Award Winners-65
Master Photos-65
01Titanium-134
Hobby Parallel-134
Premiere Date-134
Retail-134
Retail Parallel-134
Double-Sided Jerseys-55
Double-Sided Patches-55
01Titanium Draft Day Edition-92
01Topps-178
OPC Parallel-178
01UD Mask Collection-94
Gold-94
01Upper Deck-401
Exclusives-401
01Upper Deck MVP-181
01Upper Deck Victory-341
Gold-341
01Upper Deck Vintage-249
01Upper Deck Vintage-251
02Atomic-95
Blue-95
Gold-95
Red-95
Hobby Parallel-95
Power Converters-18
Super Colliders-16
02BAP First Edition-73
02BAP First Edition-371
02BAP First Edition-411H
Jerseys-73
02BAP Memorabilia-114
02BAP Memorabilia-245
Emerald-114
Emerald-245
Ruby-114
Ruby-245
Sapphire-114
Sapphire-245
He Shoots-He Scores Prizes-23
NHL All-Star Game-114
NHL All-Star Game-245
NHL All-Star Game Blue-114
NHL All-Star Game Blue-245
NHL All-Star Game Green-114
NHL All-Star Game Green-245
NHL All-Star Game Red-114
NHL All-Star Game Red-245
Stanley Cup Playoffs-SC-13
02BAP Memorabilia Toronto Fall Expo-114
02BAP Memorabilia Toronto Fall Expo-245
02BAP Signature Series-9
Autographs-9
Autograph Buybacks 1998-292
Autographs Gold-9
Golf-GS95
Jerseys-SGJ32
Jersey Autographs-SGJ32
Team Quads-TQ14
02BAP Ultimate Memorabilia Jerseys-38
02BAP Ultimate Mem Jersey and Stick-29
02Bowman YoungStars-4
Gold-4
Silver-4
02Canucks Team Issue-2
02Crown Royale-94
Blue-94
Red-94
Retail-94
02eTopps-23
02ITG Used-76
02ITG Used-176
Jerseys-GUJ32
Jersey Autographs-GUJ32
Jerseys Gold-GUJ32
Jersey and Stick-SJ32
Jersey and Stick Gold-SJ32
Teammates-T19
Teammates Gold-T19
02McDonald's Pacific-39
Clear Advantage-6
02NHL Power Play Stickers-146
02O-Pee-Chee-217
02O-Pee-Chee Jumbos-25
02O-Pee-Chee Premier Blue Parallel-217
02O-Pee-Chee Premier Red Parallel-217
02O-Pee-Chee Factory Set-217
02O-Pee-Chee Factory Set Hometown Heroes-HHC6
02Pacific-373
Blue-373
Red-373
Lamplighters-13
02Pacific Complete-102
Red-102
02Pacific Exclusive-165
02Pacific Heads-Up-119
Blue-119
Purple-119
Red-119
Inside the Numbers-22
Quad Jerseys-27
Quad Jerseys Gold-27
Stat Masters-14
02Pacific Quest for the Cup-94
Gold-94
Chasing the Cup-18
02Parkhurst-35
Bronze-35
Gold-35
Silver-35
Jerseys-GJ29
Patented Power-PP8
Stick and Jerseys-SJ29
Teammates-TT18
02Parkhurst Retro-5
Minis-5
He Shoots-He Scores Prizes-23
Jerseys-RJ29
Jersey and Sticks-RSJ20
02Private Stock Reserve-147
Red-147
Retail-147
Patches-147
02SP Authentic-87
02SP Authentic-104
Beckett Promos-87
02SPx-72
Spectrum Gold-72
Spectrum Silver-72
02Stadium Club-50
Silver Decoy Cards-50
Proofs-50
Beam Team-BT13
Lone Star Signatures Blue-LSTB
Lone Star Signatures Red-LSTB
Passport-5
02Titanium-95
Blue-95
Red-95
Retail-95
Saturday Knights-10
02Topps-217
OPC Blue Parallel-217
OPC Red Parallel-217
Topps/OPC Hometown Heroes-HHC6
Own The Game-OTG3
Factory Set-217
02Topps Chrome-120
Black Border Refractors-120
Refractors-120
02Topps Heritage-22
Chrome Parallel-22
Autographs-TB
Autographs Black-TB
Autographs Red-TB
02Topps Total-334
Production-TP14
Team Checklists-TTC29
02UD Artistic Impressions-85
Gold-85
02UD Artistic Impressions Beckett Promos-85
02UD Artistic Impressions Retrospectives-R85
02UD Artistic Impressions Retrospect Gold-R85
02UD Artistic Impress Retrospect Silver-R85
02UD Honor Roll-67
Team Warriors-TW15
02UD Piece of History-85
02UD Premier Collection-52A
02UD Top Shelf-85
02Upper Deck-168
Exclusives-168
Blow-Ups-C40
Number Crunchers-NC14
Sizzling Scorers-SS14
02Upper Deck Classic Portraits-95
02Upper Deck MVP-177
Gold-177
Classics-177
Golden Classics-177
02Upper Deck Rookie Update-95
02Upper Deck Rookie Update-149B
02Upper Deck Rookie Update-150B
Jerseys-DTB
Jerseys Gold-DTB
02Upper Deck Victory-209
Bronze-209
Gold-209
Silver-209
02Upper Deck Vintage-245
02Upper Deck Vintage-289
02Upper Deck Vintage-308
Tall Boys-T63
Tall Boys Gold-T63
02Vanguard-94
LTD-94
03McFarlane Hockey-100
03McFarlane Hockey-102
03BAP Memorabilia-94
Emerald-94
Gold-94
Ruby-94
Sapphire-94
Jersey and Stick-SJ-40
Jerseys-GJ-21
03BAP Ultimate Memorabilia Autographs-89
Gold-89
03BAP Ultimate Mem Auto Jerseys-89
03BAP Ultimate Mem Auto Emblems-89
03BAP Ultimate Memorabilia Emblems-29
03BAP Ultimate Memorabilia Emblems Gold-29
03BAP Ultimate Memorabilia Jerseys-35
03BAP Ultimate Memorabilia Jerseys Gold-35
03BAP Ultimate Memorabilia Numbers-27
03BAP Ultimate Memorabilia Numbers Gold-27
03BAP Ultimate Memorabilia Triple Threads-21
03Beehive-195
Variations-195
Gold-195
Silver-195
Jumbos-25
Jumbo Variations-25
Jumbo Jerseys-BH4
Jerseys-JT26
03Black Diamond-183
Black-183
Green-183
Red-183
Signature Gems-SG-26
03Bowman-44
Gold-44
03Bowman Chrome-44
Refractors-44
Gold Refractors-44
Xfractors-44
03Canucks Postcards-3
03Canucks Sav-on-Foods-4
03Canucks Sav-on-Foods-22
03Canucks Sav-on-Foods-NNO
03Crown Royale-96
Blue-96
Retail-96
Lords of the Rink-22
03eTopps-27
03ITG Action-512
Center of Attention-CA5
First Time All-Star-FT4
Jerseys-M152
03ITG Used Signature Series-90
Gold-90
Autographs-TB
Autographs Gold-TB
Jerseys-48
Jerseys Gold-48
Jersey Autos-48
Emblems-35
Emblems Gold-35
Jersey and Stick-48
Jersey and Stick Gold-48
Teammates-5
Teammates Gold-5
03ITG VIP Jerseys-25
03McDonald's Pacific-51
Patches Silver-24
Patches Gold-24
Patches and Sticks-24
Saturday Night Rivals-2
03NHL Sticker Collection-293
03O-Pee-Chee-200
03O-Pee-Chee-305
03OPC Blue-200
03OPC Blue-305
03OPC Gold-200
03OPC Gold-305
03OPC Red-200
03OPC Red-305
03Pacific-327
Blue-327
Red-327
Jerseys-38
Jerseys Gold-38
Maximum Impact-10
View from the Crease-8
03Pacific Calder-96
03Pacific Calder-159
Silver-96
03Pacific Complete-175
Red-175
03Pacific Exhibit-197
Blue Backs-197
History Makers-7
03Pacific Heads-Up-94
Hobby LTD-94
Retail LTD-94
In Focus-10
In Focus LTD-10
Mini Sweaters-9
03Pacific Invincible-93
Blue-93
Red-93
Retail-93
Featured Performers-29
03Pacific Luxury Suite-21A
03Pacific Luxury Suite-21B
03Pacific Luxury Suite-21C
03Pacific Luxury Suite-21D
03Pacific Prism-146
Blue-146
Patches-146
Red-146
Retail-146
Stat Masters-8
03Pacific Quest for the Cup-97
Blue-97
Chasing the Cup-9
03Pacific Supreme-94
Blue-94
Red-94
Retail-94
Team-8
03Pacific Toronto Fall Expo-1
03Private Stock Reserve-207
Blue-207
Patches-207
Red-207
Retail-207
Moments in Time-10
03SP Authentic-87
Limited-87
10th Anniversary-SP19
10th Anniversary Limited-SP19
Breakout Seasons-B6
Breakout Seasons Limited-B6
Foundations-F6
Foundations Limited-F6
Honors-H22
Honors Limited-H22
Sign of the Times-TB
Sign of the Times-NB
03SP Game Used-49
03SP Game Used-121
Gold-49
Gold-121
Authentic Fabrics-AFTB
Authentic Fabrics-DFNB
Authentic Fabrics-QNBJM
Authentic Fabrics Gold-AFTB
Authentic Fabrics Gold-DFNB
Authentic Fabrics Gold-QNBJM
Double Threads-DTNB
Limited Threads-LTTB
Limited Threads Gold-LTTB
Premium Patches-PPTB
Signers-SPSTB
Team Threads-TTNBJ
Top Threads-NBJM
03SPx-96
03SPx-137
03SPx-187
Radiance-96
Radiance-137
Radiance-187
Spectrum-96
Spectrum-137
Spectrum-187
Fantasy Franchise-FF-NBM
Fantasy Franchise Limited-FF-NBM
Signature Threads-ST-TB
Style-SPX-BS
Style-SPX-HN
Style-SPX-HT
Style Limited-SPX-BS
Style Limited-SPX-HN
Style Limited-SPX-HT
VIP-VIP-NB
VIP Limited-VIP-NB
Winning Materials-WM-TB
Winning Materials Limited-WM-TB
03Titanium-205
Patches-205
Stat Masters-9
03Topps-200
03Topps-305
Blue-200
Blue-305
Gold-200
Gold-305
Red-200
Red-305
First Round Fabrics-TB
First Round Fabrics-TBAY
Topps/OPC Idols-CI3
Own the Game-OTG5
03Topps C55-110
Minis-110
Minis American Back-110
Minis American Back Red-110
Minis Bazooka Back-110
Minis Brooklyn Back-110
Minis Hat Trick Back-110
Minis O Canada Back-110
Minis O Canada Back Red-110
Minis Stanley Cup Back-110
Autographs-TA-TB
Relics-TRTB
03Topps Pristine-32
Gold Refractor Die Cuts-32
Refractors-32
Jersey Portions-PPJ-TB
Jersey Portion Refractors-PPJ-TB
Patches-PP-TB
Patch Refractors-PP-TB
Press Plates Black-32
Press Plates Cyan-32
Press Plates Magenta-32
Press Plates Yellow-32
03Topps Traded Franchise Fabrics-FF-TB
03UD Honor Roll-87
Grade A Jerseys-TVAN
Signature Class-SC2
03UD Premier Collection-57
NHL Shields-SH-AC
NHL Shields-SH-TB
Signatures-PS-TB
Signatures Gold-PS-TB
Skills-SK-BT
Skills Patches-SK-BT
Stars-ST-TB
Stars Patches-ST-TB
Teammates-PT-VC
Teammates Patches-PT-VC
03Upper Deck-433
All-Star Class-AS-29
Big Playmakers-BP-TB
BuyBacks-19
BuyBacks-20
BuyBacks-21
BuyBacks-22
BuyBacks-23
BuyBacks-24
Canadian Exclusives-433
Fan Favorites-FF2
Franchise Fabrics-FF-TB
Gifted Greats-GG6
HG-433
Jerseys-GJ-TB
Jersey Autographs-SJ-TB
Memorable Matchups-MM-BG
Power Zone-PZ-5
Superstar Spotlight-SS11
Team Essentials-TS-TB
UD Exclusives-433
03Upper Deck Classic Portraits-96
Hockey Royalty-BNM
Starring Cast-SC-TB
03Upper Deck Ice-84
Gold-84
Authentics-IA-TB
Breakers-IB-TB
Breaker Patches-IB-TB
Frozen Fabrics-FF-TB
Frozen Fabric Patches-FF-TB
Under Glass Autographs-UG-TB
03Upper Deck MVP-409
Gold Script-409
Silver Script-409
Canadian Exclusives-409
Lethal Lineups-LL4
SportsNut-SN86
Winning Formula-WF2
03Upper Deck Rookie Update-84
03Upper Deck Rookie Update-153
Skills-SKTB
Top Draws-TD3
03Upper Deck Trilogy-96
Limited-96
Limited Threads-LT13
Scripts-S2TB
Scripts-CSTB
Scripts Limited-S2TB
Scripts Red-S2TB
03Upper Deck Victory-187
Bronze-187
Gold-187
Silver-187
Game Breakers-GB28
03Toronto Star-97
04Pacific-253
Blue-253
Red-253
04UD Toronto Fall Expo Priority Signings-TB
04Upper Deck-170
Canadian Exclusives-170
HG Glossy Gold-170
HG Glossy Silver-170
Jersey Autographs-GJA-TB
Jersey Autographs-GJA-TB/MN
NHL's Best-NB-TB
Patches-GJPA-TB
Patches-GJPL-TB
Patches-GJPN-TB
School of Hard Knocks-SHK7
05Beehive-89
Matte-89
Matted Materials-MMTB
Matted Materials Remarkable-RMTB
Signature Scrapbook-SSTB
05Hot Prospects-98
En Fuego-98
Red Hot-98
White Hot-98
05Panini Stickers-358
05Parkhurst-468
05Parkhurst-569
Facsimile Auto Parallel-468
Facsimile Auto Parallel-569
Signatures-TB
True Colors-TCVAN
True Colors-TCVAN
05SP Authentic-97
Limited-97
Sign of the Times Triples-TNMB
05SP Game Used-98
Gold-98
Authentic Fabrics-AF-TB
Authentic Fabrics Autographs-AAF-TB
Authentic Fabrics Dual-MT
Authentic Fabrics Dual Autographs-MT
Authentic Fabrics Gold-AF-TB
Authentic Fabrics Quad-KBJL
Authentic Patches Quad -KBJL
Authentic Patches-AP-TB
Authentic Patches Autographs-AAP-TB
Authentic Patches Dual-MT
Authentic Patches Dual Autographs-MT
Auto Draft-AD-TB
Significant Numbers-SN-TB
05SPx Winning Combos-WC-BM
05SPx Winning Combos Gold-WC-BM
05SPx Winning Combos Spectrum-WC-BM
05The Cup-98
Gold-98
Black Rainbow-98
Dual NHL Shields-DSNB
Dual NHL Shields Autographs-ADSNB
Emblems of Endorsement-EETB
Honorable Numbers-HNTB
Limited Logos-LLTB
Masterpiece Pressplates-98
Masterpiece Pressplates Rookie Upd Auto-261
Noble Numbers-NNPB
Noble Numbers Dual-DNNBJ
Patch Variation-P98
Patch Variation Autographs-AP98
Scripted Numbers-SNPB
Scripted Numbers Dual-DSNBN
Scripted Swatches-SSTB
Signature Patches-SPTB
05UD Artifacts Remarkable Artifacts-RA-TB
05UD Artifacts Remarkable Artifacts Dual-RA-TB
05UD Artifacts Treasured Patches-TP-TB
05UD Artifacts Treasured Patch Autos-TP-TB
05UD Artifacts Treasured Patches Dual-TPD-TB
05UD Artifacts Treasured Patch Dual Autos-TPD-TB
05UD Artifacts Treasured Patches Pewter-TP-TB
05UD Artifacts Treasured Patches Silver-TP-TB
05UD Artifacts Treasured Swatches-TS-TB
05UD Artifacts Treasured Swatch Autos-TS-TB
05UD Artifacts Treasured Swatches Blue-TS-TB
05UD Artifacts Treasured Swatches Copper-TS-TB
05UD Artifacts Treasured Swatches Dual-TSD-TB
05UD Artifacts Treasured Swatch Dual Auto-TSD-TB
05UD Artifacts Treasured Swatch Dual Blue-TSD-TB
05UD Artifact Treasure Swatch Dual Copper-TSD-TB
05UD Artifact Treasure Swatch Dual Maroon-TSD-TB
05UD Artifact Treasure Swatch Dual Pewter-TSD-TB
05UD Artifact TreasuredSwatch Dual Silver-TSD-TB
05UD Artifacts Treasured Swatches Maroon-TS-TB
05UD Artifacts Treasured Swatches Pewter-TS-TB
05UD Artifacts Treasured Swatches Silver-TS-TB
05UD PowerPlay-89
Rainbow-89
05UD Toronto Fall Expo Priority Signings-PS-TB
05Ultimate Collection-88
Gold-88
Jerseys-JTB
National Heroes Jerseys-NHJTB
National Heroes Patches-NHPTB
Premium Patches-PPTB
Premium Swatches-PSTB
Ultimate Achievements-UATB
Ultimate Patches-PTB
Ultimate Signatures-USTB
Ultimate Signatures Pairings-UPNB
05Ultra-191
Gold-191
Difference Makers-DM4
Difference Makers Jerseys-DMJ-TB
Difference Makers Patches-DMP-TB
Ice-191
05Upper Deck-189
Big Playmakers-B-TB
HG Glossy-189
Jerseys Series II-J2TB
Majestic Materials-MMTB
Notable Numbers-N-TB
Patches-P-TB
05Upper Deck Ice-96
Rainbow-96
Frozen Fabrics-FFTB
Frozen Fabrics Autographs-AFFTB
Frozen Fabrics Glass-FFTB
Frozen Fabrics Patches-FFPTB
Frozen Fabrics Patch Autographs-FAPTB
Signature Swatches-SSTB
05Upper Deck MVP-373
Gold-373
Platinum-373
Materials-M-TB
05Upper Deck Rookie Update-98
05Upper Deck Rookie Update-261
05Upper Deck Trilogy-154
Crystal-154
Honorary Patches-HP-TB
Honorary Patch Scripts-HSP-TB
Honorary Swatches-HS-TB
Honorary Swatch Scripts-HSS-TB
Scripts-SCS-TB
05Upper Deck Toronto Fall Expo-189
05Upper Deck Victory-249
Black-249
Gold-249
Silver-249
06Be A Player Portraits-50
06Beehive-58
06Beehive-200
Blue-58
Matte-58
Red Facsimile Signatures-58
Wood-58
06Black Diamond-37
Black-37
Gold-37
Ruby-37
06Flair Showcase-95
06Flair Showcase-167
06Flair Showcase-268
Parallel-95
Parallel-167
Parallel-268
Hot Numbers-HN40
Hot Numbers Parallel-HN40
Inks-ITB
06Fleer-83
Tiffany-83
06Hot Prospects-44
Red Hot-44
White Hot-44
06NHL POG-25
06O-Pee-Chee-220
Rainbow-220
06Panini Stickers-52
06SP Authentic-60
Limited-60
06SP Game Used-44
Gold-44
Rainbow-44
Authentic Fabrics Triple-AF3FLA
Authentic Fabrics Triple Patches-AF3FLA
Autographs-44
By The Letter-BLTB
06SPx-43
Spectrum-43
SPxcitement-X45
SPxcitement Spectrum-X45
06The Cup Autographed NHL Shields Duals-DASBB
06The Cup Limited Logos-LLTB
06The Cup Signature Patches-SPTB
06UD Artifacts-58
Blue-58
Gold-58
Platinum-58
Radiance-58
Red-58
Tundra Tandems-TTOT
Tundra Tandems Black-TTOT
Tundra Tandems Blue-TTOT
Tundra Tandems Gold-TTOT
Tundra Tandems Platinum-TTOT
Tundra Tandems Red-TTOT
Tundra Tandems Dual Patches Red-TTOT
06UD Mini Jersey Collection-46
06UD Powerplay-44
Impact Rainbow-44
06Ultra-83
Gold Medallion-83
Ice Medallion-83
Fresh Ink-ITB
06Upper Deck Arena Giveaways-FLA6
06Upper Deck-337
Exclusives Parallel-337
High Gloss Parallel-337
Masterpieces-337
Oversized Wal-Mart Exclusives-337
06Upper Deck MVP-127
Gold Script-127
Super Script-127
06Upper Deck Trilogy-43
Honorary Scripted Patches-HSPTB
Honorary Scripted Swatches-HSSTB
06Upper Deck Victory-250

Berube, Craig
85Kamloops Blazers-2
85Medicine Hat Tigers-7
88Flyers Postcards-13
89Flyers Postcards-2
90Flyers Postcards-3
90O-Pee-Chee-448
90Pro Set-498
90Upper Deck-450
French-450
91Maple Leafs PLAY-2
91OPC Premier-47
91Parkhurst-246
French-246
91Pro Set-495
French-495
91Score Canadian Bilingual-578
91Score Canadian English-578
91Score Rookie/Traded-28T
92Flames IGA-2
92O-Pee-Chee-147
92Score-258
Canadian-258
92Stadium Club-458
92Topps-208
Gold-208G
93Leaf-314
94Be A Player Signature Cards-64
94Leaf-343
94OPC Premier-433
Special Effects-433
94Pinnacle-515
Artist's Proofs-515
Rink Collection-515
94Topps/OPC Premier-433
Special Effects-433
95Capitals Team Issue-2
96Be A Player-115
Autographs-115
Autographs Silver-115
97Pacific Dynagon Best Kept Secrets-99
98Be A Player-298
Press Release-298
98BAP Gold-298
98BAP Autographs-298
98BAP Autographs Gold-298
98Pacific-437
Ice Blue-437
Red-437
98Pacific Omega-244
Red-244
Opening Day Issue-244
99Ultimate Victory-63
1/1-63
Parallel-63
Parallel 100-63
00BAP Memorabilia Update Tough Materials-T25
00BAP Mem Update Tough Materials Gold-T25
00Pacific-292
Copper-292
Gold-292
Ice Blue-292
Premiere Date-292
00Private Stock Game Gear-100
01BAP Update Tough Customers-TC4
01BAP Update Tough Customers-TC22
01Topps Heritage-184
02BAP Sig Series Auto Buybacks 1998-298
02NHL Power Play Stickers-3
02Topps Total-355
03Philadelphia Phantoms-5

Berube, Denis
01Quebec Remparts-16
02Val d'Or Foreurs-12

Berube, Guillaume
00Quebec Remparts-21
Signed-21
01Quebec Remparts-21
02Quebec Remparts-18
03Quebec Remparts Memorial Cup-1

Berube, Mike
05Red Deer Rebels-23

Berube, Sebastien
917th Inn. Sketch QMJHL-6

Berube, Yanick
93Quebec Pee-Wee Tournament-464

Berwanger, Markus
94German DEL-259
95German DEL-345
04German Cologne Sharks Postcards-3

Berzins, Armands
01Shawinigan Cataractes-10
02Shawinigan Cataractes-7
03ECHL Update RBI Sports-138
03Louisiana Ice Gators-1
04Wheeling Nailers Riesbeck's-3
06Czech OFS-173

Bes, Jeff
907th Inn. Sketch OHL-201
917th Inn. Sketch OHL-346
93Upper Deck-255
94Classic Pro Prospects-144
01Augusta Lynx-5
03Laredo Bucks-2

Besprosvannych, Nikolai
94German First League-645

Besser, Frank
94German First League-444

Besser, Jan
05Czech HC Kladno-1

Bessette, Marcel
51Laval Dairy QSHL-68

Bessette, Roger
51Laval Dairy QSHL-48
52St. Lawrence Sales-78

Bessey, Brent
93Waterloo Black Hawks-1

Best, Randy
93St. Cloud State Huskies-1
99Topeka Scarecrows-6

Bester, Allan
83Brantford Alexanders-17
84Maple Leafs Postcards-3
84O-Pee-Chee-297
84O-Pee-Chee Stickers-20
87Maple Leafs PLAY-12
87Maple Leafs Postcards-1
87Maple Leafs Postcards Oversized-1
87O-Pee-Chee-236
87O-Pee-Chee Stickers-162
87Panini Stickers-323
88Maple Leafs PLAY-11
88Panini Stickers-116
89O-Pee-Chee-271
89O-Pee-Chee Stickers-169
89Panini Stickers-139
90Bowman-154
Tiffany-154
90O-Pee-Chee-32
90Pro Set-275A
90Pro Set-275B
90Score-27
Canadian-27
90Topps-32
Tiffany-32
90Upper Deck-241
French-241
91Maple Leafs Panini Team Stickers-2
91ProCards-118
93San Diego Gulls-3
96Collector's Edge Ice-170
Prism-170

Beswick, Sean
92North Dakota Fighting Sioux-3

Bethard, Brian
94Anchorage Aces-24

Betik, Karel
98Cleveland Lumberjacks-5
99Paramount-213
Copper-213
Emerald-213
Gold-213
Holographic Emerald-213
Holographic Gold-213
Holographic Silver-213
Ice Blue-213
Premiere Date-213
Red-213
Silver-213
00Bakersfield Condors-3
01BC Icemen-6

Beton, Ales
93Quebec Pee-Wee Tournament-1792

Betournay, Eric
00Chicoutimi Sagueneens-5
Signed-5
01Chicoutimi Sagueneens-3
02Philadelphia Phantoms-7
03Thetford Mines Prolab-3

Betournay, Mathieu
00Chicoutimi Sagueneens-3
Signed-3
01Moncton Wildcats-6
02Moncton Wildcats-10
03Moncton Wildcats-4

Bets, Maxim
93Pinnacle-502
Canadian-502
93Spokane Chiefs-2
93Classic-15
93Classic Four-Sport *-208
Gold-208
94Donruss-33
94Parkhurst-10
Gold-10
Vintage-V37
94Pinnacle-483
Artist's Proofs-483
Rink Collection-483
Rookie Team Pinnacle-6
94Score-232
Gold-232
Platinum-232
94Upper Deck-353
Electric Ice-353
SP Inserts-SP1
SP Inserts Die Cuts-SP1
94Classic-92
Gold-92
94Classic Four-Sport *-127
Gold-127
Printers Proofs-127
99Russian Hockey League-23
99Russian Metallurg Magnetogorsk-38
99Russian Stars of Hockey-24
99Russian Stars Postcards-3
01Russian Hockey League-53

Bettens, Mike
96UK Guildford Flames-8

Bettiol, Frank
52Juniors Blue Tint-53

Betts, Blair
97Upper Deck-407
98Prince George Cougars-3
98Bowman CHL-124
Golden Anniversary-124
OPC International-124
Autographs Blue-A32
Autographs Gold-A32
Autographs Silver-A32
98Bowman Chrome CHL-124
Golden Anniversary-124
Golden Anniversary Refractors-124
OPC International-124
OPC International Refractors-124
Refractors-124
99Prince George Cougars-18
99Bowman CHL-104
Gold-104
OPC International-104
03Private Stock Reserve-15
Blue-15
Red-15
Retail-15
04Hartford Wolf Pack-2
06O-Pee-Chee-336
Rainbow-336

Betts, Kaleb
06Rockford IceHogs -2

Bety, Sebastien
93Drummondville Voltigeurs-4
95Signature Rookies-19
Signatures-19
01Thetford Mines Coyotes-1
02Thetford Mines Coyotes-3
03Thetford Mines Prolab-4

Betz, Mike
98Sioux City Musketeers-2
99Sioux City Musketeers-1
00Ohio State Buckeyes-14
01Ohio State Buckeyes-3

02Ohio State Buckeyes-3
03Ohio State Buckeyes-3
Beukeboom, Jeff
82Sault Ste. Marie Greyhounds-4
83Sault Ste. Marie Greyhounds-1
84Sault Ste. Marie Greyhounds-2
85Nova Scotia Oilers-7
86Oilers Red Rooster-6
86Oilers Team Issue-6
87Oilers Team Issue-6
88Oilers Tenth Anniversary-17
88Oilers Team Issue-2
88Panini Stickers-56
89Oilers Team Issue-2
90Oilers IGA-2
90O-Pee-Chee-471
90Pro Set-439
91Pro Set Platinum-206
91Bowman-110
91Oilers Panini Team Stickers-2
91Oilers Team Issue-2
91O-Pee-Chee-284
91Parkhurst-341
French-341
91Pinnacle-229
French-229
91Pro Set-444
French-444
91Score Canadian Bilingual-253
91Score Canadian English-253
91Stadium Club-350
91Topps-284
91Upper Deck-394
French-394
92Bowman-347
92O-Pee-Chee-237
92Pinnacle-112
French-112
92Score-137
Canadian-137
92Stadium Club-129
92Topps-57
Gold-57G
92Ultra-351
92Upper Deck-161
93OPC Premier-54
Gold-54
93Pinnacle-309
Canadian-309
93PowerPlay-389
93Score-94
Canadian-94
93Stadium Club-7
Members Only Master Set-7
OPC-7
First Day Issue-7
First Day Issue OPC-7
93Topps/OPC Premier-54
Gold-54
94Be A Player Signature Cards-107
94Finest Ring Leaders-9
94Flair-110
94Fleer-131
94Leaf-528
94OPC Premier-138
Special Effects-138
94Parkhurst-148
Gold-148
94Pinnacle-195
Artist's Proofs-195
Rink Collection-195
94Score-66
Gold-66
Platinum-66
94Topps/OPC Premier-138
Special Effects-138
94Ultra-136
94Upper Deck-339
Electric Ice-339
95Canada Games NHL POGS-185
95Collector's Choice-317
Player's Club-317
Player's Club Platinum-317
95Parkhurst International-410
Emerald Ice-410
95Pinnacle-112
Artist's Proofs-112
Rink Collection-112
95Topps-63
OPC Inserts-63
95Upper Deck-203
Electric Ice-203
Electric Ice Gold-203
96Be A Player-158
Autographs-158
Autographs Silver-158
96Donruss Elite-87
Die Cut Stars-87
96Summit-71
Artist's Proofs-71
Ice-71
Metal-71
Premium Stock-71
96Upper Deck-105
97Pacific-57
Copper-57
Emerald Green-57
Ice Blue-57
Red-57
Silver-57
97Score Rangers-20
Platinum-20
Premier-20
97Upper Deck-314
98Be A Player-242
Press Release-242
98BAP Gold-242
98BAP Autographs-242
98BAP Autographs Gold-242
98Katch-96
98OPC Chrome-87
Refractors-87
98Pacific-290
Ice Blue-290
Red-290
98Topps-87
O-Pee-Chee-87
98UD Choice-136
Prime Choice Reserve-136
Reserve-136
98Upper Deck-326
Exclusives-326
Exclusives 1 of 1-326
Gold Reserve-326
02BAP Sig Series Auto Buybacks 1998-242
02Fleer Throwbacks-31
Gold-31
Platinum-31
Beuker, Dean
01Regina Pats-4
Beuselinck, Derek
91Air Canada SJHL-E44
98Madison Monsters-6
Beuthner, Wolfgang
04German Berlin Eisbarens 50th Anniv-20
Beutler, Andreas
93Swedish Semic World Champ Stickers-112
93Swiss HNL-63
95Swiss HNL-349
96Swiss HNL-322
Bevacqua, Jeff
93Quebec Pee-Wee Tournament-767
Beveridge, Bill
33O-Pee-Chee V304B-54
33V129-25
33V357 Ice Kings-60
34Beehive Group I Photos-189
35Diamond Matchbooks Tan 1-3
37O-Pee-Chee V304E-161
37V356 Worldwide Gum-82
06ITG Ultimate Memorabilia Sensational Sens Autos-5
Beverley, Nick
72O-Pee-Chee-281
73O-Pee-Chee-239
75O-Pee-Chee NHL-279
75Topps-279
76O-Pee-Chee NHL-41
76Topps-41
77O-Pee-Chee NHL-198
77Topps-198
78O-Pee-Chee-111
78Topps-111
79Rockies Team Issue-3
Bezak, Marian
81Swedish Semic Hockey VM Stickers-68
Bezborodov, Konstantin
99Russian Hockey League-27
00Russian Hockey League-135
Bezdek, Jan
93Quebec Pee-Wee Tournament-1567
Bezeau, Andy
89Niagara Falls Thunder-4
897th Inn. Sketch OHL-147
907th Inn. Sketch OHL-253
94Muskegon Fury-17
95Fort Wayne Komets-1
96Collector's Edge Ice-125
Prism-125
98Detroit Vipers-6
98Detroit Vipers Freschetta-5
98Muskegon Fury-18
99Detroit Vipers-1
99Detroit Vipers Kid's Club-3
99Fort Wayne Komets Penalty Leaders-9
Bezeau, Billy
04P.E.I. Rocket-3
06Quebec Remparts-14
Bezhukladnikov, Vyacheslav
00Russian Hockey League-122
Bezina, Goran
98Swiss Power Play Stickers-94
99Swiss Panini Stickers-81
99Swiss Panini Stickers-281
00Swiss Panini Stickers-129
00Swiss Slapshot Mini-Cards-HCFG2
02Springfield Falcons-5
03ITG VIP Rookie Debut-136
03Parkhurst Rookie-123
03UD Premier Collection-91
03Upper Deck Rookie Update-177
03Springfield Falcons Postcards-1
Bezpalec, Roman
99Czech Score Blue 2000-116
99Czech Score Red Ice 2000-116
Bezrukov, Dmitri
98Russian Hockey League-76
99Russian Hockey League-100
Bhungal, Patrick
06Chilliwack Bruins-12
Biachin, Jordan
06Austin Ice Bats-13
Biafore, Chad
87Portland Winter Hawks-3
88Portland Winter Hawks-3
96German DEL-32
98German DEL-179
99German Bundesliga 2-85
Biagini, Chris
95Slapshot-284
95Owen Sound Platers-9
Bialowas, Dwight
74O-Pee-Chee NHL-372
75O-Pee-Chee NHL-106
75Topps-106
76O-Pee-Chee NHL-198
76Topps-198
77O-Pee-Chee NHL-271
Bialowas, Frank
92Richmond Renegades-2
93St. John's Maple Leafs-2
94Parkhurst-237
Gold-237
94St. John's Maple Leafs-3
95Portland Pirates-4
05ITG Tough Customers-FB
Autographs-FB
Complete Jerseys-FB
Emblem and Numbers-FB
Famous Battles Autographs-BB
Jerseys-FB
Signed Memorabilia-FB
05Philadelphia Phantoms All-Decade Team-2
Bialynicki, Kyrzysztof
73Finnish Jaakiekko-86
Bianchi, Tony
91Minnesota Golden Gophers-2
92Minnesota Golden Gophers-3
93Minnesota Golden Gophers-3
Bianchin, Jordan
04New Mexico Scorpions-3
Bianchin, Wayne
74NHL Action Stamps-219
77O-Pee-Chee NHL-188
77Penguins Puck Bucks-14
77Topps-188
78O-Pee-Chee-103
78Topps-103
79O-Pee-Chee-290
88Oilers Tenth Anniversary-107
Bianni, Mike
84Moncton Golden Flames-2
Biasucci, Joey
02Sault Ste. Marie Greyhounds-2
Bibeault, Paul
34Beehive Group I Photos-136
43Parade Sportive *-5
Bicanek, Radim
93Upper Deck-262
93Classic-36
94Senators Team Issue-3
94Classic-111
Gold-111
Tri-Cards-T46
95Donruss-15
95Leaf-69
95Pinnacle-217
Artist's Proofs-217
Rink Collection-217
95Score-306
Black Ice Artist's Proofs-306
Black Ice-306
95PEI Senators-2
95Classic-83
95Images-43
Gold-43
97Pacific Dynagon Best Kept Secrets-64
97Manitoba Moose-B2
96Grand Rapids Griffins-3
99Cleveland Lumberjacks-1
00Panini Stickers-139
00Syracuse Crunch-20
01Blue Jackets Donatos Pizza-17
02Syracuse Crunch-19
04Czech OFS-293
04Czech Zuma-32
05Czech HC Znojmo-1
06Czech OFS-199
Defenders-14
Bicek, Jiri
97Albany River Rats-2
98Albany River Rats-2
99Albany River Rats-2
00Upper Deck Ice-115
00Albany River Rats-2
01BAP Signature Series-239
Autographs-239
Autographs Gold-239
01O-Pee-Chee-309
01O-Pee-Chee Premier Parallel-309
01Pacific-226
Extreme LTD-226
Hobby LTD-226
Premiere Date-226
Retail LTD-226
01Pacific Arena Exclusives-226
01Parkhurst-273
01Parkhurst Beckett Promos-273
01Topps-309
OPC Parallel-309
01Albany River Rats-9
02Devils Team Issue-6
02Pacific Calder-79
Silver-79
02Pacific Complete-507
Red-507
02Albany River Rats-10
03Albany River Rats-4
03Albany River Rats Kinko's-3
05Swedish SHL Elitset-218
Gold-218
06Swedish SHL Elitset-157
Bickel, Stu
06Sioux Falls Stampede -13
Bickell, Bryan
02Ottawa 67's-12
03Ottawa 67's-7
04ITG Top Prospects Spring Expo-17
04Ottawa 67's-3
04ITG Heroes and Prospects-59
Autographs-BBI
Top Prospects-17
04ITG Heroes/Prospects Toronto Expo '05-59
04ITG Heroes/Prospects Expo Heroes/Pros-59
05Ottawa 67's-3
06Norfolk Admirals-10
06ITG Heroes and Prospects-157
Autographs-ABBI
Update Autographs-ABBI
07Upper Deck Victory-208
Black-208
Gold-208
Bickell, J.P.
83Hall of Fame-184
83Hall of Fame Postcards-J3
85Hall of Fame-184
Bidner, Todd
83Moncton Alpines-21
06London Knights-26
Biduke, Jesse
04Oshawa Generals-13
04Oshawa Generals Autographs-13
06Kingston Frontenacs-9
Bieber, Simon
93Quebec Pee-Wee Tournament-503
Biegl, Radovan
94Czech APS Extraliga-24
95Czech APS Extraliga-316
96Czech APS Extraliga-50
97Czech APS Extraliga-315
97Czech DS Extraliga-110
97Czech DS Stickers-227
98Czech DS-25
98Czech DS Stickers-267
98Czech OFS-178
00Czech DS Extraliga-145
Goalies-G13
00Czech OFS-264
00Czech OFS Star Emerald-32
00Czech OFS Star Pink-32
00Czech OFS Star Violet-32
01Czech OFS-62
Gold Inserts-G5
02Czech OFS Plus-64
Checklists-C12
02Czech OFS Plus Masks-M6
02Czech OFS Plus Trios-T20
02Czech OFS Plus Duos-D1
03Czech OFS Plus-26
03Czech OFS Plus Checklists-2
03Czech OFS Plus Insert B-B10
03Czech OFS Plus Insert P-P9
03Czech OFS Plus MS Praha-SE37
04Czech OFS-360
04Czech OFS-372
Goals-Against Leaders-7
Save Percentage Leaders-8
06Czech OFS-152
Goalies II-15
Team Cards-10
Bieksa, Kevin
03Bowling Green Falcons-15
04Manitoba Moose-1
05ITG Heroes/Prosp Toronto Expo Parallel -44
05Black Diamond-289
05Hot Prospects-271
En Fuego-271
Hot Materials-HMBI
Red Hot-271
White Hot-271
05Parkhurst-668
Facsimile Auto Parallel-668
Signatures-KB
True Colors-TCVAN
True Colors-TCVAN
05SP Authentic-205
05SP Game Used-239
05SPx-242
Spectrum-242
05The Cup-162
Autographed Rookie Patches Gold Rainbow-162
Black Rainbow Rookies-162
Masterpiece Pressplates (Artifacts)-336
Masterpiece Pressplates (Black Diamond)-289
Masterpiece Pressplates (Ice)-233
Masterpiece Pressplates (Rookie Update)-246
Masterpiece Pressplates SPA Autos-205
Masterpiece Pressplates (SP Game Used)-239
Masterpiece Pressplates SPx Autos-242
Masterpiece Pressplates (Trilogy)-313
Masterpiece Pressplates Ult Coll-231
Masterpiece Pressplates Autographs-162
Platinum Rookies-162
05UD Artifacts-336
05Ultimate Collection-231
Gold-231
05Upper Deck-478
05Upper Deck Ice-233
05Upper Deck Rookie Update-246
Inspirations Patch Rookies-246
05Upper Deck Trilogy-313
05AHL Top Prospects-3
05Manitoba Moose-3
05ITG Heroes and Prospects-44
Autographs-A-KBI
06Canucks Postcards-1
06Gatorade-90
06Hot Prospects Hotagraphs-HKE
06Upper Deck Game Jerseys-J2KB
06Upper Deck Game Patches-P2KB
Bielas, Rolf
70Finnish Jaakiekko-81
70Swedish Hockey-374
70Swedish Masterserien-172
70Swedish Masterserien-174
74Finnish Jenkki-119
74Finnish Typotor-58
Bielenink, Andrzej
94German First League-565
Bielik, Miroslav
04UK Guildford Flames-16
05UK Hull Stingrays-15
Bielke, Rene
83Swedish Semic VM Stickers-143
94German DEL-245
95German DEL-220
04German Berlin Eisbarens 50th Anniv-22
Bielmann, Andre
99Swiss Panini Stickers-106
01Swiss HNL-62
02Swiss HNL-457
Bienvenue, Daniel
97Rochester Americans-1-5
Bieri, Daniel
99Swiss Panini Stickers-139
01Swiss HNL-271
03Swiss HNL-300
Bierk, Zac
93Peterborough Petes-10
95Slapshot-307
95Slapshot-NNO
95Slapshot-NNO
95Signature Rookies Auto-Phonex-7
95Signature Rook Auto-Phonex Phone Cards-7
97Bowman CHL-19
OPC-19
98Pacific-396
Ice Blue-396
Red-396
98Pacific Omega-224
Red-224
Opening Day Issue-224
98SPx Finite-79
98SPx Finite-148
Radiance-79
Radiance-148
Spectrum-79
Spectrum-148
98Upper Deck-181
Exclusives-181
Exclusives 1 of 1-181
Gold Reserve-181
98Cleveland Lumberjacks-6
98IHL All-Star Eastern Conference-3
99Detroit Vipers-10
00O-Pee-Chee-314
00O-Pee-Chee Parallel-314
00Topps/OPC-314
Parallel-314
00Cleveland Lumberjacks-13
02Coyotes Team Issue-28
02Pacific Complete-488
Red-488
02Springfield Falcons-6
03BAP Memorabilia-170
Emerald-170
Gold-170
Ruby-170
Sapphire-170
03Coyotes Postcards-1
03ITG Action-425
03Pacific-258
Blue-258
Red-258
03Pacific Complete-445
Red-445
03Pacific Supreme Generations-7
Biesenthal, Mark
99Alexandria Warthogs-1
Biette, Karry
907th Inn. Sketch WHL-177
917th Inn. Sketch WHL-227
99UK Guildford Flames-2
99UK Guildford Flames-6
00UK Guildford Flames-1
01UK Fife Flyers-10
Bifano, Paul
83Victoria Cougars-4
Big Snake, Robin
01Vancouver Giants-6
03Portland Winter Hawks-13
04Owen Sound Attack-15
04Portland Winter Hawks-13
04Portland Winter Hawks-NNO
05Rockford Ice Hogs-2
06Rockford IceHogs -3
Biggers, Brandon
05Guelph Storm-C-03
Biggs, Don
82Oshawa Generals-9
83Oshawa Generals-8
85Nova Scotia Oilers-26
88ProCards AHL-137
89ProCards AHL-331
91ProCards-205
92Binghamton Rangers-11
93Cincinnati Cyclones-3
94Classic Pro Prospects-83
95Cincinnati Cyclones-1
96Cincinnati Cyclones-22
96Collector's Edge Ice-110
Prism-110
97Cincinnati Cyclones-1
Biggs, Kenneth
51Laval Dairy QSHL-40
Biggs, Scott
82Kitchener Rangers-28
Bigliel, Moreno
93Quebec Pee-Wee Tournament-1636
Bignell, Greg
897th Inn. Sketch OHL-86
90Hampton Roads Admirals-42
Bikkinyaev, Artem
05Russian Hockey League RHL-38
Bilek, Martin
97Czech APS Extraliga-196
98Czech DS Stickers-228
98Czech OFS-396
99Czech DS-155
Goalies-G12
99Czech OFS-2
99Czech OFS Goalie Die-Cuts-2
Bilek, Roman
03Czech OFS Plus-211
Bilek, Vitezslav
03Czech OFS Plus-216
04Czech OFS-47
06Czech OFS-247
Biles, C.
28V128-2 Paulin's Candy-59
Bilick, Craig
02Kalamazoo Wings-16
Billeck, Laurie
90Prince Albert Raiders-2
907th Inn. Sketch WHL-261
917th Inn. Sketch WHL-152
95Vancouver VooDoo RHI-4
Billieras, Marc
93Quebec Pee-Wee Tournament-1493
Billington, Craig
83Belleville Bulls-24
84Belleville Bulls-10
85Devils Postcards-3
87Panini Stickers-72
88ProCards AHL-333
89ProCards AHL-224
90Alberta International Team Canada-1
91Pro Set Platinum-197
91Parkhurst-320
French-320
91Upper Deck-559
French-559
92Bowman-102
92O-Pee-Chee-372
92Parkhurst-330
Emerald Ice-330
92Score-228
Canadian-228
92Stadium Club-343
92Topps-48
Gold-48G
92Ultra-334
92Upper Deck-315
93Donruss-226
93Leaf-354
93OPC Premier-374
Gold-374
93Parkhurst-138
Emerald Ice-138
93Pinnacle-352
Canadian-352
All-Stars-1
All-Stars Canadian-1
93PowerPlay-169
93Score-207
93Score-521
Gold-521
Canadian-207
Canadian-521
Canadian Gold-521
93Senators Kraft Sheets-2
93Stadium Club All-Stars-7
93Stadium Club All-Stars Members Only-7
93Stadium Club All-Stars OPC-7
93Topps/OPC Premier-374
Gold-374
93Ultra-378
93Upper Deck-424
SP-105
94Canada Games NHL POGS-289
94Donruss-209
94Flair-119
94Kraft-34
94Leaf-84
94OPC Premier-482
Special Effects-482
94Parkhurst-158
Gold-158
94Pinnacle-320
Artist's Proofs-320
Rink Collection-320
94Score-167
Gold-167
Platinum-167
94Select-49
Gold-49
94Senators Team Issue-4
94Topps/OPC Premier-482
Special Effects-482
94Ultra-145
94Upper Deck-370
Electric Ice-370
SP Inserts-SP53
SP Inserts Die Cuts-SP53
95Be A Player-151
Signatures-S151
Signatures Die Cuts-S151
95Donruss-381
95Parkhurst International-285
Emerald Ice-285
95Upper Deck-112
Electric Ice-112
Electric Ice Gold-112
96Score-231
Artist's Proofs-231
Dealer's Choice Artist's Proofs-231
Special Artist's Proofs-231
Golden Blades-231
97Be A Player-138
Autographs-138
Autographs Die-Cuts-138
Autographs Prismatic Die-Cuts-138
97Pacific Dynagon Best Kept Secrets-23
97Pacific Omega-54
Copper-54
Dark Gray-54
Emerald Green-54
Gold-54
Ice Blue-54
97Score-19
Artist's Proofs-19
Golden Blades-19
97Score Avalanche-2
Platinum-2
Premier-2
98Be A Player-185
Press Release-185
98BAP Gold-185
98BAP Autographs-185
98BAP Autographs Gold-185
98NHL Aces Playing Cards-47
98Pacific-157
Ice Blue-157
Red-157
98Paramount-52
Copper-52
Emerald Green-52
Holo-Electric-52
Ice Blue-52
Silver-52
99Pacific-100
Copper-100
Emerald Green-100
Gold-100
Ice Blue-100
Premiere Date-100
Red-100
00Upper Deck NHLPA-PA88
01Between the Pipes-7
01Pacific-389
Extreme LTD-389
Hobby LTD-389
Premiere Date-389
Retail LTD-389
01Pacific Arena Exclusives-389
02BAP Sig Series Auto Buybacks 1998-185
02Between the Pipes-60
Gold-60
Silver-60
02Pacific-387
Blue-387
Red-387
02Pacific Complete-61
Red-61
02UD Mask Collection-88
02UD Mask Collection-89
02UD Mask Collection Beckett Promos-88
02UD Mask Collection Beckett Promos-89
Billkvam, Arne
92Finnish Semic-35
92Norwegian Elite Series-49
93Swedish Semic World Champ Stickers-245
94Finnish Jaa Kiekko-268
Billmaier, Michael
94German First League-196
Billsten, Curtis
03Everett Silvertips-10
04Everett Silvertips-25
05Kootenay Ice-2
Bilodeau, Brent
907th Inn. Sketch WHL-1
91Upper Deck-694
French-694
91Upper Deck Czech World Juniors-81
917th Inn. Sketch WHL-180
917th Inn. Sketch Memorial Cup-99
91Arena Draft Picks-13
91Arena Draft Picks French-13
91Arena Draft Picks Autographs-13
91Arena Draft Picks Autographs French-13
91Classic-14
91Star Pics-53
91Ultimate Draft-14
91Ultimate Draft-70
91Ultimate Draft French-14
91Classic Four-Sport *-14
Autographs-14A
93Fredericton Canadiens-1
94Fredericton Canadiens-2
94Classic Pro Prospects-58
98Kansas City Blades-18
99Johnstown Chiefs-9
00Johnstown Chiefs-18
01Johnstown Chiefs-4
02Johnstown Chiefs-2
03Johnstown Chiefs-1
03Johnstown Chiefs RBI Sports-209
04Johnstown Chiefs-1
05Las Vegas Wranglers-24
06Las Vegas Wranglers-24
Bilodeau, David
93Quebec Pee-Wee Tournament-225
97Rimouski Oceanic-10
Bilodeau, Laurent
93Quebec Pee-Wee Tournament-318
Bilodeau, Luc
90Montreal-Bourassa AAA-7
03St. Jean Mission-1
Bilodeau, Martin
92Quebec Pee-Wee Tournament-843
93Quebec Pee-Wee Tournament-1603
96Halifax Mooseheads I-3
96Halifax Mooseheads II-3
97Halifax Mooseheads I-2
97Halifax Mooseheads II-3
Bilodeau, Patrice
01Val d'Or Foreurs-9
02Val d'Or Foreurs-3
03Val d'Or Foreurs-4
Bilodeau, Roland
51Bas Du Fleuve-17
52Bas Du Fleuve-56
Bilodeau, Simon
93Quebec Pee-Wee Tournament-323
Bilotto, Nicholas
93Quebec Pee-Wee Tournament-135
98Quebec Remparts-3
Signed-3
02Charlotte Checkers-79
03Charlotte Checkers-65
Bilous, Jason
91British Columbia JHL-136
Bilsen, Van
79Panini Stickers-276
Biltoft, Troels
90Danish Hockey League-198
Bilyaletinov, Zinetula
79Russian National Team-11
81Swedish Semic Hockey VM Stickers-44
82Swedish Semic VM Stickers-58
83Swedish Semic VM Stickers-58
83Russian National Team-3
87Russian National Team-3
93Jets Ruffles-5
96Coyotes Coca-Cola-34
01Swiss HNL-55
03Russian Hockey League-58
Bina, Brian
04Lincoln Stars-2
05Lincoln Stars-3
Bina, Jerod
00Wichita Thunder-1
Bina, Robbie
02Lincoln Stars-21
03North Dakota Fighting Sioux-23
04North Dakota Fighting Sioux-2
Binab, Justin
04Langley Hornets-3
Binavince, Julian
94German First League-441
Biner, Sergio
01Swiss HNL-351
Binet, Eric
92Quebec Pee-Wee Tournament-1240
93Quebec Pee-Wee Tournament-360
Binet, Francis
93Quebec Pee-Wee Tournament-371
Binette, Marc-Andre
97Halifax Mooseheads I-3
97Halifax Mooseheads II-4
98Halifax Mooseheads-23
98Halifax Mooseheads Second Edition-9
99Rouyn-Noranda Huskies-2
00Rouyn-Noranda Huskies-25
Signed-25
Bingaman, Bruce
92Quebec Pee-Wee Tournament-1445
93Quebec Pee-Wee Tournament-777
Bingham, Pat
85Kamloops Blazers-3
88Kamloops Blazers-2
89Nashville Knights-1
91Richmond Renegades-9
91Richmond Renegades Set 2-15
93Lakeland Ice Warriors-5
98Huntsville Channel Cats-6
00Asheville Smoke-15
04Wheeling Nailers SGA-4
06Fort Wayne Komets-22
Binkley, Les
52Juniors Blue Tint-174
60Cleveland Barons-2
68O-Pee-Chee-100
68Shirriff Coins-140
68Topps-100
69O-Pee-Chee-110
Four-in-One-2
Stamps-3
69Topps-110
70Colgate Stamps-75
70Dad's Cookies-7
70Esso Power Players-234
70O-Pee-Chee-200
Deckle-10
70Sargent Promotions Stamps-175
71O-Pee-Chee-192
71Penguins Postcards-2
71Sargent Promotions Stamps-166
71Toronto Sun-211
72O-Pee-Chee-300
72Finnish Semic World Championship-215
72Swedish Semic World Championship-215
04ITG Franchises US West-270
Autographs-A-LB
Binnie, Troy
897th Inn. Sketch OHL-52
907th Inn. Sketch OHL-77
92Dallas Freeze-4
93Dallas Freeze-3
94Central Hockey League-4
94Dallas Freeze-4
Binns, Craig
917th Inn. Sketch OHL-179
93Owen Sound Platers-1
98Mobile Mysticks-18
00UK Sekonda Superleague-111
03Lubbock Cotton Kings-2
Bionda, Jack
44Beehive Group II Photos-380
57Bruins Photos-2
57Topps-2
94Parkhurst Missing Link-14
Biondo, Nick
05Ohio State Buckeyes-25
06Ohio State Buckeyes-18
Biotti, Chris
88Salt Lake Golden Eagles-20
89ProCards IHL-202
Birbaum, Alain
02Swiss HNL-144
Birbraer, Max
00Albany River Rats-3
01Albany River Rats-15
02Albany River Rats-15
02Albany River Rats AAP-4
03Laredo Bucks-3
Birch, Dave
71Johnstown Jets Acme-1
72Johnstown Jets-13
Birch, Joe
95Slapshot-151
Birch, Steve
03Lubbock Cotton Kings-3
Bird, Jamie
917th Inn. Sketch QMJHL-178
95Central Hockey League-92
95Slapshot Memorial Cup-56
96Knoxville Cherokees-5
98BC Icemen-11
98BC Icemen II-12
Bird, Peter
96OCN Blizzard-6
Birk, Harald
94German DEL-318
95German DEL-23
96German DEL-269
98German DEL-334
99German DEL-203
99German DEL-165
Birk, Klaus
94German DEL-328
95German DEL-324
Birmingham, Jason
04Tulsa Oilers-2
Birner, Michael
04Barrie Colts-17
05Saginaw Spirit-2
06Peoria Rivermen-2
Birnie, Jay
03Salmon Arm Silverbacks-2
06Colorado EaglesA -4
Birnie, Scott
83North Bay Centennials-4
Birnie, Stuart
87Brockville Braves-20
88Brockville Braves-7
Biron, Martin
93Amos Les Forestiers-3
95Parkhurst International-295
Emerald Ice-295
95Classic-16
Ice Breakers-BK13
Ice Breakers Die Cuts-BK13
96Donruss Canadian Ice Les Gardiens-9
96Fleer-122
96Leaf-213
Press Proofs-213
96Pinnacle-224
Artist's Proofs-224
Foil-224
Premium Stock-224
Rink Collection-224
96SkyBox Impact-145
96Summit-179
Artist's Proofs-179
Ice-179
Metal-179
Premium Stock-179
96Upper Deck Ice-118
97Rochester Americans-5-1
98Rochester Americans-5
99BAP Memorabilia-137
Gold-137
Silver-137
99BAP Millennium-35
Emerald-35
Ruby-35
Sapphire-35
Signatures-35
Signatures Gold-35
Calder Candidates Ruby-C22
Calder Candidates Emerald-C22
Calder Candidates Sapphire-C22
99Black Diamond-14
Diamond Cut-14
Final Cut-14
99Crown Royale-17
Limited Series-17
Premiere Date-17
Prospects Parallel-17
99Pacific-34
Copper-34
Emerald Green-34
Gold-34
Ice Blue-34
Premiere Date-34
Red-34
99Pacific Dynagon Ice-28
Blue-28
Copper-28
Gold-28
Premiere Date-28
99Pacific Omega-25
Copper-25
Gold-25
Ice Blue-25
Premiere Date-25
99Pacific Prism-17
Holographic Blue-17
Holographic Gold-17
Holographic Mirror-17
Holographic Purple-17
Premiere Date-17
Ice Prospects-2
99Revolution-16
Premiere Date-16
Red-16
Shadow Series-16
Copper-16
Gold-16
CSC Silver-16
99SPx-19
Radiance-19
Spectrum-19
99Stadium Club-191
First Day Issue-191
One of a Kind-191
Printing Plates Black-191
Printing Plates Cyan-191
Printing Plates Magenta-191
Printing Plates Yellow-191
99Topps Arena Giveaways-BUF-MB
99Topps Gold Label Class 1-95
Black-95
Black One of One-95
One of One-95
Red-95
Red One of One-95
99Topps Gold Label Class 2-95
99Topps Gold Label Class 2 Black-95
99Topps Gold Label Class 2 Black 1 of 1-95
99Topps Gold Label Class 2 One of One-95
99Topps Gold Label Class 2 Red-95
99Topps Gold Label Class 2 Red One of One-95
99Topps Gold Label Class 3-95
99Topps Gold Label Class 3 Black-95
99Topps Gold Label Class 3 Black 1 of 1-95
99Topps Gold Label Class 3 One of One-95
99Topps Gold Label Class 3 Red-95
99Topps Gold Label Class 3 Red One of One-95
99Topps Gold Label Fresh Gold-FG8
99Topps Gold Label Fresh Gold Black-FG8
99Topps Gold Label Fresh Gold Black 1of1-FG8
99Topps Gold Label Fresh Gold One of One-FG8
99Topps Gold Label Fresh Gold Red-FG8
99Topps Gold Label Fresh Gold Red 1 of 1-FG8
99Topps Premier Plus-129
Parallel-129
99Upper Deck-188
Exclusives-188
Exclusives 1 of 1-188
99Upper Deck Gold Reserve-188
99Upper Deck MVP-25
Gold Script-25
Silver Script-25
Super Script-25
99Upper Deck MVP SC Edition-25
Gold Script-25
Silver Script-25
Super Script-25
ProSign-MB
99Upper Deck Victory-37
00Aurora-17
Premiere Date-17
00BAP Memorabilia-204
Emerald-204
Ruby-204
Sapphire-204
Promos-204

00BAP Mem Chicago Sportsfest Copper-204
00BAP Memorabilia Chicago Sportsfest Blue-204
00BAP Memorabilia Chicago Sportsfest Gold-204
00BAP Memorabilia Chicago Sportsfest Ruby-204
00BAP Memorabilia Chicago Sun-Times Ruby-204
00BAP Memorabilia Chicago Sun-Times Gold-204
00BAP Mem Chicago Sun-Times Sapphire-204
00BAP Mem Toronto Fall Expo Copper-204
00BAP Memorabilia Toronto Fall Expo Gold-204
00BAP Memorabilia Toronto Fall Expo Ruby-204
00BAP Parkhurst 2000-P247
00BAP Signature Series-183
Emerald-183
Ruby-183
Sapphire-183
Autographs-77
Autographs Gold-77
00Black Diamond Game Gear-LMB
00O-Pee-Chee-192
00O-Pee-Chee Parallel-192
00Pacific-48
Copper-48
Gold-48
Ice Blue-48
Premiere Date-48
2001: Ice Odyssey-3
00Pacific 2001: Ice Odyssey Anaheim Ntnl-3
00Paramount-26
Copper-26
Gold-26
Holo-Gold-26
Holo-Silver-26
Ice Blue-26
Premiere Date-26
Glove Side Net Fusions-2
Glove Side Net Fusions Platinum-2
00Revolution-15
Blue-15
Premiere Date-15
Red-15
Stat Masters-11
00SP Authentic Sign of the Times-BI
00SPx Winning Materials-WBI
00Stadium Club-53
00Topps/OPC-192
Parallel-192
00Upper Deck-19
Exclusives Tier 1-19
Exclusives Tier 2-19
Game Jersey Autographs-HMA
Game Jersey Autographs Exclusives-EMB
MVP Excellence-ME6
MVP Mark of Excellence-SGTB
00Czech Stadion-155
00Rochester Americans-3
01Atomic-10
Blue-10
Gold-10
Premiere Date-10
Red-10
01BAP Signature Series-150
Autographs-150
Autographs Gold-150
Teammates-TM-4
01Between the Pipes-13
01Between the Pipes-95
Double Memorabilia-DM18
Future Wave-FW2
Goalie Gear-GG28
He Shoots-He Saves Prizes-31
Jerseys-GJ39
Jersey and Stick Cards-GSJ27
Masks-11
Masks Silver-11
Masks Gold-11
01Crown Royale-15
Blue-15
Premiere Date-15
Red-15
Retail-15
01Pacific-46
Extreme LTD-46
Hobby LTD-46
Premiere Date-46
Retail LTD-46
01Pacific Adrenaline-19
Blue-19
Premiere Date-19
Red-19
Retail-19
Creased Lightning-1
Power Play-5
01Pacific Arena Exclusives-46
01Parkhurst-39
Gold-39
Silver-39
Teammates-T11
01Private Stock-8
Gold-8
Premiere Date-8
Retail-8
Silver-8
01Private Stock Pacific Nights-8
01Private Stock PS-2002-8
01Private Stock Reserve-G1
01SP Authentic-9
01SP Authentic-126
Limited-9
Limited-126
Limited Gold-9
Limited Gold-126
Buybacks-13
Sign of the Times-MB
01SP Game Used Authentic Fabric-DFAB
01SP Game Used Inked Sweaters-ISMB
01SP Game Used Inked Sweaters-DSBO
01SP Game Used Patches-PBI
01SP Game Used Patches Signed-SPMB
01SP Game Used Patches Signed-DSPBK
01SP Game Used Patches Signed-DSPTB
01SPx-6
Hidden Treasures-TTDBA
01Titanium-13
Hobby Parallel-13
Premiere Date-13
Retail-13
Retail Parallel-13
Double-Sided Jerseys-66
Double-Sided Patches-66
01Titanium Draft Day Edition-12
01Topps Chrome-130
Refractors-130
Black Border Refractors-130
01Topps Heritage-107
Refractors-107
01Topps Reserve-71
01UD Challenge for the Cup-8
01UD Mask Collection-104
01UD Mask Collection-172
Gold-104
Gold-172
Double Patches-DPMB
Dual Jerseys-PMGB
Goalie Jerseys-SSMB
Goalie Pads-GPMB
Jerseys-J-MB
Jersey and Patch-JPMB
01UD Playmakers-13
01UD Premier Collection Signatures-BI
01UD Premier Collection Signatures Black-BI
01UD Top Shelf-81
Goalie Gear-LPMB
01Upper Deck-250
Exclusives-250
Game Jerseys Series II-GNMB
01Upper Deck Ice-4
01Upper Deck MVP-21
01Upper Deck Victory-43
Gold-43
01Upper Deck Vintage-27
01Vanguard-9
Blue-9
Red-9
One of Ones-9
Premiere Date-9
Proofs-9
Stonewallers-3
02Atomic-9
Blue-9
Gold-9
Red-9
Hobby Parallel-9
02BAP First Edition-36
02BAP First Edition-414R
Jerseys-36
02BAP Memorabilia-9
Emerald-9
Ruby-9
Sapphire-9
NHL All-Star Game-9
NHL All-Star Game Blue-9
NHL All-Star Game Green-9
NHL All-Star Game Red-9
02BAP Memorabilia Toronto Fall Expo-9
02BAP Signature Series-80
Autographs-80
Autograph Buybacks 1999-35
Autograph Buybacks 2000-77
Autograph Buybacks 2001-150
Autographs Gold-80
02Between the Pipes-15
02Between the Pipes-124
Gold-15
Silver-15
Emblems-16
Future Wave-9
Goalie Autographs-1
Jerseys-16
Masks II-4
Masks II Gold-4
Masks II Silver-4
Numbers-16
Stick and Jerseys-16
Tandems-6
02Crown Royale-10
Blue-10
Red-10
Retail-10
Dual Patches-2
02O-Pee-Chee-115
02O-Pee-Chee Premier Blue Parallel-115
02O-Pee-Chee Premier Red Parallel-115
02O-Pee-Chee Factory Set-115
02Pacific-38
Blue-38
Red-38
02Pacific Complete-459
Red-459
02Pacific Exclusive-16
02Pacific Heads-Up-12
Blue-12
Purple-12
Red-12
Quad Jerseys-4
Quad Jerseys Gold-4
02Pacific Quest for the Cup-9
Gold-9
02Pacific Toronto Fall Expo-9
Gold-9
02Parkhurst-139
Bronze-139
Gold-139
Silver-139
02Parkhurst Retro-119
Minis-119
02Private Stock Reserve-10
Blue-10
Red-10
Retail-10
02Sabres Team Issue-2
02SP Authentic-9
Beckett Promos-9
Super Premiums-SPBI
02SP Game Used-6
Authentic Fabrics-AFBI
Authentic Fabrics Gold-AFBI
Authentic Fabrics Rainbow-AFBI
First Rounder Patches-BI
Piece of History-PHBI
Piece of History Gold-PHBI
Piece of History Rainbow-PHBI
02SPx-8
Spectrum Gold-8
Spectrum Silver-8
Winning Materials-WMBI
Winning Materials Gold-BI
Winning Materials Silver-BI
Xtreme Talents-MB
Xtreme Talents Gold-MB
Xtreme Talents Silver-MB
02Stadium Club-55
Silver Decoy Cards-55
Proofs-55
Puck Stops Here-PSH5
02Titanium-11
Blue-11
Red-11
Retail-11
Jerseys-6
Jerseys Retail-6
Patches-6
02Topps-115
OPC Blue Parallel-115
OPC Red Parallel-115
First Round Fabric-MB
First Round Fabric Autographs-MB
Factory Set-115
02Topps Chrome-74
Black Border Refractors-74
Refractors-74
First Round Fabric Patches-MB
02Topps Heritage-46
Chrome Parallel-46
02Topps Total-384
02UD Artistic Impressions-10
Gold-10
02UD Artistic Impressions Beckett Promos-10
02UD Artistic Impressions Retrospectives-R10
02UD Artistic Impressions Retrospect Gold-R10
02UD Artistic Impress Retrospect Silver-R10
02UD Honor Roll-8
02UD Mask Collection-11
02UD Mask Collection-12
02UD Mask Collection-102
02UD Mask Collection Beckett Promos-11
02UD Mask Collection Beckett Promos-12
02UD Mask Collection Great Gloves-GGMB
02UD Mask Collection Masked Marvels-MMBI
02UD Mask Collection Nation's Best-NLBT
02UD Mask Collection Patches-PWMB
02UD Mask Collection View from the Cage-VBI
02UD Piece of History-10
02UD Top Shelf-9
Dual Player Jerseys-RPB
Dual Player Jerseys-STBN
Signatures-MB
Stopper Jerseys-SSBI
Sweet Sweaters-SWMB
Triple Jerseys-TSASB
02Upper Deck Goaltender Threads-MB
02Upper Deck Goaltender Threads Gold-MB
02Upper Deck Last Line of Defense-LL2
02Upper Deck Saviors Jerseys-SVMB
02Upper Deck Super Saviors-SA1
02Upper Deck Classic Portraits-11
02Upper Deck MVP-24
Gold-24
Classics-24
Golden Classics-24
Skate Around Jerseys-SDDB
Skate Around Jerseys-STDSB
Souvenirs-S-MB
02Upper Deck Rookie Update-14
02Upper Deck Victory-23
Bronze-23
Gold-23
Silver-23
02Upper Deck Vintage-31
02Upper Deck Vintage-264
Green Backs-31
Jerseys-EEMB
Jerseys Gold-EE-MB
02Vanguard-11
LTD-11
03BAP Memorabilia-136
Emerald-136
Gold-136
Ruby-136
Sapphire-136
Deep in the Crease-D13
Tandems-T-4
03BAP Ultimate Memorabilia Autographs-47
Gold-47
03BAP Ultimate Memorabilia Triple Threads-6
03Beehive-27
Gold-27
Silver-27
03Black Diamond-19
Black-19
Green-19
Red-19
03Bowman-96
Gold-96
03Bowman Chrome-96
Refractors-96
Gold Refractors-96
Xtractors-96
03Crown Royale-10
Blue-10
Retail-10
Gauntlet of Glory-4
03ITG Action-56
Jerseys-M6
03ITG Used Signature Series-95
Gold-95
Autographs-MBI
Autographs Gold-MBI
03McDonald's Pacific-5
03NHL Sticker Collection-30
03O-Pee-Chee-71
03OPC Blue-71
03OPC Gold-71
03OPC Red-71
03Pacific-36
Blue-36
Red-36
03Pacific Calder-10
Silver-10
03Pacific Complete-447
Red-447
03Pacific Exhibit-156
03Pacific Exhibit-202
Blue Backs-156
03Pacific Heads-Up-11
Hobby LTD-11
Retail LTD-11
03Pacific Invincible-9
Blue-9
Red-9
Retail-9
Jerseys-3
03Pacific Prism-14
Blue-14
Gold-14
Red-14
03Private Stock Reserve-146
Blue-146
Patches-146
Red-146
Retail-146
03SP Authentic-11
Limited-11
03SP Game Used-107
Gold-107
03Titanium-12
Hobby Jersey Number Parallels-12
Retail-12
Retail Jersey Number Parallels-12
03Topps-71
Blue-71
Gold-71
Red-71
03Topps C55-62
Minis-62
Minis American Back-62
Minis American Back Red-62
Minis Bazooka Back-62
Minis Brooklyn Back-62
Minis Hat Trick Back-62
Minis O Canada Back-62
Minis O Canada Back Red-62
Minis Stanley Cup Back-62
03Topps Pristine-4
Gold Refractor Die Cuts-4
Refractors-4
Jersey Portions-PPJ-MB
Jersey Portion Refractors-PPJ-MB
Mini-PM-MBI
Patches-PP-MB
Patch Refractors-PP-MB
Press Plates Black-4
Press Plates Cyan-4
Press Plates Magenta-4
Press Plates Yellow-4
03Upper Deck-27
Canadian Exclusives-27
HG-27
03Upper Deck MVP-61
Gold Script-61
Silver Script-61
Canadian Exclusives-61
SportsNut-SN11
03Upper Deck Victory-24
Bronze-24
Gold-24
Silver-24
03Toronto Star-9
04Pacific-29
Blue-29
Red-29
04SP Authentic Buybacks-127
04SP Authentic Buybacks-128
04SP Authentic Buybacks-129
04SP Authentic Buybacks-130
04SP Authentic Buybacks-131
04SP Authentic Buybacks-132
04SP Authentic Sign of the Times-ST-BI
04SP Authentic Sign of the Times-DS-BD
04Upper Deck-24
Canadian Exclusives-24
HG Glossy Gold-24
HG Glossy Silver-24
05Be A Player Signatures-BI
05Be A Player Signatures Gold-BI
05Be A Player Triple Signatures-BUF
05Black Diamond-84
Emerald-84
Gold-84
Onyx-84
Ruby-84
Gemography-G-BI
Gemography Emerald-G-BI
Gemography Gold-G-BI
Gemography Onyx-G-BI
Gemography Ruby-G-BI
05Parkhurst-58
Facsimile Auto Parallel-58
Signatures-MB
05SP Authentic-14
Limited-14
Prestigious Pairings-PPMB
05SP Game Used-13
Autographs-13
Gold-13
Authentic Fabrics-AF-MB
Authentic Fabrics Autographs-AAF-MB
Authentic Fabrics Dual-BB
Authentic Fabrics Dual-BN
Authentic Fabrics Dual Autographs-BB
Authentic Fabrics Gold-AF-MB
Authentic Fabrics Quad-BADS
Authentic Patches Quad -BADS
Authentic Patches-AP-MB
Authentic Patches Autographs-AAP-MB
Authentic Patches Dual-BB
Authentic Patches Dual-BN
Authentic Patches Dual Autographs-BB
Awesome Authentics-AA-BI
05SPx Winning Combos-WC-BA
05SPx Winning Combos-WC-BN
05SPx Winning Combos Autographs-AWC-BA
05SPx Winning Combos Autographs-AWC-BN
05SPx Winning Combos Gold-WC-BA
05SPx Winning Combos Gold-WC-BN
05SPx Winning Combos Spectrum-WC-BA
05SPx Winning Combos Spectrum-WC-BN
05The Cup Honorable Numbers-HNBI
05The Cup Limited Logos-LLBI
05The Cup Master Pressplate Rookie Update-201
05UD Artifacts-12
Blue-12
Gold-12
Green-12
Pewter-12
Red-12
Auto Facts-AF-BI
Auto Facts Blue-AF-BI
Auto Facts Copper-AF-BI
Auto Facts Pewter-AF-BI
Auto Facts Silver-AF-BI
Gold Autographed-12
Remarkable Artifacts-RA-BI
Remarkable Artifacts Dual-RA-BI
05Ultimate Collection-13
Gold-13
Endorsed Emblems-EEBI
05Ultra-23
Gold-23
Ice-23
05Upper Deck-267
Big Playmakers-B-MBO
Jerseys-J-MBI
Jerseys Series II-J2BI
Notable Numbers-N-BI
05Upper Deck MVP-44
Gold-44
Platinum-44
ProSign-P-MB
05Upper Deck Rookie Update-201
Inspirations Patch Rookies-201
05Upper Deck Victory-22
Black-22
Gold-22
Silver-22
06Between The Pipes The Mask-M28
06Between The Pipes The Mask Gold-M28
06Between The Pipes The Mask Silver-M28
06Between The Pipes The Mask Game-Used-MGU01
06Between The Pipes The Mask Game-Used Gold-MGU01
06Black Diamond Jerseys-JMB
06Black Diamond Jerseys Black-JMB
06Black Diamond Jerseys Gold-JMB
06Black Diamond Jerseys Ruby-JMB
06Black Diamond Jerseys Black Autographs -JBI
06Flair Showcase Inks-IBI
06Flair Showcase Stitches-SSMB
06Fleer Fabricology-FMB
06Fleer Signing Day-SDBI
06Hot Prospects Hotgraphs-HBI
06O-Pee-Chee-68
Rainbow-68
06The Cup Autographed NHL Shields Duals-DASMB
06UD Artifacts Auto-Facts-AFBI
06UD Artifacts Auto-Facts Gold-AFBI
06UD Artifacts Tundra Tandems-TTMB
06UD Artifacts Tundra Tandems Black-TTMB
06UD Artifacts Tundra Tandems Blue-TTMB
06UD Artifacts Tundra Tandems Gold-TTMB
06UD Artifacts Tundra Tandems Red-TTMB
06UD Artifacts Tundra Tandems Dual Patches Red-TTMB
06Ultra-26
Gold Medallion-26
Ice Medallion-26
Fresh Ink-IMB
Uniformity-UMB
Uniformity Patches-UPMB
Uniformity Autographed Jerseys-UAMB
06Upper Deck-275
Exclusives Parallel-275
High Gloss Parallel-275
Game Jerseys-JBI
Game Patches-PBI
Masterpieces-275
06Upper Deck MVP-40
Gold Script-40
Super Script-40
06Upper Deck Ovation-56
06Upper Deck Sweet Shot Signature Shots/Saves-SSBI
06Upper Deck Trilogy Scripts-TSMB
06Upper Deck Victory-25
06Upper Deck Victory Black-25
06Upper Deck Victory Gold-25
07Upper Deck Victory-27
Black-27
Gold-27

Biron, Mathieu
94Quebec Pee-Wee Tournament-1752
98OPC Chrome-238
Refractors-238
98Topps-238
O-Pee-Chee-238
98Bowman CHL-154
Golden Anniversary-154
OPC International-154
Autographs Blue-A21
Autographs Gold-A21
Autographs Silver-A21
98Bowman Chrome CHL-154
Golden Anniversary-154
Golden Anniversary Refractors-154
OPC International-154
OPC International Refractors-154
Refractors-154
99BAP Memorabilia-305
Gold-305
Silver-305
99BAP Millennium Calder Candidates Ruby-C35
99BAP Millennium Calder Candidate Emerald-C35
99BAP Millennium Calder Cand Sapphire-C35
99Pacific Dynagon Ice-121
Blue-121
Copper-121
Gold-121
Premiere Date-121
99Wayne Gretzky Hockey-105
99Quebec PeeWee Tournament Coll Souv-27
99Bowman CHL-69
Gold-69
OPC International-69
00BAP Memorabilia-62
Emerald-62
Ruby-62
Sapphire-62
Promos-62
00BAP Mem Chicago Sportsfest Copper-62
00BAP Memorabilia Chicago Sportsfest Blue-62
00BAP Memorabilia Chicago Sportsfest Gold-62
00BAP Memorabilia Chicago Sportsfest Ruby-62
00BAP Memorabilia Chicago Sun-Times Ruby-62
00BAP Memorabilia Chicago Sun-Times Gold-62
00BAP Mem Chicago Sun-Times Sapphire-62
00BAP Mem Toronto Fall Expo Copper-62
00BAP Memorabilia Toronto Fall Expo Gold-62
00BAP Memorabilia Toronto Fall Expo Ruby-62
00BAP Signature Series-80
Emerald-80
Ruby-80
Sapphire-80
Autographs-50
Autographs Gold-50
00O-Pee-Chee-158
00O-Pee-Chee Parallel-158
00Topps/OPC-158
Parallel-158
00Upper Deck MVP-113
First Stars-113
Second Stars-113
Third Stars-113
00Lowell Lock Monsters-23
02BAP Sig Series Auto Buybacks 2000-50
03ITG Action-286
03Panthers Team Issue-1
04Thetford Mines Prolab-21
05Parkhurst-495

Birrer, Peter
93Quebec Pee-Wee Tournament-1637

Birukov, Eugeni
05Russian Hockey League RHL-17

Biryukov, Evgeni
04Russian Under-18 Team-2

Bisaillon, J.P.
51Laval Dairy QSHL-71
52St. Lawrence Sales-30

Bisaillon, Patrick
917th Inn. Sketch QMJHL-264
917th Inn. Sketch Memorial Cup-32
97Tucson Gila Monsters-5

Bisaillon, Sebastien
03Val d'Or Foreurs-22

Biser, Scott
01Swiss HNL-411

Bishai, Mike
01Western Michigan Broncos-2
03ITG VIP Rookie Debut-111
03Parkhurst Rookie-127
03Topps Traded-TT110
Blue-TT110
Gold-TT110
Red-TT110
03Upper Deck Rookie Update-169
04Pacific-283
Blue-283
Red-283

Bishop, Allen
82North Bay Centennials-1
83Kingston Canadians-24

Bishop, Ben
05Maine Black Bears-2

Bishop, Hunter
05Vernon Vipers-3

Bishop, Mike
84Kitchener Rangers-6
90Halifax Citadels-2
90ProCards AHL/IHL-465
93UK Humberside Hawks-4
94UK Humberside Hawks-4
01UK Hull Thunder-2
01UK Hull Thunder-5
02UK Hull Thunder-2
02UK Hull Thunder-23

Bissett, Tom
90ProCards AHL/IHL-480
91Swedish Semic Elitserien Stickers-52
92Swedish Semic Elitserien Stickers-63
93Swiss HNL-376
95Swedish World Championships Stickers-232
98Swedish UD Choice-46
99Swedish Upper Deck-30
Hands of Gold-4
00Swedish Upper Deck-37
00Swedish Upper Deck-183
SHL Signatures-TB
01Swedish Brynas Tigers-4
02Finnish Cardset-159

Bisson, Michel
98Thetford Mines Coyotes-17

Bisson, Steve
88ProCards AHL-283
89ProCards IHL-130

Bisson, Todd
01Asheville Smoke-8

Bissonette, Eric
907th Inn. Sketch QMJHL-205
907th Inn. Sketch Memorial Cup-60

Bissonnette, Paul
03Saginaw Spirit-2
04Saginaw Spirit-4

Bissonnette, Roberto
99Hull Olympiques-10
Signed-10
00Hull Olympiques-8
Signed-8

Bittner, J.B.
00Sioux Falls Stampede-2
02Ohio State Buckeyes-4
03Ohio State Buckeyes-4
04Ohio State Buckeyes-5
05Johnstown Chiefs-2

Bixby, Dustin
04Gwinnett Gladiators-3

Bizjak, Marjan
93Quebec Pee-Wee Tournament-1800

Bizub, Arkadiusz
93Quebec Pee-Wee Tournament-1500

Bizubk, Lukasz
93Quebec Pee-Wee Tournament-1502

Bizyayev, Vasily
00Kitchener Rangers-5

Bizzarro, Joey
93Quebec Pee-Wee Tournament-1437

Bizzozero, Francesco
95Swiss HNL-138
96Swiss HNL-407
01Swiss HNL-364
02Swiss HNL-415

Bizzozero, Michele
95Swiss HNL-378

Bjaarnhjelm, Patrik
02Swedish SHL-219
Parallel-219
03Swedish Elite Signatures-14

Bjargestad, Hans
55Swedish Alfabilder-32

Bjelonozkjin, Anatoli
73Swedish Stickers-128

Bjerring, Henrik
99Danish Hockey League-173

Bjerrum, Mikkel
98Danish Hockey League-5
99Danish Hockey League-6

Bjerrum, Thomas
98Danish Hockey League-17
99Danish Hockey League-17

Bjorck, Jesper
02Swedish SHL-94
Parallel-94
03Swedish Elite-147
Silver-147
05Swedish SHL Elitset-163
06Swedish SHL Elitset-17

Bjork, Anders
92Swedish Semic Elitserien Stickers-41
96Denver University Pioneers-10
98Grand Rapids Griffins-4

Bjork, Johan
02Swedish Malmo Red Hawks-2
03Swedish Elite-238
Silver-238
06Swedish SHL Elitset-227

Bjork, Kent
67Swedish Hockey-251
69Swedish Hockey-296
71Swedish Hockey-291
72Swedish Stickers-74

Bjork, Lasse
84Swedish Semic Elitserien-141

Bjork, Stefan
92Swedish Semic Elitserien Stickers-350

Bjorklof, Ann
99Finnish Cardset Aces High-H-Q

Bjorkman, Henric
89Swedish Semic Elitserien Stickers-131
90Swedish Semic Elitserien Stickers-207
91Swedish Semic Elitserien Stickers-135
92Swedish Semic Elitserien Stickers-154
93Swedish Semic Elitserien-126
97Swedish Collector's Choice-196
Crash the Game Exchange-C29
Crash the Game Redemption-R29
Stick'Ums-S9
99Swedish Upper Deck-190

Bjorkman, Tommy
64Swedish Coralli ISHockey-121
65Swedish Coralli ISHockey-121
67Swedish Hockey-60

Bjorkstrand, Todd
98Danish Hockey League-173
99Danish Hockey League-56

Bjorn, Lars
55Swedish Alfabilder-1
64Swedish Coralli ISHockey-123
65Swedish Coralli ISHockey-123
67Swedish Hockey-61
81Swedish Semic Hockey VM Stickers-125
98Swedish UD Choice-199

Bjorner, Olaf
94German First League-137

Bjornfot, Niklas
92Swedish Semic Elitserien Stickers-179
93Swedish Semic Elitserien-150

Bjornlie, Dan
00Quad-City Mallards-6
01Quad-City Mallards-2
04German Cologne Sharks Postcards-4
04German DEL-206

Bjornson, Derek
96Saskatoon Blades-4
97Saskatoon Blades-2

Bjornstad, Svenn Erik
92Norwegian Elite Series-13

Bjugstad, Scott
84North Stars Postcards-4
85North Stars 7-Eleven-2
85North Stars Postcards-5
86North Stars 7-Eleven-4
86North Stars Postcards-5
86O-Pee-Chee-23
86O-Pee-Chee Stickers-168
86Topps-23
87North Stars Postcards-7
88Panini Stickers-90
88ProCards IHL-30
89ProCards AHL-15
90Pro Set-455
91ProCards-404

Bjuhr, Thomas
85Swedish Panini Stickers-17
86Portland Winter Hawks-3
89Swedish Semic Elitserien Stickers-20
90Swedish Semic Elitserien Stickers-87
91Swedish Semic Elitserien Stickers-16
92Swedish Semic Elitserien Stickers-37

Bjurling, Bjorn
02Swedish SHL-156
Parallel-156
03Swedish Elite-156
Silver-156
04Swedish Elitset-12
Gold-12
In The Crease-2
Masks-2
Signatures-8

Blaar, Achim
94German First League-543

Black, Clint
91British Columbia JHL-133
92British Columbia JHL-27
95Central Hockey League-73
99Tupelo T-Rex-11

Black, Greg
03Peoria Rivermen-10
03Worcester Ice Cats-11

Black, Guy
62Quebec Aces-3

Black, James
87Portland Winter Hawks-4
88Portland Winter Hawks-4
89Portland Winter Hawks-1
89ProCards AHL-292
90ProCards AHL/IHL-191
91Upper Deck-580
French-580
91Whalers Jr. 7-Eleven-3
91ProCards-101
92Bowman-252
92O-Pee-Chee-388
92Stadium Club-303
92Topps-232
Gold-232G
92Upper Deck-323
93Donruss-85
93Upper Deck-517
93Rochester Americans Kodak-5
94Las Vegas Thunder-1
95Indianapolis Ice-2
96Collector's Edge Future Legends-48
97Be A Player-186
Autographs-186
Autographs Die-Cuts-186
Autographs Prismatic Die-Cuts-186
97Pacific Dynagon Best Kept Secrets-19
99Pacific-436
Copper-436
Emerald Green-436
Gold-436
Ice Blue-436
Premiere Date-436
Red-436
01Grand Rapids Griffins-7
03German DEL-139

Black, Jamie
907th Inn. Sketch WHL-318
917th Inn. Sketch WHL-172
92Tacoma Rockets-2
93Cleveland Lumberjacks-10
93Cleveland Lumberjacks Postcards-3
94Muskegon Fury-18
94Classic Pro Prospects-122
99San Diego Gulls-3
00San Diego Gulls-1

Black, Jesse
95Slapshot-187

Black, Jonathan
88Richelieu Riverains-4

Black, Jordan
02Chicago Steel-2

Black, Mason
93Quebec Pee-Wee Tournament-577

Black, Mike
89Hampton Roads Admirals-1A
89Hampton Roads Admirals-1H

Black, Ryan
907th Inn. Sketch OHL-352
91Peterborough Petes-13
917th Inn. Sketch OHL-144
93London Knights-4
96Fort Worth Fire-17
98Fort Worth Brahmas-10

Black, Stephen
44Beehive Group II Photos-154

Black, Terry
87Portland Winter Hawks-5
88Portland Winter Hawks-5

Blackadar, Raymond
94Anchorage Aces-8

Blackbird, Louie
96Sarnia Sting-2
96Sudbury Wolves-3
96Sudbury Wolves Police-5

Blackburn, Alexandre
99Shawinigan Cataractes-5
Signed-5
01Chicoutimi Sagueneens-10

Blackburn, Bob
69O-Pee-Chee-113
70Esso Power Players-220

Blackburn, Dan
00SPx Rookie Redemption-RR20
00Kootenay Ice-3
00UD CHL Prospects-53
00UD CHL Prospects-91
Autographs-A-DB
CHL Class-CC7
Destination the Show-D2
Game Jersey Autographs-S-DB
Game Jerseys-DB
Game Jerseys-B-B
Game Jerseys-B-Z
Game Jerseys-L-B
01Atomic-116
Premiere Date-116
01Atomic Toronto Fall Expo-116
01BAP Memorabilia-305
Emerald-305
Ruby-305
Sapphire-305
Draft Redemptions-10
01BAP Signature Series-201
Autographs-201
Autographs Gold-201
01Between the Pipes-57
Future Wave-FW5
01Bowman YoungStars-140
Gold-140
Ice Cubed-140
Autographs-DB
Relics-JDB
Relics-SDB
Relics-DSDB
Rivals-R1
01Crown Royale-171
Crowning Achievement-8
Rookie Royalty-14
01O-Pee-Chee-332
01Pacific-458
01Pacific Adrenaline-217
Blue-217
Premiere Date-217
Red-217
Retail-217
Rookie Report-12
01Pacific Heads-Up-112
01Pacific High Voltage-7
01Parkhurst-282
01Parkhurst Beckett Promos-282
01Private Stock-131
Gold-131
Premiere Date-131
Retail-131
Silver-131
Moments in Time-7
01Private Stock Pacific Nights-131
01Private Stock PS-2002-100
01Private Stock Reserve-R6
01SP Authentic-178
Limited-178
Limited Gold-178
01SP Game Used-88
01SPx-117
01Stadium Club-131
Award Winners-131
Master Photos-131
01Titanium-171
Retail-171
01Titanium Draft Day Edition-152
01Topps-332
01Topps Chrome-150
Refractors-150
Black Border Refractors-150
01Topps Heritage-147
01Topps Reserve-116
01UD Challenge for the Cup-121
01UD Honor Roll-96
01UD Mask Collection-155
Gold-155
01UD Playmakers-131
01UD Premier Collection-113
Signatures-BR
Signatures Black-BR
01UD Top Shelf-72
01Upper Deck-434
Exclusives-434
01Upper Deck Ice-62
01Upper Deck MVP-229
01Upper Deck Victory-449
01Vanguard-122
Blue-122
Red-122
One of Ones-122
Premiere Date-122
Prime Prospects-12
Proofs-122
01UD Prospects-2
Autographs-A-DB
Jersey Autographs-S-DB
Jerseys-J-DB
Jerseys-C-BD
Jerseys-C-BM
Jerseys-C-BS
Jerseys-C-BW
Jerseys Gold-J-DB
Jerseys Gold-C-BD
Jerseys Gold-C-BM
Jerseys Gold-C-BS
Jerseys Gold-C-BW
02Atomic-66
Blue-66
Gold-66
Red-66
Hobby Parallel-66
02BAP First Edition-254
02BAP First Edition-425H
02BAP Memorabilia-54
Emerald-54
Ruby-54
Sapphire-54
Future of the Game-FG-2
NHL All-Star Game-54
NHL All-Star Game Blue-54
NHL All-Star Game Green-54
NHL All-Star Game Red-54
02BAP Memorabilia Toronto Fall Expo-54
02BAP Signature Series-172
Autographs-172
Autograph Buybacks 2001-201
Autographs Gold-172
Defensive Wall-DW4
Jerseys-SGJ50
Jersey Autographs-SGJ50
Team Quads-TQ4
02BAP Ultimate Memorabilia Numerology-29
02Between the Pipes-6
Gold-6
Silver-6
Emblems-4
Future Wave-5
Goalie Autographs-2
He Shoots-He Saves Points-12
He Shoots-He Saves Prizes-6

Inspirations-I7
Jerseys-4
Nightmares-GN1
Numbers-4
Stick and Jerseys-4
Tandems-1
02Bowman Toronto Spring Expo-9
02Bowman YoungStars-131
Gold-131
Silver-131
02O-Pee-Chee-123
02O-Pee-Chee Premier Blue Parallel-123
02O-Pee-Chee Premier Red Parallel-123
02O-Pee-Chee Factory Set-123
02Pacific-248
Blue-248
Red-248
Shining Moments-9
02Pacific Calder Collection AS Fantasy-8
02Pacific Calder Collection All-Star Fantasy Gold-8
02Pacific Complete-168
Red-168
02Pacific Entry Draft-8
02Pacific Exclusive-112
Great Expectations-13
02Pacific Heads-Up-77
Blue-77
Purple-77
Red-77
Head First-10
02Pacific Toronto Spring Expo Rookie Coll-9
02Parkhurst-51
Bronze-51
Gold-51
Silver-51
02Parkhurst Retro-174
Minis-174
02Private Stock Reserve-65
Blue-65
Red-65
Retail-65
02Rangers Team Issue-2
02SP Authentic-124
02SP Game Used First Rounder Patches-BLA
02Stadium Club-34
Silver Decoy Cards-34
Proofs-34
YoungStars Relics-S4
YoungStars Relics-DS6
02Topps-123
OPC Blue Parallel-123
OPC Red Parallel-123
First Round Fabric-DB
Factory Set-123
02Topps Chrome-79
Black Border Refractors-79
Refractors-79
First Round Fabric Patches-DB
02Topps Heritage Crease Piece-DB
02Topps Heritage Crease Piece Patches-DB
02Topps Total-401
02Upper Deck Collectors Club-NHL20
02UD Mask Collection-54
02UD Mask Collection-55
02UD Mask Collection-56
02UD Mask Collection-111
02UD Mask Collection Beckett Promos-54
02UD Mask Collection Beckett Promos-55
02UD Mask Collection Beckett Promos-56
02UD Mask Collection Great Gloves-GGDB
02UD Mask Collection Nation's Best-NOBB
02UD Mask Collection Patches-PWDB
02UD Top Shelf Stopper Jerseys-SSDB
02Upper Deck-116
Exclusives-116
CHL Graduates-CGBL
CHL Graduates Gold-CGBL
On the Rise-ORDB
02Upper Deck Classic Portraits-67
02Upper Deck MVP-124
Gold-124
Classics-124
Golden Classics-124
02Upper Deck Victory-144
Bronze-144
Gold-144
Silver-144
02Upper Deck Vintage-172
02Upper Deck Vintage-320
Green Backs-172
02Vanguard-66
LTD-66
03BAP Memorabilia-113
Emerald-113
Gold-113
Ruby-113
Sapphire-113
Deep in the Crease-D5
Future Wave-FW-5
03Bowman Future Fabrics-FF-DB
03Bowman Future Fabric Patches-DB
03Duracell-12
03ITG Action-347
Jerseys-M94
Jerseys-M229
03ITG VIP Making the Bigs-8
03ITG VIP Netminders-9
03O-Pee-Chee-178
03OPC Blue-178
03OPC Gold-178
03OPC Red-178
03Pacific-220
Blue-220
Red-220
03Pacific Exhibit-95
Blue Backs-95
Yellow Backs-95
03Parkhurst Original Six New York-3
Memorabilia-NM8
Memorabilia-NM18
03Parkhurst Rookie Road to the NHL-RNJ-12
03Parkhurst Rookie Road to the NHL Gold-RTN-12
03Parkhurst Rookie Road to the NHL Emblem-RTNE-12
03Parkhurst Rookie Road NHL Emblem Gold-RTNE-12
03Rangers Team Issue-2
03SPx Big Futures-BF-DB
03SPx Big Futures Limited-BF-DB
03SPx Winning Materials-WM-DB
03SPx Winning Materials Limited-WM-DB
03Topps-178
Blue-178
Gold-178
Red-178
Pristine Jersey Portions-PPJ-DBL
Pristine Jersey Portion Refractors-PPJ-DBL
Pristine Patches-PP-DB
Pristine Patch Refractors-PP-DB
03Upper Deck MVP-287
Gold Script-287
Silver Script-287
Canadian Exclusives-287
SportsNut-SN56
03Upper Deck Victory-129
Bronze-129
Gold-129
Silver-129
05Be A Player-60
First Period-60
Second Period-60
Third Period-60
Overtime-60

Blackburn, Don

63Quebec Aces-2
64Quebec Aces-3
65Quebec Aces-3
68Shirriff Coins-130

Blackburn, Joe

93Quebec Pee-Wee Tournament-1756
98Black Diamond-119
Double Diamond-119
Triple Diamond-119
Quadruple Diamond-119
98SPx Top Prospects-89
Radiance-89
Spectrum-89
00Michigan State Spartans-1

Blackburn, Josh

97Dubuque Fighting Saints-30
02Columbia Inferno-97
03Columbia Inferno-98

Blacklock, Justin

03Camrose Kodiaks-20

Blacklock, Kyle

907th Inn. Sketch OHL-379
90Sudbury Wolves-5
917th Inn. Sketch OHL-254
91Sudbury Wolves-4

Blackned, Brant

917th Inn. Sketch QMJHL-244
98Thunder Bay Thunder Cats-18
99Rockford IceHogs-1
02Muskegon Fury-1
03Muskegon Fury-2

Blackwin, Everton

92Thunder Bay Thunder Hawks-13

Blad, Brian

88ProCards AHL-235
89ProCards AHL-107
90Newmarket Saints-3
90ProCards AHL/IHL-164
91ProCards-608
94Brantford Smoke-14
97Toledo Storm-11

Bladon, Tom

73Flyers Linnett-3
74NHL Action Stamps-209
74O-Pee-Chee NHL-396
75Flyers Canada Dry Cans-2
75O-Pee-Chee NHL-74
75Topps-74
76O-Pee-Chee NHL-164
76Topps-164
77O-Pee-Chee NHL-131
77Topps-131A
77Topps-131B
78O-Pee-Chee-152
78Topps-152
79O-Pee-Chee-204
79Topps-204
80O-Pee-Chee-135
80Topps-135
88Oilers Tenth Anniversary-108
04ITG Franchises US East-425
Autographs-A-TBL

Blaha, Jan

94Czech APS Extraliga-60

Blaha, Michael

91Upper Deck-669
French-669
91Upper Deck Czech World Juniors-30
93Swiss HNL-223

Blaha, Pavel

94Czech APS Extraliga-255
97Czech APS Extraliga-225
97Czech DS Extraliga-16
98Czech DS Stickers-31
98Czech OFS-84

Blaho, Stefan

03Sudbury Wolves-4
04Sudbury Wolves-8

Blain, Brady

917th Inn. Sketch OHL-194
92Windsor Spitfires-16
93Windsor Spitfires-12
98Bakersfield Condors-3

Blain, Jacques

72Nordiques Postcards-4
73Nordiques Team Issue-4

Blain, Joel

87Hull Olympiques-3
907th Inn. Sketch QMJHL-149
917th Inn. Sketch QMJHL-212
92Wheeling Thunderbirds-3

Blain, Luc-Oliver

06Chicoutimi Sagueneens-2

Blain, Robert

95Slapshot-412

Blair, Andy

32O'Keefe Maple Leafs-5
33O-Pee-Chee V304B-70
33V129-11
33V288 Hamilton Gum-9
33V357 Ice Kings-4
34Beehive Group I Photos-300
35Diamond Matchbooks Tan 4-1
37V356 Worldwide Gum-56

Blair, Bryan

96Sarnia Sting-3

Blair, Campbell

93Johnstown Chiefs-2
05Maine Black Bears-29

Blair, Danny

52Juniors Blue Tint-50

Blair, Darcy

91Air Canada SJHL-E30

Blair, Jeff

95Seattle Thunderbirds-4
96Seattle Thunderbirds-1
97Seattle Thunderbirds-10
98Tri-City Americans-1
99Alexandria Warthogs-2
03Bossier-Shreveport Mudbugs-3
05Colorado Eagles-3

Blair, Rael

93Quebec Pee-Wee Tournament-1761

Blair, Scott

94Detroit Jr. Red Wings-14
95Slapshot-64
95Slapshot Memorial Cup-88

Blair, Wren

78Saginaw Gears-1

Blais, Alexandre

03Baie Comeau Drakkar-6
04Baie-Comeau Drakkar-1
05Baie-Comeau Drakkar-6
05Cape Breton Screaming Eagles-25

Blais, Ben

04Wheeling Nailers SGA-2

Blais, Dean

03North Dakota Fighting Sioux-25

Blais, Dwayne

01Colorado Gold Kings-1

Blais, Jonathan

93Quebec Pee-Wee Tournament-1592

Blaisdell, Mike

82O-Pee-Chee-81
82Post Cereal-5
83NHL Key Tags-33
83O-Pee-Chee-242
86Penguins Kodak-2
88ProCards AHL-225
99UK Sheffield Steelers-1
00UK Sekonda Superleague-142
00UK Sheffield Steelers-8
01UK Sheffield Steelers-4
02UK Sheffield Steelers-1
03UK Sheffield Steelers-3
04UK Thommo's Top 10-5
05UK Nottingham Panthers-14

Blake, Jason

93Waterloo Black Hawks-2
99BAP Millennium-126
Emerald-126
Ruby-126
Sapphire-126
Signatures-126
Signatures Gold-126
99Pacific Dynagon Ice-94
Blue-94
Copper-94
Gold-94
Premiere Date-94
99SP Authentic-105
99Topps Premier Plus-102
Parallel-102
99Ultimate Victory-100
1/1-100
Parallel-100
Parallel 100-100
99Upper Deck-240
Exclusives-240
Exclusives 1 of 1-240
99Upper Deck Gold Reserve-240
00BAP Memorabilia-364
Emerald-364
Ruby-364
Sapphire-364
Promos-364
00BAP Mem Chicago Sportsfest Copper-364
00BAP Memorabilia Chicago Sportsfest Blue-364
00BAP Memorabilia Chicago Sportsfest Gold-364
00BAP Memorabilia Chicago Sportsfest Ruby-364
00BAP Memorabilia Chicago Sun-Times Ruby-364
00BAP Memorabilia Chicago Sun-Times Gold-364
00BAP Mem Chicago Sun-Times Sapphire-364
00BAP Mem Toronto Fall Expo Copper-364
00BAP Memorabilia Toronto Fall Expo Gold-364
00BAP Memorabilia Toronto Fall Expo Ruby-364
01Upper Deck Victory-222
Gold-222
02BAP Sig Series Auto Buybacks 1999-126
02Pacific Complete-305
Red-305
03Beehive-122
Gold-122
Silver-122
03Black Diamond-117
Black-117
Green-117
Red-117
03Crown Royale-64
Blue-64
Retail-64
03ITG Action-345
03O-Pee-Chee-181
03OPC Blue-181
03OPC Gold-181
03OPC Red-181
03Pacific-210
Blue-210
Red-210
03Pacific Complete-247
Red-247
03Pacific Exhibit-91
Blue Backs-91
Yellow Backs-91
03Pacific Prism-66
Blue-66
Gold-66
Red-66
03Pacific Supreme-61
03Pacific Supreme-62
Blue-62
Red-62
Retail-62
03Private Stock Reserve-63
Blue-63
Red-63
Retail-63
03SP Game Used-94
Gold-94
03Titanium-63
Hobby Jersey Number Parallels-63
Retail-63
Retail Jersey Number Parallels-63
03Topps-181
Blue-181
Gold-181
Red-181
03UD Honor Roll Signature Class-SC31
03Upper Deck-118
Big Playmakers-BP-JB
Canadian Exclusives-118
HG-118
03Upper Deck MVP-264
Gold Script-264
Silver Script-264
Canadian Exclusives-264
03Upper Deck Victory-115
Bronze-115
Gold-115
Silver-115
Game Breakers-GB13
04Pacific-164
Blue-164
Red-164
05Panini Stickers-94
05Parkhurst-304
Facsimile Auto Parallel-304
True Colors-TCNYI
True Colors-TCNYI
True Colors-TCNYNY
True Colors-TCNYNY
05Upper Deck-122
Big Playmakers-B-JBO
HG Glossy-122
Notable Numbers-N-JBL
Patches-P-JBL
05Upper Deck MVP-246
Gold-246
Platinum-246
Materials-M-JB
05Upper Deck Toronto Fall Expo-122
06Black Diamond-54
Black-54
Gold-54
Ruby-54
06Fleer-122
Tiffany-122
06O-Pee-Chee-308
Rainbow-308
06Panini Stickers-92
06UD Toronto Fall Expo Priority Signings -PSJB
06Ultra-125
Gold Medallion-125
Ice Medallion-125
06Upper Deck Arena Giveaways-NYI3
06Upper Deck-126
Exclusives Parallel-126
High Gloss Parallel-126
Masterpieces-126
Signature Sensations-SSJB
06Upper Deck MVP-184
Gold Script-184
Super Script-184
06Upper Deck Ovation-31
06Upper Deck Victory-125
06Upper Deck Victory Black-125
06Upper Deck Victory Gold-125
07Upper Deck Ovation-70
07Upper Deck Victory-16
Black-16
Gold-16

Blake, Rob

90Bowman-142
Tiffany-142
90Kings Smokey-3
90OPC Premier-6
90Pro Set-611
90Score-421
Canadian-421
90Upper Deck-45
French-45
91Pro Set Platinum-51
91Bowman-182
91Gillette-6
91O-Pee-Chee-6
91O-Pee-Chee-112
91OPC Premier-44
91Panini Stickers-86
91Panini Stickers-339
91Parkhurst-293
French-293
91Pinnacle-201
91Pinnacle-382
French-201
French-382
91Pro Set-92
French-92
Platinum PC-PC8
91Score American-27
91Score American-349
91Score Canadian Bilingual-27
91Score Canadian Bilingual-379
91Score Canadian English-27
91Score Canadian English-379
91Score Kellogg's-22
91Score Young Superstars-8
91Stadium Club-348
91Topps-6
91Topps-112
91Upper Deck-43
91Upper Deck-148
French-43
French-148
92Bowman-367
92O-Pee-Chee-243
92Panini Stickers-71
92Panini Stickers French-71
92Parkhurst-302
Emerald Ice-302
92Pinnacle-32
French-32
Team 2000-16
Team 2000 French-16
92Pro Set-67
92Score-177
Canadian-177
Young Superstars-38
92Stadium Club-23
92Topps-211
Gold-211G
92Ultra-79
92Upper Deck-140
93Donruss-158
93Leaf-172
93OPC Premier-56
Gold-56
93Panini Stickers-209
93Parkhurst-94
Emerald Ice-94
93Pinnacle-46
Canadian-46
93PowerPlay-113
93Score-236
Canadian-236
93Stadium Club-246
Members Only Master Set-246
OPC-246
First Day Issue-246
First Day Issue OPC-246
93Topps/OPC Premier-56
Gold-56
93Ultra-24
93Upper Deck-317
NHLPA/Roots-20
SP-68
94Be A Player-R40
99 All-Stars-G3
94Canada Games NHL POGS-129
94EA Sports-61
94Finest-45
Super Team Winners-45
Refractors-45
94Flair-77
94Fleer-93
Franchise Futures-2
94Leaf-12
Gold Stars-12
94Leaf Limited-32
94McDonald's Upper Deck-McD17
94OPC Premier-498
Special Effects-498
94Parkhurst-105
Gold-105
Vintage-V85
94Pinnacle-9
Artist's Proofs-9
Rink Collection-9
Boomers-BR10
94Score-47
Gold-47
Platinum-47
94Select-98
Gold-98
94SP-53
Die Cuts-53
94Stadium Club Members Only-8
94Stadium Club-135
Members Only Master Set-135
First Day Issue-135
Super Teams-11
Super Teams Members Only Master Set-11
Super Team Winner Cards-135
94Topps/OPC Premier-498
Special Effects-498
94Ultra-96
94Upper Deck-488
94Upper Deck-564
Electric Ice-488
Electric Ice-564
Predictor Canadian-C32
94Upper Deck Predictor Canadian Exch Gold-C32
94Upper Deck SP Inserts-SP35
94Upper Deck SP Inserts Die Cuts-SP35
95SLU Hockey American-1
95SLU Hockey Canadian-2
95Bashan Super Stickers-56
95Bashan Super Stickers-58
95Be A Player-113
Signatures-S113
Signatures Die Cuts-S113
95Canada Games NHL POGS-138
95Collector's Choice-160
Player's Club-160
Player's Club Platinum-160
95Donruss-22
95Emotion-80
95Hoyle Western Playing Cards-5
95Imperial Stickers-58
95Kenner Starting Lineup Cards-2
95Leaf-148
95Leaf Limited-71
95Metal-69
95Panini Stickers-272
95Parkhurst International-106
Emerald Ice-106
95Pinnacle-198
Artist's Proofs-198
Rink Collection-198
95Playoff One on One-48
95Post Upper Deck-24
95Pro Magnets-66
95Score-11
Black Ice Artist's Proofs-11
Black Ice-11
Check It-9
95Select Certified-74
Mirror Gold-74
95SkyBox Impact-78
95Stadium Club-56
Members Only Master Set-56
95Summit-86
Artist's Proofs-86
Ice-86
95Topps-307
OPC Inserts-307
95Ultra-73
Gold Medallion-73
95Upper Deck-478
Electric Ice-478
Electric Ice Gold-478
Special Edition-SE42
Special Edition Gold-SE42
95Zenith-88
95Finnish Semic World Championships-79
95Swedish Globe World Championships-82
95Swedish World Championships Stickers-8
96Black Diamond-144
Gold-144
96Donruss-100
Press Proofs-100
96Donruss Canadian Ice-42
Gold Press Proofs-42
Red Press Proofs-42
96Donruss Elite-48
Die Cut Stars-48
96Flair-45
Blue Ice-45
96Kraft Upper Deck-33
96Leaf-177
Press Proofs-177
96Metal Universe-73
96NHL Pro Stamps-66
96Score-130
Artist's Proofs-130
Dealer's Choice Artist's Proofs-130
Special Artist's Proofs-130
Golden Blades-130
96SP-74
96Team Out-79
96Topps Picks-159
OPC Inserts-159
96Ultra-77
Gold Medallion-77
96Upper Deck-278
Generation Next-X35
96Upper Deck Ice-29
Parallel-29
97Black Diamond-103
Double Diamond-103
Triple Diamond-103
Quadruple Diamond-103
97Collector's Choice-125
Stick'Ums-S4
World Domination-W13
97Crown Royale-62
Emerald Green-62
Ice Blue-62
Silver-62
97Donruss Canadian Ice-57
Dominion Series-57
Provincial Series-57
97Donruss Priority-49
Stamp of Approval-49
97Esso Olympic Hockey Heroes-16
97Esso Olympic Hockey Heroes French-16
97Katch-68
Gold-68
Silver-68
97Kraft Team Canada-9
97McDonald's Team Canada Coins-2
97Pacific-193
Copper-193
Emerald Green-193
Ice Blue-193
Red-193
Silver-193
Team Checklists-12
97Pacific Dynagon-58
Copper-58
Dark Grey-58
Emerald Green-58
Ice Blue-58
Red-58
Silver-58
Tandems-45
97Pacific Invincible-65
Copper-65
Emerald Green-65
Ice Blue-65
Red-65
Silver-65
97Pacific Omega-106
Copper-106
Dark Gray-106
Emerald Green-106
Gold-106
Ice Blue-106
97Panini Stickers-220
97Paramount-87
Copper-87
Dark Grey-87
Emerald Green-87
Ice Blue-87
Red-87
Silver-87
97Pinnacle-64
Artist's Proofs-64
Rink Collection-64
Press Plates Back Black-64
Press Plates Back Cyan-64
Press Plates Back Magenta-64
Press Plates Back Yellow-64
Press Plates Front Black-64
Press Plates Front Cyan-64
Press Plates Front Magenta-64
Press Plates Front Yellow-64
97Pinnacle Certified-77
Red-77
Mirror Blue-77
Mirror Gold-77
Mirror Red-77
97Pinnacle Inside-71
Coach's Collection-71
Executive Collection-71
97Pinnacle Tot Cert Platinum Blue-77
97Pinnacle Tot Certi Platinum Gold-77
97Pinnacle Totally Certified Platinum Red-77
97Pinnacle Tot Cert Mirror Platinum Gold-77
97Score-148
Artist's Proofs-148
Golden Blades-148
97SP Authentic-72
97SPx-23
Bronze-23
Gold-23
Silver-23
Steel-23
Grand Finale-23
98Aurora-85
Championship Fever-23
Championship Fever Copper-23
Championship Fever Ice Blue-23
Championship Fever Red-23
Championship Fever Silver-23
98Be A Player-212
Press Release-212
98BAP Gold-212
98BAP Autographs-212
98BAP Autographs Gold-212
98Black Diamond-41
Double Diamond-41
Triple Diamond-41
Quadruple Diamond-41
98Bowman's Best-9
Refractors-9
Atomic Refractors-9
98Crown Royale-62
Limited Series-62
98Finest-7
No Protectors-7
No Protectors Refractors-7
Refractors-7
98Katch-67
98Kings LA Times Coins-1
98Kings Power Play-LAK1
98Kraft Peanut Butter-1
98McDonalds Upper Deck Gretzkys Teammates-T11
98NHL Game Day Promotion-LAK1
98OPC Chrome-63
Refractors-63
Board Members-B11
Board Members Refractors-B11
98Pacific-4
Ice Blue-4
Red-4
98Pacific Dynagon Ice-86
Blue-86
Red-86
Team Checklists-12
98Pacific Omega-109
Red-109
Opening Day Issue-109
98Panini Photocards-9
98Panini Photocards-93
98Panini Stickers-205
98Panini Stickers-224
98Paramount-102
Copper-102
Emerald Green-102
Holo-Electric-102
Ice Blue-102
Silver-102
Team Checklists Die-Cuts-12
98Revolution-65
Ice Shadow-65
Red-65
98SP Authentic-39
Power Shift-39
Authentics-6
Authentics-7
Sign of the Times-RB
Sign of the Times Gold-RB
98SPx Finite-42
98SPx Finite-108
Radiance-42
Radiance-108
Spectrum-42
Spectrum-108
98SPx Top Prospects-30
Radiance-30
Spectrum-30
98Topps-63
O-Pee-Chee-63
Board Members-B11
98Topps Gold Label Class 1-96
Black-96
Black One of One-96
One of One-96
Red-96
Red One of One-96
98Topps Gold Label Class 2-96
98Topps Gold Label Class 2 Black-96
98Topps Gold Label Class 2 Black 1 of 1-96
98Topps Gold Label Class 2 One of One-96
98Topps Gold Label Class 2 Red-96
98Topps Gold Label Class 2 Red One of One-96
98Topps Gold Label Class 3-96
98Topps Gold Label Class 3 Black-96
98Topps Gold Label Class 3 Black 1 of 1-96
98Topps Gold Label Class 3 One of One-96
98Topps Gold Label Class 3 Red-96
98Topps Gold Label Class 3 Red One of One-96
98UD Choice-95
98UD Choice-227
98UD Choice-234
Mini Bobbing Head-BH20
98UD Choice Preview-95
98UD Choice Prime Choice Reserve-95
98UD Choice Prime Choice Reserve-227
98UD Choice Prime Choice Reserve-234
98UD Choice Reserve-95
98UD Choice Reserve-227
98UD Choice Reserve-234
98Upper Deck-285
Exclusives-285
Exclusives 1 of 1-285
Frozen In Time-FT7
Frozen In Time Quantum 1-FT7
Frozen In Time Quantum 2-FT7
Frozen In Time Quantum 3-FT7
Gold Reserve-285
98Upper Deck MVP-94
Gold Script-94
Silver Script-94
Super Script-94
99Aurora-68
Premiere Date-68
99BAP Memorabilia-297
Gold-297
Silver-297
99BAP Update Teammates Jersey Cards-TM2
99BAP Millennium-118
Emerald-118
Ruby-118
Sapphire-118
Signatures-118
Signatures Gold-118
99Crown Royale-64
Limited Series-64
Premiere Date-64
99O-Pee-Chee-22
99O-Pee-Chee Chrome-22
99O-Pee-Chee Chrome Refractors-22
99Pacific-187
Copper-187
Emerald Green-187
Gold-187
Ice Blue-187
Premiere Date-187
Red-187
99Pacific Dynagon Ice-95
Blue-95
Copper-95
Gold-95
Premiere Date-95
99Pacific Omega-106
Copper-106
Gold-106
Ice Blue-106
Premiere Date-106
99Pacific Prism-65
Holographic Blue-65
Holographic Gold-65
Holographic Mirror-65
Holographic Purple-65
Premiere Date-65
99Panini Stickers-252
99Paramount-108
Copper-108
Emerald-108
Gold-108
Holographic Emerald-108
Holographic Gold-108
Holographic Silver-108
Ice Blue-108
Premiere Date-108
Red-108
Silver-108
99Revolution-68
Premiere Date-68
Red-68
Shadow Series-68
99SP Authentic-42
99SPx-73
Radiance-73
Spectrum-73
99Stadium Club-101
First Day Issue-101
One of a Kind-101
Printing Plates Black-101
Printing Plates Cyan-101
Printing Plates Magenta-101
Printing Plates Yellow-101
99Topps/OPC-22
99Topps/OPC Chrome-22
Refractors-22
99Topps Gold Label Class 1-32
Black-32
Black One of One-32
One of One-32
Red-32
Red One of One-32
99Topps Gold Label Class 2-32
99Topps Gold Label Class 2 Black-32
99Topps Gold Label Class 2 Black 1 of 1-32
99Topps Gold Label Class 2 One of One-32
99Topps Gold Label Class 2 Red-32
99Topps Gold Label Class 2 Red One of One-32
99Topps Gold Label Class 3-32
99Topps Gold Label Class 3 Black-32
99Topps Gold Label Class 3 Black 1 of 1-32
99Topps Gold Label Class 3 One of One-32
99Topps Gold Label Class 3 Red-32
99Topps Gold Label Class 3 Red One of One-32
99Topps Premier Plus-50
Parallel-50
99Ultimate Victory-43
1/1-43
Parallel-43
Parallel 100-43
99Upper Deck-62
Exclusives-62
Exclusives 1 of 1-62
99Upper Deck Gold Reserve-62
99Upper Deck MVP-92
Gold Script-92
Silver Script-92
Super Script-92
99Upper Deck MVP SC Edition-87
Gold Script-87
Silver Script-87
Super Script-87
99Upper Deck Retro-37
Gold-37
Platinum-37
99Upper Deck Victory-130
99Upper Deck Victory-131
99Wayne Gretzky Hockey-78
00Aurora-65
Premiere Date-65
00BAP Memorabilia-22
00BAP Memorabilia-500
Emerald-22
Ruby-22
Sapphire-22
Promos-22
Jersey Cards-J39
Jersey Emblems-E39
Jersey Numbers-N39
Jersey and Stick Cards-JS39
00BAP Mem Chicago Sportsfest Copper-22
00BAP Memorabilia Chicago Sportsfest Blue-22
00BAP Memorabilia Chicago Sportsfest Gold-22
00BAP Memorabilia Chicago Sportsfest Ruby-22
00BAP Memorabilia Chicago Sun-Times Ruby-22
00BAP Memorabilia Chicago Sun-Times Gold-22
00BAP Mem Chicago Sun-Times Sapphire-22
00BAP Mem Toronto Fall Expo Copper-22
00BAP Memorabilia Toronto Fall Expo Gold-22
00BAP Memorabilia Toronto Fall Expo Ruby-22
00BAP Parkhurst 2000-P55
00BAP Signature Series-151
Emerald-151
Ruby-151
Sapphire-151
Autographs-4
Autographs Gold-4
Department of Defense-DD20
Franchise Players-F14
00BAP Ultimate Memorabilia Autographs-43
Gold-43
00BAP Ultimate Mem Game-Used Jerseys-GJ46
00BAP Ultimate Mem Game-Used Emblems-E38
00BAP Ultimate Mem Game-Used Numbers-N38
00BAP Ultimate Mem Game-Used Sticks-GS46
00BAP Ultimate Memorabilia Norris Trophy-N3
00Black Diamond-28
Gold-28
00O-Pee-Chee-103
00O-Pee-Chee Parallel-103
00Pacific-193
Copper-193
Gold-193
Ice Blue-193
Premiere Date-193
00Panini Stickers-165
00Paramount-110
Copper-110
Gold-110
Holo-Gold-110
Holo-Silver-110
Ice Blue-110
Premiere Date-110
00Private Stock Game Gear-54
00Revolution-66
Blue-66
Premiere Date-66
Red-66
00SP Authentic-21
00SPx-31
Spectrum-31
00Stadium Club-95
00Titanium-41
Blue-41
Gold-41
Premiere Date-41
Red-41
Retail-41
Game Gear-19
Game Gear-20
00Topps/OPC-103
Parallel-103
00Topps Chrome-81
OPC Refractors-81
Refractors-81
00Topps Gold Label Class 1-72
Gold-72
00Topps Gold Label Class 2-72
00Topps Gold Label Class 2 Gold-72
00Topps Gold Label Class 3-72
00Topps Gold Label Class 3 Gold-72
00Topps Heritage-60
00Topps Heritage-224
Chrome Parallel-60
00Topps Premier Plus-51
Blue Ice-51
World Premier-WP8
00Topps Stars-47
Blue-47
00UD Heroes-55
00UD Pros and Prospects-40
00Upper Deck-82
Exclusives Tier 1-82
Exclusives Tier 2-82
Triple Threat-TT8
00Upper Deck Ice-102
00Upper Deck MVP-88
First Stars-88
Second Stars-88
Third Stars-88
00Upper Deck Victory-108
00Upper Deck Victory-109
00Upper Deck Victory-306
00Upper Deck Vintage-165
00Upper Deck Vintage-172
00Czech Stadion-145
01Atomic-22
Blue-22
Gold-22
Premiere Date-22
Red-22
01Avalanche Team Issue-3
01BAP Memorabilia-278
Emerald-278
Ruby-278
Sapphire-278
All-Star Jerseys-ASJ6
All-Star Emblems-ASE6
All-Star Numbers-ASN6
All-Star Jersey Doubles-DASJ3
All-Star Starting Lineup-S9

All-Star Teammates-AST3
All-Star Teammates-AST13
Country of Origin-CO8
01BAP Signature Series Certified 100-C35
01BAP Signature Series Certified 50-C35
01BAP Signature Series Certified 1 of 1's-C35
01BAP Signature Series Autographs-LRB
01BAP Signature Series Autographs Gold-LRB
01BAP Sig Series Department of Defense-DD-1
01BAP Sig Series He Shoots/Scores Prizes-40
01BAP Sig Series International Medals-IG-2
01BAP Signature Series Jerseys-GJ-19
01BAP Signature Series Jersey Autographs-GURB
01BAP Sig Series Jersey and Stick Cards-GSJ-19
01BAP Ultimate Memorabilia Autographs-14
01BAP Ultimate Mem Autographs Gold-14
01BAP Ultimate Memorabilia Emblems-16
01BAP Ultimate Memorabilia Jerseys-16
01BAP Ultimate Mem Jerseys and Sticks-16
01BAP Ultimate Mem Journey Jerseys-6
01BAP Ultimate Mem Journey Emblems-6
01BAP Ultimate Memorabilia Numbers-13
01BAP Ultimate Memorabilia Name Plates-28
01BAP Ultimate Mem Prototypical Players-5
01BAP Update Heritage-H29
01BAP Update Travel Plans-TP6
01Bowman YoungStars-34
Gold-34
Ice Cubed-34
01Crown Royale-35
Blue-35
Premiere Date-35
Red-35
Retail-35
All-Star Honors-3
01O-Pee-Chee-71
01O-Pee-Chee Heritage Parallel-71
01O-Pee-Chee Heritage Parallel Limited-71
01O-Pee-Chee Premier Parallel-71
01Pacific-97
Extreme LTD-97
Hobby LTD-97
Premiere Date-97
Retail LTD-97
01Pacific Adrenaline-45
Blue-45
Premiere Date-45
Red-45
Retail-45
01Pacific Arena Exclusives-97
01Pacific Heads-Up-21
Blue-21
Premiere Date-21
Red-21
Silver-21
All-Star Net-2
01Parkhurst-73
Gold-73
Silver-73
He Shoots-He Scores Prizes-24
Sticks-PS33
01Private Stock-20
Gold-20
Premiere Date-20
Retail-20
Silver-20
01Private Stock Pacific Nights-20
01SP Authentic-19
Limited-19
Limited Gold-19
Buybacks-25
Sign of the Times-RB
Sign of the Times-BOB
Sign of the Times-HBB
01SP Game Used-9
01SPx Hidden Treasures-DTBN
01SPx Hidden Treasures-DTHB
01SPx Hidden Treasures-TTKBL
01Stadium Club-57
Award Winners-57
Master Photos-57
01Titanium-34
Hobby Parallel-34
Premiere Date-34
Retail-34
Retail Parallel-34
All-Stars-5
Double-Sided Jerseys-13
Double-Sided Jerseys-19
Double-Sided Patches-13
01Titanium Draft Day Edition-25
01Topps-71
Heritage Parallel-71
Heritage Parallel Limited-71
OPC Parallel-71
01Topps Chrome-71
Refractors-71
Black Border Refractors-71
01Topps Heritage-69
01Topps Heritage-117
Refractors-69
01Topps Reserve-91
01UD Challenge for the Cup-16
Jersey Autographs-UCBB
01UD Honor Roll-11
01UD Honor Roll-41
Tough Customers-TC2
01UD Mask Collection-23
Gold-23
Double Patches-DPBL
Jerseys-J-BL
Jersey and Patch-JPBL
01UD Playmakers-27
Combo Jerseys-CJRB
Combo Jerseys Gold-CJRB
01UD Premier Collection Dual Jerseys-DBB
01UD Premier Collection Dual Jerseys-DBP
01UD Premier Collection Dual Jerseys Black-DBB
01UD Premier Collection Dual Jerseys Black-DBP
01UD Premier Collection Signatures-BL
01UD Premier Collection Signatures Black-BL
01UD Stanley Cup Champs-36
Sticks-S-BK
01UD Top Shelf-86
01Upper Deck-275
Exclusives-275
01Upper Deck MVP-47
01Upper Deck Victory-90
01Upper Deck Victory-408
Gold-90
Gold-408
01Upper Deck Vintage-63
01Vanguard-23
Blue-23
Red-23
Memorabilia-49
One of Ones-23
Premiere Date-23
Proofs-23
01Czech Stadion-253
02Atomic-22
Blue-22
Gold-22
Red-22
Hobby Parallel-22
National Pride-C3
02Avalanche Postcards-16
02BAP All-Star Edition-4
Jerseys-4
Jerseys Gold-4
Jerseys Silver-4
02BAP First Edition-157
02BAP First Edition-391
Jerseys-157
02BAP Memorabilia-33
02BAP Memorabilia-251
Emerald-33
Emerald-251
Ruby-33
Ruby-251
Sapphire-33
Sapphire-251
All-Star Jerseys-ASJ-4
All-Star Starting Lineup-AS-3
All-Star Triple Jerseys-ASTJ-1
NHL All-Star Game-33
NHL All-Star Game-251
NHL All-Star Game Blue-33
NHL All-Star Game Blue-251
NHL All-Star Game Green-33
NHL All-Star Game Green-251
NHL All-Star Game Red-33
NHL All-Star Game Red-251
Teammates-TM-5
02BAP Memorabilia Toronto Fall Expo-33
02BAP Memorabilia Toronto Fall Expo-251
02BAP Signature Series-152
Autographs-152
Autograph Buybacks 1998-212
Autograph Buybacks 1999-118
Autograph Buybacks 2001-LRB
Autographs Gold-152
Defensive Wall-DW1
Golf-GS76
Jerseys-SGJ35
Jersey Autographs-SGJ35
Team Quads-TQ1
02BAP Ultimate Mem Global Dominators-3
02BAP Ultimate Memorabilia Hat Tricks-7
02BAP Ultimate Memorabilia Numerology-7
02Bowman YoungStars-70
Gold-70
Silver-70
02ITG Used-17
02ITG Used-117
Jerseys-GUJ35
Jersey Autographs-GUJ35
Jerseys Gold-GUJ35
Jersey and Stick-SJ35
Jersey and Stick Gold-SJ35
Teammates-T10
Teammates Gold-T10
Triple Memorabilia-TM18
Triple Memorabilia Gold-TM18
02McDonald's Pacific Salt Lake Gold-2
02Nextel NHL All-Star Game-1
02O-Pee-Chee-203
02O-Pee-Chee Premier Blue Parallel-203
02O-Pee-Chee Premier Red Parallel-203
02O-Pee-Chee Factory Set-203
02Pacific-87
Blue-87
Red-87
Jerseys-9
Jerseys Holo-Silver-9
02Pacific Complete-493
Red-493
02Pacific Exclusive-39
02Pacific Heads-Up-28
Blue-28
Purple-28
Red-28
Quad Jerseys-9
Quad Jerseys Gold-9
02Pacific Quest for the Cup-20
Gold-20
Jerseys-4
02Parkhurst-112
Bronze-112
Gold-112
Silver-112
College Ranks-CR5
College Ranks Jerseys-CRM5
Hardware-N3
He Shoots-He Scores Prizes-30
Jerseys-GJ38
Stick and Jerseys-SJ38
02Parkhurst Retro-66
Minis-66
Hopefuls-NH2
02Private Stock Reserve-23
Blue-23
Red-23
Retail-23
02SP Authentic-24
Beckett Promos-24
02SP Game Used Piece of History-PHRO
02SP Game Used Piece of History Gold-PHRO
02SP Game Used Piece of History Rainbow-PHRO
02SPx-20
Spectrum Gold-20
Spectrum Silver-20
02Stadium Club-30
Silver Decoy Cards-30
Proofs-30
Beam Team-BT14
Champions Fabric-FC1
Champions Patches-PC-1
02Titanium Jerseys-16
02Titanium Jerseys Retail-16
02Titanium Patches-16
02Topps-203
OPC Blue Parallel-203
OPC Red Parallel-203
Factory Set-203
02Topps Chrome-114
Black Border Refractors-114
Refractors-114
02Topps Heritage-53
02Topps Heritage-127
Chrome Parallel-53
02Topps Total-264
02UD Artistic Impressions-20
Gold-20
02UD Artistic Impressions Beckett Promos-20
02UD Artistic Impressions Common Ground-CG11
02UD Artistic Impress Common Ground Gold-CG11
02UD Artistic Impressions Retrospectives-R20
02UD Artistic Impress Retrospect Gold-R20
02UD Artistic Impress Retrospect Silver-R20
02UD Honor Roll-18
02UD Piece of History Awards Collection-AC7
02UD Piece of History Exquisite
Combos-ECBR
02UD Piece of History Patches-PHBA
02UD Premier Collection Jerseys Bronze-BR
02UD Premier Collection Jerseys Gold-BR
02UD Premier Collection Jerseys Silver-BR
02UD Top Shelf Dual Player Jerseys-RBP
02UD Top Shelf Dual Player Jerseys-STBB
02UD Top Shelf Hardware Heroes-HPMBL
02UD Top Shelf Hardware Heroes-HSRBF
02UD Top Shelf Shooting Stars-SHLE
02UD Top Shelf Signatures-BL
02Upper Deck-42
Exclusives-42
All-Star Jerseys-ASRB
All-Star Performers-ASRB
Blow-Ups-C6
Difference Makers-RB
02Upper Deck Classic Portraits-23
02Upper Deck MVP-47
Gold-47
Classics-47
Golden Classics-47
Skate Around Jerseys-SDBK
Skate Around Jerseys-SDTBL
Souvenirs-S-RB
02Upper Deck Rookie Update-28
02Upper Deck Rookie Update-151A
02Upper Deck Rookie Update-161A
02Upper Deck Victory-57
Bronze-57
Gold-57
Silver-57
National Pride-NP5
02Upper Deck Vintage-63
02Upper Deck Vintage-268
02Upper Deck Vintage-310
Green Backs-63
02UD SuperStars City AS Dual Jersey-THRB
03McFarlane Hockey Toys-R-Us-10
03McFarlane Hockey NHL 2-Pack-20
03Avalanche Team Issue-2
03BAP Memorabilia-77
Emerald-77
Gold-77
Ruby-77
Sapphire-77
All-Star Staring Lineup-9
Jersey and Stick-SJ-7
Jerseys-GJ-7
Jersey Autographs-GJ-7
Practice Jerseys-PMP6
03BAP Ultimate Memorabilia Autographs-84
Gold-84
03BAP Ultimate Memorabilia Emblems-24
03BAP Ultimate Memorabilia Emblems Gold-24
03BAP Ultimate Memorabilia Gloves Are Off-9
03BAP Ultimate Memorabilia Hat Tricks-19
03BAP Ultimate Mem Hometown Heroes-10
03BAP Ultimate Mem Hometown Heroes Gold-10
03BAP Ultimate Memorabilia Jerseys-37
03BAP Ultimate Memorabilia Jerseys Gold-37
03BAP Ultimate Memorabilia Numbers-28
03BAP Ultimate Memorabilia Numbers Gold-28
03BAP Ultimate Mem Perennial Power Jersey-5
03BAP Ult Mem Perenn Powerhouse Jsy Stick-5
03BAP Ultimate Mem Perennial Power Emblem-5
03BAP Ultimate Memorabilia Triple Threads-10
03Black Diamond-142
Black-142
Green-142
Red-142
03ITG Action-125
Jerseys-M153
03ITG Used Signature Series-7
Gold-7
Autographs-RB
Autographs Gold-RB
International Experience-10
International Experience Autographs-10
International Experience Emblems Gold-10
International Experience Emblems-10
International Experience Gold-10
Jerseys-39
Jerseys Gold-39
Jersey Autos-39
Emblems-29
Emblems Gold-29
Jersey and Stick-39
Jersey and Stick Gold-39
Norris Trophy-4
Norris Trophy Gold-4
Oh Canada-6
Oh Canada Gold-6
Oh Canada Emblems-6
Oh Canada Emblems Gold-6
Teammates-20
Teammates Gold-20
03McDonalds Pacific Hockey Root Checklist-1
03NHL Sticker Collection-187
03O-Pee-Chee-201
03OPC Blue-201
03OPC Gold-201
03OPC Red-201
03Pacific-81
Blue-81
Red-81
03Pacific Complete-166
Red-166
03Pacific Exhibit-36
Blue Backs-36
Yellow Backs-36
03Pacific Prism-27
Blue-27
Gold-27
Red-27
03Pacific Quest 4 the Cup Raising the Cup-2
03Parkhurst Rookie Retro Rookies-RR-6
03Parkhurst Rookie Retro Rookies Gold-RR-6
03Parkhurst Rookie Teammates Gold-RT17
03Parkhurst Rookie Teammates-RT17
03Private Stock Reserve-25
Blue-25
Red-25
Retail-25
03SP Game Used Authentic Fabrics-DFBJ
03SP Game Used Authentic Fabrics Gold-DFBJ
03SPx Style-SPX-JB
03SPx Style Limited-SPX-JB
03SPx Winning Materials-WM-BL
03SPx Winning Materials Limited-WM-BL
03Titanium-28
Hobby Jersey Number Parallels-28
Retail-28
Retail Jersey Number Parallels-28
03Topps-201
Blue-201
Gold-201
Red-201
03Topps C55-67
Minis-67
Minis American Back-67
Minis American Back Red-67
Minis Bazooka Back-67
Minis Brooklyn Back-67
Minis Hat Trick Back-67
Minis O Canada Back-67
Minis O Canada Back Red-67
Minis Stanley Cup Back-67
Relics-TRRB
03Topps Pristine-9
Gold Refractor Die Cuts-9
Refractors-9
Jersey Portions-PPJ-RB
Jersey Portion Refractors-PPJ-RB
Patches-PP-RB
Patch Refractors-PP-RB
Press Plates Black-9
Press Plates Cyan-9
Press Plates Magenta-9
Press Plates Yellow-9
03Upper Deck-48
Canadian Exclusives-48
HG-48
Jerseys-UD-RB
Ice Breakers-IB-RB
Ice Breaker Patches-IB-RB
Ice Clear Cut Winners-CC-RB
03Upper Deck MVP-107
Gold Script-107
Silver Script-107
Canadian Exclusives-107
Souvenirs-S4
03Upper Deck Rookie Update AS Lineup-AS11
03Upper Deck Victory-47
Bronze-47
Gold-47
Silver-47
03Bowling Green Falcons-7
03Toronto Star-25
04Pacific-65
Blue-65
Red-65
04Ultimate Collection Dual Logos-UL2-BF
04Ultimate Collection Dual Logos-UL2-NR
04Upper Deck-45
Canadian Exclusives-45
HG Glossy Gold-45
HG Glossy Silver-45
NHL's Best-NB-RB
05Be A Player-22
First Period-22
Second Period-22
Third Period-22
Overtime-22
Dual Signatures-RJ
Dual Signatures-SB
Outtakes-OT13
Quad Signatures-GDEF
Signatures-RB
Signatures Gold-RB
Triple Signatures-LBP
05Beehive-25
Beige -25
Blue -25
Gold-25
Red -25
Matte-25
Matted Materials-MMRB
Matted Materials Remarkable-RMRB
Signature Scrapbook-SSRB
05Black Diamond-23
Emerald-23
Gold-23
Onyx-23
Ruby-23
05Panini Stickers-225
05Parkhurst-124
05Parkhurst-564
Facsimile Auto Parallel-124
Facsimile Auto Parallel-564
True Colors-TCCOL
True Colors-TCCOL
True Colors-TCDECO
True Colors-TCDECO
05SP Authentic-28
Limited-28
Marks of Distinction-MDRB
Prestigious Pairings-PPBP
05SP Game Used-27
Autographs-27
Gold-27
Authentic Fabrics-AF-BL
Authentic Fabrics Autographs-AAF-BL
Authentic Fabrics Dual-SB
Authentic Fabrics Gold-AF-BL
Authentic Patches Quad -RBBF
Authentic Fabrics Quad-RBBF
Authentic Fabrics Triple-BBP
Authentic Patches-AP-BL
Authentic Patches Autographs-AAP-BL
Authentic Patches Dual-SB
Authentic Patches Triple-BBP
Auto Draft-AD-RB
Awesome Authentics-AA-RB
Awesome Authentics Gold-DA-RB
Game Gear-GG-BL
Game Gear Autographs-AG-BL
Signature Sticks-SS-RB
SIGnificance-RB
SIGnificance Gold-S-RB
Significant Numbers-SN-BL
Statscriptions-ST-RB
05SPx Winning Combos-WC-AB
05SPx Winning Combos-WC-BB
05SPx Winning Combos-WC-BP
05SPx Winning Combos Autographs-AWC-AB
05SPx Winning Combos Autographs-AWC-BB
05SPx Winning Combos Autographs-AWC-BP
05SPx Winning Combos Gold-WC-AB
05SPx Winning Combos Gold-WC-BB
05SPx Winning Combos Gold-WC-BP
05SPx Winning Combos Spectrum-WC-AB
05SPx Winning Combos Spectrum-WC-BB
05SPx Winning Combos Spectrum-WC-BP
05SPx Xcitement Superstars-XS-RB
05SPx Xcitement Superstars Gold-XS-RB
05SPx Xcitement Superstars Spectrum-XS-RB
05The Cup Dual NHL Shields Autographs-ADSPB
05The Cup Emblems of Endorsement-EERB
05The Cup Hardware Heroes-HHRO
05The Cup Honorable Numbers-HNBK
05The Cup Limited Logos-LLBL
05The Cup Master Pressplate Rookie Update-204
05The Cup Noble Numbers-NNBB
05The Cup Property of-POBL
05The Cup Scripted Numbers-SNLB
05The Cup Scripted Numbers Dual-DSNPB
05The Cup Scripted Swatches-SSBL
05The Cup Signature Patches-SPBK
05The Cup Stanley Cup Titlists-TBL
05UD Artifacts-25
05UD Artifacts-159
Blue-25
Blue-159
Gold-25
Gold-159
Green-25
Green-159
Pewter-25
Pewter-159
Red-25
Red-159
Auto Facts-AF-RB
Auto Facts Blue-AF-RB
Auto Facts Copper-AF-RB
Auto Facts Pewter-AF-RB
Auto Facts Silver-AF-RB
Gold Autographed-25
Gold Autographed-159
Remarkable Artifacts-RA-RB
Remarkable Artifacts Dual-RA-RB
05UD Powerplay Specialists-TSRB
05UD Powerplay Specialists Patches-SPRB
05Ultimate Collection-24
Gold-24
Endorsed Emblems-EEBK
National Heroes Jerseys-NHJRB
National Heroes Patches-NHPRB
05Ultra-58
Gold-58
Ice-58
05Upper Deck-44
Big Playmakers-B-ROB
HG Glossy-44
Jerseys-J-BL
Majestic Materials-MMRB
Notable Numbers-N-RBL
Patches-P-ROB
Shooting Stars-S-RB
Ice Glacial Graphs-GGRB
05Upper Deck MVP-98
Gold-98
Platinum-98
Materials-M-RB
Materials Duals-D-PB
ProSign-P-RB
05Upper Deck Rookie Update-27
05Upper Deck Rookie Update-204
Inspirations Patch Rookies-204
05Upper Deck Trilogy-24
05Upper Deck Toronto Fall Expo-44
05Upper Deck Victory-48
Black-48
Gold-48
Silver-48
Stars on Ice-SI14
06Be A Player-160
Autographs-160
Signatures-BL
Signatures 10-176
Signatures 25-176
Signatures Duals-DBC
Signatures Foursomes-FNBRB
Up Close and Personal-UC47
Up Close and Personal Autographs-UC47
06Be A Player Portraits-51
Signature Portraits-SPRB
06Beehive-56
06Beehive-195
Blue-56
Gold-56
Matte-56
Red Facsimile Signatures-56
Wood-56
06Black Diamond-106
Black-106
Gold-106
Ruby-106
Jerseys-JRO
Jerseys Black-JRO
Jerseys Gold-JRO
Jerseys Ruby-JRO
Jerseys Black Autographs -JRO
06Flair Showcase-31
06Flair Showcase-119
Parallel-31
Parallel-119
Inks-IRB
Stitches-SSBL
06Fleer-94
Tiffany-94
Fabricology-FRB
Signing Day-SDRB
06Hot Prospects-46
Red Hot-46
White Hot-46
06NHL POG-5
06O-Pee-Chee-239
06O-Pee-Chee-655
06O-Pee-Chee-684
Rainbow-239
Rainbow-655
Rainbow-684
Autographs-A-RB
06Panini Stickers-281
06SP Authentic-56
06SP Authentic-150
Limited-56
Limited-150
Sign of the Times Duals-STBM
06SP Game Used-48
Gold-48
Rainbow-48
Authentic Fabrics-AFRB
Authentic Fabrics Parallel-AFRB
Authentic Fabrics Patches-AFRB
Authentic Fabrics Dual-AF2BF
Authentic Fabrics Dual Patches-AF2BF
Authentic Fabrics Triple-AF3LAK
Authentic Fabrics Triple Patches-AF3LAK
Authentic Fabrics Quads-AF4BPJM
Authentic Fabrics Quads Patches-AF4BPJM
Authentic Fabrics Sixes-AF6NOR
Authentic Fabrics Sixes Patches-AF6NOR
06SPx-47
Spectrum-47
SPxcitement-X48
SPxcitement Spectrum-X48
SPxcitement Autographs-X48
Winning Materials-WMRO
Winning Materials Spectrum-WMRO
Winning Materials Autographs-WMRO
06The Cup-38
Autographed Foundations-CQBL
Autographed Foundations Patches-CQBL
Autographed NHL Shields Duals-DASBK
Autographed Patches-38
Black Rainbow-38
Foundations-CQBL
Foundations Patches-CQBL
Gold-38
Gold Patches-38
Honorable Numbers-HNBL
Jerseys-38
Masterpiece Pressplates-38
Property of-PORB
06UD Artifacts-55
Blue-55
Gold-55
Platinum-55
Radiance-55
Autographed Radiance Parallel-55
Red-55
Auto-Facts-AFRB
Auto-Facts Gold-AFRB
Treasured Patches Black-TSBL
Treasured Patches Blue-TSBL
Treasured Patches Gold-TSBL
Treasured Patches Platinum-TSBL
Treasured Patches Red-TSBL
Treasured Patches Autographed Black Tag
Parallel-TSBL
Treasured Swatches-TSBL
Treasured Swatches Black-TSBL
Treasured Swatches Blue-TSBL
Treasured Swatches Gold-TSBL
Treasured Swatches Platinum-TSBL
Treasured Swatches Red-TSBL
Treasured Swatches Autographed Black-TSBL
Tundra Tandems-TTFB
Tundra Tandems Black-TTFB
Tundra Tandems Blue-TTFB
Tundra Tandems Gold-TTFB
Tundra Tandems Platinum-TTFB
Tundra Tandems Red-TTFB
Tundra Tandems Dual Patches Red-TTFB
06UD Mini Jersey Collection-49
06UD Powerplay-47
Impact Rainbow-47
Specialists-SRB
Specialists Patches-PRB
06Ultimate Collection-30
Premium Patches-PS-BL
Premium Swatches-PS-BL
06Ultra-93
Gold Medallion-93
Ice Medallion-93
Uniformity-UBL
Uniformity Patches-UPBM
06Upper Deck Arena Giveaways-LAK4
06Upper Deck-339
Exclusives Parallel-339
High Gloss Parallel-339
Game Jerseys-JBL
Game Patches-PBL
Generations Duals-G2BP
Generations Triples-G3BPB
Generations Patches Dual-G2PBP
Generations Patches Triple-G3PBPB
Hometown Heroes-HH51
Masterpieces-339
Oversized Wal-Mart Exclusives-339
06Upper Deck MVP-135
Gold Script-135
Super Script-135
Jerseys-OJPB
06Upper Deck Ovation-114
06Upper Deck Sweet Shot-50
Signature Shots-STBL
Sweet Stitches-SSBL
Sweet Stitches Duals-SSBL
Sweet Stitches Triples-SSBL
06Upper Deck Trilogy-46
Honorary Scripted Patches-HSPBL
Honorary Scripted Swatches-HSSBL
Honorary Swatches-HSRB
Scripts-S3RB
06Upper Deck Victory-52
06Upper Deck Victory-253
06Upper Deck Victory Black-52
06Upper Deck Victory Gold-52
07Upper Deck Victory-191
Black-191
Gold-191

Blake, Toe
34Beehive Group I Photos-137
37O-Pee-Chee V304E-160
38Quaker Oats Photos-2
40O-Pee-Chee V301-2-101
43Parade Sportive *-8
43Parade Sportive *-77
45Quaker Oats Photos-64A
45Quaker Oats Photos-64B
45Quaker Oats Photos-64C
48Exhibits Canadian-4
51Laval Dairy QSHL-76
55Parkhurst-67
Quaker Oats-67
57Parkhurst-M16
58Parkhurst-9
59Parkhurst-27
60Shirriff Coins-40
61Shirriff/Salada Coins-101
61York Yellow Backs-22
62Shirriff Coins-31
63Chex Photos-7
63Parkhurst-34
63Parkhurst-93
64Canadiens Postcards-3
64Topps-43
65Topps-1
66Topps-1
67Canadiens IGA-NNO
83Hall of Fame Postcards-G1
85Hall of Fame-92
91Pro Set-337
French-337
93O-Pee-Chee Canadiens Hockey Fest-5
93O-Pee-Chee Canadiens Hockey Fest-59
93O-Pee-Chee Canadiens Hockey Fest-65
93Parkhurst Parkie Reprints-PR47
94Parkhurst Missing Link-84
94Parkhurst Tall Boys-87
02BAP Ultimate Mem Paper Cuts Autos-2
02Parkhurst Reprints-211
02Parkhurst Reprints-213
02Parkhurst Reprints-225
02Parkhurst Reprints-241
02Parkhurst Reprints-290
02Parkhurst Reprints-292
02Parkhurst Reprints-299
03BAP Ultimate Memorabilia Linemates-10
03BAP Ultimate Mem Linemates Autos-2
03BAP Ultimate Memorabilia Paper Cuts-8
03BAP Ultimate Mem Vintage Blade of Steel-13
03Parkhurst Original Six Montreal-46
04ITG Franchises Canadian-53
04ITG Franchises Update Linemates-ULI2
04ITG Franchises Update Linemates Gold-ULI2
04ITG Ultimate Memorabilia-159
04ITG Ultimate Memorabilia-160
Gold-159
Gold-160
Blades of Steel-10
Bleu Blanc et Rouge-5
Day In History-34
Day In History Gold-34
Nicknames-3
Paper Cuts-5
Paper Cuts Memorabilia-9
04Ultimate Collection Ultimate Cuts-UC-TB
04ITG Heroes and Prospects-178
04ITG Heroes/Prospects Toronto Expo '05-178
04ITG Heroes/Prospects Expo Heroes/Pros-178
05ITG Ultimate Memorabilia Level 1-95
05ITG Ultimate Memorabilia Level 2-95
05ITG Ultimate Memorabilia Level 3-95
05ITG Ultimate Memorabilia Level 4-95
05ITG Ultimate Memorabilia Level 5-95
05ITG Ultimate Mem Blades of Steel-9
05ITG Ultimate Mem Blades of Steel Gold-9
05ITG Ultimate Mem Bleu Blanc Rouge Autos-10
05ITG Ultimate Mem Decades Jerseys-3
05ITG Ultimate Mem Decades Jerseys Gold-3
05ITG Ultimate Mem Quad Paper Cuts Autos-4
05The Cup Legendary Cuts-LCTB
06ITG Ultimate Memorabilia-140
Artist Proof-140
Decades-3
Decades Gold-3
Retro Teammates-17
Retro Teammates Gold-17

Blanar, Michael
03Kelowna Rockets-1
04Kelowna Rockets-26

Blanchard, Guy
86Sudbury Wolves-28

Blanchard, Jean-Christophe
04Moncton Wildcats-17
05ITG Heroes/Prosp Toronto Expo Parallel -411
05Moncton Wildcats-3
05ITG Heroes and Prospects-411
06Victoriaville Tigres-3

Blanchard, Nicolas
04Chicoutimi Sagueneens-19
05ITG Heroes/Prosp Toronto Expo Parallel -150
05Chicoutimi Sagueneens-4
05ITG Heroes and Prospects-150
Autographs-A-NBL
06Chicoutimi Sagueneens-3

Blanchard, Paul
93Quebec Pee-Wee Tournament-981

Blanchard, Sean
95Slapshot-277
97Bowman CHL-13
OPC-13
98UD Choice-264
Prime Choice Reserve-264
Reserve-264
98Bowman CHL-24
Golden Anniversary-24
OPC International-24
98Bowman Chrome CHL-24
Golden Anniversary-24
Golden Anniversary Refractors-24
OPC International-24
OPC International Refractors-24
Refractors-24
99Lowell Lock Monsters-11
99Mississippi Sea Wolves Kelly Cup-6
00Florida Everblades-3
01UK London Knights-5
02UK London Knights-18
06Augusta Lynx-2

Blanchard, Trevor
99Owen Sound Platers-23
00Owen Sound Attack-2
01Sudbury Wolves-2
01Sudbury Wolves Police-20

Blanchette, Adam
03Quebec Remparts-2
04Moncton Wildcats-7
06Rio Grande Valley Killer Bees-6

Blanchette, Andre
01Brandon Wheat Kings-1
02Brandon Wheat Kings-7
03Brandon Wheat Kings-17

Blanchette, Rob
06Texas Tornados-17

Blank, Boris
99German Bundesliga 2-314
01German Berlin Polar Bears Postcards-3
01German Upper Deck-244
02German Berlin Polar Bears Postcards-5
02German DEL City Press-26
04German Cologne Sharks Postcards-5
04German DEL-207
05German DEL-221
06German DEL-131
German Forwards-GF12

Blank, Sachar
02German Adler Mannheim Eagles Postcards-7
03German Mannheim Eagles Postcards-4
04German Adler Mannheim Eagles Postcards-4
05German DEL-256

Blanke, Frank
94German First League-445

Blanshan, Cody
01Sioux Falls Stampede-1
04Medicine Hat Tigers-4
06Idaho Steelheads-14

Blasche, Reik
94German First League-598

Blasche, Thomas
94German First League-541

Blase, Billy
05Salmon Arm Silverbacks-4

Blasko, Dan
91British Columbia JHL-19
92British Columbia JHL-81

Blatak, Miroslav
00Czech OFS-376
01Czech OFS-116
02Czech DS-44
02Czech DS-65
02Czech OFS Plus-24
03Czech OFS Plus-131
04Czech OFS-273
05Czech HC Hame Zlin-4
06Czech CP Cup Postcards-1
06Czech LG Hockey Games Postcards-3
06Czech OFS All Stars-4
06Czech OFS Defenders-10

Blatchford, Ryan
02Spokane Chiefs-2
03Everett Silvertips-15
04Everett Silvertips-9

Blatek, Miroslav
06Swedish SHL Elitset-254

Blatnik, Erik
93Quebec Pee-Wee Tournament-1788

Blatny, Zdenek
00Black Diamond-73
Gold-73
00SP Authentic-126
00SP Game Used-86
00SPx-122
Spectrum-122
00UD Heroes-177
00UD Pros and Prospects-128
00UD Reserve-116
00Upper Deck-208
Exclusives Tier 1-208
Exclusives Tier 2-208
00Upper Deck Ice-53
Immortals-53
Legends-53
Stars-53
00Upper Deck Vintage-395
00Kootenay Ice-4
00UD CHL Prospects Destination the Show-D5
01Chicago Wolves-2
02Chicago Wolves-2
03Chicago Wolves-2
05Providence Bruins-1
06Springfield Falcons-11

Blatter, Florian
02Swiss HNL-250
04Swiss Davos Postcards-5

Blazek, Jakub
01Czech OFS-78

Blazek, Ladislav
94Czech APS Extraliga-2
95Czech APS Extraliga-102
96Czech APS Extraliga-265
97Czech APS Extraliga-149
97Czech DS Extraliga-74
97Czech DS Stickers-170
98Czech DS-19
98Czech DS Stickers-187
98Czech OFS-251
99Czech DS-113
Goalies-G9
99Czech OFS-3
99Czech OFS-NNO
99Czech OFS Goalie Die-Cuts-3
00Czech DS Extraliga-109
00Czech OFS-83
00Czech OFS-399
00Czech OFS Star Emerald-35
00Czech OFS Star Pink-35
00Czech OFS Star Violet-35

Blazek, Roman
94Czech APS Extraliga-264
94German First League-639
95Czech APS Extraliga-141
96Czech APS Extraliga-66
97Czech DS Stickers-239

Blazek, Tomas
93Parkhurst-517
Emerald Ice-517
94SP-156
Die Cuts-156
94Czech APS Extraliga-41
95Czech APS Extraliga-331
97Czech APS Extraliga-254
97Czech DS Extraliga-69
97Czech DS Stickers-257
98Czech DS-52
98Czech DS Stickers-137
98Czech OFS-153
99Czech DS-81
99Czech OFS-88
99Czech OFS-495
All-Star Game Blue-495
All-Star Game Gold-495
All-Star Game Red-495
All-Star Game Silver-495
00Czech DS Extraliga-92
00Czech OFS-44
01Czech OFS-246
02Czech OFS Plus-213
03Czech OFS Plus-47
03Czech Pardubice Postcards-2
04Czech OFS-111
05Czech HC Pardubice-1
06Czech HC Pardubice Postcards-2
06Czech OFS-111

Blaznek, Joe
98ECHL All-Star Northern Conference-16
99Kansas City Blades Supercuts-2
00Richmond Renegades-4
01Florida Everblades-14
02Florida Everblades-4
02Florida Everblades RBI-118
03Lubbock Cotton Kings-4

Blazyczek, Marco
94German First League-558

Bleau, Eric
99Baie-Comeau Drakkar-3

Bleicher, Marcus
94German DEL-149
95German DEL-143
98German DEL-153
99German Bundesliga 2-78

Bleiker, Sacha
93Swiss HNL-342
95Swiss HNL-418
96Swiss HNL-452

Blessman, John
88ProCards AHL-343
94Raleigh Icecaps-1
95Buffalo Stampedes RHI-43
95Wheeling Thunderbirds-16
95Wheeling Thunderbirds Series II-3
96Wheeling Nailers-4
96Wheeling Nailers Photo Pack-13

Blevins, Wes
01Rockford IceHogs-24
03Bossier-Shreveport Mudbugs-4

Blight, Chris
06Toledo Storm-12

Blight, Rick
75Canucks Royal Bank-1
76Canucks Royal Bank-1
76O-Pee-Chee NHL-238
76Topps-238
77Canucks Canada Dry Cans-1
77Canucks Royal Bank-1
77O-Pee-Chee NHL-259
77Topps-259
78Canucks Royal Bank-1
78O-Pee-Chee-7
78Topps-7
79Canucks Royal Bank-2
79O-Pee-Chee-395
80O-Pee-Chee-372

Blinco, Russ
34Beehive Group I Photos-190
34Sweet Caporal-15
35O-Pee-Chee V304C-75
36O-Pee-Chee V304D-127
37O-Pee-Chee V304E-169

37V356 Worldwide Gum-30
05ITG Ultimate Mem Marvelous Maroons Auto-1

Blindenbacher, Severin
01Swiss HNL-53
02Swiss HNL-291

Blinov, Yuri
72Finnish Jaakiekko-22
72Finnish Hellas-69
73Swedish Stickers-103
74Finnish Jenkki-62
91Future Trends Canada '72-34
91Future Trends Canada '72 French-34

Blishen, Don
907th Inn. Sketch WHL-116

Bliss, Ben
03UK Sheffield Steelers-4
03UK Sheffield Steelers Stickers-17
04UK Sheffield Steelers-16

Bliznak, Mario
05Vancouver Giants-3

Bloch, Kevin
99Kitchener Rangers-25
00Kitchener Rangers-6

Blochin, Juri
73Swedish Stickers-101

Blochliger, Bernhard
93Swiss HNL-350

Block, Brady
97Lethbridge Hurricanes-2
99Lethbridge Hurricanes-4
99Bowman CHL-102
Gold-102
OPC International-102
00Calgary Hitmen-3

Block, Grant
93Cleveland Lumberjacks-25
93Cleveland Lumberjacks Postcards-4
94Muskegon Fury-3

Block, Ken
73Quaker Oats WHA-37

Block, Kieran
02Medicine Hat Tigers-4
04Medicine Hat Tigers-5
05Medicine Hat Tigers-5

Block, Matt
94Milwaukee Admirals-3
05Chicoutimi Sagueneens-23
05Saint John's Sea Dogs-23

Bloem, Dieter
95German DEL-249
96German DEL-99

Bloemberg, Jeff
89Rangers Marine Midland Bank-38
89ProCards IHL-38
900-Pee-Chee-483
90Upper Deck-370
French-370
90ProCards AHL/IHL-10
91ProCards-210
95Adirondack Red Wings-1

Blokhin, Alexander
02Russian Hockey League-271

Blom, Bud
61Hamilton Red Wings-1

Blom, Dennis
98Danish Hockey League-191

Blom, Jamie
04Rimouski Oceanic-7
05Rimouski Oceanic-4

Blom, Tage
69Swedish Hockey-77

Blom, Thomas
83Swedish Semic Elitserien-101

Blomberg, Ake
55Swedish Alfabilder-27

Blomberg, Rune
56Swedish Alfabilder-87

Blomdahl, Patric
05Swedish SHL Elitset-227
Gold-227
06Swedish SHL Elitset-211

Blomer, Gert
56Swedish Alfabilder-40
64Swedish Coralli ISHockey-16
64Swedish Coralli ISHockey-92
65Swedish Coralli ISHockey-16
65Swedish Coralli ISHockey-92
67Swedish Hockey-283
69Swedish Hockey-330
70Swedish Hockey-245

Blomquist, Gote
55Swedish Alfabilder-10

Blomquist, Kirk
82Brandon Wheat Kings-21

Blomqvist, Alexander
02Swedish SHL-250
Parallel-250

Blomqvist, Ari
78Finnish SM-Liiga-83
80Finnish Mallasjuoma-64

Blomqvist, Lars
71Swedish Hockey-341

Blomqvist, Mats
84Swedish Semic Elitserien-170
85Swedish Panini Stickers-155
86Swedish Panini Stickers-165

Blomqvist, Timo
78Finnish SM-Liiga-67
80Finnish Mallasjuoma-70
81Capitals Team Issue-1
82Capitals Team Issue-1
86Devils Police-3
89Swedish Semic Elitserien Stickers-171
89Swedish Semic World Champ Stickers-32
90Swedish Semic Elitserien Stickers-127
91Swedish Semic Elitserien Stickers-179
92Swedish Semic Elitserien Stickers-203
94Finnish SISU-262
95Finnish SISU-86
Double Trouble-6
95Finnish SISU Limited-58
99Finnish Cardset Aces High-D-2

Blomsten, Arto
84Swedish Semic Elitserien-83
85Swedish Panini Stickers-73
86Swedish Panini Stickers-63
87Swedish Panini Stickers-72
89Swedish Semic Elitserien Stickers-53
90Swedish Semic Elitserien Stickers-276
91Swedish Semic Elitserien Stickers-59
92Upper Deck-369
92Upper Deck-376
92Swedish Semic Elitserien Stickers-78
93Donruss-506
93Jets Readers Club-4
93Jets Ruffles-6
93OPC Premier-453
Gold-453
93Parkhurst-232
Emerald Ice-232
93Topps/OPC Premier-453
Gold-453
93Upper Deck-505
SP-174
93Swedish Semic World Champ Stickers-4
94Leaf-125
95Parkhurst International-373
Emerald Ice-373
95Swedish Globe World Championships-20
97Swedish Collector's Choice-72
98Swedish UD Choice-187

Blondin, Carl
917th Inn. Sketch QMJHL-99

Bloom, Mike
74Capitals White Borders-6
74NHL Action Stamps-318
740-Pee-Chee NHL-369
750-Pee-Chee NHL-376
760-Pee-Chee NHL-56
76Topps-56
770-Pee-Chee NHL-375

Bloski, Jeff
91Air Canada SJHL-E28

Bloski, Mike
81Saskatoon Blades-20

Blouin, Donald
93Quebec Pee-Wee Tournament-1383

Blouin, Gaetan
90Saskatoon Blades-21
907th Inn. Sketch WHL-95

Blouin, Guillaume
05Moncton Wildcats-7

Blouin, Jacques
917th Inn. Sketch QMJHL-136

Blouin, Jean
907th Inn. Sketch QMJHL-56
91ProCards-290
92Atlanta Knights-15
94Thunder Bay Senators-20
98San Angelo Outlaws-2

Blouin, Maxime
96Rimouski Oceanic Quebec Police-4

Blouin, Sebastien
04Baie-Comeau Drakkar-22

Blouin, Stephane
93Quebec Pee-Wee Tournament-1057

Blouin, Sylvain
917th Inn. Sketch QMJHL-238
95Binghamton Rangers-1
95Signature Rookies-59
Signatures-59
96Binghamton Rangers-2
97Hartford Wolf Pack-2
02Atomic-114
Blue-114
Gold-114
Red-114
Hobby Parallel-114
02BAP First Edition-270
02BAP Memorabilia-359
02BAP Ultimate Memorabilia-38
02Canadiens Postcards-9
02Crown Royale-122
Blue-122
Purple-122
Red-122
Retail-122
02Pacific Heads-Up-136
02Parkhurst-238
Bronze-238
Gold-238
Silver-238
02Private Stock Reserve-167
Blue-167
Red-167
Retail-167
02SP Authentic-147
02SP Game Used-80
02SPx-164
02UD Foundations-132
02UD Honor Roll-156
02UD Mask Collection-123
02UD Piece of History-135
02UD Top Shelf-114
02Upper Deck-209
Exclusives-209
02Upper Deck Victory-103
Bronze-103
Gold-103
Silver-103
02Upper Deck Vintage-335
02Vanguard-120
LTD-120

Bloye, Damien
93North Bay Centennials-16
94North Bay Centennials-19

Blue, John
90ProCards AHL/IHL-103
91ProCards-50
92Parkhurst-245
Emerald Ice-245
Cherry Picks-CP19
93OPC Premier-209
Gold-209
93Pinnacle-335
Canadian-335
93PowerPlay-287
93Score-399
Canadian-399
93Stadium Club-334
Members Only Master Set-334
First Day Issue-334
93Topps/OPC Premier-209
Gold-209
93Upper Deck-74
94Canada Games NHL POGS-271
95Phoenix Roadrunners-3
03McFarlane Hockey-10
03McFarlane Hockey-12

Blum, Jeff
98Port Huron Border Cats-15

Blum, John
83Moncton Alpines-9
85Moncton Golden Flames-17
86Capitals Kodak-3
88Oilers Tenth Anniversary-106
88ProCards AHL-25
89ProCards AHL-73
90ProCards AHL/IHL-128
98Detroit Vipers-23

Blum, Jonathan
05Vancouver Giants-4

Blum, Ken
93Richmond Renegades-15
94Flint Generals-3

Blum, Mike
907th Inn. Sketch OHL-202

Blumer, Anthony
05Quad City Mallards-1

Blunden, Michael
03Erie Otters-2
04Erie Otters-1
05ITG Heroes/Prosp Toronto Expo Parallel -126
05Erie Otters-3
05OHL Bell All-Star Classic-22
05ITG Heroes and Prospects-126
Autographs-A-MBL
06Beehive-112
Matte-112
06Hot Prospects-153
Red Hot-153
White Hot-153
060-Pee-Chee-570
Rainbow-570
06SP Authentic-172
Limited-172
06SP Game Used-109
Gold-109
Rainbow-109
Autographs-109
Rookie Exclusives Autographs-REMB
06SPx-209
Spectrum-209
06The Cup-121
Autographed Rookie Masterpiece Pressplates-121
Gold Rainbow Autographed Rookie Patches-121
Masterpiece Pressplates (Bee Hive)-112
Masterpiece Pressplates (Marquee Rookies)-570
Masterpiece Pressplates (SP Authentic Autographs)-172
Masterpiece Pressplates (SP Game Used)-109
Masterpiece Pressplates (Sweet Beginnings)-116
Masterpiece Pressplates (Ultimate Collection Autographs)-106
Masterpiece Pressplates (Victory)-319
Rookies Black-121
Rookies Platinum-121
06UD Artifacts-266
06Ultimate Collection-106
Rookies Autographed NHL Shields-106
Rookies Autographed Patches-106
Ultimate Debut Threads Jerseys-DJ-MB
Ultimate Debut Threads Jerseys Autographs-DJ-MB
Ultimate Debut Threads Patches-DJ-MB
Ultimate Debut Threads Patches Autographs-DJ-MB
06Upper Deck-464
Exclusives Parallel-464
High Gloss Parallel-464
Masterpieces-464
Rookie Headliners-RH19
06Upper Deck Sweet Shot-116
Rookie Jerseys Autographs-116
06Upper Deck Victory-319
06Norfolk Admirals-13
07Upper Deck Rookie Class -35

Blunden, Stephen
06Belleville Bulls-4

Blundy, Chad
93Quebec Pee-Wee Tournament-1185

Blyth, Charlie
99Missouri River Otters-4
99Missouri River Otters Sheet-2
00Tacoma Sabercats-5
01Missouri River Otters-10
03Missouri River Otters-3
04Missouri River Otters-2

Blyth, Steve
83Springfield Indians-20

Boake, Peter
91Air Canada SJHL-B8

Boardman, Brent
03Yarmouth Mariners-5

Boback, Mike
92Classic-83
Gold-83
93Portland Pirates-15
94Portland Pirates-2
94Classic Pro Prospects-46
95Phoenix Roadrunners-4

Bobariko, Evgeni
00Russian Hockey League-362
00Russian Hockey League-363
01Russian Hockey League-13

Bobillier, Fredy
93Swiss HNL-37
95Swedish World Championships Stickers-120
95Swiss HNL-62
96Swiss HNL-206
98Swiss Power Play Stickers-6
99Swiss Panini Stickers-6
00Swiss Panini Stickers-8
00Swiss Slapshot Mini-Cards-HCAP2
01Swiss HNL-324
02Swiss HNL-85

Bobkin, Alexander
02Russian Hockey League-40

Bobrov, Vsevolod
73Russian National Team-23
73Swedish Stickers-97
74Russian National Team-2
91Future Trends Canada '72-10
91Future Trends Canada '72 French-10
03Czech Stadion-637

Bobyck, Brent
90ProCards AHL/IHL-59
00UK Sekonda Superleague-39
00UK Sekonda Superleague-160
00UK Sekonda Superleague-193
00UK Sheffield Steelers-9
01UK Sheffield Steelers-5
02UK Sheffield Steelers-2
03UK Sheffield Steelers-5
03UK Sheffield Steelers Stickers-10
04UK Brent Bobyck Testimonial-1
04UK Brent Bobyck Testimonial-2
04UK Brent Bobyck Testimonial-3
04UK Brent Bobyck Testimonial-4
04UK Brent Bobyck Testimonial-5
04UK Brent Bobyck Testimonial-6
04UK Brent Bobyck Testimonial-7
04UK Brent Bobyck Testimonial-8
04UK Brent Bobyck Testimonial-9
04UK Brent Bobyck Testimonial-10
04UK Brent Bobyck Testimonial-11
04UK Brent Bobyck Testimonial-12
04UK Sheffield Steelers-19

Bochatay, Didier
00Quebec Remparts-16
Signed-16
01Quebec Remparts-15
02Quebec Remparts-14
02Val d'Or Foreurs-18

Bochek, Kyle
06Kingston Frontenacs-2

Bochenski, Brandon
00Lincoln Stars-19
03North Dakota Fighting Sioux-1
04SP Authentic Rookie Redemptions-RR49
04AHL All-Stars-5
04Binghamton Senators-1
04Binghamton Senators Hess-7
05ITG Heroes/Prosp Toronto Expo Parallel -42
05Beehive-91
Matte-91
Signature Scrapbook-SSBB
05Black Diamond-150
Emerald-150
Gold-150
Onyx-150
Ruby-150
05Hot Prospects-153
En Fuego-153
Red Hot-153
White Hot-153
05Parkhurst-101
Facsimile Auto Parallel-649
Signatures-BO
05SP Authentic-175
Limited-175
05SP Game Used-102
Autographs-102
Gold-102
Rookie Exclusives-BB
Rookie Exclusives Silver-RE-BB
05SPx-179
Spectrum-179
Xcitement Rookies-XR-BB
Xcitement Rookies Gold-XR-BB
Xcitement Rookies Spectrum-XR-BB
05The Cup-149
Autographed Rookie Patches Gold Rainbow-149
Black Rainbow Rookies-149
Masterpiece Pressplates (Artifacts)-240
Masterpiece Pressplates (Bee Hive)-91
Masterpiece Pressplates (Black Diamond)-150
Masterpiece Pressplates (Ice)-175
Masterpiece Pressplates (MVP)-423
Masterpiece Pressplates (Power Play)-142
Masterpiece Pressplates (Rookie Update)-223
Masterpiece Pressplates SPA Autos-175
Masterpiece Pressplates (SP Game Used)-102
Masterpiece Pressplates SPx Autos-179
Masterpiece Pressplates (Trilogy)-206
Masterpiece Pressplates Ult Coll Autos-126
Masterpiece Pressplates Autographs-149
Platinum Rookies-149
05UD Artifacts-240
Gold-RED40
05UD PowerPlay-142
05UD Rookie Class-44
05Ultimate Collection-126
Autographed Patches-126
Ultimate Debut Threads Jerseys-DTJBB
Ultimate Debut Threads Jerseys Autos-DAJBB
Ultimate Debut Threads Patches-DTPBB
Ultimate Debut Threads Patches Autos-DAPBB
05Ultra-233
Gold-233
Ice-233
Rookie Uniformity Jerseys-RU-BB
Rookie Uniformity Jersey Autographs-ARU-BB
Rookie Uniformity Patches-RUP-BB
Rookie Uniformity Patch Autographs-ARP-BB
05Upper Deck-238
HG Glossy-238
Rookie Ink-RIBB
05Upper Deck Rookie Showcase-RS36
05Upper Deck Rookie Showcase Promos-RS36
05Upper Deck Rookie Threads-RTBB
05Upper Deck Rookie Threads Autographs-ARTBB
05Upper Deck Ice-175
Fresh Ice-FIBB
Fresh Ice Glass-FIBB
Fresh Ice Glass Patches-FIPBB
Premieres Auto Patches-AIPBB
05Upper Deck MVP-423
Gold-423
Platinum-423
05Upper Deck Rookie Update-223
Inspirations Patch Rookies-223
05Upper Deck Trilogy-206
05Upper Deck Toronto Fall Expo-238
05Binghamton Senators-17
05Binghamton Senators Quickway-17
05ITG Heroes and Prospects-42
Autographs-A-BBO
Complete Logos-AHL-2
Future Teammates-FT5
He Shoots-He Scores Prizes-33
Jerseys-GUJ-29
Jerseys Gold-GUJ-29
Emblems-GUE-29
Emblems Gold-GUE-29
Numbers-GUN-29
Numbers Gold-GUN-29
06Be A Player Portraits First Exposures-FEBB
06Black Diamond Gemography-GBB
06Black Diamond Jerseys-JBO
06Black Diamond Jerseys Black-JBO
06Black Diamond Jerseys Gold-JBO
06Black Diamond Jerseys Ruby-JBO
06Black Diamond Jerseys Black Autographs -JBO
06Hot Prospects Hot Materials -HMBB
06Hot Prospects Hot Materials Red Hot-HMBB
06Hot Prospects Hot Materials White Hot-HMBB
060-Pee-Chee-115
Rainbow-115
Swatches-S-BB
06Upper Deck Game Jerseys-J2BB
06Upper Deck Game Patches-P2BB
06Upper Deck MVP-69
Gold Script-69
Super Script-69
Jerseys-OJAB
06Binghamton Senators 5th Anniversary-3
06Norfolk Admirals-17

Bochy, David
92Quebec Pee-Wee Tournament-1402
99Swiss Panini Stickers-339
01Swiss HNL-322

Bocjun, Todd
89Peterborough Petes-122
897th Inn. Sketch OHL-122
907th Inn. Sketch OHL-353

Bockler, Robert
94German First League-193

Bodak, Bob
84Springfield Indians-23
86Moncton Golden Flames-27
88Salt Lake Golden Eagles-23
89ProCards AHL-295
90ProCards AHL/IHL-3

Boddy, Gregg
72Canucks Royal Bank-2
72Sargent Promotions Stamps-223
730-Pee-Chee-235
74Canucks Royal Bank-1
74NHL Action Stamps-286
740-Pee-Chee NHL-349
75Canucks Royal Bank-2
750-Pee-Chee NHL-285
75Topps-285

Bodger, Doug
850-Pee-Chee-38
850-Pee-Chee Stickers-99
85Topps-38
860-Pee-Chee-24
860-Pee-Chee Stickers-232
86Penguins Kodak-3
86Topps-24
870-Pee-Chee-125
87Panini Stickers-141
87Penguins Masks-1
87Penguins Kodak-1
87Topps-125
880-Pee-Chee-96
880-Pee-Chee Stickers-234
88Panini Stickers-332
88Sabres Blue Shield-4
88Sabres Wonder Bread/Hostess-4
88Topps-96
890-Pee-Chee-154
890-Pee-Chee Stickers-257
89Panini Stickers-209
89Sabres Blue Shield-3
89Sabres Campbell's-4
89Topps-154
90Bowman-245
Tiffany-245
900-Pee-Chee-282
90Panini Stickers-33
90Pro Set-19
90Sabres Blue Shield-3
90Sabres Campbell's-3
90Score-211
Canadian-211
90Topps-282
Tiffany-282
90Upper Deck-50
French-50
91Pro Set Platinum-12
91Bowman-21
910-Pee-Chee-207
91Panini Stickers-307
91Parkhurst-15
French-15
91Pinnacle-8
French-8
91Pro Set-19
French-19
Puck Candy-3
91Sabres Blue Shield-3
91Sabres Pepsi/Campbell's-3
91Score American-297
91Score Canadian Bilingual-517
91Score Canadian English-517
91Stadium Club-114
91Topps-207
91Upper Deck-477
French-477
92Bowman-13
920-Pee-Chee-146
92Panini Stickers-245
92Panini Stickers French-245
92Parkhurst-253
Emerald Ice-253
92Pinnacle-97
French-97
92Sabres Blue Shield-3
92Sabres Jubilee Foods-2
92Score-226
Canadian-226
92Stadium Club-147
92Topps-247
Gold-247G
92Ultra-258
92Upper Deck-207
93Donruss-33
93Leaf-19
93OPC Premier-29
Gold-29
93Panini Stickers-109
93Pinnacle-82
Canadian-82
93PowerPlay-26
93Sabres Limited Edition Team Issue-1
93Score-21
Canadian-21
93Stadium Club-354
Members Only Master Set-354
First Day Issue-354
93Topps/OPC Premier-29
Gold-29
93Ultra-31
93Upper Deck-187
94Be A Player Signature Cards-39
94Canada Games NHL POGS-49
94EA Sports-13
94Flair-16
94Leaf-357
94Pinnacle-357
Artist's Proofs-357
Rink Collection-357
94Score-198
Gold-198
Platinum-198
94Stadium Club-148
Members Only Master Set-148
First Day Issue-148
Super Team Winner Cards-148
94Ultra-20
94Upper Deck-494
Electric Ice-494
95Collector's Choice-77
Player's Club-77
Player's Club Platinum-77
95Donruss-226
95Parkhurst International-454
Emerald Ice-454
95Score-171
Black Ice Artist's Proofs-171
Black Ice-171
95SP-134
95Upper Deck-165
Electric Ice-165
Electric Ice Gold-165
96Be A Player-208
Autographs-208
Autographs Silver-208
96Fleer Picks-164
97Pacific Invincible NHL Regime-175
97Panini Stickers-229
97Sharks Fleer All-Star Sheet-1
990-Pee-Chee-149
990-Pee-Chee Chrome-149
990-Pee-Chee Chrome Refractors-149
99Topps/OPC-149
99Topps/OPC Chrome-149
Refractors-149
05SP Game Used Oldtimer's Challenge-OC-DB
05SP Game Used Oldtimer's Challenge Autos-OCA-DB
05SP Game Used Oldtimer's Challenge Patch-OCP-DB
05SP Game Used Oldtime Chall Patch Autoa-OAP-DB
06UD Artifacts Auto-Facts-AFDB
06UD Artifacts Auto-Facts Gold-AFDB

Bodie, Troy
02Kelowna Rockets-21
03Kelowna Rockets-2
04Kelowna Rockets-1
05Kelowna Rockets-4
06Stockton Thunder-11a

Bodin, Kent
71Swedish Hockey-136

Bodker, Kevin
06London Knights-5

Bodkin, Rick
92Sudbury Wolves-15
93Sudbury Wolves-14
93Sudbury Wolves Police-14
94Sudbury Wolves-12
94Sudbury Wolves Police-3

Bodnar, Chris
04Knoxville Ice Bears-2

Bodnar, Gus
44Beehive Group II Photos-4
44Beehive Group II Photos-81
45Quaker Oats Photos-8
51Parkhurst-40
52Parkhurst-37
53Parkhurst-75
54Parkhurst-62
91Ultimate Original Six-31
French-31
02Maple Leafs Platinum Collection-111

Bodnar, Marian
93Quebec Pee-Wee Tournament-1714

Bodnarchuk, Andrew
05Halifax Mooseheads-3
06Halifax Mooseheads-2

Bodnarchuk, Mike
87Kingston Canadians-14
90ProCards AHL/IHL-574
91ProCards-419
92Cincinnati Cyclones-3

Bodrov, Denis
05Russian Hockey League RHL-6

Bodunov, Alexander
73Finnish Jaakiekko-2
73Russian National Team-16
73Swedish Stickers-95
74Finnish Jenkki-43
74Russian National Team-3
74Swedish Stickers-59
74Swedish Semic World Champ Stickers-41
91Future Trends Canada '72-32
91Future Trends Canada '72 French-32

Body, Lou
92Harvard Crimson-3
94Richmond Renegades-15
95Richmond Renegades-5
95Signature Rookies Auto-Phonex-8
95Signature Rook Auto-Phonex Phone Cards-8

Boe, Vince
907th Inn. Sketch WHL-15

Boehm, Dave
95North Iowa Huskies-1
06Cedar Rapids RoughRiders-3

Boehm, Rick
94German DEL-374

Boehm, Ron
67Seals Team Issue-2

Boesch, Garth
44Beehive Group II Photos-381
45Quaker Oats Photos-9A
45Quaker Oats Photos-9B
45Quaker Oats Photos-9C
04ITG Franchises Update-497

Boesch, Marius
93Swiss HNL-365

Boeser, Dan
03Wisconsin Badgers-1
05Rockford Ice Hogs-3
06Rockford IceHogs -4

Boettger, Dwayne
83Moncton Alpines-5
84Nova Scotia Oilers-3
85Nova Scotia Oilers-12

Boettger, Jeff
99San Antonio Iguanas-13

Boeve, Jon
89Sudbury Wolves-9
90Rayside-Balfour Jr. Canadians-2
90Sudbury Wolves-4

Bogas, Chris
95Donruss Elite World Juniors-26
99Louisiana Ice Gators-12
02Manchester Monarchs-19
02Reading Royals-6
04Peoria Rivermen-4
06Port Huron Flags-22

Bogdanov, Anatoli
92Finnish Jyvas-Hyva Stickers-35
95Finnish SISU-392

Bogden, Shane
88Regina Pats-1

Bogelsack, Friedhelm
83Swedish Semic VM Stickers-154
94German DEL-132
95German DEL-124
04German Berlin Eisbarens 50th Anniv-37

Bogg, Hakan
04Swedish Elitset-106
Gold-106
05Swedish SHL Elitset-109
06Swedish SHL Elitset-255
Playmakers-11

Bogle, Andrew
00Michigan State Spartans-2

Bognar, Derby
93Fort Worth Fire-2
95Alaska Gold Kings-2

Bogosian, Aaron
03Cornwall Colts-1
06Cedar Rapids RoughRiders-4

Bogoslowski, Mark
89Johnstown Chiefs-27

Bogoyevac, Steve
92Dayton Bombers-2
93Dayton Bombers-7
93Richmond Renegades-16
94Los Angeles Blades RHI-14
94Richmond Renegades-4

Boguniecki, Eric
96New Hampshire Wildcats-22
97Fort Wayne Komets-19
98Fort Wayne Komets-4
99BAP Memorabilia-389
Gold-389
Silver-389
99Louisville Panthers-4
00Pacific-191
Copper-191
Gold-191
Ice Blue-191
Premiere Date-191
00Worcester Icecats-19
01Worcester Icecats-21
01Worcester Icecats-28
02BAP Signature Series-150
Autographs-150
Autographs Gold-150
02Bowman YoungStars-73
Gold-73
Silver-73
02Pacific Complete-190
Red-190
02Vanguard-82
LTD-82
02Worcester IceCats-26
03Blues Team Set-3
03ITG Action-543
03NHL Sticker Collection-279
03Pacific-279
Blue-279
Red-279
03Pacific Complete-148
Red-148
03Upper Deck-413
Canadian Exclusives-413
HG-413
UD Exclusives-413
03Upper Deck MVP-360
Gold Script-360
Silver Script-360
Canadian Exclusives-360
03Worcester Ice Cats 10th Anniversary-11
05Blues Team Set-2

Bogusevich, Yuri
00Russian Hockey League-344
02Russian Hockey League-4

Boguslawski, David
02Tri-City Stormfront-17

Boh, Aaron
917th Inn. Sketch WHL-16
93Phoenix Cobras RHI-5
95Louisiana Ice Gators Playoffs-2
95Louisiana Ice Gators Glossy-1
96Louisiana Ice Gators II-1
00UK Sekonda Superleague-188
01Colorado Gold Kings-2

Bohac, Daniel
98Spokane Chiefs-2
99Spokane Chiefs-3
00Czech DS Extraliga-153
00Czech OFS-276
01Czech OFS-276
02Czech OFS Plus-126
Trios-T3
03Colorado Eagles-4

Bohac, Jan
00Czech OFS-97
02Czech DS-54
02Czech DS-75

Bohacek, Jan
94Czech APS Extraliga-72
95Czech APS Extraliga-180
96Czech APS Extraliga-124
97Czech APS Extraliga-273
97Czech DS Stickers-59
98Czech DS Stickers-72
99Czech OFS-387
99Czech Score Blue 2000-91
99Czech Score Red Ice 2000-91
00Czech DS Extraliga-119
00Czech DS Extraliga-138
00Czech OFS-115
01Czech OFS-176

Bohlin, Sune
64Swedish Coralli ISHockey-117

Bohlmark, Hans
67Swedish Hockey-233

Bohm, Richard
95Finnish Semic World Championships-170
95German DEL-371

Bohm, Robert
94German First League-217

Bohmbach, Andy
05Waterloo Blackhawks-5

Bohme, Jorg
94German First League-435

Bohme, Rastislav
04UK Edinburgh Capitals-15

Bohonos, Lonny
93Portland Winter Hawks-2
95Bowman-93
All-Foil-93
95Images-69
Gold-69
96Syracuse Crunch-19
96Collector's Edge Ice-87
Prism-87
97Be A Player-148
Autographs-148
Autographs Die-Cuts-148
Autographs Prismatic Die-Cuts-148
97Donruss-15
Press Proofs Silver-15
Press Proofs Gold-15
97Pacific-310
Copper-310
Emerald Green-310
Ice Blue-310
Red-310
Silver-310
97Score-78
Artist's Proofs-78
Golden Blades-78
97Score Canucks-9
Platinum-9
Premier-9
97Upper Deck-172
97St. John's Maple Leafs-2
99Pacific-403
Copper-403
Emerald Green-403
Gold-403
Ice Blue-403
Premiere Date-403
Red-403
99Manitoba Moose-4
00Swiss Panini Stickers-112
00Swiss Slapshot Mini-Cards-HCD8
01Swiss HNL-110
02Swiss HNL-5
02Swiss HNL-243
02Swiss HNL-497
04Chicago Wolves-16
05German DEL-244

Bohren, Alfred
99Swiss Panini Stickers-129
02Swiss HNL-321

Bohun, Bryce
91Air Canada SJHL-A6
91Air Canada SJHL All-Stars-14

Bohunicky, Lukas
05ITG Heroes/Prosp Toronto Expo Parallel -421
05Kootenay Ice-3

Bohunicky, Peter
93Quebec Pee-Wee Tournament-1568
99Czech OFS-325
00Czech OFS-180
01Czech OFS-114
05ITG Heroes and Prospects-421
Team Orr-TO2

Boice, Tyler
04Langley Hornets-4

Boichenko, Pavel
00Russian Hockey League-325
03Russian Hockey League-81
04Russian Super League All-Stars-13

Boies, Gabriel
03Victoriaville Tigers-3
04Victoriaville Tigres-5
05Chicoutimi Sagueneens-27
05Victoriaville Tigres-8

Boiger, Elmar
94German DEL-178
95German DEL-180

Boij, Patrik
95Swedish Upper Deck-151

Boijoli, Patrice
93Quebec Pee-Wee Tournament-413

Boiko, Igor
99Greensboro Generals-9
01Russian Hockey League-7

Boikov, Alexandre
95Tri-City Americans-5
96Kentucky Thoroughblades-2
97Kentucky Thoroughblades-4
99Russian Stars Postcards-4
99Milwaukee Admirals Keebler-13
00Pacific-229
Copper-229
Gold-229
Ice Blue-229
Premiere Date-229
00Upper Deck-424
Exclusives Tier 1-424
Exclusives Tier 2-424
00Russian Hockey League-277
00Milwaukee Admirals Postcards-3
01Milwaukee Admirals-5
02Russian Hockey League-43
03Russian Hockey League-111
03Russian Metallurg Magnitogorsk-2
03Russian National Team-18

Boilard, David
00Quebec Remparts-4
Signed-4

Boilard, Ryan
93Quebec Pee-Wee Tournament-766

Boileau, Bob
82Birmingham South Stars-3

Boileau, Claude
52Juniors Blue Tint-136

Boileau, Marc
52Juniors Blue Tint-116
62Parkhurst-29
69Seattle Totems-4
740-Pee-Chee NHL-49
74Topps-49

Boileau, Patrick
95Portland Pirates-5
96Portland Pirates-27
96Collector's Edge Ice-51
Prism-51
97Portland Pirates-3
98Portland Pirates-2
99Portland Pirates-3
00Portland Pirates-5
02BAP Memorabilia-358
02BAP Ultimate Memorabilia-44
02Parkhurst-243
Bronze-243
Gold-243
Silver-243
02Upper Deck Rookie Update-120
02Grand Rapids Griffins-6
03Wilkes-Barre Scranton Penguins-5
04Swiss Lausanne HC Postcards-7
05German DEL-81
06German DEL-69

Boily, Charles
93Quebec Pee-Wee Tournament-1139

Boily, Denis
96Rimouski Oceanic-4
96Rimouski Oceanic Quebec Police-5
97Rimouski Oceanic-79
98Val d'Or Foreurs-22

Boily, Dominic
93Quebec Pee-Wee Tournament-1138

Boily, Frederic
93Quebec Pee-Wee Tournament-1353

Boily, Philippe
93Quebec Pee-Wee Tournament-402

Boimistruck, Fred
81Maple Leafs Postcards-4
82Maple Leafs Postcards-5
820-Pee-Chee-318
82Post Cereal-18

Bois, Curtis
94Thunder Bay Flyers-3
99Huntington Blizzard-24
00Rockford IceHogs-1

Bois, Danny
00London Knights-11
00London Knights-U6
01London Knights-8
02London Knights-6
03London Knights-17
04Binghamton Senators-2
05Binghamton Senators-2
05Binghamton Senators Quickway-2
06Binghamton Senators-3
06Binghamton Senators 5th Anniversary-4
07Upper Deck Victory-240
Black-240
Gold-240

Boisclair, Daniel
96Quebec Pee-Wee Tournament-16
01UD Prospects-3

Jerseys-J-BO
Jerseys-C-BG
Jerseys Gold-J-BO
Jerseys Gold-C-BG
03ECHL Update RBI Sports-128
03Greenville Grrrowl-2

Boisclair, Maxime
01Sherbrooke Castors-11
04Chicoutimi Sagueneens-18
05ITG Heroes/Prosp Toronto Expo Parallel -302
05Chicoutimi Sagueneens-5
05ITG Heroes and Prospects-302
Autographs Series II-MXB

Boissinot, David
93Quebec Pee-Wee Tournament-117

Boisvert, Andre
51Laval Dairy Lac St. Jean-18

Boisvert, Gilles
52Juniors Blue Tint-118

Boisvert, Hugo
01Grand Rapids Griffins-6
02Grand Rapids Griffins-7
03Grand Rapids Griffins-2
05German DEL-312

Boisvert, Richard
88Richelieu Riverains-5

Boisvert, Serge
82Maple Leafs Postcards-6
83Moncton Alpines-19
85Canadiens Placemats-5
85Canadiens Placemats-7
85Canadiens Postcards-1
85Canadiens Postcards-2
86Sherbrooke Canadiens-6
89Swedish Semic Elitserien Stickers-277
90Swedish Semic Elitserien Stickers-40
91Swedish Semic Elitserien Stickers-288
92Swedish Semic Elitserien Stickers-310
93Swedish Semic Elitserien-277

Boiteau, Jean-Sebastien
917th Inn. Sketch QMJHL-50

Boivin, Alexandre
04P.E.I. Rocket-1
05Gatineau Olympiques-22
05PEI Rocket-6
06Gatineau Olympiques-12

Boivin, Cedric
93Quebec Pee-Wee Tournament-378

Boivin, Claude
90ProCards AHL/IHL-48
907th Inn. Sketch Memorial Cup-69
91Pro Set Platinum-264
91Upper Deck-475
French-475
91ProCards-273
92Flyers J.C. Penney-5
92Flyers Upper Deck Sheets-9
92Pro Set-130
92Score-352
Canadian-352
92Stadium Club-16
92Topps-427
Gold-427G
92Upper Deck-57
93Flyers J.C. Penney-2
93Flyers Lineup Sheets-2
93Parkhurst-146
Emerald Ice-146
94Parkhurst-159
Gold-159
94Senators Team Issue-5
94Upper Deck-146
Electric Ice-146

Boivin, Frederic
907th Inn. Sketch QMJHL-140
917th Inn. Sketch QMJHL-220

Boivin, Leo
44Beehive Group II Photos-5
44Beehive Group II Photos-382
45Quaker Oats Photos-11
52Parkhurst-34
53Parkhurst-6
54Parkhurst-26
55Bruins Photos-3
57Bruins Photos-3
57Topps-18
58Topps-20
59Topps-26
60Shirriff Coins-107
60Topps-62
Stamps-3
61Shirriff/Salada Coins-5
61Topps-7
62Topps-5
Hockey Bucks-3
63Topps-5
63Toronto Star-5
64Beehive Group III Photos-2
64Beehive Group III Photos-65
64Coca-Cola Caps-15
64Topps-50
64Toronto Star-6
65Coca-Cola-13
65Topps-32
66Topps-50
680-Pee-Chee-101
68Shirriff Coins-141
68Topps-101
690-Pee-Chee-122
Four-in-One-5
69Topps-122
700-Pee-Chee-42
Deckle-15
70Topps-42
85Hall of Fame-252
91Bruins Sports Action Legends-2
91Bruins Sports Action Legends-35
94Parkhurst Missing Link-11
94Parkhurst Tall Boys-9
95Parkhurst '66-67-48
Coins-48
02Parkhurst Reprints-170
02Parkhurst Reprints-175
02Parkhurst Reprints-191

Boivin, Patrick
92Quebec Pee-Wee Tournament-76
93Quebec Pee-Wee Tournament-454

Boivin, Richard
907th Inn. Sketch QMJHL-27

Boivin, Robbie
93Quebec Pee-Wee Tournament-29

Boivin, Simon
93Quebec Pee-Wee Tournament-1136

Bojnic, Frantisek
03Czech OFS Plus-89

Bokal, Brad
93Quebec Pee-Wee Tournament-890

Bokenfohr, Murray
907th Inn. Sketch WHL-325

Bokoc, Jan
01Czech OFS-260

Bokros, Ernest
02Slovakian Kvarteto-26
06Czech OFS Coaches-1

Bokshowan, Lorne
81Milwaukee Admirals-9

Bokstrom, Carsten
84Swedish Semic Elitserien-124

Bolan, Eddy
51Bas Du Fleuve-52

Boland, John
81Ottawa 67's-2

Boland, Mike
79Rochester Americans-1

Bolander, Ake
67Swedish Hockey-264

Boldavesko, Sergei
94German First League-281

Boldin, Igor
92Russian Stars Red Ace-3
92Russian Stars Red Ace-12
94Finnish SISU-32
94Finnish SISU-167
94Finnish SISU Fire On Ice-2
96Swedish Brynas Tigers-17
99Russian Hockey League-41
00Russian Hockey League-6
00Russian Hockey League-364

Boldirev, Ivan
71Toronto Sun-4
720-Pee-Chee-41
72Sargent Promotions Stamps-51
72Topps-146
730-Pee-Chee-68
73Topps-68
74NHL Action Stamps-84
740-Pee-Chee NHL-16
74Topps-16
750-Pee-Chee NHL-12
75Topps-12
760-Pee-Chee NHL-251
76Topps-251
770-Pee-Chee NHL-61
77Topps-61
780-Pee-Chee-135
78Topps-135
79Flames Team Issue-2
790-Pee-Chee-127
79Topps-127
80Canucks Silverwood Dairies-2
80Canucks Team Issue-2
800-Pee-Chee-52
80Pepsi-Cola Caps-102
80Topps-52
81Canucks Team Issue-1
810-Pee-Chee-329
82Canucks Team Issue-1
820-Pee-Chee-338
820-Pee-Chee Stickers-241
82Post Cereal-19
82Topps Stickers-241
830-Pee-Chee-118
830-Pee-Chee Stickers-132
83Topps Stickers-132
840-Pee-Chee-50
840-Pee-Chee Stickers-39
84Topps-38
850-Pee-Chee-92
850-Pee-Chee Stickers-34
85Topps-92

Boldt, Max
96German DEL-19

Boldt, Tyler
00Kamloops Blazers-3
02Kamloops Blazers-15
03Brandon Wheat Kings-2
04Saskatoon Blades-10

Bolduc, Alex
37V356 Worldwide Gum-119
05Bakersfield Condors-8
06Bakersfield Condors-15
06Manitoba Moose-27

Bolduc, Dan
790-Pee-Chee-173
79Red Wings Postcards-2
79Topps-173
84Moncton Golden Flames-8
85Moncton Golden Flames-2
86Moncton Golden Flames-2

Bolduc, David
93Amos Les Forestiers-4
96Rimouski Oceanic-5

Bolduc, Francois
03Rimouski Oceanic-3
03Rimouski Oceanic Sheets-3
04Rimouski Oceanic-8
05Rimouski Oceanic-7
06Rimouski Oceanic-5

Bolduc, Jean-Michel
01Quebec Remparts-1
02Quebec Remparts-1
03Quebec Remparts Memorial Cup-2
03Rimouski Oceanic-4
03Rimouski Oceanic Sheets-5
04Rimouski Oceanic-23
05Drummondville Voltigeurs-33
05Rimouski Oceanic-3

Bolduc, Kevin
92Quebec Pee-Wee Tournament-435
97Rimouski Oceanic-17

Bolduc, Mathieu
04Chicoutimi Sagueneens-15
05Chicoutimi Sagueneens-16
06Chicoutimi Sagueneens-4

Bolduc, Michel
81Fredericton Express-4
82Fredericton Express-4
83Fredericton Express-9
84Fredericton Express-13
92Quebec Pee-Wee Tournament-797
93Quebec Pee-Wee Tournament-966

Bolduc, Patrick
92Quebec Pee-Wee Tournament-223
00Shawinigan Cataractes-6
Signed-6
03Thetford Mines Prolab-5

Bolduc, Sebastien
00Rimouski Oceanic-23
Signed-23
01Rimouski Oceanic-22

Bolduc, Simon
05PEI Rocket-25

Bolduc, Tommy
98Quebec Remparts-4
Signed-4
99Quebec Remparts-9
Signed-9
04St Georges de Beauce Garaga-12

Bolebruch, Pavol
93Quebec Pee-Wee Tournament-1566

Bolf, Lukas
03Barrie Colts-17
04Barrie Colts-19
06Czech HC Vsetin Postcards-1
06Czech OFS-174

Bolibruck, Kevin
95Slapshot-320
95Classic-94
95Signature Rookies Auto-Phonex-9
95Signature Rook Auto-Phonex Phone Cards-9
97Bowman CHL-14
OPC-14
99Hamilton Bulldogs-6
00Rochester Americans-4
03UK Sheffield Steelers-6

Bolin, Sune
57Swedish Alfabilder-82

Boling, Todd
93Quebec Pee-Wee Tournament-626

Bolke, Harald
83Swedish Semic VM Stickers-161
94German First League-567

Bolkov, Oleg
99Russian Hockey League-186

Boll, Buzz
33V129-4
34Beehive Group I Photos-301
350-Pee-Chee V304C-90
360-Pee-Chee V304D-119
370-Pee-Chee V304E-140
37V356 Worldwide Gum-40
38Quaker Oats Photos-3
390-Pee-Chee V301-1-21

Boll, Jared
03Lincoln Stars-4
04Lincoln Stars-4
04Lincoln Stars Update-39
04Lincoln Stars Update-46
05Plymouth Whalers-A-03
06Plymouth Whalers-3

Bolland, David
02London Knights-11
03London Knights-18
04London Knights-13
04ITG Heroes and Prospects-68
Autographs-DB
Combos-6
Emblems-53
Emblems Gold-53
He Shoots-He Scores Prizes-12
Jersey Autographs-53
Jerseys-53
Jerseys Gold-53
Numbers-53
Numbers Gold-53
Top Prospects-5
04ITG Heroes/Prospects Toronto Expo '05-68
04ITG Heroes/Prospects Expo Heroes/Pros-68
05ITG Heroes/Prosp Toronto Expo Parallel -121
05London Knights-10
05OHL Bell All-Star Classic-2
05ITG Heroes and Prospects-121
Autographs-A-DB
Complete Jerseys-CJ-3
Complete Jerseys Gold-CJ-3
Complete Logos-CHL-15
He Shoots-He Scores Prizes-16
Jerseys-GUJ-57
Jerseys Gold-GUJ-57
Emblems-GUE-57
Emblems Gold-GUE-57
Numbers-GUN-57
Numbers Gold-GUN-57
Memorial Cup-MC-6
Nameplates-N-35
Nameplates Gold-N-35
Oh Canada-OC-7
Oh Canada Gold-OC-7
06Be A Player-220
06Beehive-113
Matte-113
06Flair Showcase-309
06Hot Prospects-154
Red Hot-154
White Hot-154
060-Pee-Chee-569
Rainbow-569
06SP Authentic-171
Limited-171
06SP Game Used-108
Gold-108
Rainbow-108
06SPx-208
Spectrum-208
06The Cup-120
Autographed Rookie Masterpiece Pressplates-120
Gold Rainbow Autographed Rookie Patches-120
Masterpiece Pressplates (Bee Hive)-113
Masterpiece Pressplates (Marquee Rookies)-569
Masterpiece Pressplates (SP Authentic Autographs)-171
Masterpiece Pressplates (SP Game Used)-108
Masterpiece Pressplates (Sweet Beginnings)-115
Masterpiece Pressplates (Ultimate Collection Autographs)-107
Masterpiece Pressplates (Victory)-318
Rookies Black-120
Rookies Platinum-120
06UD Artifacts-237
06Ultimate Collection-107
Rookies Autographed NHL Shields-107
Rookies Autographed Patches-107
Ultimate Debut Threads Jerseys-DJ-BO
Ultimate Debut Threads Jerseys Autographs-DJ-BO
Ultimate Debut Threads Patches-DJ-BO
Ultimate Debut Threads Patches Autographs-DJ-BO
06Upper Deck-463
Exclusives Parallel-463
High Gloss Parallel-463
Masterpieces-463
Rookie Headliners-RH10
06Upper Deck Sweet Shot-115
Rookie Jerseys Autographs-115
06Upper Deck Victory-318
06Norfolk Admirals-9
07Upper Deck Rookie Class -24

Bolland, Scott
04Lethbridge Hurricanes-23

Bollig, Brandon
06Lincoln Stars-12
06Lincoln Stars Traded-11T
06Lincoln Stars Upper DeckÂ Signature Series -3

Bolonchuk, Larry
72Canucks Royal Bank-3
760-Pee-Chee NHL-322
780-Pee-Chee-387

Bolshakov, Stanislav
03Prince George Cougars-11

Bolt, Bobby
04Kingston Frontenacs-3
05Kingston Frontenacs-17
06Kingston Frontenacs-12

Bolton, Hugh
44Beehive Group II Photos-383
45Quaker Oats Photos-10
51Parkhurst-79
55Parkhurst-14
55Parkhurst-69
Quaker Oats-14
Quaker Oats-69
57Parkhurst-T13
94Parkhurst Missing Link-124

Bolton, Jordan
97Arizona Icecats-5

Bolton, Shannon
88Sudbury Wolves-19

Boltunov, Oleg
99Russian Hockey League-229
00Russian Hockey League-368
03Russian Hockey League-83

Boman, Arne
55Swedish Alfabilder-9

Boman, Johan
93Swedish Semic Elitserien-23
00Swedish Upper Deck-24

Boman, Roger
65Swedish Coralli ISHockey-145

Bombardir, Brad
91Upper Deck Czech World Juniors-55
92North Dakota Fighting Sioux-4
95Images-51
Gold-51
95Signature Rookies-66
Signatures-66
96Albany River Rats-2
96Collector's Edge Future Legends-1
97Be A Player-214
Autographs-214
Autographs Die-Cuts-214
Autographs Prismatic Die-Cuts-214
97Devils Team Issue-6
97Pacific Omega-126
Copper-126
Dark Gray-126
Emerald Green-126
Gold-126
Ice Blue-126
98Devils Team Issue-3
99Devils Team Issue-4
990-Pee-Chee-178
990-Pee-Chee Chrome-178
990-Pee-Chee Chrome Refractors-178
99Topps/OPC-178
99Topps/OPC Chrome-178
Refractors-178
00Upper Deck Vintage-181
01Upper Deck Vintage-125
02BAP First Edition-260
03ITG Action-257
03Wild Law Enforcement Cards-1

Bombic, Frantisek
02Finnish Cardset-7
04Czech OFS-90
06Czech OFS-130

Bombis, Bjorn
03German DEL-122
04German DEL-262
04German Nuremburg Ice Tigers Postcards-3
05German DEL-102
05German DEL-332

Bona, Graham
04Rimouski Oceanic-4
05Rimouski Oceanic-10
06Rimouski Oceanic-6

Bonanno, Liana
06Ohio State Buckeyes Women-9

Bonar, Dan
820-Pee-Chee-150

Bonar, Graeme
83Sault Ste. Marie Greyhounds-2
84Sault Ste. Marie Greyhounds-3
86Sherbrooke Canadiens-7
88ProCards IHL-15

Bonar, Josh
00Kamloops Blazers-4
01Vancouver Giants-7

Bond, Bertil
71Swedish Hockey-349

Bond, Bill
67Columbus Checkers-3

Bond, Joby
92North Dakota Fighting Sioux-5

Bond, Kerry
66Columbus Checkers-3

Bond, Kjell
83Swedish Semic Elitserien-136

Bond, Roland
64Swedish Coralli ISHockey-50
65Swedish Coralli ISHockey-50
67Swedish Hockey-101
70Swedish Hockey-71
71Swedish Hockey-160
72Swedish Stickers-153
73Finnish Jaakiekko-24
73Swedish Stickers-20
73Swedish Stickers-42
74Finnish Jenkki-24
74Swedish Stickers-161
74Swedish Semic World Champ Stickers-15

Bonda, Martin
96Slovakian Quebec Pee-Wee Tournament-4

Bonderer, Marco
93Quebec Pee-Wee Tournament-1635

Bonderev, Igor
98Huntsville Channel Cats-3
01Fort Wayne Komets-2
03Colorado Eagles-5

Bondra, Peter
90Capitals Kodak-3
90Capitals Postcards-3
90Capitals Smokey-3
90OPC Premier-7
90Pro Set-645
90Score Rookie/Traded-71T
90Upper Deck-536
French-536
91Pro Set Platinum-244
91Bowman-299
91Capitals Junior 5x7-3
91Capitals Kodak-3
910-Pee-Chee-362
91Parkhurst-188
French-188
91Pinnacle-87
French-87
91Pro Set-511
French-511
91Score American-216
91Score Canadian Bilingual-216
91Score Canadian English-216
91Stadium Club-37
91Topps-362
91Upper Deck-131
French-131
Euro-Stars-12
Euro-Stars French-12
92Bowman-248
92Capitals Kodak-3
920-Pee-Chee-106
92Panini Stickers-164
92Panini Stickers French-164
92Parkhurst-204
Emerald Ice-204
92Pinnacle-82
French-82
92Pro Set-209
92Score-165
Canadian-165
92Sports Illustrated for Kids II-435
92Stadium Club-286
92Topps-294
Gold-294G
92Ultra-230
92Upper Deck-115
93Donruss-366
93Leaf-79
93OPC Premier-12
Gold-12
93Panini Stickers-24
93Parkhurst-222
Emerald Ice-222
93Pinnacle-164
Canadian-164
All-Stars-12
All-Stars Canadian-12
93PowerPlay-258
93Score-344
Canadian-344
International Stars-4
International Stars Canadian-4
93Stadium Club-82
Members Only Master Set-82
OPC-82
First Day Issue-82
First Day Issue OPC-82
All-Stars-10
All-Stars Members Only-10
All-Stars OPC-10
93Topps/OPC Premier-12
Gold-12
93Ultra-46
93Upper Deck-95
93Upper Deck-308
SP-168
93Upper Deck Locker All-Stars-1
94Canada Games NHL POGS-242
94Donruss-31
94EA Sports-155
94Flair-196
94Fleer-232
94Leaf-277
94OPC Premier-283
Special Effects-283
94Parkhurst-251
Gold-251
SE Vintage-13
94Pinnacle-281
Artist's Proofs-281
Rink Collection-281
94Score-12
Gold-12
Platinum-12
94Select-89
Gold-89
94SP-129
Die Cuts-129
94Stadium Club-247
Members Only Master Set-247
First Day Issue-247
Super Team Winner Cards-247
94Topps/OPC Premier-283
Special Effects-283
94Ultra-231
94Upper Deck-135
Electric Ice-135
SP Inserts-SP85
SP Inserts Die Cuts-SP85
95Bashan Super Stickers-130
95Be A Player-210
Signatures-S210
Signatures Die Cuts-S210
95Bowman-55
All-Foil-55
95Canada Games NHL POGS-281
95Capitals Team Issue-3
95Collector's Choice-58
Player's Club-58
Player's Club Platinum-58
Crash The Game-C13A
Crash The Game-C13B
Crash The Game-C13C
Crash The Game Gold-C13A
Crash The Game Gold-C13B
Crash The Game Gold-C13C
Crash the Game Silver Redeemed-C13
Crash the Game Silver Bonus-C13
Crash the Game Gold Redeemed-C13
Crash the Game Gold Bonus-C13
95Donruss-19
Marksmen-1
95Donruss Elite-48
Die Cut Stars-48
Die Cut Uncut-48
95Finest-73
Refractors-73
95Hoyle Eastern Playing Cards-2
95Imperial Stickers-130
95Kraft-61
95Leaf-136
95Leaf Limited-30
95Metal-156
95NHL Aces Playing Cards-7D
95Panini Stickers-139
95Panini Stickers-151
95Parkhurst International-490
Emerald Ice-490
95Pinnacle Roaring 20s-14
95Playoff One on One-212
95Playoff One on One-320
95Score-53
Black Ice Artist's Proofs-53
Black Ice-53
Golden Blades-4
Lamplighters-7
95Select Certified-51
Mirror Gold-51
95SkyBox Impact-174
95SkyBox Impact-242
95SP-155
95Stadium Club-209
Members Only Master Set-209
95Summit-63
Artist's Proofs-63
Ice-63
Mad Hatters-11
95Topps-6
95Topps-310
OPC Inserts-6
OPC Inserts-310
Hidden Gems-6HG
Marquee Men Power Boosters-6
95Ultra-172
95Ultra-319
Gold Medallion-172
Extra Attackers-1
Red Light Specials-1
Red Light Specials Gold Medallion-1
95Upper Deck-232
95Upper Deck-249
95Upper Deck-339
Electric Ice-232
Electric Ice-249
Electric Ice-339
Electric Ice Gold-232
Electric Ice Gold-249
Electric Ice Gold-339
95Upper Deck All-Star Game Predictors-26
Redemption Winners-26
95Upper Deck NHL All-Stars-AS11
95Upper Deck NHL All-Stars Jumbo-AS11
95Upper Deck Special Edition-SE177
95Upper Deck Special Edition Gold-SE177
95Zenith-49
95Slovakian APS National Team-17
96Black Diamond-133
Gold-133
96Collector's Choice-279
96Collector's Choice-334
MVP-UD23
MVP Gold-UD23
Crash the Game-C4A
Crash the Game-C4B
Crash the Game-C4C
Crash the Game Gold-C4A
Crash the Game Gold-C4B
Crash the Game Gold-C4C
Crash the Game Exchange-CR4
Crash the Game Exchange Gold-CR4
96Donruss-147
Press Proofs-147
96Donruss Canadian Ice-24
Gold Press Proofs-24
Red Press Proofs-24
96Donruss Elite-11
Die Cut Stars-11
96Flair-97
Blue Ice-97
96Fleer-115
96Fleer-138
96Fleer Picks-44
Fabulous 50-2
96Kraft Upper Deck-33
96Leaf-200
Press Proofs-200
96Leaf Limited-63
Gold-63
96Leaf Preferred-29
Press Proofs-29
96Maggers-4
96Metal Universe-161
Lethal Weapons-1
Lethal Weapons Super Power-1
96Pinnacle-109
Artist's Proofs-109
Foil-109
Premium Stock-109
Rink Collection-109
96Playoff One on One-391
96Score-185
Artist's Proofs-185
Dealer's Choice Artist's Proofs-185
Special Artist's Proofs-185
Golden Blades-185
96Select Certified-78
Artist's Proofs-78
Blue-78
Mirror Blue-78
Mirror Gold-78
Mirror Red-78
Red-78
96SkyBox Impact-136
96SP-163
Holoview Collection-HC14
96SPx-49
Gold-49
96Stadium Club Members Only-31
96Summit-62
Artist's Proofs-62
Ice-62
Metal-62
Premium Stock-62
96Team Out-40
96Ultra-172
Gold Medallion-172
Mr. Momentum-1
96Upper Deck-180
96Upper Deck-364
Generation Next-X26
96Zenith-71
Artist's Proofs-71
96Swedish Semic Wien-228
96Collector's Edge Ice-120
Crucibles-C15
Prism-120
97SLU Hockey Canadian-3
97SLU Hockey American-3
97Be A Player-92
Autographs-92
Autographs Die-Cuts-92
Autographs Prismatic Die-Cuts-92
One Timers-13
97Black Diamond-87
Double Diamond-87
Triple Diamond-87
Quadruple Diamond-87
97Collector's Choice-270
Crash the Game-C25A
Crash the Game-C25B
Crash the Game-C25C
Crash the Game Exchange-CR25
Star Quest-SQ58
97Crown Royale-138
Emerald Green-138
Ice Blue-138
Silver-138
Hat Tricks Die-Cuts-20
97Donruss-135
Press Proofs Silver-135
Press Proofs Gold-135
Red Alert-10
97Donruss Canadian Ice-25
Dominion Series-25
Provincial Series-25
97Donruss Limited-129
Exposure-129
97Donruss Preferred-78
Cut to the Chase-78
97Donruss Priority-47
Stamp of Approval-47
97Katch-151
Gold-151
Silver-151
97Kenner Starting Lineup Cards-3
97Kraft-16
97Leaf-91
Fractal Matrix-91
Fractal Matrix Die Cuts-91
97Leaf International-91
Universal Ice-91
97Pacific-18
Copper-18
Emerald Green-18
Ice Blue-18
Red-18
Silver-18
Slap Shots Die-Cuts-12C
Team Checklists-26
97Pacific Dynagon-130
Copper-130
Dark Grey-130
Emerald Green-130
Ice Blue-130
Red-130
Silver-130
Best Kept Secrets-100
Tandems-15
97Pacific Invincible-145
Copper-145
Emerald Green-145
Ice Blue-145
Red-145
Silver-145
Feature Performers-36
NHL Regime-206
97Pacific Omega-236
Copper-236
Dark Gray-236
Emerald Green-236
Gold-236
Ice Blue-236
Game Face-20
97Panini Stickers-109
97Paramount-193
Copper-193
Dark Grey-193
Emerald Green-193
Ice Blue-193
Red-193
Silver-193
97Pinnacle-181
Press Plates Back Black-181
Press Plates Back Cyan-181
Press Plates Back Magenta-181
Press Plates Back Yellow-181
Press Plates Front Black-181
Press Plates Front Cyan-181
Press Plates Front Magenta-181
Press Plates Front Yellow-181
97Pinnacle Certified-46
Red-46
Mirror Blue-46
Mirror Gold-46
Mirror Red-46
97Pinnacle Inside-83
Coach's Collection-83
Executive Collection-83
97Pinnacle Tot Cert Platinum Blue-46
97Pinnacle Tot Cert Platinum Gold-46
97Pinnacle Totally Certified Platinum Red-46
97Pinnacle Tot Cert Mirror Platinum Gold-46
97Post Pinnacle-22
97Revolution-145
Copper-145
Emerald-145
Ice Blue-145
Silver-145
1998 All-Star Game Die-Cuts-20
Team Checklist Laser Cuts-26
97Score-103
Artist's Proofs-103
Golden Blades-103
97SP Authentic-164
Sign of the Times-PB
97SPx-50
Bronze-50
Gold-50
Silver-50
Steel-50
Grand Finale-50
97Studio-60
Press Proofs Silver-60
Press Proofs Gold-60
97Upper Deck The Specialists-12
97Upper Deck Specialists Level 2 Die Cuts-12
97Upper Deck Crash the All-Star Game-18
97Upper Deck Crash the All-Star Game-AR18
97Upper Deck Ice-12
Parallel-12
Power Shift-12
97Zenith-42
Z-Gold-42
Z-Silver-42
97Zenith 5 x 7-43
Gold Impulse-43
Silver Impulse-43
98SLU Hockey Extended-35
98Aurora-194
Atomic Laser Cuts-20
Championship Fever-49
Championship Fever Copper-49
Championship Fever Ice Blue-49
Championship Fever Red-49
Championship Fever Silver-49
Cubes-19
Man Advantage-20
98Be A Player-146
Press Release-146
98BAP Gold-146
98BAP Autographs-146
98BAP Autographs Gold-146
98BAP Tampa Bay All Star Game-146
98Black Diamond-88
Double Diamond-88
Triple Diamond-88
Quadruple Diamond-88
Myriad-M15
Myriad 2-M15
Winning Formula Gold-WF29
Winning Formula Platinum-WF29
98Bowman's Best-21
Refractors-21
Atomic Refractors-21
Autographs-A3A
Autographs-A3B
Autographs Refractors-A3A
Autographs Refractors-A3B
Autographs Atomic Refractors-A3A
Autographs Atomic Refractors-A3B
Mirror Image Fusion-F13
Mirror Image Fusion Refractors-F13
Mirror Image Fusion Atomic Refractors-F13
98Capitals Kids and Cops-2
98Crown Royale-140
Limited Series-140
Master Performers-20
Pillars of the Game-25
Pivotal Players-24
98Finest-52
No Protectors-52
No Protectors Refractors-52
Refractors-52
Red Lighters-R5
Red Lighters Refractors-R5
98Kenner Starting Lineup Cards-4
98Kraft Fearless Forwards-1
98OPC Chrome-126
Refractors-126
Season's Best-SB14
Season's Best Refractors-SB14
98Pacific-12
Ice Blue-12
Red-12
Dynagon Ice Inserts-19
Titanium Ice-19
Gold Crown Die-Cuts-35
98Pacific Dynagon Ice-193
Blue-193
Red-193
Forward Thinking-20
Team Checklists-27
98Pacific Omega-245
Red-245
Opening Day Issue-245
Online-36
Planet Ice-8
Planet Ice Parallel-8
98Panini Photocards-10
98Panini Photocards-99
98Panini Stickers-2
98Panini Stickers-104
98Paramount-242
Copper-242
Emerald Green-242
Holo-Electric-242
Ice Blue-242
Silver-242
Special Delivery Die-Cuts-20
Team Checklists Die-Cuts-27
98Revolution-146
Ice Shadow-146
Red-146
All-Star Die Cuts-3
Chalk Talk Laser-Cuts-20
Showstoppers-36
98SP Authentic-88
Power Shift-88
Sign of the Times-PBO
Sign of the Times Gold-PBO
Snapshots-SS28
Stat Masters-S18
98SPx Finite-87
98SPx Finite-110
98SPx Finite-168
Radiance-87
Radiance-110
Radiance-168
Spectrum-87
Spectrum-110
Spectrum-168
98SPx Top Prospects-60
Radiance-60
Spectrum-60
Highlight Heroes-H30
Lasting Impressions-L15
Premier Stars-PS15
98Topps-126
O-Pee-Chee-126
Mystery Finest Bronze-M14
Mystery Finest Bronze Refractors-M14
Mystery Finest Gold-M14
Mystery Finest Gold Refractors-M14
Mystery Finest Silver-M14
Mystery Finest Silver Refractors-M14
Season's Best-SB14
98Topps Gold Label Class 1-16
Black-16
Black One of One-16
One of One-16
Red-16
Red One of One-16
98Topps Gold Label Class 2-16
98Topps Gold Label Class 2 Black-16
98Topps Gold Label Class 2 Black 1 of 1-16
98Topps Gold Label Class 2 One of One-16
98Topps Gold Label Class 2 Red-16
98Topps Gold Label Class 2 Red One of One-16
98Topps Gold Label Class 3-16
98Topps Gold Label Class 3 Black-16
98Topps Gold Label Class 3 Black 1 of 1-16
98Topps Gold Label Class 3 One of One-16
98Topps Gold Label Class 3 Red-16
98Topps Gold Label Class 3 Red One of One-16
98UD Choice-213
98UD Choice Preview-213
98UD Choice Prime Choice Reserve-213
98UD Choice Reserve-213
98UD Choice StarQuest Blue-SQ14
98UD Choice StarQuest Gold-SQ14
98UD Choice StarQuest Green-SQ14
98UD Choice StarQuest Red-SQ14
98UD3-38
98UD3-98
98UD3-158
Die-Cuts-38
Die-Cuts-98
Die-Cuts-158
98Upper Deck-200
Exclusives-200
Exclusives 1 of 1-200
Fantastic Finishers-FF2
Fantastic Finishers Quantum 1-FF2
Fantastic Finishers Quantum 2-FF2
Fantastic Finishers Quantum 3-FF2
Gold Reserve-200
98Upper Deck MVP-209
Gold Script-209
Silver Script-209
Super Script-209
Snipers-S9

98Slovakian Eurotel-1
99Aurora-146
Striped-146
Premiere Date-146
Premiere Date Striped-146
99BAP Memorabilia-72
Gold-72
Silver-72
Jersey Cards-J28
Jersey Emblems-E28
Jersey Numbers-I28
Jersey and Stick Cards-S28
99BAP Update Teammates Jersey Cards-TM13
99BAP Millennium-245
Emerald-245
Ruby-245
Sapphire-245
Signatures-245
Signatures Gold-245
Jerseys-J17
Jersey and Stick Cards-JS17
Jersey Emblems-E17
Jersey Numbers-N17
99Black Diamond-89
Diamond Cut-89
Final Cut-89
Diamonation-D17
99Crown Royale-141
Limited Series-141
Premiere Date-141
99Jell-O Pudding Super Skills-1
99McDonald's Upper Deck Game Jerseys-GJPB
99O-Pee-Chee-67
99O-Pee-Chee Chrome-67
99O-Pee-Chee Chrome Refractors-67
99O-Pee-Chee Top of the World-TW18
99Pacific-437
Copper-437
Emerald Green-437
Gold-437
Ice Blue-437
Premiere Date-437
Red-437
Team Leaders-28
99Pacific Dynagon Ice-199
Blue-199
Copper-199
Gold-199
Premiere Date-199
2000 All-Star Preview-20
99Pacific Omega-241
Copper-241
Gold-241
Ice Blue-241
Premiere Date-241
99Pacific Prism-146
Holographic Blue-146
Holographic Gold-146
Holographic Mirror-146
Holographic Purple-146
Premiere Date-146
99Panini Stickers-167
99Paramount-242
Copper-242
Emerald-242
Gold-242
Holographic Emerald-242
Holographic Gold-242
Holographic Silver-242
Ice Blue-242
Premiere Date-242
Red-242
Silver-242
Ice Alliance-28
99Revolution-147
Premiere Date-147
Red-147
Shadow Series-147
Showstoppers-36
Top of the Line-30
Copper-147
Gold-147
CSC Silver-147
99SP Authentic-90
99SPx-159
Radiance-159
Spectrum-159
99Stadium Club-100
First Day Issue-100
One of a Kind-100
Printing Plates Black-100
Printing Plates Cyan-100
Printing Plates Magenta-100
Printing Plates Yellow-100
Chrome-33
Chrome Refractors-33
99Topps/OPC-67
Top of the World-TW18
99Topps/OPC Chrome-67
Refractors-67
99Topps Gold Label Class 1-9
Black-9
Black One of One-9
One of One-9
Red-9
Red One of One-9
99Topps Gold Label Class 2-9
99Topps Gold Label Class 2 Black-9
99Topps Gold Label Class 2 Black 1 of 1-9
99Topps Gold Label Class 2 One of One-9
99Topps Gold Label Class 2 Red-9
99Topps Gold Label Class 2 Red One of One-9
99Topps Gold Label Class 3-9
99Topps Gold Label Class 3 Black-9
99Topps Gold Label Class 3 Black 1 of 1-9
99Topps Gold Label Class 3 One of One-9
99Topps Gold Label Class 3 Red-9
99Topps Gold Label Class 3 Red One of One-9
99Topps Premier Plus-2
Parallel-2
Code Red-CR7
99Ultimate Victory-90
1/1-90
Parallel-90
Parallel 100-90
99Upper Deck-132
99Upper Deck-151
Exclusives-132
Exclusives-151
Exclusives 1 of 1-132
Exclusives 1 of 1-151
Crunch Time-CT3
Crunch Time Quantum Gold-CT3
Crunch Time Quantum Silver-CT3
99Upper Deck Century Legends-69
Century Collection-69
99Upper Deck Gold Reserve-132
99Upper Deck Gold Reserve-151
99Upper Deck HoloGrFx-59
Ausome-59
99Upper Deck MVP-215
Gold Script-215
Silver Script-215
Super Script-215
Draft Report-DR6
99Upper Deck MVP SC Edition-188
Gold Script-188
Silver Script-188
Super Script-188
Stanley Cup Talent-SC20
99Upper Deck Ovation-59
Standing Ovation-59
99Upper Deck Retro-79
Gold-79
Platinum-79
99Upper Deck Victory-303
99Upper Deck Victory-304
99Wayne Gretzky Hockey-173
Elements of the Game-EG13
00Aurora-146
Premiere Date-146
Dual Game-Worn Jerseys-4
Game-Worn Jerseys-10
Game-Worn Jersey Patches-10
00BAP Memorabilia-74
Emerald-74
Ruby-74
Sapphire-74
Promos-74
00BAP Mem Chicago Sportsfest Copper-74
00BAP Memorabilia Chicago Sportsfest Blue-74
00BAP Memorabilia Chicago Sportsfest Gold-74
00BAP Memorabilia Chicago Sportsfest Ruby-74
00BAP Memorabilia Chicago Sun-Times Ruby-74
00BAP Memorabilia Chicago Sun-Times Gold-74
00BAP Mem Chicago Sun-Times Sapphire-74
00BAP Mem Toronto Fall Expo Copper-74
00BAP Memorabilia Toronto Fall Expo Gold-74
00BAP Memorabilia Toronto Fall Expo Ruby-74
00BAP Parkhurst 2000-P236
00BAP Signature Series-121
Emerald-121
Ruby-121
Sapphire-121
Autographs-213
Autographs Gold-213
He Shoots-He Scores Prizes-6
00Crown Royale-106
Ice Blue-106
Limited Series-106
Premiere Date-106
Red-106
00Kraft-7
00O-Pee-Chee-44
00O-Pee-Chee Parallel-44
00Pacific-418
Copper-418
Gold-418
Ice Blue-418
Premiere Date-418
00Panini Stickers-102
00Paramount-243
Copper-243
Gold-243
Holo-Gold-243
Holo-Silver-243
Ice Blue-243
Premiere Date-243
00Private Stock Game Gear-101
00Private Stock Game Gear Patches-101
00Private Stock PS-2001 Action-59
00Revolution-146
Blue-146
Premiere Date-146
Red-146
NHL Game Gear-10
00SP Authentic-88
00SPx Winning Materials-PBO
00Stadium Club-160
00Titanium-98
Blue-98
Gold-98
Premiere Date-98
Red-98
Retail-98
00Titanium Draft Day Edition-98
00Topps/OPC-44
Parallel-44
00Topps Chrome-36
OPC Refractors-36
Refractors-36
00Topps Gold Label Class 1-43
Gold-43
00Topps Gold Label Class 2-43
00Topps Gold Label Class 2 Gold-43
00Topps Gold Label Class 3-43
00Topps Gold Label Class 3 Gold-43
00Topps Heritage-16
Chrome Parallel-16
00UD Heroes Signs of Greatness-PB
00UD Pros and Prospects-87
00UD Reserve-87
00Upper Deck-407
Exclusives Tier 1-407
Exclusives Tier 2-407
Game Jerseys-PE
Game Jersey Autographs Exclusives-EPE
Legends Epic Signatures-PBO
00Upper Deck MVP-182
First Stars-182
Second Stars-182
Third Stars-182
00Upper Deck Victory-234
00Upper Deck Victory-329
00Upper Deck Vintage-364
00Upper Deck Vintage-369
00Vanguard-98
High Voltage-36
High Voltage Gold-36
High Voltage Green-36
High Voltage Red-36
High Voltage Silver-36
Holographic Gold-98
Holographic Purple-98
Pacific Proofs-98
01Atomic-97
Blue-97
Gold-97
Premiere Date-97
Red-97
Power Play-35
Team Nucleus-15
01BAP Memorabilia-195
Emerald-195
Ruby-195
Sapphire-195
All-Star Jerseys-ASJ45
All-Star Emblems-ASE45
All-Star Numbers-ASN45
All-Star Teammates-AST27
Country of Origin-CO37
He Shoots-He Scores Prizes-33
01BAP Signature Series Certified 100-C31
01BAP Signature Series Certified 50-C31
01BAP Signature Series Certified 1 of 1's-C31
01BAP Signature Series Autographs-LPBO
01BAP Signature Series Autographs Gold-LPBO
01BAP Sig Series He Shoots/Scores Prizes-39
01BAP Signature Series Jerseys-GJ-64
01BAP Signature Series Jersey Autographs-GUPBO
01BAP Sig Series Jersey and Stick Cards-GSJ-64
01BAP Signature Series Emblems-GUE-32
01BAP Signature Series Numbers-ITN-32
01BAP Signature Series Teammates-TM-30
01BAP Ultimate Memorabilia Autographs-11
01BAP Ultimate Mem Autographs Gold-11
01BAP Ultimate Memorabilia Dynamic Duos-11
01BAP Ultimate Mem Scoring Leaders-14
01BAP Ultimate Mem Scoring Leaders-17
01BAP Update He Shoots-He Scores Prizes-27
01Bowman YoungStars-48
Gold-48
Ice Cubed-48
01Crown Royale-141
Blue-141
Premiere Date-141
Red-141
Retail-141
Triple Threads-20
01O-Pee-Chee-34
01O-Pee-Chee Heritage Parallel-34
01O-Pee-Chee Heritage Parallel Limited-34
01O-Pee-Chee Premier Parallel-34
01Pacific-390
01Pacific-425
01Pacific-443
Extreme LTD-390
Gold-425
Gold-443
Hobby LTD-390
Premiere Date-390
Retail LTD-390
01Pacific Adrenaline-194
Blue-194
Premiere Date-194
Red-194
Retail-194
01Pacific Arena Exclusives-390
01Pacific Arena Exclusives-425
01Pacific Arena Exclusives-443
01Pacific Heads-Up-97
Blue-97
Premiere Date-97
Red-97
Silver-97
01Parkhurst-30
Gold-30
Silver-30
Jerseys-PJ7
Milestones-M28
Sticks-PS7
Teammates-T6
01Private Stock-97
Gold-97
Premiere Date-97
Retail-97
Silver-97
Game Gear-99
Game Gear Patches-99
01Private Stock Pacific Nights-97
01Private Stock PS-2002-74
01SP Authentic-88
Limited-88
Limited Gold-88
Buybacks-23
01SP Game Used-60
Authentic Fabric-AFPB
Authentic Fabric-DFNB
Authentic Fabric Gold-AFPB
Inked Sweaters-DSKB
Inked Sweaters-DSPB
Patches-PBO
Patches-CPBA
Patches-CPJB
Patches-CPKB
Patches Signed-SPPB
Patches Signed-DSPAB
Patches Signed-DSPKBO
Tools of the Game Signed-STPB
01SPx-69
Hidden Treasures-DTBJ
Hidden Treasures-TTBSS
01Stadium Club-9
Award Winners-9
Master Photos-9
01Titanium-140
Hobby Parallel-140
Premiere Date-140
Retail-140
Retail Parallel-140
01Titanium Draft Day Edition-99
01Topps-34
Heritage Parallel-34
Heritage Parallel Limited-34
OPC Parallel-34
Shot Masters-SM12
01Topps Chrome-34
Refractors-34
Black Border Refractors-34
01Topps Heritage-35
Refractors-35
01Topps Reserve-11
01UD Challenge for the Cup-90
01UD Honor Roll Jerseys-J-PB
01UD Honor Roll Jerseys Gold-J-PB
01UD Honor Roll Pucks-P-PO
01UD Honor Roll Pucks Gold-P-PO
01UD Mask Collection-99
Gold-99
01UD Playmakers-98
01UD Premier Collection Dual Jerseys-DJB
01UD Premier Collection Dual Jersey Black-DJB
01UD Premier Collection Jerseys-BPB
01UD Premier Collection Jerseys Black-B-PB
01UD Premier Collection Signatures-PB
01UD Premier Collection Signatures Black-PB
01UD Top Shelf-120
Jerseys-PB
Sticks-SPB
Sticks Gold-SPB
01Upper Deck-173
Exclusives-173
Crunch Timers-CT15
Shooting Stars-SS20
01Upper Deck Ice-125
01Upper Deck MVP-184
Souvenirs-S-PB
Souvenirs Gold-S-PB
01Upper Deck Victory-350
01Upper Deck Victory-430
Gold-350
Gold-430
01Upper Deck Vintage-255
01Upper Deck Vintage-260
01Upper Deck Vintage-264
01Vanguard-98
Blue-98
Red-98
Memorabilia-33
One of Ones-98
Patches-33
Premiere Date-98
Proofs-98
01Czech Stadion-261
01Slovakian Kvarteto-1C
01Slovakian Kvarteto-2B
01Slovakian Kvarteto-3D
01Slovakian Kvarteto-HOKEJ
02Atomic-98
Blue-98
Gold-98
Red-98
Hobby Parallel-98
Power Converters-20
02BAP All-Star Edition-5
Jerseys-5
Jerseys Gold-5
Jerseys Silver-5
02BAP First Edition-143
02BAP First Edition-387
Jerseys-143
02BAP Memorabilia-142
Emerald-142
Ruby-142
Sapphire-142
All-Star Jerseys-ASJ-5
NHL All-Star Game-142
NHL All-Star Game Blue-142
NHL All-Star Game Green-142
NHL All-Star Game Red-142
Teammates-TM-11
02BAP Memorabilia Toronto Fall Expo-142
02BAP Signature Series-138
Autographs-138
Autograph Buybacks 1998-146
Autograph Buybacks 1999-245
Autograph Buybacks 2000-213
Autograph Buybacks 2001-LPBO
Autographs Gold-138
Golf-GS71
Jerseys-SGJ45
Jersey Autographs-SGJ45
Team Quads-TQ9
02Bowman YoungStars-61
Gold-61
Silver-61
02Capitals Team Issue-1
02Crown Royale-98
Blue-98
Red-98
Retail-98
Jerseys-24
Jerseys Gold-24
Dual Patches-23
02eTopps-26
02ITG Used-79
02ITG Used-179
Jerseys-GUJ45
Jersey Autographs-GUJ45
Jerseys Gold-GUJ45
Jersey and Stick-SJ45
Jersey and Stick Gold-SJ45
02O-Pee-Chee-129
02O-Pee-Chee Premier Blue Parallel-129
02O-Pee-Chee Premier Red Parallel-129
02O-Pee-Chee Factory Set-129
02Pacific-388
Blue-388
Red-388
02Pacific Complete-14
Red-14
02Pacific Exclusive-170
02Pacific Heads-Up-123
Blue-123
Purple-123
Red-123
Quad Jerseys-34
Quad Jerseys Gold-34
02Parkhurst-98
Bronze-98
Gold-98
Silver-98
Jerseys-GJ45
Stick and Jerseys-SJ45
Teammates-TT17
02Parkhurst Retro-24
Minis-24
02Private Stock Reserve-148
Red-148
Retail-148
Patches-148
02SP Authentic-90
02SP Authentic-105
Beckett Promos-90
02SP Game Used Authentic Fabrics-AFBD
02SP Game Used Authentic Fabrics-AFBO
02SP Game Used Authentic Fabrics-CFJB
02SP Game Used Authentic Fabrics Gold-AFBD
02SP Game Used Authentic Fabrics Gold-AFBO
02SP Game Used Authentic Fabrics Gold-CFJB
02SP Game Used Authentic Fabrics Rainbow-AFBD
02SP Game Used Authentic Fabrics Rainbow-AFBO
02SP Game Used Authentic Fabrics Rainbow-CFJB
02SP Game Used Piece of History-PHBD
02SP Game Used Piece of History-PHBO
02SP Game Used Piece of History Gold-PHBD
02SP Game Used Piece of History Gold-PHBO
02SP Game Used Piece of History Rainbow-PHBD
02SP Game Used Piece of History Rainbow-PHBO
02SP Game Used Tools of the Game-PB
02SPx-144
Milestones-MBO
Milestones Gold-BO
Milestones Silver-BO
Smooth Skaters-PB
Smooth Skaters Gold-PB
Smooth Skaters Silver-PB
Xtreme Talents-PB
Xtreme Talents Gold-PB
Xtreme Talents Silver-PB
02Stadium Club-67
Silver Decoy Cards-67
Proofs-67
World Stage-WS17
02Titanium Jerseys-73
02Titanium Jerseys Retail-73
02Topps-129
OPC Blue Parallel-129
OPC Red Parallel-129
Coast to Coast-CC5
Factory Set-129
02Topps Chrome-81
Black Border Refractors-81
Refractors-81
02Topps Heritage-51
Chrome Parallel-51
02Topps Total-172
02UD Artistic Impressions-89
Gold-89
02UD Artistic Impressions Beckett Promos-89
02UD Artistic Impressions Retrospectives-R89
02UD Artistic Impressions Retrospect Gold-R89
02UD Artistic Impress Retrospect Silver-R89
02UD Honor Roll Grade A Jerseys-TJKB
02UD Mask Collection Patches-PGPB
02UD Piece of History-89
02UD Top Shelf-89
Clutch Performers-CPBO
Dual Player Jerseys-RBZ
Dual Player Jerseys-STBJ
Goal Oriented-GOBO
Milestones Jerseys-MBBRR
Shooting Stars-SHBO
Signatures-PE
Triple Jerseys-HTBSB
Triple Jerseys-HTGHB
Triple Jerseys-TSJBK
02Upper Deck-174
Exclusives-174
Letters of Note-LNPB
Letters of Note Gold-LNPB
Reaching Fifty-50BO
Reaching Fifty Gold-50BO
Specialists-SPB
02Upper Deck Classic Portraits-99
Headliners-JB
Headliners Limited-JB
Hockey Royalty-HBK
Hockey Royalty Limited-HBK
Stitches-CBO
Stitches Limited-CBO
02Upper Deck MVP-185
Gold-185
Classics-185
Golden Classics-185
Overdrive-SO14
02Upper Deck Victory-214
Bronze-214
Gold-214
Silver-214
02Upper Deck Vintage-255
02Upper Deck Vintage-290
02Upper Deck Vintage-305
02Upper Deck Vintage-309
Green Backs-255
Jerseys-HSPB
Jerseys Gold-HS-PB
02Vanguard-98
LTD-98
Jerseys-49
Jerseys Gold-49
02Slovakian Kvarteto-2
03BAP Memorabilia-71
Emerald-71
Gold-71
Ruby-71
Sapphire-71
Jersey and Stick-SJ-17
03BAP Ultimate Memorabilia Autographs-63
Gold-63
03Beehive-200
Gold-200
Silver-200
Sticks Beige Border-BE25
Sticks Blue Border-BL9
03Black Diamond-75
Black-75
Green-75
Red-75
Threads-DT-PB
Threads Green-DT-PB
Threads Red-DT-PB
Threads Black-DT-PB
03ITG Action-589
Jerseys-M123
03ITG Used Signature Series-65
Gold-65
Autographs-PB1
Autographs-PB2
Autographs Gold-PB1
Autographs Gold-PB2
03NHL Sticker Collection-143
03O-Pee-Chee-124
03OPC Blue-124
03OPC Gold-124
03OPC Red-124
03Pacific-340
Blue-340
Red-340
03Pacific Complete-243
Red-243
03Pacific Exhibit-147
Blue Backs-147
Yellow Backs-147
03Pacific Invincible-98
Blue-98
Red-98
Retail-98
03Pacific Luxury Suite-50A
03Pacific Luxury Suite-50B
03Pacific Luxury Suite-50C
03Pacific Prism-98
Blue-98
Gold-98
Red-98
03Pacific Quest for the Cup-73
Blue-73
03Pacific Supreme-98
Blue-98
Red-98
Retail-98
03Parkhurst Rookie-53
03SP Authentic-90
Limited-90
03SP Game Used Authentic Fabrics-DFJB
03SP Game Used Authentic Fabrics Gold-DFJB
03SPx-100
Radiance-100
Spectrum-100
Winning Materials-WM-BO
Winning Materials Limited-WM-BO
03Titanium-98
Hobby Jersey Number Parallels-98
Retail-98
Retail Jersey Number Parallels-98
03Topps-124
Blue-124
Gold-124
Red-124
Topps/OPC Idols-II6
03Topps C55-16
Minis-16
Minis American Back-16
Minis American Back Red-16
Minis Bazooka Back-16
Minis Brooklyn Back-16
Minis Hat Trick Back-16
Minis O Canada Back-16
Minis O Canada Back Red-16
Minis Stanley Cup Back-16
03Topps Traded-TT26
Blue-TT26
Gold-TT26
Red-TT26
03UD Honor Roll-90
03Upper Deck-438
Canadian Exclusives-438
HG-438
UD Exclusives-438
03Upper Deck Classic Portraits-99
03Upper Deck Ice-88
Gold-88
03Upper Deck MVP-428
Gold Script-428
Silver Script-428
Canadian Exclusives-428
Souvenirs-S8
SportsNut-SN91
03Upper Deck Rookie Update-60
03Upper Deck Trilogy-99
Limited-99
03Upper Deck Victory-198
Bronze-198
Gold-198
Silver-198
03Czech Stadion-530
03Russian World Championship Stars-19
03Toronto Star-100
04Pacific-182
Blue-182
Red-182
04Upper Deck World Cup Tribute-PBPDZC
04Slovakian Poprad Team Set-15
05Be A Player Quad Signatures-OTWA
05Be A Player Signatures-PB
05Be A Player Signatures Gold-PB
05Be A Player Triple Signatures-BSH
05Black Diamond Jerseys-J-PE
05Black Diamond Jerseys Ruby-J-PE
05Black Diamond Jersey Duals-DJ-PE
05Black Diamond Jersey Triples-TJ-PE
05Black Diamond Jersey Quads-QJ-PE
05Panini Stickers-16
05Parkhurst-22
Facsimile Auto Parallel-22
True Colors-TCATL
True Colors-TCATL
05SP Game Used-7
Gold-7
Game Gear-GG-PB
05The Cup Dual NHL Shields-DSHB
05UD Powerplay Specialists-TSBO
05UD Powerplay Specialists Patches-SPBO
05Ultimate Coll National Heroes Jersey-NHJPB
05Ultimate Coll National Heroes Patch-NHPPB
05Ultra-10
Gold-10
Ice-10
05Upper Deck-251
05Upper Deck All-Time Greatest-60
05Upper Deck Big Playmakers-B-PBO
05Upper Deck Jerseys Series II-J2PB
05Upper Deck Patches-P-PBO
05Upper Deck Shooting Stars-S-PB
05Upper Deck Hockey Showcase-HS37
05Upper Deck Showcase Promos-HS37
05Upper Deck MVP-20
Gold-20
Platinum-20
05Upper Deck Victory-138
05Upper Deck Victory-204
Black-138
Black-204
Gold-138
Gold-204
Silver-138
Silver-204
Game Breakers-GB31
06Black Diamond Jerseys-JPB
06Black Diamond Jerseys Black-JPB
06Black Diamond Jerseys Gold-JPB
06Black Diamond Jerseys Ruby-JPB
06Blackhawks Postcards Glossy-2
06Fleer Fabricology-FPB
06Upper Deck Game Jerseys-JPB
06Upper Deck Game Patches-PPB
06Russian Sport Collection Olympic Stars-42

Bondy, Mike

98Flint Generals-11

Bone, Jason

99Kamloops Blazers-2
00Sudbury Wolves-20

Bonello, Brad

03Erie Otters-3
04Ottawa 67's-10

Bonello, Frank

52Juniors Blue Tint-172

Bongers, Lutz

94German First League-495

Bonhomme, Tessa

04Ohio State Buckeyes Women-9
06Ohio State Buckeyes Women-4

Bonin, Brian

92Minnesota Golden Gophers-2
93Minnesota Golden Gophers-4
94Minnesota Golden Gophers-4
95Minnesota Golden Gophers-7
96Cleveland Lumberjacks-4
96Cleveland Lumberjacks Multi-Ad-6
96Collect Edge Ice Sign Sealed Delivered-3
98Kansas City Blades-9
99Pacific-350
Copper-350
Emerald Green-350
Gold-350
Ice Blue-350
Premiere Date-350
Red-350
99Syracuse Crunch-3
00Cleveland Lumberjacks-2
01Swiss HNL-201
02Swiss HNL-328

Bonin, Marcel

44Beehive Group II Photos-155
44Beehive Group II Photos-224
51Laval Dairy QSHL-15
54Topps-59
55Bruins Photos-2
56Quebec Aces-3
57Parkhurst-M18
58Parkhurst-32
59Parkhurst-12
60Parkhurst-51
60Shirriff Coins-29
60York Photos-5
61Parkhurst-47
61Shirriff/Salada Coins-115
61York Yellow Backs-29
62Parkhurst-45
62Shirriff Coins-27
92Sport-Flash-7
92Sport-Flash Autographs-7
94Parkhurst Missing Link-19
02Parkhurst Reprints-232
02Parkhurst Reprints-269

Bonito, Jean-Daniel

93Swiss HNL-327
95Swiss HNL-472
96Swiss HNL-371
98Swiss Power Play Stickers-340

Bonk, Dave

05Bakersfield Condors-15

Bonk, Radek

93Classic-98
Class of '94-CL4
Crash Numbered-N10
94Finest-3
Super Team Winners-3
Refractors-3
Bowman's Best-R11
Bowman's Best-X23
Bowman's Best Refractors-R11
Bowman's Best Refractors-X23
94Fleer-142
Rookie Sensations-1
94Select-186
Gold-186
94Senators Team Issue-6
94SP-80
Die Cuts-80
Premier-9
Premier Die-Cuts-9
94Upper Deck-304
94Upper Deck-538
94Upper Deck-542
Electric Ice-304
Electric Ice-538
Electric Ice-542
SP Inserts-SP144
SP Inserts Die Cuts-SP144
94Las Vegas Thunder-2
94Classic-3
Gold-3
Autographs-3
Draft Day-1
Draft Day-2
Draft Day-3
Picks-CP13
Previews-HK2
ROY Sweepstakes-R2
Tri-Cards-T46
94Classic Pro Prospects-1
94Classic Pro Prospects-2
94Classic Pro Prospects-3
94Classic Pro Prospects-100
94Classic Pro Prospects-200
Autographs-AU1
International Heroes-LP21
Promo-1
94Assets *-20
94Assets *-45
Phone Cards One Minute/$2-4
94Classic Four-Sport *-117
Gold-117
BCs-BC18
High Voltage-HV12
Printers Proofs-117
Tri-Cards-TC4
94Images Chrome *-CC16
94Signature Rookies Gold Standard *-78
Signatures-GS3
95Bashan Super Stickers-84
95Bashan Super Stickers-88
95Be A Player-31
Signatures-S31
Signatures Die Cuts-S31
95Canada Games NHL POGS-194
95Collector's Choice-110
Player's Club-110
Player's Club Platinum-110
95Donruss-194
95Donruss Elite-62
Die Cut Stars-62
Die Cut Uncut-62
95Emotion-122
95Hoyle Eastern Playing Cards-3
95Imperial Stickers-88
95Leaf-263
Studio Rookies-20
95Metal-102
95Panini Stickers-50
95Parkhurst International-147
Emerald Ice-147
95Pinnacle-43
Artist's Proofs-43
Rink Collection-43
Global Gold-6
95Playoff One on One-72
95Pro Magnets-111
95Score-190
Black Ice Artist's Proofs-190
Black Ice-190
95Senators Team Issue-5
95SkyBox Impact-117
95SP-102
95Stadium Club-101
Members Only Master Set-101
95Summit-123
Artist's Proofs-123
Ice-123
95Topps-64
OPC Inserts-64
95Ultra-110
Gold Medallion-110
High Speed-4
95Upper Deck-124
Electric Ice-124
Electric Ice Gold-124
Special Edition-SE62
Special Edition Gold-SE62
95Images-25
Gold-25
Autographs-25A
Clear Excitement-CE13
95Images Four-Sport *-96
95Images Platinum Prospects-PR6
95Signature Rookies Cool Five-CF1
95Signature Rookies Cool Five Signatures-CF1
96Collector's Choice-181
96Donruss-128
Press Proofs-128
96Fleer-74
96Leaf-129
Press Proofs-129
96Metal Universe-104
96NHL Pro Stamps-111
96Pinnacle-50
Artist's Proofs-50
Foil-50
Premium Stock-50
Rink Collection-50
96Score-97
Artist's Proofs-97
Dealer's Choice Artist's Proofs-97
Special Artist's Proofs-97
Golden Blades-97
96Senators Pizza Hut-2
96SkyBox Impact-87
96SP-105
96Topps Picks-147
OPC Inserts-147
96Ultra-114
Gold Medallion-114
96Upper Deck-301
96Czech APS Extraliga-342
96Collector's Edge Ice-158
Prism-158
97Donruss Limited-12
Exposure-12
97Pacific-331
Copper-331
Emerald Green-331
Ice Blue-331
Red-331
Silver-331
97Panini Stickers-37
97Paramount-123
Copper-123
Dark Grey-123
Emerald Green-123
Ice Blue-123
Red-123
Silver-123
97Upper Deck-320
98Be A Player-94
Press Release-94
98BAP Gold-94
98BAP Autographs-94
98BAP Autographs Gold-94
98BAP Tampa Bay All Star Game-94
98Pacific-307
Ice Blue-307
Red-307
98Panini Stickers-41
98Senators Team Issue-4
99BAP Memorabilia-136
Gold-136
Silver-136
99Black Diamond-60
Diamond Cut-60
Final Cut-60
99Crown Royale-95
Limited Series-95
Premiere Date-95
99Pacific-285
Copper-285
Emerald Green-285
Gold-285
Ice Blue-285
Premiere Date-285
Red-285
99Pacific Dynagon Ice-138
Blue-138
Copper-138
Gold-138
Premiere Date-138
99Pacific Omega-158
Copper-158
Gold-158
Ice Blue-158
Premiere Date-158
99Pacific Prism-95
Holographic Blue-95
Holographic Gold-95
Holographic Mirror-95
Holographic Purple-95
Premiere Date-95
99Panini Stickers-116
99Paramount-160
Copper-160
Emerald-160
Gold-160
Holographic Emerald-160
Holographic Gold-160
Holographic Silver-160
Ice Blue-160
Premiere Date-160
Red-160
Silver-160
99Senators Team Issue-3
99SP Authentic-59
99Topps Gold Label Class 1-73
Black-73
Black One of One-73
One of One-73
Red-73
Red One of One-73
99Topps Gold Label Class 2-73
99Topps Gold Label Class 2 Black-73
99Topps Gold Label Class 2 Black 1 of 1-73
99Topps Gold Label Class 2 One of One-73
99Topps Gold Label Class 2 Red-73
99Topps Gold Label Class 2 Red One of One-73
99Topps Gold Label Class 3-73
99Topps Gold Label Class 3 Black-73
99Topps Gold Label Class 3 Black 1 of 1-73
99Topps Gold Label Class 3 One of One-73
99Topps Gold Label Class 3 Red-73
99Topps Gold Label Class 3 Red One of One-73
99Upper Deck-266
Exclusives-266
Exclusives 1 of 1-266
99Upper Deck Gold Reserve-266
99Upper Deck MVP SC Edition-125
Gold Script-125
Silver Script-125
Super Script-125
99Wayne Gretzky Hockey-117
99Czech DS-79
00Aurora-100
Premiere Date-100
00BAP Memorabilia-105
Emerald-105
Ruby-105
Sapphire-105
Promos-105
00BAP Mem Chicago Sportsfest Copper-105
00BAP Memorabilia Chicago Sportsfest Blue-105
00BAP Memorabilia Chicago Sportsfest Gold-105
00BAP Memorabilia Chicago Sportsfest Ruby-105
00BAP Memorabilia Chicago Sun-Times Ruby-105
00BAP Memorabilia Chicago Sun-Times Gold-105
00BAP Mem Chicago Sun-Times Sapphire-105
00BAP Mem Toronto Fall Expo Copper-105
00BAP Memorabilia Toronto Fall Expo Gold-105
00BAP Memorabilia Toronto Fall Expo Ruby-105
00BAP Parkhurst 2000-P115

00BAP Signature Series-166
Emerald-166
Ruby-166
Sapphire-166
Autographs-160
Autographs Gold-160
00Black Diamond-41
Gold-41
00Crown Royale-74
Ice Blue-74
Limited Series-74
Premiere Date-74
Red-74
00Kraft-9
000-Pee-Chee-134
000-Pee-Chee Parallel-134
00Pacific-276
Copper-276
Gold-276
Ice Blue-276
Premiere Date-276
00Panini Stickers-72
00Paramount-171
Copper-171
Gold-171
Holo-Gold-171
Holo-Silver-171
Ice Blue-171
Premiere Date-171
00Private Stock-69
Gold-69
Premiere Date-69
Retail-69
Silver-69
00Revolution-102
Blue-102
Premiere Date-102
Red-102
00Senators Team Issue-3
00SPx-47
Spectrum-47
00Stadium Club-72
00Titanium-64
Blue-64
Gold-64
Premiere Date-64
Red-64
Retail-64
00Topps/OPC-134
Parallel-134
00Topps Chrome-101
OPC Refractors-101
Refractors-101
00Topps Heritage-132
00UD Heroes-84
00UD Pros and Prospects-61
00Upper Deck-349
Exclusives Tier 1-349
Exclusives Tier 2-349
00Upper Deck Legends-94
00Upper Deck Legends-95
Legendary Collection Bronze-94
Legendary Collection Bronze-95
Legendary Collection Gold-94
Legendary Collection Gold-95
Legendary Collection Silver-94
Legendary Collection Silver-95
00Upper Deck MVP-127
First Stars-127
Second Stars-127
Third Stars-127
00Upper Deck Victory-160
00Upper Deck Vintage-248
01BAP Memorabilia-3
Emerald-3
Ruby-3
Sapphire-3
All-Star Jerseys-ASJ23
All-Star Emblems-ASE23
All-Star Numbers-ASN23
Country of Origin-CO26
01BAP Signature Series-164
Autographs-164
Autographs Gold-164
Jerseys-GJ-44
Jersey Autographs-GURBO
Jersey and Stick Cards-GSJ-44
01Bowman YoungStars-97
Gold-97
Ice Cubed-97
010-Pee-Chee-36
010-Pee-Chee Heritage Parallel-36
010-Pee-Chee Heritage Parallel Limited-36
010-Pee-Chee Premier Parallel-36
01Pacific-271
Extreme LTD-271
Hobby LTD-271
Premiere Date-271
Retail LTD-271
01Pacific Adrenaline-132
Blue-132
Premiere Date-132
Red-132
Retail-132
01Pacific Arena Exclusives-271
01Parkhurst-130
Jerseys-PJ47
Teammates-T16
01Private Stock PS-2002-51
01Senators Team Issue-3
01SP Authentic-58
Limited-58
Limited Gold-58
01SP Game Used-37
Authentic Fabric-AFBN
Authentic Fabric-DFFD
Authentic Fabric Gold-AFBN
01SPx-45
01Topps-36
Heritage Parallel-36
Heritage Parallel Limited-36
OPC Parallel-36
01Topps Chrome-36
Refractors-36
Black Border Refractors-36
01UD Mask Collection-69
Gold-69
01UD Playmakers-68
01Upper Deck-120
Exclusives-120
Game Jerseys Series II-GNRB
Tandems-T6
01Upper Deck MVP-130
01Upper Deck Victory-246
01Upper Deck Victory-432
Gold-246
Gold-432
01Upper Deck Vintage-175
01Upper Deck Vintage-181
01Upper Deck Vintage-182
02BAP All-Star Edition-6
Jerseys-6
Jerseys Gold-6
Jerseys Silver-6
02BAP First Edition-15
Jerseys-15
02BAP Memorabilia-177
Emerald-177
Ruby-177
Sapphire-177
NHL All-Star Game-177
NHL All-Star Game Blue-177
NHL All-Star Game Green-177
NHL All-Star Game Red-177
02BAP Memorabilia Toronto Fall Expo-177
02BAP Signature Series-68
Autographs-68
Autograph Buybacks 1998-94
Autograph Buybacks 2000-160
Autograph Buybacks 2001-164
Autographs Gold-68
02Bowman YoungStars-28
Gold-28
Silver-28
02ITG Used International Experience-IE21
02ITG Used International Experience Gold-IE21
02NHL Power Play Stickers-101
020-Pee-Chee-260
020-Pee-Chee Premier Blue Parallel-260
020-Pee-Chee Premier Red Parallel-260
020-Pee-Chee Factory Set-260
020-Pee-Chee Factory Set Hometown Heroes-HHC18
02Pacific-263
Blue-263
Red-263
02Pacific Complete-309
Red-309
02Pacific Exclusive-120
02Pacific Heads-Up-85
Blue-85
Purple-85
Red-85
02Pacific Quest for the Cup-69
Gold-69
02Parkhurst-121
Bronze-121
Gold-121
Silver-121
02Parkhurst Retro-31
Minis-31
02Private Stock Reserve-71
Blue-71
Red-71
Retail-71
02Senators Team Issue-3
02Senators Team Issue-8
02Topps-260
OPC Blue Parallel-260
OPC Red Parallel-260
Topps/OPC Hometown Heroes-HHC18
Factory Set-260
02Topps Total-116
02Upper Deck-367
Exclusives-367
02Upper Deck Beckett UD Promos-367
02Upper Deck MVP-130
Gold-130
Classics-130
Golden Classics-130
02Upper Deck Victory-150
Bronze-150
Gold-150
Silver-150
02Upper Deck Vintage-175
Green Backs-175
03ITG Action-436
Jerseys-M7
030-Pee-Chee-96
03OPC Blue-96
03OPC Gold-96
03OPC Red-96
03Pacific-234
Blue-234
Red-234
03Pacific Complete-240
Red-240
03Private Stock Reserve-72
Blue-72
Red-72
Retail-72
03Senators Postcards-9
03Titanium-70
Hobby Jersey Number Parallels-70
Retail-70
Retail Jersey Number Parallels-70
03Topps-96
Blue-96
Gold-96
Red-96
03Topps C55-35
Minis-35
Minis American Back-35
Minis American Back Red-35
Minis Bazooka Back-35
Minis Brooklyn Back-35
Minis Hat Trick Back-35
Minis O Canada Back-35
Minis O Canada Back Red-35
Minis Stanley Cup Back-35
03Upper Deck-377
Canadian Exclusives-377
HG-377
UD Exclusives-377
03Upper Deck MVP-292
Gold Script-292
Silver Script-292
Canadian Exclusives-292
04UD All-World-9
Gold-9
04Czech OFS-204
04Czech OFS-399
Checklist Cards-10
Stars-28
04Czech Zuma-28
05Canadiens Team Issue-2
05Panini Stickers-78
05Parkhurst-264
Facsimile Auto Parallel-264
05UD Powerplay Specialists-TSBK
05UD Powerplay Specialists Patches-SPBK
05Upper Deck-353
Jerseys-J-RBK
05Upper Deck MVP-203
Gold-203
Platinum-203
06Canadiens Postcards-4
06Flair Showcase Stitches-SSBO
06Gatorade-42
060-Pee-Chee-265
Rainbow-265
06Ultra Uniformity-URB
06Ultra Uniformity Patches-UPBO_
06Upper Deck-358
Exclusives Parallel-358
High Gloss Parallel-358
Masterpieces-358

Bonnard, J. Francois
94French National Team-6

Bonneau, Jimmy
04P.E.I. Rocket-9

Bonneau, Rob
97Hampton Roads Admirals-3
98Orlando Solar Bears II-13
99Utah Grizzlies-23

Bonner, Bruce
94German First League-546

Bonner, Craig
89Kamloops Blazers-2
907th Inn. Sketch WHL-298
907th Inn. Sketch Memorial Cup-23
917th Inn. Sketch WHL-91

Bonner, Doug
93Seattle Thunderbirds-2
94Finest-113
Super Team Winners-113
Refractors-113
94Leaf Limited World Juniors USA-2
95Seattle Thunderbirds-5
95Signature Rookies-62
Signatures-62
96Louisiana Ice Gators-2
96Peoria Rivermen-2
96Peoria Rivermen Photo Album-2
97Louisiana Ice Gators-19
98Louisiana Ice Gators-3

Bonner, Jim
90Michigan Tech Huskies-1
91Michigan Tech Huskies-1
91Michigan Tech Huskies-34

Bonneru, Jimmy
03P.E.I. Rocket-2

Bonnett, Joe
92Western Michigan Broncos-2

Bonney, Wayne
90Pro Set-682

Bonneyman, Art
28V128-2 Paulin's Candy-41

Bonni, Ray
97Bowman CHL-135
OPC-135
Autographs-15

Bonni, Ryan
95Saskatoon Blades-5
96Saskatoon Blades-5
97Saskatoon Blades-3
97Bowman CHL Bowman's Best-11
97Bowman CHL Bowman Best Atomic Refractor-11
97Bowman CHL Bowman's Best Refractor-11
99BAP Memorabilia-374
Gold-374
Silver-374
99Pacific Omega-238
Copper-238
Gold-238
Ice Blue-238
Premiere Date-238
99Syracuse Crunch-13
000-Pee-Chee-312
000-Pee-Chee Parallel-312
00Topps/OPC-312
Parallel-312
00Topps Chrome-207
OPC Refractors-207
Refractors-207
00Kansas City Blades-1
01Manitoba Moose-3
06Las Vegas Wranglers-2

Bono, Gene
98Phoenix Mustangs-9

Bonsignore, Jason
93Donruss Team USA-2
93Parkhurst-510
Emerald Ice-510
93Pinnacle-489
Canadian-489
93Upper Deck-560
93Niagara Falls Thunder-23
93Niagara Falls Thunder-28
93Classic-99
Class of '94-CL2
Crash Numbered-N4
Promos-2
94Slapshot Promos-7
94Finest-117
Super Team Winners-117
Refractors-117
94Leaf Limited World Juniors USA-3
94Score-209
Gold-209
Platinum-209
94SP-173
Die Cuts-173
94Upper Deck-523
Electric Ice-523
94Sudbury Wolves-17
94Classic-4
Gold-4
Autographs-4
Draft Day-4
ROY Sweepstakes-R3
Tri-Cards-T22
94Classic Pro Prospects-201
Autographs-AU2
94Classic Four-Sport *-118
Gold-118
High Voltage-HV16
Printers Proofs-118
95Be A Player-179
Signatures-S179
Signatures Die Cuts-S179
95Bowman-101
All-Foil-101
95Donruss-249
Pro Pointers-3
95Emotion generatioNext-3
95Leaf-229
Studio Rookies-12
95Leaf Limited-59
95Metal-172
95Panini Stickers-256
95Parkhurst International-80
Emerald Ice-80
95Pinnacle-207
Artist's Proofs-207
Rink Collection-207
95Playoff One on One-256
95Pro Magnets-82
95Score-308
Black Ice Artist's Proofs-308
Black Ice-308
95Select Certified-113
Mirror Gold-113
95SkyBox Impact-196
95Stadium Club-191
Members Only Master Set-191
95Topps SuperSkills Super Rookies-SR2
95Ultra-332
95Upper Deck-266
Electric Ice-266
Electric Ice Gold-266
95Zenith-136
95Classic-97
Ice Breakers-BK17
Ice Breakers Die Cuts-BK17
95Images-45
Gold-45
Autographs-45A
95Images Four-Sport *-97
95Classic Five-Sport *-127
Autographs-127
Strive For Five-HK6
96Fleer-123
96NHL Pro Stamps-82
96SkyBox Impact-146
96Upper Deck-62
96Classic Signings *-74
Blue-74
Die-Cuts-74
Red-74
96Visions *-86
98OPC Chrome-129
Refractors-129
98Pacific-64
Ice Blue-64
Red-64
98Topps-129
O-Pee-Chee-129
98Upper Deck-180
Exclusives-180
Exclusives 1 of 1-180
Gold Reserve-180
98Cleveland Lumberjacks-7
99St. John's Maple Leafs-4
02Springfield Falcons-7

Bonvie, Dennis
917th Inn. Sketch OHL-54
94Cape Breton Oilers-4
95Leaf-306
95Upper Deck-393
Electric Ice-393
Electric Ice Gold-393
97Upper Deck-277
00Stadium Club-107
00Wilkes-Barre Scranton Penguins-1
01Providence Bruins-17
02NHL Power Play Stickers-119
03Binghamton Senators-2
03Binghamton Senators Postcards-5
03Hershey Bears Patriot News-2
04Hershey Bears Patriot News-4
05WBS Penguins-2
06Binghamton Senators 5th Anniversary-5
06Wilkes-Barre Scranton Penguins-6
06Wilkes-Barre Scranton Penguins Jerseys-13

Bonvie, Herb
95Slapshot-225

Bonvie, Joe
95Madison Monsters-20

Boogaard, Aaron
02Calgary Hitmen-16

Boogaard, Derek
00Prince George Cougars-25
04Houston Aeros-1
05Beehive-93
Matte-93
05Black Diamond-253
05Hot Prospects-203
Autographed Patch Variation-203
Autographed Patch Variation Gold-203
Hot Materials-HMDB
Red Hot-203
05Parkhurst-246
Facsimile Auto Parallel-246
Signatures-DE
True Colors-TCMIN
True Colors-TCMIN
05SP Authentic-162
Limited-162
Sign of the Times-BO
05SP Game Used-171
Autographs-171
Gold-171
05SPx-206
Spectrum-206
05The Cup-144
Black Rainbow Rookies-144
Masterpiece Pressplates (Artifacts)-288
Masterpiece Pressplates (Bee Hive)-93
Masterpiece Pressplates (Black Diamond)-253
Masterpiece Pressplates (Ice)-153
Masterpiece Pressplates (Rookie Update)-146
Masterpiece Pressplates SPA Autos-162
Masterpiece Pressplates (SP Game Used)-171
Masterpiece Pressplates (SPx)-206
Masterpiece Pressplates (Trilogy)-270
Masterpiece Pressplates Ult Coll-151
Masterpiece Pressplates Autographs-144
Platinum Rookies-144
05UD Artifacts-288
05Ultimate Collection-151
Gold-151
Ultimate Debut Threads Jerseys-DTJDB
Ultimate Debut Threads Jerseys Autos-DAJDB
Ultimate Debut Threads Patches-DTPDB
Ultimate Debut Threads Patches Autos-DAPDB
05Ultra-221
Gold-221
Fresh Ink-FI-BO
Fresh Ink Blue-FI-BO
Ice-221
05Upper Deck Ice-153
Premieres Auto Patches-AIPDB
05Upper Deck Rookie Update-146
05Upper Deck Trilogy-270
06Be A Player Portraits First Exposures-FEDB
060-Pee-Chee-241
Rainbow-241
06UD Artifacts Auto-Facts-AFDE
06UD Artifacts Auto-Facts Gold-AFDE
06UD Powerplay Last Man Standing-LM2
06Upper Deck-98
Exclusives Parallel-98
High Gloss Parallel-98
Masterpieces-98
06Houston Aeros RetroÂ -5

Booker, Craig
85Kitchener Rangers-17
86Kitchener Rangers-21
87Kitchener Rangers-21

Booker, Wes
96Sault Ste. Marie Greyhounds-1
96Sault Ste. Marie Greyhounds Autographed-1

Boome, Danny
93UK Sheffield Steelers-9

Boomer, Ron
52Juniors Blue Tint-180

Boomsma, Scott
04Brampton Battalion-22

Boon, Dickie
60Topps-17
Stamps-4
83Hall of Fame-108
83Hall of Fame Postcards-H2
85Hall of Fame-108

Boon, Peter
03German DEL-46

Boone, Jonathan
99Halifax Mooseheads-6
00Halifax Mooseheads-2

Boone, Ken
93Kingston Frontenacs-11
98Peoria Rivermen-17
99Indianapolis Ice-2
00Indianapolis Ice-3
02Fort Wayne Komets-4
03Indianapolis Ice-3

Booras, Jon
00Sioux Falls Stampede-3
06Bloomington PrairieThunder-3

Boork, Leif
83Swedish Semic Elitserien-99
86Swedish Panini Stickers-56
91Swedish Semic Elitserien Stickers-313
92Swedish Semic Elitserien Stickers-335
93Swedish Semic Elitserien-300
99Norwegian National Team-24

Boorman, Bryan
95Red Deer Rebels-2

Boos, Tino
94German DEL-171
95German DEL-167
96German DEL-243
98German DEL-62
99German DEL-190
99German DEL-382
00German DEL-138
01German Upper Deck-136
02German DEL City Press-191
03German DEL-167
04German Cologne Sharks Postcards-6
04German DEL-208
05German DEL-202
05German DEL-298
06German DEL-118
German Forwards-GF11

Booth, David
06Be A Player-238
06Beehive-124
Matte-124
06Rochester Americans-2
06SP Authentic-240
Limited-240
06The Cup-133
Autographed Rookie Masterpiece Pressplates-133
Gold Rainbow Autographed Rookie Patches-133
Masterpiece Pressplates (Bee Hive)-124
Masterpiece Pressplates (Marquee Rookies)-589
Masterpiece Pressplates (SP Authentic)-240
Masterpiece Pressplates (Sweet Beginnings)-128
Masterpiece Pressplates (Ultimate Collection)-75
Rookies Black-133
Rookies Platinum-133
06Ultimate Collection-75
06Upper Deck High Gloss Parallel-470
06Upper Deck Masterpieces-470
06Upper Deck Sweet Shot-128
Rookie Jerseys Autographs-128

Booth, Derek
907th Inn. Sketch OHL-254
92Toledo Storm-23
92Toledo Storm Team Issue-19
93Rochester Americans Kodak-6
98Abilene Aviators-6
99German Bundesliga 2-146
02Peoria Rivermen-17
02Peoria Rivermen RBI Sports-153
06Bloomington PrairieThunder-22

Booth, Justin
93Quebec Pee-Wee Tournament-878

Boothman, George
34Beehive Group I Photos-302

Boothroyd, Luke
04UK U-20 Team-20

Bootland, Darryl
99UD Prospects-7
00St. Michaels Majors-6
01St. Michaels Majors-23
03Beehive-247
Gold-247
Silver-247
03ITG Action-655
03ITG Used Signature Series-151
Gold-151
Autographs-151A
Autographs Gold-151
03ITG VIP Rookie Debut-59
03Pacific Complete-577
Red-577
03Pacific Heads-Up-113
Hobby LTD-113
Retail LTD-113
03Pacific Luxury Suite-63
Gold-63
03Pacific Quest for the Cup-114
03Parkhurst Rookie-166
03SP Authentic-130
Limited-130
03Topps Traded-TT108
Blue-TT108
Gold-TT108
Red-TT108
03UD Honor Roll-133
03Upper Deck-466
Canadian Exclusives-466
HG-466
UD Exclusives-466
03Grand Rapids Griffins-3
06ITG Heroes and Prospects Jerseys-GUJ24
06ITG Heroes and Prospects Jerseys Gold-GUJ24
06ITG Heroes and Prospects Emblems-GUE24
06ITG Heroes and Prospects Emblems Gold-GUE24
06ITG Heroes and Prospects Numbers-GUN24
06ITG Heroes and Prospects Numbers Gold-GUN24

Bootland, Nick
95Slapshot-104
95Guelph Storm-6
96Guelph Storm-27
96Guelph Storm Premier Collection-12
97Guelph Storm-26
98Hershey Bears-26
00Hershey Bears-3
02Hershey Bears-2
03Kalamazoo Wings-24
04Cleveland Barons-2
05Kalamazoo Wings-22

Borba, Kevin
04Penticton Vees-13

Borbeau, Eric
01Chicoutimi Sagueneens-14

Borberg, Gordon
03German DEL-124
04German DEL-145
04German Hannover Scorpions Postcards-3

Bordeleau, Chris
69Canadiens Postcards Color-3
70Esso Power Players-251
70Sargent Promotions Stamps-185
71Blues Postcards-4
71Letraset Action Replays-24
710-Pee-Chee-51
71Sargent Promotions Stamps-187
71Topps-51
71Toronto Sun-234
720-Pee-Chee-299
727-Eleven Slurpee Cups WHA-2
730-Pee-Chee WHA Posters-17
73Quaker Oats WHA-15
750-Pee-Chee WHA-116
76Nordiques Postcards-5
760-Pee-Chee WHA-49

Bordeleau, J.P.
730-Pee-Chee-258
74NHL Action Stamps-83
740-Pee-Chee NHL-69
740-Pee-Chee NHL-309
74Topps-69
750-Pee-Chee NHL-369
760-Pee-Chee NHL-208
76Topps-208
770-Pee-Chee NHL-156
77Topps-156
780-Pee-Chee-101
78Topps-101
79Blackhawks Postcards-2
790-Pee-Chee-212
79Topps-212
80Blackhawks White Border-2
800-Pee-Chee-339

Bordeleau, Patrick
03Val d'Or Foreurs-20

Bordeleau, Paulin
73Canucks Royal Bank-1
74Canucks Royal Bank-2
74NHL Action Stamps-283
740-Pee-Chee NHL-340
75Canucks Royal Bank-3
750-Pee-Chee NHL-151
75Topps-151
76Nordiques Marie Antoinette-3
76Nordiques Postcards-6
760-Pee-Chee WHA-98
770-Pee-Chee WHA-32
90ProCards AHL/IHL-74
91ProCards-91
92Fredericton Canadiens-2
93Fredericton Canadiens-2
94Fredericton Canadiens-3
95Fredericton Canadiens-2
96Fredericton Canadiens-24
99Detroit Vipers Kid's Club-7

Bordeleau, Sebastien
917th Inn. Sketch QMJHL-210
95Fredericton Canadiens-3
95Slapshot Memorial Cup-69
96Canadiens Postcards-2
96Upper Deck-193
96Fredericton Canadiens-1
96Collector's Edge Ice-38
Prism-38
97Be A Player-211
Autographs-211
Autographs Die-Cuts-211
Autographs Prismatic Die-Cuts-211
97Canadiens Postcards-1
97Donruss Limited-195
Exposure-195
97Pacific-194
Copper-194
Emerald Green-194
Ice Blue-194
Red-194
Silver-194
97Score Canadiens-14
Platinum-14
Premier-14
97Upper Deck-87
98Predators Team Issue-3
98Upper Deck-298
Exclusives-298
Exclusives 1 of 1-298
Gold Reserve-298
98Upper Deck MVP-115
Gold Script-115
Silver Script-115
Super Script-115
990-Pee-Chee-204
990-Pee-Chee Chrome-204
990-Pee-Chee Chrome Refractors-204
99Pacific-218
Copper-218
Emerald Green-218
Gold-218
Ice Blue-218
Premiere Date-218
Red-218
99Topps/OPC-204
99Topps/OPC Chrome-204
Refractors-204
00Pacific-219
Copper-219
Gold-219
Ice Blue-219
Premiere Date-219
01Pacific-320
Extreme LTD-320
Hobby LTD-320
Premiere Date-320
Retail LTD-320
01Pacific Arena Exclusives-320
02Swiss HNL-264

Borden, Daryl
05Kingston Frontenacs-23
06Kingston Frontenacs-22

Borders, Jeff
93Omaha Lancers-2

Borders, Scott
97Lethbridge Hurricanes-3
99Lethbridge Hurricanes-5
00Lethbridge Hurricanes-3
01Lethbridge Hurricanes-16
02Fresno Falcons-9
03Fresno Falcons-1
05Bakersfield Condors-16
06Bakersfield Condors-12

Bordowski, Richard
02Czech OFS Plus-315
03Czech OFS Plus-281
04Czech OFS-205
05Czech HC Trinec-1

Bordson, Rob
06Cedar Rapids RoughRiders-5

Borega, Nathan
00Louisiana Ice Gators-3

Borek, Angela
98Minnesota Golden Gophers Women-1

Borell, Goran
69Swedish Hockey-222
71Swedish Hockey-367

Borer, Casey
03St. Cloud State Huskies-1
04St. Cloud State Huskies-2
05St. Cloud State Huskies-24
05St. Cloud State Huskies-2

Borg, Ulf
83Swedish Semic Elitserien-199
84Swedish Semic Elitserien-223
86Swedish Panini Stickers-250
87Swedish Panini Stickers-239

Borgen, Brent
02Lincoln Stars-15
03Lincoln Stars-12
03Lincoln Stars Update-41
04Minnesota Golden Gophers-2
05Lincoln Stars Update Traded-5T
05Lincoln Stars Update Traded-12T
05Minnesota Golden Gophers-3

Borges, Daniel
03Saginaw Spirit-3
04Saginaw Spirit-11

Borggaard, Andy
93Huntington Blizzard-5

Borgo, Richard
86Kitchener Rangers-15
87Kitchener Rangers-15
88Kitchener Rangers-15
89Kitchener Rangers-16
90Kitchener Rangers-14
907th Inn. Sketch OHL-228
907th Inn. Sketch Memorial Cup-35
93Thunder Bay Senators-6
93Classic Pro Prospects-103

Borgqvist, Robert
95Collector's Choice-348
Player's Club-348
Player's Club Platinum-348
02Swedish Malmo Red Hawks-16
02Swedish SHL-228
Parallel-228
04Swedish Elitset-82
Gold-82

Borgstrom, Jorma
65Finnish Hellas-52
70Finnish Jaakiekko-279
71Finnish Suomi Stickers-150
72Finnish Jaakiekko-140

Borik, Daniel
93Quebec Pee-Wee Tournament-1565

Boriskov, Igor
98Swiss Power Play Stickers-346
00Russian Hockey League-310

Borisnok, Mike
05Waterloo Blackhawks-6

Borisov, Sergei
03Russian Hockey League-281
04Russian RHL-1

Borland, Bill
23V128-1 Paulin's Candy-1
24Crescent Selkirks-14
28V128-2 Paulin's Candy-77

Born, Simon
02Swiss HNL-466

Bornand, Thierry
01Swiss HNL-272
02Swiss HNL-89

Borne, Alexandre
93Quebec Pee-Wee Tournament-992

Borner, Henrik
98Danish Hockey League-223
99Danish Hockey League-138

Bornet, Mauro
93Swiss HNL-274

Bornstrom, Bengt
64Swedish Coralli ISHockey-54
65Swedish Coralli ISHockey-54

Borodkin, Anton
98Kamloops Blazers-3
99Kamloops Blazers-3
00Prince Albert Raiders-2

Borodulin, Mikhail
98Russian Hockey League-10
99Russian Hockey League-3
99Russian Metallurg Magnetogorsk-41

Boron, Tim
03St. Cloud State Huskies-2
04St. Cloud State Huskies-3
05St. Cloud State Huskies-27
05St. Cloud State Huskies-3
06Colorado EaglesÂ -5

Borovansky, Michal
06Czech OFS-24

Borovkov, Alexander
01Russian Hockey League-8

Borozenko, Alexander
01Russian Hockey League-146

Borrett, Barry
77Nova Scotia Voyageurs-3

Borris, Kevin
95Seattle Thunderbirds-6

Borrozino, David
96Pensacola Ice Pilots-3

Borsato, Luciano
89ProCards AHL-35
91Pro Set Platinum-275
91Jets IGA-3
91Parkhurst-425
French-425
91Pinnacle-353
French-353
91Upper Deck-599
French-599
91Moncton Hawks-1
91ProCards-186
92Bowman-52
920-Pee-Chee-149
92Panini Stickers-E
92Panini Stickers French-E
92Parkhurst-439
Emerald Ice-439
92Pinnacle-218
French-218
92Pro Set Gold Team Leaders-15
92Pro Set Rookie Goal Leaders-8
92Score-256
Canadian-256
92Stadium Club-81
92Topps-239
Gold-239G
92Ultra-239
92Upper Deck-77
93Jets Readers Club-5
93Jets Ruffles-7
93OPC Premier-234
Gold-234
93Panini Stickers-195
93Parkhurst-501
Emerald Ice-501
93PowerPlay-471
93Score-401
Canadian-401
93Stadium Club-317
Members Only Master Set-317
First Day Issue-317
93Topps/OPC Premier-234
Gold-234
93Ultra-452
94OPC Premier-148
Special Effects-148
94Parkhurst SE-SE200
Gold-SE200
94Topps/OPC Premier-148
Special Effects-148
95German DEL-207
96German DEL-350
98Finnish Kerailysarja-44
99Finnish Cardset-30
00German DEL-185
01German Upper Deck-197

Borschevsky, Nikolai
92Maple Leafs Kodak-7
92OPC Premier-100
92Parkhurst-186
92Parkhurst-216
Emerald Ice-186
Emerald Ice-216
92Pinnacle-397
French-397
92Ultra-418
Imports-1
92Upper Deck-572
92Russian Stars Red Ace-4
92Russian Stars Red Ace-11
92Classic-52
Gold-52
93Donruss-332
93Leaf-137
Maple Leafs Score Black's-18
93OPC Premier-107
Gold-107
93Panini Stickers-224
93Parkhurst-203
Emerald Ice-203
93Pinnacle-12
Canadian-12
93PowerPlay-240
93Score-41
Canadian-41
International Stars-12
International Stars Canadian-12
93Stadium Club-375
Members Only Master Set-375
First Day Issue-375
93Topps/OPC Premier-107
Gold-107
93Ultra-99
93Upper Deck-164
SP-156
94Canada Games NHL POGS-230
94EA Sports-137
94Leaf-279
94Maple Leafs Gangsters-4
94Maple Leafs Kodak-5
94Maple Leafs Pin-up Posters-6
94Parkhurst-231
Gold-231
94Pinnacle-160
Artist's Proofs-160
Rink Collection-160
94Score-30
Gold-30
Platinum-30
94Stadium Club-209
Members Only Master Set-209
First Day Issue-209
Super Team Winner Cards-209
94Ultra-375
94Upper Deck-405
Electric Ice-405
95Collector's Choice-300
Player's Club-300
Player's Club Platinum-300
95Upper Deck-173
Electric Ice-173
Electric Ice-490
Electric Ice Gold-173
Electric Ice Gold-490

Borsheim, Les
96Brandon Wheat Kings-1
97Brandon Wheat Kings-3
99Brandon Wheat Kings-3
03Oklahoma City Blazers-4
05Colorado Eagles-4
06Colorado EaglesÂ -6

Bortis, Kyle
05Swift Current Broncos-9
06Swift Current Broncos-10

Bortuzzo, Robert
06Kitchener Rangers-12

Borup, Andreas
98Danish Hockey League-146
99Danish Hockey League-172

Borys, Cory
91Air Canada SJHL-D35

Borzecki, Adam
97Rimouski Oceanic-98
98Bowman CHL-120
Golden Anniversary-120
OPC International-120
98Bowman Chrome CHL-120
Golden Anniversary-120
Golden Anniversary Refractors-120
OPC International-120
OPC International Refractors-120
Refractors-120
00Idaho Steelheads-3
01Syracuse Crunch-20
02Syracuse Crunch-17
02Syracuse Crunch Sheets-14

04Reading Royals-24
Borzov, Leonid
73Swedish Stickers-114
Bosch, Brennan
05Medicine Hat Tigers-6
06Medicine Hat Tigers-3
Bosch, Bryan
88Lethbridge Hurricanes-3
89Lethbridge Hurricanes-3
Bosch, Marius
98Swiss Power Play Stickers-357
Bosch, Patrice
93Swiss HNL-300
96Swiss HNL-473
Boscher, Richard
91Air Canada SJHL-B1
92Saskatchewan JHL-130
Boschman, Joel
94Spokane Chiefs-15
95Spokane Chiefs-13
96Spokane Chiefs-11
97Red Deer Rebels-4
Boschman, Laurie
79Maple Leafs Postcards-3
80Maple Leafs Postcards-3
80Maple Leafs Postcards-4
800-Pee-Chee-179
80Pepsi-Cola Caps-82
80Topps-179
81Maple Leafs Postcards-5
810-Pee-Chee-314
810-Pee-Chee Stickers-103
82Oilers Red Rooster-14
83Jets Postcards-3
830-Pee-Chee-381
83Vachon-123
84Jets Police-4
840-Pee-Chee-335
840-Pee-Chee Stickers-288
847-Eleven Discs-57
84Topps-151
85Jets Police-2
85Jets Silverwood Dairy-1
850-Pee-Chee-251
850-Pee-Chee Stickers-254
86Jets Postcards-2
86Kraft Drawings-3
860-Pee-Chee-184
860-Pee-Chee Stickers-111
86Topps-184
87Jets Postcards-3
870-Pee-Chee-222
87Panini Stickers-368
88Jets Police-2
88Jets Postcards-4
88Oilers Tenth Anniversary-94
880-Pee-Chee-200
880-Pee-Chee Stickers-139
88Panini Stickers-153
89Jets Safeway-5
890-Pee-Chee Stickers-147
89Panini Stickers-169
90Devils Team Issue-2
900-Pee-Chee-39
90OPC Premier-8
90Panini Stickers-320
90Pro Set-324
90Pro Set-476
90Score Rookie/Traded-63T
90Topps-39
Tiffany-39
90Upper Deck-103
French-103
91Bowman-282
910-Pee-Chee-202
91Panini Stickers-215
91Parkhurst-316
French-316
91Pro Set-426
French-426
91Score Canadian Bilingual-436
91Score Canadian English-436
91Stadium Club-292
91Topps-202
91Upper Deck-279
French-279
92Parkhurst-122
Emerald Ice-122
92Pinnacle-375
French-375
92Score-374
92Score-513
Canadian-374
Canadian-513
92Stadium Club-310
92Topps-246
Gold-246G
93Score-289
Canadian-289
93Stadium Club-3
Members Only Master Set-3
OPC-3
First Day Issue-3
First Day Issue OPC-3
02Fleer Throwbacks-55
Gold-55
Platinum-55
02Maple Leafs Platinum Collection-82
04ITG Franchises Canadian-136
Autographs-LBH
Boss, Carsten
94German First League-492
Boss, Daniell
04Swiss Davos Postcards-6
Bossence, Andy
04Kootenay Ice-2
Bossio, John
99Odessa Jackalopes-13
01Odessa Jackalopes-3
02Odessa Jackalopes-1
03Odessa Jackalopes-2
Bosson, Mattias
93Swedish Semic Elitserien-182
94Swedish Leaf-252
95Swedish Leaf-94
95Swedish Upper Deck-142
97Swedish Collector's Choice-143
99Finnish Cardset-301
00Swedish Upper Deck-26
Bossy, Mike
780-Pee-Chee-1
780-Pee-Chee-63
780-Pee-Chee-67
780-Pee-Chee-115
78Topps-1
78Topps-63
78Topps-67
78Topps-115
79Islanders Transparencies-1
790-Pee-Chee-1
790-Pee-Chee-5
790-Pee-Chee-7
790-Pee-Chee-161
790-Pee-Chee-230
79Topps-1
79Topps-5
79Topps-7
79Topps-161
79Topps-230
800-Pee-Chee-25
800-Pee-Chee-204
800-Pee-Chee Super-12
80Topps-25
80Topps-204
810-Pee-Chee-198
810-Pee-Chee-208
810-Pee-Chee-219
810-Pee-Chee-382
810-Pee-Chee-386
810-Pee-Chee-388
810-Pee-Chee-390
810-Pee-Chee Stickers-150
810-Pee-Chee Stickers-158
810-Pee-Chee Stickers-253
81Post Standups-6
81Topps-4
81Topps-57
81Topps-E125
82McDonald's Stickers-6
82McDonald's Stickers-21
820-Pee-Chee-2
820-Pee-Chee-197
820-Pee-Chee-199
820-Pee-Chee Stickers-1
820-Pee-Chee Stickers-50
820-Pee-Chee Stickers-51
820-Pee-Chee Stickers-165
82Post Cereal-12
82Topps Stickers-1
82Topps Stickers-50
82Topps Stickers-51
82Topps Stickers-165
83Islanders Team Issue-1
83NHL Key Tags-80
830-Pee-Chee-1
830-Pee-Chee-3
830-Pee-Chee-205
830-Pee-Chee-210
830-Pee-Chee Stickers-10
830-Pee-Chee Stickers-78
830-Pee-Chee Stickers-79
830-Pee-Chee Stickers-176
830-Pee-Chee Stickers-306
830-Pee-Chee Stickers-321
830-Pee-Chee Stickers-322
83Puffy Stickers-19
83Topps Stickers-10
83Topps Stickers-78
83Topps Stickers-79
83Topps Stickers-176
83Topps Stickers-306
83Topps Stickers-321
83Topps Stickers-322
84Islanders News-2
84Islanders News-35
84Kellogg's Accordion Discs-1
84Kellogg's Accordion Discs Singles-2
840-Pee-Chee-122
840-Pee-Chee-209
840-Pee-Chee-362
840-Pee-Chee-376
840-Pee-Chee Stickers-82
840-Pee-Chee Stickers-83
840-Pee-Chee Stickers-235
847-Eleven Discs-33
84Topps-91
84Topps-155
85Islanders News-2
85Islanders News-32
85Islanders News Trottier-32
850-Pee-Chee-130
850-Pee-Chee Stickers-66
850-Pee-Chee Stickers-118
857-Eleven Credit Cards-12
85Topps-130
85Topps Sticker Inserts-9
86Islanders Team Issue-21
860-Pee-Chee-90
860-Pee-Chee Box Bottoms-B
860-Pee-Chee Stickers-117
860-Pee-Chee Stickers-194
860-Pee-Chee Stickers-217
86Topps-90
86Topps Box Bottoms-B
86Topps Sticker Inserts-4
870-Pee-Chee-105
870-Pee-Chee Stickers-244
87Panini Stickers-97
87Pro-Sport All-Stars-6
87Topps-105
88Esso All-Stars-2
90Pro Set-650
91Pro Set HOF Induction-1
91Upper Deck-45
920-Pee-Chee-391
25th Anniv. Inserts-11
92Pinnacle-245
French-245
93Islanders Chemical Bank Alumni-2
93Classic-116
Autographs-AU1
95Zeller's Masters of Hockey Signed-1
96Swedish Semic Wien Hockey Legends-HL3
97SLU Canadian Timeless Legends-2
98SLU Canadian Timeless Legends-1
99Topps Stanley Cup Heroes-SC2
99Topps Stanley Cup Heroes Refractors-SC2
99Topps Stanley Cup Heroes Autographs-SCA2
99Upper Deck 500 Goal Club-500MB
99Upper Deck 500 Goal Club-500MB
99Upper Deck Century Legends-20
Century Collection-20
Epic Signatures-MB
Epic Signatures 100-MB
Jerseys of the Century-JC2
99Upper Deck Retro-96
Gold-96
Platinum-96
Inkredible-MB
Inkredible Level 2-MB
00UD Heroes-133
Game-Used Twigs-T-BO
Game-Used Twigs Gold-C-HB
00Upper Deck Legends-81
Legendary Collection Bronze-81
Legendary Collection Gold-81
Legendary Collection Silver-81
Enshrined Stars-ES8
Epic Signatures-MB
Essence of the Game-EG3
Legendary Game Jerseys-JMB
Supreme Milestones-SM12
00Upper Deck Vintage Dynasty: A Piece of History-BK
00Upper Deck Vintage Dynasty: A Piece of History Gold-BK
01BAP Memorabilia 500 Goal Scorers-GS13
01BAP Signature Series 500 Goal Scorers-10
01BAP Sig Series 500 Goal Scorers Autos-10
01BAP Signature Series Vintage Autographs-VA-30
01BAP Ultimate Mem All-Star History-33
01BAP Ultimate Memorabilia Calder Trophy-18
01BAP Ultimate Memorabilia Decades-24
01BAP Ultimate Mem Dynasty Jerseys-2
01BAP Ultimate Mem Dynasty Emblems-2
01BAP Ultimate Mem Dynasty Numbers-2
01BAP Ultimate Mem 500 Goal Scorers-5
01BAP Ultimate Mem 500 Goal Scorers Autos-17
01BAP Ultimate Mem 500 Goal Jerseys/Stick-5
01BAP Ultimate Mem 500 Goal Emblems-5
01BAP Ultimate Mem Playoff Records-16
01BAP Ultimate Mem Retired Numbers-4
01BAP Ultimate Memorabilia Retro Trophies-6
01BAP Ultimate Mem Retro Teammates-5
01Fleer Legacy-32
Ultimate-32
01Greats of the Game-72
Autographs-72
Board Certified-1
01Parkhurst Autographs-PA29
01Parkhurst 500 Goal Scorers-PGS13
01Topps Archives-63
01UD Premier Collection Signatures-MB
01UD Premier Collection Signatures Black-MB
01UD Stanley Cup Champs-19
Jerseys-T-MB
Pieces of Glory-G-BO
Sticks-S-BO
01Upper Deck Legends-42
01Upper Deck Legends-96
Epic Signatures-MB
Fiorentino Collection-FCMB
Milestones-MMB
Milestones Platinum-MMB
Sticks-PHMB
01Upper Deck Vintage Jerseys-SCMB
01Upper Deck Vintage Jerseys-SDMB
02BAP Memorabilia Mini Stanley Cups-19
02BAP NHL All-Star History-33
02BAP Ultimate Memorabilia All-Star MVP-15
02BAP Ultimate Memorabilia Conn Smythe-12
02BAP Ultimate Memorabilia Emblem Attic-24
02BAP Ultimate Memorabilia Numerology-25
02BAP Ultimate Mem Playoff Scorers-12
02BAP Ultimate Mem Vintage Jerseys-28
02Parkhurst Vintage Teammates-VT10
02UD Foundations-62
02UD Foundations-119
1000 Point Club-MB
1000 Point Club-BO
1000 Point Club Gold-MB
1000 Point Club Silver-MB
Calder Winners-TMB
Calder Winners Gold-TMB
Calder Winners Silver-T-MB
Canadian Heroes-CMB
Canadian Heroes Gold-CMB
Canadian Heroes Silver-C-MB
Classic Greats-GMB
Classic Greats Gold-GMB
Classic Greats Silver-G-MB
Milestones-NMB
Milestones Gold-NMB
Milestones Silver-N-MB
Playoff Performers-PMB
Playoff Performers Gold-PMB
Playoff Performers Silver-P-MB
Power Stations-SMB
Power Stations Gold-SMB
Power Stations Silver-S-MB
Signs of Greatness-SGMB
02UD Piece of History Historical Swatches-HSMB
02UD Piece of History Hockey Beginnings-HB7
02UD Piece of History Mark of Distinction-MB
03BAP Ultimate Memorabilia Cornerstones-8
03BAP Ultimate Memorabilia Great Moments-9
03BAP Ultimate Mem Hometown Heroes-20
03BAP Ultimate Mem Hometown Heroes Gold-20
03BAP Ultimate Mem Jersey and Stick-29
03BAP Ultimate Mem Jersey and Stick Gold-29
03BAP Ultimate Memorabilia Linemates-7
03BAP Ultimate Mem Raised to the Rafters-17
03BAP Ultimate Mem Retro Teammates-6
03BAP Ultimate Memorabilia Triple Threads-26
03BAP Ultimate Mem Vintage Jerseys-26
03BAP Ultimate Mem Vintage Jerseys Gold-26
03Canada Post-23
03ITG Used Sig Series Vintage Mem -19
03ITG Used Sig Series Vintage Mem Gold-19
03ITG VIP MVP-16
03Parkhurst Rookie Jerseys-GJ-47
03Parkhurst Rookie Jerseys Gold-GJ-47
03Parkhurst Rookie Jersey and Sticks-SJ-29
03Parkhurst Rookie Jersey and Sticks Gold-SJ-29
03Parkhurst Rookie ROYalty-VR-22
03Parkhurst Rookie ROYalty Gold-VR-22
03SP Authentic Sign of the Times-BTG
03SP Game Used Limited Threads-LTMB
03SP Game Used Limited Threads Gold-LTMB
03SPx-112
Radiance-112
Spectrum-112
03UD Premier Collection Legends-PL-MB
03UD Premier Collection Legends Patches-PL-MB
03UD Premier Collection Signatures-PS-BY
03UD Premier Collection Signatures Gold-PS-BY
03Upper Deck Trilogy-124
Crest Variations-124
Limited-124
Scripts-S3BY
Scripts-S3MB
Scripts-CSBY
Scripts-CSBY2
Scripts Limited-S3BY
Scripts Limited-S3MB
Scripts Red-S3MB
04ITG NHL AS FANtasy AS History Jerseys-SB33
04ITG Franchises He Shoots/Scores Prizes-41
04ITG Franchises Update Complete Jerseys-UCJ6
04ITG Franchises Upd Complete Jersey Gold-UCJ6
04ITG Franchises Update Linemates-ULI3
04ITG Franchises Update Linemates Gold-ULI3
04ITG Franchises US East-369
Autographs-A-MBO
Barn Burners-EBB2
Barn Burners Gold-EBB2
Double Memorabilia-EDM12
Double Memorabilia Autographs-EDM-MB
Double Memorabilia Gold-EDM12
Forever Rivals-EFR2
Forever Rivals Gold-EFR2
Memorabilia-ESM16
Memorabilia Autographs-ESM-MB
Memorabilia Gold-ESM16
Teammates-ETM2
Teammates Gold-ETM2
Trophy Winners-ETW3
Trophy Winners Gold-ETW3
04ITG Ultimate Memorabilia-168
Gold-168
Autographs-44
Autographs Gold-44
Calder Trophy-2
Conn Smythe Trophy-5
Cornerstones-9
Cornerstones Gold-9
Country of Origin-9
Country of Origin Gold-9
Day In History-2
Day In History-8
Day In History-25
Day In History Gold-2
Day In History Gold-8
Day In History Gold-25
Jersey Autographs-22
Jersey Autographs Gold-22
Jersey and Sticks-6
Jersey and Sticks Gold-6
Retro Teammates-5
Seams Unbelievable-4
Stick Autographs-2
Stick Autographs Gold-2
Triple Threads-9
04SP Authentic Buybacks-151
04SP Authentic Buybacks-152
04SP Authentic Buybacks-153
04SP Authentic Sign of the Times-DS-BT
04SP Authentic Sign of the Times-TS-BTG
04SP Authentic Sign of the Times-QS-BDPB
04SP Authentic Sign of the Times-SS-RLW
04UD All-World-104
Autographs-104
04UD Legendary Signatures-57
Autographs-MB
HOF Inks-HOF-MB
Linemates-CGBTMB
04UD Legends Classics-40
04UD Legends Classics-60
04UD Legends Classics-65
Gold-40
Gold-60
Gold-65
Platinum-40
Platinum-60
Platinum-65
Silver-40
Silver-60
Silver-65
Signature Moments-M18
Signatures-CS18
Signatures-DC5
Signatures-TC5
Signatures-QC2
04Ultimate Collection Jerseys-UGJ-BO
04Ultimate Collection Jerseys Gold-UGJ-BO
04Ultimate Collection Jersey Autographs-UGJA-BO
04ITG Heroes and Prospects-158
Aspiring-7
Autographs-MBO
Hero Memorabilia-7
04ITG Heroes/Prospects Toronto Expo '05-158
04ITG Heroes/Prospects Expo Heroes/Pros-158
05ITG Heroes/Prosp Toronto Expo Parallel -22
05Beehive-221
PhotoGraphs-PGMB
Signature Scrapbook-SSBO
05Black Diamond Jerseys-J-BO
05Black Diamond Jerseys Ruby-J-BO
05Black Diamond Jersey Duals-DJ-BO
05Black Diamond Jersey Triples-TJ-BO
05Black Diamond Jersey Quads-QJ-BO
05ITG Ultimate Memorabilia Level 1-70
05ITG Ultimate Memorabilia Level 2-70
05ITG Ultimate Memorabilia Level 3-70
05ITG Ultimate Memorabilia Level 4-70
05ITG Ultimate Memorabilia Level 5-70
05ITG Ultimate Mem Cornerstones Jerseys-8
05ITG Ultimate Mem Cornerst Jerseys Gold-8
05ITG Ultimate Mem Double Mem Autos-20
05ITG Ultimate Mem Double Mem Autos Gold-20
05ITG Ultimate Memorabilia Emblems-13
05ITG Ultimate Memorabilia Emblems Gold-13
05ITG Ultimate Mem First Rounders Jerseys-4
05ITG Ultimate Mem 1st Round Jersey Gold-4
05ITG Ultimate Memorabilia In The Numbers-9
05ITG Ultimate Mem In The Numbers Gold-9
05ITG Ultimate Mem Jersey and Emblem-17
05ITG Ultimate Mem Jersey Emblems Gold-17
05ITG Ultimate Memorabilia Jerseys-26
05ITG Ultimate Memorabilia Jerseys Gold-26
05ITG Ultimate Mem Raised to the Rafters-6
05ITG Ultimate Mem Raised Rafters Gold-6
05ITG Ultimate Mem Record Breaker Jerseys-8
05ITG Ultimate Mem RecBreak Jerseys Gold-8
05ITG Ultimate Mem Retro Teammate Jerseys-1
05ITG Ult Mem Retro Teammates Jersey Gold-1
05ITG Ultimate Memorabilia Sextuple Autos-5
05ITG Ult Mem 3 Star of the Game Jsy-20
05ITG Ult Mem 3 Star of the Game Jsy Gold-20
05ITG Ultimate Memorabilia Ultimate Autos-49
05ITG Ultimate Mem Ultimate Autos Gold-49
05NHL Legends Medallions-1
05SP Authentic Exquisite Endorsements-EEMB
05SP Authentic Immortal Inks-IIMB
05SP Authentic Octographs-OH
05SP Authentic Prestigious Pairings-PPTB
05SP Authentic Sign of the Times Quads-QTBNP
05SP Game Used Authentic Fabrics-AF-BO
05SP Game Used Authentic Fabrics Autos-AAF-BO
05SP Game Used Authentic Fabrics Dual-NY
05SP Game Used Authentic Fabrics Gold-AF-BO
05SP Game Used Authentic Fabrics Quad-TBYS
05SP Game Used Authentic Patches Quad -TBYS
05SP Game Used Authentic Patches-AP-BO
05SP Game Used Authentic Patch Autos-AAP-BO
05SP Game Used Authentic Patches Dual-NY
05SP Game Used Game Gear-GG-MB
05SP Game Used Game Gear Autographs-AG-MB
05SP Game Used Signature Sticks-SS-MB
05SP Game Used Significant Numbers-SN-BY
05SP Game Used Statscriptions-ST-MB
05SPx-113
Spectrum-113
Winning Combos-WC-BK
Winning Combos-WC-NY
Winning Combos Autographs-AWC-NY
Winning Combos Gold-WC-BK
Winning Combos Gold-WC-NY
Winning Combos Spectrum-WC-BK
Winning Combos Spectrum-WC-NY
Winning Materials-WM-BY
Winning Materials Gold-WM-BY
Winning Materials Spectrum-WM-BY
Xcitement Legends-XL-MB
Xcitement Legends Gold-XL-MB
Xcitement Legends Spectrum-XL-MB
05The Cup-65
Gold-65
Black Rainbow-65
Emblems of Endorsement-EEBY
Hardware Heroes-HHBO1
Hardware Heroes-HHBO2
Hardware Heroes-HHBO3
Honorable Numbers-HNBY
Limited Logos-LLBY
Masterpiece Pressplates-65
Noble Numbers-NNBS
Noble Numbers Dual-DNNLB
Noble Numbers Dual-DNNTB
Patch Variation-P65
Patch Variation Autographs-AP65
Scripted Numbers-SNBL
Scripted Numbers-SNBS
Scripted Swatches-SSBY
Signature Patches-SPBY
Stanley Cup Titlists-TBY
05UD Artifacts-104
Blue-104
Gold-104
Green-104
Pewter-104
Red-104
Auto Facts-AF-BO
Auto Facts Blue-AF-BO
Auto Facts Copper-AF-BO
Auto Facts Pewter-AF-BO
Auto Facts Silver-AF-BO
Gold Autographed-104
Remarkable Artifacts-RA-BS
Remarkable Artifacts Dual-RA-BS
05Ultimate Collection Endorsed Emblems-EEBY
05Upper Deck All-Time Greatest-37
05Upper Deck All-Time Greatest-79
05Upper Deck Big Playmakers-B-MBI
05Upper Deck NHL Generations-TBTN
05Upper Deck Notable Numbers-N-MBY
05Upper Deck Patches-P-MB
05Upper Deck Ice Signature Swatches-SSBO
05Upper Deck Trilogy-164
Crystal-164
Ice Scripts-IS-BO
05ITG Heroes and Prospects-22
Aspiring-ASP7
Autographs-A-MBO
Hero Memorabilia-HM-32
06Beehive-182
5 X 7 Black and White-182
Signature Scrapbook-SSMB
06ITG International Ice-60
06ITG International Ice-140
Gold-60
Gold-140
Autographs-AMBO
Autographs-AMBO2
Emblems-GUE16
Emblems Gold-GUE16
International Rivals-IR09
International Rivals Gold-IR09
Jerseys-GUJ16
Jerseys Gold-GUJ16
My Country My Team-MC13
My Country My Team Gold-MC13
Numbers-GUN16
Numbers Gold-GUN16
Teammates-IT05
Teammates Gold-IT05
06ITG Ultimate Memorabilia-104
Artist Proof-104
Boys Will Be Boys-19
Boys Will Be Boys Gold-19
First Round Picks-13
First Round Picks Gold-13
Retro Teammates-15
Retro Teammates Gold-15
Road to the Cup-6
Road to the Cup Gold-6
Sensational Season-10
Sensational Season Gold-10
Stick Rack-24
Stick Rack Gold-24
06Parkhurst-20
Autographs-20
Autographs Dual-DABG
06SP Authentic Sign of the Times Duals-STBG
06SP Authentic Sign of the Times Quads-ST4BCTS
06SP Game Used Authentic Fabrics Quads-AF4NMBT
06SP Game Used Authentic Fabrics Quads Patches-AF4NMBT
06SP Game Used Authentic Fabrics Eights-AF8HOF
06SP Game Used Authentic Fabrics Eights Patches-AF8HOF
06SP Game Used By The Letter-BLBO
06SP Game Used Legendary Fabrics-LFMB
06SP Game Used Legendary Fabrics Autographs-LFMB
06SPx-132
Spectrum-132
SPxcitement-X63
SPxcitement Spectrum-X63
SPxcitement Autographs-X63
06The Cup-56
Autographed Foundations-CQMI
Autographed Foundations Patches-CQMI
Autographed Patches-56
Black Rainbow-56
Foundations-CQMI
Foundations Patches-CQMI
Gold-56
Gold Patches-56
Honorable Numbers-HNMI
Jerseys-56
Limited Logos-LLBO
Masterpiece Pressplates-56
Scripted Swatches-SSBO
Signature Patches-SPMB
Stanley Cup Signatures-CSMB
06UD Artifacts-104
Blue-104
Gold-104
Platinum-104
Radiance-104
Autographed Radiance Parallel-104
Red-104
Auto-Facts-AFBY
Auto-Facts Gold-AFBY
06Ultimate Collection-39
Autographed Jerseys-AJ-BO
Autographed Patches-AJ-BO
Jerseys-UJ-MB
Jerseys Triple-UJ3-SBG
Patches-UJ-MB
Premium Patches-PS-BO
Premium Swatches-PS-BO
Signatures-US-BM
Ultimate Achievements-UA-MI
06Upper Deck Sweet Shot-67
Signature Shots/Saves-SSMB
Signature Shots/Saves Sticks-SSSBO
Signature Sticks-STMI
Sweet Stitches-SSMI
Sweet Stitches Duals-SSMI
Sweet Stitches Triples-SSMI
06Upper Deck Trilogy Combo Autographed Jerseys-CJBS
06Upper Deck Trilogy Combo Autographed Patches-CJBS
06Upper Deck Trilogy Combo Clearcut Autographs-C3BPS
06Upper Deck Trilogy Frozen In Time-FT13
06Upper Deck Trilogy Ice Scripts-ISMB
06Upper Deck Trilogy Legendary Scripts-LSMB
06Upper Deck Trilogy Scripts-S1MB
Bostock, Bret
00Connecticut Huskies-2
Boston, Scott
87Brockville Braves-17
897th Inn. Sketch OHL-87
907th Inn. Sketch OHL-340
917th Inn. Sketch OHL-115
92Atlanta Knights-14
93Knoxville Cherokees-1
95South Carolina Stingrays-15
96South Carolina Stingrays-20
98Tacoma Sabercats-3
99Tacoma Sabercats-1
00Tacoma Sabercats-2
Bostrom, Anders
83Swedish Semic Elitserien-30
84Swedish Semic Elitserien-29
Bostrom, Gote
65Swedish Coralli ISHockey-169
Bostrom, Hans
67Swedish Hockey-85
Bostrom, Helge
33V252 Canadian Gum-4
Bostrom, Juhani
70Finnish Jaakiekko-101
71Finnish Suomi Stickers-111
72Finnish Jaakiekko-81
72Finnish Panda Toronto-1
73Finnish Jaakiekko-126
78Finnish SM-Liiga-38
Bostrom, Justin
04Sioux City Musketeers-2
05Minnesota Golden Gophers-4
06Minnesota Golden Gophers-3
Bostrom, Kent
04Sioux City Musketeers-3
Bostrom, Soren
57Swedish Alfabilder-75
67Swedish Hockey-215
Both, Brad
00Fresno Falcons-3
01Fresno Falcons-1
02Fresno Falcons-7
04Atlantic City Boardwalk Bullies-4
05Fresno Falcons-2
Bothwell, Tim
840-Pee-Chee-182
850-Pee-Chee-161
850-Pee-Chee Stickers-49
85Topps-161
87Blues Kodak-2
870-Pee-Chee-29
870-Pee-Chee Stickers-26
87Topps-29
88Blues Kodak-2
88ProCards IHL-68
89ProCards AHL-23
907th Inn. Sketch WHL-42
917th Inn. Sketch WHL-328
92Phoenix Roadrunners-1
Botteri, Stephane
92Finnish Semic-221
93Swedish Semic World Champ Stickers-251
94Finnish Jaa Kiekko-217
Botterill, Jason
93Donruss Team Canada-4
93Pinnacle-467
Canadian-467
93Upper Deck-534
93Michigan Wolverines-2
94Finest-144
Super Team Winners-144
Refractors-144
94Score-202
Gold-202
Platinum-202
94SP-143
Die Cuts-143
95Donruss Canadian World Junior Team-18
95Donruss Elite World Juniors-10
95SP-175
95Topps Canadian World Juniors-14CJ
98McDonald's Upper Deck-25
98Pacific-172
Ice Blue-172
Red-172
98Upper Deck-260
Exclusives-260
Exclusives 1 of 1-260
Gold Reserve-260
98Michigan K-Wings-2
99BAP Memorabilia-252
Gold-252
Silver-252
99BAP Millennium-18
Emerald-18
Ruby-18
Sapphire-18
Signatures-18
Signatures Gold-18
99Paramount-9
Copper-9
Emerald-9
Gold-9
Holographic Emerald-9
Holographic Gold-9
Holographic Silver-9
Ice Blue-9
Premiere Date-9
Red-9
Silver-9
99Upper Deck Victory-17
02BAP Sig Series Auto Buybacks 1999-18
02Rochester Americans-3
03Rochester Americans-4
04Rochester Americans-4
Botterill, Jennifer
04Canadian Womens World Championship Team-4
06ITG Going For Gold-11
06ITG Going For Gold Samples-11
06ITG Going For Gold Autographs-AB
06ITG Going For Gold Jerseys-GUJ11
Botterill, Scott
96Prince Albert Raiders-2
97Prince Albert Raiders-1
Bottomley, Jarret
03Yarmouth Mariners-6
Boucha, Henry
72Sargent Promotions Stamps-84
72Finnish Semic World Championship-126
72Swedish Semic World Championship-126
73North Stars Action Posters-1
730-Pee-Chee-33
73Red Wings McCarthy Postcards-3
73Topps-33
74Lipton Soup-32
74NHL Action Stamps-141
740-Pee-Chee NHL-38
74Topps-38
750-Pee-Chee WHA-79
760-Pee-Chee NHL-209
76Rockies Puck Bucks-3
76Topps-209
04ITG Franchises US West-207
04ITG Franchises US West-228
Autographs-A-HB
Bouchard, Adam
93Quebec Pee-Wee Tournament-607
Bouchard, Butch
34Beehive Group I Photos-138
43Parade Sportive *-6
43Parade Sportive *-9
43Parade Sportive *-10
43Parade Sportive *-11
44Beehive Group II Photos-225
45Quaker Oats Photos-65A
45Quaker Oats Photos-65B
45Quaker Oats Photos-65C
48Exhibits Canadian-5
51Parkhurst-3
52Parkhurst-13
53Parkhurst-32
54Parkhurst-6
54Parkhurst-97
55Parkhurst-46
55Parkhurst-71
Quaker Oats-46
83Hall of Fame-228
83Hall of Fame Postcards-M1
85Hall of Fame-228
91Ultimate Original Six-8
French-8
930-Pee-Chee Canadiens Hockey Fest-2
01BAP Memorabilia Rocket's Mates-RM9
01BAP Signature Series Vintage Autographs-VA-19
01Parkhurst Autographs-PA25
01Parkhurst Reprints-PR50
01Parkhurst Reprints-PR63
01Parkhurst Reprints-PR70
01Parkhurst Reprints-PR73
01Parkhurst Reprints-PR105
03Parkhurst Original Six Montreal-41
03Parkhurst Original Six Montreal-72
Autographs-2
04ITG Franchises Canadian-54
Autographs-BBO
04ITG Ultimate Memorabilia-3
Gold-3
Autographs-55
Autographs Gold-55
06ITG Ultimate Memorabilia-24
Artist Proof-24
06Parkhurst-71
06Parkhurst-186
Autographs-71
Autographs-186
Autographs Dual-DABL
06The Cup Stanley Cup Signatures-CSBD
Bouchard, Dan
72Flames Postcards-2
720-Pee-Chee-203
72Sargent Promotions Stamps-14
730-Pee-Chee-45
73Topps-45
74Lipton Soup-44
74NHL Action Stamps-6
740-Pee-Chee NHL-15
74Topps-15
750-Pee-Chee NHL-268
75Topps-268
760-Pee-Chee NHL-111
76Topps-111
770-Pee-Chee NHL-37
77Topps-37
78Flames Majik Market-30
780-Pee-Chee-169
78Topps-169
79Panini Stickers-53
79Flames Postcards-2
79Flames Team Issue-3
790-Pee-Chee-28
79Topps-28
80Flames Postcards-1
80Nordiques Postcards-3
800-Pee-Chee-68
80Pepsi-Cola Caps-1
80Topps-68
81Nordiques Postcards-3
810-Pee-Chee-270
810-Pee-Chee Stickers-73
810-Pee-Chee Stickers-84
82McDonald's Stickers-1
82Nordiques Postcards-3
820-Pee-Chee-278
820-Pee-Chee Stickers-27
82Topps Stickers-27
83NHL Key Tags-112
83Nordiques Postcards-3
830-Pee-Chee-290
830-Pee-Chee Stickers-245
83Puffy Stickers-18
83Topps Stickers-245
83Vachon-62
84Nordiques Postcards-4
840-Pee-Chee-277
840-Pee-Chee Stickers-172
840-Pee-Chee Stickers-173
84Topps-128
85Jets Police-3
850-Pee-Chee-246
850-Pee-Chee Stickers-143
92Nordiques Petro-Canada-2
04ITG Franchises Canadian-1
04ITG Franchises Canadian-77
Autographs-DB2
Autographs-DB3
Goalie Gear-GG8
Goalie Gear Gold-GG8
04ITG Franchises Update Complete Jerseys-UCJ2
04ITG Franchises Upd Complete Jersey Gold-UCJ2
04ITG Franchises US East-306
Autographs-A-DB1
06Between The Pipes-84
Autographs-ADB
Double Jerseys-DJ17
Double Jerseys Gold-DJ17
Bouchard, Danick
02Shawinigan Cataractes-8
03Shawinigan Cataractes-3
05Shawinigan Cataractes-10
Bouchard, Dave
04Drummondville Voltigeurs-14
05Drummondville Voltigeurs-12
06Saint Johns Sea Dogs-6
Bouchard, David
03Drummondville Voltigeurs-2
05Rimouski Oceanic-17
06Rimouski Oceanic-9
Bouchard, Eddie
23V145-1-37
24C144 Champ's Cigarettes-5
24V145-2-19
Bouchard, Emile
43Parade Sportive *-6
930-Pee-Chee Canadiens Hockey Fest-2
Bouchard, Eric
917th Inn. Sketch WHL-137
Bouchard, Francois
99Swedish Upper Deck-173
00Swedish Upper Deck-46
01St. John's Maple Leafs-3
02German DEL City Press-130
03German DEL-93
04German DEL-104
04Baie-Comeau Drakkar-6
05ITG Heroes/Prosp Toronto Expo Parallel -412
05German DEL-82
Defender-DF02
Defender Promos-DF02
05Baie-Comeau Drakkar-11
05ITG Heroes and Prospects-412
Autographs Update-A-FB
Team Cherry-TC17
06German DEL-144
All-Star Jerseys-AS2
06ITG Heroes and Prospects-117
Autographs-AFB
CHL Top Prospects-TP03
CHL Top Prospects Gold-TP03
Bouchard, Frederic
98Dayton Bombers-1
98Dayton Bombers EBK-1
99UHL All-Stars West-2T
00Fort Wayne Komets-1
00Fort Wayne Komets Shoe Carnival-13
01Fort Wayne Komets-3
01Fort Wayne Komets Shoe Carnival-9
01Milwaukee Admirals-6
02German DEL City Press-4
Bouchard, Gilles
907th Inn. Sketch QMJHL-38
917th Inn. Sketch Memorial Cup-34
Bouchard, Hughes
88Richelieu Riverains-6
917th Inn. Sketch QMJHL-152
93Roanoke Express-5
Bouchard, Joel
907th Inn. Sketch QMJHL-244
917th Inn. Sketch QMJHL-143
93Donruss Team Canada-5
93Pinnacle-461
Canadian-461
93Upper Deck-541
94Saint John Flames-1
95Saint John Flames-3
96Upper Deck Ice-8
Parallel-8
97Be A Player-129
Autographs-129
Autographs Die-Cuts-129
Autographs Prismatic Die-Cuts-129
97Pacific-338
Copper-338
Emerald Green-338
Ice Blue-338
Red-338
Silver-338
97Panini Stickers-197
98Panini Stickers-141
98Predators Team Issue-4
990-Pee-Chee-220
990-Pee-Chee Chrome-220
990-Pee-Chee Chrome Refractors-220
99Topps/OPC-220
99Topps/OPC Chrome-220
Refractors-220
00Upper Deck NHLPA-PA67
01Pacific-297
Extreme LTD-297
Hobby LTD-297
Premiere Date-297
Retail LTD-297
01Pacific Arena Exclusives-297
01Albany River Rats-23
03Parkhurst Original Six New York-9
Bouchard, Leon
51Laval Dairy Subset-25
52Bas Du Fleuve-57
52St. Lawrence Sales-41
Bouchard, Mathieu
93Quebec Pee-Wee Tournament-1350
Bouchard, Maxime
99Rouyn-Noranda Huskies-3
00Rouyn-Noranda Huskies-20
Signed-20
01Drummondville Voltigeurs-22
Bouchard, Pierre
69Canadiens Postcards Color-4
71Bazooka-20
71Canadiens Postcards-1
710-Pee-Chee-2
71Sargent Promotions Stamps-112
71Toronto Sun-147
72Canadiens Postcards-2
72Canadiens Great West Life Prints-1
72Dimanche/Derniere Heure *-133
72Dimanche/Derniere Heure *-134
720-Pee-Chee-165
72Sargent Promotions Stamps-116
73Canadiens Postcards-2
730-Pee-Chee-261
74Canadiens Postcards-1
74NHL Action Stamps-159
740-Pee-Chee NHL-178
740-Pee-Chee NHL-254
74Topps-178
74Topps-254
75Canadiens Postcards-2
750-Pee-Chee NHL-304
75Topps-304
76Canadiens Postcards-1
760-Pee-Chee NHL-177

76Topps-177
77Canadiens Postcards-1
770-Pee-Chee NHL-20
77Topps-20
780-Pee-Chee-116
78Topps-116
79Capitals Team Issue-1
790-Pee-Chee-289
800-Pee-Chee-373
93Quebec Pee-Wee Tournament-937

Bouchard, Pierre-Marc

00Chicoutimi Sagueneens-23
Signed-23
01SPx Rookie Redemption-R15
01Chicoutimi Sagueneens-23
02Atomic-113
Blue-113
Gold-113
Red-113
Hobby Parallel-113
02BAP All-Star Edition-126
Gold-126
Silver-126
02BAP First Edition-440H
02BAP Memorabilia-271
Emerald-271
Ruby-271
Sapphire-271
Draft Redemptions-8
NHL All-Star Game-271
NHL All-Star Game Blue-271
NHL All-Star Game Green-271
NHL All-Star Game Red-271
02BAP Memorabilia Toronto Fall Expo-271
02BAP Signature Series-196
Autographs-196
Autographs Gold-196
02BAP Ultimate Memorabilia-1
Autographs-9
Autographs Gold-9
02Bowman YoungStars-161
Gold-161
Silver-161
02Crown Royale-119
Blue-119
Purple-119
Red-119
Retail-119
02eTopps-46
02ITG Used-81
020-Pee-Chee-332
020-Pee-Chee Premier Blue Parallel-332
020-Pee-Chee Premier Red Parallel-332
020-Pee-Chee Factory Set-332
02Pacific-409
02Pacific Calder-124
Silver-124
Reflections-15
02Pacific Complete-516
Red-516
02Pacific Exclusive-180
Blue-180
Gold-180
02Pacific Heads-Up-137
02Pacific Quest for the Cup-124
Gold-124
02Parkhurst-201
Bronze-201
Gold-201
Silver-201
02Parkhurst Retro-201
Minis-201
02Private Stock Reserve-165
Blue-165
Red-165
Retail-165
02SP Authentic-198
Signed Patches-PPB
02SP Game Used-81
02SPx-152
02Stadium Club-132
Silver Decoy Cards-132
Proofs-132
02Titanium-119
Blue-119
Red-119
Retail-119
Right on Target-13
02Topps-332
OPC Blue Parallel-332
OPC Red Parallel-332
Factory Set-332
02Topps Chrome-180
Black Border Refractors-180
Refractors-180
02Topps Heritage-149
02Topps Total-422
02UD Artistic Impressions-124
Gold-124
Common Ground-CG8
Common Ground Gold-CG8
Retrospectives-R95
Retrospectives Gold-R95
Retrospectives Signed-R95
Retrospectives Silver-R95
02UD Foundations-156
02UD Honor Roll-155
02UD Mask Collection-160
02UD Piece of History-134
02UD Premier Collection-72B
Gold-72B
Signatures Bronze-SPM
Signatures Gold-SPM
Signatures Silver-SPM
02UD Top Shelf-130
02Upper Deck-239
Exclusives-239
02Upper Deck Classic Portraits-118
02Upper Deck Rookie Update-164
Autographs-PM
02Vanguard-118
LTD-118
Prime Prospects-14
02UD SuperStars *-283
Gold-283
03BAP Ultimate Mem Franch Present Future-15
03Beehive-100
Gold-100
Silver-100
03Black Diamond-70
Black-70
Green-70
Red-70
03Bowman-67
Gold-67
Signs of the Future-SOF-PMB
03Bowman Chrome-67
Refractors-67
Gold Refractors-67
Xfractors-67
03Crown Royale-50
Blue-50
Retail 50
03ITG Action-292
030-Pee-Chee-183
03OPC Blue-183
03OPC Gold-183
03OPC Red-183
03Pacific-161
Blue-161
Red-161
03Pacific Calder Collection NHL All-Star Block Party Gold-8
03Pacific Complete-382
Red-382
03Pacific Heads-Up-49
Hobby LTD-49
Retail LTD-49
03Pacific Prism Rookie Revolution-10
03Pacific Supreme-47
Blue-47
Red-47
Retail-47
03Private Stock Reserve-48
Blue-48
Red-48
Retail-48
Rising Stock-9
03SP Authentic-44
Limited-44
03SPx-49
03SPx-171
Radiance-49
Radiance-171
Spectrum-49
Spectrum-171
Big Futures-BF-PMB
Big Futures Limited-BF-PMB
03Topps-183
Blue-183
Gold-183
Red-183
03Topps C55-126
Minis-126
Minis American Back-126
Minis American Back Red-126
Minis Bazooka Back-126
Minis Brooklyn Back-126
Minis Hat Trick Back-126
Minis O Canada Back-126
Minis O Canada Back Red-126
Minis Stanley Cup Back-126
03UD Honor Roll-42
03Upper Deck-96
Canadian Exclusives-96
HG-96
Shooting Stars-ST-PM
03Upper Deck All-Star Promos-AS15
03Upper Deck Classic Portraits-47
03Upper Deck MVP-214
Gold Script-214
Silver Script-214
Canadian Exclusives-214
03Upper Deck Rookie Update YoungStars-YS12
03Upper Deck Trilogy-47
Limited-47
Scripts-S1PB
Scripts Limited-S1PB
03Upper Deck Victory-91
Bronze-91
Gold-91
Silver-91
03Wild Law Enforcement Cards-2
04ITG All-Star FANtasy Hall Minnesota-8
04Upper Deck-88
Canadian Exclusives-88
HG Glossy Gold-88
HG Glossy Silver-88
04AHL Top Prospects-21
04Houston Aeros-2
05Beehive Matted Materials-MMPB
05Panini Stickers-299
05Parkhurst-234
Facsimile Auto Parallel-234
Signatures-PB
True Colors-TCMIN
True Colors-TCMIN
True Colors-TCMIDA
True Colors-TCMIDA
05SP Authentic Sign of the Times-PM
05SP Game Used Authentic Fabrics Quad-GFRB
05SP Game Used Authentic Patches Quad -GFRB
05SP Game Used Game Gear-GG-PM
05SP Game Used Game Gear Autographs-AG-PM
05SP Game Used SIGnificance-PM
05SP Game Used SIGnificance Gold-S-PM
05SP Game Used Significant Numbers-SN-PM
05SP Game Used Statscriptions-ST-PM
05UD Powerplay Specialists-TSPB
05UD Powerplay Specialists Patches-SPPB
05UD Toronto Fall Expo Priority Signings-PS-PB
05Ultra-101
Gold-101
Ice-101
05Upper Deck-96
HG Glossy-96
Notable Numbers-N-PMB
05Upper Deck MVP-193
Gold-193
Platinum-193
05Upper Deck Toronto Fall Expo-96
05Upper Deck Victory-224
Black-224
Gold-224
05Wild Crime Prevention-8
05ITG Heroes and Prospects Aspiring-ASP14
05ITG Heroes/Prospects Complete Jerseys-CJ-13
05ITG Heroes/Prospects Comp Jerseys Gold-CJ-13
05ITG Heroes/Prospects Future Teammates-FT1
05ITG Heroes and Prospects Jerseys-GUJ-31
05ITG Heroes and Prospects Jerseys Gold-GUJ-31
05ITG Heroes and Prospects Emblems-GUE-31
05ITG Heroes and Prospects Emblems Gold-GUE-31
05ITG Heroes and Prospects Numbers-GUN-31
05ITG Heroes and Prospects Numbers Gold-GUN-31
05ITG Heroes and Prospects Making the Big-MTB-3
05ITG Heroes and Prospects Nameplates-N-18
05ITG Heroes and Prospects Nameplate Gold-N-18
05ITG Heroes and Prospects National Pride-NPR-7
06Be A Player-159
Autographs-159
Profiles-PP9
Profiles Autographs-PP9
Signatures-PB
Signatures 10-174
Signatures Duals-DBP
06Beehive Matted Materials-MMBO
06Beehive Remarkable Matted Materials-MMBO
06Beehive Signature Scrapbook-SSPB
06Black Diamond-43
Black-43
Gold-43
Ruby-43
06Flair Showcase Inks-IPB
06Flair Showcase Stitches-SSPB
06Fleer-99
Tiffany-99
06Hot Prospects Hotagraphs-HPB
060-Pee-Chee-247
Rainbow-247
Autographs-A-PB
06Panini Stickers-298
06SP Authentic Sign of the Times-STPB
06SP Authentic Sign of the Times Triples-ST3PGB
06SP Game Used Authentic Fabrics-AFBO
06SP Game Used Authentic Fabrics Parallel-AFBO
06SP Game Used Authentic Fabrics Patches-AFBO
06SP Game Used Authentic Fabrics Dual-AF2PB
06SP Game Used Authentic Fabrics Dual Patches-AF2PB
06SP Game Used Authentic Fabrics Triple-AF3MIN
06SP Game Used Authentic Fabrics Triple Patches-AF3MIN
06SP Game Used Inked Sweaters-ISPB
06SP Game Used Inked Sweaters Patches-ISPB
06SP Game Used Inked Sweaters Dual-IS2GB
06SP Game Used Inked Sweaters Dual Patches-IS2GB
06SP Game Used Letter Marks-LMPI
06SP Game Used SIGnificance-SPB
06SPx Winning Materials-WMBO
06SPx Winning Materials Spectrum-WMBO
06SPx Winning Materials Autographs-WMBO
06The Cup Autographed NHL Shields Duals-DASGB
06UD Artifacts Auto-Facts-AFPB
06UD Artifacts Auto-Facts Gold-AFPB
06UD Artifacts Tundra Tandems-TTBR
06UD Artifacts Tundra Tandems Black-TTBR
06UD Artifacts Tundra Tandems Blue-TTBR
06UD Artifacts Tundra Tandems Gold-TTBR
06UD Artifacts Tundra Tandems Platinum-TTBR
06UD Artifacts Tundra Tandems Red-TTBR
06UD Artifacts Tundra Tandems Dual Patches Red-TTBR
06UD Toronto Fall Expo Priority Signings -PSPB
06Ultimate Collection Signatures-US-BO
06Ultra-99
Gold Medallion-99
Ice Medallion-99
Uniformity-UPB
Uniformity Patches-UPPA
Uniformity Autographed Jerseys-UAPB
06Upper Deck Arena Giveaways-MIN2
06Upper Deck-96
Exclusives Parallel-96
High Gloss Parallel-96
Masterpieces-96
Signature Sensations-SSPB
06Upper Deck MVP-143
Gold Script-143
Super Script-143
Autographs-OABP
Jerseys-OJBK
06Upper Deck Ovation-75
06Upper Deck Sweet Shot Signature Shots/Saves-SSBO
06Upper Deck Sweet Shot Signature Shots/Saves Sticks-SSSPB
06Upper Deck Sweet Shot Signature Sticks-STPI
06Upper Deck Sweet Shot Sweet Stitches-SSBO
06Upper Deck Sweet Shot Sweet Stitches Duals-SSBO
06Upper Deck Sweet Shot Sweet Stitches Triples-SSBO
06Upper Deck Trilogy Honorary Scripted Patches-HSPPI
06Upper Deck Trilogy Honorary Scripted Swatches-HSSPI
06Upper Deck Victory-99
06Upper Deck Victory Black-99
06Upper Deck Victory Gold-99
07Upper Deck Victory-140
Black-140
Gold-140

Bouchard, Robin

917th Inn. Sketch QMJHL-48
94Roanoke Express-13
95Flint Generals-11
96Flint Generals-3
98Muskegon Fury-6
99Muskegon Fury-7
00Muskegon Fury-1
02Muskegon Fury-2
03Muskegon Fury-3
05Muskegon Fury-2

Bouchard, Simon

92Quebec Pee-Wee Tournament-868
05Drummondville Voltigeurs-29
06Drummondville Voltigeurs-5

Bouchard, Yannick

92Quebec Pee-Wee Tournament-579
93Quebec Pee-Wee Tournament-226
96Rimouski Oceanic-6
96Rimouski Oceanic Quebec Police-6

Boucher, Billy

23V145-1-16
24Anonymous NHL-1
24Anonymous NHL-2
24Anonymous NHL-19
24C144 Champ's Cigarettes-6
24V130 Maple Crispette-11
24V145-2-46

Boucher, Bob

24C144 Champ's Cigarettes-7

Boucher, Brian

94Select-155
Gold-155
94Tri-City Americans-3
95Donruss Elite World Juniors-23
95Tri-City Americans-6
95Tri-City Americans-30
95Signature Rookies Auto-Phonex-10
95Signature Rook Auto-Phonex Phone Cards-10
95Signature Rookies Tetrad *-69
95Signature Rookies Tetrad Autobilia *-94
95Signature Rookies Tetrad Signatures *-68
96Upper Deck Ice-148
97Bowman CHL-81
OPC-81
99BAP Memorabilia-336
Gold-336
Silver-336
99BAP Millennium Calder Candidates Ruby-C27
99BAP Millennium Calder Candidate Emerald-C27
99BAP Millennium Calder Cand Sapphire-C27
990-Pee-Chee Chrome-289
990-Pee-Chee Chrome Refractors-289
99Pacific Dynagon Ice-144
Blue-144
Copper-144
Gold-144
Premiere Date-144
99Pacific Omega-167
Copper-167
Gold-167
Ice Blue-167
Premiere Date-167
99Pacific Prism-100
Holographic Blue-100
Holographic Gold-100
Holographic Mirror-100
Holographic Purple-100
Premiere Date-100
99Stadium Club-196
First Day Issue-196
One of a Kind-196
Printing Plates Black-196
Printing Plates Cyan-196
Printing Plates Magenta-196
Printing Plates Yellow-196
99Topps/OPC Chrome-289
Refractors-289
99Topps Premier Plus-140
Parallel-140
99Upper Deck MVP SC Edition-137
Gold Script-137
Silver Script-137
Super Script-137
00McFarlane Hockey-70
00Aurora-104
Pinstripes-104
Pinstripes Premiere Date-104
Premiere Date-104
Championship Fever-17
Championship Fever Copper-17
Championship Fever Platinum Blue-17
Championship Fever Silver-17
Scouting Reports-16
Styrotechs-8B
00BAP Memorabilia-143
Emerald-143
Ruby-143
Sapphire-143
Promos-143
00BAP Mem Chicago Sportsfest Copper-143
00BAP Memorabilia Chicago Sportsfest Blue-143
00BAP Memorabilia Chicago Sportsfest Gold-143
00BAP Memorabilia Chicago Sportsfest Ruby-143
00BAP Memorabilia Chicago Sun-Times Ruby-143
00BAP Memorabilia Chicago Sun-Times Gold-143
00BAP Mem Chicago Sun-Times Sapphire-143
00BAP Mem Toronto Fall Expo Copper-143
00BAP Memorabilia Toronto Fall Expo Gold-143
00BAP Memorabilia Toronto Fall Expo Ruby-143
00BAP Parkhurst 2000-P89
00BAP Signature Series-217
Emerald-217
Ruby-217
Sapphire-217
Autographs-168
Autographs Gold-168
00BAP Ultimate Mem Goalie Memorabilia-GM7
00BAP Ultimate Memorabilia Goalie Sticks-G22
00BAP Ultimate Mem Plante Jersey Cards-PJ15
00BAP Ultimate Mem Plante Skate Cards-PS15
00Black Diamond-42
Gold-42
00Crown Royale-78
Ice Blue-78
Limited Series-78
Premiere Date-78
Red-78
00McDonald's Pacific-24
Blue-24
Glove Side Net Fusions-5
000-Pee-Chee-63
000-Pee-Chee Parallel-63
00Pacific-293
Copper-293
Gold-293
Ice Blue-293
Premiere Date-293
2001: Ice Odyssey-17
Gold Crown Die Cuts-22
In the Cage Net-Fusions-9
00Pacific 2001: Ice Odyssey Anaheim Ntnl-17
00Paramount-177
Copper-177
Gold-177
Holo-Gold-177
Holo-Silver-177
Ice Blue-177
Premiere Date-177
Epic Scope-15
Freeze Frame-25
Glove Side Net Fusions-14
Glove Side Net Fusions Platinum-14
00Private Stock-71
Gold-71
Premiere Date-71
Retail-71
Silver-71
PS-2001 Action-41
PS-2001 New Wave-17
00Revolution-106
Blue-106
Premiere Date-106
Red-106
HD NHL-24
Stat Masters-17
00SP Game Used-44
Patch Cards-P-BB
Tools of the Game-BB
Tools of the Game Exclusives-BB
Tools of the Game Combos-C-LB
00SPx-49
Spectrum-49
Highlight Heroes-HH10
Winning Materials-WBC
00Stadium Club-190
Beam Team-BT22
Glove Save-GS5
00Titanium-68
Blue-68
Gold-68
Premiere Date-68
Red-68
Retail-68
Three-Star Selections-6
00Topps/OPC-63
Parallel-63
00Topps Chrome-51
OPC Refractors-51
Refractors-51
00Topps Gold Label Class 1-46
Gold-46
00Topps Gold Label Class 2-46
00Topps Gold Label Class 2 Gold-46
00Topps Gold Label Class 3-46
00Topps Gold Label Class 3 Gold-46
00Topps Gold Label Autographs-GLA-BB
00Topps Gold Label Behind the Mask-BTM5
00Topps Gold Label Behind the Mask 1 to 1-BTM5
00Topps Gold Label New Generation-NG13
00Topps Gold Label New Generation 1 to 1-NG13
00Topps Heritage-101
00Topps Heritage-237
New Tradition-NT8
00Topps Premier Plus-2
Blue Ice-2
Masters of the Break-MB18
00Topps Stars-80
Blue-80
Autographs-ABB
Progression-P6
00UD Heroes-87
Timeless Moments-TM8
00Upper Deck-128
Exclusives Tier 1-128
Exclusives Tier 2-128
All-Star Class-A7
Prospects In Depth-P9
Rise to Prominence-RP6
00Upper Deck Ice-29
Immortals-29
Legends-29
Stars-29
00Upper Deck Legends-99
Legendary Collection Bronze-99
Legendary Collection Gold-99
Legendary Collection Silver-99
00Upper Deck MVP-130
First Stars-130
Masked Men-MM6
Second Stars-130
Third Stars-130
00Upper Deck Victory-172
00Upper Deck Victory-254
00Upper Deck Vintage-266
00Upper Deck Vintage-271
00Upper Deck Vintage-272
Great Gloves-GG13
Star Tandems-S5B
00Vanguard-71
Holographic Gold-71
Holographic Purple-71
Pacific Proofs-71
01BAP Memorabilia Goalies Jerseys-GJ15
01BAP Signature Series-192
Autographs-192
Autographs Gold-192
Jerseys-GJ-50
Jersey Autographs-GUBB
Jersey and Stick Cards-GSJ-50
Emblems-GUE-49
Numbers-ITN-49
Teammates-TM-23
01Between the Pipes-61
01Between the Pipes-93
Double Memorabilia-DM20
Future Wave-FW8
Goalie Gear-GG20
He Shoots-He Saves Points-1
He Shoots-He Saves Prizes-15
Jerseys-GJ24
Emblems-GUE9
Jersey and Stick Cards-GSJ23
Tandems-GT2
01Crown Royale-104
Blue-104
Premiere Date-104
Red-104
Retail-104
01Flyers Postcards-1
01Pacific-283
Extreme LTD-283
Hobby LTD-283
Premiere Date-283
Retail LTD-283
01Pacific Arena Exclusives-283
01SP Game Used Authentic Fabric-AFBB
01SP Game Used Authentic Fabric-DFLB
01SP Game Used Authentic Fabric Gold-AFBB
01SP Game Used Tools of the Game-TBB
01SP Game Used Tools of the Game-CTCB
01SP Game Used Tools of the Game-CTDB
01SP Game Used Tools of the Game-CTKB
01SP Game Used Tools of the Game-TTRBK
01SPx-188
01Topps Game-Worn Jersey-JBB
01Topps Chrome-135
Refractors-135
Black Border Refractors-135
01Topps Reserve Emblems-BB
01Topps Reserve Jerseys-BB
01Topps Reserve Name Plates-BB
01Topps Reserve Numbers-BB
01Topps Reserve Patches-BB
01UD Challenge for the Cup-60
Jerseys-UCLB
01UD Honor Roll Jerseys-J-BB
01UD Honor Roll Jerseys Gold-J-BB
01UD Mask Collection Double Patches-DPBB
01UD Mask Collection Dual Jerseys-MBBC
01UD Mask Collection Goalie Jerseys-MMBB
01UD Mask Collection Goalie Jerseys-SYBB
01UD Mask Collection Jerseys-J-BB
01UD Mask Collection Jersey and Patch-JPBB
01UD Mask Collection Sticks-SSBB
01UD Premier Collection Dual Jerseys-DCB
01UD Premier Collection Dual Jersey Black-DCB
01UD Top Shelf Goalie Gear-LPBB
01Upper Deck-357
Exclusives-357
Game Jerseys-GJBB
Goaltender Threads-TTBB
01Upper Deck Ice-113
01Upper Deck MVP Morning Skate Jerseys-J-BB
01Upper Deck MVP Morn Skate Jersey Autos-SJ-BB
01Upper Deck Victory-264
Gold-264
02BAP First Edition-79
02BAP First Edition-415R
Jerseys-79
02BAP Memorabilia-261
Emerald-261
Ruby-261
Sapphire-261
NHL All-Star Game-261
NHL All-Star Game Blue-261
NHL All-Star Game Green-261
NHL All-Star Game Red-261
02BAP Memorabilia Toronto Fall Expo-261
02BAP Signature Series-83
Autographs-83
Autograph Buybacks 2000-168
Autograph Buybacks 2001-192
Autographs Gold-83
02Between the Pipes-56
Gold-56
Silver-56
02Coyotes Team Issue-16
02ITG Used Goalie Pad and Jersey-GP17
02ITG Used Goalie Pad and Jersey Gold-GP17
020-Pee-Chee-55
020-Pee-Chee Premier Blue Parallel-55
020-Pee-Chee Premier Red Parallel-55
020-Pee-Chee Factory Set-55
02Pacific-275
Blue-275
Red-275
02Pacific Complete-460
Red-460
02Pacific Exclusive-131
02Parkhurst-154
Bronze-154
Gold-154
Silver-154
02Parkhurst Retro-90
Minis-90
02SP Authentic-128
02SP Game Used Authentic Fabrics-AFBB
02SP Game Used Authentic Fabrics Gold-AFBB
02SP Game Used Authentic Fabrics Rainbow-AFBB
02SP Game Used First Rounder Patches-BB
02SP Game Used Tools of the Game-BB
02Titanium-78
Blue-78
Red-78
Retail-78
02Topps-55
OPC Blue Parallel-55
OPC Red Parallel-55
Factory Set-55
02Topps Heritage-172
Crease Piece-BB
Crease Piece Patches-BB
02Topps Total-274
02UD Mask Collection-64
02UD Mask Collection-65
02UD Mask Collection-66
02UD Mask Collection Beckett Promos-64
02UD Mask Collection Beckett Promos-65
02UD Mask Collection Beckett Promos-66
02UD Mask Collection Great Gloves-GGBB
02UD Mask Collection Nation's Best-NDBJ
02UD Top Shelf Dual Player Jerseys-STGB
02UD Top Shelf Signatures-BB
02UD Top Shelf Stopper Jerseys-SSBB
02Upper Deck-379
Exclusives-379
02Upper Deck Beckett UD Promos-379
02Upper Deck Bright Futures-BB
02Upper Deck Saviors Jerseys-SVBB
02Upper Deck MVP Skate Around Jerseys-SDCB
02Upper Deck MVP Souvenirs-S-BB
02Upper Deck Rookie Update-77
02Upper Deck Victory-161
Bronze-161
Gold-161
Silver-161
02Upper Deck Vintage Jerseys-EEBB
02Upper Deck Vintage Jerseys Gold-EE-BB
02Vanguard-77
LTD-77
03BAP Memorabilia-105
Emerald-105
Gold-105
Ruby-105
Sapphire-105
03BAP Ultimate Mem Franch Present Future-23
03Beehive-148
Gold-148
Silver-148
Sticks Beige Border-BE30
03Bowman-92
Gold-92
03Bowman Chrome-92
Refractors-92
Gold Refractors-92
Xfractors-92
03Coyotes Postcards-2
03ITG Action-498
030-Pee-Chee-33
03OPC Blue-33
03OPC Gold-33
03OPC Red-33
03Pacific-259
Blue-259
Red-259
03Pacific Calder-76
Silver-76
03Pacific Complete-456
Red-456
03SP Game Used Game Gear-GGBB
03Topps-33
Blue-33
Gold-33
Red-33
03Topps Pristine-59
Gold Refractor Die Cuts-59
Refractors-59
Press Plates Black-59
Press Plates Cyan-59
Press Plates Magenta-59
Press Plates Yellow-59
03UD Premier Collection-44
03Upper Deck-150
Canadian Exclusives-150
HG-150
Classic Portraits Classic Stitches-CS-BB
03Upper Deck MVP-331
Gold Script-331
Silver Script-331
Canadian Exclusives-331
Souvenirs-S23
03Upper Deck Rookie Update-67
04Pacific-199
Blue-199
Red-199
04Upper Deck-137
Canadian Exclusives-137
HG Glossy Gold-137
HG Glossy Silver-137
04Swedish HV71 Postcards-1
05Be A Player Signatures-BN
05Be A Player Signatures Gold-BN
05Upper Deck MVP Materials-M-BB
05Upper Deck Victory-151
Black-151
Gold-151
Silver-151
06Blackhawks Postcards-18
06Upper Deck-295
Exclusives Parallel-295
High Gloss Parallel-295
Masterpieces-295

Boucher, Brock

95Slapshot-22
95Barrie Colts-3
96Barrie Colts-2
97Barrie Colts-2
99Hull Olympiques-15
Signed-15

Boucher, Charlie

917th Inn. Sketch QMJHL-174

Boucher, Chris

00St. Michaels Majors-7

Boucher, Claude

93Quebec Pee-Wee Tournament-285

Boucher, Denis

52Juniors Blue Tint-135

Boucher, Eric

92Quebec Pee-Wee Tournament-622
93Quebec Pee-Wee Tournament-303

Boucher, Francois

28La Presse Photos-2
30Rogers Peet Company *-22
30Rogers Peet *-22
34Beehive Group I Photos-261
34Diamond Matchbooks Silver-4
35CCM Green Border Photos-7
35Diamond Matchbooks Tan 2-3
35Diamond Matchbooks Tan 2-4
35Diamond Matchbooks Tan 3-3
37V356 Worldwide Gum-16
60Topps-29
Stamps-5
83Hall of Fame Postcards-G2
85Hall of Fame-93
93Quebec Pee-Wee Tournament-78
02BAP Ultimate Mem Paper Cuts Autos-35
03BAP Ultimate Mem Linemates Autos-5
03BAP Ultimate Memorabilia Paper Cuts-48
03Parkhurst Original Six New York-41
Inserts-N3
04ITG Franchises Update-483
04ITG Ultimate Memorabilia-90
Gold-90
Broadway Blueshirts-2
Paper Cuts-21
05ITG Ultimate Mem Broadway Bluesh Autos-7
05ITG Ultimate Mem Quad Paper Cuts Autos-5
06ITG Ultimate Memorabilia Broadway Blue Shirts Autos-3

Boucher, Frank

06ITG Ultimate Memorabilia Broadway Blue Shirts Autos-3

Boucher, Gaetan

91Pro Set Platinum-298
93Swiss HNL-197

Boucher, George

23V145-1-6
24V145-2-2
28La Presse Photos-3
83Hall of Fame Postcards-L1
85Hall of Fame-229

Boucher, Guy

99Rouyn-Noranda Huskies-23

Boucher, Jean-Francois

04P.E.I. Rocket-27

Boucher, Jesse

03Kitchener Rangers-2
03Kitchener Rangers Memorial Cup-2

Boucher, Maxime

93Quebec Pee-Wee Tournament-456

Boucher, Nick

03Wheeling Nailers-81

Boucher, Philippe

907th Inn. Sketch QMJHL-50
91Upper Deck-68
French-68
917th Inn. Sketch QMJHL-43
917th Inn. Sketch CHL Award Winners-21
917th Inn. Sketch CHL Award Winners-25
917th Inn. Sketch Memorial Cup-103
91Arena Draft Picks-10
91Arena Draft Picks French-10
91Arena Draft Picks Autographs-10
91Arena Draft Picks Autographs French-10
91Classic-11
91Star Pics-28
91Star Pics-36
91Ultimate Draft-11
91Ultimate Draft-67
91Ultimate Draft-75
91Ultimate Draft-82
91Ultimate Draft French-11
91Classic Four-Sport *-11
Autographs-11A
92OPC Premier-72
92Parkhurst-16
Emerald Ice-16
92Upper Deck-484
93Durivage Score-4
93Parkhurst-24
Emerald Ice-24
Calder Candidates-C11
Calder Candidates Gold-C11
93Pinnacle-213
Canadian-213
93PowerPlay-296
93Score-455
Canadian-455
93Ultra-70
All-Rookies-1
93Upper Deck-82
SP-14
93Rochester Americans Kodak-7
93Classic Pro Prospects-68
94Leaf-539
94OPC Premier-371
Special Effects-371
94Parkhurst SE-SE16
Gold-SE16
94Stadium Club-64
Members Only Master Set-64
First Day Issue-64
Super Team Winner Cards-64
94Topps/OPC Premier-371
Special Effects-371
94Upper Deck-71
Electric Ice-71
95Topps-136
OPC Inserts-136
96Be A Player-74
Autographs-74
Autographs Silver-74
97Pacific Invincible NHL Regime-92
98Upper Deck MVP-99
Gold Script-99
Silver Script-99
Super Script-99
00Upper Deck NHLPA-PA40
00Manitoba Moose-4
01Topps Reserve-56
02Pacific Complete-364
Red-364
02Stars Postcards-23
03ITG Action-119
030-Pee-Chee-132
03OPC Blue-132
03OPC Gold-132
03OPC Red-132
03Pacific Complete-59
Red-59
03Stars Postcards-3
03Topps-132
Blue-132
Gold-132
Red-132
05Parkhurst-159
Facsimile Auto Parallel-159
05Upper Deck-309
05Upper Deck MVP-135
Gold-135
Platinum-135
060-Pee-Chee-169
Rainbow-169
06Panini Stickers-252
06Stars Team Postcards-4
06Upper Deck-67
Exclusives Parallel-67
High Gloss Parallel-67
Masterpieces-67
07Upper Deck Victory-183
Black-183
Gold-183

Boucher, Rodrigue

01Cape Breton Screaming Eagles-14

Boucher, Scott

92British Columbia JHL-167

Boucher, Tyler

91British Columbia JHL-90
92British Columbia JHL-119
97New Mexico Scorpions-24
97New Mexico Scorpions II-7
97New Mexico Scorpions II-8
97New Mexico Scorpions II-9
99Corpus Christi IceRays-1

Bouck, Tyler

98Prince George Cougars-4
99Prince George Cougars-11
99Bowman CHL-105
Gold-105
OPC International-105
00BAP Memorabilia-430
Emerald-430
Ruby-430
Sapphire-430
00Black Diamond-66
00Black Diamond-96
Gold-66
00Private Stock-115
Gold-115
Premiere Date-115
Retail-115
Silver-115
00SP Authentic-103
00SP Game Used-68
00SPx-160
00Stars Postcards-2
00Titanium Draft Day Edition-159
00Titanium Draft Day Promos-159
00Topps Premier Plus-117
Blue Ice-117
00Topps Stars-125
Blue-125
00UD Heroes-163
00UD Pros and Prospects-103
00UD Reserve-94
00Upper Deck-201
Exclusives Tier 1-201
Exclusives Tier 2-201
00Upper Deck Ice-46
Immortals-46
Legends-46
Stars-46
00Upper Deck MVP-215
First Stars-215
Second Stars-215
Third Stars-215
00Upper Deck Vintage-378
00Vanguard-116
Pacific Proofs-116
01BAP Memorabilia-227
Emerald-227
Ruby-227
Sapphire-227
01UD Playmakers Practice Jerseys-PJTB
01UD Playmakers Practice Jerseys Gold-PJTB
01Upper Deck-365
Exclusives-365
02Manitoba Moose-25
03Manitoba Moose-8
04Finnish Cardset-309
06Manitoba Moose-20

Boudaev, Aleksei

95Red Deer Rebels-3
96Mississippi Sea Wolves-2

Boudeau, Yannis

93Quebec Pee-Wee Tournament-1641

Boudreau, Bruce

78Maple Leafs Postcards-2
780-Pee-Chee-280
790-Pee-Chee-354
85Nova Scotia Oilers-5
88ProCards AHL-302
89ProCards IHL-108
90ProCards AHL/IHL-541
91ProCards-260
93Fort Wayne Komets-23
96Mississippi Sea Wolves-21
97Mississippi Sea Wolves-8
99Lowell Lock Monsters-25
99Mississippi Sea Wolves Kelly Cup-1
00Lowell Lock Monsters-28
01Manchester Monarchs-15A
02Manchester Monarchs-3
03Manchester Monarchs-22
05Hershey Bears-18

Boudreau, Carl

907th Inn. Sketch QMJHL-97
907th Inn. Sketch Memorial Cup-56
917th Inn. Sketch QMJHL-116
92Oklahoma City Blazers-2
93Oklahoma City Blazers-2
95Central Hockey League-38
98San Angelo Outlaws-3

Boudreau, Darryl

82Kitchener Rangers-10

Boudreau, David

03Vernon Vipers-3

Boudreau, Rene

37V356 Worldwide Gum-117

Boudreault, Dave

907th Inn. Sketch QMJHL-119
917th Inn. Sketch QMJHL-117
93Quebec Pee-Wee Tournament-374

Boudreault, Patrice

93Quebec Pee-Wee Tournament-385

Boudreault, Serge

67Columbus Checkers-4

Boudrias, Andre

680-Pee-Chee-53
68Shirriff Coins-64

68Topps-53
69O-Pee-Chee-16
69Topps-16
70Canucks Royal Bank-1
70Dad's Cookies-8
70Esso Power Players-43
70O-Pee-Chee-121
70Sargent Promotions Stamps-219
70Topps-121
71Bazooka-16
71Canucks Royal Bank-16
71O-Pee-Chee-12
71Sargent Promotions Stamps-215
71Topps-12
71Toronto Sun-276
72Canucks Nalley's-1
72Canucks Royal Bank-4
72O-Pee-Chee-93
72Sargent Promotions Stamps-214
72Topps-158
72Finnish Semic World Championship-210
72Swedish Semic World Championship-210
73Canucks Royal Bank-2
73O-Pee-Chee-19
73Topps-19
74Canucks Royal Bank-3
74Lipton Soup-14
74NHL Action Stamps-277
74O-Pee-Chee NHL-117
74O-Pee-Chee NHL-191
74Topps-117
74Topps-191
75Canucks Royal Bank-4
75O-Pee-Chee NHL-60
75O-Pee-Chee NHL-329
75Topps-60
75Topps-329
76Nordiques Marie Antoinette-4
76Nordiques Postcards-7
76O-Pee-Chee WHA-87
04ITG Franchises Canadian-125
Autographs-ABO

Bouffard, Bernard
98Thetford Mines Coyotes-11

Bouffard, Marco
93Quebec Pee-Wee Tournament-942

Bouffard, Martin
93Quebec Pee-Wee Tournament-977

Bouge, Art
81Red Wings Oldtimers-20

Boughner, Bob
89Sault Ste. Marie Greyhounds-7
907th Inn. Sketch OHL-153
917th Inn. Sketch Memorial Cup-4
96Be A Player-178
Autographs-178
Autographs Silver-178
97Pacific Dynagon Best Kept Secrets-9
98Predators Team Issue-5
99O-Pee-Chee-173
99O-Pee-Chee Chrome-173
99O-Pee-Chee Chrome Refractors-173
99Pacific-219
Copper-219
Emerald Green-219
Gold-219
Ice Blue-219
Premiere Date-219
Red-219
99Topps/OPC-173
99Topps/OPC Chrome-173
Refractors-173
99Upper Deck Retro-42
Gold-42
Platinum-42
99Upper Deck Victory-160
00BAP Memorabilia Update Tough Materials-T21
00BAP Mem Update Tough Materials Gold-T21
00Upper Deck NHLPA-PA71
01O-Pee-Chee-223
01O-Pee-Chee Premier Parallel-223
01Pacific Heads-Up Quad Jerseys-28
01Titanium Double-Sided Jerseys-6
01Topps-223
OPC Parallel-223
01Vanguard Memorabilia-24
02NHL Power Play Stickers-5
02Pacific-50
Blue-50
Red-50
02Pacific Complete-433
Red-433
02Topps Total-94
03Hurricanes Postcards-4
03ITG Action-9
03NHL Sticker Collection-169
03O-Pee-Chee-232
03OPC Blue-232
03OPC Gold-232
03OPC Red-232
03Pacific Complete-493
Red-493
03Topps-232
Blue-232
Gold-232
Red-232
05Be A Player Signatures-BO
05Be A Player Signatures Gold-BO

Bougie, Georges
51Laval Dairy QSHL-77
52St. Lawrence Sales-32

Bougie, Nicolas
93Quebec Pee-Wee Tournament-441

Bouillon, Francis
96Wheeling Nailers-5
96Wheeling Nailers Photo Pack-11
99BAP Memorabilia-331
Gold-331
Silver-331
99Pacific Omega-124
Copper-124
Gold-124
Ice Blue-124
Premiere Date-124
99Pacific Prism-70
Holographic Blue-70
Holographic Gold-70
Holographic Mirror-70
Holographic Purple-70
Premiere Date-70
99Topps Premier Plus-83
Parallel-83
99Upper Deck Gold Reserve-343
99Upper Deck MVP SC Edition-96
Gold Script-96
Silver Script-96
Super Script-96
00Canadiens Postcards-1
00Upper Deck NHLPA-PA46
01BAP Signature Series-188
Autographs-188
Autographs Gold-188
01UD Mask Collection-51
Gold-51
01Quebec Citadelles-9
02BAP Sig Series Auto Buybacks 2001-188
02Hamilton Bulldogs-23
03Canadiens Postcards-3
05Canadiens Team Issue-3
05Parkhurst-262
Facsimile Auto Parallel-262
06Canadiens Postcards-5

Boulanger, Jeff
02South Carolina Stingrays-2

Boulay, Patrick
93Quebec Pee-Wee Tournament-455

Boulerice, Jesse
95Slapshot-74
96Detroit Whalers-1
97Black Diamond-98
Double Diamond-98
Triple Diamond-98
Quadruple Diamond-98
98UD Choice-305
Prime Choice Reserve-305
Reserve-305
01BAP Signature Series-242
Autographs-242
Autographs Gold-242
01Parkhurst-251
01Parkhurst Beckett Promos-251
03Hurricanes Postcards-5
05Upper Deck MVP-83
Gold-83
Platinum-83
06Albany River Rats-5

Boulet, Guillaume
93Quebec Pee-Wee Tournament-240

Boulet, Vincent
93Quebec Pee-Wee Tournament-250

Bouliane, Andre
907th Inn. Sketch QMJHL-264
917th Inn. Sketch QMJHL-149

Boulianne, Daniel
93Quebec Pee-Wee Tournament-531

Boulianne, Mathieu
93Quebec Pee-Wee Tournament-529

Boulianne, Vincent
93Quebec Pee-Wee Tournament-372

Boulin, Vladislav
91Upper Deck Czech World Juniors-2
94Flair-125
94Leaf-456
94OPC Premier-434
Special Effects-434
94Parkhurst SE-SE125
Gold-SE125
94Topps/OPC Premier-434
Special Effects-434
94Ultra-342
94Upper Deck-266
Electric Ice-266
99German DEL-149
02Russian Hockey League-59
02Russian SL-39
02Russian Transfert-19
03Russian Hockey League-40
04Russian Moscow Dynamo-4
05Russian Hockey League RHL-12

Boulton, Eric
93Oshawa Generals-21
95Slapshot-339
95Sarnia Sting-9
96Charlotte Checkers-2
97Charlotte Checkers-2
98Kentucky Thoroughblades-2
00BAP Memorabilia-438
Emerald-438
Ruby-438
Sapphire-438
00Black Diamond-92
00Crown Royale-112
21st Century Rookies-3
00Private Stock-104
Gold-104
Premiere Date-104
Retail-104
Silver-104
00SP Authentic-137
00SPx-177
00Topps Premier Plus-137
Blue Ice-137
00Upper Deck Ice-111
02Pacific Complete-440
Red-440
02Sabres Team Issue-3
03ITG Action-51

Boumedienne, Josef
97Swedish Collector's Choice-171
98Finnish Keraillysarja-207
99Finnish Cardset-120
00Albany River Rats-4
01BAP Memorabilia-346
Emerald-346
Ruby-346
Sapphire-346
01Parkhurst-298
01Parkhurst Beckett Promos-298
01SP Authentic-160
Limited-160
Limited Gold-160
01SP Game Used-85
01SPx-112
01UD Challenge for the Cup-117
01UD Playmakers-141
01UD Premier Collection-82
01Upper Deck-432
Exclusives-432
01Upper Deck Ice-82
01Upper Deck Vintage-284
04Finnish Cardset-261
04Swedish Pure Skills-128
Parallel-128

Bounds, Steve
03Camrose Kodiaks-2

Bouquet, Stephane
907th Inn. Sketch QMJHL-99

Bourassa, Bertrand
51Laval Dairy QSHL-81

Bourassa, Jarad
01Moose Jaw Warriors-2
04Oklahoma City Blazers-2
05Idaho Steelheads-3
06Bloomington PrairieThunder-4

Bourbonnais, Rick
77O-Pee-Chee NHL-312

Bourbonnais, Roger
69Swedish Hockey-349
70Swedish Masterserien-185

Bourcier, Reg
99Kitchener Rangers-23

Bourdeau, Francois
88Richelieu Riverains-7
907th Inn. Sketch QMJHL-104
917th Inn. Sketch QMJHL-68
93Johnstown Chiefs-3
94Central Hockey League-21
98Idaho Steelheads-3
99Asheville Smoke-2
01Sorel Royaux-2

Bourdon, Armand
51Laval Dairy Lac St. Jean-9

Bourdon, Luc
03Val d'Or Foreurs-6
04ITG Heroes and Prospects-224
04ITG Heroes/Prospects Toronto Expo '05-224
05ITG Heroes/Prosp Toronto Expo Parallel -139
05Moncton Wildcats-29
05ITG Heroes and Prospects-139
Autographs-A-LB
Complete Logos-CHL-17
Jerseys-GUJ-75
Jerseys Gold-GUJ-75
Emblems-GUE-75
Emblems Gold-GUE-75
Numbers-GUN-75
Numbers Gold-GUN-75
Nameplates-N-52
Nameplates Gold-N-52
06Be A Player-203
Autographs-203
Signatures 10-203
Signatures Duals-DMB
Signatures Trios-TCWB
06Be A Player Portraits-110
06Beehive-159
Blue-159
Matte-159
Red Facsimile Signatures-159
Wood-159
06Black Diamond-207
Black-207
Gold-207
Ruby-207
06Canucks Postcards-2
06Flair Showcase-329
06Hot Prospects-182
Red Hot-182
White Hot-182
Hot Materials -HMLB
Hot Materials Red Hot-HMLB
Hot Materials White Hot-HMLB
06O-Pee-Chee-558
06O-Pee-Chee-618
Rainbow-558
Rainbow-618
06SP Authentic-208
Limited-208
06SP Game Used-158
Gold-158
Rainbow-158
06SPx-192
Spectrum-192
06The Cup-165
Autographed Rookie Masterpiece Pressplates-165
Gold Rainbow Autographed Rookie Patches-165
Masterpiece Pressplates (Be A Player Portraits)-110
Masterpiece Pressplates (Bee Hive)-159
Masterpiece Pressplates (Marquee Rookies)-558
Masterpiece Pressplates (MVP)-304
Masterpiece Pressplates (SP Authentic Autographs)-208
Masterpiece Pressplates (SP Game Used)-158
Masterpiece Pressplates (SPx Autographs)-192
Masterpiece Pressplates (Sweet Beginnings)-157
Masterpiece Pressplates (Trilogy)-158
Masterpiece Pressplates (Victory)-305
NHL Shields Duals-DSHBE
NHL Shields Duals-DSHBW
Rookies Black-165
Rookies Platinum-165
Signature Patches-SPLB
06UD Artifacts-259
06UD Mini Jersey Collection-119
06Ultimate Collection Ultimate Debut Threads Jerseys-DJ-LB
06Ultimate Collection Ultimate Debut Threads Jerseys Autographs-DJ-LB
06Ultimate Collection Ultimate Debut Threads Patches-DJ-LB
06Ultimate Collection Ultimate Debut Threads Patches Autographs-DJ-LB
06Ultra-242
06Ultra-244
Gold Medallion-242
Ice Medallion-242
06Upper Deck-248
Exclusives Parallel-248
High Gloss Parallel-248
Masterpieces-248
Rookie Game Dated Moments-RGD29
Rookie Headliners-RH4
Rookie Materials-RMLB
Rookie Materials Patches-RMLB
06Upper Deck MVP-304
Gold Script-304
Super Script-304
06Upper Deck Ovation-199
06Upper Deck Sweet Shot-157
Rookie Jerseys Autographs-157
06Upper Deck Trilogy-158
06Upper Deck Victory-305
06ITG Heroes and Prospects-128
06ITG Heroes and Prospects-143
Autographs-ALB1
Autographs-ALB2
Quad Emblems-QE03
Quad Emblems Gold-QE03
Triple Memorabilia-TM06
Triple Memorabilia Gold-TM06
07Upper Deck Rookie Class -7
07ITG Going For Gold World Juniors-6
Autographs-6
Emblems-GUE6
Jerseys-GUJ6
Numbers-GUN6

Bourdreau, Matt
04Vernon Vipers-25

Boureault, Julien
93Quebec Pee-Wee Tournament-405

Bourgeault, Leo
33O-Pee-Chee V304A-28

Bourgeois, Cedric
92Quebec Pee-Wee Tournament-785
93Quebec Pee-Wee Tournament-1040

Bourgeois, Charlie
81Flames Postcards-1
85Flames Red Rooster-4
86O-Pee-Chee-239
86O-Pee-Chee Stickers-178
87Blues Kodak-3
87Panini Stickers-309
88ProCards AHL-62

Bourgeois, Mark
93Wichita Thunder-2

Bourgeois, Martin
93Quebec Pee-Wee Tournament-71

Bourgeois, Shawn
91British Columbia JHL-15
92British Columbia JHL-202
03Vernon Vipers-22

Bourgoin, Paul-Andre
01Shawinigan Cataractes-3

Bourgon, Sebastian
00Quebec Remparts-2
Signed-2
01Quebec Remparts-2
02Quebec Remparts-2
03Quebec Remparts Memorial Cup-3

Bourgouin, Paul-Andre
02Shawinigan Cataractes-3

Bourhis, Brad
02Macon Trax-11

Bourke, Peter
93Michigan Wolverines-3

Bournazakis, Mike
93Quebec Pee-Wee Tournament-1687
03Cape Fear Fire Antz-2

Bournazakis, Peter
01Indianapolis Ice-3
04Atlantic City Boardwalk Bullies-25

Bourne, Bob
75O-Pee-Chee NHL-163
75Topps-163
77O-Pee-Chee NHL-93
77Topps-93
78O-Pee-Chee-69
78O-Pee-Chee-126
78Topps-69
78Topps-126
79Islanders Transparencies-2
79O-Pee-Chee-56
79Topps-56
80O-Pee-Chee-276
81O-Pee-Chee-201
81O-Pee-Chee Stickers-163
81Topps-E87
82O-Pee-Chee-198
82O-Pee-Chee Stickers-53
82Post Cereal-12
82Topps Stickers-53
83Islanders Team Issue-2
83NHL Key Tags-83
83O-Pee-Chee-4
83O-Pee-Chee Stickers-80
83O-Pee-Chee Stickers-174
83Topps Stickers-80
83Topps Stickers-174
84Islanders News-3
84O-Pee-Chee-123
84O-Pee-Chee Stickers-89
84Topps-92
84Kelowna Wings-42
85Islanders News-3
85O-Pee-Chee-97
85O-Pee-Chee Stickers-67
85Topps-97
86Kings 20th Anniversary Team Issue-1
86O-Pee-Chee-14
86O-Pee-Chee Stickers-208
86Topps-14
87O-Pee-Chee-167
87Topps-167
88O-Pee-Chee-101
88O-Pee-Chee Minis-2
88O-Pee-Chee Stickers-213
88Panini Stickers-399
88Topps-101
93Las Vegas Thunder-3
98Las Vegas Thunder-25
99IHL All-Stars-21
99Utah Grizzlies-6
00Upper Deck Vintage Dynasty: A Piece of History-BG
00Upper Deck Vintage Dynasty: A Piece of History Gold-BG
00Utah Grizzlies-6
04ITG Franchises US East-378
Autographs-A-BBN
05SP Game Used Oldtimer's Challenge-OC-BB
05SP Game Used Oldtimer's Challenge Autos-OCA-BB
05SP Game Used Oldtimer's Challenge Patch-OCP-BB
05SP Game Used Oldtime Chall Patch Autoa-OAP-BB
06Parkhurst-19
Autographs-19
06UD Artifacts-103
Blue-103
Gold-103
Platinum-103
Radiance-103
Autographed Radiance Parallel-103
Red-103
Auto-Facts-AFBB
Auto-Facts Gold-AFBB
Treasured Patches Black-TSBB
Treasured Patches Blue-TSBB
Treasured Patches Gold-TSBB
Treasured Patches Platinum-TSBB
Treasured Patches Red-TSBB
Treasured Patches Autographed Black Tag Parallel-TSBB
Treasured Swatches-TSBB
Treasured Swatches Black-TSBB
Treasured Swatches Blue-TSBB
Treasured Swatches Gold-TSBB
Treasured Swatches Platinum-TSBB
Treasured Swatches Red-TSBB
Treasured Swatches Autographed Black-TSBB
Tundra Tandems-TTBN
Tundra Tandems Black-TTBN
Tundra Tandems Blue-TTBN
Tundra Tandems Gold-TTBN
Tundra Tandems Platinum-TTBN
Tundra Tandems Red-TTBN
Tundra Tandems Dual Patches Red-TTBN
06Upper Deck Sweet Shot Signature Sticks-STBB

Bourne, Joe
03Gwinnett Gladiators-13
03Gwinnett Gladiators RBI Sports-194
04Gwinnett Gladiators-4

Bourque, Chris
05ITG Heroes/Prosp Toronto Expo Parallel -77
05AHL Top Prospects-4
05Hershey Bears-3
05ITG Heroes and Prospects-77
Autographs-A-CBQ
Autographs-DA-BB
Complete Jerseys-CJ-8
Complete Jerseys Gold-CJ-8
Complete Logos-AHL-21
Jerseys-GUJ-64
Jerseys Gold-GUJ-64
Emblems-GUE-64
Emblems Gold-GUE-64
Numbers-GUN-64
Numbers Gold-GUN-64
Nameplates-N-42
Nameplates Gold-N-42
06ITG International Ice-152
Gold-152
Autographs-ACB
06ITG Ultimate Memorabilia Bloodlines-3
06ITG Ultimate Memorabilia Bloodlines Gold-3
06ITG Ultimate Memorabilia Bloodlines Autos-3
06ITG Ultimate Memorabilia Bloodlines Autos Gold-3

Bourque, Claude
34Beehive Group I Photos-139
39O-Pee-Chee V301-1-28

Bourque, Dave
95Slapshot-351
95Sarnia Sting-21
96Sarnia Sting-4
01Fort Worth Brahmas-3
02New Mexico Scorpions-17

Bourque, Phil
81Kingston Canadians-6
89O-Pee-Chee-19
89Panini Stickers-317
89Penguins Coke/Elby's-1
89Penguins Foodland-5
89Topps-19
90Bowman-205
Tiffany-205
90O-Pee-Chee-41
90Panini Stickers-129
90Penguins Foodland-1
90Pro Set-228A
90Pro Set-228B
90Score-234
Canadian-234
90Topps-41
Tiffany-41
90Upper Deck-31
French-31
91Bowman-94
91O-Pee-Chee-33
91Panini Stickers-272
91Parkhurst-136
French-136
91Penguins Coke/Elby's-29
91Penguins Foodland-15
91Pinnacle-227
French-227
91Pro Set-189
French-189
91Score American-69
91Score Canadian Bilingual-69
91Score Canadian English-69
91Stadium Club-168
91Topps-33
91Upper Deck-398
French-398
92Bowman-293
92OPC Premier-73
92Panini Stickers-225
92Panini Stickers French-225
92Pinnacle-353
French-353
92Score-223
Canadian-223
92Stadium Club-282
92Topps-442
Gold-442G
92Ultra-352
92Upper Deck-141
92Upper Deck-452
93Pinnacle-331
Canadian-331
93Score-308
Canadian-308
94Pinnacle-112
Artist's Proofs-112
Rink Collection-112
94Senators Team Issue-7
95Collector's Choice-86
Player's Club-86
Player's Club Platinum-86
95Swedish Globe World Championships-126
95Swedish World Championships Stickers-223
99German Bundesliga 2-156

Bourque, Ray
80Liberty Matchbooks-NNO
80O-Pee-Chee-2
80O-Pee-Chee-140
80Topps-2
80Topps-140
81O-Pee-Chee-1
81O-Pee-Chee-17
81O-Pee-Chee Stickers-49
81Post Standups-1
81Topps-5
81Topps-E126
82McDonald's Stickers-28
82O-Pee-Chee-7
82O-Pee-Chee-24
82O-Pee-Chee Stickers-86
82O-Pee-Chee Stickers-87
82O-Pee-Chee Stickers-166
82Post Cereal-1
82Topps Stickers-86
82Topps Stickers-87
82Topps Stickers-166
83Bruins Team Issue-1
83NHL Key Tags-2
83O-Pee-Chee-45
83O-Pee-Chee Stickers-46
83O-Pee-Chee Stickers-47
83O-Pee-Chee Stickers-173
83Puffy Stickers-11
83Topps Stickers-46
83Topps Stickers-47
83Topps Stickers-173
84Bruins Postcards-1
84O-Pee-Chee-1
84O-Pee-Chee-211
84O-Pee-Chee Stickers-143
84O-Pee-Chee Stickers-183
847-Eleven Discs-1
84Topps-1
84Topps-157
85O-Pee-Chee-40
85O-Pee-Chee Box Bottoms-B
85O-Pee-Chee Stickers-115
85O-Pee-Chee Stickers-157
857-Eleven Credit Cards-1
85Topps-40
85Topps Box Bottoms-B
85Topps Sticker Inserts-5
86O-Pee-Chee-1
86O-Pee-Chee Stickers-34
86O-Pee-Chee Stickers-119
86Topps-1
86Topps Sticker Inserts-11
87O-Pee-Chee-87
87O-Pee-Chee Box Bottoms-F
87O-Pee-Chee Minis-4
87O-Pee-Chee Stickers-116
87O-Pee-Chee Stickers-140
87O-Pee-Chee Stickers-178
87Panini Stickers-6
87Panini Stickers-381
87Topps-87
87Topps Box Bottoms-F
87Topps Sticker Inserts-1
88Bruins Sports Action-1
88Bruins Sports Action-24
88Bruins Postcards-1
88Esso All-Stars-3
88Frito-Lay Stickers-16
88O-Pee-Chee-73
88O-Pee-Chee Box Bottoms-I
88O-Pee-Chee Minis-3
88O-Pee-Chee Stickers-23
88O-Pee-Chee Stickers-117
88O-Pee-Chee Stickers-208
88Panini Stickers-204
88Panini Stickers-405
88Topps-73
88Topps Box Bottoms-I
88Topps Sticker Inserts-5
89Bruins Sports Action-1
89Bruins Sports Action Update-1
89Bruins Sports Action Update-12
89Kraft-52
89Kraft All-Stars Stickers-4
89O-Pee-Chee-110
89O-Pee-Chee Stickers-32
89O-Pee-Chee Stickers-72
89O-Pee-Chee Stickers-162
89O-Pee-Chee Stickers-210
89Panini Stickers-187
89Panini Stickers-201
89Sports Illustrated for Kids I-134
89Topps-110
89Topps Sticker Inserts-7
89Swedish Semic World Champ Stickers-57
90Bowman-31
Tiffany-31
90Bruins Sports Action-2
90Kraft-3
90Kraft-80
90O-Pee-Chee-43
90O-Pee-Chee-165
90O-Pee-Chee-196
90O-Pee-Chee-475
90O-Pee-Chee Box Bottoms-I
90OPC Premier-9
90Panini Stickers-17
90Panini Stickers-322
90Pro Set-1B
90Pro Set-1C
90Pro Set-357
90Pro Set-384
90Score Promos-200
90Score-200
90Score-313
90Score-363
90Score-368
Canadian-200
Canadian-313
Canadian-363
90Score Hottest/Rising Stars-35
90Topps-43
90Topps-165
90Topps-196
Tiffany-43
Tiffany-196
90Topps Box Bottoms-I
90Upper Deck-64
90Upper Deck-204
90Upper Deck-320
90Upper Deck-489
French-64
French-204
French-320
French-489
91Pro Set Platinum-2
91Pro Set Platinum-278
91Bowman-356
91Bruins Sports Action-4
91Bruins Sports Action-24
91Bruins Sports Action Legends-3
91Gillette-26
91Kraft-57
91McDonald's Upper Deck-10
91McDonald's Upper Deck-H3
91O-Pee-Chee-66
91O-Pee-Chee-170
91O-Pee-Chee-261
91O-Pee-Chee-517
91OPC Premier-119
91OPC Premier-192
91Panini Stickers-171
91Panini Stickers-335
91Parkhurst-9
91Parkhurst-221
91Parkhurst-469
91Parkhurst-472
French-9
French-221
French-469
French-472
91Pinnacle-15
91Pinnacle-368
French-15
French-368
B-B2
B French-B2
91Pro Set-9
91Pro Set-296
91Pro Set-322
91Pro Set-567
French-9
French-296
French-322
French-567
Awards Special-AC7
Puck Candy-1
91Score National-3
91Score Ntnl Candy Wholesalers Convention-3
91Score Fanfest-3
91Score American-50
91Score American-344
91Score American-415
91Score American-429
91Score Canadian Bilingual-50
91Score Canadian Bilingual-319
91Score Canadian Bilingual-331
91Score Canadian Bilingual-374
91Score Canadian English-50
91Score Canadian English-319
91Score Canadian English-331
91Score Canadian English-374
91Stadium Club Charter Member-44
91Stadium Club-233
91Topps-66
91Topps-261
91Topps-517
Topps/Bowman Preview Sheet-4
Team Scoring Leaders-19
91Upper Deck-255
91Upper Deck-633
French-255
French-633
Award Winner Holograms-AW5A
Award Winner Holograms-AW5B
91Finnish Semic World Champ Stickers-55
91Swedish Semic World Champ Stickers-55
92Bowman-3
92Bowman-223
92Bruins Postcards-1
92Durivage Panini-31
92High-5 Previews-P5
92Humpty Dumpty I-1
92Kraft-37
92McDonald's Upper Deck-H5
92O-Pee-Chee-126
92O-Pee-Chee-348
92Panini Stickers-144
92Panini Stickers-279
92Panini Stickers French-144
92Panini Stickers French-279
92Parkhurst-1
92Parkhurst-464
Emerald Ice-1
Emerald Ice-464
92Pinnacle-2
French-2
Team Pinnacle-2
Team French-2
92Pro Set-4
92Pro Set-261
92Score-100
92Score-419
92Score-447
92Score-490
92Score-520
Canadian-100
Canadian-419
Canadian-447
Canadian-490
Canadian-520
92Seasons Patches-17
92Stadium Club-249
92Stadium Club-267
92Topps-221
92Topps-262
Gold-221G
Gold-262G
92Ultra-2
All-Stars-2
Award Winners-8
92Upper Deck-265
92Upper Deck-626
92Finnish Semic-80
93SLU Hockey American-2
93SLU Hockey Canadian-2
93Donruss-24
93Durivage Score-26
93Kenner Starting Lineup Cards-2
93Kraft-29
93Leaf-215
Gold All-Stars-7
93McDonald's Upper Deck-H4
93OPC Premier-93
93OPC Premier-350
93OPC Premier-383
Gold-93
Gold-350
Gold-383
Black Gold-21
93Panini Stickers-10
93Parkhurst-14
Emerald Ice-14
93Pinnacle-250
Canadian-250
All-Stars-21
All-Stars-48
All-Stars Canadian-21
All-Stars Canadian-48
Captains-2
Captains Canadian-2
Team Pinnacle-8
Team Canadian-8
93PowerPlay-16
Slapshot Artists-2
93Score-29
Canadian-29
Dream Team-7
Franchise-1
93Stadium Club-160
Members Only Master Set-160
OPC-160
First Day Issue-160
First Day Issue OPC-160
All-Stars-2
All-Stars Members Only-2
All-Stars OPC-2
Finest-12
Finest Members Only-12
Master Photos-3
Master Photos Winners-3
93Topps Premier Promo Sheet-602
93Topps/OPC Premier-93
93Topps/OPC Premier-350
93Topps/OPC Premier-383
Gold-93
Gold-350
Gold-383
93Topps Premier Black Gold-15
93Ultra-1
All-Stars-2
93Upper Deck-116
Next In Line-NL4
SP-7
93Upper Deck Locker All-Stars-39
93Swedish Semic World Champ Stickers-192
94SLU Hockey American-2
94Be A Player-R32
Signature Cards-32
94Canada Games NHL POGS-42
94Canada Games NHL POGS-263
94Donruss-68
Dominators-2
94EA Sports-7
94EA Sports-185
94Finest-35
Super Team Winners-35
Refractors-35
Bowman's Best-B1
Bowman's Best Refractors-B1
Division's Clear Cut-2
94Flair-8
94Fleer-9
94Hockey Wit-77
94Kenner Starting Lineup Cards-2
94Kraft-57
94Kraft-67
94Leaf-77
Gold Stars-6
94Leaf Limited-84
94McDonald's Upper Deck-McD5
94OPC Premier-36
94OPC Premier-420
94OPC Premier-454
94OPC Premier-490
Special Effects-36
Special Effects-420
Special Effects-454
Special Effects-490
94Parkhurst-13
94Parkhurst-304
Gold-13
Gold-304
Crash the Game Green-2
Crash the Game Blue-2
Crash the Game Gold-2
Crash the Game Red-2
SE Vintage-18
94Pinnacle-190
Artist's Proofs-190
Rink Collection-190
Boomers-BR7
Team Pinnacle-TP3
Team Dufex Parallel-TP3
94Post Box Backs-3
94Score-180
Gold-180
Platinum-180
Dream Team-DT3
90 Plus Club-21
94Select-18
Gold-18
First Line-FL2
94SP-6
Die Cuts-6
Premier-20
Premier Die-Cuts-20
94Stadium Club Members Only-25
94Stadium Club-77
94Stadium Club-267
Members Only Master Set-77
Members Only Master Set-267
First Day Issue-77
First Day Issue-267
Finest Inserts-8
Finest Inserts Members Only-8
Super Team Winner Cards-77
Super Team Winner Cards-267
94Topps/OPC Premier-36
94Topps/OPC Premier-420
94Topps/OPC Premier-454
94Topps/OPC Premier-490
Special Effects-36
Special Effects-420
Special Effects-454
Special Effects-490
94Topps Finest Bronze-20
94Ultra-10
All-Stars-1
Award Winners-1
94Upper Deck-296
Electric Ice-296
Predictor Canadian-C26
94Upper Deck Predictor Canadian Exch Gold-C26
94Upper Deck Predictor Retail-R14
94Upper Deck Predictor Retail Exchange-R14
94Upper Deck SP Inserts-SP4
94Upper Deck SP Inserts Die Cuts-SP4
95Bashan Super Stickers-6
Die-Cut-6
95Bowman-2
All-Foil-2
95Canada Games NHL POGS-4
95Canada Games NHL POGS-18
95Canada Games NHL POGS-36
95Collector's Choice-216
95Collector's Choice-385
Player's Club-216
Player's Club-385
Player's Club Platinum-216
Player's Club Platinum-385
Crash The Game-C24A
Crash The Game-C24B
Crash The Game-C24C
Crash The Game Gold-C24A
Crash The Game Gold-C24B
Crash The Game Gold-C24C
Crash the Game Silver Redeemed-C24
Crash the Game Silver Bonus-C24
Crash the Game Gold Redeemed-C24
Crash the Game Gold Bonus-C24
95Donruss-127
Dominators-3
95Donruss Elite-9
Die Cut Stars-9
Die Cut Uncut-9
95Emotion-6
95Finest-2
95Finest-77
Refractors-2
Refractors-77
95Hoyle Eastern Playing Cards-4
95Imperial Stickers-6
Die Cut Superstars-6
95Kraft-51
95Leaf-106
Gold Stars-3
95Leaf Limited-16
95Metal-6
95NHL Aces Playing Cards-8D
95NHL Cool Trade-6
95NHL Cool Trade-RP6
95Panini Stickers-9
95Parkhurst International-11
Emerald Ice-11
Crown Collection Silver Series 2-9
Crown Collection Gold Series 2-9
NHL All-Stars-5
Parkie's Trophy Picks-PP22
95Pinnacle-56
Artist's Proofs-56
Rink Collection-56
95Pinnacle FANtasy-2
95Playoff One on One-5
95Playoff One on One-116
95Playoff One on One-226
95Post Upper Deck-1

01UD Honor Roll-5
01UD Honor Roll-35
Jerseys-J-RB
Jerseys Gold-J-RB
01UD Mask Collection Double Patches-DPRB
01UD Mask Collection Gloves-GGRB
01UD Mask Collection Jerseys-J-RB
01UD Mask Collection Jersey and Patch-JPRB
01UD Premier Collection-4
Dual Jerseys-DBB
Dual Jerseys-DBTO
Dual Jerseys Black-DBB
Dual Jerseys Black-DBTO
Jerseys-BRB
Jerseys-GRB
Jerseys Black-B-RB
Jerseys Black-G-RB
Signatures-RB
Signatures Black-RB
01UD Stanley Cup Champs-5
Jerseys-T-RB
Pieces of Glory-G-RB
Sticks-S-RB
01UD Top Shelf-10
Jerseys-RB
Jersey Autographs-RB
Sticks-SRB
Sticks-BPR
Sticks Gold-SRB
Sticks Gold-BPR
01Upper Deck-212
Exclusives-212
Game Jerseys Series II-SSRB
Game Jerseys Series II-DJBR
Game Jersey Autographs-SRB
Game Jersey Autographs-SJBO
Game Jersey Autographs-SJRB
Patches-PRB
Skilled Stars-SS14
01Upper Deck Avalanche NHL All-Star Game-CA1
01Upper Deck Avalanche NHL All-Star Game-HH3
01Upper Deck Ice-10
01Upper Deck Legends-50
Sticks-PHRA
Sticks-PHRB
01Upper Deck MVP-48
Souvenirs-S-RB
Souvenirs Gold-S-RB
01Upper Deck Victory-85
01Upper Deck Victory-411
Gold-85
Gold-411
01Upper Deck Vintage-66
Next In Line-NLBL
01Czech Stadion-217
02BAP Sig Series Auto Buybacks 1999-20
02SP Authentic Sign of the Times-RB
02SP Authentic Sign of the Times-BR
02SP Authentic Sign of the Times-CBO
02SP Authentic Sign of the Times-OBT
02SP Authentic Sign of the Times-TSB
02SP Authentic Super Premiums-TPTBN
02SP Game Used-59
Authentic Fabrics-AFBQ
Authentic Fabrics-AFRB
Authentic Fabrics Gold-AFBQ
Authentic Fabrics Gold-AFRB
Authentic Fabrics Rainbow-AFBQ
Authentic Fabrics Rainbow-AFRB
First Rounder Patches-RB
Piece of History-PHBQ
Piece of History-PHRB
Piece of History Gold-PHBQ
Piece of History Gold-PHRB
Piece of History Rainbow-PHBQ
Piece of History Rainbow-PHRB
Signature Style-RB
02SPx Winning Materials-WMBO
02SPx Winning Materials-WMRB
02SPx Winning Materials Gold-BO
02SPx Winning Materials Gold-RB
02SPx Winning Materials Silver-BO
02SPx Winning Materials Silver-RB
02SPx Xtreme Talents-RB
02SPx Xtreme Talents Gold-RB
02SPx Xtreme Talents Silver-RB
02UD Artistic Impressions-5
02UD Artistic Impressions-24
Gold-5
Gold-24
Artist's Touch-ATRB
Artist's Touch Gold-ATRB
02UD Artistic Impressions Beckett Promos-5
02UD Artistic Impressions Beckett Promos-24
02UD Artistic Impressions Common Ground-CG7
02UD Artistic Impressions Common Ground-CG14
02UD Artistic Impress Common Ground Gold-CG7
02UD Artistic Impress Common Ground Gold-CG14
02UD Artistic Impressions Flashbacks-UD7
02UD Artistic Impressions Flashbacks Gold-UD7
02UD Artistic Impress Great Depiction-GD7
02UD Artistic Impress Great Depiction Gold-GD7
02UD Artistic Impressions Retrospectives-R5
02UD Artistic Impressions Retrospectives-R24
02UD Artistic Impress Retrospect Gold-R5
02UD Artistic Impress Retrospect Gold-R24
02UD Artistic Impress Retrospect Auto-R5
02UD Artistic Impress Retrospect Auto-R24
02UD Artistic Impress Retrospect Silver-R5
02UD Artistic Impress Retrospect Silver-R24
02Upper Deck Collectors Club-NHL4
Jerseys-RB-J
02UD Foundations-6
02UD Foundations-18
02UD Foundations-108
02UD Foundations-118
1000 Point Club-BO1
1000 Point Club-BO2
Calder Winners-TRB
Calder Winners Gold-TRB
Calder Winners Silver-T-RB
Canadian Heroes-CBO
Canadian Heroes Gold-CBO
Canadian Heroes Silver-C-BO
Classic Greats-GBO
Classic Greats-GRB
Classic Greats Gold-GBO
Classic Greats Gold-GRB
Classic Greats Silver-G-BO
Classic Greats Silver-G-RB
Defense First-DBO
Defense First-DRB
Defense First Gold-DBO
Defense First Gold-DRB
Defense First Silver-D-BO
Defense First Silver-D-RB
Milestones-NBO
Milestones Gold-NBO
Milestones Silver-N-BO
Playoff Performers-PRB
Playoff Performers Gold-PRB
Playoff Performers Silver-P-RB
Signs of Greatness-SGRA
Signs of Greatness-SGRB
02UD Honor Roll Grade A Jerseys-GARB
02UD Piece of History-98
02UD Piece of History-118
02UD Piece of History-119
02UD Piece of History-120
Awards Collection-AC2
Exquisite Combos-ECNB
Historical Swatches-HSRB
Hockey Beginnings-HB2
Marks of Distinction-RA
Patches-PHRB
Simply the Best-SB1
02UD Premier Collection-59A
Jerseys Bronze-RB
Jerseys Gold-RB
Jerseys Silver-RB
Patches-PBO
Patches-PRB
Signatures Bronze-SRA
Signatures Bronze-SRB
Signatures Gold-SRA
Signatures Gold-SRB
Signatures Silver-SRA
Signatures Silver-SRB
02UD Top Shelf Clutch Performers-CPRB
02UD Top Shelf Dual Player Jerseys-STBB
02UD Top Shelf Dual Player Jerseys-STBT
02UD Top Shelf Milestones Jerseys-MBMBS
02UD Top Shelf Milestones Jerseys-MGBYM
02UD Top Shelf Shooting Stars-SHRB
02UD Top Shelf Signatures-RB
02UD Top Shelf Sweet Sweaters-SWRB
02Upper Deck Playbooks-PL2
02Upper Deck Classic Portraits Mini-Busts-115
02Upper Deck Classic Portraits Mini-Busts-116
02Upper Deck Classic Portraits Mini-Busts-117
02Upper Deck Classic Portraits Mini-Busts-118
02Upper Deck Classic Portraits Mini-Busts-119
02Upper Deck Classic Portraits Mini-Busts-120
02Upper Deck Classic Portraits Mini-Busts-121
02Upper Deck Classic Portraits Mini-Busts-122
02Upper Deck Classic Portraits Mini-Busts-123
02Upper Deck Classic Portraits Mini-Busts-124
02Upper Deck MVP Prosign-RB
02Upper Deck Rookie Update-165
Autographs-RB
02Upper Deck Vintage Jerseys-HSRB
02Upper Deck Vintage Jerseys Gold-HS-RB
02UD SuperStars *-37
Gold-37
03BAP Ultimate Memorabilia Autographs-155
Gold-155
03BAP Ultimate Mem Auto Jerseys-155
03BAP Ultimate Mem Auto Emblems-155
03BAP Ultimate Mem Always An All-Star-15
03BAP Ultimate Mem Always An AS Gold-15
03BAP Ultimate Mem Blades of Steel-6
03BAP Ultimate Memorabilia Career Year-3
03BAP Ultimate Memorabilia Cornerstones-5
03BAP Ultimate Memorabilia Emblem Attic-4
03BAP Ultimate Mem Emblem Attic Gold-4
03BAP Ultimate Memorabilia Gloves Are Off-19
03BAP Ultimate Memorabilia Great Moments-6
03BAP Ultimate Mem Hometown Heroes-3
03BAP Ultimate Mem Hometown Heroes Gold-3
03BAP Ultimate Mem Jersey and Emblems-34
03BAP Ultimate Mem Jersey and Emblem Gold-34
03BAP Ultimate Mem Jersey and Numbers-34
03BAP Ultimate Mem Jersey and Number Gold-34
03BAP Ultimate Mem Jersey and Stick-23
03BAP Ultimate Mem Jersey and Stick Gold-23
03BAP Ultimate Mem Journey Jerseys-10
03BAP Ultimate Mem Journey Jerseys Gold-10
03BAP Ultimate Mem Journey Emblems-10
03BAP Ultimate Mem Journey Emblems Gold-10
03BAP Ultimate Mem Lifetime Achievers-4
03BAP Ultimate Memorabilia Nameplates-28
03BAP Ultimate Mem Nameplates Gold-28
03BAP Ultimate Mem Perennial Power Jersey-4
03BAP Ult Mem Perenn Powerhouse Jsy Stick-4
03BAP Ultimate Mem Perennial Power Emblem-4
03BAP Ultimate Mem Raised to the Rafters-6
03BAP Ultimate Mem Retro Teammates-1
03BAP Ultimate Mem Retro-Active Trophies-4
03BAP Ultimate Mem Retro-Active Trophies-12
03BAP Ultimate Mem Seams Unbelievable-5
03BAP Ultimate Memorabilia Triple Threads-14
03BAP Ultimate Mem Ultimate Captains-1
03BAP Ultimate Mem Vint Comp Jersey-2
03BAP Ultimate Mem Vint Comp Jersey Gold-2
03BAP Ultimate Mem Vint Complete Package-4
03BAP Ultimate Mem Vint Comp Package Gold-4
03BAP Ultimate Mem Vintage Hat Tricks-3
03BAP Ultimate Mem Vintage Jerseys-33
03BAP Ultimate Mem Vintage Jerseys Gold-33
03Black Diamond Signature Gems-SG-2
03Canada Post-20
03ITG Used Signature Series-116
Gold-116
Autographs-RBO
Autographs Gold-RBO
Game-Day Jerseys-5
Game-Day Jerseys Gold-5
Jerseys-36
Jerseys Gold-36
Jersey Autos-36
Emblems-10
Emblems Gold-10
Jersey and Stick-36
Jersey and Stick Gold-36
Norris Trophy-9
Norris Trophy Gold-9
Teammates-18
Teammates Gold-18
Triple Memorabilia-3
Triple Memorabilia Gold-3
Vintage Memorabilia-2
Vintage Memorabilia Autographs-2
Vintage Memorabilia Gold-2
03Parkhurst Original Six Boston-41
03Parkhurst Original Six Boston-70
03Parkhurst Original Six Boston-73
03Parkhurst Original Six Boston-94
03Parkhurst Original Six Boston-100
Autographs-1
Inserts-B12
Inserts-B17
Memorabilia-BM36
Memorabilia-BM53
Memorabilia-BM64
Memorabilia-BM66
03Parkhurst Orig Six He Shoots/Scores-17
03Parkhurst Orig Six He Shoots/Scores-17A
03Parkhurst Rookie-57
Emblems-GUE-7
Emblem Autographs-GUE-RB
Emblems Gold-GUE-7
Jerseys-GJ-46
Jerseys Gold-GJ-46
Jersey and Sticks-SJ-27
Jersey and Sticks Gold-SJ-27
ROYalty-VR-7
ROYalty Autographs-VR-RB
ROYalty Gold-VR-7
03SP Game Used Signers-SPSRB
03SPx Hall Pass-HP-RB
03SPx Hall Pass Limited-HP-RB
03SPx Winning Materials-WM-RB
03SPx Winning Materials Limited-WM-RB
03UD Toronto Fall Expo Priority Signings-RB
03Upper Deck MVP ProSign-PS-RB
03Upper Deck MVP Threads-TC10
03Upper Deck Trilogy-136
Authentic Patches-AP15
Authentic Patches-AP41
Crest Variations-136
Limited-136
Scripts-S3RB
Scripts Limited-S3RB
Scripts Red-S3RB
03Upper Deck Victory Freshman Flashback-FF48
04ITG NHL AS FANtasy AS History Jerseys-SB35
04ITG Franchises He Shoots/Scores Prizes-23
04ITG Franchises He Shoots/Scores Prizes-34
04ITG Franchises US East-327
Autographs-A-RB1
Barn Burners-EBB6
Barn Burners Gold-EBB6
Complete Jerseys-ECJ1
Complete Jerseys Gold-ECJ1
Double Memorabilia-EDM7
Double Memorabilia Autographs-EDM-RB
Double Memorabilia Gold-EDM7
Forever Rivals-EFR6
Forever Rivals Gold-EFR6
Memorabilia-ESM3
Memorabilia Autographs-ESM-RB
Memorabilia Gold-ESM3
Original Sticks-EOS9
Original Sticks Autographs-EOS-RB
Original Sticks Gold-EOS9
Teammates-ETM4
Teammates Gold-ETM4
Triple Memorabilia-ETM4
Triple Memorabilia Autographs-ETM-RB
Triple Memorabilia Gold-ETM4
Trophy Winners-ETW5
Trophy Winners Gold-ETW5
04ITG Franchises US West-184
Autographs-A-RB2
Barn Burners-WBB3
Barn Burners Gold-WBB3
Complete Jerseys-WCJ1
Complete Jerseys Gold-WCJ1
Double Memorabilia-WDM7
Double Memorabilia Autographs-WDMRB
Double Memorabilia Gold-WDM7
Memorabilia-WSM10
Memorabilia Autographs-WSMRB
Memorabilia Gold-WSM10
Original Sticks-WOS8
Original Sticks Autographs-WOSRB
Original Sticks Gold-WOS8
Teammates-WTM4
Teammates Gold-WTM4
Triple Memorabilia Autographs-WTMRB
Triple Memorabilia Gold-WTM5
04ITG Ultimate Memorabilia-106
04ITG Ultimate Memorabilia-125
Gold-106
Gold-125
Archives 1st Edition-12
Archives 1st Edition-29
Archives 1st Edition-31
Auto Threads-9
Auto Threads-13
Autographs-4
Autographs-8
Autographs Gold-4
Autographs Gold-8
Calder Trophy-7
Complete Jerseys-4
Complete Logo-1
Complete Logo-2
Complete Logo-3
Complete Logo-4
Complete Package-9
Cornerstones-5
Cornerstones Gold-5
Country of Origin-13
Country of Origin Gold-13
Day In History-6
Day In History-27
Day In History-43
Day In History Gold-6
Day In History Gold-27
Day In History Gold-43
Gloves are Off-1
Heroes Patrick Roy-5
Jerseys-1
Jerseys Gold-1
Jersey Autographs-50
Jersey Autographs Gold-50
Jersey and Sticks-3
Jersey and Sticks Gold-3
Norris Trophy-1
Original Six-1
Original Six-13
Raised to the Rafters-3
Retro Teammates-1
Retro Teammates-14
Seams Unbelievable-9
Stick Autographs-5
Stick Autographs Gold-5
Triple Threads-6
04MasterCard Priceless Moments-8
04SP Authentic Buybacks-163
04SP Authentic Sign of the Times-DS-RP
04SP Authentic Sign of the Times-TS-BNT
04SP Authentic Sign of the Times-DS-BPBP
04SP Authentic Sign of the Times-FS-BOS
04SP Authentic Sign of the Times-SS-DEE
04UD Legends Classics Signature Moments-M53
04UD Legends Classics Signatures-CS51
04UD Legends Classics Signatures-DC4
04UD Legends Classics Signatures-DC10
04UD Legends Classics Signatures-TC9
04Ultimate Collection Buybacks-74
04Ultimate Collection Buybacks-75
04Ultimate Collection Buybacks-76
04Ultimate Collection Dual Logos-UL2-BB
04Ultimate Collection Jerseys-UGJ-RB
04Ultimate Collection Jerseys Gold-UGJ-RB
04Ultimate Collection Jersey Autographs-UGJA-RB
04Ultimate Collection Patches-UP-RB1
04Ultimate Collection Patches-UP-RB2
04Ultimate Collection Patch Autographs-UPA-RB
04Ultimate Collection Patch Autographs-UPA-CNRB
04Ultimate Collection Patch Autographs-UPA-RBJB
04Ultimate Collection Signatures-US-RB1
04Ultimate Collection Signature Logos-ULA-RB1
04Ultimate Collection Signature Logos-ULA-RB2
04Ultimate Collection Signature Patches-SP-RB
04ITG Heroes and Prospects-150
Aspiring-5
Autographs-RB
Hero Memorabilia-4
04ITG Heroes/Prospects Toronto Expo '05-150
04ITG Heroes/Prospects Expo Heroes/Pros-150
05ITG Heroes/Prosp Toronto Expo Parallel -13
05ITG Heroes/Prosp Toronto Expo Parallel -182
05Beehive PhotoGraphs-PGRB
05Black Diamond-186
Emerald-186
Gold-186
Onyx-186
Ruby-186
Gemography-G-RB
Gemography Emerald-G-RB
Gemography Gold-G-RB
Gemography Onyx-G-RB
Gemography Ruby-G-RB
05ITG Ultimate Memorabilia Level 1-82
05ITG Ultimate Memorabilia Level 2-82
05ITG Ultimate Memorabilia Level 3-82
05ITG Ultimate Memorabilia Level 4-82
05ITG Ultimate Memorabilia Level 5-82
05ITG Ultimate Mem Blades of Steel-3
05ITG Ultimate Mem Blades of Steel Gold-3
05ITG Ultimate Mem Complete Jersey-21
05ITG Ultimate Mem Complete Jersey Gold-21
05ITG Ultimate Mem Complete Package-14
05ITG Ultimate Mem Complete Package Gold-14
05ITG Ultimate Mem Cornerstones Jerseys-2
05ITG Ultimate Mem Cornerst Jerseys Gold-2
05ITG Ultimate Mem Decades Jerseys-1
05ITG Ultimate Mem Decades Jerseys-4
05ITG Ultimate Mem Decades Jerseys Gold-1
05ITG Ultimate Mem Decades Jerseys Gold-4
05ITG Ultimate Mem Double Mem-15
05ITG Ultimate Mem Double Mem Gold-15
05ITG Ultimate Memorabilia Emblems-21
05ITG Ultimate Memorabilia Emblems Gold-21
05ITG Ultimate Mem First Rounders Jerseys-8
05ITG Ultimate Mem First Rounders Jerseys-9
05ITG Ultimate Mem 1st Round Jersey Gold-8
05ITG Ultimate Mem 1st Round Jersey Gold-9
05ITG Ultimate Memorabilia Gloves Are Off-7
05ITG Ultimate Mem Gloves Are Off Gold-7
05ITG Ultimate Memorabilia In The Numbers-23
05ITG Ultimate Mem In The Numbers Gold-23
05ITG Ultimate Mem Jersey and Emblem-10
05ITG Ultimate Mem Jersey Emblems Gold-10
05ITG Ultimate Memorabilia Jerseys-31
05ITG Ultimate Memorabilia Jerseys Gold-31
05ITG Ultimate Mem Pass the Torch Jerseys-6
05ITG Ultimate Mem Passing Torch Jsy Gold-6
05ITG Ultimate Memorabilia R.O.Y. Autos-17
05ITG Ultimate Mem R.O.Y. Autos Gold-17
05ITG Ultimate Memorabilia R.O.Y. Emblems-4
05ITG Ultimate Mem R.O.Y. Emblems Gold-4
05ITG Ultimate Memorabilia R.O.Y. Jerseys-4
05ITG Ultimate Mem R.O.Y. Jerseys Gold-4
05ITG Ultimate Memorabilia R.O.Y. Numbers-4
05ITG Ultimate Mem R.O.Y. Numbers Gold-4
05ITG Ultimate Mem Raised to the Rafters-16
05ITG Ultimate Mem Raised Rafters Gold-16
05ITG Ultimate Mem Record Breaker Jerseys-18
05ITG Ultimate Mem RecBreak Jerseys Gold-18
05ITG Ultimate Mem Retro Teammate Jerseys-18
05ITG Ultimate Mem Retro Teammate Jerseys-19
05ITG Ult Mem Retro Teammates Jersey Gold-18
05ITG Ult Mem Retro Teammates Jersey Gold-19
05ITG Ultimate Mem Seams Unbelievable-3
05ITG Ultimate Mem Seam Unbelievable Gold-3
05ITG Ultimate Memorabilia Stick Autos-2
05ITG Ultimate Mem Stick Autos Gold-2
05ITG Ult Mem 3 Star of the Game Jsy-24
05ITG Ult Mem 3 Star of the Game Jsy Gold-24
05ITG Ultimate Memorabilia Triple Autos-11
05ITG Ultimate Mem Triple Autos Gold-11
05ITG Ultimate Mem Triple Threads Jerseys-5
05ITG Ultimate Mem Triple Thread Jsy Gold-5
05ITG Ultimate Memorabilia Ultimate Autos-48
05ITG Ultimate Mem Ultimate Autos Gold-48
05NHL Legends Medallions-2
05SP Authentic Exquisite Endorsements-EERB
05SP Authentic Immortal Inks-IIRB
05SP Authentic Marks of Distinction-MDBO
05SP Authentic Prestigious Pairings-PPBN
05SP Authentic Sign of the Times Quads-QTNBB
05SP Authentic Six Star Signatures-SSBO
05SP Game Used Authentic Fabrics-AF-RB
05SP Game Used Authentic Fabrics Dual-CO
05SP Game Used Authentic Fabrics Dual-NB
05SP Game Used Authentic Fabric Dual Auto-CO
05SP Game Used Authentic Fabric Dual Auto-NB
05SP Game Used Authentic Fabrics Gold-AF-RB
05SP Game Used Authentic Fabrics Quad-RBBF
05SP Game Used Authentic Patches Quad -RBBF
05SP Game Used Authentic Fabrics Triple-BBP
05SP Game Used Authentic Patches-AP-RB
05SP Game Used Authentic Patches Dual-CO
05SP Game Used Authentic Patches Dual-NB
05SP Game Used Authentic Patch Dual Autos-CO
05SP Game Used Authentic Patch Dual Autos-NB
05SP Game Used Authentic Patches Triple-BBP
05SP Game Used Auto Draft-AD-BO
05SP Game Used By the Letter-LM-RB
05SP Game Used Game Gear-GG-BB
05SP Game Used Game Gear-GG-RB
05SP Game Used Game Gear Autographs-AG-RB
05SP Game Used Heritage Classic-HC-RB
05SP Game Used Heritage Classic Autos-HCA-RB
05SP Game Used Heritage Classic Patches-HCP-RB
05SP GameUsed Heritage Classic Patch Auto-HAP-RB
05SP Game Used Oldtimer's Challenge-OC-BO
05SP Game Used Oldtimer's Challenge Autos-OCA-BO
05SP Game Used Oldtimer's Challenge Patch-OCP-BO
05SP Game Used Oldtime Chall Patch Autoa-OAP-BO
05SP Game Used Significant Numbers-SN-RB
05SPx-120
Spectrum-120
Winning Combos-WC-BB
Winning Combos-WC-BL
Winning Combos Autographs-AWC-BB
Winning Combos Gold-WC-BB
Winning Combos Gold-WC-BL
Winning Combos Spectrum-WC-BB
Winning Combos Spectrum-WC-BL
05The Cup-8
Gold-8
Black Rainbow-8
Dual NHL Shields Autographs-ADSBL
Emblems of Endorsement-EEBQ
Hardware Heroes-HHRB1
Hardware Heroes-HHRB2
Hardware Heroes-HHRB3
Honorable Numbers-HNRB
Limited Logos-LLRB
Masterpiece Pressplates-8
Noble Numbers-NNBE
Noble Numbers Dual-DNNPR
Patch Variation-P8
Patch Variation Autographs-AP8
Property of-PORB
Scripted Numbers-SNBE
Scripted Numbers Dual-DSNNB
Scripted Swatches-SSRB1
Scripted Swatches-SSRB2
Signature Patches-SPRB
05UD Artifacts Frozen Artifacts-FA-RB
05UD Artifacts Frozen Artifacts Autos-FA-RB
05UD Artifacts Frozen Artifacts Copper-FA-RB
05UD Artifacts Frozen Artifacts Dual-FAD-RB
05UD Artifact Frozen Artifact Dual Auto-FAD-RB
05UD Artifact Frozen Artifact Dual Copper-FAD-RB
05UD Artifact Frozen Artifact Dual Gold-FAD-RB
05UD Artifact Frozen Artifact Dual Maroon-FAD-RB
05UD Artifact Frozen Artifact Dual Pewter-FAD-RB
05UD Artifact Frozen Artifact Dual Silver-FAD-RB
05UD Artifacts Frozen Artifacts Gold-FA-RB
05UD Artifacts Frozen Artifacts Maroon-FA-RB
05UD Artifacts Frozen Artifacts Patches-FP-RB
05UD Artifact Frozen Artifact Patch Autos-FP-RB
05UD Artifact Frozen Artifact Patch Dual-FPD-RB
05UD Artifact Frozen Art Patch Dual Auto-FPD-RB
05UD Artifacts Frozen Art Patch Pewter-FP-RB
05UD Artifacts Frozen Art Patch Silver-FP-RB
05UD Artifacts Frozen Artifacts Pewter-FA-RB
05UD Artifacts Frozen Artifacts Silver-FA-RB
05UD Artifacts Remarkable Artifacts-RA-BQ1
05UD Artifacts Remarkable Artifacts-RA-BQ2
05UD Artifacts Remarkable Artifacts Dual-RA-BQ1
05UD Artifacts Remarkable Artifacts Dual-RA-BQ2
05Ultimate Collection Endorsed Emblems-EERB
05Ultimate Collection Jerseys-JRB
05Ultimate Collection Premium Patches-PPRB
05Ultimate Collection Premium Swatches-PSRB
05Ultimate Coll Ultimate Achievements-UARB
05Ultimate Collection Ultimate Patches-PRB
05Ultimate Collection Ultimate Signatures-USRB
05Ultimate Coll Ultimate Sigs Logos-SLRB
05Ultimate Coll Ultimate Sigs Pairings-UPBO
05Ultimate Coll Ultimate Sigs Pairings-UPBR
05Ultimate Coll Ultimate Sigs Trios-UTBNE
05Ultra Super Six-SS4
05Ultra Super Six-SS7
05Ultra Super Six Jerseys-SSJ-RB1
05Ultra Super Six Jerseys-SSJ-RB2
05Ultra Super Six Jersey Autographs-SAJ-RB1
05Ultra Super Six Jersey Autographs-SAJ-RB2
05Ultra Super Six Patches-SSP-RB1
05Ultra Super Six Patches-SSP-RB2
05Ultra Super Six Patch Autographs-SAP-RB1
05Ultra Super Six Patch Autographs-SAP-RB2
05Upper Deck All-Time Greatest-62
05Upper Deck Big Playmakers-B-RB
05Upper Deck Jerseys-J-RB
05Upper Deck NHL Generations-DBB
05Upper Deck Notable Numbers-N-RBO
05Upper Deck Patches-P-RB
05Upper Deck Ice Frozen Fabrics-FFRB
05Upper Deck Ice Frozen Fabrics Autos-AFFRB
05Upper Deck Ice Frozen Fabrics Glass-FFRB
05Upper Deck Ice Frozen Fabrics Patches-FFPRB
05Upper Deck Ice Frozen Fabric Patch Auto-FAPRB
05Upper Deck Ice Signature Swatches-SSRB
05Upper Deck Trilogy-96
Crystal-96
Crystal Autographs-96
Ice Scripts-IS-RB
Legendary Scripts-LEG-RB
Personal Scripts-PER-RB
Scripts-SSS-RB
05ITG Heroes and Prospects-13
05ITG Heroes and Prospects-182
Aspiring-ASP9
Autographs-A-RB
Autographs Series II-RB2
CHL Grads-CG-12
CHL Grads Gold-CG-12
Future Teammates-FT8
Future Teammates-FT11
He Shoots-He Scores Prizes-4
Hero Memorabilia-HM-2
Hero Memorabilia Dual-HDM-5
Spectrum-STM-08
Spectrum Gold-STM-08
06Beehive-216
5 X 7 Black and White-216
Matted Materials-MMRB
PhotoGraphs-PGRB
Remarkable Matted Materials-MMRB
06Black Diamond-149B
Gold-149B
Ruby-149B
06Flair Showcase-206
06Flair Showcase-273
Parallel-206
Parallel-273
Hot Numbers-HN3
Hot Numbers Parallel-HN3
06ITG International Ice-4
06ITG International Ice-43
06ITG International Ice-133
Gold-4
Gold-43
Gold-133
Autographs-ARB
Autographs-ARB2
Autographs-ARB3
Best of the Best-BB08
Best of the Best Gold-BB08
Canadian Dream Team-DT07
Canadian Dream Team Gold-DT07
Cornerstones-IC12
Cornerstones Gold-IC12
International Rivals-IR08
Quad Patch-QP05
Quad Patch Gold-QP05
Stick and Jersey-SJ03
Stick and Jersey Gold-SJ03
Teammates-IT06
Teammates Gold-IT06
06ITG Ultimate Memorabilia-119
Artist Proof-119
Autos Triple-1
Autos Triple Gold-1
Bloodlines-3
Bloodlines Gold-3
Bloodlines Autos-3
Bloodlines Autos Gold-3
Captain-C-6
Captain-C Gold-6
Complete Jersey-23
Complete Jersey Gold-23
Complete Package-2
Complete Package Gold-2
Decades-7
Decades Gold-7
Double Memorabilia-21
Double Memorabilia Gold-21
First Round Picks-30
First Round Picks Gold-30
Gloves Are Off-18
Gloves Are Off Gold-18
Going For Gold-22
Going For Gold Gold-22
Journey Emblem-1
Journey Emblem Gold-1
Journey Jersey-1
Journey Jersey Gold-1
Legendary Captains-8
Legendary Captains Gold-8
Passing The Torch-6
Passing The Torch Gold-6
Retro Teammates-19
Retro Teammates Gold-19
Retrospective-7
Retrospective Gold-7
Stick Rack-13
Stick Rack-27
Stick Rack Gold-13
Stick Rack Gold-27
06Parkhurst-77
06Parkhurst-163
Autographs-77
Autographs-163
Autographs Dual-DAOB
06SP Authentic-148
Limited-148
Sign of the Times-STIB
Sign of the Times Duals-STOB
Sign of the Times Triples-ST3OBE
06SP Game Used Authentic Fabrics Sixes-AF6NOR
06SP Game Used Authentic Fabrics Sixes Patches-AF6NOR
06SP Game Used Authentic Fabrics Eights-AF8HOF
06SP Game Used Authentic Fabrics Eights Patches-AF8HOF
06SP Game Used By The Letter-BLRB
06SP Game Used Inked Sweaters Dual-IS2BP
06SP Game Used Inked Sweaters Dual-IS2RB
06SP Game Used Inked Sweaters Dual Patches-IS2BP
06SP Game Used Inked Sweaters Dual Patches-IS2RB
06SP Game Used Legendary Fabrics-LFRB
06SP Game Used Legendary Fabrics Autographs-LFRB
06SP Game Used Letter Marks-LMBQ
06SPx-123
Spectrum-123
SPxcitement-X6
SPxcitement Spectrum-X6
SPxcitement Autographs-X6
06The Cup-7
Autographed Foundations-CQRB
Autographed Foundations Patches-CQRB
Autographed NHL Shields Duals-DASBM
Autographed NHL Shields Duals-DASBS
Autographed NHL Shields Duals-DASNB
Autographed Patches-7
Black Rainbow-7
Foundations-CQRB
Foundations Patches-CQRB
Enshrinements-ERB
Gold-7
Gold Patches-7
Jerseys-7
Masterpiece Pressplates-7
Scripted Swatches-SSRB
Scripted Swatches Duals-DSNB
Scripted Swatches Duals-DSPR
Signature Patches-SPBO1
Signature Patches-SPBO2
Stanley Cup Signatures-CSRB
Stanley Cup Titlists Patches-TRB
06UD Artifacts-144
Blue-144
Gold-144
Platinum-144
Radiance-144
Autographed Radiance Parallel-144
Red-144
Auto-Facts-AFRA
Auto-Facts Gold-AFRA
Treasured Patches Black-TSRB
Treasured Patches Blue-TSRB
Treasured Patches Gold-TSRB
Treasured Patches Platinum-TSRB
Treasured Patches Red-TSRB
Treasured Patches Autographed Black Tag Parallel-TSRB
Treasured Swatches-TSRB
Treasured Swatches Black-TSRB
Treasured Swatches Blue-TSRB
Treasured Swatches Gold-TSRB
Treasured Swatches Platinum-TSRB
Treasured Swatches Red-TSRB
Treasured Swatches Autographed Black-TSRB
Tundra Tandems-TTBO
Tundra Tandems-TTCR
Tundra Tandems-TTRB
Tundra Tandems Black-TTBO
Tundra Tandems Black-TTCR
Tundra Tandems Black-TTRB
Tundra Tandems Blue-TTBO
Tundra Tandems Blue-TTCR
Tundra Tandems Blue-TTRB
Tundra Tandems Gold-TTBO
Tundra Tandems Gold-TTCR
Tundra Tandems Gold-TTRB
Tundra Tandems Platinum-TTCR
Tundra Tandems Platinum-TTRB
Tundra Tandems Red-TTBO
Tundra Tandems Red-TTCR
Tundra Tandems Red-TTRB
Tundra Tandems Dual Patches Red-TTBO
Tundra Tandems Dual Patches Red-TTCR
Tundra Tandems Dual Patches Red-TTRB
06Ultimate Collection-6
Autographed Jerseys-AJ-RB
Autographed Patches-AJ-RB
Jerseys-UJ-RB
Jerseys Dual-UJ2-RB
Patches-UJ-RB
Patches Dual-UJ2-RB
Premium Patches-PS-RB
Premium Swatches-PS-RB
Signatures-US-RB
Ultimate Signatures Logos-SL-RB
06Upper Deck Game Jerseys-J2RB
06Upper Deck Game Patches-P2RB
06Upper Deck Generations Triples-G3PBPB
06Upper Deck Generations Patches Triple-G3PBPB
06Upper Deck Sweet Shot-12
Signature Shots/Saves-SSRB
Signature Shots/Saves Ice Signings-SSIRB
Signature Shots/Saves Sticks-SSSRB
Signature Sticks-STRB
Sweet Stitches-SSRB
Sweet Stitches Duals-SSRB
Sweet Stitches Triples-SSRB
06Upper Deck Trilogy Combo Clearcut Autographs-C3NOB
06Upper Deck Trilogy Frozen In Time-FT16
06Upper Deck Trilogy Honorary Scripted Patches-HSPRB
06Upper Deck Trilogy Honorary Scripted Swatches-HSSRB
06Upper Deck Trilogy Honorary Swatches-HSBO
06Upper Deck Trilogy Ice Scripts-ISRB
06Upper Deck Trilogy Legendary Scripts-LSRB
06Upper Deck Trilogy Scripts-S1RB
06Upper Deck Trilogy Scripts-S2RB

Bourque, Rene

95Bashan Super Stickers-6
03Wisconsin Badgers-2
03SP Authentic Rookie Redemptions-RR32
04AHL All-Stars-6
04Norfolk Admirals-5
05ITG Heroes/Prosp Toronto Expo Parallel -60
05Beehive-130
Beige -130
Blue -130
Gold-130
Red -130
Matte-130
05Black Diamond-166
Emerald-166
Gold-166
Onyx-166
Ruby-166
05Hot Prospects-194
Autographed Patch Variation-194
Autographed Patch Variation Gold-194
Red Hot-194
05Parkhurst-110
Facsimile Auto Parallel-110
True Colors-TCCHI
True Colors-TCCHI
05SP Authentic-148
Limited-148
Rarefied Rookies-RRRB
05SP Game Used-116
Autographs-116
Gold-116
Rookie Exclusives-RB
Rookie Exclusives Silver-RE-RB
05SPx-155
Spectrum-155
Xcitement Rookies-XR-RB
Xcitement Rookies Gold-XR-RB
Xcitement Rookies Spectrum-XR-RB
05The Cup-131
Autographed Rookie Patches Gold Rainbow-131
Black Rainbow Rookies-131
Masterpiece Pressplates (Artifacts)-232
Masterpiece Pressplates (Bee Hive)-130
Masterpiece Pressplates (Black Diamond)-166
Masterpiece Pressplates (Ice)-174
Masterpiece Pressplates (MVP)-397
Masterpiece Pressplates (Power Play)-150
Masterpiece Pressplates (Power Play)-150
Masterpiece Pressplates (Rookie Update)-118
Masterpiece Pressplates SPA Autos-148
Masterpiece Pressplates (SP Game Used)-116
Masterpiece Pressplates SPx Autos-155
Masterpiece Pressplates (Trilogy)-183
Masterpiece Pressplates Ult Coll Autos-110
Masterpiece Pressplates Autographs-131
Platinum Rookies-131
05UD Artifacts-232
Gold-RED32
05UD PowerPlay-150
05UD Rookie Class-20
05Ultimate Collection-110
Autographed Patches-110
Autographed Shields-110
Ultimate Debut Threads Jerseys-DTJRB
Ultimate Debut Threads Jerseys Autos-DAJRB
Ultimate Debut Threads Patches-DTPRB
Ultimate Debut Threads Patches Autos-DAPRB
05Ultra-210
Gold-210
Ice-210
Rookie Uniformity Jerseys-RU-RB
Rookie Uniformity Jersey Autographs-ARU-RB
Rookie Uniformity Patches-RUP-RB
Rookie Uniformity Patch Autographs-ARP-RB
05Upper Deck-221
HG Glossy-221
Rookie Ink-RIRB
Rookie Threads-RTRB
Rookie Threads Autographs-ARTRB
05Upper Deck Ice-174
Premieres Auto Patches-AIPRB
05Upper Deck MVP-397
Gold-397
Platinum-397
05Upper Deck Rookie Update-118
05Upper Deck Trilogy-183
05Upper Deck Toronto Fall Expo-221
05ITG Heroes and Prospects-60
Autographs-A-RBQ
06Beehive Signature Scrapbook-SSRB
06Black Diamond Gemography-GRB
06Blackhawks Postcards-11
06Fleer-47
Tiffany-47
06O-Pee-Chee-114
Rainbow-114
06Ultra-46
Gold Medallion-46
Ice Medallion-46
06Upper Deck-46
Exclusives Parallel-46
High Gloss Parallel-46
Masterpieces-46
Signature Sensations-SSRB
06Upper Deck MVP-64
Gold Script-64
Super Script-64
Autographs-OABK

Bourque-Leblanc, Adam

05Baie-Comeau Drakkar-13

Bourquin, Eric

93Swiss HNL-241
95Swiss HNL-370
96Swiss HNL-229
01Swiss HNL-404

Bourret, Alex

03Lewiston Maineiacs-4
04ITG Heroes and Prospects-207
04ITG Heroes/Prospects Toronto Expo '05-207
05ITG Heroes/Prosp Toronto Expo Parallel -145
05Extreme Top Prospects Signature Edition-S2
05Shawinigan Cataractes-3
05ITG Heroes and Prospects-145
Autographs-A-AB
06ITG Heroes and Prospects-109
Autographs-AAB
National Pride-NP04
National Pride Gold-NP04

Bourret, Dominic

93Quebec Pee-Wee Tournament-403

Bousek, Ladislav

99Czech Score Blue 2000-28
99Czech Score Red Ice 2000-28

Bouskill, David

98Muskegon Fury-13
99Topeka Scarecrows-12

Bousquet, Dany

99ECHL All-Star Southern Conference-5
03German DEL-47
04German DEL-185
All-Stars-AS14

Bousquet, Jarrett

89Kamloops Blazers-3
907th Inn. Sketch WHL-285
907th Inn. Sketch Memorial Cup-14
917th Inn. Sketch WHL-80

Boutet, Steve

93Quebec Pee-Wee Tournament-347

Boutette, Pat

75Maple Leafs Postcards-4
76Maple Leafs Postcards-3
76O-Pee-Chee NHL-367
77Maple Leafs Postcards-1
77O-Pee-Chee NHL-284
78Maple Leafs Postcards-3
78Maple Leafs Postcards-4
78O-Pee-Chee-374
79Maple Leafs Postcards-4
79O-Pee-Chee-319
80O-Pee-Chee-14
80Topps-14
81O-Pee-Chee-255
81Topps-E81
82O-Pee-Chee-263
82O-Pee-Chee Stickers-148
82Post Cereal-15
82Topps Stickers-148
83NHL Key Tags-103
83O-Pee-Chee-276
83O-Pee-Chee Stickers-233
83Penguins Coke-1
83Penguins Heinz Photos-2
83Topps Stickers-233
84O-Pee-Chee-171
84Penguins Heinz Photos-1

Bouthillette, Gabriel

03Gatineau Olympiques-1

Boutilier, Paul

85Islanders News-17

Boutin, Alexandre

93Quebec Pee-Wee Tournament-1137

Boutin, Frederic

93Quebec Pee-Wee Tournament-56

Boutin, J.F.

93Sherbrooke Faucons-9
97Wheeling Nailers-1
97Wheeling Nailers Photo Pack-1
98Peoria Rivermen-9
99Peoria Rivermen-15
00Peoria Rivermen-4
01Johnstown Chiefs-14
02Johnstown Chiefs-3
03Elmira Jackals-3
04German Weiden Blue Devils-3

Boutin, Jonathan

01Halifax Mooseheads-2
01Shawinigan Cataractes-19
02Halifax Mooseheads-3
02Shawinigan Cataractes-17
03P.E.I. Rocket-3
03Shawinigan Cataractes-4
04P.E.I. Rocket-10
04Quebec Remparts-21
04ITG Heroes and Prospects-213
04ITG Heroes/Prospects Toronto Expo '05-213
05Johnstown Chiefs-3
05ITG Heroes and Prospects Net Prospects-NP-19
05ITG Heroes and Prosp Net Prospects Gold-NP-19
06Between The Pipes Prospect Trios-PT12
06Between The Pipes Prospect Trios-PT19
06Between The Pipes Prospect Trios Gold-PT12
06Between The Pipes Prospect Trios Gold-PT19
06Springfield Falcons-20

Boutin, Pascal

06PEI Rocket-10

Boutin, Rollie

82Birmingham South Stars-4

Boutlier, Kevin

06Chilliwack Bruins-3

Bouvier, Joey

96Regina Pats-21
97Regina Pats-16

Bouvrette, Lionel

43Parade Sportive *-12
43Parade Sportive *-13

Bowmeester, Jay

96Quebec Pee-Wee Tournament-720
99Medicine Hat Tigers-3
99UD Prospects-50
99UD Prospects-74
CHL Class-C5
Destination the Show-DS10
Signatures of Tradition-JB
00Medicine Hat Tigers-1
00UD CHL Prospects-56
00UD CHL Prospects-100
Autographs-A-JB
CHL Class-CC4
Destination the Show-D4
Game Jersey Autographs-S-JB
Game Jerseys-JB
Game Jerseys-S-B
Great Desire-GD2
Supremacy-CS9
01SPx Rookie Redemption-R13
01UD Prospects Autographs-A-JB
02Atomic-111
Blue-111
Gold-111
Red-111
Hobby Parallel-111
02BAP All-Star Edition-142
Gold-142
Silver-142
02BAP First Edition-438R
02BAP Memorabilia-274
Emerald-274
Ruby-274
Sapphire-274
Draft Redemptions-3

Future of the Game-FG-22
NHL All-Star Game-274
NHL All-Star Game Blue-274
NHL All-Star Game Green-274
NHL All-Star Game Red-274
02BAP Memorabilia Toronto Fall Expo-274
02BAP Signature Series-191
All-Rookie-AR2
Autographs-191
Autographs Gold-191
Jerseys-SGJ55
Jersey Autographs-SGJ55
Team Quads-TQ5
02BAP Ultimate Memorabilia-4
Autographs-6
Autographs Gold-6
Calder Candidates-11
Jerseys-14
Jersey and Stick-12
Nameplates-5
02Bowman YoungStars-133
Gold-133
Silver-133
Autographs-JB
Jerseys-JB
Patches-JB
Double Stuff-JB
Triple Stuff-JB
Rivals-RNJB
Rivals Patches-3
Sticks-JB
02Crown Royale-115
Blue-115
Purple-115
Red-115
Retail-115
Rookie Royalty-11
02eTopps-43
02ITG Used-84
Calder Jerseys-C3
Calder Jerseys Gold-C3
Emblems-E39
02O-Pee-Chee-336
02O-Pee-Chee Premier Blue Parallel-336
02O-Pee-Chee Premier Red Parallel-336
02O-Pee-Chee Factory Set-336
02Pacific-407
02Pacific Calder-119
Silver-119
Reflections-11
02Pacific Complete-568
Red-568
02Pacific Exclusive-198
Blue-198
Gold-198
02Pacific Heads-Up-134
02Pacific Quest for the Cup-120
Gold-120
Calder Contenders-9
02Parkhurst-204
Bronze-204
Gold-204
Silver-204
Hardware-C4
Heroes-NH10
Jerseys-GJ51
02Parkhurst Retro-204
Minis-204
Hopefuls-CH8
Jerseys-RJ12
Memorabilia-RM26
02Private Stock Reserve-163
Blue-163
Red-163
Retail-163
Class Act-8
Moments in Time-3
02SP Authentic-187
Sign of the Times-JB
Sign of the Times-BB
Sign of the Times-SZB
Signed Patches-PJB
02SP Game Used-78
02SPx-150
02Stadium Club-128
Silver Decoy Cards-128
Proofs-128
02Titanium-116
Blue-116
Red-116
Retail-116
Right on Target-9
02Topps-336
OPC Blue Parallel-336
OPC Red Parallel-336
Factory Set-336
02Topps Chrome-177
Black Border Refractors-177
Refractors-177
02Topps Heritage-138
02Topps Total-420
02UD Artistic Impressions-94
Gold-94
Common Ground-CG4
Common Ground-CG7
Common Ground Gold-CG4
Common Ground Gold-CG7
Retrospectives-R93
Retrospectives Gold-R93
Retrospectives Signed-R93
Retrospectives Silver-R93
02UD Foundations-153
02UD Honor Roll-153
Signature Class-JB
02UD Mask Collection-172
02UD Piece of History-132
02UD Premier Collection-82
Gold-82
Signatures Bronze-SBW
Signatures Bronze-SJB
Signatures Gold-SBW
Signatures Gold-SJB
Signatures Silver-SBW
Signatures Silver-SJB
02UD Top Shelf-93
02Upper Deck-236
Exclusives-236
02Upper Deck Classic Portraits-116
02Upper Deck Rookie Update-118
Autographs-JB
02Vanguard-115
LTD-115
Prime Prospects-11
02UD SuperStars *-269
Gold-269
03BAP Memorabilia-37
Emerald-37
Gold-37
Ruby-37
Sapphire-37
Jerseys-GJ-19
03BAP Ultimate Memorabilia Autographs-52
Gold-52
03BAP Ultimate Mem Auto Jerseys-52
03BAP Ultimate Mem Franch Present Future-13
03BAP Ultimate Memorabilia Triple Threads-10
03Beehive-84
Gold-84
Silver-84
03Black Diamond-20
Black-20
Green-20
Red-20
Threads-DT-JB
Threads Green-DT-JB
Threads Red-DT-JB
Threads Black-DT-JB
03Bowman-75
Gold-75
Future Fabrics-FF-JB
Future Fabric Patches-JB
03Bowman Chrome-75
Refractors-75
Gold Refractors-75
Xfractors-75
03Crown Royale-43
Blue-43
Retail-43
Jerseys-11
Patches-11
Lords of the Rink-13
03ITG Action-264
Jerseys-M154
03ITG Toronto Fall Expo Jerseys-FE3
03ITG Used Signature Series-57
Gold-57
Autographs-JBO
Autographs Gold-JBO
Teammates-11
Teammates Gold-11
03ITG VIP International Experience-2
03ITG VIP Jerseys-15
03ITG VIP Making the Bigs-1
03ITG VIP Sophomores-2
03McDonald's Pacific-24
Canadian Pride-4
03NHL Sticker Collection-49
03O-Pee-Chee-278
03OPC Blue-278
03OPC Gold-278
03OPC Red-278
03Pacific-141
Blue-141
Red-141
03Pacific Atlantic City National-4
03Pacific Calder Contenders Entry Draft-9
03Pacific Calder-45
Silver-45
03Pacific Calder Collection NHL All-Star Block Party Gold-6
03Pacific Complete-223
Red-223
03Pacific Exhibit-62
Blue Backs-62
Yellow Backs-62
Pursuing Prominence-7
03Pacific Heads-Up-43
Hobby LTD-43
Retail LTD-43
In Focus-8
In Focus LTD-8
Jerseys-12
03Pacific Invincible-41
Blue-41
Red-41
Retail-41
New Sensations-13
03Pacific Luxury Suite-36A
03Pacific Luxury Suite-36B
03Pacific Montreal Olympic Stadium Show-5
Gold-5
03Pacific Prism-43
Blue-43
Gold-43
Red-43
Paramount Prodigies-11
Rookie Revolution-8
03Pacific Quest for the Cup-45
Blue-45
03Pacific Supreme-41
Blue-41
Red-41
Retail-41
03Pacific Toronto Spring Expo-5
Gold-5
03Panthers Team Issue-2
03Parkhurst Rookie Road to the NHL-RNJ-5
03Parkhurst Rookie Road to the NHL Gold-RTN-5
03Parkhurst Rookie Road to the NHL Emblem-RTNE-5
03Parkhurst Rookie Road NHL Emblem Gold-RTNE-5
03Parkhurst Rookie Teammates Gold-RT6
03Parkhurst Rookie Teammates-RT6
03Private Stock Reserve-40
Blue-40
Red-40
Retail-40
Rising Stock-8
03SP Authentic-36
Limited-36
03SP Game Used Authentic Fabrics-DFBL
03SP Game Used Authentic Fabrics Gold-DFBL
03SP Game Used Double Threads-DTBL
03SP Game Used Limited Threads-LTJB
03SP Game Used Limited Threads Gold-LTJB
03SPx-42
03SPx-162
Radiance-42
Radiance-162
Spectrum-42
Spectrum-162
Big Futures-BF-JB
Big Futures Limited-BF-JB
Winning Materials-WM-JB
Winning Materials Limited-WM-JB
03Titanium-156
Hobby Jersey Number Parallels-156
Patches-156
Retail-156
Right on Target-7
03Topps-278
Blue-278
Gold-278
Red-278
First Round Fabrics-JB
First Round Fabrics-JSJB
03Topps All-Star Block Party-6
03Topps C55-44
Minis-44
Minis American Back-44
Minis American Back Red-44
Minis Bazooka Back-44
Minis Brooklyn Back-44
Minis Hat Trick Back-44
Minis O Canada Back-44
Minis O Canada Back Red-44
Minis Stanley Cup Back-44
Relics-TRJB
03Topps Pristine Popular Demand Relics-PD-JB
03Topps Pristine Popular Demand Relic Ref-PD-JB
03Topps Traded Future Phenoms-FP-JB
03UD Honor Roll-33
03UD Honor Roll-100
03Upper Deck-84
All-Star Class-AS-12
Canadian Exclusives-84
HG-84
Shooting Stars-ST-JB
03Upper Deck All-Star Promos-S5
03Upper Deck All-Star Promos-AS14
03Upper Deck Classic Portraits-41
Classic Colors-CC-JB
Hockey Royalty-PLB
03Upper Deck Ice-39
Gold-39
03Upper Deck MVP-183
Gold Script-183
Silver Script-183
Canadian Exclusives-183
03Upper Deck Rookie Update-38
Super Stars-SSJB
Top Draws-TD18
03Upper Deck Trilogy-41
Limited-41
Scripts-S1JB
Scripts Limited-S1JB
Scripts Red-S1JB
03Upper Deck Victory-81
Bronze-81
Gold-81
Silver-81
Freshman Flashback-FF22
03Toronto Star-39
04Pacific-109
Blue-109
Red-109
04SP Authentic Buybacks-78
04SP Authentic Buybacks-79
04SP Authentic Buybacks-80
04SP Authentic Buybacks-81
04SP Authentic Octographs-OS-ROK
04SP Authentic Rookie Review-RR-JB
04SP Authentic Sign of the Times-ST-JB
04SP Authentic Sign of the Times-QS-BPBP
04SP Authentic Sign of the Times-SS-DEE
04UD Toronto Fall Expo Pride of Canada-4
04Ultimate Collection Buybacks-27
04Ultimate Collection Buybacks-28
04Ultimate Collection Patch Autographs-UPA-JB
04Ultimate Collection Patch Autographs-UPA-RBJB
04Ultimate Collection Signatures-US-JB
04Ultimate Collection Signature Patches-SP-JB
04Upper Deck-77
Canadian Exclusives-77
HG Glossy Gold-77
HG Glossy Silver-77
World Cup Tribute-JB
World Cup Tribute-JBAF
04AHL All-Stars-7
04AHL Top Prospects-48
04San Antonio Rampage-4
04ITG Heroes and Prospects-194
Autographs-U-JBW
04ITG Heroes/Prospects Toronto Expo '05-194
05ITG Heroes/Prosp Toronto Expo Parallel -72
05Be A Player-40
First Period-40
Second Period-40
Third Period-40
Overtime-40
Dual Signatures-RJ
Quad Signatures-GDEF
Signatures-JB
Signatures Gold-JB
Triple Signatures-PAN
05Beehive-39
Matte-39
Matted Materials-MMJB
Signature Scrapbook-SSJB
05McDonalds Upper Deck-1
05Panini Stickers-59
05Parkhurst-206
05Parkhurst-582
Facsimile Auto Parallel-206
Facsimile Auto Parallel-582
True Colors-TCFLA
True Colors-TCFLA
True Colors-TCFLTB
True Colors-TCFLTB
05SP Authentic Prestigious Pairings-PPHB
05SP Authentic Scripts to Success-SSJB
05SP Authentic Sign of the Times-BW
05SP Game Used Authentic Fabrics-AF-JB
05SP Game Used Authentic Fabrics Autos-AAF-JB
05SP Game Used Authentic Fabrics Gold-AF-JB
05SP Game Used Authentic Fabrics Quad-HLBJ
05SP Game Used Authentic Fabrics Quad-NSZB
05SP Game Used Authentic Patches Quad -HLBJ
05SP Game Used Authentic Patches Quad -NSZB
05SP Game Used Authentic Patches-AP-JB
05SP Game Used Authentic Patch Autos-AAP-JB
05SP Game Used Awesome Authentics-AA-JB
05SP Game Used Awesome Authentics Gold-DA-JB
05SP Game Used SIGnificance-JB
05SP Game Used SIGnificance Gold-S-JB
05SP Game Used Statscriptions-ST-JB
05SPx Winning Combos-WC-BH
05SPx Winning Combos-WC-FL
05SPx Winning Combos Autographs-AWC-BL
05SPx Winning Combos Gold-WC-BH
05SPx Winning Combos Gold-WC-FL
05SPx Winning Combos Spectrum-WC-BH
05SPx Winning Combos Spectrum-WC-FL
05The Cup NHL Shields-DSLB
05The Cup Emblems of Endorsement-EEBO
05The Cup Master Pressplate Rookie Update-196
05The Cup Noble Numbers-NNBB
05UD Artifacts Auto Facts-AF-JB
05UD Artifacts Auto Facts Blue-AF-JB
05UD Artifacts Auto Facts Copper-AF-JB
05UD Artifacts Auto Facts Pewter-AF-JB
05UD Artifacts Auto Facts Silver-AF-JB
05UD Artifacts Frozen Artifacts-FA-BO
05UD Artifacts Frozen Artifacts Autos-FA-BO
05UD Artifacts Frozen Artifacts Copper-FA-BO
05UD Artifacts Frozen Artifacts Dual-FAD-BO
05UD Artifact Frozen Artifact Dual Auto-FAD-BO
05UD Artifact Frozen Artifact Dual Copper-FAD-BO
05UD Artifact Frozen Artifacts Dual Gold-FAD-BO
05UD Artifact Frozen Artifact Dual Maroon-FAD-BO
05UD Artifact Frozen Artifact Dual Pewter-FAD-BO
05UD Artifact Frozen Artifact Dual Silver-FAD-BO
05UD Artifacts Frozen Artifacts Gold-FA-BO
05UD Artifacts Frozen Artifacts Maroon-FA-BO
05UD Artifacts Frozen Artifacts Patches-FP-BO
05UD Artifact Frozen Artifact Patch Autos-FP-BO
05UD Artifact Frozen Artifact Patch Dual-FPD-BO
05UD Artifacts Frozen Art Patch Dual Auto-FPD-BO
05UD Artifacts Frozen Art Patch Pewter-FP-BO
05UD Artifacts Frozen Art Patch Silver-FP-BO
05UD Artifacts Frozen Artifacts Pewter-FA-BO
05UD Artifacts Frozen Artifacts Silver-FA-BO
05UD Artifacts Remarkable Artifacts-RA-JB
05UD Artifacts Remarkable Artifacts Dual-RA-JB
05Ultimate Coll National Heroes Jersey-NHJJB
05Ultimate Coll National Heroes Patch-NHPJB
05Ultra-90
Gold-90
Fresh Ink-FI-JB
Fresh Ink Blue-FI-JB
Ice-90
05Upper Deck-83
Big Playmakers-B-JBL
HG Glossy-83
Jerseys-J-JAB
Jerseys Series II-J2JB
Majestic Materials-MMJB
NHL Generations-DBB
Notable Numbers-N-JB
Patches-P-JBO
05Upper Deck Ice-42
Rainbow-42
Cool Threads-CTJB
Cool Threads Autographs-ACTJB
Cool Threads Glass-CTJB
Cool Threads Patches-CTPJB
Cool Threads Patch Autographs-CAPJB
Fresh Ice-FIJB
Fresh Ice Glass-FIJB
Fresh Ice Glass Patches-FIPJB
Glacial Graphs-GGJB
Glacial Graphs Labels-GGJB
05Upper Deck MVP-166
Gold-166
Platinum-166
05Upper Deck Rookie Update-196
Inspirations Patch Rookies-196
05Upper Deck Trilogy Honorary Patches-HP-JB
05Upper Deck Tril Honorary Patch Script-HSP-JB
05Upper Deck Trilogy Honorary Swatches-HS-JB
05Upper Deck Tril Honorary Swatch Scripts-HSS-JB
05Upper Deck Trilogy Scripts-SFS-JB
05Upper Deck Toronto Fall Expo-83
05Upper Deck Victory-89
Black-89
Gold-89
Silver-89
05ITG Heroes and Prospects-72
Autographs-A-JBO
Autographs-DA-BL
Complete Jerseys-CJ-32
Complete Jerseys Gold-CJ-32
He Shoots-He Scores Prizes-9
He Shoots-He Scores Prizes-28
Jerseys-GUJ-3
Jerseys Gold-GUJ-03
Emblems-GUE-3
Emblems Gold-GUE-03
Numbers-GUN-3
Numbers Gold-GUN-03
Nameplates-N-29
Nameplates Gold-N-29
National Pride-NPR-5
Spectrum-STM-08
Spectrum Gold-STM-08
06Be A Player-158
Autographs-158
Profiles-PP22
Profiles Autographs-PP22
Signatures-JB
Signatures 10-173
Signatures Duals-DVB
Signatures Trios-TJBM
Signatures Foursomes-FNBRB
Portraits Dual Signature Portraits-DSJB
Portraits Signature Portraits-SPJB
06Beehive Matted Materials-MMJB
06Black Diamond-105
Black-105
Gold-105
Ruby-105
Jerseys-JJB
Jerseys Black-JJB
Jerseys Gold-JJB
Jerseys Ruby-JJB
Jerseys Black Autographs -JJB
06Flair Showcase Stitches-SSJB
06Fleer-85
Tiffany-85
Fabricology-FBO
Speed Machines-SM13
06Hot Prospects Hot Materials -HMJB
06Hot Prospects Hot Materials Red Hot-HMJB
06Hot Prospects Hot Materials White Hot-HMJB
06ITG International Ice Complete Jersey-CJ05
06ITG International Ice Complete Jersey Gold-CJ05
06ITG International Ice Emblems-GUE10
06ITG International Ice Emblems Gold-GUE10
06ITG International Ice Jerseys-GUJ10
06ITG International Ice Jerseys Gold-GUJ10
06ITG International Ice My Country My Team-MC12
06ITG International Ice My Country My Team Gold-MC12
06ITG International Ice Numbers-GUN10
06ITG International Ice Numbers Gold-GUN10
06McDonald's Upper Deck-20
06O-Pee-Chee-207
Rainbow-207
Swatches-S-JB
06Panini Stickers-59
06SP Authentic-122
Limited-122
06SP Game Used-43
Gold-43
Rainbow-43
Authentic Fabrics-AFJB
Authentic Fabrics Parallel-AFJB
Authentic Fabrics Patches-AFJB
Authentic Fabrics Dual-AF2BH
Authentic Fabrics Dual Patches-AF2BH
Authentic Fabrics Triple-AF3FLA
Authentic Fabrics Triple Patches-AF3FLA
Autographs-43
Inked Sweaters Dual-IS2OJ
Inked Sweaters Dual Patches-IS2OJ
SIGnificance-SJB
06SPx-45
Spectrum-45
SPxcitement-X42
SPxcitement Spectrum-X42
SPxcitement Autographs-X42
Winning Materials-WMJB
Winning Materials Spectrum-WMJB
Winning Materials Autographs-WMJB
06The Cup NHL Shields Duals-DSHBN
06UD Artifacts Auto-Facts-AFBO
06UD Artifacts Auto-Facts Gold-AFBO
06UD Artifacts Frozen Artifacts-FAJB
06UD Artifacts Frozen Artifacts Black-FAJB
06UD Artifacts Frozen Artifacts Blue-FAJB
06UD Artifacts Frozen Artifacts Gold-FAJB
06UD Artifacts Frozen Artifacts Platinum-FAJB
06UD Artifacts Frozen Artifacts Red-FAJB
06UD Artifacts Frozen Artifacts Autographed Black-FAJB
06UD Artifacts Frozen Artifacts Patches Black-FAJB
06UD Artifacts Frozen Artifacts Patches Blue-FAJB
06UD Artifacts Frozen Artifacts Patches Gold-FAJB
06UD Artifacts Frozen Artifacts Patches Platinum-FAJB
06UD Artifacts Frozen Artifacts Patches Red-FAJB
06UD Artifacts Frozen Artifacts Patches Autographed Black Tag Parallel-FAJB
06UD Artifacts Tundra Tandems-TTEJ
06UD Artifacts Tundra Tandems Black-TTEJ
06UD Artifacts Tundra Tandems Blue-TTEJ
06UD Artifacts Tundra Tandems Gold-TTEJ
06UD Artifacts Tundra Tandems Platinum-TTEJ
06UD Artifacts Tundra Tandems Red-TTEJ
06UD Artifacts Tundra Tandems Dual Patches Red-TTEJ
06UD Powerplay-45
Impact Rainbow-45
06UD Toronto Fall Expo Priority Signings -PSBO
06Ultimate Collection Premium Patches-PS-JB
06Ultimate Collection Premium Swatches-PS-JB
06Ultra-87
Gold Medallion-87
Ice Medallion-87
Fresh Ink-IJB
06Upper Deck Arena Giveaways-FLA1
06Upper Deck-83
Exclusives Parallel-83
High Gloss Parallel-83
Game Jerseys-JJB
Game Patches-PJB
Generations Duals-G2NB
Generations Patches Dual-G2PNB
Masterpieces-83
Signatures-SBO
Signature Sensations-SSBO
Walmart Tins Oversize-83
06Upper Deck MVP-130
Gold Script-130
Super Script-130
Jerseys-OJBJ
06Upper Deck Ovation-72
06Upper Deck Trilogy Honorary Scripted Patches-HSPJB
06Upper Deck Trilogy Honorary Scripted Swatches-HSSJB
06Upper Deck Victory-86
06Upper Deck Victory Black-86
06Upper Deck Victory Gold-86
06ITG Heroes and Prospects Complete AHL Logos-AHL08
06ITG Heroes and Prospects Jerseys-GUJ60
06ITG Heroes and Prospects Jerseys Gold-GUJ60
06ITG Heroes and Prospects Emblems-GUE60
06ITG Heroes and Prospects Emblems Gold-GUE60
06ITG Heroes and Prospects Numbers-GUN60
06ITG Heroes and Prospects Numbers Gold-GUN60
07Upper Deck Ovation-27
07Upper Deck Victory-88
Black-88
Gold-88
Stars on Ice-SI21

Bowen, Chris
98Topeka Scarecrows-9

Bowen, Curtis
907th Inn. Sketch OHL-78
917th Inn. Sketch OHL-305
92Ottawa 67's-2
92Classic-12
Gold-12
LPs-LP8
92Classic Four-Sport *-161
Gold-161
Autographs-158A
93Donruss Team Canada-6
93Flyers Lineup Sheets-40
93Pinnacle-468
Canadian-468
93Upper Deck-547
93Classic-16
93Classic Four-Sport *-256
Gold-256
94Classic-26
Gold-26
Tri-Cards-T19
95Adirondack Red Wings-2
96Collector's Edge Ice-1
Prism-1
00UK Sekonda Superleague-91
01UK Belfast Giants-12
03UK Belfast Giants-2
05UK Nottingham Panthers-10

Bowen, Eric
00Kootenay Ice-5

Bowen, Jason
907th Inn. Sketch WHL-97
917th Inn. Sketch WHL-288
92Classic-9
Gold-9
92Classic Four-Sport *-158
Gold-158
93Donruss-241
93Flyers J.C. Penney-3
93Flyers Lineup Sheets-3
93Parkhurst-418
Emerald Ice-418
93Pinnacle-215
Canadian-215
93PowerPlay-404
93Score-471
Canadian-471
93Ultra-35
93Upper Deck-240
94Donruss-32
94Leaf-248
94OPC Premier-234
Special Effects-234
94Pinnacle-111
Artist's Proofs-111
Rink Collection-111
94Topps/OPC Premier-234
Special Effects-234
94Ultra-154
00UK Sekonda Superleague-172
01UK Belfast Giants-17
02UK Guildford Flames-10
03UK Belfast Giants-3

Bower, Johnny
44Beehive Group II Photos-299
44Beehive Group II Photos-384
51Cleveland Barons-11
54Parkhurst-65
58Parkhurst-46
59Parkhurst-25
59Parkhurst-32
60Parkhurst-3
60Shirriff Coins-1
60York Photos-6
61Parkhurst-3
61Shirriff/Salada Coins-41
61York Yellow Backs-8
62Parkhurst-16
62Shirriff Coins-1
62York Iron-On Transfers-1
63Chex Photos-8
63Parkhurst-5
63Parkhurst-65
63Toronto Star-6
63York White Backs-2
64Beehive Group III Photos-154A
64Beehive Group III Photos-154B
64Coca-Cola Caps-91
64Topps-40
65Coca-Cola-91
65Coca-Cola Booklets-A
65Maple Leafs White Border-3
65Topps-77
66Maple Leafs Hockey Talks-2
66Topps-12
66Topps USA Test-12
67Post Flip Books-1
67Post Flip Books-2
67Topps-76
67York Action Octagons-16
67York Action Octagons-23
67York Action Octagons-25
67York Action Octagons-26
67York Action Octagons-27
67York Action Octagons-29
67York Action Octagons-30
67York Action Octagons-34
67York Action Octagons-36
68Maple Leafs White Border-1
68O-Pee-Chee-122
Puck Stickers-17
68Post Marbles-3
68Shirriff Coins-164
68Topps-122
69Maple Leafs White Border Glossy-2
69O-Pee-Chee-187
73Maple Leafs Postcards-1
80Maple Leafs Postcards-5
83Hall of Fame-211
83Hall of Fame Postcards-O5
85Hall of Fame-211
85Maple Leafs Postcards-4
85Maple Leafs Postcards-35
88Esso All-Stars-4
91Ultimate Original Six-32
91Ultimate Original Six-80
French-32
French-80
92Hall of Fame Legends-23
92Parkhurst Parkie Reprints-PR3
92Zeller's Masters of Hockey-1
92Zeller's Masters of Hockey Signed-1
93High Liner Greatest Goalies-9
93Parkhurst Parkie Reprints Case Inserts-8
94Parkhurst Missing Link-103
94Parkhurst Tall Boys-129
95Parkhurst '66-67-119
Coins-119
97Beehive-57
Golden Portraits-57
Golden Originals Autographs-57
99BAP Memorabilia AS Canadian Hobby-CH5
99BAP Memorabilia AS Cdn Hobby Autos-CH5
99Topps Premier Plus Club Signings-CS4
99Topps Premier Plus Club Signings-CSC2
00BAP Memorabilia Goalie Memorabilia-G13
00BAP Memorabilia Goalie Memorabilia-G19
00BAP Memorabilia Goalie Memorabilia-G24
00BAP Memorabilia Goalie Memorabilia-G29
00BAP Sig Ser Goalie Memorabilia Autos-GLS4
00BAP Ultimate Mem Goalie Memorabilia-GM6
00BAP Ultimate Mem Goalie Memorabilia-GM19
00BAP Ultimate Mem Goalie Mem Autos-UG4
01BAP Memorabilia Goalie Traditions-GT2
01BAP Memorabilia Goalie Traditions-GT20
01BAP Memorabilia Goalie Traditions-GT21
01BAP Memorabilia Goalie Traditions-GT37
01BAP Signature Series Vintage Autographs-VA-10
01BAP Ultimate Mem All-Star History-15
01BAP Ultimate Memorabilia Cornerstones-1
01BAP Ultimate Memorabilia Decades-9
01BAP Ultimate Mem Retro Teammates-8
01BAP Ultimate Mem Stanley Cup Winners-8
01BAP Update Rocket's Rivals-RR-3
01Between the Pipes-123
01Between the Pipes-149
Vintage Memorabilia-VM12
01Greats of the Game-14
Autographs-14
01Parkhurst Autographs-PA24
01Parkhurst Reprints-PR26
01Parkhurst Reprints-PR55
01Parkhurst Reprints-PR91
01Parkhurst Reprints-PR125
01Parkhurst Reprints-PR139
01Parkhurst Reprints-PR148
01Parkhurst Vintage Memorabilia-PV30
01Topps Archives-52
02BAP Memorabilia Mini Stanley Cups-1
02BAP NHL All-Star History-15
02BAP Ultimate Memorabilia Cup Duels-3
02BAP Ultimate Memorabilia Cup Duels-5
02BAP Ultimate Mem Retro Teammates-8
02Between the Pipes Goalie Autographs-26
02Between the Pipes Record Breakers-13
02Between the Pipes Vintage Memorabilia-1
02ITG Used Vintage Memorabilia-VM15
02ITG Used Vintage Memorabilia Gold-VM15
02Maple Leafs Platinum Collection-44
02Parkhurst Retro Nicknames-RN8
02Topps Heritage Reprint Autographs-JB
02Topps Heritage Reprint Relics-JB
02Topps Heritage Reprints-JB
03BAP Ultimate Memorabilia Autographs-165
Gold-165
03BAP Ultimate Mem Auto Jerseys-165
03BAP Ultimate Mem Auto Sticks-165
03BAP Ultimate Memorabilia Cornerstones-4
03BAP Ultimate Memorabilia Emblem Attic-2
03BAP Ultimate Mem Emblem Attic Gold-2
03BAP Ultimate Mem Jersey and Stick-22
03BAP Ultimate Mem Jersey and Stick Gold-22
03BAP Ultimate Mem Raised to the Rafters-5
03BAP Ultimate Mem Retro-Active Trophies-16
03BAP Ultimate Memorabilia Triple Threads-7
03BAP Ultimate Mem Vint Complete Jersey-3
03BAP Ultimate Mem Vint Comp Jersey Gold-3
03BAP Ultimate Mem Vintage Jerseys-7
03BAP Ultimate Mem Vintage Jerseys Gold-7
03ITG Toronto Fall Expo Forever Rivals-FR7
03ITG Used Signature Series-114B
03Pacific Exhibit-221
03Parkhurst Orig Six New York Mem-NM38
03Parkhurst Original Six Toronto-56
03Parkhurst Original Six Toronto-82
Autographs-2
Inserts-T14
Memorabilia-TM20
Memorabilia-TM34
Memorabilia-TM37
03Parkhurst Rookie Before the Mask-BTM-5
03Parkhurst Rookie Before the Mask Gold-BTM-5
04Canada Post-25
04Canada Post Autographs-1
04ITG NHL AS FANtasy AS History Jerseys-SB15
04ITG Franchises Canadian-94
Autographs-JB
Double Memorabilia-DM3
Double Memorabilia Autographs-DM3
Double Memorabilia Gold-DM3
Forever Rivals-FR1
Forever Rivals Gold-FR1
Goalie Gear-GG2
Goalie Gear Autographs-GG2
Goalie Gear Gold-GG2
Triple Memorabilia-TM9
Triple Memorabilia Autographs-TM9
Triple Memorabilia Gold-TM9
04ITG Franchises He Shoots/Scores Prizes-14
04ITG Franchises Update-484
04ITG Ultimate Memorabilia-192
Gold-192
Auto Threads-28
Autographs-48
Autographs Gold-48
Complete Jerseys-3
Complete Package-14
Day In History-50
Day In History Gold-50
Emblem Attic-6
Emblem Attic Gold-6
Goalie Gear-18
Jersey Autographs-28
Jersey Autographs Gold-28
Jersey and Sticks-18
Jersey and Sticks Gold-18
Nicknames-13
Nickname Autographs-13
Original Six-1
Raised to the Rafters-4
Stick Autographs-19
Stick Autographs Gold-19
Triple Threads-3
04UD Legendary Signatures-49
AKA Autographs-AKA-BO
Autographs-BO
HOF Inks-HOF-BO
04UD Legends Classics-32
04UD Legends Classics-78
Gold-32
Gold-78
Platinum-32
Platinum-78
Silver-32
Silver-78
Jersey Redemptions-JY11
Signature Moments-M25
Signatures-CS25
Signatures-DC21
Signatures-TC2
04ITG Heroes and Prospects-138
Autographs-JBO
Hero Memorabilia-10
04ITG Heroes/Prospects Toronto Expo '05-138
04ITG Heroes/Prospects Expo Heroes/Pros-138
05ITG Heroes/Prosp Toronto Expo Parallel -10
05Between the Pipes-1
Autographs-A-JB
Jersey and Sticks-SJ-5
Signed Memorabilia-SM-5
05ITG Ultimate Memorabilia Level 1-57
05ITG Ultimate Memorabilia Level 2-57
05ITG Ultimate Memorabilia Level 3-57
05ITG Ultimate Memorabilia Level 4-57
05ITG Ultimate Memorabilia Level 5-57
05ITG Ultimate Mem Decades Jerseys-8
05ITG Ultimate Mem Decades Jerseys Gold-8
05ITG Ultimate Memorabilia Emblem Attic-9
05ITG Ultimate Mem Emblem Attic Gold-9
05ITG Ultimate Memorabilia Goalie Gear-12
05ITG Ultimate Mem Goalie Gear Gold-12
05ITG Ultimate Mem Pass the Torch Jerseys-7
05ITG Ultimate Mem Passing Torch Jsy Gold-7
05ITG Ultimate Memorabilia Sextuple Autos-1
05ITG Ultimate Mem 3 Star of the Game Jsy-8
05ITG Ult Mem 3 Star of the Game Jsy Gold-8
05ITG Ultimate Mem Triple Threads Jerseys-8
05ITG Ultimate Mem Triple Thread Jsy Gold-8
05SPx Xcitement Legends-XL-BO
05SPx Xcitement Legends Gold-XL-BO
05SPx Xcitement Legends Spectrum-XL-BO
05UD Artifacts-105
Blue-105
Gold-105
Green-105
Pewter-105
Red-105
Gold Autographed-105
05ITG Heroes and Prospects-10
Autographs-A-JBW
He Shoots-He Scores Prizes-60
Hero Memorabilia-HM-40
06Between The Pipes-95
06Between The Pipes-135
Autographs-AJB
Shooting Gallery-SG02
Shooting Gallery-SG09
Shooting Gallery Gold-SG02
Shooting Gallery Gold-SG09
Stick and Jersey-SJ02
Stick and Jersey Gold-SJ02
Stick and Jersey Autographs-SJ02
Stick Work-SW06
Stick Work Gold-SW06
06ITG Ultimate Memorabilia-82
Artist Proof-82
Cornerstones-9
Cornerstones Gold-9
Decades-8
Decades Gold-8
Emblem Attic-11
Emblem Attic Gold-11
Retro Teammates-5
Retro Teammates Gold-5
Ring Leaders-14
Ring Leaders Gold-14
Road to the Cup-3
Road to the Cup Gold-3
Stick Rack-3
Stick Rack Gold-3
Triple Thread Jerseys-10
Triple Thread Jerseys Gold-10
06Parkhurst-21
Autographs-21
06SP Authentic Sign of the Times Duals-STBE
06SP Authentic Sign of the Times Triples-ST3BEK
06The Cup-85
Black Rainbow-85
Gold-85
Gold Patches-85
Masterpiece Pressplates-85
Stanley Cup Signatures-CSJO
Stanley Cup Titlists-TJB
06Ultimate Collection Signatures-US-JO
06Upper Deck All-Time Greatest-ATG28
06Upper Deck Sweet Shot-96
Signature Shots/Saves Sticks-SSSJO
06ITG Heroes and Prospects-21
Autographs-AJBO
Heroes Memorabilia-HM20
Heroes Memorabilia Gold-HM20
07Maple Leafs 1967 Commemorative-2
07Maple Leafs 1967 Commemorative-30
Autographs-AJB1
Autographs-AJB2
Jerseys-JJB

Bowers, Rodney
93Prince Albert Raiders-2
00Amarillo Rattlers-3

Bowers, Ross
04UK Milton Keynes Lightning-18

Bowie, Danny
00QMJHL All-Star Program Inserts-43

Bowie, Russell
83Hall of Fame-48
83Hall of Fame Postcards-D2
85Hall of Fame-48

Bowkus, Jack
84Saskatoon Blades Stickers-1
86Saskatoon Blades Photos-3

Bowler, Bill
917th Inn. Sketch OHL-188
92Windsor Spitfires-9
93Windsor Spitfires-8
94Windsor Spitfires-10
95Las Vegas Thunder-1
98IHL All-Star Western Conference-3
98Manitoba Moose-C2
99Manitoba Moose-7
00Syracuse Crunch-7
01SPx-110
01UD Top Shelf-51
01UD Top Shelf-51B
01Upper Deck-195
Exclusives-195
01Norfolk Admirals-2

Bowles, Scott
03Calgary Hitmen-1
06Owen Sound Attack-22

Bowman, Amber
04Ohio State Buckeyes Women-10
05Ohio State Buckeyes Women-4
06Ohio State Buckeyes Women-18

Bowman, Bill
24Crescent Selkirks-4

Bowman, David
02Windsor Spitfires-9
04Johnstown Chiefs-2

Bowman, Kirk
77O-Pee-Chee NHL-309
78O-Pee-Chee-61
78Topps-61

Bowman, Michael
01UK Hull Thunder-14

Bowman, Ralph
34Beehive Group I Photos-89
35Diamond Matchbooks Tan 1-4

Bowman, Scotty
71Canadiens Postcards-2
72Canadiens Postcards-3
72Dimanche/Derniere Heure *-135
73Canadiens Postcards-3
74Canadiens Postcards-2
74O-Pee-Chee NHL-261
74Topps-261
75Canadiens Postcards-3
76Canadiens Postcards-2
77Canadiens Postcards-2
77Sportscasters-8205
77Finnish Sportscasters-90-2162
78Canadiens Postcards-1
82Sabres Milk Panels-18
91Penguins Coke/Elby's-NNO
91Pro Set HOF Induction-4
92Penguins Coke/Clark-2
93Kraft-30
94Hockey Wit-49
95Arizona Icecats-22
95Arizona Icecats-23
96Collector's Choice-308
96Kraft Upper Deck-40
98Bowman's Best Scotty Bowman's Best-SB11
98Bowman's Best Scotty Bowman's Best-SB11S
98Bowman's Best S.Bowman's Best Refractor-SB11
98Bowman's Best S.Bowmans Best Atomic Ref-SB11
99Russian Fetisov Tribute-41
02Czech Stadion Cup Finals-484
03Beehive Jumbos-17
03Beehive Jumbo Variations-17
03SP Authentic Honors-H7
03SP Authentic Honors-H8
03SP Authentic Honors-H9
03SP Authentic Honors Limited-H7
03SP Authentic Honors Limited-H8
03SP Authentic Honors Limited-H9
03SP Authentic Sign of the Times-SB
03SP Authentic Sign of the Times-BCY
03SP Game Used Authentic Fabrics-DFSG
03SP Game Used Authentic Fabrics-QYBHH
03SP Game Used Authentic Fabrics Gold-DFSG
03SP Game Used Authentic Fabrics Gold-QYBHH
03SP Game Used Limited Threads-LTSB
03SP Game Used Limited Threads Gold-LTSB
03SP Game Used Team Threads-TTLBF
03SPx-105
Radiance-105
Spectrum-105
03UD Premier Collection Legends-PL-SB
03UD Premier Collection Legends Patches-PL-SB
03Upper Deck Trilogy-132
Crest Variations-132
Limited-132
Scripts-S3SB
Scripts-CSSB
Scripts Limited-S3SB
Scripts Red-S3SB

04MasterCard Priceless Moments-9
04SP Authentic Buybacks-176
04SP Authentic Sign of the Times-ST-BO
04SP Authentic Sign of the Times-DS-BC
05Beehive Signature Scrapbook-SSSB
05SPx-124
Spectrum-124
Xcitement Legends-XL-SB
Xcitement Legends Gold-XL-SB
Xcitement Legends Spectrum-XL-SB
05The Cup-41
Gold-41
Black Rainbow-41
Hardware Heroes-HHSB1
Hardware Heroes-HHSB2
Masterpiece Pressplates-41
Stanley Cup Titlists-TSB
05UD Artifacts-106
Blue-106
Gold-106
Green-106
Pewter-106
Red-106
Gold Autographed-106
06ITG Ultimate Memorabilia-127
Artist Proof-127
Bowman Factor Autos-1
Bowman Factor Autos-2
Bowman Factor Autos-3
Bowman Factor Autos-4
Bowman Factor Autos-5
Bowman Factor Autos-6
Bowman Factor Autos-7
Bowman Factor Autos-8
Bowman Factor Autos-9
Bowman Factor Autos-10
Bowman Factor Autos-11
Bowman Factor Autos-12
Bowman Factor Autos-13
Bowman Factor Autos-14
Bowman Factor Autos Gold-1
Bowman Factor Autos Gold-2
Bowman Factor Autos Gold-3
Bowman Factor Autos Gold-4
Bowman Factor Autos Gold-5
Bowman Factor Autos Gold-6
Bowman Factor Autos Gold-7
Bowman Factor Autos Gold-8
Bowman Factor Autos Gold-9
Bowman Factor Autos Gold-10
Bowman Factor Autos Gold-11
Bowman Factor Autos Gold-12
Bowman Factor Autos Gold-13
Bowman Factor Autos Gold-14
06Parkhurst-22
Autographs-22
Autographs Dual-DAAB
06SP Authentic Sign of the Times Quads-ST4BLSR
06The Cup-30
Black Rainbow-30
Gold-30
Masterpiece Pressplates-30
Stanley Cup Signatures-CSSB
06Upper Deck Trilogy Ice Scripts-ISSB
06Upper Deck Trilogy Legendary Scripts-LSSB

Bowman, Sean
93Omaha Lancers-3

Bownass, Jack
51Laval Dairy QSHL-61
52St. Lawrence Sales-98
61Union Oil WHL-1
69Swedish Hockey-350

Bowness, Rick
77O-Pee-Chee NHL-265
78O-Pee-Chee-173
78Topps-173
81O-Pee-Chee-361
84Jets Police-23
85Jets Police-23
86Jets Postcards-3
87Moncton Hawks-2
88ProCards AHL-189
89ProCards AHL-75
90ProCards AHL/IHL-143
93Senators Kraft Sheets-3
94Senators Team Issue-8
02Coyotes Team Issue-24

Bowness, Ryan
00Brampton Battalion-20
03Brampton Battalion-1

Bowtell, Cody
99Lowell Lock Monsters-8
99Mississippi Sea Wolves-10
99Mississippi Sea Wolves Kelly Cup-8

Boxer, Herb
95Central Hockey League-36

Boxer, Marc
98Bakersfield Condors-4

Boxma, B.J.
98Kootenay Ice-23
00Swift Current Broncos-1
01Swift Current Broncos-23

Boxma, Mike
03Kootenay Ice-10

Boyce, Arthur
12C57-40

Boyce, Darryl
01St. Michaels Majors-19
02St. Michaels Majors-18
03St. Michael's Majors-18
04St. Michael's Majors-19

Boyce, Ian
90ProCards AHL/IHL-268
91ProCards-249
91Rochester Americans Kodak-3
93Fort Wayne Komets-1
96Kansas City Blades-1
97Fort Wayne Komets-2
98Fort Wayne Komets-3
01Fort Wayne Komets Shoe Carnival-16

Boychuk, David
99Spokane Chiefs-5
00Spokane Chiefs-2
01Spokane Chiefs-3

Boychuk, John
00Calgary Hitmen-4
01Calgary Hitmen-4
01Calgary Hitmen Autographed-4
02Calgary Hitmen-23
04Hershey Bears Patriot News-5
06Albany River Rats-6

Boychuk, Zach
05Lethbridge Hurricanes-3

Boyd, Cameron
93Quebec Pee-Wee Tournament-876

Boyd, Dave
94Birmingham Bulls-4

Boyd, Don
82Regina Pats-23
83Regina Pats-23
85London Knights-4
87Sault Ste. Marie Greyhounds-22

Boyd, Dustin
04Moose Jaw Warriors-12
05ITG Heroes/Prosp Toronto Expo Parallel -322
05Moose Jaw Warriors-2
05ITG Heroes and Prospects-322
Autographs Series II-DBO
Oh Canada-OC-11
Oh Canada Gold-OC-11
06Be A Player-204
06Beehive-111
Blue-111
Gold-111
Matte-111
Red Facsimile Signatures-111
Wood-111
06Flair Showcase-307
06Hot Prospects-106
Red Hot-106
White Hot-106
06O-Pee-Chee-574
Rainbow-574
06SP Authentic-169
Limited-169
06SP Game Used-157
Gold-157
Rainbow-157
Autographs-157
Rookie Exclusives Autographs-REDU
06SPx-161
Spectrum-161
06The Cup-118
Autographed NHL Shields Duals-DASBP
Autographed Rookie Masterpiece Pressplates-118
Enshrinements-EDB
Gold Rainbow Autographed Rookie Patches-118
Masterpiece Pressplates (Bee Hive)-111
Masterpiece Pressplates (Marquee Rookies)-574
Masterpiece Pressplates (SP Authentic Autographs)-169
Masterpiece Pressplates (SP Game Used)-157
Masterpiece Pressplates (SPx Autographs)-161
Masterpiece Pressplates (Sweet Beginnings)-113
Masterpiece Pressplates (Ultimate Collection Autographs)-121
Masterpiece Pressplates (Victory)-327
NHL Shields Duals-DSHDB
NHL Shields Duals-DSHIB
Rookies Black-118
Rookies Platinum-118
06UD Artifacts-235
06Ultimate Collection-121
Rookies Autographed NHL Shields-121
Rookies Autographed Patches-121
Ultimate Debut Threads Jerseys-DJ-DU
Ultimate Debut Threads Jerseys Autographs-DJ-DU
Ultimate Debut Threads Patches-DJ-DU
Ultimate Debut Threads Patches Autographs-DJ-DU
06Upper Deck-461
Exclusives Parallel-461
High Gloss Parallel-461
Masterpieces-461
Rookie Headliners-RH29
06Upper Deck Sweet Shot-113
Rookie Jerseys Autographs-113
06Upper Deck Victory-327
06AHL Top Prospects-30
06ITG Heroes and Prospects National Pride-NP18
06ITG Heroes and Prospects National Pride Gold-NP18
07Upper Deck Rookie Class -10

Boyd, Irwin
34Beehive Group I Photos-4

Boyd, James
93Kitchener Rangers-14
95Slapshot-43
97Medicine Hat Tigers-2
98Medicine Hat Tigers-2
01Belleville Bulls-2

Boyd, Jason
96Brandon Wheat Kings-18

Boyd, Jim
75Phoenix Roadrunners WHA-2

Boyd, Kevin
95Slapshot-167
98Port Huron Border Cats-14
99Bakersfield Condors-3
00Bakersfield Condors-4

Boyd, Randy
81Ottawa 67's-3
83O-Pee-Chee-283
83Penguins Heinz Photos-3
86Islanders Team Issue-25
87Canucks Shell Oil-3
88Canucks Mohawk-4
91ProCards-609
93Memphis RiverKings-18

Boyd, Rick
88ProCards IHL-2
89Johnstown Chiefs-23

Boyd, Stephanie
94Classic Women of Hockey-W33

Boyd, Steve
89 7th Inn. Sketch OHL-37

Boyer, Don
96OCN Blizzard-14
97OCN Blizzard-13

Boyer, Wally
63Rochester Americans-5
64Beehive Group III Photos-31
64Beehive Group III Photos-155
66Topps-55
67Seals Team Issue-3
68O-Pee-Chee-105
68Shirriff Coins-146
68Topps-105
69O-Pee-Chee-118
69Topps-118
70Dad's Cookies-9
70Esso Power Players-230
70O-Pee-Chee-203
70Sargent Promotions Stamps-171
71Toronto Sun-212
72O-Pee-Chee-308

Boyer, Zac
88Kamloops Blazers-4
89Kamloops Blazers-4
90 7th Inn. Sketch WHL-284
90 7th Inn. Sketch Memorial Cup-2
91 7th Inn. Sketch WHL-84
92Indianapolis Ice-3
93Indianapolis Ice-2
94Classic Pro Prospects-114
01Colorado Gold Kings-3
02Orlando Seals-8

Boyes, Brad
99Upper Deck Sobey's Memorial Cup-15
99UD Prospects-12
99UD Prospects-69
00UD CHL Prospects-6
Future Leaders-FL3
02AHL Top Prospects-6
02St. John's Maple Leafs Atlant-4
03BAP Memorabilia-234
03ITG Action-669
03ITG VIP Rookie Debut-133
03Parkhurst Rookie-67
03SP Authentic-162
03SP Game Used-128
03UD Premier Collection-79
03Upper Deck Rookie Update-120
03AHL Top Prospects-4
03Cleveland Barons-1
03Pacific AHL Prospects-19
Gold-19
04SP Authentic Sign of the Times-ST-BB
04SP Authentic Sign of the Times-FS-NED
04Ultimate Collection Signatures-US-BB
04Providence Bruins-3
04ITG Heroes and Prospects-8
Aspiring-9
Autographs-BB
Combos-4
Complete Emblems-30
Emblems-15
Emblems Gold-15
He Shoots-He Scores Prizes-11
Jersey Autographs-15
Jerseys-15
Jerseys Gold-15
Numbers-15
Numbers Gold-15
04ITG Heroes/Prospects Toronto Expo '05-8
04ITG Heroes/Prospects Expo Heroes/Pros-8
05ITG Heroes/Prosp Toronto Expo Parallel -61
05Black Diamond Gemography-G-BB
05Black Diamond Gemography Emerald-G-BB
05Black Diamond Gemography Gold-G-BB
05Black Diamond Gemography Onyx-G-BB
05Black Diamond Gemography Ruby-G-BB
05Bruins Boston Globe-7
05Parkhurst-35
Facsimile Auto Parallel-35
Signatures-BB
05UD Artifacts Auto Facts-AF-BB
05UD Artifacts Auto Facts Blue-AF-BB
05UD Artifacts Auto Facts Copper-AF-BB
05UD Artifacts Auto Facts Pewter-AF-BB
05UD Artifacts Auto Facts Silver-AF-BB
05UD Powerplay Power Marks-PMBB
05UD Rookie Class-6
05Ultimate Collection-8
Gold-8
05Upper Deck-258
Notable Numbers-N-BB
05Upper Deck MVP-39
Gold-39
Platinum-39
05Upper Deck Trilogy Scripts-SFS-BB
05Upper Deck Victory-206
Black-206
Gold-206
Silver-206
05ITG Heroes and Prospects-61
Autographs-A-BB
Complete Jerseys-CJ-28
Complete Jerseys Gold-CJ-28
Complete Logos-AHL-13
Future Teammates-FT10
He Shoots-He Scores Prizes-20
Jerseys-GUJ-9
Jerseys Gold-GUJ-09
Emblems-GUE-9
Emblems Gold-GUE-09
Numbers-GUN-9
Numbers Gold-GUN-09
Nameplates-N-22
Nameplates Gold-N-22
06Be A Player-157
Autographs-157
Signatures-BB
Signatures 10-172
Signatures Duals-DWB
Signatures Trios-TWBS
06Be A Player Portraits-9
Dual Signature Portraits-DSBB
Signature Portraits-SPBB
Triple Signature Portraits-TBOS
06Beehive-93
06Beehive-230
Matte-93
Matted Materials-MMBB
Remarkable Matted Materials-MMBB
Signature Scrapbook-SSBB
06Black Diamond-89
Black-89
Gold-89
Ruby-89
Jerseys-JBB
Jerseys Black-JBB
Jerseys Gold-JBB
Jerseys Ruby-JBB
Jerseys Black Autographs -JBB
06Flair Showcase-17
06Flair Showcase-109
Parallel-11
Parallel-109
Inks-IBB
Wave of the Future-WF5
06Fleer-17
Tiffany-17
Signing Day-SDBB
06Hot Prospects-10
Red Hot-10
White Hot-10
Hot Materials -HMBR
Hot Materials Red Hot-HMBR
Hot Materials White Hot-HMBR
Hotagraphs-HBR
06McDonald's Upper Deck Rookie Review-RR13
06O-Pee-Chee-47
06O-Pee-Chee-623
Rainbow-47
Rainbow-623
Autographs-A-BB
06Panini Stickers-18
06SP Authentic-93
Chirography-BB
Limited-93
Sign of the Times Triples-ST3BBK
06SP Game Used-8
Gold-8
Rainbow-8
Authentic Fabrics-AFBB
Authentic Fabrics Parallel-AFBB
Authentic Fabrics Patches-AFBB
Authentic Fabrics Triple-AF3BOS
Authentic Fabrics Triple Patches-AF3BOS
Authentic Fabrics Fives-AP5RPT
Authentic Fabrics Fives Patches-AP5RPT
Autographs-8
Inked Sweaters-ISBB
Inked Sweaters Patches-ISBB
Inked Sweaters Dual-IS2BB
Inked Sweaters Dual Patches-IS2BB
Letter Marks-LMBB
06SPx-9
Spectrum-9
SPxcitement-X9
SPxcitement Spectrum-X9
Winning Materials-WMBB
Winning Materials Spectrum-WMBB
Winning Materials Autographs-WMBB
06The Cup Autographed Foundations-CQBB
06The Cup Autographed Foundations Patches-CQBB
06The Cup Autographed NHL Shields Duals-DASBO
06The Cup Foundations-CQBB
06The Cup Foundations Patches-CQBB
06The Cup Limited Logos-LLBB
06UD Artifacts-91
Blue-91
Gold-91
Platinum-91
Radiance-91
Autographed Radiance Parallel-91
Red-91
Auto-Facts-AFBR
Auto-Facts Gold-AFBR
Tundra Tandems-TTBB
Tundra Tandems Black-TTBB
Tundra Tandems Blue-TTBB
Tundra Tandems Gold-TTBB
Tundra Tandems Platinum-TTBB
Tundra Tandems Red-TTBB
Tundra Tandems Dual Patches Red-TTBB
06UD Mini Jersey Collection-8
06UD Powerplay-8
Impact Rainbow-8
Power Marks-PMBB
06UD Toronto Fall Expo Priority Signings -PSBB
06Ultimate Collection Autographed Jerseys-AJ-BB
06Ultimate Collection Autographed Patches-AJ-BB
06Ultimate Collection Signatures-US-BB
06Ultra-15
Gold Medallion-15
Ice Medallion-15
Fresh Ink-IBB
06Upper Deck Arena Giveaways-BOS1
06Upper Deck-15
Exclusives Parallel-15
High Gloss Parallel-15
Game Jerseys-JBB
Game Patches-PBB
Masterpieces-15
Signatures-SBB
Signature Sensations-SSBB
Walmart Tins Oversize-15
06Upper Deck MVP-20
Gold Script-20
Super Script-20
Autographs-OABS
06Upper Deck Ovation-4
06Upper Deck Sweet Shot Signature Shots/Saves-SSBB
06Upper Deck Sweet Shot Signature Shots/Saves Ice Signings-SSIBB
06Upper Deck Sweet Shot Signature Shots/Saves Sticks-SSSBB
06Upper Deck Trilogy-10
Combo Clearcut Autographs-C2BB
Honorary Scripted Patches-HSPBB
Honorary Scripted Swatches-HSSBB
Ice Scripts-ISBB
Scripts-TSBB
06Upper Deck Victory-16
06Upper Deck Victory Black-16
06Upper Deck Victory Gold-16
06Upper Deck Victory Next In Line-NL8
06Upper Deck Victory Oversize Cards-BB
06ITG Heroes and Prospects-23
Autographs-ABBO
Sticks and Jerseys-SJ20
Sticks and Jerseys Gold-SJ20
07Upper Deck Ovation-58
07Upper Deck Victory-113
Black-113
Gold-113

Boyes, Jeff
93Quebec Pee-Wee Tournament-1689

Boykins, Kobie
93RPI Engineers-3

Boyko, Darren
92Finnish Jyvas-Hyva Stickers-7
93Finnish SISU-96
94Finnish SISU-10
95Finnish SISU-13
95Finnish SISU-174
95Finnish SISU-369
95Finnish SISU Limited-44

Boyko, Rob
95Classic-82

Boylan, Mike
00Connecticut Huskies-3

Boyle, Alexander
93Quebec Pee-Wee Tournament-1440

Boyle, Dan
98Kentucky Thoroughblades-3
99BAP Memorabilia-285
Gold-285
Silver-285
99BAP Millennium-114
Emerald-114
Ruby-114
Sapphire-114
Signatures-114
Signatures Gold-114
99Pacific-185
Copper-185
Emerald Green-185
Gold-185
Ice Blue-185
Premiere Date-185
Red-185
99Louisville Panthers-5
00Panthers Team Issue-26
00Upper Deck NHLPA-PA38
01Upper Deck-77
Exclusives-77
02BAP Sig Series Auto Buybacks 1999-114
02Lightning Team Issue-3
02Pacific Complete-250
Red-250
03ITG Action-528
03Lightning Team Issue-23
03NHL Sticker Collection-129
03Pacific-304
Blue-304
Red-304
03Pacific Complete-257
Red-257
03Private Stock Reserve-93
Blue-93
Red-93
Retail-93
03Upper Deck-421
Canadian Exclusives-421
HG-421
UD Exclusives-421
03Upper Deck MVP-380
Gold Script-380
Silver Script-380
Canadian Exclusives-380
04Swedish Pure Skills-10
Parallel-10
05Lightning Team Issue-8
05Panini Stickers-160
05Parkhurst-435
Facsimile Auto Parallel-435
05Upper Deck Victory-180
Black-180
Gold-180
Silver-180
06Be A Player-156
Autographs-156
Signatures-BO
06Lightning Postcards-4
06NHL POG-12
06O-Pee-Chee-444
Rainbow-444
06Panini Stickers-152
06Upper Deck-176
Exclusives Parallel-176
High Gloss Parallel-176
Masterpieces-176
06Upper Deck MVP-267
Gold Script-267
Super Script-267
07Upper Deck Victory-69
Black-69
Gold-69

Boyle, Daryl
04Brandon Wheat Kings-7
05Brandon Wheat Kings-2

Boyle, Jordan
90Rayside-Balfour Jr. Canadians-3

Boyle, Matt
06Moncton Wildcats-22

Boyle, Steve
74Sioux City Musketeers-1

Boynton, John
93Quebec Pee-Wee Tournament-752

Boynton, Nick
92Quebec Pee-Wee Tournament-343
95Slapshot-262
95Slapshot-NNO
95Classic-92
96Black Diamond-22
Gold-22
96Upper Deck-373
97Collector's Choice-309
97Bowman CHL-15
97Bowman CHL-154
OPC-15
OPC-154
Autographs-34
Bowman's Best-6
Bowman's Best Atomic Refractors-6
Bowman's Best Refractor-6
98Bowman CHL-27
Golden Anniversary-27
OPC International-27
98Bowman Chrome CHL-27
Golden Anniversary-27
Golden Anniversary Refractors-27
OPC International-27
OPC International Refractors-27
Refractors-27
99SPx-173
Radiance-173
Spectrum-173
99Upper Deck-162
Exclusives-162
Exclusives 1 of 1-162
99Upper Deck Gold Reserve-162
99Upper Deck Victory-372
99Providence Bruins-4
00BAP Memorabilia-274
Emerald-274
Ruby-274
Sapphire-274
Promos-274
00BAP Mem Chicago Sportsfest Copper-274
00BAP Memorabilia Chicago Sportsfest Blue-274
00BAP Memorabilia Chicago Sportsfest Gold-274
00BAP Memorabilia Chicago Sportsfest Ruby-274
00BAP Memorabilia Chicago Sun-Times Ruby-274
00BAP Memorabilia Chicago Sun-Times Gold-274
00BAP Mem Chicago Sun-Times Sapphire-274
00BAP Mem Toronto Fall Expo Copper-274
00BAP Memorabilia Toronto Fall Expo Gold-274
00BAP Memorabilia Toronto Fall Expo Ruby-274
00BAP Parkhurst 2000-P86
00Pacific-45
Copper-45
Gold-45
Ice Blue-45
Premiere Date-45
00Providence Bruins-3
01BAP Memorabilia-223
Emerald-223
Ruby-223
Sapphire-223
01BAP Signature Series-227
Autographs-227
Autographs Gold-227
01Bowman YoungStars-127
Gold-127
Ice Cubed-127
Autographs-NB
Relics-JNB
Relics-SNB
Relics-DSNB
Rivals-R4
01Parkhurst-278
01Parkhurst Beckett Promos-278
02BAP First Edition-35
Jerseys-35
02Bruins Team Issue-2
02O-Pee-Chee-211
02O-Pee-Chee Premier Blue Parallel-211
02O-Pee-Chee Premier Red Parallel-211
02O-Pee-Chee Factory Set-211
02Pacific-23
Blue-23
Red-23
02Pacific Complete-35
Red-35
02Pacific Exclusive-10
02Parkhurst Retro-198
Minis-198
02Stadium Club YoungStars Relics-S18
02Topps-211
OPC Blue Parallel-211
OPC Red Parallel-211
Factory Set-211
02Topps Total-103
02Upper Deck-14
Exclusives-14
02Upper Deck MVP-17
Gold-17
Classics-17
Golden Classics-17
02Upper Deck Victory-19
Bronze-19
Gold-19
Silver-19
02Upper Deck Vintage-19
02Upper Deck Vintage-263
03Beehive-18
Gold-18
Silver-18
03Bruins Team Issue-1
03ITG Action-67
Jerseys-M8
03NHL Sticker Collection-19
03O-Pee-Chee-175
03OPC Blue-175
03OPC Gold-175
03OPC Red-175
03Pacific-25
Blue-25
Red-25
03Pacific Complete-150
Red-150
03Parkhurst Original Six Boston-3
Memorabilia-BM5
03Topps-175
Blue-175
Gold-175
Red-175
Traded Future Phenoms-FP-NB
03Upper Deck-262
Canadian Exclusives-262
HG-262
UD Exclusives-262
03Upper Deck MVP-38
Gold Script-38
Silver Script-38
Canadian Exclusives-38
04Upper Deck-16
Canadian Exclusives-16
HG Glossy Gold-16
HG Glossy Silver-16
04UK EIHL All-Stars-15
05Be A Player Signatures-NB
05Be A Player Signatures Gold-NB
05Black Diamond-7
Emerald-7
Gold-7
Onyx-7
Ruby-7
05Bruins Boston Globe-15
05Parkhurst-46
Facsimile Auto Parallel-46
05The Cup Master Pressplate Rookie Update-238
05Ultra-20
Gold-20
Ice-20
05Upper Deck-13
HG Glossy-13
Jerseys-J-NIB
Jerseys Series II-J2NB
NHL Generations-DNZ
Notable Numbers-N-NB
05Upper Deck MVP-36
Gold-36
Platinum-36
05Upper Deck Rookie Update-238
Inspirations Patch Rookies-238
05Upper Deck Toronto Fall Expo-13
05Upper Deck Victory-16
Black-16
Gold-16
Silver-16
06O-Pee-Chee-375
Rainbow-375
06Panini Stickers-322
06Upper Deck-400
Exclusives Parallel-400
High Gloss Parallel-400
Masterpieces-400

Boysen, Joe
00Arizona Icecats-2

Boyte, Eric
99Adirondack IceHawks-3

Bozek, Darwin
89ProCards AHL-11

Bozek, Roman
94Czech APS Extraliga-112
95Czech APS Extraliga-70

Bozek, Steve
82O-Pee-Chee-151
82O-Pee-Chee Stickers-233
82Post Cereal-8
82Topps Stickers-233
83O-Pee-Chee-77
83Vachon-3
84O-Pee-Chee-220
85Flames Red Rooster-5
86Flames Red Rooster-3
87Flames Red Rooster-2
87O-Pee-Chee-216
88Canucks Mohawk-6
89Canucks Mohawk-3
89O-Pee-Chee Stickers-67
90Bowman-64
Tiffany-64
90Canucks Mohawk-3
90O-Pee-Chee-76
90Panini Stickers-301
90Pro Set-293
90Score Rookie/Traded-89T
90Topps-76
Tiffany-76
91Bowman-325
91Canucks Panini Team Stickers-3
91O-Pee-Chee-397
91Panini Stickers-48
91Pinnacle-61
French-61
91Pro Set-486
French-486
91Score Canadian Bilingual-252
91Score Canadian Bilingual-556
91Score Canadian English-252
91Score Canadian English-556
91Score Rookie/Traded-6T
91Sharks Sports Action-3
91Stadium Club-28
91Topps-397
92Score-37
Canadian-37

Bozik, Mojmir
89Swedish Semic World Champ Stickers-188

Bozoian, A.J.
05Fort Wayne Komets Choice-20
05Fort Wayne Komets Sprint-1
06Fort Wayne Komets-1

Bozoian, Mike
93Quebec Pee-Wee Tournament-1753

Bozon, Philippe
91Parkhurst-375
French-375
92O-Pee-Chee-257
92OPC Premier-25
92Parkhurst-159
92Parkhurst-452
Emerald Ice-159
Emerald Ice-452
92Stadium Club-8
92Topps-433
Gold-433G
92Ultra-392
92Upper Deck-283
92Finnish Semic-230
93OPC Premier-68
Gold-68
93Parkhurst-179
Emerald Ice-179
93Stadium Club-214
Members Only Master Set-214
OPC-214
First Day Issue-214
First Day Issue OPC-214
93Topps/OPC Premier-68
Gold-68
93Ultra-210
93Upper Deck-113
SP-134
93Swedish Semic World Champ Stickers-268
94Donruss-261
94Leaf-321
94Parkhurst SE-SE153
Gold-SE153
94Stadium Club-233
Members Only Master Set-233
First Day Issue-233
Super Team Winner Cards-233
95Swedish Globe World Championships-205
95Swedish World Championships Stickers-112
95Swiss HNL-379
96Swedish Semic Wien-188
96Swiss HNL-259
96Swiss HNL-262
98German DEL-226
99Swiss Panini Stickers-164
00Swiss Panini Stickers-208
00Swiss Slapshot Mini-Cards-HCL10
01Swiss HNL-331
02Swiss HNL-344

Brabec, Jaroslav
94Czech APS Extraliga-105
95Czech APS Extraliga-71
95Czech APS Extraliga-266

Brabenec, Kamil
96Czech APS Extraliga-261
98Czech OFS-413
99Czech DS-42
99Czech OFS-177
00Czech DS Extraliga-84
00Czech OFS-20
01Czech DS-12
01Czech OFS-135
02Swedish SHL-224
Parallel-224
03Swedish Elite-84
Global Impact-GI8
Silver-84
04Czech OFS-243
05Czech HC Ceski Budejovice-1
06Czech OFS-1

Bracco, Jon
92Saskatchewan JHL-102

Bracco, Michael
88Brockville Braves-18

Brack, David
06Lincoln Stars-2
06Lincoln Stars Upper DeckÂ Signature Series -4

Brackenbury, Curt
76Nordiques Marie Antoinette-5
76Nordiques Postcards-8
76O-Pee-Chee WHA-4
79O-Pee-Chee-308
80Pepsi-Cola Caps-22
81Oilers Red Rooster-15
81O-Pee-Chee-109
88Oilers Tenth Anniversary-10
90Hampton Roads Admirals-59
02Fleer Throwbacks-89
Gold-89
Platinum-89
Stickwork-3

Bradertscher, Rolf
98Swiss Power Play Stickers-138

Bradette, Martin
93Amos Les Forestiers-5

Bradford, Brent
92British Columbia JHL-63

Bradley, Brian
75Roanoke Valley Rebels-11
85Moncton Golden Flames-9
86Flames Red Rooster-4
88Canucks Mohawk-6
89Canucks Mohawk-4
89O-Pee-Chee-287
89O-Pee-Chee-315
89O-Pee-Chee Stickers-63
89Panini Stickers-152
90Bowman-58
Tiffany-58
90Canucks Molson-1
90O-Pee-Chee-59
90O-Pee-Chee-115
90Panini Stickers-302
90Pro Set-294
90Score-198
Canadian-198
90Topps-59
90Topps-115
Tiffany-59
Tiffany-115
90Upper Deck-79
French-79
91Pro Set Platinum-231
91Bowman-159
91Canucks Panini Team Stickers-4
91Maple Leafs PLAY-3
91O-Pee-Chee-234
91OPC Premier-185
91OPC Premier-190
91Panini Stickers-93
91Parkhurst-171
French-171
91Pinnacle-90
French-90
91Pro Set-489
French-489
91Score Canadian Bilingual-255
91Score Canadian English-255
91Stadium Club-257
91Topps-234
92Bowman-283
92Lightning Sheraton-6
92O-Pee-Chee-27
92Parkhurst-174
Emerald Ice-174
92Pinnacle Canadian Promo Panels-2
92Pinnacle-387
French-387
92Pro Set-174
92Score-259
Canadian-259
92Stadium Club-163
92Topps-291
Gold-291G
92Ultra-408
92Upper Deck-544
93Donruss-324
93Kraft-2
93Leaf-209
93Lightning Kash n'Karry-1
93Lightning Season in Review-3
93McDonald's Upper Deck-1
93OPC Premier-117
Gold-117
93Panini Stickers-S
93Parkhurst-465
Emerald Ice-465
93Pinnacle-60
Canadian-60
All-Stars-33
All-Stars Canadian-33
93PowerPlay-228
93Score-230
Canadian-230
Franchise-20
93Stadium Club-212
Members Only Master Set-212
OPC-212
First Day Issue-212
First Day Issue OPC-212
All-Stars-11
All-Stars Members Only-11
All-Stars OPC-11
93Topps/OPC Premier-117
Gold-117
93Ultra-36
93Upper Deck-121
93Upper Deck-305
SP-148
93Upper Deck Locker All-Stars-20
94Canada Games NHL POGS-221
94Donruss-40
94EA Sports-129
94Flair-170
94Fleer-203
94Leaf-42
94Lightning Photo Album-4
94Lightning Postcards-2
94OPC Premier-247
Special Effects-247
94Parkhurst-221
Gold-221
Vintage-V71
94Pinnacle-278
Artist's Proofs-278
Rink Collection-278
94Score-179
Gold-179
Platinum-179
94Select-43
Gold-43
94SP-114
Die Cuts-114
94Stadium Club Members Only-41
94Topps/OPC Premier-247
Special Effects-247
94Ultra-202
94Upper Deck-118
Electric Ice-118
SP Inserts-SP74
SP Inserts Die Cuts-SP74
95Bashan Super Stickers-111
95Bashan Super Stickers-113
95Be A Player-117
Signatures-S117
Signatures Die Cuts-S117
95Canada Games NHL POGS-246
95Collector's Choice-128
Player's Club-128
Player's Club Platinum-128
95Donruss-139
95Donruss Elite-82
Die Cut Stars-82
Die Cut Uncut-82
95Emotion-162
95Finest-143
Refractors-143
95Hoyle Eastern Playing Cards-5
95Imperial Stickers-113
95Kraft-69
95Leaf-159
95Lightning Team Issue-4
95Metal-135
95NHL Aces Playing Cards-4C
95Panini Stickers-124
95Parkhurst International-190
Emerald Ice-190
95Playoff One on One-197
95Pro Magnets-71
95Score-232
Black Ice Artist's Proofs-232
Black Ice-232
95Select Certified-83
Mirror Gold-83
95SkyBox Impact-153
95Stadium Club-39
Members Only Master Set-39
95Summit-146
Artist's Proofs-146
Ice-146
95Topps-148
OPC Inserts-148
95Topps SuperSkills-59
Platinum-59
95Ultra-308
95Upper Deck-83
Electric Ice-83
Electric Ice Gold-83
Special Edition-SE166

Special Edition Gold-SE166
96SLU Hockey Canadian-1
96SLU Hockey American-2
96Collector's Choice-250
96Donruss-116
Press Proofs-116
96Fleer-103
96Kenner Starting Lineup Cards-2
96Leaf-58
Press Proofs-58
96Leaf Limited-76
Gold-76
96Leaf Preferred-18
Press Proofs-18
96Metal Universe-142
96NHL Pro Stamps-71
96Pinnacle-17
Artist's Proofs-17
Foil-17
Premium Stock-17
Rink Collection-17
96Score-45
Artist's Proofs-45
Dealer's Choice Artist's Proofs-45
Special Artist's Proofs-45
Golden Blades-45
96SkyBox Impact-120
BladeRunners-1
96SP-149
96Summit-18
Artist's Proofs-18
Ice-18
Metal-18
Premium Stock-18
96Topps Picks-71
OPC Inserts-71
96Ultra-155
Gold Medallion-155
96Zenith-59
Artist's Proofs-59
97Katch-133
Gold-133
Silver-133
97Pacific-64
Copper-64
Emerald Green-64
Ice Blue-64
Red-64
Silver-64
98Katch-133
03Lightning Team Issue-15
04ITG Franchises Canadian-123
04ITG Franchises US East-437
Autographs-A-BBR

Bradley, E.J.
98Johnstown Chiefs-17
99Johnstown Chiefs-21

Bradley, George
01Guelph Storm-6
01Guelph Storm Memorial Cup-6
02Guelph Storm-9
03Guelph Storm-7

Bradley, John
91Rochester Americans Kodak-4
91Rochester Americans Postcards-2
93Johnstown Chiefs-1
95Lethbridge Hurricanes-2
04Tennessee Valley AFL-1

Bradley, Les
82Kitchener Rangers-27
83Kitchener Rangers-29
84Kitchener Rangers-29

Bradley, Matt
95Bowman Draft Prospects-P3
95Slapshot-113
98UD Choice-274
Prime Choice Reserve-274
Reserve-274
98Kentucky Thoroughblades-4
98Bowman CHL-28
Golden Anniversary-28
OPC International-28
98Bowman Chrome CHL-28
Golden Anniversary-28
Golden Anniversary Refractors-28
OPC International-28
OPC International Refractors-28
Refractors-28
99Kentucky Thoroughblades-4
00BAP Memorabilia-435
Emerald-435
Ruby-435
Sapphire-435
00BAP Signature Series-256
Emerald-256
Ruby-256
Sapphire-256
Autographs-218
Autographs Gold-218
00Kentucky Thoroughblades-4
01Sharks Postcards-3
01Titanium Draft Day Edition-164
02BAP Sig Series Auto Buybacks 2000-218
02Pacific Complete-261
Red-261
02Topps Total-117
05Parkhurst-497
06O-Pee-Chee-499
Rainbow-499

Bradley, Todd
91Oshawa Generals-13
91Oshawa Generals Sheet-21
917th Inn. Sketch OHL-150
92Oshawa Generals Sheet-16
93Oshawa Generals-13

Brady, Fred
52Juniors Blue Tint-60

Brady, Lance
95Birmingham Bulls-3

Brady, Neil
85Medicine Hat Tigers-11
88ProCards AHL-337
89Devils Caretta-3
90Bowman-88
Tiffany-88
90ProCards AHL/IHL-568
92OPC Premier-82
92Parkhurst-124
Emerald Ice-124
92Senators Team Issue-3
93OPC Premier-17
Gold-17
93Panini Stickers-119
93Score-293
Canadian-293
93Stadium Club-199
Members Only Master Set-199
OPC-199
First Day Issue-199
First Day Issue OPC-199
93Topps/OPC Premier-17
Gold-17
93Upper Deck-81
96Michigan K-Wings-21
99Utah Grizzlies-26

Brady, Peter
02Austin Ice Bats-2
03Austin Ice Bats-1

Brady, Peter-Emmanuel
04Austin Ice Bats-1

Brady, Sean
98Fort Worth Brahmas-8

Braff, Eric
98Kingston Frontenacs-1
99Kingston Frontenacs-3
00Kingston Frontenacs-1
03St. Francis Xavier X-Men-21
04St. Francis Xavier X-Men-2

Bragg, Matthew
06Barrie Colts-17

Bragnalo, Christian
94Thunder Bay Flyers-4
96New Hampshire Wildcats-23
97New Hampshire Wildcats-24
98New Hampshire Wildcats-18
01Fort Wayne Komets-4

Bragnalo, Rick
77O-Pee-Chee NHL-296
78O-Pee-Chee-308
82Swedish Semic VM Stickers-134
83Swedish Semic VM Stickers-134

Braham, Dean
84Prince Albert Raiders Stickers-3

Brainerd, Michael
93Quebec Pee-Wee Tournament-631

Braithwaite, Andrew
04Williams Lake Timberwolves-1

Branch, Craig
93Quebec Pee-Wee Tournament-1206

Branch, David
907th Inn. Sketch OHL-300
95Slapshot-5

Branch, James
70Swedish Masterserien-177

Branch, Rod
93Kamloops Blazers-2
94Kamloops Blazers-17
95Prince Albert Raiders-1
95Slapshot Memorial Cup-1
99Topeka Scarecrows-13
03Tulsa Oilers-3

Brancik, Richard
94Czech APS Extraliga-21
95Czech APS Extraliga-118
97Czech APS Extraliga-120
99Czech Score Blue 2000-106
99Czech Score Red Ice 2000-106

Brand, Aaron
94Sarnia Sting-9
95Slapshot-338
95Sarnia Sting-8
95Classic-96
96St. John's Maple Leafs-3
97St. John's Maple Leafs-3
99St. John's Maple Leafs-5
03Port Huron Beacons-3
05Port Huron Flags-10

Brand, Konrad
95Kamloops Blazers-31
96Kamloops Blazers-5
97Medicine Hat Tigers-3
98Medicine Hat Tigers-3
99Medicine Hat Tigers-16

Brand, Scott
95Waterloo Blackhawks -25

Branda, Daniel
98Czech OFS-14
99Czech OFS-342
00Czech DS Extraliga-115
00Czech OFS-93
01Czech OFS All Stars-21
02Czech OFS Plus-1
02Czech OFS Plus All-Star Game-H43
03Russian Hockey League-173
03Russian SL-34
04Czech OFS-91
06Czech OFS-131
Stars-3

Brandimore, Chad
03UK Manchester Phoenix-12

Brandis, Casper
99Danish Hockey League-191

Brandl, Daniel
01Czech OFS-11

Brandl, Thomas
91Finnish Semic World Champ Stickers-165
91Swedish Semic World Champ Stickers-165
93Swedish Semic World Champ Stickers-166
94Finnish Jaa Kiekko-280
94German DEL-202
94German First League-40
95German DEL-205
95German DEL-430
95Swedish Globe World Championships-221
95Swedish World Championships Stickers-63
96German DEL-289
96Swedish Semic Wien-197
98German DEL-21
99German DEL-127
00German DEL-155
Star Attractions-S5
01German Upper Deck-153
02German DEL City Press-215

Brandner, Christoph
95Austrian National Team-1
95Swedish World Championships Stickers-275
00German DEL-151
02SPx Rookie Redemption-R201
02German DEL City Press-216
Top Scorers-TS1
03Black Diamond-167
Black-167
Green-167
Red-167
03ITG VIP Rookie Debut-9
03Parkhurst Rookie-78
03SP Authentic-96
Limited-96
03SP Game Used-65
Gold-65
03UD Honor Roll-151
03Upper Deck-222
Canadian Exclusives-222
HG-222
03Upper Deck MVP-444
03Upper Deck Rookie Update-191
03Upper Deck Trilogy-154
Limited-154
03German DEL All-Stars-AS7
04Upper Deck All-Star Promos-CB
05Swedish SHL Elitset-274
Gold-274
Series Two Signatures-23
06German DEL-78

Brandon, Bob
99Tupelo T-Rex-3

Brandon, Derek
97Prince Albert Raiders-2
98Prince Albert Raiders-1

Brandon, Howard
23Crescent Selkirks-4
23V128-1 Paulin's Candy-7
24Crescent Selkirks-1

Brandreth, Pat
00Kamloops Blazers-5
01Vancouver Giants-8

Brandstrom, Ingemar
57Swedish Alfabilder-94

Brandt, Andy
03Wisconsin Badgers-3
04Wisconsin Badgers-12
05Wisconsin Badgers-1

Brandt, Jake
00Lincoln Stars-22
03North Dakota Fighting Sioux-24
04North Dakota Fighting Sioux-3

Brandt, Mats
99Danish Hockey League-162

Branham, Tim
00Barrie Colts-2
01Guelph Storm-5
01Guelph Storm Memorial Cup-4
04Florida Everblades-10

Brannare, Stefan
92British Columbia JHL-154
97Wheeling Nailers-14
97Wheeling Nailers Photo Pack-14

Brannen, Chris
99Kitchener Rangers-19
00Kitchener Rangers-7
03St. Francis Xavier X-Men-24
05Odessa Jackalopes-2
06Odessa Jackalopes-3

Brannlund, Lars-Ake
67Swedish Hockey-232

Brannon, Scott
05Cape Breton Screaming Eagles-14
06Cape Breton Screaming Eagles-8

Brannstrom, Fabian
94German DEL-74
95German DEL-71
01German Upper Deck-167
02German DEL City Press-43
03German Deg Metro Stars-1
03German DEL-31
04German DEL-43
04German Dusseldorf Metro Stars Postcards-1
05German DEL-63

Brannstrom, Niklas
89Swedish Semic Elitserien Stickers-210
91Swedish Semic Elitserien Stickers-98
92Swedish Semic Elitserien Stickers-120
93Swedish Semic Elitserien-93
94Swedish Leaf-275
95Swedish Upper Deck 1st Division Stars-DS7
97Swedish Collector's Choice-179
99German DEL-257
02Swedish SHL-184
Parallel-184

Brant, Chris
82Kingston Canadians-18
83Sault Ste. Marie Greyhounds-3
84Sault Ste. Marie Greyhounds-4
88ProCards AHL-59
00UK Sekonda Superleague-40
01UK Sheffield Steelers-6

Brantschen, Beat
01Swiss HNL-430

Brar, Dampy
98Las Vegas Thunder-3
98Tacoma Sabercats-4
99Tacoma Sabercats-14
00Tacoma Sabercats-14

Brasar, Per Olov
70Swedish Hockey-73
71Swedish Hockey-163
72Swedish Stickers-165
73Swedish Stickers-49
74Swedish Stickers-27
74Swedish Stickers-206
78North Stars Cloverleaf Dairy-2
78O-Pee-Chee-99
78Topps-99
79Panini Stickers-195
79O-Pee-Chee-192
79Topps-192
80Canucks Silverwood Dairies-3
80Canucks Team Issue-3
80O-Pee-Chee-291
80Pepsi-Cola Caps-103
81Canucks Team Issue-2
81O-Pee-Chee-330
81O-Pee-Chee Stickers-244

Brasey, Patrice
91Finnish Semic World Champ Stickers-182
91Swedish Semic World Champ Stickers-182
92Finnish Semic-198
93Swedish Semic World Champ Stickers-113
93Swiss HNL-36
95Swiss HNL-63
96Swiss HNL-207
98Swiss Power Play Stickers-82
00Swiss Panini Stickers-303
01Swiss HNL-325
02Swiss HNL-338

Brashear, Donald
907th Inn. Sketch QMJHL-245
917th Inn. Sketch QMJHL-139
92Fredericton Canadiens-3
93Fredericton Canadiens-3
94Canadiens Postcards-2
94Donruss-146
94Leaf-227
94Ultra-310
94Fredericton Canadiens-4
94Classic Enforcers-E1
94Classic Pro Prospects-146
95Canadiens Postcards-1
95Upper Deck-411
Electric Ice-411
Electric Ice Gold-411
96Be A Player-181
96Be A Player-P181
Autographs-181
Autographs Silver-181
96Canucks Postcards-8
97Pacific Invincible NHL Regime-200
97Pacific Omega-227
Copper-227
Dark Gray-227
Emerald Green-227
Gold-227
Ice Blue-227
97Revolution-138
Copper-138
Emerald-138
Ice Blue-138
Silver-138
97Score Canucks-17
Platinum-17
Premier-17
97Upper Deck-376
98Aurora-187
98Be A Player-143
Press Release-143
98BAP Gold-143
98BAP Autographs-143
98BAP Autographs Gold-143
98BAP Tampa Bay All Star Game-143
98Crown Royale-133
Limited Series-133
98Pacific-425
Ice Blue-425
Red-425
98Pacific Dynagon Ice-186
Blue-186
Red-186
98Paramount-233
Copper-233
Emerald Green-233
Holo-Electric-233
Ice Blue-233
Silver-233
98Revolution Three Pronged Attack-10
98Revolution 3 Pronged Attack Parallel-10
99Pacific-421
Copper-421
Emerald Green-421
Gold-421
Ice Blue-421
Premiere Date-421
Red-421
99Paramount-233
Copper-233
Emerald-233
Gold-233
Holographic Emerald-233
Holographic Gold-233
Holographic Silver-233
Ice Blue-233
Premiere Date-233
Red-233
Silver-233
00BAP Memorabilia Update Tough Materials-T6
00BAP Mem Update Tough Materials Gold-T6
00Pacific-405
Copper-405
Gold-405
Ice Blue-405
Premiere Date-405
00Topps Heritage-164
00Upper Deck-401
Exclusives Tier 1-401
Exclusives Tier 2-401
00Upper Deck Vintage-351
00Upper Deck Vintage-357
01BAP Memorabilia-462
Emerald-462
Ruby-462
Sapphire-462
01BAP Update Tough Customers-TC16
01BAP Update Tough Customers-TC19
01Flyers Postcards-2
01O-Pee-Chee-190
01O-Pee-Chee Premier Parallel-190
01Pacific-378
01Pacific-424
Extreme LTD-378
Gold-424
Hobby LTD-378
Premiere Date-378
Retail LTD-378
01Pacific Arena Exclusives-378
01Pacific Arena Exclusives-424
01Parkhurst-354
01Topps-190
OPC Parallel-190
Reserve Emblems-DOB
Reserve Jerseys-DOB
Reserve Name Plates-DOB
Reserve Numbers-DOB
Reserve Patches-DOB
01Upper Deck-403
Exclusives-403
01Upper Deck Ice-110
01Upper Deck Victory-339
Gold-339
02BAP First Edition-247
02BAP Sig Series Auto Buybacks 1998-143
02BAP Signature Series Famous Scraps-FS11
02BAP Signature Series Golf-GS33
02Flyers Postcards-20
02Pacific-276
Blue-276
Red-276
02Pacific Complete-68
Red-68
02Parkhurst-177
Bronze-177
Gold-177
Silver-177
02SP Game Used Authentic Fabrics-AFDB
02SP Game Used Authentic Fabrics Gold-AFDB
02SP Game Used Authentic Fabrics Rainbow-AFDB
02Topps Total-226
02Upper Deck-373
Exclusives-373
02Upper Deck Beckett UD Promos-373
02Upper Deck Number Crunchers-NC9
02Upper Deck Vintage-191
03Flyers Postcards-2
03ITG Action-486
Jerseys-M9
03O-Pee-Chee-209
03O-Pee-Chee-282
03OPC Blue-209
03OPC Blue-282
03OPC Gold-209
03OPC Gold-282
03OPC Red-209
03OPC Red-282
03Pacific-247
Blue-247
Red-247
03Pacific Complete-1
Red-1
03SP Game Used Team Threads-TTDSS
03Topps-209
03Topps-282
Blue-209
Blue-282
Gold-209
Gold-282
Red-209
Red-282
03Upper Deck-385
Canadian Exclusives-385
HG-385
Tough Customers-TC-15
UD Exclusives-385
Classic Portraits Hockey Royalty-DSB
03Upper Deck MVP-315
Gold Script-315
Silver Script-315
Canadian Exclusives-315
05Flyers Team Issue-2
05ITG Tough Customers-DB
Autographs-DB
Complete Jerseys-DB
Double Memorabilia-DB
Emblem and Numbers-DB
Famous Battles Autographs-BB
Jerseys-DB
Signed Memorabilia-DB
05Parkhurst-366
Facsimile Auto Parallel-366
05SP Game Used Authentic Fabrics Dual-WB
05SP Game Used Authentic Fabrics Triple-DBS
05SP Game Used Authentic Patches Dual-WB
05SP Game Used Authentic Patches Triple-DBS
05Upper Deck-143
HG Glossy-143
Jerseys-J-DBR
Notable Numbers-N-DBR
Patches-P-DOB
05Upper Deck MVP-288
Gold-288
Platinum-288
05Upper Deck Toronto Fall Expo-143
05Upper Deck Victory-146
Black-146
Gold-146
Silver-146
06Black Diamond Jerseys-JDB
06Black Diamond Jerseys Black-JDB
06Black Diamond Jerseys Gold-JDB
06Black Diamond Jerseys Ruby-JDB
06Flair Showcase Stitches-SSDB
06Fleer Fabricology-FDB
06O-Pee-Chee-488
Rainbow-488
06UD Powerplay Last Man Standing-LM4
06UD Powerplay Specialists-SDB
06UD Powerplay Specialists Patches-PDB
06Upper Deck-446
Exclusives Parallel-446
High Gloss Parallel-446
Masterpieces-446

Brass, John
96OCN Blizzard-9

Brassard, Andre
89Nashville Knights-2

Brassard, Chris
93London Knights-5
94Kitchener Rangers-19
01Greensboro Generals-13
02Bossier-Shreveport Mudbugs-3
03Bossier-Shreveport Mudbugs-5
05Bossier-Shreveport Mudbugs-2

Brassard, Derick
04Drummondville Voltigeurs-4
04Drummondville Voltigeurs-NNO
05ITG Heroes/Prosp Toronto Expo Parallel -135
05Drummondville Voltigeurs-2
05Extreme Top Prospects Signature Edition-S11
05ITG Heroes and Prospects-135
Autographs-A-DBR
Oh Canada-OC-4
Oh Canada Gold-OC-4
Team Cherry-TC16
06ITG Ultimate Memorabilia Future Star-17
06ITG Ultimate Memorabilia Future Star Gold-17
06ITG Ultimate Memorabilia Future Star Autos-8
06ITG Ultimate Memorabilia Future Star Autos Gold-8
06ITG Ultimate Memorabilia Future Star Patches Autos-8
06ITG Ultimate Memorabilia Future Star Patches Autos Gold-8
06Drummondville Voltigeurs-1
06ITG Heroes and Prospects-84
Autographs-ADB
CHL Top Prospects-TP08
CHL Top Prospects Gold-TP08
Class of 2006-CL03
Complete CHL Logos-CHL05

Brassard, Joel
917th Inn. Sketch QMJHL-38

Bratash, Oleg
90O-Pee-Chee-525
98Russian Hockey League-141

Brathwaite, Frank
02Between the Pipes Tandems-15

Brathwaite, Fred
89Oshawa Generals-35
89Oshawa Generals 7th Inning Sketch-23
897th Inn. Sketch OHL-23
907th Inn. Sketch OHL-327
907th Inn. Sketch Memorial Cup-77
91Oshawa Generals Sheet-23
917th Inn. Sketch OHL-169
93Donruss-119
93PowerPlay-339
93Score-618
Gold-618
Canadian-618
Canadian Gold-618
93Ultra-313
93Upper Deck-435
94Donruss-320
94Leaf-26
94Ultra-289
96Collector's Edge Ice-31
Prism-31
97Manitoba Moose-A5
99BAP Memorabilia-360
Gold-360
Silver-360
99O-Pee-Chee-108
99O-Pee-Chee Chrome-108
99O-Pee-Chee Chrome Refractors-108
99Pacific-51
Copper-51
Emerald Green-51
Gold-51
Ice Blue-51
Premiere Date-51
Red-51
99Pacific Omega-34
Copper-34
Gold-34
Ice Blue-34
Premiere Date-34
99Revolution-23
Premiere Date-23
Red-23
Shadow Series-23
99SP Authentic-15
99Topps/OPC-108
99Topps/OPC Chrome-108
Refractors-108
99Upper Deck MVP SC Edition-32
Gold Script-32
Silver Script-32
Super Script-32
00Aurora-22
Pinstripes-22
Pinstripes Premiere Date-22
Premiere Date-22
00BAP Memorabilia-190
Emerald-190
Ruby-190
Sapphire-190
Promos-190
00BAP Mem Chicago Sportsfest Copper-190
00BAP Memorabilia Chicago Sportsfest Blue-190
00BAP Memorabilia Chicago Sportsfest Gold-190
00BAP Memorabilia Chicago Sportsfest Ruby-190
00BAP Memorabilia Chicago Sun-Times Ruby-190
00BAP Memorabilia Chicago Sun-Times Gold-190
00BAP Mem Chicago Sun-Times Sapphire-190
00BAP Mem Toronto Fall Expo Copper-190
00BAP Memorabilia Toronto Fall Expo Gold-190
00BAP Memorabilia Toronto Fall Expo Ruby-190
00BAP Parkhurst 2000-P28
00BAP Signature Series-182
Emerald-182
Ruby-182
Sapphire-182
Autographs-66
Autographs Gold-66
00O-Pee-Chee-51
00O-Pee-Chee Parallel-51
00Pacific-61
Copper-61
Gold-61
Ice Blue-61
Premiere Date-61
In the Cage Net-Fusions-2
00Paramount-33
Copper-33
Gold-33
Holo-Gold-33
Holo-Silver-33
Ice Blue-33
Premiere Date-33
Glove Side Net Fusions-4
Glove Side Net Fusions Platinum-4
00Private Stock-14
Gold-14
Premiere Date-14
Retail-14
Silver-14
00Revolution-20
Blue-20
Premiere Date-20
Red-20
00SPx-8
Spectrum-8
00Stadium Club-120
Glove Save-GS10
00Titanium Game Gear-64
00Titanium Game Gear Patches-64
00Titanium Draft Day Edition-13
Patches-13
00Topps/OPC-51
Parallel-51
Autographs-AFB
00Topps Chrome-41
OPC Refractors-41
Refractors-41
00Topps Gold Label Class 1-52
Gold-52
00Topps Gold Label Class 2-52
00Topps Gold Label Class 2 Gold-52
00Topps Gold Label Class 3-52
00Topps Gold Label Class 3 Gold-52
00Topps Heritage-156
00Topps Stars-61
Blue-61
00UD Heroes-16
00Upper Deck-30
Exclusives Tier 1-30
Exclusives Tier 2-30
00Upper Deck MVP-30
First Stars-30
Second Stars-30
Third Stars-30
00Upper Deck Victory-36
00Upper Deck Vintage-56
00Upper Deck Vintage-61
00Upper Deck Vintage-62
Great Gloves-GG4
01BAP Memorabilia-33
Emerald-33
Ruby-33
Sapphire-33
01BAP Signature Series-196
Autographs-196
Autographs Gold-196
01Between the Pipes-67
01McDonald's Pacific-32
01O-Pee-Chee-217
01O-Pee-Chee Premier Parallel-217
01Pacific-57
Extreme LTD-57
Hobby LTD-57
Premiere Date-57
Retail LTD-57
Jerseys-4
01Pacific Adrenaline-157
Blue-157
Premiere Date-157
Red-157
Retail-157
Jerseys-39
Power Play-29
01Pacific Arena Exclusives-57
01Pacific Heads-Up-79
Blue-79
Premiere Date-79
Red-79
Silver-79
01Private Stock Game Gear-86
01Private Stock Game Gear Patches-86
01Private Stock PS-2002-60
01Titanium Double-Sided Jerseys-37
01Topps-217
OPC Parallel-217
01Topps Heritage-177
01Upper Deck-382
Exclusives-382
01Vanguard Memorabilia-5
01Vanguard Patches-5
02BAP Memorabilia-141
02BAP Memorabilia-256
Emerald-141
Emerald-256
Ruby-141
Ruby-256
Sapphire-141
Sapphire-256
NHL All-Star Game-141
NHL All-Star Game-256
NHL All-Star Game Blue-141
NHL All-Star Game Blue-256
NHL All-Star Game Green-141
NHL All-Star Game Green-256
NHL All-Star Game Red-141
NHL All-Star Game Red-256
02BAP Memorabilia Toronto Fall Expo-141
02BAP Memorabilia Toronto Fall Expo-256
02BAP Sig Series Auto Buybacks 2000-66
02BAP Sig Series Auto Buybacks 2001-196
02Between the Pipes-58
Gold-58
Silver-58
Jerseys-40
02Blues Team Issue-1
02O-Pee-Chee-197
02O-Pee-Chee Premier Blue Parallel-197
02O-Pee-Chee Premier Red Parallel-197
02O-Pee-Chee Factory Set-197
02Pacific-319
Blue-319
Red-319
02Pacific Complete-159
Red-159
02Topps-197
OPC Blue Parallel-197
OPC Red Parallel-197
Factory Set-197
02Topps Total-202
02UD Mask Collection-75
02UD Mask Collection-77
02UD Mask Collection Beckett Promos-75
02UD Mask Collection Beckett Promos-77
02Upper Deck-396
Exclusives-396
02Upper Deck Beckett UD Promos-396
03BAP Memorabilia-120
Emerald-120
Gold-120
Ruby-120
Sapphire-120
03Pacific Complete-486
Red-486
03Pacific Invincible Jerseys-7
04Russian Legion-6
05Russian Hockey League RHL-13

Brauer, Cam
88Regina Pats-2
90ProCards AHL/IHL-173
91ProCards-98

Brault, Bob
51Bas Du Fleuve-22
52Bas Du Fleuve-61

Brault, Jean-Francois
03Halifax Mooseheads-18
04Halifax Mooseheads-11
05Halifax Mooseheads-20

Braun, Constantin
05German DEL-306

Braun, Frank
70Finnish Jaakiekko-82
70Swedish Hockey-367
70Swedish Masterserien-171
70Swedish Masterserien-173
70Swedish Masterserien-174
74Finnish Jenkki-113
83Swedish Semic VM Stickers-145

Braun, Manfred
94German First League-224

Braun, Ryan
99OCN Blizzard-12
00OCN Blizzard-11
01OCN Blizzard-14
02OCN Blizzard-12

Braunlich, Steffan
06Bloomington PrairieThunder-5

Bray, Josh
05Red Deer Rebels-24

Bray, Mike
98Halifax Mooseheads-8
98Halifax Mooseheads Second Edition-12
00Quebec Remparts-11
Signed-11
01Quebec Remparts-10

Brazda, Radomir
94Czech APS Extraliga-256
95Czech APS Extraliga-320
96Czech APS Extraliga-145
97Czech DS Stickers-251
99Czech Score Blue 2000-130
99Czech Score Red Ice 2000-130

Brazeau, Pascal
93Quebec Pee-Wee Tournament-1041

Brdarovich, Johnny
98San Antonio Iguanas-13
99San Antonio Iguanas-5

Brearley, Peter
93Kitchener Rangers-17
98Roanoke Express-20
99Huntington Blizzard-7
01Bakersfield Condors-2
02New Mexico Scorpions-3

Breault, Benjamin
04Baie-Comeau Drakkar-4
05ITG Heroes/Prosp Toronto Expo Parallel -415
05Baie-Comeau Drakkar-1
05ITG Heroes and Prospects-415
Team Orr-TO3

Breault, Frank
84Chicoutimi Sagueneens-5
88ProCards AHL-216
89ProCards AHL-2
90Kings Smokey-13
90Pro Set-612
91O-Pee-Chee-496
91Pro Set-541
French-541
91Topps-496
92Phoenix Roadrunners-2
02Drummondville Voltigeurs-1

Brebant, Rick
00UK Sekonda Superleague-152
00UK Sheffield Steelers-10
01UK Sheffield Steelers-7
02UK Sheffield Steelers-3
03UK Manchester Phoenix-2
04UK Thommo's Top 10-4

Brechbuhl, Bruno
96Swiss HNL-328
98Swiss Power Play Stickers-140
99Swiss Panini Stickers-140
00Swiss Panini Stickers-184
00Swiss Slapshot Mini-Cards-LT10
01Swiss HNL-202
02Swiss HNL-108

Breen, Christopher
06Saginaw Spirit-7

Breen, George
95Classic-70
Autographs-1
95Classic Five-Sport *-129
Autographs-129

Breen, Mike
79Rochester Americans-2

Breen, Neil
02New Mexico Scorpions-13

Brehm, Jean-Claude
94German First League-136

Breilin, Matti
66Finnish Jaakiekkosarja-69

Breistroff, Michel
92Harvard Crimson-4
94Finnish Jaa Kiekko-218

Breitbach, Robin
02Swiss HNL-179

Breitenbach, Ken
77O-Pee-Chee NHL-279

Breitkreuz, Adam
00Calgary Hitmen-5
01Calgary Hitmen-5
01Calgary Hitmen Autographed-5

Breitkreuz, Cameron
04Tulsa Oilers-3

Breitner, Stefan
94German First League-375

Breitschuh, Jurgen
04German Berlin Eisbarens 50th Anniv-60

Brejta, Grzegorz
93Quebec Pee-Wee Tournament-1516

Brekelmans, Cory
00Sarnia Sting-4

Brekke, Brent
92Western Michigan Broncos-3
93Western Michigan Broncos-2
95Dayton Bombers-14

Bremberg, Fredrik
03Swedish Elite-165
Silver-165
04Swedish Elitset-19
Gold-19
05Swedish SHL Elitset-168
Gold-168
Icons-9
06Swedish SHL Elitset-166
Playmakers-2

Brendl, Pavel
98Calgary Hitmen-6
98Calgary Hitmen Autographs-6
99Black Diamond-91
Diamond Cut-91
Final Cut-91
99O-Pee-Chee-271
99O-Pee-Chee Chrome-271
99O-Pee-Chee Chrome Refractors-271
99SP Authentic-122
99SPx-166
Radiance-166
Spectrum-166
99Topps/OPC-271
99Topps/OPC Chrome-271
Refractors-271
99Ultimate Victory-109
1/1-109
Parallel-109
Parallel 100-109
99Upper Deck-306
Exclusives-306
Exclusives 1 of 1-306
99Upper Deck Sobey's Memorial Cup-7
99Upper Deck Gold Reserve-306
99Upper Deck MVP SC Edition-194
Gold Script-194
Silver Script-194
Super Script-194
Game-Used Souvenirs-GUPB
Game-Used Souvenirs-SGPB
ProSign-PBR
99Upper Deck Ovation-61
Standing Ovation-61
99Upper Deck Victory-358
99Calgary Hitmen-2
99Calgary Hitmen Autographs-2
99Bowman CHL-5
99Bowman CHL-83
Gold-5
Gold-83
OPC International-5
OPC International-83
Autographs-BA25
Autographs Gold-BA25
Autographs Silver-BA25
Scout's Choice-SC3
99UD Prospects-33
CHL Class-C7
Destination the Show-DS2
International Stars-IN3
Signatures of Tradition-PB
00SP Authentic BuyBacks-11
00SP Authentic Sign of the Times-BR
00SP Authentic Sign of the Times-B/Y
00SPx-123
Spectrum-123
00UD Heroes Signs of Greatness-PA
00UD Reserve Buyback Autographs-37
00UD Reserve Buyback Autographs-38
00Upper Deck-212
Exclusives Tier 1-212
Exclusives Tier 2-212
Signs of Greatness-SPB
MVP Excellence-ME2
MVP Mark of Excellence-SGBB
00Calgary Hitmen-6
00UD CHL Prospects-46
Autographs-A-PB
CHL Class-CC6
Destination the Show-D3
Game Jersey Autographs-S-PB
Game Jerseys-PB
Supremacy-CS5
01Atomic-119
Premiere Date-119
Rookie Reaction-6
01Atomic Toronto Fall Expo-119
01BAP Memorabilia-380

Emerald-380
Ruby-380
Sapphire-380
01BAP Signature Series-220
Autographs-220
Autographs Gold-220
01Pacific Adrenaline-219
Blue-219
Premiere Date-219
Red-219
Retail-219
Rookie Report-13
01Pacific Heads-Up-114
01Parkhurst-275
01Parkhurst Beckett Promos-275
01Private Stock-106
Gold-106
Premiere Date-106
Retail-106
Silver-106
Game Gear-70
Game Gear Patches-70
Moments in Time-8
01Private Stock Pacific Nights-106
01Private Stock PS-2002-84
01Private Stock Reserve-R7
01SP Authentic-124
Limited-124
Limited Gold-124
01SP Game Used-40
01SPx-120
01Stadium Club-113
Award Winners-113
Master Photos-113
01Titanium Double-Sided Jerseys-31
01Titanium Double-Sided Jerseys-33
01Titanium Double-Sided Patches-33
01Titanium Draft Day Edition-155
01Topps Heritage-183
01Upper Deck-358
Exclusives-358
01Vanguard-71
Blue-71
Red-71
Memorabilia-19
One of Ones-71
Premiere Date-71
Prime Prospects-14
Proofs-71
01Czech Stadion-235
02BAP First Edition-82
Jerseys-82
02BAP Memorabilia-50
02BAP Memorabilia-236
Emerald-50
Emerald-236
Ruby-50
Ruby-236
Sapphire-50
Sapphire-236
NHL All-Star Game-50
NHL All-Star Game-236
NHL All-Star Game Blue-50
NHL All-Star Game Blue-236
NHL All-Star Game Green-50
NHL All-Star Game Green-236
NHL All-Star Game Red-50
NHL All-Star Game Red-236
02BAP Memorabilia Toronto Fall Expo-50
02BAP Memorabilia Toronto Fall Expo-236
02BAP Signature Series-94
Autographs-94
Autograph Buybacks 2001-220
Autographs Gold-94
02Bowman YoungStars-111
Gold-111
Silver-111
Autographs-PB
Jerseys-PB
Patches-PB
Double Stuff-PB
Triple Stuff-PB
Rivals-BRPB
Rivals Patches-1
Sticks-PB
02Flyers Postcards-19
02O-Pee-Chee-272
02O-Pee-Chee Premier Blue Parallel-272
02O-Pee-Chee Premier Red Parallel-272
02O-Pee-Chee Factory Set-272
02Pacific Calder-60
Silver-60
02Pacific Complete-532
Red-532
02Pacific Exclusive-124
02Parkhurst Retro-188
Minis-188
02SP Authentic-127
Sign of the Times-BE
Sign of the Times-GB
02SP Game Used Future Fabrics-FFPB
02SP Game Used Future Fabrics Gold-FFPB
02SP Game Used Future Fabrics Rainbow-FFPB
02SP Game Used Signature Style-BR
02Stadium Club-113
Silver Decoy Cards-113
Proofs-113
02Topps-272
OPC Blue Parallel-272
OPC Red Parallel-272
Factory Set-272
02UD Honor Roll Signature Class-BR
02UD Piece of History Mark of Distinction-PA
02UD Premier Collection Signatures Bronze-SBR
02UD Premier Collection Signatures Gold-SBR
02UD Premier Collection Signatures Silver-SBR
02UD Top Shelf Signatures-PA
02Upper Deck-372
Exclusives-372
02Upper Deck Beckett UD Promos-372
02Upper Deck Bright Futures-PB
02Upper Deck Rookie Update-19
Autographs-BR
03Hurricanes Postcards-6
03ITG Action-117
03Pacific Complete-500
Red-500
03Upper Deck-38
Big Playmakers-BP-PL
Canadian Exclusives-38
HG-38
03Upper Deck MVP-86
Gold Script-86
Silver Script-86
Canadian Exclusives-86
SportsNut-SN17
03Upper Deck Victory-36
Bronze-36
Gold-36
Silver-36
03Lowell Lock Monsters-19
03Lowell Lock Monsters Photo Album-19
06Swedish SHL Elitset-260
Performers-14

Brenk, Jake
03Minnesota State Mavericks-3

Brennan, Chad
93St. Cloud State Huskies-2

Brennan, Doug
33V357 Ice Kings-45
34Diamond Matchbooks Silver-5

Brennan, Kip
98Sudbury Wolves-17
00Lowell Lock Monsters-24
01BAP Memorabilia-329
Emerald-329
Ruby-329
Sapphire-329
01UD Playmakers-121
01Manchester Monarchs-9A
02Pacific Complete-569
Red-569
02Pacific Quest for the Cup-121
Gold-121
02Manchester Monarchs-4
03O-Pee-Chee-314
03OPC Blue-314
03OPC Gold-314
03OPC Red-314
03Topps-314
Blue-314
Gold-314
Red-314
04Chicago Wolves-18
05Ducks Team Issue-1

Brennan, Lester
37V356 Worldwide Gum-106

Brennan, Michael
91Air Canada SJHL-B50

Brennan, Rich
91Upper Deck Czech World Juniors-76
97Be A Player-236
Autographs-236
Autographs Die-Cuts-236
Autographs Prismatic Die-Cuts-236
98Pacific-377
Ice Blue-377
Red-377
98Hartford Wolf Pack-27
99Lowell Lock Monsters-5
00Lowell Lock Monsters-6
01Manchester Monarchs-5B
02Providence Bruins-5
03Providence Bruins-1
04German Augsburg Panthers Postcards-5
04German DEL Update-287
05German DEL-263
06German DEL-157

Brennan, Terry
93Quebec Pee-Wee Tournament-1302

Brenneman, John
64Beehive Group III Photos-156
64Coca-Cola Caps-27
65Maple Leafs White Border-4
68O-Pee-Chee-83
68Shirriff Coins-110
68Topps-83
07Maple Leafs 1967 Commemorative-3

Brenner, Anthony
94German First League-362

Brenner, Jordan
00Barrie Colts-3

Brenner, Matt
97Central Texas Stampede-1
98Amarillo Rattlers-1

Brent, Steve
91Air Canada SJHL-D42
92Saskatchewan JHL-6

Brent, Tim
00St. Michaels Majors-8
01St. Michaels Majors-9
02St. Michaels Majors-8
03St. Michael's Majors-6
04Cincinnati Mighty Ducks-8
04ITG Heroes and Prospects-107
Autographs-TB
04ITG Heroes/Prospects Toronto Expo '05-107
04ITG Heroes/Prospects Expo Heroes/Pros-107
05Portland Pirates-4
06Hot Prospects-190
06Portland Pirates-6

Brenton, Matthew
06Moncton Wildcats-4

Brenzavich, Dan
98Thunder Bay Thunder Cats-9
99Asheville Smoke-3

Brenzig, Thomas
94German First League-264

Bresagk, Michael
94German DEL-249
95German DEL-244
95Swedish World Championships Stickers-59
98German DEL-143
98German DEL-319
99German DEL-76
99German DEL-383
00German DEL-74
01German Upper Deck-76
02German DEL City Press-67
03German DEL-94
04German DEL-105
05German DEL-83
05German DEL-369
06German DEL-54

Bresagk, Thomas
94German DEL-409
95German DEL-407

Bresciani, Joel
03Huntsville Channel Cats-2

Breslin, Tim
91ProCards-395
92Phoenix Roadrunners-3
93Phoenix Roadrunners-1
96Chicago Wolves-11
98Chicago Wolves Turner Cup-15

Breton, Christian
87Hull Olympiques-4

Breton, Etienne
05Cape Breton Screaming Eagles-15
06Cape Breton Screaming Eagles-2

Breton, Luc
77Granby Vics-2

Brewer, Carl
44Beehive Group II Photos-385
59Parkhurst-3
60Parkhurst-18
60Shirriff Coins-3
60York Photos-7
61Parkhurst-18
61Shirriff/Salada Coins-45
61York Yellow Backs-13
62Parkhurst-8
62Shirriff Coins-5
62Shirriff Coins-51
62York Iron-On Transfers-5
63Maple Leafs Team Issue-3
63Maple Leafs Team Issue-4
63Parkhurst-8
63Parkhurst-68
63Toronto Star-7
63York White Backs-17
64Beehive Group III Photos-157
64Coca-Cola Caps-92
64Topps-75
64Toronto Star-7
65Topps-78
69O-Pee-Chee-59
Four-in-One-7
69Topps-59
70O-Pee-Chee-243
71Blues Postcards-5
71O-Pee-Chee-222
71Toronto Sun-235
727-Eleven Slurpee Cups WHA-3
79Maple Leafs Postcards-5
92Parkhurst Parkie Reprints-PR13
94Parkhurst Missing Link Future Stars-FS1
94Parkhurst Tall Boys-114

Brewer, Eric
97Black Diamond-90
Double Diamond-90
Triple Diamond-90
Quadruple Diamond-90
97Bowman CHL-153
OPC-153
Autographs-33
Bowman's Best-8
Bowman's Best Atomic Refractors-8
Bowman's Best Refractor-8
98Be A Player-235
Press Release-235
98BAP Gold-235
98BAP Autographs-235
98BAP Autographs Gold-235
98Black Diamond-52
Double Diamond-52
Triple Diamond-52
Quadruple Diamond-52
Myriad-M29
Myriad 2-M29
98Bowman's Best-115
Refractors-115
Atomic Refractors-115
Mirror Image Fusion-F17
Mirror Image Fusion Refractors-F17
Mirror Image Fusion Atomic Refractors-F17
98Pacific Dynagon Ice-114
Blue-114
Red-114
98Pacific Omega-153
Red-153
Opening Day Issue-153
98SP Authentic-102
Power Shift-102
Snapshots-SS21
98SPx Top Prospects-37
Radiance-37
Spectrum-37
98Topps Gold Label Class 1-68
Black-68
Black One of One-68
One of One-68
Red-68
Red One of One-68
98Topps Gold Label Class 2-68
98Topps Gold Label Class 2 Black-68
98Topps Gold Label Class 2 Black 1 of 1-68
98Topps Gold Label Class 2 One of One-68
98Topps Gold Label Class 2 Red-68
98Topps Gold Label Class 2 Red One of One-68
98Topps Gold Label Class 3-68
98Topps Gold Label Class 3 Black-68
98Topps Gold Label Class 3 Black 1 of 1-68
98Topps Gold Label Class 3 One of One-68
98Topps Gold Label Class 3 Red-68
98Topps Gold Label Class 3 Red One of One-68
98UD Choice-256
Prime Choice Reserve-256
Reserve-256
98Upper Deck-417
Exclusives-417
Exclusives 1 of 1-417
Game Jerseys-GJ13
Generation Next-GN18
Generation Next Quantum 1-GN18
Generation Next Quantum 2-GN18
Generation Next Quantum 3-GN18
Profiles-P5
Profiles Quantum 1-P5
Profiles Quantum 2-P5
Profiles Quantum 3-P5
Gold Reserve-417
98Upper Deck MVP-124
Gold Script-124
Silver Script-124
Super Script-124
ProSign-EB
98Prince George Cougars-5
99O-Pee-Chee-97
99O-Pee-Chee Chrome-97
99O-Pee-Chee Chrome Refractors-97
99Pacific-251
Copper-251
Emerald Green-251
Gold-251
Ice Blue-251
Premiere Date-251
Red-251
99Paramount-140
Copper-140
Emerald-140
Gold-140
Holographic Emerald-140
Holographic Gold-140
Holographic Silver-140
Ice Blue-140
Premiere Date-140
Red-140
Silver-140
99SPx-92
Radiance-92
Spectrum-92
99Stadium Club-110
First Day Issue-110
One of a Kind-110
Printing Plates Black-110
Printing Plates Cyan-110
Printing Plates Magenta-110
Printing Plates Yellow-110
Capture the Action-CA8
Capture the Action Game View-CAG8
99Topps/OPC-97
99Topps/OPC Chrome-97
Refractors-97
99Upper Deck-82
Exclusives-82
Exclusives 1 of 1-82
Crunch Time-CT10
Crunch Time Quantum Gold-CT10
Crunch Time Quantum Silver-CT10
New Ice Age-N18
New Ice Age Quantum Gold-N18
New Ice Age Quantum Silver-N18
99Upper Deck Gold Reserve-82
99Upper Deck HoloGrFx-36
Ausome-36
99Upper Deck MVP-126
Gold Script-126
Silver Script-126
Super Script-126
Draft Report-DR4
99Upper Deck Retro-53
Gold-53
Platinum-53
99Upper Deck Victory-176
99Upper Deck Victory-177
99Lowell Lock Monsters-17
00Upper Deck-297
Exclusives Tier 1-297
Exclusives Tier 2-297
00Upper Deck Vintage-140
01BAP Signature Series-184
Autographs-184
Autographs Gold-184
01Pacific Adrenaline-71
Blue-71
Premiere Date-71
Red-71
Retail-71
01Upper Deck-301
Exclusives-301
02BAP First Edition-198
02BAP First Edition-417R
02BAP Memorabilia-39
Emerald-39
Ruby-39
Sapphire-39
NHL All-Star Game-39
NHL All-Star Game Blue-39
NHL All-Star Game Green-39
NHL All-Star Game Red-39
02BAP Memorabilia Toronto Fall Expo-39
02BAP Signature Series-44
Autographs-44
Autograph Buybacks 1998-235
Autograph Buybacks 2001-184
Autographs Gold-44
Team Quads-TQ17
02McDonald's Pacific Salt Lake Gold-4
02NHL Power Play Stickers-24
02Oilers Postcards-1
02O-Pee-Chee-150
02O-Pee-Chee Premier Blue Parallel-150
02O-Pee-Chee Premier Red Parallel-150
02O-Pee-Chee Factory Set-150
02Pacific-138
Blue-138
Red-138
02Pacific Complete-63
Red-63
02Parkhurst-182
Bronze-182
Gold-182
Silver-182
02Topps-150
OPC Blue Parallel-150
OPC Red Parallel-150
Factory Set-150
02Topps Total-175
02Upper Deck MVP-74
Gold-74
Classics-74
Golden Classics-74
02Upper Deck Victory-86
Bronze-86
Gold-86
Silver-86
03BAP Ultimate Memorabilia Autographs-37
Gold-37
03BAP Ultimate Memorabilia Triple Threads-11
03Beehive-76
Gold-76
Silver-76
03Bowman-52
Gold-52
03Bowman Chrome-52
Refractors-52
Gold Refractors-52
Xfractors-52
03ITG Action-222
Jerseys-M10
03ITG Used Signature Series-4
Gold-4
Autographs-EB
Autographs Gold-EB
Oh Canada-7
Oh Canada Gold-7
Oh Canada Emblems-7
Oh Canada Emblems Gold-7
03NHL Sticker Collection-227
03Oilers Postcards-2
03O-Pee-Chee-197
03OPC Blue-197
03OPC Gold-197
03OPC Red-197
03Pacific-129
Blue-129
Red-129
03Pacific Complete-291
Red-291
03Topps-197
Blue-197
Gold-197
Red-197
03Topps C55-119
Minis-119
Minis American Back-119
Minis American Back Red-119
Minis Bazooka Back-119
Minis Brooklyn Back-119
Minis Hat Trick Back-119
Minis O Canada Back-119
Minis O Canada Back Red-119
Minis Stanley Cup Back-119
03Topps Pristine-54
Gold Refractor Die Cuts-54
Refractors-54
Press Plates Black-54
Press Plates Cyan-54
Press Plates Magenta-54
Press Plates Yellow-54
03Upper Deck-77
Canadian Exclusives-77
HG-77
03Upper Deck MVP-166
Gold Script-166
Silver Script-166
Canadian Exclusives-166
03Upper Deck Victory-75
Bronze-75
Gold-75
Silver-75
03Russian World Championship Stars-35
04UD Toronto Fall Expo Pride of Canada-5
04Upper Deck-71
Canadian Exclusives-71
Heritage Classic-CC-EB
HG Glossy Gold-71
HG Glossy Silver-71
World Cup Tribute-WREB
World Cup Tribute-EBEJWR
05Be A Player Signatures-EB
05Be A Player Signatures Gold-EB
05Blues Team Set-3
05Panini Stickers-336
05SP Game Used Authentic Fabrics Quad-SCPTB
05SP Game Used Authentic Patches Quad -SCPTB
05UD Powerplay Specialists-TSEB
05UD Powerplay Specialists Patches-SPEB
05Upper Deck-415
05Upper Deck Hockey Showcase-HS10
05Upper Deck Showcase Promos-HS10
05Upper Deck MVP-340
Gold-340
Platinum-340
06Be A Player-155
Autographs-155
Signatures-EB
Signatures 25-170
06O-Pee-Chee-429
Rainbow-429
06Panini Stickers-345

Brewer, Justin
93Quebec Pee-Wee Tournament-1754

Brewer, Michael
92Alberta International Team Canada-6
92San Diego Gulls-4

Brezeault, Reginald
907th Inn. Sketch QMJHL-182
917th Inn. Sketch QMJHL-157
93Fort Worth Fire-3
93Roanoke Express-6
99Charlotte Checkers-6

Brezgunov, Vadim
91O-Pee-Chee Inserts-11R
98Czech OFS-353
00Russian Hockey League-316
01Russian Hockey League-113
03Russian Hockey League-108

Brezik, David
98Czech OFS-276
99Czech Score Blue 2000-150
99Czech Score Red Ice 2000-150

Brezina, Robert
94German DEL-426
95German DEL-395
96German DEL-304
99German Bundesliga 2-298
04German Augsburg Panthers Postcards-6
04German DEL-24

Brian, Mark
93Quebec Pee-Wee Tournament-1755

Briand, Arnaud
92Finnish Semic-231
93Swedish Semic World Champ Stickers-259
94Finnish Jaa Kiekko-229
94French National Team-7
00German DEL-20

Briard, Travis
06Penticton Vees-2

Brice, Nathan
00Prince George Cougars-10
02Red Deer Rebels-22
03Red Deer Rebels-17

Brich, Martin
93Swiss HNL-64
95Swiss HNL-115
96Swiss HNL-276
98Swiss Power Play Stickers-229

Brick, Jeff
93RPI Engineers-4

Bricker, Harry
89ProCards AHL-357
90ProCards AHL/IHL-52

Brickley, Andy
83Penguins Coke-2
83Springfield Indians-14
84Penguins Heinz Photos-2
86Devils Police-4
87Panini Stickers-86
88Bruins Postcards-2
89Bruins Sports Action-2
89O-Pee-Chee-29
89Panini Stickers-194
89Topps-29
90Bowman-27
Tiffany-27
90Bruins Sports Action-3
90O-Pee-Chee-88
90Panini Stickers-16
90Pro Set-406
90Topps-88
Tiffany-88
90Upper Deck-84
French-84
92Bowman-17
92Score-296
Canadian-296
92Stadium Club-208
92Topps-109
Gold-109G

Brickley, Brendan
06Texas Tornados-15

Brickley, Quintan
90Knoxville Cherokees-116

Bricknell, Corey
93Niagara Falls Thunder-20

Brideau, Christian
03Quebec Remparts-3

Bridgman, Mel
75Flyers Canada Dry Cans-3
76O-Pee-Chee NHL-26
76Topps-26
77O-Pee-Chee NHL-121
77Topps-121
78O-Pee-Chee-26
78Topps-26
79O-Pee-Chee-201
79Topps-201
80O-Pee-Chee-189
80Topps-189
81Flames Postcards-2
81O-Pee-Chee-248
82Flames Dollars-1
82O-Pee-Chee-39
82O-Pee-Chee-40
82O-Pee-Chee Stickers-213
82Post Cereal-3
82Topps Stickers-213
83Devils Postcards-18
83NHL Key Tags-21
83O-Pee-Chee-226
83O-Pee-Chee Stickers-265
83Topps Stickers-265
84Devils Postcards-18
84O-Pee-Chee-109
84O-Pee-Chee-361
84O-Pee-Chee Stickers-71
847-Eleven Discs-31
84Topps-84
84Kelowna Wings-30
84Victoria Cougars-3
85O-Pee-Chee-42
85O-Pee-Chee Stickers-57
857-Eleven Credit Cards-11
85Topps-42
86Devils Police-5
86O-Pee-Chee-136
86O-Pee-Chee Stickers-203
86Topps-136
87O-Pee-Chee-17
87Panini Stickers-89
87Red Wings Little Caesars-3
87Topps-17
04ITG Franchises US East-427
06Devils Team Set-33

Briell, Lars
00Swedish Upper Deck-23

Brien, David
97Dubuque Fighting Saints-20

Briere, Daniel
94Parkhurst SE-SE261
Gold-SE261
95Bowman Draft Prospects-P4
95Classic-58
CHL All-Stars-AS17
96Upper Deck Ice-120
96All-Sport PPF *-172
96All Sport PPF Gold *-172
96Visions Signings *-68
Autographs-68A
Autographs Silver-68A
97Springfield Falcons-1
97Bowman CHL-50
OPC-50
97Players Club *-12
98Black Diamond-67
Double Diamond-67
Triple Diamond-67
Quadruple Diamond-67
98Bowman's Best-108
Refractors-108
Atomic Refractors-108
Performers-BP8
Performers Refractors-BP8
Performers Atomic Refractors-BP8
98Crown Royale Rookie Class-7
98McDonald's Upper Deck-27
98OPC Chrome-149
Refractors-149
98Pacific Omega-182
Red-182
Opening Day Issue-182
98Revolution-109
Ice Shadow-109
Red-109
98SP Authentic-104
Power Shift-104
98SPx Finite-143
Radiance-143
Spectrum-143
98SPx Top Prospects-48
Radiance-48
Spectrum-48
98Topps-149
O-Pee-Chee-149
98UD Choice-163
98UD Choice Preview-163
98UD Choice Prime Choice Reserve-163
98UD Choice Reserve-163
98Upper Deck-7
Exclusives-7
Exclusives 1 of 1-7
Generation Next-GN19
Generation Next Quantum 1-GN19
Generation Next Quantum 2-GN19
Generation Next Quantum 3-GN19
Gold Reserve-7
98Upper Deck MVP-157
Gold Script-157
Silver Script-157
Super Script-157
98Autographed Collection Autographs *-4
99O-Pee-Chee-144
99O-Pee-Chee Chrome-144
99O-Pee-Chee Chrome Refractors-144
99Topps/OPC-144
99Topps/OPC Chrome-144
Refractors-144
99Upper Deck-272
Exclusives-272
Exclusives 1 of 1-272
99Upper Deck Gold Reserve-272
99Upper Deck MVP-162
Gold Script-162
Silver Script-162
Super Script-162
99Upper Deck Victory-230
99Wayne Gretzky Hockey-131
00Upper Deck Victory-176
01Coyotes Team Issue-3
01Crown Royale-110
Blue-110
Premiere Date-110
Red-110
Retail-110
01Pacific-298
Extreme LTD-298
Hobby LTD-298
Premiere Date-298
Retail LTD-298
01Pacific Arena Exclusives-298
01Topps Reserve Emblems-DAB
01Topps Reserve Jerseys-DAB
01Topps Reserve Name Plates-DAB
01Topps Reserve Numbers-DAB
01Topps Reserve Patches-DAB
01UD Mask Collection Double Patches-DPDB
01UD Mask Collection Jerseys-J-DB
01UD Mask Collection Jersey and Patch-JPDB
01Upper Deck Victory-273
Gold-273
02Atomic-77
Blue-77
Gold-77
Red-77
Hobby Parallel-77
Power Converters-15
02BAP First Edition-64
02BAP First Edition-363
02BAP First Edition-388
Jerseys-64
02BAP Memorabilia-16
02BAP Memorabilia-223
02BAP Memorabilia-340
Emerald-16
Emerald-223
Ruby-16
Ruby-223
Sapphire-16
Sapphire-223
Franchise Players-FP-23
NHL All-Star Game-16
NHL All-Star Game-223
NHL All-Star Game Blue-16
NHL All-Star Game Blue-223
NHL All-Star Game Green-16
NHL All-Star Game Green-223
NHL All-Star Game Red-16
NHL All-Star Game Red-223
02BAP Memorabilia Toronto Fall Expo-16
02BAP Memorabilia Toronto Fall Expo-223
02BAP Signature Series-89
Autographs-89
Autographs Gold-89
Franchise Players-FJ23
02Coyotes Team Issue-34
02Crown Royale-74
Blue-74
Red-74
Retail-74
02ITG Used Franchise Players-F23
02ITG Used Franchise Players Autographs-F23
02ITG Used Franchise Players Gold-F23
02O-Pee-Chee-36
02O-Pee-Chee Premier Blue Parallel-36
02O-Pee-Chee Premier Red Parallel-36
02O-Pee-Chee Factory Set-36
02Pacific-291
Blue-291
Red-291
02Pacific Complete-406
Red-406
02Pacific Exclusive-132
02Pacific Heads-Up-94
Blue-94
Purple-94
Red-94
02Parkhurst-16
Bronze-16
Gold-16
Silver-16
Franchise Players-FP23
Teammates-TT20
02Parkhurst Retro-56
Minis-56
Franchise Players-RF23
02Private Stock Reserve-77
Blue-77
Red-77
Retail-77
02SP Authentic-71
Beckett Promos-71
Super Premiums-SPDB
02SP Game Used First Rounder Patches-DB
02SP Game Used Future Fabrics-FFDB
02SP Game Used Future Fabrics Gold-FFDB
02SP Game Used Future Fabrics Rainbow-FFDB
02Stadium Club Lone Star Signatures Blue-LSDB
02Stadium Club Lone Star Signatures Red-LSDB
02Topps-36
OPC Blue Parallel-36
OPC Red Parallel-36
Factory Set-36
02Topps Chrome-34
Black Border Refractors-34
Refractors-34
02Topps Total-277
02UD Artistic Impressions-69
02UD Artistic Impressions Beckett Promos-69
02UD Artistic Impressions Retrospectives-R69
02UD Artistic Impressions Retrospect Gold-R69
02UD Artistic Impress Retrospect Silver-R69
02UD Artistic Impressions Right Track-RTDB
02UD Artistic Impression Right Track Gold-RTDB
02UD Mask Collection Patches-PGDB
02UD Piece of History-69
02UD Top Shelf-69
Dual Player Jerseys-STBD
Goal Oriented-GODB
Shooting Stars-SHDB
Sweet Sweaters-SWDB
02Upper Deck-137
Exclusives-137
CHL Graduates-CGDB
CHL Graduates Gold-CGDB
Hot Spots-HSDB
Speed Demons-SDDB
02Upper Deck Classic Portraits-77
Hockey Royalty-BLB
Hockey Royalty Limited-BLB
02Upper Deck MVP-140
Gold-140
Classics-140
Golden Classics-140
02Upper Deck Rookie Update-75
02Upper Deck Victory-168
Bronze-168
Gold-168
Silver-168
02Upper Deck Vintage-197
02Upper Deck Vintage-283
02Upper Deck Vintage-314
Tall Boys-T50
Tall Boys Gold-T50
03BAP Memorabilia-19
Emerald-19
Gold-19
Ruby-19
Sapphire-19
03Beehive-26
Gold-26
Silver-26
03Black Diamond-38
Black-38
Green-38
Red-38
Threads-DT-DB
Threads Green-DT-DB
Threads Red-DT-DB
Threads Black-DT-DB
03eTopps-3
03ITG Action-22
Jerseys-M95
03NHL Sticker Collection-264
03O-Pee-Chee-68
03OPC Blue-68
03OPC Gold-68
03OPC Red-68
03Pacific-37
Blue-37
Red-37
03Pacific Calder-11
Silver-11
03Pacific Complete-120
Red-120
03Pacific Exhibit-17
Blue Backs-17
Yellow Backs-17
03Pacific Heads-Up-12
Hobby LTD-12
Retail LTD-12
03Pacific Prism-15
Blue-15
Gold-15
Red-15
03Pacific Quest for the Cup-11
Blue-11
03Pacific Supreme-9
Blue-9
Red-9
Retail-9
03Private Stock Reserve-12
Blue-12
Red-12
Retail-12
03SP Authentic-10
Limited-10
03Titanium-13
Hobby Jersey Number Parallels-13
Retail-13
Retail Jersey Number Parallels-13
03Topps-68
Blue-68
Gold-68
Red-68
03Topps C55-105
Minis-105
Minis American Back-105
Minis American Back Red-105
Minis Bazooka Back-105
Minis Brooklyn Back-105
Minis Hat Trick Back-105
Minis O Canada Back-105
Minis O Canada Back Red-105
Minis Stanley Cup Back-105
03UD Honor Roll-9
03Upper Deck-21
Canadian Exclusives-21
HG-21
03Upper Deck Ice-11
Gold-11
03Upper Deck MVP-52
Gold Script-52
Silver Script-52
Canadian Exclusives-52
03Upper Deck Rookie Update-10
03Upper Deck Victory-20
Bronze-20
Gold-20
Silver-20
04Pacific-30
Blue-30
Red-30
04SP Authentic Buybacks-27
04SP Authentic Buybacks-28
04SP Authentic Buybacks-29
04SP Authentic Buybacks-30
04SP Authentic Buybacks-31
04SP Authentic Buybacks-32
04SP Authentic Buybacks-33
04SP Authentic Buybacks-34
04SP Authentic Buybacks-35
04SP Authentic Rookie Review-RR-DA
04SP Authentic Sign of the Times-ST-DB
04UD All-World-84
Gold-84
Autographs-84
Quad Autographs-AQ-GSC
Six Autographs-AS-SWT
04Upper Deck-19
Canadian Exclusives-19
HG Glossy Gold-19
HG Glossy Silver-19
05Be A Player-11
First Period-11
Second Period-11
Third Period-11
Overtime-11
Dual Signatures-BD
Signatures-DB
Signatures Gold-DB
Triple Signatures-BUF
05Beehive-13
Matte-13
05McDonalds Upper Deck-22
05Panini Stickers-34
05Parkhurst-62
Facsimile Auto Parallel-62
Signatures-DB
05SP Authentic-15
Limited-15
Sign of the Times Triples-TDBV
05SP Game Used Authentic Fabrics-AF-BE
05SP Game Used Authentic Fabrics Autos-AAF-BE
05SP Game Used Authentic Fabrics Dual-BB
05SP Game Used Authentic Fabric Dual Auto-BB
05SP Game Used Authentic Fabrics Gold-AF-BE
05SP Game Used Authentic Fabrics Quad-BADS
05SP Game Used Authentic Fabrics Quad-MNDB
05SP Game Used Authentic Patches Quad -BADS
05SP Game Used Authentic Patches Quad -MNDB
05SP Game Used Authentic Patches-AP-BE
05SP Game Used Authentic Patch Autos-AAP-BE
05SP Game Used Authentic Patches Dual-BB
05SP Game Used Authentic Patch Dual Autos-BB
05SP Game Used Auto Draft-AD-DB
05SP Game Used Awesome Authentics-AA-DB
05SP Game Used Game Gear-GG-DB
05SP Game Used Game Gear Autographs-AG-DB
05SP Game Used Signature Sticks-SS-DB
05SPx Winning Combos-WC-DB
05SPx Winning Combos Autographs-AWC-DB
05SPx Winning Combos Gold-WC-DB
05SPx Winning Combos Spectrum-WC-DB
05SPx Winning Materials-WM-DB
05SPx Winning Materials Gold-WM-DB
05SPx Winning Materials Spectrum-WM-DB
05UD Artifacts Remarkable Artifacts-RA-DB
05UD Artifacts Remarkable Artifacts Dual-RA-DB
05UD PowerPlay-12
05UD PowerPlay-94
Rainbow-12

05Ultimate Collection-14
Gold-14
05Ultra-25
Gold-25
Ice-25
05Upper Deck-22
Big Playmakers-B-DB
HG Glossy-22
Jerseys-J-DB
Notable Numbers-N-DB
Patches-P-DAB
05Upper Deck MVP-46
Gold-46
Platinum-46
05Upper Deck Trilogy-12
Honorary Patches-HP-DB
Honorary Patch Scripts-HSP-DB
Honorary Swatches-HS-DB
Honorary Swatch Scripts-HSS-DB
Ice Scripts-IS-DB
05Upper Deck Toronto Fall Expo-22
05Upper Deck Victory-24
Black-24
Gold-24
Silver-24
06Be A Player-154
Autographs-154
Signatures-BD
Signatures 10-169
Signatures Duals-DBU
Signatures Trios-TDBV
Up Close and Personal-UC24
Up Close and Personal Autographs-UC24
06Be A Player Portraits-13
Dual Signature Portraits-DSDB
Signature Portraits-SPDB
Triple Signature Portraits-TBUF
06Black Diamond-10
Black-10
Gold-10
Ruby-10
06Flair Showcase Inks-IDB
06Fleer-27
Tiffany-27
Signing Day-SDDB
06Hot Prospects-13
Red Hot-13
White Hot-13
06NHL POG-21
06O-Pee-Chee-58
Rainbow-58
Autographs-A-DB
06Panini Stickers-32
06SP Authentic-91
Limited-91
Sign of the Times Triples-ST3DBM
06SP Game Used Authentic Fabrics Dual-AF2AB
06SP Game Used Authentic Fabrics Dual Patches-AF2AB
06SP Game Used Authentic Fabrics Triple-AF3BUF
06SP Game Used Authentic Fabrics Triple Patches-AF3BUF
06SP Game Used Authentic Fabrics Fives-AP5SCP
06SP Game Used Authentic Fabrics Fives Patches-AP5SCP
06SP Game Used Inked Sweaters-ISDB
06SP Game Used Inked Sweaters Patches-ISDB
06SP Game Used SIGnificance-SBR
06The Cup Autographed NHL Shields Duals-DASBD
06The Cup Limited Logos-LLDB
06The Cup Scripted Swatches-SSDB
06The Cup Signature Patches-SPDB
06UD Artifacts-90
Blue-90
Gold-90
Platinum-90
Radiance-90
Red-90
06UD Biography of a Season-BOS11
06Ultimate Collection Premium Patches-PS-DB
06Ultimate Collection Premium Swatches-PS-DB
06Ultra-27
Gold Medallion-27
Ice Medallion-27
Fresh Ink-IDB
06Upper Deck Arena Giveaways-BUF3
06Upper Deck-272
Exclusives Parallel-272
High Gloss Parallel-272
Game Dated Moments-GD30
Game Jerseys-J2DB
Game Patches-P2DB
Masterpieces-272
06Upper Deck MVP-30
Gold Script-30
Super Script-30
Jerseys-OJHB
06Upper Deck Ovation-156
06Upper Deck Sweet Shot Signature Sticks-STDB
06Upper Deck Trilogy-13
Ice Scripts-ISDB
Scripts-TSDB
06Upper Deck Victory-27
06Upper Deck Victory Black-27
06Upper Deck Victory Gold-27
07Sports Illustrated for Kids *-150
07Upper Deck Ovation-45
07Upper Deck Victory-40
Black-40
Gold-40
GameBreakers-GB12
Stars on Ice-SI47

Briere, Jean-Philippe
99Rimouski Oceanic-11
Signed-11
00Rimouski Oceanic-13
Signed-13
01Rimouski Oceanic-12

Briere, Michel
04ITG Franchises Update-489

Briere, Pierre-Luc
01Chicoutimi Sagueneens-8

Briffey, Shean
93Quebec Pee-Wee Tournament-39

Briggs, Kellen
00Sioux Falls Stampede-4
01Sioux Falls Stampede-2
03Minnesota Golden Gophers-11
04Minnesota Golden Gophers-3
05Minnesota Golden Gophers-5
06Minnesota Golden Gophers-4

Bright, Chris
90ProCards AHL/IHL-188
91ProCards-110
94Classic Pro Prospects-245
05German DEL-318

Brigley, Travis
95Lethbridge Hurricanes-3
96Lethbridge Hurricanes-1
97Saint John Flames-4
97Bowman CHL-110
OPC-110
99Pacific Omega-42
Copper-42
Gold-42
Ice Blue-42
Premiere Date-42
99Topps Premier Plus-87
Parallel-87
99Upper Deck Gold Reserve-339
00Louisville Panthers-15
01Cincinnati Mighty Ducks-5
02Cincinnati Mighty Ducks-A-8
06German DEL-1
New Arrivals-NA1

Brill, John
91Minnesota Golden Gophers-3
92Minnesota Golden Gophers-4
94Dayton Bombers-13
94Classic Pro Prospects-232
95Dayton Bombers-15

Brillant, Pierre
51Bas Du Fleuve-36
51Laval Dairy Subset-13
52St. Lawrence Sales-50

Brimanis, Aris
92Brandon Wheat Kings-1
94Donruss-65
94Leaf-123
94Classic Pro Prospects-138
95Images-76
Gold-76
Autographs-76A
98Grand Rapids Griffins-5
99Kansas City Blades Supercuts-3
00UD Heroes-76
01Cincinnati Mighty Ducks-6
02Worcester IceCats-4
03Worcester Ice Cats-7
04Worcester IceCats-4

Brimmer, Chuck
81Kingston Canadians-11
81Sault Ste. Marie Greyhounds-5

Brimmer, Kent
84Belleville Bulls-16

Brimsek, Frank
34Beehive Group I Photos-5A
34Beehive Group I Photos-5B
39O-Pee-Chee V301-1-97
43Parade Sportive *-14
44Beehive Group II Photos-6
44Beehive Group II Photos-82
83Hall of Fame-124
83Hall of Fame Postcards-I3
85Hall of Fame-124
91Bruins Sports Action Legends-4
94Parkhurst Tall Boys Greats-7
00BAP Memorabilia Goalie Memorabilia-G10
00BAP Memorabilia Goalie Memorabilia-G14
00BAP Memorabilia Goalie Memorabilia-G26
00BAP Ultimate Mem Goalie Memorabilia-GM18
01BAP Memorabilia Goalie Traditions-GT13
01BAP Memorabilia Goalie Traditions-GT31
01BAP Memorabilia Goalie Traditions-GT32
01BAP Memorabilia Goalie Traditions-GT41
01BAP Ultimate Mem All-Star History-2
01BAP Ultimate Memorabilia Calder Trophy-25
01BAP Ultimate Memorabilia Cornerstones-6
01BAP Ultimate Memorabilia Decades-2
01BAP Update Rocket's Rivals-RR-5
01Between the Pipes-128
01Between the Pipes-148
Trophy Winners-TW23
Vintage Memorabilia-VM7
02BAP NHL All-Star History-2
02BAP Ultimate Memorabilia Emblem Attic-22
02BAP Ultimate Memorabilia Retro Trophies-15
02BAP Ultimate Mem Vintage Jerseys-12
02Between the Pipes-112
Vintage Memorabilia-17
02ITG Used Vintage Memorabilia-VM19
02ITG Used Vintage Memorabilia Gold-VM19
02Parkhurst Retro Nicknames-RN1
02SP Authentic Legendary Cuts-LCFB
03BAP Ultimate Memorabilia Cornerstones-6
03BAP Ultimate Memorabilia Emblem Attic-6
03BAP Ultimate Mem Emblem Attic Gold-6
03BAP Ultimate Memorabilia Paper Cuts-4
03BAP Ultimate Memorabilia Triple Threads-9
03BAP Ultimate Mem Vintage Jerseys-9
03BAP Ultimate Mem Vintage Jerseys Gold-9
03ITG Used Signature Series Goalie Gear-32
03ITG Used Sig Series Goalie Gear Autos-32
03ITG Used Sig Series Goalie Gear Gold-32
03ITG VIP Vintage Memorabilia-8
03Parkhurst Original Six Boston-48
03Parkhurst Original Six Boston-61
03Parkhurst Original Six Boston-84
Inserts-B15
Memorabilia-BM26
03Parkhurst Orig Six Chicago Mem -CM19
03Parkhurst Orig Six Chicago Mem -CM57
03Parkhurst Rookie Before the Mask-BTM-2
03Parkhurst Rookie Before the Mask Gold-BTM-2
03Parkhurst Rookie ROYalty-VR-21
03Parkhurst Rookie ROYalty Gold-VR-21
04ITG NHL AS FANtasy AS History Jerseys-SB2
04ITG Franchises Update Double Mem-UDM3
04ITG Franchises Update Double Mem Gold-UDM3
04ITG Franchises Update Memorabilia-USM4
04ITG Franchises Update Memorabilia Gold-USM4
04ITG Franchises US East-319
04ITG Franchises US West Double Mem-WDM5
04ITG Franchises US West Double Mem Gold-WDM5
04ITG Franchises US West Goalie Gear-WGG5
04ITG Franchises US West Goalie Gear Gold-WGG5
04ITG Franchises US West Memorabilia-WSM8
04ITG Franchises US West Memorabilia Gold-WSM8
04ITG Ultimate Memorabilia-61
04ITG Ultimate Memorabilia-64
Gold-61
Gold-64
Autographs-58
Autographs Gold-58
Beantown's Best-4
Complete Jerseys-14
Day In History-4
Day In History Gold-4
Goalie Gear-7
Jerseys-13
Jerseys Gold-13
Nicknames-22
Original Six-7
Original Six-12
Original Six-18
Paper Cuts Memorabilia-16
Triple Threads-4
05ITG Ultimate Memorabilia Level 1-35
05ITG Ultimate Memorabilia Level 2-35
05ITG Ultimate Memorabilia Level 3-35
05ITG Ultimate Memorabilia Level 4-35
05ITG Ultimate Memorabilia Level 5-35
05ITG Ultimate Mem Decades Jerseys-1
05ITG Ultimate Mem Decades Jerseys-8
05ITG Ultimate Mem Decades Jerseys Gold-1
05ITG Ultimate Mem Decades Jerseys Gold-8
05ITG Ultimate Memorabilia Emblem Attic-10
05ITG Ultimate Mem Emblem Attic Gold-10
05ITG Ultimate Memorabilia Goalie Gear-5
05ITG Ultimate Mem Goalie Gear Gold-5
05ITG Ultimate Mem Quad Paper Cuts Autos-1
05ITG Ultimate Mem 3 Star of the Game Jsy-3
05ITG Ult Mem 3 Star of the Game Jsy Gold-3
06Between The Pipes Double Jerseys-DJ26
06Between The Pipes Double Jerseys Gold-DJ26
06Between The Pipes Emblems-GUE54
06Between The Pipes Emblems Gold-GUE54
06Between The Pipes Jerseys-GUJ54
06Between The Pipes Jerseys Gold-GUJ54
06Between The Pipes Numbers-GUN54
06Between The Pipes Numbers Gold-GUN54
06Between The Pipes Shooting Gallery-SG04
06Between The Pipes Shooting Gallery Gold-SG04
06ITG Ultimate Memorabilia Decades-7
06ITG Ultimate Memorabilia Decades-8
06ITG Ultimate Memorabilia Decades Gold-7
06ITG Ultimate Memorabilia Decades Gold-8
06ITG Ultimate Memorabilia Emblem Attic-2
06ITG Ultimate Memorabilia Emblem Attic Gold-2

Brincko, Dusan
06Czech OFS-196

Brind'Amour, Rod
89Blues Kodak-19
90Blues Kodak-2
90Bowman-23
Tiffany-23
90O-Pee-Chee-332
90Panini Stickers-266
90Panini Stickers-343
90Pro Set-259
90Score-131
90Score-328
Canadian-131
Canadian-328
90Score Hottest/Rising Stars-98
90Score Young Superstars-31
90Topps-332
Tiffany-332
90Upper Deck-36
90Upper Deck-347
French-36
French-347
91Pro Set Platinum-90
91Bowman-374
91Flyers J.C. Penney-2
91O-Pee-Chee-490
91OPC Premier-94
91Panini Stickers-30
91Parkhurst-124
French-124
91Pinnacle-9
French-9
91Pro Set-211
91Pro Set-453
French-211
French-453
Puck Candy-20
91Score American-85
91Score Canadian Bilingual-85
91Score Canadian Bilingual-618
91Score Canadian English-85
91Score Canadian English-618
91Score Rookie/Traded-68T
91Stadium Club-184
91Topps-490
91Upper Deck-189
91Upper Deck-547
French-189
French-547
92Bowman-224
92Bowman-268
92Flyers J.C. Penney-4
92Flyers Upper Deck Sheets-5
92Flyers Upper Deck Sheets-27
92Humpty Dumpty I-2
92McDonald's Upper Deck-16
92O-Pee-Chee-49
92OPC Premier Star Performers-9
92Panini Stickers-187
92Panini Stickers French-187
92Parkhurst-126
Emerald Ice-126
92Pinnacle-26
French-26
Team 2000-18
Team 2000 French-18
92Pro Set-132
92Score-324
Canadian-324
Young Superstars-26
92Seasons Patches-39
92Stadium Club-202
92Topps-90
Gold-90G
92Ultra-152
92Upper Deck-15
92Upper Deck-264
93Donruss-248
93Flyers J.C. Penney-4
93Flyers Lineup Sheets-4
93Flyers Lineup Sheets-5
93Leaf-26
93OPC Premier-115
Gold-115
93Panini Stickers-47
93Parkhurst-152
Emerald Ice-152
93Pinnacle-170
Canadian-170
Team 2001-11
Team 2001 Canadian-11
93PowerPlay-178
93Score-45
Canadian-45
93Stadium Club-78
Members Only Master Set-78
OPC-78
First Day Issue-78
First Day Issue OPC-78
93Topps/OPC Premier-115
Gold-115
93Ultra-74
93Upper Deck-361
SP-114
94Be A Player Signature Cards-175
94Canada Games NHL POGS-373
94Donruss-80
94EA Sports-100
94Finest-85
Super Team Winners-85
Refractors-85
94Flair-126
94Fleer-150
94Hockey Wit-59
94Leaf-150
94Leaf Limited-78
94OPC Premier-17
Special Effects-17
94Parkhurst-167
Gold-167
SE Vintage-25
94Pinnacle-273
Artist's Proofs-273
Rink Collection-273
94Score-132
Gold-132
Platinum-132
90 Plus Club-13
94Select-119
Gold-119
94SP-86
Die Cuts-86
94Topps/OPC Premier-17
Special Effects-17
94Ultra-155
94Upper Deck-111
Electric Ice-111
SP Inserts-SP57
SP Inserts Die Cuts-SP57
95Bashan Super Stickers-94
95Canada Games NHL POGS-202
95Collector's Choice-29
Player's Club-29
Player's Club Platinum-29
95Donruss-188
95Donruss Elite-91
Die Cut Stars-91
Die Cut Uncut-91
95Emotion-129
95Finest-44
Refractors-44
95Hoyle Eastern Playing Cards-6
95Imperial Stickers-94
95Leaf-154
95Leaf Limited-69
95Metal-108
95Panini Stickers-114
95Parkhurst International-158
Emerald Ice-158
95Pinnacle-109
Artist's Proofs-109
Rink Collection-109
95Playoff One on One-291
95Pro Magnets-51
95Score-244
Black Ice Artist's Proofs-244
Black Ice-244
95Select Certified-59
Mirror Gold-59
95SkyBox Impact-123
95SP-110
95Stadium Club-36
Members Only Master Set-36
95Summit-79
Artist's Proofs-79
Ice-79
95Topps-39
OPC Inserts-39
95Ultra-115
Gold Medallion-115
Crease Crashers-2
95Upper Deck-324
Electric Ice-324
Electric Ice Gold-324
Special Edition-SE64
Special Edition Gold-SE64
95Zenith-68
95Finnish Semic World Championships-90
95Swedish World Championships Stickers-19
96Be A Player-21
Autographs-21
Autographs Silver-21
96Black Diamond-117
Gold-117
96Collector's Choice-192
96Donruss-155
Press Proofs-155
96Donruss Elite-93
Die Cut Stars-93
96Fleer-78
96Fleer Picks-54
96Flyers Postcards-2
96Leaf-41
Press Proofs-41
96Leaf Preferred-64
Press Proofs-64
96Metal Universe-109
96NHL Aces Playing Cards-4
96NHL Pro Stamps-51
96Pinnacle-123
Artist's Proofs-123
Foil-123
Premium Stock-123
Rink Collection-123
96Score-102
Artist's Proofs-102
Dealer's Choice Artist's Proofs-102
Special Artist's Proofs-102
Golden Blades-102
96SkyBox Impact-92
96Summit-123
Artist's Proofs-123
Ice-123
Metal-123
Premium Stock-123
96Ultra-121
Gold Medallion-121
96Upper Deck-121
Power Performers-P26
96Upper Deck Ice-48
Parallel-48
96Swedish Semic Wien-98
97Black Diamond-61
Double Diamond-61
Triple Diamond-61
Quadruple Diamond-61
97Collector's Choice-192
World Domination-W8
97Crown Royale-95
Emerald Green-95
Ice Blue-95
Silver-95
97Donruss-157
Press Proofs Silver-157
Press Proofs Gold-157
97Donruss Canadian Ice-113
Dominion Series-113
Provincial Series-113
97Donruss Limited-82
Exposure-82
97Donruss Preferred-67
Cut to the Chase-67
97Donruss Priority-33
Stamp of Approval-33
97Esso Olympic Hockey Heroes-11
97Esso Olympic Hockey Heroes French-11
97Kraft Team Canada-7
97Leaf-125
Fractal Matrix-125
Fractal Matrix Die Cuts-125
97Leaf International-125
Universal Ice-125
97McDonald's Team Canada Coins-1
97Pacific-31
Copper-31
Emerald Green-31
Ice Blue-31
Red-31
Silver-31
Slap Shots Die-Cuts-6A
97Pacific Dynagon-88
Copper-88
Dark Grey-88
Emerald Green-88
Ice Blue-88
Red-88
Silver-88
Best Kept Secrets-68
Tandems-20
97Pacific Invincible-98
Copper-98
Emerald Green-98
Ice Blue-98
Red-98
Silver-98
NHL Regime-139
97Pacific Omega-160
Copper-160
Dark Gray-160
Emerald Green-160
Gold-160
Ice Blue-160
Team Leaders-15
97Panini Stickers-93
97Paramount-130
Copper-130
Dark Grey-130
Emerald Green-130
Ice Blue-130
Red-130
Silver-130
97Pinnacle-111
Press Plates Back Black-111
Press Plates Back Cyan-111
Press Plates Back Magenta-111
Press Plates Back Yellow-111
Press Plates Front Black-111
Press Plates Front Cyan-111
Press Plates Front Magenta-111
Press Plates Front Yellow-111
97Pinnacle Certified-93
Red-93
Mirror Blue-93
Mirror Gold-93
Mirror Red-93
97Pinnacle Inside-92
97Pinnacle Tot Cert Platinum Blue-93
97Pinnacle Tot Certi Platinum Gold-93
97Pinnacle Totally Certified Platinum Red-93
97Pinnacle Tot Cert Mirror Platinum Gold-93
97Revolution-97
Copper-97
Emerald-97
Ice Blue-97
Silver-97
97Score-127
Artist's Proofs-127
Golden Blades-127
Check It-16
97Score Flyers-5
Platinum-5
Premier-5
97SP Authentic-115
97Upper Deck-121
Game Dated Moments-121
Three Star Selects-17C
97Zenith-74
Z-Gold-74
Z-Silver-74
97Zenith 5 x 7-49
Gold Impulse-49
Silver Impulse-49
98Aurora-135
98Be A Player-251
Press Release-251
98BAP Gold-251
98BAP Autographs-251
98BAP Autographs Gold-251
98Black Diamond-65
Double Diamond-65
Triple Diamond-65
Quadruple Diamond-65
98Bowman's Best-67
Refractors-67
Atomic Refractors-67
98Crown Royale-97
Limited Series-97
98Finest-17
No Protectors-17
No Protectors Refractors-17
Refractors-17
98Jell-O Spoons-1
98Katch-108
98OPC Chrome-116
Refractors-116
98Pacific-17
Ice Blue-17
Red-17
98Pacific Dynagon Ice-133
Blue-133
Red-133
98Pacific Omega-172
Red-172
Opening Day Issue-172
98Panini Photocards-12
98Panini Stickers-90
98Paramount-169
Copper-169
Emerald Green-169
Holo-Electric-169
Ice Blue-169
Silver-169
98Revolution-103
Ice Shadow-103
Red-103
98SP Authentic-64
Power Shift-64
98SPx Finite-62
Radiance-62
Spectrum-62
98Topps-116
O-Pee-Chee-116
98Topps Gold Label Class 1-99
Black-99
Black One of One-99
One of One-99
Red-99
Red One of One-99
98Topps Gold Label Class 2-99
98Topps Gold Label Class 2 Black-99
98Topps Gold Label Class 2 Black 1 of 1-99
98Topps Gold Label Class 2 One of One-99
98Topps Gold Label Class 2 Red-99
98Topps Gold Label Class 2 Red One of One-99
98Topps Gold Label Class 3-99
98Topps Gold Label Class 3 Black-99
98Topps Gold Label Class 3 Black 1 of 1-99
98Topps Gold Label Class 3 One of One-99
98Topps Gold Label Class 3 Red-99
98Topps Gold Label Class 3 Red One of One-99
98UD Choice-149
98UD Choice Preview-149
98UD Choice Prime Choice Reserve-149
98UD Choice Reserve-149
98Upper Deck-334
Exclusives-334
Exclusives 1 of 1-334
Gold Reserve-334
98Upper Deck MVP-155
Gold Script-155
Silver Script-155
Super Script-155
99Aurora-103
Premiere Date-103
99BAP Memorabilia-59
99BAP Memorabilia-394
Gold-59
Gold-394
Silver-59
Silver-394
99BAP Millennium-181
Emerald-181
Ruby-181
Sapphire-181
Signatures-181
Signatures Gold-181
99O-Pee-Chee-238
99O-Pee-Chee Chrome-238
99O-Pee-Chee Chrome Refractors-238
99Pacific-299
Copper-299
Emerald Green-299
Gold-299
Ice Blue-299
Premiere Date-299
Red-299
99Pacific Dynagon Ice-145
Blue-145
Copper-145
Gold-145
Premiere Date-145
99Panini Stickers-124
99Paramount-168
Copper-168
Emerald-168
Gold-168
Holographic Emerald-168
Holographic Gold-168
Holographic Silver-168
Ice Blue-168
Premiere Date-168
Red-168
Silver-168
99Revolution-106
Premiere Date-106
Red-106
Shadow Series-106
Copper-106
Gold-106
CSC Silver-106
99SPx-111
Radiance-111
Spectrum-111
99Stadium Club Promos-PP4
99Stadium Club-33
First Day Issue-33
One of a Kind-33
Printing Plates Black-33
Printing Plates Cyan-33
Printing Plates Magenta-33
Printing Plates Yellow-33
Eyes of the Game-EG10
Eyes of the Game Refractors-EG10
99Topps/OPC-238
99Topps/OPC Chrome-238
Refractors-238
99Topps Gold Label Class 1-59
Black-59
Black One of One-59
One of One-59
Red-59
Red One of One-59
99Topps Gold Label Class 2-59
99Topps Gold Label Class 2 Black-59
99Topps Gold Label Class 2 Black 1 of 1-59
99Topps Gold Label Class 2 One of One-59
99Topps Gold Label Class 2 Red-59
99Topps Gold Label Class 2 Red One of One-59
99Topps Gold Label Class 3-59
99Topps Gold Label Class 3 Black-59
99Topps Gold Label Class 3 Black 1 of 1-59
99Topps Gold Label Class 3 One of One-59
99Topps Gold Label Class 3 Red-59
99Topps Gold Label Class 3 Red One of One-59
99Topps Premier Plus-62
Parallel-62
99Upper Deck-96
Exclusives-96
Exclusives 1 of 1-96
99Upper Deck Gold Reserve-96
99Upper Deck MVP-149
Gold Script-149
Silver Script-149
Super Script-149
ProSign-RBR
99Upper Deck Victory-214
99Wayne Gretzky Hockey-127
00SLU Hockey-40
00Aurora-27
Premiere Date-27
00BAP Memorabilia-200
Emerald-200
Ruby-200
Sapphire-200
Promos-200
00BAP Mem Chicago Sportsfest Copper-200
00BAP Memorabilia Chicago Sportsfest Blue-200
00BAP Memorabilia Chicago Sportsfest Gold-200
00BAP Memorabilia Chicago Sportsfest Ruby-200
00BAP Memorabilia Chicago Sun-Times Ruby-200
00BAP Memorabilia Chicago Sun-Times Gold-200
00BAP Mem Chicago Sun-Times Sapphire-200
00BAP Mem Toronto Fall Expo Copper-200
00BAP Memorabilia Toronto Fall Expo Gold-200
00BAP Memorabilia Toronto Fall Expo Ruby-200
00BAP Parkhurst 2000-P24
00BAP Signature Series-16
Emerald-16
Ruby-16
Sapphire-16
Autographs-166
Autographs Gold-166
00O-Pee-Chee-57
00O-Pee-Chee Parallel-57
00Pacific-79
Copper-79
Gold-79
Ice Blue-79
Premiere Date-79
00Paramount-41
Copper-41
Gold-41
Holo-Gold-41
Holo-Silver-41
Ice Blue-41
Premiere Date-41
00Private Stock Game Gear-12
00Revolution-25
Blue-25
Premiere Date-25
Red-25
00Stadium Club-8
00Topps/OPC-57
Parallel-57
00Topps Chrome-45
OPC Refractors-45
Refractors-45
00Topps Heritage-110
00Topps Premier Plus-76
Blue Ice-76
00Topps Stars-38
Blue-38
00Upper Deck-36
Exclusives Tier 1-36
Exclusives Tier 2-36
00Upper Deck MVP-38
First Stars-38
Second Stars-38
Third Stars-38
00Upper Deck Victory-45
00Upper Deck Vintage-71
00Vanguard-18
Holographic Gold-18
Holographic Purple-18
Pacific Proofs-18
01BAP Memorabilia-246
Emerald-246
Ruby-246
Sapphire-246
01BAP Signature Series-152
Autographs-152
Autographs Gold-152
01O-Pee-Chee-216
01O-Pee-Chee Premier Parallel-216
01Pacific-70
Extreme LTD-70
Hobby LTD-70
Premiere Date-70
Retail LTD-70
01Pacific Adrenaline-31
Blue-31
Premiere Date-31
Red-31
Retail-31
01Pacific Arena Exclusives-70
01Parkhurst-104
01Private Stock Game Gear-18
01SP Authentic Buybacks-29
01SP Authentic Sign of the Times-RB
01Stadium Club-95
Award Winners-95
Master Photos-95
01Titanium Double-Sided Jerseys-46
01Titanium Double-Sided Patches-46
01Topps-216
OPC Parallel-216
01Topps Reserve-25
01UD Playmakers Practice Jerseys-PJRB
01UD Playmakers Practice Jerseys Gold-PJRB
01Upper Deck-264
Exclusives-264
01Upper Deck MVP-32
Morning Skate Jerseys-J-RB
Morning Skate Jersey Autographs-SJ-RB
01Upper Deck Victory-60
Gold-60
01Upper Deck Vintage-48
01Upper Deck Vintage-52
02BAP First Edition-278
02BAP First Edition-386
02BAP Memorabilia-192
Emerald-192
Ruby-192
Sapphire-192
NHL All-Star Game-192
NHL All-Star Game Blue-192
NHL All-Star Game Green-192
NHL All-Star Game Red-192
02BAP Memorabilia Toronto Fall Expo-192
02BAP Sig Series Auto Buybacks 1998-251
02BAP Sig Series Auto Buybacks 1999-181
02BAP Sig Series Auto Buybacks 2000-166
02BAP Sig Series Auto Buybacks 2001-152
02Crown Royale-16
Blue-16
Red-16
Retail-16
Dual Patches-3
02Hurricanes Postcards-1
02O-Pee-Chee-130
02O-Pee-Chee Premier Blue Parallel-130
02O-Pee-Chee Premier Red Parallel-130
02O-Pee-Chee Factory Set-130
02Pacific-63
Blue-63
Red-63
02Pacific Complete-317
Red-317
02Pacific Exclusive-26
02Pacific Heads-Up Quad Jerseys-6
02Pacific Heads-Up Quad Jerseys Gold-6
02Parkhurst-1
Bronze-1
Gold-1
Silver-1
02Parkhurst Retro-99
Minis-99
02Private Stock Reserve-15
Blue-15
Red-15
Retail-15
02SP Authentic-15
Beckett Promos-15
02Titanium-17
Blue-17
Red 17
Retail-17
Jerseys-8
Jerseys Retail-8
Patches-8
02Topps-130
OPC Blue Parallel-130
OPC Red Parallel-130
Factory Set-130
02Topps Chrome-82
Black Border Refractors-82
Refractors-82
02Topps Total-38
02UD Piece of History Mark of Distinction-BR
02Upper Deck-28
Exclusives-28
02Upper Deck Classic Portraits-18
02Upper Deck MVP-37
Gold-37
Classics-37
Golden Classics-37
Skate Around Jerseys-SDBN
Souvenirs-S-BR
02Upper Deck Rookie Update-20
02Upper Deck Victory-39
Bronze-39
Gold-39
Silver-39
02Upper Deck Vintage-46
02Vanguard-17
LTD-17
Jerseys-9
Jerseys Gold-9
03Beehive-36
Gold-36
Silver-36
03Hurricanes Postcards-7
03ITG Action-127
03NHL Sticker Collection-33
03O-Pee-Chee-109
03OPC Blue-109
03OPC Gold-109
03OPC Red-109
03Pacific-59
Blue-59
Red-59
03Pacific Complete-48
Red-48
03Pacific Exhibit-26
Blue Backs-26
Yellow Backs-26
03Topps-109
Blue-109
Gold-109
Red-109
03Upper Deck-279
Canadian Exclusives-279
HG-279
UD Exclusives-279
03Upper Deck MVP-79
Gold Script-79
Silver Script-79
Canadian Exclusives-79
03Upper Deck Victory-34
Bronze-34
Gold-34
Silver-34
03Toronto Star-12
04Pacific-46
Blue-46
Red-46
05Be A Player Signatures-RA
05Be A Player Signatures Gold-RA
05Black Diamond-18
Emerald-18
Gold-18
Onyx-18
Ruby-18
05Panini Stickers-43
05Parkhurst-88
05Parkhurst-506
Facsimile Auto Parallel-88
Facsimile Auto Parallel-506
True Colors-TCCAR
True Colors-TCCAR
05SP Game Used Game Gear-GG-BA
05The Cup Master Pressplate Rookie Update-251
05Ultra-46
Gold-46
Ice-46
05Upper Deck-281
05Upper Deck All-Time Greatest-11
05Upper Deck MVP-77
Gold-77
Platinum-77
05Upper Deck Rookie Update-251
Inspirations Patch Rookies-251
05Upper Deck Victory-35
Black-35
Gold-35
Silver-35
06Be A Player-153
Autographs-153
Signatures-RB
Signatures 10-168
Signatures Duals-DSB
Signatures Trios-TSBC
Up Close and Personal-UC49
Up Close and Personal Autographs-UC49
06Be A Player Portraits-20
06Beehive-84
Matte-84
06Black Diamond-15
Black-15
Gold-15
Ruby-15
Jerseys-JRB
Jerseys Black-JRB
Jerseys Gold-JRB
Jerseys Ruby-JRB
06Flair Showcase-216
Parallel-216
Stitches-SSRB
06Fleer-39
Tiffany-39
Fabricology-FRO
06Hot Prospects-21
Red Hot-21
White Hot-21
06Hurricanes Postcards-6
06O-Pee-Chee-95
Rainbow-95
Swatches-S-RB
06Panini Stickers-41
06SP Authentic-84
Limited-84
06SP Game Used-20
Gold-20
Rainbow-20

Authentic Fabrics Dual-AF2WB
Authentic Fabrics Dual Patches-AF2WB
Authentic Fabrics Triple-AF3CAR
Authentic Fabrics Triple Patches-AF3CAR
Authentic Fabrics Sixes-AF6SEL
Authentic Fabrics Sixes Patches-AF6SEL
06SPx-18
Spectrum-18
06The Cup NHL Shields Duals-DSHWB
06UD Artifacts-83
Blue-83
Gold-83
Platinum-83
Radiance-83
Red-83
Frozen Artifacts-FARB
Frozen Artifacts Black-FARB
Frozen Artifacts Blue-FARB
Frozen Artifacts Gold-FARB
Frozen Artifacts Platinum-FARB
Frozen Artifacts Red-FARB
Frozen Artifacts Patches Black-FARB
Frozen Artifacts Patches Blue-FARB
Frozen Artifacts Patches Gold-FARB
Frozen Artifacts Patches Platinum-FARB
Frozen Artifacts Patches Red-FARB
Tundra Tandems-TTWB
Tundra Tandems Black-TTWB
Tundra Tandems Blue-TTWB
Tundra Tandems Gold-TTWB
Tundra Tandems Platinum-TTWB
Tundra Tandems Red-TTWB
Tundra Tandems Dual Patches Red-TTWB
06UD Mini Jersey Collection-20
06UD Powerplay-20
Impact Rainbow-20
06Ultra-41
Gold Medallion-41
Ice Medallion-41
06Upper Deck Arena Giveaways-CAR6
06Upper Deck-286
Exclusives Parallel-286
High Gloss Parallel-286
Award Winners-AW6
Award Winners Canadian Exclusive-OAW13
Game Dated Moments-GD26
Game Jerseys-JRB
Game Patches-PRB
Masterpieces-286
Oversized Wal-Mart Exclusives-286
06Upper Deck MVP-52
Gold Script-52
Super Script-52
Jerseys-OJRB
06Upper Deck Ovation-112
06Upper Deck Trilogy-20
06Upper Deck Victory-40
06Upper Deck Victory Black-40
06Upper Deck Victory Gold-40
07Upper Deck Victory-84
Black-84
Gold-84

Brindamour, Frederic
93Quebec Pee-Wee Tournament-301

Brindley, Ryan
94Thunder Bay Flyers-5
99Austin Ice Bats-24
01South Carolina Stingrays-3
02South Carolina Stingrays-3
04Florida Everblades-9
05Florida Everblades-11

Brine, David
03Halifax Mooseheads-21
04Halifax Mooseheads-4A
04Halifax Mooseheads-4B
05Halifax Mooseheads-23

Brink, Andy
93Donruss Team USA-3
93Pinnacle-490
Canadian-490
93Minnesota Golden Gophers-5
94Minnesota Golden Gophers-5
95Minnesota Golden Gophers-8

Brinkley, Ryan
02South Carolina Stingrays RBI-205

Brisco, Dale
84Nanaimo Clippers-3

Brisebois, Patrice
90Upper Deck-454
French-454
907th Inn. Sketch QMJHL-8
907th Inn. Sketch Memorial Cup-59
91Canadiens Postcards-2
91Parkhurst-309
French-309
91Score American-382
91Score Canadian Bilingual-272
91Score Canadian English-272
91Upper Deck-442
French-442
91ProCards-80
917th Inn. Sketch CHL Award Winners-24
917th Inn. Sketch Memorial Cup-62
92Bowman-435
92Canadiens Postcards-2
92Durivage Panini-32
92O-Pee-Chee-239
92Panini Stickers-155
92Panini Stickers French-155
92Parkhurst-320
Emerald Ice-320
92Pinnacle-153
French-153
92Score-388
Canadian-388
92Stadium Club-238
92Topps-189
Gold-189G
92Ultra-325
92Upper Deck-277
93Canadiens Postcards-2
93Donruss-171
93Durivage Score-7
93Leaf-191
93O-Pee-Chee Canadiens Hockey Fest-49
93OPC Premier-59
Gold-59
93Parkhurst-105
Emerald Ice-105
93Pinnacle-253
Canadian-253
93PowerPlay-125
93Score-163
Canadian-163
93Stadium Club-27
Members Only Master Set-27
OPC-27
First Day Issue-27
First Day Issue OPC-27
93Topps/OPC Premier-59
Gold-59
93Ultra-52
93Upper Deck-318
94Canadiens Postcards-3
94Donruss-250
94Flair-85
94Fleer-102
94Leaf-325
94Parkhurst-116
Gold-116
94Pinnacle-191
Artist's Proofs-191
Rink Collection-191
94Ultra-106
94Upper Deck-193
Electric Ice-193
95Be A Player-44
Signatures-S44
Signatures Die Cuts-S44
95Canada Games NHL POGS-152
95Canadiens Postcards-2
95Canadiens Sheets-10
95Collector's Choice-61
Player's Club-61
Player's Club Platinum-61
95Panini Stickers-44
95Parkhurst International-380
Emerald Ice-380
95Playoff One on One-272
95Score-148
Black Ice Artist's Proofs-148
Black Ice-148
95SP-77
95Topps-199
OPC Inserts-199
95Ultra-254
95Upper Deck-6
Electric Ice-6
Electric Ice Gold-6
96Canadiens Postcards-3
96Canadiens Sheets-1
96Collector's Choice-142
96Fleer Picks-160
96Upper Deck-88
97Canadiens Postcards-2
97Score Canadiens-20
Platinum-20
Premier-20
97Upper Deck-295
98Be A Player-216
Press Release-216
98BAP Gold-216
98BAP Autographs-216
98BAP Autographs Gold-216
98Kraft Peanut Butter-3
98OPC Chrome-80
Refractors-80
98Topps-80
O-Pee-Chee-80
98Upper Deck-293
Exclusives-293
Exclusives 1 of 1-293
Gold Reserve-293
99BAP Memorabilia-182
Gold-182
Silver-182
00BAP Memorabilia-240
Emerald-240
Ruby-240
Sapphire-240
Promos-240
00BAP Mem Chicago Sportsfest Copper-240
00BAP Memorabilia Chicago Sportsfest Blue-240
00BAP Memorabilia Chicago Sportsfest Gold-240
00BAP Memorabilia Chicago Sportsfest Ruby-240
00BAP Memorabilia Chicago Sun-Times Ruby-240
00BAP Memorabilia Chicago Sun-Times Gold-240
00BAP Mem Chicago Sun-Times Sapphire-240
00BAP Mem Toronto Fall Expo Copper-240
00BAP Memorabilia Toronto Fall Expo Gold-240
00BAP Memorabilia Toronto Fall Expo Ruby-240
00Canadiens Postcards-6
00Pacific-205
Copper-205
Gold-205
Ice Blue-205
Premiere Date-205
00Stadium Club-147
01Canadiens Postcards-3
01Pacific-203
Extreme LTD-203
Hobby LTD-203
Premiere Date-203
Retail LTD-203
01Pacific Arena Exclusives-203
01Upper Deck-93
Exclusives-93
01Upper Deck MVP-99
01Upper Deck Victory-189
Gold-189
02BAP Sig Series Auto Buybacks 1998-216
02Canadiens Postcards-15
02NHL Power Play Stickers-61
02O-Pee-Chee-41
02O-Pee-Chee Premier Blue Parallel-41
02O-Pee-Chee Premier Red Parallel-41
02O-Pee-Chee Factory Set-41
02Pacific-192
Blue-192
Red-192
02Pacific Complete-65
Red-65
02Topps-41
OPC Blue Parallel-41
OPC Red Parallel-41
Factory Set-41
02Topps Total-177
03Canadiens Postcards-4
03ITG Action-371
03NHL Sticker Collection-59
03O-Pee-Chee-133
03OPC Blue-133
03OPC Gold-133
03OPC Red-133
03Pacific-174
Blue-174
Red-174
03Pacific Complete-141
Red-141
03Pacific Montreal International-6
03Parkhurst Original Six Montreal-4
03Topps-133
Blue-133
Gold-133
Red-133
04Pacific-136
Blue-136
Red-136
05Parkhurst-128
Facsimile Auto Parallel-128
05Upper Deck-296
05Upper Deck MVP-105
Gold-105
Platinum-105
06Avalanche Team Postcards-2
06O-Pee-Chee-132
Rainbow-132
06Upper Deck-303
Exclusives Parallel-303
High Gloss Parallel-303
Masterpieces-303
06Upper Deck MVP-80
Gold Script-80
Super Script-80

Brisebois, Philippe
05Victoriaville Tigres-11

Brisebois, Travis
04Swift Current Broncos-1
05Vernon Vipers-4

Briske, Byron
93Red Deer Rebels-2
95Tri-City Americans-7
95Signature Rookies-58
Signatures-58
98Cincinnati Mighty Ducks-9

Briske, Shannon
93Portland Winter Hawks-3

Brisson, David
03Grand Rapids Griffins-4
04Fresno Falcons-1

Brisson, Luc
93Quebec Pee-Wee Tournament-980

Brisson, Martin
93Quebec Pee-Wee Tournament-430

Brisson, Sylvain
917th Inn. Sketch QMJHL-42

Brisson, Therese
94Classic Women of Hockey-W4
97Collector's Choice-286
04Canadian Womens World Championship Team-5

Bristow, Cam
907th Inn. Sketch WHL-246
91Air Canada SJHL-D41
92Saskatchewan JHL-49
00UK Sekonda Superleague-13
02Norfolk Admirals-5
02Roanoke Express RBI Sports-189
03Las Vegas Wranglers-3
03Las Vegas Wranglers RBI-226

Brittain, Josh
06Kingston Frontenacs-11

Brittig, Christian
94German DEL-307
95German DEL-65
96German DEL-261
98German DEL-120
99German Bundesliga 2-260
03German Deg Metro Stars-2
03German DEL-32
04German DEL-42
04German Dusseldorf Metro Stars Postcards-2

Brittle, Adam
04UK Coventry Blaze-2
04UK U-20 Team-9

Britton, Craig
02UK Peterborough Phantoms-4

Briza, Petr
89Swedish Semic World Champ Stickers-180
91Finnish Semic World Champ Stickers-102
91Finnish Jyvas-Hyva Stickers-43
91Swedish Semic World Champ Stickers-102
92Finnish Jyvas-Hyva Stickers-121
93Finnish SISU-366
93Swedish Semic World Champ Stickers-89
94Finnish Jaa Kiekko-165
94German DEL-260
94Swedish Olympics Lillehammer*-319
95Czech APS Extraliga-355
95Finnish Semic World Championships-140
95Finnish Semic World Championships-213
95German DEL-242
95Swedish Globe World Championships-146
95Swedish World Championships Stickers-186
96German DEL-135
96Swedish Semic Wien-104
98German DEL-65
99Czech DS-141
Goalies-G11
99Czech OFS-4
99Czech OFS-487
99Czech OFS-NNO
All-Star Game Blue-487
All-Star Game Gold-487
All-Star Game Red-487
All-Star Game Silver-487
99Czech OFS Goalie Die-Cuts-4
00Czech DS Extraliga-1
Goalies-G1
Top Stars-TS1
00Czech OFS-290
00Czech OFS Star Emerald-7
00Czech OFS Star Pink-7
00Czech OFS Star Violet-7
01Czech DS-51
Goalies-G3
01Czech National Team Postcards-2
01Czech OFS-16
01Czech OFS H Inserts-H15
02Czech DS-3
02Czech DS-81
02Czech OFS Plus-3
02Czech OFS Plus All-Star Game-H24
02Czech OFS Plus Trios-T14
02Czech OFS Plus Duos-D2
02Czech National Team Postcards-3
03Czech OFS Plus-152
03Czech OFS Plus Checklists-8
03Czech OFS Plus Insert B-B2
03Czech OFS Plus Insert B-B15
03Czech OFS Plus Insert H-H19
03Czech OFS Plus Insert P-P2
03Czech OFS Plus MS Praha-SE3
04Czech HC Sparta Praha Postcards-1
04Czech OFS-183
Goals-Against Leaders-3
Save Percentage Leaders-2
Team Cards-9
05Czech HC Sparta Praha-1
06Czech OFS Goalies I-13
06Czech OFS Goalies II-14

Brizhgalov, Vladislav
99Russian Hockey League-189
99Russian Hockey League-234

Brkic, Darren
90Michigan Tech Huskies-20
91Michigan Tech Huskies-2

Brklaicich, Steve
51Laval Dairy Subset-61

Brnak, Tomas
06Czech OFS-321

Broadbelt, Dave
52Juniors Blue Tint-163

Broadbent, Punch
12C57-2
23V145-1-9
24C144 Champ's Cigarettes-8
24V130 Maple Crispette-18
24V145-2-39
83Hall of Fame-3
83Hall of Fame Postcards-A2
85Hall of Fame-3

Broccoli, Peter
99Ohio State Buckeyes-2
00Ohio State Buckeyes-11
01Ohio State Buckeyes-4
02Ohio State Buckeyes-5

Brochu, Derek
04Owen Sound Attack-4
05Owen Sound Attack-9
06Owen Sound Attack-9

Brochu, Guillaume
93Quebec Pee-Wee Tournament-989

Brochu, Martin
907th Inn. Sketch QMJHL-67
917th Inn. Sketch QMJHL-44
93Fredericton Canadiens-4
94Fredericton Canadiens-5
94Classic Pro Prospects-94
95Fredericton Canadiens-4
95Wheeling Thunderbirds-20
96Portland Pirates-30
96Collector's Edge Ice-39
Prism-39
QuantumMotion-11
97Portland Pirates-4
98Portland Pirates-3
99AHL All-Stars-1
99Portland Pirates-4
00Pacific-419
Copper-419
Gold-419
Ice Blue-419
Premiere Date-419
00SP Authentic-139
00Upper Deck Ice-83
01Between the Pipes-80
02Between the Pipes-61
Gold-61
Silver-61
02Russian Hockey League-178
03BAP Memorabilia Deep in the Crease-D15
03Wilkes-Barre Scranton Penguins-6

Brochu, Stephane
90ProCards AHL/IHL-546
91ProCards-445
93Flint Generals-19
94Flint Generals-4
95Flint Generals-24
96Flint Generals-4
97Flint Generals-2
97Flint Generals EBK-4
98Flint Generals-5
98UHL All-Stars-2
99Adirondack IceHawks-2
99UHL All-Stars East-2T

Brocklehurst, Aaron
04St. Cloud State Huskies-4
05St. Cloud State Huskies-4
05St. Cloud State Huskies-4

Brocklehurst, Craig
907th Inn. Sketch OHL-27

Brockmann, Andreas
91Finnish Semic World Champ Stickers-167
91Swedish Semic World Champ Stickers-167
93Swedish Semic World Champ Stickers-156
94German DEL-93
95German DEL-95
95German DEL-436
96German DEL-282
98German DEL-176
99German Bundesliga 2-92

Broda, Mike
95Red Deer Rebels-4
96Red Deer Rebels-16

Broda, Turk
34Beehive Group I Photos-303
36O-Pee-Chee V304D-97
37O-Pee-Chee V304E-133
38Quaker Oats Photos-4
39O-Pee-Chee V301-1-2
40O-Pee-Chee V301-2-108
40O-Pee-Chee V301-2-130
43Parade Sportive *-15
43Parade Sportive *-16
44Beehive Group II Photos-386
45Quaker Oats Photos-12A
45Quaker Oats Photos-12B
45Quaker Oats Photos-12C
48Exhibits Canadian-29
51Parkhurst-75
55Parkhurst-23
Quaker Oats-23
64Beehive Group III Photos-158
83Hall of Fame-94
83Hall of Fame Postcards-G3
85Hall of Fame-94
91Kraft-37
92Parkhurst Parkie Reprints-PR6
94Parkhurst Missing Link Pop-Ups-P6
00BAP Memorabilia Goalie Memorabilia-G18
00BAP Memorabilia Goalie Memorabilia-G19
00BAP Memorabilia Goalie Memorabilia-G27
00BAP Ultimate Mem Goalie Memorabilia-GM6
00BAP Ultimate Mem Goalie Memorabilia-GM19
01BAP Memorabilia Goalie Traditions-GT3
01BAP Memorabilia Goalie Traditions-GT19
01BAP Memorabilia Goalie Traditions-GT21
01BAP Memorabilia Goalie Traditions-GT37
01BAP Ultimate Mem All-Star History-1
01BAP Ultimate Mem Stanley Cup Winners-20
01BAP Update Rocket's Rivals-RR-6
01Between the Pipes-127
01Between the Pipes-147
Trophy Winners-TW9
Vintage Memorabilia-VM2
01Parkhurst Reprints-PR106
01Parkhurst Vintage Memorabilia-PV20
02BAP NHL All-Star History-1
02BAP Ultimate Mem Paper Cuts Autos-18
02Between the Pipes-118
02Maple Leafs Platinum Collection-45
02Parkhurst Retro Nicknames-RN18
03BAP Ultimate Mem Maple Leafs Forever-3
03BAP Ultimate Memorabilia Paper Cuts-18
03ITG VIP Collages-30
03Parkhurst Original Six Toronto-57
03Parkhurst Original Six Toronto-67
03Parkhurst Original Six Toronto-83
03Parkhurst Original Six Toronto-95
Inserts-T12
Memorabilia-TM35
03Parkhurst Rookie Before the Mask-BTM-16
03Parkhurst Rookie Before the Mask Gold-BTM-16
03SP Authentic Special Cuts-TB
04ITG NHL AS FANtasy AS History Jerseys-SB1
04ITG Franchises Canadian-107
04ITG Ultimate Memorabilia-196
Gold-196
Day In History-32
Day In History-46
Day In History Gold-32
Day In History Gold-46
Maple Leafs Forever-3
Original Six-14
Original Six-15
Paper Cuts-10
Paper Cuts Memorabilia-14
05Between the Pipes-2
05ITG Ultimate Memorabilia Level 1-97
05ITG Ultimate Memorabilia Level 2-97
05ITG Ultimate Memorabilia Level 3-97
05ITG Ultimate Memorabilia Level 4-97
05ITG Ultimate Memorabilia Level 5-97
05ITG Ultimate Memorabilia Lumbergraphs-9
05ITG Ultimate Mem Leafs Forever Autos-5
05ITG Ultimate Memorabilia Vintage Lumber-21
05ITG Ultimate Mem Vintage Lumber Gold-21
06Between The Pipes-134
06ITG Ultimate Memorabilia-144
Artist Proof-144
Cornerstones-9
Cornerstones Gold-9
Maple Leafs Forever Autos-6
Stick Rack-19
Stick Rack Gold-19

Brodahl, Erik
92Norwegian Elite Series-131

Broden, Connie
94Parkhurst Missing Link-82

Broderick, Ken
69O-Pee-Chee-197
75O-Pee-Chee NHL-340
76O-Pee-Chee WHA-44
77O-Pee-Chee WHA-4

Broderick, Len
57Parkhurst-M21
57Parkhurst-M23
02Parkhurst Reprints-216

Brodeur, Denis
51Bas Du Fleuve-2
52Bas Du Fleuve-17
04Upper Deck-196
Canadian Exclusives-196
HG Glossy Gold-196
HG Glossy Silver-196

Brodeur, Martin
90Score-439
Canadian-439
907th Inn. Sketch QMJHL-222
917th Inn. Sketch QMJHL-1
92O-Pee-Chee-59
92Score-480
Canadian-480
92Sports Illustrated for Kids II-413
92Sports Illustrated for Kids II-767
92Stadium Club-233
92Topps-513
Gold-513G
92Upper Deck-408
93Donruss-195
Rated Rookies-10
93Durivage Score-5
93Leaf-345
93OPC Premier-401
Gold-401
93Parkhurst-380
Emerald Ice-380
93PowerPlay-374
93Score-648
Gold-648
Canadian-648
Canadian Gold-648
93Stadium Club-352
Members Only Master Set-352
First Day Issue-352
93Topps/OPC Premier-401
Gold-401
93Ultra-357
Wave of the Future-2
93Upper Deck-334
94Be A Player-R58
94Be A Player-R130
Signature Cards-3
94Canada Games NHL POGS-284
94Canada Games NHL POGS-326
94Donruss-24
Elite Inserts-2
Masked Marvels-2
94Finest-71
Super Team Winners-71
Refractors-71
94Flair-92
94Fleer-111
Netminders-2
94Kraft-35
94Kraft-58
94Leaf-56
Crease Patrol-9
Gold Rookies-1
Gold Stars-8
Limited Inserts-13
94Leaf Limited-70
94McDonald's Upper Deck-McD35
94OPC Premier-83
94OPC Premier-190
94OPC Premier-380
94OPC Premier-470
94O-Pee-Chee Finest Inserts-14
94OPC Premier Special Effects-83
94OPC Premier Special Effects-190
94OPC Premier Special Effects-380
94OPC Premier Special Effects-470
94Parkhurst-126
94Parkhurst-278
Gold-126
Gold-278
SE Vintage-8
94Pinnacle-145
94Pinnacle-462
Artist's Proofs-145
Artist's Proofs-462
Rink Collection-145
Rink Collection-462
Goaltending Greats-GT7
94Post Box Backs-4
94Select-78
Gold-78
94SP-63
Die Cuts-63
94Stadium Club Members Only-46
94Stadium Club-119
94Stadium Club-186
94Stadium Club-264
Members Only Master Set-119
Members Only Master Set-186
Members Only Master Set-264
First Day Issue-119
First Day Issue-186
First Day Issue-264
Super Teams-13
Super Teams Members Only Master Set-13
Super Team Winner Cards-119
Super Team Winner Cards-186
Super Team Winner Cards-264
94Topps/OPC Premier-83
94Topps/OPC Premier-190
94Topps/OPC Premier-380
94Topps/OPC Premier-470
Special Effects-83
Special Effects-190
Special Effects-380
Special Effects-470
94Topps Finest Bronze-12
94Ultra-115
All-Rookies-2
All-Rookies Parallel-2
Award Winners-2
94Upper Deck-96
Electric Ice-96
Ice Gallery-IG11
Predictor Hobby-H12
Predictor Hobby-H29
94Upper Deck Predictor Hobby Exch Gold-H12
94Upper Deck Predictor Hobby Exch Gold-H29
94Upper Deck Predictor Hobby Exch Silver-H12
94Upper Deck SP Inserts-SP43
94Upper Deck SP Inserts Die Cuts-SP43
94Classic All-Rookie Team-AR1
94Classic Pro Prospects-12
Jumbos-PP24
94Images *-101
95SLU Hockey American-2
95SLU Hockey Canadian-3
95Bashan Super Stickers-70
Die-Cut-16
95Bowman-70
All-Foil-70
Bowman's Best-BB8
Bowman's Best Refractors-BB8
95Canada Games NHL POGS-167
95Collector's Choice-204
Player's Club-204
Player's Club Platinum-204
95Donruss-149
Between The Pipes-5
Dominators-4
95Donruss Elite-43
Die Cut Stars-43
Die Cut Uncut-43
Painted Warriors-3
Painted Warriors-P3
95Emotion-94
Xcited-18
95Finest-45
95Finest-178
Refractors-45
Refractors-178
95Hoyle Eastern Playing Cards-7
95Imperial Stickers-70
Die Cut Superstars-16
95Kenner Starting Lineup Cards-3
95Kraft-21
95Leaf-66
Road To The Cup-2
95Leaf Limited-18
Stick Side-2
Stick Side-P2
95McDonald's Pinnacle-MCD-27
95Metal-81
95NHL Aces Playing Cards-9C
95NHL Cool Trade-18
95NHL Cool Trade-RP18
95Panini Stickers-90
95Parkhurst International-122
95Parkhurst International-NNO3
Emerald Ice-122
Crown Collection Silver Series 1-11
Crown Collection Gold Series 1-11
Goal Patrol-1
NHL All-Stars-6
Parkie's Trophy Picks-PP32
95Pinnacle Clear Shots-1
95Pinnacle Masks-2
95Pinnacle Roaring 20s-3
95Pinnacle FANtasy-19
95Playoff One on One-57
95Playoff One on One-275
95Post Upper Deck-2
95Pro Magnets-36
95Pro Magnets Iron Curtain Insert-2
95Score Promos-25
95Score-25
95Score-323
Black Ice Artist's Proofs-25
Black Ice Artist's Proofs-323
Black Ice-25
Black Ice-323
95Select Certified-24
Mirror Gold-24
Gold Team-9
95SkyBox Impact-90
Deflectors-11
95SP-79
Holoviews-FX12
Holoviews Special FX-FX12
Stars/Etoiles-E18
Stars/Etoiles Gold-E18
95Stadium Club-85
Members Only Master Set-85
Generation TSC-GT5
Generation TSC Members Only Master Set-GT5
Nemeses-N6
Nemeses Members Only Master Set-N6
95Summit-27
Artist's Proofs-27
Ice-27
GM's Choice-2
In The Crease-1
95Topps-9
95Topps-325
OPC Inserts-9
OPC Inserts-325
Marquee Men Power Boosters-9
Mystery Finest-M21
Mystery Finest Refractors-M21
Profiles-PF6
Young Stars-YS2
95Topps SuperSkills-80
Platinum-80
95Ultra-86
95Ultra-186
95Ultra-366
Gold Medallion-86
Gold Medallion-186
High Speed-5
Premier Pad Men-2
Premier Pad Men Gold Medallion-2
95Upper Deck-211
Electric Ice-211
Electric Ice Gold-211
95Upper Deck All-Star Game Predictors-29
Redemption Winners-29
95Upper Deck Freeze Frame-F14
95Upper Deck Freeze Frame Jumbo-F14
95Upper Deck NHL All-Stars-AS6
95Upper Deck NHL All-Stars Jumbo-AS6
95Upper Deck Predictor Hobby-H5
95Upper Deck Predictor Hobby-H11
95Upper Deck Predictor Hobby Exchange-H5
95Upper Deck Predictor Hobby Exchange-H11
95Upper Deck Predictor Retail-R57
95Upper Deck Predictor Retail Exchange-R57
95Upper Deck Special Edition-SE135
95Upper Deck Special Edition Gold-SE135
95Zenith-12
Z-Team-2
Z-Team-S2
95Signature Rookies-CS1
95Signature Rookies Tetrad Autobilia *-95
95Signature Rookies Tetrad SR Force *-F6
96Headliners Hockey-2
96Be A Player Stacking the Pads-5
96Black Diamond-134
Gold-134
96Collector's Choice-144
96Collector's Choice-306
96Collector's Choice-322
MVP-UD21
MVP Gold-UD21
Stick'Ums-S24
96Devils Team Issue-30
96Donruss-148
Press Proofs-148
Between the Pipes-2
Dominators-1
96Donruss Canadian Ice-46
Gold Press Proofs-46
Red Press Proofs-46
Les Gardiens-4
96Donruss Elite-16
Die Cut Stars-16
Painted Warriors-8
Painted Warriors Promos-P8
96Duracell L'Equipe Beliveau-JB6
96Flair-52
Blue Ice-52
Hot Gloves-2
96Fleer-58
96Fleer-145
96Fleer-146
Picks Dream Lines-3
Picks Fabulous 50-4
Picks Fantasy Force-8
96Kraft Upper Deck-14
96Leaf-6
Press Proofs-6
Shut Down-6
Sweaters Away-6
Sweaters Home-6
96Leaf Limited-87
Gold-87
Stubble-11
96Leaf Preferred-81
Press Proofs-81
Steel-2
Steel Gold-2
Masked Marauders-2
96Maggers-6
96McDonald's Pinnacle-33
96Metal Universe-86
Armor Plate-2
Armor Plate Super Power-2
Ice Carvings-1
Ice Carvings Super Power-1
96NHL Aces Playing Cards-5
96NHL Pro Stamps-36
96Pinnacle-92
Artist's Proofs-92
Foil-92
Premium Stock-92
Rink Collection-92
Masks-4
Masks Die Cuts-4
Team Pinnacle-9
96Pinnacle Mint-23
Bronze-23
Gold-23
Silver-23
Coins Brass-23
Coins Solid Gold-23
Coins Gold Plated-23
Coins Nickel-23
Coins Silver-23
96Playoff One on One-440
96Score Samples-10
96Score Samples-10
96Score Samples-10
96Score-10
Artist's Proofs-10
Dealer's Choice Artist's Proofs-10
Special Artist's Proofs-10
Golden Blades-10
Net Worth-2
Sudden Death-1
96Select Certified-6
Artist's Proofs-6
Blue-6
Mirror Blue-6
Mirror Gold-6
Mirror Red-6
Red-6
Freezers-1
96SkyBox Impact-68
96SP-86
SPx Force-3
SPx Force-5
SPx Force Autographs-3
96SPx-25
Gold-25
96Stadium Club Members Only-29
96Summit-114
Artist's Proofs-114
Ice-114
Metal-114
Premium Stock-114
In The Crease-8
In The Crease Premium Stock-8
Untouchables-16
96Team Out-61
96Topps Picks-27
Fantasy Team-FT3
Ice D-ID6
OPC Inserts-27
96Ultra-93
Gold Medallion-93
96Upper Deck-91
Generation Next-X18
Hart Hopefuls Bronze-HH10
Hart Hopefuls Gold-HH10
Hart Hopefuls Silver-HH10
Lord Stanley's Heroes Finals-LS5
Lord Stanley's Heroes Quarterfinals-LS5
Lord Stanley's Heroes Semifinals-LS5
Superstar Showdown-SS12A
96Upper Deck Ice-92
Parallel-92
96Zenith-2
Artist's Proofs-2
Champion Salute-15
Champion Salute-P15
Champion Salute Diamond-15
96Collector's Edge Ice Livin' Large-L11
97Headliners Hockey-1
97SLU Hockey American-4
97SLU Hockey Canadian-4
97Be A Player-2
Autographs-2
Autographs Die-Cuts-2
Autographs Prismatic Die-Cuts-2
Stacking the Pads-11
97Beehive-45
Golden Portraits-45
Team-6
Team Gold-6
97Black Diamond-122
Double Diamond-122
Triple Diamond-122
Quadruple Diamond-122
Premium Cut-PC24
Premium Cut Double Diamond-PC24
Premium Cut Quadruple Diamond Horiz-PC24
Premium Cut Triple Diamond-PC24
Premium Cut Quadruple Diamond Verticals-PC24
97Collector's Choice-141
Star Quest-SQ50
Stick'Ums-S3
World Domination-W20
97Crown Royale-73
Emerald Green-73
Ice Blue-73
Silver-73
Freeze Out Die-Cuts-11
97Devils Team Issue-24
97Donruss-126
Press Proofs Silver-126
Press Proofs Gold-126
Between The Pipes-2
Elite Inserts-10
97Donruss Canadian Ice-42
Dominion Series-42
Provincial Series-42
Les Gardiens-3
97Donruss Canadian Ice Les Gardiens Promo-3
97Donruss Cdn Ice Stanley Cup Scrapbook-24
97Donruss Elite-8
97Donruss Elite-137
Aspirations-8
Aspirations-137
Status-8
Status-137
Back to the Future-7
Back to the Future Autographs-7
Craftsmen-8
Master Craftsmen-8
97Donruss Limited-74
97Donruss Limited-127
97Donruss Limited-149
97Donruss Limited-150
Exposure-74
Exposure-127
Exposure-149
Exposure-150
Fabric of the Game-2
97Donruss Preferred-16
97Donruss Preferred-185
Cut to the Chase-16
Cut to the Chase-185
Color Guard-2
Color Guard Promos-2
Precious Metals-6
97Donruss Priority-7
97Donruss Priority-196
Stamp of Approval-7
Stamp of Approval-196
Postcards-24
Postcards Opening Day Issues-7
Postmaster General-10
Postmaster Generals Promos-10
Stamps-24
Stamps Bronze-24
Stamps Gold-24
Stamps Silver-24
97Highland Mint Mint-Cards Pinnacle/Score-1
97Highland Mint Mint-Cards Pinnacle/Score-2
97Katch-79
Gold-79
Silver-79
97Kenner Starting Lineup Cards-4
97Kraft Team Canada-2
97Leaf-7
97Leaf-174
97Leaf-P6
Fractal Matrix-7
Fractal Matrix-174
Fractal Matrix Die Cuts-7
Fractal Matrix Die Cuts-174
Pipe Dreams-6
97Leaf International-7
Universal Ice-7
97McDonald's Team Canada Coins-3
97McDonald's Upper Deck-25
97NHL Aces Playing Cards-38
97Pacific-30
Copper-30
Emerald Green-30
Ice Blue-30
Red-30
Silver-30
Card-Supials-10
Card-Supials Minis-10
Gold Crown Die-Cuts-14
In The Cage Laser Cuts-12
Team Checklists-14
97Pacific Dynagon-68
Copper-68
Dark Grey-68
Emerald Green-68
Ice Blue-68
Red-68
Silver-68
Best Kept Secrets-52
Best Kept Secrets-106
Stonewallers-12
Tandems-12

97Pacific Invincible-76
Copper-76
Emerald Green-76
Ice Blue-76
Red-76
Silver-76
Feature Performers-19
NHL Regime-108
97Pacific Omega-127
Copper-127
Dark Gray-127
Emerald Green-127
Gold-127
Gold-249
Ice Blue-127
No Scoring Zone-7
Silks-7
Team Leaders-13
97Panini Stickers-64
97Panini Stickers-124
97Paramount-101
Copper-101
Dark Grey-101
Emerald Green-101
Ice Blue-101
Red-101
Silver-101
Big Numbers Die-Cuts-12
Canadian Greats-9
Glove Side Laser Cuts-11
97Pinnacle-43
Artist's Proofs-43
Rink Collection-43
Epix Game Emerald-8
Epix Game Orange-8
Epix Game Purple-8
Epix Moment Emerald-8
Epix Moment Orange-8
Epix Moment Purple-8
Epix Play Emerald-8
Epix Play Orange-8
Epix Play Purple-8
Epix Season Emerald-8
Epix Season Orange-8
Epix Season Purple-8
Press Plates Back Black-43
Press Plates Back Cyan-43
Press Plates Back Magenta-43
Press Plates Back Yellow-43
Press Plates Front Black-43
Press Plates Front Cyan-43
Press Plates Front Magenta-43
Press Plates Front Yellow-43
Masks-3
Masks Die Cuts-3
Masks Jumbos-3
97Pinnacle Masks Promos-3
97Pinnacle Team Pinnacle-1
97Pinnacle Team Pinnacle Mirror-1
97Pinnacle Team Pinnacle Parallel-1
97Pinnacle Team Pinnacle Parallel Mirror-1
97Pinnacle Tins-1
97Pinnacle Certified-3
Red-3
Mirror Blue-3
Mirror Gold-3
Mirror Red-3
Team-1
Gold Team Promo-1
Gold Team-1
97Pinnacle Inside-7
Coach's Collection-7
Executive Collection-7
Stand Up Guys-2A/B
Stand Up Guys-2C/D
Stand Up Guys Promos-2A/B
Stand Up Guys Promos-2C/D
Stoppers-4
Track-6
Cans-17
Cans Gold-17
Promos-7
97Pinnacle Mint-16
Bronze-16
Gold Team-16
Silver Team-16
Coins Brass-16
Coins Brass Proofs-16
Coins Gold Plated-16
Coins Gold Plated Proofs-16
Coins Nickel Silver-16
Coins Nickel Silver Proofs-16
Coins Solid Gold-16
Coins Solid Silver-16
97Pinnacle Power Pack Blow-Ups-7
97Pinnacle Replica Masks-1
97Pinnacle Tot Cert Platinum Blue-3
97Pinnacle Tot Cert Platinum Gold-3
97Pinnacle Totally Certified Platinum Red-3
97Pinnacle Tot Cert Mirror Platinum Gold-3
97Post Pinnacle-8
97Revolution-75
Copper-75
Emerald-75
Ice Blue-75
Silver-75
1998 All-Star Game Die-Cuts-13
NHL Icons-6
Return to Sender Die-Cuts-11
Team Checklist Laser Cuts-14
97Score-30
97Score-269
Artist's Proofs-30
Golden Blades-30
Net Worth-14
97Score Devils-16
Platinum-16
Premier-16
97SP Authentic-87
Icons-I14
Icons Die-Cuts-I14
Icons Embossed-I14
Sign of the Times-MB
97SPx-27
Bronze-27
Gold-27
Silver-27
Steel-27
DuoView-3
DuoView Autographs-3
Grand Finale-27
97Studio-20
Press Proofs Silver-20
Press Proofs Gold-20
Portraits-20
Portraits-NNOA
Silhouettes-4
Silhouettes 8x10-4
97Upper Deck-300
Blow-Ups 3 x 5-2-4
Blow-Ups 5 x 7-4B

Game Dated Moments-300
Smooth Grooves-SG4
The Specialists-30
The Specialists Level 2 Die Cuts-30
Three Star Selects-10A
97Upper Deck Diamond Vision-5
Signature Moves-5
97Upper Deck Ice-7
Parallel-7
Champions-IC7
Champions 2 Die Cuts-IC7
Power Shift-7
97Zenith-21
Z-Gold-21
Z-Silver-21
97Zenith 5 x 7-5
Gold Impulse-5
Silver Impulse-5
97Zenith Chasing The Cup-11
97Zenith Z-Team-8
97Zenith Z-Team 5x7-8
97Zenith Z-Team Gold-8
97Pinnacle Collector's Club Team Pinnacle-H7
98Headliners Hockey In the Crease-1
98SLU Hockey Classic Doubles-1
98SLU Hockey-40
98Aurora-108
98Aurora-S108
Atomic Laser Cuts-12
Championship Fever-26
Championship Fever-NNO
Championship Fever Copper-26
Championship Fever Copper-NNO
Championship Fever Ice Blue-26
Championship Fever Ice Blue-NNO
Championship Fever Red-26
Championship Fever Red-NNO
Championship Fever Silver-26
Cubes-11
NHL Command-7
98Be A Player-79
Press Release-79
98BAP Gold-79
98BAP Autographs-79
98BAP Autographs Gold-79
98BAP AS Game Used Stick Cards-S8
98BAP AS Game Used Jersey Cards-AS8
98BAP Playoff Game Used Jerseys-G9
98BAP Playoff Game Used Jersey Autographs-G9
98BAP Playoff Highlights-H4
98BAP Playoff Practice Used Jerseys-P19
98BAP Tampa Bay All Star Game-79
98Black Diamond-50
Double Diamond-50
Triple Diamond-50
Quadruple Diamond-50
Myriad-M21
Myriad 2-M21
Winning Formula Gold-WF15
Winning Formula Platinum-WF15
98Bowman's Best-8
Refractors-8
Atomic Refractors-8
Mirror Image Fusion-F19
Mirror Image Fusion Refractors-F19
Mirror Image Fusion Atomic Refractors-F19
Scotty Bowman's Best-SB2
Scotty Refractors-SB2
Scotty Atomic Refractors-SB2
98Crown Royale-78
Limited Series-78
Cramer's Choice Jumbos-7
Cramer's Choice Jumbos Dark Blue-7
Cramer's Choice Jumbos Green-7
Cramer's Choice Jumbos Red-7
Cramer's Choice Jumbos Light Blue-7
Cramer's Choice Jumbos Gold-7
Cramer's Choice Jumbos Purple-7
Living Legends-7
Master Performers-13
Pillars of the Game-16
Pivotal Players-14
98Devils Power Play-NJD3
98Devils Team Issue-4
98Donruss Elite Promos-13
98Finest-35
No Protectors-35
No Protectors Refractors-35
Refractors-35
Centurion-C11
Centurion Refractors-C11
Double Sided Mystery Finest-M21
Double Sided Mystery Finest-M22
Double Sided Mystery Finest-M23
Double Sided Mystery Finest-M24
Double Sided Mystery Refractors-M21
Double Sided Mystery Refractors-M22
Double Sided Mystery Refractors-M23
Double Sided Mystery Refractors-M24
Oversize-3
Oversize Refractors-3
98Katch-79
Gold-79
Silver-79
98Kenner Starting Lineup Cards-5
98Lunchables Goalie Greats Rounds-2
98Lunchables Goalie Greats Squares-2
98McDonald's Upper Deck-17
98NHL Aces Playing Cards-52
98OPC Chrome-20
Refractors-20
Season's Best-SB2
Season's Best Refractors-SB2
98Pacific-30
Ice Blue-30
Red-30
Cramer's Choice-6
Dynagon Ice Inserts-12
Titanium Ice-12
Gold Crown Die-Cuts-18
98Pacific Martin Brodeur Show Promo-1
98Pacific Team Checklists-15
98Pacific Trophy Winners-1
98Pacific Dynagon Ice-108
Blue-108
Red-108
Watchmen-5
Preeminent Players-7
Team Checklists-15
98Pacific Omega-136
98Pacific Omega-S136
Red-136
Opening Day Issue-136
Championship Spotlight-6
Championship Spotlight Green-6
Championship Spotlight Red-6
Championship Spotlight Gold-6
EO Portraits-13
EO Portraits 1 of 1-13
Face to Face-1
Online-19

Planet Ice-19
Planet Ice Parallel-19
Prism-12
98Panini Photocards-13
98Panini Photocards-94
98Panini Stickers-67
98Paramount-132
98Paramount-NNO
Copper-132
Emerald Green-132
Holo-Electric-132
Ice Blue-132
Silver-132
Glove Side Laser Cuts-10
Hall of Fame Bound-6
Hall of Fame Bound Proofs-6
Ice Galaxy-6
Ice Galaxy Gold-6
Ice Galaxy Silver-6
Team Checklists Die-Cuts-15
98Post-2
98Revolution-83
98Revolution-S83
Ice Shadow-83
Red-83
All-Star Die Cuts-5
NHL Icons-7
Showstoppers-21
Three Pronged Attack-15
Three Pronged Attack Parallel-15
98SP Authentic-48
Power Shift-48
Snapshots-SS13
Stat Masters-S13
98SPx Finite-46
98SPx Finite-105
98SPx Finite-161
98SPx Finite-176
Radiance-46
Radiance-105
Radiance-161
Radiance-176
Spectrum-46
Spectrum-105
Spectrum-161
Spectrum-176
98SPx Top Prospects-35
Radiance-35
Spectrum-35
Highlight Heroes-H17
Lasting Impressions-L21
Premier Stars-PS5
98Topps-20
O-Pee-Chee-20
Local Legends-L6
Mystery Finest Bronze-M12
Mystery Finest Bronze Refractors-M12
Mystery Finest Gold-M12
Mystery Finest Gold Refractors-M12
Mystery Finest Silver-M12
Mystery Finest Silver Refractors-M12
Season's Best-SB2
98Topps Gold Label Class 1-10
Black-10
Black One of One-10
One of One-10
Red-10
Red One of One-10
98Topps Gold Label Class 2-10
98Topps Gold Label Class 2 Black-10
98Topps Gold Label Class 2 Black 1 of 1-10
98Topps Gold Label Class 2 One of One-10
98Topps Gold Label Class 2 Red-10
98Topps Gold Label Class 2 Red One of One-10
98Topps Gold Label Class 3-10
98Topps Gold Label Class 3 Black-10
98Topps Gold Label Class 3 Black 1 of 1-10
98Topps Gold Label Class 3 One of One-10
98Topps Gold Label Class 3 Red-10
98Topps Gold Label Class 3 Red One of One-10
98UD Choice-116
98UD Choice-245
Blow-Ups-4
Mini Bobbing Head-BH7
Prime Choice Reserve-116
Prime Choice Reserve-245
Reserve-116
Reserve-245
StarQuest Blue-SQ23
StarQuest Gold-SQ23
StarQuest Green-SQ23
StarQuest Red-SQ23
98UD3-36
98UD3-96
98UD3-156
Die-Cuts-36
Die-Cuts-96
Die-Cuts-156
98Upper Deck-118
Exclusives-118
Exclusives 1 of 1-118
Frozen In Time-FT4
Frozen In Time Quantum 1-FT4
Frozen In Time Quantum 2-FT4
Frozen In Time Quantum 3-FT4
Game Jerseys-GJ6
Lord Stanley's Heroes-LS5
Lord Stanley's Heroes Quantum 1-LS5
Lord Stanley's Heroes Quantum 2-LS5
Lord Stanley's Heroes Quantum 3-LS5
Profiles-P6
Profiles Quantum 1-P6
Profiles Quantum 2-P6
Profiles Quantum 3-P6
Gold Reserve-118
98Upper Deck MVP-117
Gold Script-117
Silver Script-117
Super Script-117
Special Forces-F9
99SLU Hockey Pro Action Deluxe-10
99Aurora-84
Striped-84
Premiere Date-84
Premiere Date Striped-84
Championship Fever-15
Championship Fever-NNO
Championship Fever Copper-15
Championship Fever Copper-NNO
Championship Fever Ice Blue-15
Championship Fever Ice Blue-NNO
Championship Fever Silver-15
Championship Fever Silver-NNO
Glove Unlimited-11
Styrotechs-12
99BAP Memorabilia-61
Gold-61
Silver-61
Jersey Cards-J8
Jersey Emblems-E8
Jersey Numbers-I8

Jersey and Stick Cards-S8
Selects Silver-SL12
Selects Gold-SL12
99BAP Update Double AS Jersey Cards-D19
99BAP Update Teammates Jersey Cards-TM9
99BAP Update Teammates Jersey Cards-TM17
99BAP Update Teammates Jersey Cards-TM35
99BAP Millennium-143
Emerald-143
Ruby-143
Sapphire-143
Signatures-143
Signatures Gold-143
Jerseys-J25
Jersey Autographs-J25
Jersey and Stick Cards-JS25
Jersey Emblems-E25
Jersey Numbers-N25
99Black Diamond-51
Diamond Cut-51
Final Cut-51
A Piece of History-MB
A Piece of History Double-MB
A Piece of History Triple-MB
Diamonation-D10
Diamond Skills-DS8
99Crown Royale-78
Limited Series-78
Premiere Date-78
Card-Supials-13
Card-Supials Minis-13
Cramer's Choice Jumbos-8
Cramer's Choice Jumbos Dark Blue-8
Cramer's Choice Jumbos Gold-8
Cramer's Choice Jumbos Green-8
Cramer's Choice Jumbos Light Blue-8
Cramer's Choice Jumbos Purple-8
Cramer's Choice Jumbos Red-8
Gold Crown Die-Cuts Jumbos-5
Ice Elite-16
Ice Elite Parallel-16
International Glory-14
International Glory Parallel-14
99Devils Team Issue-23
99Jell-O Goalie Collection-2
99Jell-O Partners of Power-1
99Kraft Peanut Butter-2
99O-Pee-Chee-20
99O-Pee-Chee All-Topps-AT2
99O-Pee-Chee Chrome-20
99O-Pee-Chee Chrome All Topps-AT2
99O-Pee-Chee Chrome All-Topps Refractors-AT2
99O-Pee-Chee Chrome Ice Masters-IM11
99O-Pee-Chee Chrome Ice Masters Refractor-IM11
99O-Pee-Chee Chrome Refractors-20
99O-Pee-Chee Chrome Postmasters-PM6
99O-Pee-Chee Chrome Postmasters Refractor-PM6
99O-Pee-Chee Ice Masters-IM11
99O-Pee-Chee Post Masters-PM6
99O-Pee-Chee Top of the World-TW15
99Pacific-235
Copper-235
Emerald Green-235
Gold-235
Ice Blue-235
Premiere Date-235
Red-235
Center Ice-14
Center Ice Proofs-14
Gold Crown Die-Cuts-21
In the Cage Net-Fusions-10
Past and Present-15
Team Leaders-16
99Pacific Dynagon Ice-114
99Pacific Dynagon Ice-NNO
Blue-114
Copper-114
Gold-114
Premiere Date-114
2000 All-Star Preview-13
Lords of the Rink-8
Masks-2
Masks-7
Masks Holographic Blue-2
Masks Holographic Blue-7
Masks Holographic Gold-2
Masks Holographic Gold-7
Masks Holographic Purple-2
Masks Holographic Purple-7
99Pacific Omega-133
99Pacific Omega-NNO
Copper-133
Gold-133
Ice Blue-133
Premiere Date-133
Cup Contenders-12
EO Portraits-11
EO Portraits 1/1-11
Game-Used Jerseys-4
North American All-Stars-7
5 Star Talents-28
5 Star Talents Parallel-28
99Pacific Prism-79
99Pacific Prism-NNO
Holographic Blue-79
Holographic Gold-79
Holographic Mirror-79
Holographic Purple-79
Premiere Date-79
Clear Advantage-12
Sno-Globe Die-Cuts-13
99Panini Stickers-79
99Panini Stickers-347
99Paramount-131
Copper-131
Emerald-131
Gold-131
Holographic Emerald-131
Holographic Gold-131
Holographic Silver-131
Ice Blue-131
Premiere Date-131
Red-131
Silver-131
Glove Side Net Fusions-11
Hall of Fame Bound-7
Hall of Fame Bound Proofs-7
Ice Advantage-14
Ice Advantage Proofs-14
Ice Alliance-16
Personal Best-21
Toronto Fall Expo '99-131
99Revolution-84
Premiere Date-84
Red-84
Shadow Series-84
Ice Sculptures-7
NHL Icons-12
Ornaments-13
Showstoppers-21
Copper-84

Gold-84
CSC Silver-84
99SP Authentic-49
Honor Roll-HR4
Supreme Skill-SS7
99SPx-85
Radiance-85
Spectrum-85
Winning Materials-WM2
99Stadium Club-16
First Day Issue-16
One of a Kind-16
Printing Plates Black-16
Printing Plates Cyan-16
Printing Plates Magenta-16
Printing Plates Yellow-16
Capture the Action-CA14
Capture the Action Game View-CAG14
Chrome-15
Chrome Refractors-15
Chrome Oversized-9
Chrome Oversized Refractors-9
Goalie Cam-GC2
99Topps/OPC-20
All-Topps-AT2
Ice Masters-IM11
Postmasters-PM6
99Topps Stanley Cup Heroes-SC14
99Topps Stanley Cup Heroes Refractors-SC14
99Topps/OPC Top of the World-TW15
99Topps/OPC Chrome-20
Refractors-20
All-Topps-AT2
All-Topps Refractors-AT2
Ice Masters-IM11
Ice Masters Refractors-IM11
Postmasters-PM6
Postmasters Refractors-PM6
99Topps Gold Label Class 1-24
Black-24
Black One of One-24
One of One-24
Red-24
Red One of One-24
99Topps Gold Label Class 2-24
99Topps Gold Label Class 2 Black-24
99Topps Gold Label Class 2 Black 1 of 1-24
99Topps Gold Label Class 2 One of One-24
99Topps Gold Label Class 2 Red-24
99Topps Gold Label Class 2 Red One of One-24
99Topps Gold Label Class 3-24
99Topps Gold Label Class 3 Black-24
99Topps Gold Label Class 3 Black 1 of 1-24
99Topps Gold Label Class 3 One of One-24
99Topps Gold Label Class 3 Red-24
99Topps Gold Label Class 3 Red One of One-24
99Topps Gold Label Quest for the Cup-QC5
99Topps Gold Label Quest for the Cup One of One -QC5
99Topps Gold Label Quest 4 the Cup Black-QC5
99Topps Gold Label Quest for the Cup Black One of One -QC5
99Topps Gold Label Quest for the Cup Red-QC5
99Topps Gold Label Quest for the Cup Red One of One -QC5
99Topps Premier Plus-66
Parallel-66
Calling All Calders-CAC5
Imperial Guard-IG3
Premier Team-PT9
Premier Team Parallel-PT9
99Ultimate Victory-50
1/1-50
Parallel-50
Parallel 100-50
Frozen Fury-FF7
Net Work-NW10
Stature-S7
The Victors-V6
99Upper Deck-77
99Upper Deck-148
Exclusives-77
Exclusives-148
Exclusives 1 of 1-77
Exclusives 1 of 1-148
All-Star Class-AS19
All-Star Class Quantum Gold-AS19
All-Star Class Quantum Silver-AS19
Crunch Time-CT24
Crunch Time Quantum Gold-CT24
Crunch Time Quantum Silver-CT24
Game Jerseys-MB
Game Jerseys Series II-MB
Game Jerseys Patch-MBP
Game Jersey Patch Series II-MBP
New Ice Age-N7
New Ice Age Quantum Gold-N7
New Ice Age Quantum Silver-N7
Sixth Sense-SS15
Sixth Sense Quantum Gold-SS15
Sixth Sense Quantum Silver-SS15
Ultimate Defense-UD9
Ultimate Defense Quantum Gold-UD9
Ultimate Defense Quantum Silver-UD9
99Upper Deck Century Legends-63
Century Collection-63
99Upper Deck Gold Reserve-77
99Upper Deck Gold Reserve-148
99Upper Deck HoloGrFx-33
Ausome-33
99Upper Deck MVP-115
Gold Script-115
Silver Script-115
Super Script-115
Draw Your Own Trading Card-W9
Last Line-LL2
Talent-MVP9
99Upper Deck MVP SC Edition-104
Gold Script-104
Silver Script-104
Super Script-104
Clutch Performers-CP6
Golden Memories-GM6
Playoff Heroes-PH7
Stanley Cup Talent-SC10
99Upper Deck Ovation-33
Standing Ovation-33
A Piece Of History-MB
Lead Performers-LP17
Superstar Theater-ST8
99Upper Deck PowerDeck-14
Auxiliary-14
Auxiliary 1 of 1-14
99Upper Deck Retro-45
Gold-45
Platinum-45
Distant Replay-DR2
Distant Replay Level 2-DR2
Turn of the Century-TC2
99Upper Deck Victory-165
99Upper Deck Victory-166

99Upper Deck Victory-346
99Upper Deck Victory-386
99Wayne Gretzky Hockey-100
Elements of the Game-EG10
99Russian Fetisov Tribute-33
99Slovakian Challengers-8
00SP Authentic Autographed Replica Jersey-1
00Aurora-81
Pinstripes-81
Pinstripes Premiere Date-81
Premiere Date-81
Canvas Creations-7
Championship Fever-14
Championship Fever Copper-14
Championship Fever Platinum Blue-14
Championship Fever Silver-14
Scouting Reports-13
Styrotechs-7B
00BAP Memorabilia-40
Emerald-40
Ruby-40
Sapphire-40
Promos-40
Jersey Cards-J4
Jersey Emblems-E4
Jersey Numbers-N4
Jersey and Stick Cards-JS4
00BAP Mem Chicago Sportsfest Copper-40
00BAP Memorabilia Chicago Sportsfest Blue-40
00BAP Memorabilia Chicago Sportsfest Gold-40
00BAP Memorabilia Chicago Sportsfest Ruby-40
00BAP Memorabilia Chicago Sun-Times Ruby-40
00BAP Memorabilia Chicago Sun-Times Gold-40
00BAP Mem Chicago Sun-Times Sapphire-40
00BAP Mem Toronto Fall Expo Copper-40
00BAP Memorabilia Toronto Fall Expo Gold-40
00BAP Memorabilia Toronto Fall Expo Ruby-40
00BAP Memorabilia Update Teammates-TM1
00BAP Memorabilia Update Teammates-TM10
00BAP Memorabilia Update Teammates Gold-TM1
00BAP Memorabilia Update Teammates Gold-TM10
00BAP Parkhurst 2000-P99
00BAP Signature Series-164
Emerald-164
Ruby-164
Sapphire-164
Autographs-139
Autographs Gold-139
Franchise Players-F18
He Shoots-He Scores Points-2
He Shoots-He Scores Prizes-7
Jersey Cards-J25
Jersey and Stick Cards-GSJ25
Jersey Cards Autographs-J25
Jersey Emblems-E25
Jersey Numbers-IN25
00BAP Ultimate Memorabilia Autographs-25
Gold-25
00BAP Ultimate Memorabilia Active Eight-AE7
00BAP Ultimate Memorabilia Active Eight-AE8
00BAP Ultimate Mem Game-Used Jerseys-GJ25
00BAP Ultimate Mem Game-Used Emblems-E23
00BAP Ultimate Mem Game-Used Numbers-N23
00BAP Ultimate Mem Game-Used Sticks-GS25
00BAP Ultimate Mem Goalie Memorabilia-GM14
00BAP Ultimate Memorabilia Goalie Sticks-G18
00BAP Ultimate Mem Plante Jersey Cards-PJ3
00BAP Ultimate Mem Plante Skate Cards-PS3
00BAP Ultimate Mem Magnificent Ones-ML3
00BAP Ultimate Mem Magnificent Ones Autos-ML3
00BAP Ultimate Memorabilia Teammates-TM30
00Black Diamond-33
00Black Diamond-89
Gold-33
Gold-89
Diamond Might-FP7
Diamond Skills-IC4
00Crown Royale-62
Ice Blue-62
Limited Series-62
Premiere Date-62
Red-62
Jewels of the Crown-17
Landmarks-7
Now Playing-11
00Devils Team Issue-2
00McDonald's Pacific-20
Blue-20
Glove Side Net Fusions-4
Game Jerseys-7
00O-Pee-Chee-131
00O-Pee-Chee-326
00O-Pee-Chee Parallel-131
00O-Pee-Chee Parallel-326
00Pacific-232
Copper-232
Gold-232
Ice Blue-232
Premiere Date-232
2001: Ice Odyssey-12
Cramer's Choice-7
Gold Crown Die Cuts-18
In the Cage Net-Fusions-7
North American Stars-7
00Pacific 2001: Ice Odyssey Anaheim Ntnl-12
00Panini Stickers-48
00Paramount-142
Copper-142
Gold-142
Holo-Gold-142
Holo-Silver-142
Ice Blue-142
Premiere Date-142
Epic Scope-13
Freeze Frame-21
Glove Side Net Fusions-12
Glove Side Net Fusions Platinum-12
Hall of Fame Bound-8
Hall of Fame Bound Canvas Proofs-8
Hall of Fame Bound Proofs-8
Sub Zero-7
Sub Zero Gold-7
Sub Zero Red-7
00Private Stock-57
Gold-57
Premiere Date-57
Retail-57
Silver-57
Artist's Canvas-14
Artist's Canvas Proofs-14
Extreme Action-13
PS-2001 Action-31
PS-2001 Stars-17
Reserve-14
00Revolution-85
Blue-85
Premiere Date-85
Red-85
HD NHL-20
Ice Immortals-13
NHL Icons-15

Stat Masters-16
00SP Authentic-53
BuyBacks-60
BuyBacks-61
BuyBacks-62
BuyBacks-63
Honor-SP4
Parents' Scrapbook-PS5
Sign of the Times-MB
Sign of the Times-B/S
Sign of the Times-BGE
Super Stoppers-SS4
00SP Game Used-36
Patch Cards-P-MB
Tools of the Game-MB
Tools of the Game Exclusives-MB
Tools of the Game Combos-C-BR
00SPx-37
00SPx-88
Spectrum-37
Spectrum-88
SPXcitement-X8
SPXtreme-S4
Winning Materials-MB
Winning Materials Autographs-SMB
00Stadium Club-16
Beam Team-BT13
Capture the Action-CA2
Capture the Action Game View-2
Co-Signers-CO2
Glove Save-GS1
Lone Star Signatures-LS2
Special Forces-SF17
11 X 14 Autographs-MB
00Titanium-54
Blue-54
Gold-54
Premiere Date-54
Red-54
Retail-54
All-Stars-7NA
Game Gear-105
Game Gear Patches-105
Three-Star Selections-4
00Topps/OPC-131
00Topps/OPC-326
Parallel-131
Parallel-326
Combos-TC8
Combos Jumbos-TC8
Hobby Masters-HM1
Own the Game-OTG11
00Topps Chrome-98
00Topps Chrome-163
OPC Refractors-98
OPC Refractors-163
Refractors-98
Refractors-163
Combos-TC8
Combos Refractors-TC8
Hobby Masters Refractors-HM1
00Topps Gold Label Class 1-71
Gold-71
00Topps Gold Label Class 2-71
00Topps Gold Label Class 2 Gold-71
00Topps Gold Label Class 3-71
00Topps Gold Label Class 3 Gold-71
00Topps Gold Label Behind the Mask-BTM4
00Topps Gold Label Behind the Mask 1 to 1-BTM4
00Topps Gold Label Bullion-B1
00Topps Gold Label Bullion One to One-B1
00Topps Gold Label Game-Worn Jerseys-GLJ-MB
00Topps Heritage-2
00Topps Heritage-231
Chrome Parallel-2
Heroes-HH6
00Topps Premier Plus-36
Blue Ice-36
Masters of the Break-MB11
Private Signings-PSMB
Team-PT5
Team Blue Ice-PR5
World Premier-WP2
00Topps Stars-17
00Topps Stars-126
Blue-17
Blue-126
Progression-P5
Walk of Fame-WF10
00UD Heroes-149
Game-Used Twigs-T-MB
Game-Used Twigs Gold-C-RB
Player Idols-PI2
Second Season Heroes-SS7
Timeless Moments-TM6
00UD Pros and Prospects-52
Championship Rings-CR6
ProMotion-PM7
00UD Reserve-52
Buyback Autographs-67
Buyback Autographs-68
Buyback Autographs-69
Buyback Autographs-70
Buyback Autographs-71
Golden Goalies-GG7
Power Portfolios-PP4
The Big Ticket-BT7
00Upper Deck-335
Exclusives Tier 1-335
Exclusives Tier 2-335
e-Cards-EC7
e-Card Prizes-AMB
e-Card Prizes-EMB
e-Card Prizes-SEMB
Game Jerseys-MB
Game Jersey Autographs Exclusives-EMB
Game Jersey Combos-DGB
Game Jersey Patches-MBP
Game Jersey Patch Autographs Exclusives-MBP
Gate Attractions-GA8
Lord Stanley's Heroes-L6
Profiles-P6
Signs of Greatness-SMB
Skilled Stars-SS13
Triple Threat-TT2
00Upper Deck Ice-24
Immortals-24
Legends-24
Stars-24
Champions-IC4
Game Jerseys-JCMB
Rink Favorites-FP7
00Upper Deck Legends-76
00Upper Deck Legends-79
Legendary Collection Bronze-76
Legendary Collection Bronze-79
Legendary Collection Gold-76
Legendary Collection Gold-79
Legendary Collection Silver-76
Legendary Collection Silver-79
Epic Signatures-MBR

Essence of the Game-EG5
Legendary Game Jerseys-JMBR
of the Cage-LC2
00Upper Deck MVP-106
First Stars-106
Masked Men-MM5
Second Stars-106
Talent-M10
Third Stars-106
Valuable Commodities-VC6
00Upper Deck Victory-134
00Upper Deck Victory-135
00Upper Deck Victory-309
00Upper Deck Vintage-211
00Upper Deck Vintage-221
00Upper Deck Vintage-222
All UD Team-UD2
National Heroes-NH14
Star Tandems-S4B
00Vanguard-57
Cosmic Force-7
High Voltage-19
High Voltage Gold-19
High Voltage Green-19
High Voltage Red-19
High Voltage Silver-19
Holographic Gold-57
Holographic Purple-57
In Focus-12
Pacific Proofs-57
Press East/West-14
00Czech Stadion-65
00Czech Stadion-156
01Atomic-57
Blue-57
Gold-57
Premiere Date-57
Red-57
Core Players-10
Statosphere-4
Team Nucleus-8
01BAP Memorabilia-40
Emerald-40
Ruby-40
Sapphire-40
All-Star Jerseys-ASJ8
All-Star Emblems-ASE8
All-Star Numbers-ASN8
All-Star Jersey Doubles-DASJ5
All-Star Teammates-AST4
All-Star Teammates-AST15
Country of Origin-CO11
Goalies Jerseys-GJ13
He Shoots-He Scores Points-11
He Shoots-He Scores Prizes-7
Stanley Cup Playoffs-SC21
01BAP Signature Series Certified 100-C24
01BAP Signature Series Certified 50-C24
01BAP Signature Series Certified 1 of 1's-C24
01BAP Signature Series Franchise Jerseys-FP-18
01BAP Sig Series International Medals-IG-1
01BAP Signature Series Jerseys-GJ-35
01BAP Sig Series Jersey and Stick Cards-GSJ-35
01BAP Signature Series Emblems-GUE-34
01BAP Signature Series Numbers-ITN-34
01BAP Signature Series Teammates-TM-17
01BAP Ultimate Memorabilia Calder Trophy-8
01BAP Ultimate Memorabilia Emblems-2
01BAP Ultimate Memorabilia Jerseys-2
01BAP Ultimate Mem Jerseys and Sticks-2
01BAP Ultimate Mem Legend Terry Sawchuk-2
01BAP Ultimate Memorabilia Name Plates-30
01BAP Ultimate Mem Prototypical Players-2
01BAP Ultimate Memorabilia Retro Trophies-12
01BAP Update He Shoots-He Scores Points-10
01BAP Update He Shoots-He Scores Prizes-36
01Between the Pipes-36
01Between the Pipes-98
All-Star Jerseys-ASJ3
Double Memorabilia-DM6
Goalie Gear-GG12
He Shoots-He Saves Points-12
He Shoots-He Saves Prizes-26
Jerseys-GJ13
Jersey and Stick Cards-GSJ12
Record Breakers-RB2
Record Breakers-RB4
Trophy Winners-TW17
01Bowman YoungStars-80
Gold-80
Ice Cubed-80
01Crown Royale-85
Blue-85
Premiere Date-85
Red-85
Retail-85
All-Star Honors-12
Crowning Achievement-17
Jewels of the Crown-18
Legendary Heroes-5
01Devils Team Issue-2
01eTopps-10
01McDonald's Pacific-24
Glove-Side Net-Fusion-4
01O-Pee-Chee-3
01O-Pee-Chee Heritage Parallel-3
01O-Pee-Chee Heritage Parallel Limited-3
01O-Pee-Chee Premier Parallel-3
01O-Pee-Chee Jumbos-3
01Pacific-227
Extreme LTD-227
Hobby LTD-227
Premiere Date-227
Retail LTD-227
All-Stars-NA9
Cramer's Choice-7
Gold Crown Die-Cuts-12
Impact Zone-12
Steel Curtain-11
01Pacific Adrenaline-111
Blue-111
Premiere Date-111
Red-111
Retail-111
Blade Runners-7
Creased Lightning-11
Jerseys-25
Power Play-22
01Pacific Arena Exclusives-227
01Pacific Heads-Up-56
Blue-56
Premiere Date-56
Red-56
Silver-56
All-Star Net-2
HD NHL-17
Rink Immortals-8
Showstoppers-12
01Pacific Montreal International-6
01Parkhurst-98

Gold-98
Silver-98
He Shoots-He Scores Points-11
He Shoots-He Scores Prizes-16
Heroes-H9
Jerseys-PJ46
Jersey and Stick-PSJ8
Milestones-M2
Milestones-M16
Milestones-M43
Sticks-PS31
Teammates-T14
Teammates-T28
Waving the Flag-6
01Private Stock-55
Gold-55
Premiere Date-55
Retail-55
Silver-55
01Private Stock Pacific Nights-55
01Private Stock PS-2002-44
01Private Stock Reserve-G7
01SP Authentic-48
01SP Authentic-102
Limited-48
Limited-102
Limited Gold-48
Limited Gold-102
Buybacks-14
Sign of the Times-BR
Sign of the Times-BB
Sign of the Times-JBB
01SP Game Used-31
Authentic Fabric-AFMB
Authentic Fabric-DFBR
Authentic Fabric Gold-AFMB
Inked Sweaters-SMB
Inked Sweaters-ISMB
Patches-PMB
Patches-CPBJ
Patches-CPHB
Patches-TPJBB
Patches Signed-SPMB
Patches Signed-DSPBJ
01SPx-37
01SPx-87
Hidden Treasures-TTBTT
Hockey Treasures-HTMB
01Sports Illustrated for Kids III-168
01Sports Illustrated for Kids III-367
01Stadium Club-1
Award Winners-1
Master Photos-1
Gallery-G23
Gallery Gold-G23
Perennials-P3
Souvenirs-MB
Souvenirs-EBMB
Souvenirs-PRMB
Souvenirs-EBMBPR
01Titanium-82
Hobby Parallel-82
Premiere Date-82
Retail-82
Retail Parallel-82
Double-Sided Jerseys-68
Saturday Knights-12
Three-Star Selections-5
01Titanium Draft Day Edition-51
01Topps-3
Heritage Parallel-3
Heritage Parallel Limited-3
OPC Parallel-3
Own The Game-OTG21
01Topps Chrome-3
Refractors-3
Black Border Refractors-3
01Topps Heritage-46
01Topps Heritage-128
Refractors-46
Jerseys-JMB
01Topps Reserve-40
Emblems-MB
Jerseys-MB
Name Plates-MB
Numbers-MB
Patches-MB
01UD Challenge for the Cup-50
Backstops-BB6
Jerseys-TMB
Jersey Autographs-TBR
01UD Honor Roll-12
01UD Honor Roll-42
Honor Society-HS-RB
Honor Society Gold-HS-RB
Jerseys-J-MB
Jerseys Gold-J-MB
Playoff Matchups-HS-RB
Playoff Matchups Gold-HS-RB
01UD Mask Collection-118
01UD Mask Collection-181
Gold-118
Gold-181
Dual Jerseys-MBBT
Dual Jerseys-PMSB
Goalie Jerseys-VCMB
Goalie Jerseys-CGMB
Sticks-SSMB
01UD Playmakers-58
Jerseys-J-MB
Jerseys Gold-J-MB
01UD Premier Collection-32
Dual Jerseys-DRB
Dual Jerseys-DBTE
Dual Jerseys Black-DRB
Dual Jerseys Black-DBTE
Jerseys-SMB
Jerseys Black-S-MB
01UD Stanley Cup Champs-78
Pieces of Glory-G-MB
Sticks-S-MB
01UD Top Shelf-25
All-Star Nets-NMB
Patches-PMB
Sticks-SMB
Sticks Gold-SMB
01Upper Deck-221
01Upper Deck-332
01Upper Deck-411
Exclusives-221
Exclusives-332
Exclusives-411
Franchise Cornerstones-FC8
Game Jerseys Series II-FJMB
Game Jerseys Series II-SSMB
Game Jerseys Series II-DJSB
Game Jersey Autographs-SJMB
Goalies in Action-GL3
Goaltender Threads-TTMB
Last Line of Defense-LL5
Patches Series II-PLMB
Pride of a Nation-PNMB
Pride of a Nation-DPSB
Skilled Stars-SS11
01Upper Deck Ice-27
Autographs-MB
01Upper Deck MVP-110
Goalie Sticks-G-MB
Masked Men-MM1
Talent-MT14
Valuable Commodities-VC4
01Upper Deck Victory-205
01Upper Deck Victory-215
01Upper Deck Victory-402
Gold-205
Gold-215
Gold-402
01Upper Deck Vintage-149
01Upper Deck Vintage-157
01Upper Deck Vintage-267
01Upper Deck Vintage-270
01Vanguard-56
Blue-56
Red-56
East Meets West-4
In Focus-7
Memorabilia-50
One of Ones-56
Premiere Date-56
Proofs-56
Stonewallers-11
V-Team-5
02McFarlane Hockey Team Canada-10
02Atomic-60
Blue-60
Gold-60
Red-60
Denied-11
Hobby Parallel-60
National Pride-C8
02BAP All-Star Edition-7
02BAP All-Star Edition-8
02BAP All-Star Edition-9
He Shoots-He Scores Points-9
He Shoots-He Score Prizes-3
Jerseys-7
Jerseys-8
Jerseys-9
Jerseys Gold-7
Jerseys Gold-8
Jerseys Gold-9
Jerseys Silver-7
Jerseys Silver-8
Jerseys Silver-9
02BAP First Edition-141
02BAP First Edition-330
02BAP First Edition-358
02BAP First Edition-380
02BAP First Edition-405H
Debut Jerseys-7
He Shoots-He Scores Prizes-24
Jerseys-141
02BAP Memorabilia-89
02BAP Memorabilia-218
Emerald-89
Emerald-218
Ruby-89
Ruby-218
Sapphire-89
Sapphire-218
All-Star Jerseys-ASJ-6
All-Star Emblems-ASE-1
All-Star Numbers-ASN-1
All-Star Teammates-AST-9
All-Star Teammates-AST-18
All-Star Teammates-AST-25
All-Star Triple Jerseys-ASTJ-2
Franchise Players-FP-18
He Shoots-He Scores Points-14
He Shoots-He Scores Prizes-7
Mini Stanley Cups-33
NHL All-Star Game-89
NHL All-Star Game-218
NHL All-Star Game Blue-89
NHL All-Star Game Blue-218
NHL All-Star Game Green-89
NHL All-Star Game Green-218
NHL All-Star Game Red-89
NHL All-Star Game Red-218
Stanley Cup Playoffs-SC-8
Teammates-TM-14
02BAP Memorabilia Toronto Fall Expo-89
02BAP Memorabilia Toronto Fall Expo-218
02BAP Sig Series Auto Buybacks 1998-79
02BAP Sig Series Auto Buybacks 1999-143
02BAP Sig Series Auto Buybacks 2000-139
02BAP Signature Series Defensive Wall-DW6
02BAP Signature Series Franchise Players-FJ18
02BAP Signature Series Golf-GS51
02BAP Signature Series Jerseys-SGJ15
02BAP Signature Series Jersey Autographs-SGJ15
02BAP Signature Series Team Quads-TQ7
02BAP Signature Series Triple Memorabilia-TM9
02BAP Ultimate Memorabilia Active Eight-3
02BAP Ultimate Memorabilia Cup Duels-16
02BAP Ultimate Memorabilia Cup Duels-19
02BAP Ultimate Memorabilia Cup Duels-20
02BAP Ultimate Memorabilia Emblems-15
02BAP Ultimate Memorabilia Jerseys-5
02BAP Ultimate Mem Jersey and Stick-6
02BAP Ultimate Mem Lifetime Achievers-12
02BAP Ultimate Mem Magnificent Ones-5
02BAP Ultimate Mem Magnificent Ones Autos-5
02BAP Ultimate Memorabilia Nameplates-17
02BAP Ultimate Memorabilia Numbers-26
02BAP Ultimate Memorabilia Retro Trophies-15
02BAP Ultimate Memorabilia Vezina Winner-1
02Between the Pipes-8
02Between the Pipes-138
Gold-8
Silver-8
All-Star Stick and Jersey-3
Behind the Mask-2
Double Memorabilia-1
Emblems-18
He Shoots-He Saves Points-18
He Shoots-He Saves Prizes-16
Inspirations-I8
Jerseys-18
Numbers-18
Pads-1
Record Breakers-9
Stick and Jerseys-18
02Bowman Toronto Spring Expo-6
02Bowman YoungStars-2
Gold-2
Silver-2
02Crown Royale-56
Blue-56
Red-56
Retail-56
Jerseys-10
Jerseys Gold-10
Dual Patches-14
Coats of Armor-6
Royal Portraits-7
02Devils Team Issue-23
02eTopps-6
02ITG Used-41
02ITG Used-141
Franchise Players-F18
Franchise Players Autographs-F18
Franchise Players Gold-F18
Goalie Pad and Jersey-GP3
Goalie Pad and Jersey Gold-GP3
International Experience-IE20
International Experience Gold-IE20
Jerseys-GUJ15
Jersey Autographs-GUJ15
Jerseys Gold-GUJ15
Emblems-E15
Jersey and Stick-SJ15
Jersey and Stick Gold-SJ15
Teammates-T14
Teammates Gold-T14
02McDonald's Pacific-23
Jersey Patches Silver-9
Jersey Patches Gold-9
Salt Lake Gold-1
02O-Pee-Chee-3
02O-Pee-Chee Jumbos-14
02O-Pee-Chee Premier Blue Parallel-3
02O-Pee-Chee Premier Red Parallel-3
02O-Pee-Chee Factory Set-3
02Pacific-218
Blue-218
Red-218
Cramer's Choice-8
Main Attractions-11
Maximum Impact-5
02Pacific Calder-16
Silver-16
Chasing Glory-6
Hart Stoppers-6
02Pacific Complete-465
Red-465
02Pacific Exclusive-102
Advantage-11
Etched in Stone-7
02Pacific Heads-Up-70
Blue-70
Purple-70
Red-70
Etched in Time-11
Inside the Numbers-13
Quad Jerseys-17
Quad Jerseys-28
Quad Jerseys Gold-17
Quad Jerseys Gold-28
Showstoppers-13
02Pacific Les Gardiens-6
Gold-6
02Pacific Quest for the Cup-56
Gold-56
Raising the Cup-9
02Pacific Toronto Fall Expo-6
Gold-6
02Parkhurst-96
Bronze-96
Gold-96
Silver-96
Franchise Players-FP18
Hardware-V4
He Shoots-He Scores Points-1
He Shoots-He Scores Prizes-11
Jerseys-GJ43
Mario's Mates-MM4
Milestones-MS2
Stick and Jerseys-SJ43
Teammates-TT5
02Parkhurst Retro-70
Minis-70
Franchise Players-RF18
He Shoots-He Scores Points-10
He Shoots-He Scores Prizes-7
Hopefuls-VH3
Jerseys-RJ6
Jersey and Sticks-RSJ6
Memorabilia-RM9
02Private Stock Reserve-129
Red-129
Retail-129
InCrease Security-13
Patches-129
02SP Authentic-53
Beckett Promos-53
Sign of the Times-MB
Sign of the Times-MM
Super Premiums-SPMB
Super Premiums-TPRBB
02SP Game Used-28
Authentic Fabrics-AFMB
Authentic Fabrics-CFNB
Authentic Fabrics-CFTB
Authentic Fabrics Gold-AFMB
Authentic Fabrics Gold-CFNB
Authentic Fabrics Gold-CFTB
Authentic Fabrics Rainbow-AFMB
Authentic Fabrics Rainbow-CFNB
Authentic Fabrics Rainbow-CFTB
First Rounder Patches-MB
Piece of History-PHMB
Piece of History Gold-PHMB
Piece of History Rainbow-PHMB
Signature Style-MB
02SPx-43
02SPx-93
Spectrum Gold-43
Spectrum Gold-93
Spectrum Silver-43
Spectrum Silver-93
Milestones-MMB
Milestones Gold-MB
Milestones Silver-MB
Winning Materials-WMMB
Winning Materials Gold-MB
Winning Materials Silver-MB
02Stadium Club-8
Silver Decoy Cards-8
Proofs-8
Champions Fabric-FC4
Champions Patches-PC-4
Puck Stops Here-PSH10
World Stage-WS3
02Titanium-62
Blue-62
Red-62
Retail-62
Masked Marauders-5
02Topps-3
OPC Blue Parallel-3
OPC Red Parallel-3
Topps/OPC Hometown Heroes-HHU1
Own The Game-OTG17
Factory Set-3
Factory Set Hometown Heroes-HHU1
02Topps Chrome-3
Black Border Refractors-3
Refractors-3
e-Topps Decoy Cards-6
02Topps Heritage-19
02Topps Heritage-115
Chrome Parallel-19
Calder Cloth-MB
Calder Cloth Patches-MB
02Topps Total-293
Team Checklists-TTC18
Topps-TT15
02UD Artistic Impressions-52
Gold-52
Artist's Touch-ATMB
Artist's Touch Gold-ATMB
02UD Artistic Impressions Beckett Promos-52
02UD Artistic Impressions Common Ground-CG22
02UD Artistic Impress Common Ground Gold-CG22
02UD Artistic Impress Great Depiction-GD3
02UD Artistic Impress Great Depiction Gld-GD3
02UD Artistic Impressions Performers-SSMB
02UD Artistic Impressions Performers Gold-SSMB
02UD Artistic Impressions Retrospectives-R52
02UD Artistic Impressions Retrospect Gold-R52
02UD Artistic Impress Retrospect Auto-R52
02UD Artistic Impress Retrospect Silver-R52
02Upper Deck Collectors Club-NHL10
02UD Foundations-58
02UD Honor Roll-41
Grade A Jerseys-GAMB
Signature Class-MB
Students of the Game-SG18
02UD Mask Collection-50
02UD Mask Collection-51
02UD Mask Collection-91
02UD Mask Collection Beckett Promos-50
02UD Mask Collection Beckett Promos-51
02UD Mask Collection Career Wins-CWMB
02UD Mask Collection Great Gloves-GGBR
02UD Mask Collection Masked Marvels-MMMB
02UD Mask Collection Mini Masks-MB
02UD Mask Collection Mini Masks Autos-MB
02UD Mask Collection Nation's Best-NRBP
02UD Mask Collection Patches-PWBR
02UD Mask Collection Super Stoppers-SSMB
02UD Mask Collection View from the Cage-VMB
02UD Piece of History-51
02UD Piece of History-101
Awards Collection-AC18
02UD Premier Collection-33
Jerseys Bronze-MB
Jerseys Gold-MB
Jerseys Silver-MB
NHL Patches-MB1
Patches-PMB
Signatures Bronze-SMB
Signatures Bronze-ASMB
Signatures Gold-SMB
Signatures Gold-ASMB
Signatures Silver-SMB
Signatures Silver-ASMB
02UD Top Shelf-52
Clutch Performers-CPMB
Dual Player Jerseys-STBS
Hardware Heroes-HBRBD
Milestones Jerseys-MRBRJ
Stopper Jerseys-SSMB
02Upper Deck-107
02Upper Deck-190
Exclusives-107
Exclusives-190
Blow-Ups-C25
Fan Favorites-MB
Game Jersey Autographs-MB
Game Jersey Series II-GJMB
Gifted Greats-GG10
Last Line of Defense-LL8
Patch Card Name Plate-MB
Patch Card Numbers-MB
Patchwork-PWMB
Super Saviors-SA8
02Upper Deck Classic Portraits-57
Etched in Time-ET10
Hockey Royalty-BPT
Hockey Royalty-RBT
Hockey Royalty Limited-BPT
Hockey Royalty Limited-RBT
Mini-Busts-83
Mini-Busts-84
Mini-Busts-85
Mini-Busts-86
Mini-Busts-87
Mini-Busts-88
Mini-Busts-89
Mini-Busts-90
Pillars of Strength-PS6
02Upper Deck MVP-108
Gold-108
Classics-108
Golden Classics-108
Masked Men-MM4
02Upper Deck Rookie Update-60
02Upper Deck Rookie Update-107
02Upper Deck Victory-127
Bronze-127
Gold-127
Silver-127
National Pride-NP8
02Upper Deck Vintage-152
02Upper Deck Vintage-278
02Upper Deck Vintage-298
02Upper Deck Vintage-316
Tall Boys-T39
Tall Boys Gold-T39
02Vanguard-60
LTD-60
East Meets West-9
Jerseys-26
Jerseys Gold-26
Stonewallers-7
V-Team-5
02UD SuperStars *-144
Gold-144
03McFarlane Hockey NHL 2-Pack-10
03McFarlane Hockey 3-Inch Duals-30
03BAP Memorabilia-137
Emerald-137
Gold-137
Ruby-137
Sapphire-137
All-Star Complete Jerseys-ASCJ9
All-Star Emblems-ASE-14
All-Star Jerseys-ASJ-21
All-Star Jerseys-ASJ-34
All-Star Numbers-ASN-14
All-Star Teammates-AST8
Brush with Greatness-2
Brush with Greatness Contest Cards-2
Deep in the Crease-D4
He Shoots-He Scores Points-20
He Shoots-He Scores Prizes-14
Jersey and Stick-SJ-33
Jerseys-GJ-42
Jersey Autographs-GJ-42
Practice Jerseys-PMP2
Stanley Cup Champions-SCC-1
Stanley Cup Playoffs-SCP-30
Tandems-T-5
03BAP Ultimate Memorabilia Autographs-137
Gold-137
03BAP Ultimate Mem Auto Jerseys-137
03BAP Ultimate Mem Auto Emblems-137
03BAP Ultimate Memorabilia Active Eight-1
03BAP Ultimate Memorabilia Active Eight-2
03BAP Ultimate Mem Always An All-Star-1
03BAP Ultimate Mem Always An AS Gold-1
03BAP Ultimate Memorabilia Career Year-1
03BAP Ultimate Mem Complete Jersey-16
03BAP Ultimate Mem Complete Jersey Gold-16
03BAP Ultimate Memorabilia Emblems-16
03BAP Ultimate Memorabilia Emblems Gold-16
03BAP Ultimate Mem Franch Present Future-18
03BAP Ultimate Memorabilia Heroes-13
03BAP Ultimate Mem Heroes Autos-7
03BAP Ultimate Mem Hometown Heroes-2
03BAP Ultimate Mem Hometown Heroes Gold-2
03BAP Ultimate Memorabilia Jerseys-15
03BAP Ultimate Memorabilia Jerseys Gold-15
03BAP Ultimate Mem Jersey and Emblems-24
03BAP Ultimate Mem Jersey and Emblem Gold-24
03BAP Ultimate Mem Jersey and Numbers-24
03BAP Ultimate Mem Jersey and Number Gold-24
03BAP Ultimate Mem Jersey and Stick-12
03BAP Ultimate Mem Jersey and Stick Gold-12
03BAP Ultimate Memorabilia Nameplates-10
03BAP Ultimate Mem Nameplates Gold-10
03BAP Ultimate Memorabilia Numbers-12
03BAP Ultimate Memorabilia Numbers Gold-12
03BAP Ultimate Mem Redemption Cards-1
03BAP Ultimate Mem Retro-Active Trophies-6
03BAP Ultimate Mem Retro-Active Trophies-15
03BAP Ultimate Mem Seams Unbelievable-6
03BAP Ultimate Memorabilia Triple Threads-1
03Beehive-115
Variations-115
Gold-115
Silver-115
Jumbos-18
Jumbo Variations-18
Jerseys-JT17
Signatures-RF1
Sticks Beige Border-BE5
Sticks Blue Border-BL13
Sticks Red Border-RE14
03Black Diamond-80
Black-80
Green-80
Red-80
Threads-DT-MB
Threads Green-DT-MB
Threads Red-DT-MB
Threads Black-DT-MB
03Bowman-30
Gold-30
03Bowman Chrome-30
Refractors-30
Gold Refractors-30
Xfractors-30
03Crown Royale-59
Blue-59
Retail-59
Gauntlet of Glory-12
Global Conquest-1
Jerseys-14
Patches-14
03Devils Team Issue-30
03Duracell-10
03eTopps-36
03ITG Action-357
Highlight Reel-HR3
Homeboys-HB10
Jerseys-M181
Jerseys-M201
Jerseys-M222
Jerseys-M258
League Leaders-L7
League Leaders-L8
Oh Canada-OC4
Trophy Winners-TW2
03ITG Toronto Fall Expo Jerseys-FE29
03ITG Used Signature Series-106
Gold-106
Autographs-MB
Autographs Gold-MB
Franchise-18
Franchise Autographs-18
Franchise Gold-18
Game-Day Jerseys-7
Game-Day Jerseys Gold-7
Goalie Gear-1
Goalie Gear Autographs-1
Goalie Gear Gold-1
International Experience-1
International Experience Autographs-1
International Experience Emblems Gold-1
International Experience Emblems-1
International Experience Gold-1
Jerseys-25
Jerseys Gold-25
Jersey Autos-25
Emblems-8
Emblems Gold-8
Jersey and Stick-25
Jersey and Stick Gold-25
Oh Canada-2
Oh Canada Gold-2
Oh Canada Emblems-2
Oh Canada Emblems Gold-2
Retrospectives-11A
Retrospectives-11B
Retrospectives-11C
Retrospectives-11D
Retrospectives-11E
Retrospectives-11F
Retrospectives Gold-11A
Retrospectives Gold-11B
Retrospectives Gold-11C
Retrospectives Gold-11D
Retrospectives Gold-11E
Retrospectives Gold-11F
Teammates-16
Teammates Gold-16
Triple Memorabilia-10
Triple Memorabilia Gold-10
03ITG VIP Brightest Stars-9
03ITG VIP Collages-2
03ITG VIP Collage Autographs-2
03ITG VIP International Experience-12
03ITG VIP Jerseys-19
03ITG VIP Jersey Autographs-19
03ITG VIP Jersey and Emblems-13
03ITG VIP Jersey and Numbers-13
03ITG VIP Netminders-1
03McDonald's Pacific-30
Patches Silver-16
Patches Gold-16
Patches and Sticks-16
Net Fusions-5
03NHL Sticker Collection-70
03O-Pee-Chee-158
03O-Pee-Chee-290
03OPC Blue-158
03OPC Blue-290
03OPC Gold-158
03OPC Gold-290
03OPC Red-158
03OPC Red-290
03Pacific-196
Blue-196
Red-196
Cramer's Choice-7
In the Crease-7
Jerseys-23
Jerseys Gold-23
03Pacific Atlantic City National-3
03Pacific Calder-62
03Pacific Calder-150
Silver-62
03Pacific Complete-461
Red-461
03Pacific Exhibit-177
03Pacific Exhibit-224
Blue Backs-177
Standing on Tradition-8
03Pacific Heads-Up-58
Hobby LTD-58
Retail LTD-58
Jerseys-18
Mini Sweaters-6
Rink Immortals-7
Rink Immortals LTD-7
Stonewallers-7
Stonewallers LTD-7
03Pacific Invincible-55
Blue-55
Red-55
Retail-55
Featured Performers-18
Freeze Frame-12
Jerseys-18
03Pacific Luxury Suite-13A
03Pacific Luxury Suite-13B
03Pacific Luxury Suite-13C
03Pacific Luxury Suite-13D
03Pacific Luxury Suite-40A
03Pacific Luxury Suite-40B
03Pacific Luxury Suite-40C
03Pacific Prism-127
Blue-127
Patches-127
Red-127
Retail-127
Crease Police-6
03Pacific Quest for the Cup-63
Blue-63
Raising the Cup-12
03Pacific Supreme-57
Blue-57
Red-57
Retail-57
Standing Guard-9
03Parkhurst Rookie-44
Jerseys-GJ-17
Jerseys Gold-GJ-17
Jersey and Sticks-SJ-4
Jersey and Sticks Gold-SJ-4
ROYalty-VR-2
ROYalty Autographs-VR-MB
ROYalty Gold-VR-2
03Private Stock Reserve-178
Blue-178
Patches-178
Red-178
Retail-178
Increase Security-9
03SP Authentic-51
Limited-51
10th Anniversary-SP18
10th Anniversary Limited-SP18
Breakout Seasons-B2
Breakout Seasons Limited-B2
Foundations-F8
Foundations Limited-F8
Honors-H24
Honors Limited-H24
Sign of the Times-MB
Sign of the Times-RGB
03SP Game Used-27
03SP Game Used-113
Gold-27
Gold-113
Authentic Fabrics-DFBP
Authentic Fabrics-DFBR
Authentic Fabrics-QRGBT
Authentic Fabrics Gold-DFBP
Authentic Fabrics Gold-DFBR
Authentic Fabrics Gold-QRGBT
Authentic Patches-APMB
Double Threads-DTBR
Game Gear-GGMB
Game Gear Combo-GCMB
Premium Patches-PPMB
Team Threads-TTBSG
03SPx-57
03SPx-117
03SPx-155
03SPx-178
Radiance-57
Radiance-117
Radiance-155
Radiance-178
Spectrum-57
Spectrum-117
Spectrum-155
Spectrum-178
Fantasy Franchise-FF-GRB
Fantasy Franchise-FF-SBJ
Fantasy Franchise Limited-FF-GRB
Fantasy Franchise Limited-FF-SBJ
Hall Pass-HP-MB
Hall Pass Limited-HP-MB
Origins-O-MB
Style-SPX-BG
Style-SPX-RB
Style Limited-SPX-BG
Style Limited-SPX-RB
VIP-VIP-SB
VIP Limited-VIP-SB
03Titanium-200
Patches-200
Highlight Reels-7
Masked Marauders-6
03Topps-158
03Topps-290
Blue-158
Blue-290
Gold-158
Gold-290
Red-158
Red-290
Box Toppers-15
Topps/OPC Idols-CI2
Own the Game-OTG11
03Topps C55-30
03Topps C55-30B
Minis-30
Minis American Back-30
Minis American Back Red-30
Minis Bazooka Back-30
Minis Brooklyn Back-30
Minis Hat Trick Back-30
Minis O Canada Back-30
Minis O Canada Back Red-30
Minis Stanley Cup Back-30
Award Winners-7
Award Winners-16
03Topps Pristine-20
Gold Refractor Die Cuts-20
Refractors-20
Mini-PM-MB
Press Plates Black-20
Press Plates Cyan-20
Press Plates Magenta-20
Press Plates Yellow-20
03Topps Traded Franchise Fabrics-FF-MB
03UD Honor Roll-48
03UD Honor Roll-129
Grade A Jerseys-GAMB
Signature Class-SC3
03UD Premier Collection-32
NHL Shields-SH-GL
NHL Shields-SH-MB
Signatures-PS-MB
Signatures Gold-PS-MB
Skills-SK-BF
Skills Patches-SK-BF
Super Stars-SS-MB
Super Stars Patches-SS-MB
Teammates-PT-ND
Teammates Patches-PT-ND
03UD Toronto Fall Expo Priority Signings-MB
03Upper Deck-117
03Upper Deck-200
All-Star Class-AS-16
All-Star Lineup-AS5
Big Playmakers-BP-MB
Canadian Exclusives-117
Canadian Exclusives-200
Franchise Fabrics-FF-MB
Gifted Greats-GG10
HG-117
HG-200
Jerseys-GJ-MB
Magic Moments-MM-12
Memorable Matchups-MM-GB
NHL Best-NB-MB
Patches-SV1
Patches-PLG-MB
Patches-PNM-MB
Patches-PNR-MB
Performers-PS8
Super Saviors-SS-MB
Superstar Spotlight-SS6
Three Stars-TS6
03Upper Deck All-Star Promos-AS6
03Upper Deck Classic Portraits-59
03Upper Deck Classic Portraits-110
03Upper Deck Classic Portraits-134
03Upper Deck Classic Portraits-145
Genuine Greatness-GG-MB
Premium Portraits-PP-MB
Starring Cast-SC-MB
03Upper Deck Ice-52
Gold-52
Authentics-IA-MB
Breakers-IB-MB
Breaker Patches-IB-MB
Clear Cut Winners-CC-MB
Icons-I-MB
Icons Jerseys-I-MB
Under Glass Autographs-UG-MB
03Upper Deck MVP-260
03Upper Deck MVP-438
Gold Script-260
Gold Script-438
Silver Script-260
Silver Script-438
Canadian Exclusives-260
Canadian Exclusives-438
Clutch Performers-CP3
Masked Men-MM1
ProSign-PS-MB
SportsNut-SN50
Talent-MT2
03Upper Deck Rookie Update-53
All-Star Lineup-AS1
Skills-SKMB
Super Stars-SSMB
03Upper Deck Trilogy-59
Authentic Patches-AP10
Limited-59
Limited Threads-LT28
Limited Threads-LT29
Scripts-S2MB
Scripts Limited-S2MB
03Upper Deck Victory-113
Bronze-113
Gold-113
Silver-113
Freshman Flashback-FF27
Game Breakers-GB4
03Czech Stadion-607
03Toronto Star-51
Foil-29
04MasterCard Priceless Moments-10
04Pacific-154
Blue-154
Red-154
All-Stars-10
Cramer's Choice-7
In The Crease-8
Milestones-2
04Pacific NHL All-Star Nets-1
Gold-1
04Pacific NHL Draft All-Star Nets-3
04SP Authentic-52
04SP Authentic-122
Limited-52
Buybacks-133
Octographs-OS-GOA
Rookie Review-RR-BR
Sign of the Times-ST-MB
Sign of the Times-DS-BR
Sign of the Times-TS-RLB
Sign of the Times-QS-FBRE
Sign of the Times-FS-GOL
Sign of the Times-SS-ALS
Sign of the Times-SS-CNP
04UD All-World-96
04UD Toronto Fall Expo Pride of Canada-1
04UD Toronto Fall Expo Priority Signings-MB
04Ultimate Collection-25
04Ultimate Collection-65
Dual Logos-UL2-BE
Dual Logos-UL2-BG
Dual Logos-UL2-LB
Dual Logos-UL2-RB
Jerseys-UGJ-MB
Jerseys Gold-UGJ-MB
Jersey Autographs-UGJA-MB
Patches-UP-MB
Patch Autographs-UPA-MB
Patch Autographs-UPA-PRMB
Signatures-US-MB
Signature Logos-ULA-MB
Signature Patches-SP-MB
04Upper Deck-107
1997 Game Jerseys-MB
Canadian Exclusives-107
Hardware Heroes-AW5
Hardware Heroes-AW12
HG Glossy Gold-107
HG Glossy Silver-107
Jersey Autographs-GJA-MB/PR
NHL's Best-NB-MB
Patches-GJPA-MB
Patches-GJPL-MB
Patches-GJPN-MB
Three Stars-AS7
World's Best-WB4
World Cup Tribute-MB
World Cup Tribute-MBRL
World Cup Tribute-MBRLJT
05ITG Heroes/Prosp Toronto Expo Parallel -1
05ITG Heroes/Prosp Toronto Expo Parallel -181
05Be A Player-52
First Period-52
Second Period-52
Third Period-52
Overtime-52
Class Action-CA15
Dual Signatures-BF
Ice Icons-ICE1
Outtakes-OT31
Quad Signatures-BLTG
Quad Signatures-GOAL
Signatures-MT
Signatures Gold-MT
Triple Signatures-DEV
World Cup Salute-WCS11
05Beehive-51
05Beehive-197
Beige -52
Blue -52
Gold-52
Red -52
Matte-52
Matted Materials-MMMB
Matted Materials Remarkable-RMMB
Signature Scrapbook-SSMB
05Between the Pipes-3
Autographs-A-MB
Double Memorabilia-DM-3
Jerseys-GUJ-3
Jersey and Sticks-SJ-3
Pads-GUP-5
Signed Memorabilia-SM-3
05Black Diamond-51
Emerald-51
Gold-51
Onyx-51
Ruby-51
Gemography-G-MB
Gemography Emerald-G-MB
Gemography Gold-G-MB
Gemography Onyx-G-MB
Gemography Ruby-G-MB
Jerseys-J-MB
Jerseys Ruby-J-MB
Jersey Duals-DJ-MB
Jersey Triples-TJ-MB
Jersey Quads-QJ-MB
05Devils Team Issue-10
05Hot Prospects-58
En Fuego-58
Red Hot-58
White Hot-58
05ITG Passing the Torch-2
05ITG Passing the Torch-3
05ITG Passing the Torch-4
05ITG Passing the Torch-5
05ITG Passing the Torch-6
05ITG Passing the Torch-7
05ITG Passing the Torch-8
05ITG Passing the Torch-9
05ITG Passing the Torch-10
05ITG Passing the Torch-11
05ITG Passing the Torch-12
05ITG Passing the Torch-13
05ITG Passing the Torch-14
05ITG Passing the Torch-15
05ITG Passing the Torch-16
Autographs-PTT1
Memorabilia-PTT1
Memorabilia-PTT2
Memorabilia-PTT3
Memorabilia-PTT4
Memorabilia-PTT5
Memorabilia-PTT6
Memorabilia-PTT15
Memorabilia-PTT16
Memorabilia-PTT17
Memorabilia-PTT18
Memorabilia-PTT19
Memorabilia-PTT20
Memorabilia-PTT23
Memorabilia-PTT24
Memorabilia-PTT25
Memorabilia-PTT26
Memorabilia Autographs-PTT1A
Memorabilia Autographs-PTT2A
Memorabilia Autographs-PTT3A
Memorabilia Autographs-PTT4A
Memorabilia Autographs-PTT5A
Memorabilia Autographs-PTT6A
Memorabilia Autographs-PTT20A
Memorabilia Autographs-PTT25A
Memorabilia Autographs-PTT26A
05ITG Ultimate Memorabilia Level 1-68
05ITG Ultimate Memorabilia Level 2-68
05ITG Ultimate Memorabilia Level 3-68

05ITG Ultimate Memorabilia Level 4-68
05ITG Ultimate Memorabilia Level 5-68
05ITG Ultimate Mem Complete Jersey-11
05ITG Ultimate Mem Complete Jersey Gold-11
05ITG Ultimate Memorabilia Double Autos-6
05ITG Ultimate Mem Double Autos Gold-6
05ITG Ultimate Mem Double Mem-1
05ITG Ultimate Mem Double Mem Autos-2
05ITG Ultimate Mem Double Mem Autos Gold-2
05ITG Ultimate Mem Double Mem Gold-1
05ITG Ultimate Memorabilia Emblems-23
05ITG Ultimate Memorabilia Emblems Gold-23
05ITG Ultimate Mem First Rounders Jerseys-5
05ITG Ultimate Mem 1st Round Jersey Gold-5
05ITG Ultimate Memorabilia Goalie Gear-13
05ITG Ultimate Mem Goalie Gear Gold-13
05ITG Ultimate Memorabilia In The Numbers-17
05ITG Ultimate Mem In The Numbers Gold-17
05ITG Ultimate Mem Jersey and Emblem-7
05ITG Ultimate Memorabilia Jersey Autos-1
05ITG Ultimate Mem Jersey Autos Gold-1
05ITG Ultimate Mem Jersey Emblems Gold-7
05ITG Ultimate Memorabilia Jerseys-25
05ITG Ultimate Memorabilia Jerseys Gold-25
05ITG Ultimate Mem Pass the Torch Jerseys-4
05ITG Ultimate Mem Pass the Torch Jerseys-18
05ITG Ultimate Mem Passing Torch Jsy Gold-4
05ITG Ultimate Mem Passing Torch Jsy Gold-18
05ITG Ultimate Memorabilia R.O.Y. Autos-14
05ITG Ultimate Mem R.O.Y. Autos Gold-14
05ITG Ultimate Memorabilia R.O.Y. Emblems-7
05ITG Ultimate Mem R.O.Y. Emblems Gold-7
05ITG Ultimate Memorabilia R.O.Y. Jerseys-7
05ITG Ultimate Mem R.O.Y. Jerseys Gold-7
05ITG Ultimate Memorabilia R.O.Y. Numbers-7
05ITG Ultimate Mem R.O.Y. Numbers Gold-7
05ITG Ultimate Mem Record Breaker Jerseys-6
05ITG Ultimate Mem RecBreak Jerseys Gold-6
05ITG Ultimate Mem Seams Unbelievable-5
05ITG Ultimate Mem Seam Unbelievable Gold-5
05ITG Ultimate Memorabilia Sextuple Autos-1
05ITG Ultimate Memorabilia Stick Autos-3
05ITG Ultimate Mem Stick Autos Gold-3
05ITG Ultimate Mem Sticks and Jerseys-28
05ITG Ultimate Mem Stick and Jerseys Gold-28
05ITG Ultimate Mem 3 Star of the Game Jsy-24
05ITG Ult Mem 3 Star of the Game Jsy Gold-24
05ITG Ultimate Memorabilia Trifecta Autos-5
05ITG Ultimate Mem Trifecta Autos Gold-5
05ITG Ultimate Memorabilia Triple Autos-9
05ITG Ultimate Mem Triple Autos Gold-9
05ITG Ultimate Mem Triple Threads Jerseys-2
05ITG Ultimate Mem Triple Thread Jsy Gold-2
05ITG Ultimate Memorabilia Ultimate Autos-47
05ITG Ultimate Mem Ultimate Autos Gold-47
05ITG Ultimate Mem Ult Hero Double Jersey-7
05ITG Ult Mem Ult Hero Double Jersey Gold-7
05ITG Ultimate Mem Ult Hero Single Jersey-7
05ITG Ult Mem Ult Hero Single Jersey Gold-7
05ITG Ultimate Mem Ult Hero Triple Jersey-7
05ITG Ult Mem Ult Hero Triple Jersey Gold-7
05McDonalds Upper Deck-48
Autographs-MA6
Goalie Factory-GF3
Jerseys-MJ6
Patches-MP6
05Panini Stickers-79
05Parkhurst-287
05Parkhurst-561
05Parkhurst-688
Facsimile Auto Parallel-287
Facsimile Auto Parallel-561
Facsimile Auto Parallel-688
True Colors-TCNJD
True Colors-TCNJD
True Colors-TCNJNY
True Colors-TCNJNY
05SP Authentic-57
05SP Authentic-113
Limited-57
Limited-113
Chirography-SPMB
Octographs-OG
Prestigious Pairings-PPRB
Sign of the Times Duals-DBR
Sign of the Times Quads-QRCEB
Six Star Signatures-SSGO
05SP Game Used-58
Autographs-58
Gold-58
Authentic Fabrics-AF-BR
Authentic Fabrics Dual-EB
Authentic Fabrics Gold-AF-BR
Authentic Fabrics Quad-BEGK
Authentic Fabrics Quad-RBLT
Authentic Patches Quad -BEGK
Authentic Patches Quad -RBLT
Authentic Fabrics Triple-BIS
Authentic Fabrics Triple-BTR
Authentic Patches-AP-BR
Authentic Patches Dual-EB
Authentic Patches Triple-BIS
Authentic Patches Triple-BTR
Auto Draft-AD-MB
Awesome Authentics-AA-MB
Awesome Authentics Gold-DA-MB
Game Gear-GG-BR
Game Gear Autographs-AG-BR
SIGnificance-MB
SIGnificance Gold-S-MB
SIGnificance Extra-BL
SIGnificance Extra Gold-BL
Significant Numbers-SN-MB
05SPx-50
05SPx-111
Spectrum-50
Spectrum-111
Winning Combos-WC-BE
Winning Combos-WC-BT
Winning Combos Autographs-AWC-BT
Winning Combos Gold-WC-BE
Winning Combos Gold-WC-BT
Winning Combos Spectrum-WC-BE
Winning Combos Spectrum-WC-BT
Winning Materials-WM-MB
Winning Materials Autographs-AWM-MB
Winning Materials Gold-WM-MB
Winning Materials Spectrum-WM-MB
Xcitement Superstars-XS-MB
Xcitement Superstars Gold-XS-MB
Xcitement Superstars Spectrum-XS-MB
05The Cup-62
Gold-62
Black Rainbow-62
Dual NHL Shields-DSBE
Dual NHL Shields-DSBG
Dual NHL Shields Autographs-ADSRB
Emblems of Endorsement-EEMB
Hardware Heroes-HHMB1
Hardware Heroes-HHMB2
Honorable Numbers-HNMB
Limited Logos-LLMB
Masterpiece Pressplates-62
Noble Numbers-NNBC
Noble Numbers Dual-DNNBE
Noble Numbers Dual-DNNRB
Patch Variation-P62
Patch Variation Autographs-AP62
Scripted Numbers-SNBC
Scripted Numbers Dual-DSNBB
Scripted Numbers Dual-DSNRB
Scripted Swatches-SSMB
Signature Patches-SPMB
Stanley Cup Titlists-TMB
05UD Artifacts-58
05UD Artifacts-175
Blue-58
Blue-175
Gold-58
Gold-175
Green-58
Green-175
Pewter-58
Pewter-175
Red-58
Red-175
Auto Facts Blue-AF-MB
Auto Facts Copper-AF-MB
Auto Facts Pewter-AF-MB
Auto Facts Silver-AF-MB
Gold Autographed-58
Gold Autographed-175
Remarkable Artifacts-RA-MB
Remarkable Artifacts Dual-RA-MB
Treasured Patches-TP-MB
Treasured Patches Autographed-TP-MB
Treasured Patches Dual-TPD-MB
Treasured Patches Dual Autographed-TPD-MB
Treasured Patches Pewter-TP-MB
Treasured Patches Silver-TP-MB
Treasured Swatches-TS-MB
Treasured Swatches Autographed-TS-MB
Treasured Swatches Blue-TS-MB
Treasured Swatches Copper-TS-MB
Treasured Swatches Dual-TSD-MB
Treasured Swatches Dual Autographed-TSD-MB
Treasured Swatches Dual Blue-TSD-MB
Treasured Swatches Dual Copper-TSD-MB
Treasured Swatches Dual Maroon-TSD-MB
Treasured Swatches Dual Pewter-TSD-MB
Treasured Swatches Dual Silver-TSD-MB
Treasured Swatches Maroon-TS-MB
Treasured Swatches Pewter-TS-MB
Treasured Swatches Silver-TS-MB
05UD PowerPlay-52
05UD PowerPlay-120
05UD PowerPlay-127
Rainbow-52
Specialists-TSMB
Specialists Patches-SPMB
05UD Toronto Fall Expo Priority Signings-PS-MB
05Ultimate Collection-54
Gold-54
Endorsed Emblems-EEMB
Jerseys-JMB
Jerseys Triple-TJRTB
Marquee Attractions-MA29
Marquee Attractions Signatures-SMA29
National Heroes Jerseys-NHJMB
National Heroes Patches-NHPMB
Premium Patches-PPMB
Premium Swatches-PSMB
Ultimate Achievements-UAMB
Ultimate Patches-PMB
Ultimate Patches Triple-TPRTB
Ultimate Signatures-USMB
Ultimate Signatures Foursomes-UFRBGL
Ultimate Signatures Pairings-UPRB
05Ultra-116
Gold-116
Fresh Ink-FI-MB
Fresh Ink Blue-FI-MB
Ice-116
Super Six-SS3
Super Six Jerseys-SSJ-MB
Super Six Jersey Autographs-SAJ-MB
Super Six Patches-SSP-MB
Super Six Patch Autographs-SAP-MB
05Upper Deck-362
05Upper Deck All-Time Greatest-35
05Upper Deck All-Time Greatest-78
05Upper Deck Big Playmakers-B-MB
05Upper Deck Destined for the Hall-DH2
05Upper Deck Hometown Heroes-HH2
05Upper Deck Jerseys-J-MB
05Upper Deck Jerseys Series II-J2MB
05Upper Deck Majestic Materials-MMMB
05Upper Deck NHL Generations-DBT
05Upper Deck NHL Generations-TBLL
05Upper Deck NHL Generations-TRBL
05Upper Deck Notable Numbers-N-MBR
05Upper Deck Scrapbooks-HS30
05Upper Deck Ice-56
Rainbow-56
Cool Threads-CTMB
Cool Threads Autographs-ACTMB
Cool Threads Glass-CTMB
Cool Threads Patches-CTPMB
Cool Threads Patch Autographs-CAPMB
Frozen Fabrics-FFMB
Frozen Fabrics Autographs-AFFMB
Frozen Fabrics Glass-FFMB
Frozen Fabrics Patches-FFPMB
Frozen Fabrics Patch Autographs-FAPMB
Glacial Graphs-GGMB
Signature Swatches-SSMB
05Upper Deck MVP-230
05Upper Deck MVP-442
Gold-230
Gold-442
Platinum-230
Platinum-442
Rising to the Occasion-RO5
05Upper Deck Rookie Update-56
05Upper Deck Trilogy-52
05Upper Deck Trilogy-117
Crystal-117
Crystal Autographs-117
Honorary Patches-HP-MB
Honorary Patch Scripts-HSP-MB
Honorary Swatches-HS-MB
Honorary Swatch Scripts-HSS-MB
Ice Scripts-IS-MB
Personal Scripts-PER-MB
Scripts-SSS-MB
05Upper Deck Victory-115
Black-115
Gold-115
Silver-115
Blow-Ups-BU22
Stars on Ice-SI26
05Czech Stadion-678
05ITG Heroes and Prospects-1
05ITG Heroes and Prospects-181
Aspiring-ASP18
Autographs-A-MB
Autographs-DA-BF
Autographs Series II-MB2
Autographs Series II-BP
CHL Grads-CG-14
CHL Grads Gold-CG-14
He Shoots-He Scores Prizes-3
He Shoots-He Scores Prizes-47
He Shoots-He Scores Prizes-57
Hero Memorabilia-HM-15
National Pride-NPR-17
Spectrum-STM-09
Spectrum Gold-STM-09
06Be A Player Portraits-62
06Beehive-41
06Beehive-185
Blue-41
Gold-41
Matte-41
Red Facsimile Signatures-41
Wood-41
5 X 7 Black and White-41
5 X 7 Cherry Wood-41
Matted Materials-MMMB
PhotoGraphs-PGMB
Remarkable Matted Materials-MMMB
06Between The Pipes-70
06Between The Pipes-114
06Between The Pipes-117
06Between The Pipes-149
Aspiring-AS01
Aspiring-AS09
Aspiring Gold-AS01
Aspiring Gold-AS09
Autographs-AMB2
Autographs-AMB
Autographs-AMB3
Complete Jersey-CJ03
Complete Jersey Gold-CJ03
Complete Package-CP09
Complete Package Gold-CP09
Double Jerseys-DJ04
Double Jerseys-DJ19
Double Jerseys-DJ22
Double Jerseys-DJ25
Double Jerseys Gold-DJ04
Double Jerseys Gold-DJ19
Double Jerseys Gold-DJ22
Double Jerseys Gold-DJ25
Double Memorabilia-DM02
Double Memorabilia Gold-DM02
Emblems-GUE70
Emblems Gold-GUE70
Emblems Autographs-GUE70
Gloves-GG01
Gloves Gold-GG01
Jerseys-GUJ70
Jerseys Gold-GUJ70
Jerseys Autographs-GUJ70
Numbers-GUN70
Numbers Gold-GUN70
Numbers Autographs-GUN70
Pads-GP01
Pads Gold-GP01
Playing For Your Country-PC02
Playing For Your Country Gold-PC02
Roy vs. Brodeur-RB01
Roy vs. Brodeur-RB02
Roy vs. Brodeur-RB03
Roy vs. Brodeur-RB04
Roy vs. Brodeur-RB05
Roy vs. Brodeur-RB06
Roy vs. Brodeur-RB07
Roy vs. Brodeur-RB08
Roy vs. Brodeur-RB09
Roy vs. Brodeur-RB10
Roy vs. Brodeur Gold-RB01
Roy vs. Brodeur Gold-RB02
Roy vs. Brodeur Gold-RB03
Roy vs. Brodeur Gold-RB04
Roy vs. Brodeur Gold-RB05
Roy vs. Brodeur Gold-RB06
Roy vs. Brodeur Gold-RB07
Roy vs. Brodeur Gold-RB08
Roy vs. Brodeur Gold-RB09
Roy vs. Brodeur Gold-RB10
Shooting Gallery-SG08
Shooting Gallery-SG10
Shooting Gallery Gold-SG08
Shooting Gallery Gold-SG10
Stick and Jersey-SJ03
Stick and Jersey Gold-SJ03
Stick and Jersey Autographs-SJ03
Stick Work-SW01
Stick Work Gold-SW01
06Black Diamond-160B
Black-156B
Gold-160B
Ruby-160B
Jerseys-JBR
Jerseys Black-JBR
Jerseys Gold-JBR
Jerseys Ruby-JBR
Jerseys Black Autographs -JMB
06Devils Team Set-1
06Flair Showcase-187
06Flair Showcase-243
06Flair Showcase-287
Parallel-187
Parallel-243
Parallel-287
Hot Gloves-HG18
Hot Numbers-HN27
Hot Numbers Parallel-HN27
Inks-IMB
Stitches-SSBR
06Fleer-115
Oversized-115
Tiffany-115
Fabricology-FMA
Hockey Headliners-HL23
Netminders-N15
Signing Day-SDMB
06Hot Prospects-57
Red Hot-57
White Hot-57
Hot Materials -HMMB
Hot Materials Red Hot-HMMB
Hot Materials White Hot-HMMB
Hotagraphs-HMB
06ITG International Ice-28
06ITG International Ice-98
Gold-28
Gold-98
Autographs-AMB
Autographs-AMB2
Best of the Best-BB07
Best of the Best Gold-BB07
Canadian Dream Team-DT03
Canadian Dream Team Gold-DT03
Complete Jersey-CJ03
Complete Jersey Gold-CJ03
Cornerstones-IC09
Cornerstones Gold-IC09
Double Memorabilia-DM03
Double Memorabilia Gold-DM03
Emblem Autographs-GUE12
Emblem Autographs Gold-GUE12
Emblems-GUE12
Emblems Gold-GUE12
Goaltending Glory-GG03
Goaltending Glory Gold-GG03
Hockey Passport-HP05
Hockey Passport Gold-HP05
International Rivals-IR17
International Rivals Gold-IR17
Jersey Autographs-GUJ12
Jersey Autographs Gold-GUJ12
Jerseys-GUJ12
Jerseys Gold-GUJ12
My Country My Team-MC26
My Country My Team Gold-MC26
Numbers-GUN12
Numbers Autographs-GUN12
Numbers Autographs Gold-GUN12
Numbers Gold-GUN12
Passing The Torch-PTT2
Passing The Torch-PTT3
Passing The Torch Gold-PTT2
Passing The Torch Gold-PTT3
Quad Patch-QP03
Quad Patch Gold-QP03
Stick and Jersey-SJ19
Stick and Jersey Gold-SJ19
Teammates-IT09
Teammates Gold-IT09
Triple Memorabilia-TM06
Triple Memorabilia Gold-TM06
06ITG Ultimate Memorabilia-98
Artist Proof-98
Autos-3
Autos Gold-3
Autos Dual-3
Autos Dual Gold-3
Autos Triple-4
Autos Triple Gold-4
Complete Jersey-4
Complete Jersey Gold-4
Complete Package-18
Complete Package Gold-18
Decades-6
Decades-8
Decades Gold-6
Decades Gold-8
Double Memorabilia-3
Double Memorabilia Gold-3
Double Memorabilia Autos-5
Double Memorabilia Autos Gold-5
Emblems-7
Emblems Gold-7
First Round Picks-19
First Round Picks Gold-19
Gloves Are Off-15
Gloves Are Off Gold-15
Going For Gold-19
Going For Gold Gold-19
In The Numbers-3
In The Numbers Gold-3
Jerseys-13
Jerseys Gold-13
Jerseys and Emblems-5
Jerseys and Emblems Gold-5
Jerseys Autos-4
Jerseys Autos Gold-4
Passing The Torch-11
Passing The Torch Gold-11
R.O.Y. Autos-12
R.O.Y. Autos Gold-12
R.O.Y. Emblems-12
R.O.Y. Emblems Gold-12
R.O.Y. Jerseys-12
R.O.Y. Jerseys Gold-12
R.O.Y. Numbers-12
R.O.Y. Numbers Gold-12
Retrospective-10
Retrospective Gold-10
Ring Leaders-7
Ring Leaders Gold-7
Sensational Season-9
Sensational Season Gold-9
Sticks and Jerseys-4
Sticks and Jerseys Gold-4
Triple Thread Jerseys-4
Triple Thread Jerseys Gold-4
06McDonald's Upper Deck-27
Autographs-AMB
Clear Cut Winners-CC6
Hot Gloves-HG1
Jerseys-JMB
Patches-PMB
06NHL POG-1
06O-Pee-Chee-291
06O-Pee-Chee-608
06O-Pee-Chee-658
06O-Pee-Chee-687
Rainbow-291
Rainbow-608
Rainbow-658
Rainbow-687
Swatches-S-MB
06Panini Stickers-76
06SP Authentic-43
06SP Authentic-133
Limited-43
Limited-133
Sign of the Times-STMB
Sign of the Times Duals-STBW
Sign of the Times Duals-STRB
Sign of the Times Triples-ST3RBW
Sign of the Times Quads-ST4RBLF
06SP Game Used-60
Gold-60
Rainbow-60
Authentic Fabrics-AFMB
Authentic Fabrics Parallel-AFMB
Authentic Fabrics Patches-AFMB
Authentic Fabrics Dual-AF2BG
Authentic Fabrics Dual Patches-AF2BG
Authentic Fabrics Triple-AF3NJD
Authentic Fabrics Triple Patches-AF3NJD
Authentic Fabrics Quads-AF4RBTL
Authentic Fabrics Quads Patches-AF4RBTL
Authentic Fabrics Sixes-AF6JEN
Authentic Fabrics Sixes-AF6WIN
Authentic Fabrics Sixes Patches-AF6JEN
Authentic Fabrics Sixes Patches-AF6WIN
Authentic Fabrics Sevens-AF7VEZ
Authentic Fabrics Sevens Patches-AF7VEZ
Authentic Fabrics Eights-AF8CAN
Authentic Fabrics Eights Patches-AF8CAN
Autographs-60
By The Letter-BLMB
Inked Sweaters-ISMB
Inked Sweaters Patches-ISMB
Inked Sweaters Dual-IS2BL
Inked Sweaters Dual Patches-IS2BL
Letter Marks-LMMB
SIGnificance-SMB
06SPx-59
06SPx-131
Spectrum-59
Spectrum-131
SPxcitement-X60
SPxcitement Spectrum-X60
SPxcitement Autographs-X60
Winning Materials-WMMB
Winning Materials Spectrum-WMMB
Winning Materials Autographs-WMMB
06The Cup-52
Autographed Foundations-CQMB
Autographed Foundations Patches-CQMB
Autographed NHL Shields Duals-DASBH
Autographed NHL Shields Duals-DASLB
Autographed NHL Shields Duals-DASNJ
Autographed NHL Shields Duals-DASRB
Autographed Patches-52
Black Rainbow-52
Foundations-CQMB
Foundations Patches-CQMB
Enshrinements-EMB
Gold-52
Gold Patches-52
Honorable Numbers-HNMB
Jerseys-52
Limited Logos-LLMB
Masterpiece Pressplates-52
NHL Shields Duals-DSHLE
Property of-POMB
Scripted Swatches-SSMB
Scripted Swatches Duals-DSRB
Signature Patches-SPBR
Stanley Cup Signatures-CSBR
06UD Artifacts-43
06UD Artifacts-179
Blue-43
Blue-179
Gold-43
Gold-179
Platinum-43
Platinum-179
Radiance-43
Radiance-179
Autographed Radiance Parallel-43
Autographed Radiance Parallel-179
Red-43
Red-179
Auto-Facts-AFMB
Auto-Facts Gold-AFMB
Treasured Patches Black-TSMB
Treasured Patches Blue-TSMB
Treasured Patches Gold-TSMB
Treasured Patches Platinum-TSMB
Treasured Patches Red-TSMB
Treasured Patches Autographed Black Tag Parallel-TSMB
Treasured Swatches-TSMB
Treasured Swatches Black-TSMB
Treasured Swatches Blue-TSMB
Treasured Swatches Gold-TSMB
Treasured Swatches Platinum-TSMB
Treasured Swatches Red-TSMB
Treasured Swatches Autographed Black-TSMB
Tundra Tandems-TTBE
Tundra Tandems Black-TTBE
Tundra Tandems Blue-TTBE
Tundra Tandems Gold-TTBE
Tundra Tandems Platinum-TTBE
Tundra Tandems Red-TTBE
Tundra Tandems Dual Patches Red-TTBE
06UD Mini Jersey Collection-60
06UD Powerplay-59
Impact Rainbow-59
Goal Robbers-GR12
In Action-IA6
Specialists-SMB
Specialists Patches-PMB
06UD Toronto Fall Expo Priority Signings -PSMB
06Ultimate Collection-37
Autographed Jerseys-AJ-MB
Autographed Patches-AJ-MB
Jerseys-UJ-BR
Jerseys Triple-UJ3-RBL
Patches-UJ-BR
Patches Triple-UJ3-RBL
Premium Patches-PS-MB
Premium Swatches-PS-MB
Signatures-US-MB
Ultimate Achievements-UA-MB
Ultimate Signatures Logos-SL-MB
06Ultra-115
Gold Medallion-115
Ice Medallion-115
Action-UA16
Difference Makers-DM20
Fresh Ink-IBR
Uniformity-UBR
Uniformity Patches-UPBR
06Upper Deck Arena Giveaways-NJD1
06Upper Deck-114
Exclusives Parallel-114
High Gloss Parallel-114
All-Time Greatest-ATG13
All World-AW25
Game Dated Moments-GD8
Game Dated Moments-GD35
Game Jerseys-JMB
Game Patches-PMB
Generations Duals-G2BL
Generations Patches Dual-G2PBL
Masterpieces-114
Signatures-SMB
Statistical Leaders-SL5
Walmart Tins Oversize-114
Zero Men-ZM1
06Upper Deck MVP-171
Gold Script-171
Super Script-171
Clutch Performers-CP4
Gotta Have Hart-HH16
International Icons-II14
Jerseys-OJBL
Jerseys-OJBN
Jerseys-OJDR
Last Line of Defense-LL1
06Upper Deck Ovation-28
06Upper Deck Sweet Shot-63
Signature Shots/Saves-SSBR
Signature Shots/Saves Ice Signings-SSIMB
Signature Shots/Saves Sticks-SSSMB
Signature Sticks-STMB
Sweet Stitches-SSMB
Sweet Stitches Duals-SSMB
Sweet Stitches Triples-SSMB
06Upper Deck Trilogy-58
Combo Autographed Jerseys-CJRB
Combo Autographed Patches-CJRB
Combo Clearcut Autographs-C3RBH
Frozen In Time-FT11
Honorary Scripted Patches-HSPMB
Honorary Scripted Swatches-HSSMB
Honorary Swatches-HSMB
Ice Scripts-ISMA
Scripts-S1BR
Scripts-S2MB
Scripts-S3MB
06Upper Deck National NHL VIP-4
06Upper Deck Victory-116
06Upper Deck Victory Black-116
06Upper Deck Victory Gold-116
06Upper Deck Victory GameBreakers-GB28
06Upper Deck Victory Oversize Cards-MB
06Russian Sport Collection Olympic Stars-34
06ITG Heroes and Prospects-15
Autographs-AMB
Double Memorabilia-DM04
Double Memorabilia Gold-DM04
Heroes Memorabilia-HM05
Heroes Memorabilia Gold-HM05
Quad Emblems-QE14
Triple Memorabilia-TM02
Triple Memorabilia Gold-TM02
07Upper Deck All-Star Game Redemptions-AS1
07Upper Deck Ovation-18
3x5s-XL12
07Upper Deck Victory-1
Black-1
Gold-1
GameBreakers-GB2
Oversize Cards-OS1
Stars on Ice-SI30

Brodeur, Mike
05ITG Heroes/Prosp Toronto Expo Parallel -353
05ITG Heroes and Prospects-353
Autographs Series II-MBR
Complete Logos-ECHL-1
Jerseys-GUJ-103
Jerseys Gold-GUJ-103
Net Prospects Dual-NPD9
Net Prospects Dual Gold-NPD9
06Toledo Storm-9

Brodeur, Richard
73Nordiques Team Issue-5
75O-Pee-Chee WHA-44
76Nordiques Marie Antoinette-6
76Nordiques Postcards-9
76O-Pee-Chee WHA-12
77O-Pee-Chee WHA-38
79O-Pee-Chee-176
79Topps-176
80Canucks Silverwood Dairies-4
80Canucks Team Issue-4
80Pepsi-Cola Caps-104
81Canucks Team Issue-3
81O-Pee-Chee-331
82Canucks Team Issue-2
82McDonald's Stickers-2
82O-Pee-Chee-339
82O-Pee-Chee-340
82O-Pee-Chee Stickers-7
82O-Pee-Chee Stickers-247
82Post Cereal-19
82Topps Stickers-7
82Topps Stickers-247
83Canucks Team Issue-1
83Esso-4
83NHL Key Tags-126
83O-Pee-Chee-346
83O-Pee-Chee Stickers-276
83O-Pee-Chee Stickers-277
83Puffy Stickers-1
83Topps Stickers-276
83Topps Stickers-277
83Vachon-101
84Canucks Team Issue-2
84Kellogg's Accordion Discs-1
84Kellogg's Accordion Discs Singles-5
84O-Pee-Chee-314
84O-Pee-Chee Stickers-277
847-Eleven Discs-48
85Canucks Team Issue-1
85O-Pee-Chee-180
86Canucks Team Issue-1
86Kraft Drawings-4
86O-Pee-Chee-246
86O-Pee-Chee Stickers-98
87Canucks Shell Oil-4
87O-Pee-Chee-257
87O-Pee-Chee Stickers-189
87Panini Stickers-340
88ProCards AHL-53
00Upper Deck Legends-127
00Upper Deck Legends-128
Legendary Collection Bronze-127
Legendary Collection Bronze-128
Legendary Collection Gold-127
Legendary Collection Gold-128
Legendary Collection Silver-127
Legendary Collection Silver-128
01Greats of the Game-48
Autographs-48
04ITG Franchises Canadian-119
Autographs-RBR
Complete Jerseys-CJ7
Complete Jerseys Gold-CJ7
Goalie Gear-GG10
Goalie Gear Autographs-GG10
Goalie Gear Gold-GG10
Memorabilia-SM22
Memorabilia Autographs-SM22
Memorabilia Gold-SM22
04ITG Franchises He Shoots/Scores Prizes-17
04ITG Ultimate Memorabilia Triple Threads-7
04UD Legendary Signatures-61
AKA Autographs-AKA-RD
Autographs-RD
05Between the Pipes-4
Autographs-A-RB
Jerseys-GUJ-12
05ITG Ultimate Mem 3 Star of the Game Jsy-19
05ITG Ult Mem 3 Star of the Game Jsy Gold-19
05SP Game Used Oldtimer's Challenge-OC-RB
05SP Game Used Oldtimer's Challenge Autos-OCA-RB
05SP Game Used Oldtimer's Challenge Patch-OCP-RB
05SP Game Used Oldtime Chall Patch Autoa-OAP-RB
06Between The Pipes-99
Autographs-ARBR
Emblems-GUE17
Emblems Gold-GUE17
Emblems Autographs-GUE17
Jerseys-GUJ17
Jerseys Gold-GUJ17
Jerseys Autographs-GUJ17
Numbers-GUN17
Numbers Gold-GUN17
Numbers Autographs-GUN17
Stick and Jersey-SJ39
Stick and Jersey Gold-SJ39
Stick and Jersey Autographs-SJ39
06Parkhurst-24
Autographs-24
Autographs Dual-DATB
06SP Authentic Sign of the Times Duals-STLB
06SP Game Used SIGnificance-SRB
06SPx-117
Spectrum-117
SPxcitement-X98
SPxcitement Spectrum-X98
06The Cup Signature Patches-SPRI
06UD Artifacts-105
Blue-105
Gold-105
Platinum-105
Radiance-105
Autographed Radiance Parallel-105
Red-105
Auto-Facts-AFRI
Auto-Facts Gold-AFRI
Tundra Tandems-TTDR
Tundra Tandems Black-TTDR
Tundra Tandems Blue-TTDR
Tundra Tandems Gold-TTDR
Tundra Tandems Platinum-TTDR
Tundra Tandems Red-TTDR
Tundra Tandems Dual Patches Red-TTDR
06Ultimate Collection Signatures-US-BR
06Upper Deck Trilogy Legendary Scripts-LSBR
06Upper Deck Trilogy Scripts-TSRB

Brodie, Andrew
897th Inn. Sketch OHL-68
907th Inn. Sketch OHL-79

Brodie, T.J.
06Saginaw Spirit-20

Brodie, Troy
03Kelowna Rockets Memorial Cup-1

Brodmann, Mario
93Swedish Semic World Champ Stickers-120
93Swiss HNL-121
95Swiss HNL-41
96Swiss HNL-188
98Swiss Power Play Stickers-310

Brodnicke, Richard
94German DEL-350

Brodt, Chelsey
04Minnesota Golden Gophers Women-12

Brodt, Winny
98Minnesota Golden Gophers Women-2

Brodziak, Kyle
01Moose Jaw Warriors-6
05Beehive-164
Matte-164
05Black Diamond-239
05Hot Prospects-127
En Fuego-127
Red Hot-127
White Hot-127
05SP Authentic-230
Limited-230
05SP Game Used-168
Gold-168
05SPx-199
05SPx-258
Spectrum-199
05The Cup Masterpiece Pressplate Artifact-277
05The Cup Masterpiece Pressplate Bee Hive-164
05The Cup Master Pressplate Black Diamond-239
05The Cup Masterpiece Pressplates (Ice)-151
05The Cup Master Pressplate Rookie Update-130
05The Cup Masterpiece Pressplates SPA-230
05The Cup Masterpiece Pressplates SP GU-168
05The Cup Masterpiece Pressplates (SPx)-199
05The Cup Masterpiece Pressplates (SPx)-258
05The Cup Masterpiece Pressplates Trilogy-256
05The Cup Masterpiece Pressplate Ult Coll-149
05The Cup Masterpiece Pressplates Victory-263
05UD Artifacts-277
05Ultimate Collection-149
Gold-149
05Ultra-219
Gold-219
Ice-219
05Upper Deck-468
05Upper Deck Ice-151
05Upper Deck Rookie Update-130
05Upper Deck Trilogy-256
05Upper Deck Victory-263
Black-263
Gold-263
Silver-263
05Iowa Stars-8
06Wilkes-Barre Scranton Penguins-10
06Wilkes-Barre Scranton Penguins Jerseys-4

Broman, Bjorn
71Swedish Hockey-249
72Swedish Stickers-232

Broman, Lennart
71Swedish Hockey-250

Bromley, Gary
74NHL Action Stamps-41
74O-Pee-Chee NHL-7
74Sabres Postcards-1
74Topps-7
75O-Pee-Chee NHL-368
77O-Pee-Chee WHA-45
78Canucks Royal Bank-2
79Canucks Royal Bank-3
79O-Pee-Chee-167
79Topps-167
80Canucks Silverwood Dairies-5
80Canucks Team Issue-5
80O-Pee-Chee-330

Broms, Anders
89Swedish Semic Elitserien Stickers-143

Broms, Niklas
05Swedish SHL Elitset-213

Broms, Sigge
57Swedish Alltabilder-132

Bromwell, Murray
83Devils Postcards-4

Bronilla, Rich
92Ottawa 67's-3
95Slapshot-260
98Huntington Blizzard-17
98Las Vegas Coyotes RHI-12
99Jacksonville Lizard Kings-3
00UK Sekonda Superleague-72
01UK London Knights-18
02UK London Knights-14

Bronniman, Ollie
06UK Guildford Flames-22

Bronsard, Christian
98Manitoba Moose-D2
99Syracuse Crunch-15
02Russian Hockey League-72
03Russian SL-19
03UK Sheffield Steelers-7

Brook, Phil
97UK Kingston Hawks Stickers-8

Brookbank, Leigh
91Air Canada SJHL-B30
92Saskatchewan JHL-157

Brookbank, Sheldon
02Grand Rapids Griffins-8
03Cincinnati Mighty Ducks-B3
04Cincinnati Mighty Ducks-17
05Milwaukee Admirals Choice-2
05Milwaukee Admirals Pepsi-3
06Milwaukee Admirals -2

Brookbank, Wade
98Anchorage Aces-13
01Grand Rapids Griffins-3
03Bowman-130
Gold-130
03Bowman Chrome-130
Refractors-130
Gold Refractors-130
Xfractors-130
03ITG Used Signature Series-197
Gold-197
03ITG VIP Rookie Debut-23
03Pacific Calder-136
Silver-136
03Pacific Complete-520
Red-520
03Parkhurst Rookie-129
03SP Game Used-69
Gold-69
03Topps Traded-TT140
Blue-TT140
Gold-TT140
Red-TT140
03UD Honor Roll-161
03Upper Deck-227
Canadian Exclusives-227
HG-227
03Upper Deck Trilogy-158
Limited-158
04Manitoba Moose-19

Brooke, Bob
85O-Pee-Chee-202
86North Stars 7-Eleven-11
86O-Pee-Chee-48
86O-Pee-Chee Stickers-219
86Topps-48
87North Stars Postcards-8
87O-Pee-Chee-64
87Panini Stickers-301
87Topps-64
88North Stars ADA-2
88O-Pee-Chee-61
88Panini Stickers-91
88Topps-61
89O-Pee-Chee-215
89Swedish Semic World Champ Stickers-171
90Bowman-79
Tiffany-79
90O-Pee-Chee-105
90Topps-105
Tiffany-105

Brooks, Alex
01Finnish Cardset-256
02Albany River Rats-2
02Albany River Rats AAP-5
03Albany River Rats-5
03Albany River Rats Kinko's-4
04Albany River Rats-3
05Albany River Rats-4
06Devils Team Set-2
06Hot Prospects-168
Red Hot-168
White Hot-168
06O-Pee-Chee-563
Rainbow-563
06SP Game Used-130
Gold-130
Rainbow-130
Autographs-130
Rookie Exclusives Autographs-REAL
06SPx-203
Spectrum-203
06The Cup-101
Autographed Rookie Masterpiece Pressplates-101
Gold Rainbow Autographed Rookies-101
Masterpiece Pressplates (Marquee Rookies)-563
Masterpiece Pressplates (SP Game Used)-130
Masterpiece Pressplates (Victory)-307
Rookies Black-101
Rookies Platinum-101
06Upper Deck-477
Exclusives Parallel-477
High Gloss Parallel-477
Masterpieces-477
Victory-307

Brooks, Brendan
97Owen Sound Platers-22
98Quad-City Mallards-2
99Quad-City Mallards-13
02Peoria Rivermen-16
02Peoria Rivermen Photo Pack-2
02Peoria Rivermen RBI Sports-154
03Peoria Rivermen-2
04Worcester IceCats-18
05Peoria Rivermen-17

Brooks, Chris
92Western Michigan Broncos-4
93Western Michigan Broncos-3
97Mobile Mysticks-10
97Mobile Mysticks Kellogg's-14
98Amarillo Rattlers-2

Brooks, Gordy
74Capitals White Borders-7
74NHL Action Stamps-316

Brooks, Herb
80USA Olympic Team Mini Pics-15
87North Stars Postcards-9
95Signature Rookies Miracle on Ice-41
95Signature Rookies Miracle on Ice-42
95Signature Rook Miracle on Ice Sigs-41
95Signature Rook Miracle on Ice Sigs-42
04Ultimate Collection-50

Brooks, Jason
95Slapshot-171
02Guelph Storm-28
03Guelph Storm-25
04Guelph Storm-27

Brooks, Mark
92Oshawa Generals Sheet-5

Brooks, Ross

74NHL Action Stamps-32
74O-Pee-Chee NHL-376
Brooks, Shaun
01Arizona Icecats-2
02Arizona Icecats-3
03Arizona Icecats-2
Brooks, Tom
06Texas Tornados-11
Brooks, W.
28V128-2 Paulin's Candy-80
Brookwell, Cody
04Williams Lake Timberwolves-2
Brophey, Evan
02Barrie Colts-1
03Barrie Colts-3
04Belleville Bulls-9
05ITG Heroes/Prosp Toronto Expo Parallel -129
05Plymouth Whalers-B-14
05ITG Heroes and Prospects-129
Autographs-A-EB
06Plymouth Whalers-4
Brophy, John
84Maple Leafs Postcards-4
87Maple Leafs PLAY-28
88Maple Leafs PLAY-28
89Hampton Roads Admirals-2
90Hampton Roads Admirals-60
91Hampton Roads Admirals-19
92Hampton Roads Admirals-20
93Hampton Roads Admirals-1
94Hampton Roads Admirals-1
95Hampton Roads Admirals-2
96Hampton Roads Admirals-HRA21
97Hampton Roads Admirals-22
98Hampton Roads Admirals-2
98Hampton Roads Admirals 10th Anniversary-1
99Hampton Roads Admirals-22
06Richmond Renegades-19
Brophy, Scott
03Gatineau Olympiques-2
04Gatineau Olympiques-4
Bros, Michal
95Upper Deck-541
Electric Ice-541
Electric Ice Gold-541
95Czech APS Extraliga-120
96Czech APS Extraliga-278
97Czech APS Extraliga-33
97Czech DS Extraliga-65
97Czech DS Stickers-181
98Czech DS-81
98Czech DS Stickers-180
98Czech OFS-110
98Czech OFS-432
99Czech DS-151
99Czech OFS-102
99Czech OFS-472
00Czech DS Extraliga-11
National Team-NT10
World Champions-WCH11
00Czech OFS-306
01Czech DS-13
01Czech OFS-15
02Czech DS-21
02Czech OFS Plus-2
03Czech OFS Plus-151
04Czech HC Sparta Praha Postcards-2
04Czech OFS-325
Assist Leaders-10
Points Leaders-15
05Finnish Cardset -275
06Czech Super Six Postcards-2
06Finnish Cardset-103
Brossart, Willie
73Maple Leafs Postcards-2
74NHL Action Stamps-254
74NHL Action Stamps Update-41
Brosseau, david
96Charlotte Checkers-3
97Charlotte Checkers-3
98Charlotte Checkers-4
99Austin Ice Bats-6
00Austin Ice Bats-2
01Macon Whoopee-5
04Richmond Riverdogs-13
Brost, Todd
90Alberta International Team Canada-12
91Alberta International Team Canada-2
92Salt Lake Golden Eagles-1
93Alberta International Team Canada-2
93OPC Premier Team Canada-8
93PowerPlay-479
93Ultra-459
93Phoenix Cobras RHI-6
94Huntington Blizzard-5
97El Paso Buzzards-20
98El Paso Buzzards-10
03Elmira Jackals-23
Brostrom, Anders
71Swedish Hockey-264
72Swedish Stickers-242
83Swedish Semic Elitserien-228
Brostrom, Bjarne
69Swedish Hockey-223
71Swedish Hockey-369
Brosz, Tyler
04Minnesota-Duluth Bulldogs-2
Broten, Aaron
81Rockies Postcards-2
82O-Pee-Chee-136
83Devils Postcards-3
83O-Pee-Chee-227
83O-Pee-Chee Stickers-226
83Topps Stickers-226
84Devils Postcards-10
85O-Pee-Chee-249
85O-Pee-Chee Stickers-62
86Devils Police-6
87O-Pee-Chee-46
87O-Pee-Chee Stickers-62
87Panini Stickers-78
87Topps-46
88Devils Caretta-3
88O-Pee-Chee-138
88O-Pee-Chee Stickers-76
88Panini Stickers-271
88Topps-138
89Devils Caretta-4
89O-Pee-Chee-180
89O-Pee-Chee-308
89O-Pee-Chee Stickers-88
89Panini Stickers-254
89Topps-180
90Bowman-185
Tiffany-185
90Maple Leafs Postcards-1
90Nordiques Petro-Canada-1
90O-Pee-Chee-118
90OPC Premier-10
90Panini Stickers-247
90Pro Set-131
90Pro Set-530
90Score-162
Canadian-162
90Score Hottest/Rising Stars-72
90Score Rookie/Traded-21T
90Topps-118
Tiffany-118
90Upper Deck-210
French-210
91Bowman-162
91Panini Stickers-105
91Score American-307
91Score Canadian Bilingual-250
91Score Canadian Bilingual-337
91Score Canadian English-250
91Score Canadian English-337
94Minnesota Golden Gophers-6
06Parkhurst-25
Autographs-25
Autographs Dual-DABB
Broten, Neal
81North Stars Postcards-4
81Swedish Semic Hockey VM Stickers-99
82North Stars Postcards-4
82North Stars Postcards-4
82O-Pee-Chee-164
82O-Pee-Chee Stickers-190
82Topps Stickers-190
83North Stars Postcards-5
83O-Pee-Chee-168
83O-Pee-Chee Stickers-120
83Puffy Stickers-13
83Topps Stickers-120
84North Stars 7-Eleven-1
84North Stars Postcards-5
84O-Pee-Chee-96
84O-Pee-Chee Stickers-46
84Topps-72
85North Stars 7-Eleven-6
85North Stars Postcards-6
85O-Pee-Chee-124
85O-Pee-Chee Stickers-40
85Topps-124
86North Stars 7-Eleven-1
86North Stars Postcards-2
86O-Pee-Chee-99
86O-Pee-Chee Stickers-166
86Topps-99
87North Stars Postcards-10
87O-Pee-Chee-11
87O-Pee-Chee Stickers-52
87Panini Stickers-297
87Topps-11
88Frito-Lay Stickers-7
88North Stars ADA-3
88O-Pee-Chee-144
88O-Pee-Chee Stickers-201
88Panini Stickers-92
88Topps-144
89O-Pee-Chee-87
89O-Pee-Chee-306
89O-Pee-Chee Stickers-202
89Panini Stickers-107
89Topps-87
89Swedish Semic World Champ Stickers-165
90Bowman-178
Tiffany-178
90O-Pee-Chee-90
90Panini Stickers-261
90Pro Set-132
90Score-144
Canadian-144
90Topps-90
Tiffany-90
90Upper Deck-48
French-48
91Pro Set Platinum-143
91Pro Set Platinum-188
91Bowman-121
91Bowman-420
91O-Pee-Chee-420
91Panini Stickers-107
91Parkhurst-80
French-80
91Pinnacle-161
French-161
91Pro Set-112
French-112
91Score American-280
91Score American-307
91Score Canadian Bilingual-337
91Score Canadian Bilingual-500
91Score Canadian English-337
91Score Canadian English-500
91Stadium Club-99
91Topps-420
91Upper Deck-232
French-232
91Finnish Semic World Champ Stickers-140
91Swedish Semic World Champ Stickers-140
92Bowman-81
92O-Pee-Chee-62
92Panini Stickers-89
92Panini Stickers French-89
92Parkhurst-313
Emerald Ice-313
92Pinnacle-209
French-209
92Score-32
Canadian-32
92Stadium Club-90
92Topps-309
Gold-309G
92Ultra-89
92Upper Deck-206
93OPC Premier-131
Gold-131
93Panini Stickers-272
93Parkhurst-54
Emerald Ice-54
93Pinnacle-334
Canadian-334
93PowerPlay-57
93Score-166
Canadian-166
93Stadium Club-28
Members Only Master Set-28
OPC-28
First Day Issue-28
First Day Issue OPC-28
93Topps/OPC Premier-131
Gold-131
93Ultra-296
93Upper Deck-109
SP-34
94Canada Games NHL POGS-76
94Donruss-67
94Flair-39
94Leaf-246
94OPC Premier-74
Special Effects-74
94Parkhurst-53
Gold-53
94Pinnacle-293
Artist's Proofs-293
Rink Collection-293
94Score-113
Gold-113
Platinum-113
94Stars HockeyKaps-3
94Stars Score Sheet-113
94Topps/OPC Premier-74
Special Effects-74
94Ultra-48
94Upper Deck-273
Electric Ice-273
SP Inserts-SP18
SP Inserts Die Cuts-SP18
94Minnesota Golden Gophers-6
95Be A Player-42
Signatures-S42
Signatures Die Cuts-S42
95Canada Games NHL POGS-157
95Collector's Choice-285
Player's Club-285
Player's Club Platinum-285
95Donruss-259
95Emotion-95
95Leaf-286
Road To The Cup-7
95Metal-82
95Panini Stickers-80
95Parkhurst International-120
Emerald Ice-120
95Pinnacle-117
Artist's Proofs-117
Rink Collection-117
95Playoff One on One-276
95Score-265
Black Ice Artist's Proofs-265
Black Ice-265
95SkyBox Impact-91
95Ultra-87
95Ultra-187
Gold Medallion-87
Gold Medallion-187
95Upper Deck-114
Electric Ice-114
Electric Ice Gold-114
95Signature Rookies Miracle on Ice-3
95Signature Rookies Miracle on Ice-4
95Signature Rook Miracle on Ice Sigs-3
95Signature Rook Miracle on Ice Sigs-4
96Collector's Choice-152
96Stars Postcards-3
97Pacific Dynagon Best Kept Secrets-28
01Fleer Legacy-29
Ultimate-29
01Greats of the Game-71
Autographs-71
01Topps Archives-15
Arena Seats-ASNB
01Topps Chrome Reprints-5
01Topps Chrome Reprint Refractors-5
01Topps Chrome Reprint Autographs-5
01Upper Deck Legends Milestones-MNB
01Upper Deck Legends Milestones Platinum-MNB
04ITG Franchises Update-473
04ITG Franchises US West-195
Autographs-A-NB
04UD Legendary Signatures-59
Autographs-NB
Linemates-BENBCI
Miracle Men-USA6
Miracle Men Autographs-USA-NB
05ITG Heroes/Prosp Toronto Expo Parallel -37
05ITG Heroes and Prospects-37
Autographs-A-NB
06ITG International Ice-79
Gold-79
Autographs-ANB
06Parkhurst-26
06Parkhurst-225
Autographs-26
Autographs-225
Autographs Dual-DABB
Autographs Dual-DACB
Broten, Paul
89Rangers Marine Midland Bank-37
89ProCards IHL-28
90Bowman-224
Tiffany-224
90Score Rookie/Traded-41T
91Parkhurst-336
French-336
91Stadium Club-376
91Upper Deck-550
French-550
92Bowman-265
92O-Pee-Chee-364
92Pinnacle-212
French-212
92Score-353
Canadian-353
92Stadium Club-109
92Topps-355
Gold-355G
92Ultra-134
92Ultra-353
92Upper Deck-148
93Parkhurst-324
Emerald Ice-324
93Score-297
93Score-658
Gold-658
Canadian-297
Canadian-658
Canadian Gold-658
93Upper Deck-468
94Leaf-409
94OPC Premier-261
Special Effects-261
94Parkhurst-60
Gold-60
94Pinnacle-433
Artist's Proofs-433
Rink Collection-433
94Stars HockeyKaps-4
94Stars Pinnacle Sheet-433
94Stars Pinnacle Sheet-NNO
94Stars Postcards-1
94Topps/OPC Premier-261
Special Effects-261
94Upper Deck-15
Electric Ice-15
94Minnesota Golden Gophers-6
97Cincinnati Cyclones-2
98German DEL-110
Brough, Tyler
98Prince George Cougars-6
Broughton, George
12C57-39
Brouillard, Daniel
93Quebec Pee-Wee Tournament-910
Brouillette, Julien
04Chicoutimi Sagueneens-11
05Chicoutimi Sagueneens-10
06Chicoutimi Sagueneens-5
Brousseau, Jason
90 7th Inn. Sketch QMJHL-57
90 7th Inn. Sketch Memorial Cup-67
91 7th Inn. Sketch QMJHL-230
92Fort Worth Fire-3
93Fort Worth Fire-4
94Johnstown Chiefs-2
Brousseau, Nicolas
94Central Hockey League-39
Brousseau, Paul
90 7th Inn. Sketch QMJHL-177
91 7th Inn. Sketch QMJHL-206
94Classic Pro Prospects-152
97Pinnacle Inside-141
99Louisville Panthers-21
00Louisville Panthers-3
02German DEL City Press-278
03German DEL-152
Brouwer, Troy
04Moose Jaw Warriors-18
05ITG Heroes/Prosp Toronto Expo Parallel -316
05Moose Jaw Warriors-3
05ITG Heroes and Prospects-316
Autographs Series II-TB
06Blackhawks Postcards Glossy-1
06Hot Prospects-202
06The Cup Masterpiece Pressplates (Ultimate Collection)-69
06Ultimate Collection-69
06AHL Top Prospects-27
06Norfolk Admirals-8
Brower, Scott
89ProCards IHL-36
90ProCards AHL/IHL-302
93Finnish SISU-256
94Central Hockey League-40
95Central Hockey League-19
99Corpus Christi IceRays-30
99Memphis RiverKings All-Time-17
Brown, Adam
34Beehive Group I Photos-90
44Beehive Group II Photos-83
51Parkhurst-30
Brown, Alan
94Huntington Blizzard-6
Brown, Andrew
99Guelph Storm-20
00Belleville Bulls-9
01Belleville Bulls-3
02Belleville Bulls-2
03Belleville Bulls-9
03Belleville Bulls-21
04Lakehead University Thunderwolves-9
Brown, Andy
72Sargent Promotions Stamps-83
74O-Pee-Chee WHA-58
Brown, Arnie
63Rochester Americans-6
64Beehive Group III Photos-121
64Coca-Cola Caps-75
64Topps-34
65Coca-Cola-76
65Topps-90
66Topps-90
66Topps USA Test-48
67Topps-89
68O-Pee-Chee-68
68Shirriff Coins-98
68Topps-68
69O-Pee-Chee-34
69Topps-34
70Colgate Stamps-76
70Dad's Cookies-10
70Esso Power Players-184
70O-Pee-Chee-66
70Sargent Promotions Stamps-116
70Topps-66
71O-Pee-Chee-14
71Sargent Promotions Stamps-57
71Topps-14
71Toronto Sun-86
72O-Pee-Chee-144
72Sargent Promotions Stamps-72
72Topps-111
73O-Pee-Chee-225
74NHL Action Stamps-14
94Parkhurst Tall Boys-97
95Parkhurst '66-67-86
Coins-86
Brown, Bob
52Juniors Blue Tint-15
91 7th Inn. Sketch CHL Award Winners-19
95Tri-City Americans-8
Brown, Bobby
93Brandon Wheat Kings-13
94Brandon Wheat Kings-1
95Brandon Wheat Kings-1
95Slapshot Memorial Cup-36
96Roanoke Express-10
97UK Guildford Flames-12
98Dayton Bombers-2
98Dayton Bombers EBK-6
98ECHL All-Star Northern Conference-10
00Austin Ice Bats-3
01Austin Ice Bats-2
02Louisiana Ice Gators-4
03Louisiana Ice Gators-2
Brown, Brad
91 7th Inn. Sketch OHL-53
93North Bay Centennials-1
93North Bay Centennials-25
93Classic-100
94North Bay Centennials-4
94Classic-16
Gold-16
94Classic Four-Sport *-132
Gold-132
Printers Proofs-132
94Signature Rookies Gold Standard *-79
95Classic-90
95Images Four-Sport *-109
95Signature Rookies Club Promos-3
95Signature Rookies Future Flash-FF2
95Signature Rook Future Flash Sigs-FF2
96Fredericton Canadiens-2
97Pacific Invincible NHL Regime-100
97Upper Deck-296
98Pacific Dynagon Ice-93
Blue-93
Red-93
98Pacific Omega-57
Red-57
Opening Day Issue-57
98Upper Deck-292
Exclusives-292
Exclusives 1 of 1-292
Gold Reserve-292
99BAP Millennium-55
Emerald-55
Ruby-55
Sapphire-55
Signatures-55
Signatures Gold-55
99Blackhawks Chicago Sun-Times-2
99Blackhawks Lineup Cards-2
00BAP Memorabilia-475
Emerald-475
Ruby-475
Sapphire-475
Update Tough Materials-T15
Update Tough Materials Gold-T15
00Topps Gold Label Class 1-99
Gold-99
00Topps Gold Label Class 2-99
00Topps Gold Label Class 2 Gold-99
00Topps Gold Label Class 3-99
00Topps Gold Label Class 3 Gold-99
01BAP Update Tough Customers-TC9
02BAP Sig Series Auto Buybacks 1999-55
06Toronto Marlies-4
Brown, Cal
90ProCards AHL/IHL-171
Brown, Cam
88Brandon Wheat Kings-23
89Brandon Wheat Kings-8
90ProCards AHL/IHL-336
91ProCards-598
94Erie Panthers-9
98Baton Rouge Kingfish-3
03Gwinnett Gladiators-9
03Gwinnett Gladiators RBI Sports-195
04Gwinnett Gladiators-5
Brown, Christophe
93Swiss HNL-45
95Swiss HNL-70
96Swiss HNL-214
98Swiss Power Play Stickers-212
99Swiss Panini Stickers-213
00Swiss Panini Stickers-255
01Swiss EV Zug Postcards-23
01Swiss HNL-178
04Swiss Lausanne HC Postcards-14
Brown, Connie
34Beehive Group I Photos-91
Brown, Craig
92Western Michigan Broncos-5
93Western Michigan Broncos-4
96Pensacola Ice Pilots-1
97Pensacola Ice Pilots-3
98Pensacola Ice Pilots-15
Brown, Curtis
95Donruss Elite World Juniors-11
95Ultra-333
95Upper Deck-531
Electric Ice-307
Electric Ice-531
Electric Ice Gold-307
Electric Ice Gold-531
95Prince Albert Raiders-2
95Signature Rookies-63
Signatures-63
96Fleer Picks-150
96Leaf Preferred-142
Press Proofs-142
96Metal Universe-172
96Pinnacle-227
Artist's Proofs-227
Foil-227
Premium Stock-227
Rink Collection-227
96SP-14
96Summit-185
Artist's Proofs-185
Ice-185
Metal-185
Premium Stock-185
96Ultra-14
Gold Medallion-14
Rookies-3
96Upper Deck-226
96Zenith-145
Artist's Proofs-145
97Be A Player-53
Autographs-53
Autographs Die-Cuts-53
Autographs Prismatic Die-Cuts-53
97Upper Deck-230
98OPC Chrome-185
Refractors-185
98Pacific-104
Ice Blue-104
Red-104
98Pacific Omega-21
Red-21
Opening Day Issue-21
98Topps-185
O-Pee-Chee-185
99Aurora-15
Premiere Date-15
99BAP Memorabilia-243
Gold-243
Silver-243
99Kraft Face Off Rivals-4
99O-Pee-Chee-86
99O-Pee-Chee Chrome-86
99O-Pee-Chee Chrome Refractors-86
99Pacific-35
Copper-35
Emerald Green-35
Gold-35
Ice Blue-35
Premiere Date-35
Red-35
99Pacific Dynagon Ice-29
Blue-29
Copper-29
Gold-29
Premiere Date-29
99Pacific Omega-26
Copper-26
Gold-26
Ice Blue-26
Premiere Date-26
99Pacific Prism-18
Holographic Blue-18
Holographic Gold-18
Holographic Mirror-18
Holographic Purple-18
Premiere Date-18
99Paramount-26
Copper-26
Emerald-26
Gold-26
Holographic Emerald-26
Holographic Gold-26
Holographic Silver-26
Ice Blue-26
Premiere Date-26
Red-26
Silver-26
99Revolution-17
Premiere Date-17
Red-17
Shadow Series-17
99Topps/OPC-86
99Topps/OPC Chrome-86
Refractors-86
99Upper Deck-190
Exclusives-190
Exclusives 1 of 1-190
99Upper Deck Gold Reserve-190
99Upper Deck MVP SC Edition-24
Gold Script-24
Silver Script-24
Super Script-24
99Wayne Gretzky Hockey-25
00BAP Memorabilia-332
Emerald-332
Ruby-332
Sapphire-332
Promos-332
00BAP Mem Chicago Sportsfest Copper-332
00BAP Memorabilia Chicago Sportsfest Blue-332
00BAP Memorabilia Chicago Sportsfest Gold-332
00BAP Memorabilia Chicago Sportsfest Ruby-332
00BAP Memorabilia Chicago Sun-Times Ruby-332
00BAP Memorabilia Chicago Sun-Times Gold-332
00BAP Mem Chicago Sun-Times Sapphire-332
00BAP Mem Toronto Fall Expo Copper-332
00BAP Memorabilia Toronto Fall Expo Gold-332
00BAP Memorabilia Toronto Fall Expo Ruby-332
00O-Pee-Chee-137
00O-Pee-Chee Parallel-137
00Pacific-49
Copper-49
Gold-49
Ice Blue-49
Premiere Date-49
00Panini Stickers-19
00Paramount-27
Copper-27
Gold-27
Holo-Gold-27
Holo-Silver-27
Ice Blue-27
Premiere Date-27
00Topps/OPC-137
Parallel-137
00Upper Deck-250
Exclusives Tier 1-250
Exclusives Tier 2-250
00Upper Deck MVP-21
First Stars-21
ProSign-CB
Second Stars-21
Third Stars-21
00Upper Deck Victory-31
00Upper Deck Vintage-43
01Upper Deck-20
Exclusives-20
Game Jerseys-NGCB
01Upper Deck Victory-37
Gold-37
01Upper Deck Vintage-33
01Upper Deck Vintage-35
02O-Pee-Chee-249
02O-Pee-Chee Premier Blue Parallel-249
02O-Pee-Chee Premier Red Parallel-249
02O-Pee-Chee Factory Set-249
02Pacific-39
Blue-39
Red-39
02Pacific Complete-243
Red-243
02Parkhurst-197
Bronze-197
Gold-197
Silver-197
02Topps-249
OPC Blue Parallel-249
OPC Red Parallel-249
Factory Set-249
02Topps Total-227
02Upper Deck-264
Exclusives-264
02Upper Deck Beckett UD Promos-264
02Upper Deck Vintage-34
03ITG Action-19
03NHL Sticker Collection-24
03Pacific-38
Blue-38
Red-38
03Pacific Complete-71
Red-71
03Upper Deck-23
Canadian Exclusives-23
HG-23
03Upper Deck MVP-55
Gold Script-55
Silver Script-55
Canadian Exclusives-55
05Parkhurst-116
Facsimile Auto Parallel-116
05Upper Deck MVP-94
Gold-94
Platinum-94
06Be A Player-152
Autographs-152
Signatures-CB
Brown, Dan
89Peterborough Petes-99
89 7th Inn. Sketch OHL-99
94Central Hockey League-41
95Central Hockey League-20
98Columbus Cottonmouths-2
99Memphis RiverKings All-Time-7
Brown, Dave
81Saskatoon Blades-7
83Springfield Indians-8
85Flyers Postcards-2
86Flyers Postcards-2
87Flyers Postcards-21
88Flyers Postcards-16
88Oilers Tenth Anniversary-145
88Oilers Team Issue-3
88Panini Stickers-319
89Oilers Team Issue-3
90Oilers IGA-3
90Pro Set-440
91Flyers J.C. Penney-3
91Oilers Panini Team Stickers-3
91Pro Set-452
French-452
91Score Canadian Bilingual-634
91Score Canadian English-634
91Score Rookie/Traded-84T
92Flyers J.C. Penney-6
92Flyers Upper Deck Sheets-6
92Flyers Upper Deck Sheets-30
93Flyers J.C. Penney-6
93Flyers Lineup Sheets-6
94Leaf-428
02Fleer Throwbacks-32
Gold-32
Platinum-32
Autographs-12
Squaring Off-8
Squaring Off Memorabilia-8
Brown, David
04Notre Dame Fighting Irish-2
Brown, Doug
88Devils Caretta-4
88O-Pee-Chee-115
88O-Pee-Chee Stickers-23
88O-Pee-Chee Stickers-80
88Panini Stickers-272
88Topps-115
89Devils Caretta-5
89O-Pee-Chee-242
90Devils Team Issue-3
90O-Pee-Chee-117
90Panini Stickers-67
90Pro Set-163
90Topps-117
Tiffany-117
90Upper Deck-159
French-159
91Bowman-285
91O-Pee-Chee-42
91Pinnacle-363
French-363
91Pro Set-138
French-138
91Score American-163
91Score Canadian Bilingual-163
91Score Canadian English-163
91Stadium Club-47
91Topps-42
91Upper Deck-214
French-214
92Bowman-126
92O-Pee-Chee-333
92Score-118
Canadian-118
92Stadium Club-331
92Topps-139
Gold-139G
92Finnish Semic-165
93Donruss-258
93Leaf-378
93Parkhurst-424
Emerald Ice-424
93Penguins Foodland-7
93PowerPlay-411
93Score-582
Gold-582
Canadian-582
Canadian Gold-582
93Ultra-393
93Upper Deck-459
94Be A Player Signature Cards-28
94Donruss-213
94Leaf-116
94OPC Premier-263
Special Effects-263
94Parkhurst SE-SE135
Gold-SE135
94Pinnacle-197
Artist's Proofs-197
Rink Collection-197
94Score-15
Gold-15
Platinum-15
94Topps/OPC Premier-263
Special Effects-263
94Upper Deck-422
Electric Ice-422
94Finnish Jaa Kiekko-117
95Collector's Choice-47
Player's Club-47
Player's Club Platinum-47
95Score-193
Black Ice Artist's Proofs-193
Black Ice-193
95Topps-81
OPC Inserts-81
Power Lines-8PL
95Upper Deck-79
Electric Ice-79
Electric Ice Gold-79
95Swedish Globe World Championships-114
96Be A Player-43
Autographs-43
Autographs Silver-43
97Pacific Invincible NHL Regime-67
97Score Red Wings-13
Platinum-13
Premier-13
98Finest-10
No Protectors-10
No Protectors Refractors-10
Refractors-10
98Pacific-187
Ice Blue-187
Red-187
98Upper Deck-267
Exclusives-267
Exclusives 1 of 1-267
Gold Reserve-267
98Upper Deck MVP-76
Gold Script-76
Silver Script-76
Super Script-76
99Pacific-134
Copper-134
Emerald Green-134
Gold-134
Ice Blue-134
Premiere Date-134
Red-134
99Russian Fetisov Tribute-30
00Pacific-144
Copper-144
Gold-144
Ice Blue-144
Premiere Date-144
Brown, Dustin
00Guelph Storm-3
01Guelph Storm-23
01Guelph Storm Memorial Cup-23
02SPx Rookie Redemption-R219
02Guelph Storm-7
03BAP Memorabilia-178
Emerald-178
Gold-178
Ruby-178
Sapphire-178
Draft Redemptions-13
Future of the Game-FG-20
Super Rookies-SR11
Super Rookies Gold-SR11
Super Rookies Silver-SR11
03BAP Ultimate Memorabilia Autographs-111
Gold-111
03BAP Ultimate Mem Auto Jerseys-111
03BAP Ultimate Mem Auto Emblems-111
03BAP Ultimate Mem Auto Numbers-111
03BAP Ultimate Mem Rookie Jersey Emblems-16
03BAP Ultimate Mem Rookie Jsy Emblem Gold-16
03BAP Ultimate Mem Rookie Jersey Numbers-16
03BAP Ultimate Mem Rookie Jsy Number Gold-16
03BAP Ultimate Memorabilia Triple Threads-33
03Beehive-214
Gold-214
Silver-214
03Black Diamond-193
Black-193
Green-193
Red-193
03Bowman-146
Gold-146
03Bowman Chrome-146
Refractors-146
Gold Refractors-146
Xfractors-146
03Crown Royale-119
Red-119
Retail-119
03eTopps-49
03ITG Action-605
03ITG Toronto Spring Expo Class of 2004-4
03ITG Used Signature Series-138
Autographs Gold-138
03ITG VIP Rookie Debut-20
03O-Pee-Chee-339
03OPC Blue-339
03OPC Gold-339
03OPC Red-339
03Pacific-356
03Pacific Calder-167
03Pacific Complete-545
Red-545
03Pacific Heads-Up-119
Hobby LTD-119
Retail LTD-119
Jerseys-14
Prime Prospects-10
Prime Prospects LTD-10
03Pacific Invincible-112
Blue-112
Red-112
Retail-112
03Pacific Luxury Suite-89
Gold-89
03Pacific Quest for the Cup-119
Calder Contenders-10
03Pacific Supreme-119
03Pacific Supreme-119A
Blue-119
Red-119
Retail-119
03Parkhurst Toronto Expo Rookie Preview-PRP-9
03Parkhurst Rookie-194
Road to the NHL-RNJ-4
Road to the NHL Gold-RTN-4
Road to the NHL Emblems-RTNE-4
Road to the NHL Emblems Gold-RTNE-4
Rookie Emblems-RE-6
Rookie Emblems Gold-RE-6
Rookie Jerseys-RJ-6
Rookie Jerseys Gold-RJ-6
Rookie Numbers-RN-6
Rookie Numbers Gold-RN-6
Teammates Gold-RT7
Teammates-RT7
03Private Stock Reserve-120
Blue-120
Red-120
Retail-120
Class Act-5
03SP Authentic-150
Limited-150
Signed Patches-DB
03SP Game Used-88
Gold-88
Rookie Exclusives-RE2
03SPx-223
Radiance-223
Spectrum-223
03Titanium-210
Patches-210
03Topps-339
Blue-339
Gold-339
Red-339
03Topps C55-140
Minis-140
Minis American Back-140
Minis American Back Red-140
Minis Bazooka Back-140
Minis Brooklyn Back-140
Minis Hat Trick Back-140
Minis O Canada Back-140
Minis O Canada Back Red-140
Minis Stanley Cup Back-140
03Topps Pristine-116
03Topps Pristine-117
03Topps Pristine-118
Gold Refractor Die Cuts-116
Gold Refractor Die Cuts-117
Gold Refractor Die Cuts-118
Refractors-116
Refractors-117
Refractors-118
Mini-PM-DB
Press Plates Black-116
Press Plates Black-117
Press Plates Black-118
Press Plates Cyan-116
Press Plates Cyan-117
Press Plates Cyan-118
Press Plates Magenta-116
Press Plates Magenta-117
Press Plates Magenta-118
Press Plates Yellow-116
Press Plates Yellow-117
Press Plates Yellow-118
03Topps Traded-TT113
Blue-TT113
Gold-TT113
Red-TT113
03UD Honor Roll-183
03UD Premier Collection-72
03Upper Deck-217
Canadian Exclusives-217
HG-217
Rookie Threads-RT-2

03Upper Deck Classic Portraits-171
03Upper Deck Ice-113
Glass Parallel-113
03Upper Deck MVP-466
03Upper Deck Rookie Update-157
03Upper Deck Trilogy-177
Limited-177
03Upper Deck Victory-205
03Guelph Storm-23
04Pacific-119
Blue-119
Red-119
04Pacific Toronto Spring Expo-4
Gold-4
04SP Authentic Rookie Review-RR-DB
04SP Authentic Sign of the Times-ST-DU
04SP Authentic Sign of the Times-TS-PBF
04SP Authentic Sign of the Times-QS-BBLK
04SP Authentic Sign of the Times-FS-PAC
04AHL All-Stars-8
04AHL Top Prospects-29
04Manchester Monarchs-8
04Manchester Monarchs Tobacco-9
05ITG Heroes/Prosp Toronto Expo Parallel -83
05Be A Player Dual Signatures-RB
05Be A Player Signatures-DU
05Be A Player Signatures Gold-DU
05Beehive Matted Materials-MMDB
05Black Diamond-75
Emerald-75
Gold-75
Onyx-75
Ruby-75
Gemography-G-DB
Gemography Emerald-G-DB
Gemography Gold-G-DB
Gemography Onyx-G-DB
Gemography Ruby-G-DB
05Kings Team Issue-13
05Parkhurst-228
Facsimile Auto Parallel-228
True Colors-TCLAK
True Colors-TCLAK
05SP Authentic Scripts to Success-SSDB
05SP Authentic Sign of the Times-DB
05SP Game Used Authentic Fabrics-AF-DB
05SP Game Used Authentic Fabrics Autos-AAF-DB
05SP Game Used Authentic Fabrics Dual-BF
05SP Game Used Authentic Fabrics Gold-AF-DB
05SP Game Used Authentic Patches-AP-DB
05SP Game Used Authentic Patch Autos-AAP-DB
05SP Game Used Authentic Patches Dual-BF
05SP Game Used Awesome Authentics-AA-DU
05SP Game Used Awesome Authentics Gold-DA-DU
05SP Game Used SIGnificance-DB
05SP Game Used SIGnificance Gold-S-DB
05SP Game Used SIGnificance Extra-FB
05SP Game Used SIGnificance Extra Gold-FB
05SP Game Used Significant Numbers-SN-DB
05SP Game Used Statscriptions-ST-DB
05SPx Winning Combos-WC-BF
05SPx Winning Combos Autographs-AWC-BF
05SPx Winning Combos Spectrum-WC-BF
05UD Artifacts-47
Blue-47
Gold-47
Green-47
Pewter-47
Red-47
Auto Facts-AF-DU
Auto Facts Blue-AF-DU
Auto Facts Copper-AF-DU
Auto Facts Pewter-AF-DU
Auto Facts Silver-AF-DU
Frozen Artifacts-FA-DU
Frozen Artifacts Autographed-FA-DU
Frozen Artifacts Copper-FA-DU
Frozen Artifacts Dual-FAD-DU
Frozen Artifacts Dual Autographed-FAD-DU
Frozen Artifacts Dual Copper-FAD-DU
Frozen Artifacts Dual Gold-FAD-DU
Frozen Artifacts Dual Maroon-FAD-DU
Frozen Artifacts Dual Pewter-FAD-DU
Frozen Artifacts Dual Silver-FAD-DU
Frozen Artifacts Gold-FA-DU
Frozen Artifacts Maroon-FA-DU
Frozen Artifacts Patches-FP-DU
Frozen Artifacts Patches Autographed-FP-DU
Frozen Artifacts Patches Dual-FPD-DU
Frozen Artifacts Patches Dual Autos-FPD-DU
Frozen Artifacts Patches Pewter-FP-DU
Frozen Artifacts Patches Silver-FP-DU
Frozen Artifacts Pewter-FA-DU
Frozen Artifacts Silver-FA-DU
Gold Autographed-47
Remarkable Artifacts-RA-DU
Remarkable Artifacts Dual-RA-DU
05UD Powerplay Power Marks-PMDB
05Ultimate Collection Endorsed Emblems-EEDB
05Ultra-96
Gold-96
Fresh Ink-FI-DB
Fresh Ink Blue-FI-DB
Ice-96
05Upper Deck-91
HG Glossy-91
Jerseys-J-BR
NHL Generations-DGB
Notable Numbers-N-DUB
Patches-P-DBN
Ice Fresh Ice-FIDB
Ice Fresh Ice Glass-FIDB
Ice Fresh Ice Glass Patches-FIPDB
05Upper Deck MVP-183
Gold-183
Platinum-183
05Upper Deck Trilogy Scripts-SFS-DB
05Upper Deck Toronto Fall Expo-91
05Manchester Monarchs-26
05ITG Heroes and Prospects-83
Aspiring-ASP11
Autographs-A-DBN
Jerseys-GUJ-17
Jerseys Gold-GUJ-17
Emblems-GUE-17
Emblems Gold-GUE-17
Numbers-GUN-17
Numbers Gold-GUN-17
Making the Bigs-MTB-11
Shooting Stars-AS-12
06Be A Player-151
Autographs-151
Signatures-DB
Signatures 25-166
06Flair Showcase Inks-IDU
06Flair Showcase Wave of the Future-WF17
06Fleer Signing Day-SDBR
06O-Pee-Chee-226
Rainbow-226
06Panini Stickers-288
06SP Game Used SIGnificance-SDB
06Ultra-95
Gold Medallion-95
Ice Medallion-95
06Upper Deck Arena Giveaways-LAK3
06Upper Deck-93
Exclusives Parallel-93
High Gloss Parallel-93
Generations Duals-G2GB
Generations Patches Dual-G2PGB
Masterpieces-93
06Upper Deck MVP-140
Gold Script-140
Super Script-140
06Upper Deck Trilogy Combo Clearcut Autographs-C3FCB
06Upper Deck Trilogy Honorary Scripted Patches-HSPDB
06Upper Deck Trilogy Honorary Scripted Swatches-HSSDB
06Upper Deck Trilogy Ice Scripts-ISBR
06Upper Deck Trilogy Scripts-TSBR
06Upper Deck Victory-90
06Upper Deck Victory Black-90
06Upper Deck Victory Gold-90

Brown, Eric
93Waterloo Black Hawks-4
98Youngstown State-3

Brown, George A.
34Beehive Group I Photos-140
37O-Pee-Chee V304E-157

Brown, George V
83Hall of Fame Postcards-L2
85Hall of Fame-152

Brown, Greg
90OPC Premier-11
90Pro Set-590
90Sabres Blue Shield-4
90Sabres Campbell's-4
90Score Rookie/Traded-96T
91Score Canadian Bilingual-518
91Score Canadian English-518
91ProCards-18
91Rochester Americans Dunkin' Donuts-1
91Rochester Americans Kodak-5
91Rochester Americans Postcards-3
92Rochester Americans Dunkin' Donuts-2
92Rochester Americans Kodak-4
93San Diego Gulls-4
95Swedish Leaf-287
95Swedish Upper Deck-176
96Swiss HNL-7
98German DEL-94
99German DEL-120

Brown, Ivan
95UK Guildford Flames-18

Brown, Jamie
95Halifax Mooseheads-4
96Halifax Mooseheads I-4
96Halifax Mooseheads II-4

Brown, Jared
06Lincoln Stars-7
06Lincoln Stars Traded-10T
06Lincoln Stars Upper DeckÂ Signature Series -5

Brown, Jason
91Air Canada SJHL-B46
92Saskatchewan JHL-18

Brown, Jeff
84Sudbury Wolves-7
85Nordiques McDonald's-2
85Nordiques Team Issue-3
85Sudbury Wolves-20
86Nordiques General Foods-3
86Nordiques McDonald's-3
86Nordiques Team Issue-1
87Nordiques General Foods-2
87Nordiques Team Issue-17
88Nordiques General Foods-4
88Nordiques Team Issue-5
88O-Pee-Chee-201
88O-Pee-Chee Stickers-192
88Panini Stickers-349
89Blues Kodak-21
89Kraft-28
89Nordiques Team Issue-3
89Nordiques General Foods-2
89Nordiques Police-1
89O-Pee-Chee-28
89O-Pee-Chee Stickers-193
89Panini Stickers-325
89Topps-28
90Blues Kodak-3
90Bowman-25
Tiffany-25
90O-Pee-Chee-220
90O-Pee-Chee-295
90Panini Stickers-274
90Pro Set-260
90Score-41
Canadian-41
90Topps-220
90Topps-295
Tiffany-295
90Upper Deck-191
French-191
91Pro Set Platinum-114
91Blues Postcards-3
91Bowman-385
91O-Pee-Chee-222
91Panini Stickers-23
91Parkhurst-156
French-156
91Pinnacle-72
French-72
91Pro Set-212
French-212
91Score American-276
91Score Canadian Bilingual-496
91Score Canadian English-496
91Stadium Club-148
91Topps-222
91Upper Deck-211
French-211
92Bowman-247
92Panini Stickers-25
92Panini Stickers French-25
92Pinnacle-13
French-13
92Pro Set-158
92Score-220
Canadian-220
92Stadium Club-263
92Topps-174
Gold-174G
92Ultra-183
92Quebec Pee-Wee Tournament-302
93Donruss-293
93Donruss-499
93Leaf-29
93OPC Premier-363
93OPC Premier-381
Gold-363
Gold-381
93Panini Stickers-165
93Parkhurst-173
Emerald Ice-173
93Pinnacle-39
Canadian-39
93PowerPlay-207
93Score-194
Canadian-194
93Stadium Club-188
Members Only Master Set-188
OPC-188
First Day Issue-188
First Day Issue OPC-188
Finest-2
Finest Members Only-2
93Topps/OPC Premier-363
93Topps/OPC Premier-381
Gold-363
Gold-381
93Ultra-223
93Upper Deck-130
SP-135
94Canada Games NHL POGS-313
94Canucks Program Inserts-4
94Donruss-109
94EA Sports-121
94Flair-188
94Fleer-222
94Leaf-247
94Leaf Limited-18
94OPC Premier-272
94OPC Premier-487
Special Effects-272
Special Effects-487
94Parkhurst-244
Gold-244
Vintage-V45
94Pinnacle-34
Artist's Proofs-34
Rink Collection-34
94Select-110
Gold-110
94SP-123
Die Cuts-123
94Topps/OPC Premier-272
94Topps/OPC Premier-487
Special Effects-272
Special Effects-487
94Ultra-221
94Upper Deck-34
Electric Ice-34
SP Inserts-SP81
SP Inserts Die Cuts-SP81
95Bashan Super Stickers-126
95Canada Games NHL POGS-276
95Canucks Building the Dream Art-8
95Collector's Choice-301
Player's Club-301
Player's Club Platinum-301
95Donruss-183
95Donruss Elite-78
Die Cut Stars-78
Die Cut Uncut-78
95Emotion-177
95Hoyle Western Playing Cards-6
95Imperial Stickers-126
95Leaf-245
95Metal-148
95Panini Stickers-297
95Parkhurst International-365
Emerald Ice-365
95Pinnacle-29
Artist's Proofs-29
Rink Collection-29
95Playoff One on One-206
95Score-23
Black Ice Artist's Proofs-23
Black Ice-23
95SkyBox Impact-166
95Stadium Club Members Only-23
95Topps-268
OPC Inserts-268
95Ultra-165
Gold Medallion-165
95Upper Deck-352
Electric Ice-352
Electric Ice Gold-352
Special Edition-SE84
Special Edition Gold-SE84
95Sarnia Sting-17
96Collector's Choice-120
96Fleer Picks-64
96Metal Universe-65
96Pinnacle-12
Artist's Proofs-12
Foil-12
Premium Stock-12
Rink Collection-12
96Playoff One on One-396
96Score-87
Artist's Proofs-87
Dealer's Choice Artist's Proofs-87
Special Artist's Proofs-87
Golden Blades-87
96SkyBox Impact-51
96Team Out-83
96Ultra-72
Gold Medallion-72
96Upper Deck-73
96Whalers Kid's Club-23
97Be A Player-89
Autographs-89
Autographs Die-Cuts-89
Autographs Prismatic Die-Cuts-89
97Hurricanes Team Issue-1
97Pacific Dynagon Best Kept Secrets-16
97Sudbury Wolves Anniversary-2
98Pacific-438
Ice Blue-438
Red-438
98Paramount-243
Copper-243
Emerald Green-243
Holo-Electric-243
Ice Blue-243
Silver-243
98Bowman CHL-4
Golden Anniversary-4
OPC International-4
98Bowman Chrome CHL-4
Golden Anniversary-4
Golden Anniversary Refractors-4
OPC International-4
OPC International Refractors-4
Refractors-4

Brown, Jeffrey
94Sarnia Sting-21
95Bowman Draft Prospects-P5
95Slapshot-347
95Slapshot-439
95Classic-96
98Hartford Wolf Pack-2
99Charlotte Checkers-20

Brown, Jeremy
92Western Michigan Broncos-6
93Western Michigan Broncos-5
97Wheeling Nailers-6
97Wheeling Nailers Photo Pack-6
99Providence Bruins-5
00Providence Bruins-16

Brown, Jerry
34Beehive Group I Photos-92

Brown, Jim
907th Inn. Sketch OHL-298
917th Inn. Sketch OHL-288
93Anaheim Bullfrogs RHI-3
93Owen Sound Platers-2
94Hampton Roads Admirals-18
96Knoxville Cherokees-14
96Knoxville Cherokees-P2
97Quad-City Mallards-20
01Kalamazoo K-Wings-8
03Florida Everblades-3

Brown, Joel
82Kingston Canadians-4
83Kingston Canadians-18
84Kitchener Rangers-14

Brown, Josh
04Penticton Vees-3

Brown, Justin
93Quebec Pee-Wee Tournament-665
01Michigan Tech Huskies-2

Brown, Keith
79Blackhawks Postcards-1
80Blackhawks Postcards-1
80Blackhawks White Border-3
80O-Pee-Chee-98
80Topps-98
81Blackhawks Borderless Postcards-2
81Blackhawks Brown Background-1
81O-Pee-Chee-55
81O-Pee-Chee Stickers-115
81Topps-W67
82Blackhawks Postcards-2
82O-Pee-Chee-62
83Blackhawks Postcards-2
83O-Pee-Chee-98
84O-Pee-Chee-33
84O-Pee-Chee Stickers-28
84Topps-28
85Blackhawks Team Issue-2
85O-Pee-Chee-59
85Topps-59
86Blackhawks Coke-3
86O-Pee-Chee-206
87Blackhawks Coke-3
87O-Pee-Chee-47
87Panini Stickers-233
87Topps-47
88Blackhawks Coke-2
89Blackhawks Coke-23
90Blackhawks Coke-23
90Bowman-10
Tiffany-10
90O-Pee-Chee-276
90Panini Stickers-192
90Pro Set-49
90Score-161
Canadian-161
90Topps-276
Tiffany-276
91Blackhawks Coke-2
91Panini Stickers-21
91Parkhurst-261
French-261
91Pinnacle-154
91Pinnacle-370
French-154
French-370
91Pro Set-371
French-371
91Score American-76
91Score Canadian Bilingual-76
91Score Canadian English-76
92Blackhawks Coke-16
92Bowman-4
92O-Pee-Chee-48
92Panini Stickers-13
92Panini Stickers French-13
92Parkhurst-274
Emerald Ice-274
92Pinnacle-92
French-92
92Score-68
Canadian-68
92Stadium Club-274
92Topps-52
Gold-52G
93Pinnacle-422
Canadian-422
93Score-384
93Score-569
Gold-569
Canadian-384
Canadian-569
Canadian Gold-569
93Stadium Club-58
93Stadium Club-281
Members Only Master Set-58
Members Only Master Set-281
OPC-58
First Day Issue-58
First Day Issue-281
First Day Issue OPC-58
93Ultra-322
94Fleer-78
94Pinnacle-368
Artist's Proofs-368
Rink Collection-368
94Ultra-295
04UD Legendary Signatures-96
Autographs-KB
Rearguard Retrospectives-DWKB

Brown, Kevin
93Detroit Jr. Red Wings-17
93Classic-17
93Classic-33
93Classic Four-Sport *-257
Gold-257
94Finest-15
Super Team Winners-15
Refractors-15
94Leaf-457
94Leaf Limited-7
94Parkhurst SE-SE77
Gold-SE77
94Upper Deck-249
Electric Ice-249
94Classic-36
Gold-36
Tri-Cards-T31
95Donruss-168
95Leaf-38
95Pinnacle-215
Artist's Proofs-215
Rink Collection-215
95Score-301
Black Ice Artist's Proofs-301
Black Ice-301
95Phoenix Roadrunners-5
95Images-28
Gold-28
96Whalers Kid's Club-26
96Springfield Falcons-44
98Upper Deck MVP-84
Gold Script-84
Silver Script-84
Super Script-84
99Hamilton Bulldogs-15
00UK Sekonda Superleague-98
01Hamilton Bulldogs-5
02Florida Everblades-5

Brown, Kevin (Minors)
907th Inn. Sketch OHL-255
917th Inn. Sketch OHL-108
917th Inn. Sketch OHL-218
94Dayton Bombers-12
95Dayton Bombers-7
96Collector's Edge Ice-182
Prism-182
97Toledo Storm-22
98Port Huron Border Cats-13

Brown, Kurt
97Wheeling Nailers-19
97Wheeling Nailers Photo Pack-19

Brown, Larry
70Esso Power Players-130
71Sargent Promotions Stamps-159
71Toronto Sun-190
72Sargent Promotions Stamps-95
74O-Pee-Chee NHL-271
75O-Pee-Chee NHL-377
76O-Pee-Chee NHL-355
77O-Pee-Chee NHL-289
78O-Pee-Chee-361
79O-Pee-Chee-323

Brown, Lisa
94Classic Women of Hockey-W24

Brown, Marc
92Quebec Pee-Wee Tournament-1886
96Spokane Chiefs-22
97Spokane Chiefs-13
98Prince Albert Raiders-2
00Worcester Icecats-6
01Worcester Icecats-2
02Worcester IceCats-11
03Worcester Ice Cats-16
04German Augsburg Panthers Postcards-7
04German DEL-25

Brown, Mike
95Red Deer Rebels-5
96Red Deer Rebels-18
97Bowman CHL-126
OPC-126
Autographs-126
Bowman's Best-13
Bowman's Best Atomic Refractors-13
Bowman's Best Refractor-13
98Kamloops Blazers-4
99Syracuse Crunch-24
99Bowman CHL-106
Gold-106
OPC International-106
00Titanium Draft Day Edition-174
00Titanium Draft Day Promos-174
00Kansas City Blades-14
01O-Pee-Chee-297
01O-Pee-Chee Premier Parallel-297
01SPx-130
01Topps-297
OPC Parallel-297
01UD Top Shelf-65
01UD Top Shelf-65B
01Upper Deck-210
Exclusives-210
01Upper Deck MVP-218
03Michigan Wolverines-19
03Saginaw Spirit-4
04Michigan Wolverines-8
04Norfolk Admirals-6
04Saginaw Spirit-23
05Manitoba Moose-4
05Norfolk Admirals-15
06Hot Prospects-144
Red Hot-144
White Hot-144
06O-Pee-Chee-582
Rainbow-582
06SP Game Used Rookie Exclusives Autographs-REBR
06The Cup-92
Autographed Rookie Masterpiece Pressplates-92
Gold Rainbow Autographed Rookies-92
Masterpiece Pressplates (Marquee Rookies)-582
Rookies Black-92
Rookies Platinum-92
06Upper Deck-454
Exclusives Parallel-454
High Gloss Parallel-454
Masterpieces-454
06Manitoba Moose-9

Brown, Mike (Goalie)
03Saginaw Spirit-4
04Saginaw Spirit-23
06Hot Prospects-144
Red Hot-144
White Hot-144
06O-Pee-Chee-582
Rainbow-582
06SP Game Used Rookie Exclusives Autographs-REBR
06The Cup-92
Autographed Rookie Masterpiece Pressplates-92
Gold Rainbow Autographed Rookies-92
Masterpiece Pressplates (Marquee Rookies)-582
Rookies Black-92
Rookies Platinum-92
06Upper Deck-454
Exclusives Parallel-454
High Gloss Parallel-454
Masterpieces-454

Brown, Mike (RW)
03Michigan Wolverines-19
04Michigan Wolverines-8
05Manitoba Moose-4
06Manitoba Moose-9

Brown, Minors
907th Inn. Sketch OHL-255
917th Inn. Sketch OHL-108
917th Inn. Sketch OHL-218
94Dayton Bombers-12
95Dayton Bombers-7
96Collector's Edge Ice-182
Prism-182
97Toledo Storm-22
98Port Huron Border Cats-13

Brown, Newell
84Fredericton Express-16
90Michigan Tech Huskies-2

Brown, Nicholas
93Quebec Pee-Wee Tournament-1087

Brown, Paul
02Kamloops Blazers-4
03Kamloops Blazers-14
04Milwaukee Admirals-7
05Milwaukee Admirals Choice-3
05Milwaukee Admirals Pepsi-4
06Rockford IceHogs -5

Brown, Rich
94Sarnia Sting-27
95Slapshot-354
95Sarnia Sting-24
96St. John's Maple Leafs-4
97St. John's Maple Leafs-4

Brown, Rick
00Sarnia Sting-5

Brown, Rob
84Kamloops Blazers-4
85Kamloops Blazers-4
86Kamloops Blazers-3
87Penguins Kodak-2
88O-Pee-Chee-109
88O-Pee-Chee Stickers-63
88O-Pee-Chee Stickers-131
88O-Pee-Chee Stickers-237
88Panini Stickers-336
88Topps-109
89O-Pee-Chee-193
89O-Pee-Chee Stickers-117
89O-Pee-Chee Stickers-163
89O-Pee-Chee Stickers-236
89O-Pee-Chee Stickers-256
89Panini Stickers-186
89Panini Stickers-310
89Penguins Coke/Elby's-2
89Penguins Foodland-1
89Topps-193
89Topps Sticker Inserts-8
90Bowman-202
Tiffany-202
90Bowman Hat Tricks-3
Tiffany-3
90O-Pee-Chee-19
90Panini Stickers-128
90Pro Set-229
90Score-105
Canadian-105
90Score Hottest/Rising Stars-51
90Score Young Superstars-5
90Topps-19
Tiffany-19
90Upper Deck-142
French-142
90Whalers Jr. 7-Eleven-3
91Pro Set Platinum-42
91Bowman-16
91O-Pee-Chee-83
91Panini Stickers-315
91Parkhurst-60
91Parkhurst-258
French-60
French-258
91Pinnacle-141
French-141
91Pro Set-80
91Pro Set-606
French-80
French-606
91Score American-246
91Score Canadian Bilingual-466
91Score Canadian English-466
91Stadium Club-200
91Topps-83
91Upper Deck-198
French-198
91Whalers Jr. 7-Eleven-4
92Blackhawks Coke-8
92Bowman-168
92O-Pee-Chee-170
92Panini Stickers-10
92Panini Stickers French-10
92Pinnacle-331
French-331
92Score-244
Canadian-244
Sharpshooters-22
Sharpshooters Canadian-22
92Stadium Club-295
92Topps-72
Gold-72G
92Ultra-33
92Upper Deck-387
94Leaf-540
94Ultra-304
94Upper Deck-403
Electric Ice-403
96Collector's Edge Future Legends-13
96Collector's Edge Ice-104
Prism-104
QuantumMotion-4
97Be A Player-48
Autographs-48
Autographs Die-Cuts-48
Autographs Prismatic Die-Cuts-48
97Pacific Omega-183
Copper-183
Dark Gray-183
Emerald Green-183
Gold-183
Ice Blue-183
97Score Penguins-19
Platinum-19
Premier-19
98Be A Player-265
Press Release-265
98BAP Gold-265
98BAP Autographs-265
98BAP Autographs Gold-265
98Pacific-349
Ice Blue-349
Red-349
99Pacific-335
Copper-335
Emerald Green-335
Gold-335
Ice Blue-335
Premiere Date-335
Red-335
99Ultimate Victory-71
1/1-71
Parallel-71
Parallel 100-71
00Chicago Wolves-4
01Chicago Wolves-3
02BAP Sig Series Auto Buybacks 1998-265
02Chicago Wolves-3

Brown, Ryan
917th Inn. Sketch WHL-127
93Classic Four-Sport *-218
Gold-218
95Atlanta Knights-4
00Columbus Cottonmouths-2

Brown, Scott
97Dubuque Fighting Saints-22
00Connecticut Huskies-4

Brown, Sean
95Sarnia Sting-22

Brown, Sean (DEF)
95Slapshot-352
95Classic-20
95Classic-83
96Oilers Postcards-8
97Donruss-208
Press Proofs Silver-208
Press Proofs Gold-208
98Pacific Omega-91
Red-91
Opening Day Issue-91
98Upper Deck-276
Exclusives-276
Exclusives 1 of 1-276
Gold Reserve-276
99BAP Millennium-101
Emerald-101
Ruby-101
Sapphire-101
Signatures-101
Signatures Gold-101
00UD Heroes-50
01BAP Memorabilia-486
Emerald-486
Ruby-486
Sapphire-486
02BAP Sig Series Auto Buybacks 1999-101
02Pacific-24
Blue-24
Red-24
03Devils Team Issue-2
05Devils Team Issue-26

Brown, Sean (FWD)
907th Inn. Sketch OHL-203
91Oshawa Generals-12
92Oshawa Generals Sheet-3
93Oshawa Generals-8
94Knoxville Cherokees-8
96Roanoke Express-18

Brown, Shayne
05Medicine Hat Tigers-7
06Medicine Hat Tigers-4

Brown, Steve
95Vancouver VooDoo RHI-20
99UK Hull Thunder-18

Brown, Tom
94Sarnia Sting-6
95Slapshot-335
95Sarnia Sting-5
96Sudbury Wolves-4
96Sudbury Wolves Police-6
98Charlotte Checkers-5
99UK Guildford Flames-7
00UK Guildford Flames-2

Brown, UK
01UK Sheffield Steelers-8
02UK Sheffield Steelers-4
03UK Cardiff Devils-10
04San Antonio Rampage-16

Brown, Walter A
83Hall of Fame Postcards-F2
85Hall of Fame-78

Browne, Bill
96Sault Ste. Marie Greyhounds-2
96Sault Ste. Marie Greyhounds Autographed-2
99Kitchener Rangers-7

Browne, Cecil
23Crescent Selkirks-7
23V128-1 Paulin's Candy-5
24Crescent Selkirks-6
25Dominion Chocolates-103
28V128-2 Paulin's Candy-63

Brownlee, Brent
907th Inn. Sketch OHL-128
917th Inn. Sketch OHL-364

Brownlee, Pat
98Charlotte Checkers-6
00Lubbock Cotton Kings-6
01Austin Ice Bats-3
02Austin Ice Bats-3
03Austin Ice Bats-2

Brownlee, Scott
06Regina Pats-2

Brownschidle, Jack
78Blues Postcards-6
78O-Pee-Chee-379
79O-Pee-Chee-278
80O-Pee-Chee-101
80Topps-101
81O-Pee-Chee-302
82O-Pee-Chee-300
82Post Cereal-17
83O-Pee-Chee-311
84Whalers Junior Wendy's-1
85Whalers Junior Wendy's-1

Broz, Jiri
98Czech OFS-415
99Czech OFS-279
00Czech OFS-25
01Czech OFS-136
02Czech OFS Plus-171

Bru, Dustin
01Brandon Wheat Kings-2

Brubaker, Jeff
81Canadiens Postcards-4
84Maple Leafs Postcards-5
85Maple Leafs Postcards-5
88Oilers Tenth Anniversary-19
88ProCards AHL-18

Bruce, David
82Kitchener Rangers-11
83Kitchener Rangers-11
84Fredericton Express-7
85Fredericton Express-2
86Fredericton Express-3
87Canucks Shell Oil-5
88Canucks Mohawk-7
88Panini Stickers-137
89ProCards IHL-173
90Blues Kodak-4
90ProCards AHL/IHL-86
91Pro Set Platinum-227
91Parkhurst-384
French-384
91Pro Set-485
French-485
91Score Canadian Bilingual-644
91Score Canadian English-644
92Bowman-358
92O-Pee-Chee-246
92Panini Stickers-126
92Panini Stickers French-126
92Pinnacle-159
French-159
92Pro Set-170
92Score-301
Canadian-301
92Stadium Club-284
92Topps-448
Gold-448G
92Ultra-191
92Upper Deck-102
93Kansas City Blades-7
94Kansas City Blades-8
95Kansas City Blades-4
96Kansas City Blades-2
97Kansas City Blades Magnets-3
98German DEL-69

Bruce, Kyle
00Prince Albert Raiders-3
01Prince Albert Raiders-2
02Prince Albert Raiders-2
03Vancouver Giants-12
06Idaho Steelheads-2

Bruckl, Franz
94German First League-247

Bruckler, Bernd
03Wisconsin Badgers-4
04Wisconsin Badgers-8
06Finnish Cardset-181
Between the Pipes-2

Brucks, Bryn
03Swift Current Broncos-1

Brucks, Derrick
91Air Canada SJHL-E41

Bruderer, Ernst
93Swiss HNL-7
95Swiss HNL-4
02Swiss HNL-464

Bruderer, Martin
93Swiss HNL-10
95Swiss HNL-8
96Swiss HNL-8
96Swiss HNL-518
96Swiss HNL-531
98Swiss Power Play Stickers-107
99Swiss Panini Stickers-107
00Swiss Panini Stickers-318

Brudzewski, Steve
03Bowling Green Falcons-10

Bruegger, Florian
02Swiss HNL-351

Bruetsch, Warren
93Swiss HNL-377
95Swiss HNL-300
96Swiss HNL-284

Bruggemann, Dieter
94German First League-440

Bruggemann, Lars
94German DEL-284
95German DEL-297
96German DEL-324
98German DEL-29
99German DEL-135
99German DEL-378
01German Upper Deck-62
02German DEL City Press-153
03German DEL-140
04German DEL-146
04German DEL Update-344
04German Hannover Scorpions Postcards-4

Brugger, Marius
01Swiss HNL-452

Bruijsten, Kevin
05Dutch Vadeko Flyers -1

Bruininks, Brett
98Florida Everblades-1

Bruininks, Brian
92Dallas Freeze-5
93Dallas Freeze-4

Bruinsma, Marcel
04Langley Hornets-5
06Westside Warriors-23

Bruk, David
94Czech APS Extraliga-86
95Czech APS Extraliga-44
95Finnish Semic World Championships-157
96Czech APS Extraliga-36
97Czech APS Extraliga-279
97Czech DS Stickers-106
98Czech DS Stickers-78
99German EV Landshut-22

Brulc, Dusan
93Quebec Pee-Wee Tournament-1782

Brule, Eric
907th Inn. Sketch QMJHL-26
91ProCards-302
917th Inn. Sketch Memorial Cup-28
92Fort Worth Fire-4
97New Orleans Brass-21
98Abilene Aviators-20

Brule, Gilbert
03Vancouver Giants-14
04SP Authentic Rookie Redemptions-RR9
04Vancouver Giants-13
04ITG Heroes and Prospects-76
Autographs-GB
04ITG Heroes/Prospects Toronto Expo '05-76
04ITG Heroes/Prospects Expo Heroes/Pros-76
05ITG Heroes/Prosp Toronto Expo Parallel -164
05Beehive-106
Beige -106
Blue -106
Gold-106
Red -106
Matte-106
Signature Scrapbook-SSGB
05Black Diamond-190
Emerald-190
Gold-190
Onyx-190
Ruby-190
05Hot Prospects-233
En Fuego-233
Hot Materials-HMGB
White Hot-233
05Parkhurst-622
Facsimile Auto Parallel-622
True Colors-TCCLB
True Colors-TCCLB

05SP Authentic-151
Limited-151
Exquisite Endorsements-EEGB
Octographs-OR
Rarefied Rookies-RRGB
Rookie Authentics-RAGB
Sign of the Times Duals-DNB
Six Star Signatures-SSRO
05SP Game Used-139
Autographs-139
Gold-139
Auto Draft-AD-GB
Game Gear-GG-GB
Game Gear Autographs-AG-GB
Rookie Exclusives-GB
Rookie Exclusives Silver-RE-GB
Significant Numbers-SN-GB
05SPx-156
Spectrum-156
Xcitement Rookies-XR-GB
Xcitement Rookies Gold-XR-GB
Xcitement Rookies Spectrum-XR-GB
05The Cup-107
Autographed Rookie Patches Gold Rainbow-107
Black Rainbow Rookies-107
Dual NHL Shields Autographs-ADSRG
Masterpiece Pressplates (Artifacts)-209
Masterpiece Pressplates (Bee Hive)-106
Masterpiece Pressplates (Black Diamond)-190
Masterpiece Pressplates (Ice)-101
Masterpiece Pressplates (MVP)-395
Masterpiece Pressplates (Power Play)-164
Masterpiece Pressplates Rookie Upd Auto-264
Masterpiece Pressplates SPA Autos-151
Masterpiece Pressplates (SP Game Used)-139
Masterpiece Pressplates SPx Autos-156
Masterpiece Pressplates (Trilogy)-187
Masterpiece Pressplates Ult Coll Autos-93
Masterpiece Pressplates (Victory)-255
Masterpiece Pressplates Autographs-107
Platinum Rookies-107
05UD Artifacts-209
Gold-RED9
05UD PowerPlay-164
05UD Rookie Class-22
05Ultimate Collection-93
Autographed Patches-93
Autographed Shields-93
Jerseys-JGB
Jerseys Dual-DJNB
Marquee Attractions-MA49
Marquee Attractions Signatures-SMA49
Premium Patches-PPGB
Premium Swatches-PSGB
Ultimate Debut Threads Jerseys-DTJGB
Ultimate Debut Threads Jerseys Autos-DAJGB
Ultimate Debut Threads Patches-DTPGB
Ultimate Debut Threads Patches Autos-DAPGB
Ultimate Patches-PGB
Ultimate Patches Dual-DPNB
Ultimate Signatures-USGB
Ultimate Signatures Foursomes-UFSOBP
Ultimate Signatures Logos-SLGB
Ultimate Signatures Pairings-UPRG
Ultimate Signatures Trios-UTNBZ
05Ultra-255
Gold-255
Fresh Ink-FI-GB
Fresh Ink Blue-FI-GB
Ice-255
Rookie Uniformity Jerseys-RU-GB
Rookie Uniformity Jersey Autographs-ARU-GB
Rookie Uniformity Patches-RUP-GB
Rookie Uniformity Patch Autographs-ARP-GB
05Upper Deck-446
Majestic Materials-MMGB
Rookie Ink-RIGB
05Upper Deck Rookie Showcase-RS9
05Upper Deck Rookie Showcase Promos-RS9
05Upper Deck Rookie Threads-RTGB
05Upper Deck Rookie Threads Autographs-ARTGB
05Upper Deck Stars in the Making-SM11
05Upper Deck Ice-101
Cool Threads-CTGB
Cool Threads Autographs-ACTGB
Cool Threads Glass-CTGB
Cool Threads Patches-CTPGB
Cool Threads Patch Autographs-CAPGB
Glacial Graphs-GGGB
Premieres Auto Patches-AIPGB
Signature Swatches-SSGB
05Upper Deck MVP-395
Gold-395
Platinum-395
Rookie Breakthrough-RB4
05Upper Deck Rookie Update-264
05Upper Deck Trilogy-187
05Upper Deck Victory-255
Black-255
Gold-255
Silver-255
05Vancouver Giants-5
05ITG Heroes and Prospects-164
Autographs-A-GB
Autographs-DA-BC
CHL Grads-CG-2
CHL Grads Gold-CG-2
Complete Jerseys-CJ-2
Complete Jerseys Gold-CJ-2
Complete Logos-CHL-12
Jerseys-GUJ-56
Jerseys Gold-GUJ-56
Emblems-GUE-56
Emblems Gold-GUE-56
Numbers-GUN-56
Numbers Gold-GUN-56
Nameplates-N-34
Nameplates Gold-N-34
Spectrum-STM-06
Spectrum Gold-STM-06
06Be A Player-150
Autographs-150
Signatures-GB
Signatures Duals-DBV
Signatures Trios-TFVB
06Be A Player Portraits-34
First Exposures-FEGB
06Beehive-73
Matte-73
06Black Diamond-99
Black-99
Gold-99
Ruby-99
06Hot Prospects Hotagraphs-HGB
06ITG Ultimate Memorabilia-55
Artist Proof-55
Future Star-9
Future Star Gold-9
Future Star Autos-23
Future Star Autos Gold-23
Future Star Patches Autos-23
Future Star Patches Autos Gold-23
R.O.Y. Autos-2
R.O.Y. Autos Gold-2
R.O.Y. Emblems-2
R.O.Y. Emblems Gold-2
R.O.Y. Jerseys-2
R.O.Y. Jerseys Gold-2
R.O.Y. Numbers-2
R.O.Y. Numbers Gold-2
06O-Pee-Chee-147
Rainbow-147
Autographs-A-GB
06SP Authentic Sign of the Times-STGB
06SP Authentic Sign of the Times Duals-STNB
06SPx SPxcitement-X28
06SPx SPxcitement Spectrum-X28
06UD Toronto Fall Expo Priority Signings -PSGB
06Ultimate Collection Signatures-US-GB
06Upper Deck Arena Giveaways-CLB5
06Upper Deck-309
Exclusives Parallel-309
High Gloss Parallel-309
Masterpieces-309
Oversized Wal-Mart Exclusives-309
Signatures-SGB
06Upper Deck MVP-83
Gold Script-83
Super Script-83
06Upper Deck Sweet Shot Signature Shots/Saves-SSGB
06Upper Deck Sweet Shot Signature Shots/Saves Sticks-SSSGB
06Upper Deck Trilogy Combo Clearcut Autographs-C3NZB
06Upper Deck Victory-241
06Upper Deck Victory Next In Line-NL18
06ITG Heroes and Prospects-99
Autographs-AGBR
Quad Emblems-QE05
Quad Emblems-QE16
Quad Emblems Gold-QE05
07Upper Deck Victory-129
Black-129
Gold-129

Brule, Steve
96Albany River Rats-3
97Albany River Rats-3
98Albany River Rats-3
99Albany River Rats-3
00SPx-101
Spectrum-101
00Upper Deck-221
Exclusives Tier 1-221
Exclusives Tier 2-221
00Manitoba Moose-5
01Cincinnati Mighty Ducks-7
02Hershey Bears-3
03Hershey Bears-14
03Hershey Bears Patriot News-3
04German DEL-224
04German Krefeld Penguins Postcards-1
05German DEL-41
05German DEL-345

Brull, Olaf
94German First League-575

Brumby, David
95Lethbridge Hurricanes-4
99ECHL All-Star Southern Conference-6
00Cleveland Lumberjacks-12
00Jackson Bandits Promos-1
02South Carolina Stingrays RBI-206
03South Carolina Stingrays-323

Brummer, Johan
89Swedish Semic Elitserien Stickers-44
90Swedish Semic Elitserien Stickers-194
91Swedish Semic Elitserien Stickers-273
92Swedish Semic Elitserien Stickers-296
93Swedish Semic Elitserien-261
94Swedish Leaf-95
95Swedish Leaf-229
95Swedish Upper Deck-93

Brummit, Nathan
06Kotoks Oilers-1

Brumwell, Murray
82Birmingham South Stars-5
83O-Pee-Chee-228
83O-Pee-Chee Stickers-179
83Topps Stickers-179
88ProCards AHL-338
89ProCards AHL-9
90ProCards AHL/IHL-435

Bruna, Miroslav
95Czech APS Extraliga-197
96Czech APS Extraliga-332
97Czech DS Stickers-158
98Czech OFS-60

Brunchk, Bedrich
71Finnish Suomi Stickers-21
72Finnish Semic World Championship-35
72Swedish Semic World Championship-35
74Swedish Semic World Champ Stickers-74

Brundin, Gunnar Nilas
56Swedish Alfabilder-38

Bruneau, Paul
89 7th Inn. Sketch OHL-141

Bruneel, Jason
93Quebec Pee-Wee Tournament-1305

Brunel, Craig
96Prince Albert Raiders-3
97Prince Albert Raiders-3
98Prince Albert Raiders-3
00Rochester Americans-5
02Reading Royals RBI Sports-170
03Florence Pride-146

Brunel, Ryan
95Neepewa Natives-2

Brunelle, Jean-Francois
01Thetford Mines Coyotes-7
02Thetford Mines Coyotes-4

Brunelle, Mathieu
00Victoriaville Tigres-20
Signed-20
02Hull Olympiques-20
03Hull Olympiques Memorial Cup-2
03Trenton Titans-356
05Bakersfield Condors-23

Brunet, Benoit
87Hull Olympiques-5
88ProCards AHL-278
89ProCards AHL-186
90Canadiens Postcards-3
91Upper Deck-469
French-469
92Bowman-414
92Canadiens Postcards-3
92Durivage Panini-19
92O-Pee-Chee-352
92Stadium Club-134
92Topps-137
Gold-137G
92Ultra-101
92Upper Deck-80
93Canadiens Molson-2
93Canadiens Postcards-3
93Donruss-166
93Durivage Score-8
93Leaf-363
93O-Pee-Chee Canadiens Hockey Fest-31
93OPC Premier-84
Gold-84
93Panini Stickers-20
93Parkhurst-375
Emerald Ice-375
93PowerPlay-366
93Stadium Club-422
Members Only Master Set-422
First Day Issue-422
93Topps/OPC Premier-84
Gold-84
93Ultra-349
93Upper Deck-415
94Canadiens Postcards-4
94Leaf-401
94OPC Premier-94
Special Effects-94
94Pinnacle-452
Artist's Proofs-452
Rink Collection-452
94Stadium Club-227
Members Only Master Set-227
First Day Issue-227
Super Team Winner Cards-227
94Topps/OPC Premier-94
Special Effects-94
95Be A Player-86
Signatures-S86
Signatures Die Cuts-S86
95Canada Games NHL POGS-146
95Canadiens Postcards-3
95Canadiens Sheets-2
95Collector's Choice-35
Player's Club-35
Player's Club Platinum-35
95Donruss-367
95Metal-75
95Panini Stickers-39
95Parkhurst International-116
Emerald Ice-116
95Playoff One on One-162
95Topps-87
OPC Inserts-87
95Ultra-255
95Upper Deck-156
Electric Ice-156
Electric Ice Gold-156
96Canadiens Postcards-4
96Canadiens Sheets-2
96Maggers-7
97Canadiens Postcards-3
97Score Canadiens-18
Platinum-18
Premier-18
98Be A Player-70
Press Release-70
98BAP Gold-70
98BAP Autographs-70
98BAP Autographs Gold-70
98BAP Tampa Bay All Star Game-70
98Canadiens Team Issue-1
98Pacific-248
Ice Blue-248
Red-248
98Pacific Omega-118
Red-118
Opening Day Issue-118
99Pacific-201
Copper-201
Emerald Green-201
Gold-201
Ice Blue-201
Premiere Date-201
Red-201
99Paramount-114
Copper-114
Emerald-114
Gold-114
Holographic Emerald-114
Holographic Gold-114
Holographic Silver-114
Ice Blue-114
Premiere Date-114
Red-114
Silver-114
00Canadiens Postcards-7
00O-Pee-Chee-260B
00O-Pee-Chee Parallel-260B
00Pacific-206
Copper-206
Gold-206
Ice Blue-206
Premiere Date-206
00Titanium Game Gear-100
00Titanium Game Gear Patches-100
00Titanium Draft Day Edition-49
Patches-49
00Topps/OPC-260B
Parallel-260B
00Upper Deck-324
Exclusives Tier 1-324
Exclusives Tier 2-324
01Atomic Jerseys-31
01BAP Memorabilia-456
Emerald-456
Ruby-456
Sapphire-456
01Canadiens Postcards-4
01Pacific Heads-Up Quad Jerseys-12
01Stars Postcards-2
02BAP Sig Series Auto Buybacks 1998-70

Brunet, Gerry
51Laval Dairy Lac St. Jean-58

Brunet, Lucien
28La Presse Photos-4

Bruneteau, Eddie
43Parade Sportive *-17

Bruneteau, Mud
34Beehive Group I Photos-93
37V356 Worldwide Gum-47
39O-Pee-Chee V301-1-43
40O-Pee-Chee V301-2-138
43Parade Sportive *-18
43Parade Sportive *-19
03BAP Ultimate Memorabilia Paper Cuts-25
04ITG Franchises US West-215
04ITG Ultimate Memorabilia Motown Heroes-3
05ITG Ultimate Mem Quad Paper Cuts Autos-3

Brunetta, Mario
87Nordiques General Foods-3
87Nordiques Team Issue-25
88Nordiques General Foods-5
88Nordiques Team Issue-6
89Halifax Citadels-3
89ProCards AHL-159
90Panini Stickers-152
96German DEL-24
98German DEL-163
99Swedish Upper Deck-69

Brunette, Andrew
90 7th Inn. Sketch OHL-277
91 7th Inn. Sketch OHL-284
93Owen Sound Platers-3
94Portland Pirates-3
95Portland Pirates-6
96Fleer-124
Calder Candidates-1
96SkyBox Impact-147
96Ultra-173
Gold Medallion-173
96Upper Deck-184
96Portland Pirates-19
96Portland Pirates Shop N' Save-7
96Collector's Edge Future Legends-47
97Pacific Invincible NHL Regime-207
97Pacific Omega-237
Copper-237
Dark Gray-237
Emerald Green-237
Gold-237
Ice Blue-237
97Pinnacle Inside-111
97Upper Deck-382
97Portland Pirates-5
98Aurora-99
98Crown Royale-72
Limited Series-72
98Pacific-439
Ice Blue-439
Red-439
98Pacific Dynagon Ice-100
Blue-100
Red-100
98Pacific Omega-127
Red-127
Opening Day Issue-127
98Panini Photocards-14
98Paramount-121
Copper-121
Emerald Green-121
Holo-Electric-121
Ice Blue-121
Silver-121
98Predators Team Issue-6
98Revolution-77
Ice Shadow-77
Red-77
98SP Authentic-46
Power Shift-46
98Upper Deck-301
Exclusives-301
Exclusives 1 of 1-301
Gold Reserve-301
98Upper Deck MVP-113
Gold Script-113
Silver Script-113
Super Script-113
98Hampton Roads Admirals 10th Anniversary-12
99Aurora-6
Premiere Date-6
99BAP Memorabilia-258
Gold-258
Silver-258
99BAP Millennium-15
Emerald-15
Ruby-15
Sapphire-15
Signatures-15
Signatures Gold-15
99Crown Royale-5
Limited Series-5
Premiere Date-5
99Pacific-220
Copper-220
Emerald Green-220
Gold-220
Ice Blue-220
Premiere Date-220
Red-220
99Pacific Omega-9
Copper-9
Gold-9
Ice Blue-9
Premiere Date-9
99Pacific Prism-6
Holographic Blue-6
Holographic Gold-6
Holographic Mirror-6
Holographic Purple-6
Premiere Date-6
99Panini Stickers-18
99Paramount-10
Copper-10
Emerald-10
Gold-10
Holographic Emerald-10
Holographic Gold-10
Holographic Silver-10
Ice Blue-10
Premiere Date-10
Red-10
Silver-10
99SP Authentic-5
99Topps Gold Label Class 1-68
Black-68
Black One of One-68
One of One-68
Red-68
Red One of One-68
99Topps Gold Label Class 2-68
99Topps Gold Label Class 2 Black-68
99Topps Gold Label Class 2 Black 1 of 1-68
99Topps Gold Label Class 2 One of One-68
99Topps Gold Label Class 2 Red-68
99Topps Gold Label Class 2 Red One of One-68
99Topps Gold Label Class 3-68
99Topps Gold Label Class 3 Black-68
99Topps Gold Label Class 3 Black 1 of 1-68
99Topps Gold Label Class 3 One of One-68
99Topps Gold Label Class 3 Red-68
99Topps Gold Label Class 3 Red One of One-68
99Wayne Gretzky Hockey-10
00Aurora-5
Premiere Date-5
00BAP Memorabilia-211
Emerald-211
Ruby-211
Sapphire-211
Promos-211
00BAP Mem Chicago Sportsfest Copper-211
00BAP Memorabilia Chicago Sportsfest Blue-211
00BAP Memorabilia Chicago Sportsfest Gold-211
00BAP Memorabilia Chicago Sportsfest Ruby-211
00BAP Memorabilia Chicago Sun-Times Ruby-211
00BAP Memorabilia Chicago Sun-Times Gold-211
00BAP Mem Chicago Sun-Times Sapphire-211
00BAP Mem Toronto Fall Expo Copper-211
00BAP Memorabilia Toronto Fall Expo Gold-211
00BAP Memorabilia Toronto Fall Expo Ruby-211
00BAP Parkhurst 2000-P22
00BAP Signature Series-63
Emerald-63
Ruby-63
Sapphire-63
Autographs-133
Autographs Gold-133
00Crown Royale-5
Ice Blue-5
Limited Series-5
Premiere Date-5
Red-5
00Kraft-19
00O-Pee-Chee-52
00O-Pee-Chee Parallel-52
00Pacific-15
Copper-15
Gold-15
Ice Blue-15
Premiere Date-15
00Panini Stickers-6
00Paramount-10
Copper-10
Gold-10
Holo-Gold-10
Holo-Silver-10
Ice Blue-10
Premiere Date-10
00Revolution-5
Blue-5
Premiere Date-5
Red-5
00Stadium Club-85
00Topps/OPC-52
Parallel-52
00Topps Chrome-42
OPC Refractors-42
Refractors-42
00Topps Heritage-197
00Topps Premier Plus-64
Blue Ice-64
00Topps Stars-60
Blue-60
00UD Heroes-7
00Upper Deck-8
Exclusives Tier 1-8
Exclusives Tier 2-8
00Upper Deck MVP-8
First Stars-8
Second Stars-8
Third Stars-8
00Upper Deck Victory-10
00Upper Deck Vintage-21
01BAP Memorabilia-255
01BAP Memorabilia-334
Emerald-255
Emerald-334
Ruby-255
Ruby-334
Sapphire-255
Sapphire-334
01Crown Royale-71
Blue-71
Premiere Date-71
Red-71
Retail-71
01O-Pee-Chee-170
01O-Pee-Chee Premier Parallel-170
01Pacific-14
Extreme LTD-14
Hobby LTD-14
Premiere Date-14
Retail LTD-14
01Pacific Arena Exclusives-14
01Parkhurst-379
01SPx-177
01Titanium-68
Hobby Parallel-68
Premiere Date-68
Retail-68
Retail Parallel-68
01Topps-170
OPC Parallel-170
01Topps Heritage-158
01UD Challenge for the Cup-43
01UD Mask Collection-45
Gold-45
01UD Playmakers-51
01Upper Deck-317
Exclusives-317
01Upper Deck Victory-14
Gold-14
01Wild Crime Prevention-20
02Atomic-51
Blue-51
Gold-51
Red-51
Hobby Parallel-51
Power Converters-11
02BAP First Edition-219
02BAP Memorabilia-31
Emerald-31
Ruby-31
Sapphire-31
NHL All-Star Game-31
NHL All-Star Game Blue-31
NHL All-Star Game Green-31
NHL All-Star Game Red-31
02BAP Memorabilia Toronto Fall Expo-31
02BAP Signature Series-51
Autographs-51
Autograph Buybacks 1999-15
Autograph Buybacks 2000-133
Autographs Gold-51
02O-Pee-Chee-47
02O-Pee-Chee Premier Blue Parallel-47
02O-Pee-Chee Premier Red Parallel-47
02O-Pee-Chee Factory Set-47
02Pacific-177
Blue-177
Red-177
02Pacific Complete-315
Red-315
02Pacific Exclusive-84
02Pacific Heads-Up-59
Blue-59
Purple-59
Red-59
02Parkhurst-158
Bronze-158
Gold-158
Silver-158
02Private Stock Reserve-48
Blue-48
Red-48
Retail-48
02Stadium Club-75
Silver Decoy Cards-75
Proofs-75
02Topps-47
OPC Blue Parallel-47
OPC Red Parallel-47
Factory Set-47
02Topps Chrome-39
Black Border Refractors-39
Refractors-39
02Topps Heritage-91
Chrome Parallel-91
02Topps Total-245
02UD Honor Roll-85
02UD Top Shelf-44
02Upper Deck-331
Exclusives-331
02Upper Deck Beckett UD Promos-331
02Upper Deck Classic Portraits-49
02Upper Deck MVP-91
Gold-91
Classics-91
Golden Classics-91
02Upper Deck Victory-102
Bronze-102
Gold-102
Silver-102
02Upper Deck Vintage-130
02Upper Deck Vintage-275
02Vanguard-51
LTD-51
03Beehive-94
Gold-94
Silver-94
03ITG Action-254
03NHL Sticker Collection-243
03O-Pee-Chee-255
03OPC Blue-255
03OPC Gold-255
03OPC Red-255
03Pacific-162
Blue-162
Red-162
03Pacific Complete-278
Red-278
03Pacific Exhibit-71
Blue Backs-71
Yellow Backs-71
03Pacific Prism-51
Blue-51
Gold-51
Red-51
03Pacific Quest for the Cup-52
Blue-52
03Private Stock Reserve-49
Blue-49
Red-49
Retail-49
03Titanium-49
Hobby Jersey Number Parallels-49
Retail-49
Retail Jersey Number Parallels-49
03Topps-255
Blue-255
Gold-255
Red-255
03Topps Pristine-18
Gold Refractor Die Cuts-18
Refractors-18
Press Plates Black-18
Press Plates Cyan-18
Press Plates Magenta-18
Press Plates Yellow-18
03Upper Deck-94
Canadian Exclusives-94
HG-94
03Upper Deck MVP-210
Gold Script-210
Silver Script-210
Canadian Exclusives-210
04Pacific-127
Blue-127
Red-127
05Be A Player Signatures-AB
05Be A Player Signatures Gold-AB
05Panini Stickers-233
05Parkhurst-121
Facsimile Auto Parallel-121
05Upper Deck MVP-107
Gold-107
Platinum-107
05Upper Deck Victory-98
Black-98
Gold-98
Silver-98
06Avalanche Team Postcards-3
06O-Pee-Chee-127
Rainbow-127
06Panini Stickers-225
06Ultra-51
Gold Medallion-51
Ice Medallion-51
06Upper Deck-51
Exclusives Parallel-51
High Gloss Parallel-51
Masterpieces-51
06Upper Deck MVP-78
Gold Script-78
Super Script-78
06Upper Deck Victory-53
06Upper Deck Victory Black-53
06Upper Deck Victory Gold-53
07Upper Deck Victory-156
Black-156
Gold-156

Brunette, Jayson
98Abilene Aviators-14

Brunner, Gerhard
98German DEL-314
99German DEL-265

Brunner, Jean-Marc
95Swiss HNL-380

Brunner, Markus
90 7th Inn. Sketch OHL-328
91Oshawa Generals-15
91Oshawa Generals Sheet-19
91 7th Inn. Sketch OHL-151

Bruns, MArc
03German Mannheim Eagles Postcards-30

Bruns, Roger
94German DEL-437

Brunsing, Frank
94German DEL-224

Brunvoll, Andreas
92Norwegian Elite Series-212

Brus, Kjell
69Swedish Hockey-114
70Swedish Hockey-74
71Swedish Hockey-164
72Finnish Semic World Championship-63
72Swedish Stickers-163
72Swedish Semic World Championship-63
73Swedish Stickers-53
74Swedish Stickers-205

Brusa, Raphael
00Swiss Panini Stickers-57
00Swiss Slapshot Mini-Cards-HCCF2
01Swiss HNL-287

Bruselinck, Derek
92Saskatchewan JHL-151

Brush, Matt
98Florida Everblades-2

Brush, Tyler
97Arizona Icecats-6
98Arizona Icecats-1
99Arizona Icecats-1
00Arizona Icecats-3

Brusseau, Mike
03Fresno Falcons-2
03Lubbock Cotton Kings-5
04Tulsa Oilers-4

Brust, Barry
00Spokane Chiefs-3
01Spokane Chiefs-4
02Spokane Chiefs-3
04Reading Royals-12
05Manchester Monarchs-1
06Between The Pipes-3
Autographs-ABB
Emblems-GUE18
Emblems Gold-GUE18
Emblems Autographs-GUE18
Jerseys-GUJ18
Jerseys Gold-GUJ18
Jerseys Autographs-GUJ18
Numbers-GUN18
Numbers Gold-GUN18
Numbers Autographs-GUN18
Prospect Trios-PT14
Prospect Trios Gold-PT14
06Hot Prospects-192
06The Cup Masterpiece Pressplates (Ultimate Collection)-77
06Ultimate Collection-77
06Upper Deck-473
Exclusives Parallel-473
High Gloss Parallel-473
Masterpieces-473
06Manchester Monarchs-1

Bruun, Antti
99Finnish Cardset-248
00Finnish Cardset-152
01Finnish Cardset-38
03Finnish Cardset-131
04Finnish Cardset-266
05Finnish Cardset -102
06Swedish SHL Elitset-252

Brux, Arno
94German DEL-333
95German DEL-237
99German Bundesliga 2-135

Bry, Mark
98Sioux City Musketeers-3

Bryan, Shawn
90ProCards AHL/IHL-496

Bryan, Tim
95Slapshot-430

Bryar, Ghislain
93Quebec Pee-Wee Tournament-1207

Bryce, Ryan
05Lethbridge Hurricanes-4

Bryden, Rob
88Flint Spirits-2
88ProCards AHL-287

Brydge, Bill
23V128-1 Paulin's Candy-19
25Dominion Chocolates-101
33V129-22
33V252 Canadian Gum-5
33V357 Ice Kings-2
34Diamond Matchbooks Silver-6
35Diamond Matchbooks Tan 1-5
35Diamond Matchbooks Tan 2-5
35Diamond Matchbooks Tan 3-4

Brydges, Paul
88ProCards AHL-246
89ProCards AHL-27
93Guelph Storm-27
94Guelph Storm-28
03Guelph Storm-26

Brydges, Scott
82Oshawa Generals-7
83Oshawa Generals-11

Brydson, Glenn
33O-Pee-Chee V304B-64
33V252 Canadian Gum-6
33V357 Ice Kings-39
34Beehive Group I Photos-42
35Diamond Matchbooks Tan 1-6
35Diamond Matchbooks Tan 4-2
35Diamond Matchbooks Tan 5-1
37Diamond Matchbooks Tan 6-1

Brylin, Sergei
92Russian Stars Red Ace-5
92Russian Stars Red Ace-23
92Classic-47
Gold-47
92Classic Four-Sport *-188
Gold-188
93Pinnacle-509
Canadian-509
93Upper Deck-276
94Upper Deck-329
Electric Ice-329
95Collector's Choice-296
Player's Club-296
Player's Club Platinum-296
95Donruss-52
95Leaf-40
95Parkhurst International-119
Emerald Ice-119
95Pinnacle-120
Artist's Proofs-120
Rink Collection-120
Global Gold-18
95Playoff One on One-277
95Score-274
Black Ice Artist's Proofs-274
Black Ice-274
95Topps-35
OPC Inserts-35
New To The Game-2NG
95Ultra-88
Gold Medallion-88
95Upper Deck-31
Electric Ice-31
Electric Ice Gold-31
96Devils Team Issue-18
97Devils Team Issue-13
97Score Devils-19
Platinum-19
Premier-19
98Be A Player-231
Press Release-231
98BAP Gold-231
98BAP Autographs-231
98BAP Autographs Gold-231
98Devils Team Issue-5
98Upper Deck-311
Exclusives-311
Exclusives 1 of 1-311
Gold Reserve-311
99BAP Memorabilia-83
Gold-83
Silver-83
99Devils Team Issue-11
99Upper Deck MVP SC Edition-110
Gold Script-110
Silver Script-110
Super Script-110
99Russian Fetisov Tribute-14
00BAP Memorabilia-66
Emerald-66
Ruby-66
Sapphire-66
Promos-66
00BAP Mem Chicago Sportsfest Copper-66
00BAP Memorabilia Chicago Sportsfest Blue-66
00BAP Memorabilia Chicago Sportsfest Gold-66
00BAP Memorabilia Chicago Sportsfest Ruby-66
00BAP Memorabilia Chicago Sun-Times Ruby-66
00BAP Memorabilia Chicago Sun-Times Gold-66
00BAP Mem Chicago Sun-Times Sapphire-66
00BAP Mem Toronto Fall Expo Copper-66
00BAP Memorabilia Toronto Fall Expo Gold-66
00BAP Memorabilia Toronto Fall Expo Ruby-66
00BAP Parkhurst 2000-P194
00BAP Signature Series-100
Emerald-100
Ruby-100
Sapphire-100
00Devils Team Issue-3
00Upper Deck-107
00Upper Deck-336
Exclusives Tier 1-107
Exclusives Tier 1-336
Exclusives Tier 2-107
Exclusives Tier 2-336
00Czech Stadion-119
01BAP Memorabilia-166
Emerald-166
Ruby-166
Sapphire-166
01Devils Team Issue-3
01Pacific-228
Extreme LTD-228
Hobby LTD-228
Premiere Date-228
Retail LTD-228
01Pacific Adrenaline-112
Blue-112
Premiere Date-112
Red-112
Retail-112
01Pacific Arena Exclusives-228
01Parkhurst-182
01UD Stanley Cup Champs-76
01Upper Deck-336
Exclusives-336
01Upper Deck Victory-213
Gold-213
02BAP Sig Series Auto Buybacks 1998-231
02Devils Team Issue-14
02O-Pee-Chee-230
02O-Pee-Chee Premier Blue Parallel-230
02O-Pee-Chee Premier Red Parallel-230
02O-Pee-Chee Factory Set-230
02Pacific-219
Blue-219
Red-219
02Pacific Complete-300
Red-300
02Topps-230
OPC Blue Parallel-230
OPC Red Parallel-230
Factory Set-230
02Topps Total-178
02Upper Deck-350
Exclusives-350
02Upper Deck Beckett UD Promos-350
02Upper Deck Vintage-147
03Devils Team Issue-18
03ITG Action-383
Jerseys-M11
03NHL Sticker Collection-66
03Pacific Complete-336
Red-336
03Upper Deck-356
Canadian Exclusives-356
HG-356
UD Exclusives-356
04Russian Back to Russia-34
05Devils Team Issue-19
05Parkhurst-290
Facsimile Auto Parallel-290
05Upper Deck-114
HG Glossy-114
05Upper Deck MVP-231
Gold-231
Platinum-231
05Upper Deck Toronto Fall Expo-114
06Devils Team Set-3
06O-Pee-Chee-301
Rainbow-301
06Upper Deck-368
Exclusives Parallel-368
High Gloss Parallel-368
Masterpieces-368
06Upper Deck MVP-177
Gold Script-177
Super Script-177

Bryner, Anders
67Swedish Hockey-216
69Swedish Hockey-258

Bryzgalov, Ilja
00SPx Rookie Redemption-RR1
00Russian Goalkeepers-3
00Russian Hockey League-155
01Atomic-101
Premiere Date-101
01Atomic Toronto Fall Expo-101
01BAP Memorabilia-301
Emerald-301
Ruby-301
Sapphire-301
01Between the Pipes-84
01Bowman YoungStars-161
Gold-161
Ice Cubed-161
01Crown Royale-145

01O-Pee-Chee-350
01Pacific Adrenaline-201
Blue-201
Premiere Date-201
Red-201
Retail-201
Rookie Report-1
01Pacific Heads-Up-101
01Parkhurst-285
01Parkhurst Beckett Promos-285
01Private Stock-111
Gold-111
Premiere Date-111
Retail-111
Silver-111
01Private Stock Pacific Nights-111
01Private Stock PS-2002-76
01SP Authentic-131
Limited-131
Limited Gold-131
01SP Game Used-61
01SPx-92
01Titanium-145
Retail-145
01Titanium Draft Day Edition-101
01Topps-350
01Topps Chrome-168
Refractors-168
Black Border Refractors-168
01UD Challenge for the Cup-91
01UD Honor Roll-61
01UD Playmakers-102
01UD Premier Collection-88
01UD Top Shelf-67
01Upper Deck-413
Exclusives-413
01Upper Deck Ice-43
01Upper Deck Vintage-272
01Vanguard-101
Blue-101
Red-101
One of Ones-101
Premiere Date-101
Proofs-101
01Cincinnati Mighty Ducks-8
02BAP First Edition-261
02Between the Pipes-83
Gold-83
Silver-83
02O-Pee-Chee-279
02O-Pee-Chee Premier Blue Parallel-279
02O-Pee-Chee Premier Red Parallel-279
02O-Pee-Chee Factory Set-279
02SP Game Used Future Fabrics-FFIB
02SP Game Used Future Fabrics Gold-FFIB
02SP Game Used Future Fabrics Rainbow-FFIB
02Topps-279
OPC Blue Parallel-279
OPC Red Parallel-279
Factory Set-279
02Upper Deck Bright Futures-IB
02Upper Deck Goaltender Threads-IB
02Upper Deck Goaltender Threads Gold-IB
02Cincinnati Mighty Ducks-B-1
03BAP Memorabilia Deep in the Crease-D7
03Pacific Complete-474
Red-474
03AHL Top Prospects-5
03Cincinnati Mighty Ducks-B4
03Pacific AHL Prospects-16
Gold-16
04Cincinnati Mighty Ducks-29
04ITG Heroes/Prospects He Shoots/Scores-38
04ITG Heroes and Prospects Net Prospects-5
04ITG Heroes and Prosp Net Prospects Gold-5
05Ducks Team Issue-2
05Parkhurst-10
Facsimile Auto Parallel-10
05Upper Deck-245
06Between The Pipes-64
Autographs-AIB
Double Jerseys-DJ20
Double Jerseys Gold-DJ20
Emblems-GUE58
Emblems Gold-GUE58
Emblems Autographs-GUE58
Jerseys-GUJ58
Jerseys Gold-GUJ58
Jerseys Autographs-GUJ58
Numbers-GUN58
Numbers Gold-GUN58
Numbers Autographs-GUN58
Playing For Your Country-PC03
Playing For Your Country Gold-PC03
Prospect Trios-PT18
The Mask-M16
The Mask Gold-M16
The Mask Silver-M16
The Mask Game-Used-MGU02
The Mask Game-Used Gold-MGU02
06Black Diamond-2
Black-2
Gold-2
Ruby-2
06Fleer-6
Tiffany-6
Hockey Headliners-HL24
Netminders-N1
06ITG International Ice-29
Gold-29
Autographs-AIB
Cornerstones-IC10
Cornerstones Gold-IC10
Emblem Autographs-GUE22
Emblem Autographs Gold-GUE22
Emblems-GUE22
Emblems Gold-GUE22
Goaltending Glory-GG17
Goaltending Glory Gold-GG17
Jersey Autographs-GUJ22
Jersey Autographs Gold-GUJ22
Jerseys-GUJ22
Jerseys Gold-GUJ22
My Country My Team-MC22
My Country My Team Gold-MC22
Numbers-GUN22
Numbers Autographs-GUN22
Numbers Autographs Gold-GUN22
Numbers Gold-GUN22
Passing The Torch-PTT5
Passing The Torch Gold-PTT5
Quad Patch-QP04
Quad Patch Gold-QP04
06O-Pee-Chee-15
06O-Pee-Chee-614
Rainbow-15
Rainbow-614
06Panini Stickers-190
06Ultra Difference Makers-DM1
06Upper Deck-2
Exclusives Parallel-2
High Gloss Parallel-2
Game Dated Moments-GD9
Masterpieces-2
06Upper Deck MVP-2
Gold Script-2
Super Script-2
06Russian Sport Collection Olympic Stars-2
06Russian Torino Olympic Team-4

Bubla, Jiri
71Finnish Suomi Stickers-22
72Finnish Jaakiekko-2
72Finnish Hellas-95
72Finnish Semic World Championship-38
72Swedish Semic World Championship-38
73Finnish Jaakiekko-44
74Finnish Jenkki-67
74Swedish Stickers-11
74Swedish Semic World Champ Stickers-53
79Panini Stickers-76
81Canucks Team Issue-4
82Canucks Team Issue-3
83Canucks Team Issue-2
83NHL Key Tags-125
83O-Pee-Chee-347
83O-Pee-Chee Stickers-143
83Topps Stickers-143
83Vachon-102
84Canucks Team Issue-3
84O-Pee-Chee-315
85Canucks Team Issue-2

Bubnick, Jonathan
03Regina Pats-17
04Regina Pats-17

Bubnick, Michael
98Calgary Hitmen-10
98Calgary Hitmen Autographs-10
99Calgary Hitmen-3
99Calgary Hitmen Autographs-3
99UD Prospects-53
00Calgary Hitmen-7
01Calgary Hitmen-6
01Calgary Hitmen Autographed-6
02Calgary Hitmen-2
02Saskatoon Blades-8

Bubnik, Vlastimil
97Czech APS Extraliga-378
01Czech DS Legends-L3
03Czech Stadion-638

Bubola, Adrian
91British Columbia JHL-9

Buccella, Dan
01London Knights-17
02Mississauga Ice Dogs-15
03Huntsville Channel Cats-3

Bucella, Dan
04Huntsville Havoc-21

Buchal, Jaroslav
95Czech APS Extraliga-164
96Czech APS Extraliga-187
97Czech APS Extraliga-239
97Czech DS Stickers-50
01Czech OFS-162

Buchanan, Bucky
51Laval Dairy QSHL-56
51Laval Dairy Subset-29

Buchanan, Greg
91British Columbia JHL-6
92British Columbia JHL-211

Buchanan, Jeff
89Saskatoon Blades-17
90Saskatoon Blades-4
907th Inn. Sketch WHL-89
91Saskatoon Blades-4
917th Inn. Sketch WHL-102
92Atlanta Knights-3
93Atlanta Knights-2
95Indianapolis Ice-3
98Hershey Bears-3

Buchanan, John
93Quebec Pee-Wee Tournament-1457

Buchanan, Kirk
92British Columbia JHL-188

Buchanan, Ron
72Cleveland Crusaders WHA-1
73Quaker Oats WHA-36
74O-Pee-Chee WHA-23
75O-Pee-Chee WHA-39

Buchanan, Trevor
88Kamloops Blazers-5
89Victoria Cougars-3
94Central Hockey League-73
94San Antonio Iguanas-1
95Central Hockey League-94
96Pensacola Ice Pilots-9
01Bossier-Shreveport Mudbugs-2
02Bossier-Shreveport Mudbugs-4
03Bossier-Shreveport Mudbugs-6
05Bossier-Shreveport Mudbugs-22

Buchberger, Kelly
88Oilers Tenth Anniversary-133
88Oilers Team Issue-4
89Oilers Team Issue-4
90Oilers IGA-4
90Pro Set-441
91Oilers Panini Team Stickers-4
91Oilers IGA-2
91Oilers Team Issue-3
91Parkhurst-275
French-275
91Pro Set-385
French-385
91Score Canadian Bilingual-429
91Score Canadian English-429
92Bowman-393
92Oilers IGA-3
92Oilers Team Issue-1
92O-Pee-Chee-125
92Pinnacle-95
French-95
92Pro Set-48
92Score-126
Canadian-126
Sharpshooters-11
Sharpshooters Canadian-11
92Stadium Club-235
92Topps-455
Gold-455G
92Ultra-291
92Upper Deck-123
93Panini Stickers-241
93Pinnacle-58
Canadian-58
93PowerPlay-340
93Score-317
Canadian-317
93Ultra-314
93Upper Deck-197
94Canada Games NHL POGS-98
94Donruss-18
94Leaf-333
94OPC Premier-404
Special Effects-404
94Pinnacle-332
Artist's Proofs-332
Rink Collection-332
94Stadium Club-121
Members Only Master Set-121
First Day Issue-121
Super Team Winner Cards-121
94Topps/OPC Premier-404
Special Effects-404
94Ultra-290
94Upper Deck-134
Electric Ice-134
95Canada Games NHL POGS-111
95Collector's Choice-310
Player's Club-310
Player's Club Platinum-310
95Panini Stickers-261
95Parkhurst International-77
Emerald Ice-77
95Topps-298
OPC Inserts-298
95Upper Deck-121
Electric Ice-121
Electric Ice Gold-121
95Swedish World Championships Stickers-15
96Collector's Choice-94
96Kraft Upper Deck-36
96Oilers Postcards-16
97Be A Player-150
Autographs-150
Autographs Die-Cuts-150
Autographs Prismatic Die-Cuts-150
97Pacific-268
Copper-268
Emerald Green-268
Ice Blue-268
Red-268
Silver-268
97Pacific Dynagon-47
Copper-47
Dark Grey-47
Emerald Green-47
Ice Blue-47
Red-47
Silver-47
Tandems-49
97Pacific Omega-89
Copper-89
Dark Gray-89
Emerald Green-89
Gold-89
Ice Blue-89
97SP Authentic-64
97Upper Deck-278
98Aurora-70
98Be A Player-201
Press Release-201
98BAP Gold-201
98BAP Autographs-201
98BAP Autographs Gold-201
98OPC Chrome-22
Refractors-22
98Pacific-205
Ice Blue-205
Red-205
98Paramount-84
Copper-84
Emerald Green-84
Holo-Electric-84
Ice Blue-84
Silver-84
98Post-13
98Topps-22
O-Pee-Chee-22
98Upper Deck-93
Exclusives-93
Exclusives 1 of 1-93
Gold Reserve-93
99Aurora-7
Premiere Date-7
99BAP Millennium-19
Emerald-19
Ruby-19
Sapphire-19
Signatures-19
Signatures Gold-19
99O-Pee-Chee-216
99O-Pee-Chee Chrome-216
99O-Pee-Chee Chrome Refractors-216
99Pacific Dynagon Ice-14
Blue-14
Copper-14
Gold-14
Premiere Date-14
99Panini Stickers-10
99Paramount-11
Copper-11
Emerald-11
Gold-11
Holographic Emerald-11
Holographic Gold-11
Holographic Silver-11
Ice Blue-11
Premiere Date-11
Red-11
Silver-11
99Revolution-6
Premiere Date-6
Red-6
Shadow Series-6
99Stadium Club-158
First Day Issue-158
One of a Kind-158
Printing Plates Black-158
Printing Plates Cyan-158
Printing Plates Magenta-158
Printing Plates Yellow-158
99Topps/OPC-216
99Topps/OPC Chrome-216
Refractors-216
99Ultimate Victory-6
1/1-6
Parallel-6
Parallel 100-6
99Upper Deck-179
Exclusives-179
Exclusives 1 of 1-179
99Upper Deck Gold Reserve-179
99Upper Deck Victory-14
99Wayne Gretzky Hockey-9
00O-Pee-Chee-259B
00O-Pee-Chee Parallel-259B
00Pacific-194
Copper-194
Gold-194
Ice Blue-194
Premiere Date-194
00Topps/OPC-259B
Parallel-259B
00Upper Deck-86
Exclusives Tier 1-86
Exclusives Tier 2-86
01O-Pee-Chee-229
01O-Pee-Chee Premier Parallel-229
01Topps-229
OPC Parallel-229
02BAP Sig Series Auto Buybacks 1998-201
02BAP Sig Series Auto Buybacks 1999-19
02Coyotes Team Issue-9
02Pacific Complete-381
Red-381
02Topps Heritage-177
02Topps Total-310
03ITG Action-484

Bucher, Laurent
91Upper Deck-668
French-668
91Upper Deck Czech World Juniors-29
93Swiss HNL-421

Buchhart, Markus
94German First League-504

Buchholz, Emily
98Minnesota Golden Gophers Women-3

Buchholz, Mark
02Topeka Scarecrows-20

Buchko, Berkeley
96Medicine Hat Tigers-1
97Medicine Hat Tigers-4
98Medicine Hat Tigers-4
99Medicine Hat Tigers-9
00Prince George Cougars-12

Buchko, Mike
75HCA Steel City Vacuum-1

Buchwieser, Hubert
94German First League-304
95German DEL-352
99German Bundesliga 2-276

Bucic, Emil
02Guelph Storm-21

Buck, Brandon
06Guelph Storm-4

Buck, David
93Minnesota-Duluth Bulldogs-3

Buckberger, Ashley
917th Inn. Sketch WHL-193
95Slapshot Memorial Cup-18
96Carolina Monarchs-4
99Tacoma Sabercats-10
00Tacoma Sabercats-11

Buckland, Frank
83Hall of Fame-216
83Hall of Fame Postcards-O6
85Hall of Fame-216

Buckland, Wyatt
907th Inn. Sketch OHL-278
917th Inn. Sketch OHL-287
94Toledo Storm-2

Buckle, Chad
92British Columbia JHL-196

Buckley, Brendan
99Quad-City Mallards-11
00Wilkes-Barre Scranton Penguins-2
01Wilkes-Barre Scranton Penguins-13
02Wilkes-Barre Scranton Penguins-16
03Wilkes-Barre Scranton Penguins-7
04Worcester IceCats-5
05Peoria Rivermen-5
06Manchester Monarchs-2

Buckley, David
89Hampton Roads Admirals-3A
89Hampton Roads Admirals-3H
90Hampton Roads Admirals-43

Buckley, Grant
00Mississauga Ice Dogs-4

Buckley, Jerry
95Dayton Bombers-26

Buckley, Mike
03Gwinnett Gladiators-11

Buckley, Tom
94Detroit Jr. Red Wings-10
95Slapshot-77
95Slapshot Memorial Cup-84
96Springfield Falcons-14
98New Haven Beast-12
99Florida Everblades-10
00Florida Everblades-4
01Florida Everblades-10
02Florida Everblades-6
02Florida Everblades RBI-119
03Florida Everblades-9

Buckman, Chris
92British Columbia JHL-139

Buckman, Jason
02UK Peterborough Phantoms-8

Buckman, Lewis
02UK Peterborough Phantoms-9

Bucyk, John
44Beehive Group II Photos-8
44Beehive Group II Photos-156
57Bruins Photos-4
57Topps-10
58Bruins Photos-2
58Topps-40
59Topps-23
60Shirriff Coins-104
60Topps-11
Stamps-6
61Shirriff/Salada Coins-7
61Topps-8
62Topps-11
Hockey Bucks-4
63Topps-11
63Toronto Star-8
64Beehive Group III Photos-3
64Coca-Cola Caps-6
64Topps-100
65Coca-Cola-6
65Topps-101
66Topps-39
66Topps USA Test-39
67Topps-42
68O-Pee-Chee-5
68O-Pee-Chee-210
68Shirriff Coins-6
68Topps-5
69O-Pee-Chee-26
69Topps-26
70Bruins Postcards-7
70Bruins Team Issue-2
70Colgate Stamps-46
70Dad's Cookies-11
70Esso Power Players-60
70O-Pee-Chee-2
70Post Shooters-1
70Sargent Promotions Stamps-8
70Topps-2
71Bruins Postcards-6
71O-Pee-Chee-35
71O-Pee-Chee-249
71O-Pee-Chee 255
71Sargent Promotions Stamps-9
71Topps-1
71Topps-2
71Topps-3
71Topps-35
71Toronto Sun-5
72O-Pee-Chee-1
72Sargent Promotions Stamps-16
72Topps-60
73Mac's Milk-2
73O-Pee-Chee-147
73Topps-26
74NHL Action Stamps-31
74O-Pee-Chee NHL-28
74O-Pee-Chee NHL-239
74O-Pee-Chee NHL-245
74Topps-28
74Topps-239
74Topps-245
75O-Pee-Chee NHL-9
75O-Pee-Chee NHL-314
75Topps-9
75Topps-314
76O-Pee-Chee NHL-95
76O-Pee-Chee NHL-381
76Topps-95
76Topps Glossy Inserts-14
77O-Pee-Chee NHL-155
77Topps-155
81TCMA-5
83Hall of Fame Postcards-J4
85Hall of Fame-181
91Bruins Sports Action Legends-5
93Zeller's Masters of Hockey-2
93Zeller's Masters of Hockey Signed-2
94Parkhurst Missing Link-56
94Parkhurst Tall Boys-1
Mail-Ins-SL1
95Parkhurst '66-67-5
Coins-5
97Beehive-58
Golden Portraits-58
Golden Originals Autographs-58
98Bruins Alumni-9
Autographs-9
99BAP Memorabilia AS American Hobby-AH5
99BAP Memorabilia AS American Hobby Autos-AH5
99Upper Deck Century Legends-46
Century Collection-46
Epic Signatures-JB
Epic Signatures 100-JB
99Upper Deck Retro-105
Gold-105
Platinum-105
Inkredible-JOB
Inkredible Level 2-JOB
00Upper Deck 500 Goal Club-500JBU
00Upper Deck 500 Goal Club-500JBU
00Upper Deck Legends-8
Legendary Collection Bronze-8
Legendary Collection Gold-8
Legendary Collection Silver-8
Epic Signatures-JB
01BAP Memorabilia 500 Goal Scorers-GS16
01BAP Signature Series 500 Goal Scorers-15
01BAP Sig Series 500 Goal Scorers Autos-15
01BAP Signature Series Vintage Autographs-VA-31
01BAP Ultimate Mem All-Star History-17
01BAP Ultimate Memorabilia Captain's C-3
01BAP Ultimate Memorabilia Cornerstones-6
01BAP Ultimate Mem 500 Goal Scorers-23
01BAP Ultimate Mem 500 Goal Scorers Autos-11
01BAP Ultimate Mem 500 Goal Jerseys/Stick-23
01BAP Ultimate Mem 500 Goal Emblems-23
01BAP Ultimate Mem Retired Numbers-5
01BAP Update Passing the Torch-PTT1
01Fleer Legacy-22
Ultimate-22
01Greats of the Game-76
Autographs-76
01Parkhurst Autographs-PA21
01Parkhurst 500 Goal Scorers-PGS16
01Topps Archives-17
Arena Seats-ASJB
Autographs-4
01Topps Heritage Arena Relics-RJBU
01Topps Heritage Arena Relics-RJB/BG
01Topps Heritage Arena Relics-RJB/HR
01Topps Heritage Arena Relics-RJB/JB
01Topps Heritage Arena Relics-ARJBU
01Topps Heritage Arena Relics-ARJB/BG
01Topps Heritage Arena Relics-ARJB/HR
01Topps Heritage Arena Relics-ARJB/JB
01Topps Heritage Autographs-AJBU
01Topps Heritage Salute-S1
01Upper Deck Legends-4
02BAP Memorabilia-233
Emerald-233
Ruby-233
Sapphire-233
NHL All-Star Game-233
NHL All-Star Game Blue-233
NHL All-Star Game Green-233
NHL All-Star Game Red-233
02BAP Memorabilia Toronto Fall Expo-233
02BAP NHL All-Star History-17
02BAP Ultimate Memorabilia Emblem Attic-9
02BAP Ultimate Memorabilia Numerology-13
02BAP Ultimate Mem Retro Teammates-2
02BAP Ultimate Mem Vintage Jerseys-23
02BAP Ultimate Mem Vintage Jersey Autos-2
02Fleer Throwbacks-18
Gold-18
Platinum-18
02Parkhurst Vintage Memorabilia-VM1
02Parkhurst Vintage Teammates-VT3
02Parkhurst Retro Nicknames-RN7
02UD Foundations 1000 Point Club-JB
02UD Foundations 1000 Point Club-BU
02UD Foundations 1000 Point Club Gold-JB
02UD Foundations 1000 Point Club Silver-JB
02UD Foundations Canadian Heroes-CJB
02UD Foundations Canadian Heroes Gold-CJB
02UD Foundations Canadian Heroes Silver-C-JB
02UD Foundations Playoff Performers-PJB
02UD Foundations Playoff Performers Gold-PJB
02UD Foundations Playoff Performers Silver-P-JB
02UD Foundations Signs of Greatness-SGJBU
02UD Piece of History Historical Swatches-HSJB
02UD Piece of History Mark of Distinction-JB
03BAP Ultimate Mem Linemates Autos-9
03BAP Ultimate Mem Retro Teammates-5
03BAP Ultimate Mem Vintage Jerseys-14
03BAP Ultimate Mem Vintage Jerseys Gold-14
03Parkhurst Original Six Boston-36
03Parkhurst Original Six Boston-68
03Parkhurst Original Six Boston-75
03Parkhurst Original Six Boston-82
03Parkhurst Original Six Boston-92
Autographs-2
Inserts-B5
Memorabilia-BM27
Memorabilia-BM37
Memorabilia-BM54
03Parkhurst Original Six Detroit-48
Autographs-OS-JB
03SP Game Used Limited Threads-LTJBU
03SP Game Used Limited Threads Gold-LTJBU
03SPx-110
Radiance-110
Spectrum-110
03Upper Deck Trilogy-125
Crest Variations-125
Limited-125
Scripts-S3BK
Scripts-S3JK
Scripts-CSJB
Scripts Limited-S3BK
Scripts Limited-S3JK
Scripts Red-S3JB
04ITG NHL AS FANtasy AS History Jerseys-SB17
04ITG Franchises He Shoots/Scores Prizes-35
04ITG Franchises Update-466
04ITG Franchises US East-314
Autographs-A-JBU
Original Sticks-EOS18
Original Sticks Autographs-EOS-JB
Original Sticks Gold-EOS18
04ITG Ultimate Memorabilia-9
Gold-9
Autographs-39
Autographs Gold-39
Cornerstones-5
Cornerstones Gold-5
Day In History-23
Day In History-44
Day In History Gold-23
Day In History Gold-44
Jersey Autographs-48
Jersey Autographs Gold-48
Original Six-9
Retro Teammates-13
Stick Autographs-28
Stick Autographs Gold-28
Vintage Lumber-4
04SP Authentic Buybacks-98
04SP Authentic Buybacks-99
04SP Authentic Sign of the Times-QS-HRBG
04SP Authentic Sign of the Times-QS-BTCR
04SP Authentic Sign of the Times-FS-BOS
04SP Authentic Sign of the Times-FS-CTR
04SP Authentic Sign of the Times-SS-RLW
04UD Legendary Signatures-50
AKA Autographs-AKA-JB
Autographs-JB
HOF Inks-HOF-JB
04UD Legends Classics-33
Gold-33
Platinum-33
Silver-33
Signature Moments-M24
Signature Moments-M67
Signatures-CS24
Signatures-DC6
Signatures-DC8
Signatures-QC3
04Ultimate Collection Jerseys-UGJ-JB
04Ultimate Collection Jerseys Gold-UGJ-JB
04Ultimate Collection Jersey Autographs-UGJA-JB
04Ultimate Collection Signature Patches-SP-BU
04ITG Heroes and Prospects-159
Autographs-JBU
04ITG Heroes/Prospects Toronto Expo '05-159
04ITG Heroes/Prospects Expo Heroes/Pros-159
05Beehive-234
05Canada Post-36
05Canada Post Autographs-36
05ITG Ultimate Memorabilia Level 1-58
05ITG Ultimate Memorabilia Level 2-58
05ITG Ultimate Memorabilia Level 3-58
05ITG Ultimate Memorabilia Level 4-58
05ITG Ultimate Memorabilia Level 5-58
05ITG Ultimate Mem Cornerstones Jerseys-2
05ITG Ultimate Mem Cornerst Jerseys Gold-2
05ITG Ultimate Mem Decades Jerseys-1
05ITG Ultimate Mem 3 Star of the Game Jsy-10
05ITG Ult Mem 3 Star of the Game Jsy Gold-10
05ITG Ultimate Memorabilia Vintage Lumber-12
05ITG Ultimate Mem Vintage Lumber Gold-12
05SP Authentic Six Star Signatures-SSBO
05SPx-108
05The Cup-9
Gold-9
Black Rainbow-9
Hardware Heroes-HHJB
Masterpiece Pressplates-9
05UD Artifacts-107
Blue-107
Gold-107
Green-107
Pewter-107
Red-107
Gold Autographed-107
05Ultimate Collection Endorsed Emblems-EEBU
06Beehive Signature Scrapbook-SSJB
06ITG Ultimate Memorabilia-80
Artist Proof-80
Blades of Steel-20
Blades of Steel Gold-20
Decades-7
Decades Gold-7
Retro Teammates-10
Retro Teammates Gold-10
Road to the Cup-4
Road to the Cup Gold-4
Stick Rack-6
Stick Rack Gold-6
06Parkhurst-28
06Parkhurst-162
Autographs-28
Autographs-162
Autographs Dual-DAEB
Autographs Dual-DASB
06SP Authentic Sign of the Times-STBU
06SP Authentic Sign of the Times Quads-ST4EBOC
06The Cup-11
Black Rainbow-11
Enshrinements-EJB
Gold-11
Masterpiece Pressplates-11
Stanley Cup Signatures-CSBU
Stanley Cup Titlists-TBU
06UD Artifacts-106
Blue-106
Gold-106
Radiance-106
Autographed Radiance Parallel-106
Red-106
Auto-Facts-AFBU
Auto-Facts Gold-AFBU
Tundra Tandems-TTBO
Tundra Tandems Black-TTBO
Tundra Tandems Blue-TTBO
Tundra Tandems Gold-TTBO
Tundra Tandems Red-TTBO
Tundra Tandems Dual Patches Red-TTBO
06Ultimate Collection Signatures-US-BU
06Upper Deck Sweet Shot Signature Shots/Saves-SSJB
06Upper Deck Sweet Shot Signature Shots/Saves Sticks-SSSBU
06Upper Deck Trilogy Ice Scripts-ISJB
06Upper Deck Trilogy Scripts-TSJB

Bucyk, Randy
85Canadiens Postcards-3
86Sherbrooke Canadiens-8
88Salt Lake Golden Eagles-16
89ProCards IHL-205
90ProCards AHL/IHL-608

Buczkowski, Paul
91Saskatoon Blades-24
917th Inn. Sketch WHL-105
93Saskatoon Blades-5
95Saskatoon Blades-6
99Tallahassee Tiger Sharks-8

Buda, Dave
89ProCards AHL-54

Budai, Jeff
917th Inn. Sketch WHL-269

Budaj, Peter
00St. Michaels Majors-9
01St. Michaels Majors-24
02Hershey Bears-4
03AHL Top Prospects-6
03Hershey Bears-1
03Hershey Bears Patriot News-4
03Pacific AHL Prospects-38
Gold-38
04SP Authentic Rookie Redemptions-RR31
04AHL Top Prospects-20
04Hershey Bears Patriot News-6
04ITG Heroes and Prospects-11
Autographs-PB
Complete Emblems-29
Emblems-43
Emblems Gold-43
He Shoots-He Scores Prizes-13
Jersey Autographs-43
Jerseys-43
Jerseys Gold-43
Net Prospects-23
Net Prospects Gold-23
Numbers-43
Numbers Gold-43
04ITG Heroes/Prospects Toronto Expo '05-11
04ITG Heroes/Prospects Expo Heroes/Pros-11
05Beehive-123
Beige -123
Blue -123
Gold-123
Red -123
Matte-123
Signature Scrapbook-SSBU
05Black Diamond-164
Emerald-164
Gold-164
Onyx-164
Ruby-164
05Hot Prospects-231
En Fuego-231
Hot Materials-HMPB
Red Hot-231
White Hot-231
05Parkhurst-619
Facsimile Auto Parallel-619
Signatures-BU
True Colors-TCCOL
True Colors-TCCOL
05SP Authentic-150
Limited-150
Rarefied Rookies-RRPB
05SP Game Used-112
Autographs-112
Gold-112
Auto Draft-AD-BU
Rookie Exclusives-PB
Rookie Exclusives Silver-RE-PB
Significant Numbers-SN-BU
05SPx-183
Spectrum-183
Xcitement Rookies-XR-PB
Xcitement Rookies Gold-XR-PB
Xcitement Rookies Spectrum-XR-PB
05The Cup-117
Autographed Rookie Patches Gold Rainbow-117
Black Rainbow Rookies-117
Masterpiece Pressplates (Artifacts)-231
Masterpiece Pressplates (Bee Hive)-123
Masterpiece Pressplates (Black Diamond)-164
Masterpiece Pressplates (Ice)-126
Masterpiece Pressplates (MVP)-430
Masterpiece Pressplates (Power Play)-169
Masterpiece Pressplates (Rookie Update)-205
Masterpiece Pressplates SPA Autos-150
Masterpiece Pressplates (SP Game Used)-112
Masterpiece Pressplates SPx Autos-183
Masterpiece Pressplates (Trilogy)-186
Masterpiece Pressplates Ult Coll Autos-111
Masterpiece Pressplates (Victory)-251
Masterpiece Pressplates Autographs-117
Platinum Rookies-117
05UD Artifacts-231
Gold-RED31
05UD PowerPlay-169
05UD Rookie Class-35
05Ultimate Collection-111
Autographed Patches-111
Autographed Shields-111
Ultimate Debut Threads Jerseys Autos-DAJPB
Ultimate Debut Threads Patches-DTPPB
Ultimate Debut Threads Patches Autos-DAPPB
05Ultra-213
Gold-213
Ice-213
Rookie Uniformity Jerseys-RU-PB
Rookie Uniformity Jersey Autographs-ARU-PB
Rookie Uniformity Patches-RUP-PB
Rookie Uniformity Patch Autographs-ARP-PB
05Upper Deck-213
HG Glossy-213
Rookie Ink-RIPB
Rookie Threads-RTPB
Rookie Threads Autographs-ARTPB
05Upper Deck Ice-126
Fresh Ice-FIBU
Fresh Ice Glass-FIBU
Fresh Ice Glass Patches-FIPBU
Premieres Auto Patches-AIPPB
05Upper Deck MVP-430
Gold-430
Platinum-430
05Upper Deck Rookie Update-205
Inspirations Patch Rookies-205
05Upper Deck Trilogy-186
05Upper Deck Toronto Fall Expo-213
05Upper Deck Victory-251
Black-251
Gold-251
Silver-251
06Avalanche Team Postcards-4
06Be A Player Portraits First Exposures-FEPB
06Between The Pipes-60
Emblems-GUE60
Emblems Gold-GUE60
Jerseys-GUJ60
Jerseys Gold-GUJ60
Numbers-GUN60
Numbers Gold-GUN60
Prospect Trios-PT02
Prospect Trios Gold-PT02
06Black Diamond-21
Black-21
Gold-21
Ruby-21
Jerseys-JBU
Jerseys Black-JBU
Jerseys Gold-JBU
Jerseys Ruby-JBU
06Fleer-55
Tiffany-55
Signing Day-SDPB
06O-Pee-Chee-122
Rainbow-122
06The Cup Property of-POBU
06Ultra-54
Gold Medallion-54
Ice Medallion-54
06Upper Deck-302
Exclusives Parallel-302
High Gloss Parallel-302
Game Jerseys-JBU
Game Patches-PBU
Masterpieces-302
06Upper Deck MVP-79
Gold Script-79
Super Script-79
06Russian Sport Collection Olympic Stars-43
07Upper Deck Ovation-89
07Upper Deck Victory-152
Black-152
Gold-152

Budeau, Dennis
91Air Canada SJHL-D18

Budish, Josh
01Lincoln Stars-3

Budkin, Alexander
05Russian Hockey League RHL-5

Budkins, Jesse
06Okotoks Oilers -2

Budy, Tim
89ProCards AHL-226
92Norwegian Elite Series-106

Buenzli, Daniel
96Swiss HNL-130

Buetow, Jason
907th Inn. Sketch OHL-279
917th Inn. Sketch OHL-286

Buettgen, Jim
85Moncton Golden Flames-13

Buffey, Vern
61Sudbury Wolves-3
62Sudbury Wolves-5

Buhler, Cyrill
02Swiss HNL-115

Buhler, Michael
93Swiss HNL-71

Buhler, Scott
95Medicine Hat Tigers-4
96Medicine Hat Tigers-2
97Medicine Hat Tigers-5
98Medicine Hat Tigers-5
99Quad-City Mallards-22

Buhlmann, Marc
98Swiss Power Play Stickers-141
99Swiss Panini Stickers-141
01Swiss HNL-352
02Swiss HNL-329

Buhrer, Marco
93Quebec Pee-Wee Tournament-1634
98Swiss Power Play Stickers-104
98Swiss Power Play Stickers-274
99Swiss Panini Stickers-279
99Swiss Panini Stickers-351
00Swiss Panini Stickers-78
01Swiss HNL-76
02Swiss HNL-249

Buie, Chris
92British Columbia JHL-107

Bujar, Krzysztof
89Swedish Semic World Champ Stickers-142
92Finnish Semic-280

Bukac, Ludek
92Finnish Semic-170
94German DEL-369
95Czech APS Extraliga-351
96Czech APS Extraliga-334
98Czech OFS Legends-10

Bukna, Matej
00UK Sekonda Superleague-33
04Slovakian Skalica Team Set-2

Bukowski, Mike
94German First League-571

Bukta, Mike
89Nashville Knights-3

Bulatov, Alexei
99Russian Hockey League-151

Buldakov, Andrei
99Russian Hockey League-136

Bulis, Jan
95Bowman Draft Prospects-P6
95Slapshot-24
95Barrie Colts-4
97Black Diamond-89
Double Diamond-89
Triple Diamond-89
Quadruple Diamond-89
97Donruss Priority-174
Stamp of Approval-174
97Katch-168
Gold-168
Silver-168
97Pinnacle-24
Artist's Proofs-24
Rink Collection-24
Press Plates Back Black-24
Press Plates Back Cyan-24
Press Plates Back Magenta-24
Press Plates Back Yellow-24
Press Plates Front Black-24
Press Plates Front Cyan-24

Press Plates Front Magenta-24
Press Plates Front Yellow-24
97SP Authentic-198
97Upper Deck-381
97Upper Deck Ice-59
Parallel-59
Power Shift-59
97Barrie Colts-3
97Bowman CHL-1
OPC-1
98Pacific-440
Ice Blue-440
Red-440
98SPx Finite-89
98SPx Finite-131
Radiance-89
Radiance-131
Spectrum-89
Spectrum-131
98UD Choice-216
Prime Choice Reserve-216
Reserve-216
98UD3-29
98UD3-89
98UD3-149
Die-Cuts-29
Die-Cuts-89
Die-Cuts-149
98Upper Deck-202
Exclusives-202
Exclusives 1 of 1-202
Gold Reserve-202
99BAP Millennium-250
Emerald-250
Ruby-250
Sapphire-250
Signatures-250
Signatures Gold-250
99Crown Royale-142
Limited Series-142
Premiere Date-142
99Pacific-438
Copper-438
Emerald Green-438
Gold-438
Ice Blue-438
Premiere Date-438
Red-438
99Pacific Dynagon Ice-200
Blue-200
Copper-200
Gold-200
Premiere Date-200
99Pacific Omega-242
Copper-242
Gold-242
Ice Blue-242
Premiere Date-242
99Pacific Prism-147
Holographic Blue-147
Holographic Gold-147
Holographic Mirror-147
Holographic Purple-147
Premiere Date-147
99Paramount-243
Copper-243
Emerald-243
Gold-243
Holographic Emerald-243
Holographic Gold-243
Holographic Silver-243
Ice Blue-243
Premiere Date-243
Red-243
Silver-243
99SPx-162
Radiance-162
Spectrum-162
99Upper Deck-133
Exclusives-133
Exclusives 1 of 1-133
99Upper Deck Gold Reserve-133
99Upper Deck MVP-218
Gold Script-218
Silver Script-218
Super Script-218
99Upper Deck Victory-306
99Wayne Gretzky Hockey-177
00BAP Memorabilia-350
Emerald-350
Ruby-350
Sapphire-350
Promos-350
00BAP Mem Chicago Sportsfest Copper-350
00BAP Memorabilia Chicago Sportsfest Blue-350
00BAP Memorabilia Chicago Sportsfest Gold-350
00BAP Memorabilia Chicago Sportsfest Ruby-350
00BAP Memorabilia Chicago Sun-Times Ruby-350
00BAP Memorabilia Chicago Sun-Times Gold-350
00BAP Mem Chicago Sun-Times Sapphire-350
00BAP Mem Toronto Fall Expo Copper-350
00BAP Memorabilia Toronto Fall Expo Gold-350
00BAP Memorabilia Toronto Fall Expo Ruby-350
00Pacific-420
Copper-420
Gold-420
Ice Blue-420
Premiere Date-420
00Upper Deck Victory-236
01BAP Memorabilia-135
Emerald-135
Ruby-135
Sapphire-135
01Canadiens Postcards-5
01Pacific-204
Extreme LTD-204
Hobby LTD-204
Premiere Date-204
Retail LTD-204
01Pacific Arena Exclusives-204
01Parkhurst-201
01Upper Deck-95
Exclusives-95
02BAP Sig Series Auto Buybacks 1999-250
02Canadiens Postcards-4
02NHL Power Play Stickers-48
02Pacific Complete-199
Red-199
03Bowman-57
Gold-57
03Bowman Chrome-57
Refractors-57
Gold Refractors-57
Xfractors-57
03Canadiens Postcards-5
03ITG Action-333
03O-Pee-Chee-23
03OPC Blue-23
03OPC Gold-23
03OPC Red-23
03Pacific-175
Blue-175
Red-175
03Pacific Complete-156
Red-156
03Pacific Montreal International-5
03Parkhurst Original Six Montreal-5
Memorabilia-MM4
03Topps-23
Blue-23
Gold-23
Red-23
03Topps C55-127
Minis-127
Minis American Back-127
Minis American Back Red-127
Minis Bazooka Back-127
Minis Brooklyn Back-127
Minis Hat Trick Back-127
Minis O Canada Back-127
Minis O Canada Back Red-127
Minis Stanley Cup Back-127
03Upper Deck-100
Canadian Exclusives-100
HG-100
03Upper Deck MVP-224
Gold Script-224
Silver Script-224
Canadian Exclusives-224
04Czech NHL ELH Postcards-1
04Czech OFS-112
Stars-10
04Czech Zuma-10
04Barrie Colts 10th Anniversary-6
05Canadiens Team Issue-4
05Parkhurst-255
Facsimile Auto Parallel-255
05Upper Deck-103
HG Glossy-103
05Upper Deck MVP-205
Gold-205
Platinum-205
05Upper Deck Toronto Fall Expo-103
06Canucks Postcards-3
06Gatorade-82
06O-Pee-Chee-473
Rainbow-473
06Panini Stickers-353
06Upper Deck-438
Exclusives Parallel-438
High Gloss Parallel-438
Masterpieces-438
06Czech IIHF World Championship Postcards-3

Bull, Max
99Sioux City Musketeers-2

Bullard, Mike
82O-Pee-Chee-262
82O-Pee-Chee-264
82O-Pee-Chee Stickers-149
82Post Cereal-15
82Topps Stickers-149
83NHL Key Tags-101
83O-Pee-Chee-277
83O-Pee-Chee Stickers-235
83Penguins Coke-3
83Penguins Heinz Photos-4
83Puffy Stickers-9
83Topps Stickers-235
84O-Pee-Chee-172
84O-Pee-Chee-365
84O-Pee-Chee Stickers-118
84Penguins Heinz Photos-3
847-Eleven Discs-39
84Topps-123
85O-Pee-Chee-67
85O-Pee-Chee Stickers-104
857-Eleven Credit Cards-15
85Topps-67
86O-Pee-Chee-83
86O-Pee-Chee Stickers-228
86Topps-83
87Blues Team Issue-2
87Flames Red Rooster-3
87O-Pee-Chee-210
87O-Pee-Chee Stickers-37
88Blues Team Issue-2
88Flyers Postcards-9
88O-Pee-Chee-152
88O-Pee-Chee Stickers-93
88O-Pee-Chee Stickers-119
88Panini Stickers-8
88Topps-152
89Flyers Postcards-3
89O-Pee-Chee-21
89O-Pee-Chee Stickers-104
89Topps-21
90Bowman-114
Tiffany-114
90O-Pee-Chee-274
90Panini Stickers-119
90Pro Set-211
90Topps-274
Tiffany-274
90Upper Deck-230
French-230
91Pro Set Platinum-233
91Maple Leafs PLAY-4
91Parkhurst-397
French-397
91Pinnacle-69
French-69
91Pro Set-496
French-496
91Score Canadian Bilingual-590
91Score Canadian English-590
91Score Rookie/Traded-40T
92Score-218
Canadian-218
92Stadium Club-494
92Topps-146
Gold-146G
94German DEL-258
95German DEL-256
96German DEL-144
98German DEL-156
99German DEL-73
00German DEL-225
Profiles-P6
01German Upper Deck-228
04ITG Franchises Update Autographs-MBU
04ITG Franchises US West-279
04German Berlin Eisbaren 50th Anniv-62

Buller, Hy
44Beehive Group II Photos-300
51Parkhurst-91
52Parkhurst-98
53Parkhurst-58

Bulley, Ted
78O-Pee-Chee-217
78Topps-217
79Blackhawks Postcards-3
79O-Pee-Chee-128
79Topps-128
80O-Pee-Chee-229
80Topps-229
81Blackhawks Borderless Postcards-3
81O-Pee-Chee-56
81Topps-W68
82Capitals Team Issue-2
82O-Pee-Chee-360
82Post Cereal-4
83Penguins Coke-4

Bullis, John
06Texas Tornados-14

Bullock, Greg
95Classic-71
Autographs-2
95Classic Five-Sport *-131
Autographs-131
96St. John's Maple Leafs-6
98German DEL-290
00UK Sekonda Superleague-99
06Port Huron Flags-13

Bulow, Johan
02Swedish SHL-49
Parallel-49
03Swedish Elite-72
Silver-72

Bultje, Mark
98UHL All-Stars-4
99UK London Knights-2
00UK Sekonda Superleague-41
01UK Manchester Storm-6
02UK Hull Thunder-15
02UK Manchester Storm-8
03UK Manchester Phoenix-8

Bumagin, Alexander
05Russian Hockey League RHL-2

Bumstead, Geoff
92Cornell Big Red-3
93Cornell Big Red-3
95Alaska Gold Kings-3
99Corpus Christi IceRays-2
99Corpus Christi IceRays-31
99Corpus Christi IceRays-33
99Corpus Christi IceRays-34

Bumstead, Larry
82Brandon Wheat Kings-20

Bundgaard, Lars
98Danish Hockey League-208
99Danish Hockey League-151

Bundi, Ralf
98Swiss Power Play Stickers-275
00Swiss Panini Stickers-249
01Swiss EV Zug Postcards-7
01Swiss HNL-170
02Swiss EV Zug Postcards-9

Bunter, Rolf
93Swiss HNL-391

Bunzli, Daniel
93Swiss HNL-368
95Swiss HNL-217
96Swiss HNL-139

Burakovsky, Mikael
95Swedish Leaf-263
Rookies-7
97Swedish Collector's Choice-148

Burakovsky, Robert
85Swedish Panini Stickers-141
86Swedish Panini Stickers-157
87Swedish Panini Stickers-157
89Swedish Semic Elitserien Stickers-16
90Swedish Semic Elitserien Stickers-85
91Finnish Semic World Champ Stickers-44
91Swedish Semic Elitserien Stickers-189
91Swedish Semic World Champ Stickers-44
92Swedish Semic Elitserien Stickers-221
93Leaf-429
93Parkhurst-144
Emerald Ice-144
93Senators Kraft Sheets-4
93Ultra-379
93Upper Deck-498
SP-106
94Classic Pro Prospects-166
95Swedish Leaf-262
Face to Face-9
95Swedish Upper Deck-149
98Swiss Power Play Stickers-327
99Swiss Panini Stickers-89
00Swedish Upper Deck-119
00Swedish Upper Deck-199

Buras, Miroslav
99Czech OFS-508
All-Star Game Blue-508
All-Star Game Gold-508
All-Star Game Red-508
All-Star Game Silver-508

Buravchikov, Vyacheslav
05Russian Hockey League RHL-33

Burch, Billy
23V145-1-35
24Anonymous NHL-79
24C144 Champ's Cigarettes-9
24V130 Maple Crispette-21
24V145-2-13
30Rogers Peet Company *-42
83Hall of Fame-64
83Hall of Fame Postcards-E3
85Hall of Fame-64
04ITG Franchises Canadian-35

Burchell, Fred
52St. Lawrence Sales-6
62Quebec Aces-4
63Quebec Aces-3

Burchill, Rick
88Johnstown Chiefs-19

Burda, Vaclav
95Czech APS Extraliga-272
96Czech APS Extraliga-127
97Czech APS Extraliga-21
97Czech DS Extraliga-81
97Czech DS Stickers-60
98Czech DS-88
98Czech DS Stickers-210
98Czech OFS-364
99Swedish Upper Deck-136

Burdick, Josh
93Quebec Pee-Wee Tournament-550

Bure, Pavel
90Upper Deck-526
French-526
91Pro Set Platinum-272
91Canucks Autograph Cards-2
91Canucks Molson-2
91Canucks Molson-3
91Canucks Team Issue 8x10-2
91Gillette-10
91OPC Premier-67
91Parkhurst-404
91Parkhurst-446
91Parkhurst-462
French-404
French-446
French-462
91Pinnacle-315
French-315
91Pro Set-564
French-564
91Score Rookie/Traded-49T
91Stadium Club Members Only-38
91Upper Deck-54
91Upper Deck-555
91Upper Deck-647
French-54
French-555
French-647
91Finnish Semic World Champ Stickers-89
91Russian Stars Red Ace-1
91Russian Tri-Globe Bure-6
91Russian Tri-Globe Bure-7
91Russian Tri-Globe Bure-8
91Russian Tri-Globe Bure-9
91Russian Tri-Globe Bure-10
91Swedish Semic World Champ Stickers-89
91Star Pics-25
92Bowman-154
92Canucks Road Trip Art-4
92O-Pee-Chee-25
92O-Pee-Chee-324
25th Anniv. Inserts-25
Trophy Winners-1
92OPC Premier Star Performers-10
92Panini Stickers-271
92Panini Stickers-290
92Panini Stickers-C
92Panini Stickers French-271
92Panini Stickers French-290
92Panini Stickers French-C
92Parkhurst-188
92Parkhurst-234
92Parkhurst-460
92Parkhurst-506
Emerald Ice-188
Emerald Ice-234
Emerald Ice-460
Emerald Ice-506
92Pinnacle Canadian Promo Panels-1
92Pinnacle-110
French-110
Team 2000-8
Team 2000 French-8
Team Pinnacle-4
Team French-4
92Pro Set-192
Award Winners-CC3
Gold Team Leaders-13
Rookie Goal Leaders-2
92Score Canadian Promo Sheets-2
92Score-14
92Score-504
92Score-523
Canadian-14
Canadian-504
Canadian-523
Young Superstars-30
92Seasons Patches-31
92Sports Illustrated for Kids II-303
92Sports Illustrated for Kids II-715
92Stadium Club-246
92Stadium Club-489
92Topps-8
92Topps-353
Gold-8G
Gold-353G
92Ultra-219
Award Winners-9
Imports-2
Rookies-3
92Upper Deck-156
92Upper Deck-362
92Upper Deck-431
92Upper Deck-SP2
Euro-Rookie Team-ERT1
Euro-Stars-E2
World Junior Grads-WG5
92Finnish Semic-116
92Russian Tri-Globe From Russia With Puck-5
92Russian Tri-Globe From Russia With Puck-6
92Classic-AU2
93Donruss-351
Ice Kings-8
Special Print-X
93Kraft-3
93Kraft-51
93Leaf-10
Gold All-Stars-8
93McDonald's Upper Deck-2
93OPC Premier-260
93OPC Premier-440
Gold-260
Gold-440
Black Gold-7
93Panini Stickers-O
93Parkhurst-211
Emerald Ice-211
East/West Stars-W2
USA/Canada Gold-G7
93Pinnacle II Samples-320
93Pinnacle-320
Canadian-320
All-Stars-31
All-Stars Canadian-31
Nifty Fifty-6
Team Pinnacle-10
Team Canadian-10
Team 2001-3
Team 2001 Canadian-3
93PowerPlay-248
Global Greats-1
Point Leaders-1
93Score-333
Canadian-333
Dream Team-19
Franchise-22
International Stars-1
International Stars Canadian-1
93Seasons Patches-2
93Stadium Club-480
Members Only Master Set-480
First Day Issue-480
All-Stars-6
All-Stars Members Only-6
All-Stars OPC-6
93Topps/OPC Premier-260
93Topps/OPC Premier-440
Gold-260
Gold-440
93Ultra-37
All-Stars-17
Red Light Specials-2
Speed Merchants-1
93Upper Deck-35
93Upper Deck-307
Future Heroes-30
NHL's Best-HB5
NHLPA/Roots-15
Silver Skates-H2
Silver Skates Gold-H2
SP-162
93Upper Deck Locker All-Stars-21
93Classic-117
Autographs-AU2
Crash Numbered-N6
Promos-3
94Hockey Canadian-1
94SLU Hockey Canadian-1
94SLU Hockey American-3
94Action Packed Mammoth-MM3
94Be A Player-R35
94Be A Player-R177
Up Close and Personal-UC3
94Canada Games NHL POGS-266
94Canada Games NHL POGS-341
94Canada Games NHL POGS-376
94Canucks Program Inserts-5
94Donruss-19
Dominators-8
Elite Inserts-3
94EA Sports-143
94Finest-24
Super Team Winners-24
Refractors-24
Bowman's Best-B11
Bowman's Best Refractors-B11
Division's Clear Cut-20
94Flair-189
Hot Numbers-1
Scoring Power-1
94Fleer-223
Headliners-1
94Hockey Wit-7
94Kenner Starting Lineup Cards-3
94Kraft-68
94Leaf-10
Fire on Ice-3
Gold Stars-4
Limited Inserts-24
94Leaf Limited-100
Gold-10
94McDonald's Upper Deck-McD23
94OPC Premier-39
94OPC Premier-151
94OPC Premier-325
94OPC Premier-415
Special Effects-39
Special Effects-151
Special Effects-325
Special Effects-415
94Parkhurst-297
Gold-297
Crash the Game Green-24
Crash the Game Blue-24
Crash the Game Gold-24
Crash the Game Red-24
Vintage-V18
94Parkhurst SE-SE187
Gold-SE187
Euro-Stars-ES15
94Pinnacle-140
94Pinnacle-MVPC
Artist's Proofs-140
Rink Collection-140
Boomers-BR13
Gamers-GR4
Northern Lights-NL17
Team Pinnacle-TP12
Team Dufex Parallel-TP12
94Post Box Backs-5
94Score-78
94Score-190
Gold-190
Platinum-78
Platinum-190
Dream Team-DT24
Franchise-TF24
90 Plus Club-5
94Select-92
Gold-92
First Line-FL6
94SP-121
Die Cuts-121
Premier-16
Premier Die-Cuts-16
94Stadium Club Members Only-4
94Stadium Club-10
Members Only Master Set-10
First Day Issue-10
Dynasty and Destiny-3
Dynasty and Destiny Members Only-3
Finest Inserts-5
Finest Inserts Members Only-5
Super Teams-24
Super Teams Members Only Master Set-24
Super Team Winner Cards-10
94Topps/OPC Premier-39
94Topps/OPC Premier-151
94Topps/OPC Premier-325
94Topps/OPC Premier-415
Special Effects-39
Special Effects-151
Special Effects-325
Special Effects-415
94Topps Finest Inserts-1
94Topps/OPC Premier The Go To Guy-5
94Topps Finest Bronze-4
94Ultra-222
All-Stars-7
Red Light Specials-2
Scoring Kings-1
Speed Merchants-1
94Upper Deck-227
94Upper Deck-469
Electric Ice-90
Electric Ice-227
Electric Ice-469
Predictor Hobby-H2
Predictor Hobby-H19
94Upper Deck Predictor Hobby Exch Gold-H2
94Upper Deck Predictor Hobby Exch Gold-H19
94Upper Deck Predictor Hobby Exch Silver-H2
94Upper Deck Predictor Hobby Exch Silver-H19
94Upper Deck Predictor Retail-R1
94Upper Deck Predictor Retail-R25
94Upper Deck Predictor Retail-R31
94Upper Deck Predictor Retail-R53
94Upper Deck Predictor Retail Exchange-R1
94Upper Deck Predictor Retail Exchange-R25
94Upper Deck Predictor Retail Exchange-R31
94Upper Deck Predictor Retail Exchange-R53
94Upper Deck SP Inserts-SP171
94Upper Deck SP Inserts Die Cuts-SP171
94Upper Deck NHLPA/Be A Player-20
94Classic Pro Prospects Intl Heroes-LP22
94Classic Pro Prospects Jumbos-PP12
95SLU Hockey American-3
95Bashan Super Stickers-123
Die-Cut-14
95Be A Player Lethal Lines-LL7
95Bowman-65
All-Foil-65
Bowman's Best-BB13
Bowman's Best Refractors-BB13
95Canada Games NHL POGS-271
95Canada Games NHL POGS-274
95Canucks Building the Dream Art-10
95Collector's Choice-45
Player's Club-45
Player's Club Platinum-45
Crash The Game-C1A
Crash The Game-C1B
Crash The Game-C1C
Crash The Game Gold-C1A
Crash The Game Gold-C1B
Crash The Game Gold-C1C
Crash the Game Silver Redeemed-C1
Crash the Game Silver Bonus-C1
Crash the Game Gold Redeemed-C1
Crash the Game Gold Bonus-C1
95Donruss-170
Dominators-6
95Donruss Elite-77
Die Cut Stars-77
Die Cut Uncut-77
95Emotion-178
Xcited-16
95Finest-75
95Finest-187
Refractors-75
Refractors-187
95Hoyle Western Playing Cards-40
95Imperial Stickers-123
Die Cut Superstars-14
95Kenner Starting Lineup Cards-4
95Kraft-77
95Leaf-135
Fire On Ice-1
Freeze Frame-8
95Leaf Limited-17
95McDonald's Pinnacle-MCD-8
95Metal-149
Heavy Metal-1
International Steel-1
95NHL Aces Playing Cards-9D
95NHL Cool Trade-10
95NHL Cool Trade-RP10
95Panini Stickers-293
95Parkhurst International-248
95Parkhurst International-482
Emerald Ice-248
Emerald Ice-482
Crown Collection Silver Series 1-5
Crown Collection Gold Series 1-5
NHL All-Stars-3
95Pinnacle-1
Artist's Proofs-1
Rink Collection-1
Clear Shots-12
Global Gold-1
Roaring 20s-8
95Pinnacle FANtasy-12
95Playoff One on One-100
95Playoff One on One-207
95Playoff One on One-316
95Pro Magnets-26
95Score-135
Black Ice Artist's Proofs-135
Black Ice-135
Border Battle-11
Dream Team-10
Lamplighters-2
95Select Certified Promos-5
95Select Certified-16
Mirror Gold-16
Gold Team-5
95SkyBox Impact-167
Countdown to Impact-9
Ice Quake-3
95SP-149
Holoviews-FX20
Holoviews Special FX-FX20
Stars/Etoiles-E29
Stars/Etoiles Gold-E29
95Stadium Club Members Only-41
95Stadium Club-186
Members Only Master Set-186
Extreme North-EN1
Extreme North Members Only Master Set-EN1
Nemeses-N4
Nemeses Members Only Master Set-N4
95Summit-7
Artist's Proofs-7
Ice-7
GM's Choice-7
Mad Hatters-7
95Topps-20
95Topps-300
OPC Inserts-20
OPC Inserts-300
Canadian Gold-5CG
Hidden Gems-5HG
Marquee Men Power Boosters-20
Mystery Finest-M15
Mystery Finest Refractors-M15
Profiles-PF11
95Topps SuperSkills-30
Platinum-30
95Ultra-166
95Ultra-379
Gold Medallion-166
95Upper Deck-214
95Upper Deck-406
Electric Ice-214
Electric Ice-406
Electric Ice Gold-214
Electric Ice Gold-406
Freeze Frame-F10
Freeze Frame Jumbo-F10
NHL All-Stars-AS4
NHL All-Stars Jumbo-AS4
Predictor Retail-R9
Predictor Retail-R26
Predictor Retail Exchange-R9
Predictor Retail Exchange-R26
Special Edition-SE172
Special Edition Gold-SE172
95Zenith-9
Z-Team-12
95German DEL-442
95Swedish Globe World Championships-174
95Swedish World Championships Stickers-281
95Images-10
95Images-100
Gold-10
Gold-100
Clear Excitement-CE10
Platinum Players-PL1
96Headliners Hockey-3
96Be A Player Biscuit In The Basket-18
96Be A Player Link to History-4B
96Be A Player Link to History Autographs-4B
96Be A Player Link to History Auto Silver-4B
96Black Diamond-176
Gold-176
Run for the Cup-RC14
96Canucks Postcards-96
96Collector's Choice-266
96Collector's Choice-333
MVP-UD22
MVP Gold-UD22
Stick'Ums-S16
Crash the Game-C17A
Crash the Game-C17B
Crash the Game-C17C
Crash the Game Gold-C17A
Crash the Game Gold-C17B
Crash the Game Gold-C17C
Crash the Game Exchange-CR17
Crash the Game Exchange Gold-CR17
96Donruss-65
Press Proofs-65
Dominators-7
Elite Inserts-1
Elite Inserts Gold-1
96Donruss Canadian Ice-59
Gold Press Proofs-59
Red Press Proofs-59
96Donruss Elite-103
Die Cut Stars-103
Status-1
96Flair-93
Blue Ice-93
Center Ice Spotlight-1
96Fleer-111
Art Ross-1
Pearson-1
Picks Dream Lines-4
Picks Fabulous 50-5
96Hockey Greats Coins-3
Gold-3
96Leaf-15
Press Proofs-15
96Leaf Leather And Laces Promos-P9
96Leaf Leather And Laces-9
96Leaf Sweaters Away-13
96Leaf Sweaters Home-13
96Leaf Limited-32
Gold-32
Stubble-10
96Leaf Preferred-94
Press Proofs-94
Steel Power-3
Vanity Plates-9
Vanity Plates Gold-9
96Maggers-8
96McDonald's Pinnacle-27
96Metal Universe-155
Ice Carvings-2
Ice Carvings Super Power-2
Lethal Weapons-2
Lethal Weapons Super Power-2
96NHL Aces Playing Cards-6
96NHL Pro Stamps-26
96Pinnacle-175
96Pinnacle-248
Artist's Proofs-175
Artist's Proofs-248
Foil-175
Foil-248
Premium Stock-175
Premium Stock-248
Rink Collection-175
Rink Collection-248
By The Numbers-15
By The Numbers Premium-15
96Pinnacle Fantasy-FC14
96Pinnacle Mint-7
Bronze-7
Gold-7
Silver-7
Coins Brass-7
Coins Solid Gold-7
Coins Gold Plated-7
Coins Nickel-7
Coins Silver-7
96Playoff One on One-438
96Score-35
Artist's Proofs-35
Dealer's Choice Artist's Proofs-35
Special Artist's Proofs-35
Golden Blades-35
Dream Team-10
Sudden Death-6
96Select Certified-34
Artist's Proofs-34
Blue-34
Mirror Blue-34
Mirror Gold-34
Mirror Red-34
Red-34
Cornerstones-7
96SkyBox Impact-131
Countdown to Impact-1
VersaTeam-1
96SP-157
Clearcut Winner-CW16
SPx Force-2
96SPx-46
Gold-46
96Summit-42
Artist's Proofs-42
Ice-42
Metal-42
Premium Stock-42
96Team Out-33
96Topps Picks-15
Fantasy Team-FT13
OPC Inserts-15
96Ultra-167
Gold Medallion-167
Mr. Momentum-2
96Upper Deck-347
Game Jerseys-GJ10
Hart Hopefuls Bronze-HH14
Hart Hopefuls Gold-HH14
Hart Hopefuls Silver-HH14
Lord Stanley's Heroes Finals-LS18
Lord Stanley's Heroes Quarterfinals-LS18
Lord Stanley's Heroes Semifinals-LS18
Superstar Showdown-SS1A
96Upper Deck Ice-105
Parallel-105
96Zenith-3
Artist's Proofs-3
Z-Team-8
96Swedish Semic Wien-142
97Headliners Hockey-2
97Be A Player One Timers-12
97Beehive-15
Golden Portraits-15
97Black Diamond-115
Double Diamond-115
Triple Diamond-115
Quadruple Diamond-115
Premium Cut-PC9
Premium Cut Double Diamond-PC9
Premium Cut Quadruple Diamond Horiz-PC9
Premium Cut Triple Diamond-PC9
Premium Cut Quadruple Diamond Verticals-PC9
97Collector's Choice-255
Crash the Game-C24A
Crash the Game-C24B
Crash the Game-C24C
Crash the Game Exchange-CR24
Star Quest-SQ59
Stick'Ums-S25
97Crown Royale-133
Emerald Green-133
Ice Blue-133
Silver-133
Blades of Steel Die-Cuts-19
Cramer's Choice Jumbos-10
Cramer's Choice Jumbos Gold-10
Cramer's Choice Jumbos Signed-10
Hat Tricks Die-Cuts-18
Lamplighters Cel-Fusion Die-Cuts-19
97Donruss-187
Press Proofs Silver-187
Press Proofs Gold-187
Line 2 Line-11
Line 2 Line Die Cut-11
Red Alert-6
97Donruss Canadian Ice-18
Dominion Series-18
Provincial Series-18
97Donruss Elite-4
97Donruss Elite-118
Aspirations-4
Aspirations-118
Status-4
Status-118
Craftsmen-20
Master Craftsmen-20
Prime Numbers-12A
Prime Numbers-12B
Prime Numbers-12C
Prime Numbers Die-Cuts-12A
Prime Numbers Die-Cuts-12B
Prime Numbers Die-Cuts-12C
Prime Numbers Promos-12A
97Donruss Limited-7
97Donruss Limited-104
97Donruss Limited-153
Exposure-7
Exposure-104
Exposure-153
Fabric of the Game-66
97Donruss Preferred-25
97Donruss Preferred-194
Cut to the Chase-25
Cut to the Chase-194
Line of the Times-4A
97Donruss Preferred Line of Times Promos-4A
97Donruss Priority-15
97Donruss Priority-211
Stamp of Approval-15
Stamp of Approval-211
Direct Deposit-3
Postcards-5
Postcards Opening Day Issues-13
Stamps-5
Stamps Bronze-5
Stamps Gold-5
Stamps Silver-5
97Esso Olympic Hockey Heroes-38
97Esso Olympic Hockey Heroes French-38
97Highland Mint Mint-Cards Topps-3
97Highland Mint Mint-Cards Topps-4
97Highland Mint Mint-Coins-2
97Katch-145
Gold-145
Silver-145
97Leaf-60
Fractal Matrix-60
Fractal Matrix Die Cuts-60
Fire On Ice-8
97Leaf International-60
Universal Ice-60
97McDonald's Upper Deck-3
97NHL Aces Playing Cards-9
97Pacific-96
Copper-96
Emerald Green-96
Ice Blue-96
Red-96
Silver-96
Card-Supials-20
Card-Supials Minis-20
Gold Crown Die-Cuts-20
Slap Shots Die-Cuts-11A
Team Checklists-25
97Pacific Dynagon-125
Copper-125
Dark Grey-125
Emerald Green-125
Ice Blue-125
Red-125
Silver-125
Best Kept Secrets-95
Dynamic Duos-15A
Kings of the NHL-10
Tandems-14
97Pacific Invincible-140
Copper-140
Emerald Green-140
Ice Blue-140
Red-140
Silver-140
Attack Zone-23
NHL Regime-201
Off The Glass-20
97Pacific Omega-228
Copper-228
Dark Gray-228
Emerald Green-228
Gold-228
Ice Blue-228
Game Face-18
Silks-11
Stick Handle Laser Cuts-19
Team Leaders-19
97Panini Stickers-236
97Paramount-186
Copper-186
Dark Grey-186
Emerald Green-186

Ice Blue-186
Red-186
Silver-186
Big Numbers Die-Cuts-19
Photoengravings-19
97Pinnacle-41
Artist's Proofs-41
Rink Collection-41
Epix Game Emerald-21
Epix Game Orange-21
Epix Game Purple-21
Epix Moment Emerald-21
Epix Moment Orange-21
Epix Moment Purple-21
Epix Play Emerald-21
Epix Play Orange-21
Epix Play Purple-21
Epix Season Emerald-21
Epix Season Orange-21
Epix Season Purple-21
Press Plates Back Black-41
Press Plates Back Cyan-41
Press Plates Back Magenta-41
Press Plates Back Yellow-41
Press Plates Front Black-41
Press Plates Front Cyan-41
Press Plates Front Magenta-41
Press Plates Front Yellow-41
97Pinnacle Certified-45
Red-45
Mirror Blue-45
Mirror Gold-45
Mirror Red-45
97Pinnacle Inside-11
Coach's Collection-11
Executive Collection-11
Track-12
Cans-13
Cans Gold-13
97Pinnacle Mint-17
Bronze-17
Gold Team-17
Silver Team-17
Coins Brass-17
Coins Brass Proofs-17
Coins Gold Plated-17
Coins Gold Plated Proofs-17
Coins Nickel Silver-17
Coins Nickel Silver Proofs-17
Coins Solid Gold-17
Coins Solid Silver-17
Minternational-6
Minternational Coins-6
97Pinnacle Power Pack Blow-Ups-14
97Pinnacle Tot Cert Platinum Blue-45
97Pinnacle Tot Certi Platinum Gold-45
97Pinnacle Totally Certified Platinum Red-45
97Pinnacle Tot Cert Mirror Platinum Gold-45
97Post Pinnacle-17
97Revolution-139
Copper-139
Emerald-139
Ice Blue-139
Silver-139
1998 All-Star Game Die-Cuts-18
NHL Icons-10
Team Checklist Laser Cuts-25
97Score-96
97Score-261
Artist's Proofs-96
Golden Blades-96
97Score Canucks-1
Platinum-1
Premier-1
97SP Authentic-156
Icons-I36
Icons Die-Cuts-I36
Icons Embossed-I36
97SPx-47
Bronze-47
Gold-47
Silver-47
Steel-47
Dimension-SPX6
Grand Finale-47
97Studio-14
Press Proofs Silver-14
Press Proofs Gold-14
Hard Hats-18
Portraits-14
Silhouettes-9
Silhouettes 8x10-9
97Upper Deck-168
Blow-Ups 3 x 5-1-5
Blow-Ups 5 x 7-5B
Game Dated Moments-168
Sixth Sense Masters-SS24
Sixth Sense Wizards-SS24
Smooth Grooves-SG58
The Specialists-10
The Specialists Level 2 Die Cuts-10
Three Star Selects-5C
97Upper Deck Crash the All-Star Game-8
97Upper Deck Crash the All-Star Game-AR8
97Upper Deck Diamond Vision-10
Signature Moves-10
97Upper Deck Ice-86
Parallel-86
Power Shift-86
97Zenith-34
Z-Gold-34
Z-Silver-34
97Zenith 5 x 7-59
Gold Impulse-59
Silver Impulse-59
98SLU Hockey One on One-1
98Aurora-188
Atomic Laser Cuts-18
Championship Fever-47
Championship Fever Copper-47
Championship Fever Ice Blue-47
Championship Fever Red-47
Championship Fever Silver-47
Cubes-17
Man Advantage-18
98Be A Player-211
Press Release-211
98BAP Gold-211
98BAP Autographs-211
98BAP Autographs Gold-211
98BAP AS Game Used Jersey Cards-AS19
98BAP Playoff Game Used Jerseys-G10
98BAP Playoff Game Used Jersey Autographs-G10
98BAP Playoff Highlights-H12
98BAP Playoff Practice Used Jerseys-P4
98Black Diamond-37
Myriad-M10
Myriad 2-M10
Winning Formula Gold-WF28
Winning Formula Platinum-WF28
98Bowman's Best-58
Refractors-58
Atomic Refractors-58
Mirror Image Fusion-F14
Mirror Image Fusion Refractors-F14
Mirror Image Fusion Atomic Refractors-F14
98Crown Royale-134
Limited Series-134
98Donruss Elite Promos-8
98Finest-105
No Protectors-105
No Protectors Refractors-105
Refractors-105
Double Sided Mystery Finest-M43
Double Sided Mystery Finest-M46
Double Sided Mystery Finest-M48
Double Sided Mystery Finest-M49
Double Sided Mystery Refractors-M43
Double Sided Mystery Refractors-M46
Double Sided Mystery Refractors-M48
Double Sided Mystery Refractors-M49
Red Lighters-R4
Red Lighters Refractors-R4
98Katch-145
98Kraft Fearless Forwards-2
98McDonald's Upper Deck-14
98OPC Chrome-180
Refractors-180
Season's Best-SB15
Season's Best Refractors-SB15
98Pacific-10
Ice Blue-10
Red-10
Cramer's Choice-10
Dynagon Ice Inserts-17
Titanium Ice-17
Gold Crown Die-Cuts-33
Team Checklists-26
Timelines-19
98Pacific Dynagon Ice-187
Blue-187
Red-187
98Pacific Omega-99
Red-99
Opening Day Issue-99
Championship Spotlight-5
Championship Spotlight Green-5
Championship Spotlight Red-5
Championship Spotlight Gold-5
EO Portraits-12
EO Portraits 1 of 1-12
Face to Face-4
Online-17
Planet Ice-20
Planet Ice Parallel-20
Prism-11
98Panini Photocards-15
98Panini Stickers-216
98Paramount-234
Copper-234
Emerald Green-234
Holo-Electric-234
Ice Blue-234
Silver-234
Special Delivery Die-Cuts-18
98Revolution-59
Ice Shadow-59
Red-59
Three Pronged Attack-30
Three Pronged Attack Parallel-30
98SP Authentic-86
Power Shift-86
Sign of the Times-PB
Sign of the Times Gold-PB
Stat Masters-S17
98SPx Finite-84
98SPx Finite-91
98SPx Finite-170
Radiance-84
Radiance-91
Radiance-170
Spectrum-84
Spectrum-91
Spectrum-170
98SPx Top Prospects-58
Radiance-58
Spectrum-58
Highlight Heroes-H29
Lasting Impressions-L10
98Topps-180
O-Pee-Chee-180
Local Legends-L14
Mystery Finest Bronze-M3
Mystery Finest Bronze Refractors-M3
Mystery Finest Gold-M3
Mystery Finest Gold Refractors-M3
Mystery Finest Silver-M3
Mystery Finest Silver Refractors-M3
Season's Best-SB15
98Topps Gold Label Class 1-74
Black-74
Black One of One-74
One of One-74
Red-74
Red One of One-74
98Topps Gold Label Class 2-74
98Topps Gold Label Class 2 Black-74
98Topps Gold Label Class 2 Black 1 of 1-74
98Topps Gold Label Class 2 One of One-74
98Topps Gold Label Class 2 Red-74
98Topps Gold Label Class 2 Red One of One-74
98Topps Gold Label Class 3-74
98Topps Gold Label Class 3 Black-74
98Topps Gold Label Class 3 Black 1 of 1-74
98Topps Gold Label Class 3 One of One-74
98Topps Gold Label Class 3 Red-74
98Topps Gold Label Class 3 Red One of One-74
98UD Choice-208
Mini Bobbing Head-BH30
Prime Choice Reserve-208
Reserve-208
StarQuest Blue-SQ2
StarQuest Gold-SQ2
StarQuest Green-SQ2
StarQuest Red-SQ2
98Upper Deck-18
98Upper Deck-193
Exclusives-18
Exclusives-193
Exclusives 1 of 1-18
Exclusives 1 of 1-193
Fantastic Finishers-FF13
Fantastic Finishers Quantum 1-FF13
Fantastic Finishers Quantum 2-FF13
Fantastic Finishers Quantum 3-FF13
Frozen In Time-FT24
Frozen In Time Quantum 1-FT24
Frozen In Time Quantum 2-FT24
Frozen In Time Quantum 3-FT24
Generation Next-GN28
Generation Next-GN29
Generation Next-GN30
Generation Next Quantum 1-GN28
Generation Next Quantum 1-GN29
Generation Next Quantum 1-GN30
Generation Next Quantum 2-GN28
Generation Next Quantum 2-GN29
Generation Next Quantum 2-GN30
Generation Next Quantum 3-GN28
Generation Next Quantum 3-GN29
Generation Next Quantum 3-GN30
Lord Stanley's Heroes-LS26
Lord Stanley's Heroes Quantum 1-LS26
Lord Stanley's Heroes Quantum 2-LS26
Lord Stanley's Heroes Quantum 3-LS26
Gold Reserve-18
Gold Reserve-193
98Upper Deck MVP-85
Gold Script-85
Silver Script-85
Super Script-85
OT Heroes-OT11
Snipers-S8
99Aurora-61
Striped-61
Premiere Date-61
Premiere Date Striped-61
Canvas Creations-7
Championship Fever-14
Championship Fever Copper-14
Championship Fever Ice Blue-14
Championship Fever Silver-14
Styrotechs-11
99BAP Memorabilia-126
Gold-126
Silver-126
Jersey Cards-J19
Jersey Emblems-E19
Jersey Numbers-I19
Jersey and Stick Cards-S19
AS Heritage Ruby-H19
AS Heritage Sapphire-H19
AS Heritage Emerald-H19
99BAP Update Double AS Jersey Cards-D13
99BAP Update Teammates Jersey Cards-TM14
99BAP Update Teammates Jersey Cards-TM19
99BAP Update Teammates Jersey Cards-TM30
99BAP Millennium-106
Emerald-106
Ruby-106
Sapphire-106
Signatures-106
Signatures Gold-106
Jerseys-J10
Jersey Autographs-J10
Jersey and Stick Cards-JS10
Jersey Emblems-E10
Jersey Numbers-N10
99Black Diamond-41
Diamond Cut-41
Final Cut-41
A Piece of History-PB
A Piece of History Double-PB
A Piece of History Triple-PB
Diamonation-D8
Diamond Skills-DS4
Myriad-M6
99Crown Royale-59
Limited Series-59
Premiere Date-59
Card-Supials-12
Card-Supials Minis-12
Century 21-5
Cramer's Choice Jumbos-7
Cramer's Choice Jumbos Dark Blue-7
Cramer's Choice Jumbos Gold-7
Cramer's Choice Jumbos Green-7
Cramer's Choice Jumbos Light Blue-7
Cramer's Choice Jumbos Purple-7
Cramer's Choice Jumbos Red-7
International Glory-11
International Glory Parallel-11
99O-Pee-Chee-10
99O-Pee-Chee All-Topps-AT15
99O-Pee-Chee Chrome-10
99O-Pee-Chee Chrome All Topps-AT15
99O-Pee-Chee Chrome All-Topps Refractors-AT15
99O-Pee-Chee Chrome Refractors-10
99O-Pee-Chee Top of the World-TW9
99Oscar Mayer Lunchables-2
99Pacific-169
Copper-169
Emerald Green-169
Gold-169
Ice Blue-169
Premiere Date-169
Red-169
Gold Crown Die-Cuts-19
Past and Present-14
Team Leaders-12
99Pacific Dynagon Ice-87
Blue-87
Copper-87
Gold-87
Premiere Date-87
2000 All-Star Preview-12
Checkmates American-10
Checkmates American-25
Checkmates Canadian-25
Lamplighter Net-Fusions-6
99Pacific Omega-97
99Pacific Omega-250
Copper-97
Copper-250
Gold-97
Gold-250
Ice Blue-97
Ice Blue-250
Premiere Date-97
Premiere Date-250
Cup Contenders-11
EO Portraits-10
EO Portraits 1/1-10
NHL Generations-7
5 Star Talents-15
5 Star Talents Parallel-15
World All-Stars-4
99Pacific Prism-60
Holographic Blue-60
Holographic Gold-60
Holographic Mirror-60
Holographic Purple-60
Premiere Date-60
Clear Advantage-10
Sno-Globe Die-Cuts-12
99Panini Stickers-56
99Paramount-98
Copper-98
Emerald-98
Gold-98
Holographic Emerald-98
Holographic Gold-98
Holographic Silver-98
Ice Blue-98
Premiere Date-98
Red-98
Silver-98
Ice Advantage-12
Ice Advantage Proofs-12
Ice Alliance-12
Personal Best-19
99Revolution-62
Premiere Date-62
Red-62
Shadow Series-62
Ice Sculptures-6
Ornaments-12
Showstoppers-19
Top of the Line-4
Copper-62
Gold-62
CSC Silver-62
99SP Authentic-37
Buyback Signatures-1
Buyback Signatures-2
Buyback Signatures-3
Buyback Signatures-4
Buyback Signatures-5
Buyback Signatures-6
Buyback Signatures-7
Buyback Signatures-8
Buyback Signatures-9
Buyback Signatures-10
Jersey Redemption-JPB
Sign of the Times-PB
Sign of the Times Gold-PB
Special Forces-SF6
Supreme Skill-SS6
99SPx-69
Radiance-69
Spectrum-69
Highlight Heroes-HH7
SPXcitement-X3
Starscape-S3
99Stadium Club-9
First Day Issue-9
One of a Kind-9
Printing Plates Black-9
Printing Plates Cyan-9
Printing Plates Magenta-9
Printing Plates Yellow-9
Capture the Action-CA18
Capture the Action Game View-CAG18
Chrome-9
Chrome Refractors-9
Chrome Oversized-7
Chrome Oversized Refractors-7
Onyx Extreme-OE10
Onyx Extreme Die-Cut-OE10
99Topps/OPC-10
All-Topps-AT15
Top of the World-TW9
99Topps/OPC Chrome-10
Refractors-10
All-Topps-AT15
All-Topps Refractors-AT15
99Topps Gold Label Class 1-10
Black-10
Black One of One-10
One of One-10
Red-10
Red One of One-10
99Topps Gold Label Class 2-10
99Topps Gold Label Class 2 Black-10
99Topps Gold Label Class 2 Black 1 of 1-10
99Topps Gold Label Class 2 One of One-10
99Topps Gold Label Class 2 Red-10
99Topps Gold Label Class 2 Red One of One-10
99Topps Gold Label Class 3-10
99Topps Gold Label Class 3 Black-10
99Topps Gold Label Class 3 Black 1 of 1-10
99Topps Gold Label Class 3 One of One-10
99Topps Gold Label Class 3 Red-10
99Topps Gold Label Class 3 Red One of One-10
99Topps Gold Label Prime Gold-PG14
99Topps Gold Label Prime Gold One of One -PG14
99Topps Gold Label Prime Gold Black-PG14
99Topps Gold Label Prime Gold Black One of One -PG14
99Topps Gold Label Prime Gold Red-PG14
99Topps Gold Label Prime Gold Red One of One -PG14
99Topps Premier Plus-71
Parallel-71
Calling All Calders-CAC7
Code Red-CR8
Feature Presentations-FP6
99Ultimate Victory-38
1/1-38
Parallel-38
Parallel 100-38
Frozen Fury-FF3
Smokin Guns-SG9
Stature-S6
UV Extra-UV3
99Upper Deck-59
99Upper Deck-149
Exclusives-59
Exclusives-149
Exclusives 1 of 1-59
Exclusives 1 of 1-149
All-Star Class-AS7
All-Star Class Quantum Gold-AS7
All-Star Class Quantum Silver-AS7
Crunch Time-CT28
Crunch Time Quantum Gold-CT28
Crunch Time Quantum Silver-CT28
Fantastic Finishers-FF9
Fantastic Finishers Quantum Gold-FF9
Fantastic Finishers Quantum Silver-FF9
Ice Gallery-IG10
Ice Gallery Quantum Gold-IG10
Ice Gallery Quantum Silver-IG10
Marquee Attractions-MA10
Marquee Attractions Quantum Gold-MA10
Marquee Attractions Quantum Silver-MA10
NHL Scrapbook-SB7
NHL Scrapbook Quantum Gold-SB7
NHL Scrapbook Quantum Silver-SB7
Sixth Sense-SS13
Sixth Sense Quantum Gold-SS13
Sixth Sense Quantum Silver-SS13
99Upper Deck Century Legends-58
Century Collection-58
Epic Signatures-PB
Epic Signatures 100-PB
Essence of the Game-E6
99Upper Deck Gold Reserve-59
99Upper Deck Gold Reserve-149
Game-Used Souvenirs-GRPB
UD Authentics-PB
99Upper Deck HoloGrFx-26
Ausome-26
UD Authentics-PB
99Upper Deck MVP-85
Gold Script-85
Silver Script-85
Super Script-85
21st Century NHL-9
90's Snapshots-S10
Game-Used Souvenirs-GU4
Game-Used Souvenirs-GU18
Game-Used Souvenirs-GUS2
Hands of Gold-H3
ProSign-PB
99Upper Deck MVP SC Edition-77
Gold Script-77
Silver Script-77
Super Script-77
Game-Used Souvenirs-GUPV
Great Combinations-GCBK
Great Combinations Parallel-GCBK
Playoff Heroes-PH6
ProSign-PB
Second Season Snipers-SS5
Stanley Cup Talent-SC8
99Upper Deck Ovation-27
99Upper Deck Ovation-88
Standing Ovation-27
Standing Ovation-88
A Piece Of History-PB
A Piece Of History-PBS
Lead Performers-LP5
Superstar Theater-ST9
99Upper Deck PowerDeck-12
Auxiliary-12
Auxiliary 1 of 1-12
99Upper Deck Retro-35
Gold-35
Platinum-35
Generation-G6B
Generation Level 2-G6B
Inkredible-PAB
Inkredible Level 2-PAB
99Upper Deck Victory-119
99Upper Deck Victory-120
99Wayne Gretzky Hockey-72
Changing The Game-CG9
Elements of the Game-EG8
Great Heroes-GH10
Signs of Greatness-PB
Tools of Greatness-TGPB
99Russian Stars of Hockey-27
99Russian Fetisov Tribute-2
00SLU Hockey One On One-20
00McFarlane Hockey-80
00Aurora-60
Pinstripes-60
Pinstripes Premiere Date-60
Premiere Date-60
Canvas Creations-6
Championship Fever-13
Championship Fever Copper-13
Championship Fever Platinum Blue-13
Championship Fever Silver-13
Scouting Reports-11
00BAP Memorabilia-161
Emerald-161
Ruby-161
Sapphire-161
Promos-161
Jersey Cards-J3
Jersey Emblems-E3
Jersey Numbers-N3
Jersey and Stick Cards-JS3
Patent Power Jerseys-PP3
00BAP Mem Chicago Sportsfest Copper-161
00BAP Memorabilia Chicago Sportsfest Blue-161
00BAP Memorabilia Chicago Sportsfest Gold-161
00BAP Memorabilia Chicago Sportsfest Ruby-161
00BAP Memorabilia Chicago Sun-Times Ruby-161
00BAP Memorabilia Chicago Sun-Times Gold-161
00BAP Mem Chicago Sun-Times Sapphire-161
00BAP Mem Toronto Fall Expo Copper-161
00BAP Memorabilia Toronto Fall Expo Gold-161
00BAP Memorabilia Toronto Fall Expo Ruby-161
00BAP Mem Update Heritage Jersey Cards-H2
00BAP Mem Update Heritage Jersey Gold-H2
00BAP Memorabilia Update Record Breakers-BB1
00BAP Mem Update Record Breakers Gold-BB1
00BAP Memorabilia Update Teammates-TM8
00BAP Memorabilia Update Teammates Gold-TM8
00BAP Parkhurst 2000-P1
00BAP Signature Series-226
Emerald-226
Ruby-226
Sapphire-226
Autographs-1
Autographs Gold-1
Franchise Players-F13
He Shoots-He Scores Points-1
He Shoots-He Scores Prizes-1
Jersey Cards-J10
Jersey and Stick Cards-GSJ10
Jersey Cards Autographs-J10
Jersey Emblems-E10
Jersey Numbers-IN10
00BAP Ultimate Memorabilia Autographs-10
Gold-10
00BAP Ultimate Memorabilia Active Eight-AE3
00BAP Ultimate Mem Game-Used Jerseys-GJ10
00BAP Ultimate Mem Game-Used Emblems-E8
00BAP Ultimate Mem Game-Used Numbers-N8
00BAP Ultimate Mem Game-Used Sticks-GS10
00BAP Ultimate Mem Journey Jerseys-JJ3
00BAP Ultimate Mem Journey Emblems-JE3
00BAP Ultimate Mem Journey Numbers-JI3
00BAP Ultimate Memorabilia Teammates-TM19
00Black Diamond-26
00Black Diamond-88
Gold-26
Gold-88
Diamonation-IG4
Diamond Might-FP6
Myriad-CC3
00Crown Royale-45
Ice Blue-45
Limited Series-45
Premiere Date-45
Red-45
Jewels of the Crown-16
Landmarks-6
Now Playing-9
00Kraft-15
00McDonald's Pacific-17
Blue-17
Dial-A-Stats-3
Game Jerseys-6
00O-Pee-Chee-6
00O-Pee-Chee-328
00O-Pee-Chee Parallel-6
00O-Pee-Chee Parallel-328
00Pacific-177
Copper-177
Gold-177
Ice Blue-177
Premiere Date-177
2001: Ice Odyssey-10
Cramer's Choice-6
Euro-Stars-5
Jerseys-9
Jersey Patches-9
Gold Crown Die Cuts-16
Reflections-11
00Pacific 2001: Ice Odyssey Anaheim Ntnl-10
00Panini Stickers-37
00Panthers Team Issue-14
00Paramount-102
Copper-102
Gold-102
Holo-Gold-102
Holo-Silver-102
Ice Blue-102
Premiere Date-102
Epic Scope-12
Freeze Frame-18
Hall of Fame Bound-7
Hall of Fame Bound Canvas Proofs-7
Hall of Fame Bound Proofs-7
Sub Zero-6
Sub Zero Gold-6
Sub Zero Red-9
00Private Stock-42
Gold-42
Premiere Date-42
Retail-42
Silver-42
Artist's Canvas-13
Artist's Canvas Proofs-13
PS-2001 Action-25
PS-2001 Stars-14
Reserve-11
00Revolution-61
Blue-61
Premiere Date-61
Red-61
HD NHL-16
Ice Immortals-12
NHL Icons-13
Stat Masters-6
00SP Authentic-38
BuyBacks-38
BuyBacks-39
BuyBacks-40
BuyBacks-41
BuyBacks-42
BuyBacks-43
BuyBacks-44
BuyBacks-45
Honor-SP3
Sign of the Times-PB
Sign of the Times-B/N
Sign of the Times-LMB
Significant Stars-ST4
Special Forces-SF4
00SP Game Used-27
Patch Cards-P-PB
Tools of the Game-PB
Tools of the Game Exclusives-PB
Tools of the Game Combos-C-BF
Tools of the Game Autographed Bronze-A-PB
Tools of the Game Autographed Silver-A-PB
Tools of the Game Autographed Gold-A-PB
00SPx-28
00SPx-87
Spectrum-28
Spectrum-87
Highlight Heroes-HH8
SPXcitement-X7
00Stadium Club-1
Beam Team-BT5
Capture the Action-CA7
Capture the Action Game View-7
Co-Signers-CO1
Lone Star Signatures-LS1
Special Forces-SF7
11 X 14 Autographs-PB
00Titanium-39
Blue-39
Gold-39
Premiere Date-39
Red-39
Retail-39
All-Stars-5W
00Titanium Draft Day Edition-46
Patches-46
00Topps/OPC-6
00Topps/OPC-328
Parallel-6
Parallel-328
Combos-TC1
Combos Jumbos-TC1
Hobby Masters-HM2
NHL Draft-D8
Own the Game-OTG2
00Topps Chrome-6
OPC Refractors-6
Refractors-6
Combos-TC1
Combos Refractors-TC1
Hobby Masters Refractors-HM2
Rocket's Flare-RF1
Rocket's Flare Refractors-RF1
00Topps Gold Label Class 1-8
Gold-8
00Topps Gold Label Class 2-8
00Topps Gold Label Class 2 Gold-8
00Topps Gold Label Class 3-8
00Topps Gold Label Class 3 Gold-8
00Topps Gold Label Golden Greats-GG1
00Topps Gold Label Golden Greats 1 to 1-GG1
00Topps Heritage-9
00Topps Heritage-220
00Topps Heritage-230
00Topps Heritage-243
Chrome Parallel-9
Heroes-HH11
00Topps Premier Plus-60
Blue Ice-60
Masters of the Break-MB3
Team-PT6
Team Blue Ice-PR6
Trophy Tribute-TT13
World Premier-WP17
00Topps Stars-34
00Topps Stars-127
Blue-34
Blue-127
All-Star Authority-ASA10
Walk of Fame-WF1
00UD Heroes-148
Player Idols-PI3
Signs of Greatness-PB
Timeless Moments-TM5
Today's Snipers-TS3
00UD Pros and Prospects-36
Game Jersey Autograph Exclusives-S-PB
Game Jersey Autographs-S-PB
Great Skates-GS5
ProMotion-PM6
00UD Reserve-36
Gold Strike-GS5
On-Ice Success-OS4
The Big Ticket-BT5
00Upper Deck-74
Exclusives Tier 1-74
Exclusives Tier 2-74
All-Star Class-A5
Dignitaries-D6
e-Cards-EC4
e-Card Prizes-APB
e-Card Prizes-EPB
e-Card Prizes-SEPB
Fantastic Finishers-FF6
Fun-Damentals-F6
Game Jerseys-PB
Game Jersey Autographs-HPB
Game Jersey Autographs Exclusives-EPB
Game Jersey Autographs Exclusives-ESPB
Game Jersey Combos-DFB
Game Jersey Doubles-DPB
Game Jersey Patches-PBP
Game Jersey Patch Autographs Exclusives-PBP
Gate Attractions-GA7
Profiles-P5
Rise to Prominence-RP2
Skilled Stars-SS11
Triple Threat-TT7
00Upper Deck Ice-20
Immortals-20
Legends-20
Stars-20
Clear Cut Autographs-PB
Cool Competitors-CC3
Gallery-IG4
Game Jerseys-JCPB
Rink Favorites-FP6
00Upper Deck Legends-55
00Upper Deck Legends-57
Legendary Collection Bronze-55
Legendary Collection Bronze-57
Legendary Collection Gold-55
Legendary Collection Gold-57
Legendary Collection Silver-55
Legendary Collection Silver-57
Epic Signatures-PB
Essence of the Game-EG3
Legendary Game Jerseys-JPB
00Upper Deck MVP-79
00Upper Deck MVP-219
Excellence-ME2
First Stars-79
Game-Used Souvenirs-GSPB
Mark of Excellence-SGBB
ProSign-PB
Second Stars-79
Super Game-Used Souvenirs-GSPB
Talent-M8
Third Stars-79
Third Stars-219
Top Draws-TD5
Top Playmakers-TP6
00Upper Deck Victory-100
00Upper Deck Victory-101
00Upper Deck Victory-241
00Upper Deck Victory-251
00Upper Deck Victory-304
00Upper Deck Victory-WCB
00Upper Deck Vintage-150
00Upper Deck Vintage-160
00Upper Deck Vintage-161
All UD Team-UD10
National Heroes-NH12
00Vanguard-45
Cosmic Force-6
High Voltage-16
High Voltage Gold-16
High Voltage Green-16
High Voltage Red-16
High Voltage Silver-16
Holographic Gold-45
Holographic Purple-45
In Focus-10
Pacific Proofs-45
Press East/West-13
00Czech Stadion-99
01Atomic-44
Blue-44
Gold-44
Premiere Date-44
Red-44
Blast-6
Core Players-6
Power Play-16
Statosphere-14
01BAP Memorabilia-104
01BAP Memorabilia-480
Emerald-104
Emerald-480
Ruby-104
Ruby-480
Sapphire-104
Sapphire-480
All-Star Jerseys-ASJ15
All-Star Emblems-ASE15
All-Star Numbers-ASN15
All-Star Jersey Doubles-DASJ14
All-Star Starting Lineup-S6
All-Star Teammates-AST5
All-Star Teammates-AST14
All-Star Teammates-AST21
All-Star Teammates-AST23
All-Star Teammates-AST36
All-Star Teammates-AST44
Country of Origin-CO34
He Shoots-He Scores Points-18
He Shoots-He Scores Prizes-25
Patented Power-PP3
01BAP Signature Series Certified 100-C32
01BAP Signature Series Certified 50-C32
01BAP Signature Series Certified 1 of 1's-C32
01BAP Signature Series Autographs-LPBU
01BAP Signature Series Autographs Gold-LPBU
01BAP Signature Series Franchise Jerseys-FP-13
01BAP Sig Series He Shoots/Scores Points-12
01BAP Sig Series International Medals-IB-6
01BAP Signature Series Jerseys-GJ-28
01BAP Signature Series Jerseys-GJ-91
01BAP Signature Series Jersey Autographs-GUPB
01BAP Sig Series Jersey and Stick Cards-GSJ-28
01BAP Signature Series Emblems-GUE-26
01BAP Signature Series Numbers-ITN-26
01BAP Signature Series Teammates-TM-13
01BAP Ultimate Mem All-Star History-50
01BAP Ultimate Memorabilia Autographs-17
01BAP Ultimate Mem Autographs Gold-17
01BAP Ultimate Memorabilia Bloodlines-1
01BAP Ultimate Memorabilia Calder Trophy-10
01BAP Ultimate Memorabilia Dynamic Duos-5
01BAP Ultimate Memorabilia Emblems-8
01BAP Ultimate Memorabilia Jerseys-8
01BAP Ultimate Mem Jerseys and Sticks-8
01BAP Ultimate Mem Journey Jerseys-7
01BAP Ultimate Mem Journey Emblems-7
01BAP Ultimate Memorabilia Made to Order-6
01BAP Ultimate Memorabilia Numbers-7
01BAP Ultimate Memorabilia Name Plates-4
01BAP Ultimate Mem Prototypical Players-14
01BAP Ultimate Mem Scoring Leaders-13
01BAP Ultimate Mem Scoring Leaders-19
01BAP Ultimate Mem Scoring Leaders-20
01BAP Update He Shoots-He Scores Points-11
01BAP Update He Shoots-He Scores Prizes-8
01BAP Update He Shoots-He Scores Prizes-33
01BAP Update Heritage-H9
01Bowman YoungStars-16
Gold-16
Ice Cubed-16
01Crown Royale-63
Blue-63
Premiere Date-63
Red-63
Retail-63
All-Star Honors-11
Crowning Achievement-16
Jewels of the Crown-14
01eTopps-17
01McDonald's Pacific-18
Cosmic Force-1
01Nortel All-Star Game Sheets-3
01O-Pee-Chee-8
01O-Pee-Chee Heritage Parallel-8
01O-Pee-Chee Heritage Parallel Limited-8
01O-Pee-Chee Premier Parallel-8
01Pacific-169
01Pacific-412
01Pacific-431
Extreme LTD-169
Gold-412
Gold-431
Hobby LTD-169
Premiere Date-169
Retail LTD-169
All-Stars-W4
Cramer's Choice-6
Gold Crown Die-Cuts-11
01Pacific Adrenaline-79
Blue-79
Premiere Date-79
Red-79
Retail-79
Blade Runners-6
World Beaters-7
01Pacific Arena Exclusives-169
01Pacific Arena Exclusives-412
01Pacific Arena Exclusives-431
01Pacific Heads-Up-43
Blue-43
Premiere Date-43
Red-43
Silver-43
All-Star Net-4
HD NHL-6
Quad Jerseys-21
Rink Immortals-7
Stat Masters-8
01Parkhurst-13
01Parkhurst-390
Gold-13
Silver-13
He Shoots-He Scores Points-17
He Shoots-He Scores Prizes-6
Heroes-H4
Jerseys-PJ19
Jersey and Stick-PSJ2
Milestones-M26
Sticks-PS19
Teammates-T10
Teammates-T20
Waving the Flag-30
01Private Stock-42
Gold-42
Premiere Date-42
Retail-42
Silver-42
01Private Stock Pacific Nights-42
01Private Stock PS-2002-34
01Private Stock Reserve-S7
01SP Authentic-35
01SP Authentic-NNO
Limited-35
Limited Gold-35
Buybacks-24
Sign of the Times-PB
Sign of the Times-BL
Sign of the Times-BKK
01SP Game Used-23
Authentic Fabric-AFBU
Authentic Fabric Gold-AFBU
Patches-PPB
Patches-CPSB
Patches-TPKYB
Patches Signed-SPPB
Patches Signed-DSPBL
Patches Signed-DSPGB
01SPx-29
01SPx-76
01SPx-86
01SPx-183
01Stadium Club-16
Award Winners-16
Master Photos-16
Gallery-G24
Gallery Gold-G24
NHL Passport-NHLP4
Perennials-P1
Souvenirs-PB
Souvenirs-SFPB
Souvenirs-SSPB
01Stadium Club Toronto Fall Expo-6
01Titanium-59
Hobby Parallel-59
Premiere Date-59
Retail-59
Retail Parallel-59
Saturday Knights-9
01Topps-8
Heritage Parallel-8
Heritage Parallel Limited-8
OPC Parallel-8
Own The Game-OTG7
Shot Masters-SM2
Stars of the Game-SG3
01Topps Chrome-8
Refractors-8
Black Border Refractors-8
01Topps Heritage-11

01Topps Heritage-121
01Topps Heritage-124
01Topps Heritage-132
Refractors-11
01Topps Reserve-8
Emblems-PB
Jerseys-PB
Name Plates-PB
Numbers-PB
Patches-PB
01UD Challenge for the Cup-37
Century Men-CM10
Cornerstones-CR6
Jersey Autographs-FPPB
01UD Honor Roll-15
01UD Honor Roll-45
Honor Society-HS-BB
Honor Society Gold-HS-BB
Pucks-P-PB
Pucks Gold-P-PB
Sharp Skaters-SS4
01UD Mask Collection-64
Gold-64
01UD Playmakers-45
01UD Premier Collection-35
Dual Jerseys-DBA
Dual Jerseys-DFB
Dual Jerseys Black-DBA
Dual Jerseys Black-DFB
Jerseys-BBU
Jerseys Black-B-BU
01UD Top Shelf-19
01UD Top Shelf-109
Sticks-SPBU
Sticks-BFJ
Sticks Gold-SPB
01Upper Deck-73
01Upper Deck-180
01Upper Deck-230
Exclusives-73
Exclusives-180
Exclusives-230
Fantastic Finishers-FF1
Franchise Cornerstones-FC2
Leaders of the Pack-LP6
Shooting Stars-SS8
Skilled Stars-SS6
Tandems-T4
01Upper Deck Ice-20
01Upper Deck MVP-78
Souvenirs-C-PB
Souvenirs Gold-C-PB
Talent-MT7
Valuable Commodities-VC2
01Upper Deck Victory-151
01Upper Deck Victory-395
Gold-151
Gold-395
01Upper Deck Vintage-106
01Upper Deck Vintage-112
01Upper Deck Vintage-113
01Upper Deck Vintage-261
01Upper Deck Vintage-264
01Vanguard-42
Blue-42
Red-42
East Meets West-8
In Focus-6
Memorabilia-46
One of Ones-42
Premiere Date-42
Proofs-42
V-Team-15
02McFarlane Hockey-10
02McFarlane Hockey-12
02Atomic-67
Blue-67
Gold-67
Red-67
Cold Fusion-16
Hobby Parallel-67
Jerseys-15
Jerseys Gold-15
Patches-15
Power Converters-13
02BAP All-Star Edition-11
02BAP All-Star Edition-12
He Shoots-He Scores Points-10
He Shoots-He Score Prizes-4
Jerseys-11
Jerseys-12
Jerseys Gold-11
Jerseys Gold-12
Jerseys Silver-11
Jerseys Silver-12
02BAP First Edition-120
02BAP First Edition-338
02BAP First Edition-360
Debut Jerseys-1
He Shoots-He Score Points-12
He Shoots-He Scores Prizes-5
Jerseys-120
02BAP Memorabilia-166
02BAP Memorabilia-220
02BAP Memorabilia-238
Emerald-166
Emerald-220
Emerald-238
Ruby-166
Ruby-220
Ruby-238
Sapphire-166
Sapphire-220
Sapphire-238
All-Star Jerseys-ASJ-7
All-Star Emblems-ASE-2
All-Star Numbers-ASN-2
All-Star Teammmates-AST-10
All-Star Teammmates-AST-24
All-Star Triple Jerseys-ASTJ-3
Franchise Players-FP-20
He Shoots-He Scores Points-10
He Shoots-He Scores Prizes-11
NHL All-Star Game-166
NHL All-Star Game-220
NHL All-Star Game-238
NHL All-Star Game Blue-166
NHL All-Star Game Blue-220
NHL All-Star Game Blue-238
NHL All-Star Game Green-166
NHL All-Star Game Green-220
NHL All-Star Game Green-238
NHL All-Star Game Red-166
NHL All-Star Game Red-220
NHL All-Star Game Red-238
Teammates-TM-6
02BAP Memorabilia Toronto Fall Expo-166
02BAP Memorabilia Toronto Fall Expo-220
02BAP Memorabilia Toronto Fall Expo-238
02BAP NHL All-Star History-50
02BAP Signature Series-176
Autographs-176
Autograph Buybacks 1998-211
Autograph Buybacks 1999-106
Autograph Buybacks 2000-1
Autograph Buybacks 2001-LPBU
Autographs Gold-176
Complete Jersey-CJ8
Franchise Players-FJ20
Jerseys-SGJ6
Jersey Autographs-SGJ6
Team Quads-TQ4
02BAP Ultimate Memorabilia All-Star MVP-18
02BAP Ultimate Memorabilia Autographs-23
02BAP Ultimate Mem Autographs Gold-23
02BAP Ultimate Memorabilia Dynamic Duos-10
02BAP Ultimate Memorabilia Emblems-4
02BAP Ultimate Memorabilia Jerseys-30
02BAP Ultimate Mem Jersey and Stick-9
02BAP Ultimate Mem Journey Jerseys-9
02BAP Ultimate Mem Journey Emblems-9
02BAP Ultimate Mem Lifetime Achievers-10
02BAP Ultimate Mem Magnificent Ones-9
02BAP Ultimate Mem Magnificent Ones Autos-9
02BAP Ultimate Memorabilia Nameplates-16
02BAP Ultimate Memorabilia Numbers-19
02BAP Ultimate Memorabilia Numerology-13
02Between the Pipes Nightmares-GN5
02Bowman YoungStars-92
Gold-92
Silver-92
02Crown Royale-63
Blue-63
Red-63
Retail-63
Lords of the Rink-14
02eTopps-2
02ITG Used-51
02ITG Used-151
Franchise Players-F20
Franchise Players Autographs-F20
Franchise Players Gold-F20
Jerseys-GUJ6
Jersey Autographs-GUJ6
Jerseys Gold-GUJ6
Emblems-E6
Jersey and Stick-SJ6
Jersey and Stick Gold-SJ6
Teammates-T4
Teammates Gold-T4
02McDonald's Pacific-26
Jersey Patches Silver-10
Jersey Patches Gold-10
02O-Pee-Chee-16
02O-Pee-Chee Premier Blue Parallel-16
02O-Pee-Chee Premier Red Parallel-16
02O-Pee-Chee Factory Set-16
02Pacific-249
Blue-249
Red-249
Jerseys-34
Jerseys Holo-Silver-34
Lamplighters-9
Main Attractions-13
02Pacific Calder-19
Silver-19
02Pacific Complete-301
Red-301
02Pacific Exclusive-113
Maximum Overdrive-14
02Pacific Heads-Up-78
Blue-78
Purple-78
Red-78
Bobble Heads-2
Quad Jerseys-30
Quad Jerseys Gold-30
Stat Masters-10
02Pacific Quest for the Cup-63
Gold-63
Chasing the Cup-10
02Parkhurst-7
Bronze-7
Gold-7
Silver-7
Franchise Players-FP20
Hardware-A6
Hardware-H7
Hardware-P6
He Shoots-He Scores Points-12
He Shoots-He Scores Prizes-2
Jerseys-GJ35
Milestones-MS10
Patented Power-PP6
Stick and Jerseys-SJ35
Teammates-TT1
02Parkhurst Retro-13
Minis-13
Franchise Players-RF20
He Shoots-He Scores Points-11
He Shoots-He Scores Prizes-11
Jerseys-RJ9
Jersey and Sticks-RSJ10
Memorabilia-RM16
Nicknames-RN28
02Private Stock Reserve-66
Blue-66
Red-66
Retail-66
02Rangers Team Issue-3
02SP Authentic-61
02SP Authentic-101
Beckett Promos-61
Sign of the Times-PB
02SP Game Used-33
02SP Game Used-63
Authentic Fabrics-AFPB
Authentic Fabrics Gold-AFPB
Authentic Fabrics Rainbow-AFPB
Piece of History-PHPB
Piece of History Gold-PHPB
Piece of History Rainbow-PHPB
Signature Style-PB
02SPx-51
02SPx-94
02SPx-143
Spectrum Gold-51
Spectrum Gold-94
Spectrum Silver-51
Spectrum Silver-94
Milestones-MPB
Milestones Gold-PB
Milestones Silver-PB
Winning Materials-WMPB
Winning Materials Gold-PB
Winning Materials Silver-PB
02Stadium Club-59
Silver Decoy Cards-59
Proofs-59
World Stage-WS18
02Titanium-68
Blue-68
Red-68
Retail-68
Jerseys-43
Jerseys Retail-43
Patches-43
02Topps-16
OPC Blue Parallel-16
OPC Red Parallel-16
Coast to Coast-CC2
Factory Set-16
02Topps Chrome-16
Black Border Refractors-16
Refractors-16
e-Topps Decoy Cards-2
02Topps Heritage-10
Chrome Parallel-10
USA Test Parallel-10
02Topps Total-68
Production-TP8
Team Checklists-TTC20
02UD Artistic Impressions-59
Gold-59
02UD Artistic Impressions Beckett Promos-59
02UD Artistic Impressions Common Ground-CG10
02UD Artistic Impress Common Ground Gold-CG10
02UD Artistic Impressions Flashbacks-UD6
02UD Artistic Impressions Flashbacks Gold-UD6
02UD Artistic Impressions Great Depiction-GD10
02UD Artistic Impress Great Depiction Gld-GD10
02UD Artistic Impressions Retrospectives-R59
02UD Artistic Impressions Retrospect Gold-R59
02UD Artistic Impress Retrospect Silver-R59
02Upper Deck Collectors Club-NHL15
02UD Foundations-95
02UD Foundations-154
Calder Winners-TPB
Calder Winners Gold-TPB
Calder Winners Silver-T-PB
Playoff Performers-PPB
Playoff Performers Gold-PPB
Playoff Performers Silver-P-PB
02UD Honor Roll-49
Signature Class-PB
Students of the Game-SG20
02UD Mask Collection-57
02UD Mask Collection Beckett Promos-57
02UD Mask Collection Instant Offense-IOPB
02UD Piece of History-60
Awards Collection-AC20
Exquisite Combos-ECBM
Marks of Distinction-PB
02UD Premier Collection-37
Jerseys Bronze-PB
Jerseys Bronze-BL
Jerseys Gold-PB
Jerseys Gold-BL
Jerseys Silver-PB
Jerseys Silver-BL
Patches-PPB
Signatures Bronze-SPB
Signatures Gold-SPB
Signatures Silver-SPB
02UD Top Shelf-58
Clutch Performers-CPPB
Dual Player Jerseys-RBK
Dual Player Jerseys-RBS
Dual Player Jerseys-STBE
Goal Oriented-GOPB
Hardware Heroes-HSSBR
Milestones Jerseys-MBBRR
Milestones Jerseys-MBMBS
Shooting Stars-SHPB
Signatures-PB
Sweet Sweaters-SWPB
Triple Jerseys-HTBSB
Triple Jerseys-HTGLB
02Upper Deck-119
02Upper Deck-194
Exclusives-119
Exclusives-194
Blow-Ups-C27
Game Jersey Autographs-PB
Game Jersey Series II-GJPB
Gifted Greats-GG12
Good Old Days-GOPB
Pinpoint Accuracy-PAPB
Reaching Fifty-50PB
Reaching Fifty Gold-50PB
Shooting Stars-SS10
Sizzling Scorers-SS11
Speed Demons-SDPB
02Upper Deck Classic Portraits-65
Etched in Time-ET11
Genuine Greatness-GG6
Hockey Royalty-KFB
Hockey Royalty-LBL
Hockey Royalty Limited-KFB
Hockey Royalty Limited-LBL
Mini-Busts-105
Mini-Busts-106
Mini-Busts-107
Mini-Busts-108
Mini-Busts-109
Mini-Busts-110
Mini-Busts-111
Mini-Busts-112
Mini-Busts-113
Mini-Busts-114
Stitches-CPB
Stitches Limited-CPB
02Upper Deck MVP-122
Gold-122
Classics-122
Golden Classics-122
Prosign-PB
02Upper Deck Rookie Update-65
02Upper Deck Rookie Update-166
Autographs-PB
Jerseys-DPB
Jerseys-SLB
Jerseys Gold-DPB
Jerseys Gold-SLB
02Upper Deck Victory-138
02Upper Deck Victory-220
Bronze-138
Bronze-220
Gold-138
Gold-220
Silver-138
Silver-220
National Pride-NP35
02Upper Deck Vintage-168
02Upper Deck Vintage-280
02Upper Deck Vintage-299
Tall Boys-T44
Tall Boys Gold-T44
02Vanguard-67
LTD-67
East Meets West-4
Jerseys-29
Jerseys Gold-29
02Russian Olympic Team-3
02UD SuperStars *-165
Gold-165
City All-Stars Dual Jersey-RCPB
City All-Stars Triple Jersey-JLP
03BAP Memorabilia-69
Emerald-69
Gold-69
Ruby-69
Sapphire-69
All-Star Emblems-ASE-15
All-Star Jerseys-ASJ-22
All-Star Jerseys-ASJ-40
All-Star Numbers-ASN-15
Brush with Greatness-16
Brush with Greatness Contest Cards-16
He Shoots-He Scores Points-8
He Shoots-He Scores Prizes-15
Jersey and Stick-SJ-34
Jerseys-GJ-43
03BAP Ultimate Mem Blades of Steel-4
03Beehive Sticks Blue Border-BL10
03Black Diamond-2
Black-2
Green-2
Red-2
Signature Gems-SG-4
03ITG Action-373
Homeboys-HB14
Jerseys-M182
Jerseys-M202
Jerseys-M260
03ITG Toronto Fall Expo Jerseys-FE14
03ITG Used Sig Series Retrospectives-8A
03ITG Used Sig Series Retrospectives-8B
03ITG Used Sig Series Retrospectives-8C
03ITG Used Sig Series Retrospectives-8D
03ITG Used Sig Series Retrospectives-8E
03ITG Used Sig Series Retrospectives-8F
03ITG Used Sig Series Retrospectives Gold-8A
03ITG Used Sig Series Retrospectives Gold-8B
03ITG Used Sig Series Retrospectives Gold-8C
03ITG Used Sig Series Retrospectives Gold-8D
03ITG Used Sig Series Retrospectives Gold-8E
03ITG Used Sig Series Retrospectives Gold-8F
03ITG VIP Collages-15
03ITG VIP Jerseys-4
03NHL Sticker Collection-83
03O-Pee-Chee-6
03OPC Blue-6
03OPC Gold-6
03OPC Red-6
03Pacific-221
Blue-221
Red-221
Jerseys-25
Jerseys Gold-25
Main Attractions-9
03Pacific Exhibit-180
Blue Backs-180
03Pacific Invincible-64
Blue-64
Red-64
Retail-64
Afterburners-7
03Pacific Prism-130
Blue-130
Patches-130
Red-130
Retail-130
03Pacific Supreme Jerseys-17
03Parkhurst Orig Six Boston Mem -BM48
03Parkhurst Orig Six Chicago Mem -CM48
03Parkhurst Orig Six Detroit Mem-DM48
03Parkhurst Orig Six Montreal Mem-MM48
03Parkhurst Original Six New York-4
Memorabilia-NM6
Memorabilia-NM17
Memorabilia-NM48
03Parkhurst Original Six Shooters-OSM8
03Parkhurst Orig Six Toronto Mem-TM48
03Parkhurst Rookie ROYalty-VR-17
03Parkhurst Rookie ROYalty Gold-VR-17
03Private Stock Reserve-182
Blue-182
Patches-182
Red-182
Retail-182
03SP Authentic Sign of the Times-BL
03SP Game Used-30
Gold-30
Premium Patches-PPPB
Signers-SPSPB
Team Threads-TTBLK
03SPx Fantasy Franchise-FF-BLK
03SPx Fantasy Franchise-FF-KFB
03SPx Fantasy Franchise Limited-FF-BLK
03SPx Fantasy Franchise Limited-FF-KFB
03SPx Origins-O-PB
03SPx Signature Threads-ST-PB
03SPx Winning Materials-WM-PB
03SPx Winning Materials Limited-WM-PB
03Titanium-201
Patches-201
03Topps-6
Blue-6
Gold-6
Red-6
Topps/OPC Idols-II11
C55 Relics-TRPB
Pristine Popular Demand Relics-PD-PB
Pristine Popular Demand Relic Refractor-PD-PB
03UD Honor Roll Grade A Jerseys-TNYR
03UD Honor Roll Signature Class-SC4
03UD Premier Collection Signatures-PS-BO
03UD Premier Collection Signatures Gold-PS-BO
03UD Toronto Fall Expo Priority Signings-PB
03Upper Deck Big Playmakers-BP-PB
03Upper Deck BuyBacks-55
03Upper Deck BuyBacks-56
03Upper Deck BuyBacks-57
03Upper Deck BuyBacks-58
03Upper Deck BuyBacks-59
03Upper Deck BuyBacks-60
03Upper Deck BuyBacks-61
03Upper Deck BuyBacks-62
03Upper Deck BuyBacks-63
03Upper Deck BuyBacks-64
03Upper Deck BuyBacks-65
03Upper Deck BuyBacks-66
03Upper Deck BuyBacks-67
03Upper Deck BuyBacks-68
03Upper Deck Highlight Heroes-HH-PB
03Upper Deck Highlight Heroes Jerseys-HH-PB
03Upper Deck Team Essentials-TS-PB
03Upper Deck Classic Portraits-64
Hockey Royalty-BLC
03Upper Deck MVP-283
Gold Script-283
Silver Script-283
Canadian Exclusives-283
SportsNut-SN58
Talent-MT10
03Upper Deck Rookie Update-154
03Upper Deck Trilogy-64
Authentic Patches-AP23
Limited-64
Limited Threads-LT12
03Upper Deck Victory-126
Bronze-126
Gold-126
Silver-126
Freshman Flashback-FF29
Game Breakers-GB29
03Toronto Star-63
Foil-12
04ITG NHL AS FANtasy AS History Jerseys-SB50
04SP Authentic-127
04UD Toronto Fall Expo Priority Signings-BU
04UD Toronto Fall Expo Priority Signings-PB
04Upper Deck Big Playmakers-BP-PB
04Upper Deck Jersey Autographs-GJA-BU
04Upper Deck Jersey Autographs-GJA-PB
04Upper Deck Jersey Autographs-GJA-PB/MN
05Black Diamond Jerseys-J-PB
05Black Diamond Jerseys Ruby-J-PB
05Black Diamond Jersey Duals-DJ-PB
05Black Diamond Jersey Triples-TJ-PB
05Black Diamond Jersey Quads-QJ-PB
05UD Powerplay Specialists-TSPB
05UD Powerplay Specialists Patches-SPPB
05UD Toronto Fall Expo Priority Signings-PS-BU
05Upper Deck Trilogy Scripts-SCS-PB

Bure, Valeri

91Upper Deck-647
French-647
917th Inn. Sketch WHL-1
92Classic-14
92Classic-AU2
Gold-14
LPs-LP9
92Classic Four-Sport *-163
Gold-163
BCs-BC8
LPs-LP24
93Parkhurst-509
93Parkhurst-528
Emerald Ice-509
Emerald Ice-528
93Pinnacle-501
Canadian-501
93Upper Deck-571
93Spokane Chiefs-3
93Classic-18
93Classic Four-Sport *-258
Gold-258
94Be A Player-R159
94Finest-48
Super Team Winners-48
Refractors-48
94Flair-86
94Leaf-471
94OPC Premier-337
Special Effects-337
94Parkhurst SE-SE87
Gold-SE87
94Pinnacle-492
Artist's Proofs-492
Rink Collection-492
94Score-215
Gold-215
Platinum-215
94Select-187
Gold-187
94SP Premier-11
94SP Premier Die-Cuts-11
94Topps/OPC Premier-337
Special Effects-337
94Ultra-311
94Upper Deck-255
Electric Ice-255
Predictor Canadian-C8
94Upper Deck Predictor Canadian Exch Gold-C8
94Upper Deck Predictor Cdn Exch Silver-C8
94Upper Deck SP Inserts-SP131
94Upper Deck SP Inserts Die Cuts-SP131
94Fredericton Canadiens-6
94Classic-30
Gold-30
ROY Sweepstakes-R4
Tri-Cards-T34
95Be A Player-34
Signatures-S34
Signatures Die Cuts-S34
95Bowman-160
All-Foil-160
Bowman's Best-BB28
Bowman's Best Refractors-BB28
95Canada Games NHL POGS-147
95Canadiens Postcards-4
95Canadiens Sheets-1
95Collector's Choice-119
Player's Club-119
Player's Club Platinum-119
95Donruss-102
95Finest-34
Refractors-34
95Leaf-39
95McDonald's Pinnacle-MCD-34
95Parkhurst International-114
95Parkhurst International-511
Emerald Ice-114
Emerald Ice-511
95Pinnacle-174
Artist's Proofs-174
Rink Collection-174
Global Gold-22
95Pro Magnets-21
95Score-138
Black Ice Artist's Proofs-138
Black Ice-138
95Select Certified-131
Mirror Gold-131
95SP-74
95Stadium Club-220
Members Only Master Set-220
95Summit-197
Artist's Proofs-197
Ice-197
95Topps-358
OPC Inserts-358
95Ultra-256
95Upper Deck-304
Electric Ice-304
Electric Ice Gold-304
Special Edition-SE46
Special Edition Gold-SE46
95Zenith-125
95Finnish Semic World Championships-134
95Images-77
Gold-77
96Canadiens Postcards-5
96Canadiens Sheets-3
96Collector's Choice-141
96Donruss Rated Rookies-3
96Donruss Canadian Ice-69
Gold Press Proofs-69
Red Press Proofs-69
96Donruss Elite-119
Die Cut Stars-119
Aspirations-8
96Fleer-52
96Fleer-136
Rookie Sensations-3
96Fleer Picks-124
96Leaf-207
Press Proofs-207
96Leaf Limited-62
Gold-62
96Leaf Preferred-88
Press Proofs-88
Steel-43
Steel Gold-43
96NHL Pro Stamps-21
96Pinnacle-209
Artist's Proofs-209
Foil-209
Premium Stock-209
Rink Collection-209
96Score-245
Artist's Proofs-245
Dealer's Choice Artist's Proofs-245
Special Artist's Proofs-245
Golden Blades-245
96Select Certified-18
Artist's Proofs-18
Blue-18
Mirror Blue-18
Mirror Gold-18
Mirror Red-18
Red-18
96SkyBox Impact-60
96SkyBox Impact-167
NHL on Fox-4
96SP-80
Holoview Collection-HC16
96Summit-160
Artist's Proofs-160
Ice-160
Metal-160
Premium Stock-160
96Topps Picks Rookie Stars-RS8
96Topps Picks Rookie Stars OPC-RS8
96Upper Deck-283
Generation Next-X29
96Zenith-9
Artist's Proofs-9
Assailants-15
96Collector's Edge Ice-40
Crucibles-C11
Prism-40
QuantumMotion-10
97Black Diamond-6
Double Diamond-6
Triple Diamond-6
Quadruple Diamond-6
97Canadiens Postcards-4
97Collector's Choice-132
97Donruss-8
Press Proofs Silver-8
Press Proofs Gold-8
97Donruss Elite-57
Aspirations-57
Status-57
97Donruss Limited-7
Exposure-7
97Donruss Preferred-75
Cut to the Chase-75
97Donruss Priority-95
Stamp of Approval-95
97Katch-73
Gold-73
Silver-73
97Pacific-116
Copper-116
Emerald Green-116
Ice Blue-116
Red-116
Silver-116
97Panini Stickers-31
97Score-231
97Score Canadiens-10
Platinum-10
Premier-10
97SP Authentic-78
98Be A Player-170
Press Release-170
98BAP Gold-170
98BAP Autographs-170
98BAP Autographs Gold-170
98Pacific Omega-30
Red-30
Opening Day Issue-30
98SPx Finite-14
Radiance-14
Spectrum-14
98UD Choice-31
98UD Choice Preview-31
98UD Choice Prime Choice Reserve-31
98UD Choice Reserve-31
98Upper Deck-52
Exclusives-52
Exclusives 1 of 1-52
Gold Reserve-52
98Upper Deck MVP-30
Gold Script-30
Silver Script-30
Super Script-30
99Aurora-20
Premiere Date-20
99BAP Memorabilia-239
Gold-239
Silver-239
99BAP Millennium-40
Emerald-40
Ruby-40
Sapphire-40
Signatures-40
Signatures Gold-40
99Black Diamond-16
Diamond Cut-16
Final Cut-16
99Crown Royale-21
Limited Series-21
Premiere Date-21
99O-Pee-Chee-31
99O-Pee-Chee Chrome-31
99O-Pee-Chee Chrome Refractors-31
99Pacific-52
Copper-52
Emerald Green-52
Gold-52
Ice Blue-52
Premiere Date-52
Red-52
99Pacific Dynagon Ice-34
Blue-34
Copper-34
Gold-34
Premiere Date-34
99Pacific Omega-35
99Pacific Omega-250
Copper-35
Copper-250
Gold-35
Gold-250
Ice Blue-35
Ice Blue-250
Premiere Date-35
Premiere Date-250
World All-Stars-2
99Pacific Prism-22
Holographic Blue-22
Holographic Gold-22
Holographic Mirror-22
Holographic Purple-22
Premiere Date-22
99Panini Stickers-189
99Paramount-35
Copper-35
Emerald-35
Gold-35
Holographic Emerald-35
Holographic Gold-35
Holographic Silver-35
Ice Blue-35
Premiere Date-35
Red-35
Silver-35
99Revolution-22
Premiere Date-22
Red-22
Shadow Series-22
Copper-22
Gold-22
CSC Silver-22
99SP Authentic-13
99SPx-21
Radiance-21
Spectrum-21
99Stadium Club-142
First Day Issue-142
One of a Kind-142
Printing Plates Black-142
Printing Plates Cyan-142
Printing Plates Magenta-142
Printing Plates Yellow-142
99Topps/OPC-31
99Topps/OPC Chrome-31
Refractors-31
99Topps Gold Label Class 1-47
Black-47
Black One of One-47
One of One-47
Red-47
Red One of One-47
99Topps Gold Label Class 2-47
99Topps Gold Label Class 2 Black-47
99Topps Gold Label Class 2 Black 1 of 1-47
99Topps Gold Label Class 2 One of One-47
99Topps Gold Label Class 2 Red-47
99Topps Gold Label Class 2 Red One of One-47
99Topps Gold Label Class 3-47
99Topps Gold Label Class 3 Black-47
99Topps Gold Label Class 3 Black 1 of 1-47
99Topps Gold Label Class 3 One of One-47
99Topps Gold Label Class 3 Red-47
99Topps Gold Label Class 3 Red One of One-47
99Topps Premier Plus-29
Parallel-29
99Ultimate Victory-13
1/1-13
Parallel-13
Parallel 100-13
99Upper Deck-26
Exclusives-26
Exclusives 1 of 1-26
99Upper Deck Gold Reserve-26
99Upper Deck MVP-29
Gold Script-29
Silver Script-29
Super Script-29
99Upper Deck MVP SC Edition-29
Gold Script-29
Silver Script-29
Super Script-29
99Upper Deck Ovation-10
Standing Ovation-10
99Upper Deck Retro-11
Gold-11
Platinum-11
99Upper Deck Victory-44
99Wayne Gretzky Hockey-29
00Aurora-23
Pinstripes-23
Pinstripes Premiere Date-23
Premiere Date-23
Autographs-23
00BAP Memorabilia-138
Emerald-138
Ruby-138
Sapphire-138
Promos-138
00BAP Mem Chicago Sportsfest Copper-138
00BAP Memorabilia Chicago Sportsfest Blue-138
00BAP Memorabilia Chicago Sportsfest Gold-138
00BAP Memorabilia Chicago Sportsfest Ruby-138
00BAP Memorabilia Chicago Sun-Times Ruby-138
00BAP Memorabilia Chicago Sun-Times Gold-138
00BAP Mem Chicago Sun-Times Sapphire-138
00BAP Mem Toronto Fall Expo Copper-138
00BAP Memorabilia Toronto Fall Expo Gold-138
00BAP Memorabilia Toronto Fall Expo Ruby-138
00BAP Memorabilia Update Record Breakers-BB1
00BAP Mem Update Record Breakers Gold-BB1
00BAP Parkhurst 2000-P44
00BAP Signature Series-201
Emerald-201
Ruby-201
Sapphire-201
Autographs-2
Autographs Gold-2
Jersey Cards-J35
Jersey and Stick Cards-GSJ35
Jersey Cards Autographs-J35
Jersey Emblems-E35
Jersey Numbers-IN35
00BAP Ultimate Memorabilia Autographs-37
Gold-37
00BAP Ultimate Mem Game-Used Jerseys-GJ36
00BAP Ultimate Mem Game-Used Sticks-GS36
00Black Diamond-8
Gold-8
00Crown Royale-17
Ice Blue-17
Limited Series-17
Premiere Date-17
Red-17
Game-Worn Jerseys-2
Game-Worn Jersey Patches-2
Premium-Sized Game-Worn Jerseys-2
00Kraft-14
00McDonald's Pacific-6
Blue-6
Checklists-1
00O-Pee-Chee-96
00O-Pee-Chee-328
00O-Pee-Chee Parallel-96
00O-Pee-Chee Parallel-328
00Pacific-62
Copper-62
Gold-62
Ice Blue-62
Premiere Date-62
Gold Crown Die Cuts-5
00Panini Stickers-116
00Paramount-34
Copper-34
Gold-34
Holo-Gold-34
Holo-Silver-34
Ice Blue-34
Premiere Date-34
Freeze Frame-5
00Private Stock-15
Gold-15
Premiere Date-15
Retail-15
Silver-15
PS-2001 New Wave-5
00Revolution-21
Blue-21
Premiere Date-21
Red-21
00SP Authentic-13
00SP Game Used-8
00SPx-9
Spectrum-9
Highlight Heroes-HH4
Winning Materials-WBU
00Stadium Club-135
Beam Team-BT16
00Titanium Game Gear-65
00Titanium Game Gear Patches-65
00Titanium Draft Day Edition-14
Patches-14
00Topps/OPC-96
00Topps/OPC-328
Parallel-96
Parallel-328
Autographs-AVB
Combos-TC1
Combos Jumbos-TC1
00Topps Chrome-76
OPC Refractors-76
Refractors-76
Combos-TC1
Combos Refractors-TC1
00Topps Gold Label Class 1-6
Gold-6
00Topps Gold Label Class 2-6
00Topps Gold Label Class 2 Gold-6
00Topps Gold Label Class 3-6
00Topps Gold Label Class 3 Gold-6
00Topps Heritage-114
00Topps Premier Plus-26
Blue Ice-26
Game-Used Memorabilia-GPVB
Game-Used Memorabilia-GPVBOS
00Topps Stars-33
Blue-33
00UD Heroes-17
00UD Pros and Prospects-14
00UD Reserve-14
00Upper Deck-26
Exclusives Tier 1-26
Exclusives Tier 2-26
All-Star Class-A2
Skilled Stars-SS4
00Upper Deck Ice-7
Immortals-7
Legends-7
Stars-7
00Upper Deck Legends-20
00Upper Deck Legends-21
Legendary Collection Bronze-20
Legendary Collection Bronze-21
Legendary Collection Gold-20
Legendary Collection Gold-21
Legendary Collection Silver-20
Legendary Collection Silver-21
00Upper Deck MVP-34
First Stars-34
Second Stars-34
Third Stars-34
00Upper Deck Victory-34
00Upper Deck Victory-35
00Upper Deck Victory-241
00Upper Deck Victory-288
00Upper Deck Vintage-51
00Upper Deck Vintage-61
00Upper Deck Vintage-62
National Heroes-NH6
00Vanguard-15
Holographic Gold-15
Holographic Purple-15
Pacific Proofs-15
01Atomic-45
Blue-45
Gold-45
Premiere Date-45
Red-45
Jerseys-27
Patches-27
01BAP Memorabilia-244
01BAP Memorabilia-379
Emerald-244
Emerald-379
Ruby-244
Ruby-379
Sapphire-244
Sapphire-379
All-Star Jerseys-ASJ26
All-Star Emblems-ASE26
All-Star Numbers-ASN26
All-Star Teammates-AST14
All-Star Teammates-AST23
Country of Origin-CO36
01BAP Ultimate Memorabilia Bloodlines-1
01Crown Royale Triple Threads-3
01O-Pee-Chee-48
01O-Pee-Chee Heritage Parallel-48
01O-Pee-Chee Heritage Parallel Limited-48
01O-Pee-Chee Premier Parallel-48
01Pacific-58

Extreme LTD-58
Hobby LTD-58
Premiere Date-58
Retail LTD-58
01Pacific Adrenaline-80
Blue-80
Premiere Date-80
Red-80
Retail-80
Jerseys-18
01Pacific Arena Exclusives-58
01Pacific Heads-Up Quad Jerseys-5
01Parkhurst-237
01Private Stock Game Gear-49
01Private Stock Game Gear Patches-49
01SP Authentic-36
Limited-36
Limited Gold-36
01SP Game Used-24
01Topps-48
Heritage Parallel-48
Heritage Parallel Limited-48
OPC Parallel-48
01Topps Chrome-48
Refractors-48
Black Border Refractors-48
01Topps Heritage-172
01UD Challenge for the Cup-36
01UD Honor Roll Honor Society-HS-BB
01UD Honor Roll Honor Society Gold-HS-BB
01UD Playmakers-43
01UD Top Shelf Jerseys-VB
01Upper Deck-302
Exclusives-302
Tandems-T4
02BAP All-Star Edition-10
Jerseys-10
Jerseys Gold-10
Jerseys Silver-10
02BAP First Edition-74
Jerseys-74
02BAP Memorabilia-145
02BAP Memorabilia-260
Emerald-145
Emerald-260
Ruby-145
Ruby-260
Sapphire-145
Sapphire-260
NHL All-Star Game-145
NHL All-Star Game-260
NHL All-Star Game Blue-145
NHL All-Star Game Blue-260
NHL All-Star Game Green-145
NHL All-Star Game Green-260
NHL All-Star Game Red-145
NHL All-Star Game Red-260
02BAP Memorabilia Toronto Fall Expo-145
02BAP Memorabilia Toronto Fall Expo-260
02BAP Sig Series Auto Buybacks 1998-170
02BAP Sig Series Auto Buybacks 1999-40
02BAP Sig Series Auto Buybacks 2000-2
02Crown Royale Jerseys-7
02Crown Royale Jerseys Gold-7
02Crown Royale Dual Patches-11
02O-Pee-Chee-54
02O-Pee-Chee Premier Blue Parallel-54
02O-Pee-Chee Premier Red Parallel-54
02O-Pee-Chee Factory Set-54
02Pacific-152
Blue-152
Red-152
02Pacific Complete-217
Red-217
02Pacific Exclusive-75
02Pacific Heads-Up Quad Jerseys-25
02Pacific Heads-Up Quad Jerseys Gold-25
02Parkhurst-36
Bronze-36
Gold-36
Silver-36
02Parkhurst Retro-130
Minis-130
02Private Stock Reserve-41
Blue-41
Red-41
Retail-41
02Titanium Jerseys-31
02Titanium Jerseys Retail-31
02Titanium Patches-31
02Topps-54
OPC Blue Parallel-54
OPC Red Parallel-54
Factory Set-54
02Topps Total-113
02UD Honor Roll-83
02UD Top Shelf Dual Player Jerseys-STBL
02Upper Deck-78
Exclusives-78
02Upper Deck MVP-81
Gold-81
Classics-81
Golden Classics-81
02Upper Deck Victory-92
Bronze-92
Gold-92
Silver-92
02Upper Deck Vintage-108
02Russian Olympic Team-5
03ITG Action-214
03NHL Sticker Collection-43
03O-Pee-Chee-108
03OPC Blue-108
03OPC Gold-108
03OPC Red-108
03Pacific Calder-30
Silver-30
03Pacific Complete-331
Red-331
03Pacific Quest for the Cup-46
Blue-46
03Panthers Team Issue-3
03Private Stock Reserve-41
Blue-41
Red-41
Retail-41
03Titanium-42
Hobby Jersey Number Parallels-42
Retail-42
Retail Jersey Number Parallels-42
03Topps-108
Blue-108
Gold-108
Red-108
Pristine Stick Portions-PPS-VB
Pristine Stick Portion Refractors-PPS-VB
03Topps Traded-TT24
Blue-TT24
Gold-TT24
Red-TT24
03Upper Deck-326
Canadian Exclusives-326
HG-326
UD Exclusives-326
Classic Portraits Headliners-HH-VB
03Upper Deck MVP-184
Gold Script-184
Silver Script-184
Canadian Exclusives-184
04Pacific-83
Blue-83
Red-83
05Upper Deck Jerseys-J-VB
05Upper Deck MVP-185
Gold-185
Platinum-185

Bureau, Marc
88Salt Lake Golden Eagles-24
89ProCards IHL-208
90Score-423
Canadian-423
90ProCards AHL/IHL-603
91Bowman-126
91O-Pee-Chee-93
91Parkhurst-302
French-302
91Pinnacle-335
French-335
91Pro Set-544
French-544
91Score Canadian Bilingual-476
91Score Canadian English-476
91Stadium Club-322
91Topps-93
91Upper Deck-274
French-274
92Bowman-382
92Lightning Sheraton-7
92O-Pee-Chee-78
92Parkhurst-400
Emerald Ice-400
92Stadium Club-30
92Topps-179
Gold-179G
93Lightning Season in Review-4
93OPC Premier-344
Gold-344
93Parkhurst-461
Emerald Ice-461
93Pinnacle-321
Canadian-321
93Stadium Club-134
Members Only Master Set-134
OPC-134
First Day Issue-134
First Day Issue OPC-134
93Topps/OPC Premier-344
Gold-344
94Lightning Photo Album-5
95Canadiens Postcards-5
96Be A Player-82
Autographs-82
Autographs Silver-82
96Canadiens Postcards-6
96Canadiens Sheets-4
97Canadiens Postcards-5
97Score Canadiens-19
Platinum-19
Premier-19
98OPC Chrome-140
Refractors-140
98Topps-140
O-Pee-Chee-140
99Wayne Gretzky Hockey-124

Bureau, Pierre-Andre
03P.E.I. Rocket-4
04P.E.I. Rocket-17

Bureaux, Peter
96Kitchener Rangers-4

Bures, Jiri
99Czech Score Blue 2000-134
99Czech Score Red Ice 2000-134

Burfant, Peter
94German First League-536

Burfoot, Scott
94Erie Panthers-17
95Flint Generals-4
96Richmond Renegades-1
98Quad-City Mallards-3
99Rockford IceHogs-22
00Rockford IceHogs-22

Burger, Jiri
95Czech APS Extraliga-88
96Czech APS Extraliga-92
97Czech APS Extraliga-210
97Czech DS Stickers-149
98Czech DS-101
98Czech DS Stickers-242
98Czech OFS-170
99Czech DS-164
99Czech OFS-326
99Czech OFS-497
All-Star Game Blue-497
All-Star Game Gold-497
All-Star Game Red-497
All-Star Game Silver-497
00Finnish Cardset-132
01Czech DS-14
01Czech OFS-75
02Czech OFS Plus-46
02Czech OFS Plus All-Star Game-H2
02Czech OFS Plus Duos-D7
03Czech OFS Plus-1
03Czech OFS Plus All-Star Game-H41
03Czech OFS Plus Insert M-M21
03Czech OFS Plus Insert S-S3
03Czech OFS Plus MS Praha-SE18
04Czech OFS-224
Assist Leaders-8
Czech/Slovak-2
Goals Leaders-5
Points Leaders-7
05Czech HC Vitkovice-1
06Czech CP Cup Postcards-2
06Czech OFS-45
All Stars-17
Team Cards-11

Burgess, Don
73Vancouver Blazers-3
74O-Pee-Chee WHA-32
77O-Pee-Chee WHA-66

Burgess, Dru
98ECHL All-Star Northern Conference-13
98Roanoke Express-24
99UK Basingstoke Bison-2
02Bossier-Shreveport Mudbugs-5
05UK Hull Stingrays-7

Burgess, Steve
03Greenville Grrrowl-3

Burgess, Tim
82Oshawa Generals-16

Burgess, Trevor
907th Inn. Sketch OHL-329
91Oshawa Generals-3
91Oshawa Generals Sheet-10
91 7th Inn. Sketch OHL-162
92Oshawa Generals Sheet-19
93Greensboro Monarchs-2
95Central Hockey League-2
95Fort Worth Fire-6
96German DEL-132
99German DEL-244
00Lubbock Cotton Kings-14
03Elmira Jackals-4

Burgess, Van
90 7th Inn. Sketch WHL-45
91 7th Inn. Sketch WHL-170
93Prince Albert Raiders-3
99Greensboro Generals-16
01El Paso Buzzards-2
02Lexington Men O'War-15

Burgio, Frank
01Guelph Storm-2

Burgoyne, Jaret
89Victoria Cougars-4

Burgoyne, Jeff
00Roanoke Express-5
03UK Cardiff Devils-2
05UK Cardiff Devils-9
Gold-9
Silver-9
05UK Cardiff Devils Challenge Cup-1

Burgoyne, Ryan
93London Knights-6
95Slapshot-162

Burillo, Thomas
93Swiss HNL-198
95Swiss HNL-273
96Swiss HNL-392

Buriola, Carlo
93Swiss HNL-390

Buriola, Marino
93Swiss HNL-214

Burish, Adam
03Wisconsin Badgers-5
04Wisconsin Badgers-28
05Wisconsin Badgers-2
06Hot Prospects-152
Red Hot-152
White Hot-152
06O-Pee-Chee-561
Rainbow-561
06SP Authentic-245
Limited-245
06SP Game Used Rookie Exclusives Autographs-REAB
06SPx-202
Spectrum-202
06The Cup-96
Autographed Rookie Masterpiece Pressplates-96
Gold Rainbow Autographed Rookies-96
Masterpiece Pressplates (Marquee Rookies)-561
Masterpiece Pressplates (SP Authentic)-245
Masterpiece Pressplates (Ultimate Collection)-70
Masterpiece Pressplates (Victory)-317
Rookies Black-96
Rookies Platinum-96
06Ultimate Collection-70
06Upper Deck-465
Exclusives Parallel-465
High Gloss Parallel-465
Masterpieces-465
Victory-317
06Norfolk Admirals-11
07Upper Deck Rookie Class -50

Burish, Nikki
04Wisconsin Badgers Women-2

Burk, Josh
02Muskegon Fury-3

Burkart, Urs
93Swiss HNL-415

Burke, Adam
95Whalers Bob's Stores-2

Burke, Brian
03Canucks Postcards-4

Burke, Claude
37V356 Worldwide Gum-112

Burke, Dave
83Pinebridge Bucks-1
92Greensboro Monarchs-15

Burke, Don
92Atlanta Knights-19
94Central Hockey League-5
94Dallas Freeze-5

Burke, Eddie
34Diamond Matchbooks Silver-7
35Diamond Matchbooks Tan 1-7

Burke, Gerry
06Toledo Storm-19

Burke, Greg
92Birmingham Bulls-17
93Birmingham Bulls-17
95Dayton Bombers-28
96German DEL-111
00UK Nottingham Panthers-14
00UK Sekonda Superleague-127
01UK Guildford Flames-13
01UK London Knights-15
02UK London Knights-12

Burke, Jim
90ProCards AHL/IHL-174
91ProCards-111

Burke, Justin
90 7th Inn. Sketch WHL-63

Burke, Marty
27La Patrie-11
28La Presse Photos-5
33V252 Canadian Gum-7
33V288 Hamilton Gum-3
33V357 Ice Kings-14
34Beehive Group I Photos-43
34Diamond Matchbooks Silver-8
35Diamond Matchbooks Tan 1-8
35Diamond Matchbooks Tan 2-6
35Diamond Matchbooks Tan 3-5
35Diamond Matchbooks Tan 4-3
35Diamond Matchbooks Tan 5-2
37Diamond Matchbooks Tan 6-2
37V356 Worldwide Gum-72
05ITG Ultimate Mem Chi-Town Immortal Auto-2

Burke, Sean
88Devils Caretta-5
88Frito-Lay Stickers-38
88O-Pee-Chee-94
88O-Pee-Chee Stickers-82
88O-Pee-Chee Stickers-158
88Panini Stickers-267
88Topps-94
89Devils Caretta-6
89Kraft-53
89Kraft All-Stars Stickers-6
89O-Pee-Chee-92
89O-Pee-Chee Stickers-34
89O-Pee-Chee Stickers-86
89O-Pee-Chee Stickers-203
89Panini Stickers-185
89Panini Stickers-256
89Sports Illustrated for Kids I-30
89Topps-92
90Devils Team Issue-4
90Kraft-4
90O-Pee-Chee-140
90Panini Stickers-77
90Pro Set-164
90Score-34
Canadian-34
90Score Hottest/Rising Stars-17
90Score Young Superstars-11
90Topps-140
Tiffany-140
90Upper Deck-66
French-66
91Alberta International Team Canada-3
91Bowman-275
91O-Pee-Chee-67
91Panini Stickers-212
91Pro Set-132
French-132
91Score American-245
91Score Canadian Bilingual-465
91Score Canadian English-465
91Stadium Club-76
91Topps-67
91Upper Deck-183
French-183
92Kraft-28
92OPC Premier-92
92Parkhurst Previews-PV2
92Parkhurst-57
Emerald Ice-57
92Pinnacle-295
French-295
92Score Canadian Olympians-13
92Ultra-68
92Upper Deck-518
92Whalers Dairymart-2
92Classic-117
Gold-117
93Donruss-141
93Leaf-132
93OPC Premier-241
Gold-241
93Panini Stickers-131
93Pinnacle-31
Canadian-31
93PowerPlay-103
93Score-126
Canadian-126
Franchise-8
93Stadium Club-207
Members Only Master Set-207
OPC-207
First Day Issue-207
First Day Issue OPC-207
93Topps/OPC Premier-241
Gold-241
93Ultra-15
93Whalers Coke-1
94Be A Player Signature Cards-53
94Canada Games NHL POGS-281
94Donruss-158
94EA Sports-60
94Flair-70
94Fleer-84
94Kraft-36
94Leaf-85
94OPC Premier-542
Special Effects-542
94Parkhurst SE-SE71
Gold-SE71
94Pinnacle-114
Artist's Proofs-114
Rink Collection-114
Goaltending Greats-GT12
94Score-84
Gold-84
Platinum-84
94Select-127
Gold-127
94SP-51
Die Cuts-51
94Stadium Club-171
Members Only Master Set-171
First Day Issue-171
Super Teams-10
Super Teams Members Only Master Set-10
Super Team Winner Cards-171
94Topps/OPC Premier-542
Special Effects-542
94Ultra-87
94Upper Deck-158
Electric Ice-158
95Bashan Super Stickers-54
95Bowman-26
All-Foil-26
95Canada Games NHL POGS-131
95Collector's Choice-199
Player's Club-199
Player's Club Platinum-199
95Donruss-28
Between The Pipes-8
95Donruss Elite-107
Die Cut Stars-107
Die Cut Uncut-107
95Emotion-73
95Finest-132
Refractors-132
95Imperial Stickers-54
95Kraft-15
95Leaf-63
95Leaf Limited-14
95Metal-63
95Panini Stickers-35
95Parkhurst International-96
Emerald Ice-96
95Pinnacle-124
Artist's Proofs-124
Rink Collection-124
Masks-9
95Playoff One on One-45
95Pro Magnets-126
95Score-32
95Score-320
Black Ice Artist's Proofs-32
Black Ice Artist's Proofs-320
Black Ice-32
Black Ice-320
95Select Certified-100
Mirror Gold-100
95SkyBox Impact-71
Deflectors-4
95SP-65
95Stadium Club-29
Members Only Master Set-29
95Summit-125
Artist's Proofs-125
Ice-125
In The Crease-13
95Topps-135
OPC Inserts-135
95Topps SuperSkills-76
Platinum-76
95Ultra-65
95Ultra-367
Gold Medallion-65
Premier Pad Men-3
Premier Pad Men Gold Medallion-3
95Upper Deck-130
Electric Ice-130
Electric Ice Gold-130
Special Edition-SE39
Special Edition Gold-SE39
95Whalers Bob's Stores-1
95Zenith-100
96Be A Player-18
Autographs-18
Autographs Silver-18
96Collector's Choice-119
96Collector's Choice-319
96Donruss-121
Press Proofs-121
96Donruss Canadian Ice-66
Gold Press Proofs-66
Red Press Proofs-66
96Donruss Elite-51
Die Cut Stars-51
96Fleer-45
Vezina-2
96Leaf-85
Press Proofs-85
96Leaf Preferred-85
Press Proofs-85
96Maggers-9
96Metal Universe-66
96NHL Pro Stamps-126
96Pinnacle-37
Artist's Proofs-37
Foil-37
Premium Stock-37
Rink Collection-37
96Score-46
Artist's Proofs-46
Dealer's Choice Artist's Proofs-46
Special Artist's Proofs-46
Golden Blades-46
96Select Certified-44
Artist's Proofs-44
Blue-44
Mirror Blue-44
Mirror Gold-44
Mirror Red-44
Red-44
96SkyBox Impact-52
Zero Heroes-2
96SP-70
96Summit-109
Artist's Proofs-109
Ice-109
Metal-109
Premium Stock-109
96Ultra-73
Gold Medallion-73
96Upper Deck-72
96Upper Deck Ice-26
Parallel-26
96Whalers Kid's Club-1
96Swedish Semic Wien-77
97Collector's Choice-111
97Donruss-128
Press Proofs Silver-128
Press Proofs Gold-128
97Donruss Canadian Ice-99
Dominion Series-99
Provincial Series-99
97Donruss Elite-39
Aspirations-39
Status-39
97Donruss Limited-119
97Donruss Limited-194
Exposure-119
Exposure-194
97Donruss Preferred-104
Cut to the Chase-104
97Donruss Priority-44
Stamp of Approval-44
97Hurricanes Team Issue-2
97Katch-25
Gold-25
Silver-25
97Leaf-63
Fractal Matrix-63
Fractal Matrix Die Cuts-63
97Leaf International-63
Universal Ice-63
97Pacific-81
Copper-81
Emerald Green-81
Ice Blue-81
Red-81
Silver-81
97Pacific Dynagon-20
Copper-20
Dark Grey-20
Emerald Green-20
Ice Blue-20
Red-20
Silver-20
Tandems-37
97Pacific Invincible-22
Copper-22
Emerald Green-22
Ice Blue-22
Red-22
Silver-22
97Pacific Omega-229
Copper-229
Dark Gray-229
Emerald Green-229
Gold-229
Ice Blue-229
97Pinnacle-42
Artist's Proofs-42
Rink Collection-42
Press Plates Back Black-42
Press Plates Back Cyan-42
Press Plates Back Magenta-42
Press Plates Back Yellow-42
Press Plates Front Black-42
Press Plates Front Cyan-42
Press Plates Front Magenta-42
Press Plates Front Yellow-42
97Pinnacle Certified-25
Red-25
Mirror Blue-25
Mirror Gold-25
Mirror Red-25
97Pinnacle Inside-30
Coach's Collection-30
Executive Collection-30
97Pinnacle Tot Cert Platinum Blue-25
97Pinnacle Tot Certi Platinum Gold-25
97Pinnacle Totally Certified Platinum Red-25
97Pinnacle Tot Cert Mirror Platinum Gold-25
97Revolution-140
Copper-140
Emerald-140
Ice Blue-140
Silver-140
97Score-1
Artist's Proofs-1
Golden Blades-1
97Studio-62
Press Proofs Silver-62
Press Proofs Gold-62
97Upper Deck-31
98Be A Player-209
Press Release-209
98BAP Gold-209
98BAP Autographs-209
98BAP Autographs Gold-209
98Crown Royale-56
Limited Series-56
98NHL Aces Playing Cards-33
98OPC Chrome-19
Refractors-19
98Pacific-321
Ice Blue-321
Red-321
98Pacific Dynagon Ice-78
Blue-78
Red-78
98Pacific Omega-100
Red-100
Opening Day Issue-100
98Panini Stickers-91
98Revolution-60
Ice Shadow-60
Red-60
98Topps-19
O-Pee-Chee-19
98UD Choice-147
98UD Choice-252
98UD Choice Preview-147
98UD Choice Prime Choice Reserve-147
98UD Choice Prime Choice Reserve-252
98UD Choice Reserve-147
98UD Choice Reserve-252
99Aurora-62
Premiere Date-62
99BAP Memorabilia-216
Gold-216
Silver-216
99O-Pee-Chee-230
99O-Pee-Chee Chrome-230
99O-Pee-Chee Chrome Refractors-230
99Pacific-170
Copper-170
Emerald Green-170
Gold-170
Ice Blue-170
Premiere Date-170
Red-170
99Pacific Dynagon Ice-88
Blue-88
Copper-88
Gold-88
Premiere Date-88
99Panini Stickers-54
99Paramount-99
Copper-99
Emerald-99
Gold-99
Holographic Emerald-99
Holographic Gold-99
Holographic Silver-99
Ice Blue-99
Premiere Date-99
Red-99
Silver-99
99Revolution-63
Premiere Date-63
Red-63
Shadow Series-63
99Topps/OPC-230
99Topps/OPC Chrome-230
Refractors-230
99Upper Deck MVP SC Edition-145
Gold Script-145
Silver Script-145
Super Script-145
00BAP Memorabilia-354
Emerald-354
Ruby-354
Sapphire-354
Promos-354
00BAP Mem Chicago Sportsfest Copper-354
00BAP Memorabilia Chicago Sportsfest Blue-354
00BAP Memorabilia Chicago Sportsfest Gold-354
00BAP Memorabilia Chicago Sportsfest Ruby-354
00BAP Memorabilia Chicago Sun-Times Ruby-354
00BAP Memorabilia Chicago Sun-Times Gold-354
00BAP Mem Chicago Sun-Times Sapphire-354
00BAP Mem Toronto Fall Expo Copper-354
00BAP Memorabilia Toronto Fall Expo Gold-354
00BAP Memorabilia Toronto Fall Expo Ruby-354
00BAP Parkhurst 2000-P246
00BAP Signature Series-74
Emerald-74
Ruby-74
Sapphire-74
00Black Diamond Game Gear-BSB
00Black Diamond Game Gear-CSB
00Crown Royale-82
Ice Blue-82
Limited Series-82
Premiere Date-82
Red-82
00O-Pee-Chee-30
00O-Pee-Chee Parallel-30
00Pacific-311
Copper-311
Gold-311
Ice Blue-311
Premiere Date-311
00Stadium Club-102
00Titanium-72
Blue-72
Gold-72
Premiere Date-72
Red-72
Retail-72
Game Gear-124
Game Gear Patches-124
00Titanium Draft Day Edition-75
Patches-75
00Topps/OPC-30
Parallel-30
00Topps Chrome-28
OPC Refractors-28
Refractors-28
00Topps Heritage-125
00UD Heroes-93
00UD Reserve-66
00Upper Deck-366
Exclusives Tier 1-366
Exclusives Tier 2-366
00Upper Deck Victory-178
00Upper Deck Vintage-281
00Upper Deck Vintage-283
00Upper Deck Vintage-284
01Atomic-75
Blue-75
Gold-75
Premiere Date-75
Red-75
01BAP Memorabilia-83
Emerald-83
Ruby-83
Sapphire-83
Country of Origin-CO51
01BAP Signature Series-22
Autographs-22
Autographs Gold-22
Franchise Jerseys-FP-23
Jerseys-GJ-80
01Between the Pipes-31
Double Memorabilia-DM17
Goalie Gear-GG4
He Shoots-He Saves Points-2
He Shoots-He Saves Prizes-20
Jerseys-GJ33
Jersey and Stick Cards-GSJ31
Masks-25
Masks Silver-25
Masks Gold-25
Tandems-GT11
01Bowman YoungStars-31
Gold-31
Ice Cubed-31
01Coyotes Team Issue-4
01Crown Royale-111
Blue-111
Premiere Date-111
Red-111
Retail-111
01O-Pee-Chee-56
01O-Pee-Chee Heritage Parallel-56
01O-Pee-Chee Heritage Parallel Limited-56
01O-Pee-Chee Premier Parallel-56
01Pacific-299
01Pacific-438
Extreme LTD-299
Gold-438
Hobby LTD-299
Premiere Date-299
Retail LTD-299
Steel Curtain-16
01Pacific Adrenaline-146
Blue-146
Premiere Date-146
Red-146
Retail-146
Creased Lightning-16
Power Play-27
01Pacific Arena Exclusives-299
01Pacific Arena Exclusives-438
01Pacific Heads-Up-75
Blue-75
Premiere Date-75
Red-75
Silver-75
Quad Jerseys-16
Quad Jerseys-26
01Parkhurst-144
01Private Stock-75
Gold-75
Premiere Date-75
Retail-75
Silver-75
Game Gear-73
Game Gear Patches-73
01Private Stock Pacific Nights-75
01Private Stock PS-2002-56
01SP Authentic-65
Limited-65
Limited Gold-65
01SP Game Used-42
01SPx-50
01Sports Illustrated for Kids III-60
01Stadium Club-45
Award Winners-45
Master Photos-45
Souvenirs-SB
01Titanium-108
Hobby Parallel-108
Premiere Date-108
Retail-108
Retail Parallel-108
01Topps-56
Heritage Parallel-56
Heritage Parallel Limited-56
OPC Parallel-56
Stars of the Game-SG2
01Topps Chrome-56
Refractors-56
Black Border Refractors-56
01Topps Heritage-15
Refractors-15
01Topps Reserve-20
Emblems-SB
Jerseys-SB
Name Plates-SB
Numbers-SB
Patches-SB
01UD Challenge for the Cup-66
Jerseys-TSB
01UD Mask Collection-123
01UD Mask Collection-185
Gold-123
Gold-185
Goalie Jerseys-MMSB
Goalie Jerseys-VCSB
Goalie Jerseys-CGSB
01UD Playmakers-77
01UD Premier Collection-40
Dual Jerseys-DTB
Dual Jerseys Black-DTB
01UD Top Shelf-32
All-Star Nets-NSB
01Upper Deck-132
Exclusives-132
Game Jerseys-GJSB
01Upper Deck Ice-34
01Upper Deck MVP-147
Masked Men-MM10
01Upper Deck Victory-265
01Upper Deck Victory-272
Gold-265
Gold-272
01Upper Deck Vintage-192
01Upper Deck Vintage-198
01Upper Deck Vintage-199
01Upper Deck Vintage-269
01Vanguard-75
Blue-75
Red-75
One of Ones-75
Premiere Date-75
Proofs-75
02Atomic-78
Blue-78
Gold-78
Red-78
Denied-16
Hobby Parallel-78
02BAP All-Star Edition-13
Jerseys-13
Jerseys Gold-13
Jerseys Silver-13
02BAP First Edition-10
Jerseys-10
02BAP Memorabilia-110
Emerald-110
Ruby-110
Sapphire-110
NHL All-Star Game-110
NHL All-Star Game Blue-110
NHL All-Star Game Green-110
NHL All-Star Game Red-110
Stanley Cup Playoffs-SC-10
02BAP Memorabilia Toronto Fall Expo-110
02BAP Signature Series-98
Autographs-98
Autograph Buybacks 1998-209
Autograph Buybacks 2001-22
Autographs Gold-98
02BAP Ultimate Memorabilia Number Ones-9
02BAP Ultimate Memorabilia Numerology-3
02Between the Pipes-31
02Between the Pipes-143
Gold-31
Silver-31
All-Star Stick and Jersey-13
Behind the Mask-7
Blockers-18
Complete Package-CP7
Double Memorabilia-2
Emblems-29
Goalie Autographs-3
He Shoots-He Saves Points-1
He Shoots-He Saves Prizes-8
Inspirations-I5
Jerseys-29
Masks II-22
Masks II Gold-22
Masks II Silver-22
Numbers-29
Pads-7
Stick and Jerseys-29
Trappers-GT17
02Bowman YoungStars-37
Gold-37
Silver-37
02Coyotes Team Issue-21
02Crown Royale-75
Blue-75
Red-75
Retail-75
02ITG Used-60
02ITG Used-160
Goalie Pad and Jersey-GP13
Goalie Pad and Jersey Gold-GP13
02O-Pee-Chee-24
02O-Pee-Chee Jumbos-18
02O-Pee-Chee Premier Blue Parallel-24
02O-Pee-Chee Premier Red Parallel-24
02O-Pee-Chee Factory Set-24
02Pacific-292
Blue-292
Red-292
Maximum Impact-6
02Pacific Complete-177
Red-177
02Pacific Exclusive-133
02Pacific Heads-Up-95
Blue-95
Purple-95
Red-95
Showstoppers-16
02Pacific Quest for the Cup-78
Gold-78
02Pacific Toronto Fall Expo-8
Gold-8
02Parkhurst-166
Bronze-166
Gold-166
Silver-166
Teammates-TT20
02Parkhurst Retro-140
Minis-140
02Private Stock Reserve-78
Blue-78
Red-78
Retail-78
InCrease Security-17
02SP Authentic-69
Beckett Promos-69
02SP Game Used-38
Piece of History-PHSB
Piece of History Gold-PHSB
Piece of History Rainbow-PHSB
02SPx-58
Spectrum Gold-58
Spectrum Silver-58
02Stadium Club-13
Silver Decoy Cards-13
Proofs-13
Puck Stops Here-PSH11
02Topps-24
OPC Blue Parallel-24
OPC Red Parallel-24
Factory Set-24
02Topps Chrome-24
Black Border Refractors-24
Refractors-24
02Topps Heritage-25
Chrome Parallel-25
Crease Piece-SB
Crease Piece Patches-SB
02Topps Total-97
02UD Artistic Impressions-68
Gold-68
Artist's Touch-ATSB
Artist's Touch Gold-ATSB
02UD Artistic Impressions Beckett Promos-68

02UD Artistic Impressions Retrospectives-R68
02UD Artistic Impressions Retrospect Gold-R68
02UD Artistic Impress Retrospect Silver-R68
02UD Foundations-158
02UD Honor Roll-55
02UD Mask Collection-64
02UD Mask Collection-65
02UD Mask Collection-67
02UD Mask Collection-105
02UD Mask Collection Beckett Promos-64
02UD Mask Collection Beckett Promos-65
02UD Mask Collection Beckett Promos-67
02UD Mask Collection Career Wins-CWSB
02UD Mask Collection Nation's Best-NJBT
02UD Mask Collection Patches-PWSB
02UD Mask Collection View from the Cage-VSB
02UD Piece of History-68
Patches-PHSB
02UD Top Shelf-68
Clutch Performers-CPSB
Milestones Jerseys-MHPBJ
Stopper Jerseys-SSSB
02Upper Deck-133
02Upper Deck-241
Exclusives-133
Exclusives-241
All-Star Jerseys-ASSB
All-Star Performers-ASSB
Blow-Ups-C31
Last Line of Defense-LL10
Patchwork-PWSB
Super Saviors-SA11
02Upper Deck Classic Portraits-76
Hockey Royalty-BLB
Hockey Royalty Limited-BLB
Starring Cast-CSB
Starring Cast Limited-CSB
02Upper Deck MVP-141
Gold-141
Classics-141
Golden Classics-141
Masked Men-MM6
02Upper Deck Pearson Awards-3
02Upper Deck Victory-163
Bronze-163
Gold-163
Silver-163
02Upper Deck Vintage-194
02Upper Deck Vintage-283
Green Backs-194
Tall Boys-T49
Tall Boys Gold-T49
02UD SuperStars *-11
Gold-11
03BAP Memorabilia-162
Emerald-162
Gold-162
Ruby-162
Sapphire-162
Masks III-6
Masks III Gold-6
Masks III Silver-6
Masks III Memorabilia-6
03BAP Ultimate Memorabilia Autographs-67
Gold-67
03Beehive-153
Variations-153
Gold-153
Silver-153
Jumbo Jerseys-BH15
Sticks Beige Border-BE32
Sticks Blue Border-BL1
03Black Diamond-113
Black-113
Green-113
Red-113
03Coyotes Postcards-3
03Crown Royale-77
Blue-77
Retail-77
Gauntlet of Glory-15
03Duracell-6
03ITG Action-432
Jerseys-M96
Jerseys-M263
03ITG Used Signature Series-62
Gold-62
Autographs-SB1
Autographs-SB2
Autographs Gold-SB1
Autographs Gold-SB2
Goalie Gear-3
Goalie Gear Autographs-3
Goalie Gear Gold-3
Triple Memorabilia-12
Triple Memorabilia Gold-12
03McDonald's Pacific-40
03NHL Sticker Collection-270
03Pacific-260
Blue-260
Red-260
In the Crease-10
03Pacific Complete-459
Red-459
03Pacific Exhibit-187
03Pacific Exhibit-213
Blue Backs-187
03Pacific Heads-Up-76
Hobby LTD-76
Retail LTD-76
03Pacific Invincible-76
Blue-76
Red-76
Retail-76
Featured Performers-23
Freeze Frame-17
Jerseys-23
03Pacific Prism-137
Blue-137
Patches-137
Red-137
Retail-137
03Pacific Supreme-76
Blue-76
Red-76
Retail-76
Generations-7
Standing Guard-11
03Parkhurst Rookie-14
03Private Stock Reserve-193
Blue-193
Patches-193
Red-193
Retail-193
Increase Security-12
03SP Authentic-68
Limited-68
03SP Game Used-36
03SP Game Used-98
Gold-36
Gold-98
03SPx-75
Radiance-75
Spectrum-75
Winning Materials-WM-SB
Winning Materials Limited-WM-SB
03Titanium-77
Hobby Jersey Number Parallels-77
Retail-77
Retail Jersey Number Parallels-77
03Topps Pristine Mini-PM-SB
03Topps Traded-TT55
Blue-TT55
Gold-TT55
Red-TT55
03UD Honor Roll-67
03Upper Deck-397
All-Star Class-AS-22
Canadian Exclusives-397
HG-397
UD Exclusives-397
03Upper Deck Classic Portraits-76
03Upper Deck Ice-64
Gold-64
03Upper Deck MVP-332
Gold Script-332
Silver Script-332
Canadian Exclusives-332
SportsNut-SN68
03Upper Deck Rookie Update-64
Skills-SKSB
03Upper Deck Trilogy-76
Limited-76
03Upper Deck Victory-148
Bronze-148
Gold-148
Silver-148
Game Breakers-GB5
03Russian World Championship Stars-13
03Toronto Star-73
04Pacific-191
Blue-191
Red-191
05Be A Player Signatures-SB
05Be A Player Signatures Gold-SB
05Parkhurst-440
Facsimile Auto Parallel-440
True Colors-TCTBL
True Colors-TCTBL
05SP Authentic-91
Limited-91
Sign of the Times-SB
05SP Game Used-90
Gold-90
Authentic Fabrics Quad-BLSR
Authentic Patches Quad -BLSR
Auto Draft-AD-SB
SIGnificance-SB
SIGnificance Gold-S-SB
Statscriptions-ST-SB
05SPx-81
Spectrum-81
05UD Powerplay Specialists-TSSB
05UD Powerplay Specialists Patches-SPSB
05Ultra-171
Gold-171
Fresh Ink-FI-SB
Fresh Ink Blue-FI-SB
Ice-171
05Upper Deck-417
Big Playmakers-B-SB
Jerseys Series II-J2SB
Notable Numbers-N-SB
05Upper Deck Hockey Showcase-HS14
05Upper Deck Showcase Promos-HS14
05Upper Deck Ice-88
Rainbow-88
05Upper Deck MVP-351
Gold-351
Platinum-351
05Upper Deck Trilogy-81
05Upper Deck Victory-244
Black-244
Gold-244
Silver-244
06Springfield Falcons-1
06UD Artifacts Tundra Tandems-TTSM
06UD Artifacts Tundra Tandems Black-TTSM
06UD Artifacts Tundra Tandems Blue-TTSM
06UD Artifacts Tundra Tandems Gold-TTSM
06UD Artifacts Tundra Tandems Platinum-TTSM
06UD Artifacts Tundra Tandems Red-TTSM
06UD Artifacts Tundra Tandems Dual Patches Red-TTSM
06Upper Deck-180
Exclusives Parallel-180
High Gloss Parallel-180
Masterpieces-180
Victory-179
Victory Black-179
Victory Gold-179

Burke, Tim
77Nova Scotia Voyageurs-4
90Devils Team Issue-5

Burkett, Michael
92Michigan State Spartans-4
93Michigan State Spartans-2
97Pensacola Ice Pilots-4

Burkhalter, Loic
96Swiss HNL-239
99Swiss Panini Stickers-187
00Swiss Panini Stickers-230
00Swiss Slapshot Mini-Cards-RJ6
01Swiss HNL-221
02Swiss HNL-58

Burkhard, Alfred
94German DEL-25
94German First League-310

Burkholder, Barry
83Kingston Canadians-17
84Kingston Canadians-12
85Kingston Canadians-12

Burkholder, Dave
95Slapshot-204

Burki, Codey
03Brandon Wheat Kings-10
04Brandon Wheat Kings-18
05ITG Heroes/Prosp Toronto Expo Parallel -318
05Brandon Wheat Kings-3
05ITG Heroes and Prospects-318
Autographs Series II-CBK
Team Orr-TO4

Burkitt, Noel
92Quebec Pee-Wee Tournament-428
95Slapshot-400
95Sudbury Wolves-13
95Sudbury Wolves Police-4
03UK London Racers-2

Burkitt, Toby
907th Inn. Sketch OHL-354
917th Inn. Sketch OHL-356

Burlimann, Yves
02Swiss HNL-376

Burlin, Borje
67Swedish Hockey-182
69Swedish Hockey-238
71Swedish Hockey-229
72Swedish Stickers-217
73Swedish Stickers-73
74Swedish Stickers-207

Burlin, Dick
89Swedish Semic Elitserien Stickers-201

Burlutski, Oleg
98Russian Hockey League-140
03Russian Hockey League-228

Burman, Michael
907th Inn. Sketch OHL-304
917th Inn. Sketch OHL-62
93North Bay Centennials-11
94Knoxville Cherokees-24
94Los Angeles Blades RHI-3
95Richmond Renegades-18

Burn, Arren
93UK Humberside Hawks-9

Burnes, Andy
02Michigan Wolverines-22
03Michigan Wolverines-7

Burnes, Ethan
02Orlando Seals-14

Burnett, Derrick
06Okotoks Oilers -3

Burnett, Garrett
94Kitchener Rangers Update-35
96Knoxville Cherokees-15
97Johnstown Chiefs-17
99Kentucky Thoroughblades-5
00Cleveland Lumberjacks-17
01Cincinnati Mighty Ducks-9
02Hartford Wolf Pack-5
03Crown Royale-101
Red-101
Retail-101
03ITG VIP Rookie Debut-10
03Pacific Complete-562
Red-562
03Pacific Luxury Suite-51
Gold-51
03Pacific Supreme-101
Blue-101
Red-101
Retail-101
03Parkhurst Rookie-152
03Private Stock Reserve-101
Blue-101
Red-101
Retail-101
03Titanium-101
Hobby Jersey Number Parallels-101
Retail-101
Retail Jersey Number Parallels-101
03Upper Deck-201
Canadian Exclusives-201
HG-201
Tough Customers-TC-11

Burnett, George
89Niagara Falls Thunder-5
897th Inn. Sketch OHL-124
917th Inn. Sketch OHL-203
917th Inn. Sketch CHL Award Winners-7
95Binghamton Rangers-2
96Binghamton Rangers-3
97Guelph Storm-27

Burnett, Mathew
92Ottawa 67's-4

Burnette, Casey
96Barrie Colts-3
97Barrie Colts-4

Burnham, Brad
91Ferris State Bulldogs-6
92Ferris State Bulldogs-6

Burnie, Stu
88ProCards AHL-306

Burns, Bob
94German DEL-416
96German DEL-291

Burns, Brent
02SPx Rookie Redemption-R200
03BAP Memorabilia-194
Emerald-194
Gold-194
Ruby-194
Sapphire-194
Draft Redemptions-20
Super Rookies-SR3
Super Rookies Gold-SR3
Super Rookies Silver-SR3
03BAP Ultimate Memorabilia Autographs-110
Gold-110
03BAP Ultimate Mem Auto Jerseys-110
03BAP Ultimate Mem Auto Emblems-110
03BAP Ultimate Mem Auto Numbers-110
03BAP Ultimate Mem Rookie Jersey Emblems-28
03BAP Ultimate Mem Rookie Jsy Emblem Gold-28
03BAP Ultimate Mem Rookie Jersey Numbers-28
03BAP Ultimate Mem Rookie Jsy Number Gold-28
03Black Diamond-150
Black-150
Green-150
Red-150
03Crown Royale-121
Red-121
Retail-121
03ITG Action-611
03ITG Used Signature Series-147
Autographs Gold-147
03ITG VIP Rookie Debut-3
03Pacific Calder-121
Silver-121
03Pacific Complete-592
Red-592
03Pacific Exhibit-232
03Pacific Heads-Up-120
Hobby LTD-120
Retail LTD-120
Prime Prospects-11
Prime Prospects LTD-11
03Pacific Invincible-114
Blue-114
Red-114
Retail-114
03Pacific Luxury Suite-90
Gold-90
03Pacific Quest for the Cup-120
Calder Contenders-11
03Pacific Supreme-122
Blue-122
Red-122
Retail-122
03Parkhurst Rookie-197
Rookie Emblems-RE-43
Rookie Emblem Autographs-RE-BB
Rookie Emblems Gold-RE-43
Rookie Jerseys-RJ-43
Rookie Jersey Autographs-RJ-BB
Rookie Jerseys Gold-RJ-43
Rookie Numbers-RN-43
Rookie Number Autographs-RN-BB
Rookie Numbers Gold-RN-43
03Private Stock Reserve-123
Blue-123
Red-123
Retail-123
03SP Authentic-125
Limited-125
03SP Game Used-64
Gold-64
03Titanium-123
Hobby Jersey Number Parallels-123
Retail-123
Retail Jersey Number Parallels-123
03Topps C55-143
Minis-143
Minis American Back-143
Minis American Back Red-143
Minis Bazooka Back-143
Minis Brooklyn Back-143
Minis Hat Trick Back-143
Minis O Canada Back-143
Minis O Canada Back Red-143
Minis Stanley Cup Back-143
03Topps Traded-TT117
Blue-TT117
Gold-TT117
Red-TT117
03UD Honor Roll-145
03Upper Deck-221
Canadian Exclusives-221
HG-221
03Upper Deck Classic Portraits-185
03Upper Deck MVP-455
03Upper Deck Rookie Update-217
03Upper Deck Trilogy-153
Limited-153
04Pacific-128
Blue-128
Red-128
04Pacific NHL All-Star FANtasy-5
04Pacific NHL All-Star FANtasy Gold-5
04Upper Deck All-Star Promos-BB
04AHL Top Prospects-22
04Houston Aeros-3
05ITG Heroes/Prosp Toronto Expo Parallel -54
05Parkhurst-247
Facsimile Auto Parallel-247
05Upper Deck-346
05ITG Heroes and Prospects-54
Autographs-A-BBU
Complete Logos-AHL-7
Jerseys-GUJ-41
Jerseys Gold-GUJ-41
Emblems-GUE-41
Emblems Gold-GUE-41
Numbers-GUN-41
Numbers Gold-GUN-41
Nameplates-N-72
Nameplates Gold-N-72
06Be A Player-149
Autographs-149
Signatures-BU
06O-Pee-Chee-254
Rainbow-254

Burns, Charlie
44Beehive Group II Photos-9
58Topps-43
59Topps-40
60NHL Ceramic Tiles-1
60Topps-24
Stamps-7
61Shirriff/Salada Coins-4
61Topps-11
62Topps-15
63Topps-9
67Seals Team Issue-4
68Bauer Ads-3
68O-Pee-Chee-108
68Topps-108
69O-Pee-Chee-129
69Topps-129
70Colgate Stamps-19
70Dad's Cookies-12
70Esso Power Players-169
70O-Pee-Chee-44
Deckle-13
70Sargent Promotions Stamps-87
70Topps-44
71O-Pee-Chee-238
71Sargent Promotions Stamps-87
71Topps-21
71Toronto Sun-127
72O-Pee-Chee-178
72Sargent Promotions Stamps-106

Burns, Darren
87Brockville Braves-10
88Brockville Braves-11

Burns, Dennis
93Quebec Pee-Wee Tournament-990

Burns, Joe
93Quebec Pee-Wee Tournament-632

Burns, Lance
907th Inn. Sketch WHL-130
917th Inn. Sketch WHL-346

Burns, Norm
34Beehive Group I Photos-263

Burns, Pat
88Canadiens Postcards-2
89Canadiens Kraft-1
89Canadiens Postcards-2
90Canadiens Postcards-4
90Pro Set-669
91Canadiens Postcards-3
93Kraft-31
94Maple Leafs Kodak-6
94Maple Leafs Pin-up Posters-30
02Devils Team Issue-26
02Maple Leafs Platinum Collection-110
03Devils Team Issue-42

Burns, R.R.
95German DEL-383

Burns, Robert
93Quebec Pee-Wee Tournament-1428

Burns, Robin
74NHL Action Stamps-289
75O-Pee-Chee NHL-104
75Topps-104

Burns, Sean
89Windsor Spitfires-1
907th Inn. Sketch OHL-177

Burr, Shawn
83Kitchener Rangers-18
84Kitchener Rangers-22
85Kitchener Rangers-21
87O-Pee-Chee-164
87O-Pee-Chee Minis-5
87O-Pee-Chee Stickers-125
87Panini Stickers-247
87Red Wings Little Caesars-4
87Topps-164
88O-Pee-Chee-78
88Panini Stickers-41
88Red Wings Little Caesars-2
88Topps-78
89O-Pee-Chee-101
89O-Pee-Chee Stickers-252
89Panini Stickers-63
89Red Wings Little Caesars-2
89Topps-101
90Bowman-232
Tiffany-232
90O-Pee-Chee-74
90Panini Stickers-213
90Pro Set-66
90Score-49
Canadian-49
90Score Hottest/Rising Stars-21
90Topps-74
Tiffany-74
90Upper Deck-111
French-111
91Bowman-43
91O-Pee-Chee-184
91Panini Stickers-135
91Parkhurst-45
French-45
91Pinnacle-86
French-86
91Pro Set-58
French-58
91Red Wings Little Caesars-1
91Score American-54
91Score Canadian Bilingual-54
91Score Canadian English-54
91Stadium Club-101
91Topps-184
91Upper Deck-315
French-315
92Bowman-122
92O-Pee-Chee-24
92Pinnacle-171
French-171
92Pro Set-45
92Score-207
Canadian-207
92Stadium Club-126
92Topps-178
Gold-178G
92Ultra-44
93Leaf-296
93OPC Premier-83
Gold-83
93Parkhurst-328
Emerald Ice-328
93Pinnacle-93
Canadian-93
93Score-175
Canadian-175
93Stadium Club-313
Members Only Master Set-313
First Day Issue-313
93Topps/OPC Premier-83
Gold-83
93Upper Deck-91
94Be A Player Signature Cards-93
94Leaf-368
94Lightning Postcards-3
94Parkhurst-62
Gold-62
94Pinnacle-318
Artist's Proofs-318
Rink Collection-318
94Upper Deck-484
Electric Ice-484
94Sarnia Sting-29
95Lightning Team Issue-5
95Parkhurst International-461
Emerald Ice-461
95Score-13
Black Ice Artist's Proofs-13
Black Ice-13
95Upper Deck-355
Electric Ice-355
Electric Ice Gold-355
96Be A Player-191
Autographs-191
Autographs Silver-191
96Collector's Choice-254
97Pacific-152
Copper-152
Emerald Green-152
Ice Blue-152
Red-152
Silver-152
97Paramount-163
Copper-163
Dark Grey-163
Emerald Green-163
Ice Blue-163
Red-163
Silver-163
98Be A Player-121
Press Release-121
98BAP Gold-121
98BAP Autographs-121
98BAP Autographs Gold-121
98BAP Tampa Bay All Star Game-121
02BAP Sig Series Auto Buybacks 1998-121

Burridge, Randy
86O-Pee-Chee-70
86Topps-70
88Bruins Sports Action-2
88O-Pee-Chee-33
88O-Pee-Chee Stickers-29
88Panini Stickers-208
88Topps-33
89Bruins Sports Action-3
89O-Pee-Chee-121
89O-Pee-Chee Stickers-28
89Panini Stickers-197
89Topps-121
90Bruins Sports Action-4
90O-Pee-Chee-190
90Pro Set-2
90Score-72
Canadian-72
90Topps-190
Tiffany-190
90Upper Deck-196
French-196
91Pro Set Platinum-241
91Bowman-349
91Capitals Junior 5x7-4
91Capitals Kodak-4
91O-Pee-Chee-358
91OPC Premier-43
91Panini Stickers-174
91Parkhurst-190
French-190
91Pinnacle-55
French-55
91Pro Set-4
91Pro Set-510
French-4
French-510
91Score American-102
91Score Canadian Bilingual-102
91Score Canadian Bilingual-564
91Score Canadian English-102
91Score Canadian English-564
91Score Rookie/Traded-14T
91Stadium Club-119
91Topps-358
91Upper Deck-567
French-567
92Bowman-29
92Bowman-225
92Capitals Kodak-4
92O-Pee-Chee-370
92Panini Stickers-163
92Panini Stickers French-163
92Pinnacle-115
French-115
92Pro Set-207
92Score-297
Canadian-297
92Stadium Club-61
92Topps-83
Gold-83G
92Upper Deck-153
93Donruss-503
93Parkhurst-492
Emerald Ice-492
93Pinnacle-418
Canadian-418
93PowerPlay-464
93Score-370
Canadian-370
93Stadium Club-416
Members Only Master Set-416
First Day Issue-416
93Ultra-444
93Upper Deck-504
94Canada Games NHL POGS-243
94Donruss-66
94Flair-197
94Leaf-291
94Pinnacle-110
Artist's Proofs-110
Rink Collection-110
94Score-90
Gold-90
Platinum-90
94Stadium Club-163
Members Only Master Set-163
First Day Issue-163
Super Team Winner Cards-163
95Be A Player-114
Signatures-S114
Signatures Die Cuts-S114
95Finest-21
Refractors-21
95Metal-13
95Parkhurst International-293
Emerald Ice-293
95Score-164
Black Ice Artist's Proofs-164
Black Ice-164
95Ultra-210
95Upper Deck-320
Electric Ice-320
Electric Ice Gold-320
Special Edition-SE99
Special Edition Gold-SE99
96Collector's Choice-28
96Donruss-127
Press Proofs-127
96Leaf-121
Press Proofs-121
96Pinnacle-198
Artist's Proofs-198
Foil-198
Premium Stock-198
Rink Collection-198
96Score-52
Artist's Proofs-52
Dealer's Choice Artist's Proofs-52
Special Artist's Proofs-52
Golden Blades-52
96Summit-26
Artist's Proofs-26
Ice-26
Metal-26
Premium Stock-26
97Be A Player-79
Autographs-79
Autographs Die-Cuts-79
Autographs Prismatic Die-Cuts-79
97Pacific Invincible NHL Regime-18
97Score Sabres-6
Platinum-6
Premier-6

Burrowes, Guy
71Rochester Americans-2

Burrows, Alexandre Menard
00Shawinigan Cataractes-19
Signed-19
01Shawinigan Cataractes-20
02Greenville Grrrowl-6
03Columbia Inferno-99
03ECHL All-Stars-242
05ITG Heroes/Prosp Toronto Expo Parallel -391
05Hot Prospects-181
En Fuego-181
Red Hot-181
White Hot-181
05SP Authentic-285
Limited-285
05SPx-289
05The Cup Masterpiece Pressplates (Ice)-235
05The Cup Master Pressplate Rookie Update-189
05The Cup Masterpiece Pressplates SPA-285
05The Cup Masterpiece Pressplates (SPx)-289
05Upper Deck Ice-235
05Upper Deck Rookie Update-189
05AHL Top Prospects-5
05Manitoba Moose-5
05ITG Heroes and Prospects-391
06Canucks Postcards-4

Burrows, Dan
83Pinebridge Bucks-2

Burrows, Dave
71Penguins Postcards-3
72O-Pee-Chee-133
72Sargent Promotions Stamps-182
72Topps-82
73O-Pee-Chee-140
73Topps-27
74NHL Action Stamps-220
74O-Pee-Chee NHL-137
74O-Pee-Chee NHL-241
74Penguins Postcards-3
74Topps-137
74Topps-241
75O-Pee-Chee NHL-186
75Topps-186
76O-Pee-Chee NHL-83
76Topps-83
77Coca-Cola-2
77O-Pee-Chee NHL-66
77Penguins Puck Bucks-4
77Topps-66
78Maple Leafs Postcards-5
78O-Pee-Chee-254
78Topps-254
79Maple Leafs Postcards-6
80O-Pee-Chee-147
80Topps-147

Burstrom, Anders
94Swedish Leaf-173
95Swedish Leaf-250
97Swedish Collector's Choice-129
98Swedish UD Choice-143
99Swedish Upper Deck-145
00Swedish Upper Deck-130
02Swedish SHL-64
Parallel-64
03Finnish Cardset-42
04Swedish Elitset-272
Gold-272
05Swedish SHL Elitset-125
06Swedish SHL Elitset-220

Burt, Adam
90Bowman-252
Tiffany-252
90O-Pee-Chee-431
90Pro Set-447
90Score-370
Canadian-370
90Upper Deck-324
French-324
91Panini Stickers-318
91Parkhurst-291
French-291
91Pinnacle-77
French-77
91Score Canadian Bilingual-449
91Score Canadian English-449
91Whalers Jr. 7-Eleven-5
92Panini Stickers-264
92Panini Stickers French-264
92Score-261
Canadian-261
92Stadium Club-139
92Topps-283
Gold-283G
92Ultra-69
92Whalers Dairymart-3
93Donruss-139
93Leaf-280
93Pinnacle-313
Canadian-313
93Score-307
Canadian-307
93Whalers Coke-2
94Pinnacle-356
Artist's Proofs-356
Rink Collection-356
95Pinnacle-200
Artist's Proofs-200
Rink Collection-200
95Playoff One on One-155
95Topps-184
OPC Inserts-184
95Upper Deck-303
Electric Ice-303
Electric Ice Gold-303
96Be A Player-117
Autographs-117
Autographs Silver-117
96Whalers Kid's Club-24
97Hurricanes Team Issue-3
97Pacific Invincible NHL Regime-34
98Hurricanes Team Issue-6
99Pacific-300
Copper-300
Emerald Green-300
Gold-300
Ice Blue-300
Premiere Date-300
Red-300
00UD Pros and Prospects-5

Burt, Scott
00Idaho Steelheads-4
01Idaho Steelheads-2
04Idaho Steelheads-9
05Idaho Steelheads-4
06Idaho Steelheads-3

Burt, Wade
96Kamloops Blazers-6
98Kootenay Ice-10

Burton, Archie
52Juniors Blue Tint-16

Burton, Cumming
52Juniors Blue Tint-8

Burton, James
95Finnish Semic World Championships-184
95Swedish Globe World Championships-188
95Phoenix Roadrunners-6
96Swedish Semic Wien-213
99Fort Wayne Komets Points Leaders-11

Burton, Joe
92Oklahoma City Blazers-3
93Oklahoma City Blazers-3
94Central Hockey League-56
94Oklahoma City Blazers-2
95Central Hockey League-39
95Oklahoma Coyotes RHI-2
98Oklahoma City Blazers-6

Burton, Nick
03UK London Racers-3

Burym, Brad
02German DEL City Press-131
04German DEL-84
04German Ingolstadt Panthers-4
05German DEL-122
05German DEL-346

Busch, B.J.
93Quebec Pee-Wee Tournament-873

Busch, Florian
03German Berlin Polar Bears Postcards-7
04German Berlin Polar Bears Postcards-4
04German DEL-81
05German DEL-39
05German DEL-15
06German DEL-183

Busch, Markus
02German DEL City Press-279

Busch, Olaf
94German First League-408

Busch, Robert
95German DEL-238
02German DEL City Press-68
04German Augsburg Panthers Postcards-8

Buschan, Andrei
93Kansas City Blades-18
94Kansas City Blades-5
94Classic Four-Sport *-152
Gold-152
Printers Proofs-152

Busenburg, Marc
02Hershey Bears-5
03Hershey Bears-19
03Hershey Bears Patriot News-5
04Springfield Falcons-16

Bush, Eddie
34Beehive Group I Photos-94
61Hamilton Red Wings-2

Bushan, Andrei
99Russian Hockey League-144

Busillo, Giuseppe
98German DEL-105
99German DEL-56

Busillo, Joe
89Oshawa Generals-5
89Oshawa Generals 7th Inning Sketch-3
897th Inn. Sketch OHL-3
897th Inn. Sketch OHL-154
907th Inn. Sketch Memorial Cup-86
917th Inn. Sketch Memorial Cup-16
96German DEL-354
01UK Manchester Storm-7

Buskas, Rod
83Penguins Coke-5
84Penguins Heinz Photos-4
86Penguins Kodak-4
87Panini Stickers-144
87Penguins Kodak-3
90Kings Smokey-23
90O-Pee-Chee-509
90Pro Set-456
90Score Rookie/Traded-12T
91Blackhawks Coke-3
91Pinnacle-417
French-417
91Score Canadian Bilingual-427
91Score Canadian English-427
92Indianapolis Ice-4
92Salt Lake Golden Eagles-2
93Las Vegas Thunder-4
98Las Vegas Thunder-3

Buskoven, Henrik
92Norwegian Elite Series-63

Busniuk, Mike
76Nova Scotia Voyageurs-2
80O-Pee-Chee-326
81O-Pee-Chee-249
917th Inn. Sketch WHL-306
95Binghamton Rangers-3
96Binghamton Rangers-4
02Muskegon Fury-4
04Binghamton Senators-25
06Binghamton Senators-22

Busniuk, Ron
74Minnesota Fighting Saints WHA-5

Busque, Yvan
01Chicoutimi Sagueneens-9

Bussiere, Carl
93Quebec Pee-Wee Tournament-283

Bussieres, Joe
93Quebec Pee-Wee Tournament-259

Bussieres, Simon
93Quebec Pee-Wee Tournament-1002

Busto, Michael
04Kootenay Ice-3
05Kootenay Ice-4

Buswell, Walter
34Beehive Group I Photos-141
35Diamond Matchbooks Tan 3-6
37O-Pee-Chee V304E-174
37V356 Worldwide Gum-32
38Quaker Oats Photos-5
39O-Pee-Chee V301-1-32

But, Anton
01Russian Hockey League-130
02Russian SL-27

Butcher, Garth
81Regina Pats-2
82Canucks Team Issue-4
83Canucks Team Issue-3
83Vachon-103
84Canucks Team Issue-4
84Kelowna Wings-49
85Canucks Team Issue-3
86Canucks Team Issue-2
87Canucks Shell Oil-6
87O-Pee-Chee Stickers-200
87Panini Stickers-343
88Canucks Mohawk-8
88O-Pee-Chee-202
88O-Pee-Chee Stickers-54
88Panini Stickers-134
89Canucks Mohawk-5
89O-Pee-Chee Stickers-72
89Panini Stickers-158
90Canucks Mohawk-4
90O-Pee-Chee-150
90Pro Set-295
90Score-18
Canadian-18
90Topps-150
Tiffany-150
90Upper Deck-98
French-98
91Pro Set Platinum-223
91Blues Postcards-4
91Bowman-383
91Canucks Panini Team Stickers-5
91O-Pee-Chee-204
91Panini Stickers-28
91Parkhurst-374
French-374
91Pinnacle-85
91Pinnacle-409
French-85
French-409
91Pro Set-210
91Pro Set-583
French-210
French-583
91Score American-24
91Score Canadian Bilingual-24
91Score Canadian English-24
91Stadium Club-223
91Topps-204

91Upper Deck-397
French-397
92Bowman-124
92O-Pee-Chee-280
92Panini Stickers-24
92Panini Stickers French-24
92Parkhurst-390
Emerald Ice-390
92Pinnacle-72
French-72
92Pro Set-160
92Score-65
Canadian-65
92Stadium Club-287
92Topps-281
Gold-281G
92Ultra-184
93Donruss-289
93Donruss-477
93Leaf-239
93OPC Premier-316
Gold-316
93Panini Stickers-164
93Parkhurst-449
Emerald Ice-449
93Pinnacle-66
Canadian-66
All-Stars-24
All-Stars Canadian-24
93PowerPlay-208
93Score-173
Canadian-173
93Stadium Club-21
Members Only Master Set-21
OPC-21
First Day Issue-21
First Day Issue OPC-21
All-Stars-19
All-Stars Members Only-19
All-Stars OPC-19
93Topps/OPC Premier-316
Gold-316
93Ultra-27
94EA Sports-122
94Leaf-466
94Maple Leafs Kodak-7
94Maple Leafs Pin-up Posters-5
94Maple Leafs Postcards-2
94OPC Premier-441
Special Effects-441
94Parkhurst-188
Gold-188
94Pinnacle-394
Artist's Proofs-394
Rink Collection-394
94Score-13
Gold-13
Platinum-13
94Topps/OPC Premier-441
Special Effects-441
95Pinnacle-53
Artist's Proofs-53
Rink Collection-53
02Fleer Throwbacks-74
Gold-74
Platinum-74
04ITG Franchises Canadian-130
Autographs-GB

Butenschon, Sven
93Brandon Wheat Kings-7
94Brandon Wheat Kings-2
94Signature Rookies Tetrad *-104
Signatures-104
95Brandon Wheat Kings-2
95Slapshot Memorial Cup-33
96Cleveland Lumberjacks-5
96Cleveland Lumberjacks Multi-Ad-7
98Upper Deck-10
Exclusives-10
Exclusives 1 of 1-10
Gold Reserve-10
00Wilkes-Barre Scranton Penguins-3
01Hamilton Bulldogs-21
04German Adler Mannheim Eagles Postcards-6
04German DEL-4
Superstars-SU01
05AHL All-Stars-2
05Manitoba Moose-6
06German DEL-145
06ITG Heroes and Prospects AHL Shooting Stars-AS02

Butera, Anthony
03Mississauga Ice Dogs-4
04Mississauga Ice Dogs-1

Butkas, Mike
86Saskatoon Blades Photos-4

Butko, Sergej
95Czech APS Extraliga-158
96Czech APS Extraliga-174
97Czech DS Stickers-40
98Czech OFS-6
00Russian Hockey League-24

Butkus, Alex
01Guelph Storm-13
01Guelph Storm Memorial Cup-13

Butler, Chris
04Sioux City Musketeers-4

Butler, Dave
00Fort Wayne Komets-2

Butler, Dustin
03Portland Winter Hawks-1
04Portland Winter Hawks-1
06Kamloops Blazers-3

Butler, Gary
04Langley Hornets-6

Butler, Goalie
93Minnesota-Duluth Bulldogs-4

Butler, Jason
03OCN Blizzard-3

Butler, Jerome (Goalie)
93Minnesota-Duluth Bulldogs-4

Butler, Jerry
74NHL Action Stamps-181
74O-Pee-Chee NHL-393
75O-Pee-Chee NHL-167
75Topps-167
75Roanoke Valley Rebels-1
76O-Pee-Chee NHL-336
77O-Pee-Chee NHL-349
78Maple Leafs Postcards-6
78O-Pee-Chee-304
79Maple Leafs Postcards-7
79O-Pee-Chee-393
80Canucks Silverwood Dairies-6
80Canucks Team Issue-6
80O-Pee-Chee-351
80Pepsi-Cola Caps-105
81Canucks Team Issue-5
81O-Pee-Chee-332
82Jets Postcards-3

Butler, Markus
93Swiss HNL-249
95Swiss HNL-146
96Swiss HNL-163
98Swiss Power Play Stickers-188
99Swiss Panini Stickers-188
00Swiss Panini Stickers-231
00Swiss Slapshot Mini-Cards-RJ7
01Swiss HNL-155
02Swiss HNL-313

Butler, Rob
95Slapshot-395
95Sudbury Wolves-16
95Sudbury Wolves Police-5
96South Carolina Stingrays-22

Butler, Rod
93Waterloo Black Hawks-5
98Fayetteville Force-3
98Oklahoma City Blazers-12

Butler, Stan
95Slapshot-255
99Brampton Battalion-28
00Brampton Battalion-26

Butler, Tyler
05Missouri River Otters-10

Butochnov, Andriy
05Dutch Vadeko Flyers -2

Butochnov, Anton
05Dutch Vadeko Flyers -3

Butorac, Ali
81Oshawa Generals-4
83Belleville Bulls-19

Butorac, Tony
80Sault Ste. Marie Greyhounds-15

Butsayev, Vyatcheslav
91O-Pee-Chee Inserts-12R
91Finnish Semic World Champ Stickers-90
91Swedish Semic World Champ Stickers-90
92Flyers Upper Deck Sheets-41
92Flyers Upper Deck Sheets-43
92OPC Premier-31
92Parkhurst-363
Emerald Ice-363
92Ultra-153
92Upper Deck-503
92Finnish Semic-114
92Russian Stars Red Ace-6
92Russian Stars Red Ace-14
93Flyers J.C. Penney-5
93Flyers Lineup Sheets-7
93Leaf-307
93OPC Premier-79
Gold-79
93Parkhurst-151
Emerald Ice-151
93Score-656
Gold-656
Canadian-656
Canadian Gold-656
93Stadium Club-94
Members Only Master Set-94
OPC-94
First Day Issue-94
First Day Issue OPC-94
93Topps/OPC Premier-79
Gold-79
93Ultra-385
93Upper Deck-406
93Classic-87
McDonalds-12
93Classic Pro Prospects-131
BCs-BC14
94Parkhurst-213
Gold-213
94Pinnacle-498
Artist's Proofs-498
Rink Collection-498
94Upper Deck-417
Electric Ice-417
94Finnish Jaa Kiekko-148
97Fort Wayne Komets-9
98Fort Wayne Komets-2
98IHL All-Star Eastern Conference-2
99Grand Rapids Griffins-1
00Grand Rapids Griffins-3
02Russian SL-14
02Russian World Championships-12
03Russian Hockey League-268
03Russian National Team-34
03Russian Postcards-1
04Russian World Championship Team-21

Butsayev, Yuri
99BAP Memorabilia-317
Gold-317
Silver-317
99BAP Millennium-94
Emerald-94
Ruby-94
Sapphire-94
Signatures-94
Signatures Gold-94
99Pacific Dynagon Ice-71
Blue-71
Copper-71
Gold-71
Premiere Date-71
99Paramount-257
99Stadium Club-175
First Day Issue-175
One of a Kind-175
Printing Plates Black-175
Printing Plates Cyan-175
Printing Plates Magenta-175
Printing Plates Yellow-175
99Topps Premier Plus-107
Parallel-107
00Upper Deck NHLPA-PA31
01Cincinnati Mighty Ducks-10
02BAP Sig Series Auto Buybacks 1999-94
02Thrashers Postcards-2
02Russian Hockey League-239
03Russian Hockey League-11
03Russian Hockey League-241
03Russian Hockey League-268

Butsenko, Konstantin
98Russian Hockey League-112

Butt, Jamie
92Tacoma Rockets-3
93Tacoma Rockets-2
98Tacoma Sabercats-5

Butt, Kevin
89Oshawa Generals-15
89Oshawa Generals 7th Inning Sketch-18
897th Inn. Sketch OHL-18
907th Inn. Sketch OHL-101
907th Inn. Sketch Memorial Cup-76

Butterfield, Cole
04Moose Jaw Warriors-4

Butterfield, Jack
83Hall of Fame-167
83Hall of Fame Postcards-M2
85Hall of Fame-167

Butters, Mike
90ProCards AHL/IHL-551
91Greensboro Monarchs-3
92Anaheim Bullfrogs RHI-20

Butterworth, Simon
04UK U-20 Team-3
05UK Sheffield Steelers-8
Gold-8
Silver-8

Buturlin, Alexander
99SP Authentic-128
99Upper Deck-322
Exclusives-322
Exclusives 1 of 1-322
99Upper Deck Gold Reserve-322
99Upper Deck MVP SC Edition-200
Gold Script-200
Silver Script-200
Super Script-200
00Russian Hockey League-292
00Sarnia Sting-6
02Russian Hockey League-39
03Russian Hockey League-115
03Russian National Team-30

Buturlin, Mikhail
99Russian Hockey League-205

Butz, Rob
94Tri-City Americans-4
95St. John's Maple Leafs-3
96St. John's Maple Leafs-7

Buzak, Mike
90Fort Saskatchewan Traders-1
92Michigan State Spartans-5
93Michigan State Spartans-3
96Collector's Edge Ice-91
Prism-91
97Long Beach Ice Dogs-4
98Albany River Rats-4

Buzan, Garrett
96Denver University Pioneers-5

Buzas, Patrick
05German DEL-301
06German DEL-4

Buzek, Petr
94SP-155
Die Cuts-155
94Czech APS Extraliga-167
95Classic-52
Autographs-3
95Classic Five-Sport *-133
96Michigan K-Wings-16
96Visions *-84
98Upper Deck-82
Exclusives-82
Exclusives 1 of 1-82
Gold Reserve-82
98Michigan K-Wings-13
99BAP Memorabilia-353
Gold-353
Silver-353
99BAP Millennium Calder Candidates Ruby-C25
99BAP Millennium Calder Candidate Emerald-C25
99BAP Millennium Calder Cand Sapphire-C25
99Pacific-452
99Pacific Omega-15
Copper-15
Gold-15
Ice Blue-15
Premiere Date-15
99Pacific Prism-7
Holographic Blue-7
Holographic Gold-7
Holographic Mirror-7
Holographic Purple-7
Premiere Date-7
99Topps Premier Plus-122
Parallel-122
00BAP Memorabilia-245
Emerald-245
Ruby-245
Sapphire-245
Promos-245
00BAP Mem Chicago Sportsfest Copper-245
00BAP Memorabilia Chicago Sportsfest Blue-245
00BAP Memorabilia Chicago Sportsfest Gold-245
00BAP Memorabilia Chicago Sportsfest Ruby-245
00BAP Memorabilia Chicago Sun-Times Ruby-245
00BAP Memorabilia Chicago Sun-Times Gold-245
00BAP Mem Chicago Sun-Times Sapphire-245
00BAP Mem Toronto Fall Expo Copper-245
00BAP Memorabilia Toronto Fall Expo Gold-245
00BAP Memorabilia Toronto Fall Expo Ruby-245
00BAP Signature Series-130
Emerald-130
Ruby-130
Sapphire-130
Autographs-48
Autographs Gold-48
00O-Pee-Chee-184
00O-Pee-Chee Parallel-184
00Pacific-16
Copper-16
Gold-16
Ice Blue-16
Premiere Date-16
00Panini Stickers-9
00Stadium Club-133
00Topps/OPC-184
Parallel-184
00Topps Chrome-123
OPC Refractors-123
Refractors-123
00Upper Deck Vintage-20
02BAP Sig Series Auto Buybacks 2000-48
02NHL Power Play Stickers-15
03Czech OFS Plus-338
03Czech OFS Plus MS Praha-SE5
04Czech OFS-3
Checklist Cards-1
Stars-45
04Czech Zuma-34

Byakin, Ilya
89Russian National Team-1
91O-Pee-Chee Inserts-13R
91Finnish Semic World Champ Stickers-83
91Swedish Semic World Champ Stickers-83
93Donruss-427
93Parkhurst-341
Emerald Ice-341
93PowerPlay-341
93Score-619
Gold-619
Canadian-619
Canadian Gold-619
93Swedish Semic World Champ Stickers-131
94OPC Premier-223
Special Effects-223
94Topps/OPC Premier-223
Special Effects-223
94Ultra-70
95Finnish Semic World Championships-124
95Swedish Leaf-261
95Swedish Upper Deck-136
96Swedish Semic Wien-138
97Las Vegas Thunder-21
00Russian Hockey League-157
02Russian Hockey League-94
02Russian Hockey League-219

Byalsin, Igor
90O-Pee-Chee Red Army-1R

Byce, John
90Bowman-38
Tiffany-38
90Bruins Sports Action-5
90Score Rookie/Traded-62T
90Upper Deck-25
French-25
91ProCards-59
93Swedish Semic Elitserien-113
97Long Beach Ice Dogs-5
98Long Beach Ice Dogs-3
99UK London Knights-3

Bye, Carlos
917th Inn. Sketch WHL-217

Bye, Gunnar
92Norwegian Elite Series-123

Bye, Jered
03Lincoln Stars Update-34

Bye, Karyn
92Sports Illustrated for Kids II-432
94Classic Women of Hockey-W27

Byers, Cole
03Vernon Vipers-4

Byers, Dane
02Prince Albert Raiders-3
03Prince Albert Raiders-7
04Prince Albert Raiders-21
05Prince Albert Raiders-2
06Hartford Wolf Pack-19

Byers, Jerry
74NHL Action Stamps-2
74O-Pee-Chee NHL-273

Byers, Lyndon
81Regina Pats-3
82Regina Pats-20
83Regina Pats-20
84Bruins Postcards-2
86Moncton Golden Flames-19
88Bruins Sports Action-3
89Bruins Sports Action-4
90Bruins Sports Action-6
90O-Pee-Chee-464
90Pro Set-3
93Las Vegas Thunder-5

Byers, Mike
68Shirriff Coins-175
70Colgate Stamps-55
70Esso Power Players-161
70O-Pee-Chee-160
71O-Pee-Chee-34
71Topps-34
71Toronto Sun-107
72Whalers New England WHA-1
72Los Angeles Sharks WHA-1

Byfuglien, Bobby John
00Lincoln Stars-11

Byfuglien, Derrick
02ECHL Update-U-2

Byfuglien, Dustin
03Prince George Cougars-5
05Norfolk Admirals-11
06Flair Showcase-26
Parallel-26
06Fleer-214
Tiffany-214
06Hot Prospects-107
Red Hot-107
White Hot-107
06O-Pee-Chee-501
Rainbow-501
06SP Authentic-173
Limited-173
06SP Game Used-110
Gold-110
Rainbow-110
Autographs-110
Rookie Exclusives Autographs-REDB
06SPx-143
Spectrum-143
06The Cup-119
Autographed Rookie Masterpiece Pressplates-119
Gold Rainbow Autographed Rookie Patches-119
Masterpiece Pressplates (Artifacts)-201
Masterpiece Pressplates (Marquee Rookies)-501
Masterpiece Pressplates (MVP)-332
Masterpiece Pressplates (Power Play)-104
Masterpiece Pressplates (SP Authentic Autographs)-173
Masterpiece Pressplates (SP Game Used)-110
Masterpiece Pressplates (SPx)-143
Masterpiece Pressplates (Sweet Beginnings)-114
Masterpiece Pressplates (Trilogy)-107
Masterpiece Pressplates (Victory)-203
Rookies Black-119
Rookies Platinum-119
06UD Artifacts-201
Blue-201
Gold-201
Platinum-201
Radiance-201
Red-201
06UD Powerplay-104
Impact Rainbow-104
06Ultimate Collection Ultimate Debut Threads Jerseys-DJ-DB
06Ultimate Collection Ultimate Debut Threads Jerseys Autographs-DJ-DB
06Ultimate Collection Ultimate Debut Threads Patches-DJ-DB
06Ultimate Collection Ultimate Debut Threads Patches Autographs-DJ-DB
06Ultra-204
Gold Medallion-204
Ice Medallion-204
06Upper Deck-206
Exclusives Parallel-206
High Gloss Parallel-206
Masterpieces-206
Rookie Materials-RMDB
Rookie Materials Patches-RMDB
06Upper Deck MVP-332
Gold Script-332
Super Script-332
06Upper Deck Ovation-61
06Upper Deck Sweet Shot-114
Rookie Jerseys Autographs-114
06Upper Deck Trilogy-107
06Upper Deck Victory-203
06Upper Deck Victory Black-203
06Upper Deck Victory Gold-203
06AHL Top Prospects-28
06Norfolk Admirals-23
07Upper Deck Rookie Class -37

Byfuglien, Jamie
91Air Canada SJHL-C21

Bykov, Dmitri
99Russian Hockey League-50
00Russian Hockey League-31
00Russian Hockey League-267
02Atomic-106
Blue-106
Gold-106
Red-106
Hobby Parallel-106
02BAP All-Star Edition-146
Gold-146
Silver-146
02BAP Memorabilia-284
Emerald-284
Ruby-284
Sapphire-284
NHL All-Star Game-284
NHL All-Star Game Blue-284
NHL All-Star Game Green-284
NHL All-Star Game Red-284
02BAP Memorabilia Toronto Fall Expo-284
02BAP Signature Series-193
Autographs-193
Autographs Gold-193
02BAP Ultimate Memorabilia-14
02Bowman YoungStars-158
Gold-158
Silver-158
02Crown Royale-112
Blue-112
Purple-112
Red-112
Retail-112
Rookie Royalty-8
02ITG Used-91
02Pacific Calder-115
Silver-115
02Pacific Complete-537
Red-537
02Pacific Exclusive-177
Blue-177
Gold-177
02Pacific Heads-Up-131
02Pacific Quest for the Cup-116
Gold-116
02Parkhurst-214
Bronze-214
Gold-214
Silver-214
02Parkhurst Retro-214
Minis-214
02Private Stock Reserve-159
Blue-159
Red-159
Retail-159
02SP Authentic-143
02SP Game Used-76
02Stadium Club-140
Silver Decoy Cards-140
Proofs-140
02Titanium-113
Blue-113
Red-113
Retail-113
02Topps Chrome-161
Black Border Refractors-161
Refractors-161
02Topps Heritage-155
02Topps Total-405
02UD Honor Roll-112
02UD Mask Collection-131
02UD Premier Collection-52B
Gold-52
02UD Top Shelf-112
02Upper Deck-435
Exclusives-435
02Upper Deck Classic Portraits-112
02Upper Deck Rookie Update-162A
02Upper Deck Rookie Update-162B
02Upper Deck Rookie Update-162C
02Vanguard-112
LTD-112
03O-Pee-Chee-97
03OPC Blue-97
03OPC Gold-97
03OPC Red-97
03Parkhurst Original Six Detroit-30
03Topps-97
Blue-97
Gold-97
Red-97
03Upper Deck Victory Freshman Flashback-FF20
04Russian World Championship Team-19
05Russian Hockey League RHL-19A

Bykov, Viacheslav
83Swedish Semic VM Stickers-69
84Russian National Team-4
87Russian National Team-4
89Russian National Team-2
89Swedish Semic World Champ Stickers-92
90O-Pee-Chee Red Army-10R
91Finnish Semic World Champ Stickers-100
91Swedish Semic World Champ Stickers-100
93Swedish Semic World Champ Stickers-147
93Swiss HNL-46
94Finnish Jaa Kiekko-145
94Swedish Olympics Lillehammer*-281
95Finnish Semic World Championships-138
95Swedish Globe World Championships-180
95Swedish World Championships Stickers-49
95Swiss HNL-71
96Swedish Semic Wien-151
96Swiss HNL-215
96Swiss HNL-575
98Swiss Power Play Stickers-336
99Russian Fetisov Tribute-22
99Swiss Panini Stickers-327

Bykovsky, Boris
98Danish Hockey League-213
99Danish Hockey League-136

Byling, Lars
64Swedish Coralli ISHockey-89

Bylow, Johan
99Swedish Upper Deck-134

Bylsma, Dan
92Greensboro Monarchs-6
93Greensboro Monarchs-3
95Phoenix Roadrunners-7
96Upper Deck-276
97Be A Player-29
Autographs-29
Autographs Die-Cuts-29
Autographs Prismatic Die-Cuts-29
97Pacific-323
Copper-323
Emerald Green-323
Ice Blue-323
Red-323
Silver-323
98Long Beach Ice Dogs-4
99BAP Millennium-124
Emerald-124
Ruby-124
Sapphire-124
Signatures-124
Signatures Gold-124
01Upper Deck Vintage-7
02BAP Sig Series Auto Buybacks 1999-124
02Ducks Team Issue-1
02Pacific Complete-282
Red-282
03ITG Action-5
04Cincinnati Mighty Ducks-2
06Wilkes-Barre Scranton Penguins-23

Bylsma, Sheldon
91Air Canada SJHL-D29
92Saskatchewan JHL-167

Bylund, Agne
69Swedish Hockey-204

Bylund, Lars
65Swedish Coralli ISHockey-89
67Swedish Hockey-43
69Swedish Hockey-57
70Swedish Hockey-20
71Swedish Hockey-97

Byng, Lady
03BAP Ultimate Memorabilia Memorialized-1
04ITG Ultimate Memorabilia-163
Gold-163
Paper Cuts-18
06Beehive 5 X 7 Cherry Wood-LBT
06ITG Ultimate Memorabilia-85
Artist Proof-85

Byram, Shawn
88ProCards AHL-323
89ProCards AHL-235
91ProCards-482
92Indianapolis Ice-5
93Indianapolis Ice-3
00UK Sekonda Superleague-14
01UK Manchester Storm Retro-8
02Bakersfield Condors-3

Byrne, Paddy
36Providence Reds-2

Byrne, Shaun
93Spokane Chiefs-4

Byrne, Trevor
03Worcester Ice Cats-6
04Peoria Rivermen-24
04Worcester IceCats-3
05Peoria Rivermen-4

Byrne, Warren
04Sioux Falls Stampede-3-2

Byrnes, Jason
94Kitchener Rangers-7
95Slapshot-146
96Kitchener Rangers-3
98Baton Rouge Kingfish-4

Byron, Paul
06Gatineau Olympiques-15

Byron, Wally
24Crescent Falcon-Tigers-2
24Holland Creameries-8

Bystrom, Lars
83Swedish Semic Elitserien-168
85Swedish Panini Stickers-217
86Swedish Panini Stickers-209
87Swedish Panini Stickers-205
89Swedish Semic Elitserien Stickers-182
90Swedish Semic Elitserien Stickers-17
91Swedish Semic Elitserien Stickers-216
92Swedish Semic Elitserien Stickers-245
93Swedish Semic Elitserien-213
94Swedish Leaf-92
Studio Signatures-9
95Swedish Leaf-109
95Swedish Upper Deck-169

Bystrom, Sven
64Swedish Coralli ISHockey-72
65Swedish Coralli ISHockey-72

Byvelds, Dean
00Barrie Colts-4

Bzdel, Gerald
88ProCards AHL-97
89Halifax Citadels-4
89ProCards AHL-174
90Halifax Citadels-3
90ProCards AHL/IHL-444
91ProCards-529

Bzdel, Mike
92British Columbia JHL-150

Cabana, Chad
917th Inn. Sketch WHL-298
94Tri-City Americans-5
96Carolina Monarchs-5
98New Haven Beast-11
99Louisville Panthers-17
01Colorado Gold Kings-4

Cabana, Clint
95Medicine Hat Tigers-5
00Fort Worth Brahmas-1
04Fresno Falcons-2

Cabana, Frederik
02Halifax Mooseheads-12
03Halifax Mooseheads-9
04Halifax Mooseheads-7
05Halifax Mooseheads-25
06Philadelphia Phantoms-28
06ITG Heroes and Prospects National Pride-NP03
06ITG Heroes and Prospects National Pride Gold-NP03

Cabana, Paul
92Quebec Pee-Wee Tournament-1337
01Michigan Tech Huskies-3
02Columbia Inferno-98
03Columbia Inferno-100
05Florida Everblades-3

Cabo, Joseph
93Quebec Pee-Wee Tournament-896

Cacciola, David
05Bossier-Shreveport Mudbugs-3
06New Mexico Scorpions-7

Caccioti, Steve
04Drummondville Voltigeurs-16

Cacciotti, Steven
04Drummondville Voltigeurs-16
05Drummondville Voltigeurs-14
06Drummondville Voltigeurs-10

Cachnin, Richard
98Czech OFS-63
99Czech Score Blue 2000-48
99Czech Score Red Ice 2000-48

Cachotsky, Tomas
04Czech OFS-4

Cada, Rostislav
01Swiss HNL-211
02Swiss HNL-174

Cadarette, Dave
03Huntsville Channel Cats-4

Cadden, Cory
93Knoxville Cherokees-2
94Knoxville Cherokees-23
96South Carolina Stingrays-30

Cadieux, Bruno
99Rouyn-Noranda Huskies-4
00Rouyn-Noranda Huskies-21
Signed-21

Cadieux, Jan Philippe
99Rimouski Oceanic-10
Signed-10
00Swiss Slapshot Mini-Cards-HCL11
00QMJHL All-Star Program Inserts-36
01Swiss HNL-36
02Swiss HNL-281

Cadieux, Paul Andre
93Swiss HNL-32
95Swiss HNL-343
96Swiss HNL-316
96Swiss HNL-524
98Swiss Power Play Stickers-299

Cadieux, Steve
90Cincinnati Cyclones-26
91Cincinnati Cyclones-3
94Anaheim Bullfrogs RHI-3

Cadisch, Leo
93Swiss HNL-475

Cadotte, Mark
95Slapshot-78
96Detroit Whalers-2
99Louisiana Ice Gators-18
02UK Nottingham Panthers-11
03UK Nottingham Panthers-13
04UK Nottingham Panthers-5
06Port Huron Flags-11

Caffery, Jack
44Beehive Group II Photos-10
52Juniors Blue Tint-154
55Parkhurst-19
Quaker Oats-19
57Topps-8
94Parkhurst Missing Link-12

Caffery, Terry
69O-Pee-Chee-135
69Swedish Hockey-351
72Whalers New England WHA-2

Cagas, Pavel
94Czech APS Extraliga-1
95Czech APS Extraliga-101
96German DEL-226
98Czech DS-18
98Czech OFS-313
99Czech DS-43
Goalies-G4
99Czech OFS-531
00German DEL-96
01Czech OFS-240
01Czech OFS H Inserts-H12

Cahan, Larry
44Beehive Group II Photos-301A
44Beehive Group II Photos-301B
44Beehive Group II Photos-387
55Parkhurst-16
Quaker Oats-16
57Topps-59
58Topps-23
60NHL Ceramic Tiles-4
61Shirriff/Salada Coins-95
61Topps-52
62Topps-48
63Topps-51
64Beehive Group III Photos-122
67Seals Team Issue-5
68O-Pee-Chee-35
68Topps-35
70Dad's Cookies-13
70Esso Power Players-147
70O-Pee-Chee-164
70Sargent Promotions Stamps-79
71Toronto Sun-108
72O-Pee-Chee-307
94Parkhurst Missing Link-87

Cahill, Chris
95Alaska Gold Kings-4

Cahill, Darcy
87Kingston Canadians-16
907th Inn. Sketch OHL-204
94UK Humberside Hawks-15

Cahill, Kelly
06Ohio State Buckeyes Women-13

Cahoon, Jim
76Nova Scotia Voyageurs-3
77Nova Scotia Voyageurs-5

Caig, T.J.
04Minnesota-Duluth Bulldogs-3

Cain, Aaron
91Air Canada SJHL-A39
92Saskatchewan JHL-23

Cain, Darren
04Knoxville Ice Bears-12

Cain, Dutch
24Anonymous NHL-91
24Anonymous NHL-91
24C144 Champ's Cigarettes-10
24V130 Maple Crispette-16
24V145-2-35

Cain, Herb
34Beehive Group I Photos-191
34Sweet Caporal-16
35O-Pee-Chee V304C-77
36O-Pee-Chee V304D-110
37O-Pee-Chee V304E-172
37V356 Worldwide Gum-46
38Quaker Oats Photos-6
39O-Pee-Chee V301-1-42
05ITG Ultimate Mem Marvelous Maroons Auto-2

Cain, Kelly
85London Knights-22
86Kitchener Rangers-20

Cain, Luke
04Salmon Arm Silverbacks-12
05Salmon Arm Silverbacks-5

Cain, Paul
90Richmond Renegades-7

Cairns, Eric
917th Inn. Sketch OHL-31
93Detroit Jr. Red Wings-7
94Binghamton Rangers-1
95Binghamton Rangers-4
97Be A Player-28
Autographs-28
Autographs Die-Cuts-28
Autographs Prismatic Die-Cuts-28
97Pacific-301
Copper-301
Emerald Green-301
Ice Blue-301
Red-301
Silver-301
97Hartford Wolf Pack-3
00BAP Memorabilia-58
Emerald-58
Ruby-58
Sapphire-58
Promos-58
00BAP Mem Chicago Sportsfest Copper-58
00BAP Memorabilia Chicago Sportsfest Blue-58
00BAP Memorabilia Chicago Sportsfest Gold-58
00BAP Memorabilia Chicago Sportsfest Ruby-58
00BAP Memorabilia Chicago Sun-Times Ruby-58
00BAP Memorabilia Chicago Sun-Times Gold-58
00BAP Mem Chicago Sun-Times Sapphire-58
00BAP Mem Toronto Fall Expo Copper-58
00BAP Memorabilia Toronto Fall Expo Gold-58
00BAP Memorabilia Toronto Fall Expo Ruby-58
00BAP Memorabilia Update Tough Materials-T4
00BAP Mem Update Tough Materials Gold-T4
01BAP Update Tough Customers-TC30
01BAP Update Tough Customers-TC40
02Upper Deck-354
Exclusives-354
02Upper Deck Beckett UD Promos-354
02Upper Deck Vintage-160
02Upper Deck Vintage-279
03O-Pee-Chee-285
03OPC Blue-285
03OPC Gold-285
03OPC Red-285
03Topps-285
Blue-285
Gold-285
Red-285
Tough Materials-EC
Tough Materials-SMEC
04UK EIHL All-Stars-14
04UK London Racers-2
04UK London Racers Playoffs-1

Cairns, Mark
03Odessa Jackalopes-3

Cairns, Trevor
93Tacoma Rockets-3

Caissie, Jeremy
917th Inn. Sketch QMJHL-279

Cajanek, Petr
94Parkhurst SE-SE214
Gold-SE214
94Upper Deck-507
Electric Ice-507
94Czech APS Extraliga-202
95Czech APS Extraliga-46
96Czech APS Extraliga-45
97Czech APS Extraliga-66
97Czech DS Extraliga-108
97Czech DS Stickers-111
98Czech DS-111
98Czech DS Stickers-298
98Czech OFS-29
98Czech OFS-488
99Czech DS-7
99Czech OFS-258
99Czech OFS-451
99Czech OFS-511
All-Star Game Blue-511
All-Star Game Gold-511
All-Star Game Red-511
All-Star Game Silver-511
00Czech DS Extraliga-56
Top Stars-TS3
Valuable Players-VP6
00Czech OFS-361
00Czech OFS Star Emerald-5
00Czech OFS Star Pink-5
00Czech OFS Star Violet-5
01Czech DS-15
01Czech DS-60
Best of the Best-BB4
01Czech OFS-93
All Stars-6
01Czech OFS Red Inserts-RE18D
02BAP Signature Series-136
Autographs-136
Autographs Gold-136
02Blues Team Issue-2
02Crown Royale Rookie Royalty-18
02Pacific Exclusive-189
Blue-189
Gold-189
02Stadium Club-118
Silver Decoy Cards-118
Proofs-118
02Vanguard Prime Prospects-19
02Czech DS-22
02Czech DS-85
02Czech OFS Plus All-Star Game-H3
02Czech Stadion Olympics-325
03Blues Team Set-4
03ITG Action-594
03Pacific Complete-300
Red-300
03Upper Deck-414
Canadian Exclusives-414
HG-414
UD Exclusives-414
03Upper Deck MVP-364
Gold Script-364
Silver Script-364
Canadian Exclusives-364
04Upper Deck-151
Canadian Exclusives-151
HG Glossy Gold-151
HG Glossy Silver-151
04Czech NHL ELH Postcards-2
04Czech OFS-274
Checklist Cards-13
Stars-40
04Czech Zuma-35
05Blues Team Set-4
05Panini Stickers-341
05Parkhurst-416
Facsimile Auto Parallel-416
05Upper Deck-411
05Upper Deck Victory-243
Black-243
Gold-243
Silver-243
05Czech World Champions Postcards-20
05Czech Kvarteto Bonaparte-8c
05Czech Pexeso Mini Blue Set-16
05Czech Pexeso Mini Red Set-13
06Fleer-169
Tiffany-169
06O-Pee-Chee-428
Rainbow-428

06Panini Stickers-348
06Ultra-172
Gold Medallion-172
Ice Medallion-172
06Upper Deck-172
Exclusives Parallel-172
High Gloss Parallel-172
Masterpieces-172
06Upper Deck MVP-255
Gold Script-255
Super Script-255
06Upper Deck Ovation-143
06Upper Deck Victory-173
06Upper Deck Victory Black-173
06Upper Deck Victory Gold-173

Cajka, Ludek
97Czech APS Extraliga-377
98Czech OFS Legends-9

Cakajik, Martin
02Czech OFS Plus-148
03Czech OFS Plus-109
03Czech OFS Plus Insert M-M16
04Czech OFS-206
04Czech OFS-403
05Czech HC Znojmo-2
06Czech OFS-200

Caladi, Erik
06Belleville Bulls-5

Calce, Luigi
917th Inn. Sketch OHL-282
93Owen Sound Platers-4

Calder, Adam
01South Carolina Stingrays-4
02South Carolina Stingrays-4
02South Carolina Stingrays RBI-207
04UK Coventry Blaze-3
04UK Coventry Blaze Champions-12
04UK EIHL All-Stars-5
05UK Coventry Blaze-16
06UK Coventry Blaze-11

Calder, Frank
83Hall of Fame-18
83Hall of Fame Postcards-B3
85Hall of Fame-18
92Hall of Fame Legends-36
01Upper Deck Legends-51
03BAP Ultimate Memorabilia Memorialized-7
03BAP Ultimate Memorabilia Paper Cuts-46
04ITG Ultimate Memorabilia Paper Cuts-11
05ITG Ultimate Memorabilia Builders Autos-3
06ITG Ultimate Memorabilia-50
Artist Proof-50

Calder, Glenn
91British Columbia JHL-79
92British Columbia JHL-98

Calder, Kyle
96Regina Pats-8
97Regina Pats-2
99BAP Memorabilia-335
Gold-335
Silver-335
99BAP Millennium Calder Candidates Ruby-C3
99BAP Millennium Calder Candidate Emerald-C3
99BAP Millennium Calder Cand Sapphire-C3
99Black Diamond-21
Diamond Cut-21
Final Cut-21
99Crown Royale-31
Limited Series-31
Premiere Date-31
Prospects Parallel-31
99SP Authentic-99
99Topps Premier Plus-103
Parallel-103
99Ultimate Victory-95
1/1-95
Parallel-95
Parallel 100-95
99Upper Deck-203
Exclusives-203
Exclusives 1 of 1-203
99Upper Deck Gold Reserve-203
99Wayne Gretzky Hockey-45
99Cleveland Lumberjacks-3
99Bowman CHL-84
Gold-84
OPC International-84
00O-Pee-Chee-317
00O-Pee-Chee Parallel-317
00Topps/OPC-317
Parallel-317
00Topps Chrome-212
OPC Refractors-212
Refractors-212
00Upper Deck Victory-275
01BAP Memorabilia-236
Emerald-236
Ruby-236
Sapphire-236
01BAP Signature Series-98
Autographs-98
Autographs Gold-98
01Bowman YoungStars-149
Gold-149
Ice Cubed-149
Autographs-KC
Relics-JKC
Relics-SKC
Relics-DSKC
Rivals-R11
01Crown Royale-31
Blue-31
Premiere Date-31
Red-31
Retail-31
Triple Threads-6
01O-Pee-Chee-172
01O-Pee-Chee Premier Parallel-172
01Pacific Heads-Up Quad Jerseys-6
01Private Stock Game Gear-21
01Private Stock Game Gear Patches-21
01SPx-166
01Titanium-30
Hobby Parallel-30
Premiere Date-30
Retail-30
Retail Parallel-30
Double-Sided Jerseys-9
Double-Sided Patches-9
01Titanium Draft Day Edition-21
01Topps-172
OPC Parallel-172
01Upper Deck Victory-80
Gold-80
01Vanguard-20
Blue-20
Red-20
One of Ones-20
Premiere Date-20
Proofs-20
02BAP First Edition-232
02BAP Memorabilia Future of the Game-FG-16
02BAP Signature Series-84
Autographs-84
Autograph Buybacks 2001-98
Autographs Gold-84
02O-Pee-Chee-169
02O-Pee-Chee Premier Blue Parallel-169
02O-Pee-Chee Premier Red Parallel-169
02O-Pee-Chee Factory Set-169
02Pacific-75
Blue-75
Red-75
02Pacific Complete-132
Red-132
02Parkhurst Retro-86
Minis-86
02SP Authentic-112
02SP Game Used Future Fabrics-FFCA
02SP Game Used Future Fabrics-FFKC
02SP Game Used Future Fabrics Gold-FFCA
02SP Game Used Future Fabrics Gold-FFKC
02SP Game Used Future Fabrics Rainbow-FFCA
02SP Game Used Future Fabrics Rainbow-FFKC
02Stadium Club YoungStars Relics-S12
02Topps-169
OPC Blue Parallel-169
OPC Red Parallel-169
Factory Set-169
02Topps Total-238
02UD Artistic Impressions Right Track-RTKC
02UD Artistic Impression Right Track Gold-RTKC
02Upper Deck-38
Exclusives-38
02Upper Deck MVP-42
Gold-42
Classics-42
Golden Classics-42
02Upper Deck Victory-48
Bronze-48
Gold-48
Silver-48
02Upper Deck Vintage-57
02Upper Deck Vintage-267
03Beehive-41
Gold-41
Silver-41
03Black Diamond-69
Black-69
Green-69
Red-69
Threads-DT-KC
Threads Green-DT-KC
Threads Red-DT-KC
Threads Black-DT-KC
03Blackhawks Postcards-5
03Bowman-32
Gold-32
03Bowman Chrome-32
Refractors-32
Gold Refractors-32
Xfractors-32
03ITG Action-151
03NHL Sticker Collection-176
03O-Pee-Chee-222
03OPC Blue-222
03OPC Gold-222
03OPC Red-222
03Pacific-71
Blue-71
Red-71
03Pacific Calder-21
Silver-21
03Pacific Complete-32
Red-32
03Pacific Exhibit-31
Blue Backs-31
Yellow Backs-31
03Pacific Quest for the Cup-21
Blue-21
03Parkhurst Original Six Chicago-4
03SPx-20
03SPx-174
Radiance-20
Radiance-174
Spectrum-20
Spectrum-174
03Titanium-25
Hobby Jersey Number Parallels-25
Retail-25
Retail Jersey Number Parallels-25
03Topps-222
Blue-222
Gold-222
Red-222
03Topps C55-48
Minis-48
Minis American Back-48
Minis American Back Red-48
Minis Bazooka Back-48
Minis Brooklyn Back-48
Minis Hat Trick Back-48
Minis O Canada Back-48
Minis O Canada Back Red-48
Minis Stanley Cup Back-48
03Topps Pristine-7
Gold Refractor Die Cuts-7
Refractors-7
Press Plates Black-7
Press Plates Cyan-7
Press Plates Magenta-7
Press Plates Yellow-7
03UD Honor Roll-14
03Upper Deck-41
Canadian Exclusives-41
HG-41
03Upper Deck Classic Portraits-18
03Upper Deck MVP-93
Gold Script-93
Silver Script-93
Canadian Exclusives-93
03Upper Deck Trilogy-17
Limited-18
03Upper Deck Victory-40
Bronze-40
Gold-40
Silver-40
04Pacific-59
Blue-59
Red-59
04Upper Deck-38
Canadian Exclusives-38
HG Glossy Gold-38
HG Glossy Silver-38
04Swedish Pure Skills-85
Parallel-85
05Panini Stickers-221
05Parkhurst-102
Facsimile Auto Parallel-102
Signatures-KC
True Colors-TCCHI
True Colors-TCCHI
True Colors-TCCHDE
True Colors-TCCHDE
05Ultra-52
Gold-52
Ice-52
05Upper Deck-40
HG Glossy-40
Jerseys Series II-J2KC
05Upper Deck MVP-88
Gold-88
Platinum-88
05Upper Deck Toronto Fall Expo-40
06Be A Player-148
Autographs-148
Signatures-KC
Signatures 25-163
06Fleer Signing Day-SDKC
06Flyers Postcards-9
06Hot Prospects Hotagraphs-HKC
06O-Pee-Chee-371
Rainbow-371
Autographs-A-KC
06Panini Stickers-125
06SPx Winning Materials-WMKC
06SPx Winning Materials Spectrum-WMKC
06SPx Winning Materials Autographs-WMKC
06Ultra-44
Gold Medallion-44
Ice Medallion-44
06Upper Deck-396
Exclusives Parallel-396
High Gloss Parallel-396
Game Jerseys-J2KC
Game Patches-P2KC
Masterpieces-396
06Upper Deck MVP-220
Gold Script-220
Super Script-220
Jerseys-OJSC
Jerseys-OJWC
06Upper Deck Ovation-60
06Upper Deck Trilogy Combo Clearcut Autographs-C2CK
06Upper Deck Trilogy Honorary Scripted Patches-HSPKC
06Upper Deck Trilogy Honorary Scripted Swatches-HSSKC
06Upper Deck Trilogy Scripts-TSKC
06Upper Deck Victory-43
06Upper Deck Victory-263
06Upper Deck Victory Black-43
06Upper Deck Victory Gold-43

Calder, Pierre
907th Inn. Sketch QMJHL-61

Calder, Shane
90Saskatoon Blades-13
907th Inn. Sketch WHL-73
91Saskatoon Blades-11
917th Inn. Sketch WHL-109
93Saskatoon Blades-6
96Pensacola Ice Pilots-18
97Pensacola Ice Pilots-5
98ECHL All-Star Southern Conference-13
98Pensacola Ice Pilots-1
01Anchorage Aces-1

Caldr, Vladimir
94Czech APS Extraliga-286
95Czech APS Extraliga-51
96Czech APS Extraliga-237
97Czech APS Extraliga-264
98Czech OFS-307
99Czech OFS-41

Caldwell, Ryan
06Fleer-229
Tiffany-229
06O-Pee-Chee-514
Rainbow-514
06SPx-199
Spectrum-199
06The Cup Masterpiece Pressplates (Marquee Rookies)-514
06The Cup Masterpiece Pressplates (MVP)-352
06The Cup Masterpiece Pressplates (Power Play)-113
06The Cup Masterpiece Pressplates (Trilogy)-132
06The Cup Masterpiece Pressplates (Victory)-314
06UD Powerplay-113
Impact Rainbow-113
06Ultra-215
Gold Medallion-215
Ice Medallion-215
06Upper Deck-227
Exclusives Parallel-227
High Gloss Parallel-227
Masterpieces-227
06Upper Deck MVP-352
Gold Script-352
Super Script-352
06Upper Deck Ovation-81
06Upper Deck Trilogy-132
06Upper Deck Victory-314
06Syracuse Crunch-17

Calen, Kenneth
69Swedish Hockey-225
71Swedish Hockey-370

Caley, Troy
00Wichita Thunder-2

Calla, Brady
04Everett Silvertips-24
05ITG Heroes/Prosp Toronto Expo Parallel -315
05Everett Silvertips-2
05ITG Heroes and Prospects-315
Autographs Series II-BCA
Team Cherry-TC15
06Moose Jaw Warriors-9
06ITG Heroes and Prospects-96
Autographs-ABCA
Sticks and Jerseys-SJ06
Sticks and Jerseys Gold-SJ06

Callaghan, Gary
92Thunder Bay Thunder Hawks-9

Callahan, Brian
97Johnstown Chiefs-24
00Jackson Bandits-14
00Jackson Bandits Promos-4

Callahan, Gary
84Belleville Bulls-24
86Kitchener Rangers-24
88ProCards AHL-64

Callahan, Greg
96Johnstown Chiefs-1
96Wheeling Nailers-6
97Johnstown Chiefs-18

Callahan, Jack
94Knoxville Cherokees-14
95Signature Rookies Auto-Phonex-11
95Signature Rook Auto-Phonex Phone Cards-11

Callahan, Jimmy
05Missouri River Otters-16

Callahan, Mike
94Los Angeles Blades RHI-17

Callahan, Ryan
02Guelph Storm-20
03Guelph Storm-19
04Guelph Storm-22
05ITG Heroes/Prosp Toronto Expo Parallel -398
05Guelph Storm-D-06
05OHL Bell All-Star Classic-23
05ITG Heroes and Prospects-398
06ITG Ultimate Memorabilia Future Star-24
06ITG Ultimate Memorabilia Future Star Gold-24
06ITG Ultimate Memorabilia Future Star Autos-13
06ITG Ultimate Memorabilia Future Star Autos Gold-13
06ITG Ultimate Memorabilia Future Star Patches Autos-13
06ITG Ultimate Memorabilia Future Star Patches Autos Gold-13
06AHL Top Prospects-14
06Hartford Wolf Pack-24
06ITG Heroes and Prospects Jerseys-GUJ32
06ITG Heroes and Prospects Jerseys Gold-GUJ32
06ITG Heroes and Prospects Emblems-GUE32
06ITG Heroes and Prospects Emblems Gold-GUE32
06ITG Heroes and Prospects Numbers-GUN32
06ITG Heroes and Prospects Numbers Gold-GUN32
07Upper Deck Victory-218
Black-218
Gold-218

Callander, Drew
79Canucks Royal Bank-4

Callander, Jock
81Regina Pats-4
87Penguins Kodak-4
88ProCards IHL-44
90ProCards AHL/IHL-371
91ProCards-291
92Pro Set-175
92Atlanta Knights-9
93Upper Deck-10
93Cleveland Lumberjacks-13
93Cleveland Lumberjacks Postcards-5
94Cleveland Lumberjacks-12
94Cleveland Lumberjacks Postcards-12
95Cleveland Lumberjacks-8
95Cleveland Lumberjacks Postcards-8
96Cleveland Lumberjacks-7
96Cleveland Lumberjacks Multi-Ad-8
96Collector's Edge Ice-115
Prism-115
97Cleveland Lumberjacks-6
97Cleveland Lumberjacks Postcards-12
98Cleveland Lumberjacks-8
99Cleveland Lumberjacks-4
00Cleveland Lumberjacks-21
05Cleveland Barons-28

Callander, Preston
00Lincoln Stars-10

Callaway, Kris
98Spokane Chiefs-3
99Spokane Chiefs-6
01Lethbridge Hurricanes-10
04Lakehead University Thunderwolves-10

Callender, Drew
01Regina Pats-5

Callesen, Morten
98Danish Hockey League-199
99Danish Hockey League-75

Callighen, Brett
79Oilers Postcards-1
79O-Pee-Chee-315
80O-Pee-Chee-114
80Pepsi-Cola Caps-23
80Topps-114
81Oilers Red Rooster-18
81O-Pee-Chee-110
81O-Pee-Chee Stickers-212
81Post Standups-20
82O-Pee-Chee-103
82Post Cereal-6
88Oilers Tenth Anniversary-50

Callinan, Jeff
91Minnesota Golden Gophers-4
92Minnesota Golden Gophers-5
93Minnesota Golden Gophers-6
94Minnesota Golden Gophers-7
95Birmingham Bulls-18

Caloun, Jan
91Upper Deck Czech World Juniors-91
92Classic-38
Gold-38
Four-Sport Autographs-NNO
94Kansas City Blades-9
95Finnish Semic World Championships-159
95Kansas City Blades-5
95Images-23
Gold-23
Platinum Prospects-PR10
96Leaf-217
Press Proofs-217
96Metal Universe-173
96Pinnacle-229
Artist's Proofs-229
Foil-229
Premium Stock-229
Rink Collection-229
96Summit-187
Artist's Proofs-187
Ice-187
Metal-187
Premium Stock-187
96Upper Deck-195
96Kentucky Thoroughblades-3
96Collector's Edge Future Legends-16
96Collector's Edge Ice-144
Prism-144
97Kansas City Blades Magnets-4
98Czech OFS-244
98Czech Bonaparte-4C
98Czech Pexeso-14
98Finnish Kerailysarja-40
99Czech OFS-259
99Finnish Cardset-26
99Finnish Cardset-158
Aces High-D-6
00Upper Deck Vintage-109
00Finnish Cardset-262
00Finnish Cardset Master Blasters-2
01Finnish Cardset-187
01Finnish Cardset Dueling Aces-3
02Czech IQ Sports Blue-3
02Czech IQ Sports Yellow-3
02Finnish Cardset-8
03Finnish Cardset-7
04Czech OFS-385
Stars II-10
05Czech HC Pardubice-2
06Czech HC Pardubice Postcards-3
06Czech OFS-112
Goals Leaders-8
Points Leaders-12

Calverley, Chris
84Nanaimo Clippers-4
84Victoria Cougars-4

Calvert, Jeff
907th Inn. Sketch WHL-159
917th Inn. Sketch WHL-153
92Tacoma Rockets-4
93Tacoma Rockets-4

Camazzola, Jim
92Finnish Semic-247
93Swedish Semic World Champ Stickers-212
98German DEL-272
99German DEL-163
00German DEL-28

Cambell, Terry
94German DEL-407

Cambio, Chris
89Nashville Knights-4

Camenzind, Andreas
01Swiss HNL-111
02Swiss HNL-119

Camenzind, Arthur
93Swiss HNL-378
95Swiss HNL-225
96Swiss HNL-138

Camenzind, Joel
01Swiss HNL-453
02Swiss HNL-458

Cameron, Al
77O-Pee-Chee NHL-48
77Topps-48
78O-Pee-Chee-396
79Jets Postcards-2
80Jets Postcards-2
80Pepsi-Cola Caps-122

Cameron, Bryan
05Belleville Bulls-9
05Belleville Bulls-15
06Belleville Bulls-2

Cameron, Connor
02St. Michaels Majors-17
03St. Michael's Majors-15
04Belleville Bulls-4
05Kingston Frontenacs-18

Cameron, Craig
72O-Pee-Chee-13
72Topps-22
73O-Pee-Chee-42
73Topps-147
74NHL Action Stamps-166
74NHL Action Stamps Update-17
74O-Pee-Chee NHL-263
74Topps-263
75O-Pee-Chee NHL-239
75Topps-239
76O-Pee-Chee NHL-327

Cameron, Dave
81Rockies Postcards-3
82Post Cereal-11
83Devils Postcards-5
96Lethbridge Hurricanes-2
98Bowman CHL-141
Golden Anniversary-141
OPC International-141
Autographs Blue-A29
Autographs Gold-A29
Autographs Silver-A29
98Bowman Chrome CHL-141
Golden Anniversary-141
Golden Anniversary Refractors-141
OPC International-141
OPC International Refractors-141
Refractors-141
00St. Michaels Majors-10
01St. Michaels Majors-26
02St. Michaels Majors-25
03St. Michael's Majors-24
06Binghamton Senators-23

Cameron, David
97Prince Albert Raiders-4
00Saskatoon Blades-20
04Binghamton Senators-23

Cameron, Dustin
06Saskatoon Blades-1

Cameron, Garett
06Port Huron Flags-24

Cameron, Harry
83Hall of Fame Postcards-G4
85Hall of Fame-95

Cameron, Jeff
03Missouri River Otters-5
04Tulsa Oilers-5

Cameron, Jordan
03Alaska Aces-1

Cameron, Julian
25Dominion Chocolates-70
907th Inn. Sketch Memorial Cup-52

Cameron, Malcolm
93Huntington Blizzard-6
96Fort Worth Fire-1

Cameron, Randy
83Brandon Wheat Kings-22
84Kelowna Wings-7
06Moncton Wildcats-5

Cameron, Scott
98Barrie Colts-11
99O-Pee-Chee-257
99O-Pee-Chee Chrome-257
99O-Pee-Chee Chrome Refractors-257
99Topps/OPC-257
99Topps/OPC Chrome-257
Refractors-257
99Bowman CHL-30
Gold-30
OPC International-30
Autographs-BA11
Autographs Gold-BA11
Autographs Silver-BA11
00UD CHL Prospects-36
01Albany River Rats-17
02Albany River Rats-21
02Albany River Rats AAP-6

Cameron, Steve
06Penticton Vees-3

Camichel, Corzin
01Swiss HNL-222
02Swiss HNL-192

Camichel, Duri
01Swiss EV Zug Postcards-18
01Swiss HNL-179
02Swiss EV Zug Postcards-18
02Swiss HNL-68
03Swiss EV Zug Postcards-3
04Swiss EV Zug Postcards-18

Cammalleri, Mike
96Quebec Pee-Wee Tournament-1174
02BAP All-Star Edition-145
Gold-145
Silver-145
02BAP Memorabilia-395
02BAP Signature Series-197
All-Rookie-AR10
Autographs-197
Autographs Gold-197
Jerseys-SGJ64
Jersey Autographs-SGJ64
02BAP Ultimate Memorabilia-46
Autographs-8
Autographs Gold-8
02Bowman YoungStars-148
Gold-148
Silver-148
02Crown Royale-117
Blue-117
Purple-117
Red-117
Retail-117
02ITG Used-184
Calder Jerseys-C20
Calder Jerseys Gold-C20
02Pacific Calder-121
Silver-121
Reflections-13
02Pacific Complete-504
Red-504
02Pacific Quest for the Cup-122
Gold-122
02Parkhurst-245
Bronze-245
Gold-245
Silver-245
02Parkhurst Retro-246
Minis-246
02SP Authentic-173
02SP Game Used-99
02SPx-190
02Titanium-117
Blue-117
Red-117
Retail-117
Right on Target-11
02UD Artistic Impressions-114
Gold-114
02UD Honor Roll-115
02UD Mask Collection-164
02UD Premier Collection-56B
Gold-56
02Upper Deck-450
Exclusives-450
02Upper Deck Classic Portraits-114
02Vanguard-116
LTD-116
02Manchester Monarchs-5
03BAP Memorabilia Future of the Game-FG-13
03ITG Action-271
Jerseys-M12
03Pacific-153
Blue-153
Red-153
03Pacific Complete-397
Red-397
03Pacific Prism-47
Blue-47
Gold-47
Red-47
03Pacific Toronto Spring Expo-6
Gold-6
03SPx Big Futures-BF-MC
03SPx Big Futures Limited-BF-MC
03Upper Deck MVP-200
Gold Script-200
Silver Script-200
Canadian Exclusives-200
04AHL All-Stars-9
04AHL Top Prospects-28
04Manchester Monarchs-15
04Manchester Monarchs Tobacco-15
04ITG Heroes and Prospects-197
Autographs-U-MCA
04ITG Heroes/Prospects Toronto Expo '05-197
05ITG Heroes/Prosp Toronto Expo Parallel -93
05ITG Heroes/Prosp Toronto Expo Parallel -343
05Beehive Signature Scrapbook-SSMC
05Hot Prospects Hot Materials-HMMC
05Kings Team Issue-14
05Panini Stickers-294
05Parkhurst-222
Facsimile Auto Parallel-222
Signatures-MC
True Colors-TCLAK
True Colors-TCLAK
05SP Game Used Auto Draft-AD-CA
05SP Game Used SIGnificance-MC
05SP Game Used SIGnificance Gold-S-MC
05UD Artifacts Auto Facts-AF-MC
05UD Artifacts Auto Facts Blue-AF-MC
05UD Artifacts Auto Facts Copper-AF-MC
05UD Artifacts Auto Facts Pewter-AF-MC
05UD Artifacts Auto Facts Silver-AF-MC
05UD Artifacts Remarkable Artifacts-RA-MC
05UD Artifacts Remarkable Artifacts Dual-RA-MC
05Ultra Fresh Ink-FI-CA
05Ultra Fresh Ink Blue-FI-CA
05Upper Deck-339
Jerseys-J-MCA
Notable Numbers-N-CA
05Upper Deck MVP-187
Gold-187
Platinum-187
ProSign-P-MC
05Upper Deck Trilogy Scripts-SFS-MC
05Upper Deck Victory-95
Black-95
Gold-95
Silver-95
05Manchester Monarchs-27
05ITG Heroes and Prospects-93
05ITG Heroes and Prospects-343
AHL Grads-AG-8
AHL Grads Gold-AG-8
Autographs-A-MC
Autographs Series II-MC2
He Shoots-He Scores Prizes-29
Jerseys-GUJ-6
Jerseys Gold-GUJ-06
Emblems-GUE-6
Emblems Gold-GUE-06
Numbers-GUN-6
Numbers Gold-GUN-06
National Pride-NPR-9
Shooting Stars-AS-5
06Be A Player-147
Autographs-147
Signatures-CM
Signatures 10-162
Signatures Duals-DBC
Signatures Trios-TFCO
06Beehive Signature Scrapbook-SSMC
06Black Diamond-38
Black-38
Gold-38
Ruby-38
Jerseys-JMC
Jerseys Black-JMC
Jerseys Gold-JMC
Jerseys Ruby-JMC
Jerseys Black Autographs -JCA
06Flair Showcase Inks-IMC
06Fleer-90
Tiffany-90
06Hot Prospects Hotagraphs-HCA
06O-Pee-Chee-235
Rainbow-235
Autographs-A-MC
Swatches-S-MC
06Panini Stickers-287
06SP Authentic Chirography-MC
06SP Game Used Authentic Fabrics-AFMC
06SP Game Used Authentic Fabrics Parallel-AFMC
06SP Game Used Authentic Fabrics Patches-AFMC
06SP Game Used Authentic Fabrics Triple-AF3LAK
06SP Game Used Authentic Fabrics Triple Patches-AF3LAK
06SP Game Used Inked Sweaters-ISMC
06SP Game Used Inked Sweaters Patches-ISMC
06SP Game Used Inked Sweaters Dual-IS2FC
06SP Game Used Inked Sweaters Dual Patches-IS2FC
06SP Game Used Letter Marks-LMMI
06SP Game Used SIGnificance-SMC
06SPx Winning Materials-WMMC
06SPx Winning Materials Spectrum-WMMC
06SPx Winning Materials Autographs-WMMC
06The Cup NHL Shields Duals-DSHKC
06UD Artifacts Auto-Facts-AFMC
06UD Artifacts Auto-Facts Gold-AFMC
06UD Powerplay-48
Impact Rainbow-48
06Ultra-92
Gold Medallion-92
Ice Medallion-92
Fresh Ink-IMC
06Upper Deck Arena Giveaways-LAK6
06Upper Deck-89
Exclusives Parallel-89
High Gloss Parallel-89
Game Jerseys-J2CA
Game Patches-P2CA
Masterpieces-89
06Upper Deck MVP-134
Gold Script-134
Super Script-134
Autographs-OAFC
Jerseys-OJGC
06Upper Deck Ovation-123
06Upper Deck Sweet Shot Signature Shots/Saves-SSMC
06Upper Deck Sweet Shot Signature Shots/Saves Sticks-SSSMC
06Upper Deck Trilogy Combo Clearcut Autographs-C3FCB
06Upper Deck Trilogy Honorary Scripted Patches-HSPMC
06Upper Deck Trilogy Honorary Scripted Swatches-HSSMC
06Upper Deck Trilogy Ice Scripts-ISMC
06Upper Deck Trilogy Scripts-TSMC
06Upper Deck Victory-94
06Upper Deck Victory Black-94
06Upper Deck Victory Gold-94
06Upper Deck Victory Next In Line-NL26
07Upper Deck Ovation-79
07Upper Deck Victory-193
Black-193
Gold-193

Cammock, Dave
917th Inn. Sketch WHL-36
93Portland Winter Hawks-4

Camp, Shawn
01Guelph Storm-26
01Guelph Storm Memorial Cup-26
02Guelph Storm-27
03Guelph Storm-24

Campbell, Adam
96Owen Sound Platers-24
97Owen Sound Platers-3
98Owen Sound Platers-25
99Owen Sound Platers-12
00Sarnia Sting-7

Campbell, Angus
10C56-9
83Hall of Fame Postcards-I4
85Hall of Fame-125

Campbell, Bill
86Sherbrooke Canadiens-9

Campbell, Brian
95Slapshot-275
98Bowman CHL-23
Golden Anniversary-23
OPC International-23
98Bowman Chrome CHL-23
Golden Anniversary-23
Golden Anniversary Refractors-23
OPC International-23
OPC International Refractors-23
Refractors-23
99BAP Memorabilia-104
Gold-104
Silver-104
99BAP Millennium-32
Emerald-32
Ruby-32
Sapphire-32
Signatures-32
Signatures Gold-32
99Pacific Omega-27
Copper-27
Gold-27
Ice Blue-27
Premiere Date-27
99SP Authentic-94
Sign of the Times-BC
Sign of the Times Gold-BC
99Topps Premier Plus-119
Parallel-119
99Ultimate Victory-92
1/1-92
Parallel-92
Parallel 100-92
99Upper Deck-189
Exclusives-189
Exclusives 1 of 1-189
99Upper Deck Gold Reserve-189
99Upper Deck HoloGrFx-7
Ausome-7
99Upper Deck Victory-367
99Wayne Gretzky Hockey-26
99Bowman CHL-137
Gold-137
OPC International-137
00BAP Memorabilia-92
Emerald-92
Ruby-92
Sapphire-92
Promos-92
00BAP Mem Chicago Sportsfest Copper-92
00BAP Memorabilia Chicago Sportsfest Blue-92
00BAP Memorabilia Chicago Sportsfest Gold-92
00BAP Memorabilia Chicago Sportsfest Ruby-92
00BAP Memorabilia Chicago Sun-Times Ruby-92
00BAP Memorabilia Chicago Sun-Times Gold-92
00BAP Mem Chicago Sun-Times Sapphire-92
00BAP Mem Toronto Fall Expo Copper-92
00BAP Memorabilia Toronto Fall Expo Gold-92
00BAP Memorabilia Toronto Fall Expo Ruby-92
00O-Pee-Chee-285
00O-Pee-Chee Parallel-285
00Topps/OPC-285
Parallel-285
00Topps Chrome-180
OPC Refractors-180
Refractors-180
00Rochester Americans-6
01BAP Memorabilia-192
Emerald-192
Ruby-192
Sapphire-192
01O-Pee-Chee-311
01O-Pee-Chee Premier Parallel-311
01Parkhurst-236
01Topps-311
OPC Parallel-311
02BAP Sig Series Auto Buybacks 1999-32
02Sabres Team Issue-4
03ITG Action-11
04Finnish Cardset-238
05Parkhurst-55
Facsimile Auto Parallel-55
05Finnish Cardset -52
06Be A Player-146
Autographs-146
Signatures-BC
Signatures 25-161
Signatures Duals-DMC
Up Close and Personal-UC9
Up Close and Personal Autographs-UC9
06O-Pee-Chee-63
Rainbow-63
06Panini Stickers-35
06Upper Deck-26
Exclusives Parallel-26
High Gloss Parallel-26
Masterpieces-26

Campbell, Bryan
69O-Pee-Chee-106
70Blackhawks Postcards-2
70Esso Power Players-120
71O-Pee-Chee-214
71Toronto Sun-64
73O-Pee-Chee WHA Posters-19
73Quaker Oats WHA-13
73Vancouver Blazers-4
74O-Pee-Chee WHA-6
75O-Pee-Chee WHA-31
75Stingers Kahn's-2
76O-Pee-Chee WHA-16
77O-Pee-Chee WHA-22

Campbell, Cameron
92British Columbia JHL-28

Campbell, Cassie
94Classic Women of Hockey-W5
97Collector's Choice-281
97Esso Olympic Hockey Heroes-59
97Esso Olympic Hockey Heroes French-59
04Canadian Womens World Championship Team-6
06ITG Going For Gold-12
06ITG Going For Gold Samples-12
06ITG Going For Gold Autographs-AC
06ITG Going For Gold Jerseys-GUJ12

Campbell, Chris
93Quebec Pee-Wee Tournament-719

Campbell, Clarence
40Play Ball-200
83Hall of Fame-4
83Hall of Fame Postcards-A3
83NHL Key Tags-30
85Hall of Fame-4
01SP Game Used Signs of Tradition-LCCC
01Upper Deck Legendary Cut Signatures-LCCC
03Backcheck: A Hockey Retrospective-10
03BAP Ultimate Memorabilia Memorialized-12
05ITG Ultimate Memorabilia Builders Autos-7
06ITG Ultimate Memorabilia-31
Artist Proof-31
Builders Autos-6

Campbell, Colin
73Vancouver Blazers-5
74Penguins Postcards-4
75O-Pee-Chee NHL-346
76O-Pee-Chee NHL-372
76Rockies Coke Cans-3
76Rockies Puck Bucks-4
77Penguins Puck Bucks-6
78O-Pee-Chee-269
79Oilers Postcards-2
79O-Pee-Chee-339
80Canucks Silverwood Dairies-7
80Canucks Team Issue-7
80O-Pee-Chee-380
80Pepsi-Cola Caps-106
81Canucks Team Issue-6
81O-Pee-Chee-333
82O-Pee-Chee-82
83O-Pee-Chee-119
84O-Pee-Chee-51
84Topps-39
88Oilers Tenth Anniversary-123
89Red Wings Little Caesars-22

Campbell, Cory
03ECHL All-Stars-243
03Johnstown Chiefs-10

Campbell, Curtis
00OCN Blizzard-16

Campbell, Dean
04UK Milton Keynes Lightning-8

Campbell, Derek
99Owen Sound Platers-24
00Kingston Frontenacs-2
05Stockton Thunder-4

Campbell, Duke
49Carrera Ltd Sports Series-46

Campbell, Earl
24C144 Champ's Cigarettes-11
99SLU Football Classic Doubles-3
06Topps DPP First and Ten AutosDual Gold-BCA

Campbell, Ed
96Binghamton Rangers-5
97Fort Wayne Komets-8
98Fort Wayne Komets-1

98Hartford Wolf Pack-3
00Worcester Icecats-1
01Worcester Icecats-3
02Grand Rapids Griffins-9
03Providence Bruins-2
03Worcester Ice Cats 10th Anniversary-8
05Danbury Trashers-19
Campbell, Gregory
96Quebec Pee-Wee Tournament-578
01Plymouth Whalers-15
01Plymouth Whalers-31
03Bowman-134
Gold-134
03Bowman Chrome-134
Refractors-134
Gold Refractors-134
Xfractors-134
03Crown Royale-117
Red-117
Retail-117
03ITG VIP Rookie Debut-46
03Pacific Complete-515
Red-515
03Pacific Luxury Suite-67
Gold-67
03Parkhurst Rookie-108
03SP Authentic-101
Limited-101
03SPx-205
03Topps Pristine-155
03Topps Pristine-156
03Topps Pristine-157
Gold Refractor Die Cuts-155
Gold Refractor Die Cuts-156
Gold Refractor Die Cuts-157
Refractors-155
Refractors-156
Refractors-157
Press Plates Black-155
Press Plates Black-156
Press Plates Black-157
Press Plates Cyan-155
Press Plates Cyan-156
Press Plates Cyan-157
Press Plates Magenta-155
Press Plates Magenta-156
Press Plates Magenta-157
Press Plates Yellow-155
Press Plates Yellow-156
Press Plates Yellow-157
03Topps Traded-TT111
Blue-TT111
Gold-TT111
Red-TT111
03UD Honor Roll-153
03Upper Deck-448
Canadian Exclusives-448
HG-448
UD Exclusives-448
03Upper Deck Ice-117
Glass Parallel-117
03Kitchener Rangers Memorial Cup-3
03San Antonio Rampage-10
04San Antonio Rampage-10
Campbell, Jason
93Owen Sound Platers-5
94Owen Sound Platers-11
95Slapshot-292
95Owen Sound Platers-15
01Bossier-Shreveport Mudbugs-3
02Bossier-Shreveport Mudbugs-6
03Bossier-Shreveport Mudbugs-7
05Bossier-Shreveport Mudbugs-4
06Donruss/Playoff Hawaii Rookie Autographs-3
06Donruss/Playoff Hawaii Rookie Autographs-17
06Donruss/Playoff Hawaii Rookie Autographs-24
Campbell, Jeff
04Gwinnett Gladiators-6
Campbell, Jim
91Upper Deck Czech World Juniors-71
917th Inn. Sketch QMJHL-209
91Arena Draft Picks-21
91Arena Draft Picks French-21
91Arena Draft Picks Autographs-21
91Arena Draft Picks Autographs French-21
91Classic-25
91Star Pics-62
91Ultimate Draft-19
91Ultimate Draft French-19
91Classic Four-Sport *-25
Autographs-25A
92Upper Deck-605
93PowerPlay-499
93Stadium Club Team USA-2
93Stadium Club Team USA Members Only-2
93Topps Premier Team USA-17
93Ultra-479
94Fredericton Canadiens-7
94Classic Pro Prospects Ice Ambassadors-IA12
94Classic Pro Prospects Intl Heroes-LP1
94Images *-46
95Swedish World Championships Stickers-233
95Fredericton Canadiens-5
96Be A Player Link to History-7A
96Be A Player Link to History Autographs-7A
96Be A Player Link to History Auto Silver-7A
96Black Diamond-142
Gold-142
96Collector's Choice-360
96Donruss Canadian Ice-132
Gold Press Proofs-132
Red Press Proofs-132
96Donruss Elite-142
Die Cut Stars-142
Aspirations-7
96Flair-123
Blue Ice-123
96Hockey Greats Coins-22
Gold-22
96Leaf Preferred-147
Press Proofs-147
96Pinnacle Mint-30
Bronze-30
Gold-30
Silver-30
Coins Brass-30
Coins Solid Gold-30
Coins Gold Plated-30
Coins Nickel-30
Coins Silver-30
96Select Certified-106
Artist's Proofs-106
Blue-106
Mirror Blue-106
Mirror Gold-106
Mirror Red-106
Red-106
96SP-187
96Ultra-144
Gold Medallion-144
Rookies-4
96Upper Deck-328
96Upper Deck Ice-64
Parallel-64
96Zenith-129
Artist's Proofs-129
97Collector's Choice-228
97Crown Royale-113
Emerald Green-113
Ice Blue-113
Silver-113
97Donruss-111
Press Proofs Silver-111
Press Proofs Gold-111
97Donruss Canadian Ice-9
Dominion Series-9
Provincial Series-9
97Donruss Elite-78
Aspirations-78
Status-78
97Donruss Limited-51
97Donruss Limited-67
97Donruss Limited-99
Exposure-51
Exposure-67
Exposure-99
97Donruss Preferred-98
Cut to the Chase-98
97Donruss Priority-94
Stamp of Approval-94
97Katch-127
Gold-127
Silver-127
97Leaf-54
Fractal Matrix-54
Fractal Matrix Die Cuts-54
97Leaf International-54
Universal Ice-54
97NHL Aces Playing Cards-22
97Pacific-332
Copper-332
Emerald Green-332
Ice Blue-332
Red-332
Silver-332
97Pacific Dynagon-105
97Pacific Dynagon-143
Copper-105
Copper-143
Dark Grey-105
Dark Grey-143
Emerald Green-105
Emerald Green-143
Ice Blue-105
Ice Blue-143
Red-105
Red-143
Silver-105
Silver-143
Dynamic Duos-14A
Tandems-18
Tandems-58
97Pacific Invincible-117
Copper-117
Emerald Green-117
Ice Blue-117
Red-117
Silver-117
Feature Performers-30
97Pacific Omega-189
Copper-189
Dark Gray-189
Emerald Green-189
Gold-189
Ice Blue-189
97Panini Stickers-248
97Paramount-155
Copper-155
Dark Grey-155
Emerald Green-155
Ice Blue-155
Red-155
Silver-155
97Pinnacle-130
Press Plates Back Black-130
Press Plates Back Cyan-130
Press Plates Back Magenta-130
Press Plates Back Yellow-130
Press Plates Front Black-130
Press Plates Front Cyan-130
Press Plates Front Magenta-130
Press Plates Front Yellow-130
97Pinnacle Certified-52
Red-52
Mirror Blue-52
Mirror Gold-52
Mirror Red-52
97Pinnacle Inside-66
Coach's Collection-66
Executive Collection-66
97Pinnacle Tot Certi Platinum Blue-52
97Pinnacle Tot Certi Platinum Gold-52
97Pinnacle Totally Certified Platinum Red-52
97Pinnacle Tot Cert Mirror Platinum Gold-52
97Revolution-117
Copper-117
Emerald-117
Ice Blue-117
Silver-117
97Score-215
97Score Blues-4
Platinum-4
Premier-4
97SP Authentic-137
97Studio-34
Press Proofs Silver-34
Press Proofs Gold-34
97Upper Deck-143
Game Dated Moments-143
Smooth Grooves-SG46
Three Star Selects-15A
97Upper Deck Ice-13
Parallel-13
Power Shift-13
98SLU Hockey-50
98Aurora-158
98Be A Player-125
Press Release-125
98BAP Gold-125
98BAP Autographs-125
98BAP Autographs Gold-125
98BAP Tampa Bay All Star Game-125
98Crown Royale-113
Limited Series-113
98Finest-118
No Protectors-118
No Protectors Refractors-118
Refractors-118
98Katch-127
98Kenner Starting Lineup Cards-6
98Pacific-362
Ice Blue-362
Red-362
98Pacific Dynagon Ice-155
Blue-155
Red-155
98Paramount-198
Copper-198
Emerald Green-198
Holo-Electric-198
Ice Blue-198
Silver-198
98UD Choice-189
98UD Choice Preview-189
98UD Choice Prime Choice Reserve-189
98UD Choice Reserve-189
98Upper Deck-178
Exclusives-178
Exclusives 1 of 1-178
Gold Reserve-178
98Upper Deck MVP-183
Gold Script-183
Silver Script-183
Super Script-183
99Upper Deck-285
Exclusives-285
Exclusives 1 of 1-285
99Upper Deck Gold Reserve-285
99Upper Deck Victory-267
00Canadiens Postcards-13
01Norfolk Admirals-10
02BAP Sig Series Auto Buybacks 1998-125
03Chicago Wolves-3
05Springfield Falcons-13
Campbell, John
01Atlantic City Boardwalk Bullies-3
Campbell, Ken
66Tulsa Oilers-1
Campbell, Michael
93Quebec Pee-Wee Tournament-163
Campbell, Pat
05Ottawa 67's-4
Campbell, Patrick
06Chicoutimi Sagueneens-6
06Moncton Wildcats-20
Campbell, Peter
92Quebec Pee-Wee Tournament-1138
96Sudbury Wolves-5
96Sudbury Wolves Police-7
97Sudbury Wolves Police-4
98Owen Sound Platers-12
Campbell, Ryan
94UK Guildford Flames-13
95UK Guildford Flames-5
96UK Guildford Flames-5
97UK Guildford Flames-6
99UK Guildford Flames-8
00UK Guildford Flames-3
02UK Guildford Flames-29
03Oklahoma City Blazers-5
Campbell, Sam
04Ohio State Buckeyes-20
05Ohio State Buckeyes-21
06Ohio State Buckeyes-22
Campbell, Scott
78Jets Postcards-2
79Jets Postcards-3
80Jets Postcards-3
80Pepsi-Cola Caps-123
89Peterborough Petes-103
897th Inn. Sketch OHL-103
907th Inn. Sketch OHL-355
917th Inn. Sketch OHL-201
93Muskegon Fury-13
94German DEL-7
94Muskegon Fury-6
95German DEL-4
96German DEL-4
99UK London Knights-4
00UK Guildford Flames-4
01UK Guildford Flames-14
Campbell, Scott (DEL)
94German DEL-7
95German DEL-4
96German DEL-4
Campbell, Scott (WHA)
78Jets Postcards-2
79Jets Postcards-3
80Jets Postcards-3
80Pepsi-Cola Caps-123
Campbell, Shane
02Greensboro Generals RBI-6
Campbell, Spiff
24V145-2-8
Campbell, Terry
96German DEL-16
99German DEL-351
99German DEL-381
00German DEL-107
02German DEL City Press-132
Campbell, Wade
82Jets Postcards-4
83Jets Postcards-4
83O-Pee-Chee-382
83Vachon-124
84O-Pee-Chee-390
86Moncton Golden Flames-16
89ProCards AHL-130
90ProCards AHL/IHL-221
Campeau, Christian
907th Inn. Sketch QMJHL-72
917th Inn. Sketch QMJHL-35
92Atlanta Knights-20
93Atlanta Knights-19
94Atlanta Knights-22
95Atlanta Knights-5
Campeau, Jason
91Oshawa Generals-17
91Oshawa Generals Sheet-25
917th Inn. Sketch OHL-152
92Oshawa Generals Sheet-25
93North Bay Centennials-7
94North Bay Centennials-8
06Donruss/Playoff Hawaii Rookie Autographs-1
Campeau, Jean Claude
43Parade Sportive *-20
43Parade Sportive *-21
Campeau, Tod
44Beehive Group II Photos-226
45Quaker Oats Photos-66
51Laval Dairy QSHL-43
52St. Lawrence Sales-77
Campeau-Charron, Eric
06Drummondville Voltigeurs-9
Camper, Carter
06Lincoln Stars-24
06Lincoln Stars Traded-18T
06Lincoln Stars Upper DeckÂ Signature Series -6
Campese, Bruno
95Swedish Globe World Championships-227
95Swedish World Championships Stickers-76
96German DEL-2
96Swedish Semic Wien-175
02Calgary Hitmen-8
04Penticton Vees-23
05Penticton Vees-23
06Penticton Vees-24
Campigatto, Vern
71Johnstown Jets Acme-2
72Johnstown Jets-11
Campoli, Chris
98Quebec Pee Wee Tournament-1225
03Erie Otters-4
04SP Authentic Rookie Redemptions-RR43
04ITG Heroes and Prospects-63
Autographs-CCA
04ITG Heroes/Prospects Toronto Expo '05-63
04ITG Heroes/Prospects Expo Heroes/Pros-63
05ITG Heroes/Prosp Toronto Expo Parallel -88
05Beehive-148
Beige -148
Blue -148
Gold-148
Red -148
Matte-148
Signature Scrapbook-SSCC
05Black Diamond-153
Emerald-153
Gold-153
Onyx-153
Ruby-153
05Hot Prospects-205
Autographed Patch Variation-205
Autographed Patch Variation Gold-205
Hot Materials-HMCC
Red Hot-205
05Parkhurst-643
Facsimile Auto Parallel-643
Signatures-CC
True Colors-TCNYI
True Colors-TCNYI
05SP Authentic-202
Limited-202
05SP Game Used-144
Autographs-144
Gold-144
Rookie Exclusives-CC
Rookie Exclusives Silver-RE-CC
05SPx-197
Spectrum-197
Xcitement Rookies-XR-CC
Xcitement Rookies Gold-XR-CC
Xcitement Rookies Spectrum-XR-CC
05The Cup-122
Black Rainbow Rookies-122
Masterpiece Pressplates (Artifacts)-300
Masterpiece Pressplates (Bee Hive)-148
Masterpiece Pressplates (Black Diamond)-153
Masterpiece Pressplates (Ice)-135
Masterpiece Pressplates (MVP)-437
Masterpiece Pressplates (Rookie Update)-220
Masterpiece Pressplates SPA Autos-202
Masterpiece Pressplates (SP Game Used)-144
Masterpiece Pressplates (SPx)-197
Masterpiece Pressplates (Trilogy)-201
Masterpiece Pressplates Ult Coll-154
Masterpiece Pressplates (Victory)-276
Masterpiece Pressplates Autographs-122
Platinum Rookies-122
05UD Artifacts-300
05UD Rookie Class-21
05Ultimate Collection-154
Gold-154
Ultimate Debut Threads Jerseys-DTJCC
Ultimate Debut Threads Patches-DTPCC
05Ultra-228
Gold-228
Ice-228
05Upper Deck-214
HG Glossy-214
Rookie Ink-RICC
05Upper Deck Ice-135
Premieres Auto Patches-AIPCC
05Upper Deck MVP-437
Gold-437
Platinum-437
05Upper Deck Rookie Update-220
05Upper Deck Trilogy-201
05Upper Deck Toronto Fall Expo-214
05Upper Deck Victory-276
Black-276
Gold-276
Silver-276
05ITG Heroes and Prospects-88
Autographs-A-CC
Complete Jerseys-CJ-40
Complete Jerseys Gold-CJ-40
Jerseys-GUJ-62
Jerseys Gold-GUJ-62
Emblems-GUE-62
Emblems Gold-GUE-62
Numbers-GUN-62
Numbers Gold-GUN-62
Nameplates-N-40
Nameplates Gold-N-40
06Beehive Signature Scrapbook-SSCC
06O-Pee-Chee Autographs-A-CC
06Upper Deck-125
Exclusives Parallel-125
High Gloss Parallel-125
Masterpieces-125
Canady, Brian
03North Dakota Fighting Sioux-22
04North Dakota Fighting Sioux-4
Canale, Joe
907th Inn. Sketch QMJHL-43
917th Inn. Sketch QMJHL-97
917th Inn. Sketch CHL Award Winners-27
917th Inn. Sketch Memorial Cup-46
96Sarnia Sting-5
00Sherbrooke Castors-23
Signed-23
Canderyd, Stefan
71Swedish Hockey-331
72Swedish Stickers-147
74Swedish Stickers-209
Caniff, Bernie
93Quebec Pee-Wee Tournament-629
Canik, Dusan
94German First League-138
Cann, David
04Johnstown Chiefs-3
Cann, Mike
04Brandon Wheat Kings-4
05Lethbridge Hurricanes-5
Cann, Trevor
06Between The Pipes-49
Autographs-ATC
Prospect Trios-PT06
Prospect Trios Gold-PT06
06ITG Heroes and Prospects Quad Emblems-QE13
Cannon, Jason
92Quebec Pee-Wee Tournament-1574
95Slapshot-15
95Barrie Colts-5
97Barrie Colts-5
Cannone, Pat
06Cedar Rapids RoughRiders-6
Canotiers, Les
93Quebec Pee-Wee Tournament-252
Cantin, David
93Quebec Pee-Wee Tournament-1018
Cantin, Francois
93Quebec Pee-Wee Tournament-1085
Cantoni, Krister
95Swiss HNL-402
96Swiss HNL-240
98Swiss Power Play Stickers-15
99Swiss Panini Stickers-13
00Swiss Panini Stickers-13
00Swiss Slapshot Mini-Cards-HCAP7
01Swiss HNL-223
02Swiss HNL-83
Cantrall, George
03Missouri River Otters-19
04Missouri River Otters-23
Cantu, Kris
94North Bay Centennials-13
95Slapshot-219
96Seattle Thunderbirds-31
98Roanoke Express-12
00Columbus Cottonmouths-3
Canzanello, Andy
05Syracuse Crunch-16
06Syracuse Crunch-19
Capaul, Marco
93Swiss HNL-291
95Swiss HNL-218
96Swiss HNL-131
98Swiss Power Play Stickers-180
99Swiss Panini Stickers-180
00Swiss Panini Stickers-224
00Swiss Slapshot Mini-Cards-RJ2
01Swiss HNL-148
02Swiss HNL-308
Capaul, Sandro
93Swiss HNL-267
96Swiss HNL-453
Capek, Ivo
94Czech APS Extraliga-71
95Czech APS Extraliga-269
96Czech APS Extraliga-311
97Czech DS Stickers-151
99Czech DS-29
Goalies-G3
99Czech OFS-5
99Czech OFS Goalie Die-Cuts-5
00Czech DS Extraliga-74
Goalies-G7
00Czech OFS-7
Capel, John
82North Bay Centennials-2
83North Bay Centennials-5
Capello, Jeff
88ProCards AHL-262
Capka, Jozef
93Quebec Pee-Wee Tournament-1563
Capla, Boris
94German DEL-391
Capla, Josef
94German First League-122
Caple, Stephen
06Westside Warriors-3
Caplette, Guy
88Richelieu Riverains-8
Caplice, Shawn
907th Inn. Sketch OHL-28
917th Inn. Sketch OHL-223
92Ottawa 67's-5
Capone, Anthony
03Arizona Icecats-3
04Arizona Icecats-2
Caponigri, Paul
93Quebec Pee-Wee Tournament-709
01Ohio State Buckeyes-5
02Ohio State Buckeyes-6
03Ohio State Buckeyes-5
04Atlantic City Boardwalk Bullies-12
Cappelletti, Anthony
99Huntington Blizzard-1
00Missouri River Otters-24
01Missouri River Otters-6
03Missouri River Otters-2
Cappiello, John
93Quebec Pee-Wee Tournament-1728
Capprini, Joe
91Richmond Renegades-13
Caprara, Marco
03Sarnia Sting-3
Caprice, Frank
81Fredericton Express-13
82Fredericton Express-13
83Fredericton Express-2
84Canucks Team Issue-5
85Canucks Team Issue-4
86Canucks Team Issue-3
86Fredericton Express-4
87Canucks Shell Oil-7
87Panini Stickers-339
89ProCards AHL-72
Capson, Greg
92Greensboro Monarchs-17
93Greensboro Monarchs-4
Capuano, Dave
89ProCards IHL-145
90Canucks Mohawk-5
90O-Pee-Chee-170
90Pro Set-543
90Score Rookie/Traded-105T
90Topps-170
Tiffany-170
91Bowman-323
91Canucks Panini Team Stickers-6
91O-Pee-Chee-318
91Panini Stickers-41
91Pro Set-237
French-237
91Score American-86
91Score Canadian Bilingual-86
91Score Canadian English-86
91Stadium Club-53
91Topps-318
91Upper Deck-202
French-202
Capuano, Jack
88ProCards AHL-232
91ProCards-55
95Tallahassee Tiger Sharks-23
Caputi, Gianluc
04Mississauga Ice Dogs-9
05Mississauga Ice Dogs-8
06Mississauga Ice Dogs-9
Caputo, Dino
89Victoria Cougars-5
907th Inn. Sketch WHL-245
Cara, Jon
03Saskatoon Blades-24
04Penticton Vees-9
Carauna, Justin
04Peterborough Petes Postcards-11
Caravaggio, Luciano
93Michigan Tech Huskies-21
01Bakersfield Condors-3
02New Mexico Scorpions-4
Carbery, Timothy
93Quebec Pee-Wee Tournament-898
Carbonneau, Guy
82Canadiens Postcards-3
82Canadiens Steinberg-2
83Canadiens Postcards-3
83O-Pee-Chee-185
83O-Pee-Chee Stickers-180
83Topps Stickers-180
83Vachon-41
84Canadiens Postcards-1
84Canadiens Postcards-2
84O-Pee-Chee-257
84O-Pee-Chee Stickers-160
85Canadiens Placemats-1
85Canadiens Placemats-7
85Canadiens Postcards-4
85Canadiens Provigo-1
85O-Pee-Chee-233
85O-Pee-Chee Stickers-135
857-Eleven Credit Cards-10
86Canadiens Postcards-1
86Kraft Drawings-5
86O-Pee-Chee-176
86O-Pee-Chee Stickers-7
86Topps-176
87Canadiens Kodak-1
87Canadiens Postcards-2
87Canadiens Vachon Stickers-14
87Canadiens Vachon Stickers-15
87Canadiens Vachon Stickers-16
87Canadiens Vachon Stickers-21
87Canadiens Vachon Stickers-23
87Canadiens Vachon Stickers-62
87Canadiens Vachon Stickers-63
87O-Pee-Chee-232
87O-Pee-Chee Stickers-7
87Panini Stickers-64
87Pro-Sport All-Stars-2
88Canadiens Postcards-3
88O-Pee-Chee-203
88O-Pee-Chee Minis-4
88O-Pee-Chee Stickers-41
88O-Pee-Chee Stickers-209
88Panini Stickers-256
88Panini Stickers-407
89Canadiens Kraft-2
89Canadiens Postcards-3
89Canadiens Provigo Figurines-21
89Kraft-19
89O-Pee-Chee-53
89O-Pee-Chee Stickers-48
89O-Pee-Chee Stickers-213
89Panini Stickers-241
89Panini Stickers-381
89Topps-53
90Bowman-44
Tiffany-44
90Canadiens Postcards-5
90O-Pee-Chee-93
90Panini Stickers-58
90Pro Set-146
90Score-91
Canadian-91
90Score Hottest/Rising Stars-43
90Topps-93
Tiffany-93
90Upper Deck-188
French-188
91Pro Set Platinum-63
91Bowman-338
91Canadiens Panini Team Stickers-2
91Canadiens Postcards-4
91Kraft-79
91O-Pee-Chee-54
91OPC Premier-152
91Panini Stickers-197
91Parkhurst-92
91Parkhurst-466
French-92
French-466
91Pinnacle-130
91Pinnacle-374
French-130
French-374
91Pro Set-130
91Pro Set-345
91Pro Set-576
French-130
French-345
French-576
Puck Candy-15
91Score American-19
91Score Canadian Bilingual-19
91Score Canadian English-19
91Stadium Club Members Only-39
91Stadium Club-41
91Topps-54
91Upper Deck-265
French-265
92Bowman-38
92Canadiens Postcards-4
92Durivage Panini-1
92O-Pee-Chee-206
92Panini Stickers-149
92Panini Stickers French-149
92Parkhurst-485
92Parkhurst-508
Emerald Ice-485
Emerald Ice-508
92Pinnacle-43
French-43
92Pro Set-88
Award Winners-CC5
92Score-269
92Score-524
Canadian-269
Canadian-524
92Stadium Club-260
92Stadium Club-289
92Topps-125
Gold-125G
92Ultra-102
Award Winners-3
92Upper Deck-260
92Upper Deck-439
93Canadiens Molson-3
93Canadiens Postcards-4
93Donruss-450
93Durivage Score-9
93Kraft-47
93O-Pee-Chee Canadiens Hockey Fest-9
93OPC Premier-250
Gold-250
93Panini Stickers-19
93Parkhurst-372
Emerald Ice-372
93Pinnacle II Samples-280
93Pinnacle-280
Canadian-280
Captains-12
Captains Canadian-12
93PowerPlay-126
93Score-51
Canadian-51
93Stadium Club-1
Members Only Master Set-1
OPC-1
First Day Issue-1
First Day Issue OPC-1
93Topps/OPC Premier-250
Gold-250
93Ultra-350
93Upper Deck NHLPA/Roots-9
94Be A Player-R67
Signature Cards-106
94Leaf-23
94OPC Premier-282
Special Effects-282
94Parkhurst SE-SE155
Gold-SE155
94Pinnacle-372
Artist's Proofs-372
Rink Collection-372
94Score-46
Gold-46
Platinum-46
94Stadium Club-174
Members Only Master Set-174
First Day Issue-174
Super Team Winner Cards-174
94Topps/OPC Premier-282
Special Effects-282
94Upper Deck-122
Electric Ice-122
95Collector's Choice-302
Player's Club-302
Player's Club Platinum-302
95Parkhurst International-332
Emerald Ice-332
95Pinnacle-144
Artist's Proofs-144
Rink Collection-144
95Score-280
Black Ice Artist's Proofs-280
Black Ice-280
95Stadium Club Metalists-M12
95Stadium Club Metalists MembersOnly Set-M12
95Ultra-228
95Upper Deck-273
Electric Ice-273
Electric Ice Gold-273
96Collector's Choice-73
96Stars Postcards-4
97Be A Player-194
Autographs-194
Autographs Die-Cuts-194
Autographs Prismatic Die-Cuts-194
97Pacific-292
Copper-292
Emerald Green-292
Ice Blue-292
Red-292
Silver-292
98Be A Player-39
Press Release-39
98BAP Gold-39
98BAP Autographs-39
98BAP Autographs Gold-39
98BAP Tampa Bay All Star Game-39
98OPC Chrome-106
Refractors-106
98Pacific-173
Ice Blue-173
Red-173
98Topps-106
O-Pee-Chee-106
99Kraft Face Off Rivals-3
99Panini Stickers-220
99Paramount-70
Copper-70
Emerald-70
Gold-70
Holographic Emerald-70
Holographic Gold-70
Holographic Silver-70
Ice Blue-70
Premiere Date-70
Red-70
Silver-70
99Stars Postcards-3
00Canadiens Postcards-32
00Pacific-127
Copper-127
Gold-127
Ice Blue-127
Premiere Date-127
01Canadiens Postcards-30
02BAP Sig Series Auto Buybacks 1998-39
04ITG Franchises Update-474
04ITG Franchises US West-193
Autographs-A-GCA
Carbonneau, Sylvain
93Quebec Pee-Wee Tournament-947
Carcillo, Daniel
03Sarnia Sting-4
04Mississauga Ice Dogs-14
05ITG Heroes/Prosp Toronto Expo Parallel -268
05WBS Penguins-3
05ITG Heroes and Prospects-268
Autographs Series II-DCA
06Wilkes-Barre Scranton Penguins-5
06Wilkes-Barre Scranton Penguins Jerseys-12
07Upper Deck Victory-232
Black-232
Gold-232
Carciola, Fabio
02German Adler Mannheim Eagles Postcards-11
03German Mannheim Eagles Postcards-27
04German Adler Mannheim Eagles Postcards-7
04German DEL Update-284
05German DEL-259
Card, Checklist
50Quebec Citadelles-3
50Quebec Citadelles-20
61Topps-66
62Parkhurst-NNO2
62Topps-66
62Sudbury Wolves-4
63Topps-66
65Topps-66
65Topps-121
66Topps-66
66Topps-120
67Topps-66
67Topps-120
68O-Pee-Chee-121
68Topps-121
69Topps-132
70Topps-132
71O-Pee-Chee-111
71O-Pee-Chee-264
71Topps-111
79Panini Stickers-249
79Panini Stickers-250
79Panini Stickers-251
79Panini Stickers-252
79Panini Stickers-253
79Panini Stickers-254
79Panini Stickers-255
79Panini Stickers-258
79Panini Stickers-259
79Panini Stickers-260
79Panini Stickers-261
79Panini Stickers-262
79Panini Stickers-263
79Panini Stickers-264
79Panini Stickers-267
79Panini Stickers-268
79Panini Stickers-269
79Panini Stickers-270
79Panini Stickers-271
79Panini Stickers-272
79Panini Stickers-273
79Panini Stickers-281
79Panini Stickers-285
79Panini Stickers-286
79Panini Stickers-287
79Panini Stickers-288
79Panini Stickers-289
79Panini Stickers-290
79Panini Stickers-291
79Panini Stickers-294
79Panini Stickers-295
79Panini Stickers-296
79Panini Stickers-297
79Panini Stickers-298
79Panini Stickers-299
79Panini Stickers-300
79Panini Stickers-303
79Panini Stickers-304
79Panini Stickers-305
79Panini Stickers-306
79Panini Stickers-307
79Panini Stickers-308
79Panini Stickers-309
79Panini Stickers-313
79Panini Stickers-314
79Panini Stickers-315
79Panini Stickers-316
79Panini Stickers-317
79Panini Stickers-318
79Panini Stickers-339
79Panini Stickers-340
79Panini Stickers-341
79Panini Stickers-342
79Panini Stickers-343
79Panini Stickers-344
79Panini Stickers-347
79Panini Stickers-348
79Panini Stickers-349
79Panini Stickers-350
79Panini Stickers-351
79Panini Stickers-352
79Panini Stickers-356
79Panini Stickers-363
79Panini Stickers-364
79Panini Stickers-365
79Panini Stickers-366
79Panini Stickers-367
79Panini Stickers-368
79Panini Stickers-371
79Panini Stickers-372
79Panini Stickers-373
79Panini Stickers-374
79Panini Stickers-375
79Panini Stickers-376
79Panini Stickers-379
79Panini Stickers-380
79Panini Stickers-381
79Panini Stickers-382
79Panini Stickers-383
79Panini Stickers-384
79Panini Stickers-387
79Panini Stickers-388
79Panini Stickers-389
79Panini Stickers-390
79Panini Stickers-391
79Panini Stickers-395
79Panini Stickers-396
79Panini Stickers-398
79Panini Stickers-399
79Panini Stickers-400
82Brandon Wheat Kings-9
83Brantford Alexanders-1
83Brantford Alexanders-2
83Brantford Alexanders-8
83Brantford Alexanders-26
83Brantford Alexanders-30
83Fredericton Express-25
83Ottawa 67's-17
84Islanders News-30
84Fredericton Express-25
85Islanders News-31
85London Knights-5
85Minnesota-Duluth Bulldogs-34
85Minnesota-Duluth Bulldogs-35
85Nova Scotia Oilers-21
86London Knights-2
86London Knights-3
86London Knights-5
86Regina Pats-11
87Maple Leafs PLAY-1
87Maple Leafs PLAY-2
87Maple Leafs PLAY-5
87Brockville Braves-4
88Maple Leafs PLAY-4
88Maple Leafs PLAY-10
88Nordiques Team Issue-3
88Oilers Tenth Anniversary-80
88Brockville Braves-5
88ProCards AHL-165
88ProCards AHL-190
88ProCards AHL-245
89Johnstown Chiefs-34
89Niagara Falls Thunder-19
89Peterborough Petes-118
89Sault Ste. Marie Greyhounds-30

897th Inn. Sketch OHL-47
897th Inn. Sketch OHL-97
897th Inn. Sketch OHL-118
90Oilers IGA-28
90Brandon Wheat Kings-6
90Cincinnati Cyclones-39
90Moncton Hawks-7
907th Inn. Sketch WHL-262
91Oilers IGA-26
91Swedish Semic Elitserien Stickers-304
91Swedish Semic Elitserien Stickers-306
91Swedish Semic Elitserien Stickers-307
91Swedish Semic Elitserien Stickers-310
91Swedish Semic Elitserien Stickers-312
91Cornwall Royals-27
91Cornwall Royals-28
91Johnstown Chiefs-2
91Knoxville Cherokees-2
91Moncton Hawks-8
91Nashville Knights-23
91Peterborough Petes-15
91ProCards-237
917th Inn. Sketch WHL-72
917th Inn. Sketch WHL-242
91Ultimate Draft-57
92Kellogg's All-Star Posters-1
92Kellogg's All-Star Posters-2
92Kellogg's All-Star Posters-3
92Swedish Semic Elitserien Stickers-326
92Swedish Semic Elitserien Stickers-328
92Swedish Semic Elitserien Stickers-334
92Hampton Roads Admirals-12
92Hampton Roads Admirals-19
92Nashville Knights-3
92Nashville Knights-24
92Nashville Knights-25
92Tacoma Rockets-5
92Wheeling Thunderbirds-21
93Finnish SISU-82
93Finnish SISU-108
93Finnish SISU-135
93Finnish SISU-160
93Finnish SISU-279
93Drummondville Voltigeurs-27
93Huntington Blizzard-20
93Huntington Blizzard-21
93Huntington Blizzard-25
93Huntington Blizzard-26
93Johnstown Chiefs-21
93Johnstown Chiefs-22
93Las Vegas Thunder-6
93Lethbridge Hurricanes-1
93Omaha Lancers-4
93Omaha Lancers-7
93Omaha Lancers-19
93Owen Sound Platers-7
93Owen Sound Platers-9
93Owen Sound Platers-17
93Raleigh Icecaps-20
93Red Deer Rebels-7
93Red Deer Rebels-17
93Roanoke Express-12
93RPI Engineers-8
93Toledo Storm-3
93Toledo Storm-4
93Toledo Storm-5
93Toledo Storm-6
93Waterloo Black Hawks-3
93Waterloo Black Hawks-8
93Waterloo Black Hawks-17
93Waterloo Black Hawks-20
93Waterloo Black Hawks-21
93Waterloo Black Hawks-27
93Western Michigan Broncos-10
93Western Michigan Broncos-24
93Wheeling Thunderbirds-19
93Wheeling Thunderbirds-21
93Wheeling Thunderbirds-UD6
93Wheeling Thunderbirds-UD7
94Slapshot Promos-2
94Finnish SISU-389
94Finnish SISU-390
94Finnish SISU-391
94Finnish SISU-392
94Finnish SISU-393
94Finnish SISU-394
94Finnish SISU-395
94Finnish SISU-399
94Swedish Leaf-297
94Swedish Leaf-298
94Swedish Leaf-299
94Swedish Leaf-301
94Swedish Leaf-303
94Swedish Leaf-305
94Swedish Leaf-306
94Birmingham Bulls-13
94Birmingham Bulls-15
94Brantford Smoke-21
94Brantford Smoke-22
94Central Hockey League-38
94Dubuque Fighting Saints-6
94Dubuque Fighting Saints-16
94Dubuque Fighting Saints-29
94Erie Panthers-2
94Erie Panthers-4
94Hampton Roads Admirals-2
94Hampton Roads Admirals-22
94Huntington Blizzard-14
94Huntington Blizzard-23
94Kitchener Rangers-28
94Knoxville Cherokees-3
94Knoxville Cherokees-4
94Las Vegas Thunder-28
94Milwaukee Admirals-1
94Milwaukee Admirals-28
94Roanoke Express-21
94Roanoke Express-23
94Saint John Flames-2
94Sudbury Wolves-25
94Toledo Storm-6
94Toledo Storm-12
94Toledo Storm-20
95Slovakian APS National Team-1
95Slovakian APS National Team-3
95Slovakian-Quebec Pee-Wee Tournament-5
95Slovakian-Quebec Pee-Wee Tournament-7
95Slovakian-Quebec Pee-Wee Tournament-10
95Slovakian-Quebec Pee-Wee Tournament-11
95Birmingham Bulls-22
95Birmingham Bulls-23
95Birmingham Bulls-24
95Birmingham Bulls-25
95Birmingham Bulls-26
95Birmingham Bulls-27
95Birmingham Bulls-28
95Birmingham Bulls-29
95Buffalo Stampedes RHI-NNO4
95Fort Worth Fire-2
95Hampton Roads Admirals-3
95Hampton Roads Admirals-24
95Hampton Roads Admirals-25
95Las Vegas Thunder-25
95Milwaukee Admirals-24
95North Iowa Huskies-12
95North Iowa Huskies-13
95North Iowa Huskies-21
95North Iowa Huskies-24
95Phoenix Roadrunners-22
95Richmond Renegades-21
95Richmond Renegades-23
95Richmond Renegades-25
95Roanoke Express-23
95Saint John Flames-4
95Seattle Thunderbirds-1
95Seattle Thunderbirds-12
95Seattle Thunderbirds-16
95South Carolina Stingrays-2
95South Carolina Stingrays-3
95South Carolina Stingrays-4
95Spokane Chiefs-26
95Spokane Chiefs-27
95Spokane Chiefs-28
95Sudbury Wolves Police-1
95Tallahassee Tiger Sharks-20
95Tallahassee Tiger Sharks-22
95Tallahassee Tiger Sharks-24
95Tallahassee Tiger Sharks-25
95Tallahassee Tiger Sharks-26
95Tallahassee Tiger Sharks-27
95Toledo Storm-23
95Toledo Storm-25
95Tri-City Americans-9
95Tri-City Americans-20
95Vancouver VooDoo RHI-8
96German DEL-182
96German DEL-225
96Slovakian Quebec Pee-Wee Tournament-3
96Slovakian Quebec Pee-Wee Tournament-8
96Slovakian Quebec Pee-Wee Tournament-12
96Slovakian Quebec Pee-Wee Tournament-24
96Cincinnati Cyclones-NNO
96Cincinnati Cyclones-NNO
96Hampton Roads Admirals-HRA23
96Louisville Riverfrogs-26
96Medicine Hat Tigers-13
96Milwaukee Admirals-1
96Peoria Rivermen Photo Album-3
96Peoria Rivermen Photo Album-13
96Roanoke Express-NNO
96Sault Ste. Marie Greyhounds-10
96Sault Ste. Marie Greyhounds Autographed-10
96South Carolina Stingrays-NNO
96South Carolina Stingrays-NNO
96South Carolina Stingrays-NNO
96South Carolina Stingrays-NNO
00London Knights-21
02Albany River Rats AAP-1
04Vernon Vipers-1
06Russian Torino Olympic Team-26

Card, Generic

51Buffalo Bison-1
55Bruins Photos-NNO
64Meadow Gold Dairy -5
68Post Marbles-xx
70Swedish Hockey-36
70Swedish Hockey-37
70Swedish Hockey-38
70Swedish Hockey-39
70Swedish Hockey-40
70Swedish Hockey-41
70Swedish Hockey-42
70Swedish Hockey-43
70Swedish Hockey-44
70Swedish Hockey-45
70Swedish Hockey-46
70Swedish Hockey-47
70Swedish Hockey-166
70Swedish Hockey-167
70Swedish Hockey-168
70Swedish Hockey-169
70Swedish Hockey-170
70Swedish Hockey-171
70Swedish Hockey-172
70Swedish Hockey-173
70Swedish Hockey-174
70Swedish Hockey-175
70Swedish Hockey-176
70Swedish Hockey-177
70Swedish Hockey-333
70Swedish Hockey-334
70Swedish Hockey-335
70Swedish Hockey-336
70Swedish Hockey-337
70Swedish Hockey-338
70Swedish Hockey-339
70Swedish Hockey-340
70Swedish Hockey-341
70Swedish Hockey-342
70Swedish Hockey-343
70Swedish Hockey-344
72Nordiques Postcards-NNO
72Sabres Pepsi Pinback Buttons-9
73Book Promotional Cards-31
74Swedish Stickers-280
74Swedish Stickers-281
74Swedish Stickers-282
74Swedish Stickers-283
74Swedish Stickers-284
74Swedish Stickers-285
74Swedish Stickers-286
74Swedish Stickers-287
74Swedish Stickers-288
74Swedish Stickers-289
74Swedish Stickers-290
74Swedish Stickers-291
74Swedish Stickers-292
74Swedish Stickers-293
74Swedish Stickers-294
74Swedish Stickers-295
74Swedish Stickers-296
74Swedish Stickers-297
74Swedish Stickers-298
74Swedish Stickers-299
74Swedish Stickers-300
74Swedish Stickers-301
74Swedish Stickers-302
74Swedish Stickers-303
74Swedish Stickers-304
74Swedish Stickers-305
74Swedish Stickers-306
74Swedish Stickers-307
74Swedish Stickers-308
74Swedish Stickers-309
74Swedish Stickers-310
74Swedish Stickers-311
74Swedish Stickers-312
76Rockies Coke Cans-22
77Rockies Coke Cans-20
77Rochester Americans-1
79Panini Stickers-1
79Panini Stickers-2
79Panini Stickers-3
79Panini Stickers-4
79Panini Stickers-5
79Panini Stickers-6
79Panini Stickers-7
79Panini Stickers-8
79Panini Stickers-9
79Panini Stickers-10
79Panini Stickers-11
79Panini Stickers-12
79Panini Stickers-13
79Panini Stickers-14
79Panini Stickers-15
79Panini Stickers-16
79Panini Stickers-17
79Panini Stickers-18
79Panini Stickers-19
79Panini Stickers-20
79Panini Stickers-224
79Panini Stickers-319
79Islanders Transparencies-22
80Pepsi-Cola Caps-NNO
81Oilers Red Rooster-xx
81Post Standups-xx
81Red Wings Oldtimers-23
81Swedish Semic Hockey VM Stickers-136
81Swedish Semic Hockey VM Stickers-137
81Swedish Semic Hockey VM Stickers-138
81Swedish Semic Hockey VM Stickers-139
81Swedish Semic Hockey VM Stickers-140
81Swedish Semic Hockey VM Stickers-141
81Swedish Semic Hockey VM Stickers-142
81Swedish Semic Hockey VM Stickers-143
81Swedish Semic Hockey VM Stickers-144
81Oshawa Generals-25
81Regina Pats-25
81Saskatoon Blades-15
81Saskatoon Blades-24
82O-Pee-Chee Stickers-8
82Sabres Milk Panels-2
82Topps Stickers-8
82Brandon Wheat Kings-24
82Kitchener Rangers-1
82Kitchener Rangers-3
82Oshawa Generals-25
82Regina Pats-25
83Oilers McDonald's-10
83Belleville Bulls-2
83Brantford Alexanders-18
83Kingston Canadians-1
83Kingston Canadians-30
83Kitchener Rangers-13
83Kitchener Rangers-23
83North Bay Centennials-1
83Oshawa Generals-12
83Oshawa Generals-18
83Oshawa Generals-30
83Regina Pats-25
84Canucks Team Issue-26
84Kingston Canadians-1
84Kingston Canadians-5
84Kingston Canadians-28
84Kitchener Rangers-1
84Kitchener Rangers-26
84Kitchener Rangers-30
84Sault Ste. Marie Greyhounds-24
84Sault Ste. Marie Greyhounds-25
85Canadiens Provigo-NNO
85Flyers Postcards-31
85Nordiques Provigo-NNO
85Kingston Canadians-1
85Kingston Canadians-5
85Kingston Canadians-28
85Kitchener Rangers-1
85Kitchener Rangers-3
85London Knights-3
85Minnesota-Duluth Bulldogs-36
85Sudbury Wolves-1
85Sudbury Wolves-2
86Kingston Canadians-5
86Kitchener Rangers-1
86Kitchener Rangers-3
86Kitchener Rangers-28
86London Knights-3
86Sherbrooke Canadiens-1
86Sherbrooke Canadiens-2
86Sherbrooke Canadiens-3
86Sudbury Wolves-19
86Sudbury Wolves-27
87Maple Leafs PLAY-3
87Nordiques General Foods-32
87Swedish Panini Stickers-127
87Swedish Panini Stickers-128
87Swedish Panini Stickers-129
87Swedish Panini Stickers-130
87Swedish Panini Stickers-131
87Swedish Panini Stickers-132
87Swedish Panini Stickers-133
87Swedish Panini Stickers-134
87Swedish Panini Stickers-135
87Swedish Panini Stickers-136
87Swedish Panini Stickers-137
87Swedish Panini Stickers-138
87Swedish Panini Stickers-139
87Swedish Panini Stickers-140
87Swedish Panini Stickers-141
87Swedish Panini Stickers-142
87Swedish Panini Stickers-143
87Swedish Panini Stickers-144
87Kingston Canadians-3
87Kitchener Rangers-1
87Kitchener Rangers-3
87Kitchener Rangers-26
87Kitchener Rangers-30
87Portland Winter Hawks-21
87Regina Pats-12
88Frito-Lay Stickers-NNO
88Maple Leafs PLAY-1
88Maple Leafs PLAY-7
88Panini Stickers-377
88Panini Stickers-378
88Panini Stickers-379
88Panini Stickers-380
88Panini Stickers-381
88Panini Stickers-382
88Panini Stickers-383
88Panini Stickers-384
88Panini Stickers-385
88Panini Stickers-386
88Panini Stickers-387
88Panini Stickers-388
88Panini Stickers-389
88Panini Stickers-390
88Panini Stickers-391
88Panini Stickers-392
88Panini Stickers-393
88Panini Stickers-394
88Panini Stickers-395
88Panini Stickers-396
88Panini Stickers-397
88Panini Stickers-398
88Sabres Blue Shield-24
88Kamloops Blazers-26
88Kamloops Blazers-27
88Kamloops Blazers-28
88Kitchener Rangers-1
88Kitchener Rangers-3
88Kitchener Rangers-26
88Kitchener Rangers-30
88Portland Winter Hawks-21
88Saskatoon Blades-2
89Panini Stickers-2
89Rangers Marine Midland Bank-NNO
89Sabres Blue Shield-22
89Kitchener Rangers-1
89Kitchener Rangers-3
89Kitchener Rangers-26
89Kitchener Rangers-30
89Nashville Knights-5
89Oshawa Generals-16
89Oshawa Generals-27
89Oshawa Generals-28
89Oshawa Generals-29
89Oshawa Generals-30
89ProCards AHL-267
89Sault Ste. Marie Greyhounds-2
89Sault Ste. Marie Greyhounds-28
90Kings Smokey-24
90Kings Smokey-NNO
90Panini Stickers-2
90Pro Set-705
90Sabres Blue Shield-20
90Upper Deck-549
French-549
90Kitchener Rangers-1
90Kitchener Rangers-26
90Kitchener Rangers-30
90Michigan Tech Huskies-30
90Montreal-Bourassa AAA-2
90Montreal-Bourassa AAA-3
90Montreal-Bourassa AAA-4
90Montreal-Bourassa AAA-5
90Newmarket Saints-14
90Prince Albert Raiders-24
90Prince Albert Raiders-25
90ProCards AHL/IHL-262
90ProCards AHL/IHL-294
907th Inn. Sketch QMJHL-19
907th Inn. Sketch WHL-340
90Sudbury Wolves-22
91Future Trends Canada '72-1
91Future Trends Canada '72-2
91Future Trends Canada '72-3
91Future Trends Canada '72-6
91Future Trends Canada '72-7
91Future Trends Canada '72-12
91Future Trends Canada '72-13
91Future Trends Canada '72-16
91Future Trends Canada '72-23
91Future Trends Canada '72-24
91Future Trends Canada '72-33
91Future Trends Canada '72-39
91Future Trends Canada '72-44
91Future Trends Canada '72-45
91Future Trends Canada '72-46
91Future Trends Canada '72-55
91Future Trends Canada '72-56
91Future Trends Canada '72-60
91Future Trends Canada '72-62
91Future Trends Canada '72-64
91Future Trends Canada '72-69
91Future Trends Canada '72-72
91Future Trends Canada '72-73
91Future Trends Canada '72-77
91Future Trends Canada '72-78
91Future Trends Canada '72-80
91Future Trends Canada '72-86
91Gillette-NNO
91Gillette-NNO
91Gillette-NNO
91Gillette-NNO
91Jets IGA-34
91Nordiques Petro-Canada-1
91Panini Stickers-5
91Pro Set-334
91Pro Set-339
91Pro Set-342
91Pro Set-589
91Pro Set-590
91Pro Set-591
91Pro Set-592
91Pro Set-598
French-339
French-342
French-589
French-590
French-592
French-598
CC-CC1
CC French-CC1
Platinum HOF 75th-HHOF1
Rink Rat-RR1
Rink Rat-RR2
91Sabres Blue Shield-26
91Sabres Pepsi/Campbell's-26
91Score Kellogg's-24
91Upper Deck French-SP1
91Upper Deck Sheets-1
91Upper Deck Sheets-2
91Upper Deck Sheets-3
91Upper Deck Sheets-4
91Upper Deck Sheets-5
91Upper Deck Sheets-6
91Upper Deck Sheets-7
91Upper Deck Sheets-8
91Upper Deck Sheets-9
91Upper Deck Sheets-10
91Upper Deck Sheets-11
91Upper Deck Sheets-12
91Upper Deck Sheets-13
91Upper Deck Sheets-14
91Upper Deck Sheets-15
91Upper Deck Sheets-16
91Upper Deck Sheets-17
91Upper Deck Sheets-18
91Upper Deck Sheets-19
91Upper Deck Czech World Juniors-1
91Swedish Semic Elitserien Stickers-334
91Swedish Semic Elitserien Stickers-335
91Ferris State Bulldogs-30
91Michigan Tech Huskies-31
91Michigan Tech Huskies-35
91Michigan Wolverines-25
91Moncton Hawks-27
91Oshawa Generals-24
91Oshawa Generals-25
91Oshawa Generals-31
91Peterborough Petes-8
91Rochester Americans Dunkin' Donuts-17
91Rochester Americans Dunkin' Donuts-18
91Rochester Americans Dunkin' Donuts-19
91Rochester Americans Dunkin' Donuts-20
917th Inn. Sketch WHL-97
917th Inn. Sketch WHL-143
917th Inn. Sketch WHL-144
917th Inn. Sketch WHL-168
917th Inn. Sketch WHL-286
917th Inn. Sketch WHL-332
91Sudbury Wolves-2
91Classic-NNO
91Star Pics-1
91Ultimate Draft-1
91Ultimate Draft-89
91Ultimate Draft-90
92Disney Mighty Ducks Movie-7
92Future Trends '76 Canada Cup-111
92Future Trends '76 Canada Cup-112
92Future Trends '76 Canada Cup-113
92Future Trends '76 Canada Cup-114
92Future Trends '76 Canada Cup-115
92Future Trends '76 Canada Cup-124
92Future Trends '76 Canada Cup-159
92Future Trends '76 Canada Cup-160
92Future Trends '76 Canada Cup-166
92Future Trends '76 Canada Cup-167
92Future Trends '76 Canada Cup-170
92Lightning Sheraton-22
92Lightning Sheraton-27
92Lightning Sheraton-28
92Nordiques Petro-Canada-1
92Panini Stickers-283
92Panini Stickers French-283
92Parkhurst Parkie Sheets-1
92Parkhurst Parkie Sheets-2
92Parkhurst Parkie Sheets-3
92Parkhurst Parkie Sheets-4
92Parkhurst Parkie Sheets-5
92Parkhurst Promo Sheets-1
92Penguins Coke/Clark-26
92Penguins Foodland-18
92Pro Set-253
92Pro Set-254
92Pro Set-255
92Sabres Blue Shield-26
92Sport-Flash-15
92Sport-Flash Autographs-NNO
92Upper Deck Sheets-1
92Upper Deck Sheets-2
92Whalers Dairymart-26
92Zeller's Masters of Hockey-7
92Zeller's Masters of Hockey Signed-7
92Binghamton Rangers-23
92Binghamton Rangers-24
92Birmingham Bulls-1
92Birmingham Bulls-19
92Birmingham Bulls-21
92Brandon Wheat Kings-24
92British Columbia JHL-17
92British Columbia JHL-40
92British Columbia JHL-86
92British Columbia JHL-205
92British Columbia JHL-242
92British Columbia JHL-243
92British Columbia JHL-244
92Dayton Bombers-1
92Dayton Bombers-3
92Dayton Bombers-6
92Fredericton Canadiens-25
92Harvard Crimson-31
92Nashville Knights-1
92Northern Michigan Wildcats-32
92Peoria Rivermen-29
92Phoenix Roadrunners-28
92Raleigh Icecaps-1
92Rochester Americans Kodak-10
92St. John's Maple Leafs-25
92Sudbury Wolves-1
92Sudbury Wolves-2
92Tacoma Rockets-30
92Toledo Storm-7
92Western Michigan Broncos-30
92Wheeling Thunderbirds-23
93Flyers J.C. Penney-NNO
93High Liner Greatest Goalies-14
93Jets Ruffles-4
93Lightning Season in Review-25
93Sabres Noco-18
93Sabres Noco-20
93Finnish Jyvas-Hyva Stickers-NNO
93Finnish SISU-301
93Finnish SISU-302
93Finnish SISU-303
93Finnish SISU-304
93Finnish SISU-305
93Finnish SISU-306
93Finnish SISU-307
93Finnish SISU-308
93Finnish SISU-309
93Finnish SISU-310
93Finnish SISU-311
93Finnish SISU-312
93Finnish SISU-313
93Finnish SISU-314
93Finnish SISU-315
93Finnish SISU-316
93Finnish SISU-317
93Finnish SISU-318
93Finnish SISU-319
93Finnish SISU-320
93Finnish SISU-321
93Finnish SISU-322
93Finnish SISU-323
93Finnish SISU-324
93Finnish SISU-325
93Finnish SISU-326
93Finnish SISU-327
93Finnish SISU-328
93Finnish SISU-329
93Finnish SISU-330
93Finnish SISU-331
93Finnish SISU-332
93Finnish SISU-333
93Finnish SISU-334
93Finnish SISU-335
93Finnish SISU-336
93Finnish SISU-337
93Finnish SISU-338
93Finnish SISU-339
93Finnish SISU-340
93Finnish SISU-341
93Finnish SISU-342
93Finnish SISU-343
93Finnish SISU-344
93Finnish SISU-345
93Finnish SISU-346
93Finnish SISU-347
93Finnish SISU-348
93Finnish SISU-349
93Finnish SISU-350
93Finnish SISU-351
93Finnish SISU-352
93Finnish SISU-353
93Finnish SISU-354
93Finnish SISU-355
93Finnish SISU-356
93Finnish SISU-357
93Finnish SISU-358
93Finnish SISU-381
93Finnish SISU-382
93Finnish SISU-383
93Swedish Semic Elitserien-291
93Swedish Semic Elitserien-295
93Swedish Semic Elitserien-299
93Dayton Bombers-18
93Dayton Bombers-19
93Dayton Bombers-20
93Dayton Bombers-21
93Dayton Bombers-23
93Dayton Bombers-24
93Dayton Bombers-25
93Dayton Bombers-28
93Drummondville Voltigeurs-28
93Fredericton Canadiens-27
93Guelph Storm-30
93Huntington Blizzard-12
93Huntington Blizzard-14
93Huntington Blizzard-18
93Huntington Blizzard-19
93Kitchener Rangers-30
93Las Vegas Thunder-2
93Las Vegas Thunder-7
93Las Vegas Thunder-27
93Las Vegas Thunder-31
93Lethbridge Hurricanes-20
93Michigan State Spartans-21
93Michigan State Spartans-31
93Michigan Tech Huskies-25
93Michigan Wolverines-28
93Peoria Rivermen-31
93Peterborough Petes-30
93Portland Pirates-2
93Red Deer Rebels-30
93Roanoke Express-24
93Roanoke Express-25
93Rochester Americans Kodak-17
93St. John's Maple Leafs-3
93Sudbury Wolves Police-1
93Sudbury Wolves Police-2
93Sudbury Wolves Police-26
93Wheeling Thunderbirds-1
93Wheeling Thunderbirds-PC1
93Windsor Spitfires-25
93Windsor Spitfires-26
93Classic-86
94Slapshot Promos-8
94Ducks Carl's Jr.-28
94EA Sports-88
94EA Sports-193
94EA Sports-198
94EA Sports-199
94EA Sports-204
94EA Sports-213
94EA Sports-214
94EA Sports-215
94EA Sports-216
94EA Sports-217
94EA Sports-218
94EA Sports-219
94EA Sports-220
94EA Sports-221
94EA Sports-222
94EA Sports-223
94EA Sports-224
94EA Sports-225
94Nordiques Burger King-1
94Nordiques Burger King-28
94Upper Deck Predictor Canadian-C15
94Upper Deck Predictor Canadian-C25
94Upper Deck Predictor Canadian-C35
94Upper Deck Predictor Canadian Exch Gold-C15
94Upper Deck Predictor Canadian Exch Gold-C25
94Upper Deck Predictor Canadian Exch Gold-C35
94Upper Deck Predictor Cdn Exch Silver-C15
94Upper Deck Predictor Hobby-H15
94Upper Deck Predictor Hobby-H35
94Upper Deck Predictor Hobby Exch Gold-H15
94Upper Deck Predictor Hobby Exch Gold-H35
94Upper Deck Predictor Retail-R10
94Upper Deck Predictor Retail-R20
94Upper Deck Predictor Retail-R30
94Upper Deck Predictor Retail-R40
94Upper Deck Predictor Retail-R50
94Upper Deck Predictor Retail-R60
94Upper Deck Predictor Retail Exchange-R10
94Upper Deck Predictor Retail Exchange-R20
94Upper Deck Predictor Retail Exchange-R30
94Upper Deck Predictor Retail Exchange-R40
94Upper Deck Predictor Retail Exchange-R50
94Upper Deck Predictor Retail Exchange-R60
94Finnish SISU-197
94Finnish SISU-198
94Finnish SISU-199
94Finnish SISU-200
94German DEL-1
94German DEL-2
94German DEL-3
94Dayton Bombers-21
94Fredericton Canadiens-29
94Greensboro Monarchs-11
94Guelph Storm-29
94Guelph Storm-30
94Huntington Blizzard-25
94Huntington Blizzard-26
94Huntington Blizzard-27
94Huntington Blizzard-29
94Huntington Blizzard-30
94Huntington Blizzard-31
94Kitchener Rangers-30
94Las Vegas Thunder-3
94Las Vegas Thunder-4
94Las Vegas Thunder-10
94Milwaukee Admirals-8
94Roanoke Express-22
94Roanoke Express-24
94Saint John Flames-21
94Sarnia Sting-30
94Sudbury Wolves Police-1
94Sudbury Wolves Police-2
94Windsor Spitfires-27
94Windsor Spitfires-28
94Classic ROY Sweepstakes-R20
95Parkhurst '66-67-133
95Parkhurst '66-67-134
95Parkhurst '66-67-135
95Parkhurst '66-67-136
95Parkhurst '66-67-137
95Parkhurst '66-67-138
95Parkhurst '66-67-139
95Parkhurst '66-67-146
95Parkhurst '66-67-147
95Parkhurst '66-67-148
95Penguins Foodland-21
95Stars Score Sheet-NNO
95Ultra-197
95Ultra-NNO
Gold Medallion-197
Gold Medallion-198
Gold Medallion-199
Gold Medallion-200
95Upper Deck All-Star Game Predictors-30
Redemption Winners-30
95Upper Deck Predictor Hobby-H10
95Upper Deck Predictor Hobby-H30
95Upper Deck Predictor Hobby-H40
95Upper Deck Predictor Hobby Exchange-H10
95Upper Deck Predictor Hobby Exchange-H20
95Upper Deck Predictor Hobby Exchange-H30
95Upper Deck Predictor Hobby Exchange-H40
95Upper Deck Predictor Retail Exchange-R10
95Upper Deck Predictor Retail Exchange-R20
95Upper Deck Predictor Retail Exchange-R30
95Upper Deck Predictor Retail Exchange-R40
95Upper Deck Predictor Retail Exchange-R50
95Upper Deck Predictor Retail Exchange-R60
95Whalers Bob's Stores-27
95Slovakian-Quebec Pee-Wee Tournament-27
95Adirondack Red Wings-25
95AHCA-1
95AHCA-4
95AHCA-5
95AHCA-7
95AHCA-9
95Birmingham Bulls-1
95Buffalo Stampedes RHI-NNO5
95Buffalo Stampedes RHI-NNO6
95Dayton Bombers-23
95Flint Generals-7
95Flint Generals-8
95Guelph Storm-5
95Guelph Storm-26
95Guelph Storm-28
95Guelph Storm-30
95Las Vegas Thunder-26
95Lethbridge Hurricanes-25
95Medicine Hat Tigers-15
95Milwaukee Admirals-23
95Milwaukee Admirals-25
95Muskegon Fury-20
95North Iowa Huskies-15
95North Iowa Huskies-32
95North Iowa Huskies-33
95Phoenix Roadrunners-24
95Portland Pirates-9
95Red Deer Rebels-23
95Richmond Renegades-22
95Roanoke Express-24
95Saskatoon Blades-25
95Saskatoon Blades-26
95Saskatoon Blades-27
95Sault Ste. Marie Greyhounds-11
95Sault Ste. Marie Greyhounds-26
95Sault Ste. Marie Greyhounds-27
95Sault Ste. Marie Greyhounds-28
95Sault Ste. Marie Greyhounds-29
95Sault Ste. Marie Greyhounds-30
95Seattle Thunderbirds-30
95Seattle Thunderbirds-32
95St. John's Maple Leafs-25
95Sudbury Wolves-22
95Sudbury Wolves-23
95Sudbury Wolves Police-2
95Toledo Storm-26
95Tri-City Americans-29
95Tri-City Americans-31
95Vancouver VooDoo RHI-23
95Vancouver VooDoo RHI-24
95Vancouver VooDoo RHI-25
95Images Platinum Premier Draft Choice-PD10
96Canadiens Sheets-27
96Canadiens Sheets-28
96Collector's Choice Stick'Ums-S26
96Collector's Choice Stick'Ums-S28
96Collector's Choice Stick'Ums-S29
96Collector's Choice Stick'Ums-S30
96Ducks Team Issue-18
96Ducks Team Issue-25
96Ducks Team Issue-26
96Frosted Flakes Masks-7
96NHL Aces Playing Cards-NNO
96NHL Aces Playing Cards-NNO
96German DEL-23
96German DEL-112
96German DEL-155
96Alaska Gold Kings-13
96Anchorage Aces-1
96Anchorage Aces-3
96Anchorage Aces-6
96Anchorage Aces-8
96Anchorage Aces-16
96Binghamton Rangers-16
96Binghamton Rangers-24
96Cincinnati Cyclones-NNO
96Cleveland Lumberjacks-6
96Detroit Whalers-23
96Detroit Whalers-25
96Grand Rapids Griffins-6
96Grand Rapids Griffins-24
96Grand Rapids Griffins-26
96Guelph Storm-30
96Guelph Storm-31
96Guelph Storm-33
96Guelph Storm-34
96Hampton Roads Admirals-HRA24
96Kamloops Blazers-9
96Kamloops Blazers-27
96Kentucky Thoroughblades-NNO
96Kentucky Thoroughblades-NNO
96Kentucky Thoroughblades-NNO
96Kentucky Thoroughblades-NNO
96Kentucky Thoroughblades-NNO
96Kitchener Rangers-29
96Las Vegas Thunder-2
96Las Vegas Thunder-20
96Las Vegas Thunder-24
96Louisville Riverfrogs-24
96Louisville Riverfrogs-25
96Louisville Riverfrogs-27
96Medicine Hat Tigers-10
96Medicine Hat Tigers-17
96Peoria Rivermen-3
96Portland Pirates-NNO
96Providence Bruins-NNO
96RHI Inaugural Edition-1
96RHI Inaugural Edition-2
96RHI Inaugural Edition-3
96RHI Inaugural Edition-4
96RHI Inaugural Edition-5
96RHI Inaugural Edition-6
96RHI Inaugural Edition-7
96RHI Inaugural Edition-8
96RHI Inaugural Edition-9
96RHI Inaugural Edition-10
96RHI Inaugural Edition-11
96RHI Inaugural Edition-12
96RHI Inaugural Edition-13
96RHI Inaugural Edition-14
96RHI Inaugural Edition-15
96RHI Inaugural Edition-16
96RHI Inaugural Edition-17
96RHI Inaugural Edition-18
96Richmond Renegades-4
96Rimouski Oceanic-23
96Rimouski Oceanic Quebec Police-26
96Rimouski Oceanic Update-6
96Roanoke Express-NNO
96Roanoke Express-NNO
96Sarnia Sting-1
96Sarnia Sting-28
96Sarnia Sting-30
96Sarnia Sting-31
96Saskatoon Blades-27
96Seattle Thunderbirds-NNO
96Seattle Thunderbirds-NNO
96Springfield Falcons-NNO
96St. John's Maple Leafs-5
96Sudbury Wolves-25
96Sudbury Wolves-26
96Sudbury Wolves Police-1
96Sudbury Wolves Police-2
96Sudbury Wolves Police-3
96Syracuse Crunch-NNO
96Syracuse Crunch-NNO
96Toledo Storm-NNO
97Beehive-R1
97Esso Olympic Hockey Heroes-1
97Esso Olympic Hockey Heroes-2
97Esso Olympic Hockey Heroes-3
97Esso Olympic Hockey Heroes-4
97Esso Olympic Hockey Heroes-5
97Esso Olympic Hockey Heroes-22
97Esso Olympic Hockey Heroes-35
97Esso Olympic Hockey Heroes-41
97Esso Olympic Hockey Heroes-47
97Esso Olympic Hockey Heroes-51
97Esso Olympic Hockey Heroes-55
97Esso Olympic Hockey Heroes French-1
97Esso Olympic Hockey Heroes French-2
97Esso Olympic Hockey Heroes French-3
97Esso Olympic Hockey Heroes French-4
97Esso Olympic Hockey Heroes French-5
97Esso Olympic Hockey Heroes French-22
97Esso Olympic Hockey Heroes French-35
97Esso Olympic Hockey Heroes French-41
97Esso Olympic Hockey Heroes French-47
97Esso Olympic Hockey Heroes French-51
97Esso Olympic Hockey Heroes French-55
97Hurricanes Team Issue-28
97Pinnacle Press Plates Back Black-198
97Pinnacle Press Plates Back Black-199
97Pinnacle Press Plates Back Black-200
97Pinnacle Press Plates Back Cyan-198
97Pinnacle Press Plates Back Cyan-199
97Pinnacle Press Plates Back Cyan-200
97Pinnacle Press Plates Back Magenta-198
97Pinnacle Press Plates Back Magenta-199
97Pinnacle Press Plates Back Magenta-200
97Pinnacle Press Plates Back Yellow-198
97Pinnacle Press Plates Back Yellow-199
97Pinnacle Press Plates Back Yellow-200
97Pinnacle Press Plates Front Black-198
97Pinnacle Press Plates Front Black-199
97Pinnacle Press Plates Front Black-200
97Pinnacle Press Plates Front Cyan-198
97Pinnacle Press Plates Front Cyan-199
97Pinnacle Press Plates Front Cyan-200
97Pinnacle Press Plates Front Magenta-198
97Pinnacle Press Plates Front Magenta-199
97Pinnacle Press Plates Front Magenta-200
97Pinnacle Press Plates Front Yellow-198
97Pinnacle Press Plates Front Yellow-199
97Pinnacle Press Plates Front Yellow-200
97SP Authentic Authentics-12
97Guelph Storm-1
97Guelph Storm-29
97Guelph Storm-30
97Guelph Storm-31
97Guelph Storm-32
97Guelph Storm-33
97Guelph Storm-34
97Louisville Riverfrogs-29
97St. John's Maple Leafs-5
97Sudbury Wolves Police-1
97Sudbury Wolves Police-25
97Bowman CHL-NNO
97Bowman CHL-NNO
97Bowman CHL-NNO
97Bowman CHL-NNO
98Bowman's Best-150
98Pacific Omega-251
98Pacific Omega-252
98Charlotte Checkers-21
98Charlotte Checkers-24
98Cincinnati Cyclones-23
98Huntsville Channel Cats-21
98Huntsville Channel Cats-22
98Las Vegas Thunder-28
99Upper Deck Retro Distant Replay Level 2-DR11
99Upper Deck Retro Generation Level 2-G2A
03Devils Team Issue-45
03Devils Team Issue-47
03London Knights-27
03Vancouver Giants-1

Card, Mike

02Kelowna Rockets-17
03Kelowna Rockets Memorial Cup-2
03Kelowna Rockets-3
04Kelowna Rockets-27
05Kelowna Rockets-5
06Hot Prospects-147
Red Hot-147
White Hot-147
06O-Pee-Chee-586
Rainbow-586
06Rochester Americans-3
06SP Authentic-247
Limited-247
06SP Game Used Rookie Exclusives Autographs-RECA
06The Cup-93
Autographed Rookie Masterpiece Pressplates-93
Gold Rainbow Autographed Rookies-93
Masterpiece Pressplates (Marquee Rookies)-586
Masterpiece Pressplates (SP Authentic)-247
Masterpiece Pressplates (Ultimate Collection)-67
Rookies Black-93
Rookies Platinum-93
06Ultimate Collection-67
06Upper Deck-458
Exclusives Parallel-458
High Gloss Parallel-458
Masterpieces-458

Card, Ryan

01Peterborough Petes-9
02Peterborough Petes-9
03Guelph Storm-17
04Guelph Storm-20

card, team

24Crescent Selkirks-8
28V128-2 Paulin's Candy-1
28V128-2 Paulin's Candy-2
28V128-2 Paulin's Candy-3
28V128-2 Paulin's Candy-4
28V128-2 Paulin's Candy-5
28V128-2 Paulin's Candy-6
28V128-2 Paulin's Candy-7
28V128-2 Paulin's Candy-8
28V128-2 Paulin's Candy-9
28V128-2 Paulin's Candy-10
28V128-2 Paulin's Candy-11
28V128-2 Paulin's Candy-12
28V128-2 Paulin's Candy-13
28V128-2 Paulin's Candy-14
28V128-2 Paulin's Candy-15
28V128-2 Paulin's Candy-16
28V128-2 Paulin's Candy-17
28V128-2 Paulin's Candy-18
28V128-2 Paulin's Candy-19
28V128-2 Paulin's Candy-20
28V128-2 Paulin's Candy-21
28V128-2 Paulin's Candy-22
28V128-2 Paulin's Candy-23
28V128-2 Paulin's Candy-24
28V128-2 Paulin's Candy-25
28V128-2 Paulin's Candy-26
28V128-2 Paulin's Candy-27
28V128-2 Paulin's Candy-28
28V128-2 Paulin's Candy-29
28V128-2 Paulin's Candy-30
28V128-2 Paulin's Candy-31
28V128-2 Paulin's Candy-32
28V128-2 Paulin's Candy-33
28V128-2 Paulin's Candy-34
28V128-2 Paulin's Candy-35
28V128-2 Paulin's Candy-36
28V128-2 Paulin's Candy-37
28V128-2 Paulin's Candy-38
28V128-2 Paulin's Candy-39
28V128-2 Paulin's Candy-40
28V128-2 Paulin's Candy-51
28V128-2 Paulin's Candy-53
28V128-2 Paulin's Candy-72
28V128-2 Paulin's Candy-75
28V128-2 Paulin's Candy-82
28V128-2 Paulin's Candy-84
28V128-2 Paulin's Candy-85
28V128-2 Paulin's Candy-86
28V128-2 Paulin's Candy-90
29Imperial Tobacco-NNO
34Beehive Group I Photos-354
34Beehive Group I Photos-355
43Parade Sportive *-85
44Beehive Group II Photos-461
45Quaker Oats Photos-59
48Exhibits Canadian-52
48Exhibits Canadian-56
48Exhibits Canadian-57
48Exhibits Canadian-58
48Exhibits Canadian-59
48Exhibits Canadian-63
48Exhibits Canadian-64
48Exhibits Canadian-65
55Parkhurst-78
55Parkhurst-79
Quaker Oats-78
Quaker Oats-79
59Parkhurst-1
59Parkhurst-30
59Parkhurst-46
59Topps-18
60Cleveland Barons-19
61Shirriff/Salada Coins-S1
61Shirriff/Salada Coins-S2
61Shirriff/Salada Coins-S3
61Shirriff/Salada Coins-S4
61Shirriff/Salada Coins-S5
61Shirriff/Salada Coins-S6
61Topps-20
61Topps-42
61Topps-63
62Topps-22
62Topps-44
62Topps-65
63Topps-21
63Topps-43
63Topps-65
65Topps-123
65Topps-124
65Topps-125
65Topps-126
65Topps-127
65Topps-128
66Topps-118
66Topps-119
69Maple Leafs White Border Glossy-39
690-Pee-Chee Team Booklets-1
690-Pee-Chee Team Booklets-2
690-Pee-Chee Team Booklets-3
690-Pee-Chee Team Booklets-4
690-Pee-Chee Team Booklets-5
690-Pee-Chee Team Booklets-6
690-Pee-Chee Team Booklets-7
690-Pee-Chee Team Booklets-8
690-Pee-Chee Team Booklets-9
690-Pee-Chee Team Booklets-10
690-Pee-Chee Team Booklets-11
690-Pee-Chee Team Booklets-12
700-Pee-Chee-232
70Swedish Hockey-261
70Swedish Hockey-262
70Swedish Hockey-263
70Swedish Hockey-264
70Swedish Hockey-265
70Swedish Hockey-266
70Swedish Hockey-267
70Swedish Hockey-268
70Swedish Hockey-269
70Swedish Hockey-270
70Swedish Hockey-271
70Swedish Hockey-272
70Swedish Masterserien-51
710-Pee-Chee Posters-24
71Toronto Sun-1
71Toronto Sun-22
71Toronto Sun-42
71Toronto Sun-62
71Toronto Sun-83
71Toronto Sun-104
71Toronto Sun-125
71Toronto Sun-146
71Toronto Sun-167
71Toronto Sun-187
71Toronto Sun-209
71Toronto Sun-231
71Toronto Sun-253
71Toronto Sun-275
720-Pee-Chee-7
720-Pee-Chee-20
720-Pee-Chee-30
720-Pee-Chee-38
720-Pee-Chee-54
720-Pee-Chee-63
720-Pee-Chee-276
Team Logos-1
Team Logos-2
Team Logos-3
Team Logos-4
Team Logos-5
Team Logos-6
Team Logos-7
Team Logos-8
Team Logos-9
Team Logos-10
Team Logos-11
Team Logos-12
Team Logos-13
Team Logos-14
Team Logos-15
Team Logos-16
Team Logos-17
Team Logos-18
Team Logos-19
Team Logos-20
Team Logos-21
Team Logos-22
Team Logos-23
Team Logos-24
Team Logos-25
Team Logos-26
Team Logos-27
Team Logos-28
Team Logos-29
Team Logos-30
72Topps-1
72Topps-2
72Topps-3
72Topps-4
72Topps-5
72Topps-6
72Topps-7
73Blues White Border-24
730-Pee-Chee-92
730-Pee-Chee-93
730-Pee-Chee-94
730-Pee-Chee-95
730-Pee-Chee-96
730-Pee-Chee-97
730-Pee-Chee-98
730-Pee-Chee-99
730-Pee-Chee-100
730-Pee-Chee-101
730-Pee-Chee-102
730-Pee-Chee-103
730-Pee-Chee-104
730-Pee-Chee-105
730-Pee-Chee-106
730-Pee-Chee-107
730-Pee-Chee-191
730-Pee-Chee-192
730-Pee-Chee-193
730-Pee-Chee-194
730-Pee-Chee-195
730-Pee-Chee-196
730-Pee-Chee-197
730-Pee-Chee-198
Rings-1
Rings-2
Rings-3
Rings-4
Rings-5
Rings-6
Rings-7
Rings-8
Rings-9
Rings-10
Rings-11
Rings-12
Rings-13
Rings-14
Rings-15
Rings-16
Rings-17
Team Logos-1
Team Logos-2
Team Logos-3
Team Logos-4
Team Logos-5
Team Logos-6
Team Logos-7
Team Logos-8
Team Logos-9
Team Logos-10
Team Logos-11
Team Logos-12
Team Logos-13
Team Logos-14
Team Logos-15
Team Logos-16
Team Logos-17
73Topps-92
73Topps-93
73Topps-94
73Topps-95
73Topps-96
73Topps-97
73Topps-98
73Topps-99
73Topps-100
73Topps-101
73Topps-102
73Topps-103
73Topps-104
73Topps-105
73Topps-106
73Topps-107
73Topps-191
73Topps-192
73Topps-193
73Topps-194
73Topps-195
73Topps-196
73Topps-197
73Topps-198
740-Pee-Chee NHL-169
740-Pee-Chee NHL-209
740-Pee-Chee NHL-210
740-Pee-Chee NHL-211
740-Pee-Chee NHL-212
740-Pee-Chee NHL-213
740-Pee-Chee NHL-214
740-Pee-Chee NHL-215
740-Pee-Chee NHL-216
740-Pee-Chee NHL-247
740-Pee-Chee NHL-250
740-Pee-Chee NHL-253
740-Pee-Chee NHL-256
740-Pee-Chee NHL-267
740-Pee-Chee NHL-274
740-Pee-Chee NHL-281
740-Pee-Chee NHL-287
740-Pee-Chee NHL-300
740-Pee-Chee NHL-307
740-Pee-Chee NHL-315
740-Pee-Chee NHL-322
740-Pee-Chee NHL-330
740-Pee-Chee NHL-337
740-Pee-Chee NHL-350
740-Pee-Chee NHL-363
740-Pee-Chee NHL-370
740-Pee-Chee NHL-377
740-Pee-Chee NHL-390
74Topps-169
74Topps-209
74Topps-210
74Topps-211
74Topps-212
74Topps-213
74Topps-214
74Topps-215
74Topps-216
74Topps-247
74Topps-250
74Topps-253
74Topps-256
74Swedish Stickers-121
74Swedish Stickers-122
74Swedish Stickers-123
74Swedish Stickers-124
74Swedish Stickers-125
74Swedish Stickers-126
74Swedish Stickers-127
74Swedish Stickers-128
74Swedish Stickers-129
74Swedish Stickers-130
74Swedish Stickers-131
74Swedish Stickers-132
74Swedish Stickers-133
74Swedish Stickers-134
74Swedish Stickers-135
74Swedish Stickers-136
74Swedish Stickers-277
74Swedish Stickers-278
74Swedish Stickers-279
75Maple Leafs Postcards-30
750-Pee-Chee NHL-1
750-Pee-Chee NHL-2
750-Pee-Chee NHL-3
750-Pee-Chee NHL-4
750-Pee-Chee NHL-5
750-Pee-Chee NHL-6
750-Pee-Chee NHL-7
750-Pee-Chee NHL-81
750-Pee-Chee NHL-82
750-Pee-Chee NHL-83
750-Pee-Chee NHL-84
750-Pee-Chee NHL-85
750-Pee-Chee NHL-86
750-Pee-Chee NHL-87
750-Pee-Chee NHL-88
750-Pee-Chee NHL-89
750-Pee-Chee NHL-90
750-Pee-Chee NHL-91
750-Pee-Chee NHL-92
750-Pee-Chee NHL-93
750-Pee-Chee NHL-94
750-Pee-Chee NHL-95
750-Pee-Chee NHL-96
750-Pee-Chee NHL-97
750-Pee-Chee NHL-98
75Popsicle-1
75Popsicle-2
75Popsicle-3
75Popsicle-4
75Popsicle-5
75Popsicle-6
75Popsicle-7
75Popsicle-8
75Popsicle-9
75Popsicle-10
75Popsicle-11
75Popsicle-12
75Popsicle-13
75Popsicle-14
75Popsicle-15
75Popsicle-16
75Popsicle-17
75Popsicle-18
75Topps-1
75Topps-2
75Topps-3
75Topps-4
75Topps-5
75Topps-6
75Topps-7
75Topps-81
75Topps-82
75Topps-83
75Topps-84
75Topps-85
75Topps-86
75Topps-87
75Topps-88
75Topps-89
75Topps-90
75Topps-91
75Topps-92
75Topps-93
75Topps-94
75Topps-95
75Topps-96
75Topps-97
75Topps-98
760-Pee-Chee NHL-132
760-Pee-Chee NHL-133
760-Pee-Chee NHL-134
760-Pee-Chee NHL-135
760-Pee-Chee NHL-136
760-Pee-Chee NHL-137
760-Pee-Chee NHL-138
760-Pee-Chee NHL-139
760-Pee-Chee NHL-140
760-Pee-Chee NHL-141
760-Pee-Chee NHL-142
760-Pee-Chee NHL-143
760-Pee-Chee NHL-144
760-Pee-Chee NHL-145
760-Pee-Chee NHL-146
760-Pee-Chee NHL-147
760-Pee-Chee NHL-148
760-Pee-Chee NHL-149
760-Pee-Chee NHL-264
760-Pee-Chee WHA-130
760-Pee-Chee WHA-131
760-Pee-Chee WHA-132
76Popsicle-1
76Popsicle-2
76Popsicle-3
76Popsicle-4
76Popsicle-5
76Popsicle-6
76Popsicle-7
76Popsicle-8
76Popsicle-9
76Popsicle-10
76Popsicle-11
76Popsicle-12
76Popsicle-13
76Popsicle-14
76Popsicle-15
76Popsicle-16
76Popsicle-17
76Popsicle-18
76Topps-132
76Topps-133
76Topps-134
76Topps-135
76Topps-136
76Topps-137
76Topps-138
76Topps-139
76Topps-140
76Topps-141
76Topps-142
76Topps-143
76Topps-144
76Topps-145
76Topps-146
76Topps-147
76Topps-148
76Topps-149
76Topps-264
770-Pee-Chee NHL-71
770-Pee-Chee NHL-72
770-Pee-Chee NHL-73
770-Pee-Chee NHL-74
770-Pee-Chee NHL-75
770-Pee-Chee NHL-76
770-Pee-Chee NHL-77
770-Pee-Chee NHL-78
770-Pee-Chee NHL-79
770-Pee-Chee NHL-80
770-Pee-Chee NHL-81
770-Pee-Chee NHL-82
770-Pee-Chee NHL-83
770-Pee-Chee NHL-84
770-Pee-Chee NHL-85
770-Pee-Chee NHL-86
770-Pee-Chee NHL-87
770-Pee-Chee NHL-88
770-Pee-Chee NHL-262
770-Pee-Chee NHL-263
770-Pee-Chee NHL-264
770-Pee-Chee NHL-322
770-Pee-Chee NHL-323
770-Pee-Chee NHL-324
770-Pee-Chee NHL-325
770-Pee-Chee NHL-326
770-Pee-Chee NHL-327
770-Pee-Chee NHL-328
770-Pee-Chee NHL-329
770-Pee-Chee NHL-330
770-Pee-Chee NHL-331
770-Pee-Chee NHL-332
770-Pee-Chee NHL-333
770-Pee-Chee NHL-334
770-Pee-Chee NHL-335
770-Pee-Chee NHL-336
770-Pee-Chee NHL-337
770-Pee-Chee NHL-338
770-Pee-Chee NHL-339
77Topps-71
77Topps-72
77Topps-73
77Topps-74
77Topps-75
77Topps-76
77Topps-77
77Topps-78
77Topps-79
77Topps-80
77Topps-81
77Topps-82
77Topps-83
77Topps-84
77Topps-85
77Topps-86
77Topps-87
77Topps-88
77Topps-262
77Topps-263
77Topps-264
78Blues Postcards-9
78Maple Leafs Postcards-25
78North Stars Cloverleaf Dairy-10
78North Stars Cloverleaf Dairy-NNO
780-Pee-Chee-192
780-Pee-Chee-193
780-Pee-Chee-194
780-Pee-Chee-195
780-Pee-Chee-196
780-Pee-Chee-197
780-Pee-Chee-198
780-Pee-Chee-199
780-Pee-Chee-200
780-Pee-Chee-201
780-Pee-Chee-202
780-Pee-Chee-203
780-Pee-Chee-204
780-Pee-Chee-205
780-Pee-Chee-206
780-Pee-Chee-207
780-Pee-Chee-208
780-Pee-Chee-262
780-Pee-Chee-263
780-Pee-Chee-264
78Topps-192
78Topps-193
78Topps-194
78Topps-195
78Topps-196
78Topps-197
78Topps-198
78Topps-199
78Topps-200
78Topps-201
78Topps-202
78Topps-203
78Topps-204
78Topps-205
78Topps-206
78Topps-207
78Topps-208
78Topps-262
78Topps-263
78Topps-264
78Topps Team Inserts-1
78Topps Team Inserts-2
78Topps Team Inserts-3
78Topps Team Inserts-4
78Topps Team Inserts-5
78Topps Team Inserts-6
78Topps Team Inserts-7
78Topps Team Inserts-8
78Topps Team Inserts-9
78Topps Team Inserts-10
78Topps Team Inserts-11
78Topps Team Inserts-12
78Topps Team Inserts-13
78Topps Team Inserts-14
78Topps Team Inserts-15
78Topps Team Inserts-16
78Topps Team Inserts-17
79Panini Stickers-21
79Panini Stickers-22
79Panini Stickers-23
79Panini Stickers-24
79Panini Stickers-25
79Panini Stickers-26
79Panini Stickers-27
79Panini Stickers-28
79Panini Stickers-29
79Panini Stickers-30
79Panini Stickers-31
79Panini Stickers-32
79Panini Stickers-33
79Panini Stickers-34
79Panini Stickers-35
79Panini Stickers-36
79Panini Stickers-37
79Panini Stickers-38
79Panini Stickers-39
79Panini Stickers-40
79Panini Stickers-41
79Panini Stickers-42
79Panini Stickers-43
79Panini Stickers-44
79Panini Stickers-45
79Panini Stickers-46
79Panini Stickers-47
79Panini Stickers-48
79Panini Stickers-49
79Panini Stickers-50
79Panini Stickers-51
79Panini Stickers-70
79Panini Stickers-71
79Panini Stickers-72
79Panini Stickers-73
79Panini Stickers-92
79Panini Stickers-93
79Panini Stickers-94
79Panini Stickers-95
79Panini Stickers-114
79Panini Stickers-115
79Panini Stickers-116
79Panini Stickers-117
79Panini Stickers-136
79Panini Stickers-137
79Panini Stickers-138
79Panini Stickers-139
79Panini Stickers-158
79Panini Stickers-159
79Panini Stickers-160
79Panini Stickers-161
79Panini Stickers-180
79Panini Stickers-181
79Panini Stickers-182
79Panini Stickers-183
79Panini Stickers-202
79Panini Stickers-203
79Panini Stickers-204
79Panini Stickers-205
79Panini Stickers-225
79Panini Stickers-226
79Panini Stickers-227
79Panini Stickers-228
79Panini Stickers-229
79Panini Stickers-230
79Panini Stickers-231
79Panini Stickers-232
79Panini Stickers-233
79Panini Stickers-234
79Panini Stickers-235
79Panini Stickers-236
79Panini Stickers-237
79Panini Stickers-238
79Panini Stickers-239
79Panini Stickers-240
79Panini Stickers-241
79Panini Stickers-242
79Panini Stickers-243
79Panini Stickers-244
79Panini Stickers-245
79Panini Stickers-246
79Panini Stickers-247
79Panini Stickers-248
79Panini Stickers-256
79Panini Stickers-257
79Panini Stickers-265
79Panini Stickers-266
79Panini Stickers-274
79Panini Stickers-275
79Panini Stickers-278
79Panini Stickers-283
79Panini Stickers-284
79Panini Stickers-292
79Panini Stickers-293
79Panini Stickers-301
79Panini Stickers-302
79Panini Stickers-310
79Panini Stickers-311
79Panini Stickers-312
79Panini Stickers-320
79Panini Stickers-321
79Panini Stickers-322
79Panini Stickers-323
79Panini Stickers-324
79Panini Stickers-325
79Panini Stickers-326
79Panini Stickers-327
79Panini Stickers-328
79Panini Stickers-329
79Panini Stickers-330
79Panini Stickers-331
79Panini Stickers-332
79Panini Stickers-333
79Panini Stickers-334
79Panini Stickers-335
79Panini Stickers-336
79Panini Stickers-337
79Panini Stickers-338
79Panini Stickers-345
79Panini Stickers-346
79Panini Stickers-353
79Panini Stickers-354
79Panini Stickers-361
79Panini Stickers-362
79Panini Stickers-369
79Panini Stickers-370
79Panini Stickers-377
79Panini Stickers-378
79Panini Stickers-385
79Panini Stickers-386
79Panini Stickers-393
79Panini Stickers-394
79Panini Stickers-397
79Maple Leafs Postcards-34
790-Pee-Chee-81
790-Pee-Chee-82
790-Pee-Chee-83
790-Pee-Chee-163
790-Pee-Chee-244
790-Pee-Chee-245
790-Pee-Chee-246
790-Pee-Chee-247
790-Pee-Chee-248
790-Pee-Chee-249
790-Pee-Chee-250
790-Pee-Chee-251
790-Pee-Chee-252
790-Pee-Chee-253
790-Pee-Chee-254
790-Pee-Chee-255
790-Pee-Chee-256
790-Pee-Chee-257
790-Pee-Chee-258
790-Pee-Chee-259
790-Pee-Chee-260
790-Pee-Chee-261
79Topps-81
79Topps-82
79Topps-83
79Topps-244
79Topps-245
79Topps-246
79Topps-247
79Topps-248
79Topps-249
79Topps-250
79Topps-251
79Topps-252
79Topps-253
79Topps-254
79Topps-255
79Topps-256
79Topps-257
79Topps-258
79Topps-259
79Topps-260
79Topps-261
79Topps Team Inserts-1
79Topps Team Inserts-2
79Topps Team Inserts-3
79Topps Team Inserts-4
79Topps Team Inserts-5
79Topps Team Inserts-6
79Topps Team Inserts-7
79Topps Team Inserts-8
79Topps Team Inserts-9
79Topps Team Inserts-10
79Topps Team Inserts-11
79Topps Team Inserts-12
79Topps Team Inserts-13
79Topps Team Inserts-14
79Topps Team Inserts-15
79Topps Team Inserts-16
79Topps Team Inserts-17
79Topps Team Inserts-18
79Topps Team Inserts-19
79Topps Team Inserts-20
79Topps Team Inserts-21
80Flames Postcards-24
800-Pee-Chee-1
800-Pee-Chee-263
800-Pee-Chee-264
80Topps-1
80Topps-262
80Topps-263
80Topps-264
80Topps Team Posters-1
80Topps Team Posters-2
80Topps Team Posters-3
80Topps Team Posters-4
80Topps Team Posters-5
80Topps Team Posters-6
80Topps Team Posters-7
80Topps Team Posters-8
80Topps Team Posters-9
80Topps Team Posters-10
80Topps Team Posters-11
80Topps Team Posters-12
80Topps Team Posters-13
80Topps Team Posters-14
80Topps Team Posters-15
80Topps Team Posters-16
81Canadiens Postcards-1
810-Pee-Chee Stickers-7
810-Pee-Chee Stickers-8
810-Pee-Chee Stickers-9
810-Pee-Chee Stickers-10
810-Pee-Chee Stickers-13
810-Pee-Chee Stickers-14
810-Pee-Chee Stickers-15
810-Pee-Chee Stickers-16
810-Pee-Chee Stickers-17
810-Pee-Chee Stickers-18
810-Pee-Chee Stickers-21
810-Pee-Chee Stickers-23
810-Pee-Chee Stickers-24
810-Pee-Chee Stickers-25
810-Pee-Chee Stickers-26
810-Pee-Chee Stickers-77
810-Pee-Chee Stickers-78
810-Pee-Chee Stickers-79
810-Pee-Chee Stickers-80
810-Pee-Chee Stickers-81
810-Pee-Chee Stickers-82
810-Pee-Chee Stickers-83
810-Pee-Chee Stickers-85
810-Pee-Chee Stickers-86
810-Pee-Chee Stickers-87
810-Pee-Chee Stickers-198
810-Pee-Chee Stickers-199
810-Pee-Chee Stickers-200
810-Pee-Chee Stickers-201
810-Pee-Chee Stickers-202
810-Pee-Chee Stickers-203
810-Pee-Chee Stickers-204
810-Pee-Chee Stickers-205
810-Pee-Chee Stickers-206
810-Pee-Chee Stickers-207
810-Pee-Chee Stickers-208
81Swedish Semic Hockey VM Stickers-127
81Swedish Semic Hockey VM Stickers-128
81Swedish Semic Hockey VM Stickers-129
81Swedish Semic Hockey VM Stickers-130
81Swedish Semic Hockey VM Stickers-131
81Swedish Semic Hockey VM Stickers-132
81Swedish Semic Hockey VM Stickers-133
81Swedish Semic Hockey VM Stickers-134
81Swedish Semic Hockey VM Stickers-135
81Fredericton Express-1
81Kingston Canadians-1
81Oshawa Generals-1
81Regina Pats-1
81Saskatoon Blades-1
82Canucks Team Issue-23
82Jets Postcards-28
82North Stars Postcards-25
820-Pee-Chee Stickers-3
820-Pee-Chee Stickers-4
820-Pee-Chee Stickers-5
820-Pee-Chee Stickers-6
820-Pee-Chee Stickers-9
820-Pee-Chee Stickers-10
820-Pee-Chee Stickers-11
820-Pee-Chee Stickers-12
820-Pee-Chee Stickers-13
820-Pee-Chee Stickers-16
820-Pee-Chee Stickers-17
820-Pee-Chee Stickers-18
82Topps Stickers-3
82Topps Stickers-4
82Topps Stickers-5
82Topps Stickers-6
82Topps Stickers-9
82Topps Stickers-10
82Topps Stickers-11
82Topps Stickers-12
82Topps Stickers-13
82Topps Stickers-16
82Topps Stickers-17
82Topps Stickers-18
82Brandon Wheat Kings-1
82Fredericton Express-1
82Kingston Canadians-26
82Kingston Canadians-27
83Canadian National Juniors-NNO
83Canadian National Juniors-NNO
83Canadian National Juniors-NNO
83Canucks Team Issue-23
83Islanders Team Issue-19
83North Stars Postcards-27
830-Pee-Chee Stickers-18
830-Pee-Chee Stickers-19
830-Pee-Chee Stickers-20
830-Pee-Chee Stickers-21
83Puffy Stickers-22
83Puffy Stickers-23
83Puffy Stickers-24
83Puffy Stickers-25
83Topps Stickers-18
83Topps Stickers-19
83Topps Stickers-20
83Topps Stickers-21
83Belleville Bulls-30
83Fredericton Express-1
83Kingston Canadians-29
83Oshawa Generals-6
84Canucks Team Issue-25
84Islanders News-24
84Islanders News-25
84Islanders News-26
84Islanders News-31
84Islanders News-32
84Islanders News-33
84Islanders News-34
84Jets Police-24
840-Pee-Chee Stickers-6
840-Pee-Chee Stickers-23
840-Pee-Chee Stickers-33
840-Pee-Chee Stickers-43
840-Pee-Chee Stickers-53
840-Pee-Chee Stickers-67
840-Pee-Chee Stickers-77
840-Pee-Chee Stickers-94
840-Pee-Chee Stickers-104
840-Pee-Chee Stickers-114
840-Pee-Chee Stickers-124
840-Pee-Chee Stickers-146
840-Pee-Chee Stickers-163
840-Pee-Chee Stickers-180
840-Pee-Chee Stickers-190
840-Pee-Chee Stickers-200
840-Pee-Chee Stickers-236
840-Pee-Chee Stickers-246
840-Pee-Chee Stickers-263
840-Pee-Chee Stickers-273
840-Pee-Chee Stickers-283
84Belleville Bulls-1
84Belleville Bulls-5
84Kitchener Rangers-5
85Canucks Team Issue-25
85Islanders News-36
85Islanders News-37
85Jets Police-24
85Maple Leafs Postcards-34
850-Pee-Chee Stickers-1
850-Pee-Chee Stickers-2
850-Pee-Chee Stickers-3
850-Pee-Chee Stickers-4
857-Eleven Credit Cards-22
85Topps Sticker Inserts-13
85Topps Sticker Inserts-14
85Topps Sticker Inserts-15
85Topps Sticker Inserts-16
85Topps Sticker Inserts-17
85Topps Sticker Inserts-18
85Topps Sticker Inserts-19
85Topps Sticker Inserts-20
85Topps Sticker Inserts-21
85Topps Sticker Inserts-22
85Topps Sticker Inserts-23
85Topps Sticker Inserts-24
85Topps Sticker Inserts-25
85Topps Sticker Inserts-26
85Topps Sticker Inserts-27
85Topps Sticker Inserts-28
85Topps Sticker Inserts-29
85Topps Sticker Inserts-30
85Topps Sticker Inserts-31
85Topps Sticker Inserts-32
85Topps Sticker Inserts-33
85Swedish Panini Stickers-1
85Swedish Panini Stickers-13
85Swedish Panini Stickers-14
85Swedish Panini Stickers-23
85Swedish Panini Stickers-24
85Swedish Panini Stickers-36
85Swedish Panini Stickers-45
85Swedish Panini Stickers-57
85Swedish Panini Stickers-58
85Swedish Panini Stickers-67
85Swedish Panini Stickers-68
85Swedish Panini Stickers-80
85Swedish Panini Stickers-89
85Swedish Panini Stickers-101
85Swedish Panini Stickers-102
85Swedish Panini Stickers-131
85Swedish Panini Stickers-143
85Swedish Panini Stickers-144
85Swedish Panini Stickers-153
85Swedish Panini Stickers-154
85Swedish Panini Stickers-166
85Swedish Panini Stickers-175
85Swedish Panini Stickers-187
85Swedish Panini Stickers-188
85Swedish Panini Stickers-197
85Swedish Panini Stickers-198
85Swedish Panini Stickers-210
85Swedish Panini Stickers-219
85Swedish Panini Stickers-231
85Swedish Panini Stickers-232
85Brandon Wheat Kings-17
85Fredericton Express-3
85Kitchener Rangers-5
85Moncton Golden Flames-28
85Nova Scotia Oilers-28
85Sudbury Wolves-3
85Sudbury Wolves-21
86Capitals Kodak-26
86Flyers Postcards-29
86Jets Postcards-26
860-Pee-Chee Stickers-1
860-Pee-Chee Stickers-2
860-Pee-Chee Stickers-3
860-Pee-Chee Stickers-4
860-Pee-Chee Stickers-58
860-Pee-Chee Stickers-59
860-Pee-Chee Stickers-60
860-Pee-Chee Stickers-61
860-Pee-Chee Stickers-62
860-Pee-Chee Stickers-63
860-Pee-Chee Stickers-64
860-Pee-Chee Stickers-65
86Penguins Kodak-NNO
86Topps Sticker Inserts-13
86Topps Sticker Inserts-14
86Topps Sticker Inserts-15
86Topps Sticker Inserts-16
86Topps Sticker Inserts-17
86Topps Sticker Inserts-18
86Topps Sticker Inserts-19
86Topps Sticker Inserts-20
86Topps Sticker Inserts-21
86Topps Sticker Inserts-22
86Topps Sticker Inserts-23
86Topps Sticker Inserts-24
86Topps Sticker Inserts-25
86Topps Sticker Inserts-26
86Topps Sticker Inserts-27
86Topps Sticker Inserts-28
86Topps Sticker Inserts-29
86Topps Sticker Inserts-30
86Topps Sticker Inserts-31
86Topps Sticker Inserts-32
86Topps Sticker Inserts-33
86Swedish Panini Stickers-1
86Swedish Panini Stickers-12
86Swedish Panini Stickers-13
86Swedish Panini Stickers-28
86Swedish Panini Stickers-37
86Swedish Panini Stickers-38
86Swedish Panini Stickers-55
86Swedish Panini Stickers-66
86Swedish Panini Stickers-67
86Swedish Panini Stickers-82
86Swedish Panini Stickers-91
86Swedish Panini Stickers-92
86Swedish Panini Stickers-109
86Swedish Panini Stickers-120
86Swedish Panini Stickers-121
86Swedish Panini Stickers-136
86Swedish Panini Stickers-145
86Swedish Panini Stickers-146
86Swedish Panini Stickers-163
86Swedish Panini Stickers-174
86Swedish Panini Stickers-175
86Swedish Panini Stickers-190
86Swedish Panini Stickers-199
86Swedish Panini Stickers-200
86Swedish Panini Stickers-217
86Swedish Panini Stickers-228
86Swedish Panini Stickers-229
86Swedish Panini Stickers-244
86Swedish Panini Stickers-253
86Swedish Panini Stickers-254
86Fredericton Express-26
86Kamloops Blazers-24
86Kingston Canadians-1
86Moncton Golden Flames-9
87Blues Team Photos-1
87Blues Team Photos-2
87Blues Team Photos-3
87Blues Team Photos-4
87Blues Team Photos-5
87Blues Team Photos-6
87Blues Team Photos-7
87Blues Team Photos-8
87Blues Team Photos-9
87Blues Team Photos-10
87Blues Team Photos-11
87Blues Team Photos-12
87Blues Team Photos-13
87Blues Team Photos-14
87Blues Team Photos-15
87Blues Team Photos-16
87Blues Team Photos-17
87Blues Team Photos-18
87Blues Team Photos-19
87Blues Team Photos-20
87Canadiens Vachon Stickers-1
87Canadiens Vachon Stickers-2
87Canadiens Vachon Stickers-3
87Canadiens Vachon Stickers-4
87Canadiens Vachon Stickers-5
87Canadiens Vachon Stickers-6
87Flyers Postcards-1
87Jets Postcards-24
87Maple Leafs Postcards-21
87Maple Leafs Postcards Oversized-21
870-Pee-Chee Stickers-2
870-Pee-Chee Stickers-3
870-Pee-Chee Stickers-4
870-Pee-Chee Stickers-5
870-Pee-Chee Stickers-67
870-Pee-Chee Stickers-68
870-Pee-Chee Stickers-70
870-Pee-Chee Stickers-71
870-Pee-Chee Stickers-72
870-Pee-Chee Stickers-73
87Panini Stickers-2
87Panini Stickers-3
87Panini Stickers-19
87Panini Stickers-20
87Panini Stickers-36
87Panini Stickers-37
87Panini Stickers-53
87Panini Stickers-54
87Panini Stickers-70
87Panini Stickers-71
87Panini Stickers-87
87Panini Stickers-88
87Panini Stickers-104
87Panini Stickers-105
87Panini Stickers-121
87Panini Stickers-122

87Panini Stickers-138
87Panini Stickers-139
87Panini Stickers-155
87Panini Stickers-156
87Panini Stickers-172
87Panini Stickers-173
87Panini Stickers-189
87Panini Stickers-195
87Panini Stickers-196
87Panini Stickers-202
87Panini Stickers-218
87Panini Stickers-219
87Panini Stickers-235
87Panini Stickers-236
87Panini Stickers-252
87Panini Stickers-253
87Panini Stickers-269
87Panini Stickers-270
87Panini Stickers-286
87Panini Stickers-287
87Panini Stickers-303
87Panini Stickers-304
87Panini Stickers-320
87Panini Stickers-321
87Panini Stickers-337
87Panini Stickers-338
87Panini Stickers-354
87Panini Stickers-355
87Panini Stickers-391
87Panini Stickers-392
87Panini Stickers-395
87Panini Stickers-396
87Penguins Kodak-NNO
87Sabres Wonder Bread/Hostess-NNO
87Topps Sticker Inserts-13
87Topps Sticker Inserts-14
87Topps Sticker Inserts-15
87Topps Sticker Inserts-16
87Topps Sticker Inserts-17
87Topps Sticker Inserts-18
87Topps Sticker Inserts-19
87Topps Sticker Inserts-20
87Topps Sticker Inserts-21
87Topps Sticker Inserts-22
87Topps Sticker Inserts-23
87Topps Sticker Inserts-24
87Topps Sticker Inserts-25
87Topps Sticker Inserts-26
87Topps Sticker Inserts-27
87Topps Sticker Inserts-28
87Topps Sticker Inserts-29
87Topps Sticker Inserts-30
87Topps Sticker Inserts-31
87Topps Sticker Inserts-32
87Topps Sticker Inserts-33
87Swedish Panini Stickers-1
87Swedish Panini Stickers-2
87Swedish Panini Stickers-3
87Swedish Panini Stickers-22
87Swedish Panini Stickers-23
87Swedish Panini Stickers-24
87Swedish Panini Stickers-43
87Swedish Panini Stickers-44
87Swedish Panini Stickers-45
87Swedish Panini Stickers-64
87Swedish Panini Stickers-65
87Swedish Panini Stickers-66
87Swedish Panini Stickers-85
87Swedish Panini Stickers-86
87Swedish Panini Stickers-87
87Swedish Panini Stickers-106
87Swedish Panini Stickers-107
87Swedish Panini Stickers-108
87Swedish Panini Stickers-145
87Swedish Panini Stickers-146
87Swedish Panini Stickers-147
87Swedish Panini Stickers-166
87Swedish Panini Stickers-167
87Swedish Panini Stickers-168
87Swedish Panini Stickers-187
87Swedish Panini Stickers-188
87Swedish Panini Stickers-189
87Swedish Panini Stickers-208
87Swedish Panini Stickers-209
87Swedish Panini Stickers-210
87Swedish Panini Stickers-229
87Swedish Panini Stickers-230
87Swedish Panini Stickers-231
87Swedish Panini Stickers-250
87Swedish Panini Stickers-251
87Swedish Panini Stickers-252
87Hull Olympiques-22
87Hull Olympiques-23
87Hull Olympiques-24
87Kamloops Blazers-22
87Kamloops Blazers-23
87Moncton Hawks-25
87Regina Pats-28
88Flames Postcards-29
88Flyers Postcards-1
88Jets Police-24
88Nordiques Team Issue-33
88Oilers Tenth Anniversary-97
88Oilers Tenth Anniversary-114
88Oilers Tenth Anniversary-126
88Oilers Tenth Anniversary-162
88O-Pee-Chee Stickers-2
88O-Pee-Chee Stickers-3
88O-Pee-Chee Stickers-4
88O-Pee-Chee Stickers-5
88O-Pee-Chee Stickers-30
88O-Pee-Chee Stickers-31
88O-Pee-Chee Stickers-32
88O-Pee-Chee Stickers-33
88O-Pee-Chee Stickers-34
88O-Pee-Chee Stickers-35
88O-Pee-Chee Stickers-36
88O-Pee-Chee Stickers-37
88O-Pee-Chee Stickers-38
88O-Pee-Chee Stickers-159
88O-Pee-Chee Stickers-160
88O-Pee-Chee Stickers-161
88O-Pee-Chee Stickers-162
88O-Pee-Chee Stickers-163
88O-Pee-Chee Stickers-164
88O-Pee-Chee Stickers-165
88O-Pee-Chee Stickers-166
88O-Pee-Chee Stickers-167
88Panini Stickers-1
88Panini Stickers-2
88Panini Stickers-3
88Panini Stickers-16
88Panini Stickers-17
88Panini Stickers-18
88Panini Stickers-19
88Panini Stickers-32
88Panini Stickers-33
88Panini Stickers-34
88Panini Stickers-35
88Panini Stickers-48
88Panini Stickers-49
88Panini Stickers-50
88Panini Stickers-51
88Panini Stickers-64
88Panini Stickers-65
88Panini Stickers-66
88Panini Stickers-67
88Panini Stickers-80
88Panini Stickers-81
88Panini Stickers-82
88Panini Stickers-83
88Panini Stickers-96
88Panini Stickers-97
88Panini Stickers-98
88Panini Stickers-99
88Panini Stickers-112
88Panini Stickers-113
88Panini Stickers-114
88Panini Stickers-115
88Panini Stickers-128
88Panini Stickers-129
88Panini Stickers-130
88Panini Stickers-131
88Panini Stickers-144
88Panini Stickers-145
88Panini Stickers-146
88Panini Stickers-147
88Panini Stickers-160
88Panini Stickers-161
88Panini Stickers-163
88Panini Stickers-164
88Panini Stickers-165
88Panini Stickers-166
88Panini Stickers-167
88Panini Stickers-168
88Panini Stickers-170
88Panini Stickers-171
88Panini Stickers-172
88Panini Stickers-173
88Panini Stickers-174
88Panini Stickers-175
88Panini Stickers-178
88Panini Stickers-179
88Panini Stickers-180
88Panini Stickers-183
88Panini Stickers-184
88Panini Stickers-185
88Panini Stickers-186
88Panini Stickers-187
88Panini Stickers-189
88Panini Stickers-192
88Panini Stickers-194
88Panini Stickers-195
88Panini Stickers-196
88Panini Stickers-197
88Panini Stickers-198
88Panini Stickers-199
88Panini Stickers-200
88Panini Stickers-201
88Panini Stickers-202
88Panini Stickers-215
88Panini Stickers-216
88Panini Stickers-217
88Panini Stickers-218
88Panini Stickers-231
88Panini Stickers-232
88Panini Stickers-233
88Panini Stickers-234
88Panini Stickers-247
88Panini Stickers-248
88Panini Stickers-249
88Panini Stickers-250
88Panini Stickers-263
88Panini Stickers-264
88Panini Stickers-265
88Panini Stickers-266
88Panini Stickers-279
88Panini Stickers-280
88Panini Stickers-281
88Panini Stickers-282
88Panini Stickers-295
88Panini Stickers-296
88Panini Stickers-297
88Panini Stickers-298
88Panini Stickers-311
88Panini Stickers-312
88Panini Stickers-313
88Panini Stickers-314
88Panini Stickers-327
88Panini Stickers-328
88Panini Stickers-329
88Panini Stickers-330
88Panini Stickers-343
88Panini Stickers-344
88Panini Stickers-345
88Panini Stickers-346
88Panini Stickers-359
88Panini Stickers-360
88Panini Stickers-361
88Panini Stickers-362
88Panini Stickers-375
88Panini Stickers-376
88Sabres Wonder Bread/Hostess-xx
88Topps Sticker Inserts-13
88Topps Sticker Inserts-14
88Topps Sticker Inserts-15
88Topps Sticker Inserts-16
88Topps Sticker Inserts-17
88Topps Sticker Inserts-18
88Topps Sticker Inserts-19
88Topps Sticker Inserts-20
88Topps Sticker Inserts-21
88Topps Sticker Inserts-22
88Topps Sticker Inserts-23
88Topps Sticker Inserts-24
88Topps Sticker Inserts-25
88Topps Sticker Inserts-26
88Topps Sticker Inserts-27
88Topps Sticker Inserts-28
88Topps Sticker Inserts-29
88Topps Sticker Inserts-30
88Topps Sticker Inserts-31
88Topps Sticker Inserts-32
88Topps Sticker Inserts-33
88Brandon Wheat Kings-17
88Kitchener Rangers-5
88Lethbridge Hurricanes-24
88ProCards IHL-75
89Bruins Sports Action-23
89Bruins Sports Action-24
89Flyers Postcards-29
89Jets Safeway-30
89Nordiques Team Issue-39
89Nordiques General Foods-30
89O-Pee-Chee-329
89O-Pee-Chee Stickers-1
89O-Pee-Chee Stickers-2
89O-Pee-Chee Stickers-3
89O-Pee-Chee Stickers-4
89O-Pee-Chee Stickers-6
89O-Pee-Chee Stickers-7
89O-Pee-Chee Stickers-8
89O-Pee-Chee Stickers-9
89O-Pee-Chee Stickers-120
89O-Pee-Chee Stickers-121
89O-Pee-Chee Stickers-122
89O-Pee-Chee Stickers-123
89O-Pee-Chee Stickers-124
89O-Pee-Chee Stickers-125
89O-Pee-Chee Stickers-126
89O-Pee-Chee Stickers-127
89O-Pee-Chee Stickers-128
89O-Pee-Chee Stickers-129
89O-Pee-Chee Stickers-130
89O-Pee-Chee Stickers-131
89O-Pee-Chee Stickers-132
89O-Pee-Chee Stickers-133
89Panini Stickers-1
89Panini Stickers-3
89Panini Stickers-4
89Panini Stickers-5
89Panini Stickers-8
89Panini Stickers-9
89Panini Stickers-10
89Panini Stickers-11
89Panini Stickers-12
89Panini Stickers-13
89Panini Stickers-14
89Panini Stickers-15
89Panini Stickers-16
89Panini Stickers-17
89Panini Stickers-18
89Panini Stickers-19
89Panini Stickers-21
89Panini Stickers-22
89Panini Stickers-23
89Panini Stickers-24
89Panini Stickers-25
89Panini Stickers-26
89Panini Stickers-31
89Panini Stickers-40
89Panini Stickers-41
89Panini Stickers-46
89Panini Stickers-55
89Panini Stickers-56
89Panini Stickers-61
89Panini Stickers-70
89Panini Stickers-71
89Panini Stickers-76
89Panini Stickers-85
89Panini Stickers-86
89Panini Stickers-91
89Panini Stickers-100
89Panini Stickers-101
89Panini Stickers-106
89Panini Stickers-115
89Panini Stickers-116
89Panini Stickers-121
89Panini Stickers-130
89Panini Stickers-131
89Panini Stickers-136
89Panini Stickers-145
89Panini Stickers-146
89Panini Stickers-151
89Panini Stickers-160
89Panini Stickers-161
89Panini Stickers-166
89Panini Stickers-175
89Panini Stickers-176
89Panini Stickers-188
89Panini Stickers-193
89Panini Stickers-202
89Panini Stickers-203
89Panini Stickers-208
89Panini Stickers-217
89Panini Stickers-218
89Panini Stickers-223
89Panini Stickers-232
89Panini Stickers-233
89Panini Stickers-238
89Panini Stickers-247
89Panini Stickers-248
89Panini Stickers-253
89Panini Stickers-262
89Panini Stickers-263
89Panini Stickers-268
89Panini Stickers-277
89Panini Stickers-278
89Panini Stickers-283
89Panini Stickers-292
89Panini Stickers-293
89Panini Stickers-298
89Panini Stickers-307
89Panini Stickers-308
89Panini Stickers-313
89Panini Stickers-322
89Panini Stickers-323
89Panini Stickers-328
89Panini Stickers-337
89Panini Stickers-338
89Panini Stickers-343
89Panini Stickers-352
89Panini Stickers-353
89Panini Stickers-354
89Panini Stickers-355
89Panini Stickers-356
89Panini Stickers-357
89Panini Stickers-358
89Panini Stickers-359
89Panini Stickers-360
89Panini Stickers-361
89Panini Stickers-362
89Panini Stickers-363
89Panini Stickers-364
89Panini Stickers-365
89Panini Stickers-366
89Panini Stickers-367
89Panini Stickers-368
89Panini Stickers-369
89Panini Stickers-370
89Panini Stickers-371
89Panini Stickers-372
89Panini Stickers-373
89Sabres Campbell's-xx
89Topps Sticker Inserts-13
89Topps Sticker Inserts-14
89Topps Sticker Inserts-15
89Topps Sticker Inserts-16
89Topps Sticker Inserts-17
89Topps Sticker Inserts-18
89Topps Sticker Inserts-19
89Topps Sticker Inserts-20
89Topps Sticker Inserts-21
89Topps Sticker Inserts-22
89Topps Sticker Inserts-23
89Topps Sticker Inserts-24
89Topps Sticker Inserts-25
89Topps Sticker Inserts-26
89Topps Sticker Inserts-27
89Topps Sticker Inserts-28
89Topps Sticker Inserts-29
89Topps Sticker Inserts-30
89Topps Sticker Inserts-31
89Topps Sticker Inserts-32
89Topps Sticker Inserts-33
89Swedish Semic Elitserien Stickers-1
89Swedish Semic Elitserien Stickers-26
89Swedish Semic Elitserien Stickers-49
89Swedish Semic Elitserien Stickers-73
89Swedish Semic Elitserien Stickers-96
89Swedish Semic Elitserien Stickers-120
89Swedish Semic Elitserien Stickers-145
89Swedish Semic Elitserien Stickers-168
89Swedish Semic Elitserien Stickers-191
89Swedish Semic Elitserien Stickers-216
89Swedish Semic Elitserien Stickers-239
89Swedish Semic Elitserien Stickers-263
89Swedish Semic World Champ Stickers-1
89Swedish Semic World Champ Stickers-26
89Swedish Semic World Champ Stickers-51
89Swedish Semic World Champ Stickers-76
89Swedish Semic World Champ Stickers-101
89Swedish Semic World Champ Stickers-126
89Swedish Semic World Champ Stickers-150
89Swedish Semic World Champ Stickers-151
89Swedish Semic World Champ Stickers-176
89Brandon Wheat Kings-24
89Kitchener Rangers-5
89ProCards AHL-87
89Rayside-Balfour Jr. Canadians-1
89Sault Ste. Marie Greyhounds-4
90Flyers Postcards-26
90Jets IGA-35
90Kraft-92
90Kraft-93
90Kraft-94
90Kraft-95
90Kraft-96
90Kraft-97
90Kraft-98
90Kraft-99
90Kraft-100
90Kraft-101
90Kraft-102
90Kraft-103
90Kraft-104
90Kraft-105
90Kraft-106
90Kraft-107
90Kraft-108
90Kraft-109
90Kraft-110
90Kraft-111
90Kraft-112
90Nordiques Petro-Canada-28
90Oilers IGA-29
90O-Pee-Chee-38
90O-Pee-Chee-326
90O-Pee-Chee-346
Red Army-12R
90Panini Stickers-1
90Panini Stickers-12
90Panini Stickers-27
90Panini Stickers-42
90Panini Stickers-57
90Panini Stickers-72
90Panini Stickers-87
90Panini Stickers-102
90Panini Stickers-117
90Panini Stickers-132
90Panini Stickers-147
90Panini Stickers-162
90Panini Stickers-171
90Panini Stickers-180
90Panini Stickers-195
90Panini Stickers-210
90Panini Stickers-225
90Panini Stickers-240
90Panini Stickers-255
90Panini Stickers-270
90Panini Stickers-285
90Panini Stickers-300
90Panini Stickers-315
90Pro Set-387
90Pro Set-392
90Pro Set-393
90Pro Set-566
90Pro Set-567
90Pro Set-569
90Pro Set-570
90Pro Set-571
90Pro Set-572
90Pro Set-573A
90Pro Set-573B
90Pro Set-574
90Pro Set-575
90Pro Set-576
90Pro Set-577
90Pro Set-578
90Pro Set-579
90Pro Set-580
90Pro Set-581
90Pro Set-582
90Pro Set-583
90Pro Set-584
90Pro Set-585
90Pro Set-586
90Pro Set-704
90Sabres Campbell's-xx
90Score Canadian-331
90Score Canadian-368
90Score Canadian-369
90Topps-38
90Topps-326
90Topps-346
Tiffany-17
Tiffany-38
Tiffany-80
Tiffany-101
Tiffany-122
Tiffany-133
Tiffany-144
Tiffany-165
Tiffany-180
Tiffany-220
Tiffany-241
Tiffany-251
Tiffany-262
Tiffany-284
Tiffany-305
Tiffany-315
Tiffany-326
Tiffany-346
Tiffany-363
Tiffany-394
90Upper Deck French-451
90Upper Deck Sheets-1
90Upper Deck Sheets-2
90Upper Deck Sheets-3
90Upper Deck Sheets-4
90Upper Deck Sheets-5
90Upper Deck Sheets-6
90Upper Deck Sheets-7
90Upper Deck Sheets-8
90Upper Deck Sheets-9
90Upper Deck Sheets-10
90Upper Deck Sheets-11
90Swedish Semic Elitserien Stickers-1
90Swedish Semic Elitserien Stickers-2
90Swedish Semic Elitserien Stickers-25
90Swedish Semic Elitserien Stickers-26
90Swedish Semic Elitserien Stickers-49
90Swedish Semic Elitserien Stickers-50
90Swedish Semic Elitserien Stickers-73
90Swedish Semic Elitserien Stickers-74
90Swedish Semic Elitserien Stickers-98
90Swedish Semic Elitserien Stickers-99
90Swedish Semic Elitserien Stickers-123
90Swedish Semic Elitserien Stickers-124
90Swedish Semic Elitserien Stickers-148
90Swedish Semic Elitserien Stickers-149
90Swedish Semic Elitserien Stickers-173
90Swedish Semic Elitserien Stickers-174
90Swedish Semic Elitserien Stickers-197
90Swedish Semic Elitserien Stickers-198
90Swedish Semic Elitserien Stickers-222
90Swedish Semic Elitserien Stickers-223
90Swedish Semic Elitserien Stickers-246
90Swedish Semic Elitserien Stickers-247
90Swedish Semic Elitserien Stickers-271
90Swedish Semic Elitserien Stickers-272
90Arizona Icecats-16
90Brandon Wheat Kings-8
90Fort Saskatchewan Traders-24
90Kitchener Rangers-5
90Michigan Tech Huskies-31
90Moncton Hawks-25
90Montreal-Bourassa AAA-1
90ProCards AHL/IHL-53
90ProCards AHL/IHL-75
90ProCards AHL/IHL-122
90ProCards AHL/IHL-145
90ProCards AHL/IHL-170
90ProCards AHL/IHL-194
90ProCards AHL/IHL-219
90ProCards AHL/IHL-242
90ProCards AHL/IHL-264
90ProCards AHL/IHL-295
90ProCards AHL/IHL-321
90ProCards AHL/IHL-342
90ProCards AHL/IHL-369
90ProCards AHL/IHL-392
90ProCards AHL/IHL-414
90ProCards AHL/IHL-441
90ProCards AHL/IHL-468
90ProCards AHL/IHL-493
90ProCards AHL/IHL-514
90ProCards AHL/IHL-535
90ProCards AHL/IHL-556
90ProCards AHL/IHL-580
90ProCards AHL/IHL-581
90ProCards AHL/IHL-602
90ProCards AHL/IHL-628
90Saskatoon Blades-26
907th Inn. Sketch QMJHL-69
907th Inn. Sketch QMJHL-112
907th Inn. Sketch QMJHL-116
907th Inn. Sketch QMJHL-117
907th Inn. Sketch QMJHL-122
907th Inn. Sketch QMJHL-123
907th Inn. Sketch QMJHL-136
907th Inn. Sketch QMJHL-137
907th Inn. Sketch QMJHL-142
907th Inn. Sketch QMJHL-143
907th Inn. Sketch QMJHL-158
907th Inn. Sketch QMJHL-160
907th Inn. Sketch QMJHL-163
907th Inn. Sketch QMJHL-164
907th Inn. Sketch QMJHL-167
907th Inn. Sketch QMJHL-168
907th Inn. Sketch QMJHL-181
907th Inn. Sketch QMJHL-198
907th Inn. Sketch QMJHL-219
907th Inn. Sketch QMJHL-239
907th Inn. Sketch QMJHL-256
907th Inn. Sketch WHL-71
907th Inn. Sketch WHL-93
907th Inn. Sketch WHL-335
907th Inn. Sketch WHL-336
907th Inn. Sketch WHL-337
907th Inn. Sketch WHL-338
907th Inn. Sketch WHL-339
907th Inn. Sketch WHL-341
907th Inn. Sketch WHL-342
907th Inn. Sketch WHL-343
907th Inn. Sketch WHL-344
907th Inn. Sketch WHL-345
907th Inn. Sketch WHL-346
907th Inn. Sketch WHL-347
907th Inn. Sketch WHL-348
91Pro Set Platinum-140
91Pro Set Platinum-145
91Pro Set Platinum-146
91Pro Set Platinum-147
91Pro Set Platinum-148
91Pro Set Platinum-149
91Pro Set Platinum-150
91Bowman-410
91Bowman-412
91Bowman-416
91Devils Teams Carvel-1
91Devils Teams Carvel-2
91Devils Teams Carvel-3
91Devils Teams Carvel-4
91Devils Teams Carvel-5
91Devils Teams Carvel-6
91Devils Teams Carvel-7
91Devils Teams Carvel-8
91Devils Teams Carvel-9
91Devils Teams Carvel-10
91Flyers J.C. Penney-26
91Future Trends Canada '72-8
91Jets IGA-35
91Kraft-89
91Kraft-90
91Kraft-91
91Maple Leafs Panini Team Stickers-24
91Oilers Panini Team Stickers-24
91O-Pee-Chee-96
91O-Pee-Chee-103
91O-Pee-Chee-123
91O-Pee-Chee-185
91O-Pee-Chee-242
91O-Pee-Chee-283
91O-Pee-Chee-412
91O-Pee-Chee-525
91O-Pee-Chee-526
91O-Pee-Chee-527
91O-Pee-Chee-528
91O-Pee-Chee Inserts-29R
91Panini Stickers-1
91Panini Stickers-2
91Panini Stickers-3
91Panini Stickers-4
91Panini Stickers-6
91Panini Stickers-7
91Panini Stickers-148
91Panini Stickers-149
91Panini Stickers-150
91Panini Stickers-151
91Panini Stickers-152
91Panini Stickers-153
91Panini Stickers-154
91Panini Stickers-155
91Panini Stickers-156
91Panini Stickers-157
91Panini Stickers-158
91Panini Stickers-159
91Panini Stickers-160
91Panini Stickers-161
91Panini Stickers-162
91Panini Stickers-163
91Panini Stickers-164
91Panini Stickers-165
91Panini Stickers-166
91Panini Stickers-167
91Panini Stickers-168
91Panini Stickers-169
91Panini Stickers-326
91Parkhurst-455
French-455
French-456
French-457
French-458
French-460
French-461
91Pro Set French-319
91Pro Set French-334
91Pro Set French-591
91Pro Set HOF Induction-7
91Pro Set HOF Induction-8
91Pro Set HOF Induction-9
91Pro Set HOF Induction-10
91Pro Set HOF Induction-11
91Pro Set HOF Induction-12
91Pro Set HOF Induction-13
91Pro Set Platinum HOF 75th-145
91Pro Set Platinum HOF 75th-146
91Pro Set Platinum HOF 75th-147
91Pro Set Platinum HOF 75th-148
91Pro Set Platinum HOF 75th-149
91Pro Set Platinum HOF 75th-150
91Red Wings Little Caesars-19
91Sabres Pepsi/Campbell's-27
91Sabres Pepsi/Campbell's-28
91Score American-414
91Score Canadian Bilingual-304
91Score Canadian Bilingual-360
91Score Canadian Bilingual-386
91Score Canadian English-304
91Score Canadian English-360
91Score Canadian English-386
91Sharks Sports Action-22
91Topps-32
91Topps-44
91Topps-60
91Topps-96
91Topps-103
91Topps-123
91Topps-158
91Topps-170
91Topps-185
91Topps-191
91Topps-215
91Topps-242
91Topps-247
91Topps-283
91Topps-298
91Topps-329
91Topps-347
91Topps-372
91Topps-384
91Topps-412
91Topps-430
91Topps-525
91Topps-526
91Topps-527
91Finnish Semic World Champ Stickers-1
91Finnish Semic World Champ Stickers-26
91Finnish Semic World Champ Stickers-51
91Finnish Semic World Champ Stickers-76
91Finnish Semic World Champ Stickers-101
91Finnish Semic World Champ Stickers-126
91Finnish Semic World Champ Stickers-151
91Finnish Semic World Champ Stickers-176
91Russian Stars in NHL-11
91Swedish Semic Elitserien Stickers-1
91Swedish Semic Elitserien Stickers-27
91Swedish Semic Elitserien Stickers-53
91Swedish Semic Elitserien Stickers-78
91Swedish Semic Elitserien Stickers-103
91Swedish Semic Elitserien Stickers-128
91Swedish Semic Elitserien Stickers-151
91Swedish Semic Elitserien Stickers-175
91Swedish Semic Elitserien Stickers-200
91Swedish Semic Elitserien Stickers-225
91Swedish Semic Elitserien Stickers-251
91Swedish Semic Elitserien Stickers-276
91Swedish Semic World Champ Stickers-1
91Swedish Semic World Champ Stickers-26
91Swedish Semic World Champ Stickers-51
91Swedish Semic World Champ Stickers-76
91Swedish Semic World Champ Stickers-101
91Swedish Semic World Champ Stickers-126
91Swedish Semic World Champ Stickers-151
91Swedish Semic World Champ Stickers-176
91Air Canada SJHL All-Stars-44
91Air Canada SJHL All-Stars-46
91Greensboro Monarchs-19
91Michigan Tech Huskies-29
91Michigan Tech Huskies-32
91Michigan Tech Huskies-33
91Michigan Tech Huskies-36
91Nashville Knights-2
91Oshawa Generals-29
91Oshawa Generals-32
917th Inn. Sketch OHL-49
917th Inn. Sketch OHL-50
917th Inn. Sketch OHL-196
917th Inn. Sketch OHL-242
917th Inn. Sketch QMJHL-195
917th Inn. Sketch QMJHL-198
917th Inn. Sketch QMJHL-223
917th Inn. Sketch QMJHL-225
917th Inn. Sketch QMJHL-267
917th Inn. Sketch QMJHL-297
917th Inn. Sketch QMJHL-298
917th Inn. Sketch WHL-25
917th Inn. Sketch WHL-74
917th Inn. Sketch WHL-96
917th Inn. Sketch WHL-146
917th Inn. Sketch WHL-147
917th Inn. Sketch WHL-173
917th Inn. Sketch Memorial Cup-3
917th Inn. Sketch Memorial Cup-47
917th Inn. Sketch Memorial Cup-48
917th Inn. Sketch Memorial Cup-70
917th Inn. Sketch Memorial Cup-128
91Sudbury Wolves-3
92Disney Mighty Ducks Movie-8
92Flames IGA-30
92Flyers J.C. Penney-23
92Flyers Upper Deck Sheets-13A
92Flyers Upper Deck Sheets-13B
92Flyers Upper Deck Sheets-37B
92Future Trends '76 Canada Cup-118
92Future Trends '76 Canada Cup-119
92Future Trends '76 Canada Cup-120
92Future Trends '76 Canada Cup-121
92Future Trends '76 Canada Cup-122
92Future Trends '76 Canada Cup-123
92Future Trends '76 Canada Cup-127
92Future Trends '76 Canada Cup-129
92Future Trends '76 Canada Cup-133
92Future Trends '76 Canada Cup-134
92Future Trends '76 Canada Cup-135
92Future Trends '76 Canada Cup-137
92Future Trends '76 Canada Cup-146
92Future Trends '76 Canada Cup-147
92Future Trends '76 Canada Cup-149
92Future Trends '76 Canada Cup-151
92Future Trends '76 Canada Cup-157
92Future Trends '76 Canada Cup-165
92Future Trends '76 Canada Cup-168
92Future Trends '76 Canada Cup-176
92Future Trends '76 Canada Cup-191
92Future Trends '76 Canada Cup-192
92Future Trends '76 Canada Cup-193
92Future Trends '76 Canada Cup-194
92High Liner Stanley Cup-1
92High Liner Stanley Cup-2
92High Liner Stanley Cup-3
92High Liner Stanley Cup-4
92High Liner Stanley Cup-5
92High Liner Stanley Cup-6
92High Liner Stanley Cup-7
92High Liner Stanley Cup-8
92High Liner Stanley Cup-9
92High Liner Stanley Cup-10
92High Liner Stanley Cup-11
92High Liner Stanley Cup-12
92High Liner Stanley Cup-13
92High Liner Stanley Cup-14
92High Liner Stanley Cup-15
92High Liner Stanley Cup-16
92High Liner Stanley Cup-17
92High Liner Stanley Cup-18
92High Liner Stanley Cup-19
92High Liner Stanley Cup-20
92High Liner Stanley Cup-21
92High Liner Stanley Cup-22
92High Liner Stanley Cup-23
92High Liner Stanley Cup-24
92High Liner Stanley Cup-25
92High Liner Stanley Cup-26
92High Liner Stanley Cup-27
92Kraft-1
92Kraft-2
92Kraft-3
92Kraft-4
92Kraft-5
92Kraft-6
92Kraft-7
92Kraft-8
92Kraft-9
92Kraft-10
92Kraft-11
92Kraft-12
92Kraft-13
92Kraft-14
92Kraft-15
92Kraft-16
92Kraft-17
92Kraft-18
92Kraft-19
92Kraft-20
92Kraft-21
92Kraft-22
92Kraft-23
92Kraft-24
92McDonald's Upper Deck Iron-Ons-1
92McDonald's Upper Deck Iron-Ons-2
92McDonald's Upper Deck Iron-Ons-3
92McDonald's Upper Deck Iron-Ons-4
92McDonald's Upper Deck Iron-Ons-5
92McDonald's Upper Deck Iron-Ons-6
92McDonald's Upper Deck Iron-Ons-7
92McDonald's Upper Deck Iron-Ons-8
92McDonald's Upper Deck Iron-Ons-9
92McDonald's Upper Deck Iron-Ons-10
92McDonald's Upper Deck Iron-Ons-11
92McDonald's Upper Deck Iron-Ons-12
92McDonald's Upper Deck Iron-Ons-13
92McDonald's Upper Deck Iron-Ons-14
92McDonald's Upper Deck Iron-Ons-15
92McDonald's Upper Deck Iron-Ons-16
92McDonald's Upper Deck Iron-Ons-17
92McDonald's Upper Deck Iron-Ons-18
92McDonald's Upper Deck Iron-Ons-19
92McDonald's Upper Deck Iron-Ons-20
92McDonald's Upper Deck Iron-Ons-21
92McDonald's Upper Deck Iron-Ons-22
92McDonald's Upper Deck Iron-Ons-23
92McDonald's Upper Deck Iron-Ons-24
92McDonald's Upper Deck Iron-Ons-25
92McDonald's Upper Deck Iron-Ons-26
92Nordiques Petro-Canada-39
92Oilers IGA-30
92OPC Premier-132
92Panini Stickers-2
92Panini Stickers-14
92Panini Stickers-26
92Panini Stickers-38
92Panini Stickers-50
92Panini Stickers-62
92Panini Stickers-74
92Panini Stickers-86
92Panini Stickers-98
92Panini Stickers-110
92Panini Stickers-122
92Panini Stickers-134
92Panini Stickers-146
92Panini Stickers-158
92Panini Stickers-170
92Panini Stickers-182
92Panini Stickers-194
92Panini Stickers-206
92Panini Stickers-218
92Panini Stickers-230
92Panini Stickers-242
92Panini Stickers-254
92Panini Stickers-266
92Panini Stickers-267
92Panini Stickers-268
92Panini Stickers-269
92Panini Stickers-276
92Panini Stickers French-2
92Panini Stickers French-14
92Panini Stickers French-26
92Panini Stickers French-38
92Panini Stickers French-50
92Panini Stickers French-62
92Panini Stickers French-74
92Panini Stickers French-86
92Panini Stickers French-98
92Panini Stickers French-110
92Panini Stickers French-122
92Panini Stickers French-134
92Panini Stickers French-146
92Panini Stickers French-158
92Panini Stickers French-170
92Panini Stickers French-182
92Panini Stickers French-194
92Panini Stickers French-206
92Panini Stickers French-218
92Panini Stickers French-230
92Panini Stickers French-242
92Panini Stickers French-254
92Panini Stickers French-266
92Panini Stickers French-267
92Panini Stickers French-268
92Panini Stickers French-269
92Panini Stickers French-276
92Parkhurst Arena Tour Sheets-1
92Parkhurst Arena Tour Sheets-2
92Parkhurst Arena Tour Sheets-3
92Parkhurst Arena Tour Sheets-4
92Parkhurst Arena Tour Sheets-5
92Parkhurst Arena Tour Sheets-6
92Parkhurst Arena Tour Sheets-7
92Parkhurst Arena Tour Sheets-8
92Score-507
92Score-512
92Score-528
Canadian-507
Canadian-512
Canadian-518
Canadian-528
92Upper Deck-237
Sheets-6
Sheets-7
Sheets-8
Sheets-9
Sheets-10
Sheets-11
Sheets-12
Sheets-13
Sheets-14
Sheets-15
Sheets-16
Sheets-17
92Swedish Semic Elitserien Stickers-1
92Swedish Semic Elitserien Stickers-2
92Swedish Semic Elitserien Stickers-3
92Swedish Semic Elitserien Stickers-4
92Swedish Semic Elitserien Stickers-5
92Swedish Semic Elitserien Stickers-6
92Swedish Semic Elitserien Stickers-7
92Swedish Semic Elitserien Stickers-8
92Swedish Semic Elitserien Stickers-9
92Swedish Semic Elitserien Stickers-10
92Swedish Semic Elitserien Stickers-11
92Swedish Semic Elitserien Stickers-12
92Swedish Semic Elitserien Stickers-13
92Swedish Semic Elitserien Stickers-14
92Swedish Semic Elitserien Stickers-15
92Swedish Semic Elitserien Stickers-16
92Swedish Semic Elitserien Stickers-17
92Swedish Semic Elitserien Stickers-18
92Swedish Semic Elitserien Stickers-19
92Swedish Semic Elitserien Stickers-20
92Swedish Semic Elitserien Stickers-21
92Swedish Semic Elitserien Stickers-22
92Swedish Semic Elitserien Stickers-23
92Swedish Semic Elitserien Stickers-24
92Swedish Semic Elitserien Stickers-25
92Swedish Semic Elitserien Stickers-50
92Swedish Semic Elitserien Stickers-74
92Swedish Semic Elitserien Stickers-100
92Swedish Semic Elitserien Stickers-124
92Swedish Semic Elitserien Stickers-149
92Swedish Semic Elitserien Stickers-174
92Swedish Semic Elitserien Stickers-198
92Swedish Semic Elitserien Stickers-222
92Swedish Semic Elitserien Stickers-248
92Swedish Semic Elitserien Stickers-273
92Swedish Semic Elitserien Stickers-299
92Binghamton Rangers-1
92Dallas Freeze-20
92Greensboro Monarchs-1
92Hamilton Canucks-30
92Lake Superior State Lakers-1
92Lake Superior State Lakers-2
92Oklahoma City Blazers-18
92Raleigh Icecaps-20
92St. John's Maple Leafs-24
92Tulsa Oilers-17
93Donruss-391
93Donruss-392
93Jets Ruffles-29
93Leaf-150
93Leaf-200
93O-Pee-Chee Canadiens Hockey Fest-1
93O-Pee-Chee Canadiens Hockey Fest-12
93O-Pee-Chee Canadiens Hockey Fest-35
93O-Pee-Chee Canadiens Hockey Fest-37
93O-Pee-Chee Canadiens Hockey Fest-41
93O-Pee-Chee Canadiens Hockey Fest-46
93Panini Stickers-1
93Panini Stickers-12
93Panini Stickers-23
93Panini Stickers-34
93Panini Stickers-45
93Panini Stickers-56
93Panini Stickers-67
93Panini Stickers-78
93Panini Stickers-89
93Panini Stickers-100
93Panini Stickers-111
93Panini Stickers-122
93Panini Stickers-134
93Panini Stickers-145
93Panini Stickers-156
93Panini Stickers-167
93Panini Stickers-178
93Panini Stickers-189
93Panini Stickers-200
93Panini Stickers-211
93Panini Stickers-222
93Panini Stickers-233
93Panini Stickers-244
93Panini Stickers-255
93Panini Stickers-266
93Pinnacle All-Stars-50
93Pinnacle All-Stars Canadian-50
93Score-452
93Score-486
93Score-487
93Score-488

93Score-491
Canadian-452
Canadian-486
Canadian-487
Canadian-488
Canadian-491
93Senators Kraft Sheets-27
93Finnish Jyvas-Hyva Stickers-1
93Finnish Jyvas-Hyva Stickers-2
93Finnish Jyvas-Hyva Stickers-3
93Finnish Jyvas-Hyva Stickers-4
93Finnish Jyvas-Hyva Stickers-5
93Finnish Jyvas-Hyva Stickers-6
93Finnish Jyvas-Hyva Stickers-7
93Finnish Jyvas-Hyva Stickers-8
93Finnish Jyvas-Hyva Stickers-9
93Finnish Jyvas-Hyva Stickers-10
93Finnish Jyvas-Hyva Stickers-11
93Finnish Jyvas-Hyva Stickers-12
93Finnish Jyvas-Hyva Stickers-31
93Finnish Jyvas-Hyva Stickers-32
93Finnish Jyvas-Hyva Stickers-33
93Finnish Jyvas-Hyva Stickers-34
93Finnish Jyvas-Hyva Stickers-35
93Finnish Jyvas-Hyva Stickers-36
93Finnish Jyvas-Hyva Stickers-37
93Finnish Jyvas-Hyva Stickers-38
93Finnish Jyvas-Hyva Stickers-39
93Finnish Jyvas-Hyva Stickers-40
93Finnish Jyvas-Hyva Stickers-41
93Finnish Jyvas-Hyva Stickers-42
93Finnish Jyvas-Hyva Stickers-61
93Finnish Jyvas-Hyva Stickers-62
93Finnish Jyvas-Hyva Stickers-63
93Finnish Jyvas-Hyva Stickers-64
93Finnish Jyvas-Hyva Stickers-65
93Finnish Jyvas-Hyva Stickers-66
93Finnish Jyvas-Hyva Stickers-67
93Finnish Jyvas-Hyva Stickers-68
93Finnish Jyvas-Hyva Stickers-69
93Finnish Jyvas-Hyva Stickers-70
93Finnish Jyvas-Hyva Stickers-71
93Finnish Jyvas-Hyva Stickers-72
93Finnish Jyvas-Hyva Stickers-91
93Finnish Jyvas-Hyva Stickers-92
93Finnish Jyvas-Hyva Stickers-93
93Finnish Jyvas-Hyva Stickers-94
93Finnish Jyvas-Hyva Stickers-95
93Finnish Jyvas-Hyva Stickers-96
93Finnish Jyvas-Hyva Stickers-97
93Finnish Jyvas-Hyva Stickers-98
93Finnish Jyvas-Hyva Stickers-99
93Finnish Jyvas-Hyva Stickers-100
93Finnish Jyvas-Hyva Stickers-101
93Finnish Jyvas-Hyva Stickers-102
93Finnish Jyvas-Hyva Stickers-121
93Finnish Jyvas-Hyva Stickers-122
93Finnish Jyvas-Hyva Stickers-123
93Finnish Jyvas-Hyva Stickers-124
93Finnish Jyvas-Hyva Stickers-125
93Finnish Jyvas-Hyva Stickers-126
93Finnish Jyvas-Hyva Stickers-127
93Finnish Jyvas-Hyva Stickers-128
93Finnish Jyvas-Hyva Stickers-129
93Finnish Jyvas-Hyva Stickers-130
93Finnish Jyvas-Hyva Stickers-131
93Finnish Jyvas-Hyva Stickers-132
93Finnish Jyvas-Hyva Stickers-151
93Finnish Jyvas-Hyva Stickers-152
93Finnish Jyvas-Hyva Stickers-153
93Finnish Jyvas-Hyva Stickers-154
93Finnish Jyvas-Hyva Stickers-155
93Finnish Jyvas-Hyva Stickers-156
93Finnish Jyvas-Hyva Stickers-157
93Finnish Jyvas-Hyva Stickers-158
93Finnish Jyvas-Hyva Stickers-159
93Finnish Jyvas-Hyva Stickers-160
93Finnish Jyvas-Hyva Stickers-161
93Finnish Jyvas-Hyva Stickers-162
93Finnish Jyvas-Hyva Stickers-181
93Finnish Jyvas-Hyva Stickers-182
93Finnish Jyvas-Hyva Stickers-183
93Finnish Jyvas-Hyva Stickers-184
93Finnish Jyvas-Hyva Stickers-185
93Finnish Jyvas-Hyva Stickers-186
93Finnish Jyvas-Hyva Stickers-187
93Finnish Jyvas-Hyva Stickers-188
93Finnish Jyvas-Hyva Stickers-189
93Finnish Jyvas-Hyva Stickers-190
93Finnish Jyvas-Hyva Stickers-191
93Finnish Jyvas-Hyva Stickers-192
93Finnish Jyvas-Hyva Stickers-211
93Finnish Jyvas-Hyva Stickers-212
93Finnish Jyvas-Hyva Stickers-213
93Finnish Jyvas-Hyva Stickers-214
93Finnish Jyvas-Hyva Stickers-215
93Finnish Jyvas-Hyva Stickers-216
93Finnish Jyvas-Hyva Stickers-217
93Finnish Jyvas-Hyva Stickers-218
93Finnish Jyvas-Hyva Stickers-219
93Finnish Jyvas-Hyva Stickers-220
93Finnish Jyvas-Hyva Stickers-221
93Finnish Jyvas-Hyva Stickers-222
93Finnish Jyvas-Hyva Stickers-241
93Finnish Jyvas-Hyva Stickers-242
93Finnish Jyvas-Hyva Stickers-243
93Finnish Jyvas-Hyva Stickers-244
93Finnish Jyvas-Hyva Stickers-245
93Finnish Jyvas-Hyva Stickers-246
93Finnish Jyvas-Hyva Stickers-247
93Finnish Jyvas-Hyva Stickers-248
93Finnish Jyvas-Hyva Stickers-249
93Finnish Jyvas-Hyva Stickers-250
93Finnish Jyvas-Hyva Stickers-251
93Finnish Jyvas-Hyva Stickers-252
93Finnish Jyvas-Hyva Stickers-271
93Finnish Jyvas-Hyva Stickers-272
93Finnish Jyvas-Hyva Stickers-273
93Finnish Jyvas-Hyva Stickers-274
93Finnish Jyvas-Hyva Stickers-275
93Finnish Jyvas-Hyva Stickers-276
93Finnish Jyvas-Hyva Stickers-277
93Finnish Jyvas-Hyva Stickers-278
93Finnish Jyvas-Hyva Stickers-279
93Finnish Jyvas-Hyva Stickers-280
93Finnish Jyvas-Hyva Stickers-281
93Finnish Jyvas-Hyva Stickers-282
93Finnish Jyvas-Hyva Stickers-301
93Finnish Jyvas-Hyva Stickers-302
93Finnish Jyvas-Hyva Stickers-303
93Finnish Jyvas-Hyva Stickers-304
93Finnish Jyvas-Hyva Stickers-305
93Finnish Jyvas-Hyva Stickers-306
93Finnish Jyvas-Hyva Stickers-307
93Finnish Jyvas-Hyva Stickers-308
93Finnish Jyvas-Hyva Stickers-309
93Finnish Jyvas-Hyva Stickers-310
93Finnish Jyvas-Hyva Stickers-311
93Finnish Jyvas-Hyva Stickers-312
93Finnish Jyvas-Hyva Stickers-331
93Finnish Jyvas-Hyva Stickers-332
93Finnish Jyvas-Hyva Stickers-333
93Finnish Jyvas-Hyva Stickers-334
93Finnish Jyvas-Hyva Stickers-335
93Finnish Jyvas-Hyva Stickers-336
93Finnish Jyvas-Hyva Stickers-337
93Finnish Jyvas-Hyva Stickers-338
93Finnish Jyvas-Hyva Stickers-339
93Finnish Jyvas-Hyva Stickers-340
93Finnish Jyvas-Hyva Stickers-341
93Finnish Jyvas-Hyva Stickers-342
93Finnish SISU-1
93Finnish SISU-27
93Finnish SISU-56
93Finnish SISU-81
93Finnish SISU-107
93Finnish SISU-134
93Finnish SISU-159
93Finnish SISU-181
93Finnish SISU-206
93Finnish SISU-232
93Finnish SISU-254
93Finnish SISU-278
93Swedish Semic Elitserien-1
93Swedish Semic Elitserien-25
93Swedish Semic Elitserien-49
93Swedish Semic Elitserien-73
93Swedish Semic Elitserien-97
93Swedish Semic Elitserien-121
93Swedish Semic Elitserien-145
93Swedish Semic Elitserien-169
93Swedish Semic Elitserien-193
93Swedish Semic Elitserien-217
93Swedish Semic Elitserien-241
93Swedish Semic Elitserien-265
93Peterborough Petes-1
93Roanoke Express-22
93RPI Engineers-30
93Saskatoon Blades-24
93Seattle Thunderbirds-30
93Tacoma Rockets-28
93Tacoma Rockets-29
93Tacoma Rockets-30
93Toledo Storm-29
94Canada Games NHL POGS-1
94Canada Games NHL POGS-2
94Canada Games NHL POGS-3
94Canada Games NHL POGS-4
94Canada Games NHL POGS-5
94Canada Games NHL POGS-6
94Canada Games NHL POGS-7
94Canada Games NHL POGS-8
94Canada Games NHL POGS-9
94Canada Games NHL POGS-10
94Canada Games NHL POGS-11
94Canada Games NHL POGS-12
94Canada Games NHL POGS-13
94Canada Games NHL POGS-14
94Canada Games NHL POGS-15
94Canada Games NHL POGS-16
94Canada Games NHL POGS-17
94Canada Games NHL POGS-18
94Canada Games NHL POGS-19
94Canada Games NHL POGS-20
94Canada Games NHL POGS-21
94Canada Games NHL POGS-22
94Canada Games NHL POGS-23
94Canada Games NHL POGS-24
94Canada Games NHL POGS-25
94Canada Games NHL POGS-26
94Canada Games NHL POGS-300
94Canada Games NHL POGS-301
94Canada Games NHL POGS-302
94Canada Games NHL POGS-303
94Canada Games NHL POGS-304
94Canada Games NHL POGS-305
94Canada Games NHL POGS-306
94Canada Games NHL POGS-307
94Canada Games NHL POGS-308
94Canada Games NHL POGS-309
94Canada Games NHL POGS-310
94Canada Games NHL POGS-311
94Canada Games NHL POGS-312
94Canada Games NHL POGS-314
94Canada Games NHL POGS-315
94Canada Games NHL POGS-316
94Canada Games NHL POGS-317
94Canada Games NHL POGS-318
94Canada Games NHL POGS-319
94Canada Games NHL POGS-320
94Canada Games NHL POGS-321
94Canada Games NHL POGS-322
94Canada Games NHL POGS-323
94Canada Games NHL POGS-324
94Canada Games NHL POGS-325
94Canada Games NHL POGS-364
94EA Sports-160
94EA Sports-161
94EA Sports-162
94EA Sports-163
94EA Sports-164
94EA Sports-165
94EA Sports-166
94EA Sports-167
94EA Sports-168
94EA Sports-169
94EA Sports-170
94EA Sports-171
94EA Sports-172
94EA Sports-173
94EA Sports-174
94EA Sports-175
94EA Sports-176
94EA Sports-177
94EA Sports-178
94EA Sports-179
94EA Sports-180
94EA Sports-181
94EA Sports-182
94EA Sports-183
94EA Sports-184
94Kraft-66
94Lightning Photo Album-29
94OPC Premier-120
Special Effects-120
94Parkhurst Missing Link-154
94Parkhurst Missing Link-155
94Parkhurst Missing Link-164
94Parkhurst Missing Link-166
94Parkhurst Missing Link-178
94Parkhurst Tall Boys-151
94Parkhurst Tall Boys-153
94Parkhurst Tall Boys-155
94Parkhurst Tall Boys-175
94Parkhurst Tall Boys-176
94Parkhurst Tall Boys-178
94Stadium Club Super Teams-16
94Stadium Club Super Team MemberOnly Set-16
94Finnish SISU-138
94Finnish SISU-139
94Finnish SISU-140
94Finnish SISU-141
94Finnish SISU-142
94Finnish SISU-143
94Finnish SISU-144
94Finnish SISU-145
94Finnish SISU-146
94Finnish SISU-147
94Finnish SISU-148
94Finnish SISU-149
94Finnish SISU-178
94Finnish SISU-179
94Finnish SISU-180
94Finnish SISU-181
94Finnish SISU-182
94Finnish SISU-183
94Finnish SISU-184
94Finnish SISU-185
94Finnish SISU-186
94Finnish SISU-187
94Finnish SISU-188
94Finnish SISU-189
94Finnish SISU-190
94Finnish SISU-191
94Finnish SISU-192
94Finnish SISU-193
94Finnish SISU-194
94Finnish SISU-195
94Finnish SISU-196
94German DEL-4
94German DEL-31
94German DEL-52
94German DEL-76
94German DEL-102
94German DEL-126
94German DEL-150
94German DEL-172
94German DEL-197
94German DEL-222
94German DEL-246
94German DEL-270
94German DEL-295
94German DEL-320
94German DEL-342
94German DEL-367
94German DEL-389
94German DEL-414
94Swedish Leaf-135
94Swedish Leaf-136
94Swedish Leaf-137
94Swedish Leaf-138
94Swedish Leaf-139
94Swedish Leaf-140
94Swedish Leaf-141
94Swedish Leaf-142
94Swedish Leaf-143
94Swedish Leaf-144
94Swedish Leaf-145
94Swedish Leaf-146
94Swedish Leaf-147
94Swedish Leaf-148
94Swedish Leaf-149
94Swedish Leaf-150
94Swedish Leaf-151
94Swedish Leaf-152
94Swedish Leaf-153
94Swedish Leaf-154
94Swedish Leaf-155
94Swedish Leaf-156
94Swedish Leaf-157
94Swedish Leaf-158
94Swedish Leaf-159
94Swedish Leaf-307
94Swedish Leaf-308
94Swedish Leaf-309
94Swedish Leaf-310
94Swedish Leaf-311
94Swedish Leaf-312
94Swedish Leaf-313
94Swedish Leaf-314
94Swedish Leaf-315
94Swedish Leaf-316
94Swedish Leaf-317
94Swedish Leaf-318
94Swedish Leaf-NNO1
94Brantford Smoke-23
94Detroit Jr. Red Wings-1
94Flint Generals-24
94Hampton Roads Admirals-23
94Indianapolis Ice-26
94Roanoke Express-1
94Toledo Storm-24
95Upper Deck World Junior Alumni-1
95Imperial Stickers-1
95Imperial Stickers-5
95Imperial Stickers-10
95Imperial Stickers-14
95Imperial Stickers-20
95Imperial Stickers-26
95Imperial Stickers-32
95Imperial Stickers-36
95Imperial Stickers-42
95Imperial Stickers-46
95Imperial Stickers-51
95Imperial Stickers-56
95Imperial Stickers-62
95Imperial Stickers-68
95Imperial Stickers-73
95Imperial Stickers-78
95Imperial Stickers-84
95Imperial Stickers-89
95Imperial Stickers-95
95Imperial Stickers-100
95Imperial Stickers-105
95Imperial Stickers-111
95Imperial Stickers-116
95Imperial Stickers-122
95Imperial Stickers-128
95Imperial Stickers-133
95Leaf Freeze Frame-6
95Topps-218
OPC Inserts-218
95Finnish SISU-1
95Finnish SISU-15
95Finnish SISU-28
95Finnish SISU-42
95Finnish SISU-55
95Finnish SISU-68
95Finnish SISU-81
95Finnish SISU-94
95Finnish SISU-107
95Finnish SISU-121
95Finnish SISU-135
95Finnish SISU-148
95Finnish SISU-192
95Finnish SISU-193
95Finnish SISU-194
95Finnish SISU-195
95Finnish SISU-196
95Finnish SISU-201
95Finnish SISU-215
95Finnish SISU-229
95Finnish SISU-246
95Finnish SISU-260
95Finnish SISU-271
95Finnish SISU-283
95Finnish SISU-297
95Finnish SISU-310
95Finnish SISU-323
95Finnish SISU-338
95Finnish SISU-351
95Slovakian-Quebec Pee-Wee Tournament-28
95Swedish Leaf-2
95Swedish Leaf-3
95Swedish Leaf-13
95Swedish Leaf-14
95Swedish Leaf-25
95Swedish Leaf-26
95Swedish Leaf-37
95Swedish Leaf-38
95Swedish Leaf-47
95Swedish Leaf-48
95Swedish Leaf-59
95Swedish Leaf-60
95Swedish Leaf-72
95Swedish Leaf-73
95Swedish Leaf-85
95Swedish Leaf-86
95Swedish Leaf-97
95Swedish Leaf-98
95Swedish Leaf-111
95Swedish Leaf-112
95Swedish Leaf-124
95Swedish Leaf-125
95Swedish Leaf-135
95Swedish Leaf-136
95Swedish Leaf-151
95Swedish Leaf-152
95Swedish Leaf-166
95Swedish Leaf-167
95Swedish Leaf-181
95Swedish Leaf-182
95Swedish Leaf-196
95Swedish Leaf-197
95Swedish Leaf-209
95Swedish Leaf-210
95Swedish Leaf-222
95Swedish Leaf-223
95Swedish Leaf-233
95Swedish Leaf-234
95Swedish Leaf-245
95Swedish Leaf-246
95Swedish Leaf-255
95Swedish Leaf-256
95Swedish Leaf-269
95Swedish Leaf-270
95Swedish Leaf-280
95Swedish Leaf-281
95Swedish Leaf-289
95Swedish Leaf-290
95Swedish Globe World Championships-244
95Swedish Globe World Championships-247
95Fort Worth Fire-1
95Hampton Roads Admirals-1
95Muskegon Fury-1
95Red Deer Rebels-24
95Roanoke Express-25
95St. John's Maple Leafs-1
95Thunder Bay Senators-1
95Signature Rookies Miracle on Ice-45
95Signature Rookies Miracle on Ice-46
95Signature Rookies Miracle on Ice-48
95Signature Rookies Miracle on Ice-49
95Signature Rookies Miracle on Ice-50
95Slapshot Memorial Cup-105
95Slapshot Memorial Cup-106
95Slapshot Memorial Cup-107
96Canucks Postcards-NNO
96Collector's Choice Stick'Ums-S27
96Flyers Postcards-1
96Frosted Flakes Masks-3
96Frosted Flakes Masks-4
96Frosted Flakes Masks-5
96Frosted Flakes Masks-6
96Pinnacle Trophies-10
96Finnish SISU Redline-163
96Slovakian Quebec Pee-Wee Tournament-30
96Grand Rapids Griffins-25
96Guelph Storm-36
96Hampton Roads Admirals-NNO
96Louisville Riverfrogs-30
96Regina Pats-24
96Roanoke Express-NNO
96Saskatoon Blades-28
96Sault Ste. Marie Greyhounds-30
96Sault Ste. Marie Greyhounds Autographed-30
98Kraft Dinners Zoomer Stickers-1
98Kraft Dinners Zoomer Stickers-2
98Kraft Dinners Zoomer Stickers-3
98Kraft Dinners Zoomer Stickers-4
98Kraft Dinners Zoomer Stickers-5
98Halifax Mooseheads Second Edition-27
98Louisiana Ice Gators-23
99Russian Metallurg Magnetogorsk-54
00Swiss Panini Stickers-27
00Swiss Panini Stickers-28
00Amarillo Rattlers-20
00Prince George Cougars-1
01Flyers Postcards-24
01Flyers Postcards-29
01Swedish Brynas Tigers-27
01Chicoutimi Sagueneens-1
01Mississauga Ice Dogs-1
02Flyers Postcards-23
02Notre Dame Fighting Irish-8
03Lightning Team Issue-2
03Saginaw Spirit-25
04Czech HC Slavia Praha Postcards-12
04South Surrey Eagles-30
04Colorado Eagles-1
04Salmon Arm Silverbacks-22
04Wheeling Nailers Riesbeck's-1
05Ohio State Buckeyes Women-20
06Colorado EaglesÂ -1
06Rockford IceHogs -27

Cardarelli, Joe
93Spokane Chiefs-5
94Spokane Chiefs-7
95Spokane Chiefs-21
96Spokane Chiefs-18
99Florida Everblades-19
00UK Sekonda Superleague-42
01UK Manchester Storm-11
02UK Manchester Storm-14
05UK Nottingham Panthers-9
06UK Nottingham Panthers-1

Carden, Rick
06Lincoln Stars-4
06Lincoln Stars Upper DeckÂ Signature Series -7

Cardiff, Jim
73Quaker Oats WHA-31
73Vancouver Blazers-6

Cardiff, Mark
907th Inn. Sketch OHL-256

Cardinal, Carson
91Air Canada SJHL-E5
92Saskatchewan JHL-13

Cardinal, Curtis
93Red Deer Rebels-3

Cardinal, Eric
907th Inn. Sketch QMJHL-110
917th Inn. Sketch QMJHL-232

Cardinal, Reg
93Maine Black Bears-59
97Johnstown Chiefs-27

Cardwell, Justin
93Western Michigan Broncos-6
99Greensboro Generals-18
00Fort Worth Brahmas-2
01Fort Worth Brahmas-4
02Kalamazoo Wings-18
03Rockford Ice Hogs-2

Careau, Sylvain
917th Inn. Sketch QMJHL-93

Caretta, Martin
93Swiss HNL-408

Carey, Jason
917th Inn. Sketch WHL-285
97El Paso Buzzards-15
00Fort Worth Brahmas-3

Carey, Jim
92Sports Illustrated for Kids II-382
94Fleer-233
94SP-128
Die Cuts-128
94Portland Pirates-4
95Bashan Super Stickers-128
95Bashan Super Stickers-131
95Be A Player-189
Signatures-S189
Signatures Die Cuts-S189
95Bowman-74
All-Foil-74
95Canada Games NHL POGS-28
95Canada Games NHL POGS-287
95Capitals Team Issue-4
95Collector's Choice-30
95Collector's Choice-369
95Collector's Choice-375
Player's Club-30
Player's Club-369
Player's Club-375
Player's Club Platinum-30
Player's Club Platinum-369
Player's Club Platinum-375
95Donruss-189
Between The Pipes-6
Dominators-4
Rookie Team-1
95Donruss Elite-69
Die Cut Stars-69
Die Cut Uncut-69
Painted Warriors-10
95Emotion-186
Xcited-19
95Finest-66
Refractors-66
95Imperial Stickers-131
95Kraft-20
95Leaf-78
Freeze Frame-1
Gold Stars-1
Studio Rookies-1
95Leaf Limited-55
Stick Side-1
95McDonald's Pinnacle-MCD-40
95Metal-157
95NHL Aces Playing Cards-6S
95Panini Stickers-145
95Panini Stickers-303
95Parkhurst International-492
Emerald Ice-492
Crown Collection Silver Series 1-16
Crown Collection Gold Series 1-16
Goal Patrol-5
Parkie's Trophy Picks-PP36
95Pinnacle-138
Artist's Proofs-138
Rink Collection-138
Masks-3
Roaring 20s-9
95Pinnacle FANtasy-20
95Playoff One on One-104
95Playoff One on One-213
95Pro Magnets-32
95Score-78
95Score-317
Black Ice Artist's Proofs-78
Black Ice Artist's Proofs-317
Black Ice-78
Black Ice-317
Dream Team-12
95Select Certified Promos-12
95Select Certified-12
Mirror Gold-12
Future-2
95SkyBox Impact-175
95SkyBox Impact-228
Deflectors-2
95SP-156
95Stadium Club Members Only-48
95Stadium Club-115
Members Only Master Set-115
Generation TSC-GT6
Generation TSC Members Only Master Set-GT6
95Summit-51
Artist's Proofs-51
Ice-51
In The Crease-6
95Topps-210
95Topps-383
OPC Inserts-210
OPC Inserts-383
Marquee Men Power Boosters-383
New To The Game-1NG
Young Stars-YS8
95Topps SuperSkills-73
Platinum-73
95Ultra-173
95Ultra-320
95Ultra-368
Gold Medallion-173
All-Rookies-1
All-Rookie Gold Medallion-1
Premier Pad Men-4
Premier Pad Men Gold Medallion-4
95Upper Deck-344
Electric Ice-344
Electric Ice Gold-344
Freeze Frame-F20
Freeze Frame Jumbo-F20
Predictor Hobby-H16
Predictor Hobby Exchange-H16
Special Edition-SE87
Special Edition Gold-SE87
95Zenith-5
Z-Team-18
95Images-4
95Images-99
Gold-4
Gold-99
Clear Excitement-CE4
Platinum Prospects-PR2
95Signature Rookies-44
Signatures-44
95Signature Rookies Tetrad Previews *-2
95Signature Rookies Tetrad SR Force *-F7
96SLU Hockey Canadian-2
96SLU Hockey American-3
96Be A Player Stacking the Pads-8
96Black Diamond-147
Gold-147
96Collector's Choice-278
96Collector's Choice-334
Stick'Ums-S17
96Donruss-33
Press Proofs-33
Between the Pipes-3
Dominators-1
96Donruss Canadian Ice-79
Gold Press Proofs-79
Red Press Proofs-79
96Donruss Elite-19
Die Cut Stars-19
Painted Warriors-3
Painted Warriors Promos-P3
96Flair-98
Blue Ice-98
Hot Gloves-3
96Fleer-116
96Fleer-144
96Fleer-145
96Fleer-146
Vezina-3
Picks Fabulous 50-6
Picks Jagged Edge-12
96Kenner Starting Lineup Cards-3
96Kraft Upper Deck-50
96Leaf-68
Press Proofs-68
Shut Down-10
Sweaters Away-9
Sweaters Home-9
96Leaf Limited-16
Gold-16
Stubble-5
96Leaf Preferred-23
Press Proofs-23
Steel-21
Steel Gold-21
Masked Marauders-1
96Maggers-10
96McDonald's Pinnacle-32
96Metal Universe-162
Armor Plate-3
Armor Plate Super Power-3
Ice Carvings-3
Ice Carvings Super Power-3
96NHL Aces Playing Cards-7
96NHL Pro Stamps-32
96Pinnacle-105
Artist's Proofs-105
Foil-105
Premium Stock-105
Rink Collection-105
Masks-2
Masks Die Cuts-2
Trophies-5
96Pinnacle Mint-28
Bronze-28
Gold-28
Silver-28
Coins Brass-28
Coins Solid Gold-28
Coins Gold Plated-28
Coins Nickel-28
Coins Silver-28
96Playoff One on One-426
96Score-74
Artist's Proofs-74
Dealer's Choice Artist's Proofs-74
Special Artist's Proofs-74
Golden Blades-74
Net Worth-3
Sudden Death-2
96Select Certified-29
Artist's Proofs-29
Blue-29
Mirror Blue-29
Mirror Gold-29
Mirror Red-29
Red-29
Freezers-3
96SkyBox Impact-137
Zero Heroes-3
96SP-164
Game Film-GF13
96SPx-48
Gold-48
96Summit-94
Artist's Proofs-94
Ice-94
Metal-94
Premium Stock-94
In The Crease-6
In The Crease Premium Stock-6
Untouchables-14
96Team Out-68
96Topps Picks-13
Ice D-ID9
OPC Inserts-13
96Ultra-174
Gold Medallion-174
Clear the Ice-1
96Upper Deck-174
Superstar Showdown-SS14A
96Upper Deck Ice-72
Parallel-72
96Zenith-7
Artist's Proofs-7
Z-Team-15
96Swedish Semic Wien-157
Super Goalies-SG5
96Collector's Edge Ice-52
Crucibles-C5
Prism-52
QuantumMotion-8
The Wall-TW7
97Collector's Choice-17
Star Quest-SQ57
97Donruss-22
Press Proofs Silver-22
Press Proofs Gold-22
97Donruss Canadian Ice-59
Dominion Series-59
Provincial Series-59
97Donruss Limited-14
97Donruss Limited-131
Exposure-14
Exposure-131
Fabric of the Game-54
97Donruss Preferred-43
Cut to the Chase-43
Color Guard-13
Color Guard Promos-13
97Katch-9
Gold-9
Silver-9
97Leaf-71
97Leaf-P10
Fractal Matrix-71
Fractal Matrix Die Cuts-71
Pipe Dreams-10
97Leaf International-71
Universal Ice-71
97Pacific-23
Copper-23
Emerald Green-23
Ice Blue-23
Red-23
Silver-23
97Pacific Dynagon-8
Copper-8
Dark Grey-8
Emerald Green-8
Ice Blue-8
Red-8
Silver-8
Best Kept Secrets-6
Dynamic Duos-2B
Stonewallers-2
Tandems-17
97Pacific Invincible-8
Copper-8
Emerald Green-8
Ice Blue-8
Red-8
Silver-8
NHL Regime-11
97Panini Stickers-8
97Paramount-10
Copper-10
Dark Grey-10
Emerald Green-10
Ice Blue-10
Red-10
Silver-10
97Pinnacle-83
Artist's Proofs-83
Rink Collection-83
Press Plates Back Black-83
Press Plates Back Cyan-83
Press Plates Back Magenta-83
Press Plates Back Yellow-83
Press Plates Front Black-83
Press Plates Front Cyan-83
Press Plates Front Magenta-83
Press Plates Front Yellow-83
97Pinnacle Certified-15
Red-15
Mirror Blue-15
Mirror Gold-15
Mirror Red-15
97Pinnacle Inside-62
Coach's Collection-62
Executive Collection-62
Stand Up Guys-3A/B
Stand Up Guys-3C/D
Stand Up Guys Promos-3A/B
Stand Up Guys Promos-3C/D
Stoppers-7
97Pinnacle Tot Cert Platinum Blue-15
97Pinnacle Tot Certi Platinum Gold-15
97Pinnacle Totally Certified Platinum Red-15
97Pinnacle Tot Cert Mirror Platinum Gold-15
97Score-14
Artist's Proofs-14
Golden Blades-14
Net Worth-2
97Score Bruins-2
Platinum-2
Premier-2
97Studio-45
Press Proofs Silver-45
Press Proofs Gold-45
98Katch-8
98Providence Bruins-7
00BAP Memorabilia Georges Vezina-V5

Carey, Matt
98Quad-City Mallards-4

Carfora, Ed
97Arizona Icecats-7
98Arizona Icecats-2
99Arizona Icecats-2
00Arizona Icecats-4

Carignan, Dominic
93Quebec Pee-Wee Tournament-1103

Carignan, Patrick
917th Inn. Sketch QMJHL-160

Carinci, Vince
93Quebec Pee-Wee Tournament-1435

Caris, Ingemar
65Swedish Coralli ISHockey-167
67Swedish Hockey-284
69Swedish Hockey-331
70Swedish Hockey-243
71Swedish Hockey-302

Carkner, Matt
99O-Pee-Chee-273
99O-Pee-Chee Chrome-273
99O-Pee-Chee Chrome Refractors-273
99Topps/OPC-273
99Topps/OPC Chrome-273
Refractors-273
99Bowman CHL-23
Gold-23
OPC International-23
Autographs-BA18
Autographs Gold-BA18
Autographs Silver-BA18
01Cleveland Barons-2
02Cleveland Barons-1
03Cleveland Barons-2
04Cleveland Barons-3
05Cleveland Barons-3
06Wilkes-Barre Scranton Penguins-12
06Wilkes-Barre Scranton Penguins Jerseys-17

Carkner, Terry
87Nordiques General Foods-4
87Nordiques Team Issue-3
88Flyers Postcards-23
89Flyers Postcards-4
89O-Pee-Chee-3
89Panini Stickers-297
89Topps-3
90Flyers Postcards-4
90O-Pee-Chee-381
90Panini Stickers-114
90Pro Set-212
90Score-47
Canadian-47
90Topps-381
Tiffany-381
90Upper Deck-398
French-398
91Pro Set Platinum-212
91Bowman-232
91Flyers J.C. Penney-4
91O-Pee-Chee-291
91Panini Stickers-235
91Parkhurst-342
French-342
91Pinnacle-51
French-51
91Pro Set-173
French-173
91Score American-64
91Score Canadian Bilingual-64
91Score Canadian English-64
91Stadium Club-219
91Topps-291
91Upper Deck-204
French-204
92Bowman-129
92Flyers J.C. Penney-7
92Flyers Upper Deck Sheets-15
92Flyers Upper Deck Sheets-25
92Flyers Upper Deck Sheets-38
92O-Pee-Chee-180
92Panini Stickers-190
92Panini Stickers French-190
92Parkhurst-362
Emerald Ice-362
92Pinnacle-63
French-63
92Pro Set-269
92Score-66
Canadian-66
92Stadium Club-463
92Topps-465
Gold-465G
92Ultra-370
93Donruss-422
93Flyers Lineup Sheets-8
93OPC Premier-152
Gold-152
93Panini Stickers-54
93Parkhurst-332
Emerald Ice-332
93Pinnacle-286
Canadian-286
93PowerPlay-328
93Score-233
93Score-508
Gold-508
Canadian-233
Canadian-508
Canadian Gold-508
93Stadium Club-252
Members Only Master Set-252
First Day Issue-252
93Topps/OPC Premier-152
Gold-152
93Ultra-304
94Be A Player-R167
Signature Cards-144
94OPC Premier-359
Special Effects-359
94Parkhurst-69
Gold-69
94Pinnacle-221
Artist's Proofs-221
Rink Collection-221
94Topps/OPC Premier-359
Special Effects-359
94Upper Deck-467
Electric Ice-467
95Collector's Choice-113
Player's Club-113
Player's Club Platinum-113
95Parkhurst International-354
Emerald Ice-354
95Upper Deck-286
Electric Ice-286
Electric Ice Gold-286
96Collector's Choice-109
97Be A Player-195
Autographs-195
Autographs Die-Cuts-195
Autographs Prismatic Die-Cuts-195
97Pacific Invincible NHL Regime-84
97Upper Deck-283
98Be A Player-207
Press Release-207
98BAP Gold-207
98BAP Autographs-207
98BAP Autographs Gold-207
02BAP Sig Series Auto Buybacks 1998-207

Carlbaum, Bertil
56Swedish Alfabilder-43
57Swedish Alfabilder-136

Carlberg, Anders
65Swedish Coralli ISHockey-138

Carle, Gabriel
05Chicoutimi Sagueneens-12

Carle, Mathieu
05ITG Heroes/Prosp Toronto Expo Parallel -307
05ITG Heroes and Prospects-307
Autographs Series II-MCL
Team Cherry-TC14
06ITG Heroes and Prospects-191
Autographs-AMCR
Update Autographs-AMCR

Carle, Matt
06Be A Player-208
Autographs-208
Signatures 10-208
Signatures Duals-DCB
Signatures Trios-TCWB
06Be A Player Portraits-125
06Beehive-151
Blue-151
Gold-151
Matte-151
Red Facsimile Signatures-151
Wood-151
06Black Diamond-198
Black-198
Gold-198
Ruby-198
06Flair Showcase-82
Parallel-82
06Fleer-205
Tiffany-205
06Hot Prospects-131
Red Hot-131

White Hot-131
Hot Materials -HMMC
Hot Materials Red Hot-HMMC
Hot Materials White Hot-HMMC
Hotagraphs-HMC
06O-Pee-Chee-531
06O-Pee-Chee-631
Rainbow-531
Rainbow-631
06SP Authentic-201
Chirography-RS
Limited-201
Sign of the Times-STMA
06SP Game Used-150
Gold-150
Rainbow-150
Autographs-150
Inked Sweaters-ISCA
Inked Sweaters Patches-ISCA
Letter Marks-LMMA
Rookie Exclusives Autographs-REMC
06SPx-177
Spectrum-177
06The Cup-153
Autographed NHL Shields Duals-DASPC
Autographed Rookie Masterpiece Pressplates-153
Gold Rainbow Autographed Rookie Patches-153
Honorable Numbers-HNMC
Masterpiece Pressplates (Artifacts)-228
Masterpiece Pressplates (Be A Player Portraits)-125
Masterpiece Pressplates (Bee Hive)-151
Masterpiece Pressplates (Marquee Rookies)-531
Masterpiece Pressplates (MVP)-346
Masterpiece Pressplates (Power Play)-125
Masterpiece Pressplates (SP Authentic Autographs)-201
Masterpiece Pressplates (SP Game Used)-150
Masterpiece Pressplates (SPx Autographs)-177
Masterpiece Pressplates (Sweet Beginnings)-149
Masterpiece Pressplates (Trilogy)-150
Masterpiece Pressplates (Ultimate Collection Autographs)-130
Masterpiece Pressplates (Victory)-219
NHL Shields Duals-DSHCV
NHL Shields Duals-DSHCW
Rookies Black-153
Rookies Platinum-153
Signature Patches-SPMC
06UD Artifacts-228
Blue-228
Gold-228
Platinum-228
Radiance-228
Red-228
06UD Mini Jersey Collection-125
06UD Powerplay-125
Impact Rainbow-125
06Ultimate Collection-130
Rookies Autographed NHL Shields-130
Rookies Autographed Patches-130
Signatures-US-MC
Ultimate Debut Threads Jerseys-DJ-MC
Ultimate Debut Threads Jerseys Autographs-DJ-MC
Ultimate Debut Threads Patches-DJ-MC
Ultimate Debut Threads Patches Autographs-DJ-MC
06Ultra-225
Gold Medallion-225
Ice Medallion-225
06Upper Deck-241
Exclusives Parallel-241
High Gloss Parallel-241
Masterpieces-241
Rookie Game Dated Moments-RGD26
Rookie Headliners-RH26
Rookie Materials-RMMC
Rookie Materials Patches-RMMC
06Upper Deck MVP-346
Gold Script-346
Super Script-346
06Upper Deck Ovation-91
06Upper Deck Sweet Shot-149
Rookie Jerseys Autographs-149
Signature Shots/Saves-SSMA
Signature Shots/Saves Sticks-SSSMA
06Upper Deck Trilogy-150
06Upper Deck Victory-219
06Upper Deck Victory Black-219
06Upper Deck Victory Gold-219
07Upper Deck Rookie Class -2
07Upper Deck Rookie Class C-Card Insert-CC5

Carleton, Wayne
67Topps-77
68Post Marbles-4
68Shirriff Coins-160
69Maple Leafs White Border Glossy-3
69O-Pee-Chee-184
70Bruins Postcards-8
70Bruins Team Issue-11
70Esso Power Players-62
70O-Pee-Chee-9
70Sargent Promotions Stamps-6
70Topps-9
Topps/OPC Sticker Stamps-3
71Letraset Action Replays-18
71O-Pee-Chee-178
71Sargent Promotions Stamps-131
71Toronto Sun-43
72O-Pee-Chee-337
727-Eleven Slurpee Cups WHA-4
73O-Pee-Chee WHA Posters-8
74O-Pee-Chee WHA-45
75O-Pee-Chee WHA-43
91Ultimate Original Six-47
French-47
04ITG Franchises US East-320
Autographs-A-WCA
04ITG Franchises US West-152
07Maple Leafs 1967 Commemorative-4

Carli, Jared
99Calgary Hitmen-4
99Calgary Hitmen Autographs-4
00Calgary Hitmen-8
01Calgary Hitmen-7
01Calgary Hitmen Autographed-7

Carlin, Stewart
04Sioux Falls Stampede-2-2

Carlisle, David
02Lincoln Stars-17
03Lincoln Stars-15
03Lincoln Stars Update-42
03Lincoln Stars Update-47
04Lincoln Stars-14
04Lincoln Stars Update-42
05St. Cloud State Huskies-5
05St. Cloud State Huskies-5

Carlon, Tom
04UK Coventry Blaze-4
04UK U-20 Team-15
05UK Coventry Blaze-18
06UK Coventry Blaze-10

Carlson, Brett
04Calgary Hitmen-2

Carlson, Dan
01Johnstown Chiefs-7
02Roanoke Express-10
02Roanoke Express RBI Sports-190
03Roanoke Express-308
04UK Coventry Blaze-5
04UK Coventry Blaze Champions-10
04UK EIHL All-Stars-10
04Minnesota-Duluth Bulldogs-4
06UK Coventry Blaze-12

Carlson, Don
90Arizona Icecats-4
91Arizona Icecats-2

Carlson, Jack
80North Stars Postcards-4
81North Stars Postcards-5
02Fleer Throwbacks-87
Gold-87
Platinum-87

Carlson, Jeff
04Green Bay Gamblers-1

Carlson, Kent
83Canadiens Postcards-4
83Vachon-42
84Canadiens Postcards-3

Carlson, Ross
04Wisconsin Badgers-19
05Wisconsin Badgers-3

Carlson, Steve
82Birmingham South Stars-6
89Johnstown Chiefs-36
91Johnstown Chiefs-1

Carlsson, Ake
69Swedish Hockey-39
71Swedish Hockey-138
72Swedish Stickers-125

Carlsson, Anders
83Swedish Semic Elitserien-62
84Swedish Semic Elitserien-239
85Swedish Panini Stickers-240
88Devils Caretta-6
88ProCards AHL-339
89Swedish Semic Elitserien Stickers-38
90Swedish Semic Elitserien Stickers-185
91Finnish Semic World Champ Stickers-48
91Swedish Semic Elitserien Stickers-354
91Swedish Semic World Champ Stickers-48
92Swedish Semic Elitserien Stickers-61
93Swedish Semic Elitserien-48
94Swedish Leaf-210
95Swedish Leaf-236
Champs-5
95Swedish Upper Deck-102
97Swedish Collector's Choice-109
Crash the Game Exchange-C9
Crash the Game Redemption-R9
98Swedish UD Choice-126
99Swedish Upper Deck-112
Hands of Gold-8
Hands of Gold-10
Lasting Impressions-6

Carlsson, Arne
65Swedish Coralli ISHockey-168
67Swedish Hockey-4
67Swedish Hockey-285
69Swedish Hockey-184
69Swedish Hockey-332
70Finnish Jaakiekko-23
70Swedish Hockey-133
70Swedish Hockey-277
70Swedish Masterserien-101
71Finnish Suomi Stickers-43
71Swedish Hockey-7
71Swedish Hockey-225
72Finnish Panda Toronto-66
72Finnish Semic World Championship-50
72Swedish Stickers-213
72Swedish Semic World Championship-50
73Finnish Jaakiekko-25
73Swedish Stickers-61
74Swedish Stickers-162
74Swedish Semic World Champ Stickers-3

Carlsson, Bjorn
83Swedish Semic Elitserien-94
84Swedish Semic Elitserien-94
85Swedish Panini Stickers-83
86Swedish Panini Stickers-73
87Swedish Panini Stickers-14
89Swedish Semic Elitserien Stickers-228
90Swedish Semic Elitserien Stickers-65
91Swedish Semic Elitserien Stickers-240

Carlsson, Calle
92Upper Deck-228
00German DEL-103
01UK Nottingham Panthers-20
02UK Sheffield Steelers-5
03UK Nottingham Panthers-16
04UK Nottingham Panthers-3
05UK Nottingham Panthers-19
06UK Nottingham Panthers-20

Carlsson, Clarence
65Swedish Coralli ISHockey-202
67Swedish Hockey-151

Carlsson, Daniel
97Swedish Collector's Choice-35

Carlsson, Hans
65Swedish Coralli ISHockey-38
65Swedish Coralli ISHockey-73
67Swedish Hockey-183
69Swedish Hockey-239
70Swedish Hockey-137
71Swedish Hockey-230
72Swedish Stickers-218
73Swedish Stickers-69
74Swedish Stickers-210

Carlsson, Herman
32Swedish Marabou-146

Carlsson, Jan
83Swedish Semic Elitserien-224

Carlsson, Kurt
73Swedish Stickers-23
83Swedish Semic Elitserien-242

Carlsson, Leif
83Swedish Semic Elitserien-108
84Swedish Semic Elitserien-108
85Swedish Panini Stickers-96
85Swedish Panini Stickers-233
86Swedish Panini Stickers-90
87Swedish Panini Stickers-94
89Swedish Semic Elitserien Stickers-268
90Swedish Semic Elitserien Stickers-29
91Swedish Semic Elitserien Stickers-84
92Swedish Semic Elitserien Stickers-106
93Swedish Semic Elitserien-78
95Swedish Leaf-219
95Swedish Upper Deck-63
96German DEL-29
98German DEL-175
99German DEL-65

Carlsson, Leif R.
83Swedish Semic Elitserien-209
84Swedish Semic Elitserien-234
04German Berlin Eisbarens 50th Anniv-49

Carlsson, Lennart
69Swedish Hockey-226
71Swedish Hockey-371

Carlsson, Mattias
02Swedish SHL-257
Parallel-257

Carlsson, Nicklas
86Swedish Panini Stickers-122

Carlsson, Nils
67Swedish Hockey-134
69Swedish Hockey-146
71Swedish Hockey-350

Carlsson, Per-Olof
83Swedish Semic Elitserien-141
84Swedish Semic Elitserien-161
85Swedish Panini Stickers-146
86Swedish Panini Stickers-153
87Swedish Panini Stickers-163
89Swedish Semic Elitserien Stickers-133
90Swedish Semic Elitserien Stickers-212
91Swedish Semic Elitserien Stickers-141
92Swedish Semic Elitserien Stickers-168

Carlsson, Robert
00Swedish Upper Deck-170
02Swedish SHL-106
02Swedish SHL-253
Parallel-106
Parallel-253
Signatures Series II-9
03Swedish Elite-116
03Swedish Elite-272
Silver-116
Silver-272
04Swedish Elitset-116
04Swedish Elitset-283
Gold-116
Gold-283
Signatures-10
05Swedish SHL Elitset-126
05Swedish SHL Elitset-138
Gold-126
Gold-138
Teammates-12
06Swedish SHL Elitset-284

Carlsson, Roland
94Finnish SISU-79
95Finnish SISU-5
98Finnish Kerailysarja-171
99Finnish Cardset-296
00Finnish Cardset-320

Carlsson, Rolf
72Swedish Stickers-139

Carlsson, Stefan
65Swedish Coralli ISHockey-81

Carlsson, Stig
55Swedish Alfabilder-11
64Swedish Coralli ISHockey-64
65Swedish Coralli ISHockey-64
67Swedish Hockey-184
69Swedish Hockey-240

Carlsson, Thomas
64Swedish Coralli ISHockey-96
67Swedish Hockey-62
69Swedish Hockey-95
70Swedish Hockey-51
70Swedish Hockey-138
71Swedish Hockey-118
71Swedish Hockey-231
72Swedish Stickers-99
73Swedish Stickers-211
74Swedish Stickers-163
89Swedish Semic Elitserien Stickers-224
91Swedish Semic Elitserien Stickers-233
93Swedish Semic Elitserien-249
94Swedish Leaf-129
99Danish Hockey League-87

Carlsson, Yngve
55Swedish Alfabilder-6

Carlstrom, P.A.
65Swedish Coralli ISHockey-46

Carlyle, Randy
76Maple Leafs Postcards-4
77Maple Leafs Postcards-2
78O-Pee-Chee-312
79O-Pee-Chee-124
79Topps-124
80O-Pee-Chee-367
81O-Pee-Chee-256
81O-Pee-Chee Stickers-183
81O-Pee-Chee Stickers-255
81Post Standups-8
81Topps-E112
82O-Pee-Chee-265
82O-Pee-Chee-266
82O-Pee-Chee Stickers-144
82Post Cereal-15
82Topps Stickers-144
83NHL Key Tags-101
83O-Pee-Chee-278
83O-Pee-Chee Stickers-227
83Penguins Coke-6
83Penguins Heinz Photos-5
83Puffy Stickers-12
83Topps Stickers-227
84Jets Police-5
84O-Pee-Chee-337
84O-Pee-Chee Stickers-291
84Penguins Heinz Photos-5
85Jets Police-4
85Jets Silverwood Dairy-2
85O-Pee-Chee-57
85O-Pee-Chee Stickers-251
85Topps-57
86Jets Postcards-4
86Kraft Drawings-6
86O-Pee-Chee-144
86O-Pee-Chee Stickers-107
86Topps-144
87Jets Postcards-4
87O-Pee-Chee-9
87O-Pee-Chee Stickers-248
87Panini Stickers-360
87Topps-9
88Jets Police-3
88Jets Postcards-5
88O-Pee-Chee-204
88O-Pee-Chee Stickers-148
88Panini Stickers-149
89Jets Safeway-6
89Kraft-47
89O-Pee-Chee-291
89O-Pee-Chee Stickers-143
89Panini Stickers-168
90Jets IGA-5
90O-Pee-Chee-51
90Panini Stickers-314
90Pro Set-325
90Score-136
Canadian-136
90Topps-51
Tiffany-51
90Upper Deck-331
French-331
91Bowman-199
91Jets Panini Team Stickers-4
91Jets IGA-4
91O-Pee-Chee-72
91Panini Stickers-76
91Parkhurst-418
French-418
91Pinnacle-288
French-288
91Pro Set-273
French-273
91Score American-125
91Score Canadian Bilingual-125
91Score Canadian English-125
91Stadium Club-94
91Topps-72
92Bowman-287
92O-Pee-Chee-12
92Pinnacle-87
French-87
92Pro Set-265
92Score-167
Canadian-167
92Stadium Club-332
92Topps-147
Gold-147G
93OPC Premier-86
Gold-86
93Pinnacle All-Stars-27
93Pinnacle All-Stars Canadian-27
93Stadium Club All-Stars-15
93Stadium Club All-Stars Members Only-15
93Stadium Club All-Stars OPC-15
93Topps/OPC Premier-86
Gold-86
95Jets Team Issue-4
97Manitoba Moose-A8
97Sudbury Wolves Anniversary-3
98IHL All-Star Western Conference-21
01Sudbury Wolves-27
02Maple Leafs Platinum Collection-83
04ITG Franchises Canadian-139
Autographs-RC2
04ITG Franchises US West-271
Autographs-A-RC1
05Ducks Team Issue-22

Carlyle, Steve
69Swedish Hockey-352

Carman, Mike
06Minnesota Golden Gophers-5

Carmichael, Bruce
61Union Oil WHL-5

Carmichael, Matt
98Port Huron Border Cats-12
03Huntsville Channel Cats-5
04Huntsville Havoc-17

Carnazzolla, Jimmy
95Swedish Globe World Championships-234

Carnback, Patrik
89Swedish Semic Elitserien Stickers-276
90Swedish Semic Elitserien Stickers-37
91Finnish Semic World Champ Stickers-46
91Swedish Semic Elitserien Stickers-287
91Swedish Semic World Champ Stickers-46
92Fredericton Canadiens-4
93Donruss-6
93OPC Premier-379
Gold-379
93Parkhurst-8
Emerald Ice-8
93PowerPlay-281
93Score-615
Gold-615
Canadian-615
Canadian Gold-615
93Stadium Club-434
Members Only Master Set-434
First Day Issue-434
93Topps/OPC Premier-379
Gold-379
93Ultra-251
93Upper Deck-463
93Swedish Semic World Champ Stickers-43
93Classic Pro Prospects-105
94Donruss-29
94Ducks Carl's Jr.-1
94Fleer-1
94Leaf-102
94O-Pee-Chee Finest Inserts-1
94Parkhurst-7
Gold-7
Vintage-V28
94Pinnacle-189
Artist's Proofs-189
Rink Collection-189
94Stadium Club-53
Members Only Master Set-53
First Day Issue-53
Super Team Winner Cards-53
94Upper Deck-475
Electric Ice-475
94Swedish Leaf-270
95Collector's Choice-42
Player's Club-42
Player's Club Platinum-42
95Hoyle Western Playing Cards-7
95Panini Stickers-224
95Parkhurst International-1
Emerald Ice-1
95Playoff One on One-111
95Pro Magnets-41
95Topps-335
OPC Inserts-335
95Upper Deck-180
Electric Ice-180
Electric Ice Gold-180
95Finnish Semic World Championships-74
95Swedish Upper Deck-241
95Swedish Globe World Championships-41
95Swedish World Championships Stickers-152
96NHL Pro Stamps-41
96German DEL-359
96Swedish Semic Wien-63
97Swedish Collector's Choice-78
Stick'Ums-S13
98Swedish UD Choice-76
99Swedish Upper Deck-81
Lasting Impressions-12
00Swedish Upper Deck-68
00Swedish Upper Deck-195
SHL Excellence-S3
SHL Signatures-PC
Top Draws-T4
02Swedish SHL-278
Parallel-278

Carnegie, Herbie
51Laval Dairy QSHL-16
52St. Lawrence Sales-53
05ITG Heroes and Prospects-185
Autographs Series II-HC
06ITG Ultimate Memorabilia-66
Artist Proof-66

Carnegie, Ossie
51Bas Du Fleuve-13

Carnegie, Rane
01Belleville Bulls-4
02Belleville Bulls-3
03Belleville Bulls-1
03Belleville Bulls-22
03Plymouth Whalers-1
04Halifax Mooseheads-22
05Halifax Mooseheads-6
06Bakersfield Condors-2

Carnelley, Todd
84Kamloops Blazers-5
85Kamloops Blazers-5

Carney, Dan
97Hampton Roads Admirals-4
98Peoria Rivermen-4
99UK Hull Thunder-6
00Jackson Bandits-16
03Roanoke Express-309

Carney, Keith
91Rochester Americans Kodak-6
91Rochester Americans Postcards-4
92OPC Premier-81
92Parkhurst-15
Emerald Ice-15
92Pinnacle-229
French-229
92Pro Set-223
92Score-461
Canadian-461
92Ultra-13
92Upper Deck-402
92Classic-102
Gold-102
93Blackhawks Coke-22
93Donruss-412
93Upper Deck-516
94Blackhawks Coke-3
94Leaf-359
94Parkhurst-50
Gold-50
94Upper Deck-449
Electric Ice-449
94Flint Generals-5
95Be A Player-9
Signatures-S9
Signatures Die Cuts-S9
95Blackhawks Coke-3
95Upper Deck-435
Electric Ice-435
Electric Ice Gold-435
97Pacific Invincible NHL Regime-41
97Pacific Omega-47
Copper-47
Dark Gray-47
Emerald Green-47
Gold-47
Ice Blue-47
98UD Choice-155
Prime Choice Reserve-155
Reserve-155
98Upper Deck-343
Exclusives-343
Exclusives 1 of 1-343
Gold Reserve-343
99Pacific-316
Copper-316
Emerald Green-316
Gold-316
Ice Blue-316
Premiere Date-316
Red-316
00Pacific-312
Copper-312
Gold-312
Ice Blue-312
Premiere Date-312
01Pacific-300
Extreme LTD-300
Hobby LTD-300
Premiere Date-300
Retail LTD-300
01Pacific Arena Exclusives-300
02Pacific Complete-80
Red-80
02Topps Total-381
03ITG Action-29
03NHL Sticker Collection-159
03Pacific Complete-201
Red-201
03Upper Deck-249
Canadian Exclusives-249
HG-249
UD Exclusives-249
03Upper Deck MVP-10
Gold Script-10
Silver Script-10
Canadian Exclusives-10
05Ducks Team Issue-3
05Parkhurst Facsimile Auto Parallel-14
05Upper Deck-249
05Upper Deck MVP-10
Gold-10
Platinum-10
06O-Pee-Chee-243
Rainbow-243
06Wild Crime Prevention-3
06Wild Postcards-3

Carney, Matt
02Odessa Jackalopes-2

Caron, Alain
67Seals Team Issue-6
72Nordiques Postcards-5
72O-Pee-Chee-324
73Nordiques Team Issue-6
73Quaker Oats WHA-38

Caron, Christian
917th Inn. Sketch QMJHL-92
02Thetford Mines Coyotes-5

Caron, Daniel
77Granby Vics-3

Caron, Francois
00Chicoutimi Sagueneens-12
Signed-12
01Moncton Wildcats-10
02Moncton Wildcats-3
03Moncton Wildcats-8

Caron, Jacques
71Blues Postcards-6
72Blues White Border-1
72O-Pee-Chee-140
Player Crests-18
72Sargent Promotions Stamps-193
72Topps-86
73Canucks Royal Bank-3
89ProCards AHL-301
96Devils Team Issue-NNO
97Devils Team Issue-30
98Devils Team Issue-6
99Devils Team Issue-28
00Devils Team Issue-28
01Devils Team Issue-4
02Devils Team Issue-29
03Devils Team Issue-46
05Devils Team Issue-2
06Devils Team Set-32

Caron, Jason
05Rimouski Oceanic-18

Caron, Jeff
05Saint John's Sea Dogs-10

Caron, Jordan
06Rimouski Oceanic-16

Caron, Martin
907th Inn. Sketch QMJHL-203

Caron, Michel
01Sorel Royaux-3

Caron, Pat
907th Inn. Sketch Memorial Cup-64
98San Antonio Iguanas-7

Caron, Reaume
93Quebec Pee-Wee Tournament-243

Caron, Sebastien
93Quebec Pee-Wee Tournament-15
93Quebec Pee-Wee Tournament-432
99Rimouski Oceanic-19
Signed-19
00Black Diamond-74
Gold-74
00Upper Deck-209
Exclusives Tier 1-209
Exclusives Tier 2-209
00Upper Deck Ice-54
Immortals-54
Legends-54
Stars-54
00QMJHL All-Star Program Inserts-3
00Wilkes-Barre Scranton Penguins-4
01Wilkes-Barre Scranton Penguins-19
02Pacific Calder-89
Silver-89
02Pacific Complete-517
Red-517
02Titanium-131
Blue-131
Red-131
Retail-131
02UD Mask Collection-71
02UD Mask Collection Beckett Promos-71
02UD Premier Collection-44A
02Upper Deck Rookie Update-81
02Wilkes-Barre Scranton Penguins-23
03BAP Memorabilia-163
Emerald-163
Gold-163
Ruby-163
Sapphire-163
Deep in the Crease-D15
03Beehive-157
Gold-157
Silver-157
03Black Diamond-17
Black-17
Green-17
Red-17
03Bowman-37
Gold-37
03Bowman Chrome-37
Refractors-37
Gold Refractors-37
Xfractors-37
03ITG Action-406
03Pacific Complete-462
Red-462
03Pacific Supreme-78
Blue-78
Red-78
Retail-78
03Private Stock Reserve-82
Blue-82
Red-82
Retail-82
03SPx-79
Radiance-79
Spectrum-79
Big Futures-BF-CN
Big Futures Limited-BF-CN
03Titanium-80
Hobby Jersey Number Parallels-80
Retail-80
Retail Jersey Number Parallels-80
03Topps Pristine Mini-PM-SC
03Upper Deck-403
Canadian Exclusives-403
HG-403
UD Exclusives-403
03Upper Deck Classic Portraits-79
03Upper Deck MVP-342
Gold Script-342
Silver Script-342
Canadian Exclusives-342
03Upper Deck Rookie Update-70
03Upper Deck Trilogy-79
Limited-79
03Upper Deck Victory-153
Bronze-153
Gold-153
Silver-153
04Rimouski Oceanic Season Ticket-2
05Parkhurst-389
Facsimile Auto Parallel-389
05Upper Deck-403
05WBS Penguins-4

Caron, Vincent
93Quebec Pee-Wee Tournament-1056

Carone, Nick
92Norwegian Elite Series-5

Carpano, Andrea
93Sault Ste. Marie Greyhounds-1

Carpenter, Bobby
81Capitals Team Issue-2
82Capitals Team Issue-3
82O-Pee-Chee-361
82O-Pee-Chee Stickers-154
82Post Cereal-20
82Topps Stickers-154
83NHL Key Tags-128
83O-Pee-Chee-366
83O-Pee-Chee Stickers-206
83Puffy Stickers-20
83Topps Stickers-206
84Capitals Pizza Hut-1
84O-Pee-Chee-194
84O-Pee-Chee Stickers-132
85Capitals Pizza Hut-1
85O-Pee-Chee-26
85O-Pee-Chee Box Bottoms-C
85O-Pee-Chee Stickers-112
85Topps-26
85Topps Box Bottoms-C
86Capitals Police-3
86O-Pee-Chee-150
86O-Pee-Chee Stickers-250
86Topps-150
87O-Pee-Chee-30
87Topps-30
88Kings Smokey-3
88O-Pee-Chee-72
88O-Pee-Chee Stickers-153
88Panini Stickers-74
88Topps-72
89Bruins Sports Action-5
89O-Pee-Chee-167
89Panini Stickers-196
89Topps-167
89Swedish Semic World Champ Stickers-168
90Bowman-30
Tiffany-30
90Bruins Sports Action-7
90O-Pee-Chee-139
90Panini Stickers-7
90Pro Set-4
90Score-16
Canadian-16
90Topps-139
Tiffany-139
90Upper Deck-158
French-158
91Pro Set Platinum-154
91Bruins Sports Action-5
91O-Pee-Chee-404
91OPC Premier-148
91Panini Stickers-181
91Parkhurst-226
French-226
91Pinnacle-99
91Pinnacle-396
French-99
French-396
91Pro Set-349
French-349
91Score American-162
91Score Canadian Bilingual-162
91Score Canadian English-162
91Stadium Club-161
91Topps-404
92Bowman-10
92Capitals Kodak-5
92O-Pee-Chee-131
92OPC Premier-78
92Panini Stickers-140
92Panini Stickers French-140
92Pinnacle-315
French-315
92Score-142
Canadian-142
92Stadium Club-122
92Topps-378
Gold-378G
92Upper Deck-478
93Leaf-421
93OPC Premier-413
Gold-413
93Score-267
93Score-578
Gold-578
Canadian-267
Canadian-578
93Stadium Club-175
Members Only Master Set-175
OPC-175
First Day Issue-175
First Day Issue OPC-175
93Topps/OPC Premier-413
Gold-413
94Hockey Wit-68
94Leaf-436
94Parkhurst SE-SE96
Gold-SE96
94Pinnacle-201
Artist's Proofs-201
Rink Collection-201
94Stadium Club-158
Members Only Master Set-158
First Day Issue-158
Super Team Winner Cards-158
95Be A Player-11
Signatures-S11
Signatures Die Cuts-S11
95Canada Games NHL POGS-156
95Ultra-188
Gold Medallion-188
95Upper Deck-183
Electric Ice-183
Electric Ice Gold-183
96Be A Player-125
Autographs-125
Autographs Silver-125
96Devils Team Issue-19
97Devils Team Issue-14
97Pacific Invincible NHL Regime-109
97Score Devils-18
Platinum-18
Premier-18
98Be A Player-228
Press Release-228
98BAP Gold-228
98BAP Autographs-228
98BAP Autographs Gold-228
98Devils Team Issue-7
99Russian Fetisov Tribute-23
99Albany River Rats-4
00Albany River Rats-25
01Albany River Rats-26
02BAP Sig Series Auto Buybacks 1998-228
02Devils Team Issue-27
03Devils Team Issue-43
04ITG Franchises US East-358
Autographs-A-BCA
06SAGE Autographs Bronze-A11

Carpenter, Doug
84Devils Postcards-NNO
88ProCards AHL-119
91ProCards-382

Carpenter, Joe
93Quebec Pee-Wee Tournament-812

Carpenter, Stephen
94North Bay Centennials-9
95Slapshot-214

Carpenter, Steven
92Northern Michigan Wildcats-2
93Northern Michigan Wildcats-3
95Richmond Renegades-12
00UK Sekonda Superleague-144
00UK Sheffield Steelers-11
02UK Coventry Blaze-3
03UK Coventry Blaze-3
03UK Coventry Blaze Calendars-3
03UK Coventry Blaze History-9
04UK Milton Keynes Lightning-2
04UK Steven Carpenter Testimonial-1
04UK Steven Carpenter Testimonial-2
04UK Steven Carpenter Testimonial-3
04UK Steven Carpenter Testimonial-4
04UK Steven Carpenter Testimonial-5
04UK Steven Carpenter Testimonial-6
04UK Steven Carpenter Testimonial-7
04UK Steven Carpenter Testimonial-8
04UK Steven Carpenter Testimonial-9
04UK Steven Carpenter Testimonial-10

Carpentier, Benjamin
92Quebec Pee-Wee Tournament-772
98Hartford Wolf Pack-4
99Hartford Wolf Pack-3
00Charlotte Checkers-31
00Hartford Wolf Pack-4
02Hamilton Bulldogs-2
04Hamilton Bulldogs-2
05Albany River Rats-5

Carpentier, David
05Fort Wayne Komets Choice-6
05Fort Wayne Komets Sprint-2

Carpentier, Yannick
03Kalamazoo Wings-16
04Kalamazoo Wings-16

Carper, Brandon
95Toledo Storm-3
97Mobile Mysticks-11
98Mobile Mysticks-17
00Lubbock Cotton Kings-13
03Austin Ice Bats-3
04Fort Worth Brahmas-3

Carr, Adam
04UK Milton Keynes Lightning-9

Carr, Allan
95Slapshot-334
95Sarnia Sting-4
03Huntsville Channel Cats-6
04Memphis RiverKings-3

Carr, Gene
71Toronto Sun-236
74NHL Action Stamps-111
74O-Pee-Chee NHL-320
75O-Pee-Chee NHL-343
76O-Pee-Chee NHL-290
77O-Pee-Chee NHL-298
78O-Pee-Chee-14
78Topps-14

Carr, Lorne
34Beehive Group I Photos-218
34Beehive Group I Photos-304
35Diamond Matchbooks Tan 1-9
35Diamond Matchbooks Tan 2-7
35Diamond Matchbooks Tan 3-7
37V356 Worldwide Gum-26
39O-Pee-Chee V301-1-62
45Quaker Oats Photos-13
03BAP Ultimate Mem Maple Leafs Forever-16
05ITG Ultimate Mem Amazing Amerks Autos-2
06ITG Ultimate Memorabilia Amazing Amerks Autos-4

Carr, Mike
92Ottawa 67's-6

Carrabba, Tina
98New Hampshire Wildcats-8

Carragher, Nathan
93Quebec Pee-Wee Tournament-1215

Carre, Dominic
93Quebec Pee-Wee Tournament-1647

Carrie, Dave
87Sudbury Wolves-15
89Sault Ste. Marie Greyhounds-19

Carrier, Eric
93Quebec Pee-Wee Tournament-427
93Quebec Pee-Wee Tournament-1035

Carrier, Johny
93Quebec Pee-Wee Tournament-943

Carrier, Jonathan
04Gatineau Olympiques-9
05Gatineau Olympiques-11
06Gatineau Olympiques-4

Carrier, Mario
93Drummondville Voltigeurs-26

Carrier, Nicolas
93Quebec Pee-Wee Tournament-1030

Carriere, Daniel
02Pee Dee Pride RBI-134
03Kalamazoo Wings-8
04Kalamazoo Wings-8
04Kalamazoo Wings-25
05Kalamazoo Wings-7

Carriere, Jason
99Indianapolis Ice-3

Carriere, Larry
72O-Pee-Chee-282
72Sabres Postcards-2
73O-Pee-Chee-260
74NHL Action Stamps-46
74O-Pee-Chee NHL-43
74Sabres Postcards-2
74Topps-43
75O-Pee-Chee NHL-154
75Topps-154
76O-Pee-Chee NHL-297
77Canucks Royal Bank-2
77O-Pee-Chee NHL-304
78O-Pee-Chee-272
92Sport-Flash-2
92Sport-Flash Autographs-2

Carriere, Patrick
05Knoxville Ice Bears-2

Carriere, Rick
97Medicine Hat Tigers-6
98Medicine Hat Tigers-6

Carriere, Tom
92Western Michigan Broncos-7
93Western Michigan Broncos-7

Carrigan, Ryan
05Rockford Ice Hogs-4
06Rio Grande Valley Killer Bees-4

Carrol, Lorne
24Crescent Falcon-Tigers-9

Carroll, Andrew
04Sioux Falls Stampede-1-1

Carroll, Billy
83Islanders Team Issue-3
83O-Pee-Chee-5

84Islanders News-4
84Oilers Red Rooster-20
84Oilers Team Issue-2
85O-Pee-Chee-203
85O-Pee-Chee Stickers-224
88Oilers Tenth Anniversary-16
00Upper Deck Vintage Dynasty: A Piece of History-GC
00Upper Deck Vintage Dynasty: A Piece of History Gold-GC

Carroll, Fred
94German First League-612

Carroll, George
24C144 Champ's Cigarettes-12
24V130 Maple Crispette-20
24V145-2-42

Carroll, Greg
78Capitals Team Issue-2
79O-Pee-Chee-184
79Topps-184

Carroll, Ken
94Sarnia Sting-2
95Slapshot-181
02Bossier-Shreveport Mudbugs-7
03Bossier-Shreveport Mudbugs-8
05Bossier-Shreveport Mudbugs-5

Carroll, Marcus
05Owen Sound Attack-16
06Owen Sound Attack-17

Carruthers, Dwight
69Seattle Totems-18

Carruthers, Robin
02Columbia Inferno-99
03Columbia Inferno-101

Carse, Bill
34Beehive Group I Photos-44
39O-Pee-Chee V301-1-80

Carse, Bob
34Beehive Group I Photos-45
43Parade Sportive *-22
45Quaker Oats Photos-67

Carsky, Milan
04Slovakian Skalica Team Set-7

Carson, Brett
03Calgary Hitmen-2
05Calgary Hitmen-2
06Albany River Rats-23

Carson, Davie
93Seattle Thunderbirds-3
95Halifax Mooseheads-14

Carson, Gerald
33V252 Canadian Gum-8
33V357 Ice Kings-24
34Beehive Group I Photos-192
34Diamond Matchbooks Silver-9
34Sweet Caporal-1
35Diamond Matchbooks Tan 1-10

Carson, Jimmy
86Kings 20th Anniversary Team Issue-2
87O-Pee-Chee-92
87O-Pee-Chee Minis-6
87O-Pee-Chee Stickers-126
87O-Pee-Chee Stickers-210
87Panini Stickers-279
87Topps-92
88Oilers Tenth Anniversary-53
88Oilers Team Issue-5
88O-Pee-Chee-9
88O-Pee-Chee Minis-5
88O-Pee-Chee Stickers-158
88Panini Stickers-75
88Topps-9
89O-Pee-Chee-127
89O-Pee-Chee Stickers-222
89Panini Stickers-72
89Red Wings Little Caesars-3
89Topps-127
89Swedish Semic World Champ Stickers-163
90Bowman-229
Tiffany-229
90Kraft-5
90O-Pee-Chee-231
90OPC Premier-12
90Panini Stickers-214
90Pro Set-67
90Score-64
Canadian-64
90Score Hottest/Rising Stars-28
90Topps-231
Tiffany-231
90Upper Deck-132
French-132
91Pro Set Platinum-33
91Bowman-52
91O-Pee-Chee-104
91OPC Premier-167
91Panini Stickers-139
91Parkhurst-43
French-43
91Pinnacle-173
French-173
91Pro Set-55
French-55
91Red Wings Little Caesars-2
91Score American-224
91Score Canadian Bilingual-224
91Score Canadian English-224
91Stadium Club-121
91Topps-104
91Upper Deck-161
French-161
91Finnish Semic World Champ Stickers-150
91Swedish Semic World Champ Stickers-150
92Bowman-108
92O-Pee-Chee-152
92Panini Stickers-114
92Panini Stickers French-114
92Parkhurst-308
Emerald Ice-308
92Pinnacle-329
French-329
92Score-9
Canadian-9
Sharpshooters-9
Sharpshooters Canadian-9
92Stadium Club-277
92Topps-398
Gold-398G
92Ultra-45
92Upper Deck-253
93Donruss-159
93Donruss-500
93Leaf-149
93OPC Premier-376
Gold-376
93Panini Stickers-204
93Parkhurst-368
Emerald Ice-368
93Pinnacle-285
Canadian-285
93PowerPlay-114
93Score-109
93Score-572
Gold-572
Canadian-109
Canadian-572
Canadian Gold-572
93Stadium Club-118
Members Only Master Set-118
OPC-118
First Day Issue-118
First Day Issue OPC-118
93Topps/OPC Premier-376
Gold-376
93Ultra-42
93Swedish Semic World Champ Stickers-187
94Fleer-85
94Hockey Wit-62
94OPC Premier-326
Special Effects-326
94Parkhurst-239
Gold-239
94Parkhurst SE-SE69
Gold-SE69
94Pinnacle-436
Artist's Proofs-436
Rink Collection-436
94Topps/OPC Premier-326
Special Effects-326
94Ultra-299
94Upper Deck-198
Electric Ice-198
95Collector's Choice-180
Player's Club-180
Player's Club Platinum-180
95Donruss-359
95Leaf-308
95Panini Stickers-26
97Detroit Vipers-12

Carson, Keith
95Neepewa Natives-19

Carson, Lindsay
83Flyers J.C. Penney-4
83O-Pee-Chee-261
83O-Pee-Chee Stickers-181
83Topps Stickers-181
85Flyers Postcards-3
86Flyers Postcards-3
87Flyers Postcards-18
88ProCards AHL-58

Carson, Pete
97Columbus Cottonmouths-24
98Columbus Cottonmouths-23

Carteciano, Guy
06Owen Sound Attack-7

Cartelli, Mario
98Czech OFS-388
99Czech OFS-192
00Czech DS Extraliga-64
00Czech OFS-214
01Czech DS-4
01Czech OFS-49
All Stars-9
02Czech OFS Plus-316
03Czech OFS Plus-200
04Czech HC Plzen Postcards-3
04Czech OFS-139
05Czech HC Plzen-2
06Czech OFS-270

Carter, Anson
92Michigan State Spartans-6
93Donruss Team Canada-7
93Pinnacle-469
Canadian-469
93Upper Deck-531
93Michigan State Spartans-4
96Leaf Preferred-146
Press Proofs-146
96Select Certified-94
Artist's Proofs-94
Blue-94
Mirror Blue-94
Mirror Gold-94
Mirror Red-94
Red-94
96Upper Deck-358
96Zenith-122
Artist's Proofs-122
96Portland Pirates-33
97Be A Player-67
Autographs-67
Autographs Die-Cuts-67
Autographs Prismatic Die-Cuts-67
97Collector's Choice-13
97Crown Royale-8
Emerald Green-8
Ice Blue-8
Silver-8
97Donruss-118
Press Proofs Silver-118
Press Proofs Gold-118
97Donruss Canadian Ice-73
Dominion Series-73
Provincial Series-73
97Donruss Limited-107
Exposure-107
97Donruss Preferred-29
Cut to the Chase-29
97Donruss Priority-89
Stamp of Approval-89
97Leaf-85
Fractal Matrix-85
Fractal Matrix Die Cuts-85
97Leaf International-85
Universal Ice-85
97Pacific-131
Copper-131
Emerald Green-131
Ice Blue-131
Red-131
Silver-131
97Pacific Omega-13
Copper-13
Dark Gray-13
Emerald Green-13
Gold-13
Ice Blue-13
97Paramount-11
Copper-11
Dark Grey-11
Emerald Green-11
Ice Blue-11
Red-11
Silver-11
97Pinnacle Inside-171
97Score-226
97Score Bruins-8
Platinum-8
Premier-8
97Studio-33
Press Proofs Silver-33
Press Proofs Gold-33
97Upper Deck-11
98Aurora-9
98Finest-21
No Protectors-21
No Protectors Refractors-21
Refractors-21
98Katch-12
98Pacific-73
Ice Blue-73
Red-73
98Pacific Dynagon Ice-10
Blue-10
Red-10
98Pacific Omega-13
Red-13
Opening Day Issue-13
98Paramount-11
Copper-11
Emerald Green-11
Holo-Electric-11
Ice Blue-11
Silver-11
98Revolution-8
Ice Shadow-8
Red-8
98Upper Deck MVP-18
Gold Script-18
Silver Script-18
Super Script-18
99Aurora-11
Premiere Date-11
99BAP Memorabilia-26
Gold-26
Silver-26
99O-Pee-Chee-203
99O-Pee-Chee Chrome-203
99O-Pee-Chee Chrome Refractors-203
99O-Pee-Chee Now Starring-NS1
99Pacific-21
Copper-21
Emerald Green-21
Gold-21
Ice Blue-21
Premiere Date-21
Red-21
99Pacific Dynagon Ice-22
Blue-22
Copper-22
Gold-22
Premiere Date-22
99Pacific Omega-19
Copper-19
Gold-19
Ice Blue-19
Premiere Date-19
99Panini Stickers-22
99Paramount-18
Copper-18
Emerald-18
Gold-18
Holographic Emerald-18
Holographic Gold-18
Holographic Silver-18
Ice Blue-18
Premiere Date-18
Red-18
Silver-18
99Revolution-12
Premiere Date-12
Red-12
Shadow Series-12
99Stadium Club-138
First Day Issue-138
One of a Kind-138
Printing Plates Black-138
Printing Plates Cyan-138
Printing Plates Magenta-138
Printing Plates Yellow-138
Chrome-38
Chrome Refractors-38
99Topps/OPC-203
Now Starring-NS1
99Topps/OPC Chrome-203
Refractors-203
99Topps Gold Label Fresh Gold-FG7
99Topps Gold Label Fresh Gold Black-FG7
99Topps Gold Label Fresh Gold Black 1of1-FG7
99Topps Gold Label Fresh Gold One of One-FG7
99Topps Gold Label Fresh Gold Red-FG7
99Topps Gold Label Fresh Gold Red 1 of 1-FG7
99Topps Premier Plus-69
Parallel-69
99Upper Deck-187
Exclusives-187
Exclusives 1 of 1-187
99Upper Deck Gold Reserve-187
99Upper Deck MVP-14
Gold Script-14
Silver Script-14
Super Script-14
99Upper Deck Victory-28
00SLU Hockey-50
00Aurora-10
Premiere Date-10
00BAP Memorabilia-43
Emerald-43
Ruby-43
Sapphire-43
Promos-43
00BAP Mem Chicago Sportsfest Copper-43
00BAP Memorabilia Chicago Sportsfest Blue-43
00BAP Memorabilia Chicago Sportsfest Gold-43
00BAP Memorabilia Chicago Sportsfest Ruby-43
00BAP Memorabilia Chicago Sun-Times Ruby-43
00BAP Memorabilia Chicago Sun-Times Gold-43
00BAP Mem Chicago Sun-Times Sapphire-43
00BAP Mem Toronto Fall Expo Copper-43
00BAP Memorabilia Toronto Fall Expo Gold-43
00BAP Memorabilia Toronto Fall Expo Ruby-43
00BAP Parkhurst 2000-P159
00BAP Signature Series-72
Emerald-72
Ruby-72
Sapphire-72
00Black Diamond-98
00O-Pee-Chee-40
00O-Pee-Chee Parallel-40
00Pacific-31
Copper-31
Gold-31
Ice Blue-31
Premiere Date-31
00Panini Stickers-13
00Paramount-17
Copper-17
Gold-17
Holo-Gold-17
Holo-Silver-17
Ice Blue-17
Premiere Date-17
00Private Stock Game Gear-48
00Private Stock Game Gear Patches-48
00Revolution-9
Blue-9
Premiere Date-9
Red-9
Game-Worn Jerseys-2
Game-Worn Jersey Patches-2
00SP Authentic Sign of the Times-AC
00SPx Winning Materials-AC
00Stadium Club-119
Co-Signers-CO4
Lone Star Signatures-LS7
00Titanium Draft Day Edition-43
00Topps/OPC-40
Parallel-40
NHL Draft-D9
00Topps Chrome-32
OPC Refractors-32
Refractors-32
00Topps Gold Label Class 1-90
Gold-90
00Topps Gold Label Class 2-90
00Topps Gold Label Class 2 Gold-90
00Topps Gold Label Class 3-90
00Topps Gold Label Class 3 Gold-90
00Topps Heritage-215
00Upper Deck Ice Game Jerseys-JCAC
00Upper Deck Victory-23
00Vanguard-42
Holographic Gold-42
Holographic Purple-42
Pacific Proofs-42
01BAP Memorabilia-16
Emerald-16
Ruby-16
Sapphire-16
01BAP Signature Series-11
Autographs-11
Autographs Gold-11
01Bowman YoungStars-105
Gold-105
Ice Cubed-105
01Crown Royale-58
Blue-58
Premiere Date-58
Red-58
Retail-58
01O-Pee-Chee-198
01O-Pee-Chee Premier Parallel-198
01Pacific-153
Extreme LTD-153
Hobby LTD-153
Premiere Date-153
Retail LTD-153
01Pacific Adrenaline-72
Blue-72
Premiere Date-72
Red-72
Retail-72
01Pacific Arena Exclusives-153
01Parkhurst-107
01Private Stock Game Gear-46
01Private Stock Game Gear Patches-46
01SP Game Used Tools of the Game-TAC
01SP Game Used Tools of the Game-CTCS
01SP Game Used Tools of the Game-TTFCF
01Titanium-55
Hobby Parallel-55
Premiere Date-55
Retail-55
Retail Parallel-55
01Topps-198
OPC Parallel-198
01Topps Chrome-125
Refractors-125
Black Border Refractors-125
01Topps Heritage-80
Refractors-80
01UD Mask Collection-38
Gold-38
01UD Playmakers-42
01Upper Deck-296
Exclusives-296
01Upper Deck MVP-73
01Upper Deck Victory-135
Gold-135
01Upper Deck Vintage-103
02BAP First Edition-197
02BAP Memorabilia-25
02BAP Memorabilia-356
Emerald-25
Ruby-25
Sapphire-25
NHL All-Star Game-25
NHL All-Star Game Blue-25
NHL All-Star Game Green-25
NHL All-Star Game Red-25
02BAP Memorabilia Toronto Fall Expo-25
02BAP Sig Series Auto Buybacks 2001-11
02Bowman YoungStars-59
Gold-59
Silver-59
02Crown Royale-38
Blue-38
Red-38
Retail-38
02McDonald's Pacific-14
02NHL Power Play Stickers-27
02Oilers Postcards-9
02O-Pee-Chee-33
02O-Pee-Chee Premier Blue Parallel-33
02O-Pee-Chee Premier Red Parallel-33
02O-Pee-Chee Factory Set-33
02O-Pee-Chee Factory Set Hometown Heroes-HHC15
02Pacific-139
Blue-139
Red-139
02Pacific Complete-319
Red-319
02Pacific Exclusive-69
02Pacific Quest for the Cup-64
Gold-64
02Parkhurst-30
Bronze-30
Gold-30
Silver-30
College Ranks-CR15
College Ranks Jerseys-CRM15
02Parkhurst Retro-71
Minis-71
02Private Stock Reserve-38
Blue-38
Red-38
Retail-38
02SP Authentic-39
Beckett Promos-39
02Titanium-41
Blue-41
Red-41
Retail-41
02Topps-33
OPC Blue Parallel-33
OPC Red Parallel-33
Topps/OPC Hometown Heroes-HHC15
Factory Set-33
02Topps Chrome-33
Black Border Refractors-33
Refractors-33
02Topps Total-174
02Upper Deck-73
Exclusives-73
02Upper Deck MVP-71
Gold-71
Classics-71
Golden Classics-71
02Upper Deck Victory-82
Bronze-82
Gold-82
Silver-82
02Upper Deck Vintage-106
02Vanguard-41
LTD-41
03McFarlane Hockey-10
03McFarlane Hockey-12
03BAP Memorabilia-10
Emerald-10
Gold-10
Ruby-10
Sapphire-10
03BAP Ultimate Memorabilia Autographs-16
Gold-16
03Beehive-128
Gold-128
Silver-128
Signatures-RF12
03Black Diamond-129
Black-129
Green-129
Red-129
03ITG Action-336
Homeboys-HB12
03ITG Used Signature Series-60
Gold-60
Autographs-AC1
Autographs-AC2
Autographs Gold-AC1
Autographs Gold-AC2
03Kraft-2
03NHL Sticker Collection-223
03O-Pee-Chee-41
03OPC Blue-41
03OPC Gold-41
03OPC Red-41
03Pacific-222
Blue-222
Red-222
03Pacific Complete-69
Red-69
03Pacific Exhibit-96
Blue Backs-96
Yellow Backs-96
03Pacific Supreme-65
Blue-65
Red-65
Retail-65
03Parkhurst Original Six Boston-59
03Parkhurst Original Six New York-5
Memorabilia-NM58
03Rangers Team Issue-3
03SP Game Used-110
Gold-110
03Topps-41
Blue-41
Gold-41
Red-41
03Topps C55-22
Minis-22
Minis American Back-22
Minis American Back Red-22
Minis Bazooka Back-22
Minis Brooklyn Back-22
Minis Hat Trick Back-22
Minis O Canada Back-22
Minis O Canada Back Red-22
Minis Stanley Cup Back-22
03Topps Traded-TT64
Blue-TT64
Gold-TT64
Red-TT64
03UD Premier Collection Signatures-PS-AC
03UD Premier Collection Signatures Gold-PS-AC
03Upper Deck-125
Canadian Exclusives-125
HG-125
03Upper Deck Ice-89
Gold-89
Authentics-IA-AC
03Upper Deck MVP-277
Gold Script-277
Silver Script-277
Canadian Exclusives-277
03Upper Deck Rookie Update-89
03Upper Deck Victory-122
Bronze-122
Gold-122
Silver-122
03Czech Stadion-529
03Russian World Championship Stars-17
03Toronto Star-59
05Black Diamond Gemography-G-AC
05Black Diamond Gemography Emerald-G-AC
05Black Diamond Gemography Gold-G-AC
05Black Diamond Gemography Onyx-G-AC
05Black Diamond Gemography Ruby-G-AC
05Parkhurst-471
Facsimile Auto Parallel-471
05UD Powerplay Power Marks-PMAC
05Ultra-195
Gold-195
Ice-195
05Upper Deck-434
Big Playmakers-B-AC
Jerseys Series II-J2AC
Notable Numbers-N-AC
05Upper Deck Hockey Showcase-HS20
05Upper Deck Showcase Promos-HS20
05Upper Deck MVP-372
Gold-372
Platinum-372
06O-Pee-Chee-152
Rainbow-152
06Upper Deck Victory-242

Carter, Billy
60Shirriff Coins-115
63Quebec Aces-4

Carter, Dan
95Toledo Storm-6
96Dayton Ice Bandits-5
97El Paso Buzzards-17

Carter, Jeff
92Quebec Pee-Wee Tournament-362
02Sault Ste. Marie Greyhounds-4
03BAP Memorabilia Draft Redemptions-11
03Sault Ste. Marie Greyhounds-9
04SP Authentic Rookie Redemptions-RR22
04Sault Ste. Marie Greyhounds-6
04ITG Heroes and Prospects-78
Aspiring-11
Autographs-JC
Combos-10
Emblems-4
Emblems Gold-4
He Shoots-He Scores Prizes-25
Jersey Autographs-4
Jerseys-4
Jerseys Gold-4
National Pride-2
Numbers-4
Numbers Gold-4
04ITG Heroes/Prospects Toronto Expo '05-78
04ITG Heroes/Prospects Expo Heroes/Pros-78
05ITG Heroes/Prosp Toronto Expo Parallel -63
05ITG Heroes/Prosp Toronto Expo Parallel -340
05ITG Heroes/Prosp Toronto Expo Parallel -365
05Beehive-103
Beige -103
Blue -103
Gold-103
Red -103
Rookie Jumbos-R3
Matte-103
PhotoGraphs-PGJC
Signature Scrapbook-SSJC
05Black Diamond-195
Emerald-195
Gold-195
Onyx-195
Ruby-195
05Flyers Team Issue-3
05Hot Prospects-257
En Fuego-257
Hot Materials-HMJC
Red Hot-257
White Hot-257
05Panini Stickers-138
05Parkhurst-653
Facsimile Auto Parallel-653
True Colors-TCPHI
True Colors-TCPHI
05SP Authentic-177
Limited-177
Exquisite Endorsements-EEJC
Octographs-OR
Prestigious Pairings-PPCR
Rarefied Rookies-RRJC
Rookie Authentics-RAJC
Sign of the Times Triples-TPGC
Sign of the Times Triples-TSOC
Sign of the Times Quads-QSOPC
Sign of the Times Fives-PEGCR
Sign of the Times Fives-POCLS
Six Star Signatures-SSRO
05SP Game Used-113
Autographs-113
Gold-113
Auto Draft-AD-JE
Game Gear-GG-JC
Game Gear Autographs-AG-JC
Rookie Exclusives-JC
Rookie Exclusives Silver-RE-JC
Significant Numbers-SN-JC
05SPx-189
Spectrum-189
Xcitement Rookies-XR-JC
Xcitement Rookies Gold-XR-JC
Xcitement Rookies Spectrum-XR-JC
05The Cup-176
Autographed Rookie Patches Gold Rainbow-176
Black Rainbow Rookies-176
Dual NHL Shields-DSJM
Dual NHL Shields Autographs-ADSJM
Honorable Numbers-HNJC
Masterpiece Pressplates (Artifacts)-222
Masterpiece Pressplates (Bee Hive)-103
Masterpiece Pressplates (Black Diamond)-195
Masterpiece Pressplates (Ice)-104
Masterpiece Pressplates (MVP)-407
Masterpiece Pressplates (Power Play)-163
Masterpiece Pressplates Rookie Upd Auto-272
Masterpiece Pressplates SPA Autos-177
Masterpiece Pressplates (SP Game Used)-113
Masterpiece Pressplates SPx Autos-189
Masterpiece Pressplates (Trilogy)-207
Masterpiece Pressplates Ult Coll Autos-95
Masterpiece Pressplates (Victory)-272
Masterpiece Pressplates Autographs-176
Noble Numbers-NNKC
Platinum Rookies-176
Scripted Numbers-SNKC
Scripted Swatches-SSJC
Signature Patches-SPJC
05UD Artifacts-222
Gold-RED22
05UD PowerPlay-163
05UD Rookie Class-13
Commemorative Boxtoppers-CC-7
05Ultimate Collection-95
Autographed Patches-95
Autographed Shields-95
Jerseys-JJC
Jerseys Dual-DJCR
Jerseys Triple-TJFGC
Marquee Attractions-MA35
Marquee Attractions Signatures-SMA35
Premium Patches-PPJC
Premium Swatches-PSJC
Ultimate Debut Threads Jerseys-DTJJC
Ultimate Debut Threads Jerseys Autos-DAJJC
Ultimate Debut Threads Patches-DTPJC
Ultimate Debut Threads Patches Autos-DAPJC
Ultimate Patches-PJC
Ultimate Patches Dual-DPCR
Ultimate Patches Triple-TPFGC
Ultimate Signatures-USJC
Ultimate Signatures Logos-SLJC
Ultimate Signatures Pairings-UPCR
Ultimate Signatures Trios-UTSOC
05Ultra-254
Gold-254
Difference Makers-DM5
Difference Makers Jerseys-DMJ-JC
Difference Makers Jersey Autographs-DAJ-JC
Difference Makers Patches-DMP-JC
Difference Makers Patch Autographs-DAP-JC
Fresh Ink-FI-JC
Fresh Ink Blue-FI-JC
Ice-254
Rookie Uniformity Jerseys-RU-JC
Rookie Uniformity Jersey Autographs-ARU-JC
Rookie Uniformity Patches-RUP-JC
Rookie Uniformity Patch Autographs-ARP-JC
05Upper Deck-444
05Upper Deck-487
Majestic Materials-MMJC
Rookie Ink-RIJC
05Upper Deck Rookie Showcase-RS22
05Upper Deck Rookie Showcase Promos-RS22
05Upper Deck Rookie Threads-RTJC
05Upper Deck Rookie Threads Autographs-ARTJC
05Upper Deck Stars in the Making-SM3
05Upper Deck Ice-104
Cool Threads-CTJC
Cool Threads Autographs-ACTJC
Cool Threads Glass-CTJC
Cool Threads Patches-CTPJC
Cool Threads Patch Autographs-CAPJC
Glacial Graphs-GGJC
Premieres Auto Patches-AIPJC
Signature Swatches-SSJC
05Upper Deck MVP-407
Gold-407
Platinum-407
Rookie Breakthrough-RB3
05Upper Deck Rookie Update-272
05Upper Deck Trilogy-207
05Upper Deck Victory-272
Black-272
Gold-272
Silver-272
05ITG Heroes and Prospects-63
05ITG Heroes and Prospects-340
05ITG Heroes and Prospects-365
Aspiring-ASP12
Autographs-A-JC
Autographs-DA-CR
Autographs Series II-JC2
Autographs Series II-JC3
CHL Grads-CG-3
CHL Grads Gold-CG-3
Complete Jerseys-CJ-6
Complete Jerseys Gold-CJ-6
He Shoots-He Scores Prizes-35
Jerseys-GUJ-60
Jerseys Gold-GUJ-60
Emblems-GUE-60
Emblems Gold-GUE-60
Numbers-GUN-60
Numbers Gold-GUN-60
Making the Bigs-MTB-15
Nameplates-N-38
Nameplates Gold-N-38
National Pride-NPR-38
Spectrum-STM-05
Spectrum Gold-STM-05
06Be A Player-145
Autographs-145
Signatures-CA
Signatures 10-160
Signatures Duals-DGC
Signatures Trios-TGCR
06Be A Player Portraits-77
Dual Signature Portraits-DSGC
First Exposures-FEJC
Signature Portraits-SPJC
06Beehive-29
Matte-29
Matted Materials-MMJC
Remarkable Matted Materials-MMJC
06Black Diamond-118
Black-118
Gold-118
Ruby-118
Gemography-GCA
06Flair Showcase-75
06Flair Showcase-152
Parallel-75
Parallel-152
Wave of the Future-WF32
06Fleer-145
Tiffany-145
06Flyers Postcards-7
06Hot Prospects-72
Hot Materials -HMJC
Hot Materials Red Hot-HMJC
Hot Materials White Hot-HMJC
Hotagraphs-HJC
06McDonald's Upper Deck Rookie Review-RR9
06O-Pee-Chee-359
06O-Pee-Chee-627
Rainbow-359
Rainbow-627
Autographs-A-JC
Swatches-S-JC
06Panini Stickers-132
06SP Authentic-30
Limited-30
Sign of the Times-STJE
Sign of the Times Duals-STCC
06SP Game Used-74
Gold-74
Rainbow-74
Authentic Fabrics-AFJC
Authentic Fabrics Parallel-AFJC
Authentic Fabrics Patches-AFJC
Authentic Fabrics Dual-AF2FC
Authentic Fabrics Dual Patches-AF2FC
Authentic Fabrics Eights-AF8CEN
Authentic Fabrics Eights Patches-AF8CEN
Autographs-74
Inked Sweaters Dual-IS2GC
Inked Sweaters Dual Patches-IS2GC
Letter Marks-LMJC
SIGnificance-SJC
06SPx-74
Spectrum-74
SPxcitement-X75
SPxcitement Spectrum-X75
Winning Materials-WMCA
Winning Materials Spectrum-WMCA
Winning Materials Autographs-WMCA
06The Cup Honorable Numbers-HNJC
06The Cup Limited Logos-LLCA
06The Cup NHL Shields Duals-DSHFC
06The Cup Scripted Swatches Duals-DSGC
06UD Artifacts-30
Blue-30
Gold-30
Platinum-30
Radiance-30
Autographed Radiance Parallel-30
Red-30
Auto-Facts-AFCA
Auto-Facts Gold-AFCA
Frozen Artifacts-FAJC
Frozen Artifacts Black-FAJC
Frozen Artifacts Blue-FAJC
Frozen Artifacts Gold-FAJC
Frozen Artifacts Platinum-FAJC
Frozen Artifacts Red-FAJC
Frozen Artifacts Autographed Black-FAJC
Frozen Artifacts Patches Black-FAJC
Frozen Artifacts Patches Blue-FAJC
Frozen Artifacts Patches Gold-FAJC
Frozen Artifacts Patches Platinum-FAJC
Frozen Artifacts Patches Red-FAJC
Frozen Artifacts Patches Autographed Black Tag Parallel-FAJC
Tundra Tandems-TTGC
Tundra Tandems Black-TTGC
Tundra Tandems Blue-TTGC
Tundra Tandems Gold-TTGC
Tundra Tandems Platinum-TTGC
Tundra Tandems Red-TTGC
Tundra Tandems Dual Patches Red-TTGC
06UD Mini Jersey Collection-76
06UD Powerplay-75
Impact Rainbow-75
06UD Toronto Fall Expo Priority Signings -PSJC
06Ultra-145
Gold Medallion-145
Ice Medallion-145
06Upper Deck Arena Giveaways-PHI6
06Upper Deck-392
Exclusives Parallel-392
High Gloss Parallel-392
Game Jerseys-J2JC
Game Patches-P2JC
Generations Triples-G3SSC
Generations Patches Triple-G3PSSC
Masterpieces-392
Oversized Wal-Mart Exclusives-392
06Upper Deck MVP-213
Gold Script-213
Super Script-213
Autographs-OACR
Jerseys-OJCG
06Upper Deck Ovation-85
06Upper Deck Sweet Shot Signature Shots/Saves-SSJC
06Upper Deck Sweet Shot Signature Shots/Saves Sticks-SSSJE
06Upper Deck Trilogy-72
Combo Clearcut Autographs-C3PGC
Honorary Scripted Patches-HSPCA
Honorary Scripted Swatches-HSSCA
06Upper Deck Victory-148
06Upper Deck Victory Black-148
06Upper Deck Victory Gold-148
06Upper Deck Victory GameBreakers-GB37
06Upper Deck Victory Next In Line-NL37
06ITG Heroes and Prospects-18
Autographs-AJCA
07Upper Deck Ovation-13
07Upper Deck Victory-28
Black-28
Gold-28

Carter, John
86Moncton Golden Flames-28
88Bruins Postcards-3
88ProCards AHL-163
89Bruins Sports Action-6
90Bowman-39
Tiffany-39
90Bruins Sports Action-8
90Panini Stickers-8
90Pro Set-5
90Score-283
Canadian-283
90Upper Deck-211
French-211
91O-Pee-Chee-300
91Score Canadian Bilingual-557
91Score Canadian English-557
91Score Rookie/Traded-7T
91Topps-300
92Ultra-399
04Sioux City Musketeers-5

Carter, Lyle
71Toronto Sun-44

Carter, Mike
05Odessa Jackalopes-3

Carter, Quinn
98Arizona Icecats-3

Carter, Ron
88Oilers Tenth Anniversary-98

Carter, Ryan
02Indianapolis Ice-3
03Indianapolis Ice-4
06Portland Pirates-21
06ITG Heroes and Prospects-169
Autographs-ARC
Update Autographs-ARC

Carter, Shawn
91British Columbia JHL-97
96St. John's Maple Leafs-8
97St. John's Maple Leafs-6
98Orlando Solar Bears-6
98Orlando Solar Bears II-3
02German DEL City Press-4
02German DEL City Press-5
02German DEL City Press-6
03German DEL-19
04German Augsburg Panthers Postcards-9
04German DEL-26
05German DEL-245
06German DEL-158

Carter, Steve
96Fort Worth Fire-2
97Fort Worth Brahmas-2
98Fort Worth Brahmas-20

Carter, Warren
95Alaska Gold Kings-5

Cartera, John
04Sioux City Musketeers-5

Caruso, Brian
93Minnesota-Duluth Bulldogs-5
95Central Hockey League-3
95Fort Worth Fire-16
96Fort Worth Fire-10
97Fort Worth Brahmas-3

Caruso, Dave
02Ohio State Buckeyes-20
03Ohio State Buckeyes-6
04Ohio State Buckeyes-6
05Ohio State Buckeyes-5

Caruso, Jamie
897th Inn. Sketch OHL-156
907th Inn. Sketch OHL-305
917th Inn. Sketch OHL-88

Caruso, Michael
04Guelph Storm-2
05Guelph Storm-C-01
06Guelph Storm-22
06ITG Heroes and Prospects-182
Autographs-AMCA
Update Autographs-AMCA

Carvel, Tim
93RPI Engineers-5

Carver, Andrew
99Hull Olympiques-2
Signed-2

99Bowman CHL-65
Gold-65
OPC International-65
00Hull Olympiques-2
Signed-2
01Moncton Wildcats-2

Carver, Orrin
52Juniors Blue Tint-97

Carveth, Joe
34Beehive Group I Photos-95
40O-Pee-Chee V301-2-123
43Parade Sportive *-23
44Beehive Group II Photos-227
45Quaker Oats Photos-68
51Cleveland Barons-9
76Old Timers-4

Carvil, Stewart
93UK Humberside Hawks-7

Casale, Agostino
96German DEL-122
99German Bundesliga 2-190

Casavant, Denys
43Parade Sportive *-24
43Parade Sportive *-25

Casavant, Mario
77Granby Vics-4

Casella, Craig
93Quebec Pee-Wee Tournament-721

Casey, Gerald
52Juniors Blue Tint-95

Casey, Jon
85North Stars Postcards-7
88North Stars ADA-4
89O-Pee-Chee-48
89O-Pee-Chee Stickers-197
89Panini Stickers-114
89Topps-48
90Bowman-183
Tiffany-183
90O-Pee-Chee-269
90O-Pee-Chee-305
90O-Pee-Chee Box Bottoms-B
90Panini Stickers-254
90Pro Set-133
90Score-182
Canadian-182
90Score Hottest/Rising Stars-80
90Topps-269
90Topps-305
Tiffany-269
90Topps Box Bottoms-B
90Upper Deck-385
French-385
91Pro Set Platinum-56
91Bowman-119
91Kraft-75
91O-Pee-Chee-237
91OPC Premier-112
91Panini Stickers-118
91Parkhurst-77
French-77
91Pinnacle-144
French-144
91Pro Set-111
French-111
91Score American-191
91Score Canadian Bilingual-191
91Score Canadian English-191
91Stadium Club-138
91Topps-237
91Upper Deck-205
French-205
92Bowman-269
92Kraft-27
92O-Pee-Chee-16
92OPC Premier Star Performers-7
92Panini Stickers-87
92Panini Stickers French-87
92Parkhurst-73
Emerald Ice-73
92Pinnacle-42
French-42
92Pro Set-82
92Score-249
Canadian-249
92Seasons Patches-64
92Stadium Club-198
92Topps-379
Gold-379G
92Ultra-90
92Upper Deck-190
92North Dakota Fighting Sioux-32
93Donruss-16
93Leaf-322
93McDonald's Upper Deck-3
93OPC Premier-437
Gold-437
93Panini Stickers-276
93Parkhurst-12
Emerald Ice-12
93Pinnacle-357
Canadian-357
All-Stars-41
All-Stars-49
All-Stars Canadian-41
All-Stars Canadian-49
93PowerPlay-17
93Score-193
93Score-526
Gold-526
Canadian-193
Canadian-526
Canadian Gold-526
93Stadium Club-303
93Stadium Club-456
Members Only Master Set-303
Members Only Master Set-456
First Day Issue-303
First Day Issue-456
All-Stars-7
All-Stars Members Only-7
All-Stars OPC-7
93Topps/OPC Premier-437
Gold-437
93Ultra-91
93Ultra-266
93Upper Deck-507
SP-8
93Upper Deck Locker All-Stars-40
94EA Sports-36
94OPC Premier-229
Special Effects-229
94Parkhurst SE-SE158
Gold-SE158
94Pinnacle-393
Artist's Proofs-393
Rink Collection-393
94Score-111
Gold-111
Platinum-111
94Stadium Club-184
Members Only Master Set-184
First Day Issue-184
Super Team Winner Cards-184
94Topps/OPC Premier-229
Special Effects-229
94Upper Deck-206
Electric Ice-206
95Panini Stickers-199
95Parkhurst International-177
Emerald Ice-177
95Playoff One on One-194
95Score-290
Black Ice Artist's Proofs-290
Black Ice-290
95Upper Deck-70
Electric Ice-70
Electric Ice Gold-70
95Peoria Rivermen-1
96Be A Player-63
Autographs-63
Autographs Silver-63
96Donruss-37
Press Proofs-37
96Leaf-89
Press Proofs-89
96Score-214
Artist's Proofs-214
Dealer's Choice Artist's Proofs-214
Special Artist's Proofs-214
Golden Blades-214
96Collector's Edge Ice-176
Prism-176
97Pacific Invincible NHL Regime-167

Cashman, Brendon
93Quebec Pee-Wee Tournament-701

Cashman, Wayne
70Bruins Postcards-4
70Bruins Team Issue-12
70Esso Power Players-63
70O-Pee-Chee-7
70O-Pee-Chee-233
70Topps-7
71Bruins Postcards-9
71O-Pee-Chee-129
71Topps-129
71Toronto Sun-6
72O-Pee-Chee-68
Team Canada-4
72Sargent Promotions Stamps-18
72Topps-29
73Mac's Milk-3
73O-Pee-Chee-85
73Topps-166
74Lipton Soup-9
74NHL Action Stamps-30
74O-Pee-Chee NHL-206
74Topps-206
75O-Pee-Chee NHL-63
75Topps-63
76O-Pee-Chee NHL-165
76Topps-165
77O-Pee-Chee NHL-234
77Topps-234
77Topps/O-Pee-Chee Glossy-1
Square-1
78O-Pee-Chee-124
78Topps-124
79O-Pee-Chee-79
79Topps-79
80O-Pee-Chee-318
81O-Pee-Chee-11
82O-Pee-Chee-8
82Post Cereal-1
91Bruins Sports Action Legends-6
91Future Trends Canada '72-25
91Future Trends Canada '72 French-25
92Lightning Sheraton-8
93Lightning Season in Review-5
94Lightning Photo Album-6
94Parkhurst Tall Boys-18
99BAP Memorabilia AS American Hobby-AH6
99BAP Memorabilia AS American Hobby Autos-AH6
01Topps Archives-31
Arena Seats-ASWC
01Topps Chrome Reprints-2
01Topps Chrome Reprint Refractors-2
01Topps Chrome Reprint Autographs-2
02Fleer Throwbacks-56
Gold-56
Platinum-56
03BAP Ultimate Memorabilia Linemates-3
03Parkhurst Original Six Boston-40
03Parkhurst Original Six Boston-79
Autographs-3
04ITG Franchises Update Original Sticks-UOS5
04ITG Franchises Upd Original Sticks Gold-UOS5
04ITG Franchises US East-318
Autographs-A-WC
04ITG Ultimate Memorabilia-109
Gold-109
Retro Teammates-13
04UD Legendary Signatures-87
Autographs-WC
Linemates-WCPEKH
Summit Stars-CDN13
Summit Stars Autographs-CDN-WC
04UD Legends Classics-53
Gold-53
Platinum-53
Silver-53
Signature Moments-M8
Signatures-CS8
Signatures-QC5
04ITG Heroes and Prospects-136
Autographs-WC
04ITG Heroes/Prospects Toronto Expo '05-136
04ITG Heroes/Prospects Expo Heroes/Pros-136
05Beehive-222
Signature Scrapbook-SSWC
05SP Authentic Exquisite Endorsements-EEWC
05SP Authentic Sign of the Times Quads-QCECS
05SP Authentic Six Star Signatures-SSBO
05SP Game Used Statscriptions-ST-WC
05SPx Xcitement Legends-XL-WC
05SPx Xcitement Legends Gold-XL-WC
05SPx Xcitement Legends Spectrum-XL-WC
05The Cup Stanley Cup Titlists-TWC
05UD Artifacts-108
Blue-108
Gold-108
Green-108
Pewter-108
Red-108
Auto Facts-AF-WC
Auto Facts Blue-AF-WC
Auto Facts Copper-AF-WC
Auto Facts Pewter-AF-WC
Auto Facts Silver-AF-WC
Gold Autographed-108
06ITG International Ice-77
Gold-77
Autographs-AWC
06ITG Ultimate Memorabilia Road to the Cup-4
06ITG Ultimate Memorabilia Road to the Cup Gold-4
06Parkhurst-99
06Parkhurst-182
06Upper Deck Trilogy Scripts-TSWC

Caslava, Petr
98Czech OFS-378
99Czech OFS-367
01Czech OFS-226
02Czech OFS Plus-228
03Czech OFS Plus-48
04Czech OFS-113
05Czech HC Pardubice-3
06Czech HC Pardubice Postcards-4
06Czech OFS-113

Casparsson, Peter
99Swedish Upper Deck-130
03Swedish Elite-212
Silver-212
04Swedish Elitset-61
Gold-61
06German DEL-170

Cass, Bill
03Trenton Titans-357

Cassebaum, Ralf
94German First League-484

Casselman, Mike
96Cincinnati Cyclones-17
97Cincinnati Cyclones-3
98German DEL-74
99German DEL-318
00German DEL-228
All-Star Class-A7
01German Upper Deck-63

Cassels, Andrew
89ProCards AHL-191
90Canadiens Postcards-6
90Pro Set-615
90Score-422
Canadian-422
90Upper Deck-265
French-265
91Bowman-340
91Canadiens Panini Team Stickers-3
91O-Pee-Chee-176
91OPC Premier-72
91Parkhurst-285
French-285
91Pro Set-395
French-395
91Score Canadian Bilingual-238
91Score Canadian Bilingual-607
91Score Canadian English-238
91Score Canadian English-607
91Score Rookie/Traded-57T
91Stadium Club-329
91Topps-176
91Upper Deck-379
91Upper Deck-551
French-379
French-551
91Whalers Jr. 7-Eleven-6
92Bowman-387
92O-Pee-Chee-222
92Parkhurst-298
Emerald Ice-298
92Score-323
Canadian-323
92Stadium Club-39
92Topps-23
Gold-23G
92Ultra-70
92Upper Deck-288
92Whalers Dairymart-4
93Donruss-142
93Leaf-50
93OPC Premier-65
Gold-65
93Panini Stickers-123
93Parkhurst-359
Emerald Ice-359
93Pinnacle-103
Canadian-103
93PowerPlay-104
93Score-164
Canadian-164
93Stadium Club-74
Members Only Master Set-74
OPC-74
First Day Issue-74
First Day Issue OPC-74
93Topps/OPC Premier-65
Gold-65
93Ultra-33
93Upper Deck-346
93Whalers Coke-3
94Canada Games NHL POGS-113
94Donruss-178
94EA Sports-57
94Flair-71
94Fleer-86
94Leaf-276
94OPC Premier-227
Special Effects-227
94Parkhurst-97
Gold-97
Vintage-V58
94Pinnacle-319
Artist's Proofs-319
Rink Collection-319
94Score-34
Gold-34
Platinum-34
94Select-141
Gold-141
94SP-50
Die Cuts-50
94Topps/OPC Premier-227
Special Effects-227
94Ultra-300
94Upper Deck-317
Electric Ice-317
SP Inserts-SP32
SP Inserts Die Cuts-SP32
95Be A Player-30
Signatures-S30
Signatures Die Cuts-S30
95Bowman-4
All-Foil-4
95Canada Games NHL POGS-124
95Collector's Choice-52
Player's Club-52
Player's Club Platinum-52
95Donruss-148
95Emotion-74
95Finest-74
Refractors-74
95Kraft-62
95Leaf-147
95Metal-64
95Panini Stickers-25
95Parkhurst International-364
Emerald Ice-364
95Playoff One on One-46
95Pro Magnets-127
95Score-136
Black Ice Artist's Proofs-136
Black Ice-136
95SkyBox Impact-72
95SP-61
95Stadium Club-61
Members Only Master Set-61
95Summit-158
Artist's Proofs-158
Ice-158
95Topps-30
OPC Inserts-30
95Topps SuperSkills-4
Platinum-4
95Ultra-66
Gold Medallion-66
95Upper Deck-492
Electric Ice-311
Electric Ice-492
Electric Ice Gold-311
Electric Ice Gold-492
Special Edition-SE36
Special Edition Gold-SE36
95Whalers Bob's Stores-3
96Black Diamond-123
Gold-123
96Collector's Choice-115
96Donruss-162
Press Proofs-162
96Flair-41
Blue Ice-41
96Fleer-46
96Fleer Picks-104
96Leaf-78
Press Proofs-78
96NHL Pro Stamps-127
96Pinnacle-82
Artist's Proofs-82
Foil-82
Premium Stock-82
Rink Collection-82
96Score-146
Artist's Proofs-146
Dealer's Choice Artist's Proofs-146
Special Artist's Proofs-146
Golden Blades-146
96SkyBox Impact-53
96SP-72
96Summit-44
Artist's Proofs-44
Ice-44
Metal-44
Premium Stock-44
96Upper Deck-74
96Whalers Kid's Club-14
97Be A Player-8
Autographs-8
Autographs Die-Cuts-8
Autographs Prismatic Die-Cuts-8
97Collector's Choice-113
97Donruss-146
Press Proofs Silver-146
Press Proofs Gold-146
97Donruss Canadian Ice-66
Dominion Series-66
Provincial Series-66
97Donruss Elite-48
Aspirations-48
Status-48
97Donruss Limited-45
Exposure-45
97Donruss Preferred-94
Cut to the Chase-94
97Donruss Priority-64
Stamp of Approval-64
97Flames Collector's Photos-10
97Katch-19
Gold-19
Silver-19
97Leaf-106
Fractal Matrix-106
Fractal Matrix Die Cuts-106
97Leaf International-106
Universal Ice-106
97Pacific-166
Copper-166
Emerald Green-166
Ice Blue-166
Red-166
Silver-166
97Pacific Dynagon-21
Copper-21
Dark Grey-21
Emerald Green-21
Ice Blue-21
Red-21
Silver-21
Tandems-39
97Pacific Invincible-23
Copper-23
Emerald Green-23
Ice Blue-23
Red-23
Silver-23
97Pacific Omega-28
Copper-28
Dark Gray-28
Emerald Green-28
Gold-28
Ice Blue-28
97Panini Stickers-21
97Paramount-26
Copper-26
Dark Grey-26
Emerald Green-26
Ice Blue-26
Red-26
Silver-26
97Pinnacle-178
Press Plates Back Black-178
Press Plates Back Cyan-178
Press Plates Back Magenta-178
Press Plates Back Yellow-178
Press Plates Front Black-178
Press Plates Front Cyan-178
Press Plates Front Magenta-178
Press Plates Front Yellow-178
97Pinnacle Certified-130
Red-130
Mirror Blue-130
Mirror Gold-130
Mirror Red-130
97Pinnacle Inside-106
97Pinnacle Tot Cert Platinum Blue-130
97Pinnacle Tot Certi Platinum Gold-130
97Pinnacle Totally Certified Platinum Red-130
97Pinnacle Tot Cert Mirror Platinum Gold-130
97Score-134
Artist's Proofs-134
Golden Blades-134
98Aurora-23
98Be A Player-20
Press Release-20
98BAP Gold-20
98BAP Autographs-20
98BAP Autographs Gold-20
98BAP Tampa Bay All Star Game-20
98Crown Royale-16
Limited Series-16
98Finest-82
No Protectors-82
No Protectors Refractors-82
Refractors-82
98Katch-19
98Pacific-115
Ice Blue-115
Red-115
98Pacific Dynagon Ice-23
Blue-23
Red-23
98Paramount-26
Copper-26
Emerald Green-26
Holo-Electric-26
Ice Blue-26
Silver-26
98Upper Deck-231
Exclusives-231
Exclusives 1 of 1-231
Gold Reserve-231
99Pacific-53
Copper-53
Emerald Green-53
Gold-53
Ice Blue-53
Premiere Date-53
Red-53
99Pacific Dynagon Ice-192
Blue-192
Copper-192
Gold-192
Premiere Date-192
99Pacific Omega-232
Copper-232
Gold-232
Ice Blue-232
Premiere Date-232
99Panini Stickers-311
99Upper Deck MVP SC Edition-185
Gold Script-185
Silver Script-185
Super Script-185
00Aurora-142
Premiere Date-142
00BAP Memorabilia-178
Emerald-178
Ruby-178
Sapphire-178
Promos-178
00BAP Mem Chicago Sportsfest Copper-178
00BAP Memorabilia Chicago Sportsfest Blue-178
00BAP Memorabilia Chicago Sportsfest Gold-178
00BAP Memorabilia Chicago Sportsfest Ruby-178
00BAP Memorabilia Chicago Sun-Times Ruby-178
00BAP Memorabilia Chicago Sun-Times Gold-178
00BAP Mem Chicago Sun-Times Sapphire-178
00BAP Mem Toronto Fall Expo Copper-178
00BAP Memorabilia Toronto Fall Expo Gold-178
00BAP Memorabilia Toronto Fall Expo Ruby-178
00BAP Parkhurst 2000-P202
00Crown Royale-103
Ice Blue-103
Limited Series-103
Premiere Date-103
Red-103
00O-Pee-Chee-270B
00O-Pee-Chee Parallel-270B
00Pacific-406
Copper-406
Gold-406
Ice Blue-406
Premiere Date-406
00Panini Stickers-207
00Paramount-237
Copper-237
Gold-237
Holo-Gold-237
Holo-Silver-237
Ice Blue-237
Premiere Date-237
00Titanium-94
Blue-94
Gold-94
Premiere Date-94
Red-94
Retail-94
Game Gear-48
00Topps/OPC-270B
Parallel-270B
00Topps Chrome-160
OPC Refractors-160
Refractors-160
00Upper Deck-168
Exclusives Tier 1-168
Exclusives Tier 2-168
00Upper Deck Victory-227
00Upper Deck Vintage-354
00Vanguard-95
Holographic Gold-95
Holographic Purple-95
Pacific Proofs-95
01BAP Memorabilia-254
Emerald-254
Ruby-254
Sapphire-254
01Crown Royale Triple Threads-9
01O-Pee-Chee-212
01O-Pee-Chee Premier Parallel-212
01Pacific-379
Extreme LTD-379
Hobby LTD-379
Premiere Date-379
Retail LTD-379
Impact Zone-20
01Pacific Adrenaline-188
Blue-188
Premiere Date-188
Red-188
Retail-188
Jerseys-49
01Pacific Arena Exclusives-379
01Parkhurst-115
01Private Stock Game Gear-98
01Private Stock Game Gear Patches-98
01Private Stock PS-2002-72
01Titanium Draft Day Edition-93
01Topps-212
OPC Parallel-212
01Upper Deck-398
Exclusives-398
01Upper Deck Victory-340
Gold-340
01Upper Deck Vintage-247
01Vanguard Memorabilia-34
02BAP Sig Series Auto Buybacks 1998-20
02Bowman YoungStars-39
Gold-39
Silver-39
02Crown Royale-27
Blue-27
Red-27
Retail-27
02Pacific-374
Blue-374
Red-374
02Pacific Complete-399
Red-399
02Pacific Exclusive-49
02Parkhurst-181
Bronze-181
Gold-181
Silver-181
02Private Stock Reserve-30
Blue-30
Red-30
Retail-30
02Titanium-28
Blue-28
Red-28
Retail-28
02Topps Heritage-178
02Topps Total-282
02Upper Deck-295
Exclusives-295
02Upper Deck Beckett UD Promos-295
02Vanguard-29
LTD-29
03Black Diamond-85
Black-85
Green-85
Red-85
03ITG Action-194
03NHL Sticker Collection-195
03O-Pee-Chee-242
03OPC Blue-242
03OPC Gold-242
03OPC Red-242
03Pacific-91
Blue-91
Red-91
03Pacific Complete-209
Red-209
03Pacific Exhibit-41
Blue Backs-41
Yellow Backs-41
03Private Stock Reserve-26
Blue-26
Red-26
Retail-26
03Topps-242
Blue-242
Gold-242
Red-242
03Upper Deck-296
Canadian Exclusives-296
HG-296
UD Exclusives-296
03Upper Deck MVP-115
Gold Script-115
Silver Script-115
Canadian Exclusives-115
03Upper Deck Victory-51
Bronze-51
Gold-51
Silver-51
04Pacific-73
Blue-73
Red-73
05Be A Player Signatures-AC
05Be A Player Signatures Gold-AC
05Panini Stickers-184
05Upper Deck-439
05Upper Deck MVP-390
Gold-390
Platinum-390

Casselstahl, Daniel
94Swedish Leaf-178
00Swedish Upper Deck-168
02Swedish SHL-103
Parallel-103
03Swedish Elite-148
Silver-148
04Swedish Elitset-4
Gold-4
05Swedish SHL Elitset-149
06Swedish SHL Elitset-150

Cassidy, Bruce
82Ottawa 67's-1
83Ottawa 67's-3
84Ottawa 67's-4
85Blackhawks Team Issue-13
88Blackhawks Coke-3
88ProCards IHL-96
89ProCards IHL-51
94Indianapolis Ice-2
95Indianapolis Ice-4
98IHL All-Star Eastern Conference-21
98Indianapolis Ice-21
00Grand Rapids Griffins-23
01Grand Rapids Griffins-24

Cassidy, Jason
04Brampton Battalion-23
05Brampton Battalion-21

Cassidy, Keith
99Huntington Blizzard-13

Cassivi, Frederic
95Thunder Bay Senators-4
96Syracuse Crunch-30
98Cincinnati Cyclones-2
98Cincinnati Cyclones 2-19
00Hershey Bears-4
01BAP Memorabilia-421
Emerald-421
Ruby-421
Sapphire-421
01Between the Pipes-161
01Parkhurst-301
01UD Mask Collection-131
Gold-131
01UD Premier Collection-53
01Chicago Wolves-4
01Hershey Bears-2
02BAP First Edition-262
02Between the Pipes-35
Gold-35
Silver-35
02Upper Deck MVP-193
Gold-193
Classics-193
Golden Classics-193
02Upper Deck Victory-14
Bronze-14
Gold-14
Silver-14
02Chicago Wolves-4
03BAP Memorabilia Deep in the Crease-D1
03Chicago Wolves-4
04Cincinnati Mighty Ducks-30
05Hershey Bears-4
06Between The Pipes-14
Autographs-AFC
Prospect Trios-PT20
Prospect Trios Gold-PT20
06ITG Heroes and Prospects Calder Cup Champions-CC01

Casslind, Yngve
55Swedish Alfabilder-22

Cast, Paul
94UK Humberside Hawks-21

Castella, Reuben
917th Inn. Sketch OHL-174

Castellan, Jason
907th Inn. Sketch OHL-280

Castelli, Nick
92Quebec Pee-Wee Tournament-1446
93Quebec Pee-Wee Tournament-789

Casten, Jens
94German First League-554

Castonguay, Alexis
99Rimouski Oceanic-12
Signed-12

Casutt, Corsin
03Swiss EV Zug Postcards-4
04Swiss EV Zug Postcards-22

Caswell, Roy
82Brandon Wheat Kings-14

Catalano, Peter
93Quebec Pee-Wee Tournament-833

Catellier, Chris
89Victoria Cougars-6
907th Inn. Sketch WHL-238
917th Inn. Sketch WHL-53

Catenacci, Maurizio
96German DEL-100

Catenaro, Angelo
84Belleville Bulls-17

Caterini, Pino
75HCA Steel City Vacuum-2

Cation, Shawn
98Barrie Colts-3

Caton, Murray
91British Columbia JHL-8

Cattarinich, Joseph
10C56-16
12C61 Lacrosse-33
27La Presse Photos-16
83Hall of Fame-168
83Hall of Fame Postcards-M3
85Hall of Fame-168

Cattaruzza, Beat
93Swiss HNL-190
95Swiss HNL-265

Cattela, Gilles
00Swiss Panini Stickers-55
01Swiss HNL-282
02Swiss HNL-352

Catto, Josh
05Owen Sound Attack-11

Caudill, Kevin
03Kalamazoo Wings-7
04Knoxville Ice Bears-1
05Knoxville Ice Bears-3

Caudron, J.F.
01Atlantic City Boardwalk Bullies-4
02Atlantic City Boardwalk Bullies-2

Caufield, Jay
89Penguins Foodland-12
90Pro Set-504
91Penguins Coke/Elby's-16
92Penguins Coke/Clark-3

Caughell, Rick
03Mississauga Ice Dogs-5
04Saginaw Spirit-7

Caulfield, Kevin
92Quebec Pee-Wee Tournament-1648
02Charlotte Checkers-80
03Charlotte Checkers-66

Cauly, Jill
93Quebec Pee-Wee Tournament-1648

Causey, Carey
91British Columbia JHL-113

Cava, Chris
99Ottawa 67's-16
00Kitchener Rangers-8
01Roanoke Express-2

Cava, Peter
95Slapshot-365
95Sault Ste. Marie Greyhounds-1
96Sault Ste. Marie Greyhounds-3
96Sault Ste. Marie Greyhounds Autographed-3
98Bowman CHL-18
Golden Anniversary-18
OPC International-18
98Bowman Chrome CHL-18
Golden Anniversary-18
Golden Anniversary Refractors-18
OPC International-18
OPC International Refractors-18
Refractors-18
99Rockford IceHogs-2
00Lubbock Cotton Kings-4
04Lakehead University Thunderwolves-25

Cavallin, Mark
94Central Hockey League-94
99UK London Knights-5
00UK Sekonda Superleague-23
01UK Belfast Giants-18
01UK Belfast Giants-32

Cavallini, Gino
84Moncton Golden Flames-26
85Flames Red Rooster-6
87Blues Kodak-5
87Blues Team Issue-3
87O-Pee-Chee-146
87Panini Stickers-315
87Topps-146
88Blues Kodak-3
88Blues Team Issue-3
88O-Pee-Chee-149
88Panini Stickers-103
88Topps-149
89Blues Kodak-17
89O-Pee-Chee-176
89Panini Stickers-123
89Topps-176
90Blues Kodak-5
90O-Pee-Chee-36
90Panini Stickers-265
90Pro Set-261
90Score-63
Canadian-63
90Score Hottest/Rising Stars-27
90Topps-36
Tiffany-36
90Upper Deck-38
French-38
91Blues Postcards-5
91Bowman-368
91O-Pee-Chee-281
91Panini Stickers-24
91Pinnacle-216
French-216
91Pro Set-218
French-218
91Score American-258
91Score American-308
91Score Canadian Bilingual-338
91Score Canadian Bilingual-478
91Score Canadian English-338
91Score Canadian English-478
91Stadium Club-34
91Topps-281
91Upper Deck-187
91Upper Deck-646
French-187
French-646
92Nordiques Petro-Canada-3
92Score-42
Canadian-42
92Stadium Club-480
92Topps-234
Gold-234G
93OPC Premier-232
Gold-232
93Score-414
Canadian-414
93Stadium Club-152
Members Only Master Set-152
OPC-152
First Day Issue-152
First Day Issue OPC-152
93Topps/OPC Premier-232
Gold-232
94Milwaukee Admirals-4
95Milwaukee Admirals-3
95Milwaukee Admirals Postcards-20
96German DEL-152
96Collector's Edge Ice-159
Prism-159
03Bowling Green Falcons-17

Cavallini, Paul
87Blues Kodak-4
87Blues Team Issue-4
88Blues Kodak-4
88Blues Team Issue-4
89Blues Kodak-14
89O-Pee-Chee-269
89O-Pee-Chee Stickers-19
89Panini Stickers-127
90Blues Kodak-6
90Bowman-22
Tiffany-22
90O-Pee-Chee-57
90Panini Stickers-276
90Pro Set-262
90Pro Set-353
90Score-185
90Score-349
Canadian-185
Canadian-349
90Topps-57
Tiffany-57
90Upper Deck-281
French-281
91Pro Set Platinum-224
91Blues Postcards-6
91Bowman-378
91O-Pee-Chee-328
91Panini Stickers-35
91Parkhurst-154
French-154
91Pinnacle-182
91Pinnacle-411
French-182
French-411
91Pro Set-214
French-214
St. Louis Midwest-2
91Score American-107
91Score American-308
91Score Canadian Bilingual-107
91Score Canadian Bilingual-338
91Score Canadian English-107
91Score Canadian English-338
91Stadium Club-48
91Topps-328
91Upper Deck-184
91Upper Deck-646
French-184
91Finnish Semic World Champ Stickers-59
91Swedish Semic World Champ Stickers-59
92Bowman-193
92Capitals Kodak-6
92O-Pee-Chee-379
92Panini Stickers-23
92Panini Stickers French-23
92Pinnacle-319
French-319
92Pro Set-159
92Score-22
Canadian-22
92Stadium Club-447
92Topps-233
Gold-233G
92Ultra-185
92Ultra-432
92Upper Deck-212
93Donruss-88
93Leaf-397
93Parkhurst-50
Emerald Ice-50
93Pinnacle-370
Canadian-370
93PowerPlay-321
93Score-172
93Score-538
Gold-538
Canadian-172
Canadian-538
Canadian Gold-538
93Upper Deck-441
SP-35
94Canada Games NHL POGS-82
94Donruss-135
94Leaf-79
94OPC Premier-246

Special Effects-246
94Parkhurst Vintage-V12
94Parkhurst SE-SE42
Gold-SE42
94Pinnacle-81
Artist's Proofs-81
Rink Collection-81
94Score-94
Gold-94
Platinum-94
94Stars HockeyKaps-5
94Stars Postcards-2
94Stars Score Sheet-94
94Topps/OPC Premier-246
Special Effects-246
94Ultra-49
94Upper Deck-311
Electric Ice-311
SP Inserts-SP108
SP Inserts Die Cuts-SP108
Cavanagh, Chad
95Slapshot-164
96Detroit Whalers-3
03Johnstown Chiefs-16
03Johnstown Chiefs RBI Sports-210
04Johnstown Chiefs-4
Cavanagh, Pat
89Hampton Roads Admirals-4A
89Hampton Roads Admirals-4H
90Hampton Roads Admirals-53
92Tulsa Oilers-2
Cavanagh, Tom
05Cleveland Barons-4
Cavanaugh, Dan
03Houston Aeros-3
03Pacific AHL Prospects-40
Gold-40
04Houston Aeros-4
06Springfield Falcons-3
Cavanaugh, David
93Quebec Pee-Wee Tournament-793
Cavanaugh, Mike
87Kingston Canadians-15
907th Inn. Sketch OHL-29
Cavegn, Severin
02Swiss HNL-213
Cavicchi, Trent
97Macon Whoopee-16
97Macon Whoopee Autographs-16
Cavosie, Marc
03Houston Aeros-4
05Philadelphia Phantoms-4
Cayford, Jamie
84Nanaimo Clippers-5
Cazacu, Trajan
94German First League-559
Ceccanese, Stephen
06Cape Breton Screaming Eagles-16
Cecco, Holger
94German First League-332
Cech, Filip
00Czech OFS-371
Cech, Jakub
02Czech OFS Plus-127
Checklists-C1
02Czech OFS Plus Masks-M24
02Czech OFS Plus Trios-T3
02Czech OFS Plus Duos-D24
04Sault Ste. Marie Greyhounds-1
06Czech OFS-221
Cech, Martin
97Czech APS Extraliga-192
98Czech DS Stickers-152
98Czech OFS-288
99Czech DS-89
99Czech OFS-118
99Czech OFS-473
00Czech DS Extraliga-28
00Czech OFS-60
01Finnish Cardset-268
02Czech OFS Plus-25
02Finnish Cardset-9
03Czech National Team-3
03Czech OFS Plus-132
03Czech OFS Plus-133
03Finnish Cardset-114
03Russian Hockey League-180
03Russian Metallurg Magnitogorsk-8
04Czech OFS-275
04Russian Legion-19
06Czech HC Zlin Hame Postcards-1
06Czech OFS-222
06Czech OFS-317
Cech, Michal
98Czech OFS-322
99Czech OFS-237
00Czech OFS-282
01Czech OFS Update-292
02Czech OFS Plus-128
Trios-T2
Cech, Roman
94Czech APS Extraliga-165
95Czech APS Extraliga-181
96Czech APS Extraliga-171
97Czech APS Extraliga-85
97Czech DS Stickers-41
98Czech DS Stickers-92
98Czech OFS-198
99Czech DS-34
99Czech OFS-178
Cech, Vratislav
96Kitchener Rangers-5
97Bowman CHL-155
OPC-155
Autographs-35
99Providence Bruins-6
01Atlantic City Boardwalk Bullies-5
02Czech OFS Plus-129
04Czech OFS-48
06Czech OFS-248
Cech, Zdenek
94Czech APS Extraliga-294
95Czech APS Extraliga-28
97Czech APS Extraliga-52
Cechmanek, Roman
94Czech APS Extraliga-228
95Czech APS Extraliga-3
95Czech APS Extraliga-353
95Czech APS Extraliga-388
96Czech APS Extraliga-214
96Czech APS Extraliga-337
97Czech APS Extraliga-28
97Czech APS Extraliga-342
97Czech APS Extraliga-370
97Czech DS Extraliga-1
97Czech DS Stickers-1
97Czech DS Stickers-18
98Czech DS-20
98Czech DS Stickers-8
98Czech DS Stickers-167
98Czech OFS-99
98Czech OFS-228
98Czech OFS-438
98Czech OFS-470
Olympic Winners-17
98Czech Bonaparte-4B
98Czech Pexeso-11
98Czech Pexeso Series Two-12
99Czech DS-127
Goalies-G10
Premium-P3
99Czech OFS-6
99Czech OFS-254
99Czech OFS-489
99Czech OFS-NNO
All-Star Game Blue-489
All-Star Game Gold-489
All-Star Game Red-489
All-Star Game Silver-489
99Czech OFS Goalie Die-Cuts-6
00BAP Memorabilia-424
Emerald-424
Ruby-424
Sapphire-424
00BAP Parkhurst 2000-P230
00BAP Signature Series-297
Emerald-297
Ruby-297
Sapphire-297
00Black Diamond-128
00SP Authentic-119
00SP Game Used-77
00SPx-169
00Titanium Draft Day Edition-169
00Titanium Draft Day Promos-169
00Topps Gold Label Class 1-115
Gold-115
00Topps Gold Label Class 2-115
00Topps Gold Label Class 2 Gold-115
00Topps Gold Label Class 3-115
00Topps Gold Label Class 3 Gold-115
00Topps Heritage-88
Chrome Parallel-88
00Topps Premier Plus-136
Blue Ice-136
00Topps Stars-105
Blue-105
00UD Heroes-175
00UD Pros and Prospects-120
00UD Reserve-111
00Upper Deck-435
Exclusives Tier 1-435
Exclusives Tier 2-435
00Upper Deck Ice-96
00Vanguard-137
Pacific Proofs-137
00Czech DS Extraliga National Team-NT2
00Czech DS Extraliga World Champions-WCH1
01Atomic-71
Blue-71
Gold-71
Premiere Date-71
Red-71
Statosphere-7
01BAP Memorabilia-42
Emerald-42
Ruby-42
Sapphire-42
All-Star Jerseys-ASJ14
All-Star Emblems-ASE14
All-Star Numbers-ASN14
All-Star Teammates-AST5
All-Star Teammates-AST9
Country of Origin-CO27
Goalies Jerseys-GJ15
He Shoots-He Scores Points-1
He Shoots-He Scores Prizes-8
Stanley Cup Playoffs-SC8
01BAP Signature Series-165
Autographs-165
Autographs Gold-165
Jerseys-GJ-47
Jersey Autographs-GURC
Jersey and Stick Cards-GSJ-47
Emblems-GUE-46
Numbers-ITN-46
01BAP Ultimate Memorabilia Name Plates-20
01Between the Pipes-19
01Between the Pipes-103
All-Star Jerseys-ASJ4
He Shoots-He Saves Prizes-25
Jerseys-GJ15
Jersey and Stick Cards-GSJ14
Masks-24
Masks Silver-24
Masks Gold-24
Tandems-GT2
01Bowman YoungStars-98
Gold-98
Ice Cubed-98
01Crown Royale-105
Blue-105
Premiere Date-105
Red-105
Retail-105
01Crown Royale Toronto Expo Rookie Coll-G5
01eTopps-27
01Flyers Postcards-3
01McDonald's Pacific-28
01O-Pee-Chee-59
01O-Pee-Chee-315
01O-Pee-Chee Heritage Parallel-59
01O-Pee-Chee Heritage Parallel Limited-59
01O-Pee-Chee Premier Parallel-59
01O-Pee-Chee Premier Parallel-315
01Pacific-284
01Pacific-437
Extreme LTD-284
Gold-437
Hobby LTD-284
Premiere Date-284
Retail LTD-284
All-Stars-W7
Impact Zone-15
Steel Curtain-15
01Pacific Adrenaline-138
Blue-138
Premiere Date-138
Red-138
Retail-138
Creased Lightning-15
Power Play-26
01Pacific Arena Exclusives-284
01Pacific Arena Exclusives-437
01Pacific Heads-Up-71
Blue-71
Premiere Date-71
Red-71
Silver-71
All-Star Net-1
HD NHL-19
Showstoppers-16
01Parkhurst-71
Gold-71
Silver-71
Jerseys-PJ44
Jersey and Stick-PSJ17
Teammates-T13
01Private Stock-70
Gold-70
Premiere Date-70
Retail-70
Silver-70
01Private Stock Pacific Nights-70
01Private Stock PS-2002-53
01Private Stock Reserve-G8
01SP Authentic-64
Limited-64
Limited Gold-64
01SP Game Used-41
Tools of the Game-TRC
Tools of the Game-CTCB
Tools of the Game-CTCH
Tools of the Game-CTFC
Tools of the Game-CTRC
Tools of the Game-TTKCH
01SPx-47
Hockey Treasures-HTRC
01Stadium Club-30
Award Winners-30
Master Photos-30
Gallery-G12
Gallery Gold-G12
New Regime-NR8
New Regime-NRARC
NHL Passport-NHLP9
01Titanium-103
Hobby Parallel-103
Premiere Date-103
Retail-103
Retail Parallel-103
Double-Sided Jerseys-49
Double-Sided Jerseys-60
Double-Sided Patches-49
Double-Sided Patches-60
01Titanium Draft Day Edition-68
01Topps-59
01Topps-315
Heritage Parallel-59
Heritage Parallel Limited-59
OPC Parallel-59
OPC Parallel-315
Own The Game-OTG28
01Topps Chrome-59
Refractors-59
Black Border Refractors-59
01Topps Heritage-59
01Topps Heritage-119
01Topps Heritage-129
Refractors-59
01Topps Reserve-85
01UD Challenge for the Cup Backstops-BB7
01UD Honor Roll Honor Society-HS-CH
01UD Honor Roll Honor Society Gold-HS-CH
01UD Mask Collection-122
01UD Mask Collection-184
Gold-122
Gold-184
Dual Jerseys-MBBC
Goalie Jerseys-SYRC
Goalie Jerseys-VCRC
01UD Playmakers-73
01UD Premier Collection Dual Jerseys-DCB
01UD Premier Collection Dual Jerseys-DHC
01UD Premier Collection Dual Jersey Black-DCB
01UD Premier Collection Dual Jersey Black-DHC
01UD Top Shelf-31
All-Star Nets-NRC
Goalie Gear-LPRC
01Upper Deck-130
01Upper Deck-224
Exclusives-130
Exclusives-224
Game Jerseys-GJRC
Game Jerseys-CPC
Goaltender Threads-TTRC
Last Line of Defense-LL6
Skilled Stars-SS16
01Upper Deck MVP-138
Goalie Sticks-G-RC
Masked Men-MM13
01Upper Deck Victory-253
01Upper Deck Victory-259
Gold-253
Gold-259
01Upper Deck Vintage-184
01Upper Deck Vintage-191
01Upper Deck Vintage-268
01Upper Deck Vintage-270
Next In Line-NLSC
01Vanguard-72
Blue-72
Red-72
One of Ones-72
Premiere Date-72
Proofs-72
Stonewallers-15
V-Team-7
01Czech DS Goalies-G4
02Atomic-73
Blue-73
Gold-73
Red-73
Denied-15
Hobby Parallel-73
02BAP All-Star Edition-14
Jerseys-14
Jerseys Gold-14
Jerseys Silver-14
02BAP First Edition-55
02BAP First Edition-376
02BAP First Edition-377
Jerseys-55
02BAP Memorabilia-196
Emerald-196
Ruby-196
Sapphire-196
NHL All-Star Game-196
NHL All-Star Game Blue-196
NHL All-Star Game Green-196
NHL All-Star Game Red-196
Stanley Cup Playoffs-SC-1
Teammates-TM-9
02BAP Memorabilia Toronto Fall Expo-196
02BAP Signature Series-164
Autographs-164
Autograph Buybacks 2001-165
Autographs Gold-164
Defensive Wall-DW3
Team Quads-TQ3
02Between the Pipes-39
02Between the Pipes-142
Gold-39
Silver-39
All-Star Stick and Jersey-14
Blockers-10
Complete Package-CP12
Emblems-27
He Shoots-He Saves Points-2
He Shoots-He Saves Prizes-9
Jerseys-27
Masks II-21
Masks II Gold-21
Masks II Silver-21
Numbers-27
Stick and Jerseys-27
Tandems-8
02Bowman YoungStars-87
Gold-87
Silver-87
02Crown Royale-69
Blue-69
Red-69
Retail-69
02Flyers Postcards-14
02ITG Used Goalie Pad and Jersey-GP12
02ITG Used Goalie Pad and Jersey Gold-GP12
02ITG Used International Experience-IE27
02ITG Used International Experience Gold-IE27
02O-Pee-Chee-137
02O-Pee-Chee Premier Blue Parallel-137
02O-Pee-Chee Premier Red Parallel-137
02O-Pee-Chee Factory Set-137
02Pacific-277
Blue-277
Red-277
02Pacific Complete-119
Red-119
02Pacific Exclusive-125
02Pacific Heads-Up-89
Blue-89
Purple-89
Red-89
Quad Jerseys-20
Quad Jerseys Gold-20
02Pacific Quest for the Cup-74
Gold-74
Jerseys-15
02Parkhurst-150
Bronze-150
Gold-150
Silver-150
02Parkhurst Retro-123
Minis-123
02Private Stock Reserve-135
Red-135
Retail-135
InCrease Security-16
Patches-135
02SP Authentic-66
Beckett Promos-66
02SP Game Used Authentic Fabrics-AFCK
02SP Game Used Authentic Fabrics-AFRC
02SP Game Used Authentic Fabrics Gold-AFCK
02SP Game Used Authentic Fabrics Gold-AFRC
02SP Game Used Authentic Fabrics Rainbow-AFCK
02SP Game Used Authentic Fabrics Rainbow-AFRC
02SP Game Used Piece of History-PHCK
02SP Game Used Piece of History-PHRC
02SP Game Used Piece of History Gold-PHCK
02SP Game Used Piece of History Gold-PHRC
02SP Game Used Piece of History Rainbow-PHCK
02SP Game Used Piece of History Rainbow-PHRC
02SP Game Used Tools of the Game-RC
02SPx-57
Spectrum Gold-57
Spectrum Silver-57
02Stadium Club-62
Silver Decoy Cards-62
Proofs-62
Puck Stops Here-PSH2
02Titanium-74
Blue-74
Red-74
Retail-74
02Topps-137
OPC Blue Parallel-137
OPC Red Parallel-137
Factory Set-137
02Topps Chrome-86
Black Border Refractors-86
Refractors-86
02Topps Heritage-88
02Topps Heritage-117
Chrome Parallel-88
02Topps Total-231
02UD Artistic Impressions Common Ground-CG5
02UD Artistic Impress Common Ground Gold-CG5
02UD Honor Roll-54
02UD Mask Collection-60
02UD Mask Collection-61
02UD Mask Collection-62
02UD Mask Collection-63
02UD Mask Collection-94
02UD Mask Collection Beckett Promos-60
02UD Mask Collection Beckett Promos-61
02UD Mask Collection Beckett Promos-62
02UD Mask Collection Beckett Promos-63
02UD Mask Collection Great Gloves-GGRC
02UD Mask Collection Masked Marvels-MMRC
02UD Mask Collection Patches-PWRC
02UD Mask Collection Super Stoppers-SSRC
02UD Mask Collection View from the Cage-VRC
02UD Piece of History-67
02UD Top Shelf-64
Stopper Jerseys-SSRC
Triple Jerseys-TSLGC
02Upper Deck-129
Exclusives-129
Goaltender Threads-RC
Goaltender Threads Gold-RC
MVP Skate Around Jerseys-SDCB
MVP Skate Around Jerseys-SDKC
MVP Skate Around Jerseys-SDLC
MVP Souvenirs-S-RC
02Upper Deck Rookie Update-76
Jerseys-DRC
Jerseys Gold-DRC
02Upper Deck Victory-154
Bronze-154
Gold-154
Silver-154
02Upper Deck Vintage-184
02Upper Deck Vintage-282
02Upper Deck Vintage-317
02Upper Deck Vintage-318
Green Backs-184
Jerseys-EERC
Jerseys Gold-EE-RC
02Vanguard-72
LTD-72
Stonewallers-10
02Czech IQ Sports Blue-4
02Czech IQ Sports Yellow-4
02Czech Stadion Olympics-326
03BAP Memorabilia-158
Emerald-158
Gold-158
Ruby-158
Sapphire-158
Masks III-2
Masks III Gold-2
Masks III Silver-2
Masks III Autographs-M-RC
Masks III Memorabilia-2
03BAP Ultimate Memorabilia Autographs-44
Gold-44
03BAP Ultimate Memorabilia Triple Threads-4
03Beehive-92
Gold-92
Silver-92
Sticks Beige Border-BE34
Sticks Blue Border-BL21
03Black Diamond-29
Black-29
Green-29
Red-29
03Bowman-81
Gold-81
03Bowman Chrome-81
Refractors-81
Gold Refractors-81
Xfractors-81
03Crown Royale-47
Blue-47
Retail-47
03ITG Action Jerseys-M97
03ITG Used Signature Series-69
Gold-69
Autographs-RC
Autographs Gold-RC
Franchise Gold-14
Goalie Gear-13
Goalie Gear Autographs-13
Goalie Gear Gold-13
Jerseys-41
Jerseys Gold-41
Jersey Autos-41
Emblems-31
Emblems Gold-31
Jersey and Stick-41
Jersey and Stick Gold-41
03NHL Sticker Collection-110
03O-Pee-Chee-179
03OPC Blue-179
03OPC Gold-179
03OPC Red-179
03Pacific-248
Blue-248
Red-248
In the Crease-9
Jerseys-29
Jerseys Gold-29
03Pacific Calder-48
03Pacific Calder-149
Silver-48
03Pacific Complete-475
Red-475
03Pacific Exhibit-67
03Pacific Exhibit-208
Blue Backs-67
Yellow Backs-67
03Pacific Heads-Up-46
Hobby LTD-46
Retail LTD-46
03Pacific Invincible-45
Blue-45
Red-45
Retail-45
Freeze Frame-9
Jerseys-13
03Pacific Prism-121
Blue-121
Patches-121
Red-121
Retail-121
03Pacific Quest for the Cup-49
Blue-49
03Pacific Supreme-44
Blue-44
Red-44
Retail-44
03Private Stock Reserve-45
Blue-45
Red-45
Retail-45
03SP Authentic-40
Limited-40
03SP Game Used Authentic Fabrics-DFPC
03SP Game Used Authentic Fabrics Gold-DFPC
03SP Game Used Game Gear-GGRC
03SPx-46
Radiance-46
Spectrum-46
03Titanium-45
Hobby Jersey Number Parallels-45
Retail-45
Retail Jersey Number Parallels-45
03Topps-179
Blue-179
Gold-179
Red-179
Pristine Mini-PM-RC
03Topps Traded-TT18
Blue-TT18
Gold-TT18
Red-TT18
03UD Honor Roll-38
03UD Premier Collection Stars-ST-RC
03UD Premier Collection Stars Patches-ST-RC
03UD Premier Collection Teammates-PT-LK
03UD Premier Collection Teammates Patches-PT-LK
03Upper Deck-91
Canadian Exclusives-91
HG-91
Patches-SV3
Super Saviors-SS-RC
03Upper Deck Classic Portraits-45
03Upper Deck Ice-41
Gold-41
03Upper Deck MVP-205
Gold Script-205
Silver Script-205
Canadian Exclusives-205
Souvenirs-S13
SportsNut-SN41
03Upper Deck Rookie Update-41
Super Stars-SSRC
03Upper Deck Trilogy-45
Limited-45
04Pacific-120
Blue-120
Red-120
04Upper Deck-84
Canadian Exclusives-84
HG Glossy Gold-84
HG Glossy Silver-84
World Cup Tribute-RCTV
04Czech OFS-244
Stars-35
Team Cards-12
04Czech Zuma-8
04Czech Zuma Stars-Z8
04Czech World Championship Postcards-2
05Czech Kvarteto Bonaparte-1b
05Czech HC Karlovy Vary-2
05German DEL-324
Goalies-G01
06Swedish SHL Elitset-203
Cechs, Jakub
03Sault Ste. Marie Greyhounds-1
Ceci, John
00Ottawa 67's-21
01Ottawa 67's-2
Cecile, Jonathan
92Quebec Pee-Wee Tournament-781
93Quebec Pee-Wee Tournament-1049
Cedergren, Henrik
83Swedish Semic Elitserien-71
84Swedish Semic Elitserien-23
Cederholm, Hans
83Swedish Semic Elitserien-5
84Swedish Semic Elitserien-6
85Swedish Panini Stickers-7
87Swedish Panini Stickers-8
Cederstrand, Chris
97Red Deer Rebels-5
Cefalo, Marco
96Prince Albert Raiders-4
Ceglarski, Len
90Pro Set-385A
90Pro Set-385B
Cej, Jeff
917th Inn. Sketch WHL-305
Celentano, Matt
93Quebec Pee-Wee Tournament-1289
Celio, Brenno
93Swiss HNL-139
95Swiss HNL-188
96Swiss HNL-80
Celio, Daniele
93Swiss HNL-399
Celio, Filippo
93Swiss HNL-140
Celio, Manuele
91Finnish Semic World Champ Stickers-192
91Swedish Semic World Champ Stickers-192
92Finnish Semic-211
93Swedish Semic World Champ Stickers-124
93Swiss HNL-18
95Swiss HNL-16
96Swiss HNL-17
96Swiss HNL-536
98Swiss Power Play Stickers-16
99Swiss Panini Stickers-14
00Swiss Panini Stickers-14
00Swiss Slapshot Mini-Cards-HCAP8
01Swiss HNL-224
02Swiss HNL-194
Celio, Nicola
91Upper Deck-665
French-665
91Upper Deck Czech World Juniors-26
93Swiss HNL-146
95Swiss HNL-198
96Swiss HNL-89
96Swiss HNL-537
98Swiss Power Play Stickers-17
99Swiss Panini Stickers-15
00Swiss Panini Stickers-15
00Swiss Slapshot Mini-Cards-HCAP9
01Swiss HNL-215
02Swiss HNL-60
Cella, Tony
80Sault Ste. Marie Greyhounds-4
81Sault Ste. Marie Greyhounds-6
82Sault Ste. Marie Greyhounds-5
Cellar, Andreas
01Swiss HNL-64
Cely, Zdenek
94Czech APS Extraliga-180
95Czech APS Extraliga-213
Ceman, Dan
97Hampton Roads Admirals-5
98ECHL All-Star Northern Conference-14
98Hampton Roads Admirals-19
99UK Sheffield Steelers-2
00UK Sekonda Superleague-43
05UK Sheffield Steelers Supplementary-3
Gold-3
Silver-3
Centomo, Sebastien
99Rouyn-Noranda Huskies-5
00Rouyn-Noranda Huskies-19
Signed-19
01BAP Memorabilia-333
Emerald-333
Ruby-333
Sapphire-333
01Between the Pipes-158
01Parkhurst-348
01SPx-215
01UD Premier Collection-84
01Memphis RiverKings-1
01Memphis RiverKings-12
02BAP First Edition-266
02Between the Pipes-95
Gold-95
Silver-95
Jerseys-44
02SPx-123
02UD Foundations-140
02UD Piece of History-148
02Upper Deck-223
Exclusives-223
02Upper Deck MVP-218
Gold-218
Classics-218
Golden Classics-218
02Upper Deck Vintage-345
02ECHL Update-U-3
03BAP Memorabilia Deep in the Crease-D9
03Pacific AHL Prospects-81
Gold-81
04Las Vegas Wranglers-18
04ITG Heroes and Prospects Net Prospects-22
04ITG Heroes and Prosp Net Prospects Gold-22
Centrone, Marc
81Regina Pats-5
82Regina Pats-18
83Regina Pats-18
Cepek, Cameron
04Portland Winter Hawks-2
Cepis, Jacob
06Cedar Rapids RoughRiders-7
Cereda, Luca
95Quebec Pee-Wee Tournament-1205
99Swiss Panini Stickers-16
99Swiss Panini Stickers-289
01St. John's Maple Leafs-4
Ceresino, Ray
44Beehive Group II Photos-388
51Cleveland Barons-15
Cermak, David
94Czech APS Extraliga-61
95Czech APS Extraliga-89
96Czech APS Extraliga-86
97Czech DS Stickers-150
Cermak, Leos
00Czech OFS-102
01Czech OFS-273
03Czech OFS Plus-194
03Czech OFS Plus-314
04Czech OFS-85
05Czech HC Liberec-1
06Czech HC Slavia Praha Postcards-3
Cermak, Peter
98BC Icemen II-16
99Asheville Smoke-4
99UHL All-Stars East-12T
Cernich, Kord
90ProCards AHL/IHL-6
91ProCards-211
91ProCards-330
94Anchorage Aces-5
97Anchorage Aces-4
98Anchorage Aces-16
99Anchorage Aces-11
Cerniglia, Mike
95North Iowa Huskies-2
Cernik, Frantisek
79Panini Stickers-91
82Swedish Semic VM Stickers-91
83Swedish Semic VM Stickers-91
97Czech APS Extraliga-376
98Czech OFS Legends-14
Cernosek, Marek
96Czech APS Extraliga-273
97Czech DS Stickers-172
98Czech DS Stickers-34
98Czech OFS-333
99Czech OFS-119
99Czech OFS-343
99Czech OFS-353
00Czech OFS-140
01Czech OFS-235
02Czech OFS Plus-47
Trios-T19
03Czech OFS Plus-2
04Czech OFS-225
05Czech HC Sparta Praha-2
06Czech HC Sparta Praha Postcards-2
06Czech OFS-86
Cerny, Ales
00Swift Current Broncos-2
01Swift Current Broncos-2
02Czech OFS Plus-130
Cerny, Frantisek
82Swedish Semic VM Stickers-88
Cerny, Jakub
06Czech OFS-132
Cerny, Josef
69Swedish Hockey-22
70Finnish Jaakiekko-42
70Swedish Hockey-353
70Swedish Masterserien-147
71Finnish Suomi Stickers-23
71Swedish Hockey-49
72Finnish Panda Toronto-80
72Finnish Semic World Championship-34
72Swedish Semic World Championship-34
74Swedish Semic World Champ Stickers-70
Cerny, Michal
92Upper Deck-603
94Czech APS Extraliga-126
97Czech APS Extraliga-229
98Czech DS Stickers-36
99Czech Score Blue 2000-124
99Czech Score Red Ice 2000-124
Cerny, Milan
94Czech APS Extraliga-150
Cerny, Otakar
94Czech APS Extraliga-54
Cerny, Robert
96Slovakian Quebec Pee-Wee Tournament-5
Cerqua, Brett
93Quebec Pee-Wee Tournament-483
Cerrella, Chris
95Waterloo Blackhawks -2
02Orlando Seals-17
Cerven, Martin
95Spokane Chiefs-10
96Seattle Thunderbirds-14
97Bowman CHL-90
OPC-90
99Charlotte Checkers-30
Cervenka, Roman
05Czech HC Slavia Praha-3
06Czech HC Slavia Praha Postcards-4
06Czech OFS-290
Cerveny, Petr
99Czech Score Blue 2000-56
99Czech Score Red Ice 2000-56
Cesar, Stephane
06London Knights-18
Cescon, Craig
03Plymouth Whalers-15
04Mississauga Ice Dogs-10
Cesky, Jaroslav
04Tulsa Oilers-6
Cesnek, Michal
93Quebec Pee-Wee Tournament-1562
Cespiva, David
04German Adler Mannheim Eagles Postcards-8
05German DEL-359
Cetkovsky, Jiri
02Calgary Hitmen-17
Cey, Morgan
03Notre Dame Fighting Irish-5
04Notre Dame Fighting Irish-25
05Johnstown Chiefs-4
Cey, Patrick
05Vernon Vipers-5
Chabada, Martin
98Czech OFS-143
00Czech DS Extraliga-9
00Czech OFS-304
01Czech OFS-19
03Czech OFS Plus-340
03Czech OFS Plus MS Praha-SE35
04Czech HC Sparta Praha Postcards-3
04Czech OFS-187
Czech/Slovak-7
05Czech HC Sparta Praha-6
06Czech CP Cup Postcards-9
06Swedish SHL Elitset-218
Chabbert, Kevin
01Missouri River Otters-27
03Missouri River Otters-15
Chabbert, Steve
01Roanoke Express-3
Chabera, Jan
03Czech OFS Plus-327
06Czech OFS-7
Goalies I-8
Goalies II-4
Chabot, Francois
05Baie-Comeau Drakkar-9
06Chicoutimi Sagueneens-7
Chabot, Frederic
89ProCards IHL-135
90ProCards AHL/IHL-66
92Fredericton Canadiens-6
95Cincinnati Cyclones-2
96Collector's Edge Future Legends-17
97Be A Player-169
Autographs-169
Autographs Die-Cuts-169
Autographs Prismatic Die-Cuts-169
99Houston Aeros-20
01German Upper Deck-198
Jersey Cards-FC-J
02German DEL City Press-260
03German DEL-197
03German Nuremberg Ice Tigers Postcards-3
05German DEL-257
06Houston Aeros RetroÂ -1
Chabot, Jean-Philip
05Moncton Wildcats-22
06Gatineau Olympiques-11
Chabot, John
83Canadiens Postcards-5
84O-Pee-Chee-258
85O-Pee-Chee-244
85O-Pee-Chee Stickers-101
86O-Pee-Chee Stickers-230
86Penguins Kodak-5
87O-Pee-Chee-32
87O-Pee-Chee Stickers-169
87Panini Stickers-151
87Red Wings Little Caesars-5
87Topps-32
88O-Pee-Chee-39
88Panini Stickers-42
88Red Wings Little Caesars-3
88Topps-39
89O-Pee-Chee-225
89Red Wings Little Caesars-4
90Bowman-236
Tiffany-236
90O-Pee-Chee-163
90Panini Stickers-216
90Pro Set-68
90Score-277
Canadian-277
90Topps-163
Tiffany-163
90Upper Deck-113
French-113
90ProCards AHL/IHL-488
91Upper Deck-393
French-393
94German DEL-67
95German DEL-67
96German DEL-263
98German DEL-134
99German DEL-82
00German Berlin Polar Bears Postcards-1
00German DEL-65
Profiles-P3
Chabot, Lorne
23V128-1 Paulin's Candy-15
32O'Keefe Maple Leafs-1
33O-Pee-Chee V304A-18
33V129-45
33V252 Canadian Gum-9
33V288 Hamilton Gum-30
33V357 Ice Kings-71
34Beehive Group I Photos-46
34Diamond Matchbooks Silver-10
34Sweet Caporal-33
35CCM Green Border Photos-8
35Diamond Matchbooks Tan 1-11
35Diamond Matchbooks Tan 2-8
35Diamond Matchbooks Tan 3-8
55Parkhurst-21
Quaker Oats-21
02Parkhurst Reprints-202
05ITG Ultimate Memorabilia Lumbergraphs-10
05ITG Ultimate Mem Paper Cut Autos-7
06Between The Pipes Forgotten Franchises-FF05
06ITG Ultimate Memorabilia Maple Leafs Forever
Autos-8
06ITG Ultimate Memorabilia Marvelous Maroons
Autos-5
Chabot, Louis
01OCN Blizzard-3
Chabot, Luc
02UK Peterborough Phantoms-1
03UK Basingstoke Bison-19
03UK Coventry Blaze History-7
04UK Coventry Blaze-6
Chabot, Martin
92Quebec Pee-Wee Tournament-1270
01Chicoutimi Sagueneens-20
Chabot, Nicolas
96Rimouski Oceanic-7
96Rimouski Oceanic Quebec Police-7
98Colorado Gold Kings-1
99Idaho Steelheads-2
Chabot, Stephane
05Brampton Battalion-9
06Brampton Battalion-8
Chad, John
34Beehive Group I Photos-47
05Quad City Mallards-19
Chadney, Randy
917th Inn. Sketch WHL-55
Chadwick, Bill
83Hall of Fame Postcards-E4
85Hall of Fame-65
Chadwick, Ed
44Beehive Group II Photos-389
52Juniors Blue Tint-157
57Parkhurst-M24
57Parkhurst-M25
57Parkhurst-T2
58Parkhurst-12
59Parkhurst-5

61Shirriff/Salada Coins-20
84Nova Scotia Oilers-25
94Parkhurst Missing Link-128
02Parkhurst Reprints-217

Chagnon, Paul
94Fredericton Canadiens-8
95Fredericton Canadiens-6
96Fredericton Canadiens-27

Chagodaev, Alexander
00Russian Hockey League-291

Chainey, Alain
87Nordiques General Foods-31
89Nordiques Team Issue-4
917th Inn. Sketch QMJHL-182

Chainlere, Philippe
00Hull Olympiques-10
Signed-10

Chaisson, Ben
03Shawinigan Cataractes-5
06Halifax Mooseheads-10

Chalanek, Miroslav
94Czech APS Extraliga-15

Chalifoux, Denis
907th Inn. Sketch QMJHL-51
907th Inn. Sketch Memorial Cup-70
91ProCards-106
96Swiss HNL-506

Chalk, Dave
78Finnish SM-Liiga-119

Challande, Jean-Philippe
95Swiss HNL-487

Challice, Ben
94UK Guildford Flames-1

Chalmers, William
52Juniors Blue Tint-52

Chaloner, Kane
917th Inn. Sketch WHL-58

Chalupa, Michal
98Czech OFS-145

Chalupa, Milan
79Panini Stickers-79
82Swedish Semic VM Stickers-80
83Swedish Semic VM Stickers-80
99Czech OFS-349
00Czech OFS-185

Chamberlain, Curtis
83Saskatoon Blades-17
84Saskatoon Blades Stickers-2

Chamberlain, Jamie
95Quebec Pee-Wee Tournament-617
99O-Pee-Chee-255
99O-Pee-Chee Chrome-255
99O-Pee-Chee Chrome Refractors-255
99Topps/OPC-255
99Topps/OPC Chrome-255
Refractors-255
99Bowman CHL-6
Gold-6
OPC International-6
Autographs-BA26
Autographs Gold-BA26
Autographs Silver-BA26

Chamberlain, Murph
34Beehive Group I Photos-143
34Beehive Group I Photos-305
37O-Pee-Chee V304E-147
38Quaker Oats Photos-7
39O-Pee-Chee V301-1-12
43Parade Sportive *-26
44Beehive Group II Photos-228
45Quaker Oats Photos-69A
45Quaker Oats Photos-69B
45Quaker Oats Photos-69C
61Sudbury Wolves-4
62Sudbury Wolves-6

Chamberland, Carl
05Victoriaville Tigres-15
06Victoriaville Tigres-6

Chamberland, Germain
93Quebec Pee-Wee Tournament-435

Chamberland, Maxim
03Drummondville Voltigeurs-3
04Drummondville Voltigeurs-25

Chambers, Dave
90Nordiques Petro-Canada-2
90Pro Set-675

Chambers, Greg
01Peterborough Petes-16
02Peterborough Petes-19
03ECHL All-Stars-263
03Pensacola Ice Pilots-338

Chambers, Josh
00London Knights-23

Chambers, Shawn
88North Stars ADA-5
89O-Pee-Chee-142
89Panini Stickers-111
89Topps-142
90Bowman-180
Tiffany-180
90O-Pee-Chee-192
90Panini Stickers-252
90Pro Set-134
90Score-57
Canadian-57
90Topps-192
Tiffany-192
90Upper Deck-106
French-106
91Capitals Junior 5x7-5
91Capitals Kodak-5
91Score Canadian Bilingual-572
91Score Canadian English-572
92Lightning Sheraton-9
92Parkhurst-406
Emerald Ice-406
92Score-508
Canadian-508
92Upper Deck-104
93Donruss-325
93Leaf-40
93Lightning Kash n'Karry-2
93Lightning Season in Review-6
93OPC Premier-101
Gold-101
93Panini Stickers-219
93Pinnacle-87
Canadian-87
93PowerPlay-229
93Score-391
Canadian-391
93Stadium Club-412
Members Only Master Set-412
First Day Issue-412
93Topps/OPC Premier-101
Gold-101
93Ultra-75
93Upper Deck-68
94Canada Games NHL POGS-227
94Donruss-72
94Flair-171
94Fleer-204
94Leaf-332
94OPC Premier-174
Special Effects-174
94Parkhurst-223
Gold-223
94Pinnacle-97
Artist's Proofs-97
Rink Collection-97
94Score-153
Gold-153
Platinum-153
94Topps/OPC Premier-174
Special Effects-174
94Ultra-203
95Donruss-126
95Emotion-96
95Leaf-234
95Panini Stickers-86
95Parkhurst International-392
Emerald Ice-392
95Score-86
Black Ice Artist's Proofs-86
Black Ice-86
95SkyBox Impact-92
95Ultra-259
95Upper Deck-148
Electric Ice-148
Electric Ice Gold-148
95Finnish Semic World Championships-109
95Swedish World Championships Stickers-213
96Be A Player-75
Autographs-75
Autographs Silver-75
96Devils Team Issue-29
96Upper Deck-287
98Pacific-174
Ice Blue-174
Red-174
99BAP Millennium-83
Emerald-83
Ruby-83
Sapphire-83
Signatures-83
Signatures Gold-83
99Stars Postcards-4
02BAP Sig Series Auto Buybacks 1999-83

Chambers, Tyler
03Quebec Remparts-4

Champagne, Andrew
66Tulsa Oilers-2

Champagne, Bruno
01Chicoutimi Sagueneens-22
03Gatineau Olympiques-3

Champagne, Dennis
79Montreal Juniors-3

Champagne, Joel
06Chicoutimi Sagueneens-8

Champagne, Michel
05Gatineau Olympiques-18

Chan, Carissa
99Finnish Cardset Aces High-D-Q

Chandler, Matt
02Greensboro Generals RBI-7
03Greensboro Generals-180

Channell, Craig
89ProCards IHL-134
99Fort Wayne Komets Penalty Leaders-11

Chant, David
99Brampton Battalion-3
00Barrie Colts-5
01Barrie Colts-1
04Barrie Colts 10th Anniversary-24

Chant, Kyle
97Portland Winter Hawks-9

Chapados, Daniel
93Quebec Pee-Wee Tournament-299

Chapdelaine, Rene
89ProCards AHL-21
90ProCards AHL/IHL-429
92Phoenix Roadrunners-4
93Peoria Rivermen-3
95Peoria Rivermen-2
99Long Beach Ice Dogs-1

Chapman, Adam
99Ottawa 67's-3
00Ottawa 67's-17
01Ottawa 67's-19

Chapman, Art
33V357 Ice Kings-32
34Beehive Group I Photos-219
34Diamond Matchbooks Silver-11
35Diamond Matchbooks Tan 1-12
35Diamond Matchbooks Tan 2-9
35Diamond Matchbooks Tan 3-9
35O-Pee-Chee V304C-94
37V356 Worldwide Gum-42
39O-Pee-Chee V301-1-18
06ITG Ultimate Memorabilia Amazing Amerks Autos-5

Chapman, Blair
77O-Pee-Chee NHL-174
77Penguins Puck Bucks-9
77Topps-174
78O-Pee-Chee-33
78Topps-33
79O-Pee-Chee-21
79Topps-21
80O-Pee-Chee-48
80Topps-48
81O-Pee-Chee-291
81Topps-W115

Chapman, Brennan
01Regina Pats-6
02Regina Pats-20
03Vancouver Giants-7
04Lethbridge Hurricanes-3
05Red Deer Rebels-1

Chapman, Brian
88ProCards AHL-67
89ProCards AHL-299
90ProCards AHL/IHL-190
91ProCards-109
93Phoenix Roadrunners-2
95Phoenix Roadrunners-8
97Long Beach Ice Dogs-6
97Manitoba Moose-B1
98Manitoba Moose-D4
99Manitoba Moose-18
00Manitoba Moose-6
01Manitoba Moose-4
02Manitoba Moose-22
03Rochester Americans-5
04Springfield Falcons-4

Chapman, Craig
907th Inn. Sketch WHL-2
917th Inn. Sketch WHL-122
99Tacoma Sabercats-9
03UK Coventry Blaze History-15

Chapman, Drew
94UK Guildford Flames-7
95UK Guildford Flames-11

Chapman, Dylan
04Moose Jaw Warriors-6
05Moose Jaw Warriors-4
06Chilliwack Bruins-4

Chapman, Phil
52Juniors Blue Tint-89

Chapman, Robert
01Owen Sound Attack-1

Chapman, Travis
00Kitchener Rangers-9
01Sudbury Wolves-3
01Sudbury Wolves Police-5
03Sault Ste. Marie Greyhounds-2

Chappell, Chris
05Saginaw Spirit-3
06Saginaw Spirit-14

Chappot, Florian
95Swiss HNL-381
96Swiss HNL-241

Chappot, Roger
72Finnish Semic World Championship-149
72Swedish Semic World Championship-149

Chaput, Dan
91Ferris State Bulldogs-7
92Ferris State Bulldogs-7
93Hampton Roads Admirals-3
96Knoxville Cherokees-4
98San Angelo Outlaws-4

Chaput, Francois
97New Mexico Scorpions-14

Chaput, Martin
907th Inn. Sketch QMJHL-46
917th Inn. Sketch QMJHL-233

Chara, Zdeno
97SP Authentic-186
97Kentucky Thoroughblades-5
98Bowman's Best-134
Refractors-134
Atomic Refractors-134
98Pacific-276
Ice Blue-276
Red-276
98SPx Finite-52
Radiance-52
Spectrum-52
98UD Choice-124
Prime Choice Reserve-124
Reserve-124
98UD3-20
98UD3-80
98UD3-140
Die-Cuts-20
Die-Cuts-80
Die-Cuts-140
98Upper Deck-126
Exclusives-126
Exclusives 1 of 1-126
Gold Reserve-126
99BAP Millennium-155
Emerald-155
Ruby-155
Sapphire-155
Signatures-155
Signatures Gold-155
99O-Pee-Chee-29
99O-Pee-Chee Chrome-29
99O-Pee-Chee Chrome Refractors-29
99Pacific-252
Copper-252
Emerald Green-252
Gold-252
Ice Blue-252
Premiere Date-252
Red-252
99Panini Stickers-89
99Topps/OPC-29
99Topps/OPC Chrome-29
Refractors-29
99Upper Deck-85
Exclusives-85
Exclusives 1 of 1-85
99Upper Deck Gold Reserve-85
99Upper Deck MVP-130
Gold Script-130
Silver Script-130
Super Script-130
99Upper Deck Victory-178
00O-Pee-Chee-263A
00O-Pee-Chee Parallel-263A
00Private Stock Game Gear-67
00Private Stock Game Gear Patches-67
00Revolution Game-Worn Jerseys-7
00Revolution Game-Worn Jersey Patches-7
00Stadium Club-167
00Topps/OPC-263A
Parallel-263A
00Upper Deck-111
Exclusives Tier 1-111
Exclusives Tier 2-111
01BAP Memorabilia-498
Emerald-498
Ruby-498
Sapphire-498
01Pacific-242
01Pacific-415
Extreme LTD-242
Gold-415
Hobby LTD-242
Premiere Date-242
Retail LTD-242
Adrenaline Jerseys-31
01Pacific Arena Exclusives-242
01Pacific Arena Exclusives-415
01Parkhurst-392
01Senators Team Issue-4
02BAP Memorabilia-130
Emerald-130
Ruby-130
Sapphire-130
NHL All-Star Game-130
NHL All-Star Game Blue-130
NHL All-Star Game Green-130
NHL All-Star Game Red-130
02BAP Memorabilia Toronto Fall Expo-130
02BAP Sig Series Auto Buybacks 1999-155
02NHL Power Play Stickers-104
02Pacific-264
Blue-264
Red-264
02Pacific Complete-56
Red-56
02Parkhurst Retro-182
Minis-182
02Senators Team Issue-4
02Senators Team Issue-1
02Topps Total-69
02Upper Deck-369
Exclusives-369
02Upper Deck Beckett UD Promos-369
02Upper Deck MVP-129
Gold-129
Classics-129
Golden Classics-129
03BAP Memorabilia-90
Emerald-90
Gold-90
Ruby-90
Sapphire-90
03BAP Ultimate Mem Hometown Heroes-5
03BAP Ultimate Mem Hometown Heroes Gold-5
03BAP Ultimate Memorabilia Triple Threads-12
03Beehive-135
Gold-135
Silver-135
03Black Diamond-84
Black-84
Green-84
Red-84
03ITG Action-422
Homeboys-HB3
03O-Pee-Chee-111
03O-Pee-Chee-281
03OPC Blue-111
03OPC Blue-281
03OPC Gold-111
03OPC Gold-281
03OPC Red-111
03OPC Red-281
03Pacific-235
Blue-235
Red-235
03Pacific Complete-193
Red-193
03Pacific Exhibit-102
Blue Backs-102
Yellow Backs-102
03Pacific Prism-73
Blue-73
Gold-73
Red-73
03Parkhurst Rookie Jerseys-GJ-36
03Parkhurst Rookie Jerseys Gold-GJ-36
03Senators Postcards-2
03SPx Style-SPX-JB
03SPx Style Limited-SPX-JB
03Titanium-71
Hobby Jersey Number Parallels-71
Retail-71
Retail Jersey Number Parallels-71
03Topps-111
03Topps-281
Blue-111
Blue-281
Gold-111
Gold-281
Red-111
Red-281
03Topps C55-108
Minis-108
Minis American Back-108
Minis American Back Red-108
Minis Bazooka Back-108
Minis Brooklyn Back-108
Minis Hat Trick Back-108
Minis O Canada Back-108
Minis O Canada Back Red-108
Minis Stanley Cup Back-108
03Upper Deck-133
Canadian Exclusives-133
HG-133
03Upper Deck Classic Portraits-143
03Upper Deck MVP-294
Gold Script-294
Silver Script-294
Canadian Exclusives-294
03Upper Deck Rookie Update AS Lineup-AS6
03Upper Deck Victory-133
Bronze-133
Gold-133
Silver-133
04Pacific-183
Blue-183
Red-183
04SP Authentic Rookie Review-RR-ZC
04SP Authentic Sign of the Times-ST-ZC
04UD All-World-54
Gold-54
Autographs-54
Dual Autographs-AD-SC
04Upper Deck-122
Canadian Exclusives-122
HG Glossy Gold-122
HG Glossy Silver-122
School of Hard Knocks-SHK5
World's Best-WB20
World Cup Tribute-ZC
World Cup Tribute-ZCMG
World Cup Tribute-PBPDZC
04Swedish Pure Skills-26
Parallel-26
Professional Power-ZC
05Beehive Signature Scrapbook-SSZC
05Black Diamond-62
Emerald-62
Gold-62
Onyx-62
Ruby-62
05Panini Stickers-121
05Parkhurst-341
Facsimile Auto Parallel-341
Signatures-ZC
True Colors-TCOTT
True Colors-TCOTT
05SP Authentic Sign of the Times Triples-THHC
05SP Game Used Authentic Fabrics-AF-ZC
05SP Game Used Authentic Fabrics Autos-AAF-ZC
05SP Game Used Authentic Fabrics Gold-AF-ZC
05SP Game Used Authentic Fabrics Triple-CNP
05SP Game Used Authentic Fabrics Triple-CRH
05SP Game Used Authentic Patches-AP-ZC
05SP Game Used Authentic Patch Autos-AAP-ZC
05SP Game Used Authentic Patches Triple-CNP
05SP Game Used Authentic Patches Triple-CRH
05SP Game Used Auto Draft-AD-ZC
05SP Game Used SIGnificance-ZC
05SP Game Used SIGnificance Gold-S-ZC
05SPx Winning Combos-WC-CH
05SPx Winning Combos-WC-RC
05SPx Winning Combos Autographs-AWC-CH
05SPx Winning Combos Gold-WC-CH
05SPx Winning Combos Gold-WC-RC
05SPx Winning Combos Spectrum-WC-CH
05SPx Winning Combos Spectrum-WC-RC
05SPx Winning Materials-WM-ZC
05SPx Winning Materials Autographs-AWM-ZC
05SPx Winning Materials Gold-WM-ZC
05SPx Winning Materials Spectrum-WM-ZC
05The Cup Emblems of Endorsement-EEZC
05The Cup Master Pressplate Rookie Update-198
05The Cup Scripted Numbers-SNPC
05The Cup Signature Patches-SPZC
05UD Artifacts Auto Facts-AF-ZC
05UD Artifacts Auto Facts Blue-AF-ZC
05UD Artifacts Auto Facts Copper-AF-ZC
05UD Artifacts Auto Facts Pewter-AF-ZC
05UD Artifacts Auto Facts Silver-AF-ZC
05Ultimate Collection Jerseys Dual-DJHC
05Ultimate Coll National Heroes Jersey-NHJZC
05Ultimate Coll National Heroes Patch-NHPZC
05Ultimate Coll Ultimate Patches Dual-DPHC
05Ultra-138
Gold-138
Fresh Ink-FI-ZC
Fresh Ink Blue-FI-ZC
Ice-138
05Upper Deck-136
Big Playmakers-B-ZC
HG Glossy-136
Jerseys Series II-J2ZC
Majestic Materials-MMZC
NHL Generations-DSC
Notable Numbers-N-ZC
Patches-P-ZC
Ice Cool Threads-CTZC
Ice Cool Threads Autographs-ACTZC
Ice Cool Threads Glass-CTZC
Ice Cool Threads Patches-CTPZC
Ice Cool Threads Patch Autographs-CAPZC
05Upper Deck MVP-272
Gold-272
Platinum-272
Materials-M-ZC
Materials Duals-D-CO
ProSign-P-ZC
05Upper Deck Rookie Update-198
Inspirations Patch Rookies-198
05Upper Deck Toronto Fall Expo-136
05Upper Deck Victory-235
Black-235
Gold-235
Silver-235
05Swedish SHL Elitset-42
Gold-42
06Be A Player-144
Autographs-144
Signatures-ZC
Signatures 10-159
Signatures Duals-DCW
Up Close and Personal-UC60
Up Close and Personal Autographs-UC60
06Be A Player Portraits-12
Dual Signature Portraits-DSCJ
Signature Portraits-SPZC
06Beehive-94
Gold-94
Matte-94
Matted Materials-MMZC
Remarkable Matted Materials-MMZC
06Black Diamond-8
Black-8
Gold-8
Ruby-8
06Flair Showcase-72
06Flair Showcase-148
Parallel-72
Parallel-148
Stitches-SSZC
06Fleer-18
Tiffany-18
Fabricology-FZC
06Hot Prospects-9
Red Hot-9
White Hot-9
Hot Materials -HMZC
Hot Materials Red Hot-HMZC
Hot Materials White Hot-HMZC
-Hotagraphs-HZC
06O-Pee-Chee-51
Rainbow-51
Swatches-S-ZC
06Panini Stickers-22
06SP Authentic-94
Limited-94
06SP Game Used Authentic Fabrics Dual-AF2SC
06SP Game Used Authentic Fabrics Dual Patches-AF2SC
06SP Game Used Authentic Fabrics Triple-AF3BOS
06SP Game Used Authentic Fabrics Triple Patches-AF3BOS
06SP Game Used Inked Sweaters-ISZC
06SP Game Used Inked Sweaters Patches-ISZC
06SP Game Used Letter Marks-LMZC
06SP Game Used SIGnificance-SZC
06SPx-8
Spectrum-8
06The Cup Autographed NHL Shields Duals-DASCT
06The Cup Honorable Numbers-HNZC
06The Cup Limited Logos-LLZC
06UD Artifacts-93
Blue-93
Gold-93
Platinum-93
Radiance-93
Autographed Radiance Parallel-93
Red-93
Auto-Facts-AFZC
Auto-Facts Gold-AFZC
Tundra Tandems-TTZM
Tundra Tandems Black-TTZM
Tundra Tandems Blue-TTZM
Tundra Tandems Gold-TTZM
Tundra Tandems Platinum-TTZM
Tundra Tandems Red-TTZM
Tundra Tandems Dual Patches Red-TTZM
06UD Mini Jersey Collection-9
06UD Powerplay-10
Impact Rainbow-10
Specialists-SZC
Specialists Patches-PZC
06Ultimate Collection Premium Patches-PS-ZC
06Ultimate Collection Premium Swatches-PS-ZC
06Ultra-20
Gold Medallion-20
Ice Medallion-20
06Upper Deck Arena Giveaways-BOS4
06Upper Deck-266
Exclusives Parallel-266
High Gloss Parallel-266
All World-AW6
Game Jerseys-J2ZC
Game Patches-P2ZC
Masterpieces-266
06Upper Deck MVP-22
Gold Script-22
Super Script-22
Autographs-OACS
Jerseys-OJCR
06Upper Deck Sweet Shot-8
Signature Shots/Saves-SSZC
Sweet Stitches-SSZC
Sweet Stitches Duals-SSZC
Sweet Stitches Triples-SSZC
06Upper Deck Trilogy-8
Combo Clearcut Autographs-C2RC
Scripts-TSZC
06Upper Deck Victory-139
06Upper Deck Victory-232
06Upper Deck Victory Black-139
06Upper Deck Victory Gold-139
06Russian Sport Collection Olympic Stars-47
07Upper Deck Victory-64
Black-64
Gold-64

Charbonneau, Alain
98Val d'Or Foreurs-5

Charbonneau, Jocelyn
917th Inn. Sketch QMJHL-66

Charbonneau, Jose
86Sherbrooke Canadiens-10
87Canadiens Postcards-3
88Canadiens Postcards-4
88ProCards AHL-295
89ProCards IHL-181
90Alberta International Team Canada-13
93Parkhurst-484
Emerald Ice-484
93PowerPlay-457
93Score-638
Gold-638
Canadian-638
Canadian Gold-638
93Ultra-438
93Upper Deck-503
95German DEL-257
96German DEL-145
98German DEL-141
99German DEL-86
00German DEL-82

Charbonneau, Louis-Philippe
95Roanoke Express-8
95Slapshot Memorial Cup-72
01Sorel Royaux-4

Charbonneau, Marc
93Quebec Pee-Wee Tournament-338
99Anchorage Aces-5

Charbonneau, Patrice
917th Inn. Sketch QMJHL-251
93Drummondville Voltigeurs-17
97Macon Whoopee-10
97Macon Whoopee Autographs-10
99Rockford IceHogs-3
00Rockford IceHogs-2

Charbonneau, Patrick
92Quebec Pee-Wee Tournament-856
93Classic Four-Sport *-255
Gold-255
95PEI Senators-3
97Wheeling Nailers-9
97Wheeling Nailers Photo Pack-9

Charbonneau, Ron
94UK Guildford Flames-10

Charbonneau, Stephane
907th Inn. Sketch QMJHL-40
91ProCards-536
917th Inn. Sketch Memorial Cup-43
93Phoenix Roadrunners-3
94Erie Panthers-19
95Portland Pirates-7

Charette, Francis
04Rimouski Oceanic-9
05Drummondville Voltigeurs-32
05Rimouski Oceanic-11
06Drummondville Voltigeurs-23

Charette, Jonathan
01Val d'Or Foreurs-17
02Val d'Or Foreurs-16
03Val d'Or Foreurs-9
05Roanoke Valley Vipers-2

Charette, Michel
02Cape Breton Screaming Eagles-17
04P.E.I. Rocket-16

Charland, Carl
95Slapshot Memorial Cup-63

Charland, Francis
03Victoriaville Tigers-4
03Victoriaville Tigers-NNO

Charlebois, Bob
72O-Pee-Chee-309
73Quaker Oats WHA-23

Charlebois, Joe
04Sioux City Musketeers-6

Charles, Richard
97UK Fife Flyers-8

Charleston, Dan
02Chicago Steel-3

Charlesworth, Todd
82Oshawa Generals-22
83Oshawa Generals-3
88ProCards IHL-45
89ProCards AHL-139
90ProCards AHL/IHL-2
93Muskegon Fury-17
94Muskegon Fury-9

Charpentier, Bryce
04Florida Everblades-15
05Florida Everblades-12

Charpentier, Marco
99Baie-Comeau Drakkar-4
00Baie-Comeau Drakkar-10
Signed-10
00QMJHL All-Star Program Inserts-16
01Trenton Titans-1-2

Charpentier, Sebastien
97Hampton Roads Admirals-6
97Portland Pirates-6
98Hampton Roads Admirals 10th Anniversary-30
99Portland Pirates-5
00Portland Pirates-8
01BAP Memorabilia-328
Emerald-328
Ruby-328
Sapphire-328
01Parkhurst-350
01UD Top Shelf-141
02Between the Pipes-97
Gold-97
Silver-97
Jerseys-33
02Pacific Calder-98
Silver-98
02Pacific Complete-505
Red-505
02SPx-125
02UD Foundations-142
02UD Mask Collection-90
02UD Mask Collection Beckett Promos-90
02Upper Deck-224
Exclusives-224
02Upper Deck MVP-220
Gold-220
Classics-220
Golden Classics-220
02Upper Deck Vintage-347
03BAP Memorabilia-164
Emerald-164
Gold-164
Ruby-164
Sapphire-164
03ITG Action-520
03Pacific-341
Blue-341
Red-341
03Pacific Complete-489
Red-489
03Pacific Exhibit-148
Blue Backs-148
Yellow Backs-148
03Upper Deck-442
Canadian Exclusives-442
HG-442
UD Exclusives-442
03Upper Deck MVP-436
Gold Script-436
Silver Script-436
Canadian Exclusives-436
04Pacific-262
Blue-262
Red-262
04ITG Heroes and Prospects Net Prospects-24
04ITG Heroes and Prosp Net Prospects Gold-24

Charrette, Michel
03Drummondville Voltigeurs-4

Charrois, Martin
907th Inn. Sketch QMJHL-9
917th Inn. Sketch Memorial Cup-52

Charrois, Yvan
907th Inn. Sketch QMJHL-105

Charron, Craig
91Cincinnati Cyclones-4
92Cincinnati Cyclones-4
94Dayton Bombers-5
95Rochester Americans-1
96Rochester Americans-3
97Rochester Americans-2-1
99St. John's Maple Leafs-6
00Rochester Americans-7

Charron, Eric
90ProCards AHL/IHL-56
91ProCards-89
92Fredericton Canadiens-5
93Atlanta Knights-3
94Fleer-205
94Lightning Photo Album-7
94OPC Premier-343
Special Effects-343
94Topps/OPC Premier-343
Special Effects-343
94Ultra-371
94Upper Deck-489
Electric Ice-489
97Saint John Flames-5
00Cleveland Lumberjacks-4
01German Adler Mannheim Eagles Postcards-2
02UK Nottingham Panthers-4
03Russian Hockey League-174

Charron, Guy
69Canadiens Postcards Color-5
71Sargent Promotions Stamps-60
71Toronto Sun-87
72O-Pee-Chee-223
72Sargent Promotions Stamps-80
73O-Pee-Chee-220
73Red Wings Team Issue-5
73Red Wings McCarthy Postcards-4
74NHL Action Stamps-94
74NHL Action Stamps Update-14
74O-Pee-Chee NHL-57
74Topps-57
75O-Pee-Chee NHL-32
75O-Pee-Chee NHL-319
75Topps-32
75Topps-319
76O-Pee-Chee NHL-186
76O-Pee-Chee NHL-384
76Topps-186
77O-Pee-Chee NHL-145
77Topps-145
78Capitals Team Issue-3
78O-Pee-Chee-22
78Topps-22
79Panini Stickers-62
79Capitals Team Issue-2
79O-Pee-Chee-152
79Topps-152
80O-Pee-Chee-352
90Flames IGA/McGavin's-2
91Flames IGA-28
92Flames IGA-27
98Grand Rapids Griffins-22
99Grand Rapids Griffins-2
02Canadiens Postcards-28

Charron, Jonathan
98Val d'Or Foreurs-26

Charron, Yanick
03Gatineau Olympiques-4
03P.E.I. Rocket-5
04P.E.I. Rocket-22
05Drummondville Voltigeurs-27

Charron, Yves
917th Inn. Sketch QMJHL-31

Charter, Richard
93Quebec Pee-Wee Tournament-1159

Chartier, Christian
96Saskatoon Blades-6
97Upper Deck-402
97Saskatoon Blades-4
00Prince George Cougars-11
01St. John's Maple Leafs-5
04Las Vegas Wranglers-6
05Las Vegas Wranglers-4

Chartier, Dave
80Jets Postcards-4
81Saskatoon Blades-6
83Saskatoon Blades-10

Chartier, Jean-Philippe
99Baie-Comeau Drakkar-5

Chartier, Scott
91British Columbia JHL-35
91British Columbia JHL-158
92Western Michigan Broncos-8
93San Diego Gulls-5
93Classic-61
94Classic Autographs-NNO
99San Angelo Outlaws-2

Chartrain, Andre
81Fredericton Express-16
82Fredericton Express-16
83Fredericton Express-17

Chartrand, Brad
92Cornell Big Red-4
93Cornell Big Red-4
99BAP Memorabilia-373
Gold-373
Silver-373
99Pacific-457
99Pacific Omega-115
Copper-115
Gold-115
Ice Blue-115
Premiere Date-115
99Topps Premier Plus-90
Parallel-90
99Upper Deck Gold Reserve-342
00Upper Deck MVP-194
First Stars-194
Second Stars-194
Third Stars-194
00Upper Deck Victory-264
00Lowell Lock Monsters-7
01Manchester Monarchs-3A
02Kings Game Sheets-17
02Kings Game Sheets-18
03ITG Action-212

Chartrand, Clayton
97Prince Albert Raiders-5
98Prince Albert Raiders-4

Chartrand, Derek
96Sudbury Wolves-27

Chartrand, Jacques
52St. Lawrence Sales-27

Chartrand, Rick
89Rayside-Balfour Jr. Canadians-4

Chartrand, Simon
89Rayside-Balfour Jr. Canadians-5

Chartrand, Steve
02UK Coventry Blaze-11
03UK Coventry Blaze-10
03UK Coventry Blaze Calendars-4
03UK Coventry Blaze History-1

Chartraw, Rick
74Canadiens Postcards-3
75O-Pee-Chee NHL-388
76Canadiens Postcards-3
76O-Pee-Chee NHL-244
76Topps-244
77Canadiens Postcards-3
77O-Pee-Chee NHL-363
78Canadiens Postcards-2
78O-Pee-Chee-238
78Topps-238
79Canadiens Postcards-1
79O-Pee-Chee-243
79Topps-243
80Canadiens Postcards-3
80O-Pee-Chee-364
82Post Cereal-8
83Oilers McDonald's-6
88Oilers Tenth Anniversary-96

Chaschukhin, Konstantin
02Russian Hockey League-69

Chase, Bob
98Fort Wayne Komets-10

Chase, Don
96Wheeling Nailers-7
96Wheeling Nailers Photo Pack-1
97Mississippi Sea Wolves-3
98Pensacola Ice Pilots-5

Chase, Kelly
86Saskatoon Blades Photos-5
88ProCards IHL-81
89Blues Kodak-39
90Bowman-14
Tiffany-14
90O-Pee-Chee-432
90ProCards AHL/IHL-87
91Blues Postcards-7
91O-Pee-Chee-23
91Topps-23
93Donruss-483
94Donruss-157
94Leaf-396
95Whalers Bob's Stores-4
96Be A Player-60
Autographs-60
Autographs Silver-60
96Collector's Choice-122
96Whalers Kid's Club-12
97Paramount-156
Copper-156
Dark Grey-156
Emerald Green-156
Ice Blue-156
Red-156
Silver-156
98Be A Player-276
Press Release-276
98BAP Gold-276
98BAP Autographs-276
98BAP Autographs Gold-276
98Pacific-363
Ice Blue-363
Red-363
98Paramount-199
Copper-199
Emerald Green-199
Holo-Electric-199
Ice Blue-199
Silver-199
99Blues Taco Bell-19
00BAP Memorabilia Update Tough Materials-T9
00BAP Mem Update Tough Materials Gold-T9
02BAP Sig Series Auto Buybacks 1998-276
02Fleer Throwbacks-63
Gold-63
Platinum-63
Autographs-20
Stickwork-1
05ITG Tough Customers-KC
Autographs-KC
Complete Jerseys-KC
Emblem and Numbers-KC
Jerseys-KC
Signed Memorabilia-KC

Chase, Mike
95Central Hockey League-57

Chase, Tim
93Knoxville Cherokees-3
96Louisville Riverfrogs-18

Chasle, Yvon
52Juniors Blue Tint-134

Chasse, Denis
907th Inn. Sketch QMJHL-13
91ProCards-535
917th Inn. Sketch Memorial Cup-54
93Classic Pro Prospects-79

94Finest Bowman's Best-R15
94Finest Bowman's Best Refractors-R15
94Fleer-184
94Upper Deck-414
Electric Ice-414
95Donruss-164
95Leaf-132
95SkyBox Impact NHL On Fox-5
95Ultra-137
Gold Medallion-137
95Upper Deck-416
Electric Ice-416
Electric Ice Gold-416
00UK Cardiff Devils-9
00UK Sekonda Superleague-59
01UK Cardiff Devils-7
02UK Cardiff Devils-7

Chateau, Brooke

98Charlotte Checkers-7
99Charlotte Checkers-2
99Charlotte Checkers-24

Chatelain, Alex

98Swiss Power Play Stickers-276
99Swiss Panini Stickers-39
00Swiss Panini Stickers-39
00Swiss Slapshot Mini-Cards-SCB12
01Swiss HNL-87
02Swiss HNL-78

Chatrnuch, Roman

04Slovakian Skalica Team Set-6

Chattington, Terrance

52Juniors Blue Tint-57

Chaulk, Colin

95Slapshot-123
99Missouri River Otters-5
99Missouri River Otters Sheet-3
99UHL All-Stars West-9T
00Missouri River Otters-4
00Missouri River Otters-26
01Colorado Gold Kings-5
02Fort Wayne Komets-5
02Fort Wayne Komets Shoe Carnival-15
03Fort Wayne Komets-2
03Fort Wayne Komets 2003 Champions-1
03Fort Wayne Komets 2003 Champions-6
03Fort Wayne Komets Shoe Carnival-6
04Fort Wayne Komets-1
04Fort Wayne Komets Shoe Carnival-1
05Fort Wayne Komets Sprint-3

Chaumont, Bobby

01Sudbury Wolves-4
01Sudbury Wolves Police-13
03Sudbury Wolves-5
04Sudbury Wolves-2

Chaytors, Ryan

99Johnstown Chiefs-7

Chebaturkin, Vladimir

93Classic-37
93Classic Four-Sport *-212
Gold-212
98Pacific-277
Ice Blue-277
Red-277
99Lowell Lock Monsters-9
00Upper Deck NHLPA-PA76
00Czech Stadion-194
01Norfolk Admirals-25
03Russian National Team-14

Checco, Nick

93Minnesota Golden Gophers-7
94Minnesota Golden Gophers-8
95Minnesota Golden Gophers-9
96Minnesota Golden Gophers-6
98Florida Everblades-3
00Rockford IceHogs-3
01Rockford IceHogs-17

Checknita, Paul

87Kamloops Blazers-2
88Lethbridge Hurricanes-4

Cheechoo, Jonathan

98OPC Chrome-230
Refractors-230
98Topps-230
O-Pee-Chee-230
98Bowman CHL-142
98Bowman CHL-164
Golden Anniversary-142
Golden Anniversary-164
OPC International-142
OPC International-164
Autographs Blue-A25
Autographs Gold-A25
Autographs Silver-A25
Scout's Choice-SC18
98Bowman Chrome CHL-142
98Bowman Chrome CHL-164
Golden Anniversary-142
Golden Anniversary-164
Golden Anniversary Refractors-142
Golden Anniversary Refractors-164
OPC International-142
OPC International-164
OPC International Refractors-142
OPC International Refractors-164
Refractors-142
Refractors-164
99Upper Deck-317
Exclusives-317
Exclusives 1 of 1-317
99Upper Deck Gold Reserve-317
99Upper Deck Ovation-78
Standing Ovation-78
00Kentucky Thoroughblades-5
00Kentucky Thoroughblades-P2
01Cleveland Barons-3
02Bowman YoungStars-120
Gold-120
Silver-120
02Crown Royale Rookie Royalty-19
02Pacific Calder-93
Silver-93
Reflections-20
02Pacific Complete-539
Red-539
02Pacific Exclusive-190
Blue-190
Gold-190
Destined-10
02Stadium Club-120
Silver Decoy Cards-120
Proofs-120
02Titanium Right on Target-19
02Topps Total-432
03BAP Ultimate Mem Franch Present Future-26
03Beehive-160
Gold-160
Silver-160
03Crown Royale-85
Blue-85
Retail-85
03ITG Action-444
03Pacific-292
Blue-292
Red-292
03Pacific Calder-86
Silver-86
03Pacific Complete-248
Red-248
03Pacific Exhibit-127
Blue Backs-127
Yellow Backs-127
03Pacific Invincible New Sensations-20
03Pacific Prism Rookie Revolution-12
03Pacific Quest for the Cup-88
Blue-88
03Pacific Supreme Generations-10
03Private Stock Reserve-88
Blue-88
Red-88
Retail-88
03Sharks Postcards-1
03Titanium-86
Hobby Jersey Number Parallels-86
Retail-86
Retail Jersey Number Parallels-86
03Upper Deck-407
Canadian Exclusives-407
HG-407
UD Exclusives-407
03Upper Deck MVP-352
Gold Script-352
Silver Script-352
Canadian Exclusives-352
03Upper Deck Rookie Update YoungStars-YS18
03Pacific AHL Prospect Destined Greatness-5
04Pacific-226
Blue-226
Red-226
Gold Crown Die-Cuts-8
04UD All-World-58
Gold-58
Autographs-58
Triple Autographs-AT-CWR
Triple Autographs-AT-RCM
Quad Autographs-AQ-YFW
Six Autographs-AS-SWD
04Upper Deck YoungStars-YS-JC
04Swedish Pure Skills-39
Parallel-39
05Be A Player-74
First Period-74
Second Period-74
Third Period-74
Overtime-74
Dual Signatures-MC
Signatures-JC
Signatures Gold-JC
05Beehive-76
05Beehive-211
Beige -76
Blue -76
Gold-76
Red -76
Matte-76
Signature Scrapbook-SSCH
05Black Diamond-113
Emerald-113
Gold-113
Onyx-113
Ruby-113
Gemography-G-JC
Gemography Emerald-G-JC
Gemography Gold-G-JC
Gemography Onyx-G-JC
Gemography Ruby-G-JC
05Hot Prospects-85
En Fuego-85
Red Hot-85
White Hot-85
05McDonalds Upper Deck-43
05Panini Stickers-347
05Parkhurst-402
Facsimile Auto Parallel-402
True Colors-TCSJS
True Colors-TCSJS
True Colors-TCSJLA
True Colors-TCSJLA
05SP Authentic-82
Limited-82
Marks of Distinction-MDJC
Prestigious Pairings-PPTC
Scripts to Success-SSJC
Sign of the Times-JC
Sign of the Times Duals-DNC
Sign of the Times Fives-TNCMC
05SP Game Used-82
Autographs-82
Gold-82
Authentic Fabrics-AF-JC
Authentic Fabrics Autographs-AAF-JC
Authentic Fabrics Dual-MC
Authentic Fabrics Gold-AF-JC
Authentic Patches-AP-JC
Authentic Patches Autographs-AAP-JC
Authentic Patches Dual-MC
Auto Draft-AD-JC
Game Gear-GG-CH
Game Gear Autographs-AG-CH
Signature Sticks-SS-JC
SIGnificance-JC
SIGnificance Gold-S-JC
SIGnificance Extra-CR
SIGnificance Extra Gold-CR
Statscriptions-ST-JC
05SPx-77
Spectrum-77
05The Cup-84
Gold-84
Black Rainbow-84
Dual NHL Shields Autographs-ADSTC
Emblems of Endorsement-EEJC
Honorable Numbers-HNCH
Limited Logos-LLJC
Masterpiece Pressplates-84
Masterpiece Pressplates (Rookie Update)-231
Noble Numbers-NNSC
Patch Variation-P84
Patch Variation Autographs-AP84
Scripted Swatches-SSCH
05UD Artifacts-85
Blue-85
Gold-85
Green-85
Pewter-85
Red-85
Auto Facts-AF-JC
Auto Facts Blue-AF-JC
Auto Facts Copper-AF-JC
Auto Facts Pewter-AF-JC
Auto Facts Silver-AF-JC
Gold Autographed-85
Remarkable Artifacts-RA-JC
Remarkable Artifacts Dual-RA-JC
05UD PowerPlay-73
05UD PowerPlay-115
Rainbow-73
Power Marks-PMJC
05UD Toronto Fall Expo Priority Signings-PS-JC
05Ultimate Collection-76
Gold-76
Endorsed Emblems-EEJC
Ultimate Achievements-UAJC
Ultimate Signatures-USCH
Ultimate Signatures Pairings-UPNC
Ultimate Signatures Pairings-UPTC
Ultimate Signatures Trios-UTTNC
05Ultra-162
Gold-162
Ice-162
05Upper Deck-156
Big Playmakers-B-JC
HG Glossy-156
Jerseys Series II-J2JC
Majestic Materials-MMCH
Notable Numbers-N-JC
05Upper Deck Ice-81
Rainbow-81
05Upper Deck MVP-318
Gold-318
Platinum-318
05Upper Deck Rookie Update-84
05Upper Deck Rookie Update-231
Inspirations Patch Rookies-231
05Upper Deck Trilogy-76
Honorary Patches-HP-JC
Honorary Patch Scripts-HSP-JC
Honorary Swatches-HS-JC
Honorary Swatch Scripts-HSS-JC
05Upper Deck Toronto Fall Expo-156
05Upper Deck Victory-162
Black-162
Gold-162
Silver-162
06Be A Player-143
Autographs-143
Profiles-PP19
Profiles Autographs-PP19
Signatures-JC
Signatures 10-158
Signatures 25-158
Signatures Trios-TTCM
Signatures Foursomes-FIBRC
Up Close and Personal-UC23
Up Close and Personal Autographs-UC23
06Be A Player Portraits-86
Dual Signature Portraits-DSCT
Signature Portraits-SPCH
Timeless Tens-TTCAN
Triple Signature Portraits-TSJS
06Beehive-17
06Beehive-168
Blue-17
Gold-17
Matte-17
Red Facsimile Signatures-17
Wood-17
5 X 7 Black and White-17
Signature Scrapbook-SSJC
06Black Diamond-144
Black-144
Gold-144
Ruby-144
Gemography-GJC
06Flair Showcase-84
06Flair Showcase-159
06Flair Showcase-261
Parallel-84
Parallel-159
Parallel-261
Inks-IJC
Stitches-SSJC
06Fleer-161
Tiffany-161
Hockey Headliners-HL22
Signing Day-SDJC
Total O-O22
06Hot Prospects-84
Red Hot-84
White Hot-84
Hotagraphs-HJO
06McDonald's Upper Deck-39
Autographs-AJC
Hardware Heroes-HH7
06O-Pee-Chee-406
06O-Pee-Chee-602
Rainbow-406
Rainbow-602
Swatches-S-CH
06Panini Stickers-331
06SP Authentic-18
06SP Authentic-126
Chirography-JC
Limited-18
Limited-126
Sign of the Times-STJC
Sign of the Times Duals-STCB
Sign of the Times Duals-STPJ
Sign of the Times Triples-ST3MTC
06SP Game Used-86
Gold-86
Rainbow-86
Authentic Fabrics Triple-AF3SJS
Authentic Fabrics Triple Patches-AF3SJS
Authentic Fabrics Quads-AF4IDCH
Authentic Fabrics Quads Patches-AF4IDCH
Authentic Fabrics Fives-AF5SGG
Authentic Fabrics Fives-AF5GWG
Authentic Fabrics Fives Patches-AF5SGG
Authentic Fabrics Fives Patches-AF5GWG
Authentic Fabrics Sixes-AF6MRT
Authentic Fabrics Sixes Patches-AF6MRT
Autographs-86
Inked Sweaters Dual-IS2MC
Inked Sweaters Dual Patches-IS2MC
06SPx-86
Spectrum-86
SPxcitement-X83
SPxcitement Spectrum-X83
SPxcitement Autographs-X83
Winning Materials-WMJC
Winning Materials Spectrum-WMJC
Winning Materials Autographs-WMJC
06The Cup-78
Autographed Foundations-CQJC
Autographed Foundations Patches-CQJC
Autographed NHL Shields Duals-DASTC
Autographed Patches-78
Black Rainbow-78
Foundations-CQJC
Foundations Patches-CQJC
Enshrinements-EJC
Gold-78
Gold Patches-78
Hardware Heroes Patches-HHJC
Honorable Numbers-HNCH
Jerseys-78
Limited Logos-LLJC
Masterpiece Pressplates-78
Scripted Swatches-SSJC
Scripted Swatches Duals-DSTC
Signature Patches-SPJC
06UD Artifacts-18
06UD Artifacts-195
Blue-18
Blue-195
Gold-18
Gold-195
Platinum-18
Platinum-195
Radiance-18
Radiance-195
Autographed Radiance Parallel-18
Autographed Radiance Parallel-195
Red-18
Red-195
Auto-Facts-AFJC
Auto-Facts Gold-AFJC
Frozen Artifacts-FAJO
Frozen Artifacts Black-FAJO
Frozen Artifacts Blue-FAJO
Frozen Artifacts Gold-FAJO
Frozen Artifacts Platinum-FAJO
Frozen Artifacts Red-FAJO
Frozen Artifacts Autographed Black-FAJO
Frozen Artifacts Patches Black-FAJO
Frozen Artifacts Patches Blue-FAJO
Frozen Artifacts Patches Gold-FAJO
Frozen Artifacts Patches Platinum-FAJO
Frozen Artifacts Patches Red-FAJO
Frozen Artifacts Patches Autographed Black Tag Parallel-FAJO
Tundra Tandems-TTTC
Tundra Tandems Black-TTTC
Tundra Tandems Blue-TTTC
Tundra Tandems Gold-TTTC
Tundra Tandems Platinum-TTTC
Tundra Tandems Red-TTTC
Tundra Tandems Dual Patches Red-TTTC
06UD Mini Jersey Collection-82
06UD PowerPlay-83
Impact Rainbow-83
06Ultimate Collection-51
Jerseys Dual-UJ2-TC
Patches Dual-UJ2-TC
Signatures-US-CH
Ultimate Achievements-UA-JC
Ultimate Signatures Logos-SL-JC
06Ultra-164
Gold Medallion-164
Ice Medallion-164
Scoring Kings-SK15
06Upper Deck Arena Giveaways-SJS6
06Upper Deck-166
Exclusives Parallel-166
High Gloss Parallel-166
Award Winners Canadian Exclusive-OAW6
Game Dated Moments-GD7
Game Jerseys-JJC
Game Patches-PJC
Goal Rush-GR1
Hometown Heroes-HH40
Masterpieces-166
Statistical Leaders-SL2
Walmart Tins Oversize-166
06Upper Deck MVP-245
Gold Script-245
Super Script-245
Autographs-OAHC
Clutch Performers-CP17
Jerseys-OJCS
06Upper Deck Ovation-141
06Upper Deck Sweet Shot-88
Signature Shots/Saves-SSCH
Signature Shots/Saves Sticks-SSSJC
Signature Sticks-STJC
Sweet Stitches-SSJC
Sweet Stitches Duals-SSJC
Sweet Stitches Triples-SSJC
06Upper Deck Trilogy-84
Combo Autographed Jerseys-CJTC
Combo Autographed Patches-CJTC
Combo Clearcut Autographs-C3MTC
Ice Scripts-ISJC
Scripts-S2JC
Scripts-S3JC
Scripts-TSJC
06Upper Deck Victory-166
06Upper Deck Victory Black-166
06Upper Deck Victory Gold-166
06Upper Deck Victory GameBreakers-GB44
06Upper Deck Victory Next In Line-NL42
06Upper Deck Victory Oversize Cards-JC
07Upper Deck Ovation-8
07Upper Deck Victory-176
Black-176
Gold-176
GameBreakers-GB18
Oversize Cards-OS39
Stars on Ice-SI14

Cheeseman, Jeff

00Amarillo Rattlers-4

Cheevers, Gerry

61Sudbury Wolves-5
62Sudbury Wolves-7
63Rochester Americans-7
65Coca-Cola-1
65Topps-31
67Topps-99
68O-Pee-Chee-140
68Shirriff Coins-4
68Topps-1
69O-Pee-Chee-22
Four-in-One-12
69Topps-22
70Bruins Postcards-3
70Bruins Team Issue-13
70Colgate Stamps-71
70Dad's Cookies-14
70Esso Power Players-72
70O-Pee-Chee-1
70Sargent Promotions Stamps-15
70Topps-1
71Bruins Postcards-20
71Letraset Action Replays-8
71O-Pee-Chee-54
71Sargent Promotions Stamps-16
71Topps-4
71Topps-54
71Toronto Sun-7
72O-Pee-Chee-340
72 7-Eleven Slurpee Cups WHA-5
72Finnish Semic World Championship-188
72Swedish Semic World Championship-188
73O-Pee-Chee WHA Posters-6
73Quaker Oats WHA-8
74O-Pee-Chee WHA-30
74Team Canada L'Equipe WHA-3
75Heroes Stand-Ups-1
75O-Pee-Chee WHA-20
75O-Pee-Chee WHA-67
76O-Pee-Chee NHL-120
76Topps-120
77O-Pee-Chee NHL-260
77Sportscasters-4420
77Topps-260
77Topps/O-Pee-Chee Glossy-2
Square-2
77Finnish Sportscasters-49-1174
78O-Pee-Chee-140
78Topps-140
79O-Pee-Chee-85
79Topps-85
80O-Pee-Chee-168
80Topps-168
81Topps Thirst Break-43
85Hall of Fame-250
91Bruins Sports Action Legends-7
91Star Pics-61
92Future Trends '76 Canada Cup-109
92O-Pee-Chee-343
25th Anniv. Inserts-5
94Hockey Wit-81
94Parkhurst Tall Boys Future Stars-FS2
94Zeller's Masters of Hockey-2
94Zeller's Masters of Hockey Signed-2
95Parkhurst '66-67 Promos-1
95Parkhurst '66-67-16
95Parkhurst '66-67-PR16
Coins-16
98Bruins Alumni-30
Autographs-30
99BAP Memorabilia AS American Hobby-AH4
99BAP Memorabilia AS American Hobby Autos-AH4
99Upper Deck Century Legends Epic Sigs-GC
99Upper Deck Century Legends Epic Sig 100-GC
99Upper Deck Retro-92
Gold-92
Platinum-92
Inkredible-GC
Inkredible Level 2-GC
00BAP Memorabilia Goalie Memorabilia-G8
00BAP Memorabilia Goalie Memorabilia-G14
00BAP Memorabilia Goalie Memorabilia-G25
00BAP Memorabilia Goalie Memorabilia-G26
00BAP Memorabilia Goalie Memorabilia-G30
00BAP Sig Ser Goalie Memorabilia Autos-GLS1
00BAP Ultimate Mem Goalie Memorabilia-GM8
00BAP Ultimate Mem Goalie Memorabilia-GM9
00BAP Ultimate Mem Goalie Memorabilia-GM18
00BAP Ultimate Mem Goalie Mem Autos-UG1
01BAP Memorabilia Goalie Traditions-GT14
01BAP Memorabilia Goalie Traditions-GT32
01BAP Memorabilia Goalie Traditions-GT33
01BAP Memorabilia Goalie Traditions-GT41
01BAP Signature Series Vintage Autographs-VA-17
01BAP Ultimate Memorabilia Decades-14
01Between the Pipes-146
Double Memorabilia-DM23
Masks-7
Masks Silver-7
Masks Gold-7
Record Breakers-RB14
Vintage Memorabilia-VM3
01Fleer Legacy-36
Ultimate-36
01Greats of the Game-60
Autographs-60
01Parkhurst Autographs-PA33
01SP Game Used Tools of the Game-CTDC
01SP Game Used Tools of the Game-CTEC
01SP Game Used Tools of the Game-TTHCR
01Topps Rookie Reprints-4
01Topps Rookie Reprint Autographs-4
01Topps Stanley Cup Heroes-SCHGC
01Topps Stanley Cup Heroes Autographs-SCHAGC
01Topps Archives-23
Arena Seats-ASGC
Autographs-1
01UD Top Shelf Goalie Gear-LPGC
01Upper Deck Legends-6
01Upper Deck Legends-79
Jerseys-TTGC
Jerseys Platinum-TTGC
Sticks-PHGC
01Upper Deck Vintage Jerseys-GGGC
01Upper Deck Vintage Next In Line-NLCO
02BAP Memorabilia Mini Stanley Cups-10
02BAP Memorabilia Stanley Cup Champions-2
02BAP Ultimate Memorabilia Cup Duels-7
02BAP Ultimate Memorabilia Emblem Attic-4
02BAP Ultimate Mem Retro Teammates-2
02BAP Ultimate Mem Seams Unbelievable-6
02BAP Ultimate Mem Vintage Jerseys-15
02Between the Pipes Goalie Autographs-9
02Between the Pipes He Shoots/Saves Prize-26
02Between the Pipes Inspirations-I9
02Between the Pipes Record Breakers-8
02Between the Pipes Vintage Memorabilia-7
02ITG Used Goalie Pad and Jersey-GP15
02ITG Used Goalie Pad and Jersey Gold-GP15
02Parkhurst Vintage Memorabilia-VM18
02Parkhurst Vintage Teammates-VT3
02Parkhurst Retro Nicknames-RN6
02UD Mask Collection Mini Masks-GC
02UD Mask Collection Mini Masks Autos-GC
03BAP Memorabilia Vintage Memorabilia-VM-4
03BAP Ultimate Memorabilia Heroes-14
03BAP Ultimate Mem Retro Teammates-5
03ITG Used Signature Series Goalie Gear-23
03ITG Used Sig Series Goalie Gear Autos-23
03ITG Used Sig Series Goalie Gear Gold-23
03ITG Used Sig Series Triple Mem-13
03ITG Used Sig Series Triple Mem Gold-13
03ITG Used Sig Series Vintage Mem-13
03ITG Used Sig Series Vintage Mem Gold-13
03Parkhurst Original Six Boston-56
03Parkhurst Original Six Boston-86
Autographs-4
Memorabilia-BM23
Memorabilia-BM28
Memorabilia-BM38
Memorabilia-BM51
03Parkhurst Orig Six He Shoots/Scores-14
03Parkhurst Orig Six He Shoots/Scores-14A
04ITG Franchises He Shoots/Scores Prizes-36
04ITG Franchises Update Teammates-UTM1
04ITG Franchises Update Teammates Gold-UTM1
04ITG Franchises US East-311
Autographs-A-GC
Barn Burners-EBB4
Barn Burners Gold-EBB4
Double Memorabilia-EDM3
Double Memorabilia Autographs-EDM-GC
Double Memorabilia Gold-EDM3
Forever Rivals-EFR5
Forever Rivals Gold-EFR5
Goalie Gear-EGG1
Goalie Gear Autographs-EGG-GC
Goalie Gear Gold-EGG1
Memorabilia-ESM5
Memorabilia Autographs-ESM-GC
Memorabilia Gold-ESM5
Original Sticks-EOS17
Original Sticks Autographs-EOS-GC
Original Sticks Gold-EOS17
Teammates-ETM8
Teammates Gold-ETM8
Triple Memorabilia-ETM1
Triple Memorabilia Autographs-ETM-GC
Triple Memorabilia Gold-ETM1
04ITG Ultimate Memorabilia-104
Gold-104
Archives 1st Edition-34
Autographs-46
Autographs Gold-46
Goalie Gear-5
Jersey Autographs-15
Jersey Autographs Gold-15
Nicknames-24
Nickname Autographs-6
Original Six-16
Original Six-18
Retro Teammates-13
Stick Autographs-13
Stick Autographs Gold-13
Triple Threads-5
04SP Authentic Buybacks-58
04SP Authentic Octographs-OS-GOA
04SP Authentic Sign of the Times-QS-BTCR
04UD Legendary Signatures-36
AKA Autographs-AKA-GC
Autographs-GC
04UD Legends Classics-23
04UD Legends Classics-95
Gold-23
Gold-95
Platinum-23
Platinum-95
Silver-23
Silver-95
Signature Moments-M30
Signature Moments-M63
Signatures-CS30
Signatures-TC3
Signatures-TC4
Signatures-QC1
04ITG Heroes and Prospects-142
Aspiring-16
Autographs-GC
Hero Memorabilia-16
04ITG Heroes/Prospects Toronto Expo '05-142
04ITG Heroes/Prospects Expo Heroes/Pros-142
05ITG Heroes/Prosp Toronto Expo Parallel -189
05Beehive-223
05Between the Pipes-5
Autographs-A-GC
Complete Package-CP-4
Double Memorabilia-DM-6
Pads-GUP-3
Signed Memorabilia-SM-6
05ITG Ultimate Memorabilia Level 1-41
05ITG Ultimate Memorabilia Level 2-41
05ITG Ultimate Memorabilia Level 3-41
05ITG Ultimate Memorabilia Level 4-41
05ITG Ultimate Memorabilia Level 5-41
05ITG Ultimate Memorabilia Double Autos-3
05ITG Ultimate Mem Double Autos Gold-3
05ITG Ultimate Mem Double Mem Autos-3
05ITG Ultimate Mem Double Mem Autos Gold-3
05ITG Ultimate Memorabilia Goalie Gear-7
05ITG Ultimate Mem Goalie Gear Gold-7
05ITG Ultimate Mem Pass the Torch Jerseys-5
05ITG Ultimate Mem Pass the Torch Jerseys-7
05ITG Ultimate Mem Passing Torch Jsy Gold-5
05ITG Ultimate Mem Passing Torch Jsy Gold-7
05ITG Ultimate Mem Retro Teammate Jerseys-17
05ITG Ult Mem Retro Teammates Jersey Gold-17
05ITG Ultimate Mem Seams Unbelievable-15
05ITG Ultimate Mem Seam Unbelievable Gold-15
05ITG Ultimate Memorabilia Sextuple Autos-1
05ITG Ultimate Memorabilia Stick Autos-7
05ITG Ultimate Mem Stick Autos Gold-7
05ITG Ultimate Mem 3 Star of the Game Jsy-11
05ITG Ult Mem 3 Star of the Game Jsy Gold-11
05ITG Ultimate Mem Triple Threads Jerseys-9
05ITG Ultimate Mem Triple Thread Jsy Gold-9
05ITG Ultimate Memorabilia Ultimate Autos-46
05ITG Ultimate Mem Ultimate Autos Gold-46
05SP Authentic Exquisite Endorsements-EEGC
05SP Authentic Prestigious Pairings-PPCE
05SP Authentic Sign of the Times Quads-QCECS
05SP Authentic Sign of the Times Quads-QRCEB
05SP Authentic Six Star Signatures-SSBO
05SPx-101
Spectrum-101
Xcitement Legends-XL-GC
Xcitement Legends Gold-XL-GC
Xcitement Legends Spectrum-XL-GC
05The Cup-13
Gold-13
Black Rainbow-13
Emblems of Endorsement-EEGC
Honorable Numbers-HNGC
Masterpiece Pressplates-13
Noble Numbers-NNBC
Noble Numbers Dual-DNNCV
Patch Variation-P13
Patch Variation Autographs-AP13
Scripted Numbers-SNBC
Scripted Swatches-SSGC
Signature Patches-SPGC
Stanley Cup Titlists-TGC
05UD Artifacts-109
Blue-109
Gold-109
Green-109
Pewter-109
Red-109
Goalie Gear-FG-GC
Goalie Gear Autographed-FG-GC
Goalie Gear Dual-FGD-GC
Goalie Gear Dual Autographed-FGD-GC
Goalie Gear Pewter-FG-GC
Goalie Gear Silver-FG-GC
Gold Autographed-109
05Upper Deck Notable Numbers-N-GC
05Upper Deck Patches-P-GC
05Upper Deck Trilogy Scripts-IS-GC
05Upper Deck Trilogy Legendary Scripts-LEG-GC
05Upper Deck Trilogy Personal Scripts-PER-GC1
05Upper Deck Trilogy Personal Scripts-PER-GC2
05ITG Heroes and Prospects-189
Autographs Series II-GC
Hero Memorabilia-HM-24
National Pride-NPR-29
06Between The Pipes-89
06Between The Pipes-150
Autographs-AGC
Complete Package-CP01
Complete Package Gold-CP01
Double Jerseys-DJ10
Double Jerseys Gold-DJ10
Double Memorabilia-DM03
Double Memorabilia Gold-DM03
Pads-GP02
Pads Gold-GP02
Shooting Gallery-SG03
Shooting Gallery-SG09
Shooting Gallery Gold-SG03
Shooting Gallery Gold-SG09
Stick and Jersey-SJ04
Stick and Jersey Gold-SJ04
Stick and Jersey Autographs-SJ04
Stick Work-SW05
Stick Work Gold-SW05
06ITG International Ice-11
Gold-11
Autographs-AGC
Cornerstones-IC09
Cornerstones Gold-IC09
Goaltending Glory-GG19
Goaltending Glory Gold-GG19
International Rivals-IR04
International Rivals Gold-IR04
Teammates-IT11
Teammates Gold-IT11
06ITG Ultimate Memorabilia-54
Artist Proof-54
Jerseys Autos-5
Jerseys Autos Gold-5
Retro Teammates-10
Retro Teammates Gold-10
Road to the Cup-4
Road to the Cup Gold-4
Stick Rack-6
Stick Rack Gold-6
Triple Thread Jerseys-11
Triple Thread Jerseys Gold-11
06Parkhurst-33
Autographs-33
Autographs Dual-DABO
06SP Authentic Sign of the Times Duals-STCT
06SP Authentic Sign of the Times Triples-ST3COS
06SP Authentic Sign of the Times Quads-ST4ECVP
06SP Game Used Inked Sweaters Dual-IS2CP
06SP Game Used Inked Sweaters Dual Patches-IS2CP
06SP Game Used Letter Marks-LMGC
06The Cup Autographed Foundations-CQGC
06The Cup Autographed Foundations Patches-CQGC
06The Cup Foundations-CQGC
06The Cup Foundations Patches-CQGC
06The Cup Scripted Swatches-SSGC
06The Cup Signature Patches-SPGC
06The Cup Stanley Cup Signatures-CSGC
06UD Artifacts-107
Blue-107
Gold-107
Platinum-107
Radiance-107
Red-107
06Ultimate Collection Autographed Jerseys-AJ-GC
06Ultimate Collection Autographed Patches-AJ-GC
06Ultimate Collection Jerseys-UJ-GC
06Ultimate Collection Patches-UJ-GC
06Ultimate Collection Signatures-US-GC
06Upper Deck Sweet Shot Endorsed Equipment-EEGC
06Upper Deck Trilogy Combo Clearcut Autographs-C3FEC
06Upper Deck Trilogy Legendary Scripts-LSGC
06Upper Deck Trilogy Scripts-S1GC

Chelios, Chris

83Canadiens Postcards-6
84Canadiens Postcards-4
84O-Pee-Chee-259
85Canadiens Placemats-4
85Canadiens Placemats-7
85Canadiens Postcards-5
85Canadiens Provigo-2
85O-Pee-Chee-51
85O-Pee-Chee Box Bottoms-D
85O-Pee-Chee Stickers-125
85Topps-51
85Topps Box Bottoms-D
86Canadiens Postcards-2
86Kraft Drawings-7
86O-Pee-Chee-171
86O-Pee-Chee Stickers-6
86Topps-171
87Canadiens Postcards-4
87Canadiens Vachon Stickers-78
87Canadiens Vachon Stickers-79
87Canadiens Vachon Stickers-82
87Canadiens Vachon Stickers-83
87O-Pee-Chee-106
87O-Pee-Chee Stickers-9
87Panini Stickers-58
87Pro-Sport All-Stars-3
87Topps-106
88Canadiens Postcards-5
88O-Pee-Chee-55
88O-Pee-Chee Stickers-51
88Panini Stickers-253
88Topps-49
89Canadiens Kraft-3
89Canadiens Postcards-4
89Canadiens Provigo Figurines-24
89Kraft-20
89O-Pee-Chee-174
89O-Pee-Chee-307
89O-Pee-Chee-323
89O-Pee-Chee Stickers-56
89O-Pee-Chee Stickers-156
89O-Pee-Chee Stickers-198
89O-Pee-Chee Stickers-212
89Panini Stickers-237
89Panini Stickers-379
89Sports Illustrated for Kids I-238
89Topps-174
89Topps Sticker Inserts-1
89Swedish Semic World Champ Stickers-157
90Blackhawks Coke-5
90Bowman-42
90Bowman-46
Tiffany-42
Tiffany-46
90Kraft-6
90Kraft-81
90O-Pee-Chee-29
90OPC Premier-13
90Panini Stickers-49
90Pro Set-147A
90Pro Set-147B
90Pro Set-368
90Pro Set-427
90Score-15
Canadian-15
90Score Hottest/Rising Stars-9
90Score Rookie/Traded-4T
90Topps-29
Tiffany-29
90Upper Deck-174
90Upper Deck-422
90Upper Deck-491
French-174
French-422
French-491
91Pro Set Platinum-25
91Blackhawks Coke-4
91Bowman-398
91Gillette-16
91Kraft-18
91McDonald's Upper Deck-22
91McDonald's Upper Deck-H2
91O-Pee-Chee-233
91O-Pee-Chee-268
91OPC Premier-17
91OPC Premier-150
91Panini Stickers-10
91Panini Stickers-329
91Parkhurst-32
91Parkhurst-461
French-32
91Pinnacle-58
French-58
B-B9
B French-B9
91Pro Set-48
91Pro Set-278
French-48
French-278
Awards Special-AC15
91Score American-235
91Score Canadian Bilingual-455
91Score Canadian English-455
91Stadium Club-6
91Topps-233
91Topps-268
91Upper Deck-37
91Upper Deck-354
French-37
French-354
91Finnish Semic World Champ Stickers-130
91Swedish Semic World Champ Stickers-130
92Bowman-43
92Bowman-201
92Humpty Dumpty I-3
92Kraft-38
92McDonald's Upper Deck-3
92O-Pee-Chee-3
92Panini Stickers-11
92Panini Stickers-286
92Panini Stickers French-11
92Panini Stickers French-286
92Parkhurst-29
92Parkhurst-457
Emerald Ice-29
Emerald Ice-457
Cherry Picks-CP16
92Pinnacle-109
French-109
Team French-2
92Pro Set-34
92Score Canadian Promo Sheets-1
92Score-2
92Score-497
Canadian-2
Canadian-497
USA Greats-2
92Seasons Patches-4
92Sports Illustrated for Kids II-585
92Stadium Club-87
92Topps-98
Gold-98G
92Ultra-34
All-Stars-7
92Upper Deck-159
92Upper Deck-629
World Junior Grads-WG3
92Finnish Semic-153
93American Licorice Sour Punch Caps-3
93Anti-Gambling Postcards-NNO
93Blackhawks Coke-2
93Donruss-65
Ice Kings-5
93Kraft-70
93Leaf-51
Gold All-Stars-2
93McDonald's Upper Deck-H5
93OPC Premier-94
93OPC Premier-237
Gold-94
Gold-237
93Panini Stickers-153
93Parkhurst-45
Emerald Ice-45
93Pinnacle-181
93Pinnacle-223
93Pinnacle-233
Canadian-181
Canadian-223
Canadian-233
All-Stars-26
All-Stars Canadian-26
93PowerPlay-47
93Score-101
Canadian-101
Dream Team-3
93Stadium Club-147
93Stadium Club-420
93Stadium Club-459
Members Only Master Set-147
Members Only Master Set-420
Members Only Master Set-459
OPC-147
First Day Issue-147
First Day Issue-420
First Day Issue-459
First Day Issue OPC-147
All-Stars-3
All-Stars Members Only-3
All-Stars OPC-3
93Topps/OPC Premier-94
93Topps/OPC Premier-237
Gold-94
Gold-237
93Ultra-40
All-Stars-14
Award Winners-2
93Upper Deck-129
Award Winners-AW5
Gretzky's Great Ones-GG2
SP-28
93Upper Deck Locker All-Stars-22
93Swedish Semic World Champ Stickers-172
93Classic-118

Autographs-AU3
94Be A Player-R97
94Be A Player-R109
94Blackhawks Coke-4
94Canada Games NHL POGS-73
94Donruss-118
Dominators-6
94EA Sports-25
94EA Sports-186
94Finest-34
Super Team Winners-34
Refractors-34
94Flair-32
94Fleer-39
94Hockey Wit-12
94Kraft-2
94Leaf-7
94Leaf Limited-83
94McDonald's Upper Deck-McD16
94OPC Premier-475
94OPC Premier-486
Special Effects-475
Special Effects-486
94Parkhurst-45
Gold-45
94Pinnacle-94
Artist's Proofs-94
Rink Collection-94
Boomers-BR4
Team Pinnacle-TP3
Team Dufex Parallel-TP3
94Post Box Backs-6
94Score-189
Gold-189
Platinum-189
Check It-CI17
Dream Team-DT8
94Select-31
Gold-31
First Line-FL9
94SP-23
Die Cuts-23
94Stadium Club Members Only-2
94Stadium Club-70
Members Only Master Set-70
First Day Issue-70
Dynasty and Destiny-5
Dynasty and Destiny Members Only-5
Super Team Winner Cards-70
94Topps/OPC Premier-475
94Topps/OPC Premier-486
Special Effects-475
Special Effects-486
94Ultra-40
All-Stars-8
94Upper Deck-26
Electric Ice-26
Predictor Canadian-C29
94Upper Deck Predictor Canadian Exch Gold-C29
94Upper Deck Predictor Hobby-H7
94Upper Deck Predictor Hobby Exch Gold-H7
94Upper Deck Predictor Hobby Exch Silver-H7
94Upper Deck SP Inserts-SP16
94Upper Deck SP Inserts Die Cuts-SP16
94Upper Deck NHLPA/Be A Player-2
94Finnish Jaa Kiekko-111
94Finnish Jaa Kiekko-338
94Swedish Olympics Lillehammer*-324
95SLU Hockey American-4
95SLU Hockey Canadian-4
95Bashan Super Stickers-22
Die-Cut-10
95Be A Player-211
Signatures-S211
Signatures Die Cuts-S211
95Blackhawks Coke-4
95Bowman-12
All-Foil-12
95Canada Games NHL POGS-12
95Canada Games NHL POGS-70
95Collector's Choice-37
95Collector's Choice-380
Player's Club-37
Player's Club-380
Player's Club Platinum-37
Player's Club Platinum-380
95Donruss-91
Dominators-7
Pro Pointers-4
95Donruss Elite-61
Die Cut Stars-61
Die Cut Uncut-61
95Emotion-28
Xcited-20
95Finest-19
95Finest-121
Refractors-19
Refractors-121
95Hoyle Western Playing Cards-8
95Imperial Stickers-22
Die Cut Superstars-10
95Kenner Starting Lineup Cards-5
95Kraft-44
95Leaf-142
Gold Stars-2
Road To The Cup-6
95Leaf Limited-40
95McDonald's Pinnacle-MCD-23
95Metal-24
International Steel-2
95NHL Aces Playing Cards-9S
95NHL Cool Trade-11
95NHL Cool Trade-RP11
95Panini Stickers-164
95Parkhurst International-38
Emerald Ice-38
Crown Collection Silver Series 2-13
Crown Collection Gold Series 2-13
NHL All-Stars-4
Parkie's Trophy Picks-PP20
95Pinnacle-50
Artist's Proofs-50
Rink Collection-50
First Strike-9
Full Contact-6
95Playoff One on One-22
95Post Upper Deck-15
95Pro Magnets-7
95Score Promos-3
95Score-3
Black Ice Artist's Proofs-3
Black Ice-3
95Select Certified-2
Mirror Gold-2
Double Strike-4
Double Strike Gold-4
95SkyBox Impact-28
95SP-23
Holoviews-FX3
Holoviews Special FX-FX3
95Stadium Club Members Only-38
95Stadium Club-10
Members Only Master Set-10
Fearless-F2
Fearless Members Only Master Set-F2
95Summit-39
Artist's Proofs-39
Ice-39
GM's Choice-3
95Topps-8
95Topps-230
OPC Inserts-8
OPC Inserts-230
Home Grown USA-HGA6
Marquee Men Power Boosters-8
Mystery Finest-M18
Mystery Finest Refractors-M18
Rink Leaders-9RL
95Topps SuperSkills-50
Platinum-50
95Ultra-31
95Ultra-380
Gold Medallion-31
95Upper Deck-170
95Upper Deck-238
Electric Ice-170
Electric Ice-238
Electric Ice Gold-170
Electric Ice Gold-238
95Upper Deck All-Star Game Predictors-9
Redemption Winners-9
95Upper Deck NHL All-Stars-AS2
95Upper Deck NHL All-Stars Jumbo-AS2
95Upper Deck Predictor Hobby-H34
95Upper Deck Predictor Hobby Exchange-H34
95Upper Deck Special Edition-SE17
95Upper Deck Special Edition Gold-SE17
95Zenith-37
95Finnish Semic World Championships-104
95Swedish Globe World Championships-107
95Swiss HNL-544
96Headliners Hockey-4
96Black Diamond-145
Gold-145
96Collector's Choice-47
96Collector's Choice-301
96Collector's Choice-313
MVP-UD31
MVP Gold-UD31
96Donruss-71
Press Proofs-71
Dominators-3
Hit List-6
96Donruss Canadian Ice-56
Gold Press Proofs-56
Red Press Proofs-56
96Donruss Elite-20
Die Cut Stars-20
Perspective-11
96Duracell All-Cherry Team-DC8
96Flair-15
Blue Ice-15
96Fleer-16
96Fleer-140
Norris-2
Picks Dream Lines-2
Picks Fabulous 50-7
96Hockey Greats Coins-4
Gold-4
96Kraft Upper Deck-27
96Kraft Upper Deck-38
96Kraft Upper Deck-42
96Leaf-46
Press Proofs-46
96Leaf Limited-1
Gold-1
96Leaf Preferred-19
Press Proofs-19
Steel-7
Steel Gold-7
96Maggers-11
96McDonald's Pinnacle-8
96Metal Universe-26
Cool Steel-1
Cool Steel Super Power-1
96NHL Aces Playing Cards-8
96NHL Pro Stamps-7
96Pinnacle-34
Artist's Proofs-34
Foil-34
Premium Stock-34
Rink Collection-34
Trophies-8
96Pinnacle Fantasy-FC11
96Pinnacle Mint-22
Bronze-22
Gold-22
Silver-22
Coins Brass-22
Coins Solid Gold-22
Coins Gold Plated-22
Coins Nickel-22
Coins Silver-22
96Playoff One on One-370
96Post Upper Deck-2
96Score-36
Artist's Proofs-36
Dealer's Choice Artist's Proofs-36
Special Artist's Proofs-36
Check It-15
Golden Blades-36
Superstitions-8
96Select Certified-27
Artist's Proofs-27
Blue-27
Mirror Blue-27
Mirror Gold-27
Mirror Red-27
Red-27
96SkyBox Impact-18
BladeRunners-2
NHL on Fox-5
96SP-27
Clearcut Winner-CW18
Holoview Collection-HC6
96SPx-6
Gold-6
96Stadium Club Members Only-4
96Summit-43
Artist's Proofs-43
Ice-43
Metal-43
Premium Stock-43
96Team Out-46
96Topps Picks-19
Fantasy Team-FT6
Ice D-ID3
OPC Inserts-19
96Ultra-30
Gold Medallion-30
Power-2
Power Blue Line-2
96Upper Deck-31
Generation Next-X11
Power Performers-P15
Superstar Showdown-SS27A
96Upper Deck Ice-10
Parallel-10
96Zenith-68
Artist's Proofs-68
Champion Salute-12
Champion Salute Diamond-12
96Swedish Semic Wien-159
97SLU Hockey Canadian-5
97SLU Hockey American-6
97Be A Player-11
Autographs-11
Autographs Die-Cuts-11
Autographs Prismatic Die-Cuts-11
97Beehive-25
Golden Portraits-25
97Black Diamond-29
Double Diamond-29
Triple Diamond-29
Quadruple Diamond-29
97Collector's Choice-46
Star Quest-SQ11
Stick'Ums-S7
97Crown Royale-28
Emerald Green-28
Ice Blue-28
Silver-28
Blades of Steel Die-Cuts-4
97Donruss-37
Press Proofs Silver-37
Press Proofs Gold-37
Line 2 Line-13
Line 2 Line Die Cut-13
97Donruss Canadian Ice-120
Dominion Series-120
Provincial Series-120
Stanley Cup Scrapbook-4
97Donruss Elite-31
Aspirations-31
Status-31
97Donruss Limited-16
97Donruss Limited-87
97Donruss Limited-166
97Donruss Limited-175
Exposure-16
Exposure-87
Exposure-166
Exposure-175
Fabric of the Game-58
97Donruss Preferred-127
97Donruss Preferred-171
Cut to the Chase-127
Cut to the Chase-171
97Donruss Priority-99
Stamp of Approval-99
Postcards-23
Postcards Opening Day Issues-24
Stamps-23
Stamps Bronze-23
Stamps Gold-23
Stamps Silver-23
97Esso Olympic Hockey Heroes-30
97Esso Olympic Hockey Heroes French-30
97Jell-O Juniors To Pros-7
97Katch-32
Gold-32
Silver-32
97Kenner Starting Lineup Cards-6
97Leaf-64
Fractal Matrix-64
Fractal Matrix Die Cuts-64
97Leaf International-64
Universal Ice-64
97NHL Aces Playing Cards-42
97Pacific-7
Copper-7
Emerald Green-7
Ice Blue-7
Red-7
Silver-7
Gold Crown Die-Cuts-6
Team Checklists-6
97Pacific Dynagon-25
Copper-25
Dark Grey-25
Emerald Green-25
Ice Blue-25
Red-25
Silver-25
Best Kept Secrets-20
Tandems-35
97Pacific Invincible-28
Copper-28
Emerald Green-28
Ice Blue-28
Red-28
Silver-28
Feature Performers-6
NHL Regime-42
97Pacific Omega-48
97Pacific Omega-245
Copper-48
Copper-245
Dark Gray-48
Dark Gray-245
Emerald Green-48
Emerald Green-245
Gold-48
Gold-245
Ice Blue-48
Ice Blue-245
Stick Handle Laser Cuts-4
97Panini Stickers-129
97Paramount-41
Copper-41
Dark Grey-41
Emerald Green-41
Ice Blue-41
Red-41
Silver-41
97Pinnacle-65
Artist's Proofs-65
Rink Collection-65
Press Plates Back Black-65
Press Plates Back Cyan-65
Press Plates Back Magenta-65
Press Plates Back Yellow-65
Press Plates Front Black-65
Press Plates Front Cyan-65
Press Plates Front Magenta-65
Press Plates Front Yellow-65
Team Pinnacle-3
Team Mirror-3
Team Parallel-3
Team Parallel Mirror-3
97Pinnacle Certified-74
Red-74
Mirror Blue-74
Mirror Gold-74
Mirror Red-74
Team-5
Gold Team Promo-5
Gold Team-5
97Pinnacle Inside-18
Coach's Collection-18
Executive Collection-18
97Pinnacle Tot Cert Platinum Blue-74
97Pinnacle Tot Certi Platinum Gold-74
97Pinnacle Totally Certified Platinum Red-74
97Pinnacle Tot Cert Mirror Platinum Gold-74
97Post Pinnacle-12
97Revolution-28
Copper-28
Emerald-28
Ice Blue-28
Silver-28
1998 All-Star Game Die-Cuts-5
Team Checklist Laser Cuts-6
97Score-90
Artist's Proofs-90
Golden Blades-90
Check It-9
97SP Authentic-30
Icons-I3
Icons Die-Cuts-I3
Icons Embossed-I3
Sign of the Times-CC
97SPx-9
Bronze-9
Gold-9
Silver-9
Steel-9
Dimension-SPX10
Grand Finale-9
97Studio-30
Press Proofs Silver-30
Press Proofs Gold-30
Portraits-28
97Upper Deck-36
97Upper Deck-394
Smooth Grooves-SG7
Three Star Selects-4C
97Upper Deck Ice-67
Parallel-67
Power Shift-67
97Zenith-14
Z-Gold-14
Z-Silver-14
97Zenith 5 x 7-39
Gold Impulse-39
Silver Impulse-39
98Headliners Hockey XL-1
98NHL Pro Zone-20
98Aurora-39
Championship Fever-10
Championship Fever Copper-10
Championship Fever Ice Blue-10
Championship Fever Red-10
Championship Fever Silver-10
98Be A Player-180
Press Release-180
98BAP Gold-180
98BAP Autographs-180
98BAP Autographs Gold-180
98BAP AS Game Used Stick Cards-S19
98BAP AS Game Used Jersey Cards-AS21
98BAP Playoff Highlights-H14
98Black Diamond-19
Double Diamond-19
Triple Diamond-19
Quadruple Diamond-19
98Blackhawks Chicago Sun-Times-1
98Bowman's Best-29
Refractors-29
Atomic Refractors-29
98Crown Royale-28
Limited Series-28
Pillars of the Game-5
98Finest-127
No Protectors-127
No Protectors Refractors-127
Refractors-127
98Katch-32
98Kraft Peanut Butter-8
98OPC Chrome-166
Refractors-166
Board Members-B2
Board Members Refractors-B2
98Pacific-7
Ice Blue-7
Red-7
Gold Crown Die-Cuts-7
Team Checklists-6
98Pacific Dynagon Ice-39
Blue-39
Red-39
Team Checklists-6
98Pacific Omega-49
Red-49
Opening Day Issue-49
Online-6
Planet Ice-2
Planet Ice Parallel-2
98Panini Photocards-16
98Panini Stickers-114
98Paramount-44
Copper-44
Emerald Green-44
Holo-Electric-44
Ice Blue-44
Silver-44
Team Checklists Die-Cuts-6
98Revolution-29
Ice Shadow-29
Red-29
Showstoppers-8
Three Pronged Attack-3
Three Pronged Attack Parallel-3
98SP Authentic-19
Power Shift-19
Authentics-8
Authentics-9
98SPx Finite-120
Radiance-120
Spectrum-120
98SPx Top Prospects-12
Radiance-12
Spectrum-12
98Topps-166
O-Pee-Chee-166
Board Members-B2
Mystery Finest Bronze-M17
Mystery Finest Bronze Refractors-M17
Mystery Finest Gold-M17
Mystery Finest Gold Refractors-M17
Mystery Finest Silver-M17
Mystery Finest Silver Refractors-M17
98Topps Gold Label Class 1-3
Black-3
Black One of One-3
One of One-3
Red-3
Red One of One-3
98Topps Gold Label Class 2-3
98Topps Gold Label Class 2 Black-3
98Topps Gold Label Class 2 Black 1 of 1-3
98Topps Gold Label Class 2 One of One-3
98Topps Gold Label Class 2 Red-3
98Topps Gold Label Class 2 Red One of One-3
98Topps Gold Label Class 3-3
98Topps Gold Label Class 3 Black-3
98Topps Gold Label Class 3 Black 1 of 1-3
98Topps Gold Label Class 3 One of One-3
98Topps Gold Label Class 3 Red-3
98Topps Gold Label Class 3 Red One of One-3
98UD Choice-46
98UD Choice-223
Mini Bobbing Head-BH23
Prime Choice Reserve-46
Prime Choice Reserve-223
Reserve-46
Reserve-223
98Upper Deck-65
Exclusives-65
Exclusives 1 of 1-65
Frozen In Time-FT21
Frozen In Time Quantum 1-FT21
Frozen In Time Quantum 2-FT21
Frozen In Time Quantum 3-FT21
Gold Reserve-65
98Upper Deck MVP-44
Gold Script-44
Silver Script-44
Super Script-44
99SLU Hockey One On One-2
99Aurora-49
Striped-49
Premiere Date-49
Premiere Date Striped-49
99BAP Memorabilia-30
Gold-30
Silver-30
Jersey Cards-J21
Jersey Emblems-E21
Jersey Numbers-I21
Jersey and Stick Cards-S21
AS Heritage Ruby-H20
AS Heritage Sapphire-H20
AS Heritage Emerald-H20
99BAP Update Teammates Jersey Cards-TM11
99BAP Update Teammates Jersey Cards-TM24
99BAP Update Teammates Jersey Cards-TM39
99BAP Millennium-91
Emerald-91
Ruby-91
Sapphire-91
Signatures-91
Signatures Gold-91
Jerseys-J14
Jersey and Stick Cards-JS14
Jersey Emblems-E14
Jersey Numbers-N14
99Crown Royale-48
Limited Series-48
Premiere Date-48
99O-Pee-Chee-219
99O-Pee-Chee Chrome-219
99O-Pee-Chee Chrome Refractors-219
99Pacific-135
Copper-135
Emerald Green-135
Gold-135
Ice Blue-135
Premiere Date-135
Red-135
Gold Crown Die-Cuts-16
99Pacific Dynagon Ice-72
Blue-72
Copper-72
Gold-72
Premiere Date-72
Checkmates American-7
Checkmates American-22
Checkmates Canadian-7
99Pacific Omega-80
Copper-80
Gold-80
Ice Blue-80
Premiere Date-80
99Pacific Prism-49
Holographic Blue-49
Holographic Gold-49
Holographic Mirror-49
Holographic Purple-49
Premiere Date-49
99Panini Stickers-238
99Paramount-79
Copper-79
Emerald-79
Gold-79
Holographic Emerald-79
Holographic Gold-79
Holographic Silver-79
Ice Blue-79
Premiere Date-79
Red-79
Silver-79
99Revolution-50
Premiere Date-50
Red-50
Shadow Series-50
99SPx-60
Radiance-60
Spectrum-60
99Stadium Club-122
First Day Issue-122
One of a Kind-122
Printing Plates Black-122
Printing Plates Cyan-122
Printing Plates Magenta-122
Printing Plates Yellow-122
99Topps/OPC-219
99Topps/OPC Chrome-219
Refractors-219
99Topps Premier Plus-67
Parallel-67
99Upper Deck-223
Exclusives-223
Exclusives 1 of 1-223
Headed for the Hall-HOF14
Headed for the Hall Quantum Gold-HOF14
Headed for the Hall Quantum Silver-HOF14
99Upper Deck Century Legends-42
Century Collection-42
99Upper Deck Gold Reserve-223
99Upper Deck MVP-73
Gold Script-73
Silver Script-73
Super Script-73
99Upper Deck Retro-30
Gold-30
Platinum-30
99Upper Deck Victory-99
99Wayne Gretzky Hockey-64
00Aurora-48
Pinstripes-48
Premiere Date-48
00BAP Memorabilia-212
Emerald-212
Ruby-212
Sapphire-212
Promos-212
00BAP Mem Chicago Sportsfest Copper-212
00BAP Memorabilia Chicago Sportsfest Blue-212
00BAP Memorabilia Chicago Sportsfest Gold-212
00BAP Memorabilia Chicago Sportsfest Ruby-212
00BAP Memorabilia Chicago Sun-Times Ruby-212
00BAP Memorabilia Chicago Sun-Times Gold-212
00BAP Mem Chicago Sun-Times Sapphire-212
00BAP Mem Toronto Fall Expo Copper-212
00BAP Memorabilia Toronto Fall Expo Gold-212
00BAP Memorabilia Toronto Fall Expo Ruby-212
00BAP Mem Update Heritage Jersey Cards-H12
00BAP Mem Update Heritage Jersey Gold-H12
00BAP Memorabilia Update Teammates-TM12
00BAP Memorabilia Update Teammates Gold-TM12
00BAP Parkhurst 2000-P128
00BAP Sig Ser Department of Defense-DD3
00BAP Ultimate Mem Journey Jerseys-JJ13
00BAP Ultimate Mem Journey Emblems-JE13
00BAP Ultimate Mem Journey Numbers-JI13
00BAP Ultimate Memorabilia Norris Trophy-N5
00BAP Ultimate Memorabilia Norris Trophy-N8
00BAP Ultimate Memorabilia Teammates-TM3
00BAP Ultimate Memorabilia Teammates-TM35
00Crown Royale Game-Worn Jerseys-13
00Crown Royale Game-Worn Jersey Patches-13
00Crown Royale Premium-Sized Jerseys-13
00O-Pee-Chee-182
00O-Pee-Chee Parallel-182
00Pacific-145
Copper-145
Gold-145
Ice Blue-145
Premiere Date-145
00Paramount-83
Copper-83
Gold-83
Holo-Gold-83
Holo-Silver-83
Ice Blue-83
Premiere Date-83
Game Used Sticks-9
00Private Stock Game Gear-43
00Private Stock PS-2001 Action-19
00Revolution-50
Blue-50
Premiere Date-50
Red-50
00Stadium Club-115
00Titanium Game Gear-16
00Titanium Game Gear-94
00Titanium Game Gear Patches-94
00Titanium Draft Day Edition-36
Patches-36
00Topps/OPC-182
Parallel-182
00Topps Chrome-121
OPC Refractors-121
Refractors-121
00Topps Stars-87
Blue-87
00Upper Deck-291
Exclusives Tier 1-291
Exclusives Tier 2-291
00Upper Deck MVP-65
First Stars-65
Game-Used Souvenirs-GSCC
Second Stars-65
Super Game-Used Souvenirs-GSCC
Third Stars-65
00Upper Deck Victory-84
00Upper Deck Vintage-132
00Vanguard Dual Game-Worn Jerseys-5
00Vanguard Dual Game-Worn Patches-5
01BAP Memorabilia-124
Emerald-124
Ruby-124
Sapphire-124
All-Star Teammates-AST38
01BAP Sig Series International Medals-IS-3
01BAP Signature Series Jerseys-GJ-79
01BAP Ultimate Memorabilia Gloves Are Off-22
01Pacific-138
Extreme LTD-138
Hobby LTD-138
Premiere Date-138
Retail LTD-138
01Pacific Adrenaline-63
Blue-63
Premiere Date-63
Red-63
Retail-63
01Pacific Arena Exclusives-138
01Pacific Heads-Up Quad Jerseys-11
01Pacific Heads-Up Quad Jerseys-22
01Parkhurst-146
Jerseys-PJ42
Sticks-PS32
01SP Authentic Jerseys-NNCC
01Upper Deck Game Jerseys-ACC
01Vanguard Memorabilia-13
02Atomic National Pride-U3
02BAP All-Star Edition-15
He Shoots-He Score Prizes-5
Jerseys-15
Jerseys Gold-15
Jerseys Silver-15
02BAP First Edition-185
02BAP First Edition-339
02BAP First Edition-374
02BAP Memorabilia-84
02BAP Memorabilia-241
Emerald-84
Emerald-241
Ruby-84
Ruby-241
Sapphire-84
Sapphire-241
All-Star Jerseys-ASJ-8
NHL All-Star Game-84
NHL All-Star Game-241
NHL All-Star Game Blue-84
NHL All-Star Game Blue-241
NHL All-Star Game Green-84
NHL All-Star Game Green-241
NHL All-Star Game Red-84
NHL All-Star Game Red-241
Stanley Cup Champions-SCC-3
02BAP Memorabilia Toronto Fall Expo-84
02BAP Memorabilia Toronto Fall Expo-241
02BAP Signature Series-144
Autographs-144
Autograph Buybacks 1998-180
Autograph Buybacks 1999-91
Autographs Gold-144
Jerseys-SGJ34
Jersey Autographs-SGJ34
02BAP Ultimate Mem Dynasty Jerseys-3
02BAP Ultimate Mem Dynasty Emblems-3
02BAP Ultimate Mem Dynasty Numbers-3
02BAP Ultimate Memorabilia Emblems-6
02BAP Ultimate Memorabilia Gloves Are Off-8
02BAP Ultimate Memorabilia Hat Tricks-20
02BAP Ultimate Mem Lifetime Achievers-18
02BAP Ultimate Memorabilia Numbers-14
02ITG Used-24
02ITG Used-124
International Experience-IE18
International Experience Gold-IE18
Jerseys-GUJ34
Jersey Autographs-GUJ34
Jerseys Gold-GUJ34
Jersey and Stick-SJ34
Jersey and Stick Gold-SJ34
Teammates-T5
Teammates Gold-T5
Triple Memorabilia-TM7
Triple Memorabilia Gold-TM7
02O-Pee-Chee-90
02O-Pee-Chee-323
02O-Pee-Chee Premier Blue Parallel-90
02O-Pee-Chee Premier Blue Parallel-323
02O-Pee-Chee Premier Red Parallel-90
02O-Pee-Chee Premier Red Parallel-323
02O-Pee-Chee Factory Set-90
02O-Pee-Chee Factory Set-323
02Pacific-123
Blue-123
Red-123
02Pacific Calder-28
Silver-28
02Pacific Complete-442
Red-442
02Pacific Exclusive-60
02Parkhurst-54
Bronze-54
Gold-54
Silver-54
College Ranks-CR7
College Ranks Jerseys-CRM7
Hardware-N7
02Parkhurst Retro-160
Minis-160
02Private Stock Reserve-35
Blue-35
Red-35
Retail-35
02SP Game Used Piece of History-PHCC
02SP Game Used Piece of History Gold-PHCC
02SP Game Used Piece of History Rainbow-PHCC
02Topps-90
02Topps-323
OPC Blue Parallel-90
OPC Blue Parallel-323
OPC Red Parallel-90
OPC Red Parallel-323
Factory Set-90
Factory Set-323
02Topps Chrome-57
Black Border Refractors-57
Refractors-57
02Topps Heritage-112
02Topps Heritage-122
02Topps Total-134
Award Winners-AW8
02Upper Deck-307
Exclusives-307
All-Star Jerseys-ASCC
02Upper Deck Beckett UD Promos-307
02Upper Deck Victory-79
Bronze-79
Gold-79
Silver-79
National Pride-NP55
02Upper Deck Vintage-312
03McFarlane Hockey-110
03McFarlane Hockey-112
03McFarlane Hockey-114
03McFarlane Hockey-210
03McFarlane Hockey-212
03BAP Memorabilia Jersey and Stick-SJ-12
03BAP Ultimate Memorabilia Hat Tricks-15
03Beehive Sticks Blue Border-BL6
03eTopps-55
03ITG Action-217
Homeboys-HB11
Jerseys-M124
03ITG Toronto Fall Expo Forever Rivals-FR3
03ITG Used Sig Series Intl Experience-29
03ITG Used Sig Ser Intl Exper Emblem Gold-29
03ITG Used Sig Ser Intl Experience Emblem-29
03ITG Used Sig Ser Intl Experience Gold-29
03ITG Used Signature Series Norris Trophy-5
03ITG Used Signature Series Norris Trophy-6
03ITG Used Sig Series Norris Trophy Gold-5
03ITG Used Sig Series Norris Trophy Gold-6
03NHL Sticker Collection-217
03O-Pee-Chee-4
03OPC Blue-4
03OPC Gold-4
03OPC Red-4
03Pacific-115
Blue-115
Red-115
03Pacific Complete-111
Red-111
03Pacific Exhibit-51
Blue Backs-51
Yellow Backs-51
03Pacific Luxury Suite-34A
03Pacific Luxury Suite-34B
03Parkhurst Original Six Chicago-31
03Parkhurst Original Six Chicago-69
03Parkhurst Original Six Chicago-72
03Parkhurst Original Six Chicago-99
Memorabilia-CM59
03Parkhurst Original Six Detroit-2
Memorabilia-DM13
03Parkhurst Original Six Montreal-31
03SPx Hall Pass-HP-CC
03SPx Hall Pass Limited-HP-CC
03Topps-4
Blue-4
Gold-4
Red-4
Topps/OPC Idols-UI6
03Upper Deck-312
Canadian Exclusives-312
HG-312
UD Exclusives-312
03Upper Deck MVP-154
Gold Script-154
Silver Script-154
Canadian Exclusives-154
03Toronto Star-31
04Pacific Philadelphia-3
04Upper Deck World's Best-WB28
04Upper Deck World Cup Tribute-CC
04Upper Deck World Cup Tribute-CCTA
04Upper Deck World Cup Tribute-CCRELDH
05Black Diamond-34
Emerald-34
Gold-34
Onyx-34
Ruby-34
Jerseys-J-CC
Jerseys Ruby-J-CC
Jersey Duals-DJ-CC
Jersey Triples-TJ-CC
Jersey Quads-QJ-CC
05Panini Stickers-269
05Parkhurst-181
Facsimile Auto Parallel-181
05SP Game Used Authentic Fabrics Quad-LZDC
05SP Game Used Authentic Patches Quad -LZDC
05The Cup Master Pressplate Rookie Update-215
05UD Powerplay Specialists-TSCC
05UD Powerplay Specialists Patches-SPCC
05Ultimate Coll National Heroes Jersey-NHJCC
05Ultimate Coll National Heroes Patch-NHPCC
05Ultra-78
Gold-78
Ice-78
05Upper Deck-315
Big Playmakers-B-CC
Jerseys-J-CC
Notable Numbers-N-CCH
05Upper Deck MVP-140
Gold-140
Platinum-140
05Upper Deck Rookie Update-215
Inspirations Patch Rookies-215
05Upper Deck Trilogy Honorary Patches-HP-CC
05Upper Deck Tril Honorary Patch Script-HSP-CC
05Upper Deck Trilogy Honorary Swatches-HS-CC
05Upper Deck Tril Honorary Swatch Scripts-HSS-CC
05Upper Deck Victory-69
Black-69
Gold-69
Silver-69
06Flair Showcase Stitches-SSCC
06Fleer Fabricology-FCC
06ITG International Ice-125
06ITG International Ice-142
Gold-125
Gold-142
Autographs-ACC
Autographs-ACC2
Emblems-GUE39
Emblems Gold-GUE39
International Rivals-IR20
Jerseys-GUJ39
Jerseys Gold-GUJ39
My Country My Team-MC1
My Country My Team Gold-MC1
Numbers-GUN39
Numbers Gold-GUN39
Quad Patch-QP02
Quad Patch Gold-QP02
Stick and Jersey-SJ24
Stick and Jersey Gold-SJ24
Teammates-IT13
Teammates Gold-IT13
06ITG Ultimate Memorabilia-30
Artist Proof-30
Autos-4
Autos Gold-4
Double Memorabilia-15
Double Memorabilia Gold-15
Jerseys-4
Jerseys Gold-4
Jerseys Autos-3
Jerseys Autos Gold-3
Retro Teammates-18
Retro Teammates Gold-18
Retrospective-1
Retrospective Gold-1
Road to the Cup-10
Road to the Cup Gold-10
Triple Thread Jerseys-6
Triple Thread Jerseys Gold-6
06O-Pee-Chee-182
06O-Pee-Chee-652
Rainbow-182
Rainbow-652
Swatches-S-CC
06Panini Stickers-258
06SP Game Used Authentic Fabrics Sixes-AF6NOR
06SP Game Used Authentic Fabrics Sixes Patches-AF6NOR
06SPx Winning Materials-WMCC
06SPx Winning Materials Spectrum-WMCC
06The Cup NHL Shields Duals-DSHLC
06UD Artifacts Frozen Artifacts-FACC
06UD Artifacts Frozen Artifacts Black-FACC
06UD Artifacts Frozen Artifacts Blue-FACC
06UD Artifacts Frozen Artifacts Gold-FACC
06UD Artifacts Frozen Artifacts Platinum-FACC
06UD Artifacts Frozen Artifacts Red-FACC
06UD Artifacts Frozen Artifacts Patches Black-FACC
06UD Artifacts Frozen Artifacts Patches Blue-FACC
06UD Artifacts Frozen Artifacts Patches Gold-FACC
06UD Artifacts Frozen Artifacts Patches Platinum-FACC
06UD Artifacts Frozen Artifacts Patches Red-FACC
06UD Artifacts Tundra Tandems-TTMC
06UD Artifacts Tundra Tandems Black-TTMC
06UD Artifacts Tundra Tandems Blue-TTMC
06UD Artifacts Tundra Tandems Gold-TTMC
06UD Artifacts Tundra Tandems Platinum-TTMC
06UD Artifacts Tundra Tandems Red-TTMC
06UD Artifacts Tundra Tandems Dual Patches Red-TTMC
06Upper Deck Arena Giveaways-DET3
06Upper Deck-320
Exclusives Parallel-320
High Gloss Parallel-320
Game Jerseys-JCC
Game Patches-PCC
Masterpieces-320
06Upper Deck MVP-109
Gold Script-109
Super Script-109

Chelios, Chris (MIN)

02Bossier-Shreveport Mudbugs-8
03Pacific Red-115

Chelios, Peter

93Quebec Pee-Wee Tournament-1326

Chelios, Steve

91Nashville Knights-13
93Wichita Thunder-3

97Quad-City Mallards-10
98Bakersfield Condors-5
Chelodi, Armando
94Finnish Jaa Kiekko-309
95Swedish World Championships Stickers-92
Chemomaz, Rich
83Devils Postcards-6
Chenard, Alain
00Chicoutimi Sagueneens-14
Signed-14
Chenier, Benoit
93Quebec Pee-Wee Tournament-88
Chenuz, Olivier
93Swiss HNL-422
Cherbayev, Alexander
91Upper Deck-657
French-657
91Upper Deck Czech World Juniors-18
92Russian Stars Red Ace-7
92Classic-49
Gold-49
92Classic Four-Sport *-190
Gold-190
93Upper Deck-279
93Swedish Semic World Champ Stickers-137
93Kansas City Blades-11
93Classic-38
94Finest-14
Super Team Winners-14
Refractors-14
94Leaf-465
94Upper Deck-263
Electric Ice-263
Predictor Canadian-C12
94Upper Deck Predictor Canadian Exch Gold-C12
94Upper Deck Predictor Cdn Exch Silver-C12
94Kansas City Blades-13
94Classic Pro Prospects-194
95Kansas City Blades-6
97Czech APS Extraliga-136
98Czech DS-106
98Czech DS Stickers-261
98Czech OFS-120
99German DEL-34
00German DEL-188
01German Upper Deck-160
02German DEL City Press-172
03Russian Hockey League-163
Cheredaryk, Steve
95Signature Rookies-43
Signatures-43
96Springfield Falcons-5
97New Orleans Brass-4
02Atlantic City Boardwalk Bullies-3
Cheremetiev, Yuri
05Halifax Mooseheads-24
06Halifax Mooseheads-20
Cherenack, Hunter
98Arizona Icecats-4
99Arizona Icecats-3
Cherepanov, Alexei
06ITG Ultimate Memorabilia Autos Triple-10
06ITG Ultimate Memorabilia Autos Triple Gold-10
06ITG Ultimate Memorabilia Future Star-23
06ITG Ultimate Memorabilia Future Star Gold-23
06ITG Ultimate Memorabilia Future Star Autos-14
06ITG Ultimate Memorabilia Future Star Autos Gold-14
06ITG Ultimate Memorabilia Future Star Patches Autos-14
06ITG Ultimate Memorabilia Future Star Patches Autos Gold-14
06ITG Ultimate Memorabilia Going For Gold-16
06ITG Ultimate Memorabilia Going For Gold Gold-16
Cherewyk, James
03Kootenay Ice-5
04Kootenay Ice-4
Chermak, Leo
02Russian Hockey League-77
Chernask, Tyson
04Langley Hornets-7
Cherneski, Stefan
92Quebec Pee-Wee Tournament-1202
95Brandon Wheat Kings-3
96Brandon Wheat Kings-20
97Beehive-63
Authentic Autographs-63
Golden Portraits-63
97Brandon Wheat Kings-4
97Bowman CHL-117
OPC-117
Bowman's Best-10
Bowman's Best Atomic Refractors-10
Bowman's Best Refractor-10
98Hartford Wolf Pack-28
98Bowman CHL-76
Golden Anniversary-76
OPC International-76
98Bowman Chrome CHL-76
Golden Anniversary-76
Golden Anniversary Refractors-76
OPC International-76
OPC International Refractors-76
Refractors-76
99Hartford Wolf Pack-4
Cherni, Valeri
95Swiss HNL-426
98Russian Hockey League-157
99Danish Hockey League-80
00Russian Hockey League-56
Chernik, Alexandr
89Russian National Team-3
89Swedish Semic World Champ Stickers-100
Chernikov, Alexei
00Russian Hockey League-254
Chernishev, Arkady
69Russian National Team Postcards-20
Cherniwchan, Al
85Brandon Wheat Kings-12
Chernoff, Mike
73Vancouver Blazers-7
Chernomaz, Rich
81Victoria Cougars-4
82Victoria Cougars-3
84Devils Postcards-14
88Salt Lake Golden Eagles-6
89ProCards IHL-198
90ProCards AHL/IHL-607
91ProCards-365
92Salt Lake Golden Eagles-3
93St. John's Maple Leafs-4
94St. John's Maple Leafs-4
95German DEL-403
96German DEL-311
98German DEL-205
99German DEL-217
00St. John's Maple Leafs-5
Chernoskutov, Andrei
99Russian Hockey League-245
Chernov, Artem
00Russian Hockey League-82
00Russian Hockey League-289
01Russian Hockey League-73
02Russian Hockey League-29
Chernov, Mikhail
03Russian Hockey League-198
03Russian Hockey League-276
Cherny, Ladislav
02Russian Hockey League-61
03Russian Hockey League-130
Chernyavski, Sergei
99Russian Hockey League-216
Chernykh, Dmitri
02Russian Future Stars-12
03Russian Hockey League-247
03Russian Young Lions-1
03Russian Under-18 Team-7
Cherrey, Scott
93North Bay Centennials-15
94North Bay Centennials-18
95Slapshot-371
95Sault Ste. Marie Greyhounds-2
95Signature Rookies-5
Signatures-5
99Mobile Mysticks-20
Cherry, Dick
690-Pee-Chee-173
Cherry, Don
52Juniors Blue Tint-100
63Rochester Americans-8
74O-Pee-Chee NHL-161
74Topps-161
92Parkhurst Cherry Picks-NNO
92Parkhurst Cherry Picks-NNO
92Parkhurst Cherry Picks-NNO
93Parkhurst Cherry's Playoff Heroes-D20
96Duracell All-Cherry Team-DC21
96Duracell All-Cherry Team-DC22
97Pinnacle Hockey Night in Canada-2
00Topps Stars Game Gear-GGDC
00Topps Stars Game Gear-GGDCA
00Mississauga Ice Dogs-5
01Mississauga Ice Dogs-23
03Beehive-17
Variations-17
Gold-17
Silver-17
Jumbos-5
Jumbos-14
Jumbo Variations-5
Jumbo Variations-14
03SP Authentic Honors-H10
03SP Authentic Honors-H11
03SP Authentic Honors Limited-H10
03SP Authentic Honors Limited-H11
03SP Authentic Sign of the Times-DC
03SP Authentic Sign of the Times-BCY
03UD Premier Collection Signatures-PS-DC
03UD Premier Collection Signatures Gold-PS-DC
03Upper Deck-474
Canadian Exclusives-474
HG-474
UD Exclusives-474
Ice Under Glass Autographs-UG-DC
03Upper Deck Trilogy-137
Crest Variations-137
Limited-137
Scripts-S3DC
Scripts-CSDC
Scripts Limited-S3DC
Scripts Red-S3DC
04SP Authentic Sign of the Times-ST-DC
04SP Authentic Sign of the Times-DS-BC
04UD Legendary Signatures-29
AKA Autographs-AKA-DC
Autographs-DC
04UD Legends Classics-19
Gold-19
Platinum-19
Silver-19
Signature Moments-M3
Signature Moments-M37
Signatures-CS3
04Upper Deck-193
Canadian Exclusives-193
HG Glossy Gold-193
HG Glossy Silver-193
05Beehive Signature Scrapbook-SSDC
05SPx Xcitement Legends-XL-DC
05SPx Xcitement Legends Gold-XL-DC
05SPx Xcitement Legends Spectrum-XL-DC
05The Cup-11
Gold-11
Black Rainbow-11
Masterpiece Pressplates-11
05UD Artifacts-110
Blue-110
Gold-110
Green-110
Pewter-110
Red-110
Auto Facts-AF-DC
Auto Facts Blue-AF-DC
Auto Facts Copper-AF-DC
Auto Facts Pewter-AF-DC
Auto Facts Silver-AF-DC
Gold Autographed-110
05Upper Deck Trilogy Ice Scripts-IS-DC
05Upper Deck Trilogy Legendary Scripts-LEG-DC
06Beehive Signature Scrapbook-SSDC
06Parkhurst-34
Autographs-34
06SP Authentic Sign of the Times-STDC
06SP Authentic Sign of the Times Quads-ST4EBOC
06SP Game Used SIGnificance-SDC
06The Cup-6
Black Rainbow-6
Gold-6
Masterpiece Pressplates-6
06UD Artifacts-108
Blue-108
Gold-108
Platinum-108
Radiance-108
Red-108
06Ultimate Collection Signatures-US-DC
06Upper Deck Sweet Shot Signature Shots/Saves-SSDC
06Upper Deck Sweet Shot Signature Shots/Saves Sticks-SSSDC
06Upper Deck Trilogy Ice Scripts-ISDC
06Upper Deck Trilogy Legendary Scripts-LSDC
Cherry, Ross
02Lincoln Stars-23
Cherry, Steve
00Mississauga Ice Dogs-6
01Mississauga Ice Dogs-24
Cherviakov, Alexei
93Swedish Semic World Champ Stickers-130
01Russian Hockey League-38
Chervyakov, Alexei
99Russian Hockey League-142
99Russian Stars of Hockey-13
00Russian Hockey League-358
Chervyakov, Denis
93Classic Pro Prospects-69
96Kentucky Thoroughblades-4
99Swedish Upper Deck-187
Snapshots-14
Cherwinski, Troy
04Vernon Vipers-24
05Vernon Vipers-6
Chesney, Mike
93Quebec Pee-Wee Tournament-705
Chesson, Lisa
04Ohio State Buckeyes Women-15
05Ohio State Buckeyes Women-10
06Ohio State Buckeyes Women-8
Chestokletov, Vasili
00Russian Hockey League-94
Chettleburgh, Mike
83Brantford Alexanders-29
Chevalier, Papa Joe
01Arizona Icecats-5
Chevalier, Robert
52Juniors Blue Tint-68
Cheveldae, Jordan
05Penticton Vees-2
Cheveldae, Tim
86Saskatoon Blades Photos-6
88ProCards AHL-19
89ProCards AHL-326
90O-Pee-Chee-430
90Panini Stickers-212
90Pro Set-602
90Score-87
Canadian-87
90Upper Deck-393
French-393
91Pro Set Platinum-31
91Pro Set Platinum-280
91Bowman-47
91O-Pee-Chee-35
91OPC Premier-175
91Panini Stickers-136
91Parkhurst-39
91Parkhurst-441
French-39
French-441
91Pinnacle-21
French-21
91Pro Set-57
French-57
Puck Candy-7
91Score American-272
91Score Canadian Bilingual-492
91Score Canadian English-492
91Score Young Superstars-25
91Stadium Club-224
91Topps-35
91Upper Deck-129
French-129
92Bowman-202
92Bowman-420
92Kraft-28
92O-Pee-Chee-128
92Panini Stickers-111
92Panini Stickers French-111
92Parkhurst-37
Emerald Ice-37
92Pinnacle-37
92Pinnacle-269
French-37
French-269
Team 2000-20
Team 2000 French-20
92Pro Set-43
92Pro Set-251
92Score-275
92Score-417
Canadian-275
Canadian-417
Young Superstars-21
92Seasons Patches-7
92Stadium Club-199
92Topps-225
92Topps-310
Gold-225G
Gold-310G
92Ultra-46
92Upper Deck-5
92Upper Deck-197
93Donruss-96
93Donruss-507
93Leaf-195
93OPC Premier-66
Gold-66
93Panini Stickers-254
93Parkhurst-59
Emerald Ice-59
93Pinnacle-282
Canadian-282
93PowerPlay-67
93Score-68
Canadian-68
93Stadium Club-166
Members Only Master Set-166
OPC-166
First Day Issue-166
First Day Issue OPC-166
93Topps/OPC Premier-66
Gold-66
93Ultra-14
93Upper Deck-9
94Canada Games NHL POGS-297
94Donruss-325
94EA Sports-42
94Flair-205
94Kraft-37
94Leaf-81
94OPC Premier-502
Special Effects-502
94Parkhurst SE-SE203
Gold-SE203
94Pinnacle-130
Artist's Proofs-130
Rink Collection-130
94Select-102
Gold-102
94Stadium Club-217
Members Only Master Set-217
First Day Issue-217
Super Team Winner Cards-217
94Topps/OPC Premier-502
Special Effects-502
94Ultra-240
94Upper Deck-75
Electric Ice-75
SP Inserts-SP178
SP Inserts Die Cuts-SP178
95Be A Player-76
Signatures-S76
Signatures Die Cuts-S76
95Canada Games NHL POGS-296
95Collector's Choice-319
Player's Club-319
Player's Club Platinum-319
95Hoyle Western Playing Cards-9
95Jets Readers Club-1
95Jets Team Issue-3
95Kraft-39
95Parkhurst International-234
Emerald Ice-234
95Pinnacle-136
Artist's Proofs-136
Rink Collection-136
95Playoff One on One-325
95Pro Magnets-61
95Score-212
Black Ice Artist's Proofs-212
Black Ice-212
95Topps-291
OPC Inserts-291
95Upper Deck-452
Electric Ice-452
Electric Ice Gold-452
Special Edition-SE179
Special Edition Gold-SE179
95Images Platinum Players-PL8
96NHL Pro Stamps-61
96Playoff One on One-406
97Las Vegas Thunder-16
00Saskatoon Blades-5
Cheveldayoff, Kevin
88Brandon Wheat Kings-1
90ProCards AHL/IHL-507
91ProCards-459
Chevrefils, Real
44Beehive Group II Photos-11
52Parkhurst-80
53Parkhurst-89
54Parkhurst-63
54Topps-6
55Bruins Photos-4
57Bruins Photos-5
57Topps-1
58Bruins Photos-3
94Parkhurst Missing Link-8
Chevrier, Alain
85Devils Postcards-4
86Devils Police-7
86O-Pee-Chee-225
87O-Pee-Chee-58
87O-Pee-Chee Stickers-63
87Panini Stickers-73
87Topps-58
88Jets Police-4
89Blackhawks Coke-19
89O-Pee-Chee-132
89Panini Stickers-54
89Topps-132
90O-Pee-Chee-436
90Pro Set-230
Chevrier, Wally
61Sudbury Wolves-6
62Sudbury Wolves-8
Cheyne, Travis
91Air Canada SJHL-E8
92Saskatchewan JHL-25
Chiarello, Gene
99Bowman CHL-161
Gold-161
OPC International-161
Chiasson, Dan
84Sudbury Wolves-6
Chiasson, Luc
00Owen Sound Attack-3
01Guelph Storm-15
01Guelph Storm Memorial Cup-15
02Barrie Colts-13
Chiasson, Michael
05Rimouski Oceanic-22
06Rimouski Oceanic-24
Chiasson, Pascal
917th Inn. Sketch QMJHL-253
Chiasson, Steve
87Red Wings Little Caesars-6
88Red Wings Little Caesars-4
89O-Pee-Chee-164
89Panini Stickers-62
89Red Wings Little Caesars-5
89Topps-164
90Bowman-234
Tiffany-234
90O-Pee-Chee-94
90Panini Stickers-207
90Pro Set-69
90Score-214
Canadian-214
90Topps-94
Tiffany-94
90Upper Deck-96
French-96
91O-Pee-Chee-508
91Panini Stickers-143
91Parkhurst-268
French-268
91Pinnacle-298
French-298
91Red Wings Little Caesars-3
91Score American-293
91Score Canadian Bilingual-513
91Score Canadian English-513
91Topps-508
91Upper Deck-283
French-283
92Bowman-91
92O-Pee-Chee-160
92Panini Stickers-120
92Panini Stickers French-120
92Parkhurst-282
Emerald Ice-282
92Pinnacle-339
French-339
92Score-185
Canadian-185
92Stadium Club-105
92Topps-37
Gold-37G
92Ultra-282
92Upper Deck-546
93Donruss-97
93Leaf-111
93OPC Premier-196
Gold-196
93Panini Stickers-251
93Parkhurst-55
Emerald Ice-55
93Pinnacle-194
Canadian-194
All-Stars-23
All-Stars Canadian-23
93PowerPlay-68
93Score-221
Canadian-221
93Stadium Club-247
Members Only Master Set-247
OPC-247
First Day Issue-247
First Day Issue OPC-247
All-Stars-8
All-Stars Members Only-8
All-Stars OPC-8
93Topps/OPC Premier-196
Gold-196
93Ultra-305
93Upper Deck-345
94Be A Player-R83
Signature Cards-130
94EA Sports-38
94Fleer-28
94Leaf-487
94OPC Premier-327
Special Effects-327
94Parkhurst-68
Gold-68
94Pinnacle-376
Artist's Proofs-376
Rink Collection-376
94Score-45
Gold-45
Platinum-45
94Topps/OPC Premier-327
94Topps/OPC Premier-348
Special Effects-327
94Ultra-268
94Upper Deck-197
Electric Ice-197
SP Inserts-SP101
SP Inserts Die Cuts-SP101
95Canada Games NHL POGS-57
95Collector's Choice-43
Player's Club-43
Player's Club Platinum-43
95Donruss-69
95Emotion-20
95Leaf-193
95Panini Stickers-239
95Parkhurst International-298
Emerald Ice-298
95Pinnacle-189
Artist's Proofs-189
Rink Collection-189
95Playoff One on One-15
95Score-146
Black Ice Artist's Proofs-146
Black Ice-146
95SkyBox Impact-20
95Topps-129
OPC Inserts-129
95Ultra-23
Gold Medallion-23
95Upper Deck-10
Electric Ice-10
Electric Ice Gold-10
96Donruss-120
Press Proofs-120
96Maggers-12
96Score-235
Artist's Proofs-235
Dealer's Choice Artist's Proofs-235
Special Artist's Proofs-235
Golden Blades-235
96SP-22
96Topps Picks-125
OPC Inserts-125
96Upper Deck-26
96Whalers Kid's Club-27
97Be A Player-202
Autographs-202
Autographs Die-Cuts-202
Autographs Prismatic Die-Cuts-202
97Hurricanes Team Issue-4
98Hurricanes Team Issue-3
98Pacific-129
Ice Blue-129
Red-129
99BAP Memorabilia-SC3
Gold-SC3
Chibi, Nick
01Lethbridge Hurricanes-22
Chibirev, Igor
90O-Pee-Chee Red Army-8R
91O-Pee-Chee Inserts-14R
93Donruss-436
93PowerPlay-350
93Classic Pro Prospects-98
93Classic Four-Sport *-228
Gold-228
94Parkhurst-98
Gold-98
94Classic Pro Prospects-61
96Swiss HNL-97
98Swiss Power Play Stickers-89
99German DEL-234
00German DEL-97
01German Upper Deck-93
Chicoine, David
99Shawinigan Cataractes-22
Signed-22
00Shawinigan Cataractes-8
Signed-8
01Shawinigan Cataractes-9
01Sherbrooke Castors-6
Chicoine, Guillaume
02Rimouski Oceanic-1
03Val d'Or Foreurs-17
Chicoine, Mathieu
93Quebec Pee-Wee Tournament-298
Chieduch, Ryan
99Prince George Cougars-3
00Medicine Hat Tigers-2
Chighisola, Mike
90Cincinnati Cyclones-24
91Hampton Roads Admirals-2
95Central Hockey League-74
Chikin, Dimitri
99Swedish Upper Deck-188
00Russian Hockey League-348
Chimera, Jason
96Medicine Hat Tigers-3
97Medicine Hat Tigers-7
98Medicine Hat Tigers-7
99Hamilton Bulldogs-17
99Bowman CHL-85
Gold-85
OPC International-85
00Hamilton Bulldogs-11
01BAP Memorabilia-218
Emerald-218
Ruby-218
Sapphire-218
01Crown Royale-158
01O-Pee-Chee-277
01O-Pee-Chee Premier Parallel-277
01Pacific-154
Extreme LTD-154
Hobby LTD-154
Premiere Date-154
Retail LTD-154
01Pacific Arena Exclusives-154
01Parkhurst-315
01Private Stock-121
Gold-121
Premiere Date-121
Retail-121
Silver-121
01Private Stock Pacific Nights-121
01SP Authentic-148
Limited-148
Limited Gold-148
01SP Game Used-77
01SPx-140
01SPx-140
Rookie Treasures-RTJC
01Stadium Club-136
Award Winners-136
Master Photos-136
01Titanium-157
Retail-157
01Titanium Draft Day Edition-128
01Topps-277
OPC Parallel-277
01Topps Heritage-156
01UD Playmakers-118
01UD Top Shelf-54
01UD Top Shelf-54B
01Upper Deck-190
Exclusives-190
01Upper Deck MVP-201
01Upper Deck Victory-370
Gold-370
01Vanguard-110
Blue-110
Red-110
One of Ones-110
Premiere Date-110
Proofs-110
01Hamilton Bulldogs-6
02NHL Power Play Stickers-34
02Oilers Postcards-113
02O-Pee-Chee-267
02O-Pee-Chee Premier Blue Parallel-267
02O-Pee-Chee Premier Red Parallel-267
02O-Pee-Chee Factory Set-267
02Pacific Calder-68
Silver-68
02Pacific Complete-383
Red-383
02Topps-267
OPC Blue Parallel-267
OPC Red Parallel-267
Factory Set-267
03ITG Action-280
03Oilers Postcards-3
03Pacific-130
Blue-130
Red-130
03Pacific Complete-100
Red-100
03Upper Deck MVP-175
Gold Script-175
Silver Script-175
Canadian Exclusives-175
05Parkhurst-143
Facsimile Auto Parallel-143
06O-Pee-Chee-148
Rainbow-148
06Panini Stickers-240
Chimienti, Chris
03Mississauga Ice Dogs-6
Chin, Colin
89ProCards IHL-123
90ProCards AHL/IHL-540
91ProCards-250
93Fort Wayne Komets-2
94Classic Pro Prospects-81
95Fort Wayne Komets-2
99Fort Wayne Komets Points Leaders-5
Chin, Michael
01Notre Dame Fighting Irish-18
02Notre Dame Fighting Irish-3
03Greenville Grrrowl-4
Chinakov, Vitali
01Russian Hockey League-39
Ching, Shu
79Panini Stickers-360
Chinn, Nicky
93Quebec Pee-Wee Tournament-1327
94Finnish Jaa Kiekko-318
95UK Sheffield Steelers-6
97UK Sheffield Steelers-7
00UK Sekonda Superleague-76
01UK Guildford Flames-15
01UK Guildford Flames-24
02UK Guildford Flames-14
Chinnink, Rick
76Saginaw Gears-1
Chinova, Todd
05Quebec Remparts-23
05Quebec Remparts Signature Series-23
Chiodo, Andy
00St. Michaels Majors-11
01St. Michaels Majors-15
02St. Michaels Majors-24
03ITG Action-665
03ITG Used Signature Series-171
Gold-171
03ITG VIP Rookie Debut-123
03Parkhurst Rookie-84
03Topps Traded-TT138
Blue-TT138
Gold-TT138
Red-TT138
03UD Premier Collection-121
03Upper Deck Rookie Update-113
03Pacific AHL Prospects-95
Gold-95
03Wilkes-Barre Scranton Penguins-8
04Wilkes-Barre Scranton Penguins-26
05ITG Heroes/Prosp Toronto Expo Parallel -273
05ITG Heroes and Prospects-273
Autographs Series II-AC
Chiodo, Wade
99Des Moines Buccaneers-15
Chipchura, Kyle
02Prince Albert Raiders-4
03Prince Albert Raiders-15
04Prince Albert Raiders-13
04ITG Heroes and Prospects-87
Autographs-KC
Combos-13
Complete Emblems-5
Emblems-22
Emblems Gold-22
He Shoots-He Scores Prizes-19
Jersey Autographs-22
Jerseys-22
Jerseys Gold-22
Numbers-22
Numbers Gold-22
04ITG Heroes/Prospects Toronto Expo '05-87
04ITG Heroes/Prospects Expo Heroes/Pros-87
05ITG Heroes/Prosp Toronto Expo Parallel -328
05Prince Albert Raiders-3
05ITG Heroes and Prospects-328
Autographs Series II-KC
He Shoots-He Scores Prizes-31
Nameplates-N-70
Nameplates Gold-N-70
Oh Canada-OC-13
Oh Canada Gold-OC-13
06Hamilton Bulldogs-5
06ITG Heroes and Prospects National Pride-NP19
06ITG Heroes and Prospects National Pride Gold-NP19
Chipitsyn, Yuri
94German First League-362
Chipman, Jason
907th Inn. Sketch OHL-53
92British Columbia JHL-208
Chipperfield, Ron
74O-Pee-Chee WHA-42
75O-Pee-Chee WHA-4
76O-Pee-Chee WHA-32
77O-Pee-Chee WHA-10
79Oilers Postcards-3
80Nordiques Postcards-4
80O-Pee-Chee-280
88Oilers Tenth Anniversary-74
Chisholm, Lex
34Beehive Group I Photos-306
40O-Pee-Chee V301-2-148
Chistokletov, Vasili
01Russian Hockey League-42
Chistov, Stanislav
00Russian Hockey League-307
01BAP Memorabilia Draft Redemptions-5
01SPx Rookie Redemption-R1
01UD Top Shelf Rookie Redemption-TS1
02Atomic-101
Blue-101
Gold-101
Red-101
Hobby Parallel-101
02BAP All-Star Edition-133
Gold-133
Silver-133
02BAP First Edition-436R
02BAP Memorabilia-275
Emerald-275
Ruby-275
Sapphire-275
NHL All-Star Game-275
NHL All-Star Game Blue-275
NHL All-Star Game Green-275
NHL All-Star Game Red-275
02BAP Memorabilia Toronto Fall Expo-275
02BAP Signature Series-194
Autographs-194
Autographs Gold-194
Golf-GS87
Jerseys-SGJ57
Jersey Autographs-SGJ57
Team Quads-TQ19
02BAP Ultimate Memorabilia-5
Autographs-13
Autographs Gold-13
Calder Candidates-20
02Bowman YoungStars-116
Gold-116
Silver-116
Autographs-SC
Jerseys-SC
Patches-SC
Double Stuff-SC
Triple Stuff-SC
Rivals-SCSW
Rivals Patches-10
Sticks-SC
02Crown Royale-101
Blue-101
Purple-101
Red-101
Retail-101
Rookie Royalty-1
02eTopps-40
02ITG Used-85
Calder Jerseys-C10
Calder Jerseys Gold-C10
02O-Pee-Chee-340
02O-Pee-Chee Premier Blue Parallel-340
02O-Pee-Chee Premier Red Parallel-340
02O-Pee-Chee Factory Set-340
02Pacific-401
02Pacific Calder-101
Silver-101
Reflections-1
02Pacific Complete-506
Red-506
02Pacific Exclusive-193
Blue-193
Gold-193
Destined-1
02Pacific Heads-Up-126
02Pacific Quest for the Cup-101
Gold-101
Calder Contenders-1
02Parkhurst-205
Bronze-205
Gold-205
Silver-205
Hardware-C8
02Parkhurst Retro-205
Minis-205
Hopefuls-CH6
02Private Stock Reserve-151
Blue-151
Red-151
Retail-151
Class Act-1
02SP Authentic-182
Signed Patches-PSC
02SP Game Used-67
Signature Style-SC
02SPx-156
02Stadium Club-121
Silver Decoy Cards-121
Proofs-121
02Titanium-101
Blue-101
Red-101
Retail-101
Right on Target-1
02Topps-340
OPC Blue Parallel-340
OPC Red Parallel-340
Factory Set-340
02Topps Chrome-173
Black Border Refractors-173
Refractors-173
02Topps Heritage-135
02Topps Total-434
02UD Artistic Impressions-123
Gold-123
Common Ground-CG13
Common Ground Gold-CG13
Retrospectives-R94
Retrospectives Gold-R94
Retrospectives Signed-R94
Retrospectives Silver-R94
Right Track-RTSC
Right Track Gold-RTSC
02UD Foundations-143
02UD Honor Roll-146
Signature Class-SC
02UD Mask Collection-169
02UD Piece of History-121
02UD Premier Collection-78
Gold-78
Signatures Bronze-SSC
Signatures Gold-SSC
Signatures Silver-SSC
02UD Top Shelf-123
02Upper Deck-226
Exclusives-226
02Upper Deck Classic Portraits-102
02Upper Deck Rookie Update-166
Autographs-SC
02Vanguard-101
LTD-101
Prime Prospects-1
02UD SuperStars *-254
Gold-254
03BAP Memorabilia Future of the Game-FG-4
03Beehive-6
Gold-6
Silver-6
03Black Diamond-109
Black-109
Green-109
Red-109
03Bowman-7
Gold-7
Future Fabrics-FF-SC
Future Fabric Patches-SC
Future Rivals-CH
Future Rivals-NC
Future Rivals Patches-CH
Future Rivals Patches-NC
Goal to Goal-GC
03Bowman Chrome-7
Refractors-7
Gold Refractors-7
Xfractors-7
03ITG Action-89
Jerseys-M125
03ITG VIP Sophomores-6
03NHL Sticker Collection-158
03Pacific-1
Blue-1
Red-1
03Pacific Atlantic City National-6
03Pacific Calder Contenders Entry Draft-1
03Pacific Calder Collection NHL All-Star Block Party Gold-1
03Pacific Complete-215
Red-215
03Pacific Exhibit-1
03Pacific Exhibit-201
Blue Backs-1
Yellow Backs-1
03Pacific Invincible-1
Blue-1
Red-1
Retail-1
New Sensations-1
03Pacific Montreal Olympic Stadium Show-1
Gold-1
03Pacific Prism-1
Blue-1
Gold-1
Red-1
Paramount Prodigies-1
Rookie Revolution-1
03Pacific Toronto Spring Expo-1
Gold-1
03Private Stock Reserve-1
Blue-1
Red-1
Retail-1
03SP Authentic-3
Limited-3
Sign of the Times-SC
Sign of the Times-CF
Sign of the Times-GCF
03SPx-2
Radiance-2
Spectrum-2
Big Futures-BF-SC
Big Futures Limited-BF-SC
Fantasy Franchise-FF-FGC
Fantasy Franchise Limited-FF-FGC
03Titanium-141
Hobby Jersey Number Parallels-141
Patches-141
Retail-141
03Topps C55-64
Minis-64
Minis American Back-64
Minis American Back Red-64
Minis Bazooka Back-64
Minis Brooklyn Back-64
Minis Hat Trick Back-64
Minis O Canada Back-64
Minis O Canada Back Red-64
Minis Stanley Cup Back-64
03Topps Pristine-17
Gold Refractor Die Cuts-17
Refractors-17
Autographs-PE-SC
Autographs Gold-PE-SC
Press Plates Black-17
Press Plates Cyan-17
Press Plates Magenta-17
Press Plates Yellow-17
03Topps Traded-TT73
Blue-TT73

Gold-TT73
Red-TT73
Future Phenoms-FP-SC
03Upper Deck-247
BuyBacks-181
BuyBacks-182
Canadian Exclusives-247
HG-247
UD Exclusives-247
03Upper Deck All-Star Promos-S2
03Upper Deck All-Star Promos-AS3
03Upper Deck Classic Portraits-2
03Upper Deck MVP-7
Gold Script-7
Silver Script-7
Canadian Exclusives-7
ProSign-PS-SC
03Upper Deck Trilogy-2
Limited-2
03Upper Deck Victory-4
Bronze-4
Gold-4
Silver-4
Freshman Flashback-FF2
03Toronto Star-3
04Pacific-1
Blue-1
Red-1
04SP Authentic Buybacks-188
04SP Authentic Rookie Review-RR-SC
04SP Authentic Sign of the Times-ST-SC
04AHL Top Prospects-10
04Cincinnati Mighty Ducks-23
05SP Game Used Authentic Fabrics Quad-SGLC
05SP Game Used Authentic Patches Quad -SGLC
05Upper Deck Jerseys-J-SC
05Upper Deck Victory-4
Black-4
Gold-4
Silver-4
05Russian Hockey League RHL-7
06O-Pee-Chee-16
Rainbow-16
06Upper Deck Game Jerseys-J2SC
06Upper Deck Game Patches-P2SC

Chistov, Viktor
99Russian Stars Postcards-5
00Russian Hockey League-234
00Russian Hockey League-340
01Russian Hockey League-58
02Russian Hockey League-175
03Russian Hockey League-146
04Russian Super League All-Stars-2

Chistyakov, Alexei
99Russian Hockey League-202

Chistyakov, Anatoli
98Danish Hockey League-227
99Danish Hockey League-142

Chitaroni, Mario
84Sudbury Wolves-5
85Sudbury Wolves-13
86Sudbury Wolves-8
87Flint Spirits-1
88ProCards AHL-198
93Swedish Semic World Champ Stickers-224
94Finnish Jaa Kiekko-307
96German DEL-44
96Swedish Semic Wien-181
98German DEL-178
99German DEL-64
00German DEL-191
01German Upper Deck-199

Chitaroni, Terry
88Sudbury Wolves-15
89Sudbury Wolves-24
907th Inn. Sketch OHL-380
90Sudbury Wolves-15
917th Inn. Sketch OHL-250
917th Inn. Sketch Memorial Cup-121
91Sudbury Wolves-15
91Star Pics-15
91Ultimate Draft-49
91Ultimate Draft French-49
93St. John's Maple Leafs-5
93Classic Pro Prospects-92
94Brantford Smoke-11

Chittley, Rich
75HCA Steel City Vacuum-3

Chivojka, Petr
00Medicine Hat Tigers-3

Chlad, Martin
94Czech APS Extraliga-47
95Czech APS Extraliga-77
96Czech APS Extraliga-75
99Czech Score Blue 2000-85
99Czech Score Red Ice 2000-85

Chlubna, Tomas
94Czech APS Extraliga-132
95Czech APS Extraliga-310
96Czech APS Extraliga-204
97Czech APS Extraliga-330
97Czech DS Extraliga-115
97Czech DS Stickers-203
98Czech DS-122
98Czech DS Stickers-276
98Czech OFS-392
99Czech DS-109
99Czech OFS-320
99Czech OFS-406
00Czech DS Extraliga-128
00Czech OFS-173
01Finnish Cardset-277
02Finnish Cardset-10
04Finnish Cardset-165

Chmelir, Lukas
02Czech OFS Plus-51
03Czech OFS Plus-7
06Czech OFS-50

Chmielewski, Mike
03Kitchener Rangers-3

Choffat, Stefan
95Swiss HNL-274
96Swiss HNL-217

Choiniere, Philippe
03Indianapolis Ice-5

Chokan, Dale
907th Inn. Sketch OHL-205
917th Inn. Sketch OHL-116

Cholette, Jules
37V356 Worldwide Gum-127

Cholewa, Marek
89Swedish Semic World Champ Stickers-132
92Finnish Semic-272

Choquette, Darin
84Victoria Cougars-5

Chorney, Grant
86Regina Pats-2
89Saskatoon Blades-18

Chorney, Marc
82Post Cereal-15
83NHL Key Tags-103
83Penguins Heinz Photos-6

Chorneyko, Adam
04Kamloops Blazers-6

Chorny, Valery
96Swiss HNL-586

Chorske, Tom
89Canadiens Postcards-5
90Canadiens Postcards-7
90O-Pee-Chee-490
90Pro Set-616
91Bowman-345
91Canadiens Panini Team Stickers-4
91O-Pee-Chee-287
91OPC Premier-91
91Parkhurst-95
French-95
91Pinnacle-295
French-295
91Score Canadian Bilingual-613
91Score Canadian English-613
91Score Rookie/Traded-63T
91Stadium Club-276
91Topps-287
91Upper Deck-427
French-427
92Pinnacle-293
French-293
92Score-184
Canadian-184
92Stadium Club-351
92Topps-313
Gold-313G
92Ultra-112
93OPC Premier-524
Gold-524
93Parkhurst-384
Emerald Ice-384
93PowerPlay-375
93Topps/OPC Premier-524
Gold-524
93Upper Deck-416
94Canada Games NHL POGS-349
94Leaf-262
94OPC Premier-131
Special Effects-131
94Pinnacle-182
Artist's Proofs-182
Rink Collection-182
94Topps/OPC Premier-131
Special Effects-131
94Upper Deck-191
Electric Ice-191
95Be A Player-43
Signatures-S43
Signatures Die Cuts-S43
95Collector's Choice-237
Player's Club-237
Player's Club Platinum-237
95Score-284
Black Ice Artist's Proofs-284
Black Ice-284
95Senators Team Issue-6
96Pinnacle-26
Artist's Proofs-26
Foil-26
Premium Stock-26
Rink Collection-26
96Senators Pizza Hut-3
97Be A Player-207
Autographs-207
Autographs Die-Cuts-207
Autographs Prismatic Die-Cuts-207
97Pacific Invincible NHL Regime-132
98Pacific-278
Ice Blue-278
Red-278

Choteborsky, Jan
00Czech OFS-66
01Czech OFS-201

Chotowetz, Kelly
89Regina Pats-1
907th Inn. Sketch WHL-172

Chouinard, Dave
907th Inn. Sketch QMJHL-240
917th Inn. Sketch QMJHL-134

Chouinard, Eric
93Quebec Pee-Wee Tournament-116
94Quebec Pee-Wee Tournament-345
97Upper Deck-408
98Bowman's Best-139
Refractors-139
Atomic Refractors-139
98Finest Futures Finest-F13
98Finest Futures Finest Refractors-F13
98Quebec Remparts-5
Signed-5
98Bowman CHL-104
98Bowman CHL-143
Golden Anniversary-104
Golden Anniversary-143
OPC International-104
OPC International-143
Autographs Blue-A15
Autographs Gold-A15
Autographs Silver-A15
98Bowman Chrome CHL-104
98Bowman Chrome CHL-143
Golden Anniversary-104
Golden Anniversary-143
Golden Anniversary Refractors-104
Golden Anniversary Refractors-143
OPC International-104
OPC International-143
OPC International Refractors-104
OPC International Refractors-143
Refractors-104
Refractors-143
99Quebec PeeWee Tournament Coll Souv-26
99Quebec Remparts-4
Signed-4
99Bowman CHL-50
Gold-50
OPC International-50
00BAP Memorabilia-510
00Canadiens Postcards-10
00QMJHL All-Star Program Inserts-21
00Quebec Citadelles-2
Signed-2
01BAP Memorabilia-273
Emerald-273
Ruby-273
Sapphire-273
01O-Pee-Chee-280
01O-Pee-Chee Premier Parallel-280
01Topps-280
OPC Parallel-280
01Quebec Citadelles-2
02Pacific Calder-87
Silver-87
02Pacific Complete-561
Red-561
02Utah Grizzlies-4
05Philadelphia Phantoms-5

Chouinard, Guy
76O-Pee-Chee NHL-316
77O-Pee-Chee NHL-237
77Topps-237
78Flames Majik Market-16
78O-Pee-Chee-340
79Flames Postcards-3
79Flames Team Issue-4
79O-Pee-Chee-60
79Topps-60
80Flames Postcards-2
80O-Pee-Chee-45
80Pepsi-Cola Caps-22
80Topps-45
81Flames Postcards-3
81O-Pee-Chee-33
81O-Pee-Chee Stickers-219
81Topps-6
82O-Pee-Chee-41
82O-Pee-Chee Stickers-215
82Post Cereal-3
82Topps Stickers-215
83NHL Key Tags-17
83O-Pee-Chee-78
93Quebec Pee-Wee Tournament Gold-NNO
93Sherbrooke Faucons-25
99Quebec PeeWee Tournament Coll Souv-2
00QMJHL All-Star Program Inserts-1
04ITG Franchises Canadian-16
Autographs-GCH
04ITG Franchises US East-303

Chouinard, Jacques
80Quebec Remparts-2

Chouinard, Marc
95Classic-29
CHL All-Stars-AS18
95Classic Five-Sport *-153
Autographs-153
96Halifax Mooseheads I-5
96Halifax Mooseheads II-5
98Cincinnati Mighty Ducks-27
99Cincinnati Mighty Ducks-26
00SP Authentic-133
00SPx-173
00Titanium Draft Day Edition-151
00Titanium Draft Day Promos-151
00Upper Deck Ice-81
01BAP Memorabilia-233
Emerald-233
Ruby-233
Sapphire-233
01BAP Signature Series-18
Autographs-18
Autographs Gold-18
02BAP Sig Series Auto Buybacks 2001-18
02Pacific Complete-288
Red-288
02Topps Total-88
03ITG Action-54
03O-Pee-Chee-139
03OPC Blue-139
03OPC Gold-139
03OPC Red-139
03Topps-139
Blue-139
Gold-139
Red-139
05Panini Stickers-297
05Parkhurst-241
Facsimile Auto Parallel-241
05Upper Deck-342
05Upper Deck MVP-198
Gold-198
Platinum-198
06Canucks Postcards-5
06O-Pee-Chee-483
Rainbow-483

Chouinard, Martin
97Pensacola Ice Pilots-6

Chouinard, Mathieu
94Quebec Pee-Wee Tournament-497
97Upper Deck-397
98Finest Futures Finest-F12
98Finest Futures Finest Refractors-F12
98Bowman CHL-82
98Bowman CHL-159
Golden Anniversary-82
Golden Anniversary-159
OPC International-82
OPC International-159
Autographs Blue-A9
Autographs Gold-A9
Autographs Silver-A9
98Bowman Chrome CHL-82
98Bowman Chrome CHL-159
Golden Anniversary-82
Golden Anniversary-159
Golden Anniversary Refractors-82
Golden Anniversary Refractors-159
OPC International-82
OPC International-159
OPC International Refractors-82
OPC International Refractors-159
Refractors-82
Refractors-159
99Black Diamond-105
Diamond Cut-105
Final Cut-105
99Upper Deck-330
Exclusives-330
Exclusives 1 of 1-330
99Upper Deck Gold Reserve-330
99Upper Deck Ovation-75
Standing Ovation-75
99Quebec PeeWee Tournament Coll Souv-25
99Shawinigan Cataractes-14
Signed-14
99Bowman CHL-64
Gold-64
OPC International-64
99UD Prospects-64
Signatures of Tradition-MC
00Grand Rapids Griffins-4
01Grand Rapids Griffins-22
03Manchester Monarchs Team Issue-2
03Pacific AHL Prospects-46
Gold-46

Chouinard, Patrick
99Quebec Remparts-2
Signed-2

Chouinard, Yan
93Quebec Pee-Wee Tournament-536

Choukalos, Donald
98Calgary Hitmen-23
98Calgary Hitmen Autographs-23
01New Mexico Scorpions-17
01Vancouver Giants-10

Choules, Gregg
84Chicoutimi Sagueneens-6

Chovan, Jan
00Belleville Bulls-18
01Belleville Bulls-5
01London Knights-23

Chowaniec, Stefan
73Finnish Jaakiekko-87
74Finnish Jenkki-93
79Panini Stickers-127

Chrapala, Jay
06Richmond Renegades-1

Chrenko, Tomas
06Czech OFS-323

Chrest, Blaine
86Saskatoon Blades Photos-7

Chretien, Claude
51Laval Dairy Lac St. Jean-19

Christ, Jerzey
94German First League-405

Christen, Bjorn
98Swiss Power Play Stickers-39
98Swiss Power Play Stickers-277
99Swiss Panini Stickers-40
99Swiss Panini Stickers-290
00Swiss Panini Stickers-40
00Swiss Slapshot Mini-Cards-SCB8
01Swiss HNL-112
02Swiss HNL-255
04Swiss Davos Postcards-7

Christen, Greg
01Swiss HNL-37

Christen, Jean-Luc
93Swiss HNL-492

Christensen, Bent
98Danish Hockey League-150
99Danish Hockey League-166

Christensen, Erik
99Kamloops Blazers-4
00Kamloops Blazers-6
00UD CHL Prospects-50
02Kamloops Blazers-17
03Brandon Wheat Kings-4
04Wilkes-Barre Scranton Penguins-14
05ITG Heroes/Prosp Toronto Expo Parallel -222
05Beehive-166
Matte-166
05Black Diamond-272
05Hot Prospects-209
Autographed Patch Variation-209
Autographed Patch Variation Gold-209
Hot Materials-HMEC
Red Hot-209
05Parkhurst-393
Facsimile Auto Parallel-393
True Colors-TCPIT
True Colors-TCPIT
True Colors-TCPHPI
True Colors-TCPHPI
05SP Authentic-208
05SP Game Used-187
Gold-187
05SPx-218
Spectrum-218
05The Cup-157
Autographed Rookie Patches Gold Rainbow-157
Black Rainbow Rookies-157
Masterpiece Pressplates (Artifacts)-314
Masterpiece Pressplates (Bee Hive)-166
Masterpiece Pressplates (Black Diamond)-272
Masterpiece Pressplates (Ice)-205
Masterpiece Pressplates (Rookie Update)-243
Masterpiece Pressplates SPA Autos-208
Masterpiece Pressplates (SP Game Used)-187
Masterpiece Pressplates (SPx)-218
Masterpiece Pressplates (Trilogy)-293
Masterpiece Pressplates Ult Coll-179
Masterpiece Pressplates Autographs-157
Platinum Rookies-157
05UD Artifacts-314
05Ultimate Collection-179
Gold-179
05Upper Deck-467
05Upper Deck Ice-205
05Upper Deck Rookie Update-243
Inspirations Patch Rookies-243
05Upper Deck Trilogy-293
05WBS Penguins-5
05ITG Heroes and Prospects-222
06Black Diamond Gemography-GEC
06Upper Deck MVP Autographs-OAMC
06Wilkes-Barre Scranton Penguins-7
06Wilkes-Barre Scranton Penguins Jerseys-15
06ITG Heroes and Prospects Jerseys-GUJ12
06ITG Heroes and Prospects Jerseys Gold-GUJ12
06ITG Heroes and Prospects Emblems-GUE12
06ITG Heroes and Prospects Emblems Gold-GUE12
06ITG Heroes and Prospects Numbers-GUN12
06ITG Heroes and Prospects Numbers Gold-GUN12

Christensen, Matt
84Minnesota-Duluth Bulldogs-19
85Minnesota-Duluth Bulldogs-15

Christensen, Ted
95Collector's Choice-349
Player's Club-349
Player's Club Platinum-349

Christensen, Terry
91Michigan Falcons-16
99Tallahassee Tiger Sharks-22

Christensen, Troy
96Dayton Bombers-19

Christian, Brandon
94Johnstown Chiefs-3
95Thunder Bay Senators-5
96Johnstown Chiefs-2
00Indianapolis Ice-4
04St Georges de Beauce Garaga-23

Christian, Dave
80USA Olympic Team Mini Pics-14
80Jets Postcards-5
80O-Pee-Chee-176
80Pepsi-Cola Caps-124
80Topps-176
81Jets Postcards-3
81O-Pee-Chee-359
81O-Pee-Chee-360
81O-Pee-Chee-378
81O-Pee-Chee Stickers-136
81Topps-7
81Topps-66
81Swedish Semic Hockey VM Stickers-96
82Jets Postcards-5
82O-Pee-Chee-377
82O-Pee-Chee Stickers-206
82Post Cereal-21
82Topps Stickers-206
83NHL Key Tags-136
83O-Pee-Chee-367
84Capitals Pizza Hut-2
84O-Pee-Chee-195
84O-Pee-Chee Stickers-133
84Topps-142
85Capitals Pizza Hut-2
85O-Pee-Chee-99
85O-Pee-Chee Stickers-110
85Topps-99
86Capitals Kodak-4
86Capitals Police-4
86O-Pee-Chee-21
86O-Pee-Chee Box Bottoms-C
86O-Pee-Chee Stickers-248
86Topps-21
86Topps Box Bottoms-C
87Capitals Kodak-27
87Capitals Team Issue-3
87O-Pee-Chee-88
87O-Pee-Chee Stickers-235
87Panini Stickers-184
87Topps-88
88Capitals Borderless-1
88Capitals Smokey-1
88O-Pee-Chee-14
88O-Pee-Chee Stickers-70
88Panini Stickers-369
88Topps-14
89Bruins Sports Action Update-2
89Capitals Team Issue-2
89O-Pee-Chee-159
89O-Pee-Chee Stickers-78
89Panini Stickers-345
89Topps-159
89Swedish Semic World Champ Stickers-166
90Bowman-40
Tiffany-40
90Bruins Sports Action-9
90O-Pee-Chee-263
90Panini Stickers-18
90Pro Set-6
90Score-295
Canadian-295
90Topps-263
Tiffany-263
90Upper Deck-61
French-61
91Pro Set Platinum-110
91Blues Postcards-8
91Bowman-358
91O-Pee-Chee-276
91OPC Premier-53
91Panini Stickers-173
91Parkhurst-159
French-159
91Pinnacle-244
French-244
91Pro Set-11
91Pro Set-297
91Pro Set-471
French-11
French-297
French-471
91Score American-292
91Score Canadian Bilingual-589
91Score Canadian English-589
91Score Rookie/Traded-39T
91Stadium Club-95
91Topps-276
91Upper Deck-541
French-541
91Finnish Semic World Champ Stickers-142
91Swedish Semic World Champ Stickers-142
92Blackhawks Coke-6
92Bowman-6
92O-Pee-Chee-289
92OPC Premier-1
92Pinnacle-193
French-193
92Score-198
Canadian-198
92Stadium Club-216
92Topps-21
Gold-21G
92Ultra-273
92Upper Deck-194
92Finnish Semic-164
92North Dakota Fighting Sioux-33
93Blackhawks Coke-9
93OPC Premier-118
Gold-118
93Score-440
Canadian-440
93Topps/OPC Premier-118
Gold-118
94Finnish Jaa Kiekko-127
94Minnesota Moose-1
95Minnesota Moose-1
95Images-26
Gold-26
95Signature Rookies Miracle on Ice-5
95Signature Rookies Miracle on Ice-6
95Signature Rook Miracle on Ice Sigs-5
95Signature Rook Miracle on Ice Sigs-6
96Collector's Edge Ice-164
Prism-164
04UD Legendary Signatures-92
Autographs-DV
Miracle Men-USA8
Miracle Men Autographs-USA-DV

Christian, Gord
93Johnstown Chiefs-7
94Johnstown Chiefs-4

Christian, Jeff
90ProCards AHL/IHL-572
91ProCards-415
94Cleveland Lumberjacks-13
94Cleveland Lumberjacks Postcards-13
95Cleveland Lumberjacks-9
95Cleveland Lumberjacks Postcards-9
96Cleveland Lumberjacks-8
96Cleveland Lumberjacks Multi-Ad-9
97Las Vegas Thunder-17
99Cleveland Lumberjacks-5
00German DEL-153
01German Upper Deck-156
02German DEL City Press-44
03German DEL-123
04UK Sheffield Steelers-18
06Houston Aeros RetroÂ -6

Christian, Lou
84Nova Scotia Oilers-26

Christian, Marc
93Minnesota-Duluth Bulldogs-7

Christian, Matt
93Minnesota-Duluth Bulldogs-6

Christian, Mike
96Barrie Colts-4
96Guelph Storm-13
98Barrie Colts-17

Christian, Tim
91Ferris State Bulldogs-8
92Ferris State Bulldogs-8
95Roanoke Express-11
96Roanoke Express-24
98Roanoke Express-23

Christian, Zachary
93Quebec Pee-Wee Tournament-1276

Christiano, Jon
00Rochester Americans-25
02Rochester Americans-24

Christiansen, Doug
03Charlotte Checkers-67
05Reading Royals-2

Christiansen, Frode
92Norwegian Elite Series-214

Christiansen, Hal
89Regina Pats-2
907th Inn. Sketch WHL-164
917th Inn. Sketch WHL-225

Christiansen, Keith
72Minnesota Fighting Saints Postcards WHA-4
72Finnish Semic World Championship-124
72Swedish Semic World Championship-124

Christiansen, Ole
98Danish Hockey League-189
99Danish Hockey League-84

Christiansen, Rasmus
98Danish Hockey League-67
98Danish Hockey League-142

Christianson, Bryce
06Lincoln Stars Traded-7T
06Lincoln Stars Upper DeckÂ Signature Series -8

Christiansson, Jan
67Swedish Hockey-234

Christiansson, Jens
84Swedish Semic Elitserien-156
86Swedish Panini Stickers-143

Christie, Jason
88Saskatoon Blades-21
89Saskatoon Blades-22
94Portland Pirates-5
95Portland Pirates-8
96Portland Pirates-21
96Portland Pirates Shop N' Save-9
97Manitoba Moose-B4
97Portland Pirates-7
99Peoria Rivermen-21
00Peoria Rivermen-21
01Peoria Rivermen-2
02ECHL Update-U-4
02Peoria Rivermen-1
03Peoria Rivermen-24
04Peoria Rivermen-25

Christie, Mike
74NHL Action Stamps-61
74O-Pee-Chee NHL-278
75O-Pee-Chee NHL-366
76O-Pee-Chee NHL-333
76O-Pee-Chee NHL-383
77O-Pee-Chee NHL-357
78O-Pee-Chee-291
79O-Pee-Chee-345
79Rockies Team Issue-4
80O-Pee-Chee-358

Christie, Ryan
95Slapshot-293
95Owen Sound Platers-21
96Owen Sound Platers-21
97Owen Sound Platers-17
98Michigan K-Wings-3
99Crown Royale-43
Limited Series-43
Premiere Date-43
Prospects Parallel-43
99Pacific Omega-78
Copper-78
Gold-78
Ice Blue-78
Premiere Date-78
99Michigan K-Wings-12
00Upper Deck Victory-263
00Utah Grizzlies-18
03Las Vegas Wranglers-4
03Las Vegas Wranglers RBI-227

Christie, Steve
03Salmon Arm Silverbacks-3
04Langley Hornets-8

Christie, Taylor
06Reading Royals-3

Christion, Scott
91Air Canada SJHL-B18
91Air Canada SJHL-D17
91Air Canada SJHL All-Stars-16
91Air Canada SJHL All-Stars-49

Christoff, Steve
80USA Olympic Team Mini Pics-13
80North Stars Postcards-5
80O-Pee-Chee-103
80Topps-103
81North Stars Postcards-6
81O-Pee-Chee-160
81Topps-W104
81Swedish Semic Hockey VM Stickers-101
82O-Pee-Chee-42
82O-Pee-Chee Stickers-194
82Post Cereal-9
82Topps Stickers-194
83O-Pee-Chee-169
84O-Pee-Chee-81
95Signature Rookies Miracle on Ice-7
95Signature Rookies Miracle on Ice-8
95Signature Rook Miracle on Ice Sigs-7
95Signature Rook Miracle on Ice Sigs-8
04UD Legendary Signatures Miracle Men-USA11
04UD Legendary Sigs Miracle Men Autos-USA-ST

Christoffer, Justin
91Air Canada SJHL-C37

Christoffersen, Magnus
92Norwegian Elite Series-65

Christopher, Des
907th Inn. Sketch WHL-207

Christopherson, Ben
01Rockford IceHogs-1

Christy, Frankie
51Buffalo Bison-3

Chrun, Mike
89Spokane Chiefs-1
907th Inn. Sketch WHL-188
917th Inn. Sketch WHL-203

Chrystal, Bob
51Cleveland Barons-17
54Parkhurst-69
54Topps-2

Chubarov, Artem
97Black Diamond-69
Double Diamond-69
Triple Diamond-69
Quadruple Diamond-69
98UD Choice-284
Prime Choice Reserve-284
Reserve-284
98Russian Hockey League-163
99BAP Memorabilia-310
Gold-310
Silver-310
99BAP Millennium-233
Emerald-233
Ruby-233
Sapphire-233
Signatures-233
Signatures Gold-233
99Pacific Dynagon Ice-193
Blue-193
Copper-193
Gold-193
Premiere Date-193
99Upper Deck MVP SC Edition-186
Gold Script-186
Silver Script-186
Super Script-186
00Panini Stickers-208
00Kansas City Blades-20
01Canucks Postcards-3
01Manitoba Moose-5
02BAP Sig Series Auto Buybacks 1999-233
02Canucks Team Issue-5
02NHL Power Play Stickers-147
02Pacific Complete-180
Red-180
03Bowman-106
Gold-106
03Bowman Chrome-106
Refractors-106
Gold Refractors-106
Xfractors-106
03Canucks Postcards-5
03Canucks Sav-on-Foods-18
03ITG Action-596
03Pacific Complete-306
Red-306
04Russian Back to Russia-9
04Russian Moscow Dynamo-33

Chucko, Kris
03Salmon Arm Silverbacks-4
04Minnesota Golden Gophers-4
05Minnesota Golden Gophers-6

Chukanov, Maxim
98Russian Hockey League-30

Chumichev, Vitali
00Russian Hockey League-81
00Russian Hockey League-351

Chun, Ta
79Panini Stickers-357

Chunchukov, Alexsandr
94Raleigh Icecaps-3
96Johnstown Chiefs-3
98Fayetteville Force-6

Chupilkin, Dmitri
03Calgary Hitmen-3

Chupin, Alexei
98Russian Hockey League-53
99Russian Hockey League-54
99Russian Stars of Hockey-1
00Russian Hockey League-37
01Russian Hockey League-109
02Russian Hockey League-24
02Russian Hockey League-208
02Russian Hockey League-231
03Russian Hockey League-37
03Russian SL-1
04Russian Moscow Dynamo-34
04Russian Super League All-Stars-16
05Russian Hockey League RHL-18

Chupp, Cody
05Waterloo Blackhawks-7

Church, Brad
93Prince Albert Raiders-4
94Prince Albert Raiders-3
95Prince Albert Raiders-3
95Classic-17
Ice Breakers-BK15
Ice Breakers Die Cuts-BK15
95Images-82
Gold-82
Platinum Premier Draft Choice-PD5
95Classic Five-Sport *-134
Strive For Five-HK3
95Signature Rookies Tetrad Autobilia *-96
96Portland Pirates-12
96Classic Signings *-78
Blue-78
Die-Cuts-78
Red-78
97Portland Pirates-8
99Hampton Roads Admirals-4
00Portland Pirates-20
03Reading Royals-26
03Reading Royals RBI Sports-289
04Florida Everblades-17
05Kalamazoo Wings-16
05Missouri River Otters-14

Church, Jack
34Beehive Group I Photos-307
39O-Pee-Chee V301-1-52

Church, Jeff
97Lethbridge Hurricanes-4

Churchill, Jason
03Halifax Mooseheads-13
04Halifax Mooseheads-10
05Saint John's Sea Dogs-1

Churchman, Travis
97Regina Pats-6

Churilov, Gennady
04Quebec Remparts-1

Churla, Shane
83Medicine Hat Tigers-2
87Flames Red Rooster-4
88Flames Postcards-16
90Pro Set-135
91Score Canadian Bilingual-542
91Score Canadian English-542
92Parkhurst-316
Emerald Ice-316
92Ultra-315
93OPC Premier-368
Gold-368
93Parkhurst-316
Emerald Ice-316
93Score-425
Canadian-425
93Topps/OPC Premier-368
Gold-368
94Be A Player Signature Cards-169
94Leaf-364
94Parkhurst SE-SE41
Gold-SE41
94Pinnacle-516
Artist's Proofs-516
Rink Collection-516
94Stadium Club-21
Members Only Master Set-21
First Day Issue-21
Super Team Winner Cards-21
94Stars HockeyKaps-6
94Stars Postcards-3
94Stars Score Sheet-NNO
94Ultra-278
94Upper Deck-186
Electric Ice-186
95Parkhurst International-61
Emerald Ice-61
95Playoff One on One-246
95Pro Magnets-121
95Upper Deck-458
Electric Ice-458
Electric Ice Gold-458
96NHL Pro Stamps-121
96Pinnacle-191
Artist's Proofs-191
Foil-191
Premium Stock-191
Rink Collection-191
96Playoff One on One-365
97Be A Player-182
Autographs-182
Autographs Die-Cuts-182
Autographs Prismatic Die-Cuts-182
97Pacific Invincible NHL Regime-123
97Upper Deck-317
02Fleer Throwbacks-79
Gold-79
Platinum-79

Churran, Chris
01Mississauga Ice Dogs-7

Chvatal, Marek
03Sarnia Sting-5

Chvatal, Petr
99German DEL-405

Chvojka, Petr
99Czech OFS-120
02Czech OFS Plus-261

Chwedoruk, Justin
06Quad City Mallards-1

Chychrun, Jeff
83Kingston Canadians-18
84Kingston Canadians-18
85Kingston Canadians-18
88Flyers Postcards-6
89Flyers Postcards-5
90Flyers Postcards-5
90O-Pee-Chee-465
90Pro Set-213
90Score-138
Canadian-138
90Upper Deck-446
French-446
91Score Canadian Bilingual-626
91Score Canadian English-626
92Bowman-257
92Durivage Panini-33
92Score-364
Canadian-364
92Stadium Club-298
92Topps-196
Gold-196G

Chynoweth, Dean
85Medicine Hat Tigers-9
89Islanders Team Issue-2
90ProCards AHL/IHL-511
91ProCards-463
94OPC Premier-45
Special Effects-45
94Topps/OPC Premier-45
Special Effects-45
97Be A Player-246
Autographs-246
Autographs Die-Cuts-246
Autographs Prismatic Die-Cuts-246
97Pacific-340
Copper-340
Emerald Green-340
Ice Blue-340
Red-340
Silver-340
97Upper Deck-222
97Providence Bruins-4
99Utah Grizzlies-20

Chynoweth, Ed
917th Inn. Sketch WHL-120
917th Inn. Sketch Memorial Cup-71

Chyzowski, Barry
89ProCards IHL-42

Chyzowski, Dave
87Kamloops Blazers-3
88Kamloops Blazers-6
89Islanders Team Issue-3
90O-Pee-Chee-146
90Pro Set-483
90Score-372
Canadian-372
90Score Young Superstars-12
90Topps-146
Tiffany-146
90Upper Deck-228
French-228
90ProCards AHL/IHL-509
907th Inn. Sketch Memorial Cup-3
91Bowman-229
91O-Pee-Chee-435
91Panini Stickers-253
91Score Canadian Bilingual-443
91Score Canadian English-443
91Stadium Club-250
91Topps-435
91Upper Deck-281
French-281
91ProCards-471
95Adirondack Red Wings-3
98Kansas City Blades-20
99Kansas City Blades Supercuts-4
00German DEL-179
01German Upper Deck-229
02German DEL City Press-280

Chyzowski, Ron
88ProCards AHL-292
99German Bundesliga 2-288

Ciancio, Matt
99Sioux City Musketeers-3
00Sioux City Musketeers-3
04Northern Michigan Wildcats-2

Cianfrini, Paul
06Belleville Bulls-15

Ciarcia, Jerry
82Swedish Semic VM Stickers-142
83Swedish Semic VM Stickers-142

Ciavaglia, Peter
91ProCards-12
91Rochester Americans Dunkin' Donuts-2

91Rochester Americans Kodak-7
91Rochester Americans Postcards-5
92Rochester Americans Dunkin' Donuts-3
92Rochester Americans Kodak-5
92Classic-103
Gold-103
92Classic Four-Sport *-215
Gold-215
93Score-474
Canadian-474
93Swedish Semic Elitserien-135
94Detroit Vipers Pogs-2
95Swedish World Championships Stickers-222
96Detroit Vipers-2
96Collector's Edge Ice-121
Prism-121
97Detroit Vipers-1
98Detroit Vipers-5
98Detroit Vipers Freschetta-2
98IHL All-Star Eastern Conference-10
99Detroit Vipers-7
99Detroit Vipers Kid's Club-2

Cibak, Martin
98Medicine Hat Tigers-8
99Medicine Hat Tigers-14
01BAP Memorabilia-323
Emerald-323
Ruby-323
Sapphire-323
01Parkhurst-346
01UD Premier Collection-81
01Upper Deck Ice-149
02Upper Deck-220
Exclusives-220
02Upper Deck MVP-217
Gold-217
Classics-217
Golden Classics-217
02Springfield Falcons-8
03Lightning Team Issue-13
04Czech HC Plzen Postcards-4
04Czech OFS-348

Ciccarelli, Dino
81North Stars Postcards-7
81O-Pee-Chee-161
81Topps-W105
82McDonald's Stickers-7
82North Stars Postcards-5
82North Stars Postcards-6
82O-Pee-Chee-162
82O-Pee-Chee-165
82O-Pee-Chee Stickers-189
82Post Cereal-9
82Topps Stickers-189
83NHL Key Tags-61
83North Stars Postcards-6
83O-Pee-Chee-164
83O-Pee-Chee-170
83O-Pee-Chee Stickers-118
83O-Pee-Chee Stickers-119
83Puffy Stickers-15
83Topps Stickers-118
83Topps Stickers-119
84Kellogg's Accordion Discs-1
84Kellogg's Accordion Discs Singles-6
84North Stars 7-Eleven-12
84North Stars Postcards-6
84O-Pee-Chee-97
84O-Pee-Chee Stickers-47
84 7-Eleven Discs-27
84Topps-73
85North Stars 7-Eleven-1
85North Stars Postcards-8
85O-Pee-Chee-13
85O-Pee-Chee Stickers-39
85 7-Eleven Credit Cards-9
85Topps-13
86North Stars 7-Eleven-6
86North Stars Postcards-20
86O-Pee-Chee-138
86O-Pee-Chee Stickers-169
86Topps-138
87North Stars Postcards-11
87O-Pee-Chee-81
87O-Pee-Chee Minis-7
87O-Pee-Chee Stickers-57
87O-Pee-Chee Stickers-118
87Panini Stickers-293
87Topps-81
88North Stars ADA-6
88O-Pee-Chee-175
88O-Pee-Chee Stickers-202
88Panini Stickers-93
88Topps-175
89Capitals Kodak-22
89Capitals Team Issue-3
89O-Pee-Chee-41
89O-Pee-Chee Stickers-75
89Panini Stickers-342
89Topps-41
90Bowman-69
Tiffany-69
90Bowman Hat Tricks-15
Tiffany-15
90Capitals Kodak-4
90Capitals Postcards-4
90Capitals Smokey-4
90Kraft-7
90O-Pee-Chee-100
90OPC Premier-14
90Panini Stickers-161
90Pro Set-308
90Score-230
Canadian-230
90Score Hottest/Rising Stars-94
90Topps-100
Tiffany-100
Team Scoring Leaders-6
Team Scoring Leaders Tiffany-6
90Upper Deck-76
French-76
91Pro Set Platinum-131
91Bowman-302
91Capitals Junior 5x7-6
91Capitals Kodak-6
91Kraft-14
91O-Pee-Chee-429
91Panini Stickers-207
91Parkhurst-193
French-193
91Pinnacle-128
French-128
91Pro Set-258
French-258
91Score American-128
91Score Canadian Bilingual-128
91Score Canadian English-128
91Stadium Club-118
91Topps-429
91Upper Deck-276
French-276
92Bowman-176
92O-Pee-Chee-249
92OPC Premier-44
92Panini Stickers-160
92Panini Stickers French-160
92Parkhurst-45
Emerald Ice-45
92Pinnacle-311
French-311
92Score-395
Canadian-395
92Stadium Club-399
92Topps-318
Gold-318G
92Ultra-47
92Ultra-283
92Upper Deck-461
93Donruss-98
93Leaf-18
93OPC Premier-49
Gold-49
93Panini Stickers-245
93Parkhurst-60
Emerald Ice-60
Cherry's Playoff Heroes-D5
93Pinnacle-127
93Pinnacle-239
Canadian-127
Canadian-239
93PowerPlay-69
93Score-214
Canadian-214
93Stadium Club-294
Members Only Master Set-294
First Day Issue-294
93Topps/OPC Premier-49
Gold-49
93Ultra-32
93Upper Deck-136
SP-41
94Be A Player-R39
94Be A Player-R129
94Canada Games NHL POGS-86
94Donruss-86
94EA Sports-41
94Flair-46
94Fleer-57
94Leaf-44
94OPC Premier-541
Special Effects-541
94Parkhurst-65
Gold-65
SE Vintage-2
94Pinnacle-241
Artist's Proofs-241
Rink Collection-241
94Score-19
94Score-243
94Score-246
Gold-19
Gold-243
Gold-246
Platinum-19
Platinum-243
Platinum-246
94Select Promos-118
94Select-118
Gold-118
94Stadium Club-191
Members Only Master Set-191
First Day Issue-191
Super Team Winner Cards-191
94Topps/OPC Premier-541
Special Effects-541
94Ultra-58
94Upper Deck-5
Electric Ice-5
SP Inserts-SP112
SP Inserts Die Cuts-SP112
94Sarnia Sting-29
95Be A Player-49
Signatures-S49
Signatures Die Cuts-S49
95Canada Games NHL POGS-99
95Collector's Choice-89
Player's Club-89
Player's Club Platinum-89
95Donruss-30
95Emotion-51
95Leaf-100
95Panini Stickers-182
95Parkhurst International-339
Emerald Ice-339
95Pinnacle-74
Artist's Proofs-74
Rink Collection-74
95Playoff One on One-251
95Score-247
Black Ice Artist's Proofs-247
Black Ice-247
95Select Certified-102
Mirror Gold-102
95SkyBox Impact-50
95Stadium Club-150
Members Only Master Set-150
Power Streak-PS7
Power Streak Members Only Master Set-PS7
95Summit-65
Artist's Proofs-65
Ice-65
95Topps-77
OPC Inserts-77
95Ultra-232
95Upper Deck-431
Electric Ice-431
Electric Ice Gold-431
Special Edition-SE28
Special Edition Gold-SE28
95Zenith-51
Gifted Grinders-16
96Black Diamond-148
Gold-148
96Collector's Choice-88
96Donruss-150
Press Proofs-150
96Flair-86
Blue Ice-86
96Leaf-16
Press Proofs-16
96Maggers-13
96Metal Universe-143
96Pinnacle-31
Artist's Proofs-31
Foil-31
Premium Stock-31
Rink Collection-31
96Score-101
Artist's Proofs-101
Dealer's Choice Artist's Proofs-101
Special Artist's Proofs-101
Golden Blades-101
96SP-147
96Topps Picks 500 Club-FC4
96Ultra-156
Gold Medallion-156
96Upper Deck-196
96Upper Deck-336
Power Performers-P22
96Upper Deck Ice-66
Parallel-66
96Zenith-87
Artist's Proofs-87
97Beehive-29
Golden Portraits-29
97Black Diamond-21
Double Diamond-21
Triple Diamond-21
Quadruple Diamond-21
97Collector's Choice-237
Crash the Game-C22A
Crash the Game-C22B
Crash the Game-C22C
Crash the Game Exchange-CR22
Star Quest-SQ22
Stick'Ums-S22
97Crown Royale-124
Emerald Green-124
Ice Blue-124
Silver-124
97Donruss-177
Press Proofs Silver-177
Press Proofs Gold-177
97Donruss Canadian Ice-77
Dominion Series-77
Provincial Series-77
97Donruss Elite-43
Aspirations-43
Status-43
97Donruss Limited-25
Exposure-25
97Donruss Preferred-51
Cut to the Chase-51
97Donruss Priority-66
Stamp of Approval-66
97Katch-134
Gold-134
Silver-134
97Leaf-83
Fractal Matrix-83
Fractal Matrix Die Cuts-83
97Leaf International-83
Universal Ice-83
97Pacific-15
Copper-15
Emerald Green-15
Ice Blue-15
Red-15
Silver-15
Team Checklists-23
97Pacific Dynagon-115
Copper-115
Dark Grey-115
Emerald Green-115
Ice Blue-115
Red-115
Silver-115
Best Kept Secrets-88
Tandems-57
97Pacific Invincible-129
Copper-129
Emerald Green-129
Ice Blue-129
Red-129
Silver-129
Attack Zone-22
NHL Regime-183
97Pacific Omega-97
Copper-97
Dark Gray-97
Emerald Green-97
Gold-97
Ice Blue-97
97Panini Stickers-100
97Paramount-171
Copper-171
Dark Grey-171
Emerald Green-171
Ice Blue-171
Red-171
Silver-171
97Pinnacle-68
Artist's Proofs-68
Rink Collection-68
Press Plates Back Black-68
Press Plates Back Cyan-68
Press Plates Back Magenta-68
Press Plates Back Yellow-68
Press Plates Front Black-68
Press Plates Front Cyan-68
Press Plates Front Magenta-68
Press Plates Front Yellow-68
97Pinnacle Certified-105
Red-105
Mirror Blue-105
Mirror Gold-105
Mirror Red-105
97Pinnacle Inside-134
97Pinnacle Tot Cert Platinum Blue-105
97Pinnacle Tot Cert Platinum Gold-105
97Pinnacle Totally Certified Platinum Red-105
97Pinnacle Tot Cert Mirror Platinum Gold-105
97Revolution-58
Copper-58
Emerald-58
Ice Blue-58
Silver-58
97Score-119
Artist's Proofs-119
Golden Blades-119
Check It-15
97SP Authentic-148
Icons-I27
Icons Die-Cuts-I27
Icons Embossed-I27
97Studio-65
Press Proofs Silver-65
Press Proofs Gold-65
97Upper Deck-154
97Upper Deck-199
Game Dated Moments-154
97Upper Deck Crash the All-Star Game-17
97Upper Deck Crash the All-Star Game-AR17
97Upper Deck Ice-22
Parallel-22
Power Shift-22
97Zenith-47
Z-Gold-47
Z-Silver-47
98Aurora-78
Championship Fever-22
Championship Fever Copper-22
Championship Fever Ice Blue-22
Championship Fever Red-22
Championship Fever Silver-22
98BAP AS Milestones-M3
98BAP AS Milestones-M9
98Bowman's Best-68
Refractors-68
Atomic Refractors-68
98Crown Royale-57
Limited Series-57
98Finest-5
No Protectors-5
No Protectors Refractors-5
Refractors-5
98Katch-65
98OPC Chrome-119
Refractors-119
98Pacific-22
Ice Blue-22
Red-22
98Pacific Dynagon Ice-79
Blue-79
Red-79
Team Checklists-11
98Pacific Omega-101
Red-101
Opening Day Issue-101
98Paramount-94
Copper-94
Emerald Green-94
Holo-Electric-94
Ice Blue-94
Silver-94
Team Checklists Die-Cuts-11
98Revolution-61
Ice Shadow-61
Red-61
98Topps-119
O-Pee-Chee-119
98UD Choice-93
98UD Choice Preview-93
98UD Choice Prime Choice Reserve-93
98UD Choice Reserve-93
99Pacific-171
Copper-171
Emerald Green-171
Gold-171
Ice Blue-171
Premiere Date-171
Red-171
99Upper Deck 500 Goal Club-500DC
99Upper Deck 500 Goal Club-500DC
00Upper Deck Legends-62
Legendary Collection Bronze-62
Legendary Collection Gold-62
Legendary Collection Silver-62
01BAP Memorabilia 500 Goal Scorers-GS10
01BAP Signature Series 500 Goal Scorers-17
01BAP Sig Series 500 Goal Scorers Autos-17
01BAP Signature Series Vintage Autographs-VA-28
01BAP Ultimate Mem 500 Goal Scorers-26
01BAP Ultimate Mem 500 Goal Scorers Autos-5
01BAP Ultimate Mem 500 Goal Jerseys/Stick-26
01BAP Ultimate Mem 500 Goal Emblems-26
01Fleer Legacy-31
Ultimate-31
In the Corners-1
Memorabilia-1
01Greats of the Game-28
Autographs-28
Jerseys-1
Patches Gold-1
01Parkhurst Autographs-PA34
01Parkhurst 500 Goal Scorers-PGS10
02Fleer Throwbacks-80
Gold-80
Platinum-80
02UD Foundations-22
02UD Foundations-47
02UD Foundations-98
1000 Point Club-DC
1000 Point Club-CI
1000 Point Club Gold-DC
1000 Point Club Silver-DC
Canadian Heroes-CDC
Canadian Heroes Gold-CDC
Canadian Heroes Silver-C-DC
Classic Greats-GDC
Classic Greats Gold-GDC
Classic Greats Silver-G-DC
Playoff Performers-PDC
Playoff Performers Gold-PDC
Playoff Performers Silver-P-DC
Power Stations-SDC
Power Stations Gold-SDC
Power Stations Silver-S-DC
Signs of Greatness-SGDC
03Parkhurst Original Six Detroit-46
Autographs-OS-DC
Memorabilia-DM27
Memorabilia-DM35
Memorabilia-DM55
04ITG All-Star FANtasy Hall Minnesota-10
04ITG Franchises Update-499
Autographs-DC2
Complete Jerseys-UCJ4
Complete Jerseys Gold-UCJ4
Double Memorabilia Autographs-WDM-DC
Memorabilia Autographs-WSM-DC
04ITG Franchises US East-439
Autographs-A-DC1
04ITG Franchises US West-252
Double Memorabilia-WDM3
Double Memorabilia Gold-WDM3
Memorabilia-WSM5
Memorabilia Gold-WSM5
Teammates-WTM8
Teammates Gold-WTM8
04ITG Ultimate Memorabilia-128
04ITG Ultimate Memorabilia-145
Gold-128
Gold-145
Autographs-32
Autographs Gold-32
Complete Logo-5
Heroes Steve Yzerman-6
Jersey Autographs-9
Jersey Autographs Gold-9
Original Six-8
Original Six-18
Stick Autographs-16
Stick Autographs Gold-16
04UD Legendary Signatures-28
Autographs-CI
Linemates-BENBCI
05ITG Heroes/Prosp Toronto Expo Parallel -34
05ITG Ultimate Mem Retro Teammate Jerseys-25
05ITG Ult Mem Retro Teammates Jersey Gold-25
05ITG Heroes and Prospects-34
Autographs-A-DC
Hero Memorabilia-HM-9
06ITG Ultimate Memorabilia Stick Rack-5
06ITG Ultimate Memorabilia Stick Rack Gold-5
06Parkhurst-37
Autographs-37
Autographs Dual-DACB
06SP Game Used Letter Marks-LMDC
06The Cup-42
Autographed Foundations Patches-CQDC
Autographed Patches-42
Black Rainbow-42
Foundations-CQDC
Foundations Patches-CQDC
Gold-42
Gold Patches-42
Honorable Numbers-HNDC
Jerseys-42
Limited Logos-LLDC
Masterpiece Pressplates-42
Property of-PODC
Scripted Swatches-SSDC
Signature Patches-SPDC
06UD Artifacts Tundra Tandems-TTCL
06UD Artifacts Tundra Tandems Black-TTCL
06UD Artifacts Tundra Tandems Blue-TTCL
06UD Artifacts Tundra Tandems Gold-TTCL
06UD Artifacts Tundra Tandems Platinum-TTCL
06UD Artifacts Tundra Tandems Red-TTCL
06UD Artifacts Tundra Tandems Dual Patches Red-TTCL
06Ultimate Collection Signatures-US-CI
06Upper Deck Sweet Shot Signature Shots/Saves-SSCI

Ciccarello, Joe
93Minnesota-Duluth Bulldogs-8
00UK Sekonda Superleague-44
03UK Basingstoke Bison-8
04UK London Racers-12
04UK London Racers Playoffs-2
04UK Sheffield Steelers-15

Ciccone, Enrico
90ProCards AHL/IHL-120
91Upper Deck-51
French-51
92OPC Premier-122
92Upper Deck-90
93Leaf-375
93Lightning Season in Review-7
93Parkhurst-219
Emerald Ice-219
93Upper Deck-528
94Be A Player-R16
Signature Cards-132
94Lightning Photo Album-8
94Upper Deck-460
Electric Ice-460
95Canada Games NHL POGS-254
95Collector's Choice-152
Player's Club-152
Player's Club Platinum-152
95Lightning Team Issue-6
95Upper Deck-382
Electric Ice-382
Electric Ice Gold-382
96Be A Player-129
Autographs-129
Autographs Silver-129
96Upper Deck-238
97Hurricanes Team Issue-5
97Pacific Invincible NHL Regime-43
98Pacific-397
Ice Blue-397
Red-397
99German DEL-359
00BAP Memorabilia Update Tough Materials-T19
00BAP Mem Update Tough Materials Gold-T19
02Fleer Throwbacks-69
Gold-69
Platinum-69
Scraps-2
Tie Downs-2
Stickwork-8

Cichocki, Chris
86O-Pee-Chee-41
86O-Pee-Chee Stickers-124
86Topps-41
88ProCards AHL-327
90ProCards AHL/IHL-14
91ProCards-206
92Binghamton Rangers-9
93Cincinnati Cyclones-4
95Cincinnati Cyclones-3
96Cincinnati Cyclones-33
96Cincinnati Cyclones-3
97Cincinnati Cyclones-21
98Cincinnati Cyclones-27
98Cincinnati Cyclones 2-25
99Cincinnati Cyclones-22
02Arkansas Riverblades-22
05Stockton Thunder-22
06Stockton Thunder-15a

Cichon, Chris
93Quebec Pee-Wee Tournament-703

Cienciala, Claude
95Swiss HNL-489

Ciernik, Ivan
99Grand Rapids Griffins-3
00SPx Rookie Redemption-RR21
00Grand Rapids Griffins-5
01Atomic-117
Premiere Date-117
01Atomic Toronto Fall Expo-117
01BAP Memorabilia-232
Emerald-232
Ruby-232
Sapphire-232
01BAP Signature Series-241
Autographs-241
Autographs Gold-241
01O-Pee-Chee-357
01Parkhurst-253
01Parkhurst-400
01Parkhurst Beckett Promos-253
01Senators Team Issue-5
01SP Authentic-165
Limited-165
Limited Gold-165
01SP Game Used-90
01SPx-119
01Stadium Club-133
Award Winners-133
Master Photos-133
01Topps-357
01Topps Chrome-175
Refractors-175
Black Border Refractors-175
01UD Challenge for the Cup-125
01UD Honor Roll-83
01UD Premier Collection-86
01Upper Deck-437
Exclusives-437
01Upper Deck Ice-63
01Upper Deck Vintage-290
03ITG Action-538
03O-Pee-Chee-318
03OPC Blue-318
03OPC Gold-318
03OPC Red-318
03Topps-318
Blue-318
Gold-318
Red-318
03Upper Deck MVP-433
Gold Script-433
Silver Script-433
Canadian Exclusives-433
04German DEL-264
05German DEL-203
All-Star Jerseys-AS07
Star Attack-ST01
06German DEL-119
All-Star Jerseys-AS3

Cierny, Jozef
92Rochester Americans Dunkin' Donuts-4
92Rochester Americans Kodak-6
92Classic-35
Gold-35
92Classic Four-Sport *-182
93Classic-127
93Classic Four-Sport *-231
94Score-217
Gold-217
Platinum-217
94Cape Breton Oilers-5
94Classic Pro Prospects-86
98German DEL-255
99German DEL-39

Cierny, Ladislav
00Czech OFS-13
01Czech OFS-124
02Slovakian Kvarteto-29

Ciesla, Hank
44Beehive Group II Photos-84
52Juniors Blue Tint-32
58Topps-49
63Parkhurst-51
94Parkhurst Missing Link-29

Cifelli, Mike
06Texas Tornados-21

Ciganovic, Oliver
94German First League-254

Ciger, Zdeno
90Devils Team Issue-6
90OPC Premier-15
90Pro Set-619
90Score Rookie/Traded-82T
90Upper Deck-429
French-429
91Bowman-280
91O-Pee-Chee-352
91Score Canadian Bilingual-405
91Score Canadian English-405
91Stadium Club-379
91Topps-352
91Upper Deck-385
French-385
92Oilers Team Issue-2
92O-Pee-Chee-88
92Panini Stickers-175
92Panini Stickers French-175
92Parkhurst-286
Emerald Ice-286
92Pinnacle-302
French-302
92Score-534
Canadian-534
92Stadium Club-228
92Topps-496
Gold-496G
92Ultra-113
92Upper Deck-457
92Finnish Semic-144
93Donruss-113
93Leaf-197
93OPC Premier-456
Gold-456
93Panini Stickers-239
93Parkhurst-336
Emerald Ice-336
93PowerPlay-78
93Score-388
Canadian-388
93Stadium Club-73
Members Only Master Set-73
OPC-73
First Day Issue-73
First Day Issue OPC-73
93Topps/OPC Premier-456
Gold-456
93Ultra-315
93Upper Deck-330
94Donruss-274
94Leaf-65
94Parkhurst-76
Gold-76
94Pinnacle-70
Artist's Proofs-70
Rink Collection-70
94Score-122
Gold-122
Platinum-122
94Stadium Club-229
Members Only Master Set-229
First Day Issue-229
Super Team Winner Cards-229
94Ultra-71
94Upper Deck-28
Electric Ice-28
94Finnish Jaa Kiekko-198
95Be A Player-137
Signatures-S137
Signatures Die Cuts-S137
95Donruss-360
95Donruss Elite-24
Die Cut Stars-24
Die Cut Uncut-24
95Finest-107
Refractors-107
95Metal-53
95Parkhurst International-79
Emerald Ice-79
95SP-53
95Stadium Club-127
Members Only Master Set-127
95Ultra-237
95Slovakian APS National Team-23
96Collector's Choice-95
96Donruss-203
Press Proofs-203
96Fleer Picks-96
96Leaf-76
Press Proofs-76
96Maggers-14
96Pinnacle-148
Artist's Proofs-148
Foil-148
Premium Stock-148
Rink Collection-148
96Score-20
Artist's Proofs-20
Dealer's Choice Artist's Proofs-20
Special Artist's Proofs-20
Golden Blades-20
96Summit-19
Artist's Proofs-19
Ice-19
Metal-19
Premium Stock-19
96Swedish Semic Wien-229
00Czech OFS-415
01Parkhurst-209
01Private Stock PS-2002-47
01Upper Deck-349
Exclusives-349
01Slovakian Kvarteto-2A
03Czech OFS Plus All-Star Game-H16
04Czech OFS Czech/Slovak-25

Cihal, Miroslav
95Czech APS Extraliga-230
96Czech APS Extraliga-57
97Czech APS Extraliga-318
98Czech OFS-182

Cihlar, Jiri
94Czech APS Extraliga-177
95Czech APS Extraliga-189
97Czech APS Extraliga-303
97Czech DS Extraliga-38
98Czech DS-40
98Czech DS Stickers-117
98Czech OFS-57
99Czech Score Blue 2000-43
99Czech Score Red Ice 2000-43

Cijan, Thomas
95Austrian National Team-2

Cikl, Igor
95Czech APS Extraliga-113
96Czech APS Extraliga-344

Cilladi, John
00Hull Olympiques-6
Signed-6

Cimadamore, Julian
06Ottawa 67s-20

Cimellaro, Tony
90 7th Inn. Sketch OHL-54
91 7th Inn. Sketch OHL-109
96German DEL-109
99Adirondack IceHawks-14

Cimetta, Rob
89Bruins Sports Action-7
90O-Pee-Chee-288
90Topps-288
Tiffany-288
91Bowman-160
91Maple Leafs PLAY-5
91O-Pee-Chee-256
91OPC Premier-160
91Stadium Club-9
91Topps-256
92Stadium Club-83
92Topps-181
Gold-181G
92St. John's Maple Leafs-3
93Indianapolis Ice-4
94German DEL-280
95German DEL-276
96German DEL-181
98German DEL-113
99German DEL-275

Cimon, Sebastien
92Quebec Pee-Wee Tournament-402
93Quebec Pee-Wee Tournament-1084

Cingel, Martin
04UK Edinburgh Capitals-12

Cinibulk, Martin
96Czech APS Extraliga-122
97Czech APS Extraliga-4
98Czech DS-22
98Czech DS Stickers-208
98Czech OFS-162

Ciolli, Mike
98Las Vegas Coyotes RHI-3

Cipolla, Jason
95South Carolina Stingrays-6
96St. John's Maple Leafs-9
97Milwaukee Admirals-7
98Milwaukee Admirals-7
98Milwaukee Admirals Postcards-7
00Rochester Americans-8
01Manitoba Moose-6
03German DEL-141
04German DEL-147
04German Hannover Scorpions Postcards-5
05German DEL-123

Cipriano, Mark
89Victoria Cougars-7
90 7th Inn. Sketch WHL-242

Ciprick, Trent
84Brandon Wheat Kings-15
85Brandon Wheat Kings-15

Cipruss, Aigars
98Finnish Keraileysarja-183
99Finnish Cardset-99
00Finnish Cardset-167
01Finnish Cardset-207
02Finnish Cardset-161
04Russian Legion-33

Circelli, Anthony
92Finnish Semic-248
93Swedish Semic World Champ Stickers-215
95Finnish Semic World Championships-173
95Swedish Globe World Championships-229
95Swedish World Championships Stickers-82

Circelli, Collin
01Moncton Wildcats-17
03St. Francis Xavier X-Men-17
04St. Francis Xavier X-Men-3

Cirella, Joe
80Oshawa Generals-12
81Rockies Postcards-4
82O-Pee-Chee-137
82Post Cereal-11
82Oshawa Generals-5
83Canadian National Juniors-2
83Devils Postcards-7
84Devils Postcards-2
84O-Pee-Chee-110
84O-Pee-Chee Stickers-74
84Topps-85
85O-Pee-Chee-98
85Topps-98
86Devils Police-8
86O-Pee-Chee-163
86O-Pee-Chee Stickers-198
86Topps-163
87O-Pee-Chee-170
87O-Pee-Chee Stickers-61
87Panini Stickers-75
87Topps-170
88Devils Caretta-7
88O-Pee-Chee-188
88O-Pee-Chee Stickers-79
88Panini Stickers-268
88Topps-188
89Nordiques Team Issue-5
89Nordiques General Foods-3
89Nordiques Police-2
89O-Pee-Chee-130
89Topps-130
90Nordiques Petro-Canada-3
90Nordiques Team Issue-1
90O-Pee-Chee-107
90Panini Stickers-141
90Pro Set-243
90Score-305C
Canadian-305C
90Topps-107
Tiffany-107
90Upper Deck-293
French-293
91Nordiques Panini Team Stickers-1
91O-Pee-Chee-502
91Parkhurst-340
French-340
91Score Canadian Bilingual-441
91Score Canadian English-441
91Topps-502
92Score-369
Canadian-369
92Stadium Club-479
92Topps-163
Gold-163G
93Leaf-269
93OPC Premier-41
93OPC Premier-414
Gold-41
Gold-414
93Panthers Team Issue-1
93Parkhurst-347
Emerald Ice-347
93Pinnacle-346
Canadian-346
Expansion-3
93PowerPlay-91
93Score-515
Gold-515
Canadian-515
Canadian Gold-515
93Stadium Club-2
Members Only Master Set-2
OPC-2
First Day Issue-2
First Day Issue OPC-2
93Topps/OPC Premier-41
93Topps/OPC Premier-414
Gold-41
Gold-414
93Upper Deck-65
94EA Sports-49
94Pinnacle-308
Artist's Proofs-308
Rink Collection-308
95Milwaukee Admirals-4
96German DEL-346

Cirelli, Anthony
96German DEL-223

Cirillo, Mike
00Louisville Panthers-21
01Florida Everblades-12
01Hershey Bears-3
02Arkansas Riverblades-2

Cirillo, Ryan
95Slapshot-191
99Jacksonville Lizard Kings-12

Cirjak, John
93Spokane Chiefs-6
94Spokane Chiefs-13
95Spokane Chiefs-16
96Spokane Chiefs-13
97Regina Pats-10
97Bowman CHL-95
OPC-95

Cirone, Frank
94Raleigh Icecaps-4
96St. Louis Vipers RHI-10

Cirone, Jason
90 7th Inn. Sketch OHL-30
90 7th Inn. Sketch OHL-178
91Upper Deck-605
French-605
91Moncton Hawks-2
91ProCards-183
93Cincinnati Cyclones-5
95Buffalo Stampedes RHI-34
96Kansas City Blades-4
98Kansas City Blades-24
99Kansas City Blades Supercuts-5
00German DEL-81
06Rio Grande Valley Killer Bees-11

Cisar, Marian
96Spokane Chiefs-17
97Beehive-67
Authentic Autographs-67
Golden Portraits-67
97Spokane Chiefs-19
98Upper Deck-303
Exclusives-303
Exclusives 1 of 1-303
Gold Reserve-303
98Milwaukee Admirals-24
98Bowman CHL-58
Golden Anniversary-58
OPC International-58
98Bowman Chrome CHL-58
Golden Anniversary-58
Golden Anniversary Refractors-58
OPC International-58
OPC International Refractors-58
Refractors-58
99Milwaukee Admirals Keebler-2
00Titanium-131
Retail-131
00Titanium Draft Day Edition-131
00Titanium Draft Day Promos-131
01BAP Memorabilia-274
Emerald-274
Ruby-274
Sapphire-274
01Pacific-215
Extreme LTD-215
Hobby LTD-215
Premiere Date-215
Retail LTD-215

01Pacific Arena Exclusives-215
01Parkhurst-158
01Milwaukee Admirals-7
03German DEL-198
03German Nuremberg Ice Tigers Postcards-4
04German DEL All-Stars-AS10
04German DEL Update-311
04German Hannover Scorpions Postcards-6

Cisecki, Jon
93Quebec Pee-Wee Tournament-1617

Cissewski, Marius
94German First League-530
99German Bundesliga 2-161

Civitarese, David
06Okotoks Oilers -4

Cizek, Martin
02Plymouth Whalers-18

Clackson, Chris
04Chicago Steel-7

Clackson, Kim
78Jets Postcards-3
80Nordiques Postcards-5
80Pepsi-Cola Caps-62
81O-Pee-Chee-271
02Fleer Throwbacks-39
Gold-39
Platinum-39

Clackson, Matt
03Chicago Steel-6

Claesson, Anders
67Swedish Hockey-217
69Swedish Hockey-259
70Swedish Hockey-148
71Swedish Hockey-241

Claesson, Jan
83Swedish Semic Elitserien-91
84Swedish Semic Elitserien-91
85Swedish Panini Stickers-234

Claesson, Stefan
89Swedish Semic Elitserien Stickers-9
90Swedish Semic Elitserien Stickers-82
91Swedish Semic Elitserien Stickers-234

Claffey, Derek
06Swift Current Broncos-18

Claffey, Dustin
03Vernon Vipers-5

Clafton, Grant
03St. Cloud State Huskies-3
04St. Cloud State Huskies-5
05St. Cloud State Huskies-11
05St. Cloud State Huskies-6

Clague, Jason
93Red Deer Rebels-4

Clague, Michael
98Red Deer Rebels-4

Clair, Fraser
00Barrie Colts-6
00Mississauga Ice Dogs-7
01Barrie Colts-21
02Lexington Men O'War-16
04Atlantic City Boardwalk Bullies-3
04Barrie Colts 10th Anniversary-17
05Fresno Falcons-3

Clancey, Derek
00Jackson Bandits-24
03Reading Royals-2
05Manchester Monarchs-22

Clancy, Chris
907th Inn. Sketch OHL-31
91Cornwall Royals-20
917th Inn. Sketch OHL-16

Clancy, Dave
03UK Manchester Phoenix-3

Clancy, Greg
897th Inn. Sketch OHL-59
907th Inn. Sketch OHL-81
97Grand Rapids Griffins-3
99UK Sheffield Steelers-3

Clancy, King
23V145-1-3
24Anonymous NHL-17
24Anonymous NHL-18
24C144 Champ's Cigarettes-13
24V145-2-3
32Keefe Maple Leafs-7
33O-Pee-Chee V304A-31
33V129-8
33V252 Canadian Gum-10
33V288 Hamilton Gum-17
33V357 Ice Kings-13
33V357-2 Ice Kings Premiums-1
34Beehive Group I Photos-308
34Sweet Caporal-44
36Champion Postcards-5
36O-Pee-Chee V304D-125
37V356 Worldwide Gum-29
55Parkhurst-33
Quaker Oats-33
59Parkhurst-50
60Topps-47
Stamps-8
61York Yellow Backs-39
63Parkhurst-20
69Maple Leafs White Border Glossy-4
80Maple Leafs Postcards-6
83Hall of Fame-33
83Hall of Fame Postcards-C3
85Hall of Fame-33
92Hall of Fame Legends-8
94Parkhurst Missing Link Pop-Ups-P4
94Parkhurst Tall Boys-132
01BAP Ultimate Memorabilia Gloves Are Off-8
01BAP Update Passing the Torch-PTT6
01Upper Deck Legendary Cut Signatures-LCKC
01Upper Deck Legends-45
02BAP Ultimate Memorabilia Gloves Are Off-20
02BAP Ultimate Mem Paper Cuts Autos-21
02ITG Used Vintage Memorabilia-VM20
02ITG Used Vintage Memorabilia Gold-VM20
02Maple Leafs Platinum Collection-46
02Parkhurst Reprints-206
02Parkhurst Reprints-245
02Parkhurst Vintage Teammates-VT18
02Parkhurst Retro Nicknames-RN14
03BAP Ultimate Memorabilia Gloves Are Off-18
03BAP Ultimate Mem Maple Leafs Forever-5
03BAP Ultimate Memorabilia Memorialized-10
03BAP Ultimate Memorabilia Paper Cuts-7
03Parkhurst Original Six Toronto-59
03Parkhurst Original Six Toronto-66
03Parkhurst Original Six Toronto-89
04ITG Franchises Canadian-105
04ITG Ultimate Memorabilia-24
Gold-24
Cornerstones-3
Cornerstones Gold-3
Gloves are Off-12
Maple Leafs Forever-5
Paper Cuts Memorabilia-17
Retro Teammates-10
04Ultimate Collection Ultimate Cuts-UC-KC
05ITG Ultimate Memorabilia Level 1-60
05ITG Ultimate Memorabilia Level 2-60
05ITG Ultimate Memorabilia Level 3-60
05ITG Ultimate Memorabilia Level 4-60
05ITG Ultimate Memorabilia Level 5-60
05ITG Ultimate Memorabilia Gloves Are Off-11
05ITG Ultimate Mem Gloves Are Off Gold-11
05ITG Ultimate Mem Leafs Forever Autos-1
05ITG Ultimate Mem Paper Cut Autos-3
05ITG Ultimate Mem Quad Paper Cuts Autos-6
05ITG Ultimate Memorabilia Vintage Lumber-27
05ITG Ultimate Mem Vintage Lumber Gold-27
05The Cup Legendary Cuts-LCKC
06Beehive 5 X 7 Cherry Wood-KCT
06ITG Ultimate Memorabilia Blades of Steel-22
06ITG Ultimate Memorabilia Blades of Steel Gold-22
06ITG Ultimate Memorabilia Sensational Sens
Autos-3
06ITG Ultimate Memorabilia Stick Rack-28
06ITG Ultimate Memorabilia Stick Rack Gold-28
06ITG Ultimate Memorabilia Vintage Lumber-5
06ITG Ultimate Memorabilia Vintage Lumber Gold-5

Clancy, Terry
67Seals Team Issue-7
69Maple Leafs White Border Glossy-5
72Maple Leafs Postcards-2

Clantara, Roland
51Laval Dairy Lac St. Jean-52

Clapper, Dit
33O-Pee-Chee V304A-8
33V129-36
33V252 Canadian Gum-11
33V357 Ice Kings-1
34Beehive Group I Photos-8
34Diamond Matchbooks Silver-12
37V356 Worldwide Gum-36
39O-Pee-Chee V301-1-95
60Topps-26
Stamps-9
83Hall of Fame-79
83Hall of Fame Postcards-F3
85Hall of Fame-79
91Bruins Sports Action Legends-8
94Parkhurst Tall Boys Greats-8
99Upper Deck Century Legends-44
Century Collection-44
03BAP Ultimate Memorabilia Paper Cuts-17
03Parkhurst Original Six Boston-34
03Parkhurst Original Six Boston-64
03Parkhurst Original Six Boston-72
03Parkhurst Original Six Boston-87
Inserts-B3
04ITG Franchises US East-334
04ITG Ultimate Memorabilia-50
Gold-50
Beantown's Best-1
Blades of Steel-17
Paper Cuts-17
Paper Cuts Memorabilia-12
Retro Teammates-7
05ITG Ultimate Memorabilia Level 1-26
05ITG Ultimate Memorabilia Level 2-26
05ITG Ultimate Memorabilia Level 3-26
05ITG Ultimate Memorabilia Level 4-26
05ITG Ultimate Memorabilia Level 5-26
05ITG Ultimate Mem Beantown's Best Autos-1
05ITG Ultimate Mem Blades of Steel-12
05ITG Ultimate Mem Blades of Steel Gold-12
05ITG Ultimate Mem Decades Jerseys-4
05ITG Ultimate Mem Decades Jerseys Gold-4
05The Cup Legendary Cuts-LCDC
06ITG Ultimate Memorabilia Beantown's Best Autos-
1
06ITG Ultimate Memorabilia Blades of Steel-7
06ITG Ultimate Memorabilia Blades of Steel Gold-7

Clapton, Marty
97Hampton Roads Admirals-7
98Hampton Roads Admirals-20
99Hampton Roads Admirals-5
01South Carolina Stingrays-5
02South Carolina Stingrays-5
02South Carolina Stingrays RBI-208
05South Carolina Stingrays-10

Clarance, Blair
03Fresno Falcons-3

Clarfield, Lawrence
93Quebec Pee-Wee Tournament-1688

Claringbull, Mike
85Medicine Hat Tigers-1

Clark, Andrew
93Sault Ste. Marie Greyhounds-18
94Guelph Storm-10
95Slapshot-90
95Guelph Storm-2
96German DEL-307
99Johnstown Chiefs-17
00Johnstown Chiefs-21
01Johnstown Chiefs-18
05Brandon Wheat Kings-4

Clark, Brett
97Canadiens Postcards-6
98Be A Player-220
Press Release-220
98BAP Gold-220
98BAP Autographs-220
98BAP Autographs Gold-220
98Canadiens Team Issue-2
98Upper Deck MVP-105
Gold Script-105
Silver Script-105
Super Script-105
01O-Pee-Chee-247
01O-Pee-Chee Premier Parallel-247
01Topps-247
OPC Parallel-247
02BAP Sig Series Auto Buybacks 1998-220
02Hershey Bears-6
03Hershey Bears-4
03Hershey Bears Patriot News-6
04Hershey Bears Patriot News-7
05Parkhurst-129
Facsimile Auto Parallel-129
06Avalanche Team Postcards-5
06O-Pee-Chee-137
Rainbow-137

Clark, Brian
00Fresno Falcons-29
05Fresno Falcons-23

Clark, Chris
99BAP Memorabilia-391
Gold-391
Silver-391
00Pacific-77
Copper-77
Gold-77
Ice Blue-77
Premiere Date-77
01BAP Memorabilia-225
Emerald-225
Ruby-225
Sapphire-225
02BAP First Edition-162
02NHL Power Play Stickers-4
02Pacific-51
Blue-51
Red-51
02Pacific Complete-285
Red-285
02Topps Total-368
03ITG Action-23
03Pacific Complete-168
Red-168
05Parkhurst-490
Facsimile Auto Parallel-490
06Be A Player-142
Autographs-142
Signatures-CL
Signatures 25-157
Signatures Duals-DOC
Signatures Trios-TOKC
06Fleer-199
Tiffany-199
06O-Pee-Chee-489
Rainbow-489
06Panini Stickers-176
06Ultra-199
Gold Medallion-199
Ice Medallion-199
06Upper Deck-197
Exclusives Parallel-197
High Gloss Parallel-197
Masterpieces-197
06Upper Deck MVP-297
Gold Script-297
Super Script-297
07Upper Deck Victory-94
Black-94
Gold-94

Clark, Darren
99Peoria Rivermen-7
00Peoria Rivermen-14
01Peoria Rivermen-19
02Peoria Rivermen-5
02Peoria Rivermen Photo Pack-3
02Peoria Rivermen RBI Sports-155

Clark, Dean
84Kamloops Blazers-6
88Oilers Tenth Anniversary-100
98Calgary Hitmen-24
98Calgary Hitmen Autographs-24
99Calgary Hitmen-5
99Calgary Hitmen Autographs-5
00Calgary Hitmen-9

Clark, Don
95Saskatoon Blades-7

Clark, Donn
81Saskatoon Blades-4
917th Inn. Sketch WHL-149
95Saskatoon Blades-7

Clark, Eric
98Calgary Hitmen-22
98Calgary Hitmen Autographs-22
99Calgary Hitmen-6
99Calgary Hitmen Autographs-6

Clark, Gary
95German DEL-359
98UK Basingstoke Bison-12
99German EV Landshut-23
99UK Basingstoke Bison-4
99UK Guildford Flames-9

Clark, George A.
23Crescent Selkirks-5

Clark, Gord
86London Knights-30

Clark, Herb
10C56-11

Clark, Jason
96Wheeling Nailers-8
96Wheeling Nailers Photo Pack-15
98German DEL-3
99German EV Landshut-17

Clark, Joe
98Odessa Jackalopes-19

Clark, Kerry
86Saskatoon Blades Photos-8
88ProCards AHL-319
89ProCards AHL-248
90ProCards AHL/IHL-620
91ProCards-584
92Salt Lake Golden Eagles-4
93Portland Pirates-18
94Portland Pirates-6
94Classic Enforcers-E7
96Collector's Edge Ice-171
Prism-171
97Milwaukee Admirals-2

Clark, Norbert
51Laval Dairy Lac St. Jean-20

Clark, Ron
89Rayside-Balfour Jr. Canadians-6

Clark, Steve
00Michigan State Spartans-3

Clark, Wendel
83Saskatoon Blades-8
84Saskatoon Blades Stickers-3
85Maple Leafs Postcards-6
86Kraft Drawings-8
86Maple Leafs Postcards-4
86O-Pee-Chee-149
86O-Pee-Chee Stickers-125
86O-Pee-Chee Stickers-141
86Topps-149
87Maple Leafs PLAY-6
87Maple Leafs Postcards-2
87Maple Leafs Postcards Oversized-2
87O-Pee-Chee-12
87O-Pee-Chee Stickers-152
87Panini Stickers-330
87Pro-Sport All-Stars-10
87Topps-12
88Frito-Lay Stickers-29
88Maple Leafs PLAY-2
88O-Pee-Chee Stickers-172
88Panini Stickers-121
89Kraft-34
89Panini Stickers-144
90Bowman-159
Tiffany-159
90O-Pee-Chee-79
90Panini Stickers-286
90Pro Set-276
90Score-171
Canadian-171
90Topps-79
Tiffany-79
90Upper Deck-3
French-3
91Pro Set Platinum-120
91Bowman-156
91Gillette-11
91Kraft-42
91Maple Leafs Panini Team Stickers-3
91Maple Leafs PLAY-6
91O-Pee-Chee-464
91OPC Premier-116
91OPC Premier-177
91Panini Stickers-102
91Parkhurst-170
French-170
91Pinnacle-250
French-250
91Pro Set-225
91Pro Set-585
French-225
French-585
91Score American-116
91Score Canadian Bilingual-116
91Score Canadian English-116
91Score Kellogg's-3
91Stadium Club-124
91Topps-464
91Upper Deck-386
French-386
92Bowman-325
92Humpty Dumpty I-4
92Maple Leafs Kodak-8
92O-Pee-Chee-96
92Panini Stickers-79
92Panini Stickers French-79
92Parkhurst-179
Emerald Ice-179
Cherry Picks-CP11
92Pinnacle-276
French-276
92Pro Set-189
92Score-110
Canadian-110
92Seasons Patches-70
92Stadium Club-204
92Topps-325
Gold-325G
92Ultra-208
92Upper Deck-89
93Donruss-337
93Kraft-34
93Leaf-166
Maple Leafs Score Black's-1
93OPC Premier-359
Gold-359
93Panini Stickers-227
93Parkhurst-475
Emerald Ice-475
First Overall-F9
93Pinnacle-157
Canadian-157
Captains-23
Captains Canadian-23
93PowerPlay-241
93Score-137
Canadian-137
93Stadium Club-192
Members Only Master Set-192
OPC-192
First Day Issue-192
First Day Issue OPC-192
93Topps/OPC Premier-359
Gold-359
93Topps Premier Finest-9
93Ultra-146
93Upper Deck-340
NHLPA/Roots-6
94Be A Player-R72
94Be A Player-R142
94Canada Games NHL POGS-194
94Finest-103
Super Team Winners-103
Refractors-103
94Flair-142
94Fleer-173
Slapshot Artists-1
94Kraft-3
94Leaf-542
94Leaf Limited-31
94McDonald's Upper Deck-McD24
94Nordiques Burger King-3
94OPC Premier-55
94OPC Premier-297
94OPC Premier-345
Special Effects-55
Special Effects-297
94Parkhurst SE-SE146
Gold-SE146
94Pinnacle-385
Artist's Proofs-385
Rink Collection-385
Gamers-GR13
Northern Lights-NL5
94Score Samples-3
94Score-3
Gold-3
Platinum-3
Check It-CI13
94Select-20
Gold-20
94SP-97
Die Cuts-97
94Topps/OPC Premier-55
94Topps/OPC Premier-297
94Topps/OPC Premier-345
Special Effects-55
Special Effects-297
94Topps Finest Inserts-10
94Ultra-172
94Ultra-354
94Upper Deck-115
Electric Ice-115
SP Inserts-SP154
SP Inserts Die Cuts-SP154
95Bashan Super Stickers-77
95Be A Player-55
Signatures-S55
Signatures Die Cuts-S55
95Bowman-45
All-Foil-45
95Canada Games NHL POGS-174
95Collector's Choice-103
Player's Club-103
Player's Club Platinum-103
95Donruss-193
95Donruss-389
95Donruss Elite-27
Die Cut Stars-27
Die Cut Uncut-27
95Finest-87
Refractors-87
95Hoyle Eastern Playing Cards-8
95Imperial Stickers-76
95Imperial Stickers-77
95Kraft-9
95Leaf-207
95Leaf Limited-70
95Metal-89
95Panini Stickers-247
95Parkhurst International-399
Emerald Ice-399
95Pinnacle First Strike-8
95Pinnacle FANtasy-21
95Playoff One on One-279
95Pro Magnets-57
95Score-57
Black Ice Artist's Proofs-57
Black Ice-57
95Select Certified-82
Mirror Gold-82
95SkyBox Impact-99
95Stadium Club Members Only-18
95Stadium Club-155
Members Only Master Set-155
Fearless-F8
Fearless Members Only Master Set-F8
Power Streak-PS8
Power Streak Members Only Master Set-PS8
95Summit-131
Artist's Proofs-131
Ice-131
Mad Hatters-8
95Topps-269
OPC Inserts-269
Home Grown Canada-HGC2
95Topps SuperSkills-45
Platinum-45
95Ultra-129
95Ultra-265
Gold Medallion-129
95Upper Deck-325
Electric Ice-325
Electric Ice Gold-325
Special Edition-SE139
Special Edition Gold-SE139
95Zenith-94
Gifted Grinders-3
96Black Diamond-107
Gold-107
96Collector's Choice-258
96Donruss-98
Press Proofs-98
Dominators-6
Hit List-2
96Donruss Canadian Ice-29
Gold Press Proofs-29
Red Press Proofs-29
96Donruss Elite-98
Die Cut Stars-98
96Flair-89
Blue Ice-89
96Fleer Picks-130
96Leaf-166
Press Proofs-166
96Leaf Limited-12
Gold-12
Stubble-20
96Leaf Preferred-87
Press Proofs-87
Steel-48
Steel Gold-48
96Maggers-15
96Maple Leafs Postcards-1
96Maple Leafs Postcards-3
96Metal Universe-148
96NHL Pro Stamps-57
96Pinnacle-196
Artist's Proofs-196
Foil-196
Premium Stock-196
Rink Collection-196
96Playoff One on One-411
96Score-42
Artist's Proofs-42
Dealer's Choice Artist's Proofs-42
Special Artist's Proofs-42
Check It-7
Golden Blades-42
96Select Certified-65
96Select Certified-P65
Artist's Proofs-65
Artist's Proofs-65B
Blue-65
Mirror Blue-65
Mirror Gold-65
Mirror Red-65
Red-65
96SkyBox Impact-125
96SP-150
96Summit-140
Artist's Proofs-140
Ice-140
Metal-140
Premium Stock-140
96Ultra-162
Gold Medallion-162
96Upper Deck-342
Generation Next-X15
96Zenith-24
Artist's Proofs-24
97Collector's Choice-246
97Crown Royale-129
Emerald Green-129
Ice Blue-129
Silver-129
97Donruss-57
Press Proofs Silver-57
Press Proofs Gold-57
97Donruss Canadian Ice-80
Dominion Series-80
Provincial Series-80
97Donruss Limited-40
Exposure-40
97Donruss Priority-150
Stamp of Approval-150
97Katch-139
Gold-139
Silver-139
97Pacific-17
Copper-17
Emerald Green-17
Ice Blue-17
Red-17
Silver-17
Slap Shots Die-Cuts-10A
97Pacific Dynagon-121
Copper-121
Dark Grey-121
Emerald Green-121
Ice Blue-121
Red-121
Silver-121
Tandems-27
97Pacific Invincible-136
Copper-136
Emerald Green-136
Ice Blue-136
Red-136
Silver-136
97Pacific Omega-218
Copper-218
Dark Gray-218
Emerald Green-218
Gold-218
Ice Blue-218
97Panini Stickers-174
97Paramount-179
Copper-179
Dark Grey-179
Emerald Green-179
Ice Blue-179
Red-179
Silver-179
97Pinnacle-185
Press Plates Back Black-185
Press Plates Back Cyan-185
Press Plates Back Magenta-185
Press Plates Back Yellow-185
Press Plates Front Black-185
Press Plates Front Cyan-185
Press Plates Front Magenta-185
Press Plates Front Yellow-185
97Pinnacle Certified-71
Red-71
Mirror Blue-71
Mirror Gold-71
Mirror Red-71
97Pinnacle Inside-89
Coach's Collection-89
Executive Collection-89
97Pinnacle Tot Cert Platinum Blue-71
97Pinnacle Tot Certi Platinum Gold-71
97Pinnacle Totally Certified Platinum Red-71
97Pinnacle Tot Cert Mirror Platinum Gold-71
97Revolution-133
Copper-133
Emerald-133
Ice Blue-133
Silver-133
97Score-128
Artist's Proofs-128
Golden Blades-128
97Score Maple Leafs-5
Platinum-5
Premier-5
97SP Authentic-152
97Upper Deck-164
98Be A Player-280
Press Release-280
98BAP Gold-280
98BAP Autographs-280
98BAP Autographs Gold-280
98Black Diamond-79
Double Diamond-79
Triple Diamond-79
Quadruple Diamond-79
98Bowman's Best-19
Refractors-19
Atomic Refractors-19
98Crown Royale-123
Limited Series-123
98OPC Chrome-142
Refractors-142
98Pacific-411
Ice Blue-411
Red-411
98Pacific Dynagon Ice-171
Blue-171
Red-171
98Pacific Omega-217
Red-217
Opening Day Issue-217
98Revolution-131
Ice Shadow-131
Red-131
98SP Authentic-79
Power Shift-79
98Topps-142
O-Pee-Chee-142
98UD Choice-202
Prime Choice Reserve-202
Reserve-202
98Upper Deck-188
98Upper Deck-369
Exclusives-188
Exclusives-369
Exclusives 1 of 1-188
Exclusives 1 of 1-369
Gold Reserve-188
Gold Reserve-369
98Upper Deck MVP-190
Gold Script-190
Silver Script-190
Super Script-190
99BAP Memorabilia-268
Gold-268
Silver-268
99Pacific-136
Copper-136
Emerald Green-136
Gold-136
Ice Blue-136
Premiere Date-136
Red-136
99Pacific Dynagon Ice-47
Blue-47
Copper-47
Gold-47
Premiere Date-47
99Panini Stickers-205
99SPx-32
Radiance-32
Spectrum-32
99Upper Deck-205
Exclusives-205
Exclusives 1 of 1-205
99Upper Deck Gold Reserve-205
99Upper Deck MVP ProSign-WC
00Pacific-386
Copper-386
Gold-386
Ice Blue-386
Premiere Date-386
01BAP Update Tough Customers-TC34
01Greats of the Game-34
Autographs-34
01Upper Deck Pride of the Leafs-MLWC
01Saskatoon Blades-31
02BAP Sig Series Auto Buybacks 1998-280
02BAP Signature Series Famous Scraps-FS2
02Maple Leafs Platinum Collection-27
02Maple Leafs Platinum Collection-84
02UD Foundations-80
02UD Foundations-92
Canadian Heroes-CWC
Canadian Heroes Gold-CWC
Canadian Heroes Silver-C-WC
Classic Greats-GWC
Classic Greats Gold-GWC
Classic Greats Silver-G-WC
Lasting Impressions Sticks-L-WC
Power Stations-SWC
Power Stations Gold-SWC
Power Stations Silver-S-WC
03BAP Memorabilia Gloves-GUG16
03ITG Toronto Fall Expo Forever Rivals-FR3
03Parkhurst Orig Six He Shoots/Scores-4
03Parkhurst Orig Six He Shoots/Scores-4A
03Parkhurst Original Six Toronto-37
03Parkhurst Original Six Toronto-73
03Parkhurst Original Six Toronto-99
Autographs-3
Inserts-T16
Memorabilia-TM25
Memorabilia-TM51
Memorabilia-TM60
03Parkhurst Rookie High Expectations-HE-3
03Parkhurst Rookie High Expectations Gold-HE-3
04ITG Franchises Canadian-111
Autographs-WCL2
Complete Jerseys-CJ5
Complete Jerseys Gold-CJ5
Double Memorabilia-DM11
Double Memorabilia Autographs-DM11
Double Memorabilia Gold-DM11
Forever Rivals-FR8
Forever Rivals Gold-FR8
Memorabilia-SM18
Memorabilia Autographs-SM18
Memorabilia Gold-SM18
Teammates-TM10
Teammates Gold-TM10
Triple Memorabilia-TM10
Triple Memorabilia Autographs-TM10
Triple Memorabilia Gold-TM10
04ITG Franchises Update-481
04ITG Franchises US East-438
Autographs-A-WCL
04ITG Ultimate Memorabilia-197
Gold-197
Auto Threads-29
Autographs-10
Autographs Gold-10
Complete Logo-6
Jersey Autographs-43
Jersey Autographs Gold-43
Original Six-6
Stick Autographs-38
Stick Autographs Gold-38
04ITG Heroes and Prospects-149
Autographs-WCL
04ITG Heroes/Prospects Toronto Expo '05-149
04ITG Heroes/Prospects Expo Heroes/Pros-149
05ITG Heroes/Prosp Toronto Expo Parallel -18
05ITG Tough Customers-WC
Autographs-WC
Complete Jerseys-WC
Double Memorabilia-WC
Famous Battles Autographs-PC
Jerseys-WC
Signed Memorabilia-WC
05ITG Ultimate Mem Complete Jersey-6
05ITG Ultimate Mem Complete Jersey Gold-6
05ITG Ultimate Mem Double Mem Autos-19
05ITG Ultimate Mem Double Mem Autos Gold-19
05ITG Ultimate Memorabilia Emblems-27
05ITG Ultimate Memorabilia Emblems Gold-27
05ITG Ultimate Mem First Overall Jerseys-6
05ITG Ultimate Mem 1st Overall Jsy Gold-6
05ITG Ultimate Memorabilia In The Numbers-13
05ITG Ultimate Mem In The Numbers Gold-13
05ITG Ultimate Mem Jersey and Emblem-13
05ITG Ultimate Memorabilia Jersey Autos-31
05ITG Ultimate Mem Jersey Autos Gold-31
05ITG Ultimate Mem Jersey Emblems Gold-13
05ITG Ultimate Memorabilia Jerseys-39
05ITG Ultimate Mem Jerseys Gold-39
05ITG Ultimate Mem Retro Teammate Jerseys-11
05ITG Ult Mem Retro Teammates Jersey Gold-11
05ITG Ultimate Memorabilia Stick Autos-36
05ITG Ultimate Mem Stick Autos Gold-36
05ITG Ultimate Mem 3 Star of the Game Jsy-22
05ITG Ult Mem 3 Star of the Game Jsy Gold-22
05SP Game Used Heritage Classic-HC-WC
05SP Game Used Heritage Classic Autos-HCA-WC
05SP Game Used Heritage Classic Patches-HCP-
WC
05SP GameUsed Heritage Classic Patch Auto-HAP-
WC
05The Cup Scripted Numbers Dual-DSNGC
05The Cup Scripted Numbers Dual-DSNRC
05ITG Heroes and Prospects-18
Autographs-A-WC
Hero Memorabilia-HM-5
Hero Memorabilia Dual-HDM-3
06ITG Ultimate Memorabilia-148
Artist Proof-148
Autos-5
Autos Gold-5
Cornerstones-3
Cornerstones Gold-3
Decades-2
Decades Gold-2
First Round Picks-18
First Round Picks Gold-18
Jerseys Autos-22
Jerseys Autos Gold-22
Retro Teammates-22
Retro Teammates Gold-22
06Parkhurst-38
06Parkhurst-212
06Parkhurst-245
Autographs-38
Autographs-212
Autographs-245
06SP Authentic Sign of the Times-STWC
06The Cup Autographed NHL Shields Duals-DASGC
06The Cup Limited Logos-LLWC
06UD Artifacts-109
Blue-109
Gold-109
Platinum-109
Radiance-109
Autographed Radiance Parallel-109
Red-109
Auto-Facts-AFWC
Auto-Facts Gold-AFWC
Frozen Artifacts-FAWC
Frozen Artifacts Black-FAWC
Frozen Artifacts Blue-FAWC
Frozen Artifacts Gold-FAWC
Frozen Artifacts Platinum-FAWC
Frozen Artifacts Red-FAWC
Frozen Artifacts Autographed Black-FAWC
Frozen Artifacts Patches Black-FAWC
Frozen Artifacts Patches Blue-FAWC
Frozen Artifacts Patches Gold-FAWC
Frozen Artifacts Patches Platinum-FAWC
Frozen Artifacts Patches Red-FAWC
Frozen Artifacts Patches Autographed Black Tag
Parallel-FAWC
Tundra Tandems-TTCG
Tundra Tandems Black-TTCG
Tundra Tandems Blue-TTCG
Tundra Tandems Gold-TTCG
Tundra Tandems Platinum-TTCG
Tundra Tandems Red-TTCG
Tundra Tandems Dual Patches Red-TTCG
06UD Toronto Fall Expo Priority Signings -PSWC
06ITG Heroes and Prospects-28
Autographs-AWC

Clark, Wes
04Maine Black Bears-19
05Maine Black Bears-3

Clarke, Bobby
70Dad's Cookies-15
70Esso Power Players-211
70O-Pee-Chee-195
70Sargent Promotions Stamps-148
71O-Pee-Chee-114
O-Pee-Chee/Topps Booklets-10
71Sargent Promotions Stamps-152
71Topps-114
71Toronto Sun-191
72Flyers Mighty Milk-2
72O-Pee-Chee-14
Team Canada-5
72Sargent Promotions Stamps-162
72Topps-90
73Flyers Linnett-4
73Mac's Milk-4
73O-Pee-Chee-50
73O-Pee-Chee-134
73O-Pee-Chee-135
73Topps-2
73Topps-3
73Topps-50
74Lipton Soup-21
74NHL Action Stamps-216
74O-Pee-Chee NHL-3
74O-Pee-Chee NHL-135
74O-Pee-Chee NHL-154
74O-Pee-Chee NHL-260
74Topps-3
74Topps-135
74Topps-154
74Topps-260
75Flyers Canada Dry Cans-4
75Heroes Stand-Ups-21
75O-Pee-Chee NHL-209
75O-Pee-Chee NHL-250
75O-Pee-Chee NHL-286
75O-Pee-Chee NHL-325
75Topps-209
75Topps-250
75Topps-286
75Topps-325
76O-Pee-Chee NHL-2
76O-Pee-Chee NHL-3
76O-Pee-Chee NHL-70
76O-Pee-Chee NHL-215
76O-Pee-Chee NHL-391
76Topps-2
76Topps-3
76Topps-70
76Topps-215
76Topps Glossy Inserts-1
77Coca-Cola-3
77O-Pee-Chee NHL-115
77Sportscasters-3103
77Sportscasters-6012
77Topps-115
77Topps/O-Pee-Chee Glossy-3
Square-3
77Finnish Sportscasters-38-891
77Finnish Sportscasters-69-1649
78O-Pee-Chee-215
78Topps-215
79O-Pee-Chee-125
79Topps-125
80O-Pee-Chee-55
80O-Pee-Chee Super-16
80Topps-55
81O-Pee-Chee-240
81O-Pee-Chee Stickers-178
81Post Standups-7
81Topps-E103
82O-Pee-Chee-248
82O-Pee-Chee Stickers-115
82Post Cereal-14
82Topps Stickers-115
83Flyers J.C. Penney-5
83NHL Key Tags-96
83O-Pee-Chee-262
83O-Pee-Chee Stickers-12
83O-Pee-Chee Stickers-198
83O-Pee-Chee Stickers-302
83Puffy Stickers-7
83Topps Stickers-12
83Topps Stickers-198
83Topps Stickers-302
84Kelowna Wings-41
85Flyers Postcards-4
85Hall of Fame-258
88Esso All-Stars-5
89Flyers Postcards-6
90Pro Set-651
90Pro Set-657
90Upper Deck-509
French-509
91Future Trends Canada '72-57
91Future Trends Canada '72 French-57
91Kraft-54
91Kraft-67
92Flyers Upper Deck Sheets-44
92Future Trends '76 Canada Cup-177
92Hall of Fame Legends-16
92O-Pee-Chee-43
25th Anniv. Inserts-3
92Parkhurst-468
Emerald Ice-468
94Hockey Wit-80
98SLU Canadian Timeless Legends-2
98SLU Hockey Classic Doubles-6
99BAP Millennium Pearson-P15
99BAP Millennium Pearson Autographs-P15
99Upper Deck Century Legends-24
Century Collection-24
Epic Signatures-BC
Epic Signatures 100-BC
Jerseys of the Century-JC1
Jerseys of the Century-JCA1
99Upper Deck Retro-99
Gold-99
Platinum-99
Generation-G2B
Generation Level 2-G2B
Inkredible-BC
Inkredible Level 2-BC

Turn of the Century-TC10
00Topps Premier Plus Club Signings-CS-4
00Topps Premier Plus Club Signings-CSC-2
00UD Heroes-134
Signs of Greatness-BC
00Upper Deck Game Jersey Combos-DLC
00Upper Deck Legends-96
00Upper Deck Legends-101
Legendary Collection Bronze-96
Legendary Collection Bronze-101
Legendary Collection Gold-96
Legendary Collection Gold-101
Legendary Collection Silver-96
Legendary Collection Silver-101
Enshrined Stars-ES9
Epic Signatures-BC
01BAP Ultimate Mem All-Star History-23
01BAP Ultimate Memorabilia Decades-16
01BAP Ultimate Mem Dynasty Jerseys-3
01BAP Ultimate Mem Dynasty Emblems-3
01BAP Ultimate Mem Dynasty Numbers-3
01BAP Ultimate Memorabilia Emblem Attic-2
01BAP Ultimate Mem Retired Numbers-6
01BAP Ultimate Memorabilia Retro Trophies-5
01BAP Ultimate Memorabilia Retro Trophies-13
01BAP Ultimate Mem Retro Teammates-6
01Fleer Legacy-39
Ultimate-39
01Flyers Postcards-27
01Greats of the Game-33
Retro Collection-10
Autographs-33
01Parkhurst Autographs-PA42
01Parkhurst He Shoots-He Scores Prizes-32
01Topps Archives-19
Autographs-16
Autoproofs-2
Relics-JBC
Relics-SBC
01UD Stanley Cup Champs-23
01Upper Deck Legends-53
Epic Signatures-BC
Fiorentino Collection-FCBC
Milestones-MBC
Milestones Platinum-MBC
Sticks-PHBC
01Upper Deck Vintage Jerseys-SDBC
02BAP Memorabilia Mini Stanley Cups-12
02BAP NHL All-Star History-23
02BAP Ultimate Memorabilia Emblem Attic-28
02BAP Ultimate Mem Retro Teammates-9
02BAP Ultimate Memorabilia Retro Trophies-3
02BAP Ultimate Mem Vintage Jerseys-6
02Fleer Throwbacks-3
Gold-3
Platinum-3
Autographs-2
Squaring Off-6
Squaring Off Memorabilia-6
Stickwork-12
02Parkhurst Vintage Teammates-VT12
02UD Foundations Signs of Greatness-SGBC
02UD Top Shelf Hardware Heroes-HFYGC
03BAP Memorabilia Vintage Memorabilia-VM-15
03BAP Ultimate Memorabilia Great Moments-7
03BAP Ultimate Mem Raised to the Rafters-14
03BAP Ultimate Mem Retro Teammates-8
03BAP Ultimate Memorabilia Triple Threads-27
03BAP Ultimate Mem Vintage Jerseys-29
03BAP Ultimate Mem Vintage Jerseys Gold-29
03Beehive-139
Variations-139
Gold-139
Silver-139
03ITG VIP MVP-11
03Parkhurst Rookie Jerseys-GJ-42
03Parkhurst Rookie Jerseys Gold-GJ-42
03SP Authentic Honors-H14
03SP Authentic Honors Limited-H14
03SP Authentic Sign of the Times-BC
03SP Authentic Sign of the Times-CR
03SP Authentic Sign of the Times-CRG
03SPx-104
Radiance-104
Spectrum-104
03Topps Stanley Cup Heroes-BC
03Topps Stanley Cup Heroes Autographs-BC
03Upper Deck Trilogy-73
03Upper Deck Trilogy-140
Crest Variations-140
Limited-73
Limited-140
Scripts-S3BC
Scripts-CSBC
Scripts-CSBC2
Scripts Limited-S3BC
Scripts Red-S3BC
03Czech Stadion-547
04ITG NHL AS FANtasy AS History Jerseys-SB23
04ITG Franchises He Shoots/Scores Prizes-44
04ITG Franchises US East-411
Autographs-A-BC
Complete Jerseys-ECJ10
Complete Jerseys Gold-ECJ10
Double Memorabilia-EDM2
Double Memorabilia Autographs-EDM-BC
Double Memorabilia Gold-EDM2
Memorabilia-ESM2
Memorabilia Autographs-ESM-BC
Memorabilia Gold-ESM2
Original Sticks-EOS3
Original Sticks Autographs-EOS-BC
Original Sticks Gold-EOS3
Teammates-ETM3
Teammates Gold-ETM3
Trophy Winners-ETW2
Trophy Winners Gold-ETW2
04ITG Ultimate Memorabilia-176
Gold-176
Auto Threads-17
Autographs-35
Autographs Gold-35
Broad Street Bullies Jerseys-1
Broad Street Bullies Jersey Autographs-1
Broad Street Bullies Emblems-1
Broad Street Bullies Emblem Autographs-1
Broad Street Bullies Numbers-1
Broad Street Bullies Number Autographs-1
Cornerstones-8
Cornerstones Gold-8
Country of Origin-17
Country of Origin Gold-17
Day In History-29
Day In History Gold-29
Jersey Autographs-46
Jersey Autographs Gold-46
Raised to the Rafters-9
Retro Teammates-11
Stick Autographs-25
Stick Autographs Gold-25
Triple Threads-8
04SP Authentic Buybacks-14
04SP Authentic Octographs-OS-CAP
04SP Authentic Sign of the Times-TS-CLR
04SP Authentic Sign of the Times-QS-GTDC
04SP Authentic Sign of the Times-QS-MHCL
04UD Legendary Signatures-8
Autographs-BC
HOF Inks-HOF-BC
Linemates-BBBCRL
Summit Stars-CDN3
Summit Stars Autographs-CDN-BC
04UD Legends Classics-7
04UD Legends Classics-70
04UD Legends Classics-84
Gold-7
Gold-70
Gold-84
Platinum-7
Platinum-70
Platinum-84
Silver-7
Silver-70
Silver-84
Jersey Redemptions-JY21
Signature Moments-M49
Signatures-CS47
Signatures-DC18
Signatures-DC20
Signatures-TC6
Signatures-QC6
04Ultimate Collection Buybacks-2
04Ultimate Collection Jerseys-UGJ-BC
04Ultimate Collection Jerseys Gold-UGJ-BC
04Ultimate Collection Jersey Autographs-UGJA-BC
04Ultimate Collection Signatures-US-BC
04ITG Heroes and Prospects-175
Aspiring-11
Autographs-BCL
04ITG Heroes/Prospects Toronto Expo '05-175
05ITG Heroes/Prosp Toronto Expo Parallel -24
05Beehive-224
Signature Scrapbook-SSBC
05ITG Ultimate Memorabilia Level 1-11
05ITG Ultimate Memorabilia Level 2-11
05ITG Ultimate Memorabilia Level 3-11
05ITG Ultimate Memorabilia Level 4-11
05ITG Ultimate Memorabilia Level 5-11
05ITG Ultimate Mem Cornerstones Jerseys-10
05ITG Ultimate Mem Cornerst Jerseys Gold-10
05ITG Ultimate Mem Double Mem-21
05ITG Ultimate Mem Double Mem Gold-21
05ITG Ultimate Memorabilia Jersey Autos-3
05ITG Ultimate Mem Jersey Autos Gold-3
05ITG Ultimate Memorabilia Jerseys-3
05ITG Ultimate Memorabilia Jerseys Gold-3
05ITG Ultimate Mem Raised to the Rafters-4
05ITG Ultimate Mem Raised Rafters Gold-4
05ITG Ultimate Mem Retro Teammate Jerseys-8
05ITG Ult Mem Retro Teammates Jersey Gold-8
05ITG Ultimate Memorabilia Sextuple Autos-5
05ITG Ultimate Mem 3 Star of the Game Jsy-15
05ITG Ult Mem 3 Star of the Game Jsy Gold-15
05ITG Ultimate Memorabilia Triple Autos-2
05ITG Ultimate Mem Triple Autos Gold-2
05ITG Ultimate Memorabilia Ultimate Autos-41
05ITG Ultimate Mem Ultimate Autos Gold-41
05SPx-93
Spectrum-93
Xcitement Legends-XL-BC
Xcitement Legends Gold-XL-BC
Xcitement Legends Spectrum-XL-BC
05The Cup-77
Gold-77
Black Rainbow-77
Masterpiece Pressplates-77
Stanley Cup Titlists-TBC
05UD Artifacts-111
Blue-111
Gold-111
Green-111
Pewter-111
Red-111
Auto Facts-AF-BC
Auto Facts Blue-AF-BC
Auto Facts Copper-AF-BC
Auto Facts Pewter-AF-BC
Auto Facts Silver-AF-BC
Frozen Artifacts-FA-BC
Frozen Artifacts Autographed-FA-BC
Frozen Artifacts Copper-FA-BC
Frozen Artifacts Dual-FAD-BC
Frozen Artifacts Dual Autographed-FAD-BC
Frozen Artifacts Dual Copper-FAD-BC
Frozen Artifacts Dual Gold-FAD-BC
Frozen Artifacts Dual Maroon-FAD-BC
Frozen Artifacts Dual Pewter-FAD-BC
Frozen Artifacts Dual Silver-FAD-BC
Frozen Artifacts Gold-FA-BC
Frozen Artifacts Maroon-FA-BC
Frozen Artifacts Patches-FP-BC
Frozen Artifacts Patches Autographed-FP-BC
Frozen Artifacts Patches Dual-FPD-BC
Frozen Artifacts Patches Dual Autos-FPD-BC
Frozen Artifacts Patches Pewter-FP-BC
Frozen Artifacts Patches Silver-FP-BC
Frozen Artifacts Pewter-FA-BC
Frozen Artifacts Silver-FA-BC
Gold Autographed-111
Remarkable Artifacts-RA-BC
Remarkable Artifacts Dual-RA-BC
05Ultimate Collection Endorsed Emblems-EEBC
05Ultimate Coll Ultimate Achievements-UABC
05Ultimate Collection Ultimate Signatures-USBC
05Ultimate Coll Ultimate Sigs Pairings-UPCP
05Upper Deck All-Time Greatest-45
05Upper Deck Big Playmakers-B-BC
05Upper Deck Jerseys-J-BC
05Upper Deck NHL Generations-TCGP
05Upper Deck Notable Numbers-N-BC
05Upper Deck Patches-P-BC
05Upper Deck Trilogy Ice Scripts-IS-BC
05Upper Deck Trilogy Legendary Scripts-LEG-BC
05Upper Deck Trilogy Personal Scripts-PER-BC
05ITG Heroes and Prospects-24
Aspiring-ASP12
Autographs-A-BCL
Hero Memorabilia-HM-29
National Pride-NPR-16
06Beehive-174
5 X 7 Black and White-174
06ITG International Ice-3
06ITG International Ice-137
Gold-3
Gold-137
Autographs-ABC
Autographs-ABC2
Canadian Dream Team-DT04
Canadian Dream Team Gold-DT04
Emblem Autographs-GUE33
Emblem Autographs Gold-GUE33
Emblems-GUE33
Emblems Gold-GUE33
Jersey Autographs-GUJ33
Jersey Autographs Gold-GUJ33
Jerseys-GUJ33
Jerseys Gold-GUJ33
My Country My Team-MC20
My Country My Team Gold-MC20
Numbers-GUN33
Numbers Autographs-GUN33
Numbers Autographs Gold-GUN33
Numbers Gold-GUN33
Stick and Jersey-SJ13
Stick and Jersey Gold-SJ13
06ITG Ultimate Memorabilia-17
Artist Proof-17
Autos-7
Autos Gold-7
Boys Will Be Boys-25
Boys Will Be Boys Gold-25
Gloves Are Off-2
Gloves Are Off Gold-2
Going For Gold-3
Going For Gold Gold-3
Jerseys Autos-7
Jerseys Autos Gold-7
Legendary Captains-7
Legendary Captains Gold-7
Passing The Torch-9
Passing The Torch Gold-9
Retro Teammates-13
Retro Teammates Gold-13
Road to the Cup-9
Road to the Cup Gold-9
Stick Rack-15
Stick Rack Gold-15
Sticks Autos-3
Sticks Autos Gold-3
Triple Thread Jerseys-2
Triple Thread Jerseys Gold-2
06Parkhurst-39
06Parkhurst-200
Autographs-39
Autographs-200
Autographs Dual-DACL
Autographs Dual-DACP
06SP Authentic-147
Limited-147
Sign of the Times Duals-STCC
Sign of the Times Quads-ST4BCTS
06SP Game Used Inked Sweaters Dual-IS2CL
06SP Game Used Inked Sweaters Dual Patches-IS2CL
06SP Game Used Legendary Fabrics-LFBC
06SP Game Used Legendary Fabrics Autographs-LFBC
06SPx-141
Spectrum-141
Winning Materials-WMBC
Winning Materials Spectrum-WMBC
Winning Materials Autographs-WMBC
06The Cup-69
Autographed Patches-69
Black Rainbow-69
Gold-69
Gold Patches-69
Honorable Numbers-HNBC
Jerseys-69
Limited Logos-LLBC
Masterpiece Pressplates-69
Property of-POSD
Signature Patches-SPBC
Stanley Cup Signatures-CSBC
06UD Artifacts-110
Blue-110
Gold-110
Platinum-110
Radiance-110
Autographed Radiance Parallel-110
Red-110
Auto-Facts-AFBC
Auto-Facts Gold-AFBC
Treasured Patches Black-TSBC
Treasured Patches Blue-TSBC
Treasured Patches Gold-TSBC
Treasured Patches Platinum-TSBC
Treasured Patches Red-TSBC
Treasured Swatches-TSBC
Treasured Swatches Black-TSBC
Treasured Swatches Blue-TSBC
Treasured Swatches Gold-TSBC
Treasured Swatches Platinum-TSBC
Treasured Swatches Red-TSBC
06Ultimate Collection Jerseys-UJ-BC
06Ultimate Collection Jerseys Dual-UJ2-CP
06Ultimate Collection Patches-UJ-BC
06Ultimate Collection Patches Dual-UJ2-CP
06Ultimate Collection Signatures-US-BC
06Ultimate Collection Ultimate Achievements-UA-BC
06Upper Deck All-Time Greatest-ATG16
06Upper Deck Game Jerseys-J2BC
06Upper Deck Game Patches-P2BC
06Upper Deck Sweet Shot-78
Signature Shots/Saves Sticks-SSSBC
Signature Sticks-STBC
06Upper Deck Trilogy Combo Autographed Jerseys-CJCL
06Upper Deck Trilogy Combo Autographed Patches-CJCL
06Upper Deck Trilogy Combo Clearcut Autographs-C3CLP
06Upper Deck Trilogy Frozen In Time-FT2
06Upper Deck Trilogy Legendary Scripts-LSBC
06Upper Deck Trilogy Scripts-S1BC
06ITG Heroes and Prospects-30
Autographs-ABC

Clarke, Bobby (Def)
99Hull Olympiques-3
Signed-3
00Hull Olympiques-3
Signed-3
01Halifax Mooseheads-4
03Halifax Mooseheads-2

Clarke, Chris
91ProCards-560
94German First League-228
95German DEL-363
99German Bundesliga 2-68

Clarke, Cosmo
96Dayton Ice Bandits-6

Clarke, Dale
92Quebec Pee-Wee Tournament-416
00Worcester Icecats-23
01Upper Deck-206
Exclusives-206
01Upper Deck MVP-216
01Worcester Icecats-7
02Hershey Bears-7
04German DEL-265
05German DEL-193
06Finnish Cardset-322

Clarke, David
01UK London Knights-8
02UK Guildford Flames-3
02UK Guildford Flames-28
03UK Nottingham Panthers-2
04UK EIHL All-Stars-17
04UK Nottingham Panthers-4
05UK Nottingham Panthers-3
06UK Nottingham Panthers-2

Clarke, Defense
99Hull Olympiques-3
Signed-3
00Hull Olympiques-3
Signed-3
01Halifax Mooseheads-4
03Halifax Mooseheads-2

Clarke, Doug
88Salt Lake Golden Eagles-14
92Quebec Pee-Wee Tournament-1601

Clarke, Gary
04UK Milton Keynes Lightning-6

Clarke, Jason
917th Inn. Sketch OHL-202
94Roanoke Express-11
95Roanoke Express-16
99Mobile Mysticks-17
01Fort Worth Brahmas-5
02UK Nottingham Panthers-16

Clarke, Jim
75Phoenix Roadrunners WHA-3

Clarke, Jim (WHL)
81Regina Pats-10

Clarke, Joe
92Norwegian Elite Series-162
93Sault Ste. Marie Greyhound Memorial Cup-8

Clarke, Jordan
00Prince Albert Raiders-4
01Spokane Chiefs-5

Clarke, Matt
05London Knights-5
06London Knights-9

Clarke, Mike
75Hamilton Fincups-2
00London Knights-15
06Fayetteville FireAntz-1

Clarke, Noah
92Quebec Pee-Wee Tournament-1279
93Quebec Pee-Wee Tournament-1247
03BAP Ultimate Memorabilia Autographs-108
Gold-108
03Beehive-242
Gold-242
Silver-242
03ITG Action-649
03ITG Used Signature Series-153
Gold-153
03ITG VIP Rookie Debut-87
03Pacific Calder-120
Silver-120
03Parkhurst Rookie-167
03Topps Traded-TT114
Blue-TT114
Gold-TT114
Red-TT114
03Upper Deck Rookie Update-100
03Manchester Monarchs-2
03Manchester Monarchs Team Issue-3
03Pacific AHL Prospects-47
Gold-47
04Manchester Monarchs-17
04Manchester Monarchs Tobacco-17
05ITG Heroes/Prosp Toronto Expo Parallel -264
05Manchester Monarchs-2
05Manchester Monarchs-28
05ITG Heroes and Prospects-264
Autographs Series II-NC
06Manchester Monarchs-16

Clarke, Taylor
96Richmond Renegades-2

Clarke, Todd
83Ottawa 67's-4
84Kingston Canadians-20
85Kingston Canadians-20

Clarke, Wayne
93RPI Engineers-6

Clarke, WHA
75Phoenix Roadrunners WHA-3

Clarke, WHL
81Regina Pats-10

Clarke, Will
96Dayton Bombers-10

Clarkson, David
01Belleville Bulls Update-1
03Kitchener Rangers-4
03Kitchener Rangers Memorial Cup-4
04Kitchener Rangers-8
05Albany River Rats-6
07Upper Deck Victory-205
Black-205
Gold-205

Classen, Bryce
02Indianapolis Ice-4

Classen, Cris
00San Diego Gulls-2
01Augusta Lynx-3

Classen, Greg
00BAP Memorabilia-442
Emerald-442
Ruby-442
Sapphire-442
00SP Authentic-149
00SP Game Used-72
00Titanium Draft Day Edition-164
00Titanium Draft Day Promos-164
00Topps Heritage-94
Chrome Parallel-94
00Topps Premier Plus-135
Blue Ice-135
00UD Pros and Prospects-110
00UD Reserve-101
00Upper Deck-427
Exclusives Tier 1-427
Exclusives Tier 2-427
00Upper Deck Ice-114
00Upper Deck Vintage-383
00Milwaukee Admirals Keebler-4
01BAP Memorabilia-230
Emerald-230
Ruby-230
Sapphire-230
02Milwaukee Admirals-21
02Milwaukee Admirals Postcards-4
03Milwaukee Admirals-23
03Milwaukee Admirals Postcards-1
04Finnish Cardset-189
05Milwaukee Admirals Choice-4
05Milwaukee Admirals Pepsi-5

Clatney, Paul
95Madison Monsters-16

Clause, Greg
75Hamilton Fincups-3

Clausen, Andre
98Danish Hockey League-89
99Danish Hockey League-223

Clausen, Nikolai
98Danish Hockey League-35
99Danish Hockey League-212

Clauson, Kevin
01Johnstown Chiefs-8

Clauss, Karl
91Knoxville Cherokees-4

Clavien, Elvis
92Quebec Pee-Wee Tournament-1388
01Swiss HNL-431
02Swiss HNL-408

Clavien, Jean-Michel
93Swiss HNL-191
96Swiss HNL-365
98Swiss Power Play Stickers-339
00Swiss Panini Stickers-315

Clayton, Chris
00Brampton Battalion-12
03Brampton Battalion-2

Clayton, Kevin
91Michigan Falcons-14

Clayton, Mike
84Moncton Golden Flames-12

Clayton, Tim
03Yarmouth Mariners-7

Clayton, Tom
03Elmira Jackals-5
05Quad City Mallards-2

Clayton, Travis
98Wichita Thunder-3
99Wichita Thunder-2
00Wichita Thunder-3

Clearwater, Ray
72Cleveland Crusaders WHA-2

Cleary, Daniel
95Slapshot-39
95Upper Deck-507
Electric Ice-507
Electric Ice Gold-507
95Classic-83
CHL All-Stars-AS11
95Signature Rookies Auto-Phonex-15
95Signature Rook Auto-Phonex Phone Cards-15
95Signature Rookies Auto-Phonex Prodigies-P3
95Signature Rookies Tetrad Autobilia *-41
96All-Sport PPF *-178
96All Sport PPF Gold *-178
97Be A Player-224
Autographs-224
Autographs Die-Cuts-224
Autographs Prismatic Die-Cuts-224
97Collector's Choice-307
97Donruss Elite-37
97Donruss Elite-123
Aspirations-37
Aspirations-123
Status-37
Status-123
Back to the Future-4
Back to the Future Autographs-4
Craftsmen-10
Master Craftsmen-10
97Donruss Limited Fabric of the Game-68
97Donruss Preferred-152
97Donruss Preferred-199
Cut to the Chase-152
Cut to the Chase-199
Line of the Times-6C
97Donruss Preferred Line of Times Promos-6C
97Donruss Priority-166
97Donruss Priority-217
Stamp of Approval-166
Stamp of Approval-217
97Katch-33
Gold-33
Silver-33
97Leaf-159
97Leaf-200
Fractal Matrix-159
Fractal Matrix-200
Fractal Matrix Die Cuts-159
Fractal Matrix Die Cuts-200
97Leaf International-150
Universal Ice-150
97McDonald's Upper Deck-36
97Pacific Dynagon-NNO
Copper-NNO
Dark Grey-NNO
Emerald Green-NNO
Ice Blue-NNO
Red-NNO
Silver-NNO
97Paramount-42
Copper-42
Dark Grey-42
Emerald Green-42
Ice Blue-42
Red-42
Silver-42
97Pinnacle-10
Artist's Proofs-10
Rink Collection-10
Press Plates Back Black-10
Press Plates Back Cyan-10
Press Plates Back Magenta-10
Press Plates Back Yellow-10
Press Plates Front Black-10
Press Plates Front Cyan-10
Press Plates Front Magenta-10
Press Plates Front Yellow-10
Certified Rookie Redemption-E
Certified Rookie Redemption Gold-E
Certified Rookie Redemption Mirror Gold-E
97Score-61
Artist's Proofs-61
Golden Blades-61
97SP Authentic-177
97Upper Deck-247
97Upper Deck Ice-38
Parallel-38
Power Shift-38
97Bowman CHL-2
97Bowman CHL-121
OPC-2
OPC-121
Autographs-121
Bowman's Best-7
Bowman's Best Atomic Refractors-7
Bowman's Best Refractor-7
97Autographed Collection *-46
Autographs-9
Autographs Gold-9
97Players Club *-57
97Visions Signings *-42
98Bowman's Best-103
Refractors-103
Atomic Refractors-103
98Finest Futures Finest-F17
98Finest Futures Finest Refractors-F17
98SPx Finite-20
98SPx Finite-128
Radiance-20
Radiance-128
Spectrum-20
Spectrum-128
98Topps Gold Label Class 1-38
Black-38
Black One of One-38
One of One-38
Red-38
Red One of One-38
98Topps Gold Label Class 2-38
98Topps Gold Label Class 2 Black-38
98Topps Gold Label Class 2 Black 1 of 1-38
98Topps Gold Label Class 2 One of One-38
98Topps Gold Label Class 2 Red-38
98Topps Gold Label Class 2 Red One of One-38
98Topps Gold Label Class 3-38
98Topps Gold Label Class 3 Black-38
98Topps Gold Label Class 3 Black 1 of 1-38
98Topps Gold Label Class 3 One of One-38
98Topps Gold Label Class 3 Red-38
98Topps Gold Label Class 3 Red One of One-38
98UD Choice-44
Prime Choice Reserve-44
Reserve-44
98Upper Deck-4
Exclusives-4
Exclusives 1 of 1-4
Gold Reserve-4
98Upper Deck MVP-47
Gold Script-47
Silver Script-47
Super Script-47
98Portland Pirates-11
98Autographed Collection Autographs *-5
99BAP Memorabilia-120
Gold-120
Silver-120
99SPx-67
Radiance-67
Spectrum-67
99Hamilton Bulldogs-7
00BAP Memorabilia-388
Emerald-388
Ruby-388
Sapphire-388
Promos-388
00BAP Mem Chicago Sportsfest Copper-388
00BAP Memorabilia Chicago Sportsfest Blue-388
00BAP Memorabilia Chicago Sportsfest Gold-388
00BAP Memorabilia Chicago Sportsfest Ruby-388
00BAP Memorabilia Chicago Sun-Times Ruby-388
00BAP Memorabilia Chicago Sun-Times Gold-388
00BAP Mem Chicago Sun-Times Sapphire-388
00BAP Mem Toronto Fall Expo Copper-388
00BAP Memorabilia Toronto Fall Expo Gold-388
00BAP Memorabilia Toronto Fall Expo Ruby-388
00BAP Signature Series-103
Emerald-103
Ruby-103
Sapphire-103
Autographs-29
Autographs Gold-29
00Topps Heritage-179
00Upper Deck-72
Exclusives Tier 1-72
Exclusives Tier 2-72
00Upper Deck Vintage-146
01BAP Memorabilia-153
Emerald-153
Ruby-153
Sapphire-153
01Crown Royale-59
Blue-59
Premiere Date-59
Red-59
Retail-59
01McDonald's Pacific Hometown Pride-8
01Pacific-155
Extreme LTD-155
Hobby LTD-155
Premiere Date-155
Retail LTD-155
01Pacific Adrenaline-73
Blue-73
Premiere Date-73
Red-73
Retail-73
01Pacific Arena Exclusives-155
01Upper Deck-298
Exclusives-298
01Upper Deck Victory-142
Gold-142
02BAP Sig Series Auto Buybacks 2000-29
02Oilers Postcards-2
02Pacific-140
Blue-140
Red-140
02Pacific Complete-155
Red-155
02Topps Total-214
02Upper Deck-316
Exclusives-316
02Upper Deck Beckett UD Promos-316
02Upper Deck Vintage-105
03Coyotes Postcards-4
04Swedish Pure Skills-75
Parallel-75
05Be A Player Signatures-DC
05Be A Player Signatures Gold-DC
06O-Pee-Chee-184
Rainbow-184
07Upper Deck Victory-102
Black-102
Gold-102

Cleary, Joe
92Indianapolis Ice-6

Cleaver, Rick
03Salmon Arm Silverbacks-5

Cleghorn, Odie
10Sweet Caporal Postcards-25
11C55-25
12C57-50
23V145-1-18
24Anonymous NHL-46
24Anonymous NHL-46
24Anonymous NHL-46
24Anonymous NHL-57
24C144 Champ's Cigarettes-14
24V145-2-45
25Dominion Chocolates-117
04ITG Franchises US West-281

Cleghorn, Sprague
10Sweet Caporal Postcards-24
11C55-24
12C57-15
23V145-1-11
24Anonymous NHL-31
24Anonymous NHL-41
24C144 Champ's Cigarettes-15
24V130 Maple Crispette-15
24V145-2-49
60Topps Stamps-10
83Hall of Fame-66
83Hall of Fame Postcards-E5
85Hall of Fame-66
04ITG Ultimate Mem Bleu Blanc et Rouge-3
06ITG Ultimate Memorabilia Lumbergraphs-6
06ITG Ultimate Memorabilia Paper Cuts Autos-9

Clemens, Kevin
87Regina Pats-1

Clement, Bill
72Sargent Promotions Stamps-168
73Flyers Linnett-5
74NHL Action Stamps-204
74O-Pee-Chee NHL-357
75O-Pee-Chee NHL-189
75Topps-189
76O-Pee-Chee NHL-82
76Topps-82
77O-Pee-Chee NHL-292
78Flames Majik Market-10
78O-Pee-Chee-364
79Flames Postcards-4
79Flames Team Issue-5
79O-Pee-Chee-295
80Flames Postcards-3
80O-Pee-Chee-376
80Pepsi-Cola Caps-3
81Flames Postcards-4
81O-Pee-Chee-39
82O-Pee-Chee-44
92Parkhurst-478
Emerald Ice-478
01Topps Archives-38
01Topps Chrome Reprints-6
01Topps Chrome Reprint Refractors-6
01Topps Chrome Reprint Autographs-6
04ITG Franchises Update-457
04ITG Franchises US East-420
Autographs-A-BCL

Clement, Patrick
917th Inn. Sketch QMJHL-85
917th Inn. Sketch Memorial Cup-31

Clement, Sean
88ProCards AHL-185

Clements, Scott
88ProCards IHL-7

Clemmensen, Scott
01Atomic-114
Premiere Date-114
01Atomic Toronto Fall Expo-114
01BAP Memorabilia-374
Emerald-374
Ruby-374
Sapphire-374
01BAP Signature Series-216
Autographs-216
Autographs Gold-216
01Between the Pipes-79
01O-Pee-Chee-343
01Pacific Adrenaline-214
Blue-214
Premiere Date-214
Red-214
Retail-214
01Pacific Heads-Up-111
01Parkhurst-281
01Parkhurst Beckett Promos-281
01Private Stock-129
Gold-129
Premiere Date-129
Retail-129
Silver-129
01Private Stock Pacific Nights-129
01Private Stock PS-2002-83
01SP Authentic-159
Limited-159
Limited Gold-159
01SP Game Used-84
01SPx-111
01Stadium Club-134
Award Winners-134
Master Photos-134
01Titanium Draft Day Edition-146
01Topps-343
01Topps Chrome-161
Refractors-161
Black Border Refractors-161
01Topps Heritage-157
01Topps Reserve-102
01UD Challenge for the Cup-119
01UD Premier Collection-69
01Upper Deck-433
Exclusives-433
01Upper Deck Ice-79
01Upper Deck Vintage-285
01Albany River Rats-25
02BAP First Edition-279
02BAP Sig Series Auto Buybacks 2001-216
02Between the Pipes-88
Gold-88
Silver-88
02AHL Top Prospects-7
02Albany River Rats-22
02Albany River Rats AAP-7
03BAP Memorabilia Deep in the Crease-D4
03Devils Team Issue-40
03Pacific Complete-455
Red-455
03Albany River Rats-6
03Albany River Rats Kinko's-5
04Albany River Rats-4
05Devils Team Issue-8
05Parkhurst-294
Facsimile Auto Parallel-294
05Upper Deck-366
05ITG Heroes and Prospects Measuring Up-MU6
05ITG Heroes/Prospects Measuring Up Gold-MU6
06Devils Team Set-4
06O-Pee-Chee-302
Rainbow-302

Clermont, Daniel
99Hull Olympiques-11
Signed-11

Cliche, Marc-Andre
03Lewiston Maineiacs-5
05ITG Heroes and Prospects-138
Autographs-A-MAC
06ITG Heroes and Prospects-185
Autographs-AMAC
Update Autographs-AMAC
07ITG Going For Gold World Juniors-12
Autographs-12
Emblems-GUE12
Jerseys-GUJ12
Numbers-GUN12

Cliche, Maxim
06PEI Rocket-20

Cliche, Philippe
93Quebec Pee-Wee Tournament-364

Clifford, Brian
92Michigan State Spartans-7
93Michigan State Spartans-5
96Toledo Storm-11
97Peoria Rivermen-8

Clifford, Chris
83Kingston Canadians-14
84Kingston Canadians-7
85Kingston Canadians-7
86Kingston Canadians-9
88ProCards IHL-97
89ProCards IHL-144
90ProCards AHL/IHL-372

Climie, Ron
72O-Pee-Chee-318
73O-Pee-Chee WHA Posters-12
74O-Pee-Chee WHA-15
75O-Pee-Chee WHA-52

Cline, Bruce
50Quebec Citadelles-4
51Laval Dairy Subset-70
52St. Lawrence Sales-23
94Parkhurst Missing Link-106

Cline, Matthew
05Red Deer Rebels-2

Cline, Walter
55Montreal Royals-1

Clinton, Shaun
63Red Sox Jay Publishing-2
03Belleville Bulls-20

Cloch, Ivano
92Finnish Semic-263

Close, Edward
93Quebec Pee-Wee Tournament-1762

Cloud, Chris
04Saskatoon Blades-8
05Saskatoon Blades-4
06Saskatoon Blades-2

Clouston, Bob
96Dayton Ice Bandits-7

Clouston, Shaun
86Portland Winter Hawks-4
87Portland Winter Hawks-6
88Portland Winter Hawks-6
89ProCards IHL-166
90ProCards AHL/IHL-333
92Tulsa Oilers-3
94Central Hockey League-95
98San Angelo Outlaws-22
04Medicine Hat Tigers-25

Clouthier, Brett
98Kingston Frontenacs-2
99Kingston Frontenacs-4
00Kingston Frontenacs-3
01Albany River Rats-19
02Albany River Rats-3
02Albany River Rats AAP-8
03Albany River Rats-7
03Albany River Rats Kinko's-6
03ECHL Update RBI Sports-61
04Albany River Rats-5
05Binghamton Senators-13
05Binghamton Senators Quickway-13

Cloutier, Andrew
06Saginaw Spirit-12

Cloutier, Colin
92Brandon Wheat Kings-2
93Brandon Wheat Kings-22
94Brandon Wheat Kings-3
95Signature Rookies-4
Signatures-4
95Slapshot Memorial Cup-45

Cloutier, Dan
93Sault Ste. Marie Greyhounds-3
93Sault Ste. Marie Greyhound Memorial Cup-27
94Finest-145
Super Team Winners-145
Refractors-145
94Parkhurst SE-SE210
Gold-SE210
94Pinnacle-522
Artist's Proofs-522
Rink Collection-522
94SP-146
Die Cuts-146
94Upper Deck-498
Electric Ice-498
94Classic-22
Gold-22
94Classic Four-Sport *-139
Gold-139
Autographs-139A
Printers Proofs-139
94Signature Rookies Gold Standard *-80
94Signature Rookies Tetrad *-105
Signatures-105
95Donruss Canadian World Junior Team-2
95Slapshot-95
95Slapshot-357
95Topps Canadian World Juniors-18CJ
95Guelph Storm-22
95Sault Ste. Marie Greyhounds-3
95Classic-95
95Images-49
Gold-49
95Images Four-Sport *-113
96Binghamton Rangers-6
97Black Diamond-78
Double Diamond-78
Triple Diamond-78
Quadruple Diamond-78
97Revolution-85
Copper-85
Emerald-85
Ice Blue-85
Silver-85
97Hartford Wolf Pack-4
98Bowman's Best-116
Refractors-116
Atomic Refractors-116
Mirror Image Fusion-F9
Mirror Image Fusion Refractors-F9
Mirror Image Fusion Atomic Refractors-F9
98Pacific-291
Ice Blue-291
Red-291
98Pacific Omega-154
Red-154
Opening Day Issue-154
98Paramount-150
Copper-150
Emerald Green-150
Holo-Electric-150

Ice Blue-150
Silver-150
98SPx Finite-125
Radiance-125
Spectrum-125
98UD Choice-131
98UD Choice Preview-131
98UD Choice Prime Choice Reserve-131
98UD Choice Reserve-131
98UD3-25
98UD3-85
98UD3-145
Die-Cuts-25
Die-Cuts-85
Die-Cuts-145
98Upper Deck-134
Exclusives-134
Exclusives 1 of 1-134
Gold Reserve-134
99BAP Memorabilia-90
Gold-90
Silver-90
99BAP Millennium-219
Emerald-219
Ruby-219
Sapphire-219
Signatures-219
Signatures Gold-219
99Black Diamond-79
Diamond Cut-79
Final Cut-79
99Crown Royale-127
Limited Series-127
Premiere Date-127
99Pacific-267
Copper-267
Emerald Green-267
Gold-267
Ice Blue-267
Premiere Date-267
Red-267
99Pacific Dynagon Ice-179
Blue-179
Copper-179
Gold-179
Premiere Date-179
99Pacific Omega-213
Copper-213
Gold-213
Ice Blue-213
Premiere Date-213
99Pacific Prism-129
Holographic Blue-129
Holographic Gold-129
Holographic Mirror-129
Holographic Purple-129
Premiere Date-129
99Panini Stickers-150
99Paramount-214
Copper-214
Emerald-214
Gold-214
Holographic Emerald-214
Holographic Gold-214
Holographic Silver-214
Ice Blue-214
Premiere Date-214
Red-214
Silver-214
99SP Authentic-79
99SPx-139
Radiance-139
Spectrum-139
99Stadium Club-161
First Day Issue-161
One of a Kind-161
Printing Plates Black-161
Printing Plates Cyan-161
Printing Plates Magenta-161
Printing Plates Yellow-161
99Ultimate Victory-80
1/1-80
Parallel-80
Parallel 100-80
99Upper Deck-120
Exclusives-120
Exclusives 1 of 1-120
99Upper Deck Gold Reserve-120
99Upper Deck MVP SC Edition-168
Gold Script-168
Silver Script-168
Super Script-168
99Upper Deck Victory-273
99Upper Deck Victory-387
00Aurora-131
Premiere Date-131
00BAP Memorabilia-145
Emerald-145
Ruby-145
Sapphire-145
Promos-145
00BAP Mem Chicago Sportsfest Copper-145
00BAP Memorabilia Chicago Sportsfest Blue-145
00BAP Memorabilia Chicago Sportsfest Gold-145
00BAP Memorabilia Chicago Sportsfest Ruby-145
00BAP Memorabilia Chicago Sun-Times Ruby-145
00BAP Memorabilia Chicago Sun-Times Gold-145
00BAP Mem Chicago Sun-Times Sapphire-145
00BAP Mem Toronto Fall Expo Copper-145
00BAP Memorabilia Toronto Fall Expo Gold-145
00BAP Memorabilia Toronto Fall Expo Ruby-145
00BAP Parkhurst 2000-P121
00BAP Signature Series-51
Emerald-51
Ruby-51
Sapphire-51
Autographs-10
Autographs Gold-10
00BAP Ultimate Memorabilia Goalie Sticks-G27
00Black Diamond-54
Gold-54
00O-Pee-Chee-35
00O-Pee-Chee Parallel-35
00Pacific-369
Copper-369
Gold-369
Ice Blue-369
Premiere Date-369
00Paramount-219
Copper-219
Gold-219
Holo-Gold-219
Holo-Silver-219
Ice Blue-219
Premiere Date-219
00Private Stock-90
Gold-90
Premiere Date-90
Retail-90
Silver-90
PS-2001 New Wave-22
00Revolution-132
Blue-132
Premiere Date-132
Red-132
00SPx-62
Spectrum-62
00Stadium Club-27
00Titanium Game Gear-148
00Titanium Game Gear Patches-148
00Topps/OPC-35
Parallel-35
00Topps Chrome-30
OPC Refractors-30
Refractors-30
00UD Heroes-106
00Upper Deck-159
Exclusives Tier 1-159
Exclusives Tier 2-159
00Upper Deck MVP-159
First Stars-159
Second Stars-159
Third Stars-159
00Upper Deck Victory-212
00Upper Deck Vintage-325
00Upper Deck Vintage-332
00Upper Deck Vintage-333
Great Gloves-GG17
01BAP Signature Series Jerseys-GJ-94
01BAP Update Travel Plans-TP16
01Between the Pipes-14
01Between the Pipes-108
01Between the Pipes-165
Future Wave-FW6
Goalie Gear-GG8
He Shoots-He Saves Prizes-9
Jerseys-GJ25
Jersey and Stick Cards-GSJ24
01Bowman YoungStars-38
Gold-38
Ice Cubed-38
01Canucks Postcards-4
01Crown Royale-136
Blue-136
Premiere Date-136
Red-136
Retail-136
01McDonald's Pacific-40
01O-Pee-Chee-233
01O-Pee-Chee Premier Parallel-233
01Pacific-380
Extreme LTD-380
Hobby LTD-380
Premiere Date-380
Retail LTD-380
01Pacific Adrenaline-189
Blue-189
Premiere Date-189
Red-189
Retail-189
Power Play-35
01Pacific Arena Exclusives-380
01Pacific Heads-Up-93
Blue-93
Premiere Date-93
Red-93
Silver-93
Quad Jerseys-19
01Parkhurst-164
01Private Stock-93
Gold-93
Premiere Date-93
Retail-93
Silver-93
01Private Stock Pacific Nights-93
01Titanium-135
Hobby Parallel-135
Premiere Date-135
Retail-135
Retail Parallel-135
Double-Sided Jerseys-56
Double-Sided Patches-56
01Titanium Draft Day Edition-94
01Topps-233
OPC Parallel-233
01Topps Chrome-75
Refractors-75
Black Border Refractors-75
01UD Mask Collection-129
Gold-129
01Upper Deck-399
Exclusives-399
01Upper Deck Victory-337
01Upper Deck Victory-346
Gold-337
Gold-346
01Vanguard-95
Blue-95
Red-95
Memorabilia-35
One of Ones-95
Premiere Date-95
Proofs-95
02McFarlane Hockey-190
02McFarlane Hockey-192
02Atomic-96
Blue-96
Gold-96
Red-96
Hobby Parallel-96
02BAP First Edition-84
02BAP First Edition-413H
Jerseys-84
02BAP Memorabilia-36
Emerald-36
Ruby-36
Sapphire-36
NHL All-Star Game-36
NHL All-Star Game Blue-36
NHL All-Star Game Green-36
NHL All-Star Game Red-36
02BAP Memorabilia Toronto Fall Expo-36
02BAP Signature Series-58
Autographs-58
Autograph Buybacks 1999-219
Autograph Buybacks 2000-10
Autographs Gold-58
Defensive Wall-DW10
02Between the Pipes-11
02Between the Pipes-149
Gold-11
Silver-11
Behind the Mask-17
Double Memorabilia-3
Emblems-5
Future Wave-8
Goalie Autographs-4
He Shoots-He Saves Points-3
He Shoots-He Saves Prizes-19
Jerseys-5
Numbers-5
Pads-8
Stick and Jerseys-5
Tandems-12
Trappers-GT3
02Bowman YoungStars-44
Gold-44
Silver-44
02Canucks Team Issue-3
02Crown Royale-95
Blue-95
Red-95
Retail-95
02ITG Used Goalie Pad and Jersey-GP8
02ITG Used Goalie Pad and Jersey Gold-GP8
02NHL Power Play Stickers-151
02O-Pee-Chee-102
02O-Pee-Chee Premier Blue Parallel-102
02O-Pee-Chee Premier Red Parallel-102
02O-Pee-Chee Factory Set-102
02Pacific-375
Blue-375
Red-375
Jerseys-49
Jerseys Holo-Silver-49
02Pacific Complete-446
Red-446
02Pacific Exclusive-166
02Pacific Heads-Up-120
Blue-120
Purple-120
Red-120
Quad Jerseys-27
Quad Jerseys Gold-27
Showstoppers-20
02Pacific Quest for the Cup-95
Gold-95
02Pacific Toronto Fall Expo-4
Gold-4
02Parkhurst-43
Bronze-43
Gold-43
Silver-43
Teammates-TT18
02Parkhurst Retro-152
Minis-152
02Private Stock Reserve-95
Blue-95
Red-95
Retail-95
02Stadium Club-25
Silver Decoy Cards-25
Proofs-25
02Titanium-96
Blue-96
Red-96
Retail-96
Jerseys-69
Jerseys Retail-69
Patches-69
Masked Marauders-8
02Topps-102
OPC Blue Parallel-102
OPC Red Parallel-102
Factory Set-102
02Topps Chrome-65
Black Border Refractors-65
Refractors-65
02Topps Heritage-77
Chrome Parallel-77
Crease Piece-DC
Crease Piece Patches-DC
02Topps Total-306
02UD Artistic Impressions-86
Gold-86
02UD Artistic Impressions Beckett Promos-86
02UD Artistic Impressions Retrospectives-R86
02UD Artistic Impressions Retrospect Gold-R86
02UD Artistic Impress Retrospect Silver-R86
02UD Mask Collection-85
02UD Mask Collection-86
02UD Mask Collection-103
02UD Mask Collection Beckett Promos-85
02UD Mask Collection Beckett Promos-86
02UD Piece of History-86
02Upper Deck-170
Exclusives-170
02Upper Deck MVP-180
Gold-180
Classics-180
Golden Classics-180
02Upper Deck Rookie Update-97
02Upper Deck Victory-208
Bronze-208
Gold-208
Silver-208
02Upper Deck Vintage-250
02Upper Deck Vintage-289
02Vanguard-95
LTD-95
Jerseys-46
Jerseys Gold-46
03BAP Memorabilia-114
Emerald-114
Gold-114
Ruby-114
Sapphire-114
Deep in the Crease-D10
03BAP Ultimate Memorabilia Autographs-85
Gold-85
03BAP Ultimate Mem Auto Jerseys-85
03BAP Ultimate Memorabilia Triple Threads-2
03Beehive-187
Gold-187
Silver-187
03Bowman-58
Gold-58
03Bowman Chrome-58
Refractors-58
Gold Refractors-58
Xfractors-58
03Canucks Postcards-6
03Canucks Sav-on-Foods-16
03Canucks Sav-on-Foods-17
03Crown Royale Gauntlet of Glory-20
03Duracell-15
03ITG Action-529
Jerseys-M13
Jerseys-M238
03ITG Used Signature Series-91
Gold-91
Autographs-DC
Autographs Gold-DC
Goalie Gear-27
Goalie Gear Autographs-27
Goalie Gear Gold-27
03NHL Sticker Collection-300
03O-Pee-Chee-27
03OPC Blue-27
03OPC Gold-27
03OPC Red-27
03Pacific-328
Blue-328
Red-328
In the Crease-12
Jerseys-39
Jerseys Gold-39
03Pacific Calder-97
Silver-97
03Pacific Complete-442
Red-442
03Pacific Exhibit-140
Blue Backs-140
Yellow Backs-140
03Pacific Heads-Up-95
Hobby LTD-95
Retail LTD-95
Stonewallers-12
Stonewallers LTD-12
03Pacific Invincible-94
Blue-94
Red-94
Retail-94
Freeze Frame-23
Jerseys-31
03Pacific Luxury Suite-49A
03Pacific Luxury Suite-49B
03Pacific Prism-147
Blue-147
Patches-147
Red-147
Retail-147
03Pacific Quest for the Cup Jerseys-19
03Pacific Supreme-95
Blue-95
Red-95
Retail-95
03Parkhurst Original Six New York-37
Memorabilia-NM63
03Parkhurst Rookie-6
03Private Stock Reserve-208
Blue-208
Patches-208
Red-208
Retail-208
03Titanium-187
Hobby Jersey Number Parallels-187
Patches-187
Retail-187
03Topps-27
Blue-27
Gold-27
Red-27
03Topps C55-114
Minis-114
Minis American Back-114
Minis American Back Red-114
Minis Bazooka Back-114
Minis Brooklyn Back-114
Minis Hat Trick Back-114
Minis O Canada Back-114
Minis O Canada Back Red-114
Minis Stanley Cup Back-114
03Topps Pristine-99
Gold Refractor Die Cuts-99
Refractors-99
Jersey Portions-PPJ-DC
Jersey Portion Refractors-PPJ-DC
Mini-PM-DC
Press Plates Black-99
Press Plates Cyan-99
Press Plates Magenta-99
Press Plates Yellow-99
03Upper Deck-435
Canadian Exclusives-435
HG-435
UD Exclusives-435
03Upper Deck MVP-423
Gold Script-423
Silver Script-423
Canadian Exclusives-423
03Upper Deck Rookie Update-88
03Upper Deck Victory-194
Bronze-194
Gold-194
Silver-194
04Pacific-254
Blue-254
Red-254
04Upper Deck-173
Canadian Exclusives-173
HG Glossy Gold-173
HG Glossy Silver-173
05Be A Player Signatures-DN
05Be A Player Signatures Gold-DN
05Beehive Matted Materials-MMDC
05Black Diamond-82
Emerald-82
Gold-82
Onyx-82
Ruby-82
05McDonalds Upper Deck Goalie Factory-GF8
05Panini Stickers-359
05Parkhurst-476
Facsimile Auto Parallel-476
Signatures-DC
True Colors-TCVAN
True Colors-TCVAN
05SP Authentic Sign of the Times-DC
05SP Authentic Sign of the Times Duals-DMC
05SP Game Used Authentic Fabrics-AF-DC
05SP Game Used Authentic Fabrics Autos-AAF-DC
05SP Game Used Authentic Fabrics Gold-AF-DC
05SP Game Used Authentic Patches-AP-DC
05SP Game Used Authentic Patch Autos-AAP-DC
05SP Game Used Auto Draft-AD-DC
05SP Game Used Awesome Authentics-AA-DC
05SP Game Used SIGnificance-DC
05SP Game Used SIGnificance Gold-S-DC
05SP Game Used Significant Numbers-SN-DC
05SP Game Used Statscriptions-ST-DC
05SPx Winning Combos-WC-CN
05SPx Winning Combos Gold-WC-CN
05SPx Winning Combos Spectrum-WC-CN
05UD Artifacts Frozen Artifacts-FA-DC
05UD Artifacts Frozen Artifacts Autos-FA-DC
05UD Artifacts Frozen Artifacts Copper-FA-DC
05UD Artifacts Frozen Artifacts Dual-FAD-DC
05UD Artifacts Frozen Artifact Dual Auto-FAD-DC
05UD Artifact Frozen Artifact Dual Copper-FAD-DC
05UD Artifacts Frozen Artifacts Dual Gold-FAD-DC
05UD Artifact Frozen Artifact Dual Maroon-FAD-DC
05UD Artifact Frozen Artifact Dual Pewter-FAD-DC
05UD Artifact Frozen Artifact Dual Silver-FAD-DC
05UD Artifacts Frozen Artifacts Gold-FA-DC
05UD Artifacts Frozen Artifacts Maroon-FA-DC
05UD Artifacts Frozen Artifacts Patches-FP-DC
05UD Artifact Frozen Artifact Patch Autos-FP-DC
05UD Artifacts Frozen Art Patch Pewter-FP-DC
05UD Artifacts Frozen Art Patch Silver-FP-DC
05UD Artifacts Frozen Artifacts Pewter-FA-DC
05UD Artifacts Frozen Artifacts Silver-FA-DC
05UD Artifacts Goalie Gear Dual-FPD-BH
05UD Artifacts Goalie Gear Dual Autos-FPD-BH
05Ultra-188
Gold-188
Ice-188
05Upper Deck-186
Big Playmakers-B-DC
HG Glossy-186
Jerseys Series II-J2DC
Notable Numbers-N-DC
Patches-P-DC
05Upper Deck MVP-370
Gold-370
Platinum-370
Materials-M-DC
Materials Duals-D-LC
05Upper Deck Trilogy Honorary Patches-HP-DC
05Upper Deck Tril Honorary Patch Script-HSP-DC
05Upper Deck Trilogy Honorary Swatches-HS-DC
05Upper Deck Tril Honorary Swatch Scripts-HSS-DC
05Upper Deck Toronto Fall Expo-186
05Upper Deck Victory-191
Black-191
Gold-191
Silver-191
06Between The Pipes The Mask-M29
06Between The Pipes The Mask Gold-M29
06Between The Pipes The Mask Silver-M29
06Black Diamond Jerseys-JDC
06Black Diamond Jerseys Black-JDC
06Black Diamond Jerseys Gold-JDC
06Black Diamond Jerseys Ruby-JDC
06Black Diamond Jerseys Black Autographs -JDC
06Flair Showcase Inks-IDC
06Flair Showcase Stitches-SSDC
06O-Pee-Chee-234
Rainbow-234
06Panini Stickers-282
06Ultra Fresh Ink-IDC
06Upper Deck-341
Exclusives Parallel-341
High Gloss Parallel-341
Game Jerseys-J2DC
Game Patches-P2DC
Masterpieces-341
Signatures-SDC
06Upper Deck MVP-133
Gold Script-133
Super Script-133
Jerseys-OJJC
06Upper Deck Trilogy Honorary Scripted Patches-HSPDC
06Upper Deck Trilogy Honorary Scripted Swatches-HSSDC
06Upper Deck Trilogy Scripts-TSDC
06Upper Deck Victory-254

Cloutier, David
92Quebec Pee-Wee Tournament-691
00Val d'Or Foreurs-6
Signed-6
01Cape Breton Screaming Eagles-4
02Cleveland Barons-2
03Cleveland Barons-3

Cloutier, Denis
907th Inn. Sketch QMJHL-111
92Quebec Pee-Wee Tournament-482

Cloutier, Eric
95Louisiana Ice Gators Playoffs-3
95Louisiana Ice Gators Glossy-2
96Louisiana Ice Gators-3
97Louisiana Ice Gators-14
98Louisiana Ice Gators-4
99Quebec Remparts-20
Signed-20

Cloutier, Francois
93Quebec Pee-Wee Tournament-233
95Slapshot Memorial Cup-65

Cloutier, Frederic
93Quebec Pee-Wee Tournament-1380
00Shawinigan Cataractes-17
Signed-17
01Louisiana Ice Gators-3
02BAP Memorabilia-373
02BAP Ultimate Memorabilia-97
02Parkhurst Retro-240
Minis-240
02Upper Deck Rookie Update-129
02Louisiana Ice Gators-5
03BAP Memorabilia Deep in the Crease-D11
03ECHL All-Stars-264
03Louisiana Ice Gators-3
06Rockford IceHogs -6

Cloutier, Jacques
82Sabres Milk Panels-9
83NHL Key Tags-8
86Sabres Blue Shield-5
86Sabres Blue Shield Small-5
87Panini Stickers-21
87Sabres Blue Shield-5
87Sabres Wonder Bread/Hostess-6
88Sabres Blue Shield-5
88Sabres Wonder Bread/Hostess-5
88ProCards AHL-248
89Blackhawks Coke-11
90Blackhawks Coke-11
90Bowman-11
Tiffany-11
90Nordiques Petro-Canada-30
90O-Pee-Chee-378
90Panini Stickers-197
90Pro Set-428
90Topps-378
Tiffany-378
90Upper Deck-114
French-114
91Pro Set Platinum-219
91Bowman-146
91Nordiques Petro-Canada-3
91O-Pee-Chee-286
91Parkhurst-368
French-368
91Score Canadian Bilingual-236
91Score Canadian English-236
91Stadium Club-166
91Topps-286
92Bowman-332
92Durivage Panini-46
92Nordiques Petro-Canada-4
92O-Pee-Chee-113
92Score-378
Canadian-378
92Stadium Club-118
92Topps-66
Gold-66G
92Upper Deck-324
93Durivage Score-18

Cloutier, Keven
93Quebec Pee-Wee Tournament-398
99Rouyn-Noranda Huskies-6

Cloutier, Kevin
01Peoria Rivermen-24
03St. Georges de Beauce Garaga-2
04St Georges de Beauce Garaga-14

Cloutier, Kim
93Quebec Pee-Wee Tournament-1003

Cloutier, Nichol
907th Inn. Sketch QMJHL-243

Cloutier, Patrick
907th Inn. Sketch QMJHL-216
92Quebec Pee-Wee Tournament-474

Cloutier, Philippe
92Quebec Pee-Wee Tournament-736
93Quebec Pee-Wee Tournament-358

Cloutier, Real
74O-Pee-Chee WHA-63
75O-Pee-Chee WHA-16
76Nordiques Marie Antoinette-7
76Nordiques Postcards-10
76O-Pee-Chee WHA-1
76O-Pee-Chee WHA-3
76O-Pee-Chee WHA-76
77O-Pee-Chee WHA-8
77Sportscasters-7804
77Finnish Sportscasters-90-2139
79O-Pee-Chee-239
79Topps-239
80Nordiques Postcards-6
80O-Pee-Chee-178
80O-Pee-Chee-238
80Pepsi-Cola Caps-63
80Topps-178
80Topps-238
81Nordiques Postcards-4
81O-Pee-Chee Stickers-74
81Post Standups-17
82Nordiques Postcards-4
82O-Pee-Chee-279
82O-Pee-Chee-280
82O-Pee-Chee Stickers-23
82Post Cereal-16
82Topps Stickers-23
83NHL Key Tags-107
83Nordiques Postcards-4
83O-Pee-Chee-62
83O-Pee-Chee Stickers-246
83Puffy Stickers-10
83Topps Stickers-246
84O-Pee-Chee-19
84Topps-15
04ITG Franchises Canadian-80
Autographs-RCL

Cloutier, Rejean
84Nova Scotia Oilers-5
86Sherbrooke Canadiens-11
92Quebec Pee-Wee Tournament-77

Cloutier, Sylvain
917th Inn. Sketch OHL-350
92Classic-22
Gold-22
92Classic Four-Sport *-171
Gold-171
93Guelph Storm-9
95Adirondack Red Wings-4
98Indianapolis Ice-10
99Albany River Rats-5
00Albany River Rats-5
01Albany River Rats-2
06UK Coventry Blaze-19

Cloux, Antoine
95Swiss HNL-497
96Swiss HNL-415

Clowe, Ryane
00Rimouski Oceanic-14
Signed-14
01Rimouski Oceanic-13
03Cleveland Barons-4
04SP Authentic Rookie Redemptions-RR25
04Cleveland Barons-4
05ITG Heroes/Prosp Toronto Expo Parallel -45
05Beehive-139
Beige -139
Blue -139
Gold-139
Red -139
Matte-139
Signature Scrapbook-SSCL
05Black Diamond-276
05Hot Prospects-212
Autographed Patch Variation-212
Autographed Patch Variation Gold-212
Red Hot-212
05Parkhurst-661
Facsimile Auto Parallel-661
Signatures-CL
True Colors-TCSJS
True Colors-TCSJS
05SP Authentic-184
Limited-184
Rarefied Rookies-RRRC
Sign of the Times Fives-TNCMC
05SP Game Used-155
Autographs-155
Gold-155
Rookie Exclusives-RC
Rookie Exclusives Silver-RE-RC
05SPx-150
Spectrum-150
Xcitement Rookies-XR-RC
Xcitement Rookies Gold-XR-RC
Xcitement Rookies Spectrum-XR-RC
05The Cup-138
Autographed Rookie Patches Gold Rainbow-138
Black Rainbow Rookies-138
Masterpiece Pressplates (Artifacts)-225
Masterpiece Pressplates (Bee Hive)-139
Masterpiece Pressplates (Black Diamond)-276
Masterpiece Pressplates (Ice)-163
Masterpiece Pressplates (MVP)-425
Masterpiece Pressplates (Rookie Update)-231
Masterpiece Pressplates SPA Autos-184
Masterpiece Pressplates (SP Game Used)-155
Masterpiece Pressplates (SPx)-150
Masterpiece Pressplates (Trilogy)-213
Masterpiece Pressplates Ult Coll Autos-131
Masterpiece Pressplates Autographs-138
Platinum Rookies-138
05UD Artifacts-225
Gold-RED25
05Ultimate Collection-131
Autographed Patches-131
Autographed Shields-131
Ultimate Debut Threads Jerseys-DTJRC
Ultimate Debut Threads Jerseys Autos-DAJRC
Ultimate Debut Threads Patches-DTPRC
Ultimate Debut Threads Patches Autos-DAPRC
05Ultra-241
Gold-241
Ice-241
Rookie Uniformity Jerseys-RU-RC
Rookie Uniformity Jersey Autographs-ARU-RC
Rookie Uniformity Patches-RUP-RC
Rookie Uniformity Patch Autographs-ARP-RC
05Upper Deck-234
HG Glossy-234
Rookie Ink-RIRC
05Upper Deck Rookie Showcase-RS25
05Upper Deck Rookie Showcase Promos-RS25
05Upper Deck Rookie Threads-RTRC
05Upper Deck Ice-163
Fresh Ice-FIRC
Fresh Ice Glass-FIRC
Fresh Ice Glass Patches-FIPRC
Premieres Auto Patches-AIPRC
05Upper Deck MVP-425
Gold-425
Platinum-425
05Upper Deck Rookie Update-231
Inspirations Patch Rookies-231
05Upper Deck Trilogy-213
05Upper Deck Toronto Fall Expo-234
05Cleveland Barons-5
05ITG Heroes and Prospects-45
Autographs-A-RC

Clower, Chad
03Minnesota State Mavericks-4

Clowes, Luke
92Windsor Spitfires-3
93Windsor Spitfires-22
94Windsor Spitfires-24

Clukey, Barry
93Maine Black Bears-43

Clune, Art
52Juniors Blue Tint-152

Clune, Richard
03Sarnia Sting-6
06Barrie Colts-12

Clune, Walter
51Laval Dairy QSHL-96
51Laval Dairy Subset-96
52St. Lawrence Sales-12

Clusiault, Jonathan
92Quebec Pee-Wee Tournament-753
93Quebec Pee-Wee Tournament-336

Clutterbuck, Cal
03St. Michael's Majors-10
04Oshawa Generals-10
04Oshawa Generals Autographs-10
04St. Michael's Majors-11
05ITG Heroes/Prosp Toronto Expo Parallel -410
05ITG Heroes and Prospects-410
Team Cherry-TC13
06Oshawa Generals-5
06ITG Heroes and Prospects-198
Autographs-ACCL
Complete CHL Logos-CHL07
Jerseys-GUJ73
Emblems-GUE73
Numbers-GUN73
Update Autographs-ACCL

Clymer, Ben
95Donruss Elite World Juniors-27
96Minnesota Golden Gophers-7
97Minnesota Golden Gophers-11
99Pacific-464
99Pacific Omega-220
Copper-220
Gold-220
Ice Blue-220
Premiere Date-220
99Pacific Prism-130
Holographic Blue-130
Holographic Gold-130
Holographic Mirror-130
Holographic Purple-130
Premiere Date-130
99Upper Deck Gold Reserve-348
00Upper Deck NHLPA-PA79
01BAP Signature Series-197
Autographs-197
Autographs Gold-197
02BAP Sig Series Auto Buybacks 2001-197
02Pacific-347
Blue-347
Red-347
02Pacific Complete-268
Red-268
02Topps Total-321
03ITG Action-508
03Lightning Team Issue-12
03Pacific Complete-106
Red-106
05Parkhurst-493
Facsimile Auto Parallel-493
06Panini Stickers-178
06Upper Deck-448
Exclusives Parallel-448
High Gloss Parallel-448
Masterpieces-448

Cmorej, Peter
05Prince Albert Raiders-4
06PEI Rocket-18

Cmunt, Jiri
99Czech Score Blue 2000-7
99Czech Score Red Ice 2000-7

Coakley, Chris
93Waterloo Black Hawks-6

Coalter, Brandon
95Slapshot-237
03Florida Everblades-4
03Florida Everblades RBI Sports-162
04Florida Everblades-11
05Florida Everblades-7

Coalter, Gary
74NHL Action Stamps-290
74O-Pee-Chee NHL-17
74Topps-17
75O-Pee-Chee NHL-334

Coates, Andrew
98Red Deer Rebels-5
01OCN Blizzard-8
02OCN Blizzard-7

Coates, Brandon
917th Inn. Sketch WHL-35

Cobb, Murray
03St. Jean Mission-2

Coburn, Andrew
05Vernon Vipers-7

Coburn, Braydon
03BAP Memorabilia Draft Redemptions-8
03Portland Winter Hawks-18
03Portland Winter Hawks-25
04SP Authentic Rookie Redemptions-RR2
04Portland Winter Hawks-3
04Portland Winter Hawks-NNO
04ITG Heroes and Prospects-57
Autographs-BC
Combos-14
He Shoots-He Scores Prizes-40
04ITG Heroes/Prospects Toronto Expo '05-57
04ITG Heroes/Prospects Expo Heroes/Pros-57
05ITG Heroes/Prosp Toronto Expo Parallel -235
05Beehive-121
Beige -121
Blue -121
Gold-121
Red -121
Matte-121
Signature Scrapbook-SSCO
05Black Diamond-209
Emerald-209
Gold-209
Onyx-209
Ruby-209
05Hot Prospects-219
En Fuego-219
Hot Materials-HMBC
Red Hot-219
White Hot-219
05Parkhurst-603
Facsimile Auto Parallel-603
Signatures-BC
05SP Authentic-133
Limited-133
Rarefied Rookies-RRBC
Rookie Authentics-RABC
05SP Game Used-109
Autographs-109
Gold-109
Rookie Exclusives-BC
Rookie Exclusives Silver-RE-BC
05SPx-181
Spectrum-181
Xcitement Rookies-XR-BC
Xcitement Rookies Gold-XR-BC
Xcitement Rookies Spectrum-XR-BC
05The Cup-139
Autographed Rookie Patches Gold Rainbow-139
Black Rainbow Rookies-139
Masterpiece Pressplates (Artifacts)-202
Masterpiece Pressplates (Bee Hive)-121
Masterpiece Pressplates (Black Diamond)-209
Masterpiece Pressplates (Ice)-119
Masterpiece Pressplates (MVP)-427
Masterpiece Pressplates (Power Play)-157
Masterpiece Pressplates (Power Play)-157
Masterpiece Pressplates (Rookie Update)-196
Masterpiece Pressplates SPA Autos-133
Masterpiece Pressplates (SP Game Used)-109
Masterpiece Pressplates SPx Autos-181
Masterpiece Pressplates (Trilogy)-173
Masterpiece Pressplates Ult Coll Autos-102
Masterpiece Pressplates (Victory)-298
Masterpiece Pressplates Autographs-139
Platinum Rookies-139
05UD Artifacts-202
Gold-RED2
05UD PowerPlay-157
05Ultimate Collection-102
Autographed Patches-102
Autographed Shields-102
Ultimate Debut Threads Jerseys-DTJBC
Ultimate Debut Threads Jerseys Autos-DAJBC
Ultimate Debut Threads Patches-DTPBC
Ultimate Debut Threads Patches Autos-DAPBC
05Ultra-201
Gold-201
Ice-201
Rookie Uniformity Jerseys-RU-BC
Rookie Uniformity Jersey Autographs-ARU-BC
Rookie Uniformity Patches-RUP-BC
Rookie Uniformity Patch Autographs-ARP-BC
05Upper Deck-233
HG Glossy-233
Rookie Ink-RIBC
05Upper Deck Rookie Showcase-RS2
05Upper Deck Rookie Showcase Promos-RS2
05Upper Deck Rookie Threads-RTBC
05Upper Deck Rookie Threads Autographs-ARTBC
05Upper Deck Ice-119
Fresh Ice-FIBC
Fresh Ice Glass-FIBC
Fresh Ice Glass Patches-FIPBC
Premieres Auto Patches-AIPBC
05Upper Deck MVP-427
Gold-427
Platinum-427
05Upper Deck Rookie Update-196
Inspirations Patch Rookies-196
05Upper Deck Trilogy-173
05Upper Deck Toronto Fall Expo-233
05Upper Deck Victory-298
Black-298
Gold-298
Silver-298
05AHL All-Stars-3
05AHL Top Prospects-6
05Chicago Wolves-4
05ITG Heroes and Prospects-235
Autographs Series II-BC
He Shoots-He Scores Prizes-19
06Upper Deck Signatures-SBC
06ITG Heroes and Prospects-66
Autographs-ABCO

Cocciolo, Vince
89Portland Winter Hawks-2

Cochrane, Glen
82Post Cereal-14
83Flyers J.C. Penney-6
83NHL Key Tags-93
85Canucks Team Issue-5
86Canucks Team Issue-4
86Kraft Drawings-9
87Blackhawks Coke-4
88Oilers Tenth Anniversary-101
02Fleer Throwbacks-41
Gold-41
Platinum-41

Coci, Eric
907th Inn. Sketch QMJHL-128

Cockburn, Bill
24Crescent Falcon-Tigers-1

Cockburn, Bryce
03Trenton Titans-358
06Rockford IceHogs -7

Cockell, Matt
96Saskatoon Blades-7
97Saskatoon Blades-5

Code, Chris
907th Inn. Sketch OHL-206

Code, Tony
93Western Michigan Broncos-8

Coffey, David
04UK Milton Keynes Lightning-20

Coffey, Paul
80Pepsi-Cola Caps-24
81Oilers Red Rooster-7
81O-Pee-Chee-111
82Oilers Red Rooster-7
82O-Pee-Chee-101
82O-Pee-Chee-102

82O-Pee-Chee Stickers-104
82O-Pee-Chee Stickers-105
82O-Pee-Chee Stickers-160
82Post Cereal-6
82Topps Stickers-104
82Topps Stickers-105
82Topps Stickers-160
83Esso-5
83NHL Key Tags-38
83Oilers McDonald's-25
83O-Pee-Chee-25
83O-Pee-Chee Stickers-94
83O-Pee-Chee Stickers-95
83Puffy Stickers-3
83Topps Stickers-94
83Topps Stickers-95
83Vachon-22
84Kellogg's Accordion Discs-5A
84Kellogg's Accordion Discs-5B
84Kellogg's Accordion Discs Singles-7
84Oilers Red Rooster-7
84Oilers Team Issue-3
84O-Pee-Chee-217
84O-Pee-Chee-239
84O-Pee-Chee Stickers-134
84O-Pee-Chee Stickers-251
84O-Pee-Chee Stickers-252
847-Eleven Discs-14
84Topps-50
84Topps-163
85Oilers Red Rooster-7
85O-Pee-Chee-85
85O-Pee-Chee Stickers-56
85O-Pee-Chee Stickers-124
85O-Pee-Chee Stickers-191
85O-Pee-Chee Stickers-217
857-Eleven Credit Cards-6
85Topps-85
85Topps Sticker Inserts-4
86Kraft Drawings-10
86Oilers Red Rooster-7
86Oilers Team Issue-7
86O-Pee-Chee-137
86O-Pee-Chee Stickers-68
86O-Pee-Chee Stickers-112
86O-Pee-Chee Stickers-188
86Topps-137
86Topps Sticker Inserts-5
87O-Pee-Chee-99
87O-Pee-Chee Minis-8
87O-Pee-Chee Stickers-89
87Panini Stickers-256
87Penguins Kodak-5
87Pro-Sport All-Stars-14
87Topps-99
88Esso All-Stars-6
88Frito-Lay Stickers-24
88Oilers Tenth Anniversary-54
88Oilers Tenth Anniversary-64
88O-Pee-Chee-179
88O-Pee-Chee Minis-6
88O-Pee-Chee Stickers-233
88Panini Stickers-333
88Topps-179
89Kraft-54
89Kraft All-Stars Stickers-3
89O-Pee-Chee-95
89O-Pee-Chee Stickers-237
89Panini Stickers-183
89Panini Stickers-311
89Penguins Foodland-4
89Sports Illustrated for Kids I-300
89Topps-95
89Swedish Semic World Champ Stickers-59
90Bowman-211
Tiffany-211
90Kraft-8
90Kraft-82
90O-Pee-Chee-116
90O-Pee-Chee-202
90O-Pee-Chee Box Bottoms-C
90OPC Premier-16
90Panini Stickers-135
90Panini Stickers-324
90Penguins Foodland-2
90Pro Set-231
90Pro Set-361
90Score-6
90Score-319
90Score-332
Canadian-6
Canadian-319
Canadian-332
90Score Hottest/Rising Stars-65
90Topps-116
90Topps-202
Tiffany-116
Tiffany-202
90Topps Box Bottoms-C
90Upper Deck-124
90Upper Deck-498
French-124
French-498
91Pro Set Platinum-94
91Bowman-81
91Gillette-37
91Kraft-74
91McDonald's Upper Deck-11
91O-Pee-Chee-183
91O-Pee-Chee-384
91O-Pee-Chee-504
91OPC Premier-79
91Panini Stickers-276
91Panini Stickers-336
91Parkhurst-140
91Parkhurst-212
91Parkhurst-225
91Parkhurst-297
French-140
French-212
French-225
French-297
91Penguins Foodland Coupon Stickers-11
91Pinnacle-186
91Pinnacle-377
French-186
French-377
91Pro Set-190
91Pro Set-312
91Pro Set-319
French-190
French-312
Platinum PC-PC12
Puck Candy-21
91Score National-9
91Score Ntnl Candy Wholesalers Convention-9
91Score Fanfest-9
91Score American-115
91Score American-372
91Score Canadian Bilingual-115
91Score Canadian Bilingual-262
91Score Canadian English-115
91Score Canadian English-262
91Stadium Club Charter Member-45
91Stadium Club Members Only-40
91Stadium Club-212
91Topps-183
91Topps-504
91Upper Deck-11
91Upper Deck-177
91Upper Deck-501
91Upper Deck-615
French-11
French-177
French-501
French-615
91Finnish Semic World Champ Stickers-58
91Swedish Semic World Champ Stickers-58
92Bowman-181
92Bowman-226
92Kraft-39
92McDonald's Upper Deck-17
92O-Pee-Chee-5
92O-Pee-Chee-187
92O-Pee-Chee-318
25th Anniv. Inserts-14
92OPC Premier Star Performers-4
92Panini Stickers-72
92Panini Stickers-278
92Panini Stickers French-72
92Panini Stickers French-278
92Parkhurst-63
92Parkhurst-276
92Parkhurst-458
Emerald Ice-63
Emerald Ice-276
Emerald Ice-458
92Pinnacle-50
French-50
Team Pinnacle-3
Team French-3
92Pro Set-71
92Score-265
92Score-441
Canadian-265
Canadian-441
92Sports Illustrated for Kids II-420
92Stadium Club-169
92Topps-5
92Topps-182
Gold-5G
Gold-182G
92Ultra-80
All-Stars-1
92Upper Deck-116
92Finnish Semic-81
93Donruss-99
93Kraft-4
93Leaf-67
Gold All-Stars-7
93McDonald's Upper Deck-4
93OPC Premier-145
Gold-145
93Panini Stickers-134
93Panini Stickers-252
93Parkhurst-56
Emerald Ice-56
Cherry's Playoff Heroes-D8
93Pinnacle-80
Canadian-80
All-Stars-43
All-Stars Canadian-43
Team Pinnacle-8
Team Canadian-8
93PowerPlay-70
93Score-106
Canadian-106
Dream Team-8
93Seasons Patches-3
93Stadium Club-450
Members Only Master Set-450
First Day Issue-450
All-Stars-2
All-Stars Members Only-2
All-Stars OPC-2
Finest-4
Finest Members Only-4
93Topps/OPC Premier-145
Gold-145
93Topps Premier Black Gold-6
93Ultra-71
93Upper Deck-315
Gretzky's Great Ones-GG6
SP-42
93Upper Deck Locker All-Stars-23
93Swedish Semic World Champ Stickers-197
94Be A Player-R91
99 All-Stars-G2
94Canada Games NHL POGS-93
94Donruss-54
Dominators-6
94EA Sports-37
94Finest-68
94Finest-99
Super Team Winners-68
Super Team Winners-99
Refractors-68
Refractors-99
Ring Leaders-6
94Flair-47
94Fleer-58
94Hockey Wit-46
94Leaf-168
Fire on Ice-8
94Leaf Limited-75
94McDonald's Upper Deck-McD19
94OPC Premier-15
94OPC Premier-489
Special Effects-15
Special Effects-489
94Parkhurst-63
Gold-63
SE Vintage-15
94Pinnacle-429
Artist's Proofs-429
Rink Collection-429
94Score Dream Team-DT6
94Select-72
Gold-72
94SP-36
Die Cuts-36
94Stadium Club Members Only-3
94Topps/OPC Premier-15
94Topps/OPC Premier-489
Special Effects-15
Special Effects-489
94Ultra-59
All-Stars-9
94Upper Deck-24
Electric Ice-24
Predictor Canadian-C31
94Upper Deck Predictor Canadian Exch Gold-C31
94Upper Deck SP Inserts-SP22
94Upper Deck SP Inserts Die Cuts-SP22
94Finnish Jaa Kiekko-86
94Finnish Jaa Kiekko-337
95Bashan Super Stickers-39
Die-Cut-5
95Bowman-41
All-Foil-41
95Canada Games NHL POGS-13
95Canada Games NHL POGS-102
95Collector's Choice-18
95Collector's Choice-379
95Collector's Choice-390
Player's Club-18
Player's Club-379
Player's Club-390
Player's Club Platinum-18
Player's Club Platinum-379
Player's Club Platinum-390
Crash The Game-C29A
Crash The Game-C29B
Crash The Game-C29C
Crash The Game Gold-C29A
Crash The Game Gold-C29B
Crash The Game Gold-C29C
Crash the Game Silver Redeemed-C29
Crash the Game Silver Bonus-C29
Crash the Game Gold Redeemed-C29
Crash the Game Gold Bonus-C29
95Donruss-119
Dominators-7
Elite Inserts-5
Igniters-2
95Donruss Elite-85
Die Cut Stars-85
Die Cut Uncut-85
Cutting Edge-13
95Emotion-52
95Finest-137
Refractors-137
95Hoyle Western Playing Cards-10
95Imperial Stickers-39
Die Cut Superstars-5
95Kraft-43
95Kraft-64
95Leaf-144
Fire On Ice-4
Gold Stars-2
Road To The Cup-5
95Leaf Limited-24
95McDonald's Pinnacle-MCD-4
95Metal-44
95NHL Aces Playing Cards-1C
95Panini Stickers-147
95Panini Stickers-184
95Parkhurst International-66
Emerald Ice-66
Crown Collection Silver Series 1-8
Crown Collection Gold Series 1-8
NHL All-Stars-5
Parkie's Trophy Picks-PP19
Trophy Winners-4
95Pinnacle-14
Artist's Proofs-14
Rink Collection-14
95Playoff One on One-33
95Playoff One on One-143
95Playoff One on One-252
95Post Upper Deck-16
95Pro Magnets-101
95Score-24
Black Ice Artist's Proofs-24
Black Ice-24
Golden Blades-5
95Select Certified-21
Mirror Gold-21
95SkyBox Impact-51
95SP-45
Holoviews-FX6
Holoviews Special FX-FX6
Stars/Etoiles-E13
Stars/Etoiles Gold-E13
95Stadium Club Members Only-30
95Stadium Club-34
Members Only Master Set-34
Metalists-M11
Metalists Members Only Master Set-M11
Power Streak-PS4
Power Streak Members Only Master Set-PS4
95Summit-16
95Summit-198
Artist's Proofs-16
Artist's Proofs-198
Ice-16
Ice-198
GM's Choice-9
95Topps-4
95Topps-265
OPC Inserts-4
OPC Inserts-265
Home Grown Canada-HGC11
Marquee Men Power Boosters-4
Profiles-PF12
95Topps SuperSkills-29
Platinum-29
95Ultra-44
Gold Medallion-44
95Upper Deck-226
95Upper Deck-248
95Upper Deck-396
Electric Ice-226
Electric Ice-248
Electric Ice-396
Electric Ice Gold-226
Electric Ice Gold-248
Electric Ice Gold-396
95Upper Deck All-Star Game Predictors-8
Redemption Winners-8
95Upper Deck Freeze Frame-F17
95Upper Deck Freeze Frame Jumbo-F17
95Upper Deck NHL All-Stars-AS1
95Upper Deck NHL All-Stars Jumbo-AS1
95Upper Deck Predictor Hobby-H3
95Upper Deck Predictor Hobby-H31
95Upper Deck Predictor Hobby Exchange-H3
95Upper Deck Predictor Hobby Exchange-H31
95Upper Deck Predictor Retail-R12
95Upper Deck Predictor Retail Exchange-R12
95Upper Deck Special Edition-SE118
95Upper Deck Special Edition Gold-SE118
95Zenith-2
95Finnish Semic World Championships-82
95Swedish Globe World Championships-76
95Swedish World Championships Stickers-10
96SLU Hockey American-4
96Black Diamond-151
Gold-151
96Collector's Choice-85
96Collector's Choice-316
MVP-UD28
MVP Gold-UD28
96Donruss-140
96Donruss-238
Press Proofs-140
Press Proofs-238
Dominators-3
96Donruss Canadian Ice-9
96Donruss Canadian Ice-149
Gold Press Proofs-9
Gold Press Proofs-149
Red Press Proofs-9
Red Press Proofs-149
96Donruss Elite-72
Die Cut Stars-72
Perspective-5
96Duracell All-Cherry Team-DC1
96Duracell L'Equipe Beliveau-JB1
96Flair-66
Blue Ice-66
Hot Numbers-2
96Fleer-29
96Fleer-140
Norris-3
96Fleer Picks-20
Fabulous 50-8
Jagged Edge-18
96Flyers Postcards-3
96Kenner Starting Lineup Cards-4
96Leaf-164
Press Proofs-164
96Leaf Leather And Laces Promos-P4
96Leaf Leather And Laces-4
96Leaf Limited-18
Gold-18
Stubble-4
96Leaf Preferred-101
Press Proofs-101
96Maggers-16
96McDonald's Pinnacle-1
96Metal Universe-67
Ice Carvings-4
Ice Carvings Super Power-4
96NHL Pro Stamps-101
96Pinnacle-14
Artist's Proofs-14
Foil-14
Premium Stock-14
Rink Collection-14
Team Pinnacle-7
96Pinnacle Fantasy-FC2
96Pinnacle Mint-20
Bronze-20
Gold-20
Silver-20
Coins Brass-20
Coins Solid Gold-20
Coins Gold Plated-20
Coins Nickel-20
Coins Silver-20
96Post Upper Deck-3
96Score-142
Artist's Proofs-142
Dealer's Choice Artist's Proofs-142
Special Artist's Proofs-142
Golden Blades-142
Superstitions-6
96Select Certified-89
Artist's Proofs-89
Blue-89
Mirror Blue-89
Mirror Gold-89
Mirror Red-89
Red-89
96SkyBox Impact-33
NHL on Fox-6
96SP Clearcut Winner-CW13
96SP Game Film-GF19
96SPx-15
Gold-15
Holoview Heroes-HH4
96Stadium Club Members Only-5
96Summit-3
Artist's Proofs-3
Ice-3
Metal-3
Premium Stock-3
96Team Out-49
96Topps Picks Fantasy Team-FT7
96Ultra-122
Gold Medallion-122
Power-3
Power Blue Line-3
96Upper Deck-268
Generation Next-X9
Lord Stanley's Heroes Finals-LS10
Lord Stanley's Heroes Quarterfinals-LS10
Lord Stanley's Heroes Semifinals-LS10
Superstar Showdown-SS20A
96Zenith-48
Artist's Proofs-48
Champion Salute-4
Champion Salute Diamond-4
96Swedish Semic Wien-79
97Headliners Hockey-4
97SLU Hockey American-5
97Be A Player-12
Autographs-12
Autographs Die-Cuts-12
Autographs Prismatic Die-Cuts-12
Take A Number-11
97Collector's Choice-189
97Donruss-63
Press Proofs Silver-63
Press Proofs Gold-63
Line 2 Line-15
Line 2 Line Die Cut-15
97Donruss Canadian Ice-64
Dominion Series-64
Provincial Series-64
National Pride-23
Stanley Cup Scrapbook-30
97Donruss Elite-63
Aspirations-63
Status-63
97Donruss Limited-6
97Donruss Limited-100
97Donruss Limited-108
Exposure-6
Exposure-100
Exposure-108
Fabric of the Game-12
97Donruss Preferred-12
Cut to the Chase-12
97Donruss Priority-110
Stamp of Approval-110
97Katch-103
Gold-103
Silver-103
97Kenner Starting Lineup Cards-5
97Leaf-21
Fractal Matrix-21
Fractal Matrix Die Cuts-21
97Leaf International-21
Universal Ice-21
97Pacific-77
Copper-77
Emerald Green-77
Ice Blue-77
Red-77
Silver-77
97Pacific Invincible-99
Copper-99
Emerald Green-99
Ice Blue-99
Red-99
Silver-99
NHL Regime-140
97Pacific Omega-161
Copper-161
Dark Gray-161
Emerald Green-161
Gold-161
Ice Blue-161
97Pinnacle-153
Press Plates Back Black-153
Press Plates Back Cyan-153
Press Plates Back Magenta-153
Press Plates Back Yellow-153
Press Plates Front Black-153
Press Plates Front Cyan-153
Press Plates Front Magenta-153
Press Plates Front Yellow-153
97Pinnacle Certified-102
Red-102
Mirror Blue-102
Mirror Gold-102
Mirror Red-102
97Pinnacle Inside-160
97Pinnacle Tot Cert Platinum Blue-102
97Pinnacle Tot Cert Platinum Gold-102
97Pinnacle Totally Certified Platinum Red-102
97Pinnacle Tot Cert Mirror Platinum Gold-102
97Revolution-98
Copper-98
Emerald-98
Ice Blue-98
Silver-98
97Score-166
97Score Flyers-11
Platinum-11
Premier-11
97SP Authentic-113
97Studio-85
Press Proofs Silver-85
Press Proofs Gold-85
97Upper Deck-329
Game Dated Moments-329
98Be A Player-177
Press Release-177
98BAP Gold-177
98BAP Autographs-177
98BAP Autographs Gold-177
98BAP AS Game Used Jersey Cards-AS11
98BAP AS Milestones-M14
98BAP Playoff Highlights-H9
98McDonalds Upper Deck Gretzkys Teammates-T10
98OPC Chrome-10
Refractors-10
98Pacific-322
Ice Blue-322
Red-322
98Pacific Omega-39
Red-39
Opening Day Issue-39
98Paramount-45
Copper-45
Emerald Green-45
Holo-Electric-45
Ice Blue-45
Silver-45
98Topps-10
O-Pee-Chee-10
98UD Choice-151
98UD Choice Preview-151
98UD Choice Prime Choice Reserve-151
98UD Choice Reserve-151
98Upper Deck-66
Exclusives-66
Exclusives 1 of 1-66
Gold Reserve-66
99BAP Memorabilia AS Heritage Ruby-H15
99BAP Memorabilia AS Heritage Sapphire-H15
99BAP Memorabilia AS Heritage Emerald-H15
99BAP Update Teammates Jersey Cards-TM17
99BAP Millennium Jerseys-J32
99BAP Millennium Jersey Autographs-J32
99BAP Millennium Jersey and Stick Cards-JS32
99BAP Millennium Jersey Emblems-E32
99BAP Millennium Jersey Numbers-N32
99Pacific-68
Copper-68
Emerald Green-68
Gold-68
Ice Blue-68
Premiere Date-68
Red-68
99Stadium Club Capture the Action-CA27
99Stadium Club Capture Action Game View-CAG27
99Upper Deck Century Legends-29
Century Collection-29
99Upper Deck Victory-60
00Aurora-11
Premiere Date-11
Game-Worn Jerseys-1
Game-Worn Jersey Patches-1
00BAP Memorabilia-221
00BAP Memorabilia-467
Emerald-221
Emerald-467
Ruby-221
Ruby-467
Sapphire-221
Sapphire-467
Promos-221
Jersey Cards-J28
Jersey Emblems-E28
Jersey Numbers-N28
Jersey and Stick Cards-JS28
00BAP Mem Chicago Sportsfest Copper-221
00BAP Memorabilia Chicago Sportsfest Blue-221
00BAP Memorabilia Chicago Sportsfest Gold-221
00BAP Memorabilia Chicago Sportsfest Ruby-221
00BAP Memorabilia Chicago Sun-Times Ruby-221
00BAP Memorabilia Chicago Sun-Times Gold-221
00BAP Mem Chicago Sun-Times Sapphire-221
00BAP Mem Toronto Fall Expo Copper-221
00BAP Memorabilia Toronto Fall Expo Gold-221
00BAP Memorabilia Toronto Fall Expo Ruby-221
00BAP Mem Update Heritage Jersey Cards-H3
00BAP Mem Update Heritage Jersey Gold-H3
00BAP Parkhurst 2000-P102
00BAP Signature Series-120
Emerald-120
Ruby-120
Sapphire-120
Autographs-202
Autographs Gold-202
Department of Defense-DD13
00BAP Ultimate Mem Dynasty Jerseys-D4
00BAP Ultimate Mem Dynasty Jerseys-D7
00BAP Ultimate Mem Dynasty Emblems-D4
00BAP Ultimate Mem Dynasty Emblems-D7
00BAP Ultimate Mem Magnificent Ones-ML10
00BAP Ultimate Mem Magnificent Ones Autos-ML10
00BAP Ultimate Memorabilia Norris Trophy-N6
00O-Pee-Chee-133
00O-Pee-Chee Parallel-133
00Pacific-80
Copper-80
Gold-80
Ice Blue-80
Premiere Date-80
00Panini Stickers-26
00Private Stock Game Gear-5
00Private Stock Game Gear-6
00Stadium Club-219
00Topps/OPC-133
Parallel-133
1000 Point Club-PC4
00Topps Chrome-100
OPC Refractors-100
Refractors-100
1000 Point Club Refractors-4
00Topps Stars-96
Blue-96
00Upper Deck-244
Exclusives Tier 1-244
Exclusives Tier 2-244
00Upper Deck Legends-52
Legendary Collection Bronze-52
Legendary Collection Gold-52
Legendary Collection Silver-52
00Upper Deck Victory-48
00Upper Deck Vintage-29
00Czech Stadion-157
01BAP Ultimate Mem All-Star History-35
01BAP Ultimate Mem Retro Teammates-4
01BAP Ultimate Mem Retro Teammates-11
02BAP NHL All-Star History-35
02BAP Sig Series Auto Buybacks 1998-177
02BAP Sig Series Auto Buybacks 2000-202
04ITG Franchises Canadian-24
Autographs-PC1
Barn Burners-BB5
Barn Burners Gold-BB5
Complete Jerseys-CJ9
Complete Jerseys Gold-CJ9
Double Memorabilia-DM20
Double Memorabilia Autographs-DM20
Double Memorabilia Gold-DM20
Forever Rivals-FR5
Forever Rivals Gold-FR5
Memorabilia-SM6
Memorabilia Autographs-SM6
Memorabilia Gold-SM6
Original Sticks-OS2
Original Sticks Autographs-OS2
Original Sticks Gold-OS2
Teammates-TM6
Teammates Gold-TM6
Trophy Winners-TW6
Trophy Winners Gold-TW6
04ITG Franchises He Shoots/Scores Prizes-33
04ITG Franchises Update-458
04ITG Franchises US East Autographs-A-PC2
04ITG Franchises US East Complete Jerseys-ECJ2
04ITG Franchises US East Comp Jersey Gold-ECJ2
04ITG Franchises US East Memorabilia-ESM7
04ITG Franchises US East Memorabilia Gold-ESM7
04ITG Franchises US West-273
Autographs-A-PC3
Complete Jerseys-WCJ3
Complete Jerseys Gold-WCJ3
Memorabilia-WSM19
Memorabilia Autographs-WSMPC
Memorabilia Gold-WSM19
Teammates-WTM5
Teammates Gold-WTM5
04ITG Ultimate Memorabilia-130
04ITG Ultimate Memorabilia-141
04ITG Ultimate Memorabilia-181
Gold-130
Gold-141
Gold-181
Archives 1st Edition-23
Archives 1st Edition-30
Auto Threads-3
Autographs-14
Autographs Gold-14
Complete Jerseys-1
Complete Logo-7
Country of Origin-18
Country of Origin Gold-18
Day In History-24
Day In History-27
Day In History-47
Day In History-49
Day In History Gold-24
Day In History Gold-27
Day In History Gold-47
Day In History Gold-49
Heroes Mario Lemieux-4
Heroes Steve Yzerman-5
Jerseys-4
Jerseys Gold-4
Jersey Autographs-5
Jersey Autographs Gold-5
Jersey and Sticks-4
Jersey and Sticks Gold-4
Norris Trophy-5
Retro Teammates-8
Stick Autographs-29
Stick Autographs Gold-29
Triple Threads-6
04UD Legendary Signatures-62
Autographs-PC
Rearguard Retrospectives-PCRG
04UD Legends Classics-42
04UD Legends Classics-63
Gold-42
Gold-63
Platinum-42
Platinum-63
Silver-42
Silver-63
Signature Moments-M17
Signatures-CS17
Signatures-TC9
04Upper Deck Heritage Classic-CC-PC
04ITG Heroes and Prospects-173
Autographs-PCO
Hero Memorabilia-28
04ITG Heroes/Prospects Toronto Expo '05-173
04ITG Heroes/Prospects Expo Heroes/Pros-173
05ITG Ultimate Memorabilia Level 1-77
05ITG Ultimate Memorabilia Level 2-77
05ITG Ultimate Memorabilia Level 3-77
05ITG Ultimate Memorabilia Level 4-77
05ITG Ultimate Memorabilia Level 5-77
05ITG Ultimate Mem Cornerstones Jerseys-7
05ITG Ultimate Mem Cornerst Jerseys Gold-7
05ITG Ultimate Memorabilia Double Autos-18
05ITG Ultimate Mem Double Autos Gold-18
05ITG Ultimate Mem Double Mem-14
05ITG Ultimate Mem Double Mem Autos-11
05ITG Ultimate Mem Double Mem Autos Gold-11
05ITG Ultimate Mem Double Mem Gold-14
05ITG Ultimate Memorabilia Gloves Are Off-4
05ITG Ultimate Mem Gloves Are Off Gold-4
05ITG Ultimate Memorabilia Jerseys-29
05ITG Ultimate Memorabilia Jerseys Gold-29
05ITG Ultimate Mem Record Breaker Jerseys-18
05ITG Ultimate Mem Record Breaker Jerseys-20
05ITG Ultimate Mem RecBreak Jerseys Gold-18
05ITG Ultimate Mem RecBreak Jerseys Gold-20
05ITG Ultimate Mem Retro Teammate Jerseys-5
05ITG Ult Mem Retro Teammates Jersey Gold-5
05ITG Ultimate Memorabilia Stick Autos-27
05ITG Ultimate Mem Stick Autos Gold-27
05ITG Ultimate Mem Sticks and Jerseys-18
05ITG Ultimate Mem Stick and Jerseys Gold-18
05ITG Ultimate Memorabilia Ultimate Autos-43
05ITG Ultimate Mem Ultimate Autos Gold-43
05NHL Legends Medallions-3
05ITG Heroes and Prospects Aspiring-ASP5
06ITG International Ice-5
06ITG International Ice-21
06ITG International Ice-66
06ITG International Ice-100
Gold-5
Gold-21
Gold-66
Gold-100
Autographs-APC
Autographs-APC2
Autographs-APC3
Autographs-APC4
Best of the Best-BB03
Best of the Best Gold-BB03
Canadian Dream Team-DT10
Canadian Dream Team Gold-DT10
Cornerstones-IC12
Cornerstones Gold-IC12
International Rivals-IR20
Teammates-IT07
Teammates Gold-IT07
06ITG Ultimate Memorabilia-112
Artist Proof-112
Autos-6
Autos Gold-6
Blades of Steel-27
Blades of Steel Gold-27
Bowman Factor-12
Bowman Factor Gold-12
Bowman Factor Autos-10
Bowman Factor Autos Gold-10
Complete Package-5
Complete Package Gold-5
Cornerstones-8
Cornerstones Gold-8
Emblems-24
Emblems Gold-24
First Round Picks-14
First Round Picks Gold-14
Jerseys Autos-8
Jerseys Autos Gold-8
Journey Emblem-17
Journey Emblem Gold-17
Journey Jersey-17
Journey Jersey Gold-17
Raised to the Rafters-5
Raised to the Rafters Gold-5
Retro Teammates-16
Retro Teammates Gold-16
Retrospective-3
Retrospective Gold-3
Ring Leaders-17
Ring Leaders Gold-17
Road to the Cup-7
Road to the Cup-8
Road to the Cup Gold-7
Road to the Cup Gold-8
Sensational Season-6
Sensational Season Gold-6
Stick Rack-27
Stick Rack Gold-27
Sticks Autos-14
Sticks Autos Gold-14

Coffin, Brodie

93London Knights-7
98Huntington Blizzard-13
99Columbus Cottonmouths-26
00Fresno Falcons-4
01Fresno Falcons-2

Coghill, Trent

89Saskatoon Blades-16
90Saskatoon Blades-15
907th Inn. Sketch WHL-81

Coghlan, Ryan

04Penticton Vees-8

Cogliano, Andrew

07ITG Going For Gold World Juniors-11
Autographs-11
Emblems-GUE11
Jerseys-GUJ11
Numbers-GUN11

Cohagen, Perry

92Harvard Crimson-5

Cohen, Colby

06Lincoln Stars-17
06Lincoln Stars Traded-17T
06Lincoln Stars Upper DeckÂ Signature Series -9

Cohen, Dan

00Sioux City Musketeers-4

Cohen, David

93Quebec Pee-Wee Tournament-748

Cohen, Paul

90ProCards AHL/IHL-505
91Nashville Knights-17
98German DEL-56

Cohen, Philip

93Quebec Pee-Wee Tournament-1663

Cohen, Sandy

00Florida Everblades-5
00Trenton Titans-2

Colagiacomo, Adam

92Quebec Pee-Wee Tournament-497
93Quebec Pee-Wee Tournament-1408
95Slapshot-170
95Slapshot-NNO
95Classic-88
96Black Diamond-24
Gold-24
96Upper Deck-369
96All-Sport PPF *-74
96All Sport PPF Gold *-74
97Bowman CHL-145
OPC-145
Autographs-25
Bowman's Best-12
Bowman's Best Atomic Refractors-12
Bowman's Best Refractor-12
97Autographed Collection *-49
Autographs-10
Autographs Gold-10
99Kentucky Thoroughblades-6
99Bowman CHL-143
Gold-143
OPC International-143
00Kentucky Thoroughblades-6
01Cleveland Barons-4
02Roanoke Express-11

Colaiacovo, Carlo

00UD CHL Prospects-4
01BAP Memorabilia Draft Redemptions-17
01SPx Rookie Redemption-R28
01UD Prospects-26
02BAP All-Star Edition-137
Gold-137
Silver-137
02BAP First Edition-438H
02BAP Memorabilia-289
Emerald-289
Ruby-289
Sapphire-289
NHL All-Star Game-289
NHL All-Star Game Blue-289
NHL All-Star Game Green-289
NHL All-Star Game Red-289
02BAP Memorabilia Toronto Fall Expo-289
02BAP Signature Series-179
Autographs-179
Autographs Gold-179
Golf-GS18
Jerseys-SGJ67
Jersey Autographs-SGJ67
02BAP Ultimate Memorabilia-28
Autographs-4
Autographs Gold-4
02Crown Royale-138
Blue-138
Purple-138
Red-138
Retail-138
02ITG Used-98
02Maple Leafs Platinum Collection-24
02Pacific Calder-147
Silver-147
02Pacific Complete-575
Red-575
02Pacific Quest for the Cup-148
Gold-148
02Parkhurst-242
Bronze-242
Gold-242
Silver-242
02Parkhurst Retro-228
Minis-228
02Private Stock Reserve-183
Blue-183
Red-183
Retail-183
02SP Authentic-163
02SP Game Used-94
02SPx-189
02Titanium-138
Blue-138
Red-138
Retail-138
02Topps Total-440
02UD Artistic Impressions-130
Gold-130
Common Ground-CG18
Common Ground Gold-CG18
02UD Honor Roll-128
02UD Mask Collection-150
02UD Premier Collection-69
Gold-69
02UD Top Shelf-102
02Upper Deck-454
Exclusives-454
02Upper Deck Classic Portraits-129
02Upper Deck Rookie Update-117
02Vanguard-135
LTD-135
03BAP Memorabilia Future of the Game-FG-15
03ITG Action-547
Jerseys-M14
03Pacific Toronto Spring Expo-8
Gold-8
03Parkhurst Original Six Toronto-13
Memorabilia-TM11
03Upper Deck All-Star Promos-AS9
03Upper Deck MVP-403
Gold Script-403
Silver Script-403
Canadian Exclusives-403
03Upper Deck Victory-184
Bronze-184
Gold-184
Silver-184
03AHL Top Prospects-7
03Pacific AHL Prospect Destined Greatness-9
03Toronto Star-88
04AHL Top Prospects-53
04ITG Heroes and Prospects-5
Autographs-CC
Combos-14
Emblems-26
Emblems Gold-26
He Shoots-He Scores Prizes-29
Jersey Autographs-26
Jerseys-26
Jerseys Gold-26
Numbers-26
Numbers Gold-26
04ITG Heroes/Prospects Toronto Expo '05-5
04ITG Heroes/Prospects Expo Heroes/Pros-5
05ITG Heroes/Prosp Toronto Expo Parallel -108
05Be A Player Signatures-CC
05Be A Player Signatures Gold-CC
05Hot Prospects Hot Materials-HMCA
05Parkhurst True Colors-TCTOR
05Parkhurst True Colors-TCTOR
05SP Authentic Scripts to Success-SSCC
05SP Authentic Sign of the Times-CC
05UD Rookie Class-49
05Upper Deck Notable Numbers-N-CCO
05ITG Heroes and Prospects-108
Autographs-A-CCO
He Shoots-He Scores Prizes-38
Jerseys-GUJ-93
Jerseys Gold-GUJ-93
Nameplates-N-57
Nameplates Gold-N-57

06Flair Showcase Stitches-SSCA
06O-Pee-Chee-467
06O-Pee-Chee-640
Rainbow-467
Rainbow-640
06Ultra Uniformity-UCC
06Ultra Uniformity Patches-UPCC
06Toronto Marlies-5
Colaiacovo, Paulo
00Belleville Bulls-2
01Belleville Bulls-6
02Barrie Colts-19
03Barrie Colts-16
04Barrie Colts 10th Anniversary-23
04Colorado Eagles-3
04ITG Heroes and Prospects-97
Autographs-PC
04ITG Heroes/Prospects Toronto Expo '05-97
04ITG Heroes/Prospects Expo Heroes/Pros-97
05Colorado Eagles-5
06Colorado EaglesA -7
Colangelo, Robbie
01London Knights-19
Colarullo, Curt
93Quebec Pee-Wee Tournament-745
Colasanto, Tom
96Dayton Ice Bandits-8
Colbert, Will
02Ottawa 67's-4
03Ottawa 67's-8
04Ottawa 67's-13
Colborne, Brett
91Air Canada SJHL-E35
92Saskatchewan JHL-105
00Asheville Smoke-20
Colborne, Howie
75Roanoke Valley Rebels-10
Colbourne, Darren
92Dayton Bombers-4
93Richmond Renegades-19
94German First League-428
94Classic Pro Prospects-243
Coldwell, Daryl
81Victoria Cougars-5
Cole, Alaine
907th Inn. Sketch QMJHL-190
Cole, Bob
97Pinnacle Hockey Night in Canada-3
04UD Legends Classics-5
Gold-5
Platinum-5
Silver-5
Signature Moments-M70
Signatures-CS54
Signatures-DC19
04Ultimate Collection-54
05UD Artifacts Auto Facts-AF-CO
05UD Artifacts Auto Facts Blue-AF-CO
05UD Artifacts Auto Facts Copper-AF-CO
05UD Artifacts Auto Facts Pewter-AF-CO
05UD Artifacts Auto Facts Silver-AF-CO
Cole, Brad
03Kootenay Ice-7
04Kootenay Ice-5
05Saskatoon Blades-5
06Saskatoon Blades-3
Cole, Danton
89ProCards AHL-30
90Jets IGA-6
90OPC Premier-17
90Upper Deck-517
French-517
91Bowman-202
91Jets Panini Team Stickers-5
91Jets IGA-5
91O-Pee-Chee-27
91Panini Stickers-72
91Pro Set-263
French-263
91Score Canadian Bilingual-240
91Score Canadian English-240
91Stadium Club-342
91Topps-27
91Upper Deck-210
French-210
92Lightning Sheraton-10
92Panini Stickers-56
92Panini Stickers French-56
92Parkhurst-408
Emerald Ice-408
93Donruss-491
93Lightning Season in Review-8
93Parkhurst-464
Emerald Ice-464
93PowerPlay-441
93Score-655
Gold-655
Canadian-655
Canadian Gold-655
93Stadium Club-239
Members Only Master Set-239
OPC-239
First Day Issue-239
First Day Issue OPC-239
94Canada Games NHL POGS-222
94Donruss-172
94Leaf-259
94OPC Premier-11
Special Effects-11
94Parkhurst SE-SE169
Gold-SE169
94Pinnacle-45
Artist's Proofs-45
Rink Collection-45
94Score-131
Gold-131
Platinum-131
94Topps/OPC Premier-11
Special Effects-11
94Ultra-204
94Upper Deck-126
Electric Ice-126
96German DEL-88
96Grand Rapids Griffins-3
97Grand Rapids Griffins-4
98Grand Rapids Griffins-6
99Grand Rapids Griffins-4
00Grand Rapids Griffins-24
02Grand Rapids Griffins-10
03Grand Rapids Griffins-22
Cole, Erik
00SPx Rookie Redemption-RR6
00Cincinnati Cyclones-12
01Atomic-106
Premiere Date-106
01Atomic Toronto Fall Expo-106
01BAP Memorabilia-302
Emerald-302
Ruby-302
Sapphire-302
01BAP Signature Series-229
Autographs-229
Autographs Gold-229
01Bowman YoungStars-156
Gold-156
Ice Cubed-156
01Crown Royale-150
Rookie Royalty-3
01O-Pee-Chee-348
01Pacific Adrenaline-205
Blue-205
Premiere Date-205
Red-205
Retail-205
Rookie Report-4
01Pacific Heads-Up-104
01Pacific High Voltage-3
01Parkhurst-308
01Private Stock-117
Gold-117
Premiere Date-117
Retail-117
Silver-117
01Private Stock Pacific Nights-117
01Private Stock PS-2002-78
01SP Authentic-139
Limited-139
Limited Gold-139
01SP Game Used-69
01SPx-99
01Stadium Club-137
Award Winners-137
Master Photos-137
01Titanium-152
Retail-152
Double-Sided Jerseys-46
Double-Sided Jerseys-62
Double-Sided Patches-46
Double-Sided Patches-62
Rookie Team-3
Three-Star Selections-23
01Titanium Draft Day Edition-18
01Titanium Draft Day Edition-113
01Topps-348
01Topps Chrome-166
Refractors-166
Black Border Refractors-166
01Topps Heritage-154
01Topps Reserve-104
01UD Challenge for the Cup-100
01UD Mask Collection-138
Gold-138
01UD Playmakers-109
01UD Premier Collection-91
01UD Top Shelf-124
01Upper Deck-419
Exclusives-419
01Upper Deck Ice-48
01Upper Deck MVP-222
01Upper Deck Victory-442
01Vanguard-106
Blue-106
Red-106
One of Ones-106
Premiere Date-106
Proofs-106
02Atomic-15
Blue-15
Gold-15
Red-15
Hobby Parallel-15
Super Colliders-4
02BAP First Edition-183
02BAP Memorabilia-73
Emerald-73
Ruby-73
Sapphire-73
NHL All-Star Game-73
NHL All-Star Game Blue-73
NHL All-Star Game Green-73
NHL All-Star Game Red-73
02BAP Memorabilia Toronto Fall Expo-73
02BAP Signature Series-175
Autographs-175
Autographs Gold-175
Golf-GS37
02Bowman YoungStars-113
Gold-113
Silver-113
02Crown Royale Dual Patches-3
02eTopps-17
02Hurricanes Postcards-2
02ITG Used-32
02ITG Used-132
02O-Pee-Chee-60
02O-Pee-Chee Premier Blue Parallel-60
02O-Pee-Chee Premier Red Parallel-60
02O-Pee-Chee Factory Set-60
02Pacific-64
Blue-64
Red-64
Shining Moments-3
02Pacific Calder Collection AS Fantasy-3
02Pacific Complete-5
Red-5
02Pacific Entry Draft-2
02Pacific Exclusive-27
Great Expectations-4
02Pacific Heads-Up-19
Blue-19
Purple-19
Red-19
Postseason Picks-1
Quad Jerseys-35
Quad Jerseys Gold-35
02Parkhurst-52
Bronze-52
Gold-52
Silver-52
College Ranks-CR2
College Ranks Jerseys-CRM2
02Parkhurst Retro-179
Minis-179
02Private Stock Reserve-16
Blue-16
Red-16
Retail-16
02SP Authentic Sign of the Times-EC
02SP Game Used Signature Style-EC
02Stadium Club-99
Silver Decoy Cards-99
Proofs-99
Lone Star Signatures Blue-LSEC
Lone Star Signatures Red-LSEC
02Topps-60
OPC Blue Parallel-60
OPC Red Parallel-60
Own The Game-OTG14
Factory Set-60
02Topps Chrome-42
Black Border Refractors-42
Refractors-42
Chromographs-CGEC
Chromograph Refractors-CGEC
02Topps Heritage-23
Chrome Parallel-23
Autographs-EC
Autographs Black-EC
Autographs Red-EC
02Topps Total-383
Signatures-EC
02UD Piece of History-12
02UD Premier Collection Signatures Bronze-SEC
02UD Premier Collection Signatures Gold-SEC
02UD Premier Collection Signatures Silver-SEC
02Upper Deck-33
Exclusives-33
02Upper Deck MVP-34
Gold-34
Classics-34
Golden Classics-34
02Upper Deck Rookie Update Autographs-EC
02Upper Deck Victory-40
Bronze-40
Gold-40
Silver-40
02Upper Deck Vintage-50
02Upper Deck Vintage-266
Green Backs-50
02UD SuperStars *-257
Gold-257
03BAP Ultimate Memorabilia Autographs-14
Gold-14
03Beehive-35
Variations-35
Gold-35
Silver-35
03Black Diamond-170
Black-170
Green-170
Red-170
Signature Gems-SG-5
03Crown Royale-16
Blue-16
Retail-16
03Hurricanes Postcards-8
03ITG Action-175
Jerseys-M98
03ITG Used Signature Series-25
Gold-25
Autographs-EC
Autographs Gold-EC
03NHL Sticker Collection-34
03O-Pee-Chee-182
03OPC Blue-182
03OPC Gold-182
03OPC Red-182
03Pacific-60
Blue-60
Red-60
03Pacific Calder-16
Silver-16
03Pacific Complete-256
Red-256
03Pacific Exhibit-27
Blue Backs-27
Yellow Backs-27
03Pacific Quest for the Cup-17
Blue-17
03Private Stock Reserve-151
Blue-151
Red-151
Retail-151
03Titanium-19
Hobby Jersey Number Parallels-19
Retail-19
Retail Jersey Number Parallels-19
03Topps-182
Blue-182
Gold-182
Red-182
Topps/OPC Idols-UI19
C55 Autographs-TA-EC
03Upper Deck-37
Canadian Exclusives-37
HG-37
03Upper Deck MVP-82
Gold Script-82
Silver Script-82
Canadian Exclusives-82
ProSign-PS-EC
03Upper Deck Trilogy Scripts-S2EC
03Upper Deck Trilogy Scripts Limited-S2EC
03Upper Deck Victory-35
Bronze-35
Gold-35
Silver-35
04Pacific-47
Blue-47
Red-47
04SP Authentic-18
Limited-18
Sign of the Times-ST-EC
04UD All-World-20
Gold-20
Autographs-20
04Upper Deck-34
Canadian Exclusives-34
HG Glossy Gold-34
HG Glossy Silver-34
04German Berlin Polar Bears Postcards-5
04German DEL Superstars-SU05
05Be A Player-15
First Period-15
Second Period-15
Third Period-15
Overtime-15
Signatures-EC
Signatures Gold-EC
05Beehive-17
Matte-17
05Black Diamond-17
Emerald-17
Gold-17
Onyx-17
Ruby-17
Gemography-G-EC
Gemography Emerald-G-EC
Gemography Gold-G-EC
Gemography Onyx-G-EC
Gemography Ruby-G-EC
05Hot Prospects-20
En Fuego-20
Red Hot-20
White Hot-20
05Panini Stickers-45
05Parkhurst-86
Facsimile Auto Parallel-86
05SP Authentic Sign of the Times Duals-DCS
05SP Game Used-18
Autographs-18
Gold-18
Auto Draft-AD-EC
SIGnificance-EC
SIGnificance Gold-S-EC
05SPx-15
Spectrum-15
05UD Artifacts-20
Blue-20
Gold-20
Green-20
Pewter-20
Red-20
Auto Facts-AF-EC
Auto Facts Blue-AF-EC
Auto Facts Copper-AF-EC
Auto Facts Pewter-AF-EC
Auto Facts Silver-AF-EC
Gold Autographed-20
05Ultimate Collection Ultimate Signatures-USEC
05Ultimate Coll Ultimate Sigs Pairings-UPSC
05Ultra-41
Gold-41
Ice-41
05Upper Deck-31
HG Glossy-31
Notable Numbers-N-EC
05Upper Deck Ice-18
Rainbow-18
05Upper Deck MVP-71
Gold-71
Platinum-71
ProSign-P-EC
05Upper Deck Rookie Update-19
05Upper Deck Trilogy-19
05Upper Deck Toronto Fall Expo-31
05Upper Deck Victory-36
Black-36
Gold-36
Silver-36
06Be A Player-141
Autographs-141
Signatures-EC
Signatures 10-156
Signatures Trios-TSBC
06Be A Player Portraits-21
06Black Diamond-93
Black-93
Gold-93
Ruby-93
06Flair Showcase-22
06Flair Showcase-114
Parallel-22
Parallel-114
06Fleer-41
Tiffany-41
Speed Machines-SM5
06Hurricanes Postcards-7
06O-Pee-Chee-90
Rainbow-90
06Panini Stickers-42
06SP Game Used-19
Gold-19
Rainbow-19
Autographs-19
Letter Marks-LMEC
SIGnificance-SEC
06The Cup Autographed NHL Shields Duals-DASSC
06UD Mini Jersey Collection-19
06UD Powerplay-21
Impact Rainbow-21
06Ultra-39
Gold Medallion-39
Ice Medallion-39
06Upper Deck Arena Giveaways-CAR4
06Upper Deck-287
Exclusives Parallel-287
High Gloss Parallel-287
Game Jerseys-J2EC
Game Patches-P2EC
Masterpieces-287
Signatures-SEC
06Upper Deck MVP-53
Gold Script-53
Super Script-53
Autographs-OACL
06Upper Deck Ovation-9
06Upper Deck Trilogy Combo Clearcut Autographs-C3CGS
06Upper Deck Victory-39
06Upper Deck Victory Black-39
06Upper Deck Victory Gold-39
06Upper Deck Victory Next In Line-NL49
07Upper Deck Ovation-41
07Upper Deck Victory-81
Black-81
Gold-81
Cole, Jeff
91Air Canada SJHL-C36
91Air Canada SJHL All-Stars-5
Cole, Lee
95Slapshot-373
95Sault Ste. Marie Greyhounds-4
97Toledo Storm-17
98Port Huron Border Cats-8
00Missouri River Otters-15
Cole, Mark
03Fort Wayne Komets-15
04Huntsville Havoc-14
Cole, Mike
92British Columbia JHL-217
Cole, Patrick
907th Inn. Sketch QMJHL-252
Cole, Phil
99Lethbridge Hurricanes-6
00Lethbridge Hurricanes-4
02Columbus Cottonmouths-2
03ECHL Update RBI Sports-62
Cole, Sharon
04Wisconsin Badgers Women-3
Cole, Tom
92Nashville Knights-4
Coleman, Gerald
02London Knights-21
03London Knights-20
04London Knights-12
04ITG Heroes and Prospects-230
04ITG Heroes/Prospects Toronto Expo '05-230
05ITG Heroes/Prosp Toronto Expo Parallel -266
05Beehive-160
Matte-160
05Black Diamond-286
05Hot Prospects-170
En Fuego-170
Red Hot-170
White Hot-170
05SP Authentic-239
Limited-239
05SPx-284
05The Cup Masterpiece Pressplate Artifact-328
05The Cup Masterpiece Pressplate Bee Hive-160
05The Cup Master Pressplate Black Diamond-286
05The Cup Masterpiece Pressplates (Ice)-209
05The Cup Master Pressplate Rookie Update-181
05The Cup Masterpiece Pressplates SPA-239
05The Cup Masterpiece Pressplates (SPx)-284
05The Cup Masterpiece Pressplates Trilogy-305
05The Cup Masterpiece Pressplate Ult Coll-228
05UD Artifacts-328
05Ultimate Collection-228
Gold-228
05Upper Deck-480
05Upper Deck Ice-209
05Upper Deck Rookie Update-181
05Upper Deck Trilogy-305
05Springfield Falcons-9
05ITG Heroes and Prospects-266
Autographs Series II-GCL
Complete Jerseys-CJ-35
Complete Jerseys Gold-CJ-35
Complete Logos-CHL-23
Jerseys-GUJ-51
Jerseys-GUJ-72
Jerseys Gold-GUJ-51
Jerseys Gold-GUJ-72
Emblems-GUE-51
Emblems-GUE-72
Emblems Gold-GUE-51
Emblems Gold-GUE-72
Numbers-GUN-51
Numbers-GUN-72
Numbers Gold-GUN-51
Numbers Gold-GUN-72
Making the Bigs-MTB-16
Measuring Up-MU13
Measuring Up Gold-MU13
Memorial Cup-MC-8
Nameplates-N-64
Nameplates Gold-N-64
Net Prospects-NP-20
Net Prospects Dual-NPD4
Net Prospects Dual Gold-NPD4
Net Prospects Gold-NP-20
06Between The Pipes-15
Prospect Trios-PT17
Prospect Trios Gold-PT17
Coleman, Jon
93Donruss Team USA-4
93Pinnacle-481
Canadian-481
93Upper Deck-563
99Kentucky Thoroughblades-7
00Providence Bruins-19
03Worcester Ice Cats-5
04German Cologne Sharks Postcards-7
04German DEL Update-322A
Coleman, Russell
02UK Peterborough Phantoms-10
Coleman, Tyler
93Quebec Pee-Wee Tournament-903
00Sarnia Sting-8
Coles, Bruce
91Johnstown Chiefs-6
94Johnstown Chiefs-5
Coles, Jason
907th Inn. Sketch OHL-257
917th Inn. Sketch OHL-209
98UK Kingston Hawks-20
Coles, Travis
04Chicoutimi Sagueneens-23
Colinar, Ales
93Quebec Pee-Wee Tournament-1734
Collard, Geoff
94Dubuque Fighting Saints-7
Collenberg, Franco
04Swiss Davos Postcards-8
Collett, Ernie
24V-122-45
25Dominion Chocolates-55
Colley, Kevin
98Bowman CHL-37
Golden Anniversary-37
OPC International-37
98Bowman Chrome CHL-37
Golden Anniversary-37
Golden Anniversary Refractors-37
OPC International-37
OPC International Refractors-37
Refractors-37
99Bowman CHL-124
Gold-124
OPC International-124
01Atlantic City Boardwalk Bullies-6
02Atlantic City Boardwalk Bullies-4
02ECHL All-Star Northern-19
03Bridgeport Sound Tigers-2B
05Hot Prospects-151
En Fuego-151
Red Hot-151
White Hot-151
05SP Authentic-232
Limited-232
05SPx-213
Spectrum-213
05The Cup Masterpiece Pressplates (Ice)-202
05The Cup Master Pressplate Rookie Update-158
05The Cup Masterpiece Pressplates SPA-232
05The Cup Masterpiece Pressplates (SPx)-213
05The Cup Masterpiece Pressplate Ult Coll-156
05Ultimate Collection-156
Gold-156
05Upper Deck Ice-202
05Upper Deck Rookie Update-158
Colley, Tom
89New Haven Nighthawks-3
Collin, Christer
71Swedish Hockey-384
72Swedish Stickers-258
Collin, Curtis
82Kingston Canadians-3
83North Bay Centennials-6
Collin, Eryc
96Rimouski Oceanic-8
96Rimouski Oceanic Quebec Police-8
Collin, Mikael
71Swedish Hockey-221
72Swedish Stickers-211
73Swedish Stickers-60
74Swedish Stickers-139
Colling, Kurtis
04Vernon Vipers-23
Collins, Adam
93Quebec Pee-Wee Tournament-544
97Owen Sound Platers-23
Collins, Bill
68Shirriff Coins-68
69Canadiens Postcards Color-6
69O-Pee-Chee-126
70Esso Power Players-7
70Sargent Promotions Stamps-104
71O-Pee-Chee-139
71Sargent Promotions Stamps-49
71Toronto Sun-88
72O-Pee-Chee-265
72Sargent Promotions Stamps-71
73O-Pee-Chee-163
73Red Wings Team Issue-6
73Red Wings McCarthy Postcards-5
73Topps-158
74NHL Action Stamps-250
74O-Pee-Chee NHL-364
81Red Wings Oldtimers-10
05Muskegon Fury-3
Collins, Bill (UHL)
05Muskegon Fury-3
Collins, Brian
03Pensacola Ice Pilots-339
06Bakersfield Condors-3
Collins, Chad
06Fayetteville FireAntz-2
Collins, Chris
06Providence Bruins-2
Collins, Clint
98Huntsville Channel Cats-16
01El Paso Buzzards-3
Collins, Cody
04Penticton Vees-14
Collins, Dan
03Plymouth Whalers-2
05Plymouth Whalers-A-14
06Plymouth Whalers-5
Collins, Delaney
04Canadian Womens World Championship Team-7
06ITG Going For Gold-22
06ITG Going For Gold Samples-22
06ITG Going For Gold Autographs-ACO
06ITG Going For Gold Jerseys-GUJ22
Collins, Dusty
04Northern Michigan Wildcats-3
Collins, Garth
03Prince Albert Raiders-10
04Prince Albert Raiders-22
Collins, Gary
52Juniors Blue Tint-121
57Parkhurst-T23
Collins, Ian
93Lakeland Ice Warriors-6
93Lakeland Ice Warriors-7
Collins, Jejuan
93Quebec Pee-Wee Tournament-1316
Collins, Ken
95German DEL-7
Collins, Kenneth
52Juniors Blue Tint-115
Collins, Kevin
72Johnstown Jets-5
90Pro Set-683
Collins, Kim
83Pinebridge Bucks-3
94German First League-169
02Swiss HNL-451
Collins, Matt
99Cornwall Colts-3
Collins, Maurice
52Juniors Blue Tint-65
Collins, Mike
99San Angelo Outlaws-26
Collins, Rob
02Grand Rapids Griffins-11
03Bridgeport Sound Tigers-3B
06Fleer-223
Tiffany-223
06O-Pee-Chee-511
Rainbow-511
06SPx-196
Spectrum-196
06The Cup Masterpiece Pressplates (Artifacts)-210
06The Cup Masterpiece Pressplates (Marquee Rookies)-511
06The Cup Masterpiece Pressplates (MVP)-351
06The Cup Masterpiece Pressplates (Power Play)-118
06The Cup Masterpiece Pressplates (Trilogy)-129
06The Cup Masterpiece Pressplates (Victory)-207
06UD Artifacts-210
Blue-210
Gold-210
Platinum-210
Radiance-210
Red-210
06UD Powerplay-118
Impact Rainbow-118
06Ultra-213
Gold Medallion-213
Ice Medallion-213
06Upper Deck MVP-351
Gold Script-351
Super Script-351
06Upper Deck Trilogy-129
06Upper Deck Victory-207
06Upper Deck Victory Black-207
06Upper Deck Victory Gold-207
06German DEL-41
Collins, Sean
97Quebec Pee-Wee Tournament-1234
03Ohio State Buckeyes-17
04Ohio State Buckeyes-7
05Ohio State Buckeyes-6
06Ohio State Buckeyes-6
Collins, Shawn
93Portland Winter Hawks-5
Colliton, Jeremy
01Prince Albert Raiders-3
02Prince Albert Raiders-5
03Prince Albert Raiders-12
04Prince Albert Raiders-17
04ITG Heroes and Prospects-211
04ITG Heroes/Prospects Toronto Expo '05-211
05ITG Heroes/Prosp Toronto Expo Parallel -238
05Beehive-157
Matte-157
05Black Diamond-261
05Hot Prospects-250
En Fuego-250
Hot Materials-HMCO
Red Hot-250
White Hot-250
05Parkhurst-644
Facsimile Auto Parallel-644
True Colors-TCNYI
True Colors-TCNYI
05SP Authentic-203
05SP Game Used-224
05SPx-236
Spectrum-236
05The Cup-166
Autographed Rookie Patches Gold Rainbow-166
Black Rainbow Rookies-166
Masterpiece Pressplates (Artifacts)-299
Masterpiece Pressplates (Bee Hive)-157
Masterpiece Pressplates (Black Diamond)-261
Masterpiece Pressplates (Ice)-203
Masterpiece Pressplates (Rookie Update)-247
Masterpiece Pressplates (SP Game Used)-224
Masterpiece Pressplates SPA Autos-203
Masterpiece Pressplates SPx Autos-236
Masterpiece Pressplates (Trilogy)-280
Masterpiece Pressplates Ult Coll-158
Masterpiece Pressplates Autographs-166
Platinum Rookies-166
05UD Artifacts-299
05Ultimate Collection-158
Gold-158
05Upper Deck-481
05Upper Deck Ice-203
05Upper Deck Rookie Update-247
05Upper Deck Trilogy-280
05AHL Top Prospects-7
05ITG Heroes and Prospects-238
Autographs Series II-JCO
06Upper Deck MVP Autographs-OASC
06ITG Heroes and Prospects-67
Autographs-AJC
Jerseys-GUJ19
Jerseys Gold-GUJ19
Emblems-GUE19
Emblems Gold-GUE19
Numbers-GUN19
Numbers Gold-GUN19
Collyard, Bob
74NHL Action Stamps-319
79Panini Stickers-216
81Milwaukee Admirals-14
Collymore, Shawn `
99Quebec Remparts-23
Signed-23
00Quebec Remparts-20
Signed-20
01Quebec Remparts-20
01UD Prospects-20
Jerseys-J-SC
Jerseys Gold-J-SC
02Quebec Remparts-17
02Val d'Or Foreurs-17
03Val d'Or Foreurs-16
05Danbury Trashers-23
06Reading Royals-7
Colman, Mike
90Kansas City Blades-14
90ProCards AHL/IHL-599
91Kansas City Blades-11
91ProCards-510
92Kansas City Blades-18
93Kansas City Blades-16
Colombi, Carlo
917th Inn. Sketch QMJHL-4
Colon, Charlie
99UK Basingstoke Bison-8
Colsant, Louie
99Ohio State Buckeyes-3
Columbus, Jeff
87Sault Ste. Marie Greyhounds-24
Colville, Mac
34Beehive Group I Photos-265
37V356 Worldwide Gum-89
39O-Pee-Chee V301-1-90
06ITG Ultimate Memorabilia Broadway Blue Shirts Autos-8
Colville, Neil
34Beehive Group I Photos-266
36O-Pee-Chee V304D-105
37V356 Worldwide Gum-91
39O-Pee-Chee V301-1-39
83Hall of Fame-5
83Hall of Fame Postcards-A4
85Hall of Fame-5
02BAP Ultimate Mem Paper Cuts Autos-23
04ITG Ultimate Memorabilia-21
Gold-21
05ITG Ultimate Mem Broadway Bluesh Autos-12
06ITG Ultimate Memorabilia Broadway Blue Shirts Autos-9
Colvin, John
89Spokane Chiefs-2
Colwill, Les
58Topps-19
Colwill, Richard
00Owen Sound Attack-4
01Owen Sound Attack-2
Combe, Philippe
92Quebec Pee-Wee Tournament-1186
93Quebec Pee-Wee Tournament-1491
Combs, Jack
04Kitchener Rangers-11
05Saginaw Spirit-4
06Saginaw Spirit-16
Comeau, Blake
02Kelowna Rockets-15
03Kelowna Rockets Memorial Cup-3
03Kelowna Rockets-4
04Kelowna Rockets-15
05ITG Heroes/Prosp Toronto Expo Parallel -330
05Kelowna Rockets-6
05ITG Heroes and Prospects-330
Autographs Series II-BCO
Complete Logos-CHL-18
He Shoots-He Scores Prizes-17
Jerseys-GUJ-48
Jerseys Gold-GUJ-48
Emblems-GUE-48
Emblems Gold-GUE-48
Numbers-GUN-48
Numbers Gold-GUN-48
Nameplates-N-69
Nameplates Gold-N-69
Oh Canada-OC-9
Oh Canada Gold-OC-9
06Be A Player-206
06Beehive-135
Matte-135
06Hot Prospects-191
06SP Authentic-228
Limited-228
06The Cup Masterpiece Pressplates (Bee Hive)-135
06The Cup Masterpiece Pressplates (SP Authentic)-228
06The Cup Masterpiece Pressplates (Ultimate Collection)-83
06UD Artifacts-249
06Ultimate Collection-83
06AHL Top Prospects-7
06ITG Heroes and Prospects-168
Autographs-ABCM
National Pride-NP17
National Pride Gold-NP17
Update Autographs-ABCM
Comeau, David
93Quebec Pee-Wee Tournament-1047
Comeau, Marcel
76Saginaw Gears-2
78Saginaw Gears-2
88Saskatoon Blades-3
90ProCards AHL/IHL-440
917th Inn. Sketch WHL-148
92Tacoma Rockets-6
93Tacoma Rockets-5
Comeau, Rey
72Flames Postcards-3
72O-Pee-Chee-239
73O-Pee-Chee-29
73Topps-29
74NHL Action Stamps-3
74O-Pee-Chee NHL-296
75O-Pee-Chee NHL-248
75Topps-248
76O-Pee-Chee NHL-343
77O-Pee-Chee NHL-346
78O-Pee-Chee-293
79O-Pee-Chee-385
Comfort, Fred
23V128-1 Paulin's Candy-8
24Crescent Selkirks-9
Cominetti, Glendon
01BC Icemen-7
02Kalamazoo Wings-12
Comley, Rick
92Northern Michigan Wildcats-28
93Northern Michigan Wildcats-32
Commodore, Mike
00Devils Team Issue-4
00SP Authentic-151
00SPx-181
00Titanium Draft Day Edition-165
00Titanium Draft Day Promos-165
00Albany River Rats-6
01BAP Memorabilia-240
Emerald-240
Ruby-240
Sapphire-240
01O-Pee-Chee-300
01O-Pee-Chee Premier Parallel-300
01Topps-300
OPC Parallel-300
01Albany River Rats-4
02Cincinnati Mighty Ducks-A-1
03BAP Memorabilia-207
03Lowell Lock Monsters-16
03Lowell Lock Monsters Photo Album-1
04Lowell Lock Monsters-2
04Lowell Lock Monsters Photo Album-2
06Black Diamond-17
Black-17
Gold-17
Ruby-17
06Fleer-40
Tiffany-40
06Hurricanes Postcards-8
06O-Pee-Chee-96
Rainbow-96
06Ultra-40
Gold Medallion-40
Ice Medallion-40
06Upper Deck-39
Exclusives Parallel-39
High Gloss Parallel-39
Game Jerseys-J2MC
Game Patches-P2MC
Masterpieces-39
06Upper Deck MVP-54
Gold Script-54
Super Script-54
06Upper Deck Ovation-40
Compeau, Todd
00Roanoke Express-10
Comploi, Giorgio
92Finnish Semic-252
93Swedish Semic World Champ Stickers-216
94Finnish Jaa Kiekko-296
94Italian Milano-3
95Swedish World Championships Stickers-79
Comrie, Dan
03Lincoln Stars-22
Comrie, Mike
93Quebec Pee-Wee Tournament-1152
00BAP Memorabilia-505
00Black Diamond-97
00SP Authentic-106
00SPx-161
00Titanium-117
Retail-117
00Titanium Draft Day Edition-117
00Titanium Draft Day Promos-117
00Topps Heritage-80
Chrome Parallel-80
00Upper Deck Ice-88
00UD CHL Prospects-70
CHL Class-CC8
Future Leaders-FL7
Great Desire-GD3
Supremacy-CS8
01Atomic-41
Blue-41
Gold-41
Premiere Date-41
Red-41
Blast-5
Power Play-15
Team Nucleus-7
01BAP Memorabilia-38
Emerald-38
Ruby-38
Sapphire-38
01BAP Signature Series-38
Autographs-38
Autographs Gold-38
01Bowman YoungStars-153
Gold-153
Ice Cubed-153
Autographs-MC
Relics-JMC
Relics-SMC
Relics-DSMC
Rivals-R6
01Crown Royale-60
Blue-60
Premiere Date-60
Red-60
Retail-60
01Crown Royale Toronto Expo Rookie Coll-G2
01eTopps-19
01McDonald's Pacific Future Legends-1
01McDonald's Pacific Hometown Pride-4
01O-Pee-Chee-293
01O-Pee-Chee Premier Parallel-293
01O-Pee-Chee Jumbos-8
01Pacific-156
Extreme LTD-156
Hobby LTD-156
Premiere Date-156

Retail LTD-156
01Pacific Adrenaline-74
Blue-74
Premiere Date-74
Red-74
Retail-74
Playmakers-5
01Pacific Arena Exclusives-156
01Pacific Heads-Up-40
Blue-40
Premiere Date-40
Red-40
Silver-40
Breaking the Glass-10
Prime Picks-1
01Parkhurst-100
Gold-100
Silver-100
01Private Stock-39
Gold-39
Premiere Date-39
Retail-39
Silver-39
01Private Stock Pacific Nights-39
01Private Stock PS-2002-31
01Private Stock Reserve-56
01SP Authentic-34
01SP Authentic-112
Limited-34
Limited-112
Limited Gold-34
Limited Gold-112
Buybacks-15
Buybacks-16
Sign of the Times-MC
Sign of the Times-CH
01SP Game Used-22
01SPx-28
Signs of Xcellence-MC
01Stadium Club-76
Award Winners-76
Master Photos-76
Gallery-G25
Gallery Gold-G25
01Titanium-56
Hobby Parallel-56
Premiere Date-56
Retail-56
Retail Parallel-56
Saturday Knights-8
01Titanium Draft Day Edition-39
01Topps-293
OPC Parallel-293
01Topps Chrome-145
Refractors-145
Black Border Refractors-145
01Topps Heritage-62
Refractors-62
01Topps Reserve-14
01UD Challenge for the Cup-32
01UD Mask Collection-36
Gold-36
01UD Playmakers-39
01UD Premier Collection Signatures-MC
01UD Premier Collection Signatures Black-MC
01UD Top Shelf-94
01Upper Deck-67
Exclusives-67
01Upper Deck Ice-19
Autographs-MC
01Upper Deck MVP-76
01Upper Deck Victory-370
Gold-370
01Upper Deck Vintage-98
01Upper Deck Vintage-105
01Vanguard-39
Blue-39
Red-39
One of Ones-39
Premiere Date-39
Prime Prospects-6
Proofs-39
02Atomic-42
Blue-42
Gold-42
Red-42
Cold Fusion-13
Hobby Parallel-42
02BAP All-Star Edition-105
Gold-105
Silver-105
02BAP First Edition-187
02BAP First Edition-352
02BAP Memorabilia-99
02BAP Memorabilia-212
Emerald-99
Emerald-212
Ruby-99
Ruby-212
Sapphire-99
Sapphire-212
Franchise Players-FP-12
Future of the Game-FG-7
NHL All-Star Game-99
NHL All-Star Game-212
NHL All-Star Game Blue-99
NHL All-Star Game Blue-212
NHL All-Star Game Green-99
NHL All-Star Game Green-212
NHL All-Star Game Red-99
NHL All-Star Game Red-212
02BAP Memorabilia Toronto Fall Expo-99
02BAP Memorabilia Toronto Fall Expo-212
02BAP Signature Series-3
Autographs-3
Autograph Buybacks 2001-38
Autographs Gold-3
Famous Scraps-FS7
Franchise Players-FJ12
Jerseys-SGJ46
Jersey Autographs-SGJ46
Team Quads-TQ17
02BAP Ultimate Memorabilia Emblems-16
02BAP Ultimate Memorabilia Numbers-27
02Bowman YoungStars-135
Gold-135
Silver-135
02Crown Royale-39
Blue-39
Red-39
Retail-39
Jerseys-6
Jerseys Gold-6
02eTopps-38
02ITG Used-31
02ITG Used-131
Franchise Players-F12
Franchise Players Autographs-F12
Franchise Players Gold-F12
Jerseys-GUJ46
Jersey Autographs-GUJ46
Jerseys Gold-GUJ46
Jersey and Stick-SJ46
Jersey and Stick Gold-SJ46
02McDonald's Pacific-15
Clear Advantage-4
Jersey Patches Silver-6
Jersey Patches Gold-6
02NHL Power Play Stickers-25
02Oilers Postcards-21
02O-Pee-Chee-22
02O-Pee-Chee Jumbos-9
02O-Pee-Chee Premier Blue Parallel-22
02O-Pee-Chee Premier Red Parallel-22
02O-Pee-Chee Factory Set-22
02O-Pee-Chee Factory Set Hometown Heroes-HHC13
02Pacific-141
Blue-141
Red-141
Main Attractions-8
02Pacific Calder-40
Silver-40
02Pacific Complete-302
Red-302
02Pacific Exclusive-70
Great Expectations-7
02Pacific Heads-Up-49
Blue-49
Purple-49
Red-49
Bobble Heads-3
Quad Jerseys-5
Quad Jerseys Gold-5
02Pacific Quest for the Cup-38
Gold-38
02Parkhurst-56
Bronze-56
Gold-56
Silver-56
Franchise Players-FP12
02Parkhurst Retro-67
Minis-67
Franchise Players-RF12
02Private Stock Reserve-122
Red-122
Retail-122
Patches-122
02SP Authentic-37
02SP Authentic-116
Beckett Promos-37
Sign of the Times-MC
Sign of the Times-CI
Sign of the Times-GC
Sign of the Times-HCI
02SP Game Used-20
Signature Style-MC
02SPx-32
02SPx-91
Spectrum Gold-32
Spectrum Gold-91
Spectrum Silver-32
Spectrum Silver-91
02Stadium Club-45
Silver Decoy Cards-45
Proofs-45
YoungStars Relics-S3
YoungStars Relics-DS5
02Titanium-42
Blue-42
Red-42
Retail-42
Jerseys-28
Jerseys Retail-28
Patches-28
02Topps-22
OPC Blue Parallel-22
OPC Red Parallel-22
Topps/OPC Hometown Heroes-HHC13
Signs of the Future-MC
Factory Set-22
02Topps Chrome-22
Black Border Refractors-22
Refractors-22
02Topps Heritage-62
Chrome Parallel-62
02Topps Total-315
02UD Artistic Impressions-37
Gold-37
02UD Artistic Impressions Beckett Promos-37
02UD Artistic Impressions Retrospectives-R37
02UD Artistic Impressions Retrospect Gold-R37
02UD Artistic Impress Retrospect Auto-R37
02UD Artistic Impress Retrospect Silver-R37
02UD Foundations-150
02UD Honor Roll-30
Students of the Game-SG15
02UD Mask Collection-36
02UD Mask Collection Beckett Promos-36
02UD Piece of History-38
Marks of Distinction-MC
02UD Premier Collection-25
Jerseys Bronze-MC
Jerseys Gold-MC
Jerseys Silver-MC
Patches-PMC
Signatures Bronze-SMC
Signatures Gold-SMC
Signatures Silver-SMC
02UD Top Shelf-35
Signatures-MC
02Upper Deck-69
Exclusives-69
Blow-Ups-C16
Shooting Stars-SS8
Sizzling Scorers-SS8
02Upper Deck Classic Portraits-39
Etched in Time-ET8
02Upper Deck MVP-72
Gold-72
Classics-72
Golden Classics-72
02Upper Deck Rookie Update-41
02Upper Deck Rookie Update-169
Autographs-MC
02Upper Deck Victory-81
Bronze-81
Gold-81
Silver-81
02Upper Deck Vintage-102
02Upper Deck Vintage-272
Tall Boys-T28
Tall Boys Gold-T28
02Vanguard-42
LTD-42
03BAP Memorabilia-55
Emerald-55
Gold-55
Ruby-55
Sapphire-55
Jersey and Stick-SJ-14
Jerseys-GJ-16
03Beehive Signatures-RF16
03Beehive Sticks Beige Border-BE16
03Black Diamond-40
Black-40
Green-40
Red-40
Signature Gems-SG-6
03Bowman-89
Gold-89
Future Rivals-CI
Future Rivals Patches-CI
03Bowman Chrome-89
Refractors-89
Gold Refractors-89
Xfractors-89
03Flyers Postcards-3
03ITG Action-256
Homeboys-HB4
Jerseys-M155
Jerseys-M252
03McDonald's Pacific-21
Patches Silver-12
Patches Gold-12
Patches and Sticks-12
Saturday Night Rivals-1
03NHL Sticker Collection-224
03O-Pee-Chee-164
03OPC Blue-164
03OPC Gold-164
03OPC Red-164
03Pacific-131
Blue-131
Red-131
03Pacific Calder-77
Silver-77
03Pacific Complete-10
Red-10
03Pacific Exhibit-57
Blue Backs-57
Yellow Backs-57
03Pacific Invincible-38
Blue-38
Red-38
Retail-38
03Pacific Luxury Suite-15A
03Pacific Luxury Suite-15B
03Pacific Luxury Suite-15C
03Pacific Luxury Suite-15D
03Pacific Prism-119
Blue-119
Patches-119
Red-119
Retail-119
Paramount Prodigies-9
03Pacific Supreme-37
Blue-37
Red-37
Retail-37
Jerseys-13
03Private Stock Reserve-167
Blue-167
Patches-167
Red-167
Retail-167
03SP Authentic Sign of the Times-MC
03SP Authentic Sign of the Times-CH
03SP Game Used-20
Gold-20
Authentic Fabrics-DFHC
Authentic Fabrics Gold-DFHC
Premium Patches-PPMC
Team Threads-TTHSC
03SPx-39
Radiance-39
Spectrum-39
Signature Threads-ST-MC
03Topps-164
Blue-164
Gold-164
Red-164
Box Toppers-17
03Topps C55-92
03Topps C55-92B
Minis-92
Minis American Back-92
Minis American Back Red-92
Minis Bazooka Back-92
Minis Brooklyn Back-92
Minis Hat Trick Back-92
Minis O Canada Back-92
Minis O Canada Back Red-92
Minis Stanley Cup Back-92
Relics-TRMC
03Topps Pristine-13
Gold Refractor Die Cuts-13
Refractors-13
Patches-PP-MC
Patch Refractors-PP-MC
Press Plates Black-13
Press Plates Cyan-13
Press Plates Magenta-13
Press Plates Yellow-13
03Topps Traded-TT75
Blue-TT75
Gold-TT75
Red-TT75
03UD Honor Roll-31
03UD Premier Collection-43
03Upper Deck-319
BuyBacks-69
BuyBacks-70
Canadian Exclusives-319
HG-319
Jerseys-GJ-MC
Jerseys-UD-MC
UD Exclusives-319
03Upper Deck Classic Portraits-36
03Upper Deck Ice-68
Gold-68
03Upper Deck MVP-163
Gold Script-163
Silver Script-163
Canadian Exclusives-163
ProSign-PS-MC
SportsNut-SN35
03Upper Deck Rookie Update-68
03Upper Deck Trilogy-36
Limited-36
Scripts-CSMC
03Upper Deck Victory-73
Bronze-73
Gold-73
Silver-73
Game Breakers-GB12
03Russian World Championship Stars-14
03Toronto Star-37
Foil-14
04Pacific-200
Blue-200
Red-200
04SP Authentic-69
04UD All-World-52
Gold-52
Autographs-52
04Upper Deck-133
Canadian Exclusives-133
HG Glossy Gold-133
HG Glossy Silver-133
Jersey Autographs-GJA-MC
05Be A Player-69
First Period-69
Second Period-69
Third Period-69
Overtime-69
Signatures-MI
Signatures Gold-MI
05Black Diamond-65
Emerald-65
Gold-65
Onyx-65
Ruby-65
Gemography-G-MC
Gemography Emerald-G-MC
Gemography Gold-G-MC
Gemography Onyx-G-MC
Gemography Ruby-G-MC
05Panini Stickers-321
05Parkhurst-370
Facsimile Auto Parallel-370
True Colors-TCPHX
True Colors-TCPHX
05UD Artifacts-78
Blue-78
Gold-78
Green-78
Pewter-78
Red-78
Gold Autographed-78
05UD Powerplay Power Marks-PMMC
05UD Powerplay Specialists-TSMC
05UD Powerplay Specialists Patches-SPMC
05Upper Deck-395
Jerseys-J-MCO
Jerseys Series II-J2CM
Notable Numbers-N-MC
05Upper Deck MVP-303
Gold-303
Platinum-303
05Upper Deck Victory-152
Black-152
Gold-152
Silver-152
06Black Diamond Jerseys-JCO
06Black Diamond Jerseys Black-JCO
06Black Diamond Jerseys Gold-JCO
06Black Diamond Jerseys Ruby-JCO
06Fleer-151
Tiffany-151
06O-Pee-Chee-378
Rainbow-378
06Panini Stickers-320
06Senators Postcards-1
06UD Artifacts Tundra Tandems-TTCN
06UD Artifacts Tundra Tandems Black-TTCN
06UD Artifacts Tundra Tandems Blue-TTCN
06UD Artifacts Tundra Tandems Gold-TTCN
06UD Artifacts Tundra Tandems Platinum-TTCN
06UD Artifacts Tundra Tandems Red-TTCN
06UD Artifacts Tundra Tandems Dual Patches Red-TTCN
06Ultra-150
Gold Medallion-150
Ice Medallion-150
06Upper Deck-399
Exclusives Parallel-399
High Gloss Parallel-399
Game Jerseys-JMC
Game Patches-PMC
Masterpieces-399
Signature Sensations-SSMC
06Upper Deck MVP-228
Gold Script-228
Super Script-228
06Upper Deck Ovation-38
06Upper Deck Victory-154
06Upper Deck Victory Black-154
06Upper Deck Victory Gold-154

Comrie, Paul

99BAP Memorabilia-392
Gold-392
Silver-392
99BAP Millennium-105
Emerald-105
Ruby-105
Sapphire-105
Signatures-105
Signatures Gold-105
Calder Candidates Ruby-C26
Calder Candidates Emerald-C26
Calder Candidates Sapphire-C26
99Black Diamond-38
Diamond Cut-38
Final Cut-38
99Pacific-456
99Pacific Dynagon Ice-80
Blue-80
Copper-80
Gold-80
Premiere Date-80
99Pacific Omega-89
Copper-89
Gold-89
Ice Blue-89
Premiere Date-89
99SP Authentic-103
99Stadium Club-184
First Day Issue-184
One of a Kind-184
Printing Plates Black-184
Printing Plates Cyan-184
Printing Plates Magenta-184
Printing Plates Yellow-184
99Topps Arena Giveaways-EDM-PC
99Topps Premier Plus-108
Parallel-108
99Ultimate Victory-98
1/1-98
Parallel-98
Parallel 100-98
99Upper Deck-226
Exclusives-226
Exclusives 1 of 1-226
99Upper Deck Arena Giveaways-EO1
99Upper Deck Gold Reserve-226
02BAP Sig Series Auto Buybacks 1999-105

Comte, Alain

93Swiss HNL-423
96Swiss HNL-475

Conacher, Brian

64Beehive Group III Photos-159
65Maple Leafs White Border-5
67Topps-17
67York Action Octagons-1
67York Action Octagons-6
68Shirriff Coins-47
69Maple Leafs White Border Glossy-6
71O-Pee-Chee-138
71Toronto Sun-89
07Maple Leafs 1967 Commemorative-5
Autographs-ABC1
Autographs-ABC2

Conacher, Charles

06ITG Ultimate Memorabilia Decades-2

Conacher, Charlie

32O'Keefe Maple Leafs-9
33O-Pee-Chee V304A-34
33V129-5
33V252 Canadian Gum-12
33V288 Hamilton Gum-49
34Beehive Group I Photos-309
34Sweet Caporal-45
35CCM Green Border Photos-9
36Champion Postcards-9
36O-Pee-Chee V304D-123
36Triumph Postcards-11
37O-Pee-Chee V304E-138
37V356 Worldwide Gum-1
39O-Pee-Chee V301-1-59
55Parkhurst-26
Quaker Oats-26
83Hall of Fame-6
83Hall of Fame Postcards-A5
85Hall of Fame-6
91Pro Set-338
French-338
92Hall of Fame Legends-14
99Upper Deck Century Legends-38
Century Collection-38
02BAP Ultimate Mem Paper Cuts Autos-34
02Maple Leafs Platinum Collection-47
03BAP Ultimate Mem Hometown Heroes-15
03BAP Ultimate Mem Hometown Heroes Gold-15
03BAP Ultimate Memorabilia Linemates-11
03BAP Ultimate Mem Linemates Autos-4
03BAP Ultimate Memorabilia Paper Cuts-30
03ITG VIP Vintage Memorabilia-5
03Parkhurst Original Six Toronto-31
03Parkhurst Original Six Toronto-78
Inserts-T10
Memorabilia-TM23
04ITG Franchises Update Linemates-ULI1
04ITG Franchises Update Linemates Gold-ULI1
04ITG Ultimate Memorabilia-77
Gold-77
Day In History-35
Day In History-37
Day In History Gold-35
Day In History Gold-37
Gloves are Off-8
Maple Leafs Forever-8
Original Six-12
Paper Cuts Memorabilia-22
05ITG Ultimate Memorabilia Level 1-17
05ITG Ultimate Memorabilia Level 2-17
05ITG Ultimate Memorabilia Level 3-17
05ITG Ultimate Memorabilia Level 4-17
05ITG Ultimate Memorabilia Level 5-17
05ITG Ultimate Mem Cornerstones Jerseys-5
05ITG Ultimate Mem Cornerst Jerseys Gold-5
05ITG Ultimate Mem Decades Jerseys-6
05ITG Ultimate Mem Decades Jerseys Gold-6
05ITG Ultimate Memorabilia Gloves Are Off-15
05ITG Ultimate Mem Gloves Are Off Gold-15
05ITG Ultimate Mem Leafs Forever Autos-12
06ITG Ultimate Memorabilia-27
Artist Proof-27
Chi-Town Immortals Autos-7
Decades-2
Decades Gold-2
Gloves Are Off-6
Gloves Are Off Gold-6
Lumbergraphs-14
Maple Leafs Forever Autos-2

Conacher, Dan

06Okotoks Oilers-5

Conacher, Jim

44Beehive Group II Photos-85
51Parkhurst-105
52Parkhurst-103

Conacher, John

44Beehive Group II Photos-157

Conacher, Lionel

25Dominion Chocolates-118
27La Presse Photos-18
30Rogers Peet Company *-10
30Rogers Peet *-10
33V252 Canadian Gum-13
34Diamond Matchbooks Silver-13
34Sweet Caporal-17
36O-Pee-Chee V304D-102
36Triumph Postcards-1
37V356 Worldwide Gum-10
62Wheaties Great Moments in Cdn Sport-22
94Parkhurst Tall Boys Greats-12
04ITG Franchises US West-280
04ITG Ultimate Memorabilia-161
Gold-161
05ITG Ultimate Memorabilia Level 1-64
05ITG Ultimate Memorabilia Level 2-64
05ITG Ultimate Memorabilia Level 3-64
05ITG Ultimate Memorabilia Level 4-64
05ITG Ultimate Memorabilia Level 5-64
05ITG Ultimate Mem Marvelous Maroons Auto-8
05ITG Ultimate Mem Paper Cut Autos-6
05ITG Ultimate Mem Quad Paper Cuts Autos-2
06ITG Ultimate Memorabilia-89
Artist Proof-89
Marvelous Maroons Autos-4
Paper Cuts Autos-3

Conacher, Pat

83Oilers McDonald's-11
83Moncton Alpines-14
84Nova Scotia Oilers-7
88Devils Caretta-8
88Oilers Tenth Anniversary-139
89Devils Caretta-7
89ProCards AHL-219
90Devils Team Issue-7
90Pro Set-477
91Pro Set-427
French-427
91Score Canadian Bilingual-654
91Score Canadian English-654
91Stadium Club-387
92OPC Premier-49
92Score-544
Canadian-544
93Donruss-153
93Leaf-380
93OPC Premier-252
Gold-252
93Parkhurst-363
Emerald Ice-363
93PowerPlay-358
93Stadium Club-179
Members Only Master Set-179
OPC-179
First Day Issue-179
First Day Issue OPC-179
93Topps/OPC Premier-252
Gold-252
93Ultra-342
94Be A Player 99 All-Stars-G4
94Canada Games NHL POGS-122
94Parkhurst-107
Gold-107
94Pinnacle-403
Artist's Proofs-403
Rink Collection-403
94Stadium Club-237
Members Only Master Set-237
First Day Issue-237
Super Team Winner Cards-237
95Be A Player-92
Signatures-S92
Signatures Die Cuts-S92
95Canada Games NHL POGS-136
95Playoff One on One-268
02Coyotes Team Issue-23

Conacher, Pete

44Beehive Group II Photos-86
44Beehive Group II Photos-390
52Parkhurst-33
53Parkhurst-70
54Parkhurst-86
54Topps-33
57Parkhurst-T14

Conacher, Roy

34Beehive Group I Photos-9
39O-Pee-Chee V301-1-91
44Beehive Group II Photos-87
48Exhibits Canadian-50
51Parkhurst-50
91Bruins Sports Action Legends-12
03BAP Ultimate Mem Linemates Autos-13
04ITG Ultimate Memorabilia-121
Gold-121
06ITG Ultimate Memorabilia Chi-Town Immortals Autos-5

Conboy, Tim

03St. Cloud State Huskies-4
04Cleveland Barons-5
05Cleveland Barons-6
06Albany River Rats-7

Concannon, Brendan

96Pensacola Ice Pilots-20
97Pensacola Ice Pilots-7
98Pensacola Ice Pilots-9

Concannon, Mark

03ECHL Update RBI Sports-129

Concannon, Rob

95South Carolina Stingrays-8
96South Carolina Stingrays-21
00Idaho Steelheads-5

Concepion, Banks

02Arizona Icecats-4
03Arizona Icecats-4

Condon, Paul

93Quebec Pee-Wee Tournament-1456

Condra, Erik

04Lincoln Stars-8
05Notre Dame Freshmen-1

Conklin, Ty

00SPx Rookie Redemption-RR12
01BAP Memorabilia-388
Emerald-388
Ruby-388
Sapphire-388
01Between the Pipes-82
01Bowman YoungStars-154
Gold-154
Ice Cubed-154
01Crown Royale-159
Rookie Royalty-9
01O-Pee-Chee-359
01Pacific Adrenaline-208
Blue-208
Premiere Date-208
Red-208
Retail-208
01Parkhurst-314
01SP Authentic-146
Limited-146
Limited Gold-146
01SP Game Used-76
01Titanium-158
Retail-158
01Titanium Draft Day Edition-129
01Topps-359
01Topps Chrome-177
Refractors-177
Black Border Refractors-177
01UD Challenge for the Cup-106
01UD Playmakers-117
01UD Premier Collection-62
01Upper Deck-423
Exclusives-423
01Upper Deck Ice-54
01Vanguard-111
Blue-111
Red-111
One of Ones-111
Premiere Date-111
Proofs-111
01Hamilton Bulldogs-16
02BAP First Edition-284
02Between the Pipes-45
Gold-45
Silver-45
02O-Pee-Chee-312
02O-Pee-Chee Premier Blue Parallel-312
02O-Pee-Chee Premier Red Parallel-312
02O-Pee-Chee Factory Set-312
02Topps-312
OPC Blue Parallel-312
OPC Red Parallel-312
Factory Set-312
02AHL Top Prospects-8
02Hamilton Bulldogs-17
03Oilers Postcards-4
03Pacific Complete-437
Red-437
03Pacific Heads-Up-40
Hobby LTD-40
Retail LTD-40
03Upper Deck-322
Canadian Exclusives-322
HG-322
UD Exclusives-322
04Pacific-100
Blue-100
Red-100
04SP Authentic-38
04Upper Deck-73
Canadian Exclusives-73
Heritage Classic-CC-TC
HG Glossy Gold-73
HG Glossy Silver-73
World Cup Tribute-TCRDRE
04German DEL Superstars-SU21
05Be A Player-37
First Period-37
Second Period-37
Third Period-37
Overtime-37
05Beehive-35
Matte-35
Matted Materials-MMTC
05Black Diamond-31
Emerald-31
Gold-31
Onyx-31
Ruby-31
05Panini Stickers-274
05Parkhurst-186
Facsimile Auto Parallel-186
Signatures-TC
True Colors-TCEDM
True Colors-TCEDM
05SP Authentic Sign of the Times Quads-QPSCW
05SP Game Used-41
Autographs-41
Gold-41
Authentic Fabrics-AF-TC
Authentic Fabrics Autographs-AAF-TC
Authentic Fabrics Dual-PC
Authentic Fabrics Dual-SC
Authentic Fabrics Dual Autographs-PC
Authentic Fabrics Gold-AF-TC
Authentic Fabrics Quad-SCPTB
Authentic Patches Quad -SCPTB
Authentic Fabrics Triple-CEA
Authentic Fabrics Triple-PCS
Authentic Patches-AP-TC
Authentic Patches Autographs-AAP-TC
Authentic Patches Dual-PC
Authentic Patches Dual-SC
Authentic Patches Dual Autographs-PC
Authentic Patches Triple-CEA
Authentic Patches Triple-PCS
Awesome Authentics-AA-TC
Awesome Authentics Gold-DA-TC
SIGnificance Extra-SC
SIGnificance Extra Gold-SC
05SPx-32
Spectrum-32
Winning Combos-WC-CP
Winning Combos-WC-SC
Winning Combos Autographs-AWC-CP
Winning Combos Autographs-AWC-SC
Winning Combos Gold-WC-CP
Winning Combos Gold-WC-SC
Winning Combos Spectrum-WC-CP
Winning Combos Spectrum-WC-SC
Winning Materials-WM-TC
Winning Materials Autographs-AWM-TC
Winning Materials Gold-WM-TC
Winning Materials Spectrum-WM-TC
05The Cup Dual NHL Shields-DSPC
05The Cup Dual NHL Shields Autographs-ADSPC
05The Cup Limited Logos-LLTC
05The Cup Master Pressplate Rookie Update-208
05UD Artifacts-41
Blue-41
Gold-41
Green-41
Pewter-41
Red-41
Auto Facts-AF-TC
Auto Facts Blue-AF-TC
Auto Facts Copper-AF-TC
Auto Facts Pewter-AF-TC
Auto Facts Silver-AF-TC
Gold Autographed-41
Remarkable Artifacts-RA-TC
Remarkable Artifacts Dual-RA-TC
05Ultimate Collection Endorsed Emblems-EETC
05Ultra-80
Gold-80
Ice-80
05Upper Deck-74
Big Playmakers-B-TC
HG Glossy-74
Jerseys-J-TC
Jerseys Series II-J2TC
Majestic Materials-MMTC
NHL Generations-DTC
Notable Numbers-N-TC
05Upper Deck Ice-37
Rainbow-37
05Upper Deck MVP-152
Gold-152
Platinum-152
05Upper Deck Rookie Update-208
Inspirations Patch Rookies-208
05Upper Deck Trilogy-37
Honorary Patches-HP-TC
Honorary Patch Scripts-HSP-TC
Honorary Swatches-HS-TC
Honorary Swatch Scripts-HSS-TC
Scripts-SFS-TC
05Upper Deck Toronto Fall Expo-74
05Upper Deck Victory-79
Black-79
Gold-79
Silver-79
06Black Diamond Gemography-GTC
06Black Diamond Jerseys-JTC
06Black Diamond Jerseys Black-JTC
06Black Diamond Jerseys Gold-JTC
06Black Diamond Jerseys Ruby-JTC
06Flair Showcase Inks-ITC
06Flair Showcase Stitches-SSTC
06Fleer Fabricology-FTY
06Fleer Signing Day-SDTC
06SP Game Used Authentic Fabrics Dual-AF2LC
06SP Game Used Authentic Fabrics Dual Patches-AF2LC
06UD Artifacts Tundra Tandems-TTPT
06UD Artifacts Tundra Tandems Black-TTPT
06UD Artifacts Tundra Tandems Blue-TTPT
06UD Artifacts Tundra Tandems Gold-TTPT
06UD Artifacts Tundra Tandems Platinum-TTPT
06UD Artifacts Tundra Tandems Red-TTPT
06UD Artifacts Tundra Tandems Dual Patches Red-TTPT
06Ultra Fresh Ink-ITC
06Upper Deck Game Jerseys-JTC
06Upper Deck Game Patches-PTC
06Upper Deck MVP Jerseys-OJOC
06Upper Deck Trilogy Scripts-TSTC
06Syracuse Crunch-23

Conlan, Wayne

93Maine Black Bears-44

Conley, Michael

92Quebec Pee-Wee Tournament-1413
93Quebec Pee-Wee Tournament-762

Conley, Scott

93Quebec Pee-Wee Tournament-635

Conn, Hugh

34Diamond Matchbooks Silver-14
35Diamond Matchbooks Tan 1-13

Conn, Joe

44Beehive Group II Photos-88

Conn, Rob

91ProCards-494
92Indianapolis Ice-7
93Indianapolis Ice-5
94Indianapolis Ice-3

Conne, Flavien

98Swiss Power Play Stickers-90
98Swiss Power Play Stickers-278
99Swiss Panini Stickers-90
99Swiss Panini Stickers-291
00Swiss Panini Stickers-209
00Swiss Panini Stickers National Team-P13
00Swiss Slapshot Mini-Cards-HCL12
01Swiss HNL-38
02Swiss HNL-28
02Swiss HNL-230

Connell, Alex

24Anonymous NHL-16
24Anonymous NHL-28
24C144 Champ's Cigarettes-16
24V145-2-10
33V252 Canadian Gum-14
34Beehive Group I Photos-194
34Sweet Caporal-18
60Topps Stamps-11
83Hall of Fame-169
83Hall of Fame Postcards-M4
85Hall of Fame-169
03SP Authentic Special Cuts-AC
05ITG Ultimate Mem Marvelous Maroons Auto-7
06Between The Pipes Forgotten Franchises-FF03
06ITG Ultimate Memorabilia-3
Artist Proof-3

Connell, Jerry

98Barrie Colts-8
00Sudbury Wolves-16
01Sudbury Wolves-5
01Sudbury Wolves Police-17

Connelly, Jack

23Crescent Selkirks-8

Connelly, Jim

52Juniors Blue Tint-51

Connelly, Shane

03Chicago Steel-3
04Chicago Steel-6
05Wisconsin Badgers-4

Connelly, Wayne

44Beehive Group II Photos-12A
44Beehive Group II Photos-12B
61Parkhurst-44
62Topps-18
64Beehive Group III Photos-4
66Topps-40
68O-Pee-Chee-50
68Shirriff Coins-54
68Topps-50
69O-Pee-Chee-60
69Topps-60
70Dad's Cookies-16
70Esso Power Players-141
70O-Pee-Chee-159
70Red Wings Marathon-2
70Sargent Promotions Stamps-54
71O-Pee-Chee-237
71Sargent Promotions Stamps-186
71Topps-127
71Toronto Sun-237
72Minnesota Fighting Saints Postcards WHA-5
72O-Pee-Chee-296
72 7-Eleven Slurpee Cups WHA-6
73Quaker Oats WHA-35
74Minnesota Fighting Saints WHA-6
74O-Pee-Chee WHA-54
76O-Pee-Chee WHA-122
95Parkhurst '66-67-20
Coins-20

Conner, Chris

06Iowa Stars-4

Conners, Kevin

03Arizona Icecats-5

Connolly, Bert

35Diamond Matchbooks Tan 1-14
35Diamond Matchbooks Tan 2-10
35Diamond Matchbooks Tan 3-10

Connolly, Brett

03Sault Ste. Marie Greyhounds-3

Connolly, Chris

93Quebec Pee-Wee Tournament-844

Connolly, Jeff

96Charlotte Checkers-4

Connolly, Ryan

98San Angelo Outlaws-5

Connolly, Sean

02Trenton Titans-B-3
03ECHL Update RBI Sports-120

Connolly, Tim

93Quebec Pee-Wee Tournament-664
94Quebec Pee-Wee Tournament-649
95Quebec Pee-Wee Tournament-516
98Black Diamond-117
Double Diamond-117
Triple Diamond-117
Quadruple Diamond-117
98SPx Top Prospects-86
Radiance-86
Spectrum-86
99BAP Memorabilia-229
Gold-229
Silver-229
99BAP Millennium-153
Emerald-153
Ruby-153
Sapphire-153
Signatures-153
Signatures Gold-153
Calder Candidates Ruby-C21
Calder Candidates Emerald-C21
Calder Candidates Sapphire-C21
99Black Diamond-54
Diamond Cut-54
Final Cut-54
A Piece of History-TC
A Piece of History Double-TC
A Piece of History Triple-TC
99Crown Royale-84
Limited Series-84
Premiere Date-84
Prospects Parallel-84

99O-Pee-Chee-259
99O-Pee-Chee Chrome-259
99O-Pee-Chee Chrome Refractors-259
99Pacific Dynagon Ice-122
Blue-122
Copper-122
Gold-122
Premiere Date-122
99Pacific Omega-146
Copper-146
Gold-146
Ice Blue-146
Premiere Date-146
99Pacific Prism-85
Holographic Blue-85
Holographic Gold-85
Holographic Mirror-85
Holographic Purple-85
Premiere Date-85
99Panini Stickers-93
99Paramount-261
99SP Authentic-52
Sign of the Times-TC
Sign of the Times Gold-TC
99SPx-174
Radiance-174
Spectrum-174
99Stadium Club-199
First Day Issue-199
One of a Kind-199
Printing Plates Black-199
Printing Plates Cyan-199
Printing Plates Magenta-199
Printing Plates Yellow-199
Chrome-49
Chrome Refractors-49
99Topps/OPC-259
99Topps/OPC Chrome-259
Refractors-259
99Topps Gold Label Class 1-88
Black-88
Black One of One-88
One of One-88
Red-88
Red One of One-88
99Topps Gold Label Class 2-88
99Topps Gold Label Class 2 Black-88
99Topps Gold Label Class 2 Black 1 of 1-88
99Topps Gold Label Class 2 One of One-88
99Topps Gold Label Class 2 Red-88
99Topps Gold Label Class 2 Red One of One-88
99Topps Gold Label Class 3-88
99Topps Gold Label Class 3 Black-88
99Topps Gold Label Class 3 Black 1 of 1-88
99Topps Gold Label Class 3 One of One-88
99Topps Gold Label Class 3 Red-88
99Topps Gold Label Class 3 Red One of One-88
99Topps Gold Label Fresh Gold-FG15
99Topps Gold Label Fresh Gold Black-FG15
99Topps Gold Label Fresh Gold Black 1of1-FG15
99Topps Gold Label Fresh Gold One of One-FG15
99Topps Gold Label Fresh Gold Red-FG15
99Topps Gold Label Fresh Gold Red 1 of 1-FG15
99Topps Premier Plus-137
Parallel-137
99Upper Deck-255
Exclusives-255
Exclusives 1 of 1-255
Sixth Sense-SS12
Sixth Sense Quantum Gold-SS12
Sixth Sense Quantum Silver-SS12
99Upper Deck Arena Giveaways-NI2
99Upper Deck Gold Reserve-255
99Upper Deck HoloGrFx-37
Ausome-37
99Upper Deck MVP SC Edition-111
Gold Script-111
Silver Script-111
Super Script-111
99Upper Deck Ovation-35
Standing Ovation-35
A Piece Of History-TC
99Upper Deck Victory-374
99Wayne Gretzky Hockey-103
99Bowman CHL-11
99Bowman CHL-144
Gold-11
Gold-144
OPC International-11
OPC International-144
Autographs-BA31
Autographs Gold-BA31
Autographs Silver-BA31
Scout's Choice-SC1
00Aurora-87
Premiere Date-87
00BAP Memorabilia-15
Emerald-15
Ruby-15
Sapphire-15
Promos-15
00BAP Mem Chicago Sportsfest Copper-15
00BAP Memorabilia Chicago Sportsfest Blue-15
00BAP Memorabilia Chicago Sportsfest Gold-15
00BAP Memorabilia Chicago Sportsfest Ruby-15
00BAP Memorabilia Chicago Sun-Times Ruby-15
00BAP Memorabilia Chicago Sun-Times Gold-15
00BAP Mem Chicago Sun-Times Sapphire-15
00BAP Mem Toronto Fall Expo Copper-15
00BAP Memorabilia Toronto Fall Expo Gold-15
00BAP Memorabilia Toronto Fall Expo Ruby-15
00BAP Parkhurst 2000-P47
00BAP Signature Series-142
Emerald-142
Ruby-142
Sapphire-142
Autographs-171
Autographs Gold-171
00Black Diamond-36
Gold-36
00Crown Royale-66
Ice Blue-66
Limited Series-66
Premiere Date-66
Red-66
00McDonald's Pacific Gold Crown Die Cuts-5
00O-Pee-Chee-217
00O-Pee-Chee Parallel-217
00Pacific-247
Copper-247
Gold-247
Ice Blue-247
Premiere Date-247
00Panini Stickers-56
00Paramount-152
Copper-152
Gold-152
Holo-Gold-152
Holo-Silver-152
Ice Blue-152
Premiere Date-152
Freeze Frame-23
00Private Stock-61
Gold-61
Premiere Date-61
Retail-61
Silver-61
Extreme Action-14
Game Gear-64
PS-2001 Action-35
PS-2001 New Wave-15
00Revolution-90
Blue-90
Premiere Date-90
Red-90
00SP Authentic-58
00SP Game Used-38
00SPx-42
Spectrum-42
00Stadium Club-83
Capture the Action-CA15
Capture the Action Game View-15
00Titanium-57
Blue-57
Gold-57
Premiere Date-57
Red-57
Retail-57
00Topps/OPC-217
Parallel-217
Own the Game-OTG29
00Topps Chrome-139
OPC Refractors-139
Refractors-139
00Topps Gold Label Class 1-15
Gold-15
00Topps Gold Label Class 2-15
00Topps Gold Label Class 2 Gold-15
00Topps Gold Label Class 3-15
00Topps Gold Label Class 3 Gold-15
00Topps Gold Label New Generation-NG15
00Topps Gold Label New Generation 1 to 1-NG15
00Topps Heritage-21
Chrome Parallel-21
00Topps Premier Plus-5
Blue Ice-5
Aspirations-PA10
00Topps Stars-28
Blue-28
00UD Heroes-75
00UD Pros and Prospects-53
00UD Reserve-53
00Upper Deck-109
Exclusives Tier 1-109
Exclusives Tier 2-109
Game Jersey Autographs-HTC
Game Jersey Autographs Exclusives-ETC
Game Jersey Combos-DCL
Game Jersey Patches-TCP
Game Jersey Patch Autographs Exclusives-TCP
Prospects In Depth-P6
Skilled Stars-SS14
UD Flashback-UD5
00Upper Deck Ice-26
Immortals-26
Legends-26
Stars-26
Clear Cut Autographs-TC
Game Jerseys-JCTC
00Upper Deck Legends-87
00Upper Deck Legends-88
Legendary Collection Bronze-87
Legendary Collection Bronze-88
Legendary Collection Gold-87
Legendary Collection Gold-88
Legendary Collection Silver-87
Legendary Collection Silver-88
00Upper Deck MVP-114
First Stars-114
Second Stars-114
Third Stars-114
00Upper Deck Victory-142
00Upper Deck Victory-144
00Upper Deck Victory-311
00Upper Deck Vintage-223
00Upper Deck Vintage-233
00Upper Deck Vintage-234
00Vanguard-61
Holographic Gold-61
Holographic Purple-61
Pacific Proofs-61
01Atomic-11
Blue-11
Gold-11
Premiere Date-11
Red-11
01BAP Memorabilia-61
01BAP Memorabilia-366
Emerald-61
Emerald-366
Ruby-61
Ruby-366
Sapphire-61
Sapphire-366
01BAP Signature Series-127
Autographs-127
Autographs Gold-127
01Bowman YoungStars-111
Gold-111
Ice Cubed-111
Autographs-TC
Relics-JTC
Relics-STC
Relics-DSTC
Rivals-R8
01Crown Royale-16
Blue-16
Premiere Date-16
Red-16
Retail-16
01O-Pee-Chee-141
01O-Pee-Chee Premier Parallel-141
01Pacific-243
Extreme LTD-243
Hobby LTD-243
Premiere Date-243
Retail LTD-243
01Pacific Adrenaline-20
Blue-20
Premiere Date-20
Red-20
Retail-20
01Pacific Arena Exclusives-243
01Parkhurst-44
Gold-44
Silver-44
01Private Stock-9
Gold-9
Premiere Date-9
Retail-9
Silver-9
01Private Stock Pacific Nights-9
01SPx Hidden Treasures-DTFC
01Titanium-14
Hobby Parallel-14
Premiere Date-14
Retail-14
Retail Parallel-14
01Topps-141
OPC Parallel-141
01Topps Heritage-173
01UD Honor Roll Jerseys-J-TC
01UD Honor Roll Jerseys Gold-J-TC
01UD Mask Collection-12
Gold-12
Double Patches-DPTC
Jerseys-J-TC
Jersey and Patch-JPTC
01UD Premier Collection-7
01Upper Deck-251
Exclusives-251
01Upper Deck Ice-88
01Vanguard-10
Blue-10
Red-10
One of Ones-10
Premiere Date-10
Proofs-10
02BAP First Edition-210
02BAP Memorabilia-174
02BAP Memorabilia-253
Emerald-174
Emerald-253
Ruby-174
Ruby-253
Sapphire-174
Sapphire-253
NHL All-Star Game-174
NHL All-Star Game-253
NHL All-Star Game Blue-174
NHL All-Star Game Blue-253
NHL All-Star Game Green-174
NHL All-Star Game Green-253
NHL All-Star Game Red-174
NHL All-Star Game Red-253
02BAP Memorabilia Toronto Fall Expo-174
02BAP Memorabilia Toronto Fall Expo-253
02BAP Signature Series-75
Autographs-75
Autograph Buybacks 1999-153
Autograph Buybacks 2000-171
Autograph Buybacks 2001-127
Autographs Gold-75
02O-Pee-Chee-53
02O-Pee-Chee Premier Blue Parallel-53
02O-Pee-Chee Premier Red Parallel-53
02O-Pee-Chee Factory Set-53
02Pacific-40
Blue-40
Red-40
02Pacific Complete-318
Red-318
02Pacific Exclusive-17
02Parkhurst-163
Bronze-163
Gold-163
Silver-163
Teammates-TT12
02Parkhurst Retro-147
Minis-147
02Private Stock Reserve-11
Blue-11
Red-11
Retail-11
02Sabres Team Issue-5
02SP Authentic-11
Beckett Promos-11
02SP Game Used Authentic Fabrics-CFCS
02SP Game Used Authentic Fabrics Gold-AFCS
02SP Game Used Authentic Fabrics Gold-CFCS
02SP Game Used Authentic Fabrics Rainbow-CFCS
02SP Game Used First Rounder Patches-TC
02SP Game Used Future Fabrics-FFTC
02SP Game Used Future Fabrics Gold-FFTC
02SP Game Used Future Fabrics Rainbow-FFTC
02SP Game Used Piece of History-PHTC
02SP Game Used Piece of History Gold-PHTC
02SP Game Used Piece of History Rainbow-PHTC
02Stadium Club YoungStars Relics-S17
02Topps-53
OPC Blue Parallel-53
OPC Red Parallel-53
Factory Set-53
02Topps Total-288
02UD Piece of History-9
02UD Top Shelf Dual Player Jerseys-RMC
02Upper Deck-18
Exclusives-18
Bright Futures-TC
02Upper Deck Classic Portraits-12
Hockey Royalty-SCA
Hockey Royalty Limited-SCA
02Upper Deck MVP-22
Gold-22
Classics-22
Golden Classics-22
02Upper Deck Victory-26
Bronze-26
Gold-26
Silver-26
02Upper Deck Vintage-28
02Upper Deck Vintage-264
Green Backs-28
03ITG Action-84
Jerseys-M15
03NHL Sticker Collection-27
03O-Pee-Chee-102
03OPC Blue-102
03OPC Gold-102
03OPC Red-102
03Pacific-39
Blue-39
Red-39
03Pacific Complete-64
Red-64
03Topps-102
Blue-102
Gold-102
Red-102
03Topps C55-32
Minis-32
Minis American Back-32
Minis American Back Red-32
Minis Bazooka Back-32
Minis Brooklyn Back-32
Minis Hat Trick Back-32
Minis O Canada Back-32
Minis O Canada Back Red-32
Minis Stanley Cup Back-32
Relics-TRTC
03Topps Pristine Popular Demand Relics-PD-TC
03Topps Pristine Popular Demand Relic Ref-PD-TC
03Upper Deck-271
Canadian Exclusives-271
HG-271
UD Exclusives-271
05Hot Prospects-13
En Fuego-13
Red Hot-13
White Hot-13
05Parkhurst-53
Facsimile Auto Parallel-53
True Colors-TCBUF
True Colors-TCBUF
05Upper Deck-270
Jerseys Series II-J2CY
05Upper Deck MVP-55
Gold-55
Platinum-55
06Fleer Fabricology-FTC
06Panini Stickers-36
06Upper Deck Victory-23
06Upper Deck Victory Black-23
06Upper Deck Victory Gold-23

Connor, Cam
74Phoenix Roadrunners WHA Pins-2
75O-Pee-Chee WHA-48
76O-Pee-Chee WHA-89
78Canadiens Postcards-3
79Oilers Postcards-4
79O-Pee-Chee-138
79Topps-138
80O-Pee-Chee-387
88Oilers Tenth Anniversary-134

Connors, Bobby
23V128-1 Paulin's Candy-12

Connors, Cam
75Phoenix Roadrunners WHA-4

Connors, Sean
99Calgary Hitmen-7
99Calgary Hitmen Autographs-7
03Oklahoma City Blazers-6
04Oklahoma City Blazers-15

Connors, Shawn
05Kingston Frontenacs-4

Conroy, Al
82Medicine Hat Tigers-1
83Medicine Hat Tigers-23
85Medicine Hat Tigers-6
89ProCards AHL-314
90ProCards AHL/IHL-473
91ProCards-267
92Topps Gold-525G
93Flyers J.C. Penney-7
93Flyers Lineup Sheets-9
93OPC Premier-352
Gold-352
93Topps/OPC Premier-352
Gold-352
94Detroit Vipers Pogs-4
95Houston Aeros-2
02Spokane Chiefs-26

Conroy, Craig
92Clarkson Knights-3
94Fredericton Canadiens-9
94Classic-51
Gold-51
All-Americans-AA1
95Donruss-169
95Leaf-85
95Pinnacle-218
Artist's Proofs-218
Rink Collection-218
95Score-297
Black Ice Artist's Proofs-297
Black Ice-297
95Topps-187
OPC Inserts-187
95Fredericton Canadiens-7
95Images-64
Gold-64
Autographs-64A
96Collector's Edge Ice-41
Prism-41
97Be A Player-59
Autographs-59
Autographs Die-Cuts-59
Autographs Prismatic Die-Cuts-59
97Pacific Invincible NHL Regime-168
98Be A Player-277
Press Release-277
98BAP Gold-277
98BAP Autographs-277
98BAP Autographs Gold-277
98OPC Chrome-47
Refractors-47
98Pacific-364
Ice Blue-364
Red-364
98Paramount-200
Copper-200
Emerald Green-200
Holo-Electric-200
Ice Blue-200
Silver-200
98Topps-47
O-Pee-Chee-47
99Blues Taco Bell-13
99O-Pee-Chee-145
99O-Pee-Chee Chrome-145
99O-Pee-Chee Chrome Refractors-145
99Pacific-353
Copper-353
Emerald Green-353
Gold-353
Ice Blue-353
Premiere Date-353
Red-353
99Panini Stickers-291
99Paramount-194
Copper-194
Emerald-194
Gold-194
Holographic Emerald-194
Holographic Gold-194
Holographic Silver-194
Ice Blue-194
Premiere Date-194
Red-194
Silver-194
99Topps/OPC-145
99Topps/OPC Chrome-145
Refractors-145
01Bowman YoungStars-92
Gold-92
Ice Cubed-92
01Crown Royale-19
Blue-19
Premiere Date-19
Red-19
Retail-19
Triple Threads-2
01Pacific-59
Extreme LTD-59
Hobby LTD-59
Premiere Date-59
Retail LTD-59
01Pacific Arena Exclusives-59
01Private Stock Game Gear-14
01Private Stock Game Gear Patches-14
01SP Authentic-13
Limited-13
Limited Gold-13
01SPx-161
01Titanium-17
Hobby Parallel-17
Premiere Date-17
Retail-17
Retail Parallel-17
01UD Challenge for the Cup-11
01UD Mask Collection-14
Gold-14
01Upper Deck-30
Exclusives-30
01Upper Deck MVP-24
01Upper Deck Victory-54
Gold-54
01Upper Deck Vintage-41
01Vanguard Memorabilia-16
01Vanguard Patches-6
02Atomic-12
Blue-12
Gold-12
Red-12
Hobby Parallel-12
02BAP First Edition-253
02BAP Memorabilia-11
Emerald-11
Ruby-11
Sapphire-11
NHL All-Star Game-11
NHL All-Star Game Blue-11
NHL All-Star Game Green-11
NHL All-Star Game Red-11
02BAP Memorabilia Toronto Fall Expo-11
02BAP Signature Series-81
Autographs-81
Autograph Buybacks 1998-277
Autographs Gold-81
02Bowman YoungStars-90
Gold-90
Silver-90
02NHL Power Play Stickers-2
02O-Pee-Chee-186
02O-Pee-Chee Premier Blue Parallel-186
02O-Pee-Chee Premier Red Parallel-186
02O-Pee-Chee Factory Set-186
02Pacific-52
Blue-52
Red-52
02Pacific Complete-310
Red-310
02Pacific Exclusive-21
02Pacific Heads-Up-15
Blue-15
Purple-15
Red-15
02Parkhurst-200
Bronze-200
Gold-200
Silver-200
02Parkhurst Retro-197
Minis-197
02Private Stock Reserve-13
Blue-13
Red-13
Retail-13
02Topps-186
OPC Blue Parallel-186
OPC Red Parallel-186
Factory Set-186
02Topps Chrome-107
Black Border Refractors-107
Refractors-107
02Topps Heritage-52
Chrome Parallel-52
02Topps Total-183
02UD Honor Roll-75
02UD Top Shelf-14
02Upper Deck-26
Exclusives-26
02Upper Deck Classic Portraits-15
02Upper Deck MVP-25
Gold-25
Classics-25
Golden Classics-25
02Upper Deck Victory-29
Bronze-29
Gold-29
Silver-29
02Upper Deck Vintage-43
03ITG Action-18
03McDonald's Pacific Saturday Night Rival-3
03NHL Sticker Collection-163
03O-Pee-Chee-105
03OPC Blue-105
03OPC Gold-105
03OPC Red-105
03Pacific-47
Blue-47
Red-47
03Pacific Complete-50
Red-50
03Pacific Exhibit-23
Blue Backs-23
Yellow Backs-23
03Pacific Invincible-12
Blue-12
Red-12
Retail-12
03Pacific Prism-18
Blue-18
Gold-18
Red-18
03Private Stock Reserve-149
Blue-149
Red-149
Retail-149
03Topps-105
Blue-105
Gold-105
Red-105
03Topps C55-118
Minis-118
Minis American Back-118
Minis American Back Red-118
Minis Bazooka Back-118
Minis Brooklyn Back-118
Minis Hat Trick Back-118
Minis O Canada Back-118
Minis O Canada Back Red-118
Minis Stanley Cup Back-118
03Upper Deck-273
Canadian Exclusives-273
HG-273
UD Exclusives-273
03Upper Deck MVP-66
Gold Script-66
Silver Script-66
Canadian Exclusives-66
04Pacific-37
Blue-37
Red-37
04Upper Deck-79
Canadian Exclusives-79
HG Glossy Gold-79
HG Glossy Silver-79
05Be A Player Signatures-CO
05Be A Player Signatures Gold-CO
05Beehive Signature Scrapbook-SSCN
05Kings Team Issue-5
05Parkhurst-220
Facsimile Auto Parallel-220
05SP Authentic Sign of the Times-CO
05SP Game Used Auto Draft-AD-CC
05SP Game Used Statscriptions-ST-CC
05Upper Deck-337
Notable Numbers-N-CRC
06Be A Player-140
Autographs-140
Signatures-CC
Signatures 25-155
Signatures Duals-DCA
06Black Diamond-39
Black-39
Gold-39
Ruby-39
06Fleer-93
Tiffany-93
06O-Pee-Chee-230
Rainbow-230
06Panini Stickers-285
06Upper Deck Arena Giveaways-LAK5
06Upper Deck-340
Exclusives Parallel-340
High Gloss Parallel-340
Masterpieces-340
06Upper Deck MVP-136
Gold Script-136
Super Script-136
06Upper Deck Victory-93
06Upper Deck Victory Black-93
06Upper Deck Victory Gold-93
07Upper Deck Victory-147
Black-147
Gold-147

Conschafter, Shawn
03Austin Ice Bats-4
05Roanoke Valley Vipers-3

Consolino, Brian
93Arizona Icecats-6
94Arizona Icecats-9
95Arizona Icecats-16
96Arizona Icecats-12

Constant, Chris
89Brandon Wheat Kings-6
90Brandon Wheat Kings-23
907th Inn. Sketch WHL-229
917th Inn. Sketch WHL-209

Constant, Ryan
02OCN Blizzard-24
03OCN Blizzard-4
06Hartford Wolf Pack-1

Constantin, Charles
76Nordiques Marie Antoinette-8
76Nordiques Postcards-11

Constantin, Paul
91Lake Superior State Lakers-7

Constantine, Kevin
90ProCards AHL/IHL-121
03Everett Silvertips-26
04Everett Silvertips-30
05Everett Silvertips-26

Constantineau, Benoit
93Quebec Pee-Wee Tournament-964

Conte, David
78Finnish SM-Liiga-74

Conti, Leonardo
96German DEL-3
98German DEL-278
99German DEL-189
00German DEL-75
01German Upper Deck-248
04German DEL-166
05German DEL-174

Contini, Joe
75Hamilton Fincups-4

Contofalsky, Jozef
93Quebec Pee-Wee Tournament-1702

Contois, Andrew
04Northern Michigan Wildcats-4

Converse, Trevor
91Air Canada SJHL-D15
91Richmond Renegades-14
95Central Hockey League-4
96Johnstown Chiefs-4
98Colorado Gold Kings-2
98Colorado Gold Kings Postcards-12
00Wichita Thunder-4

Convery, Brandon
907th Inn. Sketch OHL-381
90Sudbury Wolves-12
917th Inn. Sketch OHL-258
91Sudbury Wolves-16
93Donruss Team Canada-8
93Pinnacle-470
Canadian-470
93Upper Deck-548
93Niagara Falls Thunder-11
93Niagara Falls Thunder-28
94Leaf-483
94OPC Premier-386
Special Effects-386
94Topps/OPC Premier-386
Special Effects-386
94Upper Deck-259
Electric Ice-259
94St. John's Maple Leafs-5
94Classic-82
Gold-82
Tri-Cards-T67
94Classic Pro Prospects-59
95St. John's Maple Leafs-4
96Donruss Canadian Ice-144
Gold Press Proofs-144
Red Press Proofs-144
96Fleer Picks-146
96Leaf Gold Rookies-7
96Leaf Preferred-132
Press Proofs-132
96Pinnacle-241
Artist's Proofs-241
Foil-241
Premium Stock-241
Rink Collection-241
96Summit-174
Artist's Proofs-174
Ice-174
Metal-174
Premium Stock-174
96Upper Deck-186
96Zenith-132
Artist's Proofs-132
96St. John's Maple Leafs-10
96Collector's Edge Ice-78
Prism-78
97Donruss-85
Press Proofs Silver-85
Press Proofs Gold-85
97Donruss Limited-167
Exposure-167
97Pacific Invincible NHL Regime-192
97Pinnacle Inside-152
97Score-164
97Score Maple Leafs-14
Platinum-14
Premier-14
97Sudbury Wolves Anniversary-4

Conway, Kevin
81Sault Ste. Marie Greyhounds-7
82Sault Ste. Marie Greyhounds-6
83Kingston Canadians-16
94Finnish Jaa Kiekko-324

Conway, Neil
04Owen Sound Attack-2
05Owen Sound Attack-2
06Owen Sound Attack-3

Conz, Florian
01Swiss HNL-412
02Swiss HNL-171
04Swiss Lausanne HC Postcards-18

Cook, Bill
23V128-1 Paulin's Candy-35
24V130 Maple Crispette-6
24V145-2-24
33O-Pee-Chee V304A-38
33V129-31
33V357 Ice Kings-30
34Beehive Group I Photos-267
34Diamond Matchbooks Silver-15
34Sweet Caporal-40
35Diamond Matchbooks Tan 2-11
35Diamond Matchbooks Tan 2-12
35Diamond Matchbooks Tan 3-11
36Champion Postcards-6
60Topps-10
Stamps-12
83Hall of Fame-126
83Hall of Fame Postcards-I5
85Hall of Fame-126
94Parkhurst Missing Link Pop-Ups-P8
99Upper Deck Century Legends-45
Century Collection-45
02BAP Ultimate Mem Paper Cuts Autos-4
03BAP Ultimate Mem Linemates Autos-5
03BAP Ultimate Memorabilia Paper Cuts-42
03Parkhurst Original Six New York-89
04ITG Franchises US East-395
04ITG Ultimate Memorabilia-17
Gold-17
Broadway Blueshirts-4
05ITG Ultimate Mem Broadway Bluesh Autos-8
05The Cup Legendary Cuts-LCCO
06ITG Ultimate Memorabilia Broadway Blue Shirts Autos-11

Cook, Brad
93Detroit Jr. Red Wings-13
96Dayton Ice Bandits-9
98San Angelo Outlaws-6
01Kalamazoo K-Wings-19

Cook, Brian
94Central Hockey League-42

Cook, Bun
28La Presse Photos-6
33O-Pee-Chee V304B-72
33V129-46
33V252 Canadian Gum-15
33V357 Ice Kings-66
34Beehive Group I Photos-10
34Diamond Matchbooks Silver-16
34Sweet Caporal-41
35Diamond Matchbooks Tan 1-15
35Diamond Matchbooks Tan 2-13
35Diamond Matchbooks Tan 3-12
36Champion Postcards-10
37V356 Worldwide Gum-68
51Cleveland Barons-1
94Parkhurst Tall Boys Greats-10
02BAP Ultimate Mem Paper Cuts Autos-3
03BAP Ultimate Mem Linemates Autos-5
03Parkhurst Original Six New York-60
04ITG Ultimate Memorabilia-1
Gold-1
Broadway Blueshirts-3
05ITG Ultimate Mem Broadway Bluesh Autos-6
05ITG Ultimate Mem Quad Paper Cuts Autos-5
05The Cup Legendary Cuts-LCBC
06ITG Ultimate Memorabilia Broadway Blue Shirts Autos-6

Cook, Cam
92Saskatchewan JHL-150

Cook, Charlie
05Philadelphia Phantoms-6
06Binghamton Senators-4

Cook, Chris
99Brampton Battalion-21
99Kingston Frontenacs-5
00Kingston Frontenacs-4
01Kingston Frontenacs-2
02Kingston Frontenacs-2

Cook, Dean
86Kamloops Blazers-4
87Kamloops Blazers-4
88Kamloops Blazers-7
89ProCards IHL-187

Cook, Duncan
02UK Peterborough Phantoms-11

Cook, Jesse
02Lexington Men O'War-7
03Colorado Eagles-6
04Colorado Eagles-4

Cook, Joe
91Oshawa Generals-23
91Oshawa Generals Sheet-3
917th Inn. Sketch OHL-163
92Anaheim Bullfrogs RHI-16
92Oshawa Generals Sheet-7
93Anaheim Bullfrogs RHI-4
94Anaheim Bullfrogs RHI-4
94Classic Pro Prospects-231
95Anaheim Bullfrogs RHI-7
96Anaheim Bullfrogs RHI-17

Cook, Lloyd
24Anonymous NHL-41

Cook, Michel
91Air Canada SJHL-B42
91Air Canada SJHL All-Stars-32
91Air Canada SJHL All-Stars-45
92Saskatchewan JHL-156

Cook, Tim
03Michigan Wolverines-13
04Michigan Wolverines-9

Cook, Tom
34Beehive Group I Photos-195
34Diamond Matchbooks Silver-17
35Diamond Matchbooks Tan 1-16
35Diamond Matchbooks Tan 2-14
35Diamond Matchbooks Tan 3-13
35Diamond Matchbooks Tan 4-4
35Diamond Matchbooks Tan 5-3
37Diamond Matchbooks Tan 6-3
37O-Pee-Chee V304E-180
37V356 Worldwide Gum-43

Cook, Tyler
00St. Michaels Majors-12

Cooke, James
06UK Nottingham Panthers-3

Cooke, Jamie
91ProCards-282
95Central Hockey League-21
97Idaho Steelheads-18
98Bakersfield Condors-6
98Las Vegas Coyotes RHI-9
99Bakersfield Condors-4
99Memphis RiverKings All-Time-18
00Bakersfield Condors-5
01Bakersfield Condors-4
02Bakersfield Condors-4
03Bakersfield Condors-3

Cooke, Matt
92Quebec Pee-Wee Tournament-421
95Slapshot-415
97Bowman CHL-22
OPC-22
98Pacific Dynagon Ice-188
Blue-188
Red-188
98Pacific Omega-242
Red-242
Opening Day Issue-242
98UD Choice-268
Prime Choice Reserve-268
Reserve-268
98Upper Deck-381
Exclusives-381
Exclusives 1 of 1-381
Gold Reserve-381
98Bowman CHL-11
Golden Anniversary-11
OPC International-11
98Bowman Chrome CHL-11
Golden Anniversary-11
Golden Anniversary Refractors-11
OPC International-11
OPC International Refractors-11
Refractors-11
99Syracuse Crunch-2
00Stadium Club-192
00Topps Heritage-121
01Canucks Postcards-5
02BAP First Edition-165
02BAP Signature Series Golf-GS55
02Canucks Team Issue-4
02NHL Power Play Stickers-152
02Pacific-376
Blue-376
Red-376
02Pacific Complete-151
Red-151
02Topps Total-186
02Upper Deck-415
Exclusives-415
02Upper Deck Beckett UD Promos-415
03Canucks Postcards-5
03Canucks Sav-on-Foods-23
03ITG Action-567
03O-Pee-Chee-59
03OPC Blue-59
03OPC Gold-59
03OPC Red-59
03Pacific-329
Blue-329
Red-329
03Pacific Complete-207
Red-207
03Topps-59
Blue-59
Gold-59
Red-59
03Upper Deck-188
Canadian Exclusives-188
HG-188
03Upper Deck MVP-412
Gold Script-412
Silver Script-412
Canadian Exclusives-412
03Upper Deck Victory-190
Bronze-190
Gold-190
Silver-190
05Parkhurst-480
Facsimile Auto Parallel-480
05Upper Deck-188
HG Glossy-188
Jerseys Series II-J2CK
Notable Numbers-N-MCO
05Upper Deck MVP-383
Gold-383
Platinum-383
05Upper Deck Toronto Fall Expo-188
05Upper Deck Victory-193
Black-193
Gold-193
Silver-193
06Canucks Postcards-6
06Gatorade-88
06O-Pee-Chee-474
Rainbow-474
06Panini Stickers-360
06Upper Deck-192
Exclusives Parallel-192
High Gloss Parallel-192
Masterpieces-192
06Upper Deck MVP-280
Gold Script-280
Super Script-280

Cooke, Steve
01Belleville Bulls Update-2
02Belleville Bulls-4

Cool, Eric
917th Inn. Sketch QMJHL-192

Coole, Adam
03St. Cloud State Huskies-5

Coole, Ryan

02Arkansas Riverblades-3
03Fort Wayne Komets-22
04Bakersfield Condors-1
Cooley, Gaye
71Rochester Americans-3
Coombe, Lachlan
93Sherbrooke Faucons-10
Coombs, Joe
95Slapshot-49
98Topeka Scarecrows-10
99Topeka Scarecrows-14
Cooney, Matt
93Cornell Big Red-5
98Indianapolis Ice-2
Cooper, Bryan
93Quebec Pee-Wee Tournament-472
Cooper, Carson
24Anonymous NHL-31
24Anonymous NHL-32
24C144 Champ's Cigarettes-17
24V130 Maple Crispette-9
24V145-2-21
04ITG Franchises US West-198
Cooper, Curtis
03Prince George Cougars-4
06Saginaw Spirit-4
Cooper, David
907th Inn. Sketch WHL-38
917th Inn. Sketch WHL-319
93Rochester Americans Kodak-8
94Classic Tri-Cards-T7
94Classic Pro Prospects-210
94Classic Four-Sport *-151
Gold-151
Printers Proofs-151
95Rochester Americans-2
96St. John's Maple Leafs-11
97Upper Deck-193
97St. John's Maple Leafs-7
99German DEL-172
00St. John's Maple Leafs-6
01German Berlin Polar Bears Postcards-4
01German Upper Deck-32
Skilled Stars-SS2
02German Berlin Polar Bears Postcards-6
02German DEL City Press-27
All-Stars-AS3
03German DEL-136
Cooper, Dylan
06Texas Tornados-6
Cooper, Ian
94Finnish Jaa Kiekko-330
Cooper, Jeff
88ProCards IHL-46
Cooper, Joe
34Beehive Group I Photos-268
Cooper, John
93Windsor Spitfires-23
94Windsor Spitfires-25
Cooper, Kory
95Slapshot-31
97Indianapolis Ice-4
97Bowman CHL-20
OPC-20
99Idaho Steelheads-21
01Fort Worth Brahmas-6
03Port Huron Beacons-4
Cooper, Leon
04Lakehead University Thunderwolves-12
Cooper, Matt
00London Knights-3
Cooper, Neil
93St. Cloud State Huskies-3
Cooper, Scott
93Quebec Pee-Wee Tournament-685
Cooper, Stephen
94Finnish Jaa Kiekko-314
03UK Coventry Blaze History-16
Cooper, Vern
06Plymouth Whalers-6
Coopman, Todd
89Niagara Falls Thunder-6
89Oshawa Generals-21
897th Inn. Sketch OHL-128
907th Inn. Sketch OHL-258
Cope, Miles
05Owen Sound Attack-22
Copeland, Adam
99Tallahassee Tiger Sharks-5
01Idaho Steelheads-3
Copeland, Todd
90ProCards AHL/IHL-573
91ProCards-418
92Cincinnati Cyclones-5
Copija, Miroslaw
89Swedish Semic World Champ Stickers-141
92Finnish Semic-278
Copley, John
89Kitchener Rangers-11
907th Inn. Sketch OHL-179
907th Inn. Sketch Memorial Cup-42
917th Inn. Sketch OHL-178
Copley, Randy
98Bowman CHL-114
98Bowman CHL-125
Golden Anniversary-114
Golden Anniversary-125
OPC International-114
OPC International-125
Autographs Blue-A34
Autographs Gold-A34
Autographs Silver-A34
98Bowman Chrome CHL-114
98Bowman Chrome CHL-125
Golden Anniversary-114
Golden Anniversary-125
Golden Anniversary Refractors-114
Golden Anniversary Refractors-125
OPC International-114
OPC International-125
OPC International Refractors-114
OPC International Refractors-125
Refractors-114
Refractors-125
00Florida Everblades-6
02Columbus Cottonmouths-3
02Peoria Rivermen-10
02Peoria Rivermen RBI Sports-156
04St Georges de Beauce Garaga-24
Copp, Bob
34Beehive Group I Photos-310
Coppo, Paul
70Swedish Masterserien-179
70Swedish Masterserien-184
Coqueux, Olivier
03German DEL-48
Coram, Greg
82Ottawa 67's-2
83Ottawa 67's-5
84Ottawa 67's-5
Corazzini, Carl
93Quebec Pee-Wee Tournament-648
01Providence Bruins-14
03BAP Memorabilia-221
03Beehive-222
Gold-222
Silver-222
03ITG Used Signature Series-187
Gold-187
03ITG VIP Rookie Debut-106
03Parkhurst Rookie-110
03SP Authentic-166
03Topps Traded-TT88
Blue-TT88
Gold-TT88
Red-TT88
03UD Premier Collection-81
03Upper Deck Rookie Update-140
03Providence Bruins-3
04Hershey Bears Patriot News-8
04Providence Bruins-4
05Norfolk Admirals-5
06Norfolk Admirals-20
Corbeau, Bert
23V145-1-25
24C144 Champ's Cigarettes-18
24V145-2-58
Corbeil, Justin
86Sudbury Wolves-4
87Sudbury Wolves-5
Corbeil, Nicolas
00Sherbrooke Castors-18
Signed-18
01Sherbrooke Castors-19
01UD Prospects-13
Jerseys-J-NC
Jerseys Gold-J-NC
03Cape Breton Screaming Eagles-84
03ECHL Update RBI Sports-127
06Rockford IceHogs -8
Corbet, Rene
917th Inn. Sketch QMJHL-287
917th Inn. Sketch Memorial Cup-63
917th Inn. Sketch Memorial Cup-105
91Arena Draft Picks-18
91Arena Draft Picks French-18
91Arena Draft Picks Autographs-18
91Arena Draft Picks Autographs French-18
91Classic-21
91Star Pics-31
91Ultimate Draft-20
91Ultimate Draft French-20
91Classic Four-Sport *-21
Autographs-21A
93Parkhurst-433
Emerald Ice-433
93Pinnacle-448
Canadian-448
93Upper Deck-339
94Finest-97
Super Team Winners-97
Refractors-97
94Flair-143
94Parkhurst-193
Gold-193
94Pinnacle-460
Artist's Proofs-460
Rink Collection-460
Rookie Team Pinnacle-6
94Score-236
Gold-236
Platinum-236
94Select-197
Gold-197
94Upper Deck-179
Electric Ice-179
94Classic-98
Gold-98
Tri-Cards-T55
94Classic Pro Prospects-130
Jumbos-PP18
95Be A Player-78
Signatures-S78
Signatures Die Cuts-S78
95Donruss-371
95Emotion-35
95Upper Deck-100
Electric Ice-100
Electric Ice Gold-100
95Images-78
Gold-78
96Collector's Edge Ice-27
Prism-27
97Be A Player-205
Autographs-205
Autographs Die-Cuts-205
Autographs Prismatic Die-Cuts-205
97Pacific Invincible NHL Regime-50
97Score Avalanche-14
Platinum-14
Premier-14
98Pacific-158
Ice Blue-158
Red-158
99BAP Millennium-42
Emerald-42
Ruby-42
Sapphire-42
Signatures-42
Signatures Gold-42
99Pacific-54
Copper-54
Emerald Green-54
Gold-54
Ice Blue-54
Premiere Date-54
Red-54
99Paramount-36
Copper-36
Emerald-36
Gold-36
Holographic Emerald-36
Holographic Gold-36
Holographic Silver-36
Ice Blue-36
Premiere Date-36
Red-36
Silver-36
99Upper Deck MVP-36
Gold Script-36
Silver Script-36
Super Script-36
99Upper Deck Victory-49
00Titanium Game Gear-131
00Titanium Game Gear Patches-131
00Upper Deck NHLPA-PA72
01Atomic Jerseys-43
01Atomic Patches-43
01Upper Deck Victory-286
Gold-286
01German Adler Mannheim Eagles Postcards-7
02BAP Sig Series Auto Buybacks 1999-42
02German Adler Mannheim Eagles Postcards-12
02German DEL City Press-236
03German DEL-1
03German Mannheim Eagles Postcards-26
04German Adler Mannheim Eagles Postcards-9
04German DEL-5
All-Stars-AS12
05German DEL-258
06German DEL-146
Corbett, Jeff
98Hampton Roads Admirals-14
Corbett, Mike
63Rochester Americans-9
96Denver University Pioneers-3
Corbett, Peter
91ProCards-437
Corbett, Scott
95Slapshot-350
95Sarnia Sting-20
96Sarnia Sting-6
03Augusta Lynx-34
06Richmond Renegades-2
Corbin, Victor
51Laval Dairy Lac St. Jean-36
52Bas Du Fleuve-14
Corbin, Yvan
907th Inn. Sketch QMJHL-179
917th Inn. Sketch OHL-81
98Anchorage Aces-24
99Indianapolis Ice-4
00Indianapolis Ice-5
00Indianapolis Ice-5GJ
Corcoran, Sean
93Quebec Pee-Wee Tournament-868
Cordery, Bill
94Wheeling Thunderbirds-22
Corey, Jeff
00Sioux Falls Stampede-5
06Toronto Marlies-6
Corey, Ronald
88Canadiens Postcards-6
89Canadiens Postcards-6
90Canadiens Postcards-8
91Canadiens Postcards-5
96Canadiens Postcards-7
Corkum, Bob
89ProCards AHL-278
90Sabres Campbell's-5
90Upper Deck-35
French-35
90ProCards AHL/IHL-280
91Parkhurst-238
French-238
91ProCards-8
91Rochester Americans Dunkin' Donuts-3
91Rochester Americans Kodak-8
91Rochester Americans Postcards-6
92Sabres Blue Shield-4
92Sabres Jubilee Foods-13
92Stadium Club-179
92Topps-74
Gold-74G
93Donruss-10
93Ducks Milk Caps-5
93Parkhurst-6
Emerald Ice-6
93PowerPlay-282
93Score-637
Gold-637
Canadian-637
Canadian Gold-637
93Stadium Club-284
Members Only Master Set-284
First Day Issue-284
94Canada Games NHL POGS-28
94Donruss-96
94Ducks Carl's Jr.-2
94Finest-72
Super Team Winners-72
Refractors-72
94Flair-1
94Fleer-2
94Leaf-299
94OPC Premier-31
Special Effects-31
94Parkhurst SE-SE2
Gold-SE2
94Pinnacle-144
Artist's Proofs-144
Rink Collection-144
94Score-158
Gold-158
Platinum-158
94SP-4
Die Cuts-4
94Stadium Club Super Teams-1
94Stadium Club Super Team MemberOnly Set-1
94Topps/OPC Premier-31
Special Effects-31
94Ultra-1
94Upper Deck-413
Electric Ice-413
95SLU Hockey American-5
95Be A Player-112
Signatures-S112
Signatures Die Cuts-S112
95Collector's Choice-14
Player's Club-14
Player's Club Platinum-14
95Donruss-112
95Kenner Starting Lineup Cards-6
95Leaf-300
95Pinnacle-121
Artist's Proofs-121
Rink Collection-121
95Playoff One on One-221
95Score-42
Black Ice Artist's Proofs-42
Black Ice-42
95Topps-59
OPC Inserts-59
95Upper Deck-149
Electric Ice-149
Electric Ice Gold-149
96Coyotes Coca-Cola-1
96Playoff One on One-415
97Be A Player-117
Autographs-117
Autographs Die-Cuts-117
Autographs Prismatic Die-Cuts-117
97Coyotes Face-Off Luncheon -2
97Pacific-226
Copper-226
Emerald Green-226
Ice Blue-226
Red-226
Silver-226
98Pacific-334
Ice Blue-334
Red-334
99Pacific-317
Copper-317
Emerald Green-317
Gold-317
Ice Blue-317
Premiere Date-317
Red-317
01O-Pee-Chee-259
01O-Pee-Chee Premier Parallel-259
01Topps-259
OPC Parallel-259
Cormier, Dan
84Moncton Golden Flames-18
Cormier, Derek
98German DEL-293
99German DEL-252
00German Berlin Polar Bears Postcards-2
00German DEL-66
01German Upper Deck-213
02Swiss HNL-459
Cormier, Kevin
04Halifax Mooseheads-17
05Halifax Mooseheads-17
06Rimouski Oceanic-22
Cormier, Mario
98Abilene Aviators-19
Cormier, Michel
74Phoenix Roadrunners WHA Pins-3
75O-Pee-Chee WHA-74
75Phoenix Roadrunners WHA-5
76Phoenix Roadrunners WHA-5
Cormier, Patrice
06Rimouski Oceanic-14
Cormier, Philippe
93Quebec Pee-Wee Tournament-1204
Cornacchia, David
97Sudbury Wolves Police-17
00Belleville Bulls-20
01New Mexico Scorpions-16
03ECHL All-Stars-265
04Idaho Steelheads-24
Cornacchia, Rick
83Kingston Canadians-26
84Kingston Canadians-2
89Oshawa Generals-13
907th Inn. Sketch OHL-349
907th Inn. Sketch Memorial Cup-75
917th Inn. Sketch OHL-171
93Oshawa Generals-26
Corneau, Mike
03Port Huron Beacons-5
Cornelius, Jeff
85Kingston Canadians-10
Cornelius, Sam
01Notre Dame Fighting Irish-4
Cornet, Philippe
06Rimouski Oceanic-13
Cornforth, Mark
96Providence Bruins-2
97Cleveland Lumberjacks-7
97Cleveland Lumberjacks Postcards-15
Cornier, Sylvain
907th Inn. Sketch QMJHL-197
Cornish, Clair
89Oshawa Generals-17
89Oshawa Generals 7th Inning Sketch-5
897th Inn. Sketch OHL-5
907th Inn. Sketch OHL-330
907th Inn. Sketch Memorial Cup-98
Cornish, Jeremy
03Memphis RiverKings-1
04UK London Racers-3
04UK London Racers Playoffs-3
Coroy, Carey
84Nanaimo Clippers-6
Corpse, Keli
907th Inn. Sketch OHL-55
917th Inn. Sketch OHL-224
93Kingston Frontenacs-22
95Fredericton Canadiens-8
95Wheeling Thunderbirds-4
95Wheeling Thunderbirds Series II-4
96Grand Rapids Griffins-4
96Wheeling Nailers-9
96Wheeling Nailers Photo Pack-2
98Pensacola Ice Pilots-10
00Fort Wayne Komets-3
01Quad-City Mallards-3
Corredato, Austin
04Halifax Mooseheads-25
Correia, Mike
99Rockford IceHogs-4
02Orlando Seals-2
Corrente, Matt
04Saginaw Spirit-22
05Saginaw Spirit-5
05ITG Heroes and Prospects-407
Autographs Update-A-MCO
Team Orr-TO5
06Saginaw Spirit-10
06ITG Heroes and Prospects-116
Autographs-AMC
CHL Top Prospects-TP12
CHL Top Prospects Gold-TP12
Jerseys-GUJ51
Jerseys Gold-GUJ51
Emblems-GUE51
Emblems Gold-GUE51
Numbers-GUN51
Numbers Gold-GUN51
Corrigan, Jason
897th Inn. Sketch OHL-153
Corrigan, Mike
70Canucks Royal Bank-2
70Esso Power Players-47
70O-Pee-Chee-227
71Canucks Royal Bank-2
71O-Pee-Chee-157
71Sargent Promotions Stamps-224
72O-Pee-Chee-74
72Sargent Promotions Stamps-94
72Topps-89
73O-Pee-Chee-48
73Topps-48
74NHL Action Stamps-109
74O-Pee-Chee NHL-37
74Topps-37
75O-Pee-Chee NHL-361
76O-Pee-Chee NHL-268
76O-Pee-Chee NHL-386
77O-Pee-Chee NHL-236
77Penguins Puck Bucks-27
77Topps-236
Corrinet, Chris
01BAP Memorabilia-352
Emerald-352
Ruby-352
Sapphire-352
01Crown Royale-179
01SP Game Used-99
01Titanium-183
Retail-183
01Titanium Draft Day Edition-169
01UD Challenge for the Cup-135
01UD Honor Roll-90
01UD Premier Collection-87
01Upper Deck-441
Exclusives-441
01Upper Deck Ice-84
03Worcester Ice Cats-15
Corriveau, Andre
51Laval Dairy QSHL-74
52St. Lawrence Sales-24
55Montreal Royals-2
Corriveau, Francois
92Quebec Pee-Wee Tournament-78
93Quebec Pee-Wee Tournament-241
Corriveau, Luc
90Montreal-Bourassa AAA-8
Corriveau, Rick
897th Inn. Sketch OHL-40
90Score-396
Canadian-396
907th Inn. Sketch OHL-129
917th Inn. Sketch OHL-200
92Toledo Storm-24
92Toledo Storm Team Issue-16
93Toledo Storm-25
94Toledo Storm-3
95Buffalo Stampedes RHI-72
Corriveau, Yvon
86Capitals Police-5
88Capitals Borderless-2
88Capitals Smokey-2
89Capitals Team Issue-4
90O-Pee-Chee-364
90Pro Set-100
90Score-302A
Canadian-302A
90Topps-364
Tiffany-364
90Whalers Jr. 7-Eleven-4
91Upper Deck-407
French-407
92OPC Premier-74
92Panini Stickers-259
92Panini Stickers French-259
92Parkhurst-295
Emerald Ice-295
92Score-541
Canadian-541
92Stadium Club-476
92Topps-474
Gold-474G
92Upper Deck-460
93OPC Premier-208
Gold-208
93Stadium Club-9
Members Only Master Set-9
OPC-9
First Day Issue-9
First Day Issue OPC-9
93Topps/OPC Premier-208
Gold-208
94Minnesota Moose-7
95Minnesota Moose-7
96Detroit Vipers-3
98German DEL-170
99German DEL-57
01German Upper Deck-29
02German Berlin Polar Bears Postcards-7
02German DEL City Press-28
03German Berlin Polar Bears Postcards-8
Corsi, Jim
82Swedish Semic VM Stickers-122
83Swedish Semic VM Stickers-122
88Oilers Tenth Anniversary-115
Corso, Daniel
92Quebec Pee-Wee Tournament-604
95Bowman Draft Prospects-P7
95Upper Deck-510
Electric Ice-510
Electric Ice Gold-510
97Bowman CHL-71
OPC-71
98UD Choice-269
Prime Choice Reserve-269
Reserve-269
98Bowman CHL-89
Golden Anniversary-89
OPC International-89
98Bowman Chrome CHL-89
Golden Anniversary-89
Golden Anniversary Refractors-89
OPC International-89
OPC International Refractors-89
Refractors-89
99Quebec PeeWee Tournament Coll Souv-14
00Worcester Icecats-2
01BAP Memorabilia-23
Emerald-23
Ruby-23
Sapphire-23
01O-Pee-Chee-270
01O-Pee-Chee Premier Parallel-270
01Topps-270
OPC Parallel-270
01Topps Chrome-148
Refractors-148
Black Border Refractors-148
01Upper Deck-385
Exclusives-385
02Blues Team Issue-3
03Binghamton Senators-3
03Binghamton Senators Postcards-4
03Chicago Wolves-5
04German DEL-186
05German DEL-84
Corson, Shayne
83Brantford Alexanders-2
86Canadiens Postcards-3
87Canadiens Postcards-5
87Canadiens Vachon Stickers-49
87Canadiens Vachon Stickers-50
87O-Pee-Chee Stickers-127
88Canadiens Postcards-7
89Canadiens Kraft-4
89Canadiens Postcards-3
89Canadiens Provigo Figurines-27
89Kraft-21
89O-Pee-Chee-248
89O-Pee-Chee Stickers-49
89Panini Stickers-242
90Bowman-41
Tiffany-41
90Canadiens Postcards-9
90O-Pee-Chee-58
90Panini Stickers-54
90Pro Set-148
90Pro Set-369A
90Pro Set-369B
90Score-213
Canadian-213
90Score Hottest/Rising Stars-91
90Topps-58
Tiffany-58
90Upper Deck-280
French-280
91Bowman-328
91Canadiens Panini Team Stickers-5
91Canadiens Postcards-6
91Kraft-29
91O-Pee-Chee-157
91O-Pee-Chee-298
91OPC Premier-161
91Panini Stickers-196
91Parkhurst-86
French-86
91Pinnacle-102
French-102
91Pro Set-413
French-413
91Score American-65
91Score Canadian Bilingual-65
91Score Canadian English-65
91Stadium Club-5
91Topps-157
91Upper Deck-282
91Upper Deck-505
French-282
French-505
92Bowman-82
92Humpty Dumpty II-2
92Oilers IGA-4
92Oilers Team Issue-3
92O-Pee-Chee-231
92Panini Stickers-150
92Panini Stickers French-150
92Parkhurst-53
Emerald Ice-53
92Pinnacle-323
French-323
92Pro Set-89
92Score-158
Canadian-158
92Stadium Club-221
92Topps-201
Gold-201G
92Ultra-57
92Ultra-292
92Upper Deck-330
92Upper Deck-541
92Finnish Semic-93
93Donruss-114
93Leaf-46
93OPC Premier-38
Gold-38
93Panini Stickers-236
93Parkhurst-338
Emerald Ice-338
93Pinnacle-249
Canadian-249
93PowerPlay-79
93Score-108
Canadian-108
Dynamic Duos Canadian-7
93Stadium Club-40
Members Only Master Set-40
OPC-40
First Day Issue-40
First Day Issue OPC-40
93Topps/OPC Premier-38
Gold-38
93Ultra-51
93Upper Deck-132
NHLPA/Roots-13
SP-49
94Be A Player Signature Cards-172
94Canada Games NHL POGS-99
94Donruss-221
94EA Sports-46
94Finest-74
Super Team Winners-74
Refractors-74
94Flair-57
94Fleer-69
94Leaf-164
94OPC Premier-210
Special Effects-210
94Parkhurst-75
Gold-75
Vintage-V3
94Pinnacle-44
Artist's Proofs-44
Rink Collection-44
94Score-174
Gold-174
Platinum-174
94Select-47
Gold-47
94SP-42
Die Cuts-42
94Stadium Club Members Only-12
94Topps/OPC Premier-210
Special Effects-210
94Ultra-291
94Upper Deck-351
Electric Ice-351
SP Inserts-SP116
SP Inserts Die Cuts-SP116
94Finnish Jaa Kiekko-93
95Bowman-11
All-Foil-11
95Canada Games NHL POGS-241
95Collector's Choice-146
Player's Club-146
Player's Club Platinum-146
95Donruss-376
95Emotion-145
95Finest-18
Refractors-18
95Hoyle Western Playing Cards-11
95Leaf-123
95Metal-122
95Panini Stickers-260
95Parkhurst International-174
Emerald Ice-174
95Playoff One on One-86
95Score-245
Black Ice Artist's Proofs-245
Black Ice-245
95Select Certified-101
Mirror Gold-101
95SkyBox Impact-138
95SP-122
Holoviews-FX19
Holoviews Special FX-FX19
95Stadium Club-7
Members Only Master Set-7
95Summit-151
Artist's Proofs-151
Ice-151
95Topps-55
95Topps-229
OPC Inserts-55
OPC Inserts-229
95Ultra-53
95Ultra-296
Gold Medallion-53
95Upper Deck-101
Electric Ice-101
Electric Ice Gold-101
Special Edition-SE159
Special Edition Gold-SE159
95Zenith-98
95Finnish Semic World Championships-91
95Swedish World Championships Stickers-13
96Be A Player-62
Autographs-62
Autographs Silver-62
96Black Diamond-119
Gold-119
96Canadiens Postcards-8
96Canadiens Sheets-5
96Collector's Choice-225
96Donruss-55
Press Proofs-55
96Donruss Canadian Ice-43
Gold Press Proofs-43
Red Press Proofs-43
96Donruss Elite-58
Die Cut Stars-58
96Fleer-95
96Leaf-163
Press Proofs-163
96Leaf Limited-66
Gold-66
96Leaf Preferred-26
Press Proofs-26
96Maggers-17
96Metal Universe-130
96Pinnacle-104
Artist's Proofs-104
Foil-104
Premium Stock-104
Rink Collection-104
96Score-78
Artist's Proofs-78
Dealer's Choice Artist's Proofs-78
Special Artist's Proofs-78
Golden Blades-78
96Select Certified-73
Artist's Proofs-73
Blue-73
Mirror Blue-73
Mirror Gold-73
Mirror Red-73
Red-73
96SkyBox Impact-110
96SP-84
96Summit-137
Artist's Proofs-137
Ice-137
Metal-137
Premium Stock-137
96Team Out-11
96Topps Picks-139
OPC Inserts-139
96Ultra-85
Gold Medallion-85
96Upper Deck-139
96Zenith-107
Artist's Proofs-107
97Black Diamond-107
Double Diamond-107
Triple Diamond-107
Quadruple Diamond-107
97Canadiens Postcards-7
97Collector's Choice-137
97Crown Royale-67
Emerald Green-67
Ice Blue-67
Silver-67
97Donruss-42
Press Proofs Silver-42
Press Proofs Gold-42
97Donruss Limited-172
Exposure-172
97Kraft Team Canada-1
97McDonald's Team Canada Coins-5
97Pacific-246
Copper-246
Emerald Green-246
Ice Blue-246
Red-246
Silver-246
97Pacific Omega-116
Copper-116
Dark Gray-116
Emerald Green-116
Gold-116
Gold-248
Ice Blue-116
Team Leaders-11
97Paramount-93
Copper-93
Dark Grey-93
Emerald Green-93
Ice Blue-93
Red-93
Silver-93
97Revolution-69
Copper-69
Emerald-69
Ice Blue-69
Silver-69
97Score Canadiens-12
Platinum-12
Premier-12
97SP Authentic-84
97Upper Deck-298
97Zenith-67
Z-Gold-67
Z-Silver-67
97Zenith 5 x 7-34
Gold Impulse-34
Silver Impulse-34
98Aurora-92
Man Advantage-11
98Bowman's Best-98
Refractors-98
Atomic Refractors-98
98Canadiens Team Issue-3
98Crown Royale-67
Limited Series-67
98Pacific-249
Ice Blue-249
Red-249
98Pacific Dynagon Ice-94
Blue-94
Red-94
98Pacific Omega-119
Red-119
Opening Day Issue-119
98Paramount-111
Copper-111
Emerald Green-111
Holo-Electric-111
Ice Blue-111
Silver-111
98Revolution-71
Ice Shadow-71
Red-71
98UD Choice-103
98UD Choice Preview-103
98UD Choice Prime Choice Reserve-103
98UD Choice Reserve-103
98Upper Deck-291
Exclusives-291
Exclusives 1 of 1-291
Gold Reserve-291
98Upper Deck MVP-109
Gold Script-109
Silver Script-109
Super Script-109
99Aurora-73
Premiere Date-73
99BAP Memorabilia-29
Gold-29
Silver-29
99Kraft Dinner-1
99O-Pee-Chee-126
99O-Pee-Chee Chrome-126
99O-Pee-Chee Chrome Refractors-126
99Pacific-202
Copper-202
Emerald Green-202
Gold-202
Ice Blue-202
Premiere Date-202
Red-202
99Pacific Dynagon Ice-100
Blue-100
Copper-100
Gold-100
Premiere Date-100
99Pacific Omega-116
Copper-116
Gold-116
Ice Blue-116
Premiere Date-116
99Paramount-115
Copper-115
Emerald-115
Gold-115
Holographic Emerald-115
Holographic Gold-115
Holographic Silver-115
Ice Blue-115
Premiere Date-115
Red-115
Silver-115
99Revolution-73
Premiere Date-73
Red-73
Shadow Series-73
Copper-73
Gold-73
CSC Silver-73
99Stadium Club-49
First Day Issue-49
One of a Kind-49
Printing Plates Black-49
Printing Plates Cyan-49
Printing Plates Magenta-49
Printing Plates Yellow-49
99Topps/OPC-126
99Topps/OPC Chrome-126
Refractors-126
99Upper Deck Victory-151
99Slovakian Challengers-13
00BAP Memorabilia-426
Emerald-426
Ruby-426
Sapphire-426
00BAP Signature Series-171
Emerald-171
Ruby-171
Sapphire-171
Autographs-211
Autographs Gold-211
00O-Pee-Chee-240
00O-Pee-Chee Parallel-240
00Pacific-207
Copper-207
Gold-207
Ice Blue-207
Premiere Date-207
00Private Stock Game Gear-95
00Private Stock Game Gear Patches-95
00Titanium Draft Day Edition-94
Patches-94
00Topps/OPC-240
Parallel-240
00Topps Chrome-150
OPC Refractors-150
Refractors-150
00Upper Deck-394
Exclusives Tier 1-394
Exclusives Tier 2-394
00Upper Deck Victory-124
00Vanguard Dual Game-Worn Jerseys-18
00Vanguard Dual Game-Worn Patches-18
01Pacific-362
Extreme LTD-362
Hobby LTD-362
Premiere Date-362
Retail LTD-362
Adrenaline Jerseys-46
01Pacific Arena Exclusives-362
01Upper Deck-166
Exclusives-166
01Upper Deck Vintage-237
02BAP Memorabilia-120
Emerald-120
Ruby-120
Sapphire-120
NHL All-Star Game-120
NHL All-Star Game Blue-120
NHL All-Star Game Green-120
NHL All-Star Game Red-120
02BAP Memorabilia Toronto Fall Expo-120
02BAP Sig Series Auto Buybacks 2000-211
02Maple Leafs Platinum Collection-4
02NHL Power Play Stickers-125
02O-Pee-Chee-38
02O-Pee-Chee Premier Blue Parallel-38
02O-Pee-Chee Premier Red Parallel-38
02O-Pee-Chee Factory Set-38

02Pacific-358
Blue-358
Red-358
02Pacific Complete-64
Red-64
02Topps-38
OPC Blue Parallel-38
OPC Red Parallel-38
Factory Set-38
02Topps Total-206
02Upper Deck Vintage-236
03Topps Traded-TT8
Blue-TT8
Gold-TT8
Red-TT8

Cort, Joel
94Guelph Storm-6
95Slapshot-86
95Guelph Storm-12
96Guelph Storm-6
96Guelph Storm Premier Collection-5

Cortes, Mike
84Minnesota-Duluth Bulldogs-25
85Minnesota-Duluth Bulldogs-14

Cortez, Jesse
93Quebec Pee-Wee Tournament-861

Corthay, Nicolas
95Swiss HNL-498

Corupe, Bob
57St. Catherine's Tee Pees-18

Corupe, Kenny
99Owen Sound Platers-4
01Odessa Jackalopes-4
02Louisiana Ice Gators-6
03Louisiana Ice Gators-4
04Wheeling Nailers Riesbeck's-14
05WBS Penguins-6

Corvo, Joe
96Upper Deck Ice-145
00Lowell Lock Monsters-1
01Manchester Monarchs-12A
02Pacific Calder-73
Silver-73
02Pacific Complete-545
Red-545
02Manchester Monarchs-6
03ITG Action-227
03Upper Deck MVP-199
Gold Script-199
Silver Script-199
Canadian Exclusives-199
04Chicago Wolves-6
05Kings Team Issue-8
05Parkhurst-224
Facsimile Auto Parallel-224
06Gatorade-48
06O-Pee-Chee-350
Rainbow-350
06Senators Postcards-4
06Upper Deck-385
Exclusives Parallel-385
High Gloss Parallel-385
Masterpieces-385

Corwin, Ed
98Madison Monsters-15

Cosgrove, Blake
04Northern Michigan Wildcats-5

Cossette, Bryan
91Air Canada SJHL-D44
92Saskatchewan JHL-9

Cossette, Jean Marie
52Juniors Blue Tint-39
62Quebec Aces-5

Costanzo, Dallas
03Vernon Vipers-6
04Vernon Vipers-22

Costanzo, Ryan
05Penticton Vees-3

Costea, Mark
96Alaska Gold Kings-1
98El Paso Buzzards-16

Costello, Les
44Beehive Group II Photos-391
45Quaker Oats Photos-14

Costello, Murray
44Beehive Group II Photos-89
52Juniors Blue Tint-156
94Parkhurst Missing Link-60

Costello, Rich
84O-Pee-Chee-298

Cota, Darren
85Medicine Hat Tigers-20

Cote, Alain
79O-Pee-Chee-324
80Nordiques Postcards-7
81Nordiques Postcards-5
81O-Pee-Chee-272
82Nordiques Postcards-5
82O-Pee-Chee-281
83Nordiques Postcards-5
83O-Pee-Chee-291
83Vachon-63
84Nordiques Postcards-5
84O-Pee-Chee-278
85Nordiques General Foods-4
85Nordiques McDonald's-3
85Nordiques Placemats-6
85Nordiques Provigo-5
85Nordiques Team Issue-4
85O-Pee-Chee-205
85O-Pee-Chee Stickers-149
86Kraft Drawings-11
86Nordiques General Foods-4
86Nordiques McDonald's-4
86Nordiques Team Issue-2
86Nordiques Yum-Yum-1
86O-Pee-Chee-233
86O-Pee-Chee Stickers-20
87Nordiques General Foods-5
87Nordiques Yum-Yum-1
87O-Pee-Chee-254
87Panini Stickers-169
88Nordiques General Foods-7
88Nordiques Team Issue-7
88O-Pee-Chee-205
88O-Pee-Chee Stickers-186
88Panini Stickers-352
89ProCards AHL-102
90ProCards AHL/IHL-54
907th Inn. Sketch QMJHL-89
91Canadiens Postcards-7
91OPC Premier-188
91Pro Set-417
French-417
917th Inn. Sketch QMJHL-25
917th Inn. Sketch QMJHL-54
92Fredericton Canadiens-7
93Durivage Score-19
94Thunder Bay Senators-7

97Macon Whoopee-18
97Macon Whoopee Autographs-18
99German DEL-45
00Finnish Cardset-210
03St. Jean Mission-3

Cote, Alain (Def)
91Canadiens Postcards-7
91OPC Premier-188
91Pro Set-417
French-417
92Fredericton Canadiens-7
93Durivage Score-19
99German DEL-45
00Finnish Cardset-210
03St. Jean Mission-3

Cote, Alain (Minors)
907th Inn. Sketch QMJHL-89
917th Inn. Sketch QMJHL-25
917th Inn. Sketch QMJHL-54
94Thunder Bay Senators-7
97Macon Whoopee-18
97Macon Whoopee Autographs-18

Cote, Alexandre
93Quebec Pee-Wee Tournament-1366

Cote, Andre
81Fredericton Express-24
82Fredericton Express-24
83Fredericton Express-20

Cote, Bart
89Brandon Wheat Kings-9
90Brandon Wheat Kings-4
907th Inn. Sketch WHL-219
917th Inn. Sketch Memorial Cup-94

Cote, Benoit
92Quebec Pee-Wee Tournament-835
92Quebec Pee-Wee Tournament-1323
93Quebec Pee-Wee Tournament-1597
97Bowman CHL-128
OPC-128
Autographs-128

Cote, Brandin
97Spokane Chiefs-8
98SP Authentic-124
Power Shift-124
98Upper Deck-401
Exclusives-401
Exclusives 1 of 1-401
Gold Reserve-401
98Spokane Chiefs-4
99Spokane Chiefs-7
00Spokane Chiefs-6
01Spokane Chiefs-6
02Norfolk Admirals-6
03Norfolk Admirals-7
04Norfolk Admirals-7
05UK Nottingham Panthers-11

Cote, David
93Quebec Pee-Wee Tournament-1115

Cote, Dominic
92Quebec Pee-Wee Tournament-479
92Quebec Pee-Wee Tournament-1251
98Thetford Mines Coyotes-19

Cote, Eric
93Quebec Pee-Wee Tournament-221

Cote, Francis
93Quebec Pee-Wee Tournament-118

Cote, Frank
51Bas Du Fleuve-51
52Bas Du Fleuve-36

Cote, Frederick
93Quebec Pee-Wee Tournament-1356

Cote, Georges-Etienne
01Sorel Royaux-5

Cote, Jean-Michel
03Quebec Remparts-5

Cote, Jean-Philippe
93Quebec Pee-Wee Tournament-978
01Cape Breton Screaming Eagles-7
02Cape Breton Screaming Eagles-24
04Drummondville Voltigeurs-24
04Hamilton Bulldogs-3
05Hot Prospects-142
En Fuego-142
Red Hot-142
White Hot-142
05SP Authentic-269
Limited-269
05SP Game Used-218
05SPx-268
05The Cup Masterpiece Pressplate Artifact-291
05The Cup Masterpiece Pressplates (Ice)-213
05The Cup Master Pressplate Rookie Update-151
05The Cup Masterpiece Pressplates SPA-269
05The Cup Masterpiece Pressplates SP GU-218
05The Cup Masterpiece Pressplates (SPx)-268
05The Cup Masterpiece Pressplates Trilogy-273
05The Cup Masterpiece Pressplate Ult Coll-212
05UD Artifacts-291
05Ultimate Collection-212
Gold-212
05Upper Deck Ice-213
05Upper Deck Rookie Update-151
05Upper Deck Trilogy-273
05Hamilton Bulldogs-5
05Saint John's Sea Dogs-9
06Hamilton Bulldogs-6

Cote, Jean-Sebastien
03Rimouski Oceanic-5
03Rimouski Oceanic Sheets-2
04Rimouski Oceanic-10
05Chicoutimi Sagueneens-30
05Rimouski Oceanic-8

Cote, Ladufo
93Quebec Pee-Wee Tournament-287

Cote, Martin
84Richelieu Riverains-3
92Quebec Pee-Wee Tournament-453
92Quebec Pee-Wee Tournament-1266

Cote, Mike
907th Inn. Sketch OHL-331
91Oshawa Generals Sheet-18
917th Inn. Sketch OHL-344
93Quebec Pee-Wee Tournament-222

Cote, Patrice
92Quebec Pee-Wee Tournament-536
93Quebec Pee-Wee Tournament-1134

Cote, Patrick
95Classic-33
96Michigan K-Wings-17
97Be A Player-235
Autographs-235
Autographs Die-Cuts-235
Autographs Prismatic Die-Cuts-235
98Pacific Omega-134
Red-134
Opening Day Issue-134
98Predators Team Issue-7
98Upper Deck-304
Exclusives-304
Exclusives 1 of 1-304
Gold Reserve-304
99Pacific-221
Copper-221
Emerald Green-221
Gold-221
Ice Blue-221
Premiere Date-221
Red-221
99Upper Deck Victory-162
00Hamilton Bulldogs-8

Cote, Philippe
03Baie Comeau Drakkar-23
04Baie-Comeau Drakkar-23
05Gatineau Olympiques-27

Cote, Ray
83Moncton Alpines-23
84Nova Scotia Oilers-6
88Oilers Tenth Anniversary-140

Cote, Riley
98Prince Albert Raiders-5
00Prince Albert Raiders-4
01Prince Albert Raiders-4
03ECHL Update RBI Sports-121
04Philadelphia Phantoms-1
05Philadelphia Phantoms-7
06Philadelphia Phantoms-18

Cote, Roger
80Quebec Remparts-3

Cote, Steven
93Quebec Pee-Wee Tournament-26

Cote, Sylvain
81Fredericton Express-3
82Fredericton Express-3
84Whalers Junior Wendy's-2
85Whalers Junior Wendy's-2
86Whalers Junior Thomas'-4
87Whalers Jr. Burger King/Pepsi-3
88Panini Stickers-237
88Whalers Junior Ground Round-3
89O-Pee-Chee-162
89Panini Stickers-229
89Topps-162
89Whalers Junior Milk-3
90Pro Set-448
90Score-83
Canadian-83
90Whalers Jr. 7-Eleven-5
91Bowman-17
91Capitals Junior 5x7-7
91Capitals Kodak-7
91O-Pee-Chee-249
91Pinnacle-221
French-221
91Pro Set-82
91Pro Set-512
French-82
French-512
91Score American-129
91Score Canadian Bilingual-129
91Score Canadian Bilingual-596
91Score Canadian English-129
91Score Canadian English-596
91Score Rookie/Traded-46T
91Stadium Club-183
91Topps-249
92Bowman-115
92Capitals Kodak-7
92Durivage Panini-34
92O-Pee-Chee-277
92Parkhurst-431
Emerald Ice-431
92Pinnacle-182
French-182
92Score-78
Canadian-78
92Stadium Club-145
92Topps-428
Gold-428G
92Ultra-433
93Donruss-367
93Durivage Score-35
93Leaf-52
93OPC Premier-138
Gold-138
93Parkhurst-489
Emerald Ice-489
93Pinnacle-258
Canadian-258
93PowerPlay-259
93Score-92
93Score-450
Canadian-92
Canadian-450
93Stadium Club-66
Members Only Master Set-66
OPC-66
First Day Issue-66
First Day Issue OPC-66
93Topps/OPC Premier-138
Gold-138
93Ultra-445
94Be A Player Signature Cards-166
94Canada Games NHL POGS-249
94Donruss-153
94Flair-198
94Fleer-234
94Leaf-140
94OPC Premier-208
Special Effects-208
94Parkhurst SE-SE193
Gold-SE193
94Pinnacle-33
Artist's Proofs-33
Rink Collection-33
94Select Promos-128
94Select-128
Gold-128
94Topps/OPC Premier-208
Special Effects-208
94Ultra-232
94Upper Deck-354
Electric Ice-354
95Capitals Team Issue-5
95Collector's Choice-284
Player's Club-284
Player's Club Platinum-284
95Finest-37
Refractors-37
95Leaf-218
95Metal-158
95Parkhurst International-222
Emerald Ice-222
95Pinnacle-65
Artist's Proofs-65
Rink Collection-65
95Playoff One on One-321
95Score-183
Black Ice Artist's Proofs-183
Black Ice-183
95Stadium Club-23
Members Only Master Set-23
95Topps OPC Inserts-151
95Ultra-321
95Upper Deck-133
Electric Ice-133
Electric Ice Gold-133
Special Edition-SE176
Special Edition Gold-SE176
96Collector's Choice-287
96SkyBox Impact-138
96Topps Picks-153
OPC Inserts-153
97Pacific-207
Copper-207
Emerald Green-207
Ice Blue-207
Red-207
Silver-207
98Pacific-412
Ice Blue-412
Red-412
99Pacific-404
Copper-404
Emerald Green-404
Gold-404
Ice Blue-404
Premiere Date-404
Red-404
00BAP Memorabilia-307
00BAP Memorabilia-486
Emerald-307
Emerald-486
Ruby-307
Ruby-486
Sapphire-307
Sapphire-486
Promos-307
00BAP Mem Chicago Sportsfest Copper-307
00BAP Memorabilia Chicago Sportsfest Blue-307
00BAP Memorabilia Chicago Sportsfest Gold-307
00BAP Memorabilia Chicago Sportsfest Ruby-307
00BAP Memorabilia Chicago Sun-Times Ruby-307
00BAP Memorabilia Chicago Sun-Times Gold-307
00BAP Mem Chicago Sun-Times Sapphire-307
00BAP Mem Toronto Fall Expo Copper-307
00BAP Memorabilia Toronto Fall Expo Gold-307
00BAP Memorabilia Toronto Fall Expo Ruby-307
00Pacific-128
Copper-128
Gold-128
Ice Blue-128
Premiere Date-128
00Private Stock Game Gear-102

Cotnoir, Benoit
99Mobile Mysticks-4

Cotton, Darren
02UK Peterborough Phantoms-12

Cotton, Harold
32O'Keefe Maple Leafs-8
33O-Pee-Chee V304A-35
33V129-12
33V288 Hamilton Gum-39
33V357 Ice Kings-33
34Beehive Group I Photos-311
37V356 Worldwide Gum-35
55Parkhurst-32
Quaker Oats-32
02BAP Ultimate Mem Paper Cuts Autos-1
02Parkhurst Reprints-205
04ITG Ultimate Mem Maple Leafs Forever-12
05ITG Ultimate Mem Leafs Forever Autos-6
06ITG Ultimate Memorabilia Maple Leafs Forever Autos-3

Cotton, Jeff
01Val d'Or Foreurs-8
02Val d'Or Foreurs-20
03Val d'Or Foreurs-19

Cotton, Jon
02UK Peterborough Phantoms-13

Cotuno, Dan
93Quebec Pee-Wee Tournament-706

Coucelles, Simon
05Quebec Remparts-7
05Quebec Remparts Signature Series-7

Couch, Michael
00Halifax Mooseheads-3
01Halifax Mooseheads-13

Couette, Dany
01Sorel Royaux-6

Coughlin, Ben
92Harvard Crimson-6

Coughlin, Brian
72Johnstown Jets-2

Coughlin, Kevin
03Quebec Remparts-6
04Quebec Remparts-20
05Saint John's Sea Dogs-13

Coughlin, Matt
00Belleville Bulls-4
01Belleville Bulls-7
01Belleville Bulls-28

Coulis, Tim
84Springfield Indians-10
85North Stars Postcards-9

Coulombe, Kavin
93Quebec Pee-Wee Tournament-253

Coulombe, Patrick
02Rimouski Oceanic-2
03Rimouski Oceanic-2
03Rimouski Oceanic Sheets-3
04Rimouski Oceanic-11
05Chicoutimi Sagueneens-25
05Rimouski Oceanic-1
06Hot Prospects-183
Red Hot-183
White Hot-183
06O-Pee-Chee-580
Rainbow-580
06SP Authentic-213
Limited-213
06The Cup Masterpiece Pressplates (Marquee Rookies)-580
06The Cup Masterpiece Pressplates (SP Authentic)-213
06Upper Deck-494
Exclusives Parallel-494
High Gloss Parallel-494
Masterpieces-494
06Manitoba Moose-25

Coulombe, Serge
90Rayside-Balfour Jr. Canadians-4

Coulter, Art
34Beehive Group I Photos-269
35Diamond Matchbooks Tan 1-17
35Diamond Matchbooks Tan 2-15
35Diamond Matchbooks Tan 3-14
35O-Pee-Chee V304C-93
39O-Pee-Chee V301-1-34
83Hall of Fame-185
83Hall of Fame Postcards-J5
85Hall of Fame-185
03BAP Ultimate Memorabilia Paper Cuts-37

Coulter, Jeff
00Saskatoon Blades-17
01Kelowna Rockets-2
01Vancouver Giants-9

Coupal, Gary
92Sudbury Wolves-21
93Sudbury Wolves-17
93Sudbury Wolves Police-16
94Sudbury Wolves Police-4
99Odessa Jackalopes-15

Courcelles, Sebastien
00Sherbrooke Castors-2
Signed-2
01Sherbrooke Castors-16

Courcelles, Simon
03Quebec Remparts-7
04Quebec Remparts-6

Courchaine, Adam
03Vancouver Giants-10
04Vancouver Giants-8

Courchene, Corey
03Brandon Wheat Kings-7
04Brandon Wheat Kings-3
05Brandon Wheat Kings-5

Courchesne, Pierre-Luc
00Sherbrooke Castors-16
Signed-16
01Sherbrooke Castors-18
02ECHL All-Star Northern-20
02ECHL Update-U-5
02Johnstown Chiefs-4
03Johnstown Chiefs-13
03Johnstown Chiefs RBI Sports-211
04Johnstown Chiefs-5

Courcy, Bob
62Quebec Aces-6
69Seattle Totems-3

Cournoyer, Bertrand
88Richelieu Riverains-9

Cournoyer, Yvan
64Beehive Group III Photos-101
64Canadiens Postcards-4
64Coca-Cola Caps-63
65Coca-Cola-63
65Topps-76
66Topps-72
66Topps USA Test-13
67Canadiens IGA-12
67Topps-70
67York Action Octagons-28
67York Action Octagons-29
67York Action Octagons-30
68Canadiens IGA-12
68Canadiens Postcards BW-3
68O-Pee-Chee-62
68Post Marbles-5
68Shirriff Coins-87
68Topps-62
69Canadiens Postcards Color-7
69O-Pee-Chee-6
69O-Pee-Chee-221
Four-in-One-3
Stamps-4
69Topps-6
70Canadiens Pins-2
70Colgate Stamps-60
70Dad's Cookies-17
70Esso Power Players-9
70O-Pee-Chee-50
Deckle-23
70Sargent Promotions Stamps-109
70Topps-50
71Bazooka-15
71Canadiens Postcards-3
71Colgate Heads-1
71Frito-Lay-1
71Letraset Action Replays-15
71Mattel Mini-Records-1
71O-Pee-Chee-15
71O-Pee-Chee-260
Posters-4
71Sargent Promotions Stamps-102
71Topps-15
71Toronto Sun-148
72Canadiens Postcards-4
72Canadiens Great West Life Prints-2
72Dimanche/Derniere Heure *-136
72Dimanche/Derniere Heure *-137
72O-Pee-Chee-29
72O-Pee-Chee-44
72O-Pee-Chee-250
Team Canada-6
72Sargent Promotions Stamps-117
72Topps-10
72Topps-131
72Finnish Semic World Championship-204
72Swedish Semic World Championship-204
73Canadiens Postcards-4
73Mac's Milk-5
73O-Pee-Chee-157
73Topps-115
74Canadiens Postcards-4
74Lipton Soup-13
74NHL Action Stamps-148
74O-Pee-Chee NHL-124
74O-Pee-Chee NHL-140
74Topps-124
74Topps-140
75Canadiens Postcards-4
75Heroes Stand-Ups-8
75O-Pee-Chee NHL-70
75Topps-70
76Canadiens Postcards-4
76O-Pee-Chee NHL-30
76Topps-30
77Canadiens Postcards-4
77Coca-Cola-4
77O-Pee-Chee NHL-230
77Sportscasters-213
77Sportscasters-1513
77Topps-230
77Finnish Sportscasters-58-1392
78Canadiens Postcards-4
78O-Pee-Chee-60
78Topps-60
83Hall of Fame-136
83Hall of Fame Postcards-K1
85Hall of Fame-136
88Esso All-Stars-7
91Future Trends Canada '72-82
91Future Trends Canada '72 French-82
92Sport-Flash-12
92Sport-Flash Autographs-12
93O-Pee-Chee Canadiens Hockey Fest-23
93O-Pee-Chee Canadiens Panel-1
93Zeller's Masters of Hockey-3
93Zeller's Masters of Hockey Signed-3
94Parkhurst Tall Boys-75
94Parkhurst Tall Boys-160
Autographs-A2
95Parkhurst '66-67-60
Coins-60
96Canadiens Postcards-9
99BAP Memorabilia AS Canadian Hobby-CH11
99BAP Memorabilia AS Cdn Hobby Autos-CH11
01BAP Ultimate Mem Dynasty Jerseys-4
01BAP Ultimate Mem Dynasty Emblems-4
01BAP Ultimate Mem Dynasty Numbers-4
01BAP Ultimate Memorabilia Les Canadiens-2
01BAP Ultimate Mem Retro Teammates-10
01BAP Ultimate Mem Stanley Cup Winners-3
01Greats of the Game-25
Autographs-25
01Parkhurst Autographs-PA52
01Topps Rookie Reprints-2
01Topps Rookie Reprint Autographs-2
01Topps Stanley Cup Heroes-SCHYC
01Topps Stanley Cup Heroes Autographs-SCHAYC
01Topps Archives-29
Arena Seats-ASYC
Autographs-2
01UD Stanley Cup Champs-14
01Upper Deck Legends-35
02BAP Memorabilia Mini Stanley Cups-11
02BAP Ultimate Memorabilia Conn Smythe-5
02BAP Ultimate Memorabilia Numerology-17
02BAP Ultimate Mem Retro Teammates-4
02BAP Ultimate Mem Storied Franchise-16
02Canadiens AGF-NNO
02Canadiens Molson Export-12
02UD Foundations-57
Lasting Impressions Sticks-L-YC
03BAP Ultimate Mem Hometown Heroes-7
03BAP Ultimate Mem Hometown Heroes Gold-7
03ITG Toronto Fall Expo Forever Rivals-FR6
03Parkhurst Original Six Montreal-38
03Parkhurst Original Six Montreal-78
03Parkhurst Original Six Montreal-86
Autographs-3
04ITG Franchises Canadian-52
Autographs-YC
Memorabilia-SM8
Memorabilia Autographs-SM8
Memorabilia Gold-SM8
04ITG Franchises He Shoots/Scores Prizes-11
04ITG Ultimate Mem Country of Origin-15
04ITG Ultimate Mem Country of Origin Gold-15
04ITG Ultimate Mem Jersey Autos-25
04ITG Ultimate Mem Jersey AutosGold-25
04ITG Ultimate Memorabilia Original Six-7
04ITG Ultimate Mem Retro Teammates-15
04ITG Ultimate Mem Stick Autos-40
04ITG Ultimate Mem Stick Autos Gold-40
04UD Legendary Signatures-90
AKA Autographs-AKA-YC
Autographs-YC
Summit Stars-CDN4
Summit Stars Autographs-CDN-YC
04ITG Heroes and Prospects-137
Autographs-YC
04ITG Heroes/Prospects Toronto Expo '05-137
04ITG Heroes/Prospects Expo Heroes/Pros-137
05ITG Heroes/Prosp Toronto Expo Parallel -190
05ITG Ultimate Memorabilia Level 1-100
05ITG Ultimate Memorabilia Level 2-100
05ITG Ultimate Memorabilia Level 3-100
05ITG Ultimate Memorabilia Level 4-100
05ITG Ultimate Memorabilia Level 5-100
05ITG Ultimate Memorabilia Double Autos-20
05ITG Ultimate Mem Double Autos Gold-20
05ITG Ultimate Mem Double Mem Autos-18
05ITG Ultimate Mem Double Mem Autos Gold-18
05ITG Ultimate Mem Raised to the Rafters-12
05ITG Ultimate Mem Raised Rafters Gold-12
05ITG Ultimate Mem Retro Teammate Jerseys-13
05ITG Ult Mem Retro Teammates Jersey Gold-13
05ITG Ultimate Mem 3 Star of the Game Jsy-13
05ITG Ult Mem 3 Star of the Game Jsy Gold-13
05ITG Ultimate Memorabilia Ultimate Autos-45
05ITG Ultimate Mem Ultimate Autos Gold-45
05ITG Heroes and Prospects-190
Autographs Series II-YC
Hero Memorabilia-HM-52
06ITG International Ice-150
Gold-150
Autographs-AYC
Greatest Moments-GM03
Greatest Moments Gold-GM03
Triple Memorabilia-TM02
Triple Memorabilia Gold-TM02
06ITG Ultimate Memorabilia-150
Artist Proof-150
Autos Triple-3
Autos Triple Gold-3
Bowman Factor-3
Bowman Factor Gold-3
Bowman Factor Autos-3
Bowman Factor Autos Gold-3
Jerseys Autos-9
Jerseys Autos Gold-9
Raised to the Rafters-3
Raised to the Rafters Gold-3
Retro Teammates-12
Retro Teammates Gold-12
Ring Leaders-18
Ring Leaders Gold-18
Road to the Cup-5
Road to the Cup Gold-5
Stick Rack-1
Stick Rack Gold-1

Cournoyer, Yves
88Richelieu Riverains-10

Courteau, Maurice
51Laval Dairy Lac St. Jean-59

Courteau, Yves
84Moncton Golden Flames-17
85Moncton Golden Flames-24

Courtemanche, Dave
81Kingston Canadians-3

Courtemanche, Marc
77Granby Vics-5

Courtemanche, Yves
77Granby Vics-6

Courtenay, Ed
89ProCards IHL-80
90ProCards AHL/IHL-116
91Upper Deck-517
French-517
91Kansas City Blades-12
91ProCards-507
92OPC Premier-8
92Upper Deck-507
92Kansas City Blades-12
93Leaf-145
93Panini Stickers-261
93PowerPlay-217
93Stadium Club-72
Members Only Master Set-72
OPC-72
First Day Issue-72
First Day Issue OPC-72
93Ultra-8
93Kansas City Blades-13
96South Carolina Stingrays-27
97UK Sheffield Steelers-20
99UK Sheffield Steelers-4
00UK Sekonda Superleague-15
00UK Sheffield Steelers Centurions-1
03South Carolina Stingrays-324

Courtnall, Geoff
81Victoria Cougars-6
82Victoria Cougars-4
84Bruins Postcards-3
84Victoria Cougars-6
85Moncton Golden Flames-11
88Capitals Borderless-3
88Capitals Smokey-3
88Oilers Tenth Anniversary-88
88O-Pee-Chee Stickers-222
89Capitals Kodak-14
89Capitals Team Issue-5
89O-Pee-Chee-111
89O-Pee-Chee Stickers-80
89O-Pee-Chee Stickers-107
89O-Pee-Chee Stickers-164
89O-Pee-Chee Stickers-246
89Panini Stickers-340
89Topps-111
89Topps Sticker Inserts-9
90Blues Kodak-7
90Bowman-73
Tiffany-73
90Kraft-9
90O-Pee-Chee-273
90OPC Premier-18
90Panini Stickers-159
90Pro Set-309
90Pro Set-521
90Score-124
Canadian-124
90Score Rookie/Traded-5T
90Topps-273
Tiffany-273
90Upper Deck-238
90Upper Deck-438
French-238
French-438
91Pro Set Platinum-123
91Bowman-318
91Canucks Autograph Cards-4
91Canucks Team Issue 8x10-4
91Kraft-15
91O-Pee-Chee-305
91OPC Premier-101
91Panini Stickers-38
91Parkhurst-186
French-186
91Pinnacle-263
French-263
91Pro Set-245
French-245
91Score American-150
91Score American-380
91Score Canadian Bilingual-150
91Score Canadian Bilingual-270
91Score Canadian English-150
91Score Canadian English-270
91Stadium Club-149
91Topps-305
91Upper Deck-467
French-467
92Bowman-345
92Canucks Road Trip Art-5
92O-Pee-Chee-176
92Panini Stickers-29
92Panini Stickers French-29
92Parkhurst-189
Emerald Ice-189
92Pinnacle-187
French-187
92Pro Set-198
92Score-234
Canadian-234
92Stadium Club-265
92Topps-472
Gold-472G
92Ultra-220
92Upper Deck-39
92Upper Deck-240
93Donruss-352
93Leaf-72
93OPC Premier-337
Gold-337
93Panini Stickers-170
93Parkhurst-216
Emerald Ice-216
93Pinnacle-132
Canadian-132
93PowerPlay-249
93Score-78
Canadian-78
93Stadium Club-413
Members Only Master Set-413
First Day Issue-413
93Topps/OPC Premier-337
Gold-337
93Ultra-76
93Upper Deck-114
SP-163
94Be A Player-R6
Signature Cards-135
94Canada Games NHL POGS-329
94Canucks Program Inserts-6
94Donruss-50
94EA Sports-142
94Finest-83
Super Team Winners-83
Refractors-83
94Fleer-224
94Leaf-53
94Leaf Limited-69
94OPC Premier-186
94OPC Premier-525
Special Effects-186
Special Effects-525
94Parkhurst-240
Gold-240
94Pinnacle-276
Artist's Proofs-276
Rink Collection-276
94Post Box Backs-7
94Score-161
Gold-161
Platinum-161
94Select-137
Gold-137
94SP-125
Die Cuts-125
94Topps/OPC Premier-186
94Topps/OPC Premier-525
Special Effects-186
Special Effects-525
94Ultra-382
94Upper Deck-286
Electric Ice-286
SP Inserts-SP82
SP Inserts Die Cuts-SP82
95Canada Games NHL POGS-240
95Canucks Building the Dream Art-14
95Collector's Choice-31
Player's Club-31
Player's Club Platinum-31
95Donruss-238
95Emotion-146
95Finest-49
Refractors-49
95Hoyle Western Playing Cards-12
95Leaf-233
95Leaf Limited-3
95Panini Stickers-193
95Parkhurst International-448
Emerald Ice-448
95Playoff One on One-87
95Playoff One on One-305
95Pro Magnets-11
95Pro Magnets-128
95Score-255
Black Ice Artist's Proofs-255
Black Ice-255
95SkyBox Impact-139
95SP-128
95Summit-119
Artist's Proofs-119
Ice-119
95Topps-276
OPC Inserts-276
95Ultra-167
95Ultra-297
Gold Medallion-167
95Upper Deck-120
Electric Ice-120
Electric Ice Gold-120
95Zenith-58
96Collector's Choice-229
96Donruss-54
Press Proofs-54
96Donruss Elite-43
Die Cut Stars-43
96Leaf-158
Press Proofs-158
96NHL Pro Stamps-11
96Pinnacle-146
Artist's Proofs-146
Foil-146
Premium Stock-146
Rink Collection-146
96Score-32
Artist's Proofs-32
Dealer's Choice Artist's Proofs-32
Special Artist's Proofs-32
Golden Blades-32
96SkyBox Impact-111
96Topps Picks-149
OPC Inserts-149
96Upper Deck-327
97Collector's Choice-227
97Donruss-47
Press Proofs Silver-47
Press Proofs Gold-47
97Donruss Limited-24
Exposure-24
97Pacific-62
Copper-62
Emerald Green-62
Ice Blue-62
Red-62
Silver-62
Slap Shots Die-Cuts-9A
97Pacific Invincible-118
Copper-118
Emerald Green-118
Ice Blue-118
Red-118
Silver-118
97Pacific Omega-190
Copper-190
Dark Gray-190
Emerald Green-190
Gold-190
Ice Blue-190
97Panini Stickers-167
97Paramount-157
Copper-157
Dark Grey-157
Emerald Green-157
Ice Blue-157
Red-157
Silver-157
97Revolution-118
Copper-118
Emerald-118
Ice Blue-118
Silver-118
97Score-184
97Score Blues-15
Platinum-15
Premier-15
98Aurora-159
98Be A Player-124
Press Release-124
98BAP Gold-124
98BAP Autographs-124
98BAP Autographs Gold-124
98BAP Tampa Bay All Star Game-124
98OPC Chrome-139
Refractors-139
98Pacific-365
Ice Blue-365
Red-365
98Pacific Dynagon Ice-156
Blue-156
Red-156
98Panini Stickers-156
98Paramount-201
Copper-201
Emerald Green-201
Holo-Electric-201
Ice Blue-201
Silver-201
98Topps-139
O-Pee-Chee-139
98UD Choice-190
98UD Choice Preview-190
98UD Choice Prime Choice Reserve-190
98UD Choice Reserve-190
98Upper Deck-357
Exclusives-357
Exclusives 1 of 1-357
Gold Reserve-357

99BAP Memorabilia-183
Gold-183
Silver-183
99Pacific-354
Copper-354
Emerald Green-354
Gold-354
Ice Blue-354
Premiere Date-354
Red-354
02BAP Sig Series Auto Buybacks 1998-124
Courtnall, Russ
82Victoria Cougars-5
83Victoria Cougars-5
84Maple Leafs Postcards-6
84Kelowna Wings-37
84Victoria Cougars-7
85Maple Leafs Postcards-7
85Maple Leafs Postcards-8
85O-Pee-Chee Stickers-20
86Kraft Drawings-12
86Maple Leafs Postcards-5
86O-Pee-Chee-174
86O-Pee-Chee Stickers-149
86Topps-174
87Maple Leafs PLAY-30
87Maple Leafs Postcards-3
87Maple Leafs Postcards Oversized-3
87O-Pee-Chee-62
87O-Pee-Chee Box Bottoms-P
87O-Pee-Chee Stickers-156
87Panini Stickers-327
87Topps-62
87Topps Box Bottoms-P
88Canadiens Postcards-8
88Maple Leafs PLAY-30
88O-Pee-Chee-183
88O-Pee-Chee Stickers-175
88Panini Stickers-122
88Topps-183
89Canadiens Kraft-5
89Canadiens Postcards-8
89Canadiens Provigo Figurines-6
89Kraft-22
89O-Pee-Chee-239
89O-Pee-Chee Stickers-53
90Bowman-47
Tiffany-47
90Canadiens Postcards-10
90O-Pee-Chee-124
90Panini Stickers-56
90Pro Set-149
90Score-148
Canadian-148
90Topps-124
Tiffany-124
90Upper Deck-259
French-259
91Pro Set Platinum-62
91Bowman-346
91Bowman-414
91Canadiens Panini Team Stickers-6
91Canadiens Postcards-8
91Kraft-49
91O-Pee-Chee-119
91OPC Premier-58
91OPC Premier-194
91Panini Stickers-186
91Parkhurst-308
French-308
91Pinnacle-254
French-254
91Pro Set-126
French-126
91Score American-42
91Score American-380
91Score Canadian Bilingual-42
91Score Canadian Bilingual-270
91Score Canadian English-42
91Score Canadian English-270
91Stadium Club-43
91Topps-119
Team Scoring Leaders-18
91Upper Deck-87
91Upper Deck-168
French-87
French-168
92Bowman-45
92Humpty Dumpty II-3
92O-Pee-Chee-284
92OPC Premier-20
92Panini Stickers-154
92Panini Stickers French-154
92Parkhurst-78
Emerald Ice-78
92Pinnacle-337
French-337
92Score-4
Canadian-4
92Seasons Patches-33
92Stadium Club-152
92Topps-276
Gold-276G
92Ultra-91
92Ultra-316
92Upper Deck-94
92Upper Deck-441
92Finnish Semic-95
93Donruss-80
93Kraft-5
93Leaf-65
93OPC Premier-153
Gold-153
93Panini Stickers-268
93Parkhurst-53
Emerald Ice-53
93Pinnacle-268
Canadian-268
93PowerPlay-58
93Score-130
Canadian-130
93Stadium Club-55
Members Only Master Set-55
OPC-55
First Day Issue-55
First Day Issue OPC-55
93Topps/OPC Premier-153
Gold-153
93Ultra-50
Speed Merchants-2
93Upper Deck-32
SP-36
94Be A Player-R27
99 All-Stars-G5
94Canada Games NHL POGS-77
94Donruss-167
94EA Sports-35
94Finest-54
Super Team Winners-54
Refractors-54
94Flair-40
94Fleer-48
94Leaf-126
94Leaf Limited-35
94OPC Premier-395
Special Effects-395
94Parkhurst-52
Gold-52
SE Vintage-30
94Pinnacle-133
Artist's Proofs-133
Rink Collection-133
94Post Box Backs-8
94Score-43
Gold-43
Platinum-43
94Select-70
Gold-70
94Stadium Club Members Only-19
94Stadium Club-170
Members Only Master Set-170
First Day Issue-170
Super Team Winner Cards-170
94Stars HockeyKaps-7
94Stars Pinnacle Sheet-133
94Stars Pinnacle Sheet-NNO
94Stars Score Sheet-43
94Topps/OPC Premier-395
Special Effects-395
94Ultra-279
Speed Merchants-2
94Upper Deck-31
Electric Ice-31
SP Inserts-SP19
SP Inserts Die Cuts-SP19
94Finnish Jaa Kiekko-98
95Be A Player-65
Signatures-S65
Signatures Die Cuts-S65
95Canada Games NHL POGS-275
95Collector's Choice-267
Player's Club-267
Player's Club Platinum-267
95Donruss-199
95Emotion-179
95Hoyle Western Playing Cards-13
95Leaf-51
95Metal-150
95Panini Stickers-296
95Parkhurst International-210
Emerald Ice-210
95Score-242
Black Ice Artist's Proofs-242
Black Ice-242
95SkyBox Impact-168
95Stadium Club-9
Members Only Master Set-9
95Summit-128
Artist's Proofs-128
Ice-128
95Topps-194
OPC Inserts-194
95Topps SuperSkills-11
Platinum-11
95Ultra-168
Gold Medallion-168
95Upper Deck-317
Electric Ice-317
Electric Ice Gold-317
95Zenith-115
95Finnish Semic World Championships-95
96Canucks Postcards-9
96Collector's Choice-276
96Donruss-194
Press Proofs-194
96Leaf-29
Press Proofs-29
96Metal Universe-156
96Pinnacle-75
Artist's Proofs-75
Foil-75
Premium Stock-75
Rink Collection-75
96Score-109
Artist's Proofs-109
Dealer's Choice Artist's Proofs-109
Special Artist's Proofs-109
Golden Blades-109
96SkyBox Impact-132
96SP-161
96Summit-22
Artist's Proofs-22
Ice-22
Metal-22
Premium Stock-22
96Topps Picks-107
OPC Inserts-107
96Upper Deck-350
97Collector's Choice-166
97Pacific-275
Copper-275
Emerald Green-275
Ice Blue-275
Red-275
Silver-275
97Revolution-64
Copper-64
Emerald-64
Ice Blue-64
Silver-64
98OPC Chrome-188
Refractors-188
98Pacific-233
Ice Blue-233
Red-233
98Paramount-103
Copper-103
Emerald Green-103
Holo-Electric-103
Ice Blue-103
Silver-103
98Topps-188
O-Pee-Chee-188
99Pacific-188
Copper-188
Emerald Green-188
Gold-188
Ice Blue-188
Premiere Date-188
Red-188
Courtney, Corey
97Dubuque Fighting Saints-26
00Lincoln Stars-27
01Lincoln Stars-27
02Lincoln Stars-28
03Lincoln Stars-27
04Lincoln Stars-27
05Lincoln Stars-27
06Lincoln Stars-28
Courtney, Ken
52Juniors Blue Tint-93
Courtney, Ryan
01Owen Sound Attack-3
Courtney, Sean
03Erie Otters-5
04Saginaw Spirit-19
Courville, Ian
00Hull Olympiques-23
Signed-23
Courville, Larry
91Cornwall Royals-19
917th Inn. Sketch OHL-15
94Finest-156
Super Team Winners-156
Refractors-156
94Pinnacle-540
Artist's Proofs-540
Rink Collection-540
94SP-150
Die Cuts-150
95Donruss Canadian World Junior Team-11
95Topps Canadian World Juniors-3CJ
95Classic-50
96Pinnacle-235
Artist's Proofs-235
Foil-235
Premium Stock-235
Rink Collection-235
96Syracuse Crunch-35
96Collector's Edge Ice-88
Prism-88
97Score-57
Artist's Proofs-57
Golden Blades-57
97Score Canucks-13
Platinum-13
Premier-13
99Kentucky Thoroughblades-8
00Kentucky Thoroughblades-7
01Hershey Bears-5
03Johnstown Chiefs-18
03Johnstown Chiefs RBI Sports-212
04Reading Royals-18
05Reading Royals-3
Cousens, Deron
05Penticton Vees-4
06Penticton Vees-4
Cousineau, Bryan
91Maple Leafs PLAY-7
Cousineau, Dan
99Indianapolis Ice-5
00Indianapolis Ice-6
01Indianapolis Ice-4
Cousineau, David
03ECHL All-Stars-266
03Las Vegas Wranglers-5
03Las Vegas Wranglers RBI-228
04UK Sheffield Steelers-8
Cousineau, Marcel
907th Inn. Sketch QMJHL-133
91Classic-50
91Star Pics-47
91Ultimate Draft-45
91Ultimate Draft French-45
91Classic Four-Sport *-50
Autographs-50A
93St. John's Maple Leafs-6
94St. John's Maple Leafs-6
94Classic Pro Prospects-111
95St. John's Maple Leafs-5
96Be A Player-213
Autographs-213
Autographs Silver-213
96Black Diamond-63
Gold-63
97Donruss-198
Press Proofs Silver-198
Press Proofs Gold-198
Rated Rookies-7
Medalist-7
97Donruss Canadian Ice-147
Dominion Series-147
Provincial Series-147
Les Gardiens-10
97Donruss Canadian Ice Les Gardiens Promo-10
97Donruss Limited-86
97Donruss Limited-116
97Donruss Limited-160
Exposure-86
Exposure-116
Exposure-160
Fabric of the Game-39
97Donruss Preferred-158
Cut to the Chase-158
97Leaf-114
Fractal Matrix-114
Fractal Matrix Die Cuts-114
97Leaf International-114
Universal Ice-114
97Pacific Omega-219
Copper-219
Dark Gray-219
Emerald Green-219
Gold-219
Ice Blue-219
97Pinnacle Inside-69
Coach's Collection-69
Executive Collection-69
Stand Up Guys-4A/B
Stand Up Guys-4C/D
Stand Up Guys Promos-4A/B
Stand Up Guys Promos-4C/D
Stoppers-22
97Score-23
Artist's Proofs-23
Golden Blades-23
97Score Maple Leafs-3
Platinum-3
Premier-3
97St. John's Maple Leafs-8
98NHL Aces Playing Cards-2
00Lowell Lock Monsters-20
01Manchester Monarchs-14A
02Russian Hockey League-132
02Russian Transfert-5
Coutineir, Francis
907th Inn. Sketch QMJHL-95
Coutu, Billy
23V145-1-17
24Anonymous NHL-2
24Anonymous NHL-42
24Anonymous NHL-42
24C144 Champ's Cigarettes-19
24V145-2-44
25Dominion Chocolates-89
Coutu, Justin
04Penticton Vees-18
Couture, Alexandre
97Halifax Mooseheads I-4
97Halifax Mooseheads II-5
98Peoria Rivermen-6
99Peoria Rivermen-11
Couture, Derek
01Saskatoon Blades-2
02Saskatoon Blades-13
03Saskatoon Blades-19
Couture, Frederic
93Quebec Pee-Wee Tournament-286
Couture, Gerry
44Beehive Group II Photos-90
44Beehive Group II Photos-158
44Beehive Group II Photos-229
45Quaker Oats Photos-70
51Parkhurst-17
51Buffalo Bison-4
52Parkhurst-41
53Parkhurst-84
Couture, Guillame
97Rimouski Oceanic-44
Couture, Joel
93Quebec Pee-Wee Tournament-1055
Couture, Kevin
03Brampton Batallion-3
04Brampton Battalion-3
06Austin Ice Bats-14
Couture, Liam
02Spokane Chiefs-4
05Kelowna Rockets-7
Couture, Logan
05ITG Heroes/Prosp Toronto Expo Parallel -400
05Ottawa 67's-14
05ITG Heroes and Prospects-400
06Ottawa 67's-1
06ITG Heroes and Prospects-91
Autographs-ALC
Quad Emblems-QE13
Couture, Patrick
92Quebec Pee-Wee Tournament-631
03ECHL Update RBI Sports-288
Couture, Rosario
34Diamond Matchbooks Silver-18
35Diamond Matchbooks Tan 1-18
35Diamond Matchbooks Tan 2-16
35Diamond Matchbooks Tan 3-15
Couturier, Corey
04Green Bay Gamblers-2
Couturier, Sylvain
84Richelieu Riverains-4
88ProCards AHL-211
89ProCards AHL-7
90ProCards AHL/IHL-360
91Upper Deck-491
French-491
92Phoenix Roadrunners-5
94Milwaukee Admirals-5
95Milwaukee Admirals-5
95Milwaukee Admirals Postcards-6
96Milwaukee Admirals-3
98German DEL-127
99German DEL-281
Couvrette, Michel
93Phoenix Cobras RHI-7
94Central Hockey League-96
98Phoenix Mustangs-11
Coveny, Chris
917th Inn. Sketch OHL-302
92Ottawa 67's-7
98Peoria Rivermen-5
Coveny, Michael
95Slapshot Memorial Cup-51
Covington, Steve
02Calgary Hitmen-22
03Calgary Hitmen-4
04Calgary Hitmen-3
05Calgary Hitmen-3
Cowan, Dave
84Minnesota-Duluth Bulldogs-24
85Minnesota-Duluth Bulldogs-7
Cowan, Jeff
93Guelph Storm-20
94Guelph Storm-23
95Slapshot-23
95Barrie Colts-6
95Classic-82
96Roanoke Express-17
97Saint John Flames-6
00BAP Memorabilia-18
Emerald-18
Ruby-18
Sapphire-18
Promos-18
00BAP Mem Chicago Sportsfest Copper-18
00BAP Memorabilia Chicago Sportsfest Blue-18
00BAP Memorabilia Chicago Sportsfest Gold-18
00BAP Memorabilia Chicago Sportsfest Ruby-18
00BAP Memorabilia Chicago Sun-Times Ruby-18
00BAP Memorabilia Chicago Sun-Times Gold-18
00BAP Mem Chicago Sun-Times Sapphire-18
00BAP Mem Toronto Fall Expo Copper-18
00BAP Memorabilia Toronto Fall Expo Gold-18
00BAP Memorabilia Toronto Fall Expo Ruby-18
00Black Diamond-77
Gold-77
00SPx-94
Spectrum-94
00Titanium-107
Retail-107
00Titanium Draft Day Edition-107
00Titanium Draft Day Promos-107
00UD Heroes-160
00UD Pros and Prospects-96
00Upper Deck-220
Exclusives Tier 1-220
Exclusives Tier 2-220
00Upper Deck Vintage-375
01BAP Memorabilia-449
Emerald-449
Ruby-449
Sapphire-449
01BAP Signature Series-75
Autographs-75
Autographs Gold-75
01Upper Deck Victory-51
Gold-51
02BAP Sig Series Auto Buybacks 2001-75
02Thrashers Postcards-3
02Upper Deck Vintage-12
03Thrashers Postcards-2
Cowan, Nicolas
03Lewiston Maineiacs-6
Cowan, Sean
92Raleigh Icecaps-2
92Raleigh Icecaps-33
Cowick, Bruce
74Capitals White Borders-8
74O-Pee-Chee NHL-386
Cowick, Corey
06Oshawa Generals-9
Cowie, Rob
91Moncton Hawks-3
91ProCards-174
95Phoenix Roadrunners-9
95Images-57
Gold-56
96Swiss HNL-230
96Collector's Edge Ice-183
Prism-183
98German DEL-155
99German DEL-69
00German Berlin Polar Bears Postcards-3
00German DEL-71
01Finnish Cardset-255
04German Berlin Eisbarens 50th Anniv-46
Cowie, Scott
04Peterborough Petes Postcards-16
06Ottawa 67's-2
Cowley, Bill
34Beehive Group I Photos-11
35Diamond Matchbooks Tan 1-19
39O-Pee-Chee V301-1-98
43Parade Sportive *-27
83Hall of Fame-170
83Hall of Fame Postcards-M5
85Hall of Fame-170
91Bruins Sports Action Legends-9
91Bruins Sports Action Legends-12
02BAP Ultimate Mem Paper Cuts Autos-12
03BAP Ultimate Mem Linemates Autos-13
03BAP Ultimate Memorabilia Paper Cuts-16
04ITG Franchises US East-324
04ITG Ultimate Memorabilia-18
Gold-18
Beantown's Best-7
05ITG Ultimate Mem Quad Paper Cuts Autos-1
05The Cup Legendary Cuts-LCCW
Cowley, Russ
02UK Coventry Blaze-13
03UK Coventry Blaze-11
03UK Coventry Blaze Calendars-5
04UK Coventry Blaze-7
04UK Coventry Blaze Champions-15
Cowley, Wayne
88Salt Lake Golden Eagles-5
89ProCards IHL-206
96German DEL-204
Cowmedow, Lee
97UK Fife Flyers-7
Cox, Allan
907th Inn. Sketch OHL-306
917th Inn. Sketch OHL-56
Cox, Billy
92Quebec Pee-Wee Tournament-1174
93Quebec Pee-Wee Tournament-623
Cox, Cliff
76Nova Scotia Voyageurs-4
Cox, Danny
23V128-1 Paulin's Candy-18
33O-Pee-Chee V304A-1
33V129-48
33V252 Canadian Gum-16
33V357 Ice Kings-69
Cox, Justin
98Prince George Cougars-7
99Prince George Cougars-24
00Prince George Cougars-23
01Utah Grizzlies-30
02Utah Grizzlies-5
05Idaho Steelheads-5
Cox, Peter
907th Inn. Sketch WHL-158
917th Inn. Sketch WHL-77
Cox, Tim
90Saskatoon Blades-20
907th Inn. Sketch WHL-91
Coxe, Craig
83Belleville Bulls-22
84Fredericton Express-27
85Canucks Team Issue-6
86Canucks Team Issue-5
87Blues Team Issue-5
87Canucks Shell Oil-8
88Blues Kodak-5
88Blues Team Issue-5
89Canucks Mohawk-6
90Canucks Mohawk-6
90O-Pee-Chee-339
90Pro Set-544
90Topps-339
Tiffany-339
91Canucks Panini Team Stickers-7
91O-Pee-Chee-447
91Pro Set-329
French-329
91Score Canadian Bilingual-646
91Score Canadian English-646
91Score Rookie/Traded-96T
91Topps-447
91Upper Deck-60
French-60
91ProCards-520
99San Antonio Iguanas-21
Coyne, Colleen
94Classic Women of Hockey-W26
Craas, Morgan
84Swedish Semic Elitserien-134
Crabo, Sven
70Swedish Hockey-186
71Swedish Hockey-272
Cracknell, Adam
03Kootenay Ice-15
04Kootenay Ice-6
05Kootenay Ice-5
06Las Vegas Wranglers-3
Craievich, Dave
89Oshawa Generals-2
89Oshawa Generals 7th Inning Sketch-13
897th Inn. Sketch OHL-13
907th Inn. Sketch OHL-332
907th Inn. Sketch Memorial Cup-84
91Cincinnati Cyclones-5
91ProCards-422
92Birmingham Bulls-8
93Birmingham Bulls-8
93Birmingham Bulls Birmingham News-5
94Birmingham Bulls-5
97Mobile Mysticks-8
97Mobile Mysticks Kellogg's-13
98Chicago Wolves Turner Cup-3
98Mobile Mysticks-9
99Mobile Mysticks-1
Craig, Bob
71Rochester Americans-4
Craig, Glen
89Windsor Spitfires-2
907th Inn. Sketch OHL-102
917th Inn. Sketch OHL-30
Craig, Jim
79Flames Postcards-5
79Flames Team Issue-6
80USA Olympic Team Mini Pics-1
80O-Pee-Chee-22
80Topps-22
95Signature Rookies Miracle on Ice-9
95Signature Rookies Miracle on Ice-10
95Signature Rook Miracle on Ice Sigs-9
95Signature Rook Miracle on Ice Sigs-10
98Bruins Alumni-3
Autographs-3
04UD Legendary Signatures-95
Autographs-JC
Miracle Men-USA2
Miracle Men Autographs-USA-JC
05ITG Heroes/Prosp Toronto Expo Parallel -186
05ITG Ultimate Memorabilia Level 1-55
05ITG Ultimate Memorabilia Level 2-55
05ITG Ultimate Memorabilia Level 3-55
05ITG Ultimate Memorabilia Level 4-55
05ITG Ultimate Memorabilia Level 5-55
05ITG Ultimate Memorabilia Triple Autos-16
05ITG Ultimate Mem Triple Autos Gold-16
05ITG Ultimate Memorabilia Ultimate Autos-44
05ITG Ultimate Mem Ultimate Autos Gold-44
05ITG Heroes and Prospects-186
Autographs Series II-JCR
Autographs Series II-CM2
Autographs Series II-YC2
06ITG International Ice-83
Gold-83
Autographs-AJC
Craig, Mike
89Oshawa Generals-23
89Oshawa Generals 7th Inning Sketch-9
897th Inn. Sketch OHL-9
90OPC Premier-19
90Pro Set-613
90Score Rookie/Traded-59T
90Upper Deck-472
French-472
907th Inn. Sketch Memorial Cup-90
91Pro Set Platinum-189
91Bowman-130
91O-Pee-Chee-187
91Parkhurst-301
French-301
91Pinnacle-219
French-219
91Pro Set-405
French-405
91Score American-181
91Score Canadian Bilingual-181
91Score Canadian English-181
91Stadium Club-344
91Topps-187
91Upper Deck-125
French-125
92Bowman-334
92O-Pee-Chee-103
92Panini Stickers-95
92Panini Stickers French-95
92Parkhurst-314
Emerald Ice-314
92Pinnacle-99
French-99
92Score-271
Canadian-271
92Stadium Club-268
92Topps-238
Gold-238G
92Ultra-317
92Upper Deck-65
93Donruss-81
93Leaf-88
93OPC Premier-309
Gold-309
93Panini Stickers-271
93Parkhurst-323
Emerald Ice-323
93Pinnacle-314
Canadian-314
93PowerPlay-322
93Score-156
Canadian-156
93Stadium Club-355
Members Only Master Set-355
First Day Issue-355
93Topps/OPC Premier-309
Gold-309
93Ultra-297
93Upper Deck-191
94Canada Games NHL POGS-231
94Leaf-510
94Maple Leafs Kodak-8
94Maple Leafs Pin-up Posters-21
94OPC Premier-538
Special Effects-538
94Parkhurst-54
Gold-54
94Pinnacle-399
Artist's Proofs-399
Rink Collection-399
94Stars HockeyKaps-8
94Topps/OPC Premier-538
Special Effects-538
94Upper Deck-213
Electric Ice-213
95Be A Player-17
Signatures-S17
Signatures Die Cuts-S17
97Pacific-309
Copper-309
Emerald Green-309
Ice Blue-309
Red-309
Silver-309
97Score Maple Leafs-11
Platinum-11
Premier-11
98Kentucky Thoroughblades-5
99Kentucky Thoroughblades-9
00Hershey Bears-5
01Cleveland Barons-5
02Swiss HNL-330
Craig, Ryan
98Brandon Wheat Kings-2
99Brandon Wheat Kings-4
99UD Prospects-31
00Brandon Wheat Kings-19
00UD CHL Prospects-47
01Brandon Wheat Kings-19
02Brandon Wheat Kings-19
03Hershey Bears-10
03Hershey Bears Patriot News-7
04Springfield Falcons-23
05Black Diamond-283
05Hot Prospects-269
En Fuego-269
Hot Materials-HMRC
Red Hot-269
White Hot-269
05Parkhurst-446
Facsimile Auto Parallel-446
Signatures-RC
True Colors-TCTBL
True Colors-TCTBL
05SP Authentic-196
05SP Game Used-236
05SPx-241
Spectrum-241
05The Cup-156
Autographed Rookie Patches Gold Rainbow-156
Black Rainbow Rookies-156
Masterpiece Pressplates (Artifacts)-332
Masterpiece Pressplates (Black Diamond)-283
Masterpiece Pressplates (Ice)-246
Masterpiece Pressplates (Rookie Update)-245
Masterpiece Pressplates (SP Game Used)-236
Masterpiece Pressplates SPA Autos-196
Masterpiece Pressplates SPx Autos-241
Masterpiece Pressplates (Trilogy)-306
Masterpiece Pressplates Ult Coll-173
Masterpiece Pressplates Autographs-156
Platinum Rookies-156
05UD Artifacts-332
05Ultimate Collection-173
Gold-173
05Upper Deck-469
05Upper Deck Ice-246
05Upper Deck Rookie Update-245
Inspirations Patch Rookies-245
05Upper Deck Trilogy-306
05AHL Top Prospects-8
05Springfield Falcons-21
06Black Diamond Jerseys-JRC
06Black Diamond Jerseys Black-JRC
06Black Diamond Jerseys Gold-JRC
06Black Diamond Jerseys Ruby-JRC
06Fleer-177
Tiffany-177
06Lightning Postcards-5
06O-Pee-Chee-443
Rainbow-443
06Upper Deck-177
Exclusives Parallel-177
High Gloss Parallel-177
Masterpieces-177
06Upper Deck MVP-266
Gold Script-266
Super Script-266
Craig, Tom
06Saginaw Spirit-13
Craigdallie, Marty
91Air Canada SJHL-E31
92British Columbia JHL-66
Craigen, Joe
97Peoria Rivermen-6
98Peoria Rivermen-10
Craigen, Mike
04Knoxville Ice Bears-11
05Knoxville Ice Bears-4
Craighead, John
91British Columbia JHL-165
91British Columbia JHL-NNO
93Richmond Renegades-5
94Detroit Vipers Pogs-1
96St. John's Maple Leafs-12
97Cleveland Lumberjacks-8
97Cleveland Lumberjacks Postcards-8
99German DEL-47
00German DEL-238
01German Upper Deck-214
02BAP Memorabilia-332
03UK Nottingham Panthers-17
04UK Nottingham Panthers-6
Craigwell, Dale
89Oshawa Generals-11
89Oshawa Generals 7th Inning Sketch-4
897th Inn. Sketch OHL-4
90Upper Deck-464
French-464
907th Inn. Sketch OHL-333
907th Inn. Sketch Memorial Cup-85
91Parkhurst-389
French-389
91Kansas City Blades-15
91ProCards-516
917th Inn. Sketch CHL Award Winners-2
92Bowman-198
92O-Pee-Chee-271
92Panini Stickers-133
92Panini Stickers French-133
92Parkhurst-168
Emerald Ice-168
92Score-466
Canadian-466
92Stadium Club-464
92Topps-60
Gold-60G
92Ultra-192
92Upper Deck-40
92Kansas City Blades-15
93OPC Premier-348
Gold-348
93Topps/OPC Premier-348
Gold-348
93Upper Deck-56
94Upper Deck-380
Electric Ice-380
96Kansas City Blades-4
96Collector's Edge Ice-189
Prism-189
98German DEL-285
99UK Sheffield Steelers-5
00UK Sekonda Superleague-153
00UK Sheffield Steelers-12
Crain, Jason
99Ohio State Buckeyes-4
00Ohio State Buckeyes-4
01Ohio State Buckeyes-6
03ECHL Update RBI Sports-122
Cramer, Corson
06Texas Tornados-22
Crameri, Gian-Marco
93Swiss HNL-224
95Swedish World Championships Stickers-126
95Swiss HNL-123
96Swiss HNL-164
98Swiss Power Play Stickers-165
98Swiss Power Play Stickers-254
99Swiss Panini Stickers-165
99Swiss Panini Stickers-265
00Swiss Panini Stickers-209
00Swiss Slapshot Mini-Cards-ZSCL8
01Swiss HNL-135
01Swiss HNL-118
02Swiss HNL-479
04Swiss EV Zug Postcards-16
Crampes, Alexandre
93Quebec Pee-Wee Tournament-1652
Crampton, Steve
01Moose Jaw Warriors-8
03Wheeling Nailers-82
04Wheeling Nailers Riesbeck's-18
05Las Vegas Wranglers-5
06Las Vegas Wranglers-4
Crandall, Chip
83Oshawa Generals-29
Crane, Brian
93Michigan State Spartans-6
Crane, Corey
92Sudbury Wolves-13
Crane, Derrick
907th Inn. Sketch OHL-130
917th Inn. Sketch OHL-375
Crane, Jason
97Tucson Gila Monsters-6
Crane, Ryan
01Western Michigan Broncos-3
02Augusta Lynx-61
04Kalamazoo Wings-17
Crane, Todd
95Slapshot-163
Cranley, Mark
00Mississauga Ice Dogs-8
Cranston, Sid
82Brandon Wheat Kings-7
Cranston, Tim
93UK Sheffield Steelers-3
94Finnish Jaa Kiekko-320
94UK Sheffield Steelers-11
95UK Sheffield Steelers-16
97UK Sheffield Steelers-2
00UK Sheffield Steelers Centurions-6
Crashley, Bart
67Topps-105
72Los Angeles Sharks WHA-2
72O-Pee-Chee-295
98Guelph Storm-25
99Guelph Storm-27
Craven, Murray
82Medicine Hat Tigers-2
83O-Pee-Chee-120
83Medicine Hat Tigers-1
84Kelowna Wings-44
85Flyers Postcards-5
85O-Pee-Chee-53
85O-Pee-Chee Stickers-95
85Topps-53
86Flyers Postcards-4
86O-Pee-Chee-167
86O-Pee-Chee Stickers-244
86Topps-167
87Flyers Postcards-29
87O-Pee-Chee-22
87O-Pee-Chee Stickers-69
87Panini Stickers-133
87Topps-22
88Flyers Postcards-24
88O-Pee-Chee-79
88O-Pee-Chee Box Bottoms-J
88O-Pee-Chee Stickers-98
88Panini Stickers-320
88Topps-79
88Topps Box Bottoms-J
89Flyers Postcards-7
89O-Pee-Chee-44
89Topps-44
90Bowman-109
Tiffany-109
90Flyers Postcards-6
90O-Pee-Chee-318
90Panini Stickers-116
90Pro Set-214
90Score-56
Canadian-56
90Topps-318
Tiffany-318
90Upper Deck-6
French-6
91Pro Set Platinum-179
91Bowman-230
91O-Pee-Chee-254
91Panini Stickers-234
91Parkhurst-288
French-288
91Pinnacle-177
French-177
91Pro Set-175
91Pro Set-393
French-175
French-393
91Score American-262
91Score Canadian Bilingual-482
91Score Canadian English-482
91Stadium Club-176
91Topps-254
91Upper Deck-306
French-306
91Whalers Jr. 7-Eleven-7
92Bowman-280
92O-Pee-Chee-127
92OPC Premier Star Performers-3
92Panini Stickers-262
92Panini Stickers French-262
92Parkhurst-55
92Parkhurst-495
Emerald Ice-55
Emerald Ice-495
92Pinnacle-281
French-281
92Pro Set-60
92Score-18
Canadian-18
92Stadium Club-442
92Topps-248
Gold-248G
92Ultra-71
92Upper Deck-49
92Whalers Dairymart-5
93Donruss-353
93Leaf-5
93OPC Premier-400
Gold-400
93Panini Stickers-169
93Parkhurst-208
Emerald Ice-208
93Pinnacle-88
Canadian-88
93PowerPlay-458
93Score-49
Canadian-49
93Stadium Club-264
Members Only Master Set-264
First Day Issue-264
93Topps/OPC Premier-400
Gold-400
93Ultra-439
93Upper Deck-410
94Donruss-131
94Leaf-121
94OPC Premier-47
Special Effects-47

94Parkhurst-242
Gold-242
94Pinnacle-291
Artist's Proofs-291
Rink Collection-291
94Score-109
Gold-109
Platinum-109
94Stadium Club-255
Members Only Master Set-255
First Day Issue-255
Super Team Winner Cards-255
94Topps/OPC Premier-47
Special Effects-47
94Ultra-223
94Upper Deck-45
Electric Ice-45
95Be A Player-46
Signatures-S46
Signatures Die Cuts-S46
95Blackhawks Coke-5
95Collector's Choice-120
Player's Club-120
Player's Club Platinum-120
95Donruss-46
95Leaf-6
95Parkhurst International-313
Emerald Ice-313
95Pinnacle-179
Artist's Proofs-179
Rink Collection-179
95Score-214
Black Ice Artist's Proofs-214
Black Ice-214
95Topps-52
OPC Inserts-52
95Upper Deck-151
Electric Ice-151
Electric Ice Gold-151
96Pinnacle-162
Artist's Proofs-162
Foil-162
Premium Stock-162
Rink Collection-162
96Team Out-13
97Pacific-238
Copper-238
Emerald Green-238
Ice Blue-238
Red-238
Silver-238
98Be A Player-118
Press Release-118
98BAP Gold-118
98BAP Autographs-118
98BAP Autographs Gold-118
98BAP Tampa Bay All Star Game-118
98Pacific-378
Ice Blue-378
Red-378
02BAP Sig Series Auto Buybacks 1998-118

Craven, Terry
02Lexington Men O'War-17

Crawford, Austin
93Waterloo Black Hawks-7

Crawford, Bob
83Whalers Junior Hartford Courant-1
84O-Pee-Chee-68
84O-Pee-Chee Stickers-197
84Topps-53
84Whalers Junior Wendy's-3
85O-Pee-Chee-162
85O-Pee-Chee Stickers-167
85Topps-162
85Whalers Junior Wendy's-3
86Capitals Kodak-5

Crawford, Bruce
06Saint Johns Sea Dogs-7

Crawford, Corey
01Moncton Wildcats-18
02Moncton Wildcats-6
03Moncton Wildcats-19
04Moncton Wildcats-3
04ITG Heroes and Prospects-228
04ITG Heroes/Prospects Toronto Expo '05-228
05ITG Heroes/Prosp Toronto Expo Parallel -236
05Black Diamond-225
05Hot Prospects-116
En Fuego-116
Red Hot-116
White Hot-116
05Parkhurst-618
Facsimile Auto Parallel-618
05SP Authentic-257
Limited-257
05SP Game Used-201
05SPx-252
05The Cup Masterpiece Pressplate Artifact-262
05The Cup Master Pressplate Black Diamond-225
05The Cup Masterpiece Pressplates (Ice)-260
05The Cup Master Pressplate Rookie Update-120
05The Cup Masterpiece Pressplates SPA-257
05The Cup Masterpiece Pressplates SP GU-201
05The Cup Masterpiece Pressplates (SPx)-252
05The Cup Masterpiece Pressplates Trilogy-238
05The Cup Masterpiece Pressplate Ult Coll-185
05UD Artifacts-262
05Ultimate Collection-185
Gold-185
05Upper Deck Ice-260
05Upper Deck Rookie Update-120
05Upper Deck Trilogy-238
05Norfolk Admirals-20
05ITG Heroes and Prospects-236
Autographs Series II-CCR
He Shoots-He Scores Prizes-54
Jerseys-GUJ-37
Jerseys Gold-GUJ-37
Emblems-GUE-37
Emblems Gold-GUE-37
Numbers-GUN-37
Numbers Gold-GUN-37
Net Prospects-NP-17
Net Prospects Gold-NP-17
06Between The Pipes-9
Autographs-ACC
Emblems-GUE34
Emblems Gold-GUE34
Emblems Autographs-GUE34
Jerseys-GUJ34
Jerseys Gold-GUJ34
Jerseys Autographs-GUJ34
Numbers-GUN34
Numbers Gold-GUN34
Numbers Autographs-GUN34
Prospect Trios-PT17
Prospect Trios Gold-PT17
06AHL Top Prospects-29
06Norfolk Admirals-24
06ITG Heroes and Prospects-72
Autographs-ACC

Crawford, Derek
92Dallas Freeze-6
92Dayton Bombers-5
93Dallas Freeze-5
94Central Hockey League-6
94Dallas Freeze-6
97New Mexico Scorpions-5

Crawford, Floyd
51Laval Dairy QSHL-25
52Bas Du Fleuve-45

Crawford, Glenn
94Windsor Spitfires-8
95Slapshot-411
95Slapshot-438
95Upper Deck-520
Electric Ice-520
Electric Ice Gold-520
95Classic-98
98Sudbury Wolves-14
00Muskegon Fury-8

Crawford, Jack
36John Player & Son's Player's Cigarettes-16
39Ardath Cigarettes Cricket Tennis & Golf Celebrities-35
40O-Pee-Chee V301-2-134

Crawford, Jeff
81Regina Pats-9
82Regina Pats-22
83Moncton Alpines-18
83Regina Pats-22
94Huntington Blizzard-28

Crawford, John
34Beehive Group I Photos-12
44Beehive Group II Photos-14

Crawford, Lou
85Nova Scotia Oilers-10
88ProCards AHL-10
89ProCards AHL-56
90ProCards AHL/IHL-138
91ProCards-62
00St. John's Maple Leafs-7
01St. John's Maple Leafs-6

Crawford, Marc
52Juniors Blue Tint-181
81Fredericton Express-17
82O-Pee-Chee-342
82Post Cereal-19
82Fredericton Express-17
83Canucks Team Issue-4
84Fredericton Express-23
85Fredericton Express-4
86Fredericton Express-5
907th Inn. Sketch OHL-50
91ProCards-357
92St. John's Maple Leafs-4
93St. John's Maple Leafs-7
96Kraft Upper Deck-41
97Avalanche Pins-4
97Kraft Team Canada-3
03Canucks Postcards-8

Crawford, Nick
06Saginaw Spirit-5

Crawford, Rusty
23V128-1 Paulin's Candy-70
83Hall of Fame Postcards-E6
85Hall of Fame-67

Crawford, Scott
93Quebec Pee-Wee Tournament-1411
02Peoria Rivermen-18
02Peoria Rivermen RBI Sports-157
03Peoria Rivermen-20

Crawford, Wayne
96UK Guildford Flames-3
99UK Basingstoke Bison-9
00UK Guildford Flames-5

Creagh, Brendan
93Greensboro Monarchs-5
94Greensboro Monarchs-19
95Birmingham Bulls-12

Creamer, Bob
92Nashville Knights-7

Creamer, Pierre
907th Inn. Sketch Memorial Cup-50

Creary, Jeni
04Ohio State Buckeyes Women-3

Creightney, Nigel
92British Columbia JHL-239

Creighton, Adam
81Ottawa 67's-4
82Ottawa 67's-3
83Ottawa 67's-6
84Sabres Blue Shield-3
85Sabres Blue Shield-4
85Sabres Blue Shield Small-4
86Sabres Blue Shield-6
86Sabres Blue Shield Small-6
87Panini Stickers-31
87Sabres Blue Shield-6
87Sabres Wonder Bread/Hostess-7
88Panini Stickers-225
88Sabres Wonder Bread/Hostess-6
89Blackhawks Coke-14
89O-Pee-Chee-218
89Panini Stickers-51
90Blackhawks Coke-14
90Bowman-9
Tiffany-9
90O-Pee-Chee-83
90Panini Stickers-193
90Pro Set-50
90Score-82
Canadian-82
90Topps-83
Tiffany-83
90Upper Deck-4
French-4
91Bowman-394
91Kraft-47
91O-Pee-Chee-314
91OPC Premier-171
91Panini Stickers-13
91Parkhurst-113
French-113
91Pinnacle-82
French-82
91Pro Set-42
91Pro Set-437
French-42
French-437
Puck Candy-17
91Score American-265
91Score Canadian Bilingual-485
91Score Canadian English-485
91Score Rookie/Traded-21T
91Stadium Club-89
91Topps-314
91Upper Deck-254
French-254
92Bowman-88
92Lightning Sheraton-11
92O-Pee-Chee-85
92OPC Premier-61
92Panini Stickers-204
92Panini Stickers French-204
92Parkhurst-172
Emerald Ice-172
92Pinnacle-199
French-199
92Pro Set-103
92Score-144
Canadian-144
92Stadium Club-45
92Topps-451
Gold-451G
92Ultra-409
92Upper Deck-311
93Donruss-326
93Leaf-85
93Lightning Kash n'Karry-4
93Lightning Season in Review-9
93Panini Stickers-215
93Pinnacle-272
Canadian-272
93Score-86
Canadian-86
93Stadium Club-5
Members Only Master Set-5
OPC-5
First Day Issue-5
First Day Issue OPC-5
94Fleer-185
94Parkhurst-222
Gold-222
94Stadium Club-23
Members Only Master Set-23
First Day Issue-23
Super Team Winner Cards-23
94Upper Deck-348
Electric Ice-348
95Be A Player-142
Signatures-S142
Signatures Die Cuts-S142
95Canada Games NHL POGS-234
95Collector's Choice-229
Player's Club-229
Player's Club Platinum-229
95Donruss-336
95Parkhurst International-444
Emerald Ice-444
95Score-283
Black Ice Artist's Proofs-283
Black Ice-283
95Upper Deck-375
Electric Ice-375
Electric Ice Gold-375
96Pinnacle-80
Artist's Proofs-80
Foil-80
Premium Stock-80
Rink Collection-80

Creighton, Dave
44Beehive Group II Photos-15A
44Beehive Group II Photos-15B
44Beehive Group II Photos-392
52Parkhurst-76
53Parkhurst-85
54Parkhurst-58
57Topps-66
60Parkhurst-10
94Parkhurst Missing Link-99

Crenshaw, David
92Quebec Pee-Wee Tournament-966
93Quebec Pee-Wee Tournament-1275

Cress, Mark
02Prince Albert Raiders-6

Cressman, Glen
52Juniors Blue Tint-127

Cressman, Matt
93Western Michigan Broncos-9
01Odessa Jackalopes-5
02Odessa Jackalopes-3
03Odessa Jackalopes-4
04Odessa Jackalopes-3
05Odessa Jackalopes-4
06Odessa Jackalopes-4

Cretin, Christian
93Swiss HNL-189
95Swiss HNL-216
96Swiss HNL-496
98Swiss Power Play Stickers-297

Crettenand, Yves
92Finnish Semic-232
93Swedish Semic World Champ Stickers-260

Creurer, Jeremy
04Everett Silvertips-23

Crew, J.J.
06Lincoln Stars Traded-4T
06Lincoln Stars Upper DeckÂ Signature Series -10

Crha, Jiri
73Finnish Jaakiekko-45
74Swedish Stickers-10
79Panini Stickers-75
79Maple Leafs Postcards-8
80Maple Leafs Postcards-7
80Pepsi-Cola Caps-83
81O-Pee-Chee-315
81O-Pee-Chee Stickers-106

Crichton, Cory
88Kamloops Blazers-8

Crimin, Derek
91Air Canada SJHL-B45
91Air Canada SJHL All-Stars-27
91Air Canada SJHL All-Stars-41
92Saskatchewan JHL-65
96Wheeling Nailers Photo Pack-3
97Charlotte Checkers-7
98Columbus Cottonmouths-3
99Columbus Cottonmouths-6
00Asheville Smoke-4

Crisp, Terry
68Shirriff Coins-156
70Esso Power Players-245
70Sargent Promotions Stamps-182
71Blues Postcards-7
71O-Pee-Chee-127
71Sargent Promotions Stamps-179
71Toronto Sun-238
72O-Pee-Chee-88
72Sargent Promotions Stamps-128
72Topps-103
73Flyers Linnett-6
74NHL Action Stamps-203
74O-Pee-Chee NHL-352
75Flyers Canada Dry Cans-5
75O-Pee-Chee NHL-337
80Sault Ste. Marie Greyhounds-24
81Sault Ste. Marie Greyhounds-8
82Sault Ste. Marie Greyhounds-7
84Sault Ste. Marie Greyhounds-5
85Moncton Golden Flames-1
85Moncton Golden Flames-3
86Moncton Golden Flames-1
87Flames Red Rooster-5
88Flames Postcards-28
91Alberta International Team Canada-4
92Lightning Sheraton-12
93Lightning Season in Review-10
94Lightning Photo Album-9
94Lightning Postcards-4

Crisp, Tony
87Kitchener Rangers-13

Cristensen, Terry
00UK Sekonda Superleague-87

Cristofoli, Ed
89ProCards AHL-194
90ProCards AHL/IHL-72

Croce, Pat
85Flyers Postcards-6
86Flyers Postcards-5
87Flyers Postcards-5

Crochetiere, Serge
93Quebec Pee-Wee Tournament-106
99Baie-Comeau Drakkar-6
00San Diego Gulls-3

Crocker, Corey
95Slapshot-312

Crockett, Ken
91British Columbia JHL-31

Crockford, Ian
97Flint Generals-3

Crocock, Rob
83Belleville Bulls-21

Croghan, Morris
37V356 Worldwide Gum-103

Crombeen, B.J.
01Barrie Colts-11
02Barrie Colts-20
03Barrie Colts-18
04Barrie Colts-20
04Barrie Colts 10th Anniversary-10
05Iowa Stars-21
06Finnish Cardset-356
06Finnish Porin Assat Pelaajakortit-28

Crombeen, Mike
78Blues Postcards-7
82Post Cereal-17
83O-Pee-Chee-312
83O-Pee-Chee Stickers-126
83Topps Stickers-126
83Whalers Junior Hartford Courant-2
84Whalers Junior Wendy's-4

Crombie, Chris
897th Inn. Sketch OHL-30
907th Inn. Sketch OHL-131
917th Inn. Sketch OHL-374
98UK Basingstoke Bison-3
99UK Guildford Flames-2
99UK Guildford Flames-10
00UK Guildford Flames-6

Cronan, Earl
96Fredericton Canadiens-3

Cronin, John
03Augusta Lynx-35

Cronin, Shawn
88ProCards AHL-45
89Jets Safeway-7
90Bowman-128
Tiffany-128
90Jets IGA-7
90Pro Set-559
91Jets Panini Team Stickers-6
91Jets IGA-6
91Parkhurst-423
French-423
91Pro Set-268
French-268
91Score Canadian Bilingual-423
91Score Canadian English-423
91Upper Deck-478
French-478
92Flyers J.C. Penney-8
92Flyers Upper Deck Sheets-16
92OPC Premier-42
92Score-366
Canadian-366
92Stadium Club-471
92Topps-489
Gold-489G
95Fort Wayne Komets-3

Crook, John
02UK Coventry Blaze-22

Crook, Ken
88Brockville Braves-19

Croon, Ulf
69Swedish Hockey-129
70Swedish Hockey-89

Crosby, Sidney
03Rimouski Oceanic-7
03Rimouski Oceanic-NNO
03Rimouski Oceanic Sheets-4
04SP Authentic Rookie Redemptions-RR24
04Rimouski Oceanic-1
04Rimouski Oceanic-LE1
04Rimouski Oceanic Season Ticket-3
04ITG Heroes and Prospects-104
04ITG Heroes and Prospects-222
04ITG Heroes and Prospects-NNO
Aspiring-1
Aspiring-13
Autographs-SC
Autographs-U-SC2
Combos-2
Combos-15
Combos-16
Combos-17
Combos-18
Complete Emblems-11
Emblems-55
Emblems-60
Emblems Gold-55
Emblems Gold-60
Gloves-1
Gloves-SC
He Shoots-He Scores Prizes-2
He Shoots-He Scores Prizes-4
He Shoots-He Scores Prizes-7
Jersey Autographs-55
Jerseys-55
Jerseys-60
Jerseys Gold-55
Jerseys Gold-60
National Pride-1
Numbers-55
Numbers-60
Numbers Gold-55
Numbers Gold-60
04ITG Heroes/Prospects Toronto Expo '05-104
04ITG Heroes/Prospects Toronto Expo '05-222
04ITG Heroes/Prospects Toronto Expo '05-NNO
04ITG Heroes/Prospects Expo Heroes/Pros-104
05ITG Heroes/Prosp Toronto Expo Parallel -105
05ITG Heroes/Prosp Toronto Expo Parallel -337
05ITG Heroes/Prosp Toronto Expo Parallel -361
05Beehive-101
Beige -101
Blue -101
Gold-101
Red -101
Rookie Jumbos-R1
Matte-101
Matted Materials-MMSC
Matted Materials Remarkable-RMSC
PhotoGraphs-PGSC
Signature Scrapbook-SSSC
05Black Diamond-193
Emerald-193
Gold-193
Onyx-193
Ruby-193
05Hot Prospects-276
En Fuego-276
Hot Materials-HMSC
Red Hot-276
White Hot-276
05ITG Sidney Crosby Series-1
05ITG Sidney Crosby Series-2
05ITG Sidney Crosby Series-3
05ITG Sidney Crosby Series-4
05ITG Sidney Crosby Series-5
05ITG Sidney Crosby Series-6
05ITG Sidney Crosby Series-7
05ITG Sidney Crosby Series-8
05ITG Sidney Crosby Series-9
05ITG Sidney Crosby Series-10
05ITG Sidney Crosby Series-11
05ITG Sidney Crosby Series-12
05ITG Sidney Crosby Series-13
05ITG Sidney Crosby Series-14
05ITG Sidney Crosby Series-15
05ITG Sidney Crosby Series-16
05ITG Sidney Crosby Series-17
05ITG Sidney Crosby Series-18
05ITG Sidney Crosby Series-19
05ITG Sidney Crosby Series-20
05ITG Sidney Crosby Series-21
05ITG Sidney Crosby Series-22
05ITG Sidney Crosby Series-23
05ITG Sidney Crosby Series-24
05ITG Sidney Crosby Series-25
Gold-1
Gold-2
Gold-3
Gold-4
Gold-5
Gold-6
Gold-7
Gold-8
Gold-9
Gold-10
Gold-11
Gold-12
Gold-13
Gold-14
Gold-15
Gold-16
Gold-17
Gold-18
Gold-19
Gold-20
Gold-21
Gold-22
Gold-23
Gold-24
Gold-25
Autographs-SCA1
Autographs-SCA2
Autographs-SCA3
Autographs-SCA4
Autographs-SCA5
Autographs-SCA6
Autographs-SCA7
Autographs-SCA8
Autographs-SCA9
Autographs-SCA10
Autographs-SCA11
Autographs-SCA12
Autographs-SCA13
Autographs-SCA14
Autographs-SCA15
Autographs-SCA16
Autographs-SCA17
Autographs-SCA18
Autographs-SCA19
Autographs-SCA20
Autographs-SCA21
Autographs-SCA22
Autographs-SCA23
Autographs-SCA24
Autographs-SCA25
Autographs-SCA25-1
Memorabilia-SCM1
Memorabilia-SCM2
Memorabilia-SCM3
Memorabilia-SCM4
Memorabilia-SCM5
Memorabilia-SCM6
Memorabilia-SCM7
Memorabilia-SCM8
Memorabilia-SCM9
Memorabilia-SCM10
Memorabilia-SCM11
Memorabilia-SCM12
Memorabilia-SCM13
Memorabilia-SCM14
Memorabilia-SCM15
Memorabilia-SCM16
Memorabilia-SCM17
Memorabilia-SCM18
Memorabilia-SCM19
Memorabilia-SCM20
Signed Memorabilia-CAM1
Signed Memorabilia-CAM2
Signed Memorabilia-CAM3
Signed Memorabilia-CAM4
05ITG Ultimate Memorabilia Level 1-87
05ITG Ultimate Memorabilia Level 2-87
05ITG Ultimate Memorabilia Level 3-87
05ITG Ultimate Memorabilia Level 4-87
05ITG Ultimate Memorabilia Level 5-87
05ITG Ultimate Mem Complete Jersey-4
05ITG Ultimate Mem Complete Jersey Gold-4
05ITG Ultimate Mem Double Mem-23
05ITG Ultimate Mem Double Mem Gold-23
05ITG Ultimate Memorabilia Emblems-1
05ITG Ultimate Memorabilia Emblems Gold-1
05ITG Ultimate Mem First Overall Jerseys-9
05ITG Ultimate Mem 1st Overall Jsy Gold-9
05ITG Ultimate Mem First Rounders Jerseys-2
05ITG Ultimate Mem First Rounders Jerseys-6
05ITG Ultimate Mem 1st Round Jersey Gold-2
05ITG Ultimate Mem 1st Round Jersey Gold-6
05ITG Ultimate Mem Future Stars Autos-6
05ITG Ultimate Mem Future Star Autos Gold-6
05ITG Ultimate Mem Future Stars Jerseys-6
05ITG Ultimate Mem Fut Stars Jerseys Gold-6
05ITG Ultimate Mem Future Stars Mem Autos-6
05ITG Ultimate Mem Fut Star Mem Auto Gold-6
05ITG Ultimate Memorabilia Gloves Are Off-1
05ITG Ultimate Mem Gloves Are Off Gold-1
05ITG Ultimate Memorabilia In The Numbers-21
05ITG Ultimate Mem In The Numbers Gold-21
05ITG Ultimate Mem Jersey and Emblem-22
05ITG Ultimate Memorabilia Jersey Autos-37
05ITG Ultimate Mem Jersey Autos Gold-37
05ITG Ultimate Mem Jersey Emblems Gold-22
05ITG Ultimate Memorabilia Jerseys-34
05ITG Ultimate Memorabilia Jerseys Gold-34
05ITG Ultimate Mem Pass the Torch Jerseys-1
05ITG Ultimate Mem Passing Torch Jsy Gold-1
05ITG Ultimate Memorabilia R.O.Y. Autos-6
05ITG Ultimate Mem R.O.Y. Autos Gold-6
05ITG Ultimate Memorabilia R.O.Y. Emblems-10
05ITG Ultimate Mem R.O.Y. Emblems Gold-10
05ITG Ultimate Memorabilia R.O.Y. Jerseys-10
05ITG Ultimate Mem R.O.Y. Jerseys Gold-10
05ITG Ultimate Memorabilia R.O.Y. Numbers-10
05ITG Ultimate Mem R.O.Y. Numbers Gold-10
05ITG Ultimate Memorabilia Stick Autos-31
05ITG Ultimate Mem Stick Autos Gold-31
05ITG Ultimate Mem Sticks and Jerseys-7
05ITG Ultimate Mem Stick and Jerseys Gold-7
05ITG Ultimate Mem 3 Star of the Game Jsy-25
05ITG Ult Mem 3 Star of the Game Jsy Gold-25
05ITG Ultimate Memorabilia Trifecta Autos-6
05ITG Ultimate Mem Trifecta Autos Gold-6
05ITG Ultimate Mem Triple Threads Jerseys-1
05ITG Ultimate Mem Triple Thread Jsy Gold-1
05McDonalds Upper Deck-51
05Panini Stickers-1
05Panini Stickers-139
05Parkhurst-526
05Parkhurst-586
05Parkhurst-587
05Parkhurst-593
05Parkhurst-657
05Parkhurst-694
Facsimile Auto Parallel-526
Facsimile Auto Parallel-586
Facsimile Auto Parallel-587
Facsimile Auto Parallel-593
Facsimile Auto Parallel-657
Facsimile Auto Parallel-694
Signatures-SC
True Colors-TCPIT
True Colors-TCPIT
True Colors-TCPHPI
True Colors-TCPHPI
05SP Authentic-181
Limited-181
Exquisite Endorsements-EESC
Marks of Distinction-MDSC
Rarefied Rookies-RRSC
Sign of the Times-SC
05SP Game Used-101
Autographs-101
Gold-101
Auto Draft-AD-SC
Game Gear-GG-SC
Game Gear Autographs-AG-SC
Rookie Exclusives-SC
Rookie Exclusives Silver-RE-SC
Significant Numbers-SN-SC
05SPx-191
Spectrum-191
Winning Combos-WC-GC
Winning Combos Autographs-AWC-GC
Winning Combos Gold-WC-GC
Winning Combos Spectrum-WC-GC
Winning Materials-WM-SC
Winning Materials Gold-WM-SC
Winning Materials Spectrum-WM-SC
Xcitement Rookies-XR-SC
Xcitement Rookies Gold-XR-SC
Xcitement Rookies Spectrum-XR-SC
05The Cup-180
Autographed Rookie Patches Gold Rainbow-180
Black Rainbow Rookies-180
Dual NHL Shields-DSCO
Dual NHL Shields-DSLC
Emblems of Endorsement-EESC
Honorable Numbers-HNSC
Limited Logos-LLSC
Masterpiece Pressplates (Artifacts)-224
Masterpiece Pressplates (Bee Hive)-101
Masterpiece Pressplates (Black Diamond)-193
Masterpiece Pressplates (Ice)-106
Masterpiece Pressplates (MVP)-393
Masterpiece Pressplates (Power Play)-133
Masterpiece Pressplates Rookie Upd Auto-276
Masterpiece Pressplates SPA Autos-181
Masterpiece Pressplates (SP Game Used)-101
Masterpiece Pressplates SPx Autos-191
Masterpiece Pressplates (Trilogy)-211
Masterpiece Pressplates Ult Coll Autos-91
Masterpiece Pressplates (Victory)-285
Masterpiece Pressplates Autographs-180
Noble Numbers Dual-DNNCL
Noble Numbers Dual-DNNCO
Platinum Rookies-180
Scripted Swatches-SSSC
Signature Patches-SPSC
05UD Artifacts-224
Gold-RED24
05UD Phenomenal Beginnings-1
05UD Phenomenal Beginnings-2
05UD Phenomenal Beginnings-3
05UD Phenomenal Beginnings-4
05UD Phenomenal Beginnings-5
05UD Phenomenal Beginnings-6
05UD Phenomenal Beginnings-7
05UD Phenomenal Beginnings-8
05UD Phenomenal Beginnings-9
05UD Phenomenal Beginnings-10
05UD Phenomenal Beginnings-11
05UD Phenomenal Beginnings-12
05UD Phenomenal Beginnings-13
05UD Phenomenal Beginnings-14
05UD Phenomenal Beginnings-15
05UD Phenomenal Beginnings-16
05UD Phenomenal Beginnings-17
05UD Phenomenal Beginnings-18
05UD Phenomenal Beginnings-19
05UD Phenomenal Beginnings-20
05UD Phenomenal Beginnings-NNO
05UD PowerPlay-133
05UD Rookie Class-1
Commemorative Boxtoppers-CC-1
05Ultimate Collection-91
Autographed Patches-91
Autographed Shields-91
Jerseys-JSC
Jerseys Dual-DJGC
Jerseys Dual-DJLC
Jerseys Dual-DJOC
Jerseys Triple-TJGLC
Jerseys Triple-TJNOC
Marquee Attractions-MA39
Marquee Attractions Signatures-SMA39
Premium Patches-PPSC
Premium Swatches-PSSC
Ultimate Debut Threads Jerseys-DTJSC
Ultimate Debut Threads Jerseys Autos-DAJSC
Ultimate Debut Threads Patches-DTPSC
Ultimate Debut Threads Patches Autos-DAPSC
Ultimate Patches-PSC
Ultimate Patches Dual-DPLC
Ultimate Patches Dual-DPOC
Ultimate Patches Triple-TPNOC
Ultimate Signatures-USSC
05Ultra-251
Gold-251
Difference Makers-DM6
Difference Makers Jerseys-DMJ-SC
Difference Makers Jersey Autographs-DAJ-SC
Difference Makers Patches-DMP-SC
Difference Makers Patch Autographs-DAP-SC
Fresh Ink-FI-SC
Fresh Ink Blue-FI-SC
Ice-251
Rookie Uniformity Jerseys-RU-SC
Rookie Uniformity Jersey Autographs-ARU-SC
Rookie Uniformity Patches-RUP-SC
Rookie Uniformity Patch Autographs-ARP-SC
Scoring Kings-SK11
Scoring Kings Jerseys-SKJ-SC
Scoring Kings Jersey Autographs-KAJ-SC
Scoring Kings Patches-SKP-SC
Scoring Kings Patch Autographs-KAP-SC
05Upper Deck-201
05Upper Deck-242
05Upper Deck All-Time Greatest-84
05Upper Deck HG Glossy-201
05Upper Deck HG Glossy-242
05Upper Deck Majestic Materials-MMSC
05Upper Deck Rookie Ink-RISC
05Upper Deck Rookie Showcase-RS24
05Upper Deck Rookie Showcase Promos-RS24
05Upper Deck Rookie Threads-RTSC
05Upper Deck Rookie Threads Autographs-ARTSC
05Upper Deck Sportsfest-NHL1
05Upper Deck Sportsfest-NHLAU
05Upper Deck Stars in the Making-SM1
05Upper Deck Ice-106
Cool Threads-CTSC
Cool Threads Autographs-ACTSC
Cool Threads Glass-CTSC
Cool Threads Patches-CTPSC
Cool Threads Patch Autographs-CAPSC
Frozen Fabrics-FFSC
Frozen Fabrics Autographs-AFFSC
Frozen Fabrics Glass-FFSC
Frozen Fabrics Patches-FFPSC
Frozen Fabrics Patch Autographs-FAPSC
Glacial Graphs-GGSC
Premieres Auto Patches-AIPSC
Signature Swatches-SSSC
05Upper Deck MVP-393
Gold-393
Platinum-393
Rookie Breakthrough-RB1
05Upper Deck Rookie Update-276
05Upper Deck Trilogy-211
05Upper Deck Toronto Fall Expo-201
05Upper Deck Toronto Fall Expo-242
05Upper Deck Victory-285
Black-285
Gold-285
Silver-285
05Upper Deck Where's Sidney?-NNO
05Extreme Top Prospects Signature Edition-S1
05Extreme Top Prospects Signature Edition-SS1
05ITG Heroes and Prospects-105
05ITG Heroes and Prospects-337
05ITG Heroes and Prospects-361
Aspiring-ASP19
Autographs-A-SC
Autographs Series II-SC2
Autographs Series II-SC3
CHL Grads-CG-16
CHL Grads Gold-CG-16
Complete Jerseys-CJ-25
Complete Jerseys Gold-CJ-25
Future Teammates-FT13
He Shoots-He Scores Prizes-1
He Shoots-He Scores Prizes-36
He Shoots-He Scores Prizes-38
Jerseys-GUJ-53
Jerseys-GUJ-90
Jerseys Gold-GUJ-53
Jerseys Gold-GUJ-90
Emblems-GUE-53
Emblems-GUE-90
Emblems Gold-GUE-53
Emblems Gold-GUE-90
Numbers-GUN-53
Numbers-GUN-90
Numbers Gold-GUN-53
Numbers Gold-GUN-90
Nameplates-N-31
Nameplates Gold-N-31
National Pride-NPR-11
National Pride-NPR-36
Spectrum-STM-10
Spectrum Gold-STM-10
06Sports Illustrated for Kids *-1
06Sweet Spot Update Spokesmen Signatures-15
06Be A Player Portraits-83
First Exposures-FESC
Signature Portraits-SPSC
06Beehive-19
06Beehive-169
Blue-19
Gold-19
Matte-19
Red Facsimile Signatures-19
Wood-19
5 X 7 Black and White-19
5 X 7 Dark Wood-19
Matted Materials-MMSC
PhotoGraphs-PGSC
Remarkable Matted Materials-MMSC
06Black Diamond-164B
Black-162B
Gold-164B
Ruby-164B
Gemography-GSC
Jerseys-JSC
Jerseys Black-JSC
Jerseys Gold-JSC
Jerseys Ruby-JSC
Jerseys Black Autographs -JSC
06Flair Showcase-193
06Flair Showcase-257
06Flair Showcase-294
Parallel-193
Parallel-257
Parallel-294
Hot Numbers-HN33
Hot Numbers Parallel-HN33
Inks-ISC
Stitches-SSSC
Wave of the Future-WF35
06Fleer-154
Oversized-154
Tiffany-154
Fabricology-FSC
Hockey Headliners-HL1
Hockey Headliners-HL15
Signing Day-SDSC
Total 0-020
06Gatorade-91
06Hot Prospects-77
Red Hot-77
White Hot-77
Hot Materials -HMSC
Hot Materials Red Hot-HMSC
Hot Materials White Hot-HMSC
Hotagraphs-HSC
06ITG International Ice-10
Gold-10
Autographs-ASC
Canadian Dream Team-DT11
Canadian Dream Team Gold-DT11
Complete Jersey-CJ04
Complete Jersey Gold-CJ04
Cornerstones-IC01
Cornerstones-IC11
Cornerstones Gold-IC01
Cornerstones Gold-IC11
Double Memorabilia-DM05
Double Memorabilia Gold-DM05
Emblem Autographs-GUE13
Emblem Autographs Gold-GUE13
Emblems-GUE13
Emblems Gold-GUE13
Greatest Moments-GM10
Greatest Moments Gold-GM10
Hockey Passport-HP12
Hockey Passport Gold-HP12
International Rivals-IR18
International Rivals Gold-IR18
Jersey Autographs-GUJ13
Jersey Autographs Gold-GUJ13
Jerseys-GUJ13
Jerseys Gold-GUJ13
Numbers-GUN13
Numbers Autographs-GUN13
Numbers Autographs Gold-GUN13
Numbers Gold-GUN13
Passing The Torch-PTT10
Passing The Torch Gold-PTT10
Stick and Jersey-SJ06
Stick and Jersey Gold-SJ06
Teammates-IT10
Teammates Gold-IT10
Triple Memorabilia-TM04
Triple Memorabilia Gold-TM04
06ITG Phenoms-SC01
06ITG Phenoms-SC02
06ITG Phenoms-SC03
06ITG Phenoms-SC04
06ITG Phenoms-SC05
06ITG Phenoms-SC06
Autographs-SC01
Autographs-SC02
Autographs-SC03
Autographs-SC04
Autographs-SC05
Autographs-SC06
Double Memorabilia Gold-DMSC
Double Memorabilia Silver-DMSC
Idols Gold-IDSC
Idols Silver-IDSC
Jerseys Gold-GUJSC
Jerseys Gold Dual-DJCT
Jerseys Gold Dual-DJOC
Jerseys Gold Triple-TJCOT
Jerseys Silver-GUJSC
Jerseys Silver Dual-DJCT
Jerseys Silver Dual-DJOC
Jerseys Silver Triple-TJCOT
Patches Gold-GUPSC
Patches Gold Dual-DPCT
Patches Gold Dual-DPOC
Patches Gold Triple-TPCOT
Patches Silver-GUPSC
Patches Silver Dual-DPCT
Patches Silver Dual-DPOC
Patches Silver Triple-TPCOT
Sticks Gold-GUSSC
Sticks Gold Dual-DSCT
Sticks Gold Dual-DSOC
Sticks Gold Triple-TSCOT
Sticks Silver-GUSSC
Sticks Silver Dual-DSCT
Sticks Silver Dual-DSOC
Sticks Silver Triple-TSCOT
Teammates Gold-TMSC
Teammates Silver-TMSC
Triple Memorabilia Gold-TRSC
Triple Memorabilia Silver-TRSC
06O-Pee-Chee-405
06O-Pee-Chee-621
06O-Pee-Chee-665
06O-Pee-Chee-694
Rainbow-405
Rainbow-621
Rainbow-665
Rainbow-694
Swatches-S-SC
06Panini Stickers-136
06SP Authentic-20
06SP Authentic-155
Chirography-SC
Limited-20
Limited-155
Sign of the Times-STSC
06SP Game Used-80
Gold-80
Rainbow-80
Authentic Fabrics-AFSC
Authentic Fabrics Parallel-AFSC
Authentic Fabrics Patches-AFSC
Authentic Fabrics Dual-AF2RC
Authentic Fabrics Dual Patches-AF2RC
Authentic Fabrics Triple-AF3PIT
Authentic Fabrics Triple Patches-AF3PIT
Authentic Fabrics Quads-AF4STSC
Authentic Fabrics Quads Patches-AF4STSC
Authentic Fabrics Fives-AF51ST
Authentic Fabrics Fives-AP5RPT
Authentic Fabrics Fives Patches-AF51ST

Authentic Fabrics Fives Patches-AP5RPT
Authentic Fabrics Eights-AF8CEN
Authentic Fabrics Eights Patches-AF8CEN
Autographs-80
By The Letter-BLSC
Inked Sweaters-ISSC
Inked Sweaters Patches-ISSC
Letter Marks-LMSC
SIGnificance-SSC
06SPx-81
06SPx-134
Spectrum-81
Spectrum-134
SPxcitement-X80
SPxcitement Spectrum-X80
SPxcitement Autographs-X80
Winning Materials-WMSC
Winning Materials Spectrum-WMSC
Winning Materials Autographs-WMSC
06The Cup-73
Autographed Foundations-CQSC
Autographed Foundations Patches-CQSC
Autographed Patches-73
Black Rainbow-73
Foundations-CQSC
Foundations Patches-CQSC
Enshrinements-ESC
Gold-73
Gold Patches-73
Honorable Numbers-HNSC
Jerseys-73
Limited Logos-LLSC
Masterpiece Pressplates-73
NHL Shields Duals-DSHCO
Scripted Swatches-SSSC
Signature Patches-SPSC
06UD Artifacts-21
06UD Artifacts-191
Blue-21
Blue-191
Gold-21
Gold-191
Platinum-21
Platinum-191
Radiance-21
Radiance-191
Autographed Radiance Parallel-21
Autographed Radiance Parallel-191
Red-21
Red-191
Auto-Facts-AFSC
Auto-Facts Gold-AFSC
Treasured Patches Black-TSSC
Treasured Patches Blue-TSSC
Treasured Patches Gold-TSSC
Treasured Patches Platinum-TSSC
Treasured Patches Red-TSSC
Treasured Patches Autographed Black Tag Parallel-TSSC
Treasured Swatches-TSSC
Treasured Swatches Black-TSSC
Treasured Swatches Blue-TSSC
Treasured Swatches Gold-TSSC
Treasured Swatches Platinum-TSSC
Treasured Swatches Red-TSSC
Treasured Swatches Autographed Black-TSSC
Tundra Tandems-TTLC
Tundra Tandems Black-TTLC
Tundra Tandems Blue-TTLC
Tundra Tandems Gold-TTLC
Tundra Tandems Platinum-TTLC
Tundra Tandems Red-TTLC
Tundra Tandems Dual Patches Red-TTLC
06UD Biography of a Season-BOS9
06UD Biography of a Season-BOS15
06UD Mini Jersey Collection-80
Jerseys-SC
Jersey Variations-SC
Jersey Autographs-SC
06UD Powerplay-80
Impact Rainbow-80
In Action-IA10
Power Marks-PMSC
Specialists-SSC
Specialists Patches-PSC
06UD Toronto Fall Expo Priority Signings -PSSC
06Ultimate Collection-47
Autographed Jerseys-AJ-SC
Autographed Patches-AJ-SC
Jerseys-UJ-SC
Jerseys Dual-UJ2-CM
Jerseys Triple-UJ3-CMS
Patches-UJ-SC
Patches Dual-UJ2-CM
Patches Triple-UJ3-CMS
Signatures-US-SC
Ultimate Achievements-UA-SC
Ultimate Signatures Logos-SL-SC
06Ultra-154
Gold Medallion-154
Ice Medallion-154
Action-UA23
Difference Makers-DM28
Fresh Ink-ISC
Scoring Kings-SK28
06Upper Deck Arena Giveaways-PIT1
06Upper Deck-155
06Upper Deck-199
Exclusives Parallel-155
Exclusives Parallel-199
High Gloss Parallel-155
High Gloss Parallel-199
All World-AW28
Century Marks-CM5
Game Dated Moments-GD1
Game Dated Moments-GD19
Game Dated Moments-GD21
Game Jerseys-JSC
Game Patches-PSC
Generations Duals-G2GC
Generations Triples-G3GCL
Generations Patches Dual-G2PGC
Generations Patches Triple-G3PGCL
Goal Rush-GR14
Hometown Heroes-HH39
Masterpieces-155
Masterpieces-199
Signatures-SSC
Signature Sensations-SSSC
Walmart Tins Oversize-155
06Upper Deck Rookie Showdown-RS-SCAO
06Upper Deck Entry Draft-DR1
06Upper Deck MVP-231
Gold Script-231
Super Script-231
Clutch Performers-CP22
Gotta Have Hart-HH13
International Icons-II20
Jerseys-OJCF
Jerseys-OJCO
06Upper Deck Ovation-140
06Upper Deck Sweet Shot-82
Signature Shots/Saves-SSSC
Signature Shots/Saves Ice Signings-SSISC
Signature Shots/Saves Sticks-SSSSC
Sweet Stitches-SSSC
Sweet Stitches Duals-SSSC
Sweet Stitches Triples-SSSC
06Upper Deck Trilogy-79
Frozen In Time-FT17
Honorary Scripted Patches-HSPSC
Honorary Scripted Swatches-HSSSC
Honorary Swatches-HSSC
Ice Scripts-ISSC
Scripts-S1SC
Scripts-S2SC
Scripts-S3SC
Scripts-TSSC
06Upper Deck National NHL-NHL-1
06Upper Deck National NHL Autographs-NHL-1
06Upper Deck National NHL VIP-3
06Upper Deck Victory-157
06Upper Deck Victory Black-157
06Upper Deck Victory Gold-157
06Upper Deck Victory GameBreakers-GB40
06Upper Deck Victory Next In Line-NL41
06Upper Deck Victory Oversize Cards-SC
06ITG Heroes and Prospects-24
06ITG Heroes and Prospects-147
Autographs-ASC1
Autographs-ASC2
Complete Jerseys-CJ05
Complete Jerseys Gold-CJ05
Double Memorabilia-DM03
Double Memorabilia Gold-DM03
National Pride-NP02
National Pride Gold-NP02
Quad Emblems-QE02
Quad Emblems-QE05
Quad Emblems Gold-QE02
Quad Emblems Gold-QE05
Sticks and Jerseys-SJ10
Sticks and Jerseys Gold-SJ10
Triple Memorabilia-TM04
Triple Memorabilia Gold-TM04
07Upper Deck Goudey Sport Royalty-SC
07Upper Deck Goudey Sport Royalty Autographs-SC
07Upper Deck 1989 Reprints-SC
07Upper Deck National Convention *-NTL14
07Upper Deck National Convention VIP *-VIP14
07Upper Deck BAP Draft Redemption Premium-TY-SC
07Upper Deck All-Star Game Redemptions-AS7
07Upper Deck Ovation-11
3x5s-XL8
Autographed 3x5s-XLASC
07Upper Deck Victory-14
Black-14
Gold-14
GameBreakers-GB1
Oversize Cards-OS4
Stars on Ice-SI50

Cross, Brett
04Richmond Riverdogs-20
06Richmond Renegades-3

Cross, Cory
93Atlanta Knights-18
94Lightning Photo Album-10
94Lightning Postcards-5
94Upper Deck-340
Electric Ice-340
94Atlanta Knights-21
95Leaf-275
95Lightning Team Issue-7
95Topps-44
OPC Inserts-44
95Images-88
Gold-88
96Be A Player-143
Autographs-143
Autographs Silver-143
97Pacific Invincible NHL Regime-184
97Upper Deck-365
98Be A Player-128
Press Release-128
98BAP Gold-128
98BAP Autographs-128
98BAP Autographs Gold-128
98BAP Tampa Bay All Star Game-128
99Pacific-386
Copper-386
Emerald Green-386
Gold-386
Ice Blue-386
Premiere Date-386
Red-386
00Upper Deck-396
Exclusives Tier 1-396
Exclusives Tier 2-396
01Pacific-363
Extreme LTD-363
Hobby LTD-363
Premiere Date-363
Retail LTD-363
01Pacific Arena Exclusives-363
02BAP Sig Series Auto Buybacks 1998-128
03Oilers Postcards-5
03Pacific Complete-324
Red-324
03Upper Deck MVP-174
Gold Script-174
Silver Script-174
Canadian Exclusives-174
05Parkhurst Facsimile Auto Parallel-397
06German DEL-70
New Arrivals-NA2

Cross, Nick
96UK Guildford Flames-11
03UK Guildford Flames-18
04UK Guildford Flames-19
05UK Guildford Flames-14

Crossman, Doug
81Blackhawks Borderless Postcards-4
82Blackhawks Postcards-3
82O-Pee-Chee-63
82Post Cereal-4
83Flyers J.C. Penney-7
83NHL Key Tags-26
83O-Pee-Chee-263
84O-Pee-Chee-157
85Flyers Postcards-7
86Flyers Postcards-6
86O-Pee-Chee Stickers-237
87Flyers Postcards-10
87O-Pee-Chee-182
87Panini Stickers-125
87Topps-182
88Kings Postcards-12
88Kings Smokey-4
88O-Pee-Chee-197
88O-Pee-Chee Stickers-100
88Topps-197
89Islanders Team Issue-4
90Bowman-115
Tiffany-115
90Kraft-10
90O-Pee-Chee-72
90Panini Stickers-91
90Pro Set-179
90Score-59
Canadian-59
90Score Rookie/Traded-52T
90Topps-72
Tiffany-72
90Upper Deck-7
90Upper Deck-419
French-7
French-419
90Whalers Jr. 7-Eleven-6
91O-Pee-Chee-341
91Score American-38
91Score Canadian Bilingual-38
91Score Canadian English-38
91Topps-341
92OPC Premier-59
92Parkhurst-388
Emerald Ice-388
92Pro Set-180
92Ultra-410
93OPC Premier-159
Gold-159
93Score-25
Canadian-25
93Topps/OPC Premier-159
Gold-159
93Peoria Rivermen-4

Crosty, Paul
06Toledo Storm-6

Croteau, Gary
70Esso Power Players-104
70O-Pee-Chee-189
70Sargent Promotions Stamps-141
71Letraset Action Replays-12
71O-Pee-Chee-17
71Sargent Promotions Stamps-133
71Topps-17
71Toronto Sun-45
72O-Pee-Chee-3
72Sargent Promotions Stamps-48
72Topps-83
72Finnish Semic World Championship-180
72Swedish Semic World Championship-180
73O-Pee-Chee-228
74NHL Action Stamps-295
74O-Pee-Chee NHL-36
74Topps-36
76O-Pee-Chee NHL-283
76Rockies Coke Cans-4
76Rockies Puck Bucks-5
77O-Pee-Chee NHL-52
77Rockies Coke Cans-3
77Topps-52
78O-Pee-Chee-362
79O-Pee-Chee-158
79Rockies Team Issue-5
79Topps-158
04ITG Franchises US West-229
Autographs-A-GCR

Croteau, Paul
95Roanoke Express-6
98Baton Rouge Kingfish-5

Crouch, Ryan
05Sudbury Wolves-8
06Sudbury Wolves-17

Crowder, Bruce
82O-Pee-Chee-9
82Post Cereal-1
83Bruins Team Issue-2
83NHL Key Tags-7
83O-Pee-Chee-46
06Portland Pirates-1

Crowder, Chase
03Saginaw Spirit-5
04Saginaw Spirit-16

Crowder, Keith
82O-Pee-Chee-10
82O-Pee-Chee Stickers-80
82Topps Stickers-80
83Bruins Team Issue-3
83O-Pee-Chee-47
83O-Pee-Chee Stickers-56
83Topps Stickers-56
84Bruins Postcards-4
84O-Pee-Chee-2
84Topps-2
85O-Pee-Chee-159
85O-Pee-Chee Stickers-163
85Topps-159
86O-Pee-Chee-130
86O-Pee-Chee Stickers-37
86Topps-130
87O-Pee-Chee-194
87O-Pee-Chee Stickers-136
87Panini Stickers-14
87Topps-194
88Bruins Sports Action-4
88O-Pee-Chee-206
88Panini Stickers-209
89Kings Smokey-10
89O-Pee-Chee-199
90O-Pee-Chee-476

Crowder, Tim
04South Surrey Eagles-2
04Surrey Eagles-2
04Surrey Eagles-2

Crowder, Troy
90Devils Team Issue-8
90Pro Set-620
90Score Rookie/Traded-43T
90Upper Deck-441
French-441
91O-Pee-Chee-374
91OPC Premier-169
91Score Canadian Bilingual-602
91Score Canadian English-602
91Score Rookie/Traded-52T
91Topps-374
91Upper Deck-342
French-342
96Canucks Postcards-18
97Pacific Dynagon Best Kept Secrets-96
98Hershey Bears-13
02Fleer Throwbacks-33
Gold-33
Platinum-33

Crowdis, Lou
51Buffalo Bison-5

Crowe, Phil
92Phoenix Roadrunners-6
93Donruss-446
96Detroit Vipers-4
97Pacific Dynagon Best Kept Secrets-65
97Detroit Vipers-2
98Cincinnati Cyclones-3
98Cincinnati Cyclones 2-7
98Detroit Vipers-8
99Milwaukee Admirals Keebler-8
03Colorado Eagles-7
05Colorado Eagles-21
06Colorado EaglesA -25

Crowe, Rick
91British Columbia JHL-3

Crowell, Chris
05Vernon Vipers-8

Crowell, Matt
04Williams Lake Timberwolves-3

Crowley, Dane
03Saskatoon Blades-6
04Saskatoon Blades-18
06Swift Current Broncos-21
06Swift Current Broncos-23

Crowley, Joe
917th Inn. Sketch QMJHL-203
92Indianapolis Ice-8
93Indianapolis Ice-6

Crowley, Mike
94Minnesota Golden Gophers-9
96Minnesota Golden Gophers-8
98Pacific-47
Ice Blue-47
Red-47
98Upper Deck-8
Exclusives-8
Exclusives 1 of 1-8
Gold Reserve-8
98Upper Deck MVP-5
Gold Script-5
Silver Script-5
Super Script-5
98Cincinnati Mighty Ducks-15
99IHL All-Stars-1
99Long Beach Ice Dogs-3
00Upper Deck NHLPA-PA1

Crowley, Nick
95Minnesota Golden Gophers-10

Crowley, Paul
79Rochester Americans-3

Crowley, Ted
92St. John's Maple Leafs-5
93PowerPlay-500
93Stadium Club Team USA-3
93Stadium Club Team USA Members Only-3
93Topps Premier Team USA-12
93Ultra-480
93Classic Pro Prospects-112
94Parkhurst-93
Gold-93
94Score-233
Gold-233
Platinum-233
94Upper Deck-442
Electric Ice-442
96Cincinnati Cyclones-4
97Springfield Falcons-3
98Hershey Bears-4
99Cleveland Lumberjacks-6
00German DEL-116
01German Upper Deck-64
02German DEL City Press-89
03German DEL-153
04Memphis RiverKings-18

Crowley, Troy
06Saskatoon Blades-4

Crowley, Wayne
90ProCards AHL/IHL-609

Crowther, Cory
92British Columbia JHL-103

Crozier, Greg
00Wilkes-Barre Scranton Penguins-5
01SPx-96
01Upper Deck-204
Exclusives-204
01Upper Deck Victory-385
Gold-385
01Providence Bruins-20
02Albany River Rats-24
02Albany River Rats AAP-9
03Albany River Rats-8
03Albany River Rats Kinko's-7

Crozier, Joe
51Laval Dairy QSHL-3
52St. Lawrence Sales-43
56Quebec Aces-4
63Rochester Americans-10
80Maple Leafs Postcards-8
82Kitchener Rangers-4

Crozier, Kevin
93Quebec Pee-Wee Tournament-1217

Crozier, Roger
64Beehive Group III Photos-66
64Coca-Cola Caps-37
64Topps-47
65Coca-Cola-37
65Topps-42
66Topps-43
66Topps USA Test-43
67Topps-48
68O-Pee-Chee-23
Puck Stickers-10
68Shirriff Coins-35
68Topps-23
69O-Pee-Chee-55
Four-in-One-10
69Topps-55
70Colgate Stamps-83
70Dad's Cookies-18
70Esso Power Players-73
70O-Pee-Chee-145
Deckle-11
70Sargent Promotions Stamps-26
71Bazooka-32
71Letraset Action Replays-3
71O-Pee-Chee-36
O-Pee-Chee/Topps Booklets-5
71Sabres Postcards-70
71Sargent Promotions Stamps-27
71Topps-36
71Toronto Sun-24
72O-Pee-Chee-50
72Sabres Pepsi Pinback Buttons-1
72Sabres Postcards-3
72Sargent Promotions Stamps-32
72Topps-31
72Finnish Semic World Championship-165
72Swedish Semic World Championship-165
73O-Pee-Chee-153
73Sabres Bells-1
73Sabres Postcards-1
73Topps-108
74NHL Action Stamps-45
74Sabres Postcards-3
75O-Pee-Chee NHL-350
75Sabres Linnett-1
93Sabres Noco-1
94Parkhurst Tall Boys-53
94Parkhurst Tall Boys-157
94Parkhurst Tall Boys-158
Mail-Ins-AS1
Mail-Ins-TW5
95Parkhurst '66-67-56
Coins-56
02BAP Ultimate Memorabilia Conn Smythe-2
02BAP Ultimate Memorabilia Cup Duels-6
02BAP Ultimate Memorabilia Emblem Attic-19
02BAP Ultimate Memorabilia Number Ones-7
02BAP Ultimate Memorabilia Retro Trophies-16
02BAP Ultimate Mem Vintage Jerseys-32
02Between the Pipes Double Memorabilia-20
02Between the Pipes He Shoots/Saves Prize-23
02Between the Pipes Trappers-GT16
02Between the Pipes Vintage Memorabilia-3
02Parkhurst Vintage Teammates-VT17
03BAP Ultimate Memorabilia Emblem Attic-5
03BAP Ultimate Mem Emblem Attic Gold-5
03BAP Ultimate Memorabilia Triple Threads-7
03BAP Ultimate Mem Vintage Jerseys-10
03BAP Ultimate Mem Vintage Jerseys Gold-10
03ITG Used Signature Series Goalie Gear-36
03ITG Used Sig Series Goalie Gear Autos-36
03ITG Used Sig Series Goalie Gear Gold-36
03ITG VIP MVP-13
03Parkhurst Original Six Detroit-52
Inserts-D-10
Memorabilia-DM24
Memorabilia-DM33
Memorabilia-DM56
03Parkhurst Orig Six He Shoots/Scores-25
03Parkhurst Orig Six He Shoots/Scores-25A
03Parkhurst Rookie Before the Mask-BTM-14
03Parkhurst Rookie Before the Mask Gold-BTM-14
03Parkhurst Rookie ROYalty-VR-16
03Parkhurst Rookie ROYalty Gold-VR-16
04ITG Franchises He Shoots/Scores Prizes-31
04ITG Franchises US East-349
04ITG Franchises US West-206
Double Memorabilia-WDM19
Double Memorabilia Gold-WDM19
Goalie Gear-WGG1
Goalie Gear Gold-WGG1
Memorabilia-WSM2
Memorabilia Gold-WSM2
Original Sticks-WOS9
Original Sticks Gold-WOS9
Triple Memorabilia Gold-WTM1
Trophy Winners-WTW6
Trophy Winners Gold-WTW6
04ITG Ultimate Memorabilia-116
04ITG Ultimate Memorabilia-131
Gold-116
Gold-131
Goalie Gear-8
Original Six-13
Original Six-19
Triple Threads-5
05ITG Ultimate Mem Decades Jerseys-2
05ITG Ultimate Mem Decades Jerseys Gold-2
05ITG Ultimate Mem Sticks and Jerseys-22
05ITG Ultimate Mem Stick and Jerseys Gold-22
05ITG Ultimate Mem 3 Star of the Game Jsy-9
05ITG Ult Mem 3 Star of the Game Jsy Gold-9
05ITG Ultimate Memorabilia Vintage Lumber-30
05ITG Ultimate Mem Vintage Lumber Gold-30
06Between The Pipes-130
Shooting Gallery-SG06
Shooting Gallery Gold-SG06
Stick and Jersey-SJ33
Stick and Jersey Gold-SJ33
Stick Work-SW02
Stick Work Gold-SW02
06ITG Ultimate Memorabilia Decades-5
06ITG Ultimate Memorabilia Decades Gold-5
06ITG Ultimate Memorabilia Motown Heroes Autos-5
06ITG Ultimate Memorabilia Retro Teammates-8
06ITG Ultimate Memorabilia Retro Teammates Gold-8

Cruickshank, Curtis
97Bowman CHL-139
OPC-139
Autographs-19
Bowman's Best-19
Bowman's Best Atomic Refractors-19
Bowman's Best Refractor-19
98Kingston Frontenacs-3
99Hampton Roads Admirals-6
00Rockford IceHogs-4
02Augusta Lynx-62
03UK Basingstoke Bison-1
04UK EIHL All-Stars-13
04UK Nottingham Panthers-7
05UK Nottingham Panthers-1

Cruickshank, Gord
89ProCards AHL-62

Cruikshank, Brad
03Pensacola Ice Pilots-340

Crumb, Darryl
99OCN Blizzard-8

Crumley, Chad
92Saskatchewan JHL-66

Crummer, Bob
97Guelph Storm-17
98Guelph Storm-15

Crump, Lionel
95North Iowa Huskies-3

Crunn, Carlo
05Finnish Cardset -67

Cruse, Justin
01Prince Albert Raiders-5
02Prince Albert Raiders-7
03Prince Albert Raiders-14

Crutchfield, Nels
34Sweet Caporal-2

Cruz, Jomar
97Brandon Wheat Kings-5
98Brandon Wheat Kings-3

Crystal, Bob
44Beehive Group II Photos-302

Csata, Laszlo
94German First League-609

Csipka, Pavel
00Czech OFS-162

Csumrik, Dave
00Sudbury Wolves-5
01Fort Worth Brahmas-7
04Fort Worth Brahmas-4

Cubars, Sergejs
98Danish Hockey League-124
99Danish Hockey League-181

Cubs, Hershey
93Quebec Pee-Wee Tournament-792

Cucksey, Don
91Rayside-Balfour Jr. Canadians-2

Cucuz, Sasha
94Sarnia Sting-26
95Slapshot-179
00Trenton Titans-15
01Atlantic City Boardwalk Bullies-7

Cuddihy, Jimmy
00Shawinigan Cataractes-13
Signed-13
01Shawinigan Cataractes-12
02Shawinigan Cataractes-9
03Shawinigan Cataractes-6

Cude, Wilfred
34Beehive Group I Photos-144
34Sweet Caporal-3
35Diamond Matchbooks Tan 1-20
35Diamond Matchbooks Tan 2-17
35Diamond Matchbooks Tan 3-16
35O-Pee-Chee V304C-73
36O-Pee-Chee V304D-120
37O-Pee-Chee V304E-149
37V356 Worldwide Gum-9
38Quaker Oats Photos-8
06Between The Pipes Forgotten Franchises-FF08

Cugnet, Jason
01Idaho Steelheads-4
03UK Cardiff Devils-1

Culhane, Jim
88ProCards AHL-70
89ProCards AHL-298
90ProCards AHL/IHL-504
91ProCards-454

Culic, Chet
93Minnesota-Duluth Bulldogs-6

Cull, Dean
907th Inn. Sketch OHL-389
91Rayside-Balfour Jr. Canadians-3

Cull, Trent
907th Inn. Sketch OHL-281
917th Inn. Sketch OHL-177
93Kingston Frontenacs-19
94St. John's Maple Leafs-7
95St. John's Maple Leafs-6
96St. John's Maple Leafs-13
00Wilkes-Barre Scranton Penguins-6
02Syracuse Crunch-23
02Syracuse Crunch Sheets-9
03Syracuse Crunch-23
04Guelph Storm-28
05Guelph Storm-C-07

Cullaton, Brent
96Kansas City Blades-5
99Florida Everblades-7
99Tallahassee Tiger Sharks-16
01German Upper Deck-77
02Columbus Cottonmouths-4
03Laredo Bucks-4
03San Antonio Rampage-13

Cullen, Barry
44Beehive Group II Photos-393
57Parkhurst-T21
58Parkhurst-31
59Topps-25
60Parkhurst-32
60Shirriff Coins-47
94Parkhurst Missing Link-120

Cullen, Brandon
00UD CHL Prospects-16
02Charlotte Checkers-81
03Hartford Wolf Pack-2

Cullen, Brian
44Beehive Group II Photos-304
44Beehive Group II Photos-394
52Juniors Blue Tint-25
55Parkhurst-13
Quaker Oats-13
57Parkhurst-M22
57Parkhurst-T9
58Parkhurst-36
58Parkhurst-50
59Topps-55
60Shirriff Coins-99
94Parkhurst Missing Link-118

Cullen, David
01BAP Memorabilia-414
Emerald-414
Ruby-414
Sapphire-414
01Crown Royale-164
01Private Stock-135
Gold-135
Premiere Date-135
Retail-135
Silver-135
01Private Stock Pacific Nights-135
01SP Authentic-169
Limited-169
Limited Gold-169
01SPx-121
01Titanium-163
Retail-163
01Titanium Draft Day Edition-135
01UD Challenge for the Cup-129
01Upper Deck-203
Exclusives-203
01Upper Deck MVP-212
01Upper Deck Victory-384
Gold-384
01Upper Deck Vintage-293
01Vanguard-125
Blue-125
Red-125
One of Ones-125
Premiere Date-125
Proofs-125
03Rochester Americans-6
04Rochester Americans-5

Cullen, Joe
04San Antonio Rampage-11
05Binghamton Senators Quickway-4

Cullen, John
87Flint Spirits-2
89O-Pee-Chee-145
89O-Pee-Chee Stickers-64
89O-Pee-Chee Stickers-231
89Panini Stickers-316
89Penguins Foodland-9
89Topps-145
90Bowman-210
Tiffany-210
90O-Pee-Chee-208
90OPC Premier-20
90Panini Stickers-125
90Penguins Foodland-10
90Pro Set-232
90Score-164
Canadian-164
90Score Hottest/Rising Stars-73
90Topps-208
Tiffany-208
90Upper Deck-12
90Upper Deck-492
French-12
French-492
91Pro Set Platinum-175
91Bowman-1
91Kraft-24
91O-Pee-Chee-226
91OPC Premier-127
91Panini Stickers-314
91Parkhurst-59
French-59
91Pinnacle-125
91Pinnacle-391
French-125
French-391
91Pro Set-85
91Pro Set-302
French-85
French-302
CC-CC9
CC French-CC9
91Score American-7
91Score American-421
91Score Canadian Bilingual-7
91Score Canadian Bilingual-311
91Score Canadian English-7
91Score Canadian English-311
91Score Young Superstars-5
91Stadium Club-289
91Topps-226
91Upper Deck-84
91Upper Deck-235
French-84
French-235
91Whalers Jr. 7-Eleven-8
91Finnish Semic World Champ Stickers-72
91Swedish Semic World Champ Stickers-72
92Bowman-194
92Bowman-227
92Maple Leafs Kodak-9
92McDonald's Upper Deck-18
92O-Pee-Chee-104
92Panini Stickers-257
92Panini Stickers French-257
92Parkhurst-180
Emerald Ice-180
92Pinnacle-285
French-285
92Pro Set-57
92Score-150
92Score-425
Canadian-150
Canadian-425
92Seasons Patches-45
92Stadium Club-160
92Topps-132
Gold-132G
92Ultra-72
92Ultra-419
92Upper Deck-304
92Upper Deck-465
93Donruss-334
93Leaf-245
Maple Leafs Score Black's-16
93OPC Premier-479
Gold-479
93Panini Stickers-226
93Parkhurst-473
Emerald Ice-473
93Pinnacle-388
Canadian-388
93PowerPlay-242
93Score-189
Canadian-189
93Stadium Club-209
Members Only Master Set-209
OPC-209
First Day Issue-209
First Day Issue OPC-209
93Topps/OPC Premier-479
Gold-479
93Ultra-20
93Upper Deck-395
94Be A Player Signature Cards-105
94Leaf-412
94Lightning Postcards-6
94OPC Premier-423
Special Effects-423
94Parkhurst SE-SE140
Gold-SE140
94Penguins Foodland-7
94Pinnacle-397
Artist's Proofs-397
Rink Collection-397
94SP-91
Die Cuts-91
94Topps/OPC Premier-423
Special Effects-423
94Ultra-348
94Upper Deck-281
Electric Ice-281
95Canada Games NHL POGS-248
95Collector's Choice-181
Player's Club-181
Player's Club Platinum-181
95Donruss-156
95Leaf-181
95Lightning Team Issue-8
95Parkhurst International-463
Emerald Ice-463
95Score-105
Black Ice Artist's Proofs-105
Black Ice-105
95Topps-74
OPC Inserts-74
95Ultra-309
95Upper Deck-358
Electric Ice-358
Electric Ice Gold-358
96Flair-87
Blue Ice-87
97Pacific-282
Copper-282
Emerald Green-282
Ice Blue-282
Red-282
Silver-282
97Pacific Dynagon-116
Copper-116
Dark Grey-116
Emerald Green-116
Ice Blue-116
Red-116
Silver-116
Tandems-53
97Pacific Invincible-130
Copper-130
Emerald Green-130
Ice Blue-130
Red-130
Silver-130
97Panini Stickers-107
97Score-155
Artist's Proofs-155
Golden Blades-155
98Pacific Dynagon Ice-172
Blue-172
Red-172
98Upper Deck-365
Exclusives-365
Exclusives 1 of 1-365
Gold Reserve-365
98Cleveland Lumberjacks-9

Cullen, Jon
03Atlantic City Boardwalk Bullies-2
03Atlantic City Boardwalk Bullies RBI-17
04UK EIHL All-Stars-6
04Atlantic City Boardwalk Bullies Kinko's-26

Cullen, Justin
90Kitchener Rangers-25
907th Inn. Sketch OHL-229
917th Inn. Sketch OHL-95

Cullen, Mark
03Houston Aeros-5
04Houston Aeros-5
05Hot Prospects-118
En Fuego-118
Red Hot-118
White Hot-118
05The Cup Masterpiece Pressplates (Ice)-212
05The Cup Master Pressplate Rookie Update-117
05Upper Deck Ice-212
05Upper Deck Rookie Update-117
05Norfolk Admirals-9
06Philadelphia Phantoms-23

Cullen, Matt
95Donruss Elite World Juniors-33
97Pacific Omega-1
Copper-1
Dark Gray-1
Emerald Green-1
Gold-1
Ice Blue-1
97Score Mighty Ducks-5
Platinum-5
Premier-5
98Finest-53
No Protectors-53
No Protectors Refractors-53
Refractors-53
98Pacific-45
Ice Blue-45
Red-45
98UD Choice-7
98UD Choice Preview-7
98UD Choice Prime Choice Reserve-7
98UD Choice Reserve-7
98UD3-16
98UD3-76
98UD3-136
Die-Cuts-16
Die-Cuts-76
Die-Cuts-136
98Upper Deck-32
Exclusives-32
Exclusives 1 of 1-32
Gold Reserve-32
99BAP Memorabilia-159
Gold-159
Silver-159
99BAP Millennium-9
Emerald-9
Ruby-9
Sapphire-9
Signatures-9
Signatures Gold-9
99Pacific-1
Copper-1
Emerald Green-1
Gold-1
Ice Blue-1
Premiere Date-1
Red-1
99Pacific Omega-1
Copper-1
Gold-1
Ice Blue-1
Premiere Date-1
99Panini Stickers-177
99Paramount-1
Copper-1
Emerald-1
Gold-1
Holographic Emerald-1
Holographic Gold-1
Holographic Silver-1
Ice Blue-1
Premiere Date-1
Red-1
Silver-1
99Upper Deck-12
Exclusives-12
Exclusives 1 of 1-12
99Upper Deck Gold Reserve-12
99Upper Deck MVP-7
Gold Script-7
Silver Script-7
Super Script-7
ProSign-MC
99Upper Deck Victory-4
99Wayne Gretzky Hockey-6
99Cincinnati Mighty Ducks-22
00BAP Memorabilia-357
Emerald-357
Ruby-357
Sapphire-357
Promos-357
00BAP Mem Chicago Sportsfest Copper-357
00BAP Memorabilia Chicago Sportsfest Blue-357
00BAP Memorabilia Chicago Sportsfest Gold-357
00BAP Memorabilia Chicago Sportsfest Ruby-357
00BAP Memorabilia Chicago Sun-Times Ruby-357
00BAP Memorabilia Chicago Sun-Times Gold-357
00BAP Mem Chicago Sun-Times Sapphire-357
00BAP Mem Toronto Fall Expo Copper-357
00BAP Memorabilia Toronto Fall Expo Gold-357
00BAP Memorabilia Toronto Fall Expo Ruby-357
00BAP Signature Series-32
Emerald-32
Ruby-32
Sapphire-32
Autographs-73
Autographs Gold-73
00O-Pee-Chee-211
00O-Pee-Chee Parallel-211
00Pacific-2
Copper-2
Gold-2
Ice Blue-2
Premiere Date-2

00Paramount-3
Copper-3
Gold-3
Holo-Gold-3
Holo-Silver-3
Ice Blue-3
Premiere Date-3
00Stadium Club-91
00Topps/OPC-211
Parallel-211
00Upper Deck-232
Exclusives Tier 1-232
Exclusives Tier 2-232
00Upper Deck MVP-2
First Stars-2
Second Stars-2
Third Stars-2
00Upper Deck Vintage-3
01Crown Royale-1
Blue-1
Premiere Date-1
Red-1
Retail-1
01Pacific-1
Extreme LTD-1
Hobby LTD-1
Premiere Date-1
Retail LTD-1
01Pacific Arena Exclusives-1
01UD Mask Collection-3
Gold-3
01Upper Deck-234
Exclusives-234
01Upper Deck Victory-4
Gold-4
02BAP First Edition-171
02BAP Sig Series Auto Buybacks 1999-9
02BAP Sig Series Auto Buybacks 2000-73
02O-Pee-Chee-139
02O-Pee-Chee Premier Blue Parallel-139
02O-Pee-Chee Premier Red Parallel-139
02O-Pee-Chee Factory Set-139
02Pacific-1
Blue-1
Red-1
02Pacific Complete-157
Red-157
02Topps-139
OPC Blue Parallel-139
OPC Red Parallel-139
Factory Set-139
02Topps Total-374
02Upper Deck-250
Exclusives-250
02Upper Deck Beckett UD Promos-250
02Upper Deck MVP-3
Gold-3
Classics-3
Golden Classics-3
02Upper Deck Victory-6
Bronze-6
Gold-6
Silver-6
02Upper Deck Vintage-5
03ITG Action-253
03NHL Sticker Collection-154
03Pacific-142
Blue-142
Red-142
03Pacific Complete-365
Red-365
03Panthers Team Issue-4
03Upper Deck-330
Canadian Exclusives-330
HG-330
UD Exclusives-330
05Parkhurst-92
Facsimile Auto Parallel-92
06Fleer-132
Tiffany-132
06O-Pee-Chee-328
Rainbow-328
06Ultra-132
Gold Medallion-132
Ice Medallion-132
06Upper Deck-380
Exclusives Parallel-380
High Gloss Parallel-380
Masterpieces-380
06Upper Deck MVP-198
Gold Script-198
Super Script-198
06Upper Deck Victory-261

Cullen, Peter
95North Iowa Huskies-4

Cullen, Ray
68Bauer Ads-4
68O-Pee-Chee-54
68Shirriff Coins-71
68Topps-54
69O-Pee-Chee-130
Four-in-One-15
Stamps-5
69Topps-130
70Canucks Royal Bank-3
70Colgate Stamps-15
70Dad's Cookies-19
70Esso Power Players-45
70O-Pee-Chee-228
Deckle-31
70Sargent Promotions Stamps-216

Cullen, Thom
97Las Vegas Thunder-8
00Idaho Steelheads-6
01Idaho Steelheads-5

Cullic, Chet
96Louisville Riverfrogs-17

Culligan, Chris
04Cape Breton Screaming Eagles-6
05Cape Breton Screaming Eagles-6
06Cape Breton Screaming Eagles-5

Cullimore, Jassen
89Peterborough Petes-116
897th Inn. Sketch OHL-116
907th Inn. Sketch OHL-356
91Upper Deck-72
91Upper Deck-690
French-72
French-690
91Upper Deck Czech World Juniors-64
91Peterborough Petes-21
917th Inn. Sketch OHL-146
91Arena Draft Picks-22
91Arena Draft Picks French-22
91Arena Draft Picks Autographs-22
91Arena Draft Picks Autographs French-22
91Classic-26
91Star Pics-71
91Ultimate Draft-23
91Ultimate Draft French-23
91Classic Four-Sport *-26
Autographs-26A
92Hamilton Canucks-4
94Be A Player Signature Cards-80
94Leaf-488
94OPC Premier-477
Special Effects-477
94Parkhurst SE-SE191
Gold-SE191
94Topps/OPC Premier-477
Special Effects-477
94Upper Deck-247
Electric Ice-247
95Donruss-175
95Leaf-25
95Topps-101
OPC Inserts-101
95Images-53
Gold-53
96Canadiens Postcards-10
96Canadiens Sheets-6
96Collector's Edge Ice-89
Prism-89
97Canadiens Postcards-8
97Pacific Invincible NHL Regime-101
99Paramount-215
Copper-215
Emerald-215
Gold-215
Holographic Emerald-215
Holographic Gold-215
Holographic Silver-215
Ice Blue-215
Premiere Date-215
Red-215
Silver-215
99Providence Bruins-7
00Upper Deck Vintage-329
01Upper Deck-388
Exclusives-388
03ITG Action-588
03Lightning Team Issue-11
05Panini Stickers-213
06Blackhawks Postcards-6

Cuma, Tyler
06Ottawa 67s-12

Cumiskey, Kyle
03Kelowna Rockets-5
04Kelowna Rockets-8
05Kelowna Rockets-8
06Hot Prospects-185
06AHL Top Prospects-1
06Albany River Rats-8

Cumming, Scott
85London Knights-29

Cummings, Brent
02Topeka Scarecrows-17
06Rio Grande Valley Killer Bees-1

Cummings, Burton
91Pro Set Platinum-290
91Jets IGA-7

Cummings, Don
28V128-2 Paulin's Candy-52

Cummins, Barry
98Fort Worth Brahmas-14

Cummins, Gary
94German First League-650

Cummins, Jim
92Classic-94
Gold-94
92Classic Four-Sport *-209
Gold-209
93Lightning Season in Review-11
93Stadium Club-448
Members Only Master Set-448
First Day Issue-448
94Leaf-434
95Blackhawks Coke-6
97Be A Player-80
Autographs-80
Autographs Die-Cuts-80
Autographs Prismatic Die-Cuts-80
97Pacific Invincible NHL Regime-44
98Pacific-335
Ice Blue-335
Red-335
99Pacific-318
Copper-318
Emerald Green-318
Gold-318
Ice Blue-318
Premiere Date-318
Red-318
00Topps Heritage-174
01Pacific-2
01Pacific-401
Extreme LTD-2
Gold-401
Hobby LTD-2
Premiere Date-2
Retail LTD-2
01Pacific Arena Exclusives-2
01Pacific Arena Exclusives-401
02Fleer Throwbacks-45
Gold-45
Platinum-45
Drop the Gloves-5
Stickwork-5
03Avalanche Team Issue-3

Cunderlik, Roman
95Slovakian APS National Team-7

Cunneyworth, Randy
86Penguins Kodak-6
87O-Pee-Chee-150
87Panini Stickers-148
87Penguins Masks-2
87Penguins Kodak-6
87Topps-150
88O-Pee-Chee-19
88O-Pee-Chee Stickers-231
88Panini Stickers-337
88Topps-19
89Jets Safeway-8
89Kraft-48
89O-Pee-Chee-63
89Topps-63A
89Topps-63B
89Whalers Junior Milk-4
90O-Pee-Chee-67
90Pro Set-101
90Score-276
Canadian-276
90Topps-67
Tiffany-67
90Upper Deck-268
French-268
90Whalers Jr. 7-Eleven-7
91Panini Stickers-320
91Parkhurst-284
French-284
91Pro Set-392
French-392
91Score Canadian Bilingual-424
91Score Canadian English-424
91Whalers Jr. 7-Eleven-9
92Panini Stickers-260
92Panini Stickers French-260
92Ultra-73
92Whalers Dairymart-6
93Donruss-413
93OPC Premier-423
Gold-423
93Stadium Club-341
Members Only Master Set-341
First Day Issue-341
93Topps/OPC Premier-423
Gold-423
93Whalers Coke-4
94Pinnacle-406
Artist's Proofs-406
Rink Collection-406
94Senators Team Issue-9
94Stadium Club-38
Members Only Master Set-38
First Day Issue-38
Super Team Winner Cards-38
94Ultra-336
95Be A Player-81
Signatures-S81
Signatures Die Cuts-S81
95Parkhurst International-421
Emerald Ice-421
95Pro Magnets-112
95Senators Team Issue-7
96Collector's Choice-178
96Kraft Upper Deck-34
96NHL Pro Stamps-112
96Senators Pizza Hut-4
96Upper Deck-111
97Be A Player-175
Autographs-175
Autographs Die-Cuts-175
Autographs Prismatic Die-Cuts-175
97Pacific-198
Copper-198
Emerald Green-198
Ice Blue-198
Red-198
Silver-198
97Score-161
98Rochester Americans-4
99O-Pee-Chee-142
99O-Pee-Chee Chrome-142
99O-Pee-Chee Chrome Refractors-142
99Topps/OPC-142
99Topps/OPC Chrome-142
Refractors-142
00Rochester Americans-24
02Rochester Americans-23
03Rochester Americans-7
04Rochester Americans-30

Cunniff, David
98Albany River Rats-5
99Albany River Rats-6
02Cleveland Barons-3
03Cleveland Barons-24
04Cleveland Barons-26
05Cleveland Barons-27

Cunniff, John
72Whalers New England WHA-3
89Devils Caretta-8
90Devils Team Issue-9
90Pro Set-670
96Albany River Rats-22
97Albany River Rats-23
98Albany River Rats-23
99Albany River Rats-7
00Albany River Rats-24

Cunning, Cam
02Kamloops Blazers-9
03Kamloops Blazers-9

Cunning, Len
71Johnstown Jets Acme-3

Cunningham, Bob
61Shirriff/Salada Coins-96
97Anchorage Aces-5
98Anchorage Aces-15
99Adirondack IceHawks-16
01Anchorage Aces-2
03Greenville Grrrowl-5

Cunningham, Chris
03St. Michael's Majors-8
04St. Michael's Majors-9

Cunningham, Curtis
93Quebec Pee-Wee Tournament-1238

Cunningham, Jerry
02Odessa Jackalopes-4

Cunningham, Les
34Beehive Group I Photos-49
39O-Pee-Chee V301-1-78

Cunningham, Scott
93Quebec Pee-Wee Tournament-814

Cunningham, Wes
03Owen Sound Attack-3
04Owen Sound Attack-18
05Plymouth Whalers-B-05
06Plymouth Whalers-7

Cupp, Jason
94Thunder Bay Flyers-6

Curadeau, Mathieu
02Val d'Or Foreurs-8
03Val d'Or Foreurs-21
05Gatineau Olympiques-21

Curcio, Patrick
98German DEL-199

Curic, Ivan
04Richmond Riverdogs-7

Curilla, Marek
05Medicine Hat Tigers-8
06Czech OFS-249

Curley, Brendan
93Hampton Roads Admirals-4
94Hampton Roads Admirals-16
98Hampton Roads Admirals 10th Anniversary-25

Curley, Cindy
94Classic Women of Hockey-W31

Currah, Matthew
93Quebec Pee-Wee Tournament-1695

Curran, Brian
86Islanders Team Issue-8
87O-Pee-Chee-90
87Panini Stickers-95
87Topps-90
88Maple Leafs PLAY-26
90Pro Set-277
90Sabres Blue Shield-5
91Maple Leafs Panini Team Stickers-4
91ProCards-2
91Rochester Americans Dunkin' Donuts-4
91Rochester Americans Kodak-9
94Portland Pirates-7
95Portland Pirates-10
02Macon Trax-17
03Columbus Cottonmouths-3
05Quad City Mallards-22
06Quad City Mallards-2

Curran, Chris
02Mississauga Ice Dogs-6
03Mississauga Ice Dogs-7

Curran, Jack
63Rochester Americans-11

Curran, Mike
70Swedish Masterserien-15
70Swedish Masterserien-92
72Minnesota Fighting Saints Postcards WHA-6
72Finnish Semic World Championship-118
72Swedish Semic World Championship-118
74Minnesota Fighting Saints WHA-7
92Future Trends Promo Sheet-1

Currie, Alex
10Sweet Caporal Postcards-13
11C55-13
12C57-32

Currie, Brent
99Austin Ice Bats-16
06Quad City Mallards-3

Currie, Dan
87Sault Ste. Marie Greyhounds-2
88ProCards AHL-75
89ProCards AHL-136
90ProCards AHL/IHL-222
91Upper Deck-347
French-347
91ProCards-228
92Oilers IGA-13
93Phoenix Roadrunners-4
93Classic Pro Prospects-150
96Collector's Edge Ice-105
Prism-105
97Fort Wayne Komets-5
98German DEL-198
99Bakersfield Condors-5
00Bakersfield Condors-6
02UK Hull Thunder-19

Currie, David
01Peterborough Petes-19
02Peterborough Petes-23
03Johnstown Chiefs-14
03Johnstown Chiefs RBI Sports-213
04Johnstown Chiefs-6

Currie, Glen
81Capitals Team Issue-3
82Capitals Team Issue-4
82Post Cereal-20
83NHL Key Tags-129
84Capitals Pizza Hut-3

Currie, Jason
92Clarkson Knights-4
94Richmond Renegades-19

Currie, Paul
03Yarmouth Mariners-25

Currie, Sheldon
81Milwaukee Admirals-11

Currie, Tony
78Blues Postcards-8
80O-Pee-Chee-384
81O-Pee-Chee-292
81Topps-W116
81Fredericton Express-7
82O-Pee-Chee-341
82Fredericton Express-7
83Fredericton Express-11
84Whalers Junior Wendy's-5
84Nova Scotia Oilers-22
85Fredericton Express-9

Curry, Dave
83Brandon Wheat Kings-23
85Brandon Wheat Kings-6

Curry, Floyd James
43Parade Sportive *-28
44Beehive Group II Photos-230
45Quaker Oats Photos-60C
45Quaker Oats Photos-71A
45Quaker Oats Photos-71B
48Exhibits Canadian-27
51Parkhurst-12
52Parkhurst-7
53Parkhurst-35
54Parkhurst-15
54Parkhurst-89
55Parkhurst-40
55Parkhurst-76
Quaker Oats-40
Quaker Oats-76
57Parkhurst-M20
63Quebec Aces-5
94Parkhurst Missing Link-78
02Parkhurst Reprints-151
02Parkhurst Reprints-164
02Parkhurst Reprints-188
02Parkhurst Reprints-215

Curry, John
03Boston University Terriers-25

Curry, Mike
04Minnesota-Duluth Bulldogs-5

Curry, Sean
02Florida Everblades-7
02Lowell Lock Monsters-3
03Lowell Lock Monsters-22
03Lowell Lock Monsters Photo Album-3
04Lowell Lock Monsters-3
04Lowell Lock Monsters Photo Album-3
05Providence Bruins-2
06Providence Bruins-3

Curtale, Tony
06Texas Tornados-24

Curth, Christian
94German DEL-15
95German DEL-130
96German DEL-320
99German Bundesliga 2-25

Curth, Florian
94German First League-366

Curtin, Luke
94Select-153
Gold-153
95Bowman Draft Prospects-P8
96Visions Signings *-64
Autographs-64A
Autographs Silver-64A
98Baton Rouge Kingfish-6
98ECHL All-Star Southern Conference-16
99ECHL All-Star Southern Conference-14
00Tacoma Sabercats-12
01Atlantic City Boardwalk Bullies-8
02Atlantic City Boardwalk Bullies-5
03Atlantic City Boardwalk Bullies-3
03Atlantic City Boardwalk Bullies RBI-18
04Atlantic City Boardwalk Bullies-13
04Atlantic City Boardwalk Bullies Kinko's-25
05Fresno Falcons-4

Curtin, Scot
93Quebec Pee-Wee Tournament-1307

Curtis, Joel
83Oshawa Generals-8

Curtis, Paul
70Esso Power Players-150
71O-Pee-Chee-4
71Sargent Promotions Stamps-77
71Toronto Sun-109
72O-Pee-Chee-266
72Sargent Promotions Stamps-85

Cushenan, Ian
44Beehive Group II Photos-231
44Beehive Group II Photos-305
58Parkhurst-24
63Parkhurst-49

Cusick, Fred
04UD Legends Classics-22
Gold-22
Platinum-22
Silver-22
Signature Moments-M69
Signatures-CS53
Signatures-DC19
05Beehive Signature Scrapbook-SSFC

Cusson, Charles
87Brockville Braves-22
88Brockville Braves-8

Cusson, Mathieu
95Saskatoon Blades-8
96Saskatoon Blades-8
97Saskatoon Blades-6

Cuthbert, Brenden
02Medicine Hat Tigers-5
05Missouri River Otters-12

Cuthbert, Cam
93RPI Engineers-7

Cuthbert, Chris
97Pinnacle Hockey Night in Canada-4

Cuthbert, Craig
04Kelowna Rockets-4
05Kelowna Rockets-9
06Saskatoon Blades-5

Cuthbert, Ryan
98Kelowna Rockets-1
99Kelowna Rockets-25
00Kamloops Blazers-1
00Kelowna Rockets-6
01Kelowna Rockets-3
02Kelowna Rockets-22
03Charlotte Checkers-68
03Hartford Wolf Pack-3
03Kelowna Rockets Memorial Cup-4

Cuthbert, Tyler
04Sault Ste. Marie Greyhounds-7

Cuthbertson, Scott
93Quebec Pee-Wee Tournament-1466

Cutta, Jakub
98Swift Current Broncos-12
99Swift Current Broncos-3
99UD Prospects-47
00BAP Memorabilia-406
Emerald-406
Ruby-406
Sapphire-406
00SPx-172
00Titanium Draft Day Edition-175
00Titanium Draft Day Promos-175
00UD Pros and Prospects-125
00Swift Current Broncos-3
01O-Pee-Chee-267
01O-Pee-Chee Premier Parallel-267
01Topps-267
OPC Parallel-267
04Portland Pirates-13
05Hershey Bears-5
06Czech HC Liberec Postcards-1

Cutts, Don
88Oilers Tenth Anniversary-152

Cwik, Dave
03Arizona Icecats-6

Cyenes, Dan
04Kitchener Rangers-7

Cygan, Steve
02Rockford Ice Hogs-11
03Rockford Ice Hogs-3
05Johnstown Chiefs-5

Cyr, Denis
79Montreal Juniors-4
80Flames Postcards-4
81Flames Postcards-5
82Blackhawks Postcards-4
82O-Pee-Chee-43
82Post Cereal-3
83Blackhawks Postcards-3

Cyr, Eric
93Quebec Pee-Wee Tournament-1392

Cyr, Ghyslain
79Montreal Juniors-5

Cyr, Jean-Francois
01Drummondville Voltigeurs-18
01Halifax Mooseheads-12
02Halifax Mooseheads-13
03Cape Breton Screaming Eagles-23

Cyr, Paul
81Victoria Cougars-7
82Victoria Cougars-6
83Canadian National Juniors-3
84Sabres Blue Shield-4
84Kelowna Wings-31
85O-Pee-Chee Stickers-183
85Sabres Blue Shield-5
85Sabres Blue Shield Small-5
86O-Pee-Chee-200
86Sabres Blue Shield-7
86Sabres Blue Shield Small-7
87Panini Stickers-33
90Pro Set-449
90Score Rookie/Traded-72T
90Whalers Jr. 7-Eleven-8
91Bowman-20
91O-Pee-Chee-73
91Panini Stickers-321
91Pro Set-88
French-88
91Score Canadian Bilingual-413
91Score Canadian English-413
91Stadium Club-279
91Topps-73
91Whalers Jr. 7-Eleven-10
91ProCards-100

Cyr, Raymond
52Juniors Blue Tint-81

Cyr, Ryan
03Saskatoon Blades-15
04Saskatoon Blades-13

Cyr, Sebastien
93Quebec Pee-Wee Tournament-1342

Cyrenne, Cory
95Brandon Wheat Kings-4
96Brandon Wheat Kings-17
97Brandon Wheat Kings-6
98Bowman CHL-74
Golden Anniversary-74
OPC International-74
98Bowman Chrome CHL-74
Golden Anniversary-74
Golden Anniversary Refractors-74
OPC International-74
OPC International Refractors-74
Refractors-74
99Manitoba Moose-12
01Louisiana Ice Gators-4

Cyrwus, Stanislaw
92Finnish Semic-276

Czachovski, Ludwik
73Finnish Jaakiekko-88
74Finnish Jenkki-94
74Finnish Typotor-86

Czajka, Patrik
01German Berlin Polar Bears Postcards-5

Czapka, Ludvik
89Swedish Semic World Champ Stickers-137
92Finnish Semic-281

Czczepaniec, Andrzej
73Finnish Jaakiekko-89
74Finnish Jenkki-95

Czech, Steve
04Minnesota-Duluth Bulldogs-6

Czerkawski, Mariusz
91Swedish Semic Elitserien Stickers-73
92Finnish Semic-288
93Swedish Semic Elitserien-69
94Donruss-138
94Finest Bowman's Best-R20
94Finest Bowman's Best Refractors-R20
94Flair-9
94Fleer-10
94Leaf-82
94Leaf Limited-29
94OPC Premier-293
Special Effects-293
94Parkhurst-20
Gold-20
Vintage-V55
SE Euro-Stars-ES5
94Pinnacle I Hobby Samples-246
94Pinnacle-246
94Pinnacle-467
Artist's Proofs-246
Artist's Proofs-467
Rink Collection-246
Rink Collection-467
Rookie Team Pinnacle-12
94Score-227
Gold-227
Platinum-227
94Select-190
Gold-190
Youth Explosion-YE11
94SP-10
Die Cuts-10
94Topps/OPC Premier-293
Special Effects-293
94Ultra-11
94Upper Deck-239
94Upper Deck-534
94Upper Deck-543
Electric Ice-239
Electric Ice-534
Electric Ice-543
Predictor Canadian-C5
94Upper Deck Predictor Canadian Exch Gold-C5
94Upper Deck Predictor Cdn Exch Silver-C5
94Upper Deck SP Inserts-SP5
94Upper Deck SP Inserts Die Cuts-SP5
95Collector's Choice-50
Player's Club-50
Player's Club Platinum-50
95Donruss-21
95Leaf-55
Studio Rookies-17
95McDonald's Pinnacle-MCD-37
95Panini Stickers-5
95Parkhurst International-18
95Parkhurst International-345
Emerald Ice-18
Emerald Ice-345
95Pinnacle-185
Artist's Proofs-185
Rink Collection-185
Global Gold-24
95Pinnacle FANtasy-4
95Playoff One on One-117
95Score-143
Black Ice Artist's Proofs-143
Black Ice-143
95SkyBox Impact NHL On Fox-1
95Topps-153
OPC Inserts-153
New To The Game-19NG
Power Lines-7PL
95Ultra-9
Gold Medallion-9
All-Rookies-2
All-Rookie Gold Medallion-2
95Upper Deck-189
Electric Ice-189
Electric Ice Gold-189
Special Edition-SE6
Special Edition Gold-SE6
95Finnish SISU Limited-63
96Be A Player-166
Autographs-166
Autographs Silver-166
96Black Diamond-122
Gold-122
96Collector's Choice-93
96Donruss Canadian Ice-96
Gold Press Proofs-96
Red Press Proofs-96
96Oilers Postcards-21
96Pinnacle-167
Artist's Proofs-167
Foil-167
Premium Stock-167
Rink Collection-167
96Playoff One on One-368
96SP-59
97Collector's Choice-93
97Pacific-216
Copper-216
Emerald Green-216
Ice Blue-216
Red-216
Silver-216
97Panini Stickers-211
97Pinnacle-122
Press Plates Back Black-122
Press Plates Back Cyan-122
Press Plates Back Magenta-122
Press Plates Back Yellow-122
Press Plates Front Black-122
Press Plates Front Cyan-122
Press Plates Front Magenta-122
Press Plates Front Yellow-122
97Pinnacle Inside-158
97Score-208
98Pacific-279
Ice Blue-279
Red-279
98Paramount-141
Copper-141
Emerald Green-141
Holo-Electric-141
Ice Blue-141
Silver-141
99Aurora-89
Premiere Date-89
99BAP Memorabilia-178
Gold-178
Silver-178
99BAP Millennium-157
Emerald-157
Ruby-157
Sapphire-157
Signatures-157
Signatures Gold-157
99Crown Royale-85
Limited Series-85
Premiere Date-85
99Pacific-253
Copper-253
Emerald Green-253
Gold-253
Ice Blue-253
Premiere Date-253
Red-253
99Pacific Dynagon Ice-123
Blue-123
Copper-123
Gold-123
Premiere Date-123
99Pacific Omega-140
Copper-140
Gold-140
Ice Blue-140
Premiere Date-140
99Pacific Prism-86
Holographic Blue-86
Holographic Gold-86
Holographic Mirror-86
Holographic Purple-86
Premiere Date-86
99Panini Stickers-94
99Paramount-141
Copper-141
Emerald-141
Gold-141
Holographic Emerald-141
Holographic Gold-141
Holographic Silver-141
Ice Blue-141
Premiere Date-141
Red-141
Silver-141
99Revolution-90
Premiere Date-90
Red-90
Shadow Series-90
99Stadium Club-130
First Day Issue-130
One of a Kind-130
Printing Plates Black-130
Printing Plates Cyan-130
Printing Plates Magenta-130
Printing Plates Yellow-130
99Ultimate Victory-54
1/1-54
Parallel-54
Parallel 100-54
99Upper Deck-256
Exclusives-256
Exclusives 1 of 1-256
99Upper Deck Gold Reserve-256
99Upper Deck MVP-123
Gold Script-123
Silver Script-123
Super Script-123
99Upper Deck Victory-181
00Aurora-88
Premiere Date-88
00BAP Memorabilia-269
Emerald-269
Ruby-269
Sapphire-269
Promos-269
00BAP Mem Chicago Sportsfest Copper-269
00BAP Memorabilia Chicago Sportsfest Blue-269
00BAP Memorabilia Chicago Sportsfest Gold-269
00BAP Memorabilia Chicago Sportsfest Ruby-269
00BAP Memorabilia Chicago Sun-Times Ruby-269
00BAP Memorabilia Chicago Sun-Times Gold-269
00BAP Mem Chicago Sun-Times Sapphire-269
00BAP Mem Toronto Fall Expo Copper-269
00BAP Memorabilia Toronto Fall Expo Gold-269
00BAP Memorabilia Toronto Fall Expo Ruby-269
00BAP Parkhurst 2000-P105
00BAP Signature Series-86
Emerald-86
Ruby-86
Sapphire-86
Autographs-111
Autographs Gold-111
Franchise Players-F19
00Black Diamond-37
Gold-37
00Kraft-25
00O-Pee-Chee-114
00O-Pee-Chee Parallel-114
00Pacific-248
Copper-248
Gold-248
Ice Blue-248
Premiere Date-248
00Panini Stickers-54
00Paramount-153
Copper-153
Gold-153
Holo-Gold-153
Holo-Silver-153
Ice Blue-153
Premiere Date-153
00Private Stock-62
Gold-62
Premiere Date-62
Retail-62
Silver-62
Game Gear-69
Game Gear Patches-69
00Revolution-91
Blue-91
Premiere Date-91
Red-91
00SPx-41
Spectrum-41
00Stadium Club-132
00Titanium-58
Blue-58
Gold-58
Premiere Date-58
Red-58
Retail-58
Game Gear-31
Game Gear-108
Game Gear Patches-108
00Titanium Draft Day Edition-61
Patches-61
00Topps/OPC-114
Parallel-114
00Topps Chrome-88
OPC Refractors-88
Refractors-88
00Topps Heritage-232
00Topps Premier Plus-29
Blue Ice-29
00Topps Stars-57
Blue-57
Game Gear-GGMC
00UD Heroes-74
00Upper Deck-110
Exclusives Tier 1-110
Exclusives Tier 2-110
00Upper Deck MVP-112
First Stars-112
Second Stars-112
Third Stars-112
00Upper Deck Victory-147
00Upper Deck Vintage-226
00Vanguard-62
Dual Game-Worn Jerseys-8
Dual Game-Worn Patches-8
Holographic Gold-62
Holographic Purple-62
Pacific Proofs-62
00Czech Stadion-158
01Atomic-59
Blue-59
Gold-59
Premiere Date-59
Red-59
Jerseys-38
Patches-38
01BAP Memorabilia-289
Emerald-289
Ruby-289
Sapphire-289
01BAP Signature Series-190
Autographs-190
Autographs Gold-190
01Crown Royale Triple Threads-14
01O-Pee-Chee-10
01O-Pee-Chee Heritage Parallel-10
01O-Pee-Chee Heritage Parallel Limited-10
01O-Pee-Chee Premier Parallel-10
01Pacific-244
01Pacific-415
01Pacific-434
Extreme LTD-244
Gold-415
Gold-434
Hobby LTD-244
Premiere Date-244
Retail LTD-244
Jerseys-19
01Pacific Adrenaline-118
Blue-118
Premiere Date-118
Red-118
Retail-118
01Pacific Arena Exclusives-244
01Pacific Arena Exclusives-415
01Pacific Arena Exclusives-434
01Pacific Heads-Up-59
Blue-59
Premiere Date-59
Red-59
Silver-59
Quad Jerseys-4
01Parkhurst-173
01Private Stock Game Gear-62
01Private Stock Game Gear Patches-62
01Titanium-86
Hobby Parallel-86
Premiere Date-86
Retail-86
Retail Parallel-86
01Topps-10
Heritage Parallel-10
Heritage Parallel Limited-10
OPC Parallel-10
01Topps Chrome-10
Refractors-10
Black Border Refractors-10
01Topps Reserve Emblems-MC
01Topps Reserve Jerseys-MC
01Topps Reserve Name Plates-MC
01Topps Reserve Numbers-MC
01Topps Reserve Patches-MC
01Upper Deck-113
Exclusives-113
01Upper Deck MVP-120
01Upper Deck Victory-219
Gold-219
01Upper Deck Vintage-160
01Upper Deck Vintage-165
01Vanguard Memorabilia-18
02BAP Signature Series-108
Autographs-108
Autograph Buybacks 1999-157
Autograph Buybacks 2000-111
Autograph Buybacks 2001-190
Autographs Gold-108
02Canadiens Postcards-10
02NHL Power Play Stickers-60
02O-Pee-Chee-100
02O-Pee-Chee-100U
02O-Pee-Chee Premier Blue Parallel-100
02O-Pee-Chee Premier Red Parallel-100
02O-Pee-Chee Factory Set-100
02Pacific-234
Blue-234
Red-234
02Pacific Complete-220
Red-220
02Pacific Exclusive-89
Jerseys-14
Jerseys Gold-14
02Parkhurst-191

Bronze-191
Gold-191
Silver-191
02Private Stock Reserve-51
Blue-51
Red-51
Retail-51
02Topps-100
02Topps-100U
OPC Blue Parallel-100
OPC Red Parallel-100
Factory Set-100
02Topps Chrome-64
Black Border Refractors-64
Refractors-64
02Topps Heritage-169
02Topps Total-272
02Upper Deck-336
Exclusives-336
02Upper Deck Beckett UD Promos-336
03Beehive-120
Variations-120
Gold-120
Silver-120
03Crown Royale-63
Blue-63
Retail-63
03Pacific Complete-267
Red-267
03Pacific Heads-Up-61
Hobby LTD-61
Retail LTD-61
03Titanium-64
Hobby Jersey Number Parallels-64
Retail-64
Retail Jersey Number Parallels-64
03Upper Deck-366
Canadian Exclusives-366
HG-366
UD Exclusives-366
04Pacific-165
Blue-165
Red-165
04Swedish Djurgardens Postcards-1
04Swedish Elitset-168
Gold-168
04Swedish Pure Skills-14
Parallel-14
Professional Power-MC
05Upper Deck MVP-367
Gold-367
Platinum-367

Czerlinski, Jan
95Czech APS Extraliga-345

Czibere, Mitch
05Vancouver Giants-6

Czuy, Kelly
06Las Vegas Wranglers-5

D'Agostini, Matt
04Guelph Storm-19
05Guelph Storm-B-05
06Hamilton Bulldogs-7

D'Agostino, Mark
93Quebec Pee-Wee Tournament-803

D'Alba, Adam
02Chicago Steel-4

D'Alessandro, Mike
98Guelph Storm-2
00Barrie Colts-7

D'Alessio, Corrie
91ProCards-616

D'Alvise, Dan
81Swedish Semic Hockey VM Stickers-87

D'Amario, Peter
93Memphis RiverKings-2
99Memphis RiverKings All-Time-12

D'Amico, Bruno
01Sherbrooke Castors-20

D'Amico, John
93Action Packed HOF Induction-5

D'Amour, Claud
86Sudbury Wolves-28

D'Amour, Dominic
00Rouyn-Noranda Huskies-1
Signed-1
01Hull Olympiques-4
02Hull Olympiques-4
03Gatineau Olympiques-5
03Hull Olympiques Memorial Cup-3
06Toronto Marlies-7

D'Amour, Marc
80Sault Ste. Marie Greyhounds-25
81Sault Ste. Marie Greyhounds-9
85Flames Red Rooster-7
86Moncton Golden Flames-14
88ProCards AHL-133
89ProCards AHL-352
91ProCards-264

d'Amour, Sylvain
77Granby Vics-7

D'Angelo, Ronnie
93Quebec Pee-Wee Tournament-1730
00Connecticut Huskies-5

D'Aoust, Nicolas
05Drummondville Voltigeurs-28

D'Arcy, Bryan
04Notre Dame Fighting Irish-3

D'Arcy, Ryan
92Western Michigan Broncos-9
93Western Michigan Broncos-11

D'Arpino, Anthony
03Tulsa Oilers-4

D'Ascanio, Jason
02Drummondville Voltigeurs-17
02Rimouski Oceanic-3

D'Aversa, Jonathan
03Sudbury Wolves-6
04Sudbury Wolves-19
05ITG Heroes/Prosp Toronto Expo Parallel -291
05OHL Bell All-Star Classic-12
05Sudbury Wolves-7
05ITG Heroes and Prospects-291
Autographs Series II-JDA
06Sudbury Wolves-22

d'Entremont, Georges
03Yarmouth Mariners-8

d'Entremont, Justin
03Yarmouth Mariners-9

D'Orazio, Michael
06Owen Sound Attack-2

d'Orsonnens, Martin
92Clarkson Knights-13
92Clarkson Knights-24
93Raleigh IceCaps-8
94Johnstown Chiefs-7

D'Urso, Lionel
01Swiss HNL-425
02Swiss HNL-453

Da Corte, Luigi
94Finnish Jaa Kiekko-293
95Swedish World Championships Stickers-80

Da Costa, Stephane
06Texas Tornados-19

Da Silva, Dan
03Portland Winter Hawks-17

Dabanovich, Jamie
91Knoxville Cherokees-11

Dabrowski, Marek
93Quebec Pee-Wee Tournament-1519

Dabrowski, Paul
92Quebec Pee-Wee Tournament-1434
93Quebec Pee-Wee Tournament-1584

Dachyshyn, Dean
83Moncton Alpines-22
84Nova Scotia Oilers-13
85Nova Scotia Oilers-4

Dackell, Andreas
91Swedish Semic Elitserien Stickers-51
92Swedish Semic Elitserien Stickers-64
93Swedish Semic Elitserien-37
94Swedish Leaf-49
Gold Cards-2
95Finnish Semic World Championships-70
95Swedish Leaf-18
Champs-10
95Swedish Upper Deck-36
Ticket to North America-NA3
95Swedish Globe World Championships-44
95Swedish World Championships Stickers-147
96Be A Player-109
Autographs-109
Autographs Silver-109
96Donruss Canadian Ice-134
Gold Press Proofs-134
Red Press Proofs-134
96Flair-117
Blue Ice-117
96Metal Universe-174
96Select Certified-118
Artist's Proofs-118
Blue-118
Mirror Blue-118
Mirror Gold-118
Mirror Red-118
Red-118
96Senators Pizza Hut-5
96SP-109
96Ultra-115
Gold Medallion-115
96Upper Deck-303
96Zenith-121
Artist's Proofs-121
96Swedish Semic Wien-68
96Swedish Semic Wien Coca-Cola Dream Team-11
97Collector's Choice-175
97Donruss-113
Press Proofs Silver-113
Press Proofs Gold-113
97Donruss Limited-137
Exposure-137
97Pacific-278
Copper-278
Emerald Green-278
Ice Blue-278
Red-278
Silver-278
97Pacific Omega-154
Copper-154
Dark Gray-154
Emerald Green-154
Gold-154
Ice Blue-154
97Score-203
97SP Authentic-109
97Upper Deck-323
98Aurora-129
98Pacific-308
Ice Blue-308
Red-308
98Paramount-162
Copper-162
Emerald Green-162
Holo-Electric-162
Ice Blue-162
Silver-162
98Senators Team Issue-5
98UD Choice-146
Prime Choice Reserve-146
Reserve-146
98Upper Deck-331
Exclusives-331
Exclusives 1 of 1-331
Gold Reserve-331
99BAP Memorabilia-111
Gold-111
Silver-111
99O-Pee-Chee-245
99O-Pee-Chee Chrome-245
99O-Pee-Chee Chrome Refractors-245
99Pacific-286
Copper-286
Emerald Green-286
Gold-286
Ice Blue-286
Premiere Date-286
Red-286
99Panini Stickers-110
99Paramount-161
Copper-161
Emerald-161
Gold-161
Holographic Emerald-161
Holographic Gold-161
Holographic Silver-161
Ice Blue-161
Premiere Date-161
Red-161
Silver-161
99Senators Team Issue-4
99Topps/OPC-245
99Topps/OPC Chrome-245
Refractors-245
99Ultimate Victory-60
1/1-60
Parallel-60
Parallel 100-60
00BAP Memorabilia-107
Emerald-107
Ruby-107
Sapphire-107
Promos-107
00BAP Mem Chicago Sportsfest Copper-107
00BAP Memorabilia Chicago Sportsfest Blue-107
00BAP Memorabilia Chicago Sportsfest Gold-107
00BAP Memorabilia Chicago Sportsfest Ruby-107
00BAP Memorabilia Chicago Sun-Times Ruby-107
00BAP Memorabilia Chicago Sun-Times Gold-107
00BAP Mem Chicago Sun-Times Sapphire-107
00BAP Mem Toronto Fall Expo
Copper-107
00BAP Memorabilia Toronto Fall Expo Gold-107
00BAP Memorabilia Toronto Fall Expo Ruby-107
00Pacific-444
Copper-444
Gold-444
Ice Blue-444
Premiere Date-444
00Private Stock Game Gear-80
00Private Stock Game Gear Patches-80
00Revolution Game-Worn Jerseys-9
00Revolution Game-Worn Jersey Patches-9
00Senators Team Issue-4
00Upper Deck-352
Exclusives Tier 1-352
Exclusives Tier 2-352
00Upper Deck MVP-129
First Stars-129
Second Stars-129
Third Stars-129
00Vanguard Dual Game-Worn Jerseys-17
00Vanguard Dual Game-Worn Patches-17
01Canadiens Postcards-6
01Parkhurst-219
01Upper Deck-323
Exclusives-323
02Canadiens Postcards-7
02NHL Power Play Stickers-64
02Pacific-193
Blue-193
Red-193
02Pacific Complete-60
Red-60
02Topps Total-366
02Upper Deck Vintage-138
03Canadiens Postcards-6
03ITG Action-363
03Pacific Complete-121
Red-121
03Parkhurst Original Six Montreal-8
04Swedish Elitset-152
Gold-152
Signatures Series B-1
04Swedish Pure Skills-4
Parallel-4
Signatures Limited-1
05Swedish SHL Elitset-7
Gold-7
Teammates-1
06Swedish SHL Elitset-8

Dacosta, Jeff
93Kingston Frontenacs-6
95Slapshot-111
00Rockford IceHogs-5
01Rockford IceHogs-13
02Rockford Ice Hogs-20

Dacosta, Justin
02Barrie Colts-2
03Owen Sound Attack-5
04Mississauga Ice Dogs-20
04Owen Sound Attack-20
05Mississauga Ice Dogs-16

Dadera, Roman
99Czech DS-108

Dadswell, Doug
86Moncton Golden Flames-3
87Flames Red Rooster-6
88Flames Postcards-3
90Alberta International Team Canada-2
91Cincinnati Cyclones-6
92Cincinnati Cyclones-6

Daffner, Thomas
94German First League-41
99German Bundesliga 2-196
00German DEL-125
01German Upper Deck-122
02German DEL City Press-173

Dafoe, Byron
87Portland Winter Hawks-7
88Portland Winter Hawks-7
89Portland Winter Hawks-3
91ProCards-548
93Portland Pirates-22
93Classic Pro Prospects-73
94Donruss-175
94Leaf-283
94OPC Premier-42
Special Effects-42
94Stadium Club Super Teams-25
94Stadium Club Super Team MemberOnly Set-25
94Topps/OPC Premier-42
Special Effects-42
94Upper Deck-447
Electric Ice-447
95Bowman-97
All-Foil-97
Bowman's Best-BB23
Bowman's Best Refractors-BB23
95Donruss-362
Elite Rookies-5
95Metal-173
95Parkhurst International-375
Emerald Ice-375
95Select Certified-120
Mirror Gold-120
95SP-70
95Summit-192
Artist's Proofs-192
Ice-192
95Topps-293
OPC Inserts-293
95Ultra-334
95Upper Deck-460
Electric Ice-460
Electric Ice Gold-460
95Zenith-133
96Be A Player-30
Autographs-30
Autographs Silver-30
96Black Diamond-65
Gold-65
96Donruss-221
Press Proofs-221
96Leaf-211
Press Proofs-211
96Score-260
Artist's Proofs-260
Dealer's Choice Artist's Proofs-260
Special Artist's Proofs-260
Golden Blades-260
96SkyBox Impact-56
96Topps Picks Rookie Stars-RS14
96Topps Picks Rookie Stars OPC-RS14
96Upper Deck Ice-31
Parallel-31
97Be A Player Stacking the Pads-15
97Collector's Choice-128
97Crown Royale-9
Emerald Green-9
Ice Blue-9
Silver-9
Freeze Out Die-Cuts-2
97Donruss-20
Press Proofs Silver-20
Press Proofs Gold-20
97Donruss Elite-60
Aspirations-60
Status-60
97Donruss Limited-63
Exposure-63
97Donruss Preferred-71
Cut to the Chase-71
97Donruss Priority-104
Stamp of Approval-104
Postmaster General-14
Postmaster Generals Promos-14
97Pacific-141
Copper-141
Emerald Green-141
Ice Blue-141
Red-141
Silver-141
97Pacific Omega-14
Copper-14
Dark Gray-14
Emerald Green-14
Gold-14
Ice Blue-14
97Revolution-8
Copper-8
Emerald-8
Ice Blue-8
Silver-8
Return to Sender Die-Cuts-2
97Score-47
Artist's Proofs-47
Golden Blades-47
97Score Bruins-13
Platinum-13
Premier-13
97Zenith-40
Z-Gold-40
Z-Silver-40
98Aurora-10
Championship Fever-4
Championship Fever Copper-4
Championship Fever Ice Blue-4
Championship Fever Red-4
Championship Fever Silver-4
98Be A Player-6
Press Release-6
98BAP Gold-6
98BAP Autographs-6
98BAP Autographs Gold-6
98BAP Tampa Bay All Star Game-6
98Crown Royale-8
Limited Series-8
98NHL Aces Playing Cards-24
98OPC Chrome-3
Refractors-3
98Pacific-74
Ice Blue-74
Red-74
98Pacific Dynagon Ice-9
Blue-9
Red-9
98Pacific Omega-14
Red-14
Opening Day Issue-14
98Panini Stickers-10
98Paramount-12
Copper-12
Emerald Green-12
Holo-Electric-12
Ice Blue-12
Silver-12
Glove Side Laser Cuts-2
98Revolution-9
Ice Shadow-9
Red-9
98SP Authentic Sign of the Times-BD
98SP Authentic Sign of the Times Gold-BD
98SPx Finite-7
Radiance-7
Spectrum-7
98Topps-3
O-Pee-Chee-3
98UD Choice-10
Prime Choice Reserve-10
Reserve-10
98Upper Deck-221
Exclusives-221
Exclusives 1 of 1-221
Gold Reserve-221
98Upper Deck MVP-14
Gold Script-14
Silver Script-14
Super Script-14
98Hampton Roads Admirals 10th Anniversary-29
99Aurora-12
Striped-12
Premiere Date-12
Premiere Date Striped-12
Glove Unlimited-2
99BAP Memorabilia-41
Gold-41
Silver-41
AS Heritage Ruby-H16
AS Heritage Sapphire-H16
AS Heritage Emerald-H16
99BAP Millennium-23
Emerald-23
Ruby-23
Sapphire-23
Signatures-23
Signatures Gold-23
99Black Diamond-8
Diamond Cut-8
Final Cut-8
99Crown Royale-12
Limited Series-12
Premiere Date-12
99Jell-O Goalie Collection-6
99Jell-O Partners of Power-5
99O-Pee-Chee-186
99O-Pee-Chee Chrome-186
99O-Pee-Chee Chrome Refractors-186
99O-Pee-Chee Chrome Postmasters-PM2
99O-Pee-Chee Chrome Postmasters Refractor-PM2
99O-Pee-Chee Now Starring-NS7
99O-Pee-Chee Post Masters-PM2
99Pacific-22
Copper-22
Emerald Green-22
Gold-22
Ice Blue-22
Premiere Date-22
Red-22
Gold Crown Die-Cuts-4
In the Cage Net-Fusions-2
99Pacific Dynagon Ice-23
Blue-23
Copper-23
Gold-23
Premiere Date-23
99Pacific Omega-20
Copper-20
Gold-20
Ice Blue-20
Premiere Date-20
99Pacific Prism-13
Holographic Blue-13
Holographic Gold-13
Holographic Mirror-13
Holographic Purple-13
Premiere Date-13
99Panini Stickers-23
99Panini Stickers-351
99Paramount-19
Copper-19
Emerald-19
Gold-19
Holographic Emerald-19
Holographic Gold-19
Holographic Silver-19
Ice Blue-19
Premiere Date-19
Red-19
Silver-19
Glove Side Net Fusions-2
99Revolution-13
Premiere Date-13
Red-13
Shadow Series-13
Showstoppers-4
Copper-13
Gold-13
CSC Silver-13
99SPx-13
Radiance-13
Spectrum-13
99Stadium Club-93
First Day Issue-93
One of a Kind-93
Printing Plates Black-93
Printing Plates Cyan-93
Printing Plates Magenta-93
Printing Plates Yellow-93
Goalie Cam-GC3
99Topps/OPC-186
Now Starring-NS7
Postmasters-PM2
99Topps/OPC Chrome-186
Refractors-186
Postmasters-PM2
Postmasters Refractors-PM2
99Topps Gold Label Class 1-52
Black-52
Black One of One-52
One of One-52
Red-52
Red One of One-52
99Topps Gold Label Class 2-52
99Topps Gold Label Class 2 Black-52
99Topps Gold Label Class 2 Black 1 of 1-52
99Topps Gold Label Class 2 One of One-52
99Topps Gold Label Class 2 Red-52
99Topps Gold Label Class 2 Red One of One-52
99Topps Gold Label Class 3-52
99Topps Gold Label Class 3 Black-52
99Topps Gold Label Class 3 Black 1 of 1-52
99Topps Gold Label Class 3 One of One-52
99Topps Gold Label Class 3 Red-52
99Topps Gold Label Class 3 Red One of One-52
99Topps Premier Plus-37
Parallel-37
Imperial Guard-IG8
99Upper Deck-21
Exclusives-21
Exclusives 1 of 1-21
Ultimate Defense-UD1
Ultimate Defense Quantum Gold-UD1
Ultimate Defense Quantum Silver-UD1
99Upper Deck Gold Reserve-21
99Upper Deck MVP-17
Gold Script-17
Silver Script-17
Super Script-17
Last Line-LL4
99Upper Deck MVP SC Edition-19
Gold Script-19
Silver Script-19
Super Script-19
99Upper Deck Victory-25
99Upper Deck Victory-382
00Aurora-12
Premiere Date-12
00BAP Memorabilia-186
Emerald-186
Ruby-186
Sapphire-186
Promos-186
00BAP Mem Chicago Sportsfest Copper-186
00BAP Memorabilia Chicago Sportsfest Blue-186
00BAP Memorabilia Chicago Sportsfest Gold-186
00BAP Memorabilia Chicago Sportsfest Ruby-186
00BAP Memorabilia Chicago Sun-Times Ruby-186
00BAP Memorabilia Chicago Sun-Times Gold-186
00BAP Mem Chicago Sun-Times Sapphire-186
00BAP Mem Toronto Fall Expo Copper-186
00BAP Memorabilia Toronto Fall Expo Gold-186
00BAP Memorabilia Toronto Fall Expo Ruby-186
00BAP Memorabilia Update Teammates-TM11
00BAP Memorabilia Update Teammates Gold-TM11
00BAP Parkhurst 2000-P163
00BAP Signature Series-87
Emerald-87
Ruby-87
Sapphire-87
Autographs-122
Autographs Gold-122
00BAP Ultimate Mem Goalie Memorabilia-GM18
00BAP Ultimate Memorabilia Goalie Sticks-G3
00BAP Ultimate Mem Plante Jersey Cards-PJ9
00Black Diamond Game Gear-LBD
00Crown Royale-9
Ice Blue-9
Limited Series-9
Premiere Date-9
Red-9
Game-Worn Jerseys-1
Game-Worn Jersey Patches-1
Premium-Sized Game-Worn Jerseys-1
00O-Pee-Chee-53
00O-Pee-Chee Parallel-53
00Pacific-32
Copper-32
Gold-32
Ice Blue-32
Premiere Date-32
00Paramount-18
Copper-18
Gold-18
Holo-Gold-18
Holo-Silver-18
Ice Blue-18
Premiere Date-18
Glove Side Net Fusions-1
Glove Side Net Fusions Platinum-1
00Private Stock-7
Gold-7
Premiere Date-7
Retail-7
Silver-7
00Revolution-10
Blue-10
Premiere Date-10
Red-10
00SP Authentic BuyBacks-7
00SP Authentic Sign of the Times-BD
00SP Game Used-4
Tools of the Game-BD
Tools of the Game Exclusives-BD
Tools of the Game Combos-C-SD
00Stadium Club-18
00Titanium-5
Blue-5
Gold-5
Premiere Date-5
Red-5
Retail-5
Game Gear-56
Game Gear Patches-56
00Titanium Draft Day Edition-4
Patches-4
00Topps/OPC-53
Parallel-53
00Topps Chrome-43
OPC Refractors-43
Refractors-43
00Topps Gold Label Class 1-18
Gold-18
00Topps Gold Label Class 2-18
00Topps Gold Label Class 2 Gold-18
00Topps Gold Label Class 3-18
00Topps Gold Label Class 3 Gold-18
00Topps Heritage-140
00Topps Premier Plus-78
Blue Ice-78
00Topps Stars-75
Blue-75
00UD Heroes-11
00UD Reserve-6
00Upper Deck-242
Exclusives Tier 1-242
Exclusives Tier 2-242
00Upper Deck MVP-19
First Stars-19
Second Stars-19
Third Stars-19
00Upper Deck Victory-21
00Upper Deck Vintage-33
00Upper Deck Vintage-36
00Upper Deck Vintage-37
Great Gloves-GG2
00Vanguard Dual Game-Worn Jerseys-13
00Vanguard Dual Game-Worn Patches-13
01Atomic-6
Blue-6
Gold-6
Premiere Date-6
Red-6
Jerseys-3
Patches-3
01BAP Memorabilia-47
Emerald-47
Ruby-47
Sapphire-47
Goalies Jerseys-GJ1
Goalie Traditions-GT15
Goalie Traditions-GT31
Goalie Traditions-GT33
Goalie Traditions-GT41
01BAP Signature Series Certified 100-C3
01BAP Signature Series Certified 50-C3
01BAP Signature Series Certified 1 of 1's-C3
01BAP Signature Series Autographs-LBD
01BAP Signature Series Autographs Gold-LBD
01BAP Signature Series Jerseys-GJ-5
01BAP Signature Series Jersey Autographs-GUBD
01BAP Sig Series Jersey and Stick Cards-GSJ-5
01BAP Signature Series Emblems-GUE-5
01BAP Signature Series Numbers-ITN-5
01BAP Signature Series Teammates-TM-3
01BAP Ultimate Mem Legend Terry Sawchuk-12
01Between the Pipes-8
01Between the Pipes-106
01Between the Pipes-166
He Shoots-He Saves Points-3
He Shoots-He Saves Prizes-16
Jerseys-GJ1
Jersey and Stick Cards-GSJ1
Masks-10
Masks Silver-10
Masks Gold-10
Tandems-GT10
01Bowman YoungStars-63
Gold-63
Ice Cubed-63
01Crown Royale-9
Blue-9
Premiere Date-9
Red-9
Retail-9
01O-Pee-Chee-183
01O-Pee-Chee Premier Parallel-183
01Pacific-29
Extreme LTD-29
Hobby LTD-29
Premiere Date-29
Retail LTD-29
Impact Zone-2
Steel Curtain-2
01Pacific Adrenaline-12
Blue-12
Premiere Date-12
Red-12
Retail-12
Power Play-4
01Pacific Arena Exclusives-29
01Pacific Heads-Up-7
Blue-7
Premiere Date-7
Red-7
Silver-7
Quad Jerseys-2
Showstoppers-2
01Parkhurst-117
Jerseys-PJ48
Jersey and Stick-PSJ19
Teammates-T4
01Private Stock Game Gear-8
01Private Stock Game Gear Patches-8
01Private Stock PS-2002-5
01SP Game Used Tools of the Game-TBD
01SP Game Used Tools of the Game-TDA
01SP Game Used Tools of the Game-TDF
01SP Game Used Tools of the Game-CTDB
01SP Game Used Tools of the Game-CTDC
01SP Game Used Tools of the Game-CTHD
01SP Game Used Tools of the Game-CTTD
01SP Game Used Tools of the Game-TTDER
01Titanium-7
Hobby Parallel-7
Premiere Date-7
Retail-7
Retail Parallel-7
01Topps-183
OPC Parallel-183
01Topps Chrome-122
Refractors-122
Black Border Refractors-122
01Topps Heritage-90
Refractors-90
01UD Mask Collection-103
01UD Mask Collection-171
Gold-103
Gold-171
Gloves-GGBD
Goalie Jerseys-MMBD
Goalie Jerseys-SSBD
Goalie Pads-GPBD
01UD Playmakers-9
01UD Top Shelf-80
Goalie Gear-LPBD
01Upper Deck-18
Exclusives-18
MVP Goalie Sticks-G-BD
01Upper Deck Victory-24
01Upper Deck Victory-33
Gold-24
Gold-33
01Upper Deck Vintage-20
01Upper Deck Vintage-26
01Vanguard-5
Blue-5
Red-5
One of Ones-5
Premiere Date-5
Proofs-5
Stonewallers-2
02BAP First Edition-7
Jerseys-7
02BAP Sig Series Auto Buybacks 1998-6
02BAP Sig Series Auto Buybacks 1999-23
02BAP Sig Series Auto Buybacks 2000-122
02BAP Sig Series Auto Buybacks 2001-LBD
02Between the Pipes-72
Gold-72
Silver-72
Trappers-GT4
02O-Pee-Chee-45
02O-Pee-Chee Premier Blue Parallel-45
02O-Pee-Chee Premier Red Parallel-45
02O-Pee-Chee Factory Set-45
02Pacific-25
Blue-25
Red-25
02Pacific Complete-327
Red-327
02Pacific Heads-Up-7
Blue-7
Purple-7
Red-7
Showstoppers-2
02Parkhurst-149
Bronze-149
Gold-149
Silver-149
02Parkhurst Retro-106
Minis-106
02SP Game Used Tools of the Game-BD
02Topps-45
OPC Blue Parallel-45
OPC Red Parallel-45
Own The Game-OTG19
02Topps Promos-PP5
02Topps Factory Set-45
02Topps Heritage Crease Piece-BD
02Topps Heritage Crease Piece Patches-BD
02UD Mask Collection-3
02UD Mask Collection-4
02UD Mask Collection-5
02UD Mask Collection-6
02UD Mask Collection-7
02UD Mask Collection-108
02UD Mask Collection Beckett Promos-3
02UD Mask Collection Beckett Promos-4
02UD Mask Collection Beckett Promos-5
02UD Mask Collection Beckett Promos-6
02UD Mask Collection Beckett Promos-7
02UD Mask Collection Career Wins-CWBD
02UD Premier Collection-4
02UD Top Shelf Dual Player Jerseys-STGD
02UD Top Shelf Stopper Jerseys-SSBD
02UD Top Shelf Triple Jerseys-TSGTD
02Upper Deck Saviors Jerseys-SVBD
02Vanguard-4
LTD-4
03BAP Memorabilia-107
Emerald-107
Gold-107
Ruby-107
Sapphire-107
Deep in the Crease-D1
03Black Diamond-61
Black-61
Green-61
Red-61
03ITG Action-15
Jerseys-M16
03ITG Used Signature Series-83
Gold-83
Autographs-BD
Autographs Gold-BD
Goalie Gear-20
Goalie Gear Autographs-20
Goalie Gear Gold-20
03NHL Sticker Collection-10
03Pacific-12
Blue-12
Red-12
03Pacific Complete-402
Red-402
03Pacific Exhibit-8
Blue Backs-8
Yellow Backs-8
03Pacific Invincible Jerseys-1
03Parkhurst Original Six Boston-58
03Private Stock Reserve-5
Blue-5
Red-5
Retail-5
03SP Game Used Game Gear-GGBD
03Thrashers Postcards-3
03Upper Deck-13
Canadian Exclusives-13
HG-13
03Upper Deck MVP-28
Gold Script-28
Silver Script-28
Canadian Exclusives-28

Dafoe, Kyle
96Owen Sound Platers-7
97Owen Sound Platers-4
98Sudbury Wolves-12
99Sudbury Wolves-5

Dafoe, Scott
03Vernon Vipers-7

Dagenais, Emile
51Laval Dairy Subset-106
52St. Lawrence Sales-67

Dagenais, Eric
00Sherbrooke Castors-11
Signed-11
01Sherbrooke Castors-2
02Drummondville Voltigeurs-21

Dagenais, Mike
89Peterborough Petes-102
897th Inn. Sketch OHL-102
90ProCards AHL/IHL-407
91ProCards-528
92Cincinnati Cyclones-7
93Cleveland Lumberjacks-6
93Cleveland Lumberjacks Postcards-6
94Cleveland Lumberjacks-5
94Cleveland Lumberjacks Postcards-5
03Waterloo Blackhawks-18

Dagenais, Pierre
97Beehive-74
Authentic Autographs-74
Golden Portraits-74
98Albany River Rats-6
98Bowman CHL-100
Golden Anniversary-100
OPC International-100
98Bowman Chrome CHL-100
Golden Anniversary-100
Golden Anniversary Refractors-100
OPC International-100
OPC International Refractors-100
Refractors-100
99Albany River Rats-8
00BAP Memorabilia-517
00Albany River Rats-7
01BAP Memorabilia-155
01BAP Memorabilia-481
Emerald-155
Emerald-481
Ruby-155
Ruby-481
Sapphire-155
Sapphire-481
01BAP Signature Series-250
Autographs-250
Autographs Gold-250
01Devils Team Issue-5
01O-Pee-Chee-281
01O-Pee-Chee Premier Parallel-281
01Parkhurst-378
01Stadium Club-117
Award Winners-117
Master Photos-117
01Topps-281
OPC Parallel-281
01Upper Deck Victory-379
Gold-379
03Parkhurst Original Six Montreal-30
05Canadiens Team Issue-5
05Parkhurst-266
Facsimile Auto Parallel-266
05Upper Deck-104
HG Glossy-104
05Upper Deck MVP-206
Gold-206
Platinum-206
05Upper Deck Toronto Fall Expo-104

Dagenais, Randy
03Greenville Grrrowl-6
04Louisiana Ice Gators-4

Dahl, Bjorn Anders
92Norwegian Elite Series-110
92Norwegian Elite Series-187
95Swedish World Championships Stickers-245

Dahl, Craig
03St. Cloud State Huskies-27
04St. Cloud State Huskies-28

Dahl, Geir Tore
92Norwegian Elite Series-111

Dahl, Jan Morten
92Norwegian Elite Series-215

Dahl, Jim
06Stockton Thunder-19

Dahl, John
00Swift Current Broncos-4
01Swift Current Broncos-13
02Saskatoon Blades-19
02Swift Current Broncos-1
03Everett Silvertips-21
04Fresno Falcons-3

Dahl, Kevin
91Alberta International Team Canada-5
92Flames IGA-23
92OPC Premier-22
92Parkhurst-261
Emerald Ice-261
92Ultra-266
92Upper Deck-493
93OPC Premier-362
Gold-362
93Parkhurst-298
Emerald Ice-298
93Score-423
Canadian-423
93Stadium Club-432
Members Only Master Set-432
First Day Issue-432
93Topps/OPC Premier-362
Gold-362
93Ultra-23
96Las Vegas Thunder-3
98Chicago Wolves-19
98Chicago Wolves Turner Cup-5
99Chicago Wolves-3
00Upper Deck NHLPA-PA25
00Chicago Wolves-5
01German Upper Deck-200
02German DEL City Press-261
03German Nuremberg Ice Tigers Postcards-5

Dahl, T.J.
02Tri-City Stormfront-21

Dahlberg, Lennart
83Swedish Semic Elitserien-34

84Swedish Semic Elitserien-33

Dahlberg, Ove

57Swedish Alfabilder-104

Dahlem, Fabian

94German First League-533
99German Bundesliga 2-203

Dahlen, Chad

98Sioux City Musketeers-4
99Sioux City Musketeers-4

Dahlen, Thomas

94German First League-71

Dahlen, Ulf

85Swedish Panini Stickers-38
86Swedish Panini Stickers-27
880-Pee-Chee-47
880-Pee-Chee Minis-7
880-Pee-Chee Stickers-126
880-Pee-Chee Stickers-128
880-Pee-Chee Stickers-258
88Panini Stickers-305
88Topps-47
890-Pee-Chee-2
89Panini Stickers-288
89Rangers Marine Midland Bank-16
89Topps-2
90Bowman-176
Tiffany-176
900-Pee-Chee-12
90Pro Set-136
90Score-22
Canadian-22
90Topps-12
Tiffany-12
90Upper Deck-283
French-283
91Pro Set Platinum-186
91Bowman-127
91Bowman-422
910-Pee-Chee-177
91Panini Stickers-110
91Parkhurst-76
French-76
91Pinnacle-152
French-152
91Pro Set-106
91Pro Set-607
French-106
French-607
91Score American-164
91Score Canadian Bilingual-164
91Score Canadian English-164
91Stadium Club-55
91Topps-177
91Upper Deck-348
French-348
92Bowman-143
920-Pee-Chee-129
92Panini Stickers-92
92Panini Stickers French-92
92Parkhurst-310
Emerald Ice-310
92Pinnacle-68
French-68
92Pro Set-80
92Score-330
Canadian-330
92Stadium Club-207
92Topps-28
Gold-28G
92Ultra-92
92Upper Deck-250
93Donruss-78
93Donruss-488
93Leaf-198
93OPC Premier-75
Gold-75
93Panini Stickers-270
93Parkhurst-322
Emerald Ice-322
93Pinnacle-248
Canadian-248
93PowerPlay-59
93Score-107
Canadian-107
International Stars-13
International Stars Canadian-13
93Stadium Club-238
93Stadium Club-428
Members Only Master Set-238
Members Only Master Set-428
OPC-238
First Day Issue-238
First Day Issue-428
First Day Issue OPC-238
93Topps/OPC Premier-75
Gold-75
93Ultra-81
93Upper Deck-360
93Swedish Semic Elitserien-312
93Swedish Semic World Champ Stickers-34
94Canada Games NHL POGS-63
94Donruss-57
94Flair-161
94Fleer-194
94Leaf-25
94Leaf Limited-76
94OPC Premier-299
Special Effects-299
94Parkhurst-215
Gold-215
SE Euro-Stars-ES6
94Pinnacle-48
Artist's Proofs-48
Rink Collection-48
World Edition-WE4
94Select-123
Gold-123
94Stars HockeyKaps-9
94Topps/OPC Premier-299
Special Effects-299
94Ultra-192
94Upper Deck-16
Electric Ice-16
SP Inserts-SP70
SP Inserts Die Cuts-SP70
95Bashan Super Stickers-109
95Canada Games NHL POGS-228
95Collector's Choice-297
Player's Club-297
Player's Club Platinum-297
95Donruss-92
95Emotion-154
95Hoyle Western Playing Cards-28
95Imperial Stickers-109
95Kraft-65
95Leaf-157
95Metal-128
95Panini Stickers-281
95Parkhurst International-245
95Parkhurst International-452
Emerald Ice-245
Emerald Ice-452
95Pinnacle-13
Artist's Proofs-13
Rink Collection-13
95Playoff One on One-190
95Pro Magnets-116
95Score-137
Black Ice Artist's Proofs-137
Black Ice-137
95Select Certified-25
Mirror Gold-25
95SkyBox Impact-146
95Stadium Club Members Only-42
95Summit-15
Artist's Proofs-15
Ice-15
95Topps-227
OPC Inserts-227
95Ultra-144
Gold Medallion-144
95Upper Deck-381
Electric Ice-381
Electric Ice Gold-381
Special Edition-SE72
Special Edition Gold-SE72
95Zenith-7
95Swedish Globe World Championships-48
95Swedish World Championships Stickers-286
96Be A Player-35
Autographs-35
Autographs Silver-35
96Collector's Choice-243
96Donruss-115
Press Proofs-115
96Leaf-55
Press Proofs-55
96NHL Pro Stamps-116
96Score-234
Artist's Proofs-234
Dealer's Choice Artist's Proofs-234
Special Artist's Proofs-234
Golden Blades-234
96Swedish Semic Wien-60
97Collector's Choice-48
97Pacific-74
Copper-74
Emerald Green-74
Ice Blue-74
Red-74
Silver-74
97Panini Stickers-130
97Score-252
98Swedish UD Choice-116
99Panini Stickers-164
000-Pee-Chee-270A
000-Pee-Chee Parallel-270A
00Pacific-450
Copper-450
Gold-450
Ice Blue-450
Premiere Date-450
00Panini Stickers-105
00Private Stock Game Gear-103
00Private Stock Game Gear Patches-103
00Titanium Draft Day Edition-99
00Topps/OPC-270A
Parallel-270A
00Vanguard Dual Game-Worn Jerseys-17
00Vanguard Dual Game-Worn Patches-17
01Pacific-391
Extreme LTD-391
Hobby LTD-391
Premiere Date-391
Retail LTD-391
01Pacific Arena Exclusives-391
01Pacific Heads-Up Quad Jerseys-12
01UD Mask Collection-98
Gold-98
02BAP First Edition-285
020-Pee-Chee-52
020-Pee-Chee Premier Blue Parallel-52
020-Pee-Chee Premier Red Parallel-52
020-Pee-Chee Factory Set-52
02Pacific-389
Blue-389
Red-389
02Pacific Complete-475
Red-475
02Stars Postcards-22
02Topps-52
OPC Blue Parallel-52
OPC Red Parallel-52
Factory Set-52
03NHL Sticker Collection-203
03Pacific-103
Blue-103
Red-103

Dahlgren, Lars

67Swedish Hockey-252
69Swedish Hockey-297
70Swedish Hockey-204
71Swedish Hockey-292
72Swedish Stickers-78

Dahlin, Hakan

72Swedish Stickers-198

Dahlin, Kjell

83Swedish Semic Elitserien-113
84Swedish Semic Elitserien-113
85Canadiens Postcards-6
85Canadiens Postcards-7
85Canadiens Provigo-3
85Swedish Panini Stickers-111
85Swedish Panini Stickers-112
86Canadiens Postcards-4
86Kraft Drawings-13
860-Pee-Chee-15
860-Pee-Chee-262
860-Pee-Chee Stickers-18
860-Pee-Chee Stickers-126
86Topps-15
87Canadiens Postcards-6
87Canadiens Vachon Stickers-39
87Canadiens Vachon Stickers-40
870-Pee-Chee Stickers-14
89Swedish Semic Elitserien Stickers-88
90Swedish Semic Elitserien Stickers-262
91Swedish Semic Elitserien Stickers-95
92Swedish Semic Elitserien Stickers-123
93Swedish Semic Elitserien-95

Dahllof, Hakan

70Swedish Hockey-90
71Swedish Hockey-182
72Swedish Stickers-171
74Swedish Stickers-211

Dahllof, Hans

64Swedish Coralli ISHockey-87
65Swedish Coralli ISHockey-87
67Swedish Hockey-44
69Swedish Hockey-59
70Swedish Hockey-19

Dahlman, Toni

98Danish Hockey League-29
00Finnish Cardset-156
01BAP Memorabilia-335
Emerald-335
Ruby-335
Sapphire-335
01Bowman YoungStars-122
Gold-122
Ice Cubed-122
01SPx-211
01UD Playmakers-132
01UD Premier Collection-74
01Finnish Cardset-42
01Grand Rapids Griffins-23
02Pacific Calder-86
Silver-86
02Pacific Complete-526
Red-526
02Finnish Cardset-11
03Finnish Cardset-51
03Finnish Cardset Globetrotters-GR1
04Finnish Cardset-71
04Finnish Cardset Signatures-15
04Swedish Pure Skills-120
Parallel-120
05Finnish Cardset -59
06Finnish Cardset-288

Dahlmann, Morten

99Danish Hockey League-206

Dahlquist, Chris

87Penguins Kodak-7
900-Pee-Chee-528
90Pro Set-464
91Bowman-128
910-Pee-Chee-142
91Pro Set-408
French-408
91Score American-365
91Score Canadian Bilingual-404
91Score Canadian English-404
91Stadium Club-314
91Topps-142
91Upper Deck-307
French-307
92Bowman-359
92Flames IGA-24
920-Pee-Chee-22
92OPC Premier-38
92Pinnacle-167
French-167
92Score-294
Canadian-294
92Stadium Club-57
92Topps-231
Gold-231G
92Ultra-267
93Pinnacle-414
Canadian-414
93Score-314
Canadian-314
93Stadium Club-266
Members Only Master Set-266
First Day Issue-266
94Leaf-386
94Pinnacle-402
Artist's Proofs-402
Rink Collection-402
94Senators Team Issue-10
95Canada Games NHL POGS-197
95Cincinnati Cyclones-4
96Las Vegas Thunder-4

Dahlsten, Ronni

99Danish Hockey League-41

Dahlstrom, Cully

34Beehive Group I Photos-50
35Diamond Matchbooks Tan 5-4
37Diamond Matchbooks Tan 6-4
390-Pee-Chee V301-1-46
400-Pee-Chee V301-2-137

Dahlstrom, Lars

91Swedish Semic Elitserien Stickers-293
92Swedish Semic Elitserien Stickers-321
93Swedish Semic Elitserien-286
94Swedish Leaf-94
97Swedish Collector's Choice-178

Dahlstrom, Ole Eskild

92Finnish Semic-41
92Norwegian Elite Series-34
92Norwegian Elite Series-201
93Swedish Semic World Champ Stickers-240
94Finnish Jaa Kiekko-259
99Norwegian National Team-12

Dahlstrom, Pal

92Norwegian Elite Series-41

Dahm, Sebastian

05Belleville Bulls-3
06Sarnia Sting-6
06Sudbury Wolves-23

Daigle, Alain

750-Pee-Chee NHL-394
760-Pee-Chee NHL-156
76Topps-156
770-Pee-Chee NHL-208
77Topps-208
780-Pee-Chee-117
78Topps-117
79Blackhawks Postcards-4
790-Pee-Chee-227
79Topps-227

Daigle, Alexandre

917th Inn. Sketch QMJHL-270
92Upper Deck-587
93Donruss-237
93Donruss-393
Elite Inserts-2
Rated Rookies-1
Special Print-P
93Durivage Score-1
93Kraft-6
93Leaf-311
Freshman Phenoms-1
Studio Signature-9
93OPC Premier-405
Gold-405
93Parkhurst-244
Emerald Ice-244
Calder Candidates-C1
Calder Candidates Gold-C1
Cherry's Playoff Heroes-D11
East/West Stars-E3
First Overall-F1
USA/Canada Gold-G6
93Pinnacle Power-1
93Pinnacle II Samples-SR1
93Pinnacle-236
93Pinnacle-AU1
Canadian-236
Canadian-AU1
Super Rookies-1
Super Rookies Canadian-1
Daigle Entry Draft-1
93PowerPlay-396
Rookie Standouts-3
93Score Promo Panel-587
93Score-496
93Score-587
93Score-NNO
Gold-587
Canadian-496
Canadian-587
Canadian-NNO
Canadian Gold-587
Canadian Gold-NNO
Dynamic Duos Canadian-3
93Senators Kraft Sheets-5
93Stadium Club-300
Members Only Master Set-300
First Day Issue-300
93Topps/OPC Premier-405
Gold-405
93Topps Premier Finest-1
93Ultra-380
Wave of the Future-3
93Upper Deck-170
93Upper Deck-250
Program of Excellence-E15
Silver Skates-R3
Silver Skates Gold-R3
SP-107
93Classic-1
93Classic-34
93Classic-50
93Classic-51
93Classic-52
93Classic-53
93Classic-54
93Classic-114
Crash Numbered-N1
Previews-HK1
Promos-1
Top Ten-DP1
93Classic Four-Sport *-185
Gold-185
Acetates-11
Chromium Draft Stars-DS58
LP Jumbos-2
LPs-LP1
LPs-LP22
93Classic Four-Sport MBNA Promos *-2
93Classic Four-Sport Power Pick Bonus *-PP18
93Classic Four-Sport Previews *-CC1
93Classic Four-Sport Tri-Cards *-TC4
94Be A Player-R30
94Canada Games NHL POGS-353
94Donruss-211
94Finest-88
94Finest-155
Super Team Winners-88
Super Team Winners-155
Refractors-88
Refractors-155
94Flair-120
Scoring Power-2
94Fleer-143
94Hockey Wit-91
94Leaf-119
Gold Rookies-5
94Leaf Limited-87
94McDonald's Upper Deck-McD36
94OPC Premier-140
94OPC Premier-195
940-Pee-Chee Finest Inserts-7
94OPC Premier Special Effects-140
94OPC Premier Special Effects-195
94Parkhurst-285
Gold-285
Vintage-V42
94Parkhurst SE-SE119
Gold-SE119
94Pinnacle I Hobby Samples-2
94Pinnacle-2
94Pinnacle-461
94Pinnacle-531
Artist's Proofs-2
Artist's Proofs-461
Artist's Proofs-531
Rink Collection-2
Rink Collection-461
Rink Collection-531
Gamers-GR6
Northern Lights-NL6
94Score Samples-TF16
94Score-248
Gold-248
Platinum-248
Dream Team-DT21
Franchise-TF16
94Select-3
Gold-3
94Senators Team Issue-11
94SP-81
94SP-136
Die Cuts-81
Die Cuts-136
94Stadium Club Members Only-50
94Stadium Club-110
Members Only Master Set-110
First Day Issue-110
Super Team Winner Cards-110
94Topps/OPC Premier-140
94Topps/OPC Premier-195
Special Effects-140
Special Effects-195
94Ultra-146
All-Rookies-3
All-Rookies Parallel-3
94Upper Deck-87
Electric Ice-87
Ice Gallery-IG10
SP Inserts-SP54
SP Inserts Die Cuts-SP54
94Upper Deck NHLPA/Be A Player-3
94Classic Pro Prospects-13
94Classic C3 *-18
94Images *-4
Chrome-CC14
Sudden Impact-SI5
95Upper Deck World Junior Alumni-4
95Bashan Super Stickers-86
95Be A Player-188
Signatures-S188
Signatures Die Cuts-S188
95Canada Games NHL POGS-190
95Collector's Choice-208
Player's Club-208
Player's Club Platinum-208
95Donruss-160
Canadian World Junior Team-16
95Emotion-123
95Hoyle Eastern Playing Cards-9
95Imperial Stickers-86
95Kraft-10
95Kraft-63
95Leaf-179
95Leaf Limited-38
95McDonald's Pinnacle-MCD-38
95Metal-104
95NHL Aces Playing Cards-4D
95Panini Stickers-47
95Parkhurst International-150
Emerald Ice-150
95Pinnacle-7
Artist's Proofs-7
Rink Collection-7
95Pinnacle FANtasy-3
95Playoff One on One-73
95Playoff One on One-178
95Pro Magnets-113
95Score-18
Black Ice Artist's Proofs-18
Black Ice-18
95Select Certified-22
Mirror Gold-22
95Senators Team Issue-8
95SkyBox Impact-118
95SP-103
95Stadium Club-97
Members Only Master Set-97
95Summit-21
Artist's Proofs-21
Ice-21
95Topps-342
OPC Inserts-342
Canadian World Juniors-5CJ
Home Grown Canada-HGC14
95Topps SuperSkills-24
Platinum-24
95Ultra-111
Gold Medallion-111
High Speed-6
Rising Stars-2
Rising Stars Gold Medallion-2
95Upper Deck-271
Electric Ice-271
Electric Ice Gold-271
Special Edition-SE60
Special Edition Gold-SE60
95Zenith-22
96Black Diamond-91
Gold-91
96Collector's Choice-180
96Collector's Choice-325
96Donruss-204
Press Proofs-204
96Donruss Canadian Ice-104
Gold Press Proofs-104
Red Press Proofs-104
96Donruss Elite-84
Die Cut Stars-84
96Leaf-80
Press Proofs-80
96Maggers-18
96Metal Universe-105
96NHL Pro Stamps-113
96Pinnacle-133
Artist's Proofs-133
Foil-133
Premium Stock-133
Rink Collection-133
96Score-66
Artist's Proofs-66
Dealer's Choice Artist's Proofs-66
Special Artist's Proofs-66
Golden Blades-66
96Senators Pizza Hut-6
96SkyBox Impact-88
96SP-106
96Summit-106
Artist's Proofs-106
Ice-106
Metal-106
Premium Stock-106
96Ultra-116
Gold Medallion-116
96Upper Deck-302
97Collector's Choice-174
Star Quest-SQ25
97Crown Royale-90
Emerald Green-90
Ice Blue-90
Silver-90
97Donruss-78
Press Proofs Silver-78
Press Proofs Gold-78
97Donruss Canadian Ice-122
Dominion Series-122
Provincial Series-122
National Pride-15
97Donruss Elite-24
Aspirations-24
Status-24
97Donruss Limited-161
Exposure-161
97Donruss Preferred-48
Cut to the Chase-48
97Donruss Priority-22
Stamp of Approval-22
97Flyers Phone Cards-1
97Highland Mint Mint-Cards Pinnacle/Score-3
97Highland Mint Mint-Cards Pinnacle/Score-4
97Katch-98
Gold-98
Silver-98
97Leaf-26
Fractal Matrix-26
Fractal Matrix Die Cuts-26
97Leaf International-26
Universal Ice-26
97Pacific-250
Copper-250
Emerald Green-250
Ice Blue-250
Red-250
Silver-250
Team Checklists-17
97Pacific Dynagon-84
Copper-84
Dark Grey-84
Emerald Green-84
Ice Blue-84
Red-84
Silver-84
Tandems-54
97Pacific Invincible-93
Copper-93
Emerald Green-93
Ice Blue-93
Red-93
Silver-93
Feature Performers-23
97Panini Stickers-38
97Paramount-124
Copper-124
Dark Grey-124
Emerald Green-124
Ice Blue-124
Red-124
Silver-124
97Pinnacle-159
Press Plates Back Black-159
Press Plates Back Cyan-159
Press Plates Back Magenta-159
Press Plates Back Yellow-159
Press Plates Front Black-159
Press Plates Front Cyan-159
Press Plates Front Magenta-159
Press Plates Front Yellow-159
97Pinnacle Certified-98
Red-98
Mirror Blue-98
Mirror Gold-98
Mirror Red-98
97Pinnacle Inside-109
97Pinnacle Tot Cert Platinum Blue-98
97Pinnacle Tot Certi Platinum Gold-98
97Pinnacle Totally Certified Platinum Red-98
97Pinnacle Tot Cert Mirror Platinum Gold-98
97Revolution-99
Copper-99
Emerald-99
Ice Blue-99
Silver-99
97Score-101
Artist's Proofs-101
Golden Blades-101
97SP Authentic-107
97Studio-92
Press Proofs Silver-92
Press Proofs Gold-92
97Upper Deck-117
98Aurora-136
98Finest-24
No Protectors-24
No Protectors Refractors-24
Refractors-24
98Pacific-323
Ice Blue-323
Red-323
98Pacific Dynagon Ice-134
Blue-134
Red-134
98Panini Stickers-93
98Paramount-170
Copper-170
Emerald Green-170
Holo-Electric-170
Ice Blue-170
Silver-170
98SPx Finite-61
Radiance-61
Spectrum-61
98UD Choice-148
Prime Choice Reserve-148
Reserve-148
98Upper Deck-144
Exclusives-144
Exclusives 1 of 1-144
Gold Reserve-144
98Upper Deck MVP-189
Gold Script-189
Silver Script-189
Super Script-189
99Pacific-387
Copper-387
Emerald Green-387
Gold-387
Ice Blue-387
Premiere Date-387
Red-387
99Pacific Omega-147
Copper-147
Gold-147
Ice Blue-147
Premiere Date-147
99Upper Deck Victory-277
00BAP Memorabilia-349
Emerald-349
Ruby-349
Sapphire-349
Promos-349
00BAP Mem Chicago Sportsfest Copper-349
00BAP Memorabilia Chicago Sportsfest Blue-349
00BAP Memorabilia Chicago Sportsfest Gold-349
00BAP Memorabilia Chicago Sportsfest Ruby-349
00BAP Memorabilia Chicago Sun-Times Ruby-349
00BAP Memorabilia Chicago Sun-Times Gold-349
00BAP Mem Chicago Sun-Times Sapphire-349
00BAP Mem Toronto Fall Expo Copper-349
00BAP Memorabilia Toronto Fall Expo Gold-349
00BAP Memorabilia Toronto Fall Expo Ruby-349
00Pacific-258
Copper-258
Gold-258
Ice Blue-258
Premiere Date-258
02BAP Memorabilia-140
Emerald-140
Ruby-140
Sapphire-140
NHL All-Star Game-140
NHL All-Star Game Blue-140
NHL All-Star Game Green-140
NHL All-Star Game Red-140
02BAP Memorabilia Toronto Fall Expo-140
02BAP Ultimate Memorabilia First Overall-1
02Pacific Complete-398
Red-398
02Upper Deck-389
Exclusives-389
02Upper Deck Beckett UD Promos-389
03Pacific Calder-51
Silver-51
03Pacific Complete-246
Red-246
03Pacific Quest for the Cup-53
Blue-53
03Titanium-50
Hobby Jersey Number Parallels-50
Retail-50
Retail Jersey Number Parallels-50
03Topps Traded-TT44
Blue-TT44
Gold-TT44
Red-TT44
03Upper Deck-340
Canadian Exclusives-340
HG-340
UD Exclusives-340
03Upper Deck Ice-44
Gold-44
03Upper Deck Rookie Update-44
04Pacific-129
Blue-129
Red-129
04Upper Deck-87
Canadian Exclusives-87
HG Glossy Gold-87
HG Glossy Silver-87
05Panini Stickers-305
05Parkhurst-239
Facsimile Auto Parallel-239
05Ultra-100
Gold-100
Ice-100
05Upper Deck-97
HG Glossy-97
05Upper Deck MVP-196
Gold-196
Platinum-196
05Upper Deck Toronto Fall Expo-97
05Wild Crime Prevention-1

Daigle, Chris

93Quebec Pee-Wee Tournament-1686
97Bowman CHL-79
OPC-79
98Val d'Or Foreurs-1
99Bowman CHL-79
Gold-79
OPC International-79

Daigle, Justin

06Okotoks Oilers -6

Daigle, Phil

98Huntsville Channel Cats-5

Daigle, Sylvain

92Quebec Pee-Wee Tournament-408
93Quebec Pee-Wee 20th Anniversary-16
96Mississippi Sea Wolves-3
97Springfield Falcons-4
99Mississippi Sea Wolves-24
00Muskegon Fury-11
02Muskegon Fury-5
03Muskegon Fury-4
05Danbury Trashers-11

Daigle, Vincent

93Quebec Pee-Wee Tournament-232

Daigneau, John

06Idaho Steelheads-22

Daigneault, J.J.

84Canucks Team Issue-6
85Canucks Team Issue-7
86Flyers Postcards-7
88ProCards AHL-136
88ProCards AHL-271
89Canadiens Kraft-6
89Canadiens Postcards-9
90Canadiens Postcards-11
90Pro Set-466
91Canadiens Panini Team Stickers-7
91Canadiens Postcards-9
910-Pee-Chee-456
91Panini Stickers-192
91Parkhurst-312
French-312
91Pro Set-124
French-124
91Score Canadian Bilingual-520
91Score Canadian English-520
91Topps-456
91Upper Deck-170
French-170
92Bowman-371
92Canadiens Postcards-5
92Durivage Panini-35
920-Pee-Chee-304
92Parkhurst-324
Emerald Ice-324
92Score-311
Canadian-311
92Stadium Club-308
92Topps-334
Gold-334G
92Ultra-326
92Upper Deck-331
93Canadiens Molson-5
93Canadiens Postcards-5
93Durivage Score-10
93Leaf-437
930-Pee-Chee Canadiens Hockey Fest-25
93OPC Premier-372
Gold-372
93Parkhurst-377
Emerald Ice-377
93Pinnacle-311
Canadian-311
93PowerPlay-367
93Score-299
Canadian-299
93Stadium Club-475
Members Only Master Set-475
First Day Issue-475
93Topps/OPC Premier-372
Gold-372
93Ultra-351
94Canadiens Postcards-5
94Leaf-407
94Pinnacle-224
Artist's Proofs-224
Rink Collection-224
94Stadium Club-52
Members Only Master Set-52
First Day Issue-52
Super Team Winner Cards-52
94Upper Deck-341
Electric Ice-341
95Canada Games NHL POGS-153
95Parkhurst International-442
Emerald Ice-442
95Playoff One on One-163
96Be A Player-34
Autographs-34
Autographs Silver-34
96Playoff One on One-377
97Pacific Dynagon Best Kept Secrets-1
97Score-254
97Score Mighty Ducks-8
Platinum-8
Premier-8
97Upper Deck-212
98Be A Player-76
Press Release-76
98BAP Gold-76
98BAP Autographs-76
98BAP Autographs Gold-76
98BAP Tampa Bay All Star Game-76
98Upper Deck-305
Exclusives-305
Exclusives 1 of 1-305
Gold Reserve-305
99Wayne Gretzky Hockey-133
00Upper Deck NHLPA-PA43
00Cleveland Lumberjacks-16
02BAP Sig Series Auto Buybacks 1998-76

Daigneault, Maxime

00Val d'Or Foreurs-19
Signed-19
01Val d'Or Foreurs-20
02Val d'Or Foreurs-19
03Val d'Or Foreurs-18
04ITG Heroes and Prospects-94
Autographs-U-MD
04ITG Heroes/Prospects Toronto Expo '05-94
04ITG Heroes/Prospects Expo Heroes/Pros-94
05South Carolina Stingrays-7

Daigneault, Paul

907th Inn. Sketch QMJHL-171

Dailey, Bob

73Canucks Royal Bank-4
74Canucks Royal Bank-4
74NHL Action Stamps-280
740-Pee-Chee NHL-240
74Topps-240
75Canucks Royal Bank-5
750-Pee-Chee NHL-231
75Topps-231
76Canucks Royal Bank-2
760-Pee-Chee NHL-350
770-Pee-Chee NHL-98
77Topps-98
780-Pee-Chee-131
78Topps-131
790-Pee-Chee-226
79Topps-226
800-Pee-Chee-131
80Topps-131
810-Pee-Chee-241
81Topps-E104

Dailey, Jason

98Roanoke Express-9
99Charlotte Checkers-1
01UK Guildford Flames-18
01UK Guildford Flames-28

Dailey, Zack

05Everett Silvertips-3

Dainville, Bob

52St. Lawrence Sales-89

Dairon, Michael

92British Columbia JHL-123

Dakers, Taylor

03Kootenay Ice-1
04Kootenay Ice-8
05Kootenay Ice-7

Dale, Andrew

93Sudbury Wolves-12
93Sudbury Wolves Police-12
94Sudbury Wolves-11
94Sudbury Wolves Police-5
95Slapshot-142
95Slapshot-394
95Sudbury Wolves-21
95Sudbury Wolves Police-6
97Springfield Falcons-5
99Johnstown Chiefs-9
99Mississippi Sea Wolves Kelly Cup-13
00Johnstown Chiefs-28

Dale, Bryce

04Williams Lake Timberwolves-4

Dale, Jack

69Seattle Totems-13

Dale, Jason

06Brampton Battalion-16

Dalene, Geir

92Norwegian Elite Series-228

Dalene, Ole Petter

92Norwegian Elite Series-82

Daley, Ian

93Quebec Pee-Wee Tournament-184

Daley, Joe

680-Pee-Chee-188
690-Pee-Chee-152
70Sargent Promotions Stamps-17
710-Pee-Chee-137
71Sargent Promotions Stamps-62
71Toronto Sun-90
740-Pee-Chee WHA-38
750-Pee-Chee WHA-101
760-Pee-Chee WHA-6
760-Pee-Chee WHA-20
760-Pee-Chee WHA-61
770-Pee-Chee WHA-9
78Jets Postcards-4

Daley, Pat

05Ottawa 67's-15

Daley, Trevor

00UD CHL Prospects-26
02Sault Ste. Marie Greyhounds-3
03BAP Memorabilia-245
03Beehive-248
Gold-248
Silver-248
03Crown Royale-114
Red-114
Retail-114
03ITG Used Signature Series-161
Gold-161
03ITG VIP Rookie Debut-50
03Pacific Complete-586
Red-586
03Parkhurst Rookie-149
Rookie Emblems-RE-27
Rookie Emblems Gold-RE-27
Rookie Jerseys-RJ-27
Rookie Jerseys Gold-RJ-27
Rookie Numbers-RN-27
Rookie Numbers Gold-RN-27
Teammates Gold-RT5
Teammates-RT5
03Private Stock Reserve-116
Blue-116
Red-116
Retail-116

03SP Authentic-131
Limited-131
03SPx-240
03Stars Postcards-4
03Titanium-115
Hobby Jersey Number Parallels-115
Retail-115
Retail Jersey Number Parallels-115
03Topps Traded-TT105
Blue-TT105
Gold-TT105
Red-TT105
03UD Honor Roll-134
03UD Premier Collection-88
03Upper Deck-467
Canadian Exclusives-467
HG-467
UD Exclusives-467
03Upper Deck Ice-119
Glass Parallel-119
03Upper Deck Rookie Update-116
03Upper Deck Trilogy-183
04AHL Top Prospects-17
04Hamilton Bulldogs-4
05Parkhurst-152
Facsimile Auto Parallel-152
True Colors-TCDAL
True Colors-TCDAL
05Upper Deck-311
Jerseys Series II-J2DY
05Upper Deck MVP-137
Gold-137
Platinum-137
06Stars Team Postcards-5
06UD Artifacts Tundra Tandems-TTDO
06UD Artifacts Tundra Tandems Black-TTDO
06UD Artifacts Tundra Tandems Blue-TTDO
06UD Artifacts Tundra Tandems Gold-TTDO
06UD Artifacts Tundra Tandems Platinum-TTDO
06UD Artifacts Tundra Tandems Red-TTDO
06UD Artifacts Tundra Tandems Dual Patches Red-TTDO

Dalgard, Christer
83Swedish Semic Elitserien-102
84Swedish Semic Elitserien-100
85Swedish Panini Stickers-92
86Swedish Panini Stickers-85
87Swedish Panini Stickers-90

Dalgarno, Brad
89O-Pee-Chee-246
90Pro Set-482
91Stadium Club-371
92Parkhurst-336
Emerald Ice-336
93Donruss-197
93Leaf-320
93OPC Premier-223
Gold-223
93Parkhurst-393
Emerald Ice-393
93Pinnacle-333
Canadian-333
93Score-374
Canadian-374
93Stadium Club-167
Members Only Master Set-167
OPC-167
First Day Issue-167
First Day Issue OPC-167
93Topps/OPC Premier-223
Gold-223
93Ultra-364
93Upper Deck-219
94Canada Games NHL POGS-153
94Pinnacle-238
Artist's Proofs-238
Rink Collection-238
94Stadium Club-259
Members Only Master Set-259
First Day Issue-259
Super Team Winner Cards-259
95Be A Player-10
Signatures-S10
Signatures Die Cuts-S10

Dall-Hansen, Christian
99Danish Hockey League-183

Dalla Vecchia, Gianni
93Swiss HNL-448

Dallaire, Dany
00Halifax Mooseheads-4
01Halifax Mooseheads-1

Dallaire, G.
10Sweet Caporal Postcards-39
11C55-39
12C57-7

Dallaire, Stacy
917th Inn. Sketch QMJHL-147

Dallas, Darcy
93Northern Michigan Wildcats-4

Dalliday, David
00Mississauga Ice Dogs-9
01Owen Sound Attack-4

Dallman, Kevin
98Guelph Storm-6
99Guelph Storm-5
00Guelph Storm-4
01Guelph Storm-3
01Guelph Storm Memorial Cup-2
02Providence Bruins-2
03Providence Bruins-4
04Providence Bruins-5
05Beehive-175
Matte-175
05Black Diamond-161
Emerald-161
Gold-161
Onyx-161
Ruby-161
05Hot Prospects-215
Autographed Patch Variation-215
Autographed Patch Variation Gold-215
Hot Materials-HMKD
Red Hot-215
05Parkhurst-428
Facsimile Auto Parallel-428
True Colors-TCSTL
True Colors-TCSTL
05SP Authentic-138
Limited-138
Sign of the Times-KE
05SP Game Used-143
Autographs-143
Gold-143
Rookie Exclusives-KD
Rookie Exclusives Silver-RE-KD
05SPx-138
Spectrum-138
Xcitement Rookies-XR-KD
Xcitement Rookies Gold-XR-KD
Xcitement Rookies Spectrum-XR-KD
05The Cup-153
Autographed Rookie Patches Gold Rainbow-153
Black Rainbow Rookies-153
Masterpiece Pressplates (Bee Hive)-175
Masterpiece Pressplates (Black Diamond)-161
Masterpiece Pressplates (Ice)-145
Masterpiece Pressplates (Rookie Update)-171
Masterpiece Pressplates SPA Autos-138
Masterpiece Pressplates (SP Game Used)-143
Masterpiece Pressplates (SPx)-138
Masterpiece Pressplates (SPx)-138
Masterpiece Pressplates Ult Coll-224
Masterpiece Pressplates Autographs-153
Platinum Rookies-153
05Ultimate Collection-224
Gold-224
05Ultra-205
Gold-205
Fresh Ink-FI-KD
Fresh Ink Blue-FI-KD
Ice-205
Rookie Uniformity Jerseys-RU-KD
Rookie Uniformity Jersey Autographs-ARU-KD
Rookie Uniformity Patches-RUP-KD
Rookie Uniformity Patch Autographs-ARP-KD
05Upper Deck-219
HG Glossy-219
Rookie Ink-RIKD
Rookie Threads-RTKD
Rookie Threads Autographs-ARTKD
05Upper Deck Ice-145
Premieres Auto Patches-AIPKD
05Upper Deck Rookie Update-171
05Upper Deck Toronto Fall Expo-219

Dallman, Marty
88ProCards AHL-223
94Finnish Jaa Kiekko-250
95Swedish Globe World Championships-187
98Abilene Aviators-18
04UK Thommo's Top 10-8

Dallman, Rod
84Prince Albert Raiders Stickers-4
88ProCards AHL-316
89ProCards AHL-245
91ProCards-278

Dalman, Daddy
23V128-1 Paulin's Candy-13

Dalmao, Duncan
92Quebec Pee-Wee Tournament-1105
95Slapshot-159
01Roanoke Express-4
02Roanoke Express-12
02Roanoke Express RBI Sports-191
03Roanoke Express-310

Dalpiaz, Claus
93Swedish Semic World Champ Stickers-270
94Finnish Jaa Kiekko-231
94Swedish Olympics Lillehammer*-326
95Austrian National Team-3
95German DEL-361
95Swedish Globe World Championships-181
95Swedish World Championships Stickers-257
96German DEL-184
96Swedish Semic Wien-210
98German DEL-308
99German Bundesliga 2-15

Dalton, Jamie
92Quebec Pee-Wee Tournament-1812
93Quebec Pee-Wee Tournament-639

Dalton, Ray
98Quebec Remparts-6
Signed-6

Daly, Craig
90Cincinnati Cyclones-41

Daly, Erik
98Minnesota Golden Gophers-27

Daly, Nathan
05Knoxville Ice Bears-5

Dam, Trevor
86London Knights-21
897th Inn. Sketch OHL-25
90ProCards AHL/IHL-403
91ProCards-483
92Indianapolis Ice-9

Dame, Bunny
34Beehive Group I Photos-145

Dame, George
28V128-2 Paulin's Candy-83

Dameron, Bobby M
92Quebec Pee-Wee Tournament-969
93Quebec Pee-Wee Tournament-1265

Dameworth, Chad
92Northern Michigan Wildcats-3
93Northern Michigan Wildcats-5
96Johnstown Chiefs-5
96Wheeling Nailers-10
96Wheeling Nailers Photo Pack-14
97Mississippi Sea Wolves-7
98Port Huron Border Cats-9
02Kalamazoo Wings-20
03Atlantic City Boardwalk Bullies-4
04Atlantic City Boardwalk Bullies Kinko's-20

Damgaard, Claus
98Danish Hockey League-174

Damgaard, Jesper
97Swedish Collector's Choice-138
98Swedish UD Choice-153
01German Upper Deck-215
02Swedish SHL-239
Parallel-239
03Swedish Elite-249
Global Impact-GI10
Silver-249
04Swedish Elitset-240
Gold-240
04Swedish MoDo Postcards-30
05Swedish SHL Elitset-95
Gold-95
06German DEL-2
06Swedish SHL Elitset-106

Damon, Derek
04Maine Black Bears-21
05Maine Black Bears-4

Damphousse, Jean-Francois
92Quebec Pee-Wee Tournament-777
93Quebec Pee-Wee Tournament-348
97Bowman CHL-160
OPC-160
99Upper Deck Victory-375
99Albany River Rats-9
00Albany River Rats-22
01Between the Pipes-90
01Titanium Hobby Parallel-83
01Titanium Retail-83
01Titanium Retail Parallel-83
01Titanium Draft Day Edition-147
01Albany River Rats-3
02Between the Pipes-79
Gold-79
Silver-79
02O-Pee-Chee-313
02O-Pee-Chee Premier Blue Parallel-313
02O-Pee-Chee Premier Red Parallel-313
02O-Pee-Chee Factory Set-313
02Topps-313
OPC Blue Parallel-313
OPC Red Parallel-313
Factory Set-313
02Cincinnati Mighty Ducks-A-3
03BAP Memorabilia Deep in the Crease-D3

Damphousse, Vincent
86Maple Leafs Postcards-6
87Maple Leafs PLAY-17
87Maple Leafs Postcards-4
87Maple Leafs Postcards Oversized-4
87O-Pee-Chee-243
87O-Pee-Chee Stickers-128
87Panini Stickers-333
88Maple Leafs PLAY-17
88O-Pee-Chee-207
88O-Pee-Chee Stickers-171
88Panini Stickers-123
89Kraft-35
89O-Pee-Chee-272
89O-Pee-Chee Stickers-179
89Panini Stickers-134
90Bowman-163
Tiffany-163
90Bowman Hat Tricks-6
Tiffany-6
90Maple Leafs Postcards-2
90O-Pee-Chee-121
90O-Pee-Chee-241
90OPC Premier-21
90Panini Stickers-291
90Pro Set-278
90Score-95
Canadian-95
90Score Hottest/Rising Stars-47
90Topps-121
90Topps-241
Tiffany-121
90Upper Deck-224
90Upper Deck-484
French-224
French-484
91Pro Set Platinum-35
91Bowman-170
91Kraft-84
91Maple Leafs Panini Team Stickers-5
91McDonald's Upper Deck-16
91Oilers IGA-3
91Oilers Team Issue-4
91O-Pee-Chee-299
91OPC Premier-104
91Panini Stickers-92
91Parkhurst-48
French-48
91Pinnacle-91
French-91
91Pro Set-224
91Pro Set-293
91Pro Set-381
French-224
French-293
French-381
91Score American-300
91Score American-338
91Score Canadian Bilingual-368
91Score Canadian Bilingual-609
91Score Canadian English-368
91Score Canadian English-609
91Score Rookie/Traded-59T
91Stadium Club-146
91Topps-299
Team Scoring Leaders-9
91Upper Deck-136
91Upper Deck-535
French-136
French-535
92Bowman-203A
92Bowman-203B
92Bowman-329
92Canadiens Postcards-6
92Durivage Panini-20
92McDonald's Upper Deck-4
92O-Pee-Chee-192
92OPC Premier-3
92Panini Stickers-104
92Panini Stickers French-104
92Parkhurst-86
92Parkhurst-496
Emerald Ice-86
Emerald Ice-496
92Pinnacle-261
92Pinnacle-349
French-261
French-349
92Pro Set Gold Team Leaders-5
92Score-170
Canadian-170
92Stadium Club-191
92Topps-55
Gold-55G
92Ultra-103
92Upper Deck-6
92Upper Deck-307
92Upper Deck-476
93Canadiens Molson-4
93Canadiens Postcards-6
93Donruss-172
93Durivage Score-11
93Kraft Recipes-1
93Kraft Recipes French-1
93Leaf-4
93O-Pee-Chee Canadiens Hockey Fest-38
93OPC Premier-233
Gold-233
Black Gold-2
93Panini Stickers-13
93Parkhurst-104
Emerald Ice-104
93Pinnacle-85
93Pinnacle-232
Canadian-85
Canadian-232
Team Pinnacle-10
Team Canadian-10
93PowerPlay-127
93Score-244
Canadian-244
93Stadium Club-240
Members Only Master Set-240
OPC-240
First Day Issue-240
First Day Issue OPC-240
93Topps/OPC Premier-233
Gold-233
93Ultra-79
93Upper Deck-295
93Upper Deck-380
Hat Tricks-HT8
NHLPA/Roots-25
SP-77
94Be A Player-R102
94Be A Player-R112
Signature Cards-120
94Canada Games NHL POGS-133
94Canadiens Postcards-6
94Donruss-226
94EA Sports-70
94Finest-98
Super Team Winners-98
Refractors-98
94Flair-87
94Fleer-103
94Hockey Wit-72
94Kraft-16
94Leaf-69
94Leaf Limited-90
94McDonald's Upper Deck-McD29
94OPC Premier-65
Special Effects-65
94Parkhurst-115
Gold-115
Vintage-V23
94Pinnacle I Hobby Samples-4
94Pinnacle-4
Artist's Proofs-4
Rink Collection-4
Northern Lights-NL3
94Score-165
Gold-165
Platinum-165
90 Plus Club-20
94Select-59
Gold-59
94SP-58
Die Cuts-58
94Topps/OPC Premier-65
Special Effects-65
94Topps Finest Inserts-22
94Ultra-107
94Upper Deck-280
Electric Ice-280
SP Inserts-SP39
SP Inserts Die Cuts-SP39
95Bashan Super Stickers-62
95Bashan Super Stickers-67
95Canada Games NHL POGS-148
95Canadiens Postcards-6
95Canadiens Sheets-11
95Collector's Choice-320
Player's Club-320
Player's Club Platinum-320
95Donruss-202
95Donruss Elite-96
Die Cut Stars-96
Die Cut Uncut-96
95Emotion-87
95Finest-52
Refractors-52
95Hoyle Eastern Playing Cards-10
95Imperial Stickers-67
95Leaf-302
95Leaf Limited-4
95Metal-76
95Panini Stickers-38
95Parkhurst International-110
Emerald Ice-110
95Pinnacle-84
Artist's Proofs-84
Rink Collection-84
95Playoff One on One-53
95Post Upper Deck-4
95Pro Magnets-22
95Score-36
Black Ice Artist's Proofs-36
Black Ice-36
95Select Certified-75
Mirror Gold-75
95SkyBox Impact-84
95SP-75
95Stadium Club-159
Members Only Master Set-159
95Summit-64
Artist's Proofs-64
Ice-64
95Topps-270
OPC Inserts-270
Power Lines-9PL
95Ultra-80
Gold Medallion-80
95Upper Deck-66
Electric Ice-66
Electric Ice Gold-66
Special Edition-SE133
Special Edition Gold-SE133
95Zenith-77
95German DEL-443
96Black Diamond-25
Gold-25
96Canadiens Postcards-11
96Canadiens Sheets-7
96Collector's Choice-138
96Donruss-35
Press Proofs-35
96Donruss Canadian Ice-53
Gold Press Proofs-53
Red Press Proofs-53
96Duracell L'Equipe Beliveau-JB15
96Flair-47
Blue Ice-47
96Fleer-53
96Fleer Picks-36
96Hockey Greats Coins-5
Gold-5
96Kraft Upper Deck-37
96Leaf-79
Press Proofs-79
96Leaf Limited-84
Gold-84
96Leaf Preferred-25
Press Proofs-25
96Maggers-19
96Metal Universe-79
96NHL Aces Playing Cards-9
96NHL Pro Stamps-22
96Pinnacle-72
Artist's Proofs-72
Foil-72
Premium Stock-72
Rink Collection-72
96Post Upper Deck-4
96Score-50
Artist's Proofs-50
Dealer's Choice Artist's Proofs-50
Special Artist's Proofs-50
Golden Blades-50
96Select Certified-37
Artist's Proofs-37
Blue-37
Mirror Blue-37
Mirror Gold-37
Mirror Red-37
Red-37
96SkyBox Impact-61
96Summit-136
Artist's Proofs-136
Ice-136
Metal-136
Premium Stock-136
96Ultra-86
Gold Medallion-86
96Upper Deck-86
96Upper Deck Ice-32
Parallel-32
96Zenith-100
Artist's Proofs-100
97Be A Player-157
Autographs-157
Autographs Die-Cuts-157
Autographs Prismatic Die-Cuts-157
97Canadiens Postcards-9
97Collector's Choice-130
Star Quest-SQ32
97Crown Royale-68
Emerald Green-68
Ice Blue-68
Silver-68
97Donruss-173
Press Proofs Silver-173
Press Proofs Gold-173
97Donruss Canadian Ice-115
Dominion Series-115
Provincial Series-115
National Pride-29
97Donruss Elite-81
Aspirations-81
Status-81
97Donruss Limited-137
Exposure-137
97Donruss Preferred-140
Cut to the Chase-140
97Donruss Priority-164
Stamp of Approval-164
97Gatorade Stickers-1
97Katch-74
Gold-74
Silver-74
97Kraft-1
97Kraft 3-D World's Best-7
97Leaf-109
Fractal Matrix-109
Fractal Matrix Die Cuts-109
97Leaf International-109
Universal Ice-109
97McDonald's Upper Deck-21
97NHL Aces Playing Cards-47
97Pacific-25
Copper-25
Emerald Green-25
Ice Blue-25
Red-25
Silver-25
Slap Shots Die-Cuts-4B
97Pacific Dynagon-62
Copper-62
Dark Grey-62
Emerald Green-62
Ice Blue-62
Red-62
Silver-62
Best Kept Secrets-48
Tandems-46
97Pacific Invincible-70
Copper-70
Emerald Green-70
Ice Blue-70
Red-70
Silver-70
NHL Regime-102
97Pacific Omega-117
Copper-117
Dark Gray-117
Emerald Green-117
Gold-117
Ice Blue-117
97Panini Stickers-29
97Paramount-94
Copper-94
Dark Grey-94
Emerald Green-94
Ice Blue-94
Red-94
Silver-94
97Pinnacle-85
Artist's Proofs-85
Rink Collection-85
Press Plates Back Black-85
Press Plates Back Cyan-85
Press Plates Back Magenta-85
Press Plates Back Yellow-85
Press Plates Front Black-85
Press Plates Front Cyan-85
Press Plates Front Magenta-85
Press Plates Front Yellow-85
97Pinnacle Certified-72
Red-72
Mirror Blue-72
Mirror Gold-72
Mirror Red-72
97Pinnacle Inside-36
Coach's Collection-36
Executive Collection-36
97Pinnacle Tot Cert Platinum Blue-72
97Pinnacle Tot Cert Platinum Gold-72
97Pinnacle Totally Certified Platinum Red-72
97Pinnacle Tot Cert Mirror Platinum Gold-72
97Post Pinnacle-9
97Revolution-70
Copper-70
Emerald-70
Ice Blue-70
Silver-70
97Score-112
Artist's Proofs-112
Golden Blades-112
Check It-11
97Score Canadiens-4
Platinum-4
Premier-4
97SP Authentic-82
97Studio-76
Press Proofs Silver-76
Press Proofs Gold-76
97Upper Deck-86
97Zenith-39
Z-Gold-39
Z-Silver-39
97Zenith 5 x 7-57
Gold Impulse-57
Silver Impulse-57
98SLU Hockey-60
98Aurora-93
98Be A Player-217
Press Release-217
98BAP Gold-217
98BAP Autographs-217
98BAP Autographs Gold-217
98Black Diamond-43
Double Diamond-43
Triple Diamond-43
Quadruple Diamond-43
98Bowman's Best-14
Refractors-14
Atomic Refractors-14
98Canadiens Team Issue-4
98Crown Royale-68
Limited Series-68
98Finest-9
No Protectors-9
No Protectors Refractors-9
Refractors-9
98Katch-74
98Kenner Starting Lineup Cards-7
98Kraft Fearless Forwards-3
98OPC Chrome-118
Refractors-118
98Pacific-250
Ice Blue-250
Red-250
98Pacific Dynagon Ice-95
Blue-95
Red-95
98Pacific Omega-120
Red-120
Opening Day Issue-120
98Panini Photocards-17
98Paramount-112
Copper-112
Emerald Green-112
Holo-Electric-112
Ice Blue-112
Silver-112
98Revolution-72
Ice Shadow-72
Red-72
98SP Authentic-43
Power Shift-43
98SPx Top Prospects-32
Radiance-32
Spectrum-32
98Topps-118
O-Pee-Chee-118
98Topps Gold Label Class 1-67
Black-67
Black One of One-67
One of One-67
Red-67
Red One of One-67
98Topps Gold Label Class 2-67
98Topps Gold Label Class 2 Black-67
98Topps Gold Label Class 2 Black 1 of 1-67
98Topps Gold Label Class 2 One of One-67
98Topps Gold Label Class 2 Red-67
98Topps Gold Label Class 2 Red One of One-67
98Topps Gold Label Class 3-67
98Topps Gold Label Class 3 Black-67
98Topps Gold Label Class 3 Black 1 of 1-67
98Topps Gold Label Class 3 One of One-67
98Topps Gold Label Class 3 Red-67
98Topps Gold Label Class 3 Red One of One-67
98UD Choice-110
Prime Choice Reserve-110
Reserve-110
98Upper Deck-110
Exclusives-110
Exclusives 1 of 1-110
Gold Reserve-110
98Upper Deck MVP-101
Gold Script-101
Silver Script-101
Super Script-101
99Aurora-119
Striped-119
Premiere Date-119
Premiere Date Striped-119
99BAP Memorabilia-269
Gold-269
Silver-269
99Crown Royale-122
Limited Series-122
Premiere Date-122
99Pacific-369
Copper-369
Emerald Green-369
Gold-369
Ice Blue-369
Premiere Date-369
Red-369
99Pacific Dynagon Ice-171
Blue-171
Copper-171
Gold-171
Premiere Date-171
99Pacific Omega-204
Copper-204
Gold-204
Ice Blue-204
Premiere Date-204
99Pacific Prism-123
Holographic Blue-123
Holographic Gold-123
Holographic Mirror-123
Holographic Purple-123
Premiere Date-123
99Panini Stickers-303
99Paramount-203
Copper-203
Emerald-203
Gold-203
Holographic Emerald-203
Holographic Gold-203
Holographic Silver-203
Ice Blue-203
Premiere Date-203
Red-203
Silver-203
Ice Alliance-24
99Revolution-126
Premiere Date-126
Red-126
Shadow Series-126
99SPx-126
Radiance-126
Spectrum-126
99Stadium Club-123
First Day Issue-123
One of a Kind-123
Printing Plates Black-123
Printing Plates Cyan-123
Printing Plates Magenta-123
Printing Plates Yellow-123
99Topps Gold Label Class 1-79
Black-79
Black One of One-79
One of One-79
Red-79
Red One of One-79
99Topps Gold Label Class 2-79
99Topps Gold Label Class 2 Black-79
99Topps Gold Label Class 2 Black 1 of 1-79
99Topps Gold Label Class 2 One of One-79
99Topps Gold Label Class 2 Red-79
99Topps Gold Label Class 2 Red One of One-79
99Topps Gold Label Class 3-79
99Topps Gold Label Class 3 Black-79
99Topps Gold Label Class 3 Black 1 of 1-79
99Topps Gold Label Class 3 One of One-79
99Topps Gold Label Class 3 Red-79
99Topps Gold Label Class 3 Red One of One-79
99Upper Deck-106
Exclusives-106
Exclusives 1 of 1-106
99Upper Deck Gold Reserve-106
99Upper Deck MVP-173
Gold Script-173
Silver Script-173
Super Script-173
99Upper Deck MVP SC Edition-156
Gold Script-156
Silver Script-156
Super Script-156
99Upper Deck Retro-67
Gold-67
Platinum-67
99Upper Deck Victory-247
99Wayne Gretzky Hockey-152
00Aurora-126
Premiere Date-126
00BAP Memorabilia-270
Emerald-270
Ruby-270
Sapphire-270
Promos-270
00BAP Mem Chicago Sportsfest Copper-270
00BAP Memorabilia Chicago Sportsfest Blue-270
00BAP Memorabilia Chicago Sportsfest Gold-270
00BAP Memorabilia Chicago Sportsfest Ruby-270
00BAP Memorabilia Chicago Sun-Times Ruby-270
00BAP Memorabilia Chicago Sun-Times Gold-270
00BAP Mem Chicago Sun-Times Sapphire-270
00BAP Mem Toronto Fall Expo Copper-270
00BAP Memorabilia Toronto Fall Expo Gold-270
00BAP Memorabilia Toronto Fall Expo Ruby-270
00BAP Parkhurst 2000-P40
00BAP Signature Series-161
Emerald-161
Ruby-161
Sapphire-161
Autographs-108
Autographs Gold-108
00O-Pee-Chee-178
00O-Pee-Chee Parallel-178
00Pacific-356
Copper-356
Gold-356
Ice Blue-356
Premiere Date-356
00Panini Stickers-200
00Paramount-212
Copper-212
Gold-212
Holo-Gold-212
Holo-Silver-212
Ice Blue-212
Premiere Date-212
00Private Stock-87
Gold-87
Premiere Date-87
Retail-87
Silver-87
Game Gear-91
Game Gear-92
00Revolution-127
Blue-127
Premiere Date-127
Red-127
00Stadium Club-183
00Titanium-84
Blue-84
Gold-84
Premiere Date-84
Red-84
Retail-84
00Titanium Draft Day Edition-91
Patches-91
00Topps/OPC-178
Parallel-178
00Topps Chrome-119
OPC Refractors-119
Refractors-119
00UD Heroes-98
00Upper Deck-373
Exclusives Tier 1-373
Exclusives Tier 2-373
00Upper Deck MVP-152
First Stars-152
Second Stars-152
Third Stars-152
00Upper Deck Victory-192
00Upper Deck Vintage-300
00Vanguard-86
Holographic Gold-86
Holographic Purple-86
Pacific Proofs-86
01BAP Memorabilia-29
Emerald-29
Ruby-29
Sapphire-29
Country of Origin-CO45
01BAP Signature Series-195
Autographs-195
Autographs Gold-195
01BAP Ultimate Memorabilia Dynamic Duos-16
01Bowman YoungStars-104
Gold-104
Ice Cubed-104
01Crown Royale-123
Blue-123
Premiere Date-123
Red-123
Retail-123
01O-Pee-Chee-222
01O-Pee-Chee-323
01O-Pee-Chee Premier Parallel-222
01O-Pee-Chee Premier Parallel-323
01Pacific-336
Extreme LTD-336
Hobby LTD-336
Premiere Date-336
Retail LTD-336
Jerseys-33
01Pacific Arena Exclusives-336
01Parkhurst-175
01Private Stock Game Gear-91
01Private Stock Game Gear Patches-91
01Sharks Postcards-2
01SP Authentic-74
Limited-74
Limited Gold-74
01Titanium-121
Hobby Parallel-121
Premiere Date-121
Retail-121
Retail Parallel-121
01Topps-222
01Topps-323
OPC Parallel-222
OPC Parallel-323
01Topps Chrome-77
Refractors-77
Black Border Refractors-77
01UD Mask Collection-80
Gold-80
01Upper Deck-378
Exclusives-378
01Upper Deck MVP-157
01Upper Deck Victory-296
Gold-296
01Upper Deck Vintage-214
01Upper Deck Vintage-217
02BAP All-Star Edition-16
Jerseys-16
Jerseys Gold-16
Jerseys Silver-16
02BAP First Edition-122
02BAP First Edition-392
Jerseys-122
02BAP Memorabilia-167
Emerald-167
Ruby-167
Sapphire-167
All-Star Starting Lineup-AS-4
NHL All-Star Game-167
NHL All-Star Game Blue-167
NHL All-Star Game Green-167
NHL All-Star Game Red-167
02BAP Memorabilia Toronto Fall Expo-167
02BAP Signature Series-23
Autographs-23
Autograph Buybacks 1998-217
Autograph Buybacks 2000-108
Autograph Buybacks 2001-195
Autographs Gold-23
Team Quads-TQ18
02BAP Ultimate Memorabilia All-Star MVP-21
02Bowman YoungStars-57
Gold-57
Silver-57
02Crown Royale-84
Blue-84
Red-84
Retail-84
02Nextel NHL All-Star Game-2
02O-Pee-Chee-210
02O-Pee-Chee Premier Blue Parallel-210
02O-Pee-Chee Premier Red Parallel-210
02O-Pee-Chee Factory Set-210
02Pacific-332
Blue-332
Red-332
02Pacific Complete-214
Red-214
02Pacific Exclusive-148
02Parkhurst-9
Bronze-9
Gold-9
Silver-9
Milestones-MS6
02Parkhurst Retro-77
Minis-77
02Private Stock Reserve-86
Blue-86
Red-86
Retail-86
02Sharks Team Issue-1
02SP Game Used-56
02Topps-210
OPC Blue Parallel-210
OPC Red Parallel-210
Factory Set-210
02Topps Chrome-118
Black Border Refractors-118
Refractors-118
02Topps Heritage-68
Chrome Parallel-68
02Topps Total-269
02Upper Deck-391
Exclusives-391
All-Star Jerseys-ASVD
All-Star Performers-ASVD
02Upper Deck Beckett UD Promos-391
02Upper Deck MVP-151
Gold-151
Classics-151
Golden Classics-151
02Upper Deck Victory-176
Bronze-176
Gold-176
Silver-176
02Upper Deck Vintage-208
Green Backs-208
03BAP Ultimate Memorabilia Autographs-26
Gold-26
03Beehive-165
Gold-165
Silver-165
03ITG Action-405
Jerseys-M99
03ITG Used Signature Series-87

Gold-87
Autographs-VD
Autographs Gold-VD
03NHL Sticker Collection-283
03O-Pee-Chee-114
03OPC Blue-114
03OPC Gold-114
03OPC Red-114
03Pacific-293
Blue-293
Red-293
03Pacific Complete-139
Red-139
03Pacific Exhibit-128
Blue Backs-128
Yellow Backs-128
03Pacific Supreme Generations-10
03Parkhurst Original Six Montreal-73
03Parkhurst Original Six Toronto-34
03Private Stock Reserve-89
Blue-89
Red-89
Retail-89
03Sharks Postcards-2
03SP Authentic-73
Limited-73
03Titanium-87
Hobby Jersey Number Parallels-87
Retail-87
Retail Jersey Number Parallels-87
03Topps-114
Blue-114
Gold-114
Red-114
03UD Honor Roll-72
03Upper Deck-157
Canadian Exclusives-157
HG-157
03Upper Deck Ice-71
Gold-71
03Upper Deck MVP-344
Gold Script-344
Silver Script-344
Canadian Exclusives-344
SportsNut-SN74
03Upper Deck Rookie Update-71
03Upper Deck Victory-156
Bronze-156
Gold-156
Silver-156
04Pacific-227
Blue-227
Red-227
04SP Authentic-139
05Be A Player Quad Signatures-COLO
05Be A Player Signatures-VD
05Be A Player Signatures Gold-VD
05Upper Deck Big Playmakers-B-VD
05Upper Deck Patches-P-VD
05Upper Deck MVP Materials-M-VD

Dampier, Alex
93UK Sheffield Steelers-16
94UK Sheffield Steelers-1
95UK Sheffield Steelers-21
97UK Sheffield Steelers-24
00UK Nottingham Panthers-29
00UK Sekonda Superleague-124
01UK Nottingham Panthers-23

Dams, Jeff
04Huntsville Havoc-9

Dan, Steeler
94UK Sheffield Steelers-20
95UK Sheffield Steelers-24
97UK Sheffield Steelers-23
00UK Sheffield Steelers-13
05SP Game Used Auto Draft-AD-DF

Danby, John
72Whalers New England WHA-4

Dancause, Carl
93Quebec Pee-Wee Tournament-11

Dance, John
97Peoria Rivermen-14

Dandenault, Eric
907th Inn. Sketch QMJHL-10
91ProCards-277
917th Inn. Sketch Memorial Cup-53
96Cincinnati Cyclones-37
97Cincinnati Cyclones-4
98Cincinnati Cyclones-4
98Cincinnati Cyclones 2-13
99Cincinnati Cyclones-4
02German DEL City Press-6
03German DEL-20
04German DEL-44
04German Dusseldorf Metro Stars Postcards-3

Dandenault, Mathieu
93Sherbrooke Faucons-2
95Bowman-114
All-Foil-114
95Donruss-234
95Leaf Limited-37
95Parkhurst International-335
Emerald Ice-335
95SP-43
95Stadium Club-213
Members Only Master Set-213
95Upper Deck-497
Electric Ice-497
Electric Ice Gold-497
96Be A Player-95
Autographs-95
Autographs Silver-95
98Upper Deck-84
Exclusives-84
Exclusives 1 of 1-84
Gold Reserve-84
99BAP Millennium-95
Emerald-95
Ruby-95
Sapphire-95
Signatures-95
Signatures Gold-95
99O-Pee-Chee-165
99O-Pee-Chee Chrome-165
99O-Pee-Chee Chrome Refractors-165
99Topps Arena Giveaways-DET-MD
99Topps/OPC-165
99Topps/OPC Chrome-165
Refractors-165
00Paramount-84
Copper-84
Gold-84
Holo-Gold-84
Holo-Silver-84
Ice Blue-84
Premiere Date-84
00Titanium Game Gear-95
00Titanium Game Gear Patches-95
00Titanium Draft Day Edition-37
Patches-37
01Atomic Jerseys-21
01Atomic Patches-21
01Crown Royale Triple Threads-6
01Pacific Jerseys-13
01Pacific Heads-Up Quad Jerseys-11
01UD Stanley Cup Champs-59
01Upper Deck-293
Exclusives-293
01Upper Deck Victory-125
Gold-125
02BAP Memorabilia Stanley Cup Champions-SCC-2
02BAP Sig Series Auto Buybacks 1999-95
02BAP Ultimate Mem Dynasty Jerseys-13
02BAP Ultimate Mem Dynasty Emblems-13
02BAP Ultimate Mem Dynasty Numbers-13
02Pacific Complete-371
Red-371
02Topps Total-240
02Upper Deck-308
Exclusives-308
02Upper Deck Beckett UD Promos-308
03ITG Action-296
03Parkhurst Original Six Detroit-3
Memorabilia-DM7
05Be A Player Signatures-MD
05Be A Player Signatures Gold-MD
05Canadiens Team Issue-6
05Panini Stickers-77
05Parkhurst-267
Facsimile Auto Parallel-267
05Upper Deck MVP-212
Gold-212
Platinum-212
06Canadiens Postcards-6
06O-Pee-Chee-272
Rainbow-272
06Upper Deck-106
Exclusives Parallel-106
High Gloss Parallel-106
Masterpieces-106

Dandurand, Leo
24Anonymous NHL-15
27La Patrie-16
27La Presse Photos-16
83Hall of Fame Postcards-G5
85Hall of Fame-96

Daneau, Pierre-Luc
00Victoriaville Tigres-7
Signed-7

Danecek, Jan
04Victoriaville Tigres-4
05Shawinigan Cataractes-22
05Victoriaville Tigres-9
06Czech OFS-153
Brothers-3

Danecek, Lukas
05Czech HC Trinec-2
06Czech OFS-154
Brothers-3

Daneyko, Ken
83Devils Postcards-8
86Devils Police-9
87Panini Stickers-76
88Devils Caretta-9
89Devils Caretta-9
89O-Pee-Chee-243
89Panini Stickers-258
90Devils Team Issue-10
90Pro Set-165
90Score-178
Canadian-178
90Upper Deck-427
French-427
91Bowman-284
91O-Pee-Chee-118
91Panini Stickers-218
91Parkhurst-317
French-317
91Pinnacle-142
French-142
91Pro Set-139
French-139
91Score American-46
91Score Canadian Bilingual-46
91Score Canadian English-46
91Stadium Club-103
91Topps-118
91Upper Deck-435
French-435
92Parkhurst-332
Emerald Ice-332
92Pinnacle-354
French-354
92Score-53
Canadian-53
92Topps-357
Gold-357G
92Ultra-335
92Upper Deck-259
93OPC Premier-236
Gold-236
93Parkhurst-387
Emerald Ice-387
93Pinnacle-134
Canadian-134
93Score-286
Canadian-286
93Stadium Club-206
Members Only Master Set-206
OPC-206
First Day Issue-206
First Day Issue OPC-206
93Topps/OPC Premier-236
Gold-236
93Ultra-358
94Leaf-336
94OPC Premier-79
Special Effects-79
94Parkhurst-131
Gold-131
94Pinnacle-330
Artist's Proofs-330
Rink Collection-330
94Score-142
Gold-142
Platinum-142
94Topps/OPC Premier-79
Special Effects-79
94Ultra-318
95Be A Player-48
Signatures-S48
Signatures Die Cuts-S48
95Pinnacle-177
Artist's Proofs-177
Rink Collection-177
95Topps-188
OPC Inserts-188
95Ultra-189
Gold Medallion-189
96Devils Team Issue-3
97Devils Team Issue-3
97Pacific-325
Copper-325
Emerald Green-325
Ice Blue-325
Red-325
Silver-325
97Score Devils-20
Platinum-20
Premier-20
97Upper Deck-305
98Devils Team Issue-8
98OPC Chrome-101
Refractors-101
98Topps-101
O-Pee-Chee-101
99Devils Team Issue-3
99Pacific-236
Copper-236
Emerald Green-236
Gold-236
Ice Blue-236
Premiere Date-236
Red-236
99Panini Stickers-85
99Russian Fetisov Tribute-25
00Devils Team Issue-5
00Upper Deck NHLPA-PA52
02Devils Team Issue-1
02Topps Total-220
03ITG Action-351
03Upper Deck MVP-262
Gold Script-262
Silver Script-262
Canadian Exclusives-262
06Devils Team Set-40

Daniel, Adrian
93Quebec Pee-Wee Tournament-1559

Daniel, Jarrod
917th Inn. Sketch WHL-184
94Spokane Chiefs-2

Daniel, Tom
93Quebec Pee-Wee Tournament-1271

Daniels, Bob
91Ferris State Bulldogs-9
92Ferris State Bulldogs-9

Daniels, Jeff
88ProCards IHL-47
89ProCards IHL-146
91Penguins Coke/Elby's-43
91Score American-400
91Score Canadian Bilingual-290
91Score Canadian English-290
91Upper Deck-564
French-564
91ProCards-298
92OPC Premier-58
92Parkhurst-492
Emerald Ice-492
92Penguins Coke/Clark-4
92Ultra-377
92Upper Deck-508
93Leaf-251
93OPC Premier-343
Gold-343
93Parkhurst-429
Emerald Ice-429
93Penguins Foodland-11
93Stadium Club-483
Members Only Master Set-483
First Day Issue-483
93Topps/OPC Premier-343
Gold-343
93Upper Deck-87
96Springfield Falcons-27
98Milwaukee Admirals-2
99UK Basingstoke Bison-21
00BAP Memorabilia-90
Emerald-90
Ruby-90
Sapphire-90
Promos-90
00BAP Mem Chicago Sportsfest Copper-90
00BAP Memorabilia Chicago Sportsfest Blue-90
00BAP Memorabilia Chicago Sportsfest Gold-90
00BAP Memorabilia Chicago Sportsfest Ruby-90
00BAP Memorabilia Chicago Sun-Times Ruby-90
00BAP Memorabilia Chicago Sun-Times Gold-90
00BAP Mem Chicago Sun-Times Sapphire-90
00BAP Mem Toronto Fall Expo Copper-90
00BAP Memorabilia Toronto Fall Expo Gold-90
00BAP Memorabilia Toronto Fall Expo Ruby-90
06Hurricanes Postcards-9

Daniels, Kimbi
907th Inn. Sketch WHL-46
907th Inn. Sketch WHL-72
91Flyers J.C. Penney-5
91Parkhurst-346
French-346
91Pinnacle-336
French-336
91Score American-399
91Score Canadian Bilingual-289
91Score Canadian English-289
91Upper Deck-492
91Upper Deck-687
French-492
French-687
91Upper Deck Czech World Juniors-61
92Stadium Club-453
92Upper Deck-75
96Charlotte Checkers-5
99Tallahassee Tiger Sharks-11
01Anchorage Aces-3
03Alaska Aces-2

Daniels, Mark
91Air Canada SJHL-D21

Daniels, Ryan
05ITG Heroes/Prosp Toronto Expo Parallel -289
05Saginaw Spirit-7
05ITG Heroes and Prospects-289
Autographs Series II-RD
Team Orr-TO6
06Between The Pipes-45
Autographs-ARD
Emblems-GUE24
Emblems Gold-GUE24
Emblems Autographs-GUE24
Jerseys-GUJ24
Jerseys Gold-GUJ24
Jerseys Autographs-GUJ24
Numbers-GUN24
Numbers Gold-GUN24
Numbers Autographs-GUN24
Prospect Trios-PT11
Prospect Trios Gold-PT11
06Saginaw Spirit-5
06ITG Heroes and Prospects-114
Autographs-ARDA
CHL Top Prospects-TP13
CHL Top Prospects Gold-TP13

Daniels, Scott
86Kamloops Blazers-5
88Regina Pats-3
89Regina Pats-3
90ProCards AHL/IHL-192
91ProCards-112
95Upper Deck-328
Electric Ice-328
Electric Ice Gold-328
95Whalers Bob's Stores-5
96Be A Player-170
Autographs-170
Autographs Silver-170
96Flyers Postcards-4
97Be A Player-116
Autographs-116
Autographs Die-Cuts-116
Autographs Prismatic Die-Cuts-116
97Devils Team Issue-17
98Be A Player-229
Press Release-229
98BAP Gold-229
98BAP Autographs-229
98BAP Autographs Gold-229
02BAP Sig Series Auto Buybacks 1998-229

Daniels, Tyson
04Langley Hornets-9

Daniels, Wayne
91Oshawa Generals-22

Danielsmeier, Colin
01German Upper Deck-117
02German DEL City Press-69
04German DEL-167
05German DEL-163

Danielsson, Ake
69Swedish Hockey-115
70Swedish Hockey-72
71Swedish Hockey-161
72Swedish Stickers-156
73Swedish Stickers-209
74Swedish Stickers-165

Danielsson, Bert
69Swedish Hockey-276

Danielsson, Bjorn
95Collector's Choice-342
Player's Club-342
Player's Club Platinum-342
00Swedish Upper Deck-11
01Swedish Brynas Tigers-5
02Swedish SHL-9
Parallel-9
03Swedish Elite-10
Silver-10
04Swedish Elitset-10
Gold-10
Signatures Series A-12
05Swedish SHL Elitset-9
06Swedish SHL Elitset-154

Danielsson, Gert
69Swedish Hockey-277

Danielsson, Jan
71Swedish Hockey-209
72Swedish Stickers-186

Danielsson, Jimmy
04Swedish Elitset-278
Gold-278

Danielsson, Lars
70Swedish Hockey-3
71Swedish Hockey-77
72Swedish Stickers-52
73Swedish Stickers-182
74Swedish Stickers-164

Danielsson, Martin
92Swedish Semic Elitserien Stickers-134

Danielsson, Nicklas
03Swedish Elite-150
Silver-150
04Swedish Elitset-151
Future Stars-6
Gold-151
06Swedish SHL Elitset-169

Danilov, Alexei
98Russian Hockey League-167
02Russian Hockey League-160

Danis, Yann
04SP Authentic Rookie Redemptions-RR37
04Hamilton Bulldogs-5
04ITG Heroes and Prospects-182
04ITG Heroes/Prosp Toronto Expo '05-182
05ITG Heroes/Prosp Toronto Expo Parallel -53
05Beehive-124
Beige -124
Blue -124
Gold-124
Red -124
Matte-124
Signature Scrapbook-SSYD
05Black Diamond-206
Emerald-206
Gold-206
Onyx-206
Ruby-206
05Canadiens Team Issue-7
05Hot Prospects-245
En Fuego-245
Hot Materials-HMYD
Red Hot-245
White Hot-245
05Parkhurst-635
Facsimile Auto Parallel-635
Signatures-YD
True Colors-TCMTL
True Colors-TCMTL
05SP Authentic-164
Limited-164
Rarefied Rookies-RRYD
Rookie Authentics-RAYD
Sign of the Times Duals-DTD
Sign of the Times Triples-TRTD
Sign of the Times Fives-TWLDH
Six Star Signatures-SSGO
05SP Game Used-110
Autographs-110
Gold-110
Game Gear-GG-YD
Game Gear Autographs-AG-YD
Rookie Exclusives-YD
Rookie Exclusives Silver-RE-YD
Significant Numbers-SN-YD
05SPx-160
Spectrum-160
Xcitement Rookies-XR-YD
Xcitement Rookies Gold-XR-YD
Xcitement Rookies Spectrum-XR-YD
05The Cup-132
Autographed Rookie Patches Gold Rainbow-132
Black Rainbow Rookies-132
Masterpiece Pressplates (Artifacts)-233
Masterpiece Pressplates (Bee Hive)-124
Masterpiece Pressplates (Black Diamond)-206
Masterpiece Pressplates (Ice)-132
Masterpiece Pressplates (MVP)-400
Masterpiece Pressplates (Power Play)-145
Masterpiece Pressplates (Power Play)-145
Masterpiece Pressplates (Rookie Update)-213
Masterpiece Pressplates SPA Autos-164
Masterpiece Pressplates (SP Game Used)-110
Masterpiece Pressplates SPx Autos-160
Masterpiece Pressplates (Trilogy)-195
Masterpiece Pressplates Ult Coll Autos-120
Masterpiece Pressplates (Victory)-260
Masterpiece Pressplates Autographs-132
Platinum Rookies-132
05UD Artifacts-233
Gold-RED33
05UD PowerPlay-145
05UD Rookie Class-39
05Ultimate Collection-120
Autographed Patches-120
Autographed Shields-120
Jerseys Dual-DJTD
Ultimate Debut Threads Jerseys-DTJYD
Ultimate Debut Threads Jerseys Autos-DAJYD
Ultimate Debut Threads Patches-DTPYD
Ultimate Debut Threads Patches Autos-DAPYD
Ultimate Patches Dual-DPTD
Ultimate Signatures-USYD
Ultimate Signatures Logos-SLYD
Ultimate Signatures Pairings-UPTD
Ultimate Signatures Trios-UTLTD
05Ultra-223
Gold-223
Fresh Ink-FI-YD
Fresh Ink Blue-FI-YD
Ice-223
Rookie Uniformity Jerseys-RU-YD
Rookie Uniformity Jersey Autographs-ARU-YD
Rookie Uniformity Patches-RUP-YD
Rookie Uniformity Patch Autographs-ARP-YD
05Upper Deck-227
HG Glossy-227
Rookie Ink-RIYD
05Upper Deck Rookie Showcase-RS31
05Upper Deck Rookie Showcase Promos-RS31
05Upper Deck Rookie Threads-RTYD
05Upper Deck Rookie Threads Autographs-ARTYD
05Upper Deck Ice-132
Fresh Ice-FIYD
Fresh Ice Glass-FIYD
Fresh Ice Glass Patches-FIPYD
Premieres Auto Patches-AIPYD
05Upper Deck MVP-400
Gold-400
Platinum-400
05Upper Deck Rookie Update-213
Inspirations Patch Rookies-213
05Upper Deck Trilogy-195
05Upper Deck Toronto Fall Expo-227
05Upper Deck Victory-260
Black-260
Gold-260
Silver-260
05AHL All-Stars-4
05AHL Top Prospects-9
05Hamilton Bulldogs-6
05ITG Heroes and Prospects-53
Autographs-A-YD
Autographs-DA-DT
06Be A Player Portraits First Exposures-FEYD
06Between The Pipes-54
Autographs-AYD
Emblems-GUE25
Emblems Gold-GUE25
Emblems Autographs-GUE25
Jerseys-GUJ25
Jerseys Gold-GUJ25
Jerseys Autographs-GUJ25
Numbers-GUN25
Numbers Gold-GUN25
Numbers Autographs-GUN25
Prospect Trios-PT15
Prospect Trios Gold-PT15
06Upper Deck Signatures-SYD
06Upper Deck Victory Next In Line-NL29
06Hamilton Bulldogs-8
06ITG Heroes and Prospects-36
AHL All-Star Jerseys-AJ05
AHL All-Star Jerseys Gold-AJ05
AHL All-Star Emblems-AE05
AHL All-Star Emblems Gold-AE05
AHL All-Star Numbers-AN05
AHL All-Star Numbers Gold-AN05
Autographs-AYD
Complete AHL Logos-AHL03
Jerseys-GUJ10
Jerseys Gold-GUJ10
Emblems-GUE10
Emblems Gold-GUE10
Numbers-GUN10
Numbers Gold-GUN10

Danis-Papin, Simon
05Maine Black Bears-5

Dannel, Olivier
00Chicoutimi Sagueneens-1
Signed-1
00Hull Olympiques-22
Signed-22

Danner, David
99German Bundesliga 2-110
03German DEL-49
04German Augsburg Panthers Postcards-10
04German DEL-40
05German DEL-19

Danner, Simon
05German DEL-99

Dano, Jozef
95Slovakian APS National Team-25
96Czech APS Extraliga-68
96Swedish Semic Wien-236
97Czech APS Extraliga-328
97Czech DS Extraliga-113
97Czech DS Stickers-238
98Czech DS-121
98Czech DS Stickers-279
98Czech OFS-390
99Czech OFS-404
00Czech DS Extraliga-69
00Czech OFS-225
01Slovakian Kvarteto-1B

Danowski, Derek
04Green Bay Gamblers-3

Dansereau, Keegan
04Calgary Hitmen-4
05Calgary Hitmen-4

Danskin, Richard
96UK Fife Flyers-14

Dantinne, Luc
93Quebec Pee-Wee Tournament-1082

Danton, Mike (Jefferson)
98Barrie Colts-19
00Albany River Rats-11
01BAP Memorabilia-217
Emerald-217
Ruby-217
Sapphire-217
01SPx-114
01UD Top Shelf-58
01UD Top Shelf-58B
01Upper Deck-196
Exclusives-196
01Upper Deck MVP-206
01Upper Deck Victory-379
Gold-379
02Atomic-118
Blue-118
Gold-118
Red-118
Hobby Parallel-118
02Pacific Exclusive-184
Blue-184
Gold-184
02Pacific Heads-Up-140
03Blues Team Set-5
03Pacific Complete-589
Red-589
03Topps Traded-TT58
Blue-TT58
Gold-TT58
Red-TT58

Danyluk, Cam
89Portland Winter Hawks-4
907th Inn. Sketch WHL-210
907th Inn. Sketch WHL-320
917th Inn. Sketch WHL-335
917th Inn. Sketch Memorial Cup-84

Daoust, Andre
66Columbus Checkers-4

Daoust, Dan
82Canadiens Postcards-4
82Maple Leafs Postcards-7
83Maple Leafs Postcards-3
83NHL Key Tags-118
83O-Pee-Chee-328
83O-Pee-Chee Stickers-28
83O-Pee-Chee Stickers-29
83Topps Stickers-28
83Topps Stickers-29
83Vachon-83
84Kellogg's Accordion Discs-5B
84Kellogg's Accordion Discs Singles-8
84Maple Leafs Postcards-7
84O-Pee-Chee-299
84O-Pee-Chee Stickers-9
84O-Pee-Chee Stickers-10
84Topps-137
85Maple Leafs Postcards-9
85O-Pee-Chee-164
85O-Pee-Chee Stickers-11
85Topps-164
86Kraft Drawings-14
86O-Pee-Chee-241
86O-Pee-Chee Stickers-146
87Maple Leafs PLAY-20
87Maple Leafs Postcards-5
87Maple Leafs Postcards Oversized-5
88Maple Leafs PLAY-20
88O-Pee-Chee Stickers-169
88Panini Stickers-124
89O-Pee-Chee-277
89O-Pee-Chee Stickers-177
93Swiss HNL-449
95Swiss HNL-328
96Swiss HNL-304
96Swiss HNL-579

Daoust, Eddy
51Laval Dairy Lac St. Jean-1

Daoust, Eric
93Lakeland Ice Warriors-8
93Lakeland Ice Warriors-9

Daoust, Jean-Michel
00Hull Olympiques-17
Signed-17
01Hull Olympiques-19
02Hull Olympiques-18
03Gatineau Olympiques-6
03Hull Olympiques Memorial Cup-4
05Danbury Trashers-21

Dapuzzo, Pat
90Pro Set-684

Darbellay, Alain
95Swiss HNL-473

Darby, Craig
93Fredericton Canadiens-5
93Classic-62
94Upper Deck-452
Electric Ice-452
94Fredericton Canadiens-10
94Classic-86
Gold-86
Autographs-86
94Classic Pro Prospects-110
94Classic Four-Sport *-134
Gold-134
Autographs-134A
Printers Proofs-134
95Pinnacle-213
Artist's Proofs-213
Rink Collection-213
95Score-305
Black Ice Artist's Proofs-305
Black Ice-305
95Images-33
Gold-33
96Collector's Edge Ice-92
Prism-92
98Milwaukee Admirals-17
99Pacific Omega-117
Copper-117
Gold-117
Ice Blue-117
Premiere Date-117
00BAP Memorabilia-17
Emerald-17
Ruby-17
Sapphire-17
Promos-17
00BAP Mem Chicago Sportsfest Copper-17
00BAP Memorabilia Chicago Sportsfest Blue-17
00BAP Memorabilia Chicago Sportsfest Gold-17
00BAP Memorabilia Chicago Sportsfest Ruby-17
00BAP Memorabilia Chicago Sun-Times Ruby-17
00BAP Memorabilia Chicago Sun-Times Gold-17
00BAP Mem Chicago Sun-Times Sapphire-17
00BAP Mem Toronto Fall Expo Copper-17
00BAP Memorabilia Toronto Fall Expo Gold-17
00BAP Memorabilia Toronto Fall Expo Ruby-17
00BAP Signature Series-245
Emerald-245
Ruby-245
Sapphire-245
Autographs-197
Autographs Gold-197
00Canadiens Postcards-9
00Upper Deck-95
Exclusives Tier 1-95
Exclusives Tier 2-95
00Upper Deck Victory-191
Gold-191
01Quebec Citadelles-6
02BAP Sig Series Auto Buybacks 2000-197
02Devils Team Issue-7
02Albany River Rats-5
02Albany River Rats AAP-10
03Albany River Rats-9
03Albany River Rats Kinko's-8
04AHL All-Stars-10
04Springfield Falcons-6
05Manitoba Moose-7
06German DEL-3
Team Leaders-TL1

Darby, Kevin
93Fredericton Canadiens-6

Darby, Regan
00Kansas City Blades-7
01Manitoba Moose-7
02Columbia Inferno-101
02Manitoba Moose-8
04Las Vegas Wranglers-13
05UK Cardiff Devils-1
Gold-1
Silver-1
05UK Cardiff Devils Challenge Cup-21

Darche, Mathieu
00Syracuse Crunch-10
01BAP Memorabilia-238
Emerald-238
Ruby-238
Sapphire-238
01Crown Royale-153
01O-Pee-Chee-310
01O-Pee-Chee Premier Parallel-310
01Pacific-110
Extreme LTD-110
Hobby LTD-110
Premiere Date-110
Retail LTD-110
01Pacific Arena Exclusives-110
01SP Game Used-72
01SPx-137
01SPx-137
Rookie Treasures-RTDA
01Titanium Draft Day Edition-119
01Topps-310
OPC Parallel-310
01UD Premier Collection-59
01UD Top Shelf-53
01UD Top Shelf-53B
01Upper Deck-187
Exclusives-187
01Upper Deck MVP-197
01Upper Deck Victory-372
Gold-372
01Syracuse Crunch-8
02Syracuse Crunch-7
02Syracuse Crunch Sheets-13
03O-Pee-Chee-307
03OPC Blue-307
03OPC Gold-307
03OPC Red-307
03Topps-307
Blue-307
Gold-307
Red-307
03Milwaukee Admirals-17
03Milwaukee Admirals Postcards-2
04Hershey Bears Patriot News-9
05German DEL-42

Dark, Michael
87Blues Kodak-6
88Salt Lake Golden Eagles-2

Darling, Curtis
01Spokane Chiefs-7

Darling, Dion
93Spokane Chiefs-7
93Classic Four-Sport *-222
Gold-222
94Fredericton Canadiens-11
94Tampa Bay Tritons RHI-13
95Fredericton Canadiens-9
96Fredericton Canadiens-4
98Fort Wayne Komets-9
00Manitoba Moose-7
02UK Sheffield Steelers-6
03UK Sheffield Steelers-8
03UK Sheffield Steelers Stickers-5
04UK EIHL All-Stars-9
04UK Sheffield Steelers-7
05UK Nottingham Panthers-15

Darragh, Harold
32O'Keefe Maple Leafs-16

Darragh, Jack
10Sweet Caporal Postcards-17
11C55-17
12C57-29
23V145-1-4
83Hall of Fame-199
83Hall of Fame Postcards-N3
85Hall of Fame-199

Darrah, Mark
93Quebec Pee-Wee Tournament-168

Dartsch, David
96Richmond Renegades-3
99Adirondack IceHawks-4

Darveau, Guy
89ProCards AHL-193

Darwitz, Natalie
04Minnesota Golden Gophers Women-1

Darzins, Lauris
04Kelowna Rockets-10
05Kelowna Rockets-10
06Finnish Cardset-233
06Finnish Ilves Team Set-4

Dashney, Chris
98Wichita Thunder-4
99Wichita Thunder-3

DaSilva, Dan
04Portland Winter Hawks-4
05ITG Heroes/Prosp Toronto Expo Parallel -213
05ITG Heroes and Prospects-213
Autographs Series II-DDS
06Albany River Rats-9

DaSilva, Steven
04Kootenay Ice-7
05Kootenay Ice-6

Daskalakis, Cleon
85Moncton Golden Flames-14
86Moncton Golden Flames-18

Datsyuk, Pavel
00SPx Rookie Redemption-RR11
00Russian Hockey League-334
01Atomic-108
Premiere Date-108
01Atomic Toronto Fall Expo-108
01BAP Memorabilia-303
Emerald-303
Ruby-303
Sapphire-303
01BAP Signature Series-233
Autographs-233
Autographs Gold-233
01Bowman YoungStars-165
Gold-165
Ice Cubed-165
Autographs-PD
Relics-JPD
Relics-SPD
Relics-DSPD
Rivals-R9
01Crown Royale-157
Rookie Royalty-8
01O-Pee-Chee-349
01Pacific Adrenaline-207
Blue-207
Premiere Date-207
Red-207
Retail-207
Rookie Report-8
01Pacific Heads-Up-106
01Parkhurst-254
01Parkhurst Beckett Promos-254
01Private Stock-120
Gold-120
Premiere Date-120
Retail-120
Silver-120
01Private Stock Pacific Nights-120
01Private Stock PS-2002-80
01Private Stock Reserve-R4
01SP Authentic-145
Limited-145
Limited Gold-145
01SP Game Used-75
01SPx-104
01Stadium Club-139
Award Winners-139
Master Photos-139
01Titanium-156
Retail-156
01Titanium Draft Day Edition-126
01Topps-349
01Topps Chrome-167
Refractors-167
Black Border Refractors-167
01Topps Heritage-151
01Topps Reserve-117
01UD Challenge for the Cup-105
01UD Honor Roll-71
01UD Mask Collection-144
Gold-144
01UD Playmakers-116
01UD Premier Collection-95
01UD Top Shelf-127
01Upper Deck-422
Exclusives-422
01Upper Deck Ice-53
01Upper Deck MVP-223
01Upper Deck Victory-443
01Vanguard-109
Blue-109
Red-109
One of Ones-109
Premiere Date-109
Prime Prospects-5
Proofs-109
02Atomic-35
Blue-35
Gold-35
Red-35
Cold Fusion-10
Hobby Parallel-35
02BAP First Edition-186
02BAP Memorabilia-116
Emerald-116
Ruby-116
Sapphire-116
Future of the Game-FG-1
He Shoots-He Scores Prizes-24
NHL All-Star Game-116
NHL All-Star Game Blue-116
NHL All-Star Game Green-116
NHL All-Star Game Red-116
Stanley Cup Champions-SCC-13
02BAP Memorabilia Toronto Fall Expo-116
02BAP Signature Series-166
Autographs-166
Autographs Gold-166
Jerseys-SGJ47
Jersey Autographs-SGJ47
02BAP Ultimate Mem Dynasty Jerseys-16
02BAP Ultimate Mem Dynasty Emblems-16
02BAP Ultimate Mem Dynasty Numbers-16
02Bowman Toronto Spring Expo-3
02Bowman YoungStars-123
Gold-123
Silver-123
02eTopps-13
02ITG Used-28
02ITG Used-128
02O-Pee-Chee-235
02O-Pee-Chee Premier Blue Parallel-235
02O-Pee-Chee Premier Red Parallel-235
02O-Pee-Chee Factory Set-235
02Pacific-124
Blue-124
Red-124
Shining Moments-5
02Pacific Complete-23
Red-23
02Pacific Exclusive-61
Destined-6

Great Expectations-6
02Pacific Toronto Spring Expo Rookie Coll-6
02Parkhurst-55
Bronze-55
Gold-55
Silver-55
02Parkhurst Retro-173
Minis-173
02SP Authentic-115
02Stadium Club-33
Silver Decoy Cards-33
Proofs-33
YoungStars Relics-S2
YoungStars Relics-DS4
02Topps-235
OPC Blue Parallel-235
OPC Red Parallel-235
Own The Game-OTG15
Factory Set-235
02Topps Chrome-129
Black Border Refractors-129
Refractors-129
02Topps Heritage-14
02Topps Heritage-111
Chrome Parallel-14
02Topps Total-323
02Upper Deck-309
Exclusives-309
02Upper Deck Beckett UD Promos-309
02Upper Deck MVP-69
Gold-69
Classics-69
Golden Classics-69
02Upper Deck Victory-76
Bronze-76
Gold-76
Silver-76
02Upper Deck Vintage-90
Green Backs-90
03BAP Ultimate Memorabilia Autographs-136
Gold-136
03BAP Ultimate Mem Auto Jerseys-136
03BAP Ultimate Mem Auto Emblems-136
03BAP Ultimate Mem Auto Sticks-136
03BAP Ultimate Mem Blades of Steel-7
03BAP Ultimate Memorabilia Emblems-21
03BAP Ultimate Memorabilia Emblems Gold-21
03BAP Ultimate Mem Franch Present Future-11
03BAP Ultimate Memorabilia Hat Tricks-6
03BAP Ultimate Memorabilia Jerseys-31
03BAP Ultimate Memorabilia Jerseys Gold-31
03BAP Ultimate Mem Jersey and Emblems-32
03BAP Ultimate Mem Jersey and Emblem Gold-32
03BAP Ultimate Mem Jersey and Numbers-32
03BAP Ultimate Mem Jersey and Number Gold-32
03BAP Ultimate Memorabilia Linemates-9
03BAP Ultimate Mem Linemates Autos-17
03BAP Ultimate Memorabilia Numbers-24
03BAP Ultimate Memorabilia Numbers Gold-24
03Black Diamond-120
Black-120
Green-120
Red-120
03Bowman Future Rivals-HD
03Bowman Future Rivals-KD
03Bowman Future Rivals Patches-HD
03Bowman Future Rivals Patches-KD
03eTopps-53
03ITG Action-279
Jerseys-M126
03ITG Toronto Fall Expo Jerseys-FE1
03ITG Used Signature Series-5
Gold-5
Autographs-PD
Autographs Gold-PD
Jerseys-34
Jerseys Gold-34
Jersey Autos-34
Emblems-27
Emblems Gold-27
Jersey and Stick-34
Jersey and Stick Gold-34
Triple Memorabilia-7
Triple Memorabilia Gold-7
03O-Pee-Chee-61
03OPC Blue-61
03OPC Gold-61
03OPC Red-61
03Pacific-116
Blue-116
Red-116
03Pacific Calder-34
Silver-34
03Pacific Complete-116
Red-116
03Pacific Exhibit-52
Blue Backs-52
Yellow Backs-52
03Pacific Heads-Up-34
Hobby LTD-34
Retail LTD-34
03Pacific Invincible New Sensations-10
03Pacific Prism-36
Blue-36
Gold-36
Red-36
Paramount Prodigies-7
03Pacific Quest for the Cup-34
Blue-34
03Pacific Supreme Generations-4
03Parkhurst Original Six Detroit-4
Memorabilia-DM10
Memorabilia-DM22
Memorabilia-DM55
Memorabilia-DM61
03Parkhurst Orig Six He Shoots/Scores-30
03Parkhurst Orig Six He Shoots/Scores-30A
03Parkhurst Rookie Emblems-GUE-1
03Parkhurst Rookie Emblem Autographs-GUE-PD
03Parkhurst Rookie Emblems Gold-GUE-1
03Parkhurst Rookie Jerseys-GJ-13
03Parkhurst Rookie Jersey Autographs-GUJ-PD
03Parkhurst Rookie Jerseys Gold-GJ-13
03Private Stock Reserve-32
Blue-32
Red-32
Retail-32
03SP Game Used Limited Threads-LTPD
03SP Game Used Limited Threads Gold-LTPD
03SPx-164
Radiance-164
Spectrum-164
Big Futures-BF-PD
Big Futures Limited-BF-PD
03Titanium-35
Hobby Jersey Number Parallels-35
Retail-35
Retail Jersey Number Parallels-35
Stat Masters-5
03Topps-61
Blue-61
Gold-61
Red-61
Pristine Patches-PP-PD
Pristine Patch Refractors-PP-PD
Pristine Popular Demand Relics-PD-PD
Pristine Popular Demand Relic Refractor-PD-PD
Traded Future Phenoms-FP-PD
03UD Honor Roll-105
03UD Premier Collection-21
03Upper Deck-70
Canadian Exclusives-70
HG-70
03Upper Deck Ice-30
Gold-30
03Upper Deck MVP-146
Gold Script-146
Silver Script-146
Canadian Exclusives-146
03Upper Deck Rookie Update-29
03Upper Deck Victory-66
Bronze-66
Gold-66
Silver-66
03Russian World Championship Team 2003-5
03Russian World Championships Preview-2
03Toronto Star-35
04Pacific-91
Blue-91
Red-91
Global Connection-5
04SP Authentic-32
04UD All-World-33
Gold-33
04Ultimate Collection-14
04Upper Deck-64
Big Playmakers-BP-PD
Canadian Exclusives-64
HG Glossy Gold-64
HG Glossy Silver-64
Swatch of Six-SS-PD
World's Best-WB19
World Cup Tribute-PD
World Cup Tribute-PDMAIK
04Russian Back to Russia-2
04Russian Moscow Dynamo-10
05Be A Player-32
First Period-32
Second Period-32
Third Period-32
Overtime-32
Outtakes-OT20
05Beehive-33
Matte-33
Matted Materials-MMPD
05Black Diamond-134
Emerald-134
Gold-134
Onyx-134
Ruby-134
05Hot Prospects-35
En Fuego-35
Red Hot-35
White Hot-35
05Panini Stickers-264
05Parkhurst-167
Facsimile Auto Parallel-167
True Colors-TCDET
True Colors-TCDET
True Colors-TCCHDE
True Colors-TCCHDE
True Colors-TCDECO
True Colors-TCDECO
05SP Authentic-37
Limited-37
05SP Game Used-36
Gold-36
Authentic Fabrics-AF-PD
Authentic Fabrics Gold-AF-PD
Authentic Fabrics Quad-LZDC
Authentic Patches Quad -LZDC
Authentic Fabrics Triple-DKF
Authentic Patches-AP-PD
Authentic Patches Triple-DKF
05The Cup-42
Gold-42
Black Rainbow-42
Dual NHL Shields-DSDZ
Dual NHL Shields-DSKD
Masterpiece Pressplates-42
Noble Numbers-NNDZ
Noble Numbers-NNSD
Noble Numbers Dual-DNNDZ
Noble Numbers Dual-DNNFD
Patch Variation-P42
Property of-PDPD
05UD Artifacts-37
05UD Artifacts-168
Blue-37
Blue-168
Gold-37
Gold-168
Green-37
Green-168
Pewter-37
Pewter-168
Red-37
Red-168
Gold Autographed-37
Gold Autographed-168
Treasured Patches-TP-PD
Treasured Patches Autographed-TP-PD
Treasured Patches Dual-TPD-PD
Treasured Patches Dual Autographed-TPD-PD
Treasured Patches Pewter-TP-PD
Treasured Patches Silver-TP-PD
Treasured Swatches-TS-PD
Treasured Swatches Autographed-TS-PD
Treasured Swatches Blue-TS-PD
Treasured Swatches Copper-TS-PD
Treasured Swatches Dual-TSD-PD
Treasured Swatches Dual Autographed-TSD-PD
Treasured Swatches Dual Blue-TSD-PD
Treasured Swatches Dual Copper-TSD-PD
Treasured Swatches Dual Maroon-TSD-PD
Treasured Swatches Dual Pewter-TSD-PD
Treasured Swatches Dual Silver-TSD-PD
Treasured Swatches Maroon-TS-PD
Treasured Swatches Pewter-TS-PD
Treasured Swatches Silver-TS-PD
05UD PowerPlay-32
Rainbow-32
05Ultimate Collection-36
Gold-36
Jerseys-JPD
National Heroes Jerseys-NHJPD
National Heroes Patches-NHPPD
Premium Patches-PPPD
Premium Swatches-PSPD
Ultimate Patches-PPD
05Ultra-76
Gold-76
Difference Makers-DM2
Difference Makers Jerseys-DMJ-PD
Difference Makers Patches-DMP-PD
Ice-76
05Upper Deck-314
Big Playmakers-B-PD
Jerseys-J-PD
Majestic Materials-MMPD
NHL Generations-DFD
Patches-P-PD
05Upper Deck Ice-32
Rainbow-32
Frozen Fabrics-FFPD
Frozen Fabrics Glass-FFPD
Frozen Fabrics Patches-FFPPD
05Upper Deck MVP-151
Gold-151
Platinum-151
05Upper Deck Rookie Update-34
05Upper Deck Trilogy-33
05Upper Deck Trilogy-110
Crystal-110
05Upper Deck Victory-70
Black-70
Gold-70
Silver-70
06Sports Illustrated for Kids *-106
06Be A Player Portraits-40
06Beehive-66
Blue-66
Gold-66
Matte-66
Red Facsimile Signatures-66
Wood-66
06Black Diamond-102
Black-102
Gold-102
Ruby-102
Jerseys-JPD
Jerseys Black-JPD
Jerseys Gold-JPD
Jerseys Ruby-JPD
06Flair Showcase-41
06Flair Showcase-126
06Flair Showcase-232
Parallel-41
Parallel-126
Parallel-232
Stitches-SSPD
06Fleer-69
Tiffany-69
Fabricology-FPD
Speed Machines-SM12
Total O-08
06Hot Prospects-36
Red Hot-36
White Hot-36
06NHL POG-44
06O-Pee-Chee-183
Rainbow-183
Swatches-S-PD
06Panini Stickers-257
06SP Authentic-67
Limited-67
06SP Game Used-36
Gold-36
Rainbow-36
Authentic Fabrics-AFPD
Authentic Fabrics Parallel-AFPD
Authentic Fabrics Patches-AFPD
Authentic Fabrics Sixes-AF6BYN
Authentic Fabrics Sixes Patches-AF6BYN
Authentic Fabrics Eights-AF8RUS
Authentic Fabrics Eights Patches-AF8RUS
By The Letter-BLPD
06SPx-33
Spectrum-33
SPxcitement-X35
SPxcitement Spectrum-X35
Winning Materials-WMPD
Winning Materials Spectrum-WMPD
06The Cup Foundations-CQPD
06The Cup Foundations Patches-CQPD
06The Cup NHL Shields Duals-DSHDL
06The Cup NHL Shields Duals-DSHFD
06UD Artifacts-64
06UD Artifacts-167
Blue-64
Blue-167
Gold-64
Gold-167
Platinum-64
Platinum-167
Radiance-64
Radiance-167
Red-64
Red-167
Tundra Tandems-TTDH
Tundra Tandems Black-TTDH
Tundra Tandems Blue-TTDH
Tundra Tandems Gold-TTDH
Tundra Tandems Platinum-TTDH
Tundra Tandems Red-TTDH
Tundra Tandems Dual Patches Red-TTDH
06UD Mini Jersey Collection-40
06UD Powerplay-38
Impact Rainbow-38
Specialists-SPD
Specialists Patches-PPD
06Ultimate Collection Jerseys Dual-UJ2-ZD
06Ultimate Collection Patches Dual-UJ2-ZD
06Ultimate Collection Premium Patches-PS-PD
06Ultimate Collection Premium Swatches-PS-PD
06Ultra-72
Gold Medallion-72
Ice Medallion-72
Difference Makers-DM13
Scoring Kings-SK24
Uniformity-UPD
Uniformity Patches-UPPB
06Upper Deck Arena Giveaways-DET6
06Upper Deck-68
Exclusives Parallel-68
High Gloss Parallel-68
Award Winners Canadian Exclusive-OAW12
Game Jerseys-JPD
Game Patches-PPD
Generations Duals-G2KD
Generations Duals-G2KD
Generations Patches Dual-G2PFD
Generations Patches Dual-G2PKD
Masterpieces-68
Walmart Tins Oversize-68
06Upper Deck MVP-101
Gold Script-101
Super Script-101
Jerseys-OJFD
06Upper Deck Ovation-17
06Upper Deck Sweet Shot-39
Sweet Stitches-SSPD
Sweet Stitches Duals-SSPD
Sweet Stitches Triples-SSPD
06Upper Deck Trilogy-35
06Upper Deck Victory-69
06Upper Deck Victory Black-69
06Upper Deck Victory Gold-69
06Upper Deck Victory GameBreakers-GB17
06Upper Deck Victory Oversize Cards-PD
06Russian Sport Collection Olympic Stars-5
06Russian Torino Olympic Team-14
07Upper Deck Victory-100
Black-100
Gold-100
GameBreakers-GB44
Oversize Cards-OS26

Daubenspeck, Kirk
97Indianapolis Ice-5
98Indianapolis Ice-5
01Colorado Gold Kings-6
02South Carolina Stingrays-6
02South Carolina Stingrays RBI-210
03South Carolina Stingrays-325
05Hershey Bears-21

Daugherty, Brent
84Sudbury Wolves-4
85Sudbury Wolves-11
86Sudbury Wolves-6

Daum, Chris
93Quebec Pee-Wee Tournament-1455

Davenport, David
04Cape Breton Screaming Eagles-23
05Cape Breton Screaming Eagles-22
06Cape Breton Screaming Eagles-24

Davey, Bobby
04Belleville Bulls-2
05Belleville Bulls-10
06Sarnia Sting-22

Davey, Neil
84Prince Albert Raiders Stickers-5

Daviault, Alex
90Knoxville Cherokees-118

Daviault, Patrick
99Baie-Comeau Drakkar-25

David, Adam
93Quebec Pee-Wee Tournament-1272

David, Jean-Francois
99Shawinigan Cataractes-11
Signed-11
00Shawinigan Cataractes-18
Signed-18
01Shawinigan Cataractes-18
03Laredo Bucks-5

David, Jiri
99Czech OFS-452

David, Matthew
05Victoriaville Tigres-17

David, Richard
92Norwegian Elite Series-144

David, Sylvain
93Quebec Pee-Wee Tournament-119

Davidek, Martin
06Czech OFS-175

Davidson, Andrew
01Vancouver Giants-11

Davidson, Bob
34Beehive Group I Photos-312
36O-Pee-Chee V304D-100
37O-Pee-Chee V304E-136
37V356 Worldwide Gum-48
38Quaker Oats Photos-9
39O-Pee-Chee V301-1-5
45Quaker Oats Photos-15
91Ultimate Original Six-33
French-33
03BAP Ultimate Mem Linemates Autos-17
03BAP Ultimate Mem Maple Leafs Forever-7
04ITG Franchises Update Original Sticks-UOS10
04ITG Franchises Upd Original Sticks Gold-UOS10
04ITG Ultimate Memorabilia Vintage Lumber-12
04Ultimate Collection Ultimate Cuts-UC-BD
05ITG Ultimate Memorabilia Vintage Lumber-23
05ITG Ultimate Mem Vintage Lumber Gold-23
06ITG Ultimate Memorabilia Vintage Lumber-7
06ITG Ultimate Memorabilia Vintage Lumber Gold-7

Davidson, Chad
01Regina Pats-7

Davidson, Gord
34Beehive Group I Photos-270

Davidson, James
92Quebec Pee-Wee Tournament-910
93Quebec Pee-Wee Tournament-144

Davidson, John
73Blues White Border-3
74NHL Action Stamps-239
74O-Pee-Chee NHL-11
74Topps-11
75O-Pee-Chee NHL-183
75Topps-183
76O-Pee-Chee NHL-204
76Topps-204
77Coca-Cola-5
77O-Pee-Chee NHL-28
77Sportscasters-8018
77Topps-28
78O-Pee-Chee-211
78Topps-211
79O-Pee-Chee-110
79Topps-110
80O-Pee-Chee-190
80Topps-190
81O-Pee-Chee-222
81Topps-E95
99BAP Memorabilia AS American Hobby-AH11
99BAP Memorabilia AS American Hobby Autos-AH11
01Greats of the Game-10
Autographs-10
02Between the Pipes Goalie Autographs-33
03Parkhurst Original Six New York-49
Autographs-2
Memorabilia-NM59
04ITG Franchises US East-387
Autographs-A-JD
Original Sticks-EOS20
Original Sticks Gold-EOS20
04ITG Ultimate Memorabilia-15
Gold-15
Original Six-18
Original Six-19
06Between The Pipes-94
06Between The Pipes-140
Autographs-AJD
Double Jerseys-DJ01
Double Jerseys-DJ14
Double Jerseys Gold-DJ01
Double Jerseys Gold-DJ14
Shooting Gallery-SG05
Shooting Gallery Gold-SG05
Stick and Jersey-SJ05
Stick and Jersey Gold-SJ05
Stick and Jersey Autographs-SJ05
06ITG Ultimate Memorabilia Jerseys and Emblems-4
06ITG Ultimate Memorabilia Jerseys and Emblems Gold-4
06Parkhurst-46
Autographs-46

Davidson, Lee
90Moncton Hawks-2
90ProCards AHL/IHL-256
91Moncton Hawks-4
91ProCards-166
93Fort Wayne Komets-3
97Fort Wayne Komets-3
98German DEL-189
04Minnesota-Duluth Bulldogs-27

Davidson, Malcolm
54UK A and BC Chewing Gum-38

Davidson, Matt
93Portland Winter Hawks-6
97Rochester Americans-3-5
98Rochester Americans-3
00Syracuse Crunch-18
01BAP Memorabilia-438
Emerald-438
Ruby-438
Sapphire-438
01Pacific-111
Extreme LTD-111
Hobby LTD-111
Premiere Date-111
Retail LTD-111
01Pacific Arena Exclusives-111
01Parkhurst-200
01SP Authentic-143
Limited-143
Limited Gold-143
01SP Game Used-73
01SPx-138
01SPx-138
Rookie Treasures-RTMD
01UD Honor Roll-92
01UD Premier Collection-58
01Upper Deck-188
Exclusives-188
01Upper Deck MVP-198
01Upper Deck Victory-372
Gold-372
01Syracuse Crunch-5
02Syracuse Crunch-6
03ITG Action-158
03Lowell Lock Monsters-15
03Lowell Lock Monsters Photo Album-20
04German DEL-45
04German Dusseldorf Metro Stars Postcards-4
05German DEL-264
06Finnish Cardset-266

Davidson, Randy
97Owen Sound Platers-18
98Owen Sound Platers-19
99Ottawa 67's-5

Davidson, Rick
84Victoria Cougars-8

Davidson, Robert
99Indianapolis Ice-6
00Indianapolis Ice-7
01Indianapolis Ice-5
03Sharks Postcards-3
03Missouri River Otters-23

Davidson, Rod
99Indianapolis Ice-20
00Indianapolis Ice-21
01Indianapolis Ice-6

Davidson, Ron
81Swedish Semic Hockey VM Stickers-81

Davidson, Scotty
83Hall of Fame-137
83Hall of Fame Postcards-K2
85Hall of Fame-137

Davidson, Shawna
94Classic Women of Hockey-W25

Davidson, Ty
92British Columbia JHL-126

Davidsson, Johan
92Swedish Semic Elitserien Stickers-353
93Parkhurst-538
Emerald Ice-538
93Swedish Semic Elitserien-118
94Parkhurst SE-SE236
Gold-SE236
94Swedish Leaf-242
NHL Draft-2
94Signature Rookies Gold Standard *-81
95Swedish Leaf-53
95Swedish Upper Deck-86
Ticket to North America-NA10
95Swedish Globe World Championships-62
95Signature Rookies-57
Signatures-57
98Black Diamond-3
Double Diamond-3
Triple Diamond-3
Quadruple Diamond-3
98Bowman's Best-125
Refractors-125
Atomic Refractors-125
98Pacific Omega-9
Red-9
Opening Day Issue-9
98SP Authentic-91
Power Shift-91
98Upper Deck-211
Exclusives-211
Exclusives 1 of 1-211
Gold Reserve-211
98Upper Deck MVP-4
Gold Script-4
Silver Script-4
Super Script-4
99Pacific-2
Copper-2
Emerald Green-2
Gold-2
Ice Blue-2
Premiere Date-2
Red-2
99Upper Deck MVP-10
Gold Script-10
Silver Script-10
Super Script-10
99Cincinnati Mighty Ducks-15
00BAP Memorabilia-131
Emerald-131
Ruby-131
Sapphire-131
Promos-131
00BAP Mem Chicago Sportsfest Copper-131
00BAP Memorabilia Chicago Sportsfest Blue-131
00BAP Memorabilia Chicago Sportsfest Gold-131
00BAP Memorabilia Chicago Sportsfest Ruby-131
00BAP Memorabilia Chicago Sun-Times Ruby-131
00BAP Memorabilia Chicago Sun-Times Gold-131
00BAP Mem Chicago Sun-Times Sapphire-131
00BAP Mem Toronto Fall Expo Copper-131
00BAP Memorabilia Toronto Fall Expo Gold-131
00BAP Memorabilia Toronto Fall Expo Ruby-131
00Finnish Cardset-251
02Finnish Cardset-12
02Swedish SHL-137
02Swedish SHL-187
Parallel-137
Parallel-187
Signatures-7
Team Captains-4
03Swedish Elite-55
Signatures II-15
Silver-55
Stars of the Game-4
04Swedish Allabilder Alfa Stars-15
04Swedish Allabilder Proof Parallels-15
04Swedish Elitset-59
04Swedish Elitset-136
Gold-59
Gold-136
04Swedish Pure Skills-40
Parallel-40
05Swedish SHL Elitset-61
Gold-61
Playmakers-6
Series One Signatures-7
Series Two Jerseys-GWJD
Teammates-5
06Swedish SHL Elitset-65
Performers-7

Davidsson, Mats
65Swedish Coralli ISHockey-207
67Swedish Hockey-266
69Swedish Hockey-227
71Swedish Hockey-372

Davie, Bob
34Diamond Matchbooks Silver-19

Davies, Aaron
03UK Manchester Phoenix-16

Davies, Curly
52Juniors Blue Tint-128

Davies, Dan
92British Columbia JHL-29
99Rockford IceHogs-5
00Rockford IceHogs-6
01Rockford IceHogs-6
02Rockford Ice Hogs-18
03Rockford Ice Hogs-4

Davies, Dave
74Sioux City Musketeers-2

Davies, Greg
83Victoria Cougars-6
87Kamloops Blazers-5
88ProCards IHL-48

Davies, Jason
00London Knights-19

Davies, Mark
92British Columbia JHL-194

Davies, Paul
04Odessa Jackalopes-4
05Odessa Jackalopes-5

Davis, Aaron
02Arkansas Riverblades-4
03Fort Worth Brahmas-3
04Fort Worth Brahmas-5
06Austin Ice Bats-15

Davis, Adam
01Fort Worth Brahmas-8
02Fort Worth Brahmas-1
03Fort Worth Brahmas-4
04Fort Worth Brahmas-6
04Sioux City Musketeers-7

Davis, Adam (NCAA)
04Sioux City Musketeers-7

Davis, Andrew
00Mississauga Ice Dogs-10
05Odessa Jackalopes-5
06Odessa Jackalopes-5

Davis, Bob
23V128-1 Paulin's Candy-54

Davis, Brad
06Penticton Vees-5

Davis, Dayne
04Kingston Frontenacs-5

Davis, George
01Cape Breton Screaming Eagles-15
02Cape Breton Screaming Eagles-25
02Halifax Mooseheads-15
03Halifax Mooseheads-8

Davis, Greg
01Worcester Icecats-12
02Worcester IceCats-10
03St. Jean Mission-4

Davis, Jean-Paul
89Oshawa Generals-20
89Oshawa Generals 7th Inning Sketch-6
897th Inn. Sketch OHL-6
907th Inn. Sketch OHL-334
907th Inn. Sketch Memorial Cup-80
91Oshawa Generals-27
91Oshawa Generals Sheet-24
917th Inn. Sketch OHL-164
00Bakersfield Condors-7

Davis, Joel
02Swedish SHL-205
Parallel-205

Davis, Justin
95Slapshot-115
96Sault Ste. Marie Greyhounds-4
96Sault Ste. Marie Greyhounds Autographed-4

Davis, Kelly
81Indianapolis Checkers-3
82Indianapolis Checkers-1

Davis, Ken
97Portland Winter Hawks-5
99Medicine Hat Tigers-18
00Medicine Hat Tigers-4

Davis, Kurt
05Waterloo Blackhawks-8

Davis, Lorne
44Beehive Group II Photos-232

Davis, Malcolm
84Sabres Blue Shield-5
85O-Pee-Chee Stickers-186
85Sabres Blue Shield-6
85Sabres Blue Shield Small-6

Davis, Matt
01Moncton Wildcats-19
02Moncton Wildcats-2
03Lewiston Maineiacs-7
06Philadelphia Phantoms-24

Davis, Patrick
03Kitchener Rangers-5
04Kitchener Rangers-23
05Kitchener Rangers-5

Davis, Rick
92Cornell Big Red-5

Davis, Ryan
95Slapshot-290
95Owen Sound Platers-13
96Owen Sound Platers-13
97Owen Sound Platers-10
98Guelph Storm-19
03Columbus Cottonmouths-11

Davis, Scott
907th Inn. Sketch WHL-16
97Idaho Steelheads-9
98Idaho Steelheads-4
99Idaho Steelheads-9

Davis, Troy
92North Dakota Fighting Sioux-6

Davis, Vicki
04Wisconsin Badgers Women-4

Davis, Wade
98Calgary Hitmen-13
98Calgary Hitmen Autographs-13
99Calgary Hitmen-8
99Calgary Hitmen Autographs-8
00Calgary Hitmen-10
01Calgary Hitmen-8
01Calgary Hitmen Autographed-8
02Calgary Hitmen-12
02Kamloops Blazers-5
02Regina Pats-10

Davison, Dwayne
81Ottawa 67's-6

Davison, Rob
00Kentucky Thoroughblades-8
01Cleveland Barons-6
02BAP Memorabilia-307
02SP Authentic-214
02Upper Deck Rookie Update-142
02Cleveland Barons-4
04UK EIHL All-Stars-8

Davison, Todd
02Regina Pats-7

Davison, Wade
04Vernon Vipers-21
05Vernon Vipers-9

DaVita, David
91ProCards-17

Davletov, Andrei
03Russian Hockey League-255

Davydkin, Nikolai
89Swedish Semic Elitserien Stickers-31
91Swedish Semic Elitserien Stickers-32
92Norwegian Elite Series-35

Davydov, Evgeny
90O-Pee-Chee Red Army-18R
91Parkhurst-422
French-422
91Finnish Semic World Champ Stickers-92
91Russian Stars Red Ace-2
91Swedish Semic World Champ Stickers-92
92OPC Premier-66
92Parkhurst-211
92Parkhurst-226
Emerald Ice-211
Emerald Ice-226
92Pinnacle-226
French-226
92Pro Set-224
92Score-456
Canadian-456
92Topps-115
Gold-115G
92Ultra-441
92Upper Deck-420
Calder Candidates-CC19
Euro-Rookies-ER17
Euro-Stars-E8
93Donruss-127
93Leaf-24
93OPC Premier-200
93OPC Premier-444
Gold-200
Gold-444
93Panini Stickers-194
93Parkhurst-78
Emerald Ice-78
93Pinnacle-109
Canadian-109
93PowerPlay-269
93PowerPlay-397
93Score-114
93Score-499
Gold-499
Canadian-114
Canadian-499
Canadian Gold-499
93Stadium Club-34
93Stadium Club-487
Members Only Master Set-34
Members Only Master Set-487
OPC-34
First Day Issue-34
First Day Issue-487
First Day Issue OPC-34
93Topps/OPC Premier-200
93Topps/OPC Premier-444
Gold-200
Gold-444
93Ultra-58
93Ultra-323
93Upper Deck-443
SP-55
94OPC Premier-518
Special Effects-518
94Parkhurst-161
Gold-161
94Pinnacle-202
Artist's Proofs-202
Rink Collection-202
94Stadium Club-66
Members Only Master Set-66
First Day Issue-66
Super Team Winner Cards-66
94Topps/OPC Premier-518
Special Effects-518
94Ultra-147
94Upper Deck-49
Electric Ice-49
97Swedish Collector's Choice-29
Crash the Game Exchange-C17
Crash the Game Redemption-R17
99Swiss Panini Stickers-334

Davydov, Marat
95Swedish World Championships Stickers-30
99Russian Dynamo Moscow-11
99Russian Stars Postcards-6
00Russian Dynamo Moscow-11
01Russian Dynamo Moscow-16
01Russian Dynamo Moscow Mentos-13
02Russian Hockey League-151
03Russian Hockey League-66
04Russian Super League All-Stars-8

Davydov, Oleg
95Swedish World Championships Stickers-32
03Russian Metallurg Magnitogorsk-4

Davydov, Vitalij
69Russian National Team Postcards-2
69Swedish Hockey-2
70Finnish Jaakiekko-1
70Russian National Team Postcards-2
70Swedish Hockey-315
70Swedish Masterserien-21
70Swedish Masterserien-74
70Swedish Masterserien-121
70Swedish Masterserien-122
70Swedish Masterserien-131
71Finnish Suomi Stickers-1
71Swedish Hockey-29
72Finnish Panda Toronto-48
72Finnish Semic World Championship-2
72Swedish Semic World Championship-2
73Swedish Stickers-122
74Swedish Semic World Champ Stickers-43

Davyduke, Kent
02ECHL All-Star Southern-41
02ECHL Update-U-6
03Reading Royals-19
03Reading Royals RBI Sports-290

Daw, Jeff
96Wheeling Nailers Photo Pack-8
99Houston Aeros-5
00Lowell Lock Monsters-4
01BAP Memorabilia-427
Emerald-427
Ruby-427
Sapphire-427
01UD Mask Collection-141
Gold-141
01Hershey Bears-6
02Lowell Lock Monsters-8
05Danbury Trashers-24

Dawe, Jason
89Peterborough Petes-106
897th Inn. Sketch OHL-106
907th Inn. Sketch OHL-357
91Upper Deck-75
French-75
91Peterborough Petes-1
917th Inn. Sketch OHL-145
917th Inn. Sketch Memorial Cup-113
91Arena Draft Picks-26
91Arena Draft Picks French-26
91Arena Draft Picks Autographs-26
91Arena Draft Picks Autographs French-26
91Classic-31
91Star Pics-59
91Ultimate Draft-27
91Ultimate Draft-86
91Ultimate Draft French-27
91Classic Four-Sport *-31
Autographs-31A
93Donruss-404
93Upper Deck-254
93Peterborough Petes-27
93Classic-19
94Donruss-245
94Leaf-48
94OPC Premier-149
Special Effects-149
94Parkhurst SE-SE20
Gold-SE20
94Pinnacle-366
Artist's Proofs-366
Rink Collection-366
94Topps/OPC Premier-149
Special Effects-149
94Ultra-21
94Upper Deck-167
Electric Ice-167
94Classic Pro Prospects-88
95Be A Player-50
Signatures-S50
Signatures Die Cuts-S50
95Canada Games NHL POGS-43
95Donruss-315
95Finest-158
Refractors-158
95Leaf Limited-111
95Metal-14
95Panini Stickers-18
95Parkhurst International-24
Emerald Ice-24
95Pinnacle-123
Artist's Proofs-123
Rink Collection-123
95Playoff One on One-230
95Stadium Club-147
Members Only Master Set-147
95Topps-128
OPC Inserts-128
Power Lines-6PL
95Ultra-16
95Ultra-211
Gold Medallion-16
95Upper Deck-61
Electric Ice-61
Electric Ice Gold-61
Special Edition-SE100
Special Edition Gold-SE100
96Black Diamond-139
Gold-139
96Collector's Choice-31
96Donruss-165
Press Proofs-165
96Fleer-9
96Fleer Picks-122
96Leaf-93
Press Proofs-93
96Metal Universe-13

96Pinnacle-10
Artist's Proofs-10
Foil-10
Premium Stock-10
Rink Collection-10
96Playoff One on One-421
96Score-59
Artist's Proofs-59
Dealer's Choice Artist's Proofs-59
Special Artist's Proofs-59
Golden Blades-59
96Ultra-15
Gold Medallion-15
96Upper Deck-19
96Collector's Edge Ice Crucibles-C20
97Black Diamond-30
Double Diamond-30
Triple Diamond-30
Quadruple Diamond-30
97Collector's Choice-32
97Crown Royale-12
Emerald Green-12
Ice Blue-12
Silver-12
97Katch-14
Gold-14
Silver-14
97Pacific-314
Copper-314
Emerald Green-314
Ice Blue-314
Red-314
Silver-314
97Pacific Invincible-11
Copper-11
Emerald Green-11
Ice Blue-11
Red-11
Silver-11
97Pacific Omega-20
Copper-20
Dark Gray-20
Emerald Green-20
Gold-20
Ice Blue-20
97Paramount-18
Copper-18
Dark Grey-18
Emerald Green-18
Ice Blue-18
Red-18
Silver-18
97Revolution-13
Copper-13
Emerald-13
Ice Blue-13
Silver-13
97Score-204
97Score Sabres-7
Platinum-7
Premier-7
97SP Authentic-13
97Upper Deck-19
98Aurora-115
98OPC Chrome-202
Refractors-202
98Pacific-280
Ice Blue-280
Red-280
98Paramount-142
Copper-142
Emerald Green-142
Holo-Electric-142
Ice Blue-142
Silver-142
98Topps-202
O-Pee-Chee-202
98Upper Deck-129
Exclusives-129
Exclusives 1 of 1-129
Gold Reserve-129
99Milwaukee Admirals Keebler-10
00Hartford Wolf Pack-5
01Hartford Wolf Pack-2
02Worcester IceCats-8
03Rochester Americans-15

Dawe, Wade

92Quebec Pee-Wee Tournament-1110
95Slapshot-317

Dawes, Nigel

03Kootenay Ice-9
04Kootenay Ice-9
04ITG Heroes and Prospects-223
04ITG Heroes/Prospects Toronto Expo '05-223
05ITG Heroes/Prosp Toronto Expo Parallel -234
05AHL Top Prospects-10
05Hartford Wolf Pack-2
05ITG Heroes and Prospects-234
Autographs Series II-ND
06Be A Player-227
Autographs-227
Signatures 25-227
06Be A Player Portraits-118
06Beehive-136
Blue-137
Matte-136
Red Facsimile Signatures-137
Wood-137
06Black Diamond-204
Black-204
Gold-204
Ruby-204
06Flair Showcase-319
06Hot Prospects-124
Red Hot-124
White Hot-124
Hot Materials -HMND
Hot Materials Red Hot-HMND
Hot Materials White Hot-HMND
Hotagraphs-HND
06O-Pee-Chee-545
06O-Pee-Chee-625
Rainbow-545
Rainbow-625
06SP Authentic-191
Limited-191
06SP Game Used-136
Gold-136
Rainbow-136
Autographs-136
Rookie Exclusives Autographs-REND
06SPx-181
Spectrum-181
06The Cup-143
Autographed NHL Shields Duals-DASLD
Autographed Rookie Masterpiece Pressplates-143
Gold Rainbow Autographed Rookie Patches-143
Masterpiece Pressplates (Be A Player Portraits)-
118
Masterpiece Pressplates (Bee Hive)-136
Masterpiece Pressplates (Marquee Rookies)-545
Masterpiece Pressplates (MVP)-308
Masterpiece Pressplates (SP Authentic
Autographs)-191
Masterpiece Pressplates (SP Game Used)-136
Masterpiece Pressplates (SPx Autographs)-181
Masterpiece Pressplates (Sweet Beginnings)-138
Masterpiece Pressplates (Trilogy)-138
Masterpiece Pressplates (Ultimate Collection
Autographs)-120
Masterpiece Pressplates (Victory)-291
NHL Shields Duals-DSHSD
NHL Shields Duals-DSHZD
Rookies Black-143
Rookies Platinum-143
06UD Artifacts-250
06UD Mini Jersey Collection-118
06Ultimate Collection-120
Rookies Autographed NHL Shields-120
Rookies Autographed Patches-120
Ultimate Debut Threads Jerseys-DJ-ND
Ultimate Debut Threads Jerseys Autographs-DJ-
ND
Ultimate Debut Threads Patches-DJ-ND
Ultimate Debut Threads Patches Autographs-DJ-
ND
06Ultra-235
Gold Medallion-235
Ice Medallion-235
06Upper Deck-231
Exclusives Parallel-231
High Gloss Parallel-231
Masterpieces-231
Rookie Game Dated Moments-RGD17
Rookie Headliners-RH11
Rookie Materials-RMND
Rookie Materials Patches-RMND
06Upper Deck MVP-308
Gold Script-308
Super Script-308
06Upper Deck Sweet Shot-138
Rookie Jerseys Autographs-138
Signature Shots/Saves-SSND
06Upper Deck Trilogy-138
06Upper Deck Victory-291
06Hartford Wolf Pack-17
06ITG Heroes and Prospects-78
Autographs-AND
Complete AHL Logos-AHL09
Jerseys-GUJ06
Jerseys Gold-GUJ06
Emblems-GUE06
Emblems Gold-GUE06
Numbers-GUN06
Numbers Gold-GUN06
07Upper Deck Rookie Class -25

Dawes, Robert

44Beehive Group II Photos-395

Dawkins, Mark

917th Inn. Sketch WHL-310

Dawson, Aaron

02Peterborough Petes-3
04Peterborough Petes Postcards-15

Dawson, Mike

907th Inn. Sketch OHL-56
917th Inn. Sketch OHL-233

Dawson, Wade

91ProCards-162

Daxner, Franz

94German First League-225

Day, Clarence

24C144 Champ's Cigarettes-20
28La Presse Photos-7
32O'Keefe Maple Leafs-4
33O-Pee-Chee V304A-32
33V129-2
33V252 Canadian Gum-17
33V288 Hamilton Gum-33
33V357 Ice Kings-10
33V357-2 Ice Kings Premiums-2
34Beehive Group I Photos-313
37V356 Worldwide Gum-52
55Parkhurst-34
Quaker Oats-34
83Hall of Fame Postcards-F4
85Hall of Fame-80
94Parkhurst Missing Link-134
02BAP Ultimate Mem Paper Cuts Autos-28
02Maple Leafs Platinum Collection-48
02Parkhurst Reprints-207
03BAP Ultimate Mem Maple Leafs Forever-15
03BAP Ultimate Mem Vintage Blade of Steel-7
03Parkhurst Original Six Toronto-40
03Parkhurst Original Six Toronto-76
04ITG Franchises Canadian-116
04ITG Ultimate Memorabilia-52
Gold-52
Blades of Steel-5
Cornerstones-3
Cornerstones Gold-3
Paper Cuts Memorabilia-10
Retro Teammates-10
04Ultimate Collection Ultimate Cuts-UC-HD
05ITG Ultimate Mem Paper Cut Autos-9
05ITG Ultimate Mem Quad Paper Cuts Autos-6
05The Cup Legendary Cuts-LCHD
06ITG Ultimate Memorabilia-62
Artist Proof-62
Amazing Amerks Autos-7
Blades of Steel-14
Blades of Steel Gold-14
Builders Autos-5
06The Cup Legendary Cuts-LCHD

Day, Eric

96Minnesota Golden Gophers-9
97Minnesota Golden Gophers-8

Day, Greg

02Peoria Rivermen-7
02Peoria Rivermen RBI Sports-158
03Las Vegas Wranglers-6
03Las Vegas Wranglers RBI-229

Day, Joe

90ProCards AHL/IHL-181
91Upper Deck-516
French-516
91Whalers Jr. 7-Eleven-11
91ProCards-103
94Parkhurst-138
Gold-138
97Las Vegas Thunder-4

Day, Joshua

04Sault Ste. Marie Greyhounds-5
05Mississauga Ice Dogs-18
06Mississauga Ice Dogs-16

Day, Justin

00Owen Sound Attack-5
01Owen Sound Attack-5

Day, Lewis

04UK U-20 Team-21
05UK Hull Stingrays-13

Day, Riley

02Medicine Hat Tigers-6
03Medicine Hat Tigers-2
04Brandon Wheat Kings-17
05Brandon Wheat Kings-6

Dayley, Cory

92British Columbia JHL-112

Dayley, Wade

91British Columbia JHL-47
92British Columbia JHL-116

Dayman, Ryan

92British Columbia JHL-31

Daze, Eric

94Finest-157
Super Team Winners-157
Refractors-157
94Leaf Limited World Juniors Canada-2
94Pinnacle-529
Artist's Proofs-529
Rink Collection-529
94Upper Deck-497
Electric Ice-497
95Be A Player-170
Signatures-S170
Signatures Die Cuts-S170
Lethal Lines-LL4
95Blackhawks Coke-7
95Bowman-125
All-Foil-125
Bowman's Best-BB18
Bowman's Best Refractors-BB18
95Collector's Choice-411
95Donruss-345
Canadian World Junior Team-15
Rated Rookies-6
95Donruss Elite-63
Die Cut Stars-63
Die Cut Uncut-63
Rookies-1
95Emotion generatioNext-2
95Finest-3
Refractors-3
95Leaf-226
Studio Rookies-11
95Leaf Limited-65
Rookie Phenoms-6
95Metal-174
95Panini Stickers-159
95Parkhurst International-45
Emerald Ice-45
Crown Collection Silver Series 2-16
Crown Collection Gold Series 2-16
Parkie's Trophy Picks-PP40
95Pinnacle-203
Artist's Proofs-203
Rink Collection-203
95Playoff One on One-234
95Score-312
Black Ice Artist's Proofs-312
Black Ice-312
95Select Certified-132
Mirror Gold-132
95SkyBox Impact-193
NHL On Fox-17
95SP-22
95Stadium Club-195
Members Only Master Set-195
95Summit-190
Artist's Proofs-190
Ice-190
95Topps-26
OPC Inserts-26
Canadian World Juniors-19CJ
95Ultra-32
95Ultra-335
Gold Medallion-32
Extra Attackers-2
95Upper Deck-268
Electric Ice-268
Electric Ice Gold-268
Predictor Hobby-H29
Predictor Hobby Exchange-H29
95Zenith-122
Rookie Roll Call-13
95Images-14
Gold-14
96Collector's Choice-45
96Collector's Choice-313
MVP-UD37
MVP Gold-UD37
Crash the Game-C20A
Crash the Game-C20B
Crash the Game-C20C
Crash the Game Gold-C20A
Crash the Game Gold-C20B
Crash the Game Gold-C20C
96Donruss Dominators-10
96Donruss Hit List-12
96Donruss Rated Rookies-1
96Donruss Canadian Ice-20
Gold Press Proofs-20
Red Press Proofs-20
O Canada-14
96Donruss Elite-71
Die Cut Stars-71
Aspirations-1
96Duracell L'Equipe Beliveau-JB4
96Flair-16
Blue Ice-16
Hot Numbers-3
96Fleer-17
96Fleer-136
Rookie Sensations-4
Picks Fabulous 50-9
Picks Fantasy Force-4
Picks Jagged Edge-19
96Leaf-202
Press Proofs-202
Sweaters Away-7
Sweaters Home-7
The Best Of ...-2
96Leaf Limited-37
Gold-37
96Leaf Limited Bash the Boards Promos-P10
96Leaf Limited Bash The Boards-10
96Leaf Limited Bash The Boards Ltd Ed-10
96Leaf Preferred-61
96Leaf Preferred-149
Press Proofs-61
Press Proofs-149
Steel-25
Steel Gold-25
96Maggers-20
96McDonald's Pinnacle-3
96Metal Universe-27
96NHL Aces Playing Cards-10
96Pinnacle-212
Artist's Proofs-212
Foil-212
Premium Stock-212
Rink Collection-212
By The Numbers-11
By The Numbers-P11
By The Numbers Premium-11
Team Pinnacle-10
96Score Samples-236
96Score-236
Artist's Proofs-236
Dealer's Choice Artist's Proofs-236
Special Artist's Proofs-236
Check It-16
Golden Blades-236
96Select Certified-79
Artist's Proofs-79
Blue-79
Mirror Blue-79
Mirror Gold-79
Mirror Red-79
Red-79
96SkyBox Impact-19
96SkyBox Impact-168
NHL on Fox-7
96SP-26
Clearcut Winner-CW20
Holoview Collection-HC2
96SPx-50
96SPx-GF1
Gold-50
96Stadium Club Members Only-50
96Summit-151
Artist's Proofs-151
Ice-151
Metal-151
Premium Stock-151
High Voltage-7
High Voltage Mirage-7
96Team Out-9
96Topps Picks-77
OPC Inserts-77
Rookie Stars-RS4
Rookie Stars OPC-RS4
96Ultra-31
Gold Medallion-31
96Upper Deck-29
96Upper Deck-359
Generation Next-X19
Lord Stanley's Heroes Finals-LS15
Lord Stanley's Heroes Quarterfinals-LS15
Lord Stanley's Heroes Semifinals-LS15
Superstar Showdown-SS18B
96Upper Deck Ice-79
Parallel-79
96Zenith-99
Artist's Proofs-99
Z-Team-14
97Be A Player Take A Number-2
97Black Diamond-63
Double Diamond-63
Triple Diamond-63
Quadruple Diamond-63
97Collector's Choice-53
Star Quest-SQ15
97Crown Royale-29
Emerald Green-29
Ice Blue-29
Silver-29
97Donruss-192
Press Proofs Silver-192
Press Proofs Gold-192
97Donruss Canadian Ice-21
Dominion Series-21
Provincial Series-21
97Donruss Limited-65
Exposure-65
97Donruss Preferred-116
Cut to the Chase-116
97Donruss Priority-26
Stamp of Approval-26
97Leaf-97
Fractal Matrix-97
Fractal Matrix Die Cuts-97
97Leaf International-97
Universal Ice-97
97Pacific-108
Copper-108
Emerald Green-108
Ice Blue-108
Red-108
Silver-108
97Pacific Dynagon-26
Copper-26
Dark Grey-26
Emerald Green-26
Ice Blue-26
Red-26
Silver-26
Tandems-31
97Pacific Invincible-29
Copper-29
Emerald Green-29
Ice Blue-29
Red-29
Silver-29
97Pacific Omega-49
Copper-49
Dark Gray-49
Emerald Green-49
Gold-49
Ice Blue-49
97Panini Stickers-136
97Paramount-43
Copper-43
Dark Grey-43
Emerald Green-43
Ice Blue-43
Red-43
Silver-43
97Pinnacle-121
Press Plates Back Black-121
Press Plates Back Cyan-121
Press Plates Back Magenta-121
Press Plates Back Yellow-121
Press Plates Front Black-121
Press Plates Front Cyan-121
Press Plates Front Magenta-121
Press Plates Front Yellow-121
97Pinnacle Certified-122
Red-122
Mirror Blue-122
Mirror Gold-122
Mirror Red-122
97Pinnacle Inside-88
Coach's Collection-88
Executive Collection-88
97Pinnacle Tot Cert Platinum Blue-122
97Pinnacle Tot Certi Platinum Gold-122
97Pinnacle Totally Certified Platinum Red-122
97Pinnacle Tot Cert Mirror Platinum Gold-122
97Revolution-29
Copper-29
Emerald-29
Ice Blue-29
Silver-29
97Score-193
97SP Authentic-31
97Upper Deck-41
97Zenith-55
Z-Gold-55
Z-Silver-55
97Zenith 5 x 7-54
Gold Impulse-54
Silver Impulse-54
98Aurora-40
98Be A Player-179
Press Release-179
98BAP Gold-179
98BAP Autographs-179
98BAP Autographs Gold-179
98Crown Royale-29
Limited Series-29
98Finest-66
No Protectors-66
No Protectors Refractors-66
Refractors-66
98Katch-35
98OPC Chrome-195
Refractors-195
98Pacific-143
Ice Blue-143
Red-143
98Pacific Dynagon Ice-40
Blue-40
Red-40
98Pacific Omega-50
Red-50
Opening Day Issue-50
98Panini Photocards-18
98Panini Stickers-113
98Paramount-46
Copper-46
Emerald Green-46
Holo-Electric-46
Ice Blue-46
Silver-46
98Revolution-30
Ice Shadow-30
Red-30
98Topps-195
O-Pee-Chee-195
98Topps Gold Label Class 1-98
Black-98
Black One of One-98
One of One-98
Red-98
Red One of One-98
98Topps Gold Label Class 2-98
98Topps Gold Label Class 2 Black-98
98Topps Gold Label Class 2 Black 1 of 1-98
98Topps Gold Label Class 2 One of One-98
98Topps Gold Label Class 2 Red-98
98Topps Gold Label Class 2 Red One of One-98
98Topps Gold Label Class 3-98
98Topps Gold Label Class 3 Black-98
98Topps Gold Label Class 3 Black 1 of 1-98
98Topps Gold Label Class 3 One of One-98
98Topps Gold Label Class 3 Red-98
98Topps Gold Label Class 3 Red One of One-98
98UD Choice-45
98UD Choice Preview-45
98UD Choice Prime Choice Reserve-45
98UD Choice Reserve-45
98Upper Deck-68
Exclusives-68
Exclusives 1 of 1-68
Gold Reserve-68
98Upper Deck MVP-48
Gold Script-48
Silver Script-48
Super Script-48
99BAP Memorabilia-97
Gold-97
Silver-97
99BAP Millennium-62
Emerald-62
Ruby-62
Sapphire-62
Signatures-62
Signatures Gold-62
99Blackhawks Lineup Cards-3
99Crown Royale-32
Limited Series-32
Premiere Date-32
99O-Pee-Chee-231
99O-Pee-Chee Chrome-231
99O-Pee-Chee Chrome Refractors-231
99Pacific-85
Copper-85
Emerald Green-85
Gold-85
Ice Blue-85
Premiere Date-85
Red-85
99Pacific Dynagon Ice-48
Blue-48
Copper-48
Gold-48
Premiere Date-48
99Pacific Omega-52
Copper-52
Gold-52
Ice Blue-52
Premiere Date-52
99Panini Stickers-198
99Paramount-53
Copper-53
Emerald-53
Gold-53
Holographic Emerald-53
Holographic Gold-53
Holographic Silver-53
Ice Blue-53
Premiere Date-53
Red-53
Silver-53
99Stadium Club-50
First Day Issue-50
One of a Kind-50
Printing Plates Black-50
Printing Plates Cyan-50
Printing Plates Magenta-50
Printing Plates Yellow-50
99Topps Arena Giveaways-CHI-ED
99Topps/OPC-231
99Topps/OPC Chrome-231
Refractors-231
99Upper Deck Victory-73
99Wayne Gretzky Hockey-42
00Aurora-32
Premiere Date-32
00BAP Memorabilia-144
Emerald-144
Ruby-144
Sapphire-144
Promos-144
00BAP Mem Chicago Sportsfest Copper-144
00BAP Memorabilia Chicago Sportsfest Blue-144
00BAP Memorabilia Chicago Sportsfest Gold-144
00BAP Memorabilia Chicago Sportsfest Ruby-144
00BAP Memorabilia Chicago Sun-Times Ruby-144
00BAP Memorabilia Chicago Sun-Times Gold-144
00BAP Mem Chicago Sun-Times Sapphire-144
00BAP Mem Toronto Fall Expo Copper-144
00BAP Memorabilia Toronto Fall Expo Gold-144
00BAP Memorabilia Toronto Fall Expo Ruby-144
00BAP Memorabilia Update Teammates-TM25
00BAP Memorabilia Update Teammates Gold-TM25
00BAP Parkhurst 2000-P243
00O-Pee-Chee-113
00O-Pee-Chee Parallel-113
00Pacific-93
Copper-93
Gold-93
Ice Blue-93
Premiere Date-93
00Private Stock Game Gear-16
00Private Stock Game Gear Patches-16
00Stadium Club-84
00Titanium Draft Day Edition-17
Patches-17
00Topps/OPC-113
Parallel-113
00Upper Deck-39
Exclusives Tier 1-39
Exclusives Tier 2-39
00Upper Deck MVP-42
First Stars-42
Second Stars-42
Third Stars-42
00Upper Deck Victory-57
00Upper Deck Vintage-77
00Vanguard Dual Game-Worn Jerseys-16
00Vanguard Dual Game-Worn Patches-16
01Atomic Jerseys-9
01Atomic Patches-9
01BAP Memorabilia-167
Emerald-167
Ruby-167
Sapphire-167
Country of Origin-CO46
01BAP Signature Series-68
Autographs-68
Autographs Gold-68
He Shoots-He Scores Prizes-36
Jerseys-GJ-81
Teammates-TM-7
01Bowman YoungStars-51
Gold-51
Ice Cubed-51
01Crown Royale-32
Blue-32
Premiere Date-32
Red-32
Retail-32
Triple Threads-6
01O-Pee-Chee-234
01O-Pee-Chee Premier Parallel-234
01Pacific-84
Extreme LTD-84
Hobby LTD-84
Premiere Date-84
Retail LTD-84
01Pacific Adrenaline-39
Blue-39
Premiere Date-39
Red-39
Retail-39
01Pacific Arena Exclusives-84
01Pacific Heads-Up Quad Jerseys-6
01Parkhurst-235
Jerseys-PJ50
Teammates-T9
01Private Stock Game Gear-22
01Private Stock Game Gear Patches-22
01Private Stock PS-2002-14
01SPx Hidden Treasures-TTDSA
01Titanium-31
Hobby Parallel-31
Premiere Date-31
Retail-31
Retail Parallel-31
All-Stars-4
Double-Sided Jerseys-24
Double-Sided Patches-24
01Topps-234
OPC Parallel-234
01Topps Chrome-67
Refractors-67
Black Border Refractors-67
01Topps Heritage-64
Refractors-64
01Upper Deck-40
Exclusives-40
Game Jerseys-NGED
Ice Jerseys-J-ED
01Upper Deck MVP-40
01Upper Deck Victory-74
Gold-74
01Upper Deck Vintage-53
01Upper Deck Vintage-61
01Vanguard-21
Blue-21
Red-21
One of Ones-21
Premiere Date-21
Proofs-21
02Atomic-20
Blue-20
Gold-20
Red-20
Cold Fusion-7
Hobby Parallel-20
02BAP All-Star Edition-17
Jerseys-17
Jerseys Gold-17
Jerseys Silver-17
02BAP First Edition-78
02BAP First Edition-317
02BAP First Edition-347
Jerseys-78
Scoring Leaders-6
02BAP Memorabilia-49
02BAP Memorabilia-207
02BAP Memorabilia-240
Emerald-49
Emerald-207
Emerald-240
Ruby-49
Ruby-207
Ruby-240
Sapphire-49
Sapphire-207
Sapphire-240
All-Star Jerseys-ASJ-9
Franchise Players-FP-7
NHL All-Star Game-49
NHL All-Star Game-207
NHL All-Star Game-240
NHL All-Star Game Blue-49
NHL All-Star Game Blue-207
NHL All-Star Game Blue-240
NHL All-Star Game Green-49
NHL All-Star Game Green-207
NHL All-Star Game Green-240
NHL All-Star Game Red-49
NHL All-Star Game Red-207
NHL All-Star Game Red-240
Stanley Cup Playoffs-SC-15
02BAP Memorabilia Toronto Fall Expo-49
02BAP Memorabilia Toronto Fall Expo-207
02BAP Memorabilia Toronto Fall Expo-240
02BAP Signature Series-62
Autographs-62
Autograph Buybacks 1998-179
Autograph Buybacks 1999-62
Autograph Buybacks 2001-68
Autographs Gold-62
02BAP Ultimate Memorabilia All-Star MVP-6
02Blackhawks Postcards-1
02Crown Royale-20
Blue-20
Red-20
Retail-20
02ITG Used Franchise Players-F7
02ITG Used Franchise Players Autographs-F7
02ITG Used Franchise Players Gold-F7
02ITG Used Jerseys-GUJ39
02ITG Used Jersey Autographs-GUJ39
02ITG Used Jerseys Gold-GUJ39
02ITG Used Jersey and Stick-SJ39
02ITG Used Jersey and Stick Gold-SJ39
02O-Pee-Chee-94
02O-Pee-Chee Premier Blue Parallel-94
02O-Pee-Chee Premier Red Parallel-94
02O-Pee-Chee Factory Set-94
02Pacific-76
Blue-76
Red-76
02Pacific Calder-14
Silver-14
02Pacific Chicago National *-3
02Pacific Complete-497
Red-497
02Pacific Exclusive-35
02Pacific Heads-Up-25
Blue-25
Purple-25
Red-25
Quad Jerseys-7
Quad Jerseys Gold-7
02Pacific Quest for the Cup-16
Gold-16
02Parkhurst-38
Bronze-38
Gold-38
Silver-38
Franchise Players-FP7
He Shoots-He Scores Prizes-26
Jerseys-GJ6
Stick and Jerseys-SJ6
Teammates-TT13
02Parkhurst Retro-32
Minis-32
02Private Stock Reserve-20
Blue-20
Red-20
Retail-20
02SP Authentic-18
Beckett Promos-18
02SP Game Used-10
02SP Game Used-65
Authentic Fabrics-AFDA
Authentic Fabrics-AFED
Authentic Fabrics Gold-AFDA
Authentic Fabrics Gold-AFED
Authentic Fabrics Rainbow-AFDA
Authentic Fabrics Rainbow-AFED
Piece of History-PHED
Piece of History Gold-PHED
Piece of History Rainbow-PHED
02SPx-14
Spectrum Gold-14
Spectrum Silver-14
Smooth Skaters-ED
Smooth Skaters Gold-ED
Smooth Skaters Silver-ED
02Stadium Club-54
Silver Decoy Cards-54
Proofs-54
Lone Star Signatures Blue-LSED
Lone Star Signatures Red-LSED
02Topps-94
OPC Blue Parallel-94
OPC Red Parallel-94
Factory Set-94
02Topps Chrome-59
Black Border Refractors-59
Refractors-59
02Topps Heritage-26
Chrome Parallel-26
02Topps Total-365
Award Winners-AW7
02UD Artistic Impressions-18
Gold-18
02UD Artistic Impressions Beckett Promos-18
02UD Artistic Impressions Retrospectives-R18
02UD Artistic Impressions Retrospect Gold-R18
02UD Artistic Impress Retrospect Silver-R18
02UD Honor Roll Grade A Jerseys-GAED
02UD Mask Collection Instant Offense-IOED
02UD Mask Collection Patches-PGED
02UD Piece of History-18
02UD Top Shelf-19
Dual Player Jerseys-STDT
Goal Oriented-GOED
02Upper Deck-39
Exclusives-39
CHL Graduates-CGED
CHL Graduates Gold-CGED
Difference Makers-ED
Pinpoint Accuracy-PAED
02Upper Deck Classic Portraits-21
Headliners-DZ
Headliners Limited-DZ
Hockey Royalty-DZT
Hockey Royalty-GTD
Hockey Royalty Limited-DZT
Hockey Royalty Limited-GTD
02Upper Deck MVP-43
Gold-43
Classics-43
Golden Classics-43
02Upper Deck Victory-45
Bronze-45
Gold-45
Silver-45
02Upper Deck Vintage-59
02Upper Deck Vintage-267
Green Backs-59
Jerseys-OSED
Tall Boys-T13
Tall Boys Gold-T13
02Vanguard-22
LTD-22
02UD SuperStars Leg Leaders Triple Jersey-SEB
03BAP Memorabilia-26
Emerald-26
Gold-26
Ruby-26
Sapphire-26
All-Star Jerseys-ASJ-20
03Beehive-40
Gold-40
Silver-40
03Black Diamond-6
Black-6
Green-6
Red-6
Threads-DT-ED
Threads Green-DT-ED
Threads Red-DT-ED
Threads Black-DT-ED
03Blackhawks Postcards-6
03ITG Action-177
Jerseys-M127
03ITG Used Signature Series-29
Gold-29
Autographs-ED
Autographs Gold-ED
03NHL Sticker Collection-173
03O-Pee-Chee-119
03OPC Blue-119
03OPC Gold-119
03OPC Red-119
03Pacific-72
Blue-72
Red-72
03Pacific Complete-37
Red-37
03Pacific Exhibit-32
03Pacific Exhibit-203
Blue Backs-32
Yellow Backs-32
03Pacific Invincible-17
Blue-17
Red-17
Retail-17
03Pacific Prism-108
Blue-108
Patches-108
Red-108
Retail-108
03Pacific Supreme Jerseys-7
03Parkhurst Original Six Chicago-6
Memorabilia-CM3
Memorabilia-CM12
Memorabilia-CM55
03Parkhurst Orig Six He Shoots/Scores-21
03Parkhurst Orig Six He Shoots/Scores-21A
03Private Stock Reserve-152
Blue-152
Patches-152
Red-152
Retail-152
03Topps-119
Blue-119
Gold-119
Red-119
03Upper Deck-284
Canadian Exclusives-284
HG-284
UD Exclusives-284
03Upper Deck MVP-92
Gold Script-92
Silver Script-92
Canadian Exclusives-92
SportsNut-SN20
03Upper Deck Victory-39
Bronze-39
Gold-39
Silver-39
03Toronto Star-18
04Pacific-60
Blue-60
Red-60
04SP Authentic-104
04Upper Deck-40
Canadian Exclusives-40
HG Glossy Gold-40
HG Glossy Silver-40
05Be A Player-18
First Period-18
Second Period-18
Third Period-18
Overtime-18
Dual Signatures-DT
Quad Signatures-HAWK
Quad Signatures-SDPH
Signatures-ZE
Signatures Gold-ZE
Triple Signatures-PDL
05Beehive-21
Matte-21
Signature Scrapbook-SSED
05Black Diamond-22
Emerald-22
Gold-22
Onyx-22
Ruby-22
05Parkhurst-111
Facsimile Auto Parallel-111
True Colors-TCCHI
True Colors-TCCHI
True Colors-TCCHDE

True Colors-TCCHDE
05SP Authentic-23
Limited-23
Sign of the Times-ED
05SP Game Used Auto Draft-AD-ED
05SP Game Used SIGnificance-ED
05SP Game Used SIGnificance Gold-S-ED
05SP Game Used Significant Numbers-SN-ED
05SP Game Used Statscriptions-ST-ED
05SPx Winning Materials-WM-ED
05SPx Winning Materials Autographs-AWM-ED
05SPx Winning Materials Gold-WM-ED
05SPx Winning Materials Spectrum-WM-ED
05SPx Xcitement Superstars-XS-ED
05SPx Xcitement Superstars Gold-XS-ED
05SPx Xcitement Superstars Spectrum-XS-ED
05The Cup Honorable Numbers-HNED
05The Cup Limited Logos-LLED
05UD Artifacts-22
05UD Artifacts-157
Blue-22
Blue-157
Gold-22
Gold-157
Green-22
Green-157
Pewter-22
Pewter-157
Red-22
Red-157
Gold Autographed-22
Gold Autographed-157
Remarkable Artifacts-RA-ED
Remarkable Artifacts Dual-RA-ED
05UD PowerPlay-19
Rainbow-19
05Ultra-49
Gold-49
Ice-49
Scoring Kings-SK40
Scoring Kings Jerseys-SKJ-ED
Scoring Kings Jersey Autographs-KAJ-ED
Scoring Kings Patches-SKP-ED
Scoring Kings Patch Autographs-KAP-ED
05Upper Deck-29
Big Playmakers-B-ED
HG Glossy-39
Notable Numbers-N-ED
Patches-P-ED
05Upper Deck MVP-87
Gold-87
Platinum-87
Materials-M-ED
Materials Duals-D-PD
ProSign-P-ED
05Upper Deck Rookie Update-239
Inspirations Patch Rookies-239
05Upper Deck Trilogy Honorary Patches-HP-ED
05Upper Deck Tril Honorary Patch Script-HSP-ED
05Upper Deck Trilogy Honorary Swatches-HS-ED
05Upper Deck Tril Honorary Swatch Scripts-HSS-ED
05Upper Deck Toronto Fall Expo-39
05Upper Deck Victory-40
Black-40
Gold-40
Silver-40
Game Breakers-GB7
06Flair Showcase Inks-IED
06Flair Showcase Stitches-SSED
06Fleer Fabricology-FED
06Ultra Uniformity-UED
06Ultra Uniformity Patches-UPED
06Ultra Uniformity Autographed Jerseys-UAED
06Upper Deck Trilogy Scripts-TSED

Daze, Pascal
96Owen Sound Platers-15

De Allegri, Sebastien
96Swiss HNL-253

de Brass, Christian
96Danish Hockey League-71

de Bruijn, Brain
05Dutch Vadeko Flyers -20

de Gray, John
04Brampton Battalion-13
05Brampton Battalion-4
05ITG Heroes and Prospects-294
Team Cherry-TC12
06Brampton Battalion-9

de Heer, Jack
79Panini Stickers-282

De Jonge, Gavin
93UK Humberside Hawks-2
94UK Humberside Hawks-NNO

De Marchi, Emile
79Panini Stickers-392

De Piero, Bob
82Swedish Semic VM Stickers-140
83Swedish Semic VM Stickers-140

De Raaf, Helmut
91Finnish Semic World Champ Stickers-152
91Swedish Semic World Champ Stickers-152
93Swedish Semic World Champ Stickers-149
94German DEL-78
95German DEL-76

de Ruiter, Chris
92Clarkson Knights-18

De Santis, Mark
94Classic Pro Prospects-77

De Toni, Lino
93Swedish Semic World Champ Stickers-223
94Finnish Jaa Kiekko-306

Dea, Billy
44Beehive Group II Photos-159
44Beehive Group II Photos-306
57Topps-39
68O-Pee-Chee-190
70Esso Power Players-142
70O-Pee-Chee-30
70Sargent Promotions Stamps-53
70Topps-30
76Old Timers-5
81Red Wings Oldtimers-11
94Parkhurst Missing Link-47

Deacon, Don
39O-Pee-Chee V301-1-70

Deadmarsh, Adam
917th Inn. Sketch WHL-32
92Upper Deck-609
93Donruss Team USA-5
93Pinnacle-491
Canadian-491
93Upper Deck-562
93Portland Winter Hawks-7
93Classic-20
93Classic Four-Sport *-197
Gold-197
94Be A Player-R165
94Finest-31
94Finest-118
Super Team Winners-31
Super Team Winners-118
Refractors-31
Refractors-118
Bowman's Best-R13
Bowman's Best Refractors-R13
94Flair-144
94Fleer-174
94Leaf-442
Limited World Juniors USA-4
94Nordiques Burger King-4
94OPC Premier-449
Special Effects-449
94Parkhurst SE-SE144
94Parkhurst SE-SE246
Gold-SE144
Gold-SE246
94Pinnacle-253
Artist's Proofs-253
Rink Collection-253
94Select-179
Gold-179
94SP Premier-15
94SP Premier Die-Cuts-15
94Topps/OPC Premier-449
Special Effects-449
94Ultra-355
94Upper Deck-261
94Upper Deck-562
Electric Ice-261
Electric Ice-562
SP Inserts-SP155
SP Inserts Die Cuts-SP155
94Classic Tri-Cards-T55
95Be A Player-186
Signatures-S186
Signatures Die Cuts-S186
95Canada Games NHL POGS-81
95Collector's Choice-294
95Collector's Choice-360
Player's Club-294
Player's Club-360
Player's Club Platinum-294
Player's Club Platinum-360
95Donruss-145
95Leaf-72
95Metal-30
95Parkhurst International-54
Emerald Ice-54
95Pinnacle-72
Artist's Proofs-72
Rink Collection-72
95Playoff One on One-136
95Score-168
Black Ice Artist's Proofs-168
Black Ice-168
95SkyBox Impact NHL On Fox-4
95SP-33
95Topps-288
OPC Inserts-288
New To The Game-6NG
95Ultra-130
Gold Medallion-130
95Upper Deck-65
Electric Ice-65
Electric Ice Gold-65
Special Edition-SE22
Special Edition Gold-SE22
95Images-60
Gold-60
Autographs-60A
96Black Diamond-81
Gold-81
96Collector's Choice-58
96Donruss-145
Press Proofs-145
96Metal Universe-30
96Pinnacle-43
Artist's Proofs-43
Foil-43
Premium Stock-43
Rink Collection-43
96Score-93
Artist's Proofs-93
Dealer's Choice Artist's Proofs-93
Special Artist's Proofs-93
Golden Blades-93
96SP-36
Clearcut Winner-CW17
96Topps Picks-103
OPC Inserts-103
96Ultra-34
Gold Medallion-34
96Upper Deck-41
Generation Next-X25
Power Performers-P23
97Be A Player-52
Autographs-52
Autographs Die-Cuts-52
Autographs Prismatic Die-Cuts-52
97Black Diamond-75
Double Diamond-75
Triple Diamond-75
Quadruple Diamond-75
97Collector's Choice-57
Star Quest-SQ45
97Crown Royale-32
Emerald Green-32
Ice Blue-32
Silver-32
97Donruss-161
Press Proofs Silver-161
Press Proofs Gold-161
Red Alert-1
97Donruss Canadian Ice-126
Dominion Series-126
Provincial Series-126
97Donruss Elite-75
Aspirations-75
Status-75
97Donruss Limited-95
97Donruss Limited-132
97Donruss Limited-161
Exposure-95
Exposure-132
Exposure-161
97Donruss Preferred-53
Cut to the Chase-53
97Donruss Priority-163
Stamp of Approval-163
97Katch-37
Gold-37
Silver-37
97Leaf-57
Fractal Matrix-57
Fractal Matrix Die Cuts-57
97Leaf International-57
Universal Ice-57
97Pacific-47
Copper-47
Emerald Green-47
Ice Blue-47
Red-47
Silver-47
97Pacific Invincible-33
Copper-33
Emerald Green-33
Ice Blue-33
Red-33
Silver-33
97Pacific Omega-55
Copper-55
Dark Gray-55
Emerald Green-55
Gold-55
Ice Blue-55
97Paramount-48
Copper-48
Dark Grey-48
Emerald Green-48
Ice Blue-48
Red-48
Silver-48
97Pinnacle-114
Press Plates Back Black-114
Press Plates Back Cyan-114
Press Plates Back Magenta-114
Press Plates Back Yellow-114
Press Plates Front Black-114
Press Plates Front Cyan-114
Press Plates Front Magenta-114
Press Plates Front Yellow-114
97Pinnacle Certified-112
Red-112
Mirror Blue-112
Mirror Gold-112
Mirror Red-112
97Pinnacle Inside-170
97Pinnacle Tot Cert Platinum Blue-112
97Pinnacle Tot Cert Platinum Gold-112
97Pinnacle Totally Certified Platinum Red-112
97Pinnacle Tot Cert Mirror Platinum Gold-112
97Score-146
Artist's Proofs-146
Golden Blades-146
97Score Avalanche-8
Platinum-8
Premier-8
97SP Authentic-40
97Studio-70
Press Proofs Silver-70
Press Proofs Gold-70
97Upper Deck-46
Three Star Selects-13A
97Upper Deck Ice-18
Parallel-18
Power Shift-18
98Aurora-45
98Be A Player-36
Press Release-36
98BAP Gold-36
98BAP Autographs-36
98BAP Autographs Gold-36
98BAP Tampa Bay All Star Game-36
98Finest-79
No Protectors-79
No Protectors Refractors-79
Refractors-79
98Katch-37
98NHL Game Day Promotion-COL2
98Pacific-18
Ice Blue-18
Red-18
98Pacific Dynagon Ice-45
Blue-45
Red-45
98Pacific Omega-58
Red-58
Opening Day Issue-58
98Paramount-53
Copper-53
Emerald Green-53
Holo-Electric-53
Ice Blue-53
Silver-53
98Revolution-33
Ice Shadow-33
Red-33
98SP Authentic-23
Power Shift-23
Sign of the Times-AD
Sign of the Times Gold-AD
98UD Choice-57
98UD Choice Preview-57
98UD Choice Prime Choice Reserve-57
98UD Choice Reserve-57
98Upper Deck-72
Exclusives-72
Exclusives 1 of 1-72
Gold Reserve-72
98Upper Deck MVP-58
Gold Script-58
Silver Script-58
Super Script-58
99Aurora-35
Premiere Date-35
99Avalanche Pins-3
99Avalanche Team Issue-2
99BAP Memorabilia-169
Gold-169
Silver-169
99O-Pee-Chee-28
99O-Pee-Chee Chrome-28
99O-Pee-Chee Chrome Refractors-28
99Pacific-101
Copper-101
Emerald Green-101
Gold-101
Ice Blue-101
Premiere Date-101
Red-101
99Pacific Dynagon Ice-54
Blue-54
Copper-54
Gold-54
Premiere Date-54-
99Pacific Omega-60
Copper-60
Gold-60
Ice Blue-60
Premiere Date-60
99Panini Stickers-214
99Paramount-60
Copper-60
Emerald-60
Gold-60
Holographic Emerald-60
Holographic Gold-60
Holographic Silver-60
Ice Blue-60
Premiere Date-60
Red-60
Silver-60
99Revolution-37
Premiere Date-37
Red-37
Shadow Series-37
99SPx-45
Radiance-45
Spectrum-45
99Stadium Club-92
First Day Issue-92
One of a Kind-92
Printing Plates Black-92
Printing Plates Cyan-92
Printing Plates Magenta-92
Printing Plates Yellow-92
99Topps/OPC-28
99Topps/OPC Chrome-28
Refractors-28
99Topps Premier Plus-38
Parallel-38
99Upper Deck-214
Exclusives-214
Exclusives 1 of 1-214
99Upper Deck Gold Reserve-214
99Upper Deck MVP-57
Gold Script-57
Silver Script-57
Super Script-57
99Upper Deck Victory-81
99Wayne Gretzky Hockey-49
99Slovakian Challengers-10
00SLU Hockey-60
00BAP Memorabilia-46
Emerald-46
Ruby-46
Sapphire-46
Promos-46
00BAP Mem Chicago Sportsfest Copper-46
00BAP Memorabilia Chicago Sportsfest Blue-46
00BAP Memorabilia Chicago Sportsfest Gold-46
00BAP Memorabilia Chicago Sportsfest Ruby-46
00BAP Memorabilia Chicago Sun-Times Ruby-46
00BAP Memorabilia Chicago Sun-Times Gold-46
00BAP Mem Chicago Sun-Times Sapphire-46
00BAP Mem Toronto Fall Expo Copper-46
00BAP Memorabilia Toronto Fall Expo Gold-46
00BAP Memorabilia Toronto Fall Expo Ruby-46
00BAP Parkhurst 2000-P192
00O-Pee-Chee-152
00O-Pee-Chee Parallel-152
00Pacific-108
Copper-108
Gold-108
Ice Blue-108
Premiere Date-108
00Paramount-57
Copper-57
Gold-57
Holo-Gold-57
Holo-Silver-57
Ice Blue-57
Premiere Date-57
Game Used Sticks-3
00SP Authentic-41
00Topps/OPC-152
Parallel-152
00UD Heroes-32
00Upper Deck-276
Exclusives Tier 1-276
Exclusives Tier 2-276
00Upper Deck Ice-71
00Upper Deck MVP-53
First Stars-53
Second Stars-53
Third Stars-53
00Upper Deck Victory-64
00Upper Deck Vintage-90
01BAP Memorabilia-267
Emerald-267
Ruby-267
Sapphire-267
01BAP Signature Series-25
Autographs-25
Autographs Gold-25
01Bowman YoungStars-44
Gold-44
Ice Cubed-44
01Crown Royale-67
Blue-67
Premiere Date-67
Red-67
Retail-67
01O-Pee-Chee-110
01O-Pee-Chee Heritage Parallel-110
01O-Pee-Chee Heritage Parallel Limited-110
01O-Pee-Chee Premier Parallel-110
01Pacific-180
Extreme LTD-180
Hobby LTD-180
Premiere Date-180
Retail LTD-180
01Pacific Adrenaline-86
Blue-86
Premiere Date-86
Red-86
Retail-86
01Pacific Arena Exclusives-180
01Parkhurst-238
01SP Game Used-25
01SPx-32
Hidden Treasures-DTJD
Hidden Treasures-TTFSD
01Stadium Club-41
Award Winners-41
Master Photos-41
01Titanium-64
Hobby Parallel-64
Premiere Date-64
Retail-64
Retail Parallel-64
Double-Sided Jerseys-18
Double-Sided Patches-18
01Titanium Draft Day Edition-42
01Topps-110
Heritage Parallel-110
Heritage Parallel Limited-110
OPC Parallel-110
01Topps Chrome-110
Refractors-110
Black Border Refractors-110
01Topps Heritage-50
Refractors-50
01Topps Reserve-59
01UD Challenge for the Cup Jerseys-UCPD
01UD Mask Collection-42
Gold-42
Double Patches-DPAD
Jerseys-J-AD
Jersey and Patch-JPAD
01UD Premier Collection Dual Jerseys-DDP
01UD Premier Collection Dual Jersey Black-DDP
01UD Stanley Cup Champs-42
01Upper Deck-84
Exclusives-84
01Upper Deck Avalanche NHL All-Star Game-CA3
01Upper Deck Ice-21
01Upper Deck MVP-86
01Upper Deck Victory-165
Gold-165
01Upper Deck Vintage-116
01Upper Deck Vintage-122
01Czech Stadion-228
02Kings Team Issue-1
02BAP First Edition-29
02BAP First Edition-388
02BAP First Edition-410H
Jerseys-29
02BAP Memorabilia-29
02BAP Memorabilia-251
Emerald-29
Emerald-251
Ruby-29
Ruby-251
Sapphire-29
Sapphire-251
NHL All-Star Game-29
NHL All-Star Game-251
NHL All-Star Game Blue-29
NHL All-Star Game Blue-251
NHL All-Star Game Green-29
NHL All-Star Game Green-251
NHL All-Star Game Red-29
NHL All-Star Game Red-251
02BAP Memorabilia Toronto Fall Expo-29
02BAP Memorabilia Toronto Fall Expo-251
02BAP Signature Series-19
Autographs-19
Autograph Buybacks 1998-36
Autograph Buybacks 2001-25
Autographs Gold-19
Team Quads-TQ10
02BAP Ultimate Memorabilia Hat Tricks-3
02Crown Royale Dual Patches-12
02ITG Used Triple Memorabilia-TM20
02ITG Used Triple Memorabilia Gold-TM20
02Kings Game Sheets-37
02Kings Game Sheets-38
02O-Pee-Chee-148
02O-Pee-Chee Premier Blue Parallel-148
02O-Pee-Chee Premier Red Parallel-148
02O-Pee-Chee Factory Set-148
02Pacific-165
Blue-165
Red-165
02Pacific Complete-111
Red-111
02Pacific Exclusive-80
02Pacific Heads-Up-56
Blue-56
Purple-56
Red-56
Quad Jerseys-1
Quad Jerseys Gold-1
02Parkhurst-130
Bronze-130
Gold-130
Silver-130
02Parkhurst Retro-43
Minis-43
02Private Stock Reserve-45
Blue-45
Red-45
Retail-45
02SP Game Used First Rounder Patches-AD
02SP Game Used Piece of History-PHAD
02SP Game Used Piece of History Gold-PHAD
02SP Game Used Piece of History Rainbow-PHAD
02Topps-148
OPC Blue Parallel-148
OPC Red Parallel-148
Factory Set-148
02Topps Chrome-90
Black Border Refractors-90
Refractors-90
02Topps Total-156
02UD Honor Roll Team Warriors-TW7
02UD Top Shelf Clutch Performers-CPAD
02UD Top Shelf Dual Player Jerseys-STPD
02UD Top Shelf Goal Oriented-GOAD
02UD Top Shelf Sweet Sweaters-SWAD
02Upper Deck-82
Exclusives-82
Fan Favorites-AD
Classic Portraits Hockey Royalty-DPP
Classic Portraits Hockey Royalty Limited-DPP
Classic Portraits Stitches-CAD
Classic Portraits Stitches Limited-CAD
02Upper Deck MVP-84
Gold-84
Classics-84
Golden Classics-84
Skate Around Jerseys-SAAD
Skate Around Jerseys-SDDL
Skate Around Jerseys-STDAP
02Upper Deck Rookie Update-46
02Upper Deck Rookie Update-152B
02Upper Deck Victory-95
Bronze-95
Gold-95
Silver-95
02Upper Deck Vintage-121
02Upper Deck Vintage-274
02Upper Deck Vintage-314
Green Backs-121
02Vanguard-48
LTD-48
03Beehive-89
Gold-89
Silver-89
03Black Diamond-81
Black-81
Green-81
Red-81
03ITG Action-277
Jerseys-M17
03NHL Sticker Collection-234
03O-Pee-Chee-171
03OPC Blue-171
03OPC Gold-171
03OPC Red-171
03Pacific-154
Blue-154
Red-154
03Pacific Complete-190
Red-190
03Pacific Exhibit-68
Blue Backs-68
Yellow Backs-68
03Pacific Luxury Suite-37A
03Pacific Luxury Suite-37B
03Pacific Luxury Suite-37C
03Pacific Prism-48
Blue-48
Gold-48
Red-48
03Private Stock Reserve-46
Blue-46
Red-46
Retail-46
03SPx Winning Materials-WM-AD
03SPx Winning Materials Limited-WM-AD
03Topps-171
Blue-171
Gold-171
Red-171
03Upper Deck-331
Canadian Exclusives-331
HG-331
UD Exclusives-331
Classic Portraits Classic Stitches-CS-AD
03Upper Deck MVP-197
Gold Script-197
Silver Script-197
Canadian Exclusives-197
03Upper Deck Trilogy Limited Threads-LT21
03Upper Deck Victory-86
Bronze-86
Gold-86
Silver-86

Deadmarsh, Butch
72Sabres Postcards-4
74O-Pee-Chee NHL-73
75O-Pee-Chee WHA-59
76O-Pee-Chee WHA-53

Deadmarsh, Jake
93Portland Winter Hawks-9
95Kamloops Blazers-3
95Signature Rookies Auto-Phonex-12
95Signature Rook Auto-Phonex Phone Cards-12
96Kamloops Blazers-7
98Huntington Blizzard-18

Dean, Barry
75Phoenix Roadrunners WHA-6
76Rockies Coke Cans-5
77O-Pee-Chee NHL-183
77Topps-183
78O-Pee-Chee-142
78Topps-142
79O-Pee-Chee-318

Dean, Bob
61Hamilton Red Wings-3

Dean, Kevin
91ProCards-417
92Cincinnati Cyclones-8
95Topps-208
OPC Inserts-208
96Devils Team Issue-28
97Be A Player-57
Autographs-57
Autographs Die-Cuts-57
Autographs Prismatic Die-Cuts-57
97Devils Team Issue-22
98Be A Player-82
Press Release-82
98BAP Gold-82
98BAP Autographs-82
98BAP Autographs Gold-82
98BAP Tampa Bay All Star Game-82
98Devils Team Issue-9
99Panini Stickers-14
00Pacific-94
Copper-94
Gold-94
Ice Blue-94
Premiere Date-94
00Upper Deck NHLPA-PA19
01Upper Deck Vintage-59
01Milwaukee Admirals-8
01Milwaukee Admirals Postcards-6
02BAP Sig Series Auto Buybacks 1998-82

Dean, Leigh
02New Mexico Scorpions-5

Dean, Scott
92Michigan State Spartans-8

DeAngelis, Mike
84Minnesota-Duluth Bulldogs-28
85Minnesota-Duluth Bulldogs-3
92Finnish Semic-249
93Swedish Semic World Champ Stickers-214
95Finnish Semic World Championships-172
95Swedish World Championships Stickers-85

Dearden, Chris
99Bakersfield Condors-6
00Bakersfield Condors-8

Deasley, Bryan
90ProCards AHL/IHL-619
91ProCards-580

Deazeley, Mark
89Oshawa Generals-19
89Oshawa Generals 7th Inning Sketch-10
897th Inn. Sketch OHL-10
907th Inn. Sketch OHL-335
907th Inn. Sketch Memorial Cup-97
91Oshawa Generals-26
91Oshawa Generals Sheet-17
917th Inn. Sketch OHL-153
92Toledo Storm-12
92Toledo Storm Team Issue-13
93Toledo Storm-14
94Anaheim Bullfrogs RHI-5
95Tallahassee Tiger Sharks-6
97Toledo Storm-15

Debenedet, Nelson
74NHL Action Stamps-232
74O-Pee-Chee NHL-393
74Penguins Postcards-5
81Red Wings Oldtimers-12

DeBenedictis, Mario
03St. Jean Mission-5

Deblois, Eric
98Thetford Mines Coyotes-6

Deblois, Frederic
93Quebec Pee-Wee Tournament-922

DeBlois, Lucien
78O-Pee-Chee-136
78Topps-136
79Rockies Team Issue-6
80O-Pee-Chee-146
80Topps-146
81Jets Postcards-4
81O-Pee-Chee-74
81O-Pee-Chee Stickers-232
81Topps-W79
82Jets Postcards-5
82O-Pee-Chee-379
82O-Pee-Chee Stickers-212
82Post Cereal-21
82Topps Stickers-212
83Jets Postcards-5
83NHL Key Tags-138
83O-Pee-Chee-378
83O-Pee-Chee-383
83O-Pee-Chee Stickers-284
83Topps Stickers-284
83Vachon-125
84Canadiens Postcards-5
84O-Pee-Chee-260
84O-Pee-Chee Stickers-290
85Canadiens Postcards-8
85Canadiens Provigo-4
89Nordiques Team Issue-6
89Nordiques General Foods-4
89Nordiques Police-3
90Nordiques Petro-Canada-4
90Nordiques Team Issue-2
90O-Pee-Chee-441
90Panini Stickers-140
90Pro Set-244
90Pro Set-531
90Upper Deck-363
French-363
91Maple Leafs PLAY-8
91O-Pee-Chee-102
91Panini Stickers-100
91Pro Set-491
French-491
91Score Canadian Bilingual-395
91Score Canadian English-395
91Topps-102
92Durivage Panini-2
92Score-371
Canadian-371
96Kansas City Blades-23

Deblois, Philippe
93Quebec Pee-Wee Tournament-940
93Quebec Pee-Wee Tournament-944
99Shawinigan Cataractes-12
Signed-12
03St. Georges de Beauce Garaga-3

DeBoer, Pete
89ProCards IHL-169
90ProCards AHL/IHL-330
93Detroit Jr. Red Wings-24
95Slapshot-80
95Slapshot Memorial Cup-100
96Detroit Whalers-21

Debol, Dave
79Panini Stickers-215
79O-Pee-Chee-363
80O-Pee-Chee-381
82Birmingham South Stars-7
04Michigan Wolverines TK Legacy-H6
04Michigan Wolverines TK Legacy-VH6

Debray, Clayton
96OCN Blizzard-20

Debrie, Darren
95Slapshot-270

DeBrusk, Louie
897th Inn. Sketch OHL-28
907th Inn. Sketch OHL-132
91Oilers IGA-4
91Oilers Team Issue-5
91Parkhurst-281
French-281
91Pinnacle-347
French-347
91Pro Set-535
French-535
91Upper Deck-249
91Upper Deck-526
French-249
French-526
92Bowman-318
92Oilers IGA-5
92Oilers Team Issue-4
92Stadium Club-290
92Topps-392
Gold-392G
92Upper Deck-467
93Donruss-108
93Leaf-225
93OPC Premier-319
Gold-319
93Parkhurst-337
Emerald Ice-337
93Topps/OPC Premier-319
Gold-319
93Upper Deck-79
94Be A Player-R89
Signature Cards-29
94Leaf-532
94Upper Deck-485
Electric Ice-485
95Collector's Choice-87
Player's Club-87
Player's Club Platinum-87
95Parkhurst International-81
Emerald Ice-81
96Collector's Choice-100
96Oilers Postcards-29
97Pacific Dynagon Best Kept Secrets-37
97Pacific Omega-211
Copper-211
Dark Gray-211
Emerald Green-211
Gold-211
Ice Blue-211
98Pacific-398
Ice Blue-398
Red-398
00Pacific-313
Copper-313
Gold-313
Ice Blue-313
Premiere Date-313
00Upper Deck-365
Exclusives Tier 1-365
Exclusives Tier 2-365
01Pacific-418
Gold-418
01Pacific Arena Exclusives-418
02Norfolk Admirals-7

DeBus, Steve
94Minnesota Golden Gophers-10
95Minnesota Golden Gophers-11
96Minnesota Golden Gophers-10
97Minnesota Golden Gophers-4
98Mobile Mysticks-5
99Mobile Mysticks-19
01Rockford IceHogs-22

Debusschere, Dave
91Air Canada SJHL-D46
92Saskatchewan JHL-8

Decaen, Steve
917th Inn. Sketch QMJHL-153

DeCarle, Mike
89ProCards IHL-104
91Nashville Knights-19
92Nashville Knights-15

Decary, Ed
10C56-13

DeCecco, Brett
96Seattle Thunderbirds-16
97Upper Deck-409
97Seattle Thunderbirds-14
98Bowman's Best-149
Refractors-149
Atomic Refractors-149
98Bowman CHL-59
Golden Anniversary-59
OPC International-59
98Bowman Chrome CHL-59
Golden Anniversary-59
Golden Anniversary Refractors-59
OPC International-59
OPC International Refractors-59
Refractors-59
99Bowman CHL-107
99Bowman CHL-163
Gold-107
Gold-163
OPC International-107
OPC International-163
00Kootenay Ice-6
01Roanoke Express-5
02Peoria Rivermen-8
03Alaska Aces-3
03Peoria Rivermen-3

Decelles, Luc
93Drummondville Voltigeurs-20

Dechaine, Chris
92Saskatchewan JHL-107

DeCiantis, Rob
94Kitchener Rangers-21
95Slapshot-141
95Classic-87
96Kitchener Rangers-6
99Quad-City Mallards-20

Deck, Kim
87Kamloops Blazers-6
88Kamloops Blazers-9
89Portland Winter Hawks-5
907th Inn. Sketch WHL-156
907th Inn. Sketch WHL-323

Deck, Kyle
03Regina Pats-3
04Regina Pats-4
05Regina Pats-2
06Regina Pats-3

Decker, Todd
87Kamloops Blazers-7

Deckert, Jesse
02Regina Pats-6
03Regina Pats-22
04Salmon Arm Silverbacks-16
05Prince Albert Raiders-6
06Prince Albert Raiders-2

Decloe, Dick
93Swiss HNL-237

DeCoff, Mike
89Oshawa Generals-4
907th Inn. Sketch OHL-155
917th Inn. Sketch Memorial Cup-15

Decontie, Ronnie
99Rimouski Oceanic-14
Signed-14

Decorby, Ian
94Erie Panthers-20

DeCoste, Kyle
06Brampton Battalion-22

DeCosty, Derek
92Wheeling Thunderbirds-4
93Wheeling Thunderbirds-4
94Wheeling Thunderbirds-6
94Wheeling Thunderbirds Photo Album-2
95Wheeling Thunderbirds-9
96UK Guildford Flames-17
99UK Guildford Flames-11
00UK Guildford Flames-7
01UK Guildford Flames-6
01UK Guildford Flames-24
02UK Guildford Flames-4

Decurtins, Christoph
00Swiss Panini Stickers-130
01Swiss HNL-365
02Swiss HNL-428

Deeks, Alain
92Hamilton Canucks-5
94Knoxville Cherokees-16

Deev, Alexei
97Macon Whoopee-17
97Macon Whoopee Autographs-17
98UHL All-Stars-12
99Adirondack IceHawks-18
99UHL All-Stars East-14T
00Tacoma Sabercats-7
03Russian Hockey League-124

Deev, Yakov
99Russian Hockey League-49

Deeves, David
02Macon Trax-3
05Florida Seals Team Issue-3

DeFauw, Brad
00Cincinnati Cyclones-17
02BAP Memorabilia-348
02BAP Ultimate Memorabilia-95
02Upper Deck Rookie Update-144
02Lowell Lock Monsters-22
03ITG Action-191
03Lowell Lock Monsters-2
03Lowell Lock Monsters Photo Album-18

Defazio, Dan
82Oshawa Generals-14

DeFazio, Jerrett
897th Inn. Sketch OHL-57
907th Inn. Sketch OHL-82

Defelice, Norman
44Beehive Group II Photos-66A

52Juniors Blue Tint-18
Defoe, Marc
04Swift Current Broncos-2
Defrancescanto, Chris
04South Surrey Eagles-3
Defrenza, Frank
907th Inn. Sketch WHL-98
917th Inn. Sketch WHL-54
99Asheville Smoke-5
00UK Sekonda Superleague-185
Defty, Ian
97UK Kingston Hawks Stickers-19
98UK Kingston Hawks-2
99UK Hull Thunder-3
01UK Hull Thunder-16
Degaetano, Phil
88ProCards AHL-164
94Finnish Jaa Kiekko-294
Degagne, Dustin
04Salmon Arm Silverbacks-3
05Salmon Arm Silverbacks-6
Degagne, Rob
82North Bay Centennials-3
83North Bay Centennials-7
Degagne, Shawn
96Kitchener Rangers-7
01Atlantic City Boardwalk Bullies-9
Degenhardt, A.J.
03Wisconsin Badgers-6
04Wisconsin Badgers-20
05Wisconsin Badgers-5
Degerstedt, Patrik
93Swedish Semic Elitserien-91
98German DEL-289
DeGiacomo, Dwight
90Michigan Tech Huskies-3
Degn, Kasper
98Danish Hockey League-178
99Danish Hockey League-51
Degn, Lasse
98Danish Hockey League-169
99Danish Hockey League-64
Degner, Terry
907th Inn. Sketch WHL-99
917th Inn. Sketch WHL-290
Degon, Marvin
06Hartford Wolf Pack-14
DeGrace, Yanick
907th Inn. Sketch QMJHL-170
917th Inn. Sketch QMJHL-208
DeGray, Dale
80Oshawa Generals-11
81Oshawa Generals-14
82Oshawa Generals-4
84Moncton Golden Flames-11
85Moncton Golden Flames-20
87Maple Leafs PLAY-25
88Kings Postcards-17
88Kings Smokey-5
89O-Pee-Chee-18
89Topps-18
90ProCards AHL/IHL-279
92San Diego Gulls-5
93San Diego Gulls-6
94Cleveland Lumberjacks-25
94Cleveland Lumberjacks Postcards-24
95Cincinnati Cyclones-5
96Cincinnati Cyclones-51
96Collector's Edge Ice-111
Prism-111
98Indianapolis Ice-25
99Rockford IceHogs-23
00Rockford IceHogs-21
Deguehery, Jason
03Huntsville Channel Cats-7
04Huntsville Havoc-5
Deguise, Michel
76Saginaw Gears-3
88Richelieu Riverains-11
Degurse, Mike
98Huntsville Channel Cats-7
03Huntsville Channel Cats-8
04Huntsville Havoc-18
Dehaime, Trevor
907th Inn. Sketch QMJHL-210
Dehart, John
91British Columbia JHL-99
91British Columbia JHL-164
92Cornell Big Red-6
93Cornell Big Red-6
Dehart, Tony
06London Knights-12
Dehner, Jeremy
04Green Bay Gamblers-4
04Green Bay Gamblers-25
Deines, Kris
02Calgary Hitmen-4
03Calgary Hitmen-5
05Calgary Hitmen-5
Deis, Tyler
92Saskatchewan JHL-52
99Charlotte Checkers-11
99Charlotte Checkers-34
00Charlotte Checkers-20
02Greenville Grrrowl-5
Deisenberger, Walter
94German First League-180
Deiter, Thomas
94German DEL-432
Deitsch, Jason
05Kalamazoo Wings-6
DeJong, Eric
92Quebec Pee-Wee Tournament-1560
93Quebec Pee-Wee Tournament-1255
DeJordy, Denis
61Topps-37
62Topps-25
63Topps-24
64Beehive Group III Photos-32
64Coca-Cola Caps-36
64Topps-22
65Topps-113
66Topps-115
66Topps USA Test-50
67Topps-65
67Topps-115
68O-Pee-Chee-12
68Shirriff Coins-20
68Topps-12
69O-Pee-Chee-66
Four-in-One-7
69Topps-66
70Colgate Stamps-84
70Dad's Cookies-20
70Esso Power Players-162
70O-Pee-Chee-137
70Sargent Promotions Stamps-73
70Topps-31
71Bazooka-8
71Canadiens Postcards-4
71O-Pee-Chee-63
71Topps-63
71Toronto Sun-110
72O-Pee-Chee-184
72Sargent Promotions Stamps-130
72Topps-144
73Red Wings Team Issue-7
94Parkhurst Tall Boys-28
95Parkhurst '66-67-39
Coins-39
Del Curto, Arno
93Swiss HNL-160
98Swiss Power Play Stickers-53
99Swiss Panini Stickers-53
00Swiss Panini Stickers-101
01Swiss HNL-98
02Swiss HNL-248
04Swiss Davos Postcards-9
Del Monte, Daniel
05German DEL-360
06German DEL-30
Del Monte, Dion
96German DEL-331
97UK Sheffield Steelers-10
Del Zotto, Michael
06Oshawa Generals-16
06ITG Heroes and Prospects-119
Autographs-AMDZ
Delacoure, Robin
03Greenville Grrrowl-7
Delahey, Matt
06Regina Pats-4
Delaney, Keith
96Barrie Colts-5
97Barrie Colts-6
Delaronde, Shane
95Slapshot-10
95Barrie Colts-7
Delaronde, Terrance
04Regina Pats-15
05Kamloops Blazers-18
06Kamloops Blazers-5
Delarosbil, Raymond
907th Inn. Sketch QMJHL-178
917th Inn. Sketch QMJHL-155
93Drummondville Voltigeurs-18
97Macon Whoopee-14
97Macon Whoopee Autographs-14
99Rockford IceHogs-6
03St. Georges de Beauce Garaga-4
04St Georges de Beauce Garaga-8
Delcourt, Grant
84Kelowna Wings-18
Deleeuw, Adam
96Barrie Colts-6
00St. Michaels Majors-13
Deleeuw, Brian
84Nanaimo Clippers-7
Delesoy, Jason
92British Columbia JHL-16
Deleurme, Jason
93Tacoma Rockets-6
98Hampton Roads Admirals-11
98Bowman CHL-49
Golden Anniversary-49
OPC International-49
98Bowman Chrome CHL-49
Golden Anniversary-49
Golden Anniversary Refractors-49
OPC International-49
OPC International Refractors-49
Refractors-49
01German Upper Deck-238
04Swedish Elitset-230
Gold-230
Delfino, David
92Finnish Semic-243
93Swedish Semic World Champ Stickers-209
94Finnish Jaa Kiekko-291
DelGuidice, Matt
90ProCards AHL/IHL-125
91OPC Premier-96
91Parkhurst-1
French-1
91Pro Set-521
French-521
91Upper Deck-463
French-463
93Raleigh Icecaps-3
95Roanoke Express-3
Delianedis, Dan
88ProCards AHL-330
Delisle, Guy
51Bas Du Fleuve-12
DeLisle, Joe
84Minnesota-Duluth Bulldogs-5
85Minnesota-Duluth Bulldogs-29
Delisle, Jonathan
95Slapshot Memorial Cup-70
97Bowman CHL-55
OPC-55
99Quebec Citadelles-10
00Quebec Citadelles-12
Signed-12
01New Mexico Scorpions-12
01Quebec Citadelles-14
03St. Georges de Beauce Garaga-6
04St Georges de Beauce Garaga-10
Delisle, Miguel
99Upper Deck Sobey's Memorial Cup-16
99Ottawa 67's-4
99UD Prospects-21
00Ottawa 67's-15
00UD CHL Prospects-18
01Ottawa 67's-16
02Kingston Frontenacs-4
02Owen Sound Attack-21
03ECHL Update RBI Sports-123
Delisle, Steven
06Gatineau Olympiques-6
Delisle, Xavier
94Parkhurst SE-SE255
Gold-SE255
94SP-178
Die Cuts-178
98Cleveland Lumberjacks-10
99Quebec Citadelles-4
00Canadiens Postcards-5
00Titanium Draft Day Edition-163
00Titanium Draft Day Promos-163
00Quebec Citadelles-4
Signed-4
01Quebec Citadelles-25
03German DEL-21
04German DEL-266
Deliva, Joey
917th Inn. Sketch QMJHL-204
Dell'Anna, Marc
93Quebec Pee-Wee Tournament-1773
Dell'Jannone, Patrick
82Swedish Semic VM Stickers-133
Della Bella, Paolo
95Swiss HNL-186
96Swiss HNL-79
00Russian Hockey League-121
01Swiss HNL-26
Della Rossa, Patric
93Swiss HNL-19
95Swiss HNL-17
96Swiss HNL-18
98Swiss Power Play Stickers-237
99Swiss Panini Stickers-240
99Swiss Panini Stickers-266
00Swiss Panini Stickers-280
00Swiss Panini Stickers National Team-P16
00Swiss Slapshot Mini-Cards-ZSCL9
01Swiss HNL-14
02Swiss HNL-51
02Swiss HNL-480
04Swiss EV Zug Postcards-15
Della Vedova, Scott
99Brampton Battalion-4
00Quebec Remparts-17
Signed-17
Dellaire, Stacy
907th Inn. Sketch QMJHL-172
Dellezay, Dylan
97New Hampshire Wildcats-16
Delmonte, Dan
93Peterborough Petes-24
94Sarnia Sting-17
Delmonte, David
93Quebec Pee-Wee Tournament-499
Delmore, Andy
93North Bay Centennials-5
95Slapshot-336
95Sarnia Sting-6
95Signature Rookies Auto-Phonex-13
95Signature Rook Auto-Phonex Phone Cards-13
96Sarnia Sting-7
97Bowman CHL-34
OPC-34
99BAP Memorabilia-318
Gold-318
Silver-318
99Pacific Omega-177
Copper-177
Gold-177
Ice Blue-177
Premiere Date-177
99Upper Deck Gold Reserve-346
00BAP Memorabilia-60
Emerald-60
Ruby-60
Sapphire-60
Promos-60
00BAP Mem Chicago Sportsfest Copper-60
00BAP Memorabilia Chicago Sportsfest Blue-60
00BAP Memorabilia Chicago Sportsfest Gold-60
00BAP Memorabilia Chicago Sportsfest Ruby-60
00BAP Memorabilia Chicago Sun-Times Ruby-60
00BAP Memorabilia Chicago Sun-Times Gold-60
00BAP Mem Chicago Sun-Times Sapphire-60
00BAP Mem Toronto Fall Expo Copper-60
00BAP Memorabilia Toronto Fall Expo Gold-60
00BAP Memorabilia Toronto Fall Expo Ruby-60
00BAP Signature Series-162
Emerald-162
Ruby-162
Sapphire-162
Autographs-119
Autographs Gold-119
00O-Pee-Chee-301
00O-Pee-Chee Parallel-301
00Pacific-294
Copper-294
Gold-294
Ice Blue-294
Premiere Date-294
00Paramount-178
Copper-178
Gold-178
Holo-Gold-178
Holo-Silver-178
Ice Blue-178
Premiere Date-178
00Stadium Club-71
00Topps/OPC-301
Parallel-301
00Topps Chrome-196
OPC Refractors-196
Refractors-196
00Upper Deck-358
Exclusives Tier 1-358
Exclusives Tier 2-358
00Upper Deck MVP-201
First Stars-201
Second Stars-201
Third Stars-201
00Upper Deck Victory-277
00Upper Deck Vintage-267
01Parkhurst-383
01Upper Deck-327
Exclusives-327
02BAP First Edition-293
02BAP Signature Series-70
Autographs-70
Autographs Gold-70
02Pacific-206
Blue-206
Red-206
02Pacific Complete-148
Red-148
02Topps Total-307
02Upper Deck-97
Exclusives-97
02Upper Deck MVP-105
Gold-105
Classics-105
Golden Classics-105
02Upper Deck Victory-122
Bronze-122
Gold-122
Silver-122
02Upper Deck Vintage-146
03NHL Sticker Collection-258
03Pacific-186
Blue-186
Red-186
03Upper Deck-269
Canadian Exclusives-269
HG-269
UD Exclusives-269
04German Adler Mannheim Eagles Postcards-10
04German DEL-6
05German DEL All-Star Jerseys-AS01
05AHL All-Stars-5
05Syracuse Crunch-25
06Springfield Falcons-4
Delmore, Mark
96Louisiana Ice Gators II-3
99Anchorage Aces-26
DeLorenzo, Tony
01Michigan Tech Huskies-4
Delorimiere, Bob
94Brantford Smoke-2
96Fort Worth Fire-6
Delorme, Gilbert
81Canadiens Postcards-5
82Canadiens Postcards-5
82Canadiens Steinberg-3
83Canadiens Postcards-7
83NHL Key Tags-69
83O-Pee-Chee-186
83O-Pee-Chee Stickers-70
83Topps Stickers-70
83Vachon-43
85Nordiques General Foods-5
85Nordiques McDonald's-4
85Nordiques Provigo-6
85Nordiques Team Issue-5
86Nordiques General Foods-5
86Nordiques McDonald's-5
86Nordiques Yum-Yum-2
86O-Pee-Chee-234
86O-Pee-Chee Stickers-28
87Red Wings Little Caesars-7
88Red Wings Little Caesars-5
89Penguins Foodland-6B
90O-Pee-Chee-517
91ProCards-300
92Cleveland Lumberjacks-6
93Cleveland Lumberjacks-3
93Cleveland Lumberjacks Postcards-7
Delorme, Marc
94Brantford Smoke-19
Delorme, Rene
77Granby Vics-8
Delorme, Ron
77Rockies Coke Cans-4
78O-Pee-Chee-323
79O-Pee-Chee-284
79Rockies Team Issue-7
80O-Pee-Chee-321
81O-Pee-Chee-82
81O-Pee-Chee Stickers-231
82Canucks Team Issue-5
82O-Pee-Chee-347
82Post Cereal-19
83Canucks Team Issue-5
83O-Pee-Chee-348
83Vachon-104
84Canucks Team Issue-7
84O-Pee-Chee-316
84Kelowna Wings-39
02Fleer Throwbacks-47
Gold-47
Platinum-47
04ITG Franchises Canadian-131
Autographs-RD
DeLory, James
04Oshawa Generals-19
04Oshawa Generals Autographs-19
06Oshawa Generals-21
Delparte, Guy
71Johnstown Jets Acme-4
76Rockies Coke Cans-6
76Rockies Puck Bucks-6
Delvecchio, Alex
44Beehive Group II Photos-160
51Parkhurst-63
52Parkhurst-53
53Parkhurst-47
54Parkhurst-36
54Parkhurst-90
54Topps-39
57Topps-34
58Topps-52
59Topps-8
60Parkhurst-36
60Shirriff Coins-44
61Parkhurst-25
61Shirriff/Salada Coins-70
62Parkhurst-32
62York Iron-On Transfers-21
63Chex Photos-9
63Parkhurst-50
63Toronto Star-9
63York White Backs-50
64Beehive Group III Photos-67A
64Beehive Group III Photos-67B
64Coca-Cola Caps-45B
64Topps-95
64Toronto Star-8
65Coca-Cola-44
65Topps-47
66Topps-102
66Topps USA Test-63
67Topps-51
68O-Pee-Chee-28
68Shirriff Coins-37
68Topps-28
69O-Pee-Chee-157
69O-Pee-Chee-206
Four-in-One-18
69Topps-64
70Colgate Stamps-4
70Dad's Cookies-21
70Esso Power Players-135
70O-Pee-Chee-157
70Red Wings Marathon-3
70Sargent Promotions Stamps-59
71Bazooka-7
71O-Pee-Chee-37
O-Pee-Chee/Topps Booklets-12
71Sargent Promotions Stamps-55
71Topps-37
71Toronto Sun-91
72O-Pee-Chee-26
72Sargent Promotions Stamps-76
72Topps-141
72Finnish Semic World Championship-193
72Swedish Semic World Championship-193
73O-Pee-Chee-1
73Red Wings Team Issue-8
73Topps-141
74O-Pee-Chee NHL-222
74Topps-222
76Old Timers-6
81Red Wings Oldtimers-13
83Hall of Fame-230
83Hall of Fame Postcards-E7
85Hall of Fame-230
90Pro Set-652
90Pro Set-658
91Parkhurst PHC-PHC2
91Parkhurst PHC French-PHC2
91Ultimate Original Six-68
French-68
91Star Pics-10
92Parkhurst Parkie Reprints-PR19
94Parkhurst Missing Link-59
94Parkhurst Tall Boys-56
95Parkhurst '66-67-53
95Parkhurst '66-67-127
Coins-53
99BAP Memorabilia AS Retail-R7
99BAP Memorabilia AS Retail Autographs-R7
99Upper Deck Retro-89
Gold-89
Platinum-89
Inkredible-AD
Inkredible Level 2-AD
00Topps Heritage Autographs-HA-AD
00Topps Heritage Autoproofs-39
01Fleer Legacy-60
Ultimate-60
01Greats of the Game-40
Autographs-40
01Topps Archives-13
Arena Seats-ASAD
Autographs-13
Relics-JAD
01Upper Deck Legends-20
Epic Signatures-AD
02BAP Ultimate Memorabilia Numerology-15
02BAP Ultimate Mem Retro Teammates-10
02BAP Ultimate Mem Vintage Jerseys-2
02ITG Used Vintage Memorabilia-VM11
02ITG Used Vintage Memorabilia Gold-VM11
02Parkhurst Reprints-159
02Parkhurst Reprints-173
02Parkhurst Reprints-181
02Parkhurst Reprints-193
02Parkhurst Reprints-255
02Parkhurst Reprints-265
02Parkhurst Reprints-278
02Parkhurst Reprints-292
02Parkhurst Vintage Teammates-VT17
02UD Foundations-20
03BAP Memorabilia Vintage Memorabilia-VM-14
03BAP Ultimate Memorabilia Cornerstones-7
03BAP Ultimate Mem Hometown Heroes-8
03BAP Ultimate Mem Hometown Heroes Gold-8
03BAP Ultimate Mem Vintage Jerseys-16
03BAP Ultimate Mem Vintage Jerseys Gold-16
03Parkhurst Original Six Detroit-36
03Parkhurst Original Six Detroit-70
03Parkhurst Original Six Detroit-72
03Parkhurst Original Six Detroit-82
03Parkhurst Original Six Detroit-100
Autographs-OS-AD
Inserts-D-3
Inserts-D-11
Memorabilia-DM28
Memorabilia-DM38
Memorabilia-DM54
03Parkhurst Orig Six He Shoots/Scores-28
03Parkhurst Orig Six He Shoots/Scores-28A
04ITG Franchises He Shoots/Scores Prizes-26
04ITG Franchises US West-214
Autographs-A-AD
Forever Rivals-WFR4
Forever Rivals Gold-WFR4
Memorabilia-WSM6
Memorabilia Autographs-WSMAD
Memorabilia Gold-WSM6
Teammates-WTM10
Teammates Gold-WTM10
04ITG Ultimate Memorabilia-62
Gold-62
Auto Threads-6
Autographs-12
Autographs Gold-12
Complete Jerseys-10
Cornerstones-1
Cornerstones Gold-1
Jersey Autographs-51
Jersey Autographs Gold-51
Original Six-4
Original Six-14
Retro Teammates-6
Stick Autographs-34
Stick Autographs Gold-34
04ITG Heroes and Prospects-177
Autographs-AD
Hero Memorabilia-21
04ITG Heroes/Prospects Toronto Expo '05-177
04ITG Heroes/Prospects Expo Heroes/Pros-177
05ITG Ultimate Memorabilia Level 1-1
05ITG Ultimate Memorabilia Level 2-1
05ITG Ultimate Memorabilia Level 3-1
05ITG Ultimate Memorabilia Level 4-1
05ITG Ultimate Memorabilia Level 5-1
05ITG Ultimate Mem Cornerstones Jerseys-4
05ITG Ultimate Mem Cornerst Jerseys Gold-4
05ITG Ultimate Mem Decades Jerseys-2
05ITG Ultimate Mem Decades Jerseys Gold-2
05ITG Ultimate Mem Pass the Torch Jerseys-10
05ITG Ultimate Mem Passing Torch Jsy Gold-10
05ITG Ultimate Mem Raised to the Rafters-11
05ITG Ultimate Mem Raised Rafters Gold-11
05ITG Ultimate Mem Retro Teammate Jerseys-24
05ITG Ult Mem Retro Teammates Jersey Gold-24
05ITG Ultimate Mem 3 Star of the Game Jsy-7
05ITG Ult Mem 3 Star of the Game Jsy Gold-7
05ITG Ultimate Memorabilia Vintage Lumber-20
05ITG Ultimate Mem Vintage Lumber Gold-20
06ITG Ultimate Memorabilia-4
Artist Proof-4
Autos-8
Autos Gold-8
Boys Will Be Boys-11
Boys Will Be Boys Gold-11
Decades-5
Decades Gold-5
Jerseys Autos-23
Jerseys Autos Gold-23
Retro Teammates-8
Retro Teammates Gold-8
Road to the Cup-1
Road to the Cup Gold-1
Stick Rack-11
Stick Rack Gold-11
DeMaio, Frank
90Arizona Icecats-6
DeMarchi, Matt
99Minnesota Golden Gophers-3
00Minnesota Golden Gophers-4
01Minnesota Golden Gophers-18
02Minnesota Golden Gophers-4
03Albany River Rats-10
03Albany River Rats Kinko's-9
04Albany River Rats-6
05Albany River Rats-7
DeMarco Sr., Ab
39O-Pee-Chee V301-1-82
51Buffalo Bison-8
DeMarco, Ab
69Swedish Hockey-353
70Swedish Masterserien-32
71O-Pee-Chee-309
71Toronto Sun-169
73Blues White Border-4
73O-Pee-Chee-118
73Topps-118
74Canucks Royal Bank-5
74NHL Action Stamps-218
74NHL Action Stamps Update-38
74O-Pee-Chee NHL-89
74Topps-89
75Canucks Royal Bank-6
75O-Pee-Chee NHL-78
75Topps-78
76O-Pee-Chee NHL-374
77O-Pee-Chee NHL-283
DeMars, Donny
00Sioux Falls Stampede-6
Demarski, Matt
96Lethbridge Hurricanes-3
97Seattle Thunderbirds-20
98Florida Everblades-4
99Florida Everblades-14
00Florida Everblades-7
02Greenville Grrrowl-4
03Greenville Grrrowl-8
DeMartinis, Lucio
98Val d'Or Foreurs-11
Demel, Tomas
97Czech APS Extraliga-44
98Czech OFS-345
00Czech OFS-344
02Czech OFS Plus-65
03Czech OFS Plus-28
04Czech OFS-245
Czech/Slovak-3
05Czech HC Vsetin-2
06Czech HC Vsetin Postcards-12
06Czech OFS-176
Stars-20
Demen-Willaume, Richard
05Swedish SHL Elitset-175
06Swedish SHL Elitset-30
DeMeres, Tony
34Beehive Group I Photos-146
40O-Pee-Chee V301-2-144
Demers, Alexandre
02Drummondville Voltigeurs-9
03Drummondville Voltigeurs-5
04Drummondville Voltigeurs-8
05Drummondville Voltigeurs-17
06Drummondville Voltigeurs-15
Demers, Guillaume
01Cape Breton Screaming Eagles-13
02Cape Breton Screaming Eagles-12
03Cape Breton Screaming Eagles-18
04Cape Breton Screaming Eagles-7
Demers, Jacques
81Fredericton Express-12
82Fredericton Express-12
87Red Wings Little Caesars-8
88Red Wings Little Caesars-6
89Red Wings Little Caesars-19
89Red Wings Little Caesars-22
92Canadiens Postcards-8
93Canadiens Postcards-7
93Kraft-32
93O-Pee-Chee Canadiens Hockey Fest-10
94Canadiens Postcards-7
Demers, Jason
04Moncton Wildcats-13
05Moncton Wildcats-20
06Victoriaville Tigres-12
Demers, Jean-Francois
00Chicoutimi Sagueneens-18
Signed-18
01Chicoutimi Sagueneens-11
Demers, Julien
06Ottawa 67s-13
Demers, Maxime
93Quebec Pee-Wee Tournament-436
Demers, Michel
93Quebec Pee-Wee Tournament-333
Demers, Nicolas
93Quebec Pee-Wee Tournament-448
Demers, Normand
907th Inn. Sketch QMJHL-83
907th Inn. Sketch Memorial Cup-73
Demers, Stephane
93Quebec Pee-Wee Tournament-1083
Demers, Tony
43Parade Sportive *-29
43Parade Sportive *-30
DeMichele, Mike
93Quebec Pee-Wee Tournament-161
Demidov, Ilja
00Grand Rapids Griffins-6
Demin, Vassili
94Erie Panthers-6
Demitra, Pavol
92Upper Deck-602
93Donruss-240
93Leaf-366
93Parkhurst-140
Emerald Ice-140
93Pinnacle-446
Canadian-446
93Score-624
Gold-624
Canadian-624
Canadian Gold-624
93Senators Kraft Sheets-6
93Upper Deck-372
SP-108
94Donruss-133
94Finest-111
Super Team Winners-111
Refractors-111
94Fleer-144
94Leaf-115
94OPC Premier-336
Special Effects-336
94Parkhurst SE-SE121
Gold-SE121
94Select-185
Gold-185
94Topps/OPC Premier-336
Special Effects-336
94Ultra-337
94Upper Deck-216
Electric Ice-216
SP Inserts-SP145
SP Inserts Die Cuts-SP145
95Canada Games NHL POGS-195
95Panini Stickers-53
95Parkhurst International-149
Emerald Ice-149
95PEI Senators-4
96Grand Rapids Griffins-5
96Las Vegas Thunder-5
96Collector's Edge Ice-48
Prism-48
97Be A Player-146
Autographs-146
Autographs Die-Cuts-146
Autographs Prismatic Die-Cuts-146
97Collector's Choice-232
97Crown Royale-114
Emerald Green-114
Ice Blue-114
Silver-114
97Pacific Omega-191
Copper-191
Dark Gray-191
Emerald Green-191
Gold-191
Ice Blue-191
97Score Blues-18
Platinum-18
Premier-18
97SP Authentic-142
97Upper Deck-146
98Be A Player-126
Press Release-126
98BAP Gold-126
98BAP Autographs-126
98BAP Autographs Gold-126
98BAP Tampa Bay All Star Game-126
98Finest-62
No Protectors-62
No Protectors Refractors-62
Refractors-62
98Pacific-38
Ice Blue-38
Red-38
98Pacific Omega-201
Red-201
Opening Day Issue-201
98Panini Stickers-157
98Paramount-202
Copper-202
Emerald Green-202
Holo-Electric-202
Ice Blue-202
Silver-202
98Revolution-121
Ice Shadow-121
Red-121
98SP Authentic-74
Power Shift-74
98SPx Finite-76
Radiance-76
Spectrum-76
98Topps Gold Label Class 1-29
Black-29
Black One of One-29
One of One-29
Red-29
Red One of One-29
98Topps Gold Label Class 2-29
98Topps Gold Label Class 2 Black-29
98Topps Gold Label Class 2 Black 1 of 1-29
98Topps Gold Label Class 2 One of One-29
98Topps Gold Label Class 2 Red-29
98Topps Gold Label Class 2 Red One of One-29
98Topps Gold Label Class 3-29
98Topps Gold Label Class 3 Black-29
98Topps Gold Label Class 3 Black 1 of 1-29
98Topps Gold Label Class 3 One of One-29
98Topps Gold Label Class 3 Red-29
98Topps Gold Label Class 3 Red One of One-29
98UD Choice-186
Prime Choice Reserve-186
Reserve-186
98Upper Deck-173
Exclusives-173
Exclusives 1 of 1-173
Gold Reserve-173
98Upper Deck MVP-185
Gold Script-185
Silver Script-185
Super Script-185
99Aurora-124
Premiere Date-124
99BAP Memorabilia-164
Gold-164
Silver-164
Selects Silver-SL2
Selects Gold-SL2
AS Heritage Ruby-H23
AS Heritage Sapphire-H23
AS Heritage Emerald-H23
99BAP Millennium-204
Emerald-204
Ruby-204
Sapphire-204
Signatures-204
Signatures Gold-204
99Black Diamond-72
Diamond Cut-72
Final Cut-72
99Blues Taco Bell-8
99Crown Royale-115
Limited Series-115
Premiere Date-115
International Glory-22
International Glory Parallel-22
99O-Pee-Chee-205
99O-Pee-Chee Chrome-205
99O-Pee-Chee Chrome Refractors-205
99O-Pee-Chee Now Starring-NS15
99Pacific-355
Copper-355
Emerald Green-355
Gold-355
Ice Blue-355
Premiere Date-355
Red-355
99Pacific Dynagon Ice-165
Blue-165
Copper-165
Gold-165
Premiere Date-165
99Pacific Omega-195
Copper-195
Gold-195
Ice Blue-195
Premiere Date-195
World All-Stars-7
99Pacific Prism-117
Holographic Blue-117
Holographic Gold-117
Holographic Mirror-117
Holographic Purple-117
Premiere Date-117
99Panini Stickers-293
99Panini Stickers-328
99Paramount-195
Copper-195
Emerald-195
Gold-195
Holographic Emerald-195
Holographic Gold-195
Holographic Silver-195
Ice Blue-195
Premiere Date-195
Red-195
Silver-195
Personal Best-32
99Revolution-121
Premiere Date-121
Red-121
Shadow Series-121
Showstoppers-30
Top of the Line-9
99SP Authentic-75
99SPx-132
Radiance-132
Spectrum-132
99Stadium Club-70
First Day Issue-70
One of a Kind-70
Printing Plates Black-70
Printing Plates Cyan-70
Printing Plates Magenta-70
Printing Plates Yellow-70
99Topps/OPC-205
Now Starring-NS15
99Topps/OPC Chrome-205
Refractors-205
99Topps Gold Label Class 1-21
Black-21
Black One of One-21
One of One-21
Red-21
Red One of One-21
99Topps Gold Label Class 2-21
99Topps Gold Label Class 2 Black-21
99Topps Gold Label Class 2 Black 1 of 1-21
99Topps Gold Label Class 2 One of One-21
99Topps Gold Label Class 2 Red-21
99Topps Gold Label Class 2 Red One of One-21
99Topps Gold Label Class 3-21
99Topps Gold Label Class 3 Black-21
99Topps Gold Label Class 3 Black 1 of 1-21
99Topps Gold Label Class 3 One of One-21
99Topps Gold Label Class 3 Red-21
99Topps Gold Label Class 3 Red One of One-21
99Topps Premier Plus-64
Parallel-64
99Ultimate Victory-76
1/1-76
Parallel-76
Parallel 100-76
99Upper Deck-113
Exclusives-113
Exclusives 1 of 1-113
99Upper Deck Gold Reserve-113
99Upper Deck HoloGrFx-51
Ausome-51
99Upper Deck MVP-182
Gold Script-182
Silver Script-182
Super Script-182
ProSign-PD
99Upper Deck MVP SC Edition-160
Gold Script-160
Silver Script-160
Super Script-160
99Upper Deck Ovation-48
Standing Ovation-48
99Upper Deck Retro-69
Gold-69
Platinum-69
99Upper Deck Victory-259
99Wayne Gretzky Hockey-145
00Aurora-119
Premiere Date-119
00BAP Memorabilia-129
Emerald-129
Ruby-129
Sapphire-129
Promos-129
00BAP Mem Chicago Sportsfest Copper-129
00BAP Memorabilia Chicago Sportsfest Blue-129
00BAP Memorabilia Chicago Sportsfest Gold-129
00BAP Memorabilia Chicago Sportsfest Ruby-129
00BAP Memorabilia Chicago Sun-Times Ruby-129
00BAP Memorabilia Chicago Sun-Times Gold-129
00BAP Mem Chicago Sun-Times Sapphire-129
00BAP Mem Toronto Fall Expo Copper-129
00BAP Memorabilia Toronto Fall Expo Gold-129
00BAP Memorabilia Toronto Fall Expo Ruby-129
00BAP Parkhurst 2000-P111
00BAP Signature Series-124
Emerald-124
Ruby-124
Sapphire-124
00O-Pee-Chee-43
00O-Pee-Chee Parallel-43
00Pacific-341
Copper-341
Gold-341
Ice Blue-341
Premiere Date-341
Euro-Stars-7
00Panini Stickers-195
00Paramount-204
Copper-204
Gold-204
Holo-Gold-204
Holo-Silver-204
Ice Blue-204

Premiere Date-204
00Private Stock-82
Gold-82
Premiere Date-82
Retail-82
Silver-82
PS-2001 Action-51
00Revolution-121
Blue-121
Premiere Date-121
Red-121
00SP Game Used-53
Tools of the Game-PD
Tools of the Game Exclusives-PD
Tools of the Game Combos-C-DM
00SPx-60
Spectrum-60
Winning Materials-PD
00Stadium Club-28
Co-Signers-CO1
Lone Star Signatures-LS8
Special Forces-SF13
11 X 14 Autographs-PD
00Titanium-80
Blue-80
Gold-80
Premiere Date-80
Red-80
Retail-80
00Topps/OPC-43
Parallel-43
NHL Draft-D10
00Topps Chrome-35
OPC Refractors-35
Refractors-35
00Topps Gold Label Class 1-67
Gold-67
00Topps Gold Label Class 2-67
00Topps Gold Label Class 2 Gold-67
00Topps Gold Label Class 3-67
00Topps Gold Label Class 3 Gold-67
00Topps Gold Label Bullion-B5
00Topps Gold Label Bullion One to One-B5
00Topps Heritage-51
00Topps Heritage-242
Chrome Parallel-51
00Topps Premier Plus-45
Blue Ice-45
00Topps Stars-54
Blue-54
00UD Heroes-103
00Upper Deck-150
00Upper Deck-383
Exclusives Tier 1-150
Exclusives Tier 1-383
Exclusives Tier 2-150
Exclusives Tier 2-383
Ice Game Jerseys-JCPD
00Upper Deck Legends-117
Legendary Collection Bronze-117
Legendary Collection Gold-117
Legendary Collection Silver-117
00Upper Deck MVP-156
First Stars-156
Second Stars-156
Third Stars-156
00Upper Deck Victory-200
00Upper Deck Victory-322
00Upper Deck Vintage-310
00Upper Deck Vintage-320
01BAP Memorabilia-45
Emerald-45
Ruby-45
Sapphire-45
All-Star Jerseys-ASJ27
All-Star Emblems-ASE27
All-Star Numbers-ASN27
Country of Origin-CO38
01BAP Signature Series-169
Autographs-169
Autographs Gold-169
01Bowman YoungStars-66
Gold-66
Ice Cubed-66
01Crown Royale-118
Blue-118
Premiere Date-118
Red-118
Retail-118
01O-Pee-Chee-61
01O-Pee-Chee Heritage Parallel-61
01O-Pee-Chee Heritage Parallel Limited-61
01O-Pee-Chee Premier Parallel-61
01Pacific-321
Extreme LTD-321
Hobby LTD-321
Premiere Date-321
Retail LTD-321
01Pacific Adrenaline-158
Blue-158
Premiere Date-158
Red-158
Retail-158
01Pacific Arena Exclusives-321
01Parkhurst-16
Gold-16
Silver-16
Sticks-PS35
01SP Authentic-75
Limited-75
Limited Gold-75
01SP Game Used-50
Authentic Fabric-AFPD
Authentic Fabric Gold-AFPD
01SPx-61
01Stadium Club-36
Award Winners-36
Master Photos-36
01Titanium-115
Hobby Parallel-115
Premiere Date-115
Retail-115
Retail Parallel-115
01Topps-61
Heritage Parallel-61
Heritage Parallel Limited-61
OPC Parallel-61
01Topps Chrome-61
Refractors-61
Black Border Refractors-61
01Topps Heritage-102
Refractors-102
01UD Challenge for the Cup-76
01UD Honor Roll-98
Jerseys-J-PD
Jerseys Gold-J-PD
01UD Mask Collection-86
Gold-86
Double Patches-DPPD
Jerseys-J-PD
Jersey and Patch-JPPD
01UD Playmakers-85
01UD Top Shelf-115
01Upper Deck-151
Exclusives-151
Fantastic Finishers-FF2
Tandems-T9
01Upper Deck Ice-117
01Upper Deck MVP-165
01Upper Deck Victory-307
Gold-307
01Upper Deck Vintage-221
01Upper Deck Vintage-226
01Slovakian Kvarteto-2C
02Atomic-20
02Atomic Jerseys-20
02Atomic Jerseys Gold-20
02Atomic Patches-20
02Atomic Power Converters-16
02BAP All-Star Edition-18
Jerseys-18
Jerseys Gold-18
Jerseys Silver-18
02BAP First Edition-66
02BAP First Edition-378
Jerseys-66
02BAP Memorabilia-190
Emerald-190
Ruby-190
Sapphire-190
All-Star Jerseys-ASJ-10
NHL All-Star Game-190
NHL All-Star Game Blue-190
NHL All-Star Game Green-190
NHL All-Star Game Red-190
02BAP Memorabilia Toronto Fall Expo-190
02BAP Signature Series-129
Autographs-129
Autograph Buybacks 1998-126
Autograph Buybacks 1999-204
Autograph Buybacks 2001-169
Autographs Gold-129
02Blues Magnets-1
02Blues Team Issue-4
02Bowman YoungStars-50
Gold-50
Silver-50
02Crown Royale-80
Blue-80
Red-80
Retail-80
02O-Pee-Chee-155
02O-Pee-Chee Premier Blue Parallel-155
02O-Pee-Chee Premier Red Parallel-155
02O-Pee-Chee Factory Set-155
02Pacific-320
Blue-320
Red-320
Jerseys-43
Jerseys Holo-Silver-43
02Pacific Complete-437
Red-437
02Pacific Exclusive-141
02Pacific Heads-Up-102
Blue-102
Purple-102
Red-102
Inside the Numbers-18
Quad Jerseys-23
Quad Jerseys-34
Quad Jerseys Gold-23
Quad Jerseys Gold-34
02Pacific Quest for the Cup-81
Gold-81
02Parkhurst-18
Bronze-18
Gold-18
Silver-18
02Parkhurst Retro-20
Minis-20
02Private Stock Reserve-82
Blue-82
Red-82
Retail-82
02SP Authentic-78
Beckett Promos-78
02SP Game Used Authentic Fabrics-AFPD
02SP Game Used Authentic Fabrics-CFDT
02SP Game Used Authentic Fabrics-CFWD
02SP Game Used Authentic Fabrics Gold-AFPD
02SP Game Used Authentic Fabrics Gold-CFDT
02SP Game Used Authentic Fabrics Gold-CFWD
02SP Game Used Authentic Fabrics Rainbow-AFPD
02SP Game Used Authentic Fabrics Rainbow-CFDT
02SP Game Used Authentic Fabrics Rainbow-CFWD
02Stadium Club-94
Silver Decoy Cards-94
Proofs-94
02Titanium Jerseys-56
02Titanium Jerseys Retail-56
02Titanium Patches-56
02Topps-155
OPC Blue Parallel-155
OPC Red Parallel-155
Factory Set-155
02Topps Chrome-94
Black Border Refractors-94
Refractors-94
02Topps Heritage-99
Chrome Parallel-99
02Topps Total-26
02UD Top Shelf Hardware Heroes-HGKSD
02UD Top Shelf Triple Jerseys-TSDPJ
02Upper Deck-150
Exclusives-150
02Upper Deck MVP-163
Gold-163
Classics-163
Golden Classics-163
02Upper Deck Rookie Update Jerseys-DPD
02Upper Deck Rookie Update Jerseys Gold-DPD
02Upper Deck Victory-184
Bronze-184
Gold-184
Silver-184
National Pride-NP43
02Upper Deck Vintage-219
02Upper Deck Vintage-286
Green Backs-219
02Vanguard Jerseys-38
02Vanguard Jerseys Gold-38
03BAP Memorabilia-70
Emerald-70
Gold-70
Ruby-70
Sapphire-70
03Beehive-171
Gold-171
Silver-171
03Black Diamond-45
Black-45
Green-45
Red-45
03Blues Team Set-6
03Bowman-101
Gold-101
03Bowman Chrome-101
Refractors-101
Gold Refractors-101
Xfractors-101
03ITG Action-590
Jerseys-M100
03NHL Sticker Collection-273
03O-Pee-Chee-143
03OPC Blue-143
03OPC Gold-143
03OPC Red-143
03Pacific-280
Blue-280
Red-280
03Pacific Calder-82
Silver-82
03Pacific Complete-286
Red-286
03Pacific Exhibit-121
Blue Backs-121
Yellow Backs-121
03Pacific Invincible-79
Blue-79
Red-79
Retail-79
Featured Performers-25
03Pacific Prism-82
Blue-82
Gold-82
Red-82
03Pacific Quest for the Cup-85
Blue-85
03Pacific Supreme-80
Blue-80
Red-80
Retail-80
03Private Stock Reserve-196
Blue-196
Red-196
Retail-196
03SP Authentic-77
Limited-77
03SP Game Used-95
Gold-95
03Titanium-83
Hobby Jersey Number Parallels-83
Retail-83
Retail Jersey Number Parallels-83
03Topps-143
Blue-143
Gold-143
Red-143
Box Toppers-25
03Topps C55-115
Minis-115
Minis American Back-115
Minis American Back Red-115
Minis Bazooka Back-115
Minis Brooklyn Back-115
Minis Hat Trick Back-115
Minis O Canada Back-115
Minis O Canada Back Red-115
Minis Stanley Cup Back-115
03Topps Pristine-62
Gold Refractor Die Cuts-62
Refractors-62
Press Plates Black-62
Press Plates Cyan-62
Press Plates Magenta-62
Press Plates Yellow-62
03UD Honor Roll-77
03UD Premier Collection Stars-ST-PD
03UD Premier Collection Stars Patches-ST-PD
03Upper Deck-411
Canadian Exclusives-411
HG-411
UD Exclusives-411
03Upper Deck Ice-77
Gold-77
03Upper Deck MVP-358
Gold Script-358
Silver Script-358
Canadian Exclusives-358
03Upper Deck Rookie Update-76
Super Stars-SSPD
03Upper Deck Trilogy Authentic Patches-AP17
03Upper Deck Victory-163
Bronze-163
Gold-163
Silver-163
03Toronto Star-76
04Pacific-217
Blue-217
Red-217
04UD All-World-42
Gold-42
04Upper Deck World's Best-WB21
04Upper Deck World Cup Tribute-PBPDZC
05Beehive-43
Matte-43
Matted Materials-MMDE
05Black Diamond-119
Emerald-119
Gold-119
Onyx-119
Ruby-119
05Hot Prospects-47
En Fuego-47
Red Hot-47
White Hot-47
05Kings Team Issue-15
05Panini Stickers-286
05Parkhurst-217
Facsimile Auto Parallel-217
True Colors-TCLAK
True Colors-TCLAK
True Colors-TCSJLA
True Colors-TCSJLA
05SP Authentic-48
Limited-48
05SP Game Used-47
Gold-47
Authentic Fabrics-AF-DE
Authentic Fabrics Gold-AF-DE
Authentic Patches-AP-DE
05The Cup Dual NHL Shields-DSRD
05UD Powerplay Specialists-TSPD
05UD Powerplay Specialists Patches-SPPD
05Ultimate Collection-45
Gold-45
National Heroes Jerseys-NHJPA
National Heroes Patches-NHPPA
05Ultra-95
Gold-95
Ice-95
05Upper Deck-336
Jerseys-J-PDE
Notable Numbers-N-PD
Patches-P-PDE
05Upper Deck Hockey Showcase-HS36
05Upper Deck Showcase Promos-HS36
05Upper Deck MVP-186
Gold-186
Platinum-186
Materials-M-PD
Materials Duals-D-DR
Materials Triples-T-GPD
05Upper Deck Rookie Update-46
05Upper Deck Victory-171
05Upper Deck Victory-223
Black-171
Black-223
Gold-171
Gold-223
Silver-171
Silver-223
Game Breakers-GB38
06Be A Player Portraits-53
06Beehive-53
Matte-53
06Black Diamond-40
Black-40
Gold-40
Ruby-40
Jerseys-JDE
Jerseys Black-JDE
Jerseys Gold-JDE
Jerseys Ruby-JDE
06Flair Showcase Stitches-SSDE
06Fleer-95
Tiffany-95
Fabricology-FDE
06Hot Prospects-50
Red Hot-50
White Hot-50
06NHL POG-48
06O-Pee-Chee-256
Rainbow-256
Swatches-S-DE
06Panini Stickers-295
06SP Authentic-52
Limited-52
06SP Game Used-51
Gold-51
Rainbow-51
Authentic Fabrics-AFDE
Authentic Fabrics Parallel-AFDE
Authentic Fabrics Patches-AFDE
Authentic Fabrics Dual-AF2DG
Authentic Fabrics Dual Patches-AF2DG
Authentic Fabrics Triple-AF3MIN
Authentic Fabrics Triple Patches-AF3MIN
Authentic Fabrics Sixes-AF6BYN
Authentic Fabrics Sixes Patches-AF6BYN
06SPx-50
Spectrum-50
SPxcitement-X52
SPxcitement Spectrum-X52
06The Cup NHL Shields Duals-DSHDG
06UD Artifacts-51
Blue-51
Gold-51
Platinum-51
Radiance-51
Red-51
Frozen Artifacts-FAPD
Frozen Artifacts Black-FAPD
Frozen Artifacts Blue-FAPD
Frozen Artifacts Gold-FAPD
Frozen Artifacts Platinum-FAPD
Frozen Artifacts Red-FAPD
Frozen Artifacts Patches Black-FAPD
Frozen Artifacts Patches Blue-FAPD
Frozen Artifacts Patches Gold-FAPD
Frozen Artifacts Patches Platinum-FAPD
Frozen Artifacts Patches Red-FAPD
Tundra Tandems-TTGD
Tundra Tandems Black-TTGD
Tundra Tandems Blue-TTGD
Tundra Tandems Gold-TTGD
Tundra Tandems Platinum-TTGD
Tundra Tandems Red-TTGD
Tundra Tandems Dual Patches Red-TTGD
06UD Mini Jersey Collection-53
06UD Powerplay-51
Impact Rainbow-51
06Ultra-101
Gold Medallion-101
Ice Medallion-101
Uniformity-UDE
Uniformity Patches-UPDE
06Upper Deck Arena Giveaways-MIN4
06Upper Deck-349
Exclusives Parallel-349
High Gloss Parallel-349
Game Jerseys-JDE
Game Patches-PDE
Masterpieces-349
06Upper Deck MVP-148
Gold Script-148
Super Script-148
Jerseys-OJDH
06Upper Deck Ovation-170
06Upper Deck Sweet Shot-53
06Upper Deck Trilogy-49
06Upper Deck Victory-92
06Upper Deck Victory-255
06Upper Deck Victory Black-92
06Upper Deck Victory Gold-92
06Wild Crime Prevention-1
06Wild Postcards-1
06Russian Sport Collection Olympic Stars-45
07Upper Deck Ovation-25
07Upper Deck Victory-142
Black-142
Gold-142

Demmans, Trevor

92Saskatchewan JHL-118
02Columbia Inferno-100

Demmel, Anton

94German First League-363

Demmel, Franz

94German DEL-220
95German DEL-216
96German DEL-360
99German Bundesliga 2-35

Demone, James

01Prince Albert Raiders-6

Dempsey, Ed

95Kamloops Blazers-8
96Kamloops Blazers-8
99Prince George Cougars-20

Dempsey, Nathan

917th Inn. Sketch WHL-221
94St. John's Maple Leafs-8
95St. John's Maple Leafs-7
96St. John's Maple Leafs-14
97St. John's Maple Leafs-9
99BAP Memorabilia-306
Gold-306
Silver-306
99Upper Deck MVP SC Edition-177
Gold Script-177
Silver Script-177
Super Script-177
99St. John's Maple Leafs-7
00Upper Deck Victory-270
00St. John's Maple Leafs-8
01BAP Signature Series-71
Autographs-71
Autographs Gold-71
01St. John's Maple Leafs-7
02BAP Sig Series Auto Buybacks 2001-71
03Blackhawks Postcards-7
03ITG Action-138
03Pacific Complete-276
Red-276
03Parkhurst Original Six Chicago-8
04German Berlin Polar Bears Postcards-6
04German DEL Superstars-SU07
06O-Pee-Chee-39
Rainbow-39
06Providence Bruins-4

Dempster, Wynne

71Johnstown Jets Acme-5
72Johnstown Jets-7

Demuth, Alain

92Quebec Pee-Wee Tournament-1396
99Swiss Panini Stickers-17
99Swiss Panini Stickers-292
00Swiss Panini Stickers-16
00Swiss Panini Stickers National Team-P20
00Swiss Slapshot Mini-Cards-HCAP10
01Swiss HNL-225
02Swiss EV Zug Postcards-22
02Swiss HNL-227
02Swiss HNL-231
03Swiss EV Zug Postcards-5

Denham, Jeff

91British Columbia JHL-37

Denike, Terry

03Reading Royals-28
05Florida Seals Team Issue-4

Denis, Bradley

99Knoxville Speed-3
00Knoxville Speed-2

Denis, Louis

37V356 Worldwide Gum-125
51Laval Dairy QSHL-97
51Laval Dairy Subset-97
52St. Lawrence Sales-13

Denis, Marc

95Donruss Elite World Juniors-1
95Upper Deck-529
Electric Ice-529
Electric Ice Gold-529
96Black Diamond-130
Gold-130
96Collector's Choice-363
96Upper Deck Ice-117
97Collector's Choice-302
97Donruss-202
Press Proofs Silver-202
Press Proofs Gold-202
Rated Rookies-4
Medallist-4
97Donruss Canadian Ice-145
Dominion Series-145
Provincial Series-145
Les Gardiens-12
97Donruss Canadian Ice Les Gardiens Promo-12
97Donruss Elite Back to the Future-2
97Donruss Elite Back to the Future Autos-2
97Donruss Limited-47
97Donruss Limited-127
Exposure-47
Exposure-127
Fabric of the Game-47
97Donruss Preferred-145
97Donruss Preferred-187
Cut to the Chase-145
Cut to the Chase-187
Color Guard-10
Color Guard Promos-10
97Donruss Priority Postmaster General-18
97Donruss Priority Postmast General Promo-18
97Leaf-105
97Leaf-148
Fractal Matrix-105
Fractal Matrix-148
Fractal Matrix Die Cuts-105
Fractal Matrix Die Cuts-148
97Leaf International-105
Universal Ice-105
97Pinnacle Inside-64
Coach's Collection-64
Executive Collection-64
97Score Avalanche-3
Platinum-3
Premier-3
97Studio-25
Press Proofs Silver-25
Press Proofs Gold-25
Portraits-26
97Upper Deck Three Star Selects-12B
97Upper Deck Ice-31
Parallel-31
Power Shift-31
97Bowman CHL-61
OPC-61
98Pacific Omega-59
Red-59
Opening Day Issue-59
98Upper Deck-25
98Upper Deck-75
Exclusives-25
Exclusives-75
Exclusives 1 of 1-25
Exclusives 1 of 1-75
Generation Next-GN9
Generation Next Quantum 1-GN9
Generation Next Quantum 2-GN9
Generation Next Quantum 3-GN9
Gold Reserve-25
Gold Reserve-75
98Hershey Bears-2
99Avalanche Team Issue-3
99BAP Memorabilia-86
Gold-86
Silver-86
Selects Silver-SL24
Selects Gold-SL24
99BAP Millennium-72
Emerald-72
Ruby-72
Sapphire-72
Signatures-72
Signatures Gold-72
Calder Candidates Ruby-C43
Calder Candidates Emerald-C43
Calder Candidates Sapphire-C43
99Crown Royale-35
Limited Series-35
Premiere Date-35
Prospects Parallel-35
99O-Pee-Chee-214
99O-Pee-Chee Chrome-214
99O-Pee-Chee Chrome Refractors-214
99Pacific Omega-68
Copper-68
Gold-68
Ice Blue-68
Premiere Date-68
99Paramount-61
Copper-61
Emerald-61
Gold-61
Holographic Emerald-61
Holographic Gold-61
Holographic Silver-61
Ice Blue-61
Premiere Date-61
Red-61
Silver-61
99Topps Arena Giveaways-COL-MD
99Topps/OPC-214
99Topps/OPC Chrome-214
Refractors-214
99Upper Deck MVP Draw Your Own-W17
99Upper Deck MVP SC Edition-56
Gold Script-56
Silver Script-56
Super Script-56
00BAP Memorabilia-75
Emerald-75
Ruby-75
Sapphire-75
Promos-75
00BAP Mem Chicago Sportsfest Copper-75
00BAP Memorabilia Chicago Sportsfest Blue-75
00BAP Memorabilia Chicago Sportsfest Gold-75
00BAP Memorabilia Chicago Sportsfest Ruby-75
00BAP Memorabilia Chicago Sun-Times Ruby-75
00BAP Memorabilia Chicago Sun-Times Gold-75
00BAP Mem Chicago Sun-Times Sapphire-75
00BAP Mem Toronto Fall Expo Copper-75
00BAP Memorabilia Toronto Fall Expo Gold-75
00BAP Memorabilia Toronto Fall Expo Ruby-75
00BAP Parkhurst 2000-P164
00BAP Ultimate Memorabilia Goalie Sticks-G9
00Black Diamond Game Gear-LDE
00Crown Royale-120
21st Century Rookies-8
00O-Pee-Chee-273
00O-Pee-Chee Parallel-273
00Pacific-109
Copper-109
Gold-109
Ice Blue-109
Premiere Date-109
00Paramount-68
Copper-68
Gold-68
Holo-Gold-68
Holo-Silver-68
Ice Blue-68
Premiere Date-68
00Private Stock-27
Gold-27
Premiere Date-27
Retail-27
Silver-27
Game Gear-33
PS-2001 Action-15
PS-2001 New Wave-9
00Revolution-42
Blue-42
Premiere Date-42
Red-42
00SP Authentic Sign of the Times-MD
00Stadium Club-209
00Titanium-113
Retail-113
Game Gear-11
00Titanium Draft Day Edition-113
00Titanium Draft Day Promos-113
00Topps/OPC-273
Parallel-273
00Topps Chrome-168
OPC Refractors-168
Refractors-168
00UD Heroes-33
Signs of Greatness-MA
00UD Pros and Prospects-25
00Upper Deck-53
Exclusives Tier 1-53
Exclusives Tier 2-53
00Upper Deck Ice-68
00Upper Deck MVP-55
First Stars-55
Second Stars-55
Third Stars-55
00Upper Deck Vintage-100
00Upper Deck Vintage-110
00Vanguard-113
Pacific Proofs-113
01Atomic-29
Blue-29
Gold-29
Premiere Date-29
Red-29
01BAP Memorabilia-163
Emerald-163
Ruby-163
Sapphire-163
01BAP Signature Series-35
Autographs-35
Autographs Gold-35
01Between the Pipes-25
Jerseys-GJ30
01Blue Jackets Donatos Pizza-13
01Bowman YoungStars-88
Gold-88
Ice Cubed-88
01Crown Royale-42
Blue-42
Premiere Date-42
Red-42
Retail-42
01O-Pee-Chee-218
01O-Pee-Chee Premier Parallel-218
01Pacific-112
Extreme LTD-112
Hobby LTD-112
Premiere Date-112
Retail LTD-112
01Pacific Adrenaline-52
Blue-52
Premiere Date-52
Red-52
Retail-52
Power Play-10
01Pacific Arena Exclusives-112
01Pacific Heads-Up-27
Blue-27
Premiere Date-27
Red-27
Silver-27
Breaking the Glass-8
01Parkhurst-69
Gold-69
Silver-69
01Private Stock PS-2002-21
01Stadium Club-100
Award Winners-100
Master Photos-100
New Regime-NR5
New Regime-NRAMD
01Titanium-39
Hobby Parallel-39
Premiere Date-39
Retail-39
Retail Parallel-39
01Titanium Draft Day Edition-29
01Topps-218
OPC Parallel-218
01Topps Chrome-89
Refractors-89
Black Border Refractors-89
01Topps Heritage-86
Refractors-86
01UD Mask Collection Double Patches-DPMD
01UD Mask Collection Goalie Pads-GPMD
01UD Mask Collection Jerseys-J-MD
01UD Mask Collection Jersey and Patch-JPMD
01UD Playmakers-28
01Upper Deck-279
Exclusives-279
01Upper Deck Victory-104
Gold-104
02Atomic-28
Blue-28
Gold-28
Red-28
Hobby Parallel-28
02BAP First Edition-233
02BAP First Edition-416H
02BAP Memorabilia-19
Emerald-19
Ruby-19
Sapphire-19
NHL All-Star Game-19
NHL All-Star Game Blue-19
NHL All-Star Game Green-19
NHL All-Star Game Red-19
02BAP Memorabilia Toronto Fall Expo-19
02BAP Signature Series-20
Autographs-20
Autograph Buybacks 1999-72
Autograph Buybacks 2001-35
Autographs Gold-20
02Between the Pipes-25
02Between the Pipes-129
Gold-25
Silver-25
Behind the Mask-13
Goalie Autographs-5
Masks II-9
Masks II Gold-9
Masks II Silver-9
02Bowman YoungStars-24
Gold-24
Silver-24
02Crown Royale-28
Blue-28
Red-28
Retail-28
02O-Pee-Chee-43
02O-Pee-Chee Premier Blue Parallel-43
02O-Pee-Chee Premier Red Parallel-43
02O-Pee-Chee Factory Set-43
02Pacific-99
Blue-99
Red-99
Jerseys-12
Jerseys Holo-Silver-12
02Pacific Complete-385
Red-385
02Pacific Exclusive-50
Advantage-5
02Pacific Heads-Up-34
Blue-34
Purple-34
Red-34
Quad Jerseys-10
Quad Jerseys Gold-10
02Pacific Quest for the Cup-25
Gold-25
02Parkhurst-88
Bronze-88
Gold-88
Silver-88
02Parkhurst Retro-164
Minis-164
02Private Stock Reserve-112
Red-112
Retail-112
InCrease Security-6
Patches-112
02SP Authentic-26
Beckett Promos-26
Super Premiums-SPMD
02SP Game Used-14
Authentic Fabrics-AFMD
Authentic Fabrics Gold-AFMD
Authentic Fabrics Rainbow-AFMD
First Rounder Patches-MD
Piece of History-PHMD
Piece of History Gold-PHMD
Piece of History Rainbow-PHMD
Tools of the Game-MD
02SPx-22
Spectrum Gold-22
Spectrum Silver-22
02Stadium Club-39
Silver Decoy Cards-39
Proofs-39
02Titanium-29
Blue-29
Red-29
Retail-29
02Topps-43
OPC Blue Parallel-43
OPC Red Parallel-43
Factory Set-43
02Topps Chrome-37
Black Border Refractors-37
Refractors-37
02Topps Heritage-86
Chrome Parallel-86
02Topps Total-87
02UD Artistic Impressions-25
Gold-25
02UD Artistic Impressions Beckett Promos-25
02UD Artistic Impressions Retrospectives-R25
02UD Artistic Impressions Retrospect Gold-R25
02UD Artistic Impress Retrospect Silver-R25
02UD Honor Roll-20
02UD Mask Collection-24
02UD Mask Collection-25
02UD Mask Collection-115
02UD Mask Collection Beckett Promos-24
02UD Mask Collection Beckett Promos-25
02UD Mask Collection Great Gloves-GGMD
02UD Piece of History-23
02UD Premier Collection-17
02UD Top Shelf-24
Dual Player Jerseys-RBD
Dual Player Jerseys-STTD
Stopper Jerseys-SSMD
Sweet Sweaters-SWDE
02Upper Deck-50
Exclusives-50
Blow-Ups-C10
CHL Graduates-CGMD
CHL Graduates Gold-CGMD
Hot Spots-HSMD
02Upper Deck Classic Portraits-28
02Upper Deck MVP-53
Gold-53
Classics-53
Golden Classics-53
Skate Around Jerseys-SDTD
Souvenirs-S-MD
02Upper Deck Rookie Update-30
02Upper Deck Victory-60
Bronze-60
Gold-60
Silver-60
02Upper Deck Vintage-74
02Upper Deck Vintage-269
Green Backs-74
Jerseys-HSMD
Jerseys Gold-HS-MD
02Vanguard-30
LTD-30
03BAP Memorabilia-135
Emerald-135
Gold-135
Ruby-135
Sapphire-135
Masks III-17
Masks III Gold-17
Masks III Silver-17
Masks III Autographs-M-MDE
Masks III Memorabilia-17
03BAP Ultimate Memorabilia Autographs-62
Gold-62
03BAP Ultimate Mem Auto Jerseys-62
03Beehive-58
Gold-58
Silver-58
Sticks Beige Border-BE12
Sticks Red Border-RE5
03Black Diamond-73
Black-73
Green-73
Red-73
Threads-DT-MD
Threads Green-DT-MD
Threads Red-DT-MD
Threads Black-DT-MD
03Bowman-34
Gold-34
03Bowman Chrome-34
Refractors-34
Gold Refractors-34
Xfractors-34
03Crown Royale-28
Blue-28
Retail-28
Gauntlet of Glory-7
03ITG Action-154
Jerseys-M101
03ITG Used Signature Series-36
Gold-36
Autographs-MD
Autographs Gold-MD
03NHL Sticker Collection-200
03O-Pee-Chee-176
03OPC Blue-176
03OPC Gold-176
03OPC Red-176
03Pacific-92
Blue-92
Red-92
03Pacific Calder-28
Silver-28
03Pacific Complete-483
Red-483
03Pacific Exhibit-42
Blue Backs-42
Yellow Backs-42
03Pacific Heads-Up-28
Hobby LTD-28
Retail LTD-28
03Pacific Invincible-27
Blue-27
Red-27
Retail-27
Freeze Frame-5
Jerseys-8
03Pacific Luxury Suite-7A
03Pacific Luxury Suite-7B
03Pacific Luxury Suite-7C
03Pacific Prism-29
Blue-29
Gold-29

Red-29
03Pacific Quest for the Cup-29
Blue-29
03Pacific Supreme-26
Blue-26
Red-26
Retail-26
Standing Guard-4
03Private Stock Reserve-160
Blue-160
Patches-160
Red-160
Retail-160
03SP Authentic-23
Limited-23
03SP Game Used Authentic Fabrics-DFND
03SP Game Used Authentic Fabrics Gold-DFND
03SP Game Used Double Threads-DTND
03SP Game Used Game Gear-GGMD
03SPx-26
Radiance-26
Spectrum-26
Big Futures-BF-MD
Big Futures Limited-BF-MD
03Titanium-30
Hobby Jersey Number Parallels-30
Retail-30
Retail Jersey Number Parallels-30
03Topps-176
Blue-176
Gold-176
Red-176
03Topps Pristine-43
Gold Refractor Die Cuts-43
Refractors-43
Mini-PM-MDE
Press Plates Black-43
Press Plates Cyan-43
Press Plates Magenta-43
Press Plates Yellow-43
03UD Honor Roll-21
03UD Premier Collection Stars-ST-MD
03UD Premier Collection Stars Patches-ST-MD
03UD Premier Collection Teammates-PT-CB1
03UD Premier Collection Teammates Patches-PT-CB1
03Upper Deck-58
Canadian Exclusives-58
HG-58
03Upper Deck Classic Portraits-26
03Upper Deck Ice-25
Gold-25
03Upper Deck MVP-125
Gold Script-125
Silver Script-125
Canadian Exclusives-125
SportsNut-SN25
03Upper Deck Rookie Update-25
03Upper Deck Trilogy-26
Limited-26
03Upper Deck Victory-54
Bronze-54
Gold-54
Silver-54
04Pacific-74
Blue-74
Red-74
04Upper Deck-53
Canadian Exclusives-53
HG Glossy Gold-53
HG Glossy Silver-53
05Be A Player Dual Signatures-DR
05Be A Player Dual Signatures-ND
05Be A Player Signatures-MR
05Be A Player Signatures Gold-MR
05Beehive Matted Materials-MMMD
05Black Diamond-25
Emerald-25
Gold-25
Onyx-25
Ruby-25
05Panini Stickers-237
05Parkhurst-142
Facsimile Auto Parallel-142
True Colors-TCCLB
True Colors-TCCLB
05SP Game Used Authentic Fabrics Quad-NZDF
05SP Game Used Authentic Patches Quad -NZDL
05SPx Winning Combos-WC-DN
05SPx Winning Combos Gold-WC-DN
05SPx Winning Combos Spectrum-WC-DN
05UD Artifacts Treasured Patches-TP-MD
05UD Artifacts Treasured Patch Autos-TP-MD
05UD Artifacts Treasured Patches Dual-TPD-MD
05UD Artifacts Treasured Patch Dual Autos-TPD-MD
05UD Artifacts Treasured Patches Pewter-TP-MD
05UD Artifacts Treasured Patches Silver-TP-MD
05UD Artifacts Treasured Swatches-TS-MD
05UD Artifacts Treasured Swatch Autos-TS-MD
05UD Artifacts Treasured Swatches Blue-TS-MD
05UD Artifacts Treasured Swatches Copper-TS-MD
05UD Artifacts Treasured Swatches Dual-TSD-MD
05UD Artifacts Treasured Swatch Dual Auto-TSD-MD
05UD Artifacts Treasured Swatch Dual Blue-TSD-MD
05UD Artifact Treasure Swatch Dual Copper-TSD-MD
05UD Artifact Treasure Swatch Dual Maroon-TSD-MD
05UD Artifact Treasure Swatch Dual Pewter-TSD-MD
05UD Artifact TreasuredSwatch Dual Silver-TSD-MD
05UD Artifacts Treasured Swatches Maroon-TS-MD
05UD Artifacts Treasured Swatches Pewter-TS-MD
05UD Artifacts Treasured Swatches Silver-TS-MD
05UD PowerPlay-28
Rainbow-28
05Ultra-61
Gold-61
Ice-61
05Upper Deck-52
05Upper Deck All-Time Greatest-18
05Upper Deck Big Playmakers-B-MDE
05Upper Deck HG Glossy-52
05Upper Deck Jerseys-J-MAD
05Upper Deck Notable Numbers-N-MDE
05Upper Deck Patches-P-MD
05Upper Deck MVP-113
Gold-113
Platinum-113
Materials-M-MD
Materials Triples-T-TFD
05Upper Deck Trilogy Honorary Patches-HP-MD
05Upper Deck Tril Honorary Patch Script-HSP-MD
05Upper Deck Trilogy Honorary Swatches-HS-MD
05Upper Deck Tril Honorary Swatch Scripts-HSS-MD
05Upper Deck Toronto Fall Expo-52

05Upper Deck Victory-58
Black-58
Gold-58
Silver-58
06Be A Player-139
Autographs-139
Signatures-MD
Signatures 10-154
06Black Diamond-76
Black-76
Gold-76
Ruby-76
06Flair Showcase Hot Gloves-HG9
06Fleer-174
Tiffany-174
Netminders-N25
06Lightning Postcards-6
06O-Pee-Chee-446
Rainbow-446
Swatches-S-MD
06Panini Stickers-148
06SP Game Used Inked Sweaters Dual-IS2SD
06SP Game Used Inked Sweaters Dual Patches-IS2SD
06UD Artifacts Tundra Tandems-TTSM
06UD Artifacts Tundra Tandems Black-TTSM
06UD Artifacts Tundra Tandems Blue-TTSM
06UD Artifacts Tundra Tandems Gold-TTSM
06UD Artifacts Tundra Tandems Platinum-TTSM
06UD Artifacts Tundra Tandems Red-TTSM
06UD Artifacts Tundra Tandems Dual Patches Red-TTSM
06Ultra-178
Gold Medallion-178
Ice Medallion-178
Uniformity-UMD
Uniformity Patches-UPMG
06Upper Deck Arena Giveaways-TBL5
06Upper Deck-423
Exclusives Parallel-423
High Gloss Parallel-423
Masterpieces-423
06Upper Deck MVP-259
Gold Script-259
Super Script-259
Jerseys-OJKD
Jerseys-OJWD
06Upper Deck Victory-56
06Upper Deck Victory-275
06Upper Deck Victory Black-56
06Upper Deck Victory Gold-56

Deniset, Paul
98Kamloops Blazers-5
99Kamloops Blazers-5
00Swift Current Broncos-5
01Prince Albert Raiders-7

Denisiuk, Justyn
94German First League-620

Denisov, Denis
00Russian Hockey League-284
03Russian Hockey League-161

Denisov, Dmitri
95Swedish World Championships Stickers-38
95Swiss HNL-199
96Swedish Semic Wien-155
97Czech APS Extraliga-99
98Czech DS Stickers-102
99Russian Hockey League-165
00Russian Hockey League-372

Denisov, Mikhail
74Swedish Stickers-74

Denneny, Corbett
23V145-1-40

Denneny, Cy
23V145-1-10
24Anonymous NHL-17
24C144 Champ's Cigarettes-21
24V145-2-7
60Topps-8
Stamps-13
83Hall of Fame-138
83Hall of Fame Postcards-K3
85Hall of Fame-138
04ITG Franchises Canadian-69

Dennis, Adam
02Guelph Storm-6
03Guelph Storm-21
04Guelph Storm-25
05ITG Heroes/Prosp Toronto Expo Parallel -401
05London Knights-20
05OHL Bell All-Star Classic-24
05ITG Heroes and Prospects-401
Memorial Cup-MC-7
06Hot Prospects-148
Red Hot-148
White Hot-148
06O-Pee-Chee-584
Rainbow-584
06Rochester Americans-4
06SP Authentic-248
Limited-248
06The Cup-94
Autographed Rookie Masterpiece Pressplates-94
Gold Rainbow Autographed Rookies-94
Masterpiece Pressplates (Marquee Rookies)-584
Masterpiece Pressplates (SP Authentic)-248
Masterpiece Pressplates (Ultimate Collection)-66
Rookies Black-94
Rookies Platinum-94
06Ultimate Collection-66
06Upper Deck-457
Exclusives Parallel-457
High Gloss Parallel-457
Masterpieces-457

Dennis, Andrew
03Barrie Colts-22
04Barrie Colts-24

Dennis, Daniel
91Air Canada SJHL-E20
92Saskatchewan JHL-20
97Johnstown Chiefs-26
98Fayetteville Force-12

Dennis, Duane
94Cape Breton Oilers-6
94Tampa Bay Tritons RHI-11
99German Bundesliga 2-285

Dennison, Heath
92British Columbia JHL-158

Dennison, Joe
12C57-42

Denny, Chad
03Lewiston Maineiacs-8
05ITG Heroes/Prosp Toronto Expo Parallel -142
05ITG Heroes and Prospects-142
Autographs-A-CD

Denomme, C.J.
917th Inn. Sketch OHL-74

Denomme, Jason
89Oshawa Generals-8
907th Inn. Sketch OHL-156
917th Inn. Sketch OHL-328
917th Inn. Sketch Memorial Cup-9

Dent, Ted
93Johnstown Chiefs-5
94Johnstown Chiefs-6
06Norfolk Admirals-27

Denzin, Drew
93Michigan Wolverines-4

Deobald, Lonny
92Saskatchewan JHL-56

Deopere, Scott
97Dubuque Fighting Saints-10

DePalma, Larry
87North Stars Postcards-12
88North Stars ADA-7
89ProCards IHL-79
90ProCards AHL/IHL-111
91Kansas City Blades-18
91ProCards-524
94Cleveland Lumberjacks-14
94Cleveland Lumberjacks Postcards-14
96Milwaukee Admirals-4

Depape, Ryan
04Prince Albert Raiders-15
05Prince Albert Raiders-5
06Prince Albert Raiders-16

Depoe, Don
99UK Hull Thunder-2

DePourcq, John
94Central Hockey League-110
95Louisiana Ice Gators-2
95Louisiana Ice Gators Playoffs-4
96Louisiana Ice Gators II-2
99Louisiana Ice Gators-9
00Louisiana Ice Gators-22
01Louisiana Ice Gators-6
02Louisiana Ice Gators-7

Depper, Blaine
99Kamloops Blazers-6
00Kelowna Rockets-8

DeProfio, Chris
96Louisville Riverfrogs-13
97Louisville Riverfrogs-16

Deraspe, Patrick
917th Inn. Sketch QMJHL-185

Derecola, Mike
00Charlotte Checkers-26

DeRitz, Reynald
93Swiss HNL-199
95Swiss HNL-275
96Swiss HNL-393

Derkatch, Dale
81Regina Pats-8
82Regina Pats-13
83Canadian National Juniors-4
83Regina Pats-13
94German DEL-305
94German First League-311
95German DEL-191

Derksen, Devin
907th Inn. Sketch WHL-100
93Richmond Renegades-8

Derksen, Duane
92Classic-91
Gold-91
92Classic Four-Sport *-208
Gold-208
95Madison Monsters-1
96Madison Monsters-10
99Peoria Rivermen-6
00German DEL-108
02Peoria Rivermen-11
02Peoria Rivermen Photo Pack-4
02Peoria Rivermen RBI Sports-159

Derlago, Bill
78Canucks Royal Bank-3
79Canucks Royal Bank-5
80Maple Leafs Postcards-9
80O-Pee-Chee-11
80Pepsi-Cola Caps-84
80Topps-11
81Maple Leafs Postcards-6
81O-Pee-Chee-305
81O-Pee-Chee Stickers-99
81O-Pee-Chee Stickers-108
81Topps-8
82Maple Leafs Postcards-8
82Maple Leafs Postcards-9
82O-Pee-Chee-319
82O-Pee-Chee-320
82O-Pee-Chee Stickers-67
82O-Pee-Chee Stickers-68
82Post Cereal-18
82Topps Stickers-67
82Topps Stickers-68
83Esso-6
83Maple Leafs Postcards-4
83NHL Key Tags-116
83O-Pee-Chee-327
83O-Pee-Chee Stickers-35
83Puffy Stickers-1
83Topps Stickers-35
83Vachon-84
84Maple Leafs Postcards-8
84O-Pee-Chee-300
84O-Pee-Chee Stickers-14
847-Eleven Discs-45
84Kelowna Wings-27
85O-Pee-Chee-71
85O-Pee-Chee Stickers-7
85Topps-71
86Jets Postcards-5
86Kraft Drawings-15
86Nordiques Team Issue-3
86O-Pee-Chee-254
86O-Pee-Chee Stickers-105
87O-Pee-Chee Stickers-224
02Maple Leafs Platinum Collection-28

Derlago, Mark
03Brandon Wheat Kings-6
05Brandon Wheat Kings-7

Derner, Lukas
06Czech HC Plzen Postcards-6

Dernestal, Stefan
91Swedish Semic Elitserien Stickers-227

Derouin, Geoff
01Asheville Smoke-9

DeRouville, Philippe
917th Inn. Sketch QMJHL-131
93Upper Deck-260
94Cleveland Lumberjacks-2
94Cleveland Lumberjacks Postcards-2
95Donruss-206
95Leaf-111
95Pinnacle-214
Artist's Proofs-214
Rink Collection-214
95Score-291
Black Ice Artist's Proofs-291
Black Ice-291
95Cleveland Lumberjacks-10
95Cleveland Lumberjacks Postcards-10
96Kansas City Blades-6
96Collector's Edge Ice-116
Prism-116
97Donruss-197
Press Proofs Silver-197
Press Proofs Gold-197
Canadian Ice Les Gardiens-11
97Donruss Canadian Ice Les Gardiens Promo-11
99German Bundesliga 2-199
00UK Sekonda Superleague-4

Derraugh, Doug
95German DEL-375
96German DEL-196
99German DEL-277
01German Upper Deck-123
02German DEL City Press-174

Derrer, Ronny
93Quebec Pee-Wee Tournament-1633

Derungs, Harry
93Swiss HNL-301

Derungs, Thomas
93Swiss HNL-215
95Swiss HNL-396
00Swiss Panini Stickers-64
00Swiss Slapshot Mini-Cards-HCCF9
01Swiss HNL-293
01Swiss HNL-386
02Swiss HNL-345

Dery, Mathieu
01Quebec Remparts-7

Deryabin, Dmitri
98BC Icemen II-14

DesAlliers, Renaud
02Hull Olympiques-14
03Hull Olympiques Memorial Cup-5
03Victoriaville Tigers-5
04Victoriaville Tigres-16
05Victoriaville Tigres-10

Desaluriers, Francis
99Shawinigan Cataractes-8
Signed-8

DeSantis, Jason
04Ohio State Buckeyes-19
05Ohio State Buckeyes-18
06Ohio State Buckeyes-6

DeSantis, Mark
907th Inn. Sketch OHL-32
91Cornwall Royals-2
917th Inn. Sketch OHL-3
93San Diego Gulls-7
94Greensboro Monarchs-18
94Classic Enforcers-E10
94Classic Four-Sport *-150
Gold-150
Autographs-150A
Printers Proofs-150
95Anaheim Bullfrogs RHI-18
96Louisiana Ice Gators-4
98Louisiana Ice Gators-5

Desaulniers, Gerard
51Laval Dairy QSHL-93
51Laval Dairy Subset-93
52St. Lawrence Sales-4

Desautels, Jevon
00Spokane Chiefs-5
01Spokane Chiefs-8
02Spokane Chiefs-6
04Spokane Chiefs Magnets-2

Desbiens, Denis
01Thetford Mines Coyotes-16
02Thetford Mines Coyotes-6
03Thetford Mines Prolab-6

Desbiens, Robert
51Laval Dairy Lac St. Jean-4

Deschambeault, Kevin
97Idaho Steelheads-7

Deschamps, Benoit
04Thetford Mines Prolab-2

Deschamps, Darren
02Kelowna Rockets-10
03Kelowna Rockets-6
04Kelowna Rockets-5

Deschamps, Marc
92Wheeling Thunderbirds-5

Deschamps, Matt
04Maine Black Bears-6
05Fresno Falcons-5

Deschamps, Robert
897th Inn. Sketch OHL-158
907th Inn. Sketch OHL-282

Deschatelets, Sylvain
92Quebec Pee-Wee Tournament-788
93Quebec Pee-Wee Tournament-1048
99Baie-Comeau Drakkar-7

Deschaume, Laurent
93Swedish Semic World Champ Stickers-261
95Swedish World Championships Stickers-108

Deschenes, Christian
01Sorel Royaux-7

Deschenes, Frederic
96Rochester Americans-16
99Johnstown Chiefs-24
00Johnstown Chiefs-11
01Johnstown Chiefs-16
02Thetford Mines Coyotes-7
03Thetford Mines Prolab-7
04Thetford Mines Prolab-7
04Thetford Mines Prolab-28
04Thetford Mines Prolab Autographs-7

Deschenes, Nick
03Philadelphia Phantoms-17
03Trenton Titans-359

Deschesnes, Donat
52Bas Du Fleuve-41

Deschevvy, Sergei
99Topeka Scarecrows-5
01Kalamazoo K-Wings-3

Descloux, Antoine
93Swiss HNL-38
95Swiss HNL-64
96Swiss HNL-208
98Swiss Power Play Stickers-83
99Swiss Panini Stickers-133
00Swiss Panini Stickers-131
00Swiss Slapshot Mini-Cards-HCFG3
01Swiss HNL-125

Descoteau, Derek
93Spokane Chiefs-8
94Spokane Chiefs-16

Descoteaux, Matthieu
95Bowman Draft Prospects-P9
99Hamilton Bulldogs-16
99Quebec Citadelles-20
00Quebec Citadelles-19
Signed-19
01Quebec Citadelles-20
02Utah Grizzlies-23

Desfosses, Kevin
05Quebec Remparts-15
05Quebec Remparts Signature Series-15
06Quebec Remparts-15

Desgagne, Marc
917th Inn. Sketch QMJHL-7
92Quebec Pee-Wee Tournament-847

DesGagne, Yan
99Ohio State Buckeyes-5
00Ohio State Buckeyes-8
01Ohio State Buckeyes-7

Desharnais, David
04Chicoutimi Sagueneens-6
05ITG Heroes/Prosp Toronto Expo Parallel -309
05Chicoutimi Sagueneens-1
05ITG Heroes and Prospects-309
Autographs Series II-DDE
06Chicoutimi Sagueneens-1

Desilets, Joffre
34Beehive Group I Photos-147
36O-Pee-Chee V304D-114
37O-Pee-Chee V304E-156
39O-Pee-Chee V301-1-44

Desilets, Mike
52Juniors Blue Tint-158

Desilets, Nicolas
02Shawinigan Cataractes-23
03Shawinigan Cataractes-8
05Shawinigan Cataractes-11

DeSimone, Phil
04Sioux City Musketeers-8

Desjardine, Chris
93Quebec Pee-Wee Tournament-862

Desjardine, Ken
72Nordiques Postcards-6
73Nordiques Team Issue-7

Desjardines, Mario
86Kamloops Blazers-6

Desjardins, Andrew
03Sault Ste. Marie Greyhounds-4
04Sault Ste. Marie Greyhounds-17

Desjardins, Cedrik
03Rimouski Oceanic-8
03Rimouski Oceanic Sheets-3
04Rimouski Oceanic-12
05Quebec Remparts-14
05Quebec Remparts Signature Series-14
06ITG Heroes and Prospects Memorial Cup Champions-MC01

Desjardins, Eric
88Canadiens Postcards-9
89Canadiens Kraft-7
89Canadiens Postcards-10
90Canadiens Postcards-12
90O-Pee-Chee-425
90Pro Set-467
90Score Rookie/Traded-58T
90Upper Deck-428
French-428
91Pro Set Platinum-193
91Bowman-329
91Canadiens Panini Team Stickers-8
91Canadiens Postcards-10
91Gillette-27
91O-Pee-Chee-14
91OPC Premier-157
91Panini Stickers-189
91Parkhurst-85
French-85
91Pinnacle-73
French-73
91Pro Set-118
French-118
91Score American-119
91Score Canadian Bilingual-119
91Score Canadian English-119
91Score Young Superstars-23
91Stadium Club-214
91Topps-14
91Upper Deck-360
91Upper Deck-504
French-360
French-504
92Bowman-228
92Bowman-311
92Canadiens Postcards-7
92Durivage Panini-36
92O-Pee-Chee-360
92Panini Stickers-156
92Panini Stickers French-156
92Parkhurst-80
Emerald Ice-80
92Pinnacle-16
French-16
Team 2000-9
Team 2000 French-9
92Pro Set-86
92Score-23
Canadian-23
Young Superstars-28
92Stadium Club-326
92Topps-192
Gold-192G
92Ultra-104
92Upper Deck-268
93Canadiens Postcards-8
93Donruss-173
93Durivage Score-12
93Leaf-203
93O-Pee-Chee Canadiens Hockey Fest-20
93OPC Premier-32
Gold-32
93Panini Stickers-21
93Parkhurst-102
Emerald Ice-102
93Pinnacle-59
Canadian-59
93PowerPlay-128
93Score-128
Canadian-128
93Stadium Club-170
Members Only Master Set-170
OPC-170
First Day Issue-170
First Day Issue OPC-170
93Topps/OPC Premier-32
Gold-32
93Ultra-94
93Upper Deck-184
93Swedish Semic World Champ Stickers-195
93Quebec Pee-Wee Tournament-916
94Be A Player-R105
94Canada Games NHL POGS-139
94Canadiens Postcards-8
94Donruss-177
94EA Sports-67
94Flair-88
94Fleer-151
94Leaf-433
94Parkhurst-118
Gold-118
94Pinnacle-106
Artist's Proofs-106
Rink Collection-106
94Score-110
Gold-110
Platinum-110
94Select-113
Gold-113
94Stadium Club-263
Members Only Master Set-263
First Day Issue-263
Super Team Winner Cards-263
94Ultra-108
94Upper Deck-279
Electric Ice-279
94Finnish Jaa Kiekko-87
95Bashan Super Stickers-93
95Canada Games NHL POGS-209
95Collector's Choice-105
Player's Club-105
Player's Club Platinum-105
95Donruss-151
95Emotion-130
95Finest-174
Refractors-174
95Imperial Stickers-93
95Leaf-70
95Metal-109
95Panini Stickers-119
95Parkhurst International-428
Emerald Ice-428
95Pinnacle-110
Artist's Proofs-110
Rink Collection-110
95Playoff One on One-75
95Post Upper Deck-5
95Score-207
Black Ice Artist's Proofs-207
Black Ice-207
95SkyBox Impact-124
95SP-112
95Stadium Club-125
Members Only Master Set-125
95Topps-290
OPC Inserts-290
95Ultra-116
Gold Medallion-116
95Upper Deck-186
Electric Ice-186
Electric Ice Gold-186
NHL All-Stars-AS9
NHL All-Stars Jumbo-AS9
Special Edition-SE150
Special Edition Gold-SE150
96Be A Player-40
Autographs-40
Autographs Silver-40
96Black Diamond-37
Gold-37
96Collector's Choice-195
96Donruss-25
Press Proofs-25
96Fleer-79
Norris-4
96Flyers Postcards-5
96Leaf-27
Press Proofs-27
96Leaf Preferred-32
Press Proofs-32
96Metal Universe-110
96Pinnacle-169
Artist's Proofs-169
Foil-169
Premium Stock-169
Rink Collection-169
96Score-159
Artist's Proofs-159
Dealer's Choice Artist's Proofs-159
Special Artist's Proofs-159
Golden Blades-159
96SkyBox Impact-93
NHL on Fox-8
96SP-113
96Stadium Club Members Only-41
96Team Out-86
96Topps Picks-93
OPC Inserts-93
96Ultra-123
Gold Medallion-123
96Upper Deck-123
96Upper Deck Ice-47
Parallel-47
96Swedish Semic Wien-83
97Collector's Choice World Domination-W15
97Donruss-141
Press Proofs Silver-141
Press Proofs Gold-141
97Donruss Limited-80
Exposure-80
97Esso Olympic Hockey Heroes-13
97Esso Olympic Hockey Heroes French-13
97Kraft Team Canada-4
97McDonald's Team Canada Coins-6
97Pacific-121
Copper-121
Emerald Green-121
Ice Blue-121
Red-121
Silver-121
97Pacific Omega-162
Copper-162
Dark Gray-162
Emerald Green-162
Gold-162
Ice Blue-162
97Score-196
97Score Flyers-7
Platinum-7
Premier-7
97Upper Deck-332
98Aurora-137
98Be A Player-253
Press Release-253
98BAP Gold-253
98BAP Autographs-253
98BAP Autographs Gold-253
98Finest-102
No Protectors-102
No Protectors Refractors-102
Refractors-102
98OPC Chrome-35
Refractors-35
98Pacific-324
Ice Blue-324
Red-324
98Pacific Omega-173
Red-173
Opening Day Issue-173
98Paramount-171
Copper-171
Emerald Green-171
Holo-Electric-171
Ice Blue-171
Silver-171
98Topps-35
O-Pee-Chee-35
98Upper Deck-150
Exclusives-150
Exclusives 1 of 1-150
Gold Reserve-150
98Upper Deck MVP-154
Gold Script-154
Silver Script-154
Super Script-154
99Aurora-104
Premiere Date-104
99BAP Memorabilia-189
Gold-189
Silver-189
99BAP Millennium-180
Emerald-180
Ruby-180
Sapphire-180
Signatures-180
Signatures Gold-180
99Kraft Stanley Cup Moments-2
99O-Pee-Chee-158
99O-Pee-Chee Chrome-158
99O-Pee-Chee Chrome Refractors-158
99Pacific-301
Copper-301
Emerald Green-301
Gold-301
Ice Blue-301
Premiere Date-301
Red-301
99Pacific Omega-168
Copper-168
Gold-168
Ice Blue-168
Premiere Date-168
99Panini Stickers-127
99Paramount-169
Copper-169
Emerald-169
Gold-169
Holographic Emerald-169
Holographic Gold-169
Holographic Silver-169
Ice Blue-169
Premiere Date-169
Red-169
Silver-169
99SPx-113
Radiance-113
Spectrum-113
99Topps/OPC-158
99Topps/OPC Chrome-158
Refractors-158
99Upper Deck-98
Exclusives-98
Exclusives 1 of 1-98
99Upper Deck Gold Reserve-98
99Upper Deck MVP-152
Gold Script-152
Silver Script-152
Super Script-152
99Upper Deck Victory-215
00Aurora-105
Premiere Date-105
00BAP Memorabilia-53
Emerald-53
Ruby-53
Sapphire-53
Promos-53
00BAP Mem Chicago Sportsfest Copper-53
00BAP Memorabilia Chicago Sportsfest Blue-53
00BAP Memorabilia Chicago Sportsfest Gold-53
00BAP Memorabilia Chicago Sportsfest Ruby-53
00BAP Memorabilia Chicago Sun-Times Ruby-53
00BAP Memorabilia Chicago Sun-Times Gold-53
00BAP Mem Chicago Sun-Times Sapphire-53
00BAP Mem Toronto Fall Expo Copper-53
00BAP Memorabilia Toronto Fall Expo Gold-53
00BAP Memorabilia Toronto Fall Expo Ruby-53
00BAP Parkhurst 2000-P36
00BAP Signature Series-15
Emerald-15
Ruby-15
Sapphire-15
Autographs-156
Autographs Gold-156
Department of Defense-DD17
00BAP Ultimate Memorabilia Teammates-TM29
00Crown Royale Game-Worn Jerseys-19
00Crown Royale Game-Worn Jersey Patches-19
00Crown Royale Premium-Sized Jerseys-19
00O-Pee-Chee-167
00O-Pee-Chee Parallel-167
00Pacific-295
Copper-295
Gold-295
Ice Blue-295
Premiere Date-295
Jerseys-10
Jersey Patches-10
00Paramount-179
Copper-179
Gold-179
Holo-Gold-179
Holo-Silver-179
Ice Blue-179
Premiere Date-179
Jersey and Patches-8
00Private Stock Game Gear-81
00Private Stock Game Gear Patches-81
00Revolution-107
Blue-107
Premiere Date-107
Red-107
00Stadium Club-169
00Titanium Game Gear-121
00Titanium Game Gear Patches-121
00Titanium Draft Day Edition-72
00Topps/OPC-167
Parallel-167
00Topps Chrome-115
OPC Refractors-115
Refractors-115
00Topps Heritage-225
00Topps Heritage-236
00Topps Stars-53
Blue-53
00Upper Deck-130
Exclusives Tier 1-130
Exclusives Tier 2-130
00Upper Deck MVP-133
First Stars-133
Second Stars-133
Third Stars-133
00Upper Deck Victory-171
00Upper Deck Vintage-265
01BAP Memorabilia-159
Emerald-159
Ruby-159
Sapphire-159
01Flyers Postcards-4
01O-Pee-Chee-245
01O-Pee-Chee Premier Parallel-245
01Pacific-285
Extreme LTD-285
Hobby LTD-285
Premiere Date-285
Retail LTD-285
01Pacific Arena Exclusives-285
01Pacific Heads-Up Quad Jerseys-15
01Parkhurst-111
01Topps-245
OPC Parallel-245
Heritage Captain's Cloth-CCED
Reserve Emblems-ED
Reserve Jerseys-ED
Reserve Name Plates-ED
Reserve Numbers-ED
Reserve Patches-ED
01UD Stanley Cup Champs-68
01Upper Deck-126
Exclusives-126
01Upper Deck MVP-142
01Upper Deck Victory-263
Gold-263
01Upper Deck Vintage-189
02BAP First Edition-175
02BAP Sig Series Auto Buybacks 1998-253
02BAP Sig Series Auto Buybacks 1999-180
02BAP Sig Series Auto Buybacks 2000-156
02BAP Signature Series Defensive Wall-DW3
02Flyers Postcards-16
02Pacific-278
Blue-278
Red-278
02Pacific Complete-348
Red-348
02Topps Total-327
02Upper Deck MVP-135
Gold-135
Classics-135
Golden Classics-135
03Flyers Postcards-4
03ITG Action-466
03NHL Sticker Collection-108
03Pacific-249
Blue-249
Red-249
03Pacific Complete-386
Red-386
03Topps Pristine Jersey Portions-PPJ-ED
03Topps Pristine Jersey Portion Refractor-PPJ-ED
03Topps Pristine Stick Portions-PPS-ED
03Topps Pristine Stick Portion Refractors-PPS-ED
03Upper Deck-389
Canadian Exclusives-389
HG-389
UD Exclusives-389
03Upper Deck MVP-311
Gold Script-311
Silver Script-311
Canadian Exclusives-311
05Flyers Team Issue-4
05Panini Stickers-137
05Parkhurst-359
Facsimile Auto Parallel-359
05Upper Deck-389
05Upper Deck MVP-286
Gold-286
Platinum-286

Desjardins, Gerry
69O-Pee-Chee-99
Four-in-One-14
Stamps-6
69Topps-99
70Colgate Stamps-67
70Esso Power Players-109
70O-Pee-Chee-152
70Sargent Promotions Stamps-45
72O-Pee-Chee-119
72Sargent Promotions Stamps-129
72Topps-38
73O-Pee-Chee-178
73Topps-114
75O-Pee-Chee NHL-125
75Sabres Linnett-2
75Topps-125
76O-Pee-Chee NHL-230
76Topps-230
77O-Pee-Chee NHL-150
77Topps-150

Desjardins, Martin
88ProCards AHL-293
89Canadiens Postcards-11
90ProCards AHL/IHL-410
91ProCards-484
93Swiss HNL-424
95Swiss HNL-248
96Swiss HNL-417

Desjardins, Norman
89ProCards AHL-189
90ProCards AHL/IHL-69
91ProCards-75

Desjardins, Robert
93Wichita Thunder-4

Desjardins, Stephane
907th Inn. Sketch QMJHL-5
917th Inn. Sketch QMJHL-286
917th Inn. Sketch Memorial Cup-61
92Quebec Pee-Wee Tournament-557
94Roanoke Express-12
02Macon Trax-12

Desjardins, Steven
01Fort Wayne Komets-21

Desjardins, Valerie
93Quebec Pee-Wee Tournament-19
Desjardins, Willie
04Medicine Hat Tigers-24
06Medicine Hat Tigers-25
Desjarlais, Craig
00Knoxville Speed-3
04Knoxville Ice Bears-10
Deske, Bernd
94German First League-426
Deske, Jorg
94German First League-433
Deslauriers, Jacques
51Laval Dairy QSHL-82
52St. Lawrence Sales-25
55Montreal Royals-3
Deslauriers, Jeff
01Chicoutimi Sagueneens-13
04ITG Heroes and Prospects-79
Autographs-JD
04ITG Heroes/Prospects Toronto Expo '05-79
04ITG Heroes/Prospects Expo Heroes/Pros-79
05Hamilton Bulldogs-7
06Beehive-119
Matte-119
06Between The Pipes Autographs-AJDL
06Hot Prospects-158
Red Hot-158
White Hot-158
06O-Pee-Chee-599
Rainbow-599
06SP Authentic-243
Limited-243
06The Cup-132
Autographed Rookie Masterpiece Pressplates-132
Gold Rainbow Autographed Rookie Patches-132
Masterpiece Pressplates (Bee Hive)-119
Masterpiece Pressplates (Marquee Rookies)-599
Masterpiece Pressplates (SP Authentic)-243
Masterpiece Pressplates (Sweet Beginnings)-127
Masterpiece Pressplates (Ultimate Collection)-74
Rookies Black-132
Rookies Platinum-132
06Ultimate Collection-74
06Upper Deck-468
Exclusives Parallel-468
High Gloss Parallel-468
Masterpieces-468
06Upper Deck Sweet Shot-127
Rookie Jerseys Autographs-127
06AHL Top Prospects-48
06Wilkes-Barre Scranton Penguins-8
06Wilkes-Barre Scranton Penguins Jerseys-1
Deslauriers, Kevin
99Baie-Comeau Drakkar-8
00Baie-Comeau Drakkar-14
Signed-14
01Baie-Comeau Drakkar-12
02Baie Comeau Drakkar-13
02Shawinigan Cataractes-11
Deslauriers, Mathieu
93Quebec Pee-Wee Tournament-1120
Desloges, Marc
03Everett Silvertips-3
04Swift Current Broncos-13
05Swift Current Broncos-23
Desloges, Steve
74Sioux City Musketeers-3
Desloover, Jason
99Alexandria Warthogs-3
Desmarais, Denis
99Shawinigan Cataractes-16
Signed-16
00Shawinigan Cataractes-1
Signed-1
01Shawinigan Cataractes-1
02Odessa Jackalopes-5
Desmarais, James
93Quebec Pee-Wee Tournament-137
99Peoria Rivermen-28
99Bowman CHL-82
Gold-82
OPC International-82
Desmarais, Matt
92Saskatchewan JHL-46
Desmet, Taggart
06Idaho Steelheads-4
Desnoyers, David
90Montreal-Bourassa AAA-9
917th Inn. Sketch QMJHL-3
98Thetford Mines Coyotes-18
Desnoyers, Peron
93Quebec Pee-Wee Tournament-1237
Desnoyers, Sylvain
92Quebec Pee-Wee Tournament-225
93Quebec Pee-Wee Tournament-1121
DeSousa, Andrew
98Tri-City Americans-3
01Vancouver Giants-12
02Spokane Chiefs-5
03Regina Pats-20
Desouza, Ray
92Nashville Knights-8
94Central Hockey League-7
94Dallas Freeze-7
Despatis, Chris
95Slapshot-276
Desrochers, Eric
907th Inn. Sketch QMJHL-191
Desrochers, Frederic
06Rimouski Oceanic-20
Desrochers, Jean
04Johnstown Chiefs-7
05Johnstown Chiefs-6
DesRochers, Patrick
95Slapshot-332
95Sarnia Sting-2
96Upper Deck-371
96Sarnia Sting-8
97Bowman CHL-40
OPC-40
98Finest Futures Finest-F11
98Finest Futures Finest Refractors-F11
98Bowman CHL-139
Golden Anniversary-139
OPC International-139
Autographs Blue-A20
Autographs Gold-A20
Autographs Silver-A20
Scout's Choice-SC5
98Bowman Chrome CHL-139
Golden Anniversary-139
Golden Anniversary Refractors-139
OPC International-139
OPC International Refractors-139
Refractors-139
01Between the Pipes-88
02Between the Pipes-93
Gold-93
Silver-93
02O-Pee-Chee-283
02O-Pee-Chee Premier Blue Parallel-283
02O-Pee-Chee Premier Red Parallel-283
02O-Pee-Chee Factory Set-283
02Topps-283
OPC Blue Parallel-283
OPC Red Parallel-283
Factory Set-283
03ITG Action-183
03Upper Deck MVP-88
Gold Script-88
Silver Script-88
Canadian Exclusives-88
03Lowell Lock Monsters-18
03Lowell Lock Monsters Photo Album-25
03Pacific AHL Prospects-42
Gold-42
04San Antonio Rampage-19
Desrosiers, Dennis
78Saginaw Gears-3
90Cincinnati Cyclones-38
91Cincinnati Cyclones-7
92Cincinnati Cyclones-24
93Cincinnati Cyclones-25
01Kalamazoo K-Wings-22
Desrosiers, Francois
93Quebec Pee-Wee Tournament-120
Desrosiers, Gilles
51Laval Dairy Lac St. Jean-3
52Bas Du Fleuve-53
Desrosiers, Joe
86Sudbury Wolves-30
897th Inn. Sketch OHL-95
Desrosiers, Julien
97Rimouski Oceanic-24
Desrosiers, Louis
52Bas Du Fleuve-65
52Juniors Blue Tint-47
Desrosiers, Matt
02South Carolina Stingrays-7
02South Carolina Stingrays RBI-209
04Colorado Eagles-5
05Colorado Eagles-6
Desrosiers, Patrick
93Quebec Pee-Wee Tournament-1398
Desruisseaux, Maxime
01Moncton Wildcats-21
02Moncton Wildcats-14
03Moncton Wildcats-22
04Rimouski Oceanic-13
04Victoriaville Tigres-25
Dessner, Jeff
01Chicago Wolves-5
03German DEL-168
Desson, Jennifer
04Ohio State Buckeyes Women-2
Dessureault, Simon
93Quebec Pee-Wee Tournament-214
Dessureault, Tom
93Quebec Pee-Wee Tournament-1340
Dest, Jason
03Michigan Wolverines-28
04Michigan Wolverines-11
Desyatkov, Pavel
93Pinnacle-505
Canadian-505
00Russian Hockey League-194
Detulleo, Glen
04Missouri River Otters-25
05Quad City Mallards-3
Deubert, Harald
99German DEL-404
Deuling, Jarrett
907th Inn. Sketch WHL-308
93Kamloops Blazers-3
96Kentucky Thoroughblades-5
97Milwaukee Admirals-3
98Kentucky Thoroughblades-6
99Kentucky Thoroughblades-10
00Kentucky Thoroughblades-9
Deutscher, Torsten
94German DEL-36
95German DEL-29
04German Berlin Eisbarens 50th Anniv-16
Devaney, John
81Swedish Semic Hockey VM Stickers-85
Devaux, Olivier
02Swiss HNL-166
Devaux, Sacha
95Swiss HNL-263
Deveaux, Andre
00Belleville Bulls-10
01Belleville Bulls-8
02Belleville Bulls-5
02Belleville Bulls-27
03Owen Sound Attack-16
04Springfield Falcons-2
05Springfield Falcons-2
06Springfield Falcons-25
Devecka, Dusan
04Czech OFS-5
Devereaux, Boyd
95Bowman Draft Prospects-P10
95Slapshot-149
95Slapshot-432
95Classic-87
96Black Diamond-86
Gold-86
96Oilers Postcards-19
96Upper Deck Ice-122
96Kitchener Rangers-8
96Kitchener Rangers-9
96Coll Edge Future Legends Auto Hot Pick-2
96All-Sport PPF *-79
96All Sport PPF Gold *-79
96Visions Signings *-61
Autographs-61A
Autographs Silver-61A
97Be A Player-237
Autographs-237
Autographs Die-Cuts-237
Autographs Prismatic Die-Cuts-237
97Black Diamond-146
Double Diamond-146
Triple Diamond-146
Quadruple Diamond-146
97Collector's Choice-311
97Donruss Elite-90
Aspirations-90
Status-90
97Donruss Priority-184
Stamp of Approval-184
97Katch-56
Gold-56
Silver-56
97Leaf-149
Fractal Matrix-149
Fractal Matrix Die Cuts-149
97Paramount-73
Copper-73
Dark Grey-73
Emerald Green-73
Ice Blue-73
Red-73
Silver-73
97Pinnacle-13
Artist's Proofs-13
Rink Collection-13
Press Plates Back Black-13
Press Plates Back Cyan-13
Press Plates Back Magenta-13
Press Plates Back Yellow-13
Press Plates Front Black-13
Press Plates Front Cyan-13
Press Plates Front Magenta-13
Press Plates Front Yellow-13
Certified Rookie Redemption-J
Certified Rookie Redemption Gold-J
Certified Rookie Redemption Mirror Gold-J
97Score-73
Artist's Proofs-73
Golden Blades-73
97SP Authentic-181
97Zenith-93
Z-Gold-93
Z-Silver-93
97Bowman CHL-23
OPC-23
98OPC Chrome-21
Refractors-21
98Topps-21
O-Pee-Chee-21
99Upper Deck Arena Giveaways-EO2
99Upper Deck MVP SC Edition-75
Gold Script-75
Silver Script-75
Super Script-75
00BAP Memorabilia-450
Emerald-450
Ruby-450
Sapphire-450
00Pacific-163
Copper-163
Gold-163
Ice Blue-163
Premiere Date-163
00Stadium Club-224
01Upper Deck Victory-130
Gold-130
02Pacific-125
Blue-125
Red-125
02Pacific Complete-98
Red-98
02Upper Deck-311
Exclusives-311
02Upper Deck Beckett UD Promos-311
02Upper Deck Vintage-98
03Pacific Complete-359
Red-359
03Parkhurst Original Six Detroit-5
05Be A Player Signatures-BD
05Be A Player Signatures Gold-BD
05Parkhurst-378
Facsimile Auto Parallel-378
Devereaux, John
88Flint Spirits-3
91Greensboro Monarchs-4
97Bakersfield Fog-1
Devine, Kevin
76San Diego Mariners WHA-1
81Indianapolis Checkers-4
82Indianapolis Checkers-2
Devjatov, Vladimir
73Swedish Stickers-129
Devlin, Vince
92British Columbia JHL-216
92British Columbia JHL-227
Devos, Philippe-Michael
06Victoriaville Tigres-19
DeVries, Greg
93Niagara Falls Thunder-5
94Cape Breton Oilers-7
96Oilers Postcards-5
96Upper Deck-191
97Be A Player-78
Autographs-78
Autographs Die-Cuts-78
Autographs Prismatic Die-Cuts-78
97Pacific Invincible NHL Regime-76
98Upper Deck MVP-56
Gold Script-56
Silver Script-56
Super Script-56
99Avalanche Team Issue-1
00Pacific-110
Copper-110
Gold-110
Ice Blue-110
Premiere Date-110
00Private Stock Game Gear-20
00Private Stock Game Gear Patches-20
00Upper Deck NHLPA-PA23
01Avalanche Team Issue-22
01Crown Royale Triple Threads-7
01Pacific Heads-Up Quad Jerseys-9
01Upper Deck-277
Exclusives-277
01Vanguard Memorabilia-37
01Vanguard Patches-37
02Avalanche Postcards-6
02BAP Memorabilia-77
Emerald-77
Ruby-77
Sapphire-77
NHL All-Star Game-77
NHL All-Star Game Blue-77
NHL All-Star Game Green-77
NHL All-Star Game Red-77
02BAP Memorabilia Toronto Fall Expo-77
02Pacific Complete-358
Red-358
02Topps Total-244
02Upper Deck-290
Exclusives-290
02Upper Deck Beckett UD Promos-290
02Upper Deck Vintage-68
03Parkhurst Original Six New York-14
03Rangers Team Issue-4
05Parkhurst-24
Facsimile Auto Parallel-24
06O-Pee-Chee-20
Rainbow-20
06Upper Deck-261
Exclusives Parallel-261
High Gloss Parallel-261
Masterpieces-261
DeVuono, Len
90Kitchener Rangers-7
907th Inn. Sketch OHL-93
907th Inn. Sketch OHL-230
95Central Hockey League-75
DeWaele, Kirk
93Lethbridge Hurricanes-2
00Fresno Falcons-5
01Fresno Falcons-3
02Fresno Falcons-13
03UK Sheffield Steelers-9
03UK Sheffield Steelers Stickers-12
05UK Cardiff Devils-2
Gold-2
Silver-2
05UK Cardiff Devils Challenge Cup-18
Dewan, Adam
00Roanoke Express-22
01Hamilton Bulldogs-19
02Hamilton Bulldogs-20
03Port Huron Beacons-6
Dewar, Jeff
93Seattle Thunderbirds-4
03Lubbock Cotton Kings-6
Dewitz, Dieter
70Finnish Jaakiekko-83
70Swedish Hockey-368
74Finnish Jenkki-109
04German Berlin Eisbarens 50th Anniv-47
DeWolf, Josh
95Classic-59
98Albany River Rats-7
99Albany River Rats-10
99Quebec Citadelles-22
00Quebec Citadelles-20
Signed-20
01Cincinnati Mighty Ducks-11
02Cincinnati Mighty Ducks-B-12
03German DEL-154
03Houston Aeros-6
DeWolf, Karl
94French National Team-8
Dewsbury, Al
44Beehive Group II Photos-91
51Parkhurst-38
52Parkhurst-17
53Parkhurst-78
54Parkhurst-78
94Parkhurst Missing Link-22
02Parkhurst Reprints-156
02Parkhurst Reprints-165
02Parkhurst Reprints-198
Dexheimer, Alexander
93Quebec Pee-Wee Tournament-1774
98German DEL-218
Dextater, Bill
83Kingston Canadians-28
Dexter, Brad
99ECHL All-Star Southern Conference-2
Dexter, Jason
95Birmingham Bulls-19
99Tupelo T-Rex-16
Dey, Edgar
10C56-6
Dey, Nate
04St. Cloud State Huskies-6
05St. Cloud State Huskies-17
06St. Cloud State Huskies-7
Deyell, Mark
93Saskatoon Blades-3
93Saskatoon Blades-7
95Saskatoon Blades-9
96St. John's Maple Leafs-15
97St. John's Maple Leafs-10
Dezainde, Joel
95Slapshot-158
96Owen Sound Platers-6
98Barrie Colts-5
01Albany River Rats-8
Dezainde, Norm
90Kitchener Rangers-15
907th Inn. Sketch OHL-231
917th Inn. Sketch OHL-82
93Kitchener Rangers-8
94Tampa Bay Tritons RHI-8
94Toledo Storm-4
95Toledo Storm-14
95Signature Rookies-24
Signatures-24
96Toledo Storm-22
98Dayton Bombers-3
98Dayton Bombers EBK-19
Dhadphale, Aniket
99Greensboro Generals-13
00Trenton Titans-3
01Trenton Titans-1-3
Di Fiore, Ralph
94Finnish Jaa Kiekko-295
Di Ubaldo, Chris
00Kelowna Rockets-5
02Prince Albert Raiders-8
Diachuk, Ed
61Union Oil WHL-2
Diamond, Marty
98San Angelo Outlaws-7
Dias, Matt
05Sudbury Wolves-10
06Sudbury Wolves-4
Diaz, Rafael
03Swiss EV Zug Postcards-6
04Swiss EV Zug Postcards-11
Dibbern, Tom
98Danish Hockey League-119
DiBenedetto, Justin
04St. Michael's Majors-15
06Sarnia Sting-13
Diberius, Mats
98Danish Hockey League-188
99Danish Hockey League-22
Diblasio, Robert
93Quebec Pee-Wee Tournament-1162
Dibley, Gord
67Columbus Checkers-5
Dicaire, Gerard
00UD CHL Prospects-65
02Kootenay Ice-1
04Springfield Falcons-12
05Johnstown Chiefs-7
05Springfield Falcons-10
Dicaire, Martin
03St. Jean Mission-6
Dicasmirro, Nate
95North Iowa Huskies-5
02Hamilton Bulldogs-6
06Providence Bruins-5
Dick, Harry
51Buffalo Bison-6
Dick, Jonathan
02Drummondville Voltigeurs-15
Dick, Marco
93Swiss HNL-499
95Swiss HNL-276
96Swiss HNL-394
Dick, Mike
79Philadelphia Doubleheaders-21
97Central Texas Stampede-2
Dick, Sven
93Swiss HNL-192
95Swiss HNL-266
96Swiss HNL-385
01Swiss HNL-304
02Swiss HNL-136
Dickens, Ernie
34Beehive Group I Photos-314
44Beehive Group II Photos-92
Dickenson, Herb
52Parkhurst-57
Dickenson, Lou
99UD Prospects-25
00London Knights-5
01Guelph Storm Memorial Cup-17
01Kingston Frontenacs-3
02Guelph Storm-12
02Ottawa 67's-10
Dickie, Brett
99Brandon Wheat Kings-5
00Brandon Wheat Kings-2
01Brandon Wheat Kings-4
02Brandon Wheat Kings-5
03Prince George Cougars-6
Dickie, Gary
86Regina Pats-3
87Regina Pats-2
88Regina Pats-4
Dickie, Gord
917th Inn. Sketch OHL-289
93Kitchener Rangers-6
Dickie, J.J.
96Sault Ste. Marie Greyhounds-5
96Sault Ste. Marie Greyhounds Autographed-5
Dickie, Kevin
91Air Canada SJHL All-Stars-3
91Air Canada SJHL All-Stars-47
00Saskatoon Blades-3
01Saskatoon Blades-29
02Saskatoon Blades-27
Dickie, Ryan
02Windsor Spitfires-25
Dickie, Scott
99Kitchener Rangers-24
00Kitchener Rangers-10
01Kitchener Rangers-1
03Kitchener Rangers Memorial Cup-5
Dickinson, Brett
06Cedar Rapids RoughRiders-8
Dickinson, Brian
89Rayside-Balfour Jr. Canadians-7
Dickson, Darryl
91Air Canada SJHL-D47
92Saskatchewan JHL-24
Dickson, John-Scott
02Windsor Spitfires-27
Dickson, Scott
98Topeka Scarecrows-11
Dickson, Trent
03Memphis RiverKings-2
Didier, Olivier
03Rimouski Oceanic-9
03Rimouski Oceanic Sheets-1
Didiomete, Devin
04Sudbury Wolves-9
05Sudbury Wolves-12
06Sudbury Wolves-10
Didomenico, Chris
06Saint Johns Sea Dogs-17
Diduck, Gerald
85Islanders News-18
86Islanders Team Issue-14
89Islanders Team Issue-5
89O-Pee-Chee-182
89O-Pee-Chee Stickers-117
89Panini Stickers-274
89Topps-182
90Canadiens Postcards-13
90Canucks Mohawk-7
90O-Pee-Chee-421
90OPC Premier-22
90Panini Stickers-85
90Pro Set-180
90Pro Set-468
90Score-139
Canadian-139
90Score Rookie/Traded-23T
90Upper Deck-390
French-390
91Canadiens Panini Team Stickers-9
91Canucks Autograph Cards-5
91Canucks Team Issue 8x10-5
91O-Pee-Chee-280
91Parkhurst-407
French-407
91Pinnacle-211
French-211
91Pro Set-502
French-502
91Score Canadian Bilingual-243
91Score Canadian English-243
91Topps-280
92Bowman-65
92Canucks Road Trip Art-6
92O-Pee-Chee-309
92Parkhurst-419
Emerald Ice-419
92Pinnacle-81
French-81
92Score-34
Canadian-34
92Stadium Club-97
92Topps-44
Gold-44G
92Ultra-424
93Donruss-360
93Leaf-387
93Pinnacle-291
Canadian-291
93PowerPlay-250
93Score-356
Canadian-356
93Ultra-440
94Canucks Program Inserts-7
94Leaf-402
94Pinnacle-359
Artist's Proofs-359
Rink Collection-359
94Stadium Club-91
Members Only Master Set-91
First Day Issue-91
Super Team Winner Cards-91
95Leaf-313
95Parkhurst International-368
Emerald Ice-368
95Topps-247
OPC Inserts-247
95Ultra-245
95Whalers Bob's Stores-6
96Be A Player-167
Autographs-167
Autographs Silver-167
96Whalers Kid's Club-11
97Be A Player-55
Autographs-55
Autographs Die-Cuts-55
Autographs Prismatic Die-Cuts-55
97Coyotes Face-Off Luncheon -3
00Pacific-388
Copper-388
Gold-388
Ice Blue-388
Premiere Date-388
00Stars Postcards-3
Diduck, Judy
94Classic Women of Hockey-W12
97Collector's Choice-283
Diduck, Ryan
99Brandon Wheat Kings-6
Dieard, Jean-Francis
907th Inn. Sketch QMJHL-121
Diehl, Korey
04South Surrey Eagles-4
04South Surrey Eagles-5
04Surrey Eagles-3a
04Surrey Eagles-3b
04Surrey Eagles-3
Diener, Derek
93Lethbridge Hurricanes-3
95Lethbridge Hurricanes-2
97Peoria Rivermen-2
Diener, Michael
93Swiss HNL-20
95Swiss HNL-18
96Swiss HNL-242
01Swiss HNL-454
02Swiss HNL-191
Diethelm, Rolf
02Swiss HNL-220
Dietrich, Brandon
00Charlotte Checkers-25
00Hartford Wolf Pack-6
02Reading Royals-13
02Reading Royals RBI Sports-171
03Gwinnett Gladiators-4
03Gwinnett Gladiators RBI Sports-196
Dietrich, Don
83Springfield Indians-21
Dietrich, Jacob
04Moose Jaw Warriors-7
05Lethbridge Hurricanes-6
Dietrich, Lou
52Juniors Blue Tint-13
Dietrich, Robert
04German Nuremburg Ice Tigers Postcards-4
Dietrich, Shawn
88Spokane Chiefs-3
907th Inn. Sketch WHL-198
917th Inn. Sketch WHL-200
Dietrich, Tyler
02Medicine Hat Tigers-7
03Everett Silvertips-20
04Everett Silvertips-2
Dietz, Chris
92Quebec Pee-Wee Tournament-1441
93Quebec Pee-Wee Tournament-867
Dietz, Matthias
04German Berlin Eisbarens 50th Anniv-66
Dietzsch, Andre
94German DEL-34
95German DEL-26
04German Berlin Eisbarens 50th Anniv-29
DiFazio, Alberto
82Swedish Semic VM Stickers-136
83Swedish Semic VM Stickers-136
Difrancescantonio, Chris
04Surrey Eagles-4
04Surrey Eagles-5
DiFronzo, Michele
94Classic Women of Hockey-W32
Dijkstra, Sander
05Dutch Vadeko Flyers -4
DiLauro, Ray
02Reading Royals-5
02Reading Royals RBI Sports-172
03Columbus Cottonmouths-29
04Wheeling Nailers Riesbeck's-17
05Cleveland Barons-7
06German DEL-132
Dilio, Frank
83Hall of Fame-81
83Hall of Fame Postcards-F5
85Hall of Fame-81
Dillabough, Bob
63Parkhurst-47
64Beehive Group III Photos-5
65Coca-Cola-15
65Topps-39
66Topps-98
68O-Pee-Chee-191
69O-Pee-Chee-150
70Dad's Cookies-22
70Sargent Promotions Stamps-217
72Cleveland Crusaders WHA-3
Dillabough, Travis
98Dayton Bombers-4
98Dayton Bombers EBK-9
01Macon Whoopee-6
Dillon, Cecil
33O-Pee-Chee V304B-71
33V129-32
33V252 Canadian Gum-18
33V357 Ice Kings-15
34Beehive Group I Photos-271
34Diamond Matchbooks Silver-20
35Diamond Matchbooks Tan 2-18
35Diamond Matchbooks Tan 2-19
35Diamond Matchbooks Tan 3-17
06ITG Ultimate Memorabilia Broadway Blue Shirts Autos-4
Dillon, Spencer
03Salmon Arm Silverbacks-6
04Green Bay Gamblers-5
Dillon, Wayne
74O-Pee-Chee WHA-3
75O-Pee-Chee NHL-363
76O-Pee-Chee NHL-9
76Topps-9
77O-Pee-Chee NHL-166
77Topps-166
78O-Pee-Chee-73
78Topps-73
79Jets Postcards-4
79O-Pee-Chee-359
Dilorenzo, Michael
01Hull Olympiques-22
03Yarmouth Mariners-21
Dimaio, Rob
84Kamloops Blazers-7
85Medicine Hat Tigers-5
88ProCards AHL-310
89ProCards AHL-234
90OPC Premier-27
90Pro Set-625
90Upper Deck-225
French-225
90ProCards AHL/IHL-512
91Parkhurst-325
French-325
91Pro Set-430
French-430
91Upper Deck-481
French-481
92Bowman-403
92Lightning Sheraton-13
92OPC Premier-62
92Parkhurst-402
Emerald Ice-402
92Stadium Club-33
92Topps-488
Gold-488G
92Upper Deck-529
93Lightning Kash n'Karry-5
93OPC Premier-242
Gold-242
93Panini Stickers-218
93Parkhurst-196
Emerald Ice-196
93Stadium Club-182
Members Only Master Set-182
OPC-182
First Day Issue-182
First Day Issue OPC-182
93Topps/OPC Premier-242
Gold-242
93Upper Deck-176
94Leaf-549
94OPC Premier-114
Special Effects-114
94Pinnacle-360
Artist's Proofs-360
Rink Collection-360
94Topps/OPC Premier-114
Special Effects-114
95Be A Player-105
Signatures-S105
Signatures Die Cuts-S105
95Parkhurst International-431
Emerald Ice-431
95Topps-92
OPC Inserts-92
95Upper Deck-336
Electric Ice-336
Electric Ice Gold-336
97Be A Player-6
Autographs-6
Autographs Die-Cuts-6
Autographs Prismatic Die-Cuts-6
97Pacific-287
Copper-287
Emerald Green-287
Ice Blue-287
Red-287
Silver-287
97Panini Stickers-1
97Score Bruins-9
Platinum-9
Premier-9
98Be A Player-7
Press Release-7
98BAP Gold-7
98BAP Autographs-7
98BAP Autographs Gold-7
98BAP Tampa Bay All Star Game-7
98Finest-61
No Protectors-61
No Protectors Refractors-61
Refractors-61
98Pacific-75
Ice Blue-75
Red-75
99Panini Stickers-30
99Wayne Gretzky Hockey-19
00Upper Deck-265
Exclusives Tier 1-265
Exclusives Tier 2-265
01Stars Postcards-3
01Upper Deck-288
Exclusives-288
02BAP Sig Series Auto Buybacks 1998-7
02Pacific Complete-289
Red-289
02Stars Postcards-17
03ITG Action-126
03Pacific Complete-322
Red-322
03Stars Postcards-5
05Parkhurst-444
Facsimile Auto Parallel-444
Dimaline, Joe
98Muskegon Fury-11
98UHL All-Stars-6
99Muskegon Fury-5
99UHL All-Stars West-11T
00Muskegon Fury-21
01Quad-City Mallards-4
Dimbat, Andreas
95German DEL-68
96German DEL-264
Dimella, Nick
99Des Moines Buccaneers-7
Dimitrakos, Niko
93Quebec Pee-Wee Tournament-835
02BAP Memorabilia-365
02BAP Ultimate Memorabilia-53
02Pacific Calder-143
Silver-143
02Pacific Complete-513
Red-513
02Pacific Quest for the Cup-144
Gold-144
02SP Authentic-213
02SPx-183
02Upper Deck Rookie Update-125
02AHL Top Prospects-9
02Cleveland Barons-5
03Beehive-162
Gold-162
Silver-162
03Black Diamond-99
Black-99
Green-99
Red-99
03ITG Action-429
03Pacific-294
Blue-294
Red-294
03SP Game Used-38
Gold-38
03SPx-80
Radiance-80
Spectrum-80
03Upper Deck-161
Canadian Exclusives-161
HG-161
03Upper Deck Classic Portraits-81
03Upper Deck MVP-354
Gold Script-354
Silver Script-354
Canadian Exclusives-354
03Upper Deck Trilogy-81
Limited-81
03Upper Deck Victory-159
Bronze-159
Gold-159
Silver-159
Freshman Flashback-FF39
03Cleveland Barons-6
04Pacific-296
Blue-296
Red-296
05Be A Player Signatures-ND
05Be A Player Signatures Gold-ND
05Panini Stickers-353
05Upper Deck-409
Notable Numbers-N-ND
06Philadelphia Phantoms-4
Dimitri, Dave
93Huntington Blizzard-7
Dimme, Birley
52Juniors Blue Tint-55
Dimmers, Ralph
99German DEL-403
Dimuzio, Frank
88ProCards AHL-31
93Swedish Semic World Champ Stickers-217
94Finnish Jaa Kiekko-300
98German DEL-201
Dineen, Bill
44Beehive Group II Photos-162
52Juniors Blue Tint-147
53Parkhurst-37
54Parkhurst-48
54Topps-57
57Topps-49
60Cleveland Barons-3
62Quebec Aces-7A
62Quebec Aces-7B
63Quebec Aces-6
88ProCards AHL-2
92Flyers Upper Deck Sheets-20
92Flyers Upper Deck Sheets-34
92Score-517
Canadian-517
93Parkhurst Parkie Reprints-PR62
94Parkhurst Missing Link-50
06Parkhurst-152
Autographs-152
Dineen, Gord
80Sault Ste. Marie Greyhounds-3
81Sault Ste. Marie Greyhounds-10
82Indianapolis Checkers-3
85Islanders News-19
86Islanders Team Issue-15
89O-Pee-Chee-256
90O-Pee-Chee-470
90Pro Set-233
90Upper Deck-369
French-369
91ProCards-306
92Durivage Panini-37
92San Diego Gulls-6
93Senators Kraft Sheets-7
94Stadium Club-219
Members Only Master Set-219
First Day Issue-219
Super Team Winner Cards-219
96Collector's Edge Ice-192
Prism-192
99Utah Grizzlies-9
99Utah Grizzlies-21
00Louisville Panthers-14
01Macon Whoopee-2
02ECHL Update-U-7
03Springfield Falcons Postcards-27
Dineen, Jim
98Fort Worth Brahmas-5
Dineen, Kevin
85O-Pee-Chee-34
85O-Pee-Chee Stickers-168
85Topps-34
85Whalers Junior Wendy's-4
86O-Pee-Chee-88
86O-Pee-Chee Stickers-56
86Topps-88
86Whalers Junior Thomas'-5
87O-Pee-Chee-124
87O-Pee-Chee Stickers-202
87Panini Stickers-44
87Topps-124
87Whalers Jr. Burger King/Pepsi-4
88Frito-Lay Stickers-28
88O-Pee-Chee-36
88O-Pee-Chee Stickers-269
88Panini Stickers-240
88Topps-36
88Whalers Junior Ground Round-4
89O-Pee-Chee-20
89O-Pee-Chee-304
89O-Pee-Chee Box Bottoms-M

89O-Pee-Chee Stickers-270
89Panini Stickers-219
89Topps-20
89Topps Box Bottoms-M
89Whalers Junior Milk-5
90Bowman-261
Tiffany-261
90Bowman Hat Tricks-7
Tiffany-7
90Kraft-11
90O-Pee-Chee-213
90OPC Premier-23
90Panini Stickers-43
90Pro Set-102
90Score-212
Canadian-212
90Score Hottest/Rising Stars-90
90Topps-213
Tiffany-213
90Upper Deck-266
French-266
90Whalers Jr. 7-Eleven-9
91Pro Set Platinum-46
91Bowman-6
91Flyers J.C. Penney-6
91Kraft-86
91O-Pee-Chee-285
91Panini Stickers-323
91Parkhurst-348
French-348
91Pinnacle-246
91Pinnacle-366
French-246
French-366
91Pro Set-89
91Pro Set-451
French-89
French-451
NHL Sponsor Awards-AC17
91Score American-118
91Score Canadian Bilingual-118
91Score Canadian English-118
91Score Kellogg's-11
91Stadium Club-162
91Topps-285
91Upper Deck-105
91Upper Deck-530
French-105
French-530
91Finnish Semic World Champ Stickers-71
91Swedish Semic World Champ Stickers-71
92Bowman-121
92Durivage Panini-12
92Flyers J.C. Penney-9
92Flyers Upper Deck Sheets-1
92Flyers Upper Deck Sheets-20
92Flyers Upper Deck Sheets-25
92O-Pee-Chee-200
92Panini Stickers-186
92Panini Stickers French-186
92Parkhurst-127
Emerald Ice-127
92Pinnacle-14
French-14
92Pro Set-134
92Score-284
Canadian-284
92Stadium Club-365
92Topps-131
Gold-131G
92Ultra-154
92Upper Deck-256
93Donruss-249
93Durivage Score-37
93Flyers J.C. Penney-8
93Flyers Lineup Sheets-10
93Flyers Lineup Sheets-11
93Kraft-33
93Leaf-156
Hat Trick Artists-6
93OPC Premier-167
Gold-167
93Panini Stickers-49
93Parkhurst-421
Emerald Ice-421
93Pinnacle-276
Canadian-276
Captains-17
Captains Canadian-17
93PowerPlay-179
93Score-122
Canadian-122
93Stadium Club-43
Members Only Master Set-43
OPC-43
First Day Issue-43
First Day Issue OPC-43
93Topps/OPC Premier-167
Gold-167
93Ultra-107
93Upper Deck-212
93Classic McDonalds-13
94Canada Games NHL POGS-357
94Donruss-36
94Leaf-167
94OPC Premier-207
Special Effects-207
94Parkhurst-172
Gold-172
94Pinnacle-426
Artist's Proofs-426
Rink Collection-426
94Score-197
Gold-197
Platinum-197
94Select Promos-142
94Select-142
Gold-142
94Topps/OPC Premier-207
Special Effects-207
94Ultra-156
94Upper Deck-431
Electric Ice-431
95Canada Games NHL POGS-207
95Donruss-212
95Leaf-205
95Parkhurst International-366
Emerald Ice-366
95Pinnacle-150
Artist's Proofs-150
Rink Collection-150
95Score-277
Black Ice Artist's Proofs-277
Black Ice-277
95Topps-143
OPC Inserts-143
95Images-21
Gold-21
Platinum Players-PL3
96Black Diamond-72
Gold-72
96Kraft Upper Deck-33
96SP-71
96Upper Deck-270
96Whalers Kid's Club-3
96Collector's Edge Ice-130
Crucibles-C3
Prism-130
97Collector's Choice-109
97Crown Royale-22
Emerald Green-22
Ice Blue-22
Silver-22
97Hurricanes Team Issue-6
97Katch-26
Gold-26
Silver-26
97Pacific-218
Copper-218
Emerald Green-218
Ice Blue-218
Red-218
Silver-218
97Pacific Omega-43
Copper-43
Dark Gray-43
Emerald Green-43
Gold-43
Ice Blue-43
97Paramount-33
Copper-33
Dark Grey-33
Emerald Green-33
Ice Blue-33
Red-33
Silver-33
97Upper Deck-241
98Aurora-30
98Hurricanes Team Issue-9
98Katch-25
98OPC Chrome-173
Refractors-173
98Pacific-130
Ice Blue-130
Red-130
98Pacific Dynagon Ice-30
Blue-30
Red-30
98Paramount-34
Copper-34
Emerald Green-34
Holo-Electric-34
Ice Blue-34
Silver-34
98Topps-173
O-Pee-Chee-173
99Pacific-69
Copper-69
Emerald Green-69
Gold-69
Ice Blue-69
Premiere Date-69
Red-69
99Senators Team Issue-5
00Titanium Game Gear-12
00Topps Chrome-226
OPC Refractors-226
Refractors-226
00Upper Deck-283
Exclusives Tier 1-283
Exclusives Tier 2-283
01Blue Jackets Donatos Pizza-10
02Pacific Complete-178
Red-178
06Parkhurst-50
06Parkhurst-214
06Parkhurst-227
Autographs-50
Autographs-214
Autographs-227
Autographs Dual-DALD
06Portland Pirates-24

Dineen, Nick
06Sioux Falls Stampede -12

Dineen, Peter
83Moncton Alpines-8
88ProCards AHL-21
89ProCards AHL-327
90ProCards AHL/IHL-306

Dineen, Shawn
83Moncton Alpines-25
89ProCards IHL-120

Dingle, John
04Ohio State Buckeyes-19
05Ohio State Buckeyes-23
06Ohio State Buckeyes-7

Dingle, Ryan
02Tri-City Stormfront-10

Dingman, Chris
92Brandon Wheat Kings-3
93Brandon Wheat Kings-20
94Brandon Wheat Kings-4
94Classic-17
Gold-17
Tri-Cards-T10
94Classic Four-Sport *-133
Gold-133
Printers Proofs-133
95Brandon Wheat Kings-6
95Images Four-Sport *-110
95Signature Rookies-20
Signatures-20
95Slapshot Memorial Cup-43
96Saint John Flames-2
97Be A Player-216
Autographs-216
Autographs Die-Cuts-216
Autographs Prismatic Die-Cuts-216
97Crown Royale-17
Emerald Green-17
Ice Blue-17
Silver-17
97Leaf-158
Fractal Matrix-158
Fractal Matrix Die Cuts-158
97Paramount-27
Copper-27
Dark Grey-27
Emerald Green-27
Ice Blue-27
Red-27
Silver-27
97Pinnacle-7
Artist's Proofs-7
Rink Collection-7
Press Plates Back Black-7
Press Plates Back Cyan-7
Press Plates Back Magenta-7
Press Plates Back Yellow-7
Press Plates Front Black-7
Press Plates Front Cyan-7
Press Plates Front Magenta-7
Press Plates Front Yellow-7
97Score-55
Artist's Proofs-55
Golden Blades-55
97Upper Deck-234
99Avalanche Team Issue-4
00BAP Memorabilia-277
Emerald-277
Ruby-277
Sapphire-277
Promos-277
00BAP Mem Chicago Sportsfest Copper-277
00BAP Memorabilia Chicago Sportsfest Blue-277
00BAP Memorabilia Chicago Sportsfest Gold-277
00BAP Memorabilia Chicago Sportsfest Ruby-277
00BAP Memorabilia Chicago Sun-Times Ruby-277
00BAP Memorabilia Chicago Sun-Times Gold-277
00BAP Mem Chicago Sun-Times Sapphire-277
00BAP Mem Toronto Fall Expo Copper-277
00BAP Memorabilia Toronto Fall Expo Gold-277
00BAP Memorabilia Toronto Fall Expo Ruby-277
00BAP Memorabilia Update Tough Materials-T18
00BAP Mem Update Tough Materials Gold-T18
00Private Stock Game Gear-21
00Private Stock Game Gear Patches-21
00Titanium Draft Day Edition-23
Patches-23
00Upper Deck NHLPA-PA22
01BAP Memorabilia Stanley Cup Champions-CA7
01BAP Update Tough Customers-TC26
01BAP Update Tough Customers-TC39
01Pacific Jerseys-8
01Pacific Heads-Up Quad Jerseys-9
01Upper Deck-267
Exclusives-267
02Lightning Team Issue-4
03ITG Action-595
03Lightning Team Issue-16
03Pacific Complete-303
Red-303
03Upper Deck MVP-388
Gold Script-388
Silver Script-388
Canadian Exclusives-388
05Lightning Team Issue-6

Dingwall, Richard
96UK Fife Flyers-8

Dinsmore, Charles A
24C144 Champ's Cigarettes-22
24V130 Maple Crispette-17
24V145-2-40

Dion, Connie
43Parade Sportive *-31

Dion, Michel
76O-Pee-Chee WHA-6
76O-Pee-Chee WHA-114
77O-Pee-Chee WHA-62
79O-Pee-Chee-316
80Nordiques Postcards-8
80O-Pee-Chee-223
80Topps-223
82O-Pee-Chee-267
82O-Pee-Chee Stickers-146
82O-Pee-Chee Stickers-168
82Post Cereal-15
82Topps Stickers-146
82Topps Stickers-168
83NHL Key Tags-100
83O-Pee-Chee-279
83O-Pee-Chee Stickers-234
83Penguins Coke-7
83Penguins Heinz Photos-7
83Topps Stickers-234
84O-Pee-Chee-173
84Penguins Heinz Photos-6
06Parkhurst-151
Autographs-151

Dion, Steven
907th Inn. Sketch QMJHL-141
917th Inn. Sketch QMJHL-221

Dion, Tom
92Wheeling Thunderbirds-6

Dionne, Gilbert
88Kitchener Rangers-18
89Kitchener Rangers-19
90ProCards AHL/IHL-62
907th Inn. Sketch Memorial Cup-39
91Parkhurst-313
91Parkhurst-447
French-313
French-447
91Upper Deck-448
French-448
91ProCards-73
92Bowman-439
92Canadiens Postcards-9
92Durivage Panini-21
92Humpty Dumpty I-5
92O-Pee-Chee-307
92Panini Stickers-272
92Panini Stickers-M
92Panini Stickers French-272
92Panini Stickers French-M
92Parkhurst Previews-PV3
92Parkhurst-81
92Parkhurst-237
Emerald Ice-81
Emerald Ice-237
92Pinnacle-5
French-5
Team 2000-29
Team 2000 French-29
92Pro Set-92
Rookie Goal Leaders-6
92Score-331
Canadian-331
Sharpshooters-7
Sharpshooters Canadian-7
Young Superstars-6
92Seasons Patches-24
92Stadium Club-403
92Topps-13
92Topps-19
Gold-13G
Gold-19G
92Ultra-105
Rookies-4
92Upper Deck-356
92Upper Deck-427
92Upper Deck-625
All-Rookie Team-AR2
93Canadiens Postcards-9
93Donruss-174
93Durivage Score-13
93Leaf-117
93OPC Premier-480
Gold-480
93Panini Stickers-18
93Parkhurst-101
Emerald Ice-101
93Pinnacle-199
Canadian-199
93PowerPlay-368
93Score-178
Canadian-178
93Stadium Club-115
Members Only Master Set-115
OPC-115
First Day Issue-115
First Day Issue OPC-115
93Topps/OPC Premier-480
Gold-480
93Ultra-141
93Upper Deck-117
93Classic Pro Prospects-87
94Be A Player-R22
94Canada Games NHL POGS-134
94Canadiens Postcards-9
94Fleer-152
94OPC Premier-366
Special Effects-366
94Parkhurst Vintage-V14
94Parkhurst SE-SE91
Gold-SE91
94Pinnacle-422
Artist's Proofs-422
Rink Collection-422
94Topps/OPC Premier-366
Special Effects-366
94Ultra-109
94Upper Deck-57
94Upper Deck-384
Electric Ice-57
Electric Ice-384
96Carolina Monarchs-7
97Cincinnati Cyclones-5
98Cincinnati Cyclones-5
98Cincinnati Cyclones 2-8
98IHL All-Star Eastern Conference-19
99Cincinnati Cyclones-5
99Cincinnati Cyclones-6
99IHL All-Stars-16
00Cincinnati Cyclones-11
01German Upper Deck-157
Gate Attractions-GA8
02German DEL City Press-107

Dionne, Jonathan
93Quebec Pee-Wee Tournament-76
93Quebec Pee-Wee Tournament-1346

Dionne, Marcel
71Colgate Heads-2
71O-Pee-Chee-133
71Toronto Sun-92
72O-Pee-Chee-8
72Topps-18
73O-Pee-Chee-17
73Red Wings Team Issue-9
73Topps-17
74NHL Action Stamps-105
74O-Pee-Chee NHL-72
74O-Pee-Chee NHL-84
74Topps-72
74Topps-84
75O-Pee-Chee NHL-140
75O-Pee-Chee NHL-210
75O-Pee-Chee NHL-318
75Topps-140
75Topps-210
75Topps-318
76O-Pee-Chee NHL-91
76O-Pee-Chee NHL-386
76Topps-91
76Topps Glossy Inserts-4
77Coca-Cola-6
77O-Pee-Chee NHL-1
77O-Pee-Chee NHL-2
77O-Pee-Chee NHL-3
77O-Pee-Chee NHL-240
77Topps-1
77Topps-2
77Topps-3
77Topps-240
77Topps/O-Pee-Chee Glossy-4
Square-4
78O-Pee-Chee-120
78Topps-120
79Panini Stickers-61
79O-Pee-Chee-1
79O-Pee-Chee-2
79O-Pee-Chee-3
79O-Pee-Chee-5
79O-Pee-Chee-160
79Topps-1
79Topps-2
79Topps-3
79Topps-5
79Topps-160
80Kings Card Night-1
80O-Pee-Chee-20
80O-Pee-Chee-81
80O-Pee-Chee-162
80O-Pee-Chee-163
80O-Pee-Chee-165
80O-Pee-Chee Super-8
80Topps-20
80Topps-81
80Topps-162
80Topps-163
80Topps-165
81O-Pee-Chee-141
81O-Pee-Chee-150
81O-Pee-Chee-156
81O-Pee-Chee-391
81O-Pee-Chee Stickers-147
81O-Pee-Chee Stickers-235
81O-Pee-Chee Stickers-267
81Post Standups-12
81Topps-9
81Topps-54
81Topps-W125
82Neilson's Gretzky-12
82O-Pee-Chee-149
82O-Pee-Chee-152
82O-Pee-Chee-153
82O-Pee-Chee Stickers-230
82Post Cereal-8
82Topps Stickers-230
83NHL Key Tags-54
83O-Pee-Chee-150
83O-Pee-Chee-151
83O-Pee-Chee-152
83O-Pee-Chee-211
83O-Pee-Chee Stickers-1
83O-Pee-Chee Stickers-294
83O-Pee-Chee Stickers-295
83O-Pee-Chee Stickers-323
83O-Pee-Chee Stickers-324
83Puffy Stickers-11
83Topps Stickers-1
83Topps Stickers-294
83Topps Stickers-295
83Topps Stickers-323
83Topps Stickers-324
84Kellogg's Accordion Discs-2
84Kellogg's Accordion Discs Singles-9
84Kings Smokey-2
84O-Pee-Chee-82
84O-Pee-Chee Stickers-264
84O-Pee-Chee Stickers-265
847-Eleven Discs-24
84Topps-64
85O-Pee-Chee-90
85O-Pee-Chee Box Bottoms-E
85O-Pee-Chee Stickers-235
857-Eleven Credit Cards-8
85Topps-90
85Topps Box Bottoms-E
86O-Pee-Chee-30
86O-Pee-Chee Stickers-88
86Topps-30
87O-Pee-Chee-129
87O-Pee-Chee Stickers-34
87Panini Stickers-113
87Topps-129
88Esso All-Stars-8
88Frito-Lay Stickers-34
88O-Pee-Chee-13
88O-Pee-Chee Minis-8
88O-Pee-Chee Stickers-244
88Panini Stickers-190
88Topps-13
90Pro Set-653
91Future Trends Canada '72-91
91Future Trends Canada '72 French-91
91Kraft-85
91Pinnacle-385
French-385
91Upper Deck-636
French-636
92Future Trends '76 Canada Cup-139
92Future Trends '76 Canada Cup-179
92O-Pee-Chee-294
25th Anniv. Inserts-4
93Kings Forum-9
93Zeller's Masters of Hockey-4
93Zeller's Masters of Hockey Signed-4
97SLU Canadian Timeless Legends-3
98SLU Canadian Timeless Legends-3
98Kings LA Times Coins-2
99BAP Millennium Pearson-P11
99BAP Millennium Pearson Autographs-P11
99Upper Deck 500 Goal Club-500MD
99Upper Deck 500 Goal Club-500MD
99Upper Deck Century Legends-39
Century Collection-39
Epic Signatures-MD
Epic Signatures 100-MD
99Upper Deck Retro-103
Gold-103
Platinum-103
Inkredible-MD
Inkredible Level 2-MD
Memento-RM2
00Topps Premier Plus Club Signings-CS-6
00Topps Premier Plus Club Signings-CSC-3
00UD Heroes-127
Signs of Greatness-MD
00Upper Deck Legends-58
Legendary Collection Bronze-58
Legendary Collection Gold-58
Legendary Collection Silver-58
Enshrined Stars-ES5
Epic Signatures-MD
Legendary Game Jerseys-JMD
01BAP Memorabilia 500 Goal Scorers-GS3
01BAP Signature Series 500 Goal Scorers-7
01BAP Sig Series 500 Goal Scorers Autos-7
01BAP Signature Series Vintage Autographs-VA-37
01BAP Ultimate Mem All-Star History-31
01BAP Ultimate Memorabilia Autographs-18
01BAP Ultimate Mem Autographs Gold-18
01BAP Ultimate Mem 500 Goal Scorers-9
01BAP Ultimate Mem 500 Goal Scorers Autos-14
01BAP Ultimate Mem 500 Goal Jerseys/Stick-9
01BAP Ultimate Mem 500 Goal Emblems-9
01BAP Ultimate Memorabilia Name Plates-37
01BAP Ultimate Mem Retired Numbers-7
01Fleer Legacy-16
Ultimate-16
Memorabilia-10
01Greats of the Game-16
Retro Collection-8
Autographs-16
Sticks-1
01Parkhurst Autographs-PA31
01Parkhurst 500 Goal Scorers-PGS3
01Topps Archives-27
Arena Seats-ASMD
Autographs-15
Autoproofs-1
01Upper Deck Legends-27
01Upper Deck Legends-93
Epic Signatures-MD
Fiorentino Collection-FCMD
Sticks-PHMD
02BAP NHL All-Star History-31
02BAP Ultimate Memorabilia Emblem Attic-3
02BAP Ultimate Memorabilia Numerology-18
02BAP Ultimate Memorabilia Retro Trophies-5
02BAP Ultimate Mem Scoring Leaders-14
02BAP Ultimate Mem Vintage Jerseys-26
02BAP Ultimate Mem Vintage Jersey Autos-3
02Parkhurst Vintage Memorabilia-VM5
02UD Foundations-25
02UD Foundations-42
02UD Foundations-66
02UD Foundations-114
1000 Point Club-DI
1000 Point Club-DI2
Signs of Greatness-SGMD
03BAP Memorabilia Vintage Memorabilia-VM-17
03BAP Ultimate Memorabilia Emblem Attic-18
03BAP Ultimate Mem Emblem Attic Gold-18
03BAP Ultimate Mem Hometown Heroes-7
03BAP Ultimate Mem Hometown Heroes Gold-7
03BAP Ultimate Mem Jersey and Stick-30
03BAP Ultimate Mem Jersey and Stick Gold-30
03BAP Ultimate Memorabilia Linemates-6
03BAP Ultimate Mem Raised to the Rafters-18
03BAP Ultimate Mem Retro-Active Trophies-14
03BAP Ultimate Mem Vintage Jerseys-21
03BAP Ultimate Mem Vintage Jerseys Gold-21
03Beehive-87
Variations-87
Gold-87
Silver-87
Sticks Beige Border-BE41
Sticks Red Border-RE18
03ITG Used Sig Series Vintage Mem -20
03ITG Used Sig Series Vintage Mem Gold-20
03Pacific Exhibit-223
03Parkhurst Original Six Detroit-38
03Parkhurst Original Six Detroit-74
03Parkhurst Original Six Detroit-99
Autographs-OS-MD
Inserts-D-17
03Parkhurst Orig Six New York Mem-NM29
03Parkhurst Orig Six New York Mem-NM53
03Parkhurst Orig Six New York Mem-NM60
03Parkhurst Rookie Jerseys-GJ-44
03Parkhurst Rookie Jerseys Gold-GJ-44
03SP Authentic Honors-H15
03SP Authentic Honors Limited-H15
03SPx-109
Radiance-109
Spectrum-109
03Upper Deck Trilogy-126
Authentic Patches-AP31
Crest Variations-126
Limited-126
Scripts-S3MD
Scripts Limited-S3MD
Scripts Red-S3MD
03Czech Stadion-548
04Canada Post-26
04Canada Post Autographs-2
04ITG NHL AS FANtasy AS History Jerseys-SB31
04ITG Franchises He Shoots/Scores Prizes-27
04ITG Franchises Update-464
04ITG Franchises Update-482
Memorabilia-USM8
Memorabilia Gold-USM8
Teammates-UTM2
Teammates Gold-UTM2
04ITG Franchises US West-230
Autographs-A-MD
Barn Burners-WB86
Barn Burners Gold-WB86
Double Memorabilia-WDM4
Double Memorabilia Autographs-WDMMD
Double Memorabilia Gold-WDM4
Memorabilia-WSM7
Memorabilia Autographs-WSMMD
Memorabilia Gold-WSM7
Original Sticks-WOS10
Original Sticks Autographs-WOSMD
Original Sticks Gold-WOS10
Triple Memorabilia Autographs-WTMMD
Triple Memorabilia Gold-WTM3
Trophy Winners-WTW5
Trophy Winners Gold-WTW5
04ITG Ultimate Memorabilia-59
04ITG Ultimate Memorabilia-98
Gold-59
Gold-98
Auto Threads-8
Autographs-3
Autographs-18
Autographs Gold-3
Autographs Gold-18
Day In History-17
Day In History-38
Day In History Gold-17
Day In History Gold-38
Jersey Autographs-24
Jersey Autographs Gold-24
Jersey and Sticks-10
Jersey and Sticks Gold-10
Nicknames-21
Original Six-11
Original Six-15
Stick Autographs-10
Stick Autographs Gold-10
Triple Threads-8
04SP Authentic Buybacks-106
04SP Authentic Buybacks-107
04SP Authentic Buybacks-108
04SP Authentic Buybacks-109
04SP Authentic Octographs-OS-ART
04SP Authentic Sign of the Times-QS-BDPB
04SP Authentic Sign of the Times-QS-GTDC
04SP Authentic Sign of the Times-FS-CTR
04UD Legendary Signatures-55
Autographs-MD
HOF Inks-HOF-MD
Linemates-CSMDDT
04UD Legends Classics-39
04UD Legends Classics-64
04UD Legends Classics-100
Gold-39
Gold-64
Gold-100
Platinum-39
Platinum-64
Platinum-100
Silver-39
Silver-64
Silver-100
Signature Moments-M21
Signature Moments-M57
Signatures-CS21
Signatures-DC13
Signatures-DC17
Signatures-TC14
Signatures-QC4
04Ultimate Collection Patch Autographs-UPA-MD
04ITG Heroes and Prospects-128
Autographs-MDI
He Shoots-He Scores Prizes-6
Hero Memorabilia-8
04ITG Heroes/Prospects Toronto Expo '05-128
04ITG Heroes/Prospects Expo Heroes/Pros-128
05ITG Heroes/Prosp Toronto Expo Parallel -16
05Beehive PhotoGraphs-PGMD
05Beehive Signature Scrapbook-SSMD
05ITG Ultimate Memorabilia Level 1-66
05ITG Ultimate Memorabilia Level 2-66
05ITG Ultimate Memorabilia Level 3-66
05ITG Ultimate Memorabilia Level 4-66
05ITG Ultimate Memorabilia Level 5-66
05ITG Ultimate Mem Complete Jersey-15
05ITG Ultimate Mem Complete Jersey Gold-15
05ITG Ultimate Mem Double Mem-9
05ITG Ultimate Mem Double Mem Gold-9
05ITG Ultimate Memorabilia Emblems-14
05ITG Ultimate Memorabilia Emblems Gold-14
05ITG Ultimate Mem First Rounders Jerseys-4
05ITG Ultimate Mem 1st Round Jersey Gold-4
05ITG Ultimate Memorabilia In The Numbers-10
05ITG Ultimate Mem In The Numbers Gold-10
05ITG Ultimate Mem Jersey and Emblem-16
05ITG Ultimate Memorabilia Jersey Autos-2
05ITG Ultimate Mem Jersey Autos Gold-2
05ITG Ultimate Mem Jersey Emblems Gold-16
05ITG Ultimate Memorabilia Jerseys-23
05ITG Ultimate Memorabilia Jerseys Gold-23
05ITG Ultimate Memorabilia Sextuple Autos-5
05ITG Ultimate Memorabilia Stick Autos-4
05ITG Ultimate Mem Stick Autos Gold-4
05ITG Ultimate Mem 3 Star of the Game Jsy-19
05ITG Ult Mem 3 Star of the Game Jsy Gold-19
05ITG Ultimate Memorabilia Triple Autos-17
05ITG Ultimate Mem Triple Autos Gold-17
05ITG Ultimate Mem Triple Threads Jerseys-10
05ITG Ultimate Mem Triple Thread Jsy Gold-10
05ITG Ultimate Memorabilia Ultimate Autos-42
05ITG Ultimate Mem Ultimate Autos Gold-42
05NHL Legends Medallions-4
05SP Authentic Exquisite Endorsements-EEMD
05SP Authentic Marks of Distinction-MDMD
05SP Authentic Octographs-OH
05SP Authentic Prestigious Pairings-PPDT
05SP Authentic Sign of the Times Quads-QGTVD
05SP Authentic Six Star Signatures-SSHF
05SP Game Used Authentic Fabrics-AF-MD
05SP Game Used Authentic Fabrics Autos-AAF-MD
05SP Game Used Authentic Fabric Dual Auto-DT
05SP Game Used Authentic Fabric Dual Auto-LD
05SP Game Used Authentic Fabrics Gold-AF-MD
05SP Game Used Authentic Patches-AP-MD
05SP Game Used Authentic Patch Autos-AAP-MD
05SP Game Used Authentic Patches Dual-LD
05SP Game Used Authentic Patch Dual Autos-DT
05SP Game Used Authentic Patch Dual Autos-LD
05SP Game Used Statscriptions-ST-MD
05SPx-110
Spectrum-110
Winning Combos-WC-DR
Winning Combos Autographs-AWC-DR
Winning Combos Gold-WC-DR
Winning Combos Spectrum-WC-DR
Winning Materials-WM-MD
Winning Materials Gold-WM-MD
Winning Materials Spectrum-WM-MD
Xcitement Legends-XL-MD
Xcitement Legends Gold-XL-MD
Xcitement Legends Spectrum-XL-MD
05The Cup Hardware Heroes-HHMD
05The Cup Noble Numbers Dual-DNNDV
05UD Artifacts-114
Blue-114
Gold-114
Green-114
Pewter-114
Red-114
Gold Autographed-114
05Upper Deck Notable Numbers-N-MDI
05Upper Deck Trilogy Legendary Scripts-LEG-MD
05Upper Deck Trilogy Personal Scripts-PER-MD
05ITG Heroes and Prospects-16
Aspiring-ASP11
Autographs-A-MD
Hero Memorabilia-HM-25
06Beehive-198
5 X 7 Black and White-198
5 X 7 Dark Wood-198
06ITG International Ice-13
06ITG International Ice-78
06ITG International Ice-130
Gold-13
Gold-78
Gold-130
Autographs-AMD
Autographs-AMD2
Autographs-AMD3
Emblem Autographs-GUE34
Emblem Autographs Gold-GUE34
Emblems-GUE34
Emblems Gold-GUE34
Jersey Autographs-GUJ34
Jersey Autographs Gold-GUJ34
Jerseys-GUJ34
Jerseys Gold-GUJ34
My Country My Team-MC23
My Country My Team Gold-MC23
Numbers-GUN34
Numbers Autographs-GUN34
Numbers Autographs Gold-GUN34
Numbers Gold-GUN34
Stick and Jersey-SJ27
Stick and Jersey Gold-SJ27
Teammates-IT04
Teammates Gold-IT04
06ITG Ultimate Memorabilia-95
Artist Proof-95
Autos-9
Autos Gold-9
Boys Will Be Boys-26
Boys Will Be Boys Gold-26
Double Memorabilia Autos-3
Double Memorabilia Autos Gold-3
First Round Picks-12
First Round Picks Gold-12
Jerseys Autos-11
Jerseys Autos Gold-11
Passing The Torch-3
Passing The Torch Gold-3
Sticks Autos-1
Sticks Autos Gold-1
06Parkhurst-48
06Parkhurst-185
Autographs-48
Autographs-185
Autographs Dual-DADN
06SP Authentic Sign of the Times Duals-STDV
06The Cup-39
Autographed Foundations-CQMD
Autographed Foundations Patches-CQMD
Autographed Patches-39
Black Rainbow-39
Foundations-CQMD
Foundations Patches-CQMD
Enshrinements-EMD
Gold-39
Gold Patches-39
Honorable Numbers-HNMD
Jerseys-39
Masterpiece Pressplates-39
Property of-POMD
Scripted Swatches-SSMD
Scripted Swatches Duals-DSDR
Signature Patches-SPMD
06Ultimate Collection Jerseys-UJ-MD
06Ultimate Collection Jerseys Dual-UJ2-DV
06Ultimate Collection Patches-UJ-MD
06Ultimate Collection Patches Dual-UJ2-DV
06Ultimate Collection Signatures-US-MD
06Ultimate Collection Ultimate Achievements-UA-MD
06Upper Deck All-Time Greatest-ATG10
06Upper Deck Sweet Shot Signature Shots/Saves Ice Signings-SSIMD
06Upper Deck Sweet Shot Signature Shots/Saves Sticks-SSSMD

Dionne, Vincent
93Quebec Pee-Wee Tournament-1
99Bowman CHL-52
Gold-52
OPC International-52

Diotte, Roland
79Montreal Juniors-6

DiPalma, Anthony
01Memphis RiverKings-5
04Richmond Riverdogs-21

DiPaolo, Mauro
92Quebec Pee-Wee Tournament-544
97Halifax Mooseheads II-6
98Halifax Mooseheads-21
98Halifax Mooseheads Second Edition-8

Dipenta, Joey
99Halifax Mooseheads-4
00QMJHL All-Star Program Inserts-25
02Chicago Wolves-5
03ITG Action-45
03O-Pee-Chee-309
03OPC Blue-309
03OPC Gold-309
03OPC Red-309
03Pacific-13
Red-13
03Pacific Exhibit-9
Blue Backs-9
Yellow Backs-9
03Pacific Prism-5
Blue-5
Gold-5
Red-5
03Pacific Supreme-103
Blue-103
Red-103
Retail-103
03Parkhurst Rookie-68
03Private Stock Reserve-103
Blue-103
Red-103
Retail-103
03Topps-309
Blue-309
Gold-309
Red-309
03Topps C55-134
Minis-134
Minis American Back-134
Minis American Back Red-134
Minis Bazooka Back-134
Minis Brooklyn Back-134
Minis Hat Trick Back-134
Minis O Canada Back-134
Minis O Canada Back Red-134
Minis Stanley Cup Back-134
03Upper Deck Classic Portraits-161
03Upper Deck MVP-30
Gold Script-30
Silver Script-30
Canadian Exclusives-30
03Upper Deck Victory-11
Bronze-11
Gold-11
Silver-11
03Chicago Wolves-6
04Manitoba Moose-3
05Ducks Team Issue-4

Dipietro, Paul
86Sudbury Wolves-21
87Sudbury Wolves-22
88Sudbury Wolves-22
89Sudbury Wolves-15
90ProCards AHL/IHL-68
91Pinnacle-350
French-350
91Pro Set-546
French-546
91ProCards-70
92Parkhurst-489
Emerald Ice-489
92Stadium Club-98
92Topps-361
Gold-361G
92Fredericton Canadiens-8
93Canadiens Postcards-10
93Leaf-248
93OPC Premier-288
Gold-288
93Parkhurst-108
Emerald Ice-108
93Pinnacle-114
Canadian-114
93PowerPlay-369
93Score-494
Canadian-494
93Stadium Club-194
Members Only Master Set-194
OPC-194
First Day Issue-194
First Day Issue OPC-194
93Topps/OPC Premier-288
Gold-288
93Ultra-159
93Upper Deck-108
93Sudbury Wolves-24
93Classic Pro Prospects-104
94Canadiens Postcards-10
94Maple Leafs Kodak-9

94Maple Leafs Pin-up Posters-25
94OPC Premier-252
Special Effects-252
94Pinnacle-443
Artist's Proofs-443
Rink Collection-443
94Topps/OPC Premier-252
Special Effects-252
95Houston Aeros-3
97Sudbury Wolves Anniversary-5
98Swiss Power Play Stickers-18
99Swiss Panini Stickers-214
00Swiss Panini Stickers-256
00Swiss Slapshot Mini-Cards-EVZ8
01Swiss EV Zug Postcards-27
01Swiss HNL-180
02Swiss EV Zug Postcards-4
02Swiss HNL-229
03Swiss EV Zug Postcards-7

DiPietro, Rick

94Quebec Pee-Wee Tournament-1211
00BAP Memorabilia-497
Emerald-497
Ruby-497
Sapphire-497
00BAP Parkhurst 2000-P225
00BAP Signature Series-296
Emerald-296
Ruby-296
Sapphire-296
00Black Diamond-125
00Crown Royale-132
21st Century Rookies-15
00Private Stock-151
Gold-151
Premiere Date-151
Retail-151
Silver-151
PS-2001 New Wave-26
PS-2001 Rookies-26
00SP Authentic-114
Sign of the Times-RD
00SP Game Used-73
00SPx-166
00Titanium-133
Retail-133
Three-Star Selections-24
00Titanium Draft Day Edition-133
00Titanium Draft Day Promos-133
00Topps Chrome-251
Blue-251
Red-251
OPC Refractors-251
OPC Refractors Blue-251
OPC Refractors Red-251
Refractors-251
Refractors Blue-251
Refractors Red-251
00Topps Gold Label Class 1-112
Gold-112
00Topps Gold Label Class 2-112
00Topps Gold Label Class 2 Gold-112
00Topps Gold Label Class 3-112
00Topps Gold Label Class 3 Gold-112
00Topps Heritage-96
Chrome Parallel-96
00Topps Premier Plus-127
Blue Ice-127
00UD Heroes-170
00UD Pros and Prospects-114
Now Appearing-NA5
00UD Reserve-104
00Upper Deck-411
Exclusives Tier 1-411
Exclusives Tier 2-411
00Upper Deck Ice-94
00Vanguard-133
High Voltage-21
High Voltage Gold-21
High Voltage Green-21
High Voltage Red-21
High Voltage Silver-21
Pacific Proofs-133
00Chicago Wolves-6
01Atomic-60
Blue-60
Gold-60
Premiere Date-60
Red-60
Rookie Reaction-5
Statosphere-5
Team Nucleus-9
01BAP Memorabilia-1
Emerald-1
Ruby-1
Sapphire-1
01BAP Signature Series-1
Autographs-1
Autographs Gold-1
01Between the Pipes-4
Future Wave-FW10
Goalie Gear-GG30
Masks-38
Masks Silver-38
Masks Gold-38
01Crown Royale Calder Collection Gold Ed-5
01Crown Royale Calder Collection AS Ed-C3
01Crown Royale-89
Blue-89
Premiere Date-89
Red-89
Retail-89
Crowning Achievement-7
Rookie Royalty-13
01Crown Royale Toronto Expo Rookie Coll-G3
01eTopps-26
01McDonald's Pacific-25
Future Legends-2
01O-Pee-Chee-39
01O-Pee-Chee Heritage Parallel-39
01O-Pee-Chee Heritage Parallel Limited-39
01O-Pee-Chee Premier Parallel-39
01Pacific-245
01Pacific-434
Extreme LTD-245
Gold-434
Hobby LTD-245
Premiere Date-245
Retail LTD-245
Gold Crown Die-Cuts-13
Steel Curtain-12
Top Draft Picks-1
01Pacific Top Draft Picks Draft Day Promo-1
01Pacific Adrenaline-119
Blue-119
Premiere Date-119
Red-119
Retail-119
Creased Lightning-12
Power Play-23
Rookie Report-11
01Pacific Arena Exclusives-245
01Pacific Arena Exclusives-434
01Pacific Heads-Up-60
Blue-60
Premiere Date-60
Red-60
Silver-60
Breaking the Glass-14
Prime Picks-4
Showstoppers-13
01Parkhurst-42
Gold-42
Silver-42
Sticks-PS68
01Private Stock-105
Gold-105
Premiere Date-105
Retail-105
Silver-105
Moments in Time-6
01Private Stock Pacific Nights-105
01Private Stock PS-2002-99
01SP Authentic-128
Limited-129
Limited Gold-129
Buybacks-28
Sign of the Times-RD
Sign of the Times-DL
Sign of the Times-SDP
01SP Game Used-32
Tools of the Game-TRD
01SPx-41
01Stadium Club-19
Award Winners-19
Master Photos-19
Gallery-G34
Gallery Gold-G34
New Regime-NR11
01Titanium-87
Hobby Parallel-87
Premiere Date-87
Retail-87
Retail Parallel-87
Rookie Team-8
Three-Star Selections-28
01Topps-39
Heritage Parallel-39
Heritage Parallel Limited-39
OPC Parallel-39
01Topps Chrome-39
Refractors-39
Black Border Refractors-39
01Topps Heritage-25
Refractors-25
01Topps Reserve-58
01UD Honor Roll-30
01UD Honor Roll-60
01UD Mask Collection Gloves-GGRD
01UD Top Shelf-27
01Upper Deck-108
Exclusives-108
01Upper Deck Ice-29
01Upper Deck MVP-117
Goalie Sticks-G-RD
01Upper Deck Victory-218
01Upper Deck Victory-223
Gold-218
Gold-223
01Upper Deck Vintage-159
01Upper Deck Vintage-165
01Vanguard-58
Blue-58
Red-58
One of Ones-58
Premiere Date-58
Prime Prospects-11
Proofs-58
Quebec Tournament Heroes-20
02BAP First Edition-192
02BAP First Edition-421R
02BAP Memorabilia-146
Emerald-146
Ruby-146
Sapphire-146
Future of the Game-FG-15
NHL All-Star Game-146
NHL All-Star Game Blue-146
NHL All-Star Game Green-146
NHL All-Star Game Red-146
02BAP Memorabilia Toronto Fall Expo-146
02BAP Sig Series Auto Buybacks 2001-1
02BAP Signature Series Golf-GS75
02BAP Ultimate Memorabilia First Overall-12
02Between the Pipes-14
Gold-14
Silver-14
Behind the Mask-12
Emblems-3
Future Wave-4
Inspirations-I10
Jerseys-3
Masks II-19
Masks II Gold-19
Masks II Silver-19
Numbers-3
Stick and Jerseys-3
Tandems-16
02ITG Used-46
02ITG Used-146
02O-Pee-Chee-265
02O-Pee-Chee Premier Blue Parallel-265
02O-Pee-Chee Premier Red Parallel-265
02O-Pee-Chee Factory Set-265
02Pacific-235
Blue-235
Red-235
02Pacific Calder-81
Silver-81
Reflections-17
02Pacific Complete-19
Red-19
02Pacific Entry Draft-6
02Pacific Exclusive-106
Great Expectations-12
02Pacific Heads-Up Head First-8
02Pacific Quest for the Cup-60
Gold-60
Itech Masks-6
Jerseys-10
02Parkhurst-78
Bronze-78
Gold-78
Silver-78
College Ranks-CR4
College Ranks Jerseys-CRM4
02SP Game Used Tools of the Game-RD
02Titanium-65
Blue-65
Red-65
Retail-65
Right on Target-15
02Topps-265
OPC Blue Parallel-265
OPC Red Parallel-265
Factory Set-265
02Topps Chrome-145
Black Border Refractors-145
Refractors-145
02UD Mask Collection Nation's Best-NDBJ
02UD Top Shelf Signatures-RD
02AHL Top Prospects-10
03BAP Memorabilia-155
Emerald-155
Gold-155
Ruby-155
Sapphire-155
Future Wave-FW-4
Jersey and Stick-SJ-19
Jerseys-GJ-24
Jersey Autographs-GJ-24
03BAP Ultimate Memorabilia Autographs-10
Gold-10
03BAP Ultimate Mem Auto Jerseys-10
03BAP Ultimate Mem Franch Present Future-19
03BAP Ultimate Memorabilia Triple Threads-1
03Beehive-126
Variations-126
Gold-126
Silver-126
Signatures-RF18
Sticks Beige Border-BE24
Sticks Blue Border-BL8
03Black Diamond-24
Black-24
Green-24
Red-24
03Bowman-86
Gold-86
03Bowman Chrome-86
Refractors-86
Gold Refractors-86
Xfractors-86
03Crown Royale-65
Blue-65
Retail-65
Gauntlet of Glory-13
Jerseys-15
Patches-15
03eTopps-14
03ITG Action-358
Jerseys-M156
03ITG Used Signature Series-44
Gold-44
Autographs-RD
Autographs Gold-RD
Franchise-20
Franchise Autographs-20
Franchise Gold-20
Goalie Gear-4
Goalie Gear Autographs-4
Goalie Gear Gold-4
Jerseys-37
Jerseys Gold-37
Jersey Autos-37
Emblems-28
Emblems Gold-28
Jersey and Stick-37
Jersey and Stick Gold-37
03ITG VIP Netminders-10
03O-Pee-Chee-233
03OPC Blue-233
03OPC Gold-233
03OPC Red-233
03Pacific-211
Blue-211
Red-211
03Pacific Calder-65
Silver-65
03Pacific Complete-448
Red-448
03Pacific Exhibit-92
Blue Backs-92
Yellow Backs-92
03Pacific Heads-Up-62
Hobby LTD-62
Retail LTD-62
Jerseys-19
Stonewallers-8
Stonewallers LTD-8
03Pacific Invincible-60
Blue-60
Red-60
Retail-60
Freeze Frame-13
Jerseys-19
New Sensations-16
03Pacific Luxury Suite-41A
03Pacific Luxury Suite-41B
03Pacific Prism-67
Blue-67
Gold-67
Red-67
03Pacific Quest for the Cup-66
Blue-66
03Pacific Supreme-61
03Pacific Supreme-62
Blue-61
Red-61
Retail-61
03Parkhurst Rookie High Expectations-HE-11
03Parkhurst Rookie High Expectations Gold-HE-11
03Private Stock Reserve-179
Blue-179
Patches-179
Red-179
Retail-179
Increase Security-10
03SP Authentic-57
Limited-57
03SP Game Used Game Gear-GGRD
03SP Game Used Game Gear Combo-GCRD
03SPx-61
Radiance-61
Spectrum-61
03Titanium-167
Hobby Jersey Number Parallels-167
Patches-167
Retail-167
Masked Marauders-7
03Topps-233
Blue-233
Gold-233
Red-233
03Topps C55-24
Minis-24
Minis American Back-24
Minis American Back Red-24
Minis Bazooka Back-24
Minis Brooklyn Back-24
Minis Hat Trick Back-24
Minis O Canada Back-24
Minis O Canada Back Red-24
Minis Stanley Cup Back-24
03Topps Pristine-55
Gold Refractor Die Cuts-55
Refractors-55
Mini-PM-RD
Press Plates Black-55
Press Plates Cyan-55
Press Plates Magenta-55
Press Plates Yellow-55
03UD Honor Roll-53
03UD Honor Roll-109
03UD Premier Collection-34
03Upper Deck-122
Canadian Exclusives-122
HG-122
Shooting Stars-ST-RD
03Upper Deck Classic Portraits-61
03Upper Deck Ice-55
Gold-55
Authentics-IA-RD
Under Glass Autographs-UG-RD
03Upper Deck MVP-273
Gold Script-273
Silver Script-273
Canadian Exclusives-273
ProSign-PS-RD
03Upper Deck Rookie Update-57
Top Draws-TD7
03Upper Deck Trilogy-61
Limited-61
03Upper Deck Victory-119
Bronze-119
Gold-119
Silver-119
03Pacific AHL Prospect Destined Greatness-3
03Toronto Star-57
04Pacific-166
Blue-166
Red-166
04Pacific National Convention-4
04SP Authentic-59
04UD Toronto Fall Expo Priority Signings-RD
04Ultimate Collection Dual Logos-UL2-MD
04Upper Deck-112
Canadian Exclusives-112
HG Glossy Gold-112
HG Glossy Silver-112
Jersey Autographs-GJA-RD
World Cup Tribute-RD
World Cup Tribute-TCRDRE
04ITG Heroes/Prospects He Shoots/Scores-22
04ITG Heroes and Prospects Net Prospects-4
04ITG Heroes and Prosp Net Prospects Gold-4
05Be A Player-55
First Period-55
Second Period-55
Third Period-55
Overtime-55
Signatures-RD
Signatures Gold-RD
Triple Signatures-DRL
05Beehive-58
Matte-58
05Black Diamond-122
Emerald-122
Gold-122
Onyx-122
Ruby-122
05Hot Prospects-63
En Fuego-63
Red Hot-63
White Hot-63
05McDonalds Upper Deck Goalie Gear-MG4
05Panini Stickers-92
05Parkhurst-309
Facsimile Auto Parallel-309
True Colors-TCNYI
True Colors-TCNYI
True Colors-TCNYNY
True Colors-TCNYNY
05SP Authentic-63
Limited-63
05SP Game Used-64
Gold-64
Authentic Fabrics-AF-RD
Authentic Fabrics Gold-AF-RD
Authentic Fabrics Quad-SDYH
Authentic Patches Quad -SDYH
Authentic Patches-AP-RD
Awesome Authentics-AA-RD
05SPx-55
Spectrum-55
05UD Artifacts-66
Blue-66
Gold-66
Green-66
Pewter-66
Red-66
Frozen Artifacts-FA-RD
Frozen Artifacts Autographed-FA-RD
Frozen Artifacts Copper-FA-RD
Frozen Artifacts Dual-FAD-RD
Frozen Artifacts Dual Autographed-FAD-RD
Frozen Artifacts Dual Copper-FAD-RD
Frozen Artifacts Dual Gold-FAD-RD
Frozen Artifacts Dual Maroon-FAD-RD
Frozen Artifacts Dual Pewter-FAD-RD
Frozen Artifacts Dual Silver-FAD-RD
Frozen Artifacts Gold-FA-RD
Frozen Artifacts Maroon-FA-RD
Frozen Artifacts Pewter-FA-RD
Frozen Artifacts Silver-FA-RD
Goalie Gear-FG-RD
Goalie Gear Autographed-FG-RD
Goalie Gear Dual-FGD-RD
Goalie Gear Dual Autographed-FGD-RD
Goalie Gear Pewter-FG-RD
Goalie Gear Silver-FG-RD
Gold Autographed-66
05UD PowerPlay-59
Rainbow-59
05Ultimate Collection-56
Gold-56
National Heroes Jerseys-NHJRD
National Heroes Patches-NHPRD
05Ultra-122
Gold-122
Ice-122
05Upper Deck-370
Jerseys Series II-J2RD
Majestic Materials-MMRD
Patches-P-RD
05Upper Deck Ice-61
Rainbow-61
05Upper Deck MVP-243
Gold-243
Platinum-243
05Upper Deck Rookie Update-62
05Upper Deck Trilogy-59
05Upper Deck Trilogy-145
Crystal-145
05Upper Deck Victory-121
Black-121
Gold-121
Silver-121
06Be A Player Portraits-67
06Beehive-39
Matte-39
06Between The Pipes-74
06Between The Pipes-115
Autographs-ARDI
Double Jerseys-DJ24
Double Jerseys Gold-DJ24
Emblems-GUE69
Emblems Gold-GUE69
Gloves-GG02
Gloves Gold-GG02
Jerseys-GUJ69
Jerseys Gold-GUJ69
Numbers-GUN69
Numbers Gold-GUN69
Stick and Jersey-SJ06
Stick and Jersey Gold-SJ06
The Mask-M15
The Mask Gold-M15
The Mask Silver-M15
The Mask Game-Used-MGU03
The Mask Game-Used Gold-MGU03
06Black Diamond-52
Black-52
Gold-52
Ruby-52
Jerseys-JRD
Jerseys Black-JRD
Jerseys Gold-JRD
Jerseys Ruby-JRD
06Flair Showcase-63
06Flair Showcase-142
06Flair Showcase-246
Parallel-63
Parallel-142
Parallel-246
Hot Gloves-HG19
Wave of the Future-WF26
06Fleer-123
Tiffany-123
Netminders-N16
06Hot Prospects-60
Red Hot-60
White Hot-60
06O-Pee-Chee-307
Rainbow-307
Swatches-S-RD
06Panini Stickers-88
06SP Authentic-41
Limited-41
06SP Game Used Authentic Fabrics-AFRD
06SP Game Used Authentic Fabrics Parallel-AFRD
06SP Game Used Authentic Fabrics Patches-AFRD
06SP Game Used Authentic Fabrics Dual-AF2SD
06SP Game Used Authentic Fabrics Dual Patches-AF2SD
06SP Game Used Authentic Fabrics Triple-AF3NYI
06SP Game Used Authentic Fabrics Triple Patches-AF3NYI
06SP Game Used Authentic Fabrics Fives-AF51ST
06SP Game Used Authentic Fabrics Fives Patches-AF51ST
06SP Game Used By The Letter-BLRD
06SPx-63
Spectrum-63
Winning Materials-WMRD
Winning Materials Spectrum-WMRD
06The Cup Foundations-CQRD
06The Cup Foundations Patches-CQRD
06The Cup NHL Shields Duals-DSHDS
06The Cup NHL Shields Duals-DSHDY
06UD Artifacts-40
Blue-40
Gold-40
Platinum-40
Radiance-40
Red-40
Tundra Tandems-TTMR
Tundra Tandems Black-TTMR
Tundra Tandems Blue-TTMR
Tundra Tandems Gold-TTMR
Tundra Tandems Platinum-TTMR
Tundra Tandems Red-TTMR
Tundra Tandems Dual Patches Red-TTMR
06UD Mini Jersey Collection-64
06UD Powerplay-64
Impact Rainbow-64
06Ultra-122
Gold Medallion-122
Ice Medallion-122
06Upper Deck Arena Giveaways-NYI1
06Upper Deck-122
Exclusives Parallel-122
High Gloss Parallel-122
Game Jerseys-J2RD
Game Patches-P2RD
Masterpieces-122
06Upper Deck MVP-187
Gold Script-187
Super Script-187
International Icons-II16
Jerseys-OJLD
Last Line of Defense-LL23
06Upper Deck Ovation-180
06Upper Deck Sweet Shot-65
06Upper Deck Trilogy-62
06Upper Deck Victory-123
06Upper Deck Victory Black-123
06Upper Deck Victory Gold-123
06Upper Deck Victory Next In Line-NL32
06Russian Sport Collection Olympic Stars-50
06ITG Heroes and Prospects AHL All-Star Jerseys-AJ10
06ITG Heroes and Prospects AHL All-Star Jerseys Gold-AJ10
06ITG Heroes and Prospects AHL All-Star Emblems-AE10
06ITG Heroes and Prospects AHL All-Star Emblems Gold-AE10
06ITG Heroes and Prospects AHL All-Star Numbers-AN10
06ITG Heroes and Prospects AHL All-Star Numbers Gold-AN10
07Upper Deck Ovation-17
07Upper Deck Victory-15
Black-15
Gold-15
Oversize Cards-OS5

DiRienzo, Carlo

03Kitchener Rangers-6
03Kitchener Rangers Memorial Cup-6
04Oshawa Generals-1
04Oshawa Generals Autographs-1

Dirk, Robert

87Blues Team Issue-6
88Blues Team Issue-6
89ProCards IHL-8
90Blues Kodak-8
90Pro Set-522
91Canucks Autograph Cards-6
91Canucks Team Issue 8x10-6
91O-Pee-Chee-493
91Parkhurst-403
French-403
91Score Canadian Bilingual-508
91Score Canadian English-508
91Topps-493
92Canucks Road Trip Art-7
92Parkhurst-425
Emerald Ice-425
92Score-279
Canadian-279
92Topps-437
Gold-437G
92Ultra-425
93OPC Premier-284
Gold-284
93Pinnacle-327
Canadian-327
93Score-288
Canadian-288
93Topps/OPC Premier-284
Gold-284
94Canucks Program Inserts-8
94Ducks Carl's Jr.-3
94Pinnacle-405
Artist's Proofs-405
Rink Collection-405
95Be A Player-159
Signatures-S159
Signatures Die Cuts-S159
95Upper Deck-432
Electric Ice-432
Electric Ice Gold-432
00Tacoma Sabercats-20

Dirkes, Chris

02Lexington Men O'War-14

DiRoberto, Torrey

92Quebec Pee-Wee Tournament-1556
95Seattle Thunderbirds-7
96Seattle Thunderbirds-18
97Seattle Thunderbirds-16
99Cincinnati Mighty Ducks-27

DiSalvatore, Jon

03German Nuremberg Ice Tigers Postcards-6
03Cleveland Barons-5
04Worcester IceCats-7
05Hot Prospects-168
En Fuego-168
Red Hot-168
White Hot-168
05SP Authentic-279
Limited-279
05The Cup Masterpiece Pressplates (Ice)-230
05The Cup Master Pressplate Rookie Update-173
05The Cup Masterpiece Pressplates SPA-279
05The Cup Masterpiece Pressplates Trilogy-303
05Upper Deck Ice-230
05Upper Deck Rookie Update-173
05Upper Deck Trilogy-303
05Peoria Rivermen-8
06Peoria Rivermen-3

Disher, Jason

93Kingston Frontenacs-9
95Thunder Bay Senators-6
98Madison Monsters-4
99Fort Worth Brahmas-3
02Thetford Mines Coyotes-8

Disher, Josh

03Erie Otters-6
04Erie Otters-21
05Erie Otters-18

Disiewich, Jason

91British Columbia JHL-55
92British Columbia JHL-94
92British Columbia JHL-111
93Dayton Bombers-8

Disschops, Jake

86Sudbury Wolves-31

Dittmer, Cory

97OCN Blizzard-18

Dittmer, Tyler

05Brandon Wheat Kings-8

Dittrich, Gerhard

94German First League-108

Ditzer, Tom

04Kalamazoo Wings-11

Diviney, Norm

50Quebec Citadelles-5

Divis, Reinhard

95Austrian National Team-4
99Swedish Upper Deck-103
00Swedish Upper Deck-106
Masked Men-M4
SHL Signatures-RD
01BAP Memorabilia-341
Emerald-341
Ruby-341
Sapphire-341
01Worcester Icecats-17
02Between the Pipes-98
Gold-98
Silver-98
Jerseys-49
02UD Mask Collection-78
02UD Mask Collection Beckett Promos-78
02Worcester IceCats-25
03BAP Memorabilia Deep in the Crease-D12
03Pacific Complete-451
Red-451
03Worcester Ice Cats-26
04ITG Heroes and Prospects Net Prospects-28
04ITG Heroes and Prosp Net Prospects Gold-28
05Upper Deck-412

Divis, Richard

06Czech OFS-250

Divisek, Michal

95Seattle Thunderbirds-8
96Czech APS Extraliga-223
97Czech APS Extraliga-45
98Czech DS Stickers-172
98Czech OFS-53
99Czech DS-21
99Czech OFS-313
00Czech OFS-39
02Czech OFS Plus-302
02Czech OFS Plus-355

Divisek, Tomas

98Czech OFS-222
01BAP Memorabilia-121
Emerald-121
Ruby-121
Sapphire-121
01O-Pee-Chee-289
01O-Pee-Chee Premier Parallel-289
01Parkhurst-336
01SPx-147
01SPx-147
Rookie Treasures-RTTD
01Topps-289
OPC Parallel-289
01UD Honor Roll-97
01UD Playmakers-134
01UD Premier Collection-76
01UD Top Shelf-62
01UD Top Shelf-62B
01Upper Deck-201
Exclusives-201
01Upper Deck MVP-211
02Czech OFS Plus-214
03Czech OFS Plus-49
03Czech OFS Plus MS Praha-SE44
03Czech Pardubice Postcards-3
04Czech OFS-114
Assist Leaders-13
Goals Leaders-11
Points Leaders-12
06Czech HC Plzen Postcards-14
06Czech OFS-291

DiVita, David

91Rochester Americans Dunkin' Donuts-5
91Rochester Americans Kodak-10
91Rochester Americans Postcards-7
92Rochester Americans Dunkin' Donuts-5
92Rochester Americans Kodak-7

Divjak, Dan

90Arizona Icecats-5
91Arizona Icecats-6
91Arizona Icecats-18
92Arizona Icecats-8
93Arizona Icecats-5

Dix, Steve

03Saginaw Spirit-6
05Port Huron Flags-25

Dixon, Jason

02Windsor Spitfires-11

Dixon, Justin

93Quebec Pee-Wee Tournament-1258

Dixon, Kayser

93Quebec Pee-Wee Tournament-746

Dixon, Paul

99UK Guildford Flames-2
99UK Guildford Flames-12
00UK Guildford Flames-8
01UK Guildford Flames-11
01UK Guildford Flames-24
02UK Guildford Flames-8
02UK Guildford Flames-21
03UK Guildford Flames-11
03UK Guildford Flames-19
04UK Guildford Flames-10
04UK Guildford Flames-20
05UK Guildford Flames-12
05UK Guildford Flames-22
06UK Guildford Flames-12
06UK Guildford Flames-24

Dixon, Sean

01London Knights-2

Dixon, Stephen

02Cape Breton Screaming Eagles-8
03Cape Breton Screaming Eagles-14
04Cape Breton Screaming Eagles-3
05Extreme Top Prospects Signature Edition-S12
05WBS Penguins-7
06Wilkes-Barre Scranton Penguins-19
06Wilkes-Barre Scranton Penguins Jerseys-10

Dixon, Steve

01Cape Breton Screaming Eagles-9

Djelloul, Serge

94French National Team-9
95Swedish World Championships Stickers-98

Djian, Jean-Marc

92Finnish Semic-219

Djoos, Par

86Swedish Panini Stickers-40
87Swedish Panini Stickers-50
89Swedish Semic Elitserien Stickers-29
90OPC Premier-24
90Pro Set-603
90Score Rookie/Traded-107T
92Score-372
Canadian-372
92Stadium Club-492
92Topps-93
Gold-93G
92Binghamton Rangers-20
93Swedish Semic World Champ Stickers-30
93Swiss HNL-89
94Swedish Leaf-164
95Swedish Leaf-140
95Swedish Upper Deck-203
96Swedish Brynas Tigers-6
97Swedish Collector's Choice-18
98Swedish UD Choice-37
Day in the Life-2
99Swedish Upper Deck-22
Lasting Impressions-2
00Swedish Upper Deck-31
00Swedish Upper Deck-211
SHL Signatures-PD
01Swedish Brynas Tigers-6
02Swedish SHL-2
Dynamic Duos-1
Parallel-2

Dlouhy, Jan

94Czech APS Extraliga-53
95Czech APS Extraliga-79
96Czech APS Extraliga-79
97Czech APS Extraliga-202
97Czech DS Stickers-134
98Czech DS Stickers-234
98Czech OFS-164
99Czech DS-160
99Czech OFS-162
00Czech OFS-117
01Czech OFS-182
03Czech OFS Plus-232
03Czech OFS Plus-369

Dlouhy, Radek

02Czech OFS Plus-360
03Czech OFS Plus-173
04Czech OFS-159
05Czech HC Slavia Praha-4
06Czech HC Slavia Praha Postcards-5
06Czech OFS-292

Dmitriev, Alexei

05German DEL-180

Dmitriev, Eduard

99Russian Hockey League-265

Dmitriev, Igor

74Swedish Stickers-61
89Russian National Team-4

Dmytruk, Rob

00Belleville Bulls-21

Doak, Gary

67Topps-97
68O-Pee-Chee-138
68Shirriff Coins-14
69O-Pee-Chee-202
70Bruins Team Issue-3
70Canucks Royal Bank-4
70Dad's Cookies-23
70Esso Power Players-38
70O-Pee-Chee-114
70Sargent Promotions Stamps-218
70Topps-114
71Canucks Royal Bank-21
71O-Pee-Chee-87
71Sargent Promotions Stamps-214
71Topps-87
72O-Pee-Chee-73
72Topps-81
73Red Wings Team Issue-10
74O-Pee-Chee NHL-361
75O-Pee-Chee NHL-358
76O-Pee-Chee NHL-7
76Topps-7
77O-Pee-Chee NHL-181
77Topps-181
78O-Pee-Chee-305
80O-Pee-Chee-374
98Bruins Alumni-25
Autographs-25

Doan, Shane

93Kamloops Blazers-4
94Kamloops Blazers-11
95Be A Player-172
Signatures-S172
Signatures Die Cuts-S172
95Bowman-149
All-Foil-149
Bowman's Best-BB24
Bowman's Best Refractors-BB24
95Collector's Choice-403
95Donruss-210
Rated Rookies-8
95Donruss Elite-109
Die Cut Stars-109
Die Cut Uncut-109
Rookies-13
95Finest-22
Refractors-22
95Jets Team Issue-5
95Leaf Limited-7
95Metal-175
95Parkhurst International-267
Emerald Ice-267
95Select Certified-114
Mirror Gold-114
95SkyBox Impact-226
95Stadium Club-207
Members Only Master Set-207
95Summit-188
Artist's Proofs-188
Ice-188
95Topps-314
OPC Inserts-314
SuperSkills Super Rookies-SR8
95Ultra-336
High Speed-7
95Upper Deck-269
Electric Ice-269
Electric Ice Gold-269
Predictor Hobby-H27
Predictor Hobby Exchange-H27
95Zenith-132
Rookie Roll Call-15
95Classic-7
CHL All-Stars-AS5
Ice Breakers-BK7
Ice Breakers Die Cuts-BK7
95Images-85
Gold-85
95Signature Rookies Auto-Phonex-14
95Signature Rook Auto-Phonex Phone Cards-14
95Slapshot Memorial Cup-15
95Signature Rookies Tetrad Autobilia *-97
96Collector's Choice-205
96Coyotes Coca-Cola-2
96Score-262
Artist's Proofs-262
Dealer's Choice Artist's Proofs-262
Special Artist's Proofs-262
Golden Blades-262
96Upper Deck-314
97Coyotes Face-Off Luncheon -4
97Pacific-330
Copper-330
Emerald Green-330
Ice Blue-330
Red-330
Silver-330
Invincible NHL Regime-149
97Upper Deck-131
97Springfield Falcons-6
99Pacific-319

Copper-319
Emerald Green-319
Gold-319
Ice Blue-319
Premiere Date-319
Red-319
99Pacific Omega-178
Copper-178
Gold-178
Ice Blue-178
Premiere Date-178
99Panini Stickers-283
99Upper Deck Arena Giveaways-PC2
99Upper Deck MVP SC Edition-144
Gold Script-144
Silver Script-144
Super Script-144
00Aurora-110
Premiere Date-110
00BAP Memorabilia-192
Emerald-192
Ruby-192
Sapphire-192
Promos-192
00BAP Mem Chicago Sportsfest Copper-192
00BAP Memorabilia Chicago Sportsfest Blue-192
00BAP Memorabilia Chicago Sportsfest Gold-192
00BAP Memorabilia Chicago Sportsfest Ruby-192
00BAP Memorabilia Chicago Sun-Times Ruby-192
00BAP Memorabilia Chicago Sun-Times Gold-192
00BAP Mem Chicago Sun-Times Sapphire-192
00BAP Mem Toronto Fall Expo Copper-192
00BAP Memorabilia Toronto Fall Expo Gold-192
00BAP Memorabilia Toronto Fall Expo Ruby-192
00BAP Parkhurst 2000-P195
00Crown Royale-83
Ice Blue-83
Limited Series-83
Premiere Date-83
Red-83
00O-Pee-Chee-166
00O-Pee-Chee Parallel-166
00Pacific-314
Copper-314
Gold-314
Ice Blue-314
Premiere Date-314
Jerseys-12
Jersey Patches-12
00Paramount-187
Copper-187
Gold-187
Holo-Gold-187
Holo-Silver-187
Ice Blue-187
Premiere Date-187
Jersey and Patches-9
00Private Stock Game Gear-87
00Private Stock Game Gear Patches-87
00Revolution-112
Blue-112
Premiere Date-112
Red-112
00SP Authentic-69
00Stadium Club-187
00Titanium Game Gear-125
00Titanium Game Gear Patches-125
00Titanium Draft Day Edition-76
00Topps/OPC-166
Parallel-166
00Topps Heritage-183
00UD Heroes-91
00UD Pros and Prospects-66
00Upper Deck-136
Exclusives Tier 1-136
Exclusives Tier 2-136
00Upper Deck MVP-138
First Stars-138
Second Stars-138
Third Stars-138
00Upper Deck Victory-180
00Upper Deck Vintage-278
00Vanguard-75
Holographic Gold-75
Holographic Purple-75
Pacific Proofs-75
01BAP Memorabilia-293
Emerald-293
Ruby-293
Sapphire-293
01BAP Signature Series-47
Autographs-47
Autographs Gold-47
01Coyotes Team Issue-5
01Crown Royale-112
Blue-112
Premiere Date-112
Red-112
Retail-112
01O-Pee-Chee-156
01O-Pee-Chee Premier Parallel-156
01Pacific-301
Extreme LTD-301
Hobby LTD-301
Premiere Date-301
Retail LTD-301
Jerseys-24
01Pacific Adrenaline-147
Blue-147
Premiere Date-147
Red-147
Retail-147
Jerseys-33
01Pacific Arena Exclusives-301
01Pacific Heads-Up Quad Jerseys-16
01Parkhurst-124
01Private Stock Game Gear-74
01Private Stock Game Gear Patches-74
01Private Stock PS-2002-57
01SP Authentic-67
Limited-67
Limited Gold-67
01Topps-156
OPC Parallel-156
01Topps Reserve-88
01UD Mask Collection-76
Gold-76
Double Patches-DPSD
Jerseys-J-SD
Jersey and Patch-JPSD
01UD Playmakers-76
01Upper Deck-133
Exclusives-133
Game Jerseys-NGSD
01Upper Deck MVP-145
01Upper Deck Victory-266
Gold-266
01Upper Deck Vintage-193
01Upper Deck Vintage-199
01Vanguard-76
Blue-76
Red-76
One of Ones-76
Premiere Date-76
Proofs-76
02BAP First Edition-49
Jerseys-49
02BAP Memorabilia-137
Emerald-137
Ruby-137
Sapphire-137
NHL All-Star Game-137
NHL All-Star Game Blue-137
NHL All-Star Game Green-137
NHL All-Star Game Red-137
02BAP Memorabilia Toronto Fall Expo-137
02BAP Signature Series-77
Autographs-77
Autograph Buybacks 2001-47
Autographs Gold-77
02Bowman YoungStars-95
Gold-95
Silver-95
02Coyotes Team Issue-11
02O-Pee-Chee-131
02O-Pee-Chee Premier Blue Parallel-131
02O-Pee-Chee Premier Red Parallel-131
02O-Pee-Chee Factory Set-131
02Pacific-293
Blue-293
Red-293
02Pacific Complete-469
Red-469
02Pacific Heads-Up Quad Jerseys-21
02Pacific Heads-Up Quad Jerseys Gold-21
02Parkhurst-65
Bronze-65
Gold-65
Silver-65
02Parkhurst Retro-118
Minis-118
02SP Game Used Authentic Fabrics-AFSD
02SP Game Used Authentic Fabrics Gold-AFSD
02SP Game Used Authentic Fabrics Rainbow-AFSD
02SP Game Used First Rounder Patches-SD
02Stadium Club-98
Silver Decoy Cards-98
Proofs-98
02Titanium-79
Blue-79
Red-79
Retail-79
02Topps-131
OPC Blue Parallel-131
OPC Red Parallel-131
Factory Set-131
02Topps Chrome-83
Black Border Refractors-83
Refractors-83
02Topps Heritage-71
Chrome Parallel-71
02Topps Total-317
02UD Top Shelf Dual Player Jerseys-STBD
02UD Top Shelf Shooting Stars-SHSD
02Upper Deck-135
Exclusives-135
Fan Favorites-SD
Hot Spots-HSSD
02Upper Deck MVP-143
Gold-143
Classics-143
Golden Classics-143
02Upper Deck Rookie Update-78
02Upper Deck Victory-165
Bronze-165
Gold-165
Silver-165
02Upper Deck Vintage-193
03BAP Ultimate Memorabilia Autographs-2
Gold-2
03BAP Ultimate Mem Franch Present Future-23
03Coyotes Postcards-5
03ITG Action-473
Jerseys-M18
03ITG Used Signature Series-31
Gold-31
Autographs-SD
Autographs Gold-SD
Franchise-23
Franchise Autographs-23
Franchise Gold-23
03NHL Sticker Collection-265
03Pacific-261
Blue-261
Red-261
03Pacific Calder-78
Silver-78
03Pacific Complete-122
Red-122
03Pacific Exhibit-113
Blue Backs-113
Yellow Backs-113
03Pacific Prism-78
Blue-78
Gold-78
Red-78
03Pacific Quest for the Cup-81
Blue-81
03Private Stock Reserve-78
Blue-78
Red-78
Retail-78
03Titanium-78
Hobby Jersey Number Parallels-78
Retail-78
Retail Jersey Number Parallels-78
03Topps Traded-TT56
Blue-TT56
Gold-TT56
Red-TT56
03Upper Deck-145
Canadian Exclusives-145
HG-145
03Upper Deck MVP-321
Gold Script-321
Silver Script-321
Canadian Exclusives-321
03Upper Deck Rookie Update Super Stars-SSSD
03Upper Deck Victory-145
Bronze-145
Gold-145
Silver-145
04Pacific-201
Blue-201
Red-201
04SP Authentic-70
Limited-70
Buybacks-177
Buybacks-178
Buybacks-179
Buybacks-180
Sign of the Times-ST-SD
Sign of the Times-DS-DS
Sign of the Times-FS-PAC
04UD Toronto Fall Expo Pride of Canada-12
04Upper Deck-132
Canadian Exclusives-132
HG Glossy Gold-132
HG Glossy Silver-132
World Cup Tribute-DHPMSD
05Be A Player-68
First Period-68
Second Period-68
Third Period-68
Overtime-68
Outtakes-OT39
Signatures-SD
Signatures Gold-SD
05Beehive-70
Beige -70
Blue -70
Gold-70
Red -70
Matte-70
Signature Scrapbook-SSSD
05Black Diamond-66
Emerald-66
Gold-66
Onyx-66
Ruby-66
05Hot Prospects-76
En Fuego-76
Red Hot-76
White Hot-76
05Panini Stickers-319
05Parkhurst-369
05Parkhurst-520
05Parkhurst-570
05Parkhurst-693
Facsimile Auto Parallel-369
Facsimile Auto Parallel-520
Facsimile Auto Parallel-570
Facsimile Auto Parallel-693
True Colors-TCPHX
True Colors-TCPHX
05SP Authentic-77
Limited-77
05SP Game Used-76
Autographs-76
Gold-76
Authentic Fabrics-AF-SD
Authentic Fabrics Autographs-AAF-SD
Authentic Fabrics Dual-DH
Authentic Fabrics Gold-AF-SD
Authentic Fabrics Triple-HND
Authentic Patches-AP-SD
Authentic Patches Autographs-AAP-SD
Authentic Patches Dual-DH
Authentic Patches Triple-HND
Awesome Authentics-AA-SD
Awesome Authentics Gold-DA-SD
SIGnificance-SD
SIGnificance Gold-S-SD
Significant Numbers-SN-SD
Statscriptions-ST-SD
05SPx-69
Spectrum-69
Winning Combos-WC-HD
Winning Combos-WC-ND
Winning Combos Autographs-AWC-ND
Winning Combos Gold-WC-ND
Winning Combos Spectrum-WC-ND
Winning Materials-WM-SD
Winning Materials Autographs-AWM-SD
Winning Materials Gold-WM-SD
Winning Materials Spectrum-WM-SD
Xcitement Superstars-XS-SD
Xcitement Superstars Gold-XS-SD
Xcitement Superstars Spectrum-XS-SD
05The Cup-80
Gold-80
Black Rainbow-80
Dual NHL Shields-DSJD
Limited Logos-LLSD
Masterpiece Pressplates-80
Masterpiece Pressplates (Rookie Update)-211
Noble Numbers-NNJS
Patch Variation-P80
Patch Variation Autographs-AP80
Scripted Numbers-SNND
Scripted Swatches-SSSD
Signature Patches-SPSD
05UD Artifacts-79
05UD Artifacts-188
Blue-79
Blue-188
Gold-79
Gold-188
Green-79
Green-188
Pewter-79
Pewter-188
Red-79
Red-188
Gold Autographed-79
Gold Autographed-188
Treasured Patches-TP-SD
Treasured Patches Autographed-TP-SD
Treasured Patches Dual-TPD-SD
Treasured Patches Dual Autographed-TPD-SD
Treasured Patches Pewter-TP-SD
Treasured Patches Silver-TP-SD
Treasured Swatches-TS-SD
Treasured Swatches Autographed-TS-SD
Treasured Swatches Blue-TS-SD
Treasured Swatches Copper-TS-SD
Treasured Swatches Dual-TSD-SD
Treasured Swatches Dual Autographed-TSD-SD
Treasured Swatches Dual Blue-TSD-SD
Treasured Swatches Dual Copper-TSD-SD
Treasured Swatches Dual Maroon-TSD-SD
Treasured Swatches Dual Pewter-TSD-SD
Treasured Swatches Dual Silver-TSD-SD
Treasured Swatches Maroon-TS-SD
Treasured Swatches Pewter-TS-SD
Treasured Swatches Silver-TS-SD
05UD PowerPlay-69
Rainbow-69
05Ultimate Collection-70
Gold-70
Marquee Attractions-MA38
05Ultra-148
Gold-148
Fresh Ink-FI-SD
Fresh Ink Blue-FI-SD
Ice-148
Scoring Kings-SK26
Scoring Kings Jerseys-SKJ-SD
Scoring Kings Jersey Autographs-KAJ-SD
Scoring Kings Patches-SKP-SD
Scoring Kings Patch Autographs-KAP-SD
05Upper Deck-146
05Upper Deck All-Time Greatest-44
05Upper Deck Big Playmakers-B-SD
05Upper Deck HG Glossy-146
05Upper Deck Hometown Heroes-HH24
05Upper Deck Jerseys Series II-J2SD
05Upper Deck Majestic Materials-MMSD
05Upper Deck Notable Numbers-N-SD
05Upper Deck Ice-74
Rainbow-74
Cool Threads Autographs-ACTSD
Cool Threads Glass-CTSD
Cool Threads Patches-CTPSD
Cool Threads Patch Autographs-CAPSD
Glacial Graphs-GGSD
05Upper Deck MVP-300
Gold-300
Platinum-300
ProSign-P-SD
05Upper Deck Rookie Update-76
05Upper Deck Rookie Update-211
Inspirations Patch Rookies-211
05Upper Deck Trilogy-70
05Upper Deck Toronto Fall Expo-146
05Upper Deck Victory-149
Black-149
Gold-149
Silver-149
Game Breakers-GB35
06Be A Player-138
Autographs-138
Signatures-SD
06Be A Player Portraits-81
Signature Portraits-SPSD
06Beehive-23
06Beehive-173
Blue-23
Gold-23
Matte-23
Red Facsimile Signatures-23
Wood-23
06Black Diamond-119
Black-119
Gold-119
Ruby-119
06Flair Showcase-77
06Flair Showcase-153
06Flair Showcase-255
Parallel-77
Parallel-153
Parallel-255
06Fleer-148
Tiffany-148
06Hot Prospects-74
Red Hot-74
White Hot-74
Hot Materials -HMSD
Hot Materials Red Hot-HMSD
Hot Materials White Hot-HMSD
06McDonald's Upper Deck-36
06NHL POG-13
06O-Pee-Chee-389
06O-Pee-Chee-693
Rainbow-389
Rainbow-693
Swatches-S-SD
06Panini Stickers-319
06SP Authentic-24
06SP Authentic-154
Limited-24
Limited-154
06SP Game Used-76
Gold-76
Rainbow-76
Authentic Fabrics Dual-AF2ND
Authentic Fabrics Dual Patches-AF2ND
Authentic Fabrics Triple-AF3PHX
Authentic Fabrics Triple Patches-AF3PHX
Authentic Fabrics Quads-AF4IDCH
Authentic Fabrics Quads Patches-AF4IDCH
Autographs-76
By The Letter-BLSD
Inked Sweaters Dual-IS2RD
Inked Sweaters Dual Patches-IS2RD
06SPx-77
Spectrum-77
SPxcitement-X76
SPxcitement Spectrum-X76
SPxcitement Autographs-X76
Winning Materials-WMSD
Winning Materials Spectrum-WMSD
Winning Materials Autographs-WMSD
06The Cup-72
Black Rainbow-72
Gold-72
Gold Patches-72
Jerseys-72
Masterpiece Pressplates-72
NHL Shields Duals-DSHDJ
06UD Artifacts-24
06UD Artifacts-190
Blue-24
Blue-190
Gold-24
Gold-190
Platinum-24
Platinum-190
Radiance-24
Radiance-190
Red-24
Red-190
Tundra Tandems-TTRD
Tundra Tandems Black-TTRD
Tundra Tandems Blue-TTRD
Tundra Tandems Gold-TTRD
Tundra Tandems Platinum-TTRD
Tundra Tandems Red-TTRD
Tundra Tandems Dual Patches Red-TTRD
06UD Mini Jersey Collection-77
06UD Powerplay-76
Impact Rainbow-76
06Ultimate Collection-46
Jerseys Dual-UJ2-RD
Patches Dual-UJ2-RD
06Ultra-151
Gold Medallion-151
Ice Medallion-151
Action-UA22
06Upper Deck Arena Giveaways-PHX1
06Upper Deck-149
Exclusives Parallel-149
High Gloss Parallel-149
All-Time Greatest-ATG17
Game Jerseys-J2SD
Game Patches-P2SD
Generations Duals-G2DH
Generations Patches Dual-G2PDH
Masterpieces-149
Signature Sensations-SSSD
Walmart Tins Oversize-149
06Upper Deck MVP-222
Gold Script-222
Super Script-222
Clutch Performers-CP20
Jerseys-OJDM
06Upper Deck Ovation-188
06Upper Deck Sweet Shot-80
Sweet Stitches-SSSD
Sweet Stitches Duals-SSSD
Sweet Stitches Triples-SSSD
06Upper Deck Trilogy-75
Combo Autographed Jerseys-CJRD
Combo Autographed Patches-CJRD
Honorary Scripted Patches-HSPSD
Honorary Scripted Swatches-HSSSD
06Upper Deck Victory-151
06Upper Deck Victory Black-151
06Upper Deck Victory Gold-151
06Upper Deck Victory GameBreakers-GB39
06Upper Deck Victory Oversize Cards-SD
07Upper Deck Ovation-12
07Upper Deck Victory-197
Black-197
Gold-197
Oversize Cards-OS42

Doan, Travis
99Des Moines Buccaneers-11

Dobben, Scott
02Sault Ste. Marie Greyhounds-20
03Sault Ste. Marie Greyhounds-5
04Cleveland Barons-6

Dobbin, Brian
82Kingston Canadians-11
85London Knights-10
89ProCards AHL-341
90ProCards AHL/IHL-33
91ProCards-375
94Milwaukee Admirals-6
95Cincinnati Cyclones-6
00London Knights-13

Dobbyn, Josh
96Regina Pats-9
99Alexandria Warthogs-4

Dobek, Bob
76San Diego Mariners WHA-2

Dobek, Bryan
06Fayetteville FireAntz-3

Dobes, Zdenek
97Czech APS Extraliga-126
98Czech DS Stickers-248

Dobni, Evans
81Regina Pats-7

Dobrescu, Jay
91Air Canada SJHL-E2
92Saskatchewan JHL-7

Dobrochotov, Viktor
74Swedish Stickers-88

Dobron, Michal
98Czech OFS-366
99Czech OFS-132
00Czech DS Extraliga-6
00Czech OFS-296
01Czech OFS-194
02Czech OFS Plus-256
03Czech OFS Plus-197
04Czech HC Sparta Praha Postcards-4
04Czech OFS-184
Czech/Slovak-4
05Czech HC Sparta Praha-3
06Czech OFS-25

Dobrota, Andrej
917th Inn. Sketch QMJHL-132

Dobrovolny, Jiri
98Czech OFS-308
99Czech OFS-369
00Czech OFS-65
02Czech OFS Plus-303
03Czech OFS Plus-212
04Czech OFS-6

Dobry, Ivan
95Slovakian-Quebec Pee-Wee Tournament-4

Dobryshkin, Yuri
98Russian Hockey League-158
99Russian Hockey League-46
99Russian Stars of Hockey-18
02Russian Hockey League-165
02Russian Hockey League-216
02Russian SL-47
03Russian Hockey League-210
03Russian National Team-19

Dobrzynski, Ralf
94German DEL-209

Dobson, Adam
04UK London Racers Playoffs-4

Dobson, Drew
04Waterloo Blackhawks-1
05Waterloo Blackhawks-9

Dobson, Jim
82Birmingham South Stars-8
83Fredericton Express-6
84Fredericton Express-17

Docken, Ron
71Johnstown Jets Acme-6
72Johnstown Jets-1

Dodginghorse, Brent
98Calgary Hitmen-18
98Calgary Hitmen Autographs-18

Dodier, Michel
92Quebec Pee-Wee Tournament-1301
98Thetford Mines Coyotes-14

Dodunski, Colin
91Ferris State Bulldogs-10
92Ferris State Bulldogs-10

Doell, Curtis
98Kentucky Thoroughblades-7
99Louisville Panthers-8

Doell, Kevin
03Gwinnett Gladiators-2
03Gwinnett Gladiators RBI Sports-197
04Chicago Wolves-20
05Chicago Wolves-5

Doers, Mike
94Dayton Bombers-10
94Los Angeles Blades RHI-13

Doetzel, Jaron
01Michigan Tech Huskies-5

Doherty, John
06Port Huron Flags-17

Doherty, Kevin
88Brockville Braves-6

Doherty, Paul
907th Inn. Sketch OHL-103
93Oshawa Generals-20
99Corpus Christi IceRays-3

Doherty, Steve
03Kalamazoo Wings-9
04Kalamazoo Wings-12

Dohler, Udo
94German DEL-111
95German DEL-27
96German DEL-25
99German DEL-59
99German DEL-388
00German DEL-36
04German Berlin Eisbarens 50th Anniv-52

Doig, Jason
94Parkhurst SE-SE254
Gold-SE254
94Select-161
Gold-161
94SP-177
Die Cuts-177
94Classic CHL Previews-CP4
95Bowman-120
All-Foil-120
95Collector's Choice-407
95Donruss-253
95Jets Team Issue-6
95Parkhurst International-529
Emerald Ice-529
95Stadium Club-222
Members Only Master Set-222
95Topps-355
OPC Inserts-355
95Ultra-337
95Upper Deck-499
Electric Ice-499
Electric Ice Gold-499
95Classic-31
CHL All-Stars-AS15
95Images-12
Gold-12
Clear Excitement-CE18
Platinum Premier Draft Choice-PD9
95Classic Five-Sport *-154
Autographs-154
96Fleer-125
Calder Candidates-2
96SkyBox Impact-148
96Upper Deck Ice-119
97Coyotes Face-Off Luncheon -5
97Springfield Falcons-7
97Bowman CHL-48
OPC-48
98Pacific-336
Ice Blue-336
Red-336
99Paramount-263
99Hartford Wolf Pack-5
00Upper Deck NHLPA-PA58
00Hartford Wolf Pack-7
01Grand Rapids Griffins-20
02Capitals Team Issue-2
03Pacific Complete-399
Red-399
04Upper Deck-176
Canadian Exclusives-176
HG Glossy Gold-176
HG Glossy Silver-176

Doig, Tyler
04Guelph Storm-24
05Guelph Storm-A-04
06Guelph Storm-11

Doiron, Shane
907th Inn. Sketch QMJHL-130
917th Inn. Sketch QMJHL-201

Dokshin, Ilya
00Russian Hockey League-73

Doktorchik, Andy
02Johnstown Chiefs-5

Dolak, Thomas
92Quebec Pee-Wee Tournament-1675
93Quebec Pee-Wee Tournament-1777
94German First League-74
98German DEL-61
98German DEL-331
99German DEL-173
99German DEL-387
00German DEL-180
02German DEL City Press-90
04German DEL-148
04German Hannover Scorpions Postcards-7
05German DEL-124
06German DEL-79

Dolan, Mick
91Ferris State Bulldogs-11
92Ferris State Bulldogs-11

Dolana, Libor
91Finnish Semic World Champ Stickers-120
91Swedish Semic World Champ Stickers-120
93Swiss HNL-351
94Czech APS Extraliga-174
95Czech APS Extraliga-186
96Czech APS Extraliga-321

Dolana, Tomas
04Czech OFS-358

Dolder, Kyle
02Notre Dame Fighting Irish-10

Dolezal, Jiri
89Swedish Semic World Champ Stickers-193
91Finnish Jyvas-Hyva Stickers-28
94German DEL-334
95Finnish Semic World Championships-153
95German DEL-304
95Swedish World Championships Stickers-206
96Czech APS Extraliga-13
97Czech APS Extraliga-160
97Czech DS Extraliga-77
97Czech DS Stickers-125
98Czech DS-75
98Czech DS Stickers-197
98Czech OFS-217
99Czech DS-122
99Czech OFS-382

Dolishnya, Alexander
01Russian Hockey League-165

Doll, Andre
92Cornell Big Red-7
93Cornell Big Red-7
96Swiss HNL-261
98Swiss Power Play Stickers-166
99Swiss Panini Stickers-166

Doll, Anton
94German First League-358

Dollard, David
92British Columbia JHL-52

Dollas, Bobby
86Sherbrooke Canadiens-12
87Moncton Hawks-4
88Nordiques Team Issue-34
88ProCards AHL-100
93Ducks Milk Caps-2
93OPC Premier-491
Gold-491
93PowerPlay-283
93Stadium Club-463
Members Only Master Set-463
First Day Issue-463
93Topps/OPC Premier-491
Gold-491
94Canada Games NHL POGS-366
94Ducks Carl's Jr.-4
94Flair-2
94Leaf-383
94OPC Premier-264
Special Effects-264
94Pinnacle-41
Artist's Proofs-41
Rink Collection-41
94Topps/OPC Premier-264
Special Effects-264
94Upper Deck-13
Electric Ice-13
95Collector's Choice-289
Player's Club-289
Player's Club Platinum-289
95Ducks Team Issue-1
95Emotion-1
95Panini Stickers-228
95Playoff One on One-112
95SkyBox Impact-1
95Upper Deck-395
Electric Ice-395
Electric Ice Gold-395
96Be A Player-96
Autographs-96
Autographs Silver-96
96Ducks Team Issue-2
96Pinnacle-157
Artist's Proofs-157
Foil-157
Premium Stock-157
Rink Collection-157
97Pacific-41
Copper-41
Emerald Green-41
Ice Blue-41
Red-41
Silver-41
98Be A Player-266
Press Release-266
98BAP Gold-266
98BAP Autographs-266
98BAP Autographs Gold-266
00Pacific-63
Copper-63
Gold-63
Ice Blue-63
Premiere Date-63
00Upper Deck NHLPA-PA73
00Manitoba Moose-8
02BAP Sig Series Auto Buybacks 1998-266
03St. Jean Mission-7

Dollin, Joe
03UK Guildford Flames-14

Dolson, Derek
04Odessa Jackalopes-5
05Odessa Jackalopes-7
06Odessa Jackalopes-6

Dolyny, Rustyn
00Michigan State Spartans-4
02Muskegon Fury-6
03Muskegon Fury-5
05Muskegon Fury-4

Doman, Matt
93Quebec Pee-Wee Tournament-717

Dombkiewicz, Mike
96Guelph Storm-9
97Guelph Storm-9
98Owen Sound Platers-6
99Owen Sound Platers-14
04Missouri River Otters-6
05Kalamazoo Wings-5
06Fort Wayne Komets-2

Dombrowski, Adam
98Kamloops Blazers-6

Dome, Robert
92Quebec Pee-Wee Tournament-1741
93Quebec Pee-Wee Tournament-1560
96All-Sport PPF *-175
96All Sport PPF Gold *-175
97Black Diamond-88
Double Diamond-88
Triple Diamond-88
Quadruple Diamond-88
97Donruss Preferred-163
Cut to the Chase-163
97Donruss Priority-169
Stamp of Approval-169
97Pinnacle-21
Artist's Proofs-21
Rink Collection-21
Press Plates Back Black-21
Press Plates Back Cyan-21
Press Plates Back Magenta-21
Press Plates Back Yellow-21
Press Plates Front Black-21
Press Plates Front Cyan-21
Press Plates Front Magenta-21
Press Plates Front Yellow-21
97Score Penguins-16
Platinum-16
Premier-16
97SP Authentic-128
97Upper Deck-346
97Autographed Collection *-47
Autographs-13
Autographs Gold-13
97Players Club *-6
98Pacific-350
Ice Blue-350
Red-350
98SPx Finite-67
98SPx Finite-147
Radiance-67
Radiance-147
Spectrum-67
Spectrum-147
98UD Choice-171
98UD Choice Preview-171
98UD Choice Prime Choice Reserve-171
98UD Choice Reserve-171
98UD3-9
98UD3-69
98UD3-129
Die-Cuts-9
Die-Cuts-69
Die-Cuts-129
98Upper Deck-164
Exclusives-164
Exclusives 1 of 1-164
Generation Next-GN22
Generation Next Quantum 1-GN22
Generation Next Quantum 2-GN22
Generation Next Quantum 3-GN22
Gold Reserve-164
98Upper Deck MVP-166
Gold Script-166
Silver Script-166
Super Script-166
98Autographed Collection *-27
Parallel-27
Autographs-7
Sports City USA-SC11
99Upper Deck MVP SC Edition-151
Gold Script-151
Silver Script-151
Super Script-151
99Quebec PeeWee Tournament Coll Souv-8
00BAP Memorabilia-316
Emerald-316
Ruby-316
Sapphire-316
Promos-316
00BAP Mem Chicago Sportsfest Copper-316
00BAP Memorabilia Chicago Sportsfest Blue-316
00BAP Memorabilia Chicago Sportsfest Gold-316
00BAP Memorabilia Chicago Sportsfest Ruby-316
00BAP Memorabilia Chicago Sun-Times Ruby-316
00BAP Memorabilia Chicago Sun-Times Gold-316
00BAP Mem Chicago Sun-Times Sapphire-316
00BAP Mem Toronto Fall Expo Copper-316
00BAP Memorabilia Toronto Fall Expo Gold-316
00BAP Memorabilia Toronto Fall Expo Ruby-316
01Wilkes-Barre Scranton Penguins-21
03Lowell Lock Monsters-20
03Lowell Lock Monsters Photo Album-17
04Swedish Elitset-115
Gold-115
05German DEL-265
06Swedish SHL Elitset-247

Domenichelli, Hnat
93Kamloops Blazers-5
94Kamloops Blazers-20
95Donruss Elite World Juniors-12
95Upper Deck-539
Electric Ice-539
Electric Ice Gold-539
95Kamloops Blazers-11
95Slapshot Memorial Cup-13
96Donruss Canadian Ice-122
Gold Press Proofs-122
Red Press Proofs-122
96Leaf Limited Rookies-4
96Leaf Limited Rookies Gold-4
96Leaf Preferred-121
Press Proofs-121
96Metal Universe-175
96Ultra-74
Gold Medallion-74
96Upper Deck-272
96Whalers Kid's Club-15
96Springfield Falcons-11
97Collector's Choice-33
97Donruss-196
Press Proofs Silver-196
Press Proofs Gold-196
97Donruss Canadian Ice-131
Dominion Series-131
Provincial Series-131
97Donruss Limited-45
Exposure-45
97Leaf-79
Fractal Matrix-79
Fractal Matrix Die Cuts-79
97Leaf International-79
Universal Ice-79
97Pacific-237
Copper-237
Emerald Green-237
Ice Blue-237
Red-237
Silver-237
97Pinnacle Inside-93
97Score-68
Artist's Proofs-68
Golden Blades-68
97Upper Deck-22
97Saint John Flames-7
98Pacific-116
Ice Blue-116
Red-116
98Upper Deck-53
Exclusives-53
Exclusives 1 of 1-53
Gold Reserve-53
00BAP Memorabilia-369
Emerald-369
Ruby-369
Sapphire-369
Promos-369
00BAP Mem Chicago Sportsfest Copper-369
00BAP Memorabilia Chicago Sportsfest Blue-369
00BAP Memorabilia Chicago Sportsfest Gold-369
00BAP Memorabilia Chicago Sportsfest Ruby-369
00BAP Memorabilia Chicago Sun-Times Ruby-369
00BAP Memorabilia Chicago Sun-Times Gold-369
00BAP Mem Chicago Sun-Times Sapphire-369
00BAP Mem Toronto Fall Expo Copper-369
00BAP Memorabilia Toronto Fall Expo Gold-369
00BAP Memorabilia Toronto Fall Expo Ruby-369
00Pacific-17

Copper-17
Gold-17
Ice Blue-17
Premiere Date-17
00Upper Deck-237
Exclusives Tier 1-237
Exclusives Tier 2-237
00Upper Deck Vintage-17
01BAP Memorabilia-405
Emerald-405
Ruby-405
Sapphire-405
01BAP Signature Series-74
Autographs-74
Autographs Gold-74
01Pacific-15
Extreme LTD-15
Hobby LTD-15
Premiere Date-15
Retail LTD-15
01Pacific Arena Exclusives-15
01Upper Deck-243
Exclusives-243
01Upper Deck MVP-10
01Upper Deck Victory-15
Gold-15
02BAP Sig Series Auto Buybacks 2001-74
02Pacific-178
Blue-178
Red-178
02Upper Deck Vintage-127

Domi, Tie

89ProCards AHL-127
90OPC Premier-25
90ProCards AHL/IHL-22
91Parkhurst-333
French-333
91Pro Set-440
French-440
92Parkhurst-434
Emerald Ice-434
92Score-408
Canadian-408
92Topps-395
Gold-395G
92Upper Deck-99
93Donruss-381
93Jets Readers Club-6
93Jets Ruffles-8
93Leaf-216
93OPC Premier-513
Gold-513
93Parkhurst-230
Emerald Ice-230
93Pinnacle-295
Canadian-295
93Score-312
Canadian-312
93Topps/OPC Premier-513
Gold-513
94Be A Player-R65
94Be A Player-R168
Signature Cards-143
94Canada Games NHL POGS-250
94Canada Games NHL POGS-344
94Donruss-60
94Leaf-318
94Maple Leafs Kodak-10
94Maple Leafs Pin-up Posters-24
94OPC Premier-444
Special Effects-444
94Parkhurst SE-SE202
Gold-SE202
94Pinnacle-344
Artist's Proofs-344
Rink Collection-344
94Score-123
Gold-123
Platinum-123
94Topps/OPC Premier-444
Special Effects-444
94Ultra-392
94Upper Deck-409
Electric Ice-409
95Canada Games NHL POGS-263
95Collector's Choice-242
Player's Club-242
Player's Club Platinum-242
95Donruss-225
95Parkhurst International-205
Emerald Ice-205
95Pinnacle-159
Artist's Proofs-159
Rink Collection-159
Full Contact-9
95Playoff One on One-94
95Score-275
Black Ice Artist's Proofs-275
Black Ice-275
95Ultra-159
Gold Medallion-159
96Be A Player-47
Autographs-47
Autographs Silver-47
96Collector's Choice-261
96Duracell All-Cherry Team-DC13
96Maggers-21
96Maple Leafs Postcards-4
96Upper Deck-201
96Upper Deck Ice-68
Parallel-68
97Collector's Choice-253
97Gatorade Stickers-5
97Katch-140
Gold-140
Silver-140
97Pacific-65
Copper-65
Emerald Green-65
Ice Blue-65
Red-65
Silver-65
97Pacific Omega-220
Copper-220
Dark Gray-220
Emerald Green-220
Gold-220
Ice Blue-220
97Panini Stickers-176
97Revolution-134
Copper-134
Emerald-134
Ice Blue-134
Silver-134
97Score-219
97Score Maple Leafs-8
Platinum-8
Premier-8
97Upper Deck-196
97Upper Deck-368
98Aurora-180
Front Line Copper-10
Front Line Ice Blue-10
Front Line Red-10
98Crown Royale-129
Limited Series-129
98Katch-139
98Pacific-28
Ice Blue-28
Red-28
98Pacific Dynagon Ice-178
Blue-178
Red-178
98Pacific Omega-226
Red-226
Opening Day Issue-226
98Panini Stickers-162
98Paramount-225
Copper-225
Emerald Green-225
Holo-Electric-225
Ice Blue-225
Silver-225
98Revolution-136
Ice Shadow-136
Red-136
Three Pronged Attack-9
Three Pronged Attack Parallel-9
98UD Choice-204
Prime Choice Reserve-204
Reserve-204
98Upper Deck-189
Exclusives-189
Exclusives 1 of 1-189
Gold Reserve-189
99Crown Royale-133
Limited Series-133
Premiere Date-133
99Maple Leafs Pizza Pizza-12
99McDonald's Upper Deck Signatures-TD
99O-Pee-Chee-192
99O-Pee-Chee Chrome-192
99O-Pee-Chee Chrome Refractors-192
99Pacific-405
Copper-405
Emerald Green-405
Gold-405
Ice Blue-405
Premiere Date-405
Red-405
99Pacific Dynagon Ice-186
Blue-186
Copper-186
Gold-186
Premiere Date-186
Checkmates American-15
Checkmates American-30
Checkmates Canadian-15
99Pacific Omega-223
Copper-223
Gold-223
Ice Blue-223
Premiere Date-223
99Pacific Prism-136
Holographic Blue-136
Holographic Gold-136
Holographic Mirror-136
Holographic Purple-136
Premiere Date-136
99Panini Stickers-162
99Paramount-223
Copper-223
Emerald-223
Gold-223
Holographic Emerald-223
Holographic Gold-223
Holographic Silver-223
Ice Blue-223
Premiere Date-223
Red-223
Silver-223
99Revolution-136
Premiere Date-136
Red-136
Shadow Series-136
Copper-136
Gold-136
CSC Silver-136
99Topps/OPC-192
99Topps/OPC Chrome-192
Refractors-192
99Upper Deck Victory-289
00Aurora-137
Premiere Date-137
00BAP Memorabilia Update Teammates-TM9
00BAP Memorabilia Update Teammates-TM37
00BAP Memorabilia Update Teammates Gold-TM9
00BAP Memorabilia Update Teammates Gold-TM37
00BAP Memorabilia Update Tough Materials-T2
00BAP Mem Update Tough Materials Gold-T2
00BAP Signature Series-143
Emerald-143
Ruby-143
Sapphire-143
Autographs-181
Autographs Gold-181
00BAP Ultimate Memorabilia Teammates-TM13
00BAP Ultimate Memorabilia Teammates-TM14
00O-Pee-Chee-244
00O-Pee-Chee Parallel-244
00Pacific-387
Copper-387
Gold-387
Ice Blue-387
Premiere Date-387
00Paramount-228
Copper-228
Gold-228
Holo-Gold-228
Holo-Silver-228
Ice Blue-228
Premiere Date-228
00Revolution-137
Blue-137
Premiere Date-137
Red-137
00Stadium Club Souvenirs-SCS8
00Titanium Game Gear-144
00Titanium Game Gear Patches-144
00Titanium Draft Day Edition-95
Patches-95
00Topps/OPC-244
Parallel-244
Game-Worn Sweaters-GWTD
00Topps Chrome-153
OPC Refractors-153
Refractors-153
00Topps Gold Label Bullion-B6
00Topps Gold Label Bullion One to One-B6
00Topps Heritage-170
Original Six Relics-OSJ-TD
Original Six Relics-OSJ
00Upper Deck Victory-224
00Upper Deck Vintage-344
00Upper Deck Vintage-345
00Vanguard-92
Holographic Gold-92
Holographic Purple-92
Pacific Proofs-92
01BAP Update Tough Customers-TC2
01BAP Update Tough Customers-TC11
01BAP Update Tough Customers-TC18
01O-Pee-Chee-204
01O-Pee-Chee Premier Parallel-204
01Pacific-364
01Pacific-423
Extreme LTD-364
Gold-423
Hobby LTD-364
Premiere Date-364
Retail LTD-364
Impact Zone-17
01Pacific Adrenaline-179
Blue-179
Premiere Date-179
Red-179
Retail-179
01Pacific Arena Exclusives-364
01Pacific Arena Exclusives-423
01Pacific Heads-Up Quad Jerseys-19
01Private Stock Game Gear-94
01Private Stock Game Gear Patches-94
01SP Authentic Jerseys-NNTD
01Stadium Club-78
Award Winners-78
Master Photos-78
Souvenirs-TD
Souvenirs-TDDM
01Topps-204
OPC Parallel-204
Reserve Emblems-TD
Reserve Jerseys-TD
Reserve Name Plates-TD
Reserve Numbers-TD
Reserve Patches-TD
01Upper Deck Pride of the Leafs-MLTD
01Upper Deck Victory-334
Gold-334
02McFarlane Hockey-200
02McFarlane Hockey-202
02BAP First Edition-228
02BAP Sig Series Auto Buybacks 2000-181
02BAP Signature Series Famous Scraps-FS6
02BAP Signature Series Golf-GS94
02BAP Signature Series Team Quads-TQ2
02Fleer Throwbacks-11
Gold-11
Platinum-11
Autographs-6
02Maple Leafs Platinum Collection-5
02Maple Leafs Team Issue-3
02NHL Power Play Stickers-126
02O-Pee-Chee-81
02O-Pee-Chee Premier Blue Parallel-81
02O-Pee-Chee Premier Red Parallel-81
02O-Pee-Chee Factory Set-81
02Pacific-359
Blue-359
Red-359
02Pacific Complete-166
Red-166
02Parkhurst-180
Bronze-180
Gold-180
Silver-180
02Topps-81
OPC Blue Parallel-81
OPC Red Parallel-81
Factory Set-81
02Topps Heritage-39
Chrome Parallel-39
02Topps Total-262
02Upper Deck-165
Exclusives-165
02Upper Deck Victory-203
Bronze-203
Gold-203
Silver-203
02Upper Deck Vintage-235
02Upper Deck Vintage-288
03Beehive-180
Gold-180
Silver-180
03Black Diamond-173
Black-173
Green-173
Red-173
03ITG Action-571
Jerseys-M19
03McDonald's Pacific-47
03NHL Sticker Collection-134
03O-Pee-Chee-144
03OPC Blue-144
03OPC Gold-144
03OPC Red-144
03Pacific-316
Blue-316
Red-316
03Pacific Complete-74
Red-74
03Pacific Exhibit-135
Blue Backs-135
Yellow Backs-135
03Parkhurst Orig Six He Shoots/Scores-6
03Parkhurst Orig Six He Shoots/Scores-6A
03Parkhurst Original Six Toronto-8
Memorabilia-TM8
Memorabilia-TM54
03SP Game Used Authentic Fabrics-DFDS
03SP Game Used Authentic Fabrics Gold-DFDS
03SP Game Used Team Threads-TTDSS
03SPx-125
Radiance-125
Spectrum-125
Style-SPX-DS
Style Limited-SPX-DS
03Topps-144
Blue-144
Gold-144
Red-144
03Topps C55-85
Minis-85
Minis American Back-85
Minis American Back Red-85
Minis Bazooka Back-85
Minis Brooklyn Back-85
Minis Hat Trick Back-85
Minis O Canada Back-85
Minis O Canada Back Red-85
Minis Stanley Cup Back-85
03Topps Pristine Popular Demand Relics-PD-TD
03Topps Pristine Popular Demand Relic Ref-PD-TD
03Upper Deck-181
Canadian Exclusives-181
Fan Favorites-FF5
HG-181
Tough Customers-TC-13
Classic Portraits Hockey Royalty-DSB
Ice Icons-I-TD
Ice Icons Jerseys-I-TD
03Upper Deck MVP-398
Gold Script-398
Silver Script-398
Canadian Exclusives-398
03Upper Deck Victory-181
Bronze-181
Gold-181
Silver-181
Game Breakers-GB27
03Czech Stadion-534
03Toronto Star-93
Foil-15
05Black Diamond-79
Emerald-79
Gold-79
Onyx-79
Ruby-79
05Panini Stickers-172
05Parkhurst-462
Facsimile Auto Parallel-462
05SP Game Used Authentic Fabrics Quad-DLBN
05SP Game Used Authentic Patches Quad -DLBN
05SP Game Used Authentic Fabrics Triple-DBS
05SP Game Used Authentic Patches Triple-DBS
05Ultra-184
Gold-184
Ice-184
05Upper Deck-426
Jerseys-J-TDO
Jerseys Series II-J2TD
School of Hard Knocks-HK5
05Upper Deck MVP-355
Gold-355
Platinum-355
05Upper Deck Victory-185
Black-185
Gold-185
Silver-185
06Upper Deck Victory-182
06Upper Deck Victory Black-182
06Upper Deck Victory Gold-182

Domin, Petr

00Czech OFS-182
01Czech OFS-200

Domish, Jerramie

93Quebec Pee-Wee Tournament-1582

Domke, Henry

94German First League-298
95German DEL-348

Dommen, Thomas

03Swiss EV Zug Postcards-8

Domonsky, Brad

95Slapshot-402
95Sudbury Wolves-2
95Sudbury Wolves Police-7
96Sudbury Wolves-6
96Sudbury Wolves Police-8
00Knoxville Speed-13

Donaghue, Mike

98Wichita Thunder-5
99Wichita Thunder-4
00Wichita Thunder-5

Donaghue, Tracy

98Minnesota Golden Gophers Women-4

Donaghy, Dustin

06Penticton Vees-6

Donahue, Cam

93Quebec Pee-Wee Tournament-1269

Donahue, Frazer

98Medicine Hat Tigers-9

Donahue, Mark

907th Inn. Sketch OHL-104
93Kitchener Rangers-16

Donahue, Sean

93Quebec Pee-Wee Tournament-842

Donais, Oliver

05Baie-Comeau Drakkar-17

Donald, Darren

91Air Canada SJHL-E46

Donald, Derek

92Dayton Bombers-7
93Dayton Bombers-15
94Anchorage Aces-15
96Anchorage Aces-2
97Anchorage Aces-6

Donaldson, Craig

89Oshawa Generals-7
89Oshawa Generals 7th Inning Sketch-7
897th Inn. Sketch OHL-7
907th Inn. Sketch Memorial Cup-79

Donaldson, Dale

93Red Deer Rebels-5

Donally, Ryan

05Kitchener Rangers-22
05Sudbury Wolves-18
06Las Vegas Wranglers-6

Donatelli, Clark

90Bowman-181
Tiffany-181
90O-Pee-Chee-458
90ProCards AHL/IHL-316

Donati, Justin

03Oshawa Generals-12
05ITG Heroes/Prosp Toronto Expo Parallel -402
05OHL Bell All-Star Classic-25
05ITG Heroes and Prospects-402
06Sudbury Wolves-15

Donati, Tyler

03Oshawa Generals-10
06Belleville Bulls-6

Donato, Ted

91Parkhurst-230
French-230
92Bruins Postcards-2
92OPC Premier-30
92Parkhurst-8
Emerald Ice-8
92Pro Set-221
92Score-479
Canadian-479
92Stadium Club-271
92Ultra-251
92Upper Deck-202
92Upper Deck-393
Gordie Howe Selects-G20
93Donruss-25
93Leaf-54
93OPC Premier-146
Gold-146
93Panini Stickers-8
93Parkhurst-283
Emerald Ice-283
93Pinnacle-102
Canadian-102
93PowerPlay-18
93Score-262
Canadian-262
93Stadium Club-83
Members Only Master Set-83
OPC-83
First Day Issue-83
First Day Issue OPC-83
93Topps/OPC Premier-146
Gold-146
93Ultra-267
93Upper Deck-143
94Be A Player Signature Cards-141
94Canada Games NHL POGS-43
94Donruss-155
94Leaf-49
94OPC Premier-88
Special Effects-88
94Parkhurst SE-SE14
Gold-SE14
94Pinnacle-146
Artist's Proofs-146
Rink Collection-146
94Score-27
Gold-27
Platinum-27
94Topps/OPC Premier-88
Special Effects-88
94Ultra-12
94Upper Deck-61
Electric Ice-61
94Finnish SISU-357
94Finnish SISU Guest Specials-1
95Collector's Choice-76
Player's Club-76
Player's Club Platinum-76
95Donruss-263
95Leaf-326
95Panini Stickers-4
95Parkhurst International-17
Emerald Ice-17
95Score-28
Black Ice Artist's Proofs-28
Black Ice-28
95Topps-324
OPC Inserts-324
95Ultra-204
95Upper Deck-80
Electric Ice-80
Electric Ice Gold-80
Special Edition-SE97
Special Edition Gold-SE97
95Finnish SISU Limited-97
96Be A Player-37
Autographs-37
Autographs Silver-37
96Collector's Choice-19
96Donruss-211
Press Proofs-211
96Score-30
Artist's Proofs-30
Dealer's Choice Artist's Proofs-30
Special Artist's Proofs-30
Golden Blades-30
96SP-13
96Upper Deck-221
97Collector's Choice-14
97Crown Royale-10
Emerald Green-10
Ice Blue-10
Silver-10
97Donruss-108
Press Proofs Silver-108
Press Proofs Gold-108
97Donruss Limited-118
Exposure-118
97Katch-10
Gold-10
Silver-10
97Pacific-209
Copper-209
Emerald Green-209
Ice Blue-209
Red-209
Silver-209
97Pacific Invincible-9
Copper-9
Emerald Green-9
Ice Blue-9
Red-9
Silver-9
97Pacific Omega-15
Copper-15
Dark Gray-15
Emerald Green-15
Gold-15
Ice Blue-15
97Panini Stickers-4
97Paramount-12
Copper-12
Dark Grey-12
Emerald Green-12
Ice Blue-12
Red-12
Silver-12
97Pinnacle Certified-87
Red-87
Mirror Blue-87
Mirror Gold-87
Mirror Red-87
97Pinnacle Inside-101
97Pinnacle Tot Cert Platinum Blue-87
97Pinnacle Tot Certi Platinum Gold-87
97Pinnacle Totally Certified Platinum Red-87
97Pinnacle Tot Cert Mirror Platinum Gold-87
97Revolution-9
Copper-9
Emerald-9
Ice Blue-9
Silver-9
97Score-171
97Score Bruins-6
Platinum-6
Premier-6
97SP Authentic-7
97Upper Deck-221
98Aurora-11
98Pacific-76
Ice Blue-76
Red-76
98Pacific Omega-145
Red-145
Opening Day Issue-145
98Panini Stickers-11
98Paramount-13
Copper-13
Emerald Green-13
Holo-Electric-13
Ice Blue-13
Silver-13
98UD Choice-11
98UD Choice Preview-11
98UD Choice Prime Choice Reserve-11
98UD Choice Reserve-11
98Upper Deck-217
Exclusives-217
Exclusives 1 of 1-217
Gold Reserve-217
99BAP Memorabilia-69
Gold-69
Silver-69
99Pacific Dynagon Ice-7
Blue-7
Copper-7
Gold-7
Premiere Date-7
99Panini Stickers-178
99SPx-8
Radiance-8
Spectrum-8
99Upper Deck Victory-9
00Pacific-3
Copper-3
Gold-3
Ice Blue-3
Premiere Date-3
00Stars Postcards-4
00Titanium Game Gear-14
00Upper Deck-289
Exclusives Tier 1-289
Exclusives Tier 2-289
01Manchester Monarchs-3B
02Hartford Wolf Pack-6
03Parkhurst Original Six Boston-8

Donghi, Ralph

93Swiss HNL-250
95Swiss HNL-277

Donika, Mikhail

00Russian Dynamo Moscow-12
00Russian Hockey League-313
02Russian SL-13

Donnally, Ryan

02Windsor Spitfires-18

Donnelly, Dave

86Blackhawks Coke-4
88Oilers Tenth Anniversary-150
90ProCards AHL/IHL-131

Donnelly, Gord

84Nordiques Postcards-6
84Fredericton Express-6
85Nordiques McDonald's-5
85Nordiques Team Issue-6
85Fredericton Express-20
86Nordiques General Foods-6
86Nordiques Team Issue-4
87Nordiques General Foods-6
87Nordiques Team Issue-27
88Nordiques General Foods-8
88Nordiques Team Issue-8
89Jets Safeway-9
90Jets IGA-8
90Pro Set-560
91Jets Panini Team Stickers-7
91Pro Set-357
French-357
91Sabres Blue Shield-4
91Sabres Pepsi/Campbell's-4
91Upper Deck-305
French-305
92Durivage Panini-13
92Sabres Blue Shield-5
92Sabres Jubilee Foods-3
92Ultra-259
93Stadium Club-396
Members Only Master Set-396
First Day Issue-396
94Stars Postcards-4
95Houston Aeros-4
02Fleer Throwbacks-49
Gold-49
Platinum-49

Donnelly, Mike

87Sabres Blue Shield-7
88Sabres Blue Shield-6
88ProCards AHL-263
89ProCards AHL-274
90ProCards AHL/IHL-428
91Pro Set Platinum-183
91Parkhurst-294
French-294
91Pinnacle-299
French-299
91Pro Set-399
French-399
91Score Canadian Bilingual-499
91Score Canadian English-499
91Upper Deck-420
French-420
92Bowman-342
92O-Pee-Chee-151
92Pinnacle-98
French-98
92Score-67
Canadian-67
92Stadium Club-411
92Topps-121
Gold-121G
92Ultra-81
93Donruss-155
93Leaf-282
93OPC Premier-33
Gold-33
93Parkhurst-369
Emerald Ice-369
93Pinnacle-172
Canadian-172
93PowerPlay-359
93Score-176
Canadian-176
93Stadium Club-374
Members Only Master Set-374
First Day Issue-374
93Topps/OPC Premier-33
Gold-33
94Canada Games NHL POGS-123
94Donruss-282
94Flair-78
94Leaf-106
94OPC Premier-308
Special Effects-308
94Pinnacle-223
Artist's Proofs-223
Rink Collection-223
94Stadium Club-14
Members Only Master Set-14
First Day Issue-14
Super Team Winner Cards-14
94Stars Postcards-5
94Topps/OPC Premier-308
Special Effects-308
94Ultra-97
94Upper Deck-199
Electric Ice-199
95Be A Player-80
Signatures-S80
Signatures Die Cuts-S80
95Canada Games NHL POGS-87
95Collector's Choice-263
Player's Club-263
Player's Club Platinum-263
95Donruss-232
95Leaf-217
95Panini Stickers-170
95Parkhurst International-57
Emerald Ice-57
95Pinnacle-156
Artist's Proofs-156
Rink Collection-156
95Score-147
Black Ice Artist's Proofs-147
Black Ice-147
95Upper Deck-87
Electric Ice-87
Electric Ice Gold-87
96Detroit Vipers-5

Donnelly, Pete

73Quaker Oats WHA-29
73Vancouver Blazers-8

Donnelly, Trueman

37V356 Worldwide Gum-134

Donovan, Neil

97Mobile Mysticks-19
97Mobile Mysticks Kellogg's-3

Donovan, Olivier

05Drummondville Voltigeurs-30

Donovan, Rob

94Birmingham Bulls-6
95Birmingham Bulls-7
01UK London Knights-23

Donovan, Ryan

91British Columbia JHL-109
92British Columbia JHL-171

Donovan, Shean

92Ottawa 67's-9
94Finest-158
Super Team Winners-158
Refractors-158
94Pinnacle-539
Artist's Proofs-539
Rink Collection-539
94SP-149
Die Cuts-149
94Upper Deck-366
Electric Ice-366
95Be A Player-3
Signatures-S3
Signatures Die Cuts-S3
95Bowman-140
All-Foil-140
95Donruss-77
Canadian World Junior Team-19
95Finest-163
Refractors-163
95Leaf-47
95Parkhurst International-458
Emerald Ice-458
95Pinnacle-211
Artist's Proofs-211
Rink Collection-211
95Score-307
Black Ice Artist's Proofs-307
Black Ice-307
95Stadium Club-114
Members Only Master Set-114
95Summit-177
Artist's Proofs-177
Ice-177
95Topps-42
OPC Inserts-42
Canadian World Juniors-13CJ
95Upper Deck-131
Electric Ice-131
Electric Ice Gold-131
95Classic-92
95Images-46
Gold-46
Autographs-46A
96Collector's Choice-234
96Upper Deck-149
97Be A Player-142
Autographs-142
Autographs Die-Cuts-142
Autographs Prismatic Die-Cuts-142
97Pacific Invincible NHL Regime-176
97Upper Deck-152
98Pacific-159
Ice Blue-159
Red-159
98Upper Deck-251
Exclusives-251
Exclusives 1 of 1-251
Gold Reserve-251
99BAP Millennium-63
Emerald-63
Ruby-63
Sapphire-63
Signatures-63
Signatures Gold-63
99Upper Deck Arena Giveaways-AT2
00Paramount-11
Copper-11
Gold-11
Holo-Gold-11
Holo-Silver-11
Ice Blue-11
Premiere Date-11
01Parkhurst-194
02BAP Sig Series Auto Buybacks 1999-63
03ITG Action-87
03Pacific Complete-318
Red-318
03Pacific Quest for the Cup-14
Blue-14
03Titanium-16
Hobby Jersey Number Parallels-16
Retail-16
Retail Jersey Number Parallels-16
04Pacific-38
Blue-38
Red-38
05Be A Player Signatures-DO
05Be A Player Signatures Gold-DO
05McDonalds Upper Deck-46
05Panini Stickers-201
05Parkhurst-81
Facsimile Auto Parallel-81
05Upper Deck-29
HG Glossy-29
05Upper Deck MVP-60
Gold-60
Platinum-60
05Upper Deck Toronto Fall Expo-29
06O-Pee-Chee-42
Rainbow-42

Donovan, Stanson

04Moncton Wildcats-18
05PEI Rocket-10

Dontigny, Steve

917th Inn. Sketch QMJHL-60

Doolan, John

98Kansas City Blades-27
99Kansas City Blades Supercuts-25

Dopita, Jiri

94German DEL-43
95Czech APS Extraliga-20
95Czech APS Extraliga-369
96Czech APS Extraliga-230
96Swedish Semic Wien-122
97Czech APS Extraliga-39
97Czech APS Extraliga-358
97Czech APS Extraliga-369
97Czech DS Extraliga-7
97Czech DS Stickers-10
97Czech DS Stickers-32
98Czech DS-1
98Czech DS Stickers-175
98Czech OFS-105
98Czech OFS-241
98Czech OFS-478
Olympic Winners-1
98Czech Bonaparte-5A
98Czech Pexeso-16
99Czech DS-133
National Stars-NS22
Premium-P10
99Czech OFS-57
99Czech OFS-260
99Czech OFS-512
All-Star Game Blue-512
All-Star Game Gold-512
All-Star Game Red-512
All-Star Game Silver-512
00SPx Rookie Redemption-RR22
00Czech DS Extraliga-20
National Team-NT6
Top Stars-TS4
Valuable Players-VP5
00Czech OFS-334
00Czech OFS Star Emerald-2
00Czech OFS Star Pink-2
00Czech OFS Star Violet-2
01Atomic-120
Premiere Date-120
Rookie Reaction-7
01Atomic Toronto Fall Expo-120
01BAP Memorabilia-345
Emerald-345
Ruby-345
Sapphire-345
01BAP Signature Series-206
Autographs-206
Autographs Gold-206
01Bowman YoungStars-110
Gold-110
Ice Cubed-110
01Crown Royale-173
01Flyers Postcards-5
01O-Pee-Chee-355
01Pacific-459
01Pacific Adrenaline-220
Blue-220
Premiere Date-220
Red-220
Retail-220
01Pacific Heads-Up-115
01Parkhurst-263
01Parkhurst Beckett Promos-263
01Private Stock-134
Gold-134
Premiere Date-134
Retail-134
Silver-134
01Private Stock Pacific Nights-134
01Private Stock PS-2002-85
01SP Authentic-167
Limited-167
Limited Gold-167
01SP Game Used-93
01SPx-150
01SPx-150
Rookie Treasures-RTJD
01Stadium Club-123
Award Winners-123
Master Photos-123
01Titanium-174
Retail-174
Double-Sided Jerseys-49
Double-Sided Jerseys-63
Double-Sided Patches-49

Double-Sided Patches-63
01Titanium Draft Day Edition-69
01Titanium Draft Day Edition-156
01Topps-355
01Topps Chrome-173
Refractors-173
Black Border Refractors-173
01Topps Heritage-142
01Topps Reserve-108
01UD Challenge for the Cup-126
01UD Honor Roll-98
01UD Mask Collection-159
Gold-159
01UD Playmakers-135
01UD Premier Collection-103
01UD Top Shelf-74
01Upper Deck-438
Exclusives-438
01Upper Deck Ice-64
01Upper Deck MVP-230
01Upper Deck Victory-450
01Upper Deck Vintage-292
01Vanguard-124
Blue-124
Red-124
One of Ones-124
Premiere Date-124
Proofs-124
01Czech DS-58
Best of the Best-BB9
01Czech OFS All Stars-5
02BAP First Edition-226
02BAP Sig Series Auto Buybacks 2001-206
02NHL Power Play Stickers-35
02Oilers Postcards-16
02O-Pee-Chee-251
02O-Pee-Chee Premier Blue Parallel-251
02O-Pee-Chee Premier Red Parallel-251
02O-Pee-Chee Factory Set-251
02Pacific-279
Blue-279
Red-279
Jerseys-38
Jerseys Holo-Silver-38
Heads-Up Quad Jerseys-20
Heads-Up Quad Jerseys-36
Heads-Up Quad Jerseys Gold-20
Heads-Up Quad Jerseys Gold-36
02Topps-251
OPC Blue Parallel-251
OPC Red Parallel-251
Factory Set-251
02Topps Heritage-173
02Topps Total-149
02Czech DS-58
02Czech DS-72
02Czech IQ Sports Blue-5
02Czech IQ Sports Yellow-5
02Czech Stadion Olympics-327
03Czech OFS Plus-63
03Czech OFS Plus Insert C-C6
03Czech OFS Plus Insert M-M2
03Czech OFS Plus Insert M-M26
03Czech OFS Plus MS Praha-SE10
03Czech Pardubice Postcards-4
04Czech OFS-115
Assist Leaders-7
Czech/Slovak-5
Goals Leaders-10
Points Leaders-8
Stars-13
04Czech Zuma-12
04Czech Zuma Stars-Z2
04Czech World Championship Postcards-3
05Czech HC Znojmo-3
06Czech OFS-201
Team Cards-14

Dopita, Lubos
94Czech APS Extraliga-267

Dopp, Chris
93St. Cloud State Huskies-4

Dopson, Adam
04UK London Racers-15

Dopson, Rob
90ProCards AHL/IHL-370
91ProCards-301
92Cleveland Lumberjacks-15
93Cleveland Lumberjacks-7
93Cleveland Lumberjacks Postcards-8
95Houston Aeros-5
96Collector's Edge Ice-131
Prism-131
03UK Sheffield Steelers-10
03UK Sheffield Steelers Stickers-7

Dora, Lucas
04Tulsa Oilers-7

Doraty, Ken
32O'Keefe Maple Leafs-NNO
33O-Pee-Chee V304A-4
33V129-14
33V357 Ice Kings-49

Dorchak, Dean
89Portland Winter Hawks-6
907th Inn. Sketch WHL-321

Dore, Andre
82Post Cereal-13
83Nordiques Postcards-6
83O-Pee-Chee-313
84O-Pee-Chee-279

Dore, Daniel
88Nordiques General Foods-9
88Nordiques Team Issue-9
89Nordiques Team Issue-7
89Nordiques General Foods-5
89Nordiques Police-4
90Nordiques Team Issue-3
90Upper Deck-255
French-255
90Halifax Citadels-4
91Nordiques Panini Team Stickers-2
91ProCards-539

Dore, Mike
90Rayside-Balfour Jr. Canadians-5
91Rayside-Balfour Jr. Canadians-4

Dore, Nicolas
93Quebec Pee-Wee Tournament-466

Dorey, Jim
68Maple Leafs White Border-2
69O-Pee-Chee-45
70Colgate Stamps-79
70Esso Power Players-23
70Maple Leafs Postcards-1
70O-Pee-Chee-106
70Sargent Promotions Stamps-197
70Topps-106
71Maple Leafs Postcards-2
71O-Pee-Chee-57
71Sargent Promotions Stamps-201
71Topps-57
71Toronto Sun-255
72Whalers New England WHA-5
72O-Pee-Chee-339
72Finnish Semic World Championship-168
72Swedish Semic World Championship-168
73Quaker Oats WHA-47
75O-Pee-Chee WHA-94
76Nordiques Postcards-12
76O-Pee-Chee WHA-24

Dorey, Wes
01Idaho Steelheads-6
03Alaska Aces-4

Doria, Anthony
93Quebec Pee-Wee Tournament-1170

Doria, Brandon
03Augusta Lynx-36
04Huntsville Havoc-10

Dorian, Dan
93UK Humberside Hawks-21

Dorion, Dan
88ProCards AHL-340

Dorn, Konrad
95Austrian National Team-5

Dorn, Paul
92Quebec Pee-Wee Tournament-1431
93Quebec Pee-Wee Tournament-1574
97Arizona Icecats-8
98Arizona Icecats-5
99Arizona Icecats-4
00Arizona Icecats-5

Dorn, Peter
94German First League-282

Dornbierer, Philipp
01Swiss HNL-470
02Swiss HNL-433

Dornhoefer, Gary
64Beehive Group III Photos-6
64Coca-Cola Caps-5
64Topps-72
65Topps-38
68Bauer Ads-5
68O-Pee-Chee-94
68Shirriff Coins-126
68Topps-94
69O-Pee-Chee-94
69Topps-94
70Colgate Stamps-40
70Dad's Cookies-24
70Esso Power Players-208
70Flyers Postcards-2
70O-Pee-Chee-85
Deckle-33
70Sargent Promotions Stamps-149
70Topps-85
71Letraset Action Replays-3
71O-Pee-Chee-202
71Sargent Promotions Stamps-151
71Topps-89
71Toronto Sun-192
72Flyers Mighty Milk-3
72O-Pee-Chee-146
72Sargent Promotions Stamps-161
72Topps-41
72Topps-65
72Finnish Semic World Championship-179
72Swedish Semic World Championship-179
73O-Pee-Chee-182
73Topps-182
74NHL Action Stamps-213
74O-Pee-Chee NHL-44
74Topps-44
75Flyers Canada Dry Cans-6
75O-Pee-Chee NHL-129
75Topps-129
76O-Pee-Chee NHL-256
76Topps-256
77O-Pee-Chee NHL-202
77Topps-202
94Parkhurst Tall Boys-20
04ITG Franchises Update Memorabilia-USM5
04ITG Franchises Update Memorabilia Gold-USM5
04ITG Franchises US East-418
Autographs-A-GD
04ITG Ultimate Mem Broad St Bullie Jersey-7
04ITG Ult Mem Broad St Bullie Jersey Auto-7
04ITG Ultimate Mem Broad St Bullie Emblem-7
04ITG Ult Mem Broad St Bullie Emblem Auto-7
04ITG Ultimate Mem Broad St Bullie Number-7
04ITG Ult Mem Broad St Bullie Number Auto-7
06Parkhurst-153
06Parkhurst-241
Autographs-153
Autographs-241
Autographs Dual-DASD

Dornic, Ivan
83Swedish Semic VM Stickers-96
03Portland Winter Hawks-16
03Portland Winter Hawks-24

Dorochin, Igor
94German First League-78
95German DEL-46
99German Bundesliga 2-111
02German DEL City Press-7

Dorofeyev, Igor
91O-Pee-Chee Inserts-32R
92Upper Deck-352
98Russian Hockey League-48

Dorohoy, Eddie
44Beehive Group II Photos-233
45Quaker Oats Photos-72

Doroshuk, Rob
92Norwegian Elite Series-120

Dorsett, Derek
04Medicine Hat Tigers-6
05Medicine Hat Tigers-9
06Medicine Hat Tigers-5

Dortigny, Steve
907th Inn. Sketch QMJHL-193

Dorval, Sebastien
93Quebec Pee-Wee Tournament-42

Dosdall, Cory
907th Inn. Sketch WHL-169
917th Inn. Sketch WHL-308

Dostal, David
96Czech APS Extraliga-118

Dostie, Julien
93Quebec Pee-Wee Tournament-331

Dostoinov, Alexi
06Sioux Falls Stampede -21

Dotzauer, Donar
94German First League-68

Doucet, Benoit
85Moncton Golden Flames-26
94Finnish Jaa Kiekko-281
94German DEL-86
95German DEL-91
95Swedish World Championships Stickers-66
96German DEL-279
96Swedish Semic Wien-196
03Victoriaville Tigres-6
04Victoriaville Tigres-19
05Victoriaville Tigres-4
06Victoriaville Tigres-22

Doucet, Benoit (QMJHL)
03Victoriaville Tigres-6
04Victoriaville Tigres-19
05Victoriaville Tigres-4
06Victoriaville Tigres-22

Doucet, Dany
93Quebec Pee-Wee Tournament-10
95German DEL-431

Doucet, Dave
91Air Canada SJHL-C6
92Saskatchewan JHL-81

Doucet, Francois
93Quebec Pee-Wee Tournament-1601

Doucet, Guillaume
06PEI Rocket-13

Doucet, Kyle
02Halifax Mooseheads-8
03Victoriaville Tigres-7
04Victoriaville Tigres-21

Doucet, Ricky
93Quebec Pee-Wee Tournament-1205

Doucet, Scott
04Prince Albert Raiders-7
05Prince Albert Raiders-7
06Prince Albert Raiders-8

Doucet, Wayne
86Sudbury Wolves-20
90Score-397
Canadian-397
90ProCards AHL/IHL-497
91ProCards-461

Doucette, Cody
03Moncton Wildcats-13

Doucette, Darrell
93Quebec Pee-Wee Tournament-661

Doucette, Dave
89Sault Ste. Marie Greyhounds-27
92Dallas Freeze-7
93Dallas Freeze-6
94Central Hockey League-111
98San Antonio Iguanas-9

Dougherty, Britt
02Regina Pats-11
03Regina Pats-24
06Austin Ice Bats-16

Dougherty, Todd
97Idaho Steelheads-19
98Huntsville Channel Cats-14

Doughty, Drew
05Guelph Storm-C-02
06Guelph Storm-5
06ITG Heroes and Prospects-108
Autographs-ADDO

Douglas, Chris
99UK Hull Thunder-19

Douglas, Jordy
79O-Pee-Chee-335
80O-Pee-Chee-97
80Topps-97
81O-Pee-Chee Stickers-65
82North Stars Postcards-7
82Post Cereal-7
83NHL Key Tags-60
83North Stars Postcards-7
84O-Pee-Chee-338

Douglas, Kent
44Beehive Group II Photos-396
62York Iron-On Transfers-13
63Chex Photos-10
63Maple Leafs Team Issue-5
63Parkhurst-7
63Parkhurst-67
63Toronto Star-10
63York White Backs-13
64Beehive Group III Photos-160
64Coca-Cola Caps-102
65Coca-Cola-101
65Topps-14
66Topps-82
67Seals Team Issue-8
68Bauer Ads-6
68O-Pee-Chee-26
68Shirriff Coins-39
68Topps-26
94Parkhurst Tall Boys-109
95Parkhurst '66-67-105
Coins-105
04ITG Franchises US West-264
Autographs-A-KD
07Maple Leafs 1967 Commemorative-6

Douglas, Layne
91Air Canada SJHL-A22
91Air Canada SJHL All-Stars-19
91Air Canada SJHL All-Stars-41

Douglas, Les
34Beehive Group I Photos-99
40O-Pee-Chee V301-2-129

Douglas, Leslie
51Laval Dairy QSHL-100
51Laval Dairy Subset-100
52St. Lawrence Sales-5

Douglas, Rob
94Thunder Bay Flyers-8

Douglas, Ryan
92British Columbia JHL-157
93Peterborough Petes-21
93Sault Ste. Marie Greyhounds-2
94Flint Generals-6

Douglas, Stephen
98Amarillo Rattlers-3

Doull, Doug
917th Inn. Sketch OHL-114
98Michigan K-Wings-4
00UK Sekonda Superleague-100
01St. John's Maple Leafs-8
02St. John's Maple Leafs Aliant-1
03ITG VIP Rookie Debut-81
03Parkhurst Original Six Boston-14
03Parkhurst Rookie-103
03Upper Deck Rookie Update-92

Dourion, George
897th Inn. Sketch OHL-71
907th Inn. Sketch OHL-207
917th Inn. Sketch OHL-266
91Sudbury Wolves-12

Douris, Peter
86Sherbrooke Canadiens-13
87Moncton Hawks-5
88ProCards IHL-83
89Bruins Sports Action Update-3
90Bruins Sports Action-10
90OPC Premier-26
90Pro Set-407
91Bruins Sports Action-6
91OPC Premier-141
91Pro Set-347
French-347
91Score Canadian Bilingual-633
91Score Canadian English-633
91Upper Deck-403
91Upper Deck-601
French-403
French-601
91ProCards-64
92Panini Stickers-141
92Panini Stickers French-141
92Score-384
Canadian-384
92Stadium Club-402
92Topps-190
Gold-190G
93OPC Premier-265
Gold-265
93PowerPlay-284
93Topps/OPC Premier-265
Gold-265
94Canada Games NHL POGS-30
94Ducks Carl's Jr.-5
94Leaf-397
94OPC Premier-184
Special Effects-184
94Topps/OPC Premier-184
Special Effects-184
95Be A Player-25
Signatures-S25
Signatures Die Cuts-S25
95Panini Stickers-225
95Parkhurst International-278
Emerald Ice-278
95Playoff One on One-222
96Milwaukee Admirals-5
98German DEL-70
99German DEL-323
00German DEL-177
All-Star Class-A3
01German Upper Deck-193

Douris, Yvon
77Kalamazoo Wings-8

Dousse, David
96Swiss HNL-216
98Swiss Power Play Stickers-91

Douville, Dave
93Sherbrooke Faucons-12

Douville, Thierry
00Baie-Comeau Drakkar-9
Signed-9
01Baie-Comeau Drakkar-8
02Baie Comeau Drakkar-10
03Moncton Wildcats-12
04Fresno Falcons-4

Dow, Craig
93Quebec Pee-Wee Tournament-167

Dow, Shane
98BC Icemen-5
98BC Icemen II-2

Dowd, Bill
81Ottawa 67's-5
82Ottawa 67's-4

Dowd, Brenden
06Kamloops Blazers-5

Dowd, Gary
01UK Dundee Stars-6
02UK Dundee Stars-6

Dowd, Jim
91ProCards-423
93PowerPlay-376
93Classic Pro Prospects-22
94Be A Player Signature Cards-91
94Donruss-47
94Leaf-307
94OPC Premier-321
Special Effects-321
94Parkhurst-279
Gold-279
94Parkhurst SE-SE98
Gold-SE98
94Pinnacle-439
Artist's Proofs-439
Rink Collection-439
94Stadium Club-194
Members Only Master Set-194
First Day Issue-194
Super Team Winner Cards-194
94Topps/OPC Premier-321
Special Effects-321
94Ultra-116
94Upper Deck-410
Electric Ice-410
94Classic Pro Prospects-44
95Parkhurst International-485
Emerald Ice-485
95Stadium Club-91
Members Only Master Set-91
95Topps-316
OPC Inserts-316
95Ultra-260
97Be A Player-111
Autographs-111
Autographs Die-Cuts-111
Autographs Prismatic Die-Cuts-111
97Saint John Flames-8
00Crown Royale-52
Ice Blue-52
Limited Series-52
Premiere Date-52
Red-52
00Pacific-164
Copper-164
Gold-164
Ice Blue-164
Premiere Date-164
00Topps Chrome-235
OPC Refractors-235
Refractors-235
00UD Reserve-43
00Upper Deck-91
Exclusives Tier 1-91
Exclusives Tier 2-91
00Upper Deck Vintage-176
01Crown Royale-72
Blue-72
Premiere Date-72
Red-72
Retail-72
01O-Pee-Chee-155
01O-Pee-Chee Premier Parallel-155
01Pacific-192
Extreme LTD-192
Hobby LTD-192
Premiere Date-192
Retail LTD-192
01Pacific Arena Exclusives-192
01Titanium-69
Hobby Parallel-69
Premiere Date-69
Retail-69
Retail Parallel-69
01Topps-155
OPC Parallel-155
01Topps Chrome-117
Refractors-117
Black Border Refractors-117
01UD Mask Collection-47
Gold-47
01Upper Deck-314
Exclusives-314
01Wild Crime Prevention-22
02BAP First Edition-298
02O-Pee-Chee-141
02O-Pee-Chee Premier Blue Parallel-141
02O-Pee-Chee Premier Red Parallel-141
02O-Pee-Chee Factory Set-141
02Pacific-179
Blue-179
Red-179
02Pacific Complete-96
Red-96
02Topps-141
OPC Blue Parallel-141
OPC Red Parallel-141
Factory Set-141
02Topps Total-89
02Upper Deck MVP-88
Gold-88
Classics-88
Golden Classics-88
02Upper Deck Vintage-126
03ITG Action-289
03NHL Sticker Collection-247
03Pacific Complete-210
Red-210
04German DEL-140
05Be A Player Signatures-JI
05Be A Player Signatures Gold-JI
06Devils Team Set-5

Dowell, Greg
93Quebec Pee-Wee Tournament-1153

Dowell, Jake
03Wisconsin Badgers-7
04Wisconsin Badgers-13
05Wisconsin Badgers-6

Dowell, Rick
93Quebec Pee-Wee Tournament-1154

Dowhatko, Jamie
01Lincoln Stars-4

Dowhay, Jarrid
05Prince Albert Raiders-8
06Prince Albert Raiders-10

Dowhy, Steve
97Bakersfield Fog-2
98Bakersfield Condors-7
99Bakersfield Condors-7
99Colorado Gold Kings Taco Bell-8
00Fort Worth Brahmas-4

Down, Blaine
00Barrie Colts-8
01Barrie Colts-7
03Bridgeport Sound Tigers-11
04Barrie Colts 10th Anniversary-5

Downey, Aaron
95Hampton Roads Admirals-20
96Hampton Roads Admirals-HRA20
97Providence Bruins-5
98Hampton Roads Admirals 10th Anniversary-15
98Providence Bruins-8
99Providence Bruins-8
00BAP Memorabilia-230
Emerald-230
Ruby-230
Sapphire-230
Promos-230
00BAP Mem Chicago Sportsfest Copper-230
00BAP Memorabilia Chicago Sportsfest Blue-230
00BAP Memorabilia Chicago Sportsfest Gold-230
00BAP Memorabilia Chicago Sportsfest Ruby-230
00BAP Memorabilia Chicago Sun-Times Ruby-230
00BAP Memorabilia Chicago Sun-Times Gold-230
00BAP Mem Chicago Sun-Times Sapphire-230
00BAP Mem Toronto Fall Expo Copper-230
00BAP Memorabilia Toronto Fall Expo Gold-230
00BAP Memorabilia Toronto Fall Expo Ruby-230
02Stars Postcards-16
03ITG Action-179
03Pacific Complete-401
Red-401
03Stars Postcards-6
05Blues Team Set-5
06Canadiens Postcards-7

Downey, Brian
92Thunder Bay Thunder Hawks-15
93Thunder Bay Senators-11
95Madison Monsters-2
96Madison Monsters-11
98Madison Monsters-10
98UHL All-Stars-3

Downey, Jason
907th Inn. Sketch QMJHL-176
917th Inn. Sketch QMJHL-154
93Dayton Bombers-4
94Dayton Bombers-4
95Dayton Bombers-8
96Dayton Bombers-18
97New Orleans Brass-20

Downie, Steve
05ITG Heroes/Prosp Toronto Expo Parallel -113
05OHL Bell All-Star Classic-26
05ITG Heroes and Prospects-113
Autographs-A-SD
He Shoots-He Scores Prizes-45
Oh Canada-OC-12
Oh Canada Gold-OC-12
06ITG Heroes and Prospects-122
06ITG Heroes and Prospects-144
Autographs-ASD1
Autographs-ASD2
National Pride-NP16
National Pride-NP23
National Pride Gold-NP16
Quad Emblems-QE05
Quad Emblems Gold-QE05
07ITG Going For Gold World Juniors-10
Autographs-10
Emblems-GUE10
Jerseys-GUJ10
Numbers-GUN10

Downing, Jon
84Minnesota-Duluth Bulldogs-7

Downs, Jeremy
05Bossier-Shreveport Mudbugs-6

Downs, Jon
93Quebec Pee-Wee Tournament-667

Dowzak, Tysen
05ITG Heroes/Prosp Toronto Expo Parallel -422
05Kelowna Rockets-11
05ITG Heroes and Prospects-422
Autographs Update-A-TD
Team Orr-TO7
06ITG Heroes and Prospects CHL Top Prospects-TP14
06ITG Heroes and Prospects CHL Top Prospects Gold-TP14
06ITG Heroes and Prospects Jerseys-GUJ30
06ITG Heroes and Prospects Jerseys Gold-GUJ30
06ITG Heroes and Prospects Emblems-GUE30
06ITG Heroes and Prospects Emblems Gold-GUE30
06ITG Heroes and Prospects Numbers-GUN30
06ITG Heroes and Prospects Numbers Gold-GUN30

Doyle, Adam
01Odessa Jackalopes-6
02Odessa Jackalopes-6
03Odessa Jackalopes-5
04Odessa Jackalopes-6

Doyle, Chris
06PEI Rocket-11

Doyle, Eric
05Everett Silvertips-4

Doyle, Frank
04Idaho Steelheads-4
05Albany River Rats-8
06Between The Pipes-13
Autographs-AFD
06Fleer-224
Tiffany-224
06O-Pee-Chee-507
Rainbow-507
06SPx-145
Spectrum-145
06The Cup-102
Autographed Rookie Masterpiece Pressplates-102
Gold Rainbow Autographed Rookies-102
Masterpiece Pressplates (Marquee Rookies)-507
Masterpiece Pressplates (MVP)-336
Masterpiece Pressplates (SPx)-145
Masterpiece Pressplates (Trilogy)-126
Masterpiece Pressplates (Victory)-209
Rookies Black-102
Rookies Platinum-102
06Ultimate Collection Ultimate Debut Threads Jerseys-DJ-FD
06Ultimate Collection Ultimate Debut Threads Jerseys Autographs-DJ-FD
06Ultimate Collection Ultimate Debut Threads Patches-DJ-FD
06Ultimate Collection Ultimate Debut Threads Patches Autographs-DJ-FD
06Ultra-212
Gold Medallion-212
Ice Medallion-212
06Upper Deck-224
Exclusives Parallel-224
High Gloss Parallel-224
Masterpieces-224
06Upper Deck MVP-336
Gold Script-336
Super Script-336
06Upper Deck Trilogy-126
06Upper Deck Victory-209
06Upper Deck Victory Black-209
06Upper Deck Victory Gold-209

Doyle, Jason
92Quebec Pee-Wee Tournament-1112
95Bowman Draft Prospects-P11
95Slapshot-375
95Sault Ste. Marie Greyhounds-5
95Classic-88
96Owen Sound Platers-25
97Owen Sound Platers-21

Doyle, Jeffrey
02Sault Ste. Marie Greyhounds-7
03Sault Ste. Marie Greyhounds-6

Doyle, Joe
94Sarnia Sting-5

Doyle, Marty
03Shawinigan Cataractes-7

Doyle, Mike
00Sioux Falls Stampede-7
03St. Cloud State Huskies-6
04St. Cloud State Huskies-7
06Rockford IceHogs -9

Doyle, Paul
95Slapshot-144
95Slapshot-434

Doyle, Perry
94UK Sheffield Steelers-14
95UK Sheffield Steelers-19

Doyle, Robin
88ProCards AHL-22
93Swedish Semic World Champ Stickers-272
94Finnish Jaa Kiekko-233
95Austrian National Team-6
96Swedish Semic Wien-212
98German DEL-139
99German DEL-79
00German DEL-76
01German Upper Deck-78

Doyle, Shane
84Belleville Bulls-13
88ProCards IHL-10

Doyle, Stephen
94UK Solihull Barons-2
95UK Solihull Barons-13

Doyle, Trevor
93Kingston Frontenacs-5
96Carolina Monarchs-8
97Fort Wayne Komets-18
99Syracuse Crunch-19
00UK Sekonda Superleague-6

Doyon, Mario
88ProCards IHL-98
89ProCards IHL-66
90Halifax Citadels-5
90ProCards AHL/IHL-443
91Upper Deck-411
French-411
91ProCards-364
93Fredericton Canadiens-7
96Swiss HNL-323
98Swiss Power Play Stickers-131
99German DEL-103
01German Upper Deck-158
02German DEL City Press-217
03Indianapolis Ice-6

Doyon, Remy
93Quebec Pee-Wee Tournament-928

Drabek, Adam
96Czech APS Extraliga-285

Drabek, Josef
99Czech Score Blue 2000-139
99Czech Score Red Ice 2000-139

Drabek, Vaclav
99Czech Score Blue 2000-10
99Czech Score Red Ice 2000-10

Drader, Daryl
77Rochester Americans-6
79Rochester Americans-4

Drag, Milan
89Victoria Cougars-8

Dragan, Jaromir
95Slovakian APS National Team-5
96Swedish Semic Wien-220
01Slovakian Kvarteto-1D

Dragicevic, Milan
86Regina Pats-4
87Regina Pats-3
89Spokane Chiefs-4

Dragon, Joe
86Sudbury Wolves-11
94Classic Pro Prospects-237

Dragoun, Michal
04Czech HC Sparta Praha Postcards-5
04Czech OFS-324
06Czech OFS-85

Draguzas, David
95Brandon Wheat Kings-5

Drainville, Francois
97Rimouski Oceanic-20
02Reading Royals-2

Drainville, Robert
51Laval Dairy Subset-39

Draisaitl, Peter
89Swedish Semic World Champ Stickers-124
91Finnish Semic World Champ Stickers-166
91Swedish Semic World Champ Stickers-166
92Finnish Semic-182
94German DEL-208
95German DEL-209
96German DEL-353
98German DEL-323
99German DEL-349
00German DEL-209

Drake, Clare
83Jets Safeway-29
90Jets IGA-9

Drake, Dallas
92Classic-86
Gold-86
92Classic Four-Sport *-206
Gold-206
BCs-BC9
93Donruss-100
93Donruss-508
93Leaf-148
93OPC Premier-365
Gold-365
93Parkhurst-61
Emerald Ice-61
93Pinnacle-28
Canadian-28
93PowerPlay-71
93Score-246
Canadian-246
93Stadium Club-484
Members Only Master Set-484
First Day Issue-484
93Topps/OPC Premier-365
Gold-365
93Ultra-104
93Upper Deck-50
NHL's Best-HB4
SP-43
93Classic Pro Prospects-15
BCs-BC19
LPs-LP5
94Canada Games NHL POGS-251
94Flair-206
94Leaf-380
94OPC Premier-64
Special Effects-64
94Parkhurst-261
Gold-261
Vintage-V90
94Pinnacle-225
Artist's Proofs-225
Rink Collection-225
94Topps/OPC Premier-64
Special Effects-64
94Ultra-241
94Upper Deck-360
Electric Ice-360
94Classic Autographs-NNO
95Be A Player-83
Signatures-S83
Signatures Die Cuts-S83
95Canada Games NHL POGS-288
95Collector's Choice-269
Player's Club-269
Player's Club Platinum-269
95Jets Readers Club-2
95Jets Team Issue-7
95Leaf-268
95Panini Stickers-211
95Parkhurst International-503
Emerald Ice-503
95Pinnacle-25
Artist's Proofs-25
Rink Collection-25
95Playoff One on One-326
95Pro Magnets-62
95Topps-328
OPC Inserts-328
95Ultra-326
95Upper Deck-17
Electric Ice-17
Electric Ice Gold-17
Special Edition-SE178
Special Edition Gold-SE178
96Coyotes Coca-Cola-3
96NHL Pro Stamps-62
96Playoff One on One-405
97Collector's Choice-197
97Coyotes Face-Off Luncheon -6
97Pacific Invincible NHL Regime-150
97Pacific Omega-172
Copper-172
Dark Gray-172
Emerald Green-172
Gold-172
Ice Blue-172
97Upper Deck-338
98Be A Player-257
Press Release-257
98BAP Gold-257
98BAP Autographs-257
98BAP Autographs Gold-257
98OPC Chrome-107
Refractors-107
98Pacific-337
Ice Blue-337
Red-337
98Pacific Omega-183
Red-183
Opening Day Issue-183
98Paramount-180
Copper-180
Emerald Green-180
Holo-Electric-180
Ice Blue-180
Silver-180
98Topps-107
O-Pee-Chee-107
98Upper Deck-342
Exclusives-342
Exclusives 1 of 1-342
Gold Reserve-342
99BAP Memorabilia-282
Gold-282
Silver-282
99Pacific-320
Copper-320
Emerald Green-320
Gold-320
Ice Blue-320
Premiere Date-320
Red-320
99Pacific Omega-179
Copper-179
Gold-179
Ice Blue-179
Premiere Date-179
99Paramount-178
Copper-178
Emerald-178
Gold-178
Holographic Emerald-178
Holographic Gold-178
Holographic Silver-178
Ice Blue-178
Premiere Date-178
Red-178
Silver-178
99Ultimate Victory-66
1/1-66
Parallel-66
Parallel 100-66
99Upper Deck MVP SC Edition-142
Gold Script-142
Silver Script-142
Super Script-142
00Aurora-120
Premiere Date-120
00BAP Memorabilia-147
00BAP Memorabilia-405
Emerald-147
Emerald-405
Ruby-147
Ruby-405
Sapphire-147
Sapphire-405
Promos-147
00BAP Mem Chicago Sportsfest Copper-147
00BAP Memorabilia Chicago Sportsfest Blue-147
00BAP Memorabilia Chicago Sportsfest Gold-147
00BAP Memorabilia Chicago Sportsfest Ruby-147
00BAP Memorabilia Chicago Sun-Times Ruby-147
00BAP Memorabilia Chicago Sun-Times Gold-147
00BAP Mem Chicago Sun-Times Sapphire-147
00BAP Mem Toronto Fall Expo Copper-147
00BAP Memorabilia Toronto Fall Expo Gold-147
00BAP Memorabilia Toronto Fall Expo Ruby-147
00BAP Parkhurst 2000-P221
00O-Pee-Chee-171
00O-Pee-Chee Parallel-171
00Pacific-315
Copper-315
Gold-315
Ice Blue-315
Premiere Date-315
00Private Stock Game Gear-90
00Private Stock Game Gear Patches-90
00Titanium Draft Day Edition-89
Patches-89
00Topps/OPC-171
Parallel-171
00Upper Deck Vintage-318
01Pacific-322
Extreme LTD-322
Hobby LTD-322
Premiere Date-322
Retail LTD-322
01Pacific Arena Exclusives-322
01Upper Deck-383
Exclusives-383
01Upper Deck Victory-313
Gold-313
01Vanguard Memorabilia-28
01Vanguard Patches-28
02BAP Sig Series Auto Buybacks 1998-257
02Blues Team Issue-5
02Pacific-321
Blue-321
Red-321
02Pacific Complete-92
Red-92
02Topps Total-364
03Blues Team Set-7
03ITG Action-527
03Pacific-281
Blue-281
Red-281
03Pacific Complete-70
Red-70
03Upper Deck-416
Canadian Exclusives-416
HG-416
UD Exclusives-416
03Upper Deck MVP-369
Gold Script-369
Silver Script-369
Canadian Exclusives-369
04Pacific-218
Blue-218
Red-218

05Be A Player Signatures-DD
05Be A Player Signatures Gold-DD
05Be A Player Triple Signatures-STL
05Blues Team Set-6
05Panini Stickers-339
05Parkhurst-420
05Parkhurst-522
Facsimile Auto Parallel-420
Facsimile Auto Parallel-522
05Ultra-170
Gold-170
Ice-170
05Upper Deck-167
HG Glossy-167
05Upper Deck MVP-337
Gold-337
Platinum-337
05Upper Deck Toronto Fall Expo-167
06O-Pee-Chee-426
Rainbow-426
06Upper Deck-173
Exclusives Parallel-173
High Gloss Parallel-173
Masterpieces-173

Drake, Jonathan
93Quebec Pee-Wee Tournament-1679

Drake, Lucas
05Kalamazoo Wings-11

Drakensjo, Carl
03Elmira Jackals-6

Draney, Brett
98Kamloops Blazers-7
99Kamloops Blazers-7
00Medicine Hat Tigers-5
02Lexington Men O'War-18
04Idaho Steelheads-23

Drapeau, Etienne
92Quebec Pee-Wee Tournament-1271
95Bowman Draft Prospects-P12
95Upper Deck-514
Electric Ice-514
Electric Ice Gold-514
95Halifax Mooseheads-18
95Classic CHL All-Stars-AS16
98Johnstown Chiefs-8
00Quad-City Mallards-17

Drapeau, Gaston
80Quebec Remparts-4
907th Inn. Sketch QMJHL-180
917th Inn. Sketch QMJHL-124

Draper, Dave
83Brantford Alexanders-13

Draper, Kris
90Jets IGA-10
90Score-404
Canadian-404
90Upper Deck-466
French-466
French-473
907th Inn. Sketch OHL-83
91Jets Panini Team Stickers-8
91Moncton Hawks-5
91ProCards-177
92O-Pee-Chee-374
92OPC Premier-27
92Topps-249
Gold-249G
93Donruss-423
94Be A Player Signature Cards-25
94Donruss-182
94Leaf-28
94Stadium Club-72
Members Only Master Set-72
First Day Issue-72
Super Team Winner Cards-72
94Upper Deck-492
Electric Ice-492
95Canada Games NHL POGS-94
95Upper Deck-459
Electric Ice-459
Electric Ice Gold-459
96Black Diamond-33
Gold-33
96Donruss-169
Press Proofs-169
96Donruss Canadian Ice-92
Gold Press Proofs-92
Red Press Proofs-92
96Leaf-119
Press Proofs-119
96Red Wings Detroit News/Free Press-1
96Score-192
Artist's Proofs-192
Dealer's Choice Artist's Proofs-192
Special Artist's Proofs-192
Golden Blades-192
97Be A Player-20
Autographs-20
Autographs Die-Cuts-20
Autographs Prismatic Die-Cuts-20
97Pacific Invincible NHL Regime-68
97Score Red Wings-12
Platinum-12
Premier-12
97Upper Deck-62
98Be A Player-200
Press Release-200
98BAP Gold-200
98BAP Autographs-200
98BAP Autographs Gold-200
98OPC Chrome-168
Refractors-168
98Pacific-188
Ice Blue-188
Red-188
98Topps-168
O-Pee-Chee-168
98Upper Deck-268
Exclusives-268
Exclusives 1 of 1-268
Gold Reserve-268
99Pacific-137
Copper-137
Emerald Green-137
Gold-137
Ice Blue-137
Premiere Date-137
Red-137
99Upper Deck Victory-106
00Pacific-146
Copper-146
Gold-146
Ice Blue-146
Premiere Date-146
00Upper Deck Vintage-133
02BAP Memorabilia-184
Emerald-184
Ruby-184
Sapphire-184
NHL All-Star Game-184
NHL All-Star Game Blue-184
NHL All-Star Game Green-184
NHL All-Star Game Red-184
02BAP Memorabilia Toronto Fall Expo-184
02BAP Sig Series Auto Buybacks 1998-200
02BAP Ultimate Mem Dynasty Jerseys-9
02BAP Ultimate Mem Dynasty Emblems-9
02BAP Ultimate Mem Dynasty Numbers-9
02Pacific-126
Blue-126
Red-126
02Pacific Complete-176
Red-176
02Topps Total-95
02Upper Deck-310
Exclusives-310
02Upper Deck Beckett UD Promos-310
02Upper Deck Vintage-93
03ITG Action-290
03NHL Sticker Collection-219
03Pacific Calder-35
Silver-35
03Pacific Complete-77
Red-77
03Pacific Quest for the Cup-35
Blue-35
03Parkhurst Original Six Detroit-6
03Russian World Championship Stars-15
04Pacific-92
Blue-92
Red-92
04UD Toronto Fall Expo Pride of Canada-13
04Ultimate Collection Signatures-US-KD
04Ultimate Collection Signature Logos-ULA-KD
04Ultimate Collection Signature Patches-SP-KD
04Upper Deck-62
Canadian Exclusives-62
Hardware Heroes-AW9
HG Glossy Gold-62
HG Glossy Silver-62
05Be A Player Dual Signatures-DL
05Be A Player Signatures-KD
05Be A Player Signatures Gold-KD
05Black Diamond Gemography-G-KD
05Black Diamond Gemography Emerald-G-KD
05Black Diamond Gemography Gold-G-KD
05Black Diamond Gemography Onyx-G-KD
05Black Diamond Gemography Ruby-G-KD
05Panini Stickers-262
05Parkhurst-179
05Parkhurst-571
Facsimile Auto Parallel-179
Facsimile Auto Parallel-571
True Colors-TCDET
True Colors-TCDET
True Colors-TCCHDE
True Colors-TCCHDE
05SP Authentic Sign of the Times-KD
05SP Authentic Sign of the Times Triples-TZFD
05SP Game Used Authentic Fabrics-AF-KD
05SP Game Used Authentic Fabrics Autos-AAF-KD
05SP Game Used Authentic Fabrics Dual-ZD
05SP Game Used Authentic Fabrics Gold-AF-KD
05SP Game Used Authentic Fabrics Quad-YDSL
05SP Game Used Authentic Patches Quad -YDSL
05SP Game Used Authentic Fabrics Triple-DLP
05SP Game Used Authentic Patches-AP-KD
05SP Game Used Authentic Patch Autos-AAP-KD
05SP Game Used Authentic Patches Dual-ZD
05SP Game Used Authentic Patches Triple-DLP
05SP Game Used Auto Draft-AD-KD
05SP Game Used Awesome Authentics Gold-DA-KD
05SP Game Used SIGnificance-KD
05SP Game Used SIGnificance Gold-S-KD
05SP Game Used Significant Numbers-SN-KD
05SP Game Used Statscriptions-ST-KD
05SPx Winning Combos-WC-ZD
05SPx Winning Combos Autographs-AWC-ZD
05SPx Winning Combos Gold-WC-ZD
05SPx Winning Combos Spectrum-WC-ZD
05SPx Winning Materials-WM-KD
05SPx Winning Materials Autographs-AWM-KD
05SPx Winning Materials Gold-WM-KD
05SPx Winning Materials Spectrum-WM-KD
05SPx Xcitement Superstars-XS-KD
05SPx Xcitement Superstars Gold-XS-KD
05SPx Xcitement Superstars Spectrum-XS-KD
05The Cup Emblems of Endorsement-EEKD
05The Cup Hardware Heroes-HHKD
05The Cup Limited Logos-LLKD
05The Cup Master Pressplate Rookie Update-197
05The Cup Signature Patches-SPKD
05The Cup Stanley Cup Titlists-TKD
05UD Artifacts Auto Facts-AF-KD
05UD Artifacts Auto Facts Blue-AF-KD
05UD Artifacts Auto Facts Copper-AF-KD
05UD Artifacts Auto Facts Pewter-AF-KD
05UD Artifacts Auto Facts Silver-AF-KD
05UD Artifacts Frozen Artifacts-FA-KD
05UD Artifacts Frozen Artifacts Autos-FA-KD
05UD Artifacts Frozen Artifacts Copper-FA-KD
05UD Artifacts Frozen Artifacts Dual-FAD-KD
05UD Artifacts Frozen Artifact Dual Auto-FAD-KD
05UD Artifact Frozen Artifact Dual Copper-FAD-KD
05UD Artifacts Frozen Artifacts Dual Gold-FAD-KD
05UD Artifact Frozen Artifact Dual Maroon-FAD-KD
05UD Artifact Frozen Artifact Dual Pewter-FAD-KD
05UD Artifact Frozen Artifact Dual Silver-FAD-KD
05UD Artifacts Frozen Artifacts Gold-FA-KD
05UD Artifacts Frozen Artifacts Maroon-FA-KD
05UD Artifacts Frozen Artifacts Patches-FP-KD
05UD Artifact Frozen Artifact Patch Autos-FP-KD
05UD Artifacts Frozen Artifact Patch Dual-FPD-HO
05UD Artifacts Frozen Art Patch Dual Auto-FPD-HO
05UD Artifacts Frozen Art Patch Pewter-FP-KD
05UD Artifacts Frozen Art Patch Silver-FP-KD
05UD Artifacts Frozen Artifacts Pewter-FA-KD
05UD Artifacts Frozen Artifacts Silver-FA-KD
05UD Artifacts Remarkable Artifacts-RA-KD
05UD Artifacts Remarkable Artifacts Dual-RA-KD
05UD Powerplay Power Marks-PMKD
05Ultimate Coll National Heroes Jersey-NHJKD
05Ultimate Coll National Heroes Patch-NHPKD
05Upper Deck-71
HG Glossy-71
Jerseys-J-KD
Jerseys Series II-J2KD
Notable Numbers-N-KD
Patches-P-KD
05Upper Deck MVP-144
Gold-144
Platinum-144
05Upper Deck Rookie Update-197
Inspirations Patch Rookies-197
05Upper Deck Trilogy Honorary Patches-HP-KD
05Upper Deck Tril Honorary Patch Script-HSP-KD
05Upper Deck Trilogy Honorary Swatches-HS-KD
05Upper Deck Tril Honorary Swatch Scripts-HSS-KD
05Upper Deck Toronto Fall Expo-71
05Upper Deck Victory-74
Black-74
Gold-74
Silver-74
Game Breakers-GB18
06Beehive Signature Scrapbook-SSKD
06Black Diamond-29
Black-29
Gold-29
Ruby-29
Gemography-GKD
Jerseys-JKD
Jerseys Black-JKD
Jerseys Gold-JKD
Jerseys Ruby-JKD
Jerseys Black Autographs -JKD
06Flair Showcase-43
Parallel-43
Inks-IKD
06Fleer-75
Tiffany-75
Signing Day-SDKD
06McDonald's Upper Deck Autographs-AKD
06O-Pee-Chee-186
Rainbow-186
Autographs-A-KD
06Panini Stickers-263
06SP Authentic Chirography-KD
06SP Authentic Sign of the Times-STKD
06SP Game Used Authentic Fabrics Sixes-AF6SEL
06SP Game Used Authentic Fabrics Sixes Patches-AF6SEL
06SP Game Used By The Letter-BLKD
06SP Game Used Inked Sweaters-ISKD
06SP Game Used Inked Sweaters Patches-ISKD
06SP Game Used Letter Marks-LMKD
06SP Game Used SIGnificance-SKD
06SPx Winning Materials-WMKD
06SPx Winning Materials Spectrum-WMKD
06SPx Winning Materials Autographs-WMKD
06The Cup Autographed NHL Shields Duals-DASDP
06The Cup NHL Shields Duals-DSHRW
06UD Artifacts Auto-Facts-AFKD
06UD Artifacts Auto-Facts Gold-AFKD
06UD Artifacts Tundra Tandems-TTDW
06UD Artifacts Tundra Tandems Black-TTDW
06UD Artifacts Tundra Tandems Blue-TTDW
06UD Artifacts Tundra Tandems Gold-TTDW
06UD Artifacts Tundra Tandems Platinum-TTDW
06UD Artifacts Tundra Tandems Red-TTDW
06UD Artifacts Tundra Tandems Dual Patches Red-TTDW
06Ultra-74
Gold Medallion-74
Ice Medallion-74
06Upper Deck Arena Giveaways-DET1
06Upper Deck-71
Exclusives Parallel-71
High Gloss Parallel-71
Game Jerseys-JKD
Game Patches-PKD
Masterpieces-71
Walmart Tins Oversize-71
06Upper Deck MVP-103
Gold Script-103
Super Script-103
Autographs-OADO
Jerseys-OJDP
06Upper Deck Ovation-68
06Upper Deck Sweet Shot Signature Shots/Saves-SSKD
06Upper Deck Trilogy Combo Clearcut Autographs-C3LDZ
06Upper Deck Trilogy Honorary Scripted Patches-HSPKD
06Upper Deck Trilogy Honorary Scripted Swatches-HSSKD
06Upper Deck Trilogy Honorary Swatches-HSKD
06Upper Deck Trilogy Ice Scripts-ISKD
06Upper Deck Trilogy Scripts-TSKD
06Upper Deck Victory-75
06Upper Deck Victory Black-75
06Upper Deck Victory Gold-75
07Upper Deck Ovation-86
07Upper Deck Victory-103
Black-103
Gold-103
EA Sports Face-Off-F04

Draper, Tom
88ProCards AHL-180
89Jets Safeway-10
90ProCards AHL/IHL-554
91Parkhurst-240
91Parkhurst-448
French-240
French-448
91Pinnacle-341
French-341
91Sabres Blue Shield-5
91Sabres Pepsi/Campbell's-5
91Upper Deck-552
French-552
91ProCards-20
91Rochester Americans Dunkin' Donuts-6
91Rochester Americans Postcards-8
92Bowman-56
92O-Pee-Chee-376
92Panini Stickers-243
92Panini Stickers French-243
92Pro Set-14
92Score-530
Canadian-530
92Stadium Club-395
92Topps-278
Gold-278G
92Ultra-14
92Upper Deck-201
92Upper Deck-361
94Minnesota Moose-4
95Milwaukee Admirals-6
95Milwaukee Admirals Postcards-17
96Collector's Edge Ice-160
Prism-160
98Rochester Americans-7
99Finnish Cardset-201
99Finnish Cardset-281
00Finnish Cardset-244
00Finnish Cardset Masquerade-8
01Finnish Cardset-336
01Finnish Cardset Dueling Aces-8
02Finnish Cardset-13
02Augusta Lynx-63

Draxinger, Tobias
03German Berlin Polar Bears Postcards-9
04German Berlin Polar Bears Postcards-7
04German DEL-64
05German DEL-23

Draxler, Marcus
95German DEL-377
97Johnstown Chiefs-23
02German DEL City Press-154

Drayna, D.J.
95North Iowa Huskies-6

Drazenovic, Nicholas
03Prince George Cougars-10
06ITG Heroes and Prospects Jerseys-GUJ48
06ITG Heroes and Prospects Jerseys Gold-GUJ48
06ITG Heroes and Prospects Emblems-GUE48
06ITG Heroes and Prospects Emblems Gold-GUE48
06ITG Heroes and Prospects Numbers-GUN48
06ITG Heroes and Prospects Numbers Gold-GUN48

Drechsel, Andre
93Quebec Pee-Wee Tournament-1535

Dreger, Barry
88Brandon Wheat Kings-10
93San Diego Gulls-8
01Columbus Cottonmouths-2

Dreger, Ron
81Saskatoon Blades-12
83Saskatoon Blades-19
84Saskatoon Blades Stickers-4

Dreier, Thomas
95Swiss HNL-345
96Swiss HNL-319

Dresler, Jan
01Czech OFS Update-311
02Czech OFS Plus-308
03Czech OFS Plus-3
05Czech HC Vitkovice-2
06Czech OFS-46

Dresler, Thor
98Danish Hockey League-118
99Danish Hockey League-43

Dressler, James
94German First League-511

Dreveny, Greg
897th Inn. Sketch OHL-92
907th Inn. Sketch OHL-2
917th Inn. Sketch OHL-112
92Sudbury Wolves-25

Drevitch, Scott
88ProCards AHL-160
89ProCards AHL-76
91Richmond Renegades-4
92Richmond Renegades-3
95Oklahoma Coyotes RHI-3
98Tacoma Sabercats-6
99Tacoma Sabercats-12
00Tacoma Sabercats-17

Drevitch, Todd
91Richmond Renegades-6
91Richmond Renegades Set 2-5
92Fort Worth Fire-5

Drew, Paul
01Plymouth Whalers-10
02Plymouth Whalers-13
03Plymouth Whalers-22

Drewiske, Davis
04Wisconsin Badgers-7
05Wisconsin Badgers-7

Drewiske, Jake
06Sioux Falls Stampede -22

Drewniak, Richard
94German First League-458

Drewsen, Lars-Peter
99Danish Hockey League-185

Dreyer, Frederic
93Quebec Pee-Wee Tournament-1015

Drillon, Gordon
34Beehive Group I Photos-148
34Beehive Group I Photos-315
37O-Pee-Chee V304E-142
38Quaker Oats Photos-10
39O-Pee-Chee V301-1-4
40O-Pee-Chee V301-2-110
55Parkhurst-25
Quaker Oats-25
83Hall of Fame-109
83Hall of Fame Postcards-H3
85Hall of Fame-109
02BAP Ultimate Mem Paper Cuts Autos-30
02Maple Leafs Platinum Collection-49
02Maple Leafs Platinum Collection-102
03BAP Ultimate Mem Linemates Autos-7
03BAP Ultimate Mem Maple Leafs Forever-10
03BAP Ultimate Memorabilia Paper Cuts-15
04ITG Ultimate Memorabilia-8
Gold-8
Maple Leafs Forever-11
06ITG Ultimate Memorabilia Lumbergraphs-7

Drindeyen, Vitali
00Russian Hockey League-49

Drinkwater, C.G.
83Hall of Fame-186
83Hall of Fame Postcards-J6
85Hall of Fame-186

Driscoll, Chris
907th Inn. Sketch OHL-283

Driscoll, Peter
76O-Pee-Chee WHA-45
79Oilers Postcards-5
88Oilers Tenth Anniversary-7

Driscoll, Scott
93Quebec Pee-Wee Tournament-739

Driscoll, Steve
84Fredericton Express-15

Driver, Bruce
84Devils Postcards-23
85O-Pee-Chee-127
85Topps-127
86Devils Police-10
86O-Pee-Chee-19
86Topps-19
87O-Pee-Chee-79
87O-Pee-Chee Stickers-60
87Panini Stickers-74
87Topps-79
88Devils Caretta-10
88O-Pee-Chee-157
88O-Pee-Chee Stickers-77
88Panini Stickers-269
88Topps-157
89Devils Caretta-10
90Bowman-87
Tiffany-87
90Devils Team Issue-11
90O-Pee-Chee-172
90Panini Stickers-69
90Pro Set-166
90Score-109
Canadian-109
90Topps-172
Tiffany-172
90Upper Deck-373
French-373
91Pro Set Platinum-69
91Bowman-281
91O-Pee-Chee-294
91Panini Stickers-225
91Parkhurst-322
French-322
91Pinnacle-63
French-63
91Pro Set-140
91Pro Set-577
French-140
French-577
91Score American-89
91Score Canadian Bilingual-89
91Score Canadian English-89
91Stadium Club-122
91Topps-294
91Upper Deck-292
French-292
92Panini Stickers-178
92Panini Stickers French-178
92Parkhurst-333
Emerald Ice-333
92Pinnacle-278
French-278
92Pro Set-99
92Score-251
Canadian-251
92Stadium Club-376
92Topps-384
Gold-384G
92Ultra-336
92Upper Deck-200
93Donruss-185
93Leaf-56
93OPC Premier-377
Gold-377
93Panini Stickers-44
93Pinnacle-277
Canadian-277
93PowerPlay-135
93Score-263
Canadian-263
93Stadium Club-126
Members Only Master Set-126
OPC-126
First Day Issue-126
First Day Issue OPC-126
93Topps/OPC Premier-377
Gold-377
93Ultra-214
94Canada Games NHL POGS-150
94Leaf-377
94OPC Premier-292
Special Effects-292
94Pinnacle-126
Artist's Proofs-126
Rink Collection-126
94Score-115
Gold-115
Platinum-115
94Stadium Club-35
Members Only Master Set-35
First Day Issue-35
Super Team Winner Cards-35
94Topps/OPC Premier-292
Special Effects-292
95Be A Player-147
Signatures-S147
Signatures Die Cuts-S147
95Parkhurst International-413
Emerald Ice-413
95Score-257
Black Ice Artist's Proofs-257
Black Ice-257
95Ultra-190
Gold Medallion-190
96Fleer Picks-156
97Be A Player-87
Autographs-87
Autographs Die-Cuts-87
Autographs Prismatic Die-Cuts-87
97Pacific Invincible NHL Regime-124
97Score Rangers-11
Platinum-11
Premier-11
97Upper Deck-110
98OPC Chrome-41
Refractors-41
98Pacific-292
Ice Blue-292
Red-292
98Topps-41
O-Pee-Chee-41
04ITG Franchises US East-364
Autographs-A-BDR
06Devils Team Set-34

Drobny, Vaclav
94German First League-643
99German Bundesliga 2-60

Droeske, Chris
99Bakersfield Condors-8

Drolet, Jimmy
96Fredericton Canadiens-5
00UK Sekonda Superleague-34
01UK Nottingham Panthers-14
03Bakersfield Condors-15

Drolet, Nancy
94Classic Women of Hockey-W18
97Collector's Choice-277
97Esso Olympic Hockey Heroes-56
97Esso Olympic Hockey Heroes French-56

Drolet, Rene
77Rochester Americans-7
77Rochester Americans-8

Drongowski, Guido
94German First League-491

Dronov, Viktor
99Russian Hockey League-93

Droppa, Ivan
91Upper Deck Czech World Juniors-98
92Indianapolis Ice-10
93Donruss-414
93Parkhurst-42
Emerald Ice-42
93Ultra-288
93Indianapolis Ice-7
93Classic-128
93Classic Pro Prospects-149
93Classic Four-Sport *-232
Gold-232
94Leaf-112
94Parkhurst-49
Gold-49
94Stadium Club-252
Members Only Master Set-252
First Day Issue-252
Super Team Winner Cards-252
94Upper Deck-435
Electric Ice-435
94Indianapolis Ice-4
95Indianapolis Ice-5
96Carolina Monarchs-9
98German DEL-267
99German DEL-185
00German DEL-52
Star Attractions-S1
01German Upper Deck-48
Gate Attractions-GA7
01Slovakian Kvarteto-3A
02German DEL City Press-262
03Czech OFS Plus-195
03Czech OFS Plus-365

Droppa, Miroslav
04UK Edinburgh Capitals-16

Drouillard, Phil
82North Bay Centennials-4

Drouin, Claude
80Quebec Remparts-5

Drouin, Dominic
93Quebec Pee-Wee Tournament-939

Drouin, Eric
92Quebec Pee-Wee Tournament-200
96Rimouski Oceanic-9
96Rimouski Oceanic Quebec Police-9
97Rimouski Oceanic-22
97Bowman CHL-67
OPC-67
98Bowman CHL-111
Golden Anniversary-111
OPC International-111
98Bowman Chrome CHL-111
Golden Anniversary-111
Golden Anniversary Refractors-111
OPC International-111
OPC International Refractors-111
Refractors-111
01Thetford Mines Coyotes-12
02Thetford Mines Coyotes-9

Drouin, Jerome
93Quebec Pee-Wee Tournament-949

Drouin, Jude
70Colgate Stamps-18
70O-Pee-Chee-171
70Sargent Promotions Stamps-88
71Letraset Action Replays-21
71O-Pee-Chee-68
O-Pee-Chee/Topps Booklets-21
71Sargent Promotions Stamps-81
71Topps-68
71Toronto Sun-128
72O-Pee-Chee-47
72Sargent Promotions Stamps-100
72Topps-153
73North Stars Action Posters-2
73North Stars Postcards-3
73O-Pee-Chee-125
73Topps-125
74NHL Action Stamps-139
74NHL Action Stamps Update-24
74O-Pee-Chee NHL-255
74Topps-255
75O-Pee-Chee NHL-224
75Topps-224
76O-Pee-Chee NHL-106
76Topps-106
77O-Pee-Chee NHL-182
77Topps-182
78O-Pee-Chee-93
78Topps-93
79Jets Postcards-5
79O-Pee-Chee-329
80Jets Postcards-6
80O-Pee-Chee-285
80Pepsi-Cola Caps-125

Drouin, P.C.
92Cornell Big Red-8
96Providence Bruins-17
97Charlotte Checkers-19
00UK Nottingham Panthers-10
00UK Sekonda Superleague-133
01UK Nottingham Panthers-9
02German DEL City Press-8
03Finnish Cardset-84
04Fort Wayne Komets-2
04Fort Wayne Komets Shoe Carnival-2
05Fort Wayne Komets Choice-12
05Fort Wayne Komets Sprint-4

Drouin, Polly
34Beehive Group I Photos-149
37O-Pee-Chee V304E-158
37V356 Worldwide Gum-50
38Quaker Oats Photos-11
39O-Pee-Chee V301-1-24

Drover, Jamie
93Quebec Pee-Wee Tournament-479

Drozdetski, Alexander
99Russian Hockey League-240
01Russian Hockey League-111
02Russian Hockey League-113
02Russian Hockey League-247
03Russian Hockey League-162
03Russian National Team-11

Drozdetski, Nikolai
81Swedish Semic Hockey VM Stickers-49
82Swedish Semic VM Stickers-63
83Swedish Semic VM Stickers-63

Drozdiak, Dean
83Victoria Cougars-7

Drtina, Jiri
02Sault Ste. Marie Greyhounds-17
05Czech HC Slavia Praha-5
06Czech HC Slavia Praha Postcards-6
06Czech OFS-293

Druce, John
89Capitals Kodak-19
89ProCards AHL-100
90Bowman Hat Tricks-16
Tiffany-16
90Capitals Kodak-5
90Capitals Postcards-5
90Capitals Smokey-5
90O-Pee-Chee-298
90Pro Set-310
90Score-246
Canadian-246
90Score Young Superstars-25
90Topps-298
Tiffany-298
90Upper Deck-371
French-371
91Pro Set Platinum-129
91Bowman-293
91Bowman-413
91Capitals Junior 5x7-8
91Capitals Kodak-8
91O-Pee-Chee-206
91Panini Stickers-200
91Parkhurst-415
French-415
91Pinnacle-395
French-395
91Pro Set-251
French-251
91Score American-180
91Score Canadian Bilingual-180
91Score Canadian English-180
91Stadium Club-331
91Topps-206
91Upper Deck-151
French-151
92Bowman-180
92O-Pee-Chee-105
92OPC Premier-80
92Parkhurst-437
Emerald Ice-437
92Pinnacle-185
French-185
92Score-121
Canadian-121
92Stadium Club-405
92Topps-188
Gold-188G
92Ultra-442
92Upper Deck-205
93PowerPlay-360
94Canada Games NHL POGS-124
94Donruss-223
94Leaf-131
94OPC Premier Special Effects-549
94Pinnacle-304
Artist's Proofs-304
Rink Collection-304
94Stadium Club-71
Members Only Master Set-71
First Day Issue-71
Super Team Winner Cards-71
94Topps/OPC Premier Special Effects-549
94Ultra-98
95Canada Games NHL POGS-135
95Collector's Choice-135
Player's Club-135
Player's Club Platinum-135
95Leaf-107
95Panini Stickers-269
95Pinnacle-113
Artist's Proofs-113
Rink Collection-113
95Topps-111
OPC Inserts-111
96Flyers Postcards-6
97Pacific Dynagon Best Kept Secrets-69
97Score Flyers-19
Platinum-19
Premier-19

Druce, Kevin
03Sault Ste. Marie Greyhounds-7

Druken, Harold
96Upper Deck-380
96Detroit Whalers-4
97Bowman CHL-146
OPC-146
Autographs-26
98Black Diamond-91
Double Diamond-91
Triple Diamond-91
Quadruple Diamond-91
98SPx Top Prospects-64
Radiance-64
Spectrum-64
99BAP Memorabilia-383
Gold-383
Silver-383
99Pacific Omega-239
Copper-239
Gold-239
Ice Blue-239
Premiere Date-239
99Upper Deck Gold Reserve-350
99Syracuse Crunch-1
99Bowman CHL-145
Gold-145
OPC International-145
00BAP Memorabilia-137
Emerald-137
Ruby-137
Sapphire-137
Promos-137
00BAP Mem Chicago Sportsfest Copper-137
00BAP Memorabilia Chicago Sportsfest Blue-137
00BAP Memorabilia Chicago Sportsfest Gold-137
00BAP Memorabilia Chicago Sportsfest Ruby-137
00BAP Memorabilia Chicago Sun-Times Ruby-137
00BAP Memorabilia Chicago Sun-Times Gold-137
00BAP Mem Chicago Sun-Times Sapphire-137
00BAP Mem Toronto Fall Expo Copper-137
00BAP Memorabilia Toronto Fall Expo Gold-137
00BAP Memorabilia Toronto Fall Expo Ruby-137
00BAP Signature Series-163
Emerald-163
Ruby-163
Sapphire-163
Autographs-129
Autographs Gold-129
00O-Pee-Chee-272
00O-Pee-Chee Parallel-272
00Pacific-407
Copper-407
Gold-407
Ice Blue-407
Premiere Date-407
00Topps/OPC-272
Parallel-272
00Topps Chrome-167
OPC Refractors-167
Refractors-167
00Upper Deck MVP-175
First Stars-175
Second Stars-175
Third Stars-175
00Upper Deck Victory-232
00Kansas City Blades-9
01BAP Memorabilia-224
Emerald-224
Ruby-224
Sapphire-224
01McDonald's Pacific Hometown Pride-8
01Upper Deck-172
Exclusives-172
01Upper Deck Victory-348
Gold-348
02BAP Sig Series Auto Buybacks 2000-129
02NHL Power Play Stickers-156
02Pacific Complete-295
Red-295

Drulia, Stan
84Belleville Bulls-9
88Niagara Falls Thunder-16
89ProCards AHL-138
90Knoxville Cherokees-107
91ProCards-379
92OPC Premier-105
92Parkhurst-177
Emerald Ice-177
92Upper Deck-487
93Parkhurst-191
Emerald Ice-191
93Atlanta Knights-14
94Atlanta Knights-14
95Atlanta Knights-6
96Detroit Vipers-6
96Collector's Edge Ice-100
Prism-100
QuantumMotion-6
97Detroit Vipers-4
98Detroit Vipers-12
98Detroit Vipers Freschetta-6
98IHL All-Star Eastern Conference-12
99Pacific Omega-214
Copper-214
Gold-214
Ice Blue-214
Premiere Date-214
99Ultimate Victory-81
1/1-81
Parallel-81
Parallel 100-81
99Detroit Vipers Kid's Club-4
00BAP Memorabilia-336
Emerald-336
Ruby-336
Sapphire-336
Promos-336
00BAP Mem Chicago Sportsfest Copper-336
00BAP Memorabilia Chicago Sportsfest Blue-336
00BAP Memorabilia Chicago Sportsfest Gold-336
00BAP Memorabilia Chicago Sportsfest Ruby-336
00BAP Memorabilia Chicago Sun-Times Ruby-336
00BAP Memorabilia Chicago Sun-Times Gold-336
00BAP Mem Chicago Sun-Times Sapphire-336
00BAP Mem Toronto Fall Expo Copper-336
00BAP Memorabilia Toronto Fall Expo Gold-336
00BAP Memorabilia Toronto Fall Expo Ruby-336
00Pacific-370
Copper-370
Gold-370
Ice Blue-370
Premiere Date-370
02Orlando Seals-3

Drummond, Kurt
95Swift Current Broncos-3
96Swift Current Broncos-16
97Swift Current Broncos-23
98Swift Current Broncos-7
99Bowman CHL-95
Gold-95
OPC International-95
00Hamilton Bulldogs-4
02Greensboro Generals RBI-8
03Greensboro Generals-181

Drummond, Robbie
02London Knights-24
03London Knights-23
04London Knights-6
05London Knights-15
06London Knights-11

Drury, Bryan
907th Inn. Sketch OHL-284

Drury, Chris
93Classic-101
95Donruss Elite World Juniors-34
95Upper Deck-569
Electric Ice-569
Electric Ice Gold-569
98Avalanche Team Issue-1
98Black Diamond-24
Double Diamond-24
Triple Diamond-24
Quadruple Diamond-24
Myriad-M11
Myriad 2-M11
Winning Formula Gold-WF16
Winning Formula Platinum-WF16
98Bowman's Best-102
Refractors-102
Atomic Refractors-102
Autographs-A8A
Autographs-A8B
Autographs Refractors-A8A
Autographs Refractors-A8B
Autographs Atomic Refractors-A8A
Autographs Atomic Refractors-A8B
Performers-BP7
Performers Refractors-BP7
Performers Atomic Refractors-BP7
98Crown Royale-32
Limited Series-32
Rookie Class-1
98Pacific Dynagon Ice-46
Blue-46
Red-46
Rookies-1
98Pacific Omega-67
Red-67
Opening Day Issue-67
98Revolution-34
Ice Shadow-34
Red-34
98SP Authentic-96
Power Shift-96
Snapshots-SS20
98SPx Top Prospects-17
Radiance-17
Spectrum-17
98Upper Deck-415
Exclusives-415
Exclusives 1 of 1-415
Generation Next-GN21
Generation Next Quantum 1-GN21
Generation Next Quantum 2-GN21
Generation Next Quantum 3-GN21
Profiles-P26
Profiles Quantum 1-P26
Profiles Quantum 2-P26
Profiles Quantum 3-P26
Gold Reserve-415

98Upper Deck MVP-54
Gold Script-54
Silver Script-54
Super Script-54
ProSign-CD
99Aurora-36
Striped-36
Premiere Date-36
Premiere Date Striped-36
99Avalanche Pins-7
99Avalanche Team Issue-5
99BAP Memorabilia-184
Gold-184
Silver-184
Selects Silver-SL19
Selects Gold-SL19
99BAP Millennium-69
Emerald-69
Ruby-69
Sapphire-69
Signatures-69
Signatures Gold-69
99Black Diamond-27
Diamond Cut-27
Final Cut-27
99Crown Royale-36
Limited Series-36
Premiere Date-36
Century 21-3
International Glory-5
International Glory Parallel-5
99Kraft Whiz Kid-5
99McDonald's Upper Deck-MCD18
99O-Pee-Chee-106
99O-Pee-Chee Autographs-TA6
99O-Pee-Chee Chrome-106
99O-Pee-Chee Chrome Refractors-106
99O-Pee-Chee Chrome Ice Futures-IF2
99O-Pee-Chee Chrome Ice Futures Refractor-IF2
99O-Pee-Chee Now Starring-NS6
99O-Pee-Chee Ice Futures-IF2
99Pacific-102
Copper-102
Emerald Green-102
Gold-102
Ice Blue-102
Premiere Date-102
Red-102
Gold Crown Die-Cuts-7
99Pacific Dynagon Ice-55
Blue-55
Copper-55
Gold-55
Premiere Date-55
Checkmates American-5
Checkmates American-20
Checkmates Canadian-20
99Pacific Omega-61
Copper-61
Gold-61
Ice Blue-61
Premiere Date-61
NHL Generations-3
99Pacific Prism-37
Holographic Blue-37
Holographic Gold-37
Holographic Mirror-37
Holographic Purple-37
Premiere Date-37
99Panini Stickers-4
99Panini Stickers-215
99Paramount-62
Copper-62
Emerald-62
Gold-62
Holographic Emerald-62
Holographic Gold-62
Holographic Silver-62
Ice Blue-62
Premiere Date-62
Red-62
Silver-62
Personal Best-8
Toronto Fall Expo '99-62
99Revolution-38
Premiere Date-38
Red-38
Shadow Series-38
Showstoppers-8
Top of the Line-11
Copper-38
Gold-38
CSC Silver-38
99SP Authentic-25
99SPx-42
Radiance-42
Spectrum-42
99Stadium Club-121
First Day Issue-121
One of a Kind-121
Printing Plates Black-121
Printing Plates Cyan-121
Printing Plates Magenta-121
Printing Plates Yellow-121
Capture the Action-CA2
Capture the Action Game View-CAG2
Chrome-36
Chrome Refractors-36
Co-Signers-CS1
Co-Signers-CS3
Lone Star Signatures-LS11
99Topps/OPC-106
Autographs-TA6
Ice Futures-IF2
Now Starring-NS6
99Topps/OPC Chrome-106
Refractors-106
Ice Futures-IF2
Ice Futures Refractors-IF2
99Topps Gold Label Class 1-48
Black-48
Black One of One-48
One of One-48
Red-48
Red One of One-48
99Topps Gold Label Class 2-48
99Topps Gold Label Class 2 Black-48
99Topps Gold Label Class 2 Black 1 of 1-48
99Topps Gold Label Class 2 One of One-48
99Topps Gold Label Class 2 Red-48
99Topps Gold Label Class 2 Red One of One-48
99Topps Gold Label Class 3-48
99Topps Gold Label Class 3 Black-48
99Topps Gold Label Class 3 Black 1 of 1-48
99Topps Gold Label Class 3 One of One-48
99Topps Gold Label Class 3 Red-48
99Topps Gold Label Class 3 Red One of One-48
99Topps Gold Label Fresh Gold-FG4
99Topps Gold Label Fresh Gold Black-FG4
99Topps Gold Label Fresh Gold Black 1of1-FG4
99Topps Gold Label Fresh Gold One of One-FG4
99Topps Gold Label Fresh Gold Red-FG4
99Topps Gold Label Fresh Gold Red 1 of 1-FG4
99Topps Premier Plus-8
99Topps Premier Plus-CTW1
Parallel-8
Calling All Calders-CAC1
Game Pieces-GPCD
The Next Ones-TNO3
99Topps Premiere Plus Promos-PP5
99Ultimate Victory-25
1/1-25
Parallel-25
Parallel 100-25
99Upper Deck-41
99Upper Deck-142
Exclusives-41
Exclusives-142
Exclusives 1 of 1-41
Exclusives 1 of 1-142
New Ice Age-N15
New Ice Age Quantum Gold-N15
New Ice Age Quantum Silver-N15
99Upper Deck Arena Giveaways-CA2
99Upper Deck Century Legends-74
Century Collection-74
99Upper Deck Gold Reserve-41
99Upper Deck Gold Reserve-142
UD Authentics-CD
99Upper Deck HoloGrFx-16
Ausome-16
UD Authentics-CD
99Upper Deck MVP-54
Gold Script-54
Silver Script-54
Super Script-54
21st Century NHL-10
ProSign-CD
99Upper Deck MVP SC Edition-53
Gold Script-53
Silver Script-53
Super Script-53
Cup Contenders-CC4
99Upper Deck Retro-23
Gold-23
Platinum-23
99Upper Deck Victory-76
99Upper Deck Victory-353
99Wayne Gretzky Hockey-47
Signs of Greatness-CD
00Aurora-37
Pinstripes-37
Premiere Date-37
Autographs-37
00BAP Memorabilia-162
Emerald-162
Ruby-162
Sapphire-162
Promos-162
00BAP Mem Chicago Sportsfest Copper-162
00BAP Memorabilia Chicago Sportsfest Blue-162
00BAP Memorabilia Chicago Sportsfest Gold-162
00BAP Memorabilia Chicago Sportsfest Ruby-162
00BAP Memorabilia Chicago Sun-Times Ruby-162
00BAP Memorabilia Chicago Sun-Times Gold-162
00BAP Mem Chicago Sun-Times Sapphire-162
00BAP Mem Toronto Fall Expo Copper-162
00BAP Memorabilia Toronto Fall Expo Gold-162
00BAP Memorabilia Toronto Fall Expo Ruby-162
00BAP Parkhurst 2000-P51
00BAP Signature Series-82
Emerald-82
Ruby-82
Sapphire-82
Autographs-70
Autographs Gold-70
00BAP Ultimate Memorabilia Autographs-40
Gold-40
00Black Diamond Game Gear-GDR
00Crown Royale-27
Ice Blue-27
Limited Series-27
Premiere Date-27
Red-27
00O-Pee-Chee-77
00O-Pee-Chee Parallel-77
00Pacific-111
Copper-111
Gold-111
Ice Blue-111
Premiere Date-111
2001: Ice Odyssey-5
00Pacific 2001: Ice Odyssey Anaheim Ntnl-5
00Paramount-58
Copper-58
Gold-58
Holo-Gold-58
Holo-Silver-58
Ice Blue-58
Premiere Date-58
Game Used Sticks-4
00Private Stock Game Gear-22
00Private Stock PS-2001 Action-9
00Revolution-35
Blue-35
Premiere Date-35
Red-35
00Stadium Club-87
00Topps/OPC-77
Parallel-77
00Topps Chrome-60
OPC Refractors-60
Refractors-60
00Topps Gold Label Class 1-29
Gold-29
00Topps Gold Label Class 2-29
00Topps Gold Label Class 2 Gold-29
00Topps Gold Label Class 3-29
00Topps Gold Label Class 3 Gold-29
00Topps Gold Label New Generation-NG14
00Topps Gold Label New Generation 1 to 1-NG14
00Topps Heritage-72
Chrome Parallel-72
New Tradition-NT7
00Topps Premier Plus-82
Blue Ice-82
00UD Heroes-28
00Upper Deck-274
Exclusives Tier 1-274
Exclusives Tier 2-274
00Upper Deck Legends-33
Legendary Collection Bronze-33
Legendary Collection Gold-33
Legendary Collection Silver-33
00Upper Deck MVP-47
First Stars-47
Second Stars-47
Third Stars-47
00Upper Deck Victory-59
00Upper Deck Vintage-94
00Vanguard-26
Holographic Gold-26
Holographic Purple-26
Pacific Proofs-26
01Atomic-23
Blue-23
Gold-23
Premiere Date-23
Red-23
01Avalanche Team Issue-11
01BAP Memorabilia-49
Emerald-49
Ruby-49
Sapphire-49
Stanley Cup Champions-CA14
Stanley Cup Playoffs-SC30
01BAP Signature Series Certified 100-C7
01BAP Signature Series Certified 50-C7
01BAP Signature Series Certified 1 of 1's-C7
01BAP Signature Series Autographs-LCD
01BAP Signature Series Autographs Gold-LCD
01BAP Sig Series He Shoots/Scores Prizes-29
01BAP Signature Series Jerseys-GJ-18
01BAP Signature Series Jersey Autographs-GUCD
01BAP Sig Series Jersey and Stick Cards-GSJ-18
01BAP Signature Series Emblems-GUE-17
01BAP Signature Series Numbers-ITN-17
01BAP Signature Series Teammates-TM-9
01BAP Ultimate Memorabilia Calder Trophy-3
01Bowman YoungStars-69
Gold-69
Ice Cubed-69
01Crown Royale-36
Blue-36
Premiere Date-36
Red-36
Retail-36
01O-Pee-Chee-35
01O-Pee-Chee Heritage Parallel-35
01O-Pee-Chee Heritage Parallel Limited-35
01O-Pee-Chee Premier Parallel-35
01Pacific-99
Extreme LTD-99
Hobby LTD-99
Premiere Date-99
Retail LTD-99
01Pacific Adrenaline-46
Blue-46
Premiere Date-46
Red-46
Retail-46
World Beaters-2
01Pacific Arena Exclusives-99
01Pacific Heads-Up-22
Blue-22
Premiere Date-22
Red-22
Silver-22
Breaking the Glass-6
01Parkhurst-91
Gold-91
Silver-91
He Shoots-He Scores Prizes-26
Jerseys-PJ30
Sticks-PS30
Teammates-T5
Teammates-T22
01Private Stock-21
Gold-21
Premiere Date-21
Retail-21
Silver-21
Game Gear-28
01Private Stock Pacific Nights-21
01Private Stock PS-2002-17
01SP Authentic-20
Limited-20
Limited Gold-20
01SP Game Used-11
01SPx-82
01SPx-169
Hidden Treasures-DTTD
01Stadium Club-93
Award Winners-93
Master Photos-93
Gallery-G8
Gallery Gold-G8
NHL Passport-NHLP13
Souvenirs-JSCD
Souvenirs-PFCD
Souvenirs-JSCDPF
01Titanium Double-Sided Jerseys-11
01Titanium Double-Sided Patches-11
01Topps-35
Heritage Parallel-35
Heritage Parallel Limited-35
OPC Parallel-35
Autographs-ACD
Game-Worn Jersey-JCD
Jumbo Jersey Autographs-JJA-CD
01Topps Chrome-35
Refractors-35
Black Border Refractors-35
01Topps Heritage-66
Refractors-66
01Topps Heritage Avalanche NHL AS Game-6
01Topps Reserve-70
Emblems-CD
Jerseys-CD
Name Plates-CD
Numbers-CD
Patches-CD
01UD Challenge for the Cup-19
01UD Honor Roll-92
Jerseys-J-CD
Jerseys Gold-J-CD
01UD Mask Collection-20
Gold-20
Double Patches-DPCD
Gloves-GGCD
Jerseys-J-CD
Jersey and Patch-JPCD
01UD Playmakers-25
01UD Premier Collection-14
Dual Jerseys-DDM
Dual Jerseys-DFD
Dual Jerseys Black-DDM
Dual Jerseys Black-DFD
Jerseys-BCD
Jerseys Black-B-CD
01UD Stanley Cup Champs-35
01UD Top Shelf-88
01Upper Deck-46
Exclusives-46
Crunch Timers-CT3
Game Jerseys Series II-FJCD
Game Jerseys Series II-SSCD
Game Jerseys Series II-DJTD
Gate Attractions-GA7
01Upper Deck Avalanche NHL All-Star Game-PP4
01Upper Deck MVP-46
01Upper Deck Victory-89
Gold-89
01Upper Deck Vintage-62
01Vanguard-24
Blue-24
Red-24
One of Ones-24
Premiere Date-24
Proofs-24
Quebec Tournament Heroes-13
01Czech Stadion-229
02Atomic-23
Blue-23
Gold-23
Red-23
Hobby Parallel-23
02BAP First Edition-93
Jerseys-93
02BAP Memorabilia-47
02BAP Memorabilia-255
Emerald-47
Emerald-255
Ruby-47
Ruby-255
Sapphire-47
Sapphire-255
NHL All-Star Game-47
NHL All-Star Game-255
NHL All-Star Game Blue-47
NHL All-Star Game Blue-255
NHL All-Star Game Green-47
NHL All-Star Game Green-255
NHL All-Star Game Red-47
NHL All-Star Game Red-255
Stanley Cup Playoffs-SC-18
02BAP Memorabilia Toronto Fall Expo-47
02BAP Memorabilia Toronto Fall Expo-255
02BAP Signature Series-99
Autographs-99
Autograph Buybacks 1999-69
Autograph Buybacks 2000-70
Autograph Buybacks 2001-LCD
Autographs Gold-99
Golf-GS19
02Bowman YoungStars-17
Gold-17
Silver-17
02Crown Royale-13
Blue-13
Red-13
Retail-13
02NHL Power Play Stickers-12
02O-Pee-Chee-31
02O-Pee-Chee-31U
02O-Pee-Chee Premier Blue Parallel-31
02O-Pee-Chee Premier Red Parallel-31
02O-Pee-Chee Factory Set-31
02Pacific-88
Blue-88
Red-88
Jerseys-10
Jerseys Holo-Silver-10
02Pacific Calder-7
Silver-7
02Pacific Complete-121
Red-121
02Pacific Exclusive-22
02Pacific Heads-Up-29
Blue-29
Purple-29
Red-29
Quad Jerseys-8
Quad Jerseys Gold-8
02Pacific Quest for the Cup-11
Gold-11
02Parkhurst-49
Bronze-49
Gold-49
Silver-49
College Ranks-CR1
College Ranks Jerseys-CRM1
02Parkhurst Retro-137
Minis-137
02Private Stock Reserve-14
Blue-14
Red-14
Retail-14
02SP Authentic-20
Beckett Promos-20
Super Premiums-DPDS
02SP Game Used Authentic Fabrics-AFCD
02SP Game Used Authentic Fabrics-AFDR
02SP Game Used Authentic Fabrics Gold-AFCD
02SP Game Used Authentic Fabrics Gold-AFDR
02SP Game Used Authentic Fabrics Rainbow-AFCD
02SP Game Used Authentic Fabrics Rainbow-AFDR
02SP Game Used Piece of History-PHCD
02SP Game Used Piece of History-PHDR
02SP Game Used Piece of History Gold-PHCD
02SP Game Used Piece of History Gold-PHDR
02SP Game Used Piece of History Rainbow-PHCD
02SP Game Used Piece of History Rainbow-PHDR
02SPx-17
Spectrum Gold-17
Spectrum Silver-17
02Stadium Club-21
Silver Decoy Cards-21
Proofs-21
Champions Fabric-FC10
World Stage-WS2
02Titanium-14
Blue-14
Red-14
Retail-14
Jerseys-11
Jerseys Retail-11
Patches-11
02Topps-31
02Topps-31U
OPC Blue Parallel-31
OPC Red Parallel-31
Factory Set-31
02Topps Chrome-31
Black Border Refractors-31
Refractors-31
02Topps Heritage-100
Chrome Parallel-100
Autographs-CD
Autographs Black-CD
Autographs Red-CD
Calder Cloth-CD
02Topps Total-126
02UD Honor Roll-9
Students of the Game-SG5
02UD Mask Collection-15
02UD Mask Collection Beckett Promos-15
02UD Mask Collection Instant Offense-IOCD
02UD Piece of History-25
Awards Collection-AC5
Threads-TTCD
02UD Premier Collection Jerseys Bronze-CD
02UD Premier Collection Jerseys Gold-CD
02UD Premier Collection Jerseys Silver-CD
02UD Premier Collection Patches-PCD
02UD Top Shelf Clutch Performers-CPCD
02UD Top Shelf Sweet Sweaters-SWCD
02Upper Deck-45
02Upper Deck-231
02Upper Deck-271
Exclusives-45
Exclusives-231
Exclusives-271
02Upper Deck Beckett UD Promos-271
02Upper Deck Letters of Note-LNCD
02Upper Deck Letters of Note Gold-LNCD
02Upper Deck Patchwork-PWCD
02Upper Deck Pinpoint Accuracy-PACD
02Upper Deck Playbooks Series II-HD
02Upper Deck Specialists-SCD
02Upper Deck Classic Portraits-27
Hockey Royalty-RDF
Hockey Royalty Limited-RDF
Stitches-CCD
Stitches Limited-CCD
02Upper Deck MVP-48
Gold-48
Classics-48
Golden Classics-48
Overdrive-SO5
Skate Around Jerseys-SACD
Skate Around Jerseys-SDDG
Skate Around Jerseys-SDDH
Skate Around Jerseys-SDSD
Skate Around Jerseys-STTDG
Skate Around Jerseys-STTDH
02Upper Deck Rookie Update-16
02Upper Deck Rookie Update-153A
02Upper Deck Victory-52
Bronze-52
Gold-52
Silver-52
National Pride-NP53
02Upper Deck Vintage-69
Green Backs-69
Jerseys-FSCD
Jerseys-SOCD
Jerseys Gold-SO-CD
Jerseys Gold-FS-CD
Tall Boys-T18
Tall Boys Gold-T18
02Vanguard-14
LTD-14
Jerseys-7
Jerseys Gold-7
03BAP Memorabilia-16
Emerald-16
Gold-16
Ruby-16
Sapphire-16
03BAP Ultimate Memorabilia Autographs-7
Gold-7
03Beehive-25
Variations-25
Gold-25
Silver-25
Jumbo Jerseys-BH7
Jerseys-JT30
03Black Diamond-130
Black-130
Green-130
Red-130
03Bowman-64
Gold-64
03Bowman Chrome-64
Refractors-64
Gold Refractors-64
Xfractors-64
03ITG Action Jerseys-M102
03ITG Used Signature Series-11
Gold-11
Autographs-CD
Autographs Gold-CD
03McDonald's Pacific-6
03NHL Sticker Collection-165
03O-Pee-Chee-126
03OPC Blue-126
03OPC Gold-126
03OPC Red-126
03Pacific-48
Blue-48
Red-48
Jerseys-7
Jerseys Gold-7
03Pacific Complete-194
Red-194
03Pacific Exhibit-18
Blue Backs-18
Yellow Backs-18
03Pacific Prism-106
Blue-106
Patches-106
Red-106
Retail-106
03Pacific Supreme-10
Blue-10
Red-10
Retail-10
Jerseys-4
03Private Stock Reserve-147
Blue-147
Patches-147
Red-147
Retail-147
03SP Authentic-9
Limited-9
03SP Game Used-7
Gold-7
Authentic Fabrics-DFCM
Authentic Fabrics Gold-DFCM
Authentic Patches-APCD
Double Threads-DTDS
Limited Threads-LTCD
Limited Threads Gold-LTCD
03SPx-12
Radiance-12
Spectrum-12
Fantasy Franchise-FF-DSA
Fantasy Franchise Limited-FF-DSA
VIP-VIP-DA
VIP Limited-VIP-DA
Winning Materials-WM-CD
Winning Materials Limited-WM-CD
03Topps-126
Blue-126
Gold-126
Red-126
Topps/OPC Idols-UI4
03Topps C55-98
Minis-98
Minis American Back-98
Minis American Back Red-98
Minis Bazooka Back-98
Minis Brooklyn Back-98
Minis Hat Trick Back-98
Minis O Canada Back-98
Minis O Canada Back Red-98
Minis Stanley Cup Back-98
Autographs-TA-CD
03Topps Pristine-39
Gold Refractor Die Cuts-39
Refractors-39
Press Plates Black-39
Press Plates Cyan-39
Press Plates Magenta-39
Press Plates Yellow-39
03Topps Traded-TT2
Blue-TT2
Gold-TT2
Red-TT2
03UD Honor Roll-8
03UD Premier Collection-8
03Upper Deck-267
Canadian Exclusives-267
Franchise Fabrics-FF-CD
HG-267
Patches-SP7
UD Exclusives-267
03Upper Deck Classic Portraits-11
Classic Colors-CC-CD
Starring Cast-SC-CD
03Upper Deck Ice-10
Gold-10
03Upper Deck MVP-58
Gold Script-58
Silver Script-58
Canadian Exclusives-58
Souvenirs-S1
SportsNut-SN16
03Upper Deck Rookie Update-9
03Upper Deck Rookie Update-173
Skills-SKCD
03Upper Deck Trilogy-11
Limited-11
03Upper Deck Victory-28
Bronze-28
Gold-28
Silver-28
04Pacific-31
Blue-31
Red-31
04SP Authentic Buybacks-21
04SP Authentic Buybacks-22
04SP Authentic Buybacks-23
04SP Authentic Buybacks-24
04SP Authentic Buybacks-25
04SP Authentic Buybacks-26
04SP Authentic Rookie Review-RR-CD
04SP Authentic Sign of the Times-ST-CD
04SP Authentic Sign of the Times-DS-BD
04SP Authentic Sign of the Times-FS-NED
04SP Authentic Sign of the Times-SS-USA
04Ultimate Collection-5
Buybacks-4
Patch Autographs-UPA-CD
Signatures-US-CD
Signature Logos-ULA-CD
Signature Patches-SP-CD
04Upper Deck World Cup Tribute-CD
04Upper Deck World Cup Tribute-DWMOCD
05Be A Player-10
First Period-10
Second Period-10
Third Period-10
Overtime-10
Dual Signatures-BD
Dual Signatures-GD
Outtakes-OT7
Signatures-CD
Signatures Gold-CD
Triple Signatures-BUF
05Beehive-12
Matte-12
Matted Materials-MMCD
05Black Diamond-10
Emerald-10
Gold-10
Onyx-10
Ruby-10
Gemography-G-CD
Gemography Emerald-G-CD
Gemography Gold-G-CD
Gemography Onyx-G-CD
Gemography Ruby-G-CD
05Hot Prospects-12
En Fuego-12
Red Hot-12
White Hot-12
05Panini Stickers-33
05Parkhurst-52
05Parkhurst-504
Facsimile Auto Parallel-52
Facsimile Auto Parallel-504
True Colors-TCBUF
True Colors-TCBUF
05SP Authentic-13
Limited-13
Sign of the Times Duals-DDV
Sign of the Times Triples-TDBV
05SP Game Used-12
Autographs-12
Gold-12
Authentic Fabrics-AF-CD
Authentic Fabrics Autographs-AAF-CD
Authentic Fabrics Gold-AF-CD
Authentic Fabrics Quad-BADS
Authentic Patches Quad -BADS
Authentic Patches-AP-CD
Authentic Patches Autographs-AAP-CD
Auto Draft-AD-CD
Awesome Authentics-AA-CD
Awesome Authentics Gold-DA-CD
Game Gear-GG-CD
Game Gear Autographs-AG-CD
Signature Sticks-SS-CD
SIGnificance-CD
SIGnificance Gold-S-CD
Statscriptions-ST-CD
05SPx-11
Spectrum-11
Winning Combos-WC-DB
Winning Combos Autographs-AWC-DB
Winning Combos Gold-WC-DB
Winning Combos Spectrum-WC-DB
Winning Materials-WM-CD
Winning Materials Autographs-AWM-CD
Winning Materials Gold-WM-CD
Winning Materials Spectrum-WM-CD
05The Cup-15
Gold-15
Black Rainbow-15
Emblems of Endorsement-EECD
Hardware Heroes-HHCD
Honorable Numbers-HNCD
Limited Logos-LLCD
Masterpiece Pressplates-15
Noble Numbers-NNHD
Patch Variation-P15
Patch Variation Autographs-AP15
Scripted Numbers-SNHD
Scripted Numbers Dual-DSNDM
Scripted Swatches-SSCD
Signature Patches-SPCD
Stanley Cup Titlists-TCD
05UD Artifacts-14
Blue-14
Gold-14
Green-14
Pewter-14
Red-14
Auto Facts-AF-CD
Auto Facts Blue-AF-CD
Auto Facts Copper-AF-CD
Auto Facts Pewter-AF-CD
Auto Facts Silver-AF-CD
Gold Autographed-14
Remarkable Artifacts-RA-CD
Remarkable Artifacts Dual-RA-CD
05UD Powerplay Specialists-TSCD
05UD Powerplay Specialists Patches-SPCD
05Ultimate Collection-12
Gold-12
Endorsed Emblems-EECD
National Heroes Jerseys-NHJCD
National Heroes Patches-NHPCD
05Ultra-24
Gold-24
Fresh Ink-FI-CD
Fresh Ink Blue-FI-CD
Ice-24
05Upper Deck-19
Big Playmakers-B-CD
HG Glossy-19
Jerseys-J-CD
Notable Numbers-N-CD
Patches-P-CD
Shooting Stars-S-CD
05Upper Deck Ice-13
Rainbow-13
05Upper Deck MVP-43
Gold-43
Platinum-43
05Upper Deck Rookie Update-11
05Upper Deck Trilogy-13
05Upper Deck Trilogy-97
Crystal-97
Honorary Patches-HP-CD
Honorary Patch Scripts-HSP-CD
Honorary Swatch Scripts-HSS-CD
Scripts-SCS-CD
05Upper Deck Toronto Fall Expo-19
05Upper Deck Victory-21
Black-21
Gold-21
Silver-21
Game Breakers-GB6
06Be A Player-137
Autographs-137
Signatures-CD
Signatures 10-152
Signatures 25-152
Signatures Duals-DDR
Signatures Trios-TDBV
Up Close and Personal-UC10
Up Close and Personal Autographs-UC10
06Be A Player Portraits-14
Dual Signature Portraits-DSDB
Signature Portraits-SPCD
Triple Signature Portraits-TBUF
06Beehive-89
06Beehive-226
Blue-89
Gold-89
Matte-89
Red Facsimile Signatures-89
Wood-89
Matted Materials-MMCD
Remarkable Matted Materials-MMCD
06Black Diamond-90
Black-90
Gold-90
Ruby-90
Jerseys-JCD
Jerseys Black-JCD
Jerseys Gold-JCD
Jerseys Ruby-JCD
Jerseys Black Autographs -JCD
06Flair Showcase-13
06Flair Showcase-110
06Flair Showcase-209
Parallel-13
Parallel-110
Parallel-209
Inks-ICD
Stitches-SSCD
06Fleer-23
Tiffany-23
Fabricology-FCD
Signing Day-SDCD
Speed Machines-SM6
06Hot Prospects Hot Materials -HMCD
06Hot Prospects Hot Materials Red Hot-HMCD
06Hot Prospects Hot Materials White Hot-HMCD
06O-Pee-Chee-59
Rainbow-59
Swatches-S-CD
06Panini Stickers-29
06SP Authentic-90
Limited-90
Sign of the Times Triples-ST3DBM
06SP Game Used-12
Gold-12
Rainbow-12
Authentic Fabrics-AFCD
Authentic Fabrics Parallel-AFCD
Authentic Fabrics Patches-AFCD
Authentic Fabrics Dual-AF2DM
Authentic Fabrics Dual Patches-AF2DM
Authentic Fabrics Triple-AF3BUF
Authentic Fabrics Triple Patches-AF3BUF
Authentic Fabrics Quads-AF4MWGD
Authentic Fabrics Quads Patches-AF4MWGD
Authentic Fabrics Sevens-AF7CAL
Authentic Fabrics Sevens Patches-AF7CAL
Inked Sweaters Dual-IS2DM
Inked Sweaters Dual Patches-IS2DM
06SPx-11
Spectrum-11
SPxcitement-X13
SPxcitement Spectrum-X13
Winning Materials-WMCD
Winning Materials Spectrum-WMCD
Winning Materials Autographs-WMCD
06The Cup Autographed NHL Shields Duals-DASBD
06The Cup Autographed NHL Shields Duals-DASDS
06The Cup Autographed NHL Shields Duals-DASMD
06The Cup Enshrinements-ECD
06The Cup NHL Shields Duals-DSHDA
06The Cup NHL Shields Duals-DSHLY
06The Cup Scripted Swatches-SSCD
06UD Artifacts-89
Blue-89
Gold-89
Platinum-89
Radiance-89
Autographed Radiance Parallel-89
Red-89
Auto-Facts-AFCD
Auto-Facts Gold-AFCD
Frozen Artifacts-FACD
Frozen Artifacts Black-FACD
Frozen Artifacts Blue-FACD
Frozen Artifacts Gold-FACD
Frozen Artifacts Platinum-FACD
Frozen Artifacts Red-FACD
Frozen Artifacts Autographed Black-FACD
Frozen Artifacts Patches Black-FACD
Frozen Artifacts Patches Blue-FACD
Frozen Artifacts Patches Gold-FACD
Frozen Artifacts Patches Platinum-FACD
Frozen Artifacts Patches Red-FACD
Frozen Artifacts Patches Autographed Black Tag Parallel-FACD
Tundra Tandems-TTAD
Tundra Tandems Black-TTAD
Tundra Tandems Blue-TTAD
Tundra Tandems Gold-TTAD
Tundra Tandems Platinum-TTAD
Tundra Tandems Red-TTAD
Tundra Tandems Dual Patches Red-TTAD
06UD Mini Jersey Collection-12
06UD Powerplay-11
Impact Rainbow-11
Power Marks-PMCD
06Ultimate Collection Premium Patches-PS-CD
06Ultimate Collection Premium Swatches-PS-CD
06Ultimate Collection Ultimate Signatures Logos-SL-CD
06Ultra-25
Gold Medallion-25
Ice Medallion-25
Fresh Ink-ICD
Uniformity-UCD
Uniformity Patches-UPCD
Uniformity Autographed Jerseys-UACD
06Upper Deck Arena Giveaways-BUF6
06Upper Deck-23
Exclusives Parallel-23
High Gloss Parallel-23
Game Dated Moments-GD31
Game Jerseys-JCD
Game Patches-PCD
Masterpieces-23
06Upper Deck MVP-31
Gold Script-31
Super Script-31
Autographs-OADA
Jerseys-OJDK
Jerseys-OJSD
06Upper Deck Ovation-155
06Upper Deck Sweet Shot-15
Signature Shots/Saves Sticks-SSSCD
Signature Sticks-STCD
Sweet Stitches-SSCD
Sweet Stitches Duals-SSCD
Sweet Stitches Triples-SSCD
06Upper Deck Trilogy-12
Honorary Scripted Patches-HSPCD
Honorary Scripted Swatches-HSSCD
Honorary Swatches-HSCD
Ice Scripts-ISCD
Scripts-TSCD
06Upper Deck Victory-20
06Upper Deck Victory Black-20
06Upper Deck Victory Gold-20
07Upper Deck Victory-38
Black-38
Gold-38
GameBreakers-GB7

Drury, Ted

92Upper Deck-396
92Harvard Crimson-7
93Donruss-58
93Donruss-437
Rated Rookies-14
93Leaf-424
93Parkhurst-35
Emerald Ice-35
93Pinnacle-447
Canadian-447
93PowerPlay-303
93Score-608
Gold-608
Canadian-608
Canadian Gold-608
93Stadium Club-443
Members Only Master Set-443
First Day Issue-443

93Ultra-280
Wave of the Future-4
93Upper Deck-466
SP-20
93Classic-63
94Be A Player Signature Cards-34
94Donruss-186
94Leaf-22
94OPC Premier-157
Special Effects-157
94Parkhurst-96
Gold-96
94Pinnacle-187
Artist's Proofs-187
Rink Collection-187
94Topps/OPC Premier-157
Special Effects-157
94Ultra-88
94Upper Deck-205
Electric Ice-205
94Classic Autographs-NNO
94Classic Pro Prospects-14
International Heroes-LP2
94Images *-38
95Parkhurst International-422
Emerald Ice-422
95Senators Team Issue-9
95Upper Deck-298
Electric Ice-298
Electric Ice Gold-298
96Collector's Choice-183
96Ducks Team Issue-5
96Upper Deck-115
97Be A Player-84
Autographs-84
Autographs Die-Cuts-84
Autographs Prismatic Die-Cuts-84
97Collector's Choice-6
97Pacific-312
Copper-312
Emerald Green-312
Ice Blue-312
Red-312
Silver-312
97Score Mighty Ducks-11
Platinum-11
Premier-11
98Be A Player-5
Press Release-5
98BAP Gold-5
98BAP Autographs-5
98BAP Autographs Gold-5
98BAP Tampa Bay All Star Game-5
98OPC Chrome-212
Refractors-212
98Topps-212
O-Pee-Chee-212
99Upper Deck MVP SC Edition-116
Gold Script-116
Silver Script-116
Super Script-116
00Paramount-69
Copper-69
Gold-69
Holo-Gold-69
Holo-Silver-69
Ice Blue-69
Premiere Date-69
00Private Stock-28
Gold-28
Premiere Date-28
Retail-28
Silver-28
00Chicago Wolves-7
01Albany River Rats-14
02BAP Sig Series Auto Buybacks 1998-5
02German DEL City Press-91
03German DEL-155
04German DEL All-Stars-AS11
04German DEL Update-322B
05German DEL-355
06German DEL-133
All-Star Jerseys-AS4
Team Leaders-TL2

Dryden, Dave
64Beehive Group III Photos-33
65Coca-Cola-36
67Topps-57
68O-Pee-Chee-150
68Shirriff Coins-30
70Colgate Stamps-80
71O-Pee-Chee-159
71Sabres Postcards-90
71Sargent Promotions Stamps-32
71Toronto Sun-25
72O-Pee-Chee-241
72Sabres Postcards-5
72Sargent Promotions Stamps-34
73O-Pee-Chee-63
73Sabres Postcards-2
73Topps-187
74O-Pee-Chee WHA-20
75O-Pee-Chee WHA-104
75Sabres Linnett-3
76O-Pee-Chee WHA-85
77O-Pee-Chee WHA-28
77Sportscasters-8223
77Finnish Sportscasters-85-2024
79Oilers Postcards-6
79O-Pee-Chee-71
79Topps-71
88Oilers Tenth Anniversary-90

Dryden, Henry
99Sioux City Musketeers-5

Dryden, Ken
70Canadiens Pins-3
70Swedish Masterserien-26
70Swedish Masterserien-93
71Canadiens Postcards-5
71Colgate Heads-3
71Frito-Lay-2
71Letraset Action Replays-2
71Letraset Action Replays-22
71O-Pee-Chee-45
O-Pee-Chee/Topps Booklets-17
Posters-22
71Topps-45
71Toronto Sun-149
72Canadiens Postcards-5
72Canadiens Great West Life Prints-3
72Dimanche/Derniere Heure *-138
72O-Pee-Chee-145
72O-Pee-Chee-247
Player Crests-12
Team Canada-7
72Sargent Promotions Stamps-124
72Topps-127
72Topps-160
72Swedish Stickers-111
73O-Pee-Chee-136
73Topps-4
73Topps-10
74Canadiens Postcards-5
74Lipton Soup-19
74NHL Action Stamps-158
74O-Pee-Chee NHL-155
74Topps-155
75Canadiens Postcards-5
75O-Pee-Chee NHL-35
75O-Pee-Chee NHL-213
75Topps-35
75Topps-213
76Canadiens Postcards-5
76O-Pee-Chee NHL-6
76O-Pee-Chee NHL-200
76Topps-6
76Topps-200
76Topps Glossy Inserts-5
77Canadiens Postcards-5
77O-Pee-Chee NHL-6
77O-Pee-Chee NHL-8
77O-Pee-Chee NHL-100
77Sportscasters-1423
77Topps-6
77Topps-8
77Topps-100
77Topps/O-Pee-Chee Glossy-5
Square-5
77Finnish Sportscasters-48-1145
78Canadiens Postcards-5
78O-Pee-Chee-5
78O-Pee-Chee-68
78O-Pee-Chee-70
78O-Pee-Chee-330
78Topps-50
78Topps-68
78Topps-70
79O-Pee-Chee-6
79O-Pee-Chee-8
79O-Pee-Chee-150
79Topps-6
79Topps-8A
79Topps-8B
79Topps-150
83Hall of Fame-196
83Hall of Fame Postcards-N4
85Hall of Fame-196
88Esso All-Stars-9
91Future Trends Canada '72-85
91Future Trends Canada '72 French-85
91Finnish Semic World Champ Stickers-236
91Swedish Semic World Champ Stickers-236
93O-Pee-Chee Canadiens Hockey Fest-51
96Swedish Semic Wien Hockey Legends-HL1
99Upper Deck Retro-101
Gold-101
Platinum-101
Memento-RM5
03Czech Stadion-549
06Between The Pipes The Mask-M09
06Between The Pipes The Mask Gold-M09
06Between The Pipes The Mask Silver-M09
06Between The Pipes The Mask Game-Used-MGU04
06Between The Pipes The Mask Game-Used Gold-MGU04

Drynin, Vitali
01Russian Hockey League-140

Dshunussov, Danniar
04German DEL Update-296

Dshunussow, Danier
04German Berlin Polar Bears Postcards-8
05German DEL-24

Duba, Lukas
96Czech APS Extraliga-236
06Czech HC Vsetin Postcards-5
06Czech OFS-177

Duba, Tomas
99Czech OFS-539
00Czech OFS-292
01Finnish Cardset-325
02Finnish Cardset-14
02Finnish Cardset-150
02Finnish Cardset Dynamic Duos-8
02Czech OFS Plus-252
03Czech OFS Plus-373
03Czech OFS Plus Insert M-M19
03Czech OFS Plus MS Praha-SE38
04Czech HC Plzen Postcards-5
04Czech OFS-140
Czech/Slovak-6
Goals-Against Leaders-8
Save Percentage Leaders-10
Team Cards-7
05Swedish SHL Elitset-203
Gold-203
Series Two Signatures-14
06Swedish SHL Elitset Goal Patrol-9

Dubbin, Luke
03Sudbury Wolves-7
04Sudbury Wolves-1

Dubchek, Merv
99Fort Wayne Komets Points Leaders-8

Dube, Christian
93Sherbrooke Faucons-3
94Parkhurst SE-SE258
Gold-SE258
94Select-166
Gold-166
94SP-179
Die Cuts-179
95Donruss Elite World Juniors-13
95SP-171
95Classic-34
96Black Diamond-79
Gold-79
96Collector's Choice-357
96Donruss Canadian Ice-146
Gold Press Proofs-146
Red Press Proofs-146
96Donruss Elite-137
Die Cut Stars-137
Aspirations-25
96Leaf Preferred-135
Press Proofs-135
96Metal Universe-176
96Select Certified-95
Artist's Proofs-95
Blue-95
Mirror Blue-95
Mirror Gold-95
Mirror Red-95
Red-95
96SP-183
96Ultra-104
Gold Medallion-104
Rookies-5
96Upper Deck-296
96Upper Deck Ice-136
96Zenith-135
Artist's Proofs-135
97Donruss Limited-46
Exposure-46
97Paramount-113
Copper-113
Dark Grey-113
Emerald Green-113
Ice Blue-113
Red-113
Silver-113
97Score Rangers-14
Platinum-14
Premier-14
97Upper Deck-105
Game Dated Moments-105
97Hartford Wolf Pack-5
98Hartford Wolf Pack-5
99BAP Memorabilia-46
Gold-46
Silver-46
99Swiss Panini Stickers-167
00Swiss Panini Stickers-210
00Swiss Slapshot Mini-Cards-HCL13
01Swiss HNL-39
02Swiss HNL-267

Dube, Danielle
02Bakersfield Condors-5

Dube, Dany
92Alberta International Team Canada-7
93Alberta International Team Canada-3
97Collector's Choice-288

Dube, Gilles
44Beehive Group II Photos-234
51Laval Dairy Subset-50
52St. Lawrence Sales-75

Dube, Jim
02Reading Royals-8
02Reading Royals RBI Sports-173
03Kalamazoo Wings-6

Dube, Michel
01Moncton Wildcats-9
02Moncton Wildcats-20

Dube, Nigel
06Penticton Vees-7

Dube, Norm
77O-Pee-Chee WHA-54

Dube, Roger
93Swedish Semic World Champ Stickers-262
94French National Team-10

Dube, Serge
98Sudbury Wolves-18
03Laredo Bucks-6

Dube, Yanick
917th Inn. Sketch QMJHL-227
93Donruss Team Canada-9
93Parkhurst-512
Emerald Ice-512
93Pinnacle-471
Canadian-471
93Upper Deck-533
94Classic CHL All-Stars-C2
94Signature Rookies Gold Standard *-82
95Signature Rookies-3
Club Promos-4
Signatures-3
96Swiss HNL-437
99German Bundesliga 2-26
01Swiss HNL-372

Dubeau, Martin
93Quebec Pee-Wee Tournament-24

Dubec, Marek
02Czech OFS Plus-66
03Czech OFS Plus-25
03Czech OFS Plus-370
04Czech OFS-246
06Czech OFS-178

Dubek, Vladimir
95Slovakian-Quebec Pee-Wee Tournament-6

Dubel, Jon
00Sioux Falls Stampede-8
03Minnesota State Mavericks-5

Duben, Miroslav
97Czech APS Extraliga-300
98Czech DS-37
98Czech DS Stickers-114
98Czech OFS-298
98Czech OFS-477
99Czech Score Blue 2000-42
99Czech Score Red Ice 2000-42
00Czech OFS-37
02Czech OFS Plus-215
03Czech OFS Plus-50
04Czech OFS-85
05Czech HC Karlovy Vary-3
06Czech OFS-26

Duben, Premysl
00Baie-Comeau Drakkar-11
Signed-11

Duberman, Justin
92Cleveland Lumberjacks-18
93Donruss-471
93Cleveland Lumberjacks-11
93Cleveland Lumberjacks Postcards-9
93Classic Pro Prospects-116
95South Carolina Stingrays-22

Dubielewicz, Wade
03ITG Action-673
03ITG VIP Rookie Debut-146
03Parkhurst Rookie-99
03Upper Deck Rookie Update-187
03Bridgeport Sound Tigers-1A
03Pacific AHL Prospects-9
Gold-9
Autographs-3
Jerseys-1
06Between The Pipes-53
Autographs-AWD

Dubinin, Anton
03Russian Under-18 Team-8

Dubinsky, Brandon
03Portland Winter Hawks-15
04Portland Winter Hawks-5
06Hartford Wolf Pack-28
07Upper Deck Victory-226
Black-226
Gold-226

Dubinsky, Mike
92Brandon Wheat Kings-4
93Brandon Wheat Kings-19
94Brandon Wheat Kings-5
95Signature Rookies-42
Signatures-42
95Slapshot Memorial Cup-37

Dubinsky, Steve
92Clarkson Knights-5
92Clarkson Knights-24
93Donruss-70
93Parkhurst-40
Emerald Ice-40
93Upper Deck-477
93Indianapolis Ice-8
93Classic-64
94Donruss-26
94Leaf-426
94OPC Premier-233
Special Effects-233
94Topps/OPC Premier-233
Special Effects-233
94Indianapolis Ice-5
94Classic Pro Prospects-7
95Indianapolis Ice-6
97Be A Player-166
Autographs-166
Autographs Die-Cuts-166
Autographs Prismatic Die-Cuts-166
97Pacific Dynagon Best Kept Secrets-21
99BAP Millennium-45
Emerald-45
Ruby-45
Sapphire-45
Signatures-45
Signatures Gold-45
99Stadium Club-32
First Day Issue-32
One of a Kind-32
Printing Plates Black-32
Printing Plates Cyan-32
Printing Plates Magenta-32
Printing Plates Yellow-32
01Pacific-85
Extreme LTD-85
Hobby LTD-85
Premiere Date-85
Retail LTD-85
01Pacific Arena Exclusives-85
01Milwaukee Admirals-9
02BAP Sig Series Auto Buybacks 1999-45
02Worcester IceCats-12

Dubkov, Ilja
93Roanoke Express-7
94Roanoke Express-15
95Roanoke Express-10
96Roanoke Express-21
98Danish Hockey League-154
99Danish Hockey League-161

Dubnyk, Devan
02Kamloops Blazers-3
03Kamloops Blazers-20
04ITG Top Prospects Spring Expo-13
04Kamloops Blazers-4
04ITG Heroes and Prospects-71
Aspiring-10
Autographs-DD
Combos-3
Complete Emblems-1
Emblems-18
Emblems Gold-18
He Shoots-He Scores Prizes-16
Jersey Autographs-18
Jerseys-18
Jerseys Gold-18
Net Prospects-17
Net Prospects Gold-17
Numbers-18
Numbers Gold-18
Top Prospects-13
04ITG Heroes/Prospects Toronto Expo '05-71
04ITG Heroes/Prospects Expo Heroes/Pros-71
05ITG Heroes/Prosp Toronto Expo Parallel -178
05Kamloops Blazers-22
05ITG Heroes and Prospects-178
Autographs-A-DD
Autographs-DA-DF
Jerseys-GUJ-113
Jerseys Gold-GUJ-113
Emblems-GUE-96
Emblems Gold-GUE-96
Numbers-GUN-96
Numbers Gold-GUN-96
Measuring Up-MU14
Measuring Up Gold-MU14
Net Prospects-NP-14
Net Prospects Dual-NPD8
Net Prospects Dual Gold-NPD8
Net Prospects Gold-NP-14
06Between The Pipes Autographs-ADD
06Between The Pipes The Mask-M32
06Between The Pipes The Mask Gold-M32
06Between The Pipes The Mask Silver-M32
06Stockton Thunder-2
06ITG Heroes and Prospects Quad Emblems-QE08
06ITG Heroes and Prospects Quad Emblems Gold-QE08

Dubois, Daniel
93Swiss HNL-193
95Swiss HNL-371
96Swiss HNL-231

Dubois, Eric
907th Inn. Sketch QMJHL-55
907th Inn. Sketch Memorial Cup-68
91Greensboro Monarchs-5
93Atlanta Knights-12
94Atlanta Knights-13
95Atlanta Knights-7
98Val d'Or Foreurs-25
01German Upper Deck-230

Dubois, Gilles
95Swiss HNL-382
96Swiss HNL-243
99Swiss Panini Stickers-304

Dubois, Guy
72Finnish Semic World Championship-152
72Swedish Semic World Championship-152
74Finnish Typotor-103

Dubois, Jonathan
98Huntsville Channel Cats-4

Dubois, Mathieu
93Quebec Pee-Wee Tournament-1598

Dubois, Pierre
79Montreal Juniors-7

Dubois, Robert
93Oshawa Generals-16
95Slapshot-30
95Barrie Colts-8

Dubois, Sebastien
93Quebec Pee-Wee Tournament-316

Dubord, Jocelyn
93Quebec Pee-Wee Tournament-73

Dubreuil, Marc
93Quebec Pee-Wee Tournament-315

Dubrovski, Dmitri
98Russian Hockey League-87
99Russian Hockey League-235
01Russian Hockey League-139

Dubuc, Maxime
05Saint John's Sea Dogs-15
06Saint Johns Sea Dogs-13

Dubuc, Michael
04P.E.I. Rocket-15
05PEI Rocket-20

Duca, Paolo
99Swiss Panini Stickers-18
00Swiss Panini Stickers-17
00Swiss Slapshot Mini-Cards-HCAP11
01Swiss HNL-15
02Swiss EV Zug Postcards-20
02Swiss HNL-69
03Swiss EV Zug Postcards-9
04Swiss EV Zug Postcards-20

Duce, Brad
94Thunder Bay Flyers-9

Duce, Bryan
95Slapshot-145
96Kitchener Rangers-10

Duchaine, Kevin
02Drummondville Voltigeurs-20

Ducharme, Bruno
907th Inn. Sketch QMJHL-202
917th Inn. Sketch QMJHL-250

Ducharme, Sylvain
917th Inn. Sketch QMJHL-278
93Drummondville Voltigeurs-7

Duchesne, Alexandre
90Montreal-Bourassa AAA-10
917th Inn. Sketch QMJHL-290
93Drummondville Voltigeurs-24

Duchesne, Cliff
96OCN Blizzard-11
97OCN Blizzard-16
98OCN Blizzard-15

Duchesne, Eric
907th Inn. Sketch QMJHL-37
917th Inn. Sketch QMJHL-84

Duchesne, Gaetan
80Quebec Remparts-6
81Capitals Team Issue-4
82Post Cereal-20
84Capitals Pizza Hut-4
85Capitals Pizza Hut-3
86Capitals Kodak-6
86Capitals Police-6
87Nordiques General Foods-7
87Nordiques Team Issue-9
87Panini Stickers-183
88Nordiques General Foods-10
88Nordiques Team Issue-10
88O-Pee-Chee-208
88O-Pee-Chee Stickers-187
88Panini Stickers-353
89O-Pee-Chee Stickers-194
90O-Pee-Chee-319
90Panini Stickers-256
90Pro Set-137
90Score-375
Canadian-375
90Topps-319
Tiffany-319
90Upper Deck-108
French-108
91Bowman-120
91O-Pee-Chee-433
91Panini Stickers-117
91Parkhurst-305
French-305
91Pro Set-110
French-110
91Score Canadian Bilingual-440
91Score Canadian English-440
91Stadium Club-153
91Topps-433
91Upper Deck-207
French-207
92Bowman-266
92Durivage Panini-22
92O-Pee-Chee-143
92Pinnacle-198
French-198
92Score-338
Canadian-338
92Stadium Club-307
92Topps-406
Gold-406G
92Ultra-318
92Upper Deck-469
93Donruss-301
93Durivage Score-40
93Leaf-339
93Panini Stickers-273
93Parkhurst-456
Emerald Ice-456
93Pinnacle-377
Canadian-377
93PowerPlay-433
93Score-226
93Score-545
Gold-545
Canadian-226
Canadian-545
Canadian Gold-545
94Canada Games NHL POGS-211
94Leaf-547
94OPC Premier-232
Special Effects-232
94Pinnacle-219
Artist's Proofs-219
Rink Collection-219
94Score-196
Gold-196
Platinum-196
94Topps/OPC Premier-232
Special Effects-232
95Canada Games NHL POGS-119

Duchesne, Jeremy
03Victoriaville Tigres-8
04Halifax Mooseheads-26
04Victoriaville Tigres-2
05Halifax Mooseheads-1
06Halifax Mooseheads-1

Duchesne, Paul
51Laval Dairy Lac St. Jean-45
52Bas Du Fleuve-46

Duchesne, Steve
86Kings 20th Anniversary Team Issue-3
88Kings Postcards-3
88Kings Smokey-6
88O-Pee-Chee-182
88O-Pee-Chee Stickers-152
88Panini Stickers-70
88Topps-182
89Kings Smokey-14
89Kraft-58
89O-Pee-Chee-123
89O-Pee-Chee Stickers-65
89O-Pee-Chee Stickers-150
89O-Pee-Chee Stickers-165
89Panini Stickers-93
89Panini Stickers-176
89Topps-123
89Topps Sticker Inserts-10
90Bowman-146
Tiffany-146
90Kings Smokey-15
90Kraft-65
90O-Pee-Chee-86
90Panini Stickers-241
90Pro Set-115
90Pro Set-350
90Score-26
Canadian-26
90Score Hottest/Rising Stars-15
90Topps-86
Tiffany-86
90Upper Deck-136
French-136
91Pro Set Platinum-86
91Bowman-191
91Flyers J.C. Penney-7
91O-Pee-Chee-31
91OPC Premier-13
91Panini Stickers-80
91Parkhurst-125
French-125
91Pinnacle-42
French-42
91Pro Set-96
91Pro Set-448
French-96
French-448
91Score American-205
91Score Canadian Bilingual-205
91Score Canadian Bilingual-569
91Score Canadian English-205
91Score Canadian English-569
91Score Rookie/Traded-19T
91Stadium Club-58
91Topps-31
91Upper Deck-570
French-570
91Finnish Semic World Champ Stickers-61
91Swedish Semic World Champ Stickers-61
92Bowman-31
92Durivage Panini-38
92Nordiques Petro-Canada-5
92O-Pee-Chee-296
92OPC Premier-130
92Panini Stickers-192
92Panini Stickers French-192
92Parkhurst-143
Emerald Ice-143
92Pinnacle-320
French-320
92Pro Set-137
92Score-151
Canadian-151
92Stadium Club-313
92Topps-271
Gold-271G
92Ultra-384
92Upper Deck-513
93Donruss-276
93Donruss-484
93Leaf-176
93McDonald's Upper Deck-14
93OPC Premier-151
Gold-151
93Panini Stickers-76
93Parkhurst-168
Emerald Ice-168
93Pinnacle-78
Canadian-78
All-Stars-16
All-Stars Canadian-16
93PowerPlay-197
93Score-190
Canadian-190
93Stadium Club All-Stars-8
93Stadium Club All-Stars Members Only-8
93Stadium Club All-Stars OPC-8
93Topps/OPC Premier-151
Gold-151
93Topps Premier Black Gold-2
93Ultra-7
93Upper Deck-217
93Upper Deck Locker All-Stars-2
93Swedish Semic World Champ Stickers-194
94Be A Player-R64
Signature Cards-137
94Canada Games NHL POGS-210
94Donruss-304
94EA Sports-109
94Flair-152
94Fleer-186
94Hockey Wit-8
94Leaf-3
94Leaf Limited-93
94OPC Premier-401
Special Effects-401
94Parkhurst-205
Gold-205
Vintage-V26
94Pinnacle-108
Artist's Proofs-108
Rink Collection-108
94Post Box Backs-9
94Score-52
Gold-52
Platinum-52
94Select-145
Gold-145
94Stadium Club-81
Members Only Master Set-81
First Day Issue-81
Super Team Winner Cards-81
94Topps/OPC Premier-401
Special Effects-401
94Ultra-182
94Upper Deck-108
Electric Ice-108
SP Inserts-SP158
SP Inserts Die Cuts-SP158
95Bashan Super Stickers-87
Die-Cut-15
95Canada Games NHL POGS-196
95Collector's Choice-279
Player's Club-279
Player's Club Platinum-279
95Donruss-278
95Emotion-124
95Finest-17
Refractors-17
95Imperial Stickers-87
Die Cut Superstars-15
95Leaf-143
95Metal-105
95Panini Stickers-195
95Parkhurst International-153
Emerald Ice-153
95Playoff One on One-88
95Post Upper Deck-3
95Score-99
Black Ice Artist's Proofs-99
Black Ice-99
95Senators Team Issue-10
95SkyBox Impact-119
95Stadium Club-126
Members Only Master Set-126
95Summit-145
Artist's Proofs-145
Ice-145
95Topps-102
95Topps-337
OPC Inserts-102
OPC Inserts-337
95Ultra-138
95Ultra-279
Gold Medallion-138
95Upper Deck-49
Electric Ice-49
Electric Ice Gold-49
Special Edition-SE147
Special Edition Gold-SE147
95Zenith-111
95Swedish World Championships Stickers-3
96Be A Player-141
Autographs-141
Autographs Silver-141
96Collector's Choice-182
96Donruss-182
Press Proofs-182
96Fleer-75
96Metal Universe-106
96Playoff One on One-347
96Post Upper Deck-5
96Score-62
Artist's Proofs-62
Dealer's Choice Artist's Proofs-62
Special Artist's Proofs-62
Golden Blades-62
96Senators Pizza Hut-7
96SkyBox Impact-89
96Team Out-57
96Topps Picks-73
OPC Inserts-73
96Ultra-117
Gold Medallion-117
96Upper Deck-304
96Swedish Semic Wien-84
97Collector's Choice-179
97Crown Royale-115
Emerald Green-115
Ice Blue-115
Silver-115
97Pacific-302
Copper-302
Emerald Green-302
Ice Blue-302
Red-302
Silver-302
97Pacific Invincible-94
Copper-94
Emerald Green-94
Ice Blue-94
Red-94
Silver-94
97Pacific Omega-192
Copper-192
Dark Gray-192
Emerald Green-192
Gold-192
Ice Blue-192
97Panini Stickers-45
97Pinnacle-142
Press Plates Back Black-142
Press Plates Back Cyan-142
Press Plates Back Magenta-142
Press Plates Back Yellow-142
Press Plates Front Black-142
Press Plates Front Cyan-142
Press Plates Front Magenta-142
Press Plates Front Yellow-142
97Pinnacle Inside-136
97Revolution-119
Copper-119
Emerald-119
Ice Blue-119
Silver-119
97Score-230
97Score Blues-16
Platinum-16
Premier-16
97SP Authentic-144
97Upper Deck-114
98Be A Player-215
Press Release-215
98BAP Gold-215
98BAP Autographs-215
98BAP Autographs Gold-215
98OPC Chrome-44
Refractors-44
98Pacific-366
Ice Blue-366
Red-366
98Panini Stickers-158
98Topps-44
O-Pee-Chee-44
98UD Choice-182
Prime Choice Reserve-182
Reserve-182
98Upper Deck-286
Exclusives-286
Exclusives 1 of 1-286
Gold Reserve-286
98Upper Deck MVP-93
Gold Script-93
Silver Script-93
Super Script-93
99Panini Stickers-237
99Stadium Club-166
First Day Issue-166
One of a Kind-166
Printing Plates Black-166
Printing Plates Cyan-166
Printing Plates Magenta-166
Printing Plates Yellow-166
00BAP Memorabilia-253
Emerald-253
Ruby-253
Sapphire-253
Promos-253
00BAP Mem Chicago Sportsfest Copper-253
00BAP Memorabilia Chicago Sportsfest Blue-253
00BAP Memorabilia Chicago Sportsfest Gold-253
00BAP Memorabilia Chicago Sportsfest Ruby-253
00BAP Memorabilia Chicago Sun-Times Ruby-253
00BAP Memorabilia Chicago Sun-Times Gold-253
00BAP Mem Chicago Sun-Times Sapphire-253
00BAP Mem Toronto Fall Expo Copper-253
00BAP Memorabilia Toronto Fall Expo Gold-253
00BAP Memorabilia Toronto Fall Expo Ruby-253
02BAP Sig Series Auto Buybacks 1998-215

Duchesneau, Jonathan
03Baie Comeau Drakkar-7
04Baie-Comeau Drakkar-9
05Baie-Comeau Drakkar-7
06Drummondville Voltigeurs-7

Duck, Alexander
00German DEL-213
01German Upper Deck-270
02German DEL City Press-281
04German Krefeld Penguins Postcards-2
05German DEL-222

Duco, Michael
04Kitchener Rangers-21
05Kitchener Rangers-16
06Kitchener Rangers-5

Ducolon, Toby
88ProCards IHL-92
89ProCards IHL-12

Duda, Jason
93Saskatoon Blades-8
98Wichita Thunder-6
99Wichita Thunder-5
00Wichita Thunder-6

Duda, Radek
97Czech APS Extraliga-16
99Lethbridge Hurricanes-7
00Czech OFS-314
01Czech National Team Postcards-4
01Czech OFS-212
02Czech DS-10
02Czech DS-87
02Czech OFS Plus-257
02Czech OFS Plus-361
Trios-T10
Duos-D15
03Russian Hockey League-157
03Russian SL-2
03Russian World Championship Stars-28
04Czech HC Slavia Praha Postcards-2
04Czech OFS-160
Stars-22
05Czech HC Slavia Praha-6
06Czech OFS Goals Leaders-11
06Czech OFS Points Leaders-7

Dudacek, Jiri
83Swedish Semic VM Stickers-99

Dudarev, Dmitri
00Russian Dynamo Moscow-26
00Russian Hockey League-239
02Russian Hockey League-81
03Russian Hockey League-177
04Russian RHL-16

Dudas, Jesse
04Lethbridge Hurricanes-21

Dudek, Joe
97Dubuque Fighting Saints-13

Dudik, Dimitri
98German DEL-265
99German DEL-32
00German DEL-187

Dudley, George S
83Hall of Fame Postcards-E8
85Hall of Fame-68

Dudley, Myles
93Quebec Pee-Wee Tournament-829

Dudley, Rhett
98Wichita Thunder-7
99Wichita Thunder-6
00Wichita Thunder-7
01El Paso Buzzards-2
02El Paso Buzzards-2

Dudley, Rick
74NHL Action Stamps-39
74O-Pee-Chee NHL-268
74Sabres Postcards-4
75O-Pee-Chee WHA-58
75Stingers Kahn's-3
76O-Pee-Chee WHA-17
76Stingers Kahn's-1
79O-Pee-Chee-37
79Topps-37
80O-Pee-Chee-355
81O-Pee-Chee-362
88ProCards AHL-201
89Sabres Campbell's-5
89New Haven Nighthawks-14
90Pro Set-662
90Sabres Campbell's-6
92San Diego Gulls-7
93Sabres Noco-2
93Phoenix Roadrunners-5

Due-Boje, Christian
84Swedish Semic Elitserien-129
86Swedish Panini Stickers-64
87Swedish Panini Stickers-75
89Swedish Semic Elitserien Stickers-55
90Swedish Semic Elitserien Stickers-278
91Swedish Semic Elitserien Stickers-77
92Swedish Semic Elitserien Stickers-99
93Swedish Semic Elitserien-52
94Finnish Jaa Kiekko-55

94Swedish Leaf-109
Gold Cards-4
95Swedish Leaf-28
95Swedish Upper Deck-39
97Swedish Collector's Choice-169
98German DEL-300
99German DEL-245
00Swedish Upper Deck-139

Dueck, Alexander
04German DEL-225

Dueling, Jarrett
917th Inn. Sketch WHL-93

Duerden, Dave
95Slapshot-321
95Classic-94
97Bowman CHL-3
OPC-3
98Kentucky Thoroughblades-8
99Pacific Omega-104
Copper-104
Gold-104
Ice Blue-104
Premiere Date-104
99Louisville Panthers-7
00Hartford Wolf Pack-8
00Louisville Panthers-7

Dufalt, Pascal
907th Inn. Sketch QMJHL-76

Duff, Dick
44Beehive Group II Photos-397
55Parkhurst-18
Quaker Oats-18
57Parkhurst-T3
58Parkhurst-29
59Parkhurst-38
60Parkhurst-12
60Shirriff Coins-2
60York Photos-8
61Parkhurst-12
61Shirriff/Salada Coins-53
61York Yellow Backs-2
62Parkhurst-2
62Shirriff Coins-12
62York Iron-On Transfers-7
63Chex Photos-11
63Maple Leafs Team Issue-6
63Parkhurst-4
63Parkhurst-64
63Toronto Star-11
63York White Backs-9
64Beehive Group III Photos-102
64Beehive Group III Photos-123
64Canadiens Postcards-5
64Coca-Cola Caps-79
64Topps-46
65Coca-Cola-60
65Topps-7
66Canadiens IGA-3
66Topps-71
67Canadiens IGA-8
67Post Flip Books-6
67Topps-2
67York Action Octagons-26
68Canadiens IGA-8
68Canadiens Postcards BW-4
68O-Pee-Chee-161
68Shirriff Coins-85
69O-Pee-Chee-11
70Dad's Cookies-25
70Sargent Promotions Stamps-65
71O-Pee-Chee-164
71Sabres Postcards-77
71Sargent Promotions Stamps-24
71Toronto Sun-26
80Maple Leafs Postcards-10
92Parkhurst Parkie Reprints-PR24
94Parkhurst Missing Link-126
94Parkhurst Missing Link-167
94Parkhurst Tall Boys-106
95Parkhurst '66-67-78
Coins-78
01Topps Archives-48
02Parkhurst Reprints-201
02Parkhurst Reprints-219
02Parkhurst Reprints-231
02Parkhurst Reprints-248
02Parkhurst Reprints-261
02Parkhurst Reprints-271
02Parkhurst Reprints-294
02Topps Rookie Reprints-12
02Topps Rookie Reprint Autographs-12
03Parkhurst Original Six Toronto-48
Autographs-4
04ITG Franchises Canadian-90
Autographs-DD
06ITG Heroes and Prospects-11
Autographs-ADD

Duff, John
91Ferris State Bulldogs-12
92Ferris State Bulldogs-12

Duff, Les
52Juniors Blue Tint-155
63Rochester Americans-12

Duff, Nick
03Brampton Batallion-4
03Kitchener Rangers-7
04Brampton Battalion-7
05Brampton Battalion-3

Duffey, Ben
84Minnesota-Duluth Bulldogs-1

Duffus, Parris
91Air Canada SJHL-D49
92Peoria Rivermen-2
93Peoria Rivermen-5
94Classic Pro Prospects-68
96Las Vegas Thunder-6
97Pinnacle Inside-75
Coach's Collection-75
Executive Collection-75
98German DEL-119
00German DEL-184
01Russian Hockey League-68
02Finnish Cardset-162
02Fort Wayne Komets-6

Duffy, Ben
85Minnesota-Duluth Bulldogs-31

Duffy, Francois
93Quebec Pee-Wee Tournament-25

Duffy, Matt
05Maine Black Bears-6

Dufort, Jean-Francois
99Shawinigan Cataractes-20
Signed-20
00Shawinigan Cataractes-23
Signed-23
01Cape Breton Screaming Eagles-20
01Shawinigan Cataractes-23
02Cape Breton Screaming Eagles-19

Dufour, Christine
04Wisconsin Badgers Women-5

Dufour, Guy
72O-Pee-Chee-328
73O-Pee-Chee WHA Posters-3

Dufour, Jean-Francois
99Ohio State Buckeyes-6
00Ohio State Buckeyes-2
01Asheville Smoke-20
03Wheeling Nailers-83

Dufour, Luc
83Bruins Team Issue-4
83NHL Key Tags-6
83O-Pee-Chee-48
83O-Pee-Chee Stickers-172
83O-Pee-Chee Stickers-182
83Topps Stickers-172
83Topps Stickers-182
84Nordiques Postcards-7
84O-Pee-Chee-3

Dufour, Luc (Jrs)
84Chicoutimi Sagueneens-8

Dufour, Marc
61Sudbury Wolves-7
62Sudbury Wolves-9

Dufour, Marcel
51Laval Dairy Lac St. Jean-8

Dufour, Martin
93Quebec Pee-Wee Tournament-540

Dufour, Michel
83Fredericton Express-3

Dufour, Pierre
99Danish Hockey League-124

Dufour, Rejean
04St Georges de Beauce Garaga-22

Dufresne, Dan
91Air Canada SJHL-A36
92Cornell Big Red-9
93Cornell Big Red-8

Dufresne, Donald
88ProCards AHL-298
89Canadiens Postcards-12
90Canadiens Postcards-14
90Pro Set-469
90Score Rookie/Traded-35T
90Upper Deck-332
French-332
91Canadiens Panini Team Stickers-10
91Canadiens Postcards-11
91Pro Set-418
French-418
91Score Canadian Bilingual-392
91Score Canadian English-392
92Canadiens Postcards-10
92Durivage Panini-39
93Leaf-355
93Parkhurst-467
Emerald Ice-467
93Ultra-422
94Be A Player Signature Cards-45
96Oilers Postcards-34

Dufresne, Ken
06Gatineau Olympiques-23

Dufresne, Ross
01BC Icemen-8

Dufresne, Sylvain
01Flint Generals-2
06Springfield Falcons-7

Duggan, Ben
06UK Guildford Flames-10

Duggan, Brad
81Saskatoon Blades-5

Duggan, Chris
03Lubbock Cotton Kings-7

Dugre, Jocelyn
92Quebec Pee-Wee Tournament-748
93Quebec Pee-Wee Tournament-468

Dugre, Yvan
51Laval Dairy QSHL-49

Duguay, Olivier
93Quebec Pee-Wee Tournament-416

Duguay, Ron
78O-Pee-Chee-177
78Topps-177
79O-Pee-Chee-208
79Topps-208
80O-Pee-Chee-37
80Topps-37
81O-Pee-Chee-223
81O-Pee-Chee Stickers-171
81Topps-E96
82O-Pee-Chee-217
82O-Pee-Chee-221
82O-Pee-Chee Stickers-134
82Post Cereal-13
82Topps Stickers-134
83NHL Key Tags-87
83O-Pee-Chee-121
83Puffy Stickers-13
84O-Pee-Chee-52
84O-Pee-Chee Stickers-42
84Topps-40
85O-Pee-Chee-116
85O-Pee-Chee Stickers-32
857-Eleven Credit Cards-5
85Topps-116
86Penguins Kodak-7
87O-Pee-Chee-110
87Panini Stickers-119
87Red Wings Little Caesars-9
87Topps-110
88Kings Postcards-16
88Kings Smokey-7
89Panini Stickers-96
91ProCards-317
97Sudbury Wolves Anniversary-6
02UD Foundations-27
02UD Foundations-41
02UD Foundations-68
Canadian Heroes-CRD
Canadian Heroes Gold-CRD
Canadian Heroes Silver-C-RD
Classic Greats-GRD
Classic Greats Gold-GRD
Classic Greats Silver-G-RD
03Parkhurst Original Six New York-43
Autographs-3
04ITG Franchises US East-390
Autographs-A-RDU
Original Sticks-EOS4
Original Sticks Autographs-EOS-RD
Original Sticks Gold-EOS4
04UD Legendary Signatures-75
Autographs-DU
06Parkhurst-53
Autographs-53
06Upper Deck Game Jerseys-J2DU
06Upper Deck Game Patches-J2DU

Duguid, Lorne
33O-Pee-Chee V304B-58
33V252 Canadian Gum-19
33V357 Ice Kings-52

Duhaime, Trevor
917th Inn. Sketch QMJHL-165
92Fort Worth Fire-6
92Hampton Roads Admirals-6

Duhamel, Benoit
02Drummondville Voltigeurs-14

Duhamel, Cedrick
01Sherbrooke Castors-8

Duhart, Jim
93Flint Generals-9
94Flint Generals-7
95Flint Generals-25
98Madison Monsters-13
01Flint Generals-3
04Richmond Riverdogs-4

Duke, Ryan
93Quebec Pee-Wee Tournament-1434

Duke, Steve
98Johnstown Chiefs-21
99Mississippi Sea Wolves-7
00Charlotte Checkers-23

Dukelow, Tyler
99Brampton Battalion-16

Dukovac, Paul
93Wichita Thunder-5

Dulac-Lemelin, Alexandre
04Baie-Comeau Drakkar-2
05Baie-Comeau Drakkar-15

Dulle, Kenton
06Saskatoon Blades-6

Duma, Pavel
99Russian Hockey League-130
00Russian Hockey League-287

Dumaine, Trent
91Air Canada SJHL-E24

Dumais, Olivier
93Quebec Pee-Wee Tournament-1066

Dumart, Woody
34Beehive Group I Photos-13
36Providence Reds-3
39O-Pee-Chee V301-1-94
44Beehive Group II Photos-16
51Parkhurst-28
52Parkhurst-72
53Parkhurst-96
91Bruins Sports Action Legends-36
94Kollectorfest-1
94Parkhurst Missing Link Pop-Ups-P9
98Bruins Alumni-14
Autographs-14
01Parkhurst Autographs-PA9
01Parkhurst Reprints-PR6
01Parkhurst Reprints-PR23
01Parkhurst Reprints-PR99
03BAP Ultimate Mem Linemates Autos-3
03Parkhurst Original Six Boston-55
03Parkhurst Original Six Boston-69
03Parkhurst Original Six Boston-88
04ITG Franchises US East-310
04ITG Ultimate Memorabilia-110
Gold-110
Autographs-69
Autographs Gold-69
04ITG Heroes and Prospects-180
04ITG Heroes/Prospects Toronto Expo '05-180
04ITG Heroes/Prospects Expo Heroes/Pros-180
05ITG Ultimate Mem Beantown's Best Autos-4
06ITG Ultimate Memorabilia Beantown's Best Autos-8

Dumas Jr., Denis
77Granby Vics-9

Dumas, Alex
00Asheville Smoke-22
01Columbus Cottonmouths-3

Dumas, Claude
03UK Coventry Blaze History-14

Dumas, Mark
88ProCards AHL-69

Dumas, Mathieu
01Cape Breton Screaming Eagles-19
02Val d'Or Foreurs-11
03Val d'Or Foreurs-12

Dumas, Rob
91Nashville Knights-11
92Nashville Knights-13
95Vancouver VooDoo RHI-11
97Idaho Steelheads-1
98Idaho Steelheads-5
99Idaho Steelheads-16
00Tacoma Sabercats-6

Dumas, Roger
52Bas Du Fleuve-22

Dumba, Jared
96Saskatoon Blades-9
02Indianapolis Ice-5
03Indianapolis Ice-7
04Austin Ice Bats-17

Dumbrowski, Adam
00Swift Current Broncos-6

Dumnov, Vladimir
99Russian Hockey League-34

Dumonski, Steve
95Slapshot-67
96Detroit Whalers-5
00Rockford IceHogs-7
02Rockford Ice Hogs-14

Dumont, Benoit
93Quebec Pee-Wee Tournament-77

Dumont, Eric
93Quebec Pee-Wee Tournament-1081

Dumont, Francis
93Quebec Pee-Wee Tournament-262

Dumont, Jean-Pierre
92Quebec Pee-Wee Tournament-560
95Bowman Draft Prospects-P13
97Beehive-68
Authentic Autographs-68
Golden Portraits-68
97Bowman CHL-60
OPC-60
98SP Authentic-94
Power Shift-94
98SPx Top Prospects-11
Radiance-11
Spectrum-11
98UD Choice-271
Prime Choice Reserve-271
Reserve-271
98Portland Pirates-1
99Aurora-31
Premiere Date-31
99BAP Memorabilia-270
Gold-270
Silver-270
Selects Silver-SL21
Selects Gold-SL21
99BAP Millennium-57
Emerald-57
Ruby-57
Sapphire-57
Signatures-57
Signatures Gold-57
Calder Candidates Ruby-C18
Calder Candidates Emerald-C18
Calder Candidates Sapphire-C18
99O-Pee-Chee-121
99O-Pee-Chee Chrome-121
99O-Pee-Chee Chrome Refractors-121
99Pacific-86
Copper-86
Emerald Green-86
Gold-86
Ice Blue-86
Premiere Date-86
Red-86
99Pacific Dynagon Ice-49
Blue-49
Copper-49
Gold-49
Premiere Date-49
99Pacific Omega-58
Copper-58
Gold-58
Ice Blue-58
Premiere Date-58
99Pacific Prism-33
Holographic Blue-33
Holographic Gold-33
Holographic Mirror-33
Holographic Purple-33
Premiere Date-33
99Panini Stickers-204
99Paramount-54
Copper-54
Emerald-54
Gold-54
Holographic Emerald-54
Holographic Gold-54
Holographic Silver-54
Ice Blue-54
Premiere Date-54
Red-54
99Revolution-33
Premiere Date-33
Red-33
Shadow Series-33
Copper-33
Gold-33
CSC Silver-33
99SPx-33
Radiance-33
Spectrum-33
99Stadium Club-190
First Day Issue-190
One of a Kind-190
Printing Plates Black-190
Printing Plates Cyan-190
Printing Plates Magenta-190
Printing Plates Yellow-190
Capture the Action-CA7
Capture the Action Game View-CAG7
Chrome-45
Chrome Refractors-45
99Topps Arena Giveaways-CHI-JD
99Topps/OPC-121
99Topps/OPC Chrome-121
Refractors-121
99Topps Premier Plus-131
Parallel-131
Premier Rookies-PR9
Premier Rookies Parallel-PR9
99Topps Premiere Plus Promos-PP2
99Upper Deck-35
Exclusives-35
Exclusives 1 of 1-35
New Ice Age-N20
New Ice Age Quantum Gold-N20
New Ice Age Quantum Silver-N20
99Upper Deck Arena Giveaways-CB1
99Upper Deck Gold Reserve-35
99Upper Deck HoloGrFx-13
Ausome-13
99Upper Deck MVP-44
Gold Script-44
Silver Script-44
Super Script-44
99Upper Deck Ovation-14
Standing Ovation-14
99Upper Deck Victory-66
99Wayne Gretzky Hockey-41
00BAP Memorabilia-428
Emerald-428
Ruby-428
Sapphire-428
00BAP Parkhurst 2000-P117
00BAP Signature Series-123
Emerald-123
Ruby-123
Sapphire-123
00Titanium-8
Blue-8
Gold-8
Premiere Date-8
Red-8
Retail-8
00UD Heroes-15
00Upper Deck Ice-63
01Atomic-12
Blue-12
Gold-12
Premiere Date-12
Red-12
01BAP Memorabilia-71
Emerald-71
Ruby-71
Sapphire-71
01BAP Signature Series-4
Autographs-4
Autographs Gold-4
01Bowman YoungStars-52
Gold-52
Ice Cubed-52
01Crown Royale-17
Blue-17
Premiere Date-17
Red-17
Retail-17
Triple Threads-5
01O-Pee-Chee-21
01O-Pee-Chee Heritage Parallel-21
01O-Pee-Chee Heritage Parallel Limited-21
01O-Pee-Chee Premier Parallel-21
01Pacific-47
01Pacific-404
Extreme LTD-47
Gold-404
Hobby LTD-47
Premiere Date-47
Retail LTD-47
01Pacific Adrenaline-21
Blue-21
Premiere Date-21
Red-21
Retail-21
Jerseys-3
01Pacific Arena Exclusives-47
01Pacific Arena Exclusives-404
01Pacific Heads-Up-11
Blue-11
Premiere Date-11
Red-11
Silver-11
Breaking the Glass-3
01Parkhurst-228
01Private Stock-10
Gold-10
Premiere Date-10
Retail-10
Silver-10
Game Gear-10
Game Gear Patches-10
01Private Stock Pacific Nights-10
01SP Authentic-10
Limited-10
Limited Gold-10
01SP Game Used Authentic Fabric-AFJD
01SP Game Used Authentic Fabric-DFDS
01SP Game Used Authentic Fabric Gold-AFJD
01SPx Hidden Treasures-DTAD
01SPx Hidden Treasures-TTDBA
01Stadium Club-69
Award Winners-69
Master Photos-69
01Titanium-15
Hobby Parallel-15
Premiere Date-15
Retail-15
Retail Parallel-15
Double-Sided Jerseys-4
Double-Sided Jerseys-21
Double-Sided Patches-4
Double-Sided Patches-21
01Titanium Draft Day Edition-13
01Topps-21
Heritage Parallel-21
Heritage Parallel Limited-21
OPC Parallel-21
01Topps Chrome-21
Refractors-21
Black Border Refractors-21
01Topps Heritage-61
Refractors-61
01Topps Reserve-66
01UD Mask Collection Double Patches-DPJD
01UD Mask Collection Jerseys-J-JD
01UD Mask Collection Jersey and Patch-JPJD
01Upper Deck-254
Exclusives-254
01Upper Deck MVP-22
01Upper Deck Victory-42
Gold-42
01Upper Deck Vintage-29
01Upper Deck Vintage-35
01Vanguard-11
Blue-11
Red-11
Memorabilia-31
One of Ones-11
Premiere Date-11
Proofs-11
02Atomic-10
Blue-10
Gold-10
Red-10
Hobby Parallel-10
02BAP First Edition-76
Jerseys-76
02BAP Sig Series Auto Buybacks 1999-57
02BAP Sig Series Auto Buybacks 2001-4
02Crown Royale Dual Patches-2
02O-Pee-Chee-30
02O-Pee-Chee Premier Blue Parallel-30
02O-Pee-Chee Premier Red Parallel-30
02O-Pee-Chee Factory Set-30
02Pacific-41
Blue-41
Red-41
02Pacific Complete-122
Red-122
02Pacific Exclusive-18
02Pacific Heads-Up-13
Blue-13
Purple-13
Red-13
Quad Jerseys-4
Quad Jerseys Gold-4
02Parkhurst Teammates-TT12
02Parkhurst Retro-131
Minis-131
02Private Stock Reserve-12
Blue-12
Red-12
Retail-12
02SP Game Used First Rounder Patches-JD
02SP Game Used Piece of History-PHJD
02SP Game Used Piece of History Gold-PHJD0
02SP Game Used Piece of History Rainbow-PHJD0
02SPx Winning Materials-WMDU
02SPx Winning Materials Gold-DU
02SPx Winning Materials Silver-DU
02Stadium Club-31
Silver Decoy Cards-31
Proofs-31
02Titanium Jerseys-7
02Titanium Jerseys Retail-7
02Topps-30
OPC Blue Parallel-30
OPC Red Parallel-30
First Round Fabric-JPD
Factory Set-30
02Topps Chrome-30
Black Border Refractors-30
Refractors-30
First Round Fabric Patches-JP
02Topps Total-221
02Upper Deck-17
Exclusives-17
02Upper Deck MVP-20
Gold-20
Classics-20
Golden Classics-20
Skate Around Jerseys-SDDB
Skate Around Jerseys-STDSB
02Upper Deck Victory-24
Bronze-24
Gold-24
Silver-24
02Upper Deck Vintage-33
Jerseys-HSJD
Jerseys Gold-HS-JD
02Vanguard Jerseys-6
02Vanguard Jerseys Gold-6
03Crown Royale-11
Blue-11
Retail-11
03ITG Action-36
Jerseys-M20
03O-Pee-Chee-156
03OPC Blue-156
03OPC Gold-156
03OPC Red-156
03Pacific-40
Blue-40
Red-40
Jerseys-6
Jerseys Gold-6
03Pacific Complete-38
Red-38
03Pacific Exhibit-19
Blue Backs-19
Yellow Backs-19
03Pacific Heads-Up-13
Hobby LTD-13
Retail LTD-13
03Titanium-14
Hobby Jersey Number Parallels-14
Retail-14
Retail Jersey Number Parallels-14
03Topps-156
Blue-156
Gold-156
Red-156
Pristine Jersey Portions-PPJ-JD
Pristine Jersey Portion Refractors-PPJ-JD
Pristine Patches-PP-JD
Pristine Patch Refractors-PP-JD
03Upper Deck-24
Canadian Exclusives-24
HG-24
03Upper Deck MVP-54
Gold Script-54
Silver Script-54
Canadian Exclusives-54
Souvenirs-S19
04Pacific-32
Blue-32
Red-32
04Upper Deck-22
Canadian Exclusives-22
HG Glossy Gold-22
HG Glossy Silver-22
05Be A Player Signatures-JP
05Be A Player Signatures Gold-JP
05Panini Stickers-37
05Parkhurst-65
Facsimile Auto Parallel-65
05SP Game Used Authentic Fabrics Quad-MNDB
05SP Game Used Authentic Patches Quad -MNDB
05UD Powerplay Specialists-TSJD
05UD Powerplay Specialists Patches-SPJD
05Ultra-28
Gold-28
Ice-28
05Upper Deck-24
HG Glossy-24
05Upper Deck MVP-48
Gold-48
Platinum-48
05Upper Deck Toronto Fall Expo-24
06Be A Player-136
Autographs-136
Signatures-JD
06Hot Prospects Hot Materials -HMJD
06Hot Prospects Hot Materials Red Hot-HMJD
06Hot Prospects Hot Materials White Hot-HMJD
06O-Pee-Chee-288
Rainbow-288
06SP Game Used Authentic Fabrics-AFJD
06SP Game Used Authentic Fabrics Parallel-AFJD
06SP Game Used Authentic Fabrics Patches-AFJD
06Upper Deck-364
Exclusives Parallel-364
High Gloss Parallel-364
Masterpieces-364
06Upper Deck MVP-165
Gold Script-165
Super Script-165

Dumont, Jerome
93Quebec Pee-Wee Tournament-431

Dumont, Justin
00Mississauga Ice Dogs-11

Dumont, Louis
907th Inn. Sketch WHL-168
917th Inn. Sketch WHL-222
94Wheeling Thunderbirds Photo Album-20
95Wheeling Thunderbirds-17
95Wheeling Thunderbirds Series II-5
96Louisiana Ice Gators-5
96Louisiana Ice Gators II-4
97Louisiana Ice Gators-1
98Louisiana Ice Gators-6
03Mississippi Sea Wolves-3

Dumoulin, Mario
917th Inn. Sketch QMJHL-260
98Abilene Aviators-7
02New Mexico Scorpions-6

Dunbar, Dale
85Fredericton Express-24

Dunbar, Laurie
04UK Edinburgh Capitals-3

Dunbar, Terry
04Knoxville Ice Bears-14

Duncalfe, Darren
91Air Canada SJHL-E26
97Central Texas Stampede-3

Duncan, Bobby
97Portland Winter Hawks-14

Duncan, Brett
93Seattle Thunderbirds-5
94Raleigh Icecaps-5
95Saint John Flames-5
98Tacoma Sabercats-7
99Tacoma Sabercats-20

Duncan, David
93Quebec Pee-Wee Tournament-170

Duncan, Dillon
04Lincoln Stars-5

Duncan, Glen
81Indianapolis Checkers-5
82Indianapolis Checkers-4

Duncan, Iain
87Jets Postcards-5
87Moncton Hawks-6
88Jets Police-5
88Jets Postcards-6
88O-Pee-Chee-209
88O-Pee-Chee Stickers-108
88O-Pee-Chee Stickers-132
88O-Pee-Chee Stickers-140
88O-Pee-Chee Stickers-238
88Panini Stickers-154
89Jets Safeway-11
89O-Pee-Chee-293
89O-Pee-Chee Stickers-136
89Panini Stickers-170
90Jets IGA-11
90Moncton Hawks-3
90ProCards AHL/IHL-249
92Toledo Storm-19
92Toledo Storm Team Issue-12
94Toledo Storm-5

Duncan, Josh
03Waterloo Blackhawks-16

Duncan, Ryan
04Salmon Arm Silverbacks-13

Duncan, Trevor
89Rayside-Balfour Jr. Canadians-8

Duncan, Troy
00Sudbury Wolves-10

Duncanson, Craig
85Sudbury Wolves-19
89Kings Smokey-19
90Moncton Hawks-4
90ProCards AHL/IHL-248
91Baltimore Skipjacks-13
91ProCards-566
92Binghamton Rangers-4
94Binghamton Rangers-2
97Sudbury Wolves Anniversary-7

Duncombe, Steve
03UK Sheffield Steelers-11
03UK Sheffield Steelers Stickers-14
04UK Sheffield Steelers-5
04UK U-20 Team-7
05UK Sheffield Steelers Supplementary-4
Gold-4
Silver-4

Dundas, Rocky
82Regina Pats-7
83Regina Pats-7
84Kelowna Wings-17
88ProCards AHL-285

Dunderdale, Tom
10C56-14
10Sweet Caporal Postcards-6
11C55-6
12C57-5
83Hall of Fame-127
83Hall of Fame Postcards-I6
85Hall of Fame-127

Dunham, Jason
99German Bundesliga 2-149
02German DEL City Press-70
06German DEL-171

Dunham, Mike
91Upper Deck-693
French-693
91Upper Deck Czech World Juniors-80
92Maine Black Bears-2
92Maine Black Bears-18
93PowerPlay-501
93Stadium Club Team USA-4
93Stadium Club Team USA Members Only-4
93Topps Premier Team USA-1
93Ultra-481
93Classic-56
94Finnish Jaa Kiekko-108
94Classic Autographs-NNO
94Classic Pro Prospects Ice Ambassadors-IA13
94Classic Pro Prospects Intl Heroes-LP3
94Classic Four-Sport *-148
Gold-148
Autographs-148A
Printers Proofs-148
94Images *-20
95Images-61
Gold-61
96Be A Player-212
Autographs-212
Autographs Silver-212
96Black Diamond-3
Gold-3
96Devils Team Issue-1
96Albany River Rats-4
96Collector's Edge Future Legends-3
96Collector's Edge Ice-6
Platinum Club-1
Prism-6
96Collector's Edge Ice Promos-PR3
96Collector's Edge Ice The Wall-TW10
97Be A Player-110
Autographs-110
Autographs Die-Cuts-110
Autographs Prismatic Die-Cuts-110
97Devils Team Issue-1
97Donruss-93
Press Proofs Silver-93
Press Proofs Gold-93
97Donruss Canadian Ice-87
Dominion Series-87
Provincial Series-87
97Donruss Elite-59
Aspirations-59
Status-59
97Donruss Limited-78
97Donruss Limited-194
Exposure-78
Exposure-194
Fabric of the Game-41
97Donruss Preferred-40
Cut to the Chase-40
Color Guard-17
Color Guard Promos-17
97Donruss Priority-86
Stamp of Approval-86
97Leaf-104
Fractal Matrix-104
Fractal Matrix Die Cuts-104
Pipe Dreams-16
97Leaf International-104
Universal Ice-104
97Pacific Dynagon Best Kept Secrets-106
97Pacific Invincible NHL Regime-110
97Pinnacle-79
Artist's Proofs-79
Rink Collection-79
Press Plates Back Black-79
Press Plates Back Cyan-79
Press Plates Back Magenta-79
Press Plates Back Yellow-79
Press Plates Front Black-79
Press Plates Front Cyan-79
Press Plates Front Magenta-79
Press Plates Front Yellow-79
97Score-45
97Score-269
Artist's Proofs-45
Golden Blades-45
97Score Devils-13
Platinum-13
Premier-13
97Studio-56
Press Proofs Silver-56
Press Proofs Gold-56
98Aurora-100
98Be A Player-72
Press Release-72
98BAP Gold-72
98BAP Autographs-72
98BAP Autographs Gold-72
98BAP Tampa Bay All Star Game-72
98Black Diamond-47
Double Diamond-47
Triple Diamond-47
Quadruple Diamond-47
98Bowman's Best-75
Refractors-75
Atomic Refractors-75
98Crown Royale-73
Limited Series-73
98NHL Aces Playing Cards-42
98Pacific-262
Ice Blue-262
Red-262
98Pacific Dynagon Ice-101
Blue-101
Red-101
Team Checklists-14
98Pacific Omega-128
Red-128
Opening Day Issue-128
98Panini Photocards-20
98Paramount-122
Copper-122
Emerald Green-122
Holo-Electric-122
Ice Blue-122
Silver-122
Glove Side Laser Cuts-9
98Predators Team Issue-8
98Revolution-78
Ice Shadow-78
Red-78
98SP Authentic-44
Power Shift-44
98SPx Top Prospects-34
Radiance-34
Spectrum-34
98Topps Gold Label Class 1-83
Black-83
Black One of One-83
One of One-83
Red-83
Red One of One-83
98Topps Gold Label Class 2-83
98Topps Gold Label Class 2 Black-83
98Topps Gold Label Class 2 Black 1 of 1-83
98Topps Gold Label Class 2 One of One-83
98Topps Gold Label Class 2 Red-83
98Topps Gold Label Class 2 Red One of One-83
98Topps Gold Label Class 3-83
98Topps Gold Label Class 3 Black-83
98Topps Gold Label Class 3 Black 1 of 1-83
98Topps Gold Label Class 3 One of One-83
98Topps Gold Label Class 3 Red-83
98Topps Gold Label Class 3 Red One of One-83
98Upper Deck-210
Exclusives-210
Exclusives 1 of 1-210
Gold Reserve-210
98Upper Deck MVP-110
Gold Script-110
Silver Script-110
Super Script-110
ProSign-MD
99SLU Hockey-1
99Aurora-78
Premiere Date-78
99BAP Memorabilia-299
Gold-299
Silver-299
99BAP Millennium-142
Emerald-142
Ruby-142
Sapphire-142
Signatures-142
Signatures Gold-142
99Crown Royale-74
Limited Series-74
Premiere Date-74
99Hasbro Starting Lineup Cards-1
99O-Pee-Chee-241
99O-Pee-Chee Chrome-241
99O-Pee-Chee Chrome Refractors-241
99Pacific-222
Copper-222
Emerald Green-222
Gold-222
Ice Blue-222

Premiere Date-222
Red-222
Team Leaders-15
99Pacific Dynagon Ice-106
Blue-106
Copper-106
Gold-106
Premiere Date-106
99Pacific Omega-126
Copper-126
Gold-126
Ice Blue-126
Premiere Date-126
99Pacific Prism-75
Holographic Blue-75
Holographic Gold-75
Holographic Mirror-75
Holographic Purple-75
Premiere Date-75
99Panini Stickers-339
99Paramount-123
Copper-123
Emerald-123
Gold-123
Holographic Emerald-123
Holographic Gold-123
Holographic Silver-123
Ice Blue-123
Premiere Date-123
Red-123
Silver-123
99Revolution-78
Premiere Date-78
Red-78
Shadow Series-78
99SP Authentic-47
99SPx-83
Radiance-83
Spectrum-83
99Stadium Club-125
First Day Issue-125
One of a Kind-125
Printing Plates Black-125
Printing Plates Cyan-125
Printing Plates Magenta-125
Printing Plates Yellow-125
99Topps/OPC-241
99Topps/OPC Chrome-241
Refractors-241
99Upper Deck-76
Exclusives-76
Exclusives 1 of 1-76
99Upper Deck Gold Reserve-76
99Upper Deck MVP-113
Gold Script-113
Silver Script-113
Super Script-113
99Upper Deck MVP SC Edition-98
Gold Script-98
Silver Script-98
Super Script-98
99Upper Deck Retro-44
Gold-44
Platinum-44
99Upper Deck Victory-155
99Wayne Gretzky Hockey-94
00Aurora-76
Premiere Date-76
00BAP Memorabilia-249
Emerald-249
Ruby-249
Sapphire-249
Promos-249
00BAP Mem Chicago Sportsfest Copper-249
00BAP Memorabilia Chicago Sportsfest Blue-249
00BAP Memorabilia Chicago Sportsfest Gold-249
00BAP Memorabilia Chicago Sportsfest Ruby-249
00BAP Memorabilia Chicago Sun-Times Ruby-249
00BAP Memorabilia Chicago Sun-Times Gold-249
00BAP Mem Chicago Sun-Times Sapphire-249
00BAP Mem Toronto Fall Expo Copper-249
00BAP Memorabilia Toronto Fall Expo Gold-249
00BAP Memorabilia Toronto Fall Expo Ruby-249
00BAP Parkhurst 2000-P129
00BAP Ultimate Memorabilia Goalie Sticks-G17
00Crown Royale-59
Ice Blue-59
Limited Series-59
Premiere Date-59
Red-59
00O-Pee-Chee-102
00O-Pee-Chee Parallel-102
00Pacific-220
Copper-220
Gold-220
Ice Blue-220
Premiere Date-220
00Paramount-134
Copper-134
Gold-134
Holo-Gold-134
Holo-Silver-134
Ice Blue-134
Premiere Date-134
00Private Stock-54
Gold-54
Premiere Date-54
Retail-54
Silver-54
00Revolution-80
Blue-80
Premiere Date-80
Red-80
00SP Authentic-50
00SP Game Used-34
00Stadium Club-25
00Titanium Draft Day Edition-52
Patches-52
00Topps/OPC-102
Parallel-102
00Topps Chrome-80
OPC Refractors-80
Refractors-80
00Topps Heritage-189
00UD Heroes-69
00UD Pros and Prospects-48
00UD Reserve Golden Goalies-GG6
00Upper Deck-100
Exclusives Tier 1-100
Exclusives Tier 2-100
00Upper Deck Legends-75
Legendary Collection Bronze-75
Legendary Collection Gold-75
Legendary Collection Silver-75
00Upper Deck MVP-101
First Stars-101
Second Stars-101
Third Stars-101
00Upper Deck Victory-127
00Upper Deck Vintage-201
00Upper Deck Vintage-208
00Upper Deck Vintage-209
01Atomic-54
Blue-54
Gold-54
Premiere Date-54
Red-54
Jerseys-34
Patches-34
01BAP Memorabilia-136
Emerald-136
Ruby-136
Sapphire-136
Goalies Jerseys-GJ12
01BAP Signature Series-93
Autographs-93
Autographs Gold-93
01Between the Pipes-29
01Between the Pipes-91
Double Memorabilia-DM7
Goalie Gear-GG17
He Shoots-He Saves Prizes-3
Jerseys-GJ12
Jersey and Stick Cards-GSJ11
Masks-21
Masks Silver-21
Masks Gold-21
01Bowman YoungStars-70
Gold-70
Ice Cubed-70
01Crown Royale-80
Blue-80
Premiere Date-80
Red-80
Retail-80
Triple Threads-16
01O-Pee-Chee-84
01O-Pee-Chee Heritage Parallel-84
01O-Pee-Chee Heritage Parallel Limited-84
01O-Pee-Chee Premier Parallel-84
01Pacific-216
Extreme LTD-216
Hobby LTD-216
Premiere Date-216
Retail LTD-216
01Pacific Adrenaline-103
Blue-103
Premiere Date-103
Red-103
Retail-103
Power Play-21
01Pacific Arena Exclusives-216
01Pacific Heads-Up-53
Blue-53
Premiere Date-53
Red-53
Silver-53
Quad Jerseys-13
01Parkhurst-110
01Private Stock-52
Gold-52
Premiere Date-52
Retail-52
Silver-52
Game Gear-56
Game Gear Patches-56
01Private Stock Pacific Nights-52
01SP Authentic-46
Limited-46
Limited Gold-46
01SP Game Used-29
01SPx-36
01Stadium Club-67
Award Winners-67
Master Photos-67
01Titanium-77
Hobby Parallel-77
Premiere Date-77
Retail-77
Retail Parallel-77
01Topps-84
Heritage Parallel-84
Heritage Parallel Limited-84
OPC Parallel-84
01Topps Chrome-84
Refractors-84
Black Border Refractors-84
01Topps Heritage-71
Refractors-71
01Topps Reserve-13
01UD Challenge for the Cup-48
01UD Mask Collection-117
01UD Mask Collection-180
Gold-117
Gold-180
Dual Jerseys-MBRD
Dual Jerseys-PMAD
Goalie Jerseys-MMMD
Goalie Jerseys-SYMD
Goalie Jerseys-VCMD
01UD Playmakers-56
Combo Jerseys-CJMD
Combo Jerseys Gold-CJMD
01UD Premier Collection-31
01Upper Deck-98
Exclusives-98
Goaltender Threads-TTMD
01Upper Deck Ice-26
01Upper Deck MVP-106
01Upper Deck Victory-193
01Upper Deck Victory-199
Gold-193
Gold-199
01Upper Deck Vintage-141
01Upper Deck Vintage-148
01Upper Deck Vintage-269
01Vanguard-53
Blue-53
Red-53
One of Ones-53
Premiere Date-53
Proofs-53
02Atomic-59
Blue-59
Gold-59
Red-59
Hobby Parallel-59
02BAP First Edition-46
Jerseys-46
02BAP Memorabilia-125
02BAP Memorabilia-391
Emerald-125
Ruby-125
Sapphire-125
NHL All-Star Game-125
NHL All-Star Game Blue-125
NHL All-Star Game Green-125
NHL All-Star Game Red-125
02BAP Memorabilia Toronto Fall Expo-125
02BAP Signature Series-5
Autographs-5
Autograph Buybacks 1998-72
Autograph Buybacks 1999-142
Autograph Buybacks 2001-93
Autographs Gold-5
Golf-GS57
02Between the Pipes-12
Gold-12
Silver-12
Behind the Mask-14
Blockers-8
Double Memorabilia-11
Emblems-15
Jerseys-15
Masks II-17
Masks II Gold-17
Masks II Silver-17
Numbers-15
Pads-13
Stick and Jerseys-15
Tandems-11
02ITG Used Goalie Pad and Jersey-GP5
02ITG Used Goalie Pad and Jersey Gold-GP5
02O-Pee-Chee-195
02O-Pee-Chee Premier Blue Parallel-195
02O-Pee-Chee Premier Red Parallel-195
02O-Pee-Chee Factory Set-195
02Pacific-207
Blue-207
Red-207
02Pacific Complete-474
Red-474
02Pacific Exclusive-97
02Parkhurst-64
Bronze-64
Gold-64
Silver-64
College Ranks-CR16
College Ranks Jerseys-CRM16
Teammates-TT10
02Parkhurst Retro-110
Minis-110
02Private Stock Reserve-57
Blue-57
Red-57
Retail-57
02SP Game Used-27
Piece of History-PHDU
Piece of History Gold-PHDU
Piece of History Rainbow-PHDU
02SPx-45
Spectrum Gold-45
Spectrum Silver-45
Xtreme Talents-MD
Xtreme Talents Gold-MD
Xtreme Talents Silver-MD
02Stadium Club-71
Silver Decoy Cards-71
Proofs-71
02Topps-195
OPC Blue Parallel-195
OPC Red Parallel-195
Factory Set-195
02Topps Chrome-110
Black Border Refractors-110
Refractors-110
02Topps Heritage-48
Chrome Parallel-48
02Topps Total-400
Team Checklists-TTC17
02UD Artistic Impressions Artist's Touch-ATMD
02UD Artistic Impressio Artist Touch Gold-ATMD
02UD Honor Roll Grade A Jerseys-GAMD
02UD Mask Collection-54
02UD Mask Collection-55
02UD Mask Collection-57
02UD Mask Collection Beckett Promos-54
02UD Mask Collection Beckett Promos-55
02UD Mask Collection Beckett Promos-57
02UD Mask Collection Career Wins-CWMD
02UD Mask Collection Great Gloves-GGDU
02UD Mask Collection Masked Marvels-MMMD
02UD Mask Collection Nation's Best-NRDM
02UD Mask Collection Patches-PWMD
02UD Piece of History-54
Patches-PHMD
02UD Premier Collection-38
02UD Top Shelf-48
Dual Player Jerseys-STDE
Hardware Heroes-HBRBD
Stopper Jerseys-SSDU
Sweet Sweaters-SWMD
02Upper Deck-342
Exclusives-342
02Upper Deck Beckett UD Promos-342
02Upper Deck Difference Makers-MD
02Upper Deck Goaltender Threads-MD
02Upper Deck Goaltender Threads Gold-MD
02Upper Deck Hot Spots-HSDU
02Upper Deck Patchwork-PWMD
02Upper Deck Saviors Jerseys-SVMD
02Upper Deck Classic Portraits-56
Hockey Royalty-DLH
Hockey Royalty Limited-DLH
Stitches-CMD
Stitches Limited-CMD
02Upper Deck MVP-104
Gold-104
Classics-104
Golden Classics-104
Souvenirs-S-DU
02Upper Deck Rookie Update-66
Jerseys-DMD
Jerseys Gold-DMD
02Upper Deck Victory-119
Bronze-119
Gold-119
Silver-119
National Pride-NP56
02Upper Deck Vintage-141
02Upper Deck Vintage-277
Green Backs-141
Jerseys-EEMD
Jerseys Gold-EE-MD
Tall Boys-T37
Tall Boys Gold-T37
03BAP Memorabilia-147
Emerald-147
Gold-147
Ruby-147
Sapphire-147
Deep in the Crease-D5
Masks III-8
Masks III Gold-8
Masks III Silver-8
Masks III Autographs-M-DH
Masks III Autographs-M-MDU
Masks III Memorabilia-8
03BAP Ultimate Memorabilia Autographs-58
Gold-58
03BAP Ultimate Mem Auto Jerseys-58
03Beehive-133
Gold-133
Silver-133
Sticks Beige Border-BE23
03Black Diamond-56
Black-56
Green-56
Red-56
Threads-DT-DU
Threads Green-DT-DU
Threads Red-DT-DU
Threads Black-DT-DU
03Bowman-84
Gold-84
03Bowman Chrome-84
Refractors-84
Gold Refractors-84
Xfractors-84
03Crown Royale-66
Blue-66
Retail-66
03ITG Action-313
Jerseys-M103
03ITG Used Signature Series-72
Gold-72
Autographs-MDU
Autographs Gold-MDU
Goalie Gear-17
Goalie Gear Autographs-17
Goalie Gear Gold-17
03O-Pee-Chee-253
03OPC Blue-253
03OPC Gold-253
03OPC Red-253
03Pacific-223
Blue-223
Red-223
03Pacific Complete-458
Red-458
03Pacific Exhibit-97
Blue Backs-97
Yellow Backs-97
03Pacific Invincible Freeze Frame-15
03Pacific Prism-69
Blue-69
Gold-69
Red-69
03Parkhurst Original Six New York-13
Memorabilia-NM1
Memorabilia-NM19
03Private Stock Reserve-68
Blue-68
Red-68
Retail-68
03Rangers Team Issue-5
03SP Authentic-60
Limited-60
03SPx-63
Radiance-63
Spectrum-63
Winning Materials-WM-MD
Winning Materials Limited-WM-MD
03Titanium-67
Hobby Jersey Number Parallels-67
Retail-67
Retail Jersey Number Parallels-67
03Topps-253
Blue-253
Gold-253
Red-253
Topps/OPC Idols-UI12
03Topps C55-106
Minis-106
Minis American Back-106
Minis American Back Red-106
Minis Bazooka Back-106
Minis Brooklyn Back-106
Minis Hat Trick Back-106
Minis O Canada Back-106
Minis O Canada Back Red-106
Minis Stanley Cup Back-106
03Topps Pristine-56
Gold Refractor Die Cuts-56
Refractors-56
Mini-PM-MD
Press Plates Black-56
Press Plates Cyan-56
Press Plates Magenta-56
Press Plates Yellow-56
03UD Honor Roll-57
03Upper Deck-130
Canadian Exclusives-130
HG-130
03Upper Deck Classic Portraits-65
Classic Colors-CC-MD
03Upper Deck MVP-286
Gold Script-286
Silver Script-286
Canadian Exclusives-286
SportsNut-SN55
03Upper Deck Trilogy-65
Limited-65
03Upper Deck Victory-128
Bronze-128
Gold-128
Silver-128
03Toronto Star-62
04Pacific-172
Blue-172
Red-172
04Upper Deck-119
Canadian Exclusives-119
HG Glossy Gold-119
HG Glossy Silver-119
05Upper Deck-253
Big Playmakers-B-MDU
Jerseys-J-MD
05Upper Deck MVP-23
Gold-23
Platinum-23
05Upper Deck Victory-129
Black-129
Gold-129
Silver-129
06O-Pee-Chee-318
Rainbow-318
06Upper Deck-375
Exclusives Parallel-375
High Gloss Parallel-375
Masterpieces-375

Dunk, Brett
87Brockville Braves-21

Dunlap, Gregory
93Quebec Pee-Wee Tournament-1171

Dunlap, Kenneth
93Quebec Pee-Wee Tournament-1172

Dunlop, Blake
74NHL Action Stamps-140
74O-Pee-Chee NHL-308
75O-Pee-Chee NHL-16
75Topps-16
76O-Pee-Chee NHL-263
76Topps-263
79O-Pee-Chee-174
79Topps-174
80O-Pee-Chee-370
81O-Pee-Chee-293
81O-Pee-Chee Stickers-131
81Topps-W117
82O-Pee-Chee-301
82O-Pee-Chee Stickers-199
82Post Cereal-17
82Topps Stickers-199
83O-Pee-Chee-314
83O-Pee-Chee Stickers-131
83Puffy Stickers-13
83Topps Stickers-131
92Blues UD Best of the Blues-5

Dunlop, Cole
02Arizona Icecats-5
03Arizona Icecats-7
04Arizona Icecats-3

Dunlop, Connor
01Notre Dame Fighting Irish-8
02Notre Dame Fighting Irish-2
04Czech OFS-369
Stars II-5

Dunmar, Jon
97Pensacola Ice Pilots-8

Dunn, Alex
06Odessa Jackalopes-7

Dunn, Chris
93Quebec Pee-Wee Tournament-1291

Dunn, Dave
73Canucks Royal Bank-5
74Maple Leafs Postcards-2
74NHL Action Stamps-271
74NHL Action Stamps Update-35
74O-Pee-Chee NHL-152
74Topps-152
75Maple Leafs Postcards-5
75O-Pee-Chee NHL-187
75Topps-187

Dunn, Greg
93Quebec Pee-Wee Tournament-1413

Dunn, Jamie
91Air Canada SJHL-E48
92Saskatchewan JHL-161

Dunn, Jay
91Air Canada SJHL-A28
91Air Canada SJHL All-Stars-2

Dunn, Jimmy
83Hall of Fame Postcards-O7
85Hall of Fame-217

Dunn, Pat
92Finnish Semic-233
93Swedish Semic World Champ Stickers-263
94French National Team-11
95Swedish World Championships Stickers-110
99Corpus Christi IceRays-4

Dunn, Richie
80O-Pee-Chee-109
80Topps-109
81O-Pee-Chee-29
81Sabres Milk Panels-7
82O-Pee-Chee-45
82Post Cereal-2
83NHL Key Tags-16
83O-Pee-Chee-137
83Whalers Junior Hartford Courant-3
84O-Pee-Chee-69
88ProCards AHL-259
89ProCards AHL-259

Dunn, Stu
01Flint Generals-4
03Port Huron Beacons-7

Dunne, Jeff
02Chicago Steel-5
03Chicago Steel-11

Dunnigan, Dave
91British Columbia JHL-65

Dunphy, John
99Kitchener Rangers-14
00Kitchener Rangers-11

Dunphy, Paul
92Quebec Pee-Wee Tournament-1598
93Quebec Pee-Wee Tournament-508

Dunphy, Serge
92Oshawa Generals Sheet-21
95Slapshot-404

Dunstall, Travis
05Kamloops Blazers-11
06Kamloops Blazers-6

Dunstan, Geordie
92British Columbia JHL-102

Dunville, Doug
66Tulsa Oilers-3

DuPaul, Cosmo
93Classic Four-Sport *-215
Gold-215
95PEI Senators-5
97Fort Worth Brahmas-4
98Fort Worth Brahmas-17
99Fort Worth Brahmas-4
00Lubbock Cotton Kings-18

Dupee, Keith
01Atlantic City Boardwalk Bullies-10

Dupere, David
93Quebec Pee-Wee Tournament-14

Dupere, Denis
71Maple Leafs Postcards-3
71O-Pee-Chee-200
71Toronto Sun-256
72Maple Leafs Postcards-3
72O-Pee-Chee-167
72Sargent Promotions Stamps-210
73Maple Leafs Postcards-3
73O-Pee-Chee-210
74Capitals White Borders-9
74O-Pee-Chee NHL-105
74O-Pee-Chee NHL-219
74Topps-105
74Topps-219
75O-Pee-Chee NHL-159
75O-Pee-Chee NHL-382
75Topps-159
76O-Pee-Chee NHL-334
76Rockies Coke Cans-7
77O-Pee-Chee NHL-388
77Rockies Coke Cans-5
78O-Pee-Chee-283

Dupere, Pierre-Olivier
04Victoriaville Tigres-6
05Victoriaville Tigres-16

Duperron, Christian
84Chicoutimi Sagueneens-7

Duplain, Samuel
00Val d'Or Foreurs-15
Signed-15
01Quebec Remparts-12

Duplessis, Simon
01Anchorage Aces-4

Dupont, Andre
71Blues Postcards-8
72O-Pee-Chee-16
72Sargent Promotions Stamps-194
72Topps-19
73O-Pee-Chee-113
73Topps-183
74NHL Action Stamps-211
74O-Pee-Chee NHL-67
74Topps-67
75Flyers Canada Dry Cans-7
75O-Pee-Chee NHL-56
75O-Pee-Chee NHL-211
75Topps-56
75Topps-211
76O-Pee-Chee NHL-131
76Topps-131
77O-Pee-Chee NHL-164
77Topps-164
78O-Pee-Chee-98
78Topps-98
79O-Pee-Chee-178
79Topps-178
80Nordiques Postcards-9
80Pepsi-Cola Caps-64
81Nordiques Postcards-6
81O-Pee-Chee-273
82Nordiques Postcards-6
82O-Pee-Chee-282
82Post Cereal-16
83Nordiques Postcards-7
02Fleer Throwbacks-22
Gold-22
Platinum-22
04ITG Franchises US East-428
Autographs-A-ADU

Dupont, Brodie
04Calgary Hitmen-5
05ITG Heroes/Prosp Toronto Expo Parallel -172
05Calgary Hitmen-6
05ITG Heroes and Prospects-172
Autographs-A-BD
06ITG Heroes and Prospects-179
Autographs-ABD
Update Autographs-ABD

Dupont, George
94Central Hockey League-57
94Oklahoma City Blazers-3
94Tampa Bay Tritons RHI-18
95Central Hockey League-40
95Oklahoma Coyotes RHI-4
97New Mexico Scorpions-12
97New Mexico Scorpions II-10

Dupont, Jerome
81Blackhawks Borderless Postcards-5
83Blackhawks Postcards-4
85Blackhawks Team Issue-7
86Maple Leafs Postcards-7

Dupont, Michael
04Baie-Comeau Drakkar-15
05Baie-Comeau Drakkar-21

DuPont, Micki
96Kamloops Blazers-10
98Kamloops Blazers-8
99Kamloops Blazers-8
02BAP All-Star Edition-111
Gold-111
Silver-111
02BAP First Edition-201
02NHL Power Play Stickers-18
02SP Authentic-138
02SPx-167
02Topps Chrome-149
Black Border Refractors-149
Refractors-149
02Topps Total-431
02UD Foundations-125
02UD Honor Roll-148
02UD Mask Collection-116
02UD Piece of History-124
02UD Top Shelf-107
02Upper Deck-199
Exclusives-199
02Upper Deck Classic Portraits-106
02Upper Deck MVP-197
Gold-197
Classics-197
Golden Classics-197
02Upper Deck Victory-35
Bronze-35
Gold-35
Silver-35
02Upper Deck Vintage-324
02AHL Top Prospects-11
03German Berlin Polar Bears Postcards-10
03German DEL-64
04German Berlin Polar Bears Postcards-9
04German DEL-65
05German DEL-25
All-Star Jerseys-AS02
Defender-DF03
Defender Promos-DF03
06Wilkes-Barre Scranton Penguins-14
06Wilkes-Barre Scranton Penguins Jerseys-3

Dupont, Normand
77Nova Scotia Voyageurs-6
79Canadiens Postcards-2
80Jets Postcards-7
80Pepsi-Cola Caps-126
81Jets Postcards-5
81O-Pee-Chee-363
81O-Pee-Chee Stickers-139
82Jets Postcards-7
82O-Pee-Chee-378
82Post Cereal-21
83NHL Key Tags-139
83Whalers Junior Hartford Courant-4

Dupont, Yannick
96Rimouski Oceanic-10
96Rimouski Oceanic Quebec Police-10

Dupras, Jonathan
01Baie-Comeau Drakkar-16

Dupre, Greg
01Kalamazoo K-Wings-11

Dupre, Yanick
907th Inn. Sketch QMJHL-200
91OPC Premier-16
917th Inn. Sketch QMJHL-284
917th Inn. Sketch Memorial Cup-59
917th Inn. Sketch Memorial Cup-126
91Classic-41
91Star Pics-44
91Ultimate Draft-36
91Ultimate Draft-88
91Classic Four-Sport *-41
Autographs-41A
92Stadium Club-137
92Topps-515
Gold-515G
92Upper Deck-421

Dupuis, Bob
88Oilers Tenth Anniversary-118

Dupuis, Guy
87Hull Olympiques-6
90ProCards AHL/IHL-478
91ProCards-137
93Fort Wayne Komets-4
95Fort Wayne Komets-4
97Fort Wayne Komets-1
98Fort Wayne Komets-8
98IHL All-Star Eastern Conference-1
99Fort Wayne Komets Penalty Leaders-16
01German Upper Deck-108
02Bakersfield Condors-6
03Kalamazoo Wings-4
04Bakersfield Condors-2
05Fort Wayne Komets Choice-17
05Fort Wayne Komets Sprint-5
06Fort Wayne Komets-3

Dupuis, Lori
97Collector's Choice-291

Dupuis, Marc
95Slapshot-38
98Indianapolis Ice-8
00Amarillo Rattlers-5

Dupuis, Pascal
93Quebec Pee-Wee Tournament-1045
99Shawinigan Cataractes-6
Signed-6
00Cleveland Lumberjacks-10
01Atomic-112
Premiere Date-112
01Atomic Toronto Fall Expo-112
01BAP Memorabilia-247
Emerald-247
Ruby-247
Sapphire-247
01BAP Signature Series-236
Autographs-236
Autographs Gold-236
01Bowman YoungStars-132
Gold-132
Ice Cubed-132
01Crown Royale-165
01O-Pee-Chee-341
01Pacific Heads-Up-109
01Parkhurst-267
01Parkhurst Beckett Promos-267
01Private Stock-125
Gold-125
Premiere Date-125
Retail-125
Silver-125
01Private Stock Pacific Nights-125
01SP Authentic-153
Limited-153
Limited Gold-153
01SPx-142
01SPx-142
Rookie Treasures-RTPD
01Stadium Club-135
Award Winners-135
Master Photos-135
01Titanium-164
Retail-164
01Titanium Draft Day Edition-136
01Topps-341
01Topps Chrome-159
Refractors-159
Black Border Refractors-159
01UD Challenge for the Cup-110
01UD Playmakers-122
01UD Premier Collection-65
01UD Top Shelf-56
01UD Top Shelf-56B
01Upper Deck-193
Exclusives-193
01Upper Deck Ice-140
01Upper Deck MVP-204
01Upper Deck Victory-375
Gold-375
01Vanguard-116
Blue-116
Red-116
One of Ones-116
Premiere Date-116
Proofs-116
02BAP First Edition-272
02BAP Sig Series Auto Buybacks 2001-236
02Bowman YoungStars-129
Gold-129
Silver-129
02O-Pee-Chee-56
02O-Pee-Chee Premier Blue Parallel-56
02O-Pee-Chee Premier Red Parallel-56
02O-Pee-Chee Factory Set-56
02Pacific-180
Blue-180
Red-180
02Pacific Complete-36
Red-36
02Pacific Exclusive-85
02Pacific Quest for the Cup-46
Gold-46
02Topps-56
OPC Blue Parallel-56
OPC Red Parallel-56
Factory Set-56
02Topps Total-236
02Upper Deck Rookie Update-51
03BAP Memorabilia-64
Emerald-64
Gold-64
Ruby-64
Sapphire-64
03Beehive-96
Gold-96
Silver-96
03ITG Action-267
03O-Pee-Chee-117
03OPC Blue-117
03OPC Gold-117
03OPC Red-117
03Pacific-163
Blue-163
Red-163
03Pacific Complete-313
Red-313
03Topps-117
Blue-117
Gold-117
Red-117
03Upper Deck-93
Canadian Exclusives-93
HG-93
03Upper Deck MVP-208
Gold Script-208
Silver Script-208
Canadian Exclusives-208
03Upper Deck Victory-90
Bronze-90
Gold-90
Silver-90
04Pacific-130
Blue-130
Red-130
04Upper Deck-86
Canadian Exclusives-86
HG Glossy Gold-86
HG Glossy Silver-86
05Be A Player Signatures-PD
05Be A Player Signatures Gold-PD
05Black Diamond-42
Emerald-42
Gold-42
Onyx-42
Ruby-42
05Parkhurst-248
Facsimile Auto Parallel-248
05Upper Deck-94
HG Glossy-94
05Upper Deck MVP-195
Gold-195
Platinum-195
05Upper Deck Toronto Fall Expo-94
05Upper Deck Victory-97
Black-97
Gold-97
Silver-97
05Wild Crime Prevention-3
06O-Pee-Chee-250
Rainbow-250

Dupuis, Philippe
01Hull Olympiques-8
02Hull Olympiques-9
03Gatineau Olympiques-7
03Hull Olympiques Memorial Cup-6
05Moncton Wildcats-17
06Syracuse Crunch-10

Dupuis, Yanick
93Quebec Pee-Wee Tournament-215

Durak, Miroslav
99Des Moines Buccaneers-17
03Czech OFS Plus-331
04Czech OFS-207

Durand, Brian
84Minnesota-Duluth Bulldogs-10
85Minnesota-Duluth Bulldogs-25

Durand, Chris
05ITG Heroes/Prosp Toronto Expo Parallel -167
05ITG Heroes and Prospects-167
Autographs-A-CDU
Complete Logos-CHL-4
Jerseys-GUJ-27
Jerseys Gold-GUJ-27
Emblems-GUE-27
Emblems Gold-GUE-27
Numbers-GUN-27
Numbers Gold-GUN-27

Durand, Eric
93Swedish Semic World Champ Stickers-253

Durand, Guillaume
05Shawinigan Cataractes-12

Duras, Michal
03Czech OFS Plus-213
04Czech HC Plzen Postcards-6
04Czech OFS-141
05Czech HC Plzen-3
06Czech HC Plzen Postcards-10

Duraz, Michal
06Czech OFS-271

Durbano, Steve
72Blues White Border-2
73Blues White Border-5
73O-Pee-Chee-124
73Topps-168
74NHL Action Stamps-225
74O-Pee-Chee NHL-106
74Penguins Postcards-6
74Topps-106
76O-Pee-Chee NHL-4
76O-Pee-Chee NHL-19
76O-Pee-Chee NHL-384
76Rockies Puck Bucks-7
76Topps-4
76Topps-19

Durco, Juraj
02Czech OFS Plus-131
03Memphis RiverKings-3

Durden, Sergei
05Danbury Trashers-6

Durdin, Sergei
06Quad City Mallards-4

Durdle, Darren
96German DEL-27
98German DEL-172

Durhart, Jim
99UHL All-Stars West-3T

Duriau, Vincent
01Val d'Or Foreurs-7
02Val d'Or Foreurs-4
03Gatineau Olympiques-8
Duris, Martin
95German DEL-108
99German EHC Straubing-5
Duris, Peter
96Slovakian Quebec Pee-Wee Tournament-6
Duris, Vitezslav
80Maple Leafs Postcards-11
80Pepsi-Cola Caps-85
81O-Pee-Chee-316
82Maple Leafs Postcards-10
Durnan, Bill
43Parade Sportive *-3
43Parade Sportive *-11
43Parade Sportive *-32
43Parade Sportive *-33
44Beehive Group II Photos-235
45Quaker Oats Photos-73A
45Quaker Oats Photos-73B
45Quaker Oats Photos-73C
45Quaker Oats Photos-73D
51Berk Ross-2
55Parkhurst-63
Quaker Oats-63
83Hall of Fame-139
83Hall of Fame Postcards-K4
85Hall of Fame-139
91Kraft-37
93High Liner Greatest Goalies-12
93O-Pee-Chee Canadiens Hockey Fest-47
94Parkhurst Tall Boys Greats-6
99Upper Deck Century Legends-34
Century Collection-34
01Between the Pipes-126
01Between the Pipes-145
Trophy Winners-TW12
Vintage Memorabilia-VM17
02BAP Ultimate Mem Seams Unbelievable-7
02BAP Ultimate Mem Storied Franchise-10
02Between the Pipes Trappers-GT2
02Between the Pipes Vintage Memorabilia-5
02ITG Used Vintage Memorabilia-VM17
02ITG Used Vintage Memorabilia Gold-VM17
03BAP Memorabilia Gloves-GUG7
03BAP Memorabilia Vintage Memorabilia-VM-19
03BAP Ultimate Mem Hometown Heroes-15
03BAP Ultimate Mem Hometown Heroes Gold-15
03BAP Ultimate Memorabilia Paper Cuts-10
03Canada Post-24
03Parkhurst Original Six Montreal-51
Inserts-M13
03Parkhurst Rookie Before the Mask-BTM-9
03Parkhurst Rookie Before the Mask Gold-BTM-9
04ITG Franchises Canadian-64
Goalie Gear-GG1
Goalie Gear Gold-GG1
04ITG Franchises Update Double Mem-UDM2
04ITG Franchises Update Double Mem Gold-UDM2
04ITG Franchises Update Original Sticks-UOS3
04ITG Franchises Upd Original Sticks Gold-UOS3
04ITG Ultimate Memorabilia-99
Gold-99
Bleu Blanc et Rouge-2
Day In History-33
Day In History Gold-33
Gloves are Off-9
Goalie Gear-17
Vintage Lumber-2
05ITG Ultimate Memorabilia Level 1-9
05ITG Ultimate Memorabilia Level 2-9
05ITG Ultimate Memorabilia Level 3-9
05ITG Ultimate Memorabilia Level 4-9
05ITG Ultimate Memorabilia Level 5-9
05ITG Ultimate Mem Bleu Blanc Rouge Autos-2
05ITG Ultimate Mem Cornerstones Jerseys-3
05ITG Ultimate Mem Cornerst Jerseys Gold-3
05ITG Ultimate Memorabilia Gloves Are Off-16
05ITG Ultimate Mem Gloves Are Off Gold-16
05ITG Ultimate Memorabilia Goalie Gear-2
05ITG Ultimate Mem Goalie Gear Gold-2
05ITG Ultimate Mem 3 Star of the Game Jsy-2
05ITG Ult Mem 3 Star of the Game Jsy Gold-2
05ITG Ultimate Memorabilia Vintage Lumber-14
05ITG Ultimate Mem Vintage Lumber Gold-14
06Between The Pipes Shooting Gallery-SG10
06Between The Pipes Shooting Gallery Gold-SG10
06ITG Ultimate Memorabilia-16
Artist Proof-16
Bleu Blanc et Rouge Autos-3
Cornerstones-10
Cornerstones Gold-10
Decades-6
Decades Gold-6
Legendary Captains-15
Legendary Captains Gold-15
Stick Rack-19
Stick Rack Gold-19
Vintage Lumber-6
Vintage Lumber Gold-6
Durno, Chris
01Michigan Tech Huskies-6
03Gwinnett Gladiators-5
03Gwinnett Gladiators RBI Sports-198
04Gwinnett Gladiators-8
05ITG Heroes/Prosp Toronto Expo Parallel -357
05Milwaukee Admirals Pepsi-6
05ITG Heroes and Prospects-357
Autographs Series II-CDR
06Milwaukee Admirals -3
06Portland Pirates-10
Durocher, Alec
96OCN Blizzard-5
97OCN Blizzard-15
Durocher, Andre
907th Inn. Sketch QMJHL-257
Durocher, Mario
93Sherbrooke Faucons-26
00Victoriaville Tigres-24
Signed-24
03Lewiston Maineiacs-24
Durocher, Steve
93Quebec Pee-Wee Tournament-55
Durroulin, Mario
907th Inn. Sketch QMJHL-120
Dusablon, Benoit
92Quebec Pee-Wee Tournament-764
93Quebec Pee-Wee Tournament-349
96Halifax Mooseheads I-6
96Halifax Mooseheads II-6
98Val d'Or Foreurs-2
99Halifax Mooseheads-22
99Bowman CHL-73
Gold-73
OPC International-73
00QMJHL All-Star Program Inserts-20
01Hartford Wolf Pack-1
02Hartford Wolf Pack-7
03ITG VIP Rookie Debut-129
03Parkhurst Rookie-121
03UD Premier Collection-85
03Upper Deck Rookie Update-204
03Hartford Wolf Pack-4
04Hamilton Bulldogs-6
Dusanek, Jan
98Kelowna Rockets-2
99Czech OFS-89
Dusbabek, Joe
00Roanoke Express-3
01Roanoke Express-6
02Roanoke Express-13
02Roanoke Express RBI Sports-192
03Roanoke Express-311
Duschene, Donat
51Laval Dairy QSHL-20
Dussault, Normand
43Parade Sportive *-34
43Parade Sportive *-35
44Beehive Group II Photos-236
45Quaker Oats Photos-74A
45Quaker Oats Photos-74B
51Laval Dairy QSHL-22
52St. Lawrence Sales-96
Dustin, Bobby
92Minnesota Golden Gophers-6
93Minnesota Golden Gophers-8
94Minnesota Golden Gophers-11
95Minnesota Golden Gophers-12
Dustin, Paul
93Quebec Pee-Wee Tournament-1448
Duszenko, Wilbert
94German First League-355
Dutcher, Scott
93Quebec Pee-Wee Tournament-730
Dutchyshen, Tyler
02Sault Ste. Marie Greyhounds-10
Duthie, Ryan
917th Inn. Sketch WHL-17
93Spokane Chiefs-9
94Saint John Flames-3
95Adirondack Red Wings-5
99UK London Knights-6
Dutiaume, Mark
93Brandon Wheat Kings-18
94Brandon Wheat Kings-6
95Brandon Wheat Kings-7
95Classic-37
95Slapshot Memorial Cup-41
96Brandon Wheat Kings-7
97Rochester Americans-1-4
98BC Icemen-1
98BC Icemen II-6
01UK Fife Flyers-7
01UK Sheffield Steelers-9
02UK Sheffield Steelers-7
03UK Sheffield Steelers-12
03UK Sheffield Steelers Stickers-1
04UK Sheffield Steelers-11
05UK Sheffield Steelers-5
Gold-5
Silver-5
Dutiaume, Todd
917th Inn. Sketch WHL-198
92Brandon Wheat Kings-5
01UK Fife Flyers-4
Dutil, Christian
91Air Canada SJHL-A33
92Saskatchewan JHL-158
Dutkowski, Duke
23V128-1 Paulin's Candy-26
33V252 Canadian Gum-20
33V357 Ice Kings-56
34Diamond Matchbooks Silver-21
Dutton, Mervyn
23V128-1 Paulin's Candy-62
28La Presse Photos-8
33V129-23
33V252 Canadian Gum-21
33V357 Ice Kings-25
34Beehive Group I Photos-222
34Diamond Matchbooks Silver-22
35Diamond Matchbooks Tan 1-21
35Diamond Matchbooks Tan 2-20
35Diamond Matchbooks Tan 3-18
37V356 Worldwide Gum-14
60Topps-16
83Hall of Fame-7
83Hall of Fame Postcards-A6
85Hall of Fame-7
02BAP Ultimate Mem Paper Cuts Autos-36
03BAP Ultimate Memorabilia Paper Cuts-20
04ITG Franchises US East-365
04ITG Ultimate Memorabilia-25
Gold-25
Marvelous Maroons-6
Paper Cuts-2
05ITG Ultimate Mem Amazing Amerks Autos-4
06ITG Ultimate Memorabilia Builders Autos-3
06ITG Ultimate Memorabilia Lumbergraphs-15
06ITG Ultimate Memorabilia Marvelous Maroons Autos-7
Duus, Jesper
87Swedish Panini Stickers-95
89Swedish Semic Elitserien Stickers-79
90Swedish Semic Elitserien Stickers-254
91Swedish Semic Elitserien Stickers-85
92Swedish Semic Elitserien Stickers-105
93Swedish Semic Elitserien-77
94Swedish Leaf-122
95Swedish Leaf-217
95Swedish Upper Deck-57
96German DEL-185
98German DEL-301
99Swedish Upper Deck-172
00Swedish Upper Deck-156
Duval, Ian
04Regina Pats-13
05Regina Pats-3
06Regina Pats-5
Duval, Jon
907th Inn. Sketch WHL-39
917th Inn. Sketch WHL-315
93Birmingham Bulls Birmingham News-8
94Birmingham Bulls-7
Duval, Luc
84Chicoutimi Sagueneens-9
Duval, Murray
89Kamloops Blazers-5
907th Inn. Sketch WHL-302
907th Inn. Sketch Memorial Cup-21
91ProCards-312
93Birmingham Bulls Birmingham News-6
Dvorak, Ales
98BC Icemen-4
98BC Icemen II-1
Dvorak, Filip
96Czech APS Extraliga-283
97Czech DS Stickers-188
Dvorak, Karel
97Czech APS Extraliga-290
98Czech OFS-294
Dvorak, Marek
99Czech Score Blue 2000-52
99Czech Score Red Ice 2000-52
Dvorak, Michal
96Czech APS Extraliga-281
96Kitchener Rangers-11
99German DEL-360
00Czech OFS-77
01Czech OFS-214
02Czech OFS Plus-258
03Czech OFS Plus-198
04Czech OFS-24
05Czech HC Karlovy Vary-4
06Czech OFS-27
Dvorak, Miroslav
74Swedish Stickers-119
79Panini Stickers-78
81Swedish Semic Hockey VM Stickers-57
82Swedish Semic VM Stickers-83
83Flyers J.C. Penney-8
83NHL Key Tags-95
Dvorak, Petr
02Regina Pats-3
Dvorak, Radek
95Be A Player-163
Signatures-S163
Signatures Die Cuts-S163
95Bowman-130
All-Foil-130
Bowman's Best-BB22
Bowman's Best Refractors-BB22
95Collector's Choice-398
95Donruss-277
Rated Rookies-10
95Donruss Elite-19
Die Cut Stars-19
Die Cut Uncut-19
Rookies-10
95Finest-125
Refractors-125
95Leaf Limited-10
Rookie Phenoms-7
95Metal-176
95Parkhurst International-260
95Parkhurst International-508
Emerald Ice-260
Emerald Ice-508
Parkie's Trophy Picks-PP45
95Select Certified-133
Mirror Gold-133
95SkyBox Impact-200
95SP-59
95Stadium Club-200
Members Only Master Set-200
95Summit-169
Artist's Proofs-169
Ice-169
95Topps-319
OPC Inserts-319
SuperSkills Super Rookies-SR10
95Ultra-338
Extra Attackers-3
95Upper Deck-260
Electric Ice-260
Electric Ice Gold-260
Predictor Hobby-H26
Predictor Hobby Exchange-H26
95Zenith-147
Rookie Roll Call-2
95Classic-10
Autographs-4
Ice Breakers-BK9
Ice Breakers Die Cuts-BK9
95Signature Rookies-39
Signatures-39
95Classic Five-Sport *-156
Autographs-156
Strive For Five-HK5
95Signature Rookies Tetrad *-62
95Signature Rookies Tetrad Autobilia *-42
95Signature Rookies Tetrad Signatures *-62
96Donruss-213
Press Proofs-213
96Donruss Elite-105
Die Cut Stars-105
96Leaf-160
Press Proofs-160
96Metal Universe-57
96Score-247
Artist's Proofs-247
Dealer's Choice Artist's Proofs-247
Special Artist's Proofs-247
Golden Blades-247
96SkyBox Impact-44
96Summit-169
Artist's Proofs-169
Ice-169
Metal-169
Premium Stock-169
96Ultra-64
Gold Medallion-64
96All-Sport PPF *-99
96All-Sport PPF *-173
96All Sport PPF Gold *-99
96All Sport PPF Gold *-173
96Assets *-8
Hot Prints-8
96Classic Signings *-76
Blue-76
Die-Cuts-76
Freshly Inked-FS24
Red-76
96Clear Assets *-59
96Visions *-89
96Visions Signings *-79
97Collector's Choice-103
97Pacific-50
Copper-50
Emerald Green-50
Ice Blue-50
Red-50
Silver-50
97Panini Stickers-56
97Score-221
97Upper Deck-71
98Pacific-220
Ice Blue-220
Red-220
98Panini Stickers-56
98Upper Deck-280
Exclusives-280
Exclusives 1 of 1-280
Gold Reserve-280
98Czech Pexeso Series Two-4
99BAP Memorabilia-298
99BAP Memorabilia-400
Gold-298
Gold-400
Silver-298
Silver-400
99BAP Millennium-111
Emerald-111
Ruby-111
Sapphire-111
Signatures-111
Signatures Gold-111
99Pacific-172
Copper-172
Emerald Green-172
Gold-172
Ice Blue-172
Premiere Date-172
Red-172
99Pacific Omega-148
Copper-148
Gold-148
Ice Blue-148
Premiere Date-148
99Panini Stickers-58
99Upper Deck MVP SC Edition-122
Gold Script-122
Silver Script-122
Super Script-122
00BAP Memorabilia-142
Emerald-142
Ruby-142
Sapphire-142
Promos-142
00BAP Mem Chicago Sportsfest Copper-142
00BAP Memorabilia Chicago Sportsfest Blue-142
00BAP Memorabilia Chicago Sportsfest Gold-142
00BAP Memorabilia Chicago Sportsfest Ruby-142
00BAP Memorabilia Chicago Sun-Times Ruby-142
00BAP Memorabilia Chicago Sun-Times Gold-142
00BAP Mem Chicago Sun-Times Sapphire-142
00BAP Mem Toronto Fall Expo Copper-142
00BAP Memorabilia Toronto Fall Expo Gold-142
00BAP Memorabilia Toronto Fall Expo Ruby-142
00BAP Parkhurst 2000-P58
00BAP Signature Series-198
Emerald-198
Ruby-198
Sapphire-198
00O-Pee-Chee-141
00O-Pee-Chee Parallel-141
00Pacific-259
Copper-259
Gold-259
Ice Blue-259
Premiere Date-259
00Panini Stickers-62
00Paramount-159
Copper-159
Gold-159
Holo-Gold-159
Holo-Silver-159
Ice Blue-159
Premiere Date-159
00Titanium Game Gear-32
00Topps/OPC-141
Parallel-141
00Upper Deck-345
Exclusives Tier 1-345
Exclusives Tier 2-345
00Upper Deck Victory-156
00Upper Deck Vintage-242
00Czech OFS-387
00Czech Stadion-111
01BAP Memorabilia-2
Emerald-2
Ruby-2
Sapphire-2
01BAP Signature Series-118
Autographs-118
Autographs Gold-118
01O-Pee-Chee-161
01O-Pee-Chee Premier Parallel-161
01Pacific-255
Extreme LTD-255
Hobby LTD-255
Premiere Date-255
Retail LTD-255
01Pacific Adrenaline-124
Blue-124
Premiere Date-124
Red-124
Retail-124
01Pacific Arena Exclusives-255
01Parkhurst-112
01SP Game Used Authentic Fabric-AFRD
01SP Game Used Authentic Fabric Gold-AFRD
01Topps-161
OPC Parallel-161
01Upper Deck-116
Exclusives-116
01Upper Deck Victory-235
Gold-235
01Upper Deck Vintage-171
02BAP First Edition-67
Jerseys-67
02BAP Sig Series Auto Buybacks 1999-111
02BAP Sig Series Auto Buybacks 2001-118
02BAP Signature Series Golf-GS74
02O-Pee-Chee-178
02O-Pee-Chee Premier Blue Parallel-178
02O-Pee-Chee Premier Red Parallel-178
02O-Pee-Chee Factory Set-178
02Pacific-250
Blue-250
Red-250
02Parkhurst Retro-141
Minis-141
02Topps-178
OPC Blue Parallel-178
OPC Red Parallel-178
First Round Fabric-RD
First Round Fabric Autographs-RD
Factory Set-178
Chrome First Round Fabric Patches-RD
02Topps Total-344
02UD Top Shelf Goal Oriented-GORD
02Upper Deck-117
Exclusives-117
02Upper Deck Vintage-166
Jerseys-OSRD
02Czech Stadion Olympics-328
03ITG Action-293
03Oilers Postcards-6
03Pacific Complete-177
Red-177
03Topps Traded-TT40
Blue-TT40
Gold-TT40
Red-TT40
03Upper Deck-320
Canadian Exclusives-320
HG-320
UD Exclusives-320
03Upper Deck MVP-164
Gold Script-164
Silver Script-164
Canadian Exclusives-164
04Pacific-101
Blue-101
Red-101
04Czech World Championship Postcards-4
05Panini Stickers-282
05Parkhurst Facsimile Auto Parallel-198
05Upper Deck-77
HG Glossy-77
05Upper Deck MVP-158
Gold-158
Platinum-158
05Upper Deck Toronto Fall Expo-77
05Czech World Champions Postcards-10
05Czech Kvarteto Bonaparte-6d
05Czech Pexeso Mini Blue Set-19
05Czech Pexeso Mini Red Set-12
Dvorak, Todd
95Madison Monsters-12
Dwyer, Alan
03St. Francis Xavier X-Men-16
04St. Francis Xavier X-Men-4
Dwyer, Don
92Dallas Freeze-8
93Dallas Freeze-7
Dwyer, Gordie
92Quebec Pee-Wee Tournament-185
95Slapshot Memorial Cup-61
97Bowman CHL-53
OPC-53
00Pacific-383
Copper-383
Gold-383
Ice Blue-383
Premiere Date-383
01SPx-192
04Lowell Lock Monsters-4
04Lowell Lock Monsters Photo Album-4
Dwyer, Jeff
94Quebec Pee-Wee Tournament-1846
Dwyer, John
94Dubuque Fighting Saints-8
Dwyer, Pat
05Chicago Wolves-6
06Albany River Rats-10
Dyakiv, Igor
98Russian Hockey League-124
00Russian Hockey League-181
Dyck, Ed
72Canucks Royal Bank-5
Dyck, Joel
907th Inn. Sketch WHL-57
917th Inn. Sketch WHL-138
Dyck, Larry
88ProCards IHL-41
89ProCards IHL-93
90ProCards AHL/IHL-104
91ProCards-143
95Kansas City Blades-1
96Kansas City Blades-7
97Central Texas Stampede-4
Dyck, Matt
05Salmon Arm Silverbacks-7
Dyck, Mike
86Regina Pats-5
87Regina Pats-4
88Regina Pats-5
96Medicine Hat Tigers-4
Dyck, Paul
907th Inn. Sketch WHL-160
91ProCards-304
92Cleveland Lumberjacks-25
93Cleveland Lumberjacks-4
93Cleveland Lumberjacks Postcards-10
94Cleveland Lumberjacks-3
94Cleveland Lumberjacks Postcards-3
95Kansas City Blades-2
96Kansas City Blades-8
99Houston Aeros-1
01German Upper Deck-115
02German DEL City Press-218
04German DEL-226
04German Krefeld Penguins Postcards-3
Dyck, Randall
97Medicine Hat Tigers-8
Dyck, Tyler
02Brandon Wheat Kings-9
03Brandon Wheat Kings-22
04St. Francis Xavier X-Men-5
Dye, Babe
23V145-1-23
24C144 Champ's Cigarettes-23
24V145-2-54
83Hall of Fame Postcards-C4
85Hall of Fame-34
02Maple Leafs Platinum Collection-50
04ITG Franchises Canadian-115
Dyer, Dean
89Victoria Cougars-9
Dyer, Kelly
94Classic Women of Hockey-W22
Dyhr, Nick
92Saskatchewan JHL-70
Dyjak, Chad
97Arizona Icecats-9
Dykeman, Rob
907th Inn. Sketch OHL-33
91Cornwall Royals-26
917th Inn. Sketch OHL-20
917th Inn. Sketch Memorial Cup-36
Dykhuis, Karl
90Alberta International Team Canada-4
90Score-437
Canadian-437
90Upper Deck-471
French-471
907th Inn. Sketch QMJHL-229
91Alberta International Team Canada-6
91Blackhawks Coke-5
91O-Pee-Chee-172
91Parkhurst-262
French-262
91Topps-172
91Upper Deck-688
French-688
91Upper Deck Czech World Juniors-62
92Score-462
Canadian-462
92Ultra-274
92Upper Deck-404
93PowerPlay-48
93Upper Deck-106
93Indianapolis Ice-9
94Parkhurst SE-SE34
Gold-SE34
94Indianapolis Ice-6
95Be A Player-75
Signatures-S75
Signatures Die Cuts-S75
95Leaf-264
95Panini Stickers-122
95Topps-118
OPC Inserts-118
95Ultra-283
96Flyers Postcards-7
96Upper Deck-311
97Pacific Invincible NHL Regime-141
97Pacific Omega-209
Copper-209
Dark Gray-209
Emerald Green-209
Gold-209
Ice Blue-209
97Paramount-172
Copper-172
Dark Grey-172
Emerald Green-172
Ice Blue-172
Red-172
Silver-172
98Aurora-173
98Be A Player-255
Press Release-255
98BAP Gold-255
98BAP Autographs-255
98BAP Autographs Gold-255
98Finest-122
No Protectors-122
No Protectors Refractors-122
Refractors-122
98Pacific-399
Ice Blue-399
Red-399
98Panini Stickers-100
98Paramount-217
Copper-217
Emerald Green-217
Holo-Electric-217
Ice Blue-217
Silver-217
99Upper Deck MVP SC Edition-94
Gold Script-94
Silver Script-94
Super Script-94
00Canadiens Postcards-4
00Panini Stickers-41
00Upper Deck-323
Exclusives Tier 1-323
Exclusives Tier 2-323
01Canadiens Postcards-7
01Pacific-205
Extreme LTD-205
Hobby LTD-205
Premiere Date-205
Retail LTD-205
01Pacific Arena Exclusives-205
02BAP Sig Series Auto Buybacks 1998-255
02Canadiens Postcards-11
02NHL Power Play Stickers-55
03Canadiens Postcards-7
03Parkhurst Original Six Montreal-9
05German DEL-246
Defender-DF04
Defender Promos-DF04
Dykstra, Steve
85Sabres Blue Shield-7
85Sabres Blue Shield Small-7
86Sabres Blue Shield-8
86Sabres Blue Shield Small-8
87O-Pee-Chee Stickers-146
87Sabres Wonder Bread/Hostess-8
88Oilers Tenth Anniversary-38
90ProCards AHL/IHL-317
95Central Hockey League-5
95Fort Worth Fire-5
Dylevsky, Andrej
92Nashville Knights-18
01Russian Hockey League-87
03Russian Hockey League-106
Dylla, Eric
95German DEL-22
01German Upper Deck-3
Dyment, Chris
93Quebec Pee-Wee Tournament-606
03Houston Aeros-7
03Springfield Falcons Postcards-18
04Providence Bruins-6
05Providence Bruins-3
Dymnicki, David
93Quebec Pee-Wee Tournament-742
Dzhugelia, Adgar
04Russian Under-18 Team-1
Dziama, Justin
03Boston College Eagles-6
Dzieduszycki, Matt
00Barrie Colts-9
02Syracuse Crunch-21
03Augusta Lynx-37
03San Antonio Rampage-17
04Barrie Colts 10th Anniversary-22
05Las Vegas Wranglers-6
Dziedzic, Joe
91Minnesota Golden Gophers-5
92Minnesota Golden Gophers-7
93Minnesota Golden Gophers-9
94Cleveland Lumberjacks-15
94Cleveland Lumberjacks Postcards-15
94Classic-37
Gold-37
95Donruss-235
95Penguins Foodland-13
95Topps-336
OPC Inserts-336
95Ultra-339
95Upper Deck-429
Electric Ice-429
Electric Ice Gold-429
95Signature Rookies-67
Signatures-67
96Be A Player-149
Autographs-149
Autographs Silver-149
96Collector's Choice-216
96Upper Deck-136
97Collector's Choice-213
97Pacific-305
Copper-305
Emerald Green-305
Ice Blue-305
Red-305
Silver-305
97Cleveland Lumberjacks-9
97Cleveland Lumberjacks Postcards-13
Dzikowski, John
83Brandon Wheat Kings-4
84Brandon Wheat Kings-7
85Brandon Wheat Kings-7
Dzurilla, Vladimir
69Swedish Hockey-23
70Finnish Jaakiekko-43
70Swedish Hockey-100
70Swedish Hockey-101
70Swedish Hockey-102
70Swedish Hockey-103
70Swedish Hockey-104
70Swedish Hockey-105
70Swedish Hockey-106
70Swedish Hockey-107
70Swedish Hockey-108
70Swedish Hockey-109
70Swedish Hockey-110
70Swedish Hockey-111
70Swedish Hockey-345
70Swedish Masterserien-1
70Swedish Masterserien-156
72Finnish Jaakiekko-3
72Finnish Hellas-80
92Future Trends '76 Canada Cup-152
03Czech Stadion-640
06Between The Pipes Playing For Your Country-PC06
06Between The Pipes Playing For Your Country Gold-PC06
06ITG International Ice Complete Jersey-CJ20
06ITG International Ice Complete Jersey Gold-CJ20
06ITG International Ice Emblems-GUE24
06ITG International Ice Emblems Gold-GUE24
06ITG International Ice Goaltending Glory-GG08
06ITG International Ice Goaltending Glory Gold-GG08
06ITG International Ice Greatest Moments-GM06
06ITG International Ice Greatest Moments Gold-GM06
06ITG International Ice International Rivals-IR05
06ITG International Ice International Rivals Gold-IR05
06ITG International Ice Jerseys-GUJ24
06ITG International Ice Jerseys Gold-GUJ24
06ITG International Ice Numbers-GUN24
06ITG International Ice Numbers Gold-GUN24
06ITG International Ice Passing The Torch-PTT7
06ITG International Ice Passing The Torch Gold-PTT7
06ITG International Ice Teammates-IT20
06ITG International Ice Teammates Gold-IT20
06ITG International Ice Triple Memorabilia-TM01
06ITG International Ice Triple Memorabilia Gold-TM01
Eade, Chris
99UD Prospects-9
Eades, Carey
04North Dakota Fighting Sioux-28
Eady, Tyler
01Mississauga Ice Dogs-10
02Mississauga Ice Dogs-8
Eagan, Joe
92Dallas Freeze-9
Eager, Ben
02BAP Memorabilia Draft Redemptions-23
03Oshawa Generals-25
03Oshawa Generals-NNO
04Philadelphia Phantoms-2
04ITG Heroes and Prospects-189
04ITG Heroes/Prospects Toronto Expo '05-189
05Beehive-154
Matte-154
05Black Diamond-268
05Hot Prospects-256
Hot Materials-HMBE
Red Hot-256
White Hot-256
05Parkhurst-655
Facsimile Auto Parallel-655
Signatures-BE
05SP Authentic-215
05SP Game Used-227
05SPx-238
Spectrum-238
05The Cup-168
Autographed Rookie Patches Gold Rainbow-168
Black Rainbow Rookies-168
Masterpiece Pressplates (Artifacts)-309
Masterpiece Pressplates (Bee Hive)-154
Masterpiece Pressplates (Black Diamond)-268
Masterpiece Pressplates (Ice)-216
Masterpiece Pressplates (Rookie Update)-239
Masterpiece Pressplates SPA Autos-215
Masterpiece Pressplates (SP Game Used)-227
Masterpiece Pressplates SPx Autos-238
Masterpiece Pressplates (Trilogy)-288
Masterpiece Pressplates Ult Coll-162
Masterpiece Pressplates Autographs-168
Platinum Rookies-168
05UD Artifacts-309
05Ultimate Collection-162
Gold-162
05Upper Deck Ice-216
05Upper Deck Rookie Update-239
Inspirations Patch Rookies-239
05Upper Deck Trilogy-288
05Philadelphia Phantoms-8
06Flair Showcase Inks-IBE
06Flyers Postcards-21
06UD Powerplay Power Marks-PMBE
06Upper Deck MVP Autographs-OAEE
06Philadelphia Phantoms-16
Eagerlund, Rickard
64Swedish Coralli ISHockey-62
Eagles, Langley
93Quebec Pee-Wee Tournament-1242
Eagles, Matt
05Moncton Wildcats-4
06Moncton Wildcats-10
Eagles, Mike
82Kitchener Rangers-19
83Canadian National Juniors-5
83Fredericton Express-24
84Fredericton Express-20
85Nordiques General Foods-6
85Nordiques McDonald's-6
85Nordiques Provigo-7
85Nordiques Team Issue-7
86Nordiques General Foods-7
86Nordiques McDonald's-6
86Nordiques Team Issue-5
87Nordiques General Foods-8
87Nordiques Team Issue-7
87O-Pee-Chee-253
87Panini Stickers-170
88Blackhawks Coke-4
88O-Pee-Chee Stickers-191
88Panini Stickers-354
89ProCards IHL-68
90ProCards AHL/IHL-395
91Jets IGA-8
91Parkhurst-420
French-420
91Pro Set-518
French-518
91Score Canadian Bilingual-414
91Score Canadian English-414
91Upper Deck-523
French-523
92Score-345
Canadian-345
93Jets Readers Club-7
93Jets Ruffles-9
93OPC Premier-116
Gold-116
93Parkhurst-229
Emerald Ice-229
93Score-429
Canadian-429
93Stadium Club-14
Members Only Master Set-14
OPC-14
First Day Issue-14
First Day Issue OPC-14
93Topps/OPC Premier-116
Gold-116
94Be A Player Signature Cards-157
95Capitals Team Issue-6
97Be A Player-149
Autographs-149
Autographs Die-Cuts-149
Autographs Prismatic Die-Cuts-149
97Pacific Dynagon Best Kept Secrets-101
99O-Pee-Chee-181
99O-Pee-Chee Chrome-181
99O-Pee-Chee Chrome Refractors-181
99Topps/OPC-181
99Topps/OPC Chrome-181
Refractors-181
Eagles, Travis
98Prince George Cougars-8
99Prince George Cougars-19
00Prince George Cougars-22
01Brandon Wheat Kings-5
Eakin, Bruce
81Saskatoon Blades-9
84Moncton Golden Flames-22
85Nova Scotia Oilers-27
94German DEL-91
95German DEL-93
96German DEL-234
Eakins, Dallas
88ProCards AHL-34
89ProCards AHL-41
90Moncton Hawks-5
90ProCards AHL/IHL-253
91Moncton Hawks-6
91ProCards-170
93Cincinnati Cyclones-6
96Coyotes Coca-Cola-4
97Be A Player-86
Autographs-86
Autographs Die-Cuts-86
Autographs Prismatic Die-Cuts-86
99Chicago Wolves-4
00Upper Deck NHLPA-PA13
00Chicago Wolves-8
01Chicago Wolves-6
02Chicago Wolves-6
03Manitoba Moose-20
Earhart, Barry
86London Knights-9
Earl, Luke
93Quebec Pee-Wee Tournament-815
Earl, Robbie
03Wisconsin Badgers-8
04Wisconsin Badgers-4
05Wisconsin Badgers-8
06Toronto Marlies-9
Earl, Tom
72Whalers New England WHA-6
Eason, T.J.
01Kitchener Rangers-16
03Kitchener Rangers Memorial Cup-7
East, John
897th Inn. Sketch OHL-62
90Hampton Roads Admirals-45
91Hampton Roads Admirals-3
Easter, James
05Dutch Vadeko Flyers -5
Eastland, Mike
94Maple Leafs Pin-up Posters-4
Eastman, Derek
03Columbia Inferno-102
Eastman, Steve
02Topeka Scarecrows-13

Eastwood, Mike
92Maple Leafs Kodak-10
92Parkhurst-494
Emerald Ice-494
92St. John's Maple Leafs-6
93Maple Leafs Score Black's-19
93Upper Deck-57
94Canada Games NHL POGS-232
94Leaf-378
94Maple Leafs Gangsters-5
94Parkhurst SE-SE183
Gold-SE183
94Stadium Club-167
Members Only Master Set-167
First Day Issue-167
Super Team Winner Cards-167
95Be A Player-102
Signatures-S102
Signatures Die Cuts-S102
95Canada Games NHL POGS-290
95Donruss-207
95Jets Readers Club-3
95Jets Team Issue-8
95Leaf-299
95Panini Stickers-213
95Playoff One on One-216
95Upper Deck-292
Electric Ice-292
Electric Ice Gold-292
96Coyotes Coca-Cola-5
96Playoff One on One-399
97Pacific Invincible NHL Regime-125
99Blues Taco Bell-14
99Kraft Face Off Rivals-6
99O-Pee-Chee-185
99O-Pee-Chee Chrome-185
99O-Pee-Chee Chrome Refractors-185
99Topps/OPC-185
99Topps/OPC Chrome-185
Refractors-185
99Ultimate Victory-78
1/1-78
Parallel-78
Parallel 100-78
00Pacific-342
Copper-342
Gold-342
Ice Blue-342
Premiere Date-342
00Upper Deck-385
Exclusives Tier 1-385
Exclusives Tier 2-385
01Crown Royale Triple Threads-18
01Private Stock Game Gear-87
01Private Stock Game Gear Patches-87
01Titanium Double-Sided Jerseys-37
01Titanium Draft Day Edition-83
01Upper Deck-384
Exclusives-384
01Vanguard Memorabilia-28
01Vanguard Patches-28
02Blues Team Issue-6
02Pacific Complete-334
Red-334
03Pacific Complete-350
Red-350

Eaton, Alexander
03Sudbury Wolves-8
04Sudbury Wolves-12

Eaton, Erik
03Bowling Green Falcons-11

Eaton, J.D.
907th Inn. Sketch OHL-382
90Sudbury Wolves-20
917th Inn. Sketch OHL-42

Eaton, Mark
95Waterloo Blackhawks -3
99BAP Memorabilia-364
Gold-364
Silver-364
99BAP Millennium Calder Candidates Ruby-C47
99BAP Millennium Calder Candidate Emerald-C47
99BAP Millennium Calder Cand Sapphire-C47
99Pacific Dynagon Ice-146
Blue-146
Copper-146
Gold-146
Premiere Date-146
99Pacific Omega-177
Copper-177
Gold-177
Ice Blue-177
Premiere Date-177
99Stadium Club-169
First Day Issue-169
One of a Kind-169
Printing Plates Black-169
Printing Plates Cyan-169
Printing Plates Magenta-169
Printing Plates Yellow-169
99Topps Premier Plus-84
Parallel-84
00BAP Memorabilia-97
Emerald-97
Ruby-97
Sapphire-97
Promos-97
00BAP Mem Chicago Sportsfest Copper-97
00BAP Memorabilia Chicago Sportsfest Blue-97
00BAP Memorabilia Chicago Sportsfest Gold-97
00BAP Memorabilia Chicago Sportsfest Ruby-97
00BAP Memorabilia Chicago Sun-Times Ruby-97
00BAP Memorabilia Chicago Sun-Times Gold-97
00BAP Chicago Sun-Times Sapphire-97
00BAP Mem Toronto Fall Expo Copper-97
00BAP Memorabilia Toronto Fall Expo Gold-97
00BAP Memorabilia Toronto Fall Expo Ruby-97
00O-Pee-Chee-276
00O-Pee-Chee Parallel-276
00Topps/OPC-276
Parallel-276
00Upper Deck MVP-202
First Stars-202
Second Stars-202
Third Stars-202
00Upper Deck Victory-277
00Milwaukee Admirals Keebler-5
03Pacific Complete-371
Red-371
06O-Pee-Chee-396
Rainbow-396
06Upper Deck-407
Exclusives Parallel-407
High Gloss Parallel-407
Masterpieces-407

Eatough, Jeff
82North Bay Centennials-5

Eaves, Ben
03Boston College Eagles-1
04Wilkes-Barre Scranton Penguins-11
05WBS Penguins-8

Eaves, Mike
79Panini Stickers-222
80North Stars Postcards-6
80O-Pee-Chee-206
80Topps-206
81North Stars Postcards-8
81O-Pee-Chee-171
82North Stars Postcards-8
83O-Pee-Chee-79
83Vachon-4
84O-Pee-Chee-221
84O-Pee-Chee Stickers-244
85O-Pee-Chee-213
89Flyers Postcards-8
90ProCards AHL/IHL-26
91ProCards-286
03Wisconsin Badgers-29
04Wisconsin Badgers-16
05Wisconsin Badgers-26

Eaves, Murray
83O-Pee-Chee-384
88ProCards AHL-12
89ProCards AHL-22

Eaves, Patrick
03BAP Memorabilia Draft Redemptions-29
04SP Authentic Rookie Redemptions-RR50
05ITG Heroes/Prosp Toronto Expo Parallel -275
05Beehive-92
Matte-92
Signature Scrapbook-SSEA
05Black Diamond-266
05Hot Prospects-207
Autographed Patch Variation-207
Autographed Patch Variation Gold-207
Red Hot-207
05Parkhurst-345
05Parkhurst-649
Facsimile Auto Parallel-345
Signatures-PE
05SP Authentic-174
Limited-174
Rarefied Rookies-RRPE
05SP Game Used-108
Autographs-108
Gold-108
Auto Draft-AD-PE
Rookie Exclusives-PE
Rookie Exclusives Silver-RE-PE
Significant Numbers-SN-EA
05SPx-149
Spectrum-149
05The Cup-137
Autographed Rookie Patches Gold Rainbow-137
Black Rainbow Rookies-137
Masterpiece Pressplates (Artifacts)-241
Masterpiece Pressplates (Bee Hive)-92
Masterpiece Pressplates (Black Diamond)-266
Masterpiece Pressplates (Ice)-160
Masterpiece Pressplates (Power Play)-152
Masterpiece Pressplates (Power Play)-152
Masterpiece Pressplates (Rookie Update)-224
Masterpiece Pressplates SPA Autos-174
Masterpiece Pressplates (SP Game Used)-108
Masterpiece Pressplates (SPx)-149
Masterpiece Pressplates (SPx)-149
Masterpiece Pressplates (Trilogy)-284
Masterpiece Pressplates Ult Coll Autos-128
Masterpiece Pressplates (Victory)-295
Masterpiece Pressplates Autographs-137
Platinum Rookies-137
05UD Artifacts-241
Gold-RED41
05UD PowerPlay-152
05UD Rookie Class-42
05Ultimate Collection-128
Autographed Shields-128
Ultimate Debut Threads Jerseys Autos-DAJPE
Ultimate Debut Threads Patches Autos-DAPPE
Ultimate Signatures Logos-SLEV
05Ultra-236
Gold-236
Ice-236
Rookie Uniformity Jerseys-RU-PE
Rookie Uniformity Jersey Autographs-ARU-PE
Rookie Uniformity Patches-RUP-PE
Rookie Uniformity Patch Autographs-ARP-PE
05Upper Deck-458
Rookie Ink-RIPE
Rookie Threads-RTPE
Rookie Threads Autographs-ARTPE
05Upper Deck Ice-160
Premieres Auto Patches-AIPPE
05Upper Deck Rookie Update-224
Inspirations Patch Rookies-224
05Upper Deck Trilogy-284
05Upper Deck Victory-295
Black-295
Gold-295
Silver-295
05AHL Top Prospects-11
05Binghamton Senators-12
05Binghamton Senators Quickway-12
05ITG Heroes and Prospects-275
Complete Jerseys-CJ-38
Complete Jerseys Gold-CJ-38
Complete Logos-AHL-14
Jerseys-GUJ-69
Jerseys Gold-GUJ-69
Emblems-GUE-69
Emblems Gold-GUE-69
Numbers-GUN-69
Numbers Gold-GUN-69
Nameplates-N-47
Nameplates Gold-N-47
06Be A Player-135
Autographs-135
Signatures-EA
Signatures Duals-DEV
06Black Diamond-59
Black-59
Gold-59
Ruby-59
06Fleer-139
Tiffany-139
06Gatorade-53
06McDonald's Upper Deck Rookie Review-RR10
06O-Pee-Chee-345
06O-Pee-Chee-616
Rainbow-345
Rainbow-616
06Panini Stickers-116
06SP Authentic Sign of the Times Duals-STHE
06Ultra-138
Gold Medallion-138
Ice Medallion-138
06Upper Deck-138
Exclusives Parallel-138
High Gloss Parallel-138
Masterpieces-138
06Upper Deck MVP-204
Gold Script-204
Super Script-204
06Binghamton Senators 5th Anniversary-6

Ebbett, Andrew
02Michigan Wolverines-13
03Michigan Wolverines-23
04Michigan Wolverines-2
06AHL Top Prospects-3
06Binghamton Senators-5

Ebenburger, Martin
94German First League-349

Eberenz, Bryan
93Quebec Pee-Wee Tournament-726

Eberhard, Hans
94German First League-44

Eberhard, Stefan
93Quebec Pee-Wee Tournament-1632

Eberle, Derek
907th Inn. Sketch WHL-184
917th Inn. Sketch WHL-229
97Fort Wayne Komets-11
99Jacksonville Lizard Kings-9
00UK Sekonda Superleague-7

Eberle, Greg
97Peoria Rivermen-24
99Peoria Rivermen-3

Eberle, Jorg
91Finnish Semic World Champ Stickers-188
91Swedish Semic World Champ Stickers-188
92Upper Deck-384
92Finnish Semic-208
93Swedish Semic World Champ Stickers-122
93Swiss HNL-96
95Finnish Semic World Championships-192
95Swedish Globe World Championships-210
95Swedish World Championships Stickers-127
95Swiss HNL-147
95Swiss HNL-507
95Swiss HNL-508
96Swiss HNL-19
98Swiss Power Play Stickers-213

Eberlee, Jordan
06Regina Pats-6

Eberly, Danny
03Atlantic City Boardwalk Bullies-5
03Atlantic City Boardwalk Bullies RBI-19
04Atlantic City Boardwalk Bullies Kinko's-10

Ebermann, Bohuslav
79Panini Stickers-89
96Czech APS Extraliga-286

Ecclestone, Tim
68Bauer Ads-7
68O-Pee-Chee-178
69O-Pee-Chee-179
70Colgate Stamps-58
70Dad's Cookies-26
70Esso Power Players-246
70O-Pee-Chee-102
70Sargent Promotions Stamps-188
70Topps-102
Topps/OPC Sticker Stamps-4
71Bazooka-27
71Letraset Action Replays-9
71O-Pee-Chee-52
71Sargent Promotions Stamps-56
71Topps-52
71Toronto Sun-93
72O-Pee-Chee-55
72Sargent Promotions Stamps-78
72Topps-33
73O-Pee-Chee-144
73Red Wings Team Issue-11
73Topps-124
74NHL Action Stamps-255
74O-Pee-Chee NHL-323
76O-Pee-Chee NHL-351
77O-Pee-Chee NHL-364

Eckerblom, Nicklas
03Swedish Elite Rookies-3

Eckert, Michael
94German First League-396

Eckford, Tyler
04South Surrey Eagles-6
04South Surrey Eagles-7
04Surrey Eagles-5a
04Surrey Eagles-5b
04Surrey Eagles-5

Eckmaier, Beppi
98German DEL-313

Eckmaier, J.
95German DEL-382

Ecoeur, Olivier
93Swiss HNL-328
95Swiss HNL-474
96Swiss HNL-418

Economakos, Nick
05Bakersfield Condors-9

Edberg, Rolf
70Swedish Hockey-8
71Swedish Hockey-83
72Swedish Stickers-62
73Swedish Stickers-200
74Swedish Stickers-212
78Capitals Team Issue-4
79Panini Stickers-194
79Capitals Team Issue-3
80O-Pee-Chee-65
80Topps-65
82Swedish Semic VM Stickers-21
84Swedish Semic Elitserien-140

Eddolls, Frank
43Parade Sportive *-36
44Beehive Group II Photos-307
45Quaker Oats Photos-75
51Parkhurst-89
05ITG Ultimate Mem Broadway Bluesh Autos-2

Eddy, Justin
04Portland Pirates-6

Eden, Bjorn
98Danish Hockey League-18
99Danish Hockey League-18

Edenvik, Curt
65Swedish Coralli ISHockey-172
67Swedish Hockey-26
69Swedish Hockey-40
71Swedish Hockey-332
72Swedish Stickers-142

Edenvik, Per
71Swedish Hockey-333
72Swedish Stickers-143

Eder, Florian
94German First League-189

Eder, Hans-George
94German First League-64

Eder, Stephan
94German DEL-332

Edestrand, Darryl
71O-Pee-Chee-187
71Penguins Postcards-4
71Toronto Sun-213
72O-Pee-Chee-195
72Sargent Promotions Stamps-181
73O-Pee-Chee-216
74NHL Action Stamps-34
74O-Pee-Chee NHL-313
75O-Pee-Chee NHL-11
75Topps-11
76O-Pee-Chee NHL-179
76Topps-179
77O-Pee-Chee NHL-321
77Rochester Americans-9
78O-Pee-Chee-377
79O-Pee-Chee-280

Edgar, James
01Peterborough Petes-6

Edgar, Kevin
03New Mexico Scorpions-11

Edgar, Trevor
95Slapshot-241

Edgerly, Derek
93Lakeland Ice Warriors-10

Edgerton, Devin
92Anaheim Bullfrogs RHI-19
92Wheeling Thunderbirds-7
93Atlanta Knights-9
94Atlanta Knights-10
95Phoenix Roadrunners-10
96Swiss HNL-349
98Swiss Power Play Stickers-214
99German DEL-83
00German DEL-7
01German Adler Mannheim Eagles Postcards-3
01German Upper Deck-168
02German Adler Mannheim Eagles Postcards-18
02German DEL City Press-237
03German DEL-2
03German Mannheim Eagles Postcards-25
04German Adler Mannheim Eagles Postcards-12
04German DEL-7
05German DEL-247

Edgeworth, David
02Owen Sound Attack-22
03Belleville Bulls-16
04Kingston Frontenacs-6

Edholm, Mats
87Swedish Panini Stickers-261

Edholm, Nisse
57Swedish Allabilder-111

Edin, Lage
67Swedish Hockey-117
69Swedish Hockey-130
70Swedish Hockey-85
71Swedish Hockey-178
72Swedish Stickers-168
73Swedish Stickers-227

Edinger, Adam
02Trenton Titans-A-2
03Peoria Rivermen-1

Edler, Alexander
05Kelowna Rockets-12
06Beehive-158
Matte-158
06Hot Prospects-181
Red Hot-181
White Hot-181
06O-Pee-Chee-576
Rainbow-576
06SP Authentic-209
Limited-209
06SP Game Used Rookie Exclusives Autographs-REAE
06The Cup-167
Autographed Rookie Masterpiece Pressplates-167
Gold Rainbow Autographed Rookie Patches-167
Masterpiece Pressplates (Bee Hive)-158
Masterpiece Pressplates (Marquee Rookies)-576
Masterpiece Pressplates (Sweet Beginnings)-159
Masterpiece Pressplates (Ultimate Collection)-101
Masterpiece Pressplates (Victory)-325
NHL Shields Duals-DSHBE
Rookies Black-167
Rookies Platinum-167
06Ultimate Collection-101
06Upper Deck-491
Exclusives Parallel-491
High Gloss Parallel-491
Masterpieces-491
06Upper Deck Sweet Shot-159
Rookie Jerseys Autographs-159
06Upper Deck Victory-325
06AHL Top Prospects-24
06Manitoba Moose-3
07Upper Deck Rookie Class -46

Edlund, Hans
83Swedish Semic Elitserien-42
84Swedish Semic Elitserien-42
85Swedish Panini Stickers-37
86Swedish Panini Stickers-22
87Swedish Panini Stickers-37

Edlund, Jan
69Swedish Hockey-205

Edlund, Par
85Swedish Panini Stickers-44
86Swedish Panini Stickers-17
87Swedish Panini Stickers-40
90Swedish Semic Elitserien Stickers-46
91Swedish Semic Elitserien Stickers-297
92Swedish Semic Elitserien Stickers-322
93Swedish Semic Elitserien-287
94Swedish Leaf-106
95Swedish Leaf-142
95Swedish Upper Deck-216
97Swedish Collector's Choice-75
98Swedish UD Choice-80
99Swedish Upper Deck-75
00Swedish Upper Deck-65

Edmond, Dominic
84Richelieu Riverains-5

Edmondson, Gord
04Langley Hornets-10

Edmund, Jens
98Danish Hockey League-209

Edmund, Rasmus
98Danish Hockey League-219

Edmundson, Gary
44Beehive Group II Photos-398
59Parkhurst-48
60Parkhurst-5
60Shirriff Coins-14
61Union Oil WHL-9

Edmundson, Mark
92Ottawa 67's-10
01Bakersfield Condors-5

Edqvist, Sten
65Swedish Coralli ISHockey-90

Edstrom, Anders
67Swedish Hockey-199

Edstrom, Lars
89Swedish Semic Elitserien Stickers-166
90Swedish Semic Elitserien Stickers-244
91Swedish Semic Elitserien Stickers-191
92Swedish Semic Elitserien Stickers-192
93Swedish Semic Elitserien-163
94Swedish Leaf-176
95Swedish Leaf-202
95Swedish Upper Deck-214
98Swedish UD Choice-147
99Swedish Upper Deck-149
00Swedish Upper Deck-133

Edstrom, Peter
83Swedish Semic Elitserien-48
84Swedish Semic Elitserien-48
85Swedish Panini Stickers-42
86Swedish Panini Stickers-25
87Swedish Panini Stickers-39

Edstrom, Tomas
86Swedish Panini Stickers-189

Edur, Tom
76Rockies Coke Cans-8
76Rockies Puck Bucks-8
77O-Pee-Chee NHL-169
77Rockies Coke Cans-6
77Topps-169
78O-Pee-Chee-119
78Topps-119

Edwall, Luke
04Arizona Icecats-4

Edwards, Andrew
98Arizona Icecats-6
99Arizona Icecats-5
00Arizona Icecats-6

Edwards, Dave
89Oshawa Generals-14

Edwards, Don
77O-Pee-Chee NHL-201
77Topps-201
78O-Pee-Chee-70
78O-Pee-Chee-150
78O-Pee-Chee-336
78Topps-70
78Topps-150
79O-Pee-Chee-105
79Sabres Bells-1
79Sabres Milk Panels-1
79Topps-105
80O-Pee-Chee-92
80O-Pee-Chee-166
80O-Pee-Chee-215
80Topps-92
80Topps-166
80Topps-215
81O-Pee-Chee-21
81O-Pee-Chee-389
81O-Pee-Chee Stickers-55
81Sabres Milk Panels-3
81Topps-E75
82Flames Dollars-2
82O-Pee-Chee-46
82O-Pee-Chee Stickers-124
82Post Cereal-2
82Topps Stickers-124
83NHL Key Tags-15
83O-Pee-Chee-80
83Puffy Stickers-2
83Vachon-5
84O-Pee-Chee-222
85Maple Leafs Postcards-10
85O-Pee-Chee-183
86O-Pee-Chee Stickers-139
04ITG Franchises US East-343
Autographs-A-DE

Edwards, Gary
71Letraset Action Replays-23
71O-Pee-Chee-155
71Toronto Sun-111
72O-Pee-Chee-113
Player Crests-9
72Topps-151
73O-Pee-Chee-199
74NHL Action Stamps-113
75O-Pee-Chee NHL-105
75Topps-105
76O-Pee-Chee NHL-365
77O-Pee-Chee NHL-345
78North Stars Cloverleaf Dairy-5
78O-Pee-Chee-6
78Topps-6
79North Stars Postcards-3
80North Stars Postcards-7
80O-Pee-Chee-335
88Oilers Tenth Anniversary-78

Edwards, Jeff
93Omaha Lancers-5

Edwards, Marv
52Juniors Blue Tint-17
69Maple Leafs White Border Glossy-7
69O-Pee-Chee-185
72Sargent Promotions Stamps-49

Edwards, Paul
80Oshawa Generals-10
81Oshawa Generals-8

Edwards, Ray
92Dayton Bombers-8
93Dayton Bombers-13
94Huntington Blizzard-7
96Anaheim Bullfrogs RHI-18
98Huntington Blizzard-21
99Huntington Blizzard-21
06New Mexico Scorpions-1

Edwards, Roy
57St. Catherine's Tee Pees-1
67Topps-106
68O-Pee-Chee-144
68Shirriff Coins-40
69O-Pee-Chee-56
69Topps-56
70Dad's Cookies-27
70Esso Power Players-144
70O-Pee-Chee-21
70Red Wings Marathon-4
70Sargent Promotions Stamps-62
70Topps-21
71Bazooka-21
71O-Pee-Chee-99
71Penguins Postcards-5
71Sargent Promotions Stamps-167
71Topps-99
71Toronto Sun-214
72Sargent Promotions Stamps-174
72Finnish Semic World Championship-192
72Swedish Semic World Championship-192
73O-Pee-Chee-82
73Topps-82

Edwards, Ryan
02Odessa Jackalopes-7

Edwards, Trevor
06Port Huron Flags-16

Edwards, Troy
91Air Canada SJHL-A44
92Saskatchewan JHL-1
97Idaho Steelheads-11
98Idaho Steelheads-6
99Idaho Steelheads-3

Edwardson, Dereck
04Atlantic City Boardwalk Bullies-8
05Las Vegas Wranglers-7
06Las Vegas Wranglers-7

Efthimiou, Brad
00Belleville Bulls-15
03Mississauga Ice Dogs-8

Egan, Pat
34Beehive Group I Photos-223
44Beehive Group II Photos-17
44Beehive Group II Photos-308

Egeland, Allan
907th Inn. Sketch WHL-126
917th Inn. Sketch WHL-169
92Tacoma Rockets-8
93Tacoma Rockets-7
94Atlanta Knights-15
95Atlanta Knights-8
98Orlando Solar Bears II-14
02Charlotte Checkers-82
03Charlotte Checkers-69

Egeland, Tracy
90ProCards AHL/IHL-404
91ProCards-481
92Indianapolis Ice-11
98Huntington Blizzard-12
99Greensboro Generals-8
00Lubbock Cotton Kings-2

Egen, Ulrich
82Swedish Semic VM Stickers-109
83Swedish Semic VM Stickers-109
00German Berlin Polar Bears Postcards-4
01German Berlin Polar Bears Postcards-6

Egener, Luke
04Vancouver Giants-1
05Red Deer Rebels-3

Egener, Mike
00Calgary Hitmen-11
01Calgary Hitmen-9
01Calgary Hitmen Autographed-9
02Calgary Hitmen-24
03Calgary Hitmen-6
04Springfield Falcons-17
05ITG Heroes/Prosp Toronto Expo Parallel -58
05Johnstown Chiefs-8
05Springfield Falcons-15
05ITG Heroes and Prospects-58
Autographs-A-ME
06Springfield Falcons-13

Egers, Jack
70Esso Power Players-195
71Blues Postcards-9
71Toronto Sun-170
72Blues White Border-3
72O-Pee-Chee-107
72Sargent Promotions Stamps-196
72Topps-147
73O-Pee-Chee-79
73Topps-79
74Capitals White Borders-10
74NHL Action Stamps-315
74O-Pee-Chee NHL-93
74Topps-93
75O-Pee-Chee NHL-134
75Topps-134

Eggen, Pal Kristian
92Norwegian Elite Series-211

Egger, Andres
95Swiss HNL-372
96Swiss HNL-564

Egger, Karlheinz
72Finnish Hellas-50
72Finnish Semic World Championship-101
72Swedish Semic World Championship-101

Eggert, Andrew
04Notre Dame Fighting Irish-8

Egli, Andy
93Swiss HNL-216
95Swiss HNL-65
96Swiss HNL-209
99Swiss Panini Stickers-333
00Swiss Panini Stickers-359

Egli, Guido
93Swiss HNL-251

Egli, Philipp
93Swiss HNL-352

Ego, Klaus
72Finnish Semic World Championship-103
72Swedish Semic World Championship-103

Egorov, Egor
05Shawinigan Cataractes-19

Ehelechner, Patrick
02German DEL City Press-108
03Sudbury Wolves-9
04Sudbury Wolves-11
05German DEL-242
05German DEL-313
Goalies-G02

Ehl, Mark
04Williams Lake Timberwolves-5

Ehlers, Heinz
85Swedish Panini Stickers-150
86Swedish Panini Stickers-155
87Swedish Panini Stickers-159
89Swedish Semic Elitserien Stickers-15
90Swedish Semic Elitserien Stickers-88
92Swedish Semic Elitserien Stickers-262
98German DEL-125
99German DEL-283
00German DEL-38
01German Upper Deck-17

Ehman, Gerry
44Beehive Group II Photos-399
59Parkhurst-19
60Parkhurst-8
60Shirriff Coins-19
63Rochester Americans-13
67Seals Team Issue-9
68O-Pee-Chee-84
68Shirriff Coins-109
68Topps-84
69O-Pee-Chee-83
69Topps-83
70Dad's Cookies-28
70Esso Power Players-98
70O-Pee-Chee-187
70Sargent Promotions Stamps-144

Ehrenberger, Jiri
94German First League-372

Ehrenverth, Edgar
61Sudbury Wolves-8
62Sudbury Wolves-10

Ehrhardt, Travis
05Moose Jaw Warriors-5
06Moose Jaw Warriors-5

Ehrhoff, Christian
00German DEL-145
01German Upper Deck-257
02SPx Rookie Redemption-R209
02German DEL City Press-219
Top Stars-GT3
03BAP Ultimate Mem Rookie Jersey Emblems-26
03BAP Ultimate Mem Rookie Jsy Emblem Gold-26
03BAP Ultimate Mem Rookie Jersey Numbers-26
03BAP Ultimate Mem Rookie Jsy Number Gold-26
03Black Diamond-154
Black-154
Green-154
Red-154
03ITG Action-661
03ITG VIP Rookie Debut-27
03Pacific Complete-554
Red-554
03Parkhurst Rookie-138
Rookie Emblems-RE-26
Rookie Emblems Gold-RE-26
Rookie Jerseys-RJ-26
Rookie Jerseys Gold-RJ-26
Rookie Numbers-RN-26
Rookie Numbers Gold-RN-26
03SP Authentic-145
Limited-145
03SP Game Used-76
Gold-76
03SPx-215
Radiance-215
03Topps Traded-TT160
Blue-TT160
Gold-TT160
Red-TT160
03UD Honor Roll-175
03Upper Deck-237
Canadian Exclusives-237
HG-237
03Upper Deck Rookie Update-216
YoungStars-YS19
03Upper Deck Trilogy-165
Limited-165
03Cleveland Barons-7
04German DEL Global Players-GP2
04AHL All-Stars-11
04Cleveland Barons-7
05ITG Heroes/Prosp Toronto Expo Parallel -96
05Parkhurst-413
Facsimile Auto Parallel-413
05SP Game Used Game Gear-GG-CE
05UD Artifacts Auto Facts-AF-CE
05UD Artifacts Auto Facts Blue-AF-CE
05UD Artifacts Auto Facts Copper-AF-CE
05UD Artifacts Auto Facts Pewter-AF-CE
05UD Artifacts Auto Facts Silver-AF-CE
05UD Powerplay Specialists-TSCE
05UD Powerplay Specialists Patches-SPCE
05Ultra Fresh Ink-FI-CE
05Ultra Fresh Ink Blue-FI-CE
05Upper Deck-163
HG Glossy-163
Notable Numbers-N-CE
05Upper Deck MVP-330
Gold-330
Platinum-330
05Upper Deck Toronto Fall Expo-163
05German DEL-284
05ITG Heroes and Prospects-96
Autographs-A-CEO
06O-Pee-Chee-410
Rainbow-410
06Upper Deck-167
Exclusives Parallel-167
High Gloss Parallel-167
Masterpieces-167
06Upper Deck MVP-244
Gold Script-244
Super Script-244

Ehrman, Dan
00Calgary Hitmen-12
01Calgary Hitmen-10
01Calgary Hitmen Autographed-10
04Moose Jaw Warriors-5

Ehrmantraut, Lyle
91Air Canada SJHL-E18
92Saskatchewan JHL-57

Eibl, Michael
72Finnish Hellas-58
94German First League-51

Eichberger, Thomas
93Quebec Pee-Wee Tournament-1525

Eichelberger, John
03Wisconsin Badgers-7

Eichenmann, Zdenek
94Czech APS Extraliga-134
95Czech APS Extraliga-114
96Czech APS Extraliga-84
97Czech APS Extraliga-205
97Czech DS Extraliga-93
97Czech DS Stickers-146
98Czech DS-100
98Czech DS Stickers-236
98Czech OFS-400
99Czech DS-163
99Czech OFS-163

Eichmann, Beat
95Swiss HNL-NNO
95Swiss HNL-NNO

Eichmann, Marc
01Swiss HNL-382
02Swiss HNL-74

Eichstadt, Scott
91ProCards-99

Eickman, Mike
01Lincoln Stars-4
02Lincoln Stars-4
02Lincoln Stars-43

Eide, Eskil
92Norwegian Elite Series-130

Eide, Patric
92Norwegian Elite Series-30

Eidsness, Bradley
06Okotoks Oilers -7

Eigner, Trent
94Huntington Blizzard-8
97El Paso Buzzards-7
98El Paso Buzzards-1
01El Paso Buzzards-1

Eigner, Ty
93Fort Worth Fire-5
95Central Hockey League-76

Eilertsen, Lars
92Norwegian Elite Series-79

Eimannsberger, Johann
72Finnish Semic World Championship-100
72Swedish Semic World Championship-100

Eimansberger, Johan
72Finnish Hellas-56

Einarsson, Roland
67Swedish Hockey-63
69Swedish Hockey-96
70Swedish Hockey-48
71Swedish Hockey-115
72Swedish Stickers-96
73Swedish Stickers-208

Einhorn, Andrew
97UK Guildford Flames-11

Eirickson, Shane
85Brandon Wheat Kings-23

Eisebitt, Torsten
94German DEL-398
95German DEL-418

Eiselt, Vaclav
94Czech APS Extraliga-273
95Czech APS Extraliga-144
96Czech APS Extraliga-91
97Czech APS Extraliga-209
97Czech DS Stickers-147
98Czech DS-99
98Czech DS Stickers-241
98Czech OFS-401
98Czech OFS-462
99Czech DS-154
99Czech OFS-103
00Czech OFS-75
01Czech OFS Update-289
01Czech OFS-216
01Czech OFS Plus-339

Eisener, Dan
96Swiss HNL-232

Eisenhut, Craig
06Westside Warriors-9

Eisenhut, Gunther
94German First League-35

Eisenhut, Neil
91ProCards-599
92Hamilton Canucks-6
93PowerPlay-459
94Saint John Flames-4
94Classic Pro Prospects-199
96Flint Generals-5
96Collector's Edge Ice-172
Prism-172
98German DEL-24
99German DEL-128
00German DEL-146
01German Upper Deck-49
02German DEL City Press-45

Eisenkirch, Joel
03Saskatoon Blades-5
04Saskatoon Blades-2
05Kamloops Blazers-23
06Penticton Vees-8

Eiskonen, Markku
65Finnish Hellas-95
66Finnish Jaakiekkosarja-89

Eisler, Greg
99Colorado Gold Kings Taco Bell-9
99Colorado Gold Kings Wendy's-9

Eisler, Matt
98Johnstown Chiefs-14
99Greensboro Generals-17

Ejdeholm, Dennis
99Swedish Upper Deck-131

Ejov, Ilya
05ITG Heroes/Prosp Toronto Expo Parallel -414
05ITG Heroes and Prospects-414

Ek, Marko
92Finnish Jyvas-Hyva Stickers-165
93Finnish Jyvas-Hyva Stickers-149
93Finnish SISU-151
93Finnish SISU-174B
94Finnish SISU-131
96Finnish SISU Redline-117

Ek, Rolf
57Swedish Allabilder-129

Ekdahl, Sven-Erik
56Swedish Allabilder-103

Ekelund, Peter
89Swedish Semic Elitserien Stickers-119
90Swedish Semic Elitserien Stickers-120
91Swedish Semic Elitserien Stickers-125
92Swedish Semic Elitserien Stickers-138
93Swiss HNL-400
94Swedish Leaf-293
95Swedish Leaf-58
95Swedish Upper Deck-87
97Swedish Collector's Choice-93
98Swedish UD Choice-109
99Swedish Upper Deck-95
99Swedish Upper Deck-218
Hands of Gold-7
Hands of Gold-9
00Swedish Upper Deck-99
00Swedish Upper Deck-215
02Swedish SHL-39
Parallel-39
03Swedish Elite-51
Signatures II-13
Silver-51
04Swedish Elitset-53
Gold-53
04Swedish HV71 Postcards-7

Ekenberg, Arne
67Swedish Hockey-152

Eklind, Kjell
56Swedish Allabilder-86

Eklof, Ake
64Swedish Coralli ISHockey-161
65Swedish Coralli ISHockey-161
67Swedish Hockey-118
69Swedish Hockey-131
70Swedish Hockey-49
71Swedish Hockey-125
72Swedish Stickers-104
73Swedish Stickers-220
74Swedish Stickers-213

Eklof, Rolf
64Swedish Coralli ISHockey-104

Eklund, Brian
94Quebec Pee-Wee Tournament-1182
03Pensacola Ice Pilots-341
04Springfield Falcons-5
05Hot Prospects-104
En Fuego-104
Red Hot-104
White Hot-104
05SP Authentic-243
Limited-243
05SP Game Used-188
Gold-188
05SPx-219
Spectrum-219
05The Cup Masterpiece Pressplates (Ice)-208
05The Cup Master Pressplate Rookie Update-109
05The Cup Masterpiece Pressplates SPA-243

05The Cup Masterpiece Pressplates SP GU-188
05The Cup Masterpiece Pressplates (SPx)-219
05Upper Deck Ice-208
05Upper Deck Rookie Update-109
05Springfield Falcons-4

Eklund, Christian

02Swedish SHL-19
Parallel-19
02Swedish SHL Promos-TCC2
03Swedish Elite-20
Silver-20
04Swedish Elitset-18
Gold-18
05German DEL-2
06Swedish SHL Elitset-165

Eklund, Kjell

67Swedish Hockey-135
69Swedish Hockey-147

Eklund, Per

94Swedish Leaf-194
Rookie Rockets-5
95Swedish Leaf-34
95Swedish Upper Deck-50
95Swedish Upper Deck-222
Ticket to North America-NA5
96Swedish Semic Wien-69
98Swedish UD Choice-61
99Swedish Upper Deck-46
Hands of Gold-4
Hands of Gold-6
02Swedish SHL-53
Parallel-53
02Swedish SHL Promos-TCC5
02Swedish SHL Signatures Series II-15
03Swedish Elite-77
Signatures II-11
Silver-77
Stars of the Game-5
04Swedish Elitset-69
Gold-69
Signatures Series A-3
05Swedish SHL Elitset-170
Gold-170
06German DEL-172
New Arrivals-NA3
06Swedish SHL Elitset-25

Eklund, Per-Erik

83Swedish Semic Elitserien-16
83Swedish Semic VM Stickers-14
84Swedish Semic Elitserien-14
85Flyers Postcards-8
85Swedish Panini Stickers-119
85Swedish Panini Stickers-120
86Flyers Postcards-8
86O-Pee-Chee Stickers-127
87O-Pee-Chee-98
87O-Pee-Chee Minis-9
87Panini Stickers-132
87Topps-98
88O-Pee-Chee-211
89Flyers Postcards-9
89O-Pee-Chee Stickers-105
89Panini Stickers-296
89Swedish Semic World Champ Stickers-19
90Bowman-107
Tiffany-107
90Flyers Postcards-7
90O-Pee-Chee-254
90Panini Stickers-113
90Pro Set-215
90Score-308A
Canadian-308A
90Topps-254
Tiffany-254
90Upper Deck-138
French-138
91Pro Set Platinum-89
91Bowman-241
91Flyers J.C. Penney-8
91O-Pee-Chee-111
91Panini Stickers-228
91Parkhurst-128
French-128
91Pinnacle-134
French-134
91Pro Set-179
French-179
91Score American-91
91Score Canadian Bilingual-91
91Score Canadian English-91
91Stadium Club-182
91Topps-111
91Upper Deck-103
French-103
91Finnish Semic World Champ Stickers-210
91Swedish Semic Elitserien Stickers-358
91Swedish Semic World Champ Stickers-210
92Bowman-179
92Flyers J.C. Penney-10
92Flyers Upper Deck Sheets-29
92O-Pee-Chee-242
92Panini Stickers-189
92Panini Stickers French-189
92Pinnacle-149
French-149
92Score-173
Canadian-173
92Stadium Club-154
92Topps-117
Gold-117G
92Ultra-155
92Finnish Semic-71
93Donruss-250
93Flyers J.C. Penney-9
93Flyers Lineup Sheets-12
93Leaf-177
93OPC Premier-449
Gold-449
93Panini Stickers-51
93Parkhurst-147
Emerald Ice-147
93Pinnacle-256
Canadian-256
93PowerPlay-180
93Score-181
Canadian-181
93Stadium Club-289
Members Only Master Set-289
First Day Issue-289
93Topps/OPC Premier-449
Gold-449
93Ultra-386
93Upper Deck-120
93Swedish Semic World Champ Stickers-39
94Parkhurst-56
Gold-56
94Swedish Leaf-243
95Swedish Leaf-71
95Swedish Leaf-NNO
Champs-13
Mega-11
95Swedish Upper Deck-101
95Swedish Upper Deck-228
95Swedish Upper Deck-254
95Swedish Globe World Championships-53
95Swedish World Championships Stickers-156
96Swedish Semic Wien-66
All-Stars-AS5
96Swedish Semic Wien Coca-Cola Dream Team-10
97Swedish Collector's Choice-108
97Swedish Collector's Choice-213
Stick'Ums-S6
98Swedish UD Choice-125

Eklund, Thom

83Swedish Semic Elitserien-37
83Swedish Semic VM Stickers-25
84Swedish Semic Elitserien-231
85Swedish Panini Stickers-229
86Swedish Panini Stickers-259
87Swedish Panini Stickers-245
89Swedish Semic Elitserien Stickers-226
89Swedish Semic World Champ Stickers-13
90Swedish Semic Elitserien Stickers-61
91Swedish Semic Elitserien Stickers-238

Ekman, Kenneth

67Swedish Hockey-153
70Swedish Hockey-180
71Swedish Hockey-265
72Finnish Semic World Championship-64
72Swedish Stickers-243
72Swedish Semic World Championship-64
74Swedish Stickers-166

Ekman, Nils

98Finnish Kerailysarja-22
99BAP Memorabilia-324
Gold-324
Silver-324
99Pacific Omega-220
Copper-220
Gold-220
Ice Blue-220
Premiere Date-220
99Detroit Vipers-2
99IHL All-Stars-2
00Upper Deck NHLPA-PA80
02Swedish SHL-22
Parallel-22
Sharpshooters-SS9
Signatures-3
02Hartford Wolf Pack-8
03Pacific Complete-372
Red-372
03Sharks Postcards-4
04Pacific-228
Blue-228
Red-228
04Swedish Alfabilder Alfa Stars-29
04Swedish Alfabilder Autographs-113
04Swedish Alfabilder Limited Autographs-113
04Swedish Alfabilder Proof Parallels-29
04Swedish Elitset-161
Gold-161
04Swedish Pure Skills-11
Parallel-11
05Parkhurst-404
Facsimile Auto Parallel-404
05Upper Deck Notable Numbers-N-NE
05Upper Deck Victory-161
Black-161
Gold-161
Silver-161
06O-Pee-Chee-394
Rainbow-394
06Panini Stickers-144
06Upper Deck-405
Exclusives Parallel-405
High Gloss Parallel-405
Masterpieces-405
06Upper Deck MVP-233
Gold Script-233
Super Script-233
06Upper Deck Victory-269

Ekroth, Peter

83Swedish Semic Elitserien-202
84Swedish Semic Elitserien-226
85Swedish Panini Stickers-226
86Swedish Panini Stickers-252
89Swedish Semic Elitserien Stickers-270
90Swedish Semic Elitserien Stickers-55
91Swedish Semic Elitserien Stickers-231

Ekrt, Martin

96German DEL-329
99German Bundesliga 2-324

Eksell, Ake

84Swedish Semic Elitserien-97

Ekstrom, Rikard

99Swedish Upper Deck-215
00Swedish Upper Deck-5

Elander, Peter

83Swedish Semic Elitserien-236

Elayoubi, Romy

04Chicoutimi Sagueneens-16
04Drummondville Voltigeurs-19

Elcombe, Kelly

81Fredericton Express-11
82Fredericton Express-11

Eldebrink, Anders

81Canucks Team Issue-7
81Fredericton Express-9
82Fredericton Express-9
83Swedish Semic Elitserien-198
84Swedish Semic Elitserien-222
85Swedish Panini Stickers-121
85Swedish Panini Stickers-122
85Swedish Panini Stickers-223
86Swedish Panini Stickers-248
87Swedish Panini Stickers-235
89Swedish Semic Elitserien Stickers-219
89Swedish Semic World Champ Stickers-9
93Swedish Semic World Champ Stickers-20
93Swiss HNL-11
95Swedish Upper Deck 1st Division Stars-DS6
95Swiss HNL-515
95Swiss HNL-537
97Swedish Collector's Choice-167
97Swedish Collector's Choice-208
Crash the Game Exchange-C27
Crash the Game Redemption-R27

Elder, Brian

93Quebec Pee-Wee Tournament-885
94Brandon Wheat Kings-7
95Brandon Wheat Kings-8
95Slapshot Memorial Cup-27
96Brandon Wheat Kings-10
97Bowman CHL-102
OPC-102
99Anchorage Aces-7

Elder, Josh

04Prince Albert Raiders-18
05Prince Albert Raiders-9
06Prince Albert Raiders-19

Elder, Travis

04St. Michael's Majors-18

Elderkin, Morris

98OCN Blizzard-5

Elders, Jason

92British Columbia JHL-241
95Oklahoma Coyotes RHI-5
98ECHL All-Star Southern Conference-10
98Mobile Mysticks-10
99Mobile Mysticks-10
02UK Nottingham Panthers-8

Eldred, Matt

99Milwaukee Admirals Keebler-12
00UK Sekonda Superleague-92

Elenbaas, Dave

76Nova Scotia Voyageurs-5

Eley, Mike

95Medicine Hat Tigers-6
96Medicine Hat Tigers-5

Elezi, Charlie

01Indianapolis Ice-7
03Oklahoma City Blazers-7

Elfring, Calvin

99ECHL All-Star Northern Conference-5
00Roanoke Express-8

Elgstrom, Ake

55Swedish Alfabilder-36

Elhai, Jesse

93Quebec Pee-Wee Tournament-725

Elhokayen, Bernard

04Chicoutimi Sagueneens-3

Elias, Patrik

94Czech APS Extraliga-64
96Devils Team Issue-22
96Albany River Rats-5
97Be A Player-228
Autographs-228
Autographs Die-Cuts-228
Autographs Prismatic Die-Cuts-228
One Timers-16
97Beehive-53
Authentic Autographs-53
Golden Portraits-53
Team-20
Team Gold-20
97Black Diamond-44
Double Diamond-44
Triple Diamond-44
Quadruple Diamond-44
Premium Cut-PC8
Premium Cut Double Diamond-PC8
Premium Cut Quadruple Diamond Horiz-PC8
Premium Cut Triple Diamond-PC8
Premium Cut Quadruple Diamond Verticals-PC8
97Crown Royale-74
Emerald Green-74
Ice Blue-74
Silver-74
97Devils Team Issue-21
97Donruss Elite-65
Aspirations-65
Status-65
97Donruss Priority-170
Stamp of Approval-170
Direct Deposit-24
97Katch-80
Gold-80
Silver-80
97Pacific Invincible NHL Regime-111
97Pacific Omega-128
Copper-128
Dark Gray-128
Emerald Green-128
Gold-128
Ice Blue-128
97Revolution-76
Copper-76
Emerald-76
Ice Blue-76
Silver-76
97SP Authentic-185
Icons-I6
Icons Die-Cuts-I6
Icons Embossed-I6
97Upper Deck-189
97Upper Deck Ice-60
Parallel-60
Lethal Lines-L7A
Lethal Lines 2-L7A
Power Shift-60
97Zenith-81
Z-Gold-81
Z-Silver-81
97Zenith 5 x 7-69
Gold Impulse-69
Silver Impulse-69
97Zenith Rookie Reign-14
97Zenith Z-Team-16
97Zenith Z-Team Gold-16
98Aurora-109
Championship Fever-27
Championship Fever Copper-27
Championship Fever Ice Blue-27
Championship Fever Red-27
Championship Fever Silver-27
98Be A Player-81
Press Release-81
98BAP Gold-81
98BAP Autographs-81
98BAP Autographs Gold-81
98BAP Tampa Bay All Star Game-81
98Bowman's Best-26
Refractors-26
Atomic Refractors-26
Performers-BP3
Performers Refractors-BP3
Performers Atomic Refractors-BP3
98Crown Royale-79
Limited Series-79
98Devils Team Issue-10
98Finest-59
No Protectors-59
No Protectors Refractors-59
Refractors-59
Centurion-C1
Centurion Refractors-C1
98Katch-84
98OPC Chrome-62
Refractors-62
Season's Best-SB9
Season's Best Refractors-SB9
98Pacific-26
Ice Blue-26
Red-26
Gold Crown Die-Cuts-19
98Pacific Dynagon Ice-109
Blue-109
Red-109
98Pacific Omega-137
Red-137
Opening Day Issue-137
98Panini Stickers-70
98Paramount-133
Copper-133
Emerald Green-133
Holo-Electric-133
Ice Blue-133
Silver-133
98Revolution-84
Ice Shadow-84
Red-84
98SP Authentic-50
Power Shift-50
98SPx Finite-49
98SPx Finite-123
Radiance-49
Radiance-123
Spectrum-49
Spectrum-123
98Topps-62
O-Pee-Chee-62
Autographs-A7
Season's Best-SB9
98Topps Gold Label Class 1-37
Black-37
Black One of One-37
One of One-37
Red-37
Red One of One-37
98Topps Gold Label Class 2-37
98Topps Gold Label Class 2 Black-37
98Topps Gold Label Class 2 Black 1 of 1-37
98Topps Gold Label Class 2 One of One-37
98Topps Gold Label Class 2 Red-37
98Topps Gold Label Class 2 Red One of One-37
98Topps Gold Label Class 3-37
98Topps Gold Label Class 3 Black-37
98Topps Gold Label Class 3 Black 1 of 1-37
98Topps Gold Label Class 3 One of One-37
98Topps Gold Label Class 3 Red-37
98Topps Gold Label Class 3 Red One of One-37
98UD Choice-114
Prime Choice Reserve-114
Reserve-114
StarQuest Blue-SQ12
StarQuest Gold-SQ12
StarQuest Green-SQ12
StarQuest Red-SQ12
98UD3-10
98UD3-70
98UD3-130
Die-Cuts-10
Die-Cuts-70
Die-Cuts-130
98Upper Deck-119
Exclusives-119
Exclusives 1 of 1-119
Fantastic Finishers-FF15
Fantastic Finishers Quantum 1-FF15
Fantastic Finishers Quantum 2-FF15
Fantastic Finishers Quantum 3-FF15
Gold Reserve-119
98Upper Deck MVP-119
Gold Script-119
Silver Script-119
Super Script-119
99Aurora-85
Premiere Date-85
99BAP Memorabilia-154
Gold-154
Silver-154
99Crown Royale-79
Limited Series-79
Premiere Date-79
99Devils Team Issue-19
99O-Pee-Chee-234
99O-Pee-Chee Chrome-234
99O-Pee-Chee Chrome Refractors-234
99Pacific-237
Copper-237
Emerald Green-237
Gold-237
Ice Blue-237
Premiere Date-237
Red-237
99Pacific Dynagon Ice-115
Blue-115
Copper-115
Gold-115
Premiere Date-115
99Pacific Omega-134
Copper-134
Gold-134
Ice Blue-134
Premiere Date-134
99Pacific Prism-80
Holographic Blue-80
Holographic Gold-80
Holographic Mirror-80
Holographic Purple-80
Premiere Date-80
99Paramount-132
Copper-132
Emerald-132
Gold-132
Holographic Emerald-132
Holographic Gold-132
Holographic Silver-132
Ice Blue-132
Premiere Date-132
Red-132
Silver-132
99Revolution-85
Premiere Date-85
Red-85
Shadow Series-85
99SPx-86
Radiance-86
Spectrum-86
99Stadium Club-115
First Day Issue-115
One of a Kind-115
Printing Plates Black-115
Printing Plates Cyan-115
Printing Plates Magenta-115
Printing Plates Yellow-115
99Topps Arena Giveaways-NJ-PE
99Topps/OPC-234
99Topps/OPC Chrome-234
Refractors-234
99Upper Deck-78
Exclusives-78
Exclusives 1 of 1-78
New Ice Age-N17
New Ice Age Quantum Gold-N17
New Ice Age Quantum Silver-N17
99Upper Deck Century Legends-80
Century Collection-80
99Upper Deck Gold Reserve-78
99Upper Deck MVP-116
Gold Script-116
Silver Script-116
Super Script-116
99Upper Deck MVP SC Edition-108
Gold Script-108
Silver Script-108
Super Script-108
99Upper Deck Victory-169
99Wayne Gretzky Hockey-102
99Czech DS-77
99Czech OFS-90
99Czech Score Blue 2000-160
99Czech Score Red Ice 2000-160
00Aurora-82
Premiere Date-82
00BAP Memorabilia-266
Emerald-266
Ruby-266
Sapphire-266
Promos-266
00BAP Mem Chicago Sportsfest Copper-266
00BAP Memorabilia Chicago Sportsfest Blue-266
00BAP Memorabilia Chicago Sportsfest Gold-266
00BAP Memorabilia Chicago Sportsfest Ruby-266
00BAP Memorabilia Chicago Sun-Times Ruby-266
00BAP Memorabilia Chicago Sun-Times Gold-266
00BAP Mem Chicago Sun-Times Sapphire-266
00BAP Mem Toronto Fall Expo Copper-266
00BAP Memorabilia Toronto Fall Expo Gold-266
00BAP Memorabilia Toronto Fall Expo Ruby-266
00BAP Parkhurst 2000-P25
00BAP Signature Series-186
Emerald-186
Ruby-186
Sapphire-186
Autographs-107
Autographs Gold-107
00Crown Royale-63
Ice Blue-63
Limited Series-63
Premiere Date-63
Red-63
00Devils Team Issue-6
00O-Pee-Chee-147
00O-Pee-Chee Parallel-147
00Pacific-233
Copper-233
Gold-233
Ice Blue-233
Premiere Date-233
2001: Ice Odyssey-13
Autographs-233
00Pacific 2001: Ice Odyssey Anaheim Ntnl-13
00Panini Stickers-51
00Paramount-143
Copper-143
Gold-143
Holo-Gold-143
Holo-Silver-143
Ice Blue-143
Premiere Date-143
00Private Stock-58
Gold-58
Premiere Date-58
Retail-58
Silver-58
PS-2001 Action-32
PS-2001 New Wave-13
00Revolution-86
Blue-86
Premiere Date-86
Red-86
HD NHL-21
00SP Authentic BuyBacks-58
00SP Authentic BuyBacks-59
00SP Authentic Sign of the Times-PE
00SP Authentic Sign of the Times-E/G
00SP Authentic Sign of the Times-BGE
00SPx-38
Spectrum-38
00Stadium Club-152
Beam Team-BT26
00Titanium-55
Blue-55
Gold-55
Premiere Date-55
Red-55
Retail-55
00Topps/OPC-147
Parallel-147
00Topps Chrome-107
OPC Refractors-107
Refractors-107
Rocket's Flare-RF8
Rocket's Flare Refractors-RF8
00Topps Gold Label Class 1-10
Gold-10
00Topps Gold Label Class 2-10
00Topps Gold Label Class 2 Gold-10
00Topps Gold Label Class 3-10
00Topps Gold Label Class 3 Gold-10
00Topps Heritage-38
Chrome Parallel-38
00Topps Premier Plus-61
Blue Ice-61
Masters of the Break-MB6
00Topps Stars-36
Blue-36
00UD Heroes-71
00UD Reserve-51
00Upper Deck-331
Exclusives Tier 1-331
Exclusives Tier 2-331
00Upper Deck MVP-107
First Stars-107
Second Stars-107
Third Stars-107
00Upper Deck Victory-138
00Upper Deck Vintage-213
00Vanguard-58
Holographic Gold-58
Holographic Purple-58
Pacific Proofs-58
00Czech OFS-385
00Czech Stadion-96
01Atomic-58
Blue-58
Gold-58
Premiere Date-58
Red-58
Team Nucleus-8
01BAP Memorabilia-288
Emerald-288
Ruby-288
Sapphire-288
Country of Origin-CO41
01BAP Signature Series-189
Autographs-189
Autographs Gold-189
Jerseys-GJ-82
01BAP Update He Shoots-He Scores Prizes-2
01Bowman YoungStars-11
Gold-11
Ice Cubed-11
01Crown Royale-86
Blue-86
Premiere Date-86
Red-86
Retail-86
All-Star Honors-13
Jewels of the Crown-19
01Devils Team Issue-6
01eTopps-5
01O-Pee-Chee-91
01O-Pee-Chee-319
01O-Pee-Chee Heritage Parallel-91
01O-Pee-Chee Heritage Parallel Limited-91
01O-Pee-Chee Premier Parallel-91
01O-Pee-Chee Premier Parallel-319
01Pacific-229
01Pacific-414
01Pacific-433
Extreme LTD-229
Gold-414
Gold-433
Hobby LTD-229
Premiere Date-229
Retail LTD-229
97-98 Subset-356
97-98 Subset Gold Parallel-356
01Pacific Adrenaline-113
Blue-113
Premiere Date-113
Red-113
Retail-113
World Beaters-10
01Pacific Arena Exclusives-229
01Pacific Arena Exclusives-414
01Pacific Arena Exclusives-433
01Pacific Heads-Up-57
Blue-57
Premiere Date-57
Red-57
Silver-57
01Parkhurst-18
Gold-18
Silver-18
Jerseys-PJ34
Teammates-T14
01Private Stock-56
Gold-56
Premiere Date-56
Retail-56
Silver-56
01Private Stock Pacific Nights-56
01SP Authentic-47
Limited-47
Limited Gold-47
01SP Game Used-30
01SPx-38
01Sports Illustrated for Kids III-82
01Stadium Club-46
Award Winners-46
Master Photos-46
Gallery-G4
Gallery Gold-G4
Lone Star Signatures-LS5
NHL Passport-NHLP10
01Titanium-84
Hobby Parallel-84
Premiere Date-84
Retail-84
Retail Parallel-84
All-Stars-13
Double-Sided Jerseys-69
Double-Sided Patches-69
01Topps-91
01Topps-319
Heritage Parallel-91
Heritage Parallel Limited-91
OPC Parallel-91
OPC Parallel-319
Own The Game-OTG3
Shot Masters-SM13
Stars of the Game-SG5
01Topps Chrome-91
Refractors-91
Black Border Refractors-91
01Topps Heritage-4
01Topps Heritage-114
01Topps Heritage-125
Refractors-4
01Topps Reserve-2
01UD Challenge for the Cup-53
01UD Honor Roll Pucks-P-PE
01UD Honor Roll Pucks Gold-P-PE
01UD Honor Roll Student of the Game-SG5
01UD Mask Collection-57
Gold-57
01UD Playmakers-59
01UD Stanley Cup Champs-70
01UD Top Shelf-26
01Upper Deck-102
Exclusives-102
Shooting Stars-SS10
Tandems-T5
01Upper Deck Ice-28
01Upper Deck MVP-112
Talent-MT10
01Upper Deck Victory-207
Gold-207
01Upper Deck Vintage-150
01Upper Deck Vintage-156
01Upper Deck Vintage-263
01Upper Deck Vintage-265
01Vanguard-57
Blue-57
Red-57
One of Ones-57
Premiere Date-57
Proofs-57
01Czech DS-46
01Czech Stadion-218
02Atomic-61
Blue-61
Gold-61
Red-61
Hobby Parallel-61
02BAP All-Star Edition-19
Jerseys-19
Jerseys Gold-19
Jerseys Silver-19
02BAP First Edition-34
Jerseys-34
Scoring Leaders-10
02BAP Memorabilia-123
Emerald-123
Ruby-123
Sapphire-123
All-Star Jerseys-ASJ-11
NHL All-Star Game-123
NHL All-Star Game Blue-123
NHL All-Star Game Green-123
NHL All-Star Game Red-123
Teammates-TM-14
02BAP Memorabilia Toronto Fall Expo-123
02BAP Signature Series-157
Autographs-157
Autograph Buybacks 1998-81
Autograph Buybacks 2001-189
Autographs Gold-157
Team Quads-TQ7
02Bowman YoungStars-102
Gold-102
Silver-102
02Crown Royale-57
Blue-57
Red-57
Retail-57
Jerseys-11
Jerseys Gold-11
Dual Patches-14
02Devils Team Issue-20
02eTopps-20
02ITG Used-42
02ITG Used-142
02O-Pee-Chee-261
02O-Pee-Chee Premier Blue Parallel-261
02O-Pee-Chee Premier Red Parallel-261
02O-Pee-Chee Factory Set-261
02Pacific-220
Blue-220
Red-220
02Pacific Complete-106
Red-106
02Pacific Exclusive-103
Maximum Overdrive-12
02Pacific Heads-Up-71
Blue-71
Purple-71
Red-71
Quad Jerseys-17
Quad Jerseys-32
Quad Jerseys Gold-17
Quad Jerseys Gold-32
02Pacific Quest for the Cup-57
Gold-57
02Parkhurst-91
Bronze-91
Gold-91
Silver-91
Teammates-TT5
02Parkhurst Retro-37
Minis-37
02Private Stock Reserve-130
Red-130
Retail-130
Patches-130
02SP Authentic-54
Beckett Promos-54
02SP Game Used-29
02SPx-42
Spectrum Gold-42
Spectrum Silver-42
02Stadium Club-28
Silver Decoy Cards-28
Proofs-28
World Stage-WS16
02Topps-261
OPC Blue Parallel-261
OPC Red Parallel-261
Coast to Coast-CC10
02Topps Promos-PP6
02Topps Factory Set-261
02Topps Chrome-143
Black Border Refractors-143
Refractors-143
02Topps Heritage-50
Chrome Parallel-50
Autographs-PE
Autographs Black-PE
Autographs Red-PE
02Topps Total-208
Topps-TT14
02UD Artistic Impressions-53
Gold-53
02UD Artistic Impressions Beckett Promos-53
02UD Artistic Impressions Retrospectives-R53
02UD Artistic Impressions Retrospect Gold-R53
02UD Artistic Impress Retrospect Silver-R53
02UD Honor Roll-40
02UD Mask Collection Instant Offense-IOPE
02UD Mask Collection Patches-PGPE
02UD Piece of History-50
02UD Top Shelf-50
02Upper Deck-103
Exclusives-103
Sizzling Scorers-SS10
02Upper Deck Classic Portraits-58
02Upper Deck MVP-110
Gold-110
Classics-110
Golden Classics-110
02Upper Deck Rookie Update-158C
02Upper Deck Victory-128
Bronze-128
Gold-128
Silver-128
National Pride-NP16
02Upper Deck Vintage-151
02Upper Deck Vintage-278
Green Backs-151
Tall Boys-T40
Tall Boys Gold-T40
02Vanguard-61
LTD-61
02Czech Stadion Olympics-329
03BAP Memorabilia-66
Emerald-66
Gold-66
Ruby-66
Sapphire-66
Stanley Cup Champions-SCC-9
03BAP Ultimate Memorabilia Autographs-53
Gold-53
03BAP Ultimate Memorabilia Triple Threads-25
03Beehive-116
Gold-116
Silver-116
03Black Diamond-63
Black-63
Green-63
Red-63
03Bowman-25
Gold-25
03Bowman Chrome-25
Refractors-25
Gold Refractors-25
Xfractors-25
03Crown Royale-60
Blue-60
Retail-60
03Devils Team Issue-26
03eTopps-28
03ITG Action-342
Jerseys-M128
03ITG Used Signature Series-17
Gold-17
Autographs-PE
Autographs Gold-PE
03NHL Sticker Collection-63
03O-Pee-Chee-89
03OPC Blue-89
03OPC Gold-89
03OPC Red-89
03Pacific-197
Blue-197
Red-197
03Pacific Calder-63
Silver-63
03Pacific Complete-395
Red-395
03Pacific Exhibit-84
Blue Backs-84
Yellow Backs-84
03Pacific Heads-Up-59
Hobby LTD-59
Retail LTD-59
03Pacific Invincible-56
Blue-56
Red-56
Retail-56
03Pacific Luxury Suite-40A
03Pacific Luxury Suite-40B
03Pacific Luxury Suite-40C
03Pacific Prism-61
Blue-61
Gold-61
Red-61
03Pacific Quest for the Cup-64
Blue-64
Jerseys-12
03Pacific Supreme-58
Blue-58
Red-58
Retail-58
03Private Stock Reserve-59
Blue-59
Red-59
Retail-59
03SP Authentic-52
Limited-52
03SPx-58
Radiance-58
Spectrum-58
Fantasy Franchise-FF-EHJ
Fantasy Franchise Limited-FF-EHJ
Origins-O-PE
03Titanium-166
Hobby Jersey Number Parallels-166
Patches-166
Retail-166
03Topps-89
Blue-89
Gold-89
Red-89
Topps/OPC Idols-II3
03Topps C55-86
Minis-86
Minis American Back-86
Minis American Back Red-86
Minis Bazooka Back-86
Minis Brooklyn Back-86
Minis Hat Trick Back-86
Minis O Canada Back-86
Minis O Canada Back Red-86
Minis Stanley Cup Back-86
Autographs-TA-PE
03Topps Pristine-8
Gold Refractor Die Cuts-8
Refractors-8
Press Plates Black-8
Press Plates Cyan-8
Press Plates Magenta-8
Press Plates Yellow-8
03Upper Deck-111
Canadian Exclusives-111
HG-111
03Upper Deck Classic Portraits-56
03Upper Deck Ice-51
Gold-51
03Upper Deck MVP-247
Gold Script-247
Silver Script-247
Canadian Exclusives-247
SportsNut-SN52
03Upper Deck Rookie Update-51
03Upper Deck Trilogy-56
Limited-56
03Upper Deck Victory-107
Bronze-107
Gold-107
Silver-107
03Czech Stadion-603
03Toronto Star-52
04Pacific-155
Blue-155
Red-155
04SP Authentic-53
04SP Authentic-125
04UD All-World-36
Gold-36
04Ultimate Collection Dual Logos-UL2-BE
04Upper Deck-102
Canadian Exclusives-102
HG Glossy Gold-102
HG Glossy Silver-102
World Cup Tribute-PE
World Cup Tribute-PEJJHE
04Czech OFS-312
Checklist Cards-14
Stars-41
04Czech Zuma-6
04Russian Legion-29
05Be A Player-53
First Period-53
Second Period-53
Third Period-53
Overtime-53
World Cup Salute-WCS10
05Beehive-53
05Beehive-198
Beige -53
Blue -53
Gold-53
Red -53
Matte-53
Matted Materials-MMPA
05Black Diamond-103
Emerald-103
Gold-103
Onyx-103
Ruby-103
05Devils Team Issue-13
05Hot Prospects-59

En Fuego-59
Red Hot-59
White Hot-59
05Parkhurst-291
05Parkhurst-530
Facsimile Auto Parallel-291
Facsimile Auto Parallel-530
True Colors-TCNJD
True Colors-TCNJD
True Colors-TCNJNY
True Colors-TCNJNY
05SP Authentic-58
05SP Authentic-124
Limited-58
Limited-124
05SP Game Used-59
Gold-59
Authentic Fabrics-AF-PE
Authentic Fabrics Dual-EB
Authentic Fabrics Gold-AF-PE
Authentic Fabrics Quad-BEGK
Authentic Fabrics Quad-EMMR
Authentic Patches Quad -BEGK
Authentic Patches Quad -EMMR
Authentic Fabrics Triple-SEL
Authentic Patches-AP-PE
Authentic Patches Dual-EB
Authentic Patches Triple-SEL
Awesome Authentics-AA-PE
Awesome Authentics Gold-DA-PE
05SPx-51
Spectrum-51
Winning Combos-WC-BE
Winning Combos Gold-WC-BE
Winning Combos Spectrum-WC-BE
05The Cup-63
Gold-63
Black Rainbow-63
Dual NHL Shields-DSBE
Masterpiece Pressplates-63
Noble Numbers-NNSE
Noble Numbers Dual-DNNBE
Noble Numbers Dual-DNNEH
Patch Variation-P63
Property of-POPE
05UD Artifacts-61
05UD Artifacts-177
Blue-61
Blue-177
Gold-61
Gold-177
Green-61
Green-177
Pewter-61
Pewter-177
Red-61
Red-177
Gold Autographed-61
Gold Autographed-177
Treasured Patches-TP-PE
Treasured Patches Autographed-TP-PE
Treasured Patches Dual-TPD-PE
Treasured Patches Dual Autographed-TPD-PE
Treasured Patches Pewter-TP-PE
Treasured Patches Silver-TP-PE
Treasured Swatches-TS-PE
Treasured Swatches Autographed-TS-PE
Treasured Swatches Blue-TS-PE
Treasured Swatches Copper-TS-PE
Treasured Swatches Dual-TSD-PE
Treasured Swatches Dual Blue-TSD-PE
Treasured Swatches Dual Copper-TSD-PE
Treasured Swatches Dual Maroon-TSD-PE
Treasured Swatches Dual Pewter-TSD-PE
Treasured Swatches Dual Silver-TSD-PE
Treasured Swatches Maroon-TS-PE
Treasured Swatches Pewter-TS-PE
Treasured Swatches Silver-TS-PE
05UD PowerPlay-53
Rainbow-53
05Ultimate Collection-55
Gold-55
National Heroes Jerseys-NHJPE
National Heroes Patches-NHPPE
05Ultra-118
Gold-118
Ice-118
Scoring Kings-SK14
Scoring Kings Jerseys-SKJ-PE
Scoring Kings Patches-SKP-PE
05Upper Deck-112
05Upper Deck All-Time Greatest-36
05Upper Deck Big Playmakers-B-PE
05Upper Deck HG Glossy-112
05Upper Deck Jerseys Series II-J2PE
05Upper Deck Majestic Materials-MMPE
05Upper Deck Patches-P-PE
05Upper Deck Shooting Stars-S-PE
05Upper Deck Ice-57
Rainbow-57
Cool Threads-CTPE
Cool Threads Glass-CTPE
Cool Threads Patches-CTPPE
05Upper Deck MVP-229
Gold-229
Platinum-229
Materials-M-PE
05Upper Deck Rookie Update-57
05Upper Deck Trilogy-54
05Upper Deck Trilogy-144
Crystal-144
Honorary Patches-HP-PE
Honorary Swatches-HS-PE
05Upper Deck Toronto Fall Expo-112
05Upper Deck Victory-120
Black-120
Gold-120
Silver-120
05Czech Kvarteto Bonaparte-6a
05Czech Pexeso Mini Blue Set-25
06Be A Player-134
Autographs-134
Signatures-EL
Signatures 10-149
Signatures 25-149
Signatures Duals-DER
Up Close and Personal-UC44
Up Close and Personal Autographs-UC44
06Be A Player Portraits-63
06Beehive-42
06Beehive-186
Blue-42
Gold-42
Matte-42
Red Facsimile Signatures-42
Wood-42
Signature Scrapbook-SSPE
06Black Diamond-112
Black-112
Gold-112
Ruby-112
06Devils Team Set-6
06Devils Team Set-35
06Flair Showcase-60
06Flair Showcase-140
06Flair Showcase-244
Parallel-60
Parallel-140
Parallel-244
Stitches-SSPE
06Fleer-116
Tiffany-116
Fabricology-FEP
Total 0-014
06Hot Prospects-58
Red Hot-58
White Hot-58
Hotagraphs-HPA
06O-Pee-Chee-306
Rainbow-306
06Panini Stickers-78
06SP Authentic-44
Chirography-PE
Limited-44
Sign of the Times-STEL
Sign of the Times Duals-STEG
06SP Game Used-62
Gold-62
Rainbow-62
Authentic Fabrics-AFPE
Authentic Fabrics Parallel-AFPE
Authentic Fabrics Patches-AFPE
Authentic Fabrics Triple-AF3NJD
Authentic Fabrics Triple Patches-AF3NJD
Authentic Fabrics Quads-AF4JHEG
Authentic Fabrics Quads Patches-AF4JHEG
Autographs-62
By The Letter-BLPE
Inked Sweaters-ISEL
Inked Sweaters Patches-ISEL
Inked Sweaters Dual-IS2EG
Inked Sweaters Dual Patches-IS2EG
Letter Marks-LMEL
06SPx-61
Spectrum-61
SPxcitement-X61
SPxcitement Spectrum-X61
SPxcitement Autographs-X61
Winning Materials-WMPE
Winning Materials Spectrum-WMPE
Winning Materials Autographs-WMPE
06The Cup Autographed Foundations-CQPE
06The Cup Autographed Foundations Patches-CQPE
06The Cup Autographed NHL Shields Duals-DASEZ
06The Cup Foundations-CQPE
06The Cup Foundations Patches-CQPE
06The Cup Honorable Numbers-HNPE
06The Cup Limited Logos-LLPE
06The Cup Signature Patches-SPEL
06UD Artifacts-42
06UD Artifacts-180
Blue-42
Blue-180
Gold-42
Gold-180
Platinum-42
Platinum-180
Radiance-42
Radiance-180
Red-42
Red-180
Frozen Artifacts-FAPE
Frozen Artifacts Black-FAPE
Frozen Artifacts Blue-FAPE
Frozen Artifacts Gold-FAPE
Frozen Artifacts Platinum-FAPE
Frozen Artifacts Red-FAPE
Frozen Artifacts Patches Black-FAPE
Frozen Artifacts Patches Blue-FAPE
Frozen Artifacts Patches Gold-FAPE
Frozen Artifacts Patches Platinum-FAPE
Frozen Artifacts Patches Red-FAPE
Tundra Tandems-TTBE
Tundra Tandems Black-TTBE
Tundra Tandems Blue-TTBE
Tundra Tandems Gold-TTBE
Tundra Tandems Platinum-TTBE
Tundra Tandems Red-TTBE
Tundra Tandems Dual Patches Red-TTBE
06UD Mini Jersey Collection-61
06UD Powerplay-60
Impact Rainbow-60
06Ultimate Collection Autographed Jerseys-AJ-EL
06Ultimate Collection Autographed Patches-AJ-EL
06Ultimate Collection Premium Patches-PS-PE
06Ultimate Collection Premium Swatches-PS-PE
06Ultimate Collection Signatures-US-PE
06Ultra-117
Gold Medallion-117
Ice Medallion-117
06Upper Deck Arena Giveaways-NJD6
06Upper Deck-365
Exclusives Parallel-365
High Gloss Parallel-365
Game Jerseys-J2PE
Game Patches-P2PE
Generations Duals-G2EG
Generations Patches Dual-G2PEG
Masterpieces-365
Oversized Wal-Mart Exclusives-365
06Upper Deck MVP-176
Gold Script-176
Super Script-176
Autographs-OAEG
Jerseys-OJEP
Jerseys-OJES
06Upper Deck Ovation-179
06Upper Deck Sweet Shot-64
Signature Shots/Saves-SSPE
Signature Shots/Saves Ice Signings-SSIPE
Signature Shots/Saves Sticks-SSSPE
Signature Sticks-STPE
Sweet Stitches-SSPE
Sweet Stitches Duals-SSPE
Sweet Stitches Triples-SSPE
06Upper Deck Trilogy-59
Honorary Scripted Patches-HSPPE
Honorary Scripted Swatches-HSSPE
06Upper Deck Victory-119
06Upper Deck Victory Black-119
06Upper Deck Victory Gold-119
06Upper Deck Victory GameBreakers-GB29
07Upper Deck Victory-7
Black-7
Gold-7
GameBreakers-GB23

Eliasson, Magnus
95Swedish Upper Deck-91

Eliasson, Roger
83Swedish Semic Elitserien-154
85Swedish Panini Stickers-204

Elich, Matt
92Quebec Pee-Wee Tournament-1852
95Slapshot-418
97Bowman CHL-124
OPC-124
Autographs-4
98Kingston Frontenacs-4
99Detroit Vipers-5
00Aurora-132
Premiere Date-132
00O-Pee-Chee-290
00O-Pee-Chee Parallel-290
00Pacific-371
Copper-371
Gold-371
Ice Blue-371
Premiere Date-371
00SP Game Used-82
00SPx-117
Spectrum-117
00Topps/OPC-290
Parallel-290
00Topps Chrome-185
OPC Refractors-185
Refractors-185
00UD Pros and Prospects-124
00Upper Deck-415
Exclusives Tier 1-415
Exclusives Tier 2-415
00Upper Deck Vintage-392
03Greensboro Generals-182
04Idaho Steelheads-19

Elick, Mickey
96Charlotte Checkers-6
99German DEL-141
01German Upper Deck-4
02German DEL City Press-192
03German DEL-169

Eligh, Jarrett
88Brockville Braves-16

Elik, Todd
83Kingston Canadians-15
84Kingston Canadians-8
89ProCards AHL-10
90Bowman-151
Tiffany-151
90Kings Smokey-5
90O-Pee-Chee-352
90Pro Set-116
90Score-297
Canadian-297
90Topps-352
Tiffany-352
90Upper Deck-233
French-233
91Pro Set Platinum-57
91Bowman-185
91O-Pee-Chee-251
91OPC Premier-74
91Panini Stickers-85
91Parkhurst-300
French-300
91Pinnacle-264
French-264
91Pro Set-94
91Pro Set-410
French-94
French-410
91Score American-83
91Score Canadian Bilingual-83
91Score Canadian Bilingual-563
91Score Canadian English-83
91Score Canadian English-563
91Score Rookie/Traded-13T
91Stadium Club-310
91Topps-251
91Upper Deck-544
French-544
92Bowman-317
92Oilers Team Issue-5
92O-Pee-Chee-20
92Parkhurst-77
92Parkhurst-292
Emerald Ice-77
Emerald Ice-292
92Pinnacle-207
French-207
92Score-307
Canadian-307
92Stadium Club-226
92Topps-97
Gold-97G
92Ultra-93
92Upper Deck-210
93Donruss-489
93Panini Stickers-238
93Parkhurst-71
Emerald Ice-71
93Pinnacle-202
Canadian-202
93PowerPlay-80
93PowerPlay-434
93Score-185
93Score-581
Gold-581
Canadian-185
Canadian-581
Canadian Gold-581
93Stadium Club-363
Members Only Master Set-363
First Day Issue-363
94Canada Games NHL POGS-212
94Donruss-163
94Flair-162
94Leaf-226
94OPC Premier-76
Special Effects-76
94Parkhurst-210
Gold-210
94Pinnacle-275
Artist's Proofs-275
Rink Collection-275
94Score-125
Gold-125
Platinum-125
94Topps/OPC Premier-76
Special Effects-76
94Ultra-193
94Upper Deck-363
Electric Ice-363
95Be A Player-89
Signatures-S89
Signatures Die Cuts-S89
95Donruss-388
95Leaf-165
95Playoff One on One-118
95Score-58
Black Ice Artist's Proofs-58
Black Ice-58
95Upper Deck-479
Electric Ice-479
Electric Ice Gold-479
98Swiss Power Play Stickers-142
99Swiss Panini Stickers-142
00Swiss Panini Stickers-257
00Swiss Slapshot Mini-Cards-EVZ9
01Swiss EV Zug Postcards-25
01Swiss HNL-181
02Swiss HNL-109
02Swiss SCL Tigers-7

Eliot, Darren
84Kings Smokey-18
86Kings 20th Anniversary Team Issue-4
87Panini Stickers-272

Elkins, Corey
04Sioux City Musketeers-9
05Ohio State Buckeyes-24
06Ohio State Buckeyes-17

Ellacott, Ken
82Canucks Team Issue-6

Eller, Lars
98Danish Hockey League-215

Eller, Olaf
98Danish Hockey League-228

Ellerby, Keaton
05Kamloops Blazers-5
06Kamloops Blazers-7

Ellerman, Trevor
95Central Hockey League-58

Ellett, Bob
71Rochester Americans-5
84Ottawa 67's-6

Ellett, Dave
84Jets Police-6
85Jets Police-5
85Jets Silverwood Dairy-3
85O-Pee-Chee-185
86Jets Postcards-6
87Jets Postcards-6
87O-Pee-Chee-35
87O-Pee-Chee Stickers-251
87Panini Stickers-358
87Topps-35
88Jets Police-6
88Jets Postcards-7
88O-Pee-Chee-167
88O-Pee-Chee Stickers-150
88Panini Stickers-150
88Topps-167
89Jets Safeway-12
89Kraft-49
89O-Pee-Chee-69
89O-Pee-Chee Stickers-139
89Panini Stickers-167
89Topps-69
90Bowman-132
Tiffany-132
90Maple Leafs Postcards-3
90O-Pee-Chee-104
90Panini Stickers-310
90Pro Set-326
90Pro Set-532
90Score-65
Canadian-65
90Score Hottest/Rising Stars-29
90Score Rookie/Traded-67T
90Topps-104
Tiffany-104
90Upper Deck-71
90Upper Deck-413
French-71
French-413
91Pro Set Platinum-116
91Bowman-163
91Gillette-17
91Jets Panini Team Stickers-9
91Maple Leafs PLAY-9
91O-Pee-Chee-381
91OPC Premier-180
91Panini Stickers-94
91Parkhurst-172
French-172
91Pinnacle-111
French-111
91Pro Set-230
French-230
91Score American-275
91Score Canadian Bilingual-495
91Score Canadian English-495
91Score Kellogg's-23
91Stadium Club-274
91Topps-381
91Upper Deck-96
91Upper Deck-196
French-96
French-196
91Finnish Semic World Champ Stickers-62
91Swedish Semic World Champ Stickers-62
92Bowman-204
92Bowman-291
92Humpty Dumpty II-4
92Maple Leafs Kodak-11
92McDonald's Upper Deck-5
92O-Pee-Chee-9
92Panini Stickers-83
92Panini Stickers French-83
92Parkhurst-181
Emerald Ice-181
92Pinnacle-273
French-273
92Pro Set-186
92Score-152
Canadian-152
92Stadium Club-283
92Topps-30
Gold-30G
92Ultra-209
92Upper Deck-214
93Donruss-344
93Leaf-86
Maple Leafs Score Black's-20
93OPC Premier-297
Gold-297
93Panini Stickers-231
93Parkhurst-205
Emerald Ice-205
93Pinnacle-262
Canadian-262
93PowerPlay-243
93Score-119
Canadian-119
93Stadium Club-469
Members Only Master Set-469
First Day Issue-469
93Topps/OPC Premier-297
Gold-297
93Ultra-38
93Upper Deck-215
SP-157
94Be A Player-R50
Signature Cards-65
94Canada Games NHL POGS-238
94Donruss-230
94EA Sports-134
94Flair-178
94Fleer-213
94Leaf-35
94Maple Leafs Gangsters-6
94Maple Leafs Pin-up Posters-3
94Parkhurst-227
Gold-227
Vintage-V8
94Pinnacle-209
Artist's Proofs-209
Rink Collection-209
94Score-83
Gold-83
Platinum-83
94Stadium Club-42
Members Only Master Set-42
First Day Issue-42
Super Team Winner Cards-42
94Ultra-213
94Upper Deck-67
Electric Ice-67
94Upper Deck NHLPA/Be A Player-4
95Canada Games NHL POGS-264
95Collector's Choice-162
Player's Club-162
Player's Club Platinum-162
95Donruss-340
95Panini Stickers-205
95Parkhurst International-475
Emerald Ice-475
95Score-129
Black Ice Artist's Proofs-129
Black Ice-129
95Topps-207
OPC Inserts-207
95Upper Deck-144
Electric Ice-144
Electric Ice Gold-144
96Be A Player-177
Autographs-177
Autographs Silver-177
96Upper Deck-344
97Pacific Invincible NHL Regime-112
97Paramount-13
Copper-13
Dark Grey-13
Emerald Green-13
Ice Blue-13
Red-13
Silver-13
97Score Bruins-16
Platinum-16
Premier-16
98Aurora-12
98OPC Chrome-6
Refractors-6
98Pacific-78
Ice Blue-78
Red-78
98Paramount-14
Copper-14
Emerald Green-14
Holo-Electric-14
Ice Blue-14
Silver-14
98Topps-6
O-Pee-Chee-6
99Blues Taco Bell-6
00Pacific-343
Copper-343
Gold-343
Ice Blue-343
Premiere Date-343
03Bowling Green Falcons-14
04ITG Franchises Canadian-147
Autographs-DEL

Ellfolk, Lars
73Finnish Jaakiekko-278

Ellingsen, Age
87Swedish Panini Stickers-33
92Finnish Semic-30
92Norwegian Elite Series-29
92Norwegian Elite Series-199

Ellington, Taylor
04Everett Silvertips-22
05Everett Silvertips-5

Elliott, Brandon
03Mississauga Ice Dogs-9
05Johnstown Chiefs-9

Elliott, Brian
03Wisconsin Badgers-10
04Wisconsin Badgers-1
05Wisconsin Badgers-9

Elliott, Chaucer
83Hall of Fame Postcards-M6
85Hall of Fame-171

Elliott, Jason
99Manitoba Moose-11
01Cincinnati Mighty Ducks-12
02BAP Memorabilia-317
02Between the Pipes-109
Gold-109
Silver-109
02Finnish Cardset-163
05German SC Bietigheim-Bissingen Steelers-23

Elliott, Nate
02Indianapolis Ice-6
03Indianapolis Ice-8

Elliott, Paul
96Lethbridge Hurricanes-4
98Medicine Hat Tigers-10
99Medicine Hat Tigers-5
00Kamloops Blazers-7
01Utah Grizzlies-1
03Augusta Lynx-38
03San Antonio Rampage-7

Elliott, Warren
70Flyers Postcards-3

Ellis, Aaron
93Donruss Team USA-6
93Pinnacle-479
Canadian-479
93Upper Deck-554
93Detroit Jr. Red Wings-3

Ellis, Brendan
06Westside Warriors-17

Ellis, Chris
93Quebec Pee-Wee Tournament-666

Ellis, Dan
03ITG Action-662
03ITG Used Signature Series-182
Gold-182
03ITG VIP Rookie Debut-118
03Pacific Calder-114
Silver-114
03Parkhurst Rookie-124
03Topps Traded-TT154
Blue-TT154
Gold-TT154
Red-TT154
03UD Premier Collection-89
03Upper Deck Rookie Update-144
03ECHL All-Stars-267
03ECHL Update RBI Sports-137
04Pacific-282
Blue-282
Red-282
04Hamilton Bulldogs-7
05AHL Top Prospects-12
05Iowa Stars-27
06Iowa Stars-5

Ellis, Julien
05Shawinigan Cataractes-1
06Between The Pipes-28
Autographs-AJE
Prospect Trios-PT08
Prospect Trios-PT11
Prospect Trios Gold-PT08
Prospect Trios Gold-PT11
06Manitoba Moose-22

Ellis, Matt
00St. Michaels Majors-14
01St. Michaels Majors-18
03Grand Rapids Griffins-5
07Upper Deck Victory-236
Black-236
Gold-236

Ellis, Mike
98UK Basingstoke Bison-7
99UK Basingstoke Bison-6
06UK Nottingham Panthers-19

Ellis, Ron
63Maple Leafs Team Issue-7
64Beehive Group III Photos-161
64Coca-Cola Caps-97
65Coca-Cola-95
65Maple Leafs White Border-6
65Maple Leafs White Border-7
65Topps-82
66Maple Leafs Hockey Talks-9
66Topps-81
67Post Flip Books-8
67Topps-14
67York Action Octagons-16
67York Action Octagons-17
67York Action Octagons-22
68O-Pee-Chee-126
68Post Marbles-6
68Shirriff Coins-165
68Topps-126
69Maple Leafs White Border Glossy-8
69Maple Leafs White Border Glossy-9
69Maple Leafs White Border Glossy-10
69O-Pee-Chee-46
69Topps-46
70Colgate Stamps-54
70Dad's Cookies-29
70Esso Power Players-22
70Maple Leafs Postcards-2
70O-Pee-Chee-221
Deckle-46
70Post Shooters-2
70Sargent Promotions Stamps-200
70Topps/OPC Sticker Stamps-5
71Bazooka-34
71Frito-Lay-7
71Letraset Action Replays-22
71Maple Leafs Postcards-4
71O-Pee-Chee-113
71Sargent Promotions Stamps-203
71Topps-113
71Toronto Sun-257
72Kellogg's Iron-On Transfers-1
72Maple Leafs Postcards-4
72Maple Leafs Postcards-5
72O-Pee-Chee-36
Team Canada-8
72Sargent Promotions Stamps-201
72Topps-152
72Finnish Semic World Championship-166
72Swedish Semic World Championship-166
73Mac's Milk-6
73Maple Leafs Postcards-4
73O-Pee-Chee-55
73Topps-55
74Lipton Soup-6
74Maple Leafs Postcards-3
74NHL Action Stamps-270
74O-Pee-Chee NHL-12
74Topps-12
75O-Pee-Chee NHL-59
75Topps-59
77Maple Leafs Postcards-3
77O-Pee-Chee NHL-311
78Maple Leafs Postcards-7
78O-Pee-Chee-92
78Topps-92
79Maple Leafs Postcards-9
79O-Pee-Chee-373
80O-Pee-Chee-329
80Pepsi-Cola Caps-86
91Future Trends Canada '72-76
91Future Trends Canada '72 French-76
91Ultimate Original Six-34
French-34
94Parkhurst Tall Boys-125
94Parkhurst Tall Boys-162
94Parkhurst Tall Boys-168
95Parkhurst '66-67-106
Coins-106
02Maple Leafs Platinum Collection-72
02Maple Leafs Platinum Collection-85
Autographs-72
04UD Legendary Signatures-74
Autographs-RE
Summit Stars-CDN8
Summit Stars Autographs-CDN-RE
05SP Game Used Heritage Classic-HC-RE
05SP Game Used Heritage Classic Autos-HCA-RE
05SP Game Used Heritage Classic Patches-HCP-RE
05SP GameUsed Heritage Classic Patch Auto-HAP-RE
06Parkhurst-54
Autographs-54
Autographs Dual-DAES
06SP Authentic Sign of the Times Duals-STBE
06SP Authentic Sign of the Times Triples-ST3BEK
06The Cup Autographed Foundations-CQRE
06The Cup Autographed Foundations Patches-CQRE
06The Cup Foundations-CQRE
06The Cup Honorable Numbers-HNRE
06The Cup Scripted Swatches-SSRE
06The Cup Signature Patches-SPRE
06The Cup Stanley Cup Titlists Patches-TRE
06UD Artifacts-139
Blue-139
Gold-139
Platinum-139
Radiance-139
Autographed Radiance Parallel-139
Red-139
Auto-Facts-AFRE
Auto-Facts Gold-AFRE
Tundra Tandems-TTME
Tundra Tandems Black-TTME
Tundra Tandems Blue-TTME
Tundra Tandems Gold-TTME
Tundra Tandems Platinum-TTME
Tundra Tandems Red-TTME
Tundra Tandems Dual Patches Red-TTME
06Ultimate Collection Jerseys Dual-UJ2-ME
06Ultimate Collection Patches Dual-UJ2-ME
06Ultimate Collection Premium Patches-PS-RE
06Ultimate Collection Premium Swatches-PS-RE
06Upper Deck Game Jerseys-J2RE
06Upper Deck Game Patches-J2RE
07Maple Leafs 1967 Commemorative-7
Autographs-ARE1
Autographs-ARE2

Ellis, Steve
99Sudbury Wolves-15
00Sudbury Wolves-17
03UK Sheffield Steelers-13
03UK Sheffield Steelers Stickers-8

Ellis-Plante, Julien
02Shawinigan Cataractes-1
03Shawinigan Cataractes-9
04ITG Top Prospects Spring Expo-8
04ITG Heroes and Prospects-83
Aspiring-12
Autographs-JE
Combos-9
He Shoots-He Scores Prizes-33
Net Prospects-32
Net Prospects Gold-32
Top Prospects-8
04ITG Heroes/Prospects Toronto Expo '05-83
04ITG Heroes/Prospects Expo Heroes/Pros-83
05ITG Heroes/Prosp Toronto Expo Parallel -306
05Extreme Top Prospects Signature Edition-S25
05ITG Heroes and Prospects-306
Autographs Series II-JE
Jerseys-GUJ-85
Jerseys Gold-GUJ-85
Emblems-GUE-85
Emblems Gold-GUE-85
Numbers-GUN-85
Numbers Gold-GUN-85
Measuring Up-MU3
Measuring Up Gold-MU3
Nameplates-N-50
Nameplates Gold-N-50
Net Prospects Dual-NPD10
Net Prospects Dual Gold-NPD10
Oh Canada-OC-2
Oh Canada Gold-OC-2
06ITG Heroes and Prospects CHL Top Prospects-TP18
06ITG Heroes and Prospects CHL Top Prospects Gold-TP18

Ellis-Toddingto, Kerry
03Mississippi Sea Wolves-14

Ellison, Matt
02Red Deer Rebels-8
03BAP Memorabilia-225
03ITG Used Signature Series-162
Gold-162
03ITG VIP Rookie Debut-113
03Parkhurst Rookie-82
03Topps Traded-TT149
Blue-TT149
Gold-TT149
Red-TT149
03Upper Deck Rookie Update-171
03Norfolk Admirals-8
03Pacific AHL Prospects-62
Gold-62
04Norfolk Admirals-8
05ITG Heroes/Prosp Toronto Expo Parallel -253
05Upper Deck-290
05ITG Heroes and Prospects-253
Autographs Series II-MEL
Complete Logos-AHL-23
Jerseys-GUJ-76
Jerseys Gold-GUJ-76
Emblems-GUE-76
Emblems Gold-GUE-76
Numbers-GUN-76
Numbers Gold-GUN-76
Nameplates-N-53
Nameplates Gold-N-53
06Philadelphia Phantoms-19

Ellstrom, Sven-Allan
71Swedish Hockey-361

Ellsworth, Cam
01Michigan Tech Huskies-7
06Stockton Thunder-12a

Ellwood, James
02UK Peterborough Phantoms-14

Elm, Mattias
99Swedish Upper Deck-119
Snapshots-9

Elmer, W.D.
23V128-1 Paulin's Candy-34

Elmvall, Fredrik
99Swedish Upper Deck-129

Elmy, Chad
97Saskatoon Blades-7

Elo, Hannu
65Finnish Hellas-158

Elo, Hans-Goran
84Swedish Semic Elitserien-123
86Swedish Panini Stickers-58
87Swedish Panini Stickers-69

Elofsson, Jonas
98Swedish UD Choice-87
99Swedish Upper Deck-56
99Swedish Upper Deck-205
03Swedish Elite-56
Silver-56

Elomo, Miika
94Finest-143
Super Team Winners-143
Refractors-143
95Collector's Choice-333
Player's Club-333
Player's Club Platinum-333
95Upper Deck-546
Electric Ice-546
Electric Ice Gold-546
95Finnish SISU-336
Drafted Dozen-3
95Classic-22
Ice Breakers-BK10
Ice Breakers Die Cuts-BK10
96Finnish SISU Redline-148
Rookie Energy-5
96Portland Pirates-20
96Portland Pirates Shop N' Save-8
97Portland Pirates-9
98Finnish Kerailysarja-250
99Finnish Cardset Most Wanted-8
99Portland Pirates-6
01Finnish Cardset-358
02Finnish Cardset-15
03Finnish Cardset-11
04Finnish Cardset-205

Elomo, Teemu
97Black Diamond-15
Double Diamond-15
Triple Diamond-15
Quadruple Diamond-15
98UD Choice-276
Prime Choice Reserve-276
Reserve-276
98Finnish Kerailysarja-248
99Finnish Cardset-141
00Finnish Cardset-100
01Finnish Cardset-192
02Finnish Cardset-164
03Finnish Cardset-14
04Finnish Cardset-13
Parallel-9
05Swedish SHL Elitset-265
Gold-265
06Swedish SHL Elitset-124

Eloranta, Kari
81Swedish Semic Hockey VM Stickers-21
83NHL Key Tags-19
83O-Pee-Chee-81
83O-Pee-Chee Stickers-270
83Topps Stickers-270
83Vachon-6
84O-Pee-Chee-223
85Swedish Panini Stickers-184
86Swedish Panini Stickers-113
89Finnish Pelimiehen-1
89Swedish Semic World Champ Stickers-31
92Swedish Semic Elitserien Stickers-254
93Swedish Semic Elitserien-227
94Finnish SISU-362
94Swedish Leaf-10
99Finnish Valio World Championships-1
02Swiss HNL-93
06Finnish Ilves Team Set-27

Eloranta, Mikko
95Finnish SISU-243
96Finnish SISU Redline Rookie Energy-2
98Finnish Kerailysarja-239
Leijonat-20
99BAP Millennium-27
Emerald-27
Ruby-27
Sapphire-27
Signatures-27
Signatures Gold-27
99Crown Royale-13
Limited Series-13
Premiere Date-13
99O-Pee-Chee Chrome-292
99O-Pee-Chee Chrome Refractors-292
99Topps/OPC Chrome-292
Refractors-292
99Ultimate Victory-93
1/1-93
Parallel-93
Parallel 100-93
99Finnish Cardset-189
Aces High-D-J
Par Avion-11
00Panini Stickers-15
00Upper Deck Vintage-34
01BAP Memorabilia-478
Emerald-478
Ruby-478
Sapphire-478
01Upper Deck Victory-29
Gold-29
01Upper Deck Vintage-21
02BAP Memorabilia-129
Emerald-129
Ruby-129
Sapphire-129
NHL All-Star Game-129
NHL All-Star Game Blue-129
NHL All-Star Game Green-129
NHL All-Star Game Red-129
02BAP Memorabilia Toronto Fall Expo-129
02BAP Sig Series Auto Buybacks 1999-27
02Kings Game Sheets-21
02Kings Game Sheets-22
02Topps Total-2
02Finnish Cardset-16
03Czech Stadion-533
03Finnish Cardset-167
03Finnish Cardset Globetrotters-GR2

Elsener, Dan
93Flint Generals-6
95Swiss HNL-373
95San Diego Barracudas RHI-1

Elsner, Alexandr
95Czech APS Extraliga-206
99Czech Score Blue 2000-21
99Czech Score Red Ice 2000-21

Eltermann, Detlev
94German First League-456

Elters, Helmut
94German DEL-360

Eltner, Marco
95German DEL-177
99German EV Landshut-10

Elvenes, Roger
92Swedish Semic Elitserien Stickers-268
93Swedish Semic Elitserien-230
94Swedish Leaf-33
Studio Signatures-10
95Swedish Leaf-121
95Swedish Upper Deck-179

Elvenes, Stefan
92Swedish Semic Elitserien Stickers-267
93Swedish Semic Elitserien-237
94Finnish Jaa Kiekko-76
94Swedish Leaf-81
Top Guns-4
95Swedish Leaf-264
Face to Face-9
95Swedish Upper Deck-150

Elvenes, Tord
93Swedish Semic Elitserien-239

Elwing, Sebastian
99German DEL-67

Elynuik, Pat
84Prince Albert Raiders Stickers-6
87Jets Postcards-7
88Jets Police-7
88Jets Postcards-8
89Jets Safeway-13
89O-Pee-Chee-94

89O-Pee-Chee Stickers-35
89O-Pee-Chee Stickers-66
89O-Pee-Chee Stickers-142
89O-Pee-Chee Stickers-206
89Panini Stickers-165
89Topps-94
90Bowman-137
Tiffany-137
90Jets IGA-12
90Kraft-12
90O-Pee-Chee-71
90OPC Premier-28
90Panini Stickers-312
90Pro Set-327
90Score-205
Canadian-205
90Score Hottest/Rising Stars-86
90Score Young Superstars-28
90Topps-71
Tiffany-71
90Upper Deck-74
French-74
91Pro Set Platinum-136
91Bowman-198
91Jets Panini Team Stickers-10
91Jets IGA-9
91O-Pee-Chee-326
91Panini Stickers-66
91Parkhurst-202
French-202
91Pinnacle-117
91Pinnacle-416
French-117
French-416
91Pro Set-262
French-262
91Score American-295
91Score American-341
91Score Canadian Bilingual-371
91Score Canadian Bilingual-515
91Score Canadian English-371
91Score Canadian English-515
91Score Young Superstars-34
91Stadium Club-132
91Topps-326
91Upper Deck-109
French-109
92Bowman-270
92Capitals Kodak-8
92O-Pee-Chee-201
92OPC Premier-119
92Panini Stickers-54
92Panini Stickers French-54
92Parkhurst-205
Emerald Ice-205
92Pinnacle-53
French-53
92Pro Set-214
92Score-233
Canadian-233
Sharpshooters-23
92Stadium Club-410
92Topps-56
Gold-56G
92Ultra-434
92Upper Deck-312
92Upper Deck-537
93Donruss-368
93Leaf-6
93Lightning Season in Review-12
93OPC Premier-51
Gold-51
93Panini Stickers-29
93Parkhurst-224
Emerald Ice-224
93Pinnacle-382
Canadian-382
93PowerPlay-260
93PowerPlay-442
93Score-223
93Score-580
Gold-580
Canadian-223
Canadian-580
Canadian Gold-580
93Stadium Club-49
93Stadium Club-447
Members Only Master Set-49
Members Only Master Set-447
OPC-49
First Day Issue-49
First Day Issue-447
First Day Issue OPC-49
93Topps/OPC Premier-51
Gold-51
93Ultra-67
93Upper Deck-75
94Be A Player Signature Cards-164
94Fleer-145
94Leaf-535
94OPC Premier-107
Special Effects-107
94Pinnacle-381
Artist's Proofs-381
Rink Collection-381
94Senators Team Issue-12
94Topps/OPC Premier-107
Special Effects-107
94Ultra-338
94Upper Deck-421
Electric Ice-421
95Collector's Choice-39
Player's Club-39
Player's Club Platinum-39
95Fort Wayne Komets-5
96Michigan K-Wings-10

Elzinga, Adam
01Peterborough Petes-15
02Peterborough Petes-18
03Florence Pride-147
05Kalamazoo Wings-14

Elzinga, Josh
02Chicago Steel-6
04Kalamazoo Wings-3
05Kalamazoo Wings-3

Elzner, Falk
94German First League-531

Emanuele, Nick
05Moncton Wildcats-19
06Moncton Wildcats-14

Emberg, Eddie
51Laval Dairy QSHL-108

Embley, Colin
02Fresno Falcons-11
03Missouri River Otters-7

Emeleev, Igor
99Russian Hockey League-231
00Russian Hockey League-383
02Russian Hockey League-102
03Russian National Team-5

Emelyanov, Valeri
00Russian Hockey League-205

Emerick, Bill
93Quebec Pee-Wee Tournament-1672

Emersic, Blaz
99Peoria Rivermen-13
03Charlotte Checkers-70
05UK Nottingham Panthers-6

Emerson, Nelson
90Score-383
Canadian-383
90ProCards AHL/IHL-88
91Pro Set Platinum-269
91Blues Postcards-9
91OPC Premier-138
91Parkhurst-151
French-151
91Pinnacle-314
French-314
91Pro Set-557
French-557
91Score Canadian Bilingual-550
91Score Canadian English-550
91Score Rookie/Traded-89T
91Upper Deck-445
French-445
92Bowman-40
92O-Pee-Chee-181
92Panini Stickers-B
92Panini Stickers French-B
92Parkhurst-152
92Parkhurst-232
Emerald Ice-152
Emerald Ice-232
92Pinnacle American Promo Panel-1
92Pinnacle-36
French-36
92Pro Set-161
Gold Team Leaders-9
Rookie Goal Leaders-5
92Score-376
92Score-505
Canadian-376
Canadian-505
Young Superstars-13
92Seasons Patches-16
92Stadium Club-306
92Topps-11
92Topps-480
Gold-11G
Gold-480G
92Ultra-393
Rookies-5
92Upper Deck-18
92Upper Deck-166
93Donruss-383
93Jets Readers Club-8
93Jets Ruffles-10
93Leaf-75
93OPC Premier-35
Gold-35
93Panini Stickers-159
93Parkhurst-497
Emerald Ice-497
93Pinnacle-245
Canadian-245
93PowerPlay-209
93PowerPlay-472
93Score-28
93Score-506
Gold-506
Canadian-28
Canadian-506
Canadian Gold-506
93Stadium Club-223
Members Only Master Set-223
OPC-223
First Day Issue-223
First Day Issue OPC-223
93Topps/OPC Premier-35
Gold-35
93Ultra-45
93Ultra-453
93Upper Deck-342
SP-175
94Canada Games NHL POGS-252
94Donruss-297
94Fleer-240
94Leaf-80
94OPC Premier-352
Special Effects-352
94Parkhurst-267
Gold-267
SE Vintage-33
94Pinnacle-325
Artist's Proofs-325
Rink Collection-325
94Score-41
Gold-41
Platinum-41
94Select-125
Gold-125
94SP-135
Die Cuts-135
94Stadium Club-240
Members Only Master Set-240
First Day Issue-240
Super Team Winner Cards-240
94Topps/OPC Premier-352
Special Effects-352
94Ultra-242
94Upper Deck-47
Electric Ice-47
SP Inserts-SP179
SP Inserts Die Cuts-SP179
95Be A Player-38
Signatures-S38
Signatures Die Cuts-S38
95Collector's Choice-196
Player's Club-196
Player's Club Platinum-196
95Donruss-7
95Donruss-365
95Emotion-192
95Finest-102
Refractors-102
95Leaf-163
95Metal-65
95Panini Stickers-216
95Parkhurst International-367
Emerald Ice-367
95Playoff One on One-217
95Score-259
Black Ice Artist's Proofs-259
Black Ice-259
95SkyBox Impact-73
95SP-63
95Stadium Club-38
Members Only Master Set-38
95Summit-132
Artist's Proofs-132
Ice-132
95Topps-311
OPC Inserts-311
95Ultra-179
95Ultra-246
Gold Medallion-179
95Upper Deck-178
95Upper Deck-311
Electric Ice-178
Electric Ice-471
Electric Ice Gold-178
Electric Ice Gold-471
Special Edition-SE126
Special Edition Gold-SE126
95Whalers Bob's Stores-7
95Zenith-43
95Swedish World Championships Stickers-18
96Collector's Choice-116
96Donruss-73
Press Proofs-73
96Metal Universe-68
96Pinnacle-60
Artist's Proofs-60
Foil-60
Premium Stock-60
Rink Collection-60
96Playoff One on One-400
96Score-37
Artist's Proofs-37
Dealer's Choice Artist's Proofs-37
Special Artist's Proofs-37
Golden Blades-37
96Topps Picks-135
OPC Inserts-135
96Upper Deck-269
96Whalers Kid's Club-17
97Collector's Choice-115
97Crown Royale-23
Emerald Green-23
Ice Blue-23
Silver-23
97Donruss Priority-135
Stamp of Approval-135
97Hurricanes Team Issue-7
97Pacific-349
Copper-349
Emerald Green-349
Ice Blue-349
Red-349
Silver-349
Invincible NHL Regime-35
97Pacific Omega-39
Copper-39
Dark Gray-39
Emerald Green-39
Gold-39
Ice Blue-39
97Paramount-34
Copper-34
Dark Grey-34
Emerald Green-34
Ice Blue-34
Red-34
Silver-34
97Upper Deck-243
97Upper Deck Ice-1
Parallel-1
Power Shift-1
98Aurora-31
98OPC Chrome-218
Refractors-218
98Pacific-131
Ice Blue-131
Red-131
98Pacific Omega-51
Red-51
Opening Day Issue-51
98Panini Stickers-25
98Paramount-35
Copper-35
Emerald Green-35
Holo-Electric-35
Ice Blue-35
Silver-35
98Topps-218
O-Pee-Chee-218
98UD Choice-43
98UD Choice Preview-43
98UD Choice Prime Choice Reserve-43
98UD Choice Reserve-43
98Upper Deck-60
Exclusives-60
Exclusives 1 of 1-60
Gold Reserve-60
99BAP Memorabilia-249
Gold-249
Silver-249
99BAP Millennium-17
Emerald-17
Ruby-17
Sapphire-17
Signatures-17
Signatures Gold-17
99Pacific Dynagon Ice-15
Blue-15
Copper-15
Gold-15
Premiere Date-15
99Pacific Omega-10
Copper-10
Gold-10
Ice Blue-10
Premiere Date-10
99Panini Stickers-13
99SPx-2
Radiance-2
Spectrum-2
99Upper Deck-176
Exclusives-176
Exclusives 1 of 1-176
99Upper Deck Gold Reserve-176
99Wayne Gretzky Hockey-12
00BAP Memorabilia-337
Emerald-337
Ruby-337
Sapphire-337
Promos-337
00BAP Mem Chicago Sportsfest Copper-337
00BAP Memorabilia Chicago Sportsfest Blue-337
00BAP Memorabilia Chicago Sportsfest Gold-337
00BAP Memorabilia Chicago Sportsfest Ruby-337
00BAP Memorabilia Chicago Sun-Times Ruby-337
00BAP Memorabilia Chicago Sun-Times Gold-337
00BAP Mem Chicago Sun-Times Sapphire-337
00BAP Mem Toronto Fall Expo Copper-337
00BAP Memorabilia Toronto Fall Expo Gold-337
00BAP Memorabilia Toronto Fall Expo Ruby-337
00O-Pee-Chee-130
00O-Pee-Chee Parallel-130
00Pacific-195
Copper-195
Gold-195
Ice Blue-195
Premiere Date-195
00Titanium Game Gear-21
00Topps/OPC-130
Parallel-130
00Upper Deck Vintage-171
02BAP Sig Series Auto Buybacks 1999-17

Emery, Laurent
04Swiss Lausanne HC Postcards-17

Emery, Ray
02BAP Memorabilia-313
02BAP Ultimate Memorabilia-39
02ITG Used-183
02Pacific Calder-132
Silver-132
02Pacific Complete-566
Red-566
02Pacific Quest for the Cup-132
Gold-132
02Parkhurst Retro-225
Minis-225
02SP Authentic-207
02SPx-181
02UD Artistic Impressions-134
Gold-134
02UD Honor Roll-120
02UD Mask Collection-153
02UD Premier Collection-91
Gold-91
02Upper Deck Classic Portraits-138
02AHL Top Prospects-12
03BAP Memorabilia-154
Emerald-154
Gold-154
Ruby-154
Sapphire-154
Future of the Game-FG-2
Future Wave-FW-2
03Pacific Complete-406
Red-406
03Upper Deck-135
Canadian Exclusives-135
HG-135
03Upper Deck MVP-303
Gold Script-303
Silver Script-303
Canadian Exclusives-303
03Upper Deck Victory-136
Bronze-136
Gold-136
Silver-136
Freshman Flashback-FF32
03AHL Top Prospects-8
03Binghamton Senators-4
03Binghamton Senators Postcards-12
03Pacific AHL Prospects-5
Gold-5
04Binghamton Senators-3
04Binghamton Senators Hess-13
04ITG Heroes and Prospects-45
Autographs-RE
Combos-10
Emblems-13
Emblems Gold-13
He Shoots-He Scores Prizes-24
Jersey Autographs-13
Jerseys-13
Jerseys Gold-13
Net Prospects-11
Net Prospects Gold-11
Numbers-13
Numbers Gold-13
04ITG Heroes/Prospects Toronto Expo '05-45
04ITG Heroes/Prospects Expo Heroes/Pros-45
05ITG Heroes/Prosp Toronto Expo Parallel -66
05ITG Heroes/Prosp Toronto Expo Parallel -368
05ITG Heroes/Prosp Toronto Expo Parallel -430
05ITG Ultimate Mem Future Stars Autos-4
05ITG Ultimate Mem Future Star Autos Gold-4
05ITG Ultimate Mem Future Stars Jerseys-4
05ITG Ultimate Mem Fut Stars Jerseys Gold-4
05ITG Ultimate Mem Future Stars Mem Autos-4
05ITG Ultimate Mem Fut Star Mem Auto Gold-4
05Parkhurst-344
Facsimile Auto Parallel-344
05ITG Heroes and Prospects-66
05ITG Heroes and Prospects-368
05ITG Heroes and Prospects-430
Autographs-A-RE
Autographs Series II-RE2
Autographs Update-A-RE3
Jerseys-GUJ-19
Jerseys Gold-GUJ-19
Emblems-GUE-19
Emblems Gold-GUE-19
Numbers-GUN-19
Numbers Gold-GUN-19
Making the Bigs-MTB-8
Net Prospects-NP-7
Net Prospects Gold-NP-07
06Between The Pipes-73
Aspiring-AS07
Aspiring Gold-AS07
Autographs-ARE
Complete Jersey-CJ04
Complete Jersey Gold-CJ04
Double Jerseys-DJ23
Double Jerseys Gold-DJ23
Emblems-GUE56
Emblems Gold-GUE56
Emblems Autographs-GUE56
Jerseys-GUJ56
Jerseys Gold-GUJ56
Jerseys Autographs-GUJ56
Numbers-GUN56
Numbers Gold-GUN56
Numbers Autographs-GUN56
Prospect Trios-PT03
Prospect Trios Gold-PT03
Stick and Jersey-SJ07
Stick and Jersey Gold-SJ07
Stick and Jersey Autographs-SJ07
The Mask-M05
The Mask Gold-M05
The Mask Silver-M05
The Mask Game-Used-MGU05
The Mask Game-Used Gold-MGU05
06Fleer-140
Tiffany-140
06Gatorade-51
06ITG Ultimate Memorabilia Autos-37
06ITG Ultimate Memorabilia Autos Gold-37
06ITG Ultimate Memorabilia Double Memorabilia Autos-2
06ITG Ultimate Memorabilia Double Memorabilia Autos Gold-2
06ITG Ultimate Memorabilia Emblems-9
06ITG Ultimate Memorabilia Emblems Gold-9
06ITG Ultimate Memorabilia In The Numbers-18
06ITG Ultimate Memorabilia In The Numbers Gold-18
06ITG Ultimate Memorabilia Jerseys Autos-12
06ITG Ultimate Memorabilia Jerseys Autos Gold-12
06ITG Ultimate Memorabilia Sticks and Jerseys-5
06ITG Ultimate Memorabilia Sticks and Jerseys Gold-5
06O-Pee-Chee-343
Rainbow-343
06Panini Stickers-120
06Ultra-139
Gold Medallion-139
Ice Medallion-139
06Upper Deck-136
Exclusives Parallel-136
High Gloss Parallel-136
Masterpieces-136
06Upper Deck MVP-202
Gold Script-202
Super Script-202
06Upper Deck Ovation-84
06Upper Deck Victory-142
06Upper Deck Victory Black-142
06Upper Deck Victory Gold-142
06Binghamton Senators 5th Anniversary-7
06ITG Heroes and Prospects Making The Bigs-MTB09
06ITG Heroes and Prospects Making The Bigs Gold-MTB09
06ITG Heroes and Prospects Net Prospects-NPR07
06ITG Heroes and Prospects Net Prospects Gold-NPR07
06ITG Heroes and Prospects Quad Emblems-QE09
06ITG Heroes and Prospects Quad Emblems Gold-QE09
06ITG Heroes and Prospects Sticks and Jerseys-SJ19
06ITG Heroes and Prospects Sticks and Jerseys Gold-SJ19
07Upper Deck Ovation-67
07Upper Deck Victory-41
Black-41
Gold-41

Emilyantsev, Dmitri
98Muskegon Fury-24

Eminger, John
99Kitchener Rangers-1
00London Knights-17
01Mississauga Ice Dogs-18

Eminger, Steve
99Kitchener Rangers-4
00Kitchener Rangers-12
01SPx Rookie Redemption-R30
01Kitchener Rangers-5
02Atomic-125
Blue-125
Gold-125
Red-125
Hobby Parallel-125
02BAP All-Star Edition-144
Gold-144
Silver-144
02BAP First Edition-440R
02BAP Memorabilia-288
Emerald-288
Ruby-288
Sapphire-288
Draft Redemptions-12
NHL All-Star Game-288
NHL All-Star Game Blue-288
NHL All-Star Game Green-288
NHL All-Star Game Red-288
02BAP Memorabilia Toronto Fall Expo-288
02BAP Signature Series-200
Autographs-200
Autographs Gold-200
02BAP Ultimate Memorabilia-18
02Bowman YoungStars-128
Gold-128
Silver-128
02Crown Royale-139
Blue-139
Purple-139
Red-139
Retail-139
02ITG Used-193
02Pacific Calder-149
Silver-149
02Pacific Complete-553
Red-553
02Pacific Exclusive-192
Blue-192
Gold-192
02Pacific Heads-Up-145
02Pacific Quest for the Cup-150
Gold-150
02Parkhurst-218
Bronze-218
Gold-218
Silver-218
02Parkhurst Retro-218
Minis-218
02Private Stock Reserve-184
Blue-184
Red-184
Retail-184
02SP Authentic-160
02SP Game Used-95
02SPx-162
02Stadium Club-139
Silver Decoy Cards-139
Proofs-139
02Titanium-140
Blue-140
Red-140
Retail-140
02Topps Chrome-166
Black Border Refractors-166
Refractors-166
02Topps Heritage-152
02Topps Total-406
02UD Artistic Impressions-105
Gold-105
02UD Foundations-163
02UD Honor Roll-166
02UD Mask Collection-180
02UD Piece of History-150
02UD Premier Collection-70B
Gold-70B
02UD Top Shelf-104
02Upper Deck-246
Exclusives-246
02Upper Deck Classic Portraits-130
02Upper Deck Rookie Update-154A
02Upper Deck Rookie Update-154B
02Upper Deck Rookie Update-154C
02Vanguard-136
LTD-136
02Kitchener Rangers Postcards-1
03ITG Action-579
03Upper Deck-441
Canadian Exclusives-441
HG-441
UD Exclusives-441
03Upper Deck MVP-434
Gold Script-434
Silver Script-434
Canadian Exclusives-434
03Kitchener Rangers Memorial Cup-8
04AHL All-Stars-12
04AHL Top Prospects-41
04Portland Pirates-1
05ITG Heroes/Prosp Toronto Expo Parallel -86
05Panini Stickers-186
05Upper Deck-436
05ITG Heroes and Prospects-86
Autographs-A-SE
06Be A Player-133
Autographs-133
Signatures-EM
Signatures Duals-DGE
06O-Pee-Chee-494
Rainbow-494
06Upper Deck MVP-291
Gold Script-291
Super Script-291

Emma, David
91Score American-330
92Upper Deck-462
93OPC Premier-448
Gold-448
93PowerPlay-377
93Score-468
Canadian-468
93Topps/OPC Premier-448
Gold-448
94Flair-93
94Ultra-319
94Classic Pro Prospects-98
95Upper Deck-155
Electric Ice-155
Electric Ice Gold-155
96Providence Bruins-10
00Louisville Panthers-4
01German Upper Deck-201

Emmenegger, Mark
01Swiss HNL-366

Emmerton, Cory
04Kingston Frontenacs-7
05ITG Heroes/Prosp Toronto Expo Parallel -292
05Kingston Frontenacs-1
05OHL Bell All-Star Classic-7
05ITG Heroes and Prospects-292
Autographs Series II-CEM
Team Orr-T08
06Kingston Frontenacs-13
06ITG Heroes and Prospects-88
Autographs-ACE
Jerseys-GUJ66
Emblems-GUE66
Numbers-GUN66

Emmett, Rick
93Peterborough Petes-14
94Kitchener Rangers-13
94Windsor Spitfires-21
96Quad-City Mallards-16
97Quad-City Mallards-2
98Quad-City Mallards-5
99Quad-City Mallards-6
00Muskegon Fury-28
00Quad-City Mallards-19
01Macon Whoopee-8
02Macon Trax-7
03Gwinnett Gladiators-6
03Gwinnett Gladiators RBI Sports-199
04Gwinnett Gladiators-9

Emmons, Gary
89ProCards IHL-83
91Kansas City Blades-7
91ProCards-506
92Kansas City Blades-10
93Kansas City Blades-8
94Kansas City Blades-10
95Kansas City Blades-7
96Kansas City Blades-9
97Kansas City Blades Magnets-2
98Kansas City Blades-26
99Kansas City Blades-1
99Kansas City Blades Supercuts-26

Emmons, John
92Upper Deck-608
93Donruss Team USA-7
93Pinnacle-492
Canadian-492
93Upper Deck-557
96Dayton Bombers-13
98Detroit Vipers-9
98Detroit Vipers Freschetta-8
99BAP Memorabilia-363
Gold-363
Silver-363
99Grand Rapids Griffins-5
00Upper Deck NHLPA-PA61
01Providence Bruins-11

Emmons, Shayne
00OCN Blizzard-12

Emms, Leighton
33O-Pee-Chee V304A-40
33V252 Canadian Gum-22
33V357 Ice Kings-55
34Beehive Group I Photos-224
35Diamond Matchbooks Tan 2-21
35Diamond Matchbooks Tan 3-19
37V356 Worldwide Gum-59

Emond, Marco
03Laredo Bucks-7
06Colorado EaglesÂ -8

Emond, Patrick
84Chicoutimi Sagueneens-10

Emond, Pierre-Luc
01Cape Breton Screaming Eagles-12
02Cape Breton Screaming Eagles-11
02Hershey Bears-8

Empey, Larry
91Air Canada SJHL-E12
92Saskatchewan JHL-39
94Erie Panthers-5
99Adirondack IceHawks-6
00Amarillo Rattlers-6

Emvall, Fredrik
02Swedish SHL-52
Parallel-52
03Swedish Elite-75
Silver-75
04Swedish Elitset-66
Gold-66

Emwall, Fredrik
05Swedish SHL Elitset-79
Gold-79
Series Two Signatures-17
Teammates-7
06Swedish SHL Elitset-78

Enander, Mikael
89Swedish Semic Elitserien Stickers-36
91Swedish Semic Elitserien Stickers-36
92Swedish Semic Elitserien Stickers-57
93Swedish Semic Elitserien-33
94Swedish Leaf-182

Endean, Craig
86Regina Pats-6
87Regina Pats-5
89ProCards IHL-131

Enders, Dan
97New Hampshire Wildcats-14
98New Hampshire Wildcats-3

Endicott, Derek
01Red Deer Rebels-5
02Red Deer Rebels-14
03Red Deer Rebels-11
03Saskatoon Blades-26

Endicott, Shane
99UD Prospects-40
01BAP Memorabilia-360
Emerald-360
Ruby-360
Sapphire-360
01Parkhurst-344
01SPx-213
Rookie Redemption-R24
01UD Mask Collection-164
Gold-164
01UD Premier Collection-105
01Upper Deck Ice-146
01Wilkes-Barre Scranton Penguins-12
02O-Pee-Chee-311
02O-Pee-Chee Premier Blue Parallel-311
02O-Pee-Chee Premier Red Parallel-311
02O-Pee-Chee Factory Set-311
02SPx-121
02Topps-311
OPC Blue Parallel-311
OPC Red Parallel-311
Factory Set-311
02UD Piece of History-146
02Upper Deck Vintage-344
02AHL Top Prospects-13
02Wilkes-Barre Scranton Penguins-11
03Wilkes-Barre Scranton Penguins-9
04Wilkes-Barre Scranton Penguins-12

Endras, Dennis
04German Augsburg Panthers Postcards-11
05German DEL-3

Endrass, Stefan
05German DEL-17

Eneqvist, Johan
05Swedish SHL Elitset-165
Gold-165
06Swedish SHL Elitset-19

Enga, R.J.
98Colorado Gold Kings-3
98Colorado Gold Kings Postcards-14
99Colorado Gold Kings Taco Bell-2
99Colorado Gold Kings Wendy's-5
01Colorado Gold Kings-7

Engberg, Gary
72Finnish Panda Toronto-2

Engblom, Borje
71Swedish Hockey-389

Engblom, Brian
76Nova Scotia Voyageurs-6
77Canadiens Postcards-6
78Canadiens Postcards-6
79Canadiens Postcards-3
79O-Pee-Chee-361
80Canadiens Postcards-4
80O-Pee-Chee-304
80Pepsi-Cola Caps-42
81Canadiens Postcards-6
81O-Pee-Chee-175
81O-Pee-Chee Stickers-33
81Topps-10
82Capitals Team Issue-5
82McDonald's Stickers-29
82O-Pee-Chee-362
82Post Cereal-10
83O-Pee-Chee-368
83O-Pee-Chee Stickers-203
83Puffy Stickers-20
83Topps Stickers-203
84Kings Smokey-3
84O-Pee-Chee-83
84O-Pee-Chee Stickers-271
84Topps-65
85O-Pee-Chee-5
85O-Pee-Chee Stickers-233
85Topps-5
86Flames Red Rooster-5
86O-Pee-Chee-40
86O-Pee-Chee Stickers-46
86Topps-40

Engblom, David
95Swedish Upper Deck-11
97Swedish Collector's Choice-11

Engel, Alexander
94German DEL-154
95German DEL-151
96German DEL-228
99German Bundesliga 2-147
06German DEL-38

Engel, Josh
04Wisconsin Badgers-21
05Wisconsin Badgers-10

Engel, Peter
94German First League-240

Engelbrecht, Bernhard
79Panini Stickers-97
82Swedish Semic VM Stickers-102
83Swedish Semic VM Stickers-102
94German DEL-337

Engelhardt, Brett
01Michigan Tech Huskies-8
04Gwinnett Gladiators-10
06Toronto Marlies-10

Engelland, Deryk
01Moose Jaw Warriors-3
03Las Vegas Wranglers-7
03Las Vegas Wranglers RBI-230
04Las Vegas Wranglers-3
05Hershey Bears-22

Engels, Jurgen
94German First League-388

Engevik, Glen
89Nashville Knights-6
92Norwegian Elite Series-161

Engfer, Jon
95Tallahassee Tiger Sharks-2

Englehart, Brad
98Johnstown Chiefs-22

Engler, Yves
93Quebec Pee-Wee Tournament-1394

English, John
83Sault Ste. Marie Greyhounds-4
88ProCards AHL-193

English, Scott
01Moncton Wildcats-23
03Fort Worth Brahmas-5
04Memphis RiverKings-16

Englund, Bo
64Swedish Coralli ISHockey-17
64Swedish Coralli ISHockey-52
65Swedish Coralli ISHockey-17
65Swedish Coralli ISHockey-52
67Swedish Hockey-267
69Swedish Hockey-116

Englund, Christer
71Swedish Hockey-390
73Swedish Stickers-206

Englund, Patrik
89Swedish Semic Elitserien Stickers-21
90Swedish Semic Elitserien Stickers-92
91Swedish Semic Elitserien Stickers-22
92Swedish Semic Elitserien Stickers-47
94Swedish Leaf-96
95Swedish Leaf-164
95Swedish Upper Deck-17
97Swedish Collector's Choice-99

Englund, Thomas
98Danish Hockey League-147
99Danish Hockey League-98

Engman, Gustav
04Spokane Chiefs Magnets-7

Engman, Petri
92Finnish Jyvas-Hyva Stickers-138
94Finnish SISU-333
95Finnish SISU-17

Engqvist, Knut
92British Columbia JHL-25

Engstrom, Karl-Harry
55Swedish Alfabilder-30

Engstrom, Mikael
91Swedish Semic Elitserien Stickers-174
92Swedish Semic Elitserien Stickers-196
93Swedish Semic Elitserien-166
94Swedish Leaf-114

Engstrom, Molly
04Wisconsin Badgers Women-6

Engstrom, Tracy
98Minnesota Golden Gophers Women-5

Enio, Jim
44Beehive Group II Photos-163

Enlow, Steve
04Tulsa Oilers-8

Enlund, Jonas
06Finnish Cardset-328

Ennaffati, Alexander
04P.E.I. Rocket-25

Ennaffati, Omar
00Mississauga Ice Dogs-12
03St. Francis Xavier X-Men-20
04St. Francis Xavier X-Men-6

Ennis, Jim
88Oilers Tenth Anniversary-92
88ProCards AHL-88
89ProCards AHL-300

Ennis, Tyler
05Medicine Hat Tigers-10
06Medicine Hat Tigers-6

Enqvist, Olli
71Finnish Suomi Stickers-298

Ens, Kelly
88Lethbridge Hurricanes-5
89Lethbridge Hurricanes-4
90ProCards AHL/IHL-193
91ProCards-113

Ensom, Jim
93North Bay Centennials-8
94Kitchener Rangers Update-33
95Slapshot-285
95Owen Sound Platers-28
95Owen Sound Platers-31
96Quad-City Mallards-6

Enstrom, Tobias
02Swedish SHL-238
Parallel-238
03Swedish Elite Rookies-8
03Swedish Elite Signatures-5
04Swedish Elitset-239
Gold-239
04Swedish MoDo Postcards-28
05Swedish SHL Elitset-94
Star Potential-11
06Swedish SHL Elitset-105

Enstrom, Tommy
05Swedish SHL Elitset Rookies-7

Enzler, Rico
95Swiss HNL-403
96Swiss HNL-350
96Swiss HNL-563

Eovaldi, Brian
93Quebec Pee-Wee Tournament-1748

Epanchinsev, Vadim
94Parkhurst SE-SE231
Gold-SE231
94SP-164
Die Cuts-164
94Upper Deck-514
Electric Ice-514
94Signature Rookies Gold Standard *-100
95Signature Rookies-50
Signatures-50
97Cleveland Lumberjacks-10
97Cleveland Lumberjacks Postcards-16
98Russian Hockey League-91
99Russian Hockey League-256
00Russian Hockey League-374
01Russian Hockey League-119
02Russian Hockey League-161
02Russian Hockey League-184
03Russian Hockey League-144
04Russian Super League All-Stars-31
05Russian Hockey League RHL-20

Epaulards, Les
93Quebec Pee-Wee Tournament-1020

Epiney, Gaby
93Swiss HNL-425
95Swiss HNL-200
96Swiss HNL-419
00Swiss Panini Stickers-316
01Swiss HNL-432

Epner, Erik
93Quebec Pee-Wee Tournament-574

Epoch, Paul
86Kitchener Rangers-14

Epp, Kevin
98Anchorage Aces-3

Epp, Ryan
92Quebec Pee-Wee Tournament-1754
93Quebec Pee-Wee Tournament-169

Eppers, Henrik

93Peterborough Petes-13
Epple, Markus
94German First League-194
Epstein, Nikolai
74Swedish Stickers-50
Equale, Ryan
96Roanoke Express-12
98Odessa Jackalopes-3
Equilino, Beat
93Swiss HNL-217
95Swiss HNL-116
96Swiss HNL-106
98Swiss Power Play Stickers-56
99Swiss Panini Stickers-56
00Swiss Panini Stickers-104
00Swiss Slapshot Mini-Cards-HCD2
01Swiss HNL-101
Erasmas, Ryan
91British Columbia JHL-98
Erat, Martin
00SPx Rookie Redemption-RR17
00Saskatoon Blades-12
01Atomic-113
Premiere Date-113
01Atomic Toronto Fall Expo-113
01BAP Memorabilia-310
Emerald-310
Ruby-310
Sapphire-310
01BAP Signature Series-238
Autographs-238
Autographs Gold-238
01Bowman YoungStars-126
Gold-126
Ice Cubed-126
01Crown Royale-167
Crowning Achievement-6
Rookie Royalty-12
01O-Pee-Chee-336
01Pacific Adrenaline-213
Blue-213
Premiere Date-213
Red-213
Retail-213
01Pacific Heads-Up-110
01Pacific High Voltage-6
01Parkhurst-323
01Private Stock-128
Gold-128
Premiere Date-128
Retail-128
Silver-128
01Private Stock Pacific Nights-128
01Private Stock PS-2002-98
01SP Authentic-157
Limited-157
Limited Gold-157
01SP Game Used-83
01SPx-109
01Titanium-166
Retail-166
01Titanium Draft Day Edition-142
01Topps-336
01Topps Chrome-154
Refractors-154
Black Border Refractors-154
01UD Challenge for the Cup-115
01UD Honor Roll-78
01UD Mask Collection-152
Gold-152
01UD Playmakers-125
01UD Premier Collection-100
01UD Top Shelf-131
01Upper Deck-430
Exclusives-430
01Upper Deck Ice-59
01Upper Deck MVP-226
01Upper Deck Victory-446
01Upper Deck Vintage-283
01Vanguard-118
Blue-118
Red-118
One of Ones-118
Premiere Date-118
Prime Prospects-10
Proofs-118
02BAP First Edition-297
02BAP Memorabilia-91
Emerald-91
Ruby-91
Sapphire-91
NHL All-Star Game-91
NHL All-Star Game Blue-91
NHL All-Star Game Green-91
NHL All-Star Game Red-91
02BAP Memorabilia Toronto Fall Expo-91
02BAP Signature Series Golf-GS52
02O-Pee-Chee-236
02O-Pee-Chee Premier Blue Parallel-236
02O-Pee-Chee Premier Red Parallel-236
02O-Pee-Chee Factory Set-236
02Pacific-208
Blue-208
Red-208
Jerseys-28
Jerseys Holo-Silver-28
02Pacific Calder Collection AS Fantasy-7
02Pacific Calder Collection All-Star Fantasy Gold-7
02Pacific Complete-257
Red-257
02Pacific Heads-Up Quad Jerseys-16
02Pacific Heads-Up Quad Jerseys-36
02Pacific Heads-Up Quad Jerseys Gold-16
02Pacific Heads-Up Quad Jerseys Gold-36
02Parkhurst-189
Bronze-189
Gold-189
Silver-189
02SP Game Used Future Fabrics-FFME
02SP Game Used Future Fabrics Gold-FFME
02SP Game Used Future Fabrics Rainbow-FFME
02Topps-236
OPC Blue Parallel-236
OPC Red Parallel-236
Factory Set-236
02Topps Total-209
02UD Artistic Impressions Right Track-RTME
02UD Artistic Impression Right Track Gold-RTME
02UD Top Shelf Dual Player Jerseys-STDE
02Upper Deck-99
Exclusives-99
Bright Futures-ME
Hot Spots-HSME
02Upper Deck Vintage-142
02Upper Deck Vintage-277
02Milwaukee Admirals-13
02Milwaukee Admirals Postcards-5
03ITG Action-352
03Pacific Complete-285
Red-285
03Pacific Quest for the Cup-60
Blue-60
03Titanium-164
Hobby Jersey Number Parallels-164
Patches-164
Retail-164
04Pacific-145
Blue-145
Red-145
04Upper Deck-100
Canadian Exclusives-100
HG Glossy Gold-100
HG Glossy Silver-100
04Czech OFS-276
Stars-38
04Czech Zuma-36
05Parkhurst-276
Facsimile Auto Parallel-276
05Upper Deck-361
05Upper Deck MVP-220
Gold-220
Platinum-220
05Upper Deck Victory-114
Black-114
Gold-114
Silver-114
06O-Pee-Chee-281
Rainbow-281
06Panini Stickers-310
06SP Game Used Authentic Fabrics-AFME
06SP Game Used Authentic Fabrics Parallel-AFME
06SP Game Used Authentic Fabrics Patches-AFME
06The Cup NHL Shields Duals-DSHRE
06UD Artifacts Tundra Tandems-TTVE
06UD Artifacts Tundra Tandems Black-TTVE
06UD Artifacts Tundra Tandems Blue-TTVE
06UD Artifacts Tundra Tandems Gold-TTVE
06UD Artifacts Tundra Tandems Platinum-TTVE
06UD Artifacts Tundra Tandems Red-TTVE
06UD Artifacts Tundra Tandems Dual Patches Red-TTVE
06Upper Deck-361
Exclusives Parallel-361
High Gloss Parallel-361
Game Jerseys-JME
Game Patches-PME
Masterpieces-361
06Upper Deck MVP-169
Gold Script-169
Super Script-169
06Upper Deck Victory-112
06Upper Deck Victory Black-112
06Upper Deck Victory Gold-112
06Czech IIHF World Championship Postcards-4
Erat, Roman
02Czech OFS Plus-106
03Czech OFS Plus-240
04Czech OFS-294
05Czech HC Znojmo-4
06Czech OFS-202
Stars-22
Erb, Chad
05Brandon Wheat Kings-9
Erb, Jamie
93Raleigh Icecaps-5
Erdall, Rick
89Swedish Semic Elitserien Stickers-113
90Swedish Semic Elitserien Stickers-144
91Swedish Semic Elitserien Stickers-196
Erdman, Josh
907th Inn. Sketch WHL-330
98Huntsville Channel Cats-12
Erdmann, Alexander
96German DEL-164
Eremenko, Rick
91British Columbia JHL-17
Eremeyev, Oleg
00Russian Hockey League-120
Erhart, Sven
94German First League-265
Erholm, Mikko
65Finnish Hellas-32
70Finnish Jaakiekko-226
71Finnish Suomi Stickers-242
73Finnish Jaakiekko-305
74Finnish Typotor-19
Erickson, Autry
60Shirriff Coins-112
61Shirriff/Salada Coins-18
67Seals Team Issue-10
07Maple Leafs 1967 Commemorative-8
Erickson, Brad
04Prince Albert Raiders-10
05Prince Albert Raiders-10
Erickson, Bryan
85O-Pee-Chee-80
85Topps-80
86Kings 20th Anniversary Team Issue-5
86O-Pee-Chee-101
86O-Pee-Chee Stickers-93
86Topps-101
87O-Pee-Chee-130
87Panini Stickers-282
87Topps-130
91Jets IGA-10
91Pro Set-516
French-516
91Score Canadian Bilingual-657
91Score Canadian English-657
93Jets Readers Club-9
93Jets Ruffles-11
93OPC Premier-294
Gold-294
93Topps/OPC Premier-294
Gold-294
Erickson, Chad
91ProCards-421
92Cincinnati Cyclones-9
93Raleigh Icecaps-6
95Birmingham Bulls-21
97Austin Ice Bats-2
98San Angelo Outlaws-8
Erickson, Denis
72Johnstown Jets-10
Erickson, Grant
72Cleveland Crusaders WHA-4
Erickson, Kyle
93Minnesota-Duluth Bulldogs-9
Erickson, Luke
01Lincoln Stars-6
02Lincoln Stars-18
02Topeka Scarecrows-10
Erickson, Matt
01Lincoln Stars-7
Erickson, Mike
01Minnesota Golden Gophers-5
02Minnesota Golden Gophers-5
06Augusta Lynx-3
Erickson, Patrik
87Swedish Panini Stickers-60
89Swedish Semic Elitserien Stickers-42
90Swedish Semic Elitserien Stickers-186
91Finnish Semic World Champ Stickers-47
91Swedish Semic Elitserien Stickers-15
91Swedish Semic Elitserien Stickers-355
91Swedish Semic World Champ Stickers-47
92Swedish Semic Elitserien Stickers-43
93Swedish Semic Elitserien-72
94Swedish Leaf-98
95Swedish Leaf-36
Face to Face-13
95Swedish Upper Deck-54
95Swedish Globe World Championships-54
97Swedish Collector's Choice-47
98Swedish UD Choice-63
Ericksson, Roland
79Panini Stickers-193
Ericson, Fredrik
06Swedish SHL Elitset-163
Ericsson, Arne
65Swedish Coralli ISHockey-91
Ericsson, Bengt
93Swiss HNL-287
Ericsson, Bo
82Swedish Semic VM Stickers-11
83Swedish Semic Elitserien-6
83Swedish Semic VM Stickers-11
84Swedish Semic Elitserien-224
86Swedish Panini Stickers-251
87Swedish Panini Stickers-238
Ericsson, Jan
83Swedish Semic Elitserien-24
92Swedish Semic Elitserien Stickers-264
93Swedish Semic Elitserien-233
Ericsson, Jimmie
05Swedish SHL Elitset-216
Gold-216
Ericsson, Jonathan
04Swedish Elitset-111
Gold-111
05Swedish SHL Elitset-270
Gold-270
06AHL Top Prospects-11
Ericsson, Rolf
83Swedish Semic Elitserien-18
Erikkson, Anders
98Upper Deck-88
Exclusives-88
Exclusives 1 of 1-88
Eriksen, Jarl
92Norwegian Elite Series-2
92Norwegian Elite Series-188
Eriksen, Pal Andre
92Norwegian Elite Series-76
Eriksen, Tommie
90ProCards AHL/IHL-185
92Norwegian Elite Series-37
92Norwegian Elite Series-202
95Swedish World Championships Stickers-242
Eriksson, Anders
91Swedish Semic Elitserien Stickers-327
92Swedish Semic Elitserien Stickers-230
93Parkhurst-540
Emerald Ice-540
93Swedish Semic Elitserien-200
93Classic-129
93Classic Four-Sport *-203
Gold-203
94Parkhurst SE-SE233
Gold-SE233
94SP-170
Die Cuts-170
94Upper Deck-518
Electric Ice-518
94Swedish Leaf-32
95Swedish Globe World Championships-58
95Adirondack Red Wings-6
96Collector's Choice-356
96Donruss Canadian Ice-145
Gold Press Proofs-145
Red Press Proofs-145
96Donruss Elite-129
Die Cut Stars-129
96Fleer Picks-180
96Leaf-214
Press Proofs-214
96Leaf Preferred-125
Press Proofs-125
96Metal Universe-177
96Pinnacle-219
Artist's Proofs-219
Foil-219
Premium Stock-219
Rink Collection-219
96Select Certified-92
Artist's Proofs-92
Blue-92
Mirror Blue-92
Mirror Gold-92
Mirror Red-92
Red-92
96SP-176
SPx Force-4
96Summit-190
Artist's Proofs-190
Ice-190
Metal-190
Premium Stock-190
96Ultra-49
Gold Medallion-49
Rookies-6
96Upper Deck-183
Generation Next-X22
96Upper Deck Ice-83
Parallel-83
96Zenith-137
Artist's Proofs-137
96Swedish Semic Wien-55
96Collector's Edge Future Legends-4
96Collector's Edge Ice-2
Prism-2
97Be A Player-180
Autographs-180
Autographs Die-Cuts-180
Autographs Prismatic Die-Cuts-180
97Donruss-174
Press Proofs Silver-174
Press Proofs Gold-174
97Donruss Limited-54
Exposure-54
97Paramount-64
Copper-64
Dark Grey-64
Emerald Green-64
Ice Blue-64
Red-64
Silver-64
97SP Authentic-56
98OPC Chrome-25
Refractors-25
98Pacific-189
Ice Blue-189
Red-189
98Paramount-73
Copper-73
Emerald Green-73
Holo-Electric-73
Ice Blue-73
Silver-73
98SPx Finite-129
Radiance-129
Spectrum-129
98Topps-25
O-Pee-Chee-25
98UD3-28
98UD3-88
98UD3-148
Die-Cuts-28
Die-Cuts-88
Die-Cuts-148
98Upper Deck Gold Reserve-88
99BAP Memorabilia-91
Gold-91
Silver-91
99BAP Millennium-58
Emerald-58
Ruby-58
Sapphire-58
Signatures-58
Signatures Gold-58
99O-Pee-Chee-36
99O-Pee-Chee Chrome-36
99O-Pee-Chee Chrome Refractors-36
99Pacific-87
Copper-87
Emerald Green-87
Gold-87
Ice Blue-87
Premiere Date-87
Red-87
99Panini Stickers-199
99Topps/OPC-36
99Topps/OPC Chrome-36
Refractors-36
99Upper Deck-38
Exclusives-38
Exclusives 1 of 1-38
99Upper Deck Gold Reserve-38
99Upper Deck Victory-69
99Russian Fetisov Tribute-28
00BAP Memorabilia-293
Emerald-293
Ruby-293
Sapphire-293
Promos-293
00BAP Mem Chicago Sportsfest Copper-293
00BAP Memorabilia Chicago Sportsfest Blue-293
00BAP Memorabilia Chicago Sportsfest Gold-293
00BAP Memorabilia Chicago Sportsfest Ruby-293
00BAP Memorabilia Chicago Sun-Times Ruby-293
00BAP Memorabilia Chicago Sun-Times Gold-293
00BAP Mem Chicago Sun-Times Sapphire-293
00BAP Mem Toronto Fall Expo Copper-293
00BAP Memorabilia Toronto Fall Expo Gold-293
00BAP Memorabilia Toronto Fall Expo Ruby-293
00Panthers Team Issue-28
00SP Authentic Sign of the Times-AE
00Stadium Club-164
01BAP Memorabilia-154
Emerald-154
Ruby-154
Sapphire-154
01Pacific-170
Extreme LTD-170
Hobby LTD-170
Premiere Date-170
Retail LTD-170
01Pacific Arena Exclusives-170
01Parkhurst-240
01Upper Deck Victory-152
Gold-152
02BAP Sig Series Auto Buybacks 1999-58
03Syracuse Crunch-21
04Pacific-75
Blue-75
Red-75
04Swedish Pure Skills-35
Parallel-35
05Swedish SHL Elitset-51
Gold-51
06O-Pee-Chee-143
Rainbow-143
Eriksson, Arne
64Swedish Coralli ISHockey-91
Eriksson, Bengt
67Swedish Hockey-235
69Swedish Hockey-278
71Swedish Hockey-273
Eriksson, Bernt
56Swedish Alfabilder-47
Eriksson, Bjorn
95Swedish Leaf-212
Eriksson, Bo
57Swedish Alfabilder-79
71Swedish Hockey-391
72Swedish Stickers-259
84Swedish Semic Elitserien-178
85Swedish Panini Stickers-159
85Swedish Panini Stickers-227
86Swedish Panini Stickers-170
87Swedish Panini Stickers-173
Eriksson, Claes
90Swedish Semic Elitserien Stickers-270
91Swedish Semic Elitserien Stickers-100
92Swedish Semic Elitserien Stickers-118
93Swedish Semic Elitserien-90
94Swedish Leaf-87
95Swedish Leaf-45
95Swedish Upper Deck-71
97Swedish Collector's Choice-63
98Swedish UD Choice-97
99Swedish Upper Deck-66
00Swedish Upper Deck-89
02Swedish SHL-29
Parallel-29
03Swedish Elite-40
Silver-40
Eriksson, Eddy
89Swedish Semic Elitserien Stickers-110
90Swedish Semic Elitserien Stickers-115
91Swedish Semic Elitserien Stickers-121
92Swedish Semic Elitserien Stickers-139
Eriksson, Esko
70Finnish Jaakiekko-120
71Finnish Suomi Stickers-170
72Finnish Jaakiekko-121
72Finnish Panda Toronto-19
73Finnish Jaakiekko-175
Eriksson, Fredrik
97Swedish Collector's Choice-191
03Swedish Elite-187
Silver-187
04Swedish Elitset-35
04Swedish Elitset-190
Gold-35
Gold-190
05Swedish SHL Elitset-48
05Swedish SHL Elitset-188
Gold-48
Gold-188
Eriksson, Hakan
83Swedish Semic Elitserien-88
Eriksson, Hans
64Swedish Coralli ISHockey-35
64Swedish Coralli ISHockey-81
65Swedish Coralli ISHockey-35
67Swedish Hockey-27
69Swedish Hockey-41
73Swedish Stickers-46
83Swedish Semic Elitserien-133
Eriksson, Henrik
02Swedish SHL-268
Parallel-268
Eriksson, Jan
81Swedish Semic Hockey VM Stickers-5
82Swedish Semic VM Stickers-7
83Swedish Semic Elitserien-4
83Swedish Semic VM Stickers-7
84Swedish Semic Elitserien-3
85Swedish Panini Stickers-6
87Swedish Panini Stickers-7
89Swedish Semic Elitserien Stickers-242
90Swedish Semic Elitserien Stickers-160
Eriksson, Jimmie
06Swedish SHL Elitset-271
Eriksson, Joakim
97Swedish Collector's Choice-175
Crash the Game Exchange-C26
Crash the Game Redemption-R26
02Swedish SHL-160
Parallel-160
03Swedish Elite-262
Silver-262
04Swedish Elitset-114
Dominators-1
Gold-114
Signatures-3
04Swedish Pure Skills-84
Parallel-84
05Finnish Cardset -180
06Swedish SHL Elitset-208
Eriksson, Jonas
92Swedish Semic Elitserien Stickers-102
93Swedish Semic Elitserien-75
94Swedish Leaf-113
Clean Sweepers-4
95Swedish Upper Deck 1st Division Stars-DS11
96German DEL-227
Eriksson, Jorgen
89Swedish Semic Elitserien Stickers-178
90Swedish Semic Elitserien Stickers-10
91Swedish Semic Elitserien Stickers-206
92Swedish Semic Elitserien Stickers-229
93Swedish Semic Elitserien-7
02German DEL City Press-155
Eriksson, Karl-Olof
69Swedish Hockey-298
70Swedish Hockey-198
71Swedish Hockey-284
Eriksson, Karl-Ove
67Swedish Hockey-253
Eriksson, Kent
83Swedish Semic Elitserien-233
Eriksson, Kjell
67Swedish Hockey-86
Eriksson, Kristoffer
99Colorado Gold Kings Taco Bell-22
Eriksson, Lars
83Swedish Semic Elitserien-51
83Swedish Semic VM Stickers-3
84Swedish Semic Elitserien-50
87Swedish Panini Stickers-47
Eriksson, Lars Bertil
67Swedish Hockey-200
Eriksson, Lars Erik
73Swedish Stickers-171
85Swedish Panini Stickers-47
86Swedish Panini Stickers-31
89Swedish Semic Elitserien Stickers-27
90Swedish Semic Elitserien Stickers-176
91Swedish Semic Elitserien Stickers-29
Eriksson, Leif
65Swedish Coralli ISHockey-188
67Swedish Hockey-168
86Swedish Panini Stickers-144
Eriksson, Lennart
71Swedish Hockey-323
72Swedish Stickers-138
Eriksson, Lenny
92Norwegian Elite Series-108
Eriksson, Loui
03Swedish Elite-175
Silver-175
04Swedish Elitset-175
Future Stars-2
Gold-175
05ITG Heroes/Prosp Toronto Expo Parallel -396
05Swedish SHL Elitset Star Potential-5
05Iowa Stars-13
05ITG Heroes and Prospects-396
06Be A Player-209
06Be A Player Portraits-126
06Beehive-116
Blue-116
Gold-116
Matte-116
Red Facsimile Signatures-116
Wood-116
06Black Diamond-209
Black-209
Gold-209
Ruby-209
06Flair Showcase-311
06Hot Prospects-111
Red Hot-111
White Hot-111
Hot Materials -HMLE
Hot Materials Red Hot-HMLE
Hot Materials White Hot-HMLE
Hotagraphs-HLE
06O-Pee-Chee-554
06O-Pee-Chee-619
Rainbow-554
Rainbow-619
06SP Authentic-176
Limited-176
06SP Game Used-113
Gold-113
Rainbow-113
Autographs-113
Rookie Exclusives Autographs-RELE
06SPx-185
Spectrum-185
06Stars Team Postcards-6
06The Cup-125
Autographed Rookie Masterpiece Pressplates-125
Gold Rainbow Autographed Rookie Patches-125
Honorable Numbers-HNLE
Masterpiece Pressplates (Be A Player Portraits)-126
Masterpiece Pressplates (Bee Hive)-116
Masterpiece Pressplates (Marquee Rookies)-554
Masterpiece Pressplates (MVP)-313
Masterpiece Pressplates (SP Authentic Autographs)-176
Masterpiece Pressplates (SP Game Used)-113
Masterpiece Pressplates (SPx Autographs)-185
Masterpiece Pressplates (Sweet Beginnings)-120
Masterpiece Pressplates (Trilogy)-111
Masterpiece Pressplates (Ultimate Collection Autographs)-109
Masterpiece Pressplates (Victory)-300
Rookies Black-125
Rookies Platinum-125
06UD Artifacts-240
06UD Mini Jersey Collection-115
06Ultimate Collection-109
Rookies Autographed NHL Shields-109
Rookies Autographed Patches-109
Ultimate Debut Threads Jerseys-DJ-LE
Ultimate Debut Threads Jerseys Autographs-DJ-LE
Ultimate Debut Threads Patches-DJ-LE
Ultimate Debut Threads Patches Autographs-DJ-LE
06Ultra-241
06Ultra-243
Gold Medallion-241
Ice Medallion-241
06Upper Deck-210
Exclusives Parallel-210
High Gloss Parallel-210
Masterpieces-210
Rookie Game Dated Moments-RGD6
Rookie Headliners-RH2
Rookie Materials-RMLE
Rookie Materials Patches-RMLE
06Upper Deck MVP-313
Gold Script-313
Super Script-313
06Upper Deck Sweet Shot-120
Rookie Jerseys Autographs-120
06Upper Deck Trilogy-111
06Upper Deck Victory-300
06Iowa Stars-6
06ITG Heroes and Prospects-154
Autographs-ALE
Jerseys-GUJ67
Emblems-GUE67
Numbers-GUN67
Update Autographs-ALE
07Upper Deck Rookie Class -6
Eriksson, Magnus
98Swedish UD Choice-182
99Swedish Upper Deck-185
Lasting Impressions-11
SHL Signatures-17
00Swedish Upper Deck-76
Masked Men-M3
01German Upper Deck-5
Jersey Cards-ME-J
02German DEL City Press-9
All-Stars-AS4
03German DEL-22
Eriksson, Markus
92Swedish Semic Elitserien Stickers-354
93Swedish Semic Elitserien-142
94Swedish Leaf-289
95Swedish Leaf-66
04Swedish Elitset-258
Gold-258
05Swedish SHL Elitset-113
Eriksson, Mats
71Swedish Hockey-392
72Swedish Stickers-263
Eriksson, Niklas
89Swedish Semic Elitserien Stickers-135
90Swedish Semic Elitserien Stickers-210
91Swedish Semic Elitserien Stickers-147
92Swedish Semic Elitserien Stickers-165
93Swedish Semic Elitserien-134
94Finnish Jaa Kiekko-72
94Swedish Leaf-41
Gold Cards-16
95Swedish Leaf-70
Goldies-7
95Swedish Upper Deck-103
97Swedish Collector's Choice-112
98Swedish UD Choice-127
99Swedish Upper Deck-113
00Swedish Upper Deck-113
02Swedish SHL-196
Parallel-196
Signatures Series II-20
03Swedish Elite-61
Signatures II-20
Silver-61
05Swedish SHL Elitset-66
Gold-66
Eriksson, Owe
84Swedish Semic Elitserien-62
85Swedish Panini Stickers-62
Eriksson, Patrik
86Swedish Panini Stickers-49
Eriksson, Peter
84Swedish Semic Elitserien-71
84Swedish Semic Elitserien-72
86Swedish Panini Stickers-53
86Swedish Panini Stickers-125
86Swedish Panini Stickers-131
87Swedish Panini Stickers-62
87Swedish Panini Stickers-117
87Swedish Panini Stickers-122
89Oilers Team Issue-5
89Swedish Semic Elitserien Stickers-45
90Upper Deck-145
French-145
90Swedish Semic Elitserien Stickers-110
90Swedish Semic Elitserien Stickers-193
91Swedish Semic Elitserien Stickers-47
91Swedish Semic Elitserien Stickers-115
92Swedish Semic Elitserien Stickers-145
93Swedish Semic Elitserien-114
95Swedish Upper Deck 1st Division Stars-DS16
Eriksson, Robin
83Swedish Semic Elitserien-114
84Swedish Semic Elitserien-142
Eriksson, Roland
71Swedish Hockey-393
72Swedish Stickers-43
72Swedish Stickers-264
73Swedish Stickers-25
74Swedish Stickers-214
77O-Pee-Chee NHL-123
77Topps-123
78Canucks Royal Bank-4
78O-Pee-Chee-241
78Topps-241
79O-Pee-Chee-350
83Swedish Semic Elitserien-135
83Swedish Semic VM Stickers-15
85Swedish Panini Stickers-192
Eriksson, Thomas
82Swedish Semic VM Stickers-5
83Flyers J.C. Penney-9
83Swedish Semic VM Stickers-5
84O-Pee-Chee-158
85Flyers Postcards-9
85Swedish Panini Stickers-215
86Swedish Panini Stickers-61
87Swedish Panini Stickers-74
89Swedish Semic Elitserien Stickers-52
89Swedish Semic World Champ Stickers-12
90Swedish Semic Elitserien Stickers-275
91Finnish Semic World Champ Stickers-30
91Swedish Semic Elitserien Stickers-57
91Swedish Semic Elitserien Stickers-321
91Swedish Semic World Champ Stickers-30
92Finnish Semic-53
92Swedish Semic Elitserien Stickers-83
93Swedish Semic Elitserien-56
94Swedish Leaf-262
Eriksson, Tim
02Swedish SHL-215
Parallel-215
03Swedish Elite-74
Silver-74
04Swedish Elitset-65
Gold-65
High Expectations-6
Signatures Series A-6
05Swedish SHL Elitset-77
Gold-77
Series One Signatures-2
06Swedish SHL Elitset-76
Eriksson, Tomaz
86Swedish Panini Stickers-77
89Swedish Semic Elitserien Stickers-236
90Swedish Semic Elitserien Stickers-67
91Swedish Semic Elitserien Stickers-237
Eriksson, Tommy
67Swedish Hockey-268
69Swedish Hockey-312
70Swedish Hockey-215
71Swedish Hockey-210
71Swedish Hockey-362
72Swedish Stickers-187
72Swedish Stickers-273
Eriksson, Ulf
64Swedish Coralli ISHockey-142
65Swedish Coralli ISHockey-142
Erixon, Jan
82Swedish Semic VM Stickers-24
83Swedish Semic VM Stickers-24
87Panini Stickers-120
88O-Pee-Chee-212
88Panini Stickers-306
89O-Pee-Chee-96
89Rangers Marine Midland Bank-20
89Topps-96
90O-Pee-Chee-187
90Panini Stickers-104
90Pro Set-195
90Score-272
90Score-343
Canadian-272
Canadian-343
90Topps-187
Tiffany-187
90Upper Deck-366
French-366
91Bowman-77
91O-Pee-Chee-152
91Panini Stickers-283
91Pinnacle-187
French-187
91Score American-264
91Score Canadian Bilingual-484
91Score Canadian English-484
91Stadium Club-151
91Topps-152
91Upper Deck-178
French-178
92Bowman-253
92O-Pee-Chee-207
92Panini Stickers-241
92Panini Stickers French-241
92Pinnacle-191
French-191
92Score-362
Canadian-362
92Stadium Club-161
92Topps-153
Gold-153G
93Score-287
Canadian-287
93Swedish Semic World Champ Stickers-35
Ermakov, Alexander
99Russian Hockey League-181
Ermolin, Yuri
04Russian World Junior Team-15
Ermolov, Valeri
99Alexandria Warthogs-5
Ernest, Derek
97OCN Blizzard-19
98Hampton Roads Admirals-15
99Hampton Roads Admirals-7
Erni, Bruno
93Swiss HNL-21
95Swiss HNL-19
96Swiss HNL-165
98Swiss Power Play Stickers-352
Ernlund, Hans-Olov
70Swedish Hockey-115
71Swedish Hockey-204
72Swedish Stickers-183
Ernst, Andrew
93Lakeland Ice Warriors-11
Ernst, Bingo
51Laval Dairy QSHL-83
52St. Lawrence Sales-26
Erntgaard, Christian
99Danish Hockey League-70
Erny, David
93Swiss HNL-392
Erofeev, Dimitri
98Swedish UD Choice-89
02Russian Hockey League-255
02Russian Hockey League-257
03Russian World Championship Team 2003-18
Eronen, Anssi
71Finnish Suomi Stickers-317
Eronen, Kimmo
98Finnish Kerailysarja-229
99Finnish Cardset-132
00Finnish Cardset-96
01Finnish Cardset-139
02Swedish SHL-274
Parallel-274
03Swedish Elite-24
Silver-24
04Finnish Cardset-170
Parallel-125
05Finnish Cardset -154
Errey, Bob
83Penguins Coke-8
84Penguins Heinz Photos-7
86Penguins Kodak-8
87Panini Stickers-152
87Penguins Masks-3
87Penguins Kodak-8
89O-Pee-Chee-50
89O-Pee-Chee Stickers-233
89Panini Stickers-315
89Penguins Foodland-8
89Topps-50
90Bowman-212
Tiffany-212
90O-Pee-Chee-230
90Panini Stickers-133
90Pro Set-234
90Score-255
Canadian-255
90Topps-230
Tiffany-230
91Pro Set Platinum-215
91Bowman-85
91O-Pee-Chee-94
91Panini Stickers-279
91Parkhurst-138
French-138
91Pinnacle-257
French-257
91Pro Set-187
French-187
91Score American-169
91Score Canadian Bilingual-169
91Score Canadian English-169
91Stadium Club-191
91Topps-94
92Bowman-304
92Durivage Panini-23
92O-Pee-Chee-323
92Parkhurst-374
Emerald Ice-374
92Penguins Coke/Clark-5
92Penguins Foodland-2
92Pinnacle-310
French-310
92Score-287
Canadian-287
92Stadium Club-170
92Topps-95
Gold-95G
93Leaf-377
93Parkhurst-453
Emerald Ice-453
93Pinnacle-410
Canadian-410
Captains-21
Captains Canadian-21
93PowerPlay-435
93Score-208
93Score-566
Gold-566
Canadian-208
Canadian-566
Canadian Gold-566
93Stadium Club-404
Members Only Master Set-404
First Day Issue-404
94Canada Games NHL POGS-361
94Leaf-398
94OPC Premier-331
Special Effects-331
94Parkhurst SE-SE161
Gold-SE161
94Pinnacle-192
Artist's Proofs-192
Rink Collection-192
94Score-87
Gold-87
Platinum-87
94Stadium Club-37
Members Only Master Set-37
First Day Issue-37
Super Team Winner Cards-37
94Topps/OPC Premier-331
Special Effects-331
94Upper Deck-401
Electric Ice-401
95Leaf-315
95Score-174
Black Ice Artist's Proofs-174
Black Ice-174
96Be A Player-197
Autographs-197
Autographs Silver-197
97Pacific Invincible NHL Regime-177
98Hartford Wolf Pack-6
Ersberg, Erik
05Swedish SHL Elitset-192
Gold-192
06Swedish SHL Elitset-191
Ershov, Andrei
03Russian Hockey League-102
Erskine, John
98Bowman CHL-134
Golden Anniversary-134
OPC International-134
Autographs Blue-A24
Autographs Gold-A24
Autographs Silver-A24
98Bowman Chrome CHL-134
Golden Anniversary-134
Golden Anniversary Refractors-134
OPC International-134
OPC International Refractors-134
Refractors-134
00Utah Grizzlies-10
01BAP Memorabilia-382
Emerald-382
Ruby-382
Sapphire-382
01Bowman YoungStars-116
Gold-116
Ice Cubed-116
01SPx Rookie Redemption-R10

01Stars Postcards-4
01Stars Team Issue-3
01Titanium-154
Retail-154
01Titanium Draft Day Edition-123
01UD Playmakers-115
01Upper Deck Ice-136
01Utah Grizzlies-2
02O-Pee-Chee-290
02O-Pee-Chee Premier Blue Parallel-290
02O-Pee-Chee Premier Red Parallel-290
02O-Pee-Chee Factory Set-290
02Stars Postcards-3
02Topps-290
OPC Blue Parallel-290
OPC Red Parallel-290
Factory Set-290
02Utah Grizzlies-7
03ITG Action-146
03Stars Postcards-7
04Houston Aeros-6
05Parkhurst-312

Erskine, Wayne

84Kingston Canadians-19
85Kingston Canadians-19
86Kingston Canadians-17

Ertel, Tyler

87Kitchener Rangers-14
89 7th Inn. Sketch OHL-151
90 7th Inn. Sketch OHL-180

Ertl, Jason

01Red Deer Rebels-6
02Red Deer Rebels-12
03Red Deer Rebels-9

Eruzione, Mike

80USA Olympic Team Mini Pics-2
81Swedish Semic Hockey VM Stickers-104
91Nashville Knights-24
92Sports Illustrated for Kids II-10
95Signature Rookies Miracle on Ice-11
95Signature Rookies Miracle on Ice-12
95Signature Rookies Miracle on Ice-47
95Signature Rook Miracle on Ice Sigs-11
95Signature Rook Miracle on Ice Sigs-12
96Upper Deck US Olympic Reflect Gold Sig-RGA2
04UD Legendary Signatures Miracle Men-USA1
04UD Legendary Sigs Miracle Men Autos-USA-ME

Esau, Len

90ProCards AHL/IHL-150
91ProCards-352
94Parkhurst-37
Gold-37
94Saint John Flames-5
95Cincinnati Cyclones-7
96Detroit Vipers-7
99Cincinnati Cyclones-8
00Cincinnati Cyclones-15

Esbjorn, Lars-Erik

73Swedish Stickers-147
74Swedish Stickers-167

Esbjors, Joachim

89Swedish Semic Elitserien Stickers-267
90Swedish Semic Elitserien Stickers-32
91Swedish Semic Elitserien Stickers-281
92Swedish Semic Elitserien Stickers-303
93Swedish Semic Elitserien-269
94Finnish Jaa Kiekko-61
94Swedish Leaf-195
94Swedish Leaf-144
95Swedish Upper Deck-205
97Swedish Collector's Choice-70
98Finnish Keralysarja-253
99Swedish Upper Deck-88
00Swedish Upper Deck-93

Esbjors, Jonas

91Swedish Semic Elitserien Stickers-299
92Swedish Semic Elitserien Stickers-318
93Swedish Semic Elitserien-283
94Swedish Leaf-206
95Swedish Leaf-146
97Swedish Collector's Choice-82
98Finnish Keralysarja-259
99Swedish Upper Deck-93
00Swedish Upper Deck-102
SHL Signatures-JE
02Swedish SHL-281
Parallel-281
03Swedish Elite-176
Silver-176
04Swedish Elitset-30
Gold-30
05Swedish SHL Elitset-31
05Swedish SHL Elitset-36

Esche, Robert

95Slapshot-57
96Detroit Whalers-6
97Bowman CHL-41
OPC-41
98Bowman CHL-1
Golden Anniversary-1
OPC International-1
98Bowman Chrome CHL-1
Golden Anniversary-1
Golden Anniversary Refractors-1
OPC International-1
OPC International Refractors-1
Refractors-1
99BAP Memorabilia-332
Gold-332
Silver-332
99Pacific-332
Copper-332
Emerald Green-332
Gold-332
Ice Blue-332
Premiere Date-332
Red-332
99Pacific Omega-180
Copper-180
Gold-180
Ice Blue-180
Premiere Date-180
99SPx-117
Radiance-117
Spectrum-117
99Upper Deck-101
Exclusives-101
Exclusives 1 of 1-101
99Upper Deck Gold Reserve-101
99Upper Deck MVP-160
Gold Script-160
Silver Script-160
Super Script-160
99Upper Deck Retro-63
Gold-63
Platinum-63
99Upper Deck Victory-223
00BAP Memorabilia-389
Emerald-389
Ruby-389
Sapphire-389
Promos-389
00BAP Mem Chicago Sportsfest Copper-389
00BAP Memorabilia Chicago Sportsfest Blue-389
00BAP Memorabilia Chicago Sportsfest Gold-389
00BAP Memorabilia Chicago Sportsfest Ruby-389
00BAP Memorabilia Chicago Sun-Times Ruby-389
00BAP Memorabilia Chicago Sun-Times Gold-389
00BAP Mem Chicago Sun-Times Sapphire-389
00BAP Mem Toronto Fall Expo Copper-389
00BAP Memorabilia Toronto Fall Expo Gold-389
00BAP Memorabilia Toronto Fall Expo Ruby-389
00Crown Royale-137
00O-Pee-Chee-295
00O-Pee-Chee Parallel-295
00Pacific-323
Copper-323
Gold-323
Ice Blue-323
Premiere Date-323
00Paramount-188
Copper-188
Gold-188
Holo-Gold-188
Holo-Silver-188
Ice Blue-188
Premiere Date-188
00Private Stock-137
Gold-137
Premiere Date-137
Retail-137
Silver-137
00Titanium-139
Retail-139
00Titanium Draft Day Edition-139
00Titanium Draft Day Promos-139
00Topps/OPC-295
Parallel-295
00Topps Chrome-190
OPC Refractors-190
Refractors-190
00Vanguard-139
Pacific Proofs-139
01Between the Pipes-58
Double Memorabilia-DM15
Goalie Gear-GG7
Tandems-GT11
01Coyotes Team Issue-6
01Pacific-302
Extreme LTD-302
Hobby LTD-302
Premiere Date-302
Retail LTD-302
01Pacific Arena Exclusives-302
02Between the Pipes-49
Gold-49
Silver-49
Jerseys-34
Tandems-8
02Flyers Postcards-18
02Pacific-294
Blue-294
Red-294
02Pacific Complete-456
Red-456
02UD Mask Collection-60
02UD Mask Collection-61
02UD Mask Collection Beckett Promos-60
02UD Mask Collection Beckett Promos-61
03BAP Memorabilia-156
Emerald-156
Gold-156
Ruby-156
Sapphire-156
03Beehive-143
Gold-143
Silver-143
03Black Diamond-37
Black-37
Green-37
Red-37
03Bowman-62
Gold-62
03Bowman Chrome-62
Refractors-62
Gold Refractors-62
Xfractors-62
03Flyers Program Inserts-4
03Flyers Postcards-5
03ITG Action-416
Jerseys-M21
03Pacific-250
Blue-250
Red-250
03Pacific Complete-488
Red-488
03Pacific Heads-Up-73
Hobby LTD-73
Retail LTD-73
03SPx Big Futures-BF-RE
03SPx Big Futures Limited-BF-RE
03SPx Style-SPX-BT
03SPx Style Limited-SPX-BT
03Titanium-74
Hobby Jersey Number Parallels-74
Retail-74
Retail Jersey Number Parallels-74
03Topps Pristine Mini-PM-RE
03Upper Deck-144
Canadian Exclusives-144
HG-144
03Upper Deck MVP-319
Gold Script-319
Silver Script-319
Canadian Exclusives-319
SportsNut-SN64
03Upper Deck Victory-143
Bronze-143
Gold-143
Silver-143
04Pacific-192
Blue-192
Red-192
04SP Authentic-66
Limited-66
Rookie Review-RR-RE
Sign of the Times-ST-RE
Sign of the Times-DS-CR
Sign of the Times-TS-GRE
Sign of the Times-QS-GPRE
Sign of the Times-SS-USA
04Ultimate Collection-80
04Upper Deck-131
Canadian Exclusives-131
HG Glossy Gold-131
HG Glossy Silver-131
World's Best-WB27
World Cup Tribute-RE
World Cup Tribute-CCRELDH
World Cup Tribute-TCRDRE
05Be A Player-66
First Period-66
Second Period-66
Third Period-66
Overtime-66
Dual Signatures-PE
Signatures-ES
Signatures Gold-ES
World Cup Salute-WCS14
05Beehive-66
Matte-66
Matted Materials-MMRE
Signature Scrapbook-SSRE
05Black Diamond-64
Emerald-64
Gold-64
Onyx-64
Ruby-64
Gemography-G-RE
Gemography Emerald-G-RE
Gemography Gold-G-RE
Gemography Onyx-G-RE
Gemography Ruby-G-RE
05Flyers Team Issue-5
05Panini Stickers-132
05Parkhurst-361
Facsimile Auto Parallel-361
Signatures-RE
True Colors-TCPHI
True Colors-TCPHI
05SP Authentic-76
Limited-76
Prestigious Pairings-PPEP
Sign of the Times Fives-PEGCR
05SP Game Used-75
Autographs-75
Gold-75
Authentic Fabrics-AF-RE
Authentic Fabrics Autographs-AAF-RE
Authentic Fabrics Dual-ER
Authentic Fabrics Dual-PE
Authentic Fabrics Dual Autographs-PE
Authentic Fabrics Quad-GFEP
Authentic Patches Quad -GFEP
Authentic Fabrics Triple-CEA
Authentic Patches-AP-RE
Authentic Patches Autographs-AAP-RE
Authentic Patches Dual-ER
Authentic Patches Dual-PE
Authentic Patches Dual Autographs-PE
Authentic Patches Triple-CEA
Auto Draft-AD-RE
Awesome Authentics-AA-RO
SIGnificance-RE
SIGnificance Gold-S-RE
SIGnificance Extra-PE
SIGnificance Extra Gold-PE
Statscriptions-ST-RE
05SPx-68
Spectrum-68
Winning Combos-WC-PE
Winning Combos Autographs-AWC-PE
Winning Combos Gold-WC-PE
Winning Combos Spectrum-WC-PE
Winning Materials-WM-RE
Winning Materials Autographs-AWM-RE
Winning Materials Gold-WM-RE
Winning Materials Spectrum-WM-RE
05The Cup Honorable Numbers-HNRE
05The Cup Limited Logos-LLRE
05The Cup Master Pressplate Rookie Update-221
05The Cup Scripted Swatches-SSRE
05The Cup Signature Patches-SPRE
05UD Artifacts-73
Blue-73
Gold-73
Green-73
Pewter-73
Red-73
Auto Facts-AF-RE
Auto Facts Blue-AF-RE
Auto Facts Copper-AF-RE
Auto Facts Pewter-AF-RE
Auto Facts Silver-AF-RE
Gold Autographed-73
Remarkable Artifacts-RA-RE
Remarkable Artifacts Dual-RA-RE
05UD Powerplay Specialists-TSRE
05UD Powerplay Specialists Patches-SPRE
05Ultimate Collection-67
Gold-67
Endorsed Emblems-EERE
National Heroes Jerseys-NHJRE
National Heroes Patches-NHPRE
05Ultra-140
Gold-140
Fresh Ink-FI-RE
Fresh Ink Blue-FI-RE
Ice-140
05Upper Deck-387
Jerseys-J-RE
Jerseys Series II-J2RE
Notable Numbers-N-RE
Patches-P-RE
05Upper Deck Ice-70
Rainbow-70
05Upper Deck MVP-287
Gold-287
Platinum-287
ProSign-P-RE
05Upper Deck Rookie Update-221
Inspirations Patch Rookies-221
05Upper Deck Trilogy-67
Honorary Patches-HP-RE
Honorary Patch Scripts-HSP-RE
Honorary Swatches-HS-RE
Honorary Swatch Scripts-HSS-RE
05Upper Deck Victory-144
Black-144
Gold-144
Silver-144
06Be A Player-132
Autographs-132
Signatures-RE
Signatures Duals-DNE
Portraits Signature Portraits-SPES
06Flair Showcase Stitches-SSRE
06Fleer Fabricology-FRE
06Flyers Postcards-17
06Hot Prospects Hot Materials -HMRE
06Hot Prospects Hot Materials Red Hot-HMRE
06Hot Prospects Hot Materials White Hot-HMRE
06Hot Prospects Hotographs-HRE
06O-Pee-Chee-367
Rainbow-367
Swatches-S-RE
06Panini Stickers-130
06SP Game Used Authentic Fabrics-AFRE
06SP Game Used Authentic Fabrics Parallel-AFRE
06SP Game Used Authentic Fabrics Patches-AFRE
06SP Game Used Authentic Fabrics Triple-AF3PHI
06SP Game Used Authentic Fabrics Triple Patches-AF3PHI
06SP Game Used Authentic Fabrics Sixes-AF6JEN
06SP Game Used Authentic Fabrics Sixes Patches-AF6JEN
06SP Game Used Inked Sweaters Dual-IS2EP
06SP Game Used Inked Sweaters Dual Patches-IS2EP
06SP Game Used SIGnificance-SRE
06SPx Winning Materials-WMRE
06SPx Winning Materials Spectrum-WMRE
06SPx Winning Materials Autographs-WMRE
06UD Powerplay-74
Impact Rainbow-74
Specialists-SRE
Specialists Patches-PRE
06Ultra-146
Gold Medallion-146
Ice Medallion-146
Uniformity-URE
Uniformity Patches-UPRE
06Upper Deck Arena Giveaways-PHI2
06Upper Deck-143
Exclusives Parallel-143
High Gloss Parallel-143
Masterpieces-143
06Upper Deck MVP-219
Gold Script-219
Super Script-219
Autographs-OAEE
06Upper Deck Ovation-36
06Upper Deck Trilogy Honorary Scripted Patches-HSPRE
06Upper Deck Trilogy Honorary Scripted Swatches-HSSRE
06Upper Deck Victory-150
06Upper Deck Victory Black-150
06Upper Deck Victory Gold-150

Escher, Ayocholos

95Swiss HNL-465
96Swiss HNL-366

Escobedo, Brian

03Bowling Green Falcons-2

Escott, Colin

05Gatineau Olympiques-15

Esdale, Paul

93Quebec Pee-Wee Tournament-1155
03Florida Everblades-5
03Florida Everblades RBI Sports-163

Esipov, Andrei

02Russian Hockey League-46
02Russian SL-15
03Russian Hockey League-116
03Russian Hockey League-242

Eskeleinen, Tuomas

99Finnish Cardset-269
01Finnish Cardset-16
03Finnish Cardset-33
04Finnish Cardset-32
04Finnish Cardset Signatures-9
05Finnish Cardset -177
06Finnish Cardset-2

Eskeli, Juhani Iso

65Finnish Hellas-5

Eskelinen, Tuomas

06Finnish Cardset-2

Eskilinen, Tuomas

05Finnish Cardset -177

Eskrzycki, Andrzej

79Panini Stickers-123

Esmantovich, Igor

90O-Pee-Chee-479

Esmark, Claus

98Danish Hockey League-84
99Danish Hockey League-35

Espe, Dave

89Halifax Citadels-5
89ProCards AHL-161
90Halifax Citadels-6
90ProCards AHL/IHL-442
91ProCards-531

Esposito, Angelo

05ITG Heroes/Prosp Toronto Expo Parallel -159
05ITG Heroes/Prosp Toronto Expo Parallel -373
05ITG Ultimate Memorabilia Double Autos-2
05ITG Ultimate Mem Double Autos Gold-2
05ITG Ultimate Mem Future Stars Autos-19
05ITG Ultimate Mem Future Star Autos Gold-19
05ITG Ultimate Memorabilia Triple Autos-10
05ITG Ultimate Mem Triple Autos Gold-10
05Quebec Remparts-1
05Quebec Remparts Signature Series-1
05ITG Heroes and Prospects-159
05ITG Heroes and Prospects-373
Autographs Series II-AE2
Autographs Update-A-AE
Autographs Update-DA-ET
He Shoots-He Scores Prizes-44
06ITG International Ice-155
Gold-155
Autographs-AAE
06ITG Ultimate Memorabilia-7
Artist Proof-7
Autos-10
Autos Gold-10
Autos Triple-10
Autos Triple Gold-10
Future Star-1
Future Star Gold-1
Future Star Autos-15
Future Star Autos Gold-15
Future Star Patches Autos-15
Future Star Patches Autos Gold-15
In The Numbers-5
In The Numbers Gold-5
Jerseys Autos-13
Jerseys Autos Gold-13
Triple Thread Jerseys-12
Triple Thread Jerseys Gold-12
06Quebec Remparts-1
06ITG Heroes and Prospects-81
Autographs-AAE
Complete CHL Logos-CHL03
Complete CHL Logos-CHL13
Complete Jerseys-CJ01
Complete Jerseys Gold-CJ01
Jerseys-GUJ33
Jerseys Gold-GUJ33
Emblems-GUE33
Emblems Gold-GUE33
Numbers-GUN33
Numbers Gold-GUN33
Memorial Cup Champions-MC09
Quad Emblems-QE02
Quad Emblems-QE12
Quad Emblems-QE15
Quad Emblems Gold-QE02
Triple Memorabilia-TM11

Esposito, Matt

05Everett Silvertips-6
06Chilliwack Bruins-2

Esposito, Phil

63Chex Photos-12
64Beehive Group III Photos-34A
64Beehive Group III Photos-34B
64Coca-Cola Caps-24
65Coca-Cola-25
65Topps-116
66Topps-63
66Sherriff Coins-8
67Topps-32
68O-Pee-Chee-7
68O-Pee-Chee-208
Puck Stickers-5
68Shirriff Coins-8
68Topps-7
69Equitable Sports Hall of Fame-1
69O-Pee-Chee-30
69O-Pee-Chee-205A
69O-Pee-Chee-205B
69O-Pee-Chee-214
Four-in-One-18
Stamps-7
69Topps-30
70Bruins Postcards-13
70Bruins Team Issue-4
70Dad's Cookies-30
70Esso Power Players-58
70O-Pee-Chee-11
70O-Pee-Chee-233
70O-Pee-Chee-237
Deckle-6
70Sargent Promotions Stamps-14
70Topps-11
Topps/OPC Sticker Stamps-6
71Bazooka-1
71Bruins Postcards-4
71Mattel Mini-Records-3
71O-Pee-Chee-20
71O-Pee-Chee-247
71O-Pee-Chee-253
O-Pee-Chee/Topps Booklets-2
Posters-21
71Sargent Promotions Stamps-7
71Topps-1
71Topps-2
71Topps-3
71Topps-20
71Toronto Sun-8
71Finnish Suomi Stickers-380
71Swedish Hockey-199
72Kellogg's Iron-On Transfers-2
72O-Pee-Chee-76
72O-Pee-Chee-111
72O-Pee-Chee-230
72O-Pee-Chee-272
72O-Pee-Chee-280
72O-Pee-Chee-283
Player Crests-2
Team Canada-9
72Sargent Promotions Stamps-21
72Topps-61
72Topps-62
72Topps-63
72Topps-124
72Topps-150
72Finnish Semic World Championship-184
72Swedish Stickers-115
72Swedish Semic World Championship-184
73O-Pee-Chee-120
73O-Pee-Chee-133
73O-Pee-Chee-134
73O-Pee-Chee-135
73O-Pee-Chee-138
73Topps-1
73Topps-2
73Topps-3
73Topps-6
73Topps-120
74Nabisco Sugar Daddy-11
74NHL Action Stamps-26
74O-Pee-Chee NHL-1
74O-Pee-Chee NHL-3
74O-Pee-Chee NHL-28
74O-Pee-Chee NHL-129
74O-Pee-Chee NHL-200
74O-Pee-Chee NHL-244
74O-Pee-Chee NHL-246
74Topps-1
74Topps-3
74Topps-28
74Topps-129
74Topps-200
74Topps-244
74Topps-246
75Nabisco Sugar Daddy-11
75O-Pee-Chee NHL-200A
75O-Pee-Chee NHL-200B
75O-Pee-Chee NHL-208
75O-Pee-Chee NHL-210
75O-Pee-Chee NHL-212
75O-Pee-Chee NHL-292
75O-Pee-Chee NHL-314
75Topps-200
75Topps-208
75Topps-210
75Topps-212
75Topps-292
75Topps-314
76O-Pee-Chee NHL-5
76O-Pee-Chee NHL-245
76O-Pee-Chee NHL-390
76Topps-5
76Topps-245
76Topps Glossy Inserts-7
77O-Pee-Chee NHL-5
77O-Pee-Chee NHL-55
77Sportscasters-319
77Sportscasters-2908
77Topps-5
77Topps-55
77Finnish Sportscasters-37-869
77Finnish Sportscasters-05-105
78O-Pee-Chee-2
78O-Pee-Chee-67
78O-Pee-Chee-100
78Topps-2
78Topps-67
78Topps-100
79O-Pee-Chee-220
79Topps-220
80O-Pee-Chee-100
80O-Pee-Chee-149
80O-Pee-Chee Super-14
80Topps-100
80Topps-149
82Neilson's Gretzky-36
85Hall of Fame-244
87Sault Ste. Marie Greyhounds-15
88Esso All-Stars-10
90Pro Set-403
90Upper Deck-510
French-510
91Bruins Sports Action Legends-10
91Future Trends Canada '72 Promos-2
91Future Trends Canada '72-40
91Future Trends Canada '72-70
91Future Trends Canada '72-84
91Future Trends Canada '72 French-40
91Future Trends Canada '72 French-70
91Future Trends Canada '72 French-84
91Pro Set-594
French-594
91Finnish Semic World Champ Stickers-240
91Swedish Semic World Champ Stickers-240
92Future Trends '76 Canada Cup-102
92Future Trends '76 Canada Cup-139
92Future Trends '76 Canada Cup-153
92Hall of Fame Legends-7
92Lightning Sheraton-14
92O-Pee-Chee-283
25th Anniv. Inserts-10
92Sports Illustrated for Kids II-317
93Lightning Season in Review-13
94Lightning Photo Album-11
94Lightning Postcards-7
94Parkhurst Tall Boys-29
Autographs-A4
95Fanfest Phil Esposito-1
95Fanfest Phil Esposito-2
95Fanfest Phil Esposito-3
95Fanfest Phil Esposito-4
95Fanfest Phil Esposito-5
95Parkhurst '66-67-33
Coins-33
96SLU Canadian Timeless Legends-2
97SLU Canadian Timeless Legends-4
98OPC Chrome Blast From the Past-10
98OPC Chrome Blast From Past Refractors-10
98Topps Blast From The Past-10
98Topps Blast From The Past Autographs-10
99BAP Millennium Pearson-P14
99BAP Millennium Pearson Autographs-P14
99Upper Deck Century Legends-19
Century Collection-19
Epic Signatures-PE
Epic Signatures 100-PE
99Upper Deck Retro-94
Gold-94
Platinum-94
Generation-G9A
Generation Level 2-G9A
Inkredible-PE
Inkredible Level 2-PE
Memento-RM4
00Upper Deck 500 Goal Club-500PE
00Upper Deck 500 Goal Club-500PE
00Upper Deck Legends-7
Legendary Collection Bronze-7
Legendary Collection Gold-7
Legendary Collection Silver-7
Enshrined Stars-ES12
Epic Signatures-PE
Playoff Heroes-PH12
Supreme Milestones-SM13
01BAP Memorabilia 500 Goal Scorers-GS4
01BAP Signature Series 500 Goal Scorers-9
01BAP Sig Series 500 Goal Scorers Autos-9
01BAP Signature Series Vintage Autographs-VA-2
01BAP Ultimate Memorabilia Autographs-20
01BAP Ultimate Mem Autographs Gold-20
01BAP Ultimate Memorabilia Bloodlines-5
01BAP Ultimate Memorabilia Cornerstones-5
01BAP Ultimate Memorabilia Emblem Attic-3
01BAP Ultimate Mem 500 Goal Scorers-10
01BAP Ultimate Mem 500 Goal Scorers Autos-21
01BAP Ultimate Mem 500 Goal Jerseys/Stick-10
01BAP Ultimate Mem 500 Goal Emblems-10
01BAP Ultimate Memorabilia Name Plates-38
01Fleer Legacy-4
01Fleer Legacy-11
Ultimate-4
Ultimate-11
Memorabilia-12
Memorabilia Autographs-2
01Greats of the Game-5
Retro Collection-3
Autographs-5
Sticks-2
01Parkhurst Autographs-PA13
01Parkhurst 500 Goal Scorers-PGS4
01Parkhurst Heroes-H5
01SP Authentic Sign of the Times-ET
01Topps Rookie Reprints-3
01Topps Rookie Reprint Autographs-3
01Topps Stanley Cup Heroes-SCHPE
01Topps Stanley Cup Heroes Autographs-SCHAPE
01UD Stanley Cup Champs-1
01Upper Deck Legends-3
Epic Signatures-PE
Fiorentino Collection-FCPE
Jerseys-TTPE
Jerseys Platinum-TTPE
Sticks-PHES
Sticks-PHPE
01Upper Deck Vintage Jerseys-SDPE
02BAP Memorabilia Mini Stanley Cups-8
02BAP Ultimate Memorabilia Emblem Attic-23
02BAP Ultimate Memorabilia Numerology-9
02BAP Ultimate Mem Playoff Scorers-19
02BAP Ultimate Mem Retro Teammates-5
02BAP Ultimate Memorabilia Retro Trophies-12
02BAP Ultimate Mem Scoring Leaders-19
02BAP Ultimate Mem Scoring Leaders-20
02BAP Ultimate Mem Scoring Leaders-21
02BAP Ultimate Mem Scoring Leaders-22
02BAP Ultimate Mem Scoring Leaders-23
02BAP Ultimate Mem Vintage Jerseys-30
02BAP Ultimate Mem Vintage Jersey Autos-13
02Parkhurst Vintage Teammates-VT2
02UD Foundations-7
02UD Foundations-67
02UD Foundations-109
02UD Foundations-118
1000 Point Club-ES
1000 Point Club-ES2
03BAP Ultimate Memorabilia Autographs-164
Gold-164
03BAP Ultimate Mem Hometown Heroes-16
03BAP Ultimate Mem Hometown Heroes Gold-16
03BAP Ultimate Memorabilia Linemates-3
03BAP Ultimate Mem Redemption Cards-3
03BAP Ultimate Memorabilia Triple Threads-28
03BAP Ultimate Mem Vintage Jerseys-17
03BAP Ultimate Mem Vintage Jerseys Gold-17
03Canada Post-18
03ITG Used Signature Series-120
Gold-120
Autographs-PE
Autographs Gold-PE
Vintage Memorabilia-3
Vintage Memorabilia Autographs-3
Vintage Memorabilia Gold-3
03ITG VIP Collages-29
03ITG VIP Collage Autographs-29
03ITG VIP MVP-10
03Lightning Team Issue-9
03Parkhurst Original Six Boston-52
03Parkhurst Original Six Boston-66
03Parkhurst Original Six Boston-83
03Parkhurst Original Six Boston-96
03Parkhurst Original Six Boston-99
Autographs-5
Inserts-B4
Inserts-B8
Inserts-B10
Memorabilia-BM33
Memorabilia-BM35
Memorabilia-BM52
03Parkhurst Original Six Chicago-60
03Parkhurst Original Six Chicago-87
Autographs-1
03Parkhurst Orig Six He Shoots/Scores-13
03Parkhurst Orig Six He Shoots/Scores-13A
03Parkhurst Orig Six He Shoots/Scores-22
03Parkhurst Orig Six He Shoots/Scores-22A
03Parkhurst Original Six New York-36
03Parkhurst Original Six New York-63
03Parkhurst Original Six New York-74
03Parkhurst Original Six New York-84
Autographs-4
Inserts-N5
Memorabilia-NM31
Memorabilia-NM37
Memorabilia-NM52
03SP Authentic Sign of the Times-PE
03SP Authentic Sign of the Times-ET
03Upper Deck Trilogy-141
Crest Variations-141
Limited-141
Scripts-S3PE
Scripts Limited-S3PE
03Czech Stadion-552
04ITG Franchises He Shoots/Scores Prizes-37
04ITG Franchises Update Original Sticks-UOS6
04ITG Franchises Upd Original Sticks Gold-UOS6
04ITG Franchises US East-317
04ITG Franchises US East-393
Autographs-A-PE1
Autographs-A-PE2
Double Memorabilia-EDM20
Double Memorabilia Autographs-EDM-PE
Double Memorabilia Gold-EDM20
Forever Rivals-EFR1
Forever Rivals Gold-EFR1
Memorabilia-ESM19
Memorabilia Autographs-ESM-PE
Memorabilia Gold-ESM19
Original Sticks-EOS5
Original Sticks Autographs-EOS-PE
Original Sticks Gold-EOS5
04ITG Franchises US West-171
Autographs-A-PE3
04ITG Ultimate Memorabilia-6
04ITG Ultimate Memorabilia-51
04ITG Ultimate Memorabilia-72
Gold-6
Gold-51
Gold-72
Archives 1st Edition-22
Art Ross Trophy-6
Auto Threads-10
Autographs-20
Autographs-25
Autographs Gold-20
Autographs Gold-25
Changing the Game-1
Cornerstones-5
Cornerstones-6
Cornerstones Gold-5
Cornerstones Gold-6
Country of Origin-10
Country of Origin Gold-10
Day In History-15
Day In History-42
Day In History-44
Day In History Gold-15
Day In History Gold-42
Day In History Gold-44
Emblem Attic-5
Emblem Attic Gold-5
Hart Trophy-7
Jerseys-14
Jerseys Gold-14
Jersey Autographs-38
Jersey Autographs Gold-38
Jersey and Sticks-9
Jersey and Sticks Gold-9
Original Six-12
Original Six-15
Original Six-16
Original Six-17
Retro Teammates-13
Stick Autographs-4
Stick Autographs Gold-4
Triple Threads-8
04SP Authentic Buybacks-162
04SP Authentic Octographs-OS-CAP
04SP Authentic Sign of the Times-DS-EE
04SP Authentic Sign of the Times-FS-CTR
04SP Authentic Sign of the Times-SS-ORG
04UD Legendary Signatures-65
Autographs-PE
Linemates-WCPEKH
Summit Stars-CDN1
Summit Stars Autographs-CDN-PE
04UD Legends Classics-44
04UD Legends Classics-45
04UD Legends Classics-69
04UD Legends Classics-96
Gold-44
Gold-45
Gold-69
Gold-96
Platinum-44
Platinum-45
Platinum-69
Platinum-96
Silver-44
Silver-45
Silver-69
Silver-96
Jersey Redemptions-JY23
Jersey Redemptions-JY24
Signature Moments-M15
Signatures-CS15
Signatures-DC1
Signatures-DC11
Signatures-TC3
Signatures-TC8
Signatures-QC5
04Upper Deck Jersey Autographs-GJA-PH
04ITG Heroes and Prospects-130
Aspiring-9
Autographs-PE
Hero Memorabilia-5
04ITG Heroes/Prospects Toronto Expo '05-130
04ITG Heroes/Prospects Toronto Expo Heroes/Pros-130
05ITG Heroes/Prosp Toronto Expo Parallel -6
05Beehive-225
PhotoGraphs-PGPE
Signature Scrapbook-SSPE
05ITG Ultimate Memorabilia Level 1-81
05ITG Ultimate Memorabilia Level 2-81
05ITG Ultimate Memorabilia Level 3-81
05ITG Ultimate Memorabilia Level 4-81
05ITG Ultimate Memorabilia Level 5-81
05ITG Ultimate Mem Cornerstones Jerseys-2
05ITG Ultimate Mem Cornerst Jerseys Gold-2
05ITG Ultimate Mem Decades Jerseys-1
05ITG Ultimate Mem Decades Jerseys Gold-1
05ITG Ultimate Memorabilia Double Autos-3
05ITG Ultimate Memorabilia Double Autos-15
05ITG Ultimate Mem Double Autos Gold-3
05ITG Ultimate Mem Double Autos Gold-15
05ITG Ultimate Mem Double Mem Autos-3
05ITG Ultimate Mem Double Mem Autos-10
05ITG Ultimate Mem Double Mem Autos Gold-3
05ITG Ultimate Mem Double Mem Autos Gold-10
05ITG Ultimate Memorabilia Jersey Autos-4
05ITG Ultimate Mem Jersey Autos Gold-4
05ITG Ultimate Memorabilia Jerseys-30
05ITG Ultimate Memorabilia Jerseys Gold-30
05ITG Ultimate Mem Record Breaker Jerseys-2
05ITG Ultimate Mem Record Breaker Jerseys-16
05ITG Ultimate Mem RecBreak Jerseys Gold-2
05ITG Ultimate Mem RecBreak Jerseys Gold-16
05ITG Ultimate Mem Retro Teammate Jerseys-22
05ITG Ult Mem Retro Teammates Jersey Gold-22
05ITG Ultimate Mem Seams Unbelievable-12
05ITG Ultimate Mem Seam Unbelievable Gold-12
05ITG Ultimate Memorabilia Stick Autos-5
05ITG Ultimate Mem Stick Autos Gold-5
05ITG Ultimate Mem Sticks and Jerseys-4
05ITG Ultimate Mem Stick and Jerseys Gold-4
05ITG Ultimate Mem 3 Star of the Game Jsy-14
05ITG Ult Mem 3 Star of the Game Jsy Gold-14
05ITG Ultimate Memorabilia Triple Autos-10
05ITG Ultimate Memorabilia Triple Autos-12
05ITG Ultimate Mem Triple Autos Gold-10
05ITG Ultimate Mem Triple Autos Gold-12
05ITG Ultimate Memorabilia Ultimate Autos-40
05ITG Ultimate Mem Ultimate Autos Gold-40
05ITG Ultimate Memorabilia Vintage Lumber-25
05ITG Ultimate Mem Vintage Lumber Gold-25
05SP Authentic Marks of Distinction-MDPE
05SP Authentic Prestigious Pairings-PPCE
05SP Authentic Sign of the Times Quads-QCECS
05SP Authentic Six Star Signatures-SSBO
05SP Game Used Significant Numbers-SN-PE
05SPx-119
Spectrum-119
Xcitement Legends-XL-PE
Xcitement Legends Gold-XL-PE
Xcitement Legends Spectrum-XL-PE
05The Cup-10
Gold-10
Black Rainbow-10
Hardware Heroes-HHPE1
Hardware Heroes-HHPE2
Hardware Heroes-HHPE3
Masterpiece Pressplates-10
Noble Numbers-NNBE
Patch Variation-P10
Patch Variation Autographs-AP10
Scripted Numbers-SNBE
05UD Artifacts-115
Blue-115
Gold-115
Green-115
Pewter-115
Red-115
Gold Autographed-115
05Ultimate Collection Jerseys-JPE
05Ultimate Coll Ultimate Achievements-UAPE
05Ultimate Collection Ultimate Patches-PPE
05Ultimate Collection Ultimate Signatures-USPE
05Ultimate Coll Ultimate Sigs Pairings-UPEE
05Ultimate Coll Ultimate Sigs Trios-UTBNE
05Upper Deck Notable Numbers-N-PE
05Upper Deck Trilogy-166
Crystal-166
Legendary Scripts-LEG-PE
Personal Scripts-PER-PE
05ITG Heroes and Prospects-6
Autographs-A-PE
Hero Memorabilia-HM-26
National Pride-NPR-23
06ITG International Ice-12
06ITG International Ice-39
Gold-12
Gold-39
Autographs-APE
Autographs-APE2
Best of the Best-BB10
Best of the Best Gold-BB10
Canadian Dream Team-DT05
Canadian Dream Team Gold-DT05
Cornerstones-IC01
Cornerstones Gold-IC01
Emblem Autographs-GUE21
Emblem Autographs Gold-GUE21
Emblems-GUE21
Emblems Gold-GUE21
Greatest Moments-GM02
Greatest Moments Gold-GM02
International Rivals-IR02
International Rivals Gold-IR02
Jersey Autographs-GUJ21
Jersey Autographs Gold-GUJ21
Jerseys-GUJ21
Jerseys Gold-GUJ21
My Country My Team-MC14
My Country My Team Gold-MC14
Numbers-GUN21
Numbers Autographs-GUN21
Numbers Autographs Gold-GUN21
Numbers Gold-GUN21
Passing The Torch-PTT9
Passing The Torch Gold-PTT9
Stick and Jersey-SJ14
Stick and Jersey Gold-SJ14
Teammates-IT01
Teammates Gold-IT01
Triple Memorabilia-TM02
Triple Memorabilia Gold-TM02
06ITG Ultimate Memorabilia-116
Artist Proof-116
Autos-11
Autos Gold-11
Autos Dual-5
Autos Dual Gold-5
Autos Triple-1
Autos Triple Gold-1
Blades of Steel-28

Blades of Steel Gold-28
Bloodlines-6
Bloodlines Gold-6
Bloodlines Autos-5
Bloodlines Autos Gold-5
Captain-C-5
Captain-C Gold-5
Cornerstones-7
Cornerstones Gold-7
Decades-7
Decades Gold-7
Double Memorabilia Autos-7
Double Memorabilia Autos Gold-7
Going For Gold-21
Going For Gold Gold-21
Jerseys Autos-14
Jerseys Autos Gold-14
Legendary Captains-10
Legendary Captains Gold-10
Retro Teammates-10
Retro Teammates Gold-10
Road to the Cup-4
Road to the Cup Gold-4
Sensational Season-1
Sensational Season Gold-1
Stick Rack-6
Stick Rack Gold-6
Sticks Autos-17
Sticks Autos Gold-17
06Parkhurst-56
06Parkhurst-196
Autographs-56
Autographs-196
Autographs Dual-DAEB
Autographs Dual-DAEE
Autographs Dual-DAOE
06SP Authentic Sign of the Times Triples-ST3OBE
06SP Authentic Sign of the Times Quads-ST4EBOC
06SP Game Used Authentic Fabrics Eights-AF8HOF
06SP Game Used Authentic Fabrics Eights Patches-AF8HOF
06SP Game Used Legendary Fabrics-LFPE
06SP Game Used Legendary Fabrics Autographs-LFPE
06SPx SPxcitement-X10
06SPx SPxcitement Spectrum-X10
06The Cup-5
Black Rainbow-5
Gold-5
Gold Patches-5
Masterpiece Pressplates-5
Stanley Cup Signatures-CSPE
06UD Artifacts-111
Blue-111
Gold-111
Platinum-111
Radiance-111
Autographed Radiance Parallel-111
Red-111
Auto-Facts-AFPE
Auto-Facts Gold-AFPE
06Ultimate Collection-7
Autographed Jerseys-AJ-PE
Autographed Patches-AJ-PE
Jerseys Dual-UJ2-EE
Jerseys Triple-UJ3-ENK
Patches Dual-UJ2-EE
Patches Triple-UJ3-ENK
Signatures-US-PH
Ultimate Achievements-UA-PE
06Upper Deck Sweet Shot-11
Signature Shots/Saves Sticks-SSSPH
06Upper Deck Trilogy Combo Clearcut Autographs-C2EE
06Upper Deck Trilogy Ice Scripts-ISPE
06Upper Deck Trilogy Legendary Scripts-LSPE
06Upper Deck Trilogy Scripts-S2PE

Esposito, Tony
69O-Pee-Chee-138
70Dad's Cookies-31
70Esso Power Players-126
70O-Pee-Chee-153
70O-Pee-Chee-234
70O-Pee-Chee-247
70O-Pee-Chee-250
Deckle-32
70Sargent Promotions Stamps-33
70Topps/OPC Sticker Stamps-7
71Bazooka-29
71Letraset Action Replays-13
71Mattel Mini-Records-2
71O-Pee-Chee-110
O-Pee-Chee/Topps Booklets-13
Posters-8
71Sargent Promotions Stamps-44
71Topps-4
71Topps-5
71Topps-6
71Topps-110
71Toronto Sun-65
71Finnish Suomi Stickers-381
71Swedish Hockey-195
72O-Pee-Chee-137
72O-Pee-Chee-196
72O-Pee-Chee-226
72O-Pee-Chee-286
Team Canada-10
72Sargent Promotions Stamps-66
72Topps-20
72Topps-64
72Topps-121
72Finnish Semic World Championship-231
72Swedish Semic World Championship-231
73Blues White Border-23
73O-Pee-Chee-90
73O-Pee-Chee-136
73Topps-4
73Topps-90
74Lipton Soup-45
74NHL Action Stamps-78
74O-Pee-Chee NHL-170
74Topps-170
75O-Pee-Chee NHL-240
75Topps-240
76O-Pee-Chee NHL-100
76Topps-100
76Topps Glossy Inserts-3
77O-Pee-Chee NHL-170
77Topps-170
77Finnish Sportscasters-05-105
78O-Pee-Chee-70
78O-Pee-Chee-250
78Topps-70
78Topps-250
79Blackhawks Postcards-5
79O-Pee-Chee-8
79O-Pee-Chee-80
79Topps-8A
79Topps-8B
79Topps-80
80Blackhawks White Border-4
80O-Pee-Chee-86
80O-Pee-Chee-150
80O-Pee-Chee-168
80O-Pee-Chee Super-4
80Topps-86
80Topps-150
80Topps-168
81Blackhawks Borderless Postcards-6
81O-Pee-Chee-54
81O-Pee-Chee-67
81O-Pee-Chee Stickers-113
81Topps-11
81Topps-W126
82Blackhawks Postcards-5
82O-Pee-Chee-64
82Post Cereal-4
83Blackhawks Postcards-5
83NHL Key Tags-28
83O-Pee-Chee-99
83Puffy Stickers-13
88Esso All-Stars-11
90Pro Set-659
91Future Trends Canada '72-96
91Future Trends Canada '72 French-96
91Pinnacle-388
French-388
92Lightning Sheraton-15
92O-Pee-Chee-194
25th Anniv. Inserts-2
93High Liner Greatest Goalies-8
93Lightning Season in Review-14
94Lightning Photo Album-12
96SLU Canadian Timeless Legends-3
96Swedish Semic Wien Hockey Legends-HL7
97SLU Timeless Legends *-2
98Blackhawks Legends-1
99BAP Memorabilia AS Retail-R6
99BAP Memorabilia AS Retail Autographs-R6
99Upper Deck Century Legends Epic Sigs-TE
99Upper Deck Century Legends Epic Sig 100-TE
99Upper Deck Retro-107
Gold-107
Platinum-107
Inkredible-TE
Inkredible Level 2-TE
00BAP Memorabilia Goalie Memorabilia-G12
00BAP Memorabilia Goalie Memorabilia-G16
00BAP Memorabilia Goalie Memorabilia-G25
00BAP Memorabilia Goalie Memorabilia-G30
00BAP Sig Ser Goalie Memorabilia Autos-GLS3
00BAP Ultimate Mem Goalie Memorabilia-GM5
00BAP Ultimate Mem Goalie Memorabilia-GM8
00BAP Ultimate Mem Goalie Mem Autos-UG3
00BAP Ultimate Memorabilia NHL Records-R3
00BAP Ultimate Memorabilia Retro-Active-RA3
00BAP Ultimate Memorabilia Retro-Active-RA4
00UD Heroes-124
00Upper Deck Legends-27
Legendary Collection Bronze-27
Legendary Collection Gold-27
Legendary Collection Silver-27
Enshrined Stars-ES13
Epic Signatures-TE
of the Cage-LC10
Supreme Milestones-SM14
00Upper Deck Vintage Original 6: A Piece of History-OTE
00Upper Deck Vintage Original 6: A Piece of History Gold-OTE
01BAP Memorabilia Goalie Traditions-GT8
01BAP Memorabilia Goalie Traditions-GT26
01BAP Memorabilia Goalie Traditions-GT27
01BAP Memorabilia Goalie Traditions-GT39
01BAP Signature Series Vintage Autographs-VA-1
01BAP Ultimate Mem All-Star History-26
01BAP Ultimate Memorabilia Bloodlines-5
01BAP Ultimate Memorabilia Calder Trophy-22
01BAP Ultimate Memorabilia Decades-13
01BAP Ultimate Mem Retired Numbers-8
01BAP Ultimate Memorabilia Retro Trophies-12
01Between the Pipes-119
01Between the Pipes-144
Double Memorabilia-DM29
Jersey and Stick Cards-GSJ37
Record Breakers-RB7
Record Breakers-RB19
Trophy Winners-TW15
Vintage Memorabilia-VM9
01Fleer Legacy-17
Ultimate-17
Memorabilia-2
Memorabilia-11
01Greats of the Game-19
Retro Collection-13
Autographs-19
Jerseys-2
Patches Gold-2
Sticks-3
01Parkhurst Autographs-PA37
01SP Game Used Tools of the Game-TTE
01SP Game Used Tools of the Game-CTEC
01SP Game Used Tools of the Game-TTDER
01SP Game Used Tools of the Game-TTRFE
01Topps Archives-3
Arena Seats-ASTE
Autographs-12
Relics-STE
01Upper Deck Legends-14
01Upper Deck Legends-88
Epic Signatures-TE
Florentino Collection-FCTE
Sticks-PHTE
02BAP NHL All-Star History-26
02BAP Ultimate Memorabilia Emblem Attic-10
02BAP Ultimate Memorabilia Numerology-30
02BAP Ultimate Mem Vintage Jerseys-36
02Between the Pipes Goalie Autographs-32
02Between the Pipes He Shoots/Saves Prize-25
02Between the Pipes Record Breakers-7
02Between the Pipes Vintage Memorabilia-9
02Parkhurst Vintage Teammates-VT5
02Parkhurst Retro Nicknames-RN19
02UD Mask Collection Mini Masks-TE
02UD Mask Collection Mini Masks Autos-TE
03BAP Ultimate Memorabilia Autographs-157
Gold-157
03BAP Ultimate Mem Auto Jerseys-157
03BAP Ultimate Memorabilia Cornerstones-6
03BAP Ultimate Memorabilia Emblem Attic-16
03BAP Ultimate Mem Emblem Attic Gold-16
03BAP Ultimate Mem Hometown Heroes-16
03BAP Ultimate Mem Hometown Heroes Gold-16
03ITG Used Signature Series Goalie Gear-24
03ITG Used Sig Series Goalie Gear Autos-24
03ITG Used Sig Series Goalie Gear Gold-24
03ITG Used Sig Series Vintage Mem -4
03ITG Used Sig Series Vintage Mem Autos-4
03ITG Used Sig Series Vintage Mem Gold-4
03ITG VIP Collages-25
03ITG VIP Collage Autographs-25
03ITG VIP Vintage Memorabilia-17
03Pacific Exhibit-217
03Parkhurst Original Six Chicago-59
03Parkhurst Original Six Chicago-64
03Parkhurst Original Six Chicago-88
03Parkhurst Original Six Chicago-94
03Parkhurst Original Six Chicago-97
Autographs-2
Inserts-C3
Inserts-C8
Inserts-C10
Memorabilia-CM15
Memorabilia-CM28
Memorabilia-CM32
Memorabilia-CM39
Memorabilia-CM51
03Parkhurst Orig Six He Shoots/Scores-19
03Parkhurst Orig Six He Shoots/Scores-19A
03Parkhurst Rookie Records-RRE-6
03Parkhurst Rookie Records Gold-RRE-6
03Parkhurst Rookie ROYalty-VR-28
03Parkhurst Rookie ROYalty Autographs-VR-TE
03Parkhurst Rookie ROYalty Gold-VR-28
04ITG NHL AS FANtasy AS History Jerseys-SB26
04ITG Franchises He Shoots/Scores Prizes-20
04ITG Franchises Update-476
04ITG Franchises US West-163
Autographs-A-TE
Double Memorabilia-WDM14
Double Memorabilia Autographs-WDMTE
Double Memorabilia Gold-WDM14
Goalie Gear-WGG2
Goalie Gear Autographs-WGGTE
Goalie Gear Gold-WGG2
Memorabilia-WSM22
Memorabilia Autographs-WSMTE
Memorabilia Gold-WSM22
Original Sticks-WOS11
Original Sticks Autographs-WOSTE
Original Sticks Gold-WOS11
Teammates-WTM9
Teammates Gold-WTM9
Triple Memorabilia Autographs-WTMTE
Triple Memorabilia Gold-WTM10
04ITG Ultimate Memorabilia-122
Gold-122
Archives 1st Edition-14
Archives 1st Edition-34
Autographs-23
Autographs Gold-23
Cornerstones-2
Cornerstones Gold-2
Country of Origin-14
Country of Origin Gold-14
Day In History-31
Day In History-48
Day In History Gold-31
Day In History Gold-48
Goalie Gear-13
Jersey Autographs-42
Jersey Autographs Gold-42
Nicknames-18
Original Six-11
Original Six-12
Stick Autographs-7
Stick Autographs Gold-7
Triple Threads-5
Vezina Trophy-8
04SP Authentic Buybacks-194
04SP Authentic Octographs-OS-GOA
04SP Authentic Sign of the Times-DS-EE
04SP Authentic Sign of the Times-QS-FBRE
04UD Legendary Signatures-84
AKA Autographs-AKA-TE
Autographs-TE
HOF Inks-HOF-TE
Summit Stars-CDN20
Summit Stars Autographs-CDN-TE
04UD Legends Classics-52
04UD Legends Classics-77
04UD Legends Classics-91
Gold-52
Gold-77
Gold-91
Platinum-52
Platinum-77
Platinum-91
Silver-52
Silver-77
Silver-91
Jersey Redemptions-JY22
Signature Moments-M9
Signatures-CS9
Signatures-DC1
Signatures-DC12
Signatures-TC1
Signatures-TC4
Signatures-TC15
Signatures-QC1
04ITG Heroes and Prospects-134
Autographs-TE
Hero Memorabilia-1
04ITG Heroes/Prospects Toronto Expo '05-134
04ITG Heroes/Prospects Expo Heroes/Pros-134
05ITG Heroes/Prosp Toronto Expo Parallel -23
05Beehive-226
PhotoGraphs-PGTE
Signature Scrapbook-SSTE
05Between the Pipes-6
Autographs-A-TO
Double Memorabilia-DM-5
Gloves-GUG-1
Jerseys-GUJ-4
Jersey and Sticks-SJ-6
05ITG Ultimate Memorabilia Level 1-96
05ITG Ultimate Memorabilia Level 2-96
05ITG Ultimate Memorabilia Level 3-96
05ITG Ultimate Memorabilia Level 4-96
05ITG Ultimate Memorabilia Level 5-96
05ITG Ultimate Mem Decades Jerseys-8
05ITG Ultimate Mem Decades Jerseys Gold-8
05ITG Ultimate Memorabilia Double Autos-13
05ITG Ultimate Memorabilia Double Autos-15
05ITG Ultimate Mem Double Autos Gold-13
05ITG Ultimate Mem Double Autos Gold-15
05ITG Ultimate Mem Double Mem-25
05ITG Ultimate Mem Double Mem Autos-10
05ITG Ultimate Mem Double Mem Autos-12
05ITG Ultimate Mem Double Mem Autos Gold-10
05ITG Ultimate Mem Double Mem Autos Gold-12
05ITG Ultimate Mem Double Mem Gold-25
05ITG Ultimate Memorabilia Goalie Gear-20
05ITG Ultimate Mem Goalie Gear Gold-20
05ITG Ultimate Memorabilia Jersey Autos-5
05ITG Ultimate Mem Jersey Autos Gold-5
05ITG Ultimate Memorabilia Jerseys-38
05ITG Ultimate Memorabilia Jerseys Gold-38
05ITG Ultimate Mem Pass the Torch Jerseys-14
05ITG Ultimate Mem Passing Torch Jsy Gold-14
05ITG Ultimate Memorabilia R.O.Y. Autos-13
05ITG Ultimate Mem R.O.Y. Autos Gold-13
05ITG Ultimate Memorabilia R.O.Y. Emblems-2
05ITG Ultimate Mem R.O.Y. Emblems Gold-2
05ITG Ultimate Memorabilia R.O.Y. Jerseys-2
05ITG Ultimate Mem R.O.Y. Jerseys Gold-2
05ITG Ultimate Memorabilia R.O.Y. Numbers-2
05ITG Ultimate Mem R.O.Y. Numbers Gold-2
05ITG Ultimate Mem Record Breaker Jerseys-15
05ITG Ultimate Mem RecBreak Jerseys Gold-15
05ITG Ultimate Mem Retro Teammate Jerseys-23
05ITG Ult Mem Retro Teammates Jersey Gold-23
05ITG Ultimate Mem Seam Unbelievable-9
05ITG Ultimate Mem Seam Unbelievable Gold-9
05ITG Ultimate Memorabilia Sextuple Autos-1
05ITG Ultimate Mem Sticks and Jerseys-26
05ITG Ultimate Mem Stick and Jerseys Gold-26
05ITG Ultimate Mem 3 Star of the Game Jsy-12
05ITG Ult Mem 3 Star of the Game Jsy Gold-12
05ITG Ultimate Memorabilia Triple Autos-10
05ITG Ultimate Mem Triple Autos Gold-10
05ITG Ultimate Mem Triple Threads Jerseys-9
05ITG Ultimate Mem Triple Thread Jsy Gold-9
05ITG Ultimate Memorabilia Ultimate Autos-39
05ITG Ultimate Mem Ultimate Autos Gold-39
05SP Authentic Exquisite Endorsements-EETE
05SP Authentic Prestigious Pairings-PPHE
05SP Authentic Sign of the Times Quads-QRCEB
05SP Game Used Endorsed Equipment-EE-TE
05SP Game Used Signature Sticks-SS-TE
05SP Game Used Statscriptions-ST-TE
05SPx Xcitement Legends-XL-TE
05SPx Xcitement Legends Gold-XL-TE
05SPx Xcitement Legends Spectrum-XL-TE
05The Cup-27
Gold-27
Black Rainbow-27
Emblems of Endorsement-EETE
Hardware Heroes-HHTE1
Hardware Heroes-HHTE2
Honorable Numbers-HNTE
Limited Logos-LLTE
Masterpiece Pressplates-27
Patch Variation-P27
Patch Variation Autographs-AP27
Scripted Numbers-SNET
Scripted Swatches-SSTE
05UD Artifacts-116
Blue-116
Gold-116
Green-116
Pewter-116
Red-116
Frozen Artifacts-FA-TE
Frozen Artifacts Autographed-FA-TE
Frozen Artifacts Copper-FA-TE
Frozen Artifacts Dual-FAD-TE
Frozen Artifacts Dual Autographed-FAD-TE
Frozen Artifacts Dual Copper-FAD-TE
Frozen Artifacts Dual Gold-FAD-TE
Frozen Artifacts Dual Maroon-FAD-TE
Frozen Artifacts Dual Pewter-FAD-TE
Frozen Artifacts Dual Silver-FAD-TE
Frozen Artifacts Gold-FA-TE
Frozen Artifacts Maroon-FA-TE
Frozen Artifacts Pewter-FA-TE
Frozen Artifacts Silver-FA-TE
Goalie Gear-FG-TE
Goalie Gear Autographed-FG-TE
Goalie Gear Dual-FGD-TE
Goalie Gear Dual Autographed-FGD-TE
Goalie Gear Pewter-FG-TE
Goalie Gear Silver-FG-TE
Gold Autographed-116
05UD Toronto Fall Expo Priority Signings-PS-TE
05Ultimate Coll Ultimate Achievements-UATE
05Ultimate Collection Ultimate Signatures-USTE
05Ultimate Coll Ultimate Sigs Pairings-UPEE
05Ultimate Coll Ultimate Sigs Pairings-UPHE
05Ultimate Coll Ultimate Sigs Trios-UTEHP
05Upper Deck All-Time Greatest-13
05Upper Deck All-Time Greatest-66
05Upper Deck Notable Numbers-N-TE
05Upper Deck Trilogy-159
Crystal-159
Legendary Scripts-LEG-TE
Personal Scripts-PER-TE
05ITG Heroes and Prospects-23
Autographs-A-TE
Hero Memorabilia-HM-28
National Pride-NPR-13
06Beehive-218
5 X 7 Black and White-218
PhotoGraphs-PGTE
06Between The Pipes-103
Autographs-ATE
Complete Jersey-CJ05
Complete Jersey Gold-CJ05
Double Jerseys-DJ11
Double Jerseys Gold-DJ11
Double Memorabilia-DM04
Double Memorabilia Gold-DM04
Emblems-GUE04
Emblems Gold-GUE04
Emblems Autographs-GUE04
Gloves-GG03
Gloves Gold-GG03
Jerseys-GUJ04
Jerseys Gold-GUJ04
Jerseys Autographs-GUJ04
Numbers-GUN04
Numbers Gold-GUN04
Numbers Autographs-GUN04
Playing For Your Country-PC19
Playing For Your Country Gold-PC19
Shooting Gallery-SG04
Shooting Gallery Gold-SG04
Stick and Jersey-SJ08
Stick and Jersey Gold-SJ08
Stick and Jersey Autographs-SJ08
Stick Work-SW05
Stick Work Gold-SW05
06ITG International Ice-31
06ITG International Ice-64
Gold-31
Gold-64
Autographs-ATE
Autographs-ATE2
Cornerstones-IC08
Cornerstones Gold-IC08
Goaltending Glory-GG01
Goaltending Glory Gold-GG01
International Rivals-IR01
International Rivals Gold-IR01
Passing The Torch-PTT1
Passing The Torch Gold-PTT1
Quad Patch-QP03
Quad Patch Gold-QP03
Teammates-IT01
Teammates Gold-IT01
06ITG Ultimate Memorabilia-143
Artist Proof-143
Autos-12
Autos Gold-12
Bloodlines-6
Bloodlines Gold-6
Bloodlines Autos-5
Bloodlines Autos Gold-5
Cornerstones-4
Cornerstones Gold-4
Decades-8
Decades Gold-8
Passing The Torch-16
Passing The Torch Gold-16
R.O.Y. Autos-17
R.O.Y. Autos Gold-17
R.O.Y. Emblems-17
R.O.Y. Emblems Gold-17
R.O.Y. Jerseys-17
R.O.Y. Jerseys Gold-17
R.O.Y. Numbers-17
R.O.Y. Numbers Gold-17
Sensational Season-8
Sensational Season Gold-8
06Parkhurst-57
Autographs-57
Autographs Dual-DAEE
Autographs Dual-DAHE
06SP Authentic Sign of the Times-STTE
06SP Authentic Sign of the Times Duals-STET
06SP Authentic Sign of the Times Quads-ST4ECVP
06SP Authentic Sign of the Times Quads-ST4EHSW
06SP Game Used Authentic Fabrics Quads-AF4FCSW
06SP Game Used Authentic Fabrics Quads Patches-AF4FCSW
06The Cup-20
Autographed Foundations-CQTE
Autographed Foundations Patches-CQTE
Autographed Patches-20
Black Rainbow-20
Foundations-CQTE
Foundations Patches-CQTE
Enshrinements-ETE
Gold-20
Gold Patches-20
Honorable Numbers-HNTE
Jerseys-20
Masterpiece Pressplates-20
Scripted Swatches-SSTE
Signature Patches-SPTE
06UD Artifacts-112
Blue-112
Gold-112
Platinum-112
Radiance-112
Autographed Radiance Parallel-112
Red-112
Auto-Facts-AFTE
Auto-Facts Gold-AFTE
06Ultimate Collection Autographed Jerseys-AJ-TE
06Ultimate Collection Jerseys Dual-UJ2-EE
06Ultimate Collection Patches Dual-UJ2-EE
06Ultimate Collection Signatures-US-TE
06Upper Deck All-Time Greatest-ATG23
06Upper Deck NHLPA-PA85
06Upper Deck Sweet Shot-26
Endorsed Equipment-EETE
Signature Shots/Saves Sticks-SSSTE
Signature Sticks-STTE
06Upper Deck Trilogy Combo Clearcut Autographs-C2EE
06Upper Deck Trilogy Combo Clearcut Autographs-C3FEC
06Upper Deck Trilogy Frozen In Time-FT19
06Upper Deck Trilogy Legendary Scripts-LSTE
06Upper Deck Trilogy Scripts-TSTE

Esselmont, Ryan
92British Columbia JHL-49

Esselmont, Shea
89Kamloops Blazers-6
90 7th Inn. Sketch WHL-297
90 7th Inn. Sketch Memorial Cup-4
91 7th Inn. Sketch WHL-62

Esselmont, Todd
89Kamloops Blazers-7
90 7th Inn. Sketch WHL-65
90 7th Inn. Sketch Memorial Cup-5
01Bakersfield Condors-6

Essensa, Bob
87Moncton Hawks-7
89Jets Safeway-14
89O-Pee-Chee Stickers-63
89O-Pee-Chee Stickers-205
89Panini Stickers-173
89ProCards AHL-34
90Bowman-131
Tiffany-131
90Jets IGA-13
90O-Pee-Chee-119
90OPC Premier-29
90Panini Stickers-311
90Pro Set-328
90Score-112
90Score-324
Canadian-112
Canadian-324
90Topps-119
Tiffany-119
90Upper Deck-122
90Upper Deck-337
French-122
French-337
91Pro Set Platinum-135
91Pro Set Platinum-285
91Bowman-193
91Gillette-8
91Jets IGA-11
91O-Pee-Chee-307
91Panini Stickers-75
91Parkhurst-199
French-199
91Pinnacle-66
French-66
91Pro Set Preview-266
91Pro Set-266
91Pro Set-602
French-266
French-602
91Score American-251
91Score Canadian Bilingual-471
91Score Canadian English-471
91Score Young Superstars-17
91Stadium Club-152
91Topps-307
91Upper Deck-101
French-101
92Bowman-306
92Kraft-26
92O-Pee-Chee-226
92Panini Stickers-51
92Panini Stickers French-51
92Parkhurst-207
Emerald Ice-207
92Pinnacle-190
French-190
92Pro Set-211
92Pro Set-267
92Score-123
Canadian-123
92Stadium Club-210
92Topps-183
Gold-183G
92Ultra-240
92Upper Deck-217
93Donruss-382
93Jets Readers Club-10
93Jets Ruffles-12
93Kraft Recipes-2
93Kraft Recipes French-2
93Leaf-38
93OPC Premier-161
Gold-161
93Panini Stickers-199
93Parkhurst-234
Emerald Ice-234
93Pinnacle-133
Canadian-133
93PowerPlay-270
93Score-26
Canadian-26
93Stadium Club-254
Members Only Master Set-254
First Day Issue-254
93Topps/OPC Premier-161
Gold-161
93Ultra-89
93Upper Deck-144
94EA Sports-150
94Leaf-93
94Parkhurst-64
Gold-64
94Pinnacle-428
Artist's Proofs-428
Rink Collection-428
94Score-191
Gold-191
Platinum-191
95Fort Wayne Komets-6
96Oilers Postcards-30
96Collector's Edge Ice-126
Prism-126
97Be A Player-185
Autographs-185
Autographs Die-Cuts-185
Autographs Prismatic Die-Cuts-185
97Pacific Invincible NHL Regime-77
98Crown Royale-50
Limited Series-50
98NHL Aces Playing Cards-32
98Pacific-206
Ice Blue-206
Red-206
98Pacific Dynagon Ice-70
Blue-70
Red-70
99Wayne Gretzky Hockey-132
00Upper Deck NHLPA-PA85
01Between the Pipes-70
01Pacific-381
Extreme LTD-381
Hobby LTD-381
Premiere Date-381
Retail LTD-381
01Pacific Arena Exclusives-381
01Parkhurst-243
01Czech Stadion-230
04ITG Franchises Canadian-137
Autographs-BES

Essex, Brad
96Peoria Rivermen-4
96Peoria Rivermen Photo Album-4
97Peoria Rivermen-12
99Mississippi Sea Wolves-14
99Mississippi Sea Wolves Kelly Cup-12
01Roanoke Express-7
02Roanoke Express-14
02Roanoke Express RBI Sports-193

Essolmont, Shea
89Kamloops Blazers-6

Estabrooks, Hartley
67Columbus Checkers-12

Estevez, Emilio
92Disney Mighty Ducks Movie-2

Estola, Matti
72Finnish Jaakiekko-300

Etcher, Fred
52Juniors Blue Tint-96

Etches, Derek
89Sudbury Wolves-11
90 7th Inn. Sketch OHL-383
90Sudbury Wolves-11
91 7th Inn. Sketch OHL-43

Ethier, Martin
97Bowman CHL-47
OPC-47

Ethier, Neil
89Sudbury Wolves-16

Ethier, Trevor
93Saskatoon Blades-9

Etienne, Jean
92Quebec Pee-Wee Tournament-540
93Quebec Pee-Wee Tournament-1127

Ettinger, Trevor
00Shawinigan Cataractes-22
Signed-22
02Syracuse Crunch-20

Ettles, Blair
92Cornell Big Red-10
93Cornell Big Red-9

Etz, Mark
02German DEL City Press-282
04German DEL-181
05German DEL-164

Eustache, Eddie
52Juniors Blue Tint-167

Euverman, Chad
93Quebec Pee-Wee Tournament-1615

Evaldson, Ove
67Swedish Hockey-169

Evan, Jakub
03Czech OFS Plus-217
04Czech OFS-49

Evangelista, John
99Mississippi Sea Wolves-21
03Mississippi Sea Wolves-9
04Louisiana Ice Gators-5

Evans, Blair
93Quebec Pee-Wee Tournament-191

Evans, Blake
96Spokane Chiefs-9
98Tri-City Americans-13
00UD CHL Prospects-74
01Peoria Rivermen-6
02Worcester IceCats-9
03Worcester IceCats-13
04Worcester IceCats-9
05Peoria Rivermen-10

Evans, Brennan
00Kootenay Ice-7
03Lowell Lock Monsters-4
03Lowell Lock Monsters Photo Album-21
04SP Authentic-92
04Ultimate Collection-44
04Upper Deck-182
Canadian Exclusives-182
HG Glossy Gold-182
HG Glossy Silver-182
04Lowell Lock Monsters-5
04Lowell Lock Monsters Photo Album-5
05Binghamton Senators-18
05Binghamton Senators Quickway-18

Evans, Chris
72Blues White Border-4
72O-Pee-Chee-236
72Sargent Promotions Stamps-192
73Blues White Border-6
73O-Pee-Chee-208
74NHL Action Stamps-306
74NHL Action Stamps Update-31
74O-Pee-Chee NHL-59
74Topps-59
76O-Pee-Chee WHA-22

Evans, Cory
91 7th Inn. Sketch OHL-372
93Windsor Spitfires-16
94Windsor Spitfires-18
99Fort Worth Brahmas-5

Evans, Daryl
83NHL Key Tags-53
83O-Pee-Chee-153
83O-Pee-Chee Stickers-144
83Topps Stickers-144
84Kings Smokey-4
89ProCards AHL-23
89New Haven Nighthawks-4

Evans, David
02Charlotte Checkers-83

Evans, Doug
87Blues Kodak-7
87Blues Team Issue-7
88Blues Kodak-6
88Blues Team Issue-7
90Jets IGA-14
90O-Pee-Chee-413
90Pro Set-561
91Bowman-203
91Jets Panini Team Stickers-11
91Jets IGA-12
91O-Pee-Chee-438
91Score Canadian Bilingual-399
91Score Canadian English-399
91Stadium Club-321
91Topps-438
91Michigan Wolverines-1
92Flyers J.C. Penney-11
92Flyers Upper Deck Sheets-24
92OPC Premier-45
92Dayton Bombers-9
93OPC Premier-203
Gold-203
93Topps/OPC Premier-203
Gold-203
93Peoria Rivermen-7
94Greensboro Monarchs-17
95Peoria Rivermen-3
96Peoria Rivermen-5
96Peoria Rivermen Photo Album-5
96Collector's Edge Ice-177
Prism-177
97Peoria Rivermen-4
98Peoria Rivermen-3

Evans, Frank
89Spokane Chiefs-5
90 7th Inn. Sketch WHL-196
91 7th Inn. Sketch WHL-8
91 7th Inn. Sketch CHL Award Winners-18
91 7th Inn. Sketch Memorial Cup-76
94Las Vegas Thunder-5
00UK Cardiff Devils-12
00UK Sekonda Superleague-53
01UK Cardiff Devils-6
01UK Nottingham Panthers-7
02UK Cardiff Devils-6

Evans, Jack
44Beehive Group II Photos-93
44Beehive Group II Photos-309A
44Beehive Group II Photos-309B
51Parkhurst-90
53Parkhurst-54
54Parkhurst-72
54Topps-14
57Topps-55
58Topps-31
59Topps-30
59Topps-48
60Shirriff Coins-76
60Topps-30
Stamps-14
61Shirriff/Salada Coins-39
62Topps-26
94Parkhurst Missing Link-101

Evans, Jimmy
28V128-2 Paulin's Candy-60

Evans, Keith
92Quebec Pee-Wee Tournament-1792
93Quebec Pee-Wee Tournament-197

Evans, Kevin
89ProCards IHL-76
90ProCards AHL/IHL-100
91Score Canadian Bilingual-650
91Score Canadian English-650
91Kansas City Blades-17
91ProCards-511
93Peoria Rivermen-8
95Central Hockey League-22
96Mississippi Sea Wolves-4
97Mississippi Sea Wolves-20
99Tupelo T-Rex-17

Evans, Mike
91Air Canada SJHL-C3
92Saskatchewan JHL-100

Evans, Shawn
88ProCards AHL-300
89ProCards AHL-244
91ProCards-96
94Milwaukee Admirals-7
95Fort Wayne Komets-7

Evans, Stan
23V128-1 Paulin's Candy-60

Evans, Stephen
93Quebec Pee-Wee Tournament-552

Evans, Stewart
34Beehive Group I Photos-196
34Sweet Caporal-19
37O-Pee-Chee V304E-164
37V356 Worldwide Gum-67
38Quaker Oats Photos-12

Evans, Terry
77Kalamazoo Wings-7

Evans-Harvey, Ronnie
94UK Guildford Flames-14
95UK Guildford Flames-7

Evason, Dean
86Whalers Junior Thomas'-6
87O-Pee-Chee-166
87Panini Stickers-47
87Topps-166
87Whalers Jr. Burger King/Pepsi-5
88Whalers Junior Ground Round-5
89Whalers Junior Milk-6
90Bowman-262
Tiffany-262
90O-Pee-Chee-376
90Panini Stickers-44
90Pro Set-103
90Score-259A
90Score-259B
Canadian-259A
Canadian-259B
90Topps-376
Tiffany-376
90Upper Deck-192
French-192
90Whalers Jr. 7-Eleven-10
91Pro Set Platinum-230
91Bowman-10
91O-Pee-Chee-325
91OPC Premier-36
91Panini Stickers-312
91Parkhurst-388
French-388
91Pinnacle-153
French-153
91Pro Set-84
French-84
91Score American-17
91Score Canadian Bilingual-17
91Score Canadian Bilingual-641
91Score Canadian English-17
91Score Canadian English-641
91Score Rookie/Traded-91T
91Sharks Sports Action-4
91Stadium Club-145
91Topps-325
91Upper Deck-127
91Upper Deck-560
French-127
French-560
92Bowman-133
92O-Pee-Chee-381
92Panini Stickers-131
92Panini Stickers French-131
92Parkhurst-392
Emerald Ice-392
92Pinnacle-169
French-169
92Score-103
Canadian-103
92Stadium Club-11
92Topps-304
Gold-304G
92Ultra-193
92Upper Deck-281
93Donruss-86
93Panini Stickers-259
93Parkhurst-319
Emerald Ice-319
93Pinnacle-384
Canadian-384
93PowerPlay-323
93Score-353
93Score-550
Gold-550
Canadian-353
Canadian-550
Canadian Gold-550
93Ultra-298
94Be A Player Signature Cards-138
94Canada Games NHL POGS-78
94Leaf-45
94OPC Premier-361
Special Effects-361
94Parkhurst SE-SE46
Gold-SE46
94Pinnacle-346
Artist's Proofs-346
Rink Collection-346
94Stadium Club-82
Members Only Master Set-82
First Day Issue-82
Super Team Winner Cards-82
94Stars HockeyKaps-10
94Stars Postcards-6
94Topps/OPC Premier-361
Special Effects-361
94Ultra-50
94Upper Deck-48
Electric Ice-48
95Collector's Choice-307
Player's Club-307
Player's Club Platinum-307
95Parkhurst International-36
Emerald Ice-36
95Upper Deck-22
Electric Ice-22
Electric Ice Gold-22
98German DEL-68
03Vancouver Giants-24
04Calgary Hitmen-23

Evdokimov, Vitali
00Russian Hockey League-7

Evensen, Morten
98Danish Hockey League-26

Evensson, Conny
67Swedish Hockey-87
71Swedish Hockey-150
72Swedish Stickers-133
73Swedish Stickers-178
74Swedish Stickers-215
84Swedish Semic Elitserien-121
85Swedish Panini Stickers-90
86Swedish Panini Stickers-83
91Swedish Semic Elitserien Stickers-359
92Finnish Semic-50
93Swiss HNL-6

Evequoz, Thierry
93Swiss HNL-316
95Swiss HNL-466
96Swiss HNL-254

Everett, Chris
97Tucson Gila Monsters-7

Evoy, Sean
84Sudbury Wolves-2
85Sudbury Wolves-6
Evseev, Vladislav
02Russian Future Stars-3
03Russian Hockey League-57
04Russian Moscow Dynamo-11
Evstafiev, Andrei
98Russian Hockey League-90
99Russian Hockey League-249
00Russian Hockey League-335
03Russian Hockey League-5
04Russian Super League All-Stars-20
Evstigneev, Pavel
99San Angelo Outlaws-14
Evtushevski, Greg
84Kamloops Blazers-8
94German DEL-229
95German DEL-165
96German DEL-240
98German DEL-44
99German DEL-182
01German Upper Deck-79
Evtyiokhin, Georgi
99Russian Hockey League-221
00Russian Hockey League-104
02Russian Transfert-3
Ewacha, Rod
90Michigan Tech Huskies-4
91Michigan Tech Huskies-3
Ewasiuk, Jay
97Moose Jaw Warriors-1
Ewasko, Jeff
03Rockford Ice Hogs-5
05Odessa Jackalopes-8
06Odessa Jackalopes-8
Ewen, Dean
89ProCards AHL-242
91ProCards-452
95Kansas City Blades-8
96Kansas City Blades-10
98Las Vegas Thunder-4
99Colorado Gold Kings Taco Bell-18
99Colorado Gold Kings Wendy's-11
Ewen, Todd
87Blues Kodak-8
87Blues Team Issue-8
88Blues Kodak-7
88Blues Team Issue-8
89Canadiens Kraft-8
90Canadiens Postcards-15
90Pro Set-470A
90Pro Set-470B
91Canadiens Panini Team Stickers-11
91Canadiens Postcards-12
91Pro Set-419
French-419
91Stadium Club-340
92Canadiens Postcards-11
92Pinnacle-250
French-250
92Upper Deck-549
93Donruss-9
93Leaf-427
93OPC Premier-369
Gold-369
93Parkhurst-5
Emerald Ice-5
93Pinnacle-409
Canadian-409
93PowerPlay-285
93Score-565
Gold-565
Canadian-565
Canadian Gold-565
93Stadium Club-309
Members Only Master Set-309
First Day Issue-309
93Topps/OPC Premier-369
Gold-369
93Ultra-252
93Upper Deck-449
94Ducks Carl's Jr.-6
94OPC Premier-119
Special Effects-119
94Pinnacle-503
Artist's Proofs-503
Rink Collection-503
94Topps/OPC Premier-119
Special Effects-119
94Ultra-2
94Upper Deck-427
Electric Ice-427
95Be A Player-155
Signatures-S155
Signatures Die Cuts-S155
95Upper Deck-340
Electric Ice-340
Electric Ice Gold-340
96Collector's Choice-11
97Pacific Invincible NHL Regime-178
01Fleer Legacy-40
Ultimate-40
02Fleer Throwbacks-23
Gold-23
Platinum-23
Autographs-9
Stickwork-4
Ewing, Mark
93Quebec Pee-Wee Tournament-1239
Ewing, Steve
86Kitchener Rangers-29
Exantus, Paul-Emile
907th Inn. Sketch QMJHL-265
917th Inn. Sketch QMJHL-296
Exelby, Garnet
01Chicago Wolves-7
02BAP Memorabilia-398
02BAP Ultimate Memorabilia-54
02AHL Top Prospects-14
02Chicago Wolves-7
03ITG Action-30
03O-Pee-Chee-320
03OPC Blue-320
03OPC Gold-320
03OPC Red-320
03Pacific Complete-548
Red-548
03Thrashers Postcards-4
03Topps-320
Blue-320
Gold-320
Red-320
03Topps Pristine-146
03Topps Pristine-147
03Topps Pristine-148
Gold Refractor Die Cuts-146
Gold Refractor Die Cuts-147
Gold Refractor Die Cuts-148
Refractors-146
Refractors-147
Refractors-148
Press Plates Black-146
Press Plates Black-147
Press Plates Black-148
Press Plates Cyan-146
Press Plates Cyan-147
Press Plates Cyan-148
Press Plates Magenta-146
Press Plates Magenta-147
Press Plates Magenta-148
Press Plates Yellow-146
Press Plates Yellow-147
Press Plates Yellow-148
03Upper Deck MVP-29
Gold Script-29
Silver Script-29
Canadian Exclusives-29
05Parkhurst-30
Facsimile Auto Parallel-30
06Be A Player-131
Autographs-131
Signatures-EX
06O-Pee-Chee-30
Rainbow-30
06Upper Deck-12
Exclusives Parallel-12
High Gloss Parallel-12
Masterpieces-12
MVP Gold Script-18
MVP Super Script-18
Exelby, Randy
88ProCards AHL-272
89ProCards IHL-115
90Kansas City Blades-7
90ProCards AHL/IHL-589
Exner, Kenric
98Kamloops Blazers-9
99Bowman CHL-121
Gold-121
OPC International-121
00Peoria Rivermen-16
Exner, Nathan
04Medicine Hat Tigers-7
Exter, Joe
03ECHL Update RBI Sports-286
04Wheeling Nailers Riesbeck's-13
04Wheeling Nailers SGA-7
06Cedar Rapids RoughRiders-24
Eylert, Robert
94German First League-635
Eysselt, Jan
95German DEL-287
96German DEL-315
Ezhov, Denis
03Russian Under-18 Team-13
04Russian World Junior Team-17
Ezinicki, Bill
44Beehive Group II Photos-400
45Quaker Oats Photos-16A
45Quaker Oats Photos-16B
45Quaker Oats Photos-16C
45Quaker Oats Photos-16D
Faassen, Dan
907th Inn. Sketch WHL-205
917th Inn. Sketch WHL-19
Fabian, Erik
02Topeka Scarecrows-15
03North Dakota Fighting Sioux-27
04North Dakota Fighting Sioux-5
Fabian, Petr
94Czech APS Extraliga-13
95Czech APS Extraliga-313
96Czech APS Extraliga-108
97Czech DS Stickers-276
Fabian, Sean
91Minnesota Golden Gophers-6
Fabian, Stefan
04Slovakian Poprad Team Set-9
Fabricius, Christian
98Danish Hockey League-121
99Danish Hockey League-132
Fabricius, Karl
05Swedish Lulea Hockey Postcards-16
05Swedish SHL Elitset-91
Gold-91
Series One Signatures-13
Teammates-8
06Swedish SHL Elitset-179
Fabritius, Karl
04Swedish Elitset-223
Gold-223
Fabrizi, Morris
93Quebec Pee-Wee Tournament-504
Fabrizio, Dino
93Quebec Pee-Wee Tournament-41
Fabry, Chuck
01Michigan Tech Huskies-9
Fabus, Peter
04Czech OFS Czech/Slovak-26
05Swedish SHL Elitset-264
Gold-264
06Czech HC Plzen Postcards-12
Facca, Rob
02Lincoln Stars-27
03Lincoln Stars-26
Fadden, Mitch
05Lethbridge Hurricanes-7
Fadeev, Igor
01Russian Hockey League-166
Fadejev, Michail
95Czech APS Extraliga-166
96Czech APS Extraliga-333
97Czech DS Stickers-169
Fader, Duncan
93Kingston Frontenacs-15
95Slapshot-135
Fadeyev, Sergei
00Russian Hockey League-101
03Russian Hockey League-264
Fadrny, Jan
97Czech APS Extraliga-168
98Brandon Wheat Kings-4
99Brandon Wheat Kings-7
00Kelowna Rockets-18
01Wilkes-Barre Scranton Penguins-10
03Czech OFS Plus-174
Faeh, Michel
95Swiss HNL-291
Faeh, Pascal
93Swiss HNL-476
95Swiss HNL-301
Fafard, Dominic
94Wheeling Thunderbirds-14
94Wheeling Thunderbirds Photo Album-8
95Central Hockey League-41
98Oklahoma City Blazers-3
Fafard, Perry
84Brandon Wheat Kings-12
Fagan, Andrew
96Slapshot-165
Fagemo, Linus
98Swedish UD Choice-74
99Swedish Upper Deck-80
00Swedish Upper Deck-174
02Swedish SHL-222
Parallel-222
03Swedish Elite-230
Silver-230
04Swedish Elitset-75
Gold-75
05German DEL-165
06Swedish SHL Elitset-237
Fagerhoi, Kim
92Norwegian Elite Series-95
Fagerli, Jan Roar
92Finnish Semic-32
92Norwegian Elite Series-38
95Swedish World Championships Stickers-238
Fagerlund, Bjorn
67Swedish Hockey-88
71Swedish Hockey-137
73Swedish Stickers-172
74Swedish Stickers-140
Fagerlund, Rickard
57Swedish Alfabilder-124
65Swedish Coralli ISHockey-62
Fagerstedt, Juha
04Finnish Cardset-215
05Finnish Cardset -19
06Finnish Cardset-203
Fagerstrom, Ake
70Swedish Hockey-4
71Swedish Hockey-78
72Swedish Stickers-53
73Swedish Stickers-194
Fagerstrom, Kristian
94Finnish SISU-336
95Finnish SISU-7
Fagerstrom, Veli-Pekka
95Finnish SISU-6
Fagioli, Luciano
87Sudbury Wolves-12
Fah, Michale
98Swiss Power Play Stickers-351
Fah, Pascal
99Swiss Panini Stickers-321
Fahey, Brian
03Atlantic City Boardwalk Bullies-6
03Atlantic City Boardwalk Bullies RBI-20
03ECHL All-Stars-244
04Atlantic City Boardwalk Bullies-20
04Atlantic City Boardwalk Bullies Kinko's-5
05Idaho Steelheads-6
05Iowa Stars-4
Fahey, Jim
02BAP Memorabilia-353
02BAP Ultimate Memorabilia-86
02Pacific Calder-144
Silver-144
02Pacific Complete-531
Red-531
02Pacific Quest for the Cup-145
Gold-145
02Parkhurst Retro-237
Minis-237
02SP Authentic-169
02UD Artistic Impressions-112
Gold-112
02UD Honor Roll-141
02UD Premier Collection-51B
Gold-51
02AHL Top Prospects-15
03ITG Action-476
03Sharks Postcards-5
03Upper Deck-160
Canadian Exclusives-160
HG-160
03Upper Deck MVP-349
Gold Script-349
Silver Script-349
Canadian Exclusives-349
03Upper Deck Victory-158
Bronze-158
Gold-158
Silver-158
Freshman Flashback-FF38
04Cleveland Barons-8
06O-Pee-Chee-303
Rainbow-303
Fahey, Rebecca
97Collector's Choice-292
Fahl, Dustin
92Northern Michigan Wildcats-4
Fahrutdinov, Mishat
89Swedish Semic Elitserien Stickers-262
90Swedish Semic Elitserien Stickers-162
91Swedish Semic Elitserien Stickers-264
92Swedish Semic Elitserien Stickers-287
93Swedish Semic Elitserien-254
94Swedish Leaf-47
95Swedish Leaf-129
95Swedish Upper Deck-195
Faic, Jiri
93Swiss HNL-165
Fair, Keith
93Swedish Semic World Champ Stickers-119
93Swiss HNL-147
95Swiss HNL-148
96Swiss HNL-166
98Swiss Power Play Stickers-167
99Swiss Panini Stickers-168
00Swiss Panini Stickers-211
00Swiss Slapshot Mini-Cards-HCL16
01Swiss HNL-40
02Swiss HNL-283
Fair, Quinn
91Air Canada SJHL-C9
96Mississippi Sea Wolves-5
97Mississippi Sea Wolves-16
99Mississippi Sea Wolves Kelly Cup-16
00Bakersfield Condors-9
01Bakersfield Condors-7
02Bakersfield Condors-7
03Bakersfield Condors-14
Fairbairn, Bill
70Esso Power Players-187
70Sargent Promotions Stamps-123
71O-Pee-Chee-215
71Sargent Promotions Stamps-123
71Toronto Sun-171
72O-Pee-Chee-87
72Sargent Promotions Stamps-150
73O-Pee-Chee-41
73Topps-41
74NHL Action Stamps-184
74O-Pee-Chee NHL-231
74Topps-231
75O-Pee-Chee NHL-109
75Topps-109
76O-Pee-Chee NHL-57
76Topps-57
77O-Pee-Chee NHL-303
77Topps-255
78O-Pee-Chee-267
Fairchild, Kelly
94St. John's Maple Leafs-9
94Classic-71
Gold-71
95St. John's Maple Leafs-8
95Signature Rookies-23
Signatures-23
96Collector's Edge Future Legends-5
97Milwaukee Admirals-4
98Michigan K-Wings-5
99Michigan K-Wings-15
00Hershey Bears-6
01BAP Memorabilia-431
Emerald-431
Ruby-431
Sapphire-431
01SPx-202
01UD Honor Roll-68
01Hershey Bears-7
02Upper Deck-202
Exclusives-202
02Upper Deck Vintage-327
02German Berlin Polar Bears Postcards-8
02German DEL City Press-29
03German Berlin Polar Bears Postcards-11
03German DEL-65
All-Stars-AS13
04German Berlin Polar Bears Postcards-10
04German DEL-66
All-Stars-AS13
05German DEL-26
06German DEL-17
Fairweather, Shaun
01New Mexico Scorpions-4
03Odessa Jackalopes-6
Faistenhammer, Markus
94German First League-72
Faith, Juraj
03German DEL-50
04Slovakian Poprad Team Set-21
Fakhrutdinov, Dmitri
02Russian Hockey League-194
02Russian Hockey League-251
Falardeau, Lee
05Hartford Wolf Pack-3
06Hartford Wolf Pack-8
Falesy, Kevin
87Kingston Canadians-17
89Kitchener Rangers-27
Falk, Andreas
06Swedish SHL Elitset-198
Falk, Mike
06New Mexico Scorpions-5
Falk, Nichlas
95Swedish Leaf-186
Rookies-3
95Swedish Upper Deck-48
97Swedish Collector's Choice-44
Select-UD3
98Swedish UD Choice-57
99Swedish Upper Deck-42
00Swedish Upper Deck-53
02Swedish SHL-162
Parallel-162
Team Captains-2
03Swedish Elite-18
Hot Numbers-HN3
Silver-18
04Swedish Elitset-16
04Swedish Elitset-142
Gold-16
Gold-142
Signatures-9
05Swedish SHL Elitset-19
Gold-19
Teammates-2
06Swedish SHL Elitset-20
Falk, Stefan
86Swedish Panini Stickers-134
87Swedish Panini Stickers-125
89Swedish Semic Elitserien Stickers-117
91Swedish Semic Elitserien Stickers-126
92Swedish Semic Elitserien Stickers-147
93Swedish Semic Elitserien-116
94Swedish Leaf-52
95Swedish Leaf-54
95Swedish Upper Deck-84
97Swedish Collector's Choice-92
Falkenberg, Bob
68O-Pee-Chee-141
72O-Pee-Chee-310
Falkenhall, Hakan
99Danish Hockey League-224
Falkman, Craig
72Minnesota Fighting Saints Postcards WHA-7
72Finnish Semic World Championship-127
72Swedish Semic World Championship-127
Faller, Laurent
92Quebec Pee-Wee Tournament-1397
96Swiss HNL-420
Fallkvist, Arne
57Swedish Alfabilder-107
Fallon, Dan
00Sioux City Musketeers-6
Falloon, Chris
99Prince George Cougars-15
00Prince George Cougars-9
03Prince George Cougars-9
Falloon, Pat
89Spokane Chiefs-5
90Upper Deck-469
French-469
907th Inn. Sketch WHL-189
91Pro Set Platinum-271
91Gillette-3
91Kraft-8
91OPC Premier-56
91Parkhurst-160
French-160
91Pinnacle-329
French-329
91Pro Set-558
French-558
CC-CC3
CC French-CC3
91Score Canadian Bilingual-640
91Score Canadian English-640
91Score Rookie/Traded-90T
91Sharks Sports Action-5
91Upper Deck-593
French-593
917th Inn. Sketch CHL Award Winners-12
917th Inn. Sketch Memorial Cup-87
917th Inn. Sketch Memorial Cup-100
91Arena Draft Picks-1
91Arena Draft Picks-32
91Arena Draft Picks-HOLO
91Arena Draft Picks French-1
91Arena Draft Picks French-32
91Arena Draft Picks Autographs-1
91Arena Draft Picks Autographs French-1
91Classic-2
91Classic Promos-2
91Star Pics-2
91Star Pics-36
91Ultimate Draft-2
91Ultimate Draft-56
91Ultimate Draft-58
91Ultimate Draft-78
91Ultimate Draft-80
91Ultimate Draft French-2
91Ultimate Draft Promos-1
91Classic Four-Sport *-2
Autographs-2A
92Bowman-361
92Humpty Dumpty I-6
92O-Pee-Chee-227
92OPC Premier Star Performers-12
92Panini Stickers-273
92Panini Stickers-K
92Panini Stickers French-273
92Panini Stickers French-K
92Parkhurst-161
92Parkhurst-233
Emerald Ice-161
Emerald Ice-233
92Pinnacle-9
92Pinnacle-238
French-9
French-238
Team 2000-26
Team 2000 French-26
92Pro Set-166
Gold Team Leaders-10
Rookie Goal Leaders-4
92Score-125
92Score-436
Canadian-125
Canadian-436
Young Superstars-14
92Seasons Patches-62
92Stadium Club-52
92Stadium Club-259
92Topps-7
92Topps-418
Gold-7G
Gold-418G
92Ultra-194
Rookies-6
92Upper Deck-19
92Upper Deck-286
92Upper Deck-355
92Upper Deck-386
World Junior Grads-WG13
93Donruss-308
Special Print-T
93Kraft-7
93Leaf-49
Studio Signature-2
93OPC Premier-259
Gold-259
93Panini Stickers-W
93Parkhurst-183
Emerald Ice-183
93Pinnacle-20
Canadian-20
Team 2001-26
Team 2001 Canadian-26
93PowerPlay-218
93Score-133
Canadian-133
Franchise-19
93Stadium Club-224
Members Only Master Set-224
OPC-224
First Day Issue-224
First Day Issue OPC-224
93Topps/OPC Premier-259
Gold-259
93Ultra-49
93Upper Deck-39
Future Heroes-29
SP-141
93Upper Deck Locker All-Stars-52
94Canada Games NHL POGS-214
94Donruss-83
94EA Sports-119
94Finest-32
Super Team Winners-32
Refractors-32
94Flair-163
94Fleer-195
94Hockey Wit-98
94Leaf-95
94Leaf Limited-14
94OPC Premier-521
Special Effects-521
94Parkhurst Vintage-V70
94Parkhurst SE-SE165
Gold-SE165
94Pinnacle-173
Artist's Proofs-173
Rink Collection-173
94Score-152
Gold-152
Platinum-152
94Select-116
Gold-116
94Stadium Club-62
Members Only Master Set-62
First Day Issue-62
Super Team Winner Cards-62
94Topps/OPC Premier-521
Special Effects-521
94Ultra-364
94Upper Deck-307
Electric Ice-307
95Bashan Super Stickers-107
95Be A Player-95
Signatures-S95
Signatures Die Cuts-S95
95Canada Games NHL POGS-227
95Collector's Choice-188
Player's Club-188
Player's Club Platinum-188
95Donruss-213
95Hoyle Western Playing Cards-29
95Imperial Stickers-107
95Leaf-241
95Parkhurst International-424
Emerald Ice-424
95Playoff One on One-82
95Pro Magnets-117
95Score-184
Black Ice Artist's Proofs-184
Black Ice-184
95Topps-147
OPC Inserts-147
95Ultra-284
95Upper Deck-483
Electric Ice-483
Electric Ice Gold-483
96Collector's Choice-194
96Donruss-208
Press Proofs-208
96Fleer Picks-102
96Flyers Postcards-8
96Leaf-102
Press Proofs-102
96NHL Pro Stamps-117
96Pinnacle-115
Artist's Proofs-115
Foil-115
Premium Stock-115
Rink Collection-115
96Playoff One on One-361
96Score-21
Artist's Proofs-21
Dealer's Choice Artist's Proofs-21
Special Artist's Proofs-21
Golden Blades-21
96Upper Deck-122
97Pacific-199
Copper-199
Emerald Green-199
Ice Blue-199
Red-199
Silver-199
97Score Flyers-16
Platinum-16
Premier-16
98Be A Player-205
Press Release-205
98BAP Gold-205
98BAP Autographs-205
98BAP Autographs Gold-205
98OPC Chrome-182
Refractors-182
98Topps-182
O-Pee-Chee-182
99Pacific-153
Copper-153
Emerald Green-153
Gold-153
Ice Blue-153
Premiere Date-153
Red-153
99Paramount-90
Copper-90
Emerald-90
Gold-90
Holographic Emerald-90
Holographic Gold-90
Holographic Silver-90
Ice Blue-90
Premiere Date-90
Red-90
Silver-90
00Pacific-326
Copper-326
Gold-326
Ice Blue-326
Premiere Date-326
00Swiss Panini Stickers-113
00Swiss Slapshot Mini-Cards-HCD16
02BAP Sig Series Auto Buybacks 1998-205
04ITG Franchises Update Autographs-PF
04ITG Franchises US West-300
Falta, Pavel
94Czech APS Extraliga-163
02Czech OFS Plus-149
Checklists-C3
02Czech OFS Plus Masks-M11
02Czech OFS Plus Trios-T5
02Czech OFS Plus Duos-D22
03Czech OFS Plus-313
03Czech OFS Plus Insert B-B14
03Czech OFS Plus Insert H-H4
03Czech OFS Plus Insert P-P14
03Czech OFS Plus MS Praha-SE50
04Czech OFS-84
05Czech HC Liberec-2
Falter, Martin
01Czech OFS Update-313
02Czech OFS Plus-48
Trios-T19
03Czech OFS Plus-4
Famulare, Derek
06Chicoutimi Sagueneens-9
Fancy, Jeff
907th Inn. Sketch WHL-106
917th Inn. Sketch WHL-66
Fandul, Vjatcheslav
92Finnish Jyvas-Hyva Stickers-197
93Finnish Jyvas-Hyva Stickers-353
93Finnish SISU-220
94Finnish SISU-327
94Finnish SISU Fire On Ice-3
95Finnish SISU-127
95Finnish SISU-370
98Finnish Kerailysarja-260
00Finnish Cardset-296
01German Upper Deck-28
02Finnish Cardset-17
03Finnish Cardset-175
Fankhauser, Bernhard
02Swiss HNL-467
Fankhouser, Scott
99BAP Memorabilia-387
Gold-387
Silver-387
99Crown Royale-6
Limited Series-6
Premiere Date-6
Prospects Parallel-6
99Pacific Omega-15
Copper-15
Gold-15
Ice Blue-15
Premiere Date-15
99SP Authentic-93
00Aurora-6
Premiere Date-6
00Pacific-27
Copper-27
Gold-27
Ice Blue-27
Premiere Date-27
00Paramount-12
Copper-12
Gold-12
Holo-Gold-12
Holo-Silver-12
Ice Blue-12
Premiere Date-12
00Titanium-102
Retail-102
00Titanium Draft Day Edition-102
00Titanium Draft Day Promos-102
00Upper Deck Victory-273
02Arkansas Riverblades-5
02Reading Royals-28
Farda, Richard
69Swedish Hockey-24
70Finnish Jaakiekko-44
70Swedish Hockey-354
70Swedish Masterserien-81
70Swedish Masterserien-146
71Finnish Suomi Stickers-24
71Swedish Hockey-50
72Finnish Jaakiekko-4
72Finnish Hellas-90
72Finnish Panda Toronto-81
72Finnish Semic World Championship-31
72Swedish Semic World Championship-31
73Finnish Jaakiekko-46
74Finnish Jenkki-68
74Finnish Typotor-112
74Swedish Stickers-18
74Swedish Semic World Champ Stickers-63
95Czech APS Extraliga-123
97Czech APS Extraliga-146
97Czech APS Extraliga-375
98Czech OFS-209
99Czech OFS-16
99Czech OFS-236
99Czech OFS Jagr Team Embossed-16
Farell, Brian
92Harvard Crimson-8
Farelli, Cary
82Swedish Semic VM Stickers-137
83Swedish Semic VM Stickers-137
Farkas, Jeff
95Donruss Elite World Juniors-35
97Black Diamond-125
Double Diamond-125
Triple Diamond-125
Quadruple Diamond-125
98UD Choice-306
Prime Choice Reserve-306
Reserve-306
00Aurora-138
Premiere Date-138
00BAP Memorabilia-223
Emerald-223
Ruby-223
Sapphire-223
Promos-223
00BAP Mem Chicago Sportsfest Copper-223
00BAP Memorabilia Chicago Sportsfest Blue-223
00BAP Memorabilia Chicago Sportsfest Gold-223
00BAP Memorabilia Chicago Sportsfest Ruby-223
00BAP Memorabilia Chicago Sun-Times Ruby-223
00BAP Memorabilia Chicago Sun-Times Gold-223
00BAP Mem Chicago Sun-Times Sapphire-223
00BAP Mem Toronto Fall Expo Copper-223
00BAP Memorabilia Toronto Fall Expo Gold-223
00BAP Memorabilia Toronto Fall Expo Ruby-223
00BAP Parkhurst 2000-P76
00BAP Signature Series-261
Emerald-261
Ruby-261
Sapphire-261
Autographs-8
Autographs Gold-8
00Pacific-389
Copper-389
Gold-389
Ice Blue-389
Premiere Date-389
00Paramount-229
Copper-229
Gold-229
Holo-Gold-229
Holo-Silver-229
Ice Blue-229
Premiere Date-229
00Revolution-138
Blue-138
Premiere Date-138
Red-138
00Topps Premier Plus-99
Blue Ice-99
00Upper Deck Vintage-343
00St. John's Maple Leafs-9
01O-Pee-Chee-312
01O-Pee-Chee Premier Parallel-312
01Topps-312
OPC Parallel-312
01Upper Deck Victory-389
Gold-389
01St. John's Maple Leafs-9
02BAP Sig Series Auto Buybacks 2000-8
02Chicago Wolves-8
Farmanara, Yashar
05Lethbridge Hurricanes-8
Farmer, Sean
95Slapshot Memorial Cup-59
97Idaho Steelheads-8
99Peoria Rivermen-22
Farnham, Steve
93Quebec Pee-Wee Tournament-408
Farquhar, Bryan
01Western Michigan Broncos-4
02Kalamazoo Wings-7
Farquharson, Steve
00St. Michaels Majors-15
01Barrie Colts-18
Farr, Jeremy
98Spokane Chiefs-5
99Spokane Chiefs-8
Farr, Rocky
74Sabres Postcards-5
Farrand, Gavin
03UK Sheffield Steelers-14
03UK Sheffield Steelers Stickers-2
05UK Sheffield Steelers-6
Gold-6
Silver-6
Farrell, Arthur F
83Hall of Fame Postcards-L3
85Hall of Fame-153
Farrell, Brian
94Cleveland Lumberjacks-11
94Cleveland Lumberjacks Postcards-11
94Classic-33
Gold-33
97Mississippi Sea Wolves-18
Farrell, Mike
00Portland Pirates-16
01BAP Memorabilia-316
Emerald-316
Ruby-316
Sapphire-316
01Parkhurst-349
01Topps Chrome-182
Refractors-182
Black Border Refractors-182
01UD Playmakers-143
01Upper Deck Ice-151
03Milwaukee Admirals-27
03Milwaukee Admirals Postcards-3
06Owen Sound Attack-16
Farrell, Peter
04Penticton Vees-17
05Penticton Vees-5
Farrell, Scott
89Spokane Chiefs-7
Farris, Kevin
85Nova Scotia Oilers-23
Farrish, Dave
77O-Pee-Chee NHL-179
77Topps-179
78O-Pee-Chee-41
78Topps-41
79O-Pee-Chee-299
80Maple Leafs Postcards-12
80O-Pee-Chee-311
80Pepsi-Cola Caps-87
81O-Pee-Chee-317
83Maple Leafs Postcards-5
83O-Pee-Chee-329
83Vachon-85
84O-Pee-Chee-301
88ProCards AHL-36
89ProCards AHL-49
90Moncton Hawks-6
90ProCards AHL/IHL-263
91Moncton Hawks-7
91ProCards-187
97Springfield Falcons-23
00Louisiana Ice Gators-21
01Louisiana Ice Gators-7
02Louisiana Ice Gators-23
03Louisiana Ice Gators-22
Fast, Brad
00Michigan State Spartans-5
03Lowell Lock Monsters-3
03Lowell Lock Monsters Photo Album-9
04SP Authentic-91
04Ultimate Collection-43
04Upper Deck-181
Canadian Exclusives-181
HG Glossy Gold-181
HG Glossy Silver-181
04Lowell Lock Monsters-6
04Lowell Lock Monsters Photo Album-6
05Manchester Monarchs-3
Fata, Drew
00St. Michaels Majors-16
01St. Michaels Majors-10
02Kingston Frontenacs-5
02St. Michaels Majors-9
03Wheeling Nailers-89
03Wilkes-Barre Scranton Penguins-10
04Wilkes-Barre Scranton Penguins-21
07Upper Deck Victory-241
Black-241
Gold-241
Fata, Rico
94Quebec Pee-Wee Tournament-573
95Slapshot-369
95Sault Ste. Marie Greyhounds-6
96All-Sport PPF *-76
96All Sport PPF Gold *-76
97Upper Deck-410
97Bowman CHL-24
OPC-24
98Be A Player-171
Press Release-171
98BAP Gold-171
98BAP Autographs-171
98BAP Autographs Gold-171
98Black Diamond-11
Double Diamond-11
Triple Diamond-11
Quadruple Diamond-11
98Bowman's Best-114
Refractors-114
Atomic Refractors-114
98Crown Royale-17
Limited Series-17
98Finest Futures Finest-F6
98Finest Futures Finest Refractors-F6
98OPC Chrome-225
Refractors-225
98Pacific Dynagon Ice-24
Blue-24
Red-24
98Pacific Omega-38
Red-38
Opening Day Issue-38
98SP Authentic-92
Power Shift-92
98Topps-225
O-Pee-Chee-225
98Topps Gold Label Class 1-46
Black-46
Black One of One-46
One of One-46
Red-46
Red One of One-46
98Topps Gold Label Class 2-46
98Topps Gold Label Class 2 Black-46
98Topps Gold Label Class 2 Black 1 of 1-46
98Topps Gold Label Class 2 One of One-46
98Topps Gold Label Class 2 Red-46
98Topps Gold Label Class 2 Red One of One-46
98Topps Gold Label Class 3-46
98Topps Gold Label Class 3 Black-46
98Topps Gold Label Class 3 Black 1 of 1-46
98Topps Gold Label Class 3 One of One-46
98Topps Gold Label Class 3 Red-46
98Topps Gold Label Class 3 Red One of One-46
98Upper Deck-413
Exclusives-413
Exclusives 1 of 1-413
Generation Next-GN20
Generation Next Quantum 1-GN20
Generation Next Quantum 2-GN20
Generation Next Quantum 3-GN20
Profiles-P30
Profiles Quantum 1-P30
Profiles Quantum 2-P30
Profiles Quantum 3-P30
Gold Reserve-413
98Upper Deck MVP-27
Gold Script-27
Silver Script-27
Super Script-27
ProSign-RF
98Bowman CHL-131

Golden Anniversary-131
OPC International-131
Autographs Blue-A40
Autographs Gold-A40
Autographs Silver-A40
Scout's Choice-SC16
98Bowman Chrome CHL-131
Golden Anniversary-131
Golden Anniversary Refractors-131
OPC International-131
OPC International Refractors-131
Refractors-131
99BAP Memorabilia-149
Gold-149
Silver-149
99BAP Millennium-46
Emerald-46
Ruby-46
Sapphire-46
Signatures-46
Signatures Gold-46
99O-Pee-Chee-111
99O-Pee-Chee Chrome-111
99O-Pee-Chee Chrome Refractors-111
99Pacific-66
Copper-66
Emerald Green-66
Gold-66
Ice Blue-66
Premiere Date-66
Red-66
99Paramount-37
Copper-37
Emerald-37
Gold-37
Holographic Emerald-37
Holographic Gold-37
Holographic Silver-37
Ice Blue-37
Premiere Date-37
Red-37
Silver-37
99SPx-25
Radiance-25
Spectrum-25
99Stadium Club-192
First Day Issue-192
One of a Kind-192
Printing Plates Black-192
Printing Plates Cyan-192
Printing Plates Magenta-192
Printing Plates Yellow-192
99Topps/OPC-111
99Topps/OPC Chrome-111
Refractors-111
99Topps Premier Plus-130
Parallel-130
99Upper Deck-29
99Upper Deck-164
Exclusives-29
Exclusives-164
Exclusives 1 of 1-29
Exclusives 1 of 1-164
New Ice Age-N16
New Ice Age Quantum Gold-N16
New Ice Age Quantum Silver-N16
99Upper Deck Gold Reserve-29
99Upper Deck Gold Reserve-164
99Upper Deck MVP-34
Gold Script-34
Silver Script-34
Super Script-34
Draft Report-DR7
99Upper Deck Victory-47
99Quebec PeeWee Tournament Coll Souv-24
99Bowman CHL-146
Gold-146
OPC International-146
Scout's Choice-SC12
00BAP Memorabilia-366
Emerald-366
Ruby-366
Sapphire-366
Promos-366
00BAP Mem Chicago Sportsfest Copper-366
00BAP Memorabilia Chicago Sportsfest Blue-366
00BAP Memorabilia Chicago Sportsfest Gold-366
00BAP Memorabilia Chicago Sportsfest Ruby-366
00BAP Memorabilia Chicago Sun-Times Ruby-366
00BAP Memorabilia Chicago Sun-Times Gold-366
00BAP Mem Chicago Sun-Times Sapphire-366
00BAP Mem Toronto Fall Expo Copper-366
00BAP Memorabilia Toronto Fall Expo Gold-366
00BAP Memorabilia Toronto Fall Expo Ruby-366
00Crown Royale Game-Worn Jerseys-3
00Crown Royale Game-Worn Jersey Patches-3
00Crown Royale Premium-Sized Jerseys-3
00Titanium Game Gear-66
00Titanium Game Gear Patches-66
00Topps Premier Plus GameUsed Memorabilia-GPRF
00Topps Premier Plus GameUsed Memorabilia-GPJIRF
01BAP Memorabilia-220
Emerald-220
Ruby-220
Sapphire-220
01O-Pee-Chee-313
01O-Pee-Chee Premier Parallel-313
01Pacific Heads-Up Quad Jerseys-5
01Private Stock Game Gear-66
01Private Stock Game Gear Patches-66
01SP Game Used Authentic Fabric-AFRF
01SP Game Used Authentic Fabric Gold-AFRF
01Titanium Double-Sided Jerseys-26
01Titanium Double-Sided Patches-26
01Topps-313
OPC Parallel-313
01UD Playmakers Practice Jerseys-PJRF
01UD Playmakers Practice Jerseys Gold-PJRF
01Upper Deck Game Jerseys Series II-GNRF
01Upper Deck MVP-26
01Upper Deck Victory-365
Gold-365
01Hartford Wolf Pack-3
02BAP Sig Series Auto Buybacks 1998-171
02BAP Sig Series Auto Buybacks 1999-46
03Beehive-156
Gold-156
Silver-156
03Black Diamond-54
Black-54
Green-54
Red-54
03Crown Royale-79
Blue-79
Retail-79
03ITG Action-437
03Pacific-270
Blue-270
Red-270
03Pacific Calder-80
Silver-80
03Pacific Complete-309
Red-309
03Pacific Heads-Up-78
Hobby LTD-78
Retail LTD-78
03Pacific Quest for the Cup-83
Blue-83
03Titanium-81
Hobby Jersey Number Parallels-81
Retail-81
Retail Jersey Number Parallels-81
03Upper Deck-155
Canadian Exclusives-155
HG-155
03Upper Deck Ice-70
Gold-70
03Upper Deck MVP-339
Gold Script-339
Silver Script-339
Canadian Exclusives-339
03Upper Deck Victory-151
Bronze-151
Gold-151
Silver-151
04Pacific-209
Blue-209
Red-209
04Upper Deck-142
Canadian Exclusives-142
HG Glossy Gold-142
HG Glossy Silver-142
05Be A Player Signatures-RF
05Be A Player Signatures Gold-RF
05Parkhurst-499
Facsimile Auto Parallel-499
05Upper Deck-153
HG Glossy-153
05Upper Deck MVP-309
Gold-309
Platinum-309
05Upper Deck Toronto Fall Expo-153
05WBS Penguins-9

Fatikov, Leonid
00Russian Hockey League-165
01German Upper Deck-124
Jersey Cards-LF-J

Fatkullin, Alfred
99Russian Hockey League-259

Fatrola, Richard
897th Inn. Sketch OHL-73
907th Inn. Sketch OHL-4
95Muskegon Fury-12
96Dayton Ice Bandits-10

Fattey, Chris
92Quebec Pee-Wee Tournament-1589
00Rockford IceHogs-8

Fattey, Nik
92Quebec Pee-Wee Tournament-1591
93Quebec Pee-Wee Tournament-801

Fatticci, Rico
02Greenville Grrrowl-3
05Roanoke Valley Vipers-7

Faubert, Mario
78O-Pee-Chee-296
81O-Pee-Chee-261
81O-Pee-Chee Stickers-189

Faubert, Pierre-Luc
03Lewiston Maineiacs-9

Faucher, Bryan
01Thetford Mines Coyotes-22

Faucher, Frederic
01Drummondville Voltigeurs-14
02Quebec Remparts-12
03Quebec Remparts Memorial Cup-4

Faucher, Sebastien
93Quebec Pee-Wee Tournament-111

Faucher, Vincent
91Lake Superior State Lakers-8
92Thunder Bay Thunder Hawks-22

Faul, Perry
01Prince Albert Raiders-8
02Prince Albert Raiders-9
03Prince Albert Raiders-21

Faulk, Stephen
93Quebec Pee-Wee Tournament-1244

Faulkner, Alex
44Beehive Group II Photos-164
63Parkhurst-42
63York White Backs-49
64Beehive Group III Photos-68
04ITG Franchises US West-223
Autographs-A-AF

Faulkner, Andy
91British Columbia JHL-52
91British Columbia JHL-153
96Quad-City Mallards-13
97Quad-City Mallards-14
98Madison Monsters-12

Faulkner, Geoff
02Macon Trax-15

Faurholm, Filip
98Danish Hockey League-123
99Danish Hockey League-143

Fausel, Shane
91Arizona Icecats-13

Fauss, Ted
83Nova Scotia Voyageurs-21

Faust, Andre
92Parkhurst-365
Emerald Ice-365
93Flyers Lineup Sheets-13
93Parkhurst-419
Emerald Ice-419
93Pinnacle-209
Canadian-209
93Stadium Club-462
Members Only Master Set-462
First Day Issue-462
93Upper Deck-63
93Classic McDonalds-14
93Classic Pro Prospects-47
94Donruss-184
96German DEL-20
98German DEL-275
99German DEL-164
00German DEL-137
01German Upper Deck-137

Faust, Elliott
95Slapshot-206

Faust, Philippe
98Swiss Power Play Stickers-352
02Swiss HNL-454

Fauteux, Jonathan
98Val d'Or Foreurs-6
99Bowman CHL-25
Gold-25
OPC International-25
Autographs-BA16
Autographs Gold-BA16
Autographs Silver-BA16
00Victoriaville Tigres-13
Signed-13
01Peoria Rivermen-9

Fauth, Joshua
04Kootenay Ice-10
05Regina Pats-28

Favaro, Randy
93Spokane Chiefs-10
94Spokane Chiefs-1
95Spokane Chiefs-11

Favell, Doug
68Shirriff Coins-127
69O-Pee-Chee-88
69Topps-88
70Colgate Stamps-91
70Dad's Cookies-32
70Esso Power Players-199
70Flyers Postcards-4
70O-Pee-Chee-199
Deckle-35
70Sargent Promotions Stamps-152
71Letraset Action Replays-11
71Letraset Action Replays-21
71O-Pee-Chee-72
71Sargent Promotions Stamps-156
71Topps-72
71Toronto Sun-193
72Flyers Mighty Milk-4
72O-Pee-Chee-89
Player Crests-16
72Sargent Promotions Stamps-157
72Topps-74
73Maple Leafs Postcards-5
73Maple Leafs Postcards-6
73O-Pee-Chee-158
73Topps-119
74NHL Action Stamps-262
74O-Pee-Chee NHL-4
74O-Pee-Chee NHL-46
74Topps-4
74Topps-46
75Maple Leafs Postcards-6
75O-Pee-Chee NHL-381
76O-Pee-Chee NHL-292
76Rockies Coke Cans-9
76Rockies Puck Bucks-9
77Coca-Cola-7
77O-Pee-Chee NHL-370
77Rockies Coke Cans-7
78O-Pee-Chee-54
78Topps-54
79O-Pee-Chee-274
04ITG Franchises US East-426
Autographs-A-DF1
04ITG Franchises US West-189
Autographs-A-DF1
06Between The Pipes-85
06Between The Pipes-136
Autographs-ADF

Favot, Tim
897th Inn. Sketch OHL-166
907th Inn. Sketch OHL-307
917th Inn. Sketch OHL-262
91Sudbury Wolves-17

Favre, Cedric
92Quebec Pee-Wee Tournament-1392
01Swiss HNL-426
02Swiss HNL-210

Favreau, Jonathan
02Moncton Wildcats-17

Fawcett, Len
86Kitchener Rangers-9

Fazio, Livio
95Swiss HNL-161
96Swiss HNL-56
98Swiss Power Play Stickers-84
99Swiss Panini Stickers-82
00Swiss Panini Stickers-132
00Swiss Slapshot Mini-Cards-HCFG4
01Swiss HNL-149
02Swiss HNL-94
03Swiss EV Zug Postcards-10
04Swiss EV Zug Postcards-9

Fazzalari, Daniel
06Cape Breton Screaming Eagles-4

Feakes, Tyler
02Calgary Hitmen-20
04Swift Current Broncos-4

Feamster, Dave
82Blackhawks Postcards-6
83Blackhawks Postcards-6
83O-Pee-Chee-100

Fearns, Kent
95Classic-72
Autographs-5
95Classic Five-Sport *-151
96Knoxville Cherokees-11
97Manitoba Moose-B7
98Manitoba Moose-C3
99German DEL-325
01German Upper Deck-181
02German DEL City Press-133

Feasby, Mike
98Muskegon Fury-20
99Muskegon Fury-22
02Muskegon Fury-16

Feasby, Scott
897th Inn. Sketch OHL-88
93Muskegon Fury-12
94Muskegon Fury-5
95Muskegon Fury-9
98Muskegon Fury-26
99Muskegon Fury-4
99UHL All-Stars West-10T
00Muskegon Fury-16
02Muskegon Fury-23
03Muskegon Fury-6

Featherstone, Devin
03Prince George Cougars-3

Featherstone, Glen
88ProCards IHL-71
90Blues Kodak-9
90O-Pee-Chee-387
90Pro Set-523
90Score Rookie/Traded-25T
90Topps-387
Tiffany-387
91Bowman-371
91Bruins Sports Action-7
91O-Pee-Chee-436
91OPC Premier-66
91Score Canadian Bilingual-587
91Score Canadian English-587
91Score Rookie/Traded-37T
91Stadium Club-319
91Topps-436
93OPC Premier-14
Gold-14
93PowerPlay-288
93Stadium Club-372
Members Only Master Set-372
First Day Issue-372
93Topps/OPC Premier-14
Gold-14
94Be A Player Signature Cards-81
95Parkhurst International-363
Emerald Ice-363
95Whalers Bob's Stores-8
96Whalers Kid's Club-21
97Indianapolis Ice-6
98Chicago Wolves-15
99Chicago Wolves-13
00Chicago Wolves-9

Featherstone, Tony
70Esso Power Players-103
71Topps-106
73North Stars Postcards-4
75O-Pee-Chee WHA-122

Featherstone, Travis
03Kootenay Ice-8

Fecho, Kyle
02Regina Pats-22
05Moose Jaw Warriors-6

Federenko, Brad
91Air Canada SJHL-B32
91Air Canada SJHL All-Stars-12
93Minnesota-Duluth Bulldogs-10
99Jacksonville Lizard Kings-4

Federenko, Garvin
94Anchorage Aces-12

Federko, Bernie
77O-Pee-Chee NHL-312
78Blues Postcards-10
78O-Pee-Chee-143
78Topps-143
79O-Pee-Chee-215
79Topps-215
80O-Pee-Chee-71
80O-Pee-Chee-136
80O-Pee-Chee Super-18
80Topps-71
80Topps-136
81O-Pee-Chee-288
81O-Pee-Chee-300
81O-Pee-Chee-304
81O-Pee-Chee Stickers-128
81Topps-12
81Topps-62
81Topps-W127
82O-Pee-Chee-302
82O-Pee-Chee-303
82O-Pee-Chee Stickers-197
82Post Cereal-17
82Topps Stickers-197
83O-Pee-Chee-315
83O-Pee-Chee Stickers-125
83Puffy Stickers-18
83Topps Stickers-125
84Kellogg's Accordion Discs-4
84Kellogg's Accordion Discs Singles-10
84O-Pee-Chee-184
84O-Pee-Chee-367
84O-Pee-Chee Stickers-54
84O-Pee-Chee Stickers-55
847-Eleven Discs-42
84Topps-131
85O-Pee-Chee-104
85O-Pee-Chee Stickers-53
85Topps-104
86O-Pee-Chee-105
86O-Pee-Chee Stickers-174
86Topps-105
87Blues Kodak-9
87Blues Team Issue-9
87O-Pee-Chee-83
87O-Pee-Chee Stickers-24
87Panini Stickers-312
87Topps-83
88Blues Kodak-8
88Blues Team Issue-9
88Frito-Lay Stickers-4
88O-Pee-Chee-81
88O-Pee-Chee Box Bottoms-E
88O-Pee-Chee Stickers-21
88Panini Stickers-104
88Topps-81
88Topps Box Bottoms-E
89O-Pee-Chee-107
89O-Pee-Chee Stickers-247
89Red Wings Little Caesars-6
89Topps-107
90Bowman-238
Tiffany-238
90O-Pee-Chee-191
90Panini Stickers-209
90Pro Set-70
90Score-252
Canadian-252
90Topps-191
Tiffany-191
90Upper Deck-58
French-58
91Pro Set-597
French-597
92Blues UD Best of the Blues-14
94Hockey Wit-47
00Upper Deck Legends-114
Legendary Collection Bronze-114
Legendary Collection Gold-114
Legendary Collection Silver-114
01Greats of the Game-63
Autographs-63
01Topps Archives-60
Arena Seats-ASBF
01Topps Chrome Reprints-4
01Topps Chrome Reprint Refractors-4
01Topps Chrome Reprint Autographs-4
01Upper Deck Legends-57
02Fleer Throwbacks-7
Gold-7
Platinum-7
02UD Foundations-83
02UD Foundations-116
04ITG Franchises US West-289
Autographs-A-BF
04UD Legendary Signatures-3
Autographs-BF
Linemates-BRBFWB
06Parkhurst-58
06Parkhurst-207
Autographs-58
Autographs-207
Autographs Dual-DAFM
06SP Authentic Sign of the Times Duals-STFM
06The Cup-80
Autographed Patches-80
Black Rainbow-80
Gold-80
Gold Patches-80
Jerseys-80
Limited Logos-LLBF
Masterpiece Pressplates-80
06Ultimate Collection Signatures-US-BF
06Upper Deck Sweet Shot Signature Shots/Saves-SSBF

Fedorchuk, Dean
94Dayton Bombers-14
94Classic-52
Gold-52
99German Bundesliga 2-231

Fedorko, Mike
75Hamilton Fincups-5
91Prince Albert Raiders-1
917th Inn. Sketch WHL-262

Fedorov, Anton
91Michigan Wolverines-3
93Michigan Wolverines-5
94Raleigh Icecaps-6
95Central Hockey League-77
97Mobile Mysticks-6
97Mobile Mysticks Kellogg's-17
98Colorado Gold Kings-4
98Colorado Gold Kings Postcards-16

Fedorov, Evgeni
98Russian Hockey League-31
99Russian Hockey League-168
02Russian Hockey League-13
02Russian Hockey League-14
03Russian Hockey League-13
05Russian Hockey League RHL-23

Fedorov, Fedor
98Port Huron Border Cats-24
00SP Authentic-129
00SP Game Used-84
00SPx-125
Spectrum-125
00UD Pros and Prospects-126
00Upper Deck Vintage-399
00Sudbury Wolves-23
01SPx Rookie Redemption-R29
01Manitoba Moose-8
02NHL Power Play Stickers-157
02Pacific Calder-97
Silver-97
02Pacific Complete-586
Red-586
02Pacific Exclusive-191
Blue-191
Gold-191
02Titanium Right on Target-20
02Topps Total-436
02Manitoba Moose-10
03Manitoba Moose-24
03Pacific AHL Prospects-53
Gold-53
04UD All-World-40
Gold-40
04Russian Back to Russia-19
04ITG Heroes and Prospects Emblems-34
04ITG Heroes and Prospects Emblems Gold-34
04ITG Heroes and Prospects Jerseys-34
04ITG Heroes and Prospects Jerseys Gold-34
04ITG Heroes and Prospects Numbers-34
04ITG Heroes and Prospects Numbers Gold-34
05Hartford Wolf Pack-4

Fedorov, Juri
74Swedish Stickers-87
79Panini Stickers-146
79Russian National Team-9
80USSR Olympic Team Mini Pics-1

Fedorov, Sergei
89Russian National Team-5
90O-Pee-Chee Red Army-19R
90OPC Premier-30
90Pro Set-604
90Score Rookie/Traded-20T
90Score Young Superstars-9
90Upper Deck-521
90Upper Deck-525
French-521
French-525
91Pro Set Platinum-30
91Pro Set Platinum-277
91Bowman-50
91Gillette-12
91Kraft-51
91O-Pee-Chee-8
91O-Pee-Chee-401
91OPC Premier-68
91OPC Premier-173
91Panini Stickers-145
91Panini Stickers-340
91Parkhurst-38
French-38
PHC-PHC5
PHC French-PHC5
91Pinnacle-157
French-157
91Pro Set-53
French-53
Awards Special-AC10
Platinum PC-PC7
91Red Wings Little Caesars-4
91Score American-250
91Score American-352
91Score American-408
91Score Canadian Bilingual-298
91Score Canadian Bilingual-382
91Score Canadian Bilingual-470
91Score Canadian English-298
91Score Canadian English-382
91Score Canadian English-470
91Score Hot Cards-4
91Score Young Superstars-1
91Stadium Club-316
91Topps-8
91Topps-401
91Upper Deck-6
91Upper Deck-40
91Upper Deck-82
91Upper Deck-144
91Upper Deck-631
French-6
French-40
French-82
French-144
French-631
Euro-Stars-9
Euro-Stars French-9
91Finnish Semic World Champ Stickers-219
91Russian Stars Red Ace-3
91Russian Tri-Globe Bure-NNO
91Russian Tri-Globe Fedorov-1
91Russian Tri-Globe Fedorov-2
91Russian Tri-Globe Fedorov-3
91Russian Tri-Globe Fedorov-4
91Russian Tri-Globe Fedorov-5
91Russian Tri-Globe Irbe-NNO
91Russian Tri-Globe Kamensky-NNO
91Russian Tri-Globe Semenov-NNO
91Russian Sports Unite Hearts-1
91Russian Stars in NHL-1
91Swedish Semic World Champ Stickers-219
91Star Pics-30
92Bowman-205
92Bowman-416
92Humpty Dumpty II-5
92McDonald's Upper Deck-6
92O-Pee-Chee-195
92OPC Premier Star Performers-20
92Panini Stickers-113
92Panini Stickers-291
92Panini Stickers French-113
92Panini Stickers French-291
92Parkhurst-39
92Parkhurst-219
Emerald Ice-39
Emerald Ice-219
92Pinnacle-20
French-20
Team 2000-30
Team 2000 French-30
92Pro Set-40
92Score-252
Canadian-252
Young Superstars-5
92Seasons Patches-5
92Sports Illustrated for Kids II-259
92Sports Illustrated for Kids II-557
92Stadium Club-244
92Stadium Club-300
92Topps-252
Gold-252G
92Ultra-48
Imports-3
92Upper Deck-157
92Upper Deck-632
Euro-Stars-E1
World Junior Grads-WG16
92Finnish Semic-109
93Donruss-101
Elite Inserts-U2
93Leaf-129
93OPC Premier-318
93OPC Premier-441
Gold-318
Gold-441
93Panini Stickers-246
93Parkhurst-58
Emerald Ice-58
East/West Stars-W10
93Pinnacle-54
Canadian-54
Team 2001-24
Team 2001 Canadian-24
93PowerPlay-72
Gamebreakers-1
Global Greats-2
Slapshot Artists-3
93Score-250
Canadian-250
Dynamic Duos U.S.-9
International Stars-3
International Stars Canadian-3
93Stadium Club-45
Members Only Master Set-45
OPC-45
First Day Issue-45
First Day Issue OPC-45
93Topps/OPC Premier-318
93Topps/OPC Premier-441
Gold-318
Gold-441
93Ultra-121
Speed Merchants-3
93Upper Deck-171
NHLPA/Roots-12
SP-44
94SLU Hockey Canadian-2
94Hockey Canadian-2
94SLU Hockey American-4
94Action Packed Badge of Honor Promos-1
94Be A Player-R145
99 All-Stars-G6
Up Close and Personal-UC7
94Canada Games NHL POGS-87
94Canada Games NHL POGS-267
94Canada Games NHL POGS-331
94Canada Games NHL POGS-360
94Donruss-173
Dominators-5
Elite Inserts-4
Ice Masters-2
94EA Sports-40
94Finest-65
Super Team Winners-65
Refractors-65
Bowman's Best-B7
Bowman's Best Refractors-B7
Division's Clear Cut-13
94Flair-48
94Flair-213
94Flair-214
94Flair-215
94Flair-216
94Flair-217
94Flair-218
94Flair-219
94Flair-220
94Flair-221
94Flair-222
Center Spotlight-2
Scoring Power-3
94Fleer-59
Headliners-2
94Hockey Wit-69
94Kenner Starting Lineup Cards-4
94Kraft-59
94Kraft-69
94Leaf-155
Fire on Ice-1
Gold Stars-1
Limited Inserts-7
94Leaf Limited-81
Gold-9
94McDonald's Upper Deck-McD12
94OPC Premier-40
94OPC Premier-276
94OPC Premier-520
Special Effects-40
Special Effects-276
Special Effects-520
94Parkhurst-305
Gold-305
Crash the Game Green-7
Crash the Game Blue-7
Crash the Game Gold-7
Crash the Game Red-7
Vintage-V39
94Parkhurst SE-SE50
Gold-SE50
Euro-Stars-ES16
94Pinnacle-150
Artist's Proofs-150
Rink Collection-150
Gamers-GR3
Team Pinnacle-TP8
Team Dufex Parallel-TP8
World Edition-WE5
94Post Box Backs-10
94Score Dream Team-DT12
94Score Franchise-TF7
94Score 90 Plus Club-2
94Select-10
Gold-10
94SP-33
Die Cuts-33
Premier-24
Premier Die-Cuts-24
94Stadium Club Members Only-15
94Stadium Club-250
94Stadium Club-268
Members Only Master Set-250
Members Only Master Set-268
First Day Issue-250
First Day Issue-268
Finest Inserts-6
Finest Inserts Members Only-6
Super Teams-7
Super Teams Members Only Master Set-7
Super Team Winner Cards-250
Super Team Winner Cards-268
94Topps/OPC Premier-40
94Topps/OPC Premier-276
94Topps/OPC Premier-520
Special Effects-40
Special Effects-276
Special Effects-520
94Topps Finest Inserts-3
94Topps/OPC Premier The Go To Guy-9
94Topps Finest Bronze-7
94Ultra-60
Award Winners-3
Global Greats-1
Premier Pivots-2
Scoring Kings-2
Sergei Fedorov-1
Sergei Fedorov-1AU
Sergei Fedorov-2
Sergei Fedorov-2AU
Sergei Fedorov-3
Sergei Fedorov-3AU
Sergei Fedorov-4
Sergei Fedorov-4AU
Sergei Fedorov-5
Sergei Fedorov-5AU
Sergei Fedorov-6
Sergei Fedorov-6AU
Sergei Fedorov-7
Sergei Fedorov-7AU
Sergei Fedorov-8
Sergei Fedorov-8AU
Sergei Fedorov-9
Sergei Fedorov-9AU
Sergei Fedorov-10
Sergei Fedorov-10AU
Sergei Fedorov-11
Sergei Fedorov-12
Speed Merchants-3
94Upper Deck-37
Electric Ice-37
Predictor Canadian-C21
94Upper Deck Predictor Canadian Exch Gold-C21
94Upper Deck Predictor Hobby-H6
94Upper Deck Predictor Hobby-H18
94Upper Deck Predictor Hobby Exch Gold-H6
94Upper Deck Predictor Hobby Exch Gold-H18
94Upper Deck Predictor Hobby Exch Silver-H6
94Upper Deck Predictor Hobby Exch Silver-H18
94Upper Deck Predictor Retail-R4
94Upper Deck Predictor Retail-R23
94Upper Deck Predictor Retail-R36
94Upper Deck Predictor Retail-R52
94Upper Deck Predictor Retail Exchange-R4
94Upper Deck Predictor Retail Exchange-R23
94Upper Deck Predictor Retail Exchange-R36
94Upper Deck Predictor Retail Exchange-R52
94Upper Deck SP Inserts-SP113
94Upper Deck SP Inserts Die Cuts-SP113
94Upper Deck NHLPA/Be A Player-5
94Finnish Jaa Kiekko-146
94Finnish Jaa Kiekko-348
95SLU Hockey American-6
95Bashan Super Stickers-36
95Bashan Super Stickers-38
95Be A Player Lethal Lines-LL8
95Bowman-80
All-Foil-80
Bowman's Best-BB12
Bowman's Best Refractors-BB12
95Canada Games NHL POGS-95
95Collector's Choice-148
95Collector's Choice-365
Player's Club-148
Player's Club-365
Player's Club Platinum-148
Player's Club Platinum-365
Crash The Game-C2A
Crash The Game-C2B
Crash The Game-C2C
Crash The Game Gold-C2A
Crash The Game Gold-C2B
Crash The Game Gold-C2C
Crash the Game Silver Redeemed-C2
Crash the Game Silver Bonus-C2
Crash the Game Gold Redeemed-C2
Crash the Game Gold Bonus-C2
95Donruss-285
Dominators-5
Elite Inserts-4
95Donruss Elite-53
Die Cut Stars-53
Die Cut Uncut-53
Cutting Edge-9
95Emotion-53
Xcel-3
Xcited-4
95Finest-95
95Finest-186
Refractors-95
Refractors-186
95Hoyle Western Playing Cards-27
95Imperial Stickers-38
95Kenner Starting Lineup Cards-7
95Kraft-1
95Leaf-34
Fire On Ice-7
95Leaf Limited-49
Stars of the Game-11
95McDonald's Pinnacle-MCD-17
95Metal-45
Heavy Metal-2
International Steel-3
95NHL Aces Playing Cards-11H
95NHL Cool Trade-7
95NHL Cool Trade-RP7
95Panini Stickers-178
95Parkhurst International-238
95Parkhurst International-337
Emerald Ice-238
Emerald Ice-337
All-Stars-4
Crown Collection Silver Series 1-14
Crown Collection Gold Series 1-14
Parkie's Trophy Picks-PP3
Parkie's Trophy Picks-PP52
95Pinnacle-44
Artist's Proofs-44
Rink Collection-44
Clear Shots-7
Global Gold-7
Roaring 20s-6
95Pinnacle FANtasy-30
95Playoff One on One-34
95Playoff One on One-144
95Playoff One on One-253
95Pro Magnets-102
95Score-100
Black Ice Artist's Proofs-100
Black Ice-100
Border Battle-13
Dream Team-2
Lamplighters-5
95Select Certified-29
Mirror Gold-29
Double Strike-14
Double Strike Gold-14
95SkyBox Impact-52
Countdown to Impact-6
Ice Quake-9
95SP-44
Holoviews-FX5
Holoviews Special FX-FX5
Stars/Etoiles-E12
Stars/Etoiles Gold-E12
95Stadium Club Members Only-36
95Stadium Club-169
Members Only Master Set-169
Nemeses-N7
Nemeses Members Only Master Set-N7
95Summit-31
Artist's Proofs-31
Ice-31
GM's Choice-15
Mad Hatters-9
95Topps-185
95Topps-373
OPC Inserts-185
OPC Inserts-373
Marquee Men Power Boosters-373
Mystery Finest-M5
Mystery Finest Refractors-M5
Power Lines-8PL
Profiles-PF5
95Topps SuperSkills-34
Platinum-34
95Ultra-45
95Ultra-381
Gold Medallion-45
Extra Attackers-4
Premier Pivots-1
Premier Pivots Gold Medallion-1
Ultraview-1
Ultraview Hot Pack-1
95Upper Deck-215
95Upper Deck-279
Electric Ice-215
Electric Ice-279
Electric Ice Gold-215
Electric Ice Gold-279
95Upper Deck All-Star Game Predictors-2
Redemption Winners-2
95Upper Deck Freeze Frame-F8
95Upper Deck Freeze Frame Jumbo-F8
95Upper Deck NHL All-Stars-AS15
95Upper Deck NHL All-Stars Jumbo-AS15
95Upper Deck Predictor Hobby-H6
95Upper Deck Predictor Hobby Exchange-H6
95Upper Deck Predictor Retail-R24
95Upper Deck Predictor Retail-R34
95Upper Deck Predictor Retail-R44
95Upper Deck Predictor Retail Exchange-R24
95Upper Deck Predictor Retail Exchange-R34
95Upper Deck Predictor Retail Exchange-R44
95Upper Deck Special Edition-SE115
95Upper Deck Special Edition Gold-SE115
95Zenith-30
Z-Team-9
95Swedish Globe World Championships-175
95Swedish World Championships Stickers-282
96SLU Hockey Canadian-3
96Headliners Hockey-5
96SLU Hockey American-5
96Be A Player Biscuit In The Basket-7
96Black Diamond-155
Gold-155
Run for the Cup-RC12
96Collector's Choice-80
96Collector's Choice-316
MVP-UD13
MVP Gold-UD13
Stick'Ums-S23
96Donruss-50
Press Proofs-50
Dominators-9
Elite Inserts-8
Elite Inserts Gold-8
96Donruss Canadian Ice-55
Gold Press Proofs-55
Red Press Proofs-55
96Donruss Elite-9
Die Cut Stars-9
Status-3
96Flair-26
Blue Ice-26
Center Ice Spotlight-2
96Fleer-30
96Fleer-142
96Fleer-143
Art Ross-2
Pearson-2
Picks Dream Lines-4
Picks Fabulous 50-10
Picks Fantasy Force-9
96Hockey Greats Coins-6
Gold-6
96Kenner Starting Lineup Cards-5
96Kraft Upper Deck-25
96Kraft Upper Deck-59
96Leaf-1

Press Proofs-1
96Leaf Leather And Laces Promos-P16
96Leaf Leather And Laces-16
96Leaf Sweaters Away-11
96Leaf Sweaters Home-11
96Leaf Limited-61
Gold-61
96Leaf Preferred-65
Press Proofs-65
Steel-1
Steel Gold-1
Steel Power-7
96Maggers-22
96McDonald's Pinnacle-26
96Metal Universe-45
Ice Carvings-5
Ice Carvings Super Power-5
Lethal Weapons-3
Lethal Weapons Super Power-3
96NHL Aces Playing Cards-11
96NHL Pro Stamps-102
96Pinnacle-21
Artist's Proofs-21
Foil-21
Premium Stock-21
Rink Collection-21
By The Numbers-3
By The Numbers Premium-3
Trophies-3
96Pinnacle Fantasy-FC13
96Pinnacle Mint-8
Bronze-8
Gold-8
Silver-8
Coins Brass-8
Coins Solid Gold-8
Coins Gold Plated-8
Coins Nickel-8
Coins Silver-8
96Playoff One on One-437
96Red Wings Detroit News/Free Press-2
96Red Wings Detroit News/Free Press-5
96Score Samples-77
96Score-77
Artist's Proofs-77
Dealer's Choice Artist's Proofs-77
Special Artist's Proofs-77
Golden Blades-77
Dream Team-11
Sudden Death-14
96Select Certified-55
Artist's Proofs-55
Blue-55
Mirror Blue-55
Mirror Gold-55
Mirror Red-55
Red-55
Cornerstones-13
96SkyBox Impact-34
Countdown to Impact-2
VersaTeam-2
96SP-48
Clearcut Winner-CW4
Holoview Collection-HC5
96SPx-13
Gold-13
96Stadium Club Members Only-15
96Summit-105
Artist's Proofs-105
Ice-105
Metal-105
Premium Stock-105
High Voltage-13
High Voltage Mirage-13
Untouchables-10
96Team Out-21
96Topps Picks-17
Fantasy Team-FT17
OPC Inserts-17
Top Shelf-TS11
96Ultra-50
Gold Medallion-50
Power-4
Power Red Line-1
96Upper Deck-206
96Upper Deck-250
Generation Next-X10
Hart Hopefuls Bronze-HH4
Hart Hopefuls Gold-HH4
Hart Hopefuls Silver-HH4
Lord Stanley's Heroes Finals-LS14
Lord Stanley's Heroes Quarterfinals-LS14
Lord Stanley's Heroes Semifinals-LS14
Superstar Showdown-SS8B
96Upper Deck Ice-84
Parallel-84
96Zenith-80
Artist's Proofs-80
Z-Team-5
96Swedish Semic Wien-141
97Headliners Hockey-5
97NHL Pro Zone-10
97Be A Player Take A Number-5
97Beehive-46
Golden Portraits-46
97Black Diamond-82
Double Diamond-82
Triple Diamond-82
Quadruple Diamond-82
97Collector's Choice-79
Star Quest-SQ19
97Crown Royale-45
Emerald Green-45
Ice Blue-45
Silver-45
Blades of Steel Die-Cuts-8
97Donruss-82
Press Proofs Silver-82
Press Proofs Gold-82
Red Alert-3
97Donruss Canadian Ice-72
Dominion Series-72
Provincial Series-72
Stanley Cup Scrapbook-26
97Donruss Elite-96
Aspirations-96
Status-96
Back to the Future-5
Back to the Future Autographs-5
Craftsmen-9
Master Craftsmen-9
97Donruss Limited-98
97Donruss Limited-126
97Donruss Limited-197
Exposure-98
Exposure-126
Exposure-197
Fabric of the Game-6
97Donruss Preferred-122
97Donruss Preferred-165
Cut to the Chase-122
Cut to the Chase-165
Line of the Times-1B
97Donruss Preferred Line of Times Promos-1B
97Donruss Priority-12
97Donruss Priority-214
Stamp of Approval-12
Stamp of Approval-214
Direct Deposit-12
Postcards-15
Stamps-15
Stamps Bronze-15
Stamps Gold-15
Stamps Silver-15
97Esso Olympic Hockey Heroes-36
97Esso Olympic Hockey Heroes French-36
97Highland Mint Mint-Cards Topps-5
97Highland Mint Mint-Cards Topps-6
97Highland Mint Mint-Coins-3
97Jell-O Juniors To Pros-8
97Katch-49
Gold-49
Silver-49
97Kraft-14
97Leaf-135
Fractal Matrix-135
Fractal Matrix Die Cuts-135
Banner Season-16
97Leaf International-135
Universal Ice-135
97Pacific-91
Copper-91
Emerald Green-91
Ice Blue-91
Red-91
Silver-91
Card-Supials-6
Card-Supials Minis-6
Slap Shots Die-Cuts-3B
97Pacific Dynagon-41
Copper-41
Dark Grey-41
Emerald Green-41
Ice Blue-41
Red-41
Silver-41
Best Kept Secrets-32
Dynamic Duos-7A
Tandems-8
97Pacific Invincible-46
Copper-46
Emerald Green-46
Ice Blue-46
Red-46
Silver-46
Attack Zone-9
Feature Performers-12
NHL Regime-69
Off The Glass-7
97Panini Stickers-148
97Paramount-65
Copper-65
Dark Grey-65
Emerald Green-65
Ice Blue-65
Red-65
Silver-65
Big Numbers Die-Cuts-8
97Pinnacle-77
Artist's Proofs-77
Rink Collection-77
Epix Game Emerald-5
Epix Game Orange-5
Epix Game Purple-5
Epix Moment Emerald-5
Epix Moment Orange-5
Epix Moment Purple-5
Epix Play Emerald-5
Epix Play Orange-5
Epix Play Purple-5
Epix Season Emerald-5
Epix Season Orange-5
Epix Season Purple-5
Press Plates Back Black-77
Press Plates Back Cyan-77
Press Plates Back Magenta-77
Press Plates Back Yellow-77
Press Plates Front Black-77
Press Plates Front Cyan-77
Press Plates Front Magenta-77
Press Plates Front Yellow-77
97Pinnacle Certified-56
Red-56
Mirror Blue-56
Mirror Gold-56
Mirror Red-56
97Pinnacle Inside-42
Coach's Collection-42
Executive Collection-42
Track-13
97Pinnacle Mint-14
Bronze-14
Gold Team-14
Silver Team-14
Coins Brass-14
Coins Brass Proofs-14
Coins Gold Plated-14
Coins Gold Plated Proofs-14
Coins Nickel Silver-14
Coins Nickel Silver Proofs-14
Coins Solid Gold-14
Coins Solid Silver-14
97Pinnacle Power Pack Blow-Ups-21
97Pinnacle Tot Cert Platinum Blue-56
97Pinnacle Tot Certi Platinum Gold-56
97Pinnacle Totally Certified Platinum Red-56
97Pinnacle Tot Cert Mirror Platinum Gold-56
97Post Pinnacle-13
97Score-91
97Score-264
Artist's Proofs-91
Golden Blades-91
97Score Red Wings-3
Platinum-3
Premier-3
97SPx-15
Bronze-15
Gold-15
Silver-15
Steel-15
Dimension-SPX11
Grand Finale-15
97Studio-21
Press Proofs Silver-21
Press Proofs Gold-21
Hard Hats-21
Portraits-21
Silhouettes-14
Silhouettes 8x10-14
97Upper Deck-266
Game Dated Moments-266
Game Jerseys-GJ5
Sixth Sense Masters-SS3
Sixth Sense Wizards-SS3
The Specialists-11
The Specialists Level 2 Die Cuts-11
Three Star Selects-7A
97Upper Deck Diamond Vision-23
Signature Moves-23
97Upper Deck Ice-69
Parallel-69
Lethal Lines-L6C
Lethal Lines 2-L6C
Power Shift-69
97Zenith-22
Z-Gold-22
Z-Silver-22
97Zenith 5 x 7-44
Gold Impulse-44
Silver Impulse-44
98SLU Hockey Classic Doubles-2
98Aurora-62
Atomic Laser Cuts-9
Championship Fever-16
Championship Fever Copper-16
Championship Fever Ice Blue-16
Championship Fever Red-16
Championship Fever Silver-16
Cubes-8
98Be A Player-45
Press Release-45
98BAP Gold-45
98BAP Autographs-45
98BAP Autographs Gold-45
98BAP AS Game Used Stick Cards-S14
98BAP AS Game Used Jersey Cards-AS15
98BAP Playoff Game Used Jerseys-G16
98BAP Playoff Game Used Jersey Autographs-G16
98BAP Playoff Highlights-H17
98BAP Playoff Practice Used Jerseys-P8
98BAP Tampa Bay All Star Game-45
98Black Diamond-29
Double Diamond-29
Triple Diamond-29
Quadruple Diamond-29
Myriad-M26
Myriad 2-M26
98Bowman's Best-35
Refractors-35
Atomic Refractors-35
Autographs-A4A
Autographs-A4B
Autographs Refractors-A4A
Autographs Refractors-A4B
Autographs Atomic Refractors-A4A
Autographs Atomic Refractors-A4B
Mirror Image Fusion-F16
Mirror Image Fusion Refractors-F16
Mirror Image Fusion Atomic Refractors-F16
98Crown Royale-44
Limited Series-44
Master Performers-9
Pillars of the Game-12
Pivotal Players-8
98Finest-34
No Protectors-34
No Protectors Refractors-34
Refractors-34
Double Sided Mystery Finest-M32
Double Sided Mystery Finest-M35
Double Sided Mystery Finest-M38
Double Sided Mystery Finest-M39
Double Sided Mystery Refractors-M32
Double Sided Mystery Refractors-M35
Double Sided Mystery Refractors-M38
Double Sided Mystery Refractors-M39
Red Lighters-R6
Red Lighters Refractors-R6
98Katch-49
98OPC Chrome-67
Refractors-67
98Pacific-91
Ice Blue-91
Red-91
Dynagon Ice Inserts-9
Titanium Ice-9
Gold Crown Die-Cuts-13
Trophy Winners-5
98Pacific Dynagon Ice-62
Blue-62
Red-62
Forward Thinking-9
98Pacific Omega-79
Red-79
Opening Day Issue-79
EO Portraits-9
EO Portraits 1 of 1-9
Face to Face-4
Online-14
Planet Ice-13
Planet Ice Parallel-13
Prism-8
98Panini Photocards-21
98Panini Stickers-129
98Paramount-74
Copper-74
Emerald Green-74
Holo-Electric-74
Ice Blue-74
Silver-74
Special Delivery Die-Cuts-7
98Revolution-47
Ice Shadow-47
Red-47
Chalk Talk Laser-Cuts-8
Showstoppers-16
98SP Authentic-28
Power Shift-28
Snapshots-SS29
Stat Masters-S22
98SPx Top Prospects-23
Radiance-23
Spectrum-23
Highlight Heroes-H15
Lasting Impressions-L26
98Topps-67
O-Pee-Chee-67
Local Legends-L13
98Topps Gold Label Class 1-20
Black-20
Black One of One-20
One of One-20
Red-20
Red One of One-20
98Topps Gold Label Class 2-20
98Topps Gold Label Class 2 Black-20
98Topps Gold Label Class 2 Black 1 of 1-20
98Topps Gold Label Class 2 One of One-20
98Topps Gold Label Class 2 Red-20
98Topps Gold Label Class 2 Red One of One-20
98Topps Gold Label Class 3-20
98Topps Gold Label Class 3 Black-20
98Topps Gold Label Class 3 Black 1 of 1-20
98Topps Gold Label Class 3 One of One-20
98Topps Gold Label Class 3 Red-20
98Topps Gold Label Class 3 Red One of One-20
98UD Choice-75
98UD Choice Preview-75
98UD Choice Prime Choice Reserve-75
98UD Choice Reserve-75
98UD3-42
98UD3-102
98UD3-162
Die-Cuts-42
Die-Cuts-102
Die-Cuts-162
98Upper Deck-23
98Upper Deck-262
Exclusives-23
Exclusives-262
Exclusives 1 of 1-23
Exclusives 1 of 1-262
Lord Stanley's Heroes-LS9
Lord Stanley's Heroes Quantum 1-LS9
Lord Stanley's Heroes Quantum 2-LS9
Lord Stanley's Heroes Quantum 3-LS9
Profiles-P29
Profiles Quantum 1-P29
Profiles Quantum 2-P29
Profiles Quantum 3-P29
Gold Reserve-23
Gold Reserve-262
98Upper Deck MVP-68
Gold Script-68
Silver Script-68
Super Script-68
Game Souvenirs-SF
Snipers-S12
98Slovakian Eurotel-2
99Aurora-50
Striped-50
Premiere Date-50
Premiere Date Striped-50
99BAP Memorabilia-87
Gold-87
Silver-87
Jersey Cards-J15
Jersey Emblems-E15
Jersey Numbers-I15
Jersey and Stick Cards-S15
99BAP Update Double AS Jersey Cards-D20
99BAP Update Teammates Jersey Cards-TM5
99BAP Update Teammates Jersey Cards-TM37
99BAP Update Teammates Jersey Cards-TM38
99BAP Millennium Prototypes-4
99BAP Millennium-89
Emerald-89
Ruby-89
Sapphire-89
Signatures-89
Signatures Gold-89
Jerseys-J19
Jersey Autographs-J19
Jersey and Stick Cards-JS19
Jersey Emblems-E19
Jersey Numbers-N19
Pearson-P5
Pearson Autographs-P5
Players of the Decade-D7
Players of the Decade Autographs-D7
99Black Diamond-34
Diamond Cut-34
Final Cut-34
Diamonation-D7
Diamond Skills-DS5
99Crown Royale-49
Limited Series-49
Premiere Date-49
International Glory-9
International Glory Parallel-9
99O-Pee-Chee-120
99O-Pee-Chee Chrome-120
99O-Pee-Chee Chrome Refractors-120
99Pacific-138
Copper-138
Emerald Green-138
Gold-138
Ice Blue-138
Premiere Date-138
Red-138
99Pacific Dynagon Ice-73
Blue-73
Copper-73
Gold-73
Premiere Date-73
99Pacific Omega-81
Copper-81
Gold-81
Ice Blue-81
Premiere Date-81
Cup Contenders-8
99Pacific Prism-50
Holographic Blue-50
Holographic Gold-50
Holographic Mirror-50
Holographic Purple-50
Premiere Date-50
99Panini Stickers-232
99Paramount-80
Copper-80
Emerald-80
Gold-80
Holographic Emerald-80
Holographic Gold-80
Holographic Silver-80
Ice Blue-80
Premiere Date-80
Red-80
Silver-80
Personal Best-16
99Revolution-51
Premiere Date-51
Red-51
Shadow Series-51
Showstoppers-16
Copper-51
Gold-51
CSC Silver-51
99SP Authentic-33
Jersey Redemption-JSF
Sign of the Times-SF
Sign of the Times Gold-SF
Supreme Skill-SS5
99SPx-54
Radiance-54
Spectrum-54
99Stadium Club-38
First Day Issue-38
One of a Kind-38
Printing Plates Black-38
Printing Plates Cyan-38
Printing Plates Magenta-38
Printing Plates Yellow-38
99Topps/OPC-120
99Topps/OPC Chrome-120
Refractors-120
99Topps Gold Label Class 1-22
Black-22
Black One of One-22
One of One-22
Red-22
Red One of One-22
99Topps Gold Label Class 2-22
99Topps Gold Label Class 2 Black-22
99Topps Gold Label Class 2 Black 1 of 1-22
99Topps Gold Label Class 2 One of One-22
99Topps Gold Label Class 2 Red-22
99Topps Gold Label Class 2 Red One of One-22
99Topps Gold Label Class 3-22
99Topps Gold Label Class 3 Black-22
99Topps Gold Label Class 3 Black 1 of 1-22
99Topps Gold Label Class 3 One of One-22
99Topps Gold Label Class 3 Red-22
99Topps Gold Label Class 3 Red One of One-22
99Topps Premier Plus-70
Parallel-70
99Ultimate Victory Smokin Guns-SG3
99Upper Deck-224
Exclusives-224
Exclusives 1 of 1-224
Game Jerseys-SF
Game Jerseys Series II-SF
Game Jersey Patch-SFP
Game Jersey Patch Series II-SFP
99Upper Deck Gold Reserve-224
99Upper Deck HoloGrFx-23
Ausome-23
99Upper Deck MVP-68
Gold Script-68
Silver Script-68
Super Script-68
Draw Your Own Trading Card-W30
99Upper Deck MVP SC Edition-64
Gold Script-64
Silver Script-64
Super Script-64
Great Combinations-GCSF
Great Combinations Parallel-GCSF
Playoff Heroes-PH5
Stanley Cup Talent-SC7
99Upper Deck Ovation-22
Standing Ovation-22
Superstar Theater-ST2
99Upper Deck Retro-28
Gold-28
Platinum-28
99Upper Deck Victory-100
99Wayne Gretzky Hockey-65
Elements of the Game-EG4
99Russian Stars of Hockey-28
00SLU Hockey One On One-10
00Aurora-49
Pinstripes-49
Pinstripes Premiere Date-49
Premiere Date-49
Championship Fever-10
Championship Fever Copper-10
Championship Fever Platinum Blue-10
Championship Fever Silver-10
Scouting Reports-9
00BAP Memorabilia-237
Emerald-237
Ruby-237
Sapphire-237
Promos-237
Jersey Cards-J35
Jersey Emblems-E35
Jersey Numbers-N35
Jersey and Stick Cards-JS35
00BAP Mem Chicago Sportsfest Copper-237
00BAP Memorabilia Chicago Sportsfest Blue-237
00BAP Memorabilia Chicago Sportsfest Gold-237
00BAP Memorabilia Chicago Sportsfest Ruby-237
00BAP Memorabilia Chicago Sun-Times Ruby-237
00BAP Memorabilia Chicago Sun-Times Gold-237
00BAP Mem Chicago Sun-Times Sapphire-237
00BAP Mem Toronto Fall Expo Copper-237
00BAP Memorabilia Toronto Fall Expo Gold-237
00BAP Memorabilia Toronto Fall Expo Ruby-237
00BAP Memorabilia Update Teammates-TM16
00BAP Memorabilia Update Teammates-TM29
00BAP Memorabilia Update Teammates Gold-TM16
00BAP Memorabilia Update Teammates Gold-TM29
00BAP Parkhurst 2000-P85
00BAP Signature Series-105
Emerald-105
Ruby-105
Sapphire-105
Autographs-49
Autographs Gold-49
He Shoots-He Scores Prizes-23
Jersey Cards-J19
Jersey and Stick Cards-GSJ19
Jersey Cards Autographs-J19
Jersey Emblems-E19
Jersey Numbers-IN19
00BAP Ultimate Memorabilia Autographs-19
Gold-19
00BAP Ultimate Mem Dynasty Jerseys-D16
00BAP Ultimate Mem Dynasty Emblems-D16
00BAP Ultimate Mem Game-Used Jerseys-GJ19
00BAP Ultimate Mem Game-Used Emblems-E17
00BAP Ultimate Mem Game-Used Numbers-N17
00BAP Ultimate Mem Game-Used Sticks-GS19
00BAP Ultimate Memorabilia Hart Trophy-H7
00BAP Ultimate Memorabilia Teammates-TM1
00BAP Ultimate Memorabilia Teammates-TM6
00BAP Ultimate Memorabilia Teammates-TM9
00Black Diamond Diamonation-IG3
00Black Diamond Game Gear-GFE
00Crown Royale-38
Ice Blue-38
Limited Series-38
Premiere Date-38
Red-38
00O-Pee-Chee-125
00O-Pee-Chee Parallel-125
00Pacific-147
Copper-147
Gold-147
Ice Blue-147
Premiere Date-147
Euro-Stars-4
00Panini Stickers-151
00Paramount-85
Copper-85
Gold-85
Holo-Gold-85
Holo-Silver-85
Ice Blue-85
Premiere Date-85
Freeze Frame-14
00Private Stock-35
Gold-35
Premiere Date-35
Retail-35
Silver-35
Game Gear-44
Game Gear Patches-44
PS-2001 Action-20
PS-2001 Stars-11
00Revolution-51
Blue-51
Premiere Date-51
Red-51
HD NHL-14
NHL Game Gear-4
00SP Authentic-34
00SP Game Used-23
Patch Cards-P-SF
Tools of the Game-SF
Tools of the Game Exclusives-SF
Tools of the Game Combos-C-BF
00SPx-22
Spectrum-22
SPXcitement-X6
Winning Materials-SF
Winning Materials-WFE
00Stadium Club-184
00Titanium-31
Blue-31
Gold-31
Premiere Date-31
Red-31
Retail-31
All-Stars-3W
Three-Star Selections-14
00Topps/OPC-125
Parallel-125
00Topps Chrome-96
OPC Refractors-96
Refractors-96
00Topps Gold Label Class 1-38
Gold-38
00Topps Gold Label Class 2-38
00Topps Gold Label Class 2 Gold-38
00Topps Gold Label Class 3-38
00Topps Gold Label Class 3 Gold-38
00Topps Gold Label Bullion-B3
00Topps Gold Label Bullion One to One-B3
00Topps Gold Label Game-Worn Jerseys-GLJ-SF
00Topps Gold Label Golden Greats-GG11
00Topps Gold Label Golden Greats 1 to 1-GG11
00Topps Heritage-41
Chrome Parallel-41
Autographs-HA-SF
00Topps Premier Plus-20
Blue Ice-20
Masters of the Break-MB9
Trophy Tribute-TT10
00UD Heroes-42
00UD Pros and Prospects-31
Game Jerseys-SF
Game Jersey Exclusives-SF
ProMotion-PM4
00UD Reserve-31
Gold Strike-GS4
00Upper Deck-63
Exclusives Tier 1-63
Exclusives Tier 2-63
Fun-Damentals-F5
Game Jerseys-SF
Game Jerseys-SF
Game Jersey Autographs Exclusives-ESF
Game Jersey Autographs Exclusives-ESSF
Game Jersey Combos-DFB
Game Jersey Patches-PSF
Game Jersey Patches-SFP
Game Jersey Patch Autographs Exclusives-SFP
Game Jersey Patch Exclusives Series II-ESF
Skilled Stars-SS9
Triple Threat-TT7
00Upper Deck Ice-70
Game Jerseys-JCSF
00Upper Deck Legends Epic Signatures-SF
00Upper Deck Legends Legendary Jerseys-JSF
00Upper Deck MVP-69
First Stars-69
Game-Used Souvenirs-GSSF
Second Stars-69
Super Game-Used Souvenirs-GSSF
Talent-M7
Third Stars-69
00Upper Deck Victory-85
00Upper Deck Victory-301
00Upper Deck Vintage-127
00Vanguard-37
Dual Game-Worn Jerseys-6
Dual Game-Worn Patches-6
Holographic Gold-37
Holographic Purple-37
In Focus-8
Pacific Proofs-37
Press East/West-6
01Atomic-35
Blue-35
Gold-35
Premiere Date-35
Red-35
Power Play-12
01BAP Memorabilia-75
Emerald-75
Ruby-75
Sapphire-75
Country of Origin-CO59
He Shoots-He Scores Prizes-18
Stanley Cup Playoffs-SC12
01BAP Signature Series Certified 100-C38
01BAP Signature Series Certified 50-C38
01BAP Signature Series Certified 1 of 1's-C38
01BAP Signature Series Autographs-LSF
01BAP Signature Series Autographs Gold-LSF
01BAP Sig Series He Shoots/Scores Points-2
01BAP Sig Series He Shoots/Scores Prizes-17
01BAP Signature Series Jerseys-GJ-21
01BAP Signature Series Jersey Autographs-GUSF
01BAP Sig Series Jersey and Stick Cards-GSJ-21
01BAP Signature Series Emblems-GUE-20
01BAP Signature Series Numbers-ITN-20
01BAP Ultimate Memorabilia Autographs-34
01BAP Ultimate Mem Autographs Gold-34
01BAP Ultimate Memorabilia Dynamic Duos-16
01BAP Ultimate Memorabilia Emblems-20
01BAP Ultimate Memorabilia Gloves Are Off-21
01BAP Ultimate Memorabilia Jerseys-20
01BAP Ultimate Mem Jerseys and Sticks-20
01BAP Ultimate Memorabilia Numbers-15
01BAP Ultimate Memorabilia Name Plates-35
01Bowman YoungStars-74
Gold-74
Ice Cubed-74
01Crown Royale-51
Blue-51
Premiere Date-51
Red-51
Retail-51
01eTopps-28
01McDonald's Pacific-11
01O-Pee-Chee-53
01O-Pee-Chee Heritage Parallel-53
01O-Pee-Chee Heritage Parallel Limited-53
01O-Pee-Chee Premier Parallel-53
01Pacific-139
01Pacific-429
Extreme LTD-139
Gold-429
Hobby LTD-139
Premiere Date-139
Retail LTD-139
All-Stars-W3
Gold Crown Die-Cuts-9
01Pacific Adrenaline-64
Blue-64
Premiere Date-64
Red-64
Retail-64
01Pacific Arena Exclusives-139
01Pacific Arena Exclusives-429
01Pacific Heads-Up-34
Blue-34
Premiere Date-34
Red-34
Silver-34
01Parkhurst-96
Gold-96
Silver-96
He Shoots-He Scores Prizes-15
Jerseys-PJ55
Jersey and Stick-PSJ9
Sticks-PS40
01Private Stock-32
Gold-32
Premiere Date-32
Retail-32
Silver-32
01Private Stock Pacific Nights-32
01SP Authentic-29
Limited-29
Limited Gold-29
01SP Game Used Authentic Fabric-AFSF
01SP Game Used Authentic Fabric-DFFS
01SP Game Used Authentic Fabric-TFYSF
01SP Game Used Authentic Fabric-YSFO
01SP Game Used Authentic Fabric Gold-AFSF
01SP Game Used Patches-PSF
01SP Game Used Patches-CPYF
01SP Game Used Tools of the Game-TSF
01SP Game Used Tools of the Game-CTFF
01SP Game Used Tools of the Game-CTFR
01SP Game Used Tools of the Game-CTSF
01SP Game Used Tools of the Game-TTFCF
01SP Game Used Tools of the Game-TTFSL
01SPx-24
01SPx-74
Hockey Treasures-HTSF
01Stadium Club-32
Award Winners-32
Master Photos-32
Gallery-G22
Gallery Gold-G22
NHL Passport-NHLP5
Perennials-P12
Souvenirs-SF
Souvenirs-SFPB
01Titanium-48
Hobby Parallel-48
Premiere Date-48
Retail-48
Retail Parallel-48
All-Stars-7
01Topps-53
Heritage Parallel-53
Heritage Parallel Limited-53
OPC Parallel-53
Stars of the Game-SG9
01Topps Chrome-53
Refractors-53
Black Border Refractors-53
01Topps Heritage-44
Refractors-44
Jerseys-JSF
01Topps Reserve-28
Emblems-SF
Jerseys-SF
Name Plates-SF
Numbers-SF
Patches-SF
01UD Challenge for the Cup Century Men-CM4
01UD Honor Roll-95
Defense First-DF4
Jerseys-J-SF
Jerseys Gold-J-SF
Sharp Skaters-SS3
01UD Mask Collection-35
Gold-35
Double Patches-DPSF
Dual Jerseys-PMFT
Gloves-GGSF
Jerseys-J-SF
Jersey and Patch-JPSF
01UD Premier Collection-24
Dual Jerseys-DFB
Dual Jerseys Black-DFB
Jerseys-BSF
Jerseys Black-B-SF
01UD Stanley Cup Champs-56
Jerseys-T-SF
Pieces of Glory-G-SF
Sticks-S-SF
01UD Top Shelf-93
Jerseys-SF
Sticks-SSF
Sticks Gold-SSF
01Upper Deck-294
Exclusives-294
Game Jerseys-YSF
Game Jerseys Series II-FJSF
Game Jerseys Series II-DJFS
Game Jerseys Series II-TJYFS
Patches-PSF
Patches Series II-PLSF
Pride of a Nation-PNSF
Pride of a Nation-DPFK
Pride of a Nation-TPFKK
01Upper Deck Ice-17
Combos-C-SF
Combos Gold-G-SF
Jerseys-J-SF
01Upper Deck MVP-68
Talent-MT5
Watch-MW5
01Upper Deck Victory-122
01Upper Deck Victory-400
Gold-122
Gold-400
01Upper Deck Vintage-90
01Vanguard-34
Blue-34
Red-34
East Meets West-7
Memorabilia-14
One of Ones-34
Premiere Date-34
Proofs-34
02Atomic-36
Blue-36
Gold-36
Red-36
Hobby Parallel-36
02BAP All-Star Edition-20
02BAP All-Star Edition-21
He Shoots-He Scores Points-11
He Shoots-He Score Prizes-6
Jerseys-20
Jerseys-21
Jerseys Gold-20
Jerseys Gold-21
Jerseys Silver-20
Jerseys Silver-21
02BAP First Edition-105
02BAP First Edition-304
02BAP First Edition-398
He Shoots-He Score Points-2
He Shoots-He Scores Prizes-20
Jerseys-105
02BAP Memorabilia-133
Emerald-133
Ruby-133
Sapphire-133
All-Star Jerseys-ASJ-12
All-Star Emblems-ASE-3
All-Star Numbers-ASN-3
All-Star Starting Lineup-AS-10
All-Star Teammmates-AST-1
All-Star Teammmates-AST-30
He Shoots-He Scores Prizes-28
NHL All-Star Game-133
NHL All-Star Game Blue-133
NHL All-Star Game Green-133
NHL All-Star Game Red-133
Stanley Cup Champions-SCC-10
Stanley Cup Playoffs-SC-21
Teammates-TM-2
02BAP Memorabilia Toronto Fall Expo-133
02BAP Signature Series-148
Autographs-148
Autograph Buybacks 1998-45
Autograph Buybacks 1999-89
Autograph Buybacks 2000-49
Autographs Gold-148
Jerseys-SGJ36
Jersey Autographs-SGJ36
Team Quads-TQ13
Triple Memorabilia-TM8
02BAP Ultimate Memorabilia Autographs-14
02BAP Ultimate Mem Autographs Gold-14
02BAP Ultimate Memorabilia Dynamic Duos-3
02BAP Ultimate Mem Dynasty Jerseys-17
02BAP Ultimate Mem Dynasty Emblems-17
02BAP Ultimate Mem Dynasty Numbers-17
02BAP Ultimate Memorabilia Emblems-22
02BAP Ultimate Memorabilia Gloves Are Off-9
02BAP Ultimate Memorabilia Hat Tricks-9
02BAP Ultimate Memorabilia Jerseys-34
02BAP Ultimate Mem Jersey and Stick-28
02BAP Ultimate Mem Lifetime Achievers-1
02BAP Ultimate Memorabilia Numbers-3
02BAP Ultimate Mem Playoff Scorers-8
02Bowman YoungStars-97
Gold-97
Silver-97
02Crown Royale-32
Blue-32
Red-32
Retail-32
Dual Patches-9
02eTopps-12
02ITG Used-29
02ITG Used-129
Jerseys-GUJ36
Jersey Autographs-GUJ36
Jerseys Gold-GUJ36
Emblems-E34
Jersey and Stick-SJ36
Jersey and Stick Gold-SJ36
Teammates-T20
Teammates Gold-T20
Triple Memorabilia-TM11
Triple Memorabilia Gold-TM11
02McDonald's Pacific Cup Contenders-3
02Nextel NHL All-Star Game-3
02O-Pee-Chee-46
02O-Pee-Chee Premier Blue Parallel-46
02O-Pee-Chee Premier Red Parallel-46
02O-Pee-Chee Factory Set-46
02Pacific-127
Blue-127
Red-127
Jerseys-16
Jerseys Holo-Silver-16
02Pacific Calder-22
Silver-22
02Pacific Complete-104
Red-104
02Pacific Exclusive-62
Jerseys-7
Jerseys Gold-7
Maximum Overdrive-9
02Pacific Heads-Up-41
Blue-41
Purple-41
Red-41
Quad Jerseys-9
Quad Jerseys-30
Quad Jerseys Gold-9
Quad Jerseys Gold-30
02Pacific Quest for the Cup-32
Gold-32
Raising the Cup-5
02Parkhurst-73
Bronze-73
Gold-73
Silver-73
Jerseys-GJ28
Patented Power-PP7
Stick and Jerseys-SJ28
Teammates-TT4
02Parkhurst Retro-44
Minis-44
He Shoots-He Scores Prizes-28
Jerseys-RJ28
Jersey and Sticks-RSJ28
Memorabilia-RM13
02Private Stock Reserve-116
Red-116
Retail-116
Patches-116
02SP Authentic-35

Beckett Promos-35
Super Premiums-SPSF
02SP Game Used Authentic Fabrics-AFFV
02SP Game Used Authentic Fabrics-AFSF
02SP Game Used Authentic Fabrics Gold-AFFV
02SP Game Used Authentic Fabrics Gold-AFSF
02SP Game Used Authentic Fabrics Rainbow-AFFV
02SP Game Used Authentic Fabrics Rainbow-AFSF
02SP Game Used Piece of History-PHFV
02SP Game Used Piece of History-PHSF
02SP Game Used Piece of History Gold-PHFV
02SP Game Used Piece of History Gold-PHSF
02SP Game Used Piece of History Rainbow-PHFV
02SP Game Used Piece of History Rainbow-PHSF
02SP Game Used Tools of the Game-SF
02SPx-27
02SPx-141
Spectrum Gold-27
Spectrum Silver-27
Milestones-MSF
Milestones Gold-SF
Milestones Silver-SF
Xtreme Talents-SF
Xtreme Talents Gold-SF
Xtreme Talents Silver-SF
02Stadium Club-19
Silver Decoy Cards-19
Proofs-19
World Stage-WS1
02Titanium-35
Blue-35
Red-35
Retail-35
Jerseys-23
Jerseys Retail-23
Patches-23
02Topps-46
OPC Blue Parallel-46
OPC Red Parallel-46
Factory Set-46
02Topps Chrome-38
Black Border Refractors-38
Refractors-38
02Topps Heritage-63
Chrome Parallel-63
02Topps Total-157
Production-TP7
02UD Artistic Impressions-33
Gold-33
Artist's Touch-ATSF
Artist's Touch Gold-ATSF
02UD Artistic Impressions Beckett Promos-33
02UD Artistic Impressions Common Ground-CG16
02UD Artistic Impress Common Ground Gold-CG16
02UD Artistic Impressions Flashbacks-UD8
02UD Artistic Impressions Flashbacks Gold-UD8
02UD Artistic Impressions Retrospectives-R33
02UD Artistic Impressions Retrospect Gold-R33
02UD Artistic Impress Retrospect Silver-R33
02UD Honor Roll-25
Grade A Jerseys-TYFS
Students of the Game-SG14
02UD Mask Collection Patches-PGSF
02UD Piece of History-33
02UD Piece of History-106
Awards Collection-AC15
Patches-PHSF
Threads-TTSF
02UD Premier Collection Jerseys Bronze-SF
02UD Premier Collection Jerseys Bronze-SV
02UD Premier Collection Jerseys Bronze-FJ
02UD Premier Collection Jerseys Gold-SF
02UD Premier Collection Jerseys Gold-SV
02UD Premier Collection Jerseys Gold-FJ
02UD Premier Collection Jerseys Silver-SF
02UD Premier Collection Jerseys Silver-SV
02UD Premier Collection Jerseys Silver-FJ
02UD Premier Collection Patches-PSF
02UD Top Shelf-30
All-Stars-ASSF
Clutch Performers-CPSF
Dual Player Jerseys-RFA
Dual Player Jerseys-STFL
Goal Oriented-GOSF
Hardware Heroes-HFYGC
Shooting Stars-SHSF
Sweet Sweaters-SWSF
02Upper Deck-62
Exclusives-62
All-Star Jerseys-ASSF
Patch Card Name Plate-SF
Patchwork-PWSF
Pinpoint Accuracy-PASF
Playbooks-PL6
Playbooks Series II-YF
Reaching Fifty-50SF
Reaching Fifty Gold-50SF
Specialists-SSF
Speed Demons-SDSF
02Upper Deck Classic Portraits-36
Headliners-LF
Headliners Limited-LF
Hockey Royalty-KFB
Hockey Royalty Limited-KFB
Stitches-CSF
Stitches Limited-CSF
02Upper Deck MVP Overdrive-SO8
02Upper Deck Rookie Update-39
02Upper Deck Victory-75
Bronze-75
Gold-75
Silver-75
National Pride-NP34
02Upper Deck Vintage-89
02Upper Deck Vintage-271
Green Backs-89
Tall Boys-T26
Tall Boys Gold-T26
02Vanguard-35
LTD-35
East Meets West-4
Jerseys-17
Jerseys Gold-17
02Russian Olympic Faces-3
02Russian Olympic Faces-4
02Russian Olympic Team-2
03BAP Memorabilia-85
Emerald-85
Gold-85
Ruby-85
Sapphire-85
All-Star Jerseys-ASJ-11
He Shoots-He Scores Points-17
He Shoots-He Scores Prizes-9
Jerseys-GJ-50
03BAP Ultimate Memorabilia Autographs-32
Gold-32
03BAP Ultimate Mem Auto Sticks-32
03BAP Ultimate Mem Always An All-Star-10
03BAP Ultimate Mem Always An AS Gold-10
03BAP Ultimate Mem Complete Jersey-11
03BAP Ultimate Mem Complete Jersey Gold-11
03BAP Ultimate Memorabilia Dynamic Duos-7
03BAP Ultimate Memorabilia Emblems-27
03BAP Ultimate Memorabilia Emblems Gold-27
03BAP Ultimate Mem Franch Present Future-1
03BAP Ultimate Memorabilia Jerseys-3
03BAP Ultimate Memorabilia Jerseys Gold-3
03BAP Ultimate Mem Jersey and Emblems-37
03BAP Ultimate Mem Jersey and Emblem Gold-37
03BAP Ultimate Mem Jersey and Numbers-37
03BAP Ultimate Mem Jersey and Number Gold-37
03BAP Ultimate Mem Journey Jerseys-1
03BAP Ultimate Mem Journey Jerseys Gold-1
03BAP Ultimate Mem Journey Emblems-1
03BAP Ultimate Mem Journey Emblems Gold-1
03BAP Ultimate Memorabilia Nameplates-1
03BAP Ultimate Mem Nameplates Gold-1
03BAP Ultimate Memorabilia Numbers-2
03BAP Ultimate Memorabilia Numbers Gold-2
03Beehive-5
Variations-5
Gold-5
Silver-5
Jumbos-2
Jumbo Variations-2
Jumbo Jerseys-BH12
Jerseys-JT35
Sticks Red Border-RE20
03Black Diamond-176
Black-176
Green-176
Red-176
03Bowman-91
Gold-91
03Bowman Chrome-91
Refractors-91
Gold Refractors-91
Xfractors-91
03Crown Royale-1
Blue-1
Retail-1
Global Conquest-6
Jerseys-1
Patches-1
Lords of the Rink-1
03eTopps-22
03ITG Action-207
03ITG Action-515
03ITG Action-653
Center of Attention-CA7
Jerseys-M183
Jerseys-M203
03ITG Used Signature Series-51
Gold-51
Autographs-SF
Autographs Gold-SF
Franchise-1
Franchise Autographs-1
Franchise Gold-1
Jerseys-50
Jerseys Gold-50
Jersey Autos-50
Emblems-9
Emblems Gold-9
Jersey and Stick-50
Jersey and Stick Gold-50
Teammates-14
Teammates Gold-14
03McDonald's Pacific-17
03NHL Sticker Collection-213
03O-Pee-Chee-90
03OPC Blue-90
03OPC Gold-90
03OPC Red-90
03Pacific-117
Blue-117
Red-117
View from the Crease-5
03Pacific Calder-1
Silver-1
03Pacific Complete-360
Red-360
03Pacific Exhibit-151
Blue Backs-151
03Pacific Heads-Up-1
Hobby LTD-1
Retail LTD-1
Fast Forwards-1
Fast Forwards LTD-1
In Focus-1
In Focus LTD-1
03Pacific Invincible-2
Blue-2
Red-2
Retail-2
Top Line-1
03Pacific Luxury Suite-1A
03Pacific Luxury Suite-1B
03Pacific Luxury Suite-1C
03Pacific Luxury Suite-1D
03Pacific Luxury Suite-24A
03Pacific Luxury Suite-24B
03Pacific Luxury Suite-24C
03Pacific Prism-116
Blue-116
Patches-116
Red-116
Retail-116
03Pacific Quest for the Cup-1
Blue-1
Raising the Cup-1
03Pacific Supreme-1
Blue-1
Red-1
Retail-1
Jerseys-1
03Parkhurst Original Six Detroit-97
Memorabilia-DM3
Memorabilia-DM18
Memorabilia-DM20
03Parkhurst Rookie-35
Jerseys-GJ-30
Jersey Autographs-GUJ-SF
Jerseys Gold-GJ-30
Jersey and Sticks-SJ-20
Jersey and Sticks Gold-SJ-20
Retro Rookies-RR-14
Retro Rookies Gold-RR-14
Teammates Gold-RT2
Teammates-RT2
03Private Stock Reserve-141
Blue-141
Patches-141
Red-141
Retail-141
Moments in Time-1
03SP Authentic-2
Limited-2
10th Anniversary-SP8
10th Anniversary Limited-SP8
Breakout Seasons-B8
Breakout Seasons Limited-B8
Foundations-F1
Foundations Limited-F1
Sign of the Times-SF
Sign of the Times-CF
Sign of the Times-FG
Sign of the Times-GCF
03SP Game Used-2
Gold-2
Authentic Fabrics-AFSF
Authentic Fabrics Gold-AFSF
Authentic Patches-APSF
Double Threads-DTSF
Limited Threads-LTSF
Limited Threads Gold-LTSF
Premium Patches-PPSF
Signers-SPSSF
Team Threads-TTFGC
03SPx-3
03SPx-138
03SPx-183
Radiance-3
Radiance-138
Radiance-183
Spectrum-3
Spectrum-138
Spectrum-183
Fantasy Franchise-FF-FGC
Fantasy Franchise-FF-KFB
Fantasy Franchise Limited-FF-FGC
Fantasy Franchise Limited-FF-KFB
Origins-O-SF
Signature Threads-ST-SF
Style-SPX-LH
Style Limited-SPX-LH
VIP-VIP-FG
VIP Limited-VIP-FG
Winning Materials-WM-SF
Winning Materials Limited-WM-SF
03Titanium-142
Hobby Jersey Number Parallels-142
Retail-142
Stat Masters-1
03Topps-90
Blue-90
Gold-90
Red-90
Topps/OPC Idols-II8
03Topps Pristine-45
Gold Refractor Die Cuts-45
Refractors-45
Press Plates Black-45
Press Plates Cyan-45
Press Plates Magenta-45
Press Plates Yellow-45
03Topps Traded-TT20
Blue-TT20
Gold-TT20
Red-TT20
03UD Honor Roll-2
03UD Honor Roll-117
Signature Class-SC5
03UD Premier Collection-2
Stars-ST-SF
Stars Patches-ST-SF
Teammates-PT-AM
Teammates Patches-PT-AM
03Upper Deck-5
Big Playmakers-BP-SF
BuyBacks-71
BuyBacks-72
BuyBacks-73
BuyBacks-74
BuyBacks-75
BuyBacks-76
BuyBacks-77
BuyBacks-78
BuyBacks-79
BuyBacks-80
BuyBacks-81
BuyBacks-82
BuyBacks-83
BuyBacks-84
Canadian Exclusives-5
Franchise Fabrics-FF-SF
HG-5
Jersey Autographs-SJ-SF
Magic Moments-MM-14
Memorable Matchups-MM-FK
NHL Best-NB-PS
03Upper Deck Classic Portraits-1
03Upper Deck Ice-1
Gold-1
03Upper Deck MVP-8
03Upper Deck MVP-142
Gold Script-8
Gold Script-142
Silver Script-8
Silver Script-142
Canadian Exclusives-8
Canadian Exclusives-142
SportsNut-SN32
03Upper Deck Rookie Update-3
03Upper Deck Rookie Update-156
Skills-SKSF
Super Stars-SSSF
03Upper Deck Trilogy-1
03Upper Deck Trilogy-102
Authentic Patches-AP22
Crest Variations-102
Limited-1
Limited-102
03Upper Deck Victory-62
Bronze-62
Gold-62
Silver-62
Game Breakers-GB43
04Pacific-2
Blue-2
Red-2
Philadelphia-1
04SP Authentic-3
04SP Authentic-97
04UD Toronto Fall Expo Priority Signings-SF
04Ultimate Collection Dual Logos-UL2-FG
04Ultimate Collection Patches-UP-SF
04Upper Deck-4
1997 Game Jerseys-SF
Big Playmakers-BP-EF
Canadian Exclusives-4
HG Glossy Gold-4
HG Glossy Silver-4
Jersey Autographs-GJA-SF
05Be A Player Outtakes-OT2
05Beehive-27
05Beehive-242
Beige -27
Blue -27
Gold-27
Red -27
Matte-27
Matted Materials-MMSF
05Black Diamond-87
Emerald-87
Gold-87
Onyx-87
Ruby-87
Jerseys-J-SF
Jerseys Ruby-J-SF
Jersey Duals-DJ-SF
Jersey Triples-TJ-SF
Jersey Quads-QJ-SF
05Hot Prospects-28
En Fuego-28
Red Hot-28
White Hot-28
05McDonalds Upper Deck-3
Jerseys-MJ14
Patches-MP14
05Panini Stickers-246
05Parkhurst-138
Facsimile Auto Parallel-138
True Colors-TCCLB
True Colors-TCCLB
05SP Authentic-30
Limited-30
05SP Game Used-30
Gold-30
Authentic Fabrics-AF-SF
Authentic Fabrics Gold-AF-SF
Authentic Fabrics Quad-NZDF
Authentic Patches Quad -NZDL
Authentic Fabrics Triple-DKF
Authentic Patches-AP-SF
Authentic Patches Triple-DKF
Awesome Authentics-AA-SF
By the Letter-LM-SF
05SPx-2
Spectrum-2
Winning Combos-WC-AN
Winning Combos-WC-FG
Winning Combos-WC-FR
Winning Combos Gold-WC-AN
Winning Combos Gold-WC-FG
Winning Combos Gold-WC-FR
Winning Combos Spectrum-WC-AN
Winning Combos Spectrum-WC-FG
Winning Combos Spectrum-WC-FR
Winning Materials-WM-SF
Winning Materials Gold-WM-SF
Winning Materials Spectrum-WM-SF
Xcitement Superstars-XS-SF
Xcitement Superstars Gold-XS-SF
Xcitement Superstars Spectrum-XS-SF
05The Cup-34
Gold-34
Black Rainbow-34
Masterpiece Pressplates-34
Noble Numbers Dual-DNNFD
Noble Numbers Dual-DNNFN
Patch Variation-P34
05UD Artifacts-2
05UD Artifacts-151
Blue-2
Blue-151
Gold-2
Gold-151
Green-2
Green-151
Pewter-2
Pewter-151
Red-2
Red-151
Gold Autographed-2
Gold Autographed-151
Treasured Patches-TP-SF
Treasured Patches Autographed-TP-SF
Treasured Patches Dual-TPD-SF
Treasured Patches Dual Autographed-TPD-SF
Treasured Patches Pewter-TP-SF
Treasured Patches Silver-TP-SF
Treasured Swatches-TS-SF
Treasured Swatches Autographed-TS-SF
Treasured Swatches Blue-TS-SF
Treasured Swatches Copper-TS-SF
Treasured Swatches Dual-TSD-SF
Treasured Swatches Dual Autographed-TSD-SF
Treasured Swatches Dual Blue-TSD-SF
Treasured Swatches Dual Copper-TSD-SF
Treasured Swatches Dual Maroon-TSD-SF
Treasured Swatches Dual Pewter-TSD-SF
Treasured Swatches Dual Silver-TSD-SF
Treasured Swatches Maroon-TS-SF
Treasured Swatches Pewter-TS-SF
Treasured Swatches Silver-TS-SF
05UD PowerPlay-3
05UD PowerPlay-91
Rainbow-3
05Ultimate Collection-28
Gold-28
Premium Patches-PPSF
Ultimate Patches-PSF
05Ultra-66
Gold-66
Ice-66
Scoring Kings-SK22
Scoring Kings Jerseys-SKJ-SF
Scoring Kings Patches-SKP-SF
05Upper Deck-1
05Upper Deck-302
05Upper Deck All-Time Greatest-72
05Upper Deck Big Playmakers-B-SF
05Upper Deck HG Glossy-1
05Upper Deck Jerseys-J-SF
05Upper Deck NHL Generations-DFD
05Upper Deck NHL Generations-TFKA
05Upper Deck Patches-P-SF
05Upper Deck Scrapbooks-HS29
05Upper Deck Shooting Stars-S-SF
05Upper Deck Ice-27
Rainbow-27
05Upper Deck MVP-1
Gold-1
Platinum-1
05Upper Deck Rookie Update-29
05Upper Deck Trilogy-3
05Upper Deck Trilogy-92
Crystal-92
Honorary Patches-HP-SF
Honorary Patch Scripts-HSP-SF
Honorary Swatches-HS-SF
Honorary Swatch Scripts-HSS-SF
05Upper Deck Toronto Fall Expo-1
05Upper Deck Victory-3
05Upper Deck Victory-213
Black-3
Black-213
Gold-3
Gold-213
Silver-3
Silver-213
Game Breakers-GB1
06Be A Player-130
Autographs-130
Profiles-PP5
Profiles Autographs-PP5
Signatures-SF
Signatures 10-144
Signatures 25-144
Signatures Duals-DFZ
Signatures Trios-TFVB
Signatures Foursomes-FOFKF
Up Close and Personal-UC53
Up Close and Personal Autographs-UC53
06Be A Player Portraits-33
Dual Signature Portraits-DSFN
Sensational Six-SSSTR
Signature Portraits-SPSF
Triple Signature Portraits-TCLB
06Beehive-74
Blue-74
Gold-74
Matte-74
Red Facsimile Signatures-74
Wood-74
5 X 7 Black and White-74
06Black Diamond-98
Black-98
Gold-98
Ruby-98
Jerseys-JSF
Jerseys Black-JSF
Jerseys Gold-JSF
Jerseys Ruby-JSF
06Flair Showcase-33
06Flair Showcase-122
06Flair Showcase-224
Parallel-33
Parallel-122
Parallel-224
Hot Numbers-HN14
Hot Numbers Parallel-HN14
06Fleer-56
Tiffany-56
Fabricology-FSF
Speed Machines-SM9
06Hot Prospects-30
Red Hot-30
White Hot-30
06NHL POG-55
06O-Pee-Chee-155
Rainbow-155
Swatches-S-SF
06Panini Stickers-233
06SP Authentic-74
Limited-74
06SP Game Used-29
Gold-29
Rainbow-29
Authentic Fabrics-AFSF
Authentic Fabrics Parallel-AFSF
Authentic Fabrics Patches-AFSF
Authentic Fabrics Dual-AF2NF
Authentic Fabrics Dual Patches-AF2NF
Authentic Fabrics Triple-AF3CLB
Authentic Fabrics Triple Patches-AF3CLB
Authentic Fabrics Sixes-AF6SEL
Authentic Fabrics Sixes Patches-AF6SEL
Authentic Fabrics Eights-AF8RUS
Authentic Fabrics Eights Patches-AF8RUS
By The Letter-BLSF
06SPx-27
06SPx-107
Spectrum-27
Spectrum-107
SPxcitement-X27
SPxcitement Spectrum-X27
Winning Materials-WMSF
Winning Materials Spectrum-WMSF
06The Cup-25
Black Rainbow-25
Foundations-CQSF
Foundations Patches-CQSF
Gold-25
Gold Patches-25
Jerseys-25
Masterpiece Pressplates-25
NHL Shields Duals-DSHFD
NHL Shields Duals-DSHFZ
06UD Artifacts-73
Blue-73
Gold-73
Platinum-73
Radiance-73
Red-73
Treasured Patches Black-TSSF
Treasured Patches Blue-TSSF
Treasured Patches Gold-TSSF
Treasured Patches Platinum-TSSF
Treasured Patches Red-TSSF
Treasured Swatches-TSSF
Treasured Swatches Black-TSSF
Treasured Swatches Blue-TSSF
Treasured Swatches Gold-TSSF
Treasured Swatches Platinum-TSSF
Treasured Swatches Red-TSSF
Tundra Tandems-TTNF
Tundra Tandems Black-TTNF
Tundra Tandems Blue-TTNF
Tundra Tandems Gold-TTNF
Tundra Tandems Platinum-TTNF
Tundra Tandems Red-TTNF
Tundra Tandems Dual Patches Red-TTNF
06UD Mini Jersey Collection-30
06UD Powerplay-30
Impact Rainbow-30
Specialists-SSF
Specialists Patches-PSF
06Ultimate Collection Premium Patches-PS-SF
06Ultimate Collection Premium Swatches-PS-SF
06Ultra-58
Gold Medallion-58
Ice Medallion-58
06Upper Deck Arena Giveaways-CLB6
06Upper Deck-60
Exclusives Parallel-60
High Gloss Parallel-60
All World-AW11
Game Jerseys-J2SF
Generations Duals-G2FD
Generations Patches Dual-G2PFD
Masterpieces-60
Walmart Tins Oversize-60
06Upper Deck MVP-88
Gold Script-88
Super Script-88
Gotta Have Hart-HH11
International Icons-II6
Jerseys-OJFA
Jerseys-OJFD
06Upper Deck Ovation-64
06Upper Deck Sweet Shot-32
Sweet Stitches-SSSF
Sweet Stitches Duals-SSSF
Sweet Stitches Triples-SSSF
06Upper Deck Trilogy-31
06Upper Deck Victory-58
06Upper Deck Victory Black-58
06Upper Deck Victory Gold-58
07Upper Deck Victory-126
Black-126
Gold-126
Stars on Ice-SI7

Fedoruk, Todd

98Prince Albert Raiders-6
00BAP Memorabilia-469
Emerald-469
Ruby-469
Sapphire-469
00Black Diamond-105
00SP Authentic-157
00Titanium Draft Day Edition-170
00Titanium Draft Day Promos-170
01Flyers Postcards-6
02Flyers Postcards-13
02Pacific Complete-472
Red-472
03Flyers Postcards-6
04Philadelphia Phantoms-3
05Ducks Team Issue-5
05Parkhurst-16
Facsimile Auto Parallel-16
05Upper Deck-246
06Flyers Postcards-15
06O-Pee-Chee-4
Rainbow-4
06UD Powerplay Last Man Standing-LM7
06Upper Deck-252
Exclusives Parallel-252
High Gloss Parallel-252
Masterpieces-252

Fedosov, Vladimir

91Finnish Semic World Champ Stickers-87
91Swedish Semic World Champ Stickers-87
94German First League-289
95German DEL-338
96German DEL-313
00Russian Hockey League-93
01Russian Hockey League-37

Fedotenko, Ruslan

98Sioux City Musketeers-5
00BAP Memorabilia-477
Emerald-477
Ruby-477
Sapphire-477
00Black Diamond-130
00SP Authentic-120
00SP Game Used-78
00SPx-167
00Titanium-137
Retail-137
00Titanium Draft Day Edition-137
00Titanium Draft Day Promos-137
00Topps Premier Plus-109
Blue Ice-109
00UD Reserve-108
00Upper Deck Ice-98
01BAP Memorabilia-21
Emerald-21
Ruby-21
Sapphire-21
01Flyers Postcards-7
01Pacific-286
Extreme LTD-286
Hobby LTD-286
Premiere Date-286
Retail LTD-286
01Pacific Arena Exclusives-286
01SP Game Used Authentic Fabric-AFRF
01SP Game Used Authentic Fabric-DFRF
01SP Game Used Authentic Fabric Gold-AFRF
01SPx Hidden Treasures-DTFC
01Topps Own The Game-OTG16
01UD Mask Collection Double Patches-DPRF
01UD Mask Collection Jerseys-J-RF
01UD Mask Collection Jersey and Patch-JPRF
01Upper Deck Game Jerseys-NGRF
01Upper Deck Victory-261
Gold-261
02Pacific Complete-154
Red-154
02Topps Total-313
02UD Top Shelf Dual Player Jerseys-RSF
02UD Top Shelf Dual Player Jerseys-STFP
02Upper Deck-402
Exclusives-402
02Upper Deck Beckett UD Promos-402
02Upper Deck Classic Portraits Hockey Royalty-PGF
02Upper Deck Classic Portraits Hockey Royalty Limited-PGF
02Upper Deck MVP Skate Around Jerseys-SDWF
02Upper Deck Vintage Jerseys-HSRF
02Upper Deck Vintage Jerseys Gold-HS-RF
03ITG Action-572
03Lightning Team Issue-20
03O-Pee-Chee-82
03OPC Blue-82
03OPC Gold-82
03OPC Red-82
03Pacific-305
Blue-305
Red-305
03Pacific Complete-129
Red-129
03Topps-82
Blue-82
Gold-82
Red-82
03Upper Deck-420
Canadian Exclusives-420
HG-420
UD Exclusives-420
04Upper Deck-160
Canadian Exclusives-160
HG Glossy Gold-160
HG Glossy Silver-160
05Be A Player Dual Signatures-VR
05Be A Player Signatures-FE
05Be A Player Signatures Gold-FE
05Panini Stickers-159
05Parkhurst-437
Facsimile Auto Parallel-437
Signatures-RF
True Colors-TCTBL
True Colors-TCTBL
05SP Game Used Awesome Authentics-AA-RF
05SP Game Used Game Gear-GG-RF
05SP Game Used Game Gear Autographs-AG-RF
05SP Game Used Signature Sticks-SS-RF
05SP Game Used SIGnificance-RF
05SP Game Used SIGnificance Gold-S-RF
05SP Game Used SIGnificance Extra-SF
05SP Game Used SIGnificance Extra Gold-SF
05SP Game Used Significant Numbers-SN-RF
05SP Game Used Statscriptions-ST-RF
05SPx Winning Combos-WC-SF
05SPx Winning Combos Autographs-AWC-SF
05SPx Winning Combos Gold-WC-SF
05SPx Winning Combos Spectrum-WC-SF
05SPx Winning Materials-WM-RF
05SPx Winning Materials Gold-WM-RF
05SPx Winning Materials Spectrum-WM-RF
05The Cup Stanley Cup Titlists-TRF
05UD Artifacts Auto Facts-AF-RF
05UD Artifacts Auto Facts Blue-AF-RF
05UD Artifacts Auto Facts Copper-AF-RF
05UD Artifacts Auto Facts Pewter-AF-RF
05UD Artifacts Auto Facts Silver-AF-RF
05UD Artifacts Remarkable Artifacts-RA-RF
05UD Artifacts Remarkable Artifacts Dual-RA-RF
05Ultra-175
Gold-175
Fresh Ink-FI-RF
Fresh Ink Blue-FI-RF
Ice-175
05Upper Deck-173
Big Playmakers-B-RF
HG Glossy-173
Jerseys Series II-J2RF
Notable Numbers-N-RF
Patches-P-RF
05Upper Deck MVP-346
Gold-346
Platinum-346
Materials-M-RF
Materials Triples-T-LKF
05Upper Deck Trilogy Scripts-SFS-RF
05Upper Deck Toronto Fall Expo-173
05Upper Deck Victory-177
Black-177
Gold-177
Silver-177
05Czech Stadion-682
06Be A Player-129
Autographs-129
Signatures-RF
Signatures 25-143
Signatures Duals-DRF
06Flair Showcase Inks-IRF
06Fleer-178
Tiffany-178
Fabricology-FRF
Signing Day-SDRF
06Lightning Postcards-7
06O-Pee-Chee-439
Rainbow-439
Swatches-S-RF
06Panini Stickers-155
06SP Game Used Authentic Fabrics-AFRF
06SP Game Used Authentic Fabrics Parallel-AFRF
06SP Game Used Authentic Fabrics Patches-AFRF
06SP Game Used SIGnificance-SRF
06UD Artifacts Auto-Facts-AFRF
06UD Artifacts Auto-Facts Gold-AFRF
06UD Artifacts Tundra Tandems-TTSF
06UD Artifacts Tundra Tandems Black-TTSF
06UD Artifacts Tundra Tandems Blue-TTSF
06UD Artifacts Tundra Tandems Gold-TTSF
06UD Artifacts Tundra Tandems Red-TTSF
06UD Artifacts Tundra Tandems Dual Patches Red-TTSF
06Ultra-179
Gold Medallion-179
Ice Medallion-179
Fresh Ink-IRF
06Upper Deck Arena Giveaways-TBL3
06Upper Deck-178
Exclusives Parallel-178
High Gloss Parallel-178
Game Jerseys-JRF
Game Patches-PRF
Masterpieces-178
Signature Sensations-SSRF
06Upper Deck MVP-263
Gold Script-263
Super Script-263
Jerseys-OJHF
06Upper Deck Ovation-196
06Upper Deck Trilogy Scripts-TSRF

Fedotov, Alexander

74Swedish Stickers-94

Fedotov, Anatoli

93Upper Deck-38
93Classic-130
93Classic Pro Prospects-97
93Classic Four-Sport *-233
Gold-233
94Classic Pro Prospects-62
97Swedish Collector's Choice-90

Fedotov, Sergei

96Upper Deck Ice-140
96Detroit Whalers-7
98Florida Everblades-5
99Russian Hockey League-227
00Russian Hockey League-143

Fedulov, Igor

93Swiss HNL-148
95Finnish Semic World Championships-132
95Swiss HNL-475
96Swiss HNL-372
99Swiss Panini Stickers-169
00Swiss Panini Stickers-212
00Swiss Slapshot Mini-Cards-HCL3
01Swiss HNL-332
02Swiss HNL-346

Fedyk, Brent

88ProCards AHL-16
90OPC Premier-31
90Pro Set-435
91Bowman-51
91O-Pee-Chee-376
91Panini Stickers-140
91Parkhurst-270
French-270
91Pro Set-379
French-379
91Score Canadian Bilingual-412
91Score Canadian English-412
91Stadium Club-238
91Topps-376
91Upper Deck-373
French-373
92Flyers J.C. Penney-12
92Flyers Upper Deck Sheets-17
92Flyers Upper Deck Sheets-42
92OPC Premier-26
92Parkhurst-131
Emerald Ice-131
92Score-337
Canadian-337
92Stadium Club-390
92Topps-401
Gold-401G
92Ultra-371
92Upper Deck-443
93Flyers J.C. Penney-10
93Flyers Lineup Sheets-14
93Flyers Lineup Sheets-15
93Leaf-58
93OPC Premier-211
Gold-211
93Panini Stickers-48
93Parkhurst-148
Emerald Ice-148
93Pinnacle-119
Canadian-119
93PowerPlay-181
93Score-14
Canadian-14
93Stadium Club-181
Members Only Master Set-181
OPC-181
First Day Issue-181
First Day Issue OPC-181
93Topps/OPC Premier-211
Gold-211
93Ultra-387
93Upper Deck-373
94Canada Games NHL POGS-177
94Leaf-517
94OPC Premier-509
Special Effects-509
94Parkhurst-170
Gold-170
94Pinnacle-326
Artist's Proofs-326
Rink Collection-326
94Stadium Club-169
Members Only Master Set-169
First Day Issue-169
Super Team Winner Cards-169
94Topps/OPC Premier-509
Special Effects-509
94Upper Deck-9
Electric Ice-9
95Be A Player-100
Signatures-S100
Signatures Die Cuts-S100
95Canada Games NHL POGS-204
95Collector's Choice-324
Player's Club-324
Player's Club Platinum-324
95Leaf-290
95Parkhurst International-325
Emerald Ice-325
95Upper Deck-116
Electric Ice-116
Electric Ice Gold-116
96Donruss-163
Press Proofs-163
96Leaf-82
Press Proofs-82
96Pinnacle-116
Artist's Proofs-116
Foil-116
Premium Stock-116
Rink Collection-116
96Score-191
Artist's Proofs-191
Dealer's Choice Artist's Proofs-191
Special Artist's Proofs-191
Golden Blades-191
96Upper Deck-46
96Michigan K-Wings-9
97Detroit Vipers-18
99Pacific-268
Copper-268
Emerald Green-268
Gold-268
Ice Blue-268
Premiere Date-268
Red-268
99Upper Deck Victory-194

Fedyk, Jeff

04Vernon Vipers-20

Feeney, Scott

93Quebec Pee-Wee Tournament-621

Fees, Chris

96Knoxville Cherokees-7

Feher, Artie

84Brandon Wheat Kings-8
85Brandon Wheat Kings-8

Fehr, B.J.

98Kelowna Rockets-3
00Medicine Hat Tigers-7

Fehr, Brad

93Quebec Pee-Wee Tournament-1236

Fehr, David

99Swiss Panini Stickers-322

Fehr, Eric

01Brandon Wheat Kings-6
02Brandon Wheat Kings-12
03BAP Memorabilia Draft Redemptions-18
03Brandon Wheat Kings-16
04ITG Top Prospects Spring Expo-10
04Brandon Wheat Kings-11
04ITG Heroes and Prospects-74
Autographs-EF
Complete Emblems-8
Emblems-47
Emblems Gold-47
He Shoots-He Scores Prizes-8
Jersey Autographs-47
Jerseys-47
Jerseys Gold-47
Numbers-47
Numbers Gold-47
Top Prospects-10
04ITG Heroes/Prospects Toronto Expo '05-74
04ITG Heroes/Prospects Expo Heroes/Pros-74
05ITG Heroes/Prosp Toronto Expo Parallel -214
05AHL All-Stars-6
05AHL Top Prospects-13
05Hershey Bears-6
05ITG Heroes and Prospects-214
Autographs Series II-EF
CHL Grads-CG-15
CHL Grads Gold-CG-15
Future Teammates-FT14
He Shoots-He Scores Prizes-40
Jerseys-GUJ-82
Jerseys Gold-GUJ-82
Emblems-GUE-82
Emblems Gold-GUE-82
Numbers-GUN-82
Numbers Gold-GUN-82
Nameplates-N-58
Nameplates Gold-N-58
06Be A Player-211
06Be A Player Portraits-130
06Beehive-160
Blue-160
Matte-160
Red Facsimile Signatures-160
Wood-160

06Black Diamond-191
Black-191
Gold-191
Ruby-191
06Flair Showcase-98
06Flair Showcase-169
Parallel-98
Parallel-169
06Fleer-203
Tiffany-203
06Hot Prospects-139
Red Hot-139
White Hot-139
Hot Materials -HMEF
Hot Materials Red Hot-HMEF
Hot Materials White Hot-HMEF
Hotagraphs-HEF
06O-Pee-Chee-504
06O-Pee-Chee-642
Rainbow-504
Rainbow-642
06SP Authentic-210
Limited-210
06SP Game Used-159
Gold-159
Rainbow-159
Autographs-159
Inked Sweaters-ISEF
Inked Sweaters Patches-ISEF
Rookie Exclusives Autographs-REEF
06SPx-166
Spectrum-166
06The Cup-168
Autographed Rookie Masterpiece Pressplates-168
Gold Rainbow Autographed Rookie Patches-168
Masterpiece Pressplates (Artifacts)-204
Masterpiece Pressplates (Be A Player Portraits)-130
Masterpiece Pressplates (Bee Hive)-160
Masterpiece Pressplates (Marquee Rookies)-504
Masterpiece Pressplates (MVP)-333
Masterpiece Pressplates (Power Play)-130
Masterpiece Pressplates (SP Authentic Autographs)-210
Masterpiece Pressplates (SP Game Used)-159
Masterpiece Pressplates (SPx Autographs)-166
Masterpiece Pressplates (Sweet Beginnings)-160
Masterpiece Pressplates (Trilogy)-159
Masterpiece Pressplates (Ultimate Collection Autographs)-132
Masterpiece Pressplates (Victory)-205
NHL Shields Duals-DSHFP
Rookies Black-168
Rookies Platinum-168
06UD Artifacts-204
Blue-204
Gold-204
Platinum-204
Radiance-204
Red-204
06UD Mini Jersey Collection-130
06UD Powerplay-130
Impact Rainbow-130
06Ultimate Collection-132
Rookies Autographed NHL Shields-132
Rookies Autographed Patches-132
Ultimate Debut Threads Jerseys-DJ-EF
Ultimate Debut Threads Jerseys Autographs-DJ-EF
Ultimate Debut Threads Patches-DJ-EF
Ultimate Debut Threads Patches Autographs-DJ-EF
06Ultra-230
Gold Medallion-230
Ice Medallion-230
06Upper Deck-249
Exclusives Parallel-249
High Gloss Parallel-249
Masterpieces-249
Rookie Game Dated Moments-RGD30
Rookie Materials-RMEF
Rookie Materials Patches-RMEF
06Upper Deck MVP-333
Gold Script-333
Super Script-333
06Upper Deck Ovation-150
06Upper Deck Sweet Shot-160
Rookie Jerseys Autographs-160
06Upper Deck Trilogy-159
06Upper Deck Victory-205
06Upper Deck Victory Black-205
06Upper Deck Victory Gold-205
06ITG Heroes and Prospects-34
AHL Shooting Stars-AS12
Autographs-AEF
Calder Cup Champions-CC13
CHL Top Prospects-TP17
CHL Top Prospects Gold-TP17
07Upper Deck Rookie Class -12
07Upper Deck Victory-96
Black-96
Gold-96

Feiffer, Jason
91Air Canada SJHL-A21
91Air Canada SJHL All-Stars-31

Feigl, Mario
94German First League-471

Feil, Chris
96Barrie Colts-7
98Barrie Colts-15

Felber, Harald
74Finnish Jenkki-110

Feldmann, Jan
04Swiss EV Zug Postcards-8

Feldt, Yngve
56Swedish Alfabilder-100

Felicetti, Dino
96German DEL-124
99German Bundesliga 2-8

Felix, Chris
81Sault Ste. Marie Greyhounds-11
82Sault Ste. Marie Greyhounds-8
83Sault Ste. Marie Greyhounds-5
84Sault Ste. Marie Greyhounds-6
87Sault Ste. Marie Greyhounds-11
88ProCards AHL-29
89ProCards AHL-83
90ProCards AHL/IHL-213
95Swiss HNL-490
01Bakersfield Condors-8

Feller, Jens
94German First League-297
95German DEL-347

Felli, Christian
92Cornell Big Red-11
93Cornell Big Red-10

Fels, Ken
03Port Huron Beacons-8
05Muskegon Fury-5

Felski, Sven
94German DEL-39
95German DEL-37
96German DEL-36
98German DEL-158
98German DEL-316
99German DEL-55
99German DEL-372
00German Berlin Polar Bears Postcards-5
00German DEL-63
01German Berlin Polar Bears Postcards-7
01German Upper Deck-33
Gate Attractions-GA3
02German Berlin Polar Bears Postcards-9
02German DEL City Press-30
Top Stars-GT7
03German Berlin Polar Bears Postcards-12
03German DEL-66
04German Berlin Eisbarens 50th Anniv-39
04German Berlin Polar Bears Postcards-11
04German DEL-67
05German DEL-27
05German DEL-289
06German DEL-18
German Forwards-GF6

Felsner, Brian
97Pacific Omega-50
Copper-50
Dark Gray-50
Emerald Green-50
Gold-50
Ice Blue-50
97Indianapolis Ice-7
98Detroit Vipers-4
98Detroit Vipers Freschetta-15
99Houston Aeros-8
00Cincinnati Cyclones-16
02Swedish SHL-213
Parallel-213
03Swedish Elite Global Impact-GI7
04German Augsburg Panthers Postcards-12
04German DEL-27

Felsner, Denny
91Michigan Wolverines-2
92Parkhurst-493
Emerald Ice-493
92Pinnacle-413
French-413
92Score-481
Canadian-481
92Topps-514
Gold-514G
92Upper Deck-413
92Peoria Rivermen-5
92Classic-63
92Classic-64
Gold-63
Gold-64
92Classic Four-Sport *-194
Gold-194
93Parkhurst-267
Emerald Ice-267
93Peoria Rivermen-10
94OPC Premier-436
Special Effects-436
94Parkhurst SE-SE151
Gold-SE151
94Topps/OPC Premier-436
Special Effects-436
94Upper Deck-114
Electric Ice-114
94Classic Pro Prospects-189
96Milwaukee Admirals-6
00Jackson Bandits-19
00Jackson Bandits Promos-3

Feltendahl, Lars-Olof
69Swedish Hockey-313

Femenella, Arthur
00Sioux City Musketeers-7

Fendek, Tomas
04Baie-Comeau Drakkar-23
05Baie-Comeau Drakkar-5

Fendt, Torsten
95German DEL-9
96German DEL-7
99German Bundesliga 2-221
00German DEL-110
02German DEL City Press-10
04German Augsburg Panthers Postcards-13
04German DEL-28
05German DEL-4
06German DEL-5

Fengler, Reinhardt
83Swedish Semic VM Stickers-147
04German Berlin Eisbarens 50th Anniv-23

Feniak, Jeff
98Calgary Hitmen-3
98Calgary Hitmen Autographs-3
99Calgary Hitmen-9
99Calgary Hitmen Autographs-9
01Regina Pats-8

Fennig, Wade
89Regina Pats-4
90Fort Saskatchewan Traders-2
98Colorado Gold Kings-5
98Colorado Gold Kings Postcards-18
99Colorado Gold Kings Taco Bell-21
99Colorado Gold Kings Wendy's-4

Fenton, Eric
92Maine Black Bears-11
93Portland Pirates-13
94Classic Autographs-NNO
95Peoria Rivermen-4
96Charlotte Checkers-7
96Milwaukee Admirals-7
97Milwaukee Admirals-5
98Milwaukee Admirals-5
99Milwaukee Admirals Keebler-11
00UK Sekonda Superleague-196

Fenton, Paul
85Whalers Junior Wendy's-5
88Jets Postcards-9
88O-Pee-Chee-213
89Jets Safeway-15
90Bowman-139
Tiffany-139
90Maple Leafs Postcards-4
90O-Pee-Chee-313
90Panini Stickers-313
90Pro Set-329
90Pro Set-533A
90Pro Set-533B
90Score-156
Canadian-156
90Score Rookie/Traded-57T
90Topps-313
Tiffany-313
90Upper Deck-92
French-92
91Bowman-256
91Jets Panini Team Stickers-12
91Jets Panini Team Stickers-G
91O-Pee-Chee-331
91OPC Premier-187
91Score American-14
91Score Canadian Bilingual-14
91Score Canadian Bilingual-593
91Score Canadian English-14
91Score Canadian English-593
91Sharks Sports Action-6
91Stadium Club-327
91Topps-331
92O-Pee-Chee-380
92Score-257
Canadian-257
92Stadium Club-224
92Topps-173
Gold-173G

Fenyves, Dave
85Sabres Blue Shield-8
85Sabres Blue Shield Small-8
86Sabres Blue Shield-9
86Sabres Blue Shield Small-9
88ProCards AHL-131
89ProCards AHL-335
90ProCards AHL/IHL-32
91ProCards-283

Fera, Rick
83Sault Ste. Marie Greyhounds-6
84Kingston Canadians-13
94Finnish Jaa Kiekko-325
98UK Basingstoke Bison-11

Ferding, Curt
69Swedish Hockey-228

Ference, Andrew
96Upper Deck-374
97Portland Winter Hawks-23
97Bowman CHL-100
OPC-100
98Bowman CHL-48
Golden Anniversary-48
OPC International-48
99BAP Memorabilia-312
Gold-312
Silver-312
99BAP Millennium-196
Emerald-196
Ruby-196
Sapphire-196
Signatures-196
Signatures Gold-196
99Pacific Prism Holographic Blue-113
99Pacific Prism Holographic Gold-113
99Pacific Prism Holographic Mirror-113
99Pacific Prism Holographic Purple-113
99Pacific Prism Premiere Date-113
99Paramount-267
99Topps Arena Giveaways-PIT-AF
99Topps Premier Plus-95
Parallel-95
99Upper Deck-274
Exclusives-274
Exclusives 1 of 1-274
99Upper Deck Arena Giveaways-PP1
99Upper Deck Gold Reserve-274
99Bowman CHL-115
Gold-115
OPC International-115
00Wilkes-Barre Scranton Penguins-7
01Bowman YoungStars-138
Gold-138
Ice Cubed-138
Autographs-AF
Relics-JAF
Relics-SAF
Relics-DSAF
01Upper Deck-142
Exclusives-142
01Upper Deck Vintage-205
02BAP Sig Series Auto Buybacks 1999-196
02Stadium Club YoungStars Relics-S22
02Topps Total-302
02Upper Deck-142
Exclusives-142
02Upper Deck Vintage-205
03ITG Action-6
05Parkhurst-71
Facsimile Auto Parallel-71
06Gatorade-15
06O-Pee-Chee-84
Rainbow-84
06Upper Deck-284
Exclusives Parallel-284
High Gloss Parallel-284
Masterpieces-284

Ference, Brad
96Spokane Chiefs-2
97Spokane Chiefs-2
97Bowman CHL-133
OPC-133
Autographs-13
Bowman's Best-9
Bowman's Best Atomic Refractors-9
Bowman's Best Refractor-9
98UD Choice-261
Prime Choice Reserve-261
Reserve-261
98Spokane Chiefs-6
98Tri-City Americans-17
98Bowman CHL-43
Golden Anniversary-43
OPC International-43
Scout's Choice-SC6
98Bowman Chrome CHL-43
Golden Anniversary-43
Golden Anniversary Refractors-43
OPC International-43
OPC International Refractors-43
Refractors-43
99BAP Memorabilia-398
Gold-398
Silver-398
99Pacific Prism-113
99Louisville Panthers-23
99Bowman CHL-116
Gold-116
OPC International-116
00BAP Memorabilia-295
Emerald-295
Ruby-295
Sapphire-295
Promos-295
00BAP Mem Chicago Sportsfest Copper-295
00BAP Memorabilia Chicago Sportsfest Blue-295
00BAP Memorabilia Chicago Sportsfest Gold-295
00BAP Memorabilia Chicago Sportsfest Ruby-295
00BAP Memorabilia Chicago Sun-Times Ruby-295
00BAP Memorabilia Chicago Sun-Times Gold-295
00BAP Mem Chicago Sun-Times Sapphire-295
00BAP Mem Toronto Fall Expo Copper-295
00BAP Memorabilia Toronto Fall Expo Gold-295
00BAP Memorabilia Toronto Fall Expo Ruby-295
00BAP Parkhurst 2000-P61
00BAP Signature Series-275
Emerald-275
Ruby-275
Sapphire-275
Autographs-223
Autographs Gold-223
00O-Pee-Chee-300
00O-Pee-Chee Parallel-300
00Pacific-191
Copper-191
Gold-191
Ice Blue-191
Premiere Date-191
00Paramount-103
Copper-103
Gold-103
Holo-Gold-103
Holo-Silver-103
Ice Blue-103
Premiere Date-103
00Topps/OPC-300
Parallel-300
00Topps Chrome-195
OPC Refractors-195
Refractors-195
00Louisville Panthers-12
01Bowman YoungStars Rivals-R3
02BAP First Edition-375
02BAP Sig Series Auto Buybacks 2000-223
02Topps Total-252
02Upper Deck-79
Exclusives-79
02Upper Deck Vintage-313
03Coyotes Postcards-6
03ITG Action-495
05Upper Deck MVP-304
Gold-304
Platinum-304

Fergin, Tony
93Cornell Big Red-11

Fergus, Cam
03Kitchener Rangers-8
04Gatineau Olympiques-19
05Cape Breton Screaming Eagles-24
06Cape Breton Screaming Eagles-11

Fergus, Tom
82O-Pee-Chee-11
82O-Pee-Chee Stickers-88
82Post Cereal-1
82Topps Stickers-88
83Bruins Team Issue-5
83NHL Key Tags-6
83O-Pee-Chee-49
83O-Pee-Chee Stickers-55
83Topps Stickers-55
84Bruins Postcards-5
84O-Pee-Chee-4
84O-Pee-Chee Stickers-189
84Topps-3
85Maple Leafs Postcards-11
85O-Pee-Chee-113
85O-Pee-Chee Stickers-164
85Topps-113
86Kraft Drawings-16
86Maple Leafs Postcards-8
86O-Pee-Chee-84
86O-Pee-Chee Stickers-143
86Topps-84
87Maple Leafs PLAY-7
87Maple Leafs Postcards-6
87Maple Leafs Postcards Oversized-6
87O-Pee-Chee-120
87O-Pee-Chee Stickers-159
87Panini Stickers-332
87Topps-120
88Maple Leafs PLAY-3
88O-Pee-Chee-214
88O-Pee-Chee Stickers-170
89O-Pee-Chee-103
89O-Pee-Chee Stickers-173
89Panini Stickers-135
89Topps-103
90Bowman-157
Tiffany-157
90Maple Leafs Postcards-5
90O-Pee-Chee-63
90Panini Stickers-282
90Pro Set-279A
90Pro Set-279B
90Score-285
Canadian-285
90Topps-63
Tiffany-63
90Upper Deck-83
French-83
91Pro Set Platinum-238
91Maple Leafs PLAY-10
91Parkhurst-400
French-400
91Pro Set-234
French-234
91Score Canadian Bilingual-234
91Score Canadian English-234
91Upper Deck-384
French-384
92Bowman-273
92Canucks Road Trip Art-8
92O-Pee-Chee-356
92Score-190
Canadian-190
92Stadium Club-278
92Topps-311
Gold-311G
92Ultra-426
93Swiss HNL-122
95Swiss HNL-540

Ferguson, Bob
95Indianapolis Ice-23
97Indianapolis Ice-1
98Florida Everblades-7
99Florida Everblades-23
00Florida Everblades-8

Ferguson, Chris
99Medicine Hat Tigers-2
04Saginaw Spirit-13
05Saginaw Spirit-8

Ferguson, Craig
92Fredericton Canadiens-9
93Fredericton Canadiens-8
94Leaf-525
94Fredericton Canadiens-12
94Classic Pro Prospects-45
96Carolina Monarchs-10
98New Haven Beast-1
99AHL All-Stars-2
99Louisville Panthers-1
00Swiss Panini Stickers-136
00Swiss Slapshot Mini-Cards-HCFG8
01Swiss HNL-131
02Swiss HNL-154
03German DEL-77
04German DEL-85
04German Ingolstadt Panthers-5
05German DEL-144

Ferguson, Dallas
97Anchorage Aces-7
98Anchorage Aces-22
99Anchorage Aces-22

Ferguson, Dan
89Sault Ste. Marie Greyhounds-24
907th Inn. Sketch OHL-358

Ferguson, George
72Maple Leafs Postcards-6
74Maple Leafs Postcards-4
74Maple Leafs Postcards-5
74NHL Action Stamps Update-36
74O-Pee-Chee NHL-302
75Maple Leafs Postcards-7
75O-Pee-Chee NHL-77
75Topps-77
76Maple Leafs Postcards-5
76O-Pee-Chee NHL-286
77Maple Leafs Postcards-4
77O-Pee-Chee NHL-266
78O-Pee-Chee-395
79O-Pee-Chee-139
79Topps-139
80O-Pee-Chee-44
80Topps-44
81O-Pee-Chee-262
81O-Pee-Chee Stickers-184
82North Stars Postcards-9
82O-Pee-Chee-268
82O-Pee-Chee Stickers-150
82Post Cereal-15
82Topps Stickers-150
83North Stars Postcards-8
83O-Pee-Chee-171

Ferguson, Ian
83Oshawa Generals-4

Ferguson, Jeff
88Lethbridge Hurricanes-6
89Spokane Chiefs-8

Ferguson, Jesse
98Kootenay Ice-4
01Kelowna Rockets-4

Ferguson, John
44Beehive Group II Photos-237
60Cleveland Barons-4
63Chex Photos-13
63Parkhurst-33
63Parkhurst-92
63York White Backs-35
64Beehive Group III Photos-103
64Canadiens Postcards-6
64Coca-Cola Caps-71
64Topps-4
65Canadiens Steinberg Glasses-3
65Coca-Cola-70
65Topps-10
66Canadiens IGA-9
66Topps-70
66Topps USA Test-65
67Canadiens IGA-22
67Topps-69
67York Action Octagons-16
67York Action Octagons-21
68Canadiens IGA-22
68Canadiens Postcards BW-5
68O-Pee-Chee-20
68Post Marbles-7
68Shirriff Coins-84
69Canadiens Postcards Color-8
69O-Pee-Chee-7
69Topps-7
70Canadiens Pins-4
70Dad's Cookies-33
70Esso Power Players-15
70O-Pee-Chee-264
79Jets Postcards-6
83Jets Postcards-6
84Jets Police-7
85Jets Police-6
86Jets Postcards-7
89ProCards AHL-198
90ProCards AHL/IHL-60
91Ultimate Original Six-9
French-9
91ProCards-74
94Parkhurst Tall Boys-66
95Parkhurst '66-67-59
Coins-59
99BAP Memorabilia AS Canadian Hobby-CH9
99BAP Memorabilia AS Cdn Hobby Autos-CH9
01Topps Archives-50
02Fleer Throwbacks-48
Gold-48
Platinum-48
02Parkhurst Reprints-289
02Parkhurst Reprints-298
02Topps Stanley Cup Heroes-JF
02Topps Stanley Cup Heroes Autographs-JF
03Parkhurst Original Six Montreal-52
Autographs-4
04ITG Franchises Canadian-47
Autographs-JF
Memorabilia-SM21
Memorabilia Gold-SM21
04ITG Ultimate Memorabilia-93
Gold-93
Jersey Autographs-41
Jersey Autographs Gold-41
Original Six-9
Stick Autographs-35
Stick Autographs Gold-35
Triple Threads-10
05ITG Tough Customers-JF
Jerseys-JF
05ITG Ultimate Mem Pass the Torch Jerseys-17
05ITG Ultimate Mem Passing Torch Jsy Gold-17

Ferguson, Kyle
93Michigan Tech Huskies-19
96South Carolina Stingrays-16

Ferguson, Lorne
44Beehive Group II Photos-19
51Parkhurst-35
54Topps-31
57Topps-40
58Topps-55
94Parkhurst Missing Link-54

Ferguson, Norm
69O-Pee-Chee-146
70Colgate Stamps-56
70Dad's Cookies-34
70Sargent Promotions Stamps-142
71O-Pee-Chee-179
71Sargent Promotions Stamps-136
71Toronto Sun-46
72Finnish Semic World Championship-173
72Swedish Semic World Championship-173
75O-Pee-Chee WHA-92
76San Diego Mariners WHA-3
77O-Pee-Chee WHA-52
90ProCards AHL/IHL-241
91ProCards-236

Ferguson, Scott
917th Inn. Sketch WHL-77
93Kamloops Blazers-6
98Cincinnati Mighty Ducks-28
99Pacific-3
Copper-3
Emerald Green-3
Gold-3
Ice Blue-3
Premiere Date-3
Red-3
99Cincinnati Mighty Ducks-12
00Hamilton Bulldogs-20
02NHL Power Play Stickers-28
02Oilers Postcards-15
03ITG Action-258
03Oilers Postcards-7

Ferguson, Simon
99Lethbridge Hurricanes-8
00Lethbridge Hurricanes-5
01Lethbridge Hurricanes-2
03Kelowna Rockets Memorial Cup-5
03Kelowna Rockets-7
05Portland Pirates-21
06Portland Pirates-12

Ferguson, Tim
94German DEL-23
95German DEL-20
96German DEL-17
98Florida Everblades-6
99Florida Everblades-6

Ferguson, Troy
00Michigan State Spartans-6

Ferhi, Eddie
03Cincinnati Mighty Ducks-A2

Ferhi, Thomas
04Cincinnati Mighty Ducks-28

Ferland, Carl
93Quebec Pee-Wee Tournament-277

Ferland, Jeannot
907th Inn. Sketch QMJHL-259
917th Inn. Sketch QMJHL-187

Ferland, Jonathan
04Hamilton Bulldogs-8
05Hot Prospects-144
En Fuego-144
Red Hot-144
White Hot-144
05SP Authentic-270
Limited-270
05SPx-269
05The Cup Masterpiece Pressplate Artifact-289
05The Cup Masterpiece Pressplates (Ice)-232
05The Cup Master Pressplate Rookie Update-150
05The Cup Masterpiece Pressplates SPA-270
05The Cup Masterpiece Pressplates (SPx)-269
05The Cup Masterpiece Pressplates Trilogy-274
05UD Artifacts-289
05Upper Deck Ice-232
05Upper Deck Rookie Update-150
05Upper Deck Trilogy-274
05Hamilton Bulldogs-8
06Hamilton Bulldogs-10

Fermoyle, Andy
95North Iowa Huskies-7
00Quad-City Mallards-2
01Quad-City Mallards-5

Fermstrom, Sonny
57Swedish Alfabilder-134

Fernandez, Manny
917th Inn. Sketch QMJHL-242
93Donruss Team Canada-10
93Pinnacle-457
Canadian-457
93Upper Deck-536
95Donruss-10
95Leaf-169
95Parkhurst International-63
Emerald Ice-63
95Pinnacle-216
Artist's Proofs-216
Rink Collection-216
95Score-299
Black Ice Artist's Proofs-299
Black Ice-299
95SkyBox Impact NHL On Fox-14
95Images-24
Gold-24
Platinum Prospects-PR9
96Donruss Canadian Ice Les Gardiens-8
96Michigan K-Wings-22
96Collector's Edge Ice-139
Prism-139
QuantumMotion-1
The Wall-TW2
97Pacific Omega-68
Copper-68
Dark Gray-68
Emerald Green-68
Gold-68
Ice Blue-68
98Pacific-175
Ice Blue-175
Red-175
99Pacific Omega-71
Copper-71
Gold-71
Ice Blue-71
Premiere Date-71
99Stars Postcards-5
00BAP Memorabilia-119
Emerald-119
Ruby-119
Sapphire-119
Promos-119
00BAP Mem Chicago Sportsfest Copper-119
00BAP Memorabilia Chicago Sportsfest Blue-119
00BAP Memorabilia Chicago Sportsfest Gold-119
00BAP Memorabilia Chicago Sportsfest Ruby-119
00BAP Memorabilia Chicago Sun-Times Ruby-119
00BAP Memorabilia Chicago Sun-Times Gold-119
00BAP Mem Chicago Sun-Times Sapphire-119
00BAP Mem Toronto Fall Expo Copper-119
00BAP Memorabilia Toronto Fall Expo Gold-119
00BAP Memorabilia Toronto Fall Expo Ruby-119
00BAP Parkhurst 2000-P109
00BAP Signature Series-57
Emerald-57
Ruby-57
Sapphire-57
Autographs-71
Autographs Gold-71
00BAP Ultimate Memorabilia Goalie Sticks-G15
00O-Pee-Chee-283
00O-Pee-Chee Parallel-283
00Pacific-129
Copper-129
Gold-129
Ice Blue-129
Premiere Date-129
00Panini Stickers-177
00Paramount-118
Copper-118
Gold-118
Holo-Gold-118
Holo-Silver-118
Ice Blue-118
Premiere Date-118
00Private Stock-48
00Private Stock-124
Gold-48
Gold-124
Premiere Date-48
Premiere Date-124
Retail-48
Retail-124
Silver-48
Silver-124
00Revolution-71
Blue-71
Premiere Date-71
Red-71
00SP Authentic-45
00SP Game Used-31
00SPx-34
00SPx-140
Spectrum-34
00Stadium Club-204
00Titanium-45
Blue-45
Gold-45
Premiere Date-45
Red-45
Retail-45
00Topps/OPC-283
Parallel-283
00Topps Chrome-178
OPC Refractors-178
Refractors-178
00UD Heroes-59
00UD Pros and Prospects-42
00Upper Deck-87
00Upper Deck-314
Exclusives Tier 1-87
Exclusives Tier 1-314
Exclusives Tier 2-87
Exclusives Tier 2-314
00Upper Deck MVP-96
First Stars-96
Second Stars-96
Third Stars-96
00Upper Deck Vintage-175
00Upper Deck Vintage-184
00Upper Deck Vintage-185
00Vanguard-126
Pacific Proofs-126
01Atomic-49
Blue-49
Gold-49
Premiere Date-49
Red-49
01BAP Memorabilia-214
Emerald-214
Ruby-214
Sapphire-214
01BAP Signature Series-187
Autographs-187
Autographs Gold-187
Teammates-TM-15
01Between the Pipes-39
He Shoots-He Saves Prizes-35
Jerseys-GJ29
Jersey and Stick Cards-GSJ35
Masks-19
Masks Silver-19
Masks Gold-19
01Crown Royale-73
Blue-73
Premiere Date-73
Red-73
Retail-73
01O-Pee-Chee-175
01O-Pee-Chee Premier Parallel-175
01Pacific-193
Extreme LTD-193
Hobby LTD-193
Premiere Date-193
Retail LTD-193
01Pacific Adrenaline-91
Blue-91
Premiere Date-91
Red-91
Retail-91
Power Play-19
01Pacific Arena Exclusives-193
01Pacific Heads-Up-48
Blue-48
Premiere Date-48
Red-48
Silver-48
01Parkhurst-45
Gold-45
Silver-45
01Private Stock-47
Gold-47
Premiere Date-47
Retail-47
Silver-47
01Private Stock Pacific Nights-47
01SP Authentic-41
01SP Authentic-117
Limited-41
Limited-117
Limited Gold-41
Limited Gold-117
Sign of the Times-MF
Sign of the Times-FG
01Stadium Club-58
Award Winners-58
Master Photos-58
New Regime-NR7
New Regime-NRAMF
01Titanium Double-Sided Jerseys-67
01Titanium Double-Sided Patches-67
01Titanium Draft Day Edition-44
01Topps-175
OPC Parallel-175
01Topps Chrome-120
Refractors-120
Black Border Refractors-120
01Topps Heritage-67
Refractors-67
01Topps Reserve-53
01UD Challenge for the Cup-41
01UD Mask Collection-115
Gold-115
01UD Playmakers-49
01Upper Deck-87
Exclusives-87
01Upper Deck Ice-24
01Upper Deck MVP-94
01Upper Deck Victory-170
01Upper Deck Victory-175
Gold-170
Gold-175
01Upper Deck Vintage-124
01Upper Deck Vintage-130
01Vanguard-47
Blue-47
Red-47
One of Ones-47
Premiere Date-47
Proofs-47
01Wild Crime Prevention-23
01Wild Team Issue-1
02Atomic-52
Blue-52
Gold-52
Red-52
Hobby Parallel-52
02BAP First Edition-42
Jerseys-42
02BAP Memorabilia-92
02BAP Memorabilia-255
Emerald-92
Emerald-255
Ruby-92
Ruby-255
Sapphire-92
Sapphire-255
NHL All-Star Game-92
NHL All-Star Game-255
NHL All-Star Game Blue-92
NHL All-Star Game Blue-255
NHL All-Star Game Green-92
NHL All-Star Game Green-255
NHL All-Star Game Red-92
NHL All-Star Game Red-255
02BAP Memorabilia Toronto Fall Expo-92
02BAP Memorabilia Toronto Fall Expo-255
02BAP Sig Series Auto Buybacks 2000-71
02BAP Sig Series Auto Buybacks 2001-187
02Between the Pipes-18
02Between the Pipes-135
Gold-18
Silver-18
Emblems-9
Jerseys-9
Masks II-15
Masks II Gold-15
Masks II Silver-15
Numbers-9
Stick and Jerseys-9
02Bowman YoungStars-56
Gold-56
Silver-56
02Crown Royale-47
Blue-47
Red-47
Retail-47
Dual Patches-13
02O-Pee-Chee-74
02O-Pee-Chee Premier Blue Parallel-74
02O-Pee-Chee Premier Red Parallel-74
02O-Pee-Chee Factory Set-74
02Pacific-181
Blue-181
Red-181
Jerseys-24
Jerseys Holo-Silver-24
02Pacific Complete-17
Red-17
02Pacific Exclusive-86
Jerseys-13
Jerseys Gold-13
02Pacific Heads-Up-60
Blue-60
Purple-60
Red-60
Quad Jerseys-14
Quad Jerseys Gold-14
02Pacific Quest for the Cup-47
Gold-47
02Parkhurst-76
Bronze-76
Gold-76
Silver-76
02Parkhurst Retro-111
Minis-111
02Private Stock Reserve-49
Blue-49
Red-49
Retail-49
02SP Authentic-45
Beckett Promos-45
Sign of the Times-MF
02SP Game Used Signature Style-MF0
02SPx-39
Spectrum Gold-39
Spectrum Silver-39
02Titanium-52
Blue-52
Red-52
Retail-52
02Topps-74
OPC Blue Parallel-74
OPC Red Parallel-74
Factory Set-74
02Topps Chrome-50
Black Border Refractors-50
Refractors-50
02Topps Total-229
02UD Artistic Impressions-45
Gold-45
02UD Artistic Impressions Beckett Promos-45
02UD Artistic Impressions Retrospectives-R45
02UD Artistic Impressions Retrospect Gold-R45
02UD Artistic Impress Retrospect Silver-R45
02UD Honor Roll-37
Signature Class-MF
02UD Mask Collection-42
02UD Mask Collection-44
02UD Mask Collection-110
02UD Mask Collection Beckett Promos-42
02UD Mask Collection Beckett Promos-44
02UD Piece of History-47
02UD Premier Collection Signatures Bronze-SMF
02UD Premier Collection Signatures Gold-SMF
02UD Premier Collection Signatures Silver-SMF
02UD Top Shelf-42
02Upper Deck-333
Exclusives-333
02Upper Deck Beckett UD Promos-333
02Upper Deck Classic Portraits-48
02Upper Deck MVP-90
Gold-90
Classics-90
Golden Classics-90

Prosign-MF
02Upper Deck Victory-107
Bronze-107
Gold-107
Silver-107
02Upper Deck Vintage-129
02Upper Deck Vintage-275
03BAP Memorabilia-133
Emerald-133
Gold-133
Ruby-133
Sapphire-133
Deep in the Crease-D11
Stanley Cup Playoffs-SCP-26
Tandems-T-1
03BAP Ultimate Memorabilia Autographs-77
Gold-77
03BAP Ultimate Mem Auto Jerseys-77
03Beehive-98
Gold-98
Silver-98
03Black Diamond-8
Black-8
Green-8
Red-8
03ITG Action-246
Jerseys-M104
03ITG Used Signature Series-23
Gold-23
Autographs-MF
Autographs Gold-MF
03NHL Sticker Collection-250
03Pacific-164
Blue-164
Red-164
03Pacific Complete-409
Red-409
03Pacific Exhibit-72
Blue Backs-72
Yellow Backs-72
03Pacific Invincible-47
Blue-47
Red-47
Retail-47
Jerseys-15
03Pacific Prism-52
Blue-52
Gold-52
Red-52
03SP Authentic-42
Limited-42
03SPx-48
Radiance-48
Spectrum-48
03Titanium-51
Hobby Jersey Number Parallels-51
Retail-51
Retail Jersey Number Parallels-51
03UD Honor Roll-40
03UD Honor Roll-123
03UD Premier Collection Stars-ST-MF
03UD Premier Collection Stars Patches-ST-MF
03UD Premier Collection Teammates-PT-MW
03UD Premier Collection Teammates Patches-PT-MW
03Upper Deck-98
Canadian Exclusives-98
HG-98
03Upper Deck Classic Portraits-48
03Upper Deck Ice-45
Gold-45
03Upper Deck MVP-219
Gold Script-219
Silver Script-219
Canadian Exclusives-219
SportsNut-SN44
03Upper Deck Rookie Update-45
Skills-SKMF
Super Stars-SSMF
03Upper Deck Trilogy-48
Limited-48
03Upper Deck Victory-92
Bronze-92
Gold-92
Silver-92
03Toronto Star-47
04ITG All-Star FANtasy Hall Minnesota-5
04Pacific-131
Blue-131
Red-131
04SP Authentic-45
04Upper Deck-90
Canadian Exclusives-90
HG Glossy Gold-90
HG Glossy Silver-90
05Beehive Matted Materials-MMMF
05Hot Prospects-50
En Fuego-50
Red Hot-50
White Hot-50
05Panini Stickers-304
05Parkhurst-235
Facsimile Auto Parallel-235
True Colors-TCMIN
True Colors-TCMIN
True Colors-TCMIDA
True Colors-TCMIDA
05SP Game Used Authentic Fabrics Dual-RF
05SP Game Used Authentic Fabrics Quad-GFRB
05SP Game Used Authentic Patches Quad -GFRB
05SP Game Used Authentic Patches Dual-RF
05SP Game Used Awesome Authentics-AA-MF
05SP Game Used Awesome Authentics Gold-DA-MF
05SPx-42
Spectrum-42
Winning Combos-WC-GF
Winning Combos Gold-WC-GF
Winning Combos Spectrum-WC-GF
05Ultra-103
Gold-103
Ice-103
05Upper Deck-341
Big Playmakers-B-MF
Patches-P-MFZ
05Upper Deck MVP-189
Gold-189
Platinum-189
Materials-M-MF
Materials Triples-T-TFD
05Upper Deck Rookie Update-49
05Upper Deck Victory-100
Black-100
Gold-100
Silver-100
06Be A Player Portraits-54
06Beehive-52
06Beehive-194
Blue-52
Gold-52
Matte-52
Red Facsimile Signatures-52
Wood-52
06Between The Pipes-68
Autographs-AMFR
Complete Jersey-CJ06
Complete Jersey Gold-CJ06
Double Jerseys-DJ02
Double Jerseys Gold-DJ02
Emblems-GUE05
Emblems Gold-GUE05
Emblems Autographs-GUE05
Jerseys-GUJ05
Jerseys Gold-GUJ05
Jerseys Autographs-GUJ05
Numbers-GUN05
Numbers Gold-GUN05
Numbers Autographs-GUN05
Stick and Jersey-SJ01
Stick and Jersey Gold-SJ01
Stick and Jersey Autographs-SJ01
06Black Diamond-42
Black-42
Gold-42
Ruby-42
06Flair Showcase-52
Parallel-52
Hot Gloves-HG15
06Fleer-97
Tiffany-97
Netminders-N12
06Hot Prospects-49
Red Hot-49
White Hot-49
06ITG Ultimate Memorabilia Emblems-25
06ITG Ultimate Memorabilia Emblems Gold-25
06ITG Ultimate Memorabilia Jerseys Autos-16
06ITG Ultimate Memorabilia Jerseys Autos Gold-16
06ITG Ultimate Memorabilia Sticks Autos-2
06ITG Ultimate Memorabilia Sticks Autos Gold-2
06O-Pee-Chee-252
Rainbow-252
Swatches-S-MF
06Panini Stickers-292
06SP Authentic-54
Limited-54
06SP Game Used-50
Gold-50
Rainbow-50
Authentic Fabrics-AFMF
Authentic Fabrics Parallel-AFMF
Authentic Fabrics Patches-AFMF
By The Letter-BLMF
06SPx-49
Spectrum-49
SPxcitement-X51
SPxcitement Spectrum-X51
Winning Materials-WMMF
Winning Materials Spectrum-WMMF
06The Cup NHL Shields Duals-DSHGF
06UD Artifacts-53
Blue-53
Gold-53
Platinum-53
Radiance-53
Red-53
Treasured Patches Black-TSMF
Treasured Patches Blue-TSMF
Treasured Patches Gold-TSMF
Treasured Patches Platinum-TSMF
Treasured Patches Red-TSMF
Treasured Swatches-TSMF
Treasured Swatches Black-TSMF
Treasured Swatches Blue-TSMF
Treasured Swatches Gold-TSMF
Treasured Swatches Platinum-TSMF
Treasured Swatches Red-TSMF
Tundra Tandems-TTFP
Tundra Tandems Black-TTFP
Tundra Tandems Blue-TTFP
Tundra Tandems Gold-TTFP
Tundra Tandems Platinum-TTFP
Tundra Tandems Red-TTFP
Tundra Tandems Dual Patches Red-TTFP
06UD Mini Jersey Collection-52
06UD Powerplay-50
Impact Rainbow-50
Goal Robbers-GR10
Specialists-SMF
Specialists Patches-PMF
06Ultra-97
Gold Medallion-97
Ice Medallion-97
06Upper Deck Arena Giveaways-MIN6
06Upper Deck-345
Exclusives Parallel-345
High Gloss Parallel-345
Game Jerseys-J2MF
Game Patches-P2MF
Masterpieces-345
Oversized Wal-Mart Exclusives-345
06Upper Deck MVP-147
Gold Script-147
Super Script-147
Jerseys-OJFR
Jerseys-OJRM
Last Line of Defense-LL19
06Upper Deck Ovation-24
06Upper Deck Sweet Shot-52
Sweet Stitches-SSMF
Sweet Stitches Duals-SSMF
Sweet Stitches Triples-SSMF
06Upper Deck Trilogy-50
06Upper Deck Victory-97
06Upper Deck Victory Black-97
06Upper Deck Victory Gold-97
06Houston Aeros RetroA -7
06ITG Heroes and Prospects Heroes Memorabilia-HM26
06ITG Heroes and Prospects Triple Memorabilia-TM12
07Upper Deck Ovation-24
07Upper Deck Victory-138
Black-138
Gold-138

Ferner, Mark
84Kamloops Blazers-9
88ProCards AHL-253
89ProCards AHL-89
90ProCards AHL/IHL-208
91Baltimore Skipjacks-10
91ProCards-568
93OPC Premier-478
Gold-478
93Parkhurst-275
Emerald Ice-275
93Stadium Club-342
Members Only Master Set-342
First Day Issue-342
93Topps/OPC Premier-478
Gold-478
97Long Beach Ice Dogs-7
98Long Beach Ice Dogs-5

Fernhall, Per
99Columbus Cottonmouths-21

Fernholm, Daniel
04Swedish Djurgardens Postcards-2
04Swedish Elitset-158
Future Stars-10
Gold-158
05WBS Penguins-10

Fernqvist, Lars
83Swedish Semic Elitserien-197

Ferns, Kent
95Classic Five-Sport Autographs *-151

Fernstrom, Allan
67Swedish Hockey-136

Fernstrom, Anders
56Swedish Alfabilder-73

Fernstrom, Hans-Erik
64Swedish Coralli ISHockey-106
65Swedish Coralli ISHockey-106
67Swedish Hockey-170

Ferone, Paul
95Seattle Thunderbirds-9
96Seattle Thunderbirds-7
00UK Sekonda Superleague-173
01UK Belfast Giants-25
01UK Manchester Storm-1
02UK Hull Thunder-8

Ferrand, Chace
04UK U-20 Team-11

Ferrand, Gavin
04UK Sheffield Steelers-14

Ferranti, Steve
93Michigan State Spartans-7
97Louisville Riverfrogs-9
98Amarillo Rattlers-4

Ferrara, James
06UK Nottingham Panthers-4

Ferrari, Gillian
04Canadian Womens World Championship Team-8
06ITG Going For Gold-3
06ITG Going For Gold Samples-3
06ITG Going For Gold Autographs-AF
06ITG Going For Gold Jerseys-GUJ3

Ferrari, Lou
93Quebec Pee-Wee Tournament-866

Ferrari, Marco
93Swiss HNL-302

Ferrari, Michael
93Swiss HNL-500

Ferraro, Chris
91Upper Deck-648
French-648
91Upper Deck Czech World Juniors-74
92Maine Black Bears-25
93PowerPlay-502
93Stadium Club Team USA-5
93Stadium Club Team USA Members Only-5
93Topps Premier Team USA-9
93Ultra-482
94Finnish Jaa Kiekko-129
94Atlanta Knights-11
94Classic-39
Gold-39
Autographs-39
Pro Prospects International Heroes-LP4
95Binghamton Rangers-5
96Leaf-229
Press Proofs-229
96Pinnacle-233
Artist's Proofs-233
Foil-233
Premium Stock-233
Rink Collection-233
96Binghamton Rangers-7
96Collector's Edge Future Legends-6
96Collector's Edge Ice-18
Prism-18
97Pacific Dynagon Best Kept Secrets-60
00Albany River Rats-8
03Springfield Falcons Postcards-17
04Swedish Elitset-276
Gold-276
05German DEL-64

Ferraro, Peter
91Upper Deck-648
91Upper Deck-696
French-648
French-696
91Upper Deck Czech World Juniors-83
92Maine Black Bears-26
93PowerPlay-503
93Stadium Club Team USA-6
93Stadium Club Team USA Members Only-6
93Topps Premier Team USA-15
93Ultra-483
94Finnish Jaa Kiekko-132
94Atlanta Knights-9
94Classic-38
Gold-38
Autographs-38
Pro Prospects Ice Ambassadors-IA10
Pro Prospects International Heroes-LP5
94Images *-35
95Bowman-134
All-Foil-134
95Parkhurst International-532
Emerald Ice-532
95SkyBox Impact-211
95Swedish World Championships Stickers-235
95Binghamton Rangers-6
96Fleer Promo Sheet-3
96Fleer-126
Calder Candidates-3
96Fleer Picks-140
96Leaf Gold Rookies-4
96Metal Universe-178
96Pinnacle-218
Artist's Proofs-218
Foil-218
Premium Stock-218
Rink Collection-218
96SkyBox Impact-149
96Summit-181
Artist's Proofs-181
Ice-181
Metal-181
Premium Stock-181
96Binghamton Rangers-8
96Collector's Edge Future Legends-7
96Collector's Edge Ice-17
Prism-17
97Hartford Wolf Pack-6
98Be A Player-161
Press Release-161
98BAP Gold-161
98BAP Autographs-161
98BAP Autographs Gold-161
99AHL All-Stars-3
99Providence Bruins-9
00Providence Bruins-21
02BAP Sig Series Auto Buybacks 1998-161
03Springfield Falcons Postcards-14
04Swedish Elitset-275
Gold-275
05German DEL-70

Ferraro, Ray
83Brandon Wheat Kings-20
85Whalers Junior Wendy's-6
86O-Pee-Chee-160
86O-Pee-Chee Stickers-57
86Topps-160
86Whalers Junior Thomas'-7
87O-Pee-Chee-109
87Panini Stickers-46
87Topps-109
87Whalers Jr. Burger King/Pepsi-6
88O-Pee-Chee-114
88O-Pee-Chee Stickers-268
88Panini Stickers-241
88Topps-114
88Whalers Junior Ground Round-6
89O-Pee-Chee-70
89O-Pee-Chee Stickers-263
89Panini Stickers-222
89Topps-70
89Whalers Junior Milk-7
90Bowman-258
Tiffany-258
90O-Pee-Chee-336
90Panini Stickers-45
90Pro Set-104
90Score-134
Canadian-134
90Score Rookie/Traded-15T
90Topps-336
Tiffany-336
90Upper Deck-289
French-289
91Pro Set Platinum-76
91Bowman-212
91O-Pee-Chee-304
91Panini Stickers-250
91Parkhurst-110
French-110
91Pinnacle-123
French-123
91Pro Set-156
French-156
91Score American-48
91Score Canadian Bilingual-48
91Score Canadian English-48
91Stadium Club-3
91Topps-304
91Upper Deck-311
French-311
92Bowman-128
92Bowman-229
92Humpty Dumpty I-7
92O-Pee-Chee-42
92OPC Premier Star Performers-1
92Panini Stickers-198
92Panini Stickers French-198
92Parkhurst-98
92Parkhurst-499
Emerald Ice-98
Emerald Ice-499
92Pinnacle-154
French-154
92Pro Set-105
92Score-298
Canadian-298
Sharpshooters-3
Sharpshooters Canadian-3
92Stadium Club-123
92Topps-324
Gold-324G
92Ultra-123
92Upper Deck-12
92Upper Deck-193
93Donruss-198
93Leaf-121
93OPC Premier-349
Gold-349
93Parkhurst-123
Emerald Ice-123
93Pinnacle-48
Canadian-48
93PowerPlay-382
93Score-60
Canadian-60
93Stadium Club-50
Members Only Master Set-50
OPC-50
First Day Issue-50
First Day Issue OPC-50
Master Photos-6
Master Photos Winners-6
93Topps/OPC Premier-349
Gold-349
93Ultra-16
93Upper Deck-153
SP-90
94Be A Player Signature Cards-92
94Canada Games NHL POGS-154
94Donruss-162
94Fleer-120
94Hockey Wit-84
94Leaf-334
94OPC Premier-335
Special Effects-335
94Parkhurst-134
Gold-134
Vintage-V86
94Pinnacle-314
Artist's Proofs-314
Rink Collection-314
94Select-41
Gold-41
94SP-69
Die Cuts-69
94Stadium Club-20
Members Only Master Set-20
First Day Issue-20
Super Team Winner Cards-20
94Topps/OPC Premier-335
Special Effects-335
94Ultra-324
94Upper Deck-14
Electric Ice-14
95Canada Games NHL POGS-178
95Collector's Choice-33
Player's Club-33
Player's Club Platinum-33
95Donruss-144
95Donruss-297
95Emotion-111
95Finest-36
Refractors-36
95Hoyle Eastern Playing Cards-11
95Kraft-74
95Leaf-284
95Metal-94
95Panini Stickers-103
95Parkhurst International-409
Emerald Ice-409
95Playoff One on One-173
95Score-66
Black Ice Artist's Proofs-66
Black Ice-66
95SkyBox Impact-107
95Stadium Club-120
Members Only Master Set-120
95Summit-108
Artist's Proofs-108
Ice-108
95Topps-245
OPC Inserts-245
95Topps SuperSkills-23
Platinum-23
95Ultra-93
95Ultra-273
Gold Medallion-93
95Upper Deck-90
Electric Ice-90
Electric Ice Gold-90
Special Edition-SE143
Special Edition Gold-SE143
96Be A Player-139
Autographs-139
Autographs Silver-139
96Black Diamond-74
Gold-74
96Collector's Choice-131
96Collector's Choice-320
96Donruss-183
Press Proofs-183
96Fleer-49
96Leaf Preferred-16
Press Proofs-16
96NHL Aces Playing Cards-12
96Pinnacle-29
Artist's Proofs-29
Foil-29
Premium Stock-29
Rink Collection-29
96Playoff One on One-380
96Score-107
Artist's Proofs-107
Dealer's Choice Artist's Proofs-107
Special Artist's Proofs-107
Golden Blades-107
96SkyBox Impact-57
96Topps Picks-119
OPC Inserts-119
96Upper Deck-273
97Donruss Canadian Ice-98
Dominion Series-98
Provincial Series-98
97Pacific-53
Copper-53
Emerald Green-53
Ice Blue-53
Red-53
Silver-53
97Pacific Dynagon-59
Copper-59
Dark Grey-59
Emerald Green-59
Ice Blue-59
Red-59
Silver-59
Best Kept Secrets-45
Tandems-40
97Pacific Invincible-66
Copper-66
Emerald Green-66
Ice Blue-66
Red-66
Silver-66
97Panini Stickers-224
97Pinnacle-146
Press Plates Back Black-146
Press Plates Back Cyan-146
Press Plates Back Magenta-146
Press Plates Back Yellow-146
Press Plates Front Black-146
Press Plates Front Cyan-146
Press Plates Front Magenta-146
Press Plates Front Yellow-146
97Pinnacle Certified-82
Red-82
Mirror Blue-82
Mirror Gold-82
Mirror Red-82
97Pinnacle Inside-180
97Pinnacle Tot Cert Platinum Blue-82
97Pinnacle Tot Certi Platinum Gold-82
97Pinnacle Totally Certified Platinum Red-82
97Pinnacle Tot Cert Mirror Platinum Gold-82
97Score-169
99BAP Memorabilia-255
Gold-255
Silver-255
99BAP Millennium-14
Emerald-14
Ruby-14
Sapphire-14
Signatures-14
Signatures Gold-14
99O-Pee-Chee-237
99O-Pee-Chee Chrome-237
99O-Pee-Chee Chrome Refractors-237
99Pacific-189
Copper-189
Emerald Green-189
Gold-189
Ice Blue-189
Premiere Date-189
Red-189
99Pacific Dynagon Ice-16
Blue-16
Copper-16
Gold-16
Premiere Date-16
99Pacific Omega-11
Copper-11
Gold-11
Ice Blue-11
Premiere Date-11
99Panini Stickers-12
99Revolution-7
Premiere Date-7
Red-7
Shadow Series-7
99SP Authentic-4
99SPx-3
Radiance-3
Spectrum-3
99Stadium Club-151
First Day Issue-151
One of a Kind-151
Printing Plates Black-151
Printing Plates Cyan-151
Printing Plates Magenta-151
Printing Plates Yellow-151
99Topps/OPC-237
99Topps/OPC Chrome-237
Refractors-237
99Ultimate Victory-5
1/1-5
Parallel-5
Parallel 100-5
99Upper Deck-178
Exclusives-178
Exclusives 1 of 1-178
99Upper Deck Gold Reserve-178
99Upper Deck MVP SC Edition-8
Gold Script-8
Silver Script-8
Super Script-8
99Upper Deck Victory-19
99Wayne Gretzky Hockey-11
00BAP Memorabilia-297
Emerald-297
Ruby-297
Sapphire-297
Promos-297
00BAP Mem Chicago Sportsfest Copper-297
00BAP Memorabilia Chicago Sportsfest Blue-297
00BAP Memorabilia Chicago Sportsfest Gold-297
00BAP Memorabilia Chicago Sportsfest Ruby-297
00BAP Memorabilia Chicago Sun-Times Ruby-297
00BAP Memorabilia Chicago Sun-Times Gold-297
00BAP Mem Chicago Sun-Times Sapphire-297
00BAP Mem Toronto Fall Expo Copper-297
00BAP Memorabilia Toronto Fall Expo Gold-297
00BAP Memorabilia Toronto Fall Expo Ruby-297
00BAP Parkhurst 2000-P177
00O-Pee-Chee-69
00O-Pee-Chee Parallel-69
00Pacific-18
Copper-18
Gold-18
Ice Blue-18
Premiere Date-18
00Panini Stickers-8
00Paramount-13
Copper-13
Gold-13
Holo-Gold-13
Holo-Silver-13
Ice Blue-13
Premiere Date-13
00Private Stock-4
Gold-4
Premiere Date-4
Retail-4
Silver-4
00Revolution-6
Blue-6
Premiere Date-6
Red-6
00SPx-131
00Stadium Club-49
00Topps/OPC-69
Parallel-69
00Topps Chrome-55
OPC Refractors-55
Refractors-55
00Topps Heritage-191
00Upper Deck-9
Exclusives Tier 1-9
Exclusives Tier 2-9
00Upper Deck MVP-13
First Stars-13
Second Stars-13
Third Stars-13
00Upper Deck Victory-16
00Upper Deck Vintage-22
00Vanguard-4
Holographic Gold-4
Holographic Purple-4
Pacific Proofs-4
01BAP Memorabilia-272
01BAP Memorabilia-483
Emerald-272
Emerald-483
Ruby-272
Ruby-483
Sapphire-272
Sapphire-483
01BAP Signature Series-30
Autographs-30
Autographs Gold-30
01Bowman YoungStars-23
Gold-23
Ice Cubed-23
01Crown Royale-5
Blue-5
Premiere Date-5
Red-5
Retail-5
01O-Pee-Chee-50
01O-Pee-Chee Heritage Parallel-50
01O-Pee-Chee Heritage Parallel Limited-50
01O-Pee-Chee Premier Parallel-50
01Pacific-16
01Pacific-402
Extreme LTD-16
Gold-402
Hobby LTD-16
Premiere Date-16
Retail LTD-16
01Pacific Adrenaline-7
Blue-7
Premiere Date-7
Red-7
Retail-7
01Pacific Arena Exclusives-16
01Pacific Arena Exclusives-402
01Pacific Heads-Up-3
Blue-3
Premiere Date-3
Red-3
Silver-3
01Parkhurst-102
01Private Stock PS-2002-3
01Stadium Club-25
Award Winners-25
Master Photos-25
01Titanium Draft Day Edition-84
01Topps-50
Heritage Parallel-50
Heritage Parallel Limited-50
OPC Parallel-50
01Topps Chrome-50
Refractors-50
Black Border Refractors-50
01Topps Heritage-23
Refractors-23
01Topps Reserve-50
01UD Playmakers-4
01Upper Deck-7
Exclusives-7
01Upper Deck MVP-8
01Upper Deck Victory-21
Gold-21
01Upper Deck Vintage-14
01Upper Deck Vintage-16
01Upper Deck Vintage-17
02Atomic Jerseys-21
02Atomic Jerseys Gold-21
02Atomic Patches-21
02BAP Sig Series Auto Buybacks 1999-14
02BAP Sig Series Auto Buybacks 2001-30
02Pacific-322
Blue-322
Red-322
Jerseys-44
Jerseys Holo-Silver-44
02Titanium Jerseys-57
02Titanium Jerseys Retail-57
02Titanium Patches-57

Ferras, Joe
88ProCards AHL-24

Ferreira, Brian
91Johnstown Chiefs-12
92Nashville Knights-12

Ferry, Steve
04London Knights-3
05London Knights-14
06Sarnia Sting-5

Ferschweiler, Pat
92Western Michigan Broncos-10
93Roanoke Express-8
94Roanoke Express-18
95Kansas City Blades-9
98Kansas City Blades-10
99Kansas City Blades Supercuts-6
00UK Sekonda Superleague-77

Ferster, Ryan
96UK Guildford Flames-10

Fertich, Patrick
94German First League-174

Feser, Collin
84Prince Albert Raiders Stickers-7

Feser, Till
94German DEL-283
95German DEL-278
96German DEL-175
99German Bundesliga 2-90

Fess, Chris
94Knoxville Cherokees-18

Festa, Gerry
03Calgary Hitmen-7

Festerling, Brett
05Vancouver Giants-7

Festerling, Garrett
05Regina Pats-4
06Regina Pats-7

Fetisov, Vyacheslav
79Panini Stickers-141
79Russian National Team-10
81Swedish Semic Hockey VM Stickers-39
82Swedish Semic VM Stickers-53
83Swedish Semic VM Stickers-53
84Russian National Team-5
87Russian National Team-5
89Devils Caretta-11
89Russian National Team-6
89Swedish Semic World Champ Stickers-87
90Bowman-80
Tiffany-80
90Devils Team Issue-12
90O-Pee-Chee-277
90Panini Stickers-75
90Panini Stickers-339
90Pro Set-167A
90Pro Set-167B
90Score-62
Canadian-62
90Topps-27
Tiffany-27
90Upper Deck-176
French-176
91Pro Set Platinum-199
91Bowman-273
91O-Pee-Chee-175
91Parkhurst-96
French-96
91Pinnacle-101
French-101
91Pro Set-142
French-142
91Score American-184
91Score Canadian Bilingual-184
91Score Canadian English-184
91Stadium Club-24
91Topps-175
91Upper Deck-410
French-410
91Finnish Semic World Champ Stickers-213
91Russian Stars Red Ace-4
91Russian Stars in NHL-2
91Swedish Semic World Champ Stickers-213
92Bowman-145
92O-Pee-Chee-162
92Parkhurst-334
Emerald Ice-334
92Pinnacle-299
French-299
92Pro Set-96
92Score-97
Canadian-97
92Stadium Club-392
92Topps-458
Gold-458G
92Ultra-337
92Upper Deck-278
93Pinnacle-397
Canadian-397
93PowerPlay-136
93Score-229
Canadian-229
93Stadium Club-265
Members Only Master Set-265
First Day Issue-265
94EA Sports-74
94EA Sports-208
94Upper Deck-434
Electric Ice-434
95Canada Games NHL POGS-100
95Donruss-272
95Leaf-280
95Parkhurst International-68
95Parkhurst International-249
Emerald Ice-68
Emerald Ice-249
95Swedish Globe World Championships-236
96Black Diamond-2
Gold-2
96Donruss-28
Press Proofs-28
96Donruss Elite-99
Die Cut Stars-99
96Flair-27
Blue Ice-27
96Fleer-143
96Leaf-42
Press Proofs-42
96Leaf Limited-26
Gold-26
96Leaf Preferred-34
Press Proofs-34
96Score-73
Artist's Proofs-73
Dealer's Choice Artist's Proofs-73
Special Artist's Proofs-73
Golden Blades-73
96Summit-128
Artist's Proofs-128
Ice-128
Metal-128
Premium Stock-128
97Pacific-111
Copper-111
Emerald Green-111
Ice Blue-111
Red-111
Silver-111
97Pacific Omega-78
Copper-78
Dark Gray-78
Emerald Green-78
Gold-78
Ice Blue-78
97Post Pinnacle-24
97Revolution-46
Copper-46
Emerald-46
Ice Blue-46
Silver-46
97Score Red Wings-11
Platinum-11
Premier-11
98Devils Team Issue-11
98Pacific-190
Ice Blue-190
Red-190
99Devils Team Issue-26
99Russian Stars of Hockey-37
99Russian Fetisov Tribute-8
00Devils Team Issue-26
01Devils Team Issue-7

Fetta, Joey
98Quebec Remparts-7
Signed-7

Fetterman, Matt
95North Iowa Huskies-8

Fetzer, Matt
00Sioux City Musketeers-8

Fetzner, Cole
03Victoriaville Tigers-9

Fetzner, Matt
00Lethbridge Hurricanes-6
03Saskatoon Blades-12

Fewster, Neil
917th Inn. Sketch OHL-208
93Niagara Falls Thunder-15
94Guelph Storm-11
99ECHL All-Star Southern Conference-16

Fhinn, Kjell
72Swedish Stickers-265

Fiacconi, Adriano
93Quebec Pee-Wee Tournament-492

Fiala, Jan
99Czech OFS-377

Fiala, Lukas
98Czech OFS-323
99Sioux City Musketeers-6

Fiala, Ondrej
05ITG Heroes/Prosp Toronto Expo Parallel -418
05Everett Silvertips-7
05ITG Heroes and Prospects-418
Autographs Update-A-OF
Team Orr-TO9
06ITG Heroes and Prospects-90
Autographs-AOF
Jerseys-GUJ52
Jerseys Gold-GUJ52
Emblems-GUE52
Emblems Gold-GUE52
Numbers-GUN52
Numbers Gold-GUN52
Sticks and Jerseys-SJ08
Sticks and Jerseys Gold-SJ08

Fiala, Petr
94German First League-557
99Czech OFS-322
00Czech OFS-108

Fiala, Radek
04Czech OFS-386
06Czech OFS Goalies I-9
06Czech OFS Goalies II-9

Fiander, Craig
93Fredericton Canadiens-9

Fiatt, Brian
92Tulsa Oilers-4

Fibiger, Jesse
01Cleveland Barons-7
02BAP Memorabilia-312
02Upper Deck Rookie Update-137
02Cleveland Barons-6
03Cleveland Barons-8
04Binghamton Senators-4

Fical, Petr
97Czech APS Extraliga-241
02German DEL City Press-156
03German DEL-199
03German Nuremberg Ice Tigers Postcards-7
04German DEL-246
04German Nuremberg Ice Tigers Postcards-5
05German DEL-265
06German DEL-370
06German DEL-159
06German DEL-184
German Forwards-GF10

Ficenc, Tomas
03Czech OFS Plus-18
04Czech OFS-7

Ficenec, Jakub
95Czech APS Extraliga-129
95Anaheim Bullfrogs RHI-15
96Anaheim Bullfrogs RHI-11
98ECHL All-Star Northern Conference-11
98Las Vegas Coyotes RHI-4
99Portland Pirates-7
00Portland Pirates-17
01German Upper Deck-6
02German DEL City Press-46
03German DEL-78

04German DEL-86
All-Stars-AS6
04German Ingolstadt Panthers-6
05German DEL-145
All-Star Jerseys-AS03
Defender-DF05
Defender Promos-DF05
06German DEL-95
All-Star Jerseys-AS5

Fichaud, Eric
94Finest-77
Super Team Winners-77
Refractors-77
94Flair-179
94Leaf-443
Phenoms-7
94Leaf Limited-45
94OPC Premier-533
Special Effects-533
94Parkhurst SE-SE174
Gold-SE174
94Pinnacle-493
Artist's Proofs-493
Rink Collection-493
94Select-188
Gold-188
94Topps/OPC Premier-533
Special Effects-533
94Ultra-376
94Upper Deck-338
Electric Ice-338
94Classic-14
Gold-14
CHL All-Stars-C3
CHL Previews-CP2
Tri-Cards-T67
94Assets *-62
94Assets *-87
Die Cuts-DC24
Phone Cards One Minute/$2-28
94Classic Four-Sport *-130
Gold-130
Printers Proofs-130
94Signature Rookies Gold Standard *-83
95Bowman-155
All-Foil-155
95Canada Games NHL POGS-177
95Donruss Elite Rookies-6
95Parkhurst International-537
Emerald Ice-537
95SP-90
95Images-13
Gold-13
95Images Four-Sport *-107
Classic Performances-CP20
96Be A Player-214
Autographs-214
Autographs Silver-214
96Black Diamond-105
Gold-105
96Collector's Choice-155
96Collector's Choice-323
96Donruss Rated Rookies-8
96Donruss Canadian Ice-120
Gold Press Proofs-120
Red Press Proofs-120
Les Gardiens-6
96Donruss Elite-132
Die Cut Stars-132
Aspirations-14
96Flair-115
Blue Ice-115
96Fleer-127
Calder Candidates-4
96Islander Postcards-4
96Leaf Gold Rookies-9
96Leaf Limited-69
Gold-69
96Leaf Preferred-119
Press Proofs-119
Steel-53
Steel Gold-53
96Maggers-23
96Metal Universe-179
96Pinnacle-228
Artist's Proofs-228
Foil-228
Premium Stock-228
Rink Collection-228
96Score-256
Artist's Proofs-256
Dealer's Choice Artist's Proofs-256
Special Artist's Proofs-256
Golden Blades-256
96Select Certified-103
Artist's Proofs-103
Blue-103
Mirror Blue-103
Mirror Gold-103
Mirror Red-103
Red-103
96SkyBox Impact-150
96SP-92
96Summit-178
Artist's Proofs-178
Ice-178
Metal-178
Premium Stock-178
96Topps Picks Rookie Stars-RS15
96Topps Picks Rookie Stars OPC-RS15
96Ultra-100
Gold Medallion-100
Rookies-7
96Upper Deck-96
Generation Next-X27
Superstar Showdown-SS12B
96Zenith-116
Artist's Proofs-116
96Collector's Edge Future Legends-8
96Collector's Edge Ice-93
Platinum Club-2
Prism-93
The Wall-TW11
97Collector's Choice-153
97Donruss-183
Press Proofs Silver-183
Press Proofs Gold-183
Canadian Ice Les Gardiens-8
97Donruss Canadian Ice Les Gardiens Promo-8
97Donruss Elite-87
Aspirations-87
Status-87
97Donruss Limited-59
97Donruss Limited-124
97Donruss Limited-174
Exposure-59
Exposure-124
Exposure-174
Fabric of the Game-56
97Donruss Preferred-49
Cut to the Chase-49
Color Guard-8
Color Guard Promos-8
97Donruss Priority-40
Stamp of Approval-40
Postmaster General-12
Postmaster Generals Promos-12
97Katch-86
Gold-86
Silver-86
97Leaf-20
Fractal Matrix-20
Fractal Matrix Die Cuts-20
Pipe Dreams-15
97Leaf International-20
Universal Ice-20
97Pacific-274
Copper-274
Emerald Green-274
Ice Blue-274
Red-274
Silver-274
97Pinnacle-66
Artist's Proofs-66
Rink Collection-66
Press Plates Back Black-66
Press Plates Back Cyan-66
Press Plates Back Magenta-66
Press Plates Back Yellow-66
Press Plates Front Black-66
Press Plates Front Cyan-66
Press Plates Front Magenta-66
Press Plates Front Yellow-66
97Pinnacle Inside-31
Coach's Collection-31
Executive Collection-31
Stand Up Guys-5A/B
Stand Up Guys-5C/D
Stand Up Guys Promos-5A/B
Stand Up Guys Promos-5C/D
97Score-26
Artist's Proofs-26
Golden Blades-26
97Studio-91
Press Proofs Silver-91
Press Proofs Gold-91
97Upper Deck-102
98Be A Player-227
Press Release-227
98BAP Gold-227
98BAP Autographs-227
98BAP Autographs Gold-227
98NHL Aces Playing Cards-31
98Predators Team Issue-9
99Quebec Citadelles-15
00Upper Deck NHLPA-PA47
00Quebec Citadelles-13
Signed-13
01Between the Pipes-51
02BAP Sig Series Auto Buybacks 1998-227
02Between the Pipes-71
Gold-71
Silver-71
02Hamilton Bulldogs-18
03BAP Memorabilia Deep in the Crease-D3

Fichtner, Ambrosius
94German First League-350
99German Bundesliga 2-32

Fichuk, Pete
72Finnish Semic World Championship-131
72Swedish Semic World Championship-131

Ficorelli, Terry
93Cincinnati Cyclones-31
98Muskegon Fury-1
99Muskegon Fury-23
02Muskegon Fury-7
05Muskegon Fury-24

Fiddler, Vernon
98Kelowna Rockets-4
00Medicine Hat Tigers-8
01Roanoke Express-8
02BAP Memorabilia-314
02BAP Ultimate Memorabilia-92
02Pacific Calder-128
Silver-128
02Pacific Complete-510
Red-510
02Pacific Quest for the Cup-128
Gold-128
02SP Authentic-176
02Titanium-123
Blue-123
Red-123
Retail-123
02UD Honor Roll-119
02UD Mask Collection-127
02UD Premier Collection-59B
Gold-59
02Upper Deck-456
Exclusives-456
02Milwaukee Admirals-19
02Milwaukee Admirals Postcards-6
03ITG Action-350
03Milwaukee Admirals-13
03Milwaukee Admirals Postcards-4
04Milwaukee Admirals-28
05Parkhurst-282
Facsimile Auto Parallel-282
05Milwaukee Admirals Choice-5

Fidler, Mike
77O-Pee-Chee NHL-290
78O-Pee-Chee-84
78Topps-84
79Panini Stickers-217
79North Stars Postcards-4
79O-Pee-Chee-219
79Topps-219
81O-Pee-Chee-136

Fiebelkorn, Jed
91Minnesota Golden Gophers-7
92Minnesota Golden Gophers-8
93Minnesota Golden Gophers-10
94Minnesota Golden Gophers-12
98Grand Rapids Griffins-7

Fiedler, Jonas
01Plymouth Whalers-22
03Plymouth Whalers-3

Fiedler, Tom
03German Berlin Polar Bears Postcards-13

Field, Alec
98UK Basingstoke Bison-14
99UK Basingstoke Bison-10

Field, Wilfy
34Beehive Group I Photos-225
39O-Pee-Chee V301-1-64

Fielder, Guyle
57Topps-36

Fielder, Jonas
02Plymouth Whalers-14

Fielding, Jason
93Quebec Pee-Wee Tournament-590

Fields, Sam
97Idaho Steelheads-15
97Tucson Gila Monsters-8
99San Antonio Iguanas-15

Fields, Sean
03Boston University Terriers-10
04Gwinnett Gladiators-11

Fife, Jeff
89 7th Inn. Sketch OHL-93
89 7th Inn. Sketch OHL-197

Figliomeni, Mike
93Michigan Tech Huskies-6
99Rockford IceHogs-7
99Rockford IceHogs-25
99UHL All-Stars West-21T
00Rockford IceHogs-9

Figliuzzi, Stefano
93Swedish Semic World Champ Stickers-227
94Finnish Jaa Kiekko-302
95Swedish Globe World Championships-233
95Swedish World Championships Stickers-89
96German DEL-120
96Swedish Semic Wien-178

Fihnn, Kjell
65Swedish Coralli ISHockey-48
67Swedish Hockey-102

Filangieri, Tim
03Waterloo Blackhawks-8

Filatov, Anatoli
93Niagara Falls Thunder-22
00Russian Hockey League-95
03Russian Hockey League-127

Filbey, Kenneth
94German First League-661
99German Bundesliga 2-173

Filc, Jan
02Slovakian Kvarteto-32

Filc, Martin
04Czech OFS-409

Filewich, Jonathan
00Prince George Cougars-15
01Prince George Cougars-1
03Prince George Cougars-14
04Lethbridge Hurricanes-14
05WBS Penguins-11
06AHL Top Prospects-46
06Wilkes-Barre Scranton Penguins-9
06Wilkes-Barre Scranton Penguins Jerseys-5

Filgis, Bertil
94German First League-69

Filgis, Kenneth
94German First League-591

Filiatrault, Jean-Ian
95Central Hockey League-42
95Oklahoma Coyotes RHI-6
98Oklahoma City Blazers-16

Filiatrault, Jean-Michel
03Quebec Remparts Memorial Cup-5
03Quebec Remparts-8
04Rimouski Oceanic-22

Filimonov, Dmitri
91Upper Deck-3
French-3
91Star Pics-19
92Finnish Semic-106
92Russian Stars Red Ace-6
93Donruss-239
93Leaf-400
93OPC Premier-496
Gold-496
93Parkhurst-139
Emerald Ice-139
93Pinnacle-450
Canadian-450
93PowerPlay-398
93Score-598
Gold-598
Canadian-598
Canadian Gold-598
93Senators Kraft Sheets-8
93Stadium Club-468
Members Only Master Set-468
First Day Issue-468
93Topps/OPC Premier-496
Gold-496
93Ultra-381
93Upper Deck-405
SP-109
93Swedish Semic World Champ Stickers-132
94Donruss-97
94Parkhurst-162
Gold-162
94Upper Deck-178
Electric Ice-178
95Indianapolis Ice-7
99Russian Stars of Hockey-25

Filimonov, Oleg
98Russian Hockey League-72
99Russian Hockey League-88
00Russian Hockey League-1
03Russian Hockey League-16

Filinov, Evgeni
99Russian Hockey League-238

Filion, Francois
05Baie-Comeau Drakkar-19

Filion, Maurice
72Nordiques Postcards-7
73Nordiques Team Issue-8

Filion, Nick
06Ohio State Buckeyes-16

Filip, Jan
94Czech APS Extraliga-27

Filip, Lukas
03UK London Racers-4

Filip, Martin
96Czech APS Extraliga-111
97Czech APS Extraliga-182
97Czech DS Stickers-279
98Czech DS Stickers-158
98Czech OFS-87
99Czech DS-27
99Czech OFS-133
99Czech OFS-360
00Czech OFS-49
01Czech OFS Update-308
02Czech OFS Plus-132
02Czech OFS Plus-368
03UK Basingstoke Bison-9

Filipek, Daryl
91Ferris State Bulldogs-13
92Ferris State Bulldogs-13

Filipenko, Mark
92British Columbia JHL-132

Filipenko, Wayne
91Air Canada SJHL-A20

Filipi, Milan
94Czech APS Extraliga-39
99Czech OFS-179
00Czech OFS-24

Filipic, Fraser
03Colorado Eagles-8
04Colorado Eagles-6
05Colorado Eagles-7
06Colorado EaglesÄ -9

Filipowicz, Jayme
94Dubuque Fighting Saints-9
98New Hampshire Wildcats-16
99Milwaukee Admirals Keebler-4
00Milwaukee Admirals Keebler-6
00Milwaukee Admirals Postcards-4
01Quebec Citadelles-19
03Hartford Wolf Pack-5
04Providence Bruins-7
05German DEL-15

Filippin, J. Christophe
94French National Team-12

Filippov, Alexander
73Swedish Stickers-124
98Russian Hockey League-64
99Russian Hockey League-121
00Russian Hockey League-180

Fillion, Bob
43Parade Sportive *-37
43Parade Sportive *-38
44Beehive Group II Photos-238
45Quaker Oats Photos-76A
45Quaker Oats Photos-76B
45Quaker Oats Photos-76C
45Quaker Oats Photos-76D
48Exhibits Canadian-6

Fillion, Claude
95Hampton Roads Admirals-11
97Columbus Cottonmouths-3
97Macon Whoopee-12
97Macon Whoopee Autographs-12
98Columbus Cottonmouths-4

Fillion, Denis
51Bas Du Fleuve-57
52Bas Du Fleuve-44

Fillion, Hugues
93Quebec Pee-Wee Tournament-113

Fillion, Jean-Marie
51Bas Du Fleuve-48

Fillion, Jimmy
01Shawinigan Cataractes-4

Fillion, Marcel
51Bas Du Fleuve-58
52Bas Du Fleuve-34

Fillion, Martin
92Quebec Pee-Wee Tournament-681
98Quad-City Mallards-6
01Fort Wayne Komets-16
01Thetford Mines Coyotes-8
02Thetford Mines Coyotes-10
03Thetford Mines Prolab-8
04St Georges de Beauce Garaga-7

Fillion, Pascal
92Quebec Pee-Wee Tournament-875
93Quebec Pee-Wee Tournament-537

Fillon, Pierre
90 7th Inn. Sketch QMJHL-169

Filppula, Ilari
03Finnish Cardset-77
04Finnish Cardset-84
Parallel-64
05Finnish Cardset -237
06Finnish Cardset-257

Filppula, Valtteri
04Finnish Cardset-78
04Finnish Cardset Signatures-16
05Black Diamond-237
05Hot Prospects-237
En Fuego-237
Hot Materials-HMVF
White Hot-237
05Parkhurst-627
Facsimile Auto Parallel-627
05SP Authentic-197
05SP Game Used-208
05SPx-230
Spectrum-230
05The Cup-170
Black Rainbow Rookies-170
Masterpiece Pressplates (Artifacts)-275
Masterpiece Pressplates (Black Diamond)-237
Masterpiece Pressplates (Ice)-252
Masterpiece Pressplates Rookie Upd Auto-265
Masterpiece Pressplates SPA Autos-197
Masterpiece Pressplates (SP Game Used)-208
Masterpiece Pressplates SPx Autos-230
Masterpiece Pressplates (Trilogy)-253
Masterpiece Pressplates Ult Coll-148
Masterpiece Pressplates Autographs-170
Platinum Rookies-170
05UD Artifacts-275
05Ultimate Collection-148
Gold-148
05Upper Deck-483
05Upper Deck Ice-252
05Upper Deck Rookie Update-265
05Upper Deck Trilogy-253
05Finnish Cardset Magicmakers-11
05AHL All-Stars-7
05AHL Top Prospects-14
06Be A Player Portraits First Exposures-FEVF
06Hot Prospects Hotagraphs-HVF
06SP Game Used SIGnificance-SVF
06Upper Deck MVP Autographs-OAFQ

Fimin, Yuri
98Russian Hockey League-70
99Russian Hockey League-117

Finch, Geoff
94Wheeling Thunderbirds Photo Album-7
95Wheeling Thunderbirds-2
95Wheeling Thunderbirds Series II-6

Findlay, Tim
94Windsor Spitfires-26
95Slapshot-429
95Signature Rookies-61
Signatures-61
97Austin Ice Bats-3
01Flint Generals-5

Fines, Eddie
93Quebec Pee-Wee Tournament-485

Fines, Kevin
03Cape Fear Fire Antz-3
03Lubbock Cotton Kings-8

Finger, Jeff
03Hershey Bears-2
03Hershey Bears Patriot News-8
03Reading Royals-13
04Hershey Bears Patriot News-10
06Albany River Rats-11
07Upper Deck Victory-231
Black-231
Gold-231

Fink, Patrik
94Czech APS Extraliga-178
95Czech APS Extraliga-194
96Czech APS Extraliga-328
99Czech OFS-463
00Czech OFS-203
01Czech OFS-262

Finkbeiner, Lloyd
51Buffalo Bison-7
51Laval Dairy QSHL-90

Finlay, Andy
96UK Fife Flyers-7
97UK Fife Flyers-9
01UK Dundee Stars-9
02UK Dundee Stars-9

Finley, Brian
96Barrie Colts-8
98Black Diamond-96
Double Diamond-96
Triple Diamond-96
Quadruple Diamond-96
98OPC Chrome-240
Refractors-240
98SP Authentic-114
Power Shift-114
Sign of the Times-BF
Sign of the Times Gold-BF
98SPx Top Prospects-61
Radiance-61
Spectrum-61
98Topps-240
O-Pee-Chee-240
98Upper Deck-391
Exclusives-391
Exclusives 1 of 1-391
Gold Reserve-391
98Barrie Colts-21
98Bowman CHL-21
98Bowman CHL-161
Golden Anniversary-21
Golden Anniversary-161
OPC International-21
OPC International-161
Scout's Choice-SC17
98Bowman Chrome CHL-21
98Bowman Chrome CHL-161
Golden Anniversary-21
Golden Anniversary-161
Golden Anniversary Refractors-21
Golden Anniversary Refractors-161
OPC International-21
OPC International-161
OPC International Refractors-21
OPC International Refractors-161
Refractors-21
Refractors-161
99Black Diamond-97
Diamond Cut-97
Final Cut-97
99O-Pee-Chee-261
99O-Pee-Chee Chrome-261
99O-Pee-Chee Chrome Refractors-261
99SPx-167
Radiance-167
Spectrum-167
99Topps/OPC-261
99Topps/OPC Chrome-261
Refractors-261
99Upper Deck-316
Exclusives-316
Exclusives 1 of 1-316
99Upper Deck Sobey's Memorial Cup-12
99Upper Deck Gold Reserve-316
99Upper Deck MVP SC Edition-210
Gold Script-210
Silver Script-210
Super Script-210
ProSign-BF
99Upper Deck Ovation-69
Standing Ovation-69
99Bowman CHL-40
99Bowman CHL-141
Gold-40
Gold-141
OPC International-40
OPC International-141
Autographs-BA1
Autographs Gold-BA1
Autographs Silver-BA1
Scout's Choice-SC5
99UD Prospects-14
CHL Class-C8
Destination the Show-DS7
Signatures of Tradition-BF
00Brampton Battalion-4
00UD CHL Prospects-32
CHL Class-CC1
Supremacy-CS2
02Milwaukee Admirals-4
03BAP Memorabilia-106
Emerald-106
Gold-106
Ruby-106
Sapphire-106
Deep in the Crease-D6
Future Wave-FW-8
03ITG Action-314
03Pacific Complete-452
Red-452
03Upper Deck MVP-246
Gold Script-246
Silver Script-246
Canadian Exclusives-246
03Milwaukee Admirals-3
03Milwaukee Admirals Postcards-5
04Barrie Colts 10th Anniversary-25
04Milwaukee Admirals-1
05ITG Heroes/Prosp Toronto Expo Parallel -206
05Milwaukee Admirals Choice-6
05Milwaukee Admirals Pepsi-7
05ITG Heroes and Prospects-206
Autographs Series II-BF
06Between The Pipes-6
Autographs-ABF
Emblems-GUE27
Emblems Gold-GUE27
Emblems Autographs-GUE27
Jerseys-GUJ27
Jerseys Gold-GUJ27
Jerseys Autographs-GUJ27
Numbers-GUN27
Numbers Gold-GUN27
Numbers Autographs-GUN27
Prospect Trios-PT01
Prospect Trios Gold-PT01
06Providence Bruins-6

Finley, Jeff
86Portland Winter Hawks-5
88ProCards AHL-308
89ProCards AHL-252
90ProCards AHL/IHL-503
91ProCards-470
92Stadium Club-426
93Flyers J.C. Penney-11
93Flyers Lineup Sheets-16
93PowerPlay-405
96Be A Player-156
Autographs-156
Autographs Silver-156
96Coyotes Coca-Cola-6
97Pacific Invincible NHL Regime-151
98Hartford Wolf Pack-7
99Blues Taco Bell-10
00BAP Memorabilia-100
Emerald-100
Ruby-100
Sapphire-100
Promos-100
00BAP Mem Chicago Sportsfest Copper-100
00BAP Memorabilia Chicago Sportsfest Blue-100
00BAP Memorabilia Chicago Sportsfest Gold-100
00BAP Memorabilia Chicago Sportsfest Ruby-100
00BAP Memorabilia Chicago Sun-Times Ruby-100
00BAP Memorabilia Chicago Sun-Times Gold-100
00BAP Mem Chicago Sun-Times Sapphire-100
00BAP Mem Toronto Fall Expo Copper-100
00BAP Memorabilia Toronto Fall Expo Gold-100
00BAP Memorabilia Toronto Fall Expo Ruby-100
02Blues Team Issue-7
03Blues Team Set-8
05German DEL-137

Finley, Joe
04Sioux Falls Stampede-3-3

Finn, Michel
00Chicoutimi Sagueneens-4
Signed-4

Finn, Ron
90Pro Set-685

Finn, Sean
89Johnstown Chiefs-35

Finn, Shannon
95Peoria Rivermen-5
96Milwaukee Admirals-8
97Milwaukee Admirals-6
98Milwaukee Admirals-6

Finn, Steven
85Nordiques General Foods-7
85Nordiques Provigo-8
86Nordiques McDonald's-7
86Nordiques Team Issue-6
86Fredericton Express-6
87Nordiques General Foods-9
87Nordiques Team Issue-24
88Nordiques General Foods-11
88Nordiques Team Issue-11
88Panini Stickers-350
89Nordiques Team Issue-8
89Nordiques General Foods-6
89Nordiques Police-5
89O-Pee-Chee Stickers-191
90Nordiques Petro-Canada-5
90Nordiques Team Issue-4
90Pro Set-514
91Bowman-140
91Nordiques Panini Team Stickers-3
91Nordiques Petro-Canada-4
91O-Pee-Chee-139
91Panini Stickers-261
91Pinnacle-138
French-138
91Pro Set-204
French-204
91Score American-278
91Score Canadian Bilingual-498
91Score Canadian English-498
91Stadium Club-56
91Topps-139
91Upper Deck-340
French-340
92Bowman-185
92Durivage Panini-40
92Nordiques Petro-Canada-6
92O-Pee-Chee-7
92Panini Stickers-216
92Panini Stickers French-216
92Parkhurst-379
Emerald Ice-379
92Score-44
Canadian-44
92Stadium Club-384
92Topps-449
Gold-449G
93Durivage Score-20
93Leaf-422
93OPC Premier-326
Gold-326
93Panini Stickers-75
93Pinnacle-307
Canadian-307
93Score-322
Canadian-322
93Stadium Club-464
Members Only Master Set-464
First Day Issue-464
Master Photos-21
Master Photos Winners-21
93Topps/OPC Premier-326
Gold-326
94Nordiques Burger King-5
94OPC Premier-398
Special Effects-398
94Pinnacle-312
Artist's Proofs-312
Rink Collection-312
94Stadium Club-192
Members Only Master Set-192
First Day Issue-192
Super Team Winner Cards-192
94Topps/OPC Premier-398
Special Effects-398
96Be A Player-188
Autographs-188
Autographs Silver-188
96Collector's Choice-132
97Pacific Invincible NHL Regime-93

Finn-Olsson, Jonas
99Swedish Upper Deck-198

Finnerty, Ryan
01Peoria Rivermen-16
02Peoria Rivermen-14
02Peoria Rivermen Photo Pack-5

Finney, Mark
96UK Guildford Flames-9
03UK Belfast Giants-4

Finnie, John
90 7th Inn. Sketch Memorial Cup-28
93Lakeland Ice Warriors-12
93Lakeland Ice Warriors-13
01UK Manchester Storm Retro-11

Finnigan, Frank
24C144 Champ's Cigarettes-24
24V145-2-9
32O'Keefe Maple Leafs-12
33O-Pee-Chee V304A-25
33V129-26
33V252 Canadian Gum-23
34Beehive Group I Photos-316
35Diamond Matchbooks Tan 1-22
03BAP Ultimate Mem Maple Leafs Forever-6
04ITG Franchises Canadian-70
04ITG Franchises US West-296
06ITG Ultimate Memorabilia Sensational Sens Autos-1

Finnstrom, Johan
94Swedish Leaf-202
NHL Draft-4
94Signature Rookies Gold Standard *-84
95Swedish Leaf-115
95Swedish Upper Deck-173
95Oklahoma Coyotes RHI-7
95Signature Rookies-6
Signatures-6
97Swedish Collector's Choice-118
98Swedish UD Choice-136
99Swedish Upper Deck-138
00Swedish Upper Deck-125
02Swedish SHL-220
Parallel-220
03Swedish Elite-82
Silver-82

Finstad, Morten
92Norwegian Elite Series-64

Finsted, Morten
93Swedish Semic World Champ Stickers-248
94Finnish Jaa Kiekko-260
95Finnish Semic World Championships-180

Fiore, Ross
93Quebec Pee-Wee Tournament-1189

Fiore, Tony
92Tulsa Oilers-5

Fiorentino, Peter
87Sault Ste. Marie Greyhounds-23
89ProCards IHL-46
90ProCards AHL/IHL-5
91ProCards-190
92Binghamton Rangers-18
94Binghamton Rangers-3
95Las Vegas Thunder-2
96Binghamton Rangers-9

Fioretti, Mark
84Kelowna Wings-8
92Norwegian Elite Series-189

Fioroni, Paul
98Odessa Jackalopes-6
03Lubbock Cotton Kings-9

Firmani, Adrian
93Quebec Pee-Wee Tournament-1166

Firsanov, Konstantin
03German Nuremberg Ice Tigers Postcards-8
04German DEL-247
04German Nuremberg Ice Tigers Postcards-6
05German DEL-20

Firsov, Anatoli
69Russian National Team Postcards-11
69Swedish Hockey-3
70Finnish Jaakiekko-2
70Russian National Team Postcards-11
70Swedish Hockey-323
70Swedish Masterserien-21
70Swedish Masterserien-63
70Swedish Masterserien-68
70Swedish Masterserien-121
70Swedish Masterserien-132
70Swedish Masterserien-139
71Finnish Suomi Stickers-2
71Swedish Hockey-35
72Finnish Panda Toronto-49
72Finnish Semic World Championship-11
72Swedish Semic World Championship-11
73Swedish Stickers-99
74Swedish Semic World Champ Stickers-42
91Finnish Semic World Champ Stickers-243
91Swedish Semic World Champ Stickers-243
96Swedish Semic Wien Hockey Legends-HL5
03Czech Stadion-641

Firth, Jason
88Kitchener Rangers-13
89Kitchener Rangers-14
89 7th Inn. Sketch OHL-184
90Kitchener Rangers-12
90 7th Inn. Sketch OHL-232
90 7th Inn. Sketch Memorial Cup-33
91 7th Inn. Sketch OHL-59
92Thunder Bay Thunder Hawks-10
94Thunder Bay Senators-12
95Thunder Bay Senators-7
98Thunder Bay Thunder Cats-15
98UHL All-Stars-16
99Rockford IceHogs-8
99Rockford IceHogs-26
99UHL All-Stars West-20T
01Bakersfield Condors-9
03Port Huron Beacons-9

Fischer, Andreas
93Swiss HNL-123
95Swiss HNL-450
96Swiss HNL-459

Fischer, Cole
97Spokane Chiefs-7
98Spokane Chiefs-7
00Kootenay Ice-8
02Roanoke Express-5

Fischer, David
06Minnesota Golden Gophers-6

Fischer, Frank
94German First League-171

Fischer, Jiri
98OPC Chrome-242
Refractors-242
98Topps-242
O-Pee-Chee-242
98Bowman CHL-155
Golden Anniversary-155
OPC International-155
Autographs Blue-A19
Autographs Gold-A19
Autographs Silver-A19
98Bowman Chrome CHL-155
Golden Anniversary-155
Golden Anniversary Refractors-155
OPC International-155
OPC International Refractors-155
Refractors-155
99BAP Memorabilia-396
Gold-396
Silver-396
99BAP Millennium-86
Emerald-86
Ruby-86
Sapphire-86
Signatures-86
Signatures Gold-86
Calder Candidates Ruby-C8
Calder Candidates Emerald-C8
Calder Candidates Sapphire-C8
99O-Pee-Chee Chrome-296
99O-Pee-Chee Chrome Refractors-296
99Pacific-455
99Pacific Prism-51
Holographic Blue-51,
Holographic Gold-51
Holographic Mirror-51
Holographic Purple-51
Premiere Date-51
99Topps Arena Giveaways-DET-JF
99Topps/OPC Chrome-296
Refractors-296
99Topps Premier Plus-127
Parallel-127
99Upper Deck-225
Exclusives-225
Exclusives 1 of 1-225
99Upper Deck Arena Giveaways-DR1
99Upper Deck Gold Reserve-225
99Wayne Gretzky Hockey-61
99Bowman CHL-66
Gold-66
OPC International-66
Scout's Choice-SC16
00BAP Memorabilia-298
Emerald-298
Ruby-298
Sapphire-298
Promos-298
00BAP Mem Chicago Sportsfest Copper-298
00BAP Memorabilia Chicago Sportsfest Blue-298
00BAP Memorabilia Chicago Sportsfest Gold-298
00BAP Memorabilia Chicago Sportsfest Ruby-298
00BAP Memorabilia Chicago Sun-Times Ruby-298
00BAP Memorabilia Chicago Sun-Times Gold-298
00BAP Mem Chicago Sun-Times Sapphire-298
00BAP Mem Toronto Fall Expo Copper-298
00BAP Memorabilia Toronto Fall Expo Gold-298
00BAP Memorabilia Toronto Fall Expo Ruby-298
00O-Pee-Chee-280
00O-Pee-Chee Parallel-280
00Topps/OPC-280
Parallel-280
00Topps Chrome-175
OPC Refractors-175
Refractors-175
01BAP Signature Series-59
Autographs-59
Autographs Gold-59
02BAP Memorabilia Stanley Cup Champions-SCC-1
02BAP Sig Series Auto Buybacks 1999-86
02BAP Sig Series Auto Buybacks 2001-59
02BAP Ultimate Mem Dynasty Jerseys-7
02BAP Ultimate Mem Dynasty Emblems-7
02BAP Ultimate Mem Dynasty Numbers-7
02Topps Total-15
02Czech DS-56
02Czech DS-70
02Czech Stadion Cup Finals-485
03Parkhurst Original Six Detroit-10
Memorabilia-DM8
03Upper Deck-313
Canadian Exclusives-313
HG-313
UD Exclusives-313
03Upper Deck MVP-157
Gold Script-157
Silver Script-157
Canadian Exclusives-157
04UD All-World-2
Gold-2
04Czech OFS-336
Stars II-11
04Czech Zuma-33
05Parkhurst-184
Facsimile Auto Parallel-184
05Upper Deck-72
HG Glossy-72
05Upper Deck MVP-145
Gold-145
Platinum-145
05Upper Deck Toronto Fall Expo-72
05Czech World Champions Postcards-4
05Czech Kvarteto Bonaparte-3b
05Czech Pexeso Mini Blue Set-2

Fischer, Johann
94German First League-243

Fischer, Kai
95German DEL-77
96German DEL-271
99German DEL-303

Fischer, Lubomir
94Czech APS Extraliga-277
95Czech APS Extraliga-99

Fischer, Marco
93Swiss HNL-353
96Swiss HNL-484
98Swiss Power Play Stickers-143
01Swiss HNL-333
02Swiss HNL-445

Fischer, Patrick
93Swiss HNL-124
95Swedish World Championships Stickers-128
95Swiss HNL-171
95Swiss HNL-419
96Swiss HNL-65
96Swiss HNL-454
96Swiss HNL-538
98Swiss Power Play Stickers-168
98Swiss Power Play Stickers-255
98Swiss Power Play Stickers-279
98Swiss Power Play Stickers-309
99Swiss Panini Stickers-64
99Swiss Panini Stickers-207
99Swiss Panini Stickers-267
00Swiss Panini Stickers-114
00Swiss Panini Stickers-250
00Swiss Slapshot Mini-Cards-EVZ4
00Swiss Slapshot Mini-Cards-HCD9
01Swiss EV Zug Postcards-8
01Swiss HNL-113
01Swiss HNL-171
02Swiss EV Zug Postcards-11
02Swiss HNL-19
02Swiss HNL-217
02Swiss HNL-481
03Swiss EV Zug Postcards-11
03Swiss EV Zug Postcards-12
06Black Diamond-167A
Black-167A
Gold-167A
Ruby-167A
06Hot Prospects-175
Red Hot-175
White Hot-175
06O-Pee-Chee-555
Rainbow-555

06SP Authentic-220
Limited-220
06SP Game Used-144
Gold-144
Rainbow-144
06The Cup Masterpiece Pressplates (Black Diamond)-167
06The Cup Masterpiece Pressplates (Marquee Rookies)-555
06The Cup Masterpiece Pressplates (MVP)-320
06The Cup Masterpiece Pressplates (SP Authentic)-220
06The Cup Masterpiece Pressplates (SP Game Used)-144
06The Cup Masterpiece Pressplates (Trilogy)-144
06The Cup Masterpiece Pressplates (Victory)-301
06Upper Deck-236
Exclusives Parallel-236
High Gloss Parallel-236
Masterpieces-236
06Upper Deck MVP-320
Gold Script-320
Super Script-320
06Upper Deck Trilogy-144
06Upper Deck Victory-301

Fischer, Peter
94German First League-296

Fischer, Ron
89Swedish Semic World Champ Stickers-112
94German DEL-379
95German DEL-366
95Swedish World Championships Stickers-58

Fischer, Thomas
02German Adler Mannheim Eagles Postcards-5
04German Cologne Sharks Postcards-8
04German DEL-209

Fischer, Wolfgang
74Finnish Jenkki-112

Fischoder, Frank
94German First League-416

Fiset, Dominic
02Drummondville Voltigeurs-7

Fiset, Jasmin
93Quebec Pee-Wee Tournament-1094

Fiset, Mike
85Kingston Canadians-24
86Kingston Canadians-24
87Kingston Canadians-24

Fiset, Stephane
89Nordiques Team Issue-9
89Nordiques General Foods-7
89Nordiques Police-6
90Nordiques Team Issue-5
90O-Pee-Chee-312
90Score-415
Canadian-415
90Score Young Superstars-22
90Topps-312
Tiffany-312
90Halifax Citadels-7
90ProCards AHL/IHL-466
91Nordiques Petro-Canada-5
91Panini Stickers-258
91Parkhurst-363
French-363
91Upper Deck-452
French-452
91ProCards-530
92Bowman-398
92Durivage Panini-47
92Nordiques Petro-Canada-7
92O-Pee-Chee-75
92Panini Stickers-207
92Panini Stickers French-207
92Parkhurst-378
Emerald Ice-378
92Pro Set-152
92Score-354
Canadian-354
92Stadium Club-196
92Topps-285
Gold-285G
93Donruss-274
93Durivage Score-21
93Kraft-52
93Leaf-301
93OPC Premier-165
Gold-165
93Parkhurst-164
Emerald Ice-164
93Pinnacle-115
Canadian-115
Masks-6
93PowerPlay-198
93Score-379
Canadian-379
93Stadium Club-315
Members Only Master Set-315
First Day Issue-315
93Topps/OPC Premier-165
Gold-165
93Ultra-55
93Upper Deck-203
94Canada Games NHL POGS-292
94Donruss-225
94Flair-145
94Fleer-175
94Kraft-38
94Leaf-329
94Nordiques Burger King-6
94OPC Premier-333
Special Effects-333
94Pinnacle-102
Artist's Proofs-102
Rink Collection-102
94Score-126
Gold-126
Platinum-126
94SP-99
Die Cuts-99
94Stadium Club-246
Members Only Master Set-246
First Day Issue-246
Super Team Winner Cards-246
94Topps/OPC Premier-333
Special Effects-333
94Ultra-173
94Ultra-249
94Upper Deck-450
Electric Ice-450
95Be A Player-121
Signatures-S121
Signatures Die Cuts-S121
95Canada Games NHL POGS-82
95Collector's Choice-150
Player's Club-150
Player's Club Platinum-150
95Donruss-390
95Hoyle Eastern Playing Cards-12
95Kraft-26
95Metal-31
95Parkhurst International-317
Emerald Ice-317
95Pro Magnets-1
95Score-205
Black Ice Artist's Proofs-205
Black Ice-205
95SP-34
95Stadium Club-53
Members Only Master Set-53
95Summit-160
Artist's Proofs-160
Ice-160
In The Crease-8
95Topps-284
OPC Inserts-284
95Ultra-131
95Ultra-220
95Ultra-369
Gold Medallion-131
95Upper Deck-397
Electric Ice-397
Electric Ice Gold-397
Special Edition-SE23
Special Edition Gold-SE23
95Zenith-119
95Swedish World Championships Stickers-2
96Black Diamond-85
Gold-85
96Collector's Choice-59
96Donruss-186
Press Proofs-186
96Donruss Canadian Ice-17
Gold Press Proofs-17
Red Press Proofs-17
Les Gardiens-5
96Donruss Elite-13
Die Cut Stars-13
Painted Warriors-10
Painted Warriors Promos-P10
96Leaf-188
Press Proofs-188
96Leaf Limited-72
Gold-72
96Leaf Preferred-57
Press Proofs-57
Steel-15
Steel Gold-15
96Metal Universe-74
96NHL Pro Stamps-1
96Pinnacle Masks-8
96Pinnacle Masks Die Cuts-8
96Score-17
Artist's Proofs-17
Dealer's Choice Artist's Proofs-17
Special Artist's Proofs-17
Golden Blades-17
Net Worth-10
96Select Certified-8
Artist's Proofs-8
Blue-8
Mirror Blue-8
Mirror Gold-8
Mirror Red-8
Red-8
96SP-77
96Summit-98
Artist's Proofs-98
Ice-98
Metal-98
Premium Stock-98
96Ultra-78
Gold Medallion-78
96Upper Deck-274
96Zenith-20
Artist's Proofs-20
97Donruss-179
Press Proofs Silver-179
Press Proofs Gold-179
97Donruss Canadian Ice-30
Dominion Series-30
Provincial Series-30
Les Gardiens-5
97Donruss Canadian Ice Les Gardiens Promo-5
97Donruss Elite-54
Aspirations-54
Status-54
97Donruss Limited-150
97Donruss Limited-180
Exposure-150
Exposure-180
97Donruss Preferred-136
Cut to the Chase-136
97Donruss Priority-96
Stamp of Approval-96
97Katch-69
Gold-69
Silver-69
97Leaf-93
Fractal Matrix-93
Fractal Matrix Die Cuts-93
97Leaf International-93
Universal Ice-93
97Pacific-245
Copper-245
Emerald Green-245
Ice Blue-245
Red-245
Silver-245
97Pacific Invincible-67
Copper-67
Emerald Green-67
Ice Blue-67
Red-67
Silver-67
97Pacific Omega-107
Copper-107
Dark Gray-107
Emerald Green-107
Gold-107
Ice Blue-107
97Paramount-88
Copper-88
Dark Grey-88
Emerald Green-88
Ice Blue-88
Red-88
Silver-88
97Pinnacle-52
Artist's Proofs-52
Rink Collection-52
Press Plates Back Black-52
Press Plates Back Cyan-52
Press Plates Back Magenta-52
Press Plates Back Yellow-52
Press Plates Front Black-52
Press Plates Front Cyan-52
Press Plates Front Magenta-52
Press Plates Front Yellow-52
97Pinnacle Certified-14
Red-14
Mirror Blue-14
Mirror Gold-14
Mirror Red-14
97Pinnacle Inside-23
Coach's Collection-23
Executive Collection-23
97Pinnacle Tot Cert Platinum Blue-14
97Pinnacle Tot Certi Platinum Gold-14
97Pinnacle Totally Certified Platinum Red-14
97Pinnacle Tot Cert Mirror Platinum Gold-14
97Score-35
Artist's Proofs-35
Golden Blades-35
97SP Authentic-76
97Studio-52
Press Proofs Silver-52
Press Proofs Gold-52
98Aurora-66
98Be A Player-214
Press Release-214
98BAP Gold-214
98BAP Autographs-214
98BAP Autographs Gold-214
98Katch-68
98NHL Aces Playing Cards-50
98Pacific-234
Ice Blue-234
Red-234
98Pacific Dynagon Ice-87
Blue-87
Red-87
98Pacific Omega-110
Red-110
Opening Day Issue-110
98Panini Photocards-22
98Panini Stickers-200
98Paramount-104
Copper-104
Emerald Green-104
Holo-Electric-104
Ice Blue-104
Silver-104
98Revolution-66
Ice Shadow-66
Red-66
98UD Choice-97
98UD Choice Preview-97
98UD Choice Prime Choice Reserve-97
98UD Choice Reserve-97
98Upper Deck-288
Exclusives-288
Exclusives 1 of 1-288
Gold Reserve-288
99BAP Memorabilia-250
Gold-250
Silver-250
99BAP Millennium-119
Emerald-119
Ruby-119
Sapphire-119
Signatures-119
Signatures Gold-119
99Black Diamond-46
Diamond Cut-46
Final Cut-46
99Crown Royale-65
Limited Series-65
Premiere Date-65
99Pacific-190
Copper-190
Emerald Green-190
Gold-190
Ice Blue-190
Premiere Date-190
Red-190
99Pacific Dynagon Ice-96
Blue-96
Copper-96
Gold-96
Premiere Date-96
99Pacific Omega-107
Copper-107
Gold-107
Ice Blue-107
Premiere Date-107
99Pacific Prism-66
Holographic Blue-66
Holographic Gold-66
Holographic Mirror-66
Holographic Purple-66
Premiere Date-66
99Panini Stickers-256
99Paramount-109
Copper-109
Emerald-109
Gold-109
Holographic Emerald-109
Holographic Gold-109
Holographic Silver-109
Ice Blue-109
Premiere Date-109
Red-109
Silver-109
99Revolution-69
Premiere Date-69
Red-69
Shadow Series-69
99Stadium Club-78
First Day Issue-78
One of a Kind-78
Printing Plates Black-78
Printing Plates Cyan-78
Printing Plates Magenta-78
Printing Plates Yellow-78
99Upper Deck-239
Exclusives-239
Exclusives 1 of 1-239
99Upper Deck Gold Reserve-239
99Wayne Gretzky Hockey-84
00SLU Hockey-70
00Aurora-66
Premiere Date-66
00BAP Memorabilia-159
Emerald-159
Ruby-159
Sapphire-159
Promos-159
00BAP Mem Chicago Sportsfest Copper-159
00BAP Memorabilia Chicago Sportsfest Blue-159
00BAP Memorabilia Chicago Sportsfest Gold-159
00BAP Memorabilia Chicago Sportsfest Ruby-159
00BAP Memorabilia Chicago Sun-Times Ruby-159
00BAP Memorabilia Chicago Sun-Times Gold-159
00BAP Mem Chicago Sun-Times Sapphire-159
00BAP Mem Toronto Fall Expo Copper-159
00BAP Memorabilia Toronto Fall Expo Gold-159
00BAP Memorabilia Toronto Fall Expo Ruby-159
00BAP Parkhurst 2000-P148
00Crown Royale-48
Ice Blue-48
Limited Series-48
Premiere Date-48
Red-48
00O-Pee-Chee-70
00O-Pee-Chee Parallel-70
00Pacific-196
Copper-196
Gold-196
Ice Blue-196
Premiere Date-196
In the Cage Net-Fusions-5
00Paramount-111
Copper-111
Gold-111
Holo-Gold-111
Holo-Silver-111
Ice Blue-111
Premiere Date-111
00Private Stock-45
Gold-45
Premiere Date-45
Retail-45
Silver-45
00Revolution-67
Blue-67
Premiere Date-67
Red-67
00Stadium Club-66
00Topps/OPC-70
Parallel-70
00Upper Deck-81
Exclusives Tier 1-81
Exclusives Tier 2-81
00Upper Deck MVP-85
First Stars-85
Second Stars-85
Third Stars-85
00Upper Deck Vintage-164
00Upper Deck Vintage-173
01BAP Memorabilia-490
Emerald-490
Ruby-490
Sapphire-490
01Between the Pipes-74
01Between the Pipes-157
01Manchester Monarchs-13A
02BAP Sig Series Auto Buybacks 1998-214
02BAP Sig Series Auto Buybacks 1999-119
02Between the Pipes-20
Gold-20
Silver-20
Nightmares-GN5
02Pacific-194
Blue-194
Red-194

Fiset, Yanick
93Quebec Pee-Wee Tournament-999

Fishback, Bruce
84Minnesota-Duluth Bulldogs-23
85Minnesota-Duluth Bulldogs-16

Fisher, Cole
02Roanoke Express RBI Sports-194

Fisher, Craig
90O-Pee-Chee-126
90Score-412
Canadian-412
90Topps-126
Tiffany-126
90Upper Deck-155
French-155
90ProCards AHL/IHL-30
91ProCards-233
94Indianapolis Ice-7
95Images-22
Gold-22
96Carolina Monarchs-11
96Collector's Edge Future Legends-18
96Collector's Edge Ice-173
Prism-173
98Rochester Americans-1

Fisher, Derek
92Quebec Pee-Wee Tournament-981
93Quebec Pee-Wee Tournament-722

Fisher, Drew
06Sioux Falls Stampede -3

Fisher, Dunc
44Beehive Group II Photos-310
51Parkhurst-24

Fisher, Mike
97Sudbury Wolves Police-10
98Sudbury Wolves-9
99BAP Memorabilia-311
Gold-311
Silver-311
99BAP Millennium Calder Candidates Ruby-C20
99BAP Millennium Calder Candidate Emerald-C20
99BAP Millennium Calder Cand Sapphire-C20
99Black Diamond-61
Diamond Cut-61
Final Cut-61
99Crown Royale-96
Limited Series-96
Premiere Date-96
Prospects Parallel-96
99Pacific Dynagon Ice-3
Blue-3
Copper-3
Gold-3
Premiere Date-3
99Pacific Omega-166
Copper-166
Gold-166
Ice Blue-166
Premiere Date-166
99Paramount-264
99Senators Team Issue-6
99SP Authentic-111
99Stadium Club-182
First Day Issue-182
One of a Kind-182
Printing Plates Black-182
Printing Plates Cyan-182
Printing Plates Magenta-182
Printing Plates Yellow-182
99Topps Arena Giveaways-OTT-MF
99Topps Gold Label Class 1-96
Black-96
Black One of One-96
One of One-96
Red-96
Red One of One-96
99Topps Gold Label Class 2-96
99Topps Gold Label Class 2 Black-96
99Topps Gold Label Class 2 Black 1 of 1-96
99Topps Gold Label Class 2 One of One-96
99Topps Gold Label Class 2 Red-96
99Topps Gold Label Class 2 Red One of One-96
99Topps Gold Label Class 3-96
99Topps Gold Label Class 3 Black-96
99Topps Gold Label Class 3 Black 1 of 1-96
99Topps Gold Label Class 3 One of One-96
99Topps Gold Label Class 3 Red-96
99Topps Gold Label Class 3 Red One of One-96
99Topps Premier Plus-113
Parallel-113
99Upper Deck Arena Giveaways-OS1
99Sudbury Wolves-11
00BAP Memorabilia-3
Emerald-3
Ruby-3
Sapphire-3
Promos-3
00BAP Mem Chicago Sportsfest Copper-3
00BAP Memorabilia Chicago Sportsfest Blue-3
00BAP Memorabilia Chicago Sportsfest Gold-3
00BAP Memorabilia Chicago Sportsfest Ruby-3
00BAP Memorabilia Chicago Sun-Times Ruby-3
00BAP Memorabilia Chicago Sun-Times Gold-3
00BAP Mem Chicago Sun-Times Sapphire-3
00BAP Mem Toronto Fall Expo Copper-3
00BAP Memorabilia Toronto Fall Expo Gold-3
00BAP Memorabilia Toronto Fall Expo Ruby-3
00BAP Signature Series-68
Emerald-68
Ruby-68
Sapphire-68
Autographs-184
Autographs Gold-184
00O-Pee-Chee-289
00O-Pee-Chee Parallel-289
00Pacific-277
Copper-277
Gold-277
Ice Blue-277
Premiere Date-277
00Senators Team Issue-5
00Topps/OPC-289
Parallel-289
00Topps Chrome-184
OPC Refractors-184
Refractors-184
00Upper Deck-122
Exclusives Tier 1-122
Exclusives Tier 2-122
00Upper Deck Victory-276
01Bowman YoungStars-112
Gold-112
Ice Cubed-112
Autographs-MF
Relics-JMF
Relics-SMF
Relics-DSMF
Rivals-R9
01Senators Team Issue-6
02BAP First Edition-23
Jerseys-23
02BAP Sig Series Auto Buybacks 2000-184
02BAP Signature Series Golf-GS58
02BAP Signature Series Phenoms-YP1
02NHL Power Play Stickers-106
02Pacific-265
Blue-265
Red-265
02Pacific Complete-341
Red-341
02Parkhurst-187
Bronze-187
Gold-187
Silver-187
02Senators Team Issue-5
02Senators Team Issue-7
02Stadium Club YoungStars Relics-S16
02Topps Total-148
02Upper Deck-125
Exclusives-125
02Upper Deck Vintage-177
03ITG Action-439
Jerseys-M22
03O-Pee-Chee-54
03OPC Blue-54
03OPC Gold-54
03OPC Red-54
03Pacific-236
Blue-236
Red-236
03Pacific Exhibit-103
Blue Backs-103
Yellow Backs-103
03Senators Postcards-8
03Topps-54
Blue-54
Gold-54
Red-54
03Upper Deck-376
Canadian Exclusives-376
HG-376
UD Exclusives-376
04Swiss EV Zug Postcards-3
05Georgia Legends-35
05Panini Stickers-124
05Parkhurst-340
Facsimile Auto Parallel-340
05Upper Deck MVP-278
Gold-278
Platinum-278
06Gatorade-55
06O-Pee-Chee-342
Rainbow-342
06Panini Stickers-115
06Upper Deck-390
Exclusives Parallel-390
High Gloss Parallel-390
Masterpieces-390
06Upper Deck MVP-209
Gold Script-209
Super Script-209
07Upper Deck Victory-43
Black-43
Gold-43

Fisher, Patrick
00Swiss Panini Stickers National Team-P4
04Swiss EV Zug Postcards-17

Fisher, Shane
96Alaska Gold Kings-2

Fisher, Shaun
93Quebec Pee-Wee Tournament-1312
01Florida Everblades-18
02Trenton Titans-B-4
04Kalamazoo Wings-7

Fistric, Mark
03Vancouver Giants-6
04Vancouver Giants-2
05ITG Heroes/Prosp Toronto Expo Parallel -317
05Vancouver Giants-8
05ITG Heroes and Prospects-317
Autographs Series II-MFI
06Iowa Stars-7

Fitchner, Bob
76Nordiques Marie Antoinette-9
76Nordiques Postcards-13

Fitzgerald, Brian
89ProCards AHL-223

Fitzgerald, Eric
96New Hampshire Wildcats-24

Fitzgerald, Kevin
94Anchorage Aces-1

Fitzgerald, Randy
92Quebec Pee-Wee Tournament-298
93Quebec Pee-Wee Tournament-1404
96Detroit Whalers-8
00Jackson Bandits-4

Fitzgerald, Rob
94Owen Sound Platers-17
95Slapshot-48

Fitzgerald, Rusty
93Minnesota-Duluth Bulldogs-11
95Leaf-316
95Topps-209
OPC Inserts-209
95Upper Deck-142
Electric Ice-142
Electric Ice Gold-142
95Cleveland Lumberjacks-11
96Cleveland Lumberjacks-9
96Cleveland Lumberjacks Multi-Ad-10
97Cleveland Lumberjacks-11
97Cleveland Lumberjacks Postcards-10
98Quad-City Mallards-7
99Quad-City Mallards-14
00Manitoba Moose-9
01German Upper Deck-110

Fitzgerald, Ryan
93Quebec Pee-Wee Tournament-753

Fitzgerald, Sean
01Asheville Smoke-13

Fitzgerald, Tom
88ProCards AHL-321
89Islanders Team Issue-6
89ProCards AHL-239
90Bowman-116
Tiffany-116
91O-Pee-Chee-279
91Pro Set-431
French-431
91Topps-279
91Upper Deck-389
French-389
92Bowman-369
92O-Pee-Chee-394
92Stadium Club-102
92Topps-31
Gold-31G
92Ultra-342
92Upper Deck-52
93Donruss-121
93Leaf-221
93OPC Premier-338
Gold-338
93Panthers Team Issue-2
93Parkhurst-348
Emerald Ice-348
93Pinnacle-390
Canadian-390
93Score-493
93Score-554
Gold-554
Canadian-493
Canadian-554
Canadian Gold-554
93Stadium Club-392
Members Only Master Set-392
First Day Issue-392
93Topps/OPC Premier-338
Gold-338
93Ultra-324
94Leaf-516
94OPC Premier-53
Special Effects-53
94Parkhurst SE-SE64
Gold-SE64
94Pinnacle-207
Artist's Proofs-207
Rink Collection-207
94Score-163
Gold-163
Platinum-163
94Topps/OPC Premier-53
Special Effects-53
94Upper Deck-320
Electric Ice-320
95Parkhurst International-352
Emerald Ice-352
95Topps-294
OPC Inserts-294
95Upper Deck-436
Electric Ice-436
Electric Ice Gold-436
96Be A Player-4
Autographs-4
Autographs Silver-4
96Pinnacle-57
Artist's Proofs-57
Foil-57
Premium Stock-57
Rink Collection-57
96Upper Deck-69
97Pacific-113
Copper-113
Emerald Green-113
Ice Blue-113
Red-113
Silver-113
97Upper Deck-286
98Aurora-101
98Be A Player-73
Press Release-73
98BAP Gold-73
98BAP Autographs-73
98BAP Autographs Gold-73
98BAP Tampa Bay All Star Game-73
98Crown Royale-74
Limited Series-74
98Pacific Dynagon Ice-102
Blue-102
Red-102
98Panini Stickers-140
98Paramount-123
Copper-123
Emerald Green-123
Holo-Electric-123
Ice Blue-123
Silver-123
Team Checklists Die-Cuts-14
98Predators Team Issue-10
99O-Pee-Chee-127
99O-Pee-Chee Chrome-127
99O-Pee-Chee Chrome Refractors-127
99Pacific-223
Copper-223
Emerald Green-223
Gold-223
Ice Blue-223
Premiere Date-223
Red-223
99Panini Stickers-271
99Paramount-124
Copper-124
Emerald-124
Gold-124
Holographic Emerald-124
Holographic Gold-124
Holographic Silver-124
Ice Blue-124
Premiere Date-124
Red-124
Silver-124
99Stadium Club-73
First Day Issue-73
One of a Kind-73
Printing Plates Black-73
Printing Plates Cyan-73
Printing Plates Magenta-73
Printing Plates Yellow-73
99Topps/OPC-127
99Topps/OPC Chrome-127
Refractors-127
00O-Pee-Chee-202
00O-Pee-Chee Parallel-202
00Pacific-221
Copper-221
Gold-221
Ice Blue-221
Premiere Date-221
00Titanium Draft Day Edition-53
00Topps/OPC-202
Parallel-202
00Upper Deck Vintage-203
00Upper Deck Vintage-208
00Vanguard Dual Game-Worn Jerseys-12
00Vanguard Dual Game-Worn Patches-12
01Atomic Jerseys-35
01Atomic Patches-35
01BAP Memorabilia-411
Emerald-411
Ruby-411
Sapphire-411
01Crown Royale Triple Threads-10
01Crown Royale Triple Threads-16
01Pacific Heads-Up Quad Jerseys-13
01Private Stock Game Gear-57
01Private Stock Game Gear Patches-57
01Titanium Double-Sided Jerseys-22
01Titanium Draft Day Edition-22
01Upper Deck Victory-203
Gold-203
02BAP Sig Series Auto Buybacks 1998-73
02Maple Leafs Platinum Collection-6
02Maple Leafs Team Issue-4
02NHL Power Play Stickers-131
02Pacific Complete-389
Red-389
03Pacific Complete-105
Red-105
03Parkhurst Original Six Toronto-30
05Bruins Boston Globe-5
05Parkhurst-49
Facsimile Auto Parallel-49
05Upper Deck MVP-41
Gold-41
Platinum-41

Fitzgerald, Zack
06Peoria Rivermen-4

Fitzpatrick, Blaine
95Slapshot-377
95Sault Ste. Marie Greyhounds-7
98Peoria Rivermen-25
99ECHL All-Star Northern Conference-3
99Peoria Rivermen-9
00Peoria Rivermen-13

Fitzpatrick, Chanse
03Sudbury Wolves-10
06Binghamton Senators-6

Fitzpatrick, Mark
85Medicine Hat Tigers-23
88Kings Smokey-8
88ProCards AHL-209
89Islanders Team Issue-7
89Panini Stickers-265
90Bowman-119
Tiffany-119
90O-Pee-Chee-395
90Panini Stickers-86
90Pro Set-181
90Score-102A
90Score-102B
Canadian-102A
Canadian-102B
90Score Hottest/Rising Stars-50
90Score Young Superstars-32
90Topps-395
Tiffany-395
90Upper Deck-37
French-37
91Bowman-213
91O-Pee-Chee-47
91Score American-266
91Score Canadian Bilingual-486
91Score Canadian English-486
91Stadium Club-345
91Topps-47
91Upper Deck-602
French-602
91ProCards-472
92Bowman-394
92Kraft-32
92O-Pee-Chee-204
92Panini Stickers-195
92Panini Stickers French-195
92Parkhurst-99
Emerald Ice-99
92Pinnacle-24
French-24
92Pro Set-107
92Score-210
92Score-526
Canadian-210
Canadian-526
92Stadium Club-12
92Topps-216
Gold-216G
92Ultra-124
Award Winners-7
92Upper Deck-332
93Donruss-133
93Leaf-335
93Panini Stickers-66
93Parkhurst-344
Emerald Ice-344
93Pinnacle-369
Canadian-369
93PowerPlay-92
93Score-171
93Score-537
Gold-537
Canadian-171
Canadian-537
Canadian Gold-537
93Stadium Club-307
Members Only Master Set-307
First Day Issue-307
94Donruss-235
94EA Sports-202
94Leaf-308
94OPC Premier-82
94Parkhurst-87
Gold-87
94Pinnacle-236
Artist's Proofs-236
Rink Collection-236
94Topps/OPC Premier-82
94Ultra-296
94Upper Deck-457
Electric Ice-457
SP Inserts-SP120
SP Inserts Die Cuts-SP120
95Donruss-301
95Leaf-120
95Parkhurst International-88
Emerald Ice-88
95Pinnacle-175
Artist's Proofs-175
Rink Collection-175
Masks-7
95Score-173
Black Ice Artist's Proofs-173
Black Ice-173
95Topps-183
OPC Inserts-183
95Upper Deck-423
Electric Ice-423
Electric Ice Gold-423
96Be A Player-10
Autographs-10
Autographs Silver-10
97Score-234
98Be A Player-182
Press Release-182
98BAP Gold-182
98BAP Autographs-182
98BAP Autographs Gold-182
98Blackhawks Chicago Sun-Times-2
98NHL Aces Playing Cards-5
98OPC Chrome-194
Refractors-194
98Panini Stickers-96
98Topps-194
O-Pee-Chee-194
99Pacific-88
Copper-88
Emerald Green-88
Gold-88
Ice Blue-88
Premiere Date-88
Red-88
99Cincinnati Cyclones-7
02BAP Sig Series Auto Buybacks 1998-182

Fitzpatrick, Rory
92Sudbury Wolves-5
93Sudbury Wolves-5
93Sudbury Wolves Police-5
93Classic Four-Sport *-209
Gold-209
94Slapshot Promos-7
94Finest-115
Super Team Winners-115
Refractors-115
94Leaf Limited World Juniors USA-5
94SP-192
Die Cuts-192
94Sudbury Wolves-3
94Sudbury Wolves Police-18
95Parkhurst International-535
Emerald Ice-535
95Fredericton Canadiens-10
96Canadiens Sheets-8
97Sudbury Wolves Anniversary-8
02Rochester Americans-4
03Worcester Ice Cats 10th Anniversary-9
06Canucks Postcards-7

Fitzpatrick, Ross
83Springfield Indians-15
89ProCards AHL-340
90ProCards AHL/IHL-23
91ProCards-207

Fitzsimmons, Jason
907th Inn. Sketch WHL-162
917th Inn. Sketch WHL-280
96South Carolina Stingrays-31
01South Carolina Stingrays-6
02South Carolina Stingrays-21

Fixter, Paul
01Hershey Bears-8
02Hershey Bears-8
03Hershey Bears-23
03Hershey Bears Patriot News-28
04Hershey Bears Patriot News-11
06Rio Grande Valley Killer Bees-18

Fizzell, Bert
66Columbus Checkers-5
67Columbus Checkers-6

Fizzell, Brett
93Portland Winter Hawks-10

Fizzell, Kris
94Prince Albert Raiders-4
95Prince Albert Raiders-4

Fjallby, Claes-Ove
71Swedish Hockey-352

Fjeldstad, Morten
92Norwegian Elite Series-179
99Norwegian National Team-7

Fjeldstad, Per Christian
92Norwegian Elite Series-148

Fjeldstad, Rune
92Norwegian Elite Series-218
95Swedish World Championships Stickers-253

Fjell, Kenneth
92Norwegian Elite Series-157

Flache, Paul
99Brampton Battalion-7
00Brampton Battalion-7
02Greenville Grrrowl-2
03Gwinnett Gladiators-12
03Gwinnett Gladiators RBI Sports-200
04Chicago Wolves-8

Flache, Peter
99Guelph Storm-13
04Gwinnett Gladiators-12

Flaherty, Cullen
98Sioux City Musketeers-6

Flaherty, Joe
88ProCards AHL-169

Flaherty, Ray
80Oshawa Generals-2
Flaherty, Wade
90Kansas City Blades-3
90ProCards AHL/IHL-601
91Kansas City Blades-16
91ProCards-517
92Kansas City Blades-1
93Kansas City Blades-20
95Collector's Choice-97
Player's Club-97
Player's Club Platinum-97
95Donruss-280
95Parkhurst International-189
Emerald Ice-189
95Pinnacle-173
Artist's Proofs-173
Rink Collection-173
95Topps-249
OPC Inserts-249
95Upper Deck-57
Electric Ice-57
Electric Ice Gold-57
97Pacific Invincible NHL Regime-179
98Pacific-281
Ice Blue-281
Red-281
99Pacific-254
Copper-254
Emerald Green-254
Gold-254
Ice Blue-254
Premiere Date-254
Red-254
99Kansas City Blades-2
00Titanium Game Gear-109
00Titanium Game Gear Patches-109
01Atomic Jerseys-28
01Atomic Patches-28
01Between the Pipes-154
01Utah Grizzlies-33
02Between the Pipes-53
Gold-53
Silver-53
02Pacific Jerseys-20
02Pacific Jerseys Holo-Silver-20
03Milwaukee Admirals-18
03Milwaukee Admirals Postcards-6
04Manitoba Moose-15
05AHL All-Stars-8
05Manitoba Moose-8
06Manitoba Moose-21
06ITG Heroes and Prospects AHL Shooting Stars-AS07
Flaman, Dallas
95Prince Albert Raiders-5
96Prince Albert Raiders-5
97Prince Albert Raiders-6
98Prince Albert Raiders-7
99Kelowna Rockets-19
03St. Francis Xavier X-Men-25
Flaman, Fern
44Beehive Group II Photos-20
44Beehive Group II Photos-401
45Quaker Oats Photos-17
51Parkhurst-80
52Parkhurst-47
53Parkhurst-14
54Parkhurst-20
54Topps-25
55Bruins Photos-5
57Bruins Photos-6
57Topps-4
58Bruins Photos-4
58Topps-56
59Topps-29
60Shirriff Coins-102
60Topps-57
61Topps-21
90Score-357
Canadian-357
91Bruins Sports Action Legends-11
91Bruins Sports Action Legends-35
91Ultimate Original Six-48
91Ultimate Original Six-76
French-48
French-76
93Parkhurst Parkie Reprints-PR45
94Parkhurst Missing Link-2
98Bruins Alumni-5
Autographs-5
03Parkhurst Original Six Boston-35
03Parkhurst Original Six Boston-74
03Parkhurst Original Six Boston-85
Autographs-6
Flaman, Sheldon
00Fresno Falcons-6
Flamik, Boris
04Slovakian Skalica Team Set-21
Flanagan, Dave
91ProCards-128
98Hampton Roads Admirals 10th Anniversary-23
99German Bundesliga 2-29
Flanagan, Joe
92Birmingham Bulls-4
93Birmingham Bulls-4
93Birmingham Bulls Birmingham News-9
Flanagan, Mike
89Hampton Roads Admirals-5A
89Hampton Roads Admirals-5H
Flanagan, Patrick
99UK Guildford Flames-14
Flasar, Ales
94Czech APS Extraliga-3
95Czech APS Extraliga-338
Flatha, Jorn Arild
92Norwegian Elite Series-167
Flatley, Pat
83Canadian National Juniors-6
840-Pee-Chee-124
85Islanders News-4
850-Pee-Chee-83
850-Pee-Chee Stickers-73
85Topps-83
86Islanders Team Issue-24
860-Pee-Chee-162
860-Pee-Chee Stickers-207
86Topps-162
870-Pee-Chee-136
870-Pee-Chee Stickers-245
87Panini Stickers-101
87Topps-136
880-Pee-Chee-191
88Panini Stickers-286
88Topps-191
89Islanders Team Issue-8
890-Pee-Chee-250
89Panini Stickers-272
90Bowman-124
Tiffany-124
900-Pee-Chee-350
90Panini Stickers-82
90Pro Set-182
90Score-174
Canadian-174
90Topps-350
Tiffany-350
90Upper Deck-118
French-118
91Pro Set Platinum-77
91Bowman-218
910-Pee-Chee-343
91Panini Stickers-245
91Parkhurst-111
French-111
91Pinnacle-67
91Pinnacle-405
French-67
French-405
91Pro Set-152
91Pro Set-578
French-152
French-578
91Score American-29
91Score Canadian Bilingual-29
91Score Canadian English-29
91Stadium Club-20
91Topps-343
91Upper Deck-226
French-226
92Bowman-134
92Panini Stickers-201
92Panini Stickers French-201
92Parkhurst-342
Emerald Ice-342
92Pinnacle-44
French-44
92Pro Set-102
92Score-99
Canadian-99
92Stadium Club-477
92Topps-135
Gold-135G
92Ultra-125
93Donruss-199
93Kraft-29
93Leaf-43
93OPC Premier-28
Gold-28
93Panini Stickers-60
93Parkhurst-391
Emerald Ice-391
93Pinnacle-203
Canadian-203
Captains-14
Captains Canadian-14
93PowerPlay-146
93Score-220
Canadian-220
93Stadium Club-24
Members Only Master Set-24
OPC-24
First Day Issue-24
First Day Issue OPC-24
93Topps/OPC Premier-28
Gold-28
93Ultra-34
93Upper Deck-210
94Canada Games NHL POGS-155
94Flair-102
94Fleer-121
94Leaf-381
94OPC Premier-178
Special Effects-178
94Parkhurst SE-SE103
Gold-SE103
94Pinnacle-176
Artist's Proofs-176
Rink Collection-176
94Score-116
Gold-116
Platinum-116
94Topps/OPC Premier-178
Special Effects-178
94Ultra-125
94Upper Deck-371
Electric Ice-371
95Be A Player-13
Signatures-S13
Signatures Die Cuts-S13
95Canada Games NHL POGS-173
95Collector's Choice-202
Player's Club-202
Player's Club Platinum-202
95Donruss-227
95Emotion-104
95Leaf-151
95Panini Stickers-93
95Parkhurst International-403
Emerald Ice-403
95Pinnacle-30
Artist's Proofs-30
Rink Collection-30
95Playoff One on One-62
95Pro Magnets-58
95Score-196
Black Ice Artist's Proofs-196
Black Ice-196
95SkyBox Impact-100
95Topps-139
OPC Inserts-139
95Upper Deck-106
Electric Ice-106
Electric Ice Gold-106
96NHL Pro Stamps-58
97Pacific Invincible NHL Regime-126
97Score Rangers-12
Platinum-12
Premier-12
Flatt, Dayln
03Saskatoon Blades-16
04Saskatoon Blades-17
05Kootenay Ice-8
06Brampton Battalion-5
06Owen Sound Attack-4
Flatters, John
05Vancouver Giants-9
Flaxey, Kyle
96Owen Sound Platers-8
97Owen Sound Platers-5
98Owen Sound Platers-4
Fleck, Tyler
03Oklahoma City Blazers-8
04Oklahoma City Blazers-7
Fleenor, Brandon
99Tacoma Sabercats-16
00Tacoma Sabercats-11
03Pensacola Ice Pilots-342
Fleetwood, Brent
87Portland Winter Hawks-8
88Portland Winter Hawks-8
89Portland Winter Hawks-7
94Central Hockey League-43
95Central Hockey League-23
Fleischmann, Tomas
04Portland Pirates-24
04ITG Heroes and Prospects-108
Autographs-TF
04ITG Heroes/Prospects Toronto Expo '05-108
04ITG Heroes/Prospects Expo Heroes/Pros-108
05ITG Heroes/Prosp Toronto Expo Parallel -385
05Beehive-151
Matte-151
05Black Diamond-293
05Hot Prospects-273
En Fuego-273
Hot Materials-HMTF
Red Hot-273
White Hot-273
05Parkhurst-670
Facsimile Auto Parallel-670
Signatures-TF
True Colors-TCWAS
True Colors-TCWAS
05SP Authentic-219
Limited-219
05SP Game Used-190
Gold-190
05SPx-221
Spectrum-221
05The Cup-125
Autographed Rookie Patches Gold Rainbow-125
Black Rainbow Rookies-125
Masterpiece Pressplates (Artifacts)-340
Masterpiece Pressplates (Bee Hive)-151
Masterpiece Pressplates (Black Diamond)-293
Masterpiece Pressplates (Ice)-210
Masterpiece Pressplates (Rookie Update)-237
Masterpiece Pressplates SPA Autos-219
Masterpiece Pressplates (SP Game Used)-190
Masterpiece Pressplates (SPx)-221
Masterpiece Pressplates (Trilogy)-316
Masterpiece Pressplates Ult Coll-182
Masterpiece Pressplates Autographs-125
Platinum Rookies-125
05UD Artifacts-340
05Ultimate Collection-182
Gold-182
Ultimate Debut Threads Jerseys-DTJTF
Ultimate Debut Threads Jerseys Autos-DAJTF
Ultimate Debut Threads Patches-DTPTF
Ultimate Debut Threads Patches Autos-DAPTF
05Upper Deck-476
05Upper Deck Ice-210
Premieres Auto Patches-AIPTF
05Upper Deck Rookie Update-237
Inspirations Patch Rookies-237
05Upper Deck Trilogy-316
05AHL Top Prospects-15
05Hershey Bears-7
05ITG Heroes and Prospects-385
Autographs Update-A-TF
06Black Diamond Jerseys Black-JTF
06Black Diamond Jerseys Gold-JTF
06Black Diamond Jerseys Ruby-JTF
06Upper Deck Game Jerseys-J2TF
06Upper Deck Game Patches-J2TF
06Upper Deck MVP Jerseys-OJLF
06ITG Heroes and Prospects Calder Cup Champions-CC02
Fleming, Adam
95Slapshot-128
Fleming, Bob
83Pinebridge Bucks-4
87Flint Spirits-3
Fleming, Gavin
96UK Fife Flyers-1
Fleming, Gerry
92Fredericton Canadiens-10
93Fredericton Canadiens-10
93Classic Pro Prospects-37
94Canadiens Postcards-11
96Fredericton Canadiens-6
01Florida Everblades-2
02ECHL Update-U-8
02Florida Everblades-23
03Florida Everblades-6
04Florida Everblades-25
05Florida Everblades-25
Fleming, Jake
01Minnesota Golden Gophers-27
02Minnesota Golden Gophers-6
03Minnesota Golden Gophers-12
04Minnesota Golden Gophers-5
Fleming, Reg
44Beehive Group II Photos-94
60Shirriff Coins-78
61Shirriff/Salada Coins-24
61Topps-26
62Topps-42
Hockey Bucks-5
63Topps-31
64Beehive Group III Photos-7
64Beehive Group III Photos-124
64Coca-Cola Caps-14
64Topps-35
65Coca-Cola-12
65Topps-104
66Topps-93
66Topps USA Test-54
67Topps-30
680-Pee-Chee-167
68Shirriff Coins-96
690-Pee-Chee-95
Four-in-One-2
69Topps-95
70Dad's Cookies-35
70Esso Power Players-79
700-Pee-Chee-128
Deckle-12
70Sargent Promotions Stamps-21
70Topps-128
720-Pee-Chee-316
73Quaker Oats WHA-45
74Nabisco Sugar Daddy-13
94Parkhurst Tall Boys-8
95Parkhurst '66-67-83
Coins-83
Fleming, Ryan
92Michigan State Spartans-9
93Michigan State Spartans-8
Fleming, Shaun
97Spokane Chiefs-26
Fleming, Wayne
91Alberta International Team Canada-7
92Swedish Semic Elitserien Stickers-329
93Swedish Semic Elitserien-294
94Swedish Leaf-300
02Flyers Postcards-22
Flemming, Markus
94German DEL-288
95German DEL-265
Flemming, Michael
94German DEL-412
Flesch, John
74NHL Action Stamps Update-18
750-Pee-Chee NHL-353
81Milwaukee Admirals-5
Fletcher, Christian
97Dubuque Fighting Saints-9
Fletcher, Chuck
99Louisville Panthers-31
00Panthers Team Issue-2
Fletcher, Cliff
91Maple Leafs PLAY-11
Fletcher, Craig
917th Inn. Sketch WHL-57
92British Columbia JHL-125
Fletcher, David
96Quad-City Mallards-18
98Madison Monsters-11
Fletcher, John
90Cincinnati Cyclones-37
91Johnstown Chiefs-3
Fletcher, Justin
00Sioux City Musketeers-9
03St. Cloud State Huskies-7
04St. Cloud State Huskies-8
05St. Cloud State Huskies-6
05St. Cloud State Huskies-8
Fletcher, Scott
94Spokane Chiefs-24
95Spokane Chiefs-2
04Saginaw Spirit-10
05Saginaw Spirit-9
Fletcher, Steven
86Sherbrooke Canadiens-14
88ProCards AHL-171
89ProCards AHL-347
90ProCards AHL/IHL-537
91ProCards-256
93Fort Wayne Komets-5
95Fort Wayne Komets-8
99Fort Wayne Komets Penalty Leaders-2
01Fort Wayne Komets Shoe Carnival-4
Flett, Bill
66Tulsa Oilers-4
68Bauer Ads-8
680-Pee-Chee-159
68Shirriff Coins-57
690-Pee-Chee-102
69Topps-102
70Dad's Cookies-36
70Esso Power Players-157
700-Pee-Chee-161
70Sargent Promotions Stamps-75
70Topps/OPC Sticker Stamps-8
710-Pee-Chee-47
71Sargent Promotions Stamps-67
71Topps-47
71Toronto Sun-112
720-Pee-Chee-187
72Sargent Promotions Stamps-164
72Topps-139
72Finnish Semic World Championship-226
72Swedish Semic World Championship-226
73Flyers Linnett-7
730-Pee-Chee-20
73Topps-20
74Maple Leafs Postcards-6
74Maple Leafs Postcards-7
74NHL Action Stamps-268
740-Pee-Chee NHL-64
74Topps-64
750-Pee-Chee NHL-349
760-Pee-Chee NHL-332
79Oilers Postcards-7
790-Pee-Chee-266
88Oilers Tenth Anniversary-71
Flett, Dalyn
06Kamloops Blazers-8
Flett, Josh
92British Columbia JHL-6
96Arizona Icecats-6
Fleury, Carl
917th Inn. Sketch QMJHL-104
93Sherbrooke Faucons-20
94Roanoke Express-7
96Johnstown Chiefs-6
97Johnstown Chiefs-14
98Johnstown Chiefs-11
99Johnstown Chiefs-12
03St. Georges de Beauce Garaga-6
Fleury, Chris
95Upper Deck-518
Electric Ice-518
Electric Ice Gold-518
Fleury, Marc-Andre
01Cape Breton Screaming Eagles-21
02SPx Rookie Redemption-R222
02Cape Breton Screaming Eagles-1
02Cape Breton Screaming Eagles-26
03BAP Memorabilia-183
Emerald-183
Gold-183
Ruby-183
Sapphire-183
Deep in the Crease-D15
Draft Redemptions-1
Future of the Game-FG-18
Future Wave-FW-1
Masks III-18
Masks III Gold-18
Masks III Silver-18
Masks III Autographs-M-MF
Masks III Memorabilia-18
Super Rookies-SR16
Super Rookies Gold-SR16
Super Rookies Silver-SR16
03BAP Ultimate Memorabilia Autographs-123
Gold-123
03BAP Ultimate Mem Auto Sticks-123
03BAP Ultimate Mem Calder Candidates-4
03BAP Ultimate Mem Calder Candidates Gold-4
03BAP Ultimate Mem Franch Present Future-24
03BAP Ultimate Mem Jersey and Stick-19
03BAP Ultimate Mem Jersey and Stick Gold-19
03BAP Ultimate Mem Magnificent Prospects-1
03BAP Ultimate Mem Magnif Prospect Autos-1
03BAP Ultimate Memorabilia Nameplates-25
03BAP Ultimate Mem Nameplates Gold-25
03BAP Ultimate Mem Rookie Jersey Emblems-20
03BAP Ultimate Mem Rookie Jsy Emblem Gold-20
03BAP Ultimate Mem Rookie Jersey Numbers-20
03BAP Ultimate Mem Rookie Jsy Number Gold-20
03BAP Ultimate Memorabilia Triple Threads-34
03Beehive-229
Gold-229
Silver-229
Jumbo Variations-22
03Black Diamond-198
Black-198
Green-198
Red-198
03Bowman-152
Gold-152
Signs of the Future-SOF-MAF
03Bowman Chrome-152
Refractors-152
Gold Refractors-152
Xfractors-152
03Crown Royale-131
Red-131
Retail-131
Gauntlet of Glory-16
Royal Portraits-8
03eTopps-50
03ITG Action-601
03ITG Toronto Spring Expo Class of 2004-2
03ITG Used Signature Series-134
Autographs Gold-134
Jerseys-21
Jerseys Gold-21
Jersey Autos-21
Emblems-24
Emblems Gold-24
Teammates-9
Teammates Gold-9
03ITG VIP Rookie Debut-32
03Marc-Andre Fleury Stadium Giveaways-1
03Marc-Andre Fleury Stadium Giveaways-2
03Marc-Andre Fleury Stadium Giveaways-3
03Marc-Andre Fleury Stadium Giveaways-4
03McDonald's Pacific-61
03O-Pee-Chee-340
03OPC Blue-340
03OPC Gold-340
03OPC Red-340
03Pacific-358
03Pacific Calder-130
Silver-130
Reflections-7
03Pacific Complete-405
03Pacific Complete-507
Red-405
Red-507
03Pacific Exhibit-234
03Pacific Heads-Up-130
Hobby LTD-130
Retail LTD-130
Mini Sweaters-1
Prime Prospects-17
Prime Prospects LTD-17
03Pacific Invincible-121
Blue-121
Red-121
Retail-121
03Pacific Luxury Suite-96
Gold-96
03Pacific Prism-160
03Pacific Quest for the Cup-131
Calder Contenders-17
03Pacific Supreme-133
03Pacific Supreme-133A
Blue-133
Red-133
Retail-133
Generations-8
03Parkhurst Toronto Expo Rookie Preview-PRP-1
03Parkhurst Rookie-200
Calder Candidates-CMC-3
Calder Candidates Gold-CMC-3
High Expectations-HE-12
High Expectations Gold-HE-12
Jersey and Sticks-SJ-6
Jersey and Sticks Gold-SJ-6
Rookie Emblems-RE-50
Rookie Emblem Autographs-RE-MF
Rookie Emblems Gold-RE-50
Rookie Jerseys-RJ-50
Rookie Jersey Autographs-RJ-MF
Rookie Jerseys Gold-RJ-50
Rookie Numbers-RN-50
Rookie Number Autographs-RN-MF
Rookie Numbers Gold-RN-50
Teammates Gold-RT1
Teammates-RT1
03Private Stock Reserve-134
Blue-134
Red-134
Retail-134
Class Act-9
Increase Security-13
03SP Authentic-153
Limited-153
Sign of the Times-MAF
Sign of the Times-FS
Sign of the Times-LFR
Signed Patches-MF
03SP Game Used-91
Gold-91
Rookie Exclusives-RE3
03SPx-222
Radiance-222
Spectrum-222
03Titanium-132
Hobby Jersey Number Parallels-132
Retail-132
Retail Jersey Number Parallels-132
Right on Target-13
03Topps-340
Blue-340
Gold-340
Red-340
03Topps C55-151
Minis-151
Minis American Back-151
Minis American Back Red-151
Minis Bazooka Back-151
Minis Brooklyn Back-151
Minis Hat Trick Back-151
Minis O Canada Back-151
Minis O Canada Back Red-151
Minis Stanley Cup Back-151
03Topps Pristine-104
03Topps Pristine-105
03Topps Pristine-106
Gold Refractor Die Cuts-104
Gold Refractor Die Cuts-105
Gold Refractor Die Cuts-106
Refractors-104
Refractors-105
Refractors-106
Mini-PM-MAF
Press Plates Black-104
Press Plates Black-105
Press Plates Black-106
Press Plates Cyan-104
Press Plates Cyan-105
Press Plates Cyan-106
Press Plates Magenta-104
Press Plates Magenta-105
Press Plates Magenta-106
Press Plates Yellow-104
Press Plates Yellow-105
Press Plates Yellow-106
03UD Honor Roll-182
03UD Premier Collection-117
NHL Shields-SH-MAF
Signatures-PS-MAF
Signatures Gold-PS-MAF
Skills-SK-BF
Skills Patches-SK-BF
Stars-ST-MAF
Stars Patches-ST-MAF
Teammates-PT-PP
Teammates Patches-PT-PP
03Upper Deck-234
03Upper Deck-245
Canadian Exclusives-234
Canadian Exclusives-245
HG-234
HG-245
Magic Moments-MM-9
Rookie Threads-RT-3
03Upper Deck Classic Portraits-167
03Upper Deck Ice-130
03Upper Deck Ice-90P
Glass Parallel-130
03Upper Deck MVP-461
03Upper Deck Rookie Update-159
03Upper Deck Trilogy-180
Limited-180
03Upper Deck Victory-210
03Cape Breton Screaming Eagles-29
04ITG Top Prospects Spring Expo-18
04Pacific-210
Blue-210
Red-210
04Pacific Montreal International-8
Gold-8
04Pacific Montreal International Gold-8
04Pacific NHL All-Star FANtasy-8
04Pacific NHL All-Star FANtasy Gold-8
04Pacific National Convention-5
04Pacific Toronto Spring Expo-7
Gold-7
04SP Authentic-71
Limited-71
Octographs-OS-ROK
Sign of the Times-ST-FL
Sign of the Times-QS-FSHZ
Sign of the Times-FS-GOL
04Topps NHL All-Star FANtasy-4
04Ultimate Collection Buybacks-50
04Ultimate Collection Signatures-US-MA
04Upper Deck-143
Canadian Exclusives-143
HG Glossy Gold-143
HG Glossy Silver-143
04Upper Deck All-Star Promos-MF
04AHL Top Prospects-58
04Wilkes-Barre Scranton Penguins-23
04ITG Heroes and Prospects-34
04ITG Heroes and Prospects-120
04ITG Heroes and Prospects-121
04ITG Heroes and Prospects-122
04ITG Heroes and Prospects-NNO
Aspiring-3
Autographs-MF1
Autographs-MF2
Autographs-MF3
Autographs-MF4
Combos-1
Complete Emblems-12
Emblems-2
Emblems-16
Emblems Gold-2
Emblems Gold-16
He Shoots-He Scores Prizes-1
He Shoots-He Scores Prizes-3
He Shoots-He Scores Prizes-7
Jersey Autographs-2
Jersey Autographs-16
Jerseys-2
Jerseys-16
Jerseys Gold-2
Jerseys Gold-16
National Pride-5
Net Prospects-2
Net Prospects-20
Net Prospects Gold-2
Net Prospects Gold-20
Numbers-2
Numbers-16
Numbers Gold-2
Numbers Gold-16
Top Prospects-18
04ITG Heroes/Prospects Toronto Expo '05-34
04ITG Heroes/Prospects Toronto Expo '05-120
04ITG Heroes/Prospects Toronto Expo '05-121
04ITG Heroes/Prospects Toronto Expo '05-122
04ITG Heroes/Prospects Toronto Expo '05-NNO
04ITG Heroes/Prospects Expo Heroes/Pros-34
04ITG Heroes/Prospects Expo Heroes/Pros-120
04ITG Heroes/Prospects Expo Heroes/Pros-121
04ITG Heroes/Prospects Expo Heroes/Pros-122
05ITG Heroes/Prosp Toronto Expo Parallel -84
05Be A Player-70
First Period-70
Second Period-70
Third Period-70
Overtime-70
Dual Signatures-BF
Dual Signatures-FL
Quad Signatures-GOAL
Signatures-MF
Signatures Gold-MF
Triple Signatures-FGR
05Black Diamond-110
Emerald-110
Gold-110
Onyx-110
Ruby-110
Gemography-G-MF
Gemography Emerald-G-MF
Gemography Gold-G-MF
Gemography Onyx-G-MF
Gemography Ruby-G-MF
05Hot Prospects-79
En Fuego-79
Red Hot-79
White Hot-79
05ITG Sidney Crosby Series Memorabilia-SCM5
05ITG Ultimate Mem First Overall Jerseys-7
05ITG Ultimate Mem 1st Overall Jsy Gold-7
05ITG Ultimate Mem First Rounders Jerseys-2
05ITG Ultimate Mem First Rounders Jerseys-5
05ITG Ultimate Mem 1st Round Jersey Gold-2
05ITG Ultimate Mem 1st Round Jersey Gold-5
05ITG Ultimate Mem Future Stars Autos-1
05ITG Ultimate Mem Future Star Autos Gold-1
05ITG Ultimate Mem Future Stars Jerseys-1
05ITG Ultimate Mem Fut Stars Jerseys Gold-1
05ITG Ultimate Mem Future Stars Mem Autos-1
05ITG Ultimate Mem Fut Star Mem Auto Gold-1
05ITG Ultimate Mem Pass the Torch Jerseys-18
05ITG Ultimate Mem Passing Torch Jsy Gold-18
05ITG Ultimate Memorabilia Stick Autos-29
05ITG Ultimate Mem Stick Autos Gold-29
05ITG Ultimate Mem Sticks and Jerseys-25
05ITG Ultimate Mem Stick and Jerseys Gold-25
05ITG Ultimate Memorabilia Triple Autos-13
05ITG Ultimate Mem Triple Autos Gold-13
05ITG Ultimate Mem Triple Threads Jerseys-2
05ITG Ultimate Mem Triple Thread Jsy Gold-2
05McDonalds Upper Deck Goalie Factory-GF11
05McDonalds Upper Deck Goalie Gear-MG1
05Panini Stickers-147
05Parkhurst-385
Facsimile Auto Parallel-385
05SP Authentic Prestigious Pairings-PPTF
05SP Authentic Scripts to Success-SSMF
05SP Authentic Sign of the Times-MA
05SP Game Used Endorsed Equipment-EE-MF
05SP Game Used Statscriptions-ST-MA
05The Cup-83
Gold-83
Black Rainbow-83
Masterpiece Pressplates-83
05UD Artifacts-80
Blue-80
Gold-80
Green-80
Pewter-80
Red-80
Auto Facts-AF-MF
Auto Facts Blue-AF-MF
Auto Facts Copper-AF-MF
Auto Facts Pewter-AF-MF
Auto Facts Silver-AF-MF
Gold Autographed-80
05UD PowerPlay-70
05UD PowerPlay-114
05UD PowerPlay-130
Rainbow-70
05Ultimate Collection-73
Gold-73
Ultimate Signatures-USMF
05Ultra-159
Gold-159
Ice-159
05Upper Deck-400
Notable Numbers-N-AF
05Upper Deck Ice-79
Rainbow-79
05Upper Deck Rookie Update-80
05Upper Deck Trilogy-122
Crystal-122
Ice Scripts-IS-MF
Personal Scripts-PER-MF
Scripts-SFS-MF
05Upper Deck Victory-156
Black-156
Gold-156
Silver-156
05WBS Penguins-12
05ITG Heroes and Prospects-84
Aspiring-ASP18
Autographs-A-MAF
Complete Jerseys-CJ-22
Complete Jerseys Gold-CJ-22
Complete Logos-CHL-25
Future Teammates-FT4
He Shoots-He Scores Prizes-37
Jerseys-GUJ-24
Jerseys Gold-GUJ-24
Emblems-GUE-24
Emblems Gold-GUE-24
Numbers-GUN-24
Numbers Gold-GUN-24
Measuring Up-MU12
Measuring Up Gold-MU12
Nameplates-N-5
Nameplates Gold-N-05
National Pride-NPR-2
Net Prospects-NP-2
Net Prospects Dual-NPD7
Net Prospects Dual Gold-NPD7
Net Prospects Gold-NP-02
Spectrum-STM-01
Spectrum Gold-STM-01
06Be A Player-128
Autographs-128
Profiles-PP17
Profiles Autographs-PP17
Signatures-MF
Signatures 10-142
Signatures 25-142
Signatures Duals-DFS
Signatures Trios-TFSM
Signatures Foursomes-FLTFR
Unmasked Warriors-UM8
Unmasked Warriors Autographs-UM8
Up Close and Personal-UC29
Up Close and Personal Autographs-UC29
06Be A Player Portraits-82
Dual Signature Portraits-DSFW
Sensational Six-SS1ST
Sensational Six-SSGOL
Signature Portraits-SPMA
Triple Signature Portraits-TLWF
06Beehive-21
06Beehive-171
Blue-21
Gold-21
Matte-21
Red Facsimile Signatures-21
Wood-21
5 X 7 Black and White-21
5 X 7 Dark Wood-21
Signature Scrapbook-SSMF
06Between The Pipes-69
06Between The Pipes-112
06Between The Pipes-120
Autographs-AMF2
Autographs-AMF
Autographs-AMF3
Complete Jersey-CJ07
Complete Jersey Gold-CJ07
Complete Package-CP08
Complete Package Gold-CP08
Double Jerseys-DJ18
Double Jerseys Gold-DJ18
Double Memorabilia-DM05
Double Memorabilia Gold-DM05
Emblems-GUE02
Emblems Gold-GUE02
Emblems Autographs-GUE02
Gloves-GG04
Gloves Gold-GG04
Jerseys-GUJ02
Jerseys Gold-GUJ02
Jerseys Autographs-GUJ02
Numbers-GUN02
Numbers Gold-GUN02
Numbers Autographs-GUN02
Playing For Your Country-PC10
Playing For Your Country Gold-PC10
Prospect Trios-PT13
Prospect Trios Gold-PT13
Stick and Jersey-SJ09
Stick and Jersey Gold-SJ09
Stick and Jersey Autographs-SJ09
The Mask-M10
The Mask Gold-M10
The Mask Silver-M10
The Mask Game-Used-MGU06
The Mask Game-Used Gold-MGU06
06Black Diamond-143
Black-143
Gold-143
Ruby-143
06Flair Showcase-80
06Flair Showcase-157
06Flair Showcase-258
Parallel-80
Parallel-157
Parallel-258
Hot Gloves-HG24
Inks-IMF
Wave of the Future-WF36
06Fleer-157
Tiffany-157
Netminders-N21
06Hot Prospects-78
Hotagraphs-HFL
06ITG International Ice-127
Gold-127
Autographs-AMAF
06ITG Ultimate Memorabilia-94
Artist Proof-94
Autos-38
Autos Gold-38
First Round Picks-7
First Round Picks Gold-7
06McDonald's Upper Deck-37
Autographs-AMF
Hot Gloves-HG9
06O-Pee-Chee-390
Rainbow-390
06Panini Stickers-138
06SP Authentic-21
06SP Authentic-129
Chirography-MF
Limited-21
Limited-129
Sign of the Times-STMF
Sign of the Times Triples-ST3LFM
Sign of the Times Quads-ST4RBLF
06SP Game Used-82
Gold-82
Rainbow-82
Autographs-82
Letter Marks-LMMF
06SPx-82
Spectrum-82
SPxcitement-X81
SPxcitement Spectrum-X81
SPxcitement Autographs-X81
06The Cup-74
Autographed Patches-74
Black Rainbow-74
Enshrinements-EMF
Gold-74
Gold Patches-74
Jerseys-74
Masterpiece Pressplates-74
06UD Artifacts-22
06UD Artifacts-192
Blue-22
Blue-192
Gold-22
Gold-192
Platinum-22
Platinum-192
Radiance-22
Radiance-192
Autographed Radiance Parallel-22
Autographed Radiance Parallel-192
Red-22
Red-192
06UD Mini Jersey Collection-81
06UD Powerplay-81
Impact Rainbow-81
Goal Robbers-GR8
06Ultimate Collection-48
Signatures-US-MF
Ultimate Achievements-UA-MF
06Ultra-155
Gold Medallion-155
Ice Medallion-155
06Upper Deck Arena Giveaways-PIT6
06Upper Deck-404
Exclusives Parallel-404
High Gloss Parallel-404
Hometown Heroes-HH55
Masterpieces-404
Oversized Wal-Mart Exclusives-404
Signature Sensations-SSFL
06Upper Deck Entry Draft-DR3
06Upper Deck MVP-237
Gold Script-237
Super Script-237
Last Line of Defense-LL6
06Upper Deck Ovation-40
06Upper Deck Sweet Shot-83
Endorsed Equipment-EEMF
Signature Shots/Saves-SSMF
Signature Shots/Saves Sticks-SSSMF
06Upper Deck Trilogy-80
Ice Scripts-ISMF
Scripts-S1MF
Scripts-TSMF
06Upper Deck Victory-159
06Upper Deck Victory Black-159
06Upper Deck Victory Gold-159
06Upper Deck Victory GameBreakers-GB41
06Upper Deck Victory Next In Line-NL40
06ITG Heroes and Prospects-19
Autographs-AMAF
Quad Emblems-QE04
Quad Emblems Gold-QE04
07Upper Deck Ovation-62
07Upper Deck Victory-8
Black-8
Gold-8
GameBreakers-GB30
Oversize Cards-OS2
Stars on Ice-SI48
07ITG Going For Gold World Juniors-27
Autographs-27
Emblems-GUE27
Jerseys-GUJ27

Fleury, Romain
93Swiss HNL-268
95Swiss HNL-491
96Swiss HNL-386
98Swiss Power Play Stickers-85
99Swiss Panini Stickers-83

Fleury, Sylvain
92Oklahoma City Blazers-4
98Black Diamond Winning Formula Platinum-WF19

Fleury, Theoren
88Salt Lake Golden Eagles-8
89Kraft-2
89O-Pee-Chee-232
90Bowman-102
Tiffany-102
90Flames IGA/McGavin's-3
90O-Pee-Chee-386
90Panini Stickers-176
90Pro Set-33
90Score-226
Canadian-226
90Score Young Superstars-6
90Topps-386
Tiffany-386
90Upper Deck-47
90Upper Deck-478
French-47
French-478
91Pro Set Platinum-16
91Bowman-249
91Bowman-270
91Flames Panini Team Stickers-1
91Flames IGA-1
91Gillette-4
91Kraft-13
91McDonald's Upper Deck-18
91O-Pee-Chee-282
91O-Pee-Chee-322
91OPC Premier-92
91Panini Stickers-51
91Parkhurst-22
French-22
91Pinnacle-190
91Pinnacle-358
French-190
French-358
91Pro Set-28
91Pro Set-274
French-28
French-274
NHL Sponsor Awards-AC20
Puck Candy-4
91Score American-226
91Score American-407
91Score Canadian Bilingual-226
91Score Canadian Bilingual-297
91Score Canadian English-226
91Score Canadian English-297
91Score Hot Cards-7
91Score Young Superstars-4
91Stadium Club-355
91Topps-282
91Topps-322
Team Scoring Leaders-14
91Upper Deck-80
91Upper Deck-245
91Upper Deck-506
91Upper Deck-630
French-80
French-245
French-506
French-630
92Bowman-206
92Bowman-355
92Flames IGA-20
92Humpty Dumpty I-8
92Jofa/Koho-1
92McDonald's Upper Deck-7
92O-Pee-Chee-99
92Panini Stickers-46
92Panini Stickers French-46
92Parkhurst-19
Emerald Ice-19
92Pinnacle-125
French-125
92Pro Set-23
92Score-280
Canadian-280
92Stadium Club-2
92Topps-220
Gold-220G
92Ultra-21
92Upper Deck-285
92Finnish Semic-90
93American Licorice Sour Punch Caps-1
93Donruss-46
Special Print-D
93Kraft-8
93Leaf-154
93OPC Premier-100
Gold-100
Black Gold-13
93Panini Stickers-179
93Parkhurst-28
Emerald Ice-28
93Pinnacle-79
Canadian-79
93PowerPlay-36
93Score-191
93Score-441
Canadian-191
Canadian-441
93Stadium Club-390
Members Only Master Set-390
First Day Issue-390
Master Photos-17
Master Photos Winners-17
93Topps Premier Promo Sheet-100
93Topps/OPC Premier-100
Gold-100
93Ultra-41
93Upper Deck-3
93Upper Deck-229
93Upper Deck-288
Gretzky's Great Ones-GG7
NHLPA/Roots-28
SP-21
94Be A Player-R23
Signature Cards-123
94Canada Games NHL POGS-54
94Donruss-99
94EA Sports-23
94Finest-28
Super Team Winners-28
Refractors-28
Bowman's Best-B4
Bowman's Best-X21
Bowman's Best Refractors-B4
Bowman's Best Refractors-X21
94Flair-24
94Fleer-29
94Fleury Hockey Tips-1
94Fleury Hockey Tips-2
94Fleury Hockey Tips-3
94Fleury Hockey Tips-4
94Fleury Hockey Tips-5
94Fleury Hockey Tips-6
94Fleury Hockey Tips-7
94Fleury Hockey Tips-8
94Fleury Hockey Tips-9
94Fleury Hockey Tips-10
94Fleury Hockey Tips-11
94Fleury Hockey Tips-12
94Fleury Hockey Tips-13
94Fleury Hockey Tips-14
94Hockey Wit-94
94Kraft-4
94Leaf-55
94Leaf Limited-99
94OPC Premier-295
Special Effects-295
94Parkhurst Vintage-V20
94Parkhurst SE-SE28
Gold-SE28
94Pinnacle-38
Artist's Proofs-38
Rink Collection-38
Northern Lights-NL15
94Post Box Backs-11
94Score-69
Gold-69
Platinum-69
Check It-CI15
Franchise-TF4
94Select-109
Gold-109
94SP-17
Die Cuts-17
94Stadium Club-25
Members Only Master Set-25
First Day Issue-25
Super Teams-4
Super Teams Members Only Master Set-4
Super Team Winner Cards-25
94Topps/OPC Premier-295
Special Effects-295
94Topps Finest Inserts-19
94Topps/OPC Premier The Go To Guy-7
94Ultra-29
94Upper Deck-315
94Upper Deck-566
Electric Ice-315
Electric Ice-566
Predictor Retail-R41
Predictor Retail-R58
94Upper Deck Predictor Retail Exchange-R41
94Upper Deck Predictor Retail Exchange-R58
94Upper Deck SP Inserts-SP11
94Upper Deck SP Inserts Die Cuts-SP11
94Upper Deck NHLPA/Be A Player-21
94Finnish Jaa Kiekko-96
94Finnish Jaa Kiekko-357
95SLU Hockey Canadian-5
95SLU Hockey American-7
95Bashan Super Stickers-14
95Bashan Super Stickers-15
95Bowman-52
All-Foil-52
95Canada Games NHL POGS-17
95Canada Games NHL POGS-52
95Collector's Choice-201
95Collector's Choice-384
Player's Club-201
Player's Club-384
Player's Club Platinum-201
Player's Club Platinum-384
Crash The Game-C11A
Crash The Game-C11B
Crash The Game-C11C
Crash The Game Gold-C11A
Crash The Game Gold-C11B
Crash The Game Gold-C11C
Crash the Game Silver Redeemed-C11
Crash the Game Silver Bonus-C11
Crash the Game Gold Redeemed-C11
Crash the Game Gold Bonus-C11
95Donruss-289
Marksmen-6
Pro Pointers-12
95Donruss Elite-106
Die Cut Stars-106
Die Cut Uncut-106
95Emotion-21
Xcited-1
95Finest-30
95Finest-181
Refractors-30
Refractors-181
95Hoyle Western Playing Cards-30
95Imperial Stickers-15
95Kenner Starting Lineup Cards-8
95Kraft-49
95Kraft-58
95Leaf-115
Fire On Ice-5
Gold Stars-5
95Leaf Limited-6
95Metal-18
Heavy Metal-3
Iron Warriors-3
95Metal Promo Panel-3
95NHL Aces Playing Cards-13S
95No Fear Ad Cards-2
95Panini Stickers-237
95Parkhurst International-29
Emerald Ice-29
95Pinnacle-6
Artist's Proofs-6
Rink Collection-6
First Strike-15
95Pinnacle FANtasy-9
95Playoff One on One-16
95Pro Magnets-46
95Score-121
Black Ice Artist's Proofs-121
Black Ice-121
Golden Blades-13
Lamplighters-13
95Select Certified-5
Mirror Gold-5
Double Strike-13
Double Strike Gold-13
95SkyBox Impact Promo Panel-1
95SkyBox Impact-21
Ice Quake-13
95SP-16
Stars/Etoiles-E6
Stars/Etoiles Gold-E6
95Stadium Club Members Only-33
95Stadium Club-165
Members Only Master Set-165
Extreme North-EN5
Extreme North Members Only
Master Set-EN5
95Stadium Club Master Photo Test-2
95Summit-8
Artist's Proofs-8
Ice-8
95Topps-25
95Topps-382
OPC Inserts-25
OPC Inserts-382
Canadian Gold-6CG
Hidden Gems-1HG
Home Grown Canada-HGC5
Marquee Men Power Boosters-382
95Topps SuperSkills-35
Platinum-35
95Ultra-24
95Ultra-382
Gold Medallion-24
Crease Crashers-3
Red Light Specials-2
Red Light Specials Gold Medallion-2
95Upper Deck-179
95Upper Deck-235
Electric Ice-179
Electric Ice-235
Electric Ice Gold-179
Electric Ice Gold-235
95Upper Deck All-Star Game Predictors-13
Redemption Winners-13
95Upper Deck Freeze Frame-F12
95Upper Deck Freeze Frame Jumbo-F12
95Upper Deck NHL All-Stars-AS11
95Upper Deck NHL All-Stars Jumbo-AS11
95Upper Deck Predictor Retail-R8
95Upper Deck Predictor Retail Exchange-R8
95Upper Deck Special Edition-SE101
95Upper Deck Special Edition Gold-SE101
95Zenith-11
95Finnish SISU Limited-81
Signed and Sealed-9
95Finnish Semic World Championships-96
95Swedish Globe World Championships-83
95Swedish World Championships Stickers-24
96Be A Player-159
Autographs-159
Autographs Silver-159
Biscuit In The Basket-4
96Black Diamond-70
Gold-70
96Collector's Choice-35
96Collector's Choice-300
96Collector's Choice-312
Jumbos-1
MVP-UD11
MVP Gold-UD11
Stick'Ums-S20
96Collector's Choice Blow-Ups-35
96Collector's Choice Blow-Ups Bi-Way-2
96Donruss-159
Press Proofs-159
Hit List-20
96Donruss Canadian Ice-78
Gold Press Proofs-78
Red Press Proofs-78
O Canada-5
96Donruss Elite-54
Die Cut Stars-54
96Flair-11
Blue Ice-11
96Fleer-12
Art Ross-3
96Fleer Picks-24
Fabulous 50-11
Jagged Edge-2
96Hockey Greats Coins-7
Gold-7
96Kraft Upper Deck-8
96Kraft Upper Deck-36
96Kraft Upper Deck-65
96Leaf-61
Press Proofs-61
96Leaf Limited-67
Gold-67
96Leaf Preferred-67
Press Proofs-67
Steel-47
Steel Gold-47
96Maggers-24
96McDonald's Pinnacle-15
96Metal Universe-18
96NHL Aces Playing Cards-13
96NHL Pro Stamps-46
96Pinnacle-6
Artist's Proofs-6
Foil-6
Premium Stock-6
Rink Collection-6
96Post Upper Deck-6
96Score-12
Artist's Proofs-12
Dealer's Choice Artist's Proofs-12
Special Artist's Proofs-12
Check It-13
Golden Blades-12
96Select Certified-75
Artist's Proofs-75
Blue-75
Mirror Blue-75
Mirror Gold-75
Mirror Red-75
Red-75
96SkyBox Impact-13
96SP-20
Clearcut Winner-CW14
Game Film-GF15
96SPx-5
Gold-5
96Stadium Club Members Only-7
96Summit-91
Artist's Proofs-91
Ice-91
Metal-91
Premium Stock-91
96Team Out-4
96Topps Picks Top Shelf-TS14
96Ultra-21
Gold Medallion-21
96Upper Deck-22
96Upper Deck-208
Game Jerseys-GJ12
Generation Next-X30
Lord Stanley's Heroes Finals-LS9
Lord Stanley's Heroes Quarterfinals-LS9
Lord Stanley's Heroes Semifinals-LS9
Power Performers-P14
Superstar Showdown-SS4A
96Upper Deck Ice-9
Parallel-9
96Zenith-55
Artist's Proofs-55
Assailants-11
96Swedish Semic Wien-87
96Collector's Edge Ice Livin' Large-L9
97Beehive-18
Golden Portraits-18
97Black Diamond-143
Double Diamond-143
Triple Diamond-143
Quadruple Diamond-143
97Collector's Choice-40
Crash the Game-C14A
Crash the Game-C14B
Crash the Game-C14C
Crash the Game Exchange-CR14
Star Quest-SQ64
World Domination-W11
97Crown Royale-18
Emerald Green-18
Ice Blue-18
Silver-18
97Donruss-160
Press Proofs Silver-160
Press Proofs Gold-160
97Donruss Canadian Ice-23
Dominion Series-23
Provincial Series-23
National Pride-19
97Donruss Elite-74
Aspirations-74
Status-74
97Donruss Limited-24
97Donruss Limited-157
97Donruss Limited-177
Exposure-24
Exposure-157
Exposure-177
97Donruss Preferred-138
Cut to the Chase-138
97Donruss Priority-141
Stamp of Approval-141
97Esso Olympic Hockey Heroes-12
97Esso Olympic Hockey Heroes French-12
97Flames Collector's Photos-2
97Katch-20
Gold-20
Silver-20
97Kraft-2
97Kraft 3-D World's Best-5
97Kraft Team Canada-5
97Leaf-136
Fractal Matrix-136
Fractal Matrix Die Cuts-136
97Leaf International-136
Universal Ice-136
97McDonald's Team Canada Coins-7
97McDonald's Upper Deck-2
Game Film-9
97NHL Aces Playing Cards-46
97Pacific-45
Copper-45
Emerald Green-45
Ice Blue-45
Red-45
Silver-45
97Pacific Dynagon-15
97Pacific Dynagon-137
Copper-15
Copper-137
Dark Grey-15
Dark Grey-137
Emerald Green-15
Emerald Green-137
Ice Blue-15
Ice Blue-137
Red-15
Red-137
Silver-15
Silver-137
Dynamic Duos-4A
Tandems-23
Tandems-35
97Pacific Invincible-16
Copper-16
Emerald Green-16
Ice Blue-16
Red-16
Silver-16
97Pacific Omega-29
Copper-29
Dark Gray-29
Emerald Green-29
Gold-29
Ice Blue-29
Stick Handle Laser Cuts-3
Team Leaders-3
97Panini Stickers-199
97Paramount-28
Copper-28
Dark Grey-28
Emerald Green-28
Ice Blue-28
Red-28
Silver-28
97Pinnacle-103
Press Plates Back Black-103
Press Plates Back Cyan-103
Press Plates Back Magenta-103
Press Plates Back Yellow-103
Press Plates Front Black-103
Press Plates Front Cyan-103
Press Plates Front Magenta-103
Press Plates Front Yellow-103
97Pinnacle Certified-42
Red-42
Mirror Blue-42
Mirror Gold-42
Mirror Red-42
97Pinnacle Inside-40
Coach's Collection-40
Executive Collection-40
97Pinnacle Tot Cert Platinum Blue-42
97Pinnacle Tot Certi Platinum Gold-42
97Pinnacle Totally Certified Platinum Red-42
97Pinnacle Tot Cert Mirror Platinum Gold-42
97Revolution-17
Copper-17
Emerald-17
Ice Blue-17
Silver-17
1998 All-Star Game Die-Cuts-4
Team Checklist Laser Cuts-4
97Score-97
Artist's Proofs-97
Golden Blades-97
97SP Authentic-18
Icons-I20
Icons Die-Cuts-I20
Icons Embossed-I20
97SPx-6
Bronze-6
Gold-6
Silver-6
Steel-6
Dimension-SPX14
Grand Finale-6
97Studio-81
Press Proofs Silver-81
Press Proofs Gold-81
97Upper Deck-232
Game Dated Moments-232
97Upper Deck Diamond Vision-9
Signature Moves-9
97Upper Deck Ice-64
Parallel-64
Power Shift-64
97Zenith-12
Z-Gold-12
Z-Silver-12
97Zenith 5 x 7-46
Gold Impulse-46
Silver Impulse-46
98SLU Hockey Extended-61
98Aurora-24
Championship Fever-8
Championship Fever Copper-8
Championship Fever Ice Blue-8
Championship Fever Red-8
Championship Fever Silver-8
98Be A Player-168
Press Release-168
98BAP Gold-168
98BAP Autographs-168
98BAP Autographs Gold-168
98Black Diamond-13
Double Diamond-13
Triple Diamond-13
Quadruple Diamond-13
Winning Formula Gold-WF19
98Bowman's Best-31
Refractors-31
Atomic Refractors-31
98Crown Royale-18
Limited Series-18
Pillars of the Game-4
98Finest-2
No Protectors-2
No Protectors Refractors-2
Refractors-2
98Jell-O Spoons-2
98Katch-20
98Kenner Starting Lineup Cards-8
98McDonald's Upper Deck-2
98OPC Chrome-27
Refractors-27
98Pacific-117
Ice Blue-117
Red-117
Gold Crown Die-Cuts-6
Team Checklists-4
98Pacific Dynagon Ice-25
Blue-25
Red-25
Team Checklists-4
98Pacific Omega-31
Red-31
Opening Day Issue-31
Online-5
Toronto Spring Expo-31
98Panini Photocards-23
98Panini Stickers-176
98Paramount-27
Copper-27
Emerald Green-27
Holo-Electric-27
Ice Blue-27
Silver-27
Team Checklists Die-Cuts-4
98Post-5
98Revolution-18
Ice Shadow-18
Red-18
All-Star Die Cuts-6
Chalk Talk Laser-Cuts-3
Showstoppers-6
Three Pronged Attack-2
Three Pronged Attack Parallel-2
98SP Authentic-12
Power Shift-12
98SPx Finite-12
98SPx Finite-107
98SPx Finite-167
Radiance-12
Radiance-107
Radiance-167
Spectrum-12
Spectrum-107
Spectrum-167
98SPx Top Prospects-7
Radiance-7
Spectrum-7
Highlight Heroes-H6
Lasting Impressions-L11
Premier Stars-PS19
98Topps-27
O-Pee-Chee-27
98Topps Gold Label Class 1-8
Black-8
Black One of One-8
One of One-8
Red-8
Red One of One-8
98Topps Gold Label Class 2-8
98Topps Gold Label Class 2 Black-8
98Topps Gold Label Class 2 Black 1 of 1-8
98Topps Gold Label Class 2 One of One-8
98Topps Gold Label Class 2 Red-8
98Topps Gold Label Class 2 Red One of One-8
98Topps Gold Label Class 3-8
98Topps Gold Label Class 3 Black-8
98Topps Gold Label Class 3 Black 1 of 1-8
98Topps Gold Label Class 3 One of One-8
98Topps Gold Label Class 3 Red-8
98Topps Gold Label Class 3 Red One of One-8
98Topps Gold Label Goal Race '99-GR7
98Topps Gold Label Goal '99 Black 1 of 1-GR7
98Topps Gold Label Goal Race '99 Black-GR7
98Topps Gold Label Goal Race 99 1 of 1-GR7
98Topps Gold Label Goal Race '99 Red-GR7
98Topps Gold Label GoalRace 99 Red 1 of 1-GR7
98UD Choice-34
Mini Bobbing Head-BH25
Prime Choice Reserve-34
Reserve-34
StarQuest Blue-SQ13
StarQuest Gold-SQ13
StarQuest Green-SQ13
StarQuest Red-SQ13
98UD3-40
98UD3-100
98UD3-160
Die-Cuts-40
Die-Cuts-100
Die-Cuts-160
98Upper Deck-232
Exclusives-232
Exclusives 1 of 1-232
Fantastic Finishers-FF28
Fantastic Finishers Quantum 1-FF28
Fantastic Finishers Quantum 2-FF28
Fantastic Finishers Quantum 3-FF28
Frozen In Time-FT5
Frozen In Time Quantum 1-FT5
Frozen In Time Quantum 2-FT5
Frozen In Time Quantum 3-FT5
Lord Stanley's Heroes-LS6
Lord Stanley's Heroes Quantum 1-LS6
Lord Stanley's Heroes Quantum 2-LS6
Lord Stanley's Heroes Quantum 3-LS6
Profiles-P27
Profiles Quantum 1-P27
Profiles Quantum 2-P27
Profiles Quantum 3-P27
Gold Reserve-232
98Upper Deck MVP-57
Gold Script-57
Silver Script-57
Super Script-57
99Aurora-37
Striped-37
Premiere Date-37
Premiere Date Striped-37
Championship Fever-6
Championship Fever Copper-6
Championship Fever Ice Blue-6
Championship Fever Silver-6
Styrotechs-4
99BAP Memorabilia-226
Gold-226
Silver-226
Jersey Cards-J14
Jersey Emblems-E14
Jersey Numbers-I14
Jersey and Stick Cards-S14
99BAP Update Teammates Jersey Cards-TM16
99BAP Update Teammates Jersey Cards-TM27
99BAP Update Teammates Jersey Cards-TM50
99BAP Millennium-160
Emerald-160
Ruby-160
Sapphire-160
Signatures-160
Signatures Gold-160
Jerseys-J1
Jersey Autographs-J1
Jersey and Stick Cards-JS1
Jersey Emblems-E1
Jersey Numbers-N1
99Black Diamond-56
Diamond Cut-56
Final Cut-56
Diamonation-D11
Diamond Might-DM10
Diamond Skills-DS9
99Crown Royale-89
Limited Series-89
Premiere Date-89
Ice Elite-17
Ice Elite Parallel-17
International Glory-16
International Glory Parallel-16
99Kraft Face Off Rivals-2
99O-Pee-Chee-227
99O-Pee-Chee Chrome-227
99O-Pee-Chee Chrome Refractors-227
99Pacific-103
Copper-103
Emerald Green-103
Gold-103
Ice Blue-103
Premiere Date-103
Red-103
Center Ice-5
Center Ice Proofs-5
Gold Crown Die-Cuts-8
Past and Present-5
99Pacific Dynagon Ice-128
Blue-128
Copper-128
Gold-128
Premiere Date-128
Checkmates American-6
Checkmates American-21
Checkmates Canadian-6
Lamplighter Net-Fusions-7
99Pacific Omega-149
Copper-149
Gold-149
Ice Blue-149
Premiere Date-149
Cup Contenders-13
5 Star Talents-16
5 Star Talents Parallel-16
99Pacific Prism-89
Holographic Blue-89
Holographic Gold-89
Holographic Mirror-89
Holographic Purple-89
Premiere Date-89
Clear Advantage-13
Sno-Globe Die-Cuts-14
99Panini Stickers-99
99Panini Stickers-324
99Paramount-148
Copper-148
Emerald-148
Gold-148
Holographic Emerald-148
Holographic Gold-148
Holographic Silver-148
Ice Blue-148
Premiere Date-148
Red-148
Silver-148
Personal Best-22
99Revolution-95
Premiere Date-95
Red-95
Shadow Series-95
Ice Sculptures-8
Top of the Line-27
Copper-95
Gold-95
CSC Silver-95
99SP Authentic-56
Sign of the Times-TF
Sign of the Times Gold-TF
Supreme Skill-SS8
99SPx-96
Radiance-96
Spectrum-96
99Stadium Club-163
First Day Issue-163
One of a Kind-163
Printing Plates Black-163
Printing Plates Cyan-163
Printing Plates Magenta-163
Printing Plates Yellow-163
Chrome-42
Chrome Refractors-42
Chrome Oversized-17
Chrome Oversized Refractors-17
99Topps/OPC-227
99Topps Stanley Cup Heroes-SC17
99Topps Stanley Cup Heroes Refractors-SC17
99Topps/OPC Chrome-227
Refractors-227
99Topps Gold Label Class 1-14
Black-14
Black One of One-14
One of One-14
Red-14
Red One of One-14
99Topps Gold Label Class 2-14
99Topps Gold Label Class 2 Black-14
99Topps Gold Label Class 2 Black 1 of 1-14
99Topps Gold Label Class 2 One of One-14
99Topps Gold Label Class 2 Red-14
99Topps Gold Label Class 2 Red One of One-14
99Topps Gold Label Class 3-14
99Topps Gold Label Class 3 Black-14
99Topps Gold Label Class 3 Black 1 of 1-14
99Topps Gold Label Class 3 One of One-14
99Topps Gold Label Class 3 Red-14
99Topps Gold Label Class 3 Red One of One-14
99Topps Gold Label Prime Gold-PG3
99Topps Gold Label Prime Gold Black-PG3
99Topps Gold Label Prime Gold Red-PG3
99Topps Premier Plus-3
Parallel-3
Code Red-CR5
99Ultimate Victory-57
1/1-57
Parallel-57
Parallel 100-57
Smokin Guns-SG7
Stature-S8
The Victors-V8
99Upper Deck-260
Exclusives-260
Exclusives 1 of 1-260
99Upper Deck Gold Reserve-260
99Upper Deck HoloGrFx-38
Ausome-38
99Upper Deck MVP-53
Gold Script-53
Silver Script-53
Super Script-53
ProSign-TF
99Upper Deck MVP SC Edition-117
Gold Script-117
Silver Script-117
Super Script-117
Clutch Performers-CP7
Golden Memories-GM7
Stanley Cup Talent-SC11
99Upper Deck Ovation-36
99Upper Deck Ovation-89
Standing Ovation-36
Standing Ovation-89
Lead Performers-LP2
99Upper Deck PowerDeck-15
Auxiliary-15
Auxiliary 1 of 1-15
99Upper Deck Retro-22
Gold-22
Platinum-22
Generation-G7B
Generation Level 2-G7B
99Upper Deck Victory-190
99Wayne Gretzky Hockey-109
Changing The Game-CG7
Elements of the Game-EG9
99Finnish Cardset Aces High-C-8
00Aurora-92
Pinstripes-92
Pinstripes Premiere Date-92
Premiere Date-92
00BAP Memorabilia-44
Emerald-44
Ruby-44
Sapphire-44
Promos-44
Jersey Cards-J18
Jersey Emblems-E18
Jersey Numbers-N18
Jersey and Stick Cards-JS18
00BAP Mem Chicago Sportsfest Copper-44
00BAP Memorabilia Chicago Sportsfest Blue-44
00BAP Memorabilia Chicago Sportsfest Gold-44
00BAP Memorabilia Chicago Sportsfest Ruby-44
00BAP Memorabilia Chicago Sun-Times Ruby-44
00BAP Memorabilia Chicago Sun-Times Gold-44
00BAP Mem Chicago Sun-Times Sapphire-44
00BAP Mem Toronto Fall Expo Copper-44
00BAP Memorabilia Toronto Fall Expo Gold-44
00BAP Memorabilia Toronto Fall Expo Ruby-44
00BAP Mem Update Heritage Jersey Cards-H14
00BAP Mem Update Heritage Jersey Gold-H14
00BAP Memorabilia Update Teammates-TM19
00BAP Memorabilia Update Teammates-TM40
00BAP Memorabilia Update Teammates Gold-TM19
00BAP Memorabilia Update Teammates Gold-TM40
00BAP Parkhurst 2000-P96
00BAP Signature Series-33
Emerald-33
Ruby-33
Sapphire-33
Autographs-83
Autographs Gold-83
He Shoots-He Scores Points-3
Jersey Cards-J1
Jersey and Stick Cards-GSJ1
Jersey Cards Autographs-J1
Jersey Emblems-E1
Jersey Numbers-IN1
00BAP Ultimate Memorabilia Autographs-1
Gold-1
00BAP Ultimate Mem Game-Used Jerseys-GJ1
00BAP Ultimate Mem Game-Used Sticks-GS1
00BAP Ultimate Mem Journey Jerseys-JJ15
00BAP Ultimate Mem Journey Emblems-JE15
00BAP Ultimate Mem Journey Numbers-JN15
00BAP Ultimate Memorabilia Teammates-TM37
00Black Diamond-39
Gold-39
00Crown Royale-69
Ice Blue-69
Limited Series-69
Premiere Date-69
Red-69
Game-Worn Jersey Redemptions-6
Now Playing-12
00O-Pee-Chee-12
00O-Pee-Chee Parallel-12
00Pacific-260
Copper-260
Gold-260
Ice Blue-260
Premiere Date-260
00Panini Stickers-64
00Paramount-160
Copper-160
Gold-160
Holo-Gold-160
Holo-Silver-160
Ice Blue-160
Premiere Date-160
Game Used Sticks-14
00Private Stock-64
Gold-64
Premiere Date-64
Retail-64
Silver-64
PS-2001 Action-36
00Revolution-94
Blue-94
Premiere Date-94
Red-94
00SP Authentic-56
00SPx-45
Spectrum-45
00Stadium Club-69
00Titanium-60
Blue-60
Gold-60
Premiere Date-60
Red-60
Retail-60
All-Stars-8NA
Game Gear-33
Game Gear-111
Game Gear-112
Game Gear Patches-111
Game Gear Patches-112
Three-Star Selections-16
00Titanium Draft Day Edition-65
Patches-65
00Topps/OPC-12
Parallel-12
00Topps Chrome-12
OPC Refractors-12
Refractors-12
00Topps Gold Label Class 1-60
Gold-60
00Topps Gold Label Class 2-60
00Topps Gold Label Class 2 Gold-60
00Topps Gold Label Class 3-60
00Topps Gold Label Class 3 Gold-60
00Topps Heritage-67
Chrome Parallel-67
Original Six Relics-OSJ-TF
Original Six Relics-OSJ
00Topps Premier Plus-53
Blue Ice-53
00Topps Stars-50
Blue-50
00UD Heroes-80
Game-Used Twigs-T-TF
Game-Used Twigs Gold-C-FL
00UD Pros and Prospects-56
00UD Reserve-56
Gold Strike-GS7
Practice Session Jerseys-TF
Practice Session Jerseys Autographs-TF
00Upper Deck-114
Exclusives Tier 1-114
Exclusives Tier 2-114
00Upper Deck Legends-21
00Upper Deck Legends-91
Legendary Collection Bronze-21
Legendary Collection Bronze-91
Legendary Collection Gold-21
Legendary Collection Gold-91
Legendary Collection Silver-21
Legendary Collection Silver-91
00Upper Deck MVP-121
First Stars-121
Second Stars-121
Talent-M11
Third Stars-121
Valuable Commodities-VC7
00Upper Deck Victory-150
00Upper Deck Victory-152
00Upper Deck Victory-312
00Upper Deck Vintage-235
00Vanguard-64
High Voltage-22
High Voltage Gold-22
High Voltage Green-22
High Voltage Red-22
High Voltage Silver-22
Holographic Gold-64
Holographic Purple-64
In Focus-13
Pacific Proofs-64
00Czech Stadion-118
01Atomic-63
Blue-63
Gold-63
Premiere Date-63
Red-63
Power Play-22
Team Nucleus-10
01BAP Memorabilia-239
Emerald-239
Ruby-239
Sapphire-239
All-Star Jerseys-ASJ24
All-Star Emblems-ASE24
All-Star Numbers-ASN24
All-Star Jersey Doubles-DASJ12
All-Star Starting Lineup-SL11
All-Star Teammates-AST7
All-Star Teammates-AST10
Country of Origin-CO3
01BAP Signature Series Certified 100-C46
01BAP Signature Series Certified 50-C46
01BAP Signature Series Certified 1 of 1's-C46
01BAP Sig Series International Medals-IG-4
01BAP Signature Series Jerseys-GJ-69
01BAP Sig Series Jersey and Stick Cards-GSJ-69
01BAP Ultimate Memorabilia Dynamic Duos-11
01BAP Update He Shoots-He Scores Points-2
01BAP Update He Shoots-He Scores Prizes-29
01BAP Update Heritage-H16
01Bowman YoungStars-107
Gold-107
Ice Cubed-107
01Crown Royale-94
Blue-94
Premiere Date-94
Red-94
Retail-94
Triple Threads-15
01McDonald's Pacific Hometown Pride-6

01McDonald's Pacific Jersey Patch Silver-13
01McDonald's Pacific Jersey Patches Gold-13
01Nortel All-Star Game Sheets-9
01O-Pee-Chee-37
01O-Pee-Chee Heritage Parallel-37
01O-Pee-Chee Heritage Parallel Limited-37
01O-Pee-Chee Premier Parallel-37
01Pacific-256
01Pacific-416
01Pacific-435
Extreme LTD-256
Gold-416
Gold-435
Hobby LTD-256
Premiere Date-256
Retail LTD-256
01Pacific Adrenaline-125
Blue-125
Premiere Date-125
Red-125
Retail-125
01Pacific Arena Exclusives-256
01Pacific Arena Exclusives-416
01Pacific Arena Exclusives-435
01Pacific Heads-Up-63
Blue-63
Premiere Date-63
Red-63
Silver-63
Quad Jerseys-14
Stat Masters-11
01Parkhurst-36
Gold-36
Silver-36
Jerseys-PJ43
Milestones-M50
Teammates-T3
01Private Stock-61
Gold-61
Premiere Date-61
Retail-61
Silver-61
01Private Stock Pacific Nights-61
01SP Game Used Authentic Fabric-AFTF
01SP Game Used Authentic Fabric-DFFD
01SP Game Used Authentic Fabric Gold-AFTF
01SPx-43
01Titanium-92
Hobby Parallel-92
Premiere Date-92
Retail-92
Retail Parallel-92
Double-Sided Jerseys-25
Double-Sided Jerseys-28
Double-Sided Patches-25
01Titanium Draft Day Edition-59
01Topps-37
Heritage Parallel-37
Heritage Parallel Limited-37
OPC Parallel-37
01Topps Chrome-37
Refractors-37
Black Border Refractors-37
01Topps Reserve Emblems-TF
01Topps Reserve Jerseys-TF
01Topps Reserve Name Plates-TF
01Topps Reserve Numbers-TF
01Topps Reserve Patches-TF
01UD Challenge for the Cup-58
01UD Mask Collection-63
Gold-63
01UD Playmakers-64
01UD Premier Collection Jerseys-BTF
01UD Premier Collection Jerseys Black-B-TF
01UD Stanley Cup Champs-28
Jerseys-T-TF
Pieces of Glory-G-TF
Sticks-S-TF
01UD Top Shelf-106
Sticks-STF
Sticks-KSF
Sticks Gold-STF
Sticks Gold-KSF
01Upper Deck-115
Exclusives-115
Game Jerseys-ATF
Gate Attractions-GA2
01Upper Deck Ice-107
01Upper Deck MVP-126
01Upper Deck Victory-232
01Upper Deck Victory-420
Gold-232
Gold-420
01Upper Deck Vintage-167
01Upper Deck Vintage-172
01Upper Deck Vintage-173
01Vanguard Memorabilia-45
02BAP All-Star Edition-22
Jerseys-22
Jerseys Gold-22
Jerseys Silver-22
02BAP First Edition-191
02BAP Memorabilia All-Star Jerseys-ASJ-13
02BAP Memorabilia All-Star Teammmates-AST-8
02BAP Sig Series Auto Buybacks 1998-168
02BAP Sig Series Auto Buybacks 1999-160
02BAP Sig Series Auto Buybacks 2000-83
02BAP Ultimate Mem Global Dominators-9
02McDonald's Pacific Salt Lake Gold-6
02O-Pee-Chee-202
02O-Pee-Chee Premier Blue Parallel-202
02O-Pee-Chee Premier Red Parallel-202
02O-Pee-Chee Factory Set-202
02Pacific-251
Blue-251
Red-251
Jerseys-35
Jerseys Holo-Silver-35
02Pacific Calder-32
Silver-32
02Pacific Complete-401
Red-401
02Pacific Exclusive-36
Jerseys-4
Jerseys Gold-4
02Pacific Heads-Up-79
Blue-79
Purple-79
Red-79
Quad Jerseys-18
Quad Jerseys Gold-18
02Pacific Quest for the Cup-17
Gold-17
02Parkhurst-171
Bronze-171
Gold-171
Silver-171
02Parkhurst Retro-50
Minis-50
02Private Stock Reserve-109
Red-109
Retail-109
Patches-109
02Titanium-22
Blue-22
Red-22
Retail-22
02Topps-202
OPC Blue Parallel-202
OPC Red Parallel-202
Factory Set-202
02UD Premier Collection Jerseys Bronze-TF
02UD Premier Collection Jerseys Gold-TF
02UD Premier Collection Jerseys Silver-TF
02UD Top Shelf All-Stars-ASTF
02UD Top Shelf Dual Player Jerseys-STFR
02UD Top Shelf Milestones Jerseys-MSFRM
02UD Top Shelf Shooting Stars-SHTF
02UD Top Shelf Triple Jerseys-HTKGF
02Upper Deck-280
Exclusives-280
02Upper Deck Beckett UD Promos-280
02Upper Deck Good Old Days-GOTF
02Upper Deck Number Crunchers-NC2
02Upper Deck MVP Skate Around Jerseys-SDLF
02Upper Deck MVP Skate Around Jerseys-STKFS
02Upper Deck MVP Souvenirs-S-TF0
02Upper Deck Rookie Update-157C
02Vanguard-23
LTD-23
Jerseys-11
Jerseys Gold-11
02Finnish Cardset-18
02UD SuperStars *-53
Gold-53
03BAP Memorabilia Practice Jerseys-PMP13
03ITG Action-105
03Pacific-73
Blue-73
Red-73
03Pacific Exhibit-33
Blue Backs-33
Yellow Backs-33
03Pacific Prism-24
Blue-24
Gold-24
Red-24
03Parkhurst Orig Six New York Mem-NM27
03Private Stock Reserve-153
Blue-153
Patches-153
Red-153
Retail-153

Flichel, Marty
92Tacoma Rockets-9
93Tacoma Rockets-8
96Dayton Bombers-17
98Michigan K-Wings-6
00UK Sekonda Superleague-101
03Kalamazoo Wings-13
04Idaho Steelheads-26
05Idaho Steelheads-7
06Idaho Steelheads-5

Flichel, Todd
87Moncton Hawks-8
88ProCards AHL-170
89ProCards AHL-37
90Moncton Hawks-8
90ProCards AHL/IHL-247
91ProCards-246
92Cincinnati Cyclones-10
93Rochester Americans Kodak-9

Fliegauf, Charly
94German DEL-26

Flinck, Tapio
70Finnish Jaakiekko-189
71Finnish Suomi Stickers-81
72Finnish Jaakiekko-244
72Finnish Panda Toronto-33
73Finnish Jaakiekko-241
78Finnish SM-Liiga-222
80Finnish Mallasjuoma-201

Flink, Adam
06Texas Tornados-13

Flinn, Ryan
99Halifax Mooseheads-13
01BAP Memorabilia-399
Emerald-399
Ruby-399
Sapphire-399
01Upper Deck Ice-139
01Manchester Monarchs-10B
02Pacific Complete-508
Red-508
02Manchester Monarchs-20
02Reading Royals-27
03Manchester Monarchs-3
03Manchester Monarchs Team Issue-4
04Manchester Monarchs-19
04Manchester Monarchs Tobacco-19
05Manchester Monarchs-4
05Manchester Monarchs-29

Flinn, Tyson
95Slapshot-385
95Sudbury Wolves-4
95Sudbury Wolves Police-8
96Sudbury Wolves Police-9

Flint, Calvin
89Brandon Wheat Kings-13
90Brandon Wheat Kings-21
907th Inn. Sketch WHL-232

Flintoft, Rob
87Portland Winter Hawks-9
88Portland Winter Hawks-9

Flinton, Eric
95Classic-73
Autographs-6
95Classic Five-Sport *-160
96Binghamton Rangers-10
97Charlotte Checkers-8
97Charlotte Checkers-25

Flis, Sylvester
03BAP Memorabilia-99
Emerald-99
Gold-99
Ruby-99
Sapphire-99

Floberg, Jonas
01Swedish Brynas Tigers-7
02Swedish SHL-150
Parallel-150

Flockhart, Rob
77Canucks Royal Bank-3
84Springfield Indians-13

Flockhart, Ron
82O-Pee-Chee-249
82O-Pee-Chee Stickers-113
82Topps Stickers-113
83NHL Key Tags-97
83O-Pee-Chee-264
83O-Pee-Chee Stickers-192
83Penguins Coke-9
83Topps Stickers-192
84Canadiens Postcards-6
84O-Pee-Chee-174
84O-Pee-Chee Stickers-115
84O-Pee-Chee Stickers-116
84Penguins Heinz Photos-8
84Topps-124
84Kelowna Wings-46
85O-Pee-Chee-171
85O-Pee-Chee Stickers-128
86O-Pee-Chee-146
86O-Pee-Chee Stickers-176
86Topps-146
87Blues Kodak-10
87O-Pee-Chee-103
87O-Pee-Chee Stickers-25
87Panini Stickers-317
87Topps-103
92Dallas Freeze-10
93Dallas Freeze-18
94Central Hockey League-8
94Dallas Freeze-8

Flodell, Jordon
97Moose Jaw Warriors-2
98Kamloops Blazers-10
99Lethbridge Hurricanes-9
03Tulsa Oilers-5

Flodqvist, Thord
55Swedish Alfabilder-16

Flomenhoft, Steven
92Harvard Crimson-9
93Knoxville Cherokees-4
94Knoxville Cherokees-12

Flomo, Ruby
98Danish Hockey League-210
99Danish Hockey League-177

Flood, Mark
01Peterborough Petes-4
02Peterborough Petes-4
04Peterborough Petes Postcards-9

Florence, Andrew
98Bowman Chrome CHL-48
Golden Anniversary-48
Golden Anniversary Refractors-48
OPC International-48
OPC International Refractors-48
Refractors-48

Florence, Mark
98UK Kingston Hawks-11
99UK Hull Thunder-5
01UK Hull Thunder-8
02UK Hull Thunder-10
05UK Hull Stingrays-14

Florian, Jaromir
04Guelph Storm-10

Florian, Milota
98Czech OFS-324
99Czech Score Blue 2000-137
99Czech Score Red Ice 2000-137

Florio, Perry
91Johnstown Chiefs-20
93Johnstown Chiefs-18
94Johnstown Chiefs-8
98Roanoke Express-3
00Roanoke Express-16
01Roanoke Express-22
02Roanoke Express-6

Florio, Rocky
00Wichita Thunder-8

Floss, Roland
94German First League-185

Flowers, Darryl
04Peterborough Petes Postcards-18

Floyd, Larry
83Devils Postcards-9
88ProCards AHL-90
89ProCards IHL-113
91ProCards-314
92San Diego Gulls-8
93San Diego Gulls-9

Floyd, Lloyd
90ProCards AHL/IHL-319

Fluckiger, Michael
02Swiss HNL-401

Flueler, Gilbert
01Swiss HNL-132
02Swiss HNL-409

Flueler, Lukas
06Ottawa 67s-21

Flugge, Christian
94German DEL-327

Flynn, Billy
94German DEL-53
95German DEL-25
99Greensboro Generals-25

Flynn, Brendan
91Richmond Renegades-3
91Richmond Renegades Set 2-20
92Richmond Renegades-4
93Richmond Renegades-14
95Richmond Renegades-9

Flynn, Dan
897th Inn. Sketch OHL-96
93Sault Ste. Marie Greyhounds-30
03St. Francis Xavier X-Men-27

Flynn, Michael
97Louisville Riverfrogs-6

Flynn, Norman
907th Inn. Sketch QMJHL-238

Flynn, Patrick
03German Berlin Polar Bears Postcards-14

Flynn, Ryan
06Minnesota Golden Gophers-7

Flynn, Terry
98Odessa Jackalopes-5

Fobes, Lloyd
93Quebec Pee-Wee Tournament-1156

Focht, Dan
95Bowman Draft Prospects-P20
95Tri-City Americans-10
97Springfield Falcons-8
01BAP Memorabilia-320
Emerald-320
Ruby-320
Sapphire-320
01UD Honor Roll-85
02Coyotes Team Issue-33
02Pacific Calder-90
Silver-90
02Pacific Complete-585
Red-585
02Springfield Falcons-9
03Upper Deck MVP-340
Gold Script-340
Silver Script-340
Canadian Exclusives-340
04Hamilton Bulldogs-9

Foder, Brian
98Danish Hockey League-190
99Danish Hockey League-81

Foder, Kim
98Danish Hockey League-187
99Danish Hockey League-85

Fogal, Ron
71Rochester Americans-6

Fogarty, Bryan
85Kingston Canadians-13
86Kingston Canadians-12
87Kingston Canadians-21
88Niagara Falls Thunder-14
89Nordiques Team Issue-10
89Halifax Citadels-6
89ProCards AHL-168
90Bowman-173
Tiffany-173
90Nordiques Petro-Canada-6
90Nordiques Team Issue-6
90Panini Stickers-144
90Pro Set-515
90Score-54
Canadian-54
90Upper Deck-548
French-548
91Pro Set Platinum-103
91Bowman-149
91Nordiques Panini Team Stickers-4
91Nordiques Petro-Canada-6
91O-Pee-Chee-500
91Panini Stickers-259
91Parkhurst-146
French-146
91Pinnacle-59
French-59
91Pro Set-200
French-200
91Score American-237
91Score Canadian Bilingual-457
91Score Canadian English-457
91Topps-500
91Upper Deck-337
French-337
92Penguins Coke/Clark-6
94Canadiens Postcards-12
95Minnesota Moose-11
96Kansas City Blades-11
96Collector's Edge Ice-165
Prism-165
98Indianapolis Ice-16

Fogarty, Ron
95Central Hockey League-24

Fogelson, Jason
93Quebec Pee-Wee Tournament-740

Foglietta, Bob
86Portland Winter Hawks-6
94Finnish Jaa Kiekko-301

Foglietta, Guiseppe
92Finnish Semic-258
93Swedish Semic World Champ Stickers-220

Fogolin Jr., Lee
74NHL Action Stamps-42
74Sabres Postcards-6
75O-Pee-Chee NHL-306
75Topps-306
76O-Pee-Chee NHL-253
76Topps-253
77O-Pee-Chee NHL-94
77Topps-94
78O-Pee-Chee-27
78Topps-27
79Oilers Postcards-8
79O-Pee-Chee-183
79Topps-183
80O-Pee-Chee-63
80Pepsi-Cola Caps-25
80Topps-63
81Oilers Red Rooster-2
81Oilers West Edmonton Mall-1
81O-Pee-Chee-112
81O-Pee-Chee Stickers-215
82Oilers Red Rooster-2
82O-Pee-Chee-104
82O-Pee-Chee Stickers-106
82Post Cereal-6
82Topps Stickers-106
83NHL Key Tags-36
83Oilers Dollars-H18
83Oilers McDonald's-12
83O-Pee-Chee-26
83O-Pee-Chee Stickers-17
83O-Pee-Chee Stickers-100
83Topps Stickers-17
83Topps Stickers-100
83Vachon-23
84Oilers Red Rooster-2
84Oilers Team Issue-4
84O-Pee-Chee-240
84O-Pee-Chee Stickers-254
85Oilers Red Rooster-2
85O-Pee-Chee-235
85O-Pee-Chee Stickers-218
86Oilers Red Rooster-2
86Oilers Team Issue-2
86O-Pee-Chee-210
86O-Pee-Chee Stickers-71
88Oilers Tenth Anniversary-42
04ITG Franchises Canadian-34
Autographs-LF

Fogolin Sr., Lee
44Beehive Group II Photos-95
44Beehive Group II Photos-165
51Parkhurst-46
52Parkhurst-55
53Parkhurst-72
54Parkhurst-84
04ITG Franchises Canadian Autographs-LF

Fogolin, Mike
03Prince George Cougars-7

Fohry, Armin
94German First League-204

Fois, Jordan
87Sudbury Wolves-6
88Sudbury Wolves-6
90Richmond Renegades-12

Fojtik, Tomas
03Portland Winter Hawks-2

Fokin, Sergei
92Swedish Semic Elitserien Stickers-279
93Swedish Semic Elitserien-244
94Swedish Leaf-185
95Swedish Leaf-40
95Swedish Upper Deck-58
97Swedish Collector's Choice-53
98Swedish UD Choice-85
99Swedish Upper Deck-54
00Swedish Upper Deck-77

Folden, Brian
93Waterloo Black Hawks-10

Foley, Colin
907th Inn. Sketch WHL-319
917th Inn. Sketch WHL-37
93Portland Winter Hawks-11
96Alaska Gold Kings-3

Foley, Gerry
57Topps-57
94Parkhurst Missing Link-94

Foley, Paul
75Hamilton Fincups-6

Foley, Rick
72O-Pee-Chee-80
72Sargent Promotions Stamps-165
72Topps-98
06JOGO-150

Folghera, Philipp
93Quebec Pee-Wee Tournament-1630
98Swiss Power Play Stickers-113
99Swiss Panini Stickers-293
01Swiss HNL-311

Foligno, Mike
79Red Wings Postcards-3
80O-Pee-Chee-16
80O-Pee-Chee-187
80Topps-16
80Topps-187
81O-Pee-Chee-87
81O-Pee-Chee Stickers-122
81Topps-W87
82O-Pee-Chee-26
82O-Pee-Chee Stickers-120
82Post Cereal-2
82Sabres Milk Panels-12
82Topps Stickers-120
83NHL Key Tags-13
83O-Pee-Chee-63
83O-Pee-Chee Stickers-237
83Puffy Stickers-7
83Topps Stickers-237
84O-Pee-Chee-20
84O-Pee-Chee Stickers-212
84Sabres Blue Shield-6
84Topps-16
85O-Pee-Chee-17
85O-Pee-Chee Stickers-174
85Sabres Blue Shield-9
85Sabres Blue Shield Small-9
85Topps-17
86O-Pee-Chee-127
86O-Pee-Chee Box Bottoms-D
86O-Pee-Chee Stickers-42
86Sabres Blue Shield-10
86Sabres Blue Shield Small-10
86Topps-127
86Topps Box Bottoms-D
87O-Pee-Chee-40
87O-Pee-Chee Stickers-150
87Panini Stickers-29
87Sabres Blue Shield-8
87Sabres Wonder Bread/Hostess-9
87Topps-40
88Frito-Lay Stickers-18
88O-Pee-Chee-184
88O-Pee-Chee Stickers-257
88Panini Stickers-226
88Sabres Blue Shield-7
88Sabres Wonder Bread/Hostess-7
88Topps-184
89O-Pee-Chee-78
89O-Pee-Chee Stickers-260
89Panini Stickers-210
89Sabres Blue Shield-4
89Sabres Campbell's-6
89Topps-78
90Bowman-247
Tiffany-247
90O-Pee-Chee-123
90Panini Stickers-25
90Pro Set-20
90Sabres Campbell's-7
90Score-133
Canadian-133
90Topps-123
Tiffany-123
90Upper Deck-378
French-378
91Bowman-169
91Maple Leafs PLAY-12
91O-Pee-Chee-18
91Pinnacle-292
French-292
91Score Canadian Bilingual-248
91Score Canadian English-248
91Stadium Club-29
91Topps-18
91Upper Deck-212
French-212
92Maple Leafs Kodak-23
92Panini Stickers-84
92Panini Stickers French-84
92Parkhurst-415
Emerald Ice-415
92Ultra-420
93Donruss-433
93Maple Leafs Score Black's-21
93OPC Premier-262
Gold-262
93Panini Stickers-228
93Panthers Team Issue-3
93PowerPlay-346
93Sabres Noco-3
93Score-387
93Score-647
Gold-647
Canadian-387
Canadian-647
Canadian Gold-647
93Topps/OPC Premier-262
Gold-262
93Upper Deck-155
94Stadium Club Super Teams-9
94Stadium Club Super Team MemberOnly Set-9
95St. John's Maple Leafs-24
97Sudbury Wolves Anniversary-9
98Hershey Bears-8
01Topps Archives-61
01Hershey Bears-9
02Fleer Throwbacks-4
Gold-4
Platinum-4
02Hershey Bears-27
03Sudbury Wolves-25
04ITG Franchises US East-342
Autographs-A-MF
04Sudbury Wolves-23
05Sudbury Wolves-22
06Parkhurst-62
06Parkhurst-168
Autographs-62
Autographs-168
Autographs Dual-DAPF
06Sudbury Wolves-25

Foligno, Nicholas
04Sudbury Wolves-5
05Sudbury Wolves-11
05ITG Heroes and Prospects-280
Autographs Series II-NF
Team Cherry-TC11
06Sudbury Wolves-5
06ITG Heroes and Prospects-115
Autographs-ANF

Folk, Trevor
98Wichita Thunder-8
99Wichita Thunder-7
00Wichita Thunder-9

Folkening, Ryan
92Michigan State Spartans-10

Folkesson, Osten
67Swedish Hockey-254
69Swedish Hockey-299

Folkett, Curtis
88Brandon Wheat Kings-16
91Air Canada SJHL-C15

Follmer, Kyle
06Lincoln Stars-21
06Lincoln Stars Upper DeckÂ Signature Series -11

Folta, Petr
94Czech APS Extraliga-134
95Czech APS Extraliga-304
96Czech APS Extraliga-61
97Czech APS Extraliga-332
97Czech DS Stickers-242
98Czech DS Stickers-282
98Czech OFS-187
99Czech DS-110
99Czech OFS-405
00Czech DS Extraliga-151
00Czech OFS-274
01Czech OFS-236
02Czech OFS Plus-133

Fomin, Kauko
70Finnish Jaakiekko-293
71Finnish Suomi Stickers-224

Fomitchev, Alexandre
98Calgary Hitmen-21
98Calgary Hitmen Autographs-21
99Bowman CHL-101
Gold-101
OPC International-101
00Asheville Smoke-5
01Columbus Cottonmouths-4
02Russian Hockey League-64
03Russian Hockey League-172
04Russian Super League All-Stars-18
04Russian World Championship Team-13

Fomradas, Blaine
91Air Canada SJHL-D34

Fondado, Miguel
93Swiss HNL-303
95Swiss HNL-427
96Swiss HNL-460

Fone, Jon
02UK Peterborough Phantoms-5

Fone, Steve
06UK Coventry Blaze-13

Foneir, Sebastein
907th Inn. Sketch QMJHL-81

Fonnesbech, Kim
98Danish Hockey League-160

Fonso, Antonio
94German DEL-408

Fontaine, Charles
01Hull Olympiques-3
02Hull Olympiques-3
03Cape Breton Screaming Eagles-24
04Cape Breton Screaming Eagles-8
05Cape Breton Screaming Eagles-20

Fontaine, Dave
93Amos Les Forestiers-6

Fontaine, Len
72O-Pee-Chee-244

Fontaine, Olivier
93Quebec Pee-Wee Tournament-410

Fontaine, Simon
93Quebec Pee-Wee Tournament-450

Fontana, Philippe
02Swiss HNL-357

Fontana, Ruben
93Swiss HNL-97

Fontanel, Gautier
93Quebec Pee-Wee Tournament-1488

Fontanel, Thibault
92Quebec Pee-Wee Tournament-1190
93Quebec Pee-Wee Tournament-1490

Fontas, Jon
78Saginaw Gears-4

Fonteyne, Val
44Beehive Group II Photos-166
60Parkhurst-21
60Shirriff Coins-48
61Parkhurst-21
61Shirriff/Salada Coins-67
62Parkhurst-27
63Topps-61
64Beehive Group III Photos-69
64Coca-Cola Caps-83
65Coca-Cola-45
66Topps-108
68O-Pee-Chee-109
68Shirriff Coins-137
68Topps-109
69O-Pee-Chee-119
69Topps-119
70O-Pee-Chee-208
70Sargent Promotions Stamps-176
71O-Pee-Chee-189
71Penguins Postcards-6
71Sargent Promotions Stamps-163
72O-Pee-Chee-319
94Parkhurst Tall Boys-95
95Parkhurst '66-67-57
Coins-57

Fontinato, Lou
44Beehive Group II Photos-239
44Beehive Group II Photos-311
57Topps-64
58Topps-41
59Topps-5
60NHL Ceramic Tiles-28
60Shirriff Coins-97
60Topps-61
61Shirriff/Salada Coins-111
61York Yellow Backs-40
62Parkhurst-52
62Shirriff Coins-23
81TCMA-4
91Ultimate Original Six-19
French-19
93O-Pee-Chee Canadiens Hockey Fest-52
93Parkhurst Parkie Reprints-PR61
94Parkhurst Missing Link-93
03Parkhurst Original Six New York-54
Autographs-5
05ITG Tough Customers-LF
Autographs-LF
06Parkhurst-4
06Parkhurst-237
Autographs-4
Autographs-237
Autographs Dual-DAFG

Foord, Mark
04UK London Racers-16

Foord, Matt
04UK London Racers Playoffs-5

Foote, Adam
89Sault Ste. Marie Greyhounds-15
907th Inn. Sketch OHL-157
91Pro Set Platinum-268
91Nordiques Petro-Canada-7
91Parkhurst-371
French-371
91Pinnacle-337
French-337
91Upper Deck-529
French-529
917th Inn. Sketch Memorial Cup-5
92Nordiques Petro-Canada-8
92Score-131
Canadian-131
92Stadium Club-468
92Topps Gold-528G
93Donruss-272
93Leaf-229
93Pinnacle-26
Canadian-26
93PowerPlay-418
93Score-149
Canadian-149
93Stadium Club-496
Members Only Master Set-496
First Day Issue-496
94Be A Player-R42
Signature Cards-2
94Leaf-529
94Nordiques Burger King-7
94Pinnacle-432
Artist's Proofs-432
Rink Collection-432
94Score-151
Gold-151
Platinum-151
95Pinnacle-195
Artist's Proofs-195
Rink Collection-195
95Upper Deck-204
Electric Ice-204
Electric Ice Gold-204
96Be A Player-196
Autographs-196
Autographs Silver-196
96Black Diamond-52
Gold-52
96Metal Universe-31
96SP-38
97Avalanche Pins-9
97Collector's Choice-64
World Domination-W16
97Esso Olympic Hockey Heroes-21
97Esso Olympic Hockey Heroes French-21
97Kraft Team Canada-4
97McDonald's Team Canada Coins-6
97Pacific-135
Copper-135
Emerald Green-135
Ice Blue-135
Red-135
Silver-135
97Panini Stickers-202
97Score-257
97Score Avalanche-12
Platinum-12
Premier-12
97Upper Deck-255
98Avalanche Team Issue-2
98Be A Player-33
Press Release-33
98BAP Gold-33
98BAP Autographs-33
98BAP Autographs Gold-33
98BAP Tampa Bay All Star Game-33
98OPC Chrome-189
Refractors-189
98Pacific-52
Ice Blue-52
Red-52
98Paramount-54
Copper-54
Emerald Green-54
Holo-Electric-54
Ice Blue-54
Silver-54
98Topps-189
O-Pee-Chee-189
98UD Choice-228
Prime Choice Reserve-228
Reserve-228
99Avalanche Pins-2
99Avalanche Team Issue-6
99O-Pee-Chee-52
99O-Pee-Chee Chrome-52
99O-Pee-Chee Chrome Refractors-52
99Pacific-104
Copper-104
Emerald Green-104
Gold-104
Ice Blue-104
Premiere Date-104
Red-104
99Panini Stickers-217
99Topps/OPC-52
99Topps/OPC Chrome-52
Refractors-52
99Upper Deck-40
Exclusives-40
Exclusives 1 of 1-40
99Upper Deck Gold Reserve-40
99Upper Deck Victory-82
00BAP Memorabilia-314
Emerald-314
Ruby-314
Sapphire-314
Promos-314
00BAP Mem Chicago Sportsfest Copper-314
00BAP Memorabilia Chicago Sportsfest Blue-314
00BAP Memorabilia Chicago Sportsfest Gold-314
00BAP Memorabilia Chicago Sportsfest Ruby-314
00BAP Memorabilia Chicago Sun-Times Ruby-314
00BAP Memorabilia Chicago Sun-Times Gold-314
00BAP Mem Chicago Sun-Times Sapphire-314
00BAP Mem Toronto Fall Expo Copper-314
00BAP Memorabilia Toronto Fall Expo Gold-314
00BAP Memorabilia Toronto Fall Expo Ruby-314
00BAP Sig Ser Department of Defense-DD14
00O-Pee-Chee-140
00O-Pee-Chee Parallel-140
00Pacific-112
Copper-112
Gold-112
Ice Blue-112
Premiere Date-112
00Paramount-59
Copper-59
Gold-59
Holo-Gold-59
Holo-Silver-59
Ice Blue-59
Premiere Date-59
00Private Stock Game Gear-23
00Topps/OPC-140
Parallel-140
00Upper Deck Victory-68
00Upper Deck Vintage-96
01Avalanche Team Issue-10
01BAP Memorabilia-54
Emerald-54
Ruby-54
Sapphire-54
Stanley Cup Champions-CA2
01BAP Signature Series-153
Autographs-153
Autographs Gold-153
Jerseys-GJ-83
01Pacific-100
Extreme LTD-100
Hobby LTD-100
Premiere Date-100
Retail LTD-100
01Pacific Arena Exclusives-100
01Parkhurst-188
Jerseys-PJ49
Sticks-PS44
Teammates-T5
01Stadium Club-98
Award Winners-98
Master Photos-98
01Topps Heritage-96
Refractors-96
01UD Stanley Cup Champs-41
01Upper Deck-273
Exclusives-273
01Upper Deck Avalanche NHL All-Star Game-CA2
01Upper Deck Victory-95
01Upper Deck Victory-429
Gold-95
Gold-429
02Avalanche Postcards-11
02BAP First Edition-115
Jerseys-115
02BAP Sig Series Auto Buybacks 1998-33
02BAP Sig Series Auto Buybacks 2001-153
02BAP Signature Series Defensive Wall-DW1
02BAP Signature Series Golf-GS1
02McDonald's Pacific Salt Lake Gold-2
02O-Pee-Chee-78
02O-Pee-Chee Premier Blue Parallel-78
02O-Pee-Chee Premier Red Parallel-78
02O-Pee-Chee Factory Set-78
02Pacific-89
Blue-89
Red-89
02Pacific Complete-256
Red-256
02Parkhurst-85
Bronze-85
Gold-85
Silver-85
02Parkhurst Retro-175
Minis-175
Hopefuls-NH3
02Topps-78
OPC Blue Parallel-78
OPC Red Parallel-78
Factory Set-78
02Topps Total-22
02Upper Deck-288
Exclusives-288
02Upper Deck Beckett UD Promos-288
02Upper Deck Vintage-71
03Avalanche Team Issue-4
03BAP Ultimate Memorabilia Triple Threads-12
03ITG Action-195
Jerseys-M23
03NHL Sticker Collection-188
03O-Pee-Chee-129
03OPC Blue-129
03OPC Gold-129
03OPC Red-129
03Pacific-82
Blue-82
Red-82
03Pacific Complete-188
Red-188
03Topps-129
Blue-129
Gold-129
Red-129
03Upper Deck-292
Canadian Exclusives-292
HG-292
UD Exclusives-292
03Upper Deck MVP-108
Gold Script-108
Silver Script-108
Canadian Exclusives-108
04UD Toronto Fall Expo Pride of Canada-6
04Ultimate Collection Dual Logos-UL2-BF
04Upper Deck World Cup Tribute-JBAF
05Beehive Matted Materials-MMAF
05Panini Stickers-236
05Parkhurst-145
05Parkhurst-509
05Parkhurst-565
Facsimile Auto Parallel-145
Facsimile Auto Parallel-509
Facsimile Auto Parallel-565
True Colors-TCCLB
True Colors-TCCLB
05SP Game Used Authentic Fabrics Quad-RBBF
05SP Game Used Authentic Patches Quad -RBBF
05The Cup Master Pressplate Rookie Update-232
05Ultimate Coll National Heroes Jersey-NHJFO
05Ultimate Coll National Heroes Patch-NHPFO
05Upper Deck-301
Jerseys-J-AF
Notable Numbers-N-AFO
Patches-P-AFO
05Upper Deck Hockey Showcase-HS3
05Upper Deck Showcase Promos-HS3
05Upper Deck MVP-121
Gold-121
Platinum-121

Materials-M-AF
Materials Duals-D-JF
05Upper Deck Rookie Update-232
Inspirations Patch Rookies-232
05Upper Deck Victory-52
Black-52
Gold-52
Silver-52
06O-Pee-Chee-144
Rainbow-144
06Panini Stickers-236
06Upper Deck Arena Giveaways-CLB3
06Upper Deck-57
Exclusives Parallel-57
High Gloss Parallel-57
Masterpieces-57
06Upper Deck MVP-90
Gold Script-90
Super Script-90

Forbes, Colin
97Pacific Omega-163
Copper-163
Dark Gray-163
Emerald Green-163
Gold-163
Ice Blue-163
97Upper Deck-191
98OPC Chrome-49
Refractors-49
98Pacific-325
Ice Blue-325
Red-325
98Paramount-172
Copper-172
Emerald Green-172
Holo-Electric-172
Ice Blue-172
Silver-172
98Topps-49
O-Pee-Chee-49
98Upper Deck-335
Exclusives-335
Exclusives 1 of 1-335
Gold Reserve-335
98Upper Deck MVP-151
Gold Script-151
Silver Script-151
Super Script-151
99O-Pee-Chee-95
99O-Pee-Chee Chrome-95
99O-Pee-Chee Chrome Refractors-95
99Pacific-388
Copper-388
Emerald Green-388
Gold-388
Ice Blue-388
Premiere Date-388
Red-388
99Paramount-216
Copper-216
Emerald-216
Gold-216
Holographic Emerald-216
Holographic Gold-216
Holographic Silver-216
Ice Blue-216
Premiere Date-216
Red-216
Silver-216
99Revolution-132
Premiere Date-132
Red-132
Shadow Series-132
99Topps/OPC-95
99Topps/OPC Chrome-95
Refractors-95
00BAP Signature Series-112
Emerald-112
Ruby-112
Sapphire-112
Autographs-121
Autographs Gold-121
00Senators Team Issue-6
01Topps Reserve-80
02BAP Sig Series Auto Buybacks 2000-121
04Lowell Lock Monsters-7
04Lowell Lock Monsters Photo Album-7
05Hershey Bears-23
06German DEL-147

Forbes, Dave
74NHL Action Stamps-29
74O-Pee-Chee NHL-266
75O-Pee-Chee NHL-173
75Topps-173
76O-Pee-Chee NHL-246
76Topps-246
77O-Pee-Chee NHL-143
77Topps-143
78O-Pee-Chee-167
78Topps-167

Forbes, Ian
97Guelph Storm-10
98Guelph Storm-8
99Guelph Storm-24
00Trenton Titans-16
01Trenton Titans-2-3
02Trenton Titans-B-5
03Florida Everblades-7

Forbes, Jake
24Anonymous NHL-77
06Between The Pipes Forgotten Franchises-FF04

Forbes, Mike
81Oilers Red Rooster-26
88Oilers Tenth Anniversary-72

Forbes, Mitchell
06Erie Otters-5

Forbes, Nick
96Flint Generals-6
97Flint Generals-4
97Flint Generals EBK-7
98Flint Generals-10

Forbes, Vernon
23V145-1-29
24C144 Champ's Cigarettes-25
24V130 Maple Crispette-25
24V145-2-11
25Dominion Chocolates-82

Forch, Libor
94Czech APS Extraliga-241
95Czech APS Extraliga-14

Forconi, Mike
01Sioux Falls Stampede-3

Ford, Brian
83Vachon-64
83Fredericton Express-4
89ProCards AHL-268
93Quebec Pee-Wee Tournament-668

Ford, Chad
98Quad-City Mallards-8
99Adirondack IceHawks-21

Ford, Chris
98Fayetteville Force-13

Ford, Colin
87Sault Ste. Marie Greyhounds-18

Ford, Gary
93Quebec Pee-Wee Tournament-843

Ford, George
52St. Lawrence Sales-59

Ford, John
52Juniors Blue Tint-114

Ford, Matt
04Wisconsin Badgers-6

Ford, Matthew
05Wisconsin Badgers-11

Ford, Mike
01Kalamazoo K-Wings-5
02Kalamazoo Wings-8

Ford, Pat
92Northern Michigan Wildcats-29
93Northern Michigan Wildcats-30

Ford, Ryan
04UK Edinburgh Capitals-17

Ford, Steve
96OCN Blizzard-7

Ford, Todd
00Swift Current Broncos-7
01Swift Current Broncos-22
02Swift Current Broncos-2
03Prince George Cougars-24

Ford, WHA
76O-Pee-Chee WHA-75

Foreman, Jordan
04London Knights-17
05London Knights-8
06London Knights-21

Foremsky, Taras
03Fort Worth Brahmas-6

Forest, Jonathan
00Austin Ice Bats-4
01Greensboro Generals-16
02Bossier-Shreveport Mudbugs-9
03Austin Ice Bats-5
04St Georges de Beauce Garaga-2

Forest, Richard
93Quebec Pee-Wee Tournament-1157

Forestell, Brian
89Windsor Spitfires-3
907th Inn. Sketch OHL-181

Forget, Dominic
99Shawinigan Cataractes-18
Signed-18
99Bowman CHL-81
Gold-81
OPC International-81
00Shawinigan Cataractes-21
Signed-21
01Louisiana Ice Gators-8
02Johnstown Chiefs-6
03Johnstown Chiefs-4
03Johnstown Chiefs RBI Sports-214

Fork, Bryan
95Arizona Icecats-17

Formaz, Alexandre
93Swiss HNL-317

Fornataro, Matt
03Waterloo Blackhawks-3

Forrest, J.D.
03Boston College Eagles-5
04Finnish Cardset-141
Parallel-105

Forrest, Justin
05Finnish Cardset -341

Forrest, Kirk
05Halifax Mooseheads-9

Forsander, Johan
97Black Diamond-99
Double Diamond-99
Triple Diamond-99
Quadruple Diamond-99
97Swedish Collector's Choice-85
98UD Choice-293
Prime Choice Reserve-293
Reserve-293
98Swedish UD Choice-218
99Swedish Upper Deck-207
00Swedish Upper Deck-103
02Swedish SHL-20
Parallel-20
06German DEL-31

Forsander, Jonas
99Swedish Upper Deck-94

Forsbacka, Patrik
05Finnish Cardset -349
06Finnish Cardset-180
Playmakers Rookies-8
Playmakers Rookies Gold-8
Playmakers Rookies Silver-8
Signature Sensations-35
06Finnish Porin Assat Pelaajakortit-22

Forsberg, Bjorn
71Swedish Hockey-342

Forsberg, Henrik
06Finnish Cardset-250

Forsberg, Jonas
92Swedish Semic Elitserien Stickers-349
94Parkhurst SE-SE245
Gold-SE245
94Swedish Leaf-170
95Swedish Leaf-27
Spidermen-9
95Swedish Globe World Championships-55
98Swedish UD Choice-1

Forsberg, Kent
92Swedish Semic Elitserien Stickers-332
93Swedish Semic Elitserien-297

Forsberg, Marcus
04Knoxville Ice Bears-5
05Knoxville Ice Bears-6

Forsberg, Pasi
92Finnish Jyvas-Hyva Stickers-168
93Finnish Jyvas-Hyva Stickers-298
93Finnish SISU-74

Forsberg, Per
83Swedish Semic Elitserien-150
86Swedish Panini Stickers-201
87Swedish Panini Stickers-197

Forsberg, Peter
91Upper Deck-64
French-64
91Swedish Semic Elitserien Stickers-213
91Arena Draft Picks-4
91Arena Draft Picks French-4
91Arena Draft Picks Autographs-4
91Arena Draft Picks Autographs French-4
91Classic-5
91Star Pics-35
91Ultimate Draft-5
91Ultimate Draft-61
91Ultimate Draft-76
91Ultimate Draft French-5
91Classic Four-Sport *-5
92Sports Illustrated for Kids II-425
92Sports Illustrated for Kids II-755
92Upper Deck-235
92Upper Deck-369
92Upper Deck-375
92Upper Deck-595
92Swedish Semic Elitserien Stickers-242
92Swedish Semic Elitserien Stickers-347
93Swedish Semic Elitserien-209
93Swedish Semic Elitserien-301
93Swedish Semic Elitserien-302
93Swedish Semic Elitserien-305
93Swedish Semic Elitserien-311
93Swedish Semic World Champ Stickers-13
94Be A Player-R152
94Finest-1
Super Team Winners-1
Refractors-1
Bowman's Best-R12
Bowman's Best-X22
Bowman's Best Refractors-R12
Bowman's Best Refractors-X22
94Flair-146
94Fleer-176
Rookie Sensations-2
94Leaf-475
Limited Inserts-28
Phenoms-3
94Leaf Limited-116
94McDonald's Upper Deck-McD31
94Nordiques Burger King-8
94OPC Premier-385
94OPC Premier-425
Special Effects-385
Special Effects-425
94Parkhurst SE-SE149
Gold-SE149
Euro-Stars-ES1
94Pinnacle-266
94Pinnacle-479
Artist's Proofs-266
Artist's Proofs-479
Rink Collection-266
Rink Collection-479
Rookie Team Pinnacle-9
94Score Top Rookie Redemption-2
94Select-175
Gold-175
Youth Explosion-YE7
94SP-96
Die Cuts-96
Premier-2
Premier Die-Cuts-2
94Topps/OPC Premier-385
94Topps/OPC Premier-425
Special Effects-385
Special Effects-425
94Topps Finest Bronze-17
94Ultra-356
Prospects-1
94Upper Deck-245
94Upper Deck-528
94Upper Deck-555
Electric Ice-245
Electric Ice-528
Electric Ice-555
Predictor Canadian-C1
94Upper Deck Predictor Canadian Exch Gold-C1
94Upper Deck Predictor Cdn Exch Silver-C1
94Upper Deck Predictor Hobby-H10
94Upper Deck Predictor Hobby Exch Gold-H10
94Upper Deck Predictor Hobby Exch Silver-H10
94Upper Deck SP Inserts-SP156
94Upper Deck SP Inserts Die Cuts-SP156
94Finnish Jaa Kiekko-75
94Finnish Jaa Kiekko-355
94Swedish Leaf-189
Gold Cards-19
Guest Special-3
94Swedish Olympics Lillehammer*-291
95Bashan Super Stickers-26
95Bashan Super Stickers-28
95Bowman-85
All-Foil-85
Bowman's Best-BB1
Bowman's Best Refractors-BB1
95Canada Games NHL POGS-29
95Canada Games NHL POGS-77
95Collector's Choice-26
95Collector's Choice-371
95Collector's Choice-391
Player's Club-26
Player's Club-371
Player's Club-391
Player's Club Platinum-26
Player's Club Platinum-371
Player's Club Platinum-391
Crash The Game-C20A
Crash The Game-C20B
Crash The Game-C20C
Crash The Game Gold-C20A
Crash The Game Gold-C20B
Crash The Game Gold-C20C
Crash the Game Silver Redeemed-C20
Crash the Game Silver Bonus-C20
Crash the Game Gold Redeemed-C20
Crash the Game Gold Bonus-C20
95Donruss-65
Dominators-1
Rookie Team-2
95Donruss Elite-39
Die Cut Stars-39
Die Cut Uncut-39
Cutting Edge-4
95Emotion-36
Xcited-14
95Finest-26
95Finest-100
Refractors-26
Refractors-100
95Hoyle Eastern Playing Cards-13
95Imperial Stickers-28
95Kraft-11
95Leaf-20
Fire On Ice-6
Studio Rookies-2
95Leaf Limited-2
Stars of the Game-4
95McDonald's Pinnacle-MCD-7
95Metal-32
International Steel-4
Winners-1
95NHL Aces Playing Cards-9H
95NHL Cool Trade-12
95NHL Cool Trade-RP12
95NHL/NHLPA Playing Cards-NNO
95Panini Stickers-146
95Panini Stickers-244
95Panini Stickers-299
95Parkhurst International-237
95Parkhurst International-316
Emerald Ice-237
Emerald Ice-316
All-Stars-4
Crown Collection Silver Series 1-13
Crown Collection Gold Series 1-13
Crown Collection Silver Series 2-6
Crown Collection Gold Series 2-6
Parkie's Trophy Picks-PP4
Parkie's Trophy Picks-PP13
Trophy Winners-3
95Pinnacle Clear Shots-8
95Pinnacle First Strike-11
95Pinnacle Roaring 20s-15
95Pinnacle FANtasy-25
95Playoff One on One-25
95Playoff One on One-137
95Playoff One on One-239
95Pro Magnets-2
95Score-31
Black Ice Artist's Proofs-31
Black Ice-31
Check It-7
Dream Team-5
Golden Blades-10
95Select Certified Promos-68
95Select Certified-68
Mirror Gold-68
Future-1
95SkyBox Impact-35
95SkyBox Impact-229
Ice Quake-8
95SP-29
Holoviews-FX4
Holoviews Special FX-FX4
Stars/Etoiles-E10
Stars/Etoiles Gold-E10
95Stadium Club Members Only-47
95Stadium Club-105
Members Only Master Set-105
Generation TSC-GT4
Generation TSC Members Only Master Set-GT4
Nemeses-N9
Nemeses Members Only Master Set-N9
95Summit-117
Artist's Proofs-117
Ice-117
95Topps-359
95Topps-380
OPC Inserts-359
OPC Inserts-380
Marquee Men Power Boosters-380
New To The Game-10NG
Young Stars-YS4
95Topps SuperSkills-18
Platinum-18
95Ultra-132
95Ultra-383
Gold Medallion-132
All-Rookies-3
All-Rookie Gold Medallion-3
Extra Attackers-5
High Speed-8
95Upper Deck-430
Electric Ice-430
Electric Ice Gold-430
95Upper Deck All-Star Game Predictors-11
Redemption Winners-11
95Upper Deck Freeze Frame-F1
95Upper Deck Freeze Frame Jumbo-F1
95Upper Deck NHL All-Stars-AS17
95Upper Deck NHL All-Stars Jumbo-AS17
95Upper Deck Predictor Hobby-H8
95Upper Deck Predictor Hobby Exchange-H8
95Upper Deck Predictor Retail-R25
95Upper Deck Predictor Retail-R37
95Upper Deck Predictor Retail-R54
95Upper Deck Predictor Retail Exchange-R25
95Upper Deck Predictor Retail Exchange-R37
95Upper Deck Predictor Retail Exchange-R54
95Upper Deck Special Edition-SE21
95Upper Deck Special Edition Gold-SE21
95Zenith-70
Z-Team-8
95Finnish Semic World Championships-64
95Swedish Upper Deck-234
95Swedish Globe World Championships-21
95Swedish Globe World Championships-253
95Swedish Globe World Championships-254
95Swedish Globe World Championships-255
95Swedish Globe World Championships-270
95Swedish Globe World Championships-NNO
95Swedish World Championships Stickers-287
96Be A Player Biscuit In The Basket-5
96Be A Player Link to History-2B
96Be A Player Link to History-2B
96Be A Player Link to History Autographs-2B
96Be A Player Link to History Auto Silver-2B
96Black Diamond-171
Gold-171
Run for the Cup-RC7
96Collector's Choice-63
96Collector's Choice-298
96Collector's Choice-314
MVP-UD3
MVP Gold-UD3
Stick'Ums-S3
96Donruss-139
Press Proofs-139
Go Top Shelf-10
Hit List-14
96Donruss Canadian Ice-6
Gold Press Proofs-6
Red Press Proofs-6
96Donruss Elite-12
Die Cut Stars-12
Status-7
96Duracell L'Equipe Beliveau-JB8
96Flair-18
Blue Ice-18
Center Ice Spotlight-3
Now And Then-3
96Fleer-20
96Fleer-139
Art Ross-4
Pearson-3
Picks Dream Lines-3
Picks Fabulous 50-12
96Kraft Upper Deck-48
96Leaf-159
Press Proofs-159
96Leaf Leather And Laces Promos-P6
96Leaf Leather And Laces-6
96Leaf The Best Of ...-8
96Leaf Limited-29
Gold-29
96Leaf Limited Bash the Boards Promos-P8
96Leaf Limited Bash The Boards-8
96Leaf Limited Bash The Boards Ltd Ed-8
96Leaf Preferred-110
Press Proofs-110
Steel-60
Steel Gold-60
Steel Power-6
96Maggers-25
96McDonald's Pinnacle-28
96Metal Universe-32
Cool Steel-2
Cool Steel Super Power-2
Lethal Weapons-4
Lethal Weapons Super Power-4
96NHL Aces Playing Cards-14
96NHL Pro Stamps-2
96Pinnacle-78
96Pinnacle-249
Artist's Proofs-78
Artist's Proofs-249
Foil-78
Foil-249
Premium Stock-78
Premium Stock-249
Rink Collection-78
Rink Collection-249
Team Pinnacle-2
96Pinnacle Fantasy-FC15
96Pinnacle Mint-6
Bronze-6
Gold-6
Silver-6
Coins Brass-6
Coins Solid Gold-6
Coins Gold Plated-6
Coins Nickel-6
Coins Silver-6
96Playoff One on One-357
96Score-99
Artist's Proofs-99
Dealer's Choice Artist's Proofs-99
Special Artist's Proofs-99
Check It-2
Golden Blades-99
Dream Team-4
96Select Certified Cornerstones-15
96SkyBox Impact-22
BladeRunners-3
VersaTeam-3
96SP-33
Game Film-GF2
SPx Force-1
96SPx-8
Gold-8
96Stadium Club Members Only-20
96Summit-142
Artist's Proofs-142
Ice-142
Metal-142
Premium Stock-142
High Voltage-6
High Voltage Mirage-6
Untouchables-5
96Team Out-29
96Topps Picks-5
Fantasy Team-FT16
OPC Inserts-5
Top Shelf-TS7
96Ultra-35
Gold Medallion-35
Clear the Ice-2
96Upper Deck-239
Generation Next-X2
Hart Hopefuls Bronze-HH7
Hart Hopefuls Gold-HH7
Hart Hopefuls Silver-HH7
Lord Stanley's Heroes Finals-LS8
Lord Stanley's Heroes Quarterfinals-LS8
Lord Stanley's Heroes Semifinals-LS8
Superstar Showdown-SS8A
96Upper Deck Ice-81
Parallel-81
96Zenith-76
Artist's Proofs-76
Champion Salute-9
Champion Salute-P9
Champion Salute Diamond-9
96Swedish Semic Wien-57
96Swedish Semic Wien-74
96Swedish Semic Wien Coca-Cola Dream Team-8
96Swedish Semic Wien Nordic Stars-NS1
97Headliners Hockey-6
97SLU Hockey Canadian-6
97SLU Hockey American-7
97Avalanche Pins-5
97Be A Player One Timers-11
97Beehive-9
Golden Portraits-9
Team-9
Team Gold-9
97Black Diamond-106
Double Diamond-106
Triple Diamond-106
Quadruple Diamond-106
Premium Cut-PC11
Premium Cut Double Diamond-PC11
Premium Cut Quadruple Diamond Horiz-PC11
Premium Cut Triple Diamond-PC11
Premium Cut Quadruple Diamond Verticals-PC11
97Collector's Choice-54
Crash the Game-C21A
Crash the Game-C21B
Crash the Game-C21C
Crash the Game Exchange-CR21
Star Quest-SQ71
Stick'Ums-S21
97Crown Royale-33
Emerald Green-33
Ice Blue-33
Silver-33
Blades of Steel Die-Cuts-5
Cramer's Choice Jumbos-4
Cramer's Choice Jumbos Gold-4
Cramer's Choice Jumbos Signed-4
Hat Tricks Die-Cuts-4
Lamplighters Cel-Fusion Die-Cuts-5
97Donruss-1
Press Proofs Silver-1
Press Proofs Gold-1
Line 2 Line-4
Line 2 Line-P4
Line 2 Line Die Cut-4
97Donruss Canadian Ice-6
Dominion Series-6
Provincial Series-6
Stanley Cup Scrapbook-18
97Donruss Elite-1
Aspirations-1
Status-1
Back to the Future-5
Back to the Future Autographs-5
Craftsmen-23
Master Craftsmen-23
Prime Numbers-1A
Prime Numbers-1B
Prime Numbers-1C
Prime Numbers Die-Cuts-1A
Prime Numbers Die-Cuts-1B
Prime Numbers Die-Cuts-1C
97Donruss Limited-2
97Donruss Limited-48
97Donruss Limited-109
Exposure-2
Exposure-48
Exposure-109
Fabric of the Game-72
97Donruss Preferred-2
97Donruss Preferred-173
Cut to the Chase-2
Cut to the Chase-173
Line of the Times-7B
97Donruss Preferred Line of Times Promos-7B
97Donruss Preferred Precious Metals-12
97Donruss Priority-8
97Donruss Priority-185
Stamp of Approval-8
Stamp of Approval-185
Direct Deposit-10
Direct Deposit Promos-P10
Postcards-10
Postcards Opening Day Issues-8
Stamps-10
Stamps Bronze-10
Stamps Gold-10
Stamps Silver-10
97Esso Olympic Hockey Heroes-43
97Esso Olympic Hockey Heroes French-43
97Katch-38
Gold-38
Silver-38
97Kenner Starting Lineup Cards-7
97Kraft-19
97Leaf-3
97Leaf-170
Fractal Matrix-3
Fractal Matrix-170
Fractal Matrix Die Cuts-3
Fractal Matrix Die Cuts-170
Banner Season-13
Fire On Ice-12
97Leaf International-3
Universal Ice-3
97McDonald's Upper Deck-15
97NHL Aces Playing Cards-25
97Pacific-21
Copper-21
Emerald Green-21
Ice Blue-21
Red-21
Silver-21
Card-Supials-4
Card-Supials Minis-4
Cramer's Choice-4
Gold Crown Die-Cuts-7
Slap Shots Die-Cuts-2A
97Pacific Dynagon-29
97Pacific Dynagon-138
Copper-29
Copper-138
Dark Grey-29
Dark Grey-138
Emerald Green-29
Emerald Green-138
Ice Blue-29
Ice Blue-138
Red-29
Red-138
Silver-29
Silver-138
Best Kept Secrets-24
Dynamic Duos-5A
Kings of the NHL-2
Tandems-5
Tandems-25
97Pacific Invincible-34
Copper-34
Emerald Green-34
Ice Blue-34
Red-34
Silver-34
Attack Zone-5
Feature Performers-7
NHL Regime-51
NHL Regime-216
Off The Glass-5
97Pacific Omega-56
Copper-56
Dark Gray-56
Emerald Green-56
Gold-56
Ice Blue-56
Game Face-3
Silks-3
Stick Handle Laser Cuts-5
97Panini Stickers-201
97Paramount-49
Copper-49
Dark Grey-49
Emerald Green-49
Ice Blue-49
Red-49
Silver-49
Big Numbers Die-Cuts-5
Photoengravings-5
97Pinnacle-73
97Pinnacle-191
Artist's Proofs-73
Rink Collection-73
Epix Game Emerald-14
Epix Game Orange-14
Epix Game Purple-14
Epix Moment Emerald-14
Epix Moment Orange-14
Epix Moment Purple-14
Epix Play Emerald-14
Epix Play Orange-14
Epix Play Purple-14
Epix Season Emerald-14
Epix Season Orange-14
Epix Season Purple-14
Press Plates Back Black-73
Press Plates Back Black-191
Press Plates Back Cyan-73
Press Plates Back Cyan-191
Press Plates Back Magenta-73
Press Plates Back Magenta-191
Press Plates Back Yellow-73
Press Plates Back Yellow-191
Press Plates Front Black-73
Press Plates Front Black-191
Press Plates Front Cyan-73
Press Plates Front Cyan-191
Press Plates Front Magenta-73
Press Plates Front Magenta-191
Press Plates Front Yellow-73
Press Plates Front Yellow-191
Team Pinnacle-7
Team Mirror-7
Team Parallel-7
Team Parallel Mirror-7
97Pinnacle Certified-32
Red-32
Mirror Blue-32
Mirror Gold-32
Mirror Red-32
Team-10
Gold Team Promo-10
Gold Team-10
97Pinnacle Inside-8
Coach's Collection-8
Executive Collection-8
Track-5
Cans-16
Cans Gold-16
Promos-8
97Pinnacle Mint-3
97Pinnacle Mint-P3
Bronze-3
Gold Team-3
Silver Team-3
Coins Brass-3
Coins Brass Proofs-3
Coins Gold Plated-3
Coins Gold Plated Proofs-3
Coins Nickel Silver-3
Coins Nickel Silver Proofs-3
Coins Solid Gold-3
Coins Solid Silver-3
Minternational-2
Minternational Coins-2
97Pinnacle Power Pack Blow-Ups-19
97Pinnacle Tot Cert Platinum Blue-32
97Pinnacle Tot Certi Platinum Gold-32
97Pinnacle Totally Certified Platinum Red-32
97Pinnacle Tot Cert Mirror Platinum Gold-32
97Post Pinnacle-20
97Revolution-32
Copper-32
Emerald-32
Ice Blue-32
Silver-32
1998 All-Star Game Die-Cuts-6
NHL Icons-3
97Score-83
97Score-PR83
Artist's Proofs-83
Golden Blades-83
97Score Avalanche-4
Platinum-4
Premier-4
97SP Authentic-36
Icons-I12
Icons Die-Cuts-I12
Icons Embossed-I12
97SPx-11
Bronze-11
Gold-11
Silver-11
Steel-11
Dimension-SPX16
Grand Finale-11
97Studio-15
Press Proofs Silver-15
Press Proofs Gold-15
Hard Hats-16
Portraits-15
Silhouettes-13
Silhouettes 8x10-13
97Upper Deck-252
Blow-Ups 3 x 5-2-9
Blow-Ups 5 x 7-4A
Game Dated Moments-252
Sixth Sense Masters-SS21
Sixth Sense Wizards-SS21
Smooth Grooves-SG21
The Specialists-21
The Specialists Level 2 Die Cuts-21
Three Star Selects-1C
97Upper Deck Diamond Vision-14
Signature Moves-14
97Upper Deck Ice-61
Parallel-61
Champions-IC12
Champions 2 Die Cuts-IC12
Lethal Lines-L4B
Lethal Lines 2-L4B
Power Shift-61
97Zenith-2
Z-Gold-2
Z-Silver-2
97Zenith 5 x 7-19
Gold Impulse-19
Silver Impulse-19
97Zenith Chasing The Cup-12
97Zenith Z-Team-5
97Zenith Z-Team 5x7-5
97Zenith Z-Team Gold-5
97Swedish Collector's Choice Select-UD1
97Swedish Collector's Choice Select-NNO
97Pinnacle Collector's Club Team Pinnacle-H5
97Pinnacle Collector's Club Team Pinnacle-NNO
98Aurora-46
Atomic Laser Cuts-5
Championship Fever-11
Championship Fever Copper-11
Championship Fever Ice Blue-11
Championship Fever Red-11
Championship Fever Silver-11
Cubes-4
Front Line Copper-2
Front Line Ice Blue-2
Front Line Red-2
Man Advantage-5
NHL Command-3
98Avalanche Team Issue-3
98Be A Player-35
Press Release-35
98BAP Gold-35
98BAP Autographs-35
98BAP Autographs Gold-35
98BAP AS Game Used Stick Cards-S2
98BAP AS Game Used Jersey Cards-AS2
98BAP Playoff Game Used Jerseys-G7
98BAP Playoff Highlights-H2
98BAP Playoff Practice Used Jerseys-P22
98BAP Tampa Bay All Star Game-35
98Black Diamond-21
Double Diamond-21
Triple Diamond-21
Quadruple Diamond-21
Myriad-M28
Myriad 2-M28
Winning Formula Gold-WF7
Winning Formula Platinum-WF7
98Bowman's Best-12
Refractors-12
Atomic Refractors-12
Mirror Image Fusion-F6
Mirror Image Fusion Refractors-F6
Mirror Image Fusion Atomic Refractors-F6
Scotty Bowman's Best-SB8
Scotty Refractors-SB8
Scotty Atomic Refractors-SB8
98Crown Royale-33
Limited Series-33
Cramer's Choice Jumbos-4
Cramer's Choice Jumbos Dark Blue-4
Cramer's Choice Jumbos Green-4
Cramer's Choice Jumbos Red-4
Cramer's Choice Jumbos Light Blue-4
Cramer's Choice Jumbos Gold-4
Cramer's Choice Jumbos Purple-4
Living Legends-4
Master Performers-4
Pivotal Players-4
98Donruss Elite Promos-14
98Finest-6
No Protectors-6
No Protectors Refractors-6
Refractors-6
Centurion-C7
Centurion Refractors-C7
Double Sided Mystery Finest-M21
Double Sided Mystery Finest-M25
Double Sided Mystery Finest-M26
Double Sided Mystery Finest-M27
Double Sided Mystery Refractors-M21
Double Sided Mystery Refractors-M25
Double Sided Mystery Refractors-M26
Double Sided Mystery Refractors-M27
98Katch-38
98McDonald's Upper Deck-7
98NHL Game Day Promotion-COL3
98OPC Chrome-1
Refractors-1
Season's Best-SB21
Season's Best Refractors-SB21
98Pacific-21
Ice Blue-21
Red-21
Cramer's Choice-3
Dynagon Ice Inserts-5
Titanium Ice-5
Gold Crown Die-Cuts-8
Timelines-3
98Pacific Dynagon Ice-47
Blue-47
Red-47
Adrenaline Rush Bronze-4
Adrenaline Rush Ice Blue-4
Adrenaline Rush Red-4
Adrenaline Rush Silver-4
Forward Thinking-5
Preeminent Players-3
98Pacific Omega-60
Red-60
Opening Day Issue-60
EO Portraits-4
EO Portraits 1 of 1-4
Face to Face-8
Online-8
Planet Ice-25
Planet Ice Parallel-25
Prism-4
98Panini Photocards-24
98Panini Photocards-101
98Panini Stickers-185
98Paramount-55
Copper-55
Emerald Green-55
Holo-Electric-55
Ice Blue-55
Silver-55
Hall of Fame Bound-3
Hall of Fame Bound Proofs-3
Ice Galaxy-2
Ice Galaxy Gold-2
Ice Galaxy Silver-2
Special Delivery Die-Cuts-4
98Revolution-35
Ice Shadow-35
Red-35
All-Star Die Cuts-7
Chalk Talk Laser-Cuts-4
NHL Icons-3
Showstoppers-10
Three Pronged Attack-23
Three Pronged Attack Parallel-23
98SP Authentic-20
Power Shift-20
Snapshots-SS6
Stat Masters-S19
98SPx Finite-95
98SPx Finite-166
98SPx Finite-178
Radiance-95
Radiance-166
Radiance-178
Spectrum-95
Spectrum-166
Spectrum-178
98SPx Top Prospects-13
Radiance-13
Spectrum-13
Highlight Heroes-H10
Lasting Impressions-L28
Premier Stars-PS23
98Topps-1
O-Pee-Chee-1
Ice Age 2000-I8
Local Legends-L1
Mystery Finest Bronze-M8
Mystery Finest Bronze Refractors-M8
Mystery Finest Gold-M8
Mystery Finest Gold Refractors-M8
Mystery Finest Silver-M8
Mystery Finest Silver Refractors-M8
Season's Best-SB21
98Topps Gold Label Class 1-21
Black-21
Black One of One-21
One of One-21
Red-21
Red One of One-21
98Topps Gold Label Class 2-21
98Topps Gold Label Class 2 Black-21
98Topps Gold Label Class 2 Black 1 of 1-21
98Topps Gold Label Class 2 One of One-21
98Topps Gold Label Class 2 Red-21
98Topps Gold Label Class 2 Red One of One-21
98Topps Gold Label Class 3-21
98Topps Gold Label Class 3 Black-21
98Topps Gold Label Class 3 Black 1 of 1-21
98Topps Gold Label Class 3 One of One-21
98Topps Gold Label Class 3 Red-21

98Topps Gold Label Class 3 Red One of One-21
98UD Choice-56
98UD Choice-229
98UD Choice-241
Blow-Ups-5
Mini Bobbing Head-BH14
Prime Choice Reserve-56
Prime Choice Reserve-229
Prime Choice Reserve-241
Reserve-56
Reserve-229
Reserve-241
StarQuest Blue-SQ20
StarQuest Gold-SQ20
StarQuest Green-SQ20
StarQuest Red-SQ20
98UD3-33
98UD3-93
98UD3-153
Die-Cuts-33
Die-Cuts-93
Die-Cuts-153
98Upper Deck-29
98Upper Deck-69
Exclusives-29
Exclusives-69
Exclusives 1 of 1-29
Exclusives 1 of 1-69
Fantastic Finishers-FF17
Fantastic Finishers Quantum 1-FF17
Fantastic Finishers Quantum 2-FF17
Fantastic Finishers Quantum 3-FF17
Frozen In Time-FT2
Frozen In Time Quantum 1-FT2
Frozen In Time Quantum 2-FT2
Frozen In Time Quantum 3-FT2
Generation Next-GN25
Generation Next-GN26
Generation Next-GN27
Generation Next Quantum 1-GN25
Generation Next Quantum 1-GN26
Generation Next Quantum 1-GN27
Generation Next Quantum 2-GN25
Generation Next Quantum 2-GN26
Generation Next Quantum 2-GN27
Generation Next Quantum 3-GN25
Generation Next Quantum 3-GN26
Generation Next Quantum 3-GN27
Lord Stanley's Heroes-LS12
Lord Stanley's Heroes Quantum 1-LS12
Lord Stanley's Heroes Quantum 2-LS12
Lord Stanley's Heroes Quantum 3-LS12
Profiles-P11
Profiles Quantum 1-P11
Profiles Quantum 2-P11
Profiles Quantum 3-P11
Gold Reserve-29
Gold Reserve-69
98Upper Deck MVP-51
Gold Script-51
Silver Script-51
Super Script-51
OT Heroes-OT8
Power Game-PG9
Snipers-S5
Special Forces-F14
98Slovakian Eurotel-3
99SLU Hockey-2
99Aurora-38
Striped-38
Premiere Date-38
Premiere Date Striped-38
Canvas Creations-4
Championship Fever-7
Championship Fever Copper-7
Championship Fever Ice Favorites-7
Championship Fever Silver-7
Complete Players-4
Complete Players Parallel-4
Complete Players Retail-4
Complete Players Retail Parallel-4
Styrotechs-5
99Avalanche Pins-5
99Avalanche Team Issue-7
99BAP Memorabilia-259
Gold-259
Silver-259
Jersey Cards-J2
Jersey Emblems-E2
Jersey Numbers-I2
Jersey and Stick Cards-S2
Selects Silver-SL1
Selects Gold-SL1
99BAP Update Double AS Jersey Cards-D3
99BAP Update Teammates Jersey Cards-TM10
99BAP Update Teammates Jersey Cards-TM23
99BAP Update Teammates Jersey Cards-TM28
99BAP Update Teammates Jersey Cards-TM42
99BAP Update Teammates Jersey Cards-TM43
99BAP Millennium-65
Emerald-65
Ruby-65
Sapphire-65
Signatures-65
Signatures Gold-65
Jerseys-J20
Jersey Autographs-J20
Jersey and Stick Cards-JS20
Jersey Emblems-E20
Jersey Numbers-N20
99Black Diamond-26
Diamond Cut-26
Final Cut-26
A Piece of History-PF
A Piece of History Double-PF
A Piece of History Triple-PF
Diamonation-D18
Diamond Might-DM1
99Crown Royale-37
Limited Series-37
Premiere Date-37
Card-Supials-6
Card-Supials Minis-6
Century 21-4
Cramer's Choice Jumbos-3
Cramer's Choice Jumbos Dark Blue-3
Cramer's Choice Jumbos Gold-3
Cramer's Choice Jumbos Green-3
Cramer's Choice Jumbos Light Blue-3
Cramer's Choice Jumbos Purple-3
Cramer's Choice Jumbos Red-3
International Glory-6
International Glory Parallel-6
99Hasbro Starting Lineup Cards-2
99Kraft Peanut Butter-3
99McDonald's Upper Deck-MCD10
99McDonald's Upper Deck-MCD10R
Game Jerseys-GJPF
99O-Pee-Chee-12
99O-Pee-Chee-277A
99O-Pee-Chee-277B
99O-Pee-Chee-277C
99O-Pee-Chee-277D
99O-Pee-Chee-277E
99O-Pee-Chee All-Topps-AT11
99O-Pee-Chee Chrome-12
99O-Pee-Chee Chrome-277A
99O-Pee-Chee Chrome-277B
99O-Pee-Chee Chrome-277C
99O-Pee-Chee Chrome-277D
99O-Pee-Chee Chrome-277E
99O-Pee-Chee Chrome All-Topps-AT11
99O-Pee-Chee Chrome All-Topps Refractors-AT11
99O-Pee-Chee Chrome Ice Masters-IM9
99O-Pee-Chee Chrome Ice Masters Refractor-IM9
99O-Pee-Chee Chrome Refractors-12
99O-Pee-Chee Chrome Refractors-277A
99O-Pee-Chee Chrome Refractors-277B
99O-Pee-Chee Chrome Refractors-277C
99O-Pee-Chee Chrome Refractors-277D
99O-Pee-Chee Chrome Refractors-277E
99O-Pee-Chee Chrome A-Men-AM2
99O-Pee-Chee Chrome A-Men Refractors-AM2
99O-Pee-Chee Ice Masters-IM9
99O-Pee-Chee A-Men-AM2
99O-Pee-Chee Top of the World-TW4
99Pacific-105
Copper-105
Emerald Green-105
Gold-105
Ice Blue-105
Premiere Date-105
Red-105
Center Ice-6
Center Ice Proofs-6
Cramer's Choice-3
Gold Crown Die-Cuts-9
Home and Away-4
Home and Away-14
Past and Present-6
99Pacific Dynagon Ice-56
Blue-56
Copper-56
Gold-56
Premiere Date-56
Checkmates American-5
Checkmates American-20
Checkmates Canadian-5
Lords of the Rink-4
99Pacific Omega-62
Copper-62
Gold-62
Ice Blue-62
Premiere Date-62
Cup Contenders-3
EO Portraits-5
EO Portraits 1/1-5
NHL Generations-3
5 Star Talents-19
5 Star Talents Parallel-19
99Pacific Prism-38
Holographic Blue-38
Holographic Gold-38
Holographic Mirror-38
Holographic Purple-38
Premiere Date-38
Clear Advantage-4
Dial-a-Stats-4
Sno-Globe Die-Cuts-5
99Panini Stickers-209
99Panini Stickers-320
99Paramount-63
Copper-63
Emerald-63
Gold-63
Holographic Emerald-63
Holographic Gold-63
Holographic Silver-63
Ice Blue-63
Premiere Date-63
Red-63
Silver-63
Hall of Fame Bound-4
Hall of Fame Bound Proofs-4
Ice Advantage-5
Ice Advantage Proofs-5
Personal Best-9
Toronto Fall Expo '99-63
99Revolution-39
Premiere Date-39
Red-39
Shadow Series-39
NHL Icons-5
Ornaments-6
Showstoppers-9
Top of the Line-12
Copper-39
Gold-39
CSC Silver-39
99SP Authentic-26
Supreme Skill-SS3
99SPx-40
Radiance-40
Spectrum-40
Highlight Heroes-HH8
Prolifics-P13
SPXcitement-X14
SPXtreme-XT3
Starscape-S7
99Stadium Club-8
First Day Issue-8
One of a Kind-8
Printing Plates Black-8
Printing Plates Cyan-8
Printing Plates Magenta-8
Printing Plates Yellow-8
Capture the Action-CA12
Capture the Action Game View-CAG12
Chrome-8
Chrome Refractors-8
Chrome Oversized-6
Chrome Oversized Refractors-6
Eyes of the Game-EG2
Eyes of the Game Refractors-EG2
Onyx Extreme-OE2
Onyx Extreme Die-Cut-OE2
99Topps/OPC-12
99Topps/OPC-277A
99Topps/OPC-277B
99Topps/OPC-277C
99Topps/OPC-277D
99Topps/OPC-277E
All-Topps-AT11
A-Men-AM2
Ice Masters-IM9
99Topps Stanley Cup Heroes-SC12
99Topps Stanley Cup Heroes Refractors-SC12
99Topps/OPC Top of the World-TW4
99Topps/OPC Chrome-12
99Topps/OPC Chrome-277A
99Topps/OPC Chrome-277B
99Topps/OPC Chrome-277C
99Topps/OPC Chrome-277D
99Topps/OPC Chrome-277E
Refractors-12
Refractors-277A
Refractors-277B
Refractors-277C
Refractors-277D
Refractors-277E
All-Topps-AT11
All-Topps Refractors-AT11
A-Men-AM2
A-Men Refractors-AM2
Ice Masters-IM9
Ice Masters Refractors-IM9
99Topps Gold Label Class 1-27
Black-27
Black One of One-27
One of One-27
Red-27
Red One of One-27
99Topps Gold Label Class 2-27
99Topps Gold Label Class 2 Black-27
99Topps Gold Label Class 2 Black 1 of 1-27
99Topps Gold Label Class 2 One of One-27
99Topps Gold Label Class 2 Red-27
99Topps Gold Label Class 2 Red One of One-27
99Topps Gold Label Class 3-27
99Topps Gold Label Class 3 Black-27
99Topps Gold Label Class 3 Black 1 of 1-27
99Topps Gold Label Class 3 One of One-27
99Topps Gold Label Class 3 Red-27
99Topps Gold Label Class 3 Red One of One-27
99Topps Gold Label Prime Gold-PG10
99Topps Gold Label Prime Gold One of One -PG10
99Topps Gold Label Prime Gold Black-PG10
99Topps Gold Label Prime Gold Black One of One - PG10
99Topps Gold Label Prime Gold Red-PG10
99Topps Gold Label Prime Gold Red One of One - PG10
99Topps Premier Plus-5
Parallel-5
Calling All Calders-CAC4
Premier Team-PT6
Premier Team Parallel-PT6
99Ultimate Victory-26
1/1-26
Parallel-26
Parallel 100-26
Smokin Guns-SG5
Stature-S3
The Victors-V7
UV Extra-UV6
99Upper Deck-39
99Upper Deck-154
Exclusives-39
Exclusives-154
Exclusives 1 of 1-39
Exclusives 1 of 1-154
All-Star Class-AS11
All-Star Class Quantum Gold-AS11
All-Star Class Quantum Silver-AS11
Crunch Time-CT19
Crunch Time Quantum Gold-CT19
Crunch Time Quantum Silver-CT19
Fantastic Finishers-FF10
Fantastic Finishers Quantum Gold-FF10
Fantastic Finishers Quantum Silver-FF10
Game Jerseys-PF
Game Jerseys Series II-PF
Game Jersey Patch-PFP
Game Jersey Patch 1 of 1-PFSP
Game Jersey Patch Series II-PFP
Ice Gallery-IG3
Ice Gallery Quantum Gold-IG3
Ice Gallery Quantum Silver-IG3
Marquee Attractions-MA15
Marquee Attractions Quantum Gold-MA15
Marquee Attractions Quantum Silver-MA15
NHL Scrapbook-SB6
NHL Scrapbook Quantum Gold-SB6
NHL Scrapbook Quantum Silver-SB6
Sixth Sense-SS6
Sixth Sense Quantum Gold-SS6
Sixth Sense Quantum Silver-SS6
99Upper Deck Century Legends-53
Century Collection-53
99Upper Deck Gold Reserve-39
99Upper Deck Gold Reserve-154
99Upper Deck HoloGrFx-14
Ausome-14
Impact Zone-IZ6
Impact Zone Ausome-IZ6
Pure Skill-PS2
Pure Skill Ausome-PS2
99Upper Deck MVP-52
Gold Script-52
Silver Script-52
Super Script-52
21st Century NHL-4
90's Snapshots-S6
Draw Your Own Trading Card-W24
Game-Used Souvenirs-GU19
Hands of Gold-H6
99Upper Deck MVP SC Edition-54
Gold Script-54
Silver Script-54
Super Script-54
Game-Used Souvenirs-GUPF
Golden Memories-GM3
Great Combinations-GCRF
Great Combinations Parallel-GCRF
Second Season Snipers-SS3
99Upper Deck Ovation-18
Standing Ovation-18
Lead Performers-LP4
99Upper Deck PowerDeck-7
Auxiliary-7
Auxiliary 1 of 1-7
99Upper Deck Retro-19
Gold-19
Platinum-19
99Upper Deck Victory-75
99Upper Deck Victory-77
99Upper Deck Victory-314
99Upper Deck Victory-332
99Upper Deck Victory-339
99Wayne Gretzky Hockey-51
Changing The Game-CG1
Elements of the Game-EG5
Tools of Greatness-TGPF
99Slovakian Challengers-11
00SLU Hockey One On One-10
00Aurora-38
Pinstripes-38
Pinstripes Premiere Date-38
Premiere Date-38
Canvas Creations-2
Championship Fever-5
Championship Fever Copper-5
Championship Fever Platinum Blue-5
Championship Fever Silver-5
Scouting Reports-5
Styrotechs-3A
00BAP Memorabilia-72
Emerald-72
Ruby-72
Sapphire-72
Promos-72
Jersey Cards-J14
Jersey Emblems-E14
Jersey Numbers-N14
Jersey and Stick Cards-JS14
Patent Power Jerseys-PP4
00BAP Mem Chicago Sportsfest Copper-72
00BAP Memorabilia Chicago Sportsfest Blue-72
00BAP Memorabilia Chicago Sportsfest Gold-72
00BAP Memorabilia Chicago Sportsfest Ruby-72
00BAP Memorabilia Chicago Sun-Times Ruby-72
00BAP Memorabilia Chicago Sun-Times Gold-72
00BAP Mem Chicago Sun-Times Sapphire-72
00BAP Mem Toronto Fall Expo Copper-72
00BAP Memorabilia Toronto Fall Expo Gold-72
00BAP Memorabilia Toronto Fall Expo Ruby-72
00BAP Memorabilia Update Teammates-TM18
00BAP Memorabilia Update Teammates-TM34
00BAP Memorabilia Update Teammates Gold-TM18
00BAP Memorabilia Update Teammates Gold-TM34
00BAP Parkhurst 2000-P7
00BAP Signature Series-139
Emerald-139
Ruby-139
Sapphire-139
Autographs-110
Autographs Gold-110
Franchise Players-F8
He Shoots-He Scores Points-4
He Shoots-He Scores Points-5
He Shoots-He Scores Prizes-12
Jersey Cards-J20
Jersey and Stick Cards-GSJ20
Jersey Cards Autographs-J20
Jersey Emblems-E20
Jersey Numbers-IN20
00BAP Ultimate Memorabilia Autographs-20
Gold-20
00BAP Ultimate Mem Game-Used Jerseys-GJ20
00BAP Ultimate Mem Game-Used Emblems-E18
00BAP Ultimate Mem Game-Used Numbers-N18
00BAP Ultimate Mem Game-Used Sticks-GS20
00BAP Ultimate Memorabilia Teammates-TM15
00BAP Ultimate Memorabilia Teammates-TM16
00Black Diamond-17
Gold-17
Diamond Might-FP2
Myriad-CC2
00Crown Royale-28
Ice Blue-28
Limited Series-28
Premiere Date-28
Red-28
Game-Worn Jerseys-6
Game-Worn Jersey Patches-6
Premium-Sized Game-Worn Jerseys-6
Jewels of the Crown-8
Landmarks-3
Now Playing-5
00McDonald's Pacific-8
Blue-8
Game Jerseys-2
00O-Pee-Chee-119
00O-Pee-Chee Parallel-119
00Pacific-113
00Pacific-434
Copper-113
Copper-434
Gold-113
Gold-434
Ice Blue-113
Ice Blue-434
Premiere Date-113
Premiere Date-434
2001: Ice Odyssey-6
Cramer's Choice-3
Euro-Stars-3
Gold Crown Die Cuts-8A
Reflections-5
00Pacific 2001: Ice Odyssey Anaheim Ntnl-6
00Panini Stickers-130
00Paramount-60
Copper-60
Gold-60
Holo-Gold-60
Holo-Silver-60
Ice Blue-60
Premiere Date-60
Epic Scope-5
Freeze Frame-8
Sub Zero-2
Sub Zero Gold-2
Sub Zero Red-2
00Private Stock-23
Gold-23
Premiere Date-23
Retail-23
Silver-23
Artist's Canvas-6
Artist's Canvas Proofs-6
Game Gear-24
Game Gear-25
PS-2001 Action-10
PS-2001 Stars-6
Reserve-5
00Revolution-36
Blue-36
Premiere Date-36
Red-36
HD NHL-8
Ice Immortals-5
NHL Game Gear-1
NHL Icons-6
00SP Authentic-24
Significant Stars-ST1
00SP Game Used-15
Patch Cards-D-FR
Patch Cards-P-PF
Tools of the Game-PF
Tools of the Game Exclusives-PF
Tools of the Game Combos-C-RF
00SPx-16
00SPx-71
Spectrum-16
Spectrum-71
SPXtreme-S2
Winning Materials-PF
00Stadium Club-5
Beam Team-BT2
Capture the Action-CA11
Capture the Action Game View-11
Special Forces-SF4
00Titanium-20
Blue-20
Gold-20
Premiere Date-20
Red-20
Retail-20
All-Stars-2W
Game Gear-7
Game Gear-74
Game Gear-153
Game Gear Patches-74
00Titanium Draft Day Edition-24
Patches-24
00Topps/OPC-119
Parallel-119
Combos-TC5
Combos Jumbos-TC5
Hobby Masters-HM3
00Topps Chrome-92
OPC Refractors-92
Refractors-92
Combos-TC5
Combos Refractors-TC5
Hobby Masters Refractors-HM3
00Topps Gold Label Class 1-17
Gold-17
00Topps Gold Label Class 2-17
00Topps Gold Label Class 2 Gold-17
00Topps Gold Label Class 3-17
00Topps Gold Label Class 3 Gold-17
00Topps Gold Label Bullion-B4
00Topps Gold Label Bullion One to One-B4
00Topps Gold Label Game-Worn Jerseys-GLJ-PF
00Topps Heritage-42
Chrome Parallel-42
Heroes-HH8
00Topps Premier Plus-57
Blue Ice-57
Masters of the Break-MB8
Team-PT2
Team Blue Ice-PR2
World Premier-WP16
00Topps Stars-40
00Topps Stars-128
Blue-40
Blue-128
Progression-P2
Walk of Fame-WF4
00UD Heroes-31
00UD Heroes-143
Second Season Heroes-SS2
00UD Pros and Prospects-24
Game Jerseys-PF
Game Jersey Exclusives-PF
ProMotion-PM3
00UD Reserve-23
Practice Session Jerseys-PF
Practice Session Jerseys Autographs-PF
00Upper Deck-46
Exclusives Tier 1-46
Exclusives Tier 2-46
Fantastic Finishers-FF3
Fun-Damentals-F3
Game Jerseys-PF
Game Jersey Combos-DBF
Game Jersey Patches-PFP
Game Jersey Patches-PPF
Game Jersey Patch Autographs Exclusives-PFP
Game Jersey Patch Exclusives Series II-EPF
Number Crunchers-NC1
Skilled Stars-SS6
Triple Threat-TT3
00Upper Deck Ice-13
Immortals-13
Legends-13
Stars-13
Cool Competitors-CC2
Rink Favorites-FP2
00Upper Deck Legends-34
00Upper Deck Legends-36
Legendary Collection Bronze-34
Legendary Collection Bronze-36
Legendary Collection Gold-34
Legendary Collection Gold-36
Legendary Collection Silver-34
Legendary Collection Silver-36
Legendary Game Jerseys-JPF
Playoff Heroes-PH5
00Upper Deck MVP-51
First Stars-51
Game-Used Souvenirs-GSPF
Second Stars-51
Super Game-Used Souvenirs-GSPF
Third Stars-51
Top Draws-TD3
Top Playmakers-TP3
Valuable Commodities-VC3
00Upper Deck Victory-58
00Upper Deck Victory-60
00Upper Deck Victory-291
00Upper Deck Vintage-92
All UD Team-UD8
National Heroes-NH9
00Vanguard-27
Cosmic Force-3
Dual Game-Worn Jerseys-2
Dual Game-Worn Patches-2
High Voltage-7
High Voltage Gold-7
High Voltage Green-7
High Voltage Red-7
High Voltage Silver-7
Holographic Gold-27
Holographic Purple-27
In Focus-5
Pacific Proofs-27
Press East/West-3
00Czech Stadion-115
01McFarlane Hockey-30
01Atomic-24
Blue-24
Gold-24
Premiere Date-24
Red-24
Blast-2
Jerseys-11
Power Play-8
Statosphere-11
Team Nucleus-4
01Avalanche Team Issue-23
01BAP Memorabilia-91
Emerald-91
Ruby-91
Sapphire-91
All-Star Jerseys-ASJ21
All-Star Emblems-ASE21
All-Star Numbers-ASN21
All-Star Jersey Doubles-DASJ10
All-Star Starting Line-up-S5
All-Star Teammates-AST5
All-Star Teammates-AST11
All-Star Teammates-AST26
All-Star Teammates-AST32
All-Star Teammates-AST36
All-Star Teammates-AST48
Country of Origin-CO28
He Shoots-He Scores Points-12
He Shoots-He Scores Prizes-22
Patented Power-PP6
Stanley Cup Champions-CA9
01BAP Signature Series Certified 100-C58
01BAP Signature Series Certified 50-C58
01BAP Signature Series Certified 1 of 1's-C58
01BAP Signature Series Autographs-XLPF
01BAP Signature Series Autographs Gold-LPF
01BAP Sig Series He Shoots/Scores Prizes-28
01BAP Signature Series Jerseys-GJ-75
01BAP Signature Series Emblems-GUE-14
01BAP Signature Series Numbers-ITN-14
01BAP Ultimate Mem All-Star History-49
01BAP Ultimate Memorabilia Calder Trophy-7
01BAP Ultimate Memorabilia Dynamic Duos-7
01BAP Update He Shoots-He Scores Points-15
01BAP Update He Shoots-He Scores Prizes-21
01Bowman YoungStars-73
Gold-73
Ice Cubed-73
01Crown Royale-37
Blue-37
Premiere Date-37
Red-37
Retail-37
Jewels of the Crown-6
01EA Sports-8
01eTopps-15
01McDonald's Pacific-5
Jersey Patches Silver-2
Jersey Patches Gold-2
01Nortel All-Star Game Sheets-2
01O-Pee-Chee-87
01O-Pee-Chee Heritage Parallel-87
01O-Pee-Chee Heritage Parallel Limited-87
01O-Pee-Chee Premier Parallel-87
01Pacific-101
Extreme LTD-101
Hobby LTD-101
Premiere Date-101
Retail LTD-101
All-Stars-W2
Gold Crown Die-Cuts-5
01Pacific Adrenaline-47
Blue-47
Premiere Date-47
Red-47
Retail-47
01Pacific Arena Exclusives-101
01Pacific Heads-Up-23
Blue-23
Premiere Date-23
Red-23
Silver-23
HD NHL-2
Quad Jerseys-8
Stat Masters-3
01Parkhurst-8
Gold-8
Silver-8
He Shoots-He Scores Points-12
Jerseys-PJ13
Jersey and Stick-PSJ14
Sticks-PS13
Teammates-T8
World Class Jerseys-WCJ5
World Class Emblems-WCE5
World Class Numbers-WCN5
01Private Stock Game Gear-29
01Private Stock PS-2002-18
01SP Game Used Authentic Fabric-AFPF
01SP Game Used Authentic Fabric-DFFS
01SP Game Used Authentic Fabric-TFFSR
01SP Game Used Authentic Fabric-FSRB
01SP Game Used Authentic Fabric Gold-AFPF
01SP Game Used Patches-PPF
01SPx-14
01SPx-72
Hidden Treasures-DTSF
Hidden Treasures-TTFSD
01Sports Illustrated for Kids III-217
01Stadium Club-2
Award Winners-2
Master Photos-2
Gallery-G33
Gallery Gold-G33
Heart and Soul-HS7
NHL Passport-NHLP1
Perennials-P4
Souvenirs-PF
Souvenirs-PFCD
Souvenirs-PFJS
Souvenirs-JSCDPF
01Stadium Club Toronto Fall Expo-2
01Topps-87
Heritage Parallel-87
Heritage Parallel Limited-87
OPC Parallel-87
Own The Game-OTG9
01Topps Chrome-87
Refractors-87
Black Border Refractors-87
01Topps Heritage-39
Refractors-39
Jerseys-JPF
01Topps Heritage Avalanche NHL AS Game-3
01Topps Reserve-37
Emblems-PF
Jerseys-PF
Name Plates-PF
Numbers-PF
Patches-PF
01UD Challenge for the Cup Jerseys-FPPF
01UD Mask Collection Double Patches-DPPF
01UD Mask Collection Jerseys-J-PF
01UD Mask Collection Jersey and Patch-JPPF
01UD Playmakers Jerseys-J-PF
01UD Playmakers Jerseys Gold-J-PF
01UD Premier Collection-13
Dual Jerseys-DFD
Dual Jerseys Black-DFD
Jerseys-BPF
Jerseys Black-B-PF
01UD Stanley Cup Champs-30
Jerseys-T-PF
Pieces of Glory-G-PF
Sticks-S-PF
01UD Top Shelf-9
Jerseys-PF
Patches-PPF
Sticks-SPF
Sticks-BFJ
Sticks-RSF
Sticks Gold-SPF
Sticks Gold-RSF
01Upper Deck-47
01Upper Deck-229
Exclusives-47
Exclusives-229
Franchise Cornerstones-FC4
Game Jerseys-CFR
Game Jerseys-FSR
Game Jerseys Series II-FJPF
Game Jerseys Series II-SSPF
Game Jerseys Series II-DJSF
Gate Attractions-GA9
Patches-PPF
Patches Series II-PLPF
Patches Series II-NAPF
Pride of a Nation-PNPF
Pride of a Nation-DPFS
Pride of a Nation-TPFSL
Skilled Stars-SS9
01Upper Deck Avalanche NHL All-Star Game-HH2
01Upper Deck Avalanche NHL All-Star Game-PP3
01Upper Deck EA Sports Gold-8
01Upper Deck Ice-9
01Upper Deck MVP-44
Morning Skate Jerseys-J-PF
Souvenirs-S-PF
Souvenirs Gold-S-PF
Talent-MT1
Valuable Commodities-VC6
01Upper Deck Victory-84
01Upper Deck Victory-394
Gold-84
Gold-394
01Upper Deck Vintage-65
01Upper Deck Vintage-70
01Vanguard East Meets West-3
01Vanguard Memorabilia-9
01Vanguard Memorabilia-47
02Atomic-24
Blue-24
Gold-24
Red-24
Cold Fusion-8
Hobby Parallel-24
02Avalanche Postcards-8
02BAP All-Star Edition-23
02BAP All-Star Edition-24
02BAP All-Star Edition-25
He Shoots-He Scores Points-18
He Shoots-He Score Prizes-7
Jerseys-23
Jerseys-24
Jerseys-25
Jerseys Gold-23
Jerseys Gold-24
Jerseys Gold-25
Jerseys Silver-23
Jerseys Silver-24
Jerseys Silver-25
02BAP First Edition-144
02BAP First Edition-322
02BAP First Edition-406R
He Shoots-He Score Points-18
He Shoots-He Scores Prizes-1
Jerseys-144
02BAP Memorabilia-128
02BAP Memorabilia-231
Emerald-128
Emerald-231
Ruby-128
Ruby-231
Sapphire-128
Sapphire-231
All-Star Jerseys-ASJ-14
All-Star Emblems-ASE-4
All-Star Numbers-ASN-4
All-Star Teammmates-AST-10
All-Star Teammmates-AST-14
All-Star Teammmates-AST-24
All-Star Triple Jerseys-ASTJ-4
He Shoots-He Scores Points-11
He Shoots-He Scores Prizes-10
Mini Stanley Cups-34
NHL All-Star Game-128
NHL All-Star Game-231
NHL All-Star Game Blue-128
NHL All-Star Game Blue-231
NHL All-Star Game Green-128
NHL All-Star Game Green-231
NHL All-Star Game Red-128
NHL All-Star Game Red-231
Stanley Cup Playoffs-SC-12
Teammates-TM-4
02BAP Memorabilia Toronto Fall Expo-128
02BAP Memorabilia Toronto Fall Expo-231
02BAP NHL All-Star History-49
02BAP Signature Series-102
Autographs-102
Autograph Buybacks 1998-35
Autograph Buybacks 1999-65
Autograph Buybacks 2000-110
Autographs Gold-102
Complete Jersey-CJ7
Golf-GS72
Jerseys-SGJ3
Jersey Autographs-SGJ3
Team Quads-TQ1
02BAP Ultimate Memorabilia Active Eight-2
02BAP Ultimate Memorabilia Autographs-24
02BAP Ultimate Mem Autographs Gold-24
02BAP Ultimate Memorabilia Dynamic Duos-2
02BAP Ultimate Memorabilia Emblems-11
02BAP Ultimate Mem Global Dominators-4
02BAP Ultimate Memorabilia Jerseys-31
02BAP Ultimate Mem Jersey and Stick-3
02BAP Ultimate Mem Magnificent Ones-8
02BAP Ultimate Mem Magnificent Ones Autos-8
02BAP Ultimate Memorabilia MVP Winner-1
02BAP Ultimate Memorabilia Nameplates-8
02BAP Ultimate Memorabilia Numbers-8
02BAP Ultimate Memorabilia Numerology-24
02BAP Ultimate Mem Playoff Scorers-1
02BAP Ultimate Mem Playoff Scorers-4
02BAP Ultimate Memorabilia Retro Trophies-18
02BAP Ultimate Mem Scoring Leaders-1
02Between the Pipes Nightmares-GN7
02Bowman YoungStars-14
Gold-14
Silver-14
02Crown Royale-23
Blue-23
Red-23
Retail-23
Dual Patches-5
Lords of the Rink-6
02eTopps-15
02ITG Used-16
02ITG Used-116
International Experience-IE7
International Experience Gold-IE7
Jerseys-GUJ3
Jersey Autographs-GUJ3
Jerseys Gold-GUJ3
Emblems-E3
Jersey and Stick-SJ3
Jersey and Stick Gold-SJ3
Teammates-T2
Teammates Gold-T2
02McDonald's Pacific-8
02O-Pee-Chee-71
02O-Pee-Chee Premier Blue Parallel-71
02O-Pee-Chee Premier Red Parallel-71
02O-Pee-Chee Factory Set-71
02Pacific-90
Blue-90
Red-90
Cramer's Choice-4
Lamplighters-5
02Pacific Calder 15
Silver-15
Chasing Glory-2
Hart Stoppers-2
02Pacific Chicago National *-4
02Pacific Complete-39
Red-39
02Pacific Exclusive-40
Maximum Overdrive-6
02Pacific Heads-Up-30
Blue-30
Purple-30
Red-30
Bobble Heads-4
Etched in Time-6
Postseason Picks-3
02Pacific Quest for the Cup-21
Gold-21
Jerseys-5
Raising the Cup-1
02Parkhurst-99
Bronze-99
Gold-99
Silver-99
Hardware-A7
Hardware-H8
Hardware-P7
Heroes-NH12
He Shoots-He Scores Points-2
He Shoots-He Scores Prizes-15
Jerseys-GJ46
Milestones-MS9
Patented Power-PP7
Stick and Jerseys-SJ46
Teammates-TT19
02Parkhurst Retro-171
Minis-171
He Shoots-He Scores Points-12
He Shoots-He Scores Prizes-10
Jerseys-RJ3
Jersey and Sticks-RSJ3
Memorabilia-RM17
02Private Stock Reserve-24
Blue-24
Red-24
Retail-24
Elite-2
02SP Authentic-23
02SP Authentic-95
Beckett Promos-23
Super Premiums-SPPF
Super Premiums-DPFR
02SP Game Used-11
Authentic Fabrics-AFFO
Authentic Fabrics-CFFO
Authentic Fabrics Gold-AFFO
Authentic Fabrics Gold-CFFO
Authentic Fabrics Rainbow-AFFO
Authentic Fabrics Rainbow-CFFO
First Rounder Patches-PF
Piece of History-PHFO
Piece of History-PHPF
Piece of History Gold-PHFO
Piece of History Gold-PHPF
Piece of History Rainbow-PHFO
Piece of History Rainbow-PHPF
02SPx-19
02SPx-85
Spectrum Gold-19
Spectrum Gold-85
Spectrum Silver-19
Spectrum Silver-85
Winning Materials-WMPF
Winning Materials Gold-FO
Winning Materials Silver-FO
Xtreme Talents-PF
Xtreme Talents Gold-PF
Xtreme Talents Silver-PF
02Stadium Club-46
Silver Decoy Cards-46
Proofs-46
Beam Team-BT10
02Titanium-24
Blue-24
Red-24
Retail-24
02Topps-71
OPC Blue Parallel-71
OPC Red Parallel-71
Factory Set-71
02Topps Chrome-48
Black Border Refractors-48
Refractors-48
02Topps Heritage-17
Chrome Parallel-17
Calder Cloth-PF
Calder Cloth Patches-PF
USA Test Parallel-17
02Topps Total-122
Production-TP4
02UD Artistic Impressions-23
Gold-23
Artist's Touch-ATPF
Artist's Touch Gold-ATPF
02UD Artistic Impressions Beckett Promos-23
02UD Artistic Impress Common Ground-CG21
02UD Artistic Impress Common Ground Gold-CG21
02UD Artistic Impressions Retrospectives-R23
02UD Artistic Impressions Retrospect Gold-R23
02UD Artistic Impressions Retrospect Silver-R23
02Upper Deck Collectors Club-NHL16
02UD Honor Roll-17
Grade A Jerseys-GAPF
Grade A Jerseys-TRFS
Students of the Game-SG8
Team Warriors-TW4
02UD Mask Collection Instant Offense-IOPF
02UD Piece of History-27
02UD Piece of History-107
Awards Collection-AC8
02UD Premier Collection-13
Jerseys Bronze-PF
Jerseys Bronze-PG
Jerseys Bronze-FH
Jerseys Gold-PF
Jerseys Gold-PG
Jerseys Gold-FH

Jerseys Silver-PF
Jerseys Silver-PG
Jerseys Silver-FH
Patches-PPF
02UD Top Shelf-23
Hardware Heroes-HSRBF
Shooting Stars-SHPF
02Upper Deck-48
02Upper Deck-230
Exclusives-48
Exclusives-230
Blow-Ups-C9
Fan Favorites-PF
Gifted Greats-GG5
Patch Card Name Plate-PF
Patchwork-PWPF
Playbooks Series II-FS
02Upper Deck Classic Portraits-26
Genuine Greatness-GG2
Headliners-FS
Headliners Limited-FS
Hockey Royalty-RDF
Hockey Royalty Limited-RDF
02Upper Deck MVP-46
Gold-46
Classics-46
Golden Classics-46
Overdrive-SO6
Skate Around Jerseys-SAPF
Skate Around Jerseys-SDFL
Skate Around Jerseys-STSFR
02Upper Deck Rookie Update-26
02Upper Deck Victory-56
Bronze-56
Gold-56
Silver-56
02Upper Deck Vintage-64
02Upper Deck Vintage-268
Green Backs-64
Jerseys-SOPF
Jerseys Gold-SO-PF
Tall Boys-T16
Tall Boys Gold-T16
02Vanguard-25
LTD-25
East Meets West-6
In Focus-3
02UD SuperStars *-69
Gold-69
03McFarlane Hockey 3-Inch Duals-50
03McFarlane Hockey-120
03McFarlane Hockey-122
03McFarlane Hockey-124
03Avalanche Team Issue-5
03BAP Memorabilia-72
Emerald-72
Gold-72
Ruby-72
Sapphire-72
All-Star Complete Jerseys-ASCJ1
All-Star Emblems-ASE-6
All-Star Jerseys-ASJ-1
All-Star Jerseys-ASJ-23
All-Star Numbers-ASN-6
All-Star Teammates-AST1
All-Star Teammates-AST9
Brush with Greatness-5
Brush with Greatness Contest Cards-5
He Shoots-He Scores Points-19
He Shoots-He Scores Prizes-1
Jersey and Stick-SJ-27
Jerseys-GJ-36
Jersey Autographs-GJ-36
03BAP Ultimate Memorabilia Autographs-140
Gold-140
03BAP Ultimate Mem Auto Jerseys-140
03BAP Ultimate Mem Auto Emblems-140
03BAP Ultimate Mem Auto Sticks-140
03BAP Ultimate Memorabilia Active Eight-4
03BAP Ultimate Memorabilia Active Eight-5
03BAP Ultimate Mem Always An All-Star-12
03BAP Ultimate Mem Always An AS Gold-12
03BAP Ultimate Mem Complete Jersey-13
03BAP Ultimate Mem Complete Jersey Gold-13
03BAP Ultimate Memorabilia Dynamic Duos-2
03BAP Ultimate Memorabilia Emblems-22
03BAP Ultimate Memorabilia Emblems Gold-22
03BAP Ultimate Mem Franch Present Future-8
03BAP Ultimate Memorabilia Heroes-20
03BAP Ultimate Mem Heroes Autos-10
03BAP Ultimate Mem Hometown Heroes-4
03BAP Ultimate Mem Hometown Heroes Gold-4
03BAP Ultimate Memorabilia Jerseys-12
03BAP Ultimate Memorabilia Jerseys Gold-12
03BAP Ultimate Mem Jersey and Emblems-33
03BAP Ultimate Mem Jersey and Emblem Gold-33
03BAP Ultimate Mem Jersey and Numbers-33
03BAP Ultimate Mem Jersey and Number Gold-33
03BAP Ultimate Mem Jersey and Stick-17
03BAP Ultimate Mem Jersey and Stick Gold-17
03BAP Ultimate Memorabilia Nameplates-16
03BAP Ultimate Mem Nameplates Gold-16
03BAP Ultimate Memorabilia Numbers-9
03BAP Ultimate Memorabilia Numbers Gold-9
03BAP Ultimate Mem Perennial Power Jersey-3
03BAP Ult Mem Perenn Powerhouse Jsy Stick-3
03BAP Ultimate Mem Perennial Power Emblem-3
03BAP Ultimate Mem Retro-Active Trophies-2
03BAP Ultimate Mem Retro-Active Trophies-4
03BAP Ultimate Memorabilia Triple Threads-22
03Beehive-55
Variations-55
Gold-55
Silver-55
Jumbos-8
Jumbo Variations-8
Sticks Beige Border-BE28
Sticks Red Border-RE3
03Black Diamond-36
Black-36
Green-36
Red-36
Threads-DT-PF
Threads Green-DT-PF
Threads Red-DT-PF
Threads Black-DT-PF
03Bowman-21
Gold-21
03Bowman Chrome-21
Refractors-21
Gold Refractors-21
Xfractors-21
03Crown Royale-23
Blue-23
Retail-23
Global Conquest-8
Jerseys-6
Patches-6
Lords of the Rink-5
03eTopps-33
03ITG Action-118
Center of Attention-CA4
Homeboys-HB1
Jerseys-M184
Jerseys-M204
League Leaders-L1
League Leaders-L3
League Leaders-L4
Trophy Winners-TW1
Trophy Winners-TW6
03ITG Toronto Fall Expo Jerseys-FE27
03ITG Used Signature Series-99
Gold-99
Autographs-PF
Autographs Gold-PF
Franchise-8
Franchise Autographs-8
Franchise Gold-8
Game-Day Jerseys-8
Game-Day Jerseys Gold-8
International Experience-24
International Experience Autographs-24
International Experience Emblems Gold-24
International Experience Emblems-24
International Experience Gold-24
Jerseys-35
Jerseys Gold-35
Jersey Autos-35
Emblems-5
Emblems Gold-5
Jersey and Stick-35
Jersey and Stick Gold-35
Teammates-7
Teammates Gold-7
03ITG VIP Brightest Stars-7
03ITG VIP Collages-6
03ITG VIP Collage Autographs-6
03ITG VIP International Experience-7
03ITG VIP Jerseys-11
03ITG VIP Jersey Autographs-11
03ITG VIP Jersey and Emblems-9
03ITG VIP Jersey and Numbers-9
03McDonald's Pacific-10
Patches Silver-5
Patches Gold-5
Patches and Sticks-5
03NHL Sticker Collection-183
03O-Pee-Chee-160
03OPC Blue-160
03OPC Gold-160
03OPC Red-160
03Pacific-83
Blue-83
Red-83
Cramer's Choice-1
Jerseys-8
Jerseys Gold-8
Main Attractions-4
03Pacific Calder-22
03Pacific Calder-145
Silver-22
03Pacific Complete-254
Red-254
03Pacific Exhibit-160
Blue Backs-160
History Makers-2
03Pacific Heads-Up-24
Hobby LTD-24
Retail LTD-24
Jerseys-8
Mini Sweaters-4
Rink Immortals-2
Rink Immortals LTD-2
03Pacific Invincible-21
Blue-21
Red-21
Retail-21
Featured Performers-8
Top Line-2
03Pacific Luxury Suite-5A
03Pacific Luxury Suite-5B
03Pacific Luxury Suite-5C
03Pacific Luxury Suite-5D
03Pacific Luxury Suite-28A
03Pacific Luxury Suite-28B
03Pacific Luxury Suite-28C
03Pacific Prism-110
Blue-110
Patches-109
Red-110
Retail-109
Stat Masters-3
03Pacific Quest for the Cup-23
Blue-23
Raising the Cup-3
03Pacific Supreme-21
Blue-21
Red-21
Retail-21
Jerseys-8
Team-2
03Parkhurst Orig Six Boston Mem -BM50
03Parkhurst Orig Six Chicago Mem -CM50
03Parkhurst Orig Six Detroit Mem-DM50
03Parkhurst Orig Six Montreal Mem-MM50
03Parkhurst Orig Six New York Mem-NM50
03Parkhurst Original Six Shooters-OSM10
03Parkhurst Orig Six Toronto Mem-TM50
03Parkhurst Rookie-41
Emblems-GUE-2
Emblem Autographs-GUE-PF
Emblems Gold-GUE-2
Jerseys-GJ-6
Jerseys Gold-GJ-6
Retro Rookies-RR-2
Retro Rookies Gold-RR-2
ROYalty-VR-3
ROYalty Autographs-VR-PF
ROYalty Gold-VR-3
Teammates Gold-RT12
Teammates-RT12
03Private Stock Reserve-154
Blue-154
Patches-154
Red-154
Retail-154
Moments in Time-3
03SP Authentic-22
Limited-22
Breakout Seasons-B28
Breakout Seasons Limited-B28
Foundations-F4
Foundations Limited-F4
03SP Game Used-12
03SP Game Used-120
Gold-12
Gold-120
Authentic Fabrics-DFFS
Authentic Fabrics-DFKF
Authentic Fabrics-QFSKS
Authentic Fabrics Gold-DFFS
Authentic Fabrics Gold-DFKF
Authentic Fabrics Gold-QFSKS
Authentic Patches-APPF
Double Threads-DTFS
Limited Threads-LTPF
Limited Threads Gold-LTPF
Team Threads-TTFSK
Top Threads-FSKS
03SPx-23
03SPx-121
Radiance-23
Radiance-121
Spectrum-23
Spectrum-121
Fantasy Franchise-FF-KSF
Fantasy Franchise Limited-FF-KSF
Origins-O-PF
VIP-VIP-FS
VIP Limited-VIP-FS
Winning Materials-WM-FO
Winning Materials-WM-PF
Winning Materials Limited-WM-FO
Winning Materials Limited-WM-PF
03Titanium-194
Patches-194
Highlight Reels-3
Stat Masters-3
03Topps-160
Blue-160
Gold-160
Red-160
Box Toppers-16
Topps/OPC Idols-II18
Own the Game-OTG1
03Topps C55-1
03Topps C55-1B
Minis-1
Minis American Back-1
Minis American Back Red-1
Minis Bazooka Back-1
Minis Brooklyn Back-1
Minis Hat Trick Back-1
Minis O Canada Back-1
Minis O Canada Back Red-1
Minis Stanley Cup Back-1
Award Winners-6
Award Winners-13
03Topps Pristine-100
Gold Refractor Die Cuts-100
Refractors-100
Patches-PP-PF
Patch Refractors-PP-PF
Press Plates Black-100
Press Plates Cyan-100
Press Plates Magenta-100
Press Plates Yellow-100
03UD Honor Roll-20
03UD Honor Roll-120
03UD Honor Roll-126
Grade A Jerseys-TCOL
03UD Premier Collection-16
Skills-SK-FT
Skills Patches-SK-FT
Super Stars-SS-PF
Super Stars Patches-SS-PF
Teammates-PT-CA1
Teammates Patches-PT-CA1
03Upper Deck-45
All-Star Class-AS-5
Big Playmakers-BP-PF
Canadian Exclusives-45
Franchise Fabrics-FF-PF
HG-45
Magic Moments-MM-13
Performers-PS5
Power Zone-PZ-7
Team Essentials-TP-PF
03Upper Deck Classic Portraits-21
03Upper Deck Classic Portraits-104
03Upper Deck Classic Portraits-139
Hockey Royalty-FSK
Premium Portraits-PP-PF
03Upper Deck Ice-21
Gold-21
Breakers-IB-PF
Breaker Patches-IB-PF
Clear Cut Winners-CC-PF
03Upper Deck MVP-101
Gold Script-101
Silver Script-101
Canadian Exclusives-101
Lethal Lineups-LL1
Souvenirs-S17
SportsNut-SN22
Talent-MT11
03Upper Deck Rookie Update-21
Skills-SKPF
Super Stars-SSPF
03Upper Deck Trilogy-21
03Upper Deck Trilogy-107
Authentic Patches-AP20
Crest Variations-107
Limited-21
Limited-107
Limited Threads-LT11
03Upper Deck Victory-43
Bronze-43
Gold-43
Silver-43
Freshman Flashback-FF12
Game Breakers-GB1
03Russian World Championship Stars-7
03Toronto Star-24
Foil-3
04ITG NHL AS FANtasy AS History Jerseys-SB49
04Pacific-66
Blue-66
Red-66
Global Connection-3
04SP Authentic-23
04SP Authentic-106
04SP Game Used Hawaii Conference Patch-PP24
04UD All-World-67
04UD All-World-100
Gold-67
04Ultimate Collection-10
04Ultimate Collection-79
Dual Logos-UL2-AF
Dual Logos-UL2-FS
Dual Logos-UL2-HF
Jerseys-UGJ-PF
Jerseys Gold-UGJ-PF
Patches-UP-PF
04Upper Deck-42
04Upper Deck-185
1997 Game Jerseys-PF
Canadian Exclusives-42
Canadian Exclusives-185
HG Glossy Gold-42
HG Glossy Gold-185
HG Glossy Silver-42
HG Glossy Silver-185
NHL's Best-NB-PF
Patches-GJPA-PF
Patches-GJPL-PF
Patches-GJPN-PF
World's Best-WB25
World Cup Tribute-PF
World Cup Tribute-PFSUDA
04Swedish Alfabilder Alfa Stars-21
04Swedish Alfabilder Alfa Star Golden Ice-4
04Swedish Alfabilder Autographs-103
04Swedish Alfabilder Limited Autographs-103
04Swedish Alfabilder Next In Line-3
04Swedish Alfabilder Proof Parallels-21
04Swedish Elitset-248
Dominators-2
Dominators-9
Forsberg Tribute-1
Forsberg Tribute-2
Forsberg Tribute-3
Forsberg Tribute-4
Forsberg Tribute-5
Forsberg Tribute-6
Gold-248
Signatures Series B-15
04Swedish MoDo Postcards-1
04Swedish Pure Skills-69
Parallel-69
Professional Power-PF
Signatures Limited-2
05Be A Player-20
First Period-20
Second Period-20
Third Period-20
Overtime-20
Class Action-CA6
Ice Icons-ICE4
Outtakes-OT12
05Beehive-65
05Beehive-205
Beige -65
Blue -65
Gold-65
Red -65
Matte-65
Matted Materials-MMPF
05Black Diamond-173
Emerald-173
Gold-173
Onyx-173
Ruby-173
Jerseys-J-PF
Jerseys Ruby-J-PF
Jersey Duals-DJ-PF
Jersey Triples-TJ-PF
Jersey Quads-QJ-PF
05Flyers Team Issue-6
05Hot Prospects-71
En Fuego-71
Red Hot-71
White Hot-71
05McDonalds Upper Deck-45
Top Scorers-TS5
05Panini Stickers-129
05Parkhurst-352
05Parkhurst-692
Facsimile Auto Parallel-352
Facsimile Auto Parallel-692
True Colors-TCPHI
True Colors-TCPHI
True Colors-TCPHPI
True Colors-TCPHPI
05SP Authentic-73
05SP Authentic-115
Limited-73
Limited-115
05SP Game Used-72
Gold-72
Authentic Fabrics-AF-PF
Authentic Fabrics Dual-ER
Authentic Fabrics Gold-AF-PF
Authentic Fabrics Quad-GFEP
Authentic Patches Quad -GFEP
Authentic Fabrics Triple-SFI
Authentic Fabrics Triple-SFN
Authentic Patches-AP-PF
Authentic Patches Dual-ER
Authentic Patches Triple-SFI
Authentic Patches Triple-SFN
Awesome Authentics-AA-PF
Awesome Authentics Gold-DA-PF
Game Gear-GG-PF
05SPx-65
Spectrum-65
Winning Combos-WC-FP
Winning Combos-WC-FS
Winning Combos Gold-WC-FP
Winning Combos Gold-WC-FS
Winning Combos Spectrum-WC-FP
Winning Combos Spectrum-WC-FS
Winning Materials-WM-PF
Winning Materials Gold-WM-PF
Winning Materials Spectrum-WM-PF
05The Cup-74
Gold-74
Black Rainbow-74
Dual NHL Shields-DSFG
Dual NHL Shields-DSPM
Dual NHL Shields-DSSF
Masterpiece Pressplates-74
Noble Numbers-NNFS
Noble Numbers Dual-DNNFG
Noble Numbers Dual-DNNFS
Noble Numbers Dual-DNNPJ
Patch Variation-P74
05UD Artifacts Treasured Patches-TP-PF
05UD Artifacts Treasured Patch Autos-TP-PF
05UD Artifacts Treasured Patches Dual-TPD-PF
05UD Artifacts Treasured Patch Dual Autos-TPD-PF
05UD Artifacts Treasured Patches Pewter-TP-PF
05UD Artifacts Treasured Patches Silver-TP-PF
05UD Artifacts Treasured Swatches-TS-PF
05UD Artifacts Treasured Swatch Autos-TS-PF
05UD Artifacts Treasured Swatches Blue-TS-PF
05UD Artifacts Treasured Swatches Copper-TS-PF
05UD Artifacts Treasured Swatches Dual-TSD-PF
05UD Artifacts Treasured Swatch Dual Auto-TSD-PF
05UD Artifacts Treasured Swatch Dual Blue-TSD-PF
05UD Artifact Treasure Swatch Dual Copper-TSD-PF
05UD Artifact Treasure Swatch Dual Maroon-TSD-PF
05UD Artifact Treasure Swatch Dual Pewter-TSD-PF
05UD Artifact TreasuredSwatch Dual Silver-TSD-PF
05UD Artifacts Treasured Swatches Maroon-TS-PF
05UD Artifacts Treasured Swatches Pewter-TS-PF
05UD Artifacts Treasured Swatches Silver-TS-PF
05UD PowerPlay-25
05UD PowerPlay-107
Rainbow-25
05Ultimate Collection-65
Gold-65
Jerseys-JPF
Jerseys Dual-DJFP
Jerseys Triple-TJFGC
National Heroes Jerseys-NHJPF
National Heroes Patches-NHPPF
Premium Patches-PPPF
Premium Swatches-PSPF
Ultimate Patches-PPF
Ultimate Patches Dual-DPFP
Ultimate Patches Triple-TPFGC
05Ultra-141
Gold-141
Ice-141
Scoring Kings-SK21
Scoring Kings Jerseys-SKJ-PF
Scoring Kings Patches-SKP-PF
05Upper Deck-386
05Upper Deck-441
05Upper Deck All-Time Greatest-87
05Upper Deck Big Playmakers-B-PF
05Upper Deck Hometown Heroes-HH19
05Upper Deck Jerseys-J-PF
05Upper Deck Jerseys Series II-J2PF
05Upper Deck Majestic Materials-MMPF
05Upper Deck NHL Generations-TSFZ
05Upper Deck Patches-P-PF
05Upper Deck Playoff Performers-PP3
05Upper Deck Scrapbooks-HS13
05Upper Deck Hockey Showcase-HS1
05Upper Deck Showcase Promos-HS1
05Upper Deck Ice-71
Rainbow-71
Frozen Fabrics-FFPF
Frozen Fabrics Glass-FFPF
Frozen Fabrics Patches-FFPPF
05Upper Deck MVP-280
05Upper Deck MVP-443
Gold-280
Gold-443
Platinum-280
Platinum-443
Materials Triples-T-SKF
Rising to the Occasion-RO8
05Upper Deck Rookie Update-70
05Upper Deck Trilogy-64
05Upper Deck Trilogy-105
Crystal-105
Honorary Patches-HP-PF
Honorary Swatches-HS-PF
05Upper Deck Victory-46
05Upper Deck Victory-236
Black-46
Black-236
Gold-46
Gold-236
Silver-46
Silver-236
Blow-Ups-BU9
Game Breakers-GB9
Stars on Ice-SI12
05Swedish SHL Elitset-102
Gold-102
06Be A Player-127
Autographs-127
Profiles-PP11
Profiles Autographs-PP11
Signatures-PF
Signatures 10-141
Signatures 25-141
Signatures Duals-DFL
Signatures Trios-TFLS
Signatures Foursomes-FFLNA
Up Close and Personal-UC46
Up Close and Personal Autographs-UC46
06Be A Player Portraits-75
06Beehive-27
06Beehive-175
Blue-27
Gold-27
Matte-27
Red Facsimile Signatures-27
Wood-27
5 X 7 Black and White-27
5 X 7 Cherry Wood-27
Matted Materials-MMPF
06Black Diamond-163B
Black-161B
Gold-163B
Ruby-163B
Jerseys-JPF
Jerseys Black-JPF
Jerseys Gold-JPF
Jerseys Ruby-JPF
06Flair Showcase-76
06Flair Showcase-192
06Flair Showcase-253
06Flair Showcase-292
Parallel-76
Parallel-192
Parallel-253
Parallel-292
Hot Numbers-HN32
Hot Numbers Parallel-HN32
Stitches-SSPF
06Fleer-143
Oversized-143
Tiffany-143
Fabricology-FPF
Total O-019
06Hot Prospects-70
Red Hot-70
White Hot-70
Hot Materials -HMPF
Hot Materials Red Hot-HMPF
Hot Materials White Hot-HMPF
06McDonald's Upper Deck-34
Jerseys-JPF
Patches-PPF
06O-Pee-Chee-372
06O-Pee-Chee-662
06O-Pee-Chee-692
Rainbow-372
Rainbow-662
Rainbow-692
Swatches-S-PF
06Panini Stickers-124
06SP Authentic-59
06SP Authentic-146
Limited-28
Limited-146
06SP Game Used-73
Gold-73
Rainbow-73
Authentic Fabrics-AFPF
Authentic Fabrics Parallel-AFPF
Authentic Fabrics Patches-AFPF
Authentic Fabrics Dual-AF2FC
Authentic Fabrics Dual Patches-AF2FC
Authentic Fabrics Triple-AF3PHI
Authentic Fabrics Triple Patches-AF3PHI
Authentic Fabrics Quads-AF4SFSZ
Authentic Fabrics Quads Patches-AF4SFSZ
Authentic Fabrics Sevens-AF7ART
Authentic Fabrics Sevens-AF7MVP
Authentic Fabrics Sevens Patches-AF7ART
Authentic Fabrics Sevens Patches-AF7MVP
Authentic Fabrics Eights-AF8SWE
Authentic Fabrics Eights Patches-AF8SWE
By The Letter-BLPF
06SPx-75
06SPx-116
Spectrum-75
Spectrum-116
SPxcitement-X73
SPxcitement Spectrum-X73
Winning Materials-WMPF
Winning Materials Spectrum-WMPF
06The Cup-66
Black Rainbow-66
Foundations-CQPF
Foundations Patches-CQPF
Gold-66
Gold Patches-66
Jerseys-66
Masterpiece Pressplates-66
NHL Shields Duals-DSHFC
NHL Shields Duals-DSHFG
NHL Shields Duals-DSHFL
NHL Shields Duals-DSHSF
06UD Artifacts-28
06UD Artifacts-188
Blue-28
Blue-188
Gold-28
Gold-188
Platinum-28
Platinum-188
Radiance-28
Radiance-188
Red-28
Red-188
Treasured Patches Black-TSPF
Treasured Patches Blue-TSPF
Treasured Patches Gold-TSPF
Treasured Patches Platinum-TSPF
Treasured Patches Red-TSPF
Treasured Swatches-TSPF
Treasured Swatches Black-TSPF
Treasured Swatches Blue-TSPF
Treasured Swatches Gold-TSPF
Treasured Swatches Platinum-TSPF
Treasured Swatches Red-TSPF
Tundra Tandems-TTFG
Tundra Tandems Black-TTFG
Tundra Tandems Blue-TTFG
Tundra Tandems Gold-TTFG
Tundra Tandems Platinum-TTFG
Tundra Tandems Red-TTFG
Tundra Tandems Dual Patches Red-TTFG
06UD Mini Jersey Collection-73
Jerseys-PF
Jersey Variations-PF
06UD Powerplay-72
Impact Rainbow-72
In Action-IA9
Specialists-SPF
Specialists Patches-PPF
06Ultimate Collection-45
Jerseys-UJ-PF
Jerseys Dual-UJ2-FG
Jerseys Triple-UJ3-SFL
Patches-UJ-PF
Patches Dual-UJ2-FG
Patches Triple-UJ3-SFL
06Ultra-140
Gold Medallion-140
Ice Medallion-140
Action-UA21
Difference Makers-DM26
Scoring Kings-SK25
Uniformity-UPF
Uniformity Patches-UPPB_
06Upper Deck Arena Giveaways-PHI1
06Upper Deck-142
Exclusives Parallel-142
High Gloss Parallel-142
All World-AW27
Game Jerseys-JPF
Game Patches-PPF
Generations Duals-G2FS
Generations Patches Dual-G2PFS
Masterpieces-142
Walmart Tins Oversize-142
06Upper Deck MVP-215
06Upper Deck MVP-360
Gold Script-215
Gold Script-360
Super Script-215
Super Script-360
Clutch Performers-CP2
Gotta Have Hart-HH2
International Icons-II19
Jerseys-OJCF
Jerseys-OJJF
06Upper Deck Ovation-137
06Upper Deck Sweet Shot-76
Sweet Stitches-SSPF
Sweet Stitches Duals-SSPF
Sweet Stitches Triples-SSPF
06Upper Deck Trilogy-71
06Upper Deck Victory-143
06Upper Deck Victory Black-143
06Upper Deck Victory Gold-143
06Upper Deck Victory GameBreakers-GB38
06Upper Deck Victory Oversize Cards-PF
06Russian Sport Collection Olympic Stars-21
07Upper Deck Ovation-21
07Upper Deck Victory-111
Black-111
Gold-111
GameBreakers-GB40
Oversize Cards-OS29

Forseth, Jody
91Air Canada SJHL-E43

Forsey, Jack
34Beehive Group I Photos-317

Forslund, Bryan
95Central Hockey League-59
99Jacksonville Lizard Kings-11
03Oklahoma City Blazers-9
04Oklahoma City Blazers-11

Forslund, Tomas
89Swedish Semic Elitserien Stickers-134
90Swedish Semic Elitserien Stickers-209
91Flames IGA-2
91OPC Premier-31
91Parkhurst-20
French-20
91Pinnacle-333
French-333
91Pro Set-527
French-527
91Score Canadian Bilingual-629
91Score Canadian English-629
91Score Rookie/Traded-79T
91Upper Deck-27
91Upper Deck-586
French-27
French-586
92Bowman-384
92O-Pee-Chee-70
92Panini Stickers-D
92Panini Stickers French-D
92Stadium Club-280
92Topps-186
Gold-186G
92Upper Deck-3
92Upper Deck-429
Euro-Rookie Team-ERT6
92Salt Lake Golden Eagles-5
93Swedish Semic Elitserien-143
93Swedish Semic World Champ Stickers-41
93Classic Pro Prospects-139
BCs-BC15
94Finnish Jaa Kiekko-77
94Swedish Leaf-65
95Finnish Semic World Championships-69
95Swedish Leaf-242
Face to Face-7
95Swedish Upper Deck-112
95Swedish Globe World Championships-46
95Swedish World Championships Stickers-157
96German DEL-357
96Swedish Semic Wien-67
98German DEL-88
99German DEL-115
00German DEL-136
02Swedish SHL-202
Parallel-202

Forsman, Jonny
83Swedish Semic Elitserien-185
84Swedish Semic Elitserien-208
86Swedish Panini Stickers-232
87Swedish Panini Stickers-222
88Swedish Semic Elitserien Stickers-207

Forss, Matti
73Finnish Jaakiekko-306
78Finnish SM-Liiga-35
80Finnish Mallasjuoma-7
92Finnish Jyvas-Hyva Stickers-133
93Finnish SISU-200
93Finnish SISU-387
95Finnish SISU Limited-36

Forss, Risto
66Finnish Jaakiekkosarja-57
70Finnish Jaakiekko-294

Forsstrom, Jani
06Finnish Cardset-294

Forster, Beat
01Swiss HNL-102
04Swiss Davos Postcards-10

Forster, Erwin
94German First League-648

Forster, Mathias
03German Berlin Polar Bears Postcards-15
05German DEL-325

Forster, Nathan
96Seattle Thunderbirds-4
97Seattle Thunderbirds-8
00Richmond Renegades-3

Forster, Ruedi
01Swiss HNL-367
02Swiss HNL-416

Forsyth, Blake
05Idaho Steelheads-8
06Idaho Steelheads-15

Forsyth, Euan
04UK U-20 Team-18

Forsythe, Aaron
03Minnesota State Mavericks-6

Forsythe, Blaine
04Calgary Hitmen-24
05Calgary Hitmen-25

Forsythe, Trevor
91Knoxville Cherokees-8

Forth, Mark
97Spokane Chiefs-4
98Spokane Chiefs-8
00Lethbridge Hurricanes-7

Fortier, Dave
74O-Pee-Chee NHL-382
75O-Pee-Chee NHL-366
76Canucks Royal Bank-3
76O-Pee-Chee NHL-328

Fortier, Eric
93Quebec Pee-Wee Tournament-102
00Val d'Or Foreurs-22
Signed-2
01Val d'Or Foreurs-21
03Greensboro Generals-183

Fortier, Francois
92Quebec Pee-Wee Tournament-699
93Quebec Pee-Wee Tournament-296
98Bowman CHL-90
Golden Anniversary-90
OPC International-90
98Bowman Chrome CHL-90
Golden Anniversary-90
Golden Anniversary Refractors-90
OPC International-90
OPC International Refractors-90
Refractors-90
99Hartford Wolf Pack-6
99Bowman CHL-72
Gold-72
OPC International-72
00Charlotte Checkers-32
02German DEL City Press-283
03German DEL-23
All-Stars-AS9
04German Augsburg Panthers Postcards-14
05German DEL-29
06German DEL-103
06German DEL-71

Fortier, Karl
92Quebec Pee-Wee Tournament-1250
93Quebec Pee-Wee Tournament-361

Fortier, Marc
84Chicoutimi Sagueneens-11
88Nordiques General Foods-12
88Nordiques Team Issue-12
88ProCards AHL-114
89Nordiques Team Issue-11
89Nordiques General Foods-8
89Nordiques Police-7
89O-Pee-Chee-262
89O-Pee-Chee Stickers-189
89Panini Stickers-335
90Bowman-167
Tiffany-167
90Nordiques Petro-Canada-7
90Nordiques Team Issue-7
90O-Pee-Chee-176
90Panini Stickers-153
90Pro Set-245A
90Pro Set-245B
90Score-78
Canadian-78
90Topps-176
Tiffany-176
91Nordiques Panini Team Stickers-5
91Nordiques Petro-Canada-8
92Pro Set-128
92Stadium Club-173
92Topps-226
Gold-226G
93Phoenix Roadrunners-6
93Quebec Pee-Wee Tournament-972
95Swiss HNL-42
96Swiss HNL-189
96Swiss HNL-574
98German DEL-164
99German DEL-63
00German Berlin Polar Bears Postcards-6
00German DEL-64
Game Jersey-MF
01German Berlin Polar Bears Postcards-8
01German Upper Deck-34
02German DEL City Press-72
Top Scorers-TS6
04German Berlin Eisbarens 50th Anniv-28

Fortier, Olivier
05Drummondville Voltigeurs-23
05Rimouski Oceanic-25
06Rimouski Oceanic-1

Fortier, Sebastien
917th Inn. Sketch QMJHL-39
93Wheeling Thunderbirds-10
98Phoenix Mustangs-12

Fortier, Steve
92Quebec Pee-Wee Tournament-752
93Quebec Pee-Wee Tournament-337

Fortin, Charles
93Quebec Pee-Wee Tournament-395

Fortin, Dany
917th Inn. Sketch QMJHL-18

Fortin, Emile
37V356 Worldwide Gum-122

Fortin, Francois
93Quebec Pee-Wee Tournament-1113

Fortin, Jean-Francois
93Quebec Pee-Wee Tournament-1039
93Quebec Pee-Wee Tournament-1080
96Black Diamond-4
Gold-4
96Upper Deck-375
97Bowman CHL-46
97Bowman CHL-157
OPC-46
OPC-157
Bowman's Best-17
Bowman's Best Atomic Refractors-17
Bowman's Best Refractor-17
99Portland Pirates-8
00Portland Pirates-7
02O-Pee-Chee-266
02O-Pee-Chee Premier Blue Parallel-266
02O-Pee-Chee Premier Red Parallel-266
02O-Pee-Chee Factory Set-266
02Pacific Complete-292
Red-292
02Topps-266
OPC Blue Parallel-266
OPC Red Parallel-266
Factory Set-266
02Upper Deck-225
Exclusives-225
02Upper Deck Vintage-348
05Hershey Bears-24

Fortin, Marc
93Quebec Pee-Wee Tournament-1357

Fortin, Stephane
93Quebec Pee-Wee Tournament-1203

Fortin, Steve
93Quebec Pee-Wee Tournament-1007

Fortney, Thomas
04Waterloo Blackhawks-11

Forton, Yvan
51Laval Dairy Lac St. Jean-55

Fortunas, Maxime
03Baie Comeau Drakkar-9
03Baie Comeau Drakkar-26

Fortunus, Maxime
99Baie-Comeau Drakkar-9
00Baie-Comeau Drakkar-5
Signed-5
01Baie-Comeau Drakkar-4
02Baie-Comeau Drakkar-6
03ECHL Update RBI Sports-139
03Louisiana Ice Gators-5
04Louisiana Ice Gators-6
05Manitoba Moose-9
06Manitoba Moose-18

Foster, Aaron
99Prince George Cougars-10
00Prince George Cougars-14
03Atlantic City Boardwalk Bullies-7
03Atlantic City Boardwalk Bullies RBI-21
04Atlantic City Boardwalk Bullies Kinko's-24
05Stockton Thunder-5

Foster, Adrian
00Saskatoon Blades-11
01Brandon Wheat Kings-7
03Albany River Rats-9
03Albany River Rats Kinko's-10
03Pacific AHL Prospects-2
Gold-2
04Albany River Rats-7
04ITG Heroes and Prospects-31
Autographs-AF
Complete Emblems-17
Emblems-8
Emblems Gold-8
He Shoots-He Scores Prizes-21
Jersey Autographs-8
Jerseys-8
Jerseys Gold-8
Numbers-8
Numbers Gold-8
04ITG Heroes/Prospects Toronto Expo '05-31
04ITG Heroes/Prospects Expo Heroes/Pros-31
05Albany River Rats-9

Foster, Alex
01Sioux Falls Stampede-4
06Toronto Marlies-11

Foster, Corey
89ProCards AHL-146
90ProCards AHL/IHL-231
91Pro Set Platinum-265
91Flyers J.C. Penney-9

91Parkhurst-344
French-344
91Pinnacle-332
French-332
91Pro Set-551
French-551
91Upper Deck-591
French-591
92Upper Deck-53
95Cleveland Lumberjacks-12
95Cleveland Lumberjacks Postcards-11
96Cleveland Lumberjacks-10
96Cleveland Lumberjacks Multi-Ad-11
02Springfield Falcons-10
03St. Jean Mission-8

Foster, Craig
03Sarnia Sting-7

Foster, Darryl
93Niagara Falls Thunder-3
94Detroit Jr. Red Wings-2
95Classic-89
95Slapshot Memorial Cup-76

Foster, David
91Air Canada SJHL-D9
92Saskatchewan JHL-33

Foster, Dwight
78O-Pee-Chee-271
81O-Pee-Chee-3
81O-Pee-Chee Stickers-52
81Rockies Postcards 5
81Topps-E67
82O-Pee-Chee-138
82Post Cereal-11
83NHL Key Tags-32
83O-Pee-Chee-122
83O-Pee-Chee Stickers-133
83Topps Stickers-133
84O-Pee-Chee-53
84Topps-41
85O-Pee-Chee-14
85Topps-14
87Panini Stickers-17
87Red Wings Little Caesars-10

Foster, Greg
01Bossier-Shreveport Mudbugs-5

Foster, Jeff
01Kalamazoo K-Wings-14

Foster, Jerry
89ProCards AHL-74

Foster, Kurtis
98SP Authentic-116
Power Shift-116
Sign of the Times-KF
Sign of the Times Gold-KF
98Upper Deck-393
Exclusives-393
Exclusives 1 of 1-393
Gold Reserve-393
99UD Prospects-24
01Chicago Wolves-8
02Chicago Wolves-9
03AHL Top Prospects-9
03Chicago Wolves-7
04Cincinnati Mighty Ducks-5
05ITG Heroes/Prosp Toronto Expo Parallel -254
05Parkhurst-245
05ITG Heroes and Prospects-254
Autographs Series II-KF
06Be A Player-126
Autographs-126
Signatures-KF
06O-Pee-Chee-249
Rainbow-249
06Upper Deck-351
Exclusives Parallel-351
High Gloss Parallel-351
Masterpieces-351
06Wild Crime Prevention-6
06Wild Postcards-6

Foster, Norm
88ProCards AHL-154
89ProCards AHL-60
90ProCards AHL/IHL-135
91Upper Deck-465
French-465
91ProCards-225

Foster, Stephen
01UK Hull Thunder-3
02UK Hull Thunder-3

Fotheringham, Shawn
92Clarkson Knights-6

Fotiu, Nick
75O-Pee-Chee WHA-108
77O-Pee-Chee NHL-11
77Topps-11
78O-Pee-Chee-367
79O-Pee-Chee-286
80O-Pee-Chee-184
80Topps-184
82O-Pee-Chee-222
82Post Cereal-13
83O-Pee-Chee-243
85O-Pee-Chee-22
85Topps-22
86Flames Red Rooster-6
88Oilers Tenth Anniversary-143
89ProCards AHL-20
92Nashville Knights-2
96Johnstown Chiefs-24
97Johnstown Chiefs-7
01Fleer Legacy-44
Ultimate-44
01Topps Archives-26
01Cleveland Barons-24
02Hartford Wolf Pack-28
04ITG Franchises US East-382
Autographs-A-NF

Foucher, David
06Victoriaville Tigres-14

Fougere, Roland
93Quebec Pee-Wee Tournament-1495

Fountain, Mike
907th Inn. Sketch OHL-336
91Upper Deck Czech World Juniors-52
91Oshawa Generals-1
91Oshawa Generals Sheet-22
917th Inn. Sketch OHL-170
92Alberta International Team Canada-8
92Hamilton Canucks-7
93Classic Pro Prospects-106
94Classic Tri-Cards-T70
94Classic Pro Prospects-175
94Classic Four-Sport *-158
Gold-158
Autographs-158A
Printers Proofs-158
96Canucks Postcards-30
96SP-162
96Syracuse Crunch-1
97Donruss-218
Press Proofs Silver-218
Press Proofs Gold-218
97Donruss Canadian Ice-136
Dominion Series-136
Provincial Series-136
97Pinnacle Inside-76
Coach's Collection-76
Executive Collection-76
98New Haven Beast-14
99Grand Rapids Griffins-6
00Grand Rapids Griffins-7
01Between the Pipes-48
01Russian Ultimate Line-3
02Russian Hockey League-35
02Russian SL-12
02Russian Ultimate Line-5
03German DEL-142

Fournel, Dan
93Birmingham Bulls Birmingham News-7
94Huntington Blizzard-9
95South Carolina Stingrays-9
96South Carolina Stingrays-11
98Oklahoma City Blazers-2

Fournel, Patrick
93Quebec Pee-Wee Tournament-297

Fournier, Andrew
05Plymouth Whalers-A-13
06Plymouth Whalers-8

Fournier, Benoit
03Victoriaville Tigers 10

Fournier, Chris
00Lincoln Stars-6

Fournier, Guillaume
00Quebec Remparts-12
Signed-12
03Gatineau Olympiques-9
03Victoriaville Tigers-11

Fournier, Jack
12C57-36

Fournier, Jerome
93Quebec Pee-Wee Tournament-426

Fournier, Jonathan
93Quebec Pee-Wee Tournament-269

Fournier, Karl
03Lewiston Maineiacs-10

Fournier, Martin
93Quebec Pee-Wee Tournament-1010

Fournier, Mathieu
00Rimouski Oceanic-15
Signed-15
01Rimouski Oceanic-14
02Shawinigan Cataractes-10

Fournier, Mike
00Lincoln Stars-7
01Lincoln Stars-8
02Lincoln Stars-8

Fournier, Rob
88Niagara Falls Thunder-10
897th Inn. Sketch OHL-171

Fournier, Sebastien
92Quebec Pee-Wee Tournament-1037
93Quebec Pee-Wee Tournament-1347

Fournier, Wade
95Louisiana Ice Gators-3
95Louisiana Ice Gators Playoffs-5

Fouts, Nick
00Lincoln Stars-1

Fowler, Bob
89ProCards IHL-129

Fowler, Dan
91Michigan Falcons-6
91ProCards-32

Fowler, James
28V128-2 Paulin's Candy-74
34Beehive Group I Photos-318
36O-Pee-Chee V304D-103
37O-Pee-Chee V304E-135
38Quaker Oats Photos-13
39O-Pee-Chee V301-1-55

Fowler, Norman
24C144 Champ's Cigarettes-26
24V130 Maple Crispette-3
24V145-2-30
28V128-2 Paulin's Candy-87

Fowler, Rob
87Moncton Hawks-9

Fowler, Shawn
93Quebec Pee-Wee Tournament-879

Fowler, Teal
99German Bundesliga 2-215
00German DEL-105
Game Jersey-TF

Fox, Aaron
93Quebec Pee-Wee Tournament-1418

Fox, Greg
77Nova Scotia Voyageurs-7
78Flames Majik Market-2
79Blackhawks Postcards-6
79O-Pee-Chee-116
79Topps-116
80Blackhawks Postcards-2
80Blackhawks White Border-5
80O-Pee-Chee-268
81Blackhawks Borderless Postcards-7
81Blackhawks Brown Background-2
81O-Pee-Chee-69
82Blackhawks Postcards-8
82O-Pee-Chee-65
82Post Cereal-4
83NHL Key Tags-22
83O-Pee-Chee-101
84O-Pee-Chee-175
84Penguins Heinz Photos-9

Fox, Hughie J.
25Dominion Chocolates-56

Fox, Jim
81O-Pee-Chee-153
82O-Pee-Chee-154
82O-Pee-Chee Stickers-235
82Post Cereal-8
82Topps Stickers-235
83NHL Key Tags-54
83O-Pee-Chee-154
83O-Pee-Chee Stickers-293
83Puffy Stickers-7
83Topps Stickers-293
84Kings Smokey-5
84O-Pee-Chee-84
84O-Pee-Chee Stickers-268
84Topps-66
85O-Pee-Chee-61
85O-Pee-Chee Stickers-236
85Topps-61
86Kings 20th Anniversary Team Issue-6
86O-Pee-Chee-215
86O-Pee-Chee Stickers-89
87O-Pee-Chee-75
87O-Pee-Chee Stickers-216
87Panini Stickers-281
87Topps-75
88Kings Postcards-5
88Kings Smokey-9
88O-Pee-Chee-139
88O-Pee-Chee Stickers-154
88Panini Stickers-76
88Topps-139

Fox, Ken
93Quebec Pee-Wee Tournament-501

Fox, Mark
98Colorado Gold Kings Postcards-20

Fox, T.J.
03Chicago Steel-16
04Chicago Steel-2

Fox, Wes
03ECHL Update RBI Sports-134
03Gwinnett Gladiators-10

Foy, Chris
93Richmond Renegades-18
94Richmond Renegades-5
95South Carolina Stingrays-14

Foy, Matt
02Ottawa 67's-21
03Houston Aeros-8
04SP Authentic Rookie Redemptions-RR15
04Houston Aeros-7
04ITG Heroes and Prospects-21
Autographs-MFO
Complete Emblems-23
Emblems-50
Emblems Gold-50
He Shoots-He Scores Prizes-18
Jersey Autographs-50
Jerseys-50
Jerseys Gold-50
Numbers-50
Numbers Gold-50
04ITG Heroes/Prospects Toronto Expo '05-21
05Beehive-138
Beige -138
Blue -138
Gold-138
Red -138
Matte-138
05Black Diamond-254
05Hot Prospects-202
Autographed Patch Variation-202
Autographed Patch Variation Gold-202
Hot Materials-HMMF
Red Hot-202
05Parkhurst Signatures-MF
05Parkhurst True Colors-TCMIN
05Parkhurst True Colors-TCMIN
05SP Authentic-161
Limited-161
Rarefied Rookies-RRMF
05SP Game Used-135
Autographs-135
Gold-135
Auto Draft-AD-MF
Rookie Exclusives-MF
Rookie Exclusives Silver-RE-MF
05SPx-153
Spectrum-153
05The Cup-160
Autographed Rookie Patches Gold Rainbow-160
Black Rainbow Rookies-160
Masterpiece Pressplates (Artifacts)-215
Masterpiece Pressplates (Bee Hive)-138
Masterpiece Pressplates (Black Diamond)-254
Masterpiece Pressplates (Ice)-131
Masterpiece Pressplates (MVP)-429
Masterpiece Pressplates (Power Play)-172
Masterpiece Pressplates (Rookie Update)-147
Masterpiece Pressplates SPA Autos-161
Masterpiece Pressplates (SP Game Used)-135
Masterpiece Pressplates (SPx)-153
Masterpiece Pressplates (SPx)-153
Masterpiece Pressplates Ult Coll Autos-119
Masterpiece Pressplates (Victory)-299
Masterpiece Pressplates Autographs-160
Platinum Rookies-160
05UD Artifacts-215
Gold-RED15
05UD PowerPlay-172
05Ultimate Collection-119
Autographed Patches-119
Autographed Shields-119
05Ultra-222
Gold-222
Ice-222
Rookie Uniformity Jerseys-RU-MF
Rookie Uniformity Jersey Autographs-ARU-MF
Rookie Uniformity Patches-RUP-MF
Rookie Uniformity Patch Autographs-ARP-MF
05Upper Deck-208
HG Glossy-208
Rookie Ink-RIMF
05Upper Deck Rookie Showcase-RS15
05Upper Deck Rookie Showcase Promos-RS15
05Upper Deck Rookie Threads-RTMF
05Upper Deck Rookie Threads Autographs-ARTMF
05Upper Deck Ice-131
Premieres Auto Patches-AIPMF
05Upper Deck MVP-429
Gold-429
Platinum-429
05Upper Deck Rookie Update-147
05Upper Deck Toronto Fall Expo-208
05Upper Deck Victory-299
Black-299
Gold-299
Silver-299
05ITG Heroes and Prospects Jerseys-GUJ-104
05ITG Heroes and Prospects Jerseys Gold-GUJ-104
06Hot Prospects Hotagraphs-HMF

Foyn, Stephen
92Finnish Semic-46
92Norwegian Elite Series-88

Foyston, Frank
83Hall of Fame-20
83Hall of Fame Postcards-B4
85Hall of Fame-20
04ITG Franchises US West-197

Foyt, Scott
04North Dakota Fighting Sioux-6

Fragapane, Eric
93Quebec Pee-Wee Tournament-33

Fraipont, Spencer
05Regina Pats-5

Frajkor, Robert
93Quebec Pee-Wee Tournament-1564

Francella, Giullio
82Swedish Semic VM Stickers-130

Franceschetti, Lou
86Capitals Kodak-7
86Capitals Police-7
87Capitals Kodak-25
87Capitals Team Issue-4
87Panini Stickers-188
88Capitals Borderless-4
88Capitals Smokey-4
88ProCards AHL-39
90Bowman-164
Tiffany-164
90Maple Leafs Postcards-6
90O-Pee-Chee-303
90Panini Stickers-289
90Pro Set-280
90Sabres Blue Shield-6
90Score-266
Canadian-266
90Topps-303
Tiffany-303
90Upper Deck-396
French-396
91Maple Leafs Panini Team Stickers-6
91O-Pee-Chee-354
91Score Canadian Bilingual-388
91Score Canadian English-388
91Topps-354
91Upper Deck-399
French-399
91ProCards-360
91Rochester Americans Kodak-11
91Rochester Americans Postcards-9
93Phoenix Cobras RHI-4

Francey, Steven
04UK Edinburgh Capitals-4

Franche, Delphis
51Laval Dairy QSHL-27
52St. Lawrence Sales-91

Franchin, Peter
03Kitchener Rangers-9
04Saginaw Spirit-6

Francis, Bob
90ProCards AHL/IHL-611
92Salt Lake Golden Eagles-24
94Saint John Flames-6
96Providence Bruins-NNO
02Coyotes Team Issue-25

Francis, David
02Odessa Jackalopes-8

Francis, Emile
66Topps-21
74O-Pee-Chee NHL-9
74Topps-9
83Hall of Fame Postcards-I7
85Hall of Fame-231
92Hall of Fame Legends-10
03Parkhurst Orig Six New York Mem-NM34
05ITG Ultimate Memorabilia Vintage Lumber-26
05ITG Ultimate Mem Vintage Lumber Gold-26
06Between The Pipes-87
Autographs-AEF
Shooting Gallery-SG04
Shooting Gallery Gold-SG04

Francis, Josh
03Belleville Bulls-8

Francis, Matt
04St. Cloud State Huskies-9
05St. Cloud State Huskies-19
05St. Cloud State Huskies-9

Francis, Neil
03UK Cardiff Devils-15
05UK Cardiff Devils Challenge Cup-8

Francis, Ron
80Sault Ste. Marie Greyhounds-14
81Sault Ste. Marie Greyhounds-12
82O-Pee-Chee-123
82O-Pee-Chee Stickers-129
82Post Cereal-7
82Topps Stickers-129
82Whalers Junior Hartford Courant-3
83NHL Key Tags-45
83O-Pee-Chee-138
83O-Pee-Chee Stickers-255
83Puffy Stickers-18
83Topps Stickers-255
83Whalers Junior Hartford Courant-5
84Kellogg's Accordion Discs-4
84Kellogg's Accordion Discs Singles-11
84O-Pee-Chee-70
84O-Pee-Chee Stickers-196
847-Eleven Discs-22
84Topps-54
84Whalers Junior Wendy's-6
85O-Pee-Chee-140
85O-Pee-Chee Box Bottoms-F
85O-Pee-Chee Stickers-172
857-Eleven Credit Cards-7
85Topps-140
85Topps Box Bottoms-F
85Whalers Junior Wendy's-7
86O-Pee-Chee-43
86O-Pee-Chee Stickers-51
86Topps-43
86Whalers Junior Thomas'-8
87O-Pee-Chee-187
87O-Pee-Chee Box Bottoms-J
87O-Pee-Chee Minis-10
87O-Pee-Chee Stickers-206
87Panini Stickers-43
87Topps-187
87Topps Box Bottoms-J
87Whalers Jr. Burger King/Pepsi-7
87Sault Ste. Marie Greyhounds-8
88Frito-Lay Stickers-20
88O-Pee-Chee-52
88O-Pee-Chee Box Bottoms-A
88O-Pee-Chee Stickers-264
88Panini Stickers-242
88Topps-52
88Topps Box Bottoms-A
88Whalers Junior Ground Round-7
89O-Pee-Chee-175
89O-Pee-Chee Stickers-269
89Panini Stickers-221
89Topps-175
89Whalers Junior Milk-8
89Sault Ste. Marie Greyhounds-13
90Bowman-254
Tiffany-254
90Kraft-13
90Kraft-83
90O-Pee-Chee-311
90OPC Premier-32
90Panini Stickers-39
90Pro Set-105
90Pro Set-367
90Score-70
Canadian-70
90Score Hottest/Rising Stars-37
90Topps-311
Tiffany-311
Team Scoring Leaders-21
Team Scoring Leaders Tiffany-21
90Upper Deck-67
90Upper Deck-314
French-67
French-314
90Whalers Jr. 7-Eleven-11
91Pro Set Platinum-214
91Bowman-90
91O-Pee-Chee-130
91OPC Premier-120
91Panini Stickers-281
91Parkhurst-353
French-353
91Penguins Coke/Elby's-10
91Penguins Foodland-3
91Penguins Foodland Coupon Stickers-5
91Pinnacle-167
French-167
91Pro Set-188
French-188
91Score American-267
91Score Canadian Bilingual-487
91Score Canadian English-487
91Stadium Club-73
91Topps-130
91Upper Deck-299
French-299
92Bowman-123
92O-Pee-Chee-188
92Panini Stickers-224
92Panini Stickers French-224
92Parkhurst-141
Emerald Ice-141
92Penguins Coke/Clark-7
92Penguins Foodland-7
92Penguins Foodland Coupon Stickers-2
92Pinnacle-303
French-303
92Pro Set-144
92Score-267
92Score-518
Canadian-267
92Stadium Club-352
92Topps-322
Gold-322G
92Ultra-163
92Upper Deck-291
93Donruss-261
93Leaf-161
93OPC Premier-424
Gold-424
93Panini Stickers-81
93Parkhurst-160
Emerald Ice-160
93Penguins Foodland-14
93Pinnacle-74
Canadian-74
93PowerPlay-188
93Score-151
Canadian-151
93Stadium Club-385
Members Only Master Set-385
First Day Issue-385
93Topps/OPC Premier-424
Gold-424
93Ultra-44
93Upper Deck-351
94Canada Games NHL POGS-183
94Donruss-122
94Finest Ring Leaders-16
94Flair-134
94Fleer-162
94Hockey Wit-53
94Leaf-235
94Leaf Limited-30
94OPC Premier-139
Special Effects-139
94Parkhurst-176
Gold-176
94Penguins Foodland-9
94Pinnacle-72
Artist's Proofs-72
Rink Collection-72
94Score-244
Gold-244
Platinum-244
90 Plus Club-18
94Select-84
Gold-84
94SP-92
Die Cuts-92
94Stadium Club-96
Members Only Master Set-96
First Day Issue-96
Super Teams-18
Super Teams Members Only Master Set-18
Super Team Winner Cards-96
94Topps/OPC Premier-139
Special Effects-139
94Ultra-163
94Upper Deck-12
Electric Ice-12
SP Inserts-SP150
SP Inserts Die Cuts-SP150
95Bashan Super Stickers-95
95Bashan Super Stickers-98
95Be A Player-8
Signatures-S8
Signatures Die Cuts-S8
95Bowman-31
All-Foil-31
95Canada Games NHL POGS-215
95Collector's Choice-200
95Collector's Choice-393
Player's Club-200
Player's Club-393
Player's Club Platinum-200
Player's Club Platinum-393
95Donruss-94
Igniters-10
95Donruss Elite-40
Die Cut Stars-40
Die Cut Uncut-40
95Emotion-136
Xcel-7
Xcited-11
95Finest-127
Refractors-127
95Imperial Stickers-98
95Leaf-45
95Leaf Limited-23
95Metal-116
Iron Warriors-4
95NHL Aces Playing Cards-7C
95Panini Stickers-58
95Panini Stickers-152
95Parkhurst International-164
Emerald Ice-164
Parkie's Trophy Picks-PP47
Trophy Winners-6
95Penguins Foodland-1
95Pinnacle-39
Artist's Proofs-39
Rink Collection-39
95Playoff One on One-77
95Pro Magnets-91
95Score-187
Black Ice Artist's Proofs-187
Black Ice-187
95Select Certified-52
Mirror Gold-52
Double Strike-2
Double Strike Gold-2
95SkyBox Impact-130
95SP-115
95Stadium Club Members Only-22
95Stadium Club-22
Members Only Master Set-22
Power Streak-PS3
Power Streak Members Only Master Set-PS3
95Summit-42
Artist's Proofs-42
Ice-42
95Topps-244
OPC Inserts-244
Power Lines-5PL
95Ultra-122
95Ultra-384
Gold Medallion-122
Extra Attackers-6
Premier Pivots-2
Premier Pivots Gold Medallion-2
95Upper Deck-46
95Upper Deck-255
Electric Ice-46
Electric Ice-255
Electric Ice Gold-46
Electric Ice Gold-255
95Upper Deck All-Star Game Predictors-23
Redemption Winners-23
95Upper Deck NHL All-Stars-AS18
95Upper Deck NHL All-Stars Jumbo-AS18
95Upper Deck Predictor Retail-R11
95Upper Deck Predictor Retail Exchange-R11
95Upper Deck Special Edition-SE66
95Upper Deck Special Edition Gold-SE66
95Zenith-35
96SLU Hockey Canadian-4
96SLU Hockey American-6
96Black Diamond-101
Gold-101
96Collector's Choice-212
96Collector's Choice-328
MVP-UD2
MVP Gold-UD2
96Donruss-149
Press Proofs-149
Dominators-4
96Donruss Canadian Ice-93
Gold Press Proofs-93
Red Press Proofs-93
96Donruss Elite-40
Die Cut Stars-40
96Flair-75
Blue Ice-75
96Fleer-85
96Fleer-137
96Fleer-139
Art Ross-5
96Fleer Picks-16
Fabulous 50-13
Fantasy Force-7
Jagged Edge-16
96Kenner Starting Lineup Cards-6
96Kraft Upper Deck-44
96Leaf-11
Press Proofs-11
96Leaf Limited-52
Gold-52
96Leaf Preferred-62
Press Proofs-62
Steel-6
Steel Gold-6
96Maggers-26
96Metal Universe-125
Cool Steel-3
Cool Steel Super Power-3
Lethal Weapons-5
Lethal Weapons Super Power-5
96NHL Aces Playing Cards-15
96NHL Pro Stamps-91
96Penguins Tribune-Review-1
96Pinnacle-143
Artist's Proofs-143
Foil-143
Premium Stock-143
Rink Collection-143
96Playoff One on One-360
96Score-56
Artist's Proofs-56
Dealer's Choice Artist's Proofs-56
Special Artist's Proofs-56
Golden Blades-56
96Select Certified-12
Artist's Proofs-12
Blue-12
Mirror Blue-12
Mirror Gold-12
Mirror Red-12
Red-12
96SkyBox Impact-100
BladeRunners-4
96SP-127
96Stadium Club Members Only-45
96Summit-10
Artist's Proofs-10
Ice-10
Metal-10
Premium Stock-10
Untouchables-4
96Ultra-139
Gold Medallion-139
Mr. Momentum-3
96Upper Deck-133
96Upper Deck Ice-55
Parallel-55
96Zenith-10
Artist's Proofs-10
Champion Salute-7
Champion Salute Diamond-7
97Beehive-49
Golden Portraits-49
97Black Diamond-11
Double Diamond-11
Triple Diamond-11
Quadruple Diamond-11
97Collector's Choice-204
Star Quest-SQ54
97Crown Royale-109
Emerald Green-109
Ice Blue-109
Silver-109
97Donruss-137
Press Proofs Silver-137
Press Proofs Gold-137
97Donruss Canadian Ice-44
Dominion Series-44
Provincial Series-44
National Pride-20
97Donruss Elite-113
Aspirations-113
Status-113
97Donruss Limited-199
Exposure-199
97Donruss Preferred-142
Cut to the Chase-142
97Donruss Priority-77
Stamp of Approval-77
97Katch-116
Gold-116
Silver-116
97Kraft-3
97Leaf-44
Fractal Matrix-44
Fractal Matrix Die Cuts-44
97Leaf International-44
Universal Ice-44
97Pacific-123
Copper-123
Emerald Green-123
Ice Blue-123
Red-123
Silver-123
Slap Shots Die-Cuts-8B
97Pacific Dynagon-100
Copper-100
Dark Grey-100
Emerald Green-100
Ice Blue-100
Red-100
Silver-100
Tandems-63
97Pacific Invincible-111
Copper-111
Emerald Green-111
Ice Blue-111
Red-111
Silver-111
Attack Zone-19
97Pacific Omega-184
Copper-184
Dark Gray-184
Emerald Green-184
Gold-184
Ice Blue-184
97Panini Stickers-50
97Paramount-148
Copper-148
Dark Grey-148
Emerald Green-148
Ice Blue-148
Red-148
Silver-148
97Penguins USPS Lineup Cards-NNO
97Pinnacle-78
Artist's Proofs-78
Rink Collection-78
Press Plates Back Black-78
Press Plates Back Cyan-78
Press Plates Back Magenta-78
Press Plates Back Yellow-78
Press Plates Front Black-78
Press Plates Front Cyan-78
Press Plates Front Magenta-78
Press Plates Front Yellow-78
97Pinnacle Certified-121
Red-121
Mirror Blue-121
Mirror Gold-121
Mirror Red-121
97Pinnacle Inside-52
Coach's Collection-52
Executive Collection-52
97Pinnacle Tot Cert Platinum Blue-121
97Pinnacle Tot Certi Platinum Gold-121
97Pinnacle Totally Certified Platinum Red-121
97Pinnacle Tot Cert Mirror Platinum Gold-121
97Revolution-112
Copper-112
Emerald-112
Ice Blue-112
Silver-112
97Score-132
Artist's Proofs-132
Golden Blades-132
97Score Penguins-5
Platinum-5
Premier-5
97SP Authentic-126
97SPx-41
Bronze-41
Gold-41
Silver-41
Steel-41
Grand Finale-41
97Studio-74
Press Proofs Silver-74
Press Proofs Gold-74
97Upper Deck-135
Game Dated Moments-135
Sixth Sense Masters-SS25
Sixth Sense Wizards-SS25
97Upper Deck Ice-65
Parallel-65
Power Shift-65
97Zenith-50
Z-Gold-50
Z-Silver-50
97Zenith 5 x 7-53
Gold Impulse-53
Silver Impulse-53
98Be A Player-174
Press Release-174
98BAP Gold-174
98BAP Autographs-174
98BAP Autographs Gold-174
98BAP AS Milestones-M12
98Black Diamond-14
Double Diamond-14
Triple Diamond-14
Quadruple Diamond-14
98Bowman's Best-50
Refractors-50
Atomic Refractors-50
98Crown Royale-22
Limited Series-22
98Finest-50
No Protectors-50
No Protectors Refractors-50
Refractors-50
98Hurricanes Team Issue-13
98OPC Chrome-4
Refractors-4
Season's Best-SB22
Season's Best Refractors-SB22
98Pacific-351
Ice Blue-351
Red-351
98Pacific Dynagon Ice-31
Blue-31
Red-31
98Pacific Omega-40
Red-40
Opening Day Issue-40
98Panini Photocards-25
98Panini Photocards-95
98Panini Stickers-49
98Panini Stickers-227
98Revolution-23
Ice Shadow-23
Red-23
98SP Authentic-14
Power Shift-14
Stat Masters-S21
98Topps-4
O-Pee-Chee-4
Season's Best-SB22
98Topps Gold Label Class 1-22
Black-22
Black One of One-22
One of One-22
Red-22
Red One of One-22
98Topps Gold Label Class 2-22
98Topps Gold Label Class 2 Black-22
98Topps Gold Label Class 2 Black 1 of 1-22
98Topps Gold Label Class 2 One of One-22
98Topps Gold Label Class 2 Red-22
98Topps Gold Label Class 2 Red One of One-22
98Topps Gold Label Class 3-22
98Topps Gold Label Class 3 Black-22
98Topps Gold Label Class 3 Black 1 of 1-22
98Topps Gold Label Class 3 One of One-22
98Topps Gold Label Class 3 Red-22
98Topps Gold Label Class 3 Red One of One-22
98UD Choice-169
98UD Choice Preview-169
98UD Choice Prime Choice Reserve-169
98UD Choice Reserve-169
98Upper Deck-241
Exclusives-241
Exclusives 1 of 1-241
Lord Stanley's Heroes-LS8
Lord Stanley's Heroes Quantum 1-LS8
Lord Stanley's Heroes Quantum 2-LS8
Lord Stanley's Heroes Quantum 3-LS8
Gold Reserve-241
98Upper Deck MVP-35
Gold Script-35
Silver Script-35
Super Script-35
99Aurora-25
Premiere Date-25
99BAP Memorabilia-10
Gold-10
Silver-10
AS Heritage Ruby-H8
AS Heritage Sapphire-H8
AS Heritage Emerald-H8
99Crown Royale-26
Limited Series-26
Premiere Date-26
99O-Pee-Chee-23
99O-Pee-Chee Chrome-23
99O-Pee-Chee Chrome Refractors-23
99Pacific-70
Copper-70
Emerald Green-70
Gold-70
Ice Blue-70
Premiere Date-70
Red-70
99Pacific Dynagon Ice-40
Blue-40
Copper-40
Gold-40
Premiere Date-40
99Pacific Omega-43
Copper-43
Gold-43
Ice Blue-43
Premiere Date-43
99Pacific Prism-28
Holographic Blue-28
Holographic Gold-28
Holographic Mirror-28
Holographic Purple-28
Premiere Date-28
99Panini Stickers-44
99Paramount-44
Copper-44
Emerald-44
Gold-44
Holographic Emerald-44
Holographic Gold-44
Holographic Silver-44
Ice Blue-44
Premiere Date-44
Red-44
Silver-44
99Revolution-27
Premiere Date-27
Red-27
Shadow Series-27
Copper-27
Gold-27
CSC Silver-27
99SP Authentic-16
99SPx-31
Radiance-31
Spectrum-31
99Stadium Club-25
First Day Issue-25
One of a Kind-25
Printing Plates Black-25
Printing Plates Cyan-25
Printing Plates Magenta-25
Printing Plates Yellow-25
99Topps/OPC-23
99Topps/OPC Chrome-23
Refractors-23
99Topps Gold Label Class 1-11
Black-11
Black One of One-11
One of One-11
Red-11
Red One of One-11
99Topps Gold Label Class 2-11
99Topps Gold Label Class 2 Black-11
99Topps Gold Label Class 2 Black 1 of 1-11
99Topps Gold Label Class 2 One of One-11
99Topps Gold Label Class 2 Red-11
99Topps Gold Label Class 2 Red One of One-11
99Topps Gold Label Class 3-11
99Topps Gold Label Class 3 Black-11
99Topps Gold Label Class 3 Black 1 of 1-11
99Topps Gold Label Class 3 One of One-11

99Topps Gold Label Class 3 Red-11
99Topps Gold Label Class 3 Red One of One-11
99Topps Premier Plus-21
Parallel-21
99Topps Premier Plus Promos-PP6
99Ultimate Victory-16
1/1-16
Parallel-16
Parallel 100-16
99Upper Deck-199
Exclusives-199
Exclusives 1 of 1-199
99Upper Deck Gold Reserve-199
99Upper Deck MVP-40
Gold Script-40
Silver Script-40
Super Script-40
99Upper Deck MVP SC Edition-36
Gold Script-36
Silver Script-36
Super Script-36
99Upper Deck Ovation-11
Standing Ovation-11
99Upper Deck Victory-59
99Wayne Gretzky Hockey-37
00Aurora-28
Premiere Date-28
00BAP Memorabilia-206
Emerald-206
Ruby-206
Sapphire-206
Promos-206
00BAP Mem Chicago Sportsfest Copper-206
00BAP Memorabilia Chicago Sportsfest Blue-206
00BAP Memorabilia Chicago Sportsfest Gold-206
00BAP Memorabilia Chicago Sportsfest Ruby-206
00BAP Memorabilia Chicago Sun-Times Ruby-206
00BAP Memorabilia Chicago Sun-Times Gold-206
00BAP Mem Chicago Sun-Times Sapphire-206
00BAP Mem Toronto Fall Expo Copper-206
00BAP Memorabilia Toronto Fall Expo Gold-206
00BAP Memorabilia Toronto Fall Expo Ruby-206
00BAP Parkhurst 2000-P82
00BAP Signature Series-216
Emerald-216
Ruby-216
Sapphire-216
Autographs-158
Autographs Gold-158
00BAP Ultimate Memorabilia Active Eight-AE2
00BAP Ultimate Mem Dynasty Jerseys-D10
00BAP Ultimate Mem Dynasty Emblems-D10
00Black Diamond-10
Gold-10
00Crown Royale-20
Ice Blue-20
Limited Series-20
Premiere Date-20
Red-20
00O-Pee-Chee-5
00O-Pee-Chee Parallel-5
00Pacific-81
Copper-81
Gold-81
Ice Blue-81
Premiere Date-81
00Panini Stickers-30
00Paramount-42
Copper-42
Gold-42
Holo-Gold-42
Holo-Silver-42
Ice Blue-42
Premiere Date-42
Game Used Sticks-1
00Private Stock-16
Gold-16
Premiere Date-16
Retail-16
Silver-16
00Revolution-26
Blue-26
Premiere Date-26
Red-26
00SP Authentic-16
00SP Game Used-9
00SPx-10
Spectrum-10
00Stadium Club-30
Special Forces-SF15
00Titanium-14
Blue-14
Gold-14
Premiere Date-14
Red-14
Retail-14
00Topps/OPC-5
Parallel-5
1000 Point Club-PC3
00Topps Chrome-5
OPC Refractors-5
Refractors-5
1000 Point Club Refractors-3
00Topps Gold Label Class 1-80
Gold-80
00Topps Gold Label Class 2-80
00Topps Gold Label Class 2 Gold-80
00Topps Gold Label Class 3-80
00Topps Gold Label Class 3 Gold-80
00Topps Heritage-32
Chrome Parallel-32
00Topps Premier Plus-49
Blue Ice-49
Trophy Tribute-TT12
00UD Heroes-20
00UD Pros and Prospects-16
00UD Reserve-16
00Upper Deck-31
Exclusives Tier 1-31
Exclusives Tier 2-31
00Upper Deck Ice-8
Immortals-8
Legends-8
Stars-8
00Upper Deck Legends-22
00Upper Deck Legends-24
Legendary Collection Bronze-22
Legendary Collection Bronze-24
Legendary Collection Gold-22
Legendary Collection Gold-24
Legendary Collection Silver-22
Legendary Collection Silver-24
00Upper Deck MVP-39
First Stars-39
Second Stars-39
Third Stars-39
00Upper Deck Victory-42
00Upper Deck Victory-47
00Upper Deck Victory-289
00Upper Deck Vintage-66
00Upper Deck Vintage-73
00Upper Deck Vintage-74
00Vanguard-19
Holographic Gold-19
Holographic Purple-19
Pacific Proofs-19
01Atomic-16
Blue-16
Gold-16
Premiere Date-16
Red-16
Team Nucleus-3
01BAP Memorabilia-256
Emerald-256
Ruby-256
Sapphire-256
He Shoots-He Scores Prizes-34
01BAP Signature Series Certified 100-C36
01BAP Signature Series Certified 50-C36
01BAP Signature Series Certified 1 of 1's-C36
01BAP Signature Series Autographs-LRF
01BAP Signature Series Autographs Gold-LRF
01BAP Signature Series 500 Goal Scorers-28
01BAP Sig Series He Shoots/Scores Prizes-4
01BAP Signature Series Jerseys-GJ-10
01BAP Signature Series Jersey Autographs-GURF
01BAP Sig Series Jersey and Stick Cards-GSJ-10
01BAP Signature Series Emblems-GUE-10
01BAP Signature Series Numbers-ITN-10
01BAP Signature Series Teammates-TM-6
01BAP Ultimate Memorabilia Active Eight-3
01BAP Ultimate Memorabilia Active Eight-7
01BAP Ultimate Memorabilia Captain's C-4
01BAP Ultimate Mem 500 Goal Scorers-29
01BAP Ultimate Mem 500 Goal Jerseys/Stick-29
01BAP Ultimate Mem 500 Goal Emblems-29
01BAP Update He Shoots-He Scores Points-12
01BAP Update He Shoots-He Scores Prizes-24
01Bowman YoungStars-22
Gold-22
Ice Cubed-22
01Crown Royale-25
Blue-25
Premiere Date-25
Red-25
Retail-25
01O-Pee-Chee-23
01O-Pee-Chee Heritage Parallel-23
01O-Pee-Chee Heritage Parallel Limited-23
01O-Pee-Chee Premier Parallel-23
01Pacific-71
01Pacific-406
Extreme LTD-71
Gold-406
Hobby LTD-71
Premiere Date-71
Retail LTD-71
Impact Zone-5
01Pacific Adrenaline-32
Blue-32
Premiere Date-32
Red-32
Retail-32
01Pacific Arena Exclusives-71
01Pacific Arena Exclusives-406
01Pacific Heads-Up-15
Blue-15
Premiere Date-15
Red-15
Silver-15
01Parkhurst-153
Jerseys-PJ14
Milestones-M24
Milestones-M44
Sticks-PS14
Teammates-T18
01Private Stock-14
Gold-14
Premiere Date-14
Retail-14
Silver-14
01Private Stock Pacific Nights-14
01Sports Illustrated for Kids III-198
01Stadium Club-22
Award Winners-22
Master Photos-22
01Titanium-24
Hobby Parallel-24
Premiere Date-24
Retail-24
Retail Parallel-24
Double-Sided Jerseys-45
Double-Sided Jerseys-61
Double-Sided Patches-45
Double-Sided Patches-61
01Topps-23
Heritage Parallel-23
Heritage Parallel Limited-23
OPC Parallel-23
Autographs-ARF
Captain's Cloth-CC3
Game-Worn Jersey-JRF
Jumbo Jersey Autographs-JJA-RF
01Topps Chrome-23
Refractors-23
Black Border Refractors-23
01Topps Heritage-22
Refractors-22
01Topps Reserve Emblems-ROF
01Topps Reserve Jerseys-ROF
01Topps Reserve Name Plates-ROF
01Topps Reserve Numbers-ROF
01Topps Reserve Patches-ROF
01UD Mask Collection-16
Gold-16
01Upper Deck-262
Exclusives-262
01Upper Deck MVP-35
01Upper Deck Victory-61
Gold-61
01Upper Deck Vintage-50
01Vanguard-15
Blue-15
Red-15
One of Ones-15
Premiere Date-15
Proofs-15
02McFarlane Hockey-100
02McFarlane Hockey-102
02Atomic-16
Blue-16
Gold-16
Red-16
Hobby Parallel-16
Power Converters-5
02BAP First Edition-22
02BAP First Edition-386
He Shoots-He Scores Points-1
He Shoots-He Scores Prizes-12
Jerseys-22
Scoring Leaders-5
02BAP Memorabilia-61
02BAP Memorabilia-206
Emerald-61
Emerald-206
Ruby-61
Ruby-206
Sapphire-61
Sapphire-206
Franchise Players-FP-6
He Shoots-He Scores Points-5
He Shoots-He Scores Prizes-16
NHL All-Star Game-61
NHL All-Star Game-206
NHL All-Star Game Blue-61
NHL All-Star Game Blue-206
NHL All-Star Game Green-61
NHL All-Star Game Green-206
NHL All-Star Game Red-61
NHL All-Star Game Red-206
Stanley Cup Playoffs-SC-7
Stanley Cup Playoffs-SC-29
02BAP Memorabilia Toronto Fall Expo-61
02BAP Memorabilia Toronto Fall Expo-206
02BAP Signature Series-171
Autographs-171
Autograph Buybacks 1998-174
Autograph Buybacks 2000-158
Autograph Buybacks 2001-LRF
Autographs Gold-171
Franchise Players-FJ6
Golf-GS80
Jerseys-SGJ40
Jersey Autographs-SGJ40
02BAP Ultimate Memorabilia Active Eight-1
02BAP Ultimate Memorabilia Active Eight-5
02BAP Ultimate Mem Lifetime Achievers-19
02BAP Ultimate Memorabilia Numerology-15
02BAP Ultimate Mem Retro Teammates-6
02Bowman YoungStars-6
Gold-6
Silver-6
02Crown Royale-17
Blue-17
Red-17
Retail-17
02eTopps-33
02Hurricanes Postcards-3
02ITG Used-10
02ITG Used-110
Jerseys-GUJ40
Jersey Autographs-GUJ40
Jerseys Gold-GUJ40
Jersey and Stick-SJ40
Jersey and Stick Gold-SJ40
02McDonald's Pacific Atomic-2
02McDonald's Pacific Jersey Patch Silver-3
02McDonald's Pacific Jersey Patches Gold-3
02O-Pee-Chee-19
02O-Pee-Chee-315
02O-Pee-Chee Jumbos-4
02O-Pee-Chee Premier Blue Parallel-19
02O-Pee-Chee Premier Blue Parallel-315
02O-Pee-Chee Premier Red Parallel-19
02O-Pee-Chee Premier Red Parallel-315
02O-Pee-Chee Factory Set-19
02O-Pee-Chee Factory Set-315
02Pacific-65
Blue-65
Red-65
02Pacific Complete-210
Red-210
02Pacific Exclusive-28
Etched in Stone-2
02Pacific Heads-Up-20
Blue-20
Purple-20
Red-20
Etched in Time-5
Inside the Numbers-6
Postseason Picks-2
Quad Jerseys-6
Quad Jerseys Gold-6
Stat Masters-6
02Pacific Quest for the Cup-14
Gold-14
02Parkhurst-128
Bronze-128
Gold-128
Silver-128
Jerseys-GJ22
Mario's Mates-MM6
Milestones-MS7
Stick and Jerseys-SJ22
02Parkhurst Retro-14
Minis-14
Franchise Players-RF6
02Private Stock Reserve-108
Red-108
Retail-108
02SP Authentic-16
Beckett Promos-16
02SP Game Used-9
Tools of the Game-RF
02SPx-12
02SPx-83
02SPx-127
Spectrum Gold-12
Spectrum Gold-82
Spectrum Silver-12
Spectrum Silver-82
02Stadium Club-4
Silver Decoy Cards-4
Proofs-4
Beam Team-BT11
02Titanium-18
Blue-18
Red-18
Retail-18
02Topps-19
02Topps-315
OPC Blue Parallel-19
OPC Blue Parallel-315
OPC Red Parallel-19
OPC Red Parallel-315
Captain's Cloth-CC1
Captain's Cloth-CC4
Captain's Cloth-CC15
Topps/OPC Hometown Heroes-HHU20
Factory Set-19
Factory Set-315
Factory Set Hometown Heroes-HHU20
02Topps Chrome-19
Black Border Refractors-19
Refractors-19
02Topps Heritage-4
02Topps Heritage-107
Chrome Parallel-4
02Topps Total-362
Award Winners-AW6
Team Checklists-TTC5
02UD Artistic Impressions-15
Gold-15
02UD Artistic Impressions Beckett Promos-15
02UD Artistic Impressions Flashbacks-UD5
02UD Artistic Impressions Flashbacks Gold-UD5
02UD Artistic Impressions Retrospectives-R15
02UD Artistic Impressions Retrospect Gold-R15
02UD Artistic Impress Retrospect Silver-R15
02UD Honor Roll-11
02UD Honor Roll-76
02UD Piece of History-13
02UD Premier Collection-10
02Upper Deck-276
Exclusives-276
02Upper Deck Beckett UD Promos-276
02Upper Deck Sizzling Scorers-SS4
02Upper Deck Classic Portraits-17
02Upper Deck MVP-33
Gold-33
Classics-33
Golden Classics-33
02Upper Deck Rookie Update-21
02Upper Deck Victory-38
Bronze-38
Gold-38
Silver-38
02Upper Deck Vintage-45
02Upper Deck Vintage-266
Green Backs-45
Tall Boys-T12
Tall Boys Gold-T12
02Vanguard-18
LTD-18
02Czech Stadion Cup Finals-486
03BAP Memorabilia-78
03BAP Memorabilia-230
Emerald-78
Gold-78
Ruby-78
Sapphire-78
Jersey and Stick-SJ-4
Jerseys-GJ-4
Jersey Autographs-GJ-4
03BAP Ultimate Memorabilia Autographs-21
Gold-21
03BAP Ultimate Mem Auto Jerseys-21
03Beehive-38
Gold-38
Silver-38
Jumbos-6
Jerseys-JT40
Sticks Red Border-RE11
03Black Diamond-139
Black-139
Green-139
Red-139
03Bowman-83
Gold-83
03Bowman Chrome-83
Refractors-83
Gold Refractors-83
Xfractors-83
03Hurricanes Postcards-9
03ITG Action-133
Homeboys-HB2
Jerseys-M157
Jerseys-M246
03ITG Used Signature Series-9
Gold-9
Autographs-RF1
Autographs-RF2
Autographs Gold-RF1
Autographs Gold-RF2
Jerseys-42
Jerseys Gold-42
Jersey Autos-42
Emblems-12
Emblems Gold-12
Jersey and Stick-42
Jersey and Stick Gold-42
03NHL Sticker Collection-35
03O-Pee-Chee-250
03OPC Blue-250
03OPC Gold-250
03OPC Red-250
03Pacific-61
Blue-61
Red-61
03Pacific Complete-270
Red-270
03Pacific Exhibit-158
Blue Backs-158
03Pacific Heads-Up-17
Hobby LTD-17
Retail LTD-17
03Pacific Invincible-15
Blue-15
Red-15
Retail-15
Featured Performers-6
03Pacific Luxury Suite-4A
03Pacific Luxury Suite-4B
03Pacific Luxury Suite-4C
03Pacific Prism-20
Blue-20
Gold-20
Red-20
03Pacific Quest for the Cup-18
Blue-18
03Pacific Supreme-15
Blue-15
Red-15
Retail-15
Generations-1
03Parkhurst Orig Six Boston Mem -BM42
03Parkhurst Orig Six Chicago Mem -CM42
03Parkhurst Orig Six Detroit Mem-DM42
03Parkhurst Orig Six Montreal Mem-MM42
03Parkhurst Orig Six New York Mem-NM42
03Parkhurst Original Six Shooters-OSM2
03Parkhurst Orig Six Toronto Mem-TM42
03Parkhurst Rookie-30
03Private Stock Reserve-18
Blue-18
Red-18
Retail-18
03SP Authentic-15
Limited-15
03SP Game Used-9
Gold-9
Team Threads-TTLBF
03SPx-16
Radiance-16
Spectrum-16
Hall Pass-HP-RF
Hall Pass Limited-HP-RF
03Titanium-20
Hobby Jersey Number Parallels-20
Retail-20
Retail Jersey Number Parallels-20
03Topps-250
Blue-250
Gold-250
Red-250
Lost Rookies-RF
03Topps C55-15
Minis-15
Minis American Back-15
Minis American Back Red-15
Minis Bazooka Back-15
Minis Brooklyn Back-15
Minis Hat Trick Back-15
Minis O Canada Back-15
Minis O Canada Back Red-15
Minis Stanley Cup Back-15
03Topps Pristine-72
Gold Refractor Die Cuts-72
Refractors-72
Jersey Portions-PPJ-RF
Jersey Portion Refractors-PPJ-RF
Press Plates Black-72
Press Plates Cyan-72
Press Plates Magenta-72
Press Plates Yellow-72
03Topps Traded-TT66
Blue-TT66
Gold-TT66
Red-TT66
03UD Honor Roll-13
03UD Premier Collection-54
Teammates-PT-CH
Teammates Patches-PT-CH
03Upper Deck-35
500 Goal Club-500-RF
500 Goal Club-500-RFA
BuyBacks-85
BuyBacks-86
BuyBacks-87
BuyBacks-88
BuyBacks-89
BuyBacks-90
BuyBacks-91
BuyBacks-92
BuyBacks-93
BuyBacks-94
BuyBacks-95
BuyBacks-96
Canadian Exclusives-35
HG-35
Patches-LD6
03Upper Deck Classic Portraits-15
03Upper Deck Ice-15
Gold-15
Breakers-IB-RF
Breaker Patches-IB-RF
Clear Cut Winners-CC-RF
03Upper Deck MVP-78
Gold Script-78
Silver Script-78
Canadian Exclusives-78
03Upper Deck Rookie Update-15
03Upper Deck Trilogy-15
Limited-15
03Upper Deck Victory-33
Bronze-33
Gold-33
Silver-33
03Toronto Star-14
04Pacific Philadelphia-15
04Upper Deck-32
04Upper Deck-187
Canadian Exclusives-32
Canadian Exclusives-187
HG Glossy Gold-32
HG Glossy Gold-187
HG Glossy Silver-32
HG Glossy Silver-187
Jersey Autographs-GJA-RF
05ITG Ultimate Memorabilia Double Autos-14
05ITG Ultimate Mem Double Autos Gold-14
05ITG Ultimate Memorabilia Stick Autos-10
05ITG Ultimate Mem Stick Autos Gold-10
06ITG Ultimate Memorabilia-124
Artist Proof-124
Bowman Factor-11
Bowman Factor Gold-11
Bowman Factor Autos-9
Bowman Factor Autos Gold-9
Complete Jersey-11
Complete Jersey Gold-11
First Round Picks-15
First Round Picks Gold-15
Jerseys Autos-17
Jerseys Autos Gold-17
Journey Emblem-10
Journey Emblem Gold-10
Journey Jersey-10
Journey Jersey Gold-10
Raised to the Rafters-7
Raised to the Rafters Gold-7
Retro Teammates-21
Retro Teammates Gold-21
Road to the Cup-8
Road to the Cup Gold-8
Seams Unbelievable-8
Seams Unbelievable Gold-8
Stick Rack-8
Stick Rack Gold-8
Sticks and Jerseys-6
Sticks and Jerseys Gold-6
06ITG Heroes and Prospects-12
Autographs-ARF
Heroes Memorabilia-HM04
Heroes Memorabilia Gold-HM04

Francis, Ronny (Swede)
65Swedish Coralli ISHockey-117

Francis, Todd
83Brantford Alexanders-27
94Brantford Smoke-3

Francisco, Jon
05Reading Royals-4
06Reading Royals-10

Franck, Andy
05ITG Heroes/Prosp Toronto Expo Parallel -354
05ITG Heroes and Prospects-354
Autographs Series II-AF

Franck, Shawn
06Barrie Colts-7

Francoeur, Jonathan
00Chicoutimi Sagueneens-6
Signed-6

Francoeur, Simon
93Quebec Pee-Wee Tournament-121

Francois, Jean
88Richelieu Riverains-23
92Quebec Pee-Wee Tournament-683
92Quebec Pee-Wee Tournament-1259
97Bowman CHL Autographs-37
98Bowman CHL Autographs-160
99Quebec PeeWee Tournament Coll Souv-18
01Titanium-83
Premiere Date-83
04German DEL-32

Francon, Devin
96Red Deer Rebels-14
97Red Deer Rebels-6
98Red Deer Rebels-6
00Red Deer Rebels-5
Signed-5
03Bakersfield Condors-9

Francz, Robert
95German DEL-19
02German DEL City Press-73
04German DEL-123
04German Hamburg Freezers Postcards-2
05German DEL-43
06German DEL-32
German Forwards-GF9

Franek, Karel
97Czech APS Extraliga-100

Franek, Petr
94Czech APS Extraliga-204
95Czech APS Extraliga-151
98Las Vegas Thunder-5
99German DEL-48
00Czech DS Extraliga-121
00Czech OFS-160
00Czech OFS Star Emerald-21
00Czech OFS Star Pink-21
00Czech OFS Star Violet-21
01Czech OFS-189
Gold Inserts-G2
02Czech OFS Plus-278
Checklists-C8
Trios-T4
03Czech OFS Plus Checklists-4
03Czech OFS Plus Insert B-B7
03Czech OFS Plus Insert P-P3
03Czech OFS Plus MS Praha-SE36
04Czech HC Slavia Praha Postcards-3
04Czech OFS-161
Goals-Against Leaders-6
Save Percentage Leaders-4
Team Cards-8
05Czech HC Slavia Praha-7
06Czech OFS-294
Goalies I-3
Goalies II-3
Team Cards-8

Frank, Jeff
82Regina Pats-17
83Regina Pats-17

Frank, Mark
82Medicine Hat Tigers-3

Franke, Joe
93Fort Wayne Komets-25
02Fort Wayne Komets-7

Franke, Peter
94German DEL-410
95German DEL-408
96German DEL-70
99German Bundesliga 2-96
00German DEL-51

Franklin, Jeff
93Quebec Pee-Wee Tournament-1235

Franklin, T.
83Hall of Fame-62
85Hall of Fame-62

Frankovic, Sasha
93Quebec Pee-Wee Tournament-1183

Franks, Jim
34Beehive Group I Photos-272

Franks, Mark
90Saskatoon Blades-18
907th Inn. Sketch WHL-74
91Saskatoon Blades-17
917th Inn. Sketch WHL-116
92Brandon Wheat Kings-6
93Huntington Blizzard-8
94Huntington Blizzard-10

Frankum, Paul
94UK Solihull Barons-3
95UK Solihull Barons-6

Fransen, Aaron
98Kingston Frontenacs-5

Franson, Cody
04Vancouver Giants-3
05Vancouver Giants-10
06ITG Heroes and Prospects-197
Autographs-ACF
Update Autographs-ACF
07ITG Going For Gold World Juniors-9
Autographs-9
Emblems-GUE9
Jerseys-GUJ9
Numbers-GUN9

Fransoo, Jason
03Swift Current Broncos-2
04Swift Current Broncos-5
05Everett Silvertips-8

Fransson, Johan
02Swiss SCL Tigers-1
03Swedish Elite-225
Silver-225
04Swedish Elitset-214
Dominators-4
Future Stars-4
Gold-214
Signatures-6
05Swedish Lulea Hockey Postcards-3
05Swedish SHL Elitset-83
Gold-83
Series One Signatures-12
Star Potential-10
06Swedish SHL Elitset-83
06Swedish SHL Elitset-177

Fransson, Jonas
02Swedish SHL-188
Parallel-188
05Swedish SHL Elitset-219
Gold-219
06Swedish SHL Elitset-68
Goal Patrol-10

Frantti, Gordon
91Kansas City Blades-20
91ProCards-515
94Huntington Blizzard-11

Franz, Christian
99German DEL-226
01German Upper Deck-251
02German DEL City Press-157
04German DEL-248
04German Nuremburg Ice Tigers Postcards-7
04German Weiden Blue Devils-4
05German DEL-267

Franz, Georg
89Swedish Semic World Champ Stickers-117
91Finnish Semic World Champ Stickers-175
91Swedish Semic World Champ Stickers-175
93Swedish Semic World Champ Stickers-165
94Finnish Jaa Kiekko-283
94German DEL-254
95German DEL-252
95Swedish World Championships Stickers-68
96German DEL-141
99German EHC Straubing-16

Franzen, Johan
02Swedish SHL-214
Parallel-214
03Swedish Elite-215
Silver-215
04SP Authentic Rookie Redemptions-RR48
04Swedish Elitset-206
Gold-206
05Beehive-127
Beige -127
Blue -127
Gold-127
Red -127
Matte-127
Signature Scrapbook-SSJF
05Black Diamond-158
Emerald-158
Gold-158
Onyx-158
Ruby-158
05Hot Prospects-236
En Fuego-236
Hot Materials-HMJF
Red Hot-236
White Hot-236
05Parkhurst-182
Facsimile Auto Parallel-182
Signatures-JF
05SP Authentic-154
Limited-154
Rarefied Rookies-RRJF
Sign of the Times Duals-DZF
Sign of the Times Triples-TZFD
05SP Game Used-145
Autographs-145
Gold-145
Auto Draft-AD-JF
Rookie Exclusives-JF
Rookie Exclusives Silver-RE-JF
Significant Numbers-SN-JF
05SPx-176
Spectrum-176
Xcitement Rookies-XR-JF
Xcitement Rookies Gold-XR-JF
Xcitement Rookies Spectrum-XR-JF
05The Cup-116
Autographed Rookie Patches Gold Rainbow-116
Black Rainbow Rookies-116
Masterpiece Pressplates (Artifacts)-239
Masterpiece Pressplates (Bee Hive)-127
Masterpiece Pressplates (Black Diamond)-158
Masterpiece Pressplates (Ice)-128
Masterpiece Pressplates (MVP)-421
Masterpiece Pressplates (Power Play)-149
Masterpiece Pressplates (Power Play)-149
Masterpiece Pressplates (Rookie Update)-209
Masterpiece Pressplates SPA Autos-154
Masterpiece Pressplates (SP Game Used)-145
Masterpiece Pressplates SPx Autos-176
Masterpiece Pressplates (Trilogy)-190
Masterpiece Pressplates Ult Coll Autos-115
Masterpiece Pressplates (Victory)-291
Masterpiece Pressplates Autographs-116
Platinum Rookies-116
05UD Artifacts-239
Gold-RED39
05UD PowerPlay-149
05UD Rookie Class-47
05Ultimate Collection-115
Autographed Patches-115
Autographed Shields-115
Jerseys Dual-DJFZ
Marquee Attractions-MA20
Premium Patches-PPJF
Premium Swatches-PSJF
Ultimate Debut Threads Jerseys-DTJJF
Ultimate Debut Threads Patches-DTPJF
Ultimate Patches Dual-DPFZ
Ultimate Signatures Logos-SLJF
Ultimate Signatures Pairings-UPZF
05Ultra-217
Gold-217
Ice-217
Rookie Uniformity Jerseys-RU-JF
Rookie Uniformity Jersey Autographs-ARU-JF
Rookie Uniformity Patches-RUP-JF
Rookie Uniformity Patch Autographs-ARP-JF
05Upper Deck-456
Rookie Ink-RIJF
05Upper Deck Rookie Showcase-RS35
05Upper Deck Rookie Showcase Promos-RS35
05Upper Deck Rookie Threads-RTJF
05Upper Deck Rookie Threads Autographs-ARTJF
05Upper Deck Ice-128
Fresh Ice-FIJF
Fresh Ice Glass-FIJF
Fresh Ice Glass Patches-FIPJF
Premieres Auto Patches-AIPJF
05Upper Deck MVP-421
Gold-421
Platinum-421
05Upper Deck Rookie Update-209
Inspirations Patch Rookies-209
05Upper Deck Trilogy-190
05Upper Deck Victory-291
Black-291
Gold-291
Silver-291
06Be A Player Portraits First Exposures-FEJF
06Fleer Signing Day-SDJF
06O-Pee-Chee-175
06O-Pee-Chee-639
Rainbow-175
Rainbow-639
06Upper Deck-321
Exclusives Parallel-321
High Gloss Parallel-321
Masterpieces-321

Franzen, Rikard
87Swedish Panini Stickers-9
89Swedish Semic Elitserien Stickers-8
90Swedish Semic Elitserien Stickers-81
91Swedish Semic Elitserien Stickers-7
92Swedish Semic Elitserien Stickers-33
94Swedish Leaf-108
Studio Signatures-1
95Swedish Leaf-165
Mega-13
95Swedish Upper Deck-4
95Swedish Upper Deck-219
95Swedish Upper Deck-249
96Swedish Semic Wien-51
96Swedish Semic Wien Coca-Cola Dream Team-4
98Swedish UD Choice-2
Day in the Life-1
99Swedish Upper Deck-2
Lasting Impressions-1
SHL Signatures-2
00Swedish Upper Deck-4
01Swiss HNL-78
02Swiss HNL-252
04Swedish Elitset-160
Gold-160

Franzi, Marcel
93Quebec Pee-Wee Tournament-1631
95Swiss HNL-451
96Swiss HNL-168

Franzmeier, Lacey
98Minnesota Golden Gophers Women-6

Frappier, Shawn
92Sudbury Wolves-7
93Sudbury Wolves-7
93Sudbury Wolves Police-7
94Sudbury Wolves-6
94Sudbury Wolves Police-19
95Slapshot-12
95Barrie Colts-9
96Mississippi Sea Wolves-6
97Mississippi Sea Wolves-17
98Johnstown Chiefs-16
99Johnstown Chiefs-14

Fraschina, Nicola
93Swiss HNL-264
95Swiss HNL-135

Fraser Jr., Scott
80Quebec Remparts-7

Fraser, Alain
98Swiss Power Play Stickers-330

Fraser, Barry
88Oilers Tenth Anniversary-158

Fraser, Brad
93Quebec Pee-Wee Tournament-859

Fraser, Chas.
23V145-1-39

Fraser, Chris
89Windsor Spitfires-4

Fraser, Colin
01Red Deer Rebels-7
02Red Deer Rebels-10
03Red Deer Rebels-7
04ITG Heroes and Prospects-220
04ITG Heroes/Prospects Toronto Expo '05-220
05Norfolk Admirals-10
06Norfolk Admirals-22
07Upper Deck Victory-213
Black-213
Gold-213

Fraser, Craig
897th Inn. Sketch OHL-74
907th Inn. Sketch OHL-5
917th Inn. Sketch OHL-34

Fraser, Curt
78Canucks Royal Bank-5
79Canucks Royal Bank-6
79O-Pee-Chee-117
79Topps-117
80Canucks Silverwood Dairies-8
80Canucks Team Issue-8
80O-Pee-Chee-287
80Pepsi-Cola Caps-107
81Canucks Team Issue-8
81O-Pee-Chee-346
82Canucks Team Issue-7
82O-Pee-Chee-343
82O-Pee-Chee Stickers-244
82Post Cereal-19
82Topps Stickers-244
82Victoria Cougars-7
83Blackhawks Postcards-7
83O-Pee-Chee-102
84O-Pee-Chee-34
84Topps-29
85Blackhawks Team Issue-15
85O-Pee-Chee-3
85O-Pee-Chee Stickers-24
85Topps-3
86Blackhawks Coke-5
86O-Pee-Chee-31
86Topps-31
87Blackhawks Coke-5
87Panini Stickers-231
88North Stars ADA-8
90ProCards AHL/IHL-327
91ProCards-619
98Orlando Solar Bears-16
98Orlando Solar Bears II-11

Fraser, Eric
06Westside Warriors-4

Fraser, Gord
24Anonymous NHL-136

Fraser, Iain
89Oshawa Generals-25
89Oshawa Generals 7th Inning Sketch-19
897th Inn. Sketch OHL-19
897th Inn. Sketch OHL-186
897th Inn. Sketch OHL-198
907th Inn. Sketch Memorial Cup-89
91ProCards-468
93Donruss-478
93OPC Premier-525
Gold-525
93Parkhurst-434
Emerald Ice-434
Calder Candidates-C19
Calder Candidates Gold-C19
93PowerPlay-419
Rookie Standouts-4
93Score-625
Gold-625
Canadian-625
Canadian Gold-625
93Stadium Club-485
Members Only Master Set-485
First Day Issue-485
93Topps/OPC Premier-525
Gold-525
93Ultra-73
93Ultra-400
Prospects-1
93Upper Deck-337
93Classic Pro Prospects-49
94Donruss-270
94Leaf-105
94OPC Premier-7
94O-Pee-Chee Finest Inserts-6
94OPC Premier Special Effects-7
94Parkhurst-187
94Parkhurst-280
Gold-187
Gold-280
94Pinnacle-513
Artist's Proofs-513
Rink Collection-513
94Stadium Club-32
Members Only Master Set-32
First Day Issue-32

Super Team Winner Cards-32
94Topps/OPC Premier-7
Special Effects-7
94Ultra-174
94Upper Deck-162
Electric Ice-162
94Classic Pro Prospects-15
96Kentucky Thoroughblades-6
99German DEL-214
00German DEL-43
01German Upper Deck-85
02UK Sheffield Steelers-8

Fraser, Jamie
03Brampton Batallion-5

Fraser, Kerry
90Pro Set-686

Fraser, Kris
99Owen Sound Platers-29
00Owen Sound Attack-6

Fraser, Legs
51Laval Dairy QSHL-104

Fraser, Mark
04Kitchener Rangers-17
05Kitchener Rangers-13
07Upper Deck Victory-220
Black-220
Gold-220

Fraser, Ryan
00Sarnia Sting-9

Fraser, Scott
23V128-1 Paulin's Candy-53
94Fredericton Canadiens-13
95Fredericton Canadiens-11
96Fredericton Canadiens-7
96Saint John Flames-3
98Pacific-207
Ice Blue-207
Red-207

Fraser, Trever
917th Inn. Sketch WHL-171
92Tacoma Rockets-10
93Tacoma Rockets-9
98Hampton Roads Admirals-10
99Tacoma Sabercats-4
00Tacoma Sabercats-3

Fraser, William
25Dominion Chocolates-81

Fraszko, Adam
89Swedish Semic World Champ Stickers-146

Frawley, Dan
83Springfield Indians-9
86Penguins Kodak-9
87Panini Stickers-153
87Penguins Masks-4
87Penguins Kodak-9
88Panini Stickers-338
89ProCards IHL-160
90ProCards AHL/IHL-274
91ProCards-3
91Rochester Americans Dunkin' Donuts-8
91Rochester Americans Kodak-12
91Rochester Americans Postcards-10
92Rochester Americans Dunkin' Donuts-6
92Rochester Americans Kodak-8
95Rochester Americans-3
96Rochester Americans-15
97Rochester Americans-3-2

Frawley, David
05Fort Wayne Komets Choice-5

Frayn, Robert
897th Inn. Sketch OHL-175
907th Inn. Sketch OHL-6
917th Inn. Sketch OHL-184

Frazee, Jeff
05Minnesota Golden Gophers-7
06Minnesota Golden Gophers-8

Frazer, Fritz
51Laval Dairy QSHL-106

Freadrich, Kyle
96Regina Pats-17
97Regina Pats-12
99Detroit Vipers-14
00Pacific-382
Copper-382
Gold-382
Ice Blue-382
Premiere Date-382
00SPx-119
Spectrum-119
00Upper Deck-192
Exclusives Tier 1-192
Exclusives Tier 2-192
00Upper Deck MVP-205
First Stars-205
Second Stars-205
Third Stars-205
00Upper Deck Victory-267

Frechette, Manuel
93Quebec Pee-Wee Tournament-83

Frechette, Martin
93Quebec Pee-Wee Tournament-91
03Gatineau Olympiques-10
04Gatineau Olympiques-2
05Gatineau Olympiques-10
06Gatineau Olympiques-1

Frechette, Maxime
04Drummondville Voltigeurs-21
05Drummondville Voltigeurs-10
06Drummondville Voltigeurs-22

Frechette, Yanick
907th Inn. Sketch QMJHL-60
917th Inn. Sketch QMJHL-237

Frederick, Joe
92Northern Michigan Wildcats-5
93Classic-65
94Classic Pro Prospects-131
94Classic Four-Sport *-149
Gold-149
Autographs-149A
Printers Proofs-149
99Utah Grizzlies-16
01Fresno Falcons-4
02Fresno Falcons-18
04Las Vegas Wranglers-22

Frederick, Troy
88Brandon Wheat Kings-8
89Brandon Wheat Kings-2
90ProCards AHL/IHL-596
91ProCards-512
92Kansas City Blades-8
94Central Hockey League-22
95Central Hockey League-6
95Fort Worth Fire-9
98Topeka Scarecrows-12

Fredericks, Andrew
00Arizona Icecats-7
01Arizona Icecats-4
02Arizona Icecats-6
03Arizona Icecats-8

Fredericks, Ray
51Laval Dairy Subset-104
52St. Lawrence Sales-70

Frederickson, Frank
24Holland Creameries-5
60Topps-34
Stamps-15
83Hall of Fame-49
83Hall of Fame Postcards-D3
85Hall of Fame-49

Frederiksen, Keld
98Danish Hockey League-6
99Danish Hockey League-8

Fredriksson, David
04Swedish HV71 Postcards-4
05Swedish SHL Elitset-198
Gold-198
06Swedish SHL Elitset-61

Fredriksson, Dennis
91Swedish Semic Elitserien Stickers-300

Fredriksson, Nils-Olav
56Swedish Alfabilder-50

Freeland, Jordan
01St. Michaels Majors-11

Freeman, Jaisen
99Ohio State Buckeyes-7
00Ohio State Buckeyes-3

Freer, Mark
88ProCards AHL-126
89ProCards AHL-337
90ProCards AHL/IHL-47
91Parkhurst-343
French-343
91ProCards-279
92Parkhurst-354
Emerald Ice-354
92Pro Set-127
92Upper Deck-445
93OPC Premier-142
Gold-142
93Panini Stickers-118
93Stadium Club-29
Members Only Master Set-29
OPC-29
First Day Issue-29
First Day Issue OPC-29
93Topps/OPC Premier-142
Gold-142
95Houston Aeros-6
96Collector's Edge Ice-132
Prism-132
02Hershey Bears-9
06Houston Aeros RetroÂ -2

Fregoe, Peter
03Trenton Titans-360
05Fresno Falcons-6

Freibauer, Radim
99Czech OFS-73

Freissl, Peter
94German First League-239

Freissmann, Michael
94German First League-127

Freitag, Damian
93Swiss HNL-343
95Swiss HNL-397
96Swiss HNL-343

Freitag, Fred
04German Berlin Eisbarens 50th Anniv-35

Freitag, Wayne
63Quebec Aces-7

Frelin, Mathias
99Danish Hockey League-28

French, Chris
96Alaska Gold Kings-4

French, John
72Whalers New England WHA-7
73Quaker Oats WHA-33
74O-Pee-Chee WHA-33
76O-Pee-Chee WHA-105

Frenette, Derek
91ProCards-27
92Peoria Rivermen-6
93Peoria Rivermen-11

Frenzel, Dieter
83Swedish Semic VM Stickers-148
94German First League-628
04German Berlin Eisbarens 50th Anniv-59

Frenzel, Hanne
04German Berlin Eisbarens 50th Anniv-32

Frenzel, Matthias
02German DEL City Press-74

Frescoln, Chris
93Michigan Wolverines-6

Frestadius, Robert
83Swedish Semic Elitserien-157
86Swedish Panini Stickers-194
87Swedish Panini Stickers-196
89Swedish Semic Elitserien Stickers-173

Frew, Irv
35Diamond Matchbooks Tan 1-23
35Diamond Matchbooks Tan 2-22
35Diamond Matchbooks Tan 3-20

Frey, Erich
93Swiss HNL-369
96Swiss HNL-500

Fria, Shayne
01Barrie Colts-20

Friberg, Christian
98Idaho Steelheads-7

Frick, Matt
06New Mexico Scorpions-18

Fricke, Kevin
01Memphis RiverKings-4

Fricker, Jason
02Fort Worth Brahmas-2

Frid, Rob
93London Knights-8
97Louisville Riverfrogs-20
98Quad-City Mallards-9
99Columbus Cottonmouths-23
01Odessa Jackalopes-7
02Odessa Jackalopes-9

Friday, Bill
61Sudbury Wolves-9
62Sudbury Wolves-11
91Ultimate Original Six-85
French-85

Friday, Bob
51Laval Dairy QSHL-87

Fridfinson, Wally
24Crescent Falcon-Tigers-3
24Holland Creameries-1

Fridgen, Dan
82Whalers Junior Hartford Courant-5
93RPI Engineers-9

Friedlay, Travis
02Swift Current Broncos-3

Friedley, Travis
01Swift Current Broncos-4
03Camrose Kodiaks-7
04Camrose Kodiaks-16

Friedli, Rene
93Swiss HNL-72
95Swiss HNL-45
96Swiss HNL-38
98Swiss Power Play Stickers-189
99Swiss Panini Stickers-189
00Swiss Panini Stickers-223
00Swiss Slapshot Mini-Cards-RJ8
01Swiss HNL-156

Friedli, Sacha
93Swiss HNL-239
95Swiss HNL-159
02Swiss HNL-218

Friedman, Doug
98Milwaukee Admirals-19
98Milwaukee Admirals Postcards-1
99Kentucky Thoroughblades-11
00Worcester Icecats-28

Friedrich, Beat
95Swiss HNL-356

Friedrich, C.
74Finnish Typotor-104

Friere, Eric
05Red Deer Rebels-4

Friesen, Blake
04Sioux Falls Stampede-3-6

Friesen, Curtis
907th Inn. Sketch WHL-47

Friesen, Dustin
00Swift Current Broncos-8
01Swift Current Broncos-10
02Swift Current Broncos-4
03Swift Current Broncos-3

Friesen, Gary
03Oshawa Generals-27
04Oshawa Generals-21
04Oshawa Generals Autographs-21
05Sudbury Wolves-17
06Sudbury Wolves-8

Friesen, Jackie
04Wisconsin Badgers Women-7

Friesen, Jeff
93Donruss Team Canada-11
93Parkhurst-505
Emerald Ice-505
93Pinnacle-472
Canadian-472
93Upper Deck-532
Program of Excellence-E8
93Classic-102
Class of '94-CL3
Promos-2
94Be A Player-R164
94Finest-11
94Finest-159
Super Team Winners-11
Super Team Winners-159
Refractors-11
Refractors-159
Bowman's Best-R14
Bowman's Best Refractors-R14
94Flair-164
94Fleer-196
Rookie Sensations-3
94Leaf-482
Phenoms-9
Limited World Juniors Canada-3
94OPC Premier-547
Special Effects-547
94Parkhurst SE-SE166
Gold-SE166
94Pinnacle-252
94Pinnacle-532
Artist's Proofs-252
Artist's Proofs-532
Rink Collection-252
Rink Collection-532
Rookie Team Pinnacle-7
94Score-203
Gold-203
Platinum-203
Top Rookie Redemption-8
94Select-176
Gold-176
Youth Explosion-YE9
94SP-145
Die Cuts-145
94Topps/OPC Premier-547
Special Effects-547
94Ultra-365
94Upper Deck-237
94Upper Deck-526
Electric Ice-237
Electric Ice-526
SP Inserts-SP161
SP Inserts Die Cuts-SP161
94Classic-10
Gold-10
Autographs-10
CHL All-Stars-C4
ROY Sweepstakes-R5
Tri-Cards-T61
94Classic Pro Prospects-202
94Classic Pro Prospects-209
Autographs-AU3
94Classic Four-Sport *-125
Gold-125
Printers Proofs-125
95Upper Deck World Junior Alumni-13
95Bowman-84
All-Foil-84
95Canada Games NHL POGS-30
95Canada Games NHL POGS-223
95Collector's Choice-309
95Collector's Choice-372
Player's Club-309
Player's Club-372
Player's Club Platinum-309
Player's Club Platinum-372
95Donruss-162
Canadian World Junior Team-21
Pro Pointers-11
Rookie Team-7
95Emotion-155
95Finest-27
Refractors-27
95Leaf-21
Studio Rookies-7
95Leaf Limited-62
95McDonald's Pinnacle-MCD-31
95Metal-129
95Panini Stickers-278
95Panini Stickers-304
95Parkhurst International-182
Emerald Ice-182
95Pinnacle-55

Artist's Proofs-55
Rink Collection-55
95Playoff One on One-83
95Pro Magnets-118
95Score-91
Black Ice Artist's Proofs-91
Black Ice-91
Check It-10
Golden Blades-11
95Select Certified-56
Mirror Gold-56
95SkyBox Impact-147
95SkyBox Impact-235
95SP-133
95Stadium Club-106
Members Only Master Set-106
95Summit-68
Artist's Proofs-68
Ice-68
95Topps-360
OPC Inserts-360
Canadian World Juniors-15CJ
New To The Game-18NG
Young Stars-YS6
95Topps SuperSkills-69
Platinum-69
95Ultra-145
Gold Medallion-145
All-Rookies-4
All-Rookie Gold Medallion-4
95Upper Deck-134
Electric Ice-134
Electric Ice Gold-134
Special Edition-SE74
Special Edition Gold-SE74
95Zenith-65
95Images-2
Gold-2
Autographs-2A
Clear Excitement-CE2
95Images Four-Sport *-103
95Assets Gold *-3
95Assets Gold Phone Cards $2 *-3
96Be A Player-190
Autographs-190
Autographs Silver-190
96Collector's Choice-238
96Donruss-79
Press Proofs-79
96Donruss Elite-53
Die Cut Stars-53
96Leaf-87
Press Proofs-87
96Leaf Limited-83
Gold-83
96Leaf Preferred-97
Press Proofs-97
96NHL Pro Stamps-118
96Pinnacle-18
Artist's Proofs-18
Foil-18
Premium Stock-18
Rink Collection-18
96Playoff One on One-362
96Score-4
Artist's Proofs-4
Dealer's Choice Artist's Proofs-4
Special Artist's Proofs-4
Golden Blades-4
96Select Certified-61
Artist's Proofs-61
Blue-61
Mirror Blue-61
Mirror Gold-61
Mirror Red-61
Red-61
96SkyBox Impact-116
96SP-143
96Summit-144
Artist's Proofs-144
Ice-144
Metal-144
Premium Stock-144
96Upper Deck-332
96Upper Deck Ice-58
Parallel-58
96Zenith-89
Artist's Proofs-89
96Visions *-83
97Collector's Choice-215
Star Quest-SQ10
97Crown Royale-119
Emerald Green-119
Ice Blue-119
Silver-119
97Donruss-55
Press Proofs Silver-55
Press Proofs Gold-55
97Donruss Canadian Ice-81
Dominion Series-81
Provincial Series-81
97Donruss Elite-93
Aspirations-93
Status-93
97Donruss Limited-72
97Donruss Limited-196
Exposure-72
Exposure-196
97Donruss Preferred-14
Cut to the Chase-14
97Donruss Priority-70
Stamp of Approval-70
97Leaf-102
Fractal Matrix-102
Fractal Matrix Die Cuts-102
97Leaf International-102
Universal Ice-102
97Pacific-63
Copper-63
Emerald Green-63
Ice Blue-63
Red-63
Silver-63
97Pacific Dynagon-110
Copper-110
Dark Grey-110
Emerald Green-110
Ice Blue-110
Red-110
Silver-110
Tandems-60
97Pacific Invincible-124
Copper-124
Emerald Green-124
Ice Blue-124
Red-124
Silver-124
97Pacific Omega-200
Copper-200
Dark Gray-200
Emerald Green-200

Gold-200
Ice Blue-200
97Panini Stickers-233
97Paramount-164
Copper-164
Dark Grey-164
Emerald Green-164
Ice Blue-164
Red-164
Silver-164
97Pinnacle-119
Press Plates Back Black-119
Press Plates Back Cyan-119
Press Plates Back Magenta-119
Press Plates Back Yellow-119
Press Plates Front Black-119
Press Plates Front Cyan-119
Press Plates Front Magenta-119
Press Plates Front Yellow-119
97Pinnacle Certified-81
Red-81
Mirror Blue-81
Mirror Gold-81
Mirror Red-81
97Pinnacle Inside-121
97Pinnacle Tot Cert Platinum Blue-81
97Pinnacle Tot Cert Platinum Gold-81
97Pinnacle Totally Certified Platinum Red-81
97Pinnacle Tot Cert Mirror Platinum Gold-81
97Revolution-123
Copper-123
Emerald-123
Ice Blue-123
Silver-123
97Score-170
97SP Authentic-134
97Studio-98
Press Proofs Silver-98
Press Proofs Gold-98
97Upper Deck-358
97Zenith-33
Z-Gold-33
Z-Silver-33
98Aurora-166
98Be A Player-267
Press Release-267
98BAP Gold-267
98BAP Autographs-267
98BAP Autographs Gold-267
98Bowman's Best-41
Refractors-41
Atomic Refractors-41
98Crown Royale-118
Limited Series-118
98Finest-32
No Protectors-32
No Protectors Refractors-32
Refractors-32
98OPC Chrome-128
Refractors-128
98Pacific-379
Ice Blue-379
Red-379
98Pacific Dynagon Ice-164
Blue-164
Red-164
98Pacific Omega-209
Red-209
Opening Day Issue-209
98Panini Photocards-26
98Panini Stickers-209
98Paramount-209
Copper-209
Emerald Green-209
Holo-Electric-209
Ice Blue-209
Silver-209
98Revolution-126
Ice Shadow-126
Red-126
98SP Authentic-76
Power Shift-76
98Topps-128
O-Pee-Chee-128
98Topps Gold Label Class 1-60
Black-60
Black One of One-60
One of One-60
Red-60
Red One of One-60
98Topps Gold Label Class 2-60
98Topps Gold Label Class 2 Black-60
98Topps Gold Label Class 2 Black 1 of 1-60
98Topps Gold Label Class 2 One of One-60
98Topps Gold Label Class 2 Red-60
98Topps Gold Label Class 2 Red One of One-60
98Topps Gold Label Class 3-60
98Topps Gold Label Class 3 Black-60
98Topps Gold Label Class 3 Black 1 of 1-60
98Topps Gold Label Class 3 One of One-60
98Topps Gold Label Class 3 Red-60
98Topps Gold Label Class 3 Red One of One-60
98UD Choice-174
Prime Choice Reserve-174
Reserve-174
98Upper Deck-351
Exclusives-351
Exclusives 1 of 1-351
Gold Reserve-351
98Upper Deck MVP-174
Gold Script-174
Silver Script-174
Super Script-174
99Aurora-120
Premiere Date-120
99BAP Memorabilia-274
Gold-274
Silver-274
99BAP Millennium-211
Emerald-211
Ruby-211
Sapphire-211
Signatures-211
Signatures Gold-211
99Black Diamond-76
Diamond Cut-76
Final Cut-76
99Crown Royale-123
Limited Series-123
Premiere Date-123
International Glory-24
International Glory Parallel-24
99O-Pee-Chee-96
99O-Pee-Chee Chrome-96
99O-Pee-Chee Chrome Refractors-96
99O-Pee-Chee Now Starring-NS9
99Pacific-370
Copper-370
Emerald Green-370
Gold-370
Ice Blue-370

Premiere Date-370
Red-370
99Pacific Dynagon Ice-172
Blue-172
Copper-172
Gold-172
Premiere Date-172
99Pacific Omega-205
Copper-205
Gold-205
Ice Blue-205
Premiere Date-205
99Pacific Prism-124
Holographic Blue-124
Holographic Gold-124
Holographic Mirror-124
Holographic Purple-124
Premiere Date-124
99Panini Stickers-296
99Paramount-204
Copper-204
Emerald-204
Gold-204
Holographic Emerald-204
Holographic Gold-204
Holographic Silver-204
Ice Blue-204
Premiere Date-204
Red-204
Silver-204
99Revolution-127
Premiere Date-127
Red-127
Shadow Series-127
Top of the Line-10
99SP Authentic-74
99SPx-128
Radiance-128
Spectrum-128
99Stadium Club-18
First Day Issue-18
One of a Kind-18
Printing Plates Black-18
Printing Plates Cyan-18
Printing Plates Magenta-18
Printing Plates Yellow-18
Chrome-17
Chrome Refractors-17
99Topps/OPC-96
Now Starring-NS9
99Topps/OPC Chrome-96
Refractors-96
99Topps Gold Label Class 1-42
Black-42
Black One of One-42
One of One-42
Red-42
Red One of One-42
99Topps Gold Label Class 2-42
99Topps Gold Label Class 2 Black-42
99Topps Gold Label Class 2 Black 1 of 1-42
99Topps Gold Label Class 2 One of One-42
99Topps Gold Label Class 2 Red-42
99Topps Gold Label Class 2 Red One of One-42
99Topps Gold Label Class 3-42
99Topps Gold Label Class 3 Black-42
99Topps Gold Label Class 3 Black 1 of 1-42
99Topps Gold Label Class 3 One of One-42
99Topps Gold Label Class 3 Red-42
99Topps Gold Label Class 3 Red One of One-42
99Topps Premier Plus-53
Parallel-53
99Ultimate Victory-75
1/1-75
Parallel-75
Parallel 100-75
99Upper Deck-109
Exclusives-109
Exclusives 1 of 1-109
99Upper Deck Arena Giveaways-SS2
99Upper Deck Gold Reserve-109
99Upper Deck HoloGrFx-49
Ausome-49
99Upper Deck MVP-175
Gold Script-175
Silver Script-175
Super Script-175
Draft Report-DR10
ProSign-JF
99Upper Deck MVP SC Edition-154
Gold Script-154
Silver Script-154
Super Script-154
Cup Contenders-CC8
99Upper Deck Retro-66
Gold-66
Platinum-66
99Upper Deck Victory-246
99Upper Deck Victory-248
99Wayne Gretzky Hockey-149
00Aurora-127
Premiere Date-127
00BAP Memorabilia-49
Emerald-49
Ruby-49
Sapphire-49
Promos-49
00BAP Mem Chicago Sportsfest Copper-49
00BAP Memorabilia Chicago Sportsfest Gold-49
00BAP Memorabilia Chicago Sportsfest Ruby-49
00BAP Memorabilia Chicago Sun-Times Ruby-49
00BAP Memorabilia Chicago Sun-Times Gold-49
00BAP Mem Chicago Sun-Times Sapphire-49
00BAP Mem Toronto Fall Expo Copper-49
00BAP Memorabilia Toronto Fall Expo Gold-49
00BAP Memorabilia Toronto Fall Expo Ruby-49
00BAP Parkhurst 2000-P106
00BAP Signature Series-172
Emerald-172
Ruby-172
Sapphire-172
Jersey Cards-J28
Jersey and Stick Cards-GSJ28
Jersey Emblems-E28
Jersey Numbers-IN28
00Black Diamond-50
Gold-50
00O-Pee-Chee-186
00O-Pee-Chee Parallel-186
00Pacific-357
Copper-357
Gold-357
Ice Blue-357
Premiere Date-357
00Paramount-213
Copper-213
Gold-213
Holo-Gold-213
Holo-Silver-213
Ice Blue-213

Premiere Date-213
00Private Stock-88
Gold-88
Premiere Date-88
Retail-88
Silver-88
PS-2001 Action-49
PS-2001 New Wave-21
00Revolution-128
Blue-128
Premiere Date-128
Red-128
00SPx-56
Spectrum-56
SPXcitement-X11
00Stadium Club-106
00Topps/OPC-186
Parallel-186
00Topps Chrome-124
OPC Refractors-124
Refractors-124
00Topps Gold Label Class 1-58
Gold-58
00Topps Gold Label Class 2-58
00Topps Gold Label Class 2 Gold-58
00Topps Gold Label Class 3-58
00Topps Gold Label Class 3 Gold-58
00Topps Gold Label Bullion-B8
00Topps Gold Label Bullion One to One-B8
00Topps Heritage-138
00Topps Premier Plus-13
Blue Ice-13
00Topps Stars-56
Blue-56
00UD Heroes-156
00UD Pros and Prospects-72
00UD Reserve-72
00Upper Deck-145
Exclusives Tier 1-145
Exclusives Tier 2-145
00Upper Deck Ice-61
00Upper Deck Legends-112
00Upper Deck Legends-113
Legendary Collection Bronze-112
Legendary Collection Bronze-113
Legendary Collection Gold-112
Legendary Collection Gold-113
Legendary Collection Silver-112
Legendary Collection Silver-113
00Upper Deck MVP-148
First Stars-148
Second Stars-148
Third Stars-148
00Upper Deck Victory-191
00Upper Deck Victory-193
00Upper Deck Victory-319
00Upper Deck Vintage-299
00Upper Deck Vintage-307
00Upper Deck Vintage-308
00Vanguard-87
Holographic Gold-87
Holographic Purple-87
Pacific Proofs-87
01BAP Memorabilia-68
Emerald-68
Ruby-68
Sapphire-68
01BAP Signature Series Teammates-TM-1
01Bowman YoungStars-86
Gold-86
Ice Cubed-86
01Crown Royale-2
Blue-2
Premiere Date-2
Red-2
Retail-2
01McDonald's Pacific Hometown Pride-1
01O-Pee-Chee-57
01O-Pee-Chee Heritage Parallel-57
01O-Pee-Chee Heritage Parallel Limited-57
01O-Pee-Chee Premier Parallel-57
01Pacific-3
Extreme LTD-3
Hobby LTD-3
Premiere Date-3
Retail LTD-3
01Pacific Adrenaline-1
Blue-1
Premiere Date-1
Red-1
Retail-1
01Pacific Arena Exclusives-3
01Parkhurst-156
Jerseys-PJ8
Sticks-PS8
01Private Stock-1
Gold-1
Premiere Date-1
Retail-1
Silver-1
01Private Stock Pacific Nights-1
01SP Authentic-1
Limited-1
Limited Gold-1
01SP Game Used Tools of the Game-TJF
01SP Game Used Tools of the Game-CTFF
01SP Game Used Tools of the Game-TTFCF
01SPx-152
01Stadium Club-66
Award Winners-66
Master Photos-66
01Titanium-1
Hobby Parallel-1
Premiere Date-1
Retail-1
Retail Parallel-1
Double-Sided Jerseys-2
Double-Sided Patches-2
01Titanium Draft Day Edition-1
01Topps-57
Heritage Parallel-57
Heritage Parallel Limited-57
OPC Parallel-57
01Topps Chrome-57
Refractors-57
Black Border Refractors-57
01Topps Heritage-73
Refractors-73
01Topps Reserve-62
01UD Challenge for the Cup-2
01UD Mask Collection-2
Gold-2
Double Patches-DPJF
Jerseys-J-JF
Jersey and Patch-JPJF
01UD Playmakers-2
01Upper Deck-2
Exclusives-2
01Upper Deck MVP-3
01Upper Deck Victory-11
Gold-11

01Upper Deck Vintage-2
01Vanguard-1
Blue-1
Red-1
One of Ones-1
Premiere Date-1
Proofs-1
02Atomic Jerseys-12
02Atomic Jerseys Gold-12
02Atomic Patches-12
02BAP First Edition-63
Jerseys-63
02BAP Memorabilia-62
Emerald-62
Ruby-62
Sapphire-62
NHL All-Star Game-62
NHL All-Star Game Blue-62
NHL All-Star Game Green-62
NHL All-Star Game Red-62
02BAP Memorabilia Toronto Fall Expo-62
02BAP Signature Series-109
Autographs-109
Autograph Buybacks 1998-267
Autograph Buybacks 1999-211
Autographs Gold-109
02Devils Team Issue-10
02O-Pee-Chee-73
02O-Pee-Chee Premier Blue Parallel-73
02O-Pee-Chee Premier Red Parallel-73
02O-Pee-Chee Factory Set-73
02Pacific-2
Blue-2
Red-2
02Pacific Complete-439
Red-439
02Pacific Exclusive-104
02Pacific Heads-Up Quad Jerseys-1
02Pacific Heads-Up Quad Jerseys Gold-1
02Pacific Quest for the Cup-58
Gold-58
02Parkhurst-133
Bronze-133
Gold-133
Silver-133
02Parkhurst Retro-153
Minis-153
02Private Stock Reserve-61
Blue-61
Red-61
Retail-61
02SP Authentic-55
Beckett Promos-55
02SP Game Used Authentic Fabrics-AFJF
02SP Game Used Authentic Fabrics Gold-AFJF
02SP Game Used Authentic Fabrics Rainbow-AFJF
02SP Game Used Tools of the Game-JF
02Stadium Club-108
Silver Decoy Cards-108
Proofs-108
02Topps-73
02Topps-73U
OPC Blue Parallel-73
OPC Red Parallel-73
Factory Set-73
02Topps Chrome-49
Black Border Refractors-49
Refractors-49
02Topps Heritage-158
02Topps Total-380
02UD Top Shelf-2
Dual Player Jerseys-STKF
Sweet Sweaters-SWJF
02Upper Deck-348
Exclusives-348
02Upper Deck Beckett UD Promos-348
02Upper Deck CHL Graduates-CGJF
02Upper Deck CHL Graduates Gold-CGJF
02Upper Deck Classic Portraits Headliners-KF
02Upper Deck Classic Portraits Headliners Limited-KF
02Upper Deck Classic Portraits Hockey Royalty-KFG
02Upper Deck Classic Portraits Hockey Royalty Limited-KFG
02Upper Deck Classic Portraits Stitches-CJF
02Upper Deck Classic Portraits Stitches Limited-CJF
02Upper Deck Victory-3
Bronze-3
Gold-3
Silver-3
03BAP Memorabilia Stanley Cup Champions-SCC-7
03Beehive-112
Gold-112
Silver-112
03Crown Royale-61
Blue-61
Retail-61
03Devils Team Issue-12
03ITG Action-315
03McDonald's Pacific Hockey Root Checklist-5
03NHL Sticker Collection-64
03O-Pee-Chee-238
03OPC Blue-238
03OPC Gold-238
03OPC Red-238
03Pacific-198
Blue-198
Red-198
03Pacific Calder-64
Silver-64
03Pacific Complete-378
Red-378
03Pacific Exhibit-85
Blue Backs-85
Yellow Backs-85
03Pacific Invincible-57
Blue-57
Red-57
Retail-57
03Private Stock Reserve-60
Blue-60
Red-60
Retail-60
03SP Game Used Game Gear-GGJF
03SPx Winning Materials-WM-JF
03SPx Winning Materials Limited-WM-JF
03Titanium-60
Hobby Jersey Number Parallels-60
Retail-60
Retail Jersey Number Parallels-60
03Topps-238
Blue-238
Gold-238
Red-238
03Upper Deck-112
Canadian Exclusives-112
HG-112
03Upper Deck MVP-250
Gold Script-250
Silver Script-250

Canadian Exclusives-250
03Czech Stadion-604
03Toronto Star-50
04Pacific-156
Blue-156
Red-156
04Upper Deck-103
Canadian Exclusives-103
HG Glossy Gold-103
HG Glossy Silver-103
05Black Diamond Jerseys-J-JF
05Black Diamond Jersey Ruby-J-JF
05Black Diamond Jersey Duals-DJ-JF
05Black Diamond Jersey Triples-TJ-JF
05Black Diamond Jersey Quads-QJ-JF
05Panini Stickers-185
05Parkhurst-11
Facsimile Auto Parallel-497
True Colors-TCWAS
True Colors-TCWAS
05SP Game Used Authentic Fabrics-AF-JF
05SP Game Used Authentic Fabrics Gold-AF-JF
05SP Game Used Authentic Patches-AP-JF
05SP Game Used Game Gear-GG-JF
05UD Artifacts-60
Blue-60
Gold-60
Green-60
Pewter-60
Red-60
Gold Autographed-60
05Ultra-198
Gold-198
Ice-198
05Upper Deck-116
05Upper Deck-435
HG Glossy-116
Jerseys-J-JF
Patches-P-JF
05Upper Deck Ice-99
Rainbow-99
05Upper Deck MVP-389
Gold-389
Platinum-389
05Upper Deck Toronto Fall Expo-116
05Upper Deck Victory-250
Black-250
Gold-250
Silver-250
06Black Diamond Jerseys-JJF
06Black Diamond Jerseys Black-JJF
06Black Diamond Jerseys Gold-JJF
06Black Diamond Jerseys Ruby-JJF
06Gatorade-13
06O-Pee-Chee-86
Rainbow-86
06Upper Deck-283
Exclusives Parallel-283
High Gloss Parallel-283
Game Jerseys-JJF
Game Patches-PJF
Masterpieces-283
06Upper Deck MVP-44
Gold Script-44
Super Script-44
Jerseys-OJJJ

Friesen, Karl
83Swedish Semic VM Stickers-103
89Swedish Semic World Champ Stickers-103
91Finnish Semic World Champ Stickers-154
91Swedish Semic World Champ Stickers-154
94German DEL-314
95German DEL-360

Friesen, Rob
94UK Guildford Flames-6

Friesen, Terry
95Swift Current Broncos-4
96Swift Current Broncos-1
97Swift Current Broncos-1
98Bowman CHL-62
Golden Anniversary-62
OPC International-62
98Bowman Chrome CHL-62
Golden Anniversary-62
Golden Anniversary Refractors-62
OPC International-62
OPC International Refractors-62
Refractors-62
00Fresno Falcons-7
00Fresno Falcons-21
01Fresno Falcons-5
02Fresno Falcons-17
03Fresno Falcons-4
04Columbus Cottonmouths-1
05Quad City Mallards-4

Friest, Ron
82North Stars Postcards-10

Frig, Len
74NHL Action Stamps-69
74O-Pee-Chee NHL-242
74Topps-242
75O-Pee-Chee NHL-174
75Topps-174
76O-Pee-Chee NHL-352
77O-Pee-Chee NHL-384

Frigon, Kyle
93Quebec Pee-Wee Tournament-724

Friis, Jarle
92Norwegian Elite Series-50

Friis, Martin
92Norwegian Elite Series-59

Friman, Jerry
92Swedish Semic Elitserien Stickers-96
93Swedish Semic Elitserien-68

Friman, Kari-Pekka
92Finnish Jyvas-Hyva Stickers-127
93Finnish Jyvas-Hyva Stickers-225
93Finnish SISU-190
93Finnish SISU-190B
94Finnish SISU-104
95Finnish SISU-175
95Finnish SISU-340

Frischmon, Trevor
00Lincoln Stars-20
01Lincoln Stars-9

Fritsche, Dan
03BAP Memorabilia-177
Emerald-177
Gold-177
Ruby-177
Sapphire-177
03BAP Ultimate Memorabilia Autographs-101
Gold-101
03BAP Ultimate Mem Auto Jerseys-101
03BAP Ultimate Mem Auto Emblems-101
03BAP Ultimate Mem Auto Numbers-101
03Beehive-210
Gold-210
Silver-210
03Black Diamond-161
Black-161
Green-161
Red-161
03Bowman-121
Gold-121
03Bowman Chrome-121
Refractors-121
Gold Refractors-121
Xfractors-121
03Crown Royale-112
Red-113
Retail-112
Retail-113
03ITG Action-627
03ITG Used Signature Series-146
Autographs Gold-146
03ITG VIP Rookie Debut-17
03Pacific Calder-111
Silver-111
03Pacific Complete-504
Red-504
03Pacific Heads-Up-110
Hobby LTD-110
Retail LTD-110
03Pacific Invincible-108
Blue-108
Red-108
Retail-108
03Pacific Luxury Suite-60
Gold-60
03Pacific Quest for the Cup-111
03Pacific Supreme-114
Blue-114
Red-114
Retail-114
03Parkhurst Rookie-177
Rookie Emblems-RE-19
Rookie Emblem Autographs-RE-DF
Rookie Emblems Gold-RE-19
Rookie Jerseys-RJ-19
Rookie Jersey Autographs-RJ-DF
Rookie Jerseys Gold-RJ-19
Rookie Numbers-RN-19
Rookie Number Autographs-RN-DF
Rookie Numbers Gold-RN-19
03Private Stock Reserve-114
Blue-114
Red-114
Retail-114
03SP Authentic-97
Limited-97
03SP Game Used-60
Gold-60
03SPx-191
Radiance-191
Spectrum-191
03Titanium-112
Hobby Jersey Number Parallels-112
Retail-112
Retail Jersey Number Parallels-112
03Topps Pristine-176
03Topps Pristine-177
03Topps Pristine-178
Gold Refractor Die Cuts-176
Gold Refractor Die Cuts-177
Gold Refractor Die Cuts-178
Refractors-176
Refractors-177
Refractors-178
Press Plates Black-176
Press Plates Black-177
Press Plates Black-178
Press Plates Cyan-176
Press Plates Cyan-177
Press Plates Cyan-178
Press Plates Magenta-176
Press Plates Magenta-177
Press Plates Magenta-178
Press Plates Yellow-176
Press Plates Yellow-177
Press Plates Yellow-178
03Topps Traded-TT101
Blue-TT101
Gold-TT101
Red-TT101
03UD Premier Collection-96
03Upper Deck-214
Canadian Exclusives-214
HG-214
03Upper Deck MVP-456
03Upper Deck Rookie Update-174
03Upper Deck Trilogy-149
Limited-149
03Sarnia Sting-8
04Pacific-279
Blue-279
Red-279
05Beehive Signature Scrapbook-SSDF
05Panini Stickers-239
05Parkhurst-147
Facsimile Auto Parallel-147
05SP Authentic Scripts to Success-SSDF
05SP Authentic Sign of the Times-DF
05Upper Deck-304
Notable Numbers-N-DF
05ITG Heroes/Prospects He Shoots/Scores-15
05ITG Heroes/Prospects He Shoots/Scores-26
05ITG Heroes and Prospects Memorial Cup-MC-5
06O-Pee-Chee-154
Rainbow-154
06ITG Heroes and Prospects-55
Autographs-ADF

Fritsche, John
95Swiss HNL-201
96Swiss HNL-90
98Swiss Power Play Stickers-19
99Swiss Panini Stickers-19
00Swiss Panini Stickers-18
00Swiss Slapshot Mini-Cards-HCAP12
01Swiss HNL-226
02Swiss HNL-197

Fritsche, Marc
96Swiss HNL-512

Fritsche, Tom
04Ohio State Buckeyes-18
05Ohio State Buckeyes-7
06Ohio State Buckeyes-19

Fritshaw, Luke
01Prince Albert Raiders-9
02Prince Albert Raiders-10
03Prince Albert Raiders-16
04Prince Albert Raiders-5
06Rockford IceHogs-10

Fritz, Beau
00Lincoln Stars-24
01Lincoln Stars-10

Fritz, George
94German DEL-430
95German DEL-397

Fritz, Mitch
98Kelowna Rockets-5
99Kelowna Rockets-11
01Columbus Cottonmouths-5
02Columbus Cottonmouths-5
03Columbus Cottonmouths-9
04Springfield Falcons-18
05Springfield Falcons-16
06Springfield Falcons-8

Fritz, Tommy
89Swedish Semic Elitserien Stickers-105
90Swedish Semic Elitserien Stickers-108
91Swedish Semic Elitserien Stickers-112
92Swedish Semic Elitserien Stickers-129

Fritzmeier, Franz
04German DEL-182
04German Krefeld Penguins Postcards-4
05German DEL-223
06German DEL-134

Frizzell, Billy
93Quebec Pee-Wee Tournament-1212

Frkan, Jan
96Slovakian Quebec Pee-Wee Tournament-7

Froese, Bob
78Saginaw Gears-5
83Flyers J.C. Penney-10
83NHL Key Tags-98
83O-Pee-Chee-265
83O-Pee-Chee Stickers-183
83Topps Stickers-183
84O-Pee-Chee-159
84O-Pee-Chee Stickers-113
84Topps-117
85Flyers Postcards-10
86O-Pee-Chee-55
86O-Pee-Chee-263
86O-Pee-Chee-264
86O-Pee-Chee Stickers-182
86O-Pee-Chee Stickers-186
86O-Pee-Chee Stickers-193
86O-Pee-Chee Stickers-236
86Topps-55
86Topps Sticker Inserts-7
87O-Pee-Chee-195
87Topps-195
88Panini Stickers-299
89Panini Stickers-284
89Rangers Marine Midland Bank-33

Froese, Colin
91Air Canada SJHL-E13
92Saskatchewan JHL-37

Froese, Jeff
01OCN Blizzard-6

Frogren, Jonas
00Swedish Upper Deck-78
02Swedish SHL-25
Parallel-25
03Swedish Elite-180
Silver-180
04Swedish Elitset-37
Gold-37
05Swedish SHL Elitset-40
06Swedish SHL Elitset-43

Froh, David
93Oshawa Generals-5
95Slapshot-192

Frohlich, Thomas
94German First League-118

Frohlicher, Joel
01Swiss HNL-114

Frolik, Martin
03Czech OFS Plus-218
04Czech OFS-50
05Czech HC Kladno-2
06Czech HC Kladno Postcards-4
06Czech OFS-251

Frolik, Michael
04Czech OFS-51
05ITG Heroes/Prosp Toronto Expo Parallel -428
05ITG Ultimate Mem Future Stars Autos-20
05ITG Ultimate Mem Future Star Autos Gold-20
05Czech HC Kladno-3
05ITG Heroes and Prospects-428
Autographs Update-A-MF
He Shoots-He Scores Prizes-48
06ITG International Ice-37
Gold-37
Autographs-AMF
Complete Jersey-CJ10
Complete Jersey Gold-CJ10
Cornerstones-IC05
Cornerstones Gold-IC05
Passing The Torch-PTT16
Passing The Torch Gold-PTT16
06ITG Ultimate Memorabilia Future Star Autos-24
06ITG Ultimate Memorabilia Future Star Autos Gold-24
06ITG Ultimate Memorabilia Future Star Patches Autos-24
06ITG Ultimate Memorabilia Future Star Patches Autos Gold-24
06Rimouski Oceanic-21
06ITG Heroes and Prospects-138
06ITG Heroes and Prospects-178
Autographs-AMF
Autographs-AMF2
Class of 2006-CL06
Complete Jerseys-CJ08
Complete Jerseys Gold-CJ08
Update Autographs-AMF2

Frolikov, Alexei
90O-Pee-Chee-502

Frolkin, Andrei
00Russian Hockey League-281
02Russian Hockey League-42

Frolo, Tomas
02Czech OFS Plus-367
03Czech OFS Plus-305
04Czech OFS-247
06Czech OFS-155

Frolov, Alexander
00Russian Hockey League-63
01SPx Rookie Redemption-R14
01Russian Young Lions-7
02Atomic-112
Blue-112
Gold-112
Red-112
Hobby Parallel-112
02BAP All-Star Edition-148
Gold-148
Silver-148
02BAP First Edition-434H
02BAP Memorabilia-287
Emerald-287
Ruby-287
Sapphire-287
NHL All-Star Game-287
NHL All-Star Game Blue-287
NHL All-Star Game Green-287
NHL All-Star Game Red-287
02BAP Memorabilia Toronto Fall Expo-287
02BAP Signature Series-192
Autographs-192
Autographs Gold-192
Jerseys-SGJ63
Jersey Autographs-SGJ63
Team Quads-TQ10
02BAP Ultimate Memorabilia-17
Autographs-1
Autographs Gold-1
Calder Candidates-9
02Bowman YoungStars-124
Gold-124
Silver-124
Autographs-AF
Jerseys-AF
Patches-AF
Double Stuff-AF
Triple Stuff-AF
Rivals-AFAS
Rivals Patches-12
Sticks-AF
02Crown Royale-118
Blue-118
Purple-118
Red-118
Retail-118
Rookie Royalty-13
02ITG Used-192
Calder Jerseys-C16
Calder Jerseys Gold-C16
02Kings Game Sheets-33
02Kings Game Sheets-34
02O-Pee-Chee-333
02O-Pee-Chee Premier Blue Parallel-333
02O-Pee-Chee Premier Red Parallel-333
02O-Pee-Chee Factory Set-333
02Pacific-408
02Pacific Calder-122
Silver-122
Reflections-14
02Pacific Complete-579
Red-579
02Pacific Exclusive-199
Blue-199
Gold-199
02Pacific Heads-Up-135
02Pacific Quest for the Cup-123
Gold-123
02Parkhurst-217
Bronze-217
Gold-217
Silver-217
02Parkhurst Retro-217
Minis-217
Hopefuls-CH5
02Private Stock Reserve-164
Blue-164
Red-164
Retail-164
Moments in Time-5
02SP Authentic-188
Sign of the Times-AF
Signed Patches-PAF
02SP Game Used-79
Signature Style-AF
02SPx-161
02Stadium Club-123
Silver Decoy Cards-123
Proofs-123
02Titanium-118
Blue-118
Red-118
Retail-118
Right on Target-12
02Topps-333
OPC Blue Parallel-333
OPC Red Parallel-333
Factory Set-333
02Topps Chrome-181
Black Border Refractors-181
Refractors-181
02Topps Heritage-133
02Topps Total-416
02UD Artistic Impressions-121
Gold-121
Common Ground-CG10
Common Ground Gold-CG10
Retrospectives-R99
Retrospectives Gold-R99
Retrospectives Signed-R99
Retrospectives Silver-R99
Right Track-RTAF
Right Track Gold-RTAF
02UD Foundations-155
02UD Honor Roll-154
02UD Mask Collection-161
02UD Piece of History-133
02UD Premier Collection-101
Gold-101
02UD Top Shelf-129
02Upper Deck-238
Exclusives-238
02Upper Deck Classic Portraits-117
02Upper Deck Rookie Update-159A
02Upper Deck Rookie Update-159B
02Upper Deck Rookie Update-159C
02Vanguard-117
LTD-117
Prime Prospects-13
03BAP Memorabilia-6
Emerald-6
Gold-6
Ruby-6
Sapphire-6
Future of the Game-FG-7
03BAP Ultimate Memorabilia Autographs-5
Gold-5
03BAP Ultimate Mem Franch Present Future-14
03Beehive-88
Gold-88
Silver-88
03Black Diamond-140
Black-140
Green-140
Red-140
Signature Gems-SG-32
Threads-DT-AF
Threads Green-DT-AF
Threads Red-DT-AF
Threads Black-DT-AF
03Bowman-107
Gold-107
Future Fabrics-FF-AF
Future Fabric Patches-AF
Future Rivals-JF
Future Rivals Patches-JF
03Bowman Chrome-107
Refractors-107
Gold Refractors-107
Xfractors-107
03ITG Action-268
Jerseys-M129
03ITG Used Signature Series-3
Gold-3
Autographs-AF
Autographs Gold-AF
03ITG VIP Sophomores-8
03O-Pee-Chee-223
03OPC Blue-223
03OPC Gold-223
03OPC Red-223
03Pacific-155
Blue-155
Red-155
03Pacific Calder-49
Silver-49
03Pacific Calder Collection NHL All-Star Block Party Gold-7
03Pacific Complete-249
Red-249
03Pacific Exhibit-69
Blue Backs-69
Yellow Backs-69
03Pacific Invincible New Sensations-14
03Pacific Montreal Olympic Stadium Show-6
Gold-6
03Pacific Prism-49
Blue-49
Gold-49
Red-49
Paramount Prodigies-13
Rookie Revolution-9
03Pacific Quest for the Cup-50
Blue-50
03Pacific Supreme-45
Blue-45
Red-45
Retail-45
03Parkhurst Rookie Teammates Gold-RT7
03Parkhurst Rookie Teammates-RT7
03Private Stock Reserve-47
Blue-47
Red-47
Retail-47
03SP Authentic Sign of the Times-AF
03SP Game Used Authentic Fabrics-AFAF
03SP Game Used Authentic Fabrics-DFBT
03SP Game Used Authentic Fabrics Gold-AFAF
03SP Game Used Authentic Fabrics Gold-DFBT
03SPx-45
03SPx-168
Radiance-45
Radiance-168
Spectrum-45
Spectrum-168
Big Futures-BF-AF
Big Futures Limited-BF-AF
Signature Threads-ST-AF
VIP-VIP-PF
VIP Limited-VIP-PF
03Titanium-46
Hobby Jersey Number Parallels-46
Retail-46
Retail Jersey Number Parallels-46
03Topps-223
Blue-223
Gold-223
Red-223
03Topps C55-121
Minis-121
Minis American Back-121
Minis American Back Red-121
Minis Bazooka Back-121
Minis Brooklyn Back-121
Minis Hat Trick Back-121
Minis O Canada Back-121
Minis O Canada Back Red-121
Minis Stanley Cup Back-121
03Topps Pristine-82
Gold Refractor Die Cuts-82
Refractors-82
Press Plates Black-82
Press Plates Cyan-82
Press Plates Magenta-82
Press Plates Yellow-82
03Topps Traded Future Phenoms-FP-AF
03UD Honor Roll-36
03UD Honor Roll-99
03Upper Deck-87
BuyBacks-179
BuyBacks-180
Canadian Exclusives-87
HG-87
Jerseys-UD-AF
03Upper Deck All-Star Promos-S4
03Upper Deck All-Star Promos-AS8
03Upper Deck Classic Portraits-44
03Upper Deck MVP-193
Gold Script-193
Silver Script-193
Canadian Exclusives-193
03Upper Deck Rookie Update Super Stars-SSAF
03Upper Deck Trilogy-44
Limited-44
03Upper Deck Victory-84
Bronze-84
Gold-84
Silver-84
03Russian World Championship Team 2003-3
03Toronto Star-43
04Pacific-121
Blue-121
Red-121
04SP Authentic-42
Limited-42
Buybacks-10
Buybacks-11
Rookie Review-RR-AF
Sign of the Times-ST-FR
Sign of the Times-TS-PBF
Sign of the Times-FS-PAC
04UD All-World-30
Gold-30
Autographs-30
Dual Autographs-AD-AF
Dual Autographs-AD-FZ
Triple Autographs-AT-ZFA
Quad Autographs-AQ-YFW
Five Autographs-AF-YGN
Six Autographs-AS-RUS
04Upper Deck Jersey Autographs-GJA-AF
04Russian Back to Russia-1
05Be A Player-43
First Period-43
Second Period-43
Third Period-43
Overtime-43
05Black Diamond-38
Emerald-38
Gold-38
Onyx-38
Ruby-38
05Hot Prospects-45
En Fuego-45
Red Hot-45
White Hot-45
05Kings Team Issue-6
05Panini Stickers-285
05Parkhurst-221
Facsimile Auto Parallel-221
True Colors-TCLAK
True Colors-TCLAK
True Colors-TCSJLA
True Colors-TCSJLA
05SP Authentic-47
Limited-47
Scripts to Success-SSAF
Sign of the Times-AF
05SP Game Used-48
Autographs-48
Gold-48
Authentic Fabrics-AF-AF
Authentic Fabrics Autographs-AAF-AF
Authentic Fabrics Dual-BF
Authentic Fabrics Gold-AF-AF
Authentic Fabrics Quad-FRRG
Authentic Patches Quad -FRRG
Authentic Patches-AP-AF
Authentic Patches Autographs-AAP-AF
Authentic Patches Dual-BF
Auto Draft-AD-AF
Awesome Authentics-AA-AF
SIGnificance-AF
SIGnificance Gold-S-AF
SIGnificance Extra-FB
SIGnificance Extra Gold-FB
Significant Numbers-SN-AF
Statscriptions-ST-AF
05SPx-40
Spectrum-40
Winning Combos-WC-BF
Winning Combos Autographs-AWC-BF
Winning Combos Gold-WC-BF
Winning Combos Spectrum-WC-BF
Winning Materials-WM-AF
Winning Materials Autographs-AWM-AF
Winning Materials Gold-WM-AF
Winning Materials Spectrum-WM-AF
05The Cup Emblems of Endorsement-EEAF
05The Cup Masterpiece Pressplate Auto-269
05The Cup Scripted Swatches-SSAF
05The Cup Signature Patches-SPAF
05UD Artifacts-46
Blue-46
Gold-46
Green-46
Pewter-46
Red-46
Auto Facts-AF-AF
Auto Facts Blue-AF-AF
Auto Facts Copper-AF-AF
Auto Facts Pewter-AF-AF
Auto Facts Silver-AF-AF
Frozen Artifacts-FA-AF
Frozen Artifacts Autographed-FA-AF
Frozen Artifacts Copper-FA-AF
Frozen Artifacts Dual-FAD-AF
Frozen Artifacts Dual Autographed-FAD-AF
Frozen Artifacts Dual Copper-FAD-AF
Frozen Artifacts Dual Gold-FAD-AF
Frozen Artifacts Dual Maroon-FAD-AF
Frozen Artifacts Dual Pewter-FAD-AF
Frozen Artifacts Dual Silver-FAD-AF
Frozen Artifacts Gold-FA-AF
Frozen Artifacts Maroon-FA-AF
Frozen Artifacts Patches-FP-AF
Frozen Artifacts Patches Autographed-FP-AF
Frozen Artifacts Patches Dual-FPD-AF
Frozen Artifacts Patches Dual Autos-FPD-AF
Frozen Artifacts Patches Pewter-FP-AF
Frozen Artifacts Patches Silver-FP-AF
Frozen Artifacts Pewter-FA-AF
Frozen Artifacts Silver-FA-AF
Gold Autographed-46
Remarkable Artifacts-RA-AF
Remarkable Artifacts Dual-RA-AF
05UD Toronto Fall Expo Priority Signings-PS-AF
05Ultimate Coll National Heroes Jersey-NHJAF
05Ultimate Coll National Heroes Patch-NHPAF
05Ultra-97
Gold-97
Ice-97
05Upper Deck-335
Big Playmakers-B-AF
Jerseys Series II-J2AF
Majestic Materials-MMAF
Notable Numbers-N-FR
Patches-P-ALF
05Upper Deck Ice-46
Rainbow-46
Fresh Ice-FIAF
Fresh Ice Glass Patches-FIPAF
Glacial Graphs-GGAF
05Upper Deck MVP-184
Gold-184
Platinum-184
05Upper Deck Rookie Update-44
05Upper Deck Rookie Update-269
05Upper Deck Trilogy Honorary Patches-HP-AF
05Upper Deck Tril Honorary Patch Script-HSP-AF
05Upper Deck Trilogy Honorary Swatches-HS-AF
05Upper Deck Tril Honorary Swatch Scripts-HSS-AF
05Upper Deck Trilogy Scripts-SFS-AF
06Be A Player-125
Autographs-125
Profiles-PP30
Profiles Autographs-PP30
Signatures-AF
Signatures 10-139
Signatures Trios-TFCO
Signatures Foursomes-FOFKF
06Be A Player Portraits-52
06Beehive-55
06Beehive-196
Blue-55
Gold-55
Matte-55
Red Facsimile Signatures-55
Wood-55
Matted Materials-MMAF
Remarkable Matted Materials-MMAF
Signature Scrapbook-SSAF
06Black Diamond-107
Black-107
Gold-107
Ruby-107
Jerseys-JAF
Jerseys Black-JAF
Jerseys Gold-JAF
Jerseys Ruby-JAF
Jerseys Black Autographs -JAF
06Flair Showcase-50
06Flair Showcase-134
Parallel-50
Parallel-134
Inks-IAF
Wave of the Future-WF18
06Fleer-89
Tiffany-89
Fabricology-FAF
Signing Day-SDAF
06Hot Prospects-47
Red Hot-47
White Hot-47
Hotagraphs-HAF
06McDonald's Upper Deck-21
06O-Pee-Chee-224
Rainbow-224
Swatches-S-AF
06Panini Stickers-280
06SP Authentic-57
06SP Authentic-102
Chirography-AF
Limited-57
Limited-102
Sign of the Times-STAF
Sign of the Times Duals-STFK
06SP Game Used-47
Gold-47
Rainbow-47
Authentic Fabrics-AFAF
Authentic Fabrics Parallel-AFAF
Authentic Fabrics Patches-AFAF
Authentic Fabrics Dual-AF2BF
Authentic Fabrics Dual Patches-AF2BF
Authentic Fabrics Triple-AF3LAK
Authentic Fabrics Triple Patches-AF3LAK
Autographs-47
Inked Sweaters-ISAF
Inked Sweaters Patches-ISAF
Inked Sweaters Dual-IS2FC
Inked Sweaters Dual Patches-IS2FC
Letter Marks-LMAF
SIGnificance-SAF
06SPx-46
Spectrum-46
SPxcitement-X47
SPxcitement Spectrum-X47
SPxcitement Autographs-X47
Winning Materials-WMAF
Winning Materials Spectrum-WMAF
Winning Materials Autographs-WMAF
06The Cup Autographed NHL Shields Duals-DASFK
06The Cup Limited Logos-LLAF
06The Cup Signature Patches-SPAF
06UD Artifacts-54
06UD Artifacts-173
Blue-54
Blue-173
Gold-54
Gold-173
Platinum-54
Platinum-173
Radiance-54
Radiance-173
Autographed Radiance Parallel-54
Autographed Radiance Parallel-173
Red-54
Red-173
Treasured Patches Black-TSAF
Treasured Patches Blue-TSAF
Treasured Patches Gold-TSAF
Treasured Patches Platinum-TSAF
Treasured Patches Red-TSAF
Treasured Patches Autographed Black Tag Parallel-TSAF
Treasured Swatches-TSAF
Treasured Swatches Black-TSAF
Treasured Swatches Blue-TSAF
Treasured Swatches Gold-TSAF
Treasured Swatches Platinum-TSAF
Treasured Swatches Red-TSAF
Treasured Swatches Autographed Black-TSAF
Tundra Tandems-TTFB
Tundra Tandems Black-TTFB
Tundra Tandems Blue-TTFB
Tundra Tandems Gold-TTFB
Tundra Tandems Platinum-TTFB
Tundra Tandems Red-TTFB
Tundra Tandems Dual Patches Red-TTFB
06UD Mini Jersey Collection-50
Jerseys-AF
Jersey Variations-AF
Jersey Autographs-AF
06UD Powerplay-46
Impact Rainbow-46
Specialists-SAF
Specialists Patches-PAF
06Ultimate Collection Autographed Jerseys-AJ-AF
06Ultimate Collection Autographed Patches-AJ-AF
06Ultimate Collection Premium Patches-PS-AF
06Ultimate Collection Premium Swatches-PS-AF
06Ultra-90
Gold Medallion-90
Ice Medallion-90
06Upper Deck Arena Giveaways-LAK1
06Upper Deck-90
Exclusives Parallel-90
High Gloss Parallel-90
Game Jerseys-JAF
Generations Duals-G2FK
Masterpieces-90
Shootout Artists-SA8
Signature Sensations-SSAF
Walmart Tins Oversize-90
06Upper Deck MVP-132
Gold Script-132
Super Script-132
Autographs-OAFC
Jerseys-OJFN
Jerseys-OJSF
06Upper Deck Ovation-122
06Upper Deck Sweet Shot-51
Signature Shots/Saves-SSAF
Signature Shots/Saves Sticks-SSSAF
Sweet Stitches-SSAF
Sweet Stitches Duals-SSAF
Sweet Stitches Triples-SSAF
06Upper Deck Trilogy-47
Combo Clearcut Autographs-C3FCB
Honorary Scripted Patches-HSPAF
Honorary Scripted Swatches-HSSAF
Scripts-TSAF
06Upper Deck Victory-91
06Upper Deck Victory Black-91
06Upper Deck Victory Gold-91
06Upper Deck Victory GameBreakers-GB21
06Upper Deck Victory Next In Line-NL25
06Upper Deck Victory Oversize Cards-AF
06Russian Torino Olympic Team-18
07Upper Deck Victory-194
Black-194
Gold-194

Frolov, Anatoli
74Swedish Stickers-48

Frolov, Dmitri
90O-Pee-Chee-523
92Upper Deck-348
94Finnish Jaa Kiekko-151
95Finnish Semic World Championships-130
96German DEL-210
98Russian Hockey League-165

Frolov, Konstantin
99Russian Hockey League-206

From, Marko
98Finnish Keraílysarja-31
99Finnish Cardset-22

Frosch, Dusan
03German DEL-51

Frosch, Frantisek
94German DEL-428
95German DEL-391
96German DEL-76
98German DEL-35
99German Bundesliga 2-125

Frutel, Christian
94German DEL-315

Fry, Curtis
92British Columbia JHL-51
99German DEL-247

Fry, David
02Fort Worth Brahmas-3

Fry, Matt
93Quebec Pee-Wee Tournament-509

Fry, Rick
89Portland Winter Hawks-8

Fryar, Mike
95North Iowa Huskies-9

Frycer, Miroslav
81Nordiques Postcards-7
81Swedish Semic Hockey VM Stickers-65
82Maple Leafs Postcards-11
82Maple Leafs Postcards-12
82O-Pee-Chee-321
82O-Pee-Chee Stickers-65
82Post Cereal-18
82Topps Stickers-65
83Maple Leafs Postcards-6
83NHL Key Tags-116
83O-Pee-Chee-330
83O-Pee-Chee Stickers-38
83Topps Stickers-38
83Vachon-86
84Maple Leafs Postcards-9
85Maple Leafs Postcards-12
85O-Pee-Chee-198
85O-Pee-Chee Stickers-21
86Maple Leafs Postcards-10
86O-Pee-Chee-68
86O-Pee-Chee Stickers-142
86Topps-68
87Maple Leafs PLAY-15
87Maple Leafs Postcards-7
87Maple Leafs Postcards Oversized-7
87O-Pee-Chee Stickers-158
88Oilers Tenth Anniversary-153
88Oilers Team Issue-6

Frydl, Karel
96Czech APS Extraliga-104

Fryia, Shanye
00Barrie Colts-10

Frykbo, Anders
86Swedish Panini Stickers-266
89Swedish Semic Elitserien Stickers-233
90Swedish Semic Elitserien Stickers-72
91Swedish Semic Elitserien Stickers-245

Frylen, Edvin
92Swedish Semic Elitserien Stickers-280
92Swedish Semic Elitserien Stickers-351
93Parkhurst-536
Emerald Ice-536
93Upper Deck-572
93Swedish Semic Elitserien-245
94Swedish Leaf-105
NHL Draft-5
94Signature Rookies Gold Standard *-85
95Swedish Leaf-299
95Swedish Upper Deck-188
95Signature Rookies-17
Signatures-17
97Swedish Collector's Choice-184
Select-UD15
99Swedish Upper Deck-120
00Swedish Upper Deck-47
02German DEL City Press-109
03German DEL-125
04German DEL-149
04German Hannover Scorpions Postcards-8
06Swedish SHL Elitset-96

Frysztacki, Andreas
94German First League-366

Fryzlewicz, Piotr
93Quebec Pee-Wee Tournament-1505

Fryzlewicz, Stanislav
73Finnish Jaakiekko-90

Ftorek, Robbie
74Phoenix Roadrunners WHA Pins-4
75O-Pee-Chee WHA-19
75Phoenix Roadrunners WHA-7
76O-Pee-Chee WHA-13
76Phoenix Roadrunners WHA-3
77O-Pee-Chee WHA-35
79O-Pee-Chee-267
80Nordiques Postcards-10
80O-Pee-Chee-35
80Pepsi-Cola Caps-65
80Topps-35
81O-Pee-Chee-274
81O-Pee-Chee Stickers-72
81Post Standups-24
82O-Pee-Chee-223
82Post Cereal-13
83O-Pee-Chee-244
88Kings Postcards-21
88Kings Smokey-10
89Halifax Citadels-7
89ProCards AHL-157
90Nordiques Petro-Canada-8
92Future Trends '76 Canada Cup-189
96Devils Team Issue-NNO
97Devils Team Issue-29
98Devils Team Issue-12
99Devils Team Issue-25
04ITG Franchises Canadian-81
Autographs-RFT
04Albany River Rats-25
05Albany River Rats-28

Ftorek, Sam
02Greensboro Generals RBI-9

Fuchs, Andrej

94German DEL-351
95German DEL-323
96German DEL-101
99German DEL-298

Fuchs, Boris
94German DEL-356
95German DEL-326
96German DEL-103
99German DEL-308

Fuchs, Lothar
70Finnish Jaakiekko-84
70Swedish Hockey-375

Fuchs, Regis
93Swiss HNL-73
95Swiss HNL-97
96Swiss HNL-39
98Swiss Power Play Stickers-169
99Swiss Panini Stickers-170
00Swiss Panini Stickers-213
00Swiss Slapshot Mini-Cards-HCL14
01Swiss HNL-41
02Swiss HNL-87

Fuder, Jordan
04Regina Pats-21
05Regina Pats-6

Fugere, Boby
06Quebec Remparts-16

Fugere, Claude
93Swiss HNL-263

Fugere, Nick
01Hull Olympiques-11
02Hull Olympiques-11
03Gatineau Olympiques-11
03Hull Olympiques Memorial Cup-7
04Gatineau Olympiques-10
05Gatineau Olympiques-4

Fuher, Nick
00Lincoln Stars-9
03North Dakota Fighting Sioux-30
04North Dakota Fighting Sioux-7

Fuhr, Grant
81Oilers Red Rooster-1
81Oilers West Edmonton Mall-2
82Oilers Red Rooster-31
82O-Pee-Chee-105
82O-Pee-Chee Stickers-95
82O-Pee-Chee Stickers-161
82Post Cereal-6
82Topps Stickers-95
82Topps Stickers-161
82Victoria Cougars-8
83Oilers McDonald's-19
83O-Pee-Chee-27
83Vachon-24
84Oilers Red Rooster-31
84Oilers Team Issue-5
84O-Pee-Chee-241
84O-Pee-Chee Stickers-259
85Oilers Red Rooster-31
85O-Pee-Chee-207
85O-Pee-Chee Stickers-221
86Kraft Drawings-17
86Oilers Red Rooster-31
86Oilers Team Issue-31
86O-Pee-Chee-56
86O-Pee-Chee Stickers-67
86O-Pee-Chee Stickers-121
86Topps-56
87Oilers Team Issue-31
87O-Pee-Chee-178
87O-Pee-Chee Stickers-85
87Panini Stickers-254
87Topps-178
88Esso All-Stars-12
88Oilers Tenth Anniversary-65
88Oilers Tenth Anniversary-130
88Oilers Team Issue-7
88O-Pee-Chee-59
88O-Pee-Chee Minis-9
88O-Pee-Chee Stickers-122
88O-Pee-Chee Stickers-212
88O-Pee-Chee Stickers-223
88Panini Stickers-52
88Panini Stickers-188
88Panini Stickers-403
88Topps-59
88Topps Sticker Inserts-6
89Kraft-11
89Oilers Team Issue-6
89O-Pee-Chee-192
89O-Pee-Chee Stickers-228
89Sports Illustrated for Kids I-143
89Topps-192
89Swedish Semic World Champ Stickers-53
90Bowman-189
Tiffany-189
90O-Pee-Chee-321
90Panini Stickers-230
90Pro Set-82
90Score-275
Canadian-275
90Topps-321
Tiffany-321
90Upper Deck-264
French-264
91Pro Set Platinum-117
91Bowman-111
91Bowman-407
91Gillette-19
91Kraft-9
91Maple Leafs PLAY-13
91O-Pee-Chee-84
91OPC Premier-100
91OPC Premier-191
91Parkhurst-175
French-175
91Pinnacle-168
French-168
91Pro Set-78
91Pro Set-494
French-78
French-494
Puck Candy-27
91Score American-114
91Score Canadian Bilingual-114
91Score Canadian Bilingual-608
91Score Canadian English-114
91Score Canadian English-608
91Score Rookie/Traded-58T
91Stadium Club-258
91Topps-84
91Upper Deck-264
91Upper Deck-553
French-264
French-553
92Bowman-114
92Humpty Dumpty I-9
92Kraft-35
92Maple Leafs Kodak-24
92O-Pee-Chee-31
92O-Pee-Chee-119
25th Anniv. Inserts-15
92Panini Stickers-75
92Panini Stickers French-75
92Parkhurst Previews-PV5
92Parkhurst-182
92Parkhurst-250
92Parkhurst-497
Emerald Ice-182
Emerald Ice-250
Emerald Ice-497
92Pinnacle-267
92Pinnacle-301
French-267
French-301
92Pro Set-183
92Score-20
92Score-437
Canadian-20
Canadian-437
92Seasons Patches-54
92Stadium Club-412
92Topps-350
Gold-350G
92Ultra-210
92Upper Deck-271
93SLU Hockey American-3
93Donruss-34
93High Liner Greatest Goalies-3
93Kenner Starting Lineup Cards-3
93Leaf-66
Painted Warriors-5
93OPC Premier-218
Gold-218
93Panini Stickers-108
93Parkhurst-22
Emerald Ice-22
Cherry's Playoff Heroes-D7
93Pinnacle-65
Canadian-65
Masks-1
93PowerPlay-27
Netminders-3
93Sabres Noco-4
93Score-75
Canadian-75
93Stadium Club-260
Members Only Master Set-260
First Day Issue-260
Master Photos-15
Master Photos Winners-15
93Topps/OPC Premier-218
Gold-218
93Ultra-103
93Upper Deck-163
Gretzky's Great Ones-GG10
SP-15
94SLU Hockey Canadian-3
94Hockey Canadian-3
94Be A Player 99 All-Stars-G7
94Canada Games NHL POGS-273
94Canada Games NHL POGS-333
94Donruss-212
94EA Sports-18
94Finest Ring Leaders-4
94Hockey Wit-40
94Kenner Starting Lineup Cards-5
94Leaf-78
94OPC Premier-80
94Pinnacle-421
Artist's Proofs-421
Rink Collection-421
94Select-93
Gold-93
94Topps/OPC Premier-80
94Ultra-262
95Be A Player-196
Signatures-S196
Signatures Die Cuts-S196
95Bowman-25
All-Foil-25
95Canada Games NHL POGS-8
95Canada Games NHL POGS-245
95Donruss-310
95Donruss Elite-42
Die Cut Stars-42
Die Cut Uncut-42
Painted Warriors-9
Painted Warriors-P9
95Finest-113
Refractors-113
95Kraft-28
95Metal-123
95No Fear Ad Cards-1
95Parkhurst International-443
Emerald Ice-443
Parkie's Trophy Picks-PP9
Parkie's Trophy Picks-PP34
95Score-228
Black Ice Artist's Proofs-228
Black Ice-228
95SP-126
95Stadium Club-24
Members Only Master Set-24
95Topps-242
OPC Inserts-242
95Topps SuperSkills-88
Platinum-88
95Ultra-298
95Upper Deck-484
Electric Ice-484
Electric Ice Gold-484
Special Edition-SE158
Special Edition Gold-SE158
95Zenith-107
96Be A Player Stacking the Pads-9
96Black Diamond-128
Gold-128
96Blues Dispatch 30th Anniversary-1
96Collector's Choice-224
96Donruss-117
Press Proofs-117
96Donruss Canadian Ice-109
96Donruss Canadian Ice-148
Gold Press Proofs-109
Gold Press Proofs-148
Red Press Proofs-109
Red Press Proofs-148
96Donruss Elite-29
Die Cut Stars-29
Perspective-12
96Flair-80
Blue Ice-80
96Fleer-96
96Leaf-64
Press Proofs-64
96Leaf Limited-48
Gold-48
96Maggers-27
96Metal Universe-131
96NHL Aces Playing Cards-16
96Pinnacle-181
Artist's Proofs-181
Foil-181
Premium Stock-181
Rink Collection-181
96Score-91
Artist's Proofs-91
Dealer's Choice Artist's Proofs-91
Special Artist's Proofs-91
Golden Blades-91
96Select Certified-35
Artist's Proofs-35
Blue-35
Mirror Blue-35
Mirror Gold-35
Mirror Red-35
Red-35
96SkyBox Impact-112
96SP-133
SPx Holoview Heroes-HH10
96Summit-14
Artist's Proofs-14
Ice-14
Metal-14
Premium Stock-14
96Team Out-66
96Topps Picks Ice D-ID15
96Ultra-145
Gold Medallion-145
96Upper Deck-140
Generation Next-X33
96Upper Deck Ice-62
Parallel-62
96Zenith-82
Artist's Proofs-82
Champion Salute-3
Champion Salute-P3
Champion Salute Diamond-3
97Headliners Hockey-7
97Beehive-44
Golden Portraits-44
97Black Diamond-148
Double Diamond-148
Triple Diamond-148
Quadruple Diamond-148
97Collector's Choice-225
97Crown Royale-116
Emerald Green-116
Ice Blue-116
Silver-116
Freeze Out Die-Cuts-17
97Donruss-153
Press Proofs Silver-153
Press Proofs Gold-153
97Donruss Canadian Ice-95
Dominion Series-95
Provincial Series-95
97Donruss Elite-110
Aspirations-110
Status-110
97Donruss Limited-32
Exposure-32
Fabric of the Game-45
97Donruss Preferred-60
Cut to the Chase-60
97Donruss Priority-82
Stamp of Approval-82
Postmaster General-19
Postmaster Generals Promos-19
97Gatorade Stickers-5
97Katch-128
Gold-128
Silver-128
97Leaf-123
Fractal Matrix-123
Fractal Matrix Die Cuts-123
97Leaf International-123
Universal Ice-123
97Pacific-228
Copper-228
Emerald Green-228
Ice Blue-228
Red-228
Silver-228
In The Cage Laser Cuts-18
97Pacific Dynagon-106
Copper-106
Dark Grey-106
Emerald Green-106
Ice Blue-106
Red-106
Silver-106
Stonewallers-19
Tandems-18
97Pacific Invincible-119
Copper-119
Emerald Green-119
Ice Blue-119
Red-119
Silver-119
97Pacific Omega-193
Copper-193
Dark Gray-193
Emerald Green-193
Gold-193
Ice Blue-193
97Panini Stickers-172
97Paramount-158
Copper-158
Dark Grey-158
Emerald Green-158
Ice Blue-158
Red-158
Silver-158
Glove Side Laser Cuts-18
97Pinnacle-81
Artist's Proofs-81
Rink Collection-81
Press Plates Back Black-81
Press Plates Back Cyan-81
Press Plates Back Magenta-81
Press Plates Back Yellow-81
Press Plates Front Black-81
Press Plates Front Cyan-81
Press Plates Front Magenta-81
Press Plates Front Yellow-81
Masks-10
Masks Die Cuts-10
Masks Jumbos-10
Tins-2
97Pinnacle Certified-10
Red-10
Mirror Blue-10
Mirror Gold-10
Mirror Red-10
97Pinnacle Inside-51
Coach's Collection-51
Executive Collection-51
Stand Up Guys-6A/B
Stand Up Guys-6C/D
Stand Up Guys Promos-6A/B
Stand Up Guys Promos-6C/D
Stoppers-20
97Pinnacle Tot Cert Platinum Blue-10
97Pinnacle Tot Certi Platinum Gold-10
97Pinnacle Totally Certified Platinum Red-10
97Pinnacle Tot Cert Mirror Platinum Gold-10
97Revolution-120
Copper-120
Emerald-120
Ice Blue-120
Silver-120
Return to Sender Die-Cuts-17
97Score-5
Artist's Proofs-5
Golden Blades-5
Net Worth-10
97Score Blues-11
Platinum-11
Premier-11
97SP Authentic-143
Sign of the Times-GF
97Studio-102
Press Proofs Silver-102
Press Proofs Gold-102
97Upper Deck-145
97Zenith-60
Z-Gold-60
Z-Silver-60
97Zenith 5 x 7-14
Gold Impulse-14
Silver Impulse-14
98Headliners Hockey In the Crease-2
98NHL Pro Zone-30
98SLU Hockey Extended-62
98Aurora-160
Championship Fever-41
Championship Fever Copper-41
Championship Fever Ice Blue-41
Championship Fever Red-41
Championship Fever Silver-41
98Be A Player-122
Press Release-122
98BAP Gold-122
98BAP Autographs-122
98BAP Autographs Gold-122
98BAP Tampa Bay All Star Game-122
98Bowman's Best-22
Refractors-22
Atomic Refractors-22
98Crown Royale-114
Limited Series-114
98Finest-27
No Protectors-27
No Protectors Refractors-27
Refractors-27
98Kenner Starting Lineup Cards-9
98McDonalds Upper Deck Gretzkys Teammates-T7
98NHL Aces Playing Cards-10
98OPC Chrome-114
Refractors-114
Blast From the Past-5
Blast From the Past Refractors-5
98Pacific-31
Ice Blue-31
Red-31
98Pacific Dynagon Ice-157
Blue-157
Red-157
Watchmen-8
Team Checklists-22
98Pacific Omega-202
Red-202
Opening Day Issue-202
98Panini Photocards-27
98Panini Stickers-155
98Paramount-203
Copper-203
Emerald Green-203
Holo-Electric-203
Ice Blue-203
Silver-203
Glove Side Laser Cuts-17
Team Checklists Die-Cuts-22
98Revolution-122
Ice Shadow-122
Red-122
98SPx Finite-77
Radiance-77
Spectrum-77
98Topps-114
O-Pee-Chee-114
Blast From The Past-5
98Topps Gold Label Class 1-95
Black-95
Black One of One-95
One of One-95
Red-95
Red One of One-95
98Topps Gold Label Class 2-95
98Topps Gold Label Class 2 Black-95
98Topps Gold Label Class 2 Black 1 of 1-95
98Topps Gold Label Class 2 One of One-95
98Topps Gold Label Class 2 Red-95
98Topps Gold Label Class 2 Red One of One-95
98Topps Gold Label Class 3-95
98Topps Gold Label Class 3 Black-95
98Topps Gold Label Class 3 Black 1 of 1-95
98Topps Gold Label Class 3 One of One-95
98Topps Gold Label Class 3 Red-95
98Topps Gold Label Class 3 Red One of One-95
98Upper Deck-362
Exclusives-362
Exclusives 1 of 1-362
Gold Reserve-362
99SLU Hockey Classic Doubles-1
99Aurora-125
Striped-125
Premiere Date-125
Premiere Date Striped-125
Glove Unlimited-17
99BAP Memorabilia-179
Gold-179
Silver-179
AS Heritage Ruby-H24
AS Heritage Sapphire-H24
AS Heritage Emerald-H24
99BAP Millennium-38
Emerald-38
Ruby-38
Sapphire-38
Signatures-38
Signatures Gold-38
Goalie Memorabilia-G3
99Crown Royale-22
Limited Series-22
Premiere Date-22
99McDonald's Upper Deck Game Jerseys-GJGF
99McDonald's Upper Deck Signatures-GF
99O-Pee-Chee-24
99O-Pee-Chee Chrome-24
99O-Pee-Chee Chrome Refractors-24
99Pacific-356
Copper-356
Emerald Green-356
Gold-356
Ice Blue-356
Premiere Date-356
Red-356
In the Cage Net-Fusions-17
Team Leaders-23
99Pacific Dynagon Ice-35
Blue-35
Copper-35
Gold-35
Premiere Date-35
99Pacific Omega-36
Copper-36
Gold-36
Ice Blue-36
Premiere Date-36
99Pacific Prism-23
Holographic Blue-23
Holographic Gold-23
Holographic Mirror-23
Holographic Purple-23
Premiere Date-23
99Panini Stickers-186
99Paramount-196
Copper-196
Emerald-196
Gold-196
Holographic Emerald-196
Holographic Gold-196
Holographic Silver-196
Ice Blue-196
Premiere Date-196
Red-196
Silver-196
Glove Side Net Fusions-18
99Revolution Premiere Date-122
99Revolution Red-122
99Revolution Shadow Series-122
99Topps/OPC-24
99Topps/OPC Chrome-24
Refractors-24
99Upper Deck-194
Exclusives-194
Exclusives 1 of 1-194
99Upper Deck Gold Reserve-194
99Upper Deck MVP-185
Gold Script-185
Silver Script-185
Super Script-185
99Upper Deck Victory-264
99Wayne Gretzky Hockey-31
99Slovakian Challengers-14
00BAP Memorabilia Georges Vezina-V13
00BAP Ultimate Mem Dynasty Jerseys-D3
00BAP Ultimate Mem Dynasty Emblems-D3
00Black Diamond Game Gear-LGF
00O-Pee-Chee-252B
00O-Pee-Chee Parallel-252B
00SP Authentic Sign of the Times-GMF
00Topps/OPC-252B
Parallel-252B
00Upper Deck Legends-48
Legendary Collection Bronze-48
Legendary Collection Gold-48
Legendary Collection Silver-48
Legendary Game Jerseys-JGF
of the Cage-LC6
01BAP Ultimate Mem All-Star History-38
01BAP Ultimate Memorabilia Decades-20
01BAP Ultimate Mem Stanley Cup Winners-19
01Between the Pipes-113
Double Memorabilia-DM25
He Shoots-He Saves Points-13
He Shoots-He Saves Prizes-6
Jersey and Stick Cards-GSJ41
Masks-32
Masks Silver-32
Masks Gold-32
Record Breakers-RB9
Vintage Memorabilia-VM1
01Fleer Legacy-19
Ultimate-19
01Greats of the Game-57
Autographs-57
01SP Game Used Tools of the Game-TGF
01SP Game Used Tools of the Game-CTFC
01SP Game Used Tools of the Game-CTRF
01SP Game Used Tools of the Game-CTRF
01SP Game Used Tools of the Game-TTRFE
01SP Game Used Tools of the Game Signed-STGF
01SP Game Used Tools of the Game Signed-SCRF
01Topps Archives-33
Autographs-9
Relics-JGF
01UD Stanley Cup Champs-9
01Upper Deck Legends-24
01Upper Deck Legends-82
01Upper Deck Vintage Jerseys-GGGF
02BAP Memorabilia Mini Stanley Cups-26
02BAP NHL All-Star History-38
02BAP Sig Series Auto Buybacks 1998-122
02BAP Sig Series Auto Buybacks 1999-38
02BAP Signature Series Golf-GS39
02BAP Ultimate Memorabilia All-Star MVP-8
02BAP Ultimate Memorabilia Cup Duels-9
02BAP Ultimate Memorabilia Cup Duels-11
02BAP Ultimate Memorabilia Cup Duels-12
02BAP Ultimate Memorabilia Numerology-29
02Between the Pipes Complete Package-CP11
02Between the Pipes Trappers-GT18
02UD Foundations-9
02UD Foundations-31
02UD Foundations-85
02UD Foundations-91
02UD Foundations-110
Canadian Heroes-CGF
Canadian Heroes Gold-CGF
Canadian Heroes Silver-C-GF
Classic Greats-GGF
Classic Greats Gold-GGF
Classic Greats Silver-G-GF
Defense First-DGF
Defense First Gold-DGF
Defense First Silver-D-GF
Milestones-NGF
Milestones Gold-NGF
Milestones Silver-N-GF
Playoff Performers-PGF
Playoff Performers Gold-PGF
Playoff Performers Silver-P-GF
Signs of Greatness-SGGF
02UD Mask Collection Mini Masks-GF1
02UD Mask Collection Mini Masks-GF2
02UD Mask Collection Mini Masks Autos-GF1
02UD Mask Collection Mini Masks Autos-GF2
03Pacific Quest for the Cup Eternal Champ-2
03SP Authentic Sign of the Times-GKF
03SP Game Used Game Gear-GGGF
03SP Game Used Game Gear Combo-GCGF
03Topps Stanley Cup Heroes-GF
03Topps Stanley Cup Heroes Autographs-GF
03Upper Deck Trilogy-127
Authentic Patches-AP37
Crest Variations-127
Limited-127
Scripts-S3GF
Scripts Limited-S3GF
Scripts Red-S3GF
04ITG NHL AS FANtasy AS History Jerseys-SB38
04ITG Franchises Canadian-17
Autographs-GF
Complete Jerseys-CJ4
Complete Jerseys Gold-CJ4
Double Memorabilia-DM12
Double Memorabilia Autographs-DM12
Double Memorabilia Gold-DM12
Forever Rivals-FR3
Forever Rivals Gold-FR3
Goalie Gear-GG4
Goalie Gear Autographs-GG4
Goalie Gear Gold-GG4
Memorabilia-SM7
Memorabilia Autographs-SM7
Memorabilia Gold-SM7
Teammates-TM6
Teammates Gold-TM6
Triple Memorabilia-TM8
Triple Memorabilia Autographs-TM8
Triple Memorabilia Gold-TM0
04ITG Franchises He Shoots/Scores Prizes-2
04ITG Franchises Update-456
04ITG Franchises US West-234
Memorabilia-WSM20
Memorabilia Gold-WSM20
04ITG Ultimate Memorabilia-113
04ITG Ultimate Memorabilia-139
Gold-113
Gold-139
Archives 1st Edition-26
Auto Threads-27
Autographs-53
Autographs Gold-53
Complete Logo-8
Day In History-5
Day In History Gold-5
Jersey Autographs-26
Jersey Autographs Gold-26
Jersey and Sticks-17
Jersey and Sticks Gold-17
Retro Teammates-8
Stick Autographs-44
Stick Autographs Gold-44
Vezina Trophy-7
04SP Authentic Buybacks-62
04SP Authentic Sign of the Times-DS-FH
04SP Authentic Sign of the Times-TS-GKF
04SP Authentic Sign of the Times-QS-FBRE
04SP Authentic Sign of the Times-SS-ALS
04UD Legendary Signatures-41
Autographs-GF
HOF Inks-HOF-GF
04UD Legends Classics-28
04UD Legends Classics-93
Gold-28
Gold-93
Platinum-28
Platinum-93
Silver-28
Silver-93
Jersey Redemptions-JY30
Signature Moments-M35
Signatures-CS34
04Upper Deck Heritage Classic-CC-GF
04ITG Heroes and Prospects-154
Aspiring-10
Autographs-GF
He Shoots-He Scores Prizes-5
Hero Memorabilia-26
04ITG Heroes/Prospects Toronto Expo '05-154
04ITG Heroes/Prospects Expo Heroes/Pros-154
05ITG Heroes/Prosp Toronto Expo Parallel -27
05Beehive-227
05Between the Pipes-7
Autographs-A-GR
Complete Package-CP-1
Gloves-GUG-8
Jerseys-GUJ-10
Jersey and Sticks-SJ-10
Pads-GUP-2
Signed Memorabilia-SM-9
05Canada Post-32
05Canada Post Autographs-32
05ITG Ultimate Memorabilia Level 1-44
05ITG Ultimate Memorabilia Level 2-44
05ITG Ultimate Memorabilia Level 3-44
05ITG Ultimate Memorabilia Level 4-44
05ITG Ultimate Memorabilia Level 5-44
05ITG Ultimate Mem Cornerstones Jerseys-7
05ITG Ultimate Mem Cornerst Jerseys Gold-7
05ITG Ultimate Memorabilia Double Autos-18
05ITG Ultimate Mem Double Autos Gold-18
05ITG Ultimate Mem Double Mem-22
05ITG Ultimate Mem Double Mem Autos-11
05ITG Ultimate Mem Double Mem Autos Gold-11
05ITG Ultimate Mem Double Mem Gold-22
05ITG Ultimate Mem First Rounders Jerseys-3
05ITG Ultimate Mem 1st Round Jersey Gold-3
05ITG Ultimate Mem Pass the Torch Jerseys-4
05ITG Ultimate Mem Passing Torch Jsy Gold-4
05ITG Ultimate Mem Raised to the Rafters-3
05ITG Ultimate Mem Raised Rafters Gold-3
05ITG Ultimate Mem Record Breaker Jerseys-13
05ITG Ultimate Mem RecBreak Jerseys Gold-13
05ITG Ultimate Mem Retro Teammate Jerseys-6
05ITG Ult Mem Retro Teammates Jersey Gold-6
05ITG Ultimate Memorabilia Stick Autos-6
05ITG Ultimate Mem Stick Autos Gold-6
05ITG Ultimate Mem Sticks and Jerseys-24
05ITG Ultimate Mem Stick and Jerseys Gold-24
05ITG Ultimate Mem 3 Star of the Game Jsy-17
05ITG Ult Mem 3 Star of the Game Jsy Gold-17
05ITG Ultimate Mem Triple Threads Jerseys-4
05ITG Ultimate Mem Triple Thread Jsy Gold-4
05ITG Ultimate Memorabilia Ultimate Autos-38
05ITG Ultimate Mem Ultimate Autos Gold-38
05SP Authentic Exquisite Endorsements-EEGF
05SP Authentic Prestigious Pairings-PPFK
05SP Game Used Authentic Fabrics Quad-GMCF
05SP Game Used Endorsed Equipment-EE-GF
05SP Game Used Heritage Classic-HC-GF
05SP Game Used Heritage Classic Autos-HCA-GF
05SP Game Used Heritage Classic Patches-HCP-GF
05SP GameUsed Heritage Classic Patch Auto-HAP-GF
05SP Game Used Oldtimer's Challenge-OC-GF
05SP Game Used Oldtimer's Challenge Autos-OCA-GF
05SP Game Used Oldtimer's Challenge Patch-OCP-GF
05SP Game Used Oldtime Chall Patch Autoa-OAP-GF
05SP Game Used Statscriptions-ST-PC
05SPx-104
Spectrum-104
Xcitement Legends-XL-GF
Xcitement Legends Gold-XL-GF
Xcitement Legends Spectrum-XL-GF
05The Cup-46
Gold-46
Black Rainbow-46
Emblems of Endorsement-EEGF
Hardware Heroes-HHGF
Honorable Numbers-HNGF
Limited Logos-LLGF
Masterpiece Pressplates-46
Noble Numbers-NNFJ
Noble Numbers Dual-DNNFR
Patch Variation-P46
Patch Variation Autographs-AP46
Scripted Numbers Dual-DSNRF
Scripted Swatches-SSGF
Stanley Cup Titlists-TGF
05UD Artifacts-117
Blue-117
Gold-117
Green-117
Pewter-117
Red-117
Auto Facts-AF-GF
Auto Facts Blue AF GF
Auto Facts Copper-AF-GF
Auto Facts Pewter-AF-GF
Auto Facts Silver-AF-GF
Gold Autographed-117
Remarkable Artifacts-RA-GF
Remarkable Artifacts Dual-RA-GF
05Ultimate Collection Endorsed Emblems-EEGF
05Upper Deck Jerseys-J-GF
05Upper Deck Notable Numbers-N-GF
05Upper Deck Trilogy-161
Crystal-161
Personal Scripts-PER-GF
05ITG Heroes and Prospects-27
Autographs-A-GF
CHL Grads-CG-13
CHL Grads Gold-CG-13
Future Teammates-FT9
Hero Memorabilia-HM-22
Hero Memorabilia Dual-HDM-10
06Beehive-203
5 X 7 Black and White-203
06Between The Pipes-92
06Between The Pipes-108
06Between The Pipes-142
06Between The Pipes-148
Aspiring-AS07
Aspiring Gold-AS07
Autographs-AGF2
Autographs-AGF
Complete Package-CP02
Complete Package Gold-CP02
Double Jerseys-DJ12
Double Jerseys Gold-DJ12
Emblems-GUE45
Emblems Gold-GUE45
Emblems Autographs-GUE45
Gloves-GG05
Gloves Gold-GG05
Jerseys-GUJ45
Jerseys Gold-GUJ45
Jerseys Autographs-GUJ45
Numbers-GUN45
Numbers Gold-GUN45
Numbers Autographs-GUN45
Pads-GP03
Pads Gold-GP03
Playing For Your Country-PC07
Playing For Your Country Gold-PC07
Stick and Jersey-SJ10
Stick and Jersey Gold-SJ10
Stick and Jersey Autographs-SJ10
06ITG International Ice-14
06ITG International Ice-80
Gold-14
Gold-80
Autographs-AGF
Autographs-AGF2
Canadian Dream Team-DT09
Canadian Dream Team Gold-DT09
Goaltending Glory-GG02
Goaltending Glory Gold-GG02
International Rivals-IR07
Passing The Torch-PTT1
Passing The Torch-PTT2
Passing The Torch Gold-PTT1
Passing The Torch Gold-PTT2
Quad Patch-QP03
Quad Patch Gold-QP03
06ITG Ultimate Memorabilia-58
Artist Proof-58
Cornerstones-8
Cornerstones Gold-8
Decades-8
Decades Gold-8
Jerseys Autos-18
Jerseys Autos Gold-18
Retro Teammates-20
Retro Teammates Gold-20
Road to the Cup-7
Road to the Cup Gold-7
Stick Rack-26
Stick Rack Gold-26
06Parkhurst-5
Autographs-5
Autographs Dual-DAGC
06SP Authentic Sign of the Times Duals-STGR
06SP Game Used Authentic Fabrics Sixes-AF6WIN
06SP Game Used Authentic Fabrics Sixes Patches-AF6WIN
06SP Game Used Inked Sweaters Dual-IS2FR
06SPx-127
Spectrum-127
SPxcitement-X38
SPxcitement Spectrum-X38
SPxcitement Autographs-X38
Winning Materials-WMGF
Winning Materials Spectrum-WMGF
Winning Materials Autographs-WMGF
06The Cup-34
Autographed Foundations-CQGF
Autographed Foundations Patches-CQGF
Autographed Patches-34
Black Rainbow-34
Foundations-CQGF
Foundations Patches-CQGF
Gold-34
Gold Patches-34
Honorable Numbers-HNGF
Jerseys-34
Masterpiece Pressplates-34
Scripted Swatches-SSGF
Scripted Swatches Duals-DSKF
Signature Patches-SPGF
Stanley Cup Signatures-CSGF
06UD Artifacts-113
Blue-113
Gold-113
Platinum-113
Radiance-113
Autographed Radiance Parallel-113
Red-113
Auto-Facts-AFGF
Auto-Facts Gold-AFGF
Treasured Patches Black-TSGF
Treasured Patches Blue-TSGF
Treasured Patches Gold-TSGF
Treasured Patches Platinum-TSGF
Treasured Patches Red-TSGF
Treasured Patches Autographed Black Tag Parallel-TSGF
Treasured Swatches-TSGF
Treasured Swatches Black-TSGF
Treasured Swatches Blue-TSGF
Treasured Swatches Gold-TSGF
Treasured Swatches Platinum-TSGF
Treasured Swatches Red-TSGF
Treasured Swatches Autographed Black-TSGF
Tundra Tandems-TTFR
Tundra Tandems Black-TTFR
Tundra Tandems Blue-TTFR
Tundra Tandems Gold-TTFR
Tundra Tandems Platinum-TTFR
Tundra Tandems Red-TTFR
Tundra Tandems Dual Patches Red-TTFR
06Ultimate Collection Autographed Jerseys-AJ-GF
06Ultimate Collection Autographed Patches-AJ-GF
06Ultimate Collection Jerseys-UJ-GF
06Ultimate Collection Patches-UJ-GF
06Ultimate Collection Signatures-US-GF
06Ultimate Collection Ultimate Achievements-UA-GF
06Upper Deck Sweet Shot-47
Endorsed Equipment-EEGF
Signature Shots/Saves-SSGF
Signature Shots/Saves Sticks-SSSGF
Sweet Stitches-SSGF
Sweet Stitches Duals-SSGF
Sweet Stitches Triples-SSGF
06Upper Deck Trilogy Combo Clearcut Autographs-C3FEC
06Upper Deck Trilogy Ice Scripts-ISGF
06Upper Deck Trilogy Legendary Scripts-LSGF
06ITG Heroes and Prospects Triple Memorabilia-TM01
06ITG Heroes and Prospects Triple Memorabilia Gold-TM01

Fuhrberg, Campbell
57Swedish Alfabilder-118

Fuhrer, Riccardo
95Swiss HNL-367
96Swiss HNL-226
98Swiss Power Play Stickers-305
99Swiss Panini Stickers-320
01Swiss HNL-75

Fujita, Ryan
907th Inn. Sketch WHL-105
91Saskatoon Blades-19
917th Inn. Sketch WHL-110

Fujtsawa, Yoshifumi
96Alaska Gold Kings-5

Fukami, Scott
88Lethbridge Hurricanes-7
907th Inn. Sketch WHL-259
917th Inn. Sketch WHL-69

Fuksa, Zdenek
98Czech OFS-55
99Czech Score Blue 2000-40
99Czech Score Red Ice 2000-40

Fukufuji, Yutaka
04Bakersfield Condors-3
05Manchester Monarchs-30
05Reading Royals-5
06Between The Pipes-55
Autographs-AYFA
Autographs-AYFB
06Reading Royals-17
07Upper Deck Victory-211
Black-211
Gold-211

Fukushima, Shane
95North Iowa Huskies-10

Fullan, Larry
74NHL Action Stamps-324

Fuller, Ryan
06Texas Tornados-9

Fuller, Travis
03Barrie Colts-15
04Barrie Colts-16
06Mississauga Ice Dogs-13

Fullum, Rival
87Kitchener Rangers-12
88Kitchener Rangers-12
89Kitchener Rangers-13
907th Inn. Sketch OHL-24
907th Inn. Sketch OHL-182
907th Inn. Sketch Memorial Cup-46
91Cornwall Royals-16
917th Inn. Sketch OHL-21
93Wheeling Thunderbirds-UD4
94Thunder Bay Senators-8
95Thunder Bay Senators-8

Fultz, Ryan
92Quebec Pee-Wee Tournament-1573
02Lexington Men O'War-22

Funk Sr., Lorenz
72Finnish Hellas-51
72Finnish Semic World Championship-102
72Swedish Semic World Championship-102
79Panini Stickers-105

Funk, Florian
94German DEL-136
95German DEL-138
96German DEL-35
98German DEL-169

Funk, Franz
72Finnish Hellas-43

Funk, John
00Sioux Falls Stampede-9
03Wisconsin Badgers-11
04Wisconsin Badgers-11

Funk, Jordan
06Penticton Vees-9

Funk, Lorenz
92Finnish Semic-187
94German DEL-81
95German DEL-87
96German DEL-34
98German DEL-168
99German DEL-54
99German DEL-370

00German DEL-56
02German DEL City Press-110
03German DEL-126

Funk, Michael
03Portland Winter Hawks-4
04Portland Winter Hawks-6
05ITG Heroes/Prosp Toronto Expo Parallel -320
05ITG Heroes and Prospects-320
Autographs Series II-MFU
06Hot Prospects-149
Red Hot-149
White Hot-149
06O-Pee-Chee-587
Rainbow-587
06Rochester Americans-5
06SP Authentic-246
Limited-246
06The Cup-116
Autographed Rookie Masterpiece Pressplates-116
Gold Rainbow Autographed Rookie Patches-116
Masterpiece Pressplates (Marquee Rookies)-587
Masterpiece Pressplates (SP Authentic)-246
Masterpiece Pressplates (Sweet Beginnings)-111
Masterpiece Pressplates (Ultimate Collection)-65
Rookies Black-116
Rookies Platinum-116
06Ultimate Collection-65
06Upper Deck-459
Exclusives Parallel-459
High Gloss Parallel-459
Masterpieces-459
06Upper Deck Sweet Shot-111
Rookie Jerseys Autographs-111

Funk, Ryan
05Saskatoon Blades-6
06Saskatoon Blades-7

Furchner, Sebastian
02German DEL City Press-193
03German DEL-170
04German Cologne Sharks Postcards-9
04German DEL-223
05German DEL-204
05German DEL-371
06German DEL-120

Furd, Jan
94German First League-476

Furderer, Frank
94German First League-94

Furer, Kalle
93Swiss HNL-275

Furey, Kirk
93Owen Sound Platers-8
94Owen Sound Platers-4
01Atlantic City Boardwalk Bullies-11
02Atlantic City Boardwalk Bullies-6
03Atlantic City Boardwalk Bullies-8
04German DEL-187
04Atlantic City Boardwalk Bullies Kinko's-23
05German DEL-166
06German DEL-106

Furguson, Chris
06Fayetteville FireAntz-4

Furlan, Frank
84Nanaimo Clippers-8
89Hampton Roads Admirals-6A
89Hampton Roads Admirals-6H

Furler, Rene
98Swiss Power Play Stickers-92
99Swiss Panini Stickers-91
00Swiss Panini Stickers-233
00Swiss Slapshot Mini-Cards-RJ9
01Swiss HNL-312
02Swiss HNL-371

Furlong, Chris
93Quebec Pee-Wee Tournament-192

Furlong, Olivier
03Baie Comeau Drakkar-14

Furness, Jason
95Waterloo Blackhawks -4

Furness, Ryan
98Dayton Bombers-5

Furrer, Andreas
01Swiss HNL-389
02Swiss HNL-378

Furrer, Gaston
72Finnish Semic World Championship-140
72Swedish Semic World Championship-140

Furrer, Roman
93Swiss HNL-477
95Swiss HNL-302
96Swiss HNL-285

Furst, Carl-Erik
32Swedish Marabou-148

Fusco, Mark
84Whalers Junior Wendy's-7
85O-Pee-Chee-74
85Topps-74

Fussey, Owen
99Calgary Hitmen-10
99Calgary Hitmen Autographs-10
00Calgary Hitmen-13
00UD CHL Prospects-48
01Calgary Hitmen-11
01Calgary Hitmen Autographed-11
02Calgary Hitmen-19
03ITG VIP Rookie Debut-137
03Parkhurst Rookie-126
03Topps Traded-TT165
Blue-TT165
Gold-TT165
Red-TT165
03UD Premier Collection-94
03Upper Deck Rookie Update-178
04Portland Pirates-4
05Hershey Bears-8
06Toronto Marlies-12

Fussi, Trent
05Kootenay Ice-9

Fust, John
95Swiss HNL-404
96Swiss HNL-351
98Swiss Power Play Stickers-144
99Swiss Panini Stickers-143
00Swiss Panini Stickers-185
00Swiss Slapshot Mini-Cards-LT11
01Swiss HNL-203
02Swiss HNL-199

Fuster, Marco
91Richmond Renegades-17

Futers, Shawn
02Peterborough Petes-5
04Kingston Frontenacs-8
04London Knights-20

Futtner, Franz
94German First League-66

Fyfe, Alan
01South Carolina Stingrays-7

Fylling, Quinn
01Sioux Falls Stampede-5
03North Dakota Fighting Sioux-4
04North Dakota Fighting Sioux-8

Gaarde, Jesper
98Danish Hockey League-201

Gabinet, Mike
04Finnish Cardset-287
05Idaho Steelheads-9
06Idaho Steelheads-16

Gabler, Michael
94German DEL-293

Gaborik, Marian
00BAP Memorabilia-401
Emerald-401
Ruby-401
Sapphire-401
00BAP Parkhurst 2000-P139
00BAP Signature Series-279
Emerald-279
Ruby-279
Sapphire-279
Autographs-241
Autographs Gold-241
Franchise Players-F15
00Black Diamond-123
00Crown Royale-127
21st Century Rookies-12
Now Playing-10
00Private Stock-125
Gold-125
Premiere Date-125
Retail-125
Silver-125
PS-2001 Rookies-11
00SP Authentic-110
Sign of the Times-MG
00SP Game Used-70
00SPx-163
00Stadium Club-241
00Titanium-126
Retail-126
Three-Star Selections-23
00Titanium Draft Day Edition-126
00Titanium Draft Day Promos-126
00Topps Chrome-242
Blue-242
Red-242
OPC Refractors-242
OPC Refractors Blue-242
OPC Refractors Red-242
Refractors-242
Refractors Blue-242
Refractors Red-242
00Topps Gold Label Class 1-102
Gold-102
00Topps Gold Label Class 2-102
00Topps Gold Label Class 2 Gold-102
00Topps Gold Label Class 3-102
00Topps Gold Label Class 3 Gold-102
00Topps Gold Label Autographs-GLA-MG
00Topps Gold Label New Generation-NG8
00Topps Gold Label New Generation 1 to 1-NG8
00Topps Heritage-85
Chrome Parallel-85
New Tradition-NT10
00Topps Premier Plus-130
Blue Ice-130
Private Signings-PSMG
Rookies-PR1
Rookies Blue Ice-PR1
00Topps Stars-113
00Topps Stars-150
Blue-113
Blue-150
00UD Heroes-166
00UD Pros and Prospects-108
Now Appearing-NA2
00UD Reserve-98
The Big Ticket-BT6
00Upper Deck-229
Exclusives Tier 1-229
Exclusives Tier 2-229
00Upper Deck Ice-90
00Upper Deck Vintage-184
00Upper Deck Vintage-381
00Vanguard-127
High Voltage-18
High Voltage Gold-18
High Voltage Green-18
High Voltage Red-18
High Voltage Silver-18
In Focus-11
Pacific Proofs-127
01Atomic-50
Blue-50
Gold-50
Premiere Date-50
Red-50
Core Players-8
Power Play-18
01BAP Memorabilia-285
Emerald-285
Ruby-285
Sapphire-285
01BAP Signature Series-84
Autographs-84
Autographs Gold-84
Franchise Jerseys-FP-15
Jerseys-GJ-15
Jersey Autographs-GUMG
Jersey and Stick Cards-GSJ-15
Teammates-TM-15
01BAP Ultimate Memorabilia Made to Order-7
01BAP Update He Shoots-He Scores Points-3
01BAP Update He Shoots-He Scores Prizes-32
01Bowman YoungStars-136
Gold-136
Ice Cubed-136
Autographs-MG
Relics-JMG
Relics-SMG
Relics-DSMG
Rivals-R5
01Crown Royale Calder Collection Gold Ed-4
01Crown Royale Calder Collection AS Ed-C2
01Crown Royale-74
Blue-74
Premiere Date-74
Red-74
Retail-74
Jewels of the Crown-16
01McDonald's Pacific-20
01O-Pee-Chee-18
01O-Pee-Chee Heritage Parallel-18
01O-Pee-Chee Heritage Parallel Limited-18
01O-Pee-Chee Premier Parallel-18
01Pacific-194
01Pacific-447
Extreme LTD-194
Hobby LTD-194
Premiere Date-194
Retail LTD-194
01Pacific Adrenaline-92
Blue-92
Premiere Date-92
Red-92
Retail-92
Playmakers-6
World Beaters-9
01Pacific Arena Exclusives-194
01Pacific Heads-Up-49
Blue-49
Premiere Date-49
Red-49
Silver-49
Breaking the Glass-12
Prime Picks-3
01Parkhurst-15
Gold-15
Silver-15
01Private Stock-48
Gold-48
Premiere Date-48
Retail-48
Silver-48
01Private Stock Pacific Nights-48
01Private Stock PS-2002-38
01Private Stock Reserve-S9
01SP Authentic-42
01SP Authentic-123
Limited-42
Limited-123
Limited Gold-42
Limited Gold-123
Buybacks-17
Sign of the Times-MG
Sign of the Times-FG
Sign of the Times-PHG
01SP Game Used-27
01SPx-33
01Stadium Club-27
Award Winners-27
Master Photos-27
Gallery-G17
Gallery Gold-G17
Lone Star Signatures-LS3
01Titanium-70
Hobby Parallel-70
Premiere Date-70
Retail-70
Retail Parallel-70
Double-Sided Jerseys-67
Double-Sided Patches-67
Saturday Knights-10
01Titanium Draft Day Edition-45
01Topps-18
Heritage Parallel-18
Heritage Parallel Limited-18
OPC Parallel-18
Own The Game-OTG15
01Topps Chrome-18
Refractors-18
Black Border Refractors-18
01Topps Heritage-29
Refractors-29
Autographs-AMG
01Topps Reserve-24
01UD Challenge for the Cup-42
01UD Mask Collection-46
Gold-46
01UD Playmakers-50
01UD Premier Collection-29
Signatures-MG
Signatures Black-MG
01UD Top Shelf-22
01Upper Deck-85
Exclusives-85
01Upper Deck Ice-23
01Upper Deck MVP-91
01Upper Deck Victory-171
Gold-171
01Upper Deck Vintage-123
01Upper Deck Vintage-129
01Upper Deck Vintage-130
01Vanguard-48
Blue-48
Red-48
One of Ones-48
Premiere Date-48
Prime Prospects-9
Proofs-48
01Wild Crime Prevention-18
02Atomic-53
Blue-53
Gold-53
Red-53
Hobby Parallel-53
02BAP All-Star Edition-103
Gold-103
Silver-103
02BAP First Edition-152
02BAP First Edition-320
02BAP First Edition-355
02BAP First Edition-422R
Debut Jerseys-11
He Shoots-He Scores Prizes-22
Jerseys-152
02BAP Memorabilia-109
02BAP Memorabilia-215
Emerald-109
Emerald-215
Ruby-109
Ruby-215
Sapphire-109
Sapphire-215
Franchise Players-FP-15
Future of the Game-FG-8
He Shoots-He Scores Prizes-22
NHL All-Star Game-109
NHL All-Star Game-215
NHL All-Star Game Blue-109
NHL All-Star Game Blue-215
NHL All-Star Game Green-109
NHL All-Star Game Green-215
NHL All-Star Game Red-109
NHL All-Star Game Red-215
02BAP Memorabilia Toronto Fall Expo-109
02BAP Memorabilia Toronto Fall Expo-215
02BAP Signature Series-13
Autographs-13
Autograph Buybacks 2001-84
Autographs Gold-13
Complete Jersey-CJ6
Franchise Players-FJ15
Jerseys-SGJ19
Jersey Autographs-SGJ19
02BAP Ultimate Memorabilia Dynamic Duos-9
02BAP Ultimate Memorabilia Emblems-29
02BAP Ultimate Memorabilia Jerseys-19
02BAP Ultimate Mem Jersey and Stick-27
02BAP Ultimate Memorabilia Nameplates-15
02BAP Ultimate Memorabilia Numbers-10
02BAP Ultimate Memorabilia Numerology-14
02Bowman YoungStars-114
Gold-114
Silver-114
02Crown Royale-48
Blue-48
Red-48
Retail-48
Dual Patches-13
Lords of the Rink-12
02eTopps-49
02ITG Used-38
02ITG Used-138
Franchise Players-F15
Franchise Players Autographs-F15
Franchise Players Gold-F15
Jerseys-GUJ19
Jersey Autographs-GUJ19
Jerseys Gold-GUJ19
Emblems-E19
Jersey and Stick-SJ19
Jersey and Stick Gold-SJ19
02McDonald's Pacific-19
02O-Pee-Chee-26
02O-Pee-Chee Premier Blue Parallel-26
02O-Pee-Chee Premier Red Parallel-26
02O-Pee-Chee Factory Set-26
02Pacific-182
Blue-182
Red-182
02Pacific Calder-41
Silver-41
02Pacific Complete-206
Red-206
02Pacific Exclusive-87
Great Expectations-10
02Pacific Heads-Up-61
Blue-61
Purple-61
Red-61
Head First-6
Quad Jerseys-14
Quad Jerseys-34
Quad Jerseys Gold-14
Quad Jerseys Gold-34
02Pacific Quest for the Cup-48
Gold-48
Chasing the Cup-7
02Parkhurst-107
Bronze-107
Gold-107
Silver-107
Franchise Players-FP15
Jerseys-GJ12
Stick and Jerseys-SJ12
02Parkhurst Retro-34
Minis-34
Franchise Players-RF15
He Shoots-He Scores Points-1
He Shoots-He Scores Prizes-15
Hopefuls-HH6
Hopefuls-RR4
Jerseys-RJ36
Jersey and Sticks-RSJ24
02Private Stock Reserve-126
Red-126
Retail-126
Patches-126
02SP Authentic-46
02SP Authentic-119
Beckett Promos-46
02SP Game Used-24
02SPx-38
Spectrum Gold-38
Spectrum Silver-38
02Stadium Club-42
Silver Decoy Cards-42
Proofs-42
World Stage-WS13
YoungStars Relics-S6
YoungStars Relics-DS4
02Titanium-53
Blue-53
Red-53
Retail-53
Jerseys-34
Jerseys Retail-34
Shadows-6
02Topps-26
OPC Blue Parallel-26
OPC Red Parallel-26
Factory Set-26
02Topps Chrome-26
Black Border Refractors-26
Refractors-26
02Topps Heritage-16
Chrome Parallel-16
02Topps Total-45
Team Checklists-TTC15
02UD Artistic Impressions-46
Gold-46
02UD Artistic Impressions Beckett Promos-46
02UD Artistic Impressions Great Depiction-GD11
02UD Artistic Impress Great Depiction Gld-GD11
02UD Artistic Impressions Retrospectives-R46
02UD Artistic Impressions Retrospect Gold-R46
02UD Artistic Impress Retrospect Silver-R46
02UD Honor Roll-36
Students of the Game-SG16
02UD Mask Collection-44
02UD Mask Collection Beckett Promos-44
02UD Piece of History-46
02UD Premier Collection-29
02UD Top Shelf-43
02Upper Deck-89
Exclusives-89
Blow-Ups-C20
Sizzling Scorers-SS9
02Upper Deck Classic Portraits-50
02Upper Deck MVP-89
Gold-89
Classics-89
Golden Classics-89
02Upper Deck Rookie Update-49
02Upper Deck Rookie Update-115
02Upper Deck Victory-104
Bronze-104
Gold-104
Silver-104
02Upper Deck Vintage-125
02Upper Deck Vintage-275
Tall Boys-T34
Tall Boys Gold-T34
02Vanguard-52
LTD-52
East Meets West-8
In Focus-7
03McFarlane Hockey-130
03McFarlane Hockey-132
03BAP Memorabilia-46
Emerald-46
Gold-46
Ruby-46
Sapphire-46
Brush with Greatness-3
Brush with Greatness Contest Cards-3
Jersey and Stick-SJ-37
Jerseys-GJ-47
Stanley Cup Playoffs-SCP-6
03BAP Ultimate Memorabilia Autographs-83
Gold-83
03BAP Ultimate Mem Auto Jerseys-83
03BAP Ultimate Mem Auto Emblems-83
03BAP Ultimate Mem Complete Jersey-3
03BAP Ultimate Mem Complete Jersey Gold-3
03BAP Ultimate Memorabilia Emblems-13
03BAP Ultimate Memorabilia Emblems Gold-13
03BAP Ultimate Mem Franch Present Future-15
03BAP Ultimate Mem Hometown Heroes-5
03BAP Ultimate Mem Hometown Heroes Gold-5
03BAP Ultimate Memorabilia Jerseys-28
03BAP Ultimate Memorabilia Jerseys Gold-28
03BAP Ultimate Mem Jersey and Emblems-21
03BAP Ultimate Mem Jersey and Emblem Gold-21
03BAP Ultimate Mem Jersey and Numbers-21
03BAP Ultimate Mem Jersey and Number Gold-21
03BAP Ultimate Memorabilia Numbers-22
03BAP Ultimate Memorabilia Numbers Gold-22
03BAP Ultimate Memorabilia Triple Threads-25
03Beehive-99
Variations-99
Gold-99
Silver-99
Jumbos-15
Jumbo Variations-15
Jerseys-JT7
Signatures-RF8
03Black Diamond-122
Black-122
Green-122
Red-122
Signature Gems-SG-25
03Bowman-50
Gold-50
Future Rivals-GH
Future Rivals-NG
Future Rivals Patches-GH
Future Rivals Patches-NG
Goal to Goal-GC
03Bowman Chrome-50
Refractors-50
Gold Refractors-50
Xfractors-50
03Crown Royale-51
Blue-51
Retail-51
Global Conquest-7
03eTopps-21
03ITG Action-297
First Time All-Star-FT1
Highlight Reel-HR12
Homeboys-HB3
Jerseys-M185
Jerseys-M205
Jerseys-M255
03ITG Toronto Fall Expo Jerseys-FE28
03ITG Used Signature Series-16
Gold-16
Autographs-MG
Autographs Gold-MG
Franchise-15
Franchise Autographs-15
Franchise Gold-15
Jerseys-22
Jerseys Gold-22
Jersey Autos-22
Emblems-21
Emblems Gold-21
Jersey and Stick-22
Jersey and Stick Gold-22
03ITG VIP Brightest Stars-2
03ITG VIP Collages-8
03ITG VIP Jerseys-17
03ITG VIP Jersey and Emblems-12
03ITG VIP Jersey and Numbers-12
03McDonald's Pacific-26
03NHL Sticker Collection-244
03O-Pee-Chee-5
03O-Pee-Chee-300
03OPC Blue-5
03OPC Blue-300
03OPC Gold-5
03OPC Gold-300
03OPC Red-5
03OPC Red-300
03Pacific-165
Blue-165
Red-165
Main Attractions-7
View from the Crease-7
03Pacific Calder-52
Silver-52
03Pacific Complete-192
Red-192
03Pacific Exhibit-173
Blue Backs-173
Pursuing Prominence-8
03Pacific Heads-Up-50
Hobby LTD-50
Retail LTD-50
Fast Forwards-5
Fast Forwards LTD-5
Mini Sweaters-7
03Pacific Invincible-48
Blue-48
Red-48
Retail-48
Afterburners-6
Featured Performers-15
Top Line-7
03Pacific Prism-53
Blue-53
Gold-53
Red-53
Paramount Prodigies-14
03Pacific Quest for the Cup-54
Blue-54
03Pacific Supreme-48
Blue-48
Red-48
Retail-48
Team-6
03Parkhurst Rookie-10
Jerseys-GJ-29
Jerseys Gold-GJ-29
03Private Stock Reserve-50
Blue-50
Red-50
Retail-50
03SP Authentic-43
Limited-43
10th Anniversary-SP14
10th Anniversary Limited-SP14
Breakout Seasons-B11
Breakout Seasons Limited-B11
Honors-H23
Honors Limited-H23
Sign of the Times-MG
03SP Game Used-23
Gold-23
Signers-SPSMG
03SPx-47
03SPx-122
03SPx-132
03SPx-167
Radiance-47
Radiance-122
Radiance-132
Radiance-167
Spectrum-47
Spectrum-122
Spectrum-132
Spectrum-167
Signature Threads-ST-MG
03Titanium-52
Hobby Jersey Number Parallels-52
Retail-52
Retail Jersey Number Parallels-52
03Topps-5
03Topps-300
Blue-5
Blue-300
Gold-5
Gold-300
Red-5
Red-300
Box Toppers-2
Topps/OPC Idols-II1
03Topps C55-40
03Topps C55-40B
Minis-40
Minis American Back-40
Minis American Back Red-40
Minis Bazooka Back-40
Minis Brooklyn Back-40
Minis Hat Trick Back-40
Minis O Canada Back-40
Minis O Canada Back Red-40
Minis Stanley Cup Back-40
Relics-TRMG
03Topps Pristine-51
Gold Refractor Die Cuts-51
Refractors-51
Jersey Portions-PPJ-MG
Jersey Portion Refractors-PPJ-MG
Patches-PP-MG
Patch Refractors-PP-MG
Press Plates Black-51
Press Plates Cyan-51
Press Plates Magenta-51
Press Plates Yellow-51
03Topps Traded Franchise Fabrics-FF-MG
03UD Honor Roll-41
03UD Honor Roll-91
Signature Class-SC6
03UD Premier Collection-27
NHL Shields-SH-MG
Signatures-PS-MG
Signatures Gold-PS-MG
Super Stars-SS-MG
Super Stars Patches-SS-MG
Teammates-PT-MW
Teammates Patches-PT-MW
03Upper Deck-92
All-Star Class-AS-14
All-Star Lineup-AS1
Big Playmakers-BP-MG
BuyBacks-97
BuyBacks-98
Canadian Exclusives-92
Franchise Fabrics-FF-MG
Gifted Greats-GG7
HG-92
Highlight Heroes-HH-MG
Highlight Heroes Jerseys-HH-MG
Memorable Matchups-MM-BG
Patches-SP2
Patches-PLG-MG
Patches-PNM-MG
Patches-PNR-MG
Performers-PS7
Superstar Spotlight-SS3
Three Stars-TS7
03Upper Deck Classic Portraits-46
03Upper Deck Classic Portraits-107
03Upper Deck Classic Portraits-150
Headliners-HH-MG
03Upper Deck Ice-43
Gold-43
Under Glass Autographs-UG-MG
03Upper Deck MVP-207
Gold Script-207
Silver Script-207
Canadian Exclusives-207
Clutch Performers-CP6
SportsNut-SN45
Talent-MT4
03Upper Deck Rookie Update-43
Skills-SKMG
Super Stars-SSMG
03Upper Deck Trilogy-46
03Upper Deck Trilogy-109
Crest Variations-109
Limited-46
Limited-109
Limited Threads-LT30
03Upper Deck Victory-89
Bronze-89
Gold-89
Silver-89
Freshman Flashback-FF25
Game Breakers-GB38
03Wild Law Enforcement Cards-3
03Toronto Star-46
Foil-4
04ITG NHL AS FANtasy AS History Jerseys-SB53
04ITG All-Star FANtasy Hail Minnesota-7
04Pacific-132
Blue-132
Red-132
04Pacific NHL All-Star Nets-2
Gold-2
04SP Authentic-44
04SP Authentic-119
Limited-44
Limited-119
Rookie Review-RR-MG
Sign of the Times-ST-GA
04Topps NHL All-Star FANtasy-1
04UD All-World-51
Gold-51
Autographs-51
Six Autographs-AS-SWD
04UD Toronto Fall Expo Priority Signings-MG
04Ultimate Collection-21
04Ultimate Collection-76
04Upper Deck-85
Canadian Exclusives-85
HG Glossy Gold-85
HG Glossy Silver-85
Jersey Autographs-GJA-MG
World's Best-WB23
World Cup Tribute-ZCMG
World Cup Tribute-MGHOMI
04Upper Deck All-Star Promos-MG
04Swedish Pure Skills-33
Parallel-33
Professional Power-MG
05Be A Player-44
First Period-44
Second Period-44
Third Period-44
Overtime-44
Outtakes-OT26
05Beehive-44
05Beehive-193
Beige -44
Blue -44
Gold-44
Red -44
Matte-44
Signature Scrapbook-SSMG
05Black Diamond-176
Emerald-176
Gold-176
Onyx-176
Ruby-176
Gemography-G-MG
Gemography Emerald-G-MG
Gemography Gold-G-MG
Gemography Onyx-G-MG
Gemography Ruby-G-MG
Jerseys-J-MG
Jerseys Ruby-J-MG
Jersey Duals-DJ-MG
Jersey Triples-TJ-MG
Jersey Quads-QJ-MG
05Hot Prospects-49
En Fuego-49
Red Hot-49
White Hot-49
05McDonalds Upper Deck-47
05Panini Stickers-295
05Parkhurst-236
05Parkhurst-685
Facsimile Auto Parallel-236
Facsimile Auto Parallel-685
Signatures-MG
True Colors-TCMIN
True Colors-TCMIN
True Colors-TCMIDA
True Colors-TCMIDA
05SP Authentic-49
Limited-49
Chirography-SPMG
Prestigious Pairings-PPGR
05SP Game Used-49
Autographs-49
Gold-49
Authentic Fabrics-AF-MG
Authentic Fabrics Gold-AF-MG
Authentic Fabrics Quad-GFRB
Authentic Patches Quad -GFRB
Authentic Patches-AP-MG
Auto Draft-AD-MG
Awesome Authentics-AA-MG
Awesome Authentics Gold-DA-MG
Significant Numbers-SN-MG
05SPx-41
Spectrum-41
Winning Combos-WC-GF
Winning Combos Gold-WC-GF
Winning Combos Spectrum-WC-GF
Winning Materials-WM-MG
Winning Materials Gold-WM-MG
Winning Materials Spectrum-WM-MG
Xcitement Superstars-XS-MG
Xcitement Superstars Gold-XS-MG
Xcitement Superstars Spectrum-XS-MG
05The Cup-52
Gold-52
Black Rainbow-52
Dual NHL Shields-DSGK
Dual NHL Shields Autographs-ADSGK
Emblems of Endorsement-EEMG
Honorable Numbers-HNMG
Limited Logos-LLMG
Masterpiece Pressplates-52
Noble Numbers Dual-DNNGH
Patch Variation-P52
Patch Variation Autographs-AP52
Property of-POMG
Scripted Swatches-SSMG
Signature Patches-SPMG
05UD Artifacts-50
05UD Artifacts-171
Blue-50
Blue-171
Gold-50
Gold-171
Green-50
Green-171
Pewter-50
Pewter-171
Red-50
Red-171
Auto Facts-AF-MG
Auto Facts Blue-AF-MG
Auto Facts Copper-AF-MG
Auto Facts Pewter-AF-MG
Auto Facts Silver-AF-MG
Frozen Artifacts-FA-MG
Frozen Artifacts Autographed-FA-MG
Frozen Artifacts Copper-FA-MG
Frozen Artifacts Dual-FAD-MG
Frozen Artifacts Dual Autographed-FAD-MG
Frozen Artifacts Dual Copper-FAD-MG
Frozen Artifacts Dual Gold-FAD-MG
Frozen Artifacts Dual Maroon-FAD-MG
Frozen Artifacts Dual Pewter-FAD-MG
Frozen Artifacts Dual Silver-FAD-MG
Frozen Artifacts Gold-FA-MG
Frozen Artifacts Maroon-FA-MG
Frozen Artifacts Patches-FP-MG
Frozen Artifacts Patches Autographed-FP-MG
Frozen Artifacts Patches Dual-FPD-MG
Frozen Artifacts Patches Dual Autos-FPD-MG
Frozen Artifacts Patches Pewter-FP-MG
Frozen Artifacts Patches Silver-FP-MG
Frozen Artifacts Pewter-FA-MG
Frozen Artifacts Silver-FA-MG
Gold Autographed-50
Gold Autographed-171
Remarkable Artifacts-RA-MG
Remarkable Artifacts Dual-RA-MG
Treasured Patches-TP-MG
Treasured Patches Autographed-TP-MG
Treasured Patches Dual-TPD-MG
Treasured Patches Dual Autographed-TPD-MG
Treasured Patches Pewter-TP-MG
Treasured Patches Silver-TP-MG
Treasured Swatches-TS-MG
Treasured Swatches Autographed-TS-MG
Treasured Swatches Blue-TS-MG
Treasured Swatches Copper-TS-MG
Treasured Swatches Dual-TSD-MG
Treasured Swatches Dual Autographed-TSD-MG
Treasured Swatches Dual Blue-TSD-MG
Treasured Swatches Dual Copper-TSD-MG
Treasured Swatches Dual Maroon-TSD-MG
Treasured Swatches Dual Pewter-TSD-MG
Treasured Swatches Dual Silver-TSD-MG
Treasured Swatches Maroon-TS-MG
Treasured Swatches Pewter-TS-MG
Treasured Swatches Silver-TS-MG
05UD PowerPlay-44
Rainbow-44
Power Marks-PMMG
05UD Toronto Fall Expo Priority Signings-PS-MG
05Ultimate Collection-47
Gold-47
Jerseys-JMG
National Heroes Jerseys-NHJGA
National Heroes Patches-NHPGA
Premium Patches-PPMG
Premium Swatches-PSMG
Ultimate Patches-PMG
05Ultra-99
Gold-99
Ice-99
Scoring Kings-SK36
Scoring Kings Jerseys-SKJ-MG
Scoring Kings Patches-SKP-MG
05Upper Deck-93
05Upper Deck All-Time Greatest-29
05Upper Deck Big Playmakers-B-MG
05Upper Deck HG Glossy-93
05Upper Deck Jerseys Series II-J2MG
05Upper Deck Majestic Materials-MMMG
05Upper Deck Notable Numbers-N-MG
05Upper Deck Patches-P-MG
05Upper Deck Scrapbooks-HS17
05Upper Deck Shooting Stars-S-MG
05Upper Deck Ice-47
Rainbow-47
05Upper Deck MVP-190
Gold-190
Platinum-190
Materials Triples-T-GPD
05Upper Deck Rookie Update-48
05Upper Deck Trilogy-44
05Upper Deck Trilogy-114
Crystal-114
Crystal Autographs-114
Honorary Patches-HP-MG
Honorary Patch Scripts-HSP-MG
Honorary Swatches-HS-MG
Honorary Swatch Scripts-HSS-MG
Ice Scripts-IS-MG
Scripts-SSS-MG
05Upper Deck Toronto Fall Expo-93
05Upper Deck Victory-96
Black-96
Gold-96
Silver-96
Blow-Ups-BU18
Game Breakers-GB23
05Wild Crime Prevention-2
06Be A Player Portraits-55
06Beehive-51
06Beehive-193
Blue-51
Gold-51
Matte-51
Red Facsimile Signatures-51
Wood-51
5 X 7 Black and White-51
Matted Materials-MMMG
PhotoGraphs-PGMG
Remarkable Matted Materials-MMMG
Signature Scrapbook-SSMG
06Black Diamond-158B
Gold-158B
Ruby-158B
Gemography-GMG
06Flair Showcase-51
06Flair Showcase-135
06Flair Showcase-238
Parallel-51
Parallel-135
Parallel-238
Hot Numbers-HN23
Hot Numbers Parallel-HN23
Inks-IMG
Stitches-SSMA
Wave of the Future-WF19
06Fleer-98
Tiffany-98
Fabricology-FMG
Signing Day-SDMG
Speed Machines-SM14
06Hot Prospects-48
Red Hot-48
White Hot-48
Hot Materials -HMMG
Hot Materials Red Hot-HMMG
Hot Materials White Hot-HMMG
06McDonald's Upper Deck-22
06O-Pee-Chee-240
06O-Pee-Chee-685
Rainbow-240
Rainbow-685
Autographs-A-MG
Swatches-S-MG
06Panini Stickers-293
06SP Authentic-53
06SP Authentic-130
Limited-53
Limited-130
Sign of the Times Triples-ST3PGB
06SP Game Used-49
Gold-49
Rainbow-49
Authentic Fabrics-AFMG
Authentic Fabrics Parallel-AFMG
Authentic Fabrics Patches-AFMG
Authentic Fabrics Dual-AF2DG
Authentic Fabrics Dual Patches-AF2DG
Authentic Fabrics Triple-AF3MIN
Authentic Fabrics Triple Patches-AF3MIN
Authentic Fabrics Quads-AF4JHEG
Authentic Fabrics Quads Patches-AF4JHEG
Autographs-49
Inked Sweaters-ISMG
Inked Sweaters Patches-ISMG
Inked Sweaters Dual-IS2GB

Inked Sweaters Dual Patches-IS2GB
Letter Marks-LMMG
SIGnificance-SGA
06SPx-48
Spectrum-48
SPxcitement-X50
SPxcitement Spectrum-X50
SPxcitement Autographs-X50
Winning Materials-WMMG
Winning Materials Spectrum-WMMG
Winning Materials Autographs-WMMG
06The Cup-43
Autographed Foundations-CQMG
Autographed Foundations Patches-CQMG
Autographed NHL Shields Duals-DASGB
Autographed NHL Shields Duals-DASMN
Autographed Patches-43
Black Rainbow-43
Foundations-CQMG
Foundations Patches-CQMG
Enshrinements-EMG
Gold-43
Gold Patches-43
Honorable Numbers-HNMG
Jerseys-43
Limited Logos-LLMG
Masterpiece Pressplates-43
NHL Shields Duals-DSHDG
NHL Shields Duals-DSHGF
Scripted Swatches-SSMG
Signature Patches-SPMG
06UD Artifacts-52
06UD Artifacts-174
Blue-52
Blue-174
Gold-52
Gold-174
Platinum-52
Platinum-174
Radiance-52
Radiance-174
Autographed Radiance Parallel-52
Autographed Radiance Parallel-174
Red-52
Red-174
Auto-Facts-AFMA
Auto-Facts Gold-AFMA
Tundra Tandems-TTGD
Tundra Tandems Black-TTGD
Tundra Tandems Blue-TTGD
Tundra Tandems Gold-TTGD
Tundra Tandems Platinum-TTGD
Tundra Tandems Red-TTGD
Tundra Tandems Dual Patches Red-TTGD
06UD Mini Jersey Collection-51
06UD Powerplay-49
Impact Rainbow-49
Specialists-SMG
Specialists Patches-PMG
06UD Toronto Fall Expo Priority Signings -PSMG
06Ultimate Collection-31
Autographed Jerseys-AJ-MG
Autographed Patches-AJ-MG
Jerseys-UJ-MG
Patches-UJ-MG
Premium Patches-PS-MG
Premium Swatches-PS-MG
Signatures-US-MG
Ultimate Achievements-UA-MG
Ultimate Signatures Logos-SL-MG
06Ultra-96
Gold Medallion-96
Ice Medallion-96
Action-UA13
Fresh Ink-IMG
Scoring Kings-SK17
Uniformity-UMG
Uniformity Patches-UPMK
Uniformity Autographed Jerseys-UAMG
06Upper Deck Arena Giveaways-MIN1
06Upper Deck-94
Exclusives Parallel-94
High Gloss Parallel-94
All-Time Greatest-ATG11
All World-AW15
Game Dated Moments-GD38
Game Jerseys-JMG
Game Patches-PMG
Generations Duals-G2EG
Generations Patches Dual-G2PEG
Goal Rush-GR6
Hometown Heroes-HH52
Masterpieces-94
Signatures-SMG
Signature Sensations-SSMG
Walmart Tins Oversize-94
06Upper Deck MVP-141
Gold Script-141
Super Script-141
Clutch Performers-CP19
Gotta Have Hart-HH21
International Icons-II11
Jerseys-OJGH
06Upper Deck Ovation-125
06Upper Deck Sweet Shot-54
Signature Shots/Saves-SSMG
Signature Shots/Saves Ice Signings-SSIMG
Signature Shots/Saves Sticks-SSSMG
Signature Sticks-STMG
Sweet Stitches-SSMG
Sweet Stitches Duals-SSMG
Sweet Stitches Triples-SSMG
06Upper Deck Trilogy-48
Combo Autographed Jerseys-CJGP
Combo Autographed Patches-CJGP
Ice Scripts-ISMG
Scripts-S1MG
Scripts-S3MG
Scripts-TSMG
06Upper Deck Victory-96
06Upper Deck Victory Black-96
06Upper Deck Victory Gold-96
06Upper Deck Victory GameBreakers-GB22
06Upper Deck Victory Next In Line-NL27
06Upper Deck Victory Oversize Cards-MG
06Wild Crime Prevention-8
06Wild Postcards-8
06Russian Sport Collection Olympic Stars-44
07Upper Deck Victory-144
Black-144
Gold-144
Oversize Cards-OS33

Gabriel, Jeff
93RPI Engineers-10
94Greensboro Monarchs-16

Gabriele, Sean
93Lakeland Ice Warriors-14

Gador, Rob
90Cincinnati Cyclones-28

Gadowsky, Guy
91Richmond Renegades-18
92Richmond Renegades-5
95Oklahoma Coyotes RHI-18

Gadsby, Bill
44Beehive Group II Photos-96
44Beehive Group II Photos-167
44Beehive Group II Photos-312
51Parkhurst-37
52Parkhurst-56
53Parkhurst-76
54Parkhurst-87
54Topps-20
57Topps-65
58Topps-34
59Topps-62
60Shirriff Coins-90
60Topps-22
61Parkhurst-27
61Shirriff/Salada Coins-79
62Parkhurst-25
62York Iron-On Transfers-31
63Chex Photos-14
63Parkhurst-59
63Toronto Star-12
63York White Backs-39
64Beehive Group III Photos-70
64Coca-Cola Caps-40
64Topps-96
65Coca-Cola-40
65Topps-44
76Old Timers-7
81Red Wings Oldtimers-4
83Hall of Fame-110
83Hall of Fame Postcards-H4
85Hall of Fame-110
91Kraft-74
91Ultimate Original Six-69
French-69
92Parkhurst Parkie Reprints-PR9
94Parkhurst Missing Link-89
94Parkhurst Missing Link-137
94Parkhurst Tall Boys-54
99BAP Memorabilia AS Retail-R8
99BAP Memorabilia AS Retail Autographs-R8
00Topps Heritage Arena Relics-OSA-BG
01BAP Signature Series Vintage Autographs-VA-26
01BAP Ultimate Mem All-Star History-19
01BAP Ultimate Memorabilia Decades-6
01BAP Ultimate Memorabilia Gloves Are Off-5
01BAP Update Rocket's Rivals-RR-7
01Parkhurst Autographs-PA18
01Parkhurst Heroes-H16
01Parkhurst Reprints-PR28
01Parkhurst Reprints-PR39
01Parkhurst Reprints-PR49
01Parkhurst Reprints-PR81
01Parkhurst Reprints-PR83
01Parkhurst Reprints-PR95
01Parkhurst Reprints-PR150
01Parkhurst Vintage Memorabilia-PV9
01Topps Archives-2
02BAP NHL All-Star History-19
02BAP Ultimate Memorabilia Gloves Are Off-15
02Parkhurst Vintage Memorabilia-VM20
03BAP Memorabilia Gloves-GUG18
03BAP Ultimate Memorabilia Gloves Are Off-12
03ITG Used Sig Series Vintage Mem -16
03ITG Used Sig Series Vintage Mem Gold-16
03Parkhurst Original Six Chicago-57
03Parkhurst Original Six Chicago-74
03Parkhurst Original Six Chicago-89
03Parkhurst Original Six Detroit-45
03Parkhurst Original Six Detroit-89
Autographs-OS-BG
Memorabilia-DM23
03Parkhurst Orig Six He Shoots/Scores-29
03Parkhurst Orig Six He Shoots/Scores-29A
03Parkhurst Original Six New York-44
Memorabilia-NM23
04ITG NHL AS FANtasy AS History Jerseys-SB19
04ITG Franchises US West Memorabilia-WSM23
04ITG Franchises US West Memorabilia Gold-WSM23
04ITG Franchises US West Teammates-WTM6
04ITG Franchises US West Teammates Gold-WTM6
04ITG Ultimate Memorabilia-12
04ITG Ultimate Memorabilia-56
Gold-12
Gold-56
Autographs-51
Autographs Gold-51
Original Six-3
Original Six-7
Original Six-10
05ITG Ultimate Mem Decades Jerseys-7
05ITG Ultimate Mem Decades Jerseys Gold-7
06ITG Ultimate Memorabilia Decades-4
06ITG Ultimate Memorabilia Decades Gold-4
06Parkhurst-6
06Parkhurst-173
06Parkhurst-236
Autographs-6
Autographs-173
Autographs-236
Autographs Dual-DAFG

Gaess, Ralf
94German First League-333

Gaetz, Link
88North Stars ADA-9
89ProCards IHL-88
90OPC Premier-33
90Score-411
Canadian-411
90ProCards AHL/IHL-110
91O-Pee-Chee Inserts-1S
91Pinnacle-339
91Pinnacle-412
French-339
French-412
91Pro Set-561
French-561
91Sharks Sports Action-7
94Central Hockey League-74
94San Antonio Iguanas-2
02Fleer Throwbacks-57
Gold-57
Platinum-57
03St. Jean Mission-9
04Thetford Mines Prolab-26
05ITG Tough Customers-LG
Autographs-LG

Gaffar, Shayne
907th Inn. Sketch OHL-34
91Cornwall Royals-15
917th Inn. Sketch OHL-12

Gaffney, Mike
98Detroit Vipers-7
99Finnish Cardset-225
00Austin Ice Bats-5
02Austin Ice Bats-4

Gage, Joaquin
917th Inn. Sketch WHL-46
93Prince Albert Raiders-5
94Cape Breton Oilers-8
95Bowman-154
All-Foil-154
95Donruss-237
95Leaf-255
95Parkhurst International-343
Emerald Ice-343
00Topps Heritage-203
00Vanguard-118
Pacific Proofs-118
00Hamilton Bulldogs-24
01Between the Pipes-59
02Swedish SHL-155
02Swedish SHL-284
Parallel-155
Parallel-284
03German DEL-156
03Swedish Elite-12
Silver-12
Zero Hero-4
04German DEL-188
05German DEL-184
Goalies-G03

Gage, Jody
88ProCards AHL-266
89ProCards AHL-276
90ProCards AHL/IHL-285
91ProCards-21
91Rochester Americans Dunkin' Donuts-7
91Rochester Americans Kodak-13
92Rochester Americans Dunkin' Donuts-7
92Rochester Americans Kodak-9
93Rochester Americans Kodak-10
94Classic Pro Prospects-82
95Rochester Americans-4
96Collector's Edge Ice-63
Prism-63
98Rochester Americans-23

Gaggi, Jason
95Slapshot-32
96Sudbury Wolves-7
96Sudbury Wolves Police-10

Gagne, Art
23V128-1 Paulin's Candy-31
24Anonymous NHL-12
27La Patrie-2
27La Presse Photos-6
27La Presse Photos-8

Gagne, Dominic
90Montreal-Bourassa AAA-11

Gagne, Don
83NHL Key Tags-76
89Hampton Roads Admirals-7A
89Hampton Roads Admirals-7H
90Cincinnati Cyclones-22

Gagne, Jacque
56Quebec Aces-5

Gagne, Karl
01Moncton Wildcats-7
02Moncton Wildcats-24
03Moncton Wildcats-5
04Quebec Remparts-3

Gagne, Keven
03Drummondville Voltigeurs-6
04Drummondville Voltigeurs-9
05Drummondville Voltigeurs-20

Gagne, Luc
94Sudbury Wolves-13
94Sudbury Wolves Police-6
95Slapshot-398
95Sudbury Wolves-5
95Sudbury Wolves Police-9
96Sudbury Wolves-8
96Sudbury Wolves Police-11

Gagne, Martin
907th Inn. Sketch QMJHL-39
917th Inn. Sketch Memorial Cup-42
92Quebec Pee-Wee Tournament-192

Gagne, Mathieu
01Thetford Mines Coyotes-5

Gagne, Mausime
907th Inn. Sketch QMJHL-124

Gagne, Paul
81O-Pee-Chee-75
81O-Pee-Chee Stickers-233
81Rockies Postcards-6
81Topps-W80
82O-Pee-Chee-139
83Devils Postcards-10
84Devils Postcards-17
85Devils Postcards-5
85O-Pee-Chee-163
85O-Pee-Chee Stickers-60
85Topps-163
88ProCards AHL-237
89ProCards AHL-122
93Swiss HNL-252
95Swiss HNL-452
96Swiss HNL-395
98Swiss Power Play Stickers-298
99Swiss Panini Stickers-302

Gagne, Rejean
93Quebec Pee-Wee Tournament-1065

Gagne, Remi
83Nova Scotia Voyageurs-14

Gagne, Roger
51Bas Du Fleuve-44

Gagne, Simon
93Quebec Pee-Wee Tournament-342
94Quebec Pee-Wee Tournament-1077
97Upper Deck-411
98Bowman's Best-140
Refractors-140
Atomic Refractors-140
98Quebec Remparts-8
Signed-8
98Bowman CHL-107
98Bowman CHL-126
Golden Anniversary-107
Golden Anniversary-126
OPC International-107
OPC International-126
Autographs Blue-A36
Autographs Gold-A36
Autographs Silver-A36
98Bowman Chrome CHL-107
98Bowman Chrome CHL-126
Golden Anniversary-107
Golden Anniversary-126
Golden Anniversary Refractors-107
Golden Anniversary Refractors-126
OPC International-107
OPC International-126
OPC International Refractors-107
OPC International Refractors-126
Refractors-107
Refractors-126
99BAP Memorabilia-195
Gold-195
Silver-195
99BAP Millennium-183
Emerald-183
Ruby-183
Sapphire-183
Signatures-183
Signatures Gold-183
Calder Candidates Ruby-C2
Calder Candidates Emerald-C2
Calder Candidates Sapphire-C2
99Crown Royale-101
Limited Series-101
Premiere Date-101
Prospects Parallel-101
International Glory-17
International Glory Parallel-17
99O-Pee-Chee-251
99O-Pee-Chee Chrome-251
99O-Pee-Chee Chrome Refractors-251
99Pacific Dynagon Ice-2
Blue-2
Copper-2
Gold-2
Prémiere Date-2
99Pacific Omega-169
Copper-169
Gold-169
Ice Blue-169
Premiere Date-169
NHL Generations-8
99Pacific Prism-101
Holographic Blue-101
Holographic Gold-101
Holographic Mirror-101
Holographic Purple-101
Premiere Date-101
Ice Prospects-6
99Panini Stickers-129
99SP Authentic Sign of the Times-SG
99SP Authentic Sign of the Times Gold-SG
99Stadium Club-188
First Day Issue-188
One of a Kind-188
Printing Plates Black-188
Printing Plates Cyan-188
Printing Plates Magenta-188
Printing Plates Yellow-188
Chrome-44
Chrome Refractors-44
99Topps/OPC-251
99Topps/OPC Chrome-251
Refractors-251
99Topps Gold Label Class 1-92
Black-92
Black One of One-92
One of One-92
Red-92
Red One of One-92
99Topps Gold Label Class 2-92
99Topps Gold Label Class 2 Black-92
99Topps Gold Label Class 2 Black 1 of 1-92
99Topps Gold Label Class 2 One of One-92
99Topps Gold Label Class 2 Red-92
99Topps Gold Label Class 2 Red One of One-92
99Topps Gold Label Class 3-92
99Topps Gold Label Class 3 Black-92
99Topps Gold Label Class 3 Black 1 of 1-92
99Topps Gold Label Class 3 One of One-92
99Topps Gold Label Class 3 Red-92
99Topps Gold Label Class 3 Red One of One-92
99Topps Premier Plus-139
Parallel-139
Premier Rookies-PR10
Premier Rookies Parallel-PR10
99Upper Deck-270
Exclusives-270
Exclusives 1 of 1-270
99Upper Deck Arena Giveaways-PF1
99Upper Deck Gold Reserve-270
99Upper Deck HoloGrFx-42
Ausome-42
99Upper Deck MVP SC Edition-133
Gold Script-133
Silver Script-133
Super Script-133
ProSign-SG
99Upper Deck Ovation-43
Standing Ovation-43
99Upper Deck Victory-362
99Wayne Gretzky Hockey-125
99Quebec PeeWee Tournament Coll Souv-28
99Bowman CHL-59
Gold-59
OPC International-59
Scout's Choice-SC17
00Aurora-106
Premiere Date-106
00BAP Memorabilia-6
Emerald-6
Ruby-6
Sapphire-6
Promos-6
00BAP Mem Chicago Sportsfest Copper-6
00BAP Memorabilia Chicago Sportsfest Blue-6
00BAP Memorabilia Chicago Sportsfest Gold-6
00BAP Memorabilia Chicago Sportsfest Ruby-6
00BAP Memorabilia Chicago Sun-Times Ruby-6
00BAP Memorabilia Chicago Sun-Times Gold-6
00BAP Mem Chicago Sun-Times Sapphire-6
00BAP Mem Toronto Fall Expo Copper-6
00BAP Memorabilia Toronto Fall Expo Gold-6
00BAP Memorabilia Toronto Fall Expo Ruby-6
00BAP Parkhurst 2000-P11
00BAP Signature Series-119
Emerald-119
Ruby-119
Sapphire-119
Autographs-192
Autographs Gold-192
00Black Diamond-44
Gold-44
00Crown Royale-79
Ice Blue-79
Limited Series-79
Premiere Date-79
Red-79
00O-Pee-Chee-236
00O-Pee-Chee Parallel-236
00Pacific-296
Copper-296
Gold-296
Ice Blue-296
Premiere Date-296
Autographs-296
00Paramount-180
Copper-180
Gold-180
Holo-Gold-180
Holo-Silver-180
Ice Blue-180
Premiere Date-180
00Private Stock-72
Gold-72
Premiere Date-72
Retail-72
Silver-72
PS-2001 New Wave-18
00Revolution-108
Blue-108
Premiere Date-108
Red-108
00SP Authentic-65
00SPx-48
Spectrum-48
SPXcitement-X9
00Stadium Club-81
00Titanium-69
Blue-69
Gold-69
Premiere Date-69
Red-69
Retail-69
00Topps/OPC-236
Parallel-236
Own the Game-OTG24
00Topps Chrome-146
OPC Refractors-146
Refractors-146
00Topps Gold Label Class 1-59
Gold-59
00Topps Gold Label Class 2-59
00Topps Gold Label Class 2 Gold-59
00Topps Gold Label Class 3-59
00Topps Gold Label Class 3 Gold-59
00Topps Heritage-69
Chrome Parallel-69
00Topps Premier Plus-37
Blue Ice-37
00UD Heroes-86
00UD Pros and Prospects-64
00Upper Deck-129
Exclusives Tier 1-129
Exclusives Tier 2-129
Prospects In Depth-P8
00Upper Deck MVP-132
First Stars-132
Second Stars-132
Third Stars-132
00Upper Deck Victory-174
00Upper Deck Vintage-263
00Vanguard-72
Holographic Gold-72
Holographic Purple-72
Pacific Proofs-72
01BAP Memorabilia-82
Emerald-82
Ruby-82
Sapphire-82
All-Star Jerseys-ASJ25
All-Star Emblems-ASE25
All-Star Numbers-ASN25
All-Star Teammates-AST2
01BAP Ultimate Memorabilia Gloves Are Off-16
01Bowman YoungStars-76
Gold-76
Ice Cubed-76
01Crown Royale-106
Blue-106
Premiere Date-106
Red-106
Retail-106
01Flyers Postcards-8
01O-Pee-Chee-65
01O-Pee-Chee Heritage Parallel-65
01O-Pee-Chee Heritage Parallel Limited-65
01O-Pee-Chee Premier Parallel-65
01Pacific-287
Extreme LTD-287
Hobby LTD-287
Premiere Date-287
Retail LTD-287
01Pacific Adrenaline-139
Blue-139
Premiere Date-139
Red-139
Retail-139
01Pacific Arena Exclusives-287
01Parkhurst-82
Gold-82
Silver-82
01Private Stock-71
Gold-71
Premiere Date-71
Retail-71
Silver-71
01Private Stock Pacific Nights-71
01SP Authentic Sign of the Times-SG
01SP Game Used Inked Sweaters-SGA
01SP Game Used Inked Sweaters-ISSG
01SP Game Used Inked Sweaters-DSGO
01SP Game Used Inked Sweaters-DSIG
01SP Game Used Inked Sweaters-DSLG
01SP Game Used Patches-PSG
01SP Game Used Patches-CPGK
01SP Game Used Patches-CPPG
01SP Game Used Patches Signed-SPSG
01SP Game Used Patches Signed-DSPGP
01SPx-189
Hidden Treasures-DTGW
Hidden Treasures-DTSG
Signs of Xcellence-SG
01Stadium Club-82
Award Winners-82
Master Photos-82
01Titanium-104
Hobby Parallel-104
Premiere Date-104
Retail-104
Retail Parallel-104
Double-Sided Jerseys-51
Double-Sided Jerseys-64
Double-Sided Patches-51
Double-Sided Patches-64
01Titanium Draft Day Edition-70
01Topps-65
Heritage Parallel-65
Heritage Parallel Limited-65
OPC Parallel-65
Autographs-ASG
Game-Worn Jersey-JSG
Jumbo Jersey Autographs-JJA-SG
01Topps Chrome-65
Refractors-65
Black Border Refractors-65
01Topps Heritage-72
Refractors-72
01Topps Reserve-5
Emblems-SG
Jerseys-SG
Name Plates-SG
Numbers-SG
Patches-SG
01UD Challenge for the Cup Jersey Autos-UCLG
01UD Honor Roll Sharp Skaters-SS6
01UD Mask Collection-70
Gold-70
Double Patches-DPSG
Dual Jerseys-PMGB
Jerseys-J-SG
Jersey and Patch-JPSG
01UD Playmakers Combo Jerseys-CJSG
01UD Playmakers Combo Jerseys Gold-CJSG
01UD Playmakers Jerseys-J-SG
01UD Playmakers Jerseys Gold-J-SG
01UD Playmakers Practice Jerseys-PJSG
01UD Playmakers Practice Jerseys Gold-PJSG
01UD Premier Collection-39
Jerseys-BSG
Jerseys Black-B-SG
Signatures-SG
Signatures Black-SG
01Upper Deck-361
Exclusives-361
Game Jerseys Series II-GNSG
Game Jersey Autographs-SJSG
01Upper Deck MVP-137
Morning Skate Jerseys-J-SG
Morning Skate Jersey Autographs-SJ-SG
01Upper Deck Victory-258
01Upper Deck Victory-433
Gold-258
Gold-433
01Vanguard Quebec Tournament Heroes-18
02Atomic-74
Blue-74
Gold-74
Red-74
Cold Fusion-19
Hobby Parallel-74
02BAP All-Star Edition-26
Jerseys-26
Jerseys Gold-26
Jerseys Silver-26
02BAP First Edition-124
02BAP First Edition-362
02BAP First Edition-374
02BAP First Edition-420R
Jerseys-124
02BAP Memorabilia-200
02BAP Memorabilia-222
Emerald-200
Emerald-222
Ruby-200
Ruby-222
Sapphire-200
Sapphire-222
All-Star Jerseys-ASJ-15
Franchise Players-FP-22
Future of the Game-FG-9
NHL All-Star Game-200
NHL All-Star Game-222
NHL All-Star Game Blue-200
NHL All-Star Game Blue-222
NHL All-Star Game Green-200
NHL All-Star Game Green-222
NHL All-Star Game Red-200
NHL All-Star Game Red-222
Teammates-TM-10
02BAP Memorabilia Toronto Fall Expo-200
02BAP Memorabilia Toronto Fall Expo-222
02BAP Signature Series-6
Autographs-6
Autograph Buybacks 1999-183
Autographs Gold-6
Phenoms-YP2
02BAP Ultimate Memorabilia Hat Tricks-1
02Bowman YoungStars-43
Gold-43
Silver-43
02Crown Royale-70
Blue-70
Red-70
Retail-70
02eTopps-34
02Flyers Postcards-5
02ITG Used-58
02ITG Used-158
Franchise Players-F22
Franchise Players Autographs-F22
Franchise Players Gold-F22
Teammates-T15
Teammates Gold-T15
Triple Memorabilia-TM13
Triple Memorabilia Gold-TM13
02McDonald's Pacific-31
Salt Lake Gold-10
02O-Pee-Chee-97
02O-Pee-Chee-325
02O-Pee-Chee Premier Blue Parallel-97
02O-Pee-Chee Premier Blue Parallel-325
02O-Pee-Chee Premier Red Parallel-97
02O-Pee-Chee Premier Red Parallel-325
02O-Pee-Chee Factory Set-97
02O-Pee-Chee Factory Set-325
02Pacific-280
Blue-280
Red-280
Jerseys-39
Jerseys Holo-Silver-39
02Pacific Complete-18
Red-18
02Pacific Exclusive-126
Maximum Overdrive-15
02Pacific Heads-Up-90
Blue-90
Purple-90
Red-90
Head First-12
02Pacific Quest for the Cup-75
Gold-75
02Parkhurst-28
Bronze-28
Gold-28
Silver-28
Franchise Players-FP22
Heroes-NH5
02Parkhurst Retro-38
Minis-38
02Private Stock Reserve-136
Red-136
Retail-136
Patches-136
02SP Authentic-67
Beckett Promos-67
Sign of the Times-SG
Sign of the Times-GB
Sign of the Times-GL
Super Premiums-SPSG
Super Premiums-DPRG
02SP Game Used-36
First Rounder Patches-SG
Future Fabrics-FFSG
Future Fabrics Gold-FFSG
Future Fabrics Rainbow-FFSG
Piece of History-PHSG
Piece of History Gold-PHSG
Piece of History Rainbow-PHSG
Signature Style-SG
02SPx-56
Spectrum Gold-56
Spectrum Silver-56
Smooth Skaters-SG
Smooth Skaters Gold-SG
Smooth Skaters Silver-SG
Winning Materials-WMSG
Winning Materials Gold-SG
Winning Materials Silver-SG
Xtreme Talents-SG
Xtreme Talents Gold-SG
Xtreme Talents Silver-SG
02Stadium Club-24
Silver Decoy Cards-24
Proofs-24
Lone Star Signatures Blue-LSSG
Lone Star Signatures Red-LSSG
Passport-6
02Titanium-75
Blue-75
Red-75
Retail-75
Jerseys-49
Jerseys Retail-49
Patches-49
02Topps-97
02Topps-325
OPC Blue Parallel-97
OPC Blue Parallel-325
OPC Red Parallel-97
OPC Red Parallel-325
02Topps Promos-PP1
02Topps Factory Set-97
02Topps Factory Set-325
02Topps Chrome-61
Black Border Refractors-61
Refractors-61
02Topps Heritage-28
Chrome Parallel-28
Great Skates-SG
Great Skates Patches-SG
02Topps Total-32
02UD Artistic Impressions-66
Gold-66
Artist's Touch-ATSG
Artist's Touch Gold-ATSG
02UD Artistic Impressions Beckett Promos-66
02UD Artistic Impressions Retrospectives-R66
02UD Artistic Impressions Retrospect Gold-R66
02UD Artistic Impress Retrospect Silver-R66
02UD Honor Roll Grade A Jerseys-GASG
02UD Honor Roll Grade A Jerseys-TPRG
02UD Mask Collection Instant Offense-IOSG
02UD Mask Collection Patches-PGSG
02UD Piece of History-66
Marks of Distinction-SG
Patches-PHSG
Threads-TTSG
02UD Premier Collection Jerseys Bronze-SG
02UD Premier Collection Jerseys Bronze-RG
02UD Premier Collection Jerseys Gold-SG
02UD Premier Collection Jerseys Gold-RG
02UD Premier Collection Jerseys Silver-SG
02UD Premier Collection Jerseys Silver-RG
02UD Premier Collection Patches-PSG
02UD Premier Collection Signatures Bronze-SSG
02UD Premier Collection Signatures Gold-SSG
02UD Premier Collection Signatures Silver-SSG
02UD Top Shelf-66
Clutch Performers-CPSGA
Dual Player Jerseys-RKG
Dual Player Jerseys-STGB
Dual Player Jerseys-STGR
Dual Player Jerseys-STGS
Dual Player Jerseys-STHL
Dual Player Jerseys-STHR
Goal Oriented-GOSG
Shooting Stars-SHSG
Signatures-SG
Triple Jerseys-HTKGF
Triple Jerseys-HTSIG
Triple Jerseys-TSLGC
02Upper Deck-377
Exclusives-377
02Upper Deck Beckett UD Promos-377
02Upper Deck Bright Futures-SG
02Upper Deck Game Jersey Autographs-SG
02Upper Deck Game Jersey Series II-GJSG
02Upper Deck Patch Card Logo-SG
02Upper Deck Patchwork-PWSG
02Upper Deck Shooting Stars-SS11
02Upper Deck Speed Demons-SDSG
02Upper Deck Classic Portraits-74
Etched in Time-ET12
Headliners-RG
Headliners Limited-RG
Hockey Royalty-GTD
Hockey Royalty-PGF
Hockey Royalty Limited-GTD
Hockey Royalty Limited-PGF
Starring Cast-CSG
Starring Cast Limited-CSG
Stitches-CSG
Stitches Limited-CSG
02Upper Deck MVP-138
Gold-138
Classics-138
Golden Classics-138
Overdrive-SO11
Skate Around Jerseys-SDDG
Skate Around Jerseys-SDRG
Skate Around Jerseys-SDWG
Skate Around Jerseys-STTDG
Souvenirs-S-SG
02Upper Deck Rookie Update Autographs-SG
02Upper Deck Victory-156
Bronze-156
Gold-156
Silver-156
National Pride-NP10
02Upper Deck Vintage-182
02Upper Deck Vintage-282
02Upper Deck Vintage-312
Jerseys-HSSG
Jerseys Gold-HS-SG
Tall Boys-T48
Tall Boys Gold-T48
02Vanguard-73
LTD-73
03BAP Memorabilia-89
Emerald-89
Gold-89
Ruby-89
Sapphire-89
Jerseys-GJ-30
Jersey Autographs-GJ-30
03BAP Ultimate Memorabilia Autographs-86
Gold-86
03BAP Ultimate Mem Auto Jerseys-86
03BAP Ultimate Mem Auto Sticks-86
03Beehive-147
Gold-147
Silver-147
Sticks Blue Border-BL3
03Black Diamond-86
Black-86
Green-86
Red-86
Signature Gems-SG-7
03Bowman-77
Gold-77
Future Rivals-HG
Future Rivals Patches-HG
Goal to Goal-SG
03Bowman Chrome-77
Refractors-77
Gold Refractors-77
Xfractors-77
03Flyers Postcards-7
03ITG Action-431
Jerseys-M105
03ITG Used Signature Series-19
Gold-19
Autographs-SG
Autographs Gold-SG
03McDonald's Pacific-38
03NHL Sticker Collection-103
03O-Pee-Chee-73
03OPC Blue-73
03OPC Gold-73
03OPC Red-73
03Pacific-251
Blue-251
Red-251
03Pacific Complete-172
Red-172
03Pacific Exhibit-109
Blue Backs-109
Yellow Backs-109
03Private Stock Reserve-75
Blue-75
Red-75
Retail-75
03SP Authentic-66
Limited-66
Sign of the Times-CRG
03SP Game Used-34
Gold-34
Authentic Fabrics-AFSG
Authentic Fabrics-DFRG
Authentic Fabrics-QARGL
Authentic Fabrics Gold-AFSG
Authentic Fabrics Gold-DFRG
Authentic Fabrics Gold-QARGL
Top Threads-ARGL
03SPx-72
Radiance-72
Spectrum-72
Big Futures-BF-SG
Big Futures Limited-BF-SG
03Topps-73
Blue-73
Gold-73
Red-73
03Topps Pristine-24
Gold Refractor Die Cuts-24
Refractors-24
Patches-PP-SG
Patch Refractors-PP-SG
Popular Demand Relics-PD-SG
Popular Demand Relic Refractors-PD-SG
Press Plates Black-24
Press Plates Cyan-24
Press Plates Magenta-24
Press Plates Yellow-24
03UD Honor Roll-65
Grade A Jerseys-GASG
03Upper Deck-141
Canadian Exclusives-141
HG-141
03Upper Deck Classic Portraits-73
03Upper Deck MVP-314
Gold Script-314
Silver Script-314
Canadian Exclusives-314
ProSign-PS-SG
Souvenirs-S22
03Upper Deck Victory-142
Bronze-142
Gold-142
Silver-142
03Toronto Star-71
04Pacific-193
Blue-193
Red-193
04SP Authentic-67
Limited-67
Buybacks-181
Buybacks-182
Buybacks-183
Buybacks-184
Rookie Review-RR-SG
Sign of the Times-ST-SG
Sign of the Times-TS-GRE
Sign of the Times-QS-GPRE
Sign of the Times-FS-RGT
04UD Toronto Fall Expo Pride of Canada-14
04Ultimate Collection-32
Dual Logos-UL2-RG
Signature Logos-ULA-SG
04Upper Deck-129
Canadian Exclusives-129
HG Glossy Gold-129
HG Glossy Silver-129
World Cup Tribute-SGTHRS
05Be A Player-65
First Period-65
Second Period-65
Third Period-65
Overtime-65
Outtakes-OT38
05Beehive-68
Matte-68
Matted Materials-MMSG
Signature Scrapbook-SSSG
05Black Diamond-63
Emerald-63
Gold-63
Onyx-63
Ruby-63
05Flyers Team Issue-7
05Hot Prospects-72
En Fuego-72
Red Hot-72
White Hot-72
05McDonalds Upper Deck-16

Chasing the Cup-CC1
05Panini Stickers-131
05Parkhurst-351
05Parkhurst-572
Facsimile Auto Parallel-351
Facsimile Auto Parallel-572
True Colors-TCPHI
True Colors-TCPHI
True Colors-TCPHPI
True Colors-TCPHPI
05SP Authentic-75
Limited-75
Marks of Distinction-MDSG
Sign of the Times Triples-TPGC
Sign of the Times Fives-PEGCR
05SP Game Used-74
Autographs-74
Gold-74
Authentic Fabrics-AF-SG
Authentic Fabrics Autographs-AAF-SG
Authentic Fabrics Dual-PG
Authentic Fabrics Dual Autographs-PG
Authentic Fabrics Gold-AF-SG
Authentic Fabrics Quad-GFEP
Authentic Patches Quad -GFEP
Authentic Patches-AP-SG
Authentic Patches Autographs-AAP-SG
Authentic Patches Dual-PG
Authentic Patches Dual Autographs-PG
Auto Draft-AD-SG
Awesome Authentics-AA-SG
Game Gear-GG-SG
Game Gear Autographs-AG-SG
Significant Numbers-SN-SG
Statscriptions-ST-SG
05SPx-67
Spectrum-67
Winning Combos-WC-GR
Winning Combos-WC-PG
Winning Combos Autographs-AWC-GR
Winning Combos Gold-WC-GR
Winning Combos Gold-WC-PG
Winning Combos Spectrum-WC-GR
Winning Combos Spectrum-WC-PG
Winning Materials-WM-SG
Winning Materials Autographs-AWM-SG
Winning Materials Gold-WM-SG
Winning Materials Spectrum-WM-SG
Xcitement Superstars-XS-SG
Xcitement Superstars Gold-XS-SG
Xcitement Superstars Spectrum-XS-SG
05The Cup-76
Gold-76
Black Rainbow-76
Dual NHL Shields-DSFG
Dual NHL Shields-DSKG
Dual NHL Shields Autographs-ADSKG
Emblems of Endorsement-EESG
Honorable Numbers-HNSG
Limited Logos-LLSG
Masterpiece Pressplates-76
Masterpiece Pressplates Rookie Upd Auto-264
Noble Numbers-NNGM
Noble Numbers-NNIG
Noble Numbers Dual-DNNFG
Noble Numbers Dual-DNNLG
Patch Variation-P76
Patch Variation Autographs-AP76
Scripted Numbers-SNGM
Scripted Swatches-SSSG
Signature Patches-SPSG
05UD Artifacts-75
05UD Artifacts-186
Blue-75
Blue-186
Gold-75
Gold-186
Green-75
Green-186
Pewter-75
Pewter-186
Red-75
Red-186
Auto Facts-AF-SG
Auto Facts Blue-AF-SG
Auto Facts Copper-AF-SG
Auto Facts Pewter-AF-SG
Auto Facts Silver-AF-SG
Gold Autographed-75
Gold Autographed-186
Remarkable Artifacts-RA-SG
Remarkable Artifacts Dual-RA-SG
05Ultimate Collection-66
Gold-66
Endorsed Emblems-EESG
Jerseys-JSG
Jerseys Triple-TJFGC
National Heroes Jerseys-NHJSG
National Heroes Patches-NHPSG
Premium Patches-PPSG
Ultimate Achievements-UASG
Ultimate Patches-PSG
Ultimate Patches Triple-TPFGC
Ultimate Signatures-USSG
05Ultra-142
Gold-142
Fresh Ink-FI-SG
Fresh Ink Blue-FI-SG
Ice-142
05Upper Deck-137
Big Playmakers-B-SG
HG Glossy-137
Jerseys-J-SGA
Jerseys Series II-J2GA
Majestic Materials-MMSG
NHL Generations-DGR
NHL Generations-TCGP
Notable Numbers-N-SG
Patches-P-SGA
Shooting Stars-S-SG
05Upper Deck Ice-73
Rainbow-73
Cool Threads-CTSG
Cool Threads Autographs-ACTSG
Cool Threads Glass-CTSG
Cool Threads Patches-CTPSG
Cool Threads Patch Autographs-CAPSG
Signature Swatches-SSSG
05Upper Deck MVP-279
Gold-279
Platinum-279
ProSign-P-SG
05Upper Deck Rookie Update-71
05Upper Deck Rookie Update-264
05Upper Deck Trilogy-66
05Upper Deck Trilogy-169
Crystal-169
Honorary Patches-HP-SG
Honorary Swatches-HS-SG
05Upper Deck Toronto Fall Expo-137
05Upper Deck Victory-141
Black-141
Gold-141
Silver-141
Game Breakers-GB33
06Sports Illustrated for Kids *-47
06Be A Player-124
Autographs-124
Profiles-PP4
Profiles Autographs-PP4
Signatures-GA
Signatures 10-138
Signatures 25-138
Signatures Duals-DGC
Signatures Trios-TGCR
Up Close and Personal-UC54
Up Close and Personal Autographs-UC54
06Be A Player Portraits-78
Dual Signature Portraits-DSGC
Sensational Six-SSCDN
Signature Portraits-SPSG
Timeless Tens-TTCAN
06Beehive-28
06Beehive-176
Blue-28
Gold-28
Matte-28
Red Facsimile Signatures-28
Wood-28
5 X 7 Black and White-28
06Black Diamond-117
Black-117
Gold-117
Ruby-117
Jerseys-JGA
Jerseys Black-JGA
Jerseys Gold-JGA
Jerseys Ruby-JGA
06Flair Showcase-73
06Flair Showcase-150
06Flair Showcase-254
Parallel-73
Parallel-150
Parallel-254
Stitches-SSSG
06Fleer-141
Tiffany-141
Fabricology-FSG
Speed Machines-SM20
06Flyers Postcards-6
06Hot Prospects-71
Red Hot-71
White Hot-71
06McDonald's Upper Deck-35
06NHL POG-14
06O-Pee-Chee-356
Rainbow-356
06Panini Stickers-126
06SP Authentic-29
06SP Authentic-156
Limited-29
Limited-156
Sign of the Times Duals-STLG
06SP Game Used-72
Gold-72
Rainbow-72
Authentic Fabrics-AFGA
Authentic Fabrics Parallel-AFGA
Authentic Fabrics Patches-AFGA
Authentic Fabrics Dual-AF2KG
Authentic Fabrics Dual Patches-AF2KG
Authentic Fabrics Triple-AF3PHI
Authentic Fabrics Triple Patches-AF3PHI
Authentic Fabrics Quads-AF4SKGN
Authentic Fabrics Quads Patches-AF4SKGN
Inked Sweaters Dual-IS2GC
Inked Sweaters Dual Patches-IS2GC
06SPx-76
Spectrum-76
SPxcitement-X74
SPxcitement Spectrum-X74
Winning Materials-WMGA
Winning Materials Spectrum-WMGA
06The Cup-67
Autographed Foundations-CQSG
Autographed Foundations Patches-CQSG
Autographed NHL Shields Duals-DASGP
Autographed NHL Shields Duals-DASGS
Autographed NHL Shields Duals-DASHG
Autographed Patches-67
Black Rainbow-67
Foundations-CQSG
Foundations Patches-CQSG
Gold-67
Gold Patches-67
Honorable Numbers-HNSG
Jerseys-67
Limited Logos-LLSG
Masterpiece Pressplates-67
NHL Shields Duals-DSHFG
Scripted Swatches-SSSG
Scripted Swatches Duals-DSGC
Signature Patches-SPSG
06UD Artifacts-29
06UD Artifacts-189
Blue-29
Blue-189
Gold-29
Gold-189
Platinum-29
Platinum-189
Radiance-29
Radiance-189
Red-29
Red-189
Frozen Artifacts-FASG
Frozen Artifacts Black-FASG
Frozen Artifacts Blue-FASG
Frozen Artifacts Gold-FASG
Frozen Artifacts Platinum-FASG
Frozen Artifacts Red-FASG
Frozen Artifacts Patches Black-FASG
Frozen Artifacts Patches Blue-FASG
Frozen Artifacts Patches Gold-FASG
Frozen Artifacts Patches Platinum-FASG
Frozen Artifacts Patches Red-FASG
Tundra Tandems-TTFG
Tundra Tandems-TTGC
Tundra Tandems Black-TTFG
Tundra Tandems Black-TTGC
Tundra Tandems Blue-TTFG
Tundra Tandems Blue-TTGC
Tundra Tandems Gold-TTFG
Tundra Tandems Gold-TTGC
Tundra Tandems Platinum-TTFG
Tundra Tandems Platinum-TTGC
Tundra Tandems Red-TTFG
Tundra Tandems Red-TTGC
Tundra Tandems Dual Patches Red-TTFG
Tundra Tandems Dual Patches Red-TTGC
06UD Mini Jersey Collection-74
06UD Powerplay-73
Impact Rainbow-73
Specialists-SGA
Specialists Patches-PGA
06Ultimate Collection Autographed Jerseys-AJ-SG
06Ultimate Collection Autographed Patches-AJ-SG
06Ultimate Collection Jerseys Dual-UJ2-FG
06Ultimate Collection Patches Dual-UJ2-FG
06Ultimate Collection Signatures-US-SG
06Ultimate Collection Ultimate Signatures Logos-SL-SG
06Ultra-143
Gold Medallion-143
Ice Medallion-143
Scoring Kings-SK29
Uniformity-USG
Uniformity Patches-UPSG
06Upper Deck Arena Giveaways-PHI4
06Upper Deck-391
Exclusives Parallel-391
High Gloss Parallel-391
Game Jerseys-JGA
Game Patches-PGA
Goal Rush-GR10
Hometown Heroes-HH38
Masterpieces-391
Oversized Wal-Mart Exclusives-391
Signatures-SSG
06Upper Deck MVP-211
Gold Script-211
Super Script-211
Jerseys-OJMS
Jerseys-OJSG
06Upper Deck Ovation-35
06Upper Deck Sweet Shot-77
Signature Shots/Saves-SSSG
Signature Shots/Saves Ice Signings-SSISG
06Upper Deck Trilogy-73
Combo Clearcut Autographs-C3PGC
Honorary Scripted Patches-HSPGA
Honorary Scripted Swatches-HSSGA
Honorary Swatches-HSSG
06Upper Deck Victory-145
06Upper Deck Victory Black-145
06Upper Deck Victory Gold-145
06Upper Deck Victory GameBreakers-GB36
06Upper Deck Victory Oversize Cards-SG
07Upper Deck Ovation-65
07Upper Deck Victory-32
Black-32
Gold-32
GameBreakers-GB14
Oversize Cards-OS9
Stars on Ice-SI25

Gagne, Steve
93Quebec Pee-Wee Tournament-382

Gagne, Sylvain
79Montreal Juniors-8

Gagne, Wayne
88ProCards IHL-77
01Western Michigan Broncos-8

Gagner, Dave
87North Stars Postcards-13
88North Stars ADA-10
88O-Pee-Chee-215
89O-Pee-Chee-109
89O-Pee-Chee Box Bottoms-N
89O-Pee-Chee Stickers-203
89Panini Stickers-103
89Topps-109
89Topps Box Bottoms-N
90Bowman-186
Tiffany-186
90O-Pee-Chee-168
90Panini Stickers-248
90Pro Set-138
90Score-108
Canadian-108
90Score Hottest/Rising Stars-52
90Topps-168
Tiffany-168
90Upper Deck-248
French-248
91Pro Set Platinum-60
91Bowman-131
91Bowman-419
91O-Pee-Chee-74
91OPC Premier-128
91Panini Stickers-112
91Parkhurst-78
French-78
91Pinnacle-71
French-71
91Pro Set-108
91Pro Set-288
French-108
French-288
91Score American-72
91Score Canadian Bilingual-72
91Score Canadian English-72
91Stadium Club-117
91Topps-74
Team Scoring Leaders-7
91Upper Deck-86
91Upper Deck-180
French-86
French-180
92Bowman-171
92Humpty Dumpty II-6
92O-Pee-Chee-80
92Panini Stickers-90
92Panini Stickers French-90
92Parkhurst-311
Emerald Ice-311
92Pinnacle-85
French-85
92Pro Set-77
92Score-227
Canadian-227
92Stadium Club-121
92Topps-254
Gold-254G
92Ultra-94
92Upper Deck-174
93Donruss-83
93Leaf-128
93OPC Premier-183
Gold-183
93Panini Stickers-269
93Parkhurst-317
Emerald Ice-317
93Pinnacle-77
Canadian-77
93PowerPlay-60
93Score-98
Canadian-98
93Stadium Club-436
Members Only Master Set-436
First Day Issue-436
93Topps/OPC Premier-183
Gold-183
93Ultra-92
93Upper Deck-145
94Be A Player-R5
Signature Cards-77
94Canada Games NHL POGS-79
94Donruss-164
94EA Sports-34
94Fleer-49
94Leaf-319
94OPC Premier-298
Special Effects-298
94Parkhurst-58
Gold-58
94Pinnacle-334
Artist's Proofs-334
Rink Collection-334
94Select-6
Gold-6
94SP-30
Die Cuts-30
94Stadium Club-45
Members Only Master Set-45
First Day Issue-45
Super Team Winner Cards-45
94Stars HockeyKaps-11
94Stars Pinnacle Sheet-334
94Stars Pinnacle Sheet-NNO
94Stars Postcards-7
94Topps/OPC Premier-298
Special Effects-298
94Ultra-51
94Upper Deck-382
Electric Ice-382
95Bowman-33
All-Foil-33
95Canada Games NHL POGS-86
95Collector's Choice-7
Player's Club-7
Player's Club Platinum-7
95Donruss-58
95Emotion-45
95Finest-31
Refractors-31
95Kraft-57
95Leaf-222
95Metal-38
95Panini Stickers-167
95Parkhurst International-471
Emerald Ice-471
95Pinnacle-125
Artist's Proofs-125
Rink Collection-125
95Playoff One on One-30
95Score-93
Black Ice Artist's Proofs-93
Black Ice-93
95SkyBox Impact-44
95Stadium Club-31
Members Only Master Set-31
95Summit-53
Artist's Proofs-53
Ice-53
95Topps-254
OPC Inserts-254
95Ultra-229
95Upper Deck-370
Electric Ice-370
Electric Ice Gold-370
Special Edition-SE24
Special Edition Gold-SE24
95Zenith-56
Gifted Grinders-11
95Swedish World Championships Stickers-25
96Collector's Choice-260
96Donruss-170
Press Proofs-170
96Flair-12
Blue Ice-12
96Kraft Upper Deck-64
96Metal Universe-19
96Pinnacle-39
Artist's Proofs-39
Foil-39
Premium Stock-39
Rink Collection-39
96Playoff One on One-337
96Score-14
Artist's Proofs-14
Dealer's Choice Artist's Proofs-14
Special Artist's Proofs-14
Golden Blades-14
96Summit-80
Artist's Proofs-80
Ice-80
Metal-80
Premium Stock-80
96Ultra-22
Gold Medallion-22
97Be A Player-174
Autographs-174
Autographs Die-Cuts-174
Autographs Prismatic Die-Cuts-174
97Black Diamond-58
Double Diamond-58
Triple Diamond-58
Quadruple Diamond-58
97Collector's Choice-38
97Crown Royale-56
Emerald Green-56
Ice Blue-56
Silver-56
97Donruss-80
Press Proofs Silver-80
Press Proofs Gold-80
97Donruss Priority-103
Stamp of Approval-103
97Flames Collector's Photos-15
97Pacific-159
Copper-159
Emerald Green-159
Ice Blue-159
Red-159
Silver-159
97Pacific Invincible-17
Copper-17
Emerald Green-17
Ice Blue-17
Red-17
Silver-17
97Pacific Omega-98
Copper-98
Dark Gray-98
Emerald Green-98
Gold-98
Ice Blue-98
97Panini Stickers-191
97Paramount-79
Copper-79
Dark Grey-79
Emerald Green-79
Ice Blue-79
Red-79
Silver-79
97Pinnacle-156
Press Plates Back Black-156
Press Plates Back Cyan-156
Press Plates Back Magenta-156
Press Plates Back Yellow-156
Press Plates Front Black-156
Press Plates Front Cyan-156
Press Plates Front Magenta-156
Press Plates Front Yellow-156
97Pinnacle Certified-47
Red-47
Mirror Blue-47
Mirror Gold-47
Mirror Red-47
97Pinnacle Inside-181
97Pinnacle Tot Cert Platinum Blue-47
97Pinnacle Tot Certi Platinum Gold-47
97Pinnacle Totally Certified Platinum Red-47
97Pinnacle Tot Cert Mirror Platinum Gold-47
97Revolution-59
Copper-59
Emerald-59
Ice Blue-59
Silver-59
97Score-79
Artist's Proofs-79
Golden Blades-79
97Zenith-75
Z-Gold-75
Z-Silver-75
97Zenith 5 x 7-35
Gold Impulse-35
Silver Impulse-35
98Aurora-79
98Be A Player-57
Press Release-57
98BAP Gold-57
98BAP Autographs-57
98BAP Autographs Gold-57
98BAP Tampa Bay All Star Game-57
98Finest-114
No Protectors-114
No Protectors Refractors-114
Refractors-114
98Pacific-221
Ice Blue-221
Red-221
98Pacific Dynagon Ice-80
Blue-80
Red-80
98Panini Stickers-59
98Paramount-95
Copper-95
Emerald Green-95
Holo-Electric-95
Ice Blue-95
Silver-95
98Post-20
98UD Choice-92
Prime Choice Reserve-92
Reserve-92
99Pacific-422
Copper-422
Emerald Green-422
Gold-422
Ice Blue-422
Premiere Date-422
Red-422
02BAP Sig Series Auto Buybacks 1998-57
04ITG Franchises US West-254
Autographs-A-DGG
06London Knights-25

Gagner, Ken
83Brantford Alexanders-25

Gagner, Roger
52Bas Du Fleuve-1

Gagner, Sam
06London Knights-1
06ITG Heroes and Prospects-200
Autographs-ASG
Complete CHL Logos-CHL16
Double Memorabilia-DM10
Jerseys-GUJ70
Emblems-GUE70
Numbers-GUN70
National Pride-NP22
Quad Emblems-QE13
Triple Memorabilia-TM11
07ITG Going For Gold World Juniors-22
Autographs-22
Emblems-GUE22
Jerseys-GUJ22
Numbers-GUN22

Gagnier, Francis
93Quebec Pee-Wee Tournament-34

Gagnon, Bryn
03Salmon Arm Silverbacks-7
04Salmon Arm Silverbacks-10

Gagnon, Chad
97Rimouski Oceanic-45

Gagnon, Dave
90ProCards AHL/IHL-491
91Score American-387
91Score Canadian Bilingual-277
91Score Canadian English-277
93Quebec Pee-Wee Tournament-993
94Roanoke Express-2
95Minnesota Moose-5
96Roanoke Express-1
98Roanoke Express-5
00Roanoke Express-7

Gagnon, Erik
93Quebec Pee-Wee Tournament-1133

Gagnon, Francis
04Gatineau Olympiques-23

Gagnon, Francois
907th Inn. Sketch QMJHL-263
917th Inn. Sketch QMJHL-15
94Central Hockey League-44
00Shawinigan Cataractes-15
Signed-15
01Val d'Or Foreurs-12
02Val d'Or Foreurs-9
03Val d'Or Foreurs-10

Gagnon, Germaine
72O-Pee-Chee-200
72Sargent Promotions Stamps-133
73O-Pee-Chee-161
73Topps-178
74NHL Action Stamps-85
74O-Pee-Chee NHL-344
75O-Pee-Chee NHL-101
75Topps-101

Gagnon, Gerry
51Laval Dairy Lac St. Jean-11

Gagnon, Goalie
907th Inn. Sketch QMJHL-3
917th Inn. Sketch QMJHL-292
917th Inn. Sketch Memorial Cup-50
97Tucson Gila Monsters-9

Gagnon, Henri-Paul
52Bas Du Fleuve-27

Gagnon, Herve
92Quebec Pee-Wee Tournament-813
93Quebec Pee-Wee Tournament-955

Gagnon, Jacques
51Laval Dairy QSHL-21
52Bas Du Fleuve-40

Gagnon, Jean
93Swiss HNL-416
95Swiss HNL-240

Gagnon, Jean-Francois
917th Inn. Sketch QMJHL-169

Gagnon, Jimmy
99Kitchener Rangers-17
00Kitchener Rangers-13
01Peterborough Petes-12
02Plymouth Whalers-5

Gagnon, Joel
92Oshawa Generals Sheet-22
93Oshawa Generals-2
94North Bay Centennials-1

Gagnon, Johnny
33O-Pee-Chee V304A-19
33V129-43
33V357 Ice Kings-21
34Beehive Group I Photos-151
34Diamond Matchbooks Silver-23
35Diamond Matchbooks Tan 2-23
35Diamond Matchbooks Tan 3-21
37O-Pee-Chee V304E-154
37V356 Worldwide Gum-83
38Quaker Oats Photos-14
39O-Pee-Chee V301-1-25
43Parade Sportive *-39
43Parade Sportive *-40
55Parkhurst-65
Quaker Oats-65
05ITG Ultimate Mem Bleu Blanc Rouge Autos-13

Gagnon, Jonathan
92Quebec Pee-Wee Tournament-588
00Rouyn-Noranda Huskies-24
Signed-24
01Memphis RiverKings-20
03Augusta Lynx-39
03Memphis RiverKings-4

Gagnon, Marc
91British Columbia JHL-140
91British Columbia JHL-146
93St. Cloud State Huskies-5
93St. Cloud State Huskies-29

Gagnon, Ovila
52Juniors Blue Tint-162

Gagnon, Parice
93Quebec Pee-Wee Tournament-1362

Gagnon, Pascal
917th Inn. Sketch QMJHL-46

Gagnon, Paul
51Bas Du Fleuve-47
51Laval Dairy Lac St. Jean-6

Gagnon, Paul-Sebastien
93Amos Les Forestiers-7

Gagnon, Pierre
86Sudbury Wolves-16
87Sudbury Wolves-16
88Kitchener Rangers-21

Gagnon, Samuel
04Thetford Mines Prolab-19

Gagnon, Sean
917th Inn. Sketch OHL-264
91Sudbury Wolves-5
93Sault Ste. Marie Greyhounds-7
93Sault Ste. Marie Greyhound Memorial Cup-7
94Dayton Bombers-11
95Dayton Bombers-17
95Dayton Bombers-P1
97Springfield Falcons-9
99Finnish Cardset-260
00Grand Rapids Griffins-8
01Hartford Wolf Pack-4

Gagnon, Simon
93Quebec Pee-Wee Tournament-3
02BAP Sig Series Auto Buybacks 2000-192

Gagnon, Yannick
93Drummondville Voltigeurs-3

Gagnon, Yves
93Quebec Pee-Wee Tournament-249

Gahler, Stefan
01Swiss HNL-115
02Swiss HNL-395

Gahn, Kristian
90Swedish Semic Elitserien Stickers-95
91Swedish Semic Elitserien Stickers-24
92Upper Deck-232
92Swedish Semic Elitserien Stickers-48
94Swedish Leaf-118
95Swedish Leaf-279
95Swedish Upper Deck-159
97Swedish Collector's Choice-156
98Swedish UD Choice-9
99Swedish Upper Deck-9
00Swedish Upper Deck-14
00Swedish Upper Deck-180
SHL Signatures-KG
01Swiss HNL-246
02Swedish SHL-260
Parallel-260
03Swedish Elite-266
Silver-266
04Swedish Elitset-284
Gold-284
05Swedish SHL Elitset-141
Gold-141
Icons-6
06Swedish SHL Elitset-140

Gailer, Peter
82Swedish Semic VM Stickers-104
99German Bundesliga 2-83

Gailloux, Kris
92British Columbia JHL-224

Gainer, Clayton
93Wheeling Thunderbirds-16

Gainey, Bob
72Dimanche/Derniere Heure *-139
73Canadiens Postcards-5
74Canadiens Postcards-6
74O-Pee-Chee NHL-388
75Canadiens Postcards-6
75O-Pee-Chee NHL-278
75Topps-278
76Canadiens Postcards-6
76O-Pee-Chee NHL-44
76O-Pee-Chee NHL-217
76Topps-44
76Topps-217
77Canadiens Postcards-7
77O-Pee-Chee NHL-129
77Topps-129
78Canadiens Postcards-7
78O-Pee-Chee-76
78Topps-76
79Canadiens Postcards-4
79O-Pee-Chee-170
79Topps-170
80Canadiens Postcards-5
80O-Pee-Chee-58
80O-Pee-Chee Super-9
80Pepsi-Cola Caps-43
80Topps-58
81Canadiens Postcards-7
81O-Pee-Chee-176
81O-Pee-Chee-194
81O-Pee-Chee Stickers-30
81O-Pee-Chee Stickers-43
81O-Pee-Chee Stickers-269
81Topps-13
82Canadiens Postcards-6
82Canadiens Steinberg-4
82McDonald's Stickers-12
82O-Pee-Chee-181
82O-Pee-Chee Stickers-36
82Post Cereal-10
82Topps Stickers-36
83Canadiens Postcards-8
83Esso-7
83NHL Key Tags-67
83O-Pee-Chee-187
83O-Pee-Chee Stickers-66
83Topps Stickers-66
83Vachon-44
84Canadiens Postcards-7
84Kellogg's Accordion Discs-3A
84Kellogg's Accordion Discs Singles-12
84O-Pee-Chee-261
84O-Pee-Chee Stickers-153
847-Eleven Discs-29
85Canadiens Placemats-1
85Canadiens Placemats-7
85Canadiens Postcards-9
85Canadiens Postcards-10
85Canadiens Provigo-5
85O-Pee-Chee-169
85O-Pee-Chee Stickers-138
86Canadiens Postcards-5
86Kraft Drawings-18
86O-Pee-Chee-96
86O-Pee-Chee Stickers-12
86Topps-96
87Canadiens Kodak-2
87Canadiens Postcards-7
87Canadiens Vachon Stickers-12
87Canadiens Vachon Stickers-13
87Canadiens Vachon Stickers-18
87Canadiens Vachon Stickers-53
87Canadiens Vachon Stickers-88
87O-Pee-Chee-228
87O-Pee-Chee Stickers-12
87Panini Stickers-69
88Canadiens Postcards-10
88O-Pee-Chee-216
88O-Pee-Chee Stickers-42
89Canadiens Provigo Figurines-23
89O-Pee-Chee Stickers-58
90Pro Set-668
91Kraft-39
92Future Trends '76 Canada Cup-140
93O-Pee-Chee Canadiens Hockey Fest-16
93O-Pee-Chee Canadiens Hockey Fest-59
93Upper Deck Locker All-Stars-41
94Stars HockeyKaps-12
96Stars Postcards-5
00Topps Stanley Cup Heroes-SHBG
00Topps Stanley Cup Heroes Autographs-SHBG
01BAP Ultimate Mem Dynasty Jerseys-5
01BAP Ultimate Mem Dynasty Emblems-5
01BAP Ultimate Mem Dynasty Numbers-5
01BAP Ultimate Memorabilia Les Canadiens-5
01BAP Ultimate Mem Stanley Cup Winners-18
03Canadiens Postcards-8

Gainey, Steve
95Kamloops Blazers-24
96Kamloops Blazers-11
98Kamloops Blazers-11
99Michigan K-Wings-3
00BAP Memorabilia-509
00Utah Grizzlies-3
01Pacific-123
Extreme LTD-123
Hobby LTD-123
Premiere Date-123
Retail LTD-123
01Pacific Arena Exclusives-123
01Upper Deck MVP-200
01Upper Deck Victory-368
Gold-368
01Utah Grizzlies-10
02O-Pee-Chee-275
02O-Pee-Chee Premier Blue Parallel-275
02O-Pee-Chee Premier Red Parallel-275
02O-Pee-Chee Factory Set-275
02Topps-275
OPC Blue Parallel-275
OPC Red Parallel-275
Factory Set-275
02Utah Grizzlies-13
03Stars Postcards-8
05ITG Heroes/Prosp Toronto Expo Parallel -232
05ITG Heroes and Prospects-232
Autographs Series II-SGA

Gainor, Norman
34Sweet Caporal-20
37V356 Worldwide Gum-98

Gajda, Tyson
04Memphis RiverKings-21

Gajewski, Kyle
04Sault Ste. Marie Greyhounds-2

Gajewski, Marek
94German First League-470
99German Bundesliga 2-71

Gajic, Milan
02Michigan Wolverines-24
03Michigan Wolverines-9
04Michigan Wolverines-23

Gal, Evzen
99Czech Score Blue 2000-66
99Czech Score Red Ice 2000-66

Galan, Kevin
04Williams Lake Timberwolves-6

Galanov, Maxim
97Hartford Wolf Pack-7
98Pacific Omega-200
Red-200
Opening Day Issue-200
00Upper Deck Victory-14
02German DEL City Press-11

Galardini, Dave
99Arizona Icecats-6
00Arizona Icecats-8
01Arizona Icecats-5

Galarneau, Danny
91Air Canada SJHL-B39
92Saskatchewan JHL-160

Galarneau, Michel
82Whalers Junior Hartford Courant-4
94French National Team-13

Galasek, Tomas
03Erie Otters-7
04Erie Otters-2

Galati, Mike
95Guelph Storm-29

Galazzi, Mark
01UK Guildford Flames-16
02UK Guildford Flames-16
03UK Guildford Flames-17

Galbraith, Jade
02Atlantic City Boardwalk Bullies-7
03Pensacola Ice Pilots-344

Galbraith, Lance
99Ottawa 67's-6
00Ottawa 67's-2
04Idaho Steelheads-27
05Fort Wayne Komets Choice-14
05Fort Wayne Komets Sprint-6
05Fort Wayne Komets Sprint-7
06Idaho Steelheads-6

Galbraith, Walter
33O-Pee-Chee V304A-7
38Bruins Garden Magazine Supplement-2

Galchenyuk, Alexander
91O-Pee-Chee Inserts-33R
92Upper Deck-353
93Classic Pro Prospects-96
96Madison Monsters-4

Galiamoutsas, Hakan
98German DEL-128

Galik, Martin
93Quebec Pee-Wee Tournament-1561
99Greensboro Generals-10

Galkin, Alexander
00Russian Hockey League-209

Galkin, Andrej
94Czech APS Extraliga-239
95Czech APS Extraliga-15
96Czech APS Extraliga-232
97Czech APS Extraliga-35
97Czech DS Stickers-35
98Czech DS Stickers-182
98Czech OFS-74
98Czech OFS-485
00Russian Hockey League-55
01Russian Hockey League-14
03Russian Hockey League-105

Galkin, Igor
96Flint Generals-7
97Bakersfield Fog-3

Gallace, Richard
917th Inn. Sketch OHL-119

Gallace, Steve
95Slapshot-295
95Owen Sound Platers-17
96Owen Sound Platers-17
03UK Coventry Blaze-6
03UK Coventry Blaze Calendars-12

Gallagher, Brendon
93Quebec Pee-Wee Tournament-1586

Gallagher, John
34Beehive Group I Photos-226
36O-Pee-Chee V304D-108
37V356 Worldwide Gum-41

Gallagher, Matt
89Nashville Knights-7

Gallagher, Patrick
97Idaho Steelheads-14

Gallagher, Ray
87Brockville Braves-12
88Brockville Braves-1
93Huntington Blizzard-9
94Flint Generals-8

Gallant, Andrew
02OCN Blizzard-2

Gallant, Brad
05Cape Breton Screaming Eagles-10
06Cape Breton Screaming Eagles-9

Gallant, Brett
05Saint John's Sea Dogs-5
06Saint John's Sea Dogs-23

Gallant, Chester
94Sudbury Wolves Police-7
95Slapshot-201

Gallant, Gerard
87O-Pee-Chee-67
87O-Pee-Chee Stickers-106
87Panini Stickers-245
87Red Wings Little Caesars-11
87Topps-67
88O-Pee-Chee-12
88O-Pee-Chee Stickers-254
88Panini Stickers-43
88Red Wings Little Caesars-7
88Topps-12
89O-Pee-Chee-172
89O-Pee-Chee-302
89O-Pee-Chee Stickers-32
89O-Pee-Chee Stickers-157
89O-Pee-Chee Stickers-253
89Panini Stickers-58
89Red Wings Little Caesars-7
89Topps-172
89Topps Sticker Inserts-2
90Bowman-237
Tiffany-237
90Kraft-14
90O-Pee-Chee-322
90Panini Stickers-205
90Pro Set-71
90Score-180
Canadian-180
90Score Hottest/Rising Stars-78
90Topps-322
Tiffany-322
90Upper Deck-134
French-134
91Bowman-56
91Kraft-58
91O-Pee-Chee-443
91Panini Stickers-142
91Parkhurst-269
French-269
91Pinnacle-205
French-205
91Pro Set-63
French-63
91Red Wings Little Caesars-5
91Score American-34
91Score Canadian Bilingual-34
91Score Canadian English-34

91Stadium Club-165
91Topps-443
92Bowman-169
92O-Pee-Chee-163
92Panini Stickers-116
92Panini Stickers French-116
92Pinnacle-135
French-135
92Score-119
Canadian-119
92Stadium Club-218
92Topps-92
Gold-92G
92Ultra-284
92Upper Deck-246
93Donruss-320
93Leaf-310
93Lightning Season in Review-15
93OPC Premier-511
Gold-511
93Pinnacle-404
Canadian-404
93PowerPlay-230
93Score-402
93Score-560
Canadian-402
Canadian-560
Canadian Gold-560
93Stadium Club-16
93Stadium Club-346
Members Only Master Set-16
Members Only Master Set-346
OPC-16
First Day Issue-16
First Day Issue-346
First Day Issue OPC-16
93Topps/OPC Premier-511
Gold-511
98Fort Wayne Komets-6
99Louisville Panthers-29
03Parkhurst Original Six Detroit-60
Autographs-OS-GG

Gallant, Gordie
74Minnesota Fighting Saints WHA-8
75O-Pee-Chee WHA-96
76O-Pee-Chee WHA-4

Gallant, Jim
93Quebec Pee-Wee Tournament-1202

Gallant, Luke
04Cape Breton Screaming Eagles-9

Gallant, Ryan
93Quebec Pee-Wee Tournament-1211

Gallant, Shaun
95Slapshot-282
95Owen Sound Platers-7
96Owen Sound Platers-4

Gallant, Trevor
917th Inn. Sketch OHL-80
93Kitchener Rangers-10
94Kitchener Rangers-11
94North Bay Centennials-10
95Slapshot-217
00UK Sekonda Superleague-102
01UK Manchester Storm-3
01UK Manchester Storm Retro-3
06German DEL-174

Gallatin, Randy
99Missouri River Otters-6
99Missouri River Otters Sheet-4
00Missouri River Otters-9

Gallentine, Brian
92Western Michigan Broncos-11
93Western Michigan Broncos-12
95Roanoke Express-12

Galley, Garry
84Kings Smokey-6
86Kings 20th Anniversary Team Issue-7
87Capitals Kodak-2
87Capitals Team Issue-5
88Bruins Postcards-4
89Bruins Sports Action-8
90Bruins Sports Action-11
90O-Pee-Chee-331
90Pro Set-7A
90Pro Set-7B
90Score-253
Canadian-253
90Topps-331
Tiffany-331
90Upper Deck-379
French-379
91Pro Set Platinum-211
91Bowman-360
91O-Pee-Chee-86
91Panini Stickers-175
91Parkhurst-7
91Parkhurst-350
French-7
French-350
91Pinnacle-171
French-171
91Pro Set-7
91Pro Set-298
French-7
French-298
91Score American-71
91Score Canadian Bilingual-71
91Score Canadian English-71
91Stadium Club-175
91Topps-86
91Upper Deck-439
91Upper Deck-607
French-439
French-607
92Bowman-11
92Durivage Panini-41
92Flyers J.C. Penney-13
92Flyers Upper Deck Sheets-18
92Flyers Upper Deck Sheets-37A
92O-Pee-Chee-317
92Parkhurst-364
Emerald Ice-364
92Pinnacle-103
French-103
92Score-19
Canadian-19
92Stadium Club-424
92Topps-360
Gold-360G
92Ultra-156
92Upper Deck-319
93Donruss-251
93Durivage Score-38
93Flyers J.C. Penney-12
93Flyers Lineup Sheets-17
93Flyers Lineup Sheets-42
93Leaf-120
93OPC Premier-255
Gold-255
93Panini Stickers-53
93Parkhurst-423
Emerald Ice-423
93Pinnacle-72
Canadian-72
93PowerPlay-182
93Score-143
Canadian-143
93Stadium Club-381
Members Only Master Set-381
First Day Issue-381
93Topps/OPC Premier-255
Gold-255
93Ultra-124
93Upper Deck-90
94Be A Player Signature Cards-62
94Canada Games NHL POGS-182
94Donruss-166
94EA Sports-97
94Fleer-153
94Leaf-264
94Leaf Limited-5
94OPC Premier-535
Special Effects-535
94Parkhurst Vintage-V87
94Parkhurst SE-SE128
Gold-SE128
94Pinnacle-27
Artist's Proofs-27
Rink Collection-27
94Score-26
Gold-26
Platinum-26
94Select-117
Gold-117
94Stadium Club Members Only-29
94Topps/OPC Premier-535
Special Effects-535
94Ultra-157
94Upper Deck-19
Electric Ice-19
95Canada Games NHL POGS-46
95Collector's Choice-73
Player's Club-73
Player's Club Platinum-73
95Donruss-116
95Emotion-15
95Leaf-30
95Panini Stickers-23
95Parkhurst International-21
Emerald Ice-21
95Pinnacle-4
Artist's Proofs-4
Rink Collection-4
95Playoff One on One-124
95Score-112
Black Ice Artist's Proofs-112
Black Ice-112
95SkyBox Impact-15
95Stadium Club-3
Members Only Master Set-3
95Topps-155
OPC Inserts-155
95Topps SuperSkills-37
Platinum-37
95Ultra-17
Gold Medallion-17
95Upper Deck-198
Electric Ice-198
Electric Ice Gold-198
Special Edition-SE8
Special Edition Gold-SE8
96Donruss-106
Press Proofs-106
96Leaf-8
Press Proofs-8
96Pinnacle-69
Artist's Proofs-69
Foil-69
Premium Stock-69
Rink Collection-69
96Score-131
Artist's Proofs-131
Dealer's Choice Artist's Proofs-131
Special Artist's Proofs-131
Golden Blades-131
96Topps Picks-95
OPC Inserts-95
97Collector's Choice-30
97Pacific-288
Copper-288
Emerald Green-288
Ice Blue-288
Red-288
Silver-288
97Pacific Omega-108
Copper-108
Dark Gray-108
Emerald Green-108
Gold-108
Ice Blue-108
97Paramount-89
Copper-89
Dark Grey-89
Emerald Green-89
Ice Blue-89
Red-89
Silver-89
97SP Authentic-73
98Finest-31
No Protectors-31
No Protectors Refractors-31
Refractors-31
98Pacific-235
Ice Blue-235
Red-235
99Panini Stickers-260
99Upper Deck MVP SC Edition-90
Gold Script-90
Silver Script-90
Super Script-90
00Pacific-197
Copper-197
Gold-197
Ice Blue-197
Premiere Date-197
01Pacific-246
Extreme LTD-246
Hobby LTD-246
Premiere Date-246
Retail LTD-246
01Pacific Arena Exclusives-246
03Bowling Green Falcons-5

Gallinger, Don
34Beehive Group I Photos-14

Gallo, John
93Quebec Pee-Wee Tournament-1163

Galloway, Kyle
93Roanoke Express-9

Gallstedt, Niklas
84Swedish Semic Elitserien-228
85Swedish Panini Stickers-224
89Swedish Semic Elitserien Stickers-32
90Swedish Semic Elitserien Stickers-179
91Swedish Semic Elitserien Stickers-33
92Swedish Semic Elitserien Stickers-59
93Swedish Semic Elitserien-40
02Swedish SHL-191
Parallel-191

Galuppo, Sandy
92Dayton Bombers-10
93Birmingham Bulls Birmingham News-22
94Birmingham Bulls-8

Galushkin, Andrei
03Russian Hockey League-76

Galvas, David
96Czech APS Extraliga-105
97Czech APS Extraliga-105
97Czech DS Stickers-268
98Czech DS Stickers-50

Galvas, Davis
04Slovakian Skalica Team Set-9

Galvas, Lukas
98Czech OFS-351
99Czech DS-172
99Czech OFS-222
01Czech OFS-22
02Czech OFS Plus-26
03Czech OFS Plus-71
04Czech OFS-277
05Czech HC Hame Zlin-5
06Czech OFS-223

Galvin, Tom
02Notre Dame Fighting Irish-11
03Notre Dame Fighting Irish-10
04Reading Royals-8
05Quad City Mallards-5

Galvins, Guntis
06Czech HC Vsetin Postcards-2
06Czech OFS-179

Galway, Jerry
02Atlantic City Boardwalk Bullies-8

Gamache, Jean-Guy
52Juniors Blue Tint-35

Gamache, Simon
95Quebec Pee-Wee Tournament-234
98Val d'Or Foreurs-17
00QMJHL All-Star Program Inserts-15
00Val d'Or Foreurs-12
Signed-12
01Greenville Grrrowl-19
02BAP Memorabilia-366
02BAP Ultimate Memorabilia-76
02SP Authentic-209
02Upper Deck Rookie Update-141
02Chicago Wolves-10
03ITG Action-88
03Pacific Complete-503
Red-503
03Upper Deck MVP-27
Gold Script-27
Silver Script-27
Canadian Exclusives-27
03Upper Deck Victory-10
Bronze-10
Gold-10
Silver-10
03Milwaukee Admirals-22
03Milwaukee Admirals Postcards-7
03Pacific AHL Prospects-56
Gold-56
04AHL All-Stars-13
04Milwaukee Admirals-22
05ITG Heroes/Prosp Toronto Expo Parallel -94
05Milwaukee Admirals Pepsi-8
05ITG Heroes and Prospects-94
Autographs-A-SG

Gamalei, Evgeni
01Russian Hockey League-15

Gamble, Bruce
44Beehive Group II Photos-21
60Shirriff Coins-119
62Topps-3
64Beehive Group III Photos-162
65Maple Leafs White Border-10
67Topps-18
68O-Pee-Chee-197
68Post Marbles-8
68Shirriff Coins-173
69Maple Leafs White Border Glossy-11
69Maple Leafs White Border Glossy-12
69O-Pee-Chee-44
Four-in-One-4
69Topps-44
70Colgate Stamps-82
70Dad's Cookies-37
70Esso Power Players-36
70Maple Leafs Postcards-3
70O-Pee-Chee-105
Deckle-44
70Sargent Promotions Stamps-193
70Topps-105
71O-Pee-Chee-201
Posters-16
71Sargent Promotions Stamps-160
71Topps-104
71Toronto Sun-194
95Parkhurst '66-67-118
Coins-118

Gamble, Dick
44Beehive Group II Photos-240
45Quaker Oats Photos-77
48Exhibits Canadian-7
51Parkhurst-16
52Parkhurst-5
53Parkhurst-18
54Topps-1
63Rochester Americans-14

Gamble, Mike
98Huntsville Channel Cats-17

Gamble, Troy
85Medicine Hat Tigers-15
89ProCards IHL-178
90Canucks Mohawk-8
90Canucks Molson-2
90OPC Premier-34
90Pro Set-641
90Score Rookie/Traded-32T
90Upper Deck-434
French-434
91Pro Set Platinum-121
91Bowman-315
91Canucks Panini Team Stickers-8
91Canucks Autograph Cards-7
91Canucks Team Issue 8x10-7
91O-Pee-Chee-446
91Panini Stickers-37
91Parkhurst-402
French-402
91Pro Set-238
French-238
91Score American-282
91Score Canadian Bilingual-502
91Score Canadian English-502
91Score Young Superstars-29
91Stadium Club-218
91Topps-446
91Upper Deck-120
French-120
92Bowman-410
92Topps-412
Gold-412G
92Hamilton Canucks-8
95Houston Aeros-7
96Collector's Edge Ice-133
Prism-133
The Wall-TW4

Gambucci, Gary
70Swedish Masterserien-19
72Finnish Semic World Championship-123
72Swedish Semic World Championship-123
74Minnesota Fighting Saints WHA-9

Ganchar, Perry
81Saskatoon Blades-22
86Sherbrooke Canadiens-15
89ProCards IHL-148
90ProCards AHL/IHL-379
91ProCards-292
92Cleveland Lumberjacks-10
93Cleveland Lumberjacks-16
93Cleveland Lumberjacks Postcards-11
94Cleveland Lumberjacks-18
94Cleveland Lumberjacks Postcards-18
95Cleveland Lumberjacks-13
95Cleveland Lumberjacks Postcards-12
96Cleveland Lumberjacks Multi-Ad-12
97Cleveland Lumberjacks-2
97Cleveland Lumberjacks Postcards-1
98Cleveland Lumberjacks-2
00Spokane Chiefs-7
01Spokane Chiefs-23

Ganga, Nick
99Ohio State Buckeyes-8
00Ohio State Buckeyes-7
01Quad-City Mallards-6
03ECHL All-Stars-268

Gani, Darren
83Belleville Bulls-25
84Belleville Bulls-22

Gannon, Chris
93Quebec Pee-Wee Tournament-656

Gannon, Corey
04Vernon Vipers-19

Gannon, Korey
05Vernon Vipers-10

Gans, Dave
81Oshawa Generals-11
82Oshawa Generals-19
83Oshawa Generals-27

Ganseneder, Christian
94German First League-116

Ganster, Friedrich
93Swedish Semic World Champ Stickers-277

Gant, Kevin
85Kitchener Rangers-8

Ganz, Bryan
92Northern Michigan Wildcats-6
93Northern Michigan Wildcats-6

Garand, Francois
03St. Georges de Beauce Garaga-7

Garanin, Evgeny
92Russian Stars Red Ace-8

Garant, Alexandre
93Quebec Pee-Wee Tournament-1381

Garant, Tomas
03Russian Hockey League-51

Garatti, Jason
93Minnesota-Duluth Bulldogs-12

Garay, Justin
05ITG Heroes/Prosp Toronto Expo Parallel -297
05Plymouth Whalers-B-02
05ITG Heroes and Prospects-297
Autographs Series II-JG
06Erie Otters-23

Garber, Bruce
93Birmingham Bulls-19
97Columbus Cottonmouths-22
98Columbus Cottonmouths-22
99Columbus Cottonmouths-15
00Columbus Cottonmouths-21
01Columbus Cottonmouths-20

Garbocz, Dariusz
92Finnish Semic-275

Garbutt, Josh
01Brandon Wheat Kings-8
02Brandon Wheat Kings-6
03Kamloops Blazers-5
06New Mexico Scorpions-17

Garbutt, Murray
907th Inn. Sketch WHL-25
91Kansas City Blades-6
91ProCards-514
917th Inn. Sketch Memorial Cup-90
93Huntington Blizzard-10

Garcia, Ivan
01Spokane Chiefs-9

Garden, Graham
00UK Nottingham Panthers-22
00UK Sekonda Superleague-134

Gardin, Rolf
57Swedish Alfabilder-143

Gardiner, Bert
34Beehive Group I Photos-152

Gardiner, Bruce
96Senators Pizza Hut-8
97Be A Player-51
Autographs-51
Autographs Die-Cuts-51
Autographs Prismatic Die-Cuts-51
97Pacific-172
Copper-172
Emerald Green-172
Ice Blue-172
Red-172
Silver-172
97Upper Deck-115
98Be A Player-97
Press Release-97
98BAP Gold-97
98BAP Autographs-97
98BAP Autographs Gold-97
98BAP Tampa Bay All Star Game-97
98Pacific-309
Ice Blue-309
Red-309
98Senators Team Issue-6
99Pacific-287
Copper-287
Emerald Green-287
Gold-287
Ice Blue-287
Premiere Date-287
Red-287
99Senators Team Issue-7
00Upper Deck Vintage-108
01Upper Deck-283
Exclusives-283
01Albany River Rats-20
02BAP Sig Series Auto Buybacks 1998-97
02Russian Transfert-28
03Finnish Cardset-12

Gardiner, Charlie
28V128-2 Paulin's Candy-89
33V252 Canadian Gum-24
34Diamond Matchbooks Silver-24
60Topps-32
Stamps-16
83Hall of Fame Postcards-I8
85Hall of Fame-128
01Between the Pipes-143
02Between the Pipes Vintage Memorabilia-15
03BAP Memorabilia Vintage Memorabilia-VM-2
03ITG Used Sig Series Vintage Mem -27
03ITG Used Sig Series Vintage Mem Gold-27
03Parkhurst Original Six Chicago-36
03Parkhurst Original Six Chicago-63
Inserts-C14
Memorabilia-CM17
03Parkhurst Rookie Before the Mask-BTM-8
03Parkhurst Rookie Before the Mask Gold-BTM-8
04ITG Franchises US West-172
Goalie Gear-WGG3
Goalie Gear Gold-WGG3
Memorabilia-WSM11
Memorabilia Gold-WSM11
Trophy Winners-WTW10
Trophy Winners Gold-WTW10
04ITG Ultimate Memorabilia-39
Gold-39
Original Six-6
Seams Unbelievable-6
05ITG Ultimate Memorabilia Level 1-18
05ITG Ultimate Memorabilia Level 2-18
05ITG Ultimate Memorabilia Level 3-18
05ITG Ultimate Memorabilia Level 4-18
05ITG Ultimate Memorabilia Level 5-18
05ITG Ultimate Mem Cornerstones Jerseys-1
05ITG Ultimate Mem Cornerst Jerseys Gold-1
05ITG Ultimate Mem Decades Jerseys-8
05ITG Ultimate Mem Decades Jerseys Gold-8
05ITG Ultimate Mem Pass the Torch Jerseys-14
05ITG Ultimate Mem Passing Torch Jsy Gold-14
06Between The Pipes Shooting Gallery-SG04
06Between The Pipes Shooting Gallery Gold-SG04
06ITG Ultimate Memorabilia-28
Artist Proof-28
Chi-Town Immortals Autos-1

Gardiner, Greg
03Prince George Cougars-17

Gardiner, Herb
23V128-1 Paulin's Candy-63
27La Patrie-9
27La Presse Photos-7
27La Presse Photos-9
60Topps-44
Stamps-17
83Hall of Fame-154
83Hall of Fame Postcards-L4
85Hall of Fame-154

Gardiner, Jeff
897th Inn. Sketch OHL-159
907th Inn. Sketch OHL-105
917th Inn. Sketch OHL-44

Gardiner, Pete
01Roanoke Express-9
02Greensboro Generals RBI-10
03Greensboro Generals-184
03Rochester Americans-8

Gardiner, Scott
83Belleville Bulls-5

Gardner, Bill
81Blackhawks Borderless Postcards-8
82Blackhawks Postcards-7
82Post Cereal-4
83Blackhawks Postcards-8
83NHL Key Tags-24
83O-Pee-Chee-103
83Penguins Heinz Photos-8
84O-Pee-Chee-35
85Blackhawks Team Issue-18
86Whalers Junior Thomas'-9
88ProCards IHL-99

Gardner, Cal
44Beehive Group II Photos-22
44Beehive Group II Photos-402
45Quaker Oats Photos-18A
45Quaker Oats Photos-18B
45Quaker Oats Photos-60A
45Quaker Oats Photos-60B
45Quaker Oats Photos-60D
48Exhibits Canadian-30
51Parkhurst-85
52Parkhurst-30
53Parkhurst-99
54Parkhurst-53
54Topps-47
55Bruins Photos-6
60Cleveland Barons-5
93Parkhurst Parkie Reprints-PR57
94Parkhurst Missing Link-10

Gardner, Charlie
23Crescent Selkirks-9
01Between the Pipes Vintage Memorabilia-VM20

Gardner, Daniel
94German First League-323

Gardner, Dave
73Canadiens Postcards-6
74NHL Action Stamps-244
74NHL Action Stamps Update-6
74O-Pee-Chee NHL-47
74Topps-47
75O-Pee-Chee NHL-119
75Topps-119
76O-Pee-Chee NHL-274
77O-Pee-Chee NHL-258
77Topps-258
78O-Pee-Chee-278
91Air Canada SJHL-A23
04ITG Franchises US West-181
Autographs-A-DVG

Gardner, George
70Canucks Royal Bank-5
70O-Pee-Chee-224
70Sargent Promotions Stamps-222
71Canucks Royal Bank-18
71Letraset Action Replays-16
71O-Pee-Chee-235
71Sargent Promotions Stamps-213
71Toronto Sun-277
72Canucks Nalley's-2
72Los Angeles Sharks WHA-3
73Vancouver Blazers-9

Gardner, Greg
03Mississippi Sea Wolves-4

Gardner, James
10Sweet Caporal Postcards-36
11C55-36
12C57-24
83Hall of Fame Postcards-M7
85Hall of Fame-172

Gardner, Jared
93Quebec Pee-Wee Tournament-1683

Gardner, Joel
90ProCards AHL/IHL-381
91Knoxville Cherokees-13
92Raleigh Icecaps-3
92Raleigh Icecaps-27
99Muskegon Fury-35

Gardner, Kevin
04Northern Michigan Wildcats-6
05Idaho Steelheads-10

Gardner, Paul
76Rockies Coke Cans-10
77O-Pee-Chee NHL-24
77Rockies Coke Cans-8
77Topps-24
78O-Pee-Chee-88
78Topps-88
79Maple Leafs Postcards-10
79O-Pee-Chee-5
79Topps-5
81O-Pee-Chee-257
81O-Pee-Chee Stickers-187
81Topps-E113
82O-Pee-Chee-236
82O-Pee-Chee-269
82O-Pee-Chee Stickers-145
82Post Cereal-15
82Topps Stickers-145
83NHL Key Tags-104
83O-Pee-Chee-219
83O-Pee-Chee-275
83O-Pee-Chee-280
83O-Pee-Chee Stickers-230
83Puffy Stickers-10
83Topps Stickers-230
89ProCards AHL-113
93Portland Pirates-4
96Portland Pirates-NNO

Gardner, Ryan
95Slapshot-166
99Swiss Panini Stickers-20
00Swiss Panini Stickers-19
00Swiss Slapshot Mini-Cards-HCAP13
01Swiss HNL-42
02Swiss HNL-29

Gardon, Radek
94German First League-370
99Czech OFS-335
00Czech DS Extraliga-137
00Czech OFS-124
00Czech OFS Star Emerald-29
00Czech OFS Star Pink-29
00Czech OFS Star Violet-29
01Czech OFS-173
03Czech OFS Plus-219
03Czech OFS Plus Insert C-C3
04Czech OFS-52
05Czech HC Kladno-4
06Czech HC Kladno Postcards-10
06Czech OFS-252
All Stars-19

Gare, Danny
74Sabres Postcards-7
75O-Pee-Chee NHL-64
75Topps-64
76O-Pee-Chee NHL-222
76O-Pee-Chee NHL-380
76Topps-222
77O-Pee-Chee NHL-42
78O-Pee-Chee-209
78Topps-209
79O-Pee-Chee-61
79Sabres Bells-2
79Topps-61
80O-Pee-Chee-38
80O-Pee-Chee-88
80O-Pee-Chee-161
80O-Pee-Chee-167
80O-Pee-Chee-260
80Topps-38
80Topps-88
80Topps-161
80Topps-167
80Topps-260
81O-Pee-Chee-20
81O-Pee-Chee-27
81O-Pee-Chee-28
81O-Pee-Chee Stickers-53
81Topps-14
81Topps-47
81Topps-E127
82O-Pee-Chee-83
82O-Pee-Chee Stickers-184
82Post Cereal-5
82Topps Stickers-184
83NHL Key Tags-32
83O-Pee-Chee-123
83O-Pee-Chee Stickers-135
83Puffy Stickers-17
83Topps Stickers-135
84O-Pee-Chee-54
84Topps-42
84Kelowna Wings-23
85O-Pee-Chee-37
85O-Pee-Chee Stickers-35
85Topps-37
86Oilers Red Rooster-18
86O-Pee-Chee-69
86O-Pee-Chee Stickers-159
86Topps-69
88Oilers Tenth Anniversary-20
93Lightning Season in Review-16
93Sabres Noco-5
94Lightning Photo Album-13
01Topps Archives-46
02Fleer Throwbacks-5
Gold-5
Platinum-5
02Topps Rookie Reprints-6
02Topps Rookie Reprint Autographs-6
03Parkhurst Original Six Detroit-37
03Parkhurst Original Six Detroit-73
Autographs-OS-DG
04ITG Franchises US East-344
Autographs-A-DGA
06ITG International Ice-120
Gold-120
Autographs-ADGR
Emblems-GUE31
Emblems Gold-GUE31
Jerseys-GUJ31
Jerseys Gold-GUJ31
Numbers-GUN31
Numbers Gold-GUN31
06ITG Ultimate Memorabilia Bowman Factor-10
06ITG Ultimate Memorabilia Bowman Factor Gold-10
06Parkhurst-7
06Parkhurst-166
Autographs-7
Autographs-166
Autographs Dual-DAPG

Gare, Lanny
04Fresno Falcons-5

Gare, Morey
92Northern Michigan Wildcats-30
93Northern Michigan Wildcats-31
00Hamilton Bulldogs-26

Gareau, Guy
51Laval Dairy Lac St. Jean-2

Gareev, Alik
00Russian Hockey League-242

Gariepy, Frederic
02Shawinigan Cataractes-4
03Baie Comeau Drakkar-12

Gariepy, Ray
44Beehive Group II Photos-23
54UK A and BC Chewing Gum-39

Gariffullin, Almaz
98Russian Hockey League-105
99Russian Hockey League-73
00Russian Hockey League-38
01Russian Hockey League-161
02Russian Hockey League-266
03Russian Hockey League-3

Garis, Ryan
04Minnesota-Duluth Bulldogs-8

Garland, Corey
06Drummondville Voltigeurs-12

Garland, Scott
76Maple Leafs Postcards-6
76O-Pee-Chee NHL-243
77O-Pee-Chee NHL-302
78O-Pee-Chee-274

Garlock, Ryan
02Guelph Storm-15
03Guelph Storm-16
04ITG Heroes and Prospects-101
Autographs-RG
04ITG Heroes/Prospects Toronto Expo '05-101
04ITG Heroes/Prospects Expo Heroes/Pros-101

Garnea, Jean-Francois
93Quebec Pee-Wee Tournament-53

Garnelle, Dick
56Quebec Aces-6

Garner, Tyrone
95Slapshot-232
99Pacific-66
Copper-66
Emerald Green-66
Gold-66
Ice Blue-66
Premiere Date-66
Red-66
99Upper Deck Victory-51
99Johnstown Chiefs-26
01Greenville Grrrowl-20

Garnett, Michael
00Red Deer Rebels-6
Signed-6
00Saskatoon Blades-28
01Saskatoon Blades-25
01UD Prospects-21
Autographs-A-MG
Jersey Autographs-S-MG
Jerseys-J-MG
Jerseys-C-BG
Jerseys Gold-J-MG
Jerseys Gold-C-BG
02BAP Memorabilia-322
02BAP Ultimate Memorabilia-59
02Between the Pipes-110
Gold-110
Silver-110
02Greenville Grrrowl-1
03Chicago Wolves-8
03ECHL All-Stars-269
03Gwinnett Gladiators-15
03Gwinnett Gladiators RBI Sports-201
04Chicago Wolves-4
04ITG Heroes/Prospects Complete Emblems-15
04ITG Heroes/Prospects He Shoots/Scores-9
04ITG Heroes and Prospects Net Prospects-21
04ITG Heroes and Prosp Net Prospects Gold-21
05Parkhurst-31
Facsimile Auto Parallel-31
05Chicago Wolves-7

Garnier, Florian
93Swiss HNL-315

Garnier, Philippe
05Rimouski Oceanic-26
06Rimouski Oceanic-3

Garon, Mathieu
95Bowman Draft Prospects-P14
95Upper Deck-525
Electric Ice-525
Electric Ice Gold-525
97Beehive-71
Authentic Autographs-71
Golden Portraits-71
97Zenith-98
Z-Gold-98
Z-Silver-98
97Zenith 5 x 7-78
Gold Impulse-78
Silver Impulse-78
98Bowman's Best-145
Refractors-145
Atomic Refractors-145
98UD Choice-260
Prime Choice Reserve-260
Reserve-260
98Bowman CHL-81
Golden Anniversary-81
OPC International-81
Scout's Choice-SC21
98Bowman Chrome CHL-81
Golden Anniversary-81
Golden Anniversary Refractors-81
OPC International-81
OPC International Refractors-81
Refractors-81
99Quebec Citadelles-17
00BAP Memorabilia-422
Emerald-422
Ruby-422
Sapphire-422
00BAP Parkhurst 2000-P248
00BAP Signature Series-299
Emerald-299
Ruby-299
Sapphire-299
00Canadiens Postcards-3
00Titanium-128
Retail-128
00Titanium Draft Day Edition-128
00Titanium Draft Day Promos-128
00Topps Premier Plus-101
Blue Ice-101
00Vanguard-129
Pacific Proofs-129
00Quebec Citadelles-15
Signed-15
01BAP Memorabilia-181
Emerald-181
Ruby-181
Sapphire-181
01BAP Signature Series-41
Autographs-41
Autographs Gold-41
01Between the Pipes-12
Future Wave-FW9
Jerseys-GJ36
01Canadiens Postcards-8
01O-Pee-Chee-276
01O-Pee-Chee Premier Parallel-276
01Pacific-206
Extreme LTD-206
Hobby LTD-206
Premiere Date-206
Retail LTD-206
01Pacific Arena Exclusives-206
01Parkhurst-270
01Parkhurst Beckett Promos-270
01Titanium Draft Day Edition-138
01Topps-276
OPC Parallel-276
01Topps Chrome-142
Refractors-142
Black Border Refractors-142
01Quebec Citadelles-16
02BAP Sig Series Auto Buybacks 2001-41
02Between the Pipes-81
Gold-81
Silver-81
Future Wave-6
02Canadiens Postcards-12
02Pacific-195
Blue-195
Red-195
02Pacific Calder-75
Silver-75
02Pacific Complete-551
Red-551
02UD Mask Collection-45
02UD Mask Collection-46
02UD Mask Collection Beckett Promos-45
02UD Mask Collection Beckett Promos-46
02Upper Deck-340
Exclusives-340
02Upper Deck Beckett UD Promos-340
02Hamilton Bulldogs-21
03BAP Memorabilia-141
Emerald-141
Gold-141
Ruby-141
Sapphire-141
Deep in the Crease-D3
Future Wave-FW-6
Tandems-T-8
03Canadiens Postcards-9
03Crown Royale-53
Blue-53
Retail-53
03ITG Action-359
Jerseys-M106
03Pacific-176
Blue-176
Red-176
03Pacific Complete-466
Red-466
03Pacific Exhibit-76
Blue Backs-76
Yellow Backs-76
03Parkhurst Orig Six He Shoots/Scores-7
03Parkhurst Orig Six He Shoots/Scores-7A
03Parkhurst Original Six Montreal-22
Memorabilia-MM7
03Parkhurst Rookie Road to the NHL-RNJ-15
03Parkhurst Rookie Road to the NHL Gold-RTN-15
03Parkhurst Rookie Road to the NHL Emblem-RTNE-15
03Parkhurst Rookie Road NHL Emblem Gold-RTNE-15
03Private Stock Reserve-52
Blue-52
Red-52
Retail-52
03SPx Big Futures-BF-MG
03SPx Big Futures Limited-BF-MG
03Upper Deck-104
Canadian Exclusives-104
HG-104
03Upper Deck MVP-233
Gold Script-233
Silver Script-233
Canadian Exclusives-233
03Upper Deck Victory-100
Bronze-100
Gold-100
Silver-100
04AHL All-Stars-14
04Manchester Monarchs-13
04Manchester Monarchs Tobacco-1
04ITG Heroes and Prospects Net Prospects-19
04ITG Heroes and Prosp Net Prospects Gold-19
05ITG Heroes/Prosp Toronto Expo Parallel -80
05Beehive Matted Materials-MMGA
05Black Diamond-39
Emerald-39
Gold-39
Onyx-39
Ruby-39
05Kings Team Issue-7
05Panini Stickers-293
05Parkhurst-218
Facsimile Auto Parallel-218
True Colors-TCLAK
True Colors-TCLAK
05SP Game Used Authentic Fabrics Quad-FRRG
05SP Game Used Authentic Patches Quad -FRRG
05Ultra-92
Gold-92
Ice-92
05Upper Deck-87
HG Glossy-87
Jerseys-J-MGA
Notable Numbers-N-MGA
05Upper Deck MVP-179
Gold-179

Platinum-179
05Upper Deck Toronto Fall Expo-87
05Upper Deck Victory-92
Black-92
Gold-92
Silver-92
05Manchester Monarchs-31
05ITG Heroes and Prospects-80
Autographs-A-MG
Jerseys-GUJ-46
Jerseys Gold-GUJ-46
Emblems-GUE-46
Emblems Gold-GUE-46
Numbers-GUN-46
Numbers Gold-GUN-46
Net Prospects-NP-5
Net Prospects Gold-NP-05
06Between The Pipes Emblems-GUE28
06Between The Pipes Emblems Gold-GUE28
06Between The Pipes Jerseys-GUJ28
06Between The Pipes Jerseys Gold-GUJ28
06Between The Pipes Numbers-GUN28
06Between The Pipes Numbers Gold-GUN28
06Flair Showcase Hot Gloves-HG14
06Flair Showcase Stitches-SSGA
06Fleer-91
Tiffany-91
Fabricology-FGA
06O-Pee-Chee-225
Rainbow-225
Swatches-S-GA
06Ultra-91
Gold Medallion-91
Ice Medallion-91
06Upper Deck-88
Exclusives Parallel-88
High Gloss Parallel-88
Masterpieces-88
06Upper Deck MVP-138
Gold Script-138
Super Script-138
06Upper Deck Ovation-74
06Upper Deck Victory-89
06Upper Deck Victory Black-89
06Upper Deck Victory Gold-89
07Upper Deck Victory-189
Black-189
Gold-189

Garpenlov, Johan
86Swedish Panini Stickers-81
87Swedish Panini Stickers-79
89Swedish Semic Elitserien Stickers-67
90OPC Premier-35
90Pro Set-605
90Score Rookie/Traded-17T
90Upper Deck-521
90Upper Deck-523
French-521
French-523
91Pro Set Platinum-29
91Bowman-45
91O-Pee-Chee-278
91Panini Stickers-144
91Parkhurst-385
French-385
91Pro Set-56
French-56
91Red Wings Little Caesars-6
91Score American-204
91Score Canadian Bilingual-204
91Score Canadian English-204
91Stadium Club-268
91Topps-278
91Upper Deck-28
91Upper Deck-167
French-28
French-167
Euro-Stars-15
Euro-Stars French-15
91Finnish Semic World Champ Stickers-212
91Swedish Semic Elitserien Stickers-353
91Swedish Semic World Champ Stickers-212
92Bowman-400
92Parkhurst-397
Emerald Ice-397
92Pinnacle-122
French-122
92Score-406
Canadian-406
92Stadium Club-212
92Topps-359
Gold-359G
92Ultra-400
92Upper Deck-59
93Donruss-309
93Leaf-133
93OPC Premier-53
Gold-53
93Panini Stickers-257
93Pinnacle-63
Canadian-63
93PowerPlay-219
93Score-183
Canadian-183
93Stadium Club-44
Members Only Master Set-44
OPC-44
First Day Issue-44
First Day Issue OPC-44
93Topps/OPC Premier-53
Gold-53
93Ultra-83
93Upper Deck SP-142
93Swedish Semic World Champ Stickers-38
94Be A Player-R38
Signature Cards-61
94Canada Games NHL POGS-215
94Donruss-301
94EA Sports-118
94Flair-165
94Leaf-234
94OPC Premier-201
Special Effects-201
94Parkhurst-209
Gold-209
94Pinnacle-296
Artist's Proofs-296
Rink Collection-296
94Score-176
Gold-176
Platinum-176
94SP-45
Die Cuts-45
94Topps/OPC Premier-201
Special Effects-201
94Ultra-194
94Upper Deck-64
Electric Ice-64
95Canada Games NHL POGS-120
95Collector's Choice-240
Player's Club-240
Player's Club Platinum-240
95Donruss-322
95Leaf-282
95Parkhurst International-90
Emerald Ice-90
95Stadium Club-62
Members Only Master Set-62
95Topps-56
OPC Inserts-56
95Upper Deck-129
Electric Ice-129
Electric Ice Gold-129
95Swedish Upper Deck-242
95Swedish Globe World Championships-36
96Be A Player-67
96Be A Player-P67
Autographs-67
Autographs Silver-67
96Collector's Choice-106
97Pacific-348
Copper-348
Emerald Green-348
Ice Blue-348
Red-348
Silver-348
97Panini Stickers-62
99BAP Millennium-16
Emerald-16
Ruby-16
Sapphire-16
Signatures-16
Signatures Gold-16
99Panini Stickers-11
99Revolution-9
Premiere Date-9
Red-9
Shadow Series-9
99Upper Deck MVP SC Edition-14
Gold Script-14
Silver Script-14
Super Script-14
00Panini Stickers-4
00Swedish Upper Deck-56
00Swedish Upper Deck-189
SHL Excellence-S1
SHL Signatures-JG
02BAP Sig Series Auto Buybacks 1999-16

Garrett, John
74Minnesota Fighting Saints WHA-10
75O-Pee-Chee WHA-12
76O-Pee-Chee WHA-55
77O-Pee-Chee WHA-23
79O-Pee-Chee-293
80O-Pee-Chee-77
80Topps-77
81O-Pee-Chee-137
81O-Pee-Chee Stickers-68
82Nordiques Postcards-7
82O-Pee-Chee-283
83Canucks Team Issue-6
83Nordiques Postcards-8
83O-Pee-Chee-349
83O-Pee-Chee Stickers-275
83Topps Stickers-275
83Vachon-105
84Canucks Team Issue-8
84O-Pee-Chee-317
85O-Pee-Chee-220
97Pinnacle Hockey Night in Canada-5
04ITG Franchises Update Autographs-JG

Garrett, Red
34Beehive Group I Photos-273
04ITG Franchises US East-398

Garrick, Jamie
99San Angelo Outlaws-3

Garrity, Sean
04St. Cloud State Huskies-10
05St. Cloud State Huskies-21
05St. Cloud State Huskies-10

Garrow, Mike
01Colorado Gold Kings-8
05UK Cardiff Devils Challenge Cup-16

Garthe, Marc
95German DEL-45

Gartner, Mike
79Capitals Team Issue-4
80O-Pee-Chee-49
80O-Pee-Chee-195
80Topps-49
80Topps-195
81Capitals Team Issue-5
81O-Pee-Chee-347
81O-Pee-Chee Stickers-190
81Topps-E117
82Capitals Team Issue-6
82Neilson's Gretzky-14
82O-Pee-Chee-363
82O-Pee-Chee Stickers-153
82Post Cereal-20
82Topps Stickers-153
83NHL Key Tags-128
83O-Pee-Chee-364
83O-Pee-Chee-369
83O-Pee-Chee Stickers-207
83Puffy Stickers-21
83Topps Stickers-207
84Capitals Pizza Hut-5
84Kellogg's Accordion Discs-4
84Kellogg's Accordion Discs Singles-13
84O-Pee-Chee-197
84O-Pee-Chee-370
84O-Pee-Chee Stickers-131
847-Eleven Discs-53
84Topps-143
85Capitals Pizza Hut-4
85O-Pee-Chee-46
85O-Pee-Chee Stickers-111
857-Eleven Credit Cards-20
85Topps-46
86Capitals Kodak-8
86Capitals Police-8
86O-Pee-Chee-59
86O-Pee-Chee Stickers-251
86Topps-59
87Capitals Kodak-11
87Capitals Team Issue-6
87O-Pee-Chee-168
87O-Pee-Chee Stickers-239
87Panini Stickers-180
87Topps-168
88Capitals Borderless-5
88Capitals Smokey-5
88Frito-Lay Stickers-13
88O-Pee-Chee-50
88O-Pee-Chee Box Bottoms-N
88O-Pee-Chee Stickers-67
88Panini Stickers-370
88Topps-50
88Topps Box Bottoms-N
89O-Pee-Chee-30
89O-Pee-Chee Stickers-196
89Panini Stickers-104
89Topps-30
89Swedish Semic World Champ Stickers-75
90Bowman-220
Tiffany-220
90Bowman Hat Tricks-8
90Bowman Hat Tricks-17
Tiffany-8
Tiffany-17
90Kraft-69
90O-Pee-Chee-373
90OPC Premier-36
90Panini Stickers-103
90Pro Set-196
90Pro Set-351
90Score-130
90Score-333
Canadian-130
Canadian-333
90Score Hottest/Rising Stars-60
90Topps-373
Tiffany-373
90Upper Deck-277
French-277
91Pro Set Platinum-84
91Bowman-74
91Kraft-27
91O-Pee-Chee-46
91OPC Premier-147
91OPC Premier-164
91Panini Stickers-292
91Parkhurst-122
91Parkhurst-430
French-122
French-430
91Pinnacle-202
French-202
91Pro Set-167
91Pro Set-604
French-167
French-604
Platinum PC-PC11
91Score American-135
91Score Canadian Bilingual-135
91Score Canadian English-135
91Stadium Club Members Only-41
91Stadium Club Members Only-42
91Stadium Club-51
91Topps-46
91Upper Deck-247
French-247
92Bowman-146
92O-Pee-Chee-245
92O-Pee-Chee-300
92Panini Stickers-237
92Panini Stickers French-237
92Parkhurst-108
Emerald Ice-108
92Pinnacle-94
French-94
92Pro Set-113
92Pro Set-256
92Score-50
92Score-443
92Score-445
Canadian-50
Canadian-443
Canadian-445
92Sports Illustrated for Kids II-246
92Stadium Club Members Only-44
92Stadium Club-311
92Topps-264
92Topps-404
Gold-264G
Gold-404G
92Ultra-135
92Upper Deck-34
92Upper Deck-126
93Donruss-218
93Donruss-494
93Leaf-213
93McDonald's Upper Deck-15
93OPC Premier-375
93OPC Premier-384
Gold-375
Gold-384
93Panini Stickers-91
93Parkhurst-400
Emerald Ice-400
93Pinnacle-27
93Pinnacle-241
Canadian-27
Canadian-241
All-Stars-8
All-Stars-46
All-Stars Canadian-8
All-Stars Canadian-46
93PowerPlay-157
93Score Samples-2
93Score-2
93Score-447
Canadian-2
Canadian-447
93Stadium Club-110
Members Only Master Set-110
OPC-110
First Day Issue-110
First Day Issue OPC-110
All-Stars-22
All-Stars Members Only-22
All-Stars OPC-22
Finest-6
Finest Members Only-6
93Topps/OPC Premier-375
93Topps/OPC Premier-384
Gold-375
Gold-384
93Ultra-25
Red Light Specials-3
Speed Merchants-4
93Upper Deck-205
NHLPA/Roots-26
SP-98
93Upper Deck Locker All-Stars-38
93FCA 50*-17
94Be A Player-R127
94Canada Games NHL POGS-233
94Donruss-111
94EA Sports-89
94Finest-96
Super Team Winners-96
Refractors-96
94Flair-180
94Fleer-214
94Leaf-135
Fire on Ice-11
94Maple Leafs Gangsters-7
94Maple Leafs Kodak-11
94Maple Leafs Pin-up Posters-21A
94OPC Premier-253
Special Effects-253
94Parkhurst-228
Gold-228
SE Vintage-29
94Pinnacle-31
Artist's Proofs-31
Rink Collection-31
94Score-112
94Score-242
Gold-112
Gold-242
Platinum-112
Platinum-242
94Select-95
Gold-95
94Topps/OPC Premier-253
Special Effects-253
94Ultra-214
Red Light Specials-3
94Upper Deck-32
94Upper Deck-230
Electric Ice-32
Electric Ice-230
SP Inserts-SP78
SP Inserts Die Cuts-SP78
94Upper Deck NHLPA/Be A Player-22
95Canada Games NHL POGS-261
95Collector's Choice-149
Player's Club-149
Player's Club Platinum-149
95Donruss-293
95Emotion-169
95Finest-8
Refractors-8
95Leaf-37
95Leaf Limited-109
95Metal-142
95Panini Stickers-204
95Parkhurst International-206
Emerald Ice-206
95Pinnacle-75
Artist's Proofs-75
Rink Collection-75
95Playoff One on One-95
95Score-204
Black Ice Artist's Proofs-204
Black Ice-204
95Select Certified-54
Mirror Gold-54
95SkyBox Impact-159
95Stadium Club-162
Members Only Master Set-162
95Summit-143
Artist's Proofs-143
Ice-143
95Topps-98
OPC Inserts-98
95Topps SuperSkills-28
Platinum-28
95Ultra-311
95Upper Deck-110
Electric Ice-110
Electric Ice Gold-110
95Zenith-62
95Swedish Globe World Championships-85
96Be A Player-25
Autographs-25
Autographs Silver-25
96Black Diamond-42
Gold-42
96Coyotes Coca-Cola-7
96Coyotes Coca-Cola-8
96Donruss-206
Press Proofs-206
96Donruss Canadian Ice-18
Gold Press Proofs-18
Red Press Proofs-18
96Donruss Elite-123
Die Cut Stars-123
96Duracell L'Equipe Beliveau-JB9
96Flair Now And Then-1
96Fleer Picks-170
96Leaf-91
Press Proofs-91
96Metal Universe-116
96NHL Aces Playing Cards-17
96Pinnacle-35
Artist's Proofs-35
Foil-35
Premium Stock-35
Rink Collection-35
96Playoff One on One-349
96Score-154
Artist's Proofs-154
Dealer's Choice Artist's Proofs-154
Special Artist's Proofs-154
Golden Blades-154
96SkyBox Impact BladeRunners-5
96SP-123
96Stadium Club Members Only-22
96Summit-28
Artist's Proofs-28
Ice-28
Metal-28
Premium Stock-28
96Team Out-36
96Topps Picks 500 Club-FC2
96Ultra-130
Gold Medallion-130
96Upper Deck-316
96Upper Deck Ice-52
Parallel-52
97Collector's Choice-196
97Coyotes Face-Off Luncheon -7
97Crown Royale-102
Emerald Green-102
Ice Blue-102
Silver-102
97Donruss-110
Press Proofs Silver-110
Press Proofs Gold-110
97Donruss Canadian Ice-54
97Donruss Canadian Ice-149
Dominion Series-54
Dominion Series-149
Provincial Series-54
Provincial Series-149
97Donruss Elite-147
Aspirations-147
Status-147
97Donruss Limited-40
Exposure-40
97Donruss Preferred-47
Cut to the Chase-47
97Donruss Priority-93
Stamp of Approval-93
97Katch-109
Gold-109
Silver-109
97Pacific-22
Copper-22
Emerald Green-22
Ice Blue-22
Red-22
Silver-22
Slap Shots Die-Cuts-7C
97Pacific Dynagon-95
Copper-95
Dark Grey-95
Emerald Green-95
Ice Blue-95
Red-95
Silver-95
Best Kept Secrets-74
Tandems-65
97Pacific Invincible-106
Copper-106
Emerald Green-106
Ice Blue-106
Red-106
Silver-106
NHL Regime-152
97Pacific Omega-173
Copper-173
Dark Gray-173
Emerald Green-173
Gold-173
Ice Blue-173
97Panini Stickers-158
97Paramount-139
Copper-139
Dark Grey-139
Emerald Green-139
Ice Blue-139
Red-139
Silver-139
97Pinnacle-137
Press Plates Back Black-137
Press Plates Back Cyan-137
Press Plates Back Magenta-137
Press Plates Back Yellow-137
Press Plates Front Black-137
Press Plates Front Cyan-137
Press Plates Front Magenta-137
Press Plates Front Yellow-137
97Pinnacle Certified-85
Red-85
Mirror Blue-85
Mirror Gold-85
Mirror Red-85
97Pinnacle Inside-97
97Pinnacle Tot Cert Platinum Blue-85
97Pinnacle Tot Certi Platinum Gold-85
97Pinnacle Totally Certified Platinum Red-85
97Pinnacle Tot Cert Mirror Platinum Gold-85
97Revolution-105
Copper-105
Emerald-105
Ice Blue-105
Silver-105
97Score-139
Artist's Proofs-139
Golden Blades-139
97SP Authentic-124
97Studio-89
Press Proofs Silver-89
Press Proofs Gold-89
97Upper Deck-128
98Pacific-338
Ice Blue-338
Red-338
99Upper Deck Retro-110
Gold-110
Platinum-110
00Upper Deck 500 Goal Club-500MGA
00Upper Deck 500 Goal Club-500MGA
00Upper Deck Legends-129
00Upper Deck Legends-132
Legendary Collection Bronze-129
Legendary Collection Bronze-132
Legendary Collection Gold-129
Legendary Collection Gold-132
Legendary Collection Silver-129
Legendary Collection Silver-132
Epic Signatures-MG
Legendary Game Jerseys-JMG
01BAP Memorabilia 500 Goal Scorers-GS5
01BAP Signature Series 500 Goal Scorers-14
01BAP Sig Series 500 Goal Scorers Autos-14
01BAP Signature Series Vintage Autographs-VA-38
01BAP Ultimate Mem 500 Goal Scorers-15
01BAP Ultimate Mem 500 Goal Scorers Autos-18
01BAP Ultimate Mem 500 Goal Jerseys/Stick-15
01BAP Ultimate Mem 500 Goal Emblems-15
01Fleer Legacy-59
Ultimate-59
Memorabilia-13
01Greats of the Game-75
Autographs-75
01Parkhurst Autographs-PA23
01Parkhurst 500 Goal Scorers-PGS5
01SP Authentic Jerseys-NNMG
01Topps Archives-81
Relics-JMG
01Upper Deck Legends-68
01Upper Deck Legends-98
Jerseys-TTMG
Jerseys Platinum-TTGA
Jerseys Platinum-TTMG
Milestones-MMG
Milestones Platinum-MMG
Sticks-PHMG
02BAP Ultimate Memorabilia All-Star MVP-16
02Maple Leafs Platinum Collection-51
02Topps Rookie Reprints-2
02Topps Rookie Reprint Autographs-2
02UD Foundations 1000 Point Club-GA
02UD Foundations Signs of Greatness-SGMG
02UD Piece of History Heroes Jerseys-HHMG
02UD Piece of History Historical Swatches-HSMG
02UD Piece of History Mark of Distinction-GA
03Parkhurst Original Six New York-35
03Parkhurst Original Six Toronto-54
Autographs-15
Memorabilia-TM56
Memorabilia-TM61
Memorabilia-TM63
04ITG All-Star FANtasy Hail Minnesota-1

Gartshore, David
91Lake Superior State Lakers-9
92Lake Superior State Lakers-9

Garver, Jon
93Waterloo Black Hawks-9

Garver, Matt
99Idaho Steelheads-19

Garvey, Brendan
92Oklahoma City Blazers-5

Garvey, Liam
91Michigan Tech Huskies-30
93Michigan Tech Huskies-18
95Central Hockey League-96
96Peoria Rivermen-6
96Peoria Rivermen Photo Album-6
98German DEL-256
99German DEL-46
01German Upper Deck-65
03German DEL-200
03German Nuremberg Ice Tigers Postcards-9

Garvin, Robert
93Quebec Pee-Wee Tournament-581

Garvin, Scott
92British Columbia JHL-231

Garwasiuk, Ron
77Rochester Americans-10
79Rochester Americans-5

Garzone, Matt
96Richmond Renegades-6
97Wheeling Nailers-5
97Wheeling Nailers Photo Pack-5

Gascon, Martin
06Fort Wayne Komets-4

Gasparini, Tony
93Omaha Lancers-6

Gasper, Joel
02Lincoln Stars-22

Gasseau, Sandy
93St. Cloud State Huskies-6
95San Diego Barracudas RHI-2

Gasser, Andy
93Swiss HNL-440

Gasser, Stephane
93Swiss HNL-426
95Swiss HNL-453

Gassoff Jr., Bob
01Peoria Rivermen-4

Gassoff Sr., Bob
74NHL Action Stamps-243
75O-Pee-Chee NHL-58
75Topps-58
76O-Pee-Chee NHL-301
76O-Pee-Chee NHL-393
77O-Pee-Chee NHL-4
77Topps-4
92Blues UD Best of the Blues-13
02Fleer Throwbacks-64
Gold-64
Platinum-64

Gassoff, Brad
76Canucks Royal Bank-4
77Canucks Canada Dry Cans-2
77Canucks Royal Bank-4
78O-Pee-Chee-388
79O-Pee-Chee-353

Gastaldo, Nicolas
92Quebec Pee-Wee Tournament-1394
95Swiss HNL-476
96Swiss HNL-373
98Swiss Power Play Stickers-342
01Swiss HNL-353
02Swiss HNL-394

Gastaldo, Remo
95Swiss HNL-405

Gastrin, Magnus
02Swedish SHL-55
Parallel-55
03Swedish Elite-256
Silver-256
04Swedish Elitset-101
Gold-101
04Swedish MoDo Postcards-18
05Swedish SHL Elitset-105
06Swedish SHL Elitset-115

Gatenby, Dan
87Sudbury Wolves-3

Gates, Aaron
00Roanoke Express-13
02Pee Dee Pride RBI-135

Gates, Bobby
03Lewiston Maineiacs-11

Gates, R.J.
93Quebec Pee-Wee Tournament-816
01BC Icemen-9

Gathercole, Philip
917th Inn. Sketch QMJHL-235

Gatherum, Dave
51Laval Dairy Subset-66
52St. Lawrence Sales-107

Gatiyatulin, Anvar
99Russian Hockey League-183
00Russian Hockey League-132

Gatto, Greg
907th Inn. Sketch WHL-315
917th Inn. Sketch WHL-10
99Colorado Gold Kings Taco Bell-24
02Odessa Jackalopes-10
03Odessa Jackalopes-22
04Austin Ice Bats-21

Gattolliat, Jim
98Tacoma Sabercats-8
99Tacoma Sabercats-13

Gattuso, Xavier
01Swiss HNL-334

Gatzos, Steve
80Sault Ste. Marie Greyhounds-10
83Penguins Coke-10
84Penguins Heinz Photos-10

Gauch, Nicholas
93Swiss HNL-427
95Swiss HNL-43
96Swiss HNL-421

Gaucher, Ryan
96Saskatoon Blades-10
97Saskatoon Blades-8
99ECHL All-Star Southern Conference-20
99Mississippi Sea Wolves-16
01Cincinnati Mighty Ducks-13
02ECHL All-Star Northern-21
03Florence Pride-148
04Las Vegas Wranglers-19

Gaucher, Yves
84Richelieu Riverains-6

Gaudet, Christian
03Moncton Wildcats-6
04Moncton Wildcats-10
05Moncton Wildcats-6
06Moncton Wildcats-24

Gaudet, Denis
93North Bay Centennials-17

Gaudet, Jasmin
93Quebec Pee-Wee Tournament-122

Gaudet, Kevin
94German First League-605
96German DEL-203
98German DEL-202
99German DEL-241

Gaudet, Marc-Andre
92Quebec Pee-Wee Tournament-841
97Bowman CHL-66
OPC-66
98Bowman CHL-91
Golden Anniversary-91
OPC International-91
98Bowman Chrome CHL-91
Golden Anniversary-91
Golden Anniversary Refractors-91
OPC International-91
OPC International Refractors-91
Refractors-91
99Tallahassee Tiger Sharks-21
01Thetford Mines Coyotes-15
02Thetford Mines Coyotes-11
03Thetford Mines Prolab-9
04Thetford Mines Prolab-3

Gaudet, Pius
51Bas Du Fleuve-32

Gaudette, Andre
72Nordiques Postcards-8
73Nordiques Team Issue-9
73Quaker Oats WHA-22
74O-Pee-Chee WHA-46

Gaudette, Pete
52Bas Du Fleuve-10

Gaudette, Yan
01Sherbrooke Castors-9
04Chicoutimi Sagueneens-24

Gaudreau, Daniel
93Quebec Pee-Wee Tournament-242

Gaudreau, Rob
92Classic-82
Gold-82
92Classic Four-Sport *-204
Gold-204
93Donruss-310
93Leaf-9
93OPC Premier-199
Gold-199
93Panini Stickers-258
93Parkhurst-189
Emerald Ice-189
93Pinnacle-41
Canadian-41
93PowerPlay-220
Second Year Stars-1
93Score-247
Canadian-247
93Stadium Club-174
Members Only Master Set-174
OPC-174
First Day Issue-174
First Day Issue OPC-174
93Topps/OPC Premier-199
Gold-199
93Ultra-98
Prospects-2
93Upper Deck-149
Hat Tricks-HT9
NHL's Best-HB2
SP-143
93Classic Pro Prospects-16
93Classic Pro Prospects-140
LPs-LP3
Prototypes-PR3
94Be A Player Signature Cards-85
94Fleer-146
94Leaf-39
94OPC Premier-4
Special Effects-4
94Parkhurst-207
Gold-207
94Pinnacle-349
Artist's Proofs-349
Rink Collection-349
94Senators Team Issue-13
94Topps/OPC Premier-4
Special Effects-4
94Upper Deck-182
94Upper Deck-277
Electric Ice-182
Electric Ice-277
95Collector's Choice-158
Player's Club-158
Player's Club Platinum-158
95Score-141
Black Ice Artist's Proofs-141
Black Ice-141
95Senators Team Issue-11
95Topps-117
OPC Inserts-117
95Upper Deck-164
Electric Ice-164
Electric Ice Gold-164
96Swiss HNL-244

Gaudreault, Armand
43Parade Sportive *-41
43Parade Sportive *-42
51Laval Dairy QSHL-14

Gaudreault, Leon
27La Patrie-13
27La Presse Photos-12
51Laval Dairy Lac St. Jean-32

Gaudreault, Marc
76Saginaw Gears-4

Gaudreault, Sebastien
93Quebec Pee-Wee Tournament-1360

Gaul, Horace
10C56-31

Gaul, Michael
917th Inn. Sketch QMJHL-236
94Knoxville Cherokees-19
99AHL All-Stars-4
00Syracuse Crunch-5
01Swiss HNL-126
02Swiss HNL-46

Gaulin, Jean-Marc
81Fredericton Express-22
82Fredericton Express-22
83Fredericton Express-21
84Nordiques Postcards-8
85Nordiques General Foods-8
85Fredericton Express-26
86Fredericton Express-8

Gault, Corey
04Peterborough Petes Postcards-24

Gaulton, Mitch
06Erie Otters-16

Gaume, Dallas
88ProCards AHL-61
92Norwegian Elite Series-112
92Norwegian Elite Series-126
92Norwegian Elite Series-186
92Norwegian Elite Series-195

Gaumond, Alexandre
917th Inn. Sketch QMJHL-295

Gaus, Thomas
94German DEL-417
95German DEL-388
96German DEL-296

Gaustad, B.J.
03Muskegon Fury-7
06Bloomington PrairieThunder-8

Gaustad, Paul
02BAP Memorabilia-388
02Upper Deck Rookie Update-174
02Rochester Americans-5
03Rochester Americans-9
04Portland Winter Hawks-10
04Portland Winter Hawks-NNO
04Rochester Americans-6
05Parkhurst-61
Facsimile Auto Parallel-61
05Upper Deck-268
06O-Pee-Chee-64
Rainbow-64

Gauthier, Alain
907th Inn. Sketch QMJHL-251
917th Inn. Sketch QMJHL-249

Gauthier, Charles
02Shawinigan Cataractes-24
03Shawinigan Cataractes-10

Gauthier, Daniel
90Knoxville Cherokees-106
91ProCards-296
92Cleveland Lumberjacks-22
93Cincinnati Cyclones-7
93Classic Pro Prospects-23
94Indianapolis Ice-8
95Indianapolis Ice-8
99Swiss Panini Stickers-144
00Swiss Panini Stickers-186
00Swiss Slapshot Mini-Cards-LT12
01Swiss HNL-204

Gauthier, Denis
93Drummondville Voltigeurs-14
95Donruss Elite World Juniors-5
95Upper Deck-533
Electric Ice-533
Electric Ice Gold-533
95Classic-19
CHL All-Stars-AS14
96Saint John Flames-4
97Saint John Flames-9
98Pacific-118
Ice Blue-118
Red-118
98Upper Deck-50
Exclusives-50
Exclusives 1 of 1-50
Gold Reserve-50
99BAP Millennium-44
Emerald-44
Ruby-44
Sapphire-44
Signatures-44
Signatures Gold-44
99Topps Arena Giveaways-CAL-DG
00Upper Deck NHLPA-PA14
02BAP Sig Series Auto Buybacks 1999-44
02NHL Power Play Stickers-23
02Pacific-53
Blue-53
Red-53
02Upper Deck Vintage-41
03ITG Action-26
03NHL Sticker Collection-168
06Flyers Postcards-12

Gauthier, Derek
90Kitchener Rangers-17
907th Inn. Sketch OHL-233
917th Inn. Sketch OHL-84
94Brantford Smoke-8
97Anchorage Aces-8
98Anchorage Aces-23
99Anchorage Aces-14
00Fort Wayne Komets-4
00Fort Wayne Komets Shoe Carnival-16
01Fort Wayne Komets-5
01Fort Wayne Komets Shoe Carnival-7

Gauthier, Don
89Rayside-Balfour Jr. Canadians-9

Gauthier, Fern
43Parade Sportive *-43
43Parade Sportive *-44
43Parade Sportive *-45
44Beehive Group II Photos-168

Gauthier, Francois
02Rimouski Oceanic-4
05Cape Breton Screaming Eagles-12
06Cape Breton Screaming Eagles-15

Gauthier, Gerard
90Pro Set-687

Gauthier, Jason
93Quebec Pee-Wee Tournament-1186

Gauthier, Jean
61Shirriff/Salada Coins-120
61York Yellow Backs-42
63Chex Photos-15
63Parkhurst-28
63Parkhurst-87
63York White Backs-29
63Quebec Aces-8

Gauthier, Jean-Christophe
06Cape Breton Screaming Eagles-12

Gauthier, Jean-Philippe
02Baie Comeau Drakkar-4

Gauthier, Jonathan
99Rouyn-Noranda Huskies-7
00Rouyn-Noranda Huskies-2
Signed-2
02Greenville Grrrowl-12
03Alaska Aces-5

Gauthier, Luc
86Sherbrooke Canadiens-16
88ProCards AHL-299
89ProCards AHL-197
90ProCards AHL/IHL-55
91ProCards-76
92Fredericton Canadiens-11
93Fredericton Canadiens-11
94Fredericton Canadiens-14
95Fredericton Canadiens-29
96Fredericton Canadiens-25

Gauthier, Mike
03Prince Albert Raiders-19
04Prince Albert Raiders-2
05Prince Albert Raiders-11
06Prince Albert Raiders-3

Gauthier, Olivier
05PEI Rocket-13

Gauthier, Pascal
93Quebec Pee-Wee Tournament-1131

Gauthier, Rene
02Chicago Steel-7
03Chicago Steel-18

Gauthier, Sean
907th Inn. Sketch OHL-57
91Moncton Hawks-9
91ProCards-180
93Fort Wayne Komets-6

94Los Angeles Blades RHI-15
95South Carolina Stingrays-23
96Pensacola Ice Pilots-21
97Pensacola Ice Pilots-9
98Kentucky Thoroughblades-9
99Louisiana Ice Gators-1
99Louisville Panthers-9
00Louisville Panthers-8
02Swedish SHL-189
02Swedish SHL-287
Masks-3
Parallel-189
Parallel-287
Signatures Series II-19
02Reading Royals-18
03Swedish Elite Zero Hero-7

Gauthier, Sebastien
02Shawinigan Cataractes-14
03Shawinigan Cataractes-11

Gauthier, Simon
93Quebec Pee-Wee Tournament-294

Gauthier, Steven
84Chicoutimi Sagueneens-12

Gautier, Jonathan
99Baie-Comeau Drakkar-10
00Baie-Comeau Drakkar-24
Signed-24
00QMJHL All-Star Program Inserts-7
01Val d'Or Foreurs-6

Gautschi, Marc
01Swiss HNL-464

Gauvreau, Brent
98Bowman CHL-144
Golden Anniversary-144
OPC International-144
Autographs Blue-A37
Autographs Gold-A37
Autographs Silver-A37
98Bowman Chrome CHL-144
Golden Anniversary-144
Golden Anniversary Refractors-144
OPC International-144
OPC International Refractors-144
Refractors-144
03ECHL All-Stars-270
03Mississippi Sea Wolves-2

Gavalier, Michael
01Rimouski Oceanic-4
02Rimouski Oceanic-5
03Shawinigan Cataractes-12

Gavey, Aaron
917th Inn. Sketch OHL-316
93Donruss Team Canada-12
93Pinnacle-473
Canadian-473
93Upper Deck-545
93Sault Ste. Marie Greyhounds-20
93Sault Ste. Marie Greyhound Memorial Cup-22
93Classic-21
94Be A Player-R156
94Flair-172
94Leaf-452
94Leaf Limited-118
94OPC Premier-536
Special Effects-536
94Pinnacle-251
Artist's Proofs-251
Rink Collection-251
94Score-207
Gold-207
Platinum-207
94Select-180
Gold-180
94Topps/OPC Premier-536
Special Effects-536
94Atlanta Knights-16
94Classic-115
Gold-115
CHL All-Stars-C5
ROY Sweepstakes-R6
Tri-Cards-T64
95Be A Player-165
Signatures-S165
Signatures Die Cuts-S165
95Bowman-121
All-Foil-121
95Donruss-369
95Finest-28
Refractors-28
95Lightning Team Issue-9
95Parkhurst International-527
Emerald Ice-527
95SkyBox Impact-221
95SP-138
95Stadium Club-138
Members Only Master Set-138
95Upper Deck-417
Electric Ice-417
Electric Ice Gold-417
96Collector's Choice-249
96Donruss Elite-64
Die Cut Stars-64
96Leaf-167
Press Proofs-167
96Score-259
Artist's Proofs-259
Dealer's Choice Artist's Proofs-259
Special Artist's Proofs-259
Golden Blades-259
96Summit-158
Artist's Proofs-158
Ice-158
Metal-158
Premium Stock-158
96Collector's Edge Ice-101
Prism-101
97Flames Collector's Photos-4
97Pacific Invincible NHL Regime-27
97Upper Deck-28
98Michigan K-Wings-7
99Stars Postcards-6
99Michigan K-Wings-8
00BAP Memorabilia-390
Emerald-390
Ruby-390
Sapphire-390
Promos-390
00BAP Mem Chicago Sportsfest Copper-390
00BAP Memorabilia Chicago Sportsfest Blue-390
00BAP Memorabilia Chicago Sportsfest Gold-390
00BAP Memorabilia Chicago Sportsfest Ruby-390
00BAP Memorabilia Chicago Sun-Times Ruby-390
00BAP Memorabilia Chicago Sun-Times Gold-390
00BAP Mem Chicago Sun-Times Sapphire-390
00BAP Mem Toronto Fall Expo Copper-390
00BAP Memorabilia Toronto Fall Expo Gold-390
00BAP Memorabilia Toronto Fall Expo Ruby-390
00BAP Signature Series-43
Emerald-43
Ruby-43
Sapphire-43
Autographs-185
Autographs Gold-185
00Topps Chrome-239
OPC Refractors-239
Refractors-239
00Upper Deck Vintage-179
01Upper Deck Victory-177
Gold-177
02BAP Sig Series Auto Buybacks 2000-185
02St. John's Maple Leafs Aliant-2
03Parkhurst Original Six Toronto-27
05Portland Pirates-5

Gavin, Stewart
80Maple Leafs Postcards-13
80Pepsi-Cola Caps-88
81Maple Leafs Postcards-7
82Maple Leafs Postcards-13
82Post Cereal-18
83Maple Leafs Postcards-7
83O-Pee-Chee-331
83Vachon-87
84Maple Leafs Postcards-10
84O-Pee-Chee-302
85O-Pee-Chee Stickers-17
86Whalers Junior Thomas'-10
87O-Pee-Chee-61
87Panini Stickers-49
87Topps-61
87Whalers Jr. Burger King/Pepsi-8
88North Stars ADA-11
88O-Pee-Chee-217
89O-Pee-Chee-214
89Panini Stickers-113
90O-Pee-Chee-402
90Panini Stickers-260
90Pro Set-139
90Score-244
Canadian-244
90Upper Deck-150
French-150
91Pro Set-404
French-404
91Score Canadian Bilingual-433
91Score Canadian English-433
92Score-117
Canadian-117

Gavrylin, Andrei
00Russian Hockey League-347

Gawley, Sean
917th Inn. Sketch OHL-298

Gawlik, Christoph
04German Berlin Polar Bears Postcards-12
04German DEL Update-295
05German DEL-29

Gawryletz, Travis
04Minnesota-Duluth Bulldogs-7

Gawrys, Shawn
04Lincoln Stars-12

Gaynor, Joe
05Plymouth Whalers-B-12
06Plymouth Whalers-9

Gazdic, Luke
06Erie Otters-7

Gazzaroli, Ivan
93Swiss HNL-141
95Swiss HNL-117
96Swiss HNL-81
98Swiss Power Play Stickers-7
99Swiss Panini Stickers-7
00Swiss Panini Stickers-9
00Swiss Slapshot Mini-Cards-HCAP3
01Swiss HNL-216
02Swiss HNL-56

Gazzaroli, Oliver
93Swiss HNL-501
95Swiss HNL-428

Gazzola, Marco
93Swiss HNL-292

Gebauer, Andreas
94German First League-303
95German DEL-350

Gebel, Martin
94German DEL-237
95German DEL-240
96German DEL-73

Gecse, Derek
91British Columbia JHL-101

Gecse, Dorel
91British Columbia JHL-72

Geddes, Paul
94German DEL-323
95German DEL-299
96German DEL-325

Gedyk, Adam
94German First League-602

Gee, George
44Beehive Group II Photos-97
44Beehive Group II Photos-169
51Parkhurst-43
52Parkhurst-36
53Parkhurst-83
54Parkhurst-80
02Parkhurst Reprints-171

Geekie, Craig
917th Inn. Sketch WHL-213
92Brandon Wheat Kings-7
93Spokane Chiefs-11

Geelan, Ben
02Chicago Steel-8

Geesink, Tony
84Ottawa 67's-7

Geffert, Pavel
94Czech APS Extraliga-87
95Czech APS Extraliga-375
96Czech APS Extraliga-131
97Czech APS Extraliga-180
97Czech DS Extraliga-53
97Czech DS Stickers-72
98Czech DS-58
98Czech DS Stickers-156
98Czech OFS-40
99Czech DS-96
99Czech OFS-121
99Czech OFS-388
00Czech OFS-121
01Czech OFS-169

Gegenfurther, Christian
94German DEL-383
95German DEL-367
96German DEL-189
98German DEL-310

Gehrig, Mario
94German DEL-276
95German DEL-273
96German DEL-168
98German DEL-122
98German DEL-336
99German Bundesliga 2-164

Geier, Peter
94German First League-172

Geiger, Andrew
93Quebec Pee-Wee Tournament-886

Geiger, Trevor
03Salmon Arm Silverbacks-8
04Salmon Arm Silverbacks-11

Geisbaur, Jay
93St. Cloud State Huskies-7

Geiselmann, Uwe
94German First League-467

Geisert, Jurgen
04German Berlin Eisbarens 50th Anniv-45

Geisert, Uwe
94German First League-164
04German Berlin Eisbarens 50th Anniv-21

Geisler, Beau
06Stockton Thunder-6

Gejdos, Stanislav
93Quebec Pee-Wee Tournament-1720

Gelacek, Libor
99Czech OFS-431

Gelati, Mike
95Slapshot-300

Geldart, Greg
95Tallahassee Tiger Sharks-14

Geldart, Kaine
06Plymouth Whalers-10

Geldreich, Thomas
94German First League-81

Gelech, Randall
00Kelowna Rockets-7
01Kelowna Rockets-5
02Kelowna Rockets-12
03Kelowna Rockets Memorial Cup-6
03Kelowna Rockets-8

Gelinas, Charles
93Quebec Pee-Wee Tournament-987

Gelinas, Hugo
93Quebec Pee-Wee Tournament-213

Gelinas, Jasmin
92Quebec Pee-Wee Tournament-182
98Halifax Mooseheads-19
98Halifax Mooseheads Second Edition-2
99Halifax Mooseheads-18
03Memphis RiverKings-5

Gelinas, Martin
87Hull Olympiques-7
88Oilers Tenth Anniversary-73
89Oilers Team Issue-7
90Bowman-190
Tiffany-190
90Oilers IGA-5
90O-Pee-Chee-64
90Pro Set-83
90Score-301C
Canadian-301C
90Score Young Superstars-21
90Topps-64
Tiffany-64
90Upper Deck-23
French-23
91Bowman-102
91Oilers Panini Team Stickers-5
91Oilers IGA-5
91Oilers Team Issue-6
91O-Pee-Chee-244
91Panini Stickers-128
91Parkhurst-283
French-283
91Pinnacle-93
French-93
91Pro Set-66
French-66
91Score American-159
91Score Canadian Bilingual-159
91Score Canadian English-159
91Score Young Superstars-14
91Stadium Club-11
91Topps-244
91Upper Deck-266
French-266
92Oilers IGA-6
92O-Pee-Chee-19
92Panini Stickers-106
92Panini Stickers French-106
92Pinnacle-166
French-166
92Score-281
Canadian-281
92Stadium Club-314
92Topps-292
Gold-292G
92Upper Deck-282
93Donruss-271
93Donruss-501
93Durivage Score-22
93Leaf-396
93Parkhurst-166
Emerald Ice-166
93Pinnacle-366
Canadian-366
93Score-408
93Score-534
Gold-534
Canadian-408
Canadian-534
Canadian Gold-534
93Ultra-401
93Upper Deck-322
SP-127
94Canada Games NHL POGS-335
94Canucks Program Inserts-9
94Leaf-138
94OPC Premier-101
Special Effects-101
94Parkhurst Vintage-V36
94Parkhurst SE-SE184
Gold-SE184
94Pinnacle-324
Artist's Proofs-324
Rink Collection-324
94Topps/OPC Premier-101
Special Effects-101
94Ultra-383
94Upper Deck-54
Electric Ice-54
SP Inserts-SP172
SP Inserts Die Cuts-SP172
95Be A Player-149
Signatures-S149
Signatures Die Cuts-S149
95Canada Games NHL POGS-273
95Canucks Building the Dream Art-9
95Collector's Choice-176
Player's Club-176
Player's Club Platinum-176
95Donruss-223
95Parkhurst International-480
Emerald Ice-480
95Pinnacle-161
Artist's Proofs-161
Rink Collection-161
95Topps-176
OPC Inserts-176
95Upper Deck-359
Electric Ice-359
Electric Ice Gold-359
96Canucks Postcards-23
96Donruss-133
Press Proofs-133
96Leaf-127
Press Proofs-127
96Pinnacle-83
Artist's Proofs-83
Foil-83
Premium Stock-83
Rink Collection-83
96Score-98
Artist's Proofs-98
Dealer's Choice Artist's Proofs-98
Special Artist's Proofs-98
Golden Blades-98
96Summit-79
Artist's Proofs-79
Ice-79
Metal-79
Premium Stock-79
96Upper Deck-171
97Collector's Choice-257
Star Quest-SQ8
97Crown Royale-134
Emerald Green-134
Ice Blue-134
Silver-134
97Donruss-41
Press Proofs Silver-41
Press Proofs Gold-41
97Donruss Canadian Ice-61
Dominion Series-61
Provincial Series-61
97Donruss Limited-185
Exposure-185
97Donruss Preferred-83
Cut to the Chase-83
97Hurricanes Team Issue-8
97Leaf-37
Fractal Matrix-37
Fractal Matrix Die Cuts-37
97Leaf International-37
Universal Ice-37
97Pacific-67
Copper-67
Emerald Green-67
Ice Blue-67
Red-67
Silver-67
97Pacific Dynagon-126
Copper-126
Dark Grey-126
Emerald Green-126
Ice Blue-126
Red-126
Silver-126
Tandems-60
97Pacific Invincible-141
Copper-141
Emerald Green-141
Ice Blue-141
Red-141
Silver-141
97Pacific Omega-40
Copper-40
Dark Gray-40
Emerald Green-40
Gold-40
Ice Blue-40
97Panini Stickers-238
97Paramount-187
Copper-187
Dark Grey-187
Emerald Green-187
Ice Blue-187
Red-187
Silver-187
97Pinnacle-168
Press Plates Back Black-168
Press Plates Back Cyan-168
Press Plates Back Magenta-168
Press Plates Back Yellow-168
Press Plates Front Black-168
Press Plates Front Cyan-168
Press Plates Front Magenta-168
Press Plates Front Yellow-168
97Pinnacle Certified-113
Red-113
Mirror Blue-113
Mirror Gold-113
Mirror Red-113
97Pinnacle Inside-103
97Pinnacle Tot Cert Platinum Blue-113
97Pinnacle Tot Certi Platinum Gold-113
97Pinnacle Totally Certified Platinum Red-113
97Pinnacle Tot Cert Mirror Platinum Gold-113
97Revolution-22
Copper-22
Emerald-22
Ice Blue-22
Silver-22
97Score-133
Artist's Proofs-133
Golden Blades-133
97Score Canucks-5
Platinum-5
Premier-5
97Upper Deck-167
97Upper Deck-200
98Aurora-32
98Finest-8
No Protectors-8
No Protectors Refractors-8
Refractors-8
98Hurricanes Team Issue-15
98Pacific-132
Ice Blue-132
Red-132
98Pacific Dynagon Ice-32
Blue-32
Red-32
98Pacific Omega-41
Red-41
Opening Day Issue-41
98Paramount-36
Copper-36
Emerald Green-36
Holo-Electric-36
Ice Blue-36
Silver-36
98Upper Deck-238
Exclusives-238
Exclusives 1 of 1-238
Gold Reserve-238
98Upper Deck MVP-39
Gold Script-39
Silver Script-39
Super Script-39
99Pacific-71
Copper-71
Emerald Green-71
Gold-71
Ice Blue-71
Premiere Date-71
Red-71
99Panini Stickers-47
99Paramount-45
Copper-45
Emerald-45
Gold-45
Holographic Emerald-45
Holographic Gold-45
Holographic Silver-45
Ice Blue-45
Premiere Date-45
Red-45
Silver-45
99Upper Deck-198
Exclusives-198
Exclusives 1 of 1-198
99Upper Deck Gold Reserve-198
99Upper Deck Victory-61
00O-Pee-Chee-255B
00O-Pee-Chee Parallel-255B
00Titanium Game Gear-2
00Topps/OPC-255B
Parallel-255B
00Upper Deck-261
Exclusives Tier 1-261
Exclusives Tier 2-261
00Upper Deck Vintage-68
01Pacific-72
Extreme LTD-72
Hobby LTD-72
Premiere Date-72
Retail LTD-72
01Pacific Adrenaline-33
Blue-33
Premiere Date-33
Red-33
Retail-33
01Pacific Arena Exclusives-72
01Upper Deck-263
Exclusives-263
02NHL Power Play Stickers-13
02Pacific Complete-242
Red-242
02Topps Total-171
02Upper Deck-270
Exclusives-270
02Upper Deck Beckett UD Promos-270
03Beehive-30
Gold-30
Silver-30
03ITG Action-57
03NHL Sticker Collection-166
03O-Pee-Chee-258
03OPC Blue-258
03OPC Gold-258
03OPC Red-258
03Pacific-49
Blue-49
Red-49
03Pacific Complete-58
Red-58
03Pacific Exhibit-24
Blue Backs-24
Yellow Backs-24
03Topps-258
Blue-258
Gold-258
Red-258
03Upper Deck-30
Canadian Exclusives-30
HG-30
03Upper Deck MVP-68
Gold Script-68
Silver Script-68
Canadian Exclusives-68
04Pacific-39
Blue-39
Red-39
04UD All-World-83
Gold-83
05Be A Player-14
First Period-14
Second Period-14
Third Period-14
Overtime-14
Signatures-GL
Signatures Gold-GL
05Black Diamond-14
Emerald-14
Gold-14
Onyx-14
Ruby-14
05Parkhurst-209
Facsimile Auto Parallel-209
05Upper Deck-330
05Upper Deck MVP-176
Gold-176
Platinum-176
05Upper Deck Victory-28
Black-28
Gold-28
Silver-28
06O-Pee-Chee-217
Rainbow-217
06Upper Deck-86
Exclusives Parallel-86
High Gloss Parallel-86
Masterpieces-86

Gelinas, Philippe
99Shawinigan Cataractes-2
Signed-2

Gelinas, Ryan
95Slapshot-406
97Quad-City Mallards-19

Gelineau, Jack
44Beehive Group II Photos-24
48Exhibits Canadian-47
51Laval Dairy QSHL-4
51Laval Dairy Subset-4
52St. Lawrence Sales-37

Gellard, Mike
02Providence Bruins-17
03Providence Bruins-5

Gellard, Sam
73Vancouver Blazers-10

Gelzinus, Christoph
94German First League-502

Gendron, Bryan
89Peterborough Petes-120
897th Inn. Sketch OHL-120
907th Inn. Sketch OHL-359
91Peterborough Petes-11
917th Inn. Sketch OHL-141

Gendron, Dennis
96Albany River Rats-23
97Albany River Rats-24
99Albany River Rats-11
02Albany River Rats-25
03Albany River Rats-28

Gendron, Edgard
51Laval Dairy Lac St. Jean-50
52Bas Du Fleuve-54

Gendron, Jean-Guy
44Beehive Group II Photos-25
44Beehive Group II Photos-313
52Juniors Blue Tint-40
57Bruins Photos-7
57Topps-52
58Bruins Photos-5
58Topps-51
59Topps-24
60Shirriff Coins-109
60Topps-31
60York Photos-9
61Shirriff/Salada Coins-93
61Topps-57
62Topps-16
63Topps-16
63Toronto Star-13
64Beehive Group III Photos-8
64Quebec Aces-4
65Quebec Aces-4
68O-Pee-Chee-185
69O-Pee-Chee-169
Four-in-One-11
69Topps-96
70Dad's Cookies-38
70Esso Power Players-207
70O-Pee-Chee-86
70Sargent Promotions Stamps-157
70Topps-86
71O-Pee-Chee-204
71Sargent Promotions Stamps-153
71Toronto Sun-195
72Flyers Mighty Milk-5
72Nordiques Postcards-9
72O-Pee-Chee-302
727-Eleven Slurpee Cups WHA-7
72Finnish Semic World Championship-170
72Swedish Semic World Championship-170
73Nordiques Team Issue-10

Gendron, Martin
907th Inn. Sketch QMJHL-234
917th Inn. Sketch QMJHL-27
92Classic-23
Gold-23
92Classic Four-Sport *-172
Gold-172
93Donruss Team Canada-13
93Pinnacle-474
Canadian-474
93PowerPlay-480
93Ultra-460
93Upper Deck-259
93Upper Deck-540
93Classic-131
93Classic Four-Sport *-234
Gold-234
94Portland Pirates-8
94Classic Pro Prospects Intl Heroes-LP12
95Capitals Team Issue-7
95Donruss-47
95Parkhurst International-489
Emerald Ice-489
95Pinnacle-201
Artist's Proofs-201
Rink Collection-201
95Score-315
Black Ice Artist's Proofs-315
Black Ice-315
95SkyBox Impact-224
95Ultra-174
Gold Medallion-174
95Portland Pirates-11
96Las Vegas Thunder-7
97Indianapolis Ice-8
97Milwaukee Admirals-7
99Syracuse Crunch-11
00German DEL-85
02Swiss HNL-420

Gendron, Pierre
917th Inn. Sketch QMJHL-133
97New Orleans Brass-13
03St. Jean Mission-10

Gendron, Red
98Albany River Rats-22
02Albany River Rats AAP-12

Genesse, Benoit
00Sherbrooke Castors-15
Signed-15
02Val d'Or Foreurs-15
03Port Huron Beacons-10
04Austin Ice Bats-14

Genest, Eric
93Quebec Pee-Wee Tournament-313

Genest, Hubert
06Quebec Remparts-7

Genest, Marc
96South Carolina Stingrays-10
97Macon Whoopee-11
97Macon Whoopee Autographs-11
98Idaho Steelheads-8
99Idaho Steelheads-14

Genest, Patrick
907th Inn. Sketch QMJHL-106
917th Inn. Sketch QMJHL-188

Gengel, Ladislav
04Czech OFS-248

Genik, Jason
92British Columbia JHL-182
99Corpus Christi IceRays-5

Genovese, Dan
93Quebec Pee-Wee Tournament-657

Genovy, Al
77Kalamazoo Wings-13

Genoway, Chay
05Vernon Vipers-11

Genoway, Colby
03North Dakota Fighting Sioux-13
04North Dakota Fighting Sioux-9
05Hartford Wolf Pack-5
06AHL Top Prospects-23
06Portland Pirates-11
06ITG Heroes and Prospects-59
Autographs-ACGE

Gens, Matt
03St. Cloud State Huskies-8
04St. Cloud State Huskies-11
05Rockford Ice Hogs-5
06Rockford IceHogs -11

Gentges, Frank
94German First League-357

Gentile, Flavio
91Arizona Icecats-17

Gentile, Paul
01Saskatoon Blades-3
03Calgary Hitmen-8

Genua, Peter
93Quebec Pee-Wee Tournament-1174

Genze, Alexander
94German DEL-297
95German DEL-197
95German DEL-428
96German DEL-340
99German Bundesliga 2-145
02German DEL City Press-134
04German DEL-267

Geoffrey, Kelly
06Erie Otters-11

Geoffrion, Bernie
44Beehive Group II Photos-241
45Quaker Oats Photos-78
48Exhibits Canadian-8
48Exhibits Canadian-61
51Parkhurst-14
52Parkhurst-3
53Parkhurst-29
54Parkhurst-8
54Parkhurst-100
55Parkhurst-43
55Parkhurst-70
Quaker Oats-43
Quaker Oats-70
57Parkhurst-M2
57Parkhurst-M24
58Parkhurst-28
59Parkhurst-33
60NHL Ceramic Tiles-5
60Parkhurst-46
60Parkhurst-59
60Shirriff Coins-28
60York Photos-10
61Parkhurst-35
61Shirriff/Salada Coins-104
61York Yellow Backs-28
62Wheaties Great Moments in Cdn Sport-16
62Parkhurst-48
62Parkhurst-53
62Shirriff Coins-34
62York Iron-On Transfers-12
63Chex Photos-16
63Parkhurst-29
63Parkhurst-88
63Toronto Star-14
63York White Backs-20
64Beehive Group III Photos-125
64Beehive Group III Photos-189
64Quebec Aces-5
65Quebec Aces-5
66Topps-85
66Topps USA Test-36
67Topps-29
69Equitable Sports Hall of Fame-2
72Flames Postcards-4
74O-Pee-Chee NHL-147
74Topps-147
79Canadiens Postcards-5
83Hall of Fame Postcards-M8
85Hall of Fame-166
91Kraft-84
91Ultimate Original Six-10
91Ultimate Original Six-73
91Ultimate Original Six-83
French-10
French-73
French-83
92Hall of Fame Legends-5
92Parkhurst Parkie Reprints-PR32
92Sport-Flash-5
92Sport-Flash Autographs-5
93O-Pee-Chee Canadiens Hockey Fest-54
93Parkhurst Parkie Reprints-PR46
94Parkhurst Missing Link-68
Autographs-3
95Parkhurst '66-67-89
Coins-89
99Upper Deck Century Legends-43
Century Collection-43
99Upper Deck Retro-104
Gold-104
Platinum-104
Inkredible-BG
Inkredible Level 2-BG
00Upper Deck Legends-71
Legendary Collection Bronze-71
Legendary Collection Gold-71
Legendary Collection Silver-71
Epic Signatures-BG
01BAP Memorabilia Rocket's Mates-RM5
01BAP Signature Series Vintage Autographs-VA-22
01Fleer Legacy-50
Ultimate-50
01Greats of the Game-37
Autographs-37
01Parkhurst Autographs-PA14
01Parkhurst Reprints-PR3
01Parkhurst Reprints-PR18
01Parkhurst Reprints-PR32
01Parkhurst Reprints-PR40
01Parkhurst Reprints-PR51
01Parkhurst Reprints-PR57
01Parkhurst Reprints-PR62
01Parkhurst Reprints-PR69
01Parkhurst Reprints-PR79
01Parkhurst Reprints-PR98
01Parkhurst Reprints-PR112
01Topps Heritage Arena Relics-RBG
01Topps Heritage Arena Relics-RJB/BG
01Topps Heritage Arena Relics-ARBG
01Topps Heritage Arena Relics-ARJB/BG
01Topps Heritage Autographs-ABG
01Topps Heritage Salute-S9
01Upper Deck Legends-39
02BAP Ultimate Mem Scoring Leaders-30
02BAP Ultimate Mem Scoring Leaders-35
02BAP Ultimate Mem Storied Franchise-1
02Parkhurst Retro Nicknames-RN5
03BAP Memorabilia Gloves-GUG19
03BAP Ultimate Memorabilia Gloves Are Off-14
03BAP Ultimate Memorabilia Linemates-4
03BAP Ultimate Memorabilia Vintage Lumber-1
03Parkhurst Rookie ROYalty-VR-25
03Parkhurst Rookie ROYalty Gold-VR-25
04ITG Franchises Canadian-43
Autographs-BG
Double Memorabilia-DM13
Double Memorabilia Gold-DM13
Memorabilia-SM28
Memorabilia Gold-SM28
04ITG Franchises Update Linemates-ULI5
04ITG Franchises Update Linemates Gold-ULI5
04ITG Franchises US East-397
04ITG Ultimate Memorabilia-34
04ITG Ultimate Memorabilia-54
Gold-34
Gold-54
Day In History-12
Day In History Gold-12
Nicknames-10
Stick Autographs-23
Stick Autographs Gold-23
Vintage Lumber-13
04UD Legendary Signatures-4
AKA Autographs-AKA-GE
Autographs-GE
04UD Legends Classics-3
Gold-3
Platinum-3
Silver-3
Jersey Redemptions-JY7
Signature Moments-M45
Signatures-CS43
Signatures-TC7
05Beehive-237
05ITG Ultimate Memorabilia Level 1-6
05ITG Ultimate Memorabilia Level 2-6
05ITG Ultimate Memorabilia Level 3-6
05ITG Ultimate Memorabilia Level 4-6
05ITG Ultimate Memorabilia Level 5-6
05ITG Ultimate Mem Quad Paper Cuts Autos-4
05ITG Ultimate Mem 3 Star of the Game Jsy-5
05ITG Ult Mem 3 Star of the Game Jsy Gold-5
05ITG Ultimate Memorabilia Vintage Lumber-7
05ITG Ultimate Mem Vintage Lumber Gold-7
05SP Authentic Sign of the Times Fives-LRMMG
05SP Authentic Six Star Signatures-SSMO
05SP Game Used Statscriptions-ST-BG
05SPx-91
Spectrum-91
Xcitement Legends-XL-BG
Xcitement Legends Gold-XL-BG
Xcitement Legends Spectrum-XL-BG
05UD Artifacts-118
Blue-118
Gold-118
Green-118
Pewter-118
Red-118
Frozen Artifacts-FA-BG
Frozen Artifacts Autographed-FA-BG
Frozen Artifacts Copper-FA-BG
Frozen Artifacts Dual-FAD-BG
Frozen Artifacts Dual Autographed-FAD-BG
Frozen Artifacts Dual Copper-FAD-BG
Frozen Artifacts Dual Gold-FAD-BG
Frozen Artifacts Dual Maroon-FAD-BG
Frozen Artifacts Dual Pewter-FAD-BG
Frozen Artifacts Dual Silver-FAD-BG
Frozen Artifacts Gold-FA-BG
Frozen Artifacts Maroon-FA-BG
Frozen Artifacts Patches-FP-BG
Frozen Artifacts Patches Autographed-FP-BG
Frozen Artifacts Patches Dual-FPD-BG
Frozen Artifacts Patches Dual Autos-FPD-BG
Frozen Artifacts Patches Pewter-FP-BG
Frozen Artifacts Patches Silver-FP-BG
Frozen Artifacts Pewter-FA-BG
Frozen Artifacts Silver-FA-BG
Gold Autographed-118
05Upper Deck Jerseys-J-BGE
05Upper Deck Patches-P-BGE
06ITG Ultimate Memorabilia-12
Artist Proof-12
Raised to the Rafters-4
Raised to the Rafters Gold-4

Geoffrion, Danny
79Canadiens Postcards-6
80Jets Postcards-8
80Pepsi-Cola Caps-127
81O-Pee-Chee-364
81O-Pee-Chee Stickers-141

George, CHL
98Huntsville Channel Cats-19
01Indianapolis Ice-8

George, Chris (CHL)
98Huntsville Channel Cats-19
01Indianapolis Ice-8

George, Chris (Jrs.)
94Sarnia Sting-10
95Slapshot-7
95Barrie Colts-10
97Barrie Colts-7

George, COL
94Sarnia Sting-10
95Slapshot-7
95Barrie Colts-10
97Barrie Colts-7

George, Corey
05Brampton Battalion-24

George, Darcy
92British Columbia JHL-174

George, Justin
93Northern Michigan Wildcats-7
94UK Solihul Barons-4
95UK Solihull Barons-11
03UK Coventry Blaze History-13

George, Russell
94Thunder Bay Flyers-10

George, Zac
92British Columbia JHL-26

Gerard, Dean
91Air Canada SJHL-A32
91Air Canada SJHL-B32
91Air Canada SJHL All-Stars-8
92Saskatchewan JHL-45

Gerard, Eddie
12C57-34
23V145-1-1
60Topps Stamps-18
83Hall of Fame-200
83Hall of Fame Postcards-N5
85Hall of Fame-200

Gerasimov, Aleksandr
83Swedish Semic VM Stickers-72

Gerasimov, Yuri
99Missouri River Otters Sheet-5

Gerbe, Joseph
93Quebec Pee-Wee Tournament-1752
96Guelph Storm-12
97Guelph Storm-11
98Guelph Storm-9
99Guelph Storm-9
03Greensboro Generals-185

Gerber, Beat
00Swiss Slapshot Mini-Cards-LT4
01Swiss HNL-195
02Swiss HNL-105

Gerber, Lukas
01Swiss HNL-127
02Swiss HNL-147
Gerber, Martin
96Swiss HNL-318
98Swiss Power Play Stickers-128
99Swiss Panini Stickers-130
00Swiss Panini Stickers-174
00Swiss Panini Stickers National Team-P1
00Swiss Slapshot Mini-Cards-LT1
02Atomic-102
Blue-102
Gold-102
Red-102
Hobby Parallel-102
02BAP All-Star Edition-124
Gold-124
Silver-124
02BAP Memorabilia-293
Emerald-293
Ruby-293
Sapphire-293
NHL All-Star Game-293
NHL All-Star Game Blue-293
NHL All-Star Game Green-293
NHL All-Star Game Red-293
02BAP Memorabilia Toronto Fall Expo-293
02BAP Ultimate Memorabilia-23
02Between the Pipes-76
Gold-76
Silver-76
Jerseys-46
Tandems-13
02Bowman YoungStars-144
Gold-144
Silver-144
02Crown Royale-102
Blue-102
Purple-102
Red-102
Retail-102
Rookie Royalty-2
02ITG Used-186
02Pacific Complete-600
Red-600
02Pacific Exclusive-176
Blue-176
Gold-176
02Pacific Heads-Up-127
02Pacific Quest for the Cup-102
Gold-102
02Parkhurst-223
Bronze-223
Gold-223
Silver-223
02Parkhurst Retro-223
Minis-223
02Private Stock Reserve-152
Blue-152
Red-152
Retail-152
02SP Authentic-136
02SP Game Used-68
02SPx-166
02Stadium Club-130
Silver Decoy Cards-130
Proofs-130
02Titanium-102
Blue-102
Red-102
Retail-102
02Topps Chrome-163
Black Border Refractors-163
Refractors-163
02Topps Heritage-132
02Topps Total-429
02UD Honor Roll-102
02UD Mask Collection-1
02UD Mask Collection-151
02UD Mask Collection Beckett Promos-1
02UD Premier Collection-44B
Gold-44
02UD Top Shelf-121
02Upper Deck-427
Exclusives-427
02Upper Deck Classic Portraits-103
02Vanguard-102
LTD-102
02Swedish SHL-23
Netminders-NM1
Parallel-23
02Swedish SHL Promos-TCC3
02Swiss HNL-482
03BAP Memorabilia-138
Emerald-138
Gold-138
Ruby-138
Sapphire-138
Deep in the Crease-D7
Tandems-T-7
03Beehive-2
Gold-2
Silver-2
03Crown Royale-2
Blue-2
Retail-2
Global Conquest-9
03ITG Action-58
Jerseys-M24
03Pacific-2
Blue-2
Red-2
03Pacific Complete-450
Red-450
03Titanium-1
Hobby Jersey Number Parallels-1
Retail-1
Retail Jersey Number Parallels-1
03Upper Deck-250
Canadian Exclusives-250
HG-250
UD Exclusives-250
03Upper Deck MVP-13
Gold Script-13
Silver Script-13
Canadian Exclusives-13
04Pacific-3
Blue-3
Red-3
04Upper Deck-36
Canadian Exclusives-36
HG Glossy Gold-36
HG Glossy Silver-36
04Swedish Pure Skills-25
Parallel-25
The Wall-MG
05Beehive Matted Materials-MMMG
05Hot Prospects-18
En Fuego-18
Hot Materials-HMMG
Red Hot-18
White Hot-18
05Panini Stickers-54
05Parkhurst-89
Facsimile Auto Parallel-89
True Colors-TCCAR
True Colors-TCCAR
05SP Authentic-19
Limited-19
Sign of the Times-MG
Sign of the Times Duals-DGW
05SP Game Used Statscriptions-ST-MG
05The Cup-23
Gold-23
Black Rainbow-23
Dual NHL Shields Autographs-ADSSG
Emblems of Endorsement-EEGE
Honorable Numbers-HNGE
Limited Logos-LLGE
Masterpiece Pressplates-23
Noble Numbers-NNGV
Patch Variation-P23
Patch Variation Autographs-AP23
Scripted Numbers-SNGV
Scripted Numbers Dual-DSNGA
Scripted Swatches-SSGE
Signature Patches-SPGE
05Ultimate Collection Endorsed Emblems-EEGE
05Ultimate Coll National Heroes Jersey-NHJMG
05Ultimate Coll National Heroes Patch-NHPMG
05Ultra-39
Gold-39
Ice-39
05Upper Deck-283
Jerseys Series II-J2GE
Notable Numbers-N-MGE
05Upper Deck MVP-76
Gold-76
Platinum-76
05Upper Deck Rookie Update-17
05Upper Deck Victory-34
Black-34
Gold-34
Silver-34
05Swedish SHL Elitset-37
Gold-37
Stoppers-5
06Be A Player-123
Autographs-123
Signatures-GE
Signatures 10-137
Signatures Foursomes-FLTKG
Portraits Signature Portraits-SPMG
Portraits Timeless Tens-TTNET
06Beehive-33
Matte-33
Signature Scrapbook-SSGE
06Between The Pipes-71
Autographs-AMG
Emblems-GUE20
Emblems Gold-GUE20
Emblems Autographs-GUE20
Jerseys-GUJ20
Jerseys Gold-GUJ20
Jerseys Autographs-GUJ20
Numbers-GUN20
Numbers Gold-GUN20
Numbers Autographs-GUN20
The Mask-M08
The Mask Gold-M08
The Mask Silver-M08
06Black Diamond-57
Black-57
Gold-57
Ruby-57
06Flair Showcase-68
06Flair Showcase-191
06Flair Showcase-249
Parallel-68
Parallel-191
Parallel-249
Hot Gloves-HG6
Hot Numbers-HN6
Hot Numbers Parallel-HN6
Stitches-SSMG
06Fleer-133
Tiffany-133
Netminders-N18
06Gatorade-50
06Hot Prospects-69
Red Hot-69
White Hot-69
06O-Pee-Chee-349
Rainbow-349
06Panini Stickers-119
06SP Authentic-35
Chirography-GE
Limited-35
Sign of the Times-STGE
Sign of the Times Triples-ST3RHG
06SP Game Used-69
Gold-69
Rainbow-69
Autographs-69
Inked Sweaters-ISGE
Inked Sweaters Patches-ISGE
Inked Sweaters Dual-IS2RG
Inked Sweaters Dual Patches-IS2RG
SIGnificance-SMG
06SPx-73
Spectrum-73
SPxcitement-X72
SPxcitement Spectrum-X72
06The Cup Autographed NHL Shields Duals-DASDM
06The Cup Limited Logos-LLGE
06UD Artifacts-34
Blue-34
Gold-34
Platinum-34
Radiance-34
Autographed Radiance Parallel-34
Red-34
Auto-Facts-AFMG
Auto-Facts Gold-AFMG
06UD Mini Jersey Collection-68
06UD Powerplay-68
Impact Rainbow-68
06Ultra-133
Gold Medallion-133
Ice Medallion-133
Uniformity-UGE
Uniformity Patches-UPGA
06Upper Deck Arena Giveaways-OTT5
06Upper Deck-389
Exclusives Parallel-389
High Gloss Parallel-389
All World-AW19
Masterpieces-389
06Upper Deck MVP-206
Gold Script-206
Super Script-206
Autographs-OAGA
International Icons-II18
Last Line of Defense-LL21
06Upper Deck Sweet Shot Signature Shots/Saves-SSGE
06Upper Deck Sweet Shot Signature Shots/Saves Sticks-SSSGE
06Upper Deck Trilogy-70
Combo Clearcut Autographs-C3CGS
Honorary Scripted Patches-HSPMG
Honorary Scripted Swatches-HSSMG
06Upper Deck Victory-262
06Upper Deck Victory GameBreakers-GB8
Gerber, Michal
02Swiss HNL-160
Gerber, Patrick
94German First League-231
Gerber, Real
01Swiss HNL-413
Gerber, Soren
98Danish Hockey League-192
Gerber, Walter
95Swiss HNL-357
96Swiss HNL-330
Gerbig, Sven
99German Bundesliga 2-3
04German DEL-168
05German DEL-185
Gerden, Mikael
02Swedish SHL-166
Parallel-166
Gerebi, Nick
91Minnesota Golden Gophers-8
Geremia, Ryan
95Swift Current Broncos-5
98Calgary Hitmen-12
98Calgary Hitmen Autographs-12
Gerhardsson, Peter
94Swedish Leaf-249
95Swedish Leaf-158
02Swedish SHL-98
Parallel-98
Geric, Adam
05Saskatoon Blades-7
06Saskatoon Blades-8
Geris, Dave
93Windsor Spitfires-20
94Windsor Spitfires-22
95Slapshot-425
03UK Basingstoke Bison-3
Geris, Ryan
00Sioux City Musketeers-10
Gerlach, Adam
03Minnesota State Mavericks-7
Gerlitz, H.
28V128-2 Paulin's Candy-58
Gerlitz, J.
28V128-2 Paulin's Candy-57
Gerlitz, P.
28V128-2 Paulin's Candy-54
Germain, Claude
51Laval Dairy Lac St. Jean-57
Germain, Daniel
917th Inn. Sketch QMJHL-252
Germain, Eric
88ProCards AHL-205
89ProCards AHL-12
90ProCards AHL/IHL-19
93Amos Les Forestiers-8
93Richmond Renegades-17
97Columbus Cottonmouths-4
German, Shawn
06Reading Royals-2
Germann, Reto
93Swiss HNL-354
95Swiss HNL-406
96Swiss HNL-462
01Swiss HNL-373
02Swiss HNL-181
Germyn, Carsen
98Kelowna Rockets-6
99Kelowna Rockets-13
00Kelowna Rockets-4
02Red Deer Rebels-15
03Norfolk Admirals-9
04Lowell Lock Monsters-8
04Lowell Lock Monsters Photo Album-8
06Fleer-222
Tiffany-222
06O-Pee-Chee-508
Rainbow-508
06SPx-146
Spectrum-146
06The Cup-95
Autographed Rookie Masterpiece Pressplates-95
Gold Rainbow Autographed Rookies-95
Masterpiece Pressplates (Artifacts)-207
Masterpiece Pressplates (Marquee Rookies)-508
Masterpiece Pressplates (MVP)-327
Masterpiece Pressplates (Power Play)-103
Masterpiece Pressplates (SPx)-146
Masterpiece Pressplates (Trilogy)-106
Masterpiece Pressplates (Victory)-218
Rookies Black-95
Rookies Platinum-95
06UD Artifacts-207
Blue-207
Gold-207
Platinum-207
Radiance-207
Red-207
06UD Powerplay-103
Impact Rainbow-103
06Ultimate Collection Ultimate Debut Threads Jerseys-DJ-CG
06Ultimate Collection Ultimate Debut Threads Jerseys Autographs-DJ-CG
06Ultimate Collection Ultimate Debut Threads Patches-DJ-CG
06Ultimate Collection Ultimate Debut Threads Patches Autographs-DJ-CG
06Ultra-203
Gold Medallion-203
Ice Medallion-203
06Upper Deck-205
Exclusives Parallel-205
High Gloss Parallel-205
Masterpieces-205
Rookie Materials-RMCG
Rookie Materials Patches-RMCG
06Upper Deck MVP-327
Gold Script-327
Super Script-327
06Upper Deck Ovation-110
06Upper Deck Trilogy-106
06Upper Deck Victory-218
06Upper Deck Victory Black-218
06Upper Deck Victory Gold-218
06ITG Heroes and Prospects-35
Autographs-ACG
Gernander, Jerry
03Memphis RiverKings-6
Gernander, Ken
91Moncton Hawks-10
91ProCards-178
94Binghamton Rangers-4
95Binghamton Rangers-8
96Binghamton Rangers-12
97Hartford Wolf Pack-8
98Hartford Wolf Pack-8
99Hartford Wolf Pack-7
00Hartford Wolf Pack-9
01Hartford Wolf Pack-5
02Hartford Wolf Pack-9
03Parkhurst Rookie-64
03Hartford Wolf Pack-6
04Hartford Wolf Pack-8
05Hartford Wolf Pack-26
Gerow, Rod
85London Knights-24
Gerrits, Brian
86Portland Winter Hawks-7
88Saskatoon Blades-16
Gerse, Dave
88Regina Pats-6
Gerstberger, Holger
99German DEL-402
Gerum, Christian
94German DEL-322
95German DEL-291
96German DEL-178
Gervais, Benoit
05Gatineau Olympiques-16
06Gatineau Olympiques-16
Gervais, Bruno
05ITG Heroes/Prosp Toronto Expo Parallel -269
05Beehive-158
Matte-158
05Black Diamond-262
05Hot Prospects-150
En Fuego-150
Red Hot-150
White Hot-150
05Parkhurst-645
Facsimile Auto Parallel-645
05SP Authentic-245
Limited-245
05SP Game Used-225
05SPx-275
05The Cup Masterpiece Pressplate Artifact-301
05The Cup Masterpiece Pressplate Bee Hive-158
05The Cup Master Pressplate Black Diamond-262
05The Cup Masterpiece Pressplates (Ice)-216
05The Cup Master Pressplate Rookie Update-157
05The Cup Masterpiece Pressplates SPA-245
05The Cup Masterpiece Pressplates SP GU-225
05The Cup Masterpiece Pressplates (SPx)-275
05The Cup Masterpiece Pressplates Trilogy-281
05The Cup Masterpiece Pressplate Ult Coll-216
05UD Artifacts-301
05Ultimate Collection-216
Gold-216
05Upper Deck Ice-218
05Upper Deck Rookie Update-157
05Upper Deck Trilogy-281
05AHL All-Stars-9
05AHL Top Prospects-16
05ITG Heroes and Prospects-269
Autographs Series II-BG
Gervais, Eddy
917th Inn. Sketch QMJHL-79
Gervais, Gaston
51Laval Dairy QSHL-84
52Bas Du Fleuve-23
Gervais, George
91Air Canada SJHL-B34
Gervais, Guy
50Quebec Citadelles-6
51Laval Dairy Lac St. Jean-40
52Bas Du Fleuve-20
Gervais, Hugues
97Mobile Mysticks-20
97Mobile Mysticks Kellogg's-18
98Mobile Mysticks-16
99Mobile Mysticks-7
Gervais, Phil
06Swift Current Broncos-11
Gervais, Shawn
92British Columbia JHL-168
93Seattle Thunderbirds-6
95Seattle Thunderbirds-10
Gervais, Victor
90ProCards AHL/IHL-201
91Hampton Roads Admirals-4
91ProCards-558
92Anaheim Bullfrogs RHI-13
92Hampton Roads Admirals-9
93Anaheim Bullfrogs RHI-5
93Cleveland Lumberjacks-15
93Hampton Roads Admirals-5
94Anaheim Bullfrogs RHI-6
94Cleveland Lumberjacks-16
94Cleveland Lumberjacks Postcards-16
95Anaheim Bullfrogs RHI-4
95Cleveland Lumberjacks-14
95Cleveland Lumberjacks Postcards-13
96Anaheim Bullfrogs RHI-4
96Hampton Roads Admirals-HRA9
97Hampton Roads Admirals-8
98German DEL-140
98Hampton Roads Admirals 10th Anniversary-3
99German DEL-94
00German DEL-83
01German Upper Deck-80
02German DEL City Press-75
03St. Jean Mission-11
Gesce, Derek
92British Columbia JHL-9
Gesser, Axel
94German First League-423
Gessinger, Bernd
94German First League-130
Gessinger, Martin
94German First League-139
Getliffe, Ray
34Beehive Group I Photos-15
34Beehive Group I Photos-153
39O-Pee-Chee V301-1-29
40O-Pee-Chee V301-2-147
Getzlaf, Ryan
02Calgary Hitmen-26
03BAP Memorabilia Draft Redemptions-19
03Calgary Hitmen-9
04ITG Top Prospects Spring Expo-20
04SP Authentic Rookie Redemptions-RR45
04Calgary Hitmen-6
04Calgary Hitmen-25
04ITG Heroes and Prospects-102
Autographs-RGE
Combos-4
Complete Emblems-16
Emblems-49
Emblems Gold-49
He Shoots-He Scores Prizes-10
Jersey Autographs-49
Jerseys-49
Jerseys Gold-49
Numbers-49
Numbers Gold-49
Top Prospects-20
04ITG Heroes/Prospects Toronto Expo '05-102
04ITG Heroes/Prospects Expo Heroes/Pros-102
05ITG Heroes/Prosp Toronto Expo Parallel -333
05Beehive-113
Beige -113
Blue -113
Gold-113
Red -113
Matte-113
05Black Diamond-198
Emerald-198
Gold-198
Onyx-198
Ruby-198
05Ducks Team Issue-6
05Hot Prospects-218
En Fuego-218
Hot Materials-HMRG
Red Hot-218
White Hot-218
05ITG Ultimate Mem First Rounders Jerseys-7
05ITG Ultimate Mem 1st Round Jersey Gold-7
05ITG Ultimate Mem Future Stars Autos-13
05ITG Ultimate Mem Future Star Autos Gold-13
05ITG Ultimate Mem Future Stars Jerseys-13
05ITG Ultimate Mem Fut Stars Jerseys Gold-13
05ITG Ultimate Mem Future Stars Mem Autos-13
05ITG Ultimate Mem Fut Star Mem Auto Gold-13
05Panini Stickers-198
05Parkhurst-601
Facsimile Auto Parallel-601
Signatures-RG
True Colors-TCANA
True Colors-TCANA
05SP Authentic-131
Limited-131
Prestigious Pairings-PPPG
Rarefied Rookies-RRRG
Rookie Authentics-RARG
Sign of the Times Triples-TLPG
05SP Game Used-147
Autographs-147
Gold-147
Auto Draft-AD-RG
Game Gear-GG-RG
Game Gear Autographs-AG-RG
Rookie Exclusives-RG
Rookie Exclusives Silver-RE-RG
Significant Numbers-SN-RG
05SPx-170
Spectrum-170
Xcitement Rookies-XR-RG
Xcitement Rookies Gold-XR-RG
Xcitement Rookies Spectrum-XR-RG
05The Cup-101
Autographed Rookie Patches Gold Rainbow-101
Black Rainbow Rookies-101
Masterpiece Pressplates (Artifacts)-238
Masterpiece Pressplates (Bee Hive)-113
Masterpiece Pressplates (Black Diamond)-198
Masterpiece Pressplates (Ice)-107
Masterpiece Pressplates (MVP)-414
Masterpiece Pressplates (Power Play)-146
Masterpiece Pressplates (Power Play)-146
Masterpiece Pressplates Rookie Upd Auto-256
Masterpiece Pressplates SPA Autos-131
Masterpiece Pressplates (SP Game Used)-147
Masterpiece Pressplates SPx Autos-170
Masterpiece Pressplates (Trilogy)-172
Masterpiece Pressplates Ult Coll Autos-101
Masterpiece Pressplates (Victory)-280
Masterpiece Pressplates Autographs-101
Platinum Rookies-101
05UD Artifacts-238
Gold-RED38
05UD PowerPlay-146
05UD Rookie Class-38
05Ultimate Collection-101
Autographed Patches-101
Autographed Shields-101
Jerseys-JRG
Jerseys Dual-DJPG
Jerseys Triple-TJPGL
Marquee Attractions-MA2
Marquee Attractions Signatures-SMA2
Premium Patches-PPRG
Premium Swatches-PSRG
Ultimate Debut Threads Jerseys-DTJRG
Ultimate Debut Threads Jerseys Autos-DAJRG
Ultimate Debut Threads Patches-DTPRG
Ultimate Debut Threads Patches Autos-DAPRG
Ultimate Patches-PRG
Ultimate Patches Dual-DPPG
Ultimate Patches Triple-TPPGL
Ultimate Signatures-USRG
Ultimate Signatures Logos-SLRG
Ultimate Signatures Pairings-UPPG
05Ultra-267
Gold-267
Fresh Ink-FI-RG
Fresh Ink Blue-FI-RG
Ice-267
Rookie Uniformity Jerseys-RU-RG
Rookie Uniformity Jersey Autographs-ARU-RG
Rookie Uniformity Patches-RUP-RG
Rookie Uniformity Patch Autographs-ARP-RG
Scoring Kings-SK31
Scoring Kings Jerseys-SKJ-RG
Scoring Kings Jersey Autographs-KAJ-RG
Scoring Kings Patches-SKP-RG
Scoring Kings Patch Autographs-KAP-RG
05Upper Deck-452
Rookie Ink-RIRG
05Upper Deck Rookie Showcase-RS34
05Upper Deck Rookie Showcase Promos-RS34
05Upper Deck Rookie Threads-RTRG
05Upper Deck Rookie Threads Autographs-ARTRG
05Upper Deck Ice-107
Cool Threads-CTRG
Cool Threads Autographs-ACTRG
Cool Threads Glass-CTRG
Cool Threads Patches-CTPRG
Cool Threads Patch Autographs-CAPRG
Fresh Ice-FIRG
Fresh Ice Glass-FIRG
Fresh Ice Glass Patches-FIPRG
Premieres Auto Patches-AIPRG
05Upper Deck MVP-414
Gold-414
Platinum-414
05Upper Deck Rookie Update-256
05Upper Deck Trilogy-172
05Upper Deck Victory-280
Black-280
Gold-280
Silver-280
05Portland Pirates-15
05ITG Heroes and Prospects-333
Autograph Memorabilia-GA-03
Autograph Memorabilia Gold-GA-03
Autographs Series II-RG
CHL Grads-CG-10
CHL Grads Gold-CG-10
Future Teammates-FT3
He Shoots-He Scores Prizes-18
He Shoots-He Scores Prizes-59
Jerseys-GUJ-81
Jerseys Gold-GUJ-81
Emblems-GUE-81
Emblems Gold-GUE-81
Numbers-GUN-81
Numbers Gold-GUN-81
Nameplates-N-56
Nameplates Gold-N-56
06Be A Player Portraits First Exposures-FERG
06Fleer-7
Tiffany-7
Signing Day-SDRG
06ITG Ultimate Memorabilia Future Star-21
06ITG Ultimate Memorabilia Future Star Gold-21
06ITG Ultimate Memorabilia Future Star Autos-11
06ITG Ultimate Memorabilia Future Star Autos Gold-11
06O-Pee-Chee-10
06O-Pee-Chee-632
Rainbow-10
Rainbow-632
06Panini Stickers-191
06SP Game Used Authentic Fabrics-AFRG
06SP Game Used Authentic Fabrics Parallel-AFRG
06SP Game Used Authentic Fabrics Patches-AFRG
06SP Game Used Inked Sweaters-ISRG
06SP Game Used Inked Sweaters Patches-ISRG
06The Cup Property of-PORG
06UD Artifacts Auto-Facts-AFRG
06UD Artifacts Auto-Facts Gold-AFRG
06Ultra-6
Gold Medallion-6
Ice Medallion-6
06Upper Deck-5
Exclusives Parallel-5
High Gloss Parallel-5
Generations Duals-G2PG
Generations Patches Dual-G2PPG
Masterpieces-5
06Upper Deck MVP-9
Gold Script-9
Super Script-9
Jerseys-OJGC
06Upper Deck Ovation-102
06Upper Deck Trilogy Combo Clearcut Autographs-C2PG
06Upper Deck Trilogy Scripts-TSRG
06Upper Deck Victory Next In Line-NL3
06ITG Heroes and Prospects Jerseys-GUJ18
06ITG Heroes and Prospects Jerseys Gold-GUJ18
06ITG Heroes and Prospects Emblems-GUE18
06ITG Heroes and Prospects Emblems Gold-GUE18
06ITG Heroes and Prospects Numbers-GUN18
06ITG Heroes and Prospects Numbers Gold-GUN18
06ITG Heroes and Prospects Making The Bigs-MTB07
06ITG Heroes and Prospects Making The Bigs Gold-MTB07
06ITG Heroes and Prospects Quad Emblems-QE10
06ITG Heroes and Prospects Quad Emblems Gold-QE10
06ITG Heroes and Prospects Triple Memorabilia-TM07
06ITG Heroes and Prospects Triple Memorabilia Gold-TM07
07Upper Deck Ovation-50
07Upper Deck Victory-171
Black-171
Gold-171
Stars on Ice-SI22
Geyer, Cyrill
01Swiss HNL-238
02Swiss HNL-309
Gherson, Robert
00Sarnia Sting-10
03Owen Sound Attack-24
05Hartford Wolf Pack-6
Ghillioni, Claudio
93Swiss HNL-90
95Swiss HNL-267
96Swiss HNL-387
Giacomelli, Giorgio
93Swiss HNL-466
Giacomin, Ed
64Beehive Group III Photos-126
65Coca-Cola-73
65Topps-21
66Topps-23
67Topps-85
67Topps-123
68Bauer Ads-9
68O-Pee-Chee-67
68O-Pee-Chee-205
68Shirriff Coins-95
68Topps-67
69O-Pee-Chee-33
69O-Pee-Chee-217
Four-in-One-5
Stamps-8
69Topps-33
70Colgate Stamps-70
70Dad's Cookies-39
70Esso Power Players-181
70O-Pee-Chee-68
70O-Pee-Chee-244
Deckle-42
70Post Shooters-3
70Sargent Promotions Stamps-115
70Topps-68
Topps/OPC Sticker Stamps-9
71Letraset Action Replays-10
71Mattel Mini-Records-4
71O-Pee-Chee-220
71O-Pee-Chee-248
71O-Pee-Chee-250
O-Pee-Chee/Topps Booklets-7
71Sargent Promotions Stamps-128
71Topps-4
71Topps-5
71Topps-6
71Topps-90
71Toronto Sun-172
72O-Pee-Chee-173
72Sargent Promotions Stamps-147
72Topps-165
72Finnish Semic World Championship-213
72Swedish Semic World Championship-213
73O-Pee-Chee-160
73Topps-140
74Lipton Soup-26
74NHL Action Stamps-189
74O-Pee-Chee NHL-160
74Topps-160
75O-Pee-Chee NHL-55
75Topps-55
76O-Pee-Chee NHL-160
76Topps-160
77O-Pee-Chee NHL-70
77Sportscasters-6103
77Topps-70
77Finnish Sportscasters-74-1758
81Red Wings Oldtimers-2
85Hall of Fame-259
91Ultimate Original Six-20
French-20
Box Bottoms-1
92Hall of Fame Legends-31
95Parkhurst '66-67-93
Coins-93
95Zeller's Masters of Hockey Signed-2
99BAP Memorabilia AS American Hobby-AH10
99BAP Memorabilia AS American Hobby Autos-AH10
00Upper Deck Legends-89
Legendary Collection Bronze-89
Legendary Collection Gold-89
Legendary Collection Silver-89
01BAP Memorabilia Goalie Traditions-GT11
01BAP Memorabilia Goalie Traditions-GT34
01BAP Memorabilia Goalie Traditions-GT36
01BAP Memorabilia Goalie Traditions-GT42
01BAP Ultimate Mem All-Star History-21
01BAP Ultimate Memorabilia Cornerstones-5
01BAP Update Passing the Torch-PTT5
01Between the Pipes-142
Double Memorabilia-DM30
Masks-3
Masks Silver-3
Masks Gold-3
Vintage Memorabilia-VM15
01Greats of the Game-21
Autographs-21
01Upper Deck Legends-46
01Upper Deck Legends-85
02BAP NHL All-Star History-21
02BAP Ultimate Memorabilia Cup Duels-7
02BAP Ultimate Memorabilia Emblem Attic-20
02BAP Ultimate Memorabilia Number Ones-2
02BAP Ultimate Mem Retro Teammates-5
02BAP Ultimate Mem Vintage Jerseys-11
02BAP Ultimate Mem Vintage Jersey Autos-4
02Between the Pipes Goalie Autographs-28
02Between the Pipes He Shoots/Saves Prize-27
02Between the Pipes Vintage Memorabilia-4
02Between the Pipes Vintage Memorabilia-20
02Parkhurst Vintage Teammates-VT2
02Parkhurst Retro Nicknames-RN3
03BAP Ultimate Mem Vintage Jerseys-34
03BAP Ultimate Mem Vintage Jerseys Gold-34
03ITG Used Sig Series Vintage Mem -9
03ITG Used Sig Series Vintage Mem Gold-9
03Parkhurst Original Six Detroit-56
03Parkhurst Original Six Detroit-83
Memorabilia-DM36
03Parkhurst Original Six New York-34
03Parkhurst Original Six New York-64
03Parkhurst Original Six New York-82
03Parkhurst Original Six New York-95
Autographs-6
Inserts-N2
Inserts-N7
Memorabilia-NM26
Memorabilia-NM30
Memorabilia-NM36
Memorabilia-NM39
Memorabilia-NM51
03Parkhurst Rookie Before the Mask-BTM-13
03Parkhurst Rookie Before the Mask Gold-BTM-13
04ITG NHL AS FANtasy AS History Jerseys-SB20
04ITG Franchises He Shoots/Scores Prizes-38
04ITG Franchises US East-384
Autographs-A-EG1
Double Memorabilia-EDM9
Double Memorabilia Autographs-EDM-EG
Double Memorabilia Gold-EDM9
Goalie Gear-EGG6
Goalie Gear Autographs-EGG-EG
Goalie Gear Gold-EGG6
Memorabilia-ESM21
Memorabilia Autographs-ESM-EG
Memorabilia Gold-ESM21
Original Sticks-EOS14
Original Sticks Autographs-EOS-EG
Original Sticks Gold-EOS14
Triple Memorabilia-ETM7
Triple Memorabilia Autographs-ETM-EG
Triple Memorabilia Gold-ETM7
04ITG Franchises US West-205
Autographs-A-EG2
04ITG Ultimate Memorabilia-20
04ITG Ultimate Memorabilia-42
Gold-20
Gold-42
Auto Threads-12
Autographs-9
Autographs Gold-9
Cornerstones-6
Cornerstones Gold-6
Goalie Gear-14
Jersey Autographs-27
Jersey Autographs Gold-27
Original Six-1
Original Six-13
Retro Teammates-12
Stick Autographs-42
Stick Autographs Gold-42
04ITG Heroes and Prospects-126
Autographs-EG
Hero Memorabilia-17
04ITG Heroes/Prospects Toronto Expo '05-126
04ITG Heroes/Prospects Expo Heroes/Pros-126
05ITG Heroes/Prosp Toronto Expo Parallel -31
05Between the Pipes-8
Autographs-A-EG
Jersey and Sticks-SJ-4
Signed Memorabilia-SM-7
05ITG Ultimate Memorabilia Level 1-29
05ITG Ultimate Memorabilia Level 2-29
05ITG Ultimate Memorabilia Level 3-29
05ITG Ultimate Memorabilia Level 4-29
05ITG Ultimate Memorabilia Level 5-29
05ITG Ultimate Mem Cornerstones Jerseys-6
05ITG Ultimate Mem Cornerst Jerseys Gold-6
05ITG Ultimate Mem Decades Jerseys-7
05ITG Ultimate Mem Decades Jerseys Gold-7
05ITG Ultimate Memorabilia Double Autos-9
05ITG Ultimate Mem Double Autos Gold-9
05ITG Ultimate Mem Double Mem Autos-5
05ITG Ultimate Mem Double Mem Autos Gold-5
05ITG Ultimate Memorabilia Emblem Attic-3
05ITG Ultimate Mem Emblem Attic Gold-3
05ITG Ultimate Memorabilia Goalie Gear-4
05ITG Ultimate Mem Goalie Gear Gold-4
05ITG Ultimate Memorabilia Jersey Autos-6
05ITG Ultimate Mem Jersey Autos Gold-6
05ITG Ultimate Mem Pass the Torch Jerseys-9
05ITG Ultimate Mem Passing Torch Jsy Gold-9
05ITG Ultimate Mem Retro Teammate Jerseys-21
05ITG Ult Mem Retro Teammates Jersey Gold-21
05ITG Ultimate Memorabilia Stick Autos-32
05ITG Ultimate Mem Stick Autos Gold-32
05ITG Ultimate Mem Sticks and Jerseys-23
05ITG Ultimate Mem Stick and Jerseys Gold-23
05ITG Ultimate Mem 3 Star of the Game Jsy-10
05ITG Ult Mem 3 Star of the Game Jsy Gold-10
05ITG Ultimate Memorabilia Triple Autos-15
05ITG Ultimate Mem Triple Autos Gold-15
05ITG Ultimate Memorabilia Ultimate Autos-37
05ITG Ultimate Mem Ultimate Autos Gold-37
05ITG Ultimate Memorabilia Vintage Lumber-18
05ITG Ultimate Mem Vintage Lumber Gold-18
05ITG Heroes and Prospects-31
Autographs-A-EG
Hero Memorabilia-HM-10
06Between The Pipes-86
06Between The Pipes-140
Autographs-AEG
Double Jerseys-DJ08
Double Jerseys Gold-DJ08
Double Memorabilia-DM06
Double Memorabilia Gold-DM06
Emblems-GUE52
Emblems Gold-GUE52
Gloves-GG06
Gloves Gold-GG06
Jerseys-GUJ52
Jerseys Gold-GUJ52
Numbers-GUN52
Numbers Gold-GUN52
Shooting Gallery-SG05
Shooting Gallery-SG06
Shooting Gallery-SG09
Shooting Gallery Gold-SG05
Shooting Gallery Gold-SG06
Shooting Gallery Gold-SG09
Stick and Jersey-SJ11
Stick and Jersey Gold-SJ11
Stick Work-SW05
Stick Work Gold-SW05
06ITG Ultimate Memorabilia-44
Artist Proof-44
Boys Will Be Boys-12
Boys Will Be Boys Gold-12
Decades-4
Decades Gold-4
Jerseys Autos-19
Jerseys Autos Gold-19
Journey Emblem-6
Journey Emblem Gold-6
Journey Jersey-6
Journey Jersey Gold-6
Passing The Torch-20
Passing The Torch Gold-20
Retro Teammates-9
Retro Teammates Gold-9
Stick Rack-14
Stick Rack-25
Stick Rack Gold-14
Stick Rack Gold-25
Triple Thread Jerseys-11
Triple Thread Jerseys Gold-11
06Parkhurst-8
Autographs-8
Giallonardo, Paul
02Windsor Spitfires-19
Giammarco, Franco
86Kingston Canadians-7
87Kingston Canadians-7
Gianini, Tiziano
91Upper Deck-670
French-670
91Upper Deck Czech World Juniors-31
93Swiss HNL-142
95Swiss HNL-189
96Swiss HNL-82
96Swiss HNL-532
98Swiss Power Play Stickers-8
99Swiss Panini Stickers-8
00Swiss Panini Stickers-10
00Swiss Slapshot Mini-Cards-HCAP4
01Swiss HNL-217
02Swiss HNL-149
Giannetti, Mark
93Sudbury Wolves-13
93Sudbury Wolves Police-13
97Flint Generals-5
99Jacksonville Lizard Kings-7
Gianola, Marc
93Swiss HNL-218
95Swiss HNL-118
96Swiss HNL-107
98Swiss Power Play Stickers-57
99Swiss Panini Stickers-57
00Swiss Panini Stickers-105
00Swiss Slapshot Mini-Cards-HCD3
01Swiss HNL-103
02Swiss HNL-7
04Swiss Davos Postcards-11
Giarard, Dary
907th Inn. Sketch QMJHL-21
Giard, Stephane
917th Inn. Sketch QMJHL-52
Gibb, Myles
91Air Canada SJHL-B27
Gibb, Ryan
03Oshawa Generals-31
04Oshawa Generals-2
04Oshawa Generals Autographs-2
Gibbons, Andrew
03Oshawa Generals-11
05Belleville Bulls-23
06Belleville Bulls-7
Gibbons, Jeff
92Toledo Storm-6
92Toledo Storm Team Issue-6
Gibbons, Samuel
00Rimouski Oceanic-18
Signed-18
01Rimouski Oceanic-16
01Val d'Or Foreurs-16
03Drummondville Voltigeurs-7
Gibbs, Barry
70Esso Power Players-164
70North Stars Postcards-1
70Sargent Promotions Stamps-91

71Sargent Promotions Stamps-95
71Toronto Sun-129
720-Pee-Chee-101
72Sargent Promotions Stamps-108
72Topps-169
73North Stars Action Posters-3
73North Stars Postcards-5
730-Pee-Chee-174
73Topps-30
74NHL Action Stamps-137
74NHL Action Stamps Update-1
740-Pee-Chee NHL-203
74Topps-203
750-Pee-Chee NHL-214
75Topps-214
760-Pee-Chee NHL-341
770-Pee-Chee NHL-319
78Blues Postcards-11
780-Pee-Chee-390
790-Pee-Chee-304
800-Pee-Chee-334

Gibbs, Richard
92Saskatchewan JHL-135

Giblak, Eduard
94German First League-216

Giblin, Paul
99Asheville Smoke-6
00Charlotte Checkers-19
01Macon Whoopee-9

Gibson, Adam
03Saginaw Spirit-7

Gibson, Brent
03Wisconsin Badgers-12

Gibson, Brett
03Pensacola Ice Pilots-343

Gibson, David
93Quebec Pee-Wee Tournament-1286

Gibson, Don
90Canucks Mohawk-9
90ProCards AHL/IHL-340
91Upper Deck-495
French-495
91ProCards-610

Gibson, Doug
750-Pee-Chee NHL-375

Gibson, Jack
83Hall of Fame Postcards-N6
83Jets Postcards-7
85Hall of Fame-201

Gibson, Jason
97Anchorage Aces-9
98Anchorage Aces-19

Gibson, John
98Huntsville Channel Cats-2
03Huntsville Channel Cats-17
04Huntsville Havoc-2

Gibson, Mike
86Regina Pats-7

Gibson, Phil
02Windsor Spitfires-17

Gibson, Scott
01Hull Olympiques-9
03Victoriaville Tigers-12

Gibson, Steve
907th Inn. Sketch OHL-183
917th Inn. Sketch OHL-176
92Windsor Spitfires-25
93Wheeling Thunderbirds-UD5
94Wheeling Thunderbirds-7
94Wheeling Thunderbirds Photo Album-19
95Wheeling Thunderbirds-6
95Wheeling Thunderbirds Series II-7
97Quad-City Mallards-15
98Quad-City Mallards-10
99Quad-City Mallards-3
00Quad-City Mallards-23
01Quad-City Mallards-7

Gibson, Wade
897th Inn. Sketch OHL-66
907th Inn. Sketch OHL-84
917th Inn. Sketch OHL-73
93Phoenix Cobras RHI-8
93Sault Ste. Marie Greyhounds-21
93Sault Ste. Marie Greyhound Memorial Cup-23
98Huntsville Channel Cats-11
99San Antonio Iguanas-14

Gidlund, Lars
64Swedish Coralli ISHockey-154
65Swedish Coralli ISHockey-154

Gies, Jeff
93Sault Ste. Marie Greyhounds-14
95Slapshot-368
95Sault Ste. Marie Greyhounds-8

Giesbrecht, Brent
93Quebec Pee-Wee Tournament-1610

Giesebrecht, Bert
51Laval Dairy Subset-60

Giesebrecht, Gus
34Beehive Group I Photos-100
390-Pee-Chee V301-1-69

Giesebrecht, Jack
51Laval Dairy Subset-112
52St. Lawrence Sales-62

Gieszler, Zach
04Williams Lake Timberwolves-7

Giffin, Bob
83Ottawa 67's-7
84Ottawa 67's-8

Giffin, Lee
83Oshawa Generals-22
88ProCards IHL-49
89ProCards IHL-37
90Kansas City Blades-18
90ProCards AHL/IHL-584
91ProCards-464

Giffin, Rob
93Peterborough Petes-4
95Slapshot-311
97Peoria Rivermen-22
02Fort Worth Brahmas-4

Giger, Daniel
93Swiss HNL-125
95Swiss HNL-172
96Swiss HNL-66
98Swiss Power Play Stickers-93
99Swiss Panini Stickers-92
00Swiss Panini Stickers-234
00Swiss Slapshot Mini-Cards-RJ10
01Swiss HNL-157
02Swiss HNL-314
03Swiss EV Zug Postcards-13
04Swiss EV Zug Postcards-23

Gignac, Chris
917th Inn. Sketch OHL-307
99ECHL All-Star Northern Conference-7

Gignac, Jean-Guy
52Juniors Blue Tint-74

Gignac, Marc-Olivier
03Shawinigan Cataractes-13

Gigon, Olivier
01Swiss HNL-401

Giguere, Dominick
93Quebec Pee-Wee Tournament-463

Giguere, J-S
94Parkhurst SE-SE270
Gold-SE270
95Halifax Mooseheads-2
95Classic-13
CHL All-Stars-AS13
Ice Breakers-BK12
Ice Breakers Die Cuts-BK12
96Upper Deck Ice-25
Parallel-25
96Halifax Mooseheads I-7
96Halifax Mooseheads II-7
97Donruss-200
Press Proofs Silver-200
Press Proofs Gold-200
Rated Rookies-10
Medallist-10
97Donruss Canadian Ice-146
Dominion Series-146
Provincial Series-146
Les Gardiens-4
97Donruss Canadian Ice Les Gardiens Promo-4
97Donruss Limited-29
97Donruss Limited-102
Exposure-29
Exposure-102
Fabric of the Game-9
97Donruss Preferred-160
Cut to the Chase-160
97Pinnacle Inside-63
Coach's Collection-63
Executive Collection-63
Stoppers-13
97Studio-73
Press Proofs Silver-73
Press Proofs Gold-73
97Saint John Flames-10
97Bowman CHL-62
OPC-62
98Pacific Omega-32
Red-32
Opening Day Issue-32
98Revolution-19
Ice Shadow-19
Red-19
98Upper Deck-13
Exclusives-13
Exclusives 1 of 1-13
Generation Next-GN7
Generation Next Quantum 1-GN7
Generation Next Quantum 2-GN7
Generation Next Quantum 3-GN7
Gold Reserve-13
98Upper Deck MVP-32
Gold Script-32
Silver Script-32
Super Script-32
99Aurora-21
Premiere Date-21
99BAP Memorabilia-192
Gold-192
Silver-192
99Pacific-55
Copper-55
Emerald Green-55
Gold-55
Ice Blue-55
Premiere Date-55
Red-55
99Paramount-38
Copper-38
Emerald-38
Gold-38
Holographic Emerald-38
Holographic Gold-38
Holographic Silver-38
Ice Blue-38
Premiere Date-38
Red-38
99SPx-26
Radiance-26
Spectrum-26
99Upper Deck-30
Exclusives-30
Exclusives 1 of 1-30
Crunch Time-CT7
Crunch Time Quantum Gold-CT7
Crunch Time Quantum Silver-CT7
New Ice Age-N12
New Ice Age Quantum Gold-N12
New Ice Age Quantum Silver-N12
99Upper Deck Gold Reserve-30
99Upper Deck MVP-35
Gold Script-35
Silver Script-35
Super Script-35
99Upper Deck Retro Generation-G10C
99Upper Deck Retro Generation Level 2-G10C
99Upper Deck Victory-43
99Upper Deck Victory-45
99Upper Deck Victory-383
000-Pee-Chee-319
000-Pee-Chee Parallel-319
00Pacific-64
Copper-64
Gold-64
Ice Blue-64
Premiere Date-64
00SP Authentic-2
00Titanium Draft Day Edition-1
Patches-1
00Topps/OPC-319
Parallel-319
00Topps Chrome-214
OPC Refractors-214
Refractors-214
00Upper Deck Vintage-5
01Atomic Jerseys-1
01Atomic Patches-1
01BAP Memorabilia-32
Emerald-32
Ruby-32
Sapphire-32
01BAP Signature Series-29
Autographs-29
Autographs Gold-29
01Between the Pipes-2
Tandems-GT6
01Crown Royale-3
Blue-3
Premiere Date-3
Red-3
Retail-3
Triple Threads-4
01Pacific-4
Extreme LTD-4
Hobby LTD-4
Premiere Date-4
Retail LTD-4
01Pacific Adrenaline-2
Blue-2
Premiere Date-2
Red-2
Retail-2
Power Play-1
01Pacific Arena Exclusives-4
01Pacific Heads-Up Quad Jerseys-1
01Parkhurst-12
Gold-12
Silver-12
01Private Stock Game Gear-1
01Private Stock Game Gear Patches-1
01SPx-153
01Sports Illustrated for Kids III-300
01Titanium-2
Hobby Parallel-2
Premiere Date-2
Retail-2
Retail Parallel-2
01UD Mask Collection-101
Gold-101
Double Patches-DPJG
Goalie Jerseys-SYJG
Jerseys-J-JG
Jersey and Patch-JPJG
01Upper Deck-5
Exclusives-5
01Upper Deck MVP-1
01Upper Deck Victory-1
01Upper Deck Victory-6
Gold-1
Gold-6
01Upper Deck Vintage-1
02Atomic-1
Blue-1
Gold-1
Red-1
Denied-1
Hobby Parallel-1
02BAP First Edition-57
02BAP First Edition-414H
Jerseys-57
02BAP Memorabilia-3
Emerald-3
Ruby-3
Sapphire-3
NHL All-Star Game-3
NHL All-Star Game Blue-3
NHL All-Star Game Green-3
NHL All-Star Game Red-3
02BAP Memorabilia Toronto Fall Expo-3
02BAP Signature Series-76
Autographs-76
Autograph Buybacks 2001-29
Autographs Gold-76
Golf-GS46
Team Quads-TQ19
02Between the Pipes-51
02Between the Pipes-121
Gold-51
Silver-51
Blockers-5
Emblems-11
Goalie Autographs-6
Jerseys-11
Masks II-1
Masks II Gold-1
Masks II Silver-1
Numbers-11
Stick and Jerseys-11
Tandems-13
02Crown Royale-1
Blue-1
Red-1
Retail-1
02Ducks Team Issue-2
02O-Pee-Chee-117
02O-Pee-Chee Premier Blue Parallel-117
02O-Pee-Chee Premier Red Parallel-117
02O-Pee-Chee Factory Set-117
02Pacific-3
Blue-3
Red-3
02Pacific Complete-11
Red-11
02Pacific Exclusive-1
Advantage-1
02Pacific Heads-Up-1
Blue-1
Purple-1
Red-1
Showstoppers-1
02Pacific Les Gardiens-1
Gold-1
02Pacific Quest for the Cup-1
Gold-1
02Pacific Toronto Fall Expo-7
Gold-7
02Parkhurst-172
Bronze-172
Gold-172
Silver-172
02Parkhurst Retro-180
Minis-180
Hopefuls-VH5
02Private Stock Reserve-1
Blue-1
Red-1
Retail-1
InCrease Security-1
02SP Authentic-1
Beckett Promos-1
02SP Game Used Authentic Fabrics-AFGI
02SP Game Used Authentic Fabrics-AFJG
02SP Game Used Authentic Fabrics Gold-AFGIO
02SP Game Used Authentic Fabrics Gold-AFJG
02SP Game Used Authentic Fabrics Rainbow-AFGIO
02SP Game Used Authentic Fabrics Rainbow-AFJGO
02SP Game Used First Rounder Patches-JG
02SP Game Used Future Fabrics-FFJG
02SP Game Used Future Fabrics Gold-FFJGO
02SP Game Used Future Fabrics Rainbow-FFJGO
02SPx-2
Spectrum Gold-2
Spectrum Silver-2
Winning Materials-WMJG
Winning Materials Gold-JG
Winning Materials Silver-JG
Xtreme Talents-JG
Xtreme Talents Gold-JG
Xtreme Talents Silver-JG
02Stadium Club-92
Silver Decoy Cards-92
Proofs-92
Puck Stops Here-PSH15
02Titanium-1
Blue-1
Red-1
Retail-1
02Topps-117
OPC Blue Parallel-117
OPC Red Parallel-117
Factory Set-117
02Topps Chrome-76
Black Border Refractors-76
Refractors-76
02Topps Heritage-94
Chrome Parallel-94
02Topps Total-51
02UD Artistic Impressions-1
Gold-1
02UD Artistic Impressions Beckett Promos-1
02UD Artistic Impressions Retrospectives-R1
02UD Artistic Impressions Retrospect Gold-R1
02UD Artistic Impress Retrospect Silver-R1
02UD Honor Roll-2
02UD Mask Collection-1
02UD Mask Collection-2
02UD Mask Collection-98
02UD Mask Collection Beckett Promos-1
02UD Mask Collection Beckett Promos-2
02UD Mask Collection Great Gloves-GGJG
02UD Mask Collection Masked Marvels-MMJG
02UD Mask Collection Patches-PWJG
02UD Mask Collection View from the Cage-VJG
02UD Piece of History-2
02UD Premier Collection Jerseys Bronze-KG
02UD Premier Collection Jerseys Gold-KG
02UD Premier Collection Jerseys Silver-KG
02UD Top Shelf-1
Dual Player Jerseys-STGS
Stopper Jerseys-SSJGO
02Upper Deck-2
Exclusives-2
Bright Futures-JG
Goaltender Threads-JG
Goaltender Threads Gold-JG
Last Line of Defense-LL1
Playbooks Series II-KG
Saviors Jerseys-SVJG
02Upper Deck Classic Portraits-1
Hockey Royalty-KFG
Hockey Royalty Limited-KFG
02Upper Deck MVP-2
Gold-2
Classics-2
Golden Classics-2
02Upper Deck Rookie Update-3
Jerseys-DJG
Jerseys Gold-DJG
02Upper Deck Victory-4
Bronze-4
Gold-4
Silver-4
02Upper Deck Vintage-7
02Upper Deck Vintage-261
Green Backs-7
Tall Boys-T2
Tall Boys Gold-T2
02Vanguard-1
LTD-1
03McFarlane Hockey 3-Inch Duals-40
03McFarlane Hockey-140
03McFarlane Hockey-142
03BAP Memorabilia-124
Emerald-124
Gold-124
Ruby-124
Sapphire-124
Brush with Greatness-14
Brush with Greatness Contest Cards-14
Deep in the Crease-D7
Gloves-GUG1
Jerseys-GJ-12
Masks III-1
Masks III Gold-1
Masks III Silver-1
Masks III Memorabilia-1
Stanley Cup Playoffs-SCP-2
Stanley Cup Playoffs-SCP-25
Stanley Cup Playoffs-SCP-32
Tandems-T-7
03BAP Ultimate Memorabilia Autographs-72
Gold-72
03BAP Ultimate Mem Auto Jerseys-72
03BAP Ultimate Memorabilia Triple Threads-3
03Beehive-4
Gold-4
Silver-4
Jumbos-1
Jerseys-JT23
Sticks Beige Border-BE2
Sticks Blue Border-BL5
03Black Diamond-72
Black-72
Green-72
Red-72
Signature Gems-SG-24
Threads-DT-JG
Threads Green-DT-JG
Threads Red-DT-JG
Threads Black-DT-JG
03Bowman-100
Gold-100
03Bowman Chrome-100
Refractors-100
Gold Refractors-100
Xfractors-100
03Crown Royale-3
Blue-3
Retail-3
Gauntlet of Glory-1
03Duracell-1
03eTopps-10
03ITG Action-41
Highlight Reel-HR1
Homeboys-HB13
Jerseys-M186
Jerseys-M206
Jerseys-M221
Jerseys-M241
Oh Canada-OC8
03ITG Toronto Fall Expo Jerseys-FE22
03ITG Used Signature Series Goalie Gear-28
03ITG Used Sig Series Goalie Gear Autos-28
03ITG Used Sig Series Goalie Gear Gold-28
03ITG Used Signature Series Jerseys-49
03ITG Used Signature Series Jerseys Gold-49
03ITG Used Signature Series Jersey Autos-49
03ITG Used Signature Series Emblems-14
03ITG Used Signature Series Emblems Gold-14
03ITG Used Sig Series Jersey and Stick-49
03ITG Used Sig Ser Jersey and Stick Gold-49
03ITG Used Signature Series Teammates-14
03ITG Used Sig Series Teammates Gold-14
03ITG Used Sig Series Triple Mem-14
03ITG Used Sig Series Triple Mem Gold-14
03ITG VIP Collages-13
03ITG VIP Jerseys-23
03ITG VIP Jersey and Emblems-6
03ITG VIP Jersey and Numbers-6
03ITG VIP MVP-20
03ITG VIP Netminders-6
03McDonald's Pacific-1
Net Fusions-1
03NHL Sticker Collection-160
030-Pee-Chee-187
030-Pee-Chee-291
03OPC Blue-187
03OPC Blue-291
03OPC Gold-187
03OPC Gold-291
03OPC Red-187
03OPC Red-291
03Pacific-3
Blue-3
Red-3
In the Crease-1
03Pacific Calder-2
03Pacific Calder-141
Silver-2
03Pacific Complete-403
Red-403
03Pacific Exhibit-152
Blue Backs-152
Standing on Tradition-1
03Pacific Heads-Up-2
Hobby LTD-2
Retail LTD-2
Stonewallers-1
Stonewallers LTD-1
03Pacific Invincible-3
Blue-3
Red-3
Retail-3
Featured Performers-1
Freeze Frame-1
03Pacific Luxury Suite-24A
03Pacific Luxury Suite-24B
03Pacific Luxury Suite-24C
03Pacific Prism-2
Blue-2
Gold-2
Red-2
Crease Police-1
Paramount Prodigies-2
03Pacific Quest for the Cup-2
Blue-2
Connquest-1
03Pacific Supreme-2
Blue-2
Red-2
Retail-2
Standing Guard-1
03Private Stock Reserve-2
Blue-2
Red-2
Retail-2
Increase Security-1
03SP Authentic-1
Limited-1
10th Anniversary-SP17
10th Anniversary Limited-SP17
Breakout Seasons-B15
Breakout Seasons Limited-B15
Foundations-F1
Foundations Limited-F1
Honors-H19
Honors Limited-H19
Sign of the Times-JSG
Sign of the Times-FG
Sign of the Times-GR
Sign of the Times-GCF
Sign of the Times-RGB
03SP Game Used-1
Gold-1
Authentic Fabrics-AFJG
Authentic Fabrics-DFGR
Authentic Fabrics-QRGBT
Authentic Fabrics Gold-AFJG
Authentic Fabrics Gold-DFGR
Authentic Fabrics Gold-QRGBT
Authentic Patches-APJSG
Limited Threads-LTJSG
Limited Threads Gold-LTJSG
Premium Patches-PPJSG
Signers-SSJSG
Team Threads-TTFGC
03SPx-1
03SPx-131
03SPx-158
03SPx-189
Radiance-1
Radiance-131
Radiance-158
Radiance-189
Spectrum-1
Spectrum-131
Spectrum-158
Spectrum-189
Fantasy Franchise-FF-FGC
Fantasy Franchise-FF-GRB
Fantasy Franchise Limited-FF-FGC
Fantasy Franchise Limited-FF-GRB
Origins-O-JSG
Signature Threads-ST-JSG
Style-SPX-BG
Style-SPX-RB
Style Limited-SPX-BG
VIP-VIP-FG
VIP Limited-VIP-FG
03Titanium-143
Hobby Jersey Number Parallels-143
Patches-143
Retail-143
Masked Marauders-1
03Topps-187
03Topps-291
Blue-187
Blue-291
Gold-187
Gold-291
Red-187
Red-291
Box Toppers-18
Own the Game-OTG15
03Topps C55-120
03Topps C55-120B
Minis-120
Minis American Back-120
Minis American Back Red-120
Minis Bazooka Back-120
Minis Brooklyn Back-120
Minis Hat Trick Back-120
Minis O Canada Back-120
Minis O Canada Back Red-120
Minis Stanley Cup Back-120
Autographs-TA-JG
Award Winners-15
03Topps Pristine-1
Gold Refractor Die Cuts-1
Refractors-1
Autographs-PE-JG
Autographs Gold-PE-JG
Mini-PM-JSG
Mini-PMA-JG
Press Plates Black-1
Press Plates Cyan-1
Press Plates Magenta-1
Press Plates Yellow-1
03Topps Traded Franchise Fabrics-FF-JSG
03UD Honor Roll-1
03UD Honor Roll-93
Signature Class-SC7
03UD Premier Collection-1
NHL Shields-SH-JSG
Signatures-PS-JSG
Signatures Gold-PS-JSG
Stars-ST-JSG
Stars Patches-ST-JSG
Teammates-PT-AM
Teammates Patches-PT-AM
03Upper Deck-7
All-Star Class-AS-1
Big Playmakers-BP-JS
BuyBacks-25
Canadian Exclusives-7
Fan Favorites-FF10
Gifted Greats-GG2
HG-7
Jerseys-GJ-JG
Jerseys-UD-JSG
Jersey Autographs-SJ-JSG
Magic Moments-MM-1
Memorable Matchups-MM-GB
NHL Best-NB-JG
Patches-PLG-JG
Patches-PNM-JG
Patches-PNR-JG
Performers-PS1
Super Saviors-SS-JG
Superstar Spotlight-SS1
Three Stars-TS11
03Upper Deck Classic Portraits-3
03Upper Deck Classic Portraits-101
03Upper Deck Classic Portraits-135
03Upper Deck Classic Portraits-156
Starring Cast-SC-JG
03Upper Deck Ice-3
Gold-3
Breakers-IB-JSG
Breaker Patches-IB-JSG
Frozen Fabrics-FF-JSG
Frozen Fabric Patches-FF-JSG
03Upper Deck MVP-14
03Upper Deck MVP-440
Gold Script-14
Gold Script-440
Silver Script-14
Silver Script-440
Canadian Exclusives-14
Canadian Exclusives-440
Clutch Performers-CP5
Masked Men-MM5
SportsNut-SN1
Winning Formula-WF7
03Upper Deck Rookie Update-2
Skills-SKJSG
Top Draws-TD8
03Upper Deck Trilogy-3
03Upper Deck Trilogy-108
Authentic Patches-AP2
Crest Variations-108
Limited-3
Limited-108
Scripts-S2JG
Scripts-CSJG
Scripts Limited-S2JG
03Upper Deck Victory-5
Bronze-5
Gold-5
Silver-5
03Czech Stadion-614
03Toronto Star-1
Foil-24
04Pacific-4
Blue-4
Red-4
04SP Authentic-1
Limited-1
Buybacks-85
Buybacks-86
Buybacks-87
Buybacks-88
Buybacks-89
Buybacks-90
Sign of the Times-ST-JG
Sign of the Times-SS-CAN
04Ultimate Collection-1
Dual Logos-UL2-FG
Patches-UP-JG
04Upper Deck-6
Canadian Exclusives-6
HG Glossy Gold-6
HG Glossy Silver-6
Jersey Autographs-GJA-JG
04German DEL Superstars-SU16
04German Hamburg Freezers Postcards-3
04National Trading Card Day *-T8
05Be A Player-1
First Period-1
Second Period-1
Third Period-1
Overtime-1
Outtakes-OT1
Quad Signatures-BLTG
Quad Signatures-GOAL
Signatures-JG
Signatures Gold-JG
Triple Signatures-FGR
Triple Signatures-TGR
05Beehive-3
05Beehive-241
Beige -3
Blue -3
Gold-3
Red -3
Matte-3
Matted Materials-MMJG
05Black Diamond-86
Emerald-86
Gold-86
Onyx-86
Ruby-86
05Ducks Team Issue-7
05Hot Prospects-2
En Fuego-2
Red Hot-2
White Hot-2
05McDonalds Upper Deck-18
Goalie Factory-GF6
05Panini Stickers-187
05Parkhurst-7
05Parkhurst-671
Facsimile Auto Parallel-7
Facsimile Auto Parallel-671
True Colors-TCANA
True Colors-TCANA
05SP Authentic-1
05SP Authentic-116
Limited-1
Limited-116
Chirography-SPJG
Exquisite Endorsements-EEJG
Marks of Distinction-MDJG
Octographs-OG
Six Star Signatures-SSGO
05SP Game Used-1
Autographs-1
Gold-1
Authentic Fabrics-AF-JG
Authentic Fabrics Autographs-AAF-JG
Authentic Fabrics Dual-GS
Authentic Fabrics Gold-AF-JG
Authentic Fabrics Quad-SGLC
Authentic Patches Quad -SGLC
Authentic Patches-AP-JG
Authentic Patches Autographs-AAP-JG
Authentic Patches Dual-GS
Awesome Authentics-AA-JG
Game Gear-GG-JG
Game Gear Autographs-AG-JG
05SPx-1
Spectrum-1
Winning Combos-WC-FG
Winning Combos Gold-WC-FG
Winning Combos Spectrum-WC-FG
Winning Materials-WM-JG
05The Cup-1
Gold-1
Black Rainbow-1
Dual NHL Shields-DSGS
Emblems of Endorsement-EEJG
Hardware Heroes-HHJS
Honorable Numbers-HNJS
Limited Logos-LLJS
Masterpiece Pressplates-1
Noble Numbers-NNGT
Noble Numbers Dual-DNNGS
Patch Variation-P1
Patch Variation Autographs-AP1
Scripted Numbers-SNGT
Scripted Numbers Dual-DSNGN
Scripted Swatches-SSJS
Signature Patches-SPJS
05UD Artifacts-1
Blue-1
Gold-1
Green-1
Pewter-1
Red-1
Auto Facts-AF-JG
Auto Facts Blue-AF-JG
Auto Facts Copper-AF-JG
Auto Facts Pewter-AF-JG
Auto Facts Silver-AF-JG
Gold Autographed-1
Remarkable Artifacts-RA-JG
Remarkable Artifacts Dual-RA-JG
Treasured Patches-TP-JG
Treasured Patches Autographed-TP-JG
Treasured Patches Dual-TPD-JG
Treasured Patches Dual Autographed-TPD-JG
Treasured Patches Pewter-TP-JG
Treasured Patches Silver-TP-JG
Treasured Swatches-TS-JG
Treasured Swatches Autographed-TS-JG
Treasured Swatches Blue-TS-JG
Treasured Swatches Copper-TS-JG
Treasured Swatches Dual-TSD-JG
Treasured Swatches Dual Autographed-TSD-JG
Treasured Swatches Dual Blue-TSD-JG
Treasured Swatches Dual Copper-TSD-JG
Treasured Swatches Dual Maroon-TSD-JG
Treasured Swatches Dual Pewter-TSD-JG
Treasured Swatches Dual Silver-TSD-JG
Treasured Swatches Maroon-TS-JG
Treasured Swatches Pewter-TS-JG
Treasured Swatches Silver-TS-JG
05UD PowerPlay-1
Rainbow-1
Specialists-TSJS
Specialists Patches-SPJS
05UD Toronto Fall Expo Priority Signings-PS-JG
05Ultimate Collection-2
Gold-2
Endorsed Emblems-EEJS
Marquee Attractions-MA3
Marquee Attractions Signatures-SMA3
Ultimate Achievements-UAJG
Ultimate Signatures-USJG
Ultimate Signatures Foursomes-UFRBGL
Ultimate Signatures Pairings-UPGN
05Ultra-1
Gold-1
Ice-1
05Upper Deck-6
05Upper Deck All-Time Greatest-1
05Upper Deck Big Playmakers-B-JG
05Upper Deck HG Glossy-6
05Upper Deck Hometown Heroes-HH21
05Upper Deck Jerseys-J-JG
05Upper Deck Jerseys Series II-J2JG
05Upper Deck Majestic Materials-MMJG
05Upper Deck Notable Numbers-N-GI
05Upper Deck Patches-P-JG
05Upper Deck Ice-3
Rainbow-3
05Upper Deck MVP-6
Gold-6
Platinum-6
05Upper Deck Rookie Update-1
05Upper Deck Trilogy-1
05Upper Deck Trilogy-91
Crystal-91
Crystal Autographs-91
Honorary Patches-HP-JG
Honorary Patch Scripts-HSP-JG
Honorary Swatches-HS-JG
Honorary Swatch Scripts-HSS-JG
Ice Scripts-IS-JG
Scripts-SCS-JG
05Upper Deck Toronto Fall Expo-6
05Upper Deck Victory-1
Black-1
Gold-1
Silver-1
Blow-Ups-BU1
Stars on Ice-SI1
06Be A Player Portraits-1
Dual Signature Portraits-DSGN
Sensational Six-SSGOL
Signature Portraits-SPJG
Timeless Tens-TTNET
06Beehive-100
Blue-100
Gold-100
Matte-100
Red Facsimile Signatures-100
Wood-100
5 X 7 Black and White-100
06Black Diamond-86
Black-86
Gold-86
Ruby-86
Jerseys-JJG
Jerseys Black-JJG
Jerseys Gold-JJG
Jerseys Ruby-JJG
06Flair Showcase-1
06Flair Showcase-171
06Flair Showcase-201
06Flair Showcase-271
Parallel-1
Parallel-171
Parallel-201
Parallel-271
Hot Gloves-HG1
Stitches-SSJG
06Fleer-1
Tiffany-1
Fabricology-FJG
06Hot Prospects-2
Red Hot-2
White Hot-2
06McDonald's Upper Deck Jerseys-JJG
060-Pee-Chee-17
Rainbow-17
Swatches-S-JG
06Panini Stickers-186
06SP Authentic Sign of the Times-STJG
06SP Game Used-3
Gold-3
Rainbow-3
Authentic Fabrics Sevens-AF7CON
Authentic Fabrics Sevens Patches-AF7CON
06SPx-3
Spectrum-3
Winning Materials-WMJG
Winning Materials Spectrum-WMJG
06The Cup-2
Autographed NHL Shields Duals-DASAN
Autographed Patches-2
Black Rainbow-2
Enshrinements-EJG
Gold-2
Gold Patches-2
Honorable Numbers-HNJG
Jerseys-2
Limited Logos-LLJG
Masterpiece Pressplates-2
NHL Shields Duals-DSHSG
Scripted Swatches-SSJG
Signature Patches-SPJG
06UD Artifacts-99
Blue-99
Gold-99
Radiance-99
Red-99
Treasured Patches Platinum-TSJG
Treasured Patches Red-TSJG
Treasured Swatches-TSJG
Treasured Swatches Black-TSJG
Treasured Swatches Blue-TSJG
Treasured Swatches Red-TSJG
Tundra Tandems-TTNG
Tundra Tandems Blue-TTNG
Tundra Tandems Gold-TTNG
Tundra Tandems Red-TTNG
Tundra Tandems Dual Patches Red-TTNG
06UD Mini Jersey Collection-2
06UD Powerplay-1
Impact Rainbow-1
Goal Robbers-GR1
Specialists-SJG
Specialists Patches-PJG
06Ultimate Collection Autographed Jerseys-AJ-JG
06Ultimate Collection Autographed Patches-AJ-JG
06Ultimate Collection Premium Patches-PS-JG
06Ultimate Collection Premium Swatches-PS-JG
06Ultimate Collection Signatures-US-JG
06Ultimate Collection Ultimate Signatures Logos-SL-JG
06Ultra-1
Gold Medallion-1
Ice Medallion-1
Uniformity-UJG
Uniformity Patches-UPJG
06Upper Deck Arena Giveaways-ANA5
06Upper Deck-254
Exclusives Parallel-254
High Gloss Parallel-254
Game Jerseys-JJG
Game Patches-PJG
Masterpieces-254
Oversized Wal-Mart Exclusives-254
06Upper Deck MVP-10
Gold Script-10
Super Script-10
Jerseys-OJTG
06Upper Deck Ovation-1
06Upper Deck Sweet Shot-3
Signature Shots/Saves-SSJG
Signature Shots/Saves Ice Signings-SSIJG
Signature Sticks-STJG
Sweet Stitches-SSJG
Sweet Stitches Duals-SSJG
Sweet Stitches Triples-SSJG
06Upper Deck Trilogy-3
Honorary Swatches-HSJG
06Upper Deck National NHL VIP-6
06Upper Deck Victory-1
06Upper Deck Victory Black-1
06Upper Deck Victory Gold-1
06Upper Deck Victory GameBreakers-GB1
06Upper Deck Victory Oversize Cards-JG
07Upper Deck Victory-167
Black-167
Gold-167
GameBreakers-GB10
Oversize Cards-OS38

Giguere, Karl
93Quebec Pee-Wee Tournament-276

Giguere, Patrice
93Quebec Pee-Wee Tournament-936

Giguere, Stephane
88Flint Spirits-4

Gilbert, Ed
74NHL Action Stamps-302
750-Pee-Chee NHL-370
760-Pee-Chee NHL-329

Gilbert, Gilles

71Toronto Sun-130
73O-Pee-Chee-74
73Topps-74
74NHL Action Stamps-24
74O-Pee-Chee NHL-10
74O-Pee-Chee NHL-132
74Topps-10
74Topps-132
75O-Pee-Chee NHL-45
75Topps-45
76O-Pee-Chee NHL-255
76Topps-255
77O-Pee-Chee NHL-125
77Topps-125
78O-Pee-Chee-68
78O-Pee-Chee-95
78Topps-68
78Topps-95
79O-Pee-Chee-209
79Topps-209
80O-Pee-Chee-175
80Topps-175
81O-Pee-Chee-88
81O-Pee-Chee Stickers-123
81Topps-W88
82O-Pee-Chee-84
92Sport-Flash-6
92Sport-Flash Autographs-6
02BAP Ultimate Memorabilia Cup Duels-8
02BAP Ultimate Mem Retro Teammates-2
03Parkhurst Orig Six Boston Mem -BM22
03Parkhurst Orig Six Boston Mem -BM30
04ITG Franchises Update Teammates-UTM1
04ITG Franchises Update Teammates Gold-UTM1
04ITG Franchises US East-321
Autographs-A-GG
Double Memorabilia-EDM10
Double Memorabilia Autographs-EDM-GG
Double Memorabilia Gold-EDM10
Goalie Gear-EGG8
Goalie Gear Autographs-EGG-GG
Goalie Gear Gold-EGG8
Memorabilia-ESM18
Memorabilia Autographs-ESM-GG
Memorabilia Gold-ESM18
04ITG Ultimate Memorabilia Original Six-3
04ITG Ultimate Mem Retro Teammates-14
05Between the Pipes Gloves-GUG-3
05ITG Ultimate Mem Pass the Torch Jerseys-5
05ITG Ultimate Mem Passing Torch Jsy Gold-5
06Between The Pipes-90
Autographs-AGG
Gloves-GG07
Gloves Gold-GG07
Shooting Gallery-SG03
Shooting Gallery Gold-SG03

Gilbert, Greg
82Indianapolis Checkers-5
84Islanders News-5
84O-Pee-Chee-125
84O-Pee-Chee Stickers-90
84Topps-93
85Islanders News-5
85O-Pee-Chee-126
85O-Pee-Chee Stickers-75
85Topps-126
86Islanders Team Issue-16
88O-Pee-Chee-83
88Panini Stickers-287
88Topps-83
89Blackhawks Coke-8
90Blackhawks Coke-8
90O-Pee-Chee-255
90Panini Stickers-196
90Pro Set-429
90Score-264
Canadian-264
90Topps-255
Tiffany-255
91Blackhawks Coke-6
91Bowman-401
91O-Pee-Chee-149
91Pro Set-372
French-372
91Score Canadian Bilingual-539
91Score Canadian English-539
91Stadium Club-242
91Topps-149
92Score-134
Canadian-134
92Stadium Club-323
92Topps-218
Gold-218G
92Ultra-275
93Leaf-348
93OPC Premier-216
Gold-216
93Parkhurst-404A
Emerald Ice-404A
93Pinnacle-405
Canadian-405
93Score-305
93Score-561
Gold-561
Canadian-305
Canadian-561
Canadian Gold-561
93Stadium Club-37
Members Only Master Set-37
OPC-37
First Day Issue-37
First Day Issue OPC-37
93Topps/OPC Premier-216
Gold-216
93Upper Deck-404
94Leaf-341
94OPC Premier-169
Special Effects-169
94Parkhurst SE-SE111
Gold-SE111
94Pinnacle-415
Artist's Proofs-415
Rink Collection-415
94Topps/OPC Premier-169
Special Effects-169
95Topps-96
OPC Inserts-96
06Toronto Marlies-13

Gilbert, Greg (Minors)
74Sioux City Musketeers-4

Gilbert, Jimmy
93Quebec Pee-Wee Tournament-1676

Gilbert, Lucien
51Bas Du Fleuve-25
52Bas Du Fleuve-64

Gilbert, Patrick
99Rouyn-Noranda Huskies-8
00Rouyn-Noranda Huskies-15
Signed-15
01Halifax Mooseheads-17
02Cape Breton Screaming Eagles-20

Gilbert, Remi
93Quebec Pee-Wee Tournament-935

Gilbert, Rod
44Beehive Group II Photos-314
61Topps-62
62Topps-59
63Topps-57
64Beehive Group III Photos-127
64Coca-Cola Caps-77
64Topps-24
64Toronto Star-9
65Coca-Cola-79
65Topps-91
66Topps-26
66Topps USA Test-26
67Topps-90
68O-Pee-Chee-72
68O-Pee-Chee-209
Puck Stickers-9
68Shirriff Coins-102
68Topps-72
69O-Pee-Chee-37
Four-in-One-12
Stamps-9
69Topps-37
70Colgate Stamps-53
70Dad's Cookies-40
70Esso Power Players-185
70O-Pee-Chee-63
Deckle-39
70Sargent Promotions Stamps-122
70Topps-63
Topps/OPC Sticker Stamps-10
71Bazooka-30
71Letraset Action Replays-14
71O-Pee-Chee-123
O-Pee-Chee/Topps Booklets-18
Posters-7
71Sargent Promotions Stamps-113
71Topps-123
71Toronto Sun-173
72Kellogg's Iron-On Transfers-3
72O-Pee-Chee-153
72O-Pee-Chee-229
Team Canada-11
72Sargent Promotions Stamps-141
72Topps-80
72Topps-125
72Swedish Stickers-116
73Mac's Milk-7
73O-Pee-Chee-156
73Topps-88
74Lipton Soup-40
74NHL Action Stamps-188
74O-Pee-Chee NHL-141
74O-Pee-Chee NHL-201
74Topps-141
74Topps-201
75O-Pee-Chee NHL-225
75O-Pee-Chee NHL-324
75Topps-225
75Topps-324
76O-Pee-Chee NHL-90
76O-Pee-Chee NHL-390
76Topps-90
76Topps Glossy Inserts-18
77Coca-Cola-8
77O-Pee-Chee NHL-25
77Sportscasters-3303
77Topps-25
83Hall of Fame-111
83Hall of Fame Postcards-H5
85Hall of Fame-111
90Upper Deck-512
French-512
91Future Trends Canada '72-74
91Future Trends Canada '72 French-74
91Kraft-82
91Pro Set-593
French-593
NHL Sponsor Awards-AC23
91Star Pics-7
92Zeller's Masters of Hockey-2
92Zeller's Masters of Hockey Signed-2
94Parkhurst Tall Boys-104
Autographs-A1
Mail-Ins-SL5
95Parkhurst '66-67-79
Coins-79
99BAP Memorabilia AS American Hobby-AH12
99BAP Memorabilia AS American Hobby Autos-AH12
00Upper Deck Legends-90
Legendary Collection Bronze-90
Legendary Collection Gold-90
Legendary Collection Silver-90
01BAP Update Passing the Torch-PTT5
01Fleer Legacy-26
Ultimate-26
01Greats of the Game-23
Autographs-23
02BAP Ultimate Memorabilia Numerology-10
02BAP Ultimate Mem Retro Teammates-5
03BAP Ultimate Mem Linemates Autos-10
03BAP Ultimate Mem Raised to the Rafters-9
03Parkhurst Orig Six He Shoots/Scores-23
03Parkhurst Orig Six He Shoots/Scores-23A
03Parkhurst Orig Six He Shoots/Scores-24
03Parkhurst Original Six New York-55
03Parkhurst Original Six New York-69
03Parkhurst Original Six New York-85
03Parkhurst Original Six New York-91
Autographs-7
Inserts-N1
Inserts-N4
Memorabilia-NM32
Memorabilia-NM40
Memorabilia-NM55
04ITG Franchises US East-383
Autographs-A-RGI
04ITG Ultimate Memorabilia-40
Gold-40
Cornerstones-6
Cornerstones Gold-6
Day In History-46
Day In History Gold-46
Original Six-2
Original Six-17
Retro Teammates-12
05ITG Heroes/Prosp Toronto Expo Parallel -194
05ITG Ultimate Mem Cornerstones Jerseys-6
05ITG Ultimate Mem Cornerst Jerseys Gold-6
05ITG Ultimate Mem Decades Jerseys-7
05ITG Ultimate Mem Decades Jerseys Gold-7
05ITG Ultimate Memorabilia Emblems-7
05ITG Ultimate Memorabilia Emblems Gold-7
05ITG Ultimate Memorabilia In The Numbers-2
05ITG Ultimate Mem In The Numbers Gold-2
05ITG Ultimate Mem Jersey and Emblem-28
05ITG Ultimate Memorabilia Jersey Autos-7
05ITG Ultimate Mem Jersey Autos Gold-7
05ITG Ultimate Mem Jersey
Emblems Gold-28
05ITG Ultimate Memorabilia Jerseys-32
05ITG Ultimate Memorabilia Jerseys Gold-32
05ITG Ultimate Mem Retro Teammate Jerseys-22
05ITG Ult Mem Retro Teammates Jersey Gold-22
05ITG Ultimate Mem 3 Star of the Game Jsy-14
05ITG Ult Mem 3 Star of the Game Jsy Gold-14
05ITG Ultimate Memorabilia Ultimate Autos-36
05ITG Ultimate Mem Ultimate Autos Gold-36
05ITG Heroes and Prospects-194
Autographs Series II-RGI
Hero Memorabilia-HM-44
06ITG Ultimate Memorabilia-122
Artist Proof-122
Boys Will Be Boys-13
Boys Will Be Boys Gold-13
Cornerstones-6
Cornerstones Gold-6
Decades-4
Decades Gold-4
Retro Teammates-9
Retro Teammates Gold-9
06Parkhurst-14
Autographs-14

Gilbert, Tim
05Waterloo Blackhawks-10

Gilbert, Tom
03Wisconsin Badgers-13
04Wisconsin Badgers-22
05Wisconsin Badgers-12
06Wilkes-Barre Scranton Penguins-20
06Wilkes-Barre Scranton Penguins Jerseys-9
07Upper Deck Victory-224
Black-224
Gold-224

Gilbert, Yannick
93Quebec Pee-Wee Tournament-124

Gilbertson, Stan
71Letraset Action Replays-19
71O-Pee-Chee-183
71Toronto Sun-47
72O-Pee-Chee-70
72Sargent Promotions Stamps-52
72Topps-101
73O-Pee-Chee-212
74NHL Action Stamps-60
74O-Pee-Chee NHL-223
74Topps-223
75O-Pee-Chee NHL-382
76O-Pee-Chee NHL-187
76Topps-187
77Topps-203

Gilby, Andrew
96Halifax Mooseheads I-8
96Halifax Mooseheads II-8
97Halifax Mooseheads I-5

Gilchrist, Brent
84Kelowna Wings-16
88Canadiens Postcards-11
89Canadiens Kraft-9
89Canadiens Postcards-13
90Canadiens Postcards-16
90O-Pee-Chee-422
90Pro Set-471
90Score Rookie/Traded-87T
91Pro Set Platinum-192
91Bowman-336
91Canadiens Panini Team Stickers-12
91Canadiens Postcards-13
91O-Pee-Chee-90
91Parkhurst-315
French-315
91Pinnacle-236
French-236
91Pro Set-414
French-414
91Score Canadian Bilingual-259
91Score Canadian English-259
91Topps-90
92Bowman-322
92Oilers IGA-7
92O-Pee-Chee-221
92OPC Premier-129
92Panini Stickers-153
92Panini Stickers French-153
92Pinnacle-357
French-357
92Pro Set-90
92Score-46
Canadian-46
92Stadium Club-449
92Topps-386
Gold-386G
92Ultra-293
92Upper Deck-459
93Parkhurst-52
Emerald Ice-52
93Pinnacle-415
Canadian-415
93PowerPlay-324
93Score-206
Canadian-206
93Upper Deck-329
94Fleer-50
94Leaf-340
94Parkhurst-55
Gold-55
Vintage-V21
94Pinnacle-185
Artist's Proofs-185
Rink Collection-185
94Stadium Club-143
Members Only Master Set-143
First Day Issue-143
Super Team Winner Cards-143
94Stars HockeyKaps-13
94Stars Pinnacle Sheet-185
94Stars Pinnacle Sheet-NNO
94Stars Postcards-8
94Upper Deck-347
Electric Ice-347
95Be A Player-71
Signatures-S71
Signatures Die Cuts-S71
95Parkhurst International-326
Emerald Ice-326
95Score-261
Black Ice Artist's Proofs-261
Black Ice-261
95Stars Score Sheet-261
95Upper Deck-326
Electric Ice-326
Electric Ice Gold-326
96Score-49
Artist's Proofs-49
Dealer's Choice Artist's Proofs-49
Special Artist's Proofs-49
Golden Blades-49
96Stars Postcards-6
97Be A Player-85
Autographs-85
Autographs Die-Cuts-85
Autographs Prismatic Die-Cuts-85
97Pacific-136
Copper-136
Emerald Green-136
Ice Blue-136
Red-136
Silver-136
97Pacific Omega-79
Copper-79
Dark Gray-79
Emerald Green-79
Gold-79
Ice Blue-79
97Score Red Wings-14
Platinum-14
Premier-14
98OPC Chrome-95
Refractors-95
98Pacific-191
Ice Blue-191
Red-191
98Topps-95
O-Pee-Chee-95
00BAP Signature Series-228
Emerald-228
Ruby-228
Sapphire-228
Autographs-24
Autographs Gold-24
00Upper Deck-295
Exclusives Tier 1-295
Exclusives Tier 2-295
02Pacific Complete-189
Red-189
02Predators Team Issue-1

Giles, Andy
93UK Humberside Hawks-16

Giles, Curt
80North Stars Postcards-8
81North Stars Postcards-9
82North Stars Postcards-11
82O-Pee-Chee-166
82Post Cereal-9
83NHL Key Tags-57
83North Stars Postcards-9
84North Stars Postcards-7
84North Stars Postcards-8
85North Stars 7-Eleven-3
85North Stars Postcards-10
85O-Pee-Chee-96
85Topps-96
86O-Pee-Chee-119
86O-Pee-Chee Stickers-172
86Topps-119
87North Stars Postcards-14
87Panini Stickers-110
88North Stars ADA-12
89O-Pee-Chee-213
89Panini Stickers-112
90O-Pee-Chee-228
90Panini Stickers-250
90Pro Set-140
90Score-94
Canadian-94
90Topps-228
Tiffany-228
90Upper Deck-9
French-9
91Alberta International Team Canada-8
91O-Pee-Chee-17
91Pro Set-114
French-114
91Score American-137
91Score Canadian Bilingual-137
91Score Canadian English-137
91Topps-17
92Stadium Club-64
92Topps-202
Gold-202G

Giles, Scott
04Owen Sound Attack-21
05Owen Sound Attack-7

Gilhen, Randy
86Sherbrooke Canadiens-17
87Moncton Hawks-10
88Jets Police-8
88Jets Postcards-10
90O-Pee-Chee-250
90Pro Set-506
90Topps-250
Tiffany-250
91Bowman-84
91O-Pee-Chee-418
91OPC Premier-123
91Parkhurst-335
French-335
91Pinnacle-238
French-238
91Pro Set-403
French-403
91Score American-157
91Score Canadian Bilingual-157
91Score Canadian Bilingual-566
91Score Canadian English-157
91Score Canadian English-566
91Score Rookie/Traded-16T
91Stadium Club-275
91Topps-418
91Upper Deck-603
French-603
92Bowman-327
92O-Pee-Chee-26
92Pinnacle-126
French-126
92Score-268
Canadian-268
92Stadium Club-318
92Topps-27
Gold-27G
92Upper Deck-82
93PowerPlay-93
93PowerPlay-473
93Score-643
Gold-643
Canadian-643
Canadian Gold-643
93Upper Deck-481
95Jets Team Issue-9
97Manitoba Moose-A3

Gilje, Morten
92Norwegian Elite Series-139

Gill, Aaron
01Notre Dame Fighting Irish-14
02Notre Dame Fighting Irish-15
03Notre Dame Fighting Irish-11
04Cleveland Barons-9

Gill, Andre
06Richmond Renegades-4

Gill, Hal
97Pacific Omega-16
Copper-16
Dark Gray-16
Emerald Green-16
Gold-16
Ice Blue-16
97Providence Bruins-6
98Upper Deck MVP-17
Gold Script-17
Silver Script-17
Super Script-17
99Pacific-23
Copper-23
Emerald Green-23
Gold-23
Ice Blue-23
Premiere Date-23
Red-23
99Upper Deck MVP-20
Gold Script-20
Silver Script-20
Super Script-20
99Upper Deck Victory-29
00O-Pee-Chee-252A
00O-Pee-Chee Parallel-252A
00Pacific-33
Copper-33
Gold-33
Ice Blue-33
Premiere Date-33
00Topps/OPC-252A
Parallel-252A
00Upper Deck MVP-20
First Stars-20
Second Stars-20
Third Stars-20
00Upper Deck Victory-24
01BAP Signature Series-3
Autographs-3
Autographs Gold-3
01UD Playmakers-10
02BAP Sig Series Auto Buybacks 2001-3
02Bruins Team Issue-3
02Pacific-26
Blue-26
Red-26
02Pacific Complete-498
Red-498
02Topps Total-59
02Upper Deck Vintage-26
03Bruins Team Issue-2
03ITG Action-32
03Pacific Complete-337
Red-337
03Parkhurst Original Six Boston-9
03Upper Deck-17
Canadian Exclusives-17
HG-17
03Upper Deck MVP-42
Gold Script-42
Silver Script-42
Canadian Exclusives-42
05Bruins Boston Globe-4
05Parkhurst-47
Facsimile Auto Parallel-47
05Upper Deck-261
05Upper Deck MVP-31
Gold-31
Platinum-31
06Be A Player-122
Autographs-122
Signatures-HG
06Gatorade-73
06O-Pee-Chee-459
Rainbow-459

Gill, J.K.
06Sudbury Wolves-3

Gill, Todd
86Maple Leafs Postcards-10
87Maple Leafs PLAY-13
87Maple Leafs Postcards-8
87Maple Leafs Postcards Oversized-8
87O-Pee-Chee Stickers-163
87Panini Stickers-324
88Maple Leafs PLAY-12
89Panini Stickers-143
90Pro Set-534
91Bowman-171
91Maple Leafs Panini Team Stickers-7
91Maple Leafs PLAY-14
91O-Pee-Chee-361
91Parkhurst-393
French-393
91Pinnacle-278
French-278
91Pro Set-226
French-226
91Score Canadian Bilingual-521
91Score Canadian English-521
91Stadium Club-336
91Topps-361
92Bowman-375
92Maple Leafs Kodak-25
92Panini Stickers-82
92Panini Stickers French-82
92Pinnacle-290
French-290
92Score-196
Canadian-196
92Stadium Club-261
92Topps-374
Gold-374G
93Donruss-335
93Leaf-22
Maple Leafs Score Black's-22
93OPC Premier-4
Gold-4
93Pinnacle-68
Canadian-68
93PowerPlay-449
93Score-292
Canadian-292
93Stadium Club-62
Members Only Master Set-62
OPC-62
First Day Issue-62
First Day Issue OPC-62
93Topps/OPC Premier-4
Gold-4
93Ultra-77
94Be A Player-R24
99 All-Stars-G8
Signature Cards-104
94Canada Games NHL POGS-239
94EA Sports-133
94Leaf-497
94Maple Leafs Gangsters-8
94Maple Leafs Kodak-12
94Maple Leafs Pin-up Posters-8
94Maple Leafs Postcards-1
94OPC Premier-189
Special Effects-189
94Parkhurst-233
Gold-233
94Pinnacle-181
Artist's Proofs-181
Rink Collection-181
94Score-55
Gold-55
Platinum-55
94Topps/OPC Premier-189
Special Effects-189
94Ultra-215
94Upper Deck-440
Electric Ice-440
95Canada Games NHL POGS-265
95Collector's Choice-101
Player's Club-101
Player's Club Platinum-101
95Donruss-14
95Emotion-170
95Leaf-278
95Panini Stickers-206
95Parkhurst International-202
Emerald Ice-202
95Pinnacle-171
Artist's Proofs-171
Rink Collection-171
95Score-162
Black Ice Artist's Proofs-162
Black Ice-162
95SkyBox Impact-160
95Topps-124
OPC Inserts-124
95Upper Deck-117
Electric Ice-117
Electric Ice Gold-117
95Images Platinum Players-PL10
96Be A Player-1
Autographs-1
Autographs Silver-1
96Donruss-15
Press Proofs-15
96Donruss Elite-79
Die Cut Stars-79
96Pinnacle-176
Artist's Proofs-176
Foil-176
Premium Stock-176
Rink Collection-176
96Score-208
Artist's Proofs-208
Dealer's Choice Artist's Proofs-208
Special Artist's Proofs-208
Golden Blades-208
96Summit-4
Artist's Proofs-4
Ice-4
Metal-4
Premium Stock-4
96Zenith-14
Artist's Proofs-14
97Pacific-98
Copper-98
Emerald Green-98
Ice Blue-98
Red-98
Silver-98
97Upper Deck-151
98Be A Player-127
Press Release-127
98BAP Gold-127
98BAP Autographs-127
98BAP Autographs Gold-127
98BAP Tampa Bay All Star Game-127
98Pacific-367
Ice Blue-367
Red-367
00Stadium Club-140
01Avalanche Team Issue-21
01Pacific-140
Extreme LTD-140
Hobby LTD-140
Premiere Date-140
Retail LTD-140
01Pacific Arena Exclusives-140
02BAP Sig Series Auto Buybacks 1998-127
02Maple Leafs Platinum Collection-29

Gill, Tony
04Notre Dame Fighting Irish-19

Gillam, Sean
93Spokane Chiefs-12
94Spokane Chiefs-10
95Spokane Chiefs-19
99Mississippi Sea Wolves-8
06Rio Grande Valley Killer Bees-19

Gillen, Steven
04Moose Jaw Warriors-19
05Moose Jaw Warriors-7
06Moose Jaw Warriors-18

Gilliard, Tony
82North Bay Centennials-6

Gillies, Clark
74NHL Action Stamps-163
75O-Pee-Chee NHL-199
75O-Pee-Chee NHL-323
75Topps-199
75Topps-323
76O-Pee-Chee NHL-126
76O-Pee-Chee NHL-216
76O-Pee-Chee NHL-389
76Topps-126
76Topps-216
77O-Pee-Chee NHL-250
77Topps-250
77Topps/O-Pee-Chee Glossy-6
Square-6
77Finnish Sportscasters-54-1290
78O-Pee-Chee-220
78O-Pee-Chee-327
78Topps-220
79Islanders Transparencies-3
79O-Pee-Chee-130
79Topps-130
80O-Pee-Chee-75
80Topps-75
81O-Pee-Chee-202
81O-Pee-Chee Stickers-164
81Topps-E88
82McDonald's Stickers-13
82O-Pee-Chee-201
82O-Pee-Chee Stickers-54
82O-Pee-Chee Stickers-55
82Post Cereal-12
82Topps Stickers-54
82Topps Stickers-55
83Islanders Team Issue-4
83NHL Key Tags-83
83O-Pee-Chee-6
83O-Pee-Chee Stickers-84
83Puffy Stickers-20
83Topps Stickers-84
84Islanders News-6
84O-Pee-Chee-126
84Topps-94
84Kelowna Wings-45
85Islanders News-6
85O-Pee-Chee-81
85O-Pee-Chee Stickers-68
85Topps-81
86O-Pee-Chee-141
86O-Pee-Chee Stickers-205
86Sabres Blue Shield-11
86Sabres Blue Shield Small-11
86Topps-141
87O-Pee-Chee-96
87Panini Stickers-34
87Sabres Blue Shield-9
87Sabres Wonder Bread/Hostess-10
87Topps-96
88Esso All-Stars-13
88O-Pee-Chee-80
88Topps-80
91Upper Deck-640
French-640
93Islanders Chemical Bank Alumni-3
00Upper Deck Legends-86
Legendary Collection Bronze-86
Legendary Collection Gold-86
Legendary Collection Silver-86
Legendary Game Jerseys-JCG
00Upper Deck Vintage Dynasty: A Piece of History-BG
00Upper Deck Vintage Dynasty: A Piece of History-GH
00Upper Deck Vintage Dynasty: A Piece of History Gold-BG
00Upper Deck Vintage Dynasty: A Piece of History Gold-GH
01Fleer Legacy-18
Ultimate-18
01Greats of the Game-62
Autographs-62
01Topps Archives-35
Autographs-29
01Upper Deck Legends-44
Jerseys-TTCG
Jerseys Platinum-TTCG
02Fleer Throwbacks-6
Gold-6
Platinum-6
Autographs-3
Scraps-5
Tie Downs-5
Squaring Off-2
Squaring Off Memorabilia-2
02UD Foundations-8
02UD Foundations-61
Signs of Greatness-SGCG
03BAP Ultimate Memorabilia Linemates-7
03SP Authentic Sign of the Times-BTG
04ITG Franchises Update Linemates-ULI3
04ITG Franchises Update Linemates Gold-ULI3
04ITG Franchises Update Original Sticks-UOS8
04ITG Franchises Upd Original Sticks Gold-UOS8
04ITG Franchises US East-373
Autographs-A-CG
04ITG Ultimate Memorabilia-167
Gold-167
04SP Authentic Sign of the Times-TS-BTG
04SP Authentic Sign of the Times-QS-HRBG
04UD Legendary Signatures-18
Autographs-CG
HOF Inks-HOF-CG
Linemates-CGBTMB
04UD Legends Classics-13
Gold-13
Platinum-13
Silver-13
Signature Moments-M42
Signatures-CS40
Signatures-TC5
Signatures-QC6
05SPx-126
Spectrum-126
Xcitement Legends-XL-CG
Xcitement Legends Gold-XL-CG
Xcitement Legends Spectrum-XL-CG
05The Cup-68
Gold-68
Black Rainbow-68
Masterpiece Pressplates-68
Patch Variation-P68
05UD Artifacts-119
Blue-119
Gold-119
Green-119
Pewter-119
Red-119
Gold Autographed-119
05Upper Deck Trilogy Legendary Scripts-LEG-CG
06Parkhurst-15
06Parkhurst-190
06Parkhurst-243
Autographs-15
Autographs-190
Autographs-243
Autographs Dual-DABG
06SP Authentic Sign of the Times Duals-STBG
06SP Game Used Letter Marks-LMCG
06The Cup Property of-POCG
06The Cup Stanley Cup Signatures-CSCG
06The Cup Stanley Cup Titlists-TCG
06UD Artifacts-150
Blue-150
Gold-150
Platinum-150
Radiance-150
Autographed Radiance Parallel-150
Red-150
Auto-Facts-AFCG
Auto-Facts Gold-AFCG
06Upper Deck Sweet Shot Signature Sticks-STCG

Gillies, Colton
05Saskatoon Blades-8
06Saskatoon Blades-9
06ITG Heroes and Prospects-129
Autographs-ACGI

Gillies, Nathan
03Elmira Jackals-7

Gillies, Tanner
05Red Deer Rebels-5

Gillies, Trevor
99Mississippi Sea Wolves-6
02Peoria Rivermen-3
02Peoria Rivermen RBI Sports-160
03Springfield Falcons Postcards-2
04Hartford Wolf Pack-4
05Portland Pirates-24
06Portland Pirates-20
06ITG Heroes and Prospects-62
Autographs-ATG

Gilligan, William
79Panini Stickers-223
98Swiss Power Play Stickers-273

Gillingham, Todd
907th Inn. Sketch QMJHL-174
91ProCards-351
92Salt Lake Golden Eagles-6
93St. John's Maple Leafs-8
96Collector's Edge Ice-151
Prism-151
97St. John's Maple Leafs-11

Gillis, Bruce
00Halifax Mooseheads-5
01Halifax Mooseheads-8

Gillis, Errol
23V128-1 Paulin's Candy-4
24Crescent Selkirks-7

Gillis, Jere
77Canucks Canada Dry Cans-3
77Canucks Royal Bank-5
78Canucks Royal Bank-6
78O-Pee-Chee-109
78Topps-109
79Canucks Royal Bank-7
79O-Pee-Chee-322
80O-Pee-Chee-283
81O-Pee-Chee-232
82Post Cereal-16
83Canucks Team Issue-7
83Vachon-106
84O-Pee-Chee-318
84Fredericton Express-11
85Fredericton Express-11

Gillis, Mike
79Rockies Team Issue-8
81O-Pee-Chee-12
82Post Cereal-1
84Bruins Postcards-6

Gillis, Paul
82North Bay Centennials-7
83Nordiques Postcards-9
84Nordiques Postcards-9
85Nordiques General Foods-9
85Nordiques McDonald's-7
85Nordiques Provigo-9
85Nordiques Team Issue-8
85O-Pee-Chee Stickers-150
86Nordiques General Foods-8
86Nordiques McDonald's-8
86Nordiques Team Issue-7
86Nordiques Yum-Yum-3
86O-Pee-Chee-168
86O-Pee-Chee Stickers-24
86Topps-168
87Nordiques General Foods-10
87Nordiques Team Issue-18
87Nordiques Yum-Yum-2
87O-Pee-Chee-247
87O-Pee-Chee Stickers-221
87Panini Stickers-167
88Nordiques General Foods-13
88Nordiques Team Issue-13
89Kraft-29
89Nordiques Team Issue-12
89Nordiques General Foods-9
89Nordiques Police-8
89O-Pee-Chee-265
89O-Pee-Chee Stickers-183
89Panini Stickers-330
90Bowman-165
Tiffany-165
90Nordiques Petro-Canada-9
90Nordiques Team Issue-8
90O-Pee-Chee-22
90O-Pee-Chee-122
90Panini Stickers-143
90Pro Set-246
90Score-141
Canadian-141
90Topps-22
90Topps-122
Tiffany-22
90Upper Deck-49
French-49
91Nordiques Panini Team Stickers-6
91O-Pee-Chee-469
91Score American-364
91Score Canadian Bilingual-403
91Score Canadian English-403
91Topps-469
91Whalers Jr. 7-Eleven-12
91ProCards-489
92Whalers Dairymart-7
99Guelph Storm-26
05Danbury Trashers-26

Gillis, Ryan
93North Bay Centennials-10
94North Bay Centennials-12
95Slapshot-218
96Dayton Bombers-16
99Hampton Roads Admirals-8
00UK Nottingham Panthers-16
00UK Sekonda Superleague-128
03Missouri River Otters-21
04Bakersfield Condors-4
05Port Huron Flags-14
06Bloomington PrairieThunder-9

Gillow, Russ
72Los Angeles Sharks WHA-4

Gilmore, Dave
917th Inn. Sketch OHL-363
93London Knights-9
95Classic-88
03Indianapolis Ice-9

Gilmore, Tom
72Los Angeles Sharks WHA-5

Gilmour, Darryl
86Portland Winter Hawks-8
88ProCards AHL-122
90ProCards AHL/IHL-427
91ProCards-403
92Phoenix Roadrunners-7
93Fort Wayne Komets-7
94Muskegon Fury-12

Gilmour, Doug
84O-Pee-Chee-185
84O-Pee-Chee Stickers-60
85O-Pee-Chee-76
85O-Pee-Chee Stickers-48
85Topps-76
86O-Pee-Chee-93
86O-Pee-Chee Stickers-177
86Topps-93
87Blues Kodak-11
87O-Pee-Chee-175
87O-Pee-Chee Box Bottoms-E
87O-Pee-Chee Minis-11
87O-Pee-Chee Stickers-27
87Panini Stickers-311
87Topps-175

87Topps Box Bottoms-E
88Flames Postcards-2
88Frito-Lay Stickers-8
88O-Pee-Chee-56
88O-Pee-Chee Stickers-20
88Panini Stickers-105
88Topps-56
89Kraft-1
89O-Pee-Chee-74
89O-Pee-Chee Stickers-103
89Panini Stickers-28
89Topps-74
90Bowman-96
Tiffany-96
90Flames IGA/McGavin's-4
90O-Pee-Chee-136
90Panini Stickers-172
90Pro Set-34
90Score-155
Canadian-155
90Score Hottest/Rising Stars-69
90Topps-136
Tiffany-136
90Upper Deck-271
French-271
91Pro Set Platinum-234
91Bowman-255
91Flames Panini Team Stickers-2
91Flames IGA-3
91Kraft-78
91O-Pee-Chee-208
91Panini Stickers-59
91Parkhurst-26
91Parkhurst-396
French-26
French-396
91Pinnacle-92
French-92
91Pro Set-34
French-34
91Score American-218
91Score Canadian Bilingual-218
91Score Canadian English-218
91Stadium Club-96
91Topps-208
91Upper Deck-188
91Upper Deck-558
French-188
French-558
92Blues UD Best of the Blues-2
92Bowman-83
92Humpty Dumpty II-7
92Maple Leafs Kodak-12
92O-Pee-Chee-177
92OPC Premier Star Performers-8
92Panini Stickers-77
92Panini Stickers French-77
92Parkhurst-183
92Parkhurst-502
Emerald Ice-183
Emerald Ice-502
Cherry Picks-CP1
Cherry Picks-CP1993
92Pinnacle Canadian Promo Panels-3
92Pinnacle-279
French-279
92Pro Set-184
Gold Team Leaders-11
92Score-40
92Score-43
Canadian-40
Canadian-43
92Seasons Patches-55
92Sports Illustrated for Kids II-309
92Stadium Club-359
92Topps-122
Gold-122G
92Ultra-211
92Upper Deck-21
92Upper Deck-215
92Upper Deck-639
93Donruss-341
Elite Inserts-7
93Kraft-9
93Kraft-53
93Kraft Recipes-3
93Kraft Recipes French-3
93Leaf-93
Gold All-Stars-6
Studio Signature-1
Maple Leafs Score Black's-2
93McDonald's Upper Deck-5
93OPC Premier-390
Gold-390
Black Gold-11
93Panini Stickers-T
93Parkhurst-469
Emerald Ice-469
Cherry's Playoff Heroes-D9
East/West Stars-W4
USA/Canada Gold-G10
93Pinnacle-100
93Pinnacle-226
Canadian-100
Canadian-226
All-Stars-44
All-Stars Canadian-44
93PowerPlay-284
Gamebreakers-2
Point Leaders-2
93Score-66
Canadian-66
Dynamic Duos Canadian-1
Franchise-21
93Seasons Patches-4
93Stadium Club-140
93Stadium Club-149
Members Only Master Set-140
Members Only Master Set-149
OPC-140
OPC-149
First Day Issue-140
First Day Issue-149
First Day Issue OPC-140
First Day Issue OPC-149
All-Stars-17
All-Stars Members Only-17
All-Stars OPC-17
Master Photos-2
Master Photos Winners-2
93Topps/OPC Premier-390
Gold-390
93Ultra-110
All-Stars-16
Award Winners-3
Premier Pivots-1
93Upper Deck-306
93Upper Deck-382
Award Winners-AW6
Next In Line-NL5
NHLPA/Roots-5

NHLPA/Roots-11
NHLPA/Roots-21
Silver Skates-R7
Silver Skates Gold-R7
SP-158
93Upper Deck Locker All-Stars-24
93Classic-119
Autographs-AU4
94SLU Hockey Canadian-4
94Hockey Canadian-4
94SLU Hockey American-5
94Action Packed Badge of Honor Promos-2
94Be A Player-R1
94Be A Player-R111
94Be A Player-R180
Signature Cards-1
Up Close and Personal-UC10
94Canada Games NHL POGS-45
94Canada Games NHL POGS-234
94Donruss-8
Ice Masters-3
94EA Sports-135
94Finest-100
Super Team Winners-100
Refractors-100
Bowman's Best-B19
Bowman's Best-X22
Bowman's Best Refractors-B19
Bowman's Best Refractors-X22
94Flair-181
Center Spotlight-3
94Fleer-215
Headliners-3
94Hockey Wit-61
94Kenner Starting Lineup Cards-6
94Kraft-17
94Leaf-99
Fire on Ice-5
Gold Stars-2
Limited Inserts-23
94Leaf Limited-8
Gold-3
94Maple Leafs Gangsters-9
94Maple Leafs Kodak-13
94Maple Leafs Pin-up Posters-2
94Maple Leafs Postcards-1
94Maple Leafs Postcards-2
94McDonald's Upper Deck-McD28
94NHLPA Phone Cards-1
94OPC Premier-225
94OPC Premier-279
Special Effects-225
Special Effects-279
94Parkhurst-313
Gold-313
Crash the Game Green-23
Crash the Game Blue-23
Crash the Game Gold-23
Crash the Game Red-23
Vintage-V80
94Parkhurst SE-SE176
Gold-SE176
94Pinnacle-135
Artist's Proofs-135
Rink Collection-135
Gamers-GR11
Northern Lights-NL8
Team Pinnacle-TP10
Team Dufex Parallel-TP10
World Edition-WE2
94Post Box Backs-12
94Score-185
Gold-185
Platinum-185
Dream Team-DT13
Franchise-TF23
90 Plus Club-4
94Select-69
Gold-69
94SP-115
Die Cuts-115
Premier-21
Premier Die-Cuts-21
94Stadium Club Members Only-21
94Stadium Club Super Teams-23
94Stadium Club Super Team MemberOnly Set-23
94Topps/OPC Premier-225
94Topps/OPC Premier-279
Special Effects-225
Special Effects-279
The Go To Guy-14
94Topps Finest Bronze-6
94Ultra-216
Premier Pivots-3
Scoring Kings-3
94Upper Deck-138
Electric Ice-138
Predictor Canadian-C18
94Upper Deck Predictor Canadian Exch Gold-C18
94Upper Deck Predictor Hobby-H3
94Upper Deck Predictor Hobby-H21
94Upper Deck Predictor Hobby Exch Gold-H3
94Upper Deck Predictor Hobby Exch Gold-H21
94Upper Deck Predictor Hobby Exch Silver-H3
94Upper Deck Predictor Hobby Exch Silver-H21
94Upper Deck Predictor Retail-R11
94Upper Deck Predictor Retail-R27
94Upper Deck Predictor Retail-R49
94Upper Deck Predictor Retail-R56
94Upper Deck Predictor Retail Exchange-R11
94Upper Deck Predictor Retail Exchange-R27
94Upper Deck Predictor Retail Exchange-R49
94Upper Deck Predictor Retail Exchange-R56
94Upper Deck SP Inserts-SP167
94Upper Deck SP Inserts Die Cuts-SP167
94Upper Deck NHLPA/Be A Player-41
94Upper Deck NHLPA/Be A Player-42
94Upper Deck NHLPA/Be A Player-43
94Upper Deck NHLPA/Be A Player-44
94Upper Deck NHLPA/Be A Player-45
94Classic-AU1
Autographs-NNO
95Bashan Super Stickers-116
95Bashan Super Stickers-117
95Bowman-18
All-Foil-18
95Canada Games NHL POGS-22
95Canada Games NHL POGS-257
95Collector's Choice-5
95Collector's Choice-359
Player's Club-5
Player's Club-359
Player's Club Platinum-5
Player's Club Platinum-359
Crash The Game-C21A
Crash The Game-C21B
Crash The Game-C21C
Crash The Game Gold-C21A
Crash The Game Gold-C21B
Crash The Game Gold-C21C
Crash the Game Silver Redeemed-C21

Crash the Game Silver Bonus-C21
Crash the Game Gold Redeemed-C21
Crash the Game Gold Bonus-C21
95Donruss Dominators-5
95Donruss Igniters-3
95Donruss Elite-92
Die Cut Stars-92
Die Cut Uncut-92
95Emotion-171
95Finest-55
95Finest-170
Refractors-55
Refractors-170
95Hoyle Western Playing Cards-31
95Imperial Stickers-117
95Kraft-14
95Leaf-211
95Leaf Limited-72
95McDonald's Pinnacle-MCD-9
95Metal-143
95NHL Aces Playing Cards-3H
95NHL Cool Trade-17
95NHL Cool Trade-RP17
95Panini Stickers-200
95Parkhurst International-199
Emerald Ice-199
Crown Collection Silver Series 1-12
Crown Collection Gold Series 1-12
95Pinnacle-61
Artist's Proofs-61
Rink Collection-61
Clear Shots-6
First Strike-3
95Playoff One on One-96
95Playoff One on One-202
95Playoff One on One-315
95Post Upper Deck-18
95Pro Magnets-77
95Score-73
Black Ice Artist's Proofs-73
Black Ice-73
Border Battle-5
Dream Team-6
95Select Certified-48
Mirror Gold-48
Double Strike-1
Double Strike Gold-1
95SkyBox Impact-161
Countdown to Impact-8
95SP-144
95Stadium Club Members Only-44
95Stadium Club-184
Members Only Master Set-184
Extreme North-EN8
Extreme North Members Only Master Set-EN8
Nemeses-N7
Nemeses Members Only Master Set-N7
95Stadium Club Master Photo Test-3
95Summit-62
Artist's Proofs-62
Ice-62
95Topps-234
OPC Inserts-234
Hidden Gems-3HG
Home Grown Canada-HGC4
Profiles-PF17
Rink Leaders-8RL
95Topps SuperSkills-14
Platinum-14
95Ultra-160
Gold Medallion-160
95Upper Deck-240
95Upper Deck-291
Electric Ice-240
Electric Ice-291
Electric Ice Gold-240
Electric Ice Gold-291
95Upper Deck All-Star Game Predictors-10
Redemption Winners-10
95Upper Deck Special Edition-SE80
95Upper Deck Special Edition Gold-SE80
95Zenith-54
95Swedish Globe World Championships-93
95Swiss HNL-545
96Be A Player-22
Autographs-22
Autographs Silver-22
96Black Diamond-28
Gold-28
96Collector's Choice-256
96Collector's Choice-332
MVP-UD45
MVP Gold-UD45
Crash the Game-C2A
Crash the Game-C2B
Crash the Game-C2C
Crash the Game Gold-C2A
Crash the Game Gold-C2B
Crash the Game Gold-C2C
Crash the Game Exchange-CR2
Crash the Game Exchange Gold-CR2
96Donruss-46
96Donruss-239
Press Proofs-46
Press Proofs-239
Dominators-6
Hit List-15
96Donruss Canadian Ice-112
Gold Press Proofs-112
Red Press Proofs-112
O Canada-9
96Donruss Elite-44
Die Cut Stars-44
Perspective-6
96Duracell All-Cherry Team-DC7
96Duracell L'Equipe Beliveau-JB7
96Flair-90
Blue Ice-90
96Fleer-107
96Fleer Picks-68
Captain's Choice-8
96Hockey Greats Coins-8
Gold-8
96Kraft Upper Deck-37
96Leaf-74
Press Proofs-74
Fire On Ice-10
96Leaf Leather And Laces Promos-P14
96Leaf Leather And Laces-14
96Leaf Limited-70
Gold-70
96Leaf Limited Bash the Boards Promos-P4
96Leaf Limited Bash The Boards-4
96Leaf Limited Bash The Boards Ltd Ed-4
96Leaf Preferred-104
Press Proofs-104
Steel-10
Steel Gold-10
96Maggers-28
96Maple Leafs Postcards-1
96McDonald's Pinnacle-14

96Metal Universe-149
96NHL Aces Playing Cards-18
96NHL Pro Stamps-77
96Pinnacle-127
Artist's Proofs-127
Foil-127
Premium Stock-127
Rink Collection-127
By The Numbers-7
By The Numbers Premium-7
96Playoff One on One-356
96Post Upper Deck-7
96Score-95
Artist's Proofs-95
Dealer's Choice Artist's Proofs-95
Special Artist's Proofs-95
Check It-9
Golden Blades-95
96Select Certified-15
Artist's Proofs-15
Blue-15
Mirror Blue-15
Mirror Gold-15
Mirror Red-15
Red-15
96SkyBox Impact-126
BladeRunners-6
96SP-152
Holoview Collection-HC3
Game Film-GF16
96SPx-45
Gold-45
Holoview Heroes-HH9
96Summit-118
Artist's Proofs-118
Ice-118
Metal-118
Premium Stock-118
96Ultra-163
Gold Medallion-163
96Upper Deck-162
Game Jerseys-GJ3
Generation Next-X10
Lord Stanley's Heroes Finals-LS11
Lord Stanley's Heroes Quarterfinals-LS11
Lord Stanley's Heroes Semifinals-LS11
Power Performers-P29
Superstar Showdown-SS4B
96Upper Deck Ice-69
Parallel-69
96Zenith-47
Artist's Proofs-47
Champion Salute-13
Champion Salute Diamond-13
97Be A Player Take A Number-7
97Beehive-47
Golden Portraits-47
97Black Diamond-70
Double Diamond-70
Triple Diamond-70
Quadruple Diamond-70
97Collector's Choice-139
Crash the Game-C13A
Crash the Game-C13B
Crash the Game-C13C
Crash the Game Exchange-CR13
Star Quest-SQ70
Stick'Ums-S24
97Crown Royale-75
Emerald Green-75
Ice Blue-75
Silver-75
97Devils Team Issue-27
97Donruss-10
Press Proofs Silver-10
Press Proofs Gold-10
Line 2 Line-7
Line 2 Line Die Cut-7
97Donruss Canadian Ice-49
Dominion Series-49
Provincial Series-49
National Pride-9
Stanley Cup Scrapbook-13
97Donruss Elite-73
Aspirations-73
Status-73
97Donruss Limited-66
97Donruss Limited-82
97Donruss Limited-155
Exposure-66
Exposure-82
Exposure-155
Fabric of the Game-19
97Donruss Preferred-69
Cut to the Chase-69
97Donruss Priority-52
Stamp of Approval-52
97Flames Collector's Photos-18
97Highland Mint Mint-Cards Topps-7
97Highland Mint Mint-Cards Topps-8
97Katch-81
Gold-81
Silver-81
97Leaf-80
Fractal Matrix-80
Fractal Matrix Die Cuts-80
97Leaf International-80
Universal Ice-80
97NHL Aces Playing Cards-3
97Pacific-93
Copper-93
Emerald Green-93
Ice Blue-93
Red-93
Silver-93
Card-Supials-11
Card-Supials Minis-11
97Pacific Dynagon-69
Copper-69
Dark Grey-69
Emerald Green-69
Ice Blue-69
Red-69
Silver-69
Tandems-41
97Pacific Invincible-77
Copper-77
Emerald Green-77
Ice Blue-77
Red-77
Silver-77
NHL Regime-113
97Pacific Omega-129
Copper-129
Dark Gray-129
Emerald Green-129
Gold-129
Ice Blue-129
Stick Handle Laser Cuts-11
97Panini Stickers-66
97Paramount-102

Copper-102
Dark Grey-102
Emerald Green-102
Ice Blue-102
Red-102
Silver-102
Big Numbers Die-Cuts-13
97Pinnacle-39
Artist's Proofs-39
Rink Collection-39
Epix Game Emerald-24
Epix Game Orange-24
Epix Game Purple-24
Epix Moment Emerald-24
Epix Moment Orange-24
Epix Moment Purple-24
Epix Play Emerald-24
Epix Play Orange-24
Epix Play Purple-24
Epix Season Emerald-24
Epix Season Orange-24
Epix Season Purple-24
Press Plates Back Black-39
Press Plates Back Cyan-39
Press Plates Back Magenta-39
Press Plates Back Yellow-39
Press Plates Front Black-39
Press Plates Front Cyan-39
Press Plates Front Magenta-39
Press Plates Front Yellow-39
Team Pinnacle-9
Team Mirror-9
Team Parallel-9
Team Parallel Mirror-9
97Pinnacle Certified-51
Red-51
Mirror Blue-51
Mirror Gold-51
Mirror Red-51
97Pinnacle Inside-73
Coach's Collection-73
Executive Collection-73
97Pinnacle Tot Cert Platinum Blue-51
97Pinnacle Tot Cert Platinum Gold-51
97Pinnacle Totally Certified Platinum Red-51
97Pinnacle Tot Cert Mirror Platinum Gold-51
97Revolution-77
Copper-77
Emerald-77
Ice Blue-77
Silver-77
97Score-93
Artist's Proofs-93
Golden Blades-93
Check It-6
97Score Devils-1
Platinum-1
Premier-1
97SP Authentic-88
97SPx-25
Bronze-25
Gold-25
Silver-25
Steel-25
Dimension-SPX5
Grand Finale-25
97Studio-93
Press Proofs Silver-93
Press Proofs Gold-93
97Upper Deck-91
97Upper Deck-198
Game Dated Moments-91
Sixth Sense Masters-SS16
Sixth Sense Wizards-SS16
Smooth Grooves-SG33
Three Star Selects-18B
97Upper Deck Ice-82
Parallel-82
Power Shift-82
97Zenith-46
Z-Gold-46
Z-Silver-46
97Zenith 5 x 7-12
Gold Impulse-12
Silver Impulse-12
98SLU Hockey Extended-65
98Be A Player-178
Press Release-178
98BAP Gold-178
98BAP Autographs-178
98BAP Autographs Gold-178
98BAP AS Milestones-M19
98BAP Playoff Highlights-H18
98Black Diamond-18
Double Diamond-18
Triple Diamond-18
Quadruple Diamond-18
Myriad-M25
Myriad 2-M25
98Blackhawks Chicago Sun-Times-3
98Bowman's Best-13
Refractors-13
Atomic Refractors-13
98Crown Royale-30
Limited Series-30
Pillars of the Game-6
98Finest-54
No Protectors-54
No Protectors Refractors-54
Refractors-54
98Kenner Starting Lineup Cards-10
98Pacific-93
Ice Blue-93
Red-93
Gold Crown Die-Cuts-20
Timelines-10
98Pacific Dynagon Ice-41
Blue-41
Red-41
Forward Thinking-4
98Pacific Omega-52
Red-52
Opening Day Issue-52
Online-7
98Panini Photocards-28
98Panini Stickers-69
98Paramount-47
Copper-47
Emerald Green-47
Holo-Electric-47
Ice Blue-47
Silver-47
98Post-22
98Revolution-31
Ice Shadow-31
Red-31
Showstoppers-9
98SP Authentic-18
Power Shift-18
Authentics-5
Snapshots-SS30

Stat Masters-S4
98SPx Finite-47
Radiance-47
Spectrum-47
98SPx Top Prospects-10
Radiance-10
Spectrum-10
Highlight Heroes-H7
Lasting Impressions-L25
98Topps Gold Label Class 1-64
Black-64
Black One of One-64
One of One-64
Red-64
Red One of One-64
98Topps Gold Label Class 2-64
98Topps Gold Label Class 2 Black-64
98Topps Gold Label Class 2 Black 1 of 1-64
98Topps Gold Label Class 2 One of One-64
98Topps Gold Label Class 2 Red-64
98Topps Gold Label Class 2 Red One of One-64
98Topps Gold Label Class 3-64
98Topps Gold Label Class 3 Black-64
98Topps Gold Label Class 3 Black 1 of 1-64
98Topps Gold Label Class 3 One of One-64
98Topps Gold Label Class 3 Red-64
98Topps Gold Label Class 3 Red One of One-64
98UD Choice-117
98UD Choice Preview-117
98UD Choice Prime Choice Reserve-117
98UD Choice Reserve-117
98UD3-50
98UD3-110
98UD3-170
Die-Cuts-50
Die-Cuts-110
Die-Cuts-170
98Upper Deck-63
Exclusives-63
Exclusives 1 of 1-63
Frozen In Time-FT16
Frozen In Time Quantum 1-FT16
Frozen In Time Quantum 2-FT16
Frozen In Time Quantum 3-FT16
Game Jerseys-GJ18
Lord Stanley's Heroes-LS7
Lord Stanley's Heroes Quantum 1-LS7
Lord Stanley's Heroes Quantum 2-LS7
Lord Stanley's Heroes Quantum 3-LS7
Profiles-P15
Profiles Quantum 1-P15
Profiles Quantum 2-P15
Profiles Quantum 3-P15
Gold Reserve-63
98Upper Deck MVP-43
Gold Script-43
Silver Script-43
Super Script-43
99Aurora-32
Striped-32
Premiere Date-32
Premiere Date Striped-32
99BAP Memorabilia-82
99BAP Memorabilia-384
Gold-82
Gold-384
Silver-82
Silver-384
AS Heritage Ruby-H11
AS Heritage Sapphire-H11
AS Heritage Emerald-H11
99Black Diamond-23
Diamond Cut-23
Final Cut-23
99Blackhawks Lineup Cards-4
99Crown Royale-33
Limited Series-33
Premiere Date-33
99O-Pee-Chee-103
99O-Pee-Chee Chrome-103
99O-Pee-Chee Chrome Refractors-103
99Pacific-89
Copper-89
Emerald Green-89
Gold-89
Ice Blue-89
Premiere Date-89
Red-89
Team Leaders-7
99Pacific Dynagon Ice-50
Blue-50
Copper-50
Gold-50
Premiere Date-50
99Pacific Omega-53
Copper-53
Gold-53
Ice Blue-53
Premiere Date-53
99Pacific Prism-34
Holographic Blue-34
Holographic Gold-34
Holographic Mirror-34
Holographic Purple-34
Premiere Date-34
99Panini Stickers-201
99Paramount-55
Copper-55
Emerald-55
Gold-55
Holographic Emerald-55
Holographic Gold-55
Holographic Silver-55
Ice Blue-55
Premiere Date-55
Red-55
Silver-55
99Revolution-34
Premiere Date-34
Red-34
Shadow Series-34
NHL Icons-4
99SP Authentic-21
99SPx-37
Radiance-37
Spectrum-37
99Stadium Club-90
First Day Issue-90
One of a Kind-90
Printing Plates Black-90
Printing Plates Cyan-90
Printing Plates Magenta-90
Printing Plates Yellow-90
99Topps/OPC-103
99Topps/OPC Chrome-103
Refractors-103
99Ultimate Victory-21
1/1-21
Parallel-21
Parallel 100-21
99Upper Deck-206

Exclusives-206
Exclusives 1 of 1-206
99Upper Deck Gold Reserve-206
99Upper Deck MVP-48
Gold Script-48
Silver Script-48
Super Script-48
99Upper Deck MVP SC Edition-44
Gold Script-44
Silver Script-44
Super Script-44
99Upper Deck Retro-18
Gold-18
Platinum-18
99Upper Deck Victory-67
99Wayne Gretzky Hockey-40
00Aurora-18
Pinstripes-18
Pinstripes Premiere Date-18
Premiere Date-18
Styrotechs-2A
00BAP Memorabilia-291
Emerald-291
Ruby-291
Sapphire-291
Promos-291
00BAP Mem Chicago Sportsfest Copper-291
00BAP Memorabilia Chicago Sportsfest Blue-291
00BAP Memorabilia Chicago Sportsfest Gold-291
00BAP Memorabilia Chicago Sportsfest Ruby-291
00BAP Memorabilia Chicago Sun-Times Ruby-291
00BAP Memorabilia Chicago Sun-Times Gold-291
00BAP Mem Chicago Sun-Times Sapphire-291
00BAP Mem Toronto Fall Expo Copper-291
00BAP Memorabilia Toronto Fall Expo Gold-291
00BAP Memorabilia Toronto Fall Expo Ruby-291
00BAP Parkhurst 2000-P183
00BAP Signature Series-1
Emerald-1
Ruby-1
Sapphire-1
Autographs-12
Autographs Gold-12
00Crown Royale-13
Ice Blue-13
Limited Series-13
Premiere Date-13
Red-13
00O-Pee-Chee-58
00O-Pee-Chee Parallel-58
00Pacific-50
Copper-50
Gold-50
Ice Blue-50
Premiere Date-50
Reflections-3
00Paramount-28
Copper-28
Gold-28
Holo-Gold-28
Holo-Silver-28
Ice Blue-28
Premiere Date-28
Freeze Frame-3
00Private Stock-11
Gold-11
Premiere Date-11
Retail-11
Silver-11
PS-2001 Action-6
00Revolution-16
Blue-16
Premiere Date-16
Red-16
NHL Icons-3
Stat Masters-22
00SP Authentic-12
00SP Game Used Tools of the Game Combos-C-GS
00Stadium Club-156
00Titanium-9
Blue-9
Gold-9
Premiere Date-9
Red-9
Retail-9
00Topps/OPC-58
Parallel-58
NHL Draft-DT1
1000 Point Club-PC6
00Topps Chrome-46
OPC Refractors-46
Refractors-46
1000 Point Club Refractors-6
00Topps Gold Label Class 1-54
Gold-54
00Topps Gold Label Class 2-54
00Topps Gold Label Class 2 Gold-54
00Topps Gold Label Class 3-54
00Topps Gold Label Class 3 Gold-54
00Topps Heritage-53
Chrome Parallel-53
00Topps Premier Plus-79
Blue Ice-79
00UD Heroes-14
00UD Pros and Prospects-11
00UD Reserve-9
00Upper Deck-20
Exclusives Tier 1-20
Exclusives Tier 2-20
Frozen in Time-FT1
00Upper Deck Legends-17
Legendary Collection Bronze-17
Legendary Collection Gold-17
Legendary Collection Silver-17
Legendary Game Jerseys-JDG
00Upper Deck MVP-24
First Stars-24
Second Stars-24
Third Stars-24
00Upper Deck Victory-29
00Upper Deck Victory-287
00Upper Deck Vintage-42
00Vanguard-12
Holographic Gold-12
Holographic Purple-12
Pacific Proofs-12
01BAP Memorabilia-317
Emerald-317
Ruby-317
Sapphire-317
Stanley Cup Playoffs-SC7
01BAP Update Heritage-H5
01Canadiens Postcards-9
01Crown Royale-75
Blue-75
Premiere Date-75
Red-75
Retail-75
01Pacific-48
Extreme LTD-48
Hobby LTD-48

Premiere Date-48
Retail LTD-48
Impact Zone-3
01Pacific Arena Exclusives-48
01Parkhurst-382
Milestones-M15
01Private Stock PS-2002-39
01Titanium-72
Hobby Parallel-72
Premiere Date-72
Retail-72
Retail Parallel-72
01Upper Deck-322
Exclusives-322
Pride of the Leafs-MLDG
01Upper Deck MVP-19
01Vanguard-49
Blue-49
Red-49
One of Ones-49
Premiere Date-49
Proofs-49
01Czech Stadion-242
02Atomic-54
Blue-54
Gold-54
Red-54
Hobby Parallel-54
02BAP First Edition-188
02BAP Memorabilia-63
02BAP Memorabilia-333
Emerald-63
Ruby-63
Sapphire-63
Mini Stanley Cups-27
NHL All-Star Game-63
NHL All-Star Game Blue-63
NHL All-Star Game Green-63
NHL All-Star Game Red-63
02BAP Memorabilia Toronto Fall Expo-63
02BAP Signature Series-146
Autographs-146
Autograph Buybacks 1998-178
Autograph Buybacks 2000-12
Autographs Gold-146
Golf-GS34
Jerseys-SGJ53
Jersey Autographs-SGJ53
Team Quads-TQ6
02BAP Ultimate Mem Lifetime Achievers-5
02Canadiens Postcards-25
02Maple Leafs Platinum Collection-30
02Maple Leafs Platinum Collection-109
02McDonald's Pacific-20
02NHL Power Play Stickers-58
02O-Pee-Chee-161
02O-Pee-Chee Premier Blue Parallel-161
02O-Pee-Chee Premier Red Parallel-161
02O-Pee-Chee Factory Set-161
02O-Pee-Chee Factory Set Hometown Heroes-HHC16
02Pacific-196
Blue-196
Red-196
02Pacific Complete-46
Red-46
02Pacific Heads-Up-63
Blue-63
Purple-63
Red-63
02Parkhurst-68
Bronze-68
Gold-68
Silver-68
02Parkhurst Retro-122
Minis-122
02Topps-161
OPC Blue Parallel-161
OPC Red Parallel-161
Topps/OPC Hometown Heroes-HHC16
Factory Set-161
02Topps Chrome-96
Black Border Refractors-96
Refractors-96
02Topps Total-62
02UD Artistic Impressions-48
Gold-48
02UD Artistic Impressions Beckett Promos-48
02UD Artistic Impressions Retrospectives-R48
02UD Artistic Impressions Retrospect Gold-R48
02UD Artistic Impressions Retrospect Silver-R48
02UD Foundations-53
02UD Top Shelf Hardware Heroes-HFYGC
02UD Top Shelf Sweet Sweaters-SWDG
02Upper Deck Rookie Update-91
03ITG Action-566
Homeboys-HB6
Jerseys-M130
03ITG Toronto Fall Expo Forever Rivals-FR2
03NHL Sticker Collection-55
03O-Pee-Chee-252
03OPC Blue-252
03OPC Gold-252
03OPC Red-252
03Pacific-317
Blue-317
Red-317
03Pacific Complete-23
Red-23
03Pacific Exhibit-136
Blue Backs-136
Yellow Backs-136
03Parkhurst Original Six Chicago-35
03Parkhurst Original Six Chicago-73
03Parkhurst Original Six Toronto-32
03Parkhurst Original Six Toronto-62
03Parkhurst Original Six Toronto-72
03Parkhurst Original Six Toronto-97
03SPx Hall Pass-HP-DG
03SPx Hall Pass Limited-HP-DG
03Topps-252
Blue-252
Gold-252
Red-252
03Upper Deck-180
Canadian Exclusives-180
HG-180
Classic Portraits Hockey Royalty-LYG
03Upper Deck MVP-397
Gold Script-397
Silver Script-397
Canadian Exclusives-397
Lethal Lineups-LL5
03Upper Deck Trilogy Authentic Patches-AP18
03Upper Deck Victory-180
Bronze-180
Gold-180
Silver-180
04ITG Franchises Canadian-11
04ITG Franchises Canadian-112
Autographs-DG2

Double Memorabilia-DM22
Double Memorabilia Gold-DM22
Memorabilia-SM30
Memorabilia Autographs-SM30
Memorabilia Gold-SM30
Original Sticks-OS14
Original Sticks Gold-OS14
Teammates-TM10
Teammates Gold-TM10
Trophy Winners-TW9
Trophy Winners Gold-TW9
04ITG Franchises US East-359
Memorabilia-ESM24
Memorabilia Gold-ESM24
04ITG Franchises US West-293
Autographs-A-DG1
04ITG Ultimate Memorabilia-89
Gold-89
Auto Threads-26
Autographs-49
Autographs Gold-49
Complete Logo-9
Complete Logo-10
Complete Logo-11
Cornerstones-7
Cornerstones Gold-7
Day In History-8
Day In History-17
Day In History Gold-8
Day In History Gold-17
Jersey Autographs-44
Jersey Autographs Gold-44
Jersey and Sticks-12
Jersey and Sticks Gold-12
Nicknames-15
Nickname Autographs-1
Original Six-4
Original Six-5
Stick Autographs-39
Stick Autographs Gold-39
Triple Threads-11
04UD Legendary Signatures-31
AKA Autographs-AKA-DG
Autographs-DG
05ITG Heroes/Prosp Toronto Expo Parallel -5
05ITG Ultimate Memorabilia Level 1-27
05ITG Ultimate Memorabilia Level 2-27
05ITG Ultimate Memorabilia Level 3-27
05ITG Ultimate Memorabilia Level 4-27
05ITG Ultimate Memorabilia Level 5-27
05ITG Ultimate Mem Complete Jersey-16
05ITG Ultimate Mem Complete Jersey Gold-16
05ITG Ultimate Mem Cornerstones Jerseys-5
05ITG Ultimate Mem Cornerst Jerseys Gold-5
05ITG Ultimate Mem Double Mem Autos-19
05ITG Ultimate Mem Double Mem Autos Gold-19
05ITG Ultimate Memorabilia Emblems-17
05ITG Ultimate Memorabilia Emblems Gold-17
05ITG Ultimate Memorabilia Jersey Autos-8
05ITG Ultimate Mem Jersey Autos Gold-8
05ITG Ultimate Memorabilia Jerseys-12
05ITG Ultimate Memorabilia Jerseys Gold-12
05ITG Ultimate Mem Pass the Torch Jerseys-19
05ITG Ultimate Mem Passing Torch Jsy Gold-19
05ITG Ultimate Mem Retro Teammate Jerseys-11
05ITG Ult Mem Retro Teammates Jersey Gold-11
05ITG Ultimate Memorabilia Stick Autos-38
05ITG Ultimate Mem Stick Autos Gold-38
05ITG Ultimate Mem 3 Star of the Game Jsy-22
05ITG Ult Mem 3 Star of the Game Jsy Gold-22
05ITG Ultimate Memorabilia Triple Autos-5
05ITG Ultimate Mem Triple Autos Gold-5
05ITG Ultimate Memorabilia Ultimate Autos-35
05ITG Ultimate Mem Ultimate Autos Gold-35
05SP Game Used Heritage Classic-HC-DG
05SP Game Used Heritage Classic Autos-HCA-DG
05SP Game Used Heritage Classic Patches-HCP-DG
05SP GameUsed Heritage Classic Patch Auto-HAP-DG
05SP Game Used Oldtimer's Challenge-OC-DG
05SP Game Used Oldtimer's Challenge Autos-OCA-DG
05SP Game Used Oldtimer's Challenge Patch-OCP-DG
05SP Game Used Oldtime Chall Patch Autoa-OAP-DG
05The Cup-96
Gold-96
Black Rainbow-96
Emblems of Endorsement-EEDG
Hardware Heroes-HHDG
Honorable Numbers-HNDG
Limited Logos-LLDG
Masterpiece Pressplates-96
Patch Variation-P96
Patch Variation Autographs-AP96
Property of-PODG
Scripted Numbers Dual-DSNGC
Scripted Swatches-SSDG
Signature Patches-SPDG
Stanley Cup Titlists-TDG
05Ultimate Collection Endorsed Emblems-EEDG
05Upper Deck Notable Numbers-N-DG
05ITG Heroes and Prospects-5
Autographs-A-DGI
Hero Memorabilia-HM-4
Hero Memorabilia Dual-HDM-7
06ITG International Ice-34
Gold-34
Autographs-ADG
06ITG Ultimate Memorabilia-42
Artist Proof-42
Autos-13
Autos Gold-13
Autos Dual-10
Autos Dual Gold-10
Blades of Steel-8
Blades of Steel Gold-8
Decades-2
Decades Gold-2
Double Memorabilia Autos-6
Double Memorabilia Autos Gold-6
Jerseys-19
Jerseys Gold-19
Jerseys Autos-20
Jerseys Autos Gold-20
Journey Emblem-12
Journey Emblem Gold-12
Journey Jersey-12
Journey Jersey Gold-12
Retro Teammates-22
Retro Teammates Gold-22
Stick Rack-9
Stick Rack Gold-9
Sticks Autos-18
Sticks Autos Gold-18
Triple Thread Jerseys-9
Triple Thread Jerseys Gold-9
06Parkhurst-16
06Parkhurst-213
06Parkhurst-222
Autographs-16
Autographs-213
Autographs-222
06SP Game Used Authentic Fabrics Sixes-AF6SEL
06SP Game Used Authentic Fabrics Sixes Patches-AF6SEL
06The Cup Autographed Foundations-CQDG
06The Cup Autographed Foundations Patches-CQDG
06The Cup Autographed NHL Shields Duals-DASGC
06The Cup Foundations-CQDG
06The Cup Foundations Patches-CQDG
06The Cup Limited Logos-LLDG
06The Cup Stanley Cup Signatures-CSDG
06UD Artifacts-114
Blue-114
Gold-114
Platinum-114
Radiance-114
Red-114
Treasured Patches Black-TSDG
Treasured Patches Blue-TSDG
Treasured Patches Gold-TSDG
Treasured Patches Platinum-TSDG
Treasured Patches Red-TSDG
Treasured Swatches-TSDG
Treasured Swatches Black-TSDG
Treasured Swatches Blue-TSDG
Treasured Swatches Gold-TSDG
Treasured Swatches Platinum-TSDG
Treasured Swatches Red-TSDG
Tundra Tandems-TTCG
Tundra Tandems Black-TTCG
Tundra Tandems Blue-TTCG
Tundra Tandems Gold-TTCG
Tundra Tandems Platinum-TTCG
Tundra Tandems Red-TTCG
Tundra Tandems Dual Patches Red-TTCG
06Ultimate Collection Premium Swatches-PS-DG
06Upper Deck Sweet Shot Signature Sticks-STDG
06Upper Deck Trilogy Honorary Scripted Patches-HSPDG
06Upper Deck Trilogy Honorary Scripted Swatches-HSSDG
06Upper Deck Trilogy Honorary Swatches-HSDG

Gilmour, HL
10Sweet Caporal Postcards-22
11C55-22
83Hall of Fame Postcards-D4
85Hall of Fame-50

Gilmour, Jake
01Belleville Bulls-9
02Belleville Bulls-6
03Belleville Bulls-13

Gimaev, Irek
80USSR Olympic Team Mini Pics-2
84Russian National Team-6

Gimaev, Sergei
02Russian Hockey League-168
03Russian Hockey League-149
03Russian Hockey League-211
04Russian World Junior Team-6

Gimayev, Sergej
83Swedish Semic VM Stickers-56

Gimblett, Jesse
01Owen Sound Attack-6
02Owen Sound Attack-10
03Saginaw Spirit-8
04Saginaw Spirit-21
05Saginaw Spirit-10

Gimblett, Tyson
01St. Michaels Majors-5
02St. Michaels Majors-4
05Saginaw Spirit-11

Gines, Matt
93Arizona Icecats-7

Gingras, Gaston
80Canadiens Postcards-6
80O-Pee-Chee-322
80Pepsi-Cola Caps-44
81Canadiens Postcards-8
81O-Pee-Chee-182
82Canadiens Postcards-7
82Maple Leafs Postcards-14
82Maple Leafs Postcards-15
82O-Pee-Chee-182
83Maple Leafs Postcards-8
83NHL Key Tags-115
83O-Pee-Chee-332
83O-Pee-Chee Stickers-40
83Topps Stickers-40
83Vachon-88
84O-Pee-Chee-303
85Canadiens Postcards-11
86Kraft Drawings-19
87Blues Kodak-12
87Blues Team Issue-10
87Canadiens Postcards-9
87O-Pee-Chee-229
87O-Pee-Chee Stickers-8
88Blues Kodak-9
88Blues Team Issue-10
88O-Pee-Chee-35
88Topps-35
89O-Pee-Chee-270
89O-Pee-Chee Stickers-21
95Fredericton Canadiens-12
02Canadiens Molson Export-29

Gingras, Maxime
92Quebec Pee-Wee Tournament-1274
98ECHL All-Star Northern Conference-19
99Houston Aeros-16
99Providence Bruins-10

Gingras, Michel
907th Inn. Sketch Memorial Cup-62

Gingras, Patrick
92Quebec Pee-Wee Tournament-627
99Jacksonville Lizard Kings-8

Gingue, Michael
93Quebec Pee-Wee Tournament-1317

Ginnell, Erin
86Regina Pats-8

Gionet, Aaron
98Kamloops Blazers-12
99Kamloops Blazers-9
00Kamloops Blazers-8
02Kamloops Blazers-18
03Pensacola Ice Pilots-345

Gionet, Erik
93Quebec Pee-Wee Tournament-1200

Gionet, Martin
93Quebec Pee-Wee Tournament-452

Gionta, Brian
93Quebec Pee-Wee Tournament-877
98UD Choice-298
Prime Choice Reserve-298
Reserve-298
01Bowman YoungStars-151
Gold-151
Ice Cubed-151
01Crown Royale-152
01SPx-180
01Titanium-167
Retail-167
01Titanium Draft Day Edition-148
01UD Top Shelf-100
01Albany River Rats-11
02BAP Signature Series-86
Autographs-86
Autographs Gold-86
02Devils Team Issue-11
02O-Pee-Chee-269
02O-Pee-Chee Premier Blue Parallel-269
02O-Pee-Chee Premier Red Parallel-269
02O-Pee-Chee Factory Set-269
02Pacific-221
Blue-221
Red-221
02Pacific Complete-52
Red-52
02SP Authentic-122
02Stadium Club Lone Star Signatures Blue-LSBG
02Stadium Club Lone Star Signatures Red-LSBG
02Topps-269
OPC Blue Parallel-269
OPC Red Parallel-269
Factory Set-269
Chrome Chromographs-CGBG
Chrome Chromograph Refractors-CGBG
02Topps Total-141
Signatures-BG
02Upper Deck-105
Exclusives-105
02Upper Deck Victory-125
Bronze-125
Gold-125
Silver-125
03Beehive-119
Gold-119
Silver-119
03Devils Team Issue-14
03ITG Action-332
03O-Pee-Chee-115
03OPC Blue-115
03OPC Gold-115
03OPC Red-115
03Pacific-199
Blue-199
Red-199
03Pacific Complete-164
Red-164
03Topps-115
Blue-115
Gold-115
Red-115
Signs of Youth-BG
03Upper Deck-360
Canadian Exclusives-360
HG-360
UD Exclusives-360
03Upper Deck MVP-256
Gold Script-256
Silver Script-256
Canadian Exclusives-256
04Pacific-157
Blue-157
Red-157
05Be A Player Signatures-GI
05Be A Player Signatures Gold-GI
05Beehive Matted Materials-MMGI
05Devils Team Issue-22
05Hot Prospects-60
En Fuego-60
Red Hot-60
White Hot-60
05Panini Stickers-88
05Parkhurst-285
Facsimile Auto Parallel-285
True Colors-TCNJD
True Colors-TCNJD
05SP Authentic-60
Limited-60
05Upper Deck-364
Jerseys Series II-J2GI
Majestic Materials-MMGI
05Upper Deck Ice-58
Rainbow-58
05Upper Deck MVP-237
Gold-237
Platinum-237
05Upper Deck Rookie Update-58
05Upper Deck Victory-228
Black-228
Gold-228
Silver-228
06Be A Player Portraits-64
06Beehive-43
Blue-43
Gold-43
Matte-43
Red Facsimile Signatures-43
Wood-43
Signature Scrapbook-SSBG
06Black Diamond-50
Black-50
Gold-50
Ruby-50
06Devils Team Set-7
06Flair Showcase Inks-IBG
06Fleer-117
Tiffany-117
06Hot Prospects-59
Red Hot-59
White Hot-59
06O-Pee-Chee-292
Rainbow-292
Autographs-A-BG
06Panini Stickers-77
06SP Authentic-45
Limited-45
Sign of the Times-STBG
Sign of the Times Duals-STEG
06SP Game Used-61
Gold-61
Rainbow-61
Authentic Fabrics-AFBG
Authentic Fabrics Parallel-AFBG
Authentic Fabrics Patches-AFBG
Authentic Fabrics Dual-AF2BG
Authentic Fabrics Dual Patches-AF2BG
Authentic Fabrics Triple-AF3NJD
Authentic Fabrics Triple Patches-AF3NJD
Authentic Fabrics Fives-AF5GWG
Authentic Fabrics Fives Patches-AF5GWG
Autographs-61
Inked Sweaters-ISBG
Inked Sweaters Patches-ISBG
Inked Sweaters Dual-IS2EG
Inked Sweaters Dual Patches-IS2EG
Letter Marks-LMBG
SIGnificance-SBG
06SPx-60
Spectrum-60
SPxcitement-X62
SPxcitement Spectrum-X62
Winning Materials-WMGI
Winning Materials Spectrum-WMGI
06The Cup Autographed NHL Shields Duals-DASGG
06The Cup Limited Logos-LLBG
06UD Artifacts-44
06UD Artifacts-181
Blue-44
Blue-181
Gold-44
Gold-181
Platinum-44
Platinum-181
Radiance-44
Radiance-181
Red-44
Red-181
Frozen Artifacts-FABG
Frozen Artifacts Black-FABG
Frozen Artifacts Blue-FABG
Frozen Artifacts Gold-FABG
Frozen Artifacts Platinum-FABG
Frozen Artifacts Red-FABG
Frozen Artifacts Patches Black-FABG
Frozen Artifacts Patches Blue-FABG
Frozen Artifacts Patches Gold-FABG
Frozen Artifacts Patches Platinum-FABG
Frozen Artifacts Patches Red-FABG
Tundra Tandems-TTGG
Tundra Tandems Black-TTGG
Tundra Tandems Blue-TTGG
Tundra Tandems Gold-TTGG
Tundra Tandems Platinum-TTGG
Tundra Tandems Red-TTGG
Tundra Tandems Dual Patches Red-TTGG
06UD Powerplay-61
Impact Rainbow-61
06Ultra-118
Gold Medallion-118
Ice Medallion-118
06Upper Deck Arena Giveaways-NJD2
06Upper Deck-115
Exclusives Parallel-115
High Gloss Parallel-115
Game Jerseys-J2BG
Game Patches-P2BG
Masterpieces-115
Shootout Artists-SA11
06Upper Deck MVP-172
Gold Script-172
Super Script-172
Autographs-OAEG
06Upper Deck Ovation-29
06Upper Deck Sweet Shot-62
Signature Shots/Saves-SSBG
Signature Shots/Saves Sticks-SSSBG
Sweet Stitches-SSBG
Sweet Stitches Duals-SSBG
Sweet Stitches Triples-SSBG
06Upper Deck Trilogy-60
Honorary Scripted Patches-HSPBG
Honorary Scripted Swatches-HSSBG
06Upper Deck Victory-117
06Upper Deck Victory Black-117
06Upper Deck Victory Gold-117
07Upper Deck Victory-5
Black-5
Gold-5
Stars on Ice-SI10

Giordano, Mark
02Owen Sound Attack-5
03Owen Sound Attack-6
04Lowell Lock Monsters-9
04Lowell Lock Monsters Photo Album-9
05Hot Prospects-111
En Fuego-111
Red Hot-111
White Hot-111
05SP Authentic-255
Limited-255
05The Cup Masterpiece Pressplate Artifact-254
05The Cup Masterpiece Pressplates (Ice)-266
05The Cup Master Pressplate Rookie Update-112
05The Cup Masterpiece Pressplates SPA-255
05The Cup Masterpiece Pressplates Trilogy-232
05UD Artifacts-254
05Upper Deck Ice-266
05Upper Deck Rookie Update-112
05Upper Deck Trilogy-232
06ITG Heroes and Prospects-49
Autographs-AMGI

Giove, Patrick
99Swiss Panini Stickers-328

Gippo, Kiva
93Arizona Icecats-11
94Arizona Icecats-13

Girard, Bob
76O-Pee-Chee NHL-362
77O-Pee-Chee NHL-255
78O-Pee-Chee-339

Girard, Brett
97Brandon Wheat Kings-7
98Brandon Wheat Kings-5
99Brandon Wheat Kings-8
00Brandon Wheat Kings-10

Girard, Dany
917th Inn. Sketch QMJHL-78

Girard, Frederic
92Quebec Pee-Wee Tournament-780
93Quebec Pee-Wee Tournament-1046
96Rimouski Oceanic-11
96Rimouski Oceanic Quebec Police-11

Girard, Ian
03Quebec Remparts-9
04Quebec Remparts-8
05Moncton Wildcats-21

Girard, Jonathan
93Quebec Pee-Wee Tournament-903
94Quebec Pee-Wee Tournament-617
97Upper Deck-403
98Upper Deck-222
Exclusives-222
Exclusives 1 of 1-222
Gold Reserve-222
98Bowman CHL-97
98Bowman CHL-135
Golden Anniversary-97
Golden Anniversary-135
OPC International-97
OPC International-135
Autographs Blue-A30
Autographs Gold-A30
Autographs Silver-A30
Scout's Choice-SC13
98Bowman Chrome CHL-97
98Bowman Chrome CHL-135
Golden Anniversary-97
Golden Anniversary-135
Golden Anniversary Refractors-97
Golden Anniversary Refractors-135
OPC International-97
OPC International-135
OPC International Refractors-97
OPC International Refractors-135
Refractors-97
Refractors-135
99BAP Memorabilia-156
Gold-156
Silver-156
99BAP Millennium-28
Emerald-28
Ruby-28
Sapphire-28
Signatures-28
Signatures Gold-28
Calder Candidates Ruby-C46
Calder Candidates Emerald-C46
Calder Candidates Sapphire-C46
99Pacific-32
Copper-32
Emerald Green-32
Gold-32
Ice Blue-32
Premiere Date-32
Red-32
99Paramount-20
99Paramount-252
Copper-20
Emerald-20
Gold-20
Holographic Emerald-20
Holographic Gold-20
Holographic Silver-20
Ice Blue-20
Premiere Date-20
Red-20
Silver-20
99SPx-14
Radiance-14
Spectrum-14
99Topps Arena Giveaways-BOS-JG
99Upper Deck-19
Exclusives-19
Exclusives 1 of 1-19
99Upper Deck Arena Giveaways-BB1
99Upper Deck Gold Reserve-19
99Upper Deck MVP-19
Gold Script-19
Silver Script-19
Super Script-19
99Upper Deck Victory-26
99Quebec PeeWee Tournament Coll Souv-30
99Bowman CHL-47
Gold-47
OPC International-47
00BAP Memorabilia-177
Emerald-177
Ruby-177
Sapphire-177
Promos-177
00BAP Mem Chicago Sportsfest Copper-177
00BAP Memorabilia Chicago Sportsfest Blue-177
00BAP Memorabilia Chicago Sportsfest Gold-177
00BAP Memorabilia Chicago Sportsfest Ruby-177
00BAP Memorabilia Chicago Sun-Times Ruby-177
00BAP Memorabilia Chicago Sun-Times Gold-177
00BAP Mem Chicago Sun-Times Sapphire-177
00BAP Mem Toronto Fall Expo Copper-177
00BAP Memorabilia Toronto Fall Expo Gold-177
00BAP Memorabilia Toronto Fall Expo Ruby-177
00O-Pee-Chee-325
00O-Pee-Chee Parallel-325
00Topps/OPC-325
Parallel-325
00Topps Chrome-220
OPC Refractors-220
Refractors-220
00Providence Bruins-20
01BAP Memorabilia-191
Emerald-191
Ruby-191
Sapphire-191
01Parkhurst-135
01Upper Deck-16
Exclusives-16
01Upper Deck MVP-16
01Providence Bruins-21
02BAP Sig Series Auto Buybacks 1999-28
02Pacific Complete-417
Red-417
02Upper Deck-259
Exclusives-259
02Upper Deck Beckett UD Promos-259
03ITG Action-47
03Parkhurst Original Six Boston-10
03Upper Deck MVP-39
Gold Script-39
Silver Script-39
Canadian Exclusives-39

Girard, Ken
57Parkhurst-T18
94Parkhurst Missing Link-132

Girard, Luc
98Val d'Or Foreurs-16
00Val d'Or Foreurs-5
Signed-5

Girard, Patrick
93Quebec Pee-Wee Tournament-66
00Swiss Panini Stickers-295

Girard, Rick
917th Inn. Sketch WHL-176
93Donruss Team Canada-14
93Pinnacle-475
Canadian-475
93Upper Deck-539
94Classic Tri-Cards-T70
96Syracuse Crunch-37
98German DEL-274
99German DEL-213
00German DEL-172
01German Upper Deck-81
02German DEL City Press-76
03German DEL-24
04German Augsburg Panthers Postcards-15
04German DEL-30
05German DEL-5

Girard, Roland
51Laval Dairy Lac St. Jean-43

Girard, Stephane
93Quebec Pee-Wee Tournament-1344

Girardi, Daniel
01Barrie Colts-16
02Barrie Colts-17
03Guelph Storm-4
04Guelph Storm-5
05Hartford Wolf Pack-7
06AHL Top Prospects-15
06Hartford Wolf Pack-9
06ITG Heroes and Prospects Jerseys-GUJ04
06ITG Heroes and Prospects Jerseys Gold-GUJ04
06ITG Heroes and Prospects Emblems-GUE04
06ITG Heroes and Prospects Emblems Gold-GUE04
06ITG Heroes and Prospects Numbers-GUN04
06ITG Heroes and Prospects Numbers Gold-GUN04
07Upper Deck Victory-203
Black-203
Gold-203

Girgan, Kyle
92Saskatchewan JHL-128

Girhiny, Richard
907th Inn. Sketch OHL-259
93Birmingham Bulls Birmingham News-21
95Muskegon Fury-5
98Odessa Jackalopes-4
99Odessa Jackalopes-11

Girling, Matt
04South Surrey Eagles-8
04Surrey Eagles-6
04Surrey Eagles-6

Girouard, Gilbert
51Bas Du Fleuve-14

Girouard, Guy
92Oklahoma City Blazers-6
93Oklahoma City Blazers-5

Girouard, Pierre Olivier
02Drummondville Voltigeurs-23
03OCN Blizzard-5

Giroud, Patrick
01Swiss HNL-374
01Swiss HNL-471

Giroux, Alexandre
95Quebec Pee-Wee Tournament-1153
99O-Pee-Chee-253
99O-Pee-Chee Chrome-253
99O-Pee-Chee Chrome Refractors-253
99Topps/OPC-253
99Topps/OPC Chrome-253
Refractors-253
99Hull Olympiques-7
Signed-7
99Bowman CHL-12
Gold-12
OPC International-12
Autographs-BA32
Autographs Gold-BA32
Autographs Silver-BA32
01Grand Rapids Griffins-5
03Binghamton Senators-5
03Binghamton Senators Postcards-9
03Pacific AHL Prospects-6
Gold-6
04Hartford Wolf Pack-5
04ITG Heroes and Prospects-36
Autographs-AG
04ITG Heroes/Prospects Toronto Expo '05-36
04ITG Heroes/Prospects Expo Heroes/Pros-36
05Hartford Wolf Pack-8
06Binghamton Senators 5th Anniversary-8

Giroux, Claude
05ITG Heroes/Prosp Toronto Expo Parallel -413
05Gatineau Olympiques-7
05ITG Heroes and Prospects-413
Team Orr-TO10
06Gatineau Olympiques-13
06ITG Heroes and Prospects-113
Autographs-ACGR
CHL Top Prospects-TP02
CHL Top Prospects Gold-TP02
Class of 2006-CL13
Complete CHL Logos-CHL02

Giroux, Larry
73Blues White Border-7
74NHL Action Stamps-242
75O-Pee-Chee NHL-273
75Topps-273
78Blues Postcards-12

Giroux, Ray
99BAP Memorabilia-333
Gold-333
Silver-333
99Lowell Lock Monsters-1
00O-Pee-Chee-306
00O-Pee-Chee Parallel-306
00Topps/OPC-306
Parallel-306
00Topps Chrome-201
OPC Refractors-201
Refractors-201
00Finnish Cardset-134
02Albany River Rats-19
02Albany River Rats AAP-11
03Albany River Rats-12
03Albany River Rats Kinko's-11
04Houston Aeros-8
05Russian Hockey League RHL-35

Giroux, Rejean
72Nordiques Postcards-10
73Nordiques Team Issue-11

Girvitch, Sandis
98San Angelo Outlaws-9
99San Angelo Outlaws-4

Gislimberti, Davide
96Swiss HNL-153
01Swiss HNL-462
02Swiss HNL-22

Giudice, Gerome
05Sudbury Wolves-21
06Sudbury Wolves-6

Giuliano, Jeff
93Quebec Pee-Wee Tournament-754
02Manchester Monarchs-21
02Reading Royals-16
02Reading Royals RBI Sports-174
03Manchester Monarchs-4
03Manchester Monarchs Team Issue-5
04Manchester Monarchs-11
05Hot Prospects-138
En Fuego-138
Red Hot-138
White Hot-138
05SP Authentic-228
Limited-228
05The Cup Masterpiece Pressplates (Ice)-197
05The Cup Master Pressplate Rookie Update-142
05The Cup Masterpiece Pressplates SPA-228
05Upper Deck Ice-197
05Upper Deck Rookie Update-142
05Manchester Monarchs-5
05Manchester Monarchs-32
06Manchester Monarchs-8

Given, Jason
91British Columbia JHL-103
92British Columbia JHL-122
99Columbus Cottonmouths-7

Gizhatullin, Ilnur
98Russian Hockey League-106
99Russian Hockey League-77
00Russian Hockey League-40

Gjermundsen, Pal
92Norwegian Elite Series-55

Gjertsen, Orjan
92Norwegian Elite Series-239

Glad, Jarkko
92Finnish Jyvas-Hyva Stickers-48
93Finnish SISU-118
94Finnish SISU-231
95Finnish SISU-275
98Finnish Kerailysarja-127
99Finnish Cardset-68
00Finnish Cardset-47
01Finnish Cardset-63
02Finnish Cardset-165
03Finnish Cardset-173
05Finnish Cardset -294
06Finnish Cardset-123

Gladney, Bob
78Saginaw Gears-7

Gladney, Jason
917th Inn. Sketch OHL-92
93Kitchener Rangers-1
93Kitchener Rangers-19
95Toledo Storm-15
96Toledo Storm-23
97Toledo Storm-20

Gladskikh, Evgeni
03Russian Metallurg Magnitogorsk-3

Gladu, Fernand
52Bas Du Fleuve-3

Gladu, Jean
43Parade Sportive *-46
43Parade Sportive *-47

Gladu, Patrick
95Toledo Storm-7

Gladu, Paul
51Cleveland Barons-19

Gladue, Gary
00Prince George Cougars-6
02Calgary Hitmen-3
04Spokane Chiefs Magnets-1

Gladwish, Brad
93Quebec Pee-Wee Tournament-569

Glanzmann, Patrick
93Swiss HNL-200
95Swiss HNL-202
96Swiss HNL-91

Glaser, Marvin
94German First League-566

Glasgow, Jeremy
93Quebec Pee-Wee Tournament-1149

Glass, Frank
10C56-5
10Sweet Caporal Postcards-34
11C55-34
12C57-21

Glass, Jeff
03Kootenay Ice-2
04Kootenay Ice-11
04ITG Heroes and Prospects-80
Autographs-JG
04ITG Heroes/Prospects Toronto Expo '05-80
04ITG Heroes/Prospects Expo Heroes/Pros-80
05ITG Heroes/Prosp Toronto Expo Parallel -387
05Binghamton Senators-20
05Binghamton Senators Quickway-20
05ITG Heroes and Prospects-387
Autographs Update-A-JGL
06Between The Pipes-20
06Between The Pipes-123
Aspiring-AS09
Aspiring Gold-AS09
Autographs-AJG
Autographs-AJG2
Emblems-GUE06
Emblems Gold-GUE06
Emblems Autographs-GUE06
Jerseys-GUJ06
Jerseys Gold-GUJ06
Jerseys Autographs-GUJ06
Numbers-GUN06
Numbers Gold-GUN06
Numbers Autographs-GUN06
Prospect Trios-PT03
Prospect Trios Gold-PT03
The Mask-M35
The Mask Gold-M35
The Mask Silver-M35
06ITG International Ice-124
Gold-124
Autographs-AJG
06ITG Ultimate Memorabilia Future Star Autos-10
06ITG Ultimate Memorabilia Future Star Autos Gold-10
06ITG Ultimate Memorabilia Future Star Patches Autos-10
06ITG Ultimate Memorabilia Future Star Patches Autos Gold-10
06Binghamton Senators-7
06Binghamton Senators 5th Anniversary-9

Glass, Trevor
04Medicine Hat Tigers-8
05Medicine Hat Tigers-11
06Medicine Hat Tigers-7

Glasser, Melissa
04Ohio State Buckeyes Women-1

Glassman, Rodney
92Quebec Pee-Wee Tournament-1175
97Arizona Icecats-10
98Arizona Icecats-7

Glattenbacher, Walter
94German First League-367

Glaude, Eric
02Val d'Or Foreurs-1

Glaude, Gerard
51Laval Dairy QSHL-32

Glaude, Jean-Philippe
01Drummondville Voltigeurs-4

Glavota, John
02Muskegon Fury-8
03Rockford Ice Hogs-6
04Tulsa Oilers-9
05Port Huron Flags-12

Glazachev, Konstantin
02Russian Future Stars-4
03Russian Hockey League-168
03Russian Under-18 Team-21

Glazov, Sergei
73Swedish Stickers-106

Gleason, Jay
93Quebec Pee-Wee Tournament-686

Gleason, Tim
96Quebec Pee-Wee Tournament-668
00UD CHL Prospects-29
00UD CHL Prospects-93
01BAP Memorabilia Draft Redemptions-23
02Windsor Spitfires-7
03BAP Memorabilia-187
Emerald-187
Gold-187
Ruby-187
Sapphire-187
Super Rookies-SR12
Super Rookies Gold-SR12
Super Rookies Silver-SR12
03BAP Ultimate Memorabilia Autographs-119
Gold-119
03BAP Ultimate Mem Auto Jerseys-119
03BAP Ultimate Mem Auto Emblems-119
03BAP Ultimate Mem Auto Numbers-119
03BAP Ultimate Mem Rookie Jersey Emblems-3
03BAP Ultimate Mem Rookie Jsy Emblem Gold-3
03BAP Ultimate Mem Rookie Jersey Numbers-3
03BAP Ultimate Mem Rookie Jsy Number Gold-3
03Black Diamond-165
Black-165
Green-165
Red-165
03Bowman-131
Gold-131
03Bowman Chrome-131
Refractors-131
Gold Refractors-131
Xfractors-131
03Crown Royale-120
Red-120
Retail-120
03ITG Action-628
03ITG Used Signature Series-129
Autographs Gold-129
03ITG VIP Rookie Debut-21
03Pacific Complete-598
Red-598
03Pacific Invincible-113
Blue-113
Red-113
Retail-113
03Pacific Supreme-120
Blue-120
Red-120
Retail-120
03Parkhurst Toronto Expo Rookie Preview-PRP-11
03Parkhurst Rookie-179
Road to the NHL-RNJ-13
Road to the NHL Gold-RTN-13
Road to the NHL Emblems-RTNE-13
Road to the NHL Emblems Gold-RTNE-13
Rookie Emblems-RE-7
Rookie Emblems Gold-RE-7
Rookie Jerseys-RJ-7
Rookie Jerseys Gold-RJ-7
Rookie Numbers-RN-7
Rookie Numbers Gold-RN-7
03Private Stock Reserve-121
Blue-121
Red-121
Retail-121
03SP Authentic-114
Limited-114
03SP Game Used-63
Gold-63
03SPx-192
Radiance-192
Spectrum-192
03Titanium-121
Hobby Jersey Number Parallels-121
Retail-121
Retail Jersey Number Parallels-121
03Topps Traded-TT112
Blue-TT112
Gold-TT112
Red-TT112
03UD Honor Roll-189
03Upper Deck-220
Canadian Exclusives-220
HG-220
03Upper Deck Ice-115
Glass Parallel-115
03Upper Deck MVP-448
03Upper Deck Trilogy-152
Limited-152
04Manchester Monarchs-21
04Manchester Monarchs Tobacco-21
05ITG Heroes/Prosp Toronto Expo Parallel -228
05Parkhurst Signatures-TG
05SP Authentic Sign of the Times-TG
05SP Game Used Auto Draft-AD-TG
05Upper Deck-340
Notable Numbers-N-TG
05Manchester Monarchs-33
05ITG Heroes and Prospects-228
Autographs Series II-TG
06Hurricanes Postcards-10
06O-Pee-Chee-104
Rainbow-104
06Ultra-Fresh Ink-ITG
06Upper Deck-290
Exclusives Parallel-290
High Gloss Parallel-290
Masterpieces-290
06ITG Heroes and Prospects Making The Bigs-MTB02
06ITG Heroes and Prospects Making The Bigs Gold-MTB02

Gleason, Todd
907th Inn. Sketch OHL-208
917th Inn. Sketch OHL-339

Gleason, Trent
89Windsor Spitfires-5
907th Inn. Sketch OHL-106
95Central Hockey League-25

Gleason, Troy
907th Inn. Sketch OHL-107

Glebov, Andrei
99Russian Hockey League-82

Glebov, Oleg
99Russian Hockey League-220
00Russian Hockey League-43
02Russian Ultimate Line-8

Gleed, Jon
06Hamilton Bulldogs-11

Glencross, Curtis
04Cincinnati Mighty Ducks-20
05Portland Pirates-8
06Portland Pirates-9

Glendenning, Al
95Kamloops Blazers-12

Glennie, Brian
69Maple Leafs White Border Glossy-13
69Maple Leafs White Border Glossy-14
69Maple Leafs White Border Matte-1
70Esso Power Players-34
70O-Pee-Chee-216
70Sargent Promotions Stamps-196
71Maple Leafs Postcards-5

71O-Pee-Chee-197
71Toronto Sun-258
72Maple Leafs Postcards-7
72Maple Leafs Postcards-8
72O-Pee-Chee-216
72Sargent Promotions Stamps-205
72Topps-37
73Mac's Milk-8
73Maple Leafs Postcards-7
73O-Pee-Chee-170
73Topps-163
74Maple Leafs Postcards-8
74NHL Action Stamps-267
74O-Pee-Chee NHL-310
75Maple Leafs Postcards-8
75O-Pee-Chee NHL-365
76Maple Leafs Postcards-7
76O-Pee-Chee NHL-99
76Topps-99
77Coca-Cola-9
77Maple Leafs Postcards-5
77O-Pee-Chee NHL-275
78O-Pee-Chee-345
79O-Pee-Chee-341
91Future Trends Canada '72-88
91Future Trends Canada '72 French-88

Glennie, Donnie
06Chilliwack Bruins-13

Glennon, Matt
91Johnstown Chiefs-17
91ProCards-58
98Bruins Alumni-23
Autographs-23

Glickman, Jason
87Hull Olympiques-8
89Regina Pats-5

Glines, Matt
92Arizona Icecats-14

Gliniany, Tony
02Topeka Scarecrows-3

Globke, Jon
04Sioux Falls Stampede-4-3

Globke, Rob
96Quebec Pee-Wee Tournament-531
01Notre Dame Fighting Irish-5
02Notre Dame Fighting Irish-14
03Notre Dame Fighting Irish-8
04San Antonio Rampage-13
05Black Diamond-245
05Hot Prospects-135
En Fuego-135
Red Hot-135
White Hot-135
05Parkhurst-632
Facsimile Auto Parallel-632
05SP Authentic-262
05SP Game Used-213
05SPx-262
05The Cup Master Pressplate Black Diamond-245
05The Cup Masterpiece Pressplates (Ice)-248
05The Cup Master Pressplate Rookie Update-136
05The Cup Masterpiece Pressplates SPA-262
05The Cup Masterpiece Pressplates SP GU-213
05The Cup Masterpiece Pressplates (SPx)-262
05The Cup Masterpiece Pressplates Trilogy-261
05The Cup Masterpiece Pressplate Ult Coll-208
05Ultimate Collection-208
Gold-208
05Upper Deck Ice-248
05Upper Deck Rookie Update-136
05Upper Deck Trilogy-261
06Rochester Americans-6

Globke, Ryan
05SP Authentic-262
Limited-262
05Upper Deck Ice-248

Glode, Kevin
01Moncton Wildcats-14
02Moncton Wildcats-12
03Moncton Wildcats-11
04Moncton Wildcats-5

Gloor, Kevin
01Swiss EV Zug Postcards-12
02Swiss HNL-421

Glovatskin, Vadim
98Russian Hockey League-15
99Russian Hockey League-5
99Russian Metallurg Magnetogorsk-28
00Russian Hockey League-260
02Russian Hockey League-259

Glover, Chris
83Brantford Alexanders-21

Glover, Donny
05Danbury Trashers-2

Glover, Fred
44Beehive Group II Photos-170
51Parkhurst-60
52Parkhurst-40
60Cleveland Barons-6

Glover, Howie
44Beehive Group II Photos-171
44Beehive Group II Photos-315
60Shirriff Coins-57
61Parkhurst-19
61Shirriff/Salada Coins-65
62Parkhurst-28

Glover, Jason
95Neepewa Natives-22
96Flint Generals-8
97Flint Generals-6
97Flint Generals EBK-16
98Flint Generals-20
00UK Sekonda Superleague-103

Glover, Mike
87Sault Ste. Marie Greyhounds-3
88ProCards AHL-82
99OCN Blizzard-13

Glover, Shane
02Muskegon Fury-9

Glover, Willy
00Prince George Cougars-20
01Saskatoon Blades-4

Glowa, Jeff
02Bossier-Shreveport Mudbugs-10
05UK Hull Stingrays-9

Glowa, Kelly
82Brandon Wheat Kings-11
93Swiss HNL-329
95Swiss HNL-358
01Swiss HNL-433

Glumac, Daniel
93Quebec Pee-Wee Tournament-1791

Glumac, Mike
02ECHL All-Star Southern-42
02Pee Dee Pride RBI-136
03Worcester Ice Cats-14
04AHL Top Prospects-59
04Worcester IceCats-10
04ITG Heroes and Prospects-39
Autographs-MGL
04ITG Heroes/Prospects Toronto Expo '05-39
04ITG Heroes/Prospects Expo Heroes/Pros-39
05ITG Heroes/Prosp Toronto Expo Parallel -250
05Hot Prospects-169
En Fuego-169
Red Hot-169
White Hot-169
05SP Authentic-280
Limited-280
05The Cup Masterpiece Pressplates (Ice)-263
05The Cup Master Pressplate Rookie Update-178
05The Cup Masterpiece Pressplates SPA-280
05Upper Deck Ice-263
05Upper Deck Rookie Update-178
05AHL Top Prospects-17
05Peoria Rivermen-11
05ITG Heroes and Prospects-250
Autographs Series II-MGL
06Peoria Rivermen-5
06ITG Heroes and Prospects Making The Bigs-MTB05
06ITG Heroes and Prospects Making The Bigs Gold-MTB05

Glynn, Brian
86Saskatoon Blades Photos-9
87Flames Red Rooster-7
88Flames Postcards-5
89ProCards IHL-191
91Bowman-132
91O-Pee-Chee-506
91Panini Stickers-114
91Pro Set-406
French-406
91Score Canadian Bilingual-446
91Score Canadian English-446
91Stadium Club-388
91Topps-506
91Upper Deck-158
French-158
92Bowman-379
92Oilers IGA-8
92Oilers Team Issue-6
92Parkhurst-287
Emerald Ice-287
92Pinnacle-136
French-136
92Score-361
Canadian-361
92Stadium Club-472
92Topps-198
Gold-198G
92Ultra-58
92Upper Deck-64
93Donruss-236
93Parkhurst-141
Emerald Ice-141
93PowerPlay-399
93Senators Kraft Sheets-9
93Upper Deck-458
94Canucks Program Inserts-10
95Whalers Bob's Stores-9

Gmeinder, Herbert
94German First League-278

Gmeiner, Markus
94German First League-104

Gobbi, John
99Swiss Panini Stickers-9
01Swiss HNL-218
02Swiss HNL-182

Gobel, Eric
84Richelieu Riverains-7

Gobel, Tom
94German First League-288
95German DEL-337

Gober, Mike
88ProCards AHL-5
89ProCards AHL-313
90ProCards AHL/IHL-312
91Knoxville Cherokees-6

Goc, Marcel
97Quebec Pee-Wee Tournament-1384
99German DEL-199
00German DEL-214
01BAP Memorabilia Draft Redemptions-20
01German Upper Deck-269
02German DEL City Press-239
03Cleveland Barons-9
03Pacific AHL Prospects-20
Gold-20
04Pacific-297
Blue-297
Red-297
04SP Authentic-96
04Ultimate Collection-48
04AHL Top Prospects-11
04Cleveland Barons-10
04ITG Heroes and Prospects-25
Autographs-MC
04ITG Heroes/Prospects Toronto Expo '05-25
04ITG Heroes/Prospects Expo Heroes/Pros-25
05Parkhurst-411
Facsimile Auto Parallel-411
05Upper Deck-406
Notable Numbers-N-MGO
05Upper Deck MVP-328
Gold-328
Platinum-328
05German DEL-372
06O-Pee-Chee-409
Rainbow-409
06Upper Deck-164
Exclusives Parallel-164
High Gloss Parallel-164
Masterpieces-164

Goc, Sascha
92Quebec Pee-Wee Tournament-1688
93Quebec Pee-Wee Tournament-1775
96German DEL-294
98Albany River Rats-8
99Albany River Rats-12
99Quebec PeeWee Tournament Coll Souv-15
00BAP Memorabilia-472
Emerald-472
Ruby-472
Sapphire-472
00Devils Team Issue-7
00SP Authentic-150
00Titanium Draft Day Edition-166
00Titanium Draft Day Promos-166
00Topps Premier Plus-138
Blue Ice-138
00Topps Stars-110
Blue-110
00Albany River Rats-9
01BAP Signature Series-225
Autographs-225
Autographs Gold-225
01Parkhurst-277
01Parkhurst Beckett Promos-277
02BAP Sig Series Auto Buybacks 2001-225
02German Adler Mannheim Eagles Postcards-13
02German DEL City Press-238
03German DEL-3
03German Mannheim Eagles Postcards-24
04German Adler Mannheim Eagles Postcards-13
04German DEL-8
05German DEL-125
06German DEL-89
06German DEL-185

Goclowski, Eric
00Connecticut Huskies-6

Godard, Chris
92British Columbia JHL-207

Godard, Eric
99Lethbridge Hurricanes-10
00Louisville Panthers-20
01SPx Rookie Redemption-R19
02BAP Memorabilia-374
02BAP Ultimate Memorabilia-42
02ITG Used-199
02Pacific Calder-131
Silver-131
02Pacific Complete-567
Red-567
02Pacific Quest for the Cup-131
Gold-131
02Parkhurst-249
Bronze-249
Gold-249
Silver-249
02SP Authentic-152
02Topps Chrome-152
Black Border Refractors-152
Refractors-152
02Topps Total-433
02UD Artistic Impressions-111
Gold-111
02UD Honor Roll-121
02UD Mask Collection-137
02UD Top Shelf-97
02Upper Deck-442
Exclusives-442
03Beehive-121
Gold-121
Silver-121
03Upper Deck-123
Canadian Exclusives-123
HG-123
03Upper Deck MVP-275
Gold Script-275
Silver Script-275
Canadian Exclusives-275
05Parkhurst-308

Godbout, Brent
93Minnesota Golden Gophers-11
94Minnesota Golden Gophers-13
96Minnesota Golden Gophers-11

Godbout, Daniel
917th Inn. Sketch OHL-102
94Kitchener Rangers-4

Godbout, Jason
94Minnesota Golden Gophers-14
95Minnesota Golden Gophers-13
96Minnesota Golden Gophers-12
97Minnesota Golden Gophers-15

Godden, Ernie
92Windsor Spitfires-15

Godfrey, Josh
04Guelph Storm-6
05Guelph Storm-A-01

Godfrey, Warren
44Beehive Group II Photos-26A
44Beehive Group II Photos-26B
44Beehive Group II Photos-26C
44Beehive Group II Photos-172
52Parkhurst-85
53Parkhurst-95
54Parkhurst-56
54Topps-50
57Topps-41
58Topps-58
59Topps-27
60Parkhurst-30
60Shirriff Coins-49
61Parkhurst-30
61Shirriff/Salada Coins-62
62Parkhurst-36
62Topps-4
Hockey Bucks-6
64Beehive Group III Photos-9
64Beehive Group III Photos-71
65Coca-Cola-38
93Parkhurst Parkie Reprints-PR54
94Parkhurst Missing Link-51
94Parkhurst Tall Boys-63

Godynyuk, Alexander
91Pro Set Platinum-251
91Maple Leafs PLAY-15
91O-Pee-Chee-471
91Parkhurst-248
91Pinnacle-318
French-318
91Pro Set-563
French-563
91Score American-391
91Score Canadian Bilingual-281
91Score Canadian English-281
91Topps-471
91Upper Deck-466
91Upper Deck-609
French-466
French-609
Euro-Stars-16
Euro-Stars French-16
92Flames IGA-18
92O-Pee-Chee-10
92Stadium Club-88
92Topps-256
Gold-256G
93Donruss-135
93Donruss-438
93OPC Premier-289
Gold-289
93Parkhurst-74
Emerald Ice-74
93Stadium Club-268
Members Only Master Set-268
First Day Issue-268
93Topps/OPC Premier-289
Gold-289
93Ultra-325
93Upper Deck-469
93Whalers Coke-5
94Be A Player Signature Cards-67
94Donruss-202
94Flair-72
94Leaf-29
94Parkhurst-100
Gold-100
94Pinnacle-286
Artist's Proofs-286
Rink Collection-286
94Ultra-89
94Upper Deck-188
Electric Ice-188
96Be A Player-83
Autographs-83
Autographs Silver-83
96Whalers Kid's Club-9
97Panini Stickers-26
98Swiss Power Play Stickers-31
99German DEL-53
00German Berlin Polar Bears Postcards-7
00German DEL-61

Goebel, Bryce
91Saskatoon Blades-6
917th Inn. Sketch WHL-104

Goebel, Tommy
06Ohio State Buckeyes-8

Goegan, Grant
82Swedish Semic VM Stickers-141
83Swedish Semic VM Stickers-141

Goegan, Pete
44Beehive Group II Photos-173
58Topps-47
59Topps-4
60Parkhurst-34
60Shirriff Coins-50
61Parkhurst-23
61Shirriff/Salada Coins-75
63Parkhurst-43
63York White Backs-53
64Beehive Group III Photos-72
94Parkhurst Tall Boys-61
95Parkhurst '66-67-54
Coins-54

Goehring, Karl
02Syracuse Crunch-1
02Syracuse Crunch Sheets-18
03Syracuse Crunch-1
04Syracuse Crunch-2
06O-Pee-Chee-596
Rainbow-596
06The Cup Masterpiece Pressplates (Marquee Rookies)-596
06Milwaukee Admirals -4

Goeldner, Roman
04German Weiden Blue Devils-5

Goepfert, Bobby
05St. Cloud State Huskies-1
05St. Cloud State Huskies-11

Goeppert, Bobby
96Quebec Pee-Wee Tournament-23
97Quebec Pee-Wee Tournament-835

Goerlitz, Markus
95German DEL-303

Goertz, Dave
81Regina Pats-6
82Regina Pats-9
83Regina Pats-4
84Prince Albert Raiders Stickers-8
88ProCards IHL-50
89ProCards IHL-147
90ProCards AHL/IHL-377

Goertzen, Steven
04Syracuse Crunch-11
05Hot Prospects-121
En Fuego-121
Red Hot-121
White Hot-121
05SP Authentic-225
Limited-225
05SP Game Used-176
Gold-176
05SPx-208
Spectrum-208
05The Cup Masterpiece Pressplate Artifact-268
05The Cup Masterpiece Pressplates (Ice)-192
05The Cup Master Pressplate Rookie Update-124
05The Cup Masterpiece Pressplates SPA-225
05The Cup Masterpiece Pressplates SP GU-176
05The Cup Masterpiece Pressplates (SPx)-208
05The Cup Masterpiece Pressplates Trilogy-247
05The Cup Masterpiece Pressplate Ult Coll-143
05UD Artifacts-268
05Ultimate Collection-143
Gold-143
05Upper Deck Ice-192
05Upper Deck Rookie Update-124
05Upper Deck Trilogy-247
05Syracuse Crunch-9
06Syracuse Crunch-11

Goetz, Arnaud
93Quebec Pee-Wee Tournament-1484

Goetz, Ken
03Peoria Rivermen-13
04Memphis RiverKings-11

Goetzinger, Jeremy
96Prince Albert Raiders-6
97Prince Albert Raiders-7
98Prince Albert Raiders-8
00Medicine Hat Tigers-9
03Memphis RiverKings-7
04Memphis RiverKings-9

Gofton, John
61Hamilton Red Wings-4

Gogolev, Dmitri
99Czech OFS-223
99Russian Hockey League-237
00Russian Hockey League-263
01Russian Hockey League-120
01Russian Lightnings-5
02Russian Hockey League-23
02Russian Transfert-21
04Russian Super League All-Stars-9

Gogulla, Philip
04German Cologne Sharks Postcards-10
05German DEL-219
06German DEL-121

Gohde, Bob
97Louisville Riverfrogs-10
98Amarillo Rattlers-5

Goheen, Moose
60Topps-63
Stamps-19
83Hall of Fame Postcards-H6
85Hall of Fame-112

Goicoechea, Yannick
92Finnish Semic-234

Golabek, Marcus
94German First League-527

Golak, Tomasz
93Quebec Pee-Wee Tournament-1513

Golanov, Maxim
93Upper Deck-273
95Binghamton Rangers-7
96Binghamton Rangers-11

Golczewski, Gary
97Macon Whoopee-5
97Macon Whoopee Autographs-5

Goldade, Aaron
96Brandon Wheat Kings-21
97Brandon Wheat Kings-8
98Brandon Wheat Kings-6
99Brandon Wheat Kings-9
00Brandon Wheat Kings-13

Golden, Matt
00Peoria Rivermen-15
01Peoria Rivermen-20

Golden, Mike
89ProCards IHL-34
90ProCards AHL/IHL-11

Goldfarb, Joshua
93Quebec Pee-Wee Tournament-734

Goldham, Bob
34Beehive Group I Photos-319
44Beehive Group II Photos-98
44Beehive Group II Photos-174
45Quaker Oats Photos-19A
45Quaker Oats Photos-19B
45Quaker Oats Photos-19C
51Parkhurst-67
52Parkhurst-64
53Parkhurst-49
54Parkhurst-39
54Topps-46

Goldie, Dan
94Classic Pro Prospects-233

Goldie, Jeff
01Bakersfield Condors-10
02Bakersfield Condors-8
03Odessa Jackalopes-7

Goldie, Wes
96Owen Sound Platers-26
97Owen Sound Platers-14
98Owen Sound Platers-15
99Owen Sound Platers-17
02Pee Dee Pride RBI-137
03Florence Pride-149

Goldkind, Michael
93Quebec Pee-Wee Tournament-1270
00Connecticut Huskies-7
01Kalamazoo K-Wings-2

Goldmann, Erich
94German DEL-289
95German DEL-272
96German DEL-117
99Grand Rapids Griffins-7
00Pacific-291
Copper-291
Gold-291
Ice Blue-291
Premiere Date-291
00German DEL-168
01German Upper Deck-66
02German DEL City Press-135
03German DEL-143
04German DEL-169
05German DEL-167
06German DEL-107

Goldstein, Jesse
93Quebec Pee-Wee Tournament-738

Goldstein, Lauren
93Quebec Pee-Wee Tournament-605

Goldsworthy, Bill
68O-Pee-Chee-148
68Shirriff Coins-65
69O-Pee-Chee-195
70Colgate Stamps-52
70Dad's Cookies-41
70Esso Power Players-168
70North Stars Postcards-2
70O-Pee-Chee-46
70Sargent Promotions Stamps-95
70Topps-46
71O-Pee-Chee-55
71Sargent Promotions Stamps-86
71Topps-55
71Toronto Sun-131
72O-Pee-Chee-159
Player Crests-10
Team Canada-12
72Sargent Promotions Stamps-104
72Topps-115
72Finnish Semic World Championship-220
72Swedish Semic World Championship-220
73North Stars Action Posters-4
73North Stars Postcards-6
73O-Pee-Chee-62
73Topps-62
74NHL Action Stamps-127
74O-Pee-Chee NHL-1
74O-Pee-Chee NHL-112
74O-Pee-Chee NHL-134
74O-Pee-Chee NHL-220
74Topps-1
74Topps-112
74Topps-134
74Topps-220
75O-Pee-Chee NHL-180
75O-Pee-Chee NHL-321
75Topps-180
75Topps-321
76O-Pee-Chee NHL-169
76Topps-169
77O-Pee-Chee NHL-99
77Topps-99
91Future Trends Canada '72-79
91Future Trends Canada '72 French-79
04ITG Franchises US West-255

Goldsworthy, Leroy
34Beehive Group I Photos-53
35Diamond Matchbooks Tan 1-24
35Diamond Matchbooks Tan 2-24
35Diamond Matchbooks Tan 3-22
35O-Pee-Chee V304C-96
37V356 Worldwide Gum-73
51Buffalo Bison-9

Goldsworthy, Sean
94Central Hockey League-75
94San Antonio Iguanas-3

Goldthorpe, Bill
05ITG Tough Customers-BG
Autographs-BG
Complete Jerseys-BG
Emblem and Numbers-BG
Jerseys-BG
Signed Memorabilia-BG

Goldup, Glenn
74Canadiens Postcards-7
74O-Pee-Chee NHL-275
75O-Pee-Chee NHL-391
78O-Pee-Chee-337
79O-Pee-Chee-376
80Kings Card Night-2
80O-Pee-Chee-382

Goldup, Hank
34Beehive Group I Photos-320
39O-Pee-Chee V301-1-54

Golembiewski, Leo
90Arizona Icecats-1
90Arizona Icecats-2
91Arizona Icecats-1
91Arizona Icecats-18
92Arizona Icecats-1
93Arizona Icecats-2
94Arizona Icecats-2
94Arizona Icecats-22
95Arizona Icecats-2
96Arizona Icecats-2
96Arizona Icecats-23
97Arizona Icecats-2
98Arizona Icecats-8
99Arizona Icecats-7
99Arizona Icecats-27
00Arizona Icecats-25
01Arizona Icecats-6
02Arizona Icecats-27
03Arizona Icecats-25
04Arizona Icecats-5

Golembrosky, Frank
72Nordiques Postcards-11
73Nordiques Team Issue-12

Golicic, Jurij
93Quebec Pee-Wee Tournament-1799
98Owen Sound Platers-21

Goligoski, Alex
04Minnesota Golden Gophers-6
05Minnesota Golden Gophers-8
06Minnesota Golden Gophers-9

Golikov, Alexander
74Swedish Stickers-46
79Panini Stickers-154
79Russian National Team-21
80USSR Olympic Team Mini Pics-3

Golikov, Vladimir
74Swedish Stickers-49
79Panini Stickers-148
79Russian National Team-23
81Swedish Semic Hockey VM Stickers-52
82Swedish Semic VM Stickers-66
83Swedish Semic VM Stickers-66

Golin, Sasha
06Kamloops Blazers-9

Golleret, Nicolas
93Quebec Pee-Wee Tournament-1498

Golokhvastov, Konstantin
98Russian Hockey League-69
99Russian Hockey League-149

Golonka, Jozef
69Swedish Hockey-25
70Swedish Masterserien-2
70Swedish Masterserien-7
70Swedish Masterserien-80
91Finnish Semic World Champ Stickers-248
91Swedish Semic World Champ Stickers-248
94German DEL-321
03Czech Stadion-642

Golosjumov, Sergei
89Swedish Semic World Champ Stickers-80

Golovin, Alexander
03Russian Avangard Omsk-17

Golts, Alexander
98Russian Hockey League-16
99Russian Metallurg Magnetogorsk-52
00Russian Hockey League-108
01Russian Hockey League-116
02Russian Transfert-2

Goltz, Fred
907th Inn. Sketch OHL-58
94Central Hockey League-76
94San Antonio Iguanas-4
95Louisiana Ice Gators-4
98San Antonio Iguanas-19

Goltz, Jeremy
90Arizona Icecats-7
91Arizona Icecats-7
91Arizona Icecats-18
92Arizona Icecats-9
93Arizona Icecats-12
95Arizona Icecats-20
96Arizona Icecats-24
97Arizona Icecats-25
98Arizona Icecats-9
99Arizona Icecats-8

Golubev, Kirill
99Russian Stars Postcards-7

Golubovsky, Yan
94Classic-19
Gold-19
Tri-Cards-T19
94Classic Four-Sport *-136
Gold-136
Printers Proofs-136
95Adirondack Red Wings-7
95Images-30
Gold-30
Autographs-30A
98Bowman's Best-104
Refractors-104
Atomic Refractors-104
Mirror Image Fusion-F8
Mirror Image Fusion Refractors-F8
Mirror Image Fusion Atomic Refractors-F8
98Upper Deck-11
Exclusives-11
Exclusives 1 of 1-11
Gold Reserve-11
99BAP Memorabilia-284
Gold-284
Silver-284
02Russian Hockey League-109
03Russian Hockey League-70
03Russian Hockey League-186
05Swedish SHL Elitset-206
Gold-206

Goman, Vesa
95Finnish SISU-361
96Finnish SISU Redline-156

Gombar, Jiri
99Czech Score Blue 2000-30
99Czech Score Red Ice 2000-30
01Czech OFS-166
02Czech OFS Plus-191
03Czech OFS Plus-92
04Czech OFS-92

Gomes, Jared
06Sarnia Sting-14

Gomes, Tom
94Central Hockey League-58
94Oklahoma City Blazers-4
95Central Hockey League-43
95Oklahoma Coyotes RHI-8
98Oklahoma City Blazers-8

Gomez, Robin
99Calgary Hitmen-11
99Calgary Hitmen Autographs-11
00Calgary Hitmen-14
02South Carolina Stingrays-8
02South Carolina Stingrays RBI-211
03South Carolina Stingrays-326
04Worcester IceCats-22
05South Carolina Stingrays-6

Gomez, Scott
96Surrey Eagles-NNO
98OPC Chrome-232
Refractors-232
98Topps-232
O-Pee-Chee-232
98Tri-City Americans-10
98Bowman CHL-145
Golden Anniversary-145
OPC International-145
Autographs Blue-A27
Autographs Gold-A27
Autographs Silver-A27
Scout's Choice-SC19
98Bowman Chrome CHL-145
Golden Anniversary-145
Golden Anniversary Refractors-145
OPC International-145
OPC International Refractors-145
Refractors-145
99BAP Memorabilia-301
Gold-301
Silver-301
99BAP Millennium Calder Candidates Ruby-C6
99BAP Millennium Calder Candidate Emerald-C6
99BAP Millennium Calder Cand Sapphire-C6
99Black Diamond-52
Diamond Cut-52
Final Cut-52
99Crown Royale-80
Limited Series-80
Premiere Date-80
Prospects Parallel-80
Card-Supials-14
Card-Supials Minis-14
Century 21-6
International Glory-15
International Glory Parallel-15
99Devils Team Issue-16
99O-Pee-Chee Chrome-291
99O-Pee-Chee Chrome Refractors-291
99Pacific-458
99Pacific Dynagon Ice-116
Blue-116
Copper-116
Gold-116
Premiere Date-116
99Pacific Omega-135
Copper-135
Gold-135
Ice Blue-135
Premiere Date-135
EO Portraits-12
EO Portraits 1/1-12
NHL Generations-6
North American All-Stars-8
5 Star Talents-4
5 Star Talents Parallel-4
99Pacific Prism-81
Holographic Blue-81
Holographic Gold-81
Holographic Mirror-81
Holographic Purple-81
Premiere Date-81
Ice Prospects-5
99Panini Stickers-83
99Panini Stickers-354
99SP Authentic-51
Sign of the Times-SGO
Sign of the Times Gold-SGO
Tomorrow's Headliners-TH6
99Stadium Club-198
First Day Issue-198
One of a Kind-198
Printing Plates Black-198
Printing Plates Cyan-198
Printing Plates Magenta-198
Printing Plates Yellow-198
Chrome-48
Chrome Refractors-48
99Topps Arena Giveaways-NJ-SG
99Topps/OPC Chrome-291
Refractors-291
99Topps Gold Label Class 1-87
Black-87
Black One of One-87
One of One-87
Red-87
Red One of One-87
99Topps Gold Label Class 2-87
99Topps Gold Label Class 2 Black-87
99Topps Gold Label Class 2 Black 1 of 1-87
99Topps Gold Label Class 2 One of One-87
99Topps Gold Label Class 2 Red-87
99Topps Gold Label Class 2 Red One of One-87
99Topps Gold Label Class 3-87
99Topps Gold Label Class 3 Black-87
99Topps Gold Label Class 3 Black 1 of 1-87
99Topps Gold Label Class 3 One of One-87
99Topps Gold Label Class 3 Red-87
99Topps Gold Label Class 3 Red One of One-87
99Topps Gold Label Fresh Gold-FG14
99Topps Gold Label Fresh Gold Black-FG14
99Topps Gold Label Fresh Gold Black 1of1-FG14
99Topps Gold Label Fresh Gold One of One-FG14
99Topps Gold Label Fresh Gold Red-FG14
99Topps Gold Label Fresh Gold Red 1 of 1-FG14
99Topps Premier Plus-136
Parallel-136
Game Pieces-GPSG
Premier Rookies-PR4
Premier Rookies Parallel-PR4
Signing Bonus-SB2
99Upper Deck-251
Exclusives-251
Exclusives 1 of 1-251
99Upper Deck Arena Giveaways-ND1
99Upper Deck Gold Reserve-251
99Upper Deck HoloGrFx-32
Ausome-32
99Upper Deck MVP SC Edition-107
Gold Script-107
Silver Script-107
Super Script-107
Cup Contenders-CC6
99Upper Deck Ovation-34
Standing Ovation-34
99Upper Deck Victory-360
99Bowman CHL-108
Gold-108
OPC International-108
Scout's Choice-SC19
00SP Authentic Autographed Replica Jersey-2
00Aurora-83
Pinstripes-83
Pinstripes Premiere Date-83
Premiere Date-83
Championship Fever-15
Championship Fever Copper-15
Championship Fever Platinum Blue-15
Championship Fever Silver-15
Scouting Reports-14
Styrotechs-7A
00BAP Memorabilia-146
Emerald-146
Ruby-146
Sapphire-146
Promos-146
00BAP Mem Chicago Sportsfest Copper-146
00BAP Memorabilia Chicago Sportsfest Blue-146
00BAP Memorabilia Chicago Sportsfest Gold-146
00BAP Memorabilia Chicago Sportsfest Ruby-146
00BAP Memorabilia Chicago Sun-Times Ruby-146
00BAP Memorabilia Chicago Sun-Times Gold-146
00BAP Mem Chicago Sun-Times Sapphire-146
00BAP Mem Toronto Fall Expo Copper-146
00BAP Memorabilia Toronto Fall Expo Gold-146
00BAP Memorabilia Toronto Fall Expo Ruby-146
00BAP Parkhurst 2000-P54
00BAP Signature Series-195
Emerald-195
Ruby-195
Sapphire-195
Autographs-199
Autographs Gold-199
He Shoots-He Scores Prizes-35
00BAP Ultimate Memorabilia Autographs-17
Gold-17
00BAP Ultimate Mem Game-Used Jerseys-GJ44
00BAP Ultimate Mem Game-Used Emblems-E36
00BAP Ultimate Mem Game-Used Numbers-N36
00BAP Ultimate Mem Game-Used Sticks-GS44
00Black Diamond-34
Gold-34
Diamonation-IG5
Myriad-CC4
00Crown Royale-64
Ice Blue-64
Limited Series-64
Premiere Date-64
Red-64
00Devils Team Issue-8
00McDonald's Pacific-21
Blue-21
Gold Crown Die Cuts-4
00O-Pee-Chee-203
00O-Pee-Chee Parallel-203
00Pacific-234
Copper-234
Gold-234
Ice Blue-234
Premiere Date-234
2001: Ice Odyssey-14
Autographs-234
Cramer's Choice-8
Gold Crown Die Cuts-19
North American Stars-8
Reflections-13
00Pacific 2001: Ice Odyssey Anaheim Ntnl-14
00Panini Stickers-50
00Paramount-144
Copper-144
Gold-144
Holo-Gold-144
Holo-Silver-144
Ice Blue-144
Premiere Date-144
Epic Scope-14
Freeze Frame-22
00Private Stock-59
Gold-59
Premiere Date-59
Retail-59
Silver-59
PS-2001 Action-33
PS-2001 New Wave-14
Reserve-13
00Revolution-87
Blue-87
Premiere Date-87
Red-87
HD NHL-22
Ice Immortals-14
Stat Masters-27
00SP Authentic-52
BuyBacks-56
BuyBacks-57
Parents' Scrapbook-PS4
Sign of the Times-SG
Sign of the Times-E/G
Sign of the Times-BGE
00SP Game Used-37
Tools of the Game Combos-C-GY
Tools of the Game Autographed Bronze-A-SG
Tools of the Game Autographed Silver-A-SG
Tools of the Game Autographed Gold-A-SG
00SPx-39
Spectrum-39
00Stadium Club-57
Beam Team-BT9
Capture the Action-CA3
Capture the Action Game View-3
Co-Signers-CO2
Lone Star Signatures-LS3
11 X 14 Autographs-SG
00Topps/OPC-203
Parallel-203
Autographs-ASG
Own the Game-OTG21
00Topps Chrome-134
OPC Refractors-134
Refractors-134
00Topps Gold Label Class 1-61
Gold-61
00Topps Gold Label Class 2-61
00Topps Gold Label Class 2 Gold-61
00Topps Gold Label Class 3-61
00Topps Gold Label Class 3 Gold-61
00Topps Gold Label Autographs-GLA-SG
00Topps Gold Label Bullion-B1
00Topps Gold Label Bullion One to One-B1
00Topps Gold Label New Generation-NG1
00Topps Gold Label New Generation 1 to 1-NG1
00Topps Heritage-29
00Topps Heritage-229
00Topps Heritage-240
Chrome Parallel-29
New Tradition-NT6
00Topps Premier Plus-1
00Topps Premier Plus-NNO
Blue Ice-1
Aspirations-PA1
Private Signings-CTW1
00Topps Stars-3
00Topps Stars-129

Blue-3
Blue-129
Progression-P3
00UD Heroes-150
Signs of Greatness-SG
00UD Pros and Prospects-50
Game Jersey Autograph Exclusives-S-SG
Game Jersey Autographs-S-SG
Now Appearing-NA4
00UD Reserve-50
Buyback Autographs-24
Buyback Autographs-25
Buyback Autographs-26
Gold Strike-GS6
00Upper Deck-102
Exclusives Tier 1-102
Exclusives Tier 2-102
Game Jersey Autographs-HSG
Game Jersey Autographs Exclusives-ESG
Game Jersey Combos-DGB
Game Jersey Patches-SGP
Game Jersey Patch Autographs Exclusives-SGP
Lord Stanley's Heroes-L7
Prospects In Depth-P5
Rise to Prominence-RP4
Triple Threat-TT1
UD Flashback-UD4
00Upper Deck Ice-25
Immortals-25
Legends-25
Stars-25
Clear Cut Autographs-SG
Cool Competitors-CC4
Gallery-IG5
00Upper Deck Legends-77
Legendary Collection Bronze-77
Legendary Collection Gold-77
Legendary Collection Silver-77
00Upper Deck MVP-108
First Stars-108
Second Stars-108
Third Stars-108
Top Draws-TD6
Top Playmakers-TP7
00Upper Deck Victory-137
00Upper Deck Victory-252
00Upper Deck Victory-310
00Upper Deck Vintage-215
00Upper Deck Vintage-221
00Upper Deck Vintage-222
National Heroes-NH15
Star Tandems-S4A
00Vanguard-59
High Voltage-20
High Voltage Gold-20
High Voltage Green-20
High Voltage Red-20
High Voltage Silver-20
Holographic Gold-59
Holographic Purple-59
Pacific Proofs-59
01BAP Memorabilia-60
Emerald-60
Ruby-60
Sapphire-60
All-Star Jerseys-ASJ28
All-Star Emblems-ASE28
All-Star Numbers-ASN28
All-Star Teammates-AST15
All-Star Teammates-AST24
He Shoots-He Scores Prizes-11
Stanley Cup Playoffs-SC29
01BAP Signature Series Certified 100-C39
01BAP Signature Series Certified 50-C39
01BAP Signature Series Certified 1 of 1's-C39
01BAP Signature Series Jerseys-GJ-34
01BAP Sig Series Jersey and Stick Cards-GSJ-34
01BAP Ultimate Memorabilia Calder Trophy-2
01Devils Team Issue-8
010-Pee-Chee-76
010-Pee-Chee Heritage Parallel-76
010-Pee-Chee Heritage Parallel Limited-76
010-Pee-Chee Premier Parallel-76
01Pacific-230
Extreme LTD-230
Hobby LTD-230
Premiere Date-230
Retail LTD-230
01Pacific Adrenaline-114
Blue-114
Premiere Date-114
Red-114
Retail-114
01Pacific Arena Exclusives-230
01Parkhurst-9
Gold-9
Silver-9
Heroes-H15
Jerseys-PJ9
Sticks-PS9
Teammates-T15
01Private Stock-57
Gold-57
Premiere Date-57
Retail-57
Silver-57
01Private Stock Pacific Nights-57
01Stadium Club-90
Award Winners-90
Master Photos-90
01Titanium Double-Sided Jerseys-69
01Titanium Double-Sided Patches-69
01Titanium Draft Day Edition-52
01Topps-76
Heritage Parallel-76
Heritage Parallel Limited-76
OPC Parallel-76
01Topps Heritage-85
Refractors-85
01Topps Reserve-86
01UD Challenge for the Cup-52
01UD Stanley Cup Champs-75
01Upper Deck-105
Exclusives-105
01Upper Deck MVP-116
01Upper Deck Victory-212
Gold-212
01Upper Deck Vintage-154
01Czech Stadion-231
02BAP All-Star Edition-27
Jerseys-27
Jerseys Gold-27
Jerseys Silver-27
02BAP First Edition-114
Jerseys-114
02BAP Memorabilia-152
Emerald-152
Ruby-152
Sapphire-152
NHL All-Star Game-152
NHL All-Star Game Blue-152
NHL All-Star Game Green-152
NHL All-Star Game Red-152
02BAP Memorabilia Toronto Fall Expo-152
02BAP Sig Series Auto Buybacks 2000-199
02BAP Signature Series Phenoms-YP3
02Crown Royale-58
Blue-58
Red-58
Retail-58
02Devils Team Issue-17
02ITG Used-43
02ITG Used-143
02O-Pee-Chee-112
02O-Pee-Chee Premier Blue Parallel-112
02O-Pee-Chee Premier Red Parallel-112
02O-Pee-Chee Factory Set-112
02Pacific-222
Blue-222
Red-222
02Pacific Calder-5
Silver-5
02Pacific Complete-87
Red-87
02Pacific Heads-Up Quad Jerseys-17
02Pacific Heads-Up Quad Jerseys Gold-17
02Parkhurst-84
Bronze-84
Gold-84
Silver-84
02Parkhurst Retro-105
Minis-105
02Titanium-63
Blue-63
Red-63
Retail-63
Jerseys-39
Jerseys Retail-39
Patches-39
02Topps-112
OPC Blue Parallel-112
OPC Red Parallel-112
Factory Set-112
02Topps Chrome-72
Black Border Refractors-72
Refractors-72
02Topps Heritage Calder Cloth-SG
02Topps Total-110
02Upper Deck Rookie Update-59
02Upper Deck Victory-130
Bronze-130
Gold-130
Silver-130
02Vanguard Jerseys-27
02Vanguard Jerseys Gold-27
03BAP Memorabilia Stanley Cup Champions-SCC-3
03Beehive-117
Gold-117
Silver-117
03Black Diamond-67
Black-67
Green-67
Red-67
03Crown Royale-62
Blue-62
Retail-62
03Devils Team Issue-23
03ITG Action-389
Jerseys-M25
03O-Pee-Chee-159
03OPC Blue-159
03OPC Gold-159
03OPC Red-159
03Pacific-200
Blue-200
Red-200
03Pacific Complete-202
Red-202
03Pacific Exhibit-86
Blue Backs-86
Yellow Backs-86
03Parkhurst Rookie ROYalty-VR-24
03Parkhurst Rookie ROYalty Gold-VR-24
03SP Authentic-53
Limited-53
03SP Game Used Team Threads-TTBSG
03Titanium-61
Hobby Jersey Number Parallels-61
Retail-61
Retail Jersey Number Parallels-61
03Topps-159
Blue-159
Gold-159
Red-159
Topps/OPC Idols-UI7
03UD Honor Roll-49
03Upper Deck-358
Canadian Exclusives-358
HG-358
UD Exclusives-358
03Upper Deck Ice-54
Gold-54
Breakers-IB-SG
Breaker Patches-IB-SG
Clear Cut Winners-CC-SG
03Upper Deck MVP-249
Gold Script-249
Silver Script-249
Canadian Exclusives-249
03Upper Deck Rookie Update-52
03Upper Deck Trilogy Authentic Patches-AP21
03Upper Deck Trilogy Limited Threads-LT24
03Upper Deck Victory-109
Bronze-109
Gold-109
Silver-109
04Pacific-158
Blue-158
Red-158
04Upper Deck World Cup Tribute-TASGBG
05Be A Player-54
First Period-54
Second Period-54
Third Period-54
Overtime-54
05Beehive-54
Matte-54
Matted Materials-MMGO
05Black Diamond-102
Emerald-102
Gold-102
Onyx-102
Ruby-102
05Devils Team Issue-16
05Hot Prospects-61
En Fuego-61
Red Hot-61
White Hot-61
05Panini Stickers-80
05Parkhurst-286
Facsimile Auto Parallel-286
True Colors-TCNJD
True Colors-TCNJD
True Colors-TCNJNY
True Colors-TCNJNY
05SP Authentic-59
Limited-59
05SP Game Used-60
Gold-60
Authentic Fabrics-AF-GO
Authentic Fabrics Gold-AF-GO
Authentic Fabrics Quad-BEGK
Authentic Patches Quad -BEGK
Authentic Patches-AP-GO
05SPx-53
Spectrum-53
05The Cup Dual NHL Shields-DSBG
05The Cup Signature Patches-SPGO
05The Cup Stanley Cup Titlists-TSG
05UD Artifacts-59
05UD Artifacts-176
Blue-59
Blue-176
Gold-59
Gold-176
Green-59
Green-176
Pewter-59
Pewter-176
Red-59
Red-176
Gold Autographed-59
Gold Autographed-176
05UD Powerplay Specialists-TSSG
05UD Powerplay Specialists Patches-SPSG
05Ultra-117
Gold-117
Ice-117
05Upper Deck-111
Big Playmakers-B-GO
HG Glossy-111
Jerseys-J-SGO
Jerseys Series II-J2GO
Notable Numbers-N-SGZ
Patches-P-SGO
05Upper Deck MVP-228
Gold-228
Platinum-228
05Upper Deck Rookie Update-59
05Upper Deck Trilogy-53
05Upper Deck Toronto Fall Expo-111
05Upper Deck Victory-117
Black-117
Gold-117
Silver-117
06Beehive Matted Materials-MMSG
06Beehive Remarkable Matted Materials-MMSG
06Black Diamond-49
Black-49
Gold-49
Ruby-49
Jerseys-JSG
Jerseys Black-JSG
Jerseys Gold-JSG
Jerseys Ruby-JSG
Jerseys Black Autographs -JGO
06Devils Team Set-8
06Flair Showcase Inks-ISG
06Fleer-119
Tiffany-119
Signing Day-SDSG
06Hot Prospects Hotagraphs-HSG
06O-Pee-Chee-300
Rainbow-300
Swatches-S-SG
06Panini Stickers-79
06SP Authentic Sign of the Times-STGO
06SP Game Used Authentic Fabrics-AFSG
06SP Game Used Authentic Fabrics Parallel-AFSG
06SP Game Used Authentic Fabrics Patches-AFSG
06SP Game Used Authentic Fabrics Quads-AF4MWGD
06SP Game Used Authentic Fabrics Quads Patches-AF4MWGD
06SP Game Used Authentic Fabrics Sevens-AF7CAL
06SP Game Used Authentic Fabrics Sevens Patches-AF7CAL
06SP Game Used Inked Sweaters-ISSG
06SP Game Used Inked Sweaters Patches-ISSG
06SPx-62
Spectrum-62
Winning Materials-WMSG
Winning Materials Spectrum-WMSG
Winning Materials Autographs-WMSG
06The Cup Autographed NHL Shields Duals-DASGG
06The Cup Honorable Numbers-HNGO
06The Cup Signature Patches-SPGO
06UD Artifacts Auto-Facts-AFSG
06UD Artifacts Auto-Facts Gold-AFSG
06UD Artifacts Treasured Patches Black-TSSG
06UD Artifacts Treasured Patches Blue-TSSG
06UD Artifacts Treasured Patches Gold-TSSG
06UD Artifacts Treasured Patches Platinum-TSSG
06UD Artifacts Treasured Patches Red-TSSG
06UD Artifacts Treasured Patches Autographed Black Tag Parallel-TSSG
06UD Artifacts Treasured Swatches-TSSG
06UD Artifacts Treasured Swatches Black-TSSG
06UD Artifacts Treasured Swatches Blue-TSSG
06UD Artifacts Treasured Swatches Gold-TSSG
06UD Artifacts Treasured Swatches Platinum-TSSG
06UD Artifacts Treasured Swatches Red-TSSG
06UD Artifacts Treasured Swatches Autographed Black-TSSG
06UD Artifacts Tundra Tandems-TTGG
06UD Artifacts Tundra Tandems Black-TTGG
06UD Artifacts Tundra Tandems Blue-TTGG
06UD Artifacts Tundra Tandems Gold-TTGG
06UD Artifacts Tundra Tandems Platinum-TTGG
06UD Artifacts Tundra Tandems Red-TTGG
06UD Artifacts Tundra Tandems Dual Patches Red-TTGG
06UD Powerplay Power Marks-PMSG
06UD Powerplay Specialists-SSG
06UD Powerplay Specialists Patches-PSG
06Ultra-119
Gold Medallion-119
Ice Medallion-119
Fresh Ink-ISG
06Upper Deck Arena Giveaways-NJD5
06Upper Deck-366
Exclusives Parallel-366
High Gloss Parallel-366
Game Jerseys-JSG
Game Patches-PSG
Masterpieces-366
Signature Sensations-SSSG
06Upper Deck MVP-178
Gold Script-178
Super Script-178
Jerseys-OJCG
06Upper Deck Ovation-78
06Upper Deck Sweet Shot Signature Shots/Saves-SSGO
06Upper Deck Sweet Shot Signature Shots/Saves Sticks-SSSSG
06Upper Deck Trilogy Combo Clearcut Autographs-C2GP
06Upper Deck Trilogy Honorary Scripted Patches-HSPSG
06Upper Deck Trilogy Honorary Scripted Swatches-HSSSG
06Upper Deck Trilogy Honorary Swatches-HSGO
06Upper Deck Trilogy Scripts-TSSG
06Upper Deck Victory-118
06Upper Deck Victory Black-118
06Upper Deck Victory Gold-118
07Upper Deck Ovation-73
07Upper Deck Victory-4
Black-4
Gold-4

Gomolyako, Sergei
98Russian Hockey League-1
98Russian Hockey League-129
99Russian Hockey League-7
99Russian Metallurg Magnetogorsk-27
00Russian Hockey League-151
00Russian Hockey League-361
01Russian Hockey League-41
02Russian Hockey League-79
02Russian Hockey League-155
02Russian Hockey League-233
03Russian Hockey League-126
03Russian SL-21
04Russian Super League All-Stars-25

Gonchar, Sergei
92Russian Stars Red Ace-9
92Classic-41
92Classic-43
Gold-41
Gold-43
92Classic Four-Sport *-184
Gold-184
93Upper Deck-272
94Parkhurst SE-SE195
Gold-SE195
94Upper Deck-264
Electric Ice-264
94Portland Pirates-9
94Classic-27
Gold-27
Pro Prospects Ice Ambassadors-IA19
95Canada Games NHL POGS-286
95Capitals Team Issue-8
95Donruss-173
95Emotion-187
95Leaf-26
95Metal-159
95Panini Stickers-141
95Parkhurst International-225
Emerald Ice-225
95Pinnacle-71
Artist's Proofs-71
Rink Collection-71
95SkyBox Impact-176
95Topps-47
OPC Inserts-47
95Ultra-322
95Upper Deck-305
Electric Ice-305
Electric Ice Gold-305
95Images-55
Gold-55
96Be A Player-150
Autographs-150
Autographs Silver-150
96Collector's Choice-286
96Fleer-117
Rookie Sensations-5
Picks Fabulous 50-14
96Maggers-29
96Metal Universe-163
96Pinnacle-40
Artist's Proofs-40
Foil-40
Premium Stock-40
Rink Collection-40
96SkyBox Impact-139
NHL on Fox-9
96SP-165
96Team Out-58
96Topps Picks-91
OPC Inserts-91
96Ultra-175
Gold Medallion-175
96Upper Deck-175
96Upper Deck Ice-75
Parallel-75
96Collector's Edge Ice-53
Prism-53
97Collector's Choice-273
97Pacific-103
Copper-103
Emerald Green-103
Ice Blue-103
Red-103
Silver-103
97Panini Stickers-112
97SP Authentic-166
97Upper Deck-180
98Aurora-195
98Be A Player-299
Press Release-299
98BAP Gold-299
98BAP Autographs-299
98BAP Autographs Gold-299
98Katch-156
98Pacific-441
Ice Blue-441
Red-441
98Panini Stickers-105
98Paramount-244
Copper-244
Emerald Green-244
Holo-Electric-244
Ice Blue-244
Silver-244
98SP Authentic Sign of the Times-SG
98SP Authentic Sign of the Times Gold-SG
98SPx Finite-90
Radiance-90
Spectrum-90
98Upper Deck-201
Exclusives-201
Exclusives 1 of 1-201
Gold Reserve-201
98Upper Deck MVP-211
Gold Script-211
Silver Script-211
Super Script-211
99Aurora-147
Premiere Date-147
99BAP Memorabilia-78
Gold-78
Silver-78
99BAP Millennium-249
Emerald-249
Ruby-249
Sapphire-249
Signatures-249
Signatures Gold-249
99O-Pee-Chee-146
99O-Pee-Chee Chrome-146
99O-Pee-Chee Chrome Refractors-146
99Pacific-439
Copper-439
Emerald Green-439
Gold-439
Ice Blue-439
Premiere Date-439
Red-439
99Panini Stickers-169
99Panini Stickers-344
99Paramount-244
Copper-244
Emerald-244
Gold-244
Holographic Emerald-244
Holographic Gold-244
Holographic Silver-244
Ice Blue-244
Premiere Date-244
Red-244
Silver-244
99Revolution-148
Premiere Date-148
Red-148
Shadow Series-148
99SPx-160
Radiance-160
Spectrum-160
99Topps/OPC-146
99Topps/OPC Chrome-146
Refractors-146
99Upper Deck MVP-216
Gold Script-216
Silver Script-216
Super Script-216
ProSign-SG
99Upper Deck Victory-308
00BAP Memorabilia-126
Emerald-126
Ruby-126
Sapphire-126
Promos-126
00BAP Mem Chicago Sportsfest Copper-126
00BAP Memorabilia Chicago Sportsfest Blue-126
00BAP Memorabilia Chicago Sportsfest Gold-126
00BAP Memorabilia Chicago Sportsfest Ruby-126
00BAP Memorabilia Chicago Sun-Times Ruby-126
00BAP Memorabilia Chicago Sun-Times Gold-126
00BAP Mem Chicago Sun-Times Sapphire-126
00BAP Mem Toronto Fall Expo Copper-126
00BAP Memorabilia Toronto Fall Expo Gold-126
00BAP Memorabilia Toronto Fall Expo Ruby-126
00BAP Memorabilia Update Teammates-TM2
00BAP Memorabilia Update Teammates Gold-TM2
00BAP Parkhurst 2000-P222
00BAP Signature Series-248
Emerald-248
Ruby-248
Sapphire-248
Department of Defense-DD15
00BAP Ultimate Memorabilia Teammates-TM11
00O-Pee-Chee-71
00O-Pee-Chee Parallel-71
00Pacific-421
Copper-421
Gold-421
Ice Blue-421
Premiere Date-421
00Panini Stickers-103
00Paramount-244
Copper-244
Gold-244
Holo-Gold-244
Holo-Silver-244
Ice Blue-244
Premiere Date-244
00Stadium Club-79
00Topps/OPC-71
Parallel-71
00Topps Chrome-56
OPC Refractors-56
Refractors-56
00Topps Heritage-214
00Topps Stars-71
Blue-71
00UD Heroes-118
00Upper Deck-406
Exclusives Tier 1-406
Exclusives Tier 2-406
00Upper Deck MVP-183
First Stars-183
Second Stars-183
Third Stars-183
00Upper Deck Victory-238
00Upper Deck Vintage-367
01BAP Memorabilia-86
Emerald-86
Ruby-86
Sapphire-86
01BAP Signature Series-200
Autographs-200
Autographs Gold-200
Department of Defense-DD-8
Jerseys-GJ-67
Jersey Autographs-GUSG
Jersey and Stick Cards-GSJ-67
01O-Pee-Chee-120
01O-Pee-Chee Premier Parallel-120
01Pacific-392
Extreme LTD-392
Hobby LTD-392
Premiere Date-392
Retail LTD-392
01Pacific Adrenaline-195
Blue-195
Premiere Date-195
Red-195
Retail-195
01Pacific Arena Exclusives-392
01Parkhurst-134
Jerseys-PJ29
Sticks-PS29
Teammates-T6
01Titanium-141
Hobby Parallel-141
Premiere Date-141
Retail-141
Retail Parallel-141
01Topps-120
OPC Parallel-120
01Upper Deck-175
Exclusives-175
01Upper Deck MVP-185
01Upper Deck Victory-351
Gold-351
01Upper Deck Vintage-253
01Upper Deck Vintage-260
02BAP First Edition-2
02BAP First Edition-307
02BAP First Edition-382
Jerseys-2
02BAP Memorabilia-168
Emerald-168
Ruby-168
Sapphire-168
NHL All-Star Game-168
NHL All-Star Game Blue-168
NHL All-Star Game Green-168
NHL All-Star Game Red-168
02BAP Memorabilia Toronto Fall Expo-168
02BAP Signature Series-27
Autographs-27
Autograph Buybacks 1998-299
Autograph Buybacks 1999-249
Autograph Buybacks 2001-200
Autographs Gold-27
Defensive Wall-DW9
Team Quads-TQ9
02Capitals Team Issue-3
02O-Pee-Chee-256
02O-Pee-Chee-321
02O-Pee-Chee Premier Blue Parallel-256
02O-Pee-Chee Premier Blue Parallel-321
02O-Pee-Chee Premier Red Parallel-256
02O-Pee-Chee Premier Red Parallel-321
02O-Pee-Chee Factory Set-256
02O-Pee-Chee Factory Set-321
02Pacific-390
Blue-390
Red-390
02Pacific Complete-464
Red-464
02Pacific Exclusive-171
02Parkhurst-116
Bronze-116
Gold-116
Silver-116
Hardware-N2
02Parkhurst Retro-53
Minis-53
02Private Stock Reserve-98
Blue-98
Red-98
Retail-98
02SP Game Used First Rounder Patches-GO
02SP Game Used Piece of History-PHGO
02SP Game Used Piece of History Gold-PHGO
02SP Game Used Piece of History Rainbow-PHGO
02Topps-256
02Topps-321
OPC Blue Parallel-256
OPC Blue Parallel-321
OPC Red Parallel-256
OPC Red Parallel-321
02Topps Promos-PP3
02Topps Factory Set-256
02Topps Factory Set-321
02Topps Chrome-139
Black Border Refractors-139
Refractors-139
02Topps Heritage-113
02Topps Heritage-128
02Topps Total-378
02UD Top Shelf Clutch Performers-CPSGO
02UD Top Shelf Dual Player Jerseys-STGK
02Upper Deck-175
Exclusives-175
Classic Portraits Hockey Royalty-KGJ
Classic Portraits Hockey Royalty Limited-KGJ
02Upper Deck MVP-183
Gold-183
Classics-183
Golden Classics-183
02Upper Deck Rookie Update-154B
02Upper Deck Rookie Update-162C
02Upper Deck Victory-212
Bronze-212
Gold-212
Silver-212
National Pride-NP39
02Upper Deck Vintage-254
02Upper Deck Vintage-290
02Upper Deck Vintage-310
03BAP Memorabilia-86
03BAP Memorabilia-228
Emerald-86
Gold-86
Ruby-86
Sapphire-86
03BAP Ultimate Memorabilia Autographs-42
Gold-42
03Beehive-197
Gold-197
Silver-197
03Black Diamond-55
Black-55
Green-55
Red-55
03Bowman-54
Gold-54
03Bowman Chrome-54
Refractors-54
Gold Refractors-54
Xfractors-54
03ITG Action-577
Jerseys-M107
03ITG Used Signature Series-67
Gold-67
Autographs-SG01
Autographs-SG02
Autographs Gold-SG01
Autographs Gold-SG02
03NHL Sticker Collection-147
03O-Pee-Chee-142
03OPC Blue-142
03OPC Gold-142
03OPC Red-142
03Pacific-342
Blue-342
Red-342
03Pacific Calder-6
Silver-6
03Pacific Complete-110
Red-110
03Pacific Exhibit-149
Blue Backs-149
Yellow Backs-149
03Pacific Prism-99
Blue-99
Gold-99
Red-99
03Parkhurst Rookie-28
03Private Stock Reserve-99
Blue-99
Red-99
Retail-99
03Titanium-99
Hobby Jersey Number Parallels-99
Retail-99
Retail Jersey Number Parallels-99
03Topps-142
Blue-142
Gold-142
Red-142
03Topps C55-45
Minis-45
Minis American Back-45
Minis American Back Red-45
Minis Bazooka Back-45
Minis Brooklyn Back-45
Minis Hat Trick Back-45
Minis O Canada Back-45
Minis O Canada Back Red-45
Minis Stanley Cup Back-45
03Topps Pristine-67
Gold Refractor Die Cuts-67
Refractors-67
Press Plates Black-67
Press Plates Cyan-67
Press Plates Magenta-67
Press Plates Yellow-67
03Topps Traded-TT45
Blue-TT45
Gold-TT45
Red-TT45
03Upper Deck-194
Canadian Exclusives-194
HG-194
03Upper Deck MVP-426
Gold Script-426
Silver Script-426
Canadian Exclusives-426
03Upper Deck Victory-196
Bronze-196
Gold-196
Silver-196
04Pacific-20
Blue-20
Red-20
04UD All-World-38
Gold-38
04Upper Deck-14
Canadian Exclusives-14
HG Glossy Gold-14
HG Glossy Silver-14
NHL's Best-NB-SG
World's Best-WB17
04Russian Back to Russia-27
05Hot Prospects-80
En Fuego-80
Red Hot-80
White Hot-80
05Panini Stickers-143
05Parkhurst-384
Facsimile Auto Parallel-384
05SP Game Used Authentic Fabrics Triple-GNP
05SP Game Used Authentic Patches Triple-GNP
05Upper Deck-401
Notable Numbers-N-SGO
05Upper Deck Hockey Showcase-HS5
05Upper Deck Showcase Promos-HS5
05Upper Deck MVP-315
Gold-315
Platinum-315
05Upper Deck Victory-17
05Upper Deck Victory-240
Black-17
Black-240
Gold-17
Gold-240
Silver-17
Silver-240
06Fleer-158
Tiffany-158
06O-Pee-Chee-391
Rainbow-391
06Panini Stickers-139
06The Cup NHL Shields Duals-DSHZG
06UD Powerplay-79
Impact Rainbow-79
06Upper Deck Arena Giveaways-PIT3
06Upper Deck-158
Exclusives Parallel-158
High Gloss Parallel-158
Masterpieces-158
06Upper Deck MVP-238
Gold Script-238
Super Script-238
06Upper Deck Ovation-41
06Upper Deck Victory-160
06Upper Deck Victory Black-160
06Upper Deck Victory Gold-160
06Russian Sport Collection Olympic Stars-4
06Russian Torino Olympic Team-23
07Upper Deck Victory-13
Black-13
Gold-13

Gondek, Neil
98Amarillo Rattlers-18

Goneau, Daniel
93Upper Deck Program of Excellence-E5
96Be A Player-107
Autographs-107
Autographs Silver-107
96Collector's Choice-353
96Donruss Canadian Ice-126
Gold Press Proofs-126
Red Press Proofs-126
96Donruss Elite-143
Die Cut Stars-143
Aspirations-18
96Flair-116
Blue Ice-116
96Leaf Preferred-145
Press Proofs-145
96Metal Universe-180
96Select Certified-107
Artist's Proofs-107
Blue-107
Mirror Blue-107
Mirror Gold-107
Mirror Red-107
Red-107
96SP-184
96Ultra-105
Gold Medallion-105
Rookies-8
96Upper Deck-295
96Upper Deck Ice-42
Parallel-42
96Zenith-148
Artist's Proofs-148
97Donruss-190
Press Proofs Silver-190
Press Proofs Gold-190
97Donruss Limited-148
Exposure-148
97Pacific-327
Copper-327
Emerald Green-327
Ice Blue-327
Red-327
Silver-327
97Score Rangers-18
Platinum-18
Premier-18
97Hartford Wolf Pack-9
98SPx Finite-55
98SPx Finite-141
Radiance-55
Radiance-141
Spectrum-55
Spectrum-141
98UD Choice-137
98UD Choice Preview-137
98UD Choice Prime Choice Reserve-137
98UD Choice Reserve-137
98Hartford Wolf Pack-9
99Hartford Wolf Pack-8
00Manitoba Moose-10
02Louisiana Ice Gators-8
06Fort Wayne Komets-5

Gongalsky, Igor
04Owen Sound Attack-3
05Owen Sound Attack-8
06Oshawa Generals-4

Gonthier, Vincent
92Quebec Pee-Wee Tournament-735
93Quebec Pee-Wee Tournament-926

Gooch, Mike
01OCN Blizzard-4
02OCN Blizzard-3
03OCN Blizzard-6

Good, Brad
03Sault Ste. Marie Greyhounds-8
04Sault Ste. Marie Greyhounds-3

Good, Dale
04St. Michael's Majors-5

Good, Mikael
83Swedish Semic Elitserien-152

Goodall, Glen
90ProCards AHL/IHL-482
91ProCards-191
94German First League-173
02German DEL City Press-136
03German DEL-79
04German DEL-87
04German Ingolstadt Panthers-7
05German DEL-146
06German DEL-96
Team Leaders-TL3

Goodall, Ron
85Kitchener Rangers-29
86Kitchener Rangers-27
87Kitchener Rangers-27

Goodenough, Larry
75Flyers Canada Dry Cans-8
75O-Pee-Chee NHL-373
76O-Pee-Chee NHL-96
76Topps-96
77Canucks Canada Dry Cans-4
77Canucks Royal Bank-6
77O-Pee-Chee NHL-359
79O-Pee-Chee-383

Goodenow, Bob
04Upper Deck-198

Goodenow, Joe
00Michigan State Spartans-7

Goodfellow, Ebbie
33O-Pee-Chee V304B-52
33V129-20
33V252 Canadian Gum-25
33V288 Hamilton Gum-42
34Beehive Group I Photos-101
34Sweet Caporal-37
36O-Pee-Chee V304D-117
37V356 Worldwide Gum-11
39O-Pee-Chee V301-1-66
83Hall of Fame-35
83Hall of Fame Postcards-C5
85Hall of Fame-35
02BAP Ultimate Mem Paper Cuts Autos-16
03BAP Ultimate Memorabilia Paper Cuts-24
03Parkhurst Original Six Detroit-44
03Parkhurst Original Six Detroit-80
04ITG Franchises US West-199
04ITG Ultimate Memorabilia-65
Gold-65
Motown Heroes-2
05ITG Ultimate Mem Motown Heroes Autos-3

Goodjohn, Kris
03Gwinnett Gladiators-20
03Gwinnett Gladiators RBI Sports-202
04Gwinnett Gladiators-13

Goodkey, Mark
90Fort Saskatchewan Traders-3

Goodman, Paul
34Beehive Group I Photos-54
40O-Pee-Chee V301-2-150

Goodnough, Greg
03Ottawa 67's-9

Goodwin, John
80Sault Ste. Marie Greyhounds-16
83Nova Scotia Voyageurs-7
99Fort Wayne Komets Points Leaders-6

Goodwin, Jonathan
04Fort Wayne Komets-3
04Fort Wayne Komets Shoe Carnival-3
05Fort Wayne Komets Choice-3
05Fort Wayne Komets Sprint-8
06Fort Wayne Komets-6

Goodwin, Todd
94German First League-383
94Tampa Bay Tritons RHI-5
00UK Sekonda Superleague-174
01UK Belfast Giants-26

Goody, Matt
03Port Huron Beacons-11
06Richmond Renegades-5

Goold, Billy
51Laval Dairy QSHL-89

Gooldy, Eric
96Detroit Whalers-9

Gooley, Pat
87Brockville Braves-23
88Brockville Braves-17

Goon, Patrick
93Quebec Pee-Wee Tournament-162

Goralczyk, Felix
70Swedish Masterserien-193
70Swedish Masterserien-200

Goralczyk, Robert
73Finnish Jaakiekko-91

74Finnish Jenkki-96
Goran, Lars
65Swedish Coralli ISHockey-181
70Swedish Hockey-190
73Swedish Stickers-165
73Swedish Stickers-174
73Swedish Stickers-178
74Swedish Stickers-255
Goransson, Per
83Swedish Semic Elitserien-92
84Swedish Semic Elitserien-92
86Swedish Panini Stickers-74
Gorbachev, Eduard
96Czech APS Extraliga-114
97Czech DS Stickers-272
98Russian Hockey League-27
00Russian Hockey League-60
Gorbachev, Sergei
95Signature Rookies Future Flash-FF4
95Signature Rook Future Flash Sigs-FF4
Gorbenko, Igor
98Russian Hockey League-58
Gorbenko, Oleg
99Russian Hockey League-95
Gorbunov, Vladimir
02Russian Hockey League-117
Gorbushin, Ilya
00Russian Hockey League-230
00Russian Hockey League-339
01Russian Hockey League-97
Gordichuk, Max
03Kamloops Blazers-4
04Vancouver Giants-16
Gordiouk, Viktor
91O-Pee-Chee Inserts-15R
91Finnish Semic World Champ Stickers-97
91Swedish Semic World Champ Stickers-97
92OPC Premier-60
92Parkhurst-17
92Sabres Jubilee Foods-6
92Upper Deck-579
Euro-Rookies-ER18
92Finnish Semic-119
93PowerPlay-28
93Ultra-120
All-Rookies-2
93Rochester Americans Kodak-11
93Classic Pro Prospects-88
94Leaf-468
94OPC Premier-456
Special Effects-456
94Parkhurst SE-SE23
Gold-SE23
94Topps/OPC Premier-456
Special Effects-456
94Ultra-263
96German DEL-277
96Collector's Edge Ice-149
Prism-149
00German DEL-55
02Russian Transfert-26
Gordon, Andrew
04St. Cloud State Huskies-12
05St. Cloud State Huskies-14
05St. Cloud State Huskies-12
Gordon, Ben
02Lincoln Stars-11
03Lincoln Stars-9
03Lincoln Stars Update-40
04Minnesota Golden Gophers-7
05Topps Luxury Box 1 on 1 Dual Relics 1-GB
05Topps Luxury Box One on One Dual Relics-GB
05Topps Luxury Box 1 on 1 Dual Relics 25-GB
05Ultimate Collection Signatures Quad-QSIHOG
05Minnesota Golden Gophers-9
06Minnesota Golden Gophers-10
Gordon, Bob
93Quebec Pee-Wee Tournament-603
Gordon, Boyd
00Red Deer Rebels-7
Signed-7
01Red Deer Rebels-8
02BAP Memorabilia Draft Redemptions-17
02SPx Rookie Redemption-R213
02Red Deer Rebels-16
03BAP Memorabilia-182
Emerald-182
Gold-182
Ruby-182
Sapphire-182
Super Rookies-SR8
Super Rookies Gold-SR8
Super Rookies Silver-SR8
03BAP Ultimate Memorabilia Autographs-129
Gold-129
03BAP Ultimate Mem Auto Jerseys-129
03BAP Ultimate Mem Auto Emblems-129
03BAP Ultimate Mem Auto Numbers-129
03BAP Ultimate Memorabilia Triple Threads-30
03Black Diamond-148
Black-148
Green-148
Red-148
03Bowman-119
Gold-119
03Bowman Chrome-119
Refractors-119
Gold Refractors-119
Xfractors-119
03Crown Royale-136
Red-136
Retail-136
03ITG Action-607
03ITG Used Signature Series-144
Autographs Gold-144
03ITG VIP Rookie Debut-16
03Pacific-360
03Pacific Calder-175
03Pacific Complete-584
Red-584
03Pacific Heads-Up-135
Hobby LTD-135
Retail LTD-135
Jerseys-25
03Pacific Invincible-125
Blue-125
Red-125
Retail-125
03Pacific Luxury Suite-100
Gold-100
03Pacific Quest for the Cup-138
03Pacific Supreme-140
Blue-140
Red-140
Retail-140
03Parkhurst Rookie-147
03Private Stock Reserve-140
Blue-140
Red-140
Retail-140
03SP Authentic-142
Limited-142
03SP Game Used-82
Gold-82
03SPx-207
Radiance-207
Spectrum-207
03Titanium-215
Patches-215
03Topps Traded-TT143
Blue-TT143
Gold-TT143
Red-TT143
03UD Honor Roll-146
03Upper Deck-244
Canadian Exclusives-244
HG-244
03Upper Deck Classic Portraits-187
03Upper Deck Ice-116
Glass Parallel-116
03Upper Deck MVP-442
03Upper Deck Trilogy-171
Limited-171
04Portland Pirates-3
05Ultra Fresh Ink-FI-BG
05Ultra Fresh Ink Blue-FI-BG
05Upper Deck-198
HG Glossy-198
05Upper Deck MVP-392
Gold-392
Platinum-392
ProSign-P-BG
05Upper Deck Trilogy Scripts-SFS-BG
05Upper Deck Toronto Fall Expo-198
05ITG Heroes and Prospects Complete Logos-AHL-8
05ITG Heroes and Prospects Jerseys-GUJ-8
05ITG Heroes and Prospects Jerseys Gold-GUJ-08
05ITG Heroes and Prospects Emblems-GUE-8
05ITG Heroes and Prospects Emblems Gold-GUE-08
05ITG Heroes and Prospects Numbers-GUN-8
05ITG Heroes and Prospects Numbers Gold-GUN-08
05ITG Heroes and Prospects Making the Big-MTB-6
06ITG Heroes and Prospects Calder Cup Champions-CC07
Gordon, Bruce
81Saskatoon Blades-21
Gordon, Chris
91Michigan Wolverines-4
93Anaheim Bullfrogs RHI-6
93Michigan Wolverines-7
94Anaheim Bullfrogs RHI-7
94Huntington Blizzard-12
95Flint Generals-19
97El Paso Buzzards-13
98El Paso Buzzards-2
Gordon, Ian
95Saint John Flames-6
95Signature Rookies Auto-Phonex-16
95Signature Rook Auto-Phonex Phone Cards-16
96Saint John Flames-5
97Grand Rapids Griffins-5
98Grand Rapids Griffins-8
99Utah Grizzlies-24
00German DEL-224
01German Upper Deck-231
Jersey Cards-IG-J
02German DEL City Press-284
03German DEL-95
04German DEL-106
05German DEL-85
Goalies-G04
06German DEL-55
Gordon, Jack
51Cleveland Barons-12
60Cleveland Barons-7
74O-Pee-Chee NHL-238
74Topps-238
Gordon, Larry
92Cleveland Lumberjacks-22
Gordon, Rhett
96Springfield Falcons-17
97Springfield Falcons-10
98Manitoba Moose-D7
00UK Sekonda Superleague-17
02UK Sheffield Steelers-9
04German DEL-170
Gordon, Robb
92British Columbia JHL-147
95Donruss Elite World Juniors-14
95Upper Deck-538
Electric Ice-538
Electric Ice Gold-538
96Syracuse Crunch-9
Gordon, Scott
86Fredericton Express-9
88ProCards AHL-118
89Halifax Citadels-8
89ProCards AHL-153
90Bowman-171
Tiffany-171
90Nordiques Petro-Canada-10
90Pro Set-634
90Halifax Citadels-8
90ProCards AHL/IHL-467
91Nordiques Panini Team Stickers-7
93Knoxville Cherokees-5
94Atlanta Knights-26
95Atlanta Knights-23
98Roanoke Express-2
04Providence Bruins-23
Gordon, Todd
91Greensboro Monarchs-6
92Greensboro Monarchs-13
98San Antonio Iguanas-20
04Louisiana Ice Gators-8
Gore, Forrest
99Kansas City Blades Supercuts-7
99Missouri River Otters-7
00Richmond Renegades-6
01Asheville Smoke-6
01Rockford IceHogs-7
03Missouri River Otters-16
Gorelov, Sergei
03Russian Under-18 Team-20
Goren, Lee
00Black Diamond-113
00SP Authentic-95
00SPx-152
00Providence Bruins-10
01BAP Memorabilia-59
Emerald-59
Ruby-59
Sapphire-59
01O-Pee-Chee-286
01O-Pee-Chee Premier Parallel-286
01Topps-286
OPC Parallel-286
01Upper Deck Victory-363
Gold-363
01Providence Bruins-10
02Pacific Calder-54
Silver-54
02Pacific Complete-592
Red-592
02Providence Bruins-16
03San Antonio Rampage-22
04Manitoba Moose-18
05ITG Heroes and Prospects Jerseys-GUJ-39
05ITG Heroes and Prospects Jerseys Gold-GUJ-39
05ITG Heroes and Prospects Emblems-GUE-39
05ITG Heroes and Prospects Emblems Gold-GUE-39
05ITG Heroes and Prospects Numbers-GUN-39
05ITG Heroes and Prospects Numbers Gold-GUN-39
06Manitoba Moose-23
Gorence, Tom
79O-Pee-Chee-51
79Topps-51
80O-Pee-Chee-368
81O-Pee-Chee-250
82O-Pee-Chee-250
83Moncton Alpines-17
88Oilers Tenth Anniversary-87
Gorenko, Dmitri
98Russian Hockey League-59
99Russian Hockey League-120
Gorev, Roman
94Classic Pro Prospects-141
02Russian Hockey League-85
05Czech HC Vsetin-3
Gorewich, Ben
99Missouri River Otters-8
99Missouri River Otters Sheet-6
00Fort Worth Brahmas-5
01Memphis RiverKings-18
03New Mexico Scorpions-4
Gorgenlander, Rudi
94German DEL-120
95German DEL-109
96German DEL-54
03German DEL-52
Gorges, Josh
00Kelowna Rockets-12
01Kelowna Rockets-6
02Kelowna Rockets-18
03Kelowna Rockets Memorial Cup-7
03Kelowna Rockets-9
04Cleveland Barons-11
04ITG Heroes and Prospects-82
Autographs-JGO
04ITG Heroes/Prospects Toronto Expo '05-82
04ITG Heroes/Prospects Expo Heroes/Pros-82
05Black Diamond-277
05Hot Prospects-211
Autographed Patch Variation-211
Autographed Patch Variation Gold-211
Red Hot-211
05Parkhurst True Colors-TCSJS
05Parkhurst True Colors-TCSJS
05SP Authentic-183
Limited-183
05SP Game Used-160
Autographs-160
Gold-160
Rookie Exclusives-JG
Rookie Exclusives Silver-RE-JG
05SPx-151
Spectrum-151
05The Cup-159
Autographed Rookie Patches Gold Rainbow-159
Black Rainbow Rookies-159
Masterpiece Pressplates (Artifacts)-317
Masterpiece Pressplates (Black Diamond)-277
Masterpiece Pressplates (Ice)-164
Masterpiece Pressplates (Rookie Update)-249
Masterpiece Pressplates SPA Autos-183
Masterpiece Pressplates (SP Game Used)-160
Masterpiece Pressplates (SPx)-151
Masterpiece Pressplates (SPx)-151
Masterpiece Pressplates (Trilogy)-299
Masterpiece Pressplates Ult Coll-165
Masterpiece Pressplates Autographs-159
Platinum Rookies-159
05UD Artifacts-317
05Ultimate Collection-165
Gold-165
05Ultra-242
Gold-242
Fresh Ink-FI-JG
Fresh Ink Blue-FI-JG
Ice-242
Rookie Uniformity Jerseys-RU-JG
Rookie Uniformity Jersey Autographs-ARU-JG
Rookie Uniformity Patches-RUP-JG
Rookie Uniformity Patch Autographs-ARP-JG
05Upper Deck Rookie Ink-RIJG
05Upper Deck Rookie Threads-RTJG
05Upper Deck Rookie Threads Autographs-ARTJG
05Upper Deck Ice-164
Premieres Auto Patches-AIPJG
05Upper Deck Rookie Update-249
Inspirations Patch Rookies-249
05Upper Deck Trilogy-299
05Cleveland Barons-8
06Be A Player Portraits First Exposures-FEJG
06Black Diamond Gemography-GJG
06O-Pee-Chee-420
06O-Pee-Chee-631
Rainbow-420
Rainbow-631
06Upper Deck-412
Exclusives Parallel-412
High Gloss Parallel-412
Masterpieces-412
Gorgi, Mark
91Air Canada SJHL-C31
Goring, Butch
71O-Pee-Chee-152
71Sargent Promotions Stamps-73
71Toronto Sun-113
72O-Pee-Chee-56
72Sargent Promotions Stamps-92
72Topps-72
73O-Pee-Chee-155
73Topps-138
74NHL Action Stamps-119
74O-Pee-Chee NHL-74
74O-Pee-Chee NHL-98
74Topps-74
74Topps-98
75O-Pee-Chee NHL-221
75Topps-221
76O-Pee-Chee NHL-239
76Topps-239
77Coca-Cola-10
77O-Pee-Chee NHL-67
77Topps-67
78O-Pee-Chee-151
78Topps-151
79O-Pee-Chee-98
79Topps-98
80O-Pee-Chee-254
80Topps-254
81O-Pee-Chee-203
81O-Pee-Chee Stickers-20
81Topps-E89
82O-Pee-Chee-200
82Post Cereal-12
83NHL Key Tags-84
83O-Pee-Chee-7
83O-Pee-Chee Stickers-13
83O-Pee-Chee Stickers-177
83Topps Stickers-13
83Topps Stickers-177
84Islanders News-7
84Islanders News-38
84O-Pee-Chee-127
84O-Pee-Chee Stickers-84
84Topps-95
93Las Vegas Thunder-8
00Upper Deck Legends-83
Legendary Collection Bronze-83
Legendary Collection Gold-83
Legendary Collection Silver-83
Legendary Game Jerseys-JBG
00Upper Deck Vintage Dynasty: A Piece of History-GC
00Upper Deck Vintage Dynasty: A Piece of History Gold-GC
01Fleer Legacy-43
Ultimate-43
01Greats of the Game-82
Autographs-82
01Upper Deck Legends-28
02UD Foundations-39
02UD Foundations-60
04ITG Franchises US East-372
Autographs-A-BG02
04ITG Franchises US West-238
Autographs-A-BG01
04UD Legendary Signatures-2
Autographs-BG
04UD Legends Classics-11
Gold-11
Platinum-11
Silver-11
Signature Moments-M44
Signatures-CS42
05SPx-131
Spectrum-131
Xcitement Legends-XL-GO
Xcitement Legends Gold-XL-GO
Xcitement Legends Spectrum-XL-GO
05UD Artifacts-120
Blue-120
Gold-120
Green-120
Pewter-120
Red-120
Gold Autographed-120
Gorleau, Jason
97Bowman CHL-63
OPC-63
Gorman, Dave
74Phoenix Roadrunners WHA Pins-5
75Phoenix Roadrunners WHA-8
Gorman, Ed
24Anonymous NHL-25
Gorman, Jeff
90Prince Albert Raiders-3
907th Inn. Sketch WHL-274
91Prince Albert Raiders-2
917th Inn. Sketch WHL-260
93Prince Albert Raiders-6
97Bakersfield Fog-4
Gorman, Mike
98Bowman CHL-12
Golden Anniversary-12
OPC International-12
98Bowman Chrome CHL-12
Golden Anniversary-12
Golden Anniversary Refractors-12
OPC International-12
OPC International Refractors-12
Refractors-12
99Sudbury Wolves-25
01Odessa Jackalopes-8
02Odessa Jackalopes-11
03Odessa Jackalopes-8
04Odessa Jackalopes-7
05Odessa Jackalopes-9
06Odessa Jackalopes-9
Gorman, Rich
93Quebec Pee-Wee Tournament-1671
Gorman, Sean
92Oklahoma City Blazers-7
93Kansas City Blades-2
94Central Hockey League-59
94Oklahoma City Blazers-5
Gorman, Tommy
37V356 Worldwide Gum-17
83Hall of Fame Postcards-H7
85Hall of Fame-113
06ITG Ultimate Memorabilia Sensational Sens Autos-6
Gornick, Brian
02Cincinnati Mighty Ducks-A-9
03Cincinnati Mighty Ducks-B5
Gorokhov, Ilja
95SP-181
01Russian Hockey League-117
Gorokov, Ilya
02Russian Hockey League-55
Gorovikov, Konstantin
99Grand Rapids Griffins-8
00Grand Rapids Griffins-9
01Russian Hockey League-106
01Russian Hockey League-205
02Russian Hockey League-224
Gorowsky, Tom
04Sioux Falls Stampede-1-2
05Wisconsin Badgers-13
Gorsalitz, Logan
03Camrose Kodiaks-15
04Camrose Kodiaks-5
Gorsdorf, Alexander
94German First League-631
Gorshkov, Alexei
99Russian Stars Postcards-8
01Russian Hockey League-94
02Russian Hockey League-225
Gorski, Leroy
81Saskatoon Blades-3
Gorski, Sheldon
94Central Hockey League-77
94San Antonio Iguanas-5
96Louisville Riverfrogs-9
97Louisville Riverfrogs-7
97Louisville Riverfrogs-28
99Rockford IceHogs-9
Gorsky, Matt
97Louisville Riverfrogs-26
Gosdeck, Carsten
98German DEL-18
99German Bundesliga 2-19
00German DEL-201
01German Upper Deck-267
02German DEL City Press-158
04German DEL-227
04German Krefeld Penguins Postcards-5
Gosselin, Bruno-Pierre
05Chicoutimi Sagueneens-22
Gosselin, Carl
92Quebec Pee-Wee Tournament-231
93Quebec Pee-Wee Tournament-1109
Gosselin, Christian
97Pensacola Ice Pilots-10
98Kentucky Thoroughblades-10
99Kentucky Thoroughblades-12
00Kentucky Thoroughblades-10
01Hartford Wolf Pack-6
Gosselin, David
98Milwaukee Admirals-10
98Bowman CHL-109
Golden Anniversary-109
OPC International-109
98Bowman Chrome CHL-109
Golden Anniversary-109
Golden Anniversary Refractors-109
OPC International-109
OPC International Refractors-109
Refractors-109
99IHL All-Stars-14
99Milwaukee Admirals Keebler-18
00BAP Memorabilia-83
Emerald-83
Ruby-83
Sapphire-83
Promos-83
00BAP Mem Chicago Sportsfest Copper-83
00BAP Memorabilia Chicago Sportsfest Blue-83
00BAP Memorabilia Chicago Sportsfest Gold-83
00BAP Memorabilia Chicago Sportsfest Ruby-83
00BAP Memorabilia Chicago Sun-Times Ruby-83
00BAP Memorabilia Chicago Sun-Times Gold-83
00BAP Mem Chicago Sun-Times Sapphire-83
00BAP Mem Toronto Fall Expo Copper-83
00BAP Memorabilia Toronto Fall Expo Gold-83
00BAP Memorabilia Toronto Fall Expo Ruby-83
00Black Diamond-79
Gold-79
00O-Pee-Chee-304
00O-Pee-Chee Parallel-304
00Pacific-230
Copper-230
Gold-230
Ice Blue-230
Premiere Date-230
00Revolution-81
Blue-81
Premiere Date-81
Red-81
00SP Authentic Sign of the Times-DG
00SPx-98
Spectrum-98
00Topps/OPC-304
Parallel-304
00Topps Chrome-199
OPC Refractors-199
Refractors-199
00UD Heroes-167
00Upper Deck-186
Exclusives Tier 1-186
Exclusives Tier 2-186
00Upper Deck Ice-58
Immortals-58
Legends-58
Stars-58
00Upper Deck MVP-195
First Stars-195
Second Stars-195
Third Stars-195
00Upper Deck Victory-269
00Milwaukee Admirals Postcards-5
01Milwaukee Admirals-10
01Milwaukee Admirals Postcards-7
02Utah Grizzlies-10
03German DEL-96
04German DEL-189
05German DEL-86
Gosselin, Denis
90Rayside-Balfour Jr. Canadians-6
91Rayside-Balfour Jr. Canadians-5
Gosselin, Guy
84Minnesota-Duluth Bulldogs-18
85Minnesota-Duluth Bulldogs-10
88ProCards AHL-181
89ProCards AHL-36
Gosselin, Hugues
93Quebec Pee-Wee Tournament-1589
Gosselin, Mario
83Canadian National Juniors-7
83Nordiques Postcards-10
84Nordiques Postcards-10
85Nordiques General Foods-10
85Nordiques McDonald's-8
85Nordiques Placemats-2
85Nordiques Placemats-6
85Nordiques Provigo-10
85Nordiques Team Issue-9
85O-Pee-Chee-18
85O-Pee-Chee Stickers-146
85Topps-18
86Kraft Drawings-20
86Nordiques General Foods-9
86Nordiques McDonald's-9
86Nordiques Team Issue-8
86O-Pee-Chee-235
86O-Pee-Chee Stickers-21
87Nordiques General Foods-11
87Nordiques Team Issue-26
87Nordiques Yum-Yum-3A
87Nordiques Yum-Yum-3B
87O-Pee-Chee-250
87O-Pee-Chee Stickers-231
87Panini Stickers-157
88Nordiques General Foods-14
88Nordiques Team Issue-14
88O-Pee-Chee-173
88O-Pee-Chee Stickers-193
88Panini Stickers-347
88Topps-173
89Kings Smokey-18
89O-Pee-Chee-258
90O-Pee-Chee-442
90Upper Deck-91
French-91
90ProCards AHL/IHL-349
91ProCards-115
Gosselin, Patrick
00Sherbrooke Castors-5
Signed-5
Gosselin, Remy
93Quebec Pee-Wee Tournament-332
Gosselin, Richmond
00German Berlin Polar Bears Postcards-8
01Swiss EV Zug Postcards-3
02Swiss EV Zug Postcards-5
Gosselin, Steve
907th Inn. Sketch QMJHL-23
917th Inn. Sketch QMJHL-86
98Chicago Wolves-5
03St. Georges de Beauce Garaga-8
Gosselin, Yannick
93Wichita Thunder-6
Gossmann, Carsten
94German DEL-97
95German DEL-78
Gossweiler, Manuel
01Swiss HNL-54
Gotaas, Steve
84Prince Albert Raiders Stickers-9
88ProCards IHL-51
90ProCards AHL/IHL-112
91ProCards-157
93Las Vegas Thunder-9
Gottfried, Gerhard
93Quebec Pee-Wee Tournament-1526
Gottschalk, Ryan
06Barrie Colts-19
Gottselig, Johnny
33V252 Canadian Gum-26
34Beehive Group I Photos-55
34Diamond Matchbooks Silver-25
35Diamond Matchbooks Tan 1-25
35Diamond Matchbooks Tan 2-25
35Diamond Matchbooks Tan 3-23
35Diamond Matchbooks Tan 4-5
35Diamond Matchbooks Tan 5-5
35O-Pee-Chee V304C-80
37Diamond Matchbooks Tan 6-5
37V356 Worldwide Gum-55
39O-Pee-Chee V301-1-50
04ITG Franchises US West-177
05ITG Ultimate Mem Chi-Town Immortal Auto-5
Gottwald, Tom
93Quebec Pee-Wee Tournament-658
Gotz, Patrick
93Swiss HNL-370
Gotziaman, Chris
92North Dakota Fighting Sioux-7
95Flint Generals-16
Gouch, Michael
01St. Michaels Majors-13
Goudie, Brian
917th Inn. Sketch OHL-336
917th Inn. Sketch Memorial Cup-7
93Hampton Roads Admirals-6
94Hampton Roads Admirals-9
95Richmond Renegades-8
96Richmond Renegades-7
00Richmond Renegades-2
02Florida Everblades-8
02Florida Everblades RBI-120
04Richmond Riverdogs-6
06Richmond Renegades-6
Goudreau, Marcel
66Columbus Checkers-6
Gouett, Mark
02Greenville Grrrowl-11
04UK London Racers-7
04UK London Racers Playoffs-6
Gougeon, Maxime
06Drummondville Voltigeurs-25
Gough, Justin
93Quebec Pee-Wee Tournament-1608
Gough, Michael
00St. Michaels Majors-17
02Owen Sound Attack-11
Gouin, Dominic
93Quebec Pee-Wee Tournament-107
Goulart, Chris
93Quebec Pee-Wee Tournament-694
Gould, Bob
82Capitals Team Issue-7
82Post Cereal-20
83NHL Key Tags-131
84Capitals Pizza Hut-6
84O-Pee-Chee-196
85Capitals Pizza Hut-5
86Capitals Kodak-9
86Capitals Police-9
87Capitals Kodak-23
87Capitals Team Issue-7
87O-Pee-Chee-55
87O-Pee-Chee Stickers-237
87Topps-55
88Capitals Borderless-6
88Capitals Smokey-6
89Bruins Sports Action-9
89O-Pee-Chee-289
90O-Pee-Chee-398
90ProCards AHL/IHL-144
Gould, John
74Canucks Royal Bank-6
74NHL Action Stamps-278
74O-Pee-Chee NHL-381
75Canucks Royal Bank-7
75O-Pee-Chee NHL-266
75Topps-266
76Canucks Royal Bank-5
76O-Pee-Chee NHL-85
76Topps-85
77O-Pee-Chee NHL-382
78O-Pee-Chee-309
79O-Pee-Chee-282
Gould, Justin
96Providence Bruins-9
97Charlotte Checkers-9
Goulet, Bob
89Johnstown Chiefs-20
Goulet, Brad
99Mississippi Sea Wolves-17
Goulet, Jason
00Fort Wayne Komets-5
00Fort Wayne Komets Shoe Carnival-3
00Milwaukee Admirals Postcards-6
00Saskatoon Blades-6
01Milwaukee Admirals-11
01Milwaukee Admirals Postcards-9
02Manitoba Moose-20
04Oklahoma City Blazers-14
Goulet, Louis
02Orlando Seals-7
03Augusta Lynx-40
05UK Cardiff Devils-5
Gold-5
Silver-5
05UK Cardiff Devils Challenge Cup-15
06Augusta Lynx-4
Goulet, Marty
93Quebec Pee-Wee Tournament-159
Goulet, Michel
80Nordiques Postcards-11
80O-Pee-Chee-67
80Pepsi-Cola Caps-66
80Topps-67
81Nordiques Postcards-8
81O-Pee-Chee-275
81O-Pee-Chee Stickers-75
82McDonald's Stickers-14
82McDonald's Stickers-19
82Nordiques Postcards-8
82O-Pee-Chee-284
82O-Pee-Chee Stickers-25
82Topps Stickers-25
83Esso-8
83NHL Key Tags-108
83Nordiques Postcards-11
83O-Pee-Chee-287
83O-Pee-Chee-288
83O-Pee-Chee-292
83O-Pee-Chee Stickers-166
83O-Pee-Chee Stickers-249
83O-Pee-Chee Stickers-250
83Puffy Stickers-15
83Topps Stickers-166
83Topps Stickers-249
83Topps Stickers-250
83Vachon-65
84Kellogg's Accordion Discs-1
84Kellogg's Accordion Discs Singles-14
84Nordiques Postcards-11
84O-Pee-Chee-207
84O-Pee-Chee-280
84O-Pee-Chee-366
84O-Pee-Chee-384
84O-Pee-Chee-391
84O-Pee-Chee Stickers-64
84O-Pee-Chee Stickers-140
84O-Pee-Chee Stickers-168
84O-Pee-Chee Stickers-169
847-Eleven Discs-15
84Topps-129
84Topps-153
85Nordiques General Foods-11
85Nordiques McDonald's-9
85Nordiques Placemats-6
85Nordiques Provigo-11
85Nordiques Team Issue-10
85O-Pee-Chee-150
85O-Pee-Chee Stickers-141
857-Eleven Credit Cards-15
857-Eleven Credit Cards-16
85Topps-150
86Kraft Drawings-21
86Nordiques General Foods-10
86Nordiques McDonald's-10
86Nordiques Team Issue-9
86Nordiques Yum-Yum-4
86O-Pee-Chee-92
86O-Pee-Chee Box Bottoms-E
86O-Pee-Chee Stickers-22
86O-Pee-Chee Stickers-113
86Topps-92
86Topps Box Bottoms-E
86Topps Sticker Inserts-2
87Nordiques General Foods-12
87Nordiques Team Issue-11
87Nordiques Yum-Yum-4
87O-Pee-Chee-77
87O-Pee-Chee Box Bottoms-M
87O-Pee-Chee Minis-12
87O-Pee-Chee Stickers-113
87O-Pee-Chee Stickers-225
87Panini Stickers-163
87Pro-Sport All-Stars-11
87Topps-77
87Topps Box Bottoms-M
87Topps Sticker Inserts-6
88Esso All-Stars-14
88Frito-Lay Stickers-22
88Nordiques General Foods-15
88Nordiques Team Issue-15
88O-Pee-Chee-54
88O-Pee-Chee Minis-10
88O-Pee-Chee Stickers-188
88Panini Stickers-355
88Topps-54
88Topps Sticker Inserts-7
89Kraft-30
89Nordiques Team Issue-13
89Nordiques General Foods-10
89Nordiques Police-9
89O-Pee-Chee-57
89O-Pee-Chee Stickers-186
89Panini Stickers-326
89Topps-57
89Swedish Semic World Champ Stickers-70
90Blackhawks Coke-13
90Nordiques Team Issue-9
90O-Pee-Chee-329
90Pro Set-430
90Score-221
Canadian-221
90Topps-329
Tiffany-329
90Upper Deck-133
French-133
91Pro Set Platinum-166
91Blackhawks Coke-7
91Bowman-392
91Kraft-87
91O-Pee-Chee-336
91Panini Stickers-11
91Parkhurst-36
91Parkhurst-215
91Parkhurst-428
91Parkhurst-457
French-36
French-215
French-428
91Pinnacle-109
French-109
91Pro Set-50
French-50
Platinum PC-PC15
91Score American-201
91Score American-375
91Score Canadian Bilingual-201
91Score Canadian Bilingual-265
91Score Canadian English-201
91Score Canadian English-265
91Stadium Club Members Only-43
91Stadium Club-66
91Topps-336
91Upper Deck-374
French-374
92Bowman-310
92Durivage Panini-24
92O-Pee-Chee-358
92Panini Stickers-6
92Panini Stickers French-6
92Parkhurst-272
Emerald Ice-272
92Pinnacle American Promo Panel-1
92Pinnacle-22
French-22
92Pro Set-32
92Score-222
92Score-444
Canadian-222
Canadian-444
92Stadium Club-69
92Topps-255
92Topps-347
Gold-255G
Gold-347G
92Ultra-35
92Upper Deck-113
93Blackhawks Coke-7
93Donruss-71
93Durivage Score-42
93Leaf-373
93OPC Premier-386
Gold-386
93Panini Stickers-148
93Parkhurst-313
Emerald Ice-313
93Pinnacle-399
Canadian-399
93PowerPlay-49
93Score-153
Canadian-153
93Stadium Club-12
Members Only Master Set-12
OPC-12
First Day Issue-12
First Day Issue OPC-12
93Topps/OPC Premier-386
Gold-386
93Ultra-289
94EA Sports-28
94Hockey Wit-33
98Hall of Fame Medallions-1
99Upper Deck 500 Goal Club-500MG
99Upper Deck 500 Goal Club-500MG
00UD Heroes-137
Signs of Greatness-MG
00Upper Deck 500 Goal Club-500MG
00Upper Deck 500 Goal Club-500MG
00Upper Deck Legends-110
Legendary Collection Bronze-110
Legendary Collection Gold-110
Legendary Collection Silver-110
Epic Signatures-MGO
01BAP Memorabilia 500 Goal Scorers-GS25
01BAP Signature Series 500 Goal Scorers-16
01BAP Sig Series 500 Goal Scorers Auto-16
01BAP Signature Series Vintage Autographs-VA-32
01BAP Ultimate Mem 500 Goal Scorers-24
01BAP Ultimate Mem 500 Goal Scorers Autos-16
01BAP Ultimate Mem 500 Goal Jerseys/Stick-24
01BAP Ultimate Mem 500 Goal Emblems-24
01BAP Update Passing the Torch-PTT2
01Fleer Legacy-37
Ultimate-37
Memorabilia-3
01Greats of the Game-59
Autographs-59
Jerseys-3
Patches Gold-3
01Parkhurst 500 Goal Scorers-PGS25
01Upper Deck Legends-77
02UD Foundations 1000 Point Club-MG
02UD Foundations 1000 Point Club Gold-MG
02UD Foundations 1000 Point Club Silver-MG
02UD Foundations Canadian Heroes-CMG
02UD Foundations Canadian Heroes Gold-CMG
02UD Foundations Canadian Heroes Silver-C-MG
02UD Foundations Classic Greats-GMG
02UD Foundations Classic Greats Gold-GMG
02UD Foundations Classic Greats Silver-G-MG
02UD Foundations Playoff Performers-PMG
02UD Foundations Playoff Performers Gold-PMG
02UD Foundations Playoff Performer Silver-P-MG
02UD Foundations Signs of Greatness-SGMGU
02UD Piece of History Historical Swatches-HSMG
02UD Piece of History Mark of Distinction-MG
03Parkhurst Original Six Chicago-54
03Parkhurst Original Six Chicago-90
Autographs-3
Memorabilia-CM24
Memorabilia-CM34
Memorabilia-CM55
03Upper Deck Trilogy-128
Crest Variations-128
Limited-128
Scripts-S3GT
Scripts-S3MG
Scripts Limited-S3GT
Scripts Limited-S3MG
Scripts Red-S3MG
04ITG Franchises Canadian-78
Autographs-MG2
04ITG Franchises He Shoots/Scores Prizes-30
04ITG Franchises US West-167
Autographs-A-MG1
Double Memorabilia-WDM18
Double Memorabilia Gold-WDM18
Memorabilia-WSM24
Memorabilia Gold-WSM24
Teammates-WTM7
Teammates Gold-WTM7
04ITG Ultimate Memorabilia-184
Gold-184
Complete Logo-31
Day In History-39
Day In History Gold-39
Jersey Autographs-49
Jersey Autographs Gold-49
Original Six-5
Original Six-17
Stick Autographs-1
Stick Autographs Gold-1
04UD Legendary Signatures-100
Autographs-MG
Linemates-SLDEMG
05ITG Ultimate Mem First Rounders Jerseys-9
05ITG Ultimate Mem 1st Round Jersey Gold-9
05ITG Ultimate Mem Retro Teammates Jerseys-26
05ITG Ult Mem Retro Teammates Jersey Gold-26
06ITG International Ice-20
06ITG International Ice-72
Gold-20
Gold-72
Autographs-AMG
Autographs-AMG2
Emblem Autographs-GUE08

Emblem Autographs Gold-GUE08
Emblems-GUE08
Emblems Gold-GUE08
International Rivals-IR13
International Rivals Gold-IR13
Jersey Autographs-GUJ08
Jersey Autographs Gold-GUJ08
Jerseys-GUJ08
Jerseys Gold-GUJ08
My Country My Team-MC9
My Country My Team Gold-MC9
Numbers-GUN08
Numbers Autographs-GUN08
Numbers Autographs Gold-GUN08
Numbers Gold-GUN08
06ITG Ultimate Memorabilia-103
Artist Proof-103
Autos-14
Autos Gold-14

Goulet, Stephane
03Quebec Remparts-10
04Moncton Wildcats-12
05Moncton Wildcats-2
06Stockton Thunder-3
06ITG Heroes and Prospects National Pride-NP10
06ITG Heroes and Prospects National Pride Gold-NP10

Goumaz, Nicolas
93Swiss HNL-417
95Swiss HNL-321
96Swiss HNL-255

Goupil, Alex
05Danbury Trashers-1
06Bloomington PrairieThunder-10

Goupille, Cliff
34Beehive Group I Photos-154
37O-Pee-Chee V304E-178
39O-Pee-Chee V301-1-22
40O-Pee-Chee V301-2-120

Gourlie, Bryan
87Portland Winter Hawks-10
88Portland Winter Hawks-10
89Portland Winter Hawks-9
907th Inn. Sketch WHL-304

Gouverneurs, Les
93Quebec Pee-Wee Tournament-356

Gove, David
92Quebec Pee-Wee Tournament-1642
01Johnstown Chiefs-15
04Providence Bruins-8
05Hot Prospects-114
En Fuego-114
Red Hot-114
White Hot-114
05The Cup Masterpiece Pressplates (Ice)-267
05The Cup Master Pressplate Rookie Update-116
05Upper Deck Ice-267
05Upper Deck Rookie Update-116
06Albany River Rats-12

Govedaris, Chris
90Bowman-259
Tiffany-259
90Whalers Jr. 7-Eleven-12
90ProCards AHL/IHL-187
91Score American-325
91Score Canadian Bilingual-355
91Score Canadian English-355
91ProCards-102
93St. John's Maple Leafs-9
93Classic Pro Prospects-29
94Parkhurst-236
Gold-236
94Milwaukee Admirals-9
95Minnesota Moose-8
96German DEL-45
96Collector's Edge Ice-166
Prism-166
98German DEL-167
99German DEL-72
00German DEL-73
All-Star Class-A6

Goverde, David
88Sudbury Wolves-2
89Sudbury Wolves-19
90ProCards AHL/IHL-352
91ProCards-399
92Phoenix Roadrunners-8
93Phoenix Roadrunners-7
93Classic Pro Prospects-54
95Toledo Storm-20
96Anaheim Bullfrogs RHI-8
96Toledo Storm-35
98Phoenix Mustangs-2
02Orlando Seals-9

Gowan, Mark
92Sudbury Wolves-26
01Colorado Gold Kings-9
02Fresno Falcons-16

Gowans, Stewart
93Quebec Pee-Wee Tournament-476

Gowens, Mark
93Flint Generals-17
94Flint Generals-9

Goyens, Nicholas
05Rimouski Oceanic-19
06Rimouski Oceanic-10

Goyer, Benoit
90Montreal-Bourassa AAA-12

Goyer, Gerry
67Topps-54

Goyette, Danielle
94Classic Women of Hockey-W7
97Collector's Choice-285
04Canadian Womens World Championship Team-9
06ITG Going For Gold-13
06ITG Going For Gold Samples-13
06ITG Going For Gold Autographs-AG
06ITG Going For Gold Jerseys-GUJ13

Goyette, Phil
44Beehive Group II Photos-242
44Beehive Group II Photos-317
52Juniors Blue Tint-141
57Parkhurst-M11
58Parkhurst-47
59Parkhurst-4
60NHL Ceramic Tiles-6
60Parkhurst-50
60Parkhurst-58
60Shirriff Coins-27
60York Photos-11
61Parkhurst-46
61Shirriff/Salada Coins-116
61York Yellow Backs-30
62Parkhurst-37
62Shirriff Coins-28
63Topps-58
64Beehive Group III Photos-128
64Coca-Cola Caps-87
64Topps-87
65Coca-Cola-87
65Topps-92
66Topps-28
66Topps USA Test-28
67Topps-25
68O-Pee-Chee-73
68Shirriff Coins-97
68Topps-73
69O-Pee-Chee-21
Four-in-One-6
69Topps-21
70Colgate Stamps-10
70Dad's Cookies-42
70Esso Power Players-80
70O-Pee-Chee-127
70O-Pee-Chee-251
70Topps-127
71O-Pee-Chee-88
71Sabres Postcards-79
71Sargent Promotions Stamps-30
71Topps-88
71Toronto Sun-27
72Finnish Semic World Championship-196
72Swedish Semic World Championship-196
91Ultimate Original Six-11
French-11
93Parkhurst Parkie Reprints-PR59
94Parkhurst Missing Link-74
94Parkhurst Tall Boys-105
94Parkhurst Tall Boys-173
95Parkhurst '66-67-99
Coins-99

Gozzi, Anders
87Swedish Panini Stickers-15
89Swedish Semic Elitserien Stickers-19
90Swedish Semic Elitserien Stickers-190
91Swedish Semic Elitserien Stickers-42
92Swedish Semic Elitserien Stickers-67
93Swedish Semic Elitserien-39
94Swedish Leaf-223
95Swedish Leaf-11
95Swedish Upper Deck-10
97Swedish Collector's Choice-9
98Swedish UD Choice-12
99German Bundesliga 2-102
00Swedish Upper Deck-8
SHL Signatures-AG

Grabie, Jonathan
93Quebec Pee-Wee Tournament-1661

Grabinsky, Jeff
92British Columbia JHL-38
98Colorado Gold Kings-7
98Colorado Gold Kings Postcards-13

Grabner, Michael
05ITG Heroes/Prosp Toronto Expo Parallel -419
05ITG Heroes and Prospects-419
Team Orr-TO11
06ITG Heroes and Prospects-104
Autographs-AMGR
Class of 2006-CL09
Jerseys-GUJ71
Emblems-GUE71
Numbers-GUN71

Graboski, Tony
34Beehive Group I Photos-155

Grabovski, Mikhail
05Russian Hockey League RHL-8
06Be A Player-241
06Beehive-129
Matte-129
06Hot Prospects-187
06SP Authentic-234
Limited-234
06The Cup Masterpiece Pressplates (Bee Hive)-129
06The Cup Masterpiece Pressplates (SP Authentic)-234
06The Cup Masterpiece Pressplates (Sweet Beginnings)-134
06The Cup Masterpiece Pressplates (Ultimate Collection)-81
06UD Artifacts-265
06Ultimate Collection-81
06Czech Super Six Postcards-3
06Hamilton Bulldogs-12

Grabowskis, Ewalds
94German First League-191

Gracheev, Igor
00Russian Hockey League-206

Grachev, Oleg
99Russian Hockey League-267
01Russian Hockey League-16
03Russian Avangard Omsk-20

Grachev, Vladimir
92Russian Stars Red Ace-24

Gracie, Robert
32O'Keefe Maple Leafs-14
33O-Pee-Chee V304B-66
33V129-40
33V252 Canadian Gum-27
33V357 Ice Kings-63
34Beehive Group I Photos-197
34Diamond Matchbooks Silver-26
35Diamond Matchbooks Tan 1-26
37O-Pee-Chee V304E-171
37V356 Worldwide Gum-38
38Quaker Oats Photos-15

Gradin, David
02Regina Pats-9

Gradin, Henrik
92Swedish Semic Elitserien Stickers-247
93Swedish Semic Elitserien-216

Gradin, Peter
83Swedish Semic Elitserien-14
84Swedish Semic Elitserien-13
85Swedish Panini Stickers-16
87Swedish Panini Stickers-13
89Swedish Semic Elitserien Stickers-12
90Swedish Semic Elitserien Stickers-86
91Swedish Semic Elitserien Stickers-13

Gradin, Thomas
78Canucks Royal Bank-7
79Panini Stickers-201
79Canucks Royal Bank-8
79O-Pee-Chee-53
79Topps-53
80Canucks Silverwood Dairies-9
80Canucks Team Issue-9
80O-Pee-Chee-241
80Pepsi-Cola Caps-108
80Topps-241
81Canucks Team Issue-9
81O-Pee-Chee-327
81O-Pee-Chee-346
81O-Pee-Chee Stickers-243
81Topps-15
81Topps-64
82Canucks Team Issue-8
82O-Pee-Chee-337
82O-Pee-Chee-344
82O-Pee-Chee-345
82O-Pee-Chee Stickers-240
82Post Cereal-19
82Topps Stickers-240
82Swedish Semic VM Stickers-148
83Canucks Team Issue-8
83NHL Key Tags-124
83O-Pee-Chee-350
83O-Pee-Chee Stickers-273
83Puffy Stickers-3
83Topps Stickers-273
83Vachon-107
84Canucks Team Issue-9
84Kellogg's Accordion Discs-6
84Kellogg's Accordion Discs Singles-15
84O-Pee-Chee-319
84O-Pee-Chee Stickers-282
85Canucks Team Issue-8
85O-Pee-Chee-16
85O-Pee-Chee Stickers-240
85Topps-16
87Swedish Panini Stickers-18
89Swedish Semic Elitserien Stickers-13
04ITG Franchises Canadian-132
Autographs-TG

Grady, Nick
97Barrie Colts-8

Graesen, Mats
89Swedish Semic Elitserien Stickers-284

Graf, Colton
06Chilliwack Bruins-14

Graf, Kris
95Spokane Chiefs-8
96Spokane Chiefs-7
97Spokane Chiefs-10
98Medicine Hat Tigers-11

Graf, Marco
01Swiss HNL-472
02Swiss HNL-446

Graf, Markus
98Swiss Power Play Stickers-347
99Swiss Panini Stickers-332
01Swiss HNL-301

Graff, David
97Fort Worth Brahmas-5

Graft, Whitney
04Minnesota Golden Gophers Women-11

Gragnani, Marc-Andre
03P.E.I. Rocket-6
04P.E.I. Rocket-13
05ITG Heroes/Prosp Toronto Expo Parallel -156
05PEI Rocket-28
05ITG Heroes and Prospects-156
Autographs-A-MAG
06PEI Rocket-9
06ITG Heroes and Prospects-196
Autographs-AMAG
National Pride-NP06
National Pride Gold-NP06
Update Autographs-AMAG

Graham, Bob
03Camrose Kodiaks-22

Graham, Bruce
02Moncton Wildcats-7
03Moncton Wildcats-3
04Moncton Wildcats-20
05Hartford Wolf Pack-9
06Hartford Wolf Pack-6

Graham, Dave
95UK Guildford Flames-17

Graham, Dirk
84Springfield Indians-21
85North Stars 7-Eleven-12
85North Stars Postcards-11
86North Stars Postcards-9
86O-Pee-Chee-143
86O-Pee-Chee Stickers-171
86Topps-143
87North Stars Postcards-15
87O-Pee-Chee-184
87Panini Stickers-295
87Topps-184
88Blackhawks Coke-5
88O-Pee-Chee-135
88O-Pee-Chee Stickers-7
88Panini Stickers-25
88Topps-135
89Blackhawks Coke-16
89O-Pee-Chee-52
89O-Pee-Chee-301
89O-Pee-Chee Stickers-12
89Panini Stickers-44
89Topps-52
90Blackhawks Coke-1
90Bowman-8
Tiffany-8
90O-Pee-Chee-179
90Panini Stickers-191
90Pro Set-51
90Score-17
Canadian-17
90Topps-179
Tiffany-179
90Upper Deck-131
French-131
91Pro Set Platinum-23
91Blackhawks Coke-8
91Bowman-397
91O-Pee-Chee-217
91O-Pee-Chee-430
91O-Pee-Chee-521
91OPC Premier-131
91Panini Stickers-16
91Parkhurst-33
French-33
91Pinnacle-261
French-261
91Pro Set-51
91Pro Set-323
91Pro Set-570
French-51
French-323
French-570
Awards Special-AC12
91Score American-15
91Score American-432
91Score Canadian Bilingual-15
91Score Canadian Bilingual-322
91Score Canadian English-15
91Score Canadian English-322
91Stadium Club-181
91Topps-217
91Topps-521
91Upper Deck-271
91Upper Deck-502
French-271
French-502
Award Winner Holograms-AW8
92Bowman-68
92O-Pee-Chee-210
92Panini Stickers-7
92Panini Stickers French-7
92Parkhurst-271
Emerald Ice-271
92Pinnacle-173
French-173
92Pro Set-38
92Score-27
Canadian-27
92Stadium Club-342
92Topps-376
Gold-376G
92Ultra-36
92Upper Deck-272
93Blackhawks Coke-25
93Donruss-63
93Leaf-270
93OPC Premier-88
Gold-88
93Panini Stickers-147
93Pinnacle-24
Canadian-24
Captains-5
Captains Canadian-5
93PowerPlay-50
93Score-12
Canadian-12
93Stadium Club-90
Members Only Master Set-90
OPC-90
First Day Issue-90
First Day Issue OPC-90
93Topps/OPC Premier-88
Gold-88
93Ultra-61
93Upper Deck-328
94Be A Player Signature Cards-78
94Blackhawks Coke-5
94Canada Games NHL POGS-66
94Flair-33
94Fleer-40
94Leaf-335
94OPC Premier-67
Special Effects-67
94Pinnacle-317
Artist's Proofs-317
Rink Collection-317
94Score-56
Gold-56
Platinum-56
94Topps/OPC Premier-67
Special Effects-67
94Ultra-41
94Finnish Jaa Kiekko-97
02Fleer Throwbacks-19
Gold-19
Platinum-19
03Parkhurst Original Six Chicago-39
03Parkhurst Original Six Chicago-77
Autographs-4
04ITG Franchises US West-168
Autographs-A-DGH
04Springfield Falcons-27
05Springfield Falcons-25

Graham, Ethan
01Lincoln Stars-11
02Lincoln Stars-2
02Lincoln Stars-41

Graham, Jim
66Columbus Checkers-7

Graham, Jimmy
28V128-2 Paulin's Candy-42

Graham, John
91British Columbia JHL-77
91British Columbia JHL-157

Graham, Pat
82Post Cereal-15
83Maple Leafs Postcards-9
83Penguins Heinz Photos-9

Graham, Robb
87Sudbury Wolves-13

Graham, Rod
71Rochester Americans-7
77Rochester Americans-11
77Rochester Americans-12
82Kingston Canadians-24

Graham, Ross
52Juniors Blue Tint-7

Graham, Ryan
04Gatineau Olympiques-17

Graham, Scott
03Huntsville Channel Cats-9

Grahame, John
97Providence Bruins-7
98Providence Bruins-9
99BAP Memorabilia-393
Gold-393
Silver-393
99Pacific Dynagon Ice-24
Blue-24
Copper-24
Gold-24
Premiere Date-24
99Pacific Omega-23
Copper-23
Gold-23
Ice Blue-23
Premiere Date-23
99SP Authentic-96
99Stadium Club-179
First Day Issue-179
One of a Kind-179
Printing Plates Black-179
Printing Plates Cyan-179
Printing Plates Magenta-179
Printing Plates Yellow-179
99Topps Premier Plus-100
Parallel-100
99Upper Deck-184
Exclusives-184
Exclusives 1 of 1-184
99Upper Deck Gold Reserve-184
99Wayne Gretzky Hockey-15
99Providence Bruins-11
00Aurora-13
Premiere Date-13
00BAP Memorabilia-222
Emerald-222
Ruby-222
Sapphire-222
Promos-222
00BAP Mem Chicago Sportsfest Copper-222
00BAP Memorabilia Chicago Sportsfest Blue-222
00BAP Memorabilia Chicago Sportsfest Gold-222
00BAP Memorabilia Chicago Sportsfest Ruby-222
00BAP Memorabilia Chicago Sun-Times Ruby-222
00BAP Memorabilia Chicago Sun-Times Gold-222
00BAP Mem Chicago Sun-Times Sapphire-222
00BAP Mem Toronto Fall Expo Copper-222
00BAP Memorabilia Toronto Fall Expo Gold-222
00BAP Memorabilia Toronto Fall Expo Ruby-222
00BAP Signature Series-67
Emerald-67
Ruby-67
Sapphire-67
Autographs-174
Autographs Gold-174
00Pacific-34
Copper-34
Gold-34
Ice Blue-34
Premiere Date-34
00Paramount-19
Copper-19
Gold-19
Holo-Gold-19
Holo-Silver-19
Ice Blue-19
Premiere Date-19
00Revolution-11
Blue-11
Premiere Date-11
Red-11
00Upper Deck-15
Exclusives Tier 1-15
Exclusives Tier 2-15
01Between the Pipes-11
Double Memorabilia-DM10
Jerseys-GJ42
Tandems-GT10
01Pacific-30
Extreme LTD-30
Hobby LTD-30
Premiere Date-30
Retail LTD-30
01Pacific Arena Exclusives-30
02BAP Sig Series Auto Buybacks 2000-174
02Between the Pipes-43
Gold-43
Silver-43
Jerseys-42
Tandems-17
02Pacific-27
Blue-27
Red-27
02Pacific Complete-221
Red-221
02Topps Total-57
02Upper Deck Vintage-22
03BAP Memorabilia-128
Emerald-128
Gold-128
Ruby-128
Sapphire-128
03ITG Action-586
Jerseys-M26
03Pacific-306
Blue-306
Red-306
03Pacific Complete-428
Red-428
03Pacific Exhibit-131
Blue Backs-131
Yellow Backs-131
03Pacific Invincible-85
Blue-85
Red-85
Retail-85
Freeze Frame-20
03Titanium-91
Hobby Jersey Number Parallels-91
Retail-91
Retail Jersey Number Parallels-91
03Topps Traded-TT59
Blue-TT59
Gold-TT59
Red-TT59
03Upper Deck-176
Canadian Exclusives-176
HG-176
03Upper Deck MVP-387
Gold Script-387
Silver Script-387
Canadian Exclusives-387
04Pacific-236
Blue-236
Red-236
05Panini Stickers-156
05Parkhurst-432
Facsimile Auto Parallel-432
05Upper Deck-421
06Hurricanes Postcards-11
06O-Pee-Chee-89
Rainbow-89
06Upper Deck-289
Exclusives Parallel-289
High Gloss Parallel-289
Masterpieces-289

Grahame, Ron
75Houston Aeros WHA-1
75O-Pee-Chee WHA-50
75O-Pee-Chee WHA-61
76O-Pee-Chee WHA-107
78O-Pee-Chee-219
78Topps-219
80Nordiques Postcards-12

Grahling, Eric
92Harvard Crimson-10

Grahn, Christer
70Swedish Hockey-195
71Swedish Hockey-281
72Swedish Stickers-66
74Swedish Stickers-141

Grahn, Josh
00Sioux Falls Stampede-12

Grahn, Karl-Olov
72Swedish Stickers-67

Grahouec, Toby
93Quebec Pee-Wee Tournament-1318

Gram, Chris
93Quebec Pee-Wee Tournament-1439

Gram, Jesper
98Danish Hockey League-41
99Danish Hockey League-217

Granak, Dominik
02Czech OFS Plus-235
03Czech OFS Plus-175
04Czech HC Slavia Praha Postcards-19
04Czech OFS-162
06Czech HC Slavia Praha Postcards-7
06Czech OFS-295

Granat, Elias
05Swedish SHL Elitset-204
Gold-204

Granath, Einar
56Swedish Alfabilder-48
64Swedish Coralli ISHockey-67
67Swedish Hockey-185

Granato, Cammi
92Sports Illustrated for Kids II-527
93Classic-66
93Classic Four-Sport *-254
Gold-254
94Classic Women of Hockey-W37
94Classic Pro Prospects-248
94Images Chrome *-CC12
95AHCA-10
04Ultimate Collection-51
04Upper Deck-199
Canadian Exclusives-199
HG Glossy Gold-199
HG Glossy Silver-199

Granato, Don
99Peoria Rivermen-2
00Worcester Icecats-30
01Worcester Icecats-30
02Worcester IceCats-27
03Worcester Ice Cats-27
04Worcester IceCats-23

Granato, Kevin
01Peoria Rivermen-13
02Peoria Rivermen-12

Granato, Tony
89O-Pee-Chee-161
89O-Pee-Chee-310
89O-Pee-Chee Stickers-10
89O-Pee-Chee Stickers-36
89O-Pee-Chee Stickers-150
89O-Pee-Chee Stickers-241
89Panini Stickers-285
89Topps-161
90Bowman-140
Tiffany-140
90Bowman Hat Tricks-18
Tiffany-18
90Kings Smokey-11
90O-Pee-Chee-62
90Panini Stickers-239
90Pro Set-117
90Score-48
Canadian-48
90Score Young Superstars-33
90Topps-62
Tiffany-62
90Upper Deck-272
French-272
91Pro Set Platinum-49
91Bowman-192
91Kraft-35
91O-Pee-Chee-88
91Panini Stickers-83
91Parkhurst-66
French-66
91Pinnacle-76
French-76
91Pro Set-98
French-98
91Score American-57
91Score Canadian Bilingual-57
91Score Canadian English-57
91Stadium Club-97
91Topps-88
91Upper Deck-172
91Upper Deck-508
French-172
French-508
91Finnish Semic World Champ Stickers-147
91Swedish Semic World Champ Stickers-147
92Bowman-50
92O-Pee-Chee-65
92Panini Stickers-68
92Panini Stickers French-68
92Parkhurst-301
Emerald Ice-301
92Pinnacle-69
92Pinnacle-262
French-69
French-262
92Pro Set-74
92Score-243
Canadian-243
USA Greats-4
92Seasons Patches-11
92Stadium Club-281
92Topps-242
Gold-242G
92Ultra-82
92Upper Deck-185
92Finnish Semic-162
93Donruss-160
93Leaf-201
93OPC Premier-144
93OPC Premier-504
Gold-144
Gold-504
93Panini Stickers-203
93Parkhurst-93
Emerald Ice-93
93Pinnacle-137
Canadian-137
93PowerPlay-115
93Score-52
93Score-444
Canadian-52
Canadian-444
93Stadium Club-285
Members Only Master Set-285
First Day Issue-285
93Topps/OPC Premier-144
93Topps/OPC Premier-504
Gold-144
Gold-504
93Ultra-63
93Upper Deck-146
SP-69
93Swedish Semic World Champ Stickers-181
94Be A Player-R98
99 All-Stars-G9
Signature Cards-114
94Canada Games NHL POGS-125
94Donruss-145
94Hockey Wit-32
94Leaf-229
94OPC Premier-183
Special Effects-183
94Parkhurst Vintage-V76
94Parkhurst SE-SE83
Gold-SE83
94Pinnacle-118
Artist's Proofs-118
Rink Collection-118
94Score-71
Gold-71
Platinum-71
94SP-56
Die Cuts-56
94Stadium Club Super Teams-11
94Stadium Club Super Team MemberOnly Set-11
94Topps/OPC Premier-183
Special Effects-183
94Ultra-305
94Upper Deck-29
Electric Ice-29
SP Inserts-SP126
SP Inserts Die Cuts-SP126
94Finnish Jaa Kiekko-126
95Canada Games NHL POGS-139
95Collector's Choice-194
Player's Club-194
Player's Club Platinum-194
95Donruss-111
95Leaf-174
95Metal-70
95Panini Stickers-267
95Parkhurst International-376
Emerald Ice-376
95Playoff One on One-49
95Score-233
Black Ice Artist's Proofs-233
Black Ice-233
95Stadium Club-116
Members Only Master Set-116
95Summit-100
Artist's Proofs-100
Ice-100
95Topps-58
OPC Inserts-58
95Ultra-249
95Upper Deck-201
Electric Ice-201
Electric Ice Gold-201
95Finnish Semic World Championships-117
95Swedish Globe World Championships-120
95Images Platinum Players-PL2
96Be A Player-142
Autographs-142
Autographs Silver-142
96Black Diamond-121
Gold-121
96Flair-84
Blue Ice-84
96Maggers-30
96Playoff One on One-340
96SP-140
97Collector's Choice-218
97Donruss-121
Press Proofs Silver-121
Press Proofs Gold-121
97Donruss Limited-144
Exposure-144
97NHL Aces Playing Cards-39
97Pacific-203
Copper-203
Emerald Green-203
Ice Blue-203
Red-203
Silver-203
97Pacific Dynagon-111
Copper-111
Dark Grey-111
Emerald Green-111
Ice Blue-111
Red-111
Silver-111
Best Kept Secrets-109
Tandems-67
97Pacific Invincible-125
Copper-125
Emerald Green-125
Ice Blue-125
Red-125
Silver-125
97Pacific Omega-201
Copper-201
Dark Gray-201
Emerald Green-201
Gold-201
Ice Blue-201
97Panini Stickers-227
97Paramount-165
Copper-165
Dark Grey-165
Emerald Green-165
Ice Blue-165
Red-165
Silver-165
97Pinnacle-187
Press Plates Back Black-187
Press Plates Back Cyan-187
Press Plates Back Magenta-187
Press Plates Back Yellow-187
Press Plates Front Black-187
Press Plates Front Cyan-187
Press Plates Front Magenta-187
Press Plates Front Yellow-187
97Pinnacle Inside-142
97Score-77
Artist's Proofs-77
Golden Blades-77
97SP Authentic-135
97Upper Deck-360
Game Dated Moments-360
98Aurora-167
98Be A Player-272
Press Release-272
98BAP Gold-272
98BAP Autographs-272
98BAP Autographs Gold-272
98Katch-126
98OPC Chrome-147
Refractors-147
98Pacific-380
Ice Blue-380
Red-380
98Pacific Dynagon Ice-165
Blue-165
Red-165
98Paramount-210
Copper-210
Emerald Green-210
Holo-Electric-210
Ice Blue-210
Silver-210
98Topps-147
O-Pee-Chee-147
98Upper Deck-352
Exclusives-352
Exclusives 1 of 1-352
Gold Reserve-352
99Pacific-371
Copper-371
Emerald Green-371
Gold-371
Ice Blue-371
Premiere Date-371
Red-371
00Upper Deck NHLPA-PA74
02BAP Sig Series Auto Buybacks 1998-272

Granberg, Gunnar
69Swedish Hockey-241
70Swedish Hockey-139

Granberg, Harry
56Swedish Alfabilder-65

Granberg, Roland
56Swedish Alfabilder-55

Granbois, Travis
06Quad City Mallards-5

Grand'maison, Dominic
907th Inn. Sketch QMJHL-247
917th Inn. Sketch QMJHL-257
94Central Hockey League-45
95Flint Generals-12

Grand, John
93Lakeland Ice Warriors-15

Grand, Patrick
95Swiss HNL-461
96Swiss HNL-362

Grand-Pierre, Jean-Luc
97Rochester Americans-5-5
98Rochester Americans-10
99BAP Memorabilia-80
Gold-80
Silver-80
99Pacific Omega-33
Copper-33
Gold-33
Ice Blue-33
Premiere Date-33
00BAP Memorabilia Update Tough Materials-T24
00BAP Mem Update Tough Materials Gold-T24
00Topps Chrome-223
OPC Refractors-223
Refractors-223
00Upper Deck-281
Exclusives Tier 1-281
Exclusives Tier 2-281
01Blue Jackets Donatos Pizza-16
01Upper Deck Victory-106
Gold-106
02O-Pee-Chee-228
02O-Pee-Chee Premier Blue Parallel-228
02O-Pee-Chee Premier Red Parallel-228
02O-Pee-Chee Factory Set-228
02Topps-228
OPC Blue Parallel-228
OPC Red Parallel-228
Factory Set-228
02Topps Total-361
02Upper Deck-296
Exclusives-296
02Upper Deck Beckett UD Promos-296
02Upper Deck Vintage-77
05German DEL-55
06German DEL-42

Grandberg, Geoff
907th Inn. Sketch WHL-208
917th Inn. Sketch WHL-21
917th Inn. Sketch Memorial Cup-83

Grande, Duilio
99Baie-Comeau Drakkar-11
00Baie-Comeau Drakkar-13
Signed-13
01Baie-Comeau Drakkar-11
02Reading Royals-22
02Reading Royals RBI Sports-175

Grandfield, Jeff
99OCN Blizzard-23
00OCN Blizzard-21

Grandmaitre, Patrick
99Quebec Remparts-5
Signed-5
99Bowman CHL-78
Gold-78
OPC International-78
03St. Francis Xavier X-Men-13
04St. Francis Xavier X-Men-7

Grandmaitre, Syl
81Kingston Canadians-9
82Kingston Canadians-9

Grandmont, Etienne
03Val d'Or Foreurs-2

Granholm, Henrik
65Finnish Hellas-134
70Finnish Jaakiekko-102

Granholm, Svante
67Swedish Hockey-218
69Swedish Hockey-333
70Swedish Hockey-251
71Swedish Hockey-309
72Swedish Stickers-293
73Swedish Stickers-145
74Swedish Stickers-216

Granicher, Martin
95Swiss HNL-322
96Swiss HNL-297

Grankvist, Erik
91Swedish Semic Elitserien Stickers-153
92Swedish Semic Elitserien Stickers-176
93Swedish Semic Elitserien-147
94Swedish Leaf-27
95Swedish Leaf-247

Granlund, Lars
69Swedish Hockey-97
71Swedish Hockey-353

Granlund, Mikael
93Finnish SISU-84
99German Bundesliga 2-167

Granqvist, Daniel
93Swedish Semic Elitserien-172

Granstedt, Mikael
83Swedish Semic Elitserien-182
84Swedish Semic Elitserien-205
86Swedish Panini Stickers-234
87Swedish Panini Stickers-220
89Swedish Semic Elitserien Stickers-202

Granstrom, Alf
69Swedish Hockey-78

Granstrom, Jonathan
04Swedish Elitset-257
Gold-257
05Swedish SHL Elitset-108
Star Potential-13

Granstrom, Lars-Olof
69Swedish Hockey-229

Grant, Alex
05ITG Heroes/Prosp Toronto Expo Parallel -308
05Saint John's Sea Dogs-2
05ITG Heroes and Prospects-308
Autographs Series II-AG
06Saint Johns Sea Dogs-1
06Saint Johns Sea Dogs-LE1

Grant, Benny
32O'Keefe Maple Leafs-17

Grant, Colton
06Medicine Hat Tigers-8

Grant, Danny
64Canadiens Postcards-7
67Canadiens IGA-23
68O-Pee-Chee-52
68Topps-52
69O-Pee-Chee-125
69O-Pee-Chee-208

Four-in-One-17
Stamps-10
69Topps-125
70Colgate Stamps-36
70Dad's Cookies-43
70Esso Power Players-176
70North Stars Postcards-3
70O-Pee-Chee-47
70Sargent Promotions Stamps-92
70Topps-47
Topps/OPC Sticker Stamps-11
71Letraset Action Replays-11
71O-Pee-Chee-79
O-Pee-Chee/Topps Booklets-11
71Sargent Promotions Stamps-85
71Topps-79
71Toronto Sun-132
72O-Pee-Chee-57
72Sargent Promotions Stamps-103
72Topps-39
73North Stars Postcards-7
73O-Pee-Chee-214
73Topps-161
74NHL Action Stamps-98
74O-Pee-Chee NHL-112
74O-Pee-Chee NHL-174
74Topps-112
74Topps-174
75O-Pee-Chee NHL-49
75O-Pee-Chee NHL-212
75O-Pee-Chee NHL-318
75Topps-49
75Topps-212
75Topps-318
76O-Pee-Chee NHL-16
76Topps-16
77O-Pee-Chee NHL-147
77Topps-147
78O-Pee-Chee-306
97Halifax Mooseheads I-24
97Halifax Mooseheads II-25
04ITG Franchises US West-256
Autographs-A-DGR
06Parkhurst-17
06Parkhurst-180
Autographs-17
Autographs-180

Grant, Derek
93Niagara Falls Thunder-14
95Central Hockey League-26
99Memphis RiverKings All-Time-9

Grant, Doug
73Red Wings McCarthy Postcards-6
74NHL Action Stamps-101
74O-Pee-Chee NHL-347
77O-Pee-Chee NHL-294
78O-Pee-Chee-373

Grant, Joe
81Swedish Semic Hockey VM Stickers-79

Grant, Jordan
03Plymouth Whalers-4

Grant, Kevin
86Kitchener Rangers-8
87Kitchener Rangers-8
88Sudbury Wolves-5
89ProCards IHL-197
90ProCards AHL/IHL-606
91ProCards-575
93Phoenix Roadrunners-8
95Houston Aeros-8
98German DEL-257
99German Adler Mannheim Eagles Postcards-22
99German DEL-21
00German DEL-98
01German Upper Deck-94

Grant, Lee
92British Columbia JHL-48
05Las Vegas Wranglers-8

Grant, Michael
83Hall of Fame-218
83Hall of Fame Postcards-O8
85Hall of Fame-218

Grant, Mitch
98UK Basingstoke Bison-16
99UK Basingstoke Bison-12

Grant, Peter
90Michigan Tech Huskies-5

Grant, Tommy
06Westside Warriors-11

Grant, Triston
03Vancouver Giants-11
04Vancouver Giants-9
05Philadelphia Phantoms-9
06Hot Prospects-173
Red Hot-173
White Hot-173
06O-Pee-Chee-572
Rainbow-572
06SP Authentic-222
Limited-222
06SP Game Used-140
Gold-140
Rainbow-140
06SPx-211
Spectrum-211
06The Cup Masterpiece Pressplates (Marquee Rookies)-572
06The Cup Masterpiece Pressplates (SP Authentic)-222
06The Cup Masterpiece Pressplates (SP Game Used)-140
06The Cup Masterpiece Pressplates (Victory)-324
06Upper Deck-483
Exclusives Parallel-483
High Gloss Parallel-483
Masterpieces-483
Victory-324
06Philadelphia Phantoms-13

Grant, Vince
99Ottawa 67's-14
00Amarillo Rattlers-7

Grantham, Ryley
06Moose Jaw Warriors-13

Grassel, Corey
95Madison Monsters-6

Grassie, Chris
91Nashville Knights-4
92Nashville Knights-6

Gratchev, Max
04Quebec Remparts-13
05Quebec Remparts-11
05Quebec Remparts Signature Series-11
05Rimouski Oceanic-28
06Rimouski Oceanic-4

Gratton, Benoit
96Portland Pirates-25
96Portland Pirates Shop N' Save-10
97Portland Pirates-10
98Portland Pirates-6
99Aurora-148
Premiere Date-148
99BAP Memorabilia-266
Gold-266
Silver-266
99Pacific-440
Copper-440
Emerald Green-440
Gold-440
Ice Blue-440
Premiere Date-440
Red-440
99Upper Deck Victory-311
01Quebec Citadelles-21
02Hamilton Bulldogs-22
03Parkhurst Original Six Montreal-12
03Pacific AHL Prospects-28
Gold-28
05German DEL-104

Gratton, Brad
87Kingston Canadians-19

Gratton, Chris
917th Inn. Sketch OHL-225
92Upper Deck-590
92Upper Deck-SP3
93Donruss-330
93Donruss-393
Rated Rookies-2
Special Print-V
93Leaf-331
Freshman Phenoms-3
93Lightning Kash n'Karry-3
93Lightning Season in Review-17
93OPC Premier-410
Gold-410
93Parkhurst-250
Emerald Ice-250
Calder Candidates-C3
Calder Candidates Gold-C3
Cherry's Playoff Heroes-D12
East/West Stars-E6
93Pinnacle-443
Canadian-443
Super Rookies-3
Super Rookies Canadian-3
93PowerPlay-443
Rookie Standouts-5
93Score-596
Gold-596
Canadian-596
Canadian Gold-596
93Stadium Club-320
Members Only Master Set-320
First Day Issue-320
93Topps/OPC Premier-410
Gold-410
93Ultra-423
Wave of the Future-5
93Upper Deck-78
Silver Skates-R4
Silver Skates Gold-R4
SP-149
93Classic-3
Top Ten-DP3
93Classic Four-Sport *-187
Gold-187
Chromium Draft Stars-DS60
LPs-LP24
Power Pick Bonus-PP20
Tri-Cards-TC4
94Be A Player-R110
Signature Cards-116
94Canada Games NHL POGS-223
94Donruss-189
94Finest-58
Super Team Winners-58
Refractors-58
94Flair-173
94Fleer-206
94Leaf-86
Gold Rookies-4
Limited Inserts-22
94Leaf Limited-56
94Lightning Health Plan-2
94Lightning Photo Album-14
94Lightning Postcards-9
94OPC Premier-439
94O-Pee-Chee Finest Inserts-20
94OPC Premier Special Effects-439
94Parkhurst-220
94Parkhurst-282
Gold-220
Gold-282
Crash the Game Green-22
Crash the Game Blue-22
Crash the Game Gold-22
Crash the Game Red-22
SE Vintage-16
94Pinnacle-19
94Pinnacle-468
Artist's Proofs-19
Artist's Proofs-468
Rink Collection-19
Rink Collection-468
94Select-77
Gold-77
94SP-111
Die Cuts-111
94Stadium Club-112
94Stadium Club-195
Members Only Master Set-112
Members Only Master Set-195
First Day Issue-112
First Day Issue-195
Super Team Winner Cards-112
Super Team Winner Cards-195
94Topps/OPC Premier-439
Special Effects-439
94Ultra-205
All-Rookies-4
All-Rookies Parallel-4
Power-3
94Upper Deck-345
Electric Ice-345
SP Inserts-SP75
SP Inserts Die Cuts-SP75
94Upper Deck NHLPA/Be A Player-6
94Classic Autographs-NNO
94Classic Pro Prospects-16
94Classic C3 *-20
94Images *-86
94Images *-138
95Bashan Super Stickers-114
95Canada Games NHL POGS-247
95Collector's Choice-140
95Collector's Choice-357
Player's Club-140
Player's Club-357
Player's Club Platinum-140
Player's Club Platinum-357
95Donruss-122
95Emotion-163
95Hoyle Eastern Playing Cards-28
95Imperial Stickers-114
95Leaf-133
95Leaf Limited-8
95Lightning Team Issue-10
95Metal-136
95Panini Stickers-126
95Parkhurst International-462
Emerald Ice-462
95Pinnacle-33
Artist's Proofs-33
Rink Collection-33
95Playoff One on One-92
95Pro Magnets-72
95Score-39
Black Ice Artist's Proofs-39
Black Ice-39
Check It-4
95SkyBox Impact-154
95Stadium Club-134
Members Only Master Set-134
95Summit-45
Artist's Proofs-45
Ice-45
95Topps-70
OPC Inserts-70
95Ultra-151
Gold Medallion-151
95Upper Deck-407
Electric Ice-407
Electric Ice Gold-407
Special Edition-SE75
Special Edition Gold-SE75
95Zenith-15
96Black Diamond-77
Gold-77
96Collector's Choice-245
96Collector's Choice-331
96Donruss-173
Press Proofs-173
96Donruss Canadian Ice-62
Gold Press Proofs-62
Red Press Proofs-62
O Canada-8
96Leaf-120
Press Proofs-120
96Metal Universe-144
96NHL Pro Stamps-72
96Pinnacle-141
Artist's Proofs-141
Foil-141
Premium Stock-141
Rink Collection-141
96Score-148
Artist's Proofs-148
Dealer's Choice Artist's Proofs-148
Special Artist's Proofs-148
Golden Blades-148
96SkyBox Impact-121
96SP-145
Holoview Collection-HC12
96Team Out-23
96Upper Deck-337
Generation Next-X32
Power Performers-P10
96Upper Deck Ice-65
Parallel-65
97Be A Player-137
Autographs-137
Autographs Die-Cuts-137
Autographs Prismatic Die-Cuts-137
97Collector's Choice-236
Star Quest-SQ61
97Crown Royale-96
Emerald Green-96
Ice Blue-96
Silver-96
97Donruss-56
Press Proofs Silver-56
Press Proofs Gold-56
97Donruss Canadian Ice-39
Dominion Series-39
Provincial Series-39
97Donruss Elite-91
Aspirations-91
Status-91
97Donruss Limited-148
Exposure-148
97Donruss Preferred-130
Cut to the Chase-130
97Donruss Priority-118
Stamp of Approval-118
97Flyers Phone Cards-2
97Katch-104
Gold-104
Silver-104
97Leaf-27
Fractal Matrix-27
Fractal Matrix Die Cuts-27
97Leaf International-27
Universal Ice-27
97NHL Aces Playing Cards-18
97Pacific-308
Copper-308
Emerald Green-308
Ice Blue-308
Red-308
Silver-308
97Pacific Dynagon-117
Copper-117
Dark Grey-117
Emerald Green-117
Ice Blue-117
Red-117
Silver-117
Tandems-62
97Pacific Invincible-131
Copper-131
Emerald Green-131
Ice Blue-131
Red-131
Silver-131
97Pacific Omega-164
Copper-164
Dark Gray-164
Emerald Green-164
Gold-164
Ice Blue-164
97Panini Stickers-103
97Paramount-131
Copper-131
Dark Grey-131
Emerald Green-131
Ice Blue-131
Red-131
Silver-131
97Pinnacle-183
Press Plates Back Black-183
Press Plates Back Cyan-183
Press Plates Back Magenta-183
Press Plates Back Yellow-183
Press Plates Front Black-183
Press Plates Front Cyan-183
Press Plates Front Magenta-183
Press Plates Front Yellow-183
97Pinnacle Certified-84
Red-84
Mirror Blue-84
Mirror Gold-84
Mirror Red-84
97Pinnacle Inside-110
97Pinnacle Tot Cert Platinum Blue-84
97Pinnacle Tot Certi Platinum Gold-84
97Pinnacle Totally Certified Platinum Red-84
97Pinnacle Tot Cert Mirror Platinum Gold-84
97Revolution-100
Copper-100
Emerald-100
Ice Blue-100
Silver-100
97Score-168
97Score Flyers-6
Platinum-6
Premier-6
97SP Authentic-112
97SPx-45
Bronze-45
Gold-45
Silver-45
Steel-45
Grand Finale-45
97Studio-90
Press Proofs Silver-90
Press Proofs Gold-90
97Upper Deck-155
97Upper Deck-327
97Zenith-56
Z-Gold-56
Z-Silver-56
98Aurora-138
98Be A Player-101
Press Release-101
98BAP Gold-101
98BAP Autographs-101
98BAP Autographs Gold-101
98BAP Tampa Bay All Star Game-101
98Finest-139
No Protectors-139
No Protectors Refractors-139
Refractors-139
98Pacific-55
Ice Blue-55
Red-55
98Pacific Dynagon Ice-135
Blue-135
Red-135
98Pacific Omega-218
Red-218
Opening Day Issue-218
98Paramount-173
Copper-173
Emerald Green-173
Holo-Electric-173
Ice Blue-173
Silver-173
98UD Choice-150
Prime Choice Reserve-150
Reserve-150
98Upper Deck-149
Exclusives-149
Exclusives 1 of 1-149
Gold Reserve-149
98Upper Deck MVP-192
Gold Script-192
Silver Script-192
Super Script-192
99Aurora-129
Premiere Date-129
99BAP Memorabilia-37
99BAP Memorabilia-361
Gold-37
Gold-361
Silver-37
Silver-361
99BAP Millennium-222
Emerald-222
Ruby-222
Sapphire-222
Signatures-222
Signatures Gold-222
99Crown Royale-128
Limited Series-128
Premiere Date-128
99O-Pee-Chee-170
99O-Pee-Chee Chrome-170
99O-Pee-Chee Chrome Refractors-170
99Pacific-389
Copper-389
Emerald Green-389
Gold-389
Ice Blue-389
Premiere Date-389
Red-389
99Pacific Dynagon Ice-180
Blue-180
Copper-180
Gold-180
Premiere Date-180
99Pacific Omega-215
Copper-215
Gold-215
Ice Blue-215
Premiere Date-215
99Pacific Prism-131
Holographic Blue-131
Holographic Gold-131
Holographic Mirror-131
Holographic Purple-131
Premiere Date-131
99Panini Stickers-143
99Paramount-217
Copper-217
Emerald-217
Gold-217
Holographic Emerald-217
Holographic Gold-217
Holographic Silver-217
Ice Blue-217
Premiere Date-217
Red-217
Silver-217
99Revolution-131
Premiere Date-131
Red-131
Shadow Series-131
99SP Authentic-80
99Stadium Club-43
First Day Issue-43
One of a Kind-43
Printing Plates Black-43
Printing Plates Cyan-43
Printing Plates Magenta-43
Printing Plates Yellow-43
99Topps/OPC-170
99Topps/OPC Chrome-170
Refractors-170
99Upper Deck MVP-193
Gold Script-193
Silver Script-193
Super Script-193
99Upper Deck MVP SC Edition-169
Gold Script-169
Silver Script-169
Super Script-169
99Upper Deck Victory-274
99Wayne Gretzky Hockey-158
00BAP Memorabilia-153
Emerald-153
Ruby-153
Sapphire-153
Promos-153
00BAP Mem Chicago Sportsfest Copper-153
00BAP Memorabilia Chicago Sportsfest Blue-153
00BAP Memorabilia Chicago Sportsfest Gold-153
00BAP Memorabilia Chicago Sportsfest Ruby-153
00BAP Memorabilia Chicago Sun-Times Ruby-153
00BAP Memorabilia Chicago Sun-Times Gold-153
00BAP Mem Chicago Sun-Times Sapphire-153
00BAP Mem Toronto Fall Expo Copper-153
00BAP Memorabilia Toronto Fall Expo Gold-153
00BAP Memorabilia Toronto Fall Expo Ruby-153
00BAP Parkhurst 2000-P80
00BAP Signature Series-99
Emerald-99
Ruby-99
Sapphire-99
00Crown Royale-14
Ice Blue-14
Limited Series-14
Premiere Date-14
Red-14
00O-Pee-Chee-84
00O-Pee-Chee Parallel-84
00Pacific-51
Copper-51
Gold-51
Ice Blue-51
Premiere Date-51
00Paramount-29
Copper-29
Gold-29
Holo-Gold-29
Holo-Silver-29
Ice Blue-29
Premiere Date-29
00Topps/OPC-84
Parallel-84
00Upper Deck-21
Exclusives Tier 1-21
Exclusives Tier 2-21
00Upper Deck MVP-28
First Stars-28
Second Stars-28
Third Stars-28
00Upper Deck Victory-30
00Upper Deck Vintage-41
01BAP Memorabilia-145
Emerald-145
Ruby-145
Sapphire-145
01BAP Signature Series Certified 100-C8
01BAP Signature Series Certified 50-C8
01BAP Signature Series Certified 1 of 1's-C8
01BAP Signature Series Autographs-LCG
01BAP Signature Series Autographs Gold-LCG
01O-Pee-Chee-226
01O-Pee-Chee Premier Parallel-226
01Pacific-49
Extreme LTD-49
Hobby LTD-49
Premiere Date-49
Retail LTD-49
01Pacific Adrenaline-22
Blue-22
Premiere Date-22
Red-22
Retail-22
01Pacific Arena Exclusives-49
01Parkhurst-118
01Topps-226
OPC Parallel-226
01Upper Deck-24
Exclusives-24
01Upper Deck MVP-20
01Upper Deck Victory-46
Gold-46
01Upper Deck Vintage-30
01Upper Deck Vintage-35
01Czech Stadion-241
02BAP First Edition-104
Jerseys-104
02BAP Sig Series Auto Buybacks 1998-101
02BAP Sig Series Auto Buybacks 1999-222
02BAP Sig Series Auto Buybacks 2001-LCG
02BAP Signature Series Famous Scraps-FS4
02BAP Signature Series Golf-GS20
02Crown Royale-11
Blue-11
Red-11
Retail-11
02Pacific-42
Blue-42
Red-42
02Pacific Complete-284
Red-284
02Titanium-12
Blue-12
Red-12
Retail-12
02Topps Total-155
02Upper Deck-265
Exclusives-265
02Upper Deck Beckett UD Promos-265
02Vanguard-12
LTD-12
03Avalanche Team Issue-6
03Beehive-149
Gold-149
Silver-149
03Black Diamond-31
Black-31
Green-31
Red-31
03ITG Action-488
03NHL Sticker Collection-29
03O-Pee-Chee-234
03OPC Blue-234
03OPC Gold-234
03OPC Red-234
03Pacific-262
Blue-262
Red-262
03Pacific Complete-2
Red-2
03Pacific Exhibit-114
Blue Backs-114
Yellow Backs-114
03SPx-74
Radiance-74
Spectrum-74
03Topps-234
Blue-234
Gold-234
Red-234
03Topps C55-77
Minis-77
Minis American Back-77
Minis American Back Red-77
Minis Bazooka Back-77
Minis Brooklyn Back-77
Minis Hat Trick Back-77
Minis O Canada Back-77
Minis O Canada Back Red-77
Minis Stanley Cup Back-77
03Topps Traded-TT39
Blue-TT39
Gold-TT39
Red-TT39
03Upper Deck-146
Canadian Exclusives-146
HG-146
03Upper Deck Classic Portraits-75
03Upper Deck MVP-324
Gold Script-324
Silver Script-324
Canadian Exclusives-324
03Upper Deck Trilogy-75
Limited-75
03Upper Deck Victory-147
Bronze-147
Gold-147
Silver-147
05Parkhurst-208
Facsimile Auto Parallel-208
05Upper Deck-331
05Upper Deck MVP-171
Gold-171
Platinum-171
06O-Pee-Chee-221
Rainbow-221

Gratton, Dan
82Oshawa Generals-12
83Oshawa Generals-9
88ProCards AHL-210

Gratton, Gilles
74O-Pee-Chee WHA-65
76O-Pee-Chee NHL-28
76Topps-28
77O-Pee-Chee NHL-207
77Topps-207
01Between the Pipes Masks-4
01Between the Pipes Masks Silver-4
01Between the Pipes Masks Gold-4

Gratton, Josh
01Kingston Frontenacs-4
02Windsor Spitfires-20
04Philadelphia Phantoms-4
05Hot Prospects-158
En Fuego-158
Red Hot-158
White Hot-158
05SP Authentic-273
Limited-273
05The Cup Masterpiece Pressplates (Ice)-239
05The Cup Master Pressplate Rookie Update-163
05The Cup Masterpiece Pressplates SPA-273
05Upper Deck Ice-239
05Upper Deck Rookie Update-163
05Philadelphia Phantoms-10

Gratton, Mike
90Rayside-Balfour Jr. Canadians-7

Gratton, Norm
74NHL Action Stamps-47
74NHL Action Stamps Update-19
74O-Pee-Chee NHL-288
74Sabres Postcards-8
75O-Pee-Chee NHL-34
75Topps-34

Graul, Thomas
83Swedish Semic VM Stickers-155
94German DEL-38
95German DEL-31
04German Berlin Eisbarens 50th Anniv-38

Grauwiler, Lukas
01Swiss HNL-390
02Swiss HNL-381
03Mississauga Ice Dogs-10

Grauwiler, Stefan
95Swiss HNL-162
96Swiss HNL-57
98Swiss Panini Stickers-351

Gravel, Florian
51Laval Dairy Lac St. Jean-53

Gravel, Francois
88ProCards AHL-275
89ProCards AHL-184
98German DEL-192
99German DEL-310

Gravel, Greg
80Oshawa Generals-8
81Oshawa Generals-16

Gravel, Mathieu
01Shawinigan Cataractes-7
02Shawinigan Cataractes-5
03Shawinigan Cataractes-14
04Baie-Comeau Drakkar-13

Gravel, Vincent
93Quebec Pee-Wee Tournament-1069

Gravelding, Chris
03Kitchener Rangers-10

Gravell, D.J.
93Quebec Pee-Wee Tournament-845

Gravelle, Dan
93Greensboro Monarchs-6
94Classic Pro Prospects-234
00San Diego Gulls-4
03Tulsa Oilers-6
04Tulsa Oilers-10

Gravelle, Leo
43Parade Sportive *-48
44Beehive Group II Photos-243
45Quaker Oats Photos-79A
45Quaker Oats Photos-79B
45Quaker Oats Photos-79C
51Laval Dairy QSHL-109
52St. Lawrence Sales-61

Graves, Adam
87Red Wings Little Caesars-12
88Red Wings Little Caesars-8
89Oilers Team Issue-8
90Oilers IGA-6
90O-Pee-Chee-251
90O-Pee-Chee-480
90Pro Set-84
90Score-163
Canadian-163
90Topps-251
90Upper Deck-344
French-344
91Pro Set Platinum-207
91Bowman-97
91Oilers Panini Team Stickers-6
91O-Pee-Chee-167
91OPC Premier-28
91Panini Stickers-122
91Parkhurst-339
French-339
91Pinnacle-16
French-16
91Pro Set-67
91Pro Set-443
French-67
French-443
91Score American-358
91Score Canadian Bilingual-235
91Score Canadian Bilingual-594
91Score Canadian English-235
91Score Canadian English-594
91Score Rookie/Traded-44T
91Stadium Club-332
91Topps-167
91Upper Deck-268
91Upper Deck-574
French-268
French-574
92Bowman-373
92O-Pee-Chee-158
92Panini Stickers-238
92Panini Stickers French-238
92Parkhurst-346
Emerald Ice-346
92Pinnacle-108
French-108
92Pro Set-115
92Score-71
Canadian-71
Canadian-75
92Stadium Club-150
92Topps-329
Gold-329G
92Ultra-136
92Upper Deck-388
92Upper Deck-453
92Windsor Spitfires-5
93Donruss-219
93Kraft-10
93Leaf-130
93OPC Premier-106
Gold-106
93Panini Stickers-92
93Parkhurst-134
Emerald Ice-134
93Pinnacle-99
Canadian-99
93PowerPlay-158
93Score-35
Canadian-35
Dynamic Duos U.S.-5
93Stadium Club-270
Members Only Master Set-270
First Day Issue-270
Master Photos-18
Master Photos Winners-18
93Topps/OPC Premier-106
Gold-106
93Ultra-43
93Upper Deck-128
Hat Tricks-HT1
SP-99
93Classic Team Canada-TC7
94Be A Player-R117
94Canada Games NHL POGS-259
94Canada Games NHL POGS-352
94Donruss-43
94Finest-23
Super Team Winners-23
Refractors-23
Division's Clear Cut-9
Ring Leaders-20
94Flair-111
94Fleer-132
Franchise Futures-3
94Hockey Wit-86
94Kraft-62
94Leaf-255
94Leaf Limited-13
94McDonald's Upper Deck-McD2
94OPC Premier-128
94OPC Premier-350
Special Effects-128
Special Effects-350
94Parkhurst-147
94Parkhurst-307
Gold-147
Gold-307
Crash the Game Green-15
Crash the Game Blue-15
Crash the Game Gold-15
Crash the Game Red-15
SE Vintage-41
94Pinnacle-62
Artist's Proofs-62
Rink Collection-62
Gamers-GR15
Team Pinnacle-TP6
Team Dufex Parallel-TP6
94Score-164
Gold-164
Platinum-164
Check It-CI9
Dream Team-DT9
94Select-48
Gold-48
94SP-77
Die Cuts-77
94Stadium Club Members Only-35
94Stadium Club-9
94Stadium Club-265
Members Only Master Set-9
Members Only Master Set-265
First Day Issue-9
First Day Issue-265
Super Team Winner Cards-9
Super Team Winner Cards-265
94Topps/OPC Premier-128
94Topps/OPC Premier-350
Special Effects-128
Special Effects-350
94Topps Finest Inserts-7
94Ultra-137
Award Winners-4
Power-4
Red Light Specials-4
94Upper Deck-10
Electric Ice-10
Ice Gallery-IG7
Predictor Retail-R5
Predictor Retail-R38
94Upper Deck Predictor Retail Exchange-R5
94Upper Deck Predictor Retail Exchange-R38
94Upper Deck SP Inserts-SP140
94Upper Deck SP Inserts Die Cuts-SP140
95SLU Hockey Canadian-6
95SLU Hockey American-8
95Be A Player-212
Signatures-S212
Signatures Die Cuts-S212
95Bowman-54
All-Foil-54
95Canada Games NHL POGS-179
95Collector's Choice-277
95Collector's Choice-358
Player's Club-277
Player's Club-358
Player's Club Platinum-277
Player's Club Platinum-358
95Donruss-82
95Donruss Elite-10
Die Cut Stars-10
Die Cut Uncut-10
95Emotion-112
95Hoyle Eastern Playing Cards-29
95Kenner Starting Lineup Cards-9
95Leaf-152
95Leaf Limited-11
95Panini Stickers-105
95Parkhurst International-137
Emerald Ice-137
95Pinnacle-45
Artist's Proofs-45
Rink Collection-45
95Playoff One on One-66
95Pro Magnets-96
95Score-2
Black Ice Artist's Proofs-2
Black Ice-2
95Select Certified-47
Mirror Gold-47
95SkyBox Impact-108
95SP-98
95Stadium Club-57
Members Only Master Set-57
95Summit-66
Artist's Proofs-66
Ice-66
95Topps-295
OPC Inserts-295
Home Grown Canada-HGC26
Power Lines-3PL
95Ultra-274
95Upper Deck-224
95Upper Deck-239
95Upper Deck-329
Electric Ice-224
Electric Ice-239
Electric Ice-329
Electric Ice Gold-224
Electric Ice Gold-239
Electric Ice Gold-329
Special Edition-SE57
Special Edition Gold-SE57
95Zenith-33
Gifted Grinders-17
95Swedish Globe World Championships-96
96Black Diamond-9
Gold-9
96Collector's Choice-174
96Collector's Choice-324
96Donruss-66
Press Proofs-66
96Donruss Elite-107
Die Cut Stars-107
96Fleer-67
96Fleer Picks-90
96Kraft Upper Deck-34
96Leaf-20
Press Proofs-20
96Maggers-31
96NHL Pro Stamps-96
96Pinnacle-9
Artist's Proofs-9
Foil-9
Premium Stock-9
Rink Collection-9
96Score-81
Artist's Proofs-81
Dealer's Choice Artist's Proofs-81
Special Artist's Proofs-81
Golden Blades-81
96Select Certified-51
Artist's Proofs-51
Blue-51
Mirror Blue-51
Mirror Gold-51
Mirror Red-51
Red-51
96SkyBox Impact-78
96SP-103
96Summit-120
Artist's Proofs-120
Ice-120
Metal-120
Premium Stock-120
96Team Out-6
96Upper Deck-297
Power Performers-P5
96Upper Deck Ice-44
Parallel-44
96Collector's Edge Ice Livin' Large-L1
97Be A Player-58
Autographs-58
Autographs Die-Cuts-58
Autographs Prismatic Die-Cuts-58
97Black Diamond-2
Double Diamond-2
Triple Diamond-2
Quadruple Diamond-2
97Collector's Choice-163
97Crown Royale-83
Emerald Green-83
Ice Blue-83
Silver-83
97Donruss-70
Press Proofs Silver-70
Press Proofs Gold-70
97Donruss Canadian Ice-97
Dominion Series-97
Provincial Series-97
97Donruss Elite-47
Aspirations-47
Status-47
97Donruss Limited-18
Exposure-18

97Donruss Preferred-133
Cut to the Chase-133
97Donruss Priority-83
Stamp of Approval-83
97Katch-91
Gold-91
Silver-91
97Leaf-89
Fractal Matrix-89
Fractal Matrix Die Cuts-89
97Leaf International-89
Universal Ice-89
97Pacific-26
Copper-26
Emerald Green-26
Ice Blue-26
Red-26
Silver-26
97Pacific Dynagon-77
Copper-77
Dark Grey-77
Emerald Green-77
Ice Blue-77
Red-77
Silver-77
Best Kept Secrets-58
Tandems-69
97Pacific Invincible-85
Copper-85
Emerald Green-85
Ice Blue-85
Red-85
Silver-85
NHL Regime-127
97Pacific Omega-144
Copper-144
Dark Gray-144
Emerald Green-144
Gold-144
Ice Blue-144
97Paramount-114
Copper-114
Dark Grey-114
Emerald Green-114
Ice Blue-114
Red-114
Silver-114
97Pinnacle-174
Press Plates Back Black-174
Press Plates Back Cyan-174
Press Plates Back Magenta-174
Press Plates Back Yellow-174
Press Plates Front Black-174
Press Plates Front Cyan-174
Press Plates Front Magenta-174
Press Plates Front Yellow-174
97Pinnacle Certified-96
Red-96
Mirror Blue-96
Mirror Gold-96
Mirror Red-96
97Pinnacle Inside-104
97Pinnacle Tot Cert Platinum Blue-96
97Pinnacle Tot Certi Platinum Gold-96
97Pinnacle Totally Certified Platinum Red-96
97Pinnacle Tot Cert Mirror Platinum Gold-96
97Revolution-86
Copper-86
Emerald-86
Ice Blue-86
Silver-86
97Score-142
Artist's Proofs-142
Golden Blades-142
97Score Rangers-4
Platinum-4
Premier-4
97SP Authentic-103
97Upper Deck-108
98Aurora-121
98Be A Player-91
Press Release-91
98BAP Gold-91
98BAP Autographs-91
98BAP Autographs Gold-91
98BAP Tampa Bay All Star Game-91
98Bowman's Best-81
Refractors-81
Atomic Refractors-81
98Crown Royale-87
Limited Series-87
98Katch-91
98OPC Chrome-89
Refractors-89
98Pacific-293
Ice Blue-293
Red-293
98Pacific Dynagon Ice-120
Blue-120
Red-120
98Pacific Omega-155
Red-155
Opening Day Issue-155
98Panini Photocards-29
98Panini Stickers-81
98Paramount-151
Copper-151
Emerald Green-151
Holo-Electric-151
Ice Blue-151
Silver-151
98Topps-89
O-Pee-Chee-89
98Topps Gold Label Class 1-41
Black-41
Black One of One-41
One of One-41
Red-41
Red One of One-41
98Topps Gold Label Class 2-41
98Topps Gold Label Class 2 Black-41
98Topps Gold Label Class 2 Black 1 of 1-41
98Topps Gold Label Class 2 One of One-41
98Topps Gold Label Class 2 Red-41
98Topps Gold Label Class 2 Red One of One-41
98Topps Gold Label Class 3-41
98Topps Gold Label Class 3 Black-41
98Topps Gold Label Class 3 Black 1 of 1-41
98Topps Gold Label Class 3 One of One-41
98Topps Gold Label Class 3 Red-41
98Topps Gold Label Class 3 Red One of One-41
98UD Choice-134
Prime Choice Reserve-134
Reserve-134
99Aurora-93
Premiere Date-93
99BAP Memorabilia-15
Gold-15
Silver-15
99BAP Millennium-166
Emerald-166
Ruby-166
Sapphire-166
Signatures-166
Signatures Gold-166
99BAP Millennium All-Star Fantasy-166
99O-Pee-Chee-148
99O-Pee-Chee Chrome-148
99O-Pee-Chee Chrome Refractors-148
99Pacific-269
Copper-269
Emerald Green-269
Gold-269
Ice Blue-269
Premiere Date-269
Red-269
99Pacific Dynagon Ice-129
Blue-129
Copper-129
Gold-129
Premiere Date-129
99Pacific Omega-150
Copper-150
Gold-150
Ice Blue-150
Premiere Date-150
99Panini Stickers-100
99Paramount-149
Copper-149
Emerald-149
Gold-149
Holographic Emerald-149
Holographic Gold-149
Holographic Silver-149
Ice Blue-149
Premiere Date-149
Red-149
Silver-149
99Revolution-96
Premiere Date-96
Red-96
Shadow Series-96
99SPx-100
Radiance-100
Spectrum-100
99Stadium Club-149
First Day Issue-149
One of a Kind-149
Printing Plates Black-149
Printing Plates Cyan-149
Printing Plates Magenta-149
Printing Plates Yellow-149
99Topps/OPC-148
99Topps/OPC Chrome-148
Refractors-148
99Topps Gold Label Class 1-75
Black-75
Black One of One-75
One of One-75
Red-75
Red One of One-75
99Topps Gold Label Class 2-75
99Topps Gold Label Class 2 Black-75
99Topps Gold Label Class 2 Black 1 of 1-75
99Topps Gold Label Class 2 One of One-75
99Topps Gold Label Class 2 Red-75
99Topps Gold Label Class 2 Red One of One-75
99Topps Gold Label Class 3-75
99Topps Gold Label Class 3 Black-75
99Topps Gold Label Class 3 Black 1 of 1-75
99Topps Gold Label Class 3 One of One-75
99Topps Gold Label Class 3 Red-75
99Topps Gold Label Class 3 Red One of One-75
99Topps Premier Plus-45
Parallel-45
99Upper Deck-88
Exclusives-88
Exclusives 1 of 1-88
99Upper Deck Gold Reserve-88
99Upper Deck MVP-135
Gold Script-135
Silver Script-135
Super Script-135
99Upper Deck Victory-191
99Wayne Gretzky Hockey-112
00Aurora-93
Premiere Date-93
00BAP Memorabilia-181
Emerald-181
Ruby-181
Sapphire-181
Promos-181
00BAP Mem Chicago Sportsfest Copper-181
00BAP Memorabilia Chicago Sportsfest Blue-181
00BAP Memorabilia Chicago Sportsfest Gold-181
00BAP Memorabilia Chicago Sportsfest Ruby-181
00BAP Memorabilia Chicago Sun-Times Ruby-181
00BAP Memorabilia Chicago Sun-Times Gold-181
00BAP Mem Chicago Sun-Times Sapphire-181
00BAP Mem Toronto Fall Expo Copper-181
00BAP Memorabilia Toronto Fall Expo Gold-181
00BAP Memorabilia Toronto Fall Expo Ruby-181
00BAP Parkhurst 2000-P209
00BAP Signature Series-37
Emerald-37
Ruby-37
Sapphire-37
Autographs-124
Autographs Gold-124
00O-Pee-Chee-174
00O-Pee-Chee Parallel-174
00Pacific-261
Copper-261
Gold-261
Ice Blue-261
Premiere Date-261
00Paramount-161
Copper-161
Gold-161
Holo-Gold-161
Holo-Silver-161
Ice Blue-161
Premiere Date-161
00Private Stock Game Gear-73
00Revolution-95
Blue-95
Premiere Date-95
Red-95
00Stadium Club-116
00Titanium Game Gear-34
00Titanium Game Gear-113
00Titanium Game Gear Patches-113
00Topps/OPC-174
Parallel-174
Game-Worn Sweaters-GWAG
00Topps Chrome-117
OPC Refractors-117
Refractors-117
00Topps Heritage-134
Autographs-HA-AG
00Topps Stars Game Gear-GGAG
00Upper Deck-118
Exclusives Tier 1-118
Exclusives Tier 2-118
00Upper Deck MVP-116
First Stars-116
Second Stars-116
Third Stars-116
00Upper Deck Victory-153
00Upper Deck Vintage-238
00Upper Deck Vintage-246
00Czech Stadion-161
01BAP Signature Series-168
Autographs-168
Autographs Gold-168
01O-Pee-Chee-122
01O-Pee-Chee Premier Parallel-122
01Pacific-257
Extreme LTD-257
Hobby LTD-257
Premiere Date-257
Retail LTD-257
01Pacific Arena Exclusives-257
01Pacific Heads-Up Quad Jerseys-25
01Parkhurst-250
01Sharks Postcards-1
01Topps-122
OPC Parallel-122
01Topps Heritage-171
01Upper Deck-377
Exclusives-377
02BAP Memorabilia Mini Stanley Cups-28
02BAP Signature Series-90
Autographs-90
Autograph Buybacks 1998-91
Autograph Buybacks 1999-166
Autograph Buybacks 2000-124
Autograph Buybacks 2001-168
Autographs Gold-90
02Pacific-333
Blue-333
Red-333
02Pacific Complete-160
Red-160
02Sharks Team Issue-2
02Topps Total-13
02Upper Deck-393
Exclusives-393
02Upper Deck Beckett UD Promos-393
02Upper Deck MVP-153
Gold-153
Classics-153
Golden Classics-153
03ITG Action-500
03NHL Sticker Collection-284
03Parkhurst Original Six Detroit-55
03Parkhurst Original Six New York-31
03Parkhurst Original Six New York-100
Memorabilia-NM61
03Upper Deck MVP-351
Gold Script-351
Silver Script-351
Canadian Exclusives-351

Graves, Hilliard
73O-Pee-Chee-110
73Topps-110
74O-Pee-Chee NHL-306
75O-Pee-Chee NHL-62
75Topps-62
76O-Pee-Chee NHL-273
77Canucks Canada Dry Cans-5
77Canucks Royal Bank-7
77O-Pee-Chee NHL-286
78Canucks Royal Bank-8
78O-Pee-Chee-357
79Jets Postcards-7
79O-Pee-Chee-294

Graves, Mike
93Quebec Pee-Wee Tournament-1151
97Arizona Icecats-11
98Arizona Icecats-9
99Arizona Icecats-9
00Arizona Icecats-9

Graves, Steve
81Sault Ste. Marie Greyhounds-13
82Sault Ste. Marie Greyhounds-9
83Sault Ste. Marie Greyhounds-8
84Nova Scotia Oilers-9
85Nova Scotia Oilers-17
86Oilers Red Rooster-15
88Oilers Tenth Anniversary-32
90ProCards AHL/IHL-362

Gray, Alex
23V128-1 Paulin's Candy-20

Gray, Brandon
93Oshawa Generals-6
96Pensacola Ice Pilots-10

Gray, Joe
95Waterloo Blackhawks -5

Gray, John
75Phoenix Roadrunners WHA-9
76O-Pee-Chee WHA-25
78Jets Postcards-5

Gray, Mike
917th Inn. Sketch WHL-5
93Saskatoon Blades-10

Gray, Roy
93London Knights-10
93London Knights-24
95Slapshot-261
98San Antonio Iguanas-14
99Odessa Jackalopes-10

Gray, Terry
61Topps-16
62Topps-20
62Quebec Aces-8
63Quebec Aces-9
64Quebec Aces-6
65Quebec Aces-6
68O-Pee-Chee-44
68Topps-44

Grayling, Ted
91Air Canada SJHL-D11
92Saskatchewan JHL-75

Greaves, Simon
98UK Kingston Hawks-4
99UK Hull Thunder-4

Grebeshkov, Denis
00Russian Hockey League-303
02BAP Memorabilia Draft Redemptions-18
02Russian Future Stars-6
02Russian Hockey League-204
02Russian Young Lions-7
03ITG Action-667
03ITG Used Signature Series-181
Gold-181
03ITG VIP Rookie Debut-127
03Parkhurst Rookie-140
Rookie Emblems-RE-20
Rookie Emblems Gold-RE-20
Rookie Jerseys-RJ-20
Rookie Jerseys Gold-RJ-20
Rookie Numbers-RN-20
Rookie Numbers Gold-RN-20
03UD Premier Collection-119
03Upper Deck Rookie Update-202
03AHL Top Prospects-10
03Manchester Monarchs-5
03Manchester Monarchs Team Issue-6
03Pacific AHL Prospects-48
Gold-48
04Pacific-285
Blue-285
Red-285
04AHL All-Stars-15
04AHL Top Prospects-30
04Manchester Monarchs-6
04Manchester Monarchs Tobacco-7
04ITG Heroes and Prospects-14
Autographs-DG
Emblems-37
Emblems Gold-37
He Shoots-He Scores Prizes-31
Jersey Autographs-37
Jerseys-37
Jerseys Gold-37
Numbers-37
Numbers Gold-37
04ITG Heroes/Prospects Toronto Expo '05-14
04ITG Heroes/Prospects Expo Heroes/Pros-14
05ITG Heroes/Prosp Toronto Expo Parallel -103
05Parkhurst-311
05AHL All-Stars-10
05Manchester Monarchs-6
05Manchester Monarchs-34
05ITG Heroes and Prospects-103
Autographs-A-DG

Grecica, Jason
06Moose Jaw Warriors-21

Grecko, Peter
93Quebec Pee-Wee Tournament-1712

Greco, Brady
01Michigan Tech Huskies-10
02Chicago Steel-9
05Johnstown Chiefs-10

Greco, Gus
82Sault Ste. Marie Greyhounds-10
83Sault Ste. Marie Greyhounds-9

Greco, Piero
97UK Sheffield Steelers-21

Greco, Ron
93Quebec Pee-Wee Tournament-1444

Gredder, Mike
82Indianapolis Checkers-6

Greeley, Stephen
03Boston University Terriers-7

Green, Blake
93Quebec Pee-Wee Tournament-1668

Green, Cory
92British Columbia JHL-106

Green, Darryl
95Slapshot-366

Green, Dave
91British Columbia JHL-100
92British Columbia JHL-73
92Clarkson Knights-7
93Windsor Spitfires-9
94Windsor Spitfires-11

Green, Dustin
91British Columbia JHL-26
92British Columbia JHL-55

Green, Josh
95Bowman Draft Prospects-P15
95Medicine Hat Tigers-7
95Classic-60
Autographs-7
96Medicine Hat Tigers-6
96Collect Edge Ice Sign Sealed Delivered-4
97Portland Winter Hawks-7
98Bowman's Best-119
Refractors-119
Atomic Refractors-119
98Pacific Dynagon Ice-88
Blue-88
Red-88
98Pacific Omega-116
Red-116
Opening Day Issue-116
98SP Authentic-99
Power Shift-99
98Upper Deck-418
Exclusives-418
Exclusives 1 of 1-418
Generation Next-GN13
Generation Next Quantum 1-GN13
Generation Next Quantum 2-GN13
Generation Next Quantum 3-GN13
Gold Reserve-418
98Upper Deck MVP-98
Gold Script-98
Silver Script-98
Super Script-98
00O-Pee-Chee-172
00O-Pee-Chee Parallel-172
00Pacific-249
Copper-249
Gold-249
Ice Blue-249
Premiere Date-249
00Topps/OPC-172
Parallel-172
02NHL Power Play Stickers-26
03Lowell Lock Monsters-13
03Lowell Lock Monsters Photo Album-12
04Manitoba Moose-17
05Manitoba Moose-10
06Canucks Postcards-8

Green, Mark
91Johnstown Chiefs-16

Green, Mike
98Kootenay Ice-9
00Knoxville Speed-25
01Macon Whoopee-10
01Saskatoon Blades-18
01Saskatoon Blades-18
02Saskatoon Blades-18
02Saskatoon Blades-18
03ITG VIP Rookie Debut-117
03Parkhurst Rookie-111
03Topps Traded-TT99
Blue-TT99
Gold-TT99
Red-TT99
03Upper Deck Rookie Update-170
03Pacific AHL Prospects-73
Gold-73
03Saskatoon Blades-13
03Saskatoon Blades-13
04German DEL-249
04German Nuremburg Ice Tigers Postcards-8
04Saskatoon Blades-11
04Saskatoon Blades-11
04ITG Heroes and Prospects-95
04ITG Heroes and Prospects-95
Autographs-MGR
Autographs-MGR
Combos-12
Combos-12
Complete Emblems-2
Complete Emblems-2
Top Prospects-16
Top Prospects-16
04ITG Heroes/Prospects Toronto Expo '05-95
04ITG Heroes/Prospects Toronto Expo '05-95
04ITG Heroes/Prospects Expo Heroes/Pros-95
04ITG Heroes/Prospects Expo Heroes/Pros-95
05Black Diamond-294
05Black Diamond-294
05Hot Prospects-183
En Fuego-183
Red Hot-183
White Hot-183
05Parkhurst-498
05Parkhurst-498
Facsimile Auto Parallel-498
Facsimile Auto Parallel-498
05SP Authentic-287
05SP Authentic-287
Limited-287
Limited-287
05SP Game Used-240
05SP Game Used-240
05SPx-292
05SPx-292
05The Cup Masterpiece Pressplate Artifact-342
05The Cup Master Pressplate Black Diamond-294
05The Cup Masterpiece Pressplates (Ice)-237
05The Cup Masterpiece Pressplate Rookie Update-193
05The Cup Masterpiece Pressplates SPA-287
05The Cup Masterpiece Pressplates SP GU-240
05The Cup Masterpiece Pressplates SP GU-240
05The Cup Masterpiece Pressplates (SPx)-292
05The Cup Masterpiece Pressplates Trilogy-318
05The Cup Masterpiece Pressplate Ult Coll-184
05UD Artifacts-342
05UD Artifacts-342
05Ultimate Collection-184
Gold-184
Gold-184
05Upper Deck-438
05Upper Deck-438
05Upper Deck Ice-237
05Upper Deck Ice-237
05Upper Deck Rookie Update-193
05Upper Deck Rookie Update-193
05Upper Deck Trilogy-318
05Upper Deck Trilogy-318
05German DEL-126
05Hershey Bears-9
06Be A Player-121
Autographs-121
Signatures-MG
Signatures Duals-DGE
06Iowa Stars-8
06ITG Heroes and Prospects-162
Autographs-AMG
Calder Cup Champions-CC03
Jerseys-GUJ05
Jerseys Gold-GUJ05
Emblems-GUE05
Emblems Gold-GUE05
Numbers-GUN05
Numbers Gold-GUN05

Green, Morten
98Danish Hockey League-34
99Swedish Upper Deck-116
02Swedish SHL-247
Parallel-247
03Swedish Elite-254
Silver-254
04Swedish Elitset-100
Gold-100
04Swedish MoDo Postcards-22
05Swedish SHL Elitset-103
Gold-103
06Swedish SHL Elitset-110

Green, OHL
84Sault Ste. Marie Greyhounds-7

Green, Red
23V145-1-31
24C144 Champ's Cigarettes-27
24V130 Maple Crispette-10
24V145-2-15
25Dominion Chocolates-84

Green, Rick
77O-Pee-Chee NHL-245
77Topps-245
78Capitals Team Issue-5
78O-Pee-Chee-363
79Capitals Team Issue-5
79O-Pee-Chee-309
80O-Pee-Chee-33
80Topps-33
81Capitals Team Issue-6
81O-Pee-Chee-348
81O-Pee-Chee Stickers-193
81Topps-E118
82Canadiens Postcards-8
82Canadiens Steinberg-5
82O-Pee-Chee-183
82O-Pee-Chee Stickers-156
82Post Cereal-20
82Topps Stickers-156
83Canadiens Postcards-9
83NHL Key Tags-64
83O-Pee-Chee-188
84Canadiens Postcards-8
84O-Pee-Chee-262
85Canadiens Postcards-12
85Canadiens Postcards-13
85Canadiens Provigo-6
86Canadiens Postcards-6
86Kraft Drawings-22
87Canadiens Postcards-8
87Canadiens Vachon Stickers-65
87Canadiens Vachon Stickers-66
87Canadiens Vachon Stickers-68
87Canadiens Vachon Stickers-70
87O-Pee-Chee-234
87O-Pee-Chee Stickers-11
87Panini Stickers-60
88Canadiens Postcards-12
90OPC Premier-37
90Pro Set-436
90Score Rookie/Traded-84T
91Panini Stickers-147
91Red Wings Little Caesars-7
00Canadiens Postcards-33
01Canadiens Postcards-31
01Upper Deck Legends-37
02Canadiens Postcards-29

Green, Scott
92Northern Michigan Wildcats-7
93Northern Michigan Wildcats-8
98Tacoma Sabercats-9
99San Antonio Iguanas-6
02Odessa Jackalopes-12
03Odessa Jackalopes-9

Green, Scott (OHL)
84Sault Ste. Marie Greyhounds-7

Green, Shawn
82Victoria Cougars-9

Green, Shayne
89Victoria Cougars-10
907th Inn. Sketch WHL-256
917th Inn. Sketch WHL-89
92Dayton Bombers-11
95Vancouver VooDoo RHI-10
99Tacoma Sabercats-19

Green, Shorty
23V145-1-30
24C144 Champ's Cigarettes-28
24V130 Maple Crispette-22
24V145-2-14
25Dominion Chocolates-83
83Hall of Fame-140
83Hall of Fame Postcards-K5
85Hall of Fame-140

Green, Ted
61Shirriff/Salada Coins-16
61Topps-2
62Topps-7
Hockey Bucks-7
63Topps-7
64Beehive Group III Photos-10
64Coca-Cola Caps-3
64Topps-32
64Toronto Star-10
65Coca-Cola-3
65Topps-98
66Topps-37
66Topps USA Test-37
67Topps-94
68O-Pee-Chee-4
68Shirriff Coins-12
68Topps-4
69O-Pee-Chee-23
69O-Pee-Chee-218
Four-in-One-6
69Topps-23
70Bruins Postcards-19
70Dad's Cookies-44
70Esso Power Players-57
70O-Pee-Chee-134
70Sargent Promotions Stamps-4
71Bruins Postcards-13
71O-Pee-Chee-173
71Sargent Promotions Stamps-6
71Toronto Sun-9
72Whalers New England WHA-8
72 7-Eleven Slurpee Cups WHA-8
75O-Pee-Chee WHA-57
76O-Pee-Chee WHA-112
78Jets Postcards-6
81Oilers Red Rooster-xx
82Oilers Red Rooster-NNO
83Oilers McDonald's-20
84Oilers Red Rooster-NNO
86Oilers Red Rooster-NNO
88Oilers Tenth Anniversary-57
90Oilers IGA-7
91Oilers IGA-27
92Oilers IGA-27
94Parkhurst Tall Boys-3
95Parkhurst '66-67-6
Coins-6
02Rangers Team Issue-4
03Rangers Team Issue-24

Green, Tim
98Fort Worth Brahmas-3
98Tri-City Americans-12
00Jackson Bandits-25
00Lethbridge Hurricanes-8
01Lethbridge Hurricanes-4
04Columbus Cottonmouths-18

Green, Travis
88Spokane Chiefs-9
90ProCards AHL/IHL-510
91ProCards-467
92Parkhurst-343
Emerald Ice-343
92Ultra-343
93Donruss-200
93Leaf-127
93OPC Premier-489
Gold-489
93Parkhurst-126
Emerald Ice-126
93PowerPlay-383
93Score-661
Gold-661
Canadian-661
Canadian Gold-661
93Stadium Club-394
Members Only Master Set-394
First Day Issue-394
93Topps/OPC Premier-489
Gold-489
93Ultra-365
93Upper Deck-59
93Classic Pro Prospects-126
94Canada Games NHL POGS-156
94Donruss-75
94Leaf-288
94Parkhurst-137
Gold-137
94Pinnacle-216
Artist's Proofs-216
Rink Collection-216
94Stadium Club-236
Members Only Master Set-236
First Day Issue-236
Super Team Winner Cards-236
94Ultra-126
94Upper Deck-220
Electric Ice-220
95Be A Player-15
Signatures-S15
Signatures Die Cuts-S15
95Canada Games NHL POGS-170
95Donruss-208
95Finest-79
Refractors-79
95Leaf Limited-100
95Metal-90
95Parkhurst International-400
Emerald Ice-400
95Playoff One on One-280
95SP-87
95Summit-60
Artist's Proofs-60
Ice-60
95Topps-89
OPC Inserts-89
95Ultra-266
High Speed-12
95Upper Deck-473
Electric Ice-473
Electric Ice Gold-473
Special Edition-SE138
Special Edition Gold-SE138
96Collector's Choice-157
96Donruss-175
Press Proofs-175
96Fleer-64
96Fleer Picks-70
96Islander Postcards-5
96Leaf-131
Press Proofs-131
96Leaf Preferred-5
Press Proofs-5
96Metal Universe-92
96NHL Aces Playing Cards-19
96Pinnacle-70
Artist's Proofs-70
Foil-70
Premium Stock-70
Rink Collection-70
96Playoff One on One-418
96Score-15
Artist's Proofs-15
Dealer's Choice Artist's Proofs-15
Special Artist's Proofs-15
Golden Blades-15
96SkyBox Impact-75
96SP-94
96Summit-61
Artist's Proofs-61
Ice-61
Metal-61
Premium Stock-61
96Ultra-101
Gold Medallion-101
96Upper Deck-290
96Zenith-26
Artist's Proofs-26
97Be A Player-63
Autographs-63
Autographs Die-Cuts-63
Autographs Prismatic Die-Cuts-63
97Collector's Choice-160
Star Quest-SQ39
97Donruss-62
Press Proofs Silver-62
Press Proofs Gold-62
97Donruss Canadian Ice-65
Dominion Series-65
Provincial Series-65
97Donruss Limited-59
97Donruss Limited-110
Exposure-59
Exposure-110
97Donruss Priority-102
Stamp of Approval-102
97Katch-87
Gold-87
Silver-87
97Pacific-170
Copper-170
Emerald Green-170
Ice Blue-170
Red-170
Silver-170
97Pacific Dynagon-73
Copper-73
Dark Grey-73
Emerald Green-73
Ice Blue-73
Red-73
Silver-73
Tandems-72
97Pacific Invincible-81
Copper-81
Emerald Green-81
Ice Blue-81
Red-81
Silver-81
97Pacific Omega-137
Copper-137
Dark Gray-137
Emerald Green-137
Gold-137
Ice Blue-137
97Panini Stickers-79
97Paramount-108
Copper-108
Dark Grey-108
Emerald Green-108
Ice Blue-108
Red-108
Silver-108
97Pinnacle-167
Press Plates Back Black-167
Press Plates Back Cyan-167
Press Plates Back Magenta-167
Press Plates Back Yellow-167
Press Plates Front Black-167
Press Plates Front Cyan-167
Press Plates Front Magenta-167
Press Plates Front Yellow-167
97Pinnacle Certified-123
Red-123
Mirror Blue-123
Mirror Gold-123
Mirror Red-123
97Pinnacle Inside-130
97Pinnacle Tot Cert Platinum Blue-123
97Pinnacle Tot Certi Platinum Gold-123
97Pinnacle Totally Certified Platinum Red-123
97Pinnacle Tot Cert Mirror Platinum Gold-123
97Revolution-81
Copper-81
Emerald-81
Ice Blue-81
Silver-81
97Score-173
97SP Authentic-94
97Upper Deck-307
98Aurora-1
98Be A Player-155
Press Release-155
98BAP Gold-155
98BAP Autographs-155
98BAP Autographs Gold-155
98Crown Royale-1
Limited Series-1
98Katch-6
98OPC Chrome-162
Refractors-162
98Pacific-50
Ice Blue-50
Red-50
98Pacific Dynagon Ice-1
Blue-1
Red-1
98Pacific Omega-1
Red-1
Opening Day Issue-1
98Paramount-1
Copper-1
Emerald Green-1
Holo-Electric-1
Ice Blue-1
Silver-1
98SPx Finite-4
Radiance-4
Spectrum-4
98Topps-162
O-Pee-Chee-162
98UD Choice-5
98UD Choice Preview-5
98UD Choice Prime Choice Reserve-5
98UD Choice Reserve-5
98Upper Deck-215
Exclusives-215
Exclusives 1 of 1-215
Gold Reserve-215
99Crown Royale-107
Limited Series-107
Premiere Date-107
99Pacific-4
Copper-4
Emerald Green-4
Gold-4
Ice Blue-4
Premiere Date-4
Red-4
99Pacific Dynagon Ice-151
Blue-151
Copper-151
Gold-151
Premiere Date-151
99Pacific Omega-181
Copper-181
Gold-181
Ice Blue-181
Premiere Date-181
99Pacific Prism-107
Holographic Blue-107
Holographic Gold-107
Holographic Mirror-107
Holographic Purple-107
Premiere Date-107
99Panini Stickers-277
99Upper Deck MVP SC Edition-141
Gold Script-141
Silver Script-141
Super Script-141
99Wayne Gretzky Hockey-135
00BAP Memorabilia-327
Emerald-327
Ruby-327
Sapphire-327
Promos-327
00BAP Mem Chicago Sportsfest Copper-327
00BAP Memorabilia Chicago Sportsfest Blue-327
00BAP Memorabilia Chicago Sportsfest Gold-327
00BAP Memorabilia Chicago Sportsfest Ruby-327
00BAP Memorabilia Chicago Sun-Times Ruby-327
00BAP Memorabilia Chicago Sun-Times Gold-327
00BAP Mem Chicago Sun-Times Sapphire-327
00BAP Mem Toronto Fall Expo Copper-327
00BAP Memorabilia Toronto Fall Expo Gold-327
00BAP Memorabilia Toronto Fall Expo Ruby-327
00BAP Signature Series-66
Emerald-66
Ruby-66
Sapphire-66
Autographs-164
Autographs Gold-164
00O-Pee-Chee-204
00O-Pee-Chee Parallel-204
00Pacific-316
Copper-316
Gold-316
Ice Blue-316
Premiere Date-316
00Panini Stickers-188
00Paramount-189
Copper-189
Gold-189
Holo-Gold-189
Holo-Silver-189
Ice Blue-189
Premiere Date-189
00Stadium Club-148
00Topps/OPC-204
Parallel-204
00Upper Deck-133
Exclusives Tier 1-133
Exclusives Tier 2-133
00Upper Deck MVP-139
First Stars-139
Second Stars-139
Third Stars-139
00Upper Deck Victory-182
00Upper Deck Vintage-282
01BAP Signature Series-171
Autographs-171
Autographs Gold-171
01O-Pee-Chee-142
01O-Pee-Chee Premier Parallel-142
01Parkhurst-206
01Topps-142
OPC Parallel-142
01Upper Deck-395
Exclusives-395
02BAP Sig Series Auto Buybacks 1998-155
02BAP Sig Series Auto Buybacks 2001-171
02Maple Leafs Platinum Collection-7
02Maple Leafs Team Issue-5
02NHL Power Play Stickers-124
02Pacific-360
Blue-360
Red-360
02Pacific Complete-58
Red-58
02Topps Total-350
02Upper Deck-412
Exclusives-412
02Upper Deck Beckett UD Promos-412
03ITG Action-584
03Pacific Complete-425
Red-425
03Parkhurst Original Six Boston-30
03Upper Deck-260
Canadian Exclusives-260
HG-260
UD Exclusives-260
05Bruins Boston Globe-21
05Parkhurst-44
Facsimile Auto Parallel-44
05Upper Deck-260
05Upper Deck MVP-40

Gold-40
Platinum-40
Greenan, Chad
04Kootenay Ice-12
05Kootenay Ice-10
Greenan, Roy
52Juniors Blue Tint-122
Greenberg, Steve
89Hampton Roads Admirals-8A
89Hampton Roads Admirals-8H
90Hampton Roads Admirals-46
Greene, Andy
06AHL Top Prospects-20
07Upper Deck Victory-229
Black-229
Gold-229
Greene, Chris
04Erie Otters-7
05Erie Otters-4
Greene, Matt
93Western Michigan Broncos-13
93Western Michigan Broncos-13
03North Dakota Fighting Sioux-26
03North Dakota Fighting Sioux-26
04North Dakota Fighting Sioux-10
04North Dakota Fighting Sioux-10
05Black Diamond-242
05Black Diamond-242
05Hot Prospects-128
En Fuego-128
Red Hot-128
White Hot-128
05Parkhurst-628
Facsimile Auto Parallel-628
Facsimile Auto Parallel-628
05SP Authentic-260
05SP Authentic-260
Limited-260
Limited-260
05SP Game Used-210
05SP Game Used-210
05SPx-260
05SPx-260
05The Cup Masterpiece Pressplate Artifact-279
05The Cup Master Pressplate Black Diamond-242
05The Cup Masterpiece Pressplates (Ice)-247
05The Cup Master Pressplate Rookie Update-132
05The Cup Masterpiece Pressplates SPA-260
05The Cup Masterpiece Pressplates SP GU-210
05The Cup Masterpiece Pressplates (SPx)-260
05The Cup Masterpiece Pressplates Trilogy-255
05The Cup Masterpiece Pressplate Ult Coll-150
05UD Artifacts-279
05UD Artifacts-279
05Ultimate Collection-150
Gold-150
05Upper Deck-471
05Upper Deck-471
05Upper Deck Ice-247
05Upper Deck Ice-247
05Upper Deck Rookie Update-132
05Upper Deck Rookie Update-132
05Upper Deck Trilogy-255
05Upper Deck Trilogy-255
06O-Pee-Chee-195
Rainbow-195
Greener, Adam
99UK Basingstoke Bison-16
Greenlaw, Jeff
86Capitals Kodak-10
88ProCards AHL-30
89ProCards AHL-79
90ProCards AHL/IHL-210
91Capitals Junior 5x7-9
91ProCards-547
93Cincinnati Cyclones-8
95Cincinnati Cyclones-8
96Cincinnati Cyclones-29
97Cincinnati Cyclones-6
99Austin Ice Bats-7
00Austin Ice Bats-6
01Austin Ice Bats-4
02Austin Ice Bats-5
03Austin Ice Bats-20
Greenlay, Alex
04Williams Lake Timberwolves-8
Greenlay, Mike
88Saskatoon Blades-5
89ProCards AHL-133
90Knoxville Cherokees-119
90ProCards AHL/IHL-225
91Knoxville Cherokees-3
93Atlanta Knights-1
94Atlanta Knights-2
94Classic Four-Sport *-153
Gold-153
Printers Proofs-153
Greenough, Glenn
84Sudbury Wolves-10
85Sudbury Wolves-12
Greenough, Nick
98Val d'Or Foreurs-10
99Halifax Mooseheads-7
00Halifax Mooseheads-6
02Grand Rapids Griffins-12
03Augusta Lynx-41
04Reading Royals-20
05Stockton Thunder-6
Greenville, Chris
98BC Icemen II-10
Greenway, Dave
93Red Deer Rebels-6
Greenwood, Dale
01Flint Generals-6
Greenwood, Jeff
91Air Canada SJHL-B32
91Air Canada SJHL-D20
92Saskatchewan JHL-119
Greer, Brian
95Muskegon Fury-17
00UK Sekonda Superleague-31
Greer, Jay
93Quebec Pee-Wee Tournament-1402
Gregersen, Jens Christian
98Danish Hockey League-66
99Danish Hockey League-105
Gregg, Randy
81Swedish Semic Hockey VM Stickers-77
82Oilers Red Rooster-21
83Oilers McDonald's-14
83O-Pee-Chee-28
83O-Pee-Chee Stickers-145
83Topps Stickers-145
83Vachon-25
84Oilers Red Rooster-21
84Oilers Team Issue-6
84O-Pee-Chee-242
84O-Pee-Chee Stickers-257
85Oilers Red Rooster-21
85O-Pee-Chee-199
85O-Pee-Chee Stickers-225
86Oilers Red Rooster-21
86Oilers Team Issue-21
87O-Pee-Chee Stickers-94
88Oilers Tenth Anniversary-13
88Oilers Team Issue-8
89Oilers Team Issue-9
89O-Pee-Chee-229
90O-Pee-Chee-275
90Panini Stickers-231
90Score-306C
Canadian-306C
90Topps-275
Tiffany-275
91Canucks Autograph Cards-8
91Canucks Team Issue 8x10-8
91Pinnacle-415
French-415
91Score Canadian Bilingual-598
91Score Canadian English-598
91Score Rookie/Traded-48T
04ITG Franchises Canadian-28
Autographs-RGR
04UD Legendary Signatures-66
Autographs-RG
Rearguard Retrospectives-PCRG
Gregg, Vic
52St. Lawrence Sales-64
Gregga, Shamus
93Hampton Roads Admirals-7
Gregoire, Bill
84Victoria Cougars-9
Gregoire, Jason
06Lincoln Stars-11
06Lincoln Stars Upper DeckÂ Signature Series -12
Gregoire, Jean-Francois
907th Inn. Sketch QMJHL-82
917th Inn. Sketch QMJHL-65
98Abilene Aviators-9
Gregor, Colin
88Lethbridge Hurricanes-8
907th Inn. Sketch WHL-254
93Richmond Renegades-6
94Hampton Roads Admirals-4
95Birmingham Bulls-9
Gregorek, Petr
97Czech APS Extraliga-323
98Czech OFS-181
99Czech DS-102
99Czech OFS-193
99Czech OFS-474
00Czech DS Extraliga-70
00Czech OFS-217
01Czech OFS-48
All Stars-2
02Czech OFS Plus-172
02Czech OFS Plus All-Star Game-H4
04Czech OFS-363
05Czech HC Ceski Budejovice-2
06Czech HC Ceske Budejovice Postcards-1
06Czech OFS-2
Defenders-6
Gregory, Dave
95UK Guildford Flames-1
98Topeka Scarecrows-13
Gregory, Jim
73Maple Leafs Postcards-8
Gregory, Rick
96OCN Blizzard-1
Gregson, Terry
90Pro Set-688
Greig, Jack
96Dayton Ice Bandits-11
99Adirondack IceHawks-22
Greig, Mark
88Lethbridge Hurricanes-9
89Lethbridge Hurricanes-5
90Score-431
Canadian-431
90ProCards AHL/IHL-180
91Pinnacle-352
French-352
91Pro Set-537
French-537
91Score American-383
91Score Canadian Bilingual-273
91Score Canadian English-273
91Upper Deck-456
French-456
91Whalers Jr. 7-Eleven-13
92O-Pee-Chee-186
92OPC Premier-99
92Stadium Club-421
92Topps-175
Gold-175G
93Donruss-137
93Donruss-495
93Leaf-412
93OPC Premier-301
Gold-301
93Stadium Club-386
Members Only Master Set-386
First Day Issue-386
93Topps/OPC Premier-301
Gold-301
93Ultra-334
93Whalers Coke-6
94Leaf-522
94Saint John Flames-7
95Atlanta Knights-10
97Grand Rapids Griffins-6
00UD Heroes-89
02Philadelphia Phantoms-4
03German DEL-107
04German DEL-192
05German DEL-342
05Philadelphia Phantoms All-Decade Team-3
06German DEL-108
Greilinger, Thomas
00German DEL-223
02German DEL City Press-263
03German DEL-201
03German Nuremberg Ice Tigers Postcards-10
04German Adler Mannheim Eagles Postcards-14
04German DEL-20
Grein, Andre
94German DEL-228
95German DEL-227
96German DEL-78
Greiss, Thomas
04German Cologne Sharks Postcards-11
04German DEL-210
05German DEL-205
05German DEL-378
Goalies-G05
06German DEL-186
06AHL Top Prospects-50
Greiter, Paul
94German First League-218
Grenemo, Arne
67Swedish Hockey-236
Grenier, Blake
01Moose Jaw Warriors-22
Grenier, Dave
02Shawinigan Cataractes-2
Grenier, David
93Quebec Pee-Wee Tournament-1105
95Fredericton Canadiens-13
Grenier, Eric
93Quebec Pee-Wee Tournament-470
93Quebec Pee-Wee Tournament-933
Grenier, Jeff
05Cape Breton Screaming Eagles-16
Grenier, Lucien
71Sargent Promotions Stamps-76
71Toronto Sun-114
72Sargent Promotions Stamps-1
Grenier, Martin
94Quebec Pee-Wee Tournament-628
98Quebec Remparts-9
Signed-9
99O-Pee-Chee-263
99O-Pee-Chee Chrome-263
99O-Pee-Chee Chrome Refractors-263
99Topps/OPC-263
99Topps/OPC Chrome-263
Refractors-263
99Quebec Remparts-16
Signed-16
99Bowman CHL-26
Gold-26
OPC International-26
Autographs-BA15
Autographs Gold-BA15
Autographs Silver-BA15
02Springfield Falcons-11
03Manitoba Moose-17
04Hartford Wolf Pack-6
05Hartford Wolf Pack-10
06Philadelphia Phantoms-17
Grenier, Richard
76Nordiques Marie Antoinette-10
76Nordiques Postcards-14
76O-Pee-Chee WHA-59
Grenier, Tony
84Prince Albert Raiders Stickers-10
Grennier, Matt
99Brampton Battalion-18
00Barrie Colts-11
01Kitchener Rangers-8
03Kitchener Rangers Memorial Cup-9
Grenville, Chris
917th Inn. Sketch OHL-315
95Birmingham Bulls-8
99UHL All-Stars East-7T
01BC Icemen-10
03Laredo Bucks-8
04Fort Wayne Komets-4
04Fort Wayne Komets Shoe Carnival-4
Grenzy, Michael
02Chicago Steel-10
Greschner, Mike
93Quebec Pee-Wee Tournament-1609
Greschner, Ron
75O-Pee-Chee NHL-146
75Topps-146
76O-Pee-Chee NHL-154
76Topps-154
77O-Pee-Chee NHL-256
77Topps-256
78O-Pee-Chee-154
78Topps-154
79O-Pee-Chee-78
79Topps-78
80O-Pee-Chee-248
80Topps-248
81O-Pee-Chee-224
81O-Pee-Chee Stickers-167
81Topps-E97
82O-Pee-Chee-224
82Post Cereal-13
84O-Pee-Chee-141
85O-Pee-Chee-182
86O-Pee-Chee-18
86O-Pee-Chee Stickers-222
86Topps-18
87O-Pee-Chee-159
87Panini Stickers-108
87Topps-159
89Rangers Marine Midland Bank-4
90O-Pee-Chee-447
90Pro Set-197
03Parkhurst Original Six New York-38
03Parkhurst Original Six New York-75
Autographs-8
04ITG Franchises US East-400
Autographs-A-RG
06Parkhurst-18
06Parkhurst-198
Autographs-18
Autographs-198
Autographs Dual-DAGB
Gresdal, Mike
99Ottawa 67's-18
Gretzky, Brent
897th Inn. Sketch OHL-75
907th Inn. Sketch OHL-7
917th Inn. Sketch OHL-99
92Upper Deck-37
92Atlanta Knights-10
93Donruss-318
93Parkhurst-248
Emerald Ice-248
Calder Candidates-C14
Calder Candidates Gold-C14
93Pinnacle-429
Canadian-429
93Score-606
Gold-606
Canadian-606
Canadian Gold-606
93Ultra-424
93Upper Deck-354
SP-150
93Atlanta Knights-5
94Be A Player-R161
Signature Cards-154
94OPC Premier-209
Special Effects-209
94Parkhurst-218
94Parkhurst-295
Gold-218
Gold-295
Vintage-V62
94Topps/OPC Premier-209
Special Effects-209
94Upper Deck-69
Electric Ice-69
94Atlanta Knights-8
94Classic-99
Gold-99
Tri-Cards-T64
94Classic Four-Sport *-159
Gold-159
Printers Proofs-159
95Collector's Choice-281
Player's Club-281
Player's Club Platinum-281
95St. John's Maple Leafs-9
95Images-17
Gold-17
95Images Four-Sport *-116
96Las Vegas Thunder-8
96Pensacola Ice Pilots-12
96Collector's Edge Ice-82
Prism-82
98Chicago Wolves-1
99Asheville Smoke-7
99UHL All-Stars East-21T
00Fort Wayne Komets-6
00Fort Wayne Komets Shoe Carnival-9
01Fort Wayne Komets-22
01Fort Wayne Komets Shoe Carnival-5
03Port Huron Beacons-12
Gretzky, Keith
87Flint Spirits-4
89ProCards IHL-101
91ProCards-322
92Upper Deck-37
92San Diego Gulls-9
92Classic-118
Gold-118
93Classic Pro Prospects-99
97Bakersfield Fog-20
99Asheville Smoke-23
Gretzky, Walter
98McDonalds Upper Deck Gretzkys Teammates-T1
Gretzky, Wayne
77Sportscasters-7710
77Finnish Sportscasters-89-2127
79Oilers Postcards-9
79O-Pee-Chee-18
79Topps-18
80O-Pee-Chee-3
80O-Pee-Chee-87
80O-Pee-Chee-162
80O-Pee-Chee-163
80O-Pee-Chee-182
80O-Pee-Chee-250
80O-Pee-Chee Super-7
80Topps-3
80Topps-87
80Topps-162
80Topps-163
80Topps-182
80Topps-250
81Oilers Red Rooster-99
81Oilers Red Rooster-99B
81Oilers Red Rooster-99C
81Oilers Red Rooster-99D
81Oilers West Edmonton Mall-3
81O-Pee-Chee-106
81O-Pee-Chee-125
81O-Pee-Chee-126
81O-Pee-Chee-383
81O-Pee-Chee-384
81O-Pee-Chee-392
81O-Pee-Chee Stickers-209
81O-Pee-Chee Stickers-252
81O-Pee-Chee Stickers-264
81Topps-16
81Topps-52
82McDonald's Stickers-20
82McDonald's Stickers-22
82Neilson's Gretzky-1
82Neilson's Gretzky-2
82Neilson's Gretzky-3
82Neilson's Gretzky-4
82Neilson's Gretzky-5
82Neilson's Gretzky-6
82Neilson's Gretzky-7
82Neilson's Gretzky-8
82Neilson's Gretzky-9
82Neilson's Gretzky-10
82Neilson's Gretzky-11
82Neilson's Gretzky-12
82Neilson's Gretzky-13
82Neilson's Gretzky-14
82Neilson's Gretzky-15
82Neilson's Gretzky-16
82Neilson's Gretzky-17
82Neilson's Gretzky-18
82Neilson's Gretzky-19
82Neilson's Gretzky-20
82Neilson's Gretzky-21
82Neilson's Gretzky-22
82Neilson's Gretzky-23
82Neilson's Gretzky-24
82Neilson's Gretzky-25
82Neilson's Gretzky-26
82Neilson's Gretzky-27
82Neilson's Gretzky-28
82Neilson's Gretzky-29
82Neilson's Gretzky-30
82Neilson's Gretzky-31
82Neilson's Gretzky-32
82Neilson's Gretzky-33
82Neilson's Gretzky-34
82Neilson's Gretzky-35
82Neilson's Gretzky-36
82Neilson's Gretzky-37
82Neilson's Gretzky-38
82Neilson's Gretzky-39
82Neilson's Gretzky-40
82Neilson's Gretzky-41
82Neilson's Gretzky-42
82Neilson's Gretzky-43
82Neilson's Gretzky-44
82Neilson's Gretzky-45
82Neilson's Gretzky-46
82Neilson's Gretzky-47
82Neilson's Gretzky-48
82Neilson's Gretzky-49
82Neilson's Gretzky-50
82Oilers Red Rooster-99A
82Oilers Red Rooster-99B
82Oilers Red Rooster-99C
82Oilers Red Rooster-99D
82O-Pee-Chee-1
82O-Pee-Chee-99
82O-Pee-Chee-106
82O-Pee-Chee-107
82O-Pee-Chee-235
82O-Pee-Chee-237
82O-Pee-Chee-240
82O-Pee-Chee-242
82O-Pee-Chee-243
82O-Pee-Chee Stickers-97
82O-Pee-Chee Stickers-98
82O-Pee-Chee Stickers-162
82O-Pee-Chee Stickers-256
82O-Pee-Chee Stickers-257
82O-Pee-Chee Stickers-258
82O-Pee-Chee Stickers-259
82Post Cereal-6
82Topps Stickers-97
82Topps Stickers-98
82Topps Stickers-162
82Topps Stickers-256
82Topps Stickers-257
82Topps Stickers-258
82Topps Stickers-259
83NHL Key Tags-42
83Oilers Dollars-H14
83Oilers McDonald's-21
83O-Pee-Chee-22
83O-Pee-Chee-23
83O-Pee-Chee-29
83O-Pee-Chee-203
83O-Pee-Chee-204
83O-Pee-Chee-212
83O-Pee-Chee-215
83O-Pee-Chee-216
83O-Pee-Chee-217
83O-Pee-Chee Stickers-7
83O-Pee-Chee Stickers-89
83O-Pee-Chee Stickers-90
83O-Pee-Chee Stickers-161
83O-Pee-Chee Stickers-301
83O-Pee-Chee Stickers-307
83O-Pee-Chee Stickers-325
83O-Pee-Chee Stickers-326
83Puffy Stickers-1
83Topps Stickers-7
83Topps Stickers-89
83Topps Stickers-90
83Topps Stickers-161
83Topps Stickers-301
83Topps Stickers-307
83Topps Stickers-325
83Topps Stickers-326
83Vachon-26
83Belleville Bulls-27
84Oilers Red Rooster-99A
84Oilers Red Rooster-99B
84Oilers Red Rooster-99C
84Oilers Red Rooster-99D
84Oilers Team Issue-7
84O-Pee-Chee-208
84O-Pee-Chee-243
84O-Pee-Chee-357
84O-Pee-Chee-373
84O-Pee-Chee-374
84O-Pee-Chee-380
84O-Pee-Chee-381
84O-Pee-Chee-382
84O-Pee-Chee-383
84O-Pee-Chee-388
84O-Pee-Chee Stickers-63
84O-Pee-Chee Stickers-138
84O-Pee-Chee Stickers-226
84O-Pee-Chee Stickers-229
84O-Pee-Chee Stickers-255
84O-Pee-Chee Stickers-256
847-Eleven Discs-16
847-Eleven Discs-NNO
84Topps-51
84Topps-154
85Islanders News Trottier-21
85Islanders News Trottier-29
85Oilers Red Rooster-99A
85Oilers Red Rooster-99B
85Oilers Red Rooster-99C
85O-Pee-Chee-120
85O-Pee-Chee-257
85O-Pee-Chee-258
85O-Pee-Chee-259
85O-Pee-Chee Box Bottoms-G
85O-Pee-Chee Stickers-5
85O-Pee-Chee Stickers-54
85O-Pee-Chee Stickers-120
85O-Pee-Chee Stickers-198
85O-Pee-Chee Stickers-202
85O-Pee-Chee Stickers-222
85Topps-120
85Topps Box Bottoms-G
85Topps Sticker Inserts-5
86Kraft Drawings-23
86Oilers Red Rooster-99A
86Oilers Red Rooster-99B
86Oilers Team Issue-99
86O-Pee-Chee-3
86O-Pee-Chee-259
86O-Pee-Chee-260
86O-Pee-Chee Box Bottoms-F
86O-Pee-Chee Stickers-72
86O-Pee-Chee Stickers-115
86O-Pee-Chee Stickers-183
86O-Pee-Chee Stickers-191
86O-Pee-Chee Stickers-195
86Topps-3
86Topps Box Bottoms-F
86Topps Sticker Inserts-3
87Oilers Team Issue-99
87O-Pee-Chee-53
87O-Pee-Chee Box Bottoms-A
87O-Pee-Chee Minis-13
87O-Pee-Chee Stickers-86
87O-Pee-Chee Stickers-115
87O-Pee-Chee Stickers-174
87O-Pee-Chee Stickers-180
87O-Pee-Chee Stickers-181
87Panini Stickers-192
87Panini Stickers-197
87Panini Stickers-198
87Panini Stickers-199
87Panini Stickers-200
87Panini Stickers-261
87Panini Stickers-371
87Panini Stickers-373
87Panini Stickers-389
87Topps-53
87Topps Box Bottoms-A
87Topps Sticker Inserts-5
87Hull Olympiques-9
87Sault Ste. Marie Greyhounds-29
88Esso All-Stars-15
88Kings Postcards-1
88Kings Smokey-11
88Oilers Tenth Anniversary-46
88Oilers Tenth Anniversary-55
88Oilers Tenth Anniversary-137
88O-Pee-Chee-120
88O-Pee-Chee Box Bottoms-B
88O-Pee-Chee Minis-11
88O-Pee-Chee Stickers-1
88O-Pee-Chee Stickers-121
88O-Pee-Chee Stickers-224
88Panini Stickers-58
88Panini Stickers-178
88Panini Stickers-181
88Panini Stickers-193
88Topps-120
88Topps Box Bottoms-B
88Topps Sticker Inserts-8
89Action Packed Prototypes-1
89Kings Smokey-1
89Kings Smokey Gretzky 8x10-NNO
89Kraft-59
89Kraft All-Stars Stickers-2
89O-Pee-Chee-156
89O-Pee-Chee-320
89O-Pee-Chee-325
89O-Pee-Chee Box Bottoms-E
89O-Pee-Chee Stickers-47
89O-Pee-Chee Stickers-154
89O-Pee-Chee Stickers-166
89O-Pee-Chee Stickers-209
89Panini Stickers-87
89Panini Stickers-179
89Panini Stickers-374
89Sports Illustrated for Kids I-19
89Topps-156
89Topps Box Bottoms-E
89Topps Sticker Inserts-11
89Swedish Semic World Champ Stickers-65
90SLU Kenner Club Pieces *-16
90Bowman-143
Tiffany-143
90Kings Smokey-1
90Kraft-15
90Kraft-66
90O-Pee-Chee-1
90O-Pee-Chee-2
90O-Pee-Chee-3
90O-Pee-Chee-120
90O-Pee-Chee-199
90O-Pee-Chee-522
90O-Pee-Chee Box Bottoms-D
90OPC Premier-38
90Panini Stickers-242
90Panini Stickers-332
90Pro Set-118
90Pro Set-340
90Pro Set-388
90Pro Set-394
90Pro Set-703
90Pro Set Player of the Month-P2
90Score Promos-1A
90Score Promos-1B
90Score-1
90Score-321
90Score-336
90Score-338
90Score-347
90Score-352
90Score-353
90Score-361
Canadian-1
Canadian-321
Canadian-336
Canadian-338
Canadian-347
Canadian-352
Canadian-353
Canadian-361
90Score Hottest/Rising Stars-1
90Score Rookie/Traded-110T
90Topps-1
90Topps-2
90Topps-3
90Topps-120
90Topps-199
Tiffany-1
Tiffany-2
Tiffany-3
Tiffany-120
Tiffany-199
90Topps Box Bottoms-D
90Topps Team Scoring Leaders-12
90Topps Team Scoring Leaders Tiffany-12
90Upper Deck-54
90Upper Deck-205
90Upper Deck-307
90Upper Deck-476
90Upper Deck-545
French-54
French-205
French-307
French-476
French-545
90Upper Deck Holograms-1
90Upper Deck Holograms-2
90Upper Deck Holograms-3
90Upper Deck Promos-241A
91Pro Set Platinum-52
91Pro Set Platinum-142
91Bowman-173
91Bowman-176
91Kraft-65
91McDonald's Upper Deck-17
91McDonald's Upper Deck-H1
91O-Pee-Chee-201
91O-Pee-Chee-224
91O-Pee-Chee-257
91O-Pee-Chee-258
91O-Pee-Chee-321
91O-Pee-Chee-520
91O-Pee-Chee-522
91O-Pee-Chee-524
91OPC Premier-3
91Panini Stickers-78
91Panini Stickers-327
91Parkhurst-73
91Parkhurst-207
91Parkhurst-222
91Parkhurst-429
91Parkhurst-433
91Parkhurst-465
French-73
French-207
French-222
French-429
French-433
French-465
91Pinnacle-100
91Pinnacle-381
French-100
French-381
B-B11
B French-B11
91Pro Set-101
91Pro Set-285
91Pro Set-324
91Pro Set-574
French-101
French-285
French-324
French-574
CC-CC5
CC French-CC5
Awards Special-AC4
Platinum PC-PC4
Platinum PC-PC14
Puck Candy-11
91Pro Stars Posters-1
91Score National-1
91Score Ntnl Candy Wholesalers Convention-1
91Score Fanfest-1
91Score American-100
91Score American-346
91Score American-405
91Score American-406
91Score American-413
91Score American-422
91Score American-427
91Score American-434
91Score Canadian Bilingual-100
91Score Canadian Bilingual-295
91Score Canadian Bilingual-296
91Score Canadian Bilingual-303
91Score Canadian Bilingual-312
91Score Canadian Bilingual-317
91Score Canadian Bilingual-324
91Score Canadian Bilingual-376
91Score Canadian English-100
91Score Canadian English-295
91Score Canadian English-296
91Score Canadian English-303
91Score Canadian English-312
91Score Canadian English-317
91Score Canadian English-324
91Score Canadian English-376
91Score Hot Cards-2
91Stadium Club Charter Member-46
91Stadium Club Charter Member-47
91Stadium Club Members Only-44
91Stadium Club-1
91Topps-201
91Topps-224
91Topps-257
91Topps-258
91Topps-321
91Topps-520
91Topps-522
91Topps-524
Topps/Bowman Preview Sheet-2
Team Scoring Leaders-10
91Upper Deck-13
91Upper Deck-38
91Upper Deck-45
91Upper Deck-437
91Upper Deck-501
91Upper Deck-621
91Upper Deck-SP1
French-13
French-38
French-437
French-501
French-621
Award Winner Holograms-AW1
Award Winner Holograms-AW6
Box Bottoms-1
91Upper Deck Czech World Juniors-NNO
91Upper Deck Czech World Juniors-NNO
91Finnish Semic World Champ Stickers-64
91Swedish Semic World Champ Stickers-64
92Bowman-1
92Bowman-207
92High-5 Previews-P1
92Humpty Dumpty I-10
92Kraft-40
92O-Pee-Chee-15
92O-Pee-Chee-220
25th Anniv. Inserts-12
92Panini Stickers-64
92Panini Stickers-287
92Panini Stickers French-64
92Panini Stickers French-287
92Parkhurst-65
92Parkhurst-509
Emerald Ice-65
Emerald Ice-509
92Pinnacle-200
92Pinnacle-249
French-200
French-249
Team Pinnacle-5
Team French-5
92Pro Set-66
92Pro Set-246
Gold Team Leaders-6
92Score-1
92Score-412
92Score-426
92Score-525
Canadian-1
Canadian-412
Canadian-426
Canadian-525
92Seasons Patches-9
92Sports Illustrated for Kids II-153
92Sports Illustrated for Kids II-547
92Stadium Club-18
92Stadium Club-256
92Topps-1
92Topps-123
Gold-1G
Gold-123G
92Ultra-83
All-Stars-10
Award Winners-6
92Upper Deck-25
92Upper Deck-33
92Upper Deck-37
92Upper Deck-423
92Upper Deck-435
92Upper Deck-621
All-World Team-W1
Gordie Howe Selects-G5
Sheets-5
Wayne Gretzky Heroes-10
Wayne Gretzky Heroes-11
Wayne Gretzky Heroes-12
Wayne Gretzky Heroes-13
Wayne Gretzky Heroes-14
Wayne Gretzky Heroes-15
Wayne Gretzky Heroes-16
Wayne Gretzky Heroes-17
Wayne Gretzky Heroes-NNO
World Junior Grads-WG10
92Finnish Semic-84
93Donruss-152
93Donruss-395
Elite Inserts-10
Ice Kings-4
Special Print-K
93Kings Forum-10
93Kraft-34
93Kraft-54
93Leaf-304
Gold All-Stars-6
Studio Signature-4
93OPC Premier-330
93OPC Premier-380
Gold-330
Gold-380
Black Gold-1
93Panini Stickers-R
93Parkhurst-99
Emerald Ice-99
Cherry's Playoff Heroes-D1
East/West Stars-W1
USA/Canada Gold-G1
93Pinnacle-237
93Pinnacle-400
93Pinnacle-512
Canadian-237
Canadian-400
Canadian-512
All-Stars-45
All-Stars Canadian-45
Captains-11
Captains Canadian-11
Team Pinnacle-5
Team Canadian-5
93PowerPlay-116
Gamebreakers-3
Point Leaders-3
93Score-300
93Score-662
Gold-662
Canadian-300
Canadian-662
Canadian Gold-662
Dream Team-11
Dynamic Duos U.S.-7
Franchise-9
93Seasons Patches-5
93Stadium Club-200
Members Only Master Set-200
OPC-200
First Day Issue-200
First Day Issue OPC-200
All-Stars-23
All-Stars Members Only-23
All-Stars OPC-23
Finest-1
Finest Members Only-1
Master Photos-8
Master Photos Winners-8
93Topps/OPC Premier-330
93Topps/OPC Premier-380
Gold-330
Gold-380
93Topps Premier Black Gold-7
93Topps Premier Black Gold-A
93Ultra-114
93Ultra-C3C
All-Stars-15
Premier Pivots-2
Scoring Kings-2
93Upper Deck-99
93Upper Deck-99B1
93Upper Deck-99B2
Gretzky Box Bottom-1
Gretzky Sheet-1
Next In Line-NL1
NHL's Best-HB9
Silver Skates-R1
Silver Skates-NNO
Silver Skates-NNO
Silver Skates Gold-R1
SP-70
93Upper Deck Locker All-Stars-25
93Swedish Semic World Champ Stickers-199
93Fax Pax World of Sport*-25
94Be A Player-R99
94Be A Player-R147
94Be A Player-R176
99 All-Stars-G1
Signature Cards-108
Up Close and Personal-UC1
94Canada Games NHL POGS-126
94Canada Games NHL POGS-268
94Coca-Cola Wayne Gretzky Cups-1
94Coca-Cola Wayne Gretzky Cups-2
94Coca-Cola Wayne Gretzky Cups-3
94Coca-Cola Wayne Gretzky Cups-4
94Coca-Cola Wayne Gretzky Cups-5
94Coke/Mac's Milk Gretzky POGs-1
94Coke/Mac's Milk Gretzky POGs-2
94Coke/Mac's Milk Gretzky POGs-3
94Coke/Mac's Milk Gretzky POGs-4
94Coke/Mac's Milk Gretzky POGs-5
94Coke/Mac's Milk Gretzky POGs-6
94Coke/Mac's Milk Gretzky POGs-7
94Coke/Mac's Milk Gretzky POGs-8
94Coke/Mac's Milk Gretzky POGs-9
94Coke/Mac's Milk Gretzky POGs-10
94Coke/Mac's Milk Gretzky POGs-11
94Coke/Mac's Milk Gretzky POGs-12
94Coke/Mac's Milk Gretzky POGs-13
94Coke/Mac's Milk Gretzky POGs-14
94Coke/Mac's Milk Gretzky POGs-15
94Coke/Mac's Milk Gretzky POGs-16
94Coke/Mac's Milk Gretzky POGs-17
94Coke/Mac's Milk Gretzky POGs-18
94Donruss-127
Dominators-5
Elite Inserts-5
Ice Masters-4
94EA Sports-63
94EA Sports-192
94Finest-41
Super Team Winners-41
Refractors-41
Division's Clear Cut-18
Ring Leaders-5
94Flair-79
Center Spotlight-4
Hot Numbers-2
94Fleer-94
Headliners-4
94Hockey Wit-99
94Kings Upper Deck Season Ticket-NNO
94Kraft-5
94Kraft-63
94Leaf-345
Fire on Ice-4
Gold Stars-1
Limited Inserts-11
94Leaf Limited-10
Gold-7
94OPC Premier-130
94OPC Premier-150
94OPC Premier-154
94OPC Premier-280
94OPC Premier-375
Special Effects-130
Special Effects-150

Special Effects-154
Special Effects-280
Special Effects-375
94Panini Stickers-AA
94Parkhurst-103
94Parkhurst-306
Gold-103
Gold-306
Crash the Game Green-11
Crash the Game Green-28
Crash the Game Blue-11
Crash the Game Blue-28
Crash the Game Gold-11
Crash the Game Gold-28
Crash the Game Red-11
Crash the Game Red-28
94Parkhurst SE-NNO
Vintage-20
94Pinnacle-200
Artist's Proofs-200
Rink Collection-200
Team Pinnacle-TP9
Team Dufex Parallel-TP9
94Post Box Backs-13
94Score-241
Gold-241
Platinum-241
Dream Team-DT14
Franchise-TF11
90 Plus Club-1
94Select-83
Gold-83
First Line-FL11
94SP-54A
94SP-54B
94SP-SP1
Die Cuts-54
Premier-17
Premier Die-Cuts-17
94Stadium Club Members Only-5
94Stadium Club-99
94Stadium Club-270
Members Only Master Set-99
Members Only Master Set-270
First Day Issue-99
First Day Issue-270
Finest Inserts-4
Finest Inserts Members Only-4
Super Team Winner Cards-99
Super Team Winner Cards-270
94Topps/OPC Premier-130
94Topps/OPC Premier-150
94Topps/OPC Premier-154
94Topps/OPC Premier-280
94Topps/OPC Premier-375
Special Effects-130
Special Effects-150
Special Effects-154
Special Effects-280
Special Effects-375
The Go To Guy-1
94Ultra-306
All-Stars-10
Award Winners-5
Premier Pivots-4
Scoring Kings-4
94Upper Deck-1
94Upper Deck-226
94Upper Deck-228
94Upper Deck-541
Electric Ice-1
Electric Ice-226
Electric Ice-228
Electric Ice-541
Ice Gallery-IG15
Predictor Canadian-C16
94Upper Deck Predictor Canadian Exch Gold-C16
94Upper Deck Predictor Hobby-H1
94Upper Deck Predictor Hobby-H16
94Upper Deck Predictor Hobby Exch Gold-H1
94Upper Deck Predictor Hobby Exch Gold-H16
94Upper Deck Predictor Hobby Exch Silver-H1
94Upper Deck Predictor Hobby Exch Silver-H16
94Upper Deck Predictor Retail-R19
94Upper Deck Predictor Retail-R21
94Upper Deck Predictor Retail-R42
94Upper Deck Predictor Retail-R59
94Upper Deck Predictor Retail Exchange-R19
94Upper Deck Predictor Retail Exchange-R21
94Upper Deck Predictor Retail Exchange-R42
94Upper Deck Predictor Retail Exchange-R59
94Upper Deck SP Inserts-SP36
94Upper Deck SP Inserts Die Cuts-SP36
94Upper Deck Gretzky 24K Gold-1
94Upper Deck NHLPA/Be A Player-7
94Finnish Jaa Kiekko-99
94Finnish Jaa Kiekko-344
95Bashan Super Stickers-57
Die-Cut-21
95Be A Player-97
Signatures-S97
Signatures-*S97
Signatures Die Cuts-S97
Gretzky's Great Memories-GM1
Gretzky's Great Memories-GM2
Gretzky's Great Memories-GM3
Gretzky's Great Memories-GM4
Gretzky's Great Memories-GM5
Gretzky's Great Memories-GM6
Gretzky's Great Memories-GM7
Gretzky's Great Memories-GM8
Gretzky's Great Memories-GM9
Gretzky's Great Memories-GM10
Lethal Lines-LL2
95Bowman-1
All-Foil-1
Bowman's Best-BB5
Bowman's Best Refractors-BB5
95Canada Games NHL POGS-1
95Canada Games NHL POGS-132
95Collector's Choice-1
95Collector's Choice-361
95Collector's Choice-395
95Collector's Choice-396
Player's Club-1
Player's Club-361
Player's Club-395
Player's Club-396
Player's Club Platinum-1
Player's Club Platinum-361
Player's Club Platinum-395
Player's Club Platinum-396
Crash The Game-C3A
Crash The Game-C3B
Crash The Game-C3C
Crash The Game Gold-C3A
Crash The Game Gold-C3B
Crash The Game Gold-C3C
Crash the Game Silver Redeemed-C3
Crash the Game Silver Bonus-C3
Crash the Game Gold Redeemed-C3
Crash the Game Gold Bonus-C3
95Donruss-13
Dominators-5
Elite Inserts-7
95Donruss Elite-58
Die Cut Stars-58
Die Cut Stars-58U
Die Cut Uncut-58
Die Cut Uncut-58U
Cutting Edge-3
95Emotion-81
Xcel-4
Xcited-5
95Finest-5
95Finest-180
Refractors-5
Refractors-180
95Hoyle Western Playing Cards-14
95Imperial Stickers-57
Die Cut Superstars-21
95Kraft-53
95Leaf-89
Fire On Ice-10
95Leaf Limited-87
Stars of the Game-3
95Metal-71
Heavy Metal-4
International Steel-5
95NHL Aces Playing Cards-1D
95NHL Cool Trade-2
95NHL Cool Trade-RP2
95NHL/NHLPA Playing Cards-NNO
95Panini Stickers-266
95Parkhurst International-100
95Parkhurst International-449
Emerald Ice-100
Emerald Ice-449
Crown Collection Silver Series 1-6
Crown Collection Gold Series 1-6
Crown Collection Silver Series 2-10
Crown Collection Gold Series 2-10
NHL All-Stars-1
95Pinnacle-101
Artist's Proofs-101
Rink Collection-101
Clear Shots-9
First Strike-2
95Pinnacle FANtasy-13
95Playoff One on One-50
95Playoff One on One-159
95Playoff One on One-269
95Post Upper Deck-17
95Post Upper Deck-AU17
95Pro Magnets-67
95Score-250
Black Ice Artist's Proofs-250
Black Ice-250
Border Battle-2
Dream Team-1
Lamplighters-1
95Select Certified-23
Mirror Gold-23
Gold Team-2
95SkyBox Impact-79
Countdown to Impact-4
Ice Quake-6
95SP-66A
95SP-127
95SP-GC1
Holoviews-FX10
Holoviews Special FX-FX10
Stars/Etoiles-E17
Stars/Etoiles Gold-E17
95Stadium Club Members Only-32
95Stadium Club-173
Members Only Master Set-173
Metalists-M1
Metalists Members Only Master Set-M1
Nemeses-N2
Nemeses Members Only Master Set-N2
95Summit-24
Artist's Proofs-24
Ice-24
GM's Choice-18
95Topps-85
95Topps-375
OPC Inserts-85
OPC Inserts-375
Home Grown Canada-HGC20
Marquee Men Power Boosters-375
Mystery Finest-M1
Mystery Finest Refractors-M1
Profiles-PF1
Rink Leaders-10RL
95Topps SuperSkills-15
Platinum-15
95Ultra-74
95Ultra-385
Gold Medallion-74
Extra Attackers-7
Premier Pivots-3
Premier Pivots Gold Medallion-3
Ultraview-2
Ultraview Hot Pack-2
95Upper Deck-99
95Upper Deck-222
95Upper Deck-252
Electric Ice-99
Electric Ice-222
Electric Ice-252
Electric Ice Gold-99
Electric Ice Gold-222
Electric Ice Gold-252
95Upper Deck All-Star Game Predictors-1
Redemption Winners-1
95Upper Deck Freeze Frame-F2
95Upper Deck Freeze Frame Jumbo-F2
95Upper Deck Gretzky Collection-G1
95Upper Deck Gretzky Collection-G2
95Upper Deck Gretzky Collection-G3
95Upper Deck Gretzky Collection-G4
95Upper Deck Gretzky Collection-G5
95Upper Deck Gretzky Collection-G6
95Upper Deck Gretzky Collection-G7
95Upper Deck Gretzky Collection-G8
95Upper Deck Gretzky Collection-G9
95Upper Deck Gretzky Collection-G10
95Upper Deck Gretzky Collection-G11
95Upper Deck Gretzky Collection-G12
95Upper Deck Gretzky Collection-G13
95Upper Deck Gretzky Collection-G14
95Upper Deck Gretzky Collection-G15
95Upper Deck Gretzky Collection-G16
95Upper Deck Gretzky Collection-G17
95Upper Deck Gretzky Collection-G18
95Upper Deck Gretzky Collection-G19
95Upper Deck Gretzky Collection-G20
95Upper Deck Gretzky Collection Jumbo-G1
95Upper Deck Gretzky Collection Jumbo-G2
95Upper Deck Gretzky Collection Jumbo-G3
95Upper Deck Gretzky Collection Jumbo-G4
95Upper Deck Gretzky Collection
Jumbo-G5
95Upper Deck Gretzky Collection Jumbo-G6
95Upper Deck Gretzky Collection Jumbo-G7
95Upper Deck Gretzky Collection Jumbo-G8
95Upper Deck Gretzky Collection Jumbo-G9
95Upper Deck Gretzky Collection Jumbo-G10
95Upper Deck Gretzky Collection Jumbo-G11
95Upper Deck Gretzky Collection Jumbo-G12
95Upper Deck Gretzky Collection Jumbo-G13
95Upper Deck Gretzky Collection Jumbo-G14
95Upper Deck Gretzky Collection Jumbo-G15
95Upper Deck Gretzky Collection Jumbo-G16
95Upper Deck Gretzky Collection Jumbo-G17
95Upper Deck Gretzky Collection Jumbo-G18
95Upper Deck Gretzky Collection Jumbo-G19
95Upper Deck Gretzky Collection Jumbo-G20
95Upper Deck NHL All-Stars-AS5
95Upper Deck NHL All-Stars Jumbo-AS5
95Upper Deck Predictor Hobby-H7
95Upper Deck Predictor Hobby Exchange-H7
95Upper Deck Predictor Retail-R13
95Upper Deck Predictor Retail-R23
95Upper Deck Predictor Retail-R31
95Upper Deck Predictor Retail-R41
95Upper Deck Predictor Retail-R51
95Upper Deck Predictor Retail Exchange-R13
95Upper Deck Predictor Retail Exchange-R23
95Upper Deck Predictor Retail Exchange-R31
95Upper Deck Predictor Retail Exchange-R41
95Upper Deck Predictor Retail Exchange-R51
95Upper Deck Special Edition-SE128
95Upper Deck Special Edition Gold-SE128
95Zenith-13
Z-Team-4
95Finnish Semic World Championships-99
95Swedish Globe World Championships-99
95Swedish Globe World Championships-265
95Swedish Globe World Championships-266
95Swedish Globe World Championships-267
95Swedish World Championships Stickers-276
96Headliners Hockey-6A
96Headliners Hockey-6B
96Be A Player Biscuit In The Basket-1
96Black Diamond-180
96Black Diamond-P180
Gold-180
Run for the Cup-RC1
96Collector's Choice-222
96Collector's Choice-290
96Collector's Choice-329
96Collector's Choice-336
96Collector's Choice-P222
96Collector's Choice-NNO1
96Collector's Choice-NNO2
MVP-UD1
MVP Gold-UD1
Stick'Ums-S1
Crash the Game-C1A
Crash the Game-C1B
Crash the Game-C1C
Crash the Game Gold-C1A
Crash the Game Gold-C1B
Crash the Game Gold-C1C
Crash the Game Exchange-CR1
Crash the Game Exchange Gold-CR1
96Collector's Choice Blow-Ups-170
96Collector's Choice Blow-Ups Bi-Way-1
96Donruss-93
Press Proofs-93
Dominators-5
Elite Inserts-2
Elite Inserts Gold-2
96Donruss Canadian Ice-5
Gold Press Proofs-5
Red Press Proofs-5
O Canada-7
96Donruss Elite-10
Die Cut Stars-10
Perspective-1
96Flair-59
Blue Ice-59
Hot Numbers-4
Now And Then-1
96Fleer-68
Art Ross-6
Pearson-4
96Fleer Picks-8
Captain's Choice-4
Dream Lines-1
Fabulous 50-15
96Hockey Greats Coins-9
Gold-9
96Leaf-140
Press Proofs-140
Fire On Ice-5
96Leaf Leather And Laces Promos-P8
96Leaf Leather And Laces-8
96Leaf Limited-7
Gold-7
Stubble-3
96Leaf Preferred-112
Press Proofs-112
Steel Power-5
Vanity Plates-1
Vanity Plates Gold-1
96Maggers-32
96Metal Universe-96
Lethal Weapons-6
Lethal Weapons Super Power-6
96NHL Aces Playing Cards-20
96NHL Pro Stamps-67
96Pinnacle-1
Artist's Proofs-1
Foil-1
Premium Stock-1
Rink Collection-1
By The Numbers-9
By The Numbers Premium-9
Team Pinnacle-1
96Pinnacle Fantasy-FC5
96Playoff One on One-430
96Post Upper Deck-8
96Score-41
Artist's Proofs-41
Dealer's Choice Artist's Proofs-41
Special Artist's Proofs-41
Golden Blades-41
Dream Team-8
Sudden Death-12
96Select Certified-4
Artist's Proofs-4
Blue-4
Mirror Blue-4
Mirror Gold-4
Mirror Red-4
Red-4
Cornerstones-4
96SkyBox Impact-79
Countdown to Impact-3
VersaTeam-4
96SP-99
96SP-P99
Clearcut Winner-CW1
Holoview Collection-HC1
Inside Info-IN1
Inside Info Gold-IN1
Game Film-GF1
SPx Force-1
SPx Force-5
SPx Force Autographs-1
96SPx-39
96SPx-P39
96SPx-GF1
96SPx-GS1
96SPx-GT1
Gold-39
Holoview Heroes-HH7
96Stadium Club Members Only-1
96Summit-67
Artist's Proofs-67
Ice-67
Metal-67
Premium Stock-67
High Voltage-5
High Voltage Mirage-5
Untouchables-12
96Team Out-19
96Topps Picks 500 Club-FC1
96Topps Picks Fantasy Team-FT10
96Topps Picks Top Shelf-TS2
96Ultra-106
Gold Medallion-106
Power-5
Power Red Line-2
96Upper Deck-108
96Upper Deck-361
96Upper Deck Blow-Ups-5
96Upper Deck Generation Next-X1
96Upper Deck Hart Hopefuls Bronze-HH1
96Upper Deck Hart Hopefuls Gold-HH1
96Upper Deck Hart Hopefuls Silver-HH1
96Upper Deck Lord Stanley's Heroes Finals-LS1
96Upper Deck Lord Stanleys Heroes Qfinals-LS1
96Upper Deck Lord Stanleys Heroes Semis-LS1
96Upper Deck Superstar Showdown-SS5A
96Upper Deck Ice-112
Parallel-112
Stanley Cup Foundation-S1
Stanley Cup Foundation Dynasty-S1
96Zenith-13
Artist's Proofs-13
Champion Salute-2
Champion Salute Diamond-2
96Swedish Semic Wien-99
97SLU Hockey One on One-1
97SLU Hockey Canadian-7
97Headliners Hockey-8
97SLU Hockey American-8
97Be A Player One Timers-1
97Be A Player Take A Number-8
97Beehive-33
Golden Portraits-33
Team-7
Team Gold-7
97Black Diamond-144
Double Diamond-144
Triple Diamond-144
Quadruple Diamond-144
Premium Cut-PC1
Premium Cut Double Diamond-PC1
Premium Cut Quadruple Diamond Horiz-PC1
Premium Cut Triple Diamond-PC1
Premium Cut Quadruple Diamond Verticals-PC1
97Collector's Choice-167
97Collector's Choice-312
Blow-Ups-1
Crash the Game-C1A
Crash the Game-C1B
Crash the Game-C1C
Crash the Game Exchange-CR1
Magic Men-MM1
Magic Men-MM2
Magic Men-MM3
Magic Men-MM4
Magic Men-MM5
Star Quest-SQ90
Stick'Ums-S1
World Domination-W1
97Crown Royale-84
Emerald Green-84
Ice Blue-84
Silver-84
Blades of Steel Die-Cuts-14
Cramer's Choice Jumbos-7
Cramer's Choice Jumbos Gold-7
Cramer's Choice Jumbos Signed-7
Hat Tricks Die-Cuts-11
Lamplighters Cel-Fusion Die-Cuts-11
97Donruss-143
Press Proofs Silver-143
Press Proofs Gold-143
Elite Inserts-1
Line 2 Line-1
Line 2 Line Die Cut-1
97Donruss Canadian Ice-5
Dominion Series-5
Provincial Series-5
National Pride-1
Stanley Cup Scrapbook-28
97Donruss Elite-9
97Donruss Elite-143
Aspirations-9
Aspirations-143
Status-9
Status-143
Craftsmen-19
Master Craftsmen-19
97Donruss Limited-4
97Donruss Limited-97
97Donruss Limited-200
Exposure-4
Exposure-97
Exposure-200
Fabric of the Game-1
Fabric of the Game-34
97Donruss Preferred-4
97Donruss Preferred-172
Cut to the Chase-4
Cut to the Chase-172
Line of the Times-6A
97Donruss Preferred Line of Times Promos-6A
97Donruss Preferred Precious Metals-3
97Donruss Priority-10
97Donruss Priority-199
Stamp of Approval-10
Stamp of Approval-199
Direct Deposit-8
Direct Deposit Promos-P8
Postcards-7
Postcards Opening Day Issues-10
Stamps-7
Stamps Bronze-7
Stamps Gold-7
Stamps Silver-7
97Highland Mint Mint-Cards Topps-9
97Highland Mint Mint-Cards Topps-10
97Jell-O Juniors To Pros-1
97Katch-92
97Katch-157
Gold-92
Gold-157
Silver-92
Silver-157
97Kenner Starting Lineup Cards-8
97Kraft-4
97Kraft Team Canada-11
97Leaf-8
97Leaf-175
Fractal Matrix-8
Fractal Matrix-175
Fractal Matrix Die Cuts-8
Fractal Matrix Die Cuts-175
Banner Season-3
Fire On Ice-1
97Leaf International-8
Universal Ice-8
97McDonald's Team Canada Coins-8
97McDonald's Upper Deck-1
97McDonald's Upper Deck-NNO
97McDonald's Upper Deck-NNO
97McDonald's Upper Deck-NNO
97McDonald's Upper Deck-NNO
97McDonald's Upper Deck-NNO
97McDonald's Upper Deck-NNO
97McDonald's Upper Deck-NNO
Game Film-1
97NHL Aces Playing Cards-37
97Pacific-99
Copper-99
Emerald Green-99
Ice Blue-99
Red-99
Silver-99
Card-Supials-12
Card-Supials Minis-12
Cramer's Choice-7
Gold Crown Die-Cuts-15
Slap Shots Die-Cuts-5A
Team Checklists-15
97Pacific Dynagon-78
97Pacific Dynagon-140
Copper-78
Copper-140
Dark Grey-78
Dark Grey-140
Emerald Green-78
Emerald Green-140
Ice Blue-78
Ice Blue-140
Red-78
Red-140
Silver-78
Silver-140
Best Kept Secrets-59
Dynamic Duos-10A
Kings of the NHL-6
Tandems-1
Tandems-19
97Pacific Invincible-86
Copper-86
Emerald Green-86
Ice Blue-86
Red-86
Silver-86
Attack Zone-14
Feature Performers-21
NHL Regime-128
NHL Regime-218
Off The Glass-12
97Pacific Omega-145
97Pacific Omega-250
Copper-145
Copper-250
Dark Gray-145
Dark Gray-250
Emerald Green-145
Emerald Green-250
Gold-145
Gold-250
Ice Blue-145
Ice Blue-250
Game Face-11
Silks-8
Stick Handle Laser Cuts-13
Team Leaders-14
97Panini Stickers-82
97Paramount-115
Copper-115
Dark Grey-115
Emerald Green-115
Ice Blue-115
Red-115
Silver-115
Big Numbers Die-Cuts-14
Canadian Greats-10
Photoengravings-13
97Pinnacle-67
97Pinnacle-192
Artist's Proofs-67
Rink Collection-67
Epix Game Emerald-1
Epix Game Orange-1
Epix Game Purple-1
Epix Moment Emerald-1
Epix Moment Orange-1
Epix Moment Purple-1
Epix Play Emerald-1
Epix Play Orange-1
Epix Play Purple-1
Epix Season Emerald-1
Epix Season Orange-1
Epix Season Purple-1
Press Plates Back Black-67
Press Plates Back Black-192
Press Plates Back Cyan-67
Press Plates Back Cyan-192
Press Plates Back Magenta-67
Press Plates Back Magenta-192
Press Plates Back Yellow-67
Press Plates Back Yellow-192
Press Plates Front Black-67
Press Plates Front Black-192
Press Plates Front Cyan-67
Press Plates Front Cyan-192
Press Plates Front Magenta-67
Press Plates Front Magenta-192
Press Plates Front Yellow-67
Press Plates Front Yellow-192
Team Pinnacle-4
Team Mirror-4
Team Parallel-4
Team Parallel Mirror-4
97Pinnacle Certified-100
Red-100
Mirror Blue-100
Mirror Gold-100
Mirror Red-100
Team-7
Gold Team Promo-7
Gold Team-7
97Pinnacle Inside-3
Coach's Collection-3
Executive Collection-3
Track-1
Cans-18
Cans Gold-18
97Pinnacle Mint-18
Bronze-18
Gold Team-18
Silver Team-18
Coins Brass-18
Coins Brass Proofs-18
Coins Gold Plated-18
Coins Gold Plated Proofs-18
Coins Nickel Silver-18
Coins Nickel Silver Proofs-18
Coins Solid Gold-18
Coins Solid Silver-18
97Pinnacle Power Pack Blow-Ups-17
97Pinnacle Tot Cert Platinum Blue-100
97Pinnacle Tot Cert Platinum Gold-100
97Pinnacle Totally Certified Platinum Red-100
97Pinnacle Tot Cert Mirror Platinum Gold-100
97Revolution-87
Copper-87
Emerald-87
Ice Blue-87
Silver-87
1998 All-Star Game Die-Cuts-14
NHL Icons-7
Team Checklist Laser Cuts-16
97Score-99
Artist's Proofs-99
Golden Blades-99
97Score Rangers-1
Platinum-1
Premier-1
97SP Authentic-99
Authentics-1
Authentics-2
Authentics-3
Authentics-4
Authentics-5
Authentics-6
Authentics-7
Authentics-8
Authentics-9
Authentics-10
Authentics-11
Authentics-NNO
Icons-I26
Icons Die-Cuts-I26
Icons Embossed-I26
Mark of a Legend-M6
Sign of the Times-WG
Tradition-T1
97SPx-30
97SPx-30S
Bronze-30
Gold-30
Silver-30
Steel-30
Dimension-SPX1
DuoView-1
DuoView Autographs-1
Grand Finale-30
97Studio-1
97Studio-109
Press Proofs Silver-1
Press Proofs Silver-109
Press Proofs Gold-1
Press Proofs Gold-109
Hard Hats-1
Portraits-1
Silhouettes-1
Silhouettes 8x10-1
97Upper Deck-109
97Upper Deck-209
97Upper Deck-419
Blow-Ups 3 x 5-1-1
Game Dated Moments-109
Game Jerseys-GJ8
Game Jerseys-GJ8S
Sixth Sense Masters-SS1
Sixth Sense Wizards-SS1
Smooth Grooves-SG1
The Specialists-1
The Specialists Level 2 Die Cuts-1
Three Star Selects-18
97Upper Deck Crash the All-Star Game-20
97Upper Deck Crash the All-Star Game-AR20
97Upper Deck Diamond Vision-1
97Upper Deck Diamond Vision-RT1
Signature Moves-1
Defining Moments-DM1
97Upper Deck Ice-90
Parallel-90
Champions-IC1
Champions 2 Die Cuts-IC1
Lethal Lines-L1B
Lethal Lines 2-L1B
Power Shift-90
97Zenith-4
Z-Gold-4
Z-Silver-4
97Zenith 5 x 7-1
Gold Impulse-1
Silver Impulse-1
97Zenith Chasing The Cup-2
97Zenith Z-Team-2
97Zenith Z-Team 5x7-2
97Zenith Z-Team Gold-2
97Pinnacle Collector's Club Team Pinnacle-H1
97Pinnacle Collector's Club Team Pinnacle-NNO
98SLU Hockey Freeze Frame-1
98SLU Hockey 12" Figures-1
98SLU Hockey One on One-1
98SLU Hockey Classic Doubles-3
98SLU Hockey-70
98SLU Hockey-75
98Aurora-123
Atomic Laser Cuts-13
Championship Fever-30
Championship Fever Copper-30
Championship Fever Ice Blue-30
Championship Fever Red-30
Championship Fever Silver-30
Cubes-12
Front Line Copper-9
Front Line Ice Blue-9
Front Line Red-9
Man Advantage-13
NHL Command-8
Toronto Fall Expo '98-122
98Be A Player-90
Press Release-90
98BAP Gold-90
98BAP Autographs-90
98BAP Autographs Gold-90
98BAP AS Game Used Stick Cards-S23
98BAP AS Game Used Jersey Cards-AS25
98BAP AS Milestones-M1
98BAP AS Milestones-M7
98BAP Playoff Game Used Jerseys-G1
98BAP Playoff Game Used Jersey Autographs-G1
98BAP Playoff Highlights-H3
98BAP Playoff Practice Used Jerseys-P24
98BAP Tampa Bay All Star Game-90
98Black Diamond-55
Double Diamond-55
Triple Diamond-55
Quadruple Diamond-55
Myriad-M27
Myriad 2-M27
Winning Formula Gold-WF18
Winning Formula Platinum-WF18
Year of the Great One-1
Year of the Great One-2
Year of the Great One-3
Year of the Great One-4
Year of the Great One-5
Year of the Great One-6
Year of the Great One-7
Year of the Great One-8
Year of the Great One-9
Year of the Great One-10
Year of the Great One-11
Year of the Great One-12
Year of the Great One-13
Year of the Great One-14
Year of the Great One-15
Year of the Great One-16
Year of the Great One-17
Year of the Great One-18
Year of the Great One-19
Year of the Great One-20
Year of the Great One-21
Year of the Great One-22
Year of the Great One-23
Year of the Great One-24
Year of the Great One-25
Year of the Great One-26
Year of the Great One-27
Year of the Great One-28
Year of the Great One-29
Year of the Great One-30
Year of the Great One-31
Year of the Great One-32
Year of the Great One-33
Year of the Great One-34
Year of the Great One-35
Year of the Great One-36
Year of the Great One-37
Year of the Great One-38
Year of the Great One-39
Year of the Great One-40
Year of the Great One-41
Year of the Great One-42
Year of the Great One-43
Year of the Great One-44
Year of the Great One-45
Year of the Great One-46
Year of the Great One-47
Year of the Great One-48
Year of the Great One-49
Year of the Great One-50
Year of the Great One-51
Year of the Great One-52
Year of the Great One-53
Year of the Great One-54
Year of the Great One-55
Year of the Great One-56
Year of the Great One-57
Year of the Great One-58
Year of the Great One-59
Year of the Great One-60
Year of the Great One-61
Year of the Great One-62
Year of the Great One-63
Year of the Great One-64
Year of the Great One-65
Year of the Great One-66
Year of the Great One-67
Year of the Great One-68
Year of the Great One-69
Year of the Great One-70
Year of the Great One-71
Year of the Great One-72
Year of the Great One-73
Year of the Great One-74
Year of the Great One-75
Year of the Great One-76
Year of the Great One-77
Year of the Great One-78
Year of the Great One-79
Year of the Great One-80
Year of the Great One-81
Year of the Great One-82
Year of the Great One-83
Year of the Great One-84
Year of the Great One-85
Year of the Great One-86
Year of the Great One-87
Year of the Great One-88
Year of the Great One-89
Year of the Great One-90
Year of the Great One-91
Year of the Great One-92
Year of the Great One-93
Year of the Great One-94
Year of the Great One-95
Year of the Great One-96
Year of the Great One-97
Year of the Great One-98
Year of the Great One-99
98Bowman's Best-3
Refractors-3
Atomic Refractors-3
Mirror Image Fusion-F15
Mirror Image Fusion Refractors-F15
Mirror Image Fusion Atomic Refractors-F15
98Crown Royale-88
Limited Series-88
Cramer's Choice Jumbos-8
Cramer's Choice Jumbos Dark Blue-8
Cramer's Choice Jumbos Green-8
Cramer's Choice Jumbos Red-8
Cramer's Choice Jumbos Light Blue-8
Cramer's Choice Jumbos Gold-8
Cramer's Choice Jumbos Purple-8
Living Legends-8
Master Performers-14
Pivotal Players-16
98Donruss Elite Promos-20
98Finest-64
No Protectors-64
No Protectors Refractors-64
Refractors-64
Double Sided Mystery Finest-M1
Double Sided Mystery Finest-M5
Double Sided Mystery Finest-M8
Double Sided Mystery Finest-M9
Double Sided Mystery Refractors-M1
Double Sided Mystery Refractors-M5
Double Sided Mystery Refractors-M8
Double Sided Mystery Refractors-M9
Oversize-4
Oversize Refractors-4
Red Lighters-R9
Red Lighters Refractors-R9
98Jell-O Spoons-3
98Katch-92
98Kenner Starting Lineup Cards-11
98Kenner Starting Lineup Cards-12
98McDonald's Upper Deck-1
Gretzky's Moments-M1
Gretzky's Moments-M2
Gretzky's Moments-M3
Gretzky's Moments-M4
Gretzky's Moments-M5
Gretzky's Moments-M6
Gretzky's Moments-M7
Gretzky's Moments-M8
Gretzky's Moments-M9
Gretzky's Moments-M10
98NHL Game Day Promotion-NYR1
98OPC Chrome-219
Refractors-219
Blast From the Past-1
Blast From the Past Refractors-1
Season's Best-SB20
Season's Best Refractors-SB20
98Pacific-99
Ice Blue-99
Red-99
Cramer's Choice-7
Dynagon Ice Inserts-13
Titanium Ice-13
Gold Crown Die-Cuts-23
Team Checklists-17
Timelines-11
98Pacific Dynagon Ice-121
Blue-121
Red-121
Adrenaline Rush Bronze-8
Adrenaline Rush Ice Blue-8
Adrenaline Rush Red-8
Adrenaline Rush Silver-8
Forward Thinking-13
Preeminent Players-8
Team Checklists-17
Montreal Spring Expo '99-121
98Pacific Omega-156
Red-156
Opening Day Issue-156
Championship Spotlight-7
Championship Spotlight Green-7
Championship Spotlight Red-7
Championship Spotlight Gold-7
EO Portraits-14
EO Portraits 1 of 1-14
Face to Face-2
Online-23
Planet Ice-26
Planet Ice Parallel-26
Prism-13
Toronto Spring Expo-156
98Panini Photocards-30
98Panini Photocards-102
98Panini Stickers-3
98Panini Stickers-80
98Paramount-152
Copper-152
Emerald Green-152
Holo-Electric-152
Ice Blue-152
Silver-152
Hall of Fame Bound-7
Hall of Fame Bound Proofs-7
Ice Galaxy-7
Ice Galaxy Gold-7
Ice Galaxy Silver-7
Special Delivery Die-Cuts-12
Team Checklists Die-Cuts-17
98Post-1
98Post-G1
98Post-G2
98Post-G3
98Post-G4
98Post-G5
98Post-G6
98Rangers Power Play-NYR1
98Revolution-92
Ice Shadow-92
Red-92
All-Star Die Cuts-8
Chalk Talk Laser-Cuts-11
NHL Icons-8
Showstoppers-23
Three Pronged Attack-27
Three Pronged Attack Parallel-27
98SP Authentic-56
Power Shift-56
Authentics-1
Authentics-10
Authentics-11
Sign of the Times-WG
Sign of the Times Gold-WG
Snapshots-SS1
Stat Masters-S28
Stat Masters-S29
Stat Masters-S30
98SPx Finite-53
98SPx Finite-99
98SPx Finite-151
98SPx Finite-180
98SPx Finite-S99
Radiance-53
Radiance-99
Radiance-151
Radiance-180
Spectrum-53
Spectrum-99
Spectrum-151
Spectrum-180
98SPx Top Prospects-38
Radiance-38
Spectrum-38
Highlight Heroes-H18
Lasting Impressions-L27
Premier Stars-PS1
Premier Stars-PS16
Year of the Great One-WG1
Year of the Great One-WG2
Year of the Great One-WG3

Year of the Great One-WG4
Year of the Great One-WG5
Year of the Great One-WG6
Year of the Great One-WG7
Year of the Great One-WG8
Year of the Great One-WG9
Year of the Great One-WG10
Year of the Great One-WG11
Year of the Great One-WG12
Year of the Great One-WG13
Year of the Great One-WG14
Year of the Great One-WG15
Year of the Great One-WG16
Year of the Great One-WG17
Year of the Great One-WG18
Year of the Great One-WG19
Year of the Great One-WG20
Year of the Great One-WG21
Year of the Great One-WG22
Year of the Great One-WG23
Year of the Great One-WG24
Year of the Great One-WG25
Year of the Great One-WG26
Year of the Great One-WG27
Year of the Great One-WG28
Year of the Great One-WG29
Year of the Great One-WG30
98Topps-219
O-Pee-Chee-219
Blast From The Past-1
Local Legends-L7
Mystery Finest Bronze-M4
Mystery Finest Bronze Refractors-M4
Mystery Finest Gold-M4
Mystery Finest Gold Refractors-M4
Mystery Finest Silver-M4
Mystery Finest Silver Refractors-M4
Season's Best-SB20
98Topps Gold Label Class 1-4
Black-4
Black One of One-4
One of One-4
Red-4
Red One of One-4
98Topps Gold Label Class 2-4
98Topps Gold Label Class 2 Black-4
98Topps Gold Label Class 2 Black 1 of 1-4
98Topps Gold Label Class 2 One of One-4
98Topps Gold Label Class 2 Red-4
98Topps Gold Label Class 2 Red One of One-4
98Topps Gold Label Class 3-4
98Topps Gold Label Class 3 Black-4
98Topps Gold Label Class 3 Black 1 of 1-4
98Topps Gold Label Class 3 One of One-4
98Topps Gold Label Class 3 Red-4
98Topps Gold Label Class 3 Red One of One-4
98UD Choice-128
98UD Choice-225
98UD Choice-236
98UD Choice-308
Draw Your Own Trading Card-NNO
Mini Bobbing Head-BH1
Prime Choice Reserve-128
Prime Choice Reserve-225
Prime Choice Reserve-236
Prime Choice Reserve-308
Reserve-128
Reserve-225
Reserve-236
Reserve-308
StarQuest Blue-SQ1
StarQuest Gold-SQ1
StarQuest Green-SQ1
StarQuest Red-SQ1
98UD3-31
98UD3-91
98UD3-151
Die-Cuts-31
Die-Cuts-91
Die-Cuts-151
98Upper Deck-135
98Upper Deck-207
98Upper Deck-388
98Upper Deck-390
Exclusives-135
Exclusives-207
Exclusives-388
Exclusives-390
Exclusives 1 of 1-135
Exclusives 1 of 1-207
Exclusives 1 of 1-388
Exclusives 1 of 1-390
Fantastic Finishers-FF1
Fantastic Finishers Quantum 1-FF1
Fantastic Finishers Quantum 2-FF1
Fantastic Finishers Quantum 3-FF1
Frozen In Time-FT30
Frozen In Time Quantum 1-FT30
Frozen In Time Quantum 2-FT30
Frozen In Time Quantum 3-FT30
Game Jerseys-GJ1
Game Jerseys-GJA2
Game Jerseys-GJA4
Generation Next-GN1
Generation Next-GN2
Generation Next-GN3
Generation Next Quantum 1-GN1
Generation Next Quantum 1-GN2
Generation Next Quantum 1-GN3
Generation Next Quantum 2-GN1
Generation Next Quantum 2-GN2
Generation Next Quantum 2-GN3
Generation Next Quantum 3-GN1
Generation Next Quantum 3-GN2
Generation Next Quantum 3-GN3
Lord Stanley's Heroes-LS1
Lord Stanley's Heroes Quantum 1-LS1
Lord Stanley's Heroes Quantum 2-LS1
Lord Stanley's Heroes Quantum 3-LS1
Profiles-P9
Profiles Quantum 1-P9
Profiles Quantum 2-P9
Profiles Quantum 3-P9
98Upper Deck Gretzky Game Jersey Autos-NNO
98Upper Deck Gretzky Game Jersey Autos-NNO
98Upper Deck Gretzky Game Jersey Autos-NNO
98Upper Deck Gretzky Game Jersey Autos-NNO
98Upper Deck Year of the Great One-GO1
98Upper Deck Year of the Great One-GO2
98Upper Deck Year of the Great One-GO3
98Upper Deck Year of the Great One-GO4
98Upper Deck Year of the Great One-GO5
98Upper Deck Year of the Great One-GO6
98Upper Deck Year of the Great One-GO7
98Upper Deck Year of the Great One-GO8
98Upper Deck Year of the Great One-GO9
98Upper Deck Year of the Great One-GO10
98Upper Deck Year of the Great One-GO11
98Upper Deck Year of the Great One-GO12
98Upper Deck Year of the Great One-GO13
98Upper Deck Year of the Great One-GO14
98Upper Deck Year of the Great One-GO15
98Upper Deck Year of the Great One-GO16
98Upper Deck Year of the Great One-GO17
98Upper Deck Year of the Great One-GO18
98Upper Deck Year of the Great One-GO19
98Upper Deck Year of the Great One-GO20
98Upper Deck Year of the Great One-GO21
98Upper Deck Year of the Great One-GO22
98Upper Deck Year of the Great One-GO23
98Upper Deck Year of the Great One-GO24
98Upper Deck Year of the Great One-GO25
98Upper Deck Year of the Great One-GO26
98Upper Deck Year of the Great One-GO27
98Upper Deck Year of the Great One-GO28
98Upper Deck Year of the Great One-GO29
98Upper Deck Year of the Great One-GO30
98Upper Deck Year of the Great One Quan1-GO1
98Upper Deck Year of the Great One Quan1-GO2
98Upper Deck Year of the Great One Quan1-GO3
98Upper Deck Year of the Great One Quan1-GO4
98Upper Deck Year of the Great One Quan1-GO5
98Upper Deck Year of the Great One Quan1-GO6
98Upper Deck Year of the Great One Quan1-GO7
98Upper Deck Year of the Great One Quan1-GO8
98Upper Deck Year of the Great One Quan1-GO9
98Upper Deck Year of the Great One Quan1-GO10
98Upper Deck Year of the Great One Quan1-GO11
98Upper Deck Year of the Great One Quan1-GO12
98Upper Deck Year of the Great One Quan1-GO13
98Upper Deck Year of the Great One Quan1-GO14
98Upper Deck Year of the Great One Quan1-GO15
98Upper Deck Year of the Great One Quan1-GO16
98Upper Deck Year of the Great One Quan1-GO17
98Upper Deck Year of the Great One Quan1-GO18
98Upper Deck Year of the Great One Quan1-GO19
98Upper Deck Year of the Great One Quan1-GO20
98Upper Deck Year of the Great One Quan1-GO21
98Upper Deck Year of the Great One Quan1-GO22
98Upper Deck Year of the Great One Quan1-GO23
98Upper Deck Year of the Great One Quan1-GO24
98Upper Deck Year of the Great One Quan1-GO25
98Upper Deck Year of the Great One Quan1-GO26
98Upper Deck Year of the Great One Quan1-GO27
98Upper Deck Year of the Great One Quan1-GO28
98Upper Deck Year of the Great One Quan1-GO29
98Upper Deck Year of the Great One Quan1-GO30
98Upper Deck Year of the Great One Quan 2-GO1
98Upper Deck Year of the Great One Quan 2-GO2
98Upper Deck Year of the Great One Quan 2-GO3
98Upper Deck Year of the Great One Quan 2-GO4
98Upper Deck Year of the Great One Quan 2-GO5
98Upper Deck Year of the Great One Quan 2-GO6
98Upper Deck Year of the Great One Quan 2-GO7
98Upper Deck Year of the Great One Quan 2-GO8
98Upper Deck Year of the Great One Quan 2-GO9
98Upper Deck Year of the Great One Quan 2-GO10
98Upper Deck Year of the Great One Quan 2-GO11
98Upper Deck Year of the Great One Quan 2-GO12
98Upper Deck Year of the Great One Quan 2-GO13
98Upper Deck Year of the Great One Quan 2-GO14
98Upper Deck Year of the Great One Quan 2-GO15
98Upper Deck Year of the Great One Quan 2-GO16
98Upper Deck Year of the Great One Quan 2-GO17
98Upper Deck Year of the Great One Quan 2-GO18
98Upper Deck Year of the Great One Quan 2-GO19
98Upper Deck Year of the Great One Quan 2-GO20
98Upper Deck Year of the Great One Quan 2-GO21
98Upper Deck Year of the Great One Quan 2-GO22
98Upper Deck Year of the Great One Quan 2-GO23
98Upper Deck Year of the Great One Quan 2-GO24
98Upper Deck Year of the Great One Quan 2-GO25
98Upper Deck Year of the Great One Quan 2-GO26
98Upper Deck Year of the Great One Quan 2-GO27
98Upper Deck Year of the Great One Quan 2-GO28
98Upper Deck Year of the Great One Quan 2-GO29
98Upper Deck Year of the Great One Quan 2-GO30
98Upper Deck Year of the Great One Quan 3-GO1
98Upper Deck Year of the Great One Quan 3-GO2
98Upper Deck Year of the Great One Quan 3-GO3
98Upper Deck Year of the Great One Quan 3-GO4
98Upper Deck Year of the Great One Quan 3-GO5
98Upper Deck Year of the Great One Quan 3-GO6
98Upper Deck Year of the Great One Quan 3-GO7
98Upper Deck Year of the Great One Quan 3-GO8
98Upper Deck Year of the Great One Quan 3-GO9
98Upper Deck Year of the Great One Quan 3-GO10
98Upper Deck Year of the Great One Quan 3-GO11
98Upper Deck Year of the Great One Quan 3-GO12
98Upper Deck Year of the Great One Quan 3-GO13
98Upper Deck Year of the Great One Quan 3-GO14
98Upper Deck Year of the Great One Quan 3-GO15
98Upper Deck Year of the Great One Quan 3-GO16
98Upper Deck Year of the Great One Quan 3-GO17
98Upper Deck Year of the Great One Quan 3-GO18
98Upper Deck Year of the Great One Quan 3-GO19
98Upper Deck Year of the Great One Quan 3-GO20
98Upper Deck Year of the Great One Quan 3-GO21
98Upper Deck Year of the Great One Quan 3-GO22
98Upper Deck Year of the Great One Quan 3-GO23
98Upper Deck Year of the Great One Quan 3-GO24
98Upper Deck Year of the Great One Quan 3-GO25
98Upper Deck Year of the Great One Quan 3-GO26
98Upper Deck Year of the Great One Quan 3-GO27
98Upper Deck Year of the Great One Quan 3-GO28
98Upper Deck Year of the Great One Quan 3-GO29
98Upper Deck Year of the Great One Quan 3-GO30
98Upper Deck Gold Reserve-135
98Upper Deck Gold Reserve-207
98Upper Deck Gold Reserve-388
98Upper Deck Gold Reserve-390
98Upper Deck Gold Reserve-NNO1
98Upper Deck MVP-132
98Upper Deck MVP-218
98Upper Deck MVP-219
98Upper Deck MVP-220
98Upper Deck MVP-NNO
Gold Script-132
Gold Script-218
Gold Script-219
Gold Script-220
Silver Script-132
Silver Script-218
Silver Script-219
Silver Script-220
Super Script-132
Super Script-218
Super Script-219
Super Script-220
Dynamics-D1
Dynamics-D2
Dynamics-D3
Dynamics-D4
Dynamics-D5
Dynamics-D6
Dynamics-D7
Dynamics-D8
Dynamics-D9
Dynamics-D10
Dynamics-D11
Dynamics-D12
Dynamics-D13
Dynamics-D14
Dynamics-D15
Game Souvenirs-WG
OT Heroes-OT5
ProSign-WG
Snipers-S2
Special Forces-F12
98Slovakian Eurotel-4
99Hasbro 12" Specials *-1
99SLU Hockey 12" Figures-1
99SLU Hockey One On One-1
99SLU Hockey Classic Doubles-1
99SLU Hockey Stadium Stars-1
99SLU Hockey-3
99Upper Deck PowerDeck Athlete of Century-4
99SLU Hockey Pro Action-10
99BAP Memorabilia Jersey Cards-J25
99BAP Memorabilia Jersey Emblems-E25
99BAP Memorabilia Jersey Numbers-I25
99BAP Memorabilia Jersey and Stick Cards-S25
99BAP Memorabilia AS Heritage Ruby-H18
99BAP Memorabilia AS Heritage Sapphire-H18
99BAP Memorabilia AS Heritage Emerald-H18
99BAP Update Double AS Jersey Cards-D9
99BAP Update Teammates Jersey Cards-TM2
99BAP Update Teammates Jersey Cards-TM22
99BAP Millennium-99
Emerald-99
Ruby-99
Sapphire-99
Signatures-99
Signatures Gold-99
Jerseys-J9
Jersey and Stick Cards-JS9
Jersey Emblems-E9
Jersey Numbers-N9
Pearson-P9
Pearson Autographs-P9
Players of the Decade-D1
Players of the Decade Autographs-D1
99Black Diamond A Piece of History-WG
99Black Diamond A Piece of History Double-WG
99Black Diamond A Piece of History Triple-WG
99Hasbro Starting Lineup Cards-3
99McDonald's Upper Deck-NNO
Game Jerseys-GJWG
Game Jerseys-GJWG
Signatures-WG
The Great Career-GR81-1
The Great Career-GR81-2
The Great Career-GR81-3
The Great Career-GR81-4
The Great Career-GR81-5
99Post Wayne Gretzky-1
99Post Wayne Gretzky-2
99Post Wayne Gretzky-3
99Post Wayne Gretzky-4
99Post Wayne Gretzky-5
99Post Wayne Gretzky-6
99Post Wayne Gretzky-7
99Post Wayne Gretzky-8
99Post Wayne Gretzky-9
99Post Wayne Gretzky-10
99Post Wayne Gretzky-11
99Post Wayne Gretzky-12
99Post Wayne Gretzky-13
99Post Wayne Gretzky-14
99SP Authentic Buyback Signatures-11
99SP Authentic Buyback Signatures-12
99SP Authentic Buyback Signatures-13
99SP Authentic Buyback Signatures-14
99SP Authentic Buyback Signatures-15
99SP Authentic Buyback Signatures-16
99SP Authentic Buyback Signatures-17
99SP Authentic Buyback Signatures-18
99SP Authentic Buyback Signatures-19
99SP Authentic Jersey Redemption-JWG
99SP Authentic Legendary Heroes-LH1
99SP Authentic Sign of the Times-WG
99SP Authentic Sign of the Times Gold-WG
99SPx 99 Cheers-CH1
99SPx 99 Cheers-CH2
99SPx 99 Cheers-CH3
99SPx 99 Cheers-CH4
99SPx 99 Cheers-CH5
99SPx 99 Cheers-CH6
99SPx 99 Cheers-CH7
99SPx 99 Cheers-CH8
99SPx 99 Cheers-CH9
99SPx 99 Cheers-CH10
99SPx 99 Cheers-CH11
99SPx 99 Cheers-CH12
99SPx 99 Cheers-CH13
99SPx 99 Cheers-CH14
99SPx 99 Cheers-CH15
99SPx Highlight Heroes-HH1
99SPx SPXcitement-X1
99SPx SPXtreme-XT20
99SPx Winning Materials-WM10
99SPx Winning Materials-WM-A1
99Ultimate Victory-111
99Ultimate Victory-112
99Ultimate Victory-113
99Ultimate Victory-114
99Ultimate Victory-115
99Ultimate Victory-116
99Ultimate Victory-117
99Ultimate Victory-118
99Ultimate Victory-119
99Ultimate Victory-120
1/1-111
1/1-112
1/1-113
1/1-114
1/1-115
1/1-116
1/1-117
1/1-118
1/1-119
1/1-120
Parallel-111
Parallel-112
Parallel-113
Parallel-114
Parallel-115
Parallel-116
Parallel-117
Parallel-118
Parallel-119
Parallel-120
Parallel 100-111
Parallel 100-112
Parallel 100-113
Parallel 100-114
Parallel 100-115
Parallel 100-116
Parallel 100-117
Parallel 100-118
Parallel 100-119
Parallel 100-120
Legendary Fabrics-LFWG
Legendary Fabrics-UFS
Legendary Fabrics-UF
99Upper Deck-1
99Upper Deck-2
99Upper Deck-3
99Upper Deck-4
99Upper Deck-5
99Upper Deck-6
99Upper Deck-7
99Upper Deck-8
99Upper Deck-9
99Upper Deck-10
99Upper Deck-86
99Upper Deck-134
99Upper Deck-135
99Upper Deck-136
Exclusives-1
Exclusives-2
Exclusives-3
Exclusives-4
Exclusives-5
Exclusives-6
Exclusives-7
Exclusives-8
Exclusives-9
Exclusives-10
Exclusives-86
Exclusives-134
Exclusives-135
Exclusives-136
Exclusives 1 of 1-1
Exclusives 1 of 1-2
Exclusives 1 of 1-3
Exclusives 1 of 1-4
Exclusives 1 of 1-5
Exclusives 1 of 1-6
Exclusives 1 of 1-7
Exclusives 1 of 1-8
Exclusives 1 of 1-9
Exclusives 1 of 1-10
Exclusives 1 of 1-86
Exclusives 1 of 1-134
Exclusives 1 of 1-135
Exclusives 1 of 1-136
Game Jerseys-WG1
Game Jerseys-WG2
Game Jerseys-WG3
Game Jerseys-WGS1
Game Jerseys Series II-WG
Game Jerseys Series II-WGS
Game Jersey Patch-WG1P
Game Jersey Patch-WG2P
Game Jersey Patch 1 of 1-WG1SP
Game Jersey Patch 1 of 1-WG2SP
Game Jersey Patch Series II-WGP
Game Jersey Patch Series II 1 of 1-WG-P1
Gretzky Profiles-GP1
Gretzky Profiles-GP2
Gretzky Profiles-GP3
Gretzky Profiles-GP4
Gretzky Profiles-GP5
Gretzky Profiles-GP6
Gretzky Profiles-GP7
Gretzky Profiles-GP8
Gretzky Profiles-GP9
Gretzky Profiles-GP10
Gretzky Profiles Quantum Gold-GP1
Gretzky Profiles Quantum Gold-GP2
Gretzky Profiles Quantum Gold-GP3
Gretzky Profiles Quantum Gold-GP4
Gretzky Profiles Quantum Gold-GP5
Gretzky Profiles Quantum Gold-GP6
Gretzky Profiles Quantum Gold-GP7
Gretzky Profiles Quantum Gold-GP8
Gretzky Profiles Quantum Gold-GP9
Gretzky Profiles Quantum Gold-GP10
Gretzky Profiles Quantum Silver-GP1
Gretzky Profiles Quantum Silver-GP2
Gretzky Profiles Quantum Silver-GP3
Gretzky Profiles Quantum Silver-GP4
Gretzky Profiles Quantum Silver-GP5
Gretzky Profiles Quantum Silver-GP6
Gretzky Profiles Quantum Silver-GP7
Gretzky Profiles Quantum Silver-GP8
Gretzky Profiles Quantum Silver-GP9
Gretzky Profiles Quantum Silver-GP10
Headed for the Hall-HOF1
Headed for the Hall Quantum Gold-HOF1
Headed for the Hall Quantum Silver-HOF1
PowerDeck Inserts-PD7
PowerDeck Inserts-PD8
PowerDeck Inserts-PD9
99Upper Deck Century Legends-1
99Upper Deck Century Legends-81
99Upper Deck Century Legends-82
99Upper Deck Century Legends-83
99Upper Deck Century Legends-84
99Upper Deck Century Legends-85
99Upper Deck Century Legends-86
99Upper Deck Century Legends-87
99Upper Deck Century Legends-88
99Upper Deck Century Legends-89
99Upper Deck Century Legends-90
Century Collection-1
Century Collection-81
Century Collection-82
Century Collection-83
Century Collection-84
Century Collection-85
Century Collection-86
Century Collection-87
Century Collection-88
Century Collection-89
Century Collection-90
All Century Team-AC1
Century Artifacts-C1
Century Artifacts-C2
Century Artifacts-C3
Century Artifacts-C8
Epic Signatures 100-WG
Essence of the Game-E1
Greatest Moments-GM1
Greatest Moments-GM2
Greatest Moments-GM3
Greatest Moments-GM4
Greatest Moments-GM5
Greatest Moments-GM6
Greatest Moments-GM7
Greatest Moments-GM8
Greatest Moments-GM9
Greatest Moments-GM10
Jerseys of the Century-JC6
99Upper Deck Gold Reserve-1
99Upper Deck Gold Reserve-2
99Upper Deck Gold Reserve-3
99Upper Deck Gold Reserve-4
99Upper Deck Gold Reserve-5
99Upper Deck Gold Reserve-6
99Upper Deck Gold Reserve-7
99Upper Deck Gold Reserve-8
99Upper Deck Gold Reserve-9
99Upper Deck Gold Reserve-10
99Upper Deck Gold Reserve-86
99Upper Deck Gold Reserve-134
99Upper Deck Gold Reserve-135
99Upper Deck Gold Reserve-136
Game-Used Souvenirs-GRWG
99Upper Deck Gretzky Exclusives-1
99Upper Deck Gretzky Exclusives-2
99Upper Deck Gretzky Exclusives-3
99Upper Deck Gretzky Exclusives-4
99Upper Deck Gretzky Exclusives-5
99Upper Deck Gretzky Exclusives-6
99Upper Deck Gretzky Exclusives-7
99Upper Deck Gretzky Exclusives-8
99Upper Deck Gretzky Exclusives-9
99Upper Deck Gretzky Exclusives-10
99Upper Deck Gretzky Exclusives-11
99Upper Deck Gretzky Exclusives-12
99Upper Deck Gretzky Exclusives-13
99Upper Deck Gretzky Exclusives-14
99Upper Deck Gretzky Exclusives-15
99Upper Deck Gretzky Exclusives-16
99Upper Deck Gretzky Exclusives-17
99Upper Deck Gretzky Exclusives-18
99Upper Deck Gretzky Exclusives-19
99Upper Deck Gretzky Exclusives-20
99Upper Deck Gretzky Exclusives-21
99Upper Deck Gretzky Exclusives-22
99Upper Deck Gretzky Exclusives-23
99Upper Deck Gretzky Exclusives-24
99Upper Deck Gretzky Exclusives-25
99Upper Deck Gretzky Exclusives-26
99Upper Deck Gretzky Exclusives-27
99Upper Deck Gretzky Exclusives-28
99Upper Deck Gretzky Exclusives-29
99Upper Deck Gretzky Exclusives-30
99Upper Deck Gretzky Exclusives-31
99Upper Deck Gretzky Exclusives-32
99Upper Deck Gretzky Exclusives-33
99Upper Deck Gretzky Exclusives-34
99Upper Deck Gretzky Exclusives-35
99Upper Deck Gretzky Exclusives-36
99Upper Deck Gretzky Exclusives-37
99Upper Deck Gretzky Exclusives-38
99Upper Deck Gretzky Exclusives-39
99Upper Deck Gretzky Exclusives-40
99Upper Deck Gretzky Exclusives-41
99Upper Deck Gretzky Exclusives-42
99Upper Deck Gretzky Exclusives-43
99Upper Deck Gretzky Exclusives-44
99Upper Deck Gretzky Exclusives-45
99Upper Deck Gretzky Exclusives-46
99Upper Deck Gretzky Exclusives-47
99Upper Deck Gretzky Exclusives-48
99Upper Deck Gretzky Exclusives-49
99Upper Deck Gretzky Exclusives-50
99Upper Deck Gretzky Exclusives-51
99Upper Deck Gretzky Exclusives-52
99Upper Deck Gretzky Exclusives-53
99Upper Deck Gretzky Exclusives-54
99Upper Deck Gretzky Exclusives-55
99Upper Deck Gretzky Exclusives-56
99Upper Deck Gretzky Exclusives-57
99Upper Deck Gretzky Exclusives-58
99Upper Deck Gretzky Exclusives-59
99Upper Deck Gretzky Exclusives-60
99Upper Deck Gretzky Exclusives-61
99Upper Deck Gretzky Exclusives-62
99Upper Deck Gretzky Exclusives-63
99Upper Deck Gretzky Exclusives-64
99Upper Deck Gretzky Exclusives-65
99Upper Deck Gretzky Exclusives-66
99Upper Deck Gretzky Exclusives-67
99Upper Deck Gretzky Exclusives-68
99Upper Deck Gretzky Exclusives-69
99Upper Deck Gretzky Exclusives-70
99Upper Deck Gretzky Exclusives-71
99Upper Deck Gretzky Exclusives-72
99Upper Deck Gretzky Exclusives-73
99Upper Deck Gretzky Exclusives-74
99Upper Deck Gretzky Exclusives-75
99Upper Deck Gretzky Exclusives-76
99Upper Deck Gretzky Exclusives-77
99Upper Deck Gretzky Exclusives-78
99Upper Deck Gretzky Exclusives-79
99Upper Deck Gretzky Exclusives-80
99Upper Deck Gretzky Exclusives-81
99Upper Deck Gretzky Exclusives-82
99Upper Deck Gretzky Exclusives-83
99Upper Deck Gretzky Exclusives-84
99Upper Deck Gretzky Exclusives-85
99Upper Deck Gretzky Exclusives-86
99Upper Deck Gretzky Exclusives-87
99Upper Deck Gretzky Exclusives-88
99Upper Deck Gretzky Exclusives-89
99Upper Deck Gretzky Exclusives-90
99Upper Deck Gretzky Exclusives-91
99Upper Deck Gretzky Exclusives-92
99Upper Deck Gretzky Exclusives-93
99Upper Deck Gretzky Exclusives-94
99Upper Deck Gretzky Exclusives-95
99Upper Deck Gretzky Exclusives-96
99Upper Deck Gretzky Exclusives-97
99Upper Deck Gretzky Exclusives-98
99Upper Deck Gretzky Exclusives-99
99Upper Deck Gretzky Exclusives-NNO
99Upper Deck Gretzky Exclusives-NNO
99Upper Deck Gretzky Exclusives-NNO
99Upper Deck Gretzky Exclusives-NNO
99Upper Deck Gretzky Exclusives Gold-1
99Upper Deck Gretzky Exclusives Gold-2
99Upper Deck Gretzky Exclusives Gold-3
99Upper Deck Gretzky Exclusives Gold-4
99Upper Deck Gretzky Exclusives Gold-5
99Upper Deck Gretzky Exclusives Gold-6
99Upper Deck Gretzky Exclusives Gold-7
99Upper Deck Gretzky Exclusives Gold-8
99Upper Deck Gretzky Exclusives Gold-9
99Upper Deck Gretzky Exclusives Gold-10
99Upper Deck Gretzky Exclusives Gold-11
99Upper Deck Gretzky Exclusives Gold-12
99Upper Deck Gretzky Exclusives Gold-13
99Upper Deck Gretzky Exclusives Gold-14
99Upper Deck Gretzky Exclusives Gold-15
99Upper Deck Gretzky Exclusives Gold-16
99Upper Deck Gretzky Exclusives Gold-17
99Upper Deck Gretzky Exclusives Gold-18
99Upper Deck Gretzky Exclusives Gold-19
99Upper Deck Gretzky Exclusives Gold-20
99Upper Deck Gretzky Exclusives Gold-21
99Upper Deck Gretzky Exclusives Gold-22
99Upper Deck Gretzky Exclusives Gold-23
99Upper Deck Gretzky Exclusives Gold-24
99Upper Deck Gretzky Exclusives Gold-25
99Upper Deck Gretzky Exclusives Gold-26
99Upper Deck Gretzky Exclusives Gold-27
99Upper Deck Gretzky Exclusives Gold-28
99Upper Deck Gretzky Exclusives Gold-29
99Upper Deck Gretzky Exclusives Gold-30
99Upper Deck Gretzky Exclusives Gold-31
99Upper Deck Gretzky Exclusives Gold-32
99Upper Deck Gretzky Exclusives Gold-33
99Upper Deck Gretzky Exclusives Gold-34
99Upper Deck Gretzky Exclusives Gold-35
99Upper Deck Gretzky Exclusives Gold-36
99Upper Deck Gretzky Exclusives Gold-37
99Upper Deck Gretzky Exclusives Gold-38
99Upper Deck Gretzky Exclusives Gold-39
99Upper Deck Gretzky Exclusives Gold-40
99Upper Deck Gretzky Exclusives Gold-41
99Upper Deck Gretzky Exclusives Gold-42
99Upper Deck Gretzky Exclusives Gold-43
99Upper Deck Gretzky Exclusives Gold-44
99Upper Deck Gretzky Exclusives Gold-45
99Upper Deck Gretzky Exclusives Gold-46
99Upper Deck Gretzky Exclusives Gold-47
99Upper Deck Gretzky Exclusives Gold-48
99Upper Deck Gretzky Exclusives Gold-49
99Upper Deck Gretzky Exclusives Gold-50
99Upper Deck Gretzky Exclusives Gold-51
99Upper Deck Gretzky Exclusives Gold-52
99Upper Deck Gretzky Exclusives Gold-53
99Upper Deck Gretzky Exclusives Gold-54
99Upper Deck Gretzky Exclusives Gold-55
99Upper Deck Gretzky Exclusives Gold-56
99Upper Deck Gretzky Exclusives Gold-57
99Upper Deck Gretzky Exclusives Gold-58
99Upper Deck Gretzky Exclusives Gold-59
99Upper Deck Gretzky Exclusives Gold-60
99Upper Deck Gretzky Exclusives Gold-61
99Upper Deck Gretzky Exclusives Gold-62
99Upper Deck Gretzky Exclusives Gold-63
99Upper Deck Gretzky Exclusives Gold-64
99Upper Deck Gretzky Exclusives Gold-65
99Upper Deck Gretzky Exclusives Gold-66
99Upper Deck Gretzky Exclusives Gold-67
99Upper Deck Gretzky Exclusives Gold-68
99Upper Deck Gretzky Exclusives Gold-69
99Upper Deck Gretzky Exclusives Gold-70
99Upper Deck Gretzky Exclusives Gold-71
99Upper Deck Gretzky Exclusives Gold-72
99Upper Deck Gretzky Exclusives Gold-73
99Upper Deck Gretzky Exclusives Gold-74
99Upper Deck Gretzky Exclusives Gold-75
99Upper Deck Gretzky Exclusives Gold-76
99Upper Deck Gretzky Exclusives Gold-77
99Upper Deck Gretzky Exclusives Gold-78
99Upper Deck Gretzky Exclusives Gold-79
99Upper Deck Gretzky Exclusives Gold-80
99Upper Deck Gretzky Exclusives Gold-81
99Upper Deck Gretzky Exclusives Gold-82
99Upper Deck Gretzky Exclusives Gold-83
99Upper Deck Gretzky Exclusives Gold-84
99Upper Deck Gretzky Exclusives Gold-85
99Upper Deck Gretzky Exclusives Gold-86
99Upper Deck Gretzky Exclusives Gold-87
99Upper Deck Gretzky Exclusives Gold-88
99Upper Deck Gretzky Exclusives Gold-89
99Upper Deck Gretzky Exclusives Gold-90
99Upper Deck Gretzky Exclusives Gold-91
99Upper Deck Gretzky Exclusives Gold-92
99Upper Deck Gretzky Exclusives Gold-93
99Upper Deck Gretzky Exclusives Gold-94
99Upper Deck Gretzky Exclusives Gold-95
99Upper Deck Gretzky Exclusives Gold-96
99Upper Deck Gretzky Exclusives Gold-97
99Upper Deck Gretzky Exclusives Gold-98
99Upper Deck Gretzky Exclusives Gold-99
99Upper Deck Gretzky Exclusives Platinum-1
99Upper Deck Gretzky Exclusives Platinum-2
99Upper Deck Gretzky Exclusives Platinum-3
99Upper Deck Gretzky Exclusives Platinum-4
99Upper Deck Gretzky Exclusives Platinum-5
99Upper Deck Gretzky Exclusives Platinum-6
99Upper Deck Gretzky Exclusives Platinum-7
99Upper Deck Gretzky Exclusives Platinum-8
99Upper Deck Gretzky Exclusives Platinum-9
99Upper Deck Gretzky Exclusives Platinum-10
99Upper Deck Gretzky Exclusives Platinum-11
99Upper Deck Gretzky Exclusives Platinum-12
99Upper Deck Gretzky Exclusives Platinum-13
99Upper Deck Gretzky Exclusives Platinum-14
99Upper Deck Gretzky Exclusives Platinum-15
99Upper Deck Gretzky Exclusives Platinum-16
99Upper Deck Gretzky Exclusives Platinum-17
99Upper Deck Gretzky Exclusives Platinum-18
99Upper Deck Gretzky Exclusives Platinum-19
99Upper Deck Gretzky Exclusives Platinum-20
99Upper Deck Gretzky Exclusives Platinum-21
99Upper Deck Gretzky Exclusives Platinum-22
99Upper Deck Gretzky Exclusives Platinum-23
99Upper Deck Gretzky Exclusives Platinum-24
99Upper Deck Gretzky Exclusives Platinum-25
99Upper Deck Gretzky Exclusives Platinum-26
99Upper Deck Gretzky Exclusives Platinum-27
99Upper Deck Gretzky Exclusives Platinum-28
99Upper Deck Gretzky Exclusives Platinum-29
99Upper Deck Gretzky Exclusives Platinum-30
99Upper Deck Gretzky Exclusives Platinum-31
99Upper Deck Gretzky Exclusives Platinum-32
99Upper Deck Gretzky Exclusives Platinum-33
99Upper Deck Gretzky Exclusives Platinum-34
99Upper Deck Gretzky Exclusives Platinum-35
99Upper Deck Gretzky Exclusives Platinum-36
99Upper Deck Gretzky Exclusives Platinum-37
99Upper Deck Gretzky Exclusives Platinum-38
99Upper Deck Gretzky Exclusives Platinum-39
99Upper Deck Gretzky Exclusives Platinum-40
99Upper Deck Gretzky Exclusives Platinum-41
99Upper Deck Gretzky Exclusives Platinum-42
99Upper Deck Gretzky Exclusives Platinum-43
99Upper Deck Gretzky Exclusives Platinum-44
99Upper Deck Gretzky Exclusives Platinum-45
99Upper Deck Gretzky Exclusives Platinum-46
99Upper Deck Gretzky Exclusives Platinum-47
99Upper Deck Gretzky Exclusives Platinum-48
99Upper Deck Gretzky Exclusives Platinum-49
99Upper Deck Gretzky Exclusives Platinum-50
99Upper Deck Gretzky Exclusives Platinum-51
99Upper Deck Gretzky Exclusives Platinum-52
99Upper Deck Gretzky Exclusives Platinum-53
99Upper Deck Gretzky Exclusives Platinum-54
99Upper Deck Gretzky Exclusives Platinum-55
99Upper Deck Gretzky Exclusives Platinum-56
99Upper Deck Gretzky Exclusives Platinum-57
99Upper Deck Gretzky Exclusives Platinum-58
99Upper Deck Gretzky Exclusives Platinum-59
99Upper Deck Gretzky Exclusives Platinum-60
99Upper Deck Gretzky Exclusives Platinum-61
99Upper Deck Gretzky Exclusives Platinum-62
99Upper Deck Gretzky Exclusives Platinum-63
99Upper Deck Gretzky Exclusives Platinum-64
99Upper Deck Gretzky Exclusives Platinum-65
99Upper Deck Gretzky Exclusives Platinum-66
99Upper Deck Gretzky Exclusives Platinum-67
99Upper Deck Gretzky Exclusives Platinum-68
99Upper Deck Gretzky Exclusives Platinum-69
99Upper Deck Gretzky Exclusives Platinum-70
99Upper Deck Gretzky Exclusives Platinum-71
99Upper Deck Gretzky Exclusives Platinum-72
99Upper Deck Gretzky Exclusives Platinum-73
99Upper Deck Gretzky Exclusives Platinum-74
99Upper Deck Gretzky Exclusives Platinum-75
99Upper Deck Gretzky Exclusives Platinum-76
99Upper Deck Gretzky Exclusives Platinum-77
99Upper Deck Gretzky Exclusives Platinum-78
99Upper Deck Gretzky Exclusives Platinum-79
99Upper Deck Gretzky Exclusives Platinum-80
99Upper Deck Gretzky Exclusives Platinum-81
99Upper Deck Gretzky Exclusives Platinum-82
99Upper Deck Gretzky Exclusives Platinum-83
99Upper Deck Gretzky Exclusives Platinum-84
99Upper Deck Gretzky Exclusives Platinum-85
99Upper Deck Gretzky Exclusives Platinum-86
99Upper Deck Gretzky Exclusives Platinum-87
99Upper Deck Gretzky Exclusives Platinum-88
99Upper Deck Gretzky Exclusives Platinum-89
99Upper Deck Gretzky Exclusives Platinum-90
99Upper Deck Gretzky Exclusives Platinum-91
99Upper Deck Gretzky Exclusives Platinum-92
99Upper Deck Gretzky Exclusives Platinum-93
99Upper Deck Gretzky Exclusives Platinum-94
99Upper Deck Gretzky Exclusives Platinum-95
99Upper Deck Gretzky Exclusives Platinum-96
99Upper Deck Gretzky Exclusives Platinum-97
99Upper Deck Gretzky Exclusives Platinum-98
99Upper Deck Gretzky Exclusives Platinum-99
99Upper Deck Gretzky Game Jersey Autos-WGJ
99Upper Deck Gretzky Game Jersey Autos-WGJ
99Upper Deck Gretzky Game Jersey Autos-WGJ
99Upper Deck HoloGrFx Gretzky GrFx-GG1
99Upper Deck HoloGrFx Gretzky GrFx-GG2
99Upper Deck HoloGrFx Gretzky GrFx-GG3
99Upper Deck HoloGrFx Gretzky GrFx-GG4
99Upper Deck HoloGrFx Gretzky GrFx-GG5
99Upper Deck HoloGrFx Gretzky GrFx-GG6
99Upper Deck HoloGrFx Gretzky GrFx-GG7
99Upper Deck HoloGrFx Gretzky GrFx-GG8
99Upper Deck HoloGrFx Gretzky GrFx-GG9
99Upper Deck HoloGrFx Gretzky GrFx-GG10
99Upper Deck HoloGrFx Gretzky GrFx-GG11
99Upper Deck HoloGrFx Gretzky GrFx-GG12
99Upper Deck HoloGrFx Gretzky GrFx-GG13
99Upper Deck HoloGrFx Gretzky GrFx-GG14
99Upper Deck HoloGrFx Gretzky GrFx-GG15
99Upper Deck HoloGrFx Gretzky GrFx Ausome-GG1
99Upper Deck HoloGrFx Gretzky GrFx Ausome-GG2
99Upper Deck HoloGrFx Gretzky GrFx Ausome-GG3
99Upper Deck HoloGrFx Gretzky GrFx Ausome-GG4
99Upper Deck HoloGrFx Gretzky GrFx Ausome-GG5
99Upper Deck HoloGrFx Gretzky GrFx Ausome-GG6
99Upper Deck HoloGrFx Gretzky GrFx Ausome-GG7
99Upper Deck HoloGrFx Gretzky GrFx Ausome-GG8
99Upper Deck HoloGrFx Gretzky GrFx Ausome-GG9
99Upper Deck HoloGrFx Gretzky GrFx Ausome-GG10
99Upper Deck HoloGrFx Gretzky GrFx Ausome-GG11
99Upper Deck HoloGrFx Gretzky GrFx Ausome-GG12
99Upper Deck HoloGrFx Gretzky GrFx Ausome-GG13
99Upper Deck HoloGrFx Gretzky GrFx Ausome-GG14
99Upper Deck HoloGrFx Gretzky GrFx Ausome-GG15
99Upper Deck HoloGrFx UD Authentics-WG
99Upper Deck HoloGrFx UD Authentics-WG2
99Upper Deck MVP-1
99Upper Deck MVP-131
99Upper Deck MVP-219
99Upper Deck MVP-220
Gold Script-1
Gold Script-131
Gold Script-219
Gold Script-220
Silver Script-1
Silver Script-131
Silver Script-219
Silver Script-220
Super Script-1
Super Script-131
Super Script-219
Super Script-220
90's Snapshots-S1
Draft Report-DR3
Draw Your Own Trading Card-W3
Draw Your Own Trading Card-W8
Draw Your Own Trading Card-W11
Draw Your Own Trading Card-W13
Draw Your Own Trading Card-W15
Draw Your Own Trading Card-W29
Draw Your Own Trading Card-W31
Draw Your Own Trading Card-W32
Draw Your Own Trading Card-W33
Draw Your Own Trading Card-W34
Draw Your Own Trading Card-W35
Draw Your Own Trading Card-W36
Draw Your Own Trading Card-W37
Draw Your Own Trading Card-W38
Draw Your Own Trading Card-W39
Draw Your Own Trading Card-W40
Draw Your Own Trading Card-W41
Draw Your Own Trading Card-W42
Draw Your Own Trading Card-W43
Draw Your Own Trading Card-W44
Draw Your Own Trading Card-W45
Game-Used Souvenirs-GU6
Game-Used Souvenirs-GU20
Game-Used Souvenirs-GUS1
Hands of Gold-H1
Legendary One-LO1
Legendary One-LO2
Legendary One-LO3
Legendary One-LO4
Legendary One-LO5
Legendary One-LO6
Legendary One-LO7
Legendary One-LO8
Legendary One-LO9
Legendary One-LO10
ProSign-WG
Talent-MVP1
SC Edition Great Combinations-GCGL
SC Edition Great Combinations-GCGR
SC Edition Great Combinations Parallel-GCGL
SC Edition Great Combinations Parallel-GCGR
99Upper Deck Ovation A Piece Of History-WG
99Upper Deck Ovation Center Stage-CS1
99Upper Deck Ovation Center Stage-CS2
99Upper Deck Ovation Center Stage-CS3
99Upper Deck Ovation Center Stage-CS4
99Upper Deck Ovation Center Stage-CS5
99Upper Deck Ovation Center Stage-CS11
99Upper Deck Ovation Center Stage-CS12
99Upper Deck Ovation Center Stage-CS13
99Upper Deck Ovation Center Stage-CS14
99Upper Deck Ovation Center Stage-CS15
99Upper Deck Ovation Center Stage-CS20
99Upper Deck Ovation Center Stage-CS21
99Upper Deck Ovation Center Stage-CS22
99Upper Deck Ovation Center Stage-CS23
99Upper Deck Ovation Center Stage-CS24
99Upper Deck Ovation Center Stage-CS25
99Upper Deck Ovation Center Stage-CS28
99Upper Deck Ovation Center Stage-CS29
99Upper Deck Ovation Center Stage-CS30
99Upper Deck Ovation Super Signatures-SS1
99Upper Deck Ovation Super Signatures-SSG1
99Upper Deck Ovation Super Signatures-SSR1
99Upper Deck Ovation Super Signatures-SSRC
99Upper Deck PowerDeck Athletes of the Century-4
99Upper Deck PowerDeck-20
Auxiliary-20
Auxiliary 1 of 1-20
Powerful Moment Auxiliary-PM1
Powerful Moment Auxiliary-PM2
Powerful Moment Auxiliary-PM3
Powerful Moment Auxiliary-PM4
Powerful Moment Auxiliary 1 of 1-PM1
Powerful Moment Auxiliary 1 of 1-PM2
Powerful Moment Auxiliary 1 of 1-PM3
Powerful Moment Auxiliary 1 of 1-PM4
Powerful Moments-PM1
Powerful Moments-PM2
Powerful Moments-PM3
Powerful Moments-PM4
99Upper Deck Retro-49
Gold-49
Platinum-49
Distant Replay-DR9
Distant Replay Level 2-DR9
Epic Gretzky-EG1
Epic Gretzky-EG2
Epic Gretzky-EG3
Epic Gretzky-EG4
Epic Gretzky-EG5
Epic Gretzky-EG6
Epic Gretzky-EG7
Epic Gretzky-EG8
Epic Gretzky-EG9
Epic Gretzky-EG10
Epic Gretzky Level 2-EG1
Epic Gretzky Level 2-EG2
Epic Gretzky Level 2-EG3
Epic Gretzky Level 2-EG4
Epic Gretzky Level 2-EG5
Epic Gretzky Level 2-EG6
Epic Gretzky Level 2-EG7
Epic Gretzky Level 2-EG8
Epic Gretzky Level 2-EG9
Epic Gretzky Level 2-EG10
Inkredible-WG
Inkredible Level 2-WG
Lunchboxes-1
Lunchboxes-2
Lunchboxes-3
Lunchboxes-4
Memento-RM1
Turn of the Century-TC9
99Upper Deck Victory-391
99Upper Deck Victory-392
99Upper Deck Victory-393
99Upper Deck Victory-394
99Upper Deck Victory-395
99Upper Deck Victory-396
99Upper Deck Victory-397
99Upper Deck Victory-398
99Upper Deck Victory-399
99Upper Deck Victory-400
99Upper Deck Victory-401
99Upper Deck Victory-402
99Upper Deck Victory-403
99Upper Deck Victory-404
99Upper Deck Victory-405
99Upper Deck Victory-406
99Upper Deck Victory-407
99Upper Deck Victory-408
99Upper Deck Victory-409
99Upper Deck Victory-410
99Upper Deck Victory-411
99Upper Deck Victory-412
99Upper Deck Victory-413
99Upper Deck Victory-414
99Upper Deck Victory-415
99Upper Deck Victory-416
99Upper Deck Victory-417
99Upper Deck Victory-418
99Upper Deck Victory-419
99Upper Deck Victory-420
99Upper Deck Victory-421
99Upper Deck Victory-422
99Upper Deck Victory-423
99Upper Deck Victory-424
99Upper Deck Victory-425
99Upper Deck Victory-426
99Upper Deck Victory-427
99Upper Deck Victory-428
99Upper Deck Victory-429
99Upper Deck Victory-430
99Upper Deck Victory-431
99Upper Deck Victory-432
99Upper Deck Victory-433
99Upper Deck Victory-434
99Upper Deck Victory-435
99Upper Deck Victory-436
99Upper Deck Victory-437
99Upper Deck Victory-438
99Upper Deck Victory-439
99Upper Deck Victory-440
99Wayne Gretzky Hockey-99
99Wayne Gretzky Hockey-179
99Wayne Gretzky Hockey-GM1
Hall of Fame Career-HOF1
Hall of Fame Career-HOF2
Hall of Fame Career-HOF3
Hall of Fame Career-HOF4
Hall of Fame Career-HOF5
Hall of Fame Career-HOF6
Hall of Fame Career-HOF7
Hall of Fame Career-HOF8
Hall of Fame Career-HOF9
Hall of Fame Career-HOF10
Hall of Fame Career-HOF11
Hall of Fame Career-HOF12
Hall of Fame Career-HOF13
Hall of Fame Career-HOF14
Hall of Fame Career-HOF15
Hall of Fame Career-HOF16
Hall of Fame Career-HOF17
Hall of Fame Career-HOF18
Hall of Fame Career-HOF19
Hall of Fame Career-HOF20
Hall of Fame Career-HOF21
Hall of Fame Career-HOF22
Hall of Fame Career-HOF23
Hall of Fame Career-HOF24
Hall of Fame Career-HOF25
Hall of Fame Career-HOF26
Hall of Fame Career-HOF27
Hall of Fame Career-HOF28
Hall of Fame Career-HOF29
Hall of Fame Career-HOF30
Signs of Greatness-WG

Visionary-V1
Visionary-V2
Visionary-V3
Visionary-V4
Visionary-V5
Visionary-V6
Visionary-V7
Visionary-V8
Visionary-V9
Visionary-V10
99Wayne Gretzky Living Legend-1
99Wayne Gretzky Living Legend-2
99Wayne Gretzky Living Legend-3
99Wayne Gretzky Living Legend-4
99Wayne Gretzky Living Legend-5
99Wayne Gretzky Living Legend-6
99Wayne Gretzky Living Legend-7
99Wayne Gretzky Living Legend-8
99Wayne Gretzky Living Legend-9
99Wayne Gretzky Living Legend-10
99Wayne Gretzky Living Legend-11
99Wayne Gretzky Living Legend-12
99Wayne Gretzky Living Legend-13
99Wayne Gretzky Living Legend-14
99Wayne Gretzky Living Legend-15
99Wayne Gretzky Living Legend-16
99Wayne Gretzky Living Legend-17
99Wayne Gretzky Living Legend-18
99Wayne Gretzky Living Legend-19
99Wayne Gretzky Living Legend-20
99Wayne Gretzky Living Legend-21
99Wayne Gretzky Living Legend-22
99Wayne Gretzky Living Legend-23
99Wayne Gretzky Living Legend-24
99Wayne Gretzky Living Legend-25
99Wayne Gretzky Living Legend-26
99Wayne Gretzky Living Legend-27
99Wayne Gretzky Living Legend-28
99Wayne Gretzky Living Legend-29
99Wayne Gretzky Living Legend-30
99Wayne Gretzky Living Legend-31
99Wayne Gretzky Living Legend-32
99Wayne Gretzky Living Legend-33
99Wayne Gretzky Living Legend-34
99Wayne Gretzky Living Legend-35
99Wayne Gretzky Living Legend-36
99Wayne Gretzky Living Legend-37
99Wayne Gretzky Living Legend-38
99Wayne Gretzky Living Legend-39
99Wayne Gretzky Living Legend-40
99Wayne Gretzky Living Legend-41
99Wayne Gretzky Living Legend-42
99Wayne Gretzky Living Legend-43
99Wayne Gretzky Living Legend-44
99Wayne Gretzky Living Legend-45
99Wayne Gretzky Living Legend-46
99Wayne Gretzky Living Legend-47
99Wayne Gretzky Living Legend-48
99Wayne Gretzky Living Legend-49
99Wayne Gretzky Living Legend-50
99Wayne Gretzky Living Legend-51
99Wayne Gretzky Living Legend-52
99Wayne Gretzky Living Legend-53
99Wayne Gretzky Living Legend-54
99Wayne Gretzky Living Legend-55
99Wayne Gretzky Living Legend-56
99Wayne Gretzky Living Legend-57
99Wayne Gretzky Living Legend-58
99Wayne Gretzky Living Legend-59
99Wayne Gretzky Living Legend-60
99Wayne Gretzky Living Legend-61
99Wayne Gretzky Living Legend-62
99Wayne Gretzky Living Legend-63
99Wayne Gretzky Living Legend-64
99Wayne Gretzky Living Legend-65
99Wayne Gretzky Living Legend-66
99Wayne Gretzky Living Legend-67
99Wayne Gretzky Living Legend-68
99Wayne Gretzky Living Legend-69
99Wayne Gretzky Living Legend-70
99Wayne Gretzky Living Legend-71
99Wayne Gretzky Living Legend-72
99Wayne Gretzky Living Legend-73
99Wayne Gretzky Living Legend-74
99Wayne Gretzky Living Legend-75
99Wayne Gretzky Living Legend-76
99Wayne Gretzky Living Legend-77
99Wayne Gretzky Living Legend-78
99Wayne Gretzky Living Legend-79
99Wayne Gretzky Living Legend-80
99Wayne Gretzky Living Legend-81
99Wayne Gretzky Living Legend-82
99Wayne Gretzky Living Legend-83
99Wayne Gretzky Living Legend-84
99Wayne Gretzky Living Legend-85
99Wayne Gretzky Living Legend-86
99Wayne Gretzky Living Legend-87
99Wayne Gretzky Living Legend-88
99Wayne Gretzky Living Legend-89
99Wayne Gretzky Living Legend-90
99Wayne Gretzky Living Legend-91
99Wayne Gretzky Living Legend-92
99Wayne Gretzky Living Legend-93
99Wayne Gretzky Living Legend-94
99Wayne Gretzky Living Legend-95
99Wayne Gretzky Living Legend-96
99Wayne Gretzky Living Legend-97
99Wayne Gretzky Living Legend-98
99Wayne Gretzky Living Legend-99
A Leader by Example-L1
A Leader by Example-L2
A Leader by Example-L3
A Leader by Example-L4
A Leader by Example-L5
A Leader by Example-L6
Authentics-C1
Authentics-P1
Authentics-P2
Authentics-P3
Authentics-P4
Authentics-P5
Authentics-P6
Authentics-S1
Authentics-S2
Authentics-GJ1
Goodwill Ambassador-GW1
Goodwill Ambassador-GW2
Goodwill Ambassador-GW3
Goodwill Ambassador-GW4
Goodwill Ambassador-GW5
Goodwill Ambassador-GW6
Goodwill Ambassador-GW7
Goodwill Ambassador-GW8
Goodwill Ambassador-GW9
Great Accolades-GA1
Great Accolades-GA2
Great Accolades-GA3
Great Accolades-GA4
Great Accolades-GA5
Great Accolades-GA6
Great Accolades-GA7
Great Accolades-GA8
Great Accolades-GA9
Great Accolades-GA10
Great Accolades-GA11
Great Accolades-GA12
Great Accolades-GA13
Great Accolades-GA14
Great Accolades-GA15
Great Accolades-GA16
Great Accolades-GA17
Great Accolades-GA18
Great Accolades-GA19
Great Accolades-GA20
Great Accolades-GA21
Great Accolades-GA22
Great Accolades-GA23
Great Accolades-GA24
Great Accolades-GA25
Great Accolades-GA26
Great Accolades-GA27
Great Accolades-GA28
Great Accolades-GA29
Great Accolades-GA30
Great Accolades-GA31
Great Accolades-GA32
Great Accolades-GA33
Great Accolades-GA34
Great Accolades-GA35
Great Accolades-GA36
Great Accolades-GA37
Great Accolades-GA38
Great Accolades-GA39
Great Accolades-GA40
Great Accolades-GA41
Great Accolades-GA42
Great Accolades-GA43
Great Accolades-GA44
Great Accolades-GA45
Great Stats-GS1
Great Stats-GS2
Great Stats-GS3
Great Stats-GS4
Great Stats-GS5
Great Stats-GS6
Magic Moments-MM1
Magic Moments-MM2
Magic Moments-MM3
Magic Moments-MM4
Magic Moments-MM5
Magic Moments-MM6
More Than a Number-1
More Than a Number-2
More Than a Number-3
More Than a Number-4
More Than a Number-5
More Than a Number-6
More Than a Number-7
More Than a Number-8
More Than a Number-9
More Than a Number-10
More Than a Number-11
More Than a Number-12
More Than a Number-13
More Than a Number-14
More Than a Number-15
More Than a Number-16
More Than a Number-17
More Than a Number-18
More Than a Number-19
More Than a Number-20
More Than a Number-21
More Than a Number-22
More Than a Number-23
More Than a Number-24
More Than a Number-25
More Than a Number-26
More Than a Number-27
More Than a Number-28
More Than a Number-29
More Than a Number-30
More Than a Number-31
More Than a Number-32
More Than a Number-33
More Than a Number-34
More Than a Number-35
More Than a Number-36
More Than a Number-37
More Than a Number-38
More Than a Number-39
More Than a Number-40
More Than a Number-41
More Than a Number-42
More Than a Number-43
More Than a Number-44
More Than a Number-45
More Than a Number-46
More Than a Number-47
More Than a Number-48
More Than a Number-49
More Than a Number-50
More Than a Number-51
More Than a Number-52
More Than a Number-53
More Than a Number-54
More Than a Number-55
More Than a Number-56
More Than a Number-57
More Than a Number-58
More Than a Number-59
More Than a Number-60
More Than a Number-61
More Than a Number-62
More Than a Number-63
More Than a Number-64
More Than a Number-65
More Than a Number-66
More Than a Number-67
More Than a Number-68
More Than a Number-69
More Than a Number-70
More Than a Number-71
More Than a Number-72
More Than a Number-73
More Than a Number-74
More Than a Number-75
More Than a Number-76
More Than a Number-77
More Than a Number-78
More Than a Number-79
More Than a Number-80
More Than a Number-81
More Than a Number-82
More Than a Number-83
More Than a Number-84
More Than a Number-85
More Than a Number-86
More Than a Number-87
More Than a Number-88
More Than a Number-89
More Than a Number-90
More Than a Number-91
More Than a Number-92
More Than a Number-93
More Than a Number-94
More Than a Number-95
More Than a Number-96
More Than a Number-97
More Than a Number-98
More Than a Number-99
Only One 99-1
Only One 99-2
Only One 99-3
Only One 99-4
Only One 99-5
Only One 99-6
Only One 99-7
Only One 99-8
Only One 99-9
Only One 99-10
Only One 99-11
Only One 99-12
Only One 99-13
Only One 99-14
Only One 99-15
Only One 99-16
Only One 99-17
Only One 99-18
Only One 99-19
Only One 99-20
Only One 99-21
Only One 99-22
Only One 99-23
Only One 99-24
Only One 99-25
Only One 99-26
Only One 99-27
Only One 99-28
Only One 99-29
Only One 99-30
Only One 99-31
Only One 99-32
Only One 99-33
Only One 99-34
Only One 99-35
Only One 99-36
Only One 99-37
Only One 99-38
Only One 99-39
Only One 99-40
Only One 99-41
Only One 99-42
Only One 99-43
Only One 99-44
Only One 99-45
Only One 99-46
Only One 99-47
Only One 99-48
Only One 99-49
Only One 99-50
Only One 99-51
Only One 99-52
Only One 99-53
Only One 99-54
Only One 99-55
Only One 99-56
Only One 99-57
Only One 99-58
Only One 99-59
Only One 99-60
Only One 99-61
Only One 99-62
Only One 99-63
Only One 99-64
Only One 99-65
Only One 99-66
Only One 99-67
Only One 99-68
Only One 99-69
Only One 99-70
Only One 99-71
Only One 99-72
Only One 99-73
Only One 99-74
Only One 99-75
Only One 99-76
Only One 99-77
Only One 99-78
Only One 99-79
Only One 99-80
Only One 99-81
Only One 99-82
Only One 99-83
Only One 99-84
Only One 99-85
Only One 99-86
Only One 99-87
Only One 99-88
Only One 99-89
Only One 99-90
Only One 99-91
Only One 99-92
Only One 99-93
Only One 99-94
Only One 99-95
Only One 99-96
Only One 99-97
Only One 99-98
Only One 99-99
The Great One-GO1
The Great One-GO2
The Great One-GO3
The Great One-GO4
The Great One-GO5
The Great One-GO6
The Great One-GO7
The Great One-GO8
The Great One-GO9
Wearing the Leaf-WL1
Wearing the Leaf-WL2
Wearing the Leaf-WL3
Wearing the Leaf-WL4
Wearing the Leaf-WL5
Wearing the Leaf-WL6
Year of the Great One-1
Year of the Great One-2
Year of the Great One-3
Year of the Great One-4
Year of the Great One-5
Year of the Great One-6
Year of the Great One-7
Year of the Great One-8
Year of the Great One-9
Year of the Great One-10
Year of the Great One-11
Year of the Great One-12
Year of the Great One-13
Year of the Great One-14
Year of the Great One-15
Year of the Great One-16
Year of the Great One-17
Year of the Great One-18
Year of the Great One-19
Year of the Great One-20
Year of the Great One-21
Year of the Great One-22
Year of the Great One-23
Year of the Great One-24
Year of the Great One-25
Year of the Great One-26
Year of the Great One-27
Year of the Great One-28
Year of the Great One-29
Year of the Great One-30
Year of the Great One-31
Year of the Great One-32
Year of the Great One-33
Year of the Great One-34
Year of the Great One-35
Year of the Great One-36
Year of the Great One-37
Year of the Great One-38
Year of the Great One-39
Year of the Great One-40
Year of the Great One-41
Year of the Great One-42
Year of the Great One-43
Year of the Great One-44
Year of the Great One-45
Year of the Great One-46
Year of the Great One-47
Year of the Great One-48
Year of the Great One-49
Year of the Great One-50
Year of the Great One-51
Year of the Great One-52
Year of the Great One-53
Year of the Great One-54
Year of the Great One-55
Year of the Great One-56
Year of the Great One-57
Year of the Great One-58
Year of the Great One-59
Year of the Great One-60
Year of the Great One-61
Year of the Great One-62
Year of the Great One-63
Year of the Great One-64
Year of the Great One-65
Year of the Great One-66
Year of the Great One-67
Year of the Great One-68
Year of the Great One-69
Year of the Great One-70
Year of the Great One-71
Year of the Great One-72
Year of the Great One-73
Year of the Great One-74
Year of the Great One-75
Year of the Great One-76
Year of the Great One-77
Year of the Great One-78
Year of the Great One-79
Year of the Great One-80
Year of the Great One-81
Year of the Great One-82
Year of the Great One-83
Year of the Great One-84
Year of the Great One-85
Year of the Great One-86
Year of the Great One-87
Year of the Great One-88
Year of the Great One-89
Year of the Great One-90
Year of the Great One-91
Year of the Great One-92
Year of the Great One-93
Year of the Great One-94
Year of the Great One-95
Year of the Great One-96
Year of the Great One-97
Year of the Great One-98
Year of the Great One-99
99UD Prospects-1
Signatures of Tradition-WG
00SLU Hockey-75
00BAP Memorabilia Jersey Cards-J25
00BAP Memorabilia Jersey Emblems-E25
00BAP Memorabilia Jersey Numbers-N25
00BAP Memorabilia Jersey and Stick Cards-JS25
00BAP Memorabilia Patent Power Jerseys-PP1
00BAP Signature Series-64
Emerald-64
Ruby-64
Sapphire-64
Autographs-143
Autographs Gold-143
He Shoots-He Scores Prizes-11
00BAP Ultimate Memorabilia Autographs-9
Gold-9
00BAP Ultimate Memorabilia Captain's C-C9
00BAP Ultimate Mem Dynasty Jerseys-D1
00BAP Ultimate Mem Dynasty Emblems-D1
00BAP Ultimate Mem Game-Used Jerseys-GJ9
00BAP Ultimate Mem Game-Used Emblems-E7
00BAP Ultimate Mem Game-Used Numbers-N7
00BAP Ultimate Mem Game-Used Sticks-GS9
00BAP Ultimate Memorabilia Hart Trophy-H12
00BAP Ultimate Memorabilia Hart Trophy-H14
00BAP Ultimate Memorabilia Hart Trophy-H15
00BAP Ultimate Memorabilia Hart Trophy-H16
00BAP Ultimate Memorabilia Hart Trophy-H17
00BAP Ultimate Memorabilia Hart Trophy-H18
00BAP Ultimate Memorabilia Hart Trophy-H19
00BAP Ultimate Memorabilia Hart Trophy-H20
00BAP Ultimate Mem Journey Jerseys-JJ1
00BAP Ultimate Mem Journey Emblems-JE1
00BAP Ultimate Mem Journey Numbers-JI1
00BAP Ultimate Mem Magnificent Ones-ML9
00BAP Ultimate Mem Magnificent Ones Autos-ML9
00BAP Ultimate Memorabilia NHL Records-R10
00BAP Ultimate Memorabilia Retro-Active-RA10
00BAP Ultimate Memorabilia Teammates-TM36
00Black Diamond Game Gear-GWG
00SP Authentic BuyBacks-64
00SP Authentic BuyBacks-65
00SP Authentic BuyBacks-66
00SP Authentic BuyBacks-67
00SP Authentic BuyBacks-68
00SP Authentic Power Skaters-P4
00SP Authentic Power Skaters-P5
00SP Authentic Power Skaters-P6
00SP Authentic Power Skaters-P7
00SP Authentic Sign of the Times-WG
00SP Authentic Sign of the Times-H/G
00SP Authentic Sign of the Times-M/G
00SP Authentic Sign of the Times-GMF
00SP Authentic Sign of the Times-HOG
00SP Game Used Patch Cards-D-KG
00SP Game Used Patch Cards-D-MG
00SP Game Used Patch Cards-P-WG
00SP Game Used Tools of the Game-WG
00SP Game Used Tools of the Game Excl-WG
00SP Game Used Tools of the Game Combos-C-HG
00SP Game Used Tools of the Game Combos-C-LG
00SP Game Used Tools of the Game Combos-C-MG
00SP Game Used TOTG Auto Bronze-A-WG
00SP Game Used TOTG Auto Silver-A-WG
00SP Game Used Tool of the Game Auto Gold-A-WG
00SPx Winning Materials-WG
00SPx Winning Materials-WGR
00SPx Winning Materials Autographs-SWG
00UD Heroes-126
00UD Heroes-180
Game-Used Twigs-T-WG
Game-Used Twigs Gold-C-GM
Player Idols-PI4
Second Season Heroes-SS6
Signs of Greatness-WG
00UD Pros and Prospects Championship Ring-CR4
00UD Pros and Prospect Game Jsy Auto Excl-S-WG
00UD Pros and Prospects Game Jersey Autos-S-WG
00UD Reserve Buyback Autographs-1
00UD Reserve Buyback Autographs-2
00UD Reserve Buyback Autographs-3
00UD Reserve Buyback Autographs-4
00UD Reserve Buyback Autographs-5
00UD Reserve Buyback Autographs-6
00UD Reserve Buyback Autographs-7
00UD Reserve Buyback Autographs-8
00UD Reserve Buyback Autographs-9
00UD Reserve Buyback Autographs-10
00Upper Deck 500 Goal Club-500WG
00Upper Deck 500 Goal Club-500WG
00Upper Deck Game Jerseys-WG
00Upper Deck Game Jerseys-WG
00Upper Deck Game Jersey Autos Exclusives-EWG
00Upper Deck Game Jersey Autos Exclusives-ESWG
00Upper Deck Game Jersey Combos-DGH
00Upper Deck Game Jersey Combos-DGL
00Upper Deck Game Jersey Combos-DGM
00Upper Deck Game Jersey Doubles-DWG
00Upper Deck Game Jersey Patches-PWG
00Upper Deck Game Jersey Patches-WGP
00Upper Deck Game Jersey Patch Autos Excl-WGP
00Upper Deck Game Jersey Patch Autos Excl-PSWG
00Upper Deck Game Patch Excl Series II-EWG
00Upper Deck Signs of Greatness-SWG
00Upper Deck Legends-49
00Upper Deck Legends-54
00Upper Deck Legends-61
00Upper Deck Legends-134
Legendary Collection Bronze-49
Legendary Collection Bronze-54
Legendary Collection Bronze-61
Legendary Collection Bronze-134
Legendary Collection Gold-49
Legendary Collection Gold-54
Legendary Collection Gold-61
Legendary Collection Gold-134
Legendary Collection Silver-49
Legendary Collection Silver-54
Legendary Collection Silver-61
Legendary Collection Silver-134
Enshrined Stars-ES1
Epic Signatures-WG
Essence of the Game-EG2
Legendary Game Jerseys-JWG
Playoff Heroes-PH7
Supreme Milestones-SM1
Supreme Milestones-SM4
00Upper Deck MVP Excellence-ME10
00Upper Deck MVP Game-Used Souvenirs-GSWG
00Upper Deck MVP Super Game-Used Souvenir-GSWG
00Upper Deck Victory-260
00Upper Deck Vintage Dynasty: A Piece of History-GK
00Upper Deck Vintage Dynasty: A Piece of History Gold-GK
00Upper Deck Gretzky Master Collection-1
00Upper Deck Gretzky Master Collection-2
00Upper Deck Gretzky Master Collection-3
00Upper Deck Gretzky Master Collection-4
00Upper Deck Gretzky Master Collection-5
00Upper Deck Gretzky Master Collection-6
00Upper Deck Gretzky Master Collection-7
00Upper Deck Gretzky Master Collection-8
00Upper Deck Gretzky Master Collection-9
00Upper Deck Gretzky Master Collection-10
00Upper Deck Gretzky Master Collection-11
00Upper Deck Gretzky Master Collection-12
00Upper Deck Gretzky Master Collection-13
00Upper Deck Gretzky Master Collection-14
00Upper Deck Gretzky Master Collection-15
00Upper Deck Gretzky Master Collection-16
00Upper Deck Gretzky Master Collection-17
00Upper Deck Gretzky Master Collection-18
Inserts-1
Inserts-2
Inserts-3
Inserts-4
Inserts-5
Inserts-6
Inserts-7
Inserts-8
Inserts-9
Inserts-10
Inserts-11
Inserts-12
Inserts-13
Inserts-14
Inserts-15
Inserts-16
Inserts-17
Inserts-18
00Upper Deck Gretzky Master Coll Mystery-1
00Upper Deck Gretzky Master Coll Mystery-2
00Upper Deck Gretzky Master Coll Mystery-3
00Upper Deck Gretzky Master Coll Mystery-4
00Upper Deck Gretzky Master Coll Mystery-5
00Upper Deck Gretzky Master Coll Mystery-6
00Upper Deck Gretzky Master Coll Mystery-7
00Upper Deck Gretzky Master Coll Mystery-8
00Upper Deck Gretzky Master Coll Mystery-9
00Upper Deck Gretzky Master Coll Mystery-10
00Upper Deck Gretzky Master Coll Mystery-11
00Upper Deck Gretzky Master Coll Mystery-12
00Upper Deck Gretzky Master Coll Mystery-13
00Upper Deck Gretzky Master Coll Mystery-14
00Upper Deck Gretzky Master Coll Mystery-15
00Upper Deck Gretzky Master Coll Mystery-16
00Upper Deck Gretzky Master Coll Mystery-17
00Upper Deck Gretzky Master Coll Mystery-18
00Upper Deck Gretzky Master Coll Mystery-19
00Upper Deck Gretzky Master Coll Mystery-20
00Upper Deck Gretzky Master Coll Mystery-21
00Upper Deck Gretzky Master Coll Mystery-22
00Upper Deck Wayne Gretzky Retirement Set-1
00Upper Deck Wayne Gretzky Retirement Set-2
00Upper Deck Wayne Gretzky Retirement Set-3
00Upper Deck Wayne Gretzky Retirement Set-4
00Upper Deck Wayne Gretzky Retirement Set-5
00Upper Deck Wayne Gretzky Retirement Set-6
00Upper Deck Wayne Gretzky Retirement Set-7
00Upper Deck Wayne Gretzky Retirement Set-8
00Upper Deck Wayne Gretzky Retirement Set-9
00Upper Deck Wayne Gretzky Retirement Set-10
00Upper Deck Wayne Gretzky Retirement Set-11
00Upper Deck Wayne Gretzky Retirement Set-12
00Upper Deck Wayne Gretzky Retirement Set-13
00Upper Deck Wayne Gretzky Retirement Set-14
00Upper Deck Wayne Gretzky Retirement Set-15
00Upper Deck Wayne Gretzky Retirement Set-16
00Czech Stadion-82
00Czech Stadion-159
01BAP Memorabilia All-Star Jersey Doubles-DASJ26
01BAP Memorabilia All-Star Teammates-AST34
01BAP Memorabilia All-Star Teammates-AST37
01BAP Memorabilia All-Star Teammates-AST49
01BAP Memorabilia 500 Goal Scorers-GS1
01BAP Memorabilia He Shoots/Scores Prizes-40
01BAP Memorabilia Patented Power-PP2
01BAP Signature Series Certified 100-C60
01BAP Signature Series Certified 50-C60
01BAP Signature Series Certified 1 of 1's-C60
01BAP Signature Series Autographs-XLWG
01BAP Signature Series Autographs Gold-XLWG
01BAP Ultimate Mem All-Star History-32
01BAP Ultimate Memorabilia Autographs-35
01BAP Ultimate Mem Autographs Gold-35
01BAP Ultimate Memorabilia Captain's C-5
01BAP Ultimate Mem Complete Package-1
01BAP Ultimate Memorabilia Dynamic Duos-1
01BAP Ultimate Memorabilia Emblem Attic-4
01BAP Ultimate Mem 500 Goal Scorers-1
01BAP Ultimate Mem 500 Goal Jerseys/Stick-1
01BAP Ultimate Mem 500 Goal Emblems-1
01BAP Ultimate Memorabilia Gloves Are Off-4
01BAP Ultimate Mem Journey Jerseys-22
01BAP Ultimate Mem Journey Emblems-22
01BAP Ultimate Memorabilia Made to Order-1
01BAP Ultimate Memorabilia Made to Order-2
01BAP Ultimate Memorabilia Name Plates-1
01BAP Ultimate Memorabilia Name Plates-39
01BAP Ultimate Mem Playoff Records-5
01BAP Ultimate Mem Playoff Records-9
01BAP Ultimate Mem Playoff Records-10
01BAP Ultimate Mem Playoff Records-11
01BAP Ultimate Mem Playoff Records-12
01BAP Ultimate Mem Playoff Records-13
01BAP Ultimate Mem Playoff Records-14
01BAP Ultimate Mem Playoff Records-18
01BAP Ultimate Mem Retired Numbers-9
01BAP Ultimate Memorabilia Retro Trophies-1
01BAP Ultimate Memorabilia Retro Trophies-3
01BAP Ultimate Memorabilia Retro Trophies-4
01BAP Ultimate Memorabilia Retro Trophies-16
01BAP Ultimate Memorabilia Retro Trophies-19
01BAP Ultimate Mem Retro Teammates-4
01BAP Ultimate Mem Retro Teammates-12
01BAP Ultimate Mem Retro Teammates-13
01BAP Ultimate Mem Scoring Leaders-1
01BAP Ultimate Mem Scoring Leaders-2
01BAP Ultimate Mem Scoring Leaders-3
01BAP Ultimate Mem Scoring Leaders-4
01BAP Ultimate Mem Scoring Leaders-6
01BAP Ultimate Mem Stanley Cup Winners-23
01BAP Update Heritage-H1
01SP Authentic-101
Limited-101
Limited Gold-101
Buybacks-40
Buybacks-41
Sign of the Times-WG
Sign of the Times-HGY
01SP Game Used Authentic Fabric-AFGE
01SP Game Used Authentic Fabric-AFGR
01SP Game Used Authentic Fabric-AFWG
01SP Game Used Authentic Fabric-DFLG
01SP Game Used Authentic Fabric-GYSL
01SP Game Used Authentic Fabric-HGBL
01SP Game Used Authentic Fabric Gold-AFGE
01SP Game Used Authentic Fabric Gold-AFGR
01SP Game Used Authentic Fabric Gold-AFWG
01SP Game Used Inked Sweaters-SWG
01SP Game Used Inked Sweaters-DSGP
01SP Game Used Inked Sweaters-DSHG
01SP Game Used Patches-PWG
01SP Game Used Patches-TPLGY
01SP Game Used Patches Signed-SPWG
01SP Game Used Patches Signed-DSPGB
01SP Game Used Tools of the Game-TWG
01SPx Signs of Xcellence-WG
01Sports Illustrated for Kids III-340
01UD Challenge 4 the Cup All-Time Lineup-AT2
01UD Honor Roll-2
01UD Honor Roll-32
Original Six-OS5
01UD Premier Collection-25
Dual Jerseys-DGH
Dual Jerseys-DGK
Dual Jerseys-DGL
Dual Jerseys-DGM
Dual Jerseys-DHG
Dual Jerseys Black-DGH
Dual Jerseys Black-DGK
Dual Jerseys Black-DGL
Dual Jerseys Black-DGM
Dual Jerseys Black-DHG
Jerseys-BWG
Jerseys-GWG
Jerseys Black-B-WG
Jerseys Black-G-WG
Signatures-GR
Signatures-WG
Signatures Black-GR
Signatures Black-WG
01UD Stanley Cup Champs-10
Pieces of Glory-G-WG
Sticks-S-WG
01UD Top Shelf Sticks-SWG
01UD Top Shelf Sticks Gold-SWG
01Upper Deck-424
Exclusives-424
Game Jerseys Series II-SSWG
01Upper Deck Avalanche NHL All-Star Game-WG
01Upper Deck Gretzky Expo e-Card-NNO
01Upper Deck Ice Autographs-WG
01Upper Deck Legends-22
01Upper Deck Legends-92
01Upper Deck Legends-100
Epic Signatures-WG
Fiorentino Collection-FCWG
Jerseys-TTWG
Jerseys Platinum-TTWG
Milestones-MWG
Milestones Platinum-MWG
Sticks-PHGR
Sticks-PHWG
01Upper Deck MVP Souvenirs-C-WG
01Upper Deck MVP Souvenirs Gold-C-WG
01Upper Deck Vintage Jerseys-SCWG
01Upper Deck Vintage Next In Line-NLGS
01UD Prospects Autographs-A-WG
02BAP NHL All-Star History-32
02SP Authentic-99
Sign of the Times-WG
Sign of the Times-GC
Sign of the Times-GW
Sign of the Times-GHO
Super Premiums-DPGL
Super Premiums-TPGLY
02SP Game Used-53
02SP Game Used-55
02SP Game Used-62
Authentic Fabrics-AFGY
Authentic Fabrics-AFWG
Authentic Fabrics-CFGR
Authentic Fabrics-CFWG
Authentic Fabrics Gold-AFGY
Authentic Fabrics Gold-AFWG
Authentic Fabrics Gold-CFGR
Authentic Fabrics Gold-CFWG
Authentic Fabrics Rainbow-AFGY
Authentic Fabrics Rainbow-AFWG
Authentic Fabrics Rainbow-CFGR
Authentic Fabrics Rainbow-CFWG
Piece of History-PHGY
Piece of History Gold-PHGY
Piece of History Rainbow-PHGY
Signature Style-WG
02SPx-95
Spectrum Gold-95
Spectrum Silver-95
Smooth Skaters-WG
Smooth Skaters Gold-WG
Smooth Skaters Silver-WG
02UD Artistic Impressions-39
Gold-39
02UD Artistic Impressions Beckett Promos-39
02UD Artistic Impressions Common Ground-CG3
02UD Artistic Impress Common Ground Gold-CG3
02UD Artistic Impressions Great Depiction-GD1
02UD Artistic Impress Great Depiction Gld-GD1
02UD Artistic Impressions Retrospectives-R39
02UD Artistic Impressions Retrospect Gold-R39
02UD Artistic Impress Retrospect Auto-R39
02UD Artistic Impress Retrospect Silver-R39
02UD Chicago National Spokesmen-N8
02Upper Deck Collectors Club-NHL1
02UD Foundations-34
02UD Foundations-44
02UD Foundations-45
02UD Foundations-70
02UD Foundations-87
02UD Foundations-101
02UD Foundations-105
02UD Foundations-106
02UD Foundations-117
1000 Point Club-WG
1000 Point Club-GR
1000 Point Club Gold-WG
1000 Point Club Silver-WG
Canadian Heroes-CWG
Canadian Heroes Gold-CWG
Canadian Heroes Silver-C-WG
Classic Greats-GWG
Classic Greats Gold-GWG
Classic Greats Silver-G-WG
Milestones-NWG
Milestones Gold-NWG
Milestones Silver-N-WG
Playoff Performers-PWG
Playoff Performers Gold-PWG
Playoff Performers Silver-P-WG
Signs of Greatness-SGWG
02UD Honor Roll Signature Class-WG0
02UD Piece of History-91
02UD Piece of History-92
02UD Piece of History-109
02UD Piece of History-110
02UD Piece of History-111
Awards Collection-AC16
Historical Swatches-HSWG
Hockey Beginnings-HB5
Hockey Beginnings-HB8
Marks of Distinction-WG
Patches-PHWG
Simply the Best-SB6
02UD Premier Collection-56A
Jerseys Bronze-WG
Jerseys Bronze-GL
Jerseys Gold-WG
Jerseys Gold-GL
Jerseys Silver-WG
Jerseys Silver-GL
NHL Patches-WG1
Patches-PGR
Patches-PWG
Signatures Bronze-SWG
Signatures Gold-SWG
Signatures Silver-SWG
02UD Top Shelf All-Stars-ASGR
02UD Top Shelf All-Stars-ASWG
02UD Top Shelf Clutch Performers-CPWG
02UD Top Shelf Dual Player Jerseys-STGM
02UD Top Shelf Hardware Heroes-HGKSD
02UD Top Shelf Hardware Heroes-HGSLJ
02UD Top Shelf Hardware Heroes-HHGLJ
02UD Top Shelf Milestones Jerseys-MGBYM
02UD Top Shelf Milestones Jerseys-MGHLY
02UD Top Shelf Signatures-WG
02UD Top Shelf Sweet Sweaters-SWWG
02UD Top Shelf Triple Jerseys-HTGLB
02Upper Deck-188
02Upper Deck-189
02Upper Deck-426
Exclusives-188
Exclusives-189
Exclusives-426
All-Star Jerseys-ASWG
All-Star Performers-ASWG
02Upper Deck Beckett UD Promos-426
02Upper Deck Game Jersey Autographs-WG
02Upper Deck Game Jersey Series II-GJWG
02Upper Deck Gifted Greats-GG11
02Upper Deck Patch Card Logo-WG
02Upper Deck Patch Card Name Plate-WG
02Upper Deck Patch Card Numbers-WG
02Upper Deck Playbooks-PL8
02Upper Deck Playbooks-PL9
02Upper Deck Reaching Fifty-50WG
02Upper Deck Reaching Fifty Gold-50WG
02Upper Deck Shooting Stars-SS9
02Upper Deck Classic Portraits Genuine Greatness-GG5
02Upper Deck Classic Portraits Hockey Royalty-GLS
02Upper Deck Classic Portraits Hockey Royalty Limited-GLS
02Upper Deck Gretzky All-Star Game-AS1
02Upper Deck Gretzky All-Star Game-AS2
02Upper Deck Gretzky All-Star Game-AS3
02Upper Deck MVP Prosign-WG
02Upper Deck National Convention *-N8
02Upper Deck Rookie Update-102
02Upper Deck Rookie Update-163
Autographs-WG
02UD SuperStars *-84
Gold-84
Benchmarks-B1
City All-Stars Dual Jersey-WGJG
City All-Stars Triple Jersey-SWK
Legendary Leaders Triple Jersey-JWL
Legendary Leaders Triple Jersey-SWK
Magic Moments-MM18
Spokesmen-UD14
Spokesmen-UD29
Spokesmen Black-UD14
Spokesmen Black-UD29
Spokesmen Gold-UD14
Spokesmen Gold-UD29
03Beehive-81
Variations-81
Gold-81
Silver-81
Signatures-RF4
03Black Diamond Signature Gems-SG-9
03Canada Post-1
03SP Authentic 10th Anniversary-SP1
03SP Authentic 10th Anniversary Limited-SP1
03SP Authentic Honors-H1
03SP Authentic Honors-H2
03SP Authentic Honors-H3
03SP Authentic Honors Limited-H1
03SP Authentic Honors Limited-H2
03SP Authentic Honors Limited-H3
03SP Authentic Sign of the Times-WG
03SP Authentic Sign of the Times-GK
03SP Authentic Sign of the Times-GKF
03SP Authentic Sign of the Times-GTS
03SP Game Used Authentic Fabrics-AFWG
03SP Game Used Authentic Fabrics-DFGS
03SP Game Used Authentic Fabrics-DFHG
03SP Game Used Authentic Fabrics-DFLG
03SP Game Used Authentic Fabrics-QLGHL
03SP Game Used Authentic Fabrics Gold-AFWG
03SP Game Used Authentic Fabrics Gold-DFGS
03SP Game Used Authentic Fabrics Gold-DFHG
03SP Game Used Authentic Fabrics Gold-DFLG
03SP Game Used Authentic Fabrics Gold-QLGHL
03SP Game Used Authentic Patches-APG1
03SP Game Used Authentic Patches-APWG
03SP Game Used Double Threads-DTLG
03SP Game Used Double Threads-DTWG
03SP Game Used Limited Threads-LTG1
03SP Game Used Limited Threads-LTWGR
03SP Game Used Limited Threads-LTWG
03SP Game Used Limited Threads Gold-LTG1
03SP Game Used Limited Threads Gold-LTWGR
03SP Game Used Limited Threads Gold-LTWG
03SP Game Used Premium Patches-PPWG
03SP Game Used Signers-SPSWG
03SP Game Used Team Threads-TTLGH
03SP Game Used Top Threads-LGHL
03SPx-101
Radiance-101
Spectrum-101
Fantasy Franchise-FF-LGH
Fantasy Franchise Limited-FF-LGH
Signature Threads-ST-WG
Style-SPX-GS
Style Limited-SPX-GS
Winning Materials-WM-GR
Winning Materials-WM-GY
Winning Materials-WM-WG
Winning Materials Limited-WM-GR
Winning Materials Limited-WM-GY
Winning Materials Limited-WM-WG
03UD Honor Roll Signature Class-SC8
03UD Premier Collection Legends-PL-WG
03UD Premier Collection Legends Patches-PL-WG
03UD Premier Collection NHL Shields-SH-G1
03UD Premier Collection NHL Shields-SH-WG
03UD Premier Collection Signatures-PS-G1
03UD Premier Collection Signatures-PS-WG
03UD Premier Collection Signatures Gold-PS-G1
03UD Premier Collection Signatures Gold-PS-WG
03UD Premier Collection Teammates-PT-E01
03UD Premier Collection Teammates Patches-PT-E01
03Upper Deck-472
Big Playmakers-BP-WG
Canadian Exclusives-472
Gifted Greats-GG1
HG-472
Jersey Autographs-SJ-WG
Magic Moments-MM-8
Performers-PS14
UD Exclusives-472
03Upper Deck Classic Portraits-114
Classic Colors-CC-WG
Genuine Greatness-GG-GR
Genuine Greatness-GG-WG
Premium Portraits-PP-WG
03Upper Deck Ice Authentics-IA-WG
03Upper Deck Ice Under Glass Autographs-UG-WG
03Upper Deck Magazine-UD9
03Upper Deck MVP ProSign-PS-WG
03Upper Deck Rookie Update-161
Top Draws-TD4
03Upper Deck Trilogy-38
Authentic Patches-AP1
Authentic Patches-AP39
Crest Variations-141
Limited-38
Scripts-S3G1
Scripts-S3GR
Scripts-S3GY
Scripts-S3WA
Scripts-S3WG
Scripts-S399
Scripts Limited-S3G1
Scripts Limited-S3GR
Scripts Limited-S3GY
Scripts Limited-S3WA
Scripts Limited-S3WG
Scripts Limited-S399
Scripts Red-S3WG
03Upper Deck Victory Freshman Flashback-FF49
04Upper Deck Sportsfest *-SF5
04Upper Deck National Convention *-TN13
04Upper Deck National Convention VIP *-VIP5
04SP Authentic-129
Limited-129
Octographs-OS-ART
Octographs-OS-CAP
Rookie Review-RR-WG
Sign of the Times-ST-WG
Sign of the Times-DS-HG
Sign of the Times-TS-GKF
Sign of the Times-QS-GTDC
Sign of the Times-SS-AWS
Sign of the Times-SS-ORG
04SP Game Used Hawaii Conference Patch-PP33
04SP Game Used Hawaii Conference Patch-PPA8
04UD All-World-91

Autographs-91
04UD Legendary Signatures-88
Autographs-WG
Linemates-GAWGJK
04UD Legends Classics-54
04UD Legends Classics-79
04UD Legends Classics-80
04UD Legends Classics-82
Gold-54
Gold-79
Gold-80
Gold-82
Platinum-54
Platinum-79
Platinum-80
Platinum-82
Silver-54
Silver-79
Silver-80
Silver-82
Jersey Redemptions-JY16
Jersey Redemptions-JY26
Signature Moments-M1
Signatures-CS1
Signatures-TC11
Signatures-TC14
Signatures-QC4
04UD Toronto Fall Expo Priority Signings-GR
04UD Toronto Fall Expo Priority Signings-WG
04Ultimate Collection-17
Dual Logos-UL2-GL
Dual Logos-UL2-GM
Jerseys-UGJ-WG1
Jerseys-UGJ-WG2
Jerseys Gold-UGJ-WG1
Jerseys Gold-UGJ-WG2
Jersey Autographs-UGJA-WG1
Jersey Autographs-UGJA-WG2
Patches-UP-WG1
Patches-UP-WG2
Patch Autographs-UPA-WG1
Patch Autographs-UPA-WG2
Patch Autographs-UPA-WGGH
Patch Autographs-UPA-WGJK
Signatures-US-WG1
Signature Logos-ULA-WG1
Signature Logos-ULA-WG2
Signature Logos-ULA-WG3
Signature Patches-SP-WG1
Signature Patches-SP-WG2
Signature Patches-SP-WG3
04Upper Deck-179
04Upper Deck-183
1997 Game Jerseys-WG2
Big Playmakers-BP-WG
Canadian Exclusives-179
Canadian Exclusives-183
HG Glossy Gold-179
HG Glossy Gold-183
HG Glossy Silver-179
HG Glossy Silver-183
Jersey Autographs-GJA-WG
Jersey Autographs-GJA-WG/RN
Jersey Autographs-GJA-WG/GH
NHL's Best-NB-WG
Patches-GJPA-WG
Patches-GJPL-WG
Patches-GJPN-WG
Swatch of Six-SS-WG
Three Stars-AS13
04National Trading Card Day *-UD15
04Upper Deck Sportsfest *-SF5
05Be A Player Ice Icons-ICE5
05Beehive-236
Matted Materials-MMWG
Matted Materials Remarkable-RMWG
PhotoGraphs-PGWG
05Black Diamond-184
Emerald-184
Gold-184
Onyx-184
Ruby-184
Gemography-G-WG
Gemography Emerald-G-WG
Gemography Gold-G-WG
Gemography Onyx-G-WG
Gemography Ruby-G-WG
Jerseys-J-WG
Jerseys Ruby-J-WG
Jersey Duals-DJ-WG
Jersey Triples-TJ-WG
Jersey Quads-QJ-WG
05McDonalds Upper Deck Autographs-MA1
05McDonalds Upper Deck Patches-MP7
05McDonalds Upper Deck Top Scorers-TS1
05NHL Legends Medallions-5
05SP Authentic-42
Limited-42
Exquisite Endorsements-EEWG
Immortal Inks-IIWG
Octographs-OH
Prestigious Pairings-PPHG
Sign of the Times-WG
Sign of the Times Quads-QGTVD
Six Star Signatures-SSHF
05SP Game Used Authentic Fabrics Autos-AAF-WG
05SP Game Used Authentic Fabrics Dual-GH
05SP Game Used Authentic Fabrics Dual-GK
05SP Game Used Authentic Fabric Dual Auto-GH
05SP Game Used Authentic Fabrics Gold-AF-WG
05SP Game Used Authentic Fabrics Quad-GMCF
05SP Game Used Authentic Fabrics Triple-GLY
05SP Game Used Authentic Patches-AP-WG
05SP Game Used Authentic Patch Autos-AAP-WG
05SP Game Used Authentic Patches Dual-GH
05SP Game Used Authentic Patches Dual-GK
05SP Game Used Authentic Patches Dual-GL
05SP Game Used Authentic Patch Dual Autos-GH
05SP Game Used Authentic Patches Triple-GLY
05SP Game Used Authentic Patches Triple-KGM
05SP Game Used SIGnificance Extra-GH
05SP Game Used SIGnificance Extra Gold-GH
05SP Game Used Statscriptions-ST-WG
05SPx-125
05SPx-130
Spectrum-125
Spectrum-130
Winning Combos-WC-GC
Winning Combos-WC-GM
Winning Combos Autographs-AWC-GC
Winning Combos Gold-WC-GC
Winning Combos Gold-WC-GM
Winning Combos Spectrum-WC-GC
Winning Combos Spectrum-WC-GM
Winning Materials-WM-WG
Winning Materials Autographs-AWM-WG
Winning Materials Gold-WM-WG
Winning Materials Spectrum-WM-WG
Xcitement Legends-XL-WG
Xcitement Legends Gold-XL-WG
Xcitement Legends Spectrum-XL-WG

05The Cup-45
Gold-45
Black Rainbow-45
Dual NHL Shields-DSGL
Hardware Heroes-HHWG1
Hardware Heroes-HHWG2
Hardware Heroes-HHWG3
Hardware Heroes-HHWG4
Hardware Heroes-HHWG5
Hardware Heroes-HHWG6
Hardware Heroes-HHWG7
Hardware Heroes-HHWG8
Honorable Numbers-HNWG
Masterpiece Pressplates-45
Noble Numbers Dual-DNNGL
Patch Variation-P45
Patch Variation Autographs-AP45
Property of-POWG
Signature Patches-SPWG
Stanley Cup Titlists-TWG
05UD Artifacts-113
Blue-113
Gold-113
Green-113
Pewter-113
Red-113
Auto Facts Blue-AF-WG
Auto Facts Copper-AF-WG
Auto Facts Pewter-AF-WG
Auto Facts Silver-AF-WG
Frozen Artifacts-FA-WG
Frozen Artifacts Autographed-FA-WG
Frozen Artifacts Copper-FA-WG
Frozen Artifacts Dual-FAD-WG
Frozen Artifacts Dual Autographed-FAD-WG
Frozen Artifacts Dual Copper-FAD-WG
Frozen Artifacts Dual Gold-FAD-WG
Frozen Artifacts Dual Maroon-FAD-WG
Frozen Artifacts Dual Pewter-FAD-WG
Frozen Artifacts Dual Silver-FAD-WG
Frozen Artifacts Gold-FA-WG
Frozen Artifacts Maroon-FA-WG
Frozen Artifacts Patches-FP-WG
Frozen Artifacts Patches Autographed-FP-WG
Frozen Artifacts Patches Dual-FPD-MH
Frozen Artifacts Patches Dual Autos-FPD-MH
Frozen Artifacts Patches Pewter-FP-WG
Frozen Artifacts Patches Silver-FP-WG
Frozen Artifacts Pewter-FA-WG
Frozen Artifacts Silver-FA-WG
Gold Autographed-113
Treasured Patches-TP-WG
Treasured Swatches-TS-WG
Treasured Swatches Blue-TS-WG
Treasured Swatches Copper-TS-WG
Treasured Swatches Dual-TSD-WG
Treasured Swatches Maroon-TS-WG
Treasured Swatches Pewter-TS-WG
05UD PowerPlay-123
Power Marks-PMWG
Specialists-TSWG
Specialists Patches-SPWG
05UD Toronto Fall Expo Priority Signings-PS-WG
05UD Toronto Fall Expo Priority Signings-PS-GR
05Ultimate Collection-41
Gold-41
Endorsed Emblems-EEWG
Jerseys-JWG
Jerseys Dual-DJGC
Jerseys Triple-TJGLC
Premium Patches-PPWG
Premium Swatches-PSWG
Ultimate Achievements-UAWG
Ultimate Signatures-USWG
Ultimate Signatures Foursomes-UFGHLH
Ultimate Signatures Pairings-UPHG
05Upper Deck All-Time Greatest-23
05Upper Deck All-Time Greatest-27
05Upper Deck All-Time Greatest-73
05Upper Deck Big Playmakers-B-WG
05Upper Deck Goal Rush-GR6
05Upper Deck Jerseys-J-WG
05Upper Deck NHL Generations-DGL
05Upper Deck NHL Generations-TGYS
05Upper Deck Notable Numbers-N-WG
05Upper Deck Patches-P-WG
05Upper Deck Playoff Performers-PP4
05Upper Deck Scrapbooks-HS2
05Upper Deck Sportsfest-NHL3
05Upper Deck Hawaii Trade Conference Signature Supremacy *-SSP12
05Upper Deck Hawaii Trade Conference Signature Supremacy *-SSP13
05Upper Deck Ice Glacial Graphs-GGWG
05Upper Deck MVP Materials Triples-T-GST
05Upper Deck MVP Monumental Moments-MM1
05Upper Deck MVP ProSign-P-WG
05Upper Deck MVP Rising to the Occasion-RO13
05Upper Deck MVP Tribute to Greatness-TG1
05Upper Deck MVP Tribute to Greatness-TG2
05Upper Deck MVP Tribute to Greatness-TG3
05Upper Deck MVP Tribute to Greatness-TG4
05Upper Deck MVP Tribute to Greatness-TG5
05Upper Deck MVP Tribute to Greatness-TG6
05Upper Deck MVP Tribute to Greatness-TG7
05Upper Deck National VIP *-VIP4
05Upper Deck Trilogy-113
Crystal-113
Crystal Autographs-113
Honorary Patches-HP-WG
Honorary Patch Scripts-HSP-WG
Honorary Swatches-HS-WG
Honorary Swatch Scripts-HSS-WG
Ice Scripts-IS-WG
Legendary Scripts-LEG-WG
Scripts-SSS-WG
05Upper Deck Victory-77
Black-77
Gold-77
Silver-77
Blow-Ups-BU16
06Upper Deck Ntnl Southern California-So.Cal2
06Beehive PhotoGraphs-PGWG
06Beehive Signature Scrapbook-SSWG
06Black Diamond-157B
Gold-157B
Ruby-157B
Gemography-GWG
Jerseys-JWG
Jerseys Black-JWG
Jerseys Gold-JWG
Jerseys Ruby-JWG
Jerseys Black Autographs -JWG
06SP Authentic-55
06SP Authentic-160
Limited-55
Limited-160
Sign of the Times-STWG
Sign of the Times Duals-STGL
Sign of the Times Triples-ST3LGH
Sign of the Times Quads-ST4LOGH

06SP Game Used-46
Gold-46
Rainbow-46
Authentic Fabrics Sixes-AF6BYN
Authentic Fabrics Sixes Patches-AF6BYN
Authentic Fabrics Sevens-AF7ART
Authentic Fabrics Sevens Patches-AF7ART
Authentic Fabrics Eights-AF8HOF
Authentic Fabrics Eights Patches-AF8HOF
Autographs-46
By The Letter-BLWG
Inked Sweaters-ISWG
Inked Sweaters Patches-ISWG
Inked Sweaters Dual-IS2GL
Inked Sweaters Dual Patches-IS2GL
Legendary Fabrics-LFWG
Legendary Fabrics Autographs-LFWG
Letter Marks-LMWG
06SPx-41
06SPx-128
Spectrum-41
Spectrum-128
SPxcitement-X39
SPxcitement Spectrum-X39
SPxcitement Autographs-X39
06The Cup-37
Autographed Foundations-CQWG
Autographed Foundations Patches-CQWG
Autographed NHL Shields Duals-DASGK
Autographed NHL Shields Duals-DASGL
Autographed Patches-37
Black Rainbow-37
Foundations-CQWG
Foundations Patches-CQWG
Enshrinements-EGR
Enshrinements-EWG
Gold-37
Gold Patches-37
Honorable Numbers-HNWG
Jerseys-37
Limited Logos-LLWG
Masterpiece Pressplates-37
Property of-POWG
Scripted Swatches Duals-DSGH
Scripted Swatches Duals-DSGL
Signature Patches-SPWG
Stanley Cup Signatures-CSWG
06UD Artifacts-141
Blue-141
Gold-141
Platinum-141
Radiance-141
Autographed Radiance Parallel-141
Red-141
Auto-Facts-AFWG
Auto-Facts Gold-AFWG
Tundra Tandems-TTAG
Tundra Tandems Black-TTAG
Tundra Tandems Blue-TTAG
Tundra Tandems Gold-TTAG
Tundra Tandems Platinum-TTAG
Tundra Tandems Red-TTAG
Tundra Tandems Dual Patches Red-TTAG
06UD Powerplay Power Marks-PMWG
06UD Toronto Fall Expo Priority Signings -PSWG1
06UD Toronto Fall Expo Priority Signings -PSWG2
06Ultimate Collection-27
Autographed Jerseys-AJ-WG
Autographed Patches-AJ-WG
Jerseys Dual-UJ2-GL
Jerseys Triple-UJ3-GHL
Patches Dual-UJ2-GL
Patches Triple-UJ3-GHL
Signatures-US-WG
Ultimate Achievements-UA-WG
Ultimate Signatures Logos-SL-WG
06Upper Deck-379
06Upper Deck-450
Exclusives Parallel-379
Exclusives Parallel-450
High Gloss Parallel-379
High Gloss Parallel-450
All-Time Greatest-ATG9
All-Time Greatest-ATG27
Game Jerseys-J2WG
Game Patches-P2WG
Generations Duals-G2GC
Generations Triples-G3GCL
Generations Patches Dual-G2PGC
Generations Patches Triple-G3PGCL
Masterpieces-379
Masterpieces-450
Oversized Wal-Mart Exclusives-379
Signatures-SWG
Signature Sensations-SSWG
MVP Autographs-OAGL
MVP Gotta Have Hart-HH9
MVP Jerseys-OJGL
06Upper Deck Sweet Shot-45
Signature Shots/Saves-SSWG
Signature Shots/Saves Ice Signings-SSIWG
Signature Shots/Saves Sticks-SSSWG
Signature Sticks-STWG
Sweet Stitches-SSWG
Sweet Stitches Duals-SSWG
Sweet Stitches Triples-SSWG
06Upper Deck Trilogy Combo Autographed Jerseys-CJLG
06Upper Deck Trilogy Combo Autographed Patches-CJLG
06Upper Deck Trilogy Frozen In Time-FT20
06Upper Deck Trilogy Honorary Scripted Patches-HSPWG
06Upper Deck Trilogy Honorary Scripted Swatches-HSSWG
06Upper Deck Trilogy Honorary Swatches-HSWG
06Upper Deck Trilogy Ice Scripts-ISWG
06Upper Deck Trilogy Legendary Scripts-LSWG
06Upper Deck Trilogy Scripts-S1WG
06Upper Deck Trilogy Scripts-S2WG
06Upper Deck Trilogy Scripts-TSWG
06Upper Deck National NHL-NHL-2
06Upper Deck National NHL Autographs-NHL-2
06Upper Deck National NHL VIP-2
07Upper Deck National Convention *-NTL12
07Upper Deck National Convention VIP *-VIP12

Grey, Mike
98Danish Hockey League-155
99Danish Hockey League-154

Greyeyes, Mark
87Portland Winter Hawks-11
88Portland Winter Hawks-11

Greyeyes, Matt
04Maine Black Bears-25

Grianoli, J.P.
93Quebec Pee-Wee Tournament-1725

Gribko, Evgeni
95Swedish World Championships Stickers-33
00Russian Dynamo Moscow-10
00Russian Hockey League-323
01Russian Dynamo Moscow-6

01Russian Dynamo Moscow Mentos-16

Grieco, Scott
93Lethbridge Hurricanes-4
95Lethbridge Hurricanes-6

Grier, Mike
96Be A Player-220
Autographs-220
Autographs Silver-220
96Black Diamond-15
Gold-15
96Donruss Canadian Ice-141
Gold Press Proofs-141
Red Press Proofs-141
96Flair-110
Blue Ice-110
96Metal Universe-181
96Oilers Postcards-25
96Select Certified-101
Artist's Proofs-101
Blue-101
Mirror Blue-101
Mirror Gold-101
Mirror Red-101
Red-101
96SP-177
96Ultra-58
Gold Medallion-58
Rookies-9
96Upper Deck-259
Power Performers-P13
96Upper Deck Ice-86
Parallel-86
97Collector's Choice-88
Star Quest-SQ24
97Donruss-94
Press Proofs Silver-94
Press Proofs Gold-94
97Donruss Canadian Ice-121
Dominion Series-121
Provincial Series-121
97Donruss Elite-62
Aspirations-62
Status-62
97Donruss Limited-27
97Donruss Limited-50
97Donruss Limited-199
Exposure-27
Exposure-50
Exposure-199
Fabric of the Game-22
97Donruss Preferred-44
Cut to the Chase-44
97Donruss Priority-59
Stamp of Approval-59
97Leaf-81
Fractal Matrix-81
Fractal Matrix Die Cuts-81
Banner Season-23
97Leaf International-81
Universal Ice-81
97Pacific-164
Copper-164
Emerald Green-164
Ice Blue-164
Red-164
Silver-164
97Pacific Dynagon-48
Copper-48
Dark Grey-48
Emerald Green-48
Ice Blue-48
Red-48
Silver-48
Tandems-10
97Pacific Invincible-55
Copper-55
Emerald Green-55
Ice Blue-55
Red-55
Silver-55
Off The Glass-10
97Pacific Omega-90
Copper-90
Dark Gray-90
Emerald Green-90
Gold-90
Ice Blue-90
97Paramount-74
Copper-74
Dark Grey-74
Emerald Green-74
Ice Blue-74
Red-74
Silver-74
97Pinnacle-177
Press Plates Back Black-177
Press Plates Back Cyan-177
Press Plates Back Magenta-177
Press Plates Back Yellow-177
Press Plates Front Black-177
Press Plates Front Cyan-177
Press Plates Front Magenta-177
Press Plates Front Yellow-177
97Pinnacle Certified-73
Red-73
Mirror Blue-73
Mirror Gold-73
Mirror Red-73
97Pinnacle Inside-85
Coach's Collection-85
Executive Collection-85
Track-29
97Pinnacle Tot Cert Platinum Blue-73
97Pinnacle Tot Certi Platinum Gold-73
97Pinnacle Totally Certified Platinum Red-73
97Pinnacle Tot Cert Mirror Platinum Gold-73
97Score-153
Artist's Proofs-153
Golden Blades-153
Check It-10
97SP Authentic-63
Sign of the Times-MG
97Studio-51
Press Proofs Silver-51
Press Proofs Gold-51
Hard Hats-22
97Upper Deck-67
97Upper Deck-207
Smooth Grooves-SG25
Three Star Selects-16A
98Aurora-71
98Be A Player-54
Press Release-54
98BAP Gold-54
98BAP Autographs-54
98BAP Autographs Gold-54
98BAP Tampa Bay All Star Game-54
98OPC Chrome-31
Refractors-31
98Pacific-208
Ice Blue-208

Red-208
98Pacific Dynagon Ice-71
Blue-71
Red-71
98Paramount-85
Copper-85
Emerald Green-85
Holo-Electric-85
Ice Blue-85
Silver-85
98Topps-31
O-Pee-Chee-31
98Upper Deck-94
Exclusives-94
Exclusives 1 of 1-94
Gold Reserve-94
98Upper Deck MVP-81
Gold Script-81
Silver Script-81
Super Script-81
99Aurora-57
Premiere Date-57
99BAP Memorabilia-222
Gold-222
Silver-222
99BAP Millennium-102
Emerald-102
Ruby-102
Sapphire-102
Signatures-102
Signatures Gold-102
99O-Pee-Chee-246
99O-Pee-Chee Chrome-246
99O-Pee-Chee Chrome Refractors-246
99Pacific-154
Copper-154
Emerald Green-154
Gold-154
Ice Blue-154
Premiere Date-154
Red-154
99Pacific Dynagon Ice-81
Blue-81
Copper-81
Gold-81
Premiere Date-81
99Panini Stickers-249
99Paramount-91
Copper-91
Emerald-91
Gold-91
Holographic Emerald-91
Holographic Gold-91
Holographic Silver-91
Ice Blue-91
Premiere Date-91
Red-91
Silver-91
99Revolution-57
Premiere Date-57
Red-57
Shadow Series-57
99SPx-63
Radiance-63
Spectrum-63
99Stadium Club-61
First Day Issue-61
One of a Kind-61
Printing Plates Black-61
Printing Plates Cyan-61
Printing Plates Magenta-61
Printing Plates Yellow-61
99Topps/OPC-246
99Topps/OPC Chrome-246
Refractors-246
99Upper Deck-55
Exclusives-55
Exclusives 1 of 1-55
99Upper Deck Gold Reserve-55
99Upper Deck MVP-81
Gold Script-81
Silver Script-81
Super Script-81
99Upper Deck Victory-111
99Wayne Gretzky Hockey-68
00SLU Hockey-80
00Aurora-55
Pinstripes-55
Pinstripes Premiere Date-55
Premiere Date-55
Autographs-55
00BAP Memorabilia-79
Emerald-79
Ruby-79
Sapphire-79
Promos-79
00BAP Mem Chicago Sportsfest Copper-79
00BAP Memorabilia Chicago Sportsfest Blue-79
00BAP Memorabilia Chicago Sportsfest Gold-79
00BAP Memorabilia Chicago Sportsfest Ruby-79
00BAP Memorabilia Chicago Sun-Times Ruby-79
00BAP Memorabilia Chicago Sun-Times Gold-79
00BAP Mem Chicago Sun-Times Sapphire-79
00BAP Mem Toronto Fall Expo Copper-79
00BAP Memorabilia Toronto Fall Expo Gold-79
00BAP Memorabilia Toronto Fall Expo Ruby-79
00O-Pee-Chee-132
00O-Pee-Chee Parallel-132
00Pacific-165
Copper-165
Gold-165
Ice Blue-165
Premiere Date-165
00Paramount-94
Copper-94
Gold-94
Holo-Gold-94
Holo-Silver-94
Ice Blue-94
Premiere Date-94
00Topps/OPC-132
Parallel-132
00Topps Chrome-99
OPC Refractors-99
Refractors-99
00Upper Deck-300
Exclusives Tier 1-300
Exclusives Tier 2-300
00Upper Deck MVP-75
First Stars-75
Second Stars-75
Third Stars-75
00Upper Deck Victory-95
00Upper Deck Vintage-141
01BAP Memorabilia-116
Emerald-116
Ruby-116
Sapphire-116
01O-Pee-Chee-131
01O-Pee-Chee Premier Parallel-131
01Pacific-157

Extreme LTD-157
Hobby LTD-157
Premiere Date-157
Retail LTD-157
01Pacific Adrenaline-75
Blue-75
Premiere Date-75
Red-75
Retail-75
01Pacific Arena Exclusives-157
01Topps-131
OPC Parallel-131
01Upper Deck-70
Exclusives-70
01Upper Deck MVP-71
01Upper Deck Victory-145
Gold-145
01Upper Deck Vintage-100
02BAP Sig Series Auto Buybacks 1998-54
02BAP Sig Series Auto Buybacks 1999-102
02Pacific-142
Blue-142
Red-142
02Pacific Complete-361
Red-361
02Topps Total-329
03ITG Action-556
03Pacific-343
Blue-343
Red-343
03Pacific Complete-8
Red-8
03Topps Traded-TT27
Blue-TT27
Gold-TT27
Red-TT27
03Upper Deck-196
Canadian Exclusives-196
HG-196
03Upper Deck MVP-431
Gold Script-431
Silver Script-431
Canadian Exclusives-431
03Upper Deck Victory-199
Bronze-199
Gold-199
Silver-199
05Black Diamond-11
Emerald-11
Gold-11
Onyx-11
Ruby-11
05Parkhurst-60
Facsimile Auto Parallel-60
True Colors-TCBUF
True Colors-TCBUF
05Upper Deck-271
Jerseys-J-MGR
05Upper Deck MVP-50
Gold-50
Platinum-50
05Upper Deck Victory-26
Black-26
Gold-26
Silver-26
06Hot Prospects Hot Materials -HMMI
06Hot Prospects Hot Materials Red Hot-HMMI
06Hot Prospects Hot Materials White Hot-HMMI
06O-Pee-Chee-412
Rainbow-412
06Upper Deck-413
Exclusives Parallel-413
High Gloss Parallel-413
Game Jerseys-J2MG
Game Patches-J2MG
Masterpieces-413
06Upper Deck MVP-247
Gold Script-247
Super Script-247
06Upper Deck Victory-271

Grieve, Brent
89Oshawa Generals-26
89Oshawa Generals 7th Inning Sketch-22
89 7th Inn. Sketch OHL-22
90ProCards AHL/IHL-506
90 7th Inn. Sketch Memorial Cup-92
91ProCards-453
92Classic-100
Gold-100
92Classic Four-Sport *-213
Gold-213
94Be A Player Signature Cards-42
94Blackhawks Coke-6
94Leaf-485
94OPC Premier-99
94OPC Premier-431
Special Effects-99
Special Effects-431
94Parkhurst-79
Gold-79
94Stadium Club-257
Members Only Master Set-257
First Day Issue-257
Super Team Winner Cards-257
94Topps/OPC Premier-99
94Topps/OPC Premier-431
Special Effects-99
Special Effects-431
94Ultra-274
94Upper Deck-396
Electric Ice-396
94Classic Pro Prospects-128
95Upper Deck-307

Grieve, Brian
89Oshawa Generals-9
89Oshawa Generals 7th Inning Sketch-12
89 7th Inn. Sketch OHL-12
90 7th Inn. Sketch OHL-337
90 7th Inn. Sketch Memorial Cup-81
91Oshawa Generals-2
91Oshawa Generals-28
91Oshawa Generals Sheet-16
91 7th Inn. Sketch OHL-165

Griffin, Sean
98Kingston Frontenacs-6
99Kingston Frontenacs-6

Griffis, Si
83Hall of Fame Postcards-L5
85Hall of Fame-155

Griffith, Jesse
04Salmon Arm Silverbacks-20
05Salmon Arm Silverbacks-8

Griffith, Todd
02Belleville Bulls-7
03Belleville Bulls-15
04Kingston Frontenacs-9
05Kingston Frontenacs-15
06Bakersfield Condors-23

Griffiths, Frank
93Action Packed HOF Induction-8

Griffiths, Tuffy
37V356 Worldwide Gum-132

Griga, Thomas
93Swiss HNL-276

Griga, Yvan
93Swiss HNL-166

Grigg, Kody
94North Bay Centennials-21

Grigg, Reggie
62Quebec Aces-9

Grigg, Vic
51Laval Dairy QSHL-102

Grigorenko, Igor
01Russian Young Lions-4
02Russian Future Stars-2
02Russian Hockey League-58
02Russian Hockey League-188
02Russian SL-16
02Russian Young Lions-5
03Russian World Championship Team 2003-19
04Russian RHL-13

Grigorjevs, Konstantins
98Danish Hockey League-115

Grill, Marek
04Slovakian Skalica Team Set-15
06Czech OFS-180

Grillfors, Daniel
06Swedish SHL Elitset-194

Grillo, Dean
92North Dakota Fighting Sioux-8
94Kansas City Blades-16
94Classic-42
Gold-42
95Kansas City Blades-10
96Kentucky Thoroughblades-7
97Kansas City Blades Magnets-5

Grills, Chad
91Peterborough Petes-4
91 7th Inn. Sketch OHL-135
93Peterborough Petes-11
93Sault Ste. Marie Greyhounds-22
95Flint Generals-6
96Flint Generals-9
97Flint Generals-7
97Flint Generals EBK-12
98Flint Generals-2
99UHL All-Stars East-15T
01Fort Wayne Komets-7
02Fort Worth Brahmas-5
03Fort Worth Brahmas-7
03Memphis RiverKings-8

Grimaldi, Joe
05Ottawa 67's-24
06Ottawa 67s-14

Grimard, Ron
97Spokane Chiefs-24

Grimes, Jake
89 7th Inn. Sketch OHL-76
90 7th Inn. Sketch OHL-8
91 7th Inn. Sketch OHL-111
94Thunder Bay Senators-6
94Classic Pro Prospects-43

Grimes, Kevin
97Bowman CHL-136
OPC-136
Autographs-16
98Kingston Frontenacs-7
02Greensboro Generals RBI-11
03Greensboro Generals-186

Grimson, Stu
82Regina Pats-8
83Regina Pats-8
88Salt Lake Golden Eagles-12
89ProCards IHL-199
90Blackhawks Coke-19
91Blackhawks Coke-9
91Upper Deck-416
French-416
92Blackhawks Coke-4
93Donruss-15
93Ducks Milk Caps-3
93Kraft-11
93Leaf-330
93OPC Premier-357
Gold-357
93Parkhurst-277
Emerald Ice-277
93Pinnacle-401
Canadian-401
93PowerPlay-1
93Score-558
Gold-558
Canadian-558
Canadian Gold-558
93Topps/OPC Premier-357
Gold-357
93Ultra-253
94Canada Games NHL POGS-33
94Parkhurst-3
Gold-3
94Pinnacle-512
Artist's Proofs-512
Rink Collection-512
95Be A Player-224
Signatures-S224
Signatures Die Cuts-S224
96Whalers Kid's Club-19
97Hurricanes Team Issue-9
97Katch-27
Gold-27
Silver-27
97Pacific-296
Copper-296
Emerald Green-296
Ice Blue-296
Red-296
Silver-296
97Upper Deck-33
98Be A Player-152
Press Release-152
98BAP Gold-152
98BAP Autographs-152
98BAP Autographs Gold-152
98Katch-4
98OPC Chrome-96
Refractors-96
98Pacific-133
Ice Blue-133
Red-133
98Pacific Omega-2
Red-2
Opening Day Issue-2
98Topps-96
O-Pee-Chee-96
99BAP Millennium-6
Emerald-6
Ruby-6
Sapphire-6
Signatures-6
Signatures Gold-6

99Pacific-5
Copper-5
Emerald Green-5
Gold-5
Ice Blue-5
Premiere Date-5
Red-5
00BAP Memorabilia-343
Emerald-343
Ruby-343
Sapphire-343
Promos-343
00BAP Mem Chicago Sportsfest Copper-343
00BAP Memorabilia Chicago Sportsfest Blue-343
00BAP Memorabilia Chicago Sportsfest Gold-343
00BAP Memorabilia Chicago Sportsfest Ruby-343
00BAP Memorabilia Chicago Sun-Times Ruby-343
00BAP Memorabilia Chicago Sun-Times Gold-343
00BAP Mem Chicago Sun-Times Sapphire-343
00BAP Mem Toronto Fall Expo Copper-343
00BAP Memorabilia Toronto Fall Expo Gold-343
00BAP Memorabilia Toronto Fall Expo Ruby-343
00BAP Memorabilia Update Tough Materials-T3
00BAP Mem Update Tough Materials Gold-T3
00BAP Signature Series-193
Emerald-193
Ruby-193
Sapphire-193
Autographs-179
Autographs Gold-179
01BAP Update Tough Customers-TC3
01BAP Update Tough Customers-TC6
01Pacific-181
01Pacific-413
Extreme LTD-181
Gold-413
Hobby LTD-181
Premiere Date-181
Retail LTD-181
01Pacific Arena Exclusives-181
01Pacific Arena Exclusives-413
01Upper Deck Vintage-266
02BAP Sig Series Auto Buybacks 1998-152
02BAP Sig Series Auto Buybacks 1999-6
02Pacific-209
Blue-209
Red-209
02Pacific Complete-72
Red-72
02Upper Deck MVP-101
Gold-101
Classics-101
Golden Classics-101
02Upper Deck Vintage-139
02Upper Deck Vintage-277
04UD Legendary Signatures-81
AKA Autographs-AKA-SG
Autographs-SG
05ITG Tough Customers-SG
Autographs-SG
Complete Jerseys-SG
Double Memorabilia-SG
Emblem and Numbers-SG
Famous Battles Autographs-GP
Jerseys-SG
Signed Memorabilia-SG
Stickwork-SG
06Parkhurst-23
06Parkhurst-234
Autographs-23
Autographs-234

Grischott, Curdin
02Swiss HNL-434

Grisdale, John
72Maple Leafs Postcards-9
74Canucks Royal Bank-7
75Canucks Royal Bank-6
75O-Pee-Chee NHL-339
76Canucks Royal Bank-6
77Canucks Royal Bank-8
77O-Pee-Chee NHL-277
78Canucks Royal Bank-9
78O-Pee-Chee-318

Grise, Patrick
88Richelieu Riverains-12
90 7th Inn. Sketch QMJHL-60
91 7th Inn. Sketch QMJHL-30

Grishin, Alexander
99Russian Hockey League-37
00Russian Hockey League-9
03Russian Hockey League-125

Grnak, Marianne
94Classic Women of Hockey-W16

Grochmal, Nathan
03Kamloops Blazers-8

Groenestege, Doug
03Mississauga Ice Dogs-11
06Richmond Renegades-7

Groeneveld, Phil
95Central Hockey League-7
95Fort Worth Fire-3

Grof, Jakub
00Czech OFS-171
01Czech OFS-193
02Czech OFS Plus-279

Groff, Stefan
95Swiss HNL-278

Groger, Sascha
94German First League-326

Groger, Thomas
94German DEL-12
95German DEL-322

Grogg, Stefan
93Swiss HNL-47
95San Diego Barracudas RHI-4
96Swiss HNL-67
98Swiss Power Play Stickers-215
99Swiss Panini Stickers-215
00Swiss Panini Stickers-258
00Swiss Slapshot Mini-Cards-EVZ10
01Swiss EV Zug Postcards-22
01Swiss HNL-182
02Swiss HNL-331

Groke, Jamie
85London Knights-20

Groleau, Francois
90 7th Inn. Sketch QMJHL-225
91 7th Inn. Sketch QMJHL-55
91Arena Draft Picks-29
91Arena Draft Picks French-29
91Arena Draft Picks Autographs-29
91Arena Draft Picks Autographs French-29
91Classic-35
91Star Pics-63
91Ultimate Draft-30
91Ultimate Draft French-30
91Classic Four-Sport *-35
Autographs-35A
94Saint John Flames-8
94Classic Pro Prospects-47

96Fredericton Canadiens-8
98German DEL-281
99Quebec Citadelles-9
00German DEL-9
01German Adler Mannheim Eagles Postcards-6
01German Upper Deck-171
02German DEL City Press-240
03German DEL-4
03German Mannheim Eagles Postcards-23
04German Adler Mannheim Eagles Postcards-15
04German DEL-9
05German DEL-57
Defender-DF06

Groleau, Jason
95Slapshot Memorial Cup-54
03St. Georges de Beauce Garaga-9

Groleau, Joe
99Halifax Mooseheads-5

Groleau, Marius
51Laval Dairy Subset-36

Groleau, Samuel
917th Inn. Sketch QMJHL-159
95Wheeling Thunderbirds-3
95Wheeling Thunderbirds Series II-8
99German Bundesliga 2-198
02German DEL City Press-137
03German DEL-80
04Thetford Mines Prolab-13

Groleau, Stephane
01Sorel Royaux-8

Gromling, Dimtri
98German DEL-286

Gron, Stanislav
97Seattle Thunderbirds-22
98Kootenay Ice-19
99Albany River Rats-13
00Albany River Rats-10
01BAP Memorabilia-357
Emerald-357
Ruby-357
Sapphire-357
01Parkhurst-328
01SPx-115
01UD Premier Collection-71
01UD Top Shelf-59
01UD Top Shelf-59B
01Upper Deck-197
Exclusives-197
01Upper Deck MVP-207
01Albany River Rats-10
02Czech OFS Plus-49
03Czech OFS Plus-191
06German DEL-33

Gronau, Mark
94German DEL-72
95German DEL-51

Gronberg, Jan
86Swedish Panini Stickers-54

Gronberg, Ulf
57Swedish Alfabilder-142

Gronborg, Rikard
92Swedish Semic Elitserien Stickers-257
93Phoenix Cobras RHI-9

Grondin, Jimmy
92Quebec Pee-Wee Tournament-475
96Rimouski Oceanic-12
96Rimouski Oceanic Quebec Police-12
97Rimouski Oceanic-11

Grondin, Marco
92Quebec Pee-Wee Tournament-738
93Quebec Pee-Wee Tournament-923

Grondin, Philippe
92Quebec Pee-Wee Tournament-177
93Quebec Pee-Wee Tournament-1112
96Rimouski Oceanic Update-3
97Rimouski Oceanic-27

Grondin, Pierre
77Granby Vics-10

Gronholm, Ossi-Petteri
04Finnish Cardset-286
05Finnish Cardset -127
06Finnish Cardset-137

Groning, Olle
57Swedish Alfabilder-108

Gronman, Tuomas
91Upper Deck-677
French-677
91Upper Deck Czech World Juniors-40
917th Inn. Sketch WHL-154
93Parkhurst-523
Emerald Ice-523
93Upper Deck-270
93Finnish Jyvas-Hyva Stickers-231
93Finnish SISU-188
94Finnish SISU-314
94Finnish SISU Horoscopes-4
95Finnish SISU-126
Double Trouble-1
95Finnish SISU Limited-4
95Finnish Semic World Championships-3
95Finnish Semic World Championships-225
96Donruss Canadian Ice-139
Gold Press Proofs-139
Red Press Proofs-139
96Select Certified-105
Artist's Proofs-105
Blue-105
Mirror Blue-105
Mirror Gold-105
Mirror Red-105
Red-105
96Upper Deck-237
96Finnish SISU Redline Sledgehammers-4
98Upper Deck-163
Exclusives-163
Exclusives 1 of 1-163
Gold Reserve-163
98Kansas City Blades-6
99Finnish Cardset-262
Aces High-H-3
Most Wanted-11
00Finnish Cardset-302
01Finnish Cardset-88
02Finnish Cardset-167

Gronstrand, Jari
88Nordiques General Foods-16
88Nordiques Team Issue-16
89Nordiques Team Issue-14
89Nordiques General Foods-11
91Swedish Semic Elitserien Stickers-158
93Finnish SISU-65
94German DEL-400

Gronvall, Janne
91Upper Deck-672
French-672
91Upper Deck Czech World Juniors-35
92Finnish Jyvas-Hyva Stickers-162
92Classic-32
Gold-32
93Finnish Jyvas-Hyva Stickers-291
93Finnish SISU-64
94Finnish SISU-159
94Finnish SISU-175
94St. John's Maple Leafs-10
95Finnish SISU Limited-75
95St. John's Maple Leafs-10
96Collector's Edge Ice-80
Prism-80
98Finnish Kerailysarja-211
99Finnish Cardset-122
00Finnish Cardset-87
01Finnish Cardset-167
01Finnish Cardset-340
02Finnish Cardset-19
03Swedish Elite-181
Silver-181
04Swedish Elitset-40
Gold-40
05Finnish Cardset -321
06Finnish Cardset-149

Gropp, Roby
99Tupelo T-Rex-13

Grosch, Christian
04German Weiden Blue Devils-6

Grosek, Michal
93Tacoma Rockets-10
94Finest-64
Super Team Winners-64
Refractors-64
94Fleer-241
94OPC Premier-531
Special Effects-531
94Parkhurst-266
Gold-266
94Pinnacle-482
Artist's Proofs-482
Rink Collection-482
94Topps/OPC Premier-531
Special Effects-531
94Ultra-393
94Upper Deck-433
Electric Ice-433
94Classic Pro Prospects-9
95Donruss-125
95Leaf-53
95Parkhurst International-231
Emerald Ice-231
95Upper Deck-111
Electric Ice-111
Electric Ice Gold-111
96Collector's Edge Ice-68
Prism-68
97Be A Player-187
Autographs-187
Autographs Die-Cuts-187
Autographs Prismatic Die-Cuts-187
97Crown Royale-13
Emerald Green-13
Ice Blue-13
Silver-13
97Pacific Invincible NHL Regime-19
97Pacific Omega-21
Copper-21
Dark Gray-21
Emerald Green-21
Gold-21
Ice Blue-21
97Panini Stickers-17
97Score-255
97Score Sabres-8
Platinum-8
Premier-8
98Aurora-16
98Crown Royale-12
Limited Series-12
98Katch-18
98OPC Chrome-152
Refractors-152
98Pacific-105
Ice Blue-105
Red-105
98Pacific Dynagon Ice-17
Blue-17
Red-17
98Pacific Omega-22
Red-22
Opening Day Issue-22
98Panini Photocards-31
98Panini Stickers-18
98Paramount-18
Copper-18
Emerald Green-18
Holo-Electric-18
Ice Blue-18
Silver-18
98Revolution-13
Ice Shadow-13
Red-13
98SP Authentic-10
Power Shift-10
98Topps-152
O-Pee-Chee-152
98Upper Deck MVP-25
Gold Script-25
Silver Script-25
Super Script-25
99BAP Memorabilia-32
99BAP Memorabilia-342
Gold-32
Gold-342
Silver-32
Silver-342
99Pacific-36
Copper-36
Emerald Green-36
Gold-36
Ice Blue-36
Premiere Date-36
Red-36
99Pacific Dynagon Ice-30
Blue-30
Copper-30
Gold-30
Premiere Date-30
99Panini Stickers-39
99Paramount-27
Copper-27
Emerald-27
Gold-27
Holographic Emerald-27
Holographic Gold-27
Holographic Silver-27
Ice Blue-27
Premiere Date-27
Red-27
Silver-27
99Upper Deck MVP-28
Gold Script-28
Silver Script-28
Super Script-28
00BAP Memorabilia-281
Emerald-281
Ruby-281
Sapphire-281
Promos-281
00BAP Mem Chicago Sportsfest Copper-281
00BAP Memorabilia Chicago Sportsfest Blue-281
00BAP Memorabilia Chicago Sportsfest Gold-281
00BAP Memorabilia Chicago Sportsfest Ruby-281
00BAP Memorabilia Chicago Sun-Times Ruby-281
00BAP Memorabilia Chicago Sun-Times Gold-281
00BAP Mem Chicago Sun-Times Sapphire-281
00BAP Mem Toronto Fall Expo Copper-281
00BAP Memorabilia Toronto Fall Expo Gold-281
00BAP Memorabilia Toronto Fall Expo Ruby-281
00Black Diamond-13
Gold-13
00O-Pee-Chee-255A
00O-Pee-Chee Parallel-255A
00Pacific-95
Copper-95
Gold-95
Ice Blue-95
Premiere Date-95
00Panini Stickers-127
00Paramount-49
Copper-49
Gold-49
Holo-Gold-49
Holo-Silver-49
Ice Blue-49
Premiere Date-49
00Revolution-30
Blue-30
Premiere Date-30
Red-30
00Stadium Club-134
00Topps/OPC-255A
Parallel-255A
00Upper Deck-37
Exclusives Tier 1-37
Exclusives Tier 2-37
00Upper Deck Victory-53
00Czech Stadion-160
00Hartford Wolf Pack-10
01Hartford Wolf Pack-7
02Pacific Complete-345
Red-345
03Parkhurst Original Six Boston-2
03Upper Deck MVP-41
Gold Script-41
Silver Script-41
Canadian Exclusives-41

Gross, Cody
06Prince Albert Raiders-17

Gross, Gable
98Kamloops Blazers-13
99Kamloops Blazers-10
00Kamloops Blazers-9

Gross, Lloyd
34Diamond Matchbooks Silver-27

Gross, Oleg
03Russian Hockey League-191

Gross, Pavel
94German DEL-277
95German DEL-274
96German DEL-169
98German DEL-230
99German DEL-279
00German DEL-34
Game Jersey-PG

Gross, Remo
93Swiss HNL-225

Grosse, Erwin
51Laval Dairy QSHL-64
52St. Lawrence Sales-104

Grossi, Dino
93Indianapolis Ice-10
94Classic Pro Prospects-137

Grossman, Elias
06Penticton Vees-10

Grossman, Joe
04Waterloo Blackhawks-8
05Waterloo Blackhawks-11

Grossman, Nicklas
05Swedish SHL Elitset Gold-120
05Swedish SHL Elitset Series 1 Signatures-4
05Iowa Stars-5
06Hot Prospects-200
06UD Artifacts-270
06Iowa Stars-9

Grossman, Niklas
06Be A Player-234
06SP Authentic-180
Limited-180
06The Cup-124
Autographed Rookie Masterpiece Pressplates-124
Gold Rainbow Autographed Rookie Patches-124
Masterpiece Pressplates (Sweet Beginnings)-119
Rookies Black-124
Rookies Platinum-124
06Ultimate Collection-110
Rookies Autographed NHL Shields-110
Rookies Autographed Patches-110
06Upper Deck Sweet Shot-119
Rookie Jerseys Autographs-119

Grossmann, Vitalij
94German DEL-161
95German DEL-161
99German Bundesliga 2-118

Grosso, Don
34Beehive Group I Photos-102
40O-Pee-Chee V301-2-128
57St. Catherine's Tee Pees-17

Grosul, Aaron
03Colorado Eagles-9
04Colorado Eagles-7
05Colorado Eagles-8

Grot, Denis
04Russian World Junior Team-2

Groten, Richard
90Fort Saskatchewan Traders-4

Grotnes, Pal
93Swedish Semic Elitserien-313

Groulx, Danny
98Val d'Or Foreurs-4
00Victoriaville Tigres-23
Signed-23
02Grand Rapids Griffins-14
03Grand Rapids Griffins-6
04ITG Heroes and Prospects-15
Autographs-DGR
Complete Emblems-14
Emblems-44
Emblems Gold-44
He Shoots-He Scores Prizes-15
Jersey Autographs-44
Jerseys-44
Jerseys Gold-44
Numbers-44
Numbers Gold-44
04ITG Heroes/Prospects Toronto Expo '05-15
04ITG Heroes/Prospects Expo Heroes/Pros-15
05German DEL-194
06Hamilton Bulldogs-13

Groulx, Wayne
81Sault Ste. Marie Greyhounds-14
82Sault Ste. Marie Greyhounds-11
83Sault Ste. Marie Greyhounds-11
84Sault Ste. Marie Greyhounds-8
93Swedish Semic World Champ Stickers-278
94Finnish Jaa Kiekko-239

Growden, Dan
00Belleville Bulls-16
01Belleville Bulls-10
03Johnstown Chiefs-11

Gruba, Tony
93St. Cloud State Huskies-8
94Dayton Bombers-15

Grubb, Colin
96UK Fife Flyers-5

Gruber, Bucky
95North Iowa Huskies-11

Gruber, Garry
97Peoria Rivermen-1

Gruber, Marco
02Swiss HNL-6

Gruden, John
91Ferris State Bulldogs-14
92Ferris State Bulldogs-14
94Donruss-179
94Fleer-11
94Leaf-192
94OPC Premier-447
Special Effects-447
94Topps/OPC Premier-447
Special Effects-447
94Ultra-254
94Classic-53
Gold-53
All-Americans-AA2
95Topps-104
OPC Inserts-104
96Providence Bruins-4
97Detroit Vipers-15
98Detroit Vipers-19
98Detroit Vipers Freschetta-13
99Grand Rapids Griffins-9
99IHL All-Stars-18
00Grand Rapids Griffins-10
01Grand Rapids Griffins-2
02German Berlin Polar Bears Postcards-10
02German DEL City Press-31

Gruden, Luke
99Peoria Rivermen-25
00Peoria Rivermen-3

Gruen, Danny
75O-Pee-Chee WHA-128

Gruhl, Scott
88ProCards IHL-52
89ProCards IHL-150
90ProCards AHL/IHL-382
91ProCards-254
93Classic Pro Prospects-122
94Richmond Renegades-6
95Richmond Renegades-14
96Richmond Renegades-8
99Fort Wayne Komets Penalty Leaders-15

Gruhle, Peter
04German Weiden Blue Devils-7

Grumet-Morris, Dov
96Quebec Pee-Wee Tournament-158

Grun, David
06Sioux Falls Stampede -5

Grunauer, Georg
94German First League-301

Grundling, Martin
05Moose Jaw Warriors-8
06Moose Jaw Warriors-6

Grundmann, Olaf
94German DEL-219
95German DEL-196
96German DEL-339

Grundstrom, Goran
83Swedish Semic Elitserien-54

Grunn, Carlo
01Finnish Cardset-203
02Finnish Cardset-166
03Finnish Cardset-25
04Finnish Cardset-250
06Finnish Cardset-74

Grunthal, Christof
94German First League-600

Grunwald, Benjamin
04German Weiden Blue Devils-8

Gruth, Henryk
79Panini Stickers-121
89Swedish Semic World Champ Stickers-133
92Finnish Semic-269
98Swiss Power Play Stickers-359

Gruttaduria, Mike
95Fort Worth Fire-14

Grygiel, Adrian
01German Upper Deck-258
02German DEL City Press-220
03German DEL-184
04German DEL-242
04German Krefeld Penguins Postcards-6
05German DEL-239
06German DEL-160

Grygorasz, Paul
93Quebec Pee-Wee Tournament-150

Gryp, Bob
74NHL Action Stamps-323
75O-Pee-Chee NHL-348

Grypiuk, Shane
00Red Deer Rebels-8
Signed-8

Grzegorczyk, Miroslaw
93Quebec Pee-Wee Tournament-1506

Gschliesser, Alexander
95Swedish World Championships Stickers-94

Gschwill, Timo
94German DEL-191
95German DEL-176
99German Bundesliga 2-74

Guadagnolo, Anthony
04Ottawa 67's-2

Guard, Kelly
02Kelowna Rockets-20
03Kelowna Rockets Memorial Cup-8
03Kelowna Rockets-10
04ITG Heroes and Prospects-85
Autographs-KG
04ITG Heroes/Prospects Toronto Expo '05-85
04ITG Heroes/Prospects Expo Heroes/Pros-85
05ITG Heroes/Prosp Toronto Expo Parallel -260
05Binghamton Senators-15
05Binghamton Senators Quickway-15
05ITG Heroes and Prospects-260
Autographs Series II-KG
Measuring Up-MU16
Measuring Up Gold-MU16
Nameplates-N-65
Nameplates Gold-N-65
06Beehive-139
Matte-139
06Between The Pipes-31
Autographs-AKG
Emblems-GUE07
Emblems Gold-GUE07
Emblems Autographs-GUE07
Jerseys-GUJ07
Jerseys Gold-GUJ07
Jerseys Autographs-GUJ07
Numbers-GUN07
Numbers Gold-GUN07
Numbers Autographs-GUN07
Prospect Trios-PT03
Prospect Trios Gold-PT03
06Hot Prospects-169
Red Hot-169
White Hot-169
06O-Pee-Chee-579
Rainbow-579
06SP Authentic-192
Limited-192
06The Cup-104
Autographed Rookie Masterpiece Pressplates-104
Gold Rainbow Autographed Rookies-104
Masterpiece Pressplates (Bee Hive)-139
Masterpiece Pressplates (Marquee Rookies)-579
Masterpiece Pressplates (SP Authentic Autographs)-192
Masterpiece Pressplates (Ultimate Collection)-86
Masterpiece Pressplates (Victory)-329
Rookies Black-104
Rookies Platinum-104
06Ultimate Collection-86
06Upper Deck-479
Exclusives Parallel-479
High Gloss Parallel-479
Masterpieces-479
Victory-329
06Binghamton Senators-8
06Binghamton Senators 5th Anniversary-10
07Upper Deck Rookie Class -48

Guay, Bernard
50Quebec Citadelles-7

Guay, Christopher
06Chicoutimi Sagueneens-10

Guay, Etienne
92Quebec Pee-Wee Tournament-587
93Quebec Pee-Wee Tournament-1130

Guay, Francois
88ProCards AHL-267
89ProCards AHL-273
90ProCards AHL/IHL-291
95Swiss HNL-407
96German DEL-172
98German DEL-42
99German DEL-177
00German DEL-119

Guay, Jerome
93Quebec Pee-Wee Tournament-1032

Guay, Marc-Andre
93Quebec Pee-Wee Tournament-36

Guay, Paul
84O-Pee-Chee-160
86Kings 20th Anniversary Team Issue-8
88ProCards AHL-161
89ProCards AHL-212
90ProCards AHL/IHL-513
91ProCards-611

Guay, Roger
51Bas Du Fleuve-21

Guazzini, Bjorn
99Swiss Panini Stickers-145
01Swiss HNL-375
02Swiss HNL-422

Gubarev, Alexei
99Russian Hockey League-87

Gubernatorov, Sergei
00Russian Hockey League-117

Guchko, Patrik
02Russian Hockey League-137

Gudas, Leo
89Swedish Semic World Champ Stickers-186
91Finnish Jyvas-Hyva Stickers-30
92Finnish Semic-125
93Swiss HNL-194
94Finnish Jaa Kiekko-166
94Swedish Olympics Lillehammer*-318
95Czech APS Extraliga-202
95Swedish Globe World Championships-148
96Swedish Semic Wien-112
98German DEL-279
99Czech OFS-19
99Czech OFS Jagr Team Embossed-19
99German DEL-150

Gudmundson, Jason
01Missouri River Otters-20

Gudmundsson, Peter
72Swedish Stickers-157
73Swedish Stickers-47
74Swedish Stickers-217

Guellet, Stephane
907th Inn. Sketch QMJHL-125

Guenette, Francois-Pierre
01Halifax Mooseheads-6
02Halifax Mooseheads-6
03Cape Breton Screaming Eagles-11
04Halifax Mooseheads-5

Guenette, Luc
85Fredericton Express-17

Guenette, Steve
87Penguins Kodak-10
90ProCards AHL/IHL-627
91ProCards-150

Guenette, Sylvain
93Quebec Pee-Wee Tournament-5

Guenin, Nathan
02Ohio State Buckeyes-20
03Ohio State Buckeyes-7
04Ohio State Buckeyes-8
05Ohio State Buckeyes-8
06Philadelphia Phantoms-15

Guennelon, Gerald
94Finnish Jaa Kiekko-219
94French National Team-14
95Swedish Globe World Championships-206
95Swedish World Championships Stickers-100

Guenther, Bevin
97Brandon Wheat Kings-9

Guenther, Joe
01St. Michaels Majors-22
02ECHL All-Star Southern-43
02ECHL Update-U-9
03Indianapolis Ice-10

Guentzel, Ryan
06Sioux Falls Stampede -4

Guerard, Daniel
93Classic-132
93Classic Four-Sport *-235
Gold-235
95PEI Senators-6
03St. Jean Mission-12

Guerard, Stephane
87Nordiques General Foods-13
87Nordiques Team Issue-28
88Nordiques General Foods-17
88Nordiques Team Issue-17
89Nordiques Team Issue-15
89Nordiques General Foods-12
89Nordiques Police-10
90Nordiques Team Issue-10
90Halifax Citadels-9
91Nordiques Panini Team Stickers-8

Guerette, David
93Quebec Pee-Wee Tournament-439

Guerette-Charland, Francis
04Victoriaville Tigres-20
05Victoriaville Tigres-20
06Victoriaville Tigres-23

Guerette-Charland, Keven
05Victoriaville Tigres-1
06Victoriaville Tigres-15

Guerin, Bill
91Parkhurst-453
French-453
92O-Pee-Chee-308
92OPC Premier-120
92Parkhurst-97
Emerald Ice-97
92Pro Set-230
92Score-470
Canadian-470
92Stadium Club-17
92Topps-516
Gold-516G
92Ultra-338
92Upper Deck-411
92Classic-105
Gold-105
93Donruss-186
93Leaf-7
93OPC Premier-421
Gold-421
93Parkhurst-382
Emerald Ice-382
93Pinnacle-305
Canadian-305
93Score-395
Canadian-395
93Stadium Club-467
Members Only Master Set-467
First Day Issue-467
93Topps/OPC Premier-421
Gold-421
93Ultra-359
94Be A Player Signature Cards-50
94Canada Games NHL POGS-350
94Donruss-62
94Flair-94
94Fleer-112
94Leaf-146
94OPC Premier-231
Special Effects-231
94Parkhurst-127
Gold-127
94Pinnacle-23
Artist's Proofs-23
Rink Collection-23
94Topps/OPC Premier-231
Special Effects-231
94Ultra-117
94Upper Deck-359
Electric Ice-359
95Canada Games NHL POGS-166
95Collector's Choice-60
Player's Club-60
Player's Club Platinum-60
95Donruss-35
95Finest-82
Refractors-82
95Leaf-201
95Panini Stickers-81
95Parkhurst International-124
Emerald Ice-124
95Pinnacle-32
Artist's Proofs-32
Rink Collection-32
95Playoff One on One-58
95Score-106
Black Ice Artist's Proofs-106
Black Ice-106
95SP-82
95Stadium Club-130
Members Only Master Set-130
95Summit-111
Artist's Proofs-111
Ice-111
95Topps-88
OPC Inserts-88
95Topps SuperSkills-44
Platinum-44
95Ultra-191
95Ultra-261
Gold Medallion-191
95Upper Deck-373
Electric Ice-373
Electric Ice Gold-373
Special Edition-SE48
Special Edition Gold-SE48
96Be A Player-29
Autographs-29
Autographs Silver-29
96Black Diamond-112
Gold-112
96Collector's Choice-146
96Devils Team Issue-12
96Donruss-180
Press Proofs-180
96Donruss Elite-69
Die Cut Stars-69
96Flair-53
Blue Ice-53
96Leaf Preferred-108
Press Proofs-108
96Pinnacle-170
Artist's Proofs-170
Foil-170
Premium Stock-170
Rink Collection-170
96Score-197
Artist's Proofs-197
Dealer's Choice Artist's Proofs-197
Special Artist's Proofs-197
Golden Blades-197
96Select Certified-26
Artist's Proofs-26
Blue-26
Mirror Blue-26
Mirror Gold-26
Mirror Red-26
Red-26
96SkyBox Impact-69
96SP-91
96Topps Picks-141
OPC Inserts-141
96Upper Deck-90
Power Performers-P11
96Upper Deck Ice-35
Parallel-35
96Zenith-106
Artist's Proofs-106
97Black Diamond-38
Double Diamond-38
Triple Diamond-38
Quadruple Diamond-38
97Collector's Choice-147
Star Quest-SQ21
97Devils Team Issue-9
97Gatorade Stickers-1
97Katch-82
Gold-82
Silver-82
97Pacific-117
Copper-117
Emerald Green-117
Ice Blue-117
Red-117
Silver-117
97Pacific Omega-91
Copper-91
Dark Gray-91
Emerald Green-91
Gold-91
Ice Blue-91
97Pinnacle-136
Press Plates Back Black-136
Press Plates Back Cyan-136
Press Plates Back Magenta-136
Press Plates Back Yellow-136
Press Plates Front Black-136
Press Plates Front Cyan-136
Press Plates Front Magenta-136
Press Plates Front Yellow-136
97Pinnacle Inside-131
97Revolution-54
Copper-54
Emerald-54
Ice Blue-54
Silver-54
97Score-199
97Score Devils-5
Platinum-5
Premier-5
97SP Authentic-86
97Upper Deck Three Star Selects-13C
98Aurora-72
98Be A Player-53
Press Release-53
98BAP Gold-53
98BAP Autographs-53
98BAP Autographs Gold-53
98BAP Tampa Bay All Star Game-53
98Black Diamond-35
. Double Diamond-35
Triple Diamond-35
Quadruple Diamond-35
98Crown Royale-51
Limited Series-51
98Finest-12
No Protectors-12
No Protectors Refractors-12
Refractors-12
Promos-PP5
98Pacific-209
Ice Blue-209
Red-209
98Pacific Dynagon Ice-72
Blue-72
Red-72
98Pacific Omega-92
Red-92
Opening Day Issue-92
98Paramount-86
Copper-86
Emerald Green-86
Holo-Electric-86
Ice Blue-86
Silver-86
98Revolution-54
Ice Shadow-54
Red-54
98SP Authentic-34
Power Shift-34
98SPx Finite-36
Radiance-36
Spectrum-36
98SPx Top Prospects-26
Radiance-26
Spectrum-26
98Topps Gold Label Class 1-75
Black-75
Black One of One-75
One of One-75
Red-75
Red One of One-75
98Topps Gold Label Class 2-75
98Topps Gold Label Class 2 Black-75
98Topps Gold Label Class 2 Black 1 of 1-75
98Topps Gold Label Class 2 One of One-75
98Topps Gold Label Class 2 Red-75
98Topps Gold Label Class 2 Red One of One-75
98Topps Gold Label Class 3-75
98Topps Gold Label Class 3 Black-75
98Topps Gold Label Class 3 Black 1 of 1-75
98Topps Gold Label Class 3 One of One-75
98Topps Gold Label Class 3 Red-75
98Topps Gold Label Class 3 Red One of One-75
98UD Choice-84
Prime Choice Reserve-84
Reserve-84
98Upper Deck-92
Exclusives-92
Exclusives 1 of 1-92
Gold Reserve-92
98Upper Deck MVP-80
Gold Script-80
Silver Script-80
Super Script-80
Power Game-PG14
98Slovakian Eurotel-5
99Aurora-56
Premiere Date-56
99BAP Memorabilia-225
Gold-225
Silver-225
99BAP Millennium-97
Emerald-97
Ruby-97
Sapphire-97
Signatures-97
Signatures Gold-97
99Black Diamond-39
Diamond Cut-39
Final Cut-39
99Crown Royale-54
Limited Series-54
Premiere Date-54
99O-Pee-Chee-137
99O-Pee-Chee Chrome-137
99O-Pee-Chee Chrome Refractors-137
99Pacific-155
Copper-155
Emerald Green-155
Gold-155
Ice Blue-155
Premiere Date-155
Red-155
Team Leaders-11
99Pacific Omega-90
Copper-90
Gold-90
Ice Blue-90
Premiere Date-90
99Pacific Prism-55
Holographic Blue-55
Holographic Gold-55
Holographic Mirror-55
Holographic Purple-55
Premiere Date-55
99Panini Stickers-247
99Paramount-92
Copper-92
Emerald-92
Gold-92
Holographic Emerald-92
Holographic Gold-92
Holographic Silver-92
Ice Blue-92
Premiere Date-92
Red-92
Silver-92
Ice Alliance-11
99Revolution-58
Premiere Date-58
Red-58
Shadow Series-58
Copper-58
Gold-58
CSC Silver-58
99SP Authentic-35
99SPx-61
Radiance-61
Spectrum-61
99Stadium Club-48
First Day Issue-48
One of a Kind-48
Printing Plates Black-48
Printing Plates Cyan-48
Printing Plates Magenta-48
Printing Plates Yellow-48
99Topps/OPC-137
99Topps/OPC Chrome-137
Refractors-137
99Upper Deck-54
Exclusives-54
Exclusives 1 of 1-54
99Upper Deck Gold Reserve-54
99Upper Deck HoloGrFx-25
Ausome-25
99Upper Deck MVP-78
Gold Script-78
Silver Script-78
Super Script-78
99Upper Deck Retro-32
Gold-32
Platinum-32
99Upper Deck Victory-109
00Aurora-56
Premiere Date-56
00BAP Memorabilia-27
Emerald-27
Ruby-27
Sapphire-27
Promos-27
00BAP Mem Chicago Sportsfest Copper-27
00BAP Memorabilia Chicago Sportsfest Blue-27
00BAP Memorabilia Chicago Sportsfest Gold-27
00BAP Memorabilia Chicago Sportsfest Ruby-27
00BAP Memorabilia Chicago Sun-Times Ruby-27
00BAP Memorabilia Chicago Sun-Times Gold-27
00BAP Mem Chicago Sun-Times Sapphire-27
00BAP Mem Toronto Fall Expo Copper-27
00BAP Memorabilia Toronto Fall Expo Gold-27
00BAP Memorabilia Toronto Fall Expo Ruby-27
00BAP Parkhurst 2000-P197
00BAP Signature Series-95
Emerald-95
Ruby-95
Sapphire-95
Autographs-203
Autographs Gold-203
00Crown Royale-10
Ice Blue-10
Limited Series-10
Premiere Date-10
Red-10
00O-Pee-Chee-66
00O-Pee-Chee Parallel-66
00Pacific-166
Copper-166
Gold-166
Ice Blue-166
Premiere Date-166
00Paramount-95
Copper-95
Gold-95
Holo-Gold-95
Holo-Silver-95
Ice Blue-95
Premiere Date-95
00Private Stock Game Gear-7
00Revolution-56
Blue-56
Premiere Date-56
Red-56
00SP Authentic-9
00SPx-132
00Stadium Club-26
00Titanium-6
Blue-6
Gold-6
Premiere Date-6
Red-6

Retail-6
All-Stars-2NA
00Topps/OPC-66
Parallel-66
00Topps Chrome-53
OPC Refractors-53
Refractors-53
00Topps Gold Label Class 1-22
Gold-22
00Topps Gold Label Class 2-22
00Topps Gold Label Class 2 Gold-22
00Topps Gold Label Class 3-22
00Topps Gold Label Class 3 Gold-22
00Topps Heritage-57
Chrome Parallel-57
00Upper Deck-73
Exclusives Tier 1-73
Exclusives Tier 2-73
00Upper Deck Ice-62
00Upper Deck MVP-73
First Stars-73
Second Stars-73
Third Stars-73
00Upper Deck Victory-93
00Upper Deck Vintage-32
00Upper Deck Vintage-147
00Vanguard-8
Holographic Gold-8
Holographic Purple-8
Pacific Proofs-8
00Czech Stadion-195
01Atomic-7
Blue-7
Gold-7
Premiere Date-7
Red-7
Team Nucleus-1
01BAP Memorabilia-88
Emerald-88
Ruby-88
Sapphire-88
All-Star Jerseys-ASJ10
All-Star Emblems-ASE10
All-Star Numbers-ASN10
All-Star Teammates-AST8
Country of Origin-CO14
01BAP Signature Series Certified 100-C4
01BAP Signature Series Certified 50-C4
01BAP Signature Series Certified 1 of 1's-C4
01BAP Signature Series Autographs-LBG
01BAP Signature Series Autographs Gold-LBG
01BAP Sig Series He Shoots/Scores Points-3
01BAP Sig Series He Shoots/Scores Prizes-18
01BAP Sig Series International Medals-IS-7
01BAP Signature Series Jerseys-GJ-84
01BAP Signature Series Emblems-GUE-4
01BAP Signature Series Numbers-ITN-4
01BAP Signature Series Teammates-TM-3
01BAP Ultimate Memorabilia Emblems-5
01BAP Ultimate Memorabilia Jerseys-5
01BAP Ultimate Mem Jerseys and Sticks-5
01BAP Ultimate Memorabilia Numbers-4
01BAP Ultimate Memorabilia Name Plates-9
01BAP Update He Shoots-He Scores Points-4
01BAP Update He Shoots-He Scores Prizes-15
01BAP Update Heritage-H28
01Bowman YoungStars-53
Gold-53
Ice Cubed-53
01O-Pee-Chee-6
01O-Pee-Chee Heritage Parallel-6
01O-Pee-Chee Heritage Parallel Limited-6
01O-Pee-Chee Premier Parallel-6
01Pacific-31
Extreme LTD-31
Hobby LTD-31
Premiere Date-31
Retail LTD-31
All-Stars-NA2
01Pacific Adrenaline-13
Blue-13
Premiere Date-13
Red-13
Retail-13
01Pacific Arena Exclusives-31
01Pacific Heads-Up-8
Blue-8
Premiere Date-8
Red-8
Silver-8
All-Star Net-3
01Parkhurst-33
Gold-33
Silver-33
01Private Stock-5
Gold-5
Premiere Date-5
Retail-5
Silver-5
01Private Stock Pacific Nights-5
01SP Authentic-5
Limited-5
Limited Gold-5
Sign of the Times-BG
Sign of the Times-GWA
01SP Game Used-4
Authentic Fabric-AFBG
Authentic Fabric-DFTG
Authentic Fabric Gold-AFBG
01SPx-5
01Stadium Club-33
Award Winners-33
Master Photos-33
Gallery-G30
Gallery Gold-G30
NHL Passport-NHLP14
01Titanium-8
Hobby Parallel-8
Premiere Date-8
Retail-8
Retail Parallel-8
Double-Sided Jerseys-3
Double-Sided Jerseys-74
Double-Sided Patches-3
01Titanium Draft Day Edition-9
01Topps-6
Heritage Parallel-6
Heritage Parallel Limited-6
OPC Parallel-6
Shot Masters-SM11
01Topps Chrome-6
Refractors-6
Black Border Refractors-6
01Topps Heritage-70
Refractors-70
01Topps Reserve-7
01UD Challenge for the Cup-6
01UD Mask Collection-9
Gold-9
01UD Stanley Cup Champs Pieces of Glory-G-BG
01UD Stanley Cup Champs Sticks-S-BG
01UD Top Shelf-79
01Upper Deck-244
Exclusives-244
Pride of a Nation-PNBG
Pride of a Nation-DPAG
Shooting Stars-SS2
01Upper Deck MVP-13
01Upper Deck Victory-34
01Upper Deck Victory-421
Gold-34
Gold-421
01Upper Deck Vintage-24
01Upper Deck Vintage-26
02Atomic-32
Blue-32
Gold-32
Red-32
Hobby Parallel-32
Jerseys-4
Jerseys Gold-4
Patches-4
National Pride-U1
02BAP All-Star Edition-28
Jerseys-28
Jerseys Gold-28
Jerseys Silver-28
02BAP First Edition-132
02BAP First Edition-302
02BAP First Edition-372
02BAP First Edition-403H
Jerseys-132
02BAP Memorabilia-7
02BAP Memorabilia-247
02BAP Memorabilia-268
Emerald-7
Emerald-247
Emerald-268
Ruby-7
Ruby-247
Ruby-268
Sapphire-7
Sapphire-247
Sapphire-268
All-Star Jerseys-ASJ-16
All-Star Teammmates-AST-21
NHL All-Star Game-7
NHL All-Star Game-247
NHL All-Star Game-268
NHL All-Star Game Blue-7
NHL All-Star Game Blue-247
NHL All-Star Game Blue-268
NHL All-Star Game Green-7
NHL All-Star Game Green-247
NHL All-Star Game Green-268
NHL All-Star Game Red-7
NHL All-Star Game Red-247
NHL All-Star Game Red-268
02BAP Memorabilia Toronto Fall Expo-7
02BAP Memorabilia Toronto Fall Expo-247
02BAP Memorabilia Toronto Fall Expo-268
02BAP Signature Series-125
Autographs-125
Autograph Buybacks 1998-53
Autograph Buybacks 1999-97
Autograph Buybacks 2000-203
Autograph Buybacks 2001-LBG
Autographs Gold-125
Famous Scraps-FS3
Famous Scraps-FS5
Jerseys-SGJ52
Jersey Autographs-SGJ52
Team Quads-TQ16
02BAP Ultimate Memorabilia All-Star MVP-1
02BAP Ultimate Memorabilia Jerseys-1
02BAP Ultimate Mem Journey Jerseys-7
02BAP Ultimate Mem Journey Emblems-7
02Bowman YoungStars-29
Gold-29
Silver-29
02Crown Royale-29
Blue-29
Red-29
Retail-29
02ITG Used-22
02ITG Used-122
International Experience-IE11
International Experience Gold-IE11
02O-Pee-Chee-229
02O-Pee-Chee-229U
02O-Pee-Chee Premier Blue Parallel-229
02O-Pee-Chee Premier Red Parallel-229
02O-Pee-Chee Factory Set-229
02Pacific-28
Blue-28
Red-28
02Pacific Complete-307
Red-307
02Pacific Exclusive-55
02Pacific Heads-Up-38
Blue-38
Purple-38
Red-38
Quad Jerseys-29
Quad Jerseys Gold-29
02Pacific Quest for the Cup-27
Gold-27
02Parkhurst-108
Bronze-108
Gold-108
Silver-108
02Parkhurst Retro-40
Minis-40
Jerseys-RJ33
02Private Stock Reserve-114
Red-114
Retail-114
Patches-114
02SP Authentic-28
Beckett Promos-28
Super Premiums-SPBG
Super Premiums-DPMG
02SP Game Used-15
02SP Game Used-64
Authentic Fabrics-AFBG
Authentic Fabrics-AFGU
Authentic Fabrics Gold-AFBG
Authentic Fabrics Gold-AFGU
Authentic Fabrics Rainbow-AFBG
Authentic Fabrics Rainbow-AFGU
First Rounder Patches-BG
Piece of History-PHGU
Piece of History Gold-PHGU
Piece of History Rainbow-PHGU
02SPx-25
02SPx-86
Spectrum Gold-25
Spectrum Gold-86
Spectrum Silver-25
Spectrum Silver-86
02Stadium Club-104
Silver Decoy Cards-104
Proofs-104
02Stars Postcards-15
02Titanium-31
Blue-31
Red-31
Retail-31
02Topps-229
02Topps-229U
OPC Blue Parallel-229
OPC Red Parallel-229
Topps/OPC Hometown Heroes-HHU8
Own The Game-OTG8
Factory Set-229
Factory Set Hometown Heroes-HHU8
02Topps Chrome-125
Black Border Refractors-125
Refractors-125
02Topps Heritage-125
02Topps Heritage-163
02Topps Total-168
Production-TP5
02UD Artistic Impressions-29
Gold-29
02UD Artistic Impressions Beckett Promos-29
02UD Artistic Impressions Common Ground-CG15
02UD Artistic Impress Common Ground Gold-CG15
02UD Artistic Impressions Retrospectives-R29
02UD Artistic Impress Retrospect Gold-R29
02UD Artistic Impress Retrospect Silver-R29
02UD Honor Roll-23
Students of the Game-SG11
02UD Mask Collection-29
02UD Mask Collection Beckett Promos-29
02UD Premier Collection-19
02UD Top Shelf-8
Clutch Performers-CPBG
Dual Player Jerseys-STGD
Dual Player Jerseys-STTG
Goal Oriented-GOBG
Shooting Stars-SHBG
Signatures-BG
Sweet Sweaters-SWBG
Triple Jerseys-HTGHB
Triple Jerseys-TSGTD
02Upper Deck-55
Exclusives-55
Good Old Days-GOBG
Patchwork-PWBG
Classic Portraits Hockey Royalty-GTM
Classic Portraits Hockey Royalty-GWA
Classic Portraits Hockey Royalty Limited-GTM
Classic Portraits Hockey Royalty Limited-GWA
Classic Portraits Starring Cast-CBG
Classic Portraits Starring Cast Limited-CBG
02Upper Deck Rookie Update-32
02Upper Deck Rookie Update-160C
Jerseys-DBG
Jerseys Gold-DBG
02Upper Deck Victory National Pride-NP51
02Upper Deck Vintage-83
Green Backs-83
02Vanguard-32
LTD-32
03BAP Memorabilia-12
Emerald-12
Gold-12
Ruby-12
Sapphire-12
All-Star Jerseys-ASJ-4
All-Star Jerseys-ASJ-30
All-Star Staring Lineup-11
All-Star Teammates-AST3
He Shoots-He Scores Points-7
He Shoots-He Scores Prizes-3
Jersey and Stick-SJ-11
03BAP Ultimate Memorabilia Autographs-27
Gold-27
03BAP Ultimate Mem Auto Jerseys-27
03BAP Ultimate Mem Auto Emblems-27
03BAP Ultimate Memorabilia Jerseys-8
03BAP Ultimate Memorabilia Jerseys Gold-8
03BAP Ultimate Mem Jersey and Emblems-2
03BAP Ultimate Mem Jersey and Emblem Gold-2
03BAP Ultimate Mem Jersey and Numbers-2
03BAP Ultimate Mem Jersey and Number Gold-2
03Beehive-66
Gold-66
Silver-66
Jerseys-JT12
03Black Diamond-60
Black-60
Green-60
Red-60
03Bowman-12
Gold-12
Goal to Goal-HG
03Bowman Chrome-12
Refractors-12
Gold Refractors-12
Xfractors-12
03Crown Royale-32
Blue-32
Retail-32
03ITG Action-192
Jerseys-M158
03ITG Used Signature Series-6
Gold-6
Autographs-BG
Autographs Gold-BG
International Experience-27
International Experience Autographs-27
International Experience Emblems Gold-27
International Experience Emblems-27
International Experience Gold-27
Jerseys-3
Jerseys Gold-3
Jersey Autos-3
Emblems-38
Emblems Gold-38
Jersey and Stick-3
Jersey and Stick Gold-3
03NHL Sticker Collection-204
03O-Pee-Chee-205
03O-Pee-Chee-304
03OPC Blue-205
03OPC Blue-304
03OPC Gold-205
03OPC Gold-304
03OPC Red-205
03OPC Red-304
03Pacific-104
Blue-104
Red-104
03Pacific Calder-31
Silver-31
03Pacific Complete-299
Red-299
03Pacific Exhibit-47
03Pacific Exhibit-205
Blue Backs-47
Yellow Backs-47
03Pacific Heads-Up-31
Hobby LTD-31
Retail LTD-31
03Pacific Invincible-29
Blue-29
Red-29
Retail-29
03Pacific Prism-113
Blue-113
Patches-113
Red-113
Retail-113
03Pacific Quest for the Cup-31
Blue-31
03Parkhurst Original Six Boston-60
03Parkhurst Rookie-37
Jerseys-GJ-4
Jersey Autographs-GUJ-BG
Jerseys Gold-GJ-4
03Private Stock Reserve-162
Blue-162
Patches-162
Red-162
Retail-162
03SP Authentic-26
Limited-26
03SP Game Used Authentic Fabrics-QMGTM
03SP Game Used Authentic Fabrics Gold-QMGTM
03SP Game Used Authentic Patches-APBG
03SP Game Used Double Threads-DTMG
03SP Game Used Limited Threads-LTBG
03SP Game Used Limited Threads Gold-LTBG
03SPx-29
Radiance-29
Spectrum-29
Fantasy Franchise-FF-MGT
Fantasy Franchise Limited-FF-MGT
VIP-VIP-MG
VIP Limited-VIP-MG
03Stars Postcards-9
03Titanium-196
Patches-196
03Topps-205
03Topps-304
Blue-205
Blue-304
Gold-205
Gold-304
Red-205
Red-304
First Round Fabrics-BG
First Round Fabrics-BGJI
Topps/OPC Idols-UI1
03Topps C55-31
Minis-31
Minis American Back-31
Minis American Back Red-31
Minis Bazooka Back-31
Minis Brooklyn Back-31
Minis Hat Trick Back-31
Minis O Canada Back-31
Minis O Canada Back Red-31
Minis Stanley Cup Back-31
Relics-TRBG
03Topps Pristine-11
Gold Refractor Die Cuts-11
Refractors-11
Popular Demand Relics-PD-BG
Popular Demand Relic Refractors-PD-BG
Press Plates Black-11
Press Plates Cyan-11
Press Plates Magenta-11
Press Plates Yellow-11
03Topps Traded Franchise Fabrics-FF-BG
03UD Honor Roll-24
03UD Premier Collection Teammates-PT-DS2
03UD Premier Collection Teammates Patches-PT-DS2
03Upper Deck-305
Canadian Exclusives-305
HG-305
Jerseys-GJ-BG
Patches-SP9
UD Exclusives-305
03Upper Deck Classic Portraits-29
03Upper Deck Ice-28
Gold-28
Breakers-IB-BG
Breaker Patches-IB-BG
Frozen Fabrics-FF-BG
Frozen Fabric Patches-FF-BG
03Upper Deck MVP-129
Gold Script-129
Silver Script-129
Canadian Exclusives-129
SportsNut-SN29
Threads-TC2
03Upper Deck Rookie Update-26
Skills-SKBG
03Upper Deck Trilogy-29
Limited-29
03Upper Deck Victory-57
Bronze-57
Gold-57
Silver-57
Game Breakers-GB6
03Toronto Star-26
04Pacific-84
Blue-84
Red-84
04SP Authentic-29
04SP Authentic-111
04Ultimate Collection-82
04Upper Deck-56
Canadian Exclusives-56
HG Glossy Gold-56
HG Glossy Silver-56
World Cup Tribute-BG
World Cup Tribute-TASGBG
05Be A Player Dual Signatures-GB
05Be A Player Dual Signatures-GD
05Be A Player Signatures-BG
05Be A Player Signatures Gold-BG
05Be A Player Triple Signatures-DAL
05Be A Player Triple Signatures-HGT
05Be A Player World Cup Salute-WCS15
05Beehive-29
05Beehive-186
Beige -29
Blue -29
Gold-29
Red -29
Matte-29
Matted Materials-MMBG
05Black Diamond-133
Emerald-133
Gold-133
Onyx-133
Ruby-133
05Hot Prospects Hot Materials-HMBG
05Panini Stickers-248
05Parkhurst-160
Facsimile Auto Parallel-160
True Colors-TCDAL
True Colors-TCDAL
True Colors-TCMIDA
True Colors-TCMIDA
05SP Authentic-33
Limited-33
05SP Game Used-32
Gold-32
Authentic Fabrics-AF-BG
Authentic Fabrics Gold-AF-BG
Authentic Fabrics Quad-MTGA
Authentic Fabrics Quad-TRGL
Authentic Patches Quad -MTGA
Authentic Patches Quad -TRGL
Authentic Patches-AP-BG
Awesome Authentics-AA-BG
Game Gear-GG-BG
05SPx-26
Spectrum-26
Winning Combos-WC-DA
Winning Combos Gold-WC-DA
Winning Combos Spectrum-WC-DA
Winning Materials-WM-BG
Winning Materials Gold-WM-BG
Winning Materials Spectrum-WM-BG
Xcitement Superstars-XS-BG
Xcitement Superstars Gold-XS-BG
Xcitement Superstars Spectrum-XS-BG
05The Cup Dual NHL Shields-DSMG
05The Cup Noble Numbers Dual-DNNMG
05The Cup Noble Numbers Dual-DNNTG
05UD Artifacts-33
05UD Artifacts-164
Blue-33
Blue-164
Gold-33
Gold-164
Green-33
Green-164
Pewter-33
Pewter-164
Red-33
Red-164
Frozen Artifacts-FA-GU
Frozen Artifacts Autographed-FA-GU
Frozen Artifacts Copper-FA-GU
Frozen Artifacts Dual-FAD-GU
Frozen Artifacts Dual Autographed-FAD-GU
Frozen Artifacts Dual Copper-FAD-GU
Frozen Artifacts Dual Gold-FAD-GU
Frozen Artifacts Dual Maroon-FAD-GU
Frozen Artifacts Dual Pewter-FAD-GU
Frozen Artifacts Dual Silver-FAD-GU
Frozen Artifacts Gold-FA-GU
Frozen Artifacts Maroon-FA-GU
Frozen Artifacts Patches-FP-GU
Frozen Artifacts Patches Autographed-FP-GU
Frozen Artifacts Patches Dual-FPD-GU
Frozen Artifacts Patches Dual Autos-FPD-GU
Frozen Artifacts Patches Pewter-FP-GU
Frozen Artifacts Patches Silver-FP-GU
Frozen Artifacts Pewter-FA-GU
Frozen Artifacts Silver-FA-GU
Gold Autographed-33
Gold Autographed-164
05UD PowerPlay-30
Rainbow-30
05Ultimate Collection-30
Gold-30
National Heroes Jerseys-NHJBG
National Heroes Patches-NHPBG
05Ultra-70
Gold-70
Ice-70
Scoring Kings-SK25
Scoring Kings Jerseys-SKJ-BG
Scoring Kings Patches-SKP-BG
05Upper Deck-58
Big Playmakers-B-BG
HG Glossy-58
Jerseys-J-BG
Jerseys Series II-J2BG
Majestic Materials-MMBG
NHL Generations-DGB
Patches-P-BGU
Shooting Stars-S-BG
05Upper Deck Ice-30
Rainbow-30
05Upper Deck MVP-131
Gold-131
Platinum-131
05Upper Deck Rookie Update-217
Inspirations Patch Rookies-217
05Upper Deck Trilogy-30
05Upper Deck Trilogy-137
Crystal-137
Honorary Patches-HP-BG
Honorary Patch Scripts-HSP-BG
Honorary Swatches-HS-BG
Honorary Swatch Scripts-HSS-BG
05Upper Deck Toronto Fall Expo-58
05Upper Deck Victory-61
Black-61
Gold-61
Silver-61
Game Breakers-GB15
06Be A Player-120
Autographs-120
Signatures-BG
Signatures 10-132
Signatures 25-132
Signatures Duals-DMG
Up Close and Personal-UC7
Up Close and Personal Autographs-UC7
Portraits Dual Signature Portraits-DSWG
Portraits Signature Portraits-SPBG
06Black Diamond-73
Black-73
Gold-73
Ruby-73
Jerseys-JBG
Jerseys Black-JBG
Jerseys Gold-JBG
Jerseys Ruby-JBG
06Flair Showcase Stitches-SSBG
06Fleer-171
Tiffany-171
Fabricology-FBG
Speed Machines-SM10
06O-Pee-Chee-430
Rainbow-430
06Panini Stickers-341
06SP Game Used Authentic Fabrics Dual-AF2WG
06SP Game Used Authentic Fabrics Dual Patches-AF2WG
06SP Game Used Authentic Fabrics Fives-AF5ASG
06SP Game Used Authentic Fabrics Fives Patches-AF5ASG
06SPx Winning Materials-WMBG
06SPx Winning Materials Spectrum-WMBG
06The Cup NHL Shields Duals-DSHWG
06UD Artifacts Treasured Patches Black-TSBG
06UD Artifacts Treasured Patches Blue-TSBG
06UD Artifacts Treasured Patches Gold-TSBG
06UD Artifacts Treasured Patches Platinum-TSBG
06UD Artifacts Treasured Patches Red-TSBG
06UD Artifacts Treasured Swatches-TSBG
06UD Artifacts Treasured Swatches Black-TSBG
06UD Artifacts Treasured Swatches Blue-TSBG
06UD Artifacts Treasured Swatches Gold-TSBG
06UD Artifacts Treasured Swatches Platinum-TSBG
06UD Artifacts Treasured Swatches Red-TSBG
06UD Artifacts Tundra Tandems-TTTG
06UD Artifacts Tundra Tandems-TTWG
06UD Artifacts Tundra Tandems Black-TTTG
06UD Artifacts Tundra Tandems Black-TTWG
06UD Artifacts Tundra Tandems Blue-TTTG
06UD Artifacts Tundra Tandems Blue-TTWG
06UD Artifacts Tundra Tandems Gold-TTTG
06UD Artifacts Tundra Tandems Gold-TTWG
06UD Artifacts Tundra Tandems Platinum-TTTG
06UD Artifacts Tundra Tandems Platinum-TTWG
06UD Artifacts Tundra Tandems Red-TTTG
06UD Artifacts Tundra Tandems Red-TTWG
06UD Artifacts Tundra Tandems Dual Patches Red-TTTG
06UD Artifacts Tundra Tandems Dual Patches Red-TTWG
06UD Powerplay Specialists-SBG
06UD Powerplay Specialists Patches-PBG
06Ultra-170
Gold Medallion-170
Ice Medallion-170
06Upper Deck Arena Giveaways-STL5
06Upper Deck-420
Exclusives Parallel-420
High Gloss Parallel-420
Game Jerseys-JBG
Game Patches-PBG
Generations Duals-G2GB
Generations Patches Dual-G2PGB
Masterpieces-420
06Upper Deck MVP-253
Gold Script-253
Super Script-253
06Upper Deck Victory-66
06Upper Deck Victory-273
06Upper Deck Victory Black-66
06Upper Deck Victory Gold-66
07Upper Deck Ovation-61
07Upper Deck Victory-177
Black-177
Gold-177

Guerne, Sacha

01Swiss HNL-414
02Swiss HNL-410

Guerra, Justin

02Arizona Icecats-7

Guerrera, David

03Laredo Bucks-9

Guerriero, Jason

05Finnish Cardset -222
06Milwaukee Admirals -5

Guers, Philippe

93Quebec Pee-Wee Tournament-1492

Guetens, Vern

94Erie Panthers-16

Guevremont, Jocelyn

71Canucks Royal Bank-4
710-Pee-Chee-232
71Toronto Sun-278
72Canucks Royal Bank-6
720-Pee-Chee-37
72Sargent Promotions Stamps-222
72Topps-75
73Canucks Royal Bank-6
730-Pee-Chee-143
73Topps-142
74Lipton Soup-48
74NHL Action Stamps-276
74NHL Action Stamps Update-3
740-Pee-Chee NHL-122
74Sabres Postcards-9
74Topps-122
750-Pee-Chee NHL-216
75Topps-216
760-Pee-Chee NHL-108
76Topps-108
770-Pee-Chee NHL-242
77Topps-242
780-Pee-Chee-94
78Topps-94
790-Pee-Chee-381
91Future Trends Canada '72-35
91Future Trends Canada '72 French-35

Gugelmann, Ralph

95Swiss HNL-441
96Swiss HNL-429

Guggemos, Markus

01German Upper Deck-254
04German DEL-282

Guggisberg, Peter

04Swiss Davos Postcards-12

Guida, Nic

93Quebec Pee-Wee Tournament-610

Guidarelli, T.J.

01Rockford IceHogs-23

Guidolin, Aldo

44Beehive Group II Photos-318
52St. Lawrence Sales-17B
53Parkhurst-66
60Cleveland Barons-8

Guidolin, Bep

34Beehive Group I Photos-17
44Beehive Group II Photos-99
51Parkhurst-42
51Laval Dairy Subset-114
52St. Lawrence Sales-65
740-Pee-Chee NHL-34
74Topps-34

Guidotti, Giordano

98Swiss Power Play Stickers-9

Guidotti, Vince

92Norwegian Elite Series-160

Guieseppe, Karl

93Quebec Pee-Wee Tournament-1385

Guignard, Fabian

93Swiss HNL-418
95Swiss HNL-241
96Swiss HNL-155
98Swiss Power Play Stickers-158
99Swiss Panini Stickers-84
00Swiss Panini Stickers-58
00Swiss Slapshot Mini-Cards-HCCF3
01Swiss HNL-55
02Swiss HNL-107

Guilbault, Pierre-Marc

03Shawinigan Cataractes-15
05Shawinigan Cataractes-13
06Gatineau Olympiques-21
06PEI Rocket-6

Guilbeault, Pierre-Marc

06Gatineau Olympiques-21

Guiliano, Jeff

04Manchester Monarchs Tobacco-12

Guillaume, Olivier

917th Inn. Sketch QMJHL-248

Guillet, Robert

88Richelieu Riverains-13
907th Inn. Sketch QMJHL-241
917th Inn. Sketch QMJHL-129
92Fredericton Canadiens-12
93Fredericton Canadiens-12
95Milwaukee Admirals-7
95Milwaukee Admirals Postcards-12
98German DEL-111
99German DEL-280
00German DEL-35
01German Upper Deck-7
02German DEL City Press-264
Top Scorers-TS3
03German DEL-185
04German DEL-228
04German Krefeld Penguins Postcards-7
05German DEL-224

Guilmette, Yves

77Kalamazoo Wings-12

Guimond, Geoff

00Sudbury Wolves-9

Guinard, Martin

92Quebec Pee-Wee Tournament-82
93Quebec Pee-Wee Tournament-239

Guindon, Andrew

98Tri-City Americans-23

Guindon, Bob

72Nordiques Postcards-12
73Nordiques Team Issue-13
740-Pee-Chee WHA-26
78Jets Postcards-7

Guinn, Rob

94Sarnia Sting-20
95Slapshot-47
95Classic-96
04Fort Wayne Komets-5
04Fort Wayne Komets Shoe Carnival-5
05Fort Wayne Komets Choice-21
05Fort Wayne Komets Sprint-9
06New Mexico Scorpions-10

Guirestante, John

93London Knights-11
93London Knights-25
93North Bay Centennials-19
94North Bay Centennials-22

Guitard, Dean

87Sudbury Wolves-19

Guite, Ben

02Cincinnati Mighty Ducks-B-9
03Bridgeport Sound Tigers-2A
04Providence Bruins-9
05Hot Prospects-107
En Fuego-107
Red Hot-107
White Hot-107
05SP Authentic-251
Limited-251
05The Cup Masterpiece Pressplates (Ice)-265
05The Cup Master Pressplate Rookie Update-107
05The Cup Masterpiece Pressplates SPA-251
05Upper Deck Ice-265
05Upper Deck Rookie Update-107
05Providence Bruins-5
06Albany River Rats-13

Guite, Pierre

72Nordiques Postcards-13
73Nordiques Team Issue-14
750-Pee-Chee WHA-17
75Stingers Kahn's-4
760-Pee-Chee WHA-123

Gula, Ladislav

94Czech APS Extraliga-94

Gulas, Milan

06Czech OFS-3

Gulash, Garry

92British Columbia JHL-10
95Milwaukee Admirals Postcards-3
96Richmond Renegades-9
98Quad-City Mallards-11
98UHL All-Stars-20
99Quad-City Mallards-4
99UHL All-Stars West-16T
00Quad-City Mallards-3
01Quad-City Mallards-8

Gulasi, Michal

04Lethbridge Hurricanes-18
06Czech OFS-47

Gulda, Peter

94German DEL-262
95Finnish Semic World Championships-166
95German DEL-247
95Swedish World Championships Stickers-61
96German DEL-139
98German DEL-81
98German DEL-328
99German DEL-293
00German DEL-198
01German Upper Deck-216

Gull, Fabian

93Swiss HNL-242
95Swiss HNL-190
98Swiss Power Play Stickers-327
01Swiss HNL-326
02Swiss HNL-455

Gull, Urs

93Swiss HNL-393

Gullberg, Weine

71Swedish Hockey-334
72Swedish Stickers-144

Gulliksen, Rune

92Finnish Semic-42
92Norwegian Elite Series-24
95Swedish World Championships Stickers-249

Gullion, Brett

90Fort Saskatchewan Traders-5

Gulutzan, Glen

90Brandon Wheat Kings-24
907th Inn. Sketch WHL-222
91Saskatoon Blades-13
917th Inn. Sketch WHL-112
00Fresno Falcons-8
01Fresno Falcons-6
02Fresno Falcons-12
03Las Vegas Wranglers-22
04Las Vegas Wranglers-20
05Las Vegas Wranglers-23
06Las Vegas Wranglers-20

Gummerus, Jarmo

71Finnish Suomi Stickers-278

Guna, Rudolf

03Russian Hockey League-243

Gundersen, Carl Gunnar

92Norwegian Elite Series-4

Gundersen, Gorm

92Norwegian Elite Series-91

Gundersen, Jarle

92Norwegian Elite Series-175

Gundersen, Jon

92Norwegian Elite Series-83

Gunis, Michal

96Slovakian Quebec Pee-Wee Tournament-9

Gunko, Juri

98Russian Hockey League-121
99German DEL-221

Gunler, Joakim

92Swedish Semic Elitserien Stickers-183
93Swedish Semic Elitserien-157

Gunn, Jim

83Victoria Cougars-8

Gunn, Roydon

84Prince Albert Raiders Stickers-11
93Memphis RiverKings-3

Gunnar, Lars

79Panini Stickers-198

Gunnarsson, Carl

06Swedish SHL Elitset-205

Gunnarsson, Soren

71Swedish Hockey-266
72Swedish Stickers-244
74Swedish Stickers-168

Gunther, Petri

96Denver University Pioneers-4

Guntner, Michael

93Swedish Semic World Champ Stickers-276
94Finnish Jaa Kiekko-234
95Austrian National Team-7
95Swedish World Championships Stickers-258

Gunville, Ron

89Lethbridge Hurricanes-6
91Air Canada SJHL-D15

Guolla, Steve

92Michigan State Spartans-11
93Michigan State Spartans-11
95PEI Senators-7
96Kentucky Thoroughblades-8
97Collector's Choice-220
97Pacific-281
Copper-281
Emerald Green-281
Ice Blue-281
Red-281
Silver-281
97Pacific Dynagon-112
Copper-112
Dark Grey-112
Emerald Green-112
Ice Blue-112
Red-112
Silver-112
Tandems-66
97Pacific Invincible-126
Copper-126
Emerald Green-126
Ice Blue-126
Red-126
Silver-126
97Upper Deck-148
97Kentucky Thoroughblades-6
98Kentucky Thoroughblades-11
99Upper Deck-290
Exclusives-290
Exclusives 1 of 1-290
99Upper Deck Gold Reserve-290
00Pacific-19
Copper-19
Gold-19
Ice Blue-19
Premiere Date-19
00Upper Deck-239
Exclusives Tier 1-239
Exclusives Tier 2-239
00Upper Deck Vintage-19
01Pacific-17
Extreme LTD-17
Hobby LTD-17
Premiere Date-17
Retail LTD-17
01Pacific Arena Exclusives-17
01Upper Deck-12
Exclusives-12
01Upper Deck Victory-19
Gold-19
01Upper Deck Vintage-15
01Albany River Rats-21
02Devils Team Issue-5
05German DEL-138

Gurcik, Pavol

04Slovakian Poprad Team Set-14

Gurejev, Vladimir

73Swedish Stickers-118

Guren, Miloslav

94SP-154
Die Cuts-154
94Czech APS Extraliga-186
95Czech APS Extraliga-35
95Signature Rookies-56
Signatures-56
96Fredericton Canadiens-9
98Upper Deck-296
Exclusives-296
Exclusives 1 of 1-296
Gold Reserve-296
99BAP Memorabilia-151
Gold-151
Silver-151
99Pacific-216
Copper-216
Emerald Green-216
Gold-216
Ice Blue-216
Premiere Date-216
Red-216
99Quebec Citadelles-19
00Quebec Citadelles-9
Signed-9
01Czech OFS-50
01Czech OFS Red Inserts-RE24D
02Czech OFS Plus All-Star Game-H5
02Russian Hockey League-95
03Russian Hockey League-175
04Russian Legion-25

Gurskis, John

99Peoria Rivermen-10
05Florida Seals Team Issue-6

Gusakov, Evgeny

99Baie-Comeau Drakkar-12
00Baie-Comeau Drakkar-17
Signed-17

Gusarov, Alexei
87Russian National Team-6
89Russian National Team-7
89Swedish Semic World Champ Stickers-82
90Nordiques Petro-Canada-31
91Pro Set Platinum-221
91Bowman-145
91Nordiques Petro-Canada-9
91O-Pee-Chee-355
91Panini Stickers-260
91Parkhurst-364
French-364
91Pinnacle-230
French-230
91Pro Set-207
French-207
91Score American-326
91Score Canadian Bilingual-356
91Score Canadian English-356
91Stadium Club-330
91Topps-355
91Upper Deck-365
French-365
91Russian Stars Red Ace-5
91Russian Sports Unite Hearts-3
91Russian Stars in NHL-3
92Nordiques Petro-Canada-9
92O-Pee-Chee-389
92Panini Stickers-215
92Panini Stickers French-215
92Pinnacle-161
French-161
92Pro Set-147
92Score-264
Canadian-264
92Stadium Club-451
92Ultra-173
92Upper Deck-127
92Finnish Semic-105
93OPC Premier-293
Gold-293
93Parkhurst-441
Emerald Ice-441
93Pinnacle-261
Canadian-261
93PowerPlay-420
93Score-260
Canadian-260
93Stadium Club-424
Members Only Master Set-424
First Day Issue-424
93Topps/OPC Premier-293
Gold-293
93Upper Deck-362
94Donruss-216
94Leaf-408
94Nordiques Burger King-9
94Parkhurst SE-SE148
Gold-SE148
94Pinnacle-164
Artist's Proofs-164
Rink Collection-164
94Stadium Club-67
Members Only Master Set-67
First Day Issue-67
Super Team Winner Cards-67
94Finnish Jaa Kiekko-159
95Swedish Globe World Championships-168
96Maggers-33
97Be A Player-196
Autographs-196
Autographs Die-Cuts-196
Autographs Prismatic Die-Cuts-196
97Pacific Invincible NHL Regime-52
97Panini Stickers-207
98Be A Player-183
Press Release-183
98BAP Gold-183
98BAP Autographs-183
98BAP Autographs Gold-183
98Panini Stickers-186
99Avalanche Team Issue-8
99Panini Stickers-208
00Pacific-114
Copper-114
Gold-114
Ice Blue-114
Premiere Date-114
02BAP Sig Series Auto Buybacks 1998-183

Gusev, Alexander
72Finnish Jaakiekko-23
72Finnish Hellas-62
73Finnish Jaakiekko-3
73Russian National Team-4
73Swedish Stickers-82
74Finnish Jenkki-44
74Russian National Team-4
74Swedish Stickers-4
74Swedish Semic World Champ Stickers-30
91Future Trends Canada '72-19
91Future Trends Canada '72 French-19

Gusev, Sergei
96Michigan K-Wings-7
98Be A Player-192
Press Release-192
98BAP Gold-192
98BAP Autographs-192
98BAP Autographs Gold-192
98Pacific Dynagon Ice-54
Blue-54
Red-54
98Pacific Omega-78
Red-78
Opening Day Issue-78
01Russian Hockey League-57
02BAP Sig Series Auto Buybacks 1998-192
02Russian Hockey League-212
02Russian SL-33
02Russian World Championships-11
03Russian World Championship Team 2003-15

Gusev, Sergej
74Swedish Stickers-183

Gusev, Vadim
00Russian Hockey League-354

Gusev, Vladimir
00Russian Hockey League-26
03Florence Pride-150

Gushin, Vladislav
02Russian Hockey League-258

Guskov, Alexander
99Russian Hockey League-109
02Russian Hockey League-147
02Russian Hockey League-220
02Russian Hockey League-221
02Russian SL-4
02Russian World Championships-9
03Russian Hockey League-234
03Russian Postcards-2
03Russian World Championship Team 2003-20
04Russian World Championship Team-10

Gusmanov, Denis
03Russian National Team-6

Gusmanov, Ravil
91Upper Deck Czech World Juniors-3
94Finest-107
Super Team Winners-107
Refractors-107
94OPC Premier-323
Special Effects-323
94Parkhurst SE-SE205
Gold-SE205
94Topps/OPC Premier-323
Special Effects-323
94Upper Deck-254
Electric Ice-254
94Classic-73
Gold-73
Tri-Cards-T76
98Russian Hockey League-6
98Chicago Wolves Turner Cup-23
99Russian Hockey League-17
99Russian Metallurg Magnetogorsk-37
99Russian Stars of Hockey-11
02Russian World Championships-13

Gustafson, Chris
02Augusta Lynx-64

Gustafson, Cory
92Harvard Crimson-11

Gustafson, Derek
00BAP Memorabilia-513
00Cleveland Lumberjacks-24
00Jackson Bandits-3
00Jackson Bandits Promos-2
01O-Pee-Chee-298
01O-Pee-Chee Premier Parallel-298
01Pacific-195
Extreme LTD-195
Hobby LTD-195
Premiere Date-195
Retail LTD-195
01Pacific Arena Exclusives-195
01Topps-298
OPC Parallel-298
01Upper Deck Victory-376
Gold-376
02Between the Pipes-85
Gold-85
Silver-85
03ECHL Update RBI Sports-140
03Louisiana Ice Gators-6

Gustafson, Eric
93Quebec Pee-Wee Tournament-817

Gustafson, Jon
91Richmond Renegades-16
91Richmond Renegades Set 2-10
92Richmond Renegades-6
93Richmond Renegades-20
94Central Hockey League-9
94Dallas Freeze-9

Gustafsson, Bengt
79Capitals Team Issue-6
80O-Pee-Chee-222
80Topps-222
81O-Pee-Chee-353
82Capitals Team Issue-8
82O-Pee-Chee-364
82O-Pee-Chee Stickers-157
82Post Cereal-20
82Topps Stickers-157
83NHL Key Tags-130
83O-Pee-Chee-370
84Capitals Pizza Hut-7
84O-Pee-Chee-198
84O-Pee-Chee Stickers-130
84Topps-144
85Capitals Pizza Hut-6
87Capitals Kodak-16
87Capitals Team Issue-8
88Capitals Borderless-7
88Capitals Smokey-7
88O-Pee-Chee-151
88Panini Stickers-371
88Topps-151
89Swedish Semic Elitserien Stickers-89
90Swedish Semic Elitserien Stickers-259
91O-Pee-Chee Inserts-2S
91Finnish Semic World Champ Stickers-45
91Swedish Semic Elitserien Stickers-91
91Swedish Semic Elitserien Stickers-348
91Swedish Semic World Champ Stickers-45
92Swedish Semic Elitserien Stickers-116
93Swedish Semic World Champ Stickers-15
97Swedish Alfabilder Autographs-14

Gustafsson, Bengt-Ake
99Swiss Panini Stickers-128
00Swiss Panini Stickers-173

Gustafsson, Carl Gustav
56Swedish Alfabilder-37

Gustafsson, Claes
87Swedish Panini Stickers-263

Gustafsson, Folke
56Swedish Alfabilder-85

Gustafsson, Jan
56Swedish Alfabilder-70

Gustafsson, Juha
98Finnish Kerailysarja-15
99Finnish Cardset-17
00Finnish Cardset-126
01Finnish Cardset-183
02Finnish Cardset-168
04Finnish Cardset-153
Parallel-114
06Finnish Cardset-1

Gustafsson, Lennart
67Swedish Hockey-45

Gustafsson, Magnus
90Swedish Semic Elitserien Stickers-220

Gustafsson, Per
89Swedish Semic Elitserien Stickers-104
90Swedish Semic Elitserien Stickers-106
91Swedish Semic Elitserien Stickers-111
92Swedish Semic Elitserien Stickers-131
93Swedish Semic Elitserien-104
94Swedish Leaf-276
95Swedish Leaf-231
Face to Face-6
Mega-15
95Swedish Upper Deck-76
96Swedish Upper Deck-226
95Swedish Upper Deck-253
Ticket to North America-NA11
96Black Diamond-40
Gold-40
96Metal Universe-58
96SP-179
96Upper Deck-267
97Be A Player-69
Autographs-69
Autographs Die-Cuts-69
Autographs Prismatic Die-Cuts-69
97Pacific-165
Copper-165
Emerald Green-165
Ice Blue-165
Red-165
Silver-165
97Panini Stickers-59
97St. John's Maple Leafs-12
98Swedish UD Choice-103
99Swedish Upper Deck-89
SHL Signatures-9
Snapshots-7
00Swedish Upper Deck-94
00Swedish Upper Deck-196
02Swedish SHL-36
Parallel-36
04Swedish Elitset-194
Gold-194
04Swedish HV71 Postcards-6
04Swedish Pure Skills-36
Parallel-36
05Swedish SHL Elitset-53
Gold-53
Icons-8
Series Two Signatures-11
06Swedish SHL Elitset-55

Gustafsson, Peter
89Swedish Semic Elitserien Stickers-46
90Swedish Semic Elitserien Stickers-192
91Swedish Semic Elitserien Stickers-45
92Swedish Semic Elitserien Stickers-70

Gustafsson, Tomas
84Swedish Semic Elitserien-158

Gustavson, Ben
95Slapshot-268
00Bakersfield Condors-10
06Port Huron Flags-12

Gustavson, Stefan
90Swedish Semic Elitserien Stickers-291
94Swedish Leaf-256
95Swedish Leaf-10
95Swedish Upper Deck-9
98Swedish UD Choice-8
00Swedish Upper Deck-7
02Swedish SHL-212
Parallel-212
Team Captains-6

Gustavsson, Bengt
67Swedish Hockey-137
69Swedish Hockey-148
71Swedish Hockey-262

Gustavsson, Bengt-Ake
67Swedish Hockey-5
67Swedish Hockey-138
69Swedish Hockey-149
70Swedish Hockey-112
71Swedish Hockey-201
72Swedish Stickers-181
82Swedish Semic VM Stickers-146
89Swedish Semic World Champ Stickers-20
92Finnish Semic-65
01Swedish Alfabilder-14

Gustavsson, Charles
67Swedish Hockey-201

Gustavsson, Gote
70Swedish Hockey-219
72Swedish Stickers-279

Gustavsson, Jakob
83Swedish Semic Elitserien-27
84Swedish Semic Elitserien-27
85Swedish Panini Stickers-25
86Swedish Panini Stickers-4

Gustavsson, Kjell-Ove
64Swedish Coralli ISHockey-98
65Swedish Coralli ISHockey-98
67Swedish Hockey-286
71Swedish Hockey-310

Gustavsson, Lars Ake
70Swedish Hockey-113
71Swedish Hockey-202
72Swedish Stickers-101
73Swedish Stickers-213

Gustavsson, Lars-Anders
69Swedish Hockey-279
70Swedish Hockey-187

Gustavsson, Lennart
69Swedish Hockey-117
71Swedish Hockey-324
72Swedish Stickers-137

Gustavsson, Patrik
90Swedish Semic Elitserien Stickers-139
91Swedish Semic Elitserien Stickers-195

Gustavsson, Per
95Collector's Choice-343
Player's Club-343
Player's Club Platinum-343
04Swedish Elitset Jerseys Series 1-5
04Swedish Elitset Limited Signatures-3

Gustavsson, Peter
83Swedish Semic Elitserien-243
88Swedish Semic Elitserien Stickers-282

Gustavsson, Stefan
97Swedish Collector's Choice-8
99Swedish Upper Deck-11
SHL Signatures-1

Gustavsson, Thomas
83Swedish Semic Elitserien-211
93Swedish Semic Elitserien-109
95Swedish Leaf-225
95Swedish Upper Deck-82

Gut, Karel
95Czech APS Extraliga-398

Gutenberg, Bill
91Michigan Falcons-17

Gutierrez, Moises
02Kamloops Blazers-8
03Kamloops Blazers-19
05Kamloops Blazers-21

Gutov, Alexander
02Russian Hockey League-54
03Russian Hockey League-133

Guttler, Georg
94German DEL-165
95German DEL-155

Guttner, Tobias
03German Nuremberg Ice Tigers Postcards-11
05German DEL-105

Guy, Alexandre
92Quebec Pee-Wee Tournament-1038
93Quebec Pee-Wee Tournament-1348

Guy, Jason
05Guelph Storm-D-07
06Kingston Frontenacs-23

Guy, Kevan
82Medicine Hat Tigers-4
83Medicine Hat Tigers-14
85Moncton Golden Flames-16
86Moncton Golden Flames-10
86Canucks Mohawk-9
89ProCards IHL-177
90Canucks Mohawk-10
90Pro Set-545
91Canucks Panini Team Stickers-9
91ProCards-576

Guy, Mark
89 7th Inn. Sketch OHL-27
90 7th Inn. Sketch OHL-133

Guyaz, Gilles
93Swiss HNL-428

Guyaz, Noel
93Swiss HNL-167
95Swiss HNL-191
96Swiss HNL-83
00Swiss Panini Stickers-80
00Swiss Slapshot Mini-Cards-EHCC2
01Swiss HNL-239
02Swiss HNL-278

Guyer, Andrew
03Lincoln Stars-16

Guyer, Gino
02Minnesota Golden Gophers-7
03Minnesota Golden Gophers-13
04Minnesota Golden Gophers-8
05Minnesota Golden Gophers-10

Guzda, Brad
96Knoxville Cherokees-20
96Knoxville Cherokees-P1
97Mississippi Sea Wolves-21
98Bakersfield Condors-8
98Las Vegas Coyotes RHI-14
98Las Vegas Thunder-6
99Bakersfield Condors-9
00Knoxville Speed-4

Guze, Ray
92British Columbia JHL-120

Guzior, Russ
97New Orleans Brass-10
99Mobile Mysticks-15
03Indianapolis Ice-11

Guzior, Ryan
98Fayetteville Force-14

Guzzo, Ange
91Michigan Falcons-8

Gvora, Justin
05Mississauga Ice Dogs-10

Gyenes, Dan
05Kitchener Rangers-9
06Kitchener Rangers-13

Gygli, Marc
93Swiss HNL-35

Gylywoychuk, Dwayne
89Brandon Wheat Kings-19
90Brandon Wheat Kings-13
90 7th Inn. Sketch WHL-218
91 7th Inn. Sketch WHL-210
92Brandon Wheat Kings-8
93Brandon Wheat Kings-9
94Greensboro Monarchs-15
95Dayton Bombers-30
97Central Texas Stampede-5
00Wichita Thunder-10

Gyna, Vladimir
97Czech APS Extraliga-86
98Czech OFS-262
99Czech OFS-338
00Czech DS Extraliga-42
00Czech OFS-141
01Czech OFS-149
02Czech OFS Plus-192
02Czech OFS Plus All-Star Game-H25
03Czech OFS Plus-326
04Czech OFS-362
06Czech OFS-133

Gyori, Arpad
94Czech APS Extraliga-115
96Czech APS Extraliga-254
97Czech APS Extraliga-282
97Czech DS Stickers-93
98Czech DS Stickers-80

Gyori, Dylan
95Tri-City Americans-11
96Upper Deck-381
98Tri-City Americans-16
98Bowman CHL-51
Golden Anniversary-51
OPC International-51
98Bowman Chrome CHL-51
Golden Anniversary-51
Golden Anniversary Refractors-51
OPC International-51
OPC International Refractors-51
Refractors-51
99Bowman CHL-109
Gold-109
OPC International-109
00Wilkes-Barre Scranton Penguins-8
02Roanoke Express-15
02Roanoke Express RBI Sports-195

Haaf, Thorsten
94German First League-152

Haakana, Kari
93Finnish SISU-264
94Finnish SISU-151
95Finnish SISU-285
96Finnish SISU Redline-84
98German DEL-309
99German DEL-259
00Finnish Cardset-160
01Finnish Cardset-50
02Atomic-108
Blue-108
Gold-108
Red-108
Hobby Parallel-108
02BAP All-Star Edition-118
Gold-118
Silver-118
02BAP Memorabilia-375
02BAP Ultimate Memorabilia-13
02ITG Used-182
02Parkhurst-213
Bronze-213
Gold-213
Silver-213
02Private Stock Reserve-161
Blue-161
Red-161
Retail-161
02SP Authentic-145
02UD Honor Roll-113
02UD Mask Collection-147
02UD Top Shelf-113
02Upper Deck-437
Exclusives-437
02Finnish Cardset-20
03Swedish MoDo Postcards-2
04Finnish Cardset-3
Parallel-3
05Finnish Cardset -2
05German DEL-314
06Swedish SHL Elitset-266

Haakana, Leo
65Finnish Hellas-84
72Finnish Jaakiekko-172

Haake, Bernd
94German DEL-199
95German DEL-194
96German DEL-337

Haakensen, Mattis
92Norwegian Elite Series-100

Haakstad, Jason
92British Columbia JHL-47

Haaland, Brian
03Muskegon Fury-8

Haaland, Jon Erik
92Norwegian Elite Series-136

Haanpaa, Ari
86Islanders Team Issue-2
91Finnish Semic World Champ Stickers-13
91Finnish Jyvas-Hyva Stickers-27
91Swedish Semic World Champ Stickers-13
92Finnish Jyvas-Hyva Stickers-80
93Finnish Jyvas-Hyva Stickers-287
93Finnish SISU-76
94Finnish SISU-22
95Finnish SISU-320
95Finnish SISU Limited-79

Haanpaa, Jukka
66Finnish Jaakiekkosarja-36

Haapakoski, Mikko
92Finnish Jyvas-Hyva Stickers-173
92Finnish Semic-9
93Finnish SISU-378
93Swedish Semic World Champ Stickers-49
93Swiss HNL-65
94Finnish Jaa Kiekko-6
95Finnish Semic World Championships-48
95Swiss HNL-88
98Finnish Kerailysarja-83
00Finnish Cardset-55

Haapala, Jukka
66Finnish Jaakiekkosarja-1
70Finnish Jaakiekko-227

Haapala, Martti
71Finnish Suomi Stickers-259

Haapalainen, Hannu
70Finnish Jaakiekko-241
71Finnish Suomi Stickers-207
72Finnish Jaakiekko-155
73Finnish Jaakiekko-151
74Finnish Jenkki-5
74Finnish Typotor-26
74Swedish Semic World Champ Stickers-94
77Finnish Sportscasters-82-1949
78Finnish SM-Liiga-6
78Finnish SM-Liiga-179
83Swedish Semic VM Stickers-31
05Finnish Tappara Legendat-25

Haapalainen, Olavi
66Finnish Jaakiekkosarja-182
72Finnish Jaakiekko-156

Haapamaki, Jari
91Finnish Jyvas-Hyva Stickers-12
92Finnish Jyvas-Hyva Stickers-31
93Finnish Jyvas-Hyva Stickers-51
93Finnish SISU-240
94Finnish SISU-107
95Finnish SISU-19

Haapaniemi, Harri
80Finnish Mallasjuoma-80

Haapaniemi, Markku
78Finnish SM-Liiga-215
80Finnish Mallasjuoma-187

Haapaniemi, Miro
93Finnish SISU-103
94Finnish SISU-96
95Finnish SISU-210

Haapsaari, Tommi
92Finnish Jyvas-Hyva Stickers-156
93Finnish Jyvas-Hyva Stickers-296
93Finnish SISU-67
94Finnish SISU-60
95Finnish SISU-112

Haarmann, Mark
83Oshawa Generals-7

Haarstad, Tor
64Swedish Coralli ISHockey-155
65Swedish Coralli ISHockey-155

Haas, David
85London Knights-14
88ProCards AHL-79
89ProCards AHL-141
90ProCards AHL/IHL-220
91ProCards-224
98German DEL-186
99German DEL-232
01German Upper Deck-95
03German DEL-127

Haas, Julius
70Finnish Jaakiekko-45
70Swedish Hockey-355
70Swedish Masterserien-151
72Finnish Jaakiekko-5
72Finnish Hellas-93
74Finnish Jenkki-69

Haas, Rostislav
96Czech APS Extraliga-98
97Czech APS Extraliga-102
97Czech DS Extraliga-20
97Czech DS Stickers-265
98Czech DS Stickers-47
99German Bundesliga 2-107
03German DEL-53

Haataja, Juha-Pekka
01Finnish Cardset-287
04Finnish Cardset-262
05Finnish Cardset -97
06Finnish Cardset-289

Habacek, Jiri
98Czech OFS-405

Haberl, Siegfried
95Swedish World Championships Stickers-274

Haberlin, Sandro
99Swiss Panini Stickers-190
00Swiss Panini Stickers-235
01Swiss HNL-273

Habig, Michael
93Swiss HNL-366
95Swiss HNL-393

Habisreutinger, Bruno
93Swiss HNL-293
95Swiss HNL-420
96Swiss HNL-430

Habisreutinger, Marcel
02Swiss HNL-468

Habisreutinger, Roland
95Swiss HNL-398

Habnitt, Dietmar
94German First League-373

Habscheid, Marc
81Saskatoon Blades-14
82Oilers Red Rooster-23
83Moncton Alpines-26
84Oilers Red Rooster-23
84Nova Scotia Oilers-14
88North Stars ADA-13
88Oilers Tenth Anniversary-59
89O-Pee-Chee-151
89O-Pee-Chee Stickers-198
89Red Wings Little Caesars-8
89Topps-151
90Bowman-228
Tiffany-228
90O-Pee-Chee-342
90Panini Stickers-204
90Pro Set-437
90Score Rookie/Traded-24T
90Topps-342
Tiffany-342
90Upper Deck-374
French-374
91Flames IGA-4
91O-Pee-Chee-250
91Panini Stickers-138
91Pro Set-365
French-365
91Red Wings Little Caesars-8
91Score Canadian Bilingual-583
91Score Canadian English-583
91Score Rookie/Traded-33T
91Topps-250
92Score-546
Canadian-546
93Las Vegas Thunder-10
94Las Vegas Thunder-6
95German DEL-15
99Kelowna Rockets-24
00Kelowna Rockets-22
01Kelowna Rockets-23
02Kelowna Rockets-26
03Kelowna Rockets-24

Hachborn, Len
83Springfield Indians-4
85Flyers Postcards-11
90ProCards AHL/IHL-4
91ProCards-318

Hacker, Dan
05Idaho Steelheads-11
06Iowa Stars-10

Hackert, Axel
04German Hannover Scorpions Postcards-9
05German SC Bietigheim-Bissingen Steelers-14

Hackert, Michael
99German Bundesliga 2-216
02German DEL City Press-47
03German DEL-97
04German DEL-120
05German DEL-297
05German DEL-319
06German DEL-58
German Forwards-GF2

Hackert, Oliver
94German First League-155
99German Bundesliga 2-218

Hackett, Jeff
88ProCards AHL-304
89Panini Stickers-276
89ProCards AHL-236
90OPC Premier-39
90Pro Set-624
90Score-388
Canadian-388
91Pro Set Platinum-226
91Bowman-219
91O-Pee-Chee-382
91OPC Premier-108
91Panini Stickers-240
91Pinnacle-119
French-119
91Pro Set-331
French-331
91Score American-367
91Score Canadian Bilingual-326
91Score Canadian Bilingual-642
91Score Canadian English-326
91Score Canadian English-642
91Score Rookie/Traded-92T
91Sharks Sports Action-8
91Topps-382
91Upper Deck-58
French-58
92Bowman-348
92Kraft-29
92O-Pee-Chee-218
92Panini Stickers-123
92Panini Stickers French-123
92Parkhurst-162
Emerald Ice-162
92Pinnacle-105
French-105
92Pro Set-171
92Score-82
Canadian-82
92Stadium Club-108
92Topps-185
Gold-185G
92Ultra-195
92Upper Deck-308
93Blackhawks Coke-19
93Donruss-61
93Leaf-319
93Parkhurst-312
Emerald Ice-312
93Pinnacle-373
Canadian-373
93PowerPlay-312
93Score-38
93Score-541
Gold-541
Canadian-38
Canadian-541
Canadian Gold-541
93Stadium Club-326
Members Only Master Set-326
First Day Issue-326
94Blackhawks Coke-7
94Donruss-35
94Leaf-128
95Blackhawks Coke-8
95Parkhurst International-44
Emerald Ice-44
95Upper Deck-387
Electric Ice-387
Electric Ice Gold-387
96Be A Player-42
Autographs-42
Autographs Silver-42
96Collector's Choice-54
96Donruss-88
Press Proofs-88
96Fleer-147
96Leaf-54
Press Proofs-54
96Pinnacle-110
Artist's Proofs-110
Foil-110
Premium Stock-110
Rink Collection-110
96Score-85
Artist's Proofs-85
Dealer's Choice Artist's Proofs-85
Special Artist's Proofs-85
Golden Blades-85
96Upper Deck-30
97Collector's Choice-47
97Crown Royale-30
Emerald Green-30
Ice Blue-30
Silver-30
97Donruss-116
Press Proofs Silver-116
Press Proofs Gold-116
97Donruss Canadian Ice-101
Dominion Series-101
Provincial Series-101
97Donruss Limited-160
Exposure-160
97Donruss Preferred-139
Cut to the Chase-139
97Donruss Priority-68
Stamp of Approval-68
97Katch-34
Gold-34
Silver-34
97Leaf-32
Fractal Matrix-32
Fractal Matrix Die Cuts-32
97Leaf International-32
Universal Ice-32
97Pacific-160
Copper-160
Emerald Green-160
Ice Blue-160
Red-160
Silver-160
In The Cage Laser Cuts-4
97Pacific Dynagon-27
Copper-27
Dark Grey-27
Emerald Green-27
Ice Blue-27
Red-27
Silver-27
Stonewallers-5
Tandems-39
97Pacific Invincible-30
Copper-30
Emerald Green-30
Ice Blue-30
Red-30
Silver-30
97Pacific Omega-51
Copper-51
Dark Gray-51
Emerald Green-51
Gold-51
Ice Blue-51
97Paramount-44
Copper-44
Dark Grey-44
Emerald Green-44
Ice Blue-44
Red-44
Silver-44
Glove Side Laser Cuts-4
97Pinnacle-72
Artist's Proofs-72
Rink Collection-72
Press Plates Back Black-72
Press Plates Back Cyan-72
Press Plates Back Magenta-72
Press Plates Back Yellow-72
Press Plates Front Black-72
Press Plates Front Cyan-72
Press Plates Front Magenta-72
Press Plates Front Yellow-72
Masks-7
Masks Die Cuts-7
Masks Jumbos-7
97Pinnacle Masks Promos-7
97Pinnacle Tins-3
97Pinnacle Certified-30
Red-30
Mirror Blue-30
Mirror Gold-30
Mirror Red-30
97Pinnacle Inside-41
Coach's Collection-41
Executive Collection-41
Stand Up Guys-7A/B
Stand Up Guys-7C/D
Stand Up Guys Promos-7A/B
Stand Up Guys Promos-7C/D
Stoppers-8
97Pinnacle Tot Cert Platinum Blue-30
97Pinnacle Tot Certi Platinum Gold-30
97Pinnacle Totally Certified Platinum Red-30
97Pinnacle Tot Cert Mirror Platinum Gold-30
97Revolution-30
Copper-30
Emerald-30
Ice Blue-30
Silver-30
Return to Sender Die-Cuts-4
97Score-15
Artist's Proofs-15
Golden Blades-15
97Upper Deck-38
98SLU Hockey One on One-5
98Aurora-41
98Be A Player-27
Press Release-27
98BAP Gold-27
98BAP Autographs-27
98BAP Autographs Gold-27
98BAP Tampa Bay All Star Game-27
98Bowman's Best-63
Refractors-63
Atomic Refractors-63
98Canadiens Team Issue-5
98Crown Royale-69
Limited Series-69
98Finest-86
No Protectors-86
No Protectors Refractors-86
Refractors-86
98Katch-33
98NHL Aces Playing Cards-49
98OPC Chrome-93
Refractors-93
Season's Best-SB5
Season's Best Refractors-SB5
98Pacific-144
Ice Blue-144
Red-144
98Pacific Dynagon Ice-42
Blue-42
Red-42
98Pacific Omega-121
Red-121
Opening Day Issue-121
98Panini Stickers-115
98Paramount-48
Copper-48
Emerald Green-48
Holo-Electric-48
Ice Blue-48
Silver-48
Glove Side Laser Cuts-5
98Revolution-73
Ice Shadow-73
Red-73
98SPx Finite-21
Radiance-21
Spectrum-21
98Topps-93
O-Pee-Chee-93
Season's Best-SB5
98UD Choice-49
98UD Choice Preview-49
98UD Choice Prime Choice Reserve-49
98UD Choice Reserve-49
99SLU Hockey-4
99Aurora-74
Premiere Date-74
Glove Unlimited-10
99BAP Memorabilia-209
Gold-209
Silver-209
99BAP Millennium-134
Emerald-134
Ruby-134
Sapphire-134
Signatures-134
Signatures Gold-134
Goalie Memorabilia-G5
99Crown Royale-69
Limited Series-69
Premiere Date-69
99Hasbro Starting Lineup Cards-4
99O-Pee-Chee-82
99O-Pee-Chee Chrome-82
99O-Pee-Chee Chrome Refractors-82
99Pacific-203
Copper-203
Emerald Green-203
Gold-203
Ice Blue-203
Premiere Date-203
Red-203
In the Cage Net-Fusions-9
99Pacific Dynagon Ice-101
Blue-101
Copper-101
Gold-101
Premiere Date-101
99Pacific Omega-118
Copper-118
Gold-118
Ice Blue-118
Premiere Date-118
99Pacific Prism-71
Holographic Blue-71
Holographic Gold-71
Holographic Mirror-71
Holographic Purple-71
Premiere Date-71
99Panini Stickers-72
99Paramount-116
Copper-116
Emerald-116
Gold-116
Holographic Emerald-116
Holographic Gold-116
Holographic Silver-116
Ice Blue-116
Premiere Date-116
Red-116
Silver-116
Glove Side Net Fusions-10
Ice Advantage-13
Ice Advantage Proofs-13
Ice Alliance-14
99Revolution-74
Premiere Date-74
Red-74
Shadow Series-74
99SPx-79
Radiance-79
Spectrum-79
99Topps/OPC-82
99Topps/OPC Chrome-82
Refractors-82
99Upper Deck-69
Exclusives-69
Exclusives 1 of 1-69
99Upper Deck Gold Reserve-69
99Upper Deck MVP-104
Gold Script-104
Silver Script-104
Super Script-104
ProSign-JH
99Upper Deck Victory-145
99Wayne Gretzky Hockey-88
00Aurora-71
Premiere Date-71
00BAP Memorabilia-30
Emerald-30
Ruby-30
Sapphire-30
Promos-30
00BAP Mem Chicago Sportsfest Copper-30
00BAP Memorabilia Chicago Sportsfest Blue-30
00BAP Memorabilia Chicago Sportsfest Gold-30
00BAP Memorabilia Chicago Sportsfest Ruby-30
00BAP Memorabilia Chicago Sun-Times Ruby-30
00BAP Memorabilia Chicago Sun-Times Gold-30
00BAP Mem Chicago Sun-Times Sapphire-30
00BAP Mem Toronto Fall Expo Copper-30
00BAP Memorabilia Toronto Fall Expo Gold-30
00BAP Memorabilia Toronto Fall Expo Ruby-30
00BAP Parkhurst 2000-P119
00BAP Signature Series-173
Emerald-173
Ruby-173
Sapphire-173
00BAP Ultimate Memorabilia Goalie Sticks-G16
00BAP Ultimate Mem Plante Skate Cards-PS7

00BAP Ultimate Mem Journey Jerseys-JJ4
00BAP Ultimate Mem Journey Emblems-JE4
00BAP Ultimate Mem Journey Numbers-JN4
00Canadiens Postcards-11
00McDonald's Pacific-18
Blue-18
Checklists-3
00O-Pee-Chee-124
00O-Pee-Chee Parallel-124
00Pacific-208
Copper-208
Gold-208
Ice Blue-208
Premiere Date-208
In the Cage Net-Fusions-6
00Paramount-125
Copper-125
Gold-125
Holo-Gold-125
Holo-Silver-125
Ice Blue-125
Premiere Date-125
00Private Stock Game Gear-56
00Private Stock Game Gear Patches-56
00Revolution-75
Blue-75
Premiere Date-75
Red-75
00Stadium Club-19
Souvenirs-SCS4
00Titanium Game Gear-26
00Titanium Draft Day Edition-50
00Topps/OPC-124
Parallel-124
00Topps Chrome-95
OPC Refractors-95
Refractors-95
00Topps Gold Label Class 1-9
Gold-9
00Topps Gold Label Class 2-9
00Topps Gold Label Class 2 Gold-9
00Topps Gold Label Class 3-9
00Topps Gold Label Class 3 Gold-9
00Topps Heritage-126
Autographs-HA-JH
Original Six Relics-OSS-JH
Original Six Relics-OSJA-JH
00Topps Premier Plus-28
Blue Ice-28
00Topps Stars-23
Blue-23
00Upper Deck-321
Exclusives Tier 1-321
Exclusives Tier 2-321
00Upper Deck Vintage-191
00Vanguard Dual Game-Worn Jerseys-18
00Vanguard Dual Game-Worn Patches-18
01Atomic Jerseys-32
01BAP Memorabilia-229
Emerald-229
Ruby-229
Sapphire-229
Goalies Jerseys-GJ11
01BAP Signature Series-161
Autographs-161
Autographs Gold-161
01BAP Update Heritage-H20
01Between the Pipes-73
01Between the Pipes-100
Double Memorabilia-DM5
Goalie Gear-GG2
He Shoots-He Saves Prizes-24
Jerseys-GJ23
Jersey and Stick Cards-GSJ22
Masks-37
Masks Silver-37
Masks Gold-37
Tandems-GT3
01Canadiens Postcards-10
01Crown Royale-76
Blue-76
Premiere Date-76
Red-76
Retail-76
01O-Pee-Chee-230
01O-Pee-Chee Premier Parallel-230
01Pacific-207
Extreme LTD-207
Hobby LTD-207
Premiere Date-207
Retail LTD-207
01Pacific Arena Exclusives-207
01Parkhurst-157
01Private Stock PS-2002-40
01Stadium Club Souvenirs-JHA
01Stadium Club Souvenirs-JHSK
01Titanium Draft Day Edition-49
01Topps-230
OPC Parallel-230
Reserve Emblems-JH
Reserve Jerseys-JH
Reserve Name Plates-JH
Reserve Numbers-JH
Reserve Patches-JH
01UD Challenge for the Cup-45
02BAP First Edition-119
Jerseys-119
02BAP Sig Series Auto Buybacks 1998-27
02BAP Sig Series Auto Buybacks 1999-134
02BAP Sig Series Auto Buybacks 2001-161
02Between the Pipes-42
Gold-42
Silver-42
Jerseys-50
Masks II-29
Masks II Gold-29
Masks II Silver-29
Tandems-9
02Canadiens Postcards-13
02Crown Royale-50
Blue-50
Red-50
Retail-50
02ITG Used Goalie Pad and Jersey-GP18
02ITG Used Goalie Pad and Jersey Gold-GP18
02NHL Power Play Stickers-52
02Pacific Complete-153
Red-153
02Pacific Quest for the Cup-6
Gold-6
02Parkhurst-190
Bronze-190
Gold-190
Silver-190
02Parkhurst Retro-195
Minis-195
02UD Mask Collection-8
02UD Mask Collection-9
02UD Mask Collection-10
02UD Mask Collection Beckett Promos-8
02UD Mask Collection Beckett Promos-9
02UD Mask Collection Beckett Promos-10
02UD Premier Collection-6
02Upper Deck Rookie Update-11
02Vanguard-54
LTD-54
03BAP Memorabilia-125
Emerald-125
Gold-125
Ruby-125
Sapphire-125
Masks III-9
Masks III Gold-9
Masks III Silver-9
Masks III Autographs-M-JH
Masks III Memorabilia-9
Stanley Cup Playoffs-SCP-12
03Beehive-145
Gold-145
Silver-145
03Black Diamond-7
Black-7
Green-7
Red-7
03Crown Royale-73
Blue-73
Retail-73
03Flyers Postcards-8
03ITG Action Jerseys-M27
03ITG Used Signature Series Autographs-JH
03ITG Used Sig Series Autographs Gold-JH
03ITG Used Signature Series Goalie Gear-18
03ITG Used Sig Series Goalie Gear Autos-18
03ITG Used Sig Series Goalie Gear Gold-18
03Pacific-26
Blue-26
Red-26
03Pacific Calder-154
03Pacific Complete-410
Red-410
03Pacific Exhibit-110
03Pacific Exhibit-212
Blue Backs-110
Yellow Backs-110
03Pacific Invincible-73
Blue-73
Red-73
Retail-73
Jerseys-22
03Pacific Luxury Suite-44A
03Pacific Luxury Suite-44B
03Pacific Prism-9
Blue-9
Gold-9
Red-9
03Pacific Quest for the Cup Jerseys-15
03Parkhurst Orig Six Boston Mem -BM7
03Parkhurst Orig Six Boston Mem -BM17
03Parkhurst Orig Six Chicago Mem -CM60
03Private Stock Reserve-191
Blue-191
Patches-191
Red-191
Retail-191
03SP Authentic-64
Limited-64
03Titanium-176
Hobby Jersey Number Parallels-176
Patches-176
Retail-176
03UD Honor Roll-48
03Upper Deck-390
Canadian Exclusives-390
HG-390
UD Exclusives-390
03Upper Deck MVP-318
Gold Script-318
Silver Script-318
Canadian Exclusives-318
SportsNut-SN7
03Upper Deck Victory-17
Bronze-17
Gold-17
Silver-17

Hacquoil, Frank
23V128-1 Paulin's Candy-59

Hadamczik, Alois
94Czech APS Extraliga-287
95Czech APS Extraliga-219
96Czech APS Extraliga-48
97Czech APS Extraliga-313
98Czech OFS-383
99Czech OFS-191
00Czech OFS-236

Haddad, John
95Alaska Gold Kings-6

Haddad, Joseph
05PEI Rocket-19
06PEI Rocket-21

Hadden, Greg
92Northern Michigan Wildcats-8
93Northern Michigan Wildcats-9
95Richmond Renegades-1
00UK Nottingham Panthers-8
00UK Sekonda Superleague-135
01UK Nottingham Panthers-6
02UK Masters of the Ice-1
02UK Masters of the Ice-2
02UK Masters of the Ice-3
02UK Masters of the Ice-4
02UK Masters of the Ice-5
02UK Masters of the Ice-6
02UK Masters of the Ice-7
02UK Masters of the Ice-8
02UK Nottingham Panthers-5
04UK Thommo's Top 10-1

Haddock, Robert
97El Paso Buzzards-18
98El Paso Buzzards-3
01New Mexico Scorpions-21

Haddon, Steve
06Colorado Eagles -10

Hadelov, Andreas
99Swedish Upper Deck-151
00Swedish Upper Deck-135
Masked Men-M6
SHL Signatures-AH
02Swedish SHL-67
02Swedish SHL-290
Masks-5
Netminders-NM9
Parallel-67
Parallel-290
Signatures-10
03Swedish Elite-88
Masks-3
Masks II-3
Signatures II-18
Silver-88
Zero Hero-3
04Swedish Elitset-225
Gold-225
In The Crease-8
Jerseys Series 2-AH
Masks-5
Signatures-1
04Swedish Pure Skills-56
Parallel-56
06Swedish SHL Elitset-127

Hadfield, Vic
44Beehive Group II Photos-319
60NHL Ceramic Tiles-22
61Shirriff/Salada Coins-97
62Topps-60
63Topps-54
64Beehive Group III Photos-129
64Coca-Cola Caps-81
64Topps-62
65Coca-Cola-82
65Topps-27
66Topps-86
66Topps USA Test-19
67Topps-88
68O-Pee-Chee-171
68Shirriff Coins-105
68Topps-74
69O-Pee-Chee-38
69Topps-38
70Colgate Stamps-45
70Dad's Cookies-45
70Esso Power Players-188
70O-Pee-Chee-62
70Sargent Promotions Stamps-126
70Topps-62
71Letraset Action Replays-4
71O-Pee-Chee-9
71Sargent Promotions Stamps-121
71Topps-9
71Toronto Sun-174
72O-Pee-Chee-31
72O-Pee-Chee-250
72O-Pee-Chee-272
Team Canada-13
72Sargent Promotions Stamps-151
72Topps-90
72Topps-110
72Topps-132
72Swedish Stickers-117
73O-Pee-Chee-108
73Topps-181
74NHL Action Stamps-233
74O-Pee-Chee NHL-65
74Penguins Postcards-7
74Topps-65
75O-Pee-Chee NHL-165
75Topps-165
76O-Pee-Chee NHL-226
76Topps-226
91Future Trends Canada '72-36
91Future Trends Canada '72 French-36
91Ultimate Original Six-21
French-21
94Parkhurst Tall Boys-90
95Parkhurst '66-67-98
Coins-98
99BAP Memorabilia AS American Hobby-AH7
99BAP Memorabilia AS American Hobby Autos-AH7
01Topps Archives-41
Autographs-23
03BAP Ultimate Mem Linemates Autos-10
03Parkhurst Original Six New York-57
03Parkhurst Original Six New York-73
Autographs-9
04ITG Franchises US East-410
Original Sticks-EOS6
Original Sticks Gold-EOS6
04ITG Ultimate Memorabilia-172
Gold-172
04UD Legendary Signatures-86
Autographs-VH
Summit Stars-CDN17
Summit Stars Autographs-CDN-VH
04ITG Heroes and Prospects-135
Autographs-VH
04ITG Heroes/Prospects Toronto Expo '05-135
04ITG Heroes/Prospects Expo Heroes/Pros-135

Hadley, Jeff
00Quebec Remparts-5
Signed-5
01Quebec Remparts-4

Hadley, Phil
02UK Coventry Blaze-22

Hadraschek, Christoph
94German First League-579
95German DEL-36

Haegglund, Roger
84Fredericton Express-4

Haeller, Andrea
95Swiss HNL-119

Haelzle, Brad
98Amarillo Rattlers-6
00Amarillo Rattlers-8

Haelzle, Jason
92Windsor Spitfires-4

Hafsmoe, Christian
92Norwegian Elite Series-149

Hagan, Dion
99Alexandria Warthogs-6

Hagberg, Brett
95Neepewa Natives-18

Hagelberg, Jaakko
01Finnish Cardset-298
05Finnish Cardset -108

Hagelin, Bobbie
03Swedish Elite-265
Silver-265

Hagelsperger, Joachim
94German First League-259
95German DEL-355

Hagemo, Nate
04Minnesota Golden Gophers-9
05Minnesota Golden Gophers-11

Hagen, Morten
99Danish Hockey League-204

Hager, Anton
94German First League-235

Hager, Patrick
95Swiss HNL-34
96Swiss HNL-180

Hagerback, Jonas
02Swedish SHL-226
Parallel-226
03Swedish Elite-233
Silver-233

Hagg, Lars
64Swedish Coralli ISHockey-65
65Swedish Coralli ISHockey-65

Haggert, Bob
07Maple Leafs 1967 Commemorative-9

Haggerty, Ryan
96Wheeling Nailers-11
96Wheeling Nailers Photo Pack-12
96Collector's Edge Ice-32
Prism-32
00Prince Albert Raiders-7
04Columbus Cottonmouths-9

Haggerty, Sean
93Detroit Jr. Red Wings-21
93Classic-103
94Finest-119
Super Team Winners-119
Refractors-119
94Leaf Limited World Juniors USA-6
94SP-191
Die Cuts-191
94Detroit Jr. Red Wings-23
95Slapshot-69
95Slapshot-NNO
95Classic-84
95Signature Rookies-51
Signatures-51
95Slapshot Memorial Cup-97
96Summit Metal-177
96Kentucky Thoroughblades-9
97Kentucky Thoroughblades-7
99Kansas City Blades Supercuts-8
00Milwaukee Admirals Keebler-7
00Milwaukee Admirals Postcards-7
01Providence Bruins-16

Hagglund, Roger
83Swedish Semic Elitserien-231
83Swedish Semic VM Stickers-4
86Swedish Panini Stickers-11
87Swedish Panini Stickers-30

Haggroth, Lennart
64Swedish Coralli ISHockey-12
64Swedish Coralli ISHockey-136
65Swedish Coralli ISHockey-12
65Swedish Coralli ISHockey-136
69Swedish Hockey-79
96Swedish Semic Wien Hockey Legends-HL10
97Swedish Alfabilder Autographs-4
01Swedish Alfabilder-4

Haggstrom, Olle
84Swedish Semic Elitserien-203

Hagman, Johan
98Odessa Jackalopes-8

Hagman, Matti
73Finnish Jaakiekko-127
77Finnish Sportscasters-32-747
78Finnish SM-Liiga-39
79Panini Stickers-172
80Pepsi-Cola Caps-26
81Oilers Red Rooster-10
81O-Pee-Chee-113
81O-Pee-Chee Stickers-213
82O-Pee-Chee-108
82O-Pee-Chee Stickers-103
82Post Cereal-6
82Topps Stickers-103
82Swedish Semic VM Stickers-156
83Swedish Semic VM Stickers-46
88Oilers Tenth Anniversary-58
92Future Trends '76 Canada Cup-148
92Future Trends '76 Canada Cup-187
96Finnish SISU Redline-199
04UD All-World-13
04UD All-World-106
Gold-13
Autographs-13
Autographs-106
Dual Autographs-AD-HN
Triple Autographs-AT-KHK
Quad Autographs-AQ-ALS

Hagman, Niklas
98Finnish Kerailysarja-43
00Finnish Cardset-57
01Atomic-109
Premiere Date-109
01Atomic Toronto Fall Expo-109
01BAP Memorabilia-398
Emerald-398
Ruby-398
Sapphire-398
01BAP Signature Series-234
Autographs-234
Autographs Gold-234
01Bowman YoungStars-150
Gold-150
Ice Cubed-150
01Crown Royale-161
01O-Pee-Chee-347
01Pacific Adrenaline-209
Blue-209
Premiere Date-209
Red-209
Retail-209
01Parkhurst-274
01Parkhurst Beckett Promos-274
01Private Stock-122
Gold-122
Premiere Date-122
Retail-122
Silver-122
01Private Stock Pacific Nights-122
01SP Authentic-150
Limited-150
Limited Gold-150
01SP Game Used-78
01SPx-105
01Stadium Club-128
Award Winners-128
Master Photos-128
01Titanium-160
Retail-160
01Titanium Draft Day Edition-131
01Topps-347
01Topps Chrome-165
Refractors-165
Black Border Refractors-165
01Topps Heritage-155
01Topps Reserve-101
01UD Challenge for the Cup-107
01UD Mask Collection-146
Gold-146
01UD Playmakers-119
01UD Premier Collection-97
01UD Top Shelf-128
01Upper Deck-425
Exclusives-425
01Upper Deck Ice-76
01Vanguard-113
Blue-113
Red-113
One of Ones-113
Premiere Date-113
Proofs-113
02BAP First Edition-218
02BAP Memorabilia-37
Emerald-37
Ruby-37
Sapphire-37
NHL All-Star Game-37
NHL All-Star Game Blue-37
NHL All-Star Game Green-37
NHL All-Star Game Red-37
02BAP Memorabilia Toronto Fall Expo-37
02Bowman YoungStars-106
Gold-106
Silver-106
Autographs-NH
Jerseys-NH
Patches-NH
Double Stuff-NH
Triple Stuff-NH
Rivals-NSNH
Rivals Patches-14
Sticks-NH
02O-Pee-Chee-42
02O-Pee-Chee Premier Blue Parallel-42
02O-Pee-Chee Premier Red Parallel-42
02O-Pee-Chee Factory Set-42
02Pacific-153
Blue-153
Red-153
02Pacific Complete-85
Red-85
02Parkhurst-194
Bronze-194
Gold-194
Silver-194
02Topps-42
OPC Blue Parallel-42
OPC Red Parallel-42
Factory Set-42
02Upper Deck Victory-94
Bronze-94
Gold-94
Silver-94
02Upper Deck Vintage-113
02Finnish Cardset-21
02Finnish Cardset Solid Gold Six-Pack-4
03Bowman Future Fabrics-FF-NH
03Bowman Future Fabric Patches-NH
03Bowman Future Rivals-SH
03Bowman Future Rivals Patches-SH
03ITG Action-300
03O-Pee-Chee-76
03OPC Blue-76
03OPC Gold-76
03OPC Red-76
03Pacific Complete-225
Red-225
03Panthers Team Issue-5
03Topps-76
Blue-76
Gold-76
Red-76
03Topps C55-46
Minis-46
Minis American Back-46
Minis American Back Red-46
Minis Bazooka Back-46
Minis Brooklyn Back-46
Minis Hat Trick Back-46
Minis O Canada Back-46
Minis O Canada Back Red-46
Minis Stanley Cup Back-46
04Pacific-110
Blue-110
Red-110
04Swiss Davos Postcards-13
05Upper Deck-85
HG Glossy-85
05Upper Deck Toronto Fall Expo-85
06Stars Team Postcards-7

Hagmann, Jerome
95Swiss HNL-488

Hagmann, Marco
93Swiss HNL-478
95Swiss HNL-303
96Swiss HNL-286

Hagn, Stephan
04German Weiden Blue Devils-9

Hagos, Yared
03Swedish Elite-273
Silver-273
04Swedish Elitset-285
Gold-285
High Expectations-10
Signatures-11
04Swedish Pure Skills-93
Parallel-93
05Swedish SHL Elitset Star Potential-17
05Iowa Stars-9
06Iowa Stars-11

Hagrenius, Jonathan
92Swedish Semic Elitserien Stickers-309

Hagstrom, Anders
67Swedish Hockey-6
67Swedish Hockey-255
69Swedish Hockey-300
70Finnish Jaakiekko-24
70Swedish Hockey-199
71Swedish Hockey-285
72Swedish Stickers-68

Hagstrom, Lars
64Swedish Coralli ISHockey-160
65Swedish Coralli ISHockey-160

Hagstrom, Peter
92Swedish Semic Elitserien Stickers-122
95Swedish Upper Deck 1st Division Stars-DS13
98Swedish UD Choice-93
99Swedish Upper Deck-62

Hague, Alan
93UK Sheffield Steelers-2
94UK Sheffield Steelers-13
95UK Solihull Barons-10

Hague, David
93Quebec Pee-Wee Tournament-860

Hahl, Riku
98Finnish Kerailysarja-73
99Finnish Cardset-242
00Finnish Cardset-28
01BAP Memorabilia-356
Emerald-356
Ruby-356
Sapphire-356
01Parkhurst-311
01SPx-201
01UD Playmakers-111
01UD Premier Collection-93
01UD Top Shelf-126
01Upper Deck Ice-133
01Finnish Cardset-30
01Hershey Bears-10
02Avalanche Postcards-2
02O-Pee-Chee-285
02O-Pee-Chee Premier Blue Parallel-285
02O-Pee-Chee Premier Red Parallel-285
02O-Pee-Chee Factory Set-285
02Pacific Calder-64
Silver-64
02Pacific Complete-541
Red-541
02SPx-106
02Topps-285
OPC Blue Parallel-285
OPC Red Parallel-285
Factory Set-285
02UD Foundations-126
02Upper Deck MVP-199
Gold-199
Classics-199
Golden Classics-199
02Upper Deck Vintage-328
02Finnish Cardset-22
02Hershey Bears-10
03Avalanche Team Issue-7
03ITG Action-101
04Finnish Cardset-39
04Finnish Cardset Signatures-10
04Finnish Cardset Stars of the Game-1
04Swedish Pure Skills-110
Parallel-110
05Black Diamond-3
Emerald-3
Gold-3
Onyx-3
Ruby-3
05Upper Deck-50
HG Glossy-50
Jerseys-J-RIH
NHL Generations-DLH
Notable Numbers-N-RH
05Upper Deck MVP-109
Gold-109
Platinum-109
05Upper Deck Toronto Fall Expo-50
05Finnish Cardset -33
Finnish Cardset Magicmakers-5
06Swedish SHL Elitset-287

Hahn, Chad
93Quebec Pee-Wee Tournament-1454

Hahn, Chris
05Maine Black Bears-7

Haider, Reinhard
94German DEL-29
04German Weiden Blue Devils-10

Haidy, Sam
82Sault Ste. Marie Greyhounds-12
83Sault Ste. Marie Greyhounds-11

Haig, John
97UK Fife Flyers-15
00UK Guildford Flames-9
01UK Guildford Flames-9

Haig, Scot
93Omaha Lancers-8

Haight, Steve
92Oshawa Generals Sheet-12

Hain, Rainer
94German First League-269

Hainanen, Jokke
92Finnish Jyvas-Hyva Stickers-198
00Finnish Cardset-68

Haines, Jaclyn
04Ohio State Buckeyes Women-4

Hains, Maxime
92Quebec Pee-Wee Tournament-838
93Quebec Pee-Wee Tournament-1602

Hainsey, Ron
95Quebec Pee-Wee Tournament-1243
01SPx Rookie Redemption-R16
01Quebec Citadelles-4
02Atomic-115
Blue-115
Gold-115
Red-115
Hobby Parallel-115
02BAP All-Star Edition-141
Gold-141
Silver-141
02BAP First Edition-433R
02BAP Memorabilia-292
Emerald-292
Ruby-292
Sapphire-292
NHL All-Star Game-292
NHL All-Star Game Blue-292
NHL All-Star Game Green-292
NHL All-Star Game Red-292
02BAP Memorabilia Toronto Fall Expo-292
02BAP Signature Series-186
Autographs-186
Autographs Gold-186
Jerseys-SGJ62
Jersey Autographs-SGJ62
02BAP Ultimate Memorabilia-22
Autographs-11
Autographs Gold-11
Calder Candidates-3
02Bowman YoungStars-132
Gold-132
Silver-132
02Canadiens Postcards-20
02Crown Royale-123
Blue-123
Purple-123
Red-123
Retail-123
02ITG Used-93
Calder Jerseys-C8
Calder Jerseys Gold-C8
02NHL Power Play Stickers-51
02Pacific Calder-126
Silver-126
02Pacific Complete-581
Red-581
02Pacific Exclusive-181
Blue-181
Gold-181
02Pacific Heads-Up-138
02Pacific Quest for the Cup-126
Gold-126
02Parkhurst-222
Bronze-222
Gold-222
Silver-222
Hardware-C6
Jerseys-GJ54
02Parkhurst Retro-222
Minis-222
02Private Stock Reserve-168
Blue-168
Red-168
Retail-168
02SP Authentic-189
Signed Patches-PRH
02SP Game Used-83
02SPx-153
02Stadium Club-131
Silver Decoy Cards-131
Proofs-131
02Titanium-122
Blue-122
Red-122
Retail-122
02Topps Chrome-169
Black Border Refractors-169
Refractors-169
02Topps Heritage-144
02Topps Total-402
02UD Artistic Impressions-100
Gold-100
02UD Foundations-157
02UD Honor Roll-157
02UD Mask Collection-159
02UD Piece of History-136
02UD Premier Collection-73
Gold-73
Signatures Bronze-SRH
Signatures Gold-SRH
Signatures Silver-SRH
02UD Top Shelf-94
02Upper Deck-240
Exclusives-240
02Upper Deck Classic Portraits-119
02Upper Deck Rookie Update-165
Autographs-RH
02Vanguard-121
LTD-121
02AHL Top Prospects-16
02Hamilton Bulldogs-3
03Black Diamond-76
Black-76
Green-76
Red-76
03Canadiens Postcards-10
03ITG Action-304
Jerseys-M28
03ITG VIP Making the Bigs-5
03Pacific Montreal Olympic Stadium Show-7
Gold-7
03Parkhurst Original Six Montreal-3
Memorabilia-MM58
03Parkhurst Rookie Road to the NHL-RNJ-14
03Parkhurst Rookie Road to the NHL Gold-RTN-14
03Parkhurst Rookie Road to the NHL Emblem-RTNE-14
03Parkhurst Rookie Road NHL Emblem Gold-RTNE-14
03Upper Deck-105
Canadian Exclusives-105
HG-105
03Upper Deck MVP-234
Gold Script-234
Silver Script-234
Canadian Exclusives-234
03Upper Deck Trilogy Scripts-S1RH
03Upper Deck Trilogy Scripts Limited-S1RH
03Upper Deck Trilogy Scripts Red-S1RH
03Upper Deck Victory-101
Bronze-101
Gold-101
Silver-101
04Hamilton Bulldogs-10
04ITG Heroes and Prospects Emblems-31
04ITG Heroes and Prospects Emblems Gold-31
04ITG Heroes/Prospects He Shoots/Scores-36
04ITG Heroes and Prospects Jerseys-31
04ITG Heroes and Prospects Jerseys Gold-31
04ITG Heroes and Prospects Numbers-31
04ITG Heroes and Prospects Numbers Gold-31
05ITG Heroes/Prosp Toronto Expo Parallel -239
05Hamilton Bulldogs-9
05ITG Heroes and Prospects-239
Autographs Series II-RHA
06O-Pee-Chee-151
Rainbow-151

Hainsworth, George
23V128-1 Paulin's Candy-39
24Anonymous NHL-1
27La Patrie-8
27La Presse Photos-5
33O-Pee-Chee V304A-15
33V129-13
33V252 Canadian Gum-28
34Beehive Group I Photos-321
55Parkhurst-59
Quaker Oats-59
83Hall of Fame-187
83Hall of Fame Postcards-J7
85Hall of Fame-187
94Parkhurst Missing Link Pop-Ups-P2
01Between the Pipes-130
01Between the Pipes-141
01Parkhurst Reprints-PR25
02BAP Ultimate Memorabilia Cup Duels-1
02BAP Ultimate Memorabilia Emblem Attic-1
02BAP Ultimate Mem Great Moments-15
02BAP Ultimate Mem Seams Unbelievable-4
02BAP Ultimate Mem Storied Franchise-14
02BAP Ultimate Mem Vintage Jerseys-14
02Between the Pipes-119
He Shoots-He Saves Prizes-24
Inspirations-I2
Record Breakers-3
Vintage Memorabilia-6
02ITG Used Vintage Memorabilia-VM16
02ITG Used Vintage Memorabilia Gold-VM16
03BAP Memorabilia Vintage Memorabilia-VM-20
03BAP Ultimate Memorabilia Emblem Attic-12
03BAP Ultimate Mem Emblem Attic Gold-12
03BAP Ultimate Memorabilia Heroes-9
03BAP Ultimate Mem Hometown Heroes-6
03BAP Ultimate Mem Hometown Heroes Gold-6
03BAP Ultimate Memorabilia Triple Threads-9
03BAP Ultimate Mem Vint Complete Jersey-5
03BAP Ultimate Mem Vint Comp Jersey Gold-5
03BAP Ultimate Mem Vintage Jerseys-8
03BAP Ultimate Mem Vintage Jerseys Gold-8
03ITG Toronto Fall Expo Forever Rivals-FR10
03ITG Used Sig Series Vintage Mem -23
03ITG Used Sig Series Vintage Mem Gold-23
03ITG VIP Vintage Memorabilia-3
03Parkhurst Orig Six Montreal Mem-MM28
03Parkhurst Rookie Before the Mask-BTM-10
03Parkhurst Rookie Before the Mask Gold-BTM-10
04ITG Franchises Canadian-58
Double Memorabilia-DM1
Double Memorabilia Gold-DM1
Teammates-TM1
Teammates Gold-TM1
04ITG Ultimate Memorabilia-80
Gold-80
Bleu Blanc et Rouge-8
Cornerstones-10
Cornerstones Gold-10
Day In History-10
Day In History-15
Day In History Gold-10
Day In History Gold-15
Gloves are Off-13
Goalie Gear-3
Jerseys-5
Jerseys Gold-5
Original Six-4
Paper Cuts Memorabilia-21
Triple Threads-4
Vezina Trophy-4
05ITG Ultimate Memorabilia Level 1-39
05ITG Ultimate Memorabilia Level 2-39
05ITG Ultimate Memorabilia Level 3-39
05ITG Ultimate Memorabilia Level 4-39
05ITG Ultimate Memorabilia Level 5-39
05ITG Ultimate Mem Bleu Blanc Rouge Autos-3
05ITG Ultimate Mem Decades Jerseys-5
05ITG Ultimate Mem Decades Jerseys Gold-5
05ITG Ultimate Memorabilia Emblem Attic-6
05ITG Ultimate Mem Emblem Attic Gold-6
05ITG Ultimate Memorabilia Goalie Gear-6
05ITG Ultimate Mem Goalie Gear Gold-6
05ITG Ultimate Memorabilia Lumbergraphs-1
05ITG Ultimate Mem Leafs Forever Autos-10
05ITG Ultimate Mem Paper Cut Autos-4
05ITG Ultimate Mem Record Breaker Jerseys-11
05ITG Ultimate Mem RecBreak Jerseys Gold-11
05ITG Ultimate Mem Retro Teammate Jerseys-7
05ITG Ult Mem Retro Teammates Jersey Gold-7
05ITG Heroes and Prospects Hero Mem-HM-48
06Between The Pipes-126
06Between The Pipes-146
06ITG Ultimate Memorabilia-52
Artist Proof-52
Decades-6
Decades Gold-6
Emblem Attic-9
Emblem Attic Gold-9
Lumbergraphs-9
Paper Cuts Autos-4
Retro Teammates-1
Retro Teammates Gold-1
Sensational Season-4
Sensational Season Gold-4

Hair, Houston
99Swift Current Broncos-4

Haiti, Thomas
94German First League-43

Haiusa, Erwin
94German First League-212

Hajdu, Richard
83Victoria Cougars-9
84Victoria Cougars-10

Hajdusek, Stanislav
82Swedish Semic VM Stickers-81
83Swedish Semic VM Stickers-81

Hajek, David
98Spokane Chiefs-9
99Czech Score Blue 2000-31
99Czech Score Red Ice 2000-31
00Czech OFS-116
01Czech OFS-178
01Czech OFS-267
06Asheville Tourists Multi-Ad-27
06Czech OFS-253

Hajek, Miroslav
99Czech OFS-43
02Czech OFS Plus-150
03Czech OFS Plus-110

Hajnos, Janusz
92Finnish Semic-283

Hajt, Bill
74Sabres Postcards-10
75O-Pee-Chee NHL-233
75Topps-233
76O-Pee-Chee NHL-128
76Topps-128
77O-Pee-Chee NHL-27
77Topps-27
78O-Pee-Chee-108
78Topps-108
79O-Pee-Chee-221
79Topps-221
80O-Pee-Chee-337
81Sabres Milk Panels-9
82Post Cereal-2
83O-Pee-Chee-64
84O-Pee-Chee-21
84O-Pee-Chee Stickers-214
84Sabres Blue Shield-7
84Topps-17
84Kelowna Wings-50
85O-Pee-Chee-119
85O-Pee-Chee Stickers-176
85Sabres Blue Shield-10
85Sabres Blue Shield Small-10
85Topps-119
86O-Pee-Chee-52
86Sabres Blue Shield-12
86Sabres Blue Shield Small-12
86Topps-52
87Panini Stickers-26

Hajt, Chris
94Guelph Storm-7
95Bowman Draft Prospects-P16
95Slapshot-87
95Slapshot-436
95Guelph Storm-13
95Classic-61
95Classic-85
96Guelph Storm-7
96Guelph Storm-35
96Guelph Storm Premier Collection-11
96Collect Edge Ice Sign Sealed Delivered-5
97Guelph Storm-7
97Bowman CHL-35
OPC-35
98UD Choice-299
Prime Choice Reserve-299
Reserve-299
98Bowman CHL-2
Golden Anniversary-2
OPC International-2
98Bowman Chrome CHL-2
Golden Anniversary-2
Golden Anniversary Refractors-2
OPC International-2
OPC International Refractors-2
Refractors-2
99Hamilton Bulldogs-2
00Hamilton Bulldogs-5
01Upper Deck Victory-370
Gold-370
01Hamilton Bulldogs-2
03Pacific Complete-530
Red-530
04Portland Pirates-11

Hakala, Antero
66Finnish Jaakiekkosarja-212

Hakala, Yrjo
65Finnish Hellas-87

66Finnish Jaakiekkosarja-86
05Finnish Tappara Legendat-19
Hakamaki, Pentti
72Finnish Panda Toronto-34
Hakanen, Markku
65Finnish Hellas-118
66Finnish Jaakiekkosarja-193
70Finnish Jaakiekko-121
71Finnish Suomi Stickers-171
72Finnish Jaakiekko-122
72Finnish Panda Toronto-20
73Finnish Jaakiekko-176
Hakanen, Matti
70Finnish Jaakiekko-122
71Finnish Suomi Stickers-172
72Finnish Panda Toronto-21
73Finnish Jaakiekko-242
Hakanen, Reijo
65Finnish Hellas-128
66Finnish Jaakiekkosarja-202
70Finnish Jaakiekko-123
71Finnish Suomi Stickers-173
72Finnish Panda Toronto-22
73Finnish Jaakiekko-177
Hakanen, Timo
95Collector's Choice-327
Player's Club-327
Player's Club Platinum-327
95Finnish SISU-366
Drafted Dozen-9
96Finnish SISU Redline-159
98Finnish Kerailysarja-267
99Finnish Cardset-156
02Finnish Cardset-169
Hakanson, Mikael
95Swedish Upper Deck-164
98Swedish UD Choice-58
00St. John's Maple Leafs-10
02Swedish SHL-21
02Swedish SHL-216
Parallel-21
Parallel-216
03Swedish Elite-76
Silver-76
04Swedish Elitset-68
Gold-68
05Swedish SHL Elitset-81
Hakansson, Anders
81North Stars Postcards-10
83Penguins Heinz Photos-10
84Kings Smokey-7
84O-Pee-Chee-85
Hakansson, Jonas
91Swedish Semic Elitserien Stickers-199
92Swedish Semic Elitserien Stickers-216
Hakansson, Mikael
91Swedish Semic Elitserien Stickers-329
92Swedish Semic Elitserien Stickers-94
93Parkhurst-539
Emerald Ice-539
93Swedish Semic Elitserien-66
94Swedish Leaf-208
95Swedish Leaf-106
97Swedish Collector's Choice-39
99Swedish Upper Deck-43
02Swedish SHL Signatures Series II-7
06Swedish SHL Elitset-81
Performers-9
Hakewill, Jim
05Idaho Steelheads-12
Hakkarainen, Esa
73Finnish Jaakiekko-307
78Finnish SM-Liiga-156
80Finnish Mallasjuoma-112
Hakkarainen, Mikko
05Finnish Cardset -259
06Finnish Cardset-312
Hakkinen, Pasi
98Finnish Kerailysarja-185
99Finnish Cardset-303
00Finnish Cardset-318
01UK Nottingham Panthers-21
03Finnish Cardset-58
04Finnish Cardset-62
05Finnish Cardset -50
Hakstol, Dave
92Indianapolis Ice-12
93Indianapolis Ice-11
94Minnesota Moose-15
95Minnesota Moose-10
03North Dakota Fighting Sioux-29
04North Dakota Fighting Sioux-29
Hakulinen, Markku
77Finnish Sportscasters-82-1955
78Finnish SM-Liiga-126
82Swedish Semic VM Stickers-47
Hakulinen, Yrjo
71Finnish Suomi Stickers-260
77Finnish Sportscasters-82-1955
78Finnish SM-Liiga-128
80Finnish Mallasjuoma-83
Hala, Jiri
94Czech APS Extraliga-96
Hala, Miroslav
93Quebec Pee-Wee Tournament-1557
04Czech OFS Czech/Slovak-27
Halaj, Juraj
04Czech OFS Czech/Slovak-28
04Slovakian Poprad Team Set-18
Halak, Jaroslav
06Between The Pipes-17
Autographs-AJHA
06AHL Top Prospects-13
06Hamilton Bulldogs-14
07Upper Deck Ovation-77
07Upper Deck Victory-227
Black-227
Gold-227
Halasz, David
03Ottawa 67's-10
04Oshawa Generals-20
04Oshawa Generals Autographs-20
Hale, David
98Sioux City Musketeers-7
99Sioux City Musketeers-7
03BAP Memorabilia-185
Emerald-185
Gold-185
Ruby-185
Sapphire-185
Super Rookies-SR4
Super Rookies Gold-SR4
Super Rookies Silver-SR4
03BAP Ultimate Memorabilia Autographs-116
Gold-116
03BAP Ultimate Mem Rookie Jersey Emblems-11
03BAP Ultimate Mem Rookie Jsy Emblem Gold-11
03BAP Ultimate Mem Rookie Jersey Numbers-11
03BAP Ultimate Mem Rookie Jsy Number Gold-11
03BAP Ultimate Memorabilia Triple Threads-30
03Black Diamond-156
Black-156
Green-156
Red-156
03Bowman-145
Gold-145
03Bowman Chrome-145
Refractors-145
Gold Refractors-145
Xfractors-145
03Devils Team Issue-25
03ITG Used Signature Series-124
Autographs Gold-124
03ITG VIP Rookie Debut-4
03Pacific Complete-595
Red-595
03Pacific Luxury Suite-70
Gold-70
03Pacific Quest for the Cup-125
03Pacific Supreme-127
Blue-127
Red-127
Retail-127
03Parkhurst Rookie-189
Rookie Emblems-RE-11
Rookie Emblem Autographs-RE-DHA
Rookie Emblems Gold-RE-11
Rookie Jerseys-RJ-11
Rookie Jersey Autographs-RJ-DHA
Rookie Jerseys Gold-RJ-11
Rookie Numbers-RN-11
Rookie Number Autographs-RN-DHA
Rookie Numbers Gold-RN-11
03Private Stock Reserve-128
Blue-128
Red-128
Retail-128
03SP Authentic-98
Limited-98
03SP Game Used-70
Gold-70
03SPx-198
Radiance-198
Spectrum-198
03Titanium-126
Hobby Jersey Number Parallels-126
Retail-126
Retail Jersey Number Parallels-126
03Topps C55-153
Minis-153
Minis American Back-153
Minis American Back Red-153
Minis Bazooka Back-153
Minis Brooklyn Back-153
Minis Hat Trick Back-153
Minis O Canada Back-153
Minis O Canada Back Red-153
Minis Stanley Cup Back-153
03Topps Pristine-182
03Topps Pristine-183
03Topps Pristine-184
Gold Refractor Die Cuts-182
Gold Refractor Die Cuts-183
Gold Refractor Die Cuts-184
Refractors-182
Refractors-183
Refractors-184
Press Plates Black-182
Press Plates Black-183
Press Plates Black-184
Press Plates Cyan-182
Press Plates Cyan-183
Press Plates Cyan-184
Press Plates Magenta-182
Press Plates Magenta-183
Press Plates Magenta-184
Press Plates Yellow-182
Press Plates Yellow-183
Press Plates Yellow-184
03Topps Traded-TT124
Blue-TT124
Gold-TT124
Red-TT124
03Upper Deck-228
Canadian Exclusives-228
HG-228
03Upper Deck MVP-462
03Upper Deck Trilogy-159
Limited-159
04Albany River Rats-8
05Devils Team Issue-14
05Upper Deck-363
05Albany River Rats-10
06Devils Team Set-9
Hale, Larry
70Esso Power Players-215
70Sargent Promotions Stamps-155
71Sargent Promotions Stamps-154
71Toronto Sun-196
72O-Pee-Chee-53
72Topps-44
75Houston Aeros WHA-2
Hale, Rob
88Lethbridge Hurricanes-10
89Lethbridge Hurricanes-7
Hale, Ryan
03North Dakota Fighting Sioux-6
Hales, Megan
98New Hampshire Wildcats-9
Haley, John
90Richmond Renegades-16
Haley, Michael
03Sarnia Sting-9
Haley, Mike
94Spokane Chiefs-12
95Spokane Chiefs-17
96Spokane Chiefs-14
Haley, Ryan
93Quebec Pee-Wee Tournament-776
Halfkenny, Julius
00Sarnia Sting-11
Halfmann, Andreas
94German First League-526
Halfnight, Ashlin
93Donruss Team USA-8
93Pinnacle-482
Canadian-482
98New Haven Beast-15
99German Bundesliga 2-136
Halifax, Sean
93Red Deer Rebels-8
96Knoxville Cherokees-3
Halifax, Shane
03Portland Winter Hawks-12
05Regina Pats-7
Halischuk, Matt
04St. Michael's Majors-7
06Kitchener Rangers-9
Halkidis, Bob
85Sabres Blue Shield-11
85Sabres Blue Shield Small-11
85London Knights-7
86Sabres Blue Shield-13
86Sabres Blue Shield Small-13
87Sabres Blue Shield-10
88Sabres Blue Shield-8
88Sabres Wonder Bread/Hostess-8
89ProCards AHL-270
91Maple Leafs PLAY-16
92Pro Set-190
94Lightning Photo Album-15
95Atlanta Knights-11
96Carolina Monarchs-12
98German DEL-91
Halkidis, George
03Kitchener Rangers Memorial Cup-10
03Peoria Rivermen-9
Halko, Steve
93Michigan Wolverines-8
96Springfield Falcons-20
97Hurricanes Team Issue-10
98Hurricanes Team Issue-11
98New Haven Beast-6
99BAP Millennium-47
Emerald-47
Ruby-47
Sapphire-47
Signatures-47
Signatures Gold-47
00Upper Deck-263
Exclusives Tier 1-263
Exclusives Tier 2-263
01O-Pee-Chee-251
01O-Pee-Chee Premier Parallel-251
01Topps-251
OPC Parallel-251
01Worcester Icecats-19
02BAP Sig Series Auto Buybacks 1999-47
02Lowell Lock Monsters-9
Hall, Adam
00Michigan State Spartans-8
02Atomic-116
Blue-116
Gold-116
Red-116
Hobby Parallel-116
02BAP All-Star Edition-143
Gold-143
Silver-143
02BAP Memorabilia-294
Emerald-294
Ruby-294
Sapphire-294
NHL All-Star Game-294
NHL All-Star Game Blue-294
NHL All-Star Game Green-294
NHL All-Star Game Red-294
02BAP Memorabilia Toronto Fall Expo-294
02BAP Signature Series-181
Autographs-181
Autographs Gold-181
02BAP Ultimate Memorabilia-24
Autographs-28
Calder Candidates-19
02Bowman YoungStars-134
Gold-134
Silver-134
Autographs-AH
Jerseys-AH
Patches-AH
Double Stuff-AH
Triple Stuff-AH
Rivals-AHMW
Rivals Patches-11
Sticks-AH
02Crown Royale-124
Blue-124
Purple-124
Red-124
Retail-124
02ITG Used-187
Calder Jerseys-C14
Calder Jerseys Gold-C14
02Pacific Calder-129
Silver-129
02Pacific Complete-560
Red-560
02Pacific Exclusive-182
Blue-182
Gold-182
02Pacific Quest for the Cup-129
Gold-129
02Parkhurst-224
Bronze-224
Gold-224
Silver-224
02Parkhurst Retro-224
Minis-224
02Private Stock Reserve-169
Blue-169
Red-169
Retail-169
02SP Authentic-190
Signed Patches-PHA
02SP Game Used-84
02SPx-154
02Stadium Club-136
Silver Decoy Cards-136
Proofs-136
02Titanium-124
Blue-124
Red-124
Retail-124
02Topps Chrome-156
Black Border Refractors-156
Refractors-156
02Topps Heritage-137
02Topps Total-413
02UD Foundations-134
02UD Honor Roll-117
02UD Mask Collection-149
02UD Piece of History-137
02UD Premier Collection-68
Gold-68
Signatures Bronze-SAH
Signatures Gold-SAH
Signatures Silver-SAH
02UD Top Shelf-131
02Upper Deck-211
Exclusives-211
02Upper Deck Classic Portraits-120
02Upper Deck Rookie Update-152A
02Upper Deck Rookie Update-152B
02Upper Deck Rookie Update-152C
02Upper Deck Vintage-337
02Vanguard-122
LTD-122
03Bowman-63
Gold-63
Future Fabrics-FF-AH
Future Fabric Patches-AH
Future Rivals-HH
Future Rivals Patches-HH
03Bowman Chrome-63
Refractors-63
Gold Refractors-63
Xfractors-63
03ITG Action-328
03O-Pee-Chee-198
03OPC Blue-198
03OPC Gold-198
03OPC Red-198
03Pacific-187
Blue-187
Red-187
03Pacific Complete-233
Red-233
03SP Authentic Sign of the Times-AH
03Topps-198
Blue-198
Gold-198
Red-198
03Topps C55-14
Minis-14
Minis American Back-14
Minis American Back Red-14
Minis Bazooka Back-14
Minis Brooklyn Back-14
Minis Hat Trick Back-14
Minis O Canada Back-14
Minis O Canada Back Red-14
Minis Stanley Cup Back-14
Relics-TRAH
03Topps Traded Future Phenoms-FP-AH
03UD Honor Roll Signature Class-SC28
03Upper Deck-353
Canadian Exclusives-353
HG-353
UD Exclusives-353
03Upper Deck MVP-242
Gold Script-242
Silver Script-242
Canadian Exclusives-242
ProSign-PS-RM
03Upper Deck Trilogy Scripts-S1HL
03Upper Deck Trilogy Scripts Limited-S1HL
03Upper Deck Trilogy Scripts Red-S1HL
04Pacific-146
Blue-146
Red-146
04Upper Deck Jersey Autographs-GJA-AH
05Be A Player Signatures-AH
05Be A Player Signatures Gold-AH
05Hot Prospects Hot Materials-HMAH
05Parkhurst-278
Facsimile Auto Parallel-278
True Colors-TCNSH
True Colors-TCNSH
05SP Game Used Authentic Fabrics Dual-HL
05SP Game Used Authentic Fabrics Quad-KLHV
05SP Game Used Authentic Patches Quad -KLHV
05SP Game Used Authentic Patches Dual-HL
05Upper Deck-108
Big Playmakers-B-AH
HG Glossy-108
Patches-P-AHA
Ice Fresh Ice-FIAH
Ice Fresh Ice Glass-FIAH
Ice Fresh Ice Glass Patches-FIPAH
05Upper Deck MVP-218
Gold-218
Platinum-218
Materials-M-AH
05Upper Deck Toronto Fall Expo-108
06Fleer Fabricology-FAH
06Upper Deck-378
Exclusives Parallel-378
High Gloss Parallel-378
Masterpieces-378
Signature Sensations-SSAH
Hall, Billy
917th Inn. Sketch OHL-297
92Ottawa 67's-11
Hall, Chris
92Oshawa Generals Sheet-8
93Oshawa Generals-23
95Slapshot Memorial Cup-53
Hall, Dean
89Johnstown Chiefs-28
Hall, Del
75Phoenix Roadrunners WHA-10
76O-Pee-Chee WHA-78
76Phoenix Roadrunners WHA-4
Hall, Glenn
44Beehive Group II Photos-100
44Beehive Group II Photos-175
57Topps-20
58Topps-13
59Topps-28
59Topps-32
60Shirriff Coins-61
60Topps-25
Stamps-20
61Shirriff/Salada Coins-29
61Topps-22
61Topps-32
61Topps-44
62El Producto Discs-2
62Shirriff Coins-49
62Topps-24
Hockey Bucks-8
63Chex Photos-17
63Topps-23
63Toronto Star-15
64Beehive Group III Photos-35
64Coca-Cola Caps-19
64Topps-12
64Topps-110
64Toronto Star-11
65Coca-Cola-19
65Topps-55
66Post Cereal Box Backs-3
66Topps-54
66Topps-126
67Topps-65
67Topps-129
68O-Pee-Chee-111
68O-Pee-Chee-215
Puck Stickers-13
68Shirriff Coins-151
68Topps-111
69O-Pee-Chee-12
69O-Pee-Chee-207
69O-Pee-Chee-211
Stamps-11
69Topps-12
70Esso Power Players-235
70O-Pee-Chee-210
Deckle-27
72Finnish Semic World Championship-187
72Swedish Semic World Championship-187
83Hall of Fame-114
83Hall of Fame Postcards-H8
85Hall of Fame-114
91Arizona Icecats-19
91Star Pics-52
92Blues UD Best of the Blues-1
94Parkhurst Missing Link-46
94Parkhurst Missing Link-141
94Parkhurst Missing Link-152
94Parkhurst Missing Link-158
94Parkhurst Missing Link-159
94Parkhurst Tall Boys-32
94Parkhurst Tall Boys-133
94Parkhurst Tall Boys-165
94Parkhurst Tall Boys-166
94Arizona Icecats-21
94Arizona Icecats-23
95Parkhurst '66-67-31
95Parkhurst '66-67-121
Coins-31
97SLU Canadian Timeless Legends-5
98SLU Canadian Timeless Legends-4
98Blackhawks Legends-2
99Upper Deck Century Legends-17
Century Collection-17
99Upper Deck Retro-93
Gold-93
Platinum-93
Generation-G3A
Generation Level 2-G3A
00Upper Deck Legends-28
Legendary Collection Bronze-28
Legendary Collection Gold-28
Legendary Collection Silver-28
01BAP Memorabilia Goalie Traditions-GT7
01BAP Memorabilia Goalie Traditions-GT17
01BAP Memorabilia Goalie Traditions-GT22
01BAP Memorabilia Goalie Traditions-GT23
01BAP Memorabilia Goalie Traditions-GT25
01BAP Memorabilia Goalie Traditions-GT26
01BAP Memorabilia Goalie Traditions-GT38
01BAP Memorabilia Goalie Traditions-GT39
01BAP Signature Series Vintage Autographs-VA-13
01BAP Ultimate Mem All-Star History-12
01BAP Ultimate Memorabilia Calder Trophy-23
01BAP Ultimate Memorabilia Cornerstones-3
01BAP Ultimate Memorabilia Decades-10
01BAP Ultimate Memorabilia Emblem Attic-5
01BAP Ultimate Mem Retired Numbers-10
01BAP Ultimate Memorabilia Retro Trophies-10
01BAP Ultimate Memorabilia Retro Trophies-14
01BAP Ultimate Mem Retro Teammates-7
01BAP Update Rocket's Rivals-RR-9
01Between the Pipes-121
01Between the Pipes-140
He Shoots-He Saves Points-14
He Shoots-He Saves Prizes-5
Jersey and Stick Cards-GSJ39
Record Breakers-RB20
Trophy Winners-TW7
Trophy Winners-TW13
Trophy Winners-TW16
Vintage Memorabilia-VM8
01Greats of the Game-2
Autographs-2
01Parkhurst Autographs-PA2
01Topps Archives-8
Arena Seats-ASGHA
Autographs-5
01Topps Heritage Autographs-AGH
01Topps Heritage Salute-S3
01UD Stanley Cup Champs-3
01Upper Deck Legends-12
01Upper Deck Legends-80
02BAP NHL All-Star History-12
02BAP Ultimate Memorabilia Conn Smythe-3
02BAP Ultimate Memorabilia Cup Duels-4
02BAP Ultimate Memorabilia Emblem Attic-17
02BAP Ultimate Memorabilia Great Moments-13
02BAP Ultimate Memorabilia Number Ones-3
02BAP Ultimate Memorabilia Numerology-1
02BAP Ultimate Mem Retro Teammates-3
02BAP Ultimate Memorabilia Retro Trophies-8
02BAP Ultimate Mem Seams Unbelievable-3
02BAP Ultimate Mem Vintage Jerseys-17
02BAP Ultimate Mem Vintage Jersey Autos-5
02Between the Pipes-117
Goalie Autographs-34
He Shoots-He Saves Prizes-30
Record Breakers-6
Vintage Memorabilia-12
02Parkhurst Retro Nicknames-RN10
03BAP Ultimate Memorabilia Cornerstones-6
03BAP Ultimate Memorabilia Emblem Attic-20
03BAP Ultimate Mem Emblem Attic Gold-20
03BAP Ultimate Memorabilia The Goal-4
03BAP Ultimate Memorabilia The Goal-6
03BAP Ultimate Memorabilia The Goal-7
03BAP Ultimate Memorabilia The Goal-9
03BAP Ultimate Memorabilia The Goal-11
03BAP Ultimate Memorabilia The Goal-12
03BAP Ultimate Memorabilia The Goal-13
03BAP Ultimate Memorabilia The Goal-14
03Canada Post-16
Autographs-16
03ITG Used Signature Series Goalie Gear-30
03ITG Used Sig Series Goalie Gear Autos-30
03ITG Used Sig Series Goalie Gear Gold-30
03ITG VIP MVP-14
03ITG VIP Vintage Memorabilia-20
03Pacific Exhibit-220
03Parkhurst Original Six Chicago-50
03Parkhurst Original Six Chicago-61
03Parkhurst Original Six Chicago-85
Autographs-5
Inserts-C4
Inserts-C9
Memorabilia-CM27
Memorabilia-CM33
Memorabilia-CM40
Memorabilia-CM51
03Parkhurst Original Six Detroit-47
03Parkhurst Original Six Detroit-62
03Parkhurst Original Six Detroit-90
Autographs-OS-GH
Inserts-D-9
03Parkhurst Rookie Before the Mask-BTM-12
03Parkhurst Rookie Before the Mask Gold-BTM-12
03Parkhurst Rookie ROYalty-VR-19
03Parkhurst Rookie ROYalty Gold-VR-19
04ITG NHL AS FANtasy AS History Jerseys-SB12
04ITG Franchises He Shoots/Scores Prizes-29
04ITG Franchises US West-158
04ITG Franchises US West-211
04ITG Franchises US West-285
Autographs-A-GH1
Autographs-A-GH2
Autographs-A-GH3
Barn Burners-WBB10
Barn Burners Gold-WBB10
Double Memorabilia-WDM8
Double Memorabilia Autographs-WDMGH
Double Memorabilia Gold-WDM8
Goalie Gear-WGG6
Goalie Gear Autographs-WGGGH
Goalie Gear Gold-WGG6
Memorabilia-WSM12
Memorabilia Autographs-WSMGH
Memorabilia Gold-WSM12
Original Sticks-WOS4
Original Sticks Autographs-WOSGH
Original Sticks Gold-WOS4
Teammates-WTM3
Teammates Gold-WTM3
Triple Memorabilia Autographs-WTMGH
Triple Memorabilia Gold-WTM6
Trophy Winners-WTW7
Trophy Winners Gold-WTW7
04ITG Ultimate Memorabilia-120
04ITG Ultimate Memorabilia-129
04ITG Ultimate Memorabilia-185
Gold-120
Gold-129
Gold-185
Auto Threads-2
Autographs-16
Autographs-22
Autographs Gold-16
Autographs Gold-22
Calder Trophy-6
Conn Smythe Trophy-7
Day In History-7
Day In History Gold-7
Emblem Attic-4
Emblem Attic Gold-4
Goalie Gear-11
Nicknames-8
Nickname Autographs-14
Original Six-9
Original Six-11
Original Six-16
Retro Teammates-3
Vintage Lumber-3
04SP Authentic Buybacks-60
04SP Authentic Octographs-OS-GOA
04SP Authentic Sign of the Times-DS-FH
04UD Legendary Signatures-39
AKA Autographs-AKA-HA
Autographs-HA
HOF Inks-HOF-HA
04UD Legends Classics-26
04UD Legends Classics-74
04UD Legends Classics-88
Gold-26
Gold-74
Gold-88
Platinum-26
Platinum-74
Platinum-88
Silver-26
Silver-74
Silver-88
Signature Moments-M33
Signatures-CS33
Signatures-DC12
Signatures-TC4
Signatures-QC1
04ITG Heroes and Prospects-152
Autographs-GH
04ITG Heroes/Prospects Toronto Expo '05-152
04ITG Heroes/Prospects Expo Heroes/Pros-152
05ITG Heroes/Prosp Toronto Expo Parallel -3
05Beehive-228
05Between the Pipes-9
Autographs-A-GH
Jerseys-GUJ-6
Signed Memorabilia-SM-4
05ITG Ultimate Memorabilia Level 1-43
05ITG Ultimate Memorabilia Level 2-43
05ITG Ultimate Memorabilia Level 3-43
05ITG Ultimate Memorabilia Level 4-43
05ITG Ultimate Memorabilia Level 5-43
05ITG Ultimate Mem Decades Jerseys-5
05ITG Ultimate Mem Decades Jerseys Gold-5
05ITG Ultimate Memorabilia Double Autos-13
05ITG Ultimate Mem Double Autos Gold-13
05ITG Ultimate Mem Double Mem Autos-12
05ITG Ultimate Mem Double Mem Autos Gold-12
05ITG Ultimate Memorabilia Emblem Attic-19
05ITG Ultimate Mem Emblem Attic Gold-19
05ITG Ultimate Memorabilia Gloves Are Off-12
05ITG Ultimate Mem Gloves Are Off Gold-12
05ITG Ultimate Memorabilia Goalie Gear-8
05ITG Ultimate Mem Goalie Gear Gold-8
05ITG Ultimate Memorabilia Jersey Autos-9
05ITG Ultimate Mem Jersey Autos Gold-9
05ITG Ultimate Mem Pass the Torch Jerseys-14
05ITG Ultimate Mem Passing Torch Jsy Gold-14
05ITG Ultimate Mem Seams Unbelievable-7
05ITG Ultimate Mem Seam Unbelievable Gold-7
05ITG Ultimate Memorabilia Stick Autos-8
05ITG Ultimate Mem Stick Autos Gold-8
05ITG Ultimate Mem 3 Star of the Game Jsy-9
05ITG Ult Mem 3 Star of the Game Jsy Gold-9
05ITG Ultimate Memorabilia Triple Autos-1
05ITG Ultimate Mem Triple Autos Gold-1
05ITG Ultimate Mem Triple Threads Jerseys-8
05ITG Ultimate Mem Triple Thread Jsy Gold-8
05ITG Ultimate Memorabilia Ultimate Autos-34
05ITG Ultimate Mem Ultimate Autos Gold-34
05ITG Ultimate Memorabilia Vintage Lumber-13
05ITG Ultimate Mem Vintage Lumber Gold-13
05NHL Legends Medallions-10
05UD Artifacts-121
Blue-121
Gold-121
Green-121
Pewter-121
Red-121
Gold Autographed-121
05Ultimate Coll Ultimate Sigs Trios-UTEHP
05Upper Deck Trilogy Ice Scripts-IS-HL
05ITG Heroes and Prospects-3
Autographs-A-GH
Future Teammates-FT12
Hero Memorabilia-HM-23
06Between The Pipes-91
06Between The Pipes-141
06Between The Pipes-147
Autographs-AGH
Complete Jersey-CJ02
Complete Jersey Gold-CJ02
Double Jerseys-DJ11
Double Jerseys Gold-DJ11
Emblems-GUE55
Emblems Gold-GUE55
Emblems Autographs-GUE55
Gloves-GG19
Gloves Gold-GG19
Jerseys-GUJ55
Jerseys Gold-GUJ55
Jerseys Autographs-GUJ55
Numbers-GUN55
Numbers Gold-GUN55
Numbers Autographs-GUN55
Shooting Gallery-SG04
Shooting Gallery-SG09
Shooting Gallery-SG10
Shooting Gallery Gold-SG04
Shooting Gallery Gold-SG09
Shooting Gallery Gold-SG10
Stick and Jersey-SJ12
Stick and Jersey Gold-SJ12
Stick and Jersey Autographs-SJ12
06ITG Ultimate Memorabilia-57
Artist Proof-57
Autos-15
Autos Gold-15
Bowman Factor-1
Bowman Factor Gold-1
Bowman Factor Autos-1
Bowman Factor Autos Gold-1
Boys Will Be Boys-8
Boys Will Be Boys Gold-8
Decades-6
Decades Gold-6
Jerseys Autos-2
Jerseys Autos Gold-2
Passing The Torch-16
Passing The Torch Gold-16
R.O.Y. Autos-19
R.O.Y. Autos Gold-19
R.O.Y. Emblems-19
R.O.Y. Emblems Gold-19
R.O.Y. Jerseys-19
R.O.Y. Jerseys Gold-19
R.O.Y. Numbers-19
R.O.Y. Numbers Gold-19
Retro Teammates-7
Retro Teammates Gold-7
Stick Rack-12
Stick Rack Gold-12
Sticks Autos-19
Sticks Autos Gold-19
06UD Artifacts-116
Blue-116
Gold-116
Platinum-116
Radiance-116
Red-116
Hall, Jason
90Rayside-Balfour Jr. Canadians-8
91Rayside-Balfour Jr. Canadians-6
94German First League-315
Hall, Joe
10Sweet Caporal Postcards-2
11C55-2
12C57-16
83Hall of Fame Postcards-G6
85Hall of Fame-97
Hall, Mark
06Kamloops Blazers-10
Hall, Maurice
94Anchorage Aces-19
Hall, Mike
98Indianapolis Ice-9
00Trenton Titans-4
Hall, Murray
44Beehive Group II Photos-101
62Topps-43
64Beehive Group III Photos-36
64Beehive Group III Photos-73
66Topps-105
70Canucks Royal Bank-6
70Esso Power Players-51
70O-Pee-Chee-118
70Sargent Promotions Stamps-224
70Topps-118
71Canucks Royal Bank-3
71O-Pee-Chee-109
71Sargent Promotions Stamps-211
71Topps-109
71Toronto Sun-279
72O-Pee-Chee-294
72Sargent Promotions Stamps-212
73Quaker Oats WHA-14
75Houston Aeros WHA-3
Hall, Randy
89Niagara Falls Thunder-7
897th Inn. Sketch OHL-132
907th Inn. Sketch OHL-74
917th Inn. Sketch OHL-210
93Niagara Falls Thunder-26
Hall, Scott
92British Columbia JHL-219
Hall, Taylor
81Regina Pats-15
82Regina Pats-19
83Regina Pats-19
84Canucks Team Issue-10
85Canucks Team Issue-9
86Canucks Team Issue-6
86Fredericton Express-10
90ProCards AHL/IHL-303
92Tulsa Oilers-6
94Central Hockey League-97
95Central Hockey League-60
99Corpus Christi IceRays-28
Hall, Tobias
96OCN Blizzard-17
Hall, Todd
91Upper Deck Czech World Juniors-77
97Hartford Wolf Pack-10
98Hartford Wolf Pack-10
99Hartford Wolf Pack-9
00Hartford Wolf Pack-11
Hall, Wayne
03Odessa Jackalopes-10
04Memphis RiverKings-22
Halla, Hans Petter
92Norwegian Elite Series-154
Hallback, Mathias
92Swedish Semic Elitserien Stickers-98
93Swedish Semic Elitserien-71
94Swedish Leaf-241
Hallberg, Per
98Swedish UD Choice-168
99Swedish Upper Deck-170
00Swedish Upper Deck-155
02Swedish SHL-169
Parallel-169
03Swedish Elite-35
Signatures II-2
Silver-35
04Swedish Elitset-182
Gold-182
05Swedish SHL Elitset-183
Halldorson, Derek
97Saskatoon Blades-9
00Saskatoon Blades-21
02Pee Dee Pride RBI-138
Halldorson, Laura
98Minnesota Golden Gophers Women-7
04Minnesota Golden Gophers Women-14
Hallee, Yan
00Val d'Or Foreurs-2
Signed-2
Hallegard, Jeff
83Swedish Semic Elitserien-98
86Swedish Panini Stickers-76
Haller, Andreas
93Swiss HNL-219
98Swiss Power Play Stickers-58
99Swiss Panini Stickers-58
00Swiss Panini Stickers-106
00Swiss Slapshot Mini-Cards-HCD4
01Swiss HNL-104
02Swiss HNL-2
04Swiss Davos Postcards-14
Haller, Kevin
88Regina Pats-7
89Regina Pats-6
90ProCards AHL/IHL-265
91Pro Set Platinum-250
91Bowman-28
91O-Pee-Chee-473
91Pinnacle-307
French-307
91Pro Set-525
French-525
91Sabres Blue Shield-6
91Sabres Pepsi/Campbell's-6
91Score American-386
91Score Canadian Bilingual-276
91Score Canadian English-276
91Stadium Club-382
91Topps-473
91Upper Deck-192
French-192
91Rochester Americans Kodak-14
92Bowman-301
92Canadiens Postcards-12
92O-Pee-Chee-290
92Pinnacle-211
French-211
92Score-159
Canadian-159
92Stadium Club-38
92Topps-445
Gold-445G
92Ultra-327
92Upper Deck-479
93Canadiens Molson-6
93Canadiens Postcards-11
93Donruss-168
93Leaf-223
93O-Pee-Chee Canadiens Hockey Fest-8
93OPC Premier-339
Gold-339
93Parkhurst-376
Emerald Ice-376
93Pinnacle-193
Canadian-193
93PowerPlay-370
93Score-268
Canadian-268
93Stadium Club-53
Members Only Master Set-53
OPC-53
First Day Issue-53
First Day Issue OPC-53
93Topps/OPC Premier-339
Gold-339
93Ultra-352
93Upper Deck-333
94Be A Player-R56
Signature Cards-56
94Leaf-371
94OPC Premier-351
Special Effects-351
94Parkhurst-120
Gold-120
94Parkhurst SE-SE126
Gold-SE126
94Pinnacle-373
Artist's Proofs-373
Rink Collection-373
94Topps/OPC Premier-351
Special Effects-351
94Upper Deck-144
Electric Ice-144
94Upper Deck NHLPA/Be A Player-23
95Collector's Choice-295
Player's Club-295
Player's Club Platinum-295
95Parkhurst International-430
Emerald Ice-430
95Playoff One on One-292
95Topps-178
OPC Inserts-178
95Upper Deck-357
Electric Ice-357
Electric Ice Gold-357
97Be A Player-98
Autographs-98
Autographs Die-Cuts-98
Autographs Prismatic Die-Cuts-98
97Hurricanes Team Issue-11
97Pacific Invincible NHL Regime-36
97Upper Deck-242
99Pacific-6
Copper-6
Emerald Green-6
Gold-6
Ice Blue-6
Premiere Date-6
Red-6
00Upper Deck Vintage-224
01Pacific-247
Extreme LTD-247
Hobby LTD-247
Premiere Date-247
Retail LTD-247
01Pacific Arena Exclusives-247
Hallett, Pat
04Oklahoma City Blazers-6
Hallgren, Rolf
67Swedish Hockey-28
Hallick, Matt
05Brandon Wheat Kings-10
Hallikainen, Joonas
05Finnish Cardset -226
06Finnish Cardset-53
Signature Sensations-9
Superior Snatchers-2
Superior Snatchers Gold-2
Superior Snatchers Silver-2
Hallila, Jari
72Finnish Jaakiekko-342
Hallin, Mats
81Indianapolis Checkers-6

82Indianapolis Checkers-7
83Islanders Team Issue-5
83O-Pee-Chee-8
83O-Pee-Chee Stickers-184
83Topps Stickers-184
84Islanders News-8
85Islanders News-7
85North Stars Postcards-12
87Swedish Panini Stickers-241
90Swedish Semic Elitserien Stickers-137
91Swedish Semic Elitserien Stickers-187
00Upper Deck Vintage Dynasty: A Piece of History-GH
00Upper Deck Vintage Dynasty: A Piece of History Gold-GH

Hallin, Per
00Swedish Upper Deck-171
02Swedish SHL-107
Parallel-107
Signatures-16
03Swedish Elite-130
Silver-130
04Swedish Elitset-130
Gold-130
05Swedish SHL Elitset-140
Gold-140
06Swedish SHL Elitset-139

Halmann, Philippe
00Swiss Panini Stickers-71

Halme, Ilkka
65Finnish Hellas-119

Halme, Jari
91Finnish Jyvas-Hyva Stickers-55
94Finnish SISU-37

Halme, Jussi
05Finnish Cardset -319

Halonen, Marko
93Finnish Jyvas-Hyva Stickers-205
93Finnish SISU-262

Halonen, Mikko
93Finnish Jyvas-Hyva Stickers-208
93Finnish SISU-275
94Finnish SISU-172
94Finnish SISU-334

Halpenny, Scott
87Brockville Braves-11

Halpern, Jeff
99BAP Memorabilia-378
Gold-378
Silver-378
99Pacific-466
99Pacific Dynagon Ice-201
Blue-201
Copper-201
Gold-201
Premiere Date-201
99Pacific Omega-246
Copper-246
Gold-246
Ice Blue-246
Premiere Date-246
99SP Authentic-120
99Topps Arena Giveaways-WAS-JH
99Topps Premier Plus-96
Parallel-96
99Upper Deck Arena Giveaways-WC1
99Upper Deck MVP SC Edition-191
Gold Script-191
Silver Script-191
Super Script-191
00Aurora-147
Premiere Date-147
00BAP Memorabilia-365
Emerald-365
Ruby-365
Sapphire-365
Promos-365
00BAP Mem Chicago Sportsfest Copper-365
00BAP Memorabilia Chicago Sportsfest Blue-365
00BAP Memorabilia Chicago Sportsfest Gold-365
00BAP Memorabilia Chicago Sportsfest Ruby-365
00BAP Memorabilia Chicago Sun-Times Ruby-365
00BAP Memorabilia Chicago Sun-Times Gold-365
00BAP Mem Chicago Sun-Times Sapphire-365
00BAP Mem Toronto Fall Expo Copper-365
00BAP Memorabilia Toronto Fall Expo Gold-365
00BAP Memorabilia Toronto Fall Expo Ruby-365
00BAP Signature Series-194
Emerald-194
Ruby-194
Sapphire-194
Autographs-189
Autographs Gold-189
00Black Diamond-60
Gold-60
00O-Pee-Chee-222
00O-Pee-Chee Parallel-222
00Pacific-422
Copper-422
Gold-422
Ice Blue-422
Premiere Date-422
00Paramount-245
Copper-245
Gold-245
Holo-Gold-245
Holo-Silver-245
Ice Blue-245
Premiere Date-245
00Private Stock-98
Gold-98
Premiere Date-98
Retail-98
Silver-98
00Revolution-147
Blue-147
Premiere Date-147
Red-147
00Stadium Club-191
00Topps/OPC-222
Parallel-222
00Topps Chrome-141
OPC Refractors-141
Refractors-141
00Topps Heritage-112
00Upper Deck-178
Exclusives Tier 1-178
Exclusives Tier 2-178
00Upper Deck MVP-180
First Stars-180
Second Stars-180
Third Stars-180
00Upper Deck Victory-237
00Upper Deck Vintage-361
01BAP Memorabilia-7
Emerald-7
Ruby-7
Sapphire-7
01BAP Signature Series-172
Autographs-172
Autographs Gold-172
01O-Pee-Chee-158
01O-Pee-Chee Premier Parallel-158
01Pacific-393
Extreme LTD-393
Hobby LTD-393
Premiere Date-393
Retail LTD-393
01Pacific Adrenaline-196
Blue-196
Premiere Date-196
Red-196
Retail-196
01Pacific Arena Exclusives-393
01Parkhurst-212
01Stadium Club-63
Award Winners-63
Master Photos-63
01Topps-158
OPC Parallel-158
01Topps Heritage-103
Refractors-103
01Upper Deck-176
Exclusives-176
01Upper Deck MVP-186
01Upper Deck Victory-356
Gold-356
02BAP First Edition-267
02BAP Memorabilia-64
Emerald-64
Ruby-64
Sapphire-64
NHL All-Star Game-64
NHL All-Star Game Blue-64
NHL All-Star Game Green-64
NHL All-Star Game Red-64
02BAP Memorabilia Toronto Fall Expo-64
02BAP Sig Series Auto Buybacks 2001-172
02Pacific-391
Blue-391
Red-391
02Pacific Complete-237
Red-237
02SP Game Used Future Fabrics-FFHA
02SP Game Used Future Fabrics-FFJH
02SP Game Used Future Fabrics Gold-FFHA
02SP Game Used Future Fabrics Gold-FFJH
02SP Game Used Future Fabrics Rainbow-FFHA
02SP Game Used Future Fabrics Rainbow-FFJH
02Topps Total-300
02Upper Deck Classic Portraits Hockey Royalty-HBK
02Upper Deck Classic Portraits Hockey Royalty Limited-HBK
02Upper Deck Vintage-257
Jerseys-SOJH
Jerseys Gold-SO-JH
03ITG Action-592
03NHL Sticker Collection-146
03Pacific-344
Blue-344
Red-344
03Pacific Complete-264
Red-264
03Upper Deck-439
Canadian Exclusives-439
HG-439
UD Exclusives-439
03Upper Deck MVP-430
Gold Script-430
Silver Script-430
Canadian Exclusives-430
04Pacific-263
Blue-263
Red-263
04Upper Deck-174
Canadian Exclusives-174
HG Glossy Gold-174
HG Glossy Silver-174
05Panini Stickers-178
05Parkhurst-487
05Parkhurst-525
Facsimile Auto Parallel-487
Facsimile Auto Parallel-525
Signatures-JH
True Colors-TCWAS
True Colors-TCWAS
05Upper Deck-195
HG Glossy-195
Jerseys Series II-J2JH
05Upper Deck MVP-386
Gold-386
Platinum-386
05Upper Deck Toronto Fall Expo-195
05Upper Deck Victory-197
Black-197
Gold-197
Silver-197
06Be A Player Portraits Signature Portraits-SPHA
06Fleer Signing Day-SDJH
06O-Pee-Chee-162
Rainbow-162
06Stars Team Postcards-8
06UD Artifacts Auto-Facts-AFJH
06UD Artifacts Auto-Facts Gold-AFJH
06Ultra Fresh Ink-IJH
06Upper Deck-315
Exclusives Parallel-315
High Gloss Parallel-315
Masterpieces-315
06Upper Deck MVP-100
Gold Script-100
Super Script-100
06Upper Deck Ovation-100
06Upper Deck Trilogy Scripts-TSJH
06Upper Deck Victory-197
06Upper Deck Victory-246
06Upper Deck Victory Black-197
06Upper Deck Victory Gold-197

Haltia, Patrik
90Swedish Semic Elitserien Stickers-250
91Swedish Semic Elitserien Stickers-81
92Swedish Semic Elitserien Stickers-103
94Swedish Leaf-215
NHL Draft-7
Rookie Rockets-8
95Swedish Leaf-39
Spidermen-5
96Saint John Flames-6

Halttunen, Niko
94Finest-132
Super Team Winners-132
Refractors-132
94Parkhurst SE-SE220
Gold-SE220
95Finnish SISU-51
98Finnish Keraílysarja-172
00Swedish Upper Deck-27

Halvardsson, David
02Swedish SHL-102
Parallel-102
03Swedish Elite-123
Silver-123

Halvardsson, Johan
03Swedish Elite-193
Silver-193
04Swedish Elitset-195
Gold-195
05Swedish SHL Elitset-56
Gold-56
06Swedish SHL Elitset-58

Halverson, Brent
00Sioux City Musketeers-11

Halverson, Chris
95Halifax Mooseheads-7

Halverson, Don
95Prince Albert Raiders-6
96Prince Albert Raiders-7
97Prince Albert Raiders-8

Halverson, Trevor
897th Inn. Sketch OHL-157
907th Inn. Sketch OHL-308
91Baltimore Skipjacks-3
91ProCards-555
91Arena Draft Picks-16
91Arena Draft Picks French-16
91Arena Draft Picks Autographs-16
91Arena Draft Picks Autographs French-16
91Classic-8
91Star Pics-14
91Ultimate Draft-9
91Ultimate Draft-73
91Ultimate Draft French-17
91Classic Four-Sport *-18
Autographs-18A
93San Diego Gulls-10
94Hampton Roads Admirals-7
95Hampton Roads Admirals-16
96Portland Pirates-28
98Hampton Roads Admirals 10th Anniversary-13
98Portland Pirates-4

Halward, Doug
76O-Pee-Chee NHL-306
77Rochester Americans-13
78O-Pee-Chee-392
80Kings Card Night-3
80O-Pee-Chee-207
80Topps-207
81Canucks Team Issue-10
81O-Pee-Chee-335
82Canucks Team Issue-9
82Post Cereal-19
83Canucks Team Issue-9
83NHL Key Tags-120
83O-Pee-Chee-351
83O-Pee-Chee Stickers-278
83Topps Stickers-278
83Vachon-108
84Canucks Team Issue-11
84O-Pee-Chee-320
84O-Pee-Chee Stickers-278
85Canucks Team Issue-10
85O-Pee-Chee-189
85O-Pee-Chee Stickers-243
86Kraft Drawings-24
86O-Pee-Chee-248
86O-Pee-Chee Stickers-97
87Red Wings Little Caesars-13
88Oilers Tenth Anniversary-157
88Oilers Team Issue-9
88O-Pee-Chee-113
88Topps-113

Halyk, Chris
79Rochester Americans-6

Ham, Zach
94Dubuque Fighting Saints-10
95Waterloo Blackhawks -6
01South Carolina Stingrays-8

Hamalainen, Aatu
06Finnish Cardset-267

Hamalainen, Erik
91Finnish Jyvas-Hyva Stickers-36
92Finnish Jyvas-Hyva Stickers-60
93Finnish Jyvas-Hyva Stickers-106
93Finnish SISU-12
93Finnish SISU-362
93Finnish SISU-374
94Finnish SISU-98
94Swedish Olympics Lillehammer*-304
95Finnish Beckett Ad Cards-4
95Finnish SISU-178
Gold Cards-5
95Finnish Karjala World Champ Labels-1
95Finnish Semic World Championships-4
95Swedish Leaf-163
95Swedish Upper Deck-2
95Swedish World Championships Stickers-164
96Swedish Semic Wien-4
97Swedish Collector's Choice-3
98Finnish Keraílysarja-169
Leijonat-5
99Finnish Cardset-63
00Finnish Cardset-301
01Swiss HNL-197
02Finnish Cardset-178
03Finnish Cardset-104
04Finnish Cardset-114
Parallel-85
04Swedish Pure Skills-132
Parallel-132
05Finnish Cardset -284
06Finnish Cardset-111

Hamalainen, Jari
92Finnish Jyvas-Hyva Stickers-95

Hamalainen, Jari-Hannu
71Finnish Suomi Stickers-319

Hamalainen, Jari-Pekka
71Finnish Suomi Stickers-320

Hamalainen, Jarkko
92Finnish Jyvas-Hyva Stickers-149
93Finnish Jyvas-Hyva Stickers-265
93Finnish SISU-287

Hamalainen, Tero
95Finnish SISU-209
96Finnish SISU Redline-14
Rookie Energy-4
98Finnish Keraílysarja-17
99Finnish Cardset-115

Hamalainen, Tommi
93Finnish SISU-90
94Finest-140
Super Team Winners-140
Refractors-140
94Finnish SISU-241
95Finnish SISU-218
00Swedish Upper Deck-17

Hamalainen, Ville
99Finnish Cardset-307
00Finnish Cardset-81
01Finnish Cardset-113
05Finnish Cardset -79
06Finnish Cardset-85

Haman, Radek
95Czech APS Extraliga-215
99Czech DS-194
99Czech OFS-74
00Czech DS Extraliga-107
00Czech OFS-206
01Czech OFS-103
02Czech OFS Plus-107
03Czech OFS Plus-241
04Czech OFS-295
05Czech HC Znojmo-5
06Czech OFS-203

Hamann, Martin
05German DEL-315

Hambly, Tim
04Minnesota-Duluth Bulldogs-9
05Las Vegas Wranglers-9

Hamel, Denis
97Rochester Americans-1-3
97Bowman CHL-70
OPC-70
98Rochester Americans-9
99BAP Memorabilia-376
Gold-376
Silver-376
00Titanium-106
Retail-106
00Titanium Draft Day Edition-106
00Titanium Draft Day Promos-106
00Upper Deck NHLPA-PA10
01BAP Signature Series-31
Autographs-31
Autographs Gold-31
01Upper Deck Victory-47
Gold-47
02BAP Sig Series Auto Buybacks 2001-31
02Rochester Americans-6
03Binghamton Senators-6
03Binghamton Senators Postcards-10
04Binghamton Senators-5
04Binghamton Senators Hess-2
05ITG Heroes/Prosp Toronto Expo Parallel -52
05AHL All-Stars-11
05Binghamton Senators-1
05Binghamton Senators Quickway-1
05ITG Heroes and Prospects-52
Autographs-A-DH
Complete Logos-AHL-10
Jerseys-GUJ-4
Jerseys Gold-GUJ-04
Emblems-GUE-4
Emblems Gold-GUE-04
Numbers-GUN-4
Numbers Gold-GUN-04
06Senators Postcards-5
06Binghamton Senators 5th Anniversary-11
06ITG Heroes and Prospects AHL All-Star Jerseys-AJ07
06ITG Heroes and Prospects AHL All-Star Jerseys Gold-AJ07
06ITG Heroes and Prospects AHL All-Star Emblems-AE07
06ITG Heroes and Prospects AHL All-Star Emblems Gold-AE07
06ITG Heroes and Prospects AHL All-Star Numbers-AN07
06ITG Heroes and Prospects AHL All-Star Numbers Gold-AN07

Hamel, Gilles
84O-Pee-Chee-22
84Sabres Blue Shield-8
85O-Pee-Chee Stickers-185
85Sabres Blue Shield-12
85Sabres Blue Shield Small-12
86Jets Postcards-8
87Jets Postcards-8
87O-Pee-Chee-218
87O-Pee-Chee Stickers-253
87Panini Stickers-366
88Kings Smokey-12
88ProCards AHL-174

Hamel, Jean
72Blues White Border-5
73Blues White Border-8
74NHL Action Stamps-91
74O-Pee-Chee NHL-383
75O-Pee-Chee NHL-257
75Topps-257
76O-Pee-Chee NHL-340
77O-Pee-Chee NHL-348
78O-Pee-Chee-281
79O-Pee-Chee-262
79Red Wings Postcards-4
79Topps-262
81O-Pee-Chee-97
82Nordiques Postcards-9
83Canadiens Postcards-10
83Nordiques Postcards-12
83Vachon-45
84Canadiens Postcards-9
84O-Pee-Chee-263
84O-Pee-Chee Stickers-158
88ProCards AHL-289
89ProCards AHL-201
917th Inn. Sketch QMJHL-294
93Drummondville Voltigeurs-25
93Quebec Pee-Wee Tournament-1128

Hamel, Jean-Philippe
00Rouyn-Noranda Huskies-22
Signed-22

Hamel, Kevin
02Moncton Wildcats-15
03Moncton Wildcats-9
04P.E.I. Rocket-24

Hamel, Pierre
79Jets Postcards-8
80Jets Postcards-9
80O-Pee-Chee-205
80Pepsi-Cola Caps-128
80Topps-205
81O-Pee-Chee-365
81O-Pee-Chee Stickers-143

Hamel, Tim
99Owen Sound Platers-5

Hamelin, Craig
93RPI Engineers-11
95Central Hockey League-61
97New Mexico Scorpions-9

Hamelin, Hugo
917th Inn. Sketch QMJHL-101
93Phoenix Cobras RHI-10
93Sherbrooke Faucons-22
99Memphis RiverKings All-Time-8
03St. Jean Mission-13

Hamelin, Richard
907th Inn. Sketch QMJHL-187
917th Inn. Sketch QMJHL-56

Hamerlik, Peter
00Kingston Frontenacs-6
01Kingston Frontenacs-5
02Kingston Frontenacs-6
03Augusta Lynx-42
04Providence Bruins-21

Hamhuis, Dan
98Prince George Cougars-9
99Prince George Cougars-5
00Prince George Cougars-5
01BAP Memorabilia Draft Redemptions-12
01Prince George Cougars-2
01UD Prospects-23
Autographs-A-DH
Jersey Autographs-S-DH
Jerseys-J-DH
Jerseys-C-HW
Jerseys-C-SH
Jerseys Gold-J-DH
Jerseys Gold-C-HW
Jerseys Gold-C-SH
02SPx Rookie Redemption-R203
02Milwaukee Admirals-5
02Milwaukee Admirals Postcards-7
03BAP Memorabilia-175
Emerald-175
Gold-175
Ruby-175
Sapphire-175
Super Rookies-SR13
Super Rookies Gold-SR13
Super Rookies Silver-SR13
03BAP Ultimate Memorabilia Autographs-120
Gold-120
03BAP Ultimate Mem Auto Jerseys-120
03BAP Ultimate Mem Auto Emblems-120
03BAP Ultimate Mem Auto Numbers-120
03Beehive-220
Gold-220
Silver-220
03Black Diamond-188
Black-188
Green-188
Red-188
03Bowman-118
Gold-118
Premier Performance-PP-DH
Premier Performance Patches-PP-DH
03Bowman Chrome-118
Refractors-118
Gold Refractors-118
Xfractors-118
03Crown Royale-123
Red-123
Retail-123
03ITG Action-609
03ITG Toronto Spring Expo Class of 2004-9
03ITG Used Signature Series-177
Gold-177
03ITG VIP Rookie Debut-24
03Pacific Calder-122
Silver-122
03Pacific Complete-549
Red-549
03Pacific Heads-Up-122
Hobby LTD-122
Retail LTD-122
03Pacific Invincible-116
Blue-116
Red-116
Retail-116
03Pacific Luxury Suite-68
Gold-68
03Pacific Quest for the Cup-122
03Pacific Supreme-124
Blue-124
Red-124
Retail-124
03Parkhurst Toronto Expo Rookie Preview-PRP-10
03Parkhurst Rookie-187
All-Rookie-ART-8
All-Rookie Autographs-ART-DH
All-Rookie Gold-ART-8
Road to the NHL-RNJ-17
Road to the NHL Gold-RTN-17
Road to the NHL Emblems-RTNE-17
Road to the NHL Emblems Gold-RTNE-17
Rookie Emblems-RE-10
Rookie Emblem Autographs-RE-DH
Rookie Emblems Gold-RE-10
Rookie Jerseys-RJ-10
Rookie Jersey Autographs-RJ-DH
Rookie Jerseys Gold-RJ-10
Rookie Numbers-RN-10
Rookie Number Autographs-RN-DH
Rookie Numbers Gold-RN-10
03Private Stock Reserve-125
Blue-125
Red-125
Retail-125
03SP Authentic-147
Limited-147
Signed Patches-DH
03SP Game Used-67
Gold-67
03SPx-212
Radiance-212
Spectrum-212
03Titanium-124
Hobby Jersey Number Parallels-124
Retail-124
Retail Jersey Number Parallels-124
03Topps C55-150
Minis-150
Minis American Back-150
Minis American Back Red-150
Minis Bazooka Back-150
Minis Brooklyn Back-150
Minis Hat Trick Back-150
Minis O Canada Back-150
Minis O Canada Back Red-150
Minis Stanley Cup Back-150
03Topps Pristine-158
03Topps Pristine-159
03Topps Pristine-160
Gold Refractor Die Cuts-158
Gold Refractor Die Cuts-159
Gold Refractor Die Cuts-160
Refractors-158
Refractors-159
Refractors-160
Press Plates Black-158
Press Plates Black-159
Press Plates Black-160
Press Plates Cyan-158
Press Plates Cyan-159
Press Plates Cyan-160
Press Plates Magenta-158
Press Plates Magenta-159
Press Plates Magenta-160
Press Plates Yellow-158
Press Plates Yellow-159
Press Plates Yellow-160
03Topps Traded-TT119
Blue-TT119
Gold-TT119
Red-TT119
Future Phenoms-FP-DH
03UD Honor Roll-172
03UD Premier Collection-74
Stars-ST-DH
Stars Patches-ST-DH
03Upper Deck-224
Canadian Exclusives-224
HG-224
Rookie Threads-RT-8
03Upper Deck Classic Portraits-180
03Upper Deck Ice-94
Glass Parallel-94
03Upper Deck MVP-453
03Upper Deck Rookie Update-148
YoungStars-YS20
03Upper Deck Trilogy-156
Limited-156
04AHL All-Stars-16
04Milwaukee Admirals-18
04ITG Heroes and Prospects-184
Autographs-U-DH
04ITG Heroes/Prospects Toronto Expo '05-184
05ITG Heroes/Prosp Toronto Expo Parallel -104
05Hot Prospects Hot Materials-HMDH
05Panini Stickers-312
05Parkhurst-277
Facsimile Auto Parallel-277
True Colors-TCNSH
True Colors-TCNSH
05The Cup Master Pressplate Rookie Update-249
05Upper Deck-360
Jerseys-J-HA
05Upper Deck Rookie Update-249
Inspirations Patch Rookies-249
05ITG Heroes and Prospects-104
Autographs-A-DHA
He Shoots-He Scores Prizes-32
06Be A Player-119
Autographs-119
Signatures-DA
06Black Diamond Jerseys-JDH
06Black Diamond Jerseys Black-JDH
06Black Diamond Jerseys Gold-JDH
06Black Diamond Jerseys Ruby-JDH
06Flair Showcase Stitches-SSDH
06Fleer Fabricology-FDH
06O-Pee-Chee-287
Rainbow-287
06Ultra Uniformity-UDH
06Ultra Uniformity Patches-UPDH

Hamill, Red
34Beehive Group I Photos-18
44Beehive Group II Photos-102

Hamill, Zach
04Everett Silvertips-21
05ITG Heroes/Prosp Toronto Expo Parallel -312
05Everett Silvertips-9
05ITG Heroes and Prospects-312
Autographs Series II-ZH
06ITG Heroes and Prospects Quad Emblems-QE12

Hamilton, Al
68O-Pee-Chee-70
69O-Pee-Chee-192
70Dad's Cookies-46
70Esso Power Players-77
70Sargent Promotions Stamps-22
71O-Pee-Chee-49
71Sabres Postcards-75
71Sargent Promotions Stamps-23
71Topps-49
71Toronto Sun-28
727-Eleven Slurpee Cups WHA-9
73Quaker Oats WHA-16
74O-Pee-Chee WHA-29
74Team Canada L'Equipe WHA-4
75O-Pee-Chee WHA-49
76O-Pee-Chee WHA-97
77O-Pee-Chee WHA-40
79Oilers Postcards-10
79O-Pee-Chee-355
88Oilers Tenth Anniversary-63

Hamilton, Ben
99Minnesota Golden Gophers-6

Hamilton, Bob
61Hamilton Red Wings-5
61Hamilton Red Wings-6

Hamilton, Chad
02Columbus Cottonmouths-6

Hamilton, Colin
96UK Fife Flyers-6
97UK Fife Flyers-18

Hamilton, Curtis
93Quebec Pee-Wee Tournament-1190

Hamilton, Dave
917th Inn. Sketch WHL-51

Hamilton, Hugh
93Spokane Chiefs-13
94Parkhurst SE-SE253
Gold-SE253
94Spokane Chiefs-23
95Spokane Chiefs-3
95Signature Rookies-16
Signatures-16
96Upper Deck Ice-124
96Spokane Chiefs-3
97Bowman CHL-83
OPC-83
98Florida Everblades-8
99Florida Everblades-2
00Florida Everblades-9

Hamilton, Jack
51Laval Dairy Subset-65
52St. Lawrence Sales-101

Hamilton, Jason
03Louisiana Ice Gators-7

Hamilton, Jeff
03Beehive-238
Gold-238
Silver-238
03ITG Action-643
03ITG Used Signature Series-176
Gold-176
03ITG VIP Rookie Debut-73
03Parkhurst Rookie-165
03SP Authentic-121
Limited-121
03Upper Deck Rookie Update-135
03Bridgeport Sound Tigers-4B
03Pacific AHL Prospects-10
Gold-10
Jerseys-2
04Hartford Wolf Pack-7
06Blackhawks Postcards-3
06O-Pee-Chee-119
Rainbow-119

Hamilton, Jim
77Penguins Puck Bucks-23
83Penguins Coke-11

Hamilton, Lee
95Lethbridge Hurricanes-7
99Charlotte Checkers-7
00Charlotte Checkers-12

Hamilton, Mike
04Maine Black Bears-17
05Maine Black Bears-8

Hamilton, Reg
34Beehive Group I Photos-322
37O-Pee-Chee V304E-137
38Quaker Oats Photos-16
39O-Pee-Chee V301-1-1
40O-Pee-Chee V301-2-119

Hamilton, Ryan
03Barrie Colts-4
04Barrie Colts-5

Hamilton, Steve
92Northern Michigan Wildcats-9
93Northern Michigan Wildcats-10

Hamm, Bryan
01Peterborough Petes-3
03Erie Otters-8

Hamm, Trent
91Air Canada SJHL-C14
91Air Canada SJHL All-Stars-6

Hammar, Jan
98Swedish UD Choice-156
99Swedish Upper Deck-159
00Swedish Upper Deck-149
02Swedish SHL-233
Parallel-233
03Swedish Elite-242
Silver-242
04Swedish Elitset-229
Gold-229
04Swedish Malmo Red Hawks-4

Hammarstrom, Inge
67Swedish Hockey-7
67Swedish Hockey-219
69Swedish Hockey-58
70Swedish Hockey-26
71Finnish Suomi Stickers-44
71Swedish Hockey-13
71Swedish Hockey-103
72Finnish Jaakiekko-44
72Finnish Hellas-37
72Finnish Panda Toronto-67
72Finnish Semic World Championship-61
72Swedish Stickers-11
72Swedish Stickers-89
72Swedish Semic World Championship-61
73Maple Leafs Postcards-9
73Finnish Jaakiekko-26
73Swedish Stickers-12
73Swedish Stickers-164
74Maple Leafs Postcards-9
74NHL Action Stamps-258
74O-Pee-Chee NHL-88
74Topps-88
74Swedish Stickers-313
75Maple Leafs Postcards-9
75Maple Leafs Postcards-10
75O-Pee-Chee NHL-168
75Topps-168
76Maple Leafs Postcards-8
76O-Pee-Chee NHL-358
77Maple Leafs Postcards-6
77O-Pee-Chee NHL-320
78Blues Postcards-13
78O-Pee-Chee-53
78Topps-53

Hammarstrom, Peter
89Swedish Semic Elitserien Stickers-18
90Swedish Semic Elitserien Stickers-90
91Swedish Semic Elitserien Stickers-14
92Swedish Semic Elitserien Stickers-38
93Swedish Semic Elitserien-111
94Swedish Leaf-88
95Swedish Leaf-52
95Swedish Upper Deck-85
97Swedish Collector's Choice-12
98Swedish UD Choice-11
99German DEL-71
00German Berlin Polar Bears Postcards-9
02Swedish SHL-33
Parallel-33
03Swedish Elite-43
Silver-43
04Swedish Elitset-45
04Swedish Elitset-234
Gold-45
Gold-234
04Swedish Malmo Red Hawks-21
05Swedish SHL Elitset Icons-1

Hammell, Tim
03OCN Blizzard-7

Hammer, Dominik
05German DEL-186
05German DEL-333

Hammer, Rolf
94German DEL-189
95German DEL-189
96German DEL-128

Hammer, Trevor
01El Paso Buzzards-11
01New Mexico Scorpions-2
04New Mexico Scorpions-12
05Florida Seals Team Issue-7

Hammill, Jessie
02UK Peterborough Phantoms-7

Hammond, Brett
04Minnesota-Duluth Bulldogs-10
05Fresno Falcons-7

Hammond, Ken
88Oilers Tenth Anniversary-52
89ProCards AHL-128
90ProCards AHL/IHL-141
91Pro Set-484
French-484
91Score Canadian Bilingual-647
91Score Canadian English-647
91Score Rookie/Traded-97T
91Sharks Sports Action-9
92Parkhurst Previews-PV4
92Parkhurst-358
Emerald Ice-358
92Senators Team Issue-4
94Kansas City Blades-2
95Kansas City Blades-11

Hammond, Russ
92Cornell Big Red-12
98Guelph Storm-27
99Guelph Storm-29
01Guelph Storm-29
01Guelph Storm Memorial Cup-29
02Guelph Storm-30

Hammond, Scott
82Ottawa 67's-6
83Ottawa 67's-10

Hamonic, Travis
06Moose Jaw Warriors-2

Hampe, Kevin
92Harvard Crimson-12

Hampeis, Lada
93Tacoma Rockets-11
99Anchorage Aces-27

Hampl, Peter
94German First League-46

Hampson, Ted
44Beehive Group II Photos-320
44Beehive Group II Photos-403
59Parkhurst-34
60NHL Ceramic Tiles-30
60Shirriff Coins-98
61Shirriff/Salada Coins-92
61Topps-59
62Topps-55
63York White Backs-52
64Beehive Group III Photos-74
67Topps-108
68O-Pee-Chee-85
68Shirriff Coins-111
68Topps-85
69O-Pee-Chee-86
Four-in-One-7
Stamps-12
69Topps-86
70Colgate Stamps-9
70Dad's Cookies-47
70Esso Power Players-100
70O-Pee-Chee-190
70Sargent Promotions Stamps-137
71O-Pee-Chee-101
71Sargent Promotions Stamps-94
71Topps-101
71Toronto Sun-133
72Minnesota Fighting Saints Postcards WHA-8
72Finnish Semic World Championship-176
72Swedish Semic World Championship-176
73Quaker Oats WHA-4
95Parkhurst '66-67-47
Coins-47
04ITG Franchises US West-262
Autographs-A-THA

Hampton, Rick
74NHL Action Stamps-68
74O-Pee-Chee NHL-329
75O-Pee-Chee NHL-65
75Topps-65
76O-Pee-Chee NHL-113
76O-Pee-Chee NHL-383
76Topps-113
77O-Pee-Chee NHL-63
77Topps-63
78O-Pee-Chee-174
78Topps-174
79Panini Stickers-54
79O-Pee-Chee-330

Hamr, Radek
93Leaf-265
93Parkhurst-143
Emerald Ice-143
93Score-476
Canadian-476
93Upper Deck-34
93Classic Pro Prospects-142
94Classic Pro Prospects-87
95Czech APS Extraliga-276
95Oklahoma Coyotes RHI-9
96Czech APS Extraliga-128
97Czech DS Stickers-57
98Swedish UD Choice-71
99Swedish Upper Deck-57
00Swedish Upper Deck-81
00Swedish Upper Deck-192
00Swedish Upper Deck-214
01Czech OFS-17
02Swedish SHL-170
Parallel-170
03Swedish Elite-38
Silver-38
04Czech World Championship Postcards-5
04Swedish Elitset-39
Gold-39
05Swedish SHL Elitset-41
Gold-41
06Czech CP Cup Postcards-3

Hamrla, Robert
97Czech APS Extraliga-54
98Czech OFS-332
99Czech Score Blue 2000-144
99Czech Score Red Ice 2000-144
01Czech OFS Update-293
02Czech OFS Plus-259
Checklists-C6
02Czech OFS Plus Masks-M17
02Czech OFS Plus Trios-T11
02Czech OFS Plus Duos-D15

Hamrlik, Martin
91Classic-27
91Star Pics-18
91Classic Four-Sport *-27
93Classic Pro Prospects-62
95Peoria Rivermen-6
97Czech APS Extraliga-59
98Czech DS-109
98Czech DS Stickers-291
98Czech OFS-21
99Czech DS-4
99Czech OFS-453
99Czech OFS-513
All-Star Game Blue-513
All-Star Game Gold-513
All-Star Game Red-513
All-Star Game Silver-513
00Czech DS Extraliga-53
00Czech OFS-354
01Czech OFS-83
All Stars-1
02Czech OFS Plus-27
02Czech OFS Plus All-Star Game-H6
02Czech OFS Plus Trios-T22
02Czech OFS Plus Duos-D16
03Czech OFS Plus-134
03Czech OFS Plus Insert M-M18
04Czech OFS-367
Assist Leaders-9
Defence Points-1
Stars II-15
05Czech HC Hame Zlin-6
06Czech HC Zlin Hame Postcards-2
06Czech OFS-224
Defenders-1
Stars-8

Hamrlik, Petr
00UD CHL Prospects-7

Hamrlik, Roman

91Upper Deck Czech World Juniors-88
92Lightning Sheraton-16
92OPC Premier-46
Top Rookies-2
92Parkhurst-173
92Parkhurst-443
Emerald Ice-173
Emerald Ice-443
92Pinnacle-408
French-408
92Ultra-201
Imports-4
92Upper Deck-555
92Upper Deck-631
Calder Candidates-CC8
Euro-Rookies-ER11
92Classic-1
92Classic-60
Gold-1
Gold-60
LPs-LP1
Promos-1
92Classic Four-Sport *-151
Gold-151
Autographs-151A
BCs-BC7
BCs-FS1
LPs-LP15
LPs-LP22
Previews-CC3
93Donruss-327
93Leaf-151
93Lightning Season in Review-18
93OPC Premier-281
93OPC Premier-323
Gold-281
Gold-323
93Parkhurst-190
Emerald Ice-190
First Overall-F2
93Pinnacle-34
Canadian-34
Team 2001-18
Team 2001 Canadian-18
93PowerPlay-231
93Score-131
Canadian-131
93Stadium Club-75
Members Only Master Set-75
OPC-75
First Day Issue-75
First Day Issue OPC-75
93Topps/OPC Premier-281
93Topps/OPC Premier-323
Gold-281
Gold-323
93Topps Premier Finest-2
93Ultra-108
93Upper Deck-158
SP-151
93Swedish Semic World Champ Stickers-101
93Classic-120
McDonalds-15
93Classic Pro Prospects-50
BCs-BC3
93Classic C3 *-21
94Be A Player-R9
94Donruss-130
94EA Sports-128
94Fleer-207
94Leaf-132
94Lightning Photo Album-16
94Lightning Postcards-10
94OPC Premier-54
Special Effects-54
94Parkhurst Vintage-V53
94Parkhurst SE-SE171
Gold-SE171
94Pinnacle-123
Artist's Proofs-123
Rink Collection-123
94Score-48
Gold-48
Platinum-48
94SP-112
Die Cuts-112
94Topps/OPC Premier-54
Special Effects-54
94Ultra-206
94Upper Deck-174
Electric Ice-174
SP Inserts-SP164
SP Inserts Die Cuts-SP164
95Bashan Super Stickers-112
Die-Cut-20
95Be A Player-133
Signatures-S133
Signatures Die Cuts-S133
95Bowman-82
All-Foil-82
95Canada Games NHL POGS-255
95Collector's Choice-92
Player's Club-92
Player's Club Platinum-92
95Donruss-256
95Donruss Elite-36
Die Cut Stars-36
Die Cut Uncut-36
95Emotion-164
95Finest-93
Refractors-93
95Imperial Stickers-112
Die Cut Superstars-20
95Leaf-295
95Leaf Limited-33
95Lightning Team Issue-11
95Metal-137
International Steel-6
95Panini Stickers-133
95Parkhurst International-198
Emerald Ice-198
Parkie's Trophy Picks-PP25
95Pinnacle-59
Artist's Proofs-59
Rink Collection-59
95Pinnacle FANtasy-11
95Playoff One on One-310
95Pro Magnets-73
95Score-185
Black Ice Artist's Proofs-185
Black Ice-185
95Select Certified-20
Mirror Gold-20
95SkyBox Impact-155
95SP-135
Stars/Etoiles-E25
Stars/Etoiles Gold-E25
95Stadium Club Members Only-11
95Stadium Club-89
Members Only Master Set-89
95Summit-56
Artist's Proofs-56
Ice-56
95Topps-193
OPC Inserts-193
Young Stars-YS13
95Ultra-152
Gold Medallion-152
High Speed-9
Rising Stars-3
Rising Stars Gold Medallion-3
95Upper Deck-152
Electric Ice-152
Electric Ice Gold-152
NHL All-Stars-AS8
NHL All-Stars Jumbo-AS8
Predictor Hobby-H39
Predictor Hobby Exchange-H39
Special Edition-SE76
Special Edition Gold-SE76
95Zenith-112
95Swedish Globe World Championships-149
95Swedish World Championships Stickers-192
96Black Diamond-143
Gold-143
96Collector's Choice-244
96Collector's Choice-331
MVP-UD25
MVP Gold-UD25
StickUms-S18
96Collector's Choice Blow-Ups-244
96Donruss-84
Press Proofs-84
Hit List-16
96Donruss Canadian Ice-44
Gold Press Proofs-44
Red Press Proofs-44
96Donruss Elite-23
Die Cut Stars-23
96Flair-88
Blue Ice-88
96Fleer-104
Picks Dream Lines-6
Picks Fabulous 50-16
96Leaf-118
Press Proofs-118
96Leaf Limited-4
Gold-4
96Leaf Preferred-90
Press Proofs-90
Steel-44
Steel Gold-44
96Metal Universe-145
96NHL Aces Playing Cards-21
96NHL Pro Stamps-73
96Pinnacle-178
Artist's Proofs-178
Foil-178
Premium Stock-178
Rink Collection-178
96Playoff One on One-416
96Score-127
Artist's Proofs-127
Dealer's Choice Artist's Proofs-127
Special Artist's Proofs-127
Golden Blades-127
96Select Certified-48
Artist's Proofs-48
Blue-48
Mirror Blue-48
Mirror Gold-48
Mirror Red-48
Red-48
96SkyBox Impact-122
96SP-144
Holoview Collection-HC22
96SPx-42
Gold-42
96Stadium Club Members Only-37
96Summit-132
Artist's Proofs-132
Ice-132
Metal-132
Premium Stock-132
96Team Out-75
96Topps Picks-35
Fantasy Team-FT9
OPC Inserts-35
96Ultra-157
Gold Medallion-157
Power-6
Power Blue Line-4
96Upper Deck-153
96Upper Deck-367
Generation Next-X8
Superstar Showdown-SS13A
96Upper Deck Ice-102
Parallel-102
96Zenith-92
Artist's Proofs-92
97Be A Player-147
Autographs-147
Autographs Die-Cuts-147
Autographs Prismatic Die-Cuts-147
97Black Diamond-142
Double Diamond-142
Triple Diamond-142
Quadruple Diamond-142
97Collector's Choice-240
Star Quest-SQ44
97Crown Royale-125
Emerald Green-125
Ice Blue-125
Silver-125
97Donruss-112
Press Proofs Silver-112
Press Proofs Gold-112
97Donruss Canadian Ice-123
Dominion Series-123
Provincial Series-123
97Donruss Elite-94
Aspirations-94
Status-94
97Donruss Limited-146
Exposure-146
97Donruss Preferred-141
Cut to the Chase-141
97Donruss Priority-120
Stamp of Approval-120
97Esso Olympic Hockey Heroes-53
97Esso Olympic Hockey Heroes French-53
97Katch-135
Gold-135
Silver-135
97Leaf-76
Fractal Matrix-76
Fractal Matrix Die Cuts-76
97Leaf International-76
Universal Ice-76
97NHL Aces Playing Cards-45
97Pacific-100
Copper-100
Emerald Green-100
Ice Blue-100
Red-100
Silver-100
97Pacific Dynagon-118
Copper-118
Dark Grey-118
Emerald Green-118
Ice Blue-118
Red-118
Silver-118
Tandems-61
97Pacific Invincible-132
Copper-132
Emerald Green-132
Ice Blue-132
Red-132
Silver-132
97Pacific Omega-92
Copper-92
Dark Gray-92
Emerald Green-92
Gold-92
Ice Blue-92
97Panini Stickers-101
97Paramount-173
Copper-173
Dark Grey-173
Emerald Green-173
Ice Blue-173
Red-173
Silver-173
97Pinnacle-175
Press Plates Back Black-175
Press Plates Back Cyan-175
Press Plates Back Magenta-175
Press Plates Back Yellow-175
Press Plates Front Black-175
Press Plates Front Cyan-175
Press Plates Front Magenta-175
Press Plates Front Yellow-175
97Pinnacle Inside-162
97Revolution-53
Copper-53
Emerald-53
Ice Blue-53
Silver-53
97Score-214
97SP Authentic-149
97Studio-75
Press Proofs Silver-75
Press Proofs Gold-75
97Upper Deck-157
97Upper Deck-363
Smooth Grooves-SG47
98Aurora-73
98Be A Player-52
Press Release-52
98BAP Gold-52
98BAP Autographs-52
98BAP Autographs Gold-52
98BAP Tampa Bay All Star Game-52
98Pacific-219
Ice Blue-219
Red-219
98Pacific Dynagon Ice-73
Blue-73
Red-73
98Pacific Omega-93
Red-93
Opening Day Issue-93
98Panini Stickers-196
98Paramount-87
Copper-87
Emerald Green-87
Holo-Electric-87
Ice Blue-87
Silver-87
98UD Choice-80
Prime Choice Reserve-80
Reserve-80
98Upper Deck-96
Exclusives-96
Exclusives 1 of 1-96
Gold Reserve-96
98Upper Deck MVP-83
Gold Script-83
Silver Script-83
Super Script-83
98Czech OFS-232
Olympic Winners-15
98Czech Bonaparte-8C
98Czech Pexeso-27
98Czech Spaghetti-4
99BAP Memorabilia-254
Gold-254
Silver-254
99O-Pee-Chee-110
99O-Pee-Chee Chrome-110
99O-Pee-Chee Chrome Refractors-110
99Pacific-156
Copper-156
Emerald Green-156
Gold-156
Ice Blue-156
Premiere Date-156
Red-156
99Panini Stickers-246
99Topps/OPC-110
99Topps/OPC Chrome-110
Refractors-110
99Upper Deck Victory-116
99Czech DS-3
National Stars-NS7
99Czech OFS-208
00BAP Memorabilia-117
00BAP Memorabilia-492
Emerald-117
Emerald-492
Ruby-117
Ruby-492
Sapphire-117
Sapphire-492
Promos-117
00BAP Mem Chicago Sportsfest Copper-117
00BAP Memorabilia Chicago Sportsfest Blue-117
00BAP Memorabilia Chicago Sportsfest Gold-117
00BAP Memorabilia Chicago Sportsfest Ruby-117
00BAP Memorabilia Chicago Sun-Times Ruby-117
00BAP Memorabilia Chicago Sun-Times Gold-117
00BAP Mem Chicago Sun-Times Sapphire-117
00BAP Mem Toronto Fall Expo Copper-117
00BAP Memorabilia Toronto Fall Expo Gold-117
00BAP Memorabilia Toronto Fall Expo Ruby-117
00BAP Parkhurst 2000-P90
00BAP Parkhurst 2000-P214
00BAP Signature Series-197
Emerald-197
Ruby-197
Sapphire-197
00Pacific-167
Copper-167
Gold-167
Ice Blue-167
Premiere Date-167
00Panini Stickers-161
00Stadium Club-221
00Topps Heritage-171
00UD Pros and Prospects-55
00UD Reserve-54
00Upper Deck-338
Exclusives Tier 1-338
Exclusives Tier 2-338
00Upper Deck Vintage-227
00Czech DS Extraliga Team Jagr-JT4
00Czech DS Extraliga Team Jagr Parallel-JT4
00Czech OFS-382
01BAP Memorabilia-180
Emerald-180
Ruby-180
Sapphire-180
01BAP Signature Series-43
Autographs-43
Autographs Gold-43
01Pacific-248
Extreme LTD-248
Hobby LTD-248
Premiere Date-248
Retail LTD-248
01Pacific Arena Exclusives-248
01Parkhurst-176
01Upper Deck-339
Exclusives-339
01Upper Deck MVP-119
01Upper Deck Victory-221
Gold-221
01Upper Deck Vintage-161
01Upper Deck Vintage-165
01Czech DS-3
02BAP Sig Series Auto Buybacks 1998-52
02BAP Sig Series Auto Buybacks 2001-43
02BAP Signature Series Golf-GS78
02BAP Ultimate Memorabilia First Overall-14
02Pacific-236
Blue-236
Red-236
02Pacific Complete-336
Red-336
02Parkhurst Retro-161
Minis-161
02Topps Total-147
02Upper Deck-108
Exclusives-108
02Upper Deck Vintage-155
02Czech IQ Sports Blue-6
02Czech IQ Sports Yellow-6
02Czech IQ Sports Yellow-7
02Czech Stadion Olympics-330
03ITG Action-394
03NHL Sticker Collection-79
03O-Pee-Chee-87
03OPC Blue-87
03OPC Gold-87
03OPC Red-87
03Pacific-212
Blue-212
Red-212
03Pacific Complete-200
Red-200
03Pacific Exhibit-93
Blue Backs-93
Yellow Backs-93
03Topps-87
Blue-87
Gold-87
Red-87
03Topps C55-63
Minis-63
Minis American Back-63
Minis American Back Red-63
Minis Bazooka Back-63
Minis Brooklyn Back-63
Minis Hat Trick Back-63
Minis O Canada Back-63
Minis O Canada Back Red-63
Minis Stanley Cup Back-63
03Upper Deck-367
Canadian Exclusives-367
HG-367
UD Exclusives-367
03Upper Deck MVP-268
Gold Script-268
Silver Script-268
Canadian Exclusives-268
04UD All-World-10
Gold-10
04Czech NHL ELH Postcards-3
04Czech OFS-278
Stars-39
04Czech Zuma-37
04Czech World Championship Postcards-6
05Panini Stickers-202
05Parkhurst-75
Facsimile Auto Parallel-75
05Upper Deck-278
05Upper Deck MVP-61
Gold-61
Platinum-61
05Czech Kvarteto Bonaparte-2a
05Czech Pexeso Mini Blue Set-4
06Gatorade-9
06O-Pee-Chee-73
Rainbow-73
06Upper Deck-281
Exclusives Parallel-281
High Gloss Parallel-281
Masterpieces-281

Hamula, Richard
00Kootenay Ice-9

Hamway, Mark
84Springfield Indians-18

Hana, Matti
04Finnish Cardset-285

Hanas, Trevor
917th Inn. Sketch WHL-218
93Saskatoon Blades-11
95Lethbridge Hurricanes-8
96Peoria Rivermen-7
96Peoria Rivermen Photo Album-7
97Peoria Rivermen-16
98Topeka Scarecrows-14
99Topeka Scarecrows-11

Hanchuck, Tyler
99Brampton Battalion-5
00Barrie Colts-13
01Barrie Colts-10
03Albany River Rats-13
03Albany River Rats Kinko's-12
05Reading Royals-6

Hanchuk, Jason
93Michigan Tech Huskies-5
96Louisville Riverfrogs-5

Hancock, Quinn
98Peoria Rivermen-13
98Bowman CHL-57
Golden Anniversary-57
OPC International-57
98Bowman Chrome CHL-57
Golden Anniversary-57
Golden Anniversary Refractors-57
OPC International-57
OPC International Refractors-57
Refractors-57
99Muskegon Fury-9
99UHL All-Stars West-12T
00Muskegon Fury-17
02Finnish Cardset-170
03Finnish Cardset-111
04Finnish Cardset-76
Parallel-58
05Finnish Cardset -326
06Finnish Cardset-155

Hand, Ryan James
03Baie Comeau Drakkar-1
04Baie-Comeau Drakkar-21

Hand, Tony
94Finnish Jaa Kiekko-323
95UK Sheffield Steelers-7
97UK Sheffield Steelers-9
00UK Sekonda Superleague-16
00UK Sekonda Superleague-171
00UK Sheffield Steelers Centurions-11
01UK Dundee Stars-4
02UK Dundee Stars-4
04UK EIHL All-Stars-4
04UK Thommo's Top 10-2

Handley, Pete
82North Bay Centennials-8

Handrahan, Nate
00Roanoke Express-17

Handrick, Jorg
95German DEL-259
95Swedish World Championships Stickers-69
96German DEL-147
99German DEL-333
00German DEL-181

Hands, Dennis
93Arizona Icecats-17
94Arizona Icecats-15

Handy, Ron
80Sault Ste. Marie Greyhounds-17
82Kingston Canadians-5
84Springfield Indians-14
88ProCards IHL-16
89ProCards IHL-140
90Kansas City Blades-5
90ProCards AHL/IHL-582
91Kansas City Blades-9
91ProCards-513
92Peoria Rivermen-7
93Wichita Thunder-7
94UK Sheffield Steelers-6
94Central Hockey League-112
95Louisiana Ice Gators-5
95Louisiana Ice Gators Playoffs-6
96Louisiana Ice Gators II-5

Handzus, Michal
98Bowman's Best-132
Refractors-132
Atomic Refractors-132
98Pacific Dynagon Ice-158
Blue-158
Red-158
98SP Authentic-108
Power Shift-108
98Upper Deck-363
Exclusives-363
Exclusives 1 of 1-363
Gold Reserve-363
98Upper Deck MVP-182
Gold Script-182
Silver Script-182
Super Script-182
99Blues Taco Bell-9
99O-Pee-Chee-191
99O-Pee-Chee Chrome-191
99O-Pee-Chee Chrome Refractors-191
99Pacific-357
Copper-357
Emerald Green-357
Gold-357
Ice Blue-357
Premiere Date-357
Red-357
99Panini Stickers-294
99Topps/OPC-191
99Topps/OPC Chrome-191
Refractors-191
99Upper Deck-286
Exclusives-286
Exclusives 1 of 1-286
99Upper Deck Arena Giveaways-SB2
99Upper Deck Gold Reserve-286
99Upper Deck MVP-189
Gold Script-189
Silver Script-189
Super Script-189
99Upper Deck Victory-265
00Aurora-121
Premiere Date-121
00BAP Memorabilia-198
Emerald-198
Ruby-198
Sapphire-198
Promos-198
00BAP Mem Chicago Sportsfest Copper-198
00BAP Memorabilia Chicago Sportsfest Blue-198
00BAP Memorabilia Chicago Sportsfest Gold-198
00BAP Memorabilia Chicago Sportsfest Ruby-198
00BAP Memorabilia Chicago Sun-Times Ruby-198
00BAP Memorabilia Chicago Sun-Times Gold-198
00BAP Mem Chicago Sun-Times Sapphire-198
00BAP Mem Toronto Fall Expo Copper-198
00BAP Memorabilia Toronto Fall Expo Gold-198
00BAP Memorabilia Toronto Fall Expo Ruby-198
00BAP Parkhurst 2000-P187
00BAP Signature Series-39
Emerald-39
Ruby-39
Sapphire-39
Autographs-144
Autographs Gold-144
00O-Pee-Chee-164
00O-Pee-Chee Parallel-164
00Pacific-344
Copper-344
Gold-344
Ice Blue-344
Premiere Date-344
00Panini Stickers-197
00Paramount-205
Copper-205
Gold-205
Holo-Gold-205
Holo-Silver-205
Ice Blue-205
Premiere Date-205
00Revolution-122
Blue-122
Premiere Date-122
Red-122
00SP Game Used Tools of the Game-MH
00SP Game Used Tools of the Game Excl-MH
00Stadium Club-73
00Topps/OPC-164
Parallel-164
00Topps Heritage-180
00Upper Deck-384
Exclusives Tier 1-384
Exclusives Tier 2-384
Ice Game Jerseys-JCMH
00Upper Deck Victory-206
00Upper Deck Vintage-313
01BAP Memorabilia-241
Emerald-241
Ruby-241
Sapphire-241
01Coyotes Team Issue-7
01O-Pee-Chee-188
01O-Pee-Chee Premier Parallel-188
01Pacific-303
Extreme LTD-303
Hobby LTD-303
Premiere Date-303
Retail LTD-303
01Pacific Adrenaline-148
Blue-148
Premiere Date-148
Red-148
Retail-148
01Pacific Arena Exclusives-303
01Parkhurst-152
01SP Authentic-66
Limited-66
Limited Gold-66
01Titanium Double-Sided Jerseys-72
01Titanium Double-Sided Patches-72
01Titanium Draft Day Edition-73
01Topps-188
OPC Parallel-188
01UD Challenge for the Cup-64
01UD Mask Collection-74
Gold-74
01UD Playmakers-75
01Upper Deck-135
Exclusives-135
01Upper Deck MVP-148
01Upper Deck Victory-268
Gold-268
01Upper Deck Vintage-194
01Upper Deck Vintage-199
02BAP Memorabilia-261
Emerald-261
Ruby-261
Sapphire-261
NHL All-Star Game-261
NHL All-Star Game Blue-261
NHL All-Star Game Green-261
NHL All-Star Game Red-261
02BAP Memorabilia Toronto Fall Expo-261
02BAP Signature Series-88
Autographs-88
Autograph Buybacks 2000-144
Autographs Gold-88
02Flyers Postcards-12
02O-Pee-Chee-69
02O-Pee-Chee Premier Blue Parallel-69
02O-Pee-Chee Premier Red Parallel-69
02O-Pee-Chee Factory Set-69
02Pacific-295
Blue-295
Red-295
02Pacific Complete-234
Red-234
02Pacific Exclusive Jerseys-19
02Pacific Exclusive Jerseys Gold-19
02Pacific Heads-Up Quad Jerseys-21
02Pacific Heads-Up Quad Jerseys Gold-21
02Titanium Jerseys-50
02Titanium Jerseys Retail-50
02Titanium Patches-50
02Topps-69
OPC Blue Parallel-69
OPC Red Parallel-69
Factory Set-69
02Topps Total-318
02Upper Deck-374
Exclusives-374
02Upper Deck Beckett UD Promos-374
02Slovakian Kvarteto-13
03Flyers Postcards-9
03ITG Action-442
03O-Pee-Chee-63
03OPC Blue-63
03OPC Gold-63
03OPC Red-63
03Pacific-252
Blue-252
Red-252
03Pacific Complete-103
Red-103
03Titanium-75
Hobby Jersey Number Parallels-75
Retail-75
Retail Jersey Number Parallels-75
03Topps-63
Blue-63
Gold-63
Red-63
03Upper Deck-384
Canadian Exclusives-384
HG-384
UD Exclusives-384
03Upper Deck MVP-309
Gold Script-309
Silver Script-309
Canadian Exclusives-309
03Worcester Ice Cats 10th Anniversary-19
04Pacific-194
Blue-194
Red-194
05Flyers Team Issue-8
05Parkhurst-354
Facsimile Auto Parallel-354
Signatures-MH
05UD Artifacts-76
Blue-76
Gold-76
Green-76
Pewter-76
Red-76
Gold Autographed-76
05Ultimate Coll National Heroes Jersey-NHJHA
05Ultimate Coll National Heroes Patch-NHPHA
05Upper Deck-140
HG Glossy-140
Jerseys Series II-J2HZ
Notable Numbers-N-MHA
05Upper Deck MVP-292
Gold-292
Platinum-292
05Upper Deck Toronto Fall Expo-140
05Upper Deck Victory-147
Black-147
Gold-147
Silver-147
06Black Diamond-18
Black-18
Gold-18
Ruby-18
06Blackhawks Postcards-15
06Flair Showcase Inks-IHA
06Fleer-43
Tiffany-43
06Hot Prospects Hotagraphs-HMI
06O-Pee-Chee-107
Rainbow-107
06Panini Stickers-211
06SP Game Used Inked Sweaters Dual-IS2HH
06SP Game Used SIGnificance-SMH
06The Cup Autographed NHL Shields Duals-DASHH
06UD Powerplay-24
Impact Rainbow-24
06Ultra Fresh Ink-IMH
06Upper Deck-298
Exclusives Parallel-298
High Gloss Parallel-298
Game Jerseys-J2MH
Game Patches-P2MH
Masterpieces-298
Signature Sensations-SSHA
06Upper Deck MVP-62
Gold Script-62
Super Script-62
Autographs-OAHH
06Upper Deck Victory-237

Hanemann, Roland
94German First League-213

Haner, Andreas
01Swiss HNL-473
02Swiss HNL-203

Haney, Merv
91Prince Albert Raiders-3
917th Inn. Sketch WHL-251
93Prince Albert Raiders-7

Hanft, Jorg
89Swedish Semic World Champ Stickers-111
95German DEL-271
96German DEL-436

Hanger, Trevor
95Waterloo Blackhawks -7

Hanggi, Martin
93Swiss HNL-226
96Swiss HNL-352

Hangsleben, Al
79O-Pee-Chee-307
81O-Pee-Chee-354
81O-Pee-Chee Stickers-197

Hanig, Gustav
72Finnish Hellas-53
72Finnish Semic World Championship-108
72Swedish Semic World Championship-108

Hanisz, Andrezej
89Swedish Semic World Champ Stickers-129
92Finnish Semic-267
94German DEL-361

Hanke, Armin
94German First League-319

Hankela, Timo
93Finnish Jyvas-Hyva Stickers-284
93Finnish SISU-59

Hankinson, Ben
91ProCards-413
93Pinnacle-210
Canadian-210
94Lightning Photo Album-17
95Adirondack Red Wings-8
96Grand Rapids Griffins-7

Hankinson, Casey
94Minnesota Golden Gophers-15
95Donruss Elite World Juniors-36
95Minnesota Golden Gophers-14
96Minnesota Golden Gophers-13
97Minnesota Golden Gophers-12
98Portland Pirates-8
99Cleveland Lumberjacks-7
00SPx Rookie Redemption-RR7
01SP Authentic-140
Limited-140
Limited Gold-140
01SPx-100
01UD Top Shelf-50
01UD Top Shelf-50B
01Upper Deck-184
Exclusives-184
01Upper Deck Ice-49
01Upper Deck MVP-194
01Upper Deck Victory-366
Gold-366
01Norfolk Admirals-4
02Norfolk Admirals-8
03Cincinnati Mighty Ducks-B6

Hankinson, Peter
90Moncton Hawks-9
90ProCards AHL/IHL-254
90ProCards AHL/IHL-547
91ProCards-239
92San Diego Gulls-10

Hankkio, Greg
85Kitchener Rangers-14
86London Knights-25

Hanko, Denis
94German First League-271

Hanley, Colin
04Owen Sound Attack-8

Hanley, Tim
89ProCards AHL-238
91Lake Superior State Lakers-10
92Lake Superior State Lakers-10
95Roanoke Express-17

Hanley, William
85Hall of Fame-251

Hanlon, Glen
78Canucks Royal Bank-10
79Canucks Royal Bank-9
79O-Pee-Chee-337
80Canucks Silverwood Dairies-10
80Canucks Team Issue-10
80O-Pee-Chee-141
80O-Pee-Chee Super-22
80Topps-141
81Canucks Team Issue-11
81O-Pee-Chee-336
81O-Pee-Chee Stickers-245
83NHL Key Tags-85
84O-Pee-Chee-142
84O-Pee-Chee Stickers-98
84Topps-106
85O-Pee-Chee-149
85O-Pee-Chee Stickers-87
85Topps-149
87O-Pee-Chee-89
87O-Pee-Chee Minis-14
87O-Pee-Chee Stickers-109
87Panini Stickers-238
87Red Wings Little Caesars-14
87Topps-89
88O-Pee-Chee-150
88Panini Stickers-36
88Red Wings Little Caesars-10
88Topps-150
89O-Pee-Chee-144
89Panini Stickers-65
89Red Wings Little Caesars-9
89Topps-144
90O-Pee-Chee-266
90Panini Stickers-203
90Pro Set-72
90Score-228
Canadian-228
90Topps-266
Tiffany-266
90Upper Deck-395
French-395
90ProCards AHL/IHL-305
99Portland Pirates-12

Hanlon, James
99Sporting News Supplements M101-1-12
90Knoxville Cherokees-112
94German DEL-244
95German DEL-229
96German DEL-80
00UK Sekonda Superleague-60

Hanna, John
44Beehive Group II Photos-244
58Topps-7
59Topps-31
59Topps-53
60Shirriff Coins-85
62Quebec Aces-10
63Quebec Aces-10
64Beehive Group III Photos-104
64Quebec Aces-7
65Quebec Aces-7
69Seattle Totems-11

Hanna, John B.
83Ottawa 67's-11
84Ottawa 67's-9
88ProCards AHL-74

Hannah, Andrew
97UK Guildford Flames-3

Hannah, Shaun
92Cornell Big Red-13
93Cornell Big Red-12

Hannan, Dave
83NHL Key Tags-100
83O-Pee-Chee-281
83Penguins Coke-12
83Penguins Heinz Photos-11
86Penguins Kodak-10
87Oilers Team Issue-12
87Panini Stickers-154
88Oilers Tenth Anniversary-83
89O-Pee-Chee-257
90O-Pee-Chee-449
90Pro Set-535
91Bowman-155
91Maple Leafs Panini Team Stickers-8
91Maple Leafs PLAY-17
91O-Pee-Chee-360
91Pinnacle-413
French-413
91Score Canadian Bilingual-241
91Score Canadian English-241
91Stadium Club-220
91Topps-360
91Upper Deck-312
French-312
92Sabres Blue Shield-6
92Score-538
Canadian-538
92Senators Team Issue-5
93Stadium Club-47
Members Only Master Set-47
OPC-47
First Day Issue-47
First Day Issue OPC-47
94OPC Premier-118
Special Effects-118
94Pinnacle-446
Artist's Proofs-446
Rink Collection-446
94Topps/OPC Premier-118
Special Effects-118
96Senators Pizza Hut-9

Hannan, Scott
92Quebec Pee-Wee Tournament-1015
98Pacific Dynagon Ice-166
Blue-166
Red-166
98Upper Deck-353
Exclusives-353
Exclusives 1 of 1-353
Gold Reserve-353
98Kelowna Rockets-7
99Pacific-385
Copper-385
Emerald Green-385
Gold-385
Ice Blue-385
Premiere Date-385
Red-385
99Upper Deck-112
Exclusives-112
Exclusives 1 of 1-112
99Upper Deck Gold Reserve-112
99Upper Deck MVP-180
Gold Script-180
Silver Script-180
Super Script-180
99Upper Deck Victory-249
99Kentucky Thoroughblades-13
99Bowman CHL-117
Gold-117
OPC International-117
00O-Pee-Chee-278
00O-Pee-Chee Parallel-278
00Topps/OPC-278
Parallel-278
00Topps Chrome-173
OPC Refractors-173

Refractors-173
00Upper Deck Victory-278
01Sharks Postcards-13
02Pacific Complete-333
Red-333
02Upper Deck-395
Exclusives-395
02Upper Deck Beckett UD Promos-395
03ITG Action-423
03Pacific Complete-376
Red-376
03Sharks Postcards-6
03Upper Deck MVP-348
Gold Script-348
Silver Script-348
Canadian Exclusives-348
04UD Toronto Fall Expo Pride of Canada-7
04Upper Deck-147
Canadian Exclusives-147
HG Glossy Gold-147
HG Glossy Silver-147
05Panini Stickers-348
05Parkhurst-410
Facsimile Auto Parallel-410
06NHL POG-9
06O-Pee-Chee-414
Rainbow-414
06Panini Stickers-335
06Upper Deck-411
Exclusives Parallel-411
High Gloss Parallel-411
Masterpieces-411

Hannesson, Doug
82Victoria Cougars-24

Hanni, Andreas
01Swiss HNL-219
02Swiss HNL-75

Hannigan, Gord
44Beehive Group II Photos-404
45Quaker Oats Photos-20
52Parkhurst-54
53Parkhurst-3
54Parkhurst-27

Hannigan, Pat
61Shirriff/Salada Coins-83
61Topps-58
62Topps-64
68Shirriff Coins-134

Hannon, Brian
89ProCards IHL-136
94German DEL-170
95German DEL-120

Hannula, Mika
02Swedish SHL-76
Dynamic Duos-6
Parallel-76
02Swedish SHL Promos-TCC7
03Swedish Elite-98
Silver-98
03Houston Aeros-9
04Swedish Elitset-233
Gold-233
04Swedish Malmo Red Hawks-18
04Swedish Pure Skills-61
Parallel-61
Signatures-8
05Swedish SHL Elitset-202
Gold-202
06Swedish SHL Elitset-67
Performers-6

Hannus, Tommi
01Finnish Cardset-361
03Finnish Cardset-119
04Finnish Cardset-280
05Finnish Cardset -105
06Finnish Cardset-112

Hansch, Hans
94German First League-133

Hansch, Randy
83Victoria Cougars-10
84Victoria Cougars-11
85Kamloops Blazers-6
90ProCards AHL/IHL-490

Hansen, Anders
99Danish Hockey League-202

Hansen, Andre Manscov
92Norwegian Elite Series-213
99Norwegian National Team-6

Hansen, Frode
92Norwegian Elite Series-47

Hansen, Ivan
83Swedish Semic Elitserien-138
85Swedish Panini Stickers-194
86Swedish Panini Stickers-123
87Swedish Panini Stickers-160

Hansen, Jannik
06Manitoba Moose-11
07Upper Deck Victory-245
Black-245
Gold-245

Hansen, Jeff
04Knoxville Ice Bears-18

Hansen, Justin
97Moose Jaw Warriors-3
99Prince George Cougars-16

Hansen, Kevin
92Quebec Pee-Wee Tournament-1584
95Slapshot-388
95Sudbury Wolves-8
95Sudbury Wolves Police-10
96Sudbury Wolves-9
96Sudbury Wolves Police-12
02Odessa Jackalopes-13
06Fort Wayne Komets-7

Hansen, Kristian L.
98Danish Hockey League-68

Hansen, Lars
92Norwegian Elite Series-232

Hansen, Mads
06Swedish SHL Elitset-155

Hansen, Mark
91Air Canada SJHL-E33

Hansen, Matt
92Lake Superior State Lakers-11

Hansen, Matthew
05Moose Jaw Warriors-9
05Red Deer Rebels-6

Hansen, Peter F.
98Danish Hockey League-125

Hansen, Rene
92Norwegian Elite Series-58

Hansen, Rick
91Pro Set Platinum-296

Hansen, Ronny
89Swedish Semic Elitserien Stickers-261
90Swedish Semic Elitserien Stickers-169

Hansen, Rune
92Norwegian Elite Series-70
92Norwegian Elite Series-168

Hansen, Tavis
93Tacoma Rockets-12
95Leaf-214
96Springfield Falcons-19
96Collector's Edge Ice-69
Prism-69
97Springfield Falcons-11
00O-Pee-Chee-305
00O-Pee-Chee Parallel-305
00Topps/OPC-305
Parallel-305
00Topps Chrome-200
OPC Refractors-200
Refractors-200
02Cleveland Barons-7
03Cleveland Barons-10

Hansen, Thomas
92Norwegian Elite Series-230
99Danish Hockey League-188

Hansen, Ulrich
98Danish Hockey League-130
99Danish Hockey League-144

Hansen, Zach
06Sioux Falls Stampede -18

Hanson, Carl
97Dubuque Fighting Saints-21

Hanson, Christian
05Notre Dame Freshmen-5

Hanson, Dave
82Indianapolis Checkers-8

Hanson, Devon
93Saskatoon Blades-12

Hanson, Greg
93Minnesota-Duluth Bulldogs-13

Hanson, Joel
03Waterloo Blackhawks-1

Hanson, John
01El Paso Buzzards-20
02El Paso Buzzards-4

Hanson, Keith
82Birmingham South Stars-10
84Moncton Golden Flames-16

Hanson, Michael
95Slapshot-342
95Sarnia Sting-12
96Sarnia Sting-9
98Windsor Spitfires-4

Hanson, Mike
03Columbia Inferno Update-50
04Odessa Jackalopes-8

Hanson, Tom
85Minnesota-Duluth Bulldogs-13

Hansson, Bo
64Swedish Coralli ISHockey-37
65Swedish Coralli ISHockey-37
67Swedish Hockey-29
69Swedish Hockey-42
70Swedish Hockey-9
71Swedish Hockey-84

Hansson, Bror
99German Bundesliga 2-309
02Swiss HNL-363

Hansson, Gote
64Swedish Coralli ISHockey-103
65Swedish Coralli ISHockey-103
67Swedish Hockey-139
69Swedish Hockey-150
70Swedish Hockey-117
71Swedish Hockey-211
72Swedish Stickers-188

Hansson, Hans
69Swedish Hockey-151
70Swedish Hockey-121
71Swedish Hockey-212
72Swedish Stickers-189
74Swedish Stickers-218
98Danish Hockey League-111

Hansson, Johan
96Swedish Brynas Tigers-16
97Swedish Collector's Choice-21
98Swedish UD Choice-36

Hansson, Jonas
98Danish Hockey League-100

Hansson, Mats
03Swedish Elite-271
Silver-271
04Swedish Elitset-280
Future Stars-12
Gold-280
Signatures Series A-9
05Swedish SHL Elitset-135
Gold-135
Series Two Signatures-29
Star Potential-18
06Finnish Cardset-261

Hansson, Patrick
93Northern Michigan Wildcats-11

Hansson, Roger
91Swedish Semic Elitserien Stickers-194
92Swedish Semic Elitserien Stickers-211
93Swedish Semic Elitserien-183
93Swedish Semic World Champ Stickers-18
94Swedish Leaf-207
Gold Cards-20
95Finnish Semic World Championships-65
95Swedish Leaf-93
95Swedish Upper Deck-144
95Swedish Globe World Championships-32
95Swedish World Championships Stickers-158
96German DEL-236
98German DEL-50
99German DEL-176

Hansson, Rolf
69Swedish Hockey-230
71Swedish Hockey-373

Hantschke, Ralf
91Finnish Semic World Champ Stickers-169
91Swedish Semic World Champ Stickers-169
94German DEL-263
98German DEL-151
99German DEL-89

Hanuljak, Miroslav
04Czech OFS-370

Hanus, Tim
93Johnstown Chiefs-8

Hanusch, Torsten
94German DEL-129
95German DEL-127
99German Bundesliga 2-290

Hanzal, Marcel
99Czech OFS-306
03Czech OFS Plus All-Star Game-H4

Hanzlik, Jan
00Czech OFS-301
01Czech OFS-97
02Czech DS-45
02Czech DS-66
02Czech OFS Plus-4
03Czech OFS Plus-153
04Czech HC Sparta Praha Postcards-6
04Czech OFS-185
05Czech HC Sparta Praha-4
05Czech HC Sparta Praha Postcards-6
06Czech OFS-84

Hanzlik, Jiri
95Czech APS Extraliga-248
96Czech APS Extraliga-295
97Czech APS Extraliga-177
97Czech DS Stickers-213
98Czech DS Stickers-153
98Czech OFS-37
99Czech DS-90
99Czech OFS-122
99Czech OFS-475
00Czech DS Extraliga-30
00Czech OFS-62
01Czech OFS-204
01Czech OFS Plus-260
02Czech OFS Plus-351
03Czech OFS Plus-201
03Czech OFS Plus-391
03Czech OFS Plus Insert C-C7
04Czech OFS-88
05Czech HC Liberec-3
06Czech OFS-28

Happola, Toni
01Finnish Cardset-21
01Finnish Cardset Dueling Aces-4
02Finnish Cardset-179
03Finnish Cardset-24
05Finnish Cardset -18
06Finnish Cardset-351
06Finnish Porin Assat Pelaajakortit-14

Hapson, Ted
74Minnesota Fighting Saints WHA-11

Harand, Christoph
06Czech OFS-204

Harant, Tomas
00Czech OFS-222
02Czech OFS Plus-134
Trios-T3
03Russian SL-4
04Czech OFS-378
Stars II-14
04Russian Legion-7
04Russian Moscow Dynamo-9
05Czech HC Ceski Budejovice-3

Harazim, Karel
99Czech Score Blue 2000-105
99Czech Score Red Ice 2000-105

Harazim, Marek
96Czech APS Extraliga-117

Harbaruk, Nick
66Tulsa Oilers-5
70Esso Power Players-226
70Sargent Promotions Stamps-172
71O-Pee-Chee-191
71Penguins Postcards-7
71Sargent Promotions Stamps-171
71Toronto Sun-215
72O-Pee-Chee-106
72Sargent Promotions Stamps-171
73Blues White Border-9
75O-Pee-Chee WHA-11

Harbinson, Fred
04St. Cloud State Huskies-29
05St. Cloud State Huskies-29
06St. Cloud State Huskies-29

Harbour, Jonathan
93Quebec Pee-Wee Tournament-1009

Hard, Veli-Pekka
92Finnish Jyvas-Hyva Stickers-82
93Finnish Jyvas-Hyva Stickers-141
93Finnish SISU-141
94Finnish SISU-36
95Finnish SISU-341
98Finnish Keräilysarja-77
00Finnish Cardset-346

Hardegger, Jurg
95Swiss HNL-421
96Swiss HNL-368
02Swiss HNL-178

Harder, Graeme
91British Columbia JHL-21
92British Columbia JHL-67

Harder, Mike
91Air Canada SJHL-C35
92Saskatchewan JHL-145
97Milwaukee Admirals-8
98Rochester Americans-8
99Hartford Wolf Pack-10
00Louisville Panthers-18
03German DEL-98
04German DEL Update-300
04German Ingolstadt Panthers-8

Harder, Tyler
04Calgary Hitmen-7

Hardill, Chris
01Kingston Frontenacs-6
02Ottawa 67's-1

Hardin, Per-Olaf
65Swedish Coralli ISHockey-107
67Swedish Hockey-172

Harding, D.J.
98Huntington Blizzard-5

Harding, Jason
04Penticton Vees-12

Harding, Jeff
88ProCards AHL-120

Harding, Josh
01Regina Pats-9
02BAP Memorabilia-369
02Upper Deck Rookie Update-123
02Regina Pats-23
03BAP Memorabilia-130
Emerald-130
Gold-130
Ruby-130
Sapphire-130
Deep in the Crease-D11
03Brandon Wheat Kings-1
03Regina Pats-23
04Houston Aeros-9
05ITG Heroes/Prosp Toronto Expo Parallel -55
05AHL Top Prospects-18
05ITG Heroes and Prospects-55
Autographs-A-JH
06Between The Pipes-26
Autographs-AJHR
Emblems-GUE37
Emblems Gold-GUE37
Emblems Autographs-GUE37
Jerseys-GUJ37
Jerseys Gold-GUJ37
Jerseys Autographs-GUJ37
Numbers-GUN37
Numbers Gold-GUN37
Numbers Autographs-GUN37
Prospect Trios-PT02
Prospect Trios Gold-PT02
06ITG Heroes and Prospects Jerseys-GUJ15
06ITG Heroes and Prospects Jerseys Gold-GUJ15
06ITG Heroes and Prospects Emblems-GUE15
06ITG Heroes and Prospects Emblems Gold-GUE15
06ITG Heroes and Prospects Numbers-GUN15
06ITG Heroes and Prospects Numbers Gold-GUN15

Harding, Mike
90 7th Inn. Sketch OHL-360
91Peterborough Petes-6
91 7th Inn. Sketch OHL-136
93Detroit Jr. Red Wings-12
93Peterborough Petes-5
93Peterborough Petes-28

Harding, UK
92Northern Michigan Wildcats-10
93Northern Michigan Wildcats-12
96Richmond Renegades-10
97UK Guildford Flames-15
00UK Sekonda Superleague-18

Hardmeier, Roman
01Swiss HNL-56

Hardouin, Ludovic
93Quebec Pee-Wee Tournament-1644

Hardwick, Kyle
04Lincoln Stars Update-32
05Lincoln Stars-20
05Lincoln Stars Update Traded-14T

Hardy, Bill
84Nanaimo Clippers-9

Hardy, Bruce
94German DEL-73
95German DEL-136

Hardy, Damon
93Oshawa Generals-7
94Sarnia Sting-23

Hardy, Francois
98Val d'Or Foreurs-13

Hardy, Joe
70Esso Power Players-102

Hardy, Mark
82O-Pee-Chee-155
82Post Cereal-8
83NHL Key Tags-55
83O-Pee-Chee-155
84Kings Smokey-8
84O-Pee-Chee-86
84O-Pee-Chee Stickers-272
85O-Pee-Chee Stickers-234
86Kings 20th Anniversary Team Issue-9
87Panini Stickers-275
88North Stars ADA-14
89O-Pee-Chee-252
89Rangers Marine Midland Bank-14
90Pro Set-489
90Score Rookie/Traded-104T
90Upper Deck-416
French-416
91O-Pee-Chee-406
91Pinnacle-420
French-420
91Pro Set-442
French-442
91Score Canadian Bilingual-453
91Score Canadian English-453
91Topps-406
92Pinnacle-220
French-220
92Score-247
Canadian-247
92Ultra-354
93Score-415
Canadian-415
93Stadium Club-414
Members Only Master Set-414
First Day Issue-414
93Ultra-343
93Phoenix Roadrunners-9
06Blackhawks Postcards-22

Hare, Ryan
99UD Prospects-72
00Sarnia Sting-12
02London Knights-7

Harfaoui, Nordin
98German DEL-284

Hargreaves, James
72Canucks Royal Bank-7

Hargreaves, Richard
03UK Basingstoke Bison-10
04UK London Racers-17
04UK London Racers Playoffs-7

Hargreaves, Ted
69Swedish Hockey-354
70Swedish Masterserien-186

Harikkala, Jaakko
98Finnish Keräilysarja-164
99Finnish Cardset-81
01Finnish Cardset-293
02Finnish Cardset-23
03Finnish Cardset-101
04Finnish Cardset-265

Harila, Kari
92Finnish Jyvas-Hyva Stickers-174
93Finnish Jyvas-Hyva Stickers-325
93Finnish SISU-36
93Swedish Semic World Champ Stickers-50
94Finnish Jaa Kiekko-9
95Finnish SISU-125
98Swedish UD Choice-151
99Finnish Cardset-330

Haringer, Paul
94German First League-211

Harju, Erkki
65Finnish Hellas-45

Harju, Johan
05Swedish Lulea Hockey Postcards-10
05Swedish SHL Elitset-234
Gold-234
06Swedish SHL Elitset-222

Harju, Matti
65Finnish Hellas-70
66Finnish Jaakiekkosarja-24
69Swedish Hockey-366
70Finnish Jaakiekko-103

Harju, Pentti
66Finnish Jaakiekkosarja-116

Harjula, Tuomo
00Finnish Cardset-182
01Finnish Cardset-284

Harjumaki, Jari
93Finnish SISU-62
94Finnish SISU-358

Harkala, Jari
06Finnish Porin Assat Pelaajakortit-32

Harkin, Wes
93Quebec Pee-Wee Tournament-1467

Harkins, Brett
87Brockville Braves-14
94Classic Autographs-NNO
94Classic Pro Prospects-221
95Leaf-303
96Providence Bruins-44
97Pacific Invincible NHL Regime-12
97Cleveland Lumberjacks-12
97Cleveland Lumberjacks Postcards-23
98Cleveland Lumberjacks-11
99Cleveland Lumberjacks-8
01Syracuse Crunch-22
03Finnish Cardset-27
04Finnish Cardset-27
04Finnish Cardset Signatures-7
04Swedish Pure Skills-107
Parallel-107
06Swedish SHL Elitset-133

Harkins, Todd
90ProCards AHL/IHL-624
91ProCards-589
92Salt Lake Golden Eagles-7
92Classic-113
Gold-113
93Upper Deck-80
98German DEL-208
99German DEL-209
00German Berlin Polar Bears Postcards-10

Harkonen, Marko
94Finnish SISU-332

Harkonen, Timo
71Finnish Suomi Stickers-321
80Finnish Mallasjuoma-72

Harlock, David
90Upper Deck-470
French-470
91Michigan Wolverines-5
93Alberta International Team Canada-4
93Donruss-496
93PowerPlay-481
93Ultra-461
94Maple Leafs Kodak-14
94Score Team Canada-CT15
94Finnish Jaa Kiekko-102
94St. John's Maple Leafs-11
94Classic Pro Prospects Ice Ambassadors-IA4
94Classic Pro Prospects Intl Heroes-LP13
95St. John's Maple Leafs-11
97Portland Pirates-11
99Ultimate Victory-4
1/1-4
Parallel-4
Parallel 100-4
00BAP Signature Series-114
Emerald-114
Ruby-114
Sapphire-114
Autographs-141
Autographs Gold-141
00Upper Deck NHLPA-PA4
01Topps Reserve-89
02BAP Sig Series Auto Buybacks 2000-141
02Philadelphia Phantoms-22

Harloff, Nick
06Quad City Mallards-6

Harlow, Scott
86Sherbrooke Canadiens-18
88ProCards IHL-82
89ProCards AHL-66
90ProCards AHL/IHL-421

Harlton, Tyler
99St. John's Maple Leafs-8
00St. John's Maple Leafs-11

Harmer, Duane
91 7th Inn. Sketch OHL-345
93Detroit Jr. Red Wings-18
93Guelph Storm-8
94Detroit Jr. Red Wings-21
95Roanoke Express-15
95Slapshot Memorial Cup-95
96Roanoke Express-8
98ECHL All-Star Northern Conference-2
98Roanoke Express-9
99ECHL All-Star Northern Conference-10
01Florida Everblades-6
02Florida Everblades-9
02Florida Everblades RBI-121

Harmon, Glen
43Parade Sportive *-49
43Parade Sportive *-50
43Parade Sportive *-51
44Beehive Group II Photos-245
45Quaker Oats Photos-80A
45Quaker Oats Photos-80B
45Quaker Oats Photos-80C
51Laval Dairy QSHL-86
51Laval Dairy Subset-86
52St. Lawrence Sales-2

Harney, Jake
00Fort Worth Brahmas-6

Harney, Joe
97Wheeling Nailers-7
97Wheeling Nailers Photo Pack-7
98Providence Bruins-10

Harney, Justin
00Charlotte Checkers-6
02German DEL City Press-159
03German DEL-81
All-Stars-AS4
04German DEL-88
04German Ingolstadt Panthers-9
05German DEL-187

Harpe, Daryl
90Cincinnati Cyclones-25

Harper, Chris
98Spokane Chiefs-10
00Prince Albert Raiders-17

Harper, Derrek
91British Columbia JHL-76
92British Columbia JHL-87
92British Columbia JHL-90
00Wichita Thunder-11

Harper, Kelly
92Michigan State Spartans-12
93Michigan State Spartans-10
94Huntington Blizzard-13
98Huntington Blizzard-9
99Huntington Blizzard-23

Harper, Regan
97New Mexico Scorpions-2
99Corpus Christi IceRays-6
99Tupelo T-Rex-8
03Tulsa Oilers-7

Harper, Shane
05Everett Silvertips-10

Harper, Terry
44Beehive Group II Photos-246
63Chex Photos-18
63Parkhurst-32
63Parkhurst-91
63York White Backs-11
64Beehive Group III Photos-105A
64Beehive Group III Photos-105B
64Canadiens Postcards-8
64Coca-Cola Caps-68
64Topps-3
65Coca-Cola-68
65Topps-68
66Canadiens IGA-7
66Topps-68
67Canadiens IGA-19
67Topps-6
67York Action Octagons-2
67York Action Octagons-7
67York Action Octagons-33
68Canadiens IGA-19
68Canadiens Postcards BW-6
68O-Pee-Chee-57
68Post Marbles-9
68Shirriff Coins-86
68Topps-57
69Canadiens Postcards Color-9
69O-Pee-Chee-164
70Canadiens Pins-5
70Dad's Cookies-48
70Esso Power Players-13
70O-Pee-Chee-50
70Sargent Promotions Stamps-111
70Topps-53
71Canadiens Postcards-6
71O-Pee-Chee-59
71Sargent Promotions Stamps-107
71Topps-59
71Toronto Sun-150
72O-Pee-Chee-172
72Sargent Promotions Stamps-96
72Topps-119
73O-Pee-Chee-80
73Topps-80
74NHL Action Stamps-126
74O-Pee-Chee NHL-55
74Topps-55
75O-Pee-Chee NHL-255
75Topps-255
76O-Pee-Chee NHL-262
76Topps-262
77O-Pee-Chee NHL-16
77Topps-16
78O-Pee-Chee-214
78Topps-214
94Parkhurst Tall Boys-83
95Parkhurst '66-67-66
Coins-66

Harper, Trent
91Air Canada SJHL-E21
92Saskatchewan JHL-74

Harper, Warren
88ProCards AHL-124

Harpwood, Matt
01Kitchener Rangers-18
02Mississauga Ice Dogs-14

Harrer, Johann
94German First League-359

Harrer, Peter
94German First League-124

Harrigan, Jana
04Ohio State Buckeyes Women-6
05Ohio State Buckeyes Women-1

Harrington Sr., Bill
52Juniors Blue Tint-112

Harrington, Bill
86Kamloops Blazers-7
87Kamloops Blazers-8

Harrington, Brandon
04Sioux Falls Stampede-4-6

Harrington, Chris
02Minnesota Golden Gophers-8
03Minnesota Golden Gophers-14
04Minnesota Golden Gophers-10
05Minnesota Golden Gophers-12
06ITG Heroes and Prospects-152
Autographs-ACHA
Update Autographs-ACHA

Harrington, Hugo
24Anonymous NHL-36

Harrington, John
80USA Olympic Team Mini Pics-3
81Swedish Semic Hockey VM Stickers-108
95Signature Rookies Miracle on Ice-13
95Signature Rookies Miracle on Ice-14
95Signature Rook Miracle on Ice Sigs-13
95Signature Rook Miracle on Ice Sigs-14
04UD Legendary Signatures Miracle Men-USA14
04UD Legendary Sigs Miracle Men Autos-USA-JH

Harrington, Nathan
00Sudbury Wolves-14

Harrington, Steve
93Quebec Pee-Wee Tournament-1229

Harris, Billy Edward
44Beehive Group II Photos-405
55Parkhurst-20
Quaker Oats-20
57Parkhurst-T15
58Parkhurst-4
59Parkhurst-9
60Parkhurst-15
60Shirriff Coins-8
60York Photos-12
61Parkhurst-15
61Shirriff/Salada Coins-54
61York Yellow Backs-15
62Parkhurst-1
62Shirriff Coins-13
62York Iron-On Transfers-26
63Chex Photos-19
63Maple Leafs Team Issue-8
63Maple Leafs Team Issue-9
63Parkhurst-11
63Parkhurst-71
63York White Backs-10
64Beehive Group III Photos-75
64Beehive Group III Photos-163A
64Beehive Group III Photos-163B
64Topps-27
64Toronto Star-12
65Coca-Cola-47
65Topps-53
67Seals Team Issue-11
67York Action Octagons-8
68O-Pee-Chee-80
68Shirriff Coins-112
68Topps-80
91Ultimate Original Six-35
French-35
93Parkhurst Parkie Reprints-PR39
94Parkhurst Missing Link-129
94Parkhurst Tall Boys-126
02Maple Leafs Platinum Collection-31
02Parkhurst Reprints-221
02Parkhurst Reprints-224
02Parkhurst Reprints-236
02Parkhurst Reprints-249
02Parkhurst Reprints-262
02Parkhurst Reprints-270

Harris, Billy NYI
72Sargent Promotions Stamps-131
73O-Pee-Chee-130
73Topps-130
74Lipton Soup-35
74NHL Action Stamps-175
74O-Pee-Chee NHL-228
74O-Pee-Chee NHL-233
74Team Canada L'Equipe WHA-5
74Topps-228
74Topps-233
75Heroes Stand-Ups-14
75O-Pee-Chee NHL-242
75Topps-242
76O-Pee-Chee NHL-216
76O-Pee-Chee NHL-252
76Topps-216
76Topps-252
77O-Pee-Chee NHL-126
77Topps-126
78O-Pee-Chee-182
78Topps-182
79Islanders Transparencies-4
79O-Pee-Chee-115
79Topps-115
80Kings Card Night-4
80O-Pee-Chee-46
80Topps-46
81Oilers Red Rooster-xx
81Oilers West Edmonton Mall-4
81O-Pee-Chee-144
81O-Pee-Chee Stickers-242
81Topps-W96
82Maple Leafs Postcards-16
82O-Pee-Chee-322
83Maple Leafs Postcards-10
83O-Pee-Chee-333
83O-Pee-Chee Stickers-27
83Topps Stickers-27
83Vachon-89
88Oilers Tenth Anniversary-104

Harris, Brian
04Langley Hornets-11
05Langley Hornets-22

Harris, Casey
00Indianapolis Ice-8
01Indianapolis Ice-9
03Port Huron Beacons-13

Harris, Darcy
96Kitchener Rangers-12
99Quebec Citadelles-5

Harris, Gord
90 7th Inn. Sketch OHL-59
91 7th Inn. Sketch OHL-226

Harris, Hugh
75O-Pee-Chee WHA-118
76O-Pee-Chee WHA-39

Harris, Joe
93Owen Sound Platers-10
94Owen Sound Platers-7
01Odessa Jackalopes-9

Harris, Keith
91Air Canada SJHL-B35
92Saskatchewan JHL-76

Harris, Kelly
90 7th Inn. Sketch WHL-324
91 7th Inn. Sketch WHL-41

Harris, Kevin
99Brandon Wheat Kings-10
00Brandon Wheat Kings-21
01Brandon Wheat Kings-9
02Prince Albert Raiders-11
04Oklahoma City Blazers-16

Harris, Kris
95Waterloo Blackhawks -8
97Dubuque Fighting Saints-16

Harris, Kyle
01Saskatoon Blades-5

Harris, Marc
93Quebec Pee-Wee Tournament-711
97Arizona Icecats-12
98Arizona Icecats-11
99Arizona Icecats-10
00Arizona Icecats-10

Harris, Paul
01Notre Dame Fighting Irish-13

Harris, Peter
90Richmond Renegades-17

Harris, Rick
83Pinebridge Bucks-5

Harris, Ron
61Hamilton Red Wings-7
67Seals Team Issue-12
68O-Pee-Chee-27
68Topps-27
69O-Pee-Chee-64
70Esso Power Players-140
70O-Pee-Chee-26
70Sargent Promotions Stamps-52
70Topps-23
71O-Pee-Chee-70
71Sargent Promotions Stamps-58
71Toronto Sun-94
72O-Pee-Chee-5
72Topps-138
74NHL Action Stamps-183
74O-Pee-Chee NHL-276
85Nordiques General Foods-12

Harris, Ross
90 7th Inn. Sketch WHL-244
91 7th Inn. Sketch WHL-59
94Central Hockey League-78
94San Antonio Iguanas-6
95Oklahoma Coyotes RHI-10
98San Angelo Outlaws-10
99Fort Worth Brahmas-6
00Russian Hockey League-28
00Fort Worth Brahmas-7

Harris, Ryan
97New Hampshire Wildcats-23
98New Hampshire Wildcats-16

Harris, Shawn
98Colorado Gold Kings-8
98Colorado Gold Kings Postcards-15

Harris, Smokey
24V130 Maple Crispette-7
24V145-2-22
28V128-2 Paulin's Candy-71

Harris, T.C.
93Quebec Pee-Wee Tournament-834

Harris, Ted
64Beehive Group III Photos-106
64Canadiens Postcards-9
64Coca-Cola Caps-61
65Coca-Cola-61
65Topps-5
66Canadiens IGA-4
66Topps-69
66Topps USA Test-41
67Canadiens IGA-10
67Topps-10
68Bauer Ads-10
68Canadiens IGA-10
68Canadiens Postcards BW-7
68O-Pee-Chee-162
68Post Marbles-10
68Shirriff Coins-77
69Canadiens Postcards Color-10
69O-Pee-Chee-2
69O-Pee-Chee-219
69Topps-2
70Canadiens Pins-18
70Dad's Cookies-49
70Esso Power Players-166
70North Stars Postcards-4
70O-Pee-Chee-166
70Sargent Promotions Stamps-82
71Bazooka-9
71Letraset Action Replays-24
71O-Pee-Chee-32
71Sargent Promotions Stamps-91
71Topps-32
71Toronto Sun-134
72O-Pee-Chee-118
72Sargent Promotions Stamps-109
72Topps-23
73O-Pee-Chee-154
73Red Wings McCarthy Postcards-7
73Topps-14
75O-Pee-Chee NHL-244
75Topps-244
94Parkhurst Tall Boys-78
95Parkhurst '66-67-63
Coins-63

Harris, Tim
91ProCards-587
92British Columbia JHL-149
92Salt Lake Golden Eagles-8

Harris, Toby
00Amarillo Rattlers-9

Harris, Todd
89Kamloops Blazers-8
90 7th Inn. Sketch WHL-239
90 7th Inn. Sketch Memorial Cup-15
91 7th Inn. Sketch WHL-307
93Birmingham Bulls Birmingham News-10
94Birmingham Bulls-9
95Central Hockey League-44
97Austin Ice Bats-4

Harrison, Brad
89Portland Winter Hawks-10
90 7th Inn. Sketch WHL-316
93Huntington Blizzard-11
94Erie Panthers-8
94Classic Pro Prospects-236

Harrison, Bruce
98Kelowna Rockets-8

Harrison, Dan
96Johnstown Chiefs-7
97Johnstown Chiefs-13

Harrison, David
93Quebec Pee-Wee Tournament-1696A

Harrison, Ed
44Beehive Group II Photos-27

Harrison, Jay
99Brampton Battalion-22
99UD Prospects-82
00Brampton Battalion-19
00Brampton Battalion-30
00UD CHL Prospects-1
00UD CHL Prospects-97
01UD Prospects-16
Autographs-A-JH
Jersey Autographs-S-JH
Jerseys-J-JH
Jerseys-C-HM
Jerseys Gold-J-JH
Jerseys Gold-C-HM
05Black Diamond-288
05Hot Prospects-176
En Fuego-176
Red Hot-176
White Hot-176
05Parkhurst-666
Facsimile Auto Parallel-666
05SP Authentic-283
Limited-283
05SP Game Used-237
05SPx-287
05The Cup Masterpiece Pressplate Artifact-335
05The Cup Master Pressplate Black Diamond-288
05The Cup Masterpiece Pressplates (Ice)-264
05The Cup Master Pressplate Rookie Update-186
05The Cup Masterpiece Pressplates SPA-283
05The Cup Masterpiece Pressplates SP GU-237
05The Cup Masterpiece Pressplates (SPx)-287
05The Cup Masterpiece Pressplates Trilogy-312
05The Cup Masterpiece Pressplate Ult Coll-230
05UD Artifacts-335
05Ultimate Collection-230
Gold-230
05Upper Deck Ice-264
05Upper Deck Rookie Update-186
05Upper Deck Trilogy-312
06Toronto Marlies-14

Harrison, Jim
69Maple Leafs White Border Glossy-15
70Esso Power Players-26
70Maple Leafs Postcards-4
70O-Pee-Chee-220
70Sargent Promotions Stamps-194
71Maple Leafs Postcards-6
71O-Pee-Chee-10
71Sargent Promotions Stamps-202
71Toronto Sun-259
72O-Pee-Chee-292
Player Crests-20
72 7-Eleven Slurpee Cups WHA-10
73O-Pee-Chee WHA Posters-11
73Quaker Oats WHA-10
74Team Canada L'Equipe WHA-6
75O-Pee-Chee WHA-47
76O-Pee-Chee NHL-183
77O-Pee-Chee NHL-243
77Topps-243
88Oilers Tenth Anniversary-119

Harrison, Paul
78Maple Leafs Postcards-8
78O-Pee-Chee-123
78Topps-123
79Maple Leafs Postcards-11
80Maple Leafs Postcards-14
80O-Pee-Chee-391

Harrison, Ryan

88Kamloops Blazers-10
89Victoria Cougars-11
907th Inn. Sketch WHL-290
94Central Hockey League-98
95Central Hockey League-62
95Vancouver VooDoo RHI-17
95Vancouver VooDoo RHI-21

Harrison, Steve
88Flint Spirits-5
88Flint Spirits-19
92Fort Worth Fire-7
93Fort Worth Fire-18
94Central Hockey League-23

Harrison, Terry
03Columbia Inferno-103

Harrison, Thomas
01Kitchener Rangers-3
03Kitchener Rangers-11
04Saginaw Spirit-18

Harrison, Tyler
03Brampton Battalion-6
04Brampton Battalion-20

Harrold, Josh
99Mobile Mysticks-14

Harrold, Peter
06Hot Prospects-162
Red Hot-162
White Hot-162
06O-Pee-Chee-594
Rainbow-594
06SP Authentic-239
Limited-239
06The Cup Masterpiece Pressplates (Marquee Rookies)-594
06The Cup Masterpiece Pressplates (SP Authentic)-239
06Upper Deck-472
Exclusives Parallel-472
High Gloss Parallel-472
Masterpieces-472
06AHL Top Prospects-22
06Manchester Monarchs-17

Harstad, Wade
02Topeka Scarecrows-11

Harsulla, Nick
02Medicine Hat Tigers-8

Hart, Andre
99Quebec Remparts-17
Signed-17
99Rouyn-Noranda Huskies-9

Hart, Cecil M
27La Patrie-15
27La Presse Photos-16
37V356 Worldwide Gum-97
03BAP Ultimate Memorabilia Memorialized-14
04ITG Ultimate Memorabilia Paper Cuts-22
05ITG Ultimate Memorabilia Lumbergraphs-2
06ITG Ultimate Memorabilia Builders Autos-1
06ITG Ultimate Memorabilia Paper Cuts Autos-5

Hart, Dan
84Brandon Wheat Kings-14

Hart, Gerry
71Toronto Sun-95
72O-Pee-Chee-139
72Sargent Promotions Stamps-138
72Topps-92
73O-Pee-Chee-34
73Topps-34
74NHL Action Stamps-173
74O-Pee-Chee NHL-199
74Topps-199
75Heroes Stand-Ups-15
75O-Pee-Chee NHL-18
75Topps-18
76O-Pee-Chee NHL-77
76Topps-77
77O-Pee-Chee NHL-162
77Topps-162
78O-Pee-Chee-77
78Topps-77
79O-Pee-Chee-365
80O-Pee-Chee-349
93Islanders Chemical Bank Alumni-4

Hart, Gizzy
27La Patrie-6
27La Presse Photos-13

Hart, Greg
93Kamloops Blazers-7
94Kamloops Blazers-10
95Kamloops Blazers-10
95Slapshot Memorial Cup-8

Hart, Jon
03Minnesota State Mavericks-8

Hart, Matthias
02German DEL City Press-48
03German Deg Metro Stars-3
04German Cologne Sharks Postcards-12
04German DEL-211
05German SC Bietigheim-Bissingen Steelers-12

Hart, Shane
03Guelph Storm-15

Hartfuss, Ralf
94German First League-166

Hartigan, Mark
01BAP Memorabilia-436
Emerald-436
Ruby-436
Sapphire-436
01Parkhurst-302
01SPx Rookie Redemption-R2
01UD Mask Collection-134
01UD Top Shelf-136
02BAP First Edition-299
02SPx-102
02UD Foundations-123
02Upper Deck-196
Exclusives-196
02Upper Deck MVP-191
Gold-191
Classics-191
Golden Classics-191
02Upper Deck Victory-13
Bronze-13
Gold-13
Silver-13
02Upper Deck Vintage-322
02Chicago Wolves-11
03Syracuse Crunch-3
04Syracuse Crunch-4
05ITG Heroes/Prosp Toronto Expo Parallel -212
05AHL All-Stars-12
05Syracuse Crunch-3
05ITG Heroes and Prospects-212
Autographs Series II-MHA
06Syracuse Crunch-3
06ITG Heroes and Prospects-63
Autographs-AMHA

Hartin, Pentti
70Finnish Jaakiekko-124

Hartinger, Vladimir
03New Mexico Scorpions-9
04New Mexico Scorpions-4
06New Mexico Scorpions-21

Hartje, Todd
91Upper Deck-568
French-568
91Moncton Hawks-11
91ProCards-179

Hartley, Bob
03Thrashers Postcards-5
06Thrashers Postcards-3

Hartley, Brad
03Ottawa 67's-11

Hartley, Jon
89Windsor Spitfires-6

Hartlieb, Ernie
93Quebec Pee-Wee Tournament-1749
02Arkansas Riverblades-6
03Worcester Ice Cats-21
05Florida Everblades-8

Hartman, John
01Michigan Tech Huskies-11

Hartman, Matt
04St. Cloud State Huskies-13
05St. Cloud State Huskies-20
06St. Cloud State Huskies-13

Hartman, Mike
84Belleville Bulls-30
87Sabres Blue Shield-11
88Sabres Blue Shield-9
88Sabres Wonder Bread/Hostess-9
89Sabres Blue Shield-5
89Sabres Campbell's-7
90O-Pee-Chee-16
90Panini Stickers-32
90Pro Set-414
90Sabres Blue Shield-7
90Sabres Campbell's-8
90Topps-16
Tiffany-16
91Jets IGA-13
91O-Pee-Chee-363
91Pro Set-519
French-519
91Score Canadian Bilingual-454
91Score Canadian English-454
91Stadium Club-341
91Topps-363
92Parkhurst-407
Emerald Ice-407
92Stadium Club-497
92Topps-518
Gold-518G
97Charlotte Checkers-11
98German DEL-107

Hartmann, Eduard
91Finnish Semic World Champ Stickers-104
91Swedish Semic World Champ Stickers-104
94Finnish Jaa Kiekko-191
95Slovakian APS National Team-6
96Swedish Semic Wien-219

Hartmann, Gunther
94German First League-279

Hartmann, Richard
04Czech OFS Czech/Slovak-29
04Slovakian Skalica Team Set-11

Hartmann, Urs
93Swiss HNL-355

Hartnell, Devin
00Florida Everblades-10

Hartnell, Rob
907th Inn. Sketch WHL-124
917th Inn. Sketch WHL-340
94Dayton Bombers-9
94Los Angeles Blades RHI-6
97Austin Ice Bats-5
99Idaho Steelheads-17

Hartnell, Scott
98Prince Albert Raiders-9
99UD Prospects-28
99UD Prospects-73
00BAP Memorabilia-452
Emerald-452
Ruby-452
Sapphire-452
00BAP Parkhurst 2000-P160
00BAP Signature Series-300
Emerald-300
Ruby-300
Sapphire-300
Autographs-237
Autographs Gold-237
00Black Diamond-124
00Crown Royale-130
00Private Stock-129
Gold-129
Premiere Date-129
Retail-129
Silver-129
00SP Authentic-112
Sign of the Times-SH
00SP Game Used-71
00SPx-164
00Stadium Club-250
00Titanium-132
Retail-132
00Titanium Draft Day Edition-132
00Titanium Draft Day Promos-132
00Topps Chrome-247
Blue-247
Red-247
OPC Refractors-247
OPC Refractors Blue-247
OPC Refractors Red-247
Refractors-247
Refractors Blue-247
Refractors Red-247
00Topps Gold Label Class 1-104
Gold-104
00Topps Gold Label Class 2-104
00Topps Gold Label Class 2 Gold-104
00Topps Gold Label Class 3-104
00Topps Gold Label Class 3 Gold-104
00Topps Gold Label Autographs-GLA-SH
00Topps Heritage-99
Chrome Parallel-99
00Topps Premier Plus-121
Blue Ice-121
Private Signings-PSSH
00UD Heroes-168
00UD Pros and Prospects-109
Now Appearing-NA3
00UD Reserve-100
00Upper Deck-226
Exclusives Tier 1-226
Exclusives Tier 2-226
00Upper Deck Ice-92
00Upper Deck Vintage-382
00Vanguard-131
Pacific Proofs-131
01BAP Memorabilia-182
Emerald-182
Ruby-182
Sapphire-182
01BAP Signature Series-39
Autographs-39
Autographs Gold-39
01Bowman YoungStars-145
Gold-145
Ice Cubed-145
Autographs-SH
Relics-JSH
Relics-SSH
Relics-DSSH
Rivals-R10
01O-Pee-Chee-140
01O-Pee-Chee Premier Parallel-140
01Pacific-217
Extreme LTD-217
Hobby LTD-217
Premiere Date-217
Retail LTD-217
01Pacific Adrenaline-104
Blue-104
Premiere Date-104
Red-104
Retail-104
01Pacific Arena Exclusives-217
01Parkhurst-77
Gold-77
Silver-77
01SP Authentic Buybacks-31
01SP Authentic Sign of the Times-SH
01Titanium-78
Hobby Parallel-78
Premiere Date-78
Retail-78
Retail Parallel-78
01Topps-140
OPC Parallel-140
01Topps Chrome-113
Refractors-113
Black Border Refractors-113
01UD Mask Collection-54
Gold-54
01Upper Deck MVP Souvenirs-S-SH
01Upper Deck MVP Souvenirs Gold-S-SH
01Upper Deck Victory-202
Gold-202
02BAP First Edition-211
02BAP First Edition-357
02BAP First Edition-423R
02BAP Memorabilia-185
02BAP Memorabilia-217
Emerald-185
Emerald-217
Ruby-185
Ruby-217
Sapphire-185
Sapphire-217
Franchise Players-FP-17
Future of the Game-FG-13
NHL All-Star Game-185
NHL All-Star Game-217
NHL All-Star Game Blue-185
NHL All-Star Game Blue-217
NHL All-Star Game Green-185
NHL All-Star Game Green-217
NHL All-Star Game Red-185
NHL All-Star Game Red-217
02BAP Memorabilia Toronto Fall Expo-185
02BAP Memorabilia Toronto Fall Expo-217
02BAP Signature Series-66
Autographs-66
Autograph Buybacks 2000-237
Autograph Buybacks 2001-39
Autographs Gold-66
Golf-GS83
02ITG Used Franchise Players-F17
02ITG Used Franchise Players Autographs-F17
02ITG Used Franchise Players Gold-F17
02O-Pee-Chee-206
02O-Pee-Chee Premier Blue Parallel-206
02O-Pee-Chee Premier Red Parallel-206
02O-Pee-Chee Factory Set-206
02Pacific-210
Blue-210
Red-210
02Pacific Complete-125
Red-125
02Pacific Exclusive-98
02Pacific Heads-Up-68
Blue-68
Purple-68
Red-68
Head First-7
02Parkhurst-86
Bronze-86
Gold-86
Silver-86
Franchise Players-FP17
Teammates-TT10
02Parkhurst Retro-165
Minis-165
02Predators Team Issue-2
02Private Stock Reserve-58
Blue-58
Red-58
Retail-58
02SP Authentic-52
02SP Authentic-121
Beckett Promos-52
02SP Game Used First Rounder Patches-SH
02SP Game Used Future Fabrics-FFSH
02SP Game Used Future Fabrics Gold-FFSH
02SP Game Used Future Fabrics Rainbow-FFSH
02SP Game Used Signature Style-SH
02SPx-44
Spectrum Gold-44
Spectrum Silver-44
02Stadium Club-23
Silver Decoy Cards-23
Proofs-23
YoungStars Relics-S15
YoungStars Relics-DS2
02Topps-206
OPC Blue Parallel-206
OPC Red Parallel-206
Factory Set-206
02Topps Chrome-116
Black Border Refractors-116
Refractors-116
02Topps Total-255
02UD Piece of History-53
Threads-TTSH
02UD Premier Collection Signatures Bronze-SSH
02UD Premier Collection Signatures Gold-SSH
02UD Premier Collection Signatures Silver-SSH
02UD Top Shelf Dual Player Jerseys-RSH
02UD Top Shelf Shooting Stars-SHSH
02UD Top Shelf Signatures-SH
02Upper Deck-101
Exclusives-101
Blow-Ups-C23
Game Jersey Autographs-SH
Game Jersey Series II-GJSH
Hot Spots-HSSH
Number Crunchers-NC7
02Upper Deck Classic Portraits-55
Hockey Royalty-DLH
Hockey Royalty Limited-DLH
02Upper Deck MVP-103
Gold-103
Classics-103
Golden Classics-103
02Upper Deck Rookie Update-56
02Upper Deck Victory-117
Bronze-117
Gold-117
Silver-117
02Upper Deck Vintage-140
02Upper Deck Vintage-277
Green Backs-140
Tall Boys-T38
Tall Boys Gold-T38
03BAP Memorabilia-82
Emerald-82
Gold-82
Ruby-82
Sapphire-82
03Beehive Signatures-RF24
03Black Diamond Signature Gems-SG-10
03Bowman Future Fabrics-FF-SH
03Bowman Future Fabric Patches-SH
03ITG Action-393
Jerseys-M29
03O-Pee-Chee-113
03OPC Blue-113
03OPC Gold-113
03OPC Red-113
03Pacific-188
Blue-188
Red-188
03Pacific Calder-59
Silver-59
03Pacific Complete-53
Red-53
03Pacific Exhibit-80
Blue Backs-80
Yellow Backs-80
03Pacific Heads-Up-56
Hobby LTD-56
Retail LTD-56
03Pacific Quest for the Cup-61
Blue-61
03SP Authentic Sign of the Times-SH
03Topps-113
Blue-113
Gold-113
Red-113
03Topps C55-53
Minis-53
Minis American Back-53
Minis American Back Red-53
Minis Bazooka Back-53
Minis Brooklyn Back-53
Minis Hat Trick Back-53
Minis O Canada Back-53
Minis O Canada Back Red-53
Minis Stanley Cup Back-53
03UD Honor Roll Signature Class-SC9
03Upper Deck-108
Canadian Exclusives-108
HG-108
Jersey Autographs-SJ-SH
03Upper Deck MVP-240
Gold Script-240
Silver Script-240
Canadian Exclusives-240
ProSign-PS-SH
03Upper Deck Victory-104
Bronze-104
Gold-104
Silver-104
04Pacific-147
Blue-147
Red-147
04UD Toronto Fall Expo Priority Signings-SH
05Parkhurst-275
Facsimile Auto Parallel-275
Signatures-SH
True Colors-TCNSH
True Colors-TCNSH
05Upper Deck-357
Big Playmakers-B-SH
Jerseys-J-SH
05Upper Deck MVP-222
Gold-222
Platinum-222
05Upper Deck Victory-227
Black-227
Gold-227
Silver-227
06Black Diamond-48
Black-48
Gold-48
Ruby-48
Gemography-GHA
06Fleer-114
Tiffany-114
Signing Day-SDSH
06O-Pee-Chee-276
Rainbow-276
06Panini Stickers-312
06UD Artifacts Auto-Facts-AFSH
06UD Artifacts Auto-Facts Gold-AFSH
06UD Artifacts Tundra Tandems-TTHU
06UD Artifacts Tundra Tandems Black-TTHU
06UD Artifacts Tundra Tandems Blue-TTHU
06UD Artifacts Tundra Tandems Gold-TTHU
06UD Artifacts Tundra Tandems Platinum-TTHU
06UD Artifacts Tundra Tandems Red-TTHU
06UD Artifacts Tundra Tandems Dual Patches Red-TTHU
06UD Powerplay Power Marks-PMSH
06Ultra Fresh Ink-ISH
06Upper Deck-360
Exclusives Parallel-360
High Gloss Parallel-360
Masterpieces-360
06Upper Deck MVP-170
Gold Script-170
Super Script-170
06Upper Deck Ovation-129
06Upper Deck Trilogy Scripts-TSSH
06Upper Deck Victory-114
06Upper Deck Victory Black-114
06Upper Deck Victory Gold-114

Hartnett, Jamie
94German First League-652

Hartnett, Tim
90Michigan Tech Huskies-6
91Michigan Tech Huskies-4

Hartogs, Tommie
98German DEL-34
99German DEL-136
00German DEL-234
Game Jersey-TH
01German Upper Deck-125

Hartsburg, Chris
02Albany River Rats-6
02Albany River Rats AAP-13
03Albany River Rats-14
03Albany River Rats Kinko's-13
04Colorado Eagles-8
05Colorado Eagles-9
06Colorado EaglesA -11

Hartsburg, Craig
79North Stars Postcards-5
80North Stars Postcards-9
80O-Pee-Chee-317
81North Stars Postcards-11
81O-Pee-Chee-162
81O-Pee-Chee Stickers-91
81Topps-W106
82McDonald's Stickers-30
82North Stars Postcards-12
82O-Pee-Chee-167
82O-Pee-Chee Stickers-192
82Post Cereal-9
82Topps Stickers-192
83NHL Key Tags-58
83North Stars Postcards-10
83O-Pee-Chee-172
83O-Pee-Chee Stickers-117
83Puffy Stickers-16
83Topps Stickers-117
84North Stars 7-Eleven-3
84North Stars Postcards-9
84O-Pee-Chee-98
85North Stars 7-Eleven-8
85North Stars Postcards-13
85O-Pee-Chee-242
86North Stars 7-Eleven-7
86North Stars Postcards-16
86O-Pee-Chee-12
86O-Pee-Chee Stickers-173
86Topps-12
87North Stars Postcards-16
87O-Pee-Chee-165
87O-Pee-Chee Stickers-54
87Panini Stickers-290
87Topps-165
87Sault Ste. Marie Greyhounds-21
88North Stars ADA-15
88O-Pee-Chee-159
88O-Pee-Chee Stickers-199
88Panini Stickers-86
88Topps-159
92Flyers Upper Deck Sheets-34
94Guelph Storm-27
02Flyers Postcards-22
04ITG Franchises US West-257
Autographs-A-CHA
Memorabilia-WSM18
Memorabilia Gold-WSM18
04UD Legendary Signatures-19
Autographs-CH
Rearguard Retrospectives-CHMT

Hartung, Peter
94German First League-110

Hartung, Rasmus
98Danish Hockey League-177
99Danish Hockey League-55

Hartung, Ryan
01Bakersfield Condors-11

Hartung, Tim
04Northern Michigan Wildcats-7

Hartwick, Mike
907th Inn. Sketch OHL-210
917th Inn. Sketch OHL-354
92Windsor Spitfires-26

Hartwick, Shaun
93Quebec Pee-Wee Tournament-543

Hartwig, Geoff
93Quebec Pee-Wee Tournament-894

Harty, Jonathan
04Everett Silvertips-20

Hartzell, Kevin
06Sioux Falls Stampede -23

Harvela, Harri
65Finnish Hellas-153

Harvey, Alain
94Toledo Storm-7

Harvey, Chris
91Nashville Knights-3

Harvey, Doug
43Parade Sportive *-52
44Beehive Group II Photos-247
44Beehive Group II Photos-321
45Quaker Oats Photos-60B
45Quaker Oats Photos-81A
45Quaker Oats Photos-81B
48Exhibits Canadian-9
51Parkhurst-10
52Parkhurst-14
53Parkhurst-26
54Parkhurst-14
54Parkhurst-95
54Parkhurst-98
55Parkhurst-45
55Parkhurst-77
Quaker Oats-45
Quaker Oats-77
57Parkhurst-M1
57Parkhurst-M23
58Parkhurst-49
59Parkhurst-8
60NHL Ceramic Tiles-7
60Parkhurst-48
60Shirriff Coins-26
60Topps Stamps-21
60York Photos-13
61Shirriff/Salada Coins-81
61Topps-45
62Shirriff Coins-45
62Shirriff Coins-60
63Topps-47
63Toronto Star-16
63Quebec Aces-11
64Beehive Group III Photos-130
64Quebec Aces-8
68O-Pee-Chee-1
Puck Stickers-14
83Hall of Fame-219
83Hall of Fame Postcards-O9
85Hall of Fame-219
91Kraft-71
91Ultimate Original Six-12
French-12
92Parkhurst Parkie Reprints-PR14
93O-Pee-Chee Canadiens Hockey Fest-22
93O-Pee-Chee Canadiens Hockey Fest-59
93Parkhurst Parkie Reprints-PR40
94Parkhurst Missing Link-67
94Parkhurst Missing Link-136
94Parkhurst Missing Link-148
97Donruss Limited-49
Exposure-49
99Upper Deck Century Legends-7
Century Collection-7
All Century Team-AC5
00Upper Deck Legends-65
Legendary Collection Bronze-65
Legendary Collection Gold-65
Legendary Collection Silver-65
01BAP Memorabilia Rocket's Mates-RM2
01BAP Ultimate Mem All-Star History-8
01BAP Ultimate Memorabilia Decades-5
01BAP Ultimate Memorabilia Emblem Attic-6
01BAP Ultimate Memorabilia Gloves Are Off-6
01BAP Ultimate Memorabilia Les Canadiens-12
01BAP Ultimate Mem Prototypical Players-4
01BAP Ultimate Mem Prototypical Players-5
01BAP Ultimate Mem Prototypical Players-6
01BAP Ultimate Mem Retired Numbers-11
01BAP Ultimate Memorabilia Retro Trophies-18
01BAP Ultimate Mem Retro Teammates-2
01BAP Ultimate Mem Retro Teammates-14
01BAP Ultimate Mem Stanley Cup Winners-13
01Parkhurst He Shoots-He Scores Points-2
01Parkhurst Heroes-H7
01Parkhurst Reprints-PR7
01Parkhurst Reprints-PR27
01Parkhurst Reprints-PR41
01Parkhurst Reprints-PR65
01Parkhurst Reprints-PR100
01Parkhurst Reprints-PR115
01Parkhurst Reprints-PR121
01Parkhurst Reprints-PR131
01Parkhurst Vintage Memorabilia-PV10
01Parkhurst Vintage Memorabilia-PV11
01Parkhurst Vintage Memorabilia-PV12
01SP Game Used Signs of Tradition-LCDH
01Upper Deck Legendary Cut Signatures-LCDH
02BAP NHL All-Star History-8
02BAP Ultimate Memorabilia Emblem Attic-8
02BAP Ultimate Memorabilia Gloves Are Off-14
02BAP Ultimate Memorabilia Legend-6
02BAP Ultimate Memorabilia Numerology-5
02BAP Ultimate Mem Paper Cuts Autos-8
02BAP Ultimate Mem Storied Franchise-19
02BAP Ultimate Mem Vintage Jerseys-10
02ITG Used Vintage Memorabilia-VM14
02ITG Used Vintage Memorabilia Gold-VM14
02Parkhurst Vintage Memorabilia-VM8
02Parkhurst Vintage Teammates-VT8
03BAP Memorabilia Vintage Memorabilia-VM-9
03BAP Ultimate Memorabilia Cornerstones-2
03BAP Ultimate Memorabilia Gloves Are Off-17
03BAP Ultimate Mem Hometown Heroes-3
03BAP Ultimate Mem Hometown Heroes Gold-3
03BAP Ultimate Memorabilia Paper Cuts-21
03BAP Ultimate Mem Raised to the Rafters-2
03BAP Ultimate Mem Retro Teammates-2
03BAP Ultimate Mem Retro-Active Trophies-10
03BAP Ultimate Memorabilia Triple Threads-14
03BAP Ultimate Mem Vintage Jerseys-3
03BAP Ultimate Mem Vintage Jerseys Gold-3
03BAP Ultimate Memorabilia Vintage Lumber-8
03Canada Post-4
03ITG Toronto Fall Expo Forever Rivals-FR8
03ITG Used Signature Series Norris Trophy-8
03ITG Used Sig Series Norris Trophy Gold-8
03ITG Used Sig Series Vintage Mem -28
03ITG Used Sig Series Vintage Mem Gold-28
03ITG VIP Collages-35
03ITG VIP Vintage Memorabilia-14
03Parkhurst Orig Six He Shoots/Scores-10
03Parkhurst Orig Six He Shoots/Scores-10A
03Parkhurst Original Six Montreal-66
03Parkhurst Original Six Montreal-79
03Parkhurst Original Six Montreal-87
Inserts-M2
Inserts-M11
Memorabilia-MM19
Memorabilia-MM25
Memorabilia-MM40
Memorabilia-MM53
03Parkhurst Original Six New York-47
Inserts-N8
Memorabilia-NM24
04ITG NHL AS FANtasy AS History Jerseys-SB8
04ITG Franchises Canadian-41
04ITG Franchises Update Original Sticks-UOS1
04ITG Franchises Upd Original Sticks Gold-UOS1
04ITG Franchises US East-402
04ITG Franchises US West-290
04ITG Ultimate Memorabilia-2
Gold-2
Bleu Blanc et Rouge-4
Broadway Blueshirts-7
Changing the Game-12
Day In History-33
Day In History Gold-33
Gloves are Off-11
Jersey and Sticks-1
Jersey and Sticks Gold-1
Norris Trophy-3
Original Six-8
Original Six-9
Paper Cuts-9
Paper Cuts Memorabilia-2
Raised to the Rafters-5
Retro Teammates-2
Vintage Lumber-10
04UD Legends Classics Jersey Redemptions-JY5
04Ultimate Collection Ultimate Cuts-UC-DH
04ITG Heroes and Prospects-167
Hero Memorabilia-29
04ITG Heroes/Prospects Toronto Expo '05-167
04ITG Heroes/Prospects Expo Heroes/Pros-167
05ITG Ultimate Memorabilia Level 1-28
05ITG Ultimate Memorabilia Level 2-28
05ITG Ultimate Memorabilia Level 3-28
05ITG Ultimate Memorabilia Level 4-28
05ITG Ultimate Memorabilia Level 5-28
05ITG Ultimate Mem Bleu Blanc Rouge Autos-7
05ITG Ultimate Mem Decades Jerseys-4
05ITG Ultimate Mem Decades Jerseys Gold-4
05ITG Ultimate Memorabilia Emblem Attic-13
05ITG Ultimate Mem Emblem Attic Gold-13
05ITG Ultimate Mem Pass the Torch Jerseys-8
05ITG Ultimate Mem Passing Torch Jsy Gold-8
05ITG Ultimate Mem Quad Paper Cuts Autos-4
05ITG Ultimate Mem Retro Teammate Jerseys-15
05ITG Ult Mem Retro Teammates Jersey Gold-15
05ITG Ultimate Mem Sticks and Jerseys-8
05ITG Ultimate Mem Stick and Jerseys Gold-8
05ITG Ultimate Mem 3 Star of the Game Jsy-2
05ITG Ult Mem 3 Star of the Game Jsy Gold-2
05ITG Ultimate Memorabilia Vintage Lumber-10
05ITG Ultimate Mem Vintage Lumber Gold-10
05The Cup Legendary Cuts-LCDH
06ITG Ultimate Memorabilia Bleu Blanc et Rouge Autos-4
06ITG Ultimate Memorabilia Double Memorabilia-27
06ITG Ultimate Memorabilia Double Memorabilia Gold-27
06ITG Ultimate Memorabilia Emblem Attic-3
06ITG Ultimate Memorabilia Emblem Attic Gold-3
06ITG Ultimate Memorabilia Retro Teammates-4
06ITG Ultimate Memorabilia Retro Teammates Gold-4
06ITG Ultimate Memorabilia Road to the Cup-2
06ITG Ultimate Memorabilia Road to the Cup Gold-2
06ITG Ultimate Memorabilia Stick Rack-2
06ITG Ultimate Memorabilia Stick Rack-7
06ITG Ultimate Memorabilia Stick Rack Gold-2
06ITG Ultimate Memorabilia Stick Rack Gold-7
06ITG Ultimate Memorabilia Vintage Lumber-8
06ITG Ultimate Memorabilia Vintage Lumber Gold-8

Harvey, Fred
70Esso Power Players-174
71Toronto Sun-135
72O-Pee-Chee-246
73North Stars Postcards-8
73O-Pee-Chee-190
73Topps-78
74NHL Action Stamps-11
74O-Pee-Chee NHL-319
75O-Pee-Chee NHL-298
75Topps-298
76O-Pee-Chee NHL-212
76Topps-212
77O-Pee-Chee NHL-122
77Topps-122

Harvey, Frederic
93Quebec Pee-Wee Tournament-533

Harvey, Graeme
88Sault Ste. Marie Greyhounds-29

Harvey, Greg
93Prince Albert Raiders-8

Harvey, Jeff
00Kootenay Ice-10
02Swift Current Broncos-5
03Everett Silvertips-22

Harvey, Kevin
03Owen Sound Attack-13
06New Mexico Scorpions-13

Harvey, Lloyd
23V128-1 Paulin's Candy-11

Harvey, Luke
91Ferris State Bulldogs-15
92Ferris State Bulldogs-15

Harvey, Michael
93Quebec Pee-Wee Tournament-377

Harvey, Michel
62Quebec Aces-11

Harvey, Paul
99Louisville Panthers-26
00Louisville Panthers-23

Harvey, Rene
51Laval Dairy Lac St. Jean-15

Harvey, Sebastien
92Quebec Pee-Wee Tournament-870
93Quebec Pee-Wee Tournament-528

Harvey, Todd
917th Inn. Sketch OHL-33
93Donruss Team Canada-15
93Parkhurst-513
Emerald Ice-513
93Pinnacle-476
Canadian-476
93Upper Deck-535
93Detroit Jr. Red Wings-1
93Classic-9
Top Ten-DP9
93Classic Four-Sport *-193
Gold-193
94Be A Player-R162
Signature Cards-152
94Finest-47
94Finest-160
Super Team Winners-47
Super Team Winners-160
Refractors-47
Refractors-160
Bowman's Best-R4
Bowman's Best Refractors-R4
94Flair-41
94Fleer-51
Rookie Sensations-4
94Leaf-467
Limited World Juniors Canada-4
94OPC Premier-473
Special Effects-473
94Parkhurst SE-SE39
94Parkhurst SE-SE206
Gold-SE39
Gold-SE206
94Pinnacle-262
94Pinnacle-533
Artist's Proofs-262
Artist's Proofs-533
Rink Collection-262
Rink Collection-533
Rookie Team Pinnacle-10
94Score-204
Gold-204
Platinum-204
Top Rookie Redemption-9
94Select-182
Gold-182
94SP-138
Die Cuts-138
Premier-6
Premier Die-Cuts-6
94Stars Pinnacle Sheet-262
94Stars Pinnacle Sheet-NNO
94Stars Postcards-9
94Topps/OPC Premier-473
Special Effects-473
94Ultra Prospects-2
94Upper Deck-267
94Upper Deck-500
94Upper Deck-536
94Upper Deck-546
Electric Ice-267
Electric Ice-500
Electric Ice-536
Electric Ice-546
SP Inserts-SP109
SP Inserts Die Cuts-SP109
94Classic-40
Gold-40
ROY Sweepstakes-R7
Tri-Cards-T16
95Upper Deck World Junior Alumni-14
95Bowman-78
All-Foil-78
95Collector's Choice-251
Player's Club-251
Player's Club Platinum-251
95Donruss-103
Canadian World Junior Team-17
Pro Pointers-20
Rookie Team-9
95Donruss Elite-34
Die Cut Stars-34
Die Cut Uncut-34
95Emotion-46
95Finest-97
Refractors-97
95Hoyle Western Playing Cards-32
95Leaf-2
Studio Rookies-9
95Leaf Limited-26
95McDonald's Pinnacle-MCD-32
95Metal-39
95Panini Stickers-169
95Parkhurst International-62
Emerald Ice-62
95Pinnacle-48
Artist's Proofs-48
Rink Collection-48
95Playoff One on One-247
95Pro Magnets-122
95Score-38
Black Ice Artist's Proofs-38
Black Ice-38
95Select Certified-62
Mirror Gold-62
Future-7
95SkyBox Impact-45
95SkyBox Impact-233
95SP-39
95Stadium Club-103
Members Only Master Set-103
95Stars Score Sheet-38
95Summit-148
Artist's Proofs-148
Ice-148
Mad Hatters-15
95Topps-356
OPC Inserts-356
Canadian World Juniors-10CJ
Home Grown Canada-HGC17
New To The Game-17NG
95Topps SuperSkills-68
Platinum-68
95Ultra-37
Gold Medallion-37
Crease Crashers-4
High Speed-10
95Upper Deck-199
Electric Ice-199
Electric Ice Gold-199
Special Edition-SE114
Special Edition Gold-SE114
95Zenith-75
Gifted Grinders-10
96Collector's Choice-67
96Collector's Choice-315
96Donruss-94
Press Proofs-94
96Leaf-145
Press Proofs-145
96Leaf Preferred-114
Press Proofs-114
96NHL Pro Stamps-122
96Pinnacle-52
Artist's Proofs-52
Foil-52
Premium Stock-52
Rink Collection-52
96Score-86
Artist's Proofs-86
Dealer's Choice Artist's Proofs-86
Special Artist's Proofs-86
Golden Blades-86
96SP-42
96Stars Postcards-7
96Stars Score Sheet-86
96Summit-46
Artist's Proofs-46
Ice-46
Metal-46
Premium Stock-46
96Upper Deck-45
Power Performers-P30
97Be A Player-96
Autographs-96
Autographs Die-Cuts-96
Autographs Prismatic Die-Cuts-96
97Collector's Choice-75
97Donruss-68
Press Proofs Silver-68
Press Proofs Gold-68
97Donruss Preferred-144
Cut to the Chase-144
97Donruss Priority-157
Stamp of Approval-157
97Pacific Invincible NHL Regime-60
97Upper Deck-55
98NHL Game Day Promotion-NYR2
98Pacific Omega-157
Red-157
Opening Day Issue-157
98Rangers Power Play-NYR2
98Revolution-93
Ice Shadow-93
Red-93
98Upper Deck-323
Exclusives-323
Exclusives 1 of 1-323
Gold Reserve-323
98Upper Deck MVP-138
Gold Script-138
Silver Script-138
Super Script-138
99BAP Memorabilia-176
Gold-176
Silver-176
99O-Pee-Chee-211
99O-Pee-Chee Chrome-211
99O-Pee-Chee Chrome Refractors-211
99Pacific-270
Copper-270
Emerald Green-270
Gold-270
Ice Blue-270
Premiere Date-270
Red-270
99Pacific Omega-206
Copper-206
Gold-206
Ice Blue-206
Premiere Date-206
99Paramount-150
Copper-150
Emerald-150

Gold-150
Holographic Emerald-150
Holographic Gold-150
Holographic Silver-150
Ice Blue-150
Premiere Date-150
Red-150
Silver-150
99Topps/OPC-211
99Topps/OPC Chrome-211
Refractors-211
99Upper Deck MVP SC Edition-159
Gold Script-159
Silver Script-159
Super Script-159
00O-Pee-Chee-94
00O-Pee-Chee Parallel-94
00Pacific-358
Copper-358
Gold-358
Ice Blue-358
Premiere Date-358
00Topps/OPC-94
Parallel-94
00Upper Deck-149
Exclusives Tier 1-149
Exclusives Tier 2-149
01Sharks Postcards-14
01Upper Deck-149
Exclusives-149
02Pacific Complete-382
Red-382
02Upper Deck-149
Exclusives-149
03ITG Action-421
03Sharks Postcards-7
03Upper Deck MVP-350
Gold Script-350
Silver Script-350
Canadian Exclusives-350
03Cleveland Barons-11
05Upper Deck MVP-162
Gold-162
Platinum-162

Hasanen, Pertti

72Finnish Jaakiekko-226
73Finnish Jaakiekko-259
78Finnish SM-Liiga-175
92Finnish Jyvas-Hyva Stickers-154

Hasani, Adam

06London Knights-17

Hasanov, Renat

00Russian Hockey League-218

Hascak, Marek

02Shawinigan Cataractes-19
03Shawinigan Cataractes-16

Hascak, Oto

90Swedish Semic Elitserien Stickers-62
91Finnish Semic World Champ Stickers-116
91Swedish Semic Elitserien Stickers-235
91Swedish Semic World Champ Stickers-116
93Swedish Semic Elitserien-288
94German DEL-179
95German DEL-181
95Slovakian APS National Team-16
96Czech APS Extraliga-226
96Swedish Semic Wien-235
97Czech DS Stickers-36
01Slovakian Kvarteto-38

Hasek, Dominik

89Swedish Semic World Champ Stickers-178
90ProCards AHL/IHL-409
91Pro Set Platinum-252
91Parkhurst-263
91Parkhurst-449
French-263
French-449
91Pro Set-529
French-529
91Score American-316
91Score Canadian Bilingual-346
91Score Canadian English-346
91Upper Deck-335
French-335
Euro-Stars-14
Euro-Stars French-14
91Finnish Semic World Champ Stickers-103
91Swedish Semic World Champ Stickers-103
91ProCards-500
92Bowman-428
92Kraft-30
92O-Pee-Chee-301
92OPC Premier-50
92Panini Stickers-292
92Panini Stickers French-292
92Sabres Blue Shield-7
92Sabres Jubilee Foods-4
92Score-373
Canadian-373
92Sports Illustrated for Kids II-442
92Stadium Club-107
92Topps-136
Gold-136G
92Upper Deck-92
92Upper Deck-366
92Upper Deck-506
All-Rookie Team-AR6
All-Rookie Team-AR7
Euro-Rookie Team-ERT3
Euro-Stars-E3
92Finnish Semic-124
93Leaf-256
93OPC Premier-320
93OPC Premier-463
Gold-320
Gold-463
93Pinnacle-403
Canadian-403
93PowerPlay-297
93Sabres Limited Edition Team Issue-2
93Sabres Noco-6
93Score-281
Canadian-281
93Stadium Club-178
Members Only Master Set-178
OPC-178
First Day Issue-178
First Day Issue OPC-178
93Topps/OPC Premier-320
93Topps/OPC Premier-463
Gold-320
Gold-463
93Ultra-274
93Upper Deck-387
94Canada Games NHL POGS-274
94Canada Games NHL POGS-332
94Canada Games NHL POGS-333
94Donruss-94
Dominators-3
Masked Marvels-3
94EA Sports-211
94Finest-43
Super Team Winners-43
Refractors-43
94Flair-17
Hot Numbers-3
94Fleer-20
Netminders-3
94Kraft-39
94Kraft-60
94Kraft-70
94Leaf-120
Crease Patrol-6
Gold Stars-8
Limited Inserts-3
94Leaf Limited-102
94OPC Premier-35
94OPC Premier-80
94OPC Premier-152
94OPC Premier-156
94OPC Premier-312
94OPC Premier-440
Special Effects-35
Special Effects-80
Special Effects-152
Special Effects-156
Special Effects-312
Special Effects-440
94Parkhurst-24
Gold-24
Vintage-V1
SE Euro-Stars-ES19
94Pinnacle-175
94Pinnacle-MVPU
Artist's Proofs-175
Rink Collection-175
Goaltending Greats-GT1
World Edition-WE6
94Score-78
Gold-78
Platinum-78
94Select-52
Gold-52
94SP-14
Die Cuts-14
Premier-19
Premier Die-Cuts-19
94Stadium Club-125
94Stadium Club-179
94Stadium Club-269
Members Only Master Set-125
Members Only Master Set-179
Members Only Master Set-269
First Day Issue-125
First Day Issue-179
First Day Issue-269
Super Teams-3
Super Teams Members Only Master Set-3
Super Team Winner Cards-125
Super Team Winner Cards-179
Super Team Winner Cards-269
94Topps/OPC Premier-35
94Topps/OPC Premier-80
94Topps/OPC Premier-152
94Topps/OPC Premier-156
94Topps/OPC Premier-312
94Topps/OPC Premier-440
Special Effects-35
Special Effects-80
Special Effects-152
Special Effects-156
Special Effects-312
Special Effects-440
94Ultra-22
Award Winners-6
Global Greats-2
Premier Pad Men-1
94Upper Deck-233
94Upper Deck-285
94Upper Deck-545
Electric Ice-233
Electric Ice-285
Electric Ice-545
Predictor Hobby-H31
94Upper Deck Predictor Hobby Exch Gold-H31
94Upper Deck SP Inserts-SP8
94Upper Deck SP Inserts Die Cuts-SP8
94Finnish Jaa Kiekko-163
94Finnish Jaa Kiekko-333
95SLU Hockey Canadian-7
95SLU Hockey American-9
95Bashan Super Stickers-10
95Bashan Super Stickers-12
95Be A Player-192
Signatures-S192
Signatures Die Cuts-S192
95Bowman-56
All-Foil-56
95Canada Games NHL POGS-45
95Canada Games NHL POGS-48
95Collector's Choice-258
95Collector's Choice-367
95Collector's Choice-381
95Collector's Choice-394
Player's Club-258
Player's Club-367
Player's Club-381
Player's Club-394
Player's Club Platinum-258
Player's Club Platinum-367
Player's Club Platinum-381
Player's Club Platinum-394
95Donruss-33
Between The Pipes-2
Dominators-4
95Donruss Elite-30
Die Cut Stars-30
Die Cut Uncut-30
95Emotion-16
95Finest-72
95Finest-90
Refractors-72
Refractors-90
95Hoyle Eastern Playing Cards-30
95Imperial Stickers-12
95Kenner Starting Lineup Cards-10
95Kraft-16
95Kraft-45
95Leaf-56
Gold Stars-1
95Leaf Limited-76
Stick Side-5
95McDonald's Pinnacle-MCD-28
95Metal-15
International Steel-7
95NHL Aces Playing Cards-13D
95Panini Stickers-24
95Panini Stickers-149
95Panini Stickers-154
95Parkhurst International-236
95Parkhurst International-291
Emerald Ice-236
Emerald Ice-291
All-Stars-1
Crown Collection Silver Series 2-5
Crown Collection Gold Series 2-5
Goal Patrol-4
Parkie's Trophy Picks-PP28
Trophy Winners-5
95Pinnacle-139
Artist's Proofs-139
Rink Collection-139
Clear Shots-15
First Strike-14
Global Gold-19
95Pinnacle FANtasy-17
95Playoff One on One-12
95Playoff One on One-125
95Pro Magnets-107
95Score-200
95Score-325
Black Ice Artist's Proofs-200
Black Ice Artist's Proofs-325
Black Ice-200
Black Ice-325
95Select Certified-89
Mirror Gold-89
95SkyBox Impact-16
Deflectors-1
95SP-13
95Stadium Club Members Only-12
95Stadium Club-60
Members Only Master Set-60
Metalists-M10
Metalists Members Only Master Set-M10
Nemeses-N6
Nemeses Members Only Master Set-N6
95Summit-159
Artist's Proofs-159
Ice-159
In The Crease-2
95Topps-2
95Topps-302
OPC Inserts-2
OPC Inserts-302
Hidden Gems-4HG
Marquee Men Power Boosters-2
Mystery Finest-M19
Mystery Finest Refractors-M19
Profiles-PF14
95Topps SuperSkills-75
Platinum-75
95Ultra-18
95Ultra-370
Gold Medallion-18
Premier Pad Men-5
Premier Pad Men Gold Medallion-5
Ultraview-3
Ultraview Hot Pack-3
95Upper Deck-104
Electric Ice-104
Electric Ice Gold-104
Freeze Frame-F11
Freeze Frame Jumbo-F11
NHL All-Stars-AS20
NHL All-Stars Jumbo-AS20
Predictor Hobby-H13
Predictor Hobby Exchange-H13
Special Edition-SE98
Special Edition Gold-SE98
95Zenith-109
95Czech APS Extraliga-392
95Finnish Semic World Championships-141
95Finnish Semic World Championships-214
95Swedish Globe World Championships-145
95Swedish World Championships Stickers-296
96SLU Hockey American-7
96Be A Player Stacking the Pads-11
96Black Diamond-156
Gold-156
96Collector's Choice-30
96Collector's Choice-311
96Donruss-192
Press Proofs-192
96Donruss Canadian Ice-60
Gold Press Proofs-60
Red Press Proofs-60
96Donruss Elite-37
Die Cut Stars-37
96Flair-8
Blue Ice-8
Hot Gloves-4
96Fleer-10
96Fleer-147
Vezina-4
Picks Dream Lines-6
96Kenner Starting Lineup Cards-7
96Kraft Upper Deck-18
96Leaf-19
Press Proofs-19
96Leaf Limited-21
Gold-21
96Leaf Preferred-91
Press Proofs-91
Steel-52
Steel Gold-52
Masked Marauders-7
96Metal Universe-14
Armor Plate-4
Armor Plate Super Power-4
Cool Steel-4
Cool Steel Super Power-4
96NHL Pro Stamps-107
96Pinnacle-106
Artist's Proofs-106
Foil-106
Premium Stock-106
Rink Collection-106
96Pinnacle Mint-2
Bronze-2
Gold-2
Silver-2
Coins Brass-2
Coins Solid Gold-2
Coins Gold Plated-2
Coins Nickel-2
Coins Silver-2
96Score-18
Artist's Proofs-18
Dealer's Choice Artist's Proofs-18
Special Artist's Proofs-18
Golden Blades-18
Net Worth-4
Sudden Death-3
96Select Certified-74
Artist's Proofs-74
Blue-74
Mirror Blue-74
Mirror Gold-74
Mirror Red-74
Red-74
Freezers-5
96SkyBox Impact-10
Zero Heroes-4
96SP-17
Holoview Collection-HC30
SPx Force-3
96Stadium Club Members Only-42
96Summit-2
Artist's Proofs-2
Ice-2
Metal-2
Premium Stock-2
In The Crease-14
In The Crease Premium Stock-14
96Team Out-69
96Topps Picks Ice D-ID10
96Ultra-16
Gold Medallion-16
Clear the Ice-3
96Upper Deck-222
Generation Next-X28
Superstar Showdown-SS26A
96Upper Deck Ice-5
Parallel-5
96Zenith-15
Artist's Proofs-15
96Swedish Semic Wien-103
Super Goalies-SG1
97SLU Hockey One on One-1
97Be A Player Stacking the Pads-2
97Beehive-24
Golden Portraits-24
97Black Diamond-20
Double Diamond-20
Triple Diamond-20
Quadruple Diamond-20
97Collector's Choice-22
Star Quest-SQ81
Stick'Ums-S30
97Crown Royale-14
Emerald Green-14
Ice Blue-14
Silver-14
Freeze Out Die-Cuts-3
97Donruss-9
Press Proofs Silver-9
Press Proofs Gold-9
Between The Pipes-4
Elite Inserts-11
97Donruss Canadian Ice-10
Dominion Series-10
Provincial Series-10
Stanley Cup Scrapbook-22
97Donruss Elite-30
Aspirations-30
Status-30
Craftsmen-6
Master Craftsmen-6
97Donruss Limited-76
97Donruss Limited-86
97Donruss Limited-147
Exposure-76
Exposure-86
Exposure-147
Fabric of the Game-65
97Donruss Preferred-1
97Donruss Preferred-169
Cut to the Chase-1
Cut to the Chase-169
Color Guard-6
Color Guard Promos-6
97Donruss Priority-80
Stamp of Approval-80
Postcards-31
Postcards Opening Day Issues-22
Postmaster General-13
Postmaster Generals Promos-13
Stamps-31
Stamps Bronze-31
Stamps Gold-31
Stamps Silver-31
97Esso Olympic Hockey Heroes-54
97Esso Olympic Hockey Heroes French-54
97Katch-15
Gold-15
Silver-15
97Leaf-2
97Leaf-169
Fractal Matrix-2
Fractal Matrix-169
Fractal Matrix Die Cuts-2
Fractal Matrix Die Cuts-169
Pipe Dreams-1
97Leaf International-2
Universal Ice-2
97McDonald's Upper Deck-26
97NHL Aces Playing Cards-1
97Pacific-39
Copper-39
Emerald Green-39
Ice Blue-39
Red-39
Silver-39
Cramer's Choice-2
Gold Crown Die-Cuts-3
In The Cage Laser Cuts-2
Team Checklists-3
97Pacific Dynagon-10
97Pacific Dynagon-136
Copper-10
Copper-136
Dark Grey-10
Dark Grey-136
Emerald Green-10
Emerald Green-136
Ice Blue-10
Ice Blue-136
Red-10
Red-136
Silver-10
Silver-136
Best Kept Secrets-10
Best Kept Secrets-104
Dynamic Duos-3A
Stonewallers-3
Tandems-4
Tandems-21
97Pacific Invincible-12
Copper-12
Emerald Green-12
Ice Blue-12
Red-12
Silver-12
Feature Performers-4
NHL Regime-20
97Pacific Omega-22
Copper-22
Dark Gray-22
Emerald Green-22
Gold-22
Ice Blue-22
No Scoring Zone-1
97Panini Stickers-10
97Panini Stickers-118
97Paramount-19
Copper-19
Dark Grey-19
Emerald Green-19
Ice Blue-19
Red-19
Silver-19
Big Numbers Die-Cuts-4
Glove Side Laser Cuts-2
Photoengravings-4
97Pinnacle-28
Artist's Proofs-28
Rink Collection-28
Epix Game Emerald-22
Epix Game Orange-22
Epix Game Purple-22
Epix Moment Emerald-22
Epix Moment Orange-22
Epix Moment Purple-22
Epix Play Emerald-22
Epix Play Orange-22
Epix Play Purple-22
Epix Season Emerald-22
Epix Season Orange-22
Epix Season Purple-22
Press Plates Back Black-28
Press Plates Back Cyan-28
Press Plates Back Magenta-28
Press Plates Back Yellow-28
Press Plates Front Black-28
Press Plates Front Cyan-28
Press Plates Front Magenta-28
Press Plates Front Yellow-28
Team Pinnacle-2
Team Mirror-2
Team Parallel-2
Team Parallel Mirror-2
97Pinnacle Certified-1
Red-1
Mirror Blue-1
Mirror Gold-1
Mirror Red-1
Team-4
Gold Team Promo-4
Gold Team-4
97Pinnacle Inside-2
Coach's Collection-2
Executive Collection-2
Stoppers-3
Track-15
97Pinnacle Mint-8
Bronze-8
Gold Team-8
Silver Team-8
Coins Brass-8
Coins Brass Proofs-8
Coins Gold Plated-8
Coins Gold Plated Proofs-8
Coins Nickel Silver-8
Coins Nickel Silver Proofs-8
Coins Solid Gold-8
Coins Solid Silver-8
Minternational-5
Minternational Coins-5
97Pinnacle Power Pack Blow-Ups-4
97Pinnacle Tot Certi Platinum Blue-1
97Pinnacle Tot Certi Platinum Gold-1
97Pinnacle Totally Certified Platinum Red-1
97Pinnacle Tot Cert Mirror Platinum Gold-1
97Post Pinnacle-16
97Revolution-14
Copper-14
Emerald-14
Ice Blue-14
Silver-14
1998 All-Star Game Die-Cuts-3
Return to Sender Die-Cuts-3
97Score-39
97Score-266
Artist's Proofs-39
Golden Blades-39
Net Worth-17
97Score Sabres-1
Platinum-1
Premier-1
97SP Authentic-14
Icons-I34
Icons Die-Cuts-I34
Icons Embossed-I34
97SPx-4
Bronze-4
Gold-4
Silver-4
Steel-4
DuoView-9
Grand Finale-4
97Studio-2
Press Proofs Silver-2
Press Proofs Gold-2
Portraits-2
Silhouettes-7
Silhouettes 8x10-7
97Upper Deck-225
Game Dated Moments-225
Game Jerseys-GJ3
Smooth Grooves-SG39
The Specialists-18
The Specialists Level 2 Die Cuts-18
Three Star Selects-2A
97Upper Deck Diamond Vision-24
Signature Moves-24
97Upper Deck Ice-87
Parallel-87
Champions-IC5
Champions 2 Die Cuts-IC5
Power Shift-87
97Zenith-20
Z-Gold-20
Z-Silver-20
97Zenith 5 x 7-62
Gold Impulse-62
Silver Impulse-62
97Czech APS Extraliga-368
98SLU Hockey-80
98Aurora-17
Atomic Laser Cuts-4
Championship Fever-6
Championship Fever Copper-6
Championship Fever Ice Blue-6
Championship Fever Red-6
Championship Fever Silver-6
Cubes-3
Front Line Copper-1
Front Line Ice Blue-1
Front Line Red-1
NHL Command-2
98Be A Player-162
Press Release-162
98BAP Gold-162
98BAP Autographs-162
98BAP Autographs Gold-162
98BAP AS Game Used Stick Cards-S18
98BAP AS Game Used Jersey Cards-AS20
98Black Diamond-10
Double Diamond-10
Triple Diamond-10
Quadruple Diamond-10
Myriad-M6
Myriad 2-M6
Winning Formula Gold-WF4
Winning Formula Platinum-WF4
98Bowman's Best-11
Refractors-11
Atomic Refractors-11
Autographs-A1A
Autographs-A1B
Autographs Refractors-A1A
Autographs Refractors-A1B
Autographs Atomic Refractors-A1A
Autographs Atomic Refractors-A1B
Mirror Image Fusion-F9
Mirror Image Fusion Refractors-F9
Mirror Image Fusion Atomic Refractors-F9
Scotty Bowman's Best-SB1
Scotty Refractors-SB1
Scotty Atomic Refractors-SB1
98Crown Royale-13
Limited Series-13
Cramer's Choice Jumbos-3
Cramer's Choice Jumbos Dark Blue-3
Cramer's Choice Jumbos Green-3
Cramer's Choice Jumbos Red-3
Cramer's Choice Jumbos Light Blue-3
Cramer's Choice Jumbos Gold-3
Cramer's Choice Jumbos Purple-3
Living Legends-3
Master Performers-3
Pivotal Players-2
98Donruss Elite Promos-10
98Finest-4
No Protectors-4
No Protectors Refractors-4
Refractors-4
Double Sided Mystery Finest-M2
Double Sided Mystery Finest-M5
Double Sided Mystery Finest-M6
Double Sided Mystery Finest-M7
Double Sided Mystery Refractors-M2
Double Sided Mystery Refractors-M5
Double Sided Mystery Refractors-M6
Double Sided Mystery Refractors-M7
Oversize-2
Oversize Refractors-2
98Katch-14
98Kenner Starting Lineup Cards-13
98Lunchables Goalie Greats Rounds-3
98Lunchables Goalie Greats Squares-3
98McDonald's Upper Deck-16
98NHL Aces Playing Cards-27
98OPC Chrome-163
Refractors-163
Season's Best-SB1
Season's Best Refractors-SB1
98Pacific-39
Ice Blue-39
Red-39
Cramer's Choice-2
Dynagon Ice Inserts-4
Titanium Ice-4
Gold Crown Die-Cuts-4
Team Checklists-3
Timelines-2
Trophy Winners-2
98Pacific Dynagon Ice-18
Blue-18
Red-18
Adrenaline Rush Bronze-3
Adrenaline Rush Ice Blue-3
Adrenaline Rush Red-3
Adrenaline Rush Silver-3
Watchmen-1
Preeminent Players-2
Team Checklists-3
98Pacific Omega-23
Red-23
Opening Day Issue-23
Championship Spotlight-2
Championship Spotlight Green-2
Championship Spotlight Red-2
Championship Spotlight Gold-2
EO Portraits-3
EO Portraits 1 of 1-3
Face to Face-3
Online-4
Planet Ice-21
Planet Ice Parallel-21
Prism-3
98Panini Photocards-32
98Panini Photocards-96
98Panini Stickers-19
98Panini Stickers-223
98Paramount-19
Copper-19
Emerald Green-19
Holo-Electric-19
Ice Blue-19
Silver-19
Glove Side Laser Cuts-3
Hall of Fame Bound-2
Hall of Fame Bound Proofs-2
Team Checklists Die-Cuts-3
98Revolution-14
Ice Shadow-14
Red-14
All-Star Die Cuts-9
NHL Icons-2
Showstoppers-4
Three Pronged Attack-11
Three Pronged Attack Parallel-11
98SP Authentic-8
Power Shift-8
Snapshots-SS7
Stat Masters-S3
98SPx Finite-8
98SPx Finite-103
98SPx Finite-159
98SPx Finite-173
Radiance-8
Radiance-103
Radiance-159
Radiance-173
Spectrum-8
Spectrum-103
Spectrum-159
Spectrum-173
98SPx Top Prospects-6
Radiance-6
Spectrum-6
Highlight Heroes-H5
Lasting Impressions-L6
Premier Stars-PS4
98Topps-163
O-Pee-Chee-163
Autographs-A8
Local Legends-L5
Mystery Finest Bronze-M7
Mystery Finest Bronze Refractors-M7
Mystery Finest Gold-M7
Mystery Finest Gold Refractors-M7
Mystery Finest Silver-M7
Mystery Finest Silver Refractors-M7
Season's Best-SB1
98Topps Gold Label Class 1-34
Black-34
Black One of One-34
One of One-34
Red-34
Red One of One-34
98Topps Gold Label Class 2-34
98Topps Gold Label Class 2 Black-34
98Topps Gold Label Class 2 Black 1 of 1-34
98Topps Gold Label Class 2 One of One-34
98Topps Gold Label Class 2 Red-34
98Topps Gold Label Class 2 Red One of One-34
98Topps Gold Label Class 3-34
98Topps Gold Label Class 3 Black-34
98Topps Gold Label Class 3 Black 1 of 1-34
98Topps Gold Label Class 3 One of One-34
98Topps Gold Label Class 3 Red-34
98Topps Gold Label Class 3 Red One of One-34
98UD Choice-23
98UD Choice-221
98UD Choice-244
Mini Bobbing Head-BH18
98UD Choice Preview-23
98UD Choice Prime Choice Reserve-23
98UD Choice Prime Choice Reserve-221
98UD Choice Prime Choice Reserve-244
98UD Choice Reserve-23
98UD Choice Reserve-221
98UD Choice Reserve-244
98UD Choice StarQuest Blue-SQ4
98UD Choice StarQuest Gold-SQ4
98UD Choice StarQuest Green-SQ4
98UD Choice StarQuest Red-SQ4
98UD3-57
98UD3-117
98UD3-177
Die-Cuts-57
Die-Cuts-117
Die-Cuts-177
98Upper Deck-20
98Upper Deck-44
Exclusives-20
Exclusives-44
Exclusives 1 of 1-20
Exclusives 1 of 1-44
Frozen In Time-FT10
Frozen In Time Quantum 1-FT10
Frozen In Time Quantum 2-FT10
Frozen In Time Quantum 3-FT10
Game Jerseys-GJ17
Lord Stanley's Heroes-LS27
Lord Stanley's Heroes Quantum 1-LS27
Lord Stanley's Heroes Quantum 2-LS27
Lord Stanley's Heroes Quantum 3-LS27
Profiles-P17
Profiles Quantum 1-P17
Profiles Quantum 2-P17
Profiles Quantum 3-P17
Gold Reserve-20
Gold Reserve-44
98Upper Deck MVP-21
Gold Script-21
Silver Script-21
Super Script-21
OT Heroes-OT7
Special Forces-F4
98Czech OFS-227
Olympic Winners-2
98Czech Bonaparte-2D
98Czech Bonaparte-8D
98Czech Bonaparte Tall-1
98Czech Pexeso-7
98Czech Pexeso-28
98Czech Spaghetti-2
98SLU Hockey 12" Figures-3
99SLU Hockey-5
99SLU Hockey Pro Action Deluxe-20
99Aurora-16
Striped-16
Premiere Date-16
Premiere Date Striped-16
Canvas Creations-3
Championship Fever-4
Championship Fever Copper-4
Championship Fever Ice Blue-4
Championship Fever Silver-4
Complete Players-3
Complete Players Parallel-3
Complete Players Retail-3
Complete Players Retail Parallel-3
Glove Unlimited-3
Styrotechs-3
99BAP Memorabilia-134
Gold-134
Silver-134
Jersey Cards-J20
Jersey Emblems-E20
Jersey Numbers-I20
Jersey and Stick Cards-S20
Selects Silver-SL6
Selects Gold-SL6
AS Heritage Ruby-H5
AS Heritage Sapphire-H5
AS Heritage Emerald-H5
99BAP Update Double AS Jersey Cards-D12
99BAP Update Teammates Jersey Cards-TM13
99BAP Update Teammates Jersey Cards-TM20
99BAP Millennium-29
Emerald-29
Ruby-29
Sapphire-29
Signatures-29
Signatures Gold-29
Goalie Memorabilia-G7
Jerseys-J5
Jersey Autographs-J5
Jersey and Stick Cards-JS5
Jersey Emblems-E5
Jersey Numbers-N5
Pearson-P2
Pearson Autographs-P2
Players of the Decade-D4
Players of the Decade Autographs-D4
99Black Diamond-11
Diamond Cut-11
Final Cut-11
A Piece of History-DH
A Piece of History Double-DH
A Piece of History Triple-DH
99Crown Royale-18
Limited Series-18
Premiere Date-18
Card-Supials-5
Card-Supials Minis-5
Gold Crown Die-Cuts Jumbos-2
Ice Elite-4
Ice Elite Parallel-4
International Glory-3
International Glory Parallel-3
99Hasbro Starting Lineup Cards-5
99Jell-O Goalie Collection-4
99Jell-O Partners of Power-4
99Kraft Peanut Butter-4
99McDonald's Upper Deck-MCD3
99McDonald's Upper Deck-MCD3R
99O-Pee-Chee-9
99O-Pee-Chee-279A
99O-Pee-Chee-279B
99O-Pee-Chee-279C
99O-Pee-Chee-279D
99O-Pee-Chee-279E
99O-Pee-Chee All-Topps-AT1
99O-Pee-Chee Autographs-TA2
99O-Pee-Chee Chrome-9
99O-Pee-Chee Chrome-279A
99O-Pee-Chee Chrome-279B
99O-Pee-Chee Chrome-279C
99O-Pee-Chee Chrome-279D
99O-Pee-Chee Chrome-279E
99O-Pee-Chee Chrome All-Topps-AT1
99O-Pee-Chee Chrome All-Topps Refractors-AT1
99O-Pee-Chee Chrome Ice Masters-IM2
99O-Pee-Chee Chrome Ice Masters Refractor-IM2
99O-Pee-Chee Chrome Refractors-9
99O-Pee-Chee Chrome Refractors-279A
99O-Pee-Chee Chrome Refractors-279B
99O-Pee-Chee Chrome Refractors-279C
99O-Pee-Chee Chrome Refractors-279D
99O-Pee-Chee Chrome Refractors-279E
99O-Pee-Chee Chrome Postmasters-PM1
99O-Pee-Chee Chrome Postmasters Refractor-PM1
99O-Pee-Chee Ice Masters-IM2
99O-Pee-Chee Post Masters-PM1
99O-Pee-Chee Top of the World-TW16
99Oscar Mayer Lunchables-3
99Pacific-37
Copper-37
Emerald Green-37
Gold-37
Ice Blue-37
Premiere Date-37
Red-37
Center Ice-3
Center Ice Proofs-3
Cramer's Choice-2
Gold Crown Die-Cuts-5
Home and Away-3
Home and Away-13
In the Cage Net-Fusions-3
Past and Present-4
Team Leaders-4
99Pacific Dynagon Ice-31
Blue-31
Copper-31
Gold-31
Premiere Date-31
2000 All-Star Preview-4
Lords of the Rink-3
99Pacific Omega-28
Copper-28
Gold-28
Ice Blue-28
Premiere Date-28
Cup Contenders-2
EO Portraits-4
EO Portraits 1/1-4
5 Star Talents-25
5 Star Talents Parallel-25
99Pacific Prism-19
Holographic Blue-19
Holographic Gold-19
Holographic Mirror-19
Holographic Purple-19
Premiere Date-19
Clear Advantage-3
Dial-a-Stats-3
Sno-Globe Die-Cuts-4
99Panini Stickers-6
99Panini Stickers-32
99Panini Stickers-349
99Paramount-28
Copper-28
Emerald-28
Gold-28
Holographic Emerald-28
Holographic Gold-28
Holographic Silver-28
Ice Blue-28
Premiere Date-28
Red-28
Silver-28
Glove Side Net Fusions-3
Hall of Fame Bound-3
Hall of Fame Bound Proofs-3
Ice Advantage-3
Ice Advantage Proofs-3
Ice Alliance-4
Personal Best-5
99Revolution-18
Premiere Date-18
Red-18
Shadow Series-18
Ice Sculptures-2
NHL Icons-3
Ornaments-4
Showstoppers-5
Copper-18
Gold-18
CSC Silver-18
99SP Authentic-10
99SPx-15
Radiance-15
Spectrum-15
Highlight Heroes-HH3
SPXcitement-X6
SPXtreme-XT14
Starscape-S4
Winning Materials-WM5
99Stadium Club-7
First Day Issue-7
One of a Kind-7
Printing Plates Black-7
Printing Plates Cyan-7
Printing Plates Magenta-7
Printing Plates Yellow-7
Capture the Action-CA22
Capture the Action Game View-CAG22
Chrome-7
Chrome Refractors-7
Chrome Oversized-5
Chrome Oversized Refractors-5

Goalie Cam-GC1
Onyx Extreme-OE3
Onyx Extreme Die-Cut-OE3
99Topps/OPC-9
99Topps/OPC-279A
99Topps/OPC-279B
99Topps/OPC-279C
99Topps/OPC-279D
99Topps/OPC-279E
All-Topps-AT1
Autographs-TA2
Ice Masters-IM2
Postmasters-PM1
Top of the World-TW16
99Topps/OPC Chrome-9
99Topps/OPC Chrome-279A
99Topps/OPC Chrome-279B
99Topps/OPC Chrome-279C
99Topps/OPC Chrome-279D
99Topps/OPC Chrome-279E
Refractors-9
Refractors-279A
Refractors-279B
Refractors-279C
Refractors-279D
Refractors-279E
All-Topps-AT1
All-Topps Refractors-AT1
Ice Masters-IM2
Ice Masters Refractors-IM2
Postmasters-PM1
Postmasters Refractors-PM1
99Topps Gold Label Class 1-1
Black-1
Black One of One-1
One of One-1
Red-1
Red One of One-1
99Topps Gold Label Class 2-1
99Topps Gold Label Class 2 Black-1
99Topps Gold Label Class 2 Black 1 of 1-1
99Topps Gold Label Class 2 One of One-1
99Topps Gold Label Class 2 Red-1
99Topps Gold Label Class 2 Red One of One-1
99Topps Gold Label Class 3-1
99Topps Gold Label Class 3 Black-1
99Topps Gold Label Class 3 Black 1 of 1-1
99Topps Gold Label Class 3 One of One-1
99Topps Gold Label Class 3 Red-1
99Topps Gold Label Class 3 Red One of One-1
99Topps Gold Label Prime Gold-PG1
99Topps Gold Label Prime Gold One of One -PG1
99Topps Gold Label Prime Gold Black-PG1
99Topps Gold Label Prime Gold Black One of One -PG1
99Topps Gold Label Prime Gold Red-PG1
99Topps Gold Label Prime Gold Red One of One -PG1
99Topps Premier Plus-7
Parallel-7
Imperial Guard-IG4
Premier Team-PT10
Premier Team Parallel-PT10
99Ultimate Victory-10
1/1-10
Parallel-10
Parallel 100-10
Net Work-NW1
99Upper Deck-22
99Upper Deck-145
Exclusives-22
Exclusives-145
Exclusives 1 of 1-22
Exclusives 1 of 1-145
All-Star Class-AS1
All-Star Class Quantum Gold-AS1
All-Star Class Quantum Silver-AS1
Crunch Time-CT23
Crunch Time Quantum Gold-CT23
Crunch Time Quantum Silver-CT23
Game Jerseys-DH
Game Jerseys Series II-DH
Game Jersey Patch-DHP
Game Jersey Patch 1 of 1-DHSP
Game Jersey Patch Series II-DHP
Game Jersey Patch Series II 1 of 1-DH-P1
Headed for the Hall-HOF2
Headed for the Hall Quantum Gold-HOF2
Headed for the Hall Quantum Silver-HOF2
Ice Gallery-IG4
Ice Gallery Quantum Gold-IG4
Ice Gallery Quantum Silver-IG4
Marquee Attractions-MA5
Marquee Attractions Quantum Gold-MA5
Marquee Attractions Quantum Silver-MA5
PowerDeck Inserts-PD1
Sixth Sense-SS16
Sixth Sense Quantum Gold-SS16
Sixth Sense Quantum Silver-SS16
Ultimate Defense-UD2
Ultimate Defense Quantum Gold-UD2
Ultimate Defense Quantum Silver-UD2
99Upper Deck Century Legends-51
Century Collection-51
99Upper Deck Gold Reserve-22
99Upper Deck Gold Reserve-145
99Upper Deck HoloGrFx-6
Ausome-6
Impact Zone-IZ1
Impact Zone Ausome-IZ1
Pure Skill-PS3
Pure Skill Ausome-PS3
99Upper Deck MVP-21
Gold Script-21
Silver Script-21
Super Script-21
90's Snapshots-S9
Draw Your Own Trading Card-W4
Draw Your Own Trading Card-W18
Game-Used Souvenirs-GU17
Last Line-LL1
Talent-MVP3
99Upper Deck MVP SC Edition-22
Gold Script-22
Silver Script-22
Super Script-22
Great Combinations-GCHP
Great Combinations Parallel-GCHP
Playoff Heroes-PH2
99Upper Deck Ovation-6
99Upper Deck Ovation-83
Standing Ovation-6
Standing Ovation-83
Lead Performers-LP16
Superstar Theater-ST5
99Upper Deck PowerDeck-6
Auxiliary-6
Auxiliary 1 of 1-6
Time Capsule-T5
Time Capsule Auxiliary-T5
Time Capsule Auxiliary 1 of 1-T5
99Upper Deck Retro-7
Gold-7
Platinum-7
Distant Replay-DR8
Distant Replay Level 2-DR8
Generation-G10B
Generation Level 2-G10B
Turn of the Century-TC8
99Upper Deck Victory-32
99Upper Deck Victory-33
99Upper Deck Victory-319
99Upper Deck Victory-381
99Wayne Gretzky Hockey-21
Changing The Game-CG5
Great Heroes-GH4
Will to Win-W4
99Czech DS National Stars-NS1
99Czech DS Premium-P1
99Slovakian Challengers-23
00McFarlane Hockey-90
00Aurora-19
Pinstripes-19
Pinstripes Premiere Date-19
Premiere Date-19
Championship Fever-3
Championship Fever Copper-3
Championship Fever Platinum Blue-3
Championship Fever Silver-3
Styrotechs-2B
00BAP Memorabilia-199
Emerald-199
Ruby-199
Sapphire-199
Promos-199
Georges Vezina-V2
Georges Vezina-V3
Georges Vezina-V4
Georges Vezina-V6
Georges Vezina-V7
Goalie Memorabilia-G3
Jersey Cards-J13
Jersey Emblems-E13
Jersey Numbers-N13
Jersey and Stick Cards-JS13
00BAP Mem Chicago Sportsfest Copper-199
00BAP Memorabilia Chicago Sportsfest Blue-199
00BAP Memorabilia Chicago Sportsfest Gold-199
00BAP Memorabilia Chicago Sportsfest Ruby-199
00BAP Memorabilia Chicago Sun-Times Ruby-199
00BAP Memorabilia Chicago Sun-Times Gold-199
00BAP Mem Chicago Sun-Times Sapphire-199
00BAP Mem Toronto Fall Expo Copper-199
00BAP Memorabilia Toronto Fall Expo Gold-199
00BAP Memorabilia Toronto Fall Expo Ruby-199
00BAP Memorabilia Update Teammates-TM6
00BAP Memorabilia Update Teammates Gold-TM6
00BAP Parkhurst 2000-P41
00BAP Signature Series-50
Emerald-50
Ruby-50
Sapphire-50
Franchise Players-F4
He Shoots-He Scores Points-6
He Shoots-He Scores Prizes-19
Jersey Cards-J5
Jersey and Stick Cards-GSJ5
Jersey Cards Autographs-J5
Jersey Emblems-E5
Jersey Numbers-IN5
00BAP Ultimate Memorabilia Active Eight-AE6
00BAP Ultimate Memorabilia Active Eight-AE7
00BAP Ultimate Memorabilia Active Eight-AE8
00BAP Ultimate Mem Game-Used Jerseys-GJ5
00BAP Ultimate Mem Game-Used Emblems-E4
00BAP Ultimate Mem Game-Used Numbers-N4
00BAP Ultimate Mem Game-Used Sticks-GS5
00BAP Ultimate Mem Goalie Memorabilia-GM12
00BAP Ultimate Memorabilia Goalie Sticks-G4
00BAP Ultimate Memorabilia Hart Trophy-H3
00BAP Ultimate Memorabilia Hart Trophy-H4
00BAP Ultimate Mem Plante Jersey Cards-PJ4
00BAP Ultimate Mem Plante Skate Cards-PS4
00BAP Ultimate Mem Magnificent Ones-ML8
00BAP Ultimate Mem Magnificent Ones Autos-ML8
00BAP Ultimate Memorabilia Teammates-TM20
00Black Diamond-6
Gold-6
Game Gear-LDH
00Crown Royale-15
Ice Blue-15
Limited Series-15
Premiere Date-15
Red-15
Jewels of the Crown-6
Landmarks-2
00Kraft-17
00McDonald's Pacific-5
Blue-5
Glove Side Net Fusions-1
00O-Pee-Chee-21
00O-Pee-Chee Parallel-21
00Pacific-52
Copper-52
Gold-52
Ice Blue-52
Premiere Date-52
Euro-Stars-2
Gold Crown Die Cuts-4
In the Cage Net-Fusions-1
00Panini Stickers-18
00Paramount-30
Copper-30
Gold-30
Holo-Gold-30
Holo-Silver-30
Ice Blue-30
Premiere Date-30
Epic Scope-3
Freeze Frame-4
Glove Side Net Fusions-3
Glove Side Net Fusions Platinum-3
Hall of Fame Bound-2
Hall of Fame Bound Canvas Proofs-2
Hall of Fame Bound Proofs-2
00Private Stock-12
Gold-12
Premiere Date-12
Retail-12
Silver-12
Artist's Canvas-5
Artist's Canvas Proofs-5
Extreme Action-3
Game Gear-9
PS-2001 Action-7
PS-2001 Stars-4
Reserve-4
00Revolution-17
Blue-17
Premiere Date-17
Red-17
HD NHL-5
Ice Immortals-3
NHL Icons-4
Stat Masters-12
00SP Authentic-10
Super Stoppers-SS1
00SP Game Used-6
Tools of the Game Combos-C-HP
00SPx-6
00SPx-82
Spectrum-6
Spectrum-82
Prolifics-P1
Winning Materials-DH
00Stadium Club-12
Beam Team-BT14
Capture the Action-CA5
Capture the Action Game View-5
Glove Save-GS8
Special Forces-SF18
00Titanium-10
Blue-10
Gold-10
Premiere Date-10
Red-10
Retail-10
All-Stars-1W
Game Gear-59
Game Gear Patches-59
Three-Star Selections-1
00Titanium Draft Day Edition-11
00Topps/OPC-21
Parallel-21
Combos-TC4
Combos Jumbos-TC4
Hobby Masters-HM4
NHL Draft-D12
00Topps Chrome-20
OPC Refractors-20
Refractors-20
Combos-TC4
Combos Refractors-TC4
Hobby Masters Refractors-HM4
00Topps Gold Label Class 1-66
Gold-66
00Topps Gold Label Class 2-66
00Topps Gold Label Class 2 Gold-66
00Topps Gold Label Class 3-66
00Topps Gold Label Class 3 Gold-66
00Topps Gold Label Behind the Mask-BTM3
00Topps Gold Label Behind the Mask 1 to 1-BTM3
00Topps Heritage-26
Chrome Parallel-26
Heroes-HH19
00Topps Premier Plus-17
Blue Ice-17
Masters of the Break-MB15
Trophy Tribute-TT1
00Topps Stars-6
00Topps Stars-130
Blue-6
Blue-130
All-Star Authority-ASA6
Walk of Fame-WF8
00UD Heroes-12
Game-Used Twigs-T-DH
Game-Used Twigs Gold-C-HP
Player Idols-PI6
Timeless Moments-TM2
00UD Pros and Prospects-10
ProMotion-PM2
00UD Reserve-10
Golden Goalies-GG2
The Big Ticket-BT2
00Upper Deck-248
Exclusives Tier 1-248
Exclusives Tier 2-248
Fun-Damentals-F2
Game Jersey Combos-DBH
Game Jersey Doubles-DDH
Game Jersey Patches-DHP
Game Jersey Patch Autographs Exclusives-DHP
Gate Attractions-GA2
Profiles-P1
Skilled Stars-SS3
Triple Threat-TT10
00Upper Deck Ice-5
Immortals-5
Legends-5
Stars-5
00Upper Deck Legends-16
00Upper Deck Legends-18
Legendary Collection Bronze-16
Legendary Collection Bronze-18
Legendary Collection Gold-16
Legendary Collection Gold-18
Legendary Collection Silver-16
Legendary Collection Silver-18
Legendary Game Jerseys-JDH
of the Cage-LC3
00Upper Deck MVP-23
First Stars-23
Game-Used Souvenirs-GSDH
Masked Men-MM1
Second Stars-23
Super Game-Used Souvenirs-GSDH
Third Stars-23
Top Draws-TD2
Top Playmakers-TP2
00Upper Deck Victory-25
00Upper Deck Victory-26
00Upper Deck Victory-243
00Upper Deck Victory-286
00Upper Deck Vintage-39
00Upper Deck Vintage-49
00Upper Deck Vintage-50
Great Gloves-GG3
National Heroes-NH5
00Vanguard-13
Cosmic Force-2
High Voltage-5
High Voltage Gold-5
High Voltage Green-5
High Voltage Red-5
High Voltage Silver-5
Holographic Gold-13
Holographic Purple-13
Pacific Proofs-13
Press East/West-12
00Czech DS Extraliga Best of the Best-BBH1
00Czech DS Extraliga Best of the Best-BBH2
00Czech DS Extraliga Best of the Best-BBH1
00Czech Stadion-5
00Czech Stadion-190
01McFarlane Hockey-65
01McFarlane Hockey-66
01Atomic-36
Blue-36
Gold-36
Premiere Date-36
Red-36
Jerseys-22
Patches-22
Statosphere-3
Team Nucleus-6
01BAP Memorabilia-198
01BAP Memorabilia-373
Emerald-198
Emerald-373
Ruby-198
Ruby-373
Sapphire-198
Sapphire-373
All-Star Jerseys-ASJ11
All-Star Emblems-ASE11
All-Star Numbers-ASN11
All-Star Jersey Doubles-DASJ6
All-Star Starting Lineup-S1
All-Star Teammates-AST6
All-Star Teammates-AST9
All-Star Teammates-AST28
All-Star Teammates-AST40
All-Star Teammates-AST42
Country of Origin-CO23
Goalies Jerseys-GJ2
Stanley Cup Playoffs-SC23
01BAP Signature Series Certified 100-C52
01BAP Signature Series Certified 50-C52
01BAP Signature Series Certified 1 of 1's-C52
01BAP Signature Series Autographs-XLDH
01BAP Signature Series Autographs Gold-XLDH
01BAP Signature Series Jerseys-GJ-6
01BAP Signature Series Jersey Autographs-GUDH
01BAP Sig Series Jersey and Stick Cards-GSJ-6
01BAP Signature Series Emblems-GUE-6
01BAP Signature Series Numbers-ITN-6
01BAP Signature Series Teammates-TM-12
01BAP Ultimate Memorabilia Emblems-6
01BAP Ultimate Memorabilia Jerseys-6
01BAP Ultimate Mem Jerseys and Sticks-6
01BAP Ultimate Mem Journey Jerseys-19
01BAP Ultimate Mem Journey Emblems-19
01BAP Ultimate Mem Legend Terry Sawchuk-3
01BAP Ultimate Memorabilia Numbers-5
01BAP Ultimate Memorabilia Name Plates-7
01BAP Ultimate Mem Prototypical Players-3
01BAP Ultimate Memorabilia Retro Trophies-9
01BAP Update He Shoots-He Scores Points-16
01BAP Update He Shoots-He Scores Prizes-14
01BAP Update He Shoots-He Scores Prizes-39
01BAP Update Travel Plans-TP2
01Between the Pipes-56
01Between the Pipes-109
01Between the Pipes-163
All-Star Jerseys-ASJ5
All-Star Jerseys-ASJ13
Goalie Gear-GG22
He Shoots-He Saves Points-17
He Shoots-He Saves Prizes-1
Jerseys-GJ2
Emblems-GUE1
Jersey and Stick Cards-GSJ2
Tandems-GT9
Trophy Winners-TW2
Trophy Winners-TW19
Trophy Winners-TW24
01Bowman YoungStars-21
Gold-21
Ice Cubed-21
01Crown Royale-52
Blue-52
Premiere Date-52
Red-52
Retail-52
All-Star Honors-7
Crowning Achievement-14
Jewels of the Crown-10
Legendary Heroes-3
01eTopps-33
01McDonald's Pacific-12
Hockey Greats-4
Jersey Patches Silver-9
Jersey Patches Gold-9
01Nortel All-Star Game Sheets-5
01O-Pee-Chee-49
01O-Pee-Chee-49U
01O-Pee-Chee Heritage Parallel-49
01O-Pee-Chee Heritage Parallel Limited-49
01O-Pee-Chee Premier Parallel-49
01Pacific-50
Extreme LTD-50
Hobby LTD-50
Premiere Date-50
Retail LTD-50
All-Stars-W1
Gold Crown Die-Cuts-3
Impact Zone-4
Steel Curtain-3
01Pacific Adrenaline-65
Blue-65
Premiere Date-65
Red-65
Retail-65
Blade Runners-4
Creased Lightning-6
Power Play-14
01Pacific Arena Exclusives-50
01Pacific Heads-Up-35
Blue-35
Premiere Date-35
Red-35
Silver-35
Quad Jerseys-4
Quad Jerseys-20
Rink Immortals-5
Showstoppers-6
01Parkhurst-92
Gold-92
Silver-92
He Shoots-He Scores Prizes-34
Milestones-M11
Milestones-M38
Sticks-PS60
Teammates-T23
Teammates-T27
Waving the Flag-11
01Private Stock-33
Gold-33
Premiere Date-33
Retail-33
Silver-33
Game Gear-42
01Private Stock Pacific Nights-33
01Private Stock PS-2002-27
01Private Stock Reserve-G4
01SP Authentic-27
01SP Authentic-98
Limited-27
Limited-98
Limited Gold-27
Limited Gold-98
01SP Game Used-20
Authentic Fabric-AFDH
Authentic Fabric Gold-AFDH
01SPx-26
Hockey Treasures-HTDH
01Stadium Club-103
Award Winners-103
Master Photos-103
01Titanium-49
Hobby Parallel-49
Premiere Date-49
Retail-49
Retail Parallel-49
All-Stars-8
Saturday Knights-5
Three-Star Selections-4
01Titanium Draft Day Edition-37
01Topps-49
01Topps-49U
Heritage Parallel-49
Heritage Parallel Limited-49
OPC Parallel-49
Own The Game-OTG23
01Topps Chrome-49
Refractors-49
Black Border Refractors-49
01Topps Heritage-116
01Topps Heritage-135
01Topps Heritage-159
01Topps Reserve-92
01UD Challenge for the Cup-27
Backstops-BB4
Jerseys-TDH
01UD Honor Roll-18
01UD Honor Roll-48
Honor Society-HS-CH
Honor Society Gold-HS-CH
Playoff Matchups-HS-LH
Playoff Matchups Gold-HS-LH
01UD Mask Collection-111
01UD Mask Collection-177
Gold-111
Gold-177
Goalie Jerseys-CGDH
Goalie Pads-GPDH
Sticks-SSDH
01UD Playmakers-35
01UD Premier Collection-23
Dual Jerseys-DHC
Dual Jerseys-DLH
Dual Jerseys Black-DHC
Dual Jerseys Black-DLH
Jerseys-SDH
Jerseys Black-S-DH
01UD Top Shelf-17
All-Star Nets-NDH
Goalie Gear-LPDH
Sticks-SDH
Sticks-LOH
Sticks Gold-SDH
Sticks Gold-LOH
01Upper Deck-66
01Upper Deck-214
Exclusives-66
Exclusives-214
Game Jerseys-GJDH
Game Jerseys Series II-DJSH
Last Line of Defense-LL3
Pride of a Nation-PNDH
Pride of a Nation-DPHJ
Pride of a Nation-TPHJL
01Upper Deck Ice-16
01Upper Deck MVP-69
Goalie Sticks-G-DH
01Upper Deck Victory-36
01Upper Deck Victory-39
01Upper Deck Victory-398
Gold-36
Gold-39
Gold-398
01Upper Deck Vintage-92
01Upper Deck Vintage-267
01Upper Deck Vintage-270
01Vanguard-35
Blue-35
Red-35
East Meets West-2
In Focus-3
Memorabilia-35
One of Ones-35
Premiere Date-35
Proofs-35
Stonewallers-7
V-Team-4
01Czech DS-1
Best of the Best-BB1
Goalies-G1
01Czech Stadion-249
02Atomic-5
02Atomic Jerseys-6
02Atomic Jerseys Gold-6
02Atomic Patches-6
02BAP First Edition-136
02BAP First Edition-328
02BAP First Edition-380
02BAP First Edition-395
He Shoots-He Scores Prizes-26
Jerseys-136
02BAP Memorabilia-101
02BAP Memorabilia-240
02BAP Memorabilia-243
Emerald-101
Emerald-240
Emerald-243
Ruby-101
Ruby-240
Ruby-243
Sapphire-101
Sapphire-240
Sapphire-243
All-Star Jerseys-ASJ-17
All-Star Emblems-ASE-5
All-Star Numbers-ASN-5
All-Star Starting Lineup-AS-7
All-Star Teammmates-AST-9
All-Star Teammmates-AST-11
All-Star Teammmates-AST-14
All-Star Teammmates-AST-17
All-Star Triple Jerseys-ASTJ-5
He Shoots-He Scores Points-13
He Shoots-He Scores Prizes-8
Mini Stanley Cups-40
NHL All-Star Game-101
NHL All-Star Game-240
NHL All-Star Game-243
NHL All-Star Game Blue-101
NHL All-Star Game Blue-240
NHL All-Star Game Blue-243
NHL All-Star Game Green-101
NHL All-Star Game Green-240
NHL All-Star Game Green-243
NHL All-Star Game Red-101
NHL All-Star Game Red-240
NHL All-Star Game Red-243
Stanley Cup Champions-SCC-4
Stanley Cup Playoffs-SC-27
Stanley Cup Playoffs-SC-30
Teammates-TM-1
02BAP Memorabilia Toronto Fall Expo-101
02BAP Memorabilia Toronto Fall Expo-240
02BAP Memorabilia Toronto Fall Expo-243
02BAP Sig Series Auto Buybacks 1998-162
02BAP Sig Series Auto Buybacks 1999-29
02BAP Sig Series Auto Buybacks 2001-XLDH
02McDonald's Pacific-11
Glove Side Net-Fusions-2
Jersey Patches Silver-5
Jersey Patches Gold-5
02Nextel NHL All-Star Game-4
02O-Pee-Chee-143
02O-Pee-Chee Premier Blue Parallel-143
02O-Pee-Chee Premier Red Parallel-143
02O-Pee-Chee Factory Set-143
02Pacific-128
Blue-128
Red-128
Cramer's Choice-6
Jerseys-17
Jerseys Holo-Silver-17
Maximum Impact-3
02Pacific Heads-Up-42
Blue-42
Purple-42
Red-42
Etched in Time-9
Inside the Numbers-10
Postseason Picks-6
Quad Jerseys-12
Quad Jerseys-32
Quad Jerseys Gold-12
Quad Jerseys Gold-32
Showstoppers-8
02Private Stock Reserve-117
Red-117
Retail-117
02SP Game Used Tools of the Game-DH
02SPx Winning Materials-WMDH
02SPx Winning Materials Gold-DH
02SPx Winning Materials Silver-DH
02Titanium Jerseys-24
02Titanium Jerseys Retail-24
02Titanium Patches-24
02Topps-143
OPC Blue Parallel-143
OPC Red Parallel-143
Own The Game-OTG16
Factory Set-143
02Topps Chrome All-Star Fantasy-5
02Upper Deck Collectors Club-NHL9
02UD Piece of History Awards Collection-AC13
02UD Top Shelf-31
Hardware Heroes-HHBRK
Milestones Jerseys-MHPBJ
Stopper Jerseys-SSDH
Triple Jerseys-TSSYH
02Upper Deck Gifted Greats-GG7
02Upper Deck Good Old Days-GODM
02Upper Deck Playbooks-PL7
02Upper Deck Super Saviors-SA6
02Upper Deck Classic Portraits Headliners-YH
02Upper Deck Classic Portraits Headliners Limited-YH
02Upper Deck Classic Portraits Mini-Busts-21
02Upper Deck Classic Portraits Mini-Busts-22
02Upper Deck Classic Portraits Mini-Busts-23
02Upper Deck Classic Portraits Mini-Busts-24
02Upper Deck Classic Portraits Mini-Busts-25
02Upper Deck MVP-63
Gold-63
Classics-63
Golden Classics-63
Masked Men-MM2
Vital Forces-VF8
02Upper Deck Victory-74
Bronze-74
Gold-74
Silver-74
National Pride-NP15
02Upper Deck Vintage-95
02Upper Deck Vintage-316
02Czech DS-97
02Czech DS-98
02Czech DS-99
02Czech IQ Sports Blue-1
02Czech IQ Sports Blue-7
02Czech IQ Sports Blue-8
02Czech IQ Sports Blue-9
02Czech IQ Sports Yellow-9
02Czech IQ Sports Yellow-10
02Czech IQ Sports Yellow-11
02Czech IQ Sports Yellow-12
02Czech Stadion Cup Finals-487
02Czech Stadion Olympics-333
03McFarlane Hockey-150
03McFarlane Hockey-152
03BAP Memorabilia Brush with Greatness-21
03BAP Mem Brush with Greatness Contest C-21
03BAP Memorabilia Deep in the Crease-D8
03BAP Memorabilia Jersey and Stick-SJ-39
03BAP Memorabilia Jerseys-GJ-2
03BAP Memorabilia Jersey Autographs-GJ-2
03BAP Memorabilia Masks III-3
03BAP Memorabilia Masks III Gold-3
03BAP Memorabilia Masks III Silver-3
03BAP Memorabilia Masks III Memorabilia-3
03BAP Memorabilia Tandems-T-3
03BAP Ultimate Memorabilia Autographs-144
Gold-144
03BAP Ultimate Mem Auto Jerseys-144
03BAP Ultimate Mem Auto Emblems-144
03BAP Ultimate Memorabilia Active Eight-1
03BAP Ultimate Mem Always An All-Star-19
03BAP Ultimate Mem Always An AS Gold-19
03BAP Ultimate Mem Complete Jersey-15
03BAP Ultimate Mem Complete Jersey Gold-15
03BAP Ultimate Memorabilia Emblems-2
03BAP Ultimate Memorabilia Emblems Gold-2
03BAP Ultimate Memorabilia Jerseys-24
03BAP Ultimate Memorabilia Jerseys Gold-24
03BAP Ultimate Mem Jersey and Emblems-10
03BAP Ultimate Mem Jersey and Emblem Gold-10
03BAP Ultimate Mem Jersey and Numbers-10
03BAP Ultimate Mem Jersey and Number Gold-10
03BAP Ultimate Mem Jersey and Stick-13
03BAP Ultimate Mem Jersey and Stick Gold-13
03BAP Ultimate Mem Nameplates-2
03BAP Ultimate Mem Nameplates Gold-2
03BAP Ultimate Memorabilia Numbers-19
03BAP Ultimate Memorabilia Numbers Gold-19
03BAP Ultimate Mem Retro-Active Trophies-7
03BAP Ultimate Memorabilia Triple Threads-2
03Beehive-73
Gold-73
Silver-73
Jumbo Jerseys-BH6
Jerseys-JT14
Sticks Beige Border-BE37
Sticks Red Border-RE1
03Black Diamond-180
Black-180
Green-180
Red-180
03Bowman-39
Gold-39
03Bowman Chrome-39
Refractors-39
Gold Refractors-39
Xfractors-39
03Crown Royale-35
Blue-35
Retail-35
Gauntlet of Glory-9
Global Conquest-2
03ITG Action-202
Jerseys-M197
Jerseys-M217
03ITG Used Signature Series-105
Gold-105
Autographs-DH
Autographs Gold-DH
Goalie Gear-22
Goalie Gear Autographs-22
Goalie Gear Gold-22
Jerseys-7
Jerseys Gold-7
Jersey Autos-7
Emblems-39
Emblems Gold-39
Jersey and Stick-7
Jersey and Stick Gold-7
Retrospectives-12A
Retrospectives-12B
Retrospectives-12C
Retrospectives-12D
Retrospectives-12E
Retrospectives-12F
Retrospectives Gold-12A
Retrospectives Gold-12B
Retrospectives Gold-12C
Retrospectives Gold-12D
Retrospectives Gold-12E
Retrospectives Gold-12F
Teammates-13
Teammates Gold-13
03ITG VIP Brightest Stars-6
03ITG VIP Collages-19
03ITG VIP Collage Autographs-19
03ITG VIP Jerseys-12
03ITG VIP Jersey Autographs-12
03ITG VIP Jersey and Emblems-14
03ITG VIP Jersey and Numbers-14
03ITG VIP MVP-12
03Pacific Calder-36
Silver-36
03Pacific Complete-482
Red-482
03Pacific Exhibit-167
Blue Backs-167
Standing on Tradition-5
03Pacific Heads-Up-35
Hobby LTD-35
Retail LTD-35
Rink Immortals-4
Rink Immortals LTD-4
Stonewallers-5
Stonewallers LTD-5
03Pacific Invincible-32
Blue-32
Red-32
Retail-32
Freeze Frame-7
Jerseys-11
03Pacific Luxury Suite-9A
03Pacific Luxury Suite-9B
03Pacific Luxury Suite-9C
03Pacific Quest for the Cup-36
Blue-36
Raising the Cup-7
03Pacific Supreme-32
Blue-32
Red-32
Retail-32
Standing Guard-6
03Parkhurst Original Six Chicago-32
03Parkhurst Original Six Detroit-15
Memorabilia-DM52
Memorabilia-DM58
Memorabilia-DM62
03Parkhurst Orig Six He Shoots/Scores-26
03Parkhurst Orig Six He Shoots/Scores-26A
03Parkhurst Rookie-16
Jerseys-GJ-25
Jersey Autographs-GUJ-DH
Jerseys Gold-GJ-25
Jersey and Sticks-SJ-25
Jersey and Sticks Gold-SJ-25
03Private Stock Reserve-34
Blue-34
Red-34
Retail-34
Increase Security-7
03SP Authentic-29
Limited-29
Breakout Seasons-B21
Breakout Seasons Limited-B21
Foundations-F5
Foundations Limited-F5
03SP Game Used-18
Gold-18
Authentic Fabrics-DFHL
Authentic Fabrics-QYBHH
Authentic Fabrics Gold-DFHL
Authentic Fabrics Gold-QYBHH
Authentic Patches-APDH
Game Gear-GGDH
Game Gear Combo-GCDH
Limited Threads-LTDHA
Limited Threads Gold-LTDHA
Team Threads-TTYZH
Top Threads-YZHH
03SPx-35
Radiance-35
Spectrum-35
Hall Pass-HP-DH
Hall Pass Limited-HP-DH
Winning Materials-WM-DH
Winning Materials Limited-WM-DH
03Titanium-36
Hobby Jersey Number Parallels-36
Retail-36
Retail Jersey Number Parallels-36
Highlight Reels-5
Masked Marauders-4
03Topps C55-38
Minis-38
Minis American Back-38
Minis American Back Red-38
Minis Bazooka Back-38
Minis Brooklyn Back-38
Minis Hat Trick Back-38
Minis O Canada Back-38
Minis O Canada Back Red-38
Minis Stanley Cup Back-38
03Topps Pristine-41
Gold Refractor Die Cuts-41
Refractors-41
Mini-PM-DH
Press Plates Black-41
Press Plates Cyan-41
Press Plates Magenta-41
Press Plates Yellow-41
03UD Honor Roll-27
Grade A Jerseys-TDET
03UD Premier Collection Teammates-PT-DR1
03UD Premier Collection Teammates Patches-PT-DR1
03Upper Deck-314
All-Star Class-AS-10
Canadian Exclusives-314
HG-314
Magic Moments-MM-11
Memorable Matchups-MM-HH
Patches-SV9
UD Exclusives-314
03Upper Deck Classic Portraits-34
03Upper Deck Ice Breakers-IB-DH
03Upper Deck Ice Breaker Patches-IB-DH
03Upper Deck Ice Clear Cut Winners-CC-DH
03Upper Deck MVP-155
Gold Script-155
Silver Script-155
Canadian Exclusives-155
SportsNut-SN30
03Upper Deck Trilogy-34
Authentic Patches-AP11
Limited-34
03Toronto Star-32
Foil-5
04Pacific In The Crease-5
04Pacific Philadelphia-4
04SP Authentic-64
04SP Authentic-130
Limited-64
Limited-130
Buybacks-43
Sign of the Times-ST-HA
Sign of the Times-DS-HS
Sign of the Times-FS-SEN
04Ultimate Collection-29
Buybacks-5
Buybacks-6
Buybacks-7
Buybacks-8
Buybacks-9
Dual Logos-UL2-HA
Dual Logos-UL2-HJ
Jerseys-UGJ-DO
Jerseys Gold-UGJ-DO
Jersey Autographs-UGJA-DO
Patches-UP-HA
Patch Autographs-UPA-DO
Signatures-US-HA
Signature Logos-ULA-HA
Signature Patches-SP-HA
04Upper Deck-125
Canadian Exclusives-125
HG Glossy Gold-125
HG Glossy Silver-125
05Be A Player Dual Signatures-HH
05Be A Player Quad Signatures-OTWA
05Be A Player Signatures-HA
05Be A Player Signatures Gold-HA
05Beehive-60
05Beehive-202
Beige -60
Blue -60
Gold-60
Red -60
Matte-60
05Black Diamond-180
Emerald-180
Gold-180
Onyx-180
Ruby-180
Gemography-G-HA
Gemography Emerald-G-HA
Gemography Gold-G-HA
Gemography Onyx-G-HA
Gemography Ruby-G-HA
Jerseys-J-HA
Jerseys Ruby-J-HA
Jersey Duals-DJ-HA
Jersey Triples-TJ-HA
Jersey Quads-QJ-HA
05Hot Prospects-68
En Fuego-68
Red Hot-68
White Hot-68
05McDonalds Upper Deck Autographs-MA4
05McDonalds Upper Deck Goalie Factory-GF1
05McDonalds Upper Deck Goalie Gear-MG9
05Panini Stickers-117
05Parkhurst-333
05Parkhurst-691
Facsimile Auto Parallel-333
Facsimile Auto Parallel-691
True Colors-TCOTT
True Colors-TCOTT
True Colors-TCOTTO
True Colors-TCOTTO
05SP Authentic-67
05SP Authentic-105
Limited-67
Limited-105
Chirography-SPHK
Exquisite Endorsements-EEHK
Octographs-OG
Prestigious Pairings-PPHV
Sign of the Times Triples-THHC
05SP Game Used-69
Autographs-69
Gold-69
Authentic Fabrics-AF-HA
Authentic Fabrics Autographs-AAF-HA
Authentic Fabrics Dual-HH
Authentic Fabrics Dual Autographs-HH
Authentic Fabrics Gold-AF-HA
Authentic Fabrics Triple-CRH
Authentic Fabrics Triple-HJH
Authentic Patches-AP-HA
Authentic Patches Autographs-AAP-HA
Authentic Patches Dual-HH
Authentic Patches Dual Autographs-HH
Authentic Patches Triple-CRH
Authentic Patches Triple-HJH
Awesome Authentics-AA-HK
Game Gear-GG-HA
Game Gear Autographs-AG-HA

Significant Numbers-SN-HK
05SPx-63
05SPx-98
Spectrum-63
Spectrum-98
Winning Combos-WC-VH
Winning Combos Gold-WC-VH
Winning Combos Spectrum-WC-VH
Winning Materials-WM-HA
Winning Materials Autographs-AWM-HA
Winning Materials Gold-WM-HA
Winning Materials Spectrum-WM-HA
Xcitement Superstars-XS-HA
Xcitement Superstars Gold-XS-HA
Xcitement Superstars Spectrum-XS-HA
05The Cup-70
Gold-70
Black Rainbow-70
Emblems of Endorsement-EEHK
Hardware Heroes-HHDO1
Hardware Heroes-HHDO2
Hardware Heroes-HHDO3
Honorable Numbers-HNHK
Limited Logos-LLHA
Masterpiece Pressplates-70
Masterpiece Pressplates Rookie Upd Auto-270
Noble Numbers Dual-DNNJH
Patch Variation-P70
Patch Variation Autographs-AP70
Property of-POHA
Scripted Numbers Dual-DSNHV
Scripted Swatches-SSHK
Signature Patches-SPDO
Stanley Cup Titlists-TDH
05UD Artifacts-69
05UD Artifacts-182
Blue-69
Blue-182
Gold-69
Gold-182
Green-69
Green-182
Pewter-69
Pewter-182
Red-69
Red-182
Auto Facts Blue-AF-DH
Auto Facts Copper-AF-DH
Auto Facts Pewter-AF-DH
Auto Facts Silver-AF-DH
Frozen Artifacts-FA-DH
Frozen Artifacts Autographed-FA-DH
Frozen Artifacts Copper-FA-DH
Frozen Artifacts Dual-FAD-DH
Frozen Artifacts Dual Autographed-FAD-DH
Frozen Artifacts Dual Copper-FAD-DH
Frozen Artifacts Dual Gold-FAD-DH
Frozen Artifacts Dual Maroon-FAD-DH
Frozen Artifacts Dual Pewter-FAD-DH
Frozen Artifacts Dual Silver-FAD-DH
Frozen Artifacts Gold-FA-DH
Frozen Artifacts Maroon-FA-DH
Frozen Artifacts Patches-FP-DH
Frozen Artifacts Patches Autographed-FP-DH
Frozen Artifacts Patches Pewter-FP-DH
Frozen Artifacts Patches Silver-FP-DH
Frozen Artifacts Pewter-FA-DH
Frozen Artifacts Silver-FA-DH
Goalie Gear-FG-DH
Goalie Gear Autographed-FG-DH
Goalie Gear Dual-FGD-DH
Goalie Gear Dual Autographed-FGD-DH
Goalie Gear Pewter-FG-DH
Goalie Gear Silver-FG-DH
Gold Autographed-69
Gold Autographed-182
Remarkable Artifacts-RA-HA1
Remarkable Artifacts-RA-HA2
Remarkable Artifacts Dual-RA-HA1
Remarkable Artifacts Dual-RA-HA2
Treasured Patches-TP-HA
Treasured Patches Autographed-TP-HA
Treasured Patches Dual-TPD-HA
Treasured Patches Dual Autographed-TPD-HA
Treasured Patches Pewter-TP-HA
Treasured Patches Silver-TP-HA
Treasured Swatches-TS-HA
Treasured Swatches Autographed-TS-HA
Treasured Swatches Blue-TS-HA
Treasured Swatches Copper-TS-HA
Treasured Swatches Dual-TSD-HA
Treasured Swatches Dual Autographed-TSD-HA
Treasured Swatches Dual Blue-TSD-HA
Treasured Swatches Dual Copper-TSD-HA
Treasured Swatches Dual Maroon-TSD-HA
Treasured Swatches Dual Pewter-TSD-HA
Treasured Swatches Dual Silver-TSD-HA
Treasured Swatches Maroon-TS-HA
Treasured Swatches Pewter-TS-HA
Treasured Swatches Silver-TS-HA
05UD PowerPlay-63
Rainbow-63
Specialists-TSDO
Specialists Patches-SPDO
05UD Toronto Fall Expo Priority Signings-PS-DH
05Ultimate Collection-60
Gold-60
Endorsed Emblems-EEHK
Jerseys-JDH
Jerseys Dual-DJHC
Jerseys Triple-TJHSH
Marquee Attractions-MA32
Marquee Attractions Signatures-SMA32
National Heroes Jerseys-NHJHK
National Heroes Patches-NHPHK
Premium Patches-PPHK
Ultimate Achievements-UAHK
Ultimate Patches-PDH
Ultimate Patches Dual-DPHC
Ultimate Patches Triple-TPHSH
Ultimate Signatures-USHK
Ultimate Signatures Foursomes-UFHHSH
Ultimate Signatures Logos-SLHK
Ultimate Signatures Pairings-UPHH
05Ultra-133
Gold-133
Ice-133
05Upper Deck-131
05Upper Deck All-Time Greatest-7
05Upper Deck Big Playmakers-B-DHA
05Upper Deck Destined for the Hall-DH4
05Upper Deck HG Glossy-131
05Upper Deck Jerseys-J-DO
05Upper Deck Majestic Materials-MMHK
05Upper Deck NHL Generations-DHV
05Upper Deck Notable Numbers-N-DH
05Upper Deck Patches-P-DHA
05Upper Deck Scrapbooks-HS5
05Upper Deck Ice-66
Rainbow-66
Signature Swatches-SSDH
05Upper Deck MVP-267
Gold-267
Platinum-267
Monumental Moments-MM7
Rising to the Occasion-RO7
05Upper Deck Rookie Update-65
05Upper Deck Rookie Update-270
05Upper Deck Trilogy-167
Crystal-167
Honorary Patches-HP-HK
Honorary Patch Scripts-HSP-HK
Honorary Swatches-HS-HK
Honorary Swatch Scripts-HSS-HK
Scripts-SSS-DH
05Upper Deck Toronto Fall Expo-131
05Upper Deck Victory-135
Black-135
Gold-135
Silver-135
Blow-Ups-BU25
Stars on Ice-SI29
05Czech Kvarteto Bonaparte-1a
05Czech Pexeso Mini Blue Set-14
06Sports Illustrated for Kids *-41
06Be A Player Portraits-39
Dual Signature Portraits-DSHL
Quadruple Signature Portraits-QHVHH
Sensational Six-SSGOL
Sensational Six-SSSTR
Signature Portraits-SPHK
Timeless Tens-TTNET
06Beehive-65
06Beehive-207
Blue-65
Gold-65
Matte-65
Red Facsimile Signatures-65
Wood-65
5 X 7 Black and White-65
5 X 7 Cherry Wood-65
PhotoGraphs-PGDH
06Between The Pipes-61
06Between The Pipes-139
06Between The Pipes-142
Aspiring-AS03
Aspiring-AS06
Aspiring Gold-AS03
Aspiring Gold-AS06
Autographs-ADH
Complete Jersey-CJ08
Complete Jersey Gold-CJ08
Complete Package-CP10
Complete Package Gold-CP10
Double Jerseys-DJ06
Double Jerseys-DJ07
Double Jerseys-DJ23
Double Jerseys Gold-DJ06
Double Jerseys Gold-DJ07
Double Jerseys Gold-DJ23
Double Memorabilia-DM07
Double Memorabilia Gold-DM07
Emblems-GUE61
Emblems Gold-GUE61
Emblems Autographs-GUE61
Gloves-GG09
Gloves Gold-GG09
Jerseys-GUJ61
Jerseys Gold-GUJ61
Jerseys Autographs-GUJ61
Numbers-GUN61
Numbers Gold-GUN61
Numbers Autographs-GUN61
Playing For Your Country-PC08
Playing For Your Country Gold-PC08
Shooting Gallery-SG06
Shooting Gallery-SG08
Shooting Gallery-SG10
Shooting Gallery Gold-SG06
Shooting Gallery Gold-SG08
Shooting Gallery Gold-SG10
Stick and Jersey-SJ13
Stick and Jersey Gold-SJ13
Stick and Jersey Autographs-SJ13
Stick Work-SW02
Stick Work Gold-SW02
The Mask-M18
The Mask-M23
The Mask Gold-M18
The Mask Gold-M23
The Mask Silver-M18
The Mask Silver-M23
The Mask Game-Used-MGU07
The Mask Game-Used Gold-MGU07
06Black Diamond-155B
Black-158B
Gold-155B
Ruby-155B
06Flair Showcase Hot Numbers-HN30
06Flair Showcase Hot Numbers Parallel-HN30
06Fleer-73
Tiffany-73
Netminders-N4
06Hot Prospects-37
Red Hot-37
White Hot-37
Hot Materials -HMDH
Hot Materials Red Hot-HMDH
Hot Materials White Hot-HMDH
06ITG Ultimate Memorabilia-41
Artist Proof-41
Autos-39
Autos Gold-39
Autos Dual-12
Autos Dual Gold-12
Autos Triple-4
Autos Triple Gold-4
Complete Jersey-16
Complete Jersey Gold-16
Complete Package-1
Complete Package Gold-1
Decades-6
Decades Gold-6
Double Memorabilia-16
Double Memorabilia Gold-16
Gloves Are Off-8
Gloves Are Off Gold-8
Going For Gold-26
Going For Gold Gold-26
In The Numbers-11
In The Numbers Gold-11
Jerseys-7
Jerseys Gold-7
Jerseys and Emblems-12
Jerseys and Emblems Gold-12
Jerseys Autos-6
Jerseys Autos Gold-6
Journey Emblem-16
Journey Emblem Gold-16
Journey Jersey-16
Journey Jersey Gold-16
Passing The Torch-15
Passing The Torch Gold-15
Retro Teammates-24
Retro Teammates Gold-24
Retrospective-6
Retrospective Gold-6
Road to the Cup-10
Road to the Cup Gold-10
Sticks and Jerseys-7
Sticks and Jerseys Gold-7
Triple Thread Jerseys-4
Triple Thread Jerseys Gold-4
06McDonald's Upper Deck Hot Gloves-HG2
06NHL POG-39
06O-Pee-Chee-173
06O-Pee-Chee-650
Rainbow-173
Rainbow-650
Autographs-A-HA
Swatches-S-DH
06Panini Stickers-256
06SP Authentic-66
06SP Authentic-110
Chirography-HA
Limited-66
Limited-110
Sign of the Times-STDH
Sign of the Times Duals-STVH
06SP Game Used-37
Gold-37
Rainbow-37
Authentic Fabrics-AFDH
Authentic Fabrics Parallel-AFDH
Authentic Fabrics Patches-AFDH
Authentic Fabrics Dual-AF2HO
Authentic Fabrics Dual Patches-AF2HO
Authentic Fabrics Triple-AF3DET
Authentic Fabrics Triple Patches-AF3DET
Authentic Fabrics Fives-AF5GAA
Authentic Fabrics Fives Patches-AF5GAA
Authentic Fabrics Sixes-AF6JEN
Authentic Fabrics Sixes-AF6WIN
Authentic Fabrics Sixes Patches-AF6JEN
Authentic Fabrics Sixes Patches-AF6WIN
Authentic Fabrics Sevens-AF7LBP
Authentic Fabrics Sevens-AF7VEZ
Authentic Fabrics Sevens Patches-AF7LBP
Authentic Fabrics Sevens Patches-AF7VEZ
Autographs-37
By The Letter-BLHA
Inked Sweaters-ISDH
Inked Sweaters Patches-ISDH
Inked Sweaters Dual-IS2HO
Inked Sweaters Dual-IS2HV
Inked Sweaters Dual Patches-IS2HO
Inked Sweaters Dual Patches-IS2HV
Letter Marks-LMHA
06SPx-37
06SPx-133
Spectrum-37
Spectrum-133
Winning Materials-WMHK
Winning Materials Spectrum-WMHK
Winning Materials Autographs-WMHK
06The Cup-27
Autographed Foundations-CQHA
Autographed Foundations Patches-CQHA
Autographed NHL Shields Duals-DASBH
Autographed NHL Shields Duals-DASHL
Autographed NHL Shields Duals-DASHO
Autographed NHL Shields Duals-DASHV
Autographed NHL Shields Duals-DASHZ
Autographed Patches-27
Black Rainbow-27
Foundations-CQHA
Foundations Patches-CQHA
Enshrinements-EDH
Gold-27
Gold Patches-27
Honorable Numbers-HNHA
Jerseys-27
Limited Logos-LLDO
Masterpiece Pressplates-27
Property of-POHA
Scripted Swatches-SSHA
Signature Patches-SPHA
Stanley Cup Signatures-CSDH
06UD Artifacts-66
Blue-66
Gold-66
Platinum-66
Radiance-66
Autographed Radiance Parallel-66
Red-66
Tundra Tandems-TTHO
Tundra Tandems Black-TTHO
Tundra Tandems Blue-TTHO
Tundra Tandems Gold-TTHO
Tundra Tandems Platinum-TTHO
Tundra Tandems Red-TTHO
Tundra Tandems Dual Patches Red-TTHO
06UD Mini Jersey Collection-38
06UD Powerplay-39
Impact Rainbow-39
Cup Celebrations-CC3
Specialists-SDH
Specialists Patches-PDH
06Ultimate Collection-23
Autographed Jerseys-AJ-HA
Autographed Patches-AJ-HA
Jerseys-UJ-DH
Jerseys Dual-UJ2-HL
Patches-UJ-DH
Patches Dual-UJ2-HL
Premium Patches-PS-DH
Premium Swatches-PS-DH
Signatures-US-DH
Ultimate Achievements-UA-HA
Ultimate Signatures Logos-SL-HA
06Ultra Action-UA19
06Ultra Uniformity-UHA
06Ultra Uniformity Patches-UPHA
06Upper Deck Arena Giveaways-DET2
06Upper Deck-319
Exclusives Parallel-319
High Gloss Parallel-319
All World-AW24
Game Jerseys-J2DH
Game Patches-P2DH
Generations Duals-G2VH
Generations Patches Dual-G2PVH
Masterpieces-319
Oversized Wal-Mart Exclusives-319
Zero Men-ZM2
06Upper Deck MVP-104
Gold Script-104
Super Script-104
Clutch Performers-CP24
Gotta Have Hart-HH20
International Icons-II9
Jerseys-OJHV
Last Line of Defense-LL20
06Upper Deck Sweet Shot-40
Signature Shots/Saves-SSDH
Signature Shots/Saves Ice Signings-SSIDH
Signature Shots/Saves Sticks-SSSDH
Signature Sticks-STDH
Sweet Stitches-SSDH
Sweet Stitches Duals-SSDH
Sweet Stitches Triples-SSDH
06Upper Deck Trilogy-38
Combo Autographed Jerseys-CJVH
Combo Autographed Patches-CJVH
Combo Clearcut Autographs-C3RBH
Frozen In Time-FT5
Honorary Scripted Patches-HSPHA
Honorary Scripted Swatches-HSSHA
Honorary Swatches-HSHA
Ice Scripts-ISDH
Scripts-S1HA
Scripts-S2DH
Scripts-S3HA
06Upper Deck Victory-137
06Upper Deck Victory-247
06Upper Deck Victory Black-137
06Upper Deck Victory Gold-137
06Upper Deck Victory GameBreakers-GB35
07Upper Deck Ovation-85
07Upper Deck Victory-98
Black-98
Gold-98
GameBreakers-GB17
Oversize Cards-OS25
Stars on Ice-SI23

Hasek, Jaroslav
02Czech OFS Plus-328

Hasek, Jiri
00Czech OFS-234
01Czech OFS-128
02Czech OFS Plus-82
03Czech OFS Plus-40
03Czech OFS Plus-392
03Czech OFS Plus Insert M-M10
04Czech OFS-208
05Czech HC Trinec-3
06Czech OFS-156

Hasenzahl, Tom
97Dubuque Fighting Saints-25

Haskett, Chris
95Slapshot-189
97Austin Ice Bats-6

Haskins, Tyler
02Guelph Storm-23
03St. Michael's Majors-12
04St. Michael's Majors-13
05OHL Bell All-Star Classic-27
06Saginaw Spirit-11

Haslach, Norbert
94German First League-150

Hasler, Stevan
02Swiss HNL-256
04Swiss Davos Postcards-15

Hass, W.
52Juniors Blue Tint-27

Hassan, Sana
95German DEL-405
96German DEL-301

Hassard, Bob
44Beehive Group II Photos-406
45Quaker Oats Photos-21
52Parkhurst-105
53Parkhurst-4

Hasselblad, Peter
89Swedish Semic Elitserien Stickers-78
90Swedish Semic Elitserien Stickers-253
92Swedish Semic Elitserien Stickers-206
93Swedish Semic Elitserien-176
94Swedish Leaf-31
95Swedish Leaf-267
95Swedish Upper Deck-135
02Swedish SHL-68
Parallel-68

Hasselqvist, Bertil
57Swedish Alfabilder-135

Hassinen, Jani
93Finnish Jyvas-Hyva Stickers-57
93Finnish SISU-246
94Finest-136
Super Team Winners-136
Refractors-136
94Finnish SISU-42
95Finnish SISU-23
98Finnish Keraliysarja-216
99Finnish Cardset-127
00Finnish Cardset-92
01Finnish Cardset-347
02Finnish Cardset-24
02Swedish SHL-182
Parallel-182
03Swedish Elite-50
Silver-50
04Finnish Cardset-37
Parallel-27
05Finnish Cardset -206
06Finnish Cardset-31

Hassleblad, Peter
95Swedish Leaf Face to Face-14

Hassman, Jeff
91Air Canada SJHL-A14

Hastings, Ryan
01Sudbury Wolves-6
01Sudbury Wolves Police-23
03Sudbury Wolves-11
04Sudbury Wolves-14
05Sudbury Wolves-4

Hastman, Darren
907th Inn. Sketch WHL-112
917th Inn. Sketch WHL-294

Hasumi, Taisuke
93Quebec Pee-Wee Tournament-160

Hatch, Chris
91Air Canada SJHL-B48
92Saskatchewan JHL-15

Hatcher, Derian
897th Inn. Sketch OHL-154
90Score-430
Canadian-430
90Upper Deck-359
French-359
907th Inn. Sketch OHL-309
91Pro Set Platinum-258
91OPC Premier-143
91Parkhurst-75
French-75
91Pinnacle-328
French-328
91Pro Set-543
French-543
91Score Canadian Bilingual-656
91Score Canadian English-656
91Score Rookie/Traded-106T
91Upper Deck-546
French-546
92Bowman-365
92O-Pee-Chee-123
92Panini Stickers-H
92Panini Stickers French-H
92Parkhurst-72
Emerald Ice-72
92Pinnacle-34
French-34
92Pro Set-75
92Score-51
Canadian-51
92Stadium Club-414
92Topps-405
Gold-405G
92Ultra-319
92Upper Deck-287
93Donruss-77
93Leaf-212
93OPC Premier-520
Gold-520
93Panini Stickers-274
93Parkhurst-46
Emerald Ice-46
93Pinnacle-57
Canadian-57
93PowerPlay-61
93Score-168
Canadian-168
93Stadium Club-494
Members Only Master Set-494
First Day Issue-494
93Topps/OPC Premier-520
Gold-520
93Ultra-139
93Upper Deck-204
SP-37
94Be A Player-R15
94Be A Player-R136
Signature Cards-125
94Canada Games NHL POGS-83
94Donruss-317
94EA Sports-194
94Fleer-52
94Leaf-286
94Leaf Limited-25
94OPC Premier-332
Special Effects-332
94Parkhurst Vintage-V30
94Parkhurst SE-SE45
Gold-SE45
94Pinnacle-55
Artist's Proofs-55
Rink Collection-55
94Score-148
Gold-148
Platinum-148
94Select-50
Gold-50
94Stadium Club-107
Members Only Master Set-107
First Day Issue-107
Super Team Winner Cards-107
94Stars HockeyKaps-14
94Stars Pinnacle Sheet-55
94Stars Pinnacle Sheet-NNO
94Stars Postcards-10
94Stars Score Sheet-148
94Topps/OPC Premier-332
Special Effects-332
94Ultra-52
94Upper Deck-127
Electric Ice-127
SP Inserts-SP20
SP Inserts Die Cuts-SP20
94Upper Deck NHLPA/Be A Player-24
95Collector's Choice-224
Player's Club-224
Player's Club Platinum-224
95Donruss-326
95Emotion-47
95Leaf-279
95Metal-40
95Panini Stickers-173
95Parkhurst International-58
Emerald Ice-58
95Pinnacle-70
Artist's Proofs-70
Rink Collection-70
95Playoff One on One-140
95Pro Magnets-123
95Score-225
Black Ice Artist's Proofs-225
Black Ice-225
Check It-8
95SkyBox Impact-46
95SP-40
95Stadium Club-78
Members Only Master Set-78
95Stars Score Sheet-225
95Summit-72
Artist's Proofs-72
Ice-72
95Topps-197
OPC Inserts-197
95Ultra-38
Gold Medallion-38
95Upper Deck-3
Electric Ice-3
Electric Ice Gold-3
Special Edition-SE112
Special Edition Gold-SE112
95Swedish Globe World Championships-109
96Collector's Choice-70
96Donruss Canadian Ice-4
Gold Press Proofs-4
Red Press Proofs-4
96Donruss Elite-28
Die Cut Stars-28
96Flair-22
Blue Ice-22
96Fleer-26
96Leaf Preferred-80
Press Proofs-80
96Maggers-34
96Metal Universe-39
96NHL Pro Stamps-123
96SkyBox Impact-29
96SP-45
96Stars Postcards-8
96Stars Score Sheet-NNO
96Summit Metal-29
96Team Out-80
96Ultra-42
Gold Medallion-42
96Upper Deck-44
Power Performers-P27
96Zenith-19
Artist's Proofs-19
97Black Diamond-94
Double Diamond-94
Triple Diamond-94
Quadruple Diamond-94
97Collector's Choice-70
97Crown Royale-40
Emerald Green-40
Ice Blue-40
Silver-40
97Donruss-168
Press Proofs Silver-168
Press Proofs Gold-168
97Donruss Canadian Ice-124
Dominion Series-124
Provincial Series-124
97Donruss Elite-32
Aspirations-32
Status-32
97Donruss Limited-21
Exposure-21
97Donruss Preferred-21
Cut to the Chase-21
97Donruss Priority-30
Stamp of Approval-30
97Esso Olympic Hockey Heroes-32
97Esso Olympic Hockey Heroes French-32
97Katch-44
Gold-44
Silver-44
97Leaf-144
Fractal Matrix-144
Fractal Matrix Die Cuts-144
97Leaf International-144
Universal Ice-144
97Pacific-214
Copper-214
Emerald Green-214
Ice Blue-214
Red-214
Silver-214
97Pacific Dynagon-35
Copper-35
Dark Grey-35
Emerald Green-35
Ice Blue-35
Red-35
Silver-35
Tandems-38
97Pacific Omega-69
Copper-69
Dark Gray-69
Emerald Green-69
Gold-69
Ice Blue-69
97Paramount-57
Copper-57
Dark Grey-57
Emerald Green-57
Ice Blue-57
Red-57
Silver-57
97Pinnacle-182
Press Plates Back Black-182
Press Plates Back Cyan-182
Press Plates Back Magenta-182
Press Plates Back Yellow-182
Press Plates Front Black-182
Press Plates Front Cyan-182
Press Plates Front Magenta-182
Press Plates Front Yellow-182
97Pinnacle Certified-54
Red-54
Mirror Blue-54
Mirror Gold-54
Mirror Red-54
97Pinnacle Inside-138
97Pinnacle Tot Cert Platinum Blue-54
97Pinnacle Tot Certi Platinum Gold-54
97Pinnacle Totally Certified Platinum Red-54
97Pinnacle Tot Cert Mirror Platinum Gold-54
97Score-198
97SP Authentic-45
97Studio-96
Press Proofs Silver-96
Press Proofs Gold-96
97Upper Deck-51
97Upper Deck-397
Three Star Selects-20A
97Upper Deck Ice-2
Parallel-2
Power Shift-2
98Aurora-54
98Be A Player-194
Press Release-194
98BAP Gold-194
98BAP Autographs-194
98BAP Autographs Gold-194
98Finest-39
No Protectors-39
No Protectors Refractors-39
Refractors-39
98OPC Chrome-148
Refractors-148
Board Members-B13
Board Members Refractors-B13
98Pacific-176
Ice Blue-176
Red-176
98Pacific Dynagon Ice-55
Blue-55
Red-55
98Pacific Omega-69
Red-69
Opening Day Issue-69
98Paramount-63
Copper-63
Emerald Green-63
Holo-Electric-63
Ice Blue-63
Silver-63
98Topps-148
O-Pee-Chee-148
Board Members-B13
98UD Choice-65
98UD Choice Preview-65
98UD Choice Prime Choice Reserve-65
98UD Choice Reserve-65
98Upper Deck-259
Exclusives-259
Exclusives 1 of 1-259
Game Jerseys-GJ10
Gold Reserve-259
98Upper Deck MVP-66
Gold Script-66
Silver Script-66
Super Script-66
99BAP Memorabilia-17
Gold-17
Silver-17
99BAP Millennium-77
Emerald-77
Ruby-77
Sapphire-77
Signatures-77
Signatures Gold-77
99Jell-O Partners of Power-7
99O-Pee-Chee-105
99O-Pee-Chee Chrome-105
99O-Pee-Chee Chrome Refractors-105
99Pacific-118
Copper-118
Emerald Green-118
Gold-118
Ice Blue-118
Premiere Date-118
Red-118
99Pacific Dynagon Ice-64
Blue-64
Copper-64
Gold-64
Premiere Date-64
Checkmates American-9
Checkmates American-24
Checkmates Canadian-9
99Panini Stickers-224
99Paramount-71
Copper-71
Emerald-71
Gold-71
Holographic Emerald-71
Holographic Gold-71
Holographic Silver-71
Ice Blue-71
Premiere Date-71
Red-71
Silver-71
99Stadium Club-54
First Day Issue-54
One of a Kind-54
Printing Plates Black-54
Printing Plates Cyan-54
Printing Plates Magenta-54
Printing Plates Yellow-54
99Stars Postcards-7
99Topps/OPC-105
99Topps/OPC Chrome-105
Refractors-105
99Topps Gold Label Class 1-70
Black-70
Black One of One-70
One of One-70
Red-70
Red One of One-70
99Topps Gold Label Class 2-70
99Topps Gold Label Class 2 Black-70
99Topps Gold Label Class 2 Black 1 of 1-70
99Topps Gold Label Class 2 One of One-70
99Topps Gold Label Class 2 Red-70
99Topps Gold Label Class 2 Red One of One-70
99Topps Gold Label Class 3-70
99Topps Gold Label Class 3 Black-70
99Topps Gold Label Class 3 Black 1 of 1-70
99Topps Gold Label Class 3 One of One-70
99Topps Gold Label Class 3 Red-70
99Topps Gold Label Class 3 Red One of One-70
99Topps Premier Plus-56
Parallel-56
99Upper Deck-46
Exclusives-46
Exclusives 1 of 1-46
99Upper Deck Gold Reserve-46
99Upper Deck MVP-65
Gold Script-65
Silver Script-65
Super Script-65
99Upper Deck Victory-89
00SLU Hockey-90
00BAP Memorabilia-202
Emerald-202
Ruby-202
Sapphire-202
Promos-202
00BAP Mem Chicago Sportsfest Copper-202
00BAP Memorabilia Chicago Sportsfest Blue-202
00BAP Memorabilia Chicago Sportsfest Gold-202
00BAP Memorabilia Chicago Sportsfest Ruby-202
00BAP Memorabilia Chicago Sun-Times Ruby-202
00BAP Memorabilia Chicago Sun-Times Gold-202
00BAP Mem Chicago Sun-Times Sapphire-202
00BAP Mem Toronto Fall Expo Copper-202
00BAP Memorabilia Toronto Fall Expo Gold-202
00BAP Memorabilia Toronto Fall Expo Ruby-202
00BAP Parkhurst 2000-P123
00BAP Signature Series-147
Emerald-147
Ruby-147
Sapphire-147
00O-Pee-Chee-87
00O-Pee-Chee Parallel-87
00Pacific-130
Copper-130
Gold-130
Ice Blue-130
Premiere Date-130
00Paramount-74
Copper-74
Gold-74
Holo-Gold-74
Holo-Silver-74
Ice Blue-74
Premiere Date-74
00Private Stock Game Gear-35
00Private Stock Game Gear-36
00Private Stock Game Gear Patches-35
00Private Stock Game Gear Patches-36
00Stadium Club-41
Souvenirs-SCS3
00Stars Postcards-5
00Titanium Game Gear-82
00Titanium Game Gear Patches-82
00Titanium Draft Day Edition-29
Patches-29
00Topps/OPC-87
Parallel-87
00Topps Chrome-69
OPC Refractors-69
Refractors-69
00Topps Heritage-128
00Topps Premier Plus-59
Blue Ice-59
00Topps Stars-39
Blue-39
00Upper Deck-61
Exclusives Tier 1-61
Exclusives Tier 2-61
00Upper Deck MVP-58
First Stars-58
Second Stars-58
Third Stars-58
00Upper Deck Victory-78
00Upper Deck Vintage-122
00Upper Deck Vintage-123
00Vanguard Dual Game-Worn Jerseys-4
00Vanguard Dual Game-Worn Patches-4
01BAP Memorabilia-118
Emerald-118
Ruby-118
Sapphire-118
01Crown Royale Triple Threads-8
01O-Pee-Chee-164
01O-Pee-Chee Premier Parallel-164
01Pacific-124
Extreme LTD-124
Hobby LTD-124
Premiere Date-124
Retail LTD-124
Jerseys-10
Impact Zone-9
Adrenaline Jerseys-12
01Pacific Arena Exclusives-124
01Pacific Heads-Up Quad Jerseys-10
01Pacific Heads-Up Quad Jerseys-22
01Parkhurst-149
01Private Stock Game Gear-35
01Private Stock Game Gear Patches-35
01Stars Postcards-5
01Stars Team Issue-2
01Titanium Draft Day Edition-33
01Topps-164
OPC Parallel-164
Heritage Captain's Cloth-CCDH
Reserve Emblems-DH
Reserve Jerseys-DH
Reserve Name Plates-DH
Reserve Numbers-DH
Reserve Patches-DH
01UD Stanley Cup Champs-51
01Upper Deck Victory-115
Gold-115
01Vanguard Memorabilia-11
02BAP First Edition-47
02BAP First Edition-381
Jerseys-47
02BAP Sig Series Auto Buybacks 1998-194
02BAP Sig Series Auto Buybacks 1999-77
02BAP Signature Series Defensive Wall-DW5
02O-Pee-Chee-220
02O-Pee-Chee Premier Blue Parallel-220
02O-Pee-Chee Premier Red Parallel-220
02O-Pee-Chee Factory Set-220
02Pacific-112
Blue-112
Red-112
02Pacific Complete-170
Red-170
02Parkhurst Retro Hopefuls-NH8
02Stadium Club Champions Fabric-FC2
02Stadium Club Champions Patches-PC-2
02Stars Postcards-12
02Topps-220
OPC Blue Parallel-220
OPC Red Parallel-220
Captain's Cloth-CC3
Captain's Cloth-CC16
Factory Set-220
02Topps Total-291
02UD Honor Roll-80
02Upper Deck-303
Exclusives-303
02Upper Deck Beckett UD Promos-303
02Upper Deck MVP-60
Gold-60
Classics-60
Golden Classics-60
02Upper Deck Victory-72
Bronze-72
Gold-72
Silver-72
02Upper Deck Vintage-86
02Upper Deck Vintage-270
03BAP Memorabilia-23
Emerald-23
Gold-23
Ruby-23
Sapphire-23
03Black Diamond-87
Black-87
Green-87
Red-87
03Bowman-97
Gold-97
03Bowman Chrome-97
Refractors-97
Gold Refractors-97
Xfractors-97
03ITG Action Jerseys-M30
03O-Pee-Chee-170
03OPC Blue-170
03OPC Gold-170
03OPC Red-170
03Pacific-105
Blue-105
Red-105
03Pacific Exhibit-53
Blue Backs-53
Yellow Backs-53
03Parkhurst Original Six Detroit-25
03Topps-170
Blue-170
Gold-170
Red-170
03Topps C55-76
Minis-76
Minis American Back-76
Minis American Back Red-76
Minis Bazooka Back-76
Minis Brooklyn Back-76
Minis Hat Trick Back-76
Minis O Canada Back-76
Minis O Canada Back Red-76
Minis Stanley Cup Back-76
03Topps Pristine-77
Gold Refractor Die Cuts-77
Refractors-77
Press Plates Black-77
Press Plates Cyan-77
Press Plates Magenta-77
Press Plates Yellow-77
03Upper Deck-71
Canadian Exclusives-71
HG-71
03Upper Deck MVP-153
Gold Script-153
Silver Script-153
Canadian Exclusives-153
04ITG All-Star FANtasy Hall Minnesota-2
05Be A Player Signatures-DE
05Be A Player Signatures Gold-DE
05Black Diamond-67
Emerald-67
Gold-67
Onyx-67
Ruby-67
05Flyers Team Issue-9

05Panini Stickers-135
05Parkhurst-360
Facsimile Auto Parallel-360
True Colors-TCPHI
True Colors-TCPHI
05The Cup Master Pressplate Rookie Update-235
05UD Powerplay Specialists-TSHA
05UD Powerplay Specialists Patches-SPHA
05Upper Deck Hockey Showcase-HS13
05Upper Deck Showcase Promos-HS13
05Upper Deck MVP-282
Gold-282
Platinum-282
Materials-M-DH
05Upper Deck Rookie Update-235
Inspirations Patch Rookies-235
06Flyers Postcards-1
06O-Pee-Chee-363
Rainbow-363
06Panini Stickers-128
06The Cup NHL Shields Duals-DSHPH

Hatcher, Kevin

83North Bay Centennials-8
86Capitals Kodak-11
86Capitals Police-10
87Capitals Kodak-4
87Capitals Team Issue-9
87O-Pee-Chee-68
87Panini Stickers-179
87Topps-68
88Capitals Borderless-8
88Capitals Smokey-8
88O-Pee-Chee-86
88Panini Stickers-365
88Topps-86
89Capitals Kodak-4
89Capitals Team Issue-6
89O-Pee-Chee-146
89Panini Stickers-347
89Topps-146
90Bowman-70
Tiffany-70
90Capitals Kodak-6
90Capitals Postcards-6
90Capitals Smokey-6
90O-Pee-Chee-147
90Panini Stickers-167
90Pro Set-311
90Pro Set-376
90Score-90
Canadian-90
90Score Hottest/Rising Stars-42
90Topps-147
Tiffany-147
90Upper Deck-109
90Upper Deck-486
French-109
French-486
91Pro Set Platinum-127
91Pro Set Platinum-281
91Bowman-296
91Bowman-409
91Capitals Junior 5x7-10
91Capitals Kodak-9
91Gillette-36
91Kraft-20
91O-Pee-Chee-310
91OPC Premier-88
91Panini Stickers-198
91Parkhurst-191
French-191
91Pinnacle-131
French-131
91Pro Set-249
91Pro Set-316
French-249
French-316
Puck Candy-29
91Score American-20
91Score American-340
91Score Canadian Bilingual-20
91Score Canadian Bilingual-370
91Score Canadian English-20
91Score Canadian English-370
91Score Kellogg's-7
91Stadium Club-140
91Topps-310
Team Scoring Leaders-16
91Upper Deck-98
91Upper Deck-361
91Upper Deck-511
French-98
French-361
French-511
91Finnish Semic World Champ Stickers-136
91Swedish Semic World Champ Stickers-136
92Bowman-230
92Bowman-271
92Capitals Kodak-9
92Humpty Dumpty I-11
92McDonald's Upper Deck-19
92O-Pee-Chee-145
92Panini Stickers-167
92Panini Stickers French-167
92Parkhurst-198
Emerald Ice-198
92Pinnacle-11
French-11
92Pro Set-204
92Score-273
92Score-439
Canadian-273
Canadian-439
USA Greats-13
92Seasons Patches-48
92Stadium Club-301
92Topps-149
Gold-149G
92Ultra-231
92Upper Deck-198
92Finnish Semic-151
93Donruss-369
93Kraft-33
93Leaf-34
93OPC Premier-435
Gold-435
93Panini Stickers-C
93Parkhurst-221
Emerald Ice-221
93Pinnacle-90
Canadian-90
Captains-25
Captains Canadian-25
93PowerPlay-261
93Score-136
93Score-450
Canadian-136
Canadian-450
Franchise-23
93Stadium Club-153
Members Only Master Set-153
OPC-153
First Day Issue-153
First Day Issue OPC-153
93Topps/OPC Premier-435
Gold-435
93Ultra-118
93Upper Deck-140
SP-169
93Swedish Semic World Champ Stickers-175
94Be A Player-R131
Signature Cards-48
94Canada Games NHL POGS-363
94Donruss-199
94EA Sports-151
94Finest-17
Super Team Winners-17
Refractors-17
94Fleer-53
94Hockey Wit-17
94Leaf-369
94Parkhurst-259
Gold-259
Vintage-V54
94Pinnacle-345
Artist's Proofs-345
Rink Collection-345
94Select-148
Gold-148
94SP-31
Die Cuts-31
94Stadium Club-220
Members Only Master Set-220
First Day Issue-220
Super Team Winner Cards-220
94Stars Postcards-11
94Ultra-233
94Upper Deck-332
Electric Ice-332
SP Inserts-SP86
SP Inserts-SP110
SP Inserts Die Cuts-SP86
SP Inserts Die Cuts-SP110
94Finnish Jaa Kiekko-114
94Finnish Jaa Kiekko-342
95Bashan Super Stickers-34
95Bowman-48
All-Foil-48
95Canada Games NHL POGS-89
95Collector's Choice-186
Player's Club-186
Player's Club Platinum-186
95Donruss-95
95Donruss Elite-17
Die Cut Stars-17
Die Cut Uncut-17
95Emotion-48
95Finest-148
Refractors-148
95Hoyle Western Playing Cards-33
95Imperial Stickers-34
95Leaf-117
95Metal-41
95Panini Stickers-175
95Parkhurst International-56
Emerald Ice-56
95Pinnacle-10
Artist's Proofs-10
Rink Collection-10
95Playoff One on One-248
95Score-12
Black Ice Artist's Proofs-12
Black Ice-12
95Select Certified-41
Mirror Gold-41
95SkyBox Impact-47
95SP-37
95Stadium Club Members Only-28
95Stadium Club-42
Members Only Master Set-42
95Stars Score Sheet-12
95Summit-41
Artist's Proofs-41
Ice-41
95Topps-273
OPC Inserts-273
95Topps SuperSkills-53
Platinum-53
95Ultra-230
95Upper Deck-256
95Upper Deck-309
Electric Ice-256
Electric Ice-309
Electric Ice Gold-256
Electric Ice Gold-309
Special Edition-SE25
Special Edition Gold-SE25
95Zenith-44
95Finnish Semic World Championships-106
95Swedish Globe World Championships-105
96Be A Player-14
Autographs-14
Autographs Silver-14
96Black Diamond-54
Gold-54
96Collector's Choice-71
96Donruss-29
Press Proofs-29
96Donruss Elite-24
Die Cut Stars-24
96Flair-76
Blue Ice-76
96Fleer Picks Fabulous 50-17
96Leaf-48
Press Proofs-48
96Metal Universe-126
96Pinnacle-3
Artist's Proofs-3
Foil-3
Premium Stock-3
Rink Collection-3
96Playoff One on One-408
96Score-117
Artist's Proofs-117
Dealer's Choice Artist's Proofs-117
Special Artist's Proofs-117
Golden Blades-117
96SP-130
96Stadium Club Members Only-11
96Topps Picks-33
OPC Inserts-33
96Ultra-140
Gold Medallion-140
96Upper Deck-319
Power Performers-P21
96Swedish Semic Wien-163
97Collector's Choice-207
97Donruss-26
Press Proofs Silver-26
Press Proofs Gold-26
97Donruss Limited-21
Exposure-21
97Donruss Preferred-70
Cut to the Chase-70
97Donruss Priority-100
Stamp of Approval-100
97Esso Olympic Hockey Heroes-31
97Esso Olympic Hockey Heroes French-31
97Katch-117
Gold-117
Silver-117
97Leaf-129
Fractal Matrix-129
Fractal Matrix Die Cuts-129
97Leaf International-129
Universal Ice-129
97Pacific-227
Copper-227
Emerald Green-227
Ice Blue-227
Red-227
Silver-227
97Pacific Dynagon-101
Copper-101
Dark Grey-101
Emerald Green-101
Ice Blue-101
Red-101
Silver-101
Tandems-62
97Pacific Invincible-112
Copper-112
Emerald Green-112
Ice Blue-112
Red-112
Silver-112
97Pacific Omega-185
Copper-185
Dark Gray-185
Emerald Green-185
Gold-185
Ice Blue-185
97Panini Stickers-49
97Paramount-149
Copper-149
Dark Grey-149
Emerald Green-149
Ice Blue-149
Red-149
Silver-149
97Pinnacle-171
Press Plates Back Black-171
Press Plates Back Cyan-171
Press Plates Back Magenta-171
Press Plates Back Yellow-171
Press Plates Front Black-171
Press Plates Front Cyan-171
Press Plates Front Magenta-171
Press Plates Front Yellow-171
97Pinnacle Certified-86
Red-86
Mirror Blue-86
Mirror Gold-86
Mirror Red-86
97Pinnacle Inside-98
97Pinnacle Tot Cert Platinum Blue-86
97Pinnacle Tot Certi Platinum Gold-86
97Pinnacle Totally Certified Platinum Red-86
97Pinnacle Tot Cert Mirror Platinum Gold-86
97Score-222
97Score Penguins-8
Platinum-8
Premier-8
97SP Authentic-127
97Upper Deck-343
98Aurora-153
98Be A Player-112
Press Release-112
98BAP Gold-112
98BAP Autographs-112
98BAP Autographs Gold-112
98BAP Tampa Bay All Star Game-112
98Bowman's Best-24
Refractors-24
Atomic Refractors-24
98Katch-117
98OPC Chrome-73
Refractors-73
Board Members-B14
Board Members Refractors-B14
98Pacific-352
Ice Blue-352
Red-352
98Pacific Dynagon Ice-149
Blue-149
Red-149
98Panini Photocards-33
98Paramount-191
Copper-191
Emerald Green-191
Holo-Electric-191
Ice Blue-191
Silver-191
98Topps-73
O-Pee-Chee-73
Board Members-B14
98UD Choice-172
Prime Choice Reserve-172
Reserve-172
98Upper Deck-159
98Upper Deck-348
Exclusives-159
Exclusives-348
Exclusives 1 of 1-159
Exclusives 1 of 1-348
Gold Reserve-159
Gold Reserve-348
99BAP Memorabilia-68
Gold-68
Silver-68
99Pacific-336
Copper-336
Emerald Green-336
Gold-336
Ice Blue-336
Premiere Date-336
Red-336
99Panini Stickers-107
99Upper Deck-261
Exclusives-261
Exclusives 1 of 1-261
99Upper Deck Gold Reserve-261
99Upper Deck Victory-243
99Slovakian Challengers-28
00BAP Memorabilia-466
Emerald-466
Ruby-466
Sapphire-466
00Private Stock Game Gear-13
01Pacific-73
Extreme LTD-73
Hobby LTD-73
Premiere Date-73
Retail LTD-73
01Pacific Arena Exclusives-73
02BAP Sig Series Auto Buybacks 1998-112

Hatcher, Mark

82North Bay Centennials-9
83North Bay Centennials-9
88ProCards AHL-35

Hatinen, Markus

94Finnish SISU-253
99Finnish Cardset-271

Hatinger, Josh

04Northern Michigan Wildcats-8

Hatkevitsch, Sergej

94German First League-486

Hatoum, Ed

73Vancouver Blazers-11

Hatskin, Ben

74Team Canada L'Equipe WHA-7

Hatteland, Jone

92Norwegian Elite Series-207

Hatterscheid, Daniel

05German DEL-352

Hatziioannou, Fred

01Owen Sound Attack-7
02Owen Sound Attack-19
03Oshawa Generals-8

Hauck, Robert

94German First League-257

Hauer, Brett

93PowerPlay-504
93Stadium Club Team USA-7
93Stadium Club Team USA Members Only-7
93Topps Premier Team USA-20
93Ultra-484
93Las Vegas Thunder-11
93Minnesota-Duluth Commemorative-3
93Classic-67
94Swedish Leaf-268
94Classic Autographs-NNO
95Swedish World Championships Stickers-221
98IHL All-Star Western Conference-2
98Manitoba Moose-C4
99IHL All-Stars-13
99Manitoba Moose-10
00Manitoba Moose-11
01Manchester Monarchs-6A
01Milwaukee Admirals-13
02Swiss HNL-114
04Swiss EV Zug Postcards-1

Haueter, Marc

93Swiss HNL-371
95Swiss HNL-292
96Swiss HNL-277
98Swiss Power Play Stickers-230
00Swiss Slapshot Mini-Cards-EHCC12
01Swiss HNL-240

Haugen, Geir

92Norwegian Elite Series-113

Haugh, Tom

67Swedish Hockey-154

Hauhtonen, Janne

00Finnish Cardset-175
01Finnish Cardset-67
04Finnish Cardset-88
Parallel-65
05Finnish Cardset -196
06Finnish Cardset-21
06Syracuse Crunch-12

Haukali, Terje

92Norwegian Elite Series-227

Haun, David

96Brandon Wheat Kings-23
97Brandon Wheat Kings-10
98Spokane Chiefs-11

Haun, Tim

000CN Blizzard-24

Haupt, Kevin

97Portland Winter Hawks-18
02Fresno Falcons-2

Hauser, Adam

98Minnesota Golden Gophers-22
99Minnesota Golden Gophers-7
00Minnesota Golden Gophers-6
01Minnesota Golden Gophers-15
02ECHL All-Star Southern-44
02ECHL Update-U-10
03Manchester Monarchs-6
03Pacific AHL Prospects-49
Gold-49
03Reading Royals-3
04Manchester Monarchs-1
04Manchester Monarchs Tobacco-2
04ITG Heroes and Prospects-22
Autographs-AH
04ITG Heroes/Prospects Toronto Expo '05-22
04ITG Heroes/Prospects Expo Heroes/Pros-22
05ITG Heroes/Prosp Toronto Expo Parallel -47
05Hot Prospects-130
En Fuego-130
Red Hot-130
White Hot-130
05SP Authentic-229
Limited-229
05The Cup Masterpiece Pressplates (Ice)-198
05The Cup Master Pressplate Rookie Update-138
05The Cup Masterpiece Pressplates SPA-229
05Upper Deck Ice-198
05Upper Deck Rookie Update-138
05Manchester Monarchs-7
05Manchester Monarchs-35
05ITG Heroes and Prospects-47
Autographs-A-AH
Jerseys-GUJ-108
Jerseys Gold-GUJ-108
Emblems-GUE-93
Emblems Gold-GUE-93
Numbers-GUN-93
Numbers Gold-GUN-93
Net Prospects-NP-4
Net Prospects Dual-NPD2
Net Prospects Dual Gold-NPD2
Net Prospects Gold-NP-04
06German DEL-122

Hauserer, Christian

94German First League-107

Hausler, Oliver

94German DEL-382

Hauswirth, Mike

90Michigan Tech Huskies-7
91Michigan Tech Huskies-5

Hautamaa, Juha

93Finnish SISU-130
94Finnish SISU-120
95Finnish SISU-41
95Finnish SISU Limited-105
95Finnish SISU Spotlights-8
98Finnish Kerailysarja-86
Off Duty-4
99Finnish Cardset-51
00Finnish Cardset-36

Havel, Jan

69Swedish Hockey-26
70Swedish Masterserien-10
71Finnish Suomi Stickers-25
71Swedish Hockey-51
72Finnish Semic World Championship-29
72Swedish Semic World Championship-29
74Swedish Semic World Champ Stickers-71
01Czech DS Legends-L8

Havel, Lukas

99Brampton Battalion-14
00Brampton Battalion-14
01Czech OFS-161
02Czech OFS Plus-193
03Czech OFS Plus-93
03Czech OFS Plus MS Praha-SE29
04Czech HC Slavia Praha Postcards-20
04Czech OFS-93
Goals Leaders-9

Havel, Marek

93Quebec Pee-Wee Tournament-1558

Havel, Marian

01Vancouver Giants-13
02Swift Current Broncos-6
04Czech OFS-8

Havel, Michal

99Czech Score Blue 2000-94
99Czech Score Red Ice 2000-94
00Czech OFS-130
01Czech OFS-177
06Czech HC Kladno Postcards-7
06Czech OFS-254

Havelid, Niclas

91Swedish Semic Elitserien Stickers-11
92Swedish Semic Elitserien Stickers-35
94Swedish Leaf-36
95Swedish Leaf-5
95Swedish Upper Deck-5
97Swedish Collector's Choice-6
97Swedish Collector's Choice-209
98Swedish UD Choice-152
99BAP Memorabilia-193
Gold-193
Silver-193
99BAP Millennium-4
Emerald-4
Ruby-4
Sapphire-4
Signatures-4
Signatures Gold-4
99Pacific Dynagon Ice-8
Blue-8
Copper-8
Gold-8
Premiere Date-8
99Panini Stickers-179
99Stadium Club-183
First Day Issue-183
One of a Kind-183
Printing Plates Black-183
Printing Plates Cyan-183
Printing Plates Magenta-183
Printing Plates Yellow-183
99Topps Premier Plus-110
Parallel-110
99Upper Deck-172
Exclusives-172
Exclusives 1 of 1-172
99Upper Deck Gold Reserve-172
01Topps Reserve-79
02BAP Sig Series Auto Buybacks 1999-4
02Pacific Complete-418
Red-418
03ITG Action-68
03Pacific-4
Blue-4
Red-4
03Pacific Complete-61
Red-61
04Swedish Elitset-266
Gold-266
Limited Signatures-5
Signatures Series B-14
05Parkhurst-25
Facsimile Auto Parallel-25
05Upper Deck-12
HG Glossy-12
05Upper Deck MVP-22
Gold-22
Platinum-22
05Upper Deck Toronto Fall Expo-12
06O-Pee-Chee-27
Rainbow-27
06Panini Stickers-10
06Upper Deck-14
Exclusives Parallel-14
High Gloss Parallel-14
Masterpieces-14

Havelka, Petr

99Czech OFS-104
00Czech OFS-311
01Czech OFS-96
02Czech OFS Plus-5
03Czech OFS Plus-322
04Czech OFS-142

Havenhand, Andy

93UK Sheffield Steelers-1
94UK Sheffield Steelers-23
94UK Solihul Barons-5
95UK Solihull Barons-5

Haviland, Kyle

93Memphis RiverKings-4
94Central Hockey League-46
95Muskegon Fury-3
97Austin Ice Bats-7
98Topeka Scarecrows-15
99Memphis RiverKings All-Time-15

Haviland, Mike

00Trenton Titans-11
01Atlantic City Boardwalk Bullies-22
02Atlantic City Boardwalk Bullies-9
03Atlantic City Boardwalk Bullies-27
04Atlantic City Boardwalk Bullies Kinko's-28
06Norfolk Admirals-25

Haviland, Shawn

04Guelph Storm-3
05Guelph Storm-D-01

Havir, David

99Czech OFS-75
00Czech DS Extraliga-104
00Czech OFS-195
01Czech OFS-109
02Czech OFS Plus-108
03Czech OFS Plus-242
04Czech OFS-116
Defence Points-2
05Czech HC Pardubice-4
06Czech HC Pardubice Postcards-5
06Czech OFS-114
06Czech Super Six Postcards-4

Havlat, Martin

98Czech OFS-393
99Czech DS-107
99Czech OFS-194
00BAP Memorabilia-403
Emerald-403
Ruby-403
Sapphire-403
00BAP Parkhurst 2000-P240
00BAP Signature Series-276
Emerald-276
Ruby-276
Sapphire-276
Autographs-238
Autographs Gold-238
00Black Diamond-127
00Crown Royale-134
21st Century Rookies-17
00Private Stock-132
Gold-132
Premiere Date-132
Retail-132
Silver-132
PS-2001 Rookies-14
00Senators Team Issue-7
00SP Authentic-115
Sign of the Times-HA
00SP Game Used-75
00SPx-110
Spectrum-110
00Stadium Club-249
00Titanium-134
Retail-134
Three-Star Selections-25
00Titanium Draft Day Edition-134
00Titanium Draft Day Promos-134
00Topps Chrome-248
Blue-248
Red-248
OPC Refractors-248
OPC Refractors Blue-248
OPC Refractors Red-248
Refractors-248
Refractors Blue-248
Refractors Red-248
00Topps Gold Label Class 1-109
Gold-109
00Topps Gold Label Class 2-109
00Topps Gold Label Class 2 Gold-109
00Topps Gold Label Class 3-109
00Topps Gold Label Class 3 Gold-109
00Topps Heritage-77
Chrome Parallel-77
00Topps Premier Plus-120
Blue Ice-120
00Topps Stars-101
Blue-101
00UD Heroes-173
00UD Pros and Prospects-116
00UD Reserve-107
00Upper Deck-414
Exclusives Tier 1-414
Exclusives Tier 2-414
00Upper Deck Ice-95
00Upper Deck Vintage-388
00Vanguard-135
Pacific Proofs-135
00Czech DS Extraliga National Team-NT8
00Czech DS Extraliga World Champions-WCH7
00Czech Stadion-116
01Atomic-68
Blue-68
Gold-68
Premiere Date-68
Red-68
01BAP Memorabilia-41
Emerald-41
Ruby-41
Sapphire-41
He Shoots-He Scores Points-2
01BAP Signature Series-140
Autographs-140
Autographs Gold-140
Jerseys-GJ-4
Jersey Autographs-GUMHA
Jersey and Stick Cards-GSJ-4
01BAP Update He Shoots-He Scores Points-5
01BAP Update He Shoots-He Scores Prizes-35
01Bowman YoungStars-142
Gold-142
Ice Cubed-142
01Crown Royale Calder Collection Gold Ed-6
01Crown Royale Calder Collection AS Ed-C4
01Crown Royale-100
Blue-100
Premiere Date-100
Red-100
Retail-100
01Crown Royale Toronto Expo Rookie Coll-G4
01eTopps-13
01McDonald's Pacific Future Legends-3
01O-Pee-Chee-93
01O-Pee-Chee Heritage Parallel-93
01O-Pee-Chee Heritage Parallel Limited-93
01O-Pee-Chee Premier Parallel-93
01O-Pee-Chee Jumbos-7
01Pacific-272
01Pacific-448
Extreme LTD-272
Hobby LTD-272
Premiere Date-272
Retail LTD-272
01Pacific Adrenaline-133
Blue-133
Premiere Date-133
Red-133
Retail-133
Playmakers-7
World Beaters-13
01Pacific Arena Exclusives-272
01Pacific Heads-Up-68
Blue-68
Premiere Date-68
Red-68
Silver-68
Breaking the Glass-15
Prime Picks-5
01Parkhurst-97
Gold-97
Silver-97
Waving the Flag-12
01Private Stock-67
Gold-67
Premiere Date-67
Retail-67
Silver-67
01Private Stock Pacific Nights-67
01Private Stock PS-2002-52
01Private Stock Reserve-S12
01Senators Team Issue-7
01SP Authentic-118
Limited-118
Limited Gold-118
Buybacks-18
Sign of the Times-HA
Sign of the Times-HH
Sign of the Times-HHS
01SPx-187
01Stadium Club-79
Award Winners-79
Master Photos-79
Gallery-G5
Gallery Gold-G5
Lone Star Signatures-LS4
01Titanium-99
Hobby Parallel-99
Premiere Date-99
Retail-99
Retail Parallel-99
Double-Sided Jerseys-47
Double-Sided Jerseys-60
Double-Sided Patches-47
Double-Sided Patches-60
Saturday Knights-16
01Titanium Draft Day Edition-65
01Topps-93
Heritage Parallel-93
Heritage Parallel Limited-93
OPC Parallel-93
Autographs-AMHA
Own The Game-OTG13
01Topps Chrome-93
Refractors-93
Black Border Refractors-93
01Topps Heritage-43
Refractors-43
01Topps Reserve-12
01UD Mask Collection-66
Gold-66
01UD Playmakers-70
01UD Premier Collection Signatures-MH
01UD Premier Collection Signatures Black-MH
01UD Top Shelf-110
01Upper Deck-125
Exclusives-125
01Upper Deck Ice-31
01Upper Deck MVP-136
01Upper Deck Victory-247
Gold-247
01Upper Deck Vintage-176
01Vanguard-68
Blue-68
Red-68
One of Ones-68
Premiere Date-68
Prime Prospects-13
Proofs-68
02BAP First Edition-98
02BAP First Edition-421H
Jerseys-98
02BAP Memorabilia-115
Emerald-115
Ruby-115
Sapphire-115
Future of the Game-FG-12
NHL All-Star Game-115
NHL All-Star Game Blue-115
NHL All-Star Game Green-115
NHL All-Star Game Red-115
02BAP Memorabilia Toronto Fall Expo-115
02BAP Signature Series-67
Autographs-67
Autograph Buybacks 2001-140
Autographs Gold-67
Jerseys-SGJ39
Jersey Autographs-SGJ39
Team Quads-TQ20
02Bowman YoungStars-48
Gold-48
Silver-48
02Crown Royale Jerseys-14
02Crown Royale Jerseys Gold-14
02ITG Used-54
02ITG Used-154
02McDonald's Pacific Clear Advantage-5
02NHL Power Play Stickers-108
02O-Pee-Chee-49
02O-Pee-Chee Jumbos-17
02O-Pee-Chee Premier Blue Parallel-49
02O-Pee-Chee Premier Red Parallel-49
02O-Pee-Chee Factory Set-49
02Pacific-266
Blue-266
Red-266
Jerseys-37
Jerseys Holo-Silver-37
02Pacific Complete-444
Red-444
02Pacific Exclusive-121
02Pacific Heads-Up-86
Blue-86
Purple-86
Red-86
Head First-11
Quad Jerseys-19
Quad Jerseys Gold-19
02Pacific Quest for the Cup-70
Gold-70
02Parkhurst-59
Bronze-59
Gold-59
Silver-59
Teammates-TT11
02Parkhurst Retro-85
Minis-85
02Private Stock Reserve-72
Blue-72
Red-72
Retail-72
02Senators Team Issue-6
02Senators Team Issue-5
02SP Authentic Sign of the Times-MH
02SP Game Used-34
Signature Style-MH
02Stadium Club-27
Silver Decoy Cards-27
Proofs-27
02Titanium Jerseys-47
02Titanium Jerseys Retail-47
02Titanium Patches-47
02Topps-49
OPC Blue Parallel-49
OPC Red Parallel-49
Signs of the Future-MH
Factory Set-49
02Topps Chrome-40
Black Border Refractors-40
Refractors-40
02Topps Heritage-49
Chrome Parallel-49
02Topps Total-388
02UD Artistic Impressions-61
Gold-61
02UD Artistic Impressions Beckett Promos-61
02UD Artistic Impressions Retrospectives-R61
02UD Artistic Impressions Retrospect Gold-R61
02UD Artistic Impress Retrospect Silver-R61
02UD Premier Collection Signatures Bronze-SMH
02UD Premier Collection Signatures Gold-SMH
02UD Premier Collection Signatures Silver-SMH
02UD Top Shelf-60
Signatures-HA
02Upper Deck-366
Exclusives-366
02Upper Deck Beckett UD Promos-366
02Upper Deck Classic Portraits-68
02Upper Deck MVP-128
Gold-128
Classics-128
Golden Classics-128
02Upper Deck Rookie Update Autographs-MH
02Upper Deck Victory-146
Bronze-146
Gold-146
Silver-146
National Pride-NP19
02Upper Deck Vintage-178
02Upper Deck Vintage-281
Green Backs-178
02Czech Stadion Olympics-332
03BAP Memorabilia-51
Emerald-51
Gold-51
Ruby-51
Sapphire-51
03Black Diamond Signature Gems-SG-11
03Bowman-109
Gold-109
03Bowman Chrome-109
Refractors-109
Gold Refractors-109
Xfractors-109
03ITG Action-446
Jerseys-M131
03NHL Sticker Collection-97
03O-Pee-Chee-225
03OPC Blue-225
03OPC Gold-225
03OPC Red-225
03Pacific-237
Blue-237
Red-237
03Pacific Calder-71
Silver-71
03Pacific Complete-35
Red-35
03Pacific Exhibit-104
Blue Backs-104
Yellow Backs-104
03Pacific Prism-74
Blue-74
Gold-74
Red-74
Paramount Prodigies-16
03Pacific Quest for the Cup-74
Blue-74
Jerseys-14
03Senators Postcards-6
03SP Game Used Signers-SPSHV
03Topps-225
Blue-225
Gold-225
Red-225
03Topps C55-112
Minis-112
Minis American Back-112
Minis American Back Red-112
Minis Bazooka Back-112
Minis Brooklyn Back-112
Minis Hat Trick Back-112
Minis O Canada Back-112
Minis O Canada Back Red-112
Minis Stanley Cup Back-112
03UD Honor Roll Signature Class-SC10
03Upper Deck-132
Canadian Exclusives-132
HG-132
03Upper Deck MVP-291
Gold Script-291
Silver Script-291
Canadian Exclusives-291
ProSign-PS-MH
03Upper Deck Trilogy Scripts-S2MH
03Upper Deck Trilogy Scripts Limited-S2MH
03Czech OFS Plus-345
03Czech OFS Plus-400
03Czech OFS Plus MS Praha-SE1
03Toronto Star-67
04Pacific-184
Blue-184
Red-184
Global Connection-7
04SP Authentic-63
Limited-63
Rookie Review-RR-HV
Sign of the Times-DS-SH
Sign of the Times-FS-SEN
04UD All-World-11
Gold-11
Autographs-11
Five Autographs-AF-YAO
04UD Toronto Fall Expo Priority Signings-MH
04Upper Deck-121
Canadian Exclusives-121
HG Glossy Gold-121
HG Glossy Silver-121
Jersey Autographs-GJA-MH
World Cup Tribute-MHSKTV
04Czech OFS-313
Stars-42
04Czech Zuma-7
04Russian Legion-5
04Russian Moscow Dynamo-8
05Be A Player World Cup Salute-WCS5
05Beehive-62
Matte-62
Signature Scrapbook-SSHV
05Black Diamond-106
Emerald-106
Gold-106
Onyx-106
Ruby-106
Gemography-G-MH
Gemography Emerald-G-MH
Gemography Gold-G-MH
Gemography Onyx-G-MH
Gemography Ruby-G-MH
05McDonalds Upper Deck Jerseys-MJ13
05McDonalds Upper Deck Patches-MP13
05Panini Stickers-122
05Parkhurst-347
Facsimile Auto Parallel-347

True Colors-TCOTT
True Colors-TCOTT
05SP Authentic-70
Limited-70
Chirography-SPHV
Marks of Distinction-MDHV
Sign of the Times-HV
Sign of the Times Triples-THHC
Sign of the Times Quads-QSHAH
05SP Game Used-71
Autographs-71
Gold-71
Authentic Fabrics-AF-HV
Authentic Fabrics Autographs-AAF-HV
Authentic Fabrics Dual-HH
Authentic Fabrics Dual Autographs-HH
Authentic Fabrics Gold-AF-HV
Authentic Fabrics Quad-SAHH
Authentic Patches Quad -SAHH
Authentic Fabrics Triple-HJH
Authentic Patches-AP-HV
Authentic Patches Autographs-AAP-HV
Authentic Patches Dual-HH
Authentic Patches Dual Autographs-HH
Authentic Patches Triple-HJH
Auto Draft-AD-HV
Awesome Authentics-AA-HV
Awesome Authentics Gold-DA-HV
SIGnificance-MH
SIGnificance Gold-S-MH
SIGnificance Extra-HH
SIGnificance Extra Gold-HH
Significant Numbers-SN-HV
Statscriptions-ST-HV
05SPx-62
Spectrum-62
Winning Combos-WC-CH
Winning Combos-WC-OT
Winning Combos Autographs-AWC-CH
Winning Combos Autographs-AWC-HH
Winning Combos Gold-WC-CH
Winning Combos Gold-WC-OT
Winning Combos Spectrum-WC-CH
Winning Combos Spectrum-WC-OT
Winning Materials-WM-HV
Winning Materials Autographs-AWM-HV
Winning Materials Gold-WM-HV
Winning Materials Spectrum-WM-HV
Xcitement Superstars-XS-HV
Xcitement Superstars Gold-XS-HV
Xcitement Superstars Spectrum-XS-HV
05The Cup Dual NHL Shields-DSHA
05The Cup Emblems of Endorsement-EEHV
05The Cup Honorable Numbers-HNHV
05The Cup Limited Logos-LLHV
05The Cup Masterpiece Pressplate Auto-266
05The Cup Noble Numbers Dual-DNNEH
05The Cup Scripted Numbers-SNMH
05The Cup Scripted Swatches-SSHV
05The Cup Signature Patches-SPHV
05UD Artifacts-72
Blue-72
Gold-72
Green-72
Pewter-72
Red-72
Auto Facts-AF-MH
Auto Facts Blue-AF-MH
Auto Facts Copper-AF-MH
Auto Facts Pewter-AF-MH
Auto Facts Silver-AF-MH
Frozen Artifacts-FA-MH
Frozen Artifacts Autographed-FA-MH
Frozen Artifacts Copper-FA-MH
Frozen Artifacts Dual-FAD-MH
Frozen Artifacts Dual Autographed-FAD-MH
Frozen Artifacts Dual Copper-FAD-MH
Frozen Artifacts Dual Gold-FAD-MH
Frozen Artifacts Dual Maroon-FAD-MH
Frozen Artifacts Dual Pewter-FAD-MH
Frozen Artifacts Dual Silver-FAD-MH
Frozen Artifacts Gold-FA-MH
Frozen Artifacts Maroon-FA-MH
Frozen Artifacts Patches-FP-MH
Frozen Artifacts Patches Autographed-FP-MH
Frozen Artifacts Patches Dual-FGD-KL
Frozen Artifacts Patches Dual Autos-FGD-KL
Frozen Artifacts Patches Pewter-FP-MH
Frozen Artifacts Patches Silver-FP-MH
Frozen Artifacts Pewter-FA-MH
Frozen Artifacts Silver-FA-MH
Gold Autographed-72
Remarkable Artifacts-RA-MH
Remarkable Artifacts Dual-RA-MH
05UD PowerPlay-98
Power Marks-PMHA
05UD Toronto Fall Expo Priority Signings-PS-MH
05Ultimate Collection-63
Gold-63
Endorsed Emblems-EEHV
Ultimate Achievements-UAHV
Ultimate Signatures-USHV
Ultimate Signatures Foursomes-UFHHSH
Ultimate Signatures Pairings-UPHH
05Ultra-136
Gold-136
Fresh Ink-FI-HV
Fresh Ink Blue-FI-HV
Ice-136
Scoring Kings-SK28
Scoring Kings Jerseys-SKJ-HV
Scoring Kings Jersey Autographs-KAJ-HV
Scoring Kings Patches-SKP-HV
Scoring Kings Patch Autographs-KAP-HV
05Upper Deck-381
Big Playmakers-B-MHA
Jerseys Series II-J2MH
Majestic Materials-MMHV
NHL Generations-DJH
Notable Numbers-N-HV
Patches-P-MAH
Shooting Stars-S-MHA
05Upper Deck Ice-67
Rainbow-67
Cool Threads-CTMV
Cool Threads Autographs-ACTMV
Cool Threads Glass-CTMV
Cool Threads Patches-CTPMV
Cool Threads Patch Autographs-CAPMV
Fresh Ice-FIHV
Fresh Ice Glass-FIHV
Fresh Ice Glass Patches-FIPHV
Glacial Graphs-GGHV
05Upper Deck MVP-274
Gold-274
Platinum-274
Materials Duals-D-HH
05Upper Deck Rookie Update-266
05Upper Deck Trilogy-63
05Upper Deck Trilogy-168
Crystal-168
Honorary Patches-HP-HA
Honorary Patch Scripts-HSP-HA
Honorary Swatches-HS-HA
Honorary Swatch Scripts-HSS-HA
Ice Scripts-IS-HA
Scripts-SFS-MH
05Upper Deck Victory-134
Black-134
Gold-134
Silver-134
Game Breakers-GB30
05Czech Kvarteto Bonaparte-6c
05Czech Pexeso Mini Blue Set-21
05Czech Stadion-675
06Be A Player-118
Autographs-118
Signatures-HA
Up Close and Personal-UC41
Up Close and Personal Autographs-UC41
06Be A Player Portraits-25
06Beehive-81
06Beehive-219
Blue-81
Gold-81
Matte-81
Red Facsimile Signatures-81
Wood-81
Matted Materials-MMHA
Remarkable Matted Materials-MMHA
Signature Scrapbook-SSMH
06Black Diamond-95
Black-95
Gold-95
Ruby-95
06Blackhawks Postcards-7
06Flair Showcase-71
06Flair Showcase-149
Parallel-71
Parallel-149
Inks-IMH
Wave of the Future-WF31
06Fleer-46
Tiffany-46
Hockey Headliners-HL18
06Hot Prospects-24
Red Hot-24
White Hot-24
Hot Materials -HMHA
Hot Materials Red Hot-HMHA
Hot Materials White Hot-HMHA
Hotagraphs-HHA
06O-Pee-Chee-111
Rainbow-111
Swatches-S-HA
06Panini Stickers-209
06SP Authentic-79
06SP Authentic-135
Chirography-MH
Limited-79
Limited-135
Sign of the Times-STMH
Sign of the Times Duals-STHK
06SP Game Used-22
Gold-22
Rainbow-22
Authentic Fabrics Dual-AF2HK
Authentic Fabrics Dual Patches-AF2HK
Authentic Fabrics Triple-AF3CHI
Authentic Fabrics Triple Patches-AF3CHI
Autographs-22
By The Letter-BLMH
Inked Sweaters-ISHA
Inked Sweaters Patches-ISHA
Inked Sweaters Dual-IS2HH
06SPx-20
Spectrum-20
SPxcitement-X20
SPxcitement Spectrum-X20
SPxcitement Autographs-X20
Winning Materials-WMHA
Winning Materials Spectrum-WMHA
Winning Materials Autographs-WMHA
06The Cup Autographed NHL Shields Duals-DASHH
06The Cup Honorable Numbers-HNMH
06The Cup Limited Logos-LLMH
06The Cup NHL Shields Duals-DSHHR
06The Cup Scripted Swatches-SSMH
06UD Artifacts-78
Blue-78
Gold-78
Platinum-78
Radiance-78
Autographed Radiance Parallel-78
Red-78
Tundra Tandems-TTKH
Tundra Tandems Black-TTKH
Tundra Tandems Blue-TTKH
Tundra Tandems Gold-TTKH
Tundra Tandems Platinum-TTKH
Tundra Tandems Red-TTKH
Tundra Tandems Dual Patches Red-TTKH
06UD Mini Jersey Collection-21
06UD Powerplay-25
Impact Rainbow-25
06Ultimate Collection-15
Premium Patches-PS-HA
Premium Swatches-PS-HA
Signatures-US-MH
Ultimate Signatures Logos-SL-MH
06Ultra-45
Gold Medallion-45
Ice Medallion-45
06Upper Deck Arena Giveaways-CHI2
06Upper Deck-292
Exclusives Parallel-292
High Gloss Parallel-292
All World-AW9
Game Dated Moments-GD33
Game Jerseys-JHA
Game Patches-PHA
Generations Duals-G2PSH
Generations Patches Dual-G2PSH
Masterpieces-292
Oversized Wal-Mart Exclusives-292
Signature Sensations-SSMH
06Upper Deck MVP-65
Gold Script-65
Super Script-65
Autographs-OAHH
Jerseys-OJGH
Jerseys-OJTH
06Upper Deck Ovation-186
06Upper Deck Sweet Shot-24
Signature Shots/Saves-SSMH
Signature Shots/Saves Ice Signings-SSIMH
Signature Shots/Saves Sticks-SSSMH
Sweet Stitches-SSMH
Sweet Stitches Duals-SSMH
Sweet Stitches Triples-SSMH
06Upper Deck Trilogy-21
Combo Clearcut Autographs-C3RHH
Honorary Scripted Patches-HSPHV
Honorary Scripted Swatches-HSSHV
06Upper Deck Victory-141
06Upper Deck Victory-236
06Upper Deck Victory Black-141
06Upper Deck Victory Gold-141
06Czech NHL ELH Postcards-1
07Upper Deck Victory-123
Black-123
Gold-123
Stars on Ice-SI42

Havukainen, Ari
71Finnish Suomi Stickers-360

Haw, Evan
02Saskatoon Blades-1
03Saskatoon Blades-7
04Saskatoon Blades-19

Hawco, Justin
01Cape Breton Screaming Eagles-11

Hawerchuk, Dale
81Jets Postcards-6
82Jets Postcards-8
82Jets Postcards-9
82O-Pee-Chee-3
82O-Pee-Chee-374
82O-Pee-Chee-380
82O-Pee-Chee-381
82O-Pee-Chee Stickers-204
82O-Pee-Chee Stickers-249
82Post Cereal-21
82Topps Stickers-204
82Topps Stickers-249
83Esso-9
83Jets Postcards-8
83NHL Key Tags-135
83O-Pee-Chee-377
83O-Pee-Chee-385
83O-Pee-Chee Stickers-282
83Puffy Stickers-5
83Topps Stickers-282
83Vachon-126
84Jets Police-8
84Kellogg's Accordion Discs-5A
84Kellogg's Accordion Discs-5B
84Kellogg's Accordion Discs Singles-16
84O-Pee-Chee-339
84O-Pee-Chee-393
84O-Pee-Chee Stickers-284
84O-Pee-Chee Stickers-285
847-Eleven Discs-58
84Topps-152
85Jets Police-7
85Jets Silverwood Dairy-4
85O-Pee-Chee-109
85O-Pee-Chee Stickers-248
857-Eleven Credit Cards-21
85Topps-109
85Topps Sticker Inserts-8
86Jets Postcards-9
86Kraft Drawings-25
86O-Pee-Chee-74
86O-Pee-Chee Stickers-104
86Topps-74
87Jets Postcards-9
87O-Pee-Chee-149
87O-Pee-Chee Box Bottoms-I
87O-Pee-Chee Stickers-255
87Panini Stickers-363
87Pro-Sport All-Stars-7
87Topps-149
87Topps Box Bottoms-I
88Esso All-Stars-16
88Frito-Lay Stickers-9
88Jets Police-9
88Jets Postcards-11
88O-Pee-Chee-65
88O-Pee-Chee Box Bottoms-K
88O-Pee-Chee Minis-12
88O-Pee-Chee Stickers-143
88Panini Stickers-155
88Topps-65
88Topps Box Bottoms-K
89Jets Safeway-16
89Kraft-50
89O-Pee-Chee-122
89O-Pee-Chee Stickers-134
89Panini Stickers-162
89Sports Illustrated for Kids I-126
89Topps-122
89Swedish Semic World Champ Stickers-67
90Bowman-129
Tiffany-129
90Kraft-16
90O-Pee-Chee-141
90OPC Premier-40
90Panini Stickers-317
90Pro Set-330A
90Pro Set-330B
90Pro Set-415
90Sabres Blue Shield-8
90Sabres Campbell's-9
90Score-50
Canadian-50
90Score Hottest/Rising Stars-22
90Score Rookie/Traded-2T
90Topps-141
Tiffany-141
Team Scoring Leaders-11
Team Scoring Leaders Tiffany-11
90Upper Deck-53
90Upper Deck-443
French-53
French-443
91Pro Set Platinum-11
91Bowman-31
91Kraft-36
91O-Pee-Chee-32
91O-Pee-Chee-65
91OPC Premier-1
91Panini Stickers-296
91Parkhurst-18
91Parkhurst-216
French-18
French-216
91Pinnacle-80
French-80
91Pro Set-24
French-24
91Sabres Blue Shield-7
91Sabres Pepsi/Campbell's-7
91Score American-259
91Score American-376
91Score Canadian Bilingual-266
91Score Canadian Bilingual-479
91Score Canadian English-266
91Score Canadian English-479
91Stadium Club-312
91Topps-65
Team Scoring Leaders-2
91Upper Deck-12
91Upper Deck-79
91Upper Deck-126
French-12
French-79
French-126
92Bowman-308
92O-Pee-Chee-212
92Panini Stickers-247
92Panini Stickers French-247
92Parkhurst-11
Emerald Ice-11
92Pinnacle-316
French-316
92Pro Set-12
92Sabres Blue Shield-8
92Sabres Jubilee Foods-5
92Score-272
Canadian-272
92Seasons Patches-68
92Stadium Club-419
92Topps-296
Gold-296G
92Ultra-15
92Upper Deck-302
92Finnish Semic-94
93Donruss-35
93Leaf-71
93OPC Premier-7
Gold-7
93Panini Stickers-102
93Parkhurst-23
Emerald Ice-23
93Pinnacle-260
Canadian-260
93PowerPlay-29
93Sabres Limited Edition Team Issue-3
93Sabres Noco-7
93Score-159
Canadian-159
93Stadium Club-220
Members Only Master Set-220
OPC-220
First Day Issue-220
First Day Issue OPC-220
93Topps/OPC Premier-7
Gold-7
93Topps Premier Finest-11
93Ultra-149
93Upper Deck-411
SP-16
94Be A Player-R7
Signature Cards-5
94Canada Games NHL POGS-46
94Donruss-44
94EA Sports-16
94Flair-18
94Fleer-21
94Hockey Wit-22
94Leaf-313
94Leaf Limited-94
94OPC Premier-320
Special Effects-320
94Parkhurst-29
Gold-29
Vintage-V82
94Pinnacle-43
Artist's Proofs-43
Rink Collection-43
94Score-192
Gold-192
Platinum-192
94Select-42
Gold-42
94SP-15
Die Cuts-15
94Stadium Club-248
Members Only Master Set-248
First Day Issue-248
Super Team Winner Cards-248
94Topps/OPC Premier-320
Special Effects-320
94Ultra-23
94Upper Deck-102
Electric Ice-102
SP Inserts-SP9
SP Inserts Die Cuts-SP9
94Finnish Jaa Kiekko-89
95Bashan Super Stickers-103
95Canada Games NHL POGS-238
95Collector's Choice-245
Player's Club-245
Player's Club Platinum-245
95Donruss-384
95Donruss Elite-100
Die Cut Stars-100
Die Cut Uncut-100
95Emotion-147
95Finest-153
Refractors-153
95Imperial Stickers-103
95Leaf-184
95Metal-124
95Panini Stickers-189
95Parkhurst International-180
Emerald Ice-180
95Playoff One on One-306
95Score-222
Black Ice Artist's Proofs-222
Black Ice-222
95Select Certified-97
Mirror Gold-97
95SkyBox Impact-140
95SP-123
95Stadium Club-46
Members Only Master Set-46
95Summit-95
Artist's Proofs-95
Ice-95
95Topps-271
OPC Inserts-271
95Ultra-299
95Upper Deck-38
Electric Ice-38
Electric Ice Gold-38
96Be A Player-203
Autographs-203
Autographs Silver-203
96Collector's Choice-196
96Donruss-90
Press Proofs-90
96Flair-67
Blue Ice-67
96Fleer Picks-120
96Flyers Postcards-9
96Leaf-124
Press Proofs-124
96Maggers-35
96Metal Universe-111
96Pinnacle-44
Artist's Proofs-44
Foil-44
Premium Stock-44
Rink Collection-44
96Playoff One on One-409
96Score-51
Artist's Proofs-51
Dealer's Choice Artist's Proofs-51
Special Artist's Proofs-51
Golden Blades-51
96SkyBox Impact-94
96Topps Picks 500 Club-FC8
96Upper Deck-120
96Upper Deck Ice-50
Parallel-50
97Collector's Choice-190
97Donruss-36
97Pacific-225
Copper-225
Emerald Green-225
Ice Blue-225
Red-225
Silver-225
00Upper Deck 500 Goal Club-500DH
00Upper Deck 500 Goal Club-500DH
00Upper Deck Legends-133
Legendary Collection Bronze-133
Legendary Collection Gold-133
Legendary Collection Silver-133
Epic Signatures-DH
01BAP Memorabilia 500 Goal Scorers-GS21
01BAP Signature Series 500 Goal Scorers-20
01BAP Sig Series 500 Goal Scorers Auto-20
01BAP Signature Series Vintage Autographs-VA-35
01BAP Ultimate Memorabilia Calder Trophy-17
01BAP Ultimate Mem 500 Goal Scorers-20
01BAP Ultimate Mem 500 Goal Scorers Autos-3
01BAP Ultimate Mem 500 Goal Jerseys/Stick-20
01BAP Ultimate Mem 500 Goal Emblems-20
01Parkhurst Autographs-PA22
01Parkhurst 500 Goal Scorers-PGS21
01Topps Archives Relics-SDH
01Upper Deck Legends-78
02UD Foundations-10
02UD Foundations-84
02UD Foundations-100
1000 Point Club-HA
1000 Point Club-HA2
Signs of Greatness-SGDH
04ITG Franchises Canadian-140
Autographs-DHA
Original Sticks-OS12
Original Sticks Autographs-OS12
Original Sticks Gold-OS12
04ITG Franchises Update Complete Jerseys-UCJ5
04ITG Franchises Upd Complete Jersey Gold-UCJ5
04ITG Franchises US East Complete Jerseys-ECJ8
04ITG Franchises US East Comp Jersey Gold-ECJ8
04ITG Franchises US East Memorabilia-ESM25
04ITG Franchises US East Memorabilia Gold-ESM25
04ITG Ultimate Memorabilia-27
Gold-27
Complete Logo-29
Day In History-9
Day In History-43
Day In History Gold-9
Day In History Gold-43
Gloves are Off-6
Jersey Autographs-12
Jersey Autographs Gold-12
Stick Autographs-6
Stick Autographs Gold-6
05ITG Ultimate Mem First Overall Jerseys-4
05ITG Ultimate Mem 1st Overall Jsy Gold-4
05ITG Ultimate Mem First Rounders Jerseys-1
05ITG Ultimate Mem First Rounders Jerseys-9
05ITG Ultimate Mem 1st Round Jersey Gold-1
05ITG Ultimate Mem 1st Round Jersey Gold-9
05ITG Ultimate Mem Record Breaker Jerseys-5
05ITG Ultimate Mem RecBreak Jerseys Gold-5
06ITG International Ice-27
06ITG International Ice-50
Gold-27
Gold-50
Autographs-ADH
Autographs-ADH2
Emblems-GUE14
Emblems Gold-GUE14
Jerseys-GUJ14
Jerseys Gold-GUJ14
My Country My Team-MC19
My Country My Team Gold-MC19
Numbers-GUN14
Numbers Gold-GUN14
06ITG Ultimate Memorabilia Gloves Are Off-7
06ITG Ultimate Memorabilia Gloves Are Off Gold-7
06Parkhurst-27
06Parkhurst-202
Autographs-27
Autographs-202
Autographs Dual-DAHS
06The Cup-90
Autographed Foundations-CQDH
Autographed Foundations Patches-CQDH
Autographed NHL Shields Duals-DASDA
Autographed Patches-90
Black Rainbow-90
Foundations-CQDH
Foundations Patches-CQDH
Gold-90
Gold Patches-90
Honorable Numbers-HNDH
Jerseys-90
Limited Logos-LLDH
Masterpiece Pressplates-90
Property of-PODH
Scripted Swatches-SSDH
Signature Patches-SPDH
06Ultimate Collection Signatures-US-HA
06Upper Deck Sweet Shot Signature Shots/Saves-SSHA
06Upper Deck Sweet Shot Signature Sticks-STHA
06Upper Deck Sweet Shot Sweet Stitches-SSHA
06Upper Deck Sweet Shot Sweet Stitches Duals-SSHA
06Upper Deck Sweet Shot Sweet Stitches Triples-SSHA

Hawes, Chris
917th Inn. Sketch WHL-71

Hawes, Mike
89Spokane Chiefs-10

Hawes, Tyler
03P.E.I. Rocket-7
04P.E.I. Rocket-20
05PEI Rocket-14
06PEI Rocket-17

Hawgood, Greg
84Kamloops Blazers-10
85Kamloops Blazers-7
86Kamloops Blazers-8
88ProCards AHL-168
89Bruins Sports Action-10
89O-Pee-Chee-81
89O-Pee-Chee Stickers-67
89O-Pee-Chee Stickers-207
89Panini Stickers-189
89Topps-81
90O-Pee-Chee-236
90Panini Stickers-10
90Pro Set-442
90Score Rookie/Traded-79T
90Topps-236
Tiffany-236
90Upper Deck-391
French-391
91ProCards-226
92Flyers Upper Deck Sheets-40
92Oilers IGA-9
92Parkhurst-361
Emerald Ice-361
92Stadium Club-495
92Topps-358
Gold-358G
93Donruss-245
93Flyers Lineup Sheets-18
93Leaf-266
93OPC Premier-422
Gold-422
93PowerPlay-347
93Score-396
93Score-642
Gold-642
Canadian-396
Canadian-642
Canadian Gold-642
93Topps/OPC Premier-422
Gold-422
93Ultra-388
94Leaf-534
94Parkhurst-181
Gold-181
94Penguins Foodland-2
95Las Vegas Thunder-3
96Collector's Edge Future Legends-25
96Collector's Edge Ice-152
Prism-152
98IHL All-Star Western Conference-18
99BAP Millennium-240
Emerald-240
Ruby-240
Sapphire-240
Signatures-240
Signatures Gold-240
00UD Heroes-115
01Utah Grizzlies-8
02BAP Sig Series Auto Buybacks 1999-240
02Utah Grizzlies-16
03Chicago Wolves-9
04Chicago Wolves-5
05Finnish Cardset -320

Hawkins, Manny
93Lakeland Ice Warriors-16

Hawkins, Richard
85Kitchener Rangers-27

Hawkins, Ryan
03Chicago Steel-15

Hawkins, Shawn
89Rayside-Balfour Jr. Canadians-10

Hawkins, Todd
84Belleville Bulls-26
87Flint Spirits-5
89ProCards IHL-183
90ProCards AHL/IHL-324
91ProCards-342
92St. John's Maple Leafs-7
93Cleveland Lumberjacks-9
93Cleveland Lumberjacks Postcards-12
95Cincinnati Cyclones-9
96Cincinnati Cyclones-12
97Cincinnati Cyclones-7
98Cincinnati Cyclones-6
98Cincinnati Cyclones 2-1
99Cincinnati Cyclones-9
01German Upper Deck-67
02German DEL City Press-111

Hawley, Chris
01Mississauga Ice Dogs-13
02Mississauga Ice Dogs-10

Hawley, Joe
89Peterborough Petes-105
897th Inn. Sketch OHL-105
907th Inn. Sketch OHL-361
91ProCards-44
92Peoria Rivermen-8
93Muskegon Fury-14

Hawley, Kent
88ProCards AHL-138
89ProCards AHL-348
90ProCards AHL/IHL-40
95Madison Monsters-9
96Madison Monsters-3
98Hampton Roads Admirals 10th Anniversary-22
98Madison Monsters-1

Haworth, Alan
81Sabres Milk Panels-5
82Capitals Team Issue-9
83NHL Key Tags-129
83NHL Key Tags-130
84Capitals Pizza Hut-8
84O-Pee-Chee-199
85Capitals Pizza Hut-7
85O-Pee-Chee-117
85O-Pee-Chee Stickers-108
85Topps-117
86Capitals Kodak-12
86Capitals Police-11
86O-Pee-Chee-107
86O-Pee-Chee Stickers-255
86Topps-107
87Nordiques General Foods-14
87Nordiques Team Issue-10
87Nordiques Yum-Yum-5
87Panini Stickers-187
88O-Pee-Chee-131
88O-Pee-Chee Stickers-195
88Topps-131

Haworth, Gordon
50Quebec Citadelles-8
51Laval Dairy Subset-68
52St. Lawrence Sales-22
61Union Oil WHL-6

Hawryliw, Neil
81Indianapolis Checkers-7

Hawryliw, Nigel
05Muskegon Fury-6

Hawryluk, Neil
89Lethbridge Hurricanes-8

Hay, Bill
44Beehive Group II Photos-103
60Shirriff Coins-77
60Topps-6
Stamps-22
61Shirriff/Salada Coins-34
61Topps-35
62Topps-35
Hockey Bucks-9
63Chex Photos-20
63Topps-34
63Toronto Star-17
64Beehive Group III Photos-37
64Coca-Cola Caps-26
64Topps-7
64Toronto Star-13
65Coca-Cola-28
65Topps-62
94Parkhurst Tall Boys-42
95Parkhurst '66-67-30
Coins-30

Hay, Charles
83Hall of Fame-36
83Hall of Fame Postcards-C6
85Hall of Fame-36

Hay, Darrell
98Tri-City Americans-4
99Bowman CHL-118
Gold-118
OPC International-118
00Florida Everblades-11
00Kansas City Blades-10
01Manitoba Moose-9
02Manitoba Moose-13
04Idaho Steelheads-25
06Idaho Steelheads-17

Hay, Don
95Slapshot Memorial Cup-25
96Coyotes Coca-Cola-34
98Tri-City Americans-27
01Utah Grizzlies-34
02Utah Grizzlies-12

Hay, Dwayne
94Guelph Storm-9
95Slapshot-89
95Guelph Storm-3
95Classic-38
96Upper Deck Ice-123
96Guelph Storm-22
96Guelph Storm-35
96Guelph Storm Premier Collection-9
97Portland Pirates-12
97Bowman CHL-25
OPC-25
98New Haven Beast-10
99Louisville Panthers-19
00Upper Deck NHLPA-PA15
03Pensacola Ice Pilots-346

Hay, George
23V128-1 Paulin's Candy-28
60Topps-15
Stamps-23
83Hall of Fame Postcards-G7
85Hall of Fame-98

Hay, Neil
04UK Edinburgh Capitals-11

Hay, Peter
03Reading Royals-17
03Reading Royals RBI Sports-291

Hay, Ross
04UK Edinburgh Capitals-8

Hay, Scott
94Sarnia Sting-3
01Bakersfield Condors-12
05Port Huron Flags-20

Haydar, Darren
02BAP Memorabilia-326
02BAP Ultimate Memorabilia-49
02SP Authentic-175
02SP Game Used-101
02UD Mask Collection-140
02UD Premier Collection-60B
Gold-60B
02AHL Top Prospects-17
02Milwaukee Admirals-23
02Milwaukee Admirals Postcards-8
03ITG Action-370
03Upper Deck MVP-239
Gold Script-239
Silver Script-239
Canadian Exclusives-239
03Milwaukee Admirals-6
03Milwaukee Admirals Postcards-8
03Pacific AHL Prospects-57
Gold-57
04Milwaukee Admirals-26
05Milwaukee Admirals Choice-7
05Milwaukee Admirals Pepsi-9

Haydar, Jeff
01Odessa Jackalopes-10

Hayden, Brian
95Slapshot-153

Hayden, Craig
97Fort Worth Brahmas-6
98Fort Worth Brahmas-19

Hayden, Jamie
907th Inn. Sketch WHL-171
92Thunder Bay Thunder Hawks-6
93Thunder Bay Senators-2

Hayden, Steve
92Cornell Big Red-14

Hayek, Matt
02Lincoln Stars-16
03Lincoln Stars-11
03Lincoln Stars Update-42

Hayek, Peter
82Birmingham South Stars-11

Hayes, Andrew
02Hull Olympiques-15

Hayes, Bobby
93Waterloo Black Hawks-11
00Idaho Steelheads-7

Hayes, Bryan
00Barrie Colts-12

Hayes, Harlin
95Halifax Mooseheads-1

Hayes, James
51Laval Dairy Lac St. Jean-5
51Laval Dairy QSHL-8

Hayes, Jeff
06Guelph Storm-9

Hayes, Jim
52Bas Du Fleuve-29

Hayfield, Roger
51Bas Du Fleuve-39
52Bas Du Fleuve-12

Hayko, Rick
85Minnesota-Duluth Bulldogs-9

Hayman, Kevin
03Vancouver Giants-15
05Kamloops Blazers-17

Haynes, Paul
33V357 Ice Kings-6
34Beehive Group I Photos-157
34Sweet Caporal-21
35Diamond Matchbooks Tan 2-26
35Diamond Matchbooks Tan 3-24
35O-Pee-Chee V304C-95
37O-Pee-Chee V304E-155
37V356 Worldwide Gum-33
38Quaker Oats Photos-17
39O-Pee-Chee V301-1-31
40O-Pee-Chee V301-2-112

Hayton, Bryan
96Kitchener Rangers-13

Hayward, Brian
83Jets Postcards-9
83Vachon-127
84Jets Police-9
85Jets Police-8
85O-Pee-Chee-226
86Canadiens Postcards-7
86Kraft Drawings-26
86O-Pee-Chee-255
87Canadiens Postcards-10
87Canadiens Vachon Stickers-61
87Canadiens Vachon Stickers-64
87Canadiens Vachon Stickers-67
87Canadiens Vachon Stickers-84
87O-Pee-Chee-230
87O-Pee-Chee Minis-15
87O-Pee-Chee Stickers-175
87O-Pee-Chee Stickers-184
87Panini Stickers-55
87Panini Stickers-376A
88Canadiens Postcards-13
88O-Pee-Chee-195
88O-Pee-Chee Minis-13
88O-Pee-Chee Stickers-52
88O-Pee-Chee Stickers-214
88Panini Stickers-251
88Panini Stickers-402
88Topps-195
89Canadiens Kraft-10
89Canadiens Postcards-14
89O-Pee-Chee-237
89O-Pee-Chee Stickers-50
89Panini Stickers-246
90O-Pee-Chee-23
90Panini Stickers-61
90Pro Set-150
90Score-304C
Canadian-304C
90Score Rookie/Traded-78T
90Topps-23
Tiffany-23
90Upper Deck-171
90Upper Deck-449
French-171
French-449
91Bowman-122
91O-Pee-Chee-178
91Panini Stickers-106
91Pinnacle-83
French-83
91Pro Set-327
French-327
91Score American-211
91Score Canadian Bilingual-211
91Score Canadian Bilingual-554
91Score Canadian English-211
91Score Canadian English-554
91Score Rookie/Traded-4T
91Sharks Sports Action-10
91Stadium Club-19
91Topps-178
91Upper Deck-59
French-59
92Bowman-60
92Pinnacle-266
French-266
92Stadium Club-364
92Topps-436
Gold-436G
93Panini Stickers-265
01Between the Pipes Masks-33
01Between the Pipes Masks Silver-33
01Between the Pipes Masks Gold-33
04ITG Franchises US West-298
Autographs-A-BHA
06Between The Pipes-81
Autographs-ABH

Hayward, Leon
03Manchester Monarchs-7
03Reading Royals-8
03Reading Royals RBI Sports-292

Hayward, Rick
86Sherbrooke Canadiens-19
89ProCards IHL-207
90ProCards AHL/IHL-345
91ProCards-469
93Cincinnati Cyclones-9
94Cleveland Lumberjacks-4
94Cleveland Lumberjacks Postcards-4
95Cleveland Lumberjacks-15
95Cleveland Lumberjacks Postcards-14
96Cleveland Lumberjacks-13
96Cleveland Lumberjacks Multi-Ad-13
97Cleveland Lumberjacks-13
97Cleveland Lumberjacks Postcards-4
98German DEL-144
99German DEL-78

Hazelhurst, Mark
96UK Guildford Flames-18

Head, Barry
74Sioux City Musketeers-5

Head, Don
44Beehive Group II Photos-28
61Shirriff/Salada Coins-11
61Topps-17
69Seattle Totems-1

Head, Galen
71Johnstown Jets Acme-7
72Johnstown Jets-14
93Fort Wayne Komets-26

Headley, Curly
23V128-1 Paulin's Candy-37
24C144 Champ's Cigarettes-29
24V130 Maple Crispette-4

Headley, Gopher
24V145-2-23

Healey, Chuckie
93Quebec Pee-Wee Tournament-875

Healey, Eric
01Manchester Monarchs-6B
02Manchester Monarchs-7
03Chicago Wolves-10
04German Adler Mannheim Eagles Postcards-16
04German DEL-10
04ITG Heroes/Prospects Complete Emblems-18
04ITG Heroes and Prospects Emblems-17
04ITG Heroes and Prospects Emblems Gold-17
04ITG Heroes and Prospects Jerseys-17
04ITG Heroes and Prospects Jerseys Gold-17

04ITG Heroes and Prospects Numbers-17
04ITG Heroes and Prospects Numbers Gold-17
05Hot Prospects-106
En Fuego-106
Red Hot-106
White Hot-106
05SP Authentic-250
Limited-250
05SPx-246
05The Cup Masterpiece Pressplates (Ice)-224
05The Cup Master Pressplate Rookie Update-106
05The Cup Masterpiece Pressplates SPA-250
05The Cup Masterpiece Pressplates (SPx)-246
05Upper Deck Ice-224
05Upper Deck Rookie Update-106
05AHL All-Stars-13
05Providence Bruins-6
06Springfield Falcons-5

Healey, Grant

90Rayside-Balfour Jr. Canadians-9
91Rayside-Balfour Jr. Canadians-7

Healey, Paul

93Prince Albert Raiders-9
94Prince Albert Raiders-5
96Collector's Edge Ice-44
Prism-44
97Donruss-205
Press Proofs Silver-205
Press Proofs Gold-205
99Milwaukee Admirals Keebler-15
00Hamilton Bulldogs-10
01St. John's Maple Leafs-10
03Hartford Wolf Pack-7

Healy, Glenn

88Kings Postcards-8
88Kings Smokey-13
88O-Pee-Chee Stickers-123
88O-Pee-Chee Stickers-255
88Panini Stickers-68
89Islanders Team Issue-9
89Panini Stickers-97
90O-Pee-Chee-400
90Panini Stickers-88
90Pro Set-183
90Score-294
Canadian-294
90Upper Deck-18
French-18
91Pro Set Platinum-73
91Bowman-224
91O-Pee-Chee-368
91Panini Stickers-249
91Parkhurst-107
French-107
91Pinnacle-185
French-185
91Pro Set-153
French-153
Puck Candy-18
91Score American-68
91Score Canadian Bilingual-68
91Score Canadian English-68
91Stadium Club-369
91Topps-368
91Upper Deck-224
French-224
92Bowman-434
92O-Pee-Chee-262
92Parkhurst-341
92Parkhurst-505
Emerald Ice-341
Emerald Ice-505
92Pinnacle-121
French-121
92Score-188
Canadian-188
92Stadium Club-356
92Topps-305
Gold-305G
92Ultra-126
93Donruss-211
93Leaf-327
93OPC Premier-486
Gold-486
93Panini Stickers-65
93Parkhurst-405
Emerald Ice-405
93Pinnacle-365
Canadian-365
93PowerPlay-390
93Score-177
93Score-533
Gold-533
Canadian-177
Canadian-533
Canadian Gold-533
93Stadium Club-453
Members Only Master Set-453
First Day Issue-453
93Topps/OPC Premier-486
Gold-486
93Ultra-106
93Ultra-371
93Upper Deck-321
94Be A Player-R13
Signature Cards-128
94Canada Games NHL POGS-287
94Donruss-283
94EA Sports-84
94Leaf-310
94OPC Premier-388
Special Effects-388
94Parkhurst SE-SE117
Gold-SE117
94Pinnacle-430
Artist's Proofs-430
Rink Collection-430
94Topps/OPC Premier-388
Special Effects-388
94Upper Deck-455
Electric Ice-455
95Collector's Choice-272
Player's Club-272
Player's Club Platinum-272
95Donruss-54
95Parkhurst International-406
Emerald Ice-406
95Pinnacle-91
Artist's Proofs-91
Rink Collection-91
95Score-273
Black Ice Artist's Proofs-273
Black Ice-273
95Topps-292
OPC Inserts-292
95Ultra-101
Gold Medallion-101
95Upper Deck-30
Electric Ice-30
Electric Ice Gold-30
96Be A Player-140
Autographs-140
Autographs Silver-140
96Donruss-212
Press Proofs-212
96Score-34
Artist's Proofs-34
Dealer's Choice Artist's Proofs-34
Special Artist's Proofs-34
Golden Blades-34
96Upper Deck-202
97Pacific Dynagon Best Kept Secrets-61
97Paramount-180
Copper-180
Dark Grey-180
Emerald Green-180
Ice Blue-180
Red-180
Silver-180
97Score-22
Artist's Proofs-22
Golden Blades-22
97Score Maple Leafs-2
Platinum-2
Premier-2
98NHL Aces Playing Cards-41
99Maple Leafs Pizza Pizza-18
00Pacific-390
Copper-390
Gold-390
Ice Blue-390
Premiere Date-390
00Titanium Game Gear-145
00Titanium Game Gear Patches-145
00Upper Deck NHLPA-PA84
01Pacific-365
Extreme LTD-365
Hobby LTD-365
Premiere Date-365
Retail LTD-365
01Pacific Arena Exclusives-365
01Pacific Heads-Up Quad Jerseys-19
01Titanium Double-Sided Jerseys-41
01Titanium Double-Sided Patches-41

Heaney, Geraldine

94Classic Women of Hockey-W19
97Collector's Choice-282
97Esso Olympic Hockey Heroes-57
97Esso Olympic Hockey Heroes French-57

Heaney, Mike

95Louisiana Ice Gators-6
95Louisiana Ice Gators Playoffs-7

Heaphy, Shawn

91ProCards-588
92Salt Lake Golden Eagles-9
93Las Vegas Thunder-12
93Classic Pro Prospects-141
95PEI Senators-8
96Swiss HNL-397
98Swiss Power Play Stickers-300
99Swiss Panini Stickers-340
01Swiss HNL-415
04Fresno Falcons-6

Hearn, Don

91British Columbia JHL-36
92British Columbia JHL-58

Hearn, Jamie

92Oklahoma City Blazers-8
93Wichita Thunder-8
94Central Hockey League-47
95Flint Generals-22
95Muskegon Fury-16

Hearon, Tim

93Quebec Pee-Wee Tournament-1303

Heaslip, Mark

76O-Pee-Chee NHL-376
79O-Pee-Chee-320

Heasty, John

93Flint Generals-10
96Flint Generals-10
97Flint Generals-8
97Flint Generals EBK-9

Heath, Randy

86Swedish Panini Stickers-235

Heathwood, Steve

74Sioux City Musketeers-6

Heatley, Dany

99UD Prospects-71
00Black Diamond-63
Gold-63
00Upper Deck-198
Exclusives Tier 1-198
Exclusives Tier 2-198
00Upper Deck Ice-43
Immortals-43
Legends-43
Stars-43
00Upper Deck MVP-211
First Stars-211
Second Stars-211
Third Stars-211
00Upper Deck Victory-279
01Atomic-103
Premiere Date-103
Rookie Reaction-1
01Atomic Toronto Fall Expo-103
01BAP Memorabilia-385
Emerald-385
Ruby-385
Sapphire-385
01BAP Signature Series-226
Autographs-226
Autographs Gold-226
01BAP Ultimate Memorabilia ROY-1
01Bowman YoungStars-134
Gold-134
Ice Cubed-134
Autographs-DH
Relics-JDH
Relics-SDH
Relics-DSDH
Rivals-R6
01Crown Royale-6
Blue-6
Premiere Date-6
Red-6
Retail-6
Crowning Achievement-1
Rookie Royalty-1
01Pacific Adrenaline Rookie Report-2
01Pacific High Voltage-1
01Parkhurst-286
01Parkhurst Beckett Promos-286
01Private Stock-101
Gold-101
Premiere Date-101
Retail-101
Silver-101
Moments in Time-1
01Private Stock Pacific Nights-101
01Private Stock PS-2002-93
01Private Stock Reserve-R1
01SP Authentic-3
01SP Authentic-111
Limited-3
Limited-111
Limited Gold-3
Limited Gold-111
Buybacks-7
Sign of the Times-DH
01SP Game Used-2
01SPx-94
01SPx-154
01Sports Illustrated for Kids III-232
01Stadium Club-111
Award Winners-111
Master Photos-111
01Titanium-4
Hobby Parallel-4
Premiere Date-4
Retail-4
Retail Parallel-4
Double-Sided Jerseys-23
Rookie Team-1
Three-Star Selections-21
01Titanium Draft Day Edition-4
01Titanium Draft Day Edition-104
01Topps Chrome-127
Refractors-127
Black Border Refractors-127
01Topps Heritage-185
01UD Challenge for the Cup-3
01UD Honor Roll-25
01UD Honor Roll-55
01UD Mask Collection-4
Gold-4
01UD Playmakers-6
01UD Premier Collection-2
Signatures-DH
Signatures Black-DH
01UD Top Shelf-77
01Upper Deck-239
Exclusives-239
01Upper Deck Ice-85
01Vanguard-3
Blue-3
Red-3
One of Ones-3
Premiere Date-3
Prime Prospects-1
Proofs-3
02Atomic-4
Blue-4
Gold-4
Red-4
Cold Fusion-2
Hobby Parallel-4
Power Converters-1
02BAP All-Star Edition-101
Gold-101
Silver-101
02BAP First Edition-24
02BAP First Edition-383
02BAP First Edition-384
02BAP First Edition-422H
He Shoots-He Score Points-4
He Shoots-He Scores Prizes-17
Jerseys-24
Scoring Leaders-2
02BAP Memorabilia-5
Emerald-5
Ruby-5
Sapphire-5
Future of the Game-FG-5
He Shoots-He Scores Points-8
He Shoots-He Scores Prizes-13
NHL All-Star Game-5
NHL All-Star Game Blue-5
NHL All-Star Game Green-5
NHL All-Star Game Red-5
02BAP Memorabilia Toronto Fall Expo-5
02BAP Signature Series-1
Autographs-1
Autographs Gold-1
Franchise Players-FJ2
Golf-GS79
Jerseys-SGJ30
Jersey Autographs-SGJ30
Team Quads-TQ12
02BAP Ultimate Memorabilia All-Star MVP-5
02BAP Ultimate Memorabilia Autographs-18
02BAP Ultimate Mem Autographs Gold-18
02BAP Ultimate Memorabilia Dynamic Duos-4
02BAP Ultimate Memorabilia Emblems-5
02BAP Ultimate Memorabilia Jerseys-8
02BAP Ultimate Mem Jersey and Stick-23
02BAP Ultimate Memorabilia Numbers-15
02BAP Ultimate Memorabilia Retro Trophies-1
02Bowman Toronto Spring Expo-8
02Bowman YoungStars-141
Gold-141
Silver-141
02Crown Royale-4
Blue-4
Red-4
Retail-4
Jerseys-1
Jerseys Gold-1
Dual Patches-1
Lords of the Rink-2
02eTopps-16
02ITG Used-4
02ITG Used-104
Jerseys-GUJ30
Jersey Autographs-GUJ30
Jerseys Gold-GUJ30
Emblems-E30
Jersey and Stick-SJ30
Jersey and Stick Gold-SJ30
Teammates-T7
Teammates Gold-T7
02McDonald's Pacific-2
Clear Advantage-1
Jersey Patches Silver-1
Jersey Patches Gold-1
02O-Pee-Chee-205
02O-Pee-Chee Premier Blue Parallel-205
02O-Pee-Chee Premier Red Parallel-205
02O-Pee-Chee Factory Set-205
02Pacific-13
Blue-13
Red-13
Cramer's Choice-1
Jerseys-1
Jerseys Holo-Silver-1
Lamplighters-1
Shining Moments-1
02Pacific Calder Collection AS Fantasy-1
02Pacific Calder Collection All-Star Fantasy Gold-1
02Pacific Calder-1
Silver-1
Hardware Heroes-1
02Pacific Complete-15
Red-15
02Pacific Exclusive-5
Destined-2
Great Expectations-1
Maximum Overdrive-2
02Pacific Heads-Up-4
Blue-4
Purple-4
Red-4
Head First-1
Inside the Numbers-2
Quad Jerseys-35
Quad Jerseys Gold-35
Stat Masters-2
02Pacific Quest for the Cup-4
Gold-4
Chasing the Cup-2
Jerseys-1
02Pacific Toronto Spring Expo Rookie Coll-1
02Parkhurst-125
Bronze-125
Gold-125
Silver-125
College Ranks-CR12
College Ranks Jerseys-CRM12
Heroes-NH11
He Shoots-He Scores Prizes-24
Jerseys-GJ24
Patented Power-PP6
Stick and Jerseys-SJ24
Teammates-TT9
02Parkhurst Retro-52
Minis-52
Franchise Players-RF2
He Shoots-He Scores Points-2
He Shoots-He Scores Prizes-13
Jerseys-RJ23
Jersey and Sticks-RSJ16
Memorabilia-RM10
02Private Stock Reserve-102
Red-102
Retail-102
Patches-102
02SP Authentic-4
02SP Authentic-107
Beckett Promos-4
Sign of the Times-DH
Sign of the Times-KH
Sign of the Times-HCI
02SP Game Used-3
Signature Style-DH
02SPx-4
Spectrum Gold-4
Spectrum Silver-4
02Stadium Club-47
Silver Decoy Cards-47
Proofs-47
Beam Team-BT8
YoungStars Relics-S5
YoungStars Relics-DS1
02Thrashers Postcards-4
02Titanium-4
Blue-4
Red-4
Retail-4
Jerseys-2
Jerseys Retail-2
Patches-2
02Topps-205
OPC Blue Parallel-205
OPC Red Parallel-205
Own The Game-OTG11
Factory Set-205
02Topps Chrome-115
Black Border Refractors-115
Refractors-115
02Topps Heritage-9
02Topps Heritage-103
02Topps Heritage-111
Chrome Parallel-9
Calder Cloth-DH
Calder Cloth Patches-DH
02Topps Total-6
Award Winners-AW5
02UD Artistic Impressions-3
Gold-3
Artist's Touch-ATDH
Artist's Touch Gold-ATDH
02UD Artistic Impressions Beckett Promos-3
02UD Artistic Impressions Retrospectives-R3
02UD Artistic Impressions Retrospect Gold-R3
02UD Artistic Impress Retrospect Auto-R3
02UD Artistic Impress Retrospect Silver-R3
02UD Artistic Impressions Right Track-RTDH
02UD Artistic Impression Right Track Gold-RTDH
02UD Honor Roll-4
Signature Class-DH
Students of the Game-SG2
02UD Mask Collection-5
02UD Mask Collection Beckett Promos-5
02UD Piece of History-4
Marks of Distinction-DH
02UD Premier Collection-3
Signatures Bronze-SDH
Signatures Bronze-ASDH
Signatures Gold-SDH
Signatures Gold-ASDH
Signatures Silver-SDH
Signatures Silver-ASDH
02UD Top Shelf-5
Signatures-DH
02Upper Deck-253
Exclusives-253
02Upper Deck Beckett UD Promos-253
02Upper Deck Classic Portraits-4
Mini-Busts-13
Mini-Busts-14
Mini-Busts-15
Mini-Busts-16
Mini-Busts-17
Mini-Busts-18
Mini-Busts-19
Mini-Busts-20
02Upper Deck MVP-8
Gold-8
Classics-8
Golden Classics-8
Prosign-DH
02Upper Deck Rookie Update-5
Autographs-DH
Jerseys-DDH
Jerseys-SKH
Jerseys Gold-DDH
Jerseys Gold-SKH
02Upper Deck Victory-9
Bronze-9
Gold-9
Silver-9
02Upper Deck Vintage-15
02Upper Deck Vintage-262
02Upper Deck Vintage-315
Green Backs-15
Tall Boys-T3
Tall Boys Gold-T3
02Vanguard-5
LTD-5
Jerseys-2
Jerseys Gold-2
02UD SuperStars *-255
Gold-255
03BAP Memorabilia-20
Emerald-20
Gold-20
Ruby-20
Sapphire-20
All-Star Complete Jerseys-ASCJ4
All-Star Emblems-ASE-5
All-Star Jerseys-ASJ-10
All-Star Numbers-ASN-5
All-Star Teammates-AST2
Brush with Greatness-23
Brush with Greatness Contest Cards-23
He Shoots-He Scores Points-6
He Shoots-He Scores Prizes-8
Jersey and Stick-SJ-24
Jerseys-GJ-33
03BAP Ultimate Memorabilia Autographs-151
Gold-151
03BAP Ultimate Mem Auto Jerseys-151
03BAP Ultimate Mem Auto Emblems-151
03BAP Ultimate Mem Auto Sticks-151
03BAP Ultimate Mem Complete Jersey-5
03BAP Ultimate Mem Complete Jersey Gold-5
03BAP Ultimate Memorabilia Emblems-1
03BAP Ultimate Memorabilia Emblems Gold-1
03BAP Ultimate Mem Franch Present Future-2
03BAP Ultimate Memorabilia Heroes-7
03BAP Ultimate Mem Heroes Autos-4
03BAP Ultimate Memorabilia Jerseys-5
03BAP Ultimate Memorabilia Jerseys Gold-5
03BAP Ultimate Mem Jersey and Emblems-9
03BAP Ultimate Mem Jersey and Emblem Gold-9
03BAP Ultimate Mem Jersey and Numbers-9
03BAP Ultimate Mem Jersey and Number Gold-9
03BAP Ultimate Mem Jersey and Stick-3
03BAP Ultimate Mem Jersey and Stick Gold-3
03BAP Ultimate Memorabilia Nameplates-3
03BAP Ultimate Mem Nameplates Gold-3
03BAP Ultimate Memorabilia Numbers-4
03BAP Ultimate Memorabilia Numbers Gold-4
03BAP Ultimate Memorabilia Triple Threads-18
03Beehive-11
Gold-11
Silver-11
03Black Diamond-138
Black-138
Green-138
Red-138
Threads-DT-DH
Threads Green-DT-DH
Threads Red-DT-DH
Threads Black-DT-DH
03Bowman-15
Gold-15
Future Rivals-GH
Future Rivals Patches-GH
Goal to Goal-HG
03Bowman Chrome-15
Refractors-15
Gold Refractors-15
Xfractors-15
03eTopps-16
03ITG Action-2
First Time All-Star-FT2
Highlight Reel-HR5
Jerseys-M187
Jerseys-M207
Jerseys-M234
Jerseys-M242
League Leaders-L10
Oh Canada-OC10
03ITG Toronto Fall Expo Jerseys-FE23
03ITG Used Signature Series-73
Gold-73
Autographs-DHE
Autographs Gold-DHE
International Experience-14
International Experience Autographs-14
International Experience Emblems Gold-14
International Experience Emblems-14
International Experience Gold-14
03ITG VIP Brightest Stars-3
03ITG VIP Collages-16
03ITG VIP International Experience-11
03ITG VIP Jerseys-5
03ITG VIP Jersey and Emblems-3
03ITG VIP Jersey and Numbers-3
03ITG VIP Making the Bigs-7
03McDonald's Pacific-2
Canadian Pride-1
Hockey Roots Checklists-8
Patches Silver-2
Patches Gold-2
Patches and Sticks-2
03NHL Sticker Collection-3
03O-Pee-Chee-240
03O-Pee-Chee-301
03OPC Blue-240
03OPC Blue-301
03OPC Gold-240
03OPC Gold-301
03OPC Red-240
03OPC Red-301
03Pacific-14
Blue-14
Red-14
Jerseys-2
Jerseys Gold-2
03Pacific Calder-3
Silver-3
03Pacific Complete-16
Red-16
03Pacific Exhibit-153
03Pacific Exhibit-220
Blue Backs-153
Pursuing Prominence-1
03Pacific Invincible-4
Blue-4
Red-4
Retail-4
Featured Performers-2
New Sensations-2
03Pacific Luxury Suite-25A
03Pacific Luxury Suite-25B
03Pacific Luxury Suite-25C
03Pacific Prism-102
Blue-102
Patches-102
Red-102
Retail-102
Paramount Prodigies-3
03Pacific Quest for the Cup-3
Blue-3
Chasing the Cup-1
03Pacific Supreme-4
Blue-4
Red-4
Retail-4
03Parkhurst Rookie-45
Emblems-GUE-6
Emblem Autographs-GUE-DH
Emblems Gold-GUE-6
Jerseys-GJ-21
Jerseys Gold-GJ-21
Jersey and Sticks-SJ-5
Jersey and Sticks Gold-SJ-5
Road to the NHL-RNJ-8
Road to the NHL Gold-RTN-8
Road to the NHL Emblems-RTNE-8
Road to the NHL Emblems Gold-RTNE-8
ROYalty-VR-1
ROYalty Autographs-VR-DH
ROYalty Gold-VR-1
03Private Stock Reserve-142
Blue-142
Patches-142
Red-142
Retail-142
03SP Authentic-4
Limited-4
03SP Game Used-3
Gold-3
Authentic Fabrics-DFHK
Authentic Fabrics Gold-DFHK
Limited Threads-LTDH
Limited Threads Gold-LTDH
Premium Patches-PPDH
Team Threads-TTKHK
03SPx-4
03SPx-135
03SPx-156
Radiance-4
Radiance-135
Radiance-156
Spectrum-4
Spectrum-135
Spectrum-156
Big Futures-BF-DH
Big Futures Limited-BF-DH
Fantasy Franchise-FF-KTH
Fantasy Franchise Limited-FF-KTH
Origins-O-DH
Style-SPX-LH
Style Limited-SPX-LH
03Titanium-192
Patches-192
03Topps-240
03Topps-301
Blue-240
Blue-301
Gold-240
Gold-301
Red-240
Red-301
Box Toppers-21
Topps/OPC Idols-CI1
03Topps C55-90
Minis-90
Minis American Back-90
Minis American Back Red-90
Minis Bazooka Back-90
Minis Brooklyn Back-90
Minis Hat Trick Back-90
Minis O Canada Back-90
Minis O Canada Back Red-90
Minis Stanley Cup Back-90
Relics-TRDH
03Topps Pristine-50
Gold Refractor Die Cuts-50
Refractors-50
Jersey Portions-PPJ-DH
Jersey Portion Refractors-PPJ-DH
Patches-PP-DH
Patch Refractors-PP-DH
Press Plates Black-50
Press Plates Cyan-50
Press Plates Magenta-50
Press Plates Yellow-50
03UD Honor Roll-3
03UD Premier Collection-3
03UD Toronto Fall Expo Priority Signings-DH
03Upper Deck-8
All-Star Lineup-AS2
Big Playmakers-BP-DH
Canadian Exclusives-8
Franchise Fabrics-FF-DH
Gifted Greats-GG8
HG-8
NHL Best-NB-DH
Patches-SP5
Superstar Spotlight-SS12
Team Essentials-TP-DH
Team Essentials-TS-DH
Three Stars-TS3
03Upper Deck Classic Portraits-4
Genuine Greatness-GG-DH
03Upper Deck Ice-4
Gold-4
03Upper Deck MVP-15
03Upper Deck MVP-439
Gold Script-15
Gold Script-439
Silver Script-15
Silver Script-439
Canadian Exclusives-15
Canadian Exclusives-439
ProSign-PS-DH
SportsNut-SN6
Talent-MT5
03Upper Deck Rookie Update-4
Skills-SKDH
Super Stars-SSDH
03Upper Deck Trilogy-4
03Upper Deck Trilogy-103
Authentic Patches-AP24
Crest Variations-103
Limited-4
Limited-103
03Upper Deck Victory-6
Bronze-6
Gold-6
Silver-6
Freshman Flashback-FF4
Game Breakers-GB10
03Russian World Championship Stars-12
03Toronto Star-4
Foil-27
04Pacific-10
Blue-10
Red-10
Global Connection-1
04SP Authentic-4
04SP Authentic-98
Limited-4
Limited-98
Buybacks-36
Sign of the Times-ST-DH
Sign of the Times-TS-HLK
Sign of the Times-QS-NHKS
Sign of the Times-FS-RGT
Sign of the Times-FS-SES
04UD All-World-85
Gold-85
Autographs-85
Quad Autographs-AQ-GSC
Six Autographs-AS-SWT
04UD Toronto Fall Expo Pride of Canada-15
04Ultimate Collection-2
04Ultimate Collection-61
Jerseys-UGJ-DH
Jerseys Gold-UGJ-DH
Jersey Autographs-UGJA-DH
Patches-UP-DHA
Patches-UP-DHB
Patch Autographs-UPA-DH
Signatures-US-DH
Signature Logos-ULA-DH
Signature Patches-SP-DH
04Upper Deck-7
Canadian Exclusives-7
HG Glossy Gold-7
HG Glossy Silver-7
World's Best-WB7
World Cup Tribute-DH
World Cup Tribute-DHPMSD
04Russian Legion-37
05ITG Heroes/Prosp Toronto Expo Parallel -184
05Be A Player-4
First Period-4
Second Period-4
Third Period-4
Overtime-4
Class Action-CA2
Dual Signatures-DK
Outtakes-OT3
Quad Signatures-HSNT
Quad Signatures-SHSL
Signatures-HT
Signatures Gold-HT
05Beehive-61
05Beehive-203
Beige -61
Blue -61
Gold-61
Red -61
Matte-61
Matted Materials-MMDH
Matted Materials Remarkable-RMDH
Signature Scrapbook-SSDH
05Black Diamond-127
Emerald-127
Gold-127
Onyx-127
Ruby-127
Gemography-G-DH
Gemography Emerald-G-DH
Gemography Gold-G-DH
Gemography Onyx-G-DH
Gemography Ruby-G-DH
Jerseys Ruby-J-DH
Jersey Duals-DJ-DH
Jersey Triples-TJ-DH
Jersey Quads-QJ-DH
05Hot Prospects-70
En Fuego-70
Red Hot-70
White Hot-70
05ITG Ultimate Memorabilia Level 1-21
05ITG Ultimate Memorabilia Level 2-21
05ITG Ultimate Memorabilia Level 3-21
05ITG Ultimate Memorabilia Level 4-21
05ITG Ultimate Memorabilia Level 5-21
05ITG Ultimate Memorabilia Double Autos-19
05ITG Ultimate Mem Double Autos Gold-19
05ITG Ultimate Memorabilia Jersey Autos-10
05ITG Ultimate Mem Jersey Autos Gold-10
05ITG Ultimate Memorabilia R.O.Y. Autos-11
05ITG Ultimate Mem R.O.Y. Autos Gold-11
05ITG Ultimate Memorabilia R.O.Y. Emblems-8
05ITG Ultimate Mem R.O.Y. Emblems Gold-8
05ITG Ultimate Memorabilia R.O.Y. Jerseys-8
05ITG Ultimate Mem R.O.Y. Jerseys Gold-8
05ITG Ultimate Memorabilia R.O.Y. Numbers-8
05ITG Ultimate Mem R.O.Y. Numbers Gold-8
05ITG Ultimate Memorabilia Sextuple Autos-3
05ITG Ultimate Memorabilia Stick Autos-9
05ITG Ultimate Mem Stick Autos Gold-9
05ITG Ultimate Mem Sticks and Jerseys-9
05ITG Ultimate Mem Stick and Jerseys Gold-9
05ITG Ultimate Memorabilia Triple Autos-7
05ITG Ultimate Mem Triple Autos Gold-7
05ITG Ultimate Memorabilia Ultimate Autos-33
05ITG Ultimate Mem Ultimate Autos Gold-33
05McDonalds Upper Deck-25
Jerseys-MJ5
Patches-MP5
05Panini Stickers-115
05Parkhurst-335
05Parkhurst-573
Facsimile Auto Parallel-335
Facsimile Auto Parallel-573
True Colors-TCOTT
True Colors-TCOTT
True Colors-TCOTTO
True Colors-TCOTTO
05SP Authentic-68
05SP Authentic-121
Limited-68
Limited-121
Chirography-SPDH
Exquisite Endorsements-EEDH
Marks of Distinction-MDDH
Octographs-OF
Prestigious Pairings-PPAH
Sign of the Times-DH
Sign of the Times Duals-DSH
Sign of the Times Triples-THAS
Sign of the Times Quads-QSHAH
05SP Game Used-68
Autographs-68
Gold-68
Authentic Fabrics-AF-DH
Authentic Fabrics Autographs-AAF-DH
Authentic Fabrics Dual-AH
Authentic Fabrics Dual-DJ
Authentic Fabrics Dual Autographs-AH
Authentic Fabrics Dual Autographs-DJ
Authentic Fabrics Gold-AF-DH
Authentic Fabrics Quad-SAHH
Authentic Patches Quad -SAHH
Authentic Patches-AP-DH
Authentic Patches Autographs-AAP-DH
Authentic Patches Dual-AH
Authentic Patches Dual-DJ
Authentic Patches Dual Autographs-AH
Authentic Patches Dual Autographs-DJ
Awesome Authentics-AA-DH
Game Gear-GG-DH
Game Gear Autographs-AG-DH
SIGnificance-DH
SIGnificance Gold-S-DH
SIGnificance Extra-HH
SIGnificance Extra Gold-HH
Significant Numbers-SN-DH
Statscriptions-ST-DH
05SPx-60
Spectrum-60
Winning Combos-WC-HA
Winning Combos-WC-OT
Winning Combos Autographs-AWC-HA
Winning Combos Autographs-AWC-HH
Winning Combos Gold-WC-HA
Winning Combos Gold-WC-OT
Winning Combos Spectrum-WC-HA
Winning Combos Spectrum-WC-OT
Winning Materials-WM-DH
Winning Materials Autographs-AWM-DH
Winning Materials Gold-WM-DH
Winning Materials Spectrum-WM-DH
Xcitement Superstars-XS-DH
Xcitement Superstars Gold-XS-DH
Xcitement Superstars Spectrum-XS-DH
05The Cup-71
Gold-71
Black Rainbow-71
Dual NHL Shields-DSHS
Emblems of Endorsement-EEDH
Hardware Heroes-HHDH
Honorable Numbers-HNDH
Limited Logos-LLDH
Masterpiece Pressplates-71
Masterpiece Pressplates (Rookie Update)-230
Noble Numbers-NNHR
Noble Numbers Dual-DNNHI
Patch Variation-P71
Patch Variation Autographs-AP71
Property of-PODH
Scripted Numbers Dual-DSNTH
Scripted Swatches-SSDH
Signature Patches-SPDH
05UD Artifacts-4
05UD Artifacts-153
Blue-4
Blue-153
Gold-4
Gold-153
Green-4
Green-153
Pewter-4
Pewter-153
Red-4
Red-153
Gold Autographed-4
Gold Autographed-153
Remarkable Artifacts-RA-DH
Remarkable Artifacts Dual-RA-DH
Treasured Patches-TP-DH
Treasured Patches Autographed-TP-DH
Treasured Patches Dual-TPD-DH
Treasured Patches Dual Autographed-TPD-DH
Treasured Patches Pewter-TP-DH
Treasured Patches Silver-TP-DH
Treasured Swatches-TS-DH
Treasured Swatches Autographed-TS-DH
Treasured Swatches Blue-TS-DH
Treasured Swatches Copper-TS-DH
Treasured Swatches Dual-TSD-DH
Treasured Swatches Dual Autographed-TSD-DH
Treasured Swatches Dual Blue-TSD-DH
Treasured Swatches Dual Copper-TSD-DH
Treasured Swatches Dual Maroon-TSD-DH
Treasured Swatches Dual Pewter-TSD-DH
Treasured Swatches Dual Silver-TSD-DH
Treasured Swatches Maroon-TS-DH
Treasured Swatches Pewter-TS-DH
Treasured Swatches Silver-TS-DH
05UD PowerPlay-4
05UD PowerPlay-92
Rainbow-4
Specialists-TSDH
Specialists Patches-SPDH
05Ultimate Collection-61
Gold-61
Endorsed Emblems-EEDH
Jerseys-JHE
Jerseys Dual-DJJD
Jerseys Triple-TJHSH
Marquee Attractions-MA33
Marquee Attractions Signatures-SMA33
National Heroes Patches-NHPDH
Premium Patches-PPDH
Premium Swatches-PSDH
Ultimate Achievements-UADH
Ultimate Patches-PHE
Ultimate Patches Dual-DPJD
Ultimate Patches Triple-TPHSH
Ultimate Signatures-USDH
Ultimate Signatures Foursomes-UFHHSH
Ultimate Signatures Logos-SLDH
Ultimate Signatures Pairings-UPHS
Ultimate Signatures Trios-UTHAS
05Ultra-135
Gold-135
Ice-135
Scoring Kings-SK10
Scoring Kings Jerseys-SKJ-DH
Scoring Kings Jersey Autographs-KAJ-DH
Scoring Kings Patches-SKP-DH
Scoring Kings Patch Autographs-KAP-DH
05Upper Deck-380
05Upper Deck-442
05Upper Deck All-Time Greatest-4
05Upper Deck All-Time Greatest-61
05Upper Deck Big Playmakers-B-DHE
05Upper Deck Goal Celebrations-GC2
05Upper Deck Goal Rush-GR14
05Upper Deck Hometown Heroes-HH26
05Upper Deck Jerseys-J-DH
05Upper Deck Notable Numbers-N-HE
05Upper Deck Patches-P-DHE
05Upper Deck Scrapbooks-HS15
05Upper Deck Shooting Stars-S-DH
05Upper Deck Hockey Showcase-HS26
05Upper Deck Showcase Promos-HS26
05Upper Deck Ice-65
Rainbow-65
Frozen Fabrics-FFDH
Frozen Fabrics Autographs-AFFDH
Frozen Fabrics Glass-FFDH
Frozen Fabrics Patches-FFPDH
Frozen Fabrics Patch Autographs-FAPDH
Signature Swatches-SSHE
05Upper Deck MVP-266
Gold-266

Platinum-266
ProSign-P-DH
05Upper Deck Rookie Update-66
05Upper Deck Rookie Update-230
Inspirations Patch Rookies-230
05Upper Deck Trilogy-61
05Upper Deck Trilogy-93
Crystal-93
Crystal Autographs-93
Honorary Patches-HP-DH
Honorary Patch Scripts-HSP-DH
Honorary Swatch Scripts-HSS-DH
Ice Scripts-IS-DH
05Upper Deck Victory-7
05Upper Deck Victory-234
Black-7
Black-234
Gold-7
Gold-234
Silver-7
Silver-234
Blow-Ups-BU2
Game Breakers-GB2
Stars on Ice-SI2
05ITG Heroes and Prospects-184
Autographs Series II-DHE
Autographs Series II-HK
Hero Memorabilia-HM-47
National Pride-NPR-25
06Be A Player-117
Autographs-117
Profiles-PP27
Profiles Autographs-PP27
Signatures-DH
Signatures 10-129
Signatures 25-129
Signatures Duals-DHS
Signatures Duals-DIH
Signatures Trios-TSAH
Up Close and Personal-UC12
Up Close and Personal Autographs-UC12
06Be A Player Portraits-71
Dual Signature Portraits-DSDJ
Quadruple Signature Portraits-QKIHN
Sensational Six-SSCDN
Signature Portraits-SPDH
Timeless Tens-TTCAN
Triple Signature Portraits-TOTT
06Beehive-32
06Beehive-178
Blue-32
Gold-32
Matte-32
Red Facsimile Signatures-32
Wood-32
5 X 7 Black and White-32
5 X 7 Dark Wood-32
Matted Materials-MMDH
PhotoGraphs-PGHE
Remarkable Matted Materials-MMDH
06Black Diamond-142
Black-142
Black-160B
Gold-142
Ruby-142
06Flair Showcase-70
06Flair Showcase-190
06Flair Showcase-250
06Flair Showcase-290
Parallel-70
Parallel-190
Parallel-250
Parallel-290
Hot Numbers-HN31
Hot Numbers Parallel-HN31
Inks-IHE
Wave of the Future-WF30
06Fleer-137
Oversized-137
Tiffany-137
Hockey Headliners-HL17
Speed Machines-SM18
Total 0-016
06Gatorade-47
06Hot Prospects-68
Red Hot-68
White Hot-68
Hot Materials -HMHE
Hot Materials Red Hot-HMHE
Hot Materials White Hot-HMHE
06ITG International Ice Cornerstones-IC11
06ITG International Ice Cornerstones Gold-IC11
06ITG Ultimate Memorabilia-35
Artist Proof-35
Autos-40
Autos Gold-40
Double Memorabilia Autos-2
Double Memorabilia Autos Gold-2
Journey Emblem-4
Journey Emblem Gold-4
Journey Jersey-4
Journey Jersey Gold-4
R.O.Y. Autos-11
R.O.Y. Autos Gold-11
R.O.Y. Emblems-11
R.O.Y. Emblems Gold-11
R.O.Y. Jerseys-11
R.O.Y. Jerseys Gold-11
R.O.Y. Numbers-11
R.O.Y. Numbers Gold-11
06McDonald's Upper Deck-32
Clear Cut Winners-CC7
Jerseys-JDH
Patches-PDH
06NHL POG-15
06O-Pee-Chee-339
Rainbow-339
Autographs-A-DH
06Panini Stickers-114
06Senators Postcards-6
06SP Authentic-34
06SP Authentic-108
Chirography-DH
Limited-34
Limited-108
Sign of the Times-STHE
Sign of the Times Duals-STHE
Sign of the Times Triples-ST3HNS
Sign of the Times Triples-ST3RHG
06SP Game Used-68
Gold-68
Rainbow-68
Authentic Fabrics-AFHE
Authentic Fabrics Parallel-AFHE
Authentic Fabrics Patches-AFHE
Authentic Fabrics Dual-AF2SH
Authentic Fabrics Dual Patches-AF2SH
Authentic Fabrics Triple-AF3OTT
Authentic Fabrics Triple Patches-AF3OTT
Authentic Fabrics Quads-AF4IDCH
Authentic Fabrics Quads Patches-AF4IDCH
Authentic Fabrics Fives-AF550G
Authentic Fabrics Fives-AF5ASG
Authentic Fabrics Fives-AF5PTS
Authentic Fabrics Fives Patches-AF550G
Authentic Fabrics Fives Patches-AF5ASG
Authentic Fabrics Fives Patches-AF5PTS
Authentic Fabrics Sevens-AF7CAL
Authentic Fabrics Sevens Patches-AF7CAL
Autographs-68
By The Letter-BLDH
Inked Sweaters-ISDA
Inked Sweaters Patches-ISDA
Inked Sweaters Dual-IS2NH
Inked Sweaters Dual Patches-IS2NH
06SPx-72
Spectrum-72
SPxcitement-X69
SPxcitement Spectrum-X69
SPxcitement Autographs-X69
Winning Materials-WMDH
Winning Materials Spectrum-WMDH
Winning Materials Autographs-WMDH
06The Cup-65
Autographed Foundations-CQHE
Autographed Foundations Patches-CQHE
Autographed NHL Shields Duals-DASDJ
Autographed NHL Shields Duals-DASDM
Autographed NHL Shields Duals-DASHG
Autographed NHL Shields Duals-DASHN
Autographed NHL Shields Duals-DASHR
Autographed Patches-65
Black Rainbow-65
Foundations-CQHE
Foundations Patches-CQHE
Enshrinements-EHE
Gold-65
Gold Patches-65
Honorable Numbers-HNHE
Jerseys-65
Limited Logos-LLHE
Masterpiece Pressplates-65
NHL Shields Duals-DSHJD
Property of-POHE
Scripted Swatches-SSHE
Scripted Swatches Duals-DSHS
Signature Patches-SPHE
06UD Artifacts-32
06UD Artifacts-185
Blue-32
Blue-185
Gold-32
Gold-185
Platinum-32
Platinum-185
Radiance-32
Radiance-185
Autographed Radiance Parallel-32
Autographed Radiance Parallel-185
Red-32
Red-185
Tundra Tandems-TTDD
Tundra Tandems-TTJH
Tundra Tandems Black-TTDD
Tundra Tandems Black-TTJH
Tundra Tandems Blue-TTDD
Tundra Tandems Blue-TTJH
Tundra Tandems Gold-TTDD
Tundra Tandems Gold-TTJH
Tundra Tandems Platinum-TTDD
Tundra Tandems Platinum-TTJH
Tundra Tandems Red-TTDD
Tundra Tandems Red-TTJH
Tundra Tandems Dual Patches Red-TTDD
Tundra Tandems Dual Patches Red-TTJH
06UD Mini Jersey Collection-70
Jerseys-DH
Jersey Variations-DH
Jersey Autographs-DH
06UD Powerplay-70
Impact Rainbow-70
In Action-IA8
06Ultimate Collection-43
Autographed Jerseys-AJ-DH
Autographed Patches-AJ-DH
Jerseys-UJ-HE
Jerseys Dual-UJ2-SH
Patches-UJ-HE
Patches Dual-UJ2-SH
Signatures-US-HE
Ultimate Achievements-UA-DH
Ultimate Signatures Logos-SL-DH
06Ultra-136
Gold Medallion-136
Ice Medallion-136
Action-UA20
Difference Makers-DM24
Scoring Kings-SK6
06Upper Deck Arena Giveaways-OTT3
06Upper Deck-384
Exclusives Parallel-384
High Gloss Parallel-384
Century Marks-CM3
Game Jerseys-J2HE
Game Patches-P2HE
Generations Duals-G2PJD
Generations Patches Dual-G2PJD
Goal Rush-GR3
Masterpieces-384
Oversized Wal-Mart Exclusives-384
Signatures-SDH
06Upper Deck MVP-207
Gold Script-207
Super Script-207
Autographs-OAHC
Clutch Performers-CP8
Gotta Have Hart-HH25
Jerseys-OJHB
Jerseys-OJHS
06Upper Deck Ovation-33
06Upper Deck Sweet Shot-73
Signature Shots/Saves-SSHE
Signature Shots/Saves Ice Signings-SSIHE
Signature Shots/Saves Sticks-SSSHE
Signature Sticks-STHE
Sweet Stitches-SSDA
Sweet Stitches Duals-SSDA
Sweet Stitches Triples-SSDA
06Upper Deck Trilogy-69
Combo Autographed Jerseys-CJHN
Combo Autographed Patches-CJHN
Combo Clearcut Autographs-C3RHH
Honorary Scripted Patches-HSPDH
Honorary Scripted Swatches-HSSDH
Honorary Swatches-HSDH
Ice Scripts-ISHE
Scripts-S1DH
Scripts-S3DH
06Upper Deck Victory-136
06Upper Deck Victory Black-136
06Upper Deck Victory Gold-136
06Upper Deck Victory GameBreakers-GB33
06Upper Deck Victory Next In Line-NL36
06Upper Deck Victory Oversize Cards-DH
06Russian Sport Collection Olympic Stars-41
07Sports Illustrated for Kids *-159
07Upper Deck Victory-46
Black-46
Gold-46
GameBreakers-GB35
Oversize Cards-OS13
Stars on Ice-SI11
07ITG Going For Gold World Juniors Emblems-GUE28
07ITG Going For Gold World Juniors Jerseys-GUJ28

Heatley, Mark

03Wisconsin Badgers-14
04Wisconsin Badgers-27

Heatley, Murray

74Minnesota Fighting Saints WHA-12
75O-Pee-Chee WHA-53

Heaton, Scott

94UK Sheffield Steelers-18
95UK Sheffield Steelers-15

Hebenton, Andy

44Beehive Group II Photos-29
44Beehive Group II Photos-322
57Topps-58
58Topps-46
59Topps-16
60NHL Ceramic Tiles-10
60Shirriff Coins-91
60Topps-42
Stamps-24
61Shirriff/Salada Coins-90
61Topps-55
62Topps-54
Hockey Bucks-10
63Topps-15
64Beehive Group III Photos-11
94Parkhurst Missing Link-97

Hebenton, Clay

76Phoenix Roadrunners WHA-5

Heberlein, Marc

99Swiss Panini Stickers-65
00Swiss Panini Stickers-115
01Swiss HNL-116
02Swiss HNL-23
04Swiss Davos Postcards-16

Hebert, Andre

77Granby Vics-11

Hebert, Guy

89ProCards IHL-5
90ProCards AHL/IHL-89
91ProCards-29
92Bowman-32
92O-Pee-Chee-116
92OPC Premier-40
92Parkhurst-386
Emerald Ice-386
92Score-460
Canadian-460
92Stadium Club-401
92Topps-112
Gold-112G
92Ultra-394
92Upper Deck-501
93Donruss-13
93Leaf-356
93OPC Premier-519
Gold-519
93Parkhurst-279
Emerald Ice-279
93Pinnacle-167
Canadian-167
Expansion-1
93PowerPlay-2
93Score-426
93Score-489
93Score-502
Gold-502
Canadian-426
Canadian-489
Canadian-502
Canadian Gold-502
93Stadium Club-295
Members Only Master Set-295
First Day Issue-295
93Topps/OPC Premier-519
Gold-519
93Ultra-254
93Upper Deck-1
94Be A Player-R47
Signature Cards-99
94Canada Games NHL POGS-269
94Donruss-81
94Ducks Carl's Jr.-9
94EA Sports-6
94Finest-20
Super Team Winners-20
Refractors-20
94Flair-3
94Kraft-40
94Kraft Goalie Masks-2
94Leaf-142
Limited Inserts-1
94OPC Premier-338
Special Effects-338
94Parkhurst SE-SE1
Gold-SE1
94Pinnacle-15
Artist's Proofs-15
Rink Collection-15
Masks-MA4
94Score-42
Gold-42
Platinum-42
Franchise-TF1
94Select-79
Gold-79
94SP-5
Die Cuts-5
94Stadium Club-6
Members Only Master Set-6
First Day Issue-6
Super Team Winner Cards-6
94Topps/OPC Premier-338
Special Effects-338
94Ultra-3
94Upper Deck-3
Electric Ice-3
95Collector's Choice-287
Player's Club-287
Player's Club Platinum-287
95Donruss-71
Elite Painted Warriors-5
95Emotion-2
95Finest-122
Refractors-122
95Hoyle Western Playing Cards-34
95Kraft-37
95Leaf-271
95Metal-1
95Panini Stickers-232
95Parkhurst International-4
Emerald Ice-4
95Pinnacle-143
Artist's Proofs-143
Rink Collection-143
95Playoff One on One-1
95Playoff One on One-113
95Pro Magnets-42
95Score-94
Black Ice Artist's Proofs-94
Black Ice-94
95SkyBox Impact-2
95SP-3
95Stadium Club-82
Members Only Master Set-82
95Summit-58
Artist's Proofs-58
Ice-58
95Topps-112
OPC Inserts-112
95Ultra-1
Gold Medallion-1
95Upper Deck-467
Electric Ice-467
Electric Ice Gold-467
Special Edition-SE3
Special Edition Gold-SE3
95Zenith-99
95Finnish Semic World Championships-210
95Swedish World Championships Stickers-211
96Be A Player-61
Autographs-61
Autographs Silver-61
96Black Diamond-53
Gold-53
96Collector's Choice-5
96Collector's Choice-309
96Donruss-164
Press Proofs-164
96Ducks Team Issue-21
96Flair-1
Blue Ice-1
96Fleer-1
96Fleer-147
96Kraft Upper Deck-16
96Leaf-88
Press Proofs-88
96Maggers-36
96Metal Universe-1
96NHL Pro Stamps-42
96Pinnacle-88
Artist's Proofs-88
Foil-88
Premium Stock-88
Rink Collection-88
96Score-13
Artist's Proofs-13
Dealer's Choice Artist's Proofs-13
Special Artist's Proofs-13
Golden Blades-13
96SkyBox Impact-1
96SP-5
96Summit-75
Artist's Proofs-75
Ice-75
Metal-75
Premium Stock-75
96Team Out-72
96Ultra-1
Gold Medallion-1
96Upper Deck-2
97Be A Player Stacking the Pads-1
97Black Diamond-34
Double Diamond-34
Triple Diamond-34
Quadruple Diamond-34
97Collector's Choice-1
Star Quest-SQ42
97Crown Royale-1
Emerald Green-1
Ice Blue-1
Silver-1
Freeze Out Die-Cuts-1
97Donruss-167
Press Proofs Silver-167
Press Proofs Gold-167
97Donruss Canadian Ice-37
Dominion Series-37
Provincial Series-37
97Donruss Elite-45
Aspirations-45
Status-45
97Donruss Limited-102
Exposure-102
97Donruss Preferred-129
Cut to the Chase-129
97Donruss Priority-124
Stamp of Approval-124
Postmaster General-20
Postmaster Generals Promos-20
97Katch-1
Gold-1
Silver-1
97Leaf-72
Fractal Matrix-72
Fractal Matrix Die Cuts-72
Pipe Dreams-7
97Leaf International-72
Universal Ice-72
97Pacific-260
Copper-260
Emerald Green-260
Ice Blue-260
Red-260
Silver-260
In The Cage Laser Cuts-1
97Pacific Dynagon-2
Copper-2
Dark Grey-2
Emerald Green-2
Ice Blue-2
Red-2
Silver-2
Stonewallers-1
Tandems-24
97Pacific Invincible-2
Copper-2
Emerald Green-2
Ice Blue-2
Red-2
Silver-2
97Pacific Omega-2
Copper-2
Dark Gray-2
Emerald Green-2
Gold-2
Ice Blue-2
97Paramount-1
Copper-1
Dark Grey-1
Emerald Green-1
Ice Blue-1
Red-1
Silver-1
Glove Side Laser Cuts-1
97Pinnacle-90
Artist's Proofs-90
Rink Collection-90
Press Plates Back Black-90
Press Plates Back Cyan-90
Press Plates Back Magenta-90
Press Plates Back Yellow-90
Press Plates Front Black-90
Press Plates Front Cyan-90
Press Plates Front Magenta-90
Press Plates Front Yellow-90
Masks-6
Masks Die Cuts-6
Masks Jumbos-6
97Pinnacle Masks Promos-6
97Pinnacle Tins-4
97Pinnacle Certified-19
Red-19
Mirror Blue-19
Mirror Gold-19
Mirror Red-19
97Pinnacle Inside-70
Coach's Collection-70
Executive Collection-70
Stand Up Guys-8A/B
Stand Up Guys-8C/D
Stand Up Guys Promos-8A/B
Stand Up Guys Promos-8C/D
Stoppers-6
Cans-11
Cans Gold-11
Promos-70
97Pinnacle Replica Masks-2
97Pinnacle Tot Cert Platinum Blue-19
97Pinnacle Tot Cert Platinum Gold-19
97Pinnacle Totally Certified Platinum Red-19
97Pinnacle Tot Cert Mirror Platinum Gold-19
97Revolution-1
Copper-1
Emerald-1
Ice Blue-1
Silver-1
Return to Sender Die-Cuts-1
97Score-6
Artist's Proofs-6
Golden Blades-6
Net Worth-1
97Score Mighty Ducks-14
Platinum-14
Premier-14
97SP Authentic Sign of the Times-GH
97Studio-37
Press Proofs Silver-37
Press Proofs Gold-37
97Upper Deck-6
97Zenith-66
Z-Gold-66
Z-Silver-66
97Zenith 5 x 7-11
Gold Impulse-11
Silver Impulse-11
98Aurora-2
98Be A Player-4
Press Release-4
98BAP Gold-4
98BAP Autographs-4
98BAP Autographs Gold-4
98BAP Tampa Bay All Star Game-4
98Crown Royale-2
Limited Series-2
98Ducks Power Play-ANA3
98Finest-58
No Protectors-58
No Protectors Refractors-58
Refractors-58
98Katch-1
98NHL Aces Playing Cards-6
98NHL Game Day Promotion-ANA3
98OPC Chrome-48
Refractors-48
98Pacific-54
Ice Blue-54
Red-54
98Pacific Dynagon Ice-2
Blue-2
Red-2
98Pacific Omega-3
Red-3
Opening Day Issue-3
98Panini Stickers-166
98Paramount-2
Copper-2
Emerald Green-2
Holo-Electric-2
Ice Blue-2
Silver-2
Glove Side Laser Cuts-1
98Revolution-1
Ice Shadow-1
Red-1
98SP Authentic-3
Power Shift-3
98SPx Finite-2
Radiance-2
Spectrum-2
98Topps-48
O-Pee-Chee-48
98Topps Gold Label Class 1-57
Black-57
Black One of One-57
One of One-57
Red-57
Red One of One-57
98Topps Gold Label Class 2-57
98Topps Gold Label Class 2 Black-57
98Topps Gold Label Class 2 Black 1 of 1-57
98Topps Gold Label Class 2 One of One-57
98Topps Gold Label Class 2 Red-57
98Topps Gold Label Class 2 Red One of One-57
98Topps Gold Label Class 3-57
98Topps Gold Label Class 3 Black-57
98Topps Gold Label Class 3 Black 1 of 1-57
98Topps Gold Label Class 3 One of One-57
98Topps Gold Label Class 3 Red-57
98Topps Gold Label Class 3 Red One of One-57
98UD Choice-1
98UD Choice Preview-1
98UD Choice Prime Choice Reserve-1
98UD Choice Reserve-1
98Upper Deck-212
Exclusives-212
Exclusives 1 of 1-212
Gold Reserve-212
98Upper Deck MVP-6
Gold Script-6
Silver Script-6
Super Script-6
99Aurora-1
Premiere Date-1
Glove Unlimited-1
99BAP Memorabilia-168
Gold-168
Silver-168
99BAP Millennium-5
Emerald-5
Ruby-5
Sapphire-5
Signatures-5
Signatures Gold-5
99Black Diamond-3
Diamond Cut-3
Final Cut-3
99Crown Royale-1
Limited Series-1
Premiere Date-1
99Jell-O Partners of Power-11
99O-Pee-Chee-58
99O-Pee-Chee Chrome-58
99O-Pee-Chee Chrome Refractors-58
99Pacific-7
Copper-7
Emerald Green-7
Gold-7
Ice Blue-7
Premiere Date-7
Red-7
In the Cage Net-Fusions-1
99Pacific Dynagon Ice-9
Blue-9
Copper-9
Gold-9
Premiere Date-9
99Pacific Omega-2
Copper-2
Gold-2
Ice Blue-2
Premiere Date-2
99Pacific Prism-1
Holographic Blue-1
Holographic Gold-1
Holographic Mirror-1
Holographic Purple-1
Premiere Date-1
99Panini Stickers-181
99Panini Stickers-350
99Paramount-2
Copper-2
Emerald-2
Gold-2
Holographic Emerald-2
Holographic Gold-2
Holographic Silver-2
Ice Blue-2
Premiere Date-2
Red-2
Silver-2
Glove Side Net Fusions-1
99Revolution-1
Premiere Date-1
Red-1
Shadow Series-1
Copper-1
Gold-1
CSC Silver-1
99SP Authentic-3
99SPx-6
Radiance-6
Spectrum-6
99Stadium Club-96
First Day Issue-96
One of a Kind-96
Printing Plates Black-96
Printing Plates Cyan-96
Printing Plates Magenta-96
Printing Plates Yellow-96
99Topps/OPC-58
99Topps/OPC Chrome-58
Refractors-58
99Topps Gold Label Class 1-38
Black-38
Black One of One-38
One of One-38
Red-38
Red One of One-38
99Topps Gold Label Class 2-38
99Topps Gold Label Class 2 Black-38
99Topps Gold Label Class 2 Black 1 of 1-38
99Topps Gold Label Class 2 One of One-38
99Topps Gold Label Class 2 Red-38
99Topps Gold Label Class 2 Red One of One-38
99Topps Gold Label Class 3-38
99Topps Gold Label Class 3 Black-38
99Topps Gold Label Class 3 Black 1 of 1-38
99Topps Gold Label Class 3 One of One-38
99Topps Gold Label Class 3 Red-38
99Topps Gold Label Class 3 Red One of One-38
99Topps Premier Plus-74
Parallel-74
99Ultimate Victory Net Work-NW9
99Upper Deck-171
Exclusives-171
Exclusives 1 of 1-171
99Upper Deck Gold Reserve-171
99Upper Deck MVP-6
Gold Script-6
Silver Script-6
Super Script-6
99Upper Deck MVP SC Edition-3
Gold Script-3
Silver Script-3
Super Script-3
99Upper Deck Victory-7
99Wayne Gretzky Hockey-2
00SLU Hockey-100
00Aurora-1
Premiere Date-1
00BAP Memorabilia-65
Emerald-65
Ruby-65
Sapphire-65
Promos-65
00BAP Mem Chicago Sportsfest Copper-65
00BAP Memorabilia Chicago Sportsfest Blue-65
00BAP Memorabilia Chicago Sportsfest Gold-65
00BAP Memorabilia Chicago Sportsfest Ruby-65
00BAP Memorabilia Chicago Sun-Times Ruby-65
00BAP Memorabilia Chicago Sun-Times Gold-65
00BAP Mem Chicago Sun-Times Sapphire-65
00BAP Mem Toronto Fall Expo Copper-65
00BAP Memorabilia Toronto Fall Expo Gold-65
00BAP Memorabilia Toronto Fall Expo Ruby-65
00BAP Memorabilia Update Teammates-TM23
00BAP Memorabilia Update Teammates-TM39
00BAP Memorabilia Update Teammates Gold-TM23
00BAP Memorabilia Update Teammates Gold-TM39
00BAP Parkhurst 2000-P136
00BAP Signature Series-48
Emerald-48
Ruby-48
Sapphire-48
00BAP Ultimate Memorabilia Active Eight-AE8
00BAP Ultimate Memorabilia Goalie Sticks-G1
00BAP Ultimate Mem Plante Skate Cards-PS9
00BAP Ultimate Memorabilia Teammates-TM22
00BAP Ultimate Memorabilia Teammates-TM23
00Crown Royale-1
Ice Blue-1
Limited Series-1
Premiere Date-1
Red-1
00O-Pee-Chee-46
00O-Pee-Chee Parallel-46
00Pacific-4
Copper-4
Gold-4
Ice Blue-4
Premiere Date-4
00Panini Stickers-110
00Paramount-4
Copper-4
Gold-4
Holo-Gold-4
Holo-Silver-4
Ice Blue-4
Premiere Date-4
00Private Stock-1
Gold-1
Premiere Date-1
Retail-1
Silver-1
Game Gear-1
Game Gear Patches-1
00Revolution-1
Blue-1
Premiere Date-1
Red-1
00Stadium Club-118
00Titanium Game Gear-51
00Titanium Game Gear-52
00Titanium Game Gear Patches-51
00Titanium Game Gear Patches-52
00Topps/OPC-46
Parallel-46
Own the Game-OTG19
00Topps Chrome-38
OPC Refractors-38
Refractors-38
00Topps Gold Label Class 1-62
Gold-62
00Topps Gold Label Class 2-62
00Topps Gold Label Class 2 Gold-62
00Topps Gold Label Class 3-62
00Topps Gold Label Class 3 Gold-62
00Topps Heritage-149
00Topps Premier Plus-80
Blue Ice-80
00UD Heroes-4
00UD Pros and Prospects-3
00UD Reserve Golden Goalies-GG1
00Upper Deck-6
Exclusives Tier 1-6
Exclusives Tier 2-6
00Upper Deck Victory-6
00Upper Deck Vintage-6
00Upper Deck Vintage-11
00Upper Deck Vintage-12
Great Gloves-GG1
00Vanguard-1
Dual Game-Worn Jerseys-19
Dual Game-Worn Patches-19
Holographic Gold-1
Holographic Purple-1
Pacific Proofs-1
01Atomic Jerseys-40
01Atomic Patches-40
01Pacific-258
Extreme LTD-258
Hobby LTD-258
Premiere Date-258
Retail LTD-258
Jerseys-21
01Pacific Arena Exclusives-258
01Pacific Heads-Up Quad Jerseys-1
01Vanguard Memorabilia-2
02BAP Sig Series Auto Buybacks 1998-4
02BAP Sig Series Auto Buybacks 1999-5
04ITG Franchises US West-151
Autographs-A-GHE

Hebert, Ian

94Birmingham Bulls-10
95Birmingham Bulls-16
98Danish Hockey League-200

Hebert, Jay

99Missouri River Otters-6
99Missouri River Otters Sheet-7
00Missouri River Otters-8
02Rockford Ice Hogs-17

Hebert, Patrick

907th Inn. Sketch QMJHL-195
92Quebec Pee-Wee Tournament-1261

Hebert, Roland

51Laval Dairy QSHL-19

Hebig, Harald

94German First League-629
99German Bundesliga 2-312

Hebky, David

917th Inn. Sketch WHL-56
92British Columbia JHL-215

Hecht, Jochen

94German DEL-282
95German DEL-277
95Signature Rookies Auto-Phonex-17
95Signature Rook Auto-Phonex Phone Cards-17
96German DEL-173
99BAP Memorabilia-152
Gold-152
Silver-152
99BAP Millennium Calder Candidates Ruby-C34
99BAP Millennium Calder Candidate Emerald-C34
99BAP Millennium Calder Cand Sapphire-C34
99Black Diamond-71
Diamond Cut-71
Final Cut-71
99Blues Taco Bell-2
99Crown Royale-116
Limited Series-116
Premiere Date-116
Prospects Parallel-116
International Glory-23
International Glory Parallel-23
99Pacific-367
Copper-367
Emerald Green-367
Gold-367
Ice Blue-367
Premiere Date-367
Red-367
99Pacific Omega-203
Copper-203
Gold-203
Ice Blue-203
Premiere Date-203
99Pacific Prism-118
Holographic Blue-118
Holographic Gold-118
Holographic Mirror-118
Holographic Purple-118
Premiere Date-118
99Panini Stickers-290
99Paramount-197
Copper-197
Emerald-197
Gold-197
Holographic Emerald-197
Holographic Gold-197
Holographic Silver-197
Ice Blue-197
Premiere Date-197
Red-197
Silver-197
99Revolution-122
99SP Authentic-116
Sign of the Times-JH
Sign of the Times Gold-JH
Tomorrow's Headliners-TH8
99SPx-136
Radiance-136
Spectrum-136
99Stadium Club-173
First Day Issue-173
One of a Kind-173
Printing Plates Black-173
Printing Plates Cyan-173
Printing Plates Magenta-173
Printing Plates Yellow-173
99Topps Arena Giveaways-STL-JH
99Topps Gold Label Class 1-99
Black-99
Black One of One-99
One of One-99
Red-99
Red One of One-99
99Topps Gold Label Class 2-99
99Topps Gold Label Class 2 Black-99
99Topps Gold Label Class 2 Black 1 of 1-99
99Topps Gold Label Class 2 One of One-99
99Topps Gold Label Class 2 Red-99
99Topps Gold Label Class 2 Red One of One-99
99Topps Gold Label Class 3-99
99Topps Gold Label Class 3 Black-99
99Topps Gold Label Class 3 Black 1 of 1-99
99Topps Gold Label Class 3 One of One-99
99Topps Gold Label Class 3 Red-99
99Topps Gold Label Class 3 Red One of One-99
99Topps Gold Label Fresh Gold-FG19
99Topps Gold Label Fresh Gold Black-FG19
99Topps Gold Label Fresh Gold Black 1of1-FG19
99Topps Gold Label Fresh Gold One of One-FG19
99Topps Gold Label Fresh Gold Red-FG19
99Topps Gold Label Fresh Gold Red 1 of 1-FG19
99Topps Premier Plus-116
Parallel-116
Premier Rookies-PR6
Premier Rookies Parallel-PR6
99Ultimate Victory-106
1/1-106
Parallel-106
Parallel 100-106
99Upper Deck-116
Exclusives-116
Exclusives 1 of 1-116
99Upper Deck Arena Giveaways-SB1
99Upper Deck Gold Reserve-116
99Upper Deck MVP-188
Gold Script-188
Silver Script-188
Super Script-188
99Upper Deck MVP SC Edition-164
Gold Script-164
Silver Script-164
Super Script-164
ProSign-JH
99Upper Deck Victory-262
99Wayne Gretzky Hockey-148
00BAP Memorabilia-9
Emerald-9
Ruby-9
Sapphire-9
Promos-9
00BAP Mem Chicago Sportsfest Copper-9
00BAP Memorabilia Chicago Sportsfest Blue-9
00BAP Memorabilia Chicago Sportsfest Gold-9
00BAP Memorabilia Chicago Sportsfest Ruby-9
00BAP Memorabilia Chicago Sun-Times Ruby-9
00BAP Memorabilia Chicago Sun-Times Gold-9
00BAP Mem Chicago Sun-Times Sapphire-9
00BAP Mem Toronto Fall Expo Copper-9
00BAP Memorabilia Toronto Fall Expo Gold-9
00BAP Memorabilia Toronto Fall Expo Ruby-9
00BAP Parkhurst 2000-P91
00BAP Signature Series-155
Emerald-155
Ruby-155
Sapphire-155
Autographs-47
Autographs Gold-47
00O-Pee-Chee-149
00O-Pee-Chee Parallel-149
00Pacific-345
Copper-345
Gold-345
Ice Blue-345
Premiere Date-345
00Stadium Club-186
00Topps/OPC-149
Parallel-149
Own the Game-OTG30
00Topps Chrome-108
OPC Refractors-108
Refractors-108
00Topps Heritage-113
00Upper Deck-381
Exclusives Tier 1-381
Exclusives Tier 2-381
Game Jersey Autographs-HJH
Game Jersey Autographs Exclusives-EJH
Game Jersey Patches-JHP
Game Jersey Patch Autographs Exclusives-JHP
Prospects In Depth-P10
00Upper Deck MVP-155
First Stars-155
Second Stars-155
Third Stars-155
00Upper Deck Victory-203
00Upper Deck Vintage-312
01BAP Memorabilia-30
Emerald-30

Ruby-30
Sapphire-30
01BAP Signature Series-157
Autographs-157
Autographs Gold-157
01Crown Royale Triple Threads-9
01Crown Royale Triple Threads-19
01O-Pee-Chee-43
01O-Pee-Chee Heritage Parallel-43
01O-Pee-Chee Heritage Parallel Limited-43
01O-Pee-Chee Premier Parallel-43
01Pacific-323
Extreme LTD-323
Hobby LTD-323
Premiere Date-323
Retail LTD-323
01Pacific Adrenaline-76
Blue-76
Premiere Date-76
Red-76
Retail-76
Jerseys-17
01Pacific Arena Exclusives-323
01Parkhurst-210
01Private Stock Game Gear-47
01Private Stock Game Gear Patches-47
01SP Authentic Sign of the Times-JH
01SP Authentic Sign of the Times-CH
01Titanium Double-Sided Jerseys-38
01Titanium Double-Sided Patches-38
01Titanium Draft Day Edition-40
01Topps-43
Heritage Parallel-43
Heritage Parallel Limited-43
OPC Parallel-43
01Topps Heritage-176
01UD Honor Roll Jerseys-J-JH
01UD Honor Roll Jerseys Gold-J-JH
01Upper Deck-297
Exclusives-297
01Upper Deck Victory-309
Gold-309
01Vanguard Memorabilia-29
02BAP Memorabilia-86
Emerald-86
Ruby-86
Sapphire-86
NHL All-Star Game-86
NHL All-Star Game Blue-86
NHL All-Star Game Green-86
NHL All-Star Game Red-86
02BAP Memorabilia Toronto Fall Expo-86
02BAP Sig Series Auto Buybacks 2000-47
02BAP Sig Series Auto Buybacks 2001-157
02O-Pee-Chee-176
02O-Pee-Chee Premier Blue Parallel-176
02O-Pee-Chee Premier Red Parallel-176
02O-Pee-Chee Factory Set-176
02Pacific-143
Blue-143
Red-143
02Pacific Complete-298
Red-298
02Sabres Team Issue-6
02Topps-176
OPC Blue Parallel-176
OPC Red Parallel-176
Factory Set-176
02Topps Heritage-166
02Topps Total-118
02UD Top Shelf Dual Player Jerseys-STYH
02Upper Deck-267
Exclusives-267
02Upper Deck Beckett UD Promos-267
02Upper Deck Victory-85
Bronze-85
Gold-85
Silver-85
National Pride-NP28
02Vanguard-13
LTD-13
03ITG Action-44
03NHL Sticker Collection-26
03Pacific Complete-369
Red-369
03Upper Deck-266
Canadian Exclusives-266
HG-266
UD Exclusives-266
03Upper Deck MVP-57
Gold Script-57
Silver Script-57
Canadian Exclusives-57
03Worcester Ice Cats 10th Anniversary-17
04Pacific-33
Blue-33
Red-33
04UD All-World-89
Gold-89
04Upper Deck World's Best-WB16
04Upper Deck World Cup Tribute-JH
04Upper Deck World Cup Tribute-JHOK
04German Adler Mannheim Eagles Postcards-17
04German DEL-11
Global Players-GP3
Superstars-SU02
05Panini Stickers-39
05Parkhurst-56
Facsimile Auto Parallel-56
True Colors-TCBUF
True Colors-TCBUF
05SP Authentic Sign of the Times-JH
05SP Game Used Auto Draft-AD-HE
05SP Game Used Statscriptions-ST-JH
05Ultra Fresh Ink-FI-JH
05Ultra Fresh Ink Blue-FI-JH
05Upper Deck-266
Notable Numbers-N-JH
05Upper Deck MVP-51
Gold-51
Platinum-51
05Upper Deck Victory-23
Black-23
Gold-23
Silver-23
05German DEL-290
DEB-Jerseys-TR02
Star Attack-ST02
06O-Pee-Chee-66
Rainbow-66
06Upper Deck-25
Exclusives Parallel-25
High Gloss Parallel-25
Masterpieces-25
06Upper Deck MVP-39
Gold Script-39
Super Script-39
06German DEL-187

Hecht, Oliver
94German First League-360

Hecimovic, John
00Sarnia Sting-13
03Sarnia Sting-10
04Mississauga Ice Dogs-15

Heckendorn, B.J.
93Quebec Pee-Wee Tournament-784
04Missouri River Otters-4
05Missouri River Otters-9

Hecker, Benjamin
99German DEL-289
01German Upper Deck-265

Hecker, Jochen
94German First League-422
99German Bundesliga 2-129

Hecl, Radoslav
02BAP Memorabilia-370
02BAP Ultimate Memorabilia-78
02Upper Deck Rookie Update-127
02Slovakian Kvarteto-6
02Rochester Americans-7

Hecquet, Fabien
02Swiss HNL-113

Hedberg, Anders
69Swedish Hockey-132
70Finnish Jaakiekko-25
70Swedish Hockey-91
70Swedish Hockey-282
70Swedish Masterserien-112
71Finnish Suomi Stickers-45
71Swedish Hockey-14
71Swedish Hockey-183
72Finnish Jaakiekko-45
72Finnish Hellas-38
72Finnish Semic World Championship-69
72Swedish Stickers-12
72Swedish Stickers-172
72Swedish Semic World Championship-69
73Finnish Jaakiekko-27
73Swedish Stickers-17
73Swedish Stickers-215
74O-Pee-Chee WHA-17
74Finnish Jenkki-25
74Finnish Typotor-96
74Swedish Stickers-23
74Swedish Stickers-219
74Swedish Semic World Champ Stickers-12
75O-Pee-Chee WHA-40
75O-Pee-Chee WHA-72
76O-Pee-Chee WHA-66
76O-Pee-Chee WHA-125
77O-Pee-Chee WHA-3
77Finnish Sportscasters-80-1911
78O-Pee-Chee-25
78Topps-25
79O-Pee-Chee-240
79Topps-240
80O-Pee-Chee-73
80O-Pee-Chee Super-15
80Topps-73
81O-Pee-Chee-225
81O-Pee-Chee-237
81O-Pee-Chee Stickers-166
81Topps-58
81Topps-E98
82O-Pee-Chee-225
83NHL Key Tags-88
83O-Pee-Chee-245
83O-Pee-Chee Stickers-215
83Puffy Stickers-19
83Topps Stickers-215
84O-Pee-Chee-143
84O-Pee-Chee Stickers-102
84Topps-107
85O-Pee-Chee Stickers-200
91Finnish Semic World Champ Stickers-235
91Swedish Semic World Champ Stickers-235
92Future Trends '76 Canada Cup-141
95Swedish Globe World Championships-70
97Swedish Alfabilder Autographs-10
01Swedish Alfabilder-10
04UD All-World-68
04UD All-World-111
Gold-68
Autographs-68
Autographs-111
06ITG International Ice-55
Gold-55
Autographs-AAH
06ITG Ultimate Memorabilia-6
Artist Proof-6

Hedberg, Goran
69Swedish Hockey-206

Hedberg, Jan
64Swedish Coralli ISHockey-137
65Swedish Coralli ISHockey-137

Hedberg, Johan
92Swedish Semic Elitserien Stickers-152
93Swedish Semic Elitserien-122
94Swedish Leaf-40
Clean Sweepers-7
95Swedish Leaf-61
Spidermen-7
95Swedish Upper Deck-94
95Swedish Globe World Championships-6
97Detroit Vipers-11
98Swedish UD Choice-117
Day in the Life-6
99Kentucky Thoroughblades-14
00BAP Memorabilia-502
00Titanium Draft Day Edition-176
00Titanium Draft Day Promos-176
00Upper Deck Ice-120
00Manitoba Moose-12
01Atomic-77
Blue-77
Gold-77
Premiere Date-77
Red-77
Rookie Reaction-9
Statosphere-8
Team Nucleus-11
01BAP Memorabilia-28
Emerald-28
Ruby-28
Sapphire-28
Goalies Jerseys-GJ9
Stanley Cup Playoffs-SC26
01BAP Signature Series-69
Autographs-69
Autographs Gold-69
01BAP Ultimate Mem Legend Terry Sawchuk-6
01Between the Pipes-42
01Between the Pipes-107
Double Memorabilia-DM3
Future Wave-FW1
Goalie Gear-GG5
He Shoots-He Saves Prizes-33
Jerseys-GJ9
Emblems-GUE4
Jersey and Stick Cards-GSJ8
Masks-26
Masks Silver-26
Masks Gold-26
Tandems-GT13
01Bowman YoungStars-79
Gold-79
Ice Cubed-79
01Crown Royale-114
Blue-114
Premiere Date-114
Red-114
Retail-114
Crowning Achievement-10
Rookie Royalty-17
01eTopps-7
01McDonald's Pacific-30
Glove-Side Net-Fusion-5
01O-Pee-Chee-294
01O-Pee-Chee Premier Parallel-294
01Pacific-452
01Pacific Adrenaline-151
Blue-151
Premiere Date-151
Red-151
Retail-151
Creased Lightning-17
Power Play-28
Rookie Report-16
01Pacific Arena Exclusives-452
01Pacific Heads-Up-76
Blue-76
Premiere Date-76
Red-76
Silver-76
Breaking the Glass-16
Prime Picks-6
Showstoppers-17
01Parkhurst-84
Gold-84
Silver-84
01Private Stock-108
Gold-108
Premiere Date-108
Retail-108
Silver-108
Moments in Time-10
01Private Stock Pacific Nights-108
01Private Stock PS-2002-102
01SP Authentic-70
Limited-70
Limited Gold-70
Sign of the Times-HE
Sign of the Times-HS
01SP Game Used-44
Tools of the Game-TJH
Tools of the Game-CTCH
Tools of the Game-CTHD
Tools of the Game-TTHCR
Tools of the Game-TTKCH
Tools of the Game Signed-STJH
Tools of the Game Signed-SCRH
01SPx-53
01Stadium Club-39
Award Winners-39
Master Photos-39
New Regime-NR10
New Regime-NRAJHE
01Titanium-111
Hobby Parallel-111
Premiere Date-111
Retail-111
Retail Parallel-111
01Titanium Draft Day Edition-78
01Topps-294
OPC Parallel-294
01Topps Chrome-146
Refractors-146
Black Border Refractors-146
01Topps Heritage-37
Refractors-37
Autographs-AJH
01Topps Reserve-35
01UD Challenge for the Cup-69
01UD Mask Collection-124
01UD Mask Collection-186
Gold-124
Gold-186
Goalie Pads-GPJH
01UD Playmakers-80
01UD Premier Collection Signatures-JH
01UD Premier Collection Signatures Black-JH
01UD Top Shelf-35
Goalie Gear-BJH
Goalie Gear-GGJH
Goalie Gear-LPJH
01Upper Deck-143
Exclusives-143
Goalies in Action-GL5
Last Line of Defense-LL7
01Upper Deck Ice-35
01Upper Deck MVP-152
Masked Men-MM7
01Upper Deck Victory-277
01Upper Deck Victory-385
Gold-277
Gold-385
01Upper Deck Vintage-202
01Upper Deck Vintage-208
01Vanguard-79
Blue-79
Red-79
East Meets West-4
One of Ones-79
Premiere Date-79
Proofs-79
Stonewallers-16
V-Team-8
02Atomic-79
Blue-79
Gold-79
Red-79
Hobby Parallel-79
02BAP First Edition-189
02BAP Memorabilia-107
Emerald-107
Ruby-107
Sapphire-107
NHL All-Star Game-107
NHL All-Star Game Blue-107
NHL All-Star Game Green-107
NHL All-Star Game Red-107
02BAP Memorabilia Toronto Fall Expo-107
02BAP Signature Series-22
Autographs-22
Autograph Buybacks 2001-69
Autographs Gold-22
Golf-GS44
Team Quads-TQ8
02BAP Ultimate Memorabilia Number Ones-5
02BAP Ultimate Memorabilia Numerology-1
02Between the Pipes-40
02Between the Pipes-144
Gold-40
Silver-40
Behind the Mask-15
Blockers-9
Complete Package-CP6
Double Memorabilia-15
Emblems-17
Future Wave-7
Goalie Autographs-7
He Shoots-He Saves Points-4
He Shoots-He Saves Prizes-14
Jerseys-17
Masks II-23
Masks II Gold-23
Masks II Silver-23
Numbers-17
Stick and Jerseys-17
Tandems-7
Trappers-GT5
02Bowman YoungStars-63
Gold-63
Silver-63
02Crown Royale-76
Blue-76
Red-76
Retail-76
02ITG Used-61
02ITG Used-161
International Experience-IE26
International Experience Gold-IE26
02O-Pee-Chee-106
02O-Pee-Chee Premier Blue Parallel-106
02O-Pee-Chee Premier Red Parallel-106
02O-Pee-Chee Factory Set-106
02Pacific-307
Blue-307
Red-307
02Pacific Complete-188
Red-188
02Pacific Exclusive-136
02Pacific Heads-Up-98
Blue-98
Purple-98
Red-98
Quad Jerseys-22
Quad Jerseys-31
Quad Jerseys Gold-22
Quad Jerseys Gold-31
02Pacific Quest for the Cup-79
Gold-79
02Parkhurst-69
Bronze-69
Gold-69
Silver-69
Teammates-TT14
02Parkhurst Retro-112
Minis-112
02Private Stock Reserve-79
Blue-79
Red-79
Retail-79
02Stadium Club-68
Silver Decoy Cards-68
Proofs-68
02Titanium-80
Blue-80
Red-80
Retail-80
Jerseys-53
Jerseys Retail-53
Patches-53
02Topps-106
OPC Blue Parallel-106
OPC Red Parallel-106
Factory Set-106
02Topps Chrome-67
Black Border Refractors-67
Refractors-67
02Topps Heritage-56
Chrome Parallel-56
02Topps Total-371
02UD Artistic Impressions-71
Gold-71
02UD Artistic Impressions Beckett Promos-71
02UD Artistic Impressions Retrospectives-R71
02UD Artistic Impressions Retrospect Gold-R71
02UD Artistic Impress Retrospect Silver-R71
02UD Mask Collection-68
02UD Mask Collection-69
02UD Mask Collection-70
02UD Mask Collection-71
02UD Mask Collection-101
02UD Mask Collection Beckett Promos-68
02UD Mask Collection Beckett Promos-69
02UD Mask Collection Beckett Promos-70
02UD Mask Collection Beckett Promos-71
02UD Mask Collection Masked Marvels-MMJH
02UD Mask Collection Mini Masks-JH
02UD Mask Collection Patches-PWJH
02UD Mask Collection View from the Cage-VJH
02UD Piece of History-73
02UD Top Shelf-70
Signatures-JH
02Upper Deck-143
Exclusives-143
02Upper Deck Classic Portraits-79
02Upper Deck MVP-146
Gold-146
Classics-146
Golden Classics-146
02Upper Deck Victory-170
Bronze-170
Gold-170
Silver-170
02Upper Deck Vintage-203
02Upper Deck Vintage-284
Green Backs-203
Tall Boys-T53
Tall Boys Gold-T53
02Vanguard-79
LTD-79
Jerseys-36
Jerseys Gold-36
03BAP Memorabilia-127
Emerald-127
Gold-127
Ruby-127
Sapphire-127
Deep in the Crease-D10
Masks III-14
Masks III Gold-14
Masks III Silver-14
Masks III Memorabilia-14
03BAP Ultimate Memorabilia Autographs-66
Gold-66
03BAP Ultimate Mem Auto Jerseys-66
03Beehive-193
Gold-193
Silver-193
Sticks Beige Border-BE8
03Black Diamond-47
Black-47
Green-47
Red-47
03Canucks Postcards-9
03Canucks Sav-on-Foods-2
03ITG Action-471
Jerseys-M108
03ITG Used Signature Series Autographs-JHE
03ITG Used Sig Series Autographs Gold-JHE
03NHL Sticker Collection-120
03O-Pee-Chee-206
03OPC Blue-206
03OPC Gold-206
03OPC Red-206
03Pacific-271
Blue-271
Red-271
03Pacific Complete-424
Red-424
03Pacific Exhibit-117
Blue Backs-117
Yellow Backs-117
03Pacific Invincible-95
Blue-95
Red-95
Retail-95
Jerseys-24
03Pacific Prism-80
Blue-80
Gold-80
Red-80
03SP Game Used Game Gear-GGJH
03SPx-95
Radiance-95
Spectrum-95
03Topps-206
Blue-206
Gold-206
Red-206
03Topps Pristine-36
Gold Refractor Die Cuts-36
Refractors-36
Press Plates Black-36
Press Plates Cyan-36
Press Plates Magenta-36
Press Plates Yellow-36
03Topps Traded-TT31
Blue-TT31
Gold-TT31
Red-TT31
03UD Honor Roll-85
03Upper Deck-436
Canadian Exclusives-436
HG-436
UD Exclusives-436
Classic Portraits Starring Cast-SC-JH
03Upper Deck MVP-341
Gold Script-341
Silver Script-341
Canadian Exclusives-341
SportsNut-SN70
03Upper Deck Victory-152
Bronze-152
Gold-152
Silver-152
04Swedish Alfabilder Alfa Stars-1
04Swedish Alfabilder Autographs-109
04Swedish Alfabilder Limited Autographs-109
04Swedish Alfabilder Proof Parallels-1
05Parkhurst-151
Facsimile Auto Parallel-151
05Upper Deck-308
05Upper Deck MVP-136
Gold-136
Platinum-136
06Between The Pipes The Mask-M38
06Between The Pipes The Mask Gold-M38
06Between The Pipes The Mask Silver-M38
06O-Pee-Chee-26
Rainbow-26
06Upper Deck-262
Exclusives Parallel-262
High Gloss Parallel-262
Masterpieces-262
06Upper Deck MVP-19
Gold Script-19
Super Script-19

Hedberg, Jon
99Guelph Storm-7

Hedberg, Niclas
99Finnish Cardset-207
00Finnish Cardset-8
01Finnish Cardset-5

Hedberg, Ove
65Swedish Coralli ISHockey-44
67Swedish Hockey-30
69Swedish Hockey-43

Hedbys, Gunnar
57Swedish Alfabilder-86

Hede, Niklas
94Finnish SISU-328
95Finnish SISU-223
96German DEL-43
98German DEL-161
99German DEL-271
00Finnish Cardset-230
05German DEL-326

Hedell, Jan
85Swedish Panini Stickers-182
86Swedish Panini Stickers-114
87Swedish Panini Stickers-113

Hedenstrom, Lars
64Swedish Coralli ISHockey-83
65Swedish Coralli ISHockey-83
67Swedish Hockey-46
69Swedish Hockey-60
70Swedish Hockey-21

Hedenstrom, Per
83Swedish Semic Elitserien-64
84Swedish Semic Elitserien-64
85Swedish Panini Stickers-56

Hedges, Jason
03Yarmouth Mariners-10

Hedican, Bret
92Parkhurst-385
Emerald Ice-385
92Pinnacle-228
French-228
92Pro Set-240
92Score-471
Canadian-471
92Stadium Club-203
92Topps-517
Gold-517G
92Upper Deck-414
92Classic-87
Gold-87
93Donruss-291
93Leaf-286
93OPC Premier-224
Gold-224
93Parkhurst-177
Emerald Ice-177
93Pinnacle-315
Canadian-315
93PowerPlay-210
93Stadium Club-81
Members Only Master Set-81
OPC-81
First Day Issue-81
First Day Issue OPC-81
93Topps/OPC Premier-224
Gold-224
93Ultra-66
93Upper Deck-185
94Leaf-425
94OPC Premier-162
Special Effects-162
94Parkhurst-243
Gold-243
94Pinnacle-369
Artist's Proofs-369
Rink Collection-369
94Stadium Club-27
Members Only Master Set-27
First Day Issue-27
Super Team Winner Cards-27
94Topps/OPC Premier-162
Special Effects-162
94Ultra-224
94Upper Deck-398
Electric Ice-398
95Be A Player-19
Signatures-S19
Signatures Die Cuts-S19
95Canucks Building the Dream Art-3
95Collector's Choice-255
Player's Club-255
Player's Club Platinum-255
95Parkhurst International-216
Emerald Ice-216
95Playoff One on One-317
95Topps-72
OPC Inserts-72
95Ultra-316
95Upper Deck-95
Electric Ice-95
Electric Ice Gold-95
96Canucks Postcards-3
96Upper Deck-173
97Pacific-284
Copper-284
Emerald Green-284
Ice Blue-284
Red-284
Silver-284
97SP Authentic-158
98OPC Chrome-81
Refractors-81
98Pacific-426
Ice Blue-426
Red-426
98Pacific Omega-102
Red-102
Opening Day Issue-102
98Topps-81
O-Pee-Chee-81
98Upper Deck-196
Exclusives-196
Exclusives 1 of 1-196
Gold Reserve-196
99Upper Deck Victory-126
00Panthers Team Issue-10
00Upper Deck MVP-78
First Stars-78
Second Stars-78
Third Stars-78
01O-Pee-Chee-258
01O-Pee-Chee Premier Parallel-258
01Topps-258
OPC Parallel-258
01Upper Deck Vintage-110
02Pacific-66
Blue-66
Red-66
02Pacific Complete-356
Red-356
02Topps Total-136
02Upper Deck-275
Exclusives-275
02Upper Deck Beckett UD Promos-275
03Hurricanes Postcards-10
03ITG Action-189
03NHL Sticker Collection-38
03Pacific Complete-332
Red-332
03Upper Deck-281
Canadian Exclusives-281
HG-281
UD Exclusives-281
05Be A Player Signatures-HE
05Be A Player Signatures Gold-HE
05Parkhurst-94
Facsimile Auto Parallel-94
05Upper Deck-32
HG Glossy-32
05Upper Deck MVP-82
Gold-82
Platinum-82
05Upper Deck Toronto Fall Expo-32
06Hurricanes Postcards-12
06O-Pee-Chee-103
Rainbow-103
06Panini Stickers-48

Hedican, Tom
93London Knights-27

Hedin, Pierre
97Black Diamond-36
Double Diamond-36
Triple Diamond-36
Quadruple Diamond-36
97Swedish Collector's Choice-150
98UD Choice-291
Prime Choice Reserve-291
Reserve-291
98Swedish UD Choice-167
98Swedish UD Choice-216
99Swedish Upper Deck-169
99Swedish Upper Deck-213
00Swedish Upper Deck-152
02Swedish SHL-79
Parallel-79
Team Captains-8
03Pacific Complete-506
Red-506
04Swedish Elitset-242
Gold-242
04Swedish MoDo Postcards-15
05German DEL-248

Hedin, Thomas
83Swedish Semic Elitserien-46
84Swedish Semic Elitserien-46
86Swedish Panini Stickers-233
87Swedish Panini Stickers-225

Hedington, Steve
83Oshawa Generals-10
86Sudbury Wolves-14

Hedlund, Anders
65Swedish Coralli ISHockey-166
71Swedish Hockey-343

Hedlund, Andy
02Trenton Titans-A-3
03Binghamton Senators-7
04Binghamton Senators-6
04Binghamton Senators Hess-8
05German DEL-238
Defender-DF07
06German DEL All-Star Jerseys-AS6
06Binghamton Senators-9
06Binghamton Senators 5th Anniversary-12

Hedlund, Henrik
64Swedish Coralli ISHockey-144
65Swedish Coralli ISHockey-144
67Swedish Hockey-287
69Swedish Hockey-334
70Swedish Hockey-252
71Swedish Hockey-311
72Swedish Stickers-294
73Swedish Stickers-141
74Swedish Stickers-220

Hedlund, Karl-Soren
64Swedish Coralli ISHockey-138
65Swedish Coralli ISHockey-201
67Swedish Hockey-269
69Swedish Hockey-314
70Swedish Hockey-216

Hedlund, Leif
83Swedish Semic Elitserien-190
84Swedish Semic Elitserien-213

Hedlund, Magnus
02Swedish SHL-86
Next Generation-NG3
Parallel-86
03Swedish Elite-102
Silver-102
04Swedish Elitset-99
Gold-99
04Swedish MoDo Postcards-24
05Swedish SHL Elitset-214
Gold-214

Hedlund, Mattias
93Swedish Semic Elitserien-4
98Swedish UD Choice-19
00Swedish Upper Deck-16
03Swedish Bjorkloven Umea-2

Hedlund, Soren
56Swedish Alfabilder-60

Hedlund, Tommy
89Swedish Semic Elitserien Stickers-10
95Swedish Leaf-160
95Swedish Upper Deck-7

Hedman, Anton
05Sudbury Wolves-13
06Guelph Storm-14
06Owen Sound Attack-20

Hedman, Glenn
89Swedish Semic Elitserien Stickers-200
93Swedish Semic Elitserien-11

Hedman, Kjell
67Swedish Hockey-31
69Swedish Hockey-44
70Swedish Hockey-2

Hedman, Oscar
04Swedish Elitset-241
Gold-241
04Swedish MoDo Postcards-27
05Swedish SHL Elitset-96
Gold-96
Series One Signatures-5
Star Potential-12
06Swedish SHL Elitset-107

Hedqvist, Nils-Arne
71Swedish Hockey-335
72Swedish Stickers-149
74Swedish Stickers-221

Hedson, David
72Sargent Promotions Stamps-134

Hedstrom, Jonathan
99Swedish Upper Deck-142
99Swedish Upper Deck-211
00Swedish Upper Deck-127
SHL Signatures-JO
Top Draws-T8
02BAP Memorabilia-339
02BAP Ultimate Memorabilia-99
02SP Authentic-170
02UD Artistic Impressions-91
Gold-91
02UD Honor Roll-145
02UD Mask Collection-122
02UD Premier Collection-97
Gold-97
02Swedish SHL-62
Parallel-62
Signatures Series II-13
02AHL Top Prospects-18
02Cincinnati Mighty Ducks-A-5
03Swedish Elite-162
Silver-162
04Swedish Elitset-288
Gold-288
04Swedish Pure Skills-96
Parallel-96
Signatures-14
05Ducks Team Issue-8
05Parkhurst-9
Facsimile Auto Parallel-9
05Swedish SHL Elitset-144
06Swedish SHL Elitset-288
Performers-18

Hedstrom, Kjell-Ake
67Swedish Hockey-186

Heed, Jonas
84Swedish Semic Elitserien-229
85Swedish Panini Stickers-225
86Swedish Panini Stickers-255
87Swedish Panini Stickers-237
89Swedish Semic Elitserien Stickers-221
90Swedish Semic Elitserien Stickers-30
91Swedish Semic Elitserien Stickers-280
92Swedish Semic Elitserien Stickers-305
97Swedish Collector's Choice-170

Heed, Klas
85Swedish Panini Stickers-185
86Swedish Panini Stickers-116
89Swedish Semic Elitserien Stickers-102
90Swedish Semic Elitserien Stickers-105
91Swedish Semic Elitserien Stickers-109
92Swedish Semic Elitserien Stickers-128

Heeney, Bob
85Brandon Wheat Kings-4

Heerema, Jeff
98Bowman's Best-147
Refractors-147
Atomic Refractors-147
98Finest Futures Finest-F9
98Finest Futures Finest Refractors-F9
98OPC Chrome-233
Refractors-233
98Topps-233
O-Pee-Chee-233
98Bowman CHL-146
Golden Anniversary-146
OPC International-146
Autographs Blue-A31
Autographs Gold-A31
Autographs Silver-A31
98Bowman Chrome CHL-146
Golden Anniversary-146
Golden Anniversary Refractors-146
OPC International-146
OPC International Refractors-146
Refractors-146
99Black Diamond-110
Diamond Cut-110
Final Cut-110
99Upper Deck-333
Exclusives-333
Exclusives 1 of 1-333
99Upper Deck Gold Reserve-333
99Upper Deck Ovation-65
Standing Ovation-65
00Cincinnati Cyclones-8
02Pacific Calder-61
Silver-61
02Pacific Complete-536
Red-536
02AHL Top Prospects-19
02Lowell Lock Monsters-10
03Blues Team Set-9
03Pacific-62
Blue-62
Red-62
03Hartford Wolf Pack-8
04Manitoba Moose-7
05Binghamton Senators-3
05Binghamton Senators Quickway-3
06Binghamton Senators-10
06Binghamton Senators 5th Anniversary-13

Heerema, Jesse
03Missouri River Otters-4

Heffernan, Gerry
34Beehive Group I Photos-158
43Parade Sportive *-53

Heffernan, Jimmy
37V356 Worldwide Gum-130

Heffernan, Scott
00Sarnia Sting-14
01St. Michaels Majors-4

Heffler, Eric
99Hamilton Bulldogs-24
01BC Icemen-11
03BAP Memorabilia-222

Heffler, Zsolt
94German First League-413

Hefford, Jayna
97Collector's Choice-289
04Canadian Womens World Championship Team-10
06ITG Going For Gold-14
06ITG Going For Gold Samples-14
06ITG Going For Gold Autographs-AH
06ITG Going For Gold Jerseys-GUJ14

Hefford, Warren
99Sudbury Wolves-16

Hegberg, Jason
96Lethbridge Hurricanes-5
97Lethbridge Hurricanes-5
99Lethbridge Hurricanes-11

Hegberg, Rob
94Prince Albert Raiders-6

Hegegy, Alexander
06Czech OFS-157

Hegen, Dieter
83Swedish Semic VM Stickers-115
89Swedish Semic World Champ Stickers-114
91Finnish Semic World Champ Stickers-173
91Swedish Semic World Champ Stickers-173
92Upper Deck-370
93Swedish Semic World Champ Stickers-158
94Finnish Jaa Kiekko-287
94German DEL-311
95German DEL-94
95German DEL-433
95Swedish Globe World Championships-225
95Swedish World Championships Stickers-70
96German DEL-281
96Swedish Semic Wien-198
98German DEL-292
98German DEL-338
99German DEL-254

Hegen, Gerhard
94German DEL-169
95German DEL-148

Hegland, Amber
98Minnesota Golden Gophers Women-8

Hegland, Jackson
99Columbus Cottonmouths-22

Hehr, Jason
92Northern Michigan Wildcats-11
93Northern Michigan Wildcats-13

Heick, Dirk
94German First League-179

Heickert, Robert
03Brampton Batallion-7

Heid, Chris
99Spokane Chiefs-10
00Spokane Chiefs-8
01Spokane Chiefs-10
02Spokane Chiefs-7
03Houston Aeros-10

Heidt, Michael
89Swedish Semic World Champ Stickers-113
91Finnish Semic World Champ Stickers-159
91Swedish Semic World Champ Stickers-159
92Finnish Semic-174
93Swedish Semic World Champ Stickers-151
94German DEL-275
95German DEL-246
96German DEL-138

Heidt, Robert
94German DEL-24
95German DEL-21

Heikkaranta, Aarno
65Finnish Hellas-55

Heikkeri, Esko
80Finnish Mallasjuoma-147

Heikkeri, Pertti
80Finnish Mallasjuoma-146

Heikkila, Antti

65Finnish Hellas-36
66Finnish Jaakiekkosarja-47
70Finnish Jaakiekko-191
71Finnish Suomi Stickers-82
72Finnish Jaakiekko-245
72Finnish Panda Toronto-35
73Finnish Jaakiekko-243
74Finnish Typotor-43
78Finnish SM-Liiga-63
78Finnish SM-Liiga-221
80Finnish Mallasjuoma-39
80Finnish Mallasjuoma-200

Heikkila, Kari
71Finnish Suomi Stickers-339
80Finnish Mallasjuoma-29
82Swedish Semic VM Stickers-28
84Swedish Semic Elitserien-175
85Swedish Panini Stickers-161

Heikkila, Lasse
65Finnish Hellas-37

Heikkila, Matti
78Finnish SM-Liiga-77
80Finnish Mallasjuoma-53

Heikkinen, Eetu
06Finnish Cardset-348
06Finnish Porin Assat Pelaajakortit-11

Heikkinen, Ilkka
05Finnish Cardset -104
06Finnish Cardset-109

Heikkinen, Kari
91Finnish Jyvas-Hyva Stickers-56
92Finnish Jyvas-Hyva Stickers-164
93Finnish Jyvas-Hyva Stickers-292
93Finnish SISU-70
94Finnish SISU-11

Heikkinen, Markku
92Finnish Jyvas-Hyva Stickers-77
93Finnish Jyvas-Hyva Stickers-136
93Finnish SISU-139
94Finnish SISU-3

Heikkinen, Pertti
66Finnish Jaakiekkosarja-120

Heikkonen, Hannu
66Finnish Jaakiekkosarja-163

Heil, Jeff
97Charlotte Checkers-12
98Charlotte Checkers-8

Heiland, Jason
94Central Hockey League-10
94Dallas Freeze-10

Heim, Axel
93Swiss HNL-98
95Swiss HNL-73
96Swiss HNL-190
98Swiss Power Play Stickers-238
99Swiss Panini Stickers-191
00Swiss Panini Stickers-236
00Swiss Slapshot Mini-Cards-RJ11
01Swiss HNL-158
02Swiss HNL-98

Heimo, Heikki
65Finnish Hellas-15

Heinanen, Jokke
93Finnish Jyvas-Hyva Stickers-352
93Finnish SISU-224
94Finnish SISU-116
94Finnish SISU Junior-2
95Finnish SISU-356
95Finnish SISU Limited-24
95Finnish SISU Painkillers-1
95Swedish World Championships Stickers-181
96Finnish SISU Redline-154
98Finnish Kerailysarja-262
99Finnish Cardset-290

Heindl, Bill
69Swedish Hockey-355

Heine, Pete
92Wheeling Thunderbirds-8

Heine, Thorsten
02German Berlin Polar Bears Postcards-11

Heiniger, Mario
02Swiss HNL-223

Heinisch, Martin
04Czech OFS-387

Heinisto, Pasi
92Finnish Jyvas-Hyva Stickers-115
93Finnish SISU-269
94Finnish SISU-288

Heino, Aki
98Finnish Kerailysarja-53
99Finnish Cardset-31
03Finnish Cardset-32
04Finnish Cardset-314

Heino, Heikko
66Finnish Jaakiekkosarja-73

Heino, Henri
05Finnish Cardset -119
06Finnish Cardset-130

Heino, Kimmo
65Finnish Hellas-130
70Finnish Jaakiekko-104
71Finnish Suomi Stickers-112
72Finnish Jaakiekko-82
72Finnish Panda Toronto-3
73Finnish Jaakiekko-128

Heino, Timo
78Finnish SM-Liiga-129
80Finnish Mallasjuoma-87

Heino-Lindberg, Christopher
05Swedish SHL Elitset-181
Gold-181
Rookies-3
06Swedish SHL Elitset-183
Goal Patrol-6

Heinola, Arto
87Swedish Panini Stickers-267

Heinold, Peter
94German DEL-434

Heinonen, Ismo
71Finnish Suomi Stickers-361

Heinonen, Markku
72Finnish Jaakiekko-301

Heinonen, Mauri
72Finnish Jaakiekko-302

Heinonen, Raine
73Finnish Jaakiekko-216

Heinonen, Rauno
65Finnish Hellas-9
65Finnish Hellas-99
66Finnish Jaakiekkosarja-72
70Finnish Jaakiekko-155

Heinonen, Reijo
71Finnish Suomi Stickers-85
72Finnish Jaakiekko-246
72Finnish Panda Toronto-36
73Finnish Jaakiekko-244
74Finnish Typotor-44

Heinonen, Sami
03Finnish Cardset-2

Heinrich, Alexander
05German DEL-198

Heinrich, Jamie
01Swiss HNL-294
02Swiss HNL-358

Heinrich, Lionel
55Bruins Photos-7

Heinrichs, Marco
94German DEL-213
99German Bundesliga 2-11

Heins, Shawn
91Peterborough Petes-25
917th Inn. Sketch OHL-131
92Windsor Spitfires-27
99BAP Memorabilia-227
Gold-227
Silver-227
99Pacific-385
Copper-385
Emerald Green-385
Gold-385
Ice Blue-385
Premiere Date-385
Red-385
99Kentucky Thoroughblades-15
00Stadium Club-233
00Topps Premier Plus-91
Blue Ice-91
03Chicago Wolves-11
04German Berlin Polar Bears Postcards-13
04German DEL-68
05German DEL-127
Defender-DF08

Heintz, Davin
00Saskatoon Blades-14
01Saskatoon Blades-6
03Swift Current Broncos-4

Heintz, Dustan
98Swift Current Broncos-23
04Atlantic City Boardwalk Bullies-10

Heinvirta, Risto
66Finnish Jaakiekkosarja-94

Heinze, Steve
91Parkhurst-232
French-232
92O-Pee-Chee-92
92OPC Premier-24
92Parkhurst-247
Emerald Ice-247
92Pro Set-220
92Score-476
Canadian-476
92Stadium Club-166
92Topps-519
Gold-519G
92Ultra-3
92Upper Deck-400
Ameri/Can Holograms-3
93Leaf-116
93OPC Premier-378
Gold-378
93Pinnacle-53
Canadian-53
93PowerPlay-289
93Score-251
Canadian-251
93Stadium Club-15
Members Only Master Set-15
OPC-15
First Day Issue-15
First Day Issue OPC-15
93Topps/OPC Premier-378
Gold-378
94Be A Player Signature Cards-161
94Canada Games NHL POGS-348
94Leaf-404
94OPC Premier-387
Special Effects-387
94Pinnacle-341
Artist's Proofs-341
Rink Collection-341
94Stadium Club-137
Members Only Master Set-137
First Day Issue-137
Super Team Winner Cards-137
94Topps/OPC Premier-387
Special Effects-387
94Upper Deck-327
Electric Ice-327
95Summit-87
Artist's Proofs-87
Ice-87
95Topps-278
OPC Inserts-278
95Upper Deck-293
Electric Ice-293
Electric Ice Gold-293
96Be A Player-154
Autographs-154
Autographs Silver-154
97Collector's Choice-20
97Pacific-261
Copper-261
Emerald Green-261
Ice Blue-261
Red-261
Silver-261
97Score Bruins-10
Platinum-10
Premier-10
98Be A Player-157
Press Release-157
98BAP Gold-157
98BAP Autographs-157
98BAP Autographs Gold-157
98Pacific-79
Ice Blue-79
Red-79
98Pacific Omega-15
Red-15
Opening Day Issue-15
98Upper Deck-42
Exclusives-42
Exclusives 1 of 1-42
Gold Reserve-42
99O-Pee-Chee-56
99O-Pee-Chee Chrome-56
99O-Pee-Chee Chrome Refractors-56
99Pacific-24
Copper-24
Emerald Green-24
Gold-24
Ice Blue-24
Premiere Date-24
Red-24
99Paramount-21
Copper-21
Emerald-21
Gold-21
Holographic Emerald-21
Holographic Gold-21
Holographic Silver-21
Ice Blue-21
Premiere Date-21
Red-21
Silver-21
99Topps/OPC-56
99Topps/OPC Chrome-56
Refractors-56
99Upper Deck MVP SC Edition-20
Gold Script-20
Silver Script-20
Super Script-20
00Pacific-35
Copper-35
Gold-35
Ice Blue-35
Premiere Date-35
00Paramount-70
Copper-70
Gold-70
Holo-Gold-70
Holo-Silver-70
Ice Blue-70
Premiere Date-70
00UD Reserve-26
00Upper Deck-280
Exclusives Tier 1-280
Exclusives Tier 2-280
00Upper Deck Vintage-106
01Crown Royale-68
Blue-68
Premiere Date-68
Red-68
Retail-68
01O-Pee-Chee-239
01O-Pee-Chee Premier Parallel-239
01Pacific-51
Extreme LTD-51
Hobby LTD-51
Premiere Date-51
Retail LTD-51
01Pacific Arena Exclusives-51
01Pacific Heads-Up-45
Blue-45
Premiere Date-45
Red-45
Silver-45
01Parkhurst-246
01Titanium-65
Hobby Parallel-65
Premiere Date-65
Retail-65
Retail Parallel-65
01Topps-239
OPC Parallel-239
01Upper Deck-313
Exclusives-313
02BAP Sig Series Auto Buybacks 1998-157
02O-Pee-Chee-77
02O-Pee-Chee Premier Blue Parallel-77
02O-Pee-Chee Premier Red Parallel-77
02O-Pee-Chee Factory Set-77
02Pacific-166
Blue-166
Red-166
02Topps-77
OPC Blue Parallel-77
OPC Red Parallel-77
Factory Set-77
02Manchester Monarchs-8

Heinzle, Karl
94Finnish Jaa Kiekko-248
95Austrian National Team-8

Heinzman, Franziskus
99Swiss Panini Stickers-358

Heisig, Branjo
94German DEL-394
95German DEL-164
96German DEL-238

Heiskala, Earl
61Hamilton Red Wings-8
69O-Pee-Chee-170
70Esso Power Players-212
70Flyers Postcards-5
70O-Pee-Chee-193
72Los Angeles Sharks WHA-6

Heiskanen, Arto
92Finnish Jyvas-Hyva Stickers-194
93Finnish Jyvas-Hyva Stickers-347
93Finnish SISU-230
94Finnish SISU-30
95Finnish SISU-176
95Finnish SISU Limited-27

Heiskanen, Mikko
06Finnish Cardset-295

Heiskanen, Santeri
99Finnish Cardset-20
00Finnish Cardset-162
03Finnish Cardset-116
04Finnish Cardset-125
05Finnish Cardset -115

Heisler, Jake
93Quebec Pee-Wee Tournament-857

Heiss, Joseph
91Finnish Semic World Champ Stickers-153
91Swedish Semic World Champ Stickers-153
92Finnish Semic-172
94Finnish Jaa Kiekko-272
94German DEL-200
95Finnish Semic World Championships-165
95German DEL-195
95German DEL-429
95Swedish Globe World Championships-218
95Swedish World Championships Stickers-51
96German DEL-338
98German DEL-93
98German DEL-325
99German DEL-101
00German DEL-135

Heistad, Jeramie
917th Inn. Sketch WHL-324

Heisten, Barrett
98Black Diamond-116
Double Diamond-116
Triple Diamond-116
Quadruple Diamond-116
98SPx Top Prospects-85
Radiance-85
Spectrum-85
00UD CHL Prospects-64
Supremacy-CS7
01BAP Signature Series-218
Autographs-218
Autographs Gold-218
01Parkhurst-265
01Parkhurst Beckett Promos-265
01Stadium Club-114
Award Winners-114
Master Photos-114
01Upper Deck-348
Exclusives-348
01Upper Deck Ice-108
01Hartford Wolf Pack-8
02BAP Sig Series Auto Buybacks 2001-218
02Utah Grizzlies-9

Heisten, Chris
03Florida Everblades-8

Heitsenrether, John
92Quebec Pee-Wee Tournament-1442
93Quebec Pee-Wee Tournament-787

Heittola, Steve
83Pinebridge Bucks-6

Heitzer, Christian
94German First League-345

Heiz, Patrice
93Swiss HNL-277

Hejcik, Franz
94German First League-335

Hejda, Jan
97Czech APS Extraliga-157
98Czech DS Stickers-194
98Czech OFS-253
99Czech OFS-383
00Czech OFS-90
01Czech OFS-271
02Czech OFS Plus-236
02Czech National Team-2
03Czech OFS Plus All-Star Game-H28
03Czech OFS Plus MS Praha-SE33
03Czech National Team Postcards-2
03Russian Hockey League-219
04Czech World Championship Postcards-7
04Russian Legion-23
05Czech World Champions Postcards-23
05Czech Kvarteto Bonaparte-3c
05Czech Pexeso Mini Blue Set-7
05Czech Pexeso Mini Red Set-6
06Hot Prospects-157
Red Hot-157
White Hot-157
06O-Pee-Chee-577
Rainbow-577
06SP Authentic-242
Limited-242
06The Cup Masterpiece Pressplates (Marquee Rookies)-577
06The Cup Masterpiece Pressplates (SP Authentic)-242
06The Cup Masterpiece Pressplates (Victory)-322
06Upper Deck-469
Exclusives Parallel-469
High Gloss Parallel-469
Masterpieces-469
Victory-322
06Czech IIHF World Championship Postcards-5

Hejduk, Milan
94Czech APS Extraliga-34
95Czech APS Extraliga-330
95Signature Rookies-52A
95Signature Rookies-52B
Signatures-69
96Czech APS Extraliga-157
97Czech APS Extraliga-255
97Czech DS Extraliga-70
97Czech DS Stickers-259
98Avalanche Team Issue-4
98Be A Player-187
Press Release-187
98BAP Gold-187
98BAP Autographs-187
98BAP Autographs Gold-187
98Bowman's Best-110
Refractors-110
Atomic Refractors-110
98Crown Royale-34
Limited Series-34
Rookie Class-2
98Pacific Dynagon Ice-48
Blue-48
Red-48
Rookies-2
98Pacific Omega-67
Red-67
Opening Day Issue-67
98Revolution-36
Ice Shadow-36
Red-36
98SP Authentic-95
Power Shift-95
98SPx Top Prospects-16
Radiance-16
Spectrum-16
98Topps Gold Label Class 1-90
Black-90
Black One of One-90
One of One-90
Red-90
Red One of One-90
98Topps Gold Label Class 2-90
98Topps Gold Label Class 2 Black-90
98Topps Gold Label Class 2 Black 1 of 1-90
98Topps Gold Label Class 2 One of One-90
98Topps Gold Label Class 2 Red-90
98Topps Gold Label Class 2 Red One of One-90
98Topps Gold Label Class 3-90
98Topps Gold Label Class 3 Black-90
98Topps Gold Label Class 3 Black 1 of 1-90
98Topps Gold Label Class 3 One of One-90
98Topps Gold Label Class 3 Red-90
98Topps Gold Label Class 3 Red One of One-90
98Upper Deck-247
Exclusives-247
Exclusives 1 of 1-247
Gold Reserve-247
98Upper Deck MVP-55
Gold Script-55
Silver Script-55
Super Script-55
98Czech DS Stickers-136
98Czech OFS-249
98Czech Bonaparte-1D
98Czech Pexeso-4
99Aurora-39
Premiere Date-39
99Avalanche Pins-8
99Avalanche Team Issue-9
99BAP Memorabilia-130
Gold-130
Silver-130
99BAP Millennium-70
Emerald-70
Ruby-70
Sapphire-70
Signatures-70
Signatures Gold-70
99Black Diamond-28
Diamond Cut-28
Final Cut-28
99Crown Royale-38
Limited Series-38
Premiere Date-38
Ice Elite-6
Ice Elite Parallel-6
99Kraft Overtime Winners-6
99Kraft Whiz Kid-1
99McDonald's Upper Deck-MCD19
99O-Pee-Chee-88
99O-Pee-Chee Autographs-TA7
99O-Pee-Chee Chrome-88
99O-Pee-Chee Chrome Refractors-88
99O-Pee-Chee Chrome Ice Futures-IF5
99O-Pee-Chee Chrome Ice Futures Refractor-IF5
99O-Pee-Chee Ice Futures-IF5
99Pacific-106
Copper-106
Gold Crown Die-Cuts-10
99Pacific Dynagon Ice-57
Blue-57
Copper-57
Gold-57
Premiere Date-57
99Pacific Omega-63
Copper-63
Gold-63
Ice Blue-63
Premiere Date-63
NHL Generations-2
99Pacific Prism-39
Holographic Blue-39
Holographic Gold-39
Holographic Mirror-39
Holographic Purple-39
Premiere Date-39
99Panini Stickers-212
99Paramount-64
Copper-64
Emerald-64
Gold-64
Holographic Emerald-64
Holographic Gold-64
Holographic Silver-64
Ice Blue-64
Premiere Date-64
Red-64
Silver-64
99Revolution-40
Premiere Date-40
Red-40
Shadow Series-40
Top of the Line-25
Copper-40
Gold-40
CSC Silver-40
99SP Authentic-22
Tomorrow's Headliners-TH4
99SPx-46
Radiance-46
Spectrum-46
99Stadium Club-60
First Day Issue-60
One of a Kind-60
Printing Plates Black-60
Printing Plates Cyan-60
Printing Plates Magenta-60
Printing Plates Yellow-60
Capture the Action-CA3
Capture the Action Game View-CAG3
99Topps/OPC-88
Autographs-TA7
Ice Futures-IF5
99Topps/OPC Chrome-88
Refractors-88
Ice Futures-IF5
Ice Futures Refractors-IF5
99Topps Gold Label Fresh Gold-FG10
99Topps Gold Label Fresh Gold Black-FG10
99Topps Gold Label Fresh Gold Black 1of1-FG10
99Topps Gold Label Fresh Gold One of One-FG10
99Topps Gold Label Fresh Gold Red-FG10
99Topps Gold Label Fresh Gold Red 1 of 1-FG10
99Topps Premier Plus-81
Parallel-81
The Next Ones-TNO8
99Ultimate Victory-22
1/1-22
Parallel-22
Parallel 100-22
99Upper Deck-42
Exclusives-42
Exclusives 1 of 1-42
New Ice Age-N14
New Ice Age Quantum Gold-N14
New Ice Age Quantum Silver-N14
99Upper Deck Century Legends-75
Century Collection-75
99Upper Deck Gold Reserve-42
99Upper Deck MVP-58
Gold Script-58
Silver Script-58
Super Script-58
99Upper Deck MVP SC Edition-50
Gold Script-50
Silver Script-50
Super Script-50
Cup Contenders-CC3
99Upper Deck Victory-80
99Upper Deck Victory-351
99Wayne Gretzky Hockey-48
00Aurora-39
Pinstripes-39
Pinstripes Premiere Date-39
Premiere Date-39
Scouting Reports-6
00BAP Memorabilia-239
Emerald-239
Ruby-239
Sapphire-239
Promos-239
00BAP Mem Chicago Sportsfest Copper-239
00BAP Memorabilia Chicago Sportsfest Blue-239
00BAP Memorabilia Chicago Sportsfest Gold-239
00BAP Memorabilia Chicago Sportsfest Ruby-239
00BAP Memorabilia Chicago Sun-Times Ruby-239
00BAP Memorabilia Chicago Sun-Times Gold-239
00BAP Mem Chicago Sun-Times Sapphire-239
00BAP Mem Toronto Fall Expo Copper-239
00BAP Memorabilia Toronto Fall Expo Gold-239
00BAP Memorabilia Toronto Fall Expo Ruby-239
00BAP Parkhurst 2000-P77
00BAP Signature Series-60
Emerald-60
Ruby-60
Sapphire-60
Autographs-102
Autographs Gold-102
He Shoots-He Scores Prizes-2
00BAP Ultimate Memorabilia Autographs-12
Gold-12
00BAP Ultimate Mem Game-Used Jerseys-GJ32
00BAP Ultimate Mem Game-Used Emblems-E28
00BAP Ultimate Mem Game-Used Numbers-N28
00BAP Ultimate Mem Game-Used Sticks-GS32
00Black Diamond-16
Gold-16
00Crown Royale-29
Ice Blue-29
Limited Series-29
Premiere Date-29
Red-29
00O-Pee-Chee-136
00O-Pee-Chee Parallel-136
00Pacific-115
Copper-115
Gold-115
Ice Blue-115
Premiere Date-115
2001: Ice Odyssey-7
Gold Crown Die Cuts-8B
00Pacific 2001: Ice Odyssey Anaheim Ntnl-7
00Panini Stickers-135
00Paramount-61
Copper-61
Gold-61
Holo-Gold-61
Holo-Silver-61
Ice Blue-61
Premiere Date-61
00Private Stock-24
Gold-24
Premiere Date-24
Retail-24
Silver-24
PS-2001 Action-11
PS-2001 New Wave-8
00Revolution-37
Blue-37
Premiere Date-37
Red-37
HD NHL-9
Stat Masters-3
00SP Authentic BuyBacks-13
00SP Authentic BuyBacks-14
00SP Authentic Sign of the Times-MH
00SPx-14
Spectrum-14
Highlight Heroes-HH5
00Stadium Club-114
Beam Team-BT24
00Titanium-21
Blue-21
Gold-21
Premiere Date-21
Red-21
Retail-21
00Topps/OPC-136
Parallel-136
00Topps Chrome-102
OPC Refractors-102
Refractors-102
Rocket's Flare-RF6
Rocket's Flare Refractors-RF6
00Topps Gold Label Class 1-81
Gold-81
00Topps Gold Label Class 2-81
00Topps Gold Label Class 2 Gold-81
00Topps Gold Label Class 3-81
00Topps Gold Label Class 3 Gold-81
00Topps Heritage-62
Chrome Parallel-62
New Tradition-NT3
00Topps Premier Plus-75
Blue Ice-75
Aspirations-PA4
Masters of the Break-MB5
00Topps Stars-49
Blue-49
00UD Heroes-29
00Upper Deck-43
Exclusives Tier 1-43
Exclusives Tier 2-43
All-Star Class-A3
Triple Threat-TT1
UD Flashback-UD3
00Upper Deck Ice-12
Immortals-12
Legends-12
Stars-12
00Upper Deck Legends-35
Legendary Collection Bronze-35
Legendary Collection Gold-35
Legendary Collection Silver-35
00Upper Deck MVP-49
Excellence-ME4
First Stars-49
Mark of Excellence-SGHN
Second Stars-49
Third Stars-49
00Upper Deck Victory-65
00Upper Deck Victory-295
00Upper Deck Vintage-93
00Vanguard-28
Holographic Gold-28
Holographic Purple-28
Pacific Proofs-28
00Czech DS Extraliga Team Jagr-JT11
00Czech DS Extraliga Team Jagr Parallel-JT7
00Czech OFS-386
00Czech Stadion-71
01Atomic-25
Blue-25
Gold-25
Premiere Date-25
Red-25
Power Play-9
01Avalanche Team Issue-20
01BAP Memorabilia-73
Emerald-73
Ruby-73
Sapphire-73
All-Star Jerseys-ASJ4
All-Star Emblems-ASE4
All-Star Numbers-ASN4
All-Star Starting Lineup-S4
All-Star Teammates-AST1
All-Star Teammates-AST11
Country of Origin-CO25
He Shoots-He Scores Points-3
He Shoots-He Scores Prizes-17
Patented Power-PP3
Stanley Cup Champions-CA8
01BAP Signature Series Certified 100-C25
01BAP Signature Series Certified 50-C25
01BAP Signature Series Certified 1 of 1's-C25
01BAP Signature Series Autographs-LMH
01BAP Signature Series Autographs Gold-LMH
01BAP Sig Series He Shoots/Scores Prizes-27
01BAP Signature Series Jerseys-GJ-24
01BAP Signature Series Jersey Autographs-GUMH
01BAP Sig Series Jersey and Stick Cards-GSJ-24
01BAP Signature Series Teammates-TM-9
01BAP Ultimate Mem All-Star History-51
01BAP Ultimate Memorabilia Autographs-5
01BAP Ultimate Mem Autographs Gold-5
01BAP Ultimate Memorabilia Dynamic Duos-4
01Bowman YoungStars-25
Gold-25
Ice Cubed-25
01Crown Royale-38
Blue-38
Premiere Date-38
Red-38
Retail-38
01eTopps-25
01O-Pee-Chee-51
01O-Pee-Chee Heritage Parallel-51
01O-Pee-Chee Heritage Parallel Limited-51
01O-Pee-Chee Premier Parallel-51
01Pacific-102
Extreme LTD-102
Hobby LTD-102
Premiere Date-102
Retail LTD-102
01Pacific Adrenaline-48
Blue-48
Premiere Date-48
Red-48
Retail-48
Playmakers-2
01Pacific Arena Exclusives-102
01Pacific Heads-Up-24
Blue-24
Premiere Date-24
Red-24
Silver-24
01Parkhurst-38
Gold-38
Silver-38
He Shoots-He Scores Prizes-17
Jerseys-PJ2
Sticks-PS2
Teammates-T8
Waving the Flag-10
01Private Stock-22
Gold-22
Premiere Date-22
Retail-22
Silver-22
01Private Stock Pacific Nights-22
01SP Authentic-17
Limited-17
Limited Gold-17
Sign of the Times-MH
Sign of the Times-IH
Sign of the Times-HBB
Sign of the Times-HHS
01SP Game Used Inked Sweaters-DSBH
01SPx-16
Hidden Treasures-DTHB
01Sports Illustrated for Kids III-296
01Stadium Club-51
Award Winners-51
Master Photos-51
Gallery-G27
Gallery Gold-G27
Lone Star Signatures-LS1
NHL Passport-NHLP11
01Titanium-35
Hobby Parallel-35
Premiere Date-35
Retail-35
Retail Parallel-35
Double-Sided Jerseys-11
Double-Sided Patches-11
01Topps-51
Heritage Parallel-51
Heritage Parallel Limited-51
OPC Parallel-51
Autographs-AMHE
Shot Masters-SM7
01Topps Chrome-51
Refractors-51
Black Border Refractors-51
01Topps Heritage-17
Refractors-17
01Topps Heritage Avalanche NHL AS Game-5
01Topps Reserve-48
01UD Challenge for the Cup-18
Jerseys-UCSH
01UD Honor Roll Honor Society-HS-HK
01UD Honor Roll Honor Society Gold-HS-HK
01UD Mask Collection-21
Gold-21
Double Patches-DPMH
Jerseys-J-MH
Jersey and Patch-JPMH
01UD Playmakers-24
Combo Jerseys-CJMH
Combo Jerseys Gold-CJMH
Practice Jerseys-PJMH
Practice Jerseys Gold-PJMH
01UD Premier Collection-15
Dual Jerseys-DHJ
Dual Jerseys Black-DHJ
Jerseys-BMH
Jerseys Black-B-MH
Signatures-HE
Signatures Black-HE
01UD Stanley Cup Champs-32
01UD Top Shelf-11
01Upper Deck-45
Exclusives-45
Crunch Timers-CT2
Game Jerseys Series II-FJMH
Game Jerseys Series II-TJRBH
Shooting Stars-SS4
Tandems-T2
01Upper Deck Avalanche NHL All-Star Game-HH2
01Upper Deck Avalanche NHL All-Star Game-PP5
01Upper Deck Ice-92
01Upper Deck MVP-45
Morning Skate Jerseys-J-MH
Morning Skate Jersey Autographs-SJ-MH
01Upper Deck Victory-86
01Upper Deck Victory-418
Gold-86
Gold-418
01Upper Deck Vintage-67
01Upper Deck Vintage-70
01Vanguard-25
Blue-25
Red-25
Memorabilia-49
One of Ones-25
Premiere Date-25
Proofs-25
01Czech DS-45
01Czech Stadion-219
02Avalanche Postcards-15
02BAP All-Star Edition-29
Jerseys-29
Jerseys Gold-29
Jerseys Silver-29
02BAP First Edition-16
He Shoots-He Score Points-3
He Shoots-He Scores Prizes-11
Jerseys-16
02BAP Memorabilia-149
Emerald-149
Ruby-149
Sapphire-149
All-Star Jerseys-ASJ-18
NHL All-Star Game-149
NHL All-Star Game Blue-149
NHL All-Star Game Green-149
NHL All-Star Game Red-149
02BAP Memorabilia Toronto Fall Expo-149
02BAP NHL All-Star History-51
02BAP Sig Series Auto Buybacks 1998-187
02BAP Sig Series Auto Buybacks 1999-70
02BAP Sig Series Auto Buybacks 2000-102
02BAP Sig Series Auto Buybacks 2001-LMH
02BAP Signature Series Golf-GS62
02BAP Signature Series Jerseys-SGJ29
02BAP Signature Series Jersey Autographs-SGJ29
02BAP Ultimate Memorabilia Jerseys-26
02BAP Ultimate Memorabilia Numerology-26
02Bowman YoungStars-46
Gold-46
Silver-46
02Crown Royale-24
Blue-24
Red-24
Retail-24
02ITG Used-14
02ITG Used-114
Jerseys-GUJ29
Jersey Autographs-GUJ29
Jerseys Gold-GUJ29
Emblems-E29
Jersey and Stick-SJ29
Jersey and Stick Gold-SJ29
02O-Pee-Chee-99
02O-Pee-Chee Premier Blue Parallel-99
02O-Pee-Chee Premier Red Parallel-99
02O-Pee-Chee Factory Set-99
02Pacific-91
Blue-91
Red-91
02Pacific Calder-33
Silver-33
02Pacific Complete-110
Red-110
02Pacific Exclusive-41
Jerseys-5
Jerseys Gold-5
02Pacific Heads-Up-31
Blue-31
Purple-31
Red-31
Quad Jerseys-8
Quad Jerseys-32
Quad Jerseys Gold-8
Quad Jerseys Gold-32
02Pacific Quest for the Cup-22
Gold-22
02Parkhurst-122
Bronze-122
Gold-122
Silver-122
He Shoots-He Scores Prizes-29
Jerseys-GJ16
Stick and Jerseys-SJ16
02Parkhurst Retro-79
Minis-79
He Shoots-He Scores Prizes-29
Hopefuls-RR8
02Private Stock Reserve-25
Blue-25
Red-25
Retail-25
02SP Game Used Authentic Fabrics-AFHE
02SP Game Used Authentic Fabrics Gold-AFHE
02SP Game Used Authentic Fabrics Rainbow-AFHE
02SP Game Used Piece of History-PHMH
02SP Game Used Piece of History Gold-PHMH
02SP Game Used Piece of History Rainbow-PHMH
02Stadium Club-37
Silver Decoy Cards-37
Proofs-37
Champions Fabric-FC5
Champions Patches-PC-5
02Titanium-25
Blue-25
Red-25
Retail-25
Jerseys-17
Jerseys Retail-17
Patches-17
02Topps-99
OPC Blue Parallel-99
OPC Red Parallel-99
Factory Set-99
02Topps Chrome-63
Black Border Refractors-63
Refractors-63
02Topps Heritage Great Skates-MH
02Topps Heritage Great Skates Patches-MH
02Topps Total-219
02UD Premier Collection-16
Jerseys Bronze-MH
Jerseys Bronze-FH
Jerseys Gold-MH
Jerseys Gold-FH
Jerseys Silver-MH
Jerseys Silver-FH
Patches-PMH
02UD Top Shelf Clutch Performers-CPMH
02UD Top Shelf Dual Player Jerseys-STHR
02UD Top Shelf Goal Oriented-GOMH
02UD Top Shelf Shooting Stars-SHMH
02UD Top Shelf Signatures-MH
02UD Top Shelf Triple Jerseys-HTJHS
02UD Top Shelf Triple Jerseys-HTNTH
02Upper Deck-46
Exclusives-46
Patchwork-PWMH
Pinpoint Accuracy-PAMH
Playbooks Series II-HD
Classic Portraits Hockey Royalty-JHL
Classic Portraits Hockey Royalty Limited-JHL
02Upper Deck MVP-45
Gold-45
Classics-45
Golden Classics-45
Skate Around Jerseys-SDDH
Skate Around Jerseys-SDHP
Skate Around Jerseys-STSHP
Skate Around Jerseys-STTDH
02Upper Deck Rookie Update-158B
Jerseys-DMH
Jerseys Gold-DMH
02Upper Deck Victory-54

Bronze-54
Gold-54
Silver-54
National Pride-NP14
02Upper Deck Vintage-66
Green Backs-66
Jerseys-FSMH
Jerseys Gold-FS-MH
02Vanguard-26
LTD-26
02Czech DS-57
02Czech DS-71
02Czech IQ Sports Blue-10
02Czech IQ Sports Yellow-12
02Czech Stadion Olympics-331
03McFarlane Hockey-160
03McFarlane Hockey-162
03Avalanche Team Issue-8
03BAP Memorabilia-59
Emerald-59
Gold-59
Ruby-59
Sapphire-59
He Shoots-He Scores Prizes-30
Jerseys-GJ-9
Jersey Autographs-GJ-9
03BAP Ultimate Memorabilia Autographs-78
Gold-78
03BAP Ultimate Mem Auto Jerseys-78
03BAP Ultimate Mem Auto Emblems-78
03BAP Ultimate Memorabilia Hat Tricks-9
03BAP Ultimate Memorabilia Jerseys-34
03BAP Ultimate Memorabilia Jerseys Gold-34
03BAP Ultimate Mem Perennial Power Jersey-7
03BAP Ult Mem Perenn Powerhouse Jsy Stick-7
03BAP Ultimate Mem Perennial Power Emblem-7
03Beehive-50
Gold-50
Silver-50
Sticks Beige Border-BE17
03Bowman-110
Gold-110
Future Rivals-CH
Future Rivals-HD
Future Rivals Patches-CH
Future Rivals Patches-HD
Goal to Goal-JH
03Bowman Chrome-110
Refractors-110
Gold Refractors-110
Xfractors-110
03Crown Royale-24
Blue-24
Retail-24
Lords of the Rink-6
03eTopps-13
03ITG Action-166
Jerseys-M159
League Leaders-L1
League Leaders-L2
03ITG Used Signature Series-50
Gold-50
Autographs-MHE
Autographs Gold-MHE
Jerseys-29
Jerseys Gold-29
Jersey Autos-29
Emblems-18
Emblems Gold-18
Jersey and Stick-29
Jersey and Stick Gold-29
Triple Memorabilia-15
Triple Memorabilia Gold-15
03ITG VIP Jerseys-20
03ITG VIP Jersey Autographs-20
03McDonald's Pacific-11
03NHL Sticker Collection-184
03O-Pee-Chee-272
03OPC Blue-272
03OPC Gold-272
03OPC Red-272
03Pacific-84
Blue-84
Red-84
03Pacific Calder-23
03Pacific Calder-146
Silver-23
03Pacific Complete-288
Red-288
03Pacific Exhibit-37
03Pacific Exhibit-204
Blue Backs-37
Yellow Backs-37
03Pacific Invincible-22
Blue-22
Red-22
Retail-22
03Pacific Luxury Suite-30A
03Pacific Luxury Suite-30B
03Pacific Luxury Suite-30C
03Pacific Prism-109
Blue-109
Patches-110
Red-109
Retail-110
Stat Masters-4
03Pacific Quest for the Cup-24
Blue-24
Raising the Cup-4
03Pacific Supreme-22
Blue-22
Red-22
Retail-22
03Parkhurst Rookie Jerseys-GJ-8
03Parkhurst Rookie Jerseys Gold-GJ-8
03Private Stock Reserve-155
Blue-155
Patches-155
Red-155
Retail-155
03SP Game Used-106
Gold-106
03SPx Style-SPX-HH
03SPx Style Limited-SPX-HH
03Titanium-148
Hobby Jersey Number Parallels-148
Patches-148
Retail-148
03Topps-272
Blue-272
Gold-272
Red-272
Topps/OPC Idols-II7
Own the Game-OTG4
03Topps C55-50
Minis-50
Minis American Back-50
Minis American Back Red-50
Minis Bazooka Back-50
Minis Brooklyn Back-50
Minis Hat Trick Back-50
Minis O Canada Back-50
Minis O Canada Back Red-50
Minis Stanley Cup Back-50
Award Winners-12
Relics-TRMHE
03Topps Pristine-60
Gold Refractor Die Cuts-60
Refractors-60
Autographs-PE-MH
Autographs Gold-PE-MH
Jersey Portions-PPJ-MHE
Jersey Portion Refractors-PPJ-MHE
Patches-PP-MHE
Patch Refractors-PP-MHE
Press Plates Black-60
Press Plates Cyan-60
Press Plates Magenta-60
Press Plates Yellow-60
03UD Premier Collection Stars-ST-MH
03UD Premier Collection Stars Patches-ST-MH
03Upper Deck-291
Canadian Exclusives-291
HG-291
Magic Moments-MM-10
Team Essentials-TS-MH
UD Exclusives-291
Ice Breakers-IB-HK
Ice Breaker Patches-IB-HK
Ice Clear Cut Winners-CC-MH
03Upper Deck MVP-102
Gold Script-102
Silver Script-102
Canadian Exclusives-102
Lethal Lineups-LL1
SportsNut-SN24
03Upper Deck Rookie Update Super Stars-SSHJK
03Upper Deck Trilogy Authentic Patches-AP13
03Upper Deck Victory-44
Bronze-44
Gold-44
Silver-44
03Czech National Team Postcards-3
03Russian World Championship Stars-24
03Toronto Star-22
04ITG NHL AS FANtasy AS History Jerseys-SB51
04Pacific-67
Blue-67
Red-67
04SP Authentic-24
04SP Authentic-109
Limited-24
Limited-109
Buybacks-157
Buybacks-158
Buybacks-159
Rookie Review-RR-HE
Sign of the Times-ST-MH
Sign of the Times-TS-HTA
Sign of the Times-QS-HINS
Sign of the Times-QS-IKHL
Sign of the Times-QS-TAHS
Sign of the Times-FS-RGT
04UD All-World-5
Gold-5
Autographs-5
Dual Autographs-AD-HH
Triple Autographs-AT-SHH
04Ultimate Collection-67
Buybacks-65
Buybacks-66
Buybacks-67
Buybacks-68
Buybacks-69
Dual Logos-UL2-HF
Jerseys-UGJ-HE
Jerseys Gold-UGJ-HE
Jersey Autographs-UGJA-HE
Patches-UP-HE
Patch Autographs-UPA-MH
Patch Autographs-UPA-ATMH
Signatures-US-MH
Signature Logos-ULA-MH
Signature Patches-SP-MH
04Upper Deck-44
Big Playmakers-BP-HE
Canadian Exclusives-44
HG Glossy Gold-44
HG Glossy Silver-44
World's Best-WB8
World Cup Tribute-HE
World Cup Tribute-PEJJHE
04Czech NHL ELH Postcards-4
04Czech OFS-117
Checklist Cards-6
Stars-11
04Czech Zuma-11
05Be A Player-21
First Period-21
Second Period-21
Third Period-21
Overtime-21
05Beehive-23
05Beehive-183
Beige -23
Blue -23
Gold-23
Red -23
Matte-23
Matted Materials-MMHJ
Matted Materials Remarkable-RMHJ
05Black Diamond-93
Emerald-93
Gold-93
Onyx-93
Ruby-93
Jerseys-J-MH
Jerseys Ruby-J-MH
Jersey Duals-DJ-MH
Jersey Triples-TJ-MH
Jersey Quads-QJ-MH
05Hot Prospects-25
En Fuego-25
Red Hot-25
White Hot-25
05Panini Stickers-224
05Parkhurst-122
Facsimile Auto Parallel-122
True Colors-TCCOL
True Colors-TCCOL
True Colors-TCDECO
True Colors-TCDECO
05SP Authentic-26
Limited-26
Chirography-SPMH
Marks of Distinction-MDMH
Sign of the Times Triples-TTHW
05SP Game Used-24
Autographs-24
Gold-24
Authentic Fabrics-AF-HJ
Authentic Fabrics Autographs-AAF-HJ
Authentic Fabrics Dual-TH
Authentic Fabrics Dual Autographs-TH
Authentic Fabrics Gold-AF-HJ
Authentic Fabrics Quad-SATH
Authentic Patches Quad -SATH
Authentic Patches-AP-HJ
Authentic Patches Autographs-AAP-HJ
Authentic Patches Dual-TH
Authentic Patches Dual Autographs-TH
Auto Draft-AD-MH
Awesome Authentics-AA-HJ
SIGnificance Extra-IH
SIGnificance Extra Gold-IH
Significant Numbers-SN-MH
05SPx-21
Spectrum-21
Winning Combos-WC-SH
Winning Combos-WC-TH
Winning Combos Autographs-AWC-TH
Winning Combos Gold-WC-SH
Winning Combos Gold-WC-TH
Winning Combos Spectrum-WC-SH
Winning Combos Spectrum-WC-TH
Winning Materials-WM-MH
Winning Materials Autographs-AWM-MH
Winning Materials Gold-WM-MH
Winning Materials Spectrum-WM-MH
Xcitement Superstars-XS-HK
Xcitement Superstars Gold-XS-HK
Xcitement Superstars Spectrum-XS-HK
05The Cup-30
Gold-30
Black Rainbow-30
Emblems of Endorsement-EEMH
Hardware Heroes-HHMH
Honorable Numbers-HNMH
Limited Logos-LLHJ
Masterpiece Pressplates-30
Masterpiece Pressplates (Rookie Update)-237
Noble Numbers-NNHD
Patch Variation-P30
Patch Variation Autographs-AP30
Property of-POHJ
Scripted Numbers-SNHD
Scripted Numbers Dual-DSNCO
Scripted Numbers Dual-DSNCZ
Scripted Swatches-SSMH
Signature Patches-SPHJ
Stanley Cup Titlists-THJ
05UD Artifacts-27
05UD Artifacts-160
Blue-27
Blue-160
Gold-27
Gold-160
Green-27
Green-160
Pewter-27
Pewter-160
Red-27
Red-160
Auto Facts-AF-HE
Auto Facts Blue-AF-HE
Auto Facts Copper-AF-HE
Auto Facts Pewter-AF-HE
Auto Facts Silver-AF-HE
Gold Autographed-27
Gold Autographed-160
Remarkable Artifacts-RA-HE
Remarkable Artifacts Dual-RA-HE
Treasured Patches-TP-MH
Treasured Patches Autographed-TP-MH
Treasured Patches Dual-TPD-MH
Treasured Patches Dual Autographed-TPD-MH
Treasured Patches Pewter-TP-MH
Treasured Patches Silver-TP-MH
Treasured Swatches-TS-MH
Treasured Swatches Autographed-TS-MH
Treasured Swatches Blue-TS-MH
Treasured Swatches Copper-TS-MH
Treasured Swatches Dual-TSD-MH
Treasured Swatches Dual Autographed-TSD-MH
Treasured Swatches Dual Blue-TSD-MH
Treasured Swatches Dual Copper-TSD-MH
Treasured Swatches Dual Maroon-TSD-MH
Treasured Swatches Dual Pewter-TSD-MH
Treasured Swatches Dual Silver-TSD-MH
Treasured Swatches Maroon-TS-MH
Treasured Swatches Pewter-TS-MH
Treasured Swatches Silver-TS-MH
05UD PowerPlay-24
Rainbow-24
Power Marks-PMHE
Specialists-TSMH
Specialists Patches-SPMH
05Ultimate Collection-26
Gold-26
Endorsed Emblems-EEHJ
Jerseys-JMH
Jerseys Dual-DJSH
Marquee Attractions-MA15
Marquee Attractions Signatures-SMA15
National Heroes Jerseys-NHJHJ
National Heroes Patches-NHPHJ
Premium Patches-PPMH
Premium Swatches-PSMH
Ultimate Achievements-UAMH
Ultimate Patches-PMH
Ultimate Patches Dual-DPSH
Ultimate Signatures-USMH
Ultimate Signatures Logos-SLMH
Ultimate Signatures Pairings-UPTH
Ultimate Signatures Trios-UTTHS
05Ultra-56
Gold-56
Ice-56
Scoring Kings-SK24
Scoring Kings Jerseys-SKJ-MH
Scoring Kings Jersey Autographs-KAJ-MH
Scoring Kings Patches-SKP-MH
Scoring Kings Patch Autographs-KAP-MH
05Upper Deck-292
Big Playmakers-B-HJ
Goal Rush-GR3
Jerseys-J-MHE
Jerseys Series II-J2HJ
Majestic Materials-MMHE
NHL Generations-TSHT
Notable Numbers-N-HJ
Patches-P-MHK
Shooting Stars-S-MH
05Upper Deck Ice-23
Rainbow-23
Cool Threads-CTMH
Cool Threads Autographs-ACTMH
Cool Threads Glass-CTMH
Cool Threads Patches-CTPMH
Cool Threads Patch Autographs-CAPMH
Signature Swatches-SSMH
05Upper Deck MVP-100
Gold-100
Platinum-100
Materials Duals-D-HH
ProSign-P-MH
05Upper Deck Rookie Update-26
05Upper Deck Rookie Update-237
Inspirations Patch Rookies-237
05Upper Deck Trilogy-25
05Upper Deck Trilogy-135
Crystal-135
Honorary Patches-HP-MH
Honorary Patch Scripts-HSP-MH
Honorary Swatches-HS-MH
Honorary Swatch Scripts-HSS-MH
Ice Scripts-IS-MH
05Upper Deck Victory-49
Black-49
Gold-49
Silver-49
Game Breakers-GB11
05Czech Kvarteto Bonaparte-8a
05Czech Pexeso Mini Blue Set-24
06Avalanche Team Postcards-6
06Be A Player Portraits-30
Dual Signature Portraits-DSHS
Quadruple Signature Portraits-QHVHH
Signature Portraits-SPHE
Triple Signature Portraits-TCOL
06Beehive-76
06Beehive-214
Blue-76
Gold-76
Matte-76
Red Facsimile Signatures-76
Wood-76
Matted Materials-MMMH
Remarkable Matted Materials-MMMH
Signature Scrapbook-SSHE
06Black Diamond-133
Black-133
Gold-133
Ruby-133
Jerseys-JHE
Jerseys Black-JHE
Jerseys Gold-JHE
Jerseys Ruby-JHE
Jerseys Black Autographs -JMH
06Flair Showcase-27
06Flair Showcase-120
06Flair Showcase-220
Parallel-27
Parallel-120
Parallel-220
Hot Numbers-HN12
Hot Numbers Parallel-HN12
Inks-IHJ
06Fleer-51
Tiffany-51
Signing Day-SDMH
06Hot Prospects-27
Red Hot-27
White Hot-27
Hot Materials -HMHJ
Hot Materials Red Hot-HMHJ
Hot Materials White Hot-HMHJ
06McDonald's Upper Deck-11
06O-Pee-Chee-126
Rainbow-126
Swatches-S-HE
06Panini Stickers-222
06SP Authentic-77
06SP Authentic-141
Chirography-HE
Limited-77
Limited-141
Sign of the Times-STHJ
Sign of the Times Duals-STHS
Sign of the Times Triples-ST3HTS
06SP Game Used-26
Gold-26
Rainbow-26
Authentic Fabrics-AFMH
Authentic Fabrics Parallel-AFMH
Authentic Fabrics Patches-AFMH
Authentic Fabrics Dual-AF2HS
Authentic Fabrics Dual Patches-AF2HS
Authentic Fabrics Triple-AF3COL
Authentic Fabrics Triple Patches-AF3COL
Authentic Fabrics Sixes-AF6MRT
Authentic Fabrics Sixes Patches-AF6MRT
Autographs-26
By The Letter-BLHE
Inked Sweaters-ISHE
Inked Sweaters Patches-ISHE
Inked Sweaters Dual-IS2HT
Inked Sweaters Dual Patches-IS2HT
Letter Marks-LMHE
06SPx-25
Spectrum-25
SPxcitement-X24
SPxcitement Spectrum-X24
SPxcitement Autographs-X24
Winning Materials-WMHE
Winning Materials Spectrum-WMHE
Winning Materials Autographs-WMHE
06The Cup Autographed Foundations-CQHM
06The Cup Autographed Foundations Patches-CQHM
06The Cup Autographed NHL Shields Duals-DASCO
06The Cup Autographed NHL Shields Duals-DASHS
06The Cup Autographed NHL Shields Duals-DASHT
06The Cup Foundations-CQHM
06The Cup Foundations Patches-CQHM
06The Cup Honorable Numbers-HNHM
06The Cup Limited Logos-LLMI
06The Cup NHL Shields Duals-DSHSH
06The Cup Scripted Swatches-SSMI
06The Cup Signature Patches-SPMI
06The Cup Stanley Cup Signatures-CSHE
06UD Artifacts-75
Blue-75
Gold-75
Platinum-75
Radiance-75
Autographed Radiance Parallel-75
Red-75
Frozen Artifacts-FAMH
Frozen Artifacts Black-FAMH
Frozen Artifacts Blue-FAMH
Frozen Artifacts Gold-FAMH
Frozen Artifacts Platinum-FAMH
Frozen Artifacts Red-FAMH
Frozen Artifacts Autographed Black-FAMH
Frozen Artifacts Patches Black-FAMH
Frozen Artifacts Patches Blue-FAMH
Frozen Artifacts Patches Gold-FAMH
Frozen Artifacts Patches Platinum-FAMH
Frozen Artifacts Patches Red-FAMH
Frozen Artifacts Patches Autographed Black Tag Parallel-FAMH
Tundra Tandems-TTHS
Tundra Tandems Black-TTHS
Tundra Tandems Blue-TTHS
Tundra Tandems Gold-TTHS
Tundra Tandems Platinum-TTHS
Tundra Tandems Red-TTHS
Tundra Tandems Dual Patches Red-TTHS
06UD Mini Jersey Collection-26
06UD Powerplay-27
Impact Rainbow-27
06Ultimate Collection Jerseys-UJ-MH
06Ultimate Collection Jerseys Dual-UJ2-TH
06Ultimate Collection Patches-UJ-MH
06Ultimate Collection Patches Dual-UJ2-TH
06Ultimate Collection Premium Patches-PS-HE
06Ultimate Collection Premium Swatches-PS-HE
06Ultimate Collection Signatures-US-MI
06Ultimate Collection Ultimate Achievements-UA-MH
06Ultimate Collection Ultimate Signatures Logos-SL-HE
06Ultra-50
Gold Medallion-50
Ice Medallion-50
Fresh Ink-IHE
06Upper Deck Arena Giveaways-COL6
06Upper Deck-49
Exclusives Parallel-49
High Gloss Parallel-49
All World-AW10
Game Jerseys-JHE
Game Patches-PHE
Generations Duals-G2HS
Generations Triples-G3HSS
Generations Patches Dual-G2PHS
Generations Patches Triple-G3PHSS
Hometown Heroes-HH43
Masterpieces-49
Signature Sensations-SSHE
Walmart Tins Oversize-49
06Upper Deck MVP-76
Gold Script-76
Super Script-76
Autographs-OAHT
International Icons-II5
Jerseys-OJHH
06Upper Deck Ovation-62
06Upper Deck Sweet Shot-29
Signature Shots/Saves-SSMI
Signature Shots/Saves Sticks-SSSMI
Signature Sticks-STMH
Sweet Stitches-SSHE
Sweet Stitches Duals-SSHE
Sweet Stitches Triples-SSHE
06Upper Deck Trilogy-26
Combo Autographed Jerseys-CJHT
Combo Autographed Patches-CJHT
Combo Clearcut Autographs-C2HS
Combo Clearcut Autographs-C3HTT
Honorary Scripted Patches-HSPHE
Honorary Scripted Swatches-HSSHE
Honorary Swatches-HSMH
Ice Scripts-ISMH
06Upper Deck Victory-50
06Upper Deck Victory Black-50
06Upper Deck Victory Gold-50
06Russian Sport Collection Olympic Stars-31
07Upper Deck Victory-154
Black-154
Gold-154
GameBreakers-GB16
Stars on Ice-SI32

Hejl, Pavel
99Czech Score Blue 2000-117
99Czech Score Red Ice 2000-117

Hejma, Peter
94German First League-80

Hejna, Tony
90ProCards AHL/IHL-90

Helander, Hannu
78Finnish SM-Liiga-45
80Finnish Mallasjuoma-157
82Swedish Semic VM Stickers-34
83Swedish Semic VM Stickers-34

Helander, Pekka
71Finnish Suomi Stickers-340

Helander, Peter
81Swedish Semic Hockey VM Stickers-8
82Swedish Semic VM Stickers-9

Helanen, Markus
01Finnish Cardset-246
02Finnish Cardset-171
03Finnish Cardset-57
04Finnish Cardset-275

Helber, Christian
94German First League-82

Helber, Mike
91Michigan Wolverines-6
99Swedish Upper Deck-133
Lasting Impressions-7

Helbling, Timo
98Swiss Power Play Stickers-75
99Swiss Panini Stickers-59
01Milwaukee Admirals-14
01Milwaukee Admirals Postcards-4
02Milwaukee Admirals-22
03Milwaukee Admirals-4
03Milwaukee Admirals Postcards-9
05Hot Prospects-267
En Fuego-267
Hot Materials-HMTH
Red Hot-267
White Hot-267
05SP Authentic-195
Limited-195
Sign of the Times-HE
05SP Game Used-127
Autographs-127
Gold-127
05SPx-205
Spectrum-205
05The Cup Masterpiece Pressplates (Ice)-170
05The Cup Master Pressplate Rookie Update-179
05The Cup Masterpiece Pressplates SP GU-127
05The Cup Masterpiece Pressplates (SPx)-205
05The Cup Masterpiece Pressplate Ult Coll-171
05UD Artifacts-227
Gold-RED27
05Ultimate Collection-171
Gold-171
05Ultra-247
Gold-247
Fresh Ink-FI-TI
Fresh Ink Blue-FI-TI
Ice-247
Rookie Uniformity Jerseys-RU-TH
Rookie Uniformity Jersey Autographs-ARU-TH
Rookie Uniformity Patches-RUP-TH
Rookie Uniformity Patch Autographs-ARP-TH
05Upper Deck-231
HG Glossy-231
Rookie Threads-RTTH
Rookie Threads Autographs-ARTTH
05Upper Deck Ice-170
Premieres Auto Patches-AIPTH
05Upper Deck Rookie Update-179
05Upper Deck Toronto Fall Expo-231
05Springfield Falcons-23

Helbstab, Beat
98Swiss Power Play Stickers-74

Held, Daniel
89Swedish Semic World Champ Stickers-125
94German DEL-46
95German DEL-16
99German Bundesliga 2-50
04German Berlin Eisbarens 50th Anniv-72

Held, John
75Roanoke Valley Rebels-7

Held, Ryan
99Kitchener Rangers-13
00UD CHL Prospects-40

Heldner, Thomas
93Swiss HNL-330
95Swiss HNL-203
96Swiss HNL-92
98Swiss Power Play Stickers-114
99Swiss Panini Stickers-114
00Swiss Panini Stickers-187
00Swiss Slapshot Mini-Cards-LT13
01Swiss HNL-205
02Swiss HNL-332

Heldstab, Beat
99Swiss Panini Stickers-60
01Swiss HNL-344
02Swiss HNL-156

Helenefors, Allan
69Swedish Hockey-242
70Swedish Hockey-134

Helenius, Riku
06Finnish Cardset-223
Between the Pipes-7
06Finnish Ilves Team Set-5

Helenius, Sami
93Finnish Jyvas-Hyva Stickers-266
94Saint John Flames-9
95Saint John Flames-7
96Saint John Flames-7
97Saint John Flames-11
98Las Vegas Thunder-7
99Avalanche Team Issue-10
99BAP Memorabilia-354
Gold-354
Silver-354
99BAP Millennium Calder Candidates Ruby-C32
99BAP Millennium Calder Candidate Emerald-C32
99BAP Millennium Calder Cand Sapphire-C32
99Pacific Omega-69
Copper-69
Gold-69
Ice Blue-69
Premiere Date-69
99Topps Premier Plus-86
Parallel-86
00Stars Postcards-6
00Upper Deck NHLPA-PA28
01Pacific-125
Extreme LTD-125
Hobby LTD-125
Premiere Date-125
Retail LTD-125
01Pacific Arena Exclusives-125
01Stars Postcards-6
02Stars Postcards-2
03ITG Action-124
03Finnish Cardset-59
03Finnish Cardset Globetrotters-GR3
04Finnish Cardset-50
Parallel-37
04Swedish Pure Skills-113
Parallel-113
05Finnish Cardset -293
06Finnish Cardset-122
Enforcers-1

Helenius, Teuvo
66Finnish Jaakiekkosarja-37

Helfenstein, Sven
00Swiss Panini Stickers-158
00Swiss Slapshot Mini-Cards-EHCK8
01Swiss HNL-88
02Swiss HNL-269

Helin, Jimi
92Finnish Jyvas-Hyva Stickers-111
93Finnish Jyvas-Hyva Stickers-206
93Finnish SISU-263

Helinski, Jon
84Kitchener Rangers-18

Helisten, Mikko
94Finest-131
Super Team Winners-131
Refractors-131
94Parkhurst SE-SE219
Gold-SE219
95Finnish SISU-319

Heljemo, Claes
89Swedish Semic Elitserien Stickers-98

Helle, Jari
72Finnish Jaakiekko-343

Helle, Martti
71Finnish Suomi Stickers-174
73Finnish Jaakiekko-178

Helleher, Chris
93Classic Four-Sport *-223
Gold-223

Hellenberg, Par
89Swedish Semic Elitserien Stickers-241
90Swedish Semic Elitserien Stickers-151
91Swedish Semic Elitserien Stickers-253

Heller, Jacob
03Erie Otters-9
04Erie Otters-10

Heller, Jake
05Erie Otters-14

Heller, Ott
33O-Pee-Chee V304A-16
33V129-34
33V252 Canadian Gum-29
34Beehive Group I Photos-275
34Diamond Matchbooks Silver-28
35Diamond Matchbooks Tan 1-27
35Diamond Matchbooks Tan 2-27
35Diamond Matchbooks Tan 3-25
37V356 Worldwide Gum-87
39O-Pee-Chee V301-1-33
40O-Pee-Chee V301-2-142
04ITG Ultimate Mem Broadway Blueshirts-9
05ITG Ultimate Mem Broadway Bluesh Autos-5
06ITG Ultimate Memorabilia Broadway Blue Shirts Autos-7

Hellgren, Ari
78Finnish SM-Liiga-131
80Finnish Mallasjuoma-89
81Swedish Semic Hockey VM Stickers-19
82Finnish Skopbank-2

Hellgren, Jens
83Swedish Semic Elitserien-240
84Swedish Semic Elitserien-184
85Swedish Panini Stickers-173
86Swedish Panini Stickers-185
87Swedish Panini Stickers-186
89Swedish Semic Elitserien Stickers-164
90Swedish Semic Elitserien Stickers-243
91Swedish Semic Elitserien Stickers-173

Hellgren, Roger
84Swedish Semic Elitserien-8
85Swedish Panini Stickers-10

Hellgren, Roland
57Swedish Alfabilder-114

Helling, Kjell
71Swedish Hockey-95

Hellkvist, Stefan
89Swedish Semic Elitserien Stickers-253
90Swedish Semic Elitserien Stickers-166
91Swedish Semic Elitserien Stickers-271
92Swedish Semic Elitserien Stickers-291
93Swedish Semic Elitserien-257
94Swedish Leaf-71
95Swedish Leaf-239
Face to Face-7
95Swedish Upper Deck-107
97Swedish Collector's Choice-114
98Swedish UD Choice-128
99Swedish Upper Deck-114
SHL Signatures-11
00Swedish Upper Deck-9
00Swedish Upper Deck-179
SHL Signatures-SH
02German DEL City Press-112
03Swedish Elite-194
Silver-194
04Swedish Elitset-51
Gold-51

Hellman, Bjorn
83Swedish Semic Elitserien-7
84Swedish Semic Elitserien-5
85Swedish Panini Stickers-8
87Swedish Panini Stickers-12

Hellmann, Kenneth
69Swedish Hockey-167

Hellsing, Torbjorn
70Swedish Hockey-131

Hellsten, Jens
98Danish Hockey League-95
99Danish Hockey League-115

Hellstrom, Lars
83Swedish Semic Elitserien-169

Hellstrom, Mattias
04Swedish MoDo Postcards-19
05Swedish SHL Elitset-245
06Swedish SHL Elitset-241

Hellwig, Wolfgang
99German DEL-408

Hellyer, Mike
03Prince Albert Raiders-20
04Prince Albert Raiders-8
05Prince Albert Raiders-12
06Prince Albert Raiders-9

Helm, Darren
04Medicine Hat Tigers-9
05Medicine Hat Tigers-12
06Medicine Hat Tigers-9
07ITG Going For Gold World Juniors-14
Autographs-14
Emblems-GUE14
Jerseys-GUJ14
Numbers-GUN14

Helman, Harry
23V145-1-5

Helmer, Bryan
96Albany River Rats-6
97Albany River Rats-4
98Bowman's Best-131
Refractors-131
Atomic Refractors-131
98Las Vegas Thunder-8
00Topps Heritage-205
00Kansas City Blades-19
01Manitoba Moose-10
02NHL Power Play Stickers-158
02Manitoba Moose-4
03Springfield Falcons Postcards-12

Helmer, Jayme
02London Knights-23

Helmer, Tim
82North Bay Centennials-10
83North Bay Centennials-10
83Ottawa 67's-12
84Ottawa 67's-10

Helmersson, Per
06Swedish SHL Elitset-262

Helminen, Bob
04Northern Michigan Wildcats-9

Helminen, Dwight
02Michigan Wolverines-23
03Michigan Wolverines-8
04Hartford Wolf Pack-8
05Hartford Wolf Pack-11
06Hartford Wolf Pack-20

Helminen, Raimo
89Swedish Semic World Champ Stickers-39
90Swedish Semic Elitserien Stickers-135
91Finnish Semic World Champ Stickers-24
91Swedish Semic Elitserien Stickers-186
91Swedish Semic World Champ Stickers-24
92Swedish Semic Elitserien Stickers-210
93Swedish Semic Elitserien-180
93Swedish Semic World Champ Stickers-63
94Finnish SISU-363
94Finnish Jaa Kiekko-30
94Swedish Leaf-67
Playmakers-4
95Finnish SISU Gold Cards-12
95Finnish Karjala World Champ Labels-2
95Finnish Semic World Championships-14
95Swedish Leaf-96
Champs-6
Mega-10
95Swedish Upper Deck-141
95Swedish Upper Deck-232
95Swedish Globe World Championships-141
95Swedish World Championships Stickers-179
96Swedish Semic Wien-14
98Finnish Kerailysarja-87
Leijonat-21
99Finnish Cardset-52
99Finnish Cardset-164
99Finnish Cardset-190
Aces High-S-7
00Finnish Cardset-35
00Finnish Cardset-235
01Finnish Cardset-168
01Finnish Cardset-244
01Finnish Cardset Dueling Aces-5
01Finnish Cardset Salt Lake City-11
02Finnish Cardset-172
03Finnish Cardset-56
04Finnish Cardset-60
Parallel-45
04Swedish Pure Skills Professional Power-RH
05Finnish Cardset -48
06Finnish Cardset-52

Helmuth, Andy
84Ottawa 67's-11

Helperl, Jeff
00Jackson Bandits-2
01Norfolk Admirals-9
01Roanoke Express-10
02Norfolk Admirals-9

Helppolainen, Raimo
65Finnish Hellas-81
66Finnish Jaakiekkosarja-97

Helstedt, Eric
99Sioux City Musketeers-8
02Chicago Steel-11

Hem, Morten
92Norwegian Elite Series-158

Hemenway, Ken
93Omaha Lancers-9

Hemingway, Colin
94Quebec Int. Pee-Wees-1171
03Peoria Rivermen-6
03Worcester Ice Cats-20
04Peoria Rivermen-23
05Black Diamond-280
05Hot Prospects-166
En Fuego-166
Red Hot-166
White Hot-166
05SP Authentic-237
Limited-237
05SP Game Used-174
Gold-174
05SPx-194
Spectrum-194
05The Cup Masterpiece Pressplate Artifact-324
05The Cup Master Pressplate Black Diamond-280
05The Cup Masterpiece Pressplates (Ice)-169
05The Cup Master Pressplate Rookie Update-176
05The Cup Masterpiece Pressplates SPA-237
05The Cup Masterpiece Pressplates SP GU-174
05The Cup Masterpiece Pressplates (SPx)-194
05The Cup Masterpiece Pressplates Trilogy-302
05The Cup Masterpiece Pressplate Ult Coll-223
05UD Artifacts-324
05Ultimate Collection-223
Gold-223
05Upper Deck Ice-169
05Upper Deck Rookie Update-176
05Upper Deck Trilogy-302
05Peoria Rivermen-7

Hemming, Jonas
96Finnish SISU Redline-120

Hemmings, Andrew
04UK Guildford Flames-11
05UK Guildford Flames-8
06UK Guildford Flames-7

Hemmingsson, Anders
57Swedish Alfabilder-103

Hemsky, Ales
99Czech OFS-350
00Hull Olympiques-9
Signed-9
01BAP Memorabilia Draft Redemptions-13
01SPx Rookie Redemption-R12
01Hull Olympiques-10
02Atomic-109
Blue-109
Gold-109
Red-109
Hobby Parallel-109
02BAP All-Star Edition-128
Gold-128
Silver-128
02BAP First Edition-437R
02BAP Memorabilia-281
Emerald-281
Ruby-281
Sapphire-281
NHL All-Star Game-281
NHL All-Star Game Blue-281
NHL All-Star Game Green-281
NHL All-Star Game Red-281
02BAP Memorabilia Toronto Fall Expo-281
02BAP Ultimate Memorabilia-11
Calder Candidates-12
02Bowman YoungStars-159
Gold-159
Silver-159
02Crown Royale-114
Blue-114
Purple-114
Red-114
Retail-114
Rookie Royalty-10
02eTopps-42
02ITG Used-89
Calder Jerseys-C6
Calder Jerseys Gold-C6
02NHL Power Play Stickers-46
02Oilers Postcards-20
02O-Pee-Chee-337
02O-Pee-Chee Premier Blue Parallel-337
02O-Pee-Chee Premier Red Parallel-337
02O-Pee-Chee Factory Set-337
02Pacific-406
02Pacific Calder-117
Silver-117
Reflections-10
02Pacific Complete-523
Red-523
02Pacific Exclusive-178
Blue-178
Gold-178
02Pacific Heads-Up-133
02Pacific Quest for the Cup-118
Gold-118
Calder Contenders-8
02Parkhurst-211
Bronze-211
Gold-211
Silver-211
02Parkhurst Retro-211
Minis-211
02Private Stock Reserve-162
Blue-162
Red-162
Retail-162
02SP Authentic-197
Sign of the Times-HE
Signed Patches-PAH
02SP Game Used-77

02SPx-160
02Stadium Club-129
Silver Decoy Cards-129
Proofs-129
02Titanium-115
Blue-115
Red-115
Retail-115
Right on Target-8
02Topps-337
OPC Blue Parallel-337
OPC Red Parallel-337
Factory Set-337
02Topps Chrome-176
Black Border Refractors-176
Refractors-176
02Topps Heritage-139
02Topps Total-409
02UD Artistic Impressions-104
Gold-104
Common Ground-CG2
Common Ground Gold-CG2
02UD Foundations-152
02UD Honor Roll-152
02UD Mask Collection-168
02UD Piece of History-129
02UD Premier Collection-99
Gold-99
02UD Top Shelf-128
02Upper Deck-235
Exclusives-235
02Upper Deck Classic Portraits-113
02Upper Deck Rookie Update-158A
02Upper Deck Rookie Update-158B
02Upper Deck Rookie Update-158C
02Vanguard-114
LTD-114
Prime Prospects-10
02Czech DS-47
02Czech DS-68
03BAP Memorabilia-3
Emerald-3
Gold-3
Ruby-3
Sapphire-3
Future of the Game-FG-17
03BAP Ultimate Memorabilia Autographs-3
Gold-3
03BAP Ultimate Mem Franch Present Future-12
03Beehive-79
Variations-79
Gold-79
Silver-79
Signatures-RF25
03Black Diamond-182
Black-182
Green-182
Red-182
03Bowman-61
Gold-61
03Bowman Chrome-61
Refractors-61
Gold Refractors-61
Xfractors-61
03Crown Royale Jerseys-10
03Crown Royale Patches-10
03ITG Action-249
Jerseys-M109
03ITG Used Signature Series-28
Gold-28
Autographs-AH
Autographs Gold-AH
03Oilers Postcards-8
03Pacific-132
Blue-132
Red-132
03Pacific Calder Contenders Entry Draft-8
03Pacific Complete-155
Red-155
03Pacific Exhibit-58
Blue Backs-58
Yellow Backs-58
Pursuing Prominence-6
03Pacific Heads-Up-41
Hobby LTD-41
Retail LTD-41
Jerseys-11
03Pacific Invincible-39
Blue-39
Red-39
Retail-39
Featured Performers-12
New Sensations-12
03Pacific Luxury Suite-35A
03Pacific Luxury Suite-35B
03Pacific Luxury Suite-35C
03Pacific Prism-40
Blue-40
Gold-40
Red-40
Paramount Prodigies-10
Rookie Revolution-7
03Pacific Quest for the Cup-42
Blue-42
03Pacific Supreme-38
Blue-38
Red-38
Retail-38
03Private Stock Reserve-36
Blue-36
Red-36
Retail-36
Rising Stock-7
03SP Authentic-32
Limited-32
10th Anniversary-SP15
10th Anniversary Limited-SP15
Sign of the Times-AHY
Sign of the Times-CH
03SP Game Used-19
Gold-19
Authentic Fabrics-DFHC
Authentic Fabrics-QSNZH
Authentic Fabrics Gold-DFHC
Authentic Fabrics Gold-QSNZH
Authentic Patches-APAH
Limited Threads-LTAH
Limited Threads Gold-LTAH
Team Threads-TTHSC
03SPx-37
03SPx-151
03SPx-166
Radiance-37
Radiance-151
Radiance-166
Spectrum-37
Spectrum-151
Spectrum-166
Big Futures-BF-AH
Big Futures Limited-BF-AH
Signature Threads-ST-AH
03Titanium-154
Hobby Jersey Number Parallels-154
Patches-154
Retail-154
Right on Target-6
03UD Honor Roll-30
03UD Honor Roll-95
03UD Premier Collection-24
NHL Shields-SH-AH
Signatures-PS-AH
Signatures Gold-PS-AH
Teammates-PT-E02
Teammates Patches-PT-E02
03Upper Deck-76
All-Star Lineup-AS9
Canadian Exclusives-76
HG-76
Jerseys-UD-AH
Jersey Autographs-SJ-AH
Memorable Matchups-MM-TH
Shooting Stars-ST-AH
03Upper Deck Classic Portraits-37
03Upper Deck Ice-36
Gold-36
Authentics-IA-AH
Breakers-IB-AH
Breaker Patches-IB-AH
Frozen Fabrics-FF-AH
Frozen Fabric Patches-FF-AH
Under Glass Autographs-UG-AH
03Upper Deck MVP-165
Gold Script-165
Silver Script-165
Canadian Exclusives-165
SportsNut-SN37
03Upper Deck Rookie Update-36
Skills-SKAH
Top Draws-TD10
03Upper Deck Trilogy-37
Limited-37
Scripts-S1AH
Scripts Limited-S1AH
03Upper Deck Victory-74
Bronze-74
Gold-74
Silver-74
04Pacific-102
Blue-102
Red-102
04SP Authentic Buybacks-1
04SP Authentic Buybacks-2
04SP Authentic Buybacks-3
04SP Authentic Sign of the Times-ST-AH
04SP Authentic Sign of the Times-DS-RA
04UD All-World-4
Gold-4
Autographs-4
Dual Autographs-AD-HH
Triple Autographs-AT-SHH
Five Autographs-AF-YAO
04UD Toronto Fall Expo Priority Signings-AH
04Upper Deck-70
Canadian Exclusives-70
Heritage Classic-CC-AH
HG Glossy Gold-70
HG Glossy Silver-70
Jersey Autographs-GJA-AL
04Czech NHL ELH Postcards-5
04Czech OFS-134
Stars-12
04Czech Zuma-13
05Beehive Matted Materials-MMAH
05Hot Prospects-41
En Fuego-41
Red Hot-41
White Hot-41
05Panini Stickers-279
05Parkhurst-187
Facsimile Auto Parallel-187
True Colors-TCEDM
True Colors-TCEDM
True Colors-TCEDCA
True Colors-TCEDCA
05SP Authentic Scripts to Success-SSAH
05SP Authentic Sign of the Times Duals-DPH
05SP Game Used Authentic Fabrics Dual-RA
05SP Game Used Authentic Patches Dual-RA
05SP Game Used Awesome Authentics-AA-AH
05SP Game Used Statscriptions-ST-AH
05SPx Winning Combos-WC-ED
05SPx Winning Combos-WC-PH
05SPx Winning Combos Autographs-AWC-PH
05SPx Winning Combos Autographs-AWC-SH
05SPx Winning Combos Gold-WC-ED
05SPx Winning Combos Gold-WC-PH
05SPx Winning Combos Spectrum-WC-ED
05SPx Winning Combos Spectrum-WC-PH
05SPx Winning Materials-WM-AH
05SPx Winning Materials Gold-WM-AH
05SPx Winning Materials Spectrum-WM-AH
05The Cup Dual NHL Shields Autographs-ADSAR
05The Cup Honorable Numbers-HNAH
05The Cup Master Pressplate Rookie Update-236
05The Cup Scripted Swatches-SSAH
05The Cup Signature Patches-SPAH
05UD Artifacts Auto Facts-AF-AH
05UD Artifacts Auto Facts Blue-AF-AH
05UD Artifacts Auto Facts Copper-AF-AH
05UD Artifacts Auto Facts Pewter-AF-AH
05UD Artifacts Auto Facts Silver-AF-AH
05UD Artifacts Remarkable Artifacts-RA-AH
05UD Artifacts Remarkable Artifacts Dual-RA-AH
05UD PowerPlay-36
Rainbow-36
Specialists-TSAH
Specialists Patches-SPAH
05UD Toronto Fall Expo Priority Signings-PS-AH
05Ultimate Collection-40
Gold-40
05Ultra-85
Gold-85
Ice-85
05Upper Deck-78
HG Glossy-78
Jerseys-J-AHE
Notable Numbers-N-AH
Patches-P-ALH
Ice Fresh Ice-FIHE
Ice Fresh Ice Glass-FIHE
Ice Fresh Ice Glass Patches-FIPHE
05Upper Deck MVP-155
Gold-155
Platinum-155
05Upper Deck Rookie Update-40
05Upper Deck Rookie Update-236
Inspirations Patch Rookies-236
05Upper Deck Trilogy Honorary Patches-HP-AH
05Upper Deck Tril Honorary Patch Script-HSP-AH
05Upper Deck Trilogy Honorary Swatches-HS-AH
05Upper Deck Tril Honorary Swatch Scripts-HSS-AH
05Upper Deck Trilogy Ice Scripts-IS-AH
05Upper Deck Trilogy Scripts-SFS-AH
05Upper Deck Toronto Fall Expo-78
05Upper Deck Victory-219
Black-219
Gold-219
Silver-219
05Czech World Champions Postcards-11
05Czech Pexeso Mini Red Set-22
06Be A Player Portraits-43
06Beehive-60
06Beehive-202
Blue-60
Gold-60
Matte-60
Red Facsimile Signatures-60
Wood-60
Matted Materials-MMAH
Signature Scrapbook-SSAH
06Black Diamond-103
Black-103
Gold-103
Ruby-103
Jerseys-JAH
Jerseys Black-JAH
Jerseys Gold-JAH
Jerseys Ruby-JAH
Jerseys Black Autographs -JAH
06Flair Showcase-45
06Flair Showcase-129
Parallel-45
Parallel-129
Hot Numbers-HN20
Hot Numbers Parallel-HN20
Inks-IAH
Stitches-SSAH
Wave of the Future-WF14
06Fleer-76
Tiffany-76
Signing Day-SDAH
Total 0-010
06Gatorade-17
06Hot Prospects-41
Red Hot-41
White Hot-41
06McDonald's Upper Deck-18
Autographs-AAH
Jerseys-JAH
Patches-PAH
06O-Pee-Chee-191
Rainbow-191
Autographs-A-AH
Swatches-S-AH
06Panini Stickers-272
06SP Authentic-62
06SP Authentic-101
Chirography-AH
Limited-62
Limited-101
Sign of the Times-STAH
Sign of the Times Triples-ST3SSH
06SP Game Used-39
Gold-39
Rainbow-39
Authentic Fabrics-AFAH
Authentic Fabrics Parallel-AFAH
Authentic Fabrics Patches-AFAH
Authentic Fabrics Dual-AF2HL
Authentic Fabrics Dual Patches-AF2HL
Authentic Fabrics Triple-AF3EDM
Authentic Fabrics Triple Patches-AF3EDM
Autographs-39
Inked Sweaters-ISAH
Inked Sweaters Patches-ISAH
Inked Sweaters Dual-IS2HS
Inked Sweaters Dual Patches-IS2HS
SIGnificance-SAH
06SPx-39
Spectrum-39
SPxcitement-X40
SPxcitement Spectrum-X40
SPxcitement Autographs-X40
Winning Materials-WMAH
Winning Materials Spectrum-WMAH
Winning Materials Autographs-WMAH
06The Cup-33
Autographed Foundations-CQAH
Autographed Foundations Patches-CQAH
Autographed NHL Shields Duals-DASAD
Autographed NHL Shields Duals-DASEO
Autographed Patches-33
Black Rainbow-33
Foundations-CQAH
Foundations Patches-CQAH
Gold-33
Gold Patches-33
Honorable Numbers-HNAH
Jerseys-33
Limited Logos-LLAH
Masterpiece Pressplates-33
Scripted Swatches Duals-DSAR
Signature Patches-SPAH
06UD Artifacts-60
06UD Artifacts-169
Blue-60
Blue-169
Gold-60
Gold-169
Platinum-60
Platinum-169
Radiance-60
Radiance-169
Autographed Radiance Parallel-60
Autographed Radiance Parallel-169
Red-60
Red-169
Auto-Facts-AFAH
Auto-Facts Gold-AFAH
Treasured Patches Black-TSAH
Treasured Patches Blue-TSAH
Treasured Patches Gold-TSAH
Treasured Patches Platinum-TSAH
Treasured Patches Red-TSAH
Treasured Patches Autographed Black Tag Parallel-TSAH
Treasured Swatches-TSAH
Treasured Swatches Black-TSAH
Treasured Swatches Blue-TSAH
Treasured Swatches Gold-TSAH
Treasured Swatches Platinum-TSAH
Treasured Swatches Red-TSAH
Treasured Swatches Autographed Black-TSAH
06UD Mini Jersey Collection-43
06UD Powerplay-41
Impact Rainbow-41
Specialists-SAH
Specialists Patches-PAH
06Ultimate Collection-26
Autographed Jerseys-AJ-AH
Autographed Patches-AJ-AH
Jerseys Dual-UJ2-HS
Patches Dual-UJ2-HS
Premium Patches-PS-AH
Premium Swatches-PS-AH
Signatures-US-AH
06Ultra-76
Gold Medallion-76
Ice Medallion-76
Uniformity-UAH
Uniformity Patches-UPAH
Uniformity Autographed Jerseys-UAAH
06Upper Deck Arena Giveaways-EDM1
06Upper Deck-75
Exclusives Parallel-75
High Gloss Parallel-75
Game Jerseys-JAH
Game Patches-PAH
Generations Duals-G2HH
Generations Patches Dual-G2PHH
Masterpieces-75
Shootout Artists-SA6
Walmart Tins Oversize-75
06Upper Deck MVP-113
Gold Script-113
Super Script-113
Jerseys-OJDH
Jerseys-OJHH
06Upper Deck Ovation-167
06Upper Deck Sweet Shot-43
Signature Shots/Saves-SSAH
Signature Shots/Saves Ice Signings-SSIAH
Signature Shots/Saves Sticks-SSSAH
Sweet Stitches-SSAH
Sweet Stitches Duals-SSAH
Sweet Stitches Triples-SSAH
06Upper Deck Trilogy-41
Combo Autographed Jerseys-CJHL
Combo Autographed Patches-CJHL
Combo Clearcut Autographs-C2AR
Honorary Scripted Patches-HSAH
Honorary Scripted Swatches-HSAH
Honorary Swatches-HSAH
Ice Scripts-ISAH
Scripts-TSAH
06Upper Deck Victory-78
06Upper Deck Victory Black-78
06Upper Deck Victory Gold-78
06Upper Deck Victory Next In Line-NL21
06Upper Deck Victory Oversize Cards-AH
06Russian Sport Collection Olympic Stars-32
07Upper Deck Ovation-28
07Upper Deck Victory-166
Black-166
Gold-166
GameBreakers-GB28

Hemsky, Petr
94Czech APS Extraliga-280
99Czech OFS-348
00Czech OFS-30
00London Knights-8
01Kitchener Rangers-12

Hemstrom, Jens
90Swedish Semic Elitserien Stickers-147
93Swedish Semic Elitserien-187
94Swedish Leaf-219
95Swedish Upper Deck-181

Henchberger, Lloyd
51Laval Dairy QSHL-66

Henckle, James
87Kingston Canadians-13

Hendelis, Andris
74Swedish Stickers-72

Henderson, Archie
82Whalers Junior Hartford Courant-6
84Nova Scotia Oilers-12
88ProCards IHL-17
89Nashville Knights-8

Henderson, Brian
95Kamloops Blazers-21

Henderson, Burt
92British Columbia JHL-70
93Tacoma Rockets-13
97Cincinnati Cyclones-8
98Cincinnati Cyclones-8
98Cincinnati Cyclones 2-14

Henderson, Charlie
02Michigan Wolverines-5
03Michigan Wolverines-26
04Michigan Wolverines-24

Henderson, Garfield
917th Inn. Sketch WHL-0
92Saskatchewan JHL-55

Henderson, Jay
95Red Deer Rebels-6
98Providence Bruins-11
98Bowman CHL-77
Golden Anniversary-77
OPC International-77
98Bowman Chrome CHL-77
Golden Anniversary-77
Golden Anniversary Refractors-77
OPC International-77
OPC International Refractors-77
Refractors-77
99BAP Memorabilia-358
Gold-358
Silver-358
99Pacific Omega-23
Copper-23
Gold-23
Ice Blue-23
Premiere Date-23
99Upper Deck MVP SC Edition-18
Gold Script-18
Silver Script-18
Super Script-18
99Providence Bruins-12
00Upper Deck NHLPA-PA8
00Providence Bruins-9
02Providence Bruins-10
03Milwaukee Admirals-2
03Milwaukee Admirals Postcards-10
04Providence Bruins-10
05German DEL-302
06German DEL-6

Henderson, John
51Parkhurst-23

Henderson, Kevin
04Kitchener Rangers-16
05Kitchener Rangers-11
06Kitchener Rangers-19

Henderson, Matt
98Milwaukee Admirals-20
98Milwaukee Admirals Postcards-4
01Norfolk Admirals-12
02BAP First Edition-215
02BAP Memorabilia-390
02SP Authentic-140
02SPx-171
02UD Honor Roll-109
02UD Mask Collection-134
02UD Top Shelf-109
02Norfolk Admirals-10
03German DEL-144

Henderson, Mike
98Thunder Bay Thunder Cats-10
00Barrie Colts-14
00Knoxville Speed-19
02Greenville Grrrowl-9
03Greenville Grrrowl-9

Henderson, Murray
44Beehive Group II Photos-30

Henderson, Paul
61Hamilton Red Wings-9
63Chex Photos-21
64Beehive Group III Photos-76
64Coca-Cola Caps-52
64Toronto Star-14
65Coca-Cola-50
65Topps-51
66Topps-46
66Topps USA Test-46
67Topps-103
68Bauer Ads-11
68Maple Leafs White Border-3
68O-Pee-Chee-127
68Post Marbles-11
68Shirriff Coins-161
68Topps-127
69O-Pee-Chee-47
69Topps-47
70Dad's Cookies-50
70Esso Power Players-30
70Maple Leafs Postcards-5
70O-Pee-Chee-217
70Post Shooters-4
70Sargent Promotions Stamps-195
71Colgate Heads-4
71Frito-Lay-8
71Letraset Action Replays-22
71Maple Leafs Postcards-7
71O-Pee-Chee-67
71Sargent Promotions Stamps-200
71Topps-67
71Toronto Sun-260
72Maple Leafs Postcards-10
72Maple Leafs Postcards-11
72O-Pee-Chee-126
Player Crests-19
Team Canada-14
72Sargent Promotions Stamps-203
72Topps-73
72Finnish Semic World Championship-167
72Swedish Semic World Championship-167
73Mac's Milk-9
73Maple Leafs Postcards-10
73O-Pee-Chee-7
73Topps-7
74O-Pee-Chee NHL-219
74O-Pee-Chee WHA-57
74Team Canada L'Equipe WHA-8
74Topps-219
75O-Pee-Chee WHA-42
76O-Pee-Chee WHA-84
77O-Pee-Chee WHA-31
91Future Trends Canada '72 Promos-1
91Future Trends Canada '72 Promos-3
91Future Trends Canada '72-63
91Future Trends Canada '72-71
91Future Trends Canada '72-81
91Future Trends Canada '72-98
91Future Trends Canada '72 French-71
91Future Trends Canada '72 French-98
92Future Trends '76 Canada Cup-105
94Parkhurst Tall Boys-50
95Parkhurst '66-67-40
Coins-40
97Pinnacle Certified Summit Silver-S1
97Pinnacle Certified Summit Silver-S2
97Pinnacle Certified Summit Silver-S3
97Pinnacle Certified Summit Silver-S4
97Pinnacle Certified Summit Silver-S5
97Pinnacle Certified Summit Silver-NNO
97Pinnacle Certified Summit Silver-NNO
97Pinnacle Certified Summit Silver-NNO
01Fleer Legacy-42
Ultimate-42
01Greats of the Game-42
Autographs-42
02Maple Leafs Platinum Collection-75
Autographs-75
04UD Legendary Signatures-63
Autographs-PH
Summit Stars-CDN2
Summit Stars Autographs-CDN-PH
04UD Legends Classics-43
04UD Legends Classics-58
Gold-43
Gold-58
Platinum-43
Platinum-58
Silver-43
Silver-58
Signature Moments-M16
Signatures-CS16
Signatures-TC2
05ITG Heroes/Prosp Toronto Expo Parallel -17
05ITG Ultimate Memorabilia Level 1-78
05ITG Ultimate Memorabilia Level 2-78
05ITG Ultimate Memorabilia Level 3-78
05ITG Ultimate Memorabilia Level 4-78
05ITG Ultimate Memorabilia Level 5-78
05ITG Ultimate Memorabilia Double Autos-4
05ITG Ultimate Memorabilia Double Autos-20
05ITG Ultimate Mem Double Autos Gold-4
05ITG Ultimate Mem Double Autos Gold-20
05ITG Ultimate Memorabilia Triple Autos-12
05ITG Ultimate Mem Triple Autos Gold-12
05ITG Ultimate Memorabilia Ultimate Autos-32
05ITG Ultimate Mem Ultimate Autos Gold-32
05UD Artifacts-122
Blue-122
Gold-122
Green-122
Pewter-122
Red-122
Gold Autographed-122
05ITG Heroes and Prospects-17
Autographs-A-PH
06ITG International Ice-101
06ITG International Ice-129
Gold-101
Gold-129
Autographs-APH
Autographs-APH2
06ITG Ultimate Memorabilia-113
Artist Proof-113
Autos-67
Autos Gold-67
Autos Dual-9
Autos Dual Gold-9
Autos Triple-3
Autos Triple Gold-3
06Parkhurst-29
Autographs-29
06The Cup Honorable Numbers-HNPA
06The Cup Limited Logos-LLPA
06The Cup Signature Patches-SPPH
06Ultimate Collection Jerseys Triple-UJ3-SSH
06Ultimate Collection Patches Triple-UJ3-SSH

Henderson, Ryan
96Saskatoon Blades-11

Henderson, Todd
95Alaska Gold Kings-7
96Alaska Gold Kings-6

Hendle, Philip
05German DEL-237

Hendrick, Jorg
94German DEL-266
98German DEL-72

Hendricks, Matt
03St. Cloud State Huskies-9
04Florida Everblades-12

Hendrickson, Dan
93Minnesota Golden Gophers-12
94Minnesota Golden Gophers-16
95Minnesota Golden Gophers-15
96Minnesota Golden Gophers-14
98Dayton Bombers-6
98Dayton Bombers EBK-11

Hendrickson, Darby
91Minnesota Golden Gophers-9
92Minnesota Golden Gophers-9
93PowerPlay-505
93Stadium Club Team USA-8
93Stadium Club Team USA Members Only-8
93Topps Premier Team USA-4
93Ultra-485
94Maple Leafs Pin-up Posters-29
94St. John's Maple Leafs-12
94Classic-104
Gold-104
Pro Prospects International Heroes-LP6
94Classic Four-Sport *-135
Gold-135
Printers Proofs-135
95Bowman-129
All-Foil-129
95Donruss-184
95Leaf-76
95Select Certified-142
Mirror Gold-142
95SkyBox Impact-223
95SP-145
95Summit-178
Artist's Proofs-178
Ice-178
95Ultra-340
95Upper Deck-505
Electric Ice-505
Electric Ice Gold-505
96Collector's Choice-158
96Upper Deck-100
96Collector's Edge Ice-79
Prism-79
97Be A Player-178
Autographs-178
Autographs Die-Cuts-178
Autographs Prismatic Die-Cuts-178
97Collector's Choice-250
97Pacific Invincible NHL Regime-193
97Score Maple Leafs-12
Platinum-12
Premier-12
97Upper Deck-166
99O-Pee-Chee-151
99O-Pee-Chee Chrome-151
99O-Pee-Chee Chrome Refractors-151
99Topps/OPC-151
99Topps/OPC Chrome-151
Refractors-151
00BAP Memorabilia-121
Emerald-121
Ruby-121
Sapphire-121
Promos-121
00BAP Mem Chicago Sportsfest Copper-121
00BAP Memorabilia Chicago Sportsfest Blue-121
00BAP Memorabilia Chicago Sportsfest Gold-121
00BAP Memorabilia Chicago Sportsfest Ruby-121
00BAP Memorabilia Chicago Sun-Times Ruby-121
00BAP Memorabilia Chicago Sun-Times Gold-121
00BAP Mem Chicago Sun-Times Sapphire-121
00BAP Mem Toronto Fall Expo Copper-121
00BAP Memorabilia Toronto Fall Expo Gold-121
00BAP Memorabilia Toronto Fall Expo Ruby-121
00SP Authentic-44
00Stadium Club-205
00Topps Chrome-234
OPC Refractors-234
Refractors-234
01Pacific Adrenaline-93
Blue-93
Premiere Date-93
Red-93
Retail-93
01Upper Deck-88
Exclusives-88
01Upper Deck Victory-176
Gold-176
01Wild Crime Prevention-19
02Pacific-183
Blue-183
Red-183
02Upper Deck-87
Exclusives-87
03Upper Deck MVP-217
Gold Script-217
Silver Script-217
Cánadian Exclusives-217

Hendrikx, Trevor
01Peterborough Petes-5
02Peterborough Petes-6
04Peterborough Petes Postcards-8

Hendry, Gian-Carlo
02Swiss HNL-17

Hendry, Grant
02UK Peterborough Phantoms-15

Hendry, John
91Lake Superior State Lakers-11
92Lake Superior State Lakers-12
93Toledo Storm-18
94Toledo Storm-8
95Buffalo Stampedes RHI-14

Hendry, Jordan
06Norfolk Admirals-5

Hendy, James
83Hall of Fame Postcards-B5
85Hall of Fame-19

Henegan, Kyell
05Shawinigan Cataractes-14

Hengen, Billy
00Lincoln Stars-15
01Lincoln Stars-12
03St. Cloud State Huskies-10
04St. Cloud State Huskies-14
05St. Cloud State Huskies-12
05St. Cloud State Huskies-14

Hengen, Michael
03Swift Current Broncos-5
04Swift Current Broncos-6
05Saskatoon Blades-9
05Swift Current Broncos-2
06Moose Jaw Warriors-17

Henituik, Joel
02Kelowna Rockets-4

Henkel, Andreas
94German First League-654

Henkel, Jimmy
93Quebec Pee-Wee Tournament-1577
02Atlantic City Boardwalk Bullies-10
02ECHL All-Star Northern-22
03Atlantic City Boardwalk Bullies-9
04Atlantic City Boardwalk Bullies Kinko's-11
04Lowell Lock Monsters-10
04Lowell Lock Monsters Photo Album-10

Henkelman, Derek
95Neepewa Natives-15

Henkelman, Jeff
94Kamloops Blazers-22
95Swift Current Broncos-6
96Swift Current Broncos-4
97Swift Current Broncos-5

Henkelman, Scott
99Swift Current Broncos-5
00Swift Current Broncos-9

Henley, Brent
01Colorado Gold Kings-10
02South Carolina Stingrays-9
02South Carolina Stingrays RBI-212
06Fort Wayne Komets-20

Hennes, Ty
03Boston College Eagles-4
04Bakersfield Condors-5

Hennessey, Derek
99Guelph Storm-19
01Guelph Storm-16
01Guelph Storm Memorial Cup-16

Hennessy, Josh
01Quebec Remparts-5
02Quebec Remparts-4
03Quebec Remparts Memorial Cup-6
03Quebec Remparts-11
04Quebec Remparts-14
05ITG Heroes/Prosp Toronto Expo Parallel -388
05Cleveland Barons-9
05Extreme Top Prospects Signature Edition-S23
05ITG Heroes and Prospects-388
06Be A Player-225
06Beehive-138
Blue-138
Matte-138
Red Facsimile Signatures-138
Wood-138
06Flair Showcase-320
06Hot Prospects-199
06SP Authentic-227
Limited-227
06The Cup-145
Autographed Rookie Masterpiece Pressplates-145
Gold Rainbow Autographed Rookie Patches-145
Masterpiece Pressplates (Bee Hive)-138
Masterpiece Pressplates (SP Authentic)-227
Masterpiece Pressplates (Sweet Beginnings)-140
Masterpiece Pressplates (Ultimate Collection)-85
Rookies Black-145
Rookies Platinum-145
06UD Artifacts-236
06Ultimate Collection-85
06Upper Deck Sweet Shot-140
Rookie Jerseys Autographs-140
06AHL Top Prospects-4
06Binghamton Senators-11
06ITG Heroes and Prospects-172
Autographs-AJHE
Update Autographs-AJHE

Hennigar, Rob
02Windsor Spitfires-12

Hennigar, Stan
83Nova Scotia Voyageurs-5

Henning, Chris
93Quebec Pee-Wee Tournament-708

Henning, Lorne
72Sargent Promotions Stamps-135
73O-Pee-Chee-218
74NHL Action Stamps-168
74O-Pee-Chee NHL-367
75O-Pee-Chee NHL-354
76O-Pee-Chee NHL-193
76Topps-193
77Coca-Cola-11
77O-Pee-Chee NHL-219
77Topps-219
78O-Pee-Chee-313
79Islanders Transparencies-5
79O-Pee-Chee-193
79Topps-193
84Islanders News-27
84Springfield Indians-24

Hennings, Brett
93Quebec Pee-Wee Tournament-1732

Henrich, Adam
00Brampton Battalion-10
00Brampton Battalion-32
00UD CHL Prospects-3
03Brampton Batallion-8
04AHL Top Prospects-50
04Springfield Falcons-1
05Johnstown Chiefs-11
05Springfield Falcons-1
06Springfield Falcons-26

Henrich, Ed
92Clarkson Knights-8
94Toledo Storm-9

Henrich, Michael
96Barrie Colts-9
97Barrie Colts-9
98OPC Chrome-223
Refractors-223
98Topps-223
O-Pee-Chee-223
98Barrie Colts-16
98Bowman CHL-30
98Bowman CHL-127
Golden Anniversary-30
Golden Anniversary-127
OPC International-30
OPC International-127
Autographs Blue-A6
Autographs Gold-A6
Autographs Silver-A6
98Bowman Chrome CHL-30
98Bowman Chrome CHL-127
Golden Anniversary-30
Golden Anniversary-127
Golden Anniversary Refractors-30
Golden Anniversary Refractors-127
OPC International-30
OPC International-127
OPC International Refractors-30
OPC International Refractors-127
Refractors-30
Refractors-127
99Upper Deck Sobey's Memorial Cup-3
99UD Prospects-11
00Hamilton Bulldogs-14
01Hamilton Bulldogs-14
02Hamilton Bulldogs-16
04Barrie Colts 10th Anniversary-3
05German DEL-316

Henrikson, Gunnar
91British Columbia JHL-141

Henriksson, Daniel
02Swedish SHL-56
02Swedish SHL-289
Netminders-NM6
Parallel-56
Parallel-289
Signatures Series II-2
02Swiss SCL Tigers-6
03Swedish Elite-223
Hot Numbers-HN9
Jerseys-3
Signatures-4
Silver-223
04Swedish Elitset-180
Gold-180
In The Crease-7
Limited Signatures-1
Signatures Series A-8
Signatures Series B-3
05Swedish SHL Elitset-38
Catchers-4
Catchers Gold-4
Gold-38
Series One Signatures-11
Stoppers-6
06Swedish SHL Elitset-40
Goal Patrol-7
In The Crease-4

Henriksson, Hannu
91Finnish Semic World Champ Stickers-11
91Finnish Jyvas-Hyva Stickers-11
91Swedish Semic World Champ Stickers-11
93Finnish Jyvas-Hyva Stickers-76
93Finnish SISU-114
94Finnish SISU-128
95Finnish SISU-30
95Finnish SISU-177
95Finnish SISU Limited-102
96Finnish SISU Redline Sledgehammers-1
99Finnish Cardset-246

Henriksson, Kristian
84Swedish Semic Elitserien-82

Henriksson, Lars-Olof
67Swedish Hockey-237

Henriksson, Leif
67Swedish Hockey-8
67Swedish Hockey-288
69Swedish Hockey-185
69Swedish Hockey-335
70Swedish Hockey-253
70Swedish Masterserien-104
71Swedish Hockey-312
72Swedish Stickers-295
73Swedish Stickers-140
74Swedish Stickers-222

Henriksson, Lennart
91Swedish Semic Elitserien Stickers-219

Henriksson, Olle
71Swedish Hockey-394
72Swedish Stickers-266

Henry, Alex
98Bowman CHL-156
Golden Anniversary-156
OPC International-156
Autographs Blue-A17
Autographs Gold-A17
Autographs Silver-A17
98Bowman Chrome CHL-156
Golden Anniversary-156
Golden Anniversary Refractors-156
OPC International-156
OPC International Refractors-156
Refractors-156
99Hamilton Bulldogs-18
99Bowman CHL-155
Gold-155
OPC International-155
00Hamilton Bulldogs-9
01Hamilton Bulldogs-3
02Atomic-110
Blue-110
Gold-110
Red-110
Hobby Parallel-110
02BAP All-Star Edition-108
Gold-108
Silver-108
02BAP Memorabilia-285
Emerald-285
Ruby-285
Sapphire-285
NHL All-Star Game-285
NHL All-Star Game Blue-285
NHL All-Star Game Green-285
NHL All-Star Game Red-285
02BAP Memorabilia Toronto Fall Expo-285
02BAP Ultimate Memorabilia-15
02Crown Royale-140
Blue-140
Purple-140
Red-140
Retail-140
02NHL Power Play Stickers-44
02Pacific Calder-150
Silver-150
02Pacific Complete-571
Red-571
02Pacific Exclusive-179A
Blue-179A
02Private Stock Reserve-185
Blue-185
Red-185
Retail-185
02SP Authentic-144
02UD Mask Collection-145
02UD Top Shelf-105
06Milwaukee Admirals -6

Henry, Burke
95Brandon Wheat Kings-9
96Brandon Wheat Kings-3

97Brandon Wheat Kings-11
98Brandon Wheat Kings-7
98Bowman CHL-67
Golden Anniversary-67
OPC International-67
98Bowman Chrome CHL-67
Golden Anniversary-67
Golden Anniversary Refractors-67
OPC International-67
OPC International Refractors-67
Refractors-67
99Hartford Wolf Pack-11
99Bowman CHL-96
Gold-96
OPC International-96
00Hartford Wolf Pack-12
02BAP Memorabilia-382
02BAP Ultimate Memorabilia-94
02Upper Deck Rookie Update-128
02Norfolk Admirals-11
03ITG Action-188
03Pacific Complete-531
Red-531
03Parkhurst Original Six Chicago-19
03Norfolk Admirals-10
04Milwaukee Admirals-8
06Finnish Cardset-319
Enforcers-5

Henry, Camille
44Beehive Group II Photos-323
50Quebec Citadelles-9
52Juniors Blue Tint-73A
52Juniors Blue Tint-73B
54Parkhurst-73
54Topps-32
57Topps-63
58Topps-54
59Topps-28
59Topps-46
60Shirriff Coins-83
60Topps-53
Stamps-25
61Shirriff/Salada Coins-87
61Topps-50
62Topps-62
63Topps-56
63Toronto Star-18
64Beehive Group III Photos-38
64Beehive Group III Photos-131
64Coca-Cola Caps-88
64Topps-14
65Topps-58
66Topps-55
67Topps-20
68O-Pee-Chee-116
68Topps-116
69O-Pee-Chee-17
69Topps-17
91Ultimate Original Six-22
French-22
93Parkhurst Parkie Reprints-PR50
94Parkhurst Missing Link-100
94Parkhurst Tall Boys-107
02Parkhurst Reprints-196
04ITG Franchises US East-405

Henry, Dale
83Saskatoon Blades-11
84Springfield Indians-17
86Islanders Team Issue-11
88ProCards AHL-322
89ProCards AHL-231
90ProCards AHL/IHL-529
94Central Hockey League-79
94San Antonio Iguanas-7
94Classic Enforcers-E3
95Central Hockey League-97

Henry, Daryl
83Medicine Hat Tigers-19

Henry, Frederic
97Bowman CHL-43
OPC-43
98Albany River Rats-9
99Albany River Rats-14
00Albany River Rats-23
03BAP Memorabilia-216
04Thetford Mines Prolab-17

Henry, Jim
34Beehive Group I Photos-276A
34Beehive Group I Photos-276B
43Parade Sportive *-54
44Beehive Group II Photos-31
44Beehive Group II Photos-104
51Parkhurst-19
52Parkhurst-74
53Parkhurst-86
54Parkhurst-49
54Topps-37
92Parkhurst Parkie Reprints-PR7
02BAP Ultimate Memorabilia Great Moments-3
02Parkhurst Reprints-153

Henry, Joe
06UK Coventry Blaze-2

Henry, Jordan
04Moose Jaw Warriors-2

Henry, Nick
94UK Solihul Barons-6
95UK Solihull Barons-2

Henry, Patrick
93Swiss HNL-441
98Swiss Power Play Stickers-357

Henry, Ross
06Lincoln Stars-14
06Lincoln Stars Upper DeckÂ Signature Series -13

Henry, Ryan
06Erie Otters-21

Henry, Shane
94Richmond Renegades-2

Hensick, T.J.
03Michigan Wolverines-15
04Michigan Wolverines-13

Henttonen, Juha
80Finnish Mallasjuoma-154

Hentuik, Chase
04Lethbridge Hurricanes-15

Hentunen, Jukka
99Finnish Cardset-39
00Finnish Cardset-238
00Finnish Cardset-283
01BAP Memorabilia-381
Emerald-381
Ruby-381
Sapphire-381
01Bowman YoungStars-54
Gold-54
Ice Cubed-54
01Crown Royale-149
01O-Pee-Chee-340
01Parkhurst-307
01Private Stock-116
Gold-116
Premiere Date-116
Retail-116
Silver-116
01Private Stock Pacific Nights-116
01SP Authentic-138
Limited-138
Limited Gold-138
01Stadium Club-125
Award Winners-125
Master Photos-125
01Titanium-151
Retail-151
01Titanium Draft Day Edition-50
01Titanium Draft Day Edition-143
01Topps-340
01Topps Chrome-158
Refractors-158
Black Border Refractors-158
01Topps Reserve-110
01UD Challenge for the Cup-98
01UD Playmakers-107
01Upper Deck-418
Exclusives-418
01Upper Deck Ice-75
01Vanguard-105
Blue-105
Red-105
One of Ones-105
Premiere Date-105
Proofs-105
01Finnish Cardset-173
02Pacific Jerseys-29
02Pacific Jerseys Holo-Silver-29
02Pacific Heads-Up Quad Jerseys-16
02Pacific Heads-Up Quad Jerseys-36
02Pacific Heads-Up Quad Jerseys Gold-16
02Pacific Heads-Up Quad Jerseys Gold-36
02Finnish Cardset-173

Henwood, Steve
02Owen Sound Attack-14

Henzen, Charly
72Finnish Semic World Championship-150
72Swedish Semic World Championship-150
74Finnish Typotor-105

Heon, Corey
92Saskatchewan JHL-42
97El Paso Buzzards-11
98El Paso Buzzards-4

Hepditch, Joshua
02Moncton Wildcats-16
03Moncton Wildcats-14
04Moncton Wildcats-23
05Moncton Wildcats-10

Hepple, Alan
81Ottawa 67's-7
82Ottawa 67's-7
82Ottawa 67's-8
88ProCards AHL-234
89ProCards AHL-117
90Newmarket Saints-5
90ProCards AHL/IHL-157
91ProCards-316
92Cincinnati Cyclones-11

Heppner, Ken
81Regina Pats-14

Herauf, Brad
03Oklahoma City Blazers-10
04Oklahoma City Blazers-8

Herauf, Lance
06New Mexico Scorpions-16

Herbers, Ian
84Kelowna Wings-10
93Leaf-423
93Parkhurst-70
Emerald Ice-70
94Cape Breton Oilers-9
96Detroit Vipers-8
97Detroit Vipers-6
98Detroit Vipers-17
98Detroit Vipers Freschetta-7
99Detroit Vipers Kid's Club-6
00Cleveland Lumberjacks-9
02UK Guildford Flames-1
03San Antonio Rampage-2

Herbert, Bjorn
71Finnish Suomi Stickers-279
73Finnish Jaakiekko-195

Herbert, Brian
03Louisiana Ice Gators-8
04Richmond Riverdogs-16

Herbert, Rick
82Regina Pats-10
83Regina Pats-10

Herberts, Jim
24C144 Champ's Cigarettes-30
24V130 Maple Crispette-8
24V145-2-25

Herbison, Alex
98El Paso Buzzards-5

Herbst, Abe
96Sarnia Sting-10
97Upper Deck-404
98Sudbury Wolves-22
99Sudbury Wolves-6

Herbst, Alexander
95German DEL-179
99German Bundesliga 2-327
04German Weiden Blue Devils-11

Herbst, Marco
94German DEL-141
95German DEL-125
96German DEL-205

Herczeg, Don
83Medicine Hat Tigers-3

Hergesheimer, Phil
34Beehive Group I Photos-56
40O-Pee-Chee V301-2-143

Hergesheimer, Walter
44Beehive Group II Photos-324
51Parkhurst-100
52Parkhurst-20
53Parkhurst-67
54Parkhurst-71
54Topps-22
57Topps-33
94Parkhurst Missing Link-26

Herget, Jens
94German First League-532

Hergott, Orrin
91Air Canada SJHL-B51
04Columbus Cottonmouths-7

Herhal, Matt
97Dubuque Fighting Saints-18
00Connecticut Huskies-8

Herlea, Daniel
95Swiss HNL-492
96Swiss HNL-408

Herlick, Darcy
91Air Canada SJHL-D1
92Saskatchewan JHL-147

Herlofsky, Derek
95Dayton Bombers-3
96Dayton Bombers-20
00UK Cardiff Devils-1
00UK Sekonda Superleague-52
01UK Cardiff Devils-17
02UK Cardiff Devils-17

Herman, Andre
03Red Deer Rebels-6
05Moose Jaw Warriors-10

Herman, Jan
06Czech OFS-272
Brothers-1

Herman, Martin
Brothers-1

Herman, Patrick
96OCN Blizzard-25

Herman, Tom
98OCN Blizzard-18
99OCN Blizzard-20

Hermanson, Andre
04Moose Jaw Warriors-13

Hermansson, Dan
83Swedish Semic Elitserien-207
84Swedish Semic Elitserien-232

Hermansson, Daniel
06Swedish SHL Elitset-151

Hermansson, Goran
99Swedish Upper Deck-27
02Swedish SHL-201
Parallel-201
03Swedish Elite-65
Silver-65

Hermansson, Hakan
83Swedish Semic Elitserien-100
93Swedish Semic Elitserien-20

Hermansson, Jorgen
93Swedish Semic Elitserien-8
98Swedish UD Choice-20
00Swedish Upper Deck-18
00Swedish Upper Deck-210
SHL Signatures-JH
03Swedish Bjorkloven Umea-11

Hermansson, Lennart
90Swedish Semic Elitserien Stickers-142
92Swedish Semic Elitserien Stickers-238
93Swedish Semic Elitserien-207
94Swedish Leaf-80

Hermsdorf, Steve
92Harvard Crimson-13

Hern, Bobby
93Quebec Pee-Wee Tournament-884

Hern, Jay
99Indianapolis Ice-7
01Indianapolis Ice-10

Hern, Riley
10C56-22
10Sweet Caporal Postcards-32
11C55-32
83Hall of Fame Postcards-K6
85Hall of Fame-232

Herneisen, Matthew
93Quebec Pee-Wee Tournament-1677
01Peterborough Petes-14
02Sault Ste. Marie Greyhounds-6

Herniman, Scott
88Sudbury Wolves-25

Herniman, Steve
87Sault Ste. Marie Greyhounds-19
88Kitchener Rangers-27
91ProCards-146
93Muskegon Fury-20
94Muskegon Fury-16
95Muskegon Fury-18

Heron, Bob
34Beehive Group I Photos-323
39O-Pee-Chee V301-1-53
40O-Pee-Chee V301-2-140

Heron, Chris
92Quebec Pee-Wee Tournament-498
93Quebec Pee-Wee Tournament-1405
96Upper Deck-382

Heroux, Benoit
93Quebec Pee-Wee Tournament-1386

Heroux, Patrick
93Quebec Pee-Wee Tournament-1390

Heroux, Yves
84Chicoutimi Sagueneens-13
86Fredericton Express-11
88Flint Spirits-6
90ProCards AHL/IHL-96
90ProCards AHL/IHL-518
91ProCards-34
93Indianapolis Ice-21
94Atlanta Knights-17
96German DEL-18

Herperger, Chris
907th Inn. Sketch WHL-67
917th Inn. Sketch WHL-189
93Seattle Thunderbirds-7
96Collector's Edge Ice-45
Prism-45
98Indianapolis Ice-13
99BAP Memorabilia-367
Gold-367
Silver-367
99Pacific Omega-59
Copper-59
Gold-59
Ice Blue-59
Premiere Date-59
99Cleveland Lumberjacks-9
00Upper Deck MVP-189
First Stars-189
Second Stars-189
Third Stars-189
01BAP Signature Series-119
Autographs-119
Autographs Gold-119
01Pacific-86
Extreme LTD-86
Hobby LTD-86
Premiere Date-86
Retail LTD-86
01Pacific Arena Exclusives-86
01Parkhurst-137
01Senators Team Issue-8
01Upper Deck Victory-81
Gold-81
02BAP Sig Series Auto Buybacks 2001-119
04German DEL-229
04German Krefeld Penguins Postcards-8
05German DEL-225

Herr, Craig
95Roanoke Express-21

Herr, Kelan
06Moncton Wildcats-23

Herr, Matt
95Donruss Elite World Juniors-37
98Crown Royale-141
Limited Series-141
98Pacific Dynagon Ice-194
Blue-194
Red-194
98Pacific Omega-246
Red-246
Opening Day Issue-246
98SP Authentic-113
Power Shift-113
98Upper Deck-386
Exclusives-386
Exclusives 1 of 1-386
Gold Reserve-386
98Upper Deck MVP-214
Gold Script-214
Silver Script-214
Super Script-214
98Portland Pirates-5
99Upper Deck Victory-312
99Portland Pirates-9
01Hershey Bears-11
02Providence Bruins-7
03Providence Bruins-6
04German DEL-46
04German Dusseldorf Metro Stars Postcards-5

Herrera, Mike
94Dubuque Fighting Saints-11

Herriman, Don
73Quaker Oats WHA-46

Herring, David
03Erie Otters-10
04Erie Otters-22

Herrington, Jamie
02ECHL All-Star Northern-23
06New Mexico Scorpions-15

Herrington, Nathan
98Guelph Storm-14

Herrington, Rob
92British Columbia JHL-183

Herron, Denis
74NHL Action Stamps-234
74NHL Action Stamps Update-16
74O-Pee-Chee NHL-45
74Topps-45
75O-Pee-Chee NHL-68
75Topps-68
76O-Pee-Chee NHL-55
76Topps-55
77O-Pee-Chee NHL-119
77Penguins Puck Bucks-1
77Topps-119
78O-Pee-Chee-172
78Topps-172
79Panini Stickers-52
79Canadiens Postcards-7
79O-Pee-Chee-94
79Topps-94
80Canadiens Postcards-7
80O-Pee-Chee-130
80O-Pee-Chee-166
80Pepsi-Cola Caps-45
80Topps-130
80Topps-166
81Canadiens Postcards-9
81O-Pee-Chee Stickers-258
82O-Pee-Chee-239
82O-Pee-Chee-241
82O-Pee-Chee-270
82O-Pee-Chee Stickers-41
82O-Pee-Chee Stickers-252
82Topps Stickers-41
82Topps Stickers-252
83Penguins Coke-13
83Penguins Heinz Photos-12
84Kellogg's Accordion Discs-8
84Kellogg's Accordion Discs Singles-17
84O-Pee-Chee-176
84O-Pee-Chee Stickers-122
84Penguins Heinz Photos-11
85O-Pee-Chee-186
04ITG Franchises US West-227
Autographs-A-DHE

Hersh, Harold
917th Inn. Sketch QMJHL-219A
917th Inn. Sketch QMJHL-219B
95Fredericton Canadiens-14
95Slapshot Memorial Cup-57
96Fredericton Canadiens-10
97Johnstown Chiefs-9
98Kentucky Thoroughblades-12
01Rockford IceHogs-9

Hersley, Patrik
06Swedish SHL Elitset-226

Herter, Jason
90Upper Deck-325
French-325
91ProCards-600
91UND Fighting Sioux Sports Collectors Card Set - 15
92Hamilton Canucks-9
93Classic Pro Prospects-58
96Kansas City Blades-12
98German DEL-71
99German DEL-334
00German DEL-182
01German Upper Deck-182

Hervey, Matt
83Victoria Cougars-11
87Moncton Hawks-11
88ProCards AHL-186
89ProCards AHL-40
90Moncton Hawks-10
90ProCards AHL/IHL-251
91ProCards-63
92Atlanta Knights-4

Herzig, Falk
94German DEL-402
95German DEL-421
99German Bundesliga 2-304

Herzig, Tom
84Minnesota-Duluth Bulldogs-29

Hes, Jiri
94Czech APS Extraliga-257
95Czech APS Extraliga-130
96Czech APS Extraliga-8
97Czech APS Extraliga-151
97Czech DS Stickers-116
99Czech DS-188
99Czech OFS-76
00Czech DS Extraliga-100
00Czech OFS-191
01Czech OFS-110
03Czech OFS Plus All-Star Game-H3
04Czech OFS Czech/Slovak-30

Heschuk, Brad
88Kamloops Blazers-11

Heshka, Scott
92Saskatchewan JHL-159

Heshka, Shaun
03Everett Silvertips-12
04Everett Silvertips-19
05Everett Silvertips-12
06Manitoba Moose-26

Heshmatpour, Devereaux
03Kitchener Rangers-12
04Oshawa Generals-14
04Oshawa Generals Autographs-14

Hess, Bob
75O-Pee-Chee NHL-264
75Topps-264
76O-Pee-Chee NHL-277
77O-Pee-Chee NHL-394
78O-Pee-Chee-358

Hess, Manuel
94German DEL-190
95German DEL-190
96German DEL-129

Hesse, Thomas
94German First League-453

Hessel, Bo
56Swedish Alfabilder-97

Hessel, Mats
83Swedish Semic Elitserien-13
84Swedish Semic Elitserien-12
85Swedish Panini Stickers-10
87Swedish Panini Stickers-21

Hessler, Corey
02Columbia Inferno-102
02ECHL All-Star Southern-45
03Columbia Inferno-104
05Rockford Ice Hogs-6
06Rockford IceHogs-12

Hettle, Fred
907th Inn. Sketch WHL-300
917th Inn. Sketch WHL-271

Heubach, Gert
94German First League-63

Hevonkorpi, Risto
72Finnish Jaakiekko-279

Heward, Jamie
87Regina Pats-7
88Regina Pats-8
89Regina Pats-7
907th Inn. Sketch WHL-167
91ProCards-308
92Cleveland Lumberjacks-7
93Cleveland Lumberjacks-20
93Cleveland Lumberjacks Postcards-13
93Classic Pro Prospects-107
95St. John's Maple Leafs-12
96St. John's Maple Leafs-16
98Bowman's Best-74
Refractors-74
Atomic Refractors-74
98Predators Team Issue-11
99Pacific-224
Copper-224
Emerald Green-224
Gold-224
Ice Blue-224
Premiere Date-224
Red-224
99Ultimate Victory-53
1/1-53
Parallel-53
Parallel 100-53
01Blue Jackets Donatos Pizza-24
01Upper Deck Vintage-76
02Swiss HNL-339
05Parkhurst-492
Facsimile Auto Parallel-492
05Upper Deck-437
06O-Pee-Chee-492
Rainbow-492

Hewer, Oak
96Sault Ste. Marie Greyhounds-6
96Sault Ste. Marie Greyhounds Autographed-6
01Rockford IceHogs-18
02Rockford Ice Hogs-6

Hewitson, Bobby
83Hall of Fame Postcards-F6
85Hall of Fame-82

Hewitt, Foster
34Beehive Group I Photos-356
35CCM Green Border Photos-10
38Quaker Oats Photos-18
83Hall of Fame Postcards-A7
85Hall of Fame-8
92Hall of Fame Legends-13
03BAP Ultimate Mem Maple Leafs Forever-19
03BAP Ultimate Memorabilia Paper Cuts-13
04ITG Ultimate Memorabilia-22
Gold-22
04Ultimate Collection-52
04Upper Deck-200
Canadian Exclusives-200
HG Glossy Gold-200
HG Glossy Silver-200
05ITG Ultimate Mem Leafs Forever Autos-8
06ITG Ultimate Memorabilia-49
Artist Proof-49
Builders Autos-4

Hewitt, Greg
03Columbus Stars-3

Hewitt, Jason
03UK Manchester Phoenix-15
04UK London Racers-14
04UK London Racers Playoffs-8
05UK Sheffield Steelers-16
Gold-16
Silver-16

Hewitt, John
00Asheville Smoke-6

Hewitt, William A
83Hall of Fame Postcards-G8
85Hall of Fame-99

Hewson, Ashton
05Prince Albert Raiders-13
06Prince Albert Raiders-20

Hewson, Russell
01Louisiana Ice Gators-9

Hextall Sr., Bryan
34Beehive Group I Photos-277
39O-Pee-Chee V301-1-86
83Hall of Fame Postcards-K7
85Hall of Fame-141
92Hall of Fame Legends-28
02BAP Ultimate Mem Paper Cuts Autos-7
03BAP Ultimate Memorabilia Paper Cuts-28
04Ultimate Collection Ultimate Cuts-UC-BH
05ITG Ultimate Mem Broadway Bluesh Autos-11
05ITG Ultimate Mem Quad Paper Cuts Autos-5
05The Cup Legendary Cuts-LCBH

Hextall, Brett
06Penticton Vees-12

Hextall, Bryan
69O-Pee-Chee-154
70Dad's Cookies-51
70Esso Power Players-223
70O-Pee-Chee-94
70Topps-94
71Letraset Action Replays-13
71O-Pee-Chee-16
71Penguins Postcards-8
71Sargent Promotions Stamps-173
71Topps-16
71Toronto Sun-216
72O-Pee-Chee-174
72Sargent Promotions Stamps-173
72Topps-157
73O-Pee-Chee-43
73Topps-43
75O-Pee-Chee NHL-26A
75O-Pee-Chee NHL-26B
75Topps-26
76O-Pee-Chee NHL-13
76Topps-13
04ITG Ultimate Memorabilia-68
Gold-68
Broadway Blueshirts-5
Cornerstones-8
Cornerstones Gold-8

Hextall, Dennis
69O-Pee-Chee-107
69Topps-107
70Esso Power Players-107
70O-Pee-Chee-186
70Sargent Promotions Stamps-133
71O-Pee-Chee-244
71Topps-128
72O-Pee-Chee-225
72Finnish Semic World Championship-172
72Swedish Semic World Championship-172
73North Stars Action Posters-5
73North Stars Postcards-9
73O-Pee-Chee-115
73Topps-136
74NHL Action Stamps-129
74O-Pee-Chee NHL-2
74O-Pee-Chee NHL-112
74O-Pee-Chee NHL-115
74Topps-2
74Topps-112
74Topps-115
75O-Pee-Chee NHL-310
75O-Pee-Chee NHL-321
75Topps-310
75Topps-321
76O-Pee-Chee NHL-32
76Topps-32
77O-Pee-Chee NHL-197
77Topps-197
78O-Pee-Chee-48
78Topps-48
79Capitals Team Issue-7
79O-Pee-Chee-392
81Red Wings Oldtimers-14

Hextall, Donevan
90Prince Albert Raiders-4
907th Inn. Sketch WHL-277
91Prince Albert Raiders-4
917th Inn. Sketch WHL-266
917th Inn. Sketch CHL Award Winners-15
91Arena Draft Picks-24
91Arena Draft Picks French-24
91Arena Draft Picks Autographs-24
91Arena Draft Picks Autographs French-24
91Classic-29
91Star Pics-11
91Ultimate Draft-25
91Ultimate Draft French-25
91Classic Four-Sport *-29
Autographs-29A
93Raleigh Icecaps-7

Hextall, Ron
82Brandon Wheat Kings-23
83Brandon Wheat Kings-24
86Flyers Postcards-9
87Flyers Postcards-27
87O-Pee-Chee-169
87O-Pee-Chee Minis-16
87O-Pee-Chee Stickers-1
87O-Pee-Chee Stickers-101
87O-Pee-Chee Stickers-114
87O-Pee-Chee Stickers-129
87O-Pee-Chee Stickers-182
87Panini Stickers-123
87Panini Stickers-191
87Panini Stickers-378
87Topps-169
87Topps Sticker Inserts-2
88Esso All-Stars-17
88Flyers Postcards-21
88Frito-Lay Stickers-37
88O-Pee-Chee-34
88O-Pee-Chee Minis-14
88O-Pee-Chee Stickers-103
88Panini Stickers-315
88Topps-34
89Flyers Postcards-10
89O-Pee-Chee-155
89O-Pee-Chee-311
89O-Pee-Chee Stickers-111
89Panini Stickers-302
89Sports Illustrated for Kids I-224
89Topps-155
89Swedish Semic World Champ Stickers-55
90Bowman-105
Tiffany-105
90Flyers Postcards-8
90Kraft-17
90O-Pee-Chee-243
90OPC Premier-41
90Panini Stickers-118
90Pro Set-216
90Score-25
Canadian-25
90Score Hottest/Rising Stars-14
90Topps-243
Tiffany-243
90Upper Deck-227
French-227
91Pro Set Platinum-87
91Bowman-234
91Flyers J.C. Penney-10
91O-Pee-Chee-470
91OPC Premier-38
91Panini Stickers-227
91Parkhurst-126
French-126
91Pinnacle-118
French-118
91Pro Set-176
French-176
91Score American-239
91Score Canadian Bilingual-459
91Score Canadian English-459
91Stadium Club-173
91Topps-470
91Upper Deck-327
French-327
92Bowman-195
92Kraft-31
92Nordiques Petro-Canada-10
92O-Pee-Chee-84
92OPC Premier-57
92Parkhurst-144
Emerald Ice-144
Cherry Picks-CP20
92Pinnacle-340
French-340
92Pro Set-129
92Score-104
Canadian-104
92Stadium Club-288
92Topps-40
Gold-40G
92Ultra-174
92Ultra-385
92Upper Deck-532
93Donruss-196
93High Liner Greatest Goalies-4
93Leaf-341
93OPC Premier-468
Gold-468
93Panini Stickers-77
93Parkhurst-118
Emerald Ice-118
93Pinnacle-376
Canadian-376
Masks-8
93PowerPlay-147
93Score-152
93Score-544
Gold-544
Canadian-152
Canadian-544
Canadian Gold-544
93Stadium Club-433
Members Only Master Set-433
First Day Issue-433
93Topps/OPC Premier-468
Gold-468
93Ultra-366
93Upper Deck-434
94Canada Games NHL POGS-372
94Donruss-147
94EA Sports-114
94Flair-127
94Fleer-154
94Kraft-41
94Leaf-50
94Leaf-495
94Parkhurst-136
Gold-136
94Parkhurst SE-SE130
Gold-SE130
94Pinnacle-274
Artist's Proofs-274
Rink Collection-274
Masks-MA6
94Score-140
Gold-140
Platinum-140
94Select-67
Gold-67
94SP-87
Die Cuts-87
94Stadium Club-51
94Stadium Club-182
Members Only Master Set-51
Members Only Master Set-182
First Day Issue-51
First Day Issue-182
Super Team Winner Cards-51
Super Team Winner Cards-182
94Ultra-127
94Ultra-343
94Upper Deck-170
Electric Ice-170
SP Inserts-SP147
SP Inserts Die Cuts-SP147
95Be A Player-198
Signatures-S198
Signatures Die Cuts-S198
95Bowman-38
All-Foil-38
95Canada Games NHL POGS-210
95Collector's Choice-203
Player's Club-203
Player's Club Platinum-203
95Donruss-147
95Donruss Elite-108
Die Cut Stars-108
Die Cut Uncut-108
Painted Warriors-8
95Emotion-131
95Finest-86
Refractors-86
95Hoyle Eastern Playing Cards-31
95Kraft-27
95Leaf-192
Limited Stick Side-7
95Metal-110
95Panini Stickers-123
95Parkhurst International-159
Emerald Ice-159
Parkie's Trophy Picks-PP33
95Pinnacle-95
Artist's Proofs-95
Rink Collection-95
Masks-8
95Playoff One on One-181
95Pro Magnets-52
95Pro Magnets Iron Curtain Insert-6
95Score-195
95Score-AD4
Black Ice Artist's Proofs-195
Black Ice-195
95Select Certified-78
Mirror Gold-78
95SkyBox Impact-125
95SP-109
95Stadium Club-33
Members Only Master Set-33
95Summit-133
Artist's Proofs-133
Ice-133
In The Crease-10
95Topps-167
OPC Inserts-167
Hidden Gems-12HG
95Topps SuperSkills-77
Platinum-77
95Ultra-117
95Ultra-371
Gold Medallion-117
95Upper Deck-428
Electric Ice-428
Electric Ice Gold-428
Special Edition-SE65
Special Edition Gold-SE65
95Zenith-97
95Images Platinum Players-PL4
96Be A Player Stacking the Pads-3
96Collector's Choice-191
96Collector's Choice-326
96Donruss-61
Press Proofs-61
96Donruss Canadian Ice-51
Gold Press Proofs-51
Red Press Proofs-51
96Donruss Elite-2
Die Cut Stars-2
96Flair-68
Blue Ice-68
96Fleer-80
96Fleer-144
96Fleer-145
Vezina-5
96Fleer Picks-80
Fabulous 50-18
Fantasy Force-3
96Flyers Postcards-10
96Leaf-194
Press Proofs-194
Shut Down-14
96Leaf Limited-35
Gold-35
96Leaf Preferred-77
Press Proofs-77
Steel-9
Steel Gold-9
96Maggers-37
96Metal Universe-112
Armor Plate-5
Armor Plate Super Power-5
96NHL Pro Stamps-52
96Pinnacle-101
Artist's Proofs-101
Foil-101
Premium Stock-101
Rink Collection-101
Masks-6
Masks Die Cuts-6
96Score-80
Artist's Proofs-80
Dealer's Choice Artist's Proofs-80
Special Artist's Proofs-80
Golden Blades-80
Net Worth-11
Sudden Death-14
Superstitions-9
96Select Certified-63
Artist's Proofs-63
Blue-63
Mirror Blue-63
Mirror Gold-63
Mirror Red-63
Red-63
Freezers-13
96SkyBox Impact-95
Zero Heroes-5
96SP-116
96Summit-100
Artist's Proofs-100
Ice-100
Metal-100
Premium Stock-100
In The Crease-16
In The Crease Premium Stock-16
Untouchables-18
96Team Out-64
96Topps Picks Ice D-ID11
96Ultra-124
Gold Medallion-124
96Upper Deck-119
96Upper Deck-197
Superstar Showdown-SS22B
96Zenith-46
Artist's Proofs-46
97SLU Hockey Canadian-8
97SLU Hockey American-9
97Collector's Choice-188
97Crown Royale-97
Emerald Green-97
Ice Blue-97
Silver-97
Freeze Out Die-Cuts-13
97Donruss-114
Press Proofs Silver-114
Press Proofs Gold-114
97Donruss Canadian Ice-48
Dominion Series-48
Provincial Series-48
National Pride-26
97Donruss Elite-35
Aspirations-35
Status-35
97Donruss Limited-89
Exposure-89
Fabric of the Game-52
97Donruss Preferred-96
Cut to the Chase-96
Color Guard-14
Color Guard Promos-14
97Donruss Priority-48
Stamp of Approval-48
Postmaster General-9
Postmaster Generals Promos-9
97Katch-105
Gold-105
Silver-105
97Kenner Starting Lineup Cards-9
97Leaf-52
Fractal Matrix-52
Fractal Matrix Die Cuts-52
97Leaf International-52
Universal Ice-52
97Pacific-27
Copper-27
Emerald Green-27
Ice Blue-27
Red-27
Silver-27
In The Cage Laser Cuts-14
97Pacific Dynagon-89
Copper-89
Dark Grey-89
Emerald Green-89
Ice Blue-89
Red-89
Silver-89
Stonewallers-15
Tandems-55
97Pacific Invincible-100
Copper-100
Emerald Green-100
Ice Blue-100

Red-100
Silver-100
97Pacific Omega-165
Copper-165
Dark Gray-165
Emerald Green-165
Gold-165
Ice Blue-165
No Scoring Zone-9
97Panini Stickers-91
97Paramount-132
Copper-132
Dark Grey-132
Emerald Green-132
Ice Blue-132
Red-132
Silver-132
Glove Side Laser Cuts-14
97Pinnacle-100
Artist's Proofs-100
Rink Collection-100
Press Plates Back Black-100
Press Plates Back Cyan-100
Press Plates Back Magenta-100
Press Plates Back Yellow-100
Press Plates Front Black-100
Press Plates Front Cyan-100
Press Plates Front Magenta-100
Press Plates Front Yellow-100
97Pinnacle Inside-22
Coach's Collection-22
Executive Collection-22
Stoppers-18
97Revolution-101
Copper-101
Emerald-101
Ice Blue-101
Silver-101
Return to Sender Die-Cuts-14
97Score-27
Artist's Proofs-27
Golden Blades-27
97Score Flyers-1
Platinum-1
Premier-1
97SP Authentic-116
97Studio-43
Press Proofs Silver-43
Press Proofs Gold-43
98Aurora-139
98Be A Player-99
Press Release-99
98BAP Gold-99
98BAP Autographs-99
98BAP Autographs Gold-99
98BAP Tampa Bay All Star Game-99
98Crown Royale-98
Limited Series-98
98NHL Aces Playing Cards-35
98Pacific-326
Ice Blue-326
Red-326
98Pacific Dynagon Ice-136
Blue-136
Red-136
98Pacific Omega-174
Red-174
Opening Day Issue-174
98Paramount-174
Copper-174
Emerald Green-174
Holo-Electric-174
Ice Blue-174
Silver-174
Glove Side Laser Cuts-14
98Revolution-104
Ice Shadow-104
Red-104
99Pacific-302
Copper-302
Emerald Green-302
Gold-302
Ice Blue-302
Premiere Date-302
Red-302
01Between the Pipes-114
Double Memorabilia-DM27
He Shoots-He Saves Prizes-34
Trophy Winners-TW10
Vintage Memorabilia-VM14
01Fleer Legacy-61
Ultimate-61
01Flyers Postcards-28
01Parkhurst Autographs-PA50
02BAP Sig Series Auto Buybacks 1998-99
02BAP Signature Series Famous Scraps-FS8
02BAP Ultimate Memorabilia Conn Smythe-16
02BAP Ultimate Memorabilia Cup Duels-11
02BAP Ultimate Memorabilia Retro Trophies-14
02Between the Pipes Inspirations-I10
02Fleer Throwbacks-78
Gold-78
Platinum-78
Drop the Gloves-2
Squaring Off-9
02ITG Used Goalie Pad and Jersey-GP19
02ITG Used Goalie Pad and Jersey Gold-GP19
02UD Foundations-74
02UD Foundations-79
Signs of Greatness-SGRH
04ITG Franchises US East-415
Autographs-A-RH
Double Memorabilia-EDM8
Double Memorabilia Autographs-EDM-RH
Double Memorabilia Gold-EDM8
Memorabilia-ESM6
Memorabilia Autographs-ESM-RH
Memorabilia Gold-ESM6
Original Sticks-EOS15
Original Sticks Autographs-EOS-RH
Original Sticks Gold-EOS15
Triple Memorabilia-ETM6
Triple Memorabilia Autographs-ETM-RH
Triple Memorabilia Gold-ETM6
Trophy Winners-ETW7
Trophy Winners Gold-ETW7
04ITG Ultimate Memorabilia Auto Threads-18
04ITG Ultimate Memorabilia Autographs-37
04ITG Ultimate Mem Autographs Gold-37
04ITG Ultimate Memorabilia Complete Logo-12
04ITG Ultimate Memorabilia Goalie Gear-6
05ITG Heroes/Prosp Toronto Expo Parallel -188
05ITG Heroes/Prosp Toronto Expo Parallel -347
05Between the Pipes-10
Autographs-A-RH
Double Memorabilia-DM-4
Jersey and Sticks-SJ-8
Pads-GUP-4
05ITG Ultimate Memorabilia Level 1-85
05ITG Ultimate Memorabilia Level 2-85
05ITG Ultimate Memorabilia Level 3-85
05ITG Ultimate Memorabilia Level 4-85
05ITG Ultimate Memorabilia Level 5-85
05ITG Ultimate Mem Complete Jersey-1
05ITG Ultimate Mem Complete Jersey Gold-1
05ITG Ultimate Mem Complete Package-11
05ITG Ultimate Mem Complete Package Gold-11
05ITG Ultimate Mem Cornerstones Jerseys-10
05ITG Ultimate Mem Cornerst Jerseys Gold-10
05ITG Ultimate Mem Double Mem Autos-16
05ITG Ultimate Mem Double Mem Autos Gold-16
05ITG Ultimate Memorabilia Emblems-15
05ITG Ultimate Memorabilia Emblems Gold-15
05ITG Ultimate Memorabilia Goalie Gear-18
05ITG Ultimate Mem Goalie Gear Gold-18
05ITG Ultimate Mem Jersey and Emblem-3
05ITG Ultimate Mem Jersey Emblems Gold-3
05ITG Ultimate Memorabilia Jerseys-33
05ITG Ultimate Memorabilia Jerseys Gold-33
05ITG Ultimate Mem Pass the Torch Jerseys-15
05ITG Ultimate Mem Passing Torch Jsy Gold-15
05ITG Ultimate Mem Seams Unbelievable-10
05ITG Ultimate Mem Seam Unbelievable Gold-10
05ITG Ultimate Mem Sticks and Jerseys-29
05ITG Ultimate Mem Stick and Jerseys Gold-29
05ITG Ultimate Mem Triple Threads Jerseys-4
05ITG Ultimate Mem Triple Thread Jsy Gold-4
05SPx-123
Spectrum-123
Xcitement Legends-XL-RH
Xcitement Legends Gold-XL-RH
Xcitement Legends Spectrum-XL-RH
05The Cup-75
Gold-75
Black Rainbow-75
Emblems of Endorsement-EERH
Hardware Heroes-HHRH
Honorable Numbers-HNRH
Masterpiece Pressplates-75
Patch Variation-P75
Patch Variation Autographs-AP75
Scripted Swatches-SSRH
Signature Patches-SPRH
05UD Artifacts-123
Blue-123
Gold-123
Green-123
Pewter-123
Red-123
Auto Facts-AF-RH
Auto Facts Blue-AF-RH
Auto Facts Copper-AF-RH
Auto Facts Pewter-AF-RH
Auto Facts Silver-AF-RH
Frozen Artifacts-FA-RH
Frozen Artifacts Autographed-FA-RH
Frozen Artifacts Copper-FA-RH
Frozen Artifacts Dual-FAD-RH
Frozen Artifacts Dual Autographed-FAD-RH
Frozen Artifacts Dual Copper-FAD-RH
Frozen Artifacts Dual Gold-FAD-RH
Frozen Artifacts Dual Maroon-FAD-RH
Frozen Artifacts Dual Pewter-FAD-RH
Frozen Artifacts Dual Silver-FAD-RH
Frozen Artifacts Gold-FA-RH
Frozen Artifacts Maroon-FA-RH
Frozen Artifacts Patches-FP-RH
Frozen Artifacts Patches Autographed-FP-RH
Frozen Artifacts Patches Pewter-FP-RH
Frozen Artifacts Patches Silver-FP-RH
Frozen Artifacts Pewter-FA-RH
Frozen Artifacts Silver-FA-RH
Goalie Gear Dual-FPD-RH
Goalie Gear Dual Autographed-FPD-RH
Gold Autographed-123
Remarkable Artifacts-RA-RH
Remarkable Artifacts Dual-RA-RH
05Upper Deck All-Time Greatest-46
05Upper Deck All-Time Greatest-82
05Upper Deck Big Playmakers-B-RH
05Upper Deck Jerseys-J-RHX
05Upper Deck Trilogy Personal Scripts-PER-RH
05ITG Heroes and Prospects-188
05ITG Heroes and Prospects-347
AHL Grads-AG-7
AHL Grads Gold-AG-7
Autographs Series II-RH
Autographs Series II-RH2
Hero Memorabilia Dual-HDM-17
06Between The Pipes-101
Autographs-ARH
Double Jerseys-DJ03
Double Jerseys Gold-DJ03
Double Memorabilia-DM08
Double Memorabilia Gold-DM08
Emblems-GUE08
Emblems Gold-GUE08
Emblems Autographs-GUE08
Jerseys-GUJ08
Jerseys Gold-GUJ08
Jerseys Autographs-GUJ08
Numbers-GUN08
Numbers Gold-GUN08
Numbers Autographs-GUN08
Pads-GP10
Pads Gold-GP10
Shooting Gallery-SG07
Shooting Gallery Gold-SG07
Stick and Jersey-SJ14
Stick and Jersey Gold-SJ14
Stick and Jersey Autographs-SJ14
Stick Work-SW03
Stick Work Gold-SW03
06ITG Ultimate Memorabilia-125
Artist Proof-125
Jerseys Autos-10
Jerseys Autos Gold-10
Passing The Torch-8
Passing The Torch Gold-8
Stick Rack-23
Stick Rack Gold-23
06Parkhurst-30
Autographs-30
06SP Game Used By The Letter-BLRH
06SP Game Used Inked Sweaters-ISRH
06SP Game Used Inked Sweaters Patches-ISRH
06SP Game Used Letter Marks-LMRH
06SP Game Used SIGnificance-SRH
06SPx-119
Spectrum-119
06The Cup-70
Autographed Foundations-CQRH
Autographed Foundations Patches-CQRH
Autographed Patches-70
Black Rainbow-70
Foundations-CQRH
Foundations Patches-CQRH
Enshrinements-ERH
Gold-70
Gold Patches-70
Honorable Numbers-HNRH
Jerseys-70
Masterpiece Pressplates-70
Scripted Swatches-SSRH
Signature Patches-SPRH
06UD Artifacts-117
Blue-117
Gold-117
Platinum-117
Radiance-117
Autographed Radiance Parallel-117
Red-117
Auto-Facts-AFRH
Auto-Facts Gold-AFRH
06Ultimate Collection Signatures-US-RH
06Upper Deck Sweet Shot Signature Shots/Saves-SSRH
06Upper Deck Sweet Shot Signature Shots/Saves Sticks-SSSRH
06Upper Deck Sweet Shot Signature Sticks-STRH
06Upper Deck Sweet Shot Sweet Stitches-SSRH
06Upper Deck Sweet Shot Sweet Stitches Duals-SSRH
06Upper Deck Sweet Shot Sweet Stitches Triples-SSRH
06Upper Deck Trilogy Combo Clearcut Autographs-C2SH
06Upper Deck Trilogy Legendary Scripts-LSRH
06Upper Deck Trilogy Scripts-TSRH

Heyliger, Vic
35Diamond Matchbooks Tan 5-6
37Diamond Matchbooks Tan 6-6

Heywood, Jason
00UK Sekonda Superleague-184

Heywood, Jody
04Ohio State Buckeyes Women-16
05Ohio State Buckeyes Women-11
06Ohio State Buckeyes Women-10

Hiadlovsky, Vladimir
93Quebec Pee-Wee Tournament-1555

Hibbert, Jimmy
93Niagara Falls Thunder-2
97UK Sheffield Steelers-1
00UK Sekonda Superleague-109

Hicke, Bill
44Beehive Group II Photos-248
59Parkhurst-31
60NHL Ceramic Tiles-33
60Parkhurst-40
60Parkhurst-56
60Shirriff Coins-38
60York Photos-14
61Parkhurst-38
61Shirriff/Salada Coins-108
61York Yellow Backs-16
62Parkhurst-40
62Shirriff Coins-38
63Chex Photos-22
63Parkhurst-25
63Parkhurst-84
63York White Backs-30
64Beehive Group III Photos-107
64Beehive Group III Photos-132
64Coca-Cola Caps-60
64Topps-98
65Coca-Cola-83
65Topps-30
67Seals Team Issue-13
68O-Pee-Chee-86
68Shirriff Coins-118
68Topps-86
69O-Pee-Chee-145
Four-in-One-6
69Topps-84
70Dad's Cookies-52
70Esso Power Players-99
70O-Pee-Chee-76
Deckle-38
70Sargent Promotions Stamps-143
70Topps-76
Topps/OPC Sticker Stamps-12
71O-Pee-Chee-142
71Sargent Promotions Stamps-175
71Toronto Sun-217
72O-Pee-Chee-327
94Parkhurst Tall Boys-86
95Parkhurst '66-67-91
Coins-91
04ITG Franchises US West-260
Autographs-A-BHI

Hicke, Ernie
70Esso Power Players-105
71O-Pee-Chee-61
71Sargent Promotions Stamps-139
71Topps-61
71Toronto Sun-48
72O-Pee-Chee-72
72Sargent Promotions Stamps-3
72Topps-154
73O-Pee-Chee-18
73Topps-18
74NHL Action Stamps-165
74NHL Action Stamps Update-20
74O-Pee-Chee NHL-387
75O-Pee-Chee NHL-71
75Topps-71
76O-Pee-Chee NHL-87
76Topps-87
77O-Pee-Chee NHL-132
77Topps-132

Hickel, Vern
94Anchorage Aces-14

Hickey, Greg
75Hamilton Fincups-7

Hickey, Les
51Buffalo Bison-10

Hickey, Pat
74O-Pee-Chee WHA-24
75O-Pee-Chee NHL-345
76O-Pee-Chee NHL-107
76Topps-107
77O-Pee-Chee NHL-221
77Topps-221
78O-Pee-Chee-112
78Topps-112
79Panini Stickers-68
79O-Pee-Chee-86
79Topps-86
80Maple Leafs Postcards-15
80O-Pee-Chee-28
80Pepsi-Cola Caps-89
80Topps-28
81O-Pee-Chee-318
81O-Pee-Chee Stickers-104
82O-Pee-Chee-304
88ProCards AHL-212
92Hamilton Canucks-10

Hickmott, Jordan
06Medicine Hat Tigers-10

Hicks, Alex
92Toledo Storm-21
92Toledo Storm Team Issue-9
93Toledo Storm-23
94Las Vegas Thunder-7
95Parkhurst International-271
Emerald Ice-271
95Buffalo Stampedes RHI-94
96Collector's Choice-9
96Upper Deck-6
97Be A Player-177
Autographs-177
Autographs Die-Cuts-177
Autographs Prismatic Die-Cuts-177
97Pacific Invincible NHL Regime-159
97Score Penguins-15
Platinum-15
Premier-15
98Pacific-353
Ice Blue-353
Red-353
00German Berlin Polar Bears Postcards-11
01German Upper Deck-138
02German DEL City Press-194
All-Stars-AS1
03German DEL-171
04German Cologne Sharks Postcards-13
04German DEL-212
05German DEL-218

Hicks, Brad
97OCN Blizzard-8
98OCN Blizzard-8

Hicks, Doug
77O-Pee-Chee NHL-361
78O-Pee-Chee-228
78Topps-228
79Oilers Postcards-11
79O-Pee-Chee-379
80O-Pee-Chee-221
80Topps-221
81Oilers Red Rooster-5
81O-Pee-Chee-114
82O-Pee-Chee-365
82Post Cereal-20
88Oilers Tenth Anniversary-95

Hicks, Glen
78Jets Postcards-8
79Red Wings Postcards-5
81O-Pee-Chee-98
82Birmingham South Stars-12

Hicks, Greg
52Juniors Blue Tint-124
52Cleveland Barons-9

Hicks, Jamey
98ECHL All-Star Southern Conference-6

Hicks, Jason
00Sudbury Wolves-6

Hicks, Wayne
63Quebec Aces-12
64Quebec Aces-9
65Quebec Aces-8
70O-Pee-Chee-95
70Topps-95

Hidlebaugh, Mike
91Air Canada SJHL-C50

Hiebert, James
99Swift Current Broncos-6
00Swift Current Broncos-10
01Swift Current Broncos-7
02Swift Current Broncos-7
03Laredo Bucks-10

Hiebert, Mike
00Lubbock Cotton Kings-11
00Wichita Thunder-12

Hiemer, Manuel
96German DEL-186

Hiemer, Uli
84Devils Postcards-28
86Devils Police-11
86O-Pee-Chee-226
89Swedish Semic World Champ Stickers-108
91Finnish Semic World Champ Stickers-155
91Swedish Semic World Champ Stickers-155
93Swedish Semic World Champ Stickers-153
94Finnish Jaa Kiekko-277
94German DEL-94
95German DEL-84
95Swedish World Championships Stickers-54

Hietala, Tommi
93Thunder Bay Senators-16

Hietamaki, Juhamatti
06Finnish Cardset-172
06Finnish Porin Assat Pelaajakortit-9

Hietanen, Jorma
65Finnish Hellas-89

Hietanen, Juuso
05Finnish Cardset -203
06Finnish Cardset-28
Playmakers Rookies-5
Playmakers Rookies Gold-5
Playmakers Rookies Silver-5
Signature Sensations-4

Hietanen, Olli J.
71Finnish Suomi Stickers-98
72Finnish Jaakiekko-141
73Finnish Jaakiekko-106

Hietanen, Olli T.
73Finnish Jaakiekko-107

Higdon, Henry
98Hampton Roads Admirals-12

Higgins, Chris
97Quebec Pee-Wee Tournament-831
02BAP Memorabilia Draft Redemptions-14
02SPx Rookie Redemption-R202
03BAP Memorabilia-179
Emerald-179
Gold-179
Ruby-179
Sapphire-179
Super Rookies-SR17
Super Rookies Gold-SR17
Super Rookies Silver-SR17
03BAP Ultimate Memorabilia Autographs-107
Gold-107
03BAP Ultimate Mem Auto Jerseys-107
03BAP Ultimate Mem Auto Emblems-107
03BAP Ultimate Mem Auto Numbers-107
03BAP Ultimate Mem Rookie Jersey Emblems-4
03BAP Ultimate Mem Rookie Jsy Emblem Gold-4
03BAP Ultimate Mem Rookie Jersey Numbers-4
03BAP Ultimate Mem Rookie Jsy Number Gold-4
03Beehive-219
Gold-219
Silver-219
03Black Diamond-197
Black-197
Green-197
Red-197
03Bowman-128
Gold-128
03Bowman Chrome-128
Refractors-128
Gold Refractors-128
Xfractors-128
03Canadiens Postcards-11
03Crown Royale-122
Red-122
Retail-122
03ITG Action-622
03ITG Used Signature Series-122
Autographs Gold-122
03ITG VIP Rookie Debut-37
03McDonald's Pacific-59
03Pacific Calder-168
03Pacific Complete-505
Red-505
03Pacific Heads-Up-121
Hobby LTD-121
Jerseys-16
Prime Prospects-12
Prime Prospects LTD-12
03Pacific Invincible-115
Blue-115
Red-115
Retail-115
03Pacific Luxury Suite-91
Gold-91
03Pacific Quest for the Cup-121
03Pacific Supreme-123
03Pacific Supreme-123A
Blue-123
Red-123
Retail-123
03Parkhurst Rookie-180
Rookie Emblems-RE-8
Rookie Emblem Autographs-RE-CH
Rookie Emblems Gold-RE-8
Rookie Jerseys-RJ-8
Rookie Jersey Autographs-RJ-CH
Rookie Jerseys Gold-RJ-8
Rookie Numbers-RN-8
Rookie Number Autographs-RN-CH
Rookie Numbers Gold-RN-8
Teammates Gold-RT20
Teammates-RT20
03Private Stock Reserve-124
Blue-124
Red-124
Retail-124
Class Act-6
03SP Authentic-151
Limited-151
Signed Patches-CH
03SP Game Used-66
Gold-66
03SPx-213
Radiance-213
Spectrum-213
03Titanium-211
Patches-211
03Topps Pristine-122
03Topps Pristine-123
03Topps Pristine-124
Gold Refractor Die Cuts-122
Gold Refractor Die Cuts-123
Gold Refractor Die Cuts-124
Refractors-122
Refractors-123
Refractors-124
Press Plates Black-122
Press Plates Black-123
Press Plates Black-124
Press Plates Cyan-122
Press Plates Cyan-123
Press Plates Cyan-124
Press Plates Magenta-122
Press Plates Magenta-123
Press Plates Magenta-124
Press Plates Yellow-122
Press Plates Yellow-123
Press Plates Yellow-124
03Topps Traded-TT118
Blue-TT118
Gold-TT118
Red-TT118
03UD Honor Roll-173
03UD Premier Collection-73
03Upper Deck-223
Canadian Exclusives-223
HG-223
03Upper Deck Classic Portraits-183
03Upper Deck Ice-93
Glass Parallel-93
03Upper Deck MVP-467
03Upper Deck Rookie Update-155
03Upper Deck Trilogy-155
Limited-155
03AHL Top Prospects-11
04Pacific Montreal International-4
Gold-4
04SP Authentic Sign of the Times-ST-CH
04Hamilton Bulldogs-11
05Canadiens Team Issue-8
05Parkhurst-263
Facsimile Auto Parallel-263
05Upper Deck-354
06Be A Player-116
Autographs-116
Signatures-HI
Signatures 25-128
Signatures Duals-DRH
Signatures Trios-THHK
06Beehive Signature Scrapbook-SSCH
06Canadiens Postcards-8
06Flair Showcase Wave of the Future-WF24
06Fleer-107
Tiffany-107
06Gatorade-32
06Hot Prospects Hotagraphs-HCH
06McDonald's Upper Deck Rookie Review-RR14
06O-Pee-Chee-263
06O-Pee-Chee-622
Rainbow-263
Rainbow-622
06Panini Stickers-66
06SP Authentic-51
Limited-51
Sign of the Times Triples-ST3RKH
06SP Game Used Inked Sweaters-ISCH
06SP Game Used Inked Sweaters Patches-ISCH
06SP Game Used SIGnificance-SHI
06The Cup Autographed NHL Shields Duals-DASMC
06UD Toronto Fall Expo Priority Signings -PSCH
06Ultra-108
Gold Medallion-108
Ice Medallion-108
06Upper Deck-103
Exclusives Parallel-103
High Gloss Parallel-103
Masterpieces-103
Signature Sensations-SSCH
06Upper Deck MVP-153
Gold Script-153
Super Script-153
06Upper Deck Ovation-27
06Upper Deck Sweet Shot Signature Shots/Saves-SSHI
06Upper Deck Victory-106
06Upper Deck Victory Black-106
06Upper Deck Victory Gold-106
07Upper Deck Victory-52
Black-52
Gold-52

Higgins, Jack
52Juniors Blue Tint-105

Higgins, Matt
95Bowman Draft Prospects-P17
98Bowman's Best-135
Refractors-135
Atomic Refractors-135
98Canadiens Team Issue-6
98Pacific Omega-122
Red-122
Opening Day Issue-122
98SPx Finite-45
Radiance-45
Spectrum-45
98UD Choice-107
98UD Choice Preview-107
98UD Choice Prime Choice Reserve-107
98UD Choice Reserve-107
99BAP Memorabilia-36
Gold-36
Silver-36
99BAP Millennium-131
Emerald-131
Ruby-131
Sapphire-131
Signatures-131
Signatures Gold-131
99Pacific-204
Copper-204
Emerald Green-204
Gold-204
Ice Blue-204
Premiere Date-204
Red-204
99Quebec Citadelles-24
00Quebec Citadelles-7
Signed-7
02BAP Sig Series Auto Buybacks 1999-131
03German DEL-145
04German DEL-171
05German DEL-169
06German DEL-97
All-Star Jerseys-AS7

Higgins, Mike
93Quebec Pee-Wee Tournament-604

Higgins, Paul
82Maple Leafs Postcards-17

Higgins, Tim
79Blackhawks Postcards-7
80Blackhawks White Border-6
81Blackhawks Borderless Postcards-9
81O-Pee-Chee-57
81Topps-W69
82Blackhawks Postcards-9
82O-Pee-Chee-66
82O-Pee-Chee Stickers-177
82Post Cereal-4
82Topps Stickers-177
83O-Pee-Chee-104
84Devils Postcards-20
84O-Pee-Chee-111
86O-Pee-Chee-227
87Panini Stickers-250
87Red Wings Little Caesars-15

Higgs, Reg
98Sudbury Wolves-7

Hiiros, Pentti
71Finnish Suomi Stickers-99
72Finnish Jaakiekko-142
73Finnish Jaakiekko-108

Hiirros, Pertti
70Finnish Jaakiekko-173

Hiitela, Seppo
78Finnish SM-Liiga-64

Hilbert, Andy
95Quebec Pee-Wee Tournament-762
98Black Diamond-118
Double Diamond-118
Triple Diamond-118
Quadruple Diamond-118
98SPx Top Prospects-87
Radiance-87
Spectrum-87
01Bowman YoungStars-141
Gold-141
Ice Cubed-141
01SPx-156
01Titanium-150
Retail-150
01Titanium Draft Day Edition-110
01Providence Bruins-12
02O-Pee-Chee-268
02O-Pee-Chee Premier Blue Parallel-268
02O-Pee-Chee Premier Red Parallel-268
02O-Pee-Chee Factory Set-268
02SPx-103
02Topps-268
OPC Blue Parallel-268
OPC Red Parallel-268
Factory Set-268
02Upper Deck-15
Exclusives-15
02Upper Deck MVP-194
Gold-194
Classics-194
Golden Classics-194
02AHL Top Prospects-20
02Providence Bruins-12
03ITG Action-7
03Providence Bruins-7
04AHL All-Stars-17
04Providence Bruins-11
05ITG Heroes/Prosp Toronto Expo Parallel -87
05ITG Heroes and Prospects-87
Autographs-A-AHI
Complete Logos-AHL-6
Jerseys-GUJ-5
Jerseys Gold-GUJ-05
Emblems-GUE-5
Emblems Gold-GUE-05
Numbers-GUN-5
Numbers Gold-GUN-05
Nameplates-N-28
Nameplates Gold-N-28
Shooting Stars-AS-11

Hildebrand, Ike
44Beehive Group II Photos-325
51Cleveland Barons-4
54Parkhurst-83

Hildebrand, Rolf
01Swiss HNL-391
02Swiss HNL-270

Hildebrand, Steve
06Port Huron Flags-21

Hildebrandt, Garrett
00OCN Blizzard-3
01OCN Blizzard-5
02OCN Blizzard-4

Hildebrandt, Roy
89Rayside-Balfour Jr. Canadians-11

Hilden, Antti
99Finnish Cardset-256
00Finnish Cardset-157
01Finnish Cardset-47
05Finnish Cardset -209

Hildenbrand, Steve
02Johnstown Chiefs-7
03Johnstown Chiefs-6
03Johnstown Chiefs RBI Sports-215
04Johnstown Chiefs-8

Hilger, Raimond
92Upper Deck-373
92Finnish Semic-180
93Swedish Semic World Champ Stickers-163
94Finnish Jaa Kiekko-288
94German DEL-380
95Finnish Semic World Championships-169
95German DEL-378
95Swedish World Championships Stickers-67
96German DEL-199
98German DEL-299
99German DEL-256

Hill, Al
79O-Pee-Chee-166
79Topps-166
80O-Pee-Chee-348
88ProCards AHL-140
89ProCards AHL-359
90ProCards AHL/IHL-20
91ProCards-213
95Cincinnati Cyclones-23
96Cincinnati Cyclones-NNO

Hill, Blue
93Quebec Pee-Wee Tournament-796

Hill, Brent
04Regina Pats-16

Hill, Edward
98Barrie Colts-4
99O-Pee-Chee-266
99O-Pee-Chee Chrome-266
99O-Pee-Chee Chrome Refractors-266
99Topps/OPC-266
99Topps/OPC Chrome-266
Refractors-266
99Bowman CHL-37
Gold-37
OPC International-37
Autographs-BA4
Autographs Gold-BA4
Autographs Silver-BA4
00Barrie Colts-15
02Florida Everblades-10
02Lowell Lock Monsters-4
04Peoria Rivermen-14

Hill, Jeff
90Michigan Tech Huskies-10
91Michigan Tech Huskies-6
93Michigan Tech Huskies-13

Hill, Keith
90Fort Saskatchewan Traders-6

Hill, Kiley
917th Inn. Sketch OHL-314
93Sault Ste. Marie Greyhound Memorial Cup-24
94Sudbury Wolves Police-8
98Dayton Bombers EBK-20
99Missouri River Otters-10
99Missouri River Otters Sheet-8
00Missouri River Otters-5
00Missouri River Otters-25

Hill, Kirt
04Kelowna Rockets-23
05Kelowna Rockets-13

Hill, Mel
34Beehive Group I Photos-19
34Beehive Group I Photos-324
39O-Pee-Chee V301-1-96
45Quaker Oats Photos-22
91Bruins Sports Action Legends-12
03BAP Ultimate Memorabilia Paper Cuts-11
04ITG Franchises US East-337
05ITG Ultimate Mem Quad Paper Cuts Autos-1

Hill, Phil
03UK Cardiff Devils-8
05UK Cardiff Devils Challenge Cup-20

Hill, Richmond
92Quebec Pee-Wee Tournament-361
93Quebec Pee-Wee Tournament-1175

Hill, Sean
91ProCards-84
92Canadiens Postcards-13
92Parkhurst-487
Emerald Ice-487
92Ultra-328
92Upper Deck-392
92Upper Deck-523
92Classic-101
Gold-101
92Classic Four-Sport *-214
Gold-214
93Donruss-7
93Leaf-353
93O-Pee-Chee Canadiens Hockey Fest-19
93OPC Premier-312
Gold-312
93Parkhurst-2
Emerald Ice-2
93Pinnacle-147
Canadian-147
93PowerPlay-3
93Score-490
93Score-500
Gold-500
Canadian-490
Canadian-500
Canadian Gold-500
93Stadium Club-387
Members Only Master Set-387
First Day Issue-387
93Topps/OPC Premier-312
Gold-312
93Ultra-182
93Ultra-255
93Upper Deck-16
SP-1
94Flair-121
94Fleer-147
94Leaf-476
94OPC Premier-545
94Parkhurst-6
Gold-6
94Parkhurst SE-SE124
Gold-SE124
94Pinnacle-395
Artist's Proofs-395
Rink Collection-395
94Senators Team Issue-14
94Stadium Club-28
Members Only Master Set-28
First Day Issue-28
Super Team Winner Cards-28
94Topps/OPC Premier-545
94Ultra-339
94Upper Deck-161
Electric Ice-161
95Be A Player-74
Signatures-S74
Signatures Die Cuts-S74
95Canada Games NHL POGS-198
95Collector's Choice-65
Player's Club-65
Player's Club Platinum-65
95Panini Stickers-56
95Parkhurst International-416
Emerald Ice-416
95Pinnacle-93
Artist's Proofs-93
Rink Collection-93
95Playoff One on One-287
95Senators Team Issue-12
95Topps-329
OPC Inserts-329
95Upper Deck-323
Electric Ice-323
Electric Ice Gold-323
95Swedish World Championships Stickers-214
96Senators Pizza Hut-10
96Upper Deck-117
97Hurricanes Team Issue-12
97Pacific Invincible NHL Regime-133
98Be A Player-173
Press Release-173
98BAP Gold-173
98BAP Autographs-173
98BAP Autographs Gold-173
98Hurricanes Team Issue-14
99Pacific Omega-44
Copper-44
Gold-44
Ice Blue-44
Premiere Date-44
99Upper Deck MVP SC Edition-40
Gold Script-40
Silver Script-40
Super Script-40
00BAP Memorabilia-339
00BAP Memorabilia-445
Emerald-339
Emerald-445
Ruby-339
Ruby-445
Sapphire-339
Sapphire-445
Promos-339
00BAP Mem Chicago Sportsfest Copper-339
00BAP Memorabilia Chicago Sportsfest Blue-339
00BAP Memorabilia Chicago Sportsfest Gold-339
00BAP Memorabilia Chicago Sportsfest Ruby-339
00BAP Memorabilia Chicago Sun-Times Ruby-339
00BAP Memorabilia Chicago Sun-Times Gold-339
00BAP Mem Chicago Sun-Times Sapphire-339
00BAP Mem Toronto Fall Expo Copper-339
00BAP Memorabilia Toronto Fall Expo Gold-339
00BAP Memorabilia Toronto Fall Expo Ruby-339
00O-Pee-Chee-254A
00O-Pee-Chee Parallel-254A
00Pacific-82
Copper-82
Gold-82
Ice Blue-82
Premiere Date-82
00Topps/OPC-254A
Parallel-254A
00Upper Deck-382
Exclusives Tier 1-382
Exclusives Tier 2-382
01BAP Memorabilia-487
Emerald-487
Ruby-487
Sapphire-487
02BAP Sig Series Auto Buybacks 1998-173
02Pacific Complete-270
Red-270
02Topps Total-104
03Hurricanes Postcards-11
03ITG Action-136
03NHL Sticker Collection-39
03O-Pee-Chee-246
03OPC Blue-246
03OPC Gold-246
03OPC Red-246
03Pacific-63
Blue-63
Red-63
03Pacific Complete-114
Red-114
03Topps-246
Blue-246
Gold-246
Red-246
03Upper Deck-36
Canadian Exclusives-36
HG-36
03Upper Deck MVP-81
Gold Script-81
Silver Script-81
Canadian Exclusives-81
04Pacific-48
Blue-48
Red-48
05Parkhurst-215
Facsimile Auto Parallel-215
05Upper Deck MVP-168
Gold-168
Platinum-168

Hill, Shaun
97Medicine Hat Tigers-9
98Medicine Hat Tigers-12
98Prince Albert Raiders-10

Hill, Tim
93Peterborough Petes-6
98Fayetteville Force-18
01Bossier-Shreveport Mudbugs-6

Hillas, Richard
94UK Solihul Barons-7

Hillblom, Niklas
90Swedish Semic Elitserien Stickers-219

Hillebrandt, Jon
93Stadium Club Team USA-9
93Stadium Club Team USA Members Only-9

93Topps Premier Team USA-10
93Classic-68
94Classic Autographs-NNO
94Classic Pro Prospects-162
95Binghamton Rangers-14
96Peoria Rivermen-8
96Peoria Rivermen Photo Album-8
98BC Icemen-16
98BC Icemen II-18

Hiller, Bernd
70Finnish Jaakiekko-85
70Swedish Hockey-376

Hiller, Dutch
34Beehive Group I Photos-278
39O-Pee-Chee V301-1-89
43Parade Sportive *-45
43Parade Sportive *-55
43Parade Sportive *-56
45Quaker Oats Photos-82
94Kollectorfest-2

Hiller, Guido
94German DEL-45
04German Berlin Eisbarens 50th Anniv-63

Hiller, Jim
92OPC Premier-34
92Parkhurst-70
92Parkhurst-281
Emerald Ice-70
Emerald Ice-281
92Pinnacle-399
French-399
92Ultra-307
92Upper Deck-560
94Binghamton Rangers-5
94Classic Pro Prospects-117
96German DEL-195
98German DEL-294
99German DEL-276
00German DEL-33

Hiller, Jonas
01Swiss HNL-99
02Swiss HNL-3
04Swiss Davos Postcards-17

Hiller, Peter
94German First League-578

Hillgren, Egon
56Swedish Alfabilder-41

Hillgren, Kenneth
67Swedish Hockey-171

Hillier, Craig
95Bowman Draft Prospects-P18
95Slapshot-257
97Beehive-64
Authentic Autographs-64
Golden Portraits-64

Hillier, Justin
99Sioux City Musketeers-9

Hillier, Randy
83Bruins Team Issue-6
83NHL Key Tags-4
85O-Pee-Chee-212
86Penguins Kodak-11
87Panini Stickers-145
87Penguins Kodak-11
88O-Pee-Chee-158
88Topps-158
89O-Pee-Chee-130
89Penguins Foodland-11
89Topps-126
90O-Pee-Chee-408
90Panini Stickers-137
90Penguins Foodland-3
90Pro Set-507
90Score-76
Canadian-76
91Pro Set Platinum-158
91OPC Premier-122
91Pinnacle-281
French-281
91Pro Set-360
French-360
91Sabres Blue Shield-8
91Sabres Pepsi/Campbell's-8
91Score Canadian Bilingual-580
91Score Canadian English-580
91Score Rookie/Traded-30T

Hillier, Rick
04South Surrey Eagles-29
04Surrey Eagles-7

Hillier, Robert
04Lakehead University Thunderwolves-7

Hillier, Ryan
04Halifax Mooseheads-24
05ITG Heroes/Prosp Toronto Expo Parallel -304
05Halifax Mooseheads-11
05ITG Heroes and Prospects-304
Autographs Series II-RHI
Team Cherry-TC10
06Halifax Mooseheads-13
06ITG Heroes and Prospects-93
Autographs-ARH

Hillman, Floyd
52Juniors Blue Tint-83
56Quebec Aces-7

Hillman, Jim
93Minnesota Golden Gophers-13

Hillman, John
93Minnesota Golden Gophers-14

Hillman, Larry
44Beehive Group II Photos-32
44Beehive Group II Photos-176
44Beehive Group II Photos-407
52Juniors Blue Tint-3
57Bruins Photos-8
57Topps-17
58Bruins Photos-6
58Topps-25
60York Photos-15
61Parkhurst-14
61Shirriff/Salada Coins-59
61York Yellow Backs-31
62Parkhurst-17
62Shirriff Coins-17
63Maple Leafs Team Issue-10
63York White Backs-11
63Rochester Americans-15
64Beehive Group III Photos-164
65Maple Leafs White Border-8
67Topps-60
67York Action Octagons-29
68O-Pee-Chee-48
68Shirriff Coins-74
68Topps-48
69Maple Leafs White Border Glossy-16
69O-Pee-Chee-90
Four-in-One-4
69Topps-90
70Dad's Cookies-53
70Esso Power Players-201
70Flyers Postcards-6
70O-Pee-Chee-81
70Sargent Promotions Stamps-158
70Topps-81
71O-Pee-Chee-168
71Sargent Promotions Stamps-75
71Toronto Sun-115
72O-Pee-Chee-176
72Sabres Postcards-6
72Sargent Promotions Stamps-39
72Finnish Semic World Championship-178
72Swedish Semic World Championship-178
78Jets Postcards-9
91Ultimate Original Six-36
French-36
94Parkhurst Missing Link-55
94Parkhurst Tall Boys-118
95Parkhurst '66-67-104
Coins-104
07Maple Leafs 1967 Commemorative-10

Hillman, Scott
01Odessa Jackalopes-11
02Odessa Jackalopes-14
03Odessa Jackalopes-11
04Odessa Jackalopes-9
05Odessa Jackalopes-10
06Odessa Jackalopes-10

Hillman, Wayne
44Beehive Group II Photos-105
61Shirriff/Salada Coins-21
61Topps-38
62Topps-31
63Chex Photos-23
63Topps-27
64Beehive Group III Photos-39
64Beehive Group III Photos-133
64Coca-Cola Caps-34
64Topps-41
64Toronto Star-15
65Coca-Cola-74
66Topps-87
66Topps USA Test-34
67Post Flip Books-12
67Topps-22
68O-Pee-Chee-47
68Topps-47
69O-Pee-Chee-91
69Topps-91
70Dad's Cookies-54
70Esso Power Players-203
70O-Pee-Chee-198
70Sargent Promotions Stamps-160
71Bazooka-26
71O-Pee-Chee-62
71Sargent Promotions Stamps-146
71Topps-62
71Toronto Sun-197
72O-Pee-Chee-255
72Sargent Promotions Stamps-156
94Parkhurst Tall Boys-41
95Parkhurst '66-67-84
Coins-84

Hillock, Mike
91Air Canada SJHL-C12
92Saskatchewan JHL-67
93Northern Michigan Wildcats-14

Hillstrom, Anders
96Swedish Brynas Tigers-4
00UK Sekonda Superleague-8

Hilpert, Daniel
04German DEL-100
04German Ingolstadt Panthers-10
05German DEL-147

Hilshey, Joel
95Arizona Icecats-18

Hiltebrand, Christof
01Swiss HNL-133

Hiltner, Mike
90Kansas City Blades-13
90ProCards AHL/IHL-594
91Nashville Knights-15

Hilton, Brant
03Prince Albert Raiders-3

Hilton, Kevin
93Donruss Team USA-9
93Pinnacle-493
Canadian-493
93Upper Deck-567
93Michigan Wolverines-9
96Mississippi Sea Wolves-7
97Mobile Mysticks-14
99Charlotte Checkers-5
99Mississippi Sea Wolves Kelly Cup-15
00Charlotte Checkers-9

Hilton, Mark
93Nashville Knights-8
94Central Hockey League-113
95Central Hockey League-8
95Fort Worth Fire-15
97El Paso Buzzards-19

Hiltunen, Hannu
71Finnish Suomi Stickers-299
80Finnish Mallasjuoma-93

Hiltunen, Harri
70Finnish Jaakiekko-328

Himelfarb, Eric
00Sarnia Sting-15
02Barrie Colts-11
04ITG Heroes and Prospects-75
Autographs-EH
04ITG Heroes/Prospects Toronto Expo '05-75
04ITG Heroes/Prospects Expo Heroes/Pros-75

Himes, Normie
33O-Pee-Chee V304A-29
33V129-21
33V252 Canadian Gum-30
33V357 Ice Kings-44
34Diamond Matchbooks Silver-29
35Diamond Matchbooks Tan 1-28
37V356 Worldwide Gum-92

Hindelang, Marc
99German DEL-394

Hindmarch, Dave
81Swedish Semic Hockey VM Stickers-89
83O-Pee-Chee-82
83Vachon-7
84O-Pee-Chee-224

Hindrikes, Yngve
71Swedish Hockey-395
72Swedish Stickers-267

Hinka, Jaroslav
96Czech APS Extraliga-139

Hinks, Rod
907th Inn. Sketch OHL-384
90Sudbury Wolves-10
917th Inn. Sketch OHL-252
91Sudbury Wolves-18
92Sudbury Wolves-18
93Owen Sound Platers-6
93Owen Sound Platers-11
94Johnstown Chiefs-9

Hinni, Marc
95Swiss HNL-499

Hinote, Dan
98Hershey Bears-14
99Avalanche Team Issue-11
99BAP Memorabilia-337
Gold-337
Silver-337
99Pacific Dynagon Ice-58
Blue-58
Copper-58
Gold-58
Premiere Date-58
99SP Authentic-100
99Stadium Club-177
First Day Issue-177
One of a Kind-177
Printing Plates Black-177
Printing Plates Cyan-177
Printing Plates Magenta-177
Printing Plates Yellow-177
99Topps Premier Plus-105
Parallel-105
99Upper Deck-209
Exclusives-209
Exclusives 1 of 1-209
99Upper Deck Gold Reserve-209
00BAP Memorabilia-345
Emerald-345
Ruby-345
Sapphire-345
Promos-345
00BAP Mem Chicago Sportsfest Copper-345
00BAP Memorabilia Chicago Sportsfest Blue-345
00BAP Memorabilia Chicago Sportsfest Gold-345
00BAP Memorabilia Chicago Sportsfest Ruby-345
00BAP Memorabilia Chicago Sun-Times Ruby-345
00BAP Memorabilia Chicago Sun-Times Gold-345
00BAP Mem Chicago Sun-Times Sapphire-345
00BAP Mem Toronto Fall Expo Copper-345
00BAP Memorabilia Toronto Fall Expo Gold-345
00BAP Memorabilia Toronto Fall Expo Ruby-345
00Upper Deck Victory-261
01Avalanche Team Issue-13
01Parkhurst-205
01SPx Hidden Treasures-TTTHN
01UD Stanley Cup Champs-31
01Upper Deck-278
Exclusives-278
02Avalanche Postcards-17
02SP Authentic Super Premiums-SPDH
02Topps Total-246
02UD Top Shelf Dual Player Jerseys-STSH
02Upper Deck-291
Exclusives-291
02Upper Deck Beckett UD Promos-291
02Upper Deck Classic Portraits Hockey Royalty-TSH
02Upper Deck Classic Portraits Hockey Royalty
Limited-TSH
02Upper Deck MVP Skate Around Jerseys-SDHR
02Upper Deck MVP Souvenirs-S-DH
03Avalanche Team Issue-9
03ITG Action-186
03Pacific Complete-134
Red-134
03Upper Deck-293
Canadian Exclusives-293
HG-293
UD Exclusives-293
03Upper Deck MVP-111
Gold Script-111
Silver Script-111
Canadian Exclusives-111
04Swedish MoDo Postcards-16
04Swedish Pure Skills-72
Parallel-72
05Parkhurst-132
Facsimile Auto Parallel-132
05Upper Deck-46
HG Glossy-46
05Upper Deck MVP-110
Gold-110
Platinum-110
Materials Duals-D-SH
05Upper Deck Toronto Fall Expo-46

Hinse, Andre
75Houston Aeros WHA-7
75O-Pee-Chee WHA-35
76Phoenix Roadrunners WHA-6

Hinse, Jerome
93Quebec Pee-Wee Tournament-314

Hinterstocker, Benjamin
99German DEL-191
01German Upper Deck-256
05German DEL-106

Hinterstocker, Herman
79Panini Stickers-109

Hinterstocker, Martin
79Panini Stickers-106
05German DEL-107

Hintz, Cory
97Moose Jaw Warriors-4

Hinz, Chad
96Upper Deck-383
97Moose Jaw Warriors-5
98Bowman CHL-80
Golden Anniversary-80
OPC International-80
98Bowman Chrome CHL-80
Golden Anniversary-80
Golden Anniversary Refractors-80
OPC International-80
OPC International Refractors-80
Refractors-80
99Hamilton Bulldogs-14
99Tallahassee Tiger Sharks-15
99Bowman CHL-86
Gold-86
OPC International-86
00Hamilton Bulldogs-23
01Hamilton Bulldogs-22
02Hamilton Bulldogs-5

Hirche, Klaus
70Finnish Jaakiekko-86
70Swedish Hockey-365
70Swedish Masterserien-170
70Swedish Masterserien-174

Hirsch, Corey
88Kamloops Blazers-12
89Kamloops Blazers-9
907th Inn. Sketch WHL-306
907th Inn. Sketch Memorial Cup-25
917th Inn. Sketch WHL-76
92Parkhurst-344
Emerald Ice-344
92Upper Deck-463
92Binghamton Rangers-22
93Alberta International Team Canada-5
93Donruss-216
93Leaf-313
93OPC Premier Team Canada-18
93Pinnacle-220
Canadian-220
93PowerPlay-482
93Score-453
Canadian-453
93Ultra-64
93Ultra-462
All-Rookies-3
93Classic-133
93Classic Pro Prospects-65
93Classic Pro Prospects-74
BCs-BC5
93Classic Four-Sport *-236
Gold-236
94Parkhurst-149
Gold-149
94Pinnacle Rookie Team Pinnacle-1
94Score Team Canada-CT4
94Ultra-330
94Upper Deck-218
Electric Ice-218
94Finnish Jaa Kiekko-80
94Binghamton Rangers-6
94Classic-85
Gold-85
Tri-Cards-T43
Pro Prospects Ice Ambassadors-IA2
Pro Prospects International Heroes-LP14
95Bowman-145
All-Foil-145
95Parkhurst International-483
Emerald Ice-483
95Select Certified-143
Mirror Gold-143
95SP-151
95Summit-184
Artist's Proofs-184
Ice-184
95Upper Deck-405
Electric Ice-405
Electric Ice Gold-405
95Zenith-134
95Images-62
Gold-62
96Be A Player-51
Autographs-51
Autographs Silver-51
96Black Diamond-131
Gold-131
96Canucks Postcards-31
96Collector's Choice-272
96Donruss-179
Press Proofs-179
96Donruss Canadian Ice-73
Gold Press Proofs-73
Red Press Proofs-73
96Donruss Elite-34
Die Cut Stars-34
96Flair-94
Blue Ice-94
96Leaf-152
Press Proofs-152
Shut Down-12
96Leaf Limited-89
Gold-89
96Leaf Preferred-33
Press Proofs-33
Steel-3
Steel Gold-3
96Maggers-38
96Pinnacle-211
Artist's Proofs-211
Foil-211
Premium Stock-211
Rink Collection-211
96Score-149
Artist's Proofs-149
Dealer's Choice Artist's Proofs-149
Special Artist's Proofs-149
Golden Blades-149
Net Worth-16
Sudden Death-13
96Select Certified-71
Artist's Proofs-71
Blue-71
Mirror Blue-71
Mirror Gold-71
Mirror Red-71
Red-71
96SP-159
96Summit-125
Artist's Proofs-125
Ice-125
Metal-125
Premium Stock-125
In The Crease-15
In The Crease Premium Stock-15
96Topps Picks Rookie Stars-RS16
96Topps Picks Rookie Stars OPC-RS16
96Upper Deck-168
96Upper Deck Ice-71
Parallel-71
96Zenith-75
Artist's Proofs-75
96Collector's Edge Ice-19
Prism-19
97Collector's Choice-258
97Donruss-162
Press Proofs Silver-162
Press Proofs Gold-162
97Donruss Canadian Ice-109
Dominion Series-109
Provincial Series-109
97Donruss Limited-10
Exposure-10
97Leaf-146
Fractal Matrix-146
Fractal Matrix Die Cuts-146
97Leaf International-146
Universal Ice-146
97Pacific-180
Copper-180
Emerald Green-180
Ice Blue-180
Red-180
Silver-180
97Pinnacle Inside-29
Coach's Collection-29
Executive Collection-29
Stand Up Guys-9A/B
Stand Up Guys-9C/D
Stand Up Guys Promos-9A/B
Stand Up Guys Promos-9C/D
97Score-12
Artist's Proofs-12
Golden Blades-12
97Score Canucks-11
Platinum-11
Premier-11
97Upper Deck-171
98Pacific Omega-235
Red-235
Opening Day Issue-235
99Milwaukee Admirals Keebler-1
00Cincinnati Cyclones-21
00Portland Pirates-13
01Between the Pipes-70
02Between the Pipes-70
Gold-70
Silver-70
02Utah Grizzlies-8
04German DEL Update-323B

Hirsch, Greg
92Maine Black Bears-35

Hirsch, Peter
02Swedish SHL-78
02Swedish SHL-291
Masks-6
Netminders-NM5
Parallel-78
Parallel-291
03Bakersfield Condors-8

Hirsch, Tom
84North Stars Postcards-10
84O-Pee-Chee-99
85North Stars Postcards-14
87North Stars Postcards-17

Hirsch, Tyler
02Minnesota Golden Gophers-9
03Minnesota Golden Gophers-15
04Minnesota Golden Gophers-11

Hirschfeld, Bert
45Quaker Oats Photos-83

Hirschi, Alan
95Swiss HNL-359
96Swiss HNL-367
02Swiss HNL-221

Hirschi, Markus
95Swiss HNL-360
96Swiss HNL-331

Hirschi, Steve
99Swiss Panini Stickers-134
00Swiss Panini Stickers-178
00Swiss Slapshot Mini-Cards-LT5
01Swiss HNL-196
02Swiss HNL-325

Hirschi, Urs
93Swiss HNL-243
95Swiss HNL-350
96Swiss HNL-388

Hirschovits, Kim
01Finnish Cardset-210
03Finnish Cardset-21
04Finnish Cardset-20
Parallel-13
05Finnish Cardset -16
06Finnish Cardset-244

Hirschvogel, Rainer
94German First League-276

Hirsimaki, Jari
71Finnish Suomi Stickers-341
72Finnish Jaakiekko-344
94Finnish SISU-240
95Finnish SISU-143
95Finnish SISU Limited-99
95Finnish SISU Spotlights-7

Hirsimaki, Jukka
72Finnish Jaakiekko-303
78Finnish SM-Liiga-182
80Finnish Mallasjuoma-173
83Swedish Semic Elitserien-203

Hirsimaki, Timo
66Finnish Jaakiekkosarja-188
70Finnish Jaakiekko-125
71Finnish Suomi Stickers-175
72Finnish Jaakiekko-123
72Finnish Panda Toronto-23

Hirvonen, Pentti
71Finnish Suomi Stickers-261

Hirvonen, Petteri
06Finnish Ilves Team Set-28

Hirvonen, Raimo
78Finnish SM-Liiga-26
80Finnish Mallasjuoma-9
82Finnish Skopbank-3
82Swedish Semic VM Stickers-31

Hirvonen, Seppo
71Finnish Suomi Stickers-318

Hirvonen, Timo
93Finnish Jyvas-Hyva Stickers-207
93Finnish SISU-193
94Finnish SISU-106
95Finnish SISU-294
96Finnish SISU Redline-94
96Finnish SISU Redline Foil Parallels-95
98Finnish Kerailysarja-20
99Finnish Cardset-22
00Finnish Cardset-11
01Finnish Cardset-10
02Finnish Cardset-25
03Finnish Cardset-140
04Finnish Cardset-147
Parallel-110
05Finnish Cardset -185

Hirvonen, Tomi
95Collector's Choice-338
Player's Club-338
Player's Club Platinum-338
95Finnish SISU-242
Drafted Dozen-11
96Finnish SISU Redline-36
98Finnish Kerailysarja-88
99Finnish Cardset-53
00Finnish Cardset-288
01Finnish Cardset-69
05Finnish Cardset -223
06Finnish Cardset-50
06Finnish Ilves Team Set-6

Hirvonen, Ville
01Finnish Cardset-240
03Finnish Cardset-122
04Finnish Cardset-131
Parallel-96
06Finnish Cardset-355
06Finnish Porin Assat Pelaajakortit-27

Hisey, Rob
03Erie Otters-11
05Finnish Cardset -348
06Finnish Cardset-179
06German DEL-80

Hislop, Jamie
79O-Pee-Chee-380
80Nordiques Postcards-13
80O-Pee-Chee-327
80Pepsi-Cola Caps-67
81Flames Postcards-6
81O-Pee-Chee-40
82O-Pee-Chee-47
82Post Cereal-3
83NHL Key Tags-19
83O-Pee-Chee-83
83Vachon-8
89ProCards IHL-200
90ProCards AHL/IHL-612
92Flames IGA-29

Hitchcock, Ken
84Kamloops Blazers-11
85Kamloops Blazers-8
92Flyers Upper Deck Sheets-34
96Stars Postcards-9
00Stars Postcards-7
01Stars Postcards-7
02Flyers Postcards-22
04Ultimate Collection-57

Hitchen, Allan
92Quebec Pee-Wee Tournament-1117
95Slapshot-306
98Baton Rouge Kingfish-7

Hitchings, Trevor
97Prince Albert Raiders-9
98Kelowna Rockets-9

Hitchins, Kelly
85Brandon Wheat Kings-1
88Brandon Wheat Kings-20

Hitchman, Fred
24C144 Champ's Cigarettes-31
33O-Pee-Chee V304A-5

Hitchman, Lionel
23V145-1-8
24V145-2-4
33V357 Ice Kings-34
34Diamond Matchbooks Silver-30
38Bruins Garden Magazine Supplement-3
91Bruins Sports Action Legends-13
03Parkhurst Original Six Boston-51
03Parkhurst Original Six Boston-80
04ITG Franchises Update-454
06ITG Ultimate Memorabilia Beantown's Best Autos-
5

Hiti, Rudi
93Quebec Pee-Wee Tournament-1804

Hjalm, Michael
83Swedish Semic Elitserien-162
84Swedish Semic Elitserien-37
85Swedish Panini Stickers-39
86Swedish Panini Stickers-21
87Swedish Panini Stickers-198
89Swedish Semic Elitserien Stickers-180
90Swedish Semic Elitserien Stickers-13
91Swedish Semic Elitserien Stickers-263
93Swedish Semic Elitserien-231
94Swedish Leaf-263
95Swedish Leaf-123
Face to Face-11
95Swedish Upper Deck-180

Hjalmar, Hans
86Swedish Panini Stickers-243
87Swedish Panini Stickers-219
89Swedish Semic Elitserien Stickers-204
90Swedish Semic Elitserien Stickers-242

Hjalmarsson, Mats
91Swedish Semic Elitserien Stickers-301
92Swedish Semic Elitserien Stickers-316

Hjelm, Hans
70Swedish Hockey-220

Hjelm, Jan
56Swedish Alfabilder-104

Hjerpe, Hakan
78Finnish SM-Liiga-218
82Swedish Semic VM Stickers-36
85Swedish Panini Stickers-211

Hjerppe, Hukan
80Finnish Mallasjuoma-193

Hjertaas, Troy
90Prince Albert Raiders-5
907th Inn. Sketch WHL-282
91Prince Albert Raiders-5
917th Inn. Sketch WHL-252

Hjort, Peter
98Danish Hockey League-74

Hlady, Scott
92Brandon Wheat Kings-9
93Brandon Wheat Kings-10
00Muskegon Fury-26

Hlavac, Jan
94Parkhurst SE-SE213
Gold-SE213
94SP-158
Die Cuts-158
94Upper Deck-508
Electric Ice-508
94Czech APS Extraliga-84
95Czech APS Extraliga-288
95Classic-25
95Classic Five-Sport *-136
Strive For Five-HK2
96Czech APS Extraliga-138
96Visions *-87
97Czech APS Extraliga-18
97Czech DS Extraliga-86
98Czech DS-93
98Czech DS Stickers-219
98Czech OFS-140
98Czech OFS-434
98Czech OFS-457
98Czech Pexeso Series Two-13
98Czech Pexeso Series Two-27
99BAP Memorabilia-157
Gold-157
Silver-157
99BAP Millennium-164
Emerald-164
Ruby-164
Sapphire-164
Signatures-164
Signatures Gold-164
Calder Candidates Ruby-C49
Calder Candidates Emerald-C49
Calder Candidates Sapphire-C49
99Pacific Omega-155
Copper-155
Gold-155
Ice Blue-155
Premiere Date-155
99Pacific Prism-90
Holographic Blue-90
Holographic Gold-90
Holographic Mirror-90
Holographic Purple-90
Premiere Date-90
99Stadium Club-193
First Day Issue-193
One of a Kind-193
Printing Plates Black-193
Printing Plates Cyan-193
Printing Plates Magenta-193
Printing Plates Yellow-193
99Topps Premier Plus-138
Parallel-138
99Upper Deck MVP SC Edition-123
Gold Script-123
Silver Script-123
Super Script-123
99Czech DS National Stars-NS20
00Aurora-94
Premiere Date-94
00BAP Memorabilia-187
Emerald-187
Ruby-187
Sapphire-187
Promos-187
00BAP Mem Chicago Sportsfest Copper-187
00BAP Memorabilia Chicago Sportsfest Blue-187
00BAP Memorabilia Chicago Sportsfest Gold-187
00BAP Memorabilia Chicago Sportsfest Ruby-187
00BAP Memorabilia Chicago Sun-Times Ruby-187
00BAP Memorabilia Chicago Sun-Times Gold-187
00BAP Mem Chicago Sun-Times Sapphire-187
00BAP Mem Toronto Fall Expo Copper-187
00BAP Memorabilia Toronto Fall Expo Gold-187
00BAP Memorabilia Toronto Fall Expo Ruby-187
00BAP Parkhurst 2000-P186
00BAP Signature Series-215
Emerald-215
Ruby-215
Sapphire-215
Autographs-147
Autographs Gold-147
00O-Pee-Chee-221
00O-Pee-Chee Parallel-221
00Pacific-262
Copper-262
Gold-262
Ice Blue-262
Premiere Date-262
Autographs-262
00Panini Stickers-65
00Paramount-162
Copper-162
Gold-162
Holo-Gold-162
Holo-Silver-162
Ice Blue-162
Premiere Date-162
00Topps/OPC-221
Parallel-221
Own the Game-OTG25
00Upper Deck-117
Exclusives Tier 1-117
Exclusives Tier 2-117
00Upper Deck Vintage-244
00Czech DS Extraliga Team Jagr-JT13
00Czech DS Extraliga Team Jagr Parallel-JT9
01BAP Memorabilia-137
01BAP Memorabilia-466
Emerald-137
Emerald-466
Ruby-137
Ruby-466
Sapphire-137
Sapphire-466
01BAP Signature Series-82
Autographs-82
Autographs Gold-82
01O-Pee-Chee-220
01O-Pee-Chee Premier Parallel-220
01Pacific-259
Extreme LTD-259
Hobby LTD-259
Premiere Date-259
Retail LTD-259
01Pacific Arena Exclusives-259
01Parkhurst-211
01Parkhurst-398
01SP Game Used Authentic Fabric-AFJH
01SP Game Used Authentic Fabric Gold-AFJH
01Stadium Club Souvenirs-JHL
01Topps-220
OPC Parallel-220
Reserve Numbers-JAH
01Upper Deck-359
Exclusives-359
01Upper Deck Ice-123
01Upper Deck MVP-125
01Upper Deck Victory-236
Gold-236
02BAP Sig Series Auto Buybacks 1999-164
02BAP Sig Series Auto Buybacks 2001-82
02NHL Power Play Stickers-148
02Pacific-377
Blue-377
Red-377
02Pacific Complete-432
Red-432
02Topps Total-285
02Upper Deck-172
Exclusives-172
02Czech DS-55
02Czech DS-69
02Czech DS-94
02Czech National Team Postcards-4
03ITG Action-173
03O-Pee-Chee-37
03OPC Blue-37
03OPC Gold-37
03OPC Red-37
03Parkhurst Original Six New York-21
03Rangers Team Issue-6
03Topps-37
Blue-37
Gold-37
Red-37
03Upper Deck-371
Canadian Exclusives-371
HG-371
UD Exclusives-371
03Upper Deck MVP-83
Gold Script-83
Silver Script-83
Canadian Exclusives-83
03Czech National Team Postcards-4
04Pacific-173
Blue-173
Red-173
04Czech HC Sparta Praha Postcards-7
04Czech NHL ELH Postcards-6
04Czech OFS-186
Stars-23
04Czech Zuma-38
04Czech World Championship Postcards-8
05Czech World Champions Postcards-5
05Czech Kvarteto Bonaparte-7d
05Czech Pexeso Mini Blue Set-27
05Czech Pexeso Mini Red Set-4
06Czech HC Sparta Praha Postcards-7
06Czech IIHF World Championship Postcards-6
06Czech OFS-83

Hlavacka, Martin
01Czech OFS Update-298
02Czech OFS Plus-280
02Czech OFS Plus All-Star Game-H26
03Czech OFS Plus All-Star Game-H38
03Finnish Cardset-47
03Russian Hockey League-233
04Czech OFS-25
Stars-47
05Czech HC Sparta Praha-5
06Czech HC Slavia Praha Postcards-8

Hlavka, Dan
01Czech OFS-137

Hlinka, Ivan
70Finnish Jaakiekko-46
70Swedish Hockey-356
71Swedish Hockey-52
72Finnish Jaakiekko-6
72Finnish Hellas-99
72Finnish Panda Toronto-82
72Finnish Semic World Championship-40
72Swedish Semic World Championship-40
73Finnish Jaakiekko-47
74Finnish Jenkki-70
74Finnish Typotor-113
74Swedish Hockey-358
74Swedish Semic World Champ Stickers-66
77Finnish Sportscasters-103-2455
79Panini Stickers-83
81Swedish Semic Hockey VM Stickers-72
82Canucks Team Issue-10
82O-Pee-Chee-346
82Post Cereal-19
83NHL Key Tags-122
91Finnish Semic World Champ Stickers-250
91Swedish Semic World Champ Stickers-250
92Future Trends '76 Canada Cup-128
92Finnish Semic-122
95Czech APS Extraliga-395
97Czech APS Extraliga-340
98Czech OFS-225
98Czech OFS-437
Legends-5
Olympic Winners-16
98Czech Bonaparte-6B
98Czech Pexeso-20
98Czech Pexeso Series Two-3
99Czech OFS-252
01Czech DS Legends-L7
01Czech Stadion-257
02Russian SL-22
03Czech National Team Postcards-5

Hlinka, Jaroslav
95Czech APS Extraliga-287
97Czech APS Extraliga-13
98Czech DS Stickers-221
98Czech OFS-142
99Czech DS-149
99Czech OFS-396
99Czech OFS-476
00Czech DS Extraliga-8
00Czech OFS-303
01Czech DS-16
01Czech OFS-18
All Stars-32
02Czech DS-23
02Czech OFS Plus All-Star Game-H27
02Swiss HNL-40
04Czech World Championship Postcards-9
04Russian Legion-20
06Czech CP Cup Postcards-4
06Czech HC Sparta Praha Postcards-8
06Czech IIHF World Championship Postcards-7
06Czech OFS-82
Jagr Team-14
Team Cards-9

Hlinka, Jiri
94Czech APS Extraliga-262
95Czech APS Extraliga-142
96Czech APS Extraliga-17
97Czech APS Extraliga-164
98Czech DS Stickers-201

Hlinka, Martin
99Quad-City Mallards-12
00Portland Pirates-12
00Quad-City Mallards-18
04Hershey Bears Patriot News-12
05German DEL-347
06German DEL-81
All-Star Jerseys-AS8

Hlinka, Michal
94Czech APS Extraliga-117
95Czech APS Extraliga-221

Hlinka, Miroslav
94Czech APS Extraliga-90
95Czech APS Extraliga-286
96Czech APS Extraliga-136
97Czech APS Extraliga-19
98Czech DS Stickers-220
98Czech OFS-141
02Slovakian Kvarteto-19
02Swedish SHL-248
Parallel-248
03Czech OFS Plus-371
03Russian Hockey League-47
03Russian SL-5
03Russian World Championship Stars-4
06Czech HC Pardubice Postcards-6
06Czech OFS-115
Stars-12
06Czech Super Six Postcards-5

Hlouch, Roman
99Czech Score Blue 2000-159
99Czech Score Red Ice 2000-159
04Czech OFS-9

Hlubna, Tomas
03Russian Hockey League-147
03Russian SL-6

Hluchy, Milan
03Belleville Bulls-18
04Czech OFS-334
06Czech HC Kladno Postcards-8
06Czech OFS-255

Hlusek, Stefan
96Slovakian Quebec Pee-Wee Tournament-10

Hlushko, Todd
897th Inn. Sketch OHL-41
90ProCards AHL/IHL-202
91Baltimore Skipjacks-9
91ProCards-567
92Alberta International Team Canada-9
93Alberta International Team Canada-6
93Donruss-469
93OPC Premier Team Canada-12
93PowerPlay-483
93Ultra-463
94Parkhurst SE-SE25
Gold-SE25
94Score Team Canada-CT9
94Saint John Flames-10

95Saint John Flames-8
96Summit-194
Artist's Proofs-194
Ice-194
Metal-194
Premium Stock-194
97Pacific Invincible NHL Regime-28
98Grand Rapids Griffins-9
99German DEL-117
00German DEL-10
01German Upper Deck-169
02German Adler Mannheim Eagles Postcards-1
02German DEL City Press-241
03German Mannheim Eagles Postcards-22
04German DEL Update-310
04German Hannover Scorpions Postcards-10

Hlynsky, Bill
81Saskatoon Blades-18

Hnat, David
01Czech OFS-100

Hnidy, Shane
917th Inn. Sketch WHL-177
93Prince Albert Raiders-10
94Prince Albert Raiders-7
95Prince Albert Raiders-7
97Grand Rapids Griffins-7
99Cincinnati Mighty Ducks-29
00BAP Memorabilia-414
Emerald-414
Ruby-414
Sapphire-414
00SP Authentic-156
00Titanium Draft Day Edition-168
00Titanium Draft Day Promos-168
00Upper Deck-429
Exclusives Tier 1-429
Exclusives Tier 2-429
00Upper Deck Ice-118
01Senators Team Issue-9
02NHL Power Play Stickers-109
02Senators Team Issue-22
03Senators Postcards-22
04Florida Everblades-4

Hnilicka, Ivan
71Finnish Suomi Stickers-26

Hnilicka, Milan
91Upper Deck Czech World Juniors-87
93Richmond Renegades-12
95Czech APS Extraliga-337
96Czech APS Extraliga-74
97Czech APS Extraliga-3
97Czech APS Extraliga-343
97Czech DS Extraliga-2
97Czech DS Stickers-132
98Czech DS-21
98Czech DS Stickers-207
98Czech OFS-130
98Czech OFS-229
98Czech OFS-439
98Czech OFS-446
98Czech Bonaparte-4D
98Czech Pexeso-15
98Czech Pexeso Series Two-1
98Czech Pexeso Series Two-10
98Czech Pexeso Series Two-15
98Czech Pexeso Series Two-16
98Czech Pexeso Series Two-20
98Czech Pexeso Series Two-26
99BAP Memorabilia-370
Gold-370
Silver-370
99BAP Millennium Calder Candidates Ruby-C30
99BAP Millennium Calder Candidate Emerald-C30
99BAP Millennium Calder Cand Sapphire-C30
99Crown Royale-90
Limited Series-90
Premiere Date-90
99Czech DS National Stars-NS2
99Czech DS Premium-P4
99Czech OFS-20
99Czech OFS Jagr Team Embossed-20
99Hartford Wolf Pack-12
00Vanguard-103
Pacific Proofs-102
00Czech DS Extraliga Team Jagr-JT2
00Czech DS Extraliga Team Jagr Parallel-JT2
00Czech OFS-379
00Czech Stadion-191
01Atomic-3
Blue-3
Gold-3
Premiere Date-3
Red-3
01BAP Signature Series-88
Autographs-88
Autographs Gold-88
01Between the Pipes-5
Masks-34
Masks Silver-34
01Crown Royale-7
Blue-7
Premiere Date-7
Red-7
Retail-7
01Pacific-18
Extreme LTD-18
Hobby LTD-18
Premiere Date-18
Retail LTD-18
01Pacific Adrenaline-8
Blue-8
Premiere Date-8
Red-8
Retail-8
Power Play-3
01Pacific Arena Exclusives-18
01Pacific Heads-Up-4
Blue-4
Premiere Date-4
Red-4
Silver-4
Breaking the Glass-1
01Private Stock-3
Gold-3
Premiere Date-3
Retail-3
Silver-3
01Private Stock Pacific Nights-3
01SP Authentic-4
Limited-4
Limited Gold-4
01Titanium-5
Hobby Parallel-5
Premiere Date-5
Retail-5
Retail Parallel-5
01Titanium Draft Day Edition-5
01UD Challenge for the Cup-4
01UD Mask Collection-102
Gold-102
01UD Playmakers-5
01Upper Deck-8
Exclusives-8
01Upper Deck MVP-6
01Upper Deck Victory-12
01Upper Deck Victory-20
Gold-12
Gold-20
01Upper Deck Vintage-13
01Upper Deck Vintage-17
01Vanguard-4
Blue-4
Red-4
One of Ones-4
Premiere Date-4
Proofs-4
Stonewallers-1
01Czech DS-27
Goalies-G2
01Czech Stadion-259
02BAP First Edition-229
02BAP Memorabilia-124
Emerald-124
Ruby-124
Sapphire-124
NHL All-Star Game-124
NHL All-Star Game Blue-124
NHL All-Star Game Green-124
NHL All-Star Game Red-124
02BAP Memorabilia Toronto Fall Expo-124
02BAP Signature Series-49
Autographs-49
Autograph Buybacks 2001-88
Autographs Gold-49
02Between the Pipes-32
02Between the Pipes-122
Gold-32
Silver-32
Goalie Autographs-8
Jerseys-36
Masks II-2
Masks II Gold-2
Masks II Silver-2
02O-Pee-Chee-183
02O-Pee-Chee Premier Blue Parallel-183
02O-Pee-Chee Premier Red Parallel-183
02O-Pee-Chee Factory Set-183
02Pacific-14
Blue-14
Red-14
Jerseys-2
Jerseys Holo-Silver-2
02Pacific Exclusive-6
02Pacific Heads-Up-5
Blue-5
Purple-5
Red-5
Quad Jerseys-2
Quad Jerseys Gold-2
02Parkhurst-4
Bronze-4
Gold-4
Silver-4
02Private Stock Reserve-4
Blue-4
Red-4
Retail-4
02Thrashers Postcards-5
02Topps-183
OPC Blue Parallel-183
OPC Red Parallel-183
Factory Set-183
02Topps Chrome-106
Black Border Refractors-106
Refractors-106
02Topps Total-347
02UD Mask Collection-3
02UD Mask Collection-4
02UD Mask Collection Beckett Promos-3
02UD Mask Collection Beckett Promos-4
02Upper Deck-9
Exclusives-9
02Upper Deck Classic Portraits-6
02Upper Deck Vintage-10
02Upper Deck Vintage-262
Green Backs-10
02Czech DS-1
02Czech DS-41
02Czech DS-55
02Czech DS-76
02Czech IQ Sports Yellow-8
02Chicago Wolves-12
03Pacific-15
Blue-15
Red-15
Jerseys-3
Jerseys Gold-3
03Pacific Complete-471
Red-471
03Pacific Invincible Jerseys-2
03Manchester Monarchs Team Issue-7
04Czech OFS-87
Team Cards-4
05Czech World Champions Postcards-17
05Czech Kvarteto Bonaparte-1c
05Czech Pexeso Mini Blue Set-23
05Czech Pexeso Mini Red Set-10
05Czech HC Liberec-4
06Czech CP Cup Postcards-5
06Czech IIHF World Championship Postcards-8
06Czech OFS All Stars-1
06Czech OFS Goalies I-4
06Czech OFS Goalies II-1
06Czech NHL ELH Postcards-2

Hoack, Ruediger
74Finnish Jenkki-115

Hoad, Jeff
89Brandon Wheat Kings-10
90Brandon Wheat Kings-1
907th Inn. Sketch WHL-221
917th Inn. Sketch WHL-215
92Brandon Wheat Kings-10
99UK London Knights-7
00UK Sekonda Superleague-28
01UK Belfast Giants-10
02UK London Knights-9

Hoard, Brian
87Sault Ste. Marie Greyhounds-34
88ProCards AHL-239
89ProCards AHL-111

Hobbs, Cody
06Chilliwack Bruins-5

Hobday, Brent
97Moose Jaw Warriors-6

Hobek, Thomas
94German First League-314

Hober, Dan
86Swedish Panini Stickers-245
00Swiss Panini Stickers-53

Hobin, Mike
76Phoenix Roadrunners WHA-7
77Nova Scotia Voyageurs-8

Hobson, Chris
93UK Humberside Hawks-3
94UK Humberside Hawks-16
97UK Kingston Hawks Stickers-10
98UK Kingston Hawks-13

Hobson, Doug
84Prince Albert Raiders Stickers-12
88ProCards IHL-53

Hobson, Jonathan
96Kamloops Blazers-12
98Kamloops Blazers-14
99Kamloops Blazers-11
00Kamloops Blazers-10

Hocicka, Petr
99Czech Score Blue 2000-77
99Czech Score Red Ice 2000-77

Hock, Michael
94German First League-226
05German DEL-140

Hock, Robert
94Finnish Jaa Kiekko-282
94German DEL-375
95German DEL-356
99German DEL-301
00German DEL-204
01German Upper Deck-217
Skilled Stars-SS1
02German DEL City Press-195
All-Stars-AS10
03German DEL-5
03German Mannheim Eagles Postcards-21
04German DEL-150
04German Hannover Scorpions Postcards-11
05German DEL-128
06German DEL-109
German Forwards-GF8

Hocking, Justin
90Fort Saskatchewan Traders-7
917th Inn. Sketch WHL-12
92Classic-16
Gold-16
92Classic Four-Sport *-165
Gold-165
Autographs-165A
94Leaf-479
94Upper Deck-210
Electric Ice-210
95PEI Senators-9
98Indianapolis Ice-23
99St. John's Maple Leafs-9
01UK Manchester Storm-16

Hodek, Daniel
97Czech APS Extraliga-312
98Czech OFS-302
99Czech Score Blue 2000-45
99Czech Score Red Ice 2000-45

Hodek, Petr
94Czech APS Extraliga-99

Hodge Jr., Ken
88ProCards IHL-28
89ProCards IHL-89
90Bruins Sports Action-12
90Pro Set-587
90Score Rookie/Traded-85T
90Upper Deck-529
French-529
90ProCards AHL/IHL-134
91Pro Set Platinum-6
91Bowman-347
91Bowman-362
91Bruins Sports Action-8
91Kraft-17
91O-Pee-Chee-5
91O-Pee-Chee-440
91OPC Premier-41
91OPC Premier-154
91Panini Stickers-178
91Panini Stickers-341
91Parkhurst-2
French-2
PHC-PHC3
PHC French-PHC3
91Pinnacle-203
French-203
91Pro Set-3
French-3
Awards Special-AC11
Platinum PC-PC9
91Score American-113
91Score American-353
91Score Canadian Bilingual-113
91Score Canadian Bilingual-383
91Score Canadian English-113
91Score Canadian English-383
91Score Young Superstars-9
91Stadium Club-357
91Topps-5
91Topps-440
91Upper Deck-41
91Upper Deck-251
French-41
French-251
92Pinnacle-390
French-390
92Pro Set-182
92Score-274
Canadian-274
92Topps-306
Gold-306G
92Ultra-411
92Upper Deck-254
94Kansas City Blades-7
96German DEL-110

Hodge, Brendon
03Wheeling Nailers-85
04Wheeling Nailers Riesbeck's-11
04Wheeling Nailers SGA-3
06Stockton Thunder-13a

Hodge, Charlie
44Beehive Group II Photos-251A
44Beehive Group II Photos-251B
52Juniors Blue Tint-129
55Parkhurst-69
Quaker Oats-69
57Parkhurst-M17
58Parkhurst-17
59Parkhurst-16
60Shirriff Coins-39
60York Photos-16
62Quebec Aces-12
63Chex Photos-24
63Quebec Aces-13
63Quebec Aces-14
64Beehive Group III Photos-108
64Coca-Cola Caps-55
64Topps-17
64Toronto Star-16
65Canadiens Steinberg Glasses-4
65Coca-Cola-55
65Topps-67
66Topps-65
67Seals Team Issue-14
68O-Pee-Chee-78
Puck Stickers-12
68Shirriff Coins-116
68Topps-78
69O-Pee-Chee-77
Four-in-One-8
69Topps-77
70Canucks Royal Bank-7
70Colgate Stamps-68
70Dad's Cookies-55
70Esso Power Players-37
70O-Pee-Chee-229
70Sargent Promotions Stamps-211
94Parkhurst Missing Link Future Stars-FS6
94Parkhurst Tall Boys-82
94Parkhurst Tall Boys-139
94Parkhurst Tall Boys-148
95Parkhurst '66-67-70
Coins-70
02BAP Ultimate Mem Storied Franchise-2
02Between the Pipes Goalie Autographs-35
02Between the Pipes Trappers-GT6
02Between the Pipes Vintage Memorabilia-11
02Parkhurst Reprints-214
02Parkhurst Reprints-228
02Parkhurst Reprints-238
03BAP Memorabilia Gloves-GUG10
03BAP Ultimate Memorabilia Linemates-3
03Parkhurst Orig Six Montreal Autos-5
03Parkhurst Orig Six Montreal Mem-MM20
04ITG Franchises US West-263
Autographs-A-CH
04ITG Ultimate Memorabilia Original Six-13
05Between the Pipes-11
Autographs-A-CH
Gloves-GUG-7
06Between The Pipes-82
Autographs-ACHO
Gloves-GG10
Gloves Gold-GG10

Hodge, Dan
96Peoria Rivermen-9
96Peoria Rivermen Photo Album-9
98Peoria Rivermen-2
99Peoria Rivermen-24
00Peoria Rivermen-11
01Peoria Rivermen-14
02UK Manchester Storm-17

Hodge, Ken
64Beehive Group III Photos-40
65Coca-Cola-29
65Topps-65
66Topps-114
67Topps-98
68Bauer Ads-12
68O-Pee-Chee-8
68Shirriff Coins-10
68Topps-8
69O-Pee-Chee-27
Four-in-One-2
Stamps-13
69Topps-27
70Bruins Postcards-10
70Bruins Team Issue-14
70Colgate Stamps-62
70Dad's Cookies-56
70Esso Power Players-59
70O-Pee-Chee-8
70O-Pee-Chee-233
70Post Shooters-5
70Sargent Promotions Stamps-10
70Topps-8
71Bruins Postcards-5
71O-Pee-Chee-115
71O-Pee-Chee-254
71Sargent Promotions Stamps-8
71Topps-115
71Toronto Sun-10
72O-Pee-Chee-49
72O-Pee-Chee-169
72Sargent Promotions Stamps-22
72Topps-166
73O-Pee-Chee-26
73Topps-133
74Lipton Soup-28
74NHL Action Stamps-28
74O-Pee-Chee NHL-128
74O-Pee-Chee NHL-230
74Topps-128
74Topps-230
75O-Pee-Chee NHL-215
75Topps-215
76O-Pee-Chee NHL-25
76Topps-25
77O-Pee-Chee NHL-192
77Topps-192
91Ultimate Original Six-49
French-49
917th Inn. Sketch WHL-44
94Parkhurst Tall Boys Future Stars-FS3
95Parkhurst '66-67-23
Coins-23
98Bruins Alumni-7
Autographs-7
99BAP Memorabilia AS American Hobby-AH1
99BAP Memorabilia AS American Hobby Autos-AH1
01Greats of the Game-67
Autographs-67
01Topps Archives-55
Arena Seats-ASKH
01Topps Chrome Reprints-10
01Topps Chrome Reprint Refractors-10
01Topps Chrome Reprint Autographs-10
03Parkhurst Original Six Boston-50
Autographs-7
03Parkhurst Original Six Chicago-53
Autographs-6
04UD Legendary Signatures-51
Autographs-KH
Linemates-WCPEKH
04UD Legends Classics-34
Gold-34
Platinum-34
Silver-34
Signature Moments-M23
Signature Moments-M58
Signatures-CS23
Signatures-TC8
05UD Artifacts Auto Facts-AF-KH
05UD Artifacts Auto Facts Blue-AF-KH
05UD Artifacts Auto Facts Copper-AF-KH
05UD Artifacts Auto Facts Pewter-AF-KH
05UD Artifacts Auto Facts Silver-AF-KH
06ITG Ultimate Memorabilia Road to the Cup-4
06ITG Ultimate Memorabilia Road to the Cup Gold-4

Hodge, Rob
92Quebec Pee-Wee Tournament-1568
93Western Michigan Broncos-14

Hodgen, Jeff
897th Inn. Sketch OHL-46

Hodges, Bob
77Sportscasters-1119
90Pro Set-689

Hodges, Mark
93Quebec Pee-Wee Tournament-881

Hodges, Matthew
97Sudbury Wolves Police-21

Hodges, Sean
93Quebec Pee-Wee Tournament-1160

Hodgins, Justin
00Owen Sound Attack-7

Hodgman, Justin
05Erie Otters-5
06Erie Otters-8

Hodgson, Chris
01Shawinigan Cataractes-13
05Port Huron Flags-24

Hodgson, Cody
06Brampton Battalion-18

Hodgson, Dan
84Kelowna Wings-56
84Prince Albert Raiders Stickers-13
85Maple Leafs Postcards-13
93Swiss HNL-429
95Swiss HNL-124
95Swiss HNL-521
96Swiss HNL-113
98Swiss Power Play Stickers-239
99Swiss Panini Stickers-241
00Swiss Panini Stickers-281
00Swiss Slapshot Mini-Cards-ZSCL10
01Swiss HNL-16
02Swiss HNL-55

Hodgson, Gavin
00Tacoma Sabercats-13
06Fayetteville FireAntz-5

Hodgson, Ted
51Laval Dairy QSHL-62
52St. Lawrence Sales-106
72Cleveland Crusaders WHA-5
75Roanoke Valley Rebels-13

Hodson, Jamie
97Brandon Wheat Kings-12
98Brandon Wheat Kings-8
99Brandon Wheat Kings-11
00Brandon Wheat Kings-2
01South Carolina Stingrays-9
02BAP Memorabilia-361
02BAP Ultimate Memorabilia-79
02UD Mask Collection-152
02UD Premier Collection-71A
Gold-71A
02ECHL Update-U-11
03BAP Memorabilia Deep in the Crease-D9
03Parkhurst Original Six Toronto-12
03Greensboro Generals-187
06Bakersfield Condors-19

Hodson, Jason
92British Columbia JHL-104

Hodson, Kevin
907th Inn. Sketch OHL-158
917th Inn. Sketch OHL-320
917th Inn. Sketch Memorial Cup-2
92Indianapolis Ice-13
93Sault Ste. Marie Greyhound Memorial Cup-28
94Classic Tri-Cards-T19
94Classic Pro Prospects-218
95Parkhurst International-525
Emerald Ice-525
95Adirondack Red Wings-9
96Be A Player-218
96Be A Player-P218
Autographs-218
Autographs Silver-218
96Donruss-230
Press Proofs-230
96Donruss Canadian Ice-136
Gold Press Proofs-136
Red Press Proofs-136
96Flair-108
Blue Ice-108
96Leaf Gold Rookies-2
96Leaf Preferred-137
Press Proofs-137
96Pinnacle-238
Artist's Proofs-238
Foil-238
Premium Stock-238
Rink Collection-238
96Summit-183
Artist's Proofs-183
Ice-183
Metal-183
Premium Stock-183
96Upper Deck-253
96Zenith-136
Artist's Proofs-136
96Collector's Edge Ice-3
Prism-3
The Wall-TW12
97Donruss-199
Press Proofs Silver-199
Press Proofs Gold-199
97Donruss Limited-17
97Donruss Limited-89
Exposure-17
Exposure-89
97Donruss Priority-65
Stamp of Approval-65
97Pacific Omega-80
Copper-80
Dark Gray-80
Emerald Green-80
Gold-80
Ice Blue-80
97Pinnacle-47
Artist's Proofs-47
Rink Collection-47
Press Plates Back Black-47
Press Plates Back Cyan-47
Press Plates Back Magenta-47
Press Plates Back Yellow-47
Press Plates Front Black-47
Press Plates Front Cyan-47
Press Plates Front Magenta-47
Press Plates Front Yellow-47
Inside Stoppers-10
97Score-24
Artist's Proofs-24
Golden Blades-24
97Score Red Wings-18
Platinum-18
Premier-18
97SP Authentic-179
97Upper Deck-272
97Upper Deck Ice-33
Parallel-33
Power Shift-33
98NHL Aces Playing Cards-46
98Pacific-192
Ice Blue-192
Red-192
98Paramount-75
Copper-75
Emerald Green-75
Holo-Electric-75
Ice Blue-75
Silver-75
99Aurora-130
Premiere Date-130
99O-Pee-Chee-199
99O-Pee-Chee Chrome-199
99O-Pee-Chee Chrome Refractors-199
99Pacific-390
Copper-390
Emerald Green-390
Gold-390
Ice Blue-390
Premiere Date-390
Red-390
99SPx-142
Radiance-142
Spectrum-142
99Topps/OPC-199
99Topps/OPC Chrome-199
Refractors-199
99Upper Deck-119
Exclusives-119
Exclusives 1 of 1-119
99Upper Deck Gold Reserve-119
99Upper Deck MVP-195
Gold Script-195
Silver Script-195
Super Script-195
99Upper Deck Victory-272
02Between the Pipes-66
Gold-66
Silver-66
02UD Mask Collection-79
02UD Mask Collection-80
02UD Mask Collection Beckett Promos-79
02UD Mask Collection Beckett Promos-80

Hoeck, Michael
04German Weiden Blue Devils-12

Hoekstra, Cecil
55Montreal Royals-4
60Shirriff Coins-79

Hoekstra, Ed
57St. Catherine's Tee Pees-NNO
62Quebec Aces-13
63Quebec Aces-15
64Quebec Aces-10
65Quebec Aces-9
68O-Pee-Chee-98
68Shirriff Coins-124
68Topps-98

Hoelzer, Brad
05Waterloo Blackhawks-12

Hoey, Duane
95Neepewa Natives-8

Hofbauer, Patrik
93Swedish Semic Elitserien-2
95Swedish Leaf-184

Hofbauer, Wolfgang
94German First League-466

Hofer, Michael
01Swiss HNL-387
02Swiss HNL-146

Hoff, Geir
92Finnish Semic-37
92Norwegian Elite Series-43
93Swedish Semic World Champ Stickers-237
94Finnish Jaa Kiekko-263
95Swedish Globe World Championships-193
95Swedish World Championships Stickers-244

Hoffart, Randy
84Saskatoon Blades Stickers-5
85Brandon Wheat Kings-24

Hoffe, Gregory
02Cape Breton Screaming Eagles-13
03Cape Breton Screaming Eagles-19

Hoffman, Aaron
91British Columbia JHL-66
92British Columbia JHL-80

Hoffman, Kevin
95Vancouver VooDoo RHI-17
00UK Nottingham Panthers-5

Hoffman, Matt
89Oshawa Generals-6
89Oshawa Generals 7th Inning Sketch-15
897th Inn. Sketch OHL-15
907th Inn. Sketch OHL-338
907th Inn. Sketch Memorial Cup-94
91Oshawa Generals-7
91Oshawa Generals Sheet-9
917th Inn. Sketch OHL-154
93Johnstown Chiefs-6
94Johnstown Chiefs-10
99UK Sheffield Steelers-6

Hoffman, Mike
87Flint Spirits-6
88Flint Spirits-7
88Flint Spirits-19
04Cleveland Barons-12

Hoffmann, Jim
94German DEL-187
95German DEL-187
96German DEL-126

Hoffmann, Lars
95German DEL-73

Hoffmann, Martin
02German Berlin Polar Bears Postcards-12
03German Berlin Polar Bears Postcards-16
04German Berlin Polar Bears Postcards-14

Hoffmann, Oliver
91Finnish Semic World Champ Stickers-199
91Swedish Semic World Champ Stickers-199
93Swiss HNL-22
95Swiss HNL-20
96Swiss HNL-139
98Swiss Power Play Stickers-190
99Swiss Panini Stickers-192

Hoffmeyer, Bob
84Devils Postcards-21
88Devils Caretta-11
89ProCards AHL-208
91ProCards-161

Hofford, Jim
86Sabres Blue Shield-14
86Sabres Blue Shield Small-14
88ProCards AHL-256
89ProCards AHL-281

Hofford, Lindsay
92Quebec Pee-Wee Tournament-358
00London Knights-6
01London Knights-27

Hoffort, Bruce
89ProCards AHL-350
90OPC Premier-42
90Score-413
Canadian-413
90Upper Deck-135
French-135
90ProCards AHL/IHL-36
91ProCards-326

Hofherr, Anton
72Finnish Hellas-60
72Finnish Semic World Championship-104
72Swedish Semic World Championship-104

Hofherr, Franz
72Finnish Semic World Championship-112
72Swedish Semic World Championship-112

Hofmann, Peter
93Swiss HNL-479
94German DEL-406

Hofmann, Ueli
74Finnish Typotor-106
93Swiss HNL-161
95Swiss HNL-57

Hofner, Ernst
82Swedish Semic VM Stickers-114
83Swedish Semic VM Stickers-114
94German DEL-368
95German DEL-358
98German DEL-341

Hofstetter, Christian
93Swiss HNL-39
93Swiss HNL-99
95Swiss HNL-66
95Swiss HNL-226
96Swiss HNL-140
96Swiss HNL-210
98Swiss Power Play Stickers-191

Hofstrand, Mike
04Bakersfield Condors-6
05Bakersfield Condors-14
06Bakersfield Condors-13

Hofverberg, Sture
65Swedish Coralli ISHockey-140

Hogaboam, Bill
73Red Wings McCarthy Postcards-8
74NHL Action Stamps-99
74O-Pee-Chee NHL-84
74O-Pee-Chee NHL-116
74Topps-84
74Topps-116
75O-Pee-Chee NHL-67
75Topps-67
76O-Pee-Chee NHL-73
76O-Pee-Chee NHL-387
76Topps-73
77O-Pee-Chee NHL-148
77Topps-148
79O-Pee-Chee-362

Hogan, Bryan
06Lincoln Stars-22
06Lincoln Stars Traded-14T
06Lincoln Stars Upper DeckÂ Signature Series -14

Hogan, Matt
94Sarnia Sting-25

Hogan, Peter
95Slapshot-242
98Bowman CHL-26
Golden Anniversary-26
OPC International-26
98Bowman Chrome CHL-26
Golden Anniversary-26
Golden Anniversary Refractors-26
OPC International-26
OPC International Refractors-26
Refractors-26
00Florida Everblades-12
03Columbus Cottonmouths-24

Hogan, Tim
91Michigan Wolverines-7
93Michigan Wolverines-10

Hoganson, Dale
70Esso Power Players-146
70Sargent Promotions Stamps-68
71Canadiens Postcards-7
71O-Pee-Chee-149
71Toronto Sun-116
72Dimanche/Derniere Heure *-140
75O-Pee-Chee WHA-2
80Nordiques Postcards-14
80O-Pee-Chee-155
80Pepsi-Cola Caps-68
80Topps-155
81O-Pee-Chee-276

Hogardh, Peter
95Swedish Leaf-200
95Swedish Upper Deck-215
00Swedish Upper Deck-161
02Swedish SHL-83
Parallel-83
Sharpshooters-SS1
Signatures-12
03Swedish Elite-107
Silver-107
04Swedish Elitset-173
Gold-173
05Swedish SHL Elitset-28
06Swedish SHL Elitset-33

Hogasta, Goran
79Panini Stickers-184

Hogberg, Anders
86Sudbury Wolves-34

Hogden, Jeff
91Cincinnati Cyclones-9

Hogeboom, Greg
04Manchester Monarchs-10
04Manchester Monarchs Tobacco-11
05ITG Heroes/Prosp Toronto Expo Parallel -350
05Manchester Monarchs-36
05ITG Heroes and Prospects-350
Autographs Series II-GHO
06Reading Royals-14

Hogemark, Sverre
92Norwegian Elite Series-140

Hogg, Jean-Sebastien
05Baie-Comeau Drakkar-12

Hogg, Jeff
82Oshawa Generals-2
83Kingston Canadians-25

Hogg, Kris
02Kamloops Blazers-19
03Kamloops Blazers-10
05Lethbridge Hurricanes-9

Hogg, Murray
93Guelph Storm-21
94Owen Sound Platers-23
95Slapshot-53
96Fort Worth Fire-5
97Fort Worth Brahmas-7
98Fort Worth Brahmas-9
99Fort Worth Brahmas-7

Hogg, Steve
87Brockville Braves-18
92Thunder Bay Thunder Hawks-27
93Peterborough Petes-17
95Slapshot-319

Hoggan, Jeff
03Houston Aeros-11
04Worcester IceCats-20
05Blues Team Set-7
05Hot Prospects-265
En Fuego-265
Red Hot-265
White Hot-265
05Parkhurst-422
True Colors-TCSTL
True Colors-TCSTL
05SP Authentic-186
Limited-186
Sign of the Times-HG
05SP Game Used-104
Autographs-104
Gold-104
05SPx-136
Spectrum-136
05The Cup-165
Autographed Rookie Patches Gold Rainbow-165
Black Rainbow Rookies-165
Masterpiece Pressplates (Artifacts)-323
Masterpiece Pressplates (Ice)-167
Masterpiece Pressplates (Rookie Update)-175
Masterpiece Pressplates SPA Autos-186
Masterpiece Pressplates (SP Game Used)-104
Masterpiece Pressplates (SPx)-136
Masterpiece Pressplates (SPx)-136
Masterpiece Pressplates (Trilogy)-217
Masterpiece Pressplates Ult Coll-168
Masterpiece Pressplates Autographs-165
Platinum Rookies-165
05UD Artifacts-323
05Ultimate Collection-168
Gold-168
05Ultra-244
Gold-244
Fresh Ink-FI-HO
Fresh Ink Blue-FI-HO
Ice-244
Rookie Uniformity Jerseys-RU-HO
Rookie Uniformity Jersey Autographs-ARU-HO
Rookie Uniformity Patches-RUP-HO
Rookie Uniformity Patch Autographs-ARP-HO
05Upper Deck-210
HG Glossy-210
Rookie Ink-RIHO
Rookie Threads-RTJH
Rookie Threads Autographs-ARTJH
05Upper Deck Ice-167
Premieres Auto Patches-AIPHO
05Upper Deck Rookie Update-175
05Upper Deck Trilogy-217
05Upper Deck Toronto Fall Expo-210
06Black Diamond Jerseys-JJH
06Black Diamond Jerseys Black-JJH
06Black Diamond Jerseys Gold-JJH
06Black Diamond Jerseys Ruby-JJH
06Black Diamond Jerseys Black Autographs -JJH
06UD Powerplay Power Marks-PMJH

Hoggarth, Ron
90Pro Set-690

Hogl, Michael
94German First League-131

Hoglund, Bengt
04Swedish Elitset-102
Gold-102

Hoglund, Jonas
90Swedish Semic Elitserien Stickers-269
91Swedish Semic Elitserien Stickers-99
92Upper Deck-222
92Swedish Semic Elitserien Stickers-115
93Swedish Semic Elitserien-96
94Swedish Leaf-292
95Swedish Leaf-213
95Swedish Upper Deck-68
Ticket to North America-NA8
96Be A Player Link to History-8A
96Be A Player Link to History Autographs-8A
96Be A Player Link to History Auto Silver-8A
96Black Diamond-44
Gold-44
96Collector's Choice-355
96Donruss Canadian Ice-140
Gold Press Proofs-140
Red Press Proofs-140
96Donruss Elite-146
Die Cut Stars-146
Aspirations-12
96Leaf Limited Rookies-10
96Leaf Limited Rookies Gold-10
96Leaf Preferred-124
Press Proofs-124
96Select Certified-102
Artist's Proofs-102
Blue-102
Mirror Blue-102
Mirror Gold-102
Mirror Red-102
Red-102
96SP-172
96Ultra-23
Gold Medallion-23
96Upper Deck-232
Generation Next-X38
96Zenith-117
Artist's Proofs-117
97Collector's Choice-43
97Donruss-169
Press Proofs Silver-169
Press Proofs Gold-169
97Donruss Canadian Ice-36
Dominion Series-36
Provincial Series-36
97Donruss Limited-88
Exposure-88
97Pacific-185
Copper-185
Emerald Green-185
Ice Blue-185
Red-185
Silver-185
97Pacific Dynagon-16
Copper-16
Dark Grey-16
Emerald Green-16
Ice Blue-16
Red-16
Silver-16
Tandems-36
97Pacific Invincible-18
Copper-18
Emerald Green-18
Ice Blue-18
Red-18

Silver-18
97Panini Stickers-198
97Paramount-29
Copper-29
Dark Grey-29
Emerald Green-29
Ice Blue-29
Red-29
Silver-29
97Pinnacle Inside-129
97Score-181
97Upper Deck-27
98Canadiens Team Issue-7
98Panini Stickers-38
98Upper Deck-116
Exclusives-116
Exclusives 1 of 1-116
Gold Reserve-116
99Maple Leafs Pizza Pizza-2
99Pacific Dynagon Ice-187
Blue-187
Copper-187
Gold-187
Premiere Date-187
99Pacific Omega-224
Copper-224
Gold-224
Ice Blue-224
Premiere Date-224
99Panini Stickers-156
99SP Authentic-84
99Upper Deck-292
Exclusives-292
Exclusives 1 of 1-292
99Upper Deck Gold Reserve-292
99Upper Deck MVP SC Edition-175
Gold Script-175
Silver Script-175
Super Script-175
00BAP Memorabilia-313
Emerald-313
Ruby-313
Sapphire-313
Promos-313
00BAP Mem Chicago Sportsfest Copper-313
00BAP Memorabilia Chicago Sportsfest Blue-313
00BAP Memorabilia Chicago Sportsfest Gold-313
00BAP Memorabilia Chicago Sportsfest Ruby-313
00BAP Memorabilia Chicago Sun-Times Ruby-313
00BAP Memorabilia Chicago Sun-Times Gold-313
00BAP Mem Chicago Sun-Times Sapphire-313
00BAP Mem Toronto Fall Expo Copper-313
00BAP Memorabilia Toronto Fall Expo Gold-313
00BAP Memorabilia Toronto Fall Expo Ruby-313
00BAP Parkhurst 2000-P196
000-Pee-Chee-37
000-Pee-Chee Parallel-37
00Pacific-391
Copper-391
Gold-391
Ice Blue-391
Premiere Date-391
00Panini Stickers-98
00Stadium Club-126
00Topps/OPC-37
Parallel-37
00Topps Heritage-201
00Upper Deck Victory-221
00Upper Deck Vintage-339
010-Pee-Chee-177
010-Pee-Chee Premier Parallel-177
01Pacific-366
Extreme LTD-366
Hobby LTD-366
Premiere Date-366
Retail LTD-366
01Pacific Adrenaline-180
Blue-180
Premiere Date-180
Red-180
Retail-180
01Pacific Arena Exclusives-366
01Topps-177
OPC Parallel-177
01Upper Deck-162
Exclusives-162
01Upper Deck MVP-178
01Upper Deck Victory-331
Gold-331
02Maple Leafs Platinum Collection-8
02NHL Power Play Stickers-135
020-Pee-Chee-126
020-Pee-Chee Premier Blue Parallel-126
020-Pee-Chee Premier Red Parallel-126
020-Pee-Chee Factory Set-126
02Pacific Complete-360
Red-360
02Topps-126
OPC Blue Parallel-126
OPC Red Parallel-126
Factory Set-126
02Topps Total-197
04Swedish Elitset-187
Gold-187
Signatures Series B-4
04Swedish Pure Skills-30
Parallel-30
05Swedish SHL Elitset-45
Series One Signatures-10
Teammates-3
06Swedish SHL Elitset-46

Hoglund, Patrik
91Swedish Semic Elitserien Stickers-160
92Swedish Semic Elitserien Stickers-178
93Swedish Semic Elitserien-149
94Swedish Leaf-266
95Swedish Upper Deck-115
97Swedish Collector's Choice-187
98Swedish UD Choice-185

Hogosta, Goran
71Swedish Hockey-381
72Swedish Stickers-256
74Swedish Stickers-143
81Swedish Semic Hockey VM Stickers-1
97Swedish Alfabilder Autographs-13
01Swedish Alfabilder-13

Hogstrom, Jerk
91Swedish Semic Elitserien Stickers-285

Hogue, Benoit
88Sabres Blue Shield-10
88Sabres Wonder Bread/Hostess-10
890-Pee-Chee-201
890-Pee-Chee Stickers-37
890-Pee-Chee Stickers-77
890-Pee-Chee Stickers-216
89Sabres Blue Shield-6
89Sabres Campbell's-8
900-Pee-Chee-215
90Pro Set-416
90Sabres Blue Shield-9
90Sabres Campbell's-10
90Topps-215
Tiffany-215
90Upper Deck-402
French-402
91Pro Set Platinum-200
91Bowman-38
91Nordiques Panini Team Stickers-E
91Nordiques Panini Team Stickers-F
910-Pee-Chee-292
91OPC Premier-179
91Panini Stickers-300
91Parkhurst-332
French-332
91Pinnacle-146
French-146
91Pro Set-17
91Pro Set-435
French-17
French-435
91Score American-134
91Score Canadian Bilingual-134
91Score Canadian English-134
91Score Rookie/Traded-108T
91Score Young Superstars-31
91Stadium Club-157
91Topps-292
91Upper Deck-159
French-159
92Bowman-28
92Durivage Panini-3
920-Pee-Chee-132
92Panini Stickers-197
92Panini Stickers French-197
92Parkhurst-104
Emerald Ice-104
92Pinnacle-62
French-62
92Pro Set-108
92Score-276
Canadian-276
Sharpshooters-21
Sharpshooters Canadian-21
92Stadium Club-425
92Topps-103
Gold-103G
92Ultra-127
92Upper Deck-325
93Donruss-201
93Durivage Score-29
93Leaf-155
93OPC Premier-140
Gold-140
93Panini Stickers-59
93Parkhurst-396
Emerald Ice-396
93Pinnacle-18
Canadian-18
93PowerPlay-148
93Score-16
Canadian-16
93Stadium Club-76
Members Only Master Set-76
OPC-76
First Day Issue-76
First Day Issue OPC-76
93Topps/OPC Premier-140
Gold-140
93Ultra-123
93Upper Deck-456
94Canada Games NHL POGS-374
94Donruss-188
94EA Sports-83
94Leaf-124
94Leaf Limited-20
94Maple Leafs Kodak-15
94Maple Leafs Pin-up Posters-28
94OPC Premier-26
Special Effects-26
94Parkhurst SE-SE106
Gold-SE106
94Pinnacle-129
Artist's Proofs-129
Rink Collection-129
94Select-130
Gold-130
94Topps/OPC Premier-26
Special Effects-26
94Ultra-128
94Upper Deck-436
Electric Ice-436
95Be A Player-126
Signatures-S126
Signatures Die Cuts-S126
95Canada Games NHL POGS-258
95Collector's Choice-72
Player's Club-72
Player's Club Platinum-72
95Donruss-70
95Leaf-134
95Panini Stickers-202
95Parkhurst International-330
Emerald Ice-330
95Pinnacle-186
Artist's Proofs-186
Rink Collection-186
95Score-262
Black Ice Artist's Proofs-262
Black Ice-262
95Topps-71
OPC Inserts-71
95Ultra-312
95Upper Deck-351
Electric Ice-351
Electric Ice Gold-351
Special Edition-SE171
Special Edition Gold-SE171
95Images Platinum Players-PL7
96Collector's Choice-72
96Donruss-135
Press Proofs-135
96Fleer Picks-136
96Leaf-137
Press Proofs-137
96Pinnacle-73
Artist's Proofs-73
Foil-73
Premium Stock-73
Rink Collection-73
96Score-141
Artist's Proofs-141
Dealer's Choice Artist's Proofs-141
Special Artist's Proofs-141
Golden Blades-141
96Stars Postcards-10
96Summit-56
Artist's Proofs-56
Ice-56
Metal-56
Premium Stock-56
96Upper Deck-247
97Be A Player-152
Autographs-152
Autographs Die-Cuts-152
Autographs Prismatic Die-Cuts-152
97Pacific-240
Copper-240
Emerald Green-240
Ice Blue-240
Red-240
Silver-240
97Panini Stickers-143
97Score-217
98Pacific-177
Ice Blue-177
Red-177
99Pacific-119
Copper-119
Emerald Green-119
Gold-119
Ice Blue-119
Premiere Date-119
Red-119
00Titanium Game Gear-83
00Titanium Game Gear Patches-83
01Atomic Jerseys-17
01Atomic Patches-17
01BAP Memorabilia-457
Emerald-457
Ruby-457
Sapphire-457
01Pacific Heads-Up Quad Jerseys-24
01Stars Postcards-8

Hogue, Russell
93Prince Albert Raiders-11
94Prince Albert Raiders-8
95Prince Albert Raiders-8
96Prince Albert Raiders-8

Hohenadl, Frank
94German DEL-212
95German DEL-340
98German DEL-304
99German DEL-249

Hohenberger, Herbert
87Hull Olympiques-10
90ProCards AHL/IHL-63
94German DEL-216
95Austrian National Team-9
95German DEL-204
95Swedish Globe World Championships-186
95Swedish World Championships Stickers-262
96German DEL-345
96Swedish Semic Wien-214
00German DEL-26

Hohenberger, Martin
95Signature Rookies Auto-Phonex-18
95Signature Rook Auto-Phonex Phone Cards-18
96Lethbridge Hurricanes-6
01German Upper Deck-218

Hohener, Martin
93Quebec Pee-Wee Tournament-1628
99Swiss Panini Stickers-108
00Swiss Panini Stickers-151
00Swiss Slapshot Mini-Cards-EHCK2
01Swiss HNL-57
02Swiss HNL-36
02Swiss HNL-233

Hohenleitner, Christoph
05German DEL-159

Hohl, Ryan
04Lincoln Stars-11

Hoiness, Brent
91Air Canada SJHL-A43
92Saskatchewan JHL-91
99Corpus Christi IceRays-7

Hokanson, Jeff
91British Columbia JHL-139

Hokegard, Joakim
83Swedish Semic Elitserien-221

Hokkanen, Iivo
06Finnish Cardset-34

Holan, Milos
93Donruss-244
93Parkhurst-268
Emerald Ice-268
93Pinnacle-427
Canadian-427
93Ultra-389
Wave of the Future-6
93Upper Deck-523
SP-115
93Swedish Semic World Champ Stickers-91
93Classic-134
94Donruss-10
94Leaf-289
94Classic Pro Prospects-70
95Collector's Choice-265
Player's Club-265
Player's Club Platinum-265
95Donruss-339
95Leaf-324
95Panini Stickers-230
95Parkhurst International-2
Emerald Ice-2
95Topps-173
OPC Inserts-173
95Ultra-2
Gold Medallion-2
95Upper Deck-77
Electric Ice-77
Electric Ice Gold-77
95Swedish World Championships Stickers-188
96Donruss-20
Press Proofs-20
96Score-211
Artist's Proofs-211
Dealer's Choice Artist's Proofs-211
Special Artist's Proofs-211
Golden Blades-211
98Czech OFS-359
98Czech OFS-473
99Czech DS-103
99Czech OFS-21
99Czech OFS Jagr Team Embossed-21
06Czech OFS Coaches-2

Holdan, Juri
99Czech DS-167

Holden, Barney
10C56-4
10Sweet Caporal Postcards-3
11C55-3

Holden, Cory
94German First League-653
95German DEL-315
96German DEL-97
99German Bundesliga 2-200

Holden, Jamie
05ITG Heroes/Prosp Toronto Expo Parallel -383
05Cleveland Barons-10
05Fresno Falcons-8
05ITG Heroes and Prospects-383
Autographs Update-A-JHO

Holden, Jerry
05Vernon Vipers-12

Holden, Josh
95Bowman Draft Prospects-P19
95Upper Deck-513
Electric Ice-513
Electric Ice Gold-513
95Classic-62
Autographs-8
96Regina Pats-1
96Collect Edge Ice Sign Sealed Delivered-6
96All-Sport PPF *-78
96All Sport PPF Gold *-78
97Beehive-66
Authentic Autographs-66
Golden Portraits-66
97Black Diamond-45
Double Diamond-45
Triple Diamond-45
Quadruple Diamond-45
97Zenith-100
Z-Gold-100
Z-Silver-100
97Zenith 5 x 7-80
Gold Impulse-80
Silver Impulse-80
97Regina Pats-25
97Bowman CHL-114
OPC-114
97Visions Signings Autographs *-28
98SP Authentic-112
Power Shift-112
98UD Choice-253
Prime Choice Reserve-253
Reserve-253
98Upper Deck MVP-207
Gold Script-207
Silver Script-207
Super Script-207
98Bowman CHL-73
Golden Anniversary-73
OPC International-73
98Bowman Chrome CHL-73
Golden Anniversary-73
Golden Anniversary Refractors-73
OPC International-73
OPC International Refractors-73
Refractors-73
990-Pee-Chee-44
990-Pee-Chee Chrome-44
990-Pee-Chee Chrome Refractors-44
99Pacific-423
Copper-423
Emerald Green-423
Gold-423
Ice Blue-423
Premiere Date-423
Red-423
99SPx-155
Radiance-155
Spectrum-155
99Topps/OPC-44
99Topps/OPC Chrome-44
Refractors-44
99Upper Deck-129
Exclusives-129
Exclusives 1 of 1-129
99Upper Deck Gold Reserve-129
99Upper Deck MVP-211
Gold Script-211
Silver Script-211
Super Script-211
99Upper Deck Victory-295
00BAP Signature Series-239
Emerald-239
Ruby-239
Sapphire-239
Autographs-136
Autographs Gold-136
00Kansas City Blades-13
010-Pee-Chee-265
010-Pee-Chee Premier Parallel-265
01Topps-265
OPC Parallel-265
01Manitoba Moose-11
02BAP Sig Series Auto Buybacks 2000-136
02St. John's Maple Leafs Aliant-5
03Parkhurst Original Six Toronto-28
04Finnish Cardset-222
04Swedish Pure Skills-109
Parallel-109
05Finnish Cardset Magicmakers-6

Holden, Mark
83Nova Scotia Voyageurs-1
84Nova Scotia Oilers-1

Holden, Nick
06Chilliwack Bruins-6

Holden, Paul
897th Inn. Sketch OHL-24
90ProCards AHL/IHL-431
91ProCards-396
92Salt Lake Golden Eagles-10
93St. John's Maple Leafs-10

Holdien, Dean
88Saskatoon Blades-10
89Saskatoon Blades-10

Holdridge, Kevin
96Detroit Whalers-10
03Florida Everblades RBI Sports-164
04Kalamazoo Wings-5

Holdschick, Peter
94German First League-165

Holdsworth, Brent
93London Knights-12

Holecek, Jiri
71Finnish Suomi Stickers-27
71Swedish Hockey-43
72Finnish Jaakiekko-7
72Finnish Hellas-81
72Finnish Panda Toronto-83
72Finnish Semic World Championship-22
72Swedish Stickers-21
72Swedish Stickers-45
72Swedish Semic World Championship-22
73Finnish Jaakiekko-48
73Swedish Stickers-27
74Finnish Jenkki-71
74Finnish Typotor-114
74Swedish Stickers-109
74Swedish Semic World Champ Stickers-51
77Finnish Sportscasters-83-1983
79Panini Stickers-74
91Finnish Semic World Champ Stickers-246
91Swedish Semic World Champ Stickers-246
96Swedish Semic Wien Hockey Legends-HL16
98Czech OFS Legends-8
03Czech Stadion-643

Holecko, Peter
96Slovakian Quebec Pee-Wee Tournament-11

Holeczy, Roger
94Dubuque Fighting Saints-12

Holeczy, Steve
94Dubuque Fighting Saints-13
95Waterloo Blackhawks -9

Holes, Michal
03Czech OFS Plus-282

Holfeld, Ryan
06Medicine Hat Tigers-11

Holick, Mark
84Saskatoon Blades Stickers-6
86Saskatoon Blades Photos-10
93Dallas Freeze-8

Holik, Bobby
90OPC Premier-43
90Pro Set-609
90Score Rookie/Traded-10T
90Score Young Superstars-34
90Upper Deck-534
French-534
90Whalers Jr. 7-Eleven-13
91Pro Set Platinum-43
91Bowman-18
910-Pee-Chee-7
910-Pee-Chee-56
91Panini Stickers-316
91Panini Stickers-342
91Parkhurst-290
French-290
91Pinnacle-65
French-65
91Pro Set-79
French-79
91Score American-153
91Score Canadian Bilingual-153
91Score Canadian English-153
91Score Young Superstars-36
91Stadium Club-299
91Topps-7
91Topps-56
91Upper Deck-233
French-233
Euro-Stars-3
Euro-Stars French-3
91Whalers Jr. 7-Eleven-14
91Finnish Semic World Champ Stickers-224
91Swedish Semic World Champ Stickers-224
92Bowman-407
920-Pee-Chee-254
92OPC Premier-77
92Panini Stickers-261
92Panini Stickers-293
92Panini Stickers French-261
92Panini Stickers French-293
92Parkhurst-96
Emerald Ice-96
92Pinnacle-277
French-277
92Pro Set-61
92Score-128
Canadian-128
92Stadium Club-106
92Topps-330
Gold-330G
92Ultra-339
92Upper Deck-252
92Upper Deck-500
93Donruss-183
93Leaf-227
93OPC Premier-52
93OPC Premier-322
Gold-52
Gold-322
93Parkhurst-385
Emerald Ice-385
93Pinnacle-71
Canadian-71
93PowerPlay-378
93Score-198
Canadian-198
93Stadium Club-159
Members Only Master Set-159
OPC-159
First Day Issue-159
First Day Issue OPC-159
93Topps/OPC Premier-52
93Topps/OPC Premier-322
Gold-52
Gold-322
93Ultra-360
93Upper Deck-218
94Canada Games NHL POGS-144
94Donruss-90
94Leaf-252
94OPC Premier-315
Special Effects-315
94Parkhurst-128
Gold-128
94Pinnacle-347
Artist's Proofs-347
Rink Collection-347
94Stadium Club-129
Members Only Master Set-129
First Day Issue-129
Super Team Winner Cards-129
94Topps/OPC Premier-315
Special Effects-315
94Upper Deck-314
Electric Ice-314
95Be A Player-202
Signatures-S202
Signatures Die Cuts-S202
95Canada Games NHL POGS-159
95Collector's Choice-185
Player's Club-185
Player's Club Platinum-185
95Donruss-220
95Parkhurst International-125
Emerald Ice-125
95Topps-303
OPC Inserts-303
Power Lines-10PL
95Ultra-262
95Upper Deck-365
Electric Ice-365
Electric Ice Gold-365
95Swedish World Championships Stickers-204
96Devils Team Issue-16
96SP-87
97Be A Player-201
Autographs-201
Autographs Die-Cuts-201
Autographs Prismatic Die-Cuts-201
97Collector's Choice-143
97Crown Royale-76
Emerald Green-76
Ice Blue-76
Silver-76
97Devils Team Issue-11
97Donruss-140
Press Proofs Silver-140
Press Proofs Gold-140
97Donruss Priority-158
Stamp of Approval-158
97Pacific-55
Copper-55
Emerald Green-55
Ice Blue-55
Red-55
Silver-55
97Pacific Dynagon-70
Copper-70
Dark Grey-70
Emerald Green-70
Ice Blue-70
Red-70
Silver-70
Tandems-45
97Pacific Invincible-78
Copper-78
Emerald Green-78
Ice Blue-78
Red-78
Silver-78
97Pacific Omega-130
Copper-130
Dark Gray-130
Emerald Green-130
Gold-130
Ice Blue-130
97Panini Stickers-65
97Paramount-103
Copper-103
Dark Grey-103
Emerald Green-103
Ice Blue-103
Red-103
Silver-103
97Revolution-78
Copper-78
Emerald-78
Ice Blue-78
Silver-78
97Score-183
97Score Devils-2
Platinum-2
Premier-2
97SP Authentic-89
97Upper Deck-304
97Zenith-68
Z-Gold-68
Z-Silver-68
98Aurora-110
98Bowman's Best-53
Refractors-53
Atomic Refractors-53
98Crown Royale-80
Limited Series-80
98Devils Power Play-NJD4
98Devils Team Issue-13
98Finest-95
No Protectors-95
No Protectors Refractors-95
Refractors-95
98Katch-83
98OPC Chrome-131
Refractors-131
98Pacific-263
Ice Blue-263
Red-263
98Pacific Dynagon Ice-110
Blue-110
Red-110
98Pacific Omega-138
Red-138
Opening Day Issue-138
98Panini Stickers-68
98Paramount-134
Copper-134
Emerald Green-134
Holo-Electric-134
Ice Blue-134
Silver-134
98Revolution-85
Ice Shadow-85
Red-85
All-Star Die Cuts-10
98Topps-131
O-Pee-Chee-131
98UD Choice-115
98UD Choice Preview-115
98UD Choice Prime Choice Reserve-115
98UD Choice Reserve-115
98Upper Deck-313
Exclusives-313
Exclusives 1 of 1-313
Gold Reserve-313
98Upper Deck MVP-121
Gold Script-121
Silver Script-121
Super Script-121
99Aurora-86
Premiere Date-86
99BAP Memorabilia-142
Gold-142
Silver-142
99BAP Millennium-150
Emerald-150
Ruby-150
Sapphire-150
Signatures-150
Signatures Gold-150
99Crown Royale-81
Limited Series-81
Premiere Date-81
99Devils Team Issue-9
990-Pee-Chee-119
990-Pee-Chee Chrome-119
990-Pee-Chee Chrome Refractors-119
99Pacific-238
Copper-238
Emerald Green-238
Gold-238
Ice Blue-238
Premiere Date-238
Red-238
99Pacific Dynagon Ice-117
Blue-117
Copper-117
Gold-117
Premiere Date-117
99Pacific Omega-136
Copper-136
Gold-136
Ice Blue-136
Premiere Date-136
99Pacific Prism-82
Holographic Blue-82
Holographic Gold-82
Holographic Mirror-82
Holographic Purple-82
Premiere Date-82
99Panini Stickers-81
99Paramount-133
Copper-133
Emerald-133
Gold-133
Holographic Emerald-133
Holographic Gold-133
Holographic Silver-133
Ice Blue-133
Premiere Date-133
Red-133
Silver-133
99Revolution-86
Premiere Date-86
Red-86
Shadow Series-86
99Stadium Club-108
First Day Issue-108
One of a Kind-108
Printing Plates Black-108
Printing Plates Cyan-108
Printing Plates Magenta-108
Printing Plates Yellow-108
99Topps/OPC-119
99Topps/OPC Chrome-119
Refractors-119
99Topps Gold Label Class 1-39
Black-39
Black One of One-39
One of One-39
Red-39
Red One of One-39
99Topps Gold Label Class 2-39
99Topps Gold Label Class 2 Black-39
99Topps Gold Label Class 2 Black 1 of 1-39
99Topps Gold Label Class 2 One of One-39
99Topps Gold Label Class 2 Red-39
99Topps Gold Label Class 2 Red One of One-39
99Topps Gold Label Class 3-39
99Topps Gold Label Class 3 Black-39
99Topps Gold Label Class 3 Black 1 of 1-39
99Topps Gold Label Class 3 One of One-39
99Topps Gold Label Class 3 Red-39
99Topps Gold Label Class 3 Red One of One-39
99Topps Premier Plus-12
Parallel-12
99Upper Deck Victory-175
00BAP Memorabilia-12
Emerald-12
Ruby-12
Sapphire-12
Promos-12
00BAP Mem Chicago Sportsfest Copper-12
00BAP Memorabilia Chicago Sportsfest Blue-12
00BAP Memorabilia Chicago Sportsfest Gold-12
00BAP Memorabilia Chicago Sportsfest Ruby-12
00BAP Memorabilia Chicago Sun-Times Ruby-12
00BAP Memorabilia Chicago Sun-Times Gold-12
00BAP Mem Chicago Sun-Times Sapphire-12
00BAP Mem Toronto Fall Expo Copper-12
00BAP Memorabilia Toronto Fall Expo Gold-12
00BAP Memorabilia Toronto Fall Expo Ruby-12
00BAP Parkhurst 2000-P245
00BAP Signature Series-224
Emerald-224
Ruby-224
Sapphire-224
00Devils Team Issue-9
000-Pee-Chee-106
000-Pee-Chee Parallel-106
00Pacific-235
Copper-235
Gold-235
Ice Blue-235
Premiere Date-235
00Panini Stickers-49
00Private Stock Game Gear-63
00Private Stock Game Gear Patches-63
00Stadium Club-77
00Titanium Draft Day Edition-59
Patches-59
00Topps/OPC-106
Parallel-106
Game-Worn Sweaters-GWBH
00Topps Heritage-188
00UD Heroes-72
00Upper Deck-332
Exclusives Tier 1-332
Exclusives Tier 2-332
00Upper Deck Vintage-217
00Vanguard Dual Game-Worn Jerseys-8
00Vanguard Dual Game-Worn Patches-8
01Devils Team Issue-9
010-Pee-Chee-174
010-Pee-Chee Premier Parallel-174
01Pacific-231
Extreme LTD-231
Hobby LTD-231
Premiere Date-231
Retail LTD-231
Jerseys-18
01Pacific Arena Exclusives-231
01Pacific Heads-Up Quad Jerseys-3
01Parkhurst-195
Teammates-T15
01Private Stock Game Gear-60
01Private Stock Game Gear Patches-60
01Titanium Draft Day Edition-53
01Topps-174
OPC Parallel-174
01UD Mask Collection-55
Gold-55
01UD Stanley Cup Champs-77
01Upper Deck-333
Exclusives-333
01Upper Deck Victory-214
Gold-214
01Upper Deck Vintage-157
01Vanguard Memorabilia-17
01Czech Stadion-220
02BAP First Edition-110
Jerseys-110
02BAP Memorabilia-263
Emerald-263
Ruby-263
Sapphire-263
NHL All-Star Game-263
NHL All-Star Game Blue-263
NHL All-Star Game Green-263
NHL All-Star Game Red-263
02BAP Memorabilia Toronto Fall Expo-263
02BAP Signature Series-174
Autographs-174
Autograph Buybacks 1999-150
Autographs Gold-174
Golf-GS11
02ITG Used International Experience-IE15
02ITG Used International Experience Gold-IE15
02ITG Used Emblems-E37
02Pacific-223
Blue-223
Red-223
02Pacific Complete-494
Red-494
02Pacific Exclusive-114
Jerseys-16
Jerseys Gold-16
02Pacific Heads-Up-80
Blue-80
Purple-80
Red-80
02Parkhurst-117
Bronze-117
Gold-117
Silver-117
02Parkhurst Retro-94
Minis-94
02Private Stock Reserve-67
Blue-67
Red-67
Retail-67
02Rangers Team Issue-5
02SP Authentic-60
Beckett Promos-60
02Stadium Club-102
Silver Decoy Cards-102
Proofs-102
02Topps Heritage-156
02Topps Total-316
02Upper Deck-360
Exclusives-360
02Upper Deck Beckett UD Promos-360
03ITG Action-326
Jerseys-M31
03NHL Sticker Collection-84
030-Pee-Chee-256
03OPC Blue-256
03OPC Gold-256
03OPC Red-256
03Pacific-224
Blue-224
Red-224
03Pacific Complete-232
Red-232
03Pacific Exhibit-98
Blue Backs-98
Yellow Backs-98
03Parkhurst Original Six New York-11
Memorabilia-NM10
03Rangers Team Issue-7
03Topps-256
Blue-256
Gold-256
Red-256
03Upper Deck MVP-281
Gold Script-281
Silver Script-281
Canadian Exclusives-281
03Czech Stadion-565
04Pacific-174
Blue-174
Red-174
04Upper Deck-118
Canadian Exclusives-118
HG Glossy Gold-118
HG Glossy Silver-118
05Be A Player-59
First Period-59
Second Period-59
Third Period-59
Overtime-59
Quad Signatures-SDPH
Signatures-BH
Signatures Gold-BH
05Black Diamond-55
Emerald-55
Gold-55
Onyx-55
Ruby-55
05Panini Stickers-9
05Parkhurst-32
Facsimile Auto Parallel-32
True Colors-TCATL
True Colors-TCATL
05Ultra-13
Gold-13
Ice-13
05Upper Deck-252
Jerseys-J-BHO
05Upper Deck Hockey Showcase-HS9
05Upper Deck Showcase Promos-HS9
05Upper Deck MVP-16
Gold-16
Platinum-16
05Upper Deck Victory-127
Black-127
Gold-127
Silver-127
06Be A Player-115
Autographs-115
Signatures-BH
Signatures 25-127
Signatures Trios-THKH
Portraits Signature Portraits-SPBH
06Fleer-13
Tiffany-13
060-Pee-Chee-29
Rainbow-29
06Panini Stickers-4
06Ultra-13
Gold Medallion-13
Ice Medallion-13
06Upper Deck Arena Giveaways-ATL3
06Upper Deck-13
Exclusives Parallel-13
High Gloss Parallel-13
Masterpieces-13
06Upper Deck MVP-15
Gold Script-15
Super Script-15

Holik, Jaroslav
69Swedish Hockey-27
70Finnish Jaakiekko-47
70Swedish Hockey-357
70Swedish Masterserien-6
70Swedish Masterserien-78
70Swedish Masterserien-149
72Finnish Jaakiekko-8
72Finnish Hellas-84
72Swedish Stickers-24
73Finnish Jaakiekko-49
74Finnish Jenkki-72
74Swedish Stickers-115
74Swedish Semic World Champ Stickers-60
77Sportscasters-5514
77Finnish Sportscasters-51-1218
94Czech APS Extraliga-291
01Czech DS Legends-L10
03Czech Stadion-644

Holik, Jiri
69Swedish Hockey-28
70Finnish Jaakiekko-48
70Swedish Hockey-358

70Swedish Masterserien-3
70Swedish Masterserien-150
71Finnish Suomi Stickers-28
71Swedish Hockey-53
72Finnish Jaakiekko-9
72Finnish Hellas-98
72Finnish Panda Toronto-84
72Finnish Semic World Championship-39
72Swedish Stickers-25
72Swedish Semic World Championship-39
73Finnish Jaakiekko-50
74Finnish Jenkki-73
74Finnish Typotor-115
74Swedish Stickers-116
74Swedish Semic World Champ Stickers-61
77Finnish Sportscasters-51-1218
95Czech APS Extraliga-196
95Czech APS Extraliga-393
96Czech APS Extraliga-331
03Czech Stadion-645

Holik, Vladimir
98Czech OFS-69
99Czech OFS-238
00Czech OFS-197
01Czech OFS-107

Holk, Brian
907th Inn. Sketch OHL-260

Holland, Bob
77Nova Scotia Voyageurs-9
81Indianapolis Checkers-8
82Indianapolis Checkers-9

Holland, Cory
98Madison Monsters-7

Holland, Dennis
86Portland Winter Hawks-9
87Portland Winter Hawks-12
88Portland Winter Hawks-12
89ProCards AHL-322
90ProCards AHL/IHL-471
91ProCards-593
92Cincinnati Cyclones-12
97Toledo Storm-14
99Louisiana Ice Gators-24

Holland, Derek
96Medicine Hat Tigers-7
97Lethbridge Hurricanes-6
97Medicine Hat Tigers-10
00Lubbock Cotton Kings-16
03Lubbock Cotton Kings-10

Holland, Jason
93Kamloops Blazers-8
94Kamloops Blazers-9
95Donruss Elite World Juniors-6
95Upper Deck-537
Electric Ice-537
Electric Ice Gold-537
95Kamloops Blazers-28
95Signature Rookies-11
Signatures-11
95Slapshot Memorial Cup-3
96Kentucky Thoroughblades-10
97Donruss-214
Press Proofs Silver-214
Press Proofs Gold-214
97Donruss Canadian Ice-144
Dominion Series-144
Provincial Series-144
97Kentucky Thoroughblades-8
98Upper Deck-224
Exclusives-224
Exclusives 1 of 1-224
Gold Reserve-224
98Rochester Americans-15
00Upper Deck NHLPA-PA11
00Rochester Americans-9
01Upper Deck Vintage-119
01Manchester Monarchs-7B
02Manchester Monarchs-22
05German DEL-148
06German DEL-98

Holland, Jerry
75O-Pee-Chee NHL-392
76O-Pee-Chee NHL-315

Holland, Steve
03Yarmouth Mariners-11

Hollenbush, Kevin
93Quebec Pee-Wee Tournament-791

Hollenstein, Felix
91Finnish Semic World Champ Stickers-194
91Swedish Semic World Champ Stickers-194
92Finnish Semic-209
93Swedish Semic World Champ Stickers-127
93Swiss HNL-23
95Finnish Semic World Championships-191
95Swiss HNL-21
96Swiss HNL-20
96Swiss HNL-519
96Swiss HNL-539
98Swiss Power Play Stickers-115
99Swiss Panini Stickers-115
00Swiss Panini Stickers-159
00Swiss Slapshot Mini-Cards-EHCK9
01Swiss HNL-65
02Swiss HNL-499

Holler, Christian
93Quebec Pee-Wee Tournament-1531

Hollet, Danny
04Victoriaville Tigres-7

Hollett, Frank
34Beehive Group I Photos-325
35O-Pee-Chee V304C-83
37V356 Worldwide Gum-62
39O-Pee-Chee V301-1-41
02BAP Ultimate Mem Paper Cuts Autos-13
03BAP Ultimate Memorabilia Paper Cuts-12
04ITG Ultimate Mem Beantown's Best-3
05ITG Ultimate Mem Leafs Forever Autos-11

Hollett, Steve
84Sault Ste. Marie Greyhounds-9
89ProCards AHL-97

Holley, Pat
87Sudbury Wolves-20

Holli, Antti
06Finnish Cardset-329

Holliday, Kevin
98Thunder Bay Thunder Cats-8
01Fort Wayne Komets-8
01Fort Wayne Komets Shoe Carnival-3

Hollinger, Terry
88Regina Pats-9
89Regina Pats-8
907th Inn. Sketch WHL-165
917th Inn. Sketch WHL-354
92Peoria Rivermen-9
93Peoria Rivermen-12
94Parkhurst-204
Gold-204
94Classic Pro Prospects-171
95Rochester Americans-5
96Rochester Americans-7
00Providence Bruins-14
01German Upper Deck-111
02Swiss HNL-456

Hollinger, Todd
91Air Canada SJHL-A27

Hollingshead, Kelly
91Air Canada SJHL-B20
96Knoxville Cherokees-8

Hollingworth, Bucky
54Topps-12
94Parkhurst Missing Link-62

Hollinworth, Gordie
52Juniors Blue Tint-131

Hollis, Scott
89Oshawa Generals-3
89Oshawa Generals 7th Inning Sketch-11
897th Inn. Sketch OHL-11
907th Inn. Sketch OHL-339
907th Inn. Sketch Memorial Cup-96
91Oshawa Generals-11
91Oshawa Generals Sheet-1
917th Inn. Sketch OHL-155
92Oshawa Generals Sheet-20
93Las Vegas Thunder-13
95Adirondack Red Wings-10
98Las Vegas Thunder-9
98Orlando Solar Bears-11
00Syracuse Crunch-16
01Flint Generals-7
02Muskegon Fury-10
03Muskegon Fury-9

Holloway, Bruce
81Regina Pats-13
83Fredericton Express-13
84Fredericton Express-3
05ITG Heroes and Prospects-425

Holloway, Bud
06ITG Heroes and Prospects-100
Autographs-ABHO
Jerseys-GUJ36
Jerseys Gold-GUJ36
Emblems-GUE36
Emblems Gold-GUE36
Numbers-GUN36
Numbers Gold-GUN36

Holloway, Travis
05Salmon Arm Silverbacks-9

Hollweg, Ryan
99Medicine Hat Tigers-8
00Medicine Hat Tigers-10
00UD CHL Prospects-55
02Medicine Hat Tigers-9
03Medicine Hat Tigers-3
04Hartford Wolf Pack-9
05Beehive-146
Beige -146
Blue -146
Gold-146
Red -146
Matte-146
05Black Diamond-168
Emerald-168
Gold-168
Onyx-168
Ruby-168
05Hot Prospects-206
Autographed Patch Variation-206
Autographed Patch Variation Gold-206
Red Hot-206
05Parkhurst Signatures-RH
05SP Authentic-173
Limited-173
Sign of the Times-RH
05SP Game Used-133
Autographs-133
Gold-133
Rookie Exclusives-RH
Rookie Exclusives Silver-RE-RH
05SPx-147
Spectrum-147
05The Cup-190
Black Rainbow Rookies-190
Masterpiece Pressplates (Artifacts)-303
Masterpiece Pressplates (Bee Hive)-146
Masterpiece Pressplates (Black Diamond)-168
Masterpiece Pressplates (Ice)-156
Masterpiece Pressplates (Rookie Update)-159
Masterpiece Pressplates SPA Autos-173
Masterpiece Pressplates (SP Game Used)-133
Masterpiece Pressplates (SPx)-147
Masterpiece Pressplates (SPx)-147
Masterpiece Pressplates (Trilogy)-282
Masterpiece Pressplates Ult Coll-157
Masterpiece Pressplates Autographs-190
Platinum Rookies-190
05UD Artifacts-303
05Ultimate Collection-157
Gold-157
05Ultra-229
Gold-229
Fresh Ink-FI-RH
Fresh Ink Blue-FI-RH
Ice-229
Rookie Uniformity Jerseys-RU-RH
Rookie Uniformity Jersey Autographs-ARU-RH
Rookie Uniformity Patches-RUP-RH
Rookie Uniformity Patch Autographs-ARP-RH
05Upper Deck-235
HG Glossy-235
Rookie Ink-RIRH
Rookie Threads-RTRH
Rookie Threads Autographs-ARTRH
05Upper Deck Ice-156
Premieres Auto Patches-AIPRH
05Upper Deck Rookie Update-159
05Upper Deck Trilogy-282
05Upper Deck Toronto Fall Expo-235
06Black Diamond Jerseys-JRH
06Black Diamond Jerseys Black-JRH
06Black Diamond Jerseys Gold-JRH
06Black Diamond Jerseys Ruby-JRH
06Fleer Fabricology-FRH
06UD Artifacts Auto-Facts-AFHR
06UD Artifacts Auto-Facts Gold-AFHR
06Upper Deck-132
Exclusives Parallel-132
High Gloss Parallel-132
Game Jerseys-JRH
Game Patches-PRH
Masterpieces-132
Signatures-SRH

Holly, Jan
93Quebec Pee-Wee Tournament-1556

Holly, Tyson
02Augusta Lynx-65

Holm, Tobias
02Swedish SHL-199
Parallel-199
03Swedish Elite-63
Silver-63

Holma, Eetu
04Finnish Cardset-28
Parallel-20
05Finnish Cardset -22
06Finnish Cardset-314

Holman, Jim
92Western Michigan Broncos-12
93Western Michigan Broncos-15

Holmberg, Erik
83Swedish Semic Elitserien-167
84Swedish Semic Elitserien-68
85Swedish Panini Stickers-64
86Swedish Panini Stickers-269
89Swedish Semic Elitserien Stickers-237
90Swedish Semic Elitserien Stickers-14
91Swedish Semic Elitserien Stickers-212
92Swedish Semic Elitserien Stickers-246
93Swedish Semic Elitserien-215

Holmberg, Jorgen
83Swedish Semic Elitserien-89
84Swedish Semic Elitserien-89
85Swedish Panini Stickers-81
89Swedish Semic Elitserien Stickers-260
90Swedish Semic Elitserien Stickers-165
91Swedish Semic Elitserien Stickers-270

Holmberg, Mikael
85Swedish Panini Stickers-108
86Swedish Panini Stickers-106
87Swedish Panini Stickers-104
89Swedish Semic Elitserien Stickers-92
90Swedish Semic Elitserien Stickers-266
94Swedish Leaf-198
95Swedish Leaf-68
95Swedish Upper Deck-109

Holmberg, Niklas
83Swedish Semic Elitserien-125
84Swedish Semic Elitserien-148

Holmes, Bill
24Anonymous NHL-14

Holmes, Chuck
69Seattle Totems-2

Holmes, Daril
84Kingston Canadians-25
85Kingston Canadians-25
86Kingston Canadians-13

Holmes, Darren
91British Columbia JHL-46

Holmes, Ethan
93Quebec Pee-Wee Tournament-783

Holmes, Harry
24Anonymous NHL-121
83Hall of Fame Postcards-L6
85Hall of Fame-156
06Between The Pipes Forgotten Franchises-FF02

Holmes, James
52Juniors Blue Tint-54

Holmes, Mark
88Salt Lake Golden Eagles-22

Holmes, Matt
04Thetford Mines Prolab-22

Holmes, Randy
96Madison Monsters-6
01Kalamazoo K-Wings-4
02Indianapolis Ice-7

Holmes, Samantha
98New Hampshire Wildcats-11

Holmes, Tom
92Harvard Crimson-14
96Richmond Renegades-11

Holmes, Warren
78Saginaw Gears-8
95Slapshot-243

Holmgren, Adam
06Austin Ice Bats-2

Holmgren, Arne
57Swedish Alfabilder-98

Holmgren, Erik
57Swedish Alfabilder-96

Holmgren, Leif
72Swedish Stickers-64
73Swedish Stickers-196
74Swedish Stickers-223
79Panini Stickers-192
81Swedish Semic Hockey VM Stickers-14
82Swedish Semic VM Stickers-23
83Swedish Semic Elitserien-20
83Swedish Semic VM Stickers-23
91Swedish Semic Elitserien Stickers-302
92Swedish Semic Elitserien Stickers-324

Holmgren, Niclas
86Swedish Panini Stickers-10

Holmgren, Paul
77O-Pee-Chee NHL-307
78O-Pee-Chee-234
78Topps-234
79O-Pee-Chee-156
79Topps-156
80O-Pee-Chee-164
80O-Pee-Chee-172
80Topps-164
80Topps-172
81O-Pee-Chee-242
81O-Pee-Chee Stickers-179
81Topps-E105
82O-Pee-Chee-251
82O-Pee-Chee Stickers-116
82Post Cereal-14
82Topps Stickers-116
83NHL Key Tags-96
83O-Pee-Chee-266
84North Stars 7-Eleven-7
84North Stars Postcards-11
84O-Pee-Chee-100
84Topps-74
85Flyers Postcards-12
85Islanders News Trottier-11
86Flyers Postcards-10
87Flyers Postcards-6
88Flyers Postcards-2
89Flyers Postcards-11
90Pro Set-673
92Whalers Dairymart-8
01Topps Archives-74
02Fleer Throwbacks-73
Gold-73
Platinum-73
04ITG Franchises US East-434
Autographs-A-PHO

Holmgren, Rune
57Swedish Alfabilder-97
69Swedish Hockey-231

Holmgren, Sune
55Swedish Alfabilder-29

Holmqvist, Andreas
02Swedish SHL-210
Parallel-210
03Swedish Elite-70
Silver-70
03Pensacola Ice Pilots-347
04Springfield Falcons-3
06Swedish SHL Elitset-206

Holmqvist, Johan
96Swedish Brynas Tigers-1
98Swedish UD Choice-33
99Swedish Upper Deck-18
SHL Signatures-3
Snapshots-2
00BAP Memorabilia-493
Emerald-493
Ruby-493
Sapphire-493
00SP Authentic-152
00SPx-182
00UD Heroes-171
00Upper Deck Ice-117
00Hartford Wolf Pack-13
01Between the Pipes-34
Future Wave-FW5
Jerseys-GJ38
01Hartford Wolf Pack-9
02Between the Pipes-80
Gold-80
Silver-80
02Hartford Wolf Pack-10
03BAP Memorabilia Deep in the Crease-D11
03Houston Aeros-12
04Swedish Elitset-145
Dominators-3
Gold-145
Masks-1
Signatures Series B-2
04Swedish Pure Skills-1
Parallel-1
05Swedish SHL Elitset-1
Catchers-1
Catchers Gold-1
Gold-1
Stoppers-1
06Between The Pipes-66
Autographs-AJHO
Emblems-GUE29
Emblems Gold-GUE29
Emblems Autographs-GUE29
Jerseys-GUJ29
Jerseys Gold-GUJ29
Jerseys Autographs-GUJ29
Numbers-GUN29
Numbers Gold-GUN29
Numbers Autographs-GUN29
06Lightning Postcards-9
06O-Pee-Chee-440
Rainbow-440
06Swedish SHL Elitset-1
Goal Patrol-1
In The Crease-1
07Upper Deck Victory-68
Black-68
Gold-68

Holmqvist, Leif
64Swedish Coralli ISHockey-6
64Swedish Coralli ISHockey-107
65Swedish Coralli ISHockey-6
65Swedish Coralli ISHockey-31
67Swedish Hockey-9
67Swedish Hockey-32
69Swedish Hockey-45
69Swedish Hockey-186
70Finnish Jaakiekko-26
70Swedish Hockey-1
70Swedish Hockey-62
70Swedish Hockey-63
70Swedish Hockey-64
70Swedish Hockey-65
70Swedish Hockey-120
70Swedish Hockey-273
70Swedish Masterserien-38
70Swedish Masterserien-44
70Swedish Masterserien-53
70Swedish Masterserien-103
71Finnish Suomi Stickers-46
71Swedish Hockey-2
71Swedish Hockey-75
72Finnish Jaakiekko-46
72Finnish Hellas-23
72Finnish Panda Toronto-68
72Finnish Semic World Championship-42
72Swedish Stickers-2
72Swedish Stickers-51
72Swedish Semic World Championship-42
73Swedish Stickers-190
74Swedish Stickers-316
81Swedish Semic Hockey VM Stickers-109
91Finnish Semic World Champ Stickers-231
91Swedish Semic World Champ Stickers-231
95Swedish Globe World Championships-64
97Swedish Alfabilder Autographs-7
98Swedish UD Choice-201
98Swedish UD Choice-212
01Swedish Alfabilder-7
03Czech Stadion-639
04Swedish Alfabilder Alfa Stars-46
04Swedish Alfabilder Next In Line-1
04Swedish Alfabilder Proof Parallels-46

Holmqvist, Mikael
98UD Choice-289
Prime Choice Reserve-289
Reserve-289
98Swedish UD Choice-96
98Swedish UD Choice-214
99Finnish Cardset-334
01Finnish Cardset-144
02Finnish Cardset-174
03Finnish Cardset D-Day-DD2
03Cincinnati Mighty Ducks-B7
04AHL All-Stars-18
04Cincinnati Mighty Ducks-18
06Blackhawks Postcards-9
06O-Pee-Chee-113
Rainbow-113

Holmroos, Rainer
73Finnish Jaakiekko-260

Holmstedt, Kenneth
71Swedish Hockey-321
72Swedish Stickers-136
74Swedish Stickers-142

Holmstrom, Ben
04Sioux Falls Stampede-3-5
05Sioux Falls Stampede-11

Holmstrom, Borje
67Swedish Hockey-220

Holmstrom, Christer
72Swedish Stickers-274

Holmstrom, Rune
57Swedish Alfabilder-121

Holmstrom, Tomas
94Swedish Leaf-218
NHL Draft-9
Rookie Rockets-3
95Swedish Leaf-84
Face to Face-8
95Swedish Upper Deck-123
Ticket to North America-NA15
95Swedish Globe World Championships-50
95Signature Rookies Auto-Phonex-19
95Signature Rook Auto-Phonex Phone Cards-19
96Donruss Canadian Ice-129
Gold Press Proofs-129
Red Press Proofs-129
96Flair-107
Blue Ice-107
96Leaf Limited Rookies-9
96Leaf Limited Rookies Gold-9
96Select Certified-97
Artist's Proofs-97
Blue-97
Mirror Blue-97
Mirror Gold-97
Mirror Red-97
Red-97
96Upper Deck-255
96Zenith-118
Artist's Proofs-118
96Swedish Semic Wien-70
97Be A Player-188
Autographs-188
Autographs Die-Cuts-188
Autographs Prismatic Die-Cuts-188
97Pacific-319
Copper-319
Emerald Green-319
Ice Blue-319
Red-319
Silver-319
97Score Red Wings-16
Platinum-16
Premier-16
98Be A Player-196
Press Release-196
98BAP Gold-196
98BAP Autographs-196
98BAP Autographs Gold-196
98Pacific-193
Ice Blue-193
Red-193
98SP Authentic Sign of the Times-TH
98SP Authentic Sign of the Times Gold-TH
98Upper Deck-89
Exclusives-89
Exclusives 1 of 1-89
Gold Reserve-89
98Upper Deck MVP-74
Gold Script-74
Silver Script-74
Super Script-74
99BAP Memorabilia-132
Gold-132
Silver-132
99Pacific-139
Copper-139
Emerald Green-139
Gold-139
Ice Blue-139
Premiere Date-139
Red-139
99Upper Deck-222
Exclusives-222
Exclusives 1 of 1-222
99Upper Deck Gold Reserve-222
99Upper Deck MVP-75
Gold Script-75
Silver Script-75
Super Script-75
99Upper Deck Victory-104
00BAP Memorabilia-381
Emerald-381
Ruby-381
Sapphire-381
Promos-381
00BAP Mem Chicago Sportsfest Copper-381
00BAP Memorabilia Chicago Sportsfest Blue-381
00BAP Memorabilia Chicago Sportsfest Gold-381
00BAP Memorabilia Chicago Sportsfest Ruby-381
00BAP Memorabilia Chicago Sun-Times Ruby-381
00BAP Memorabilia Chicago Sun-Times Gold-381
00BAP Mem Chicago Sun-Times Sapphire-381
00BAP Mem Toronto Fall Expo Copper-381
00BAP Memorabilia Toronto Fall Expo Gold-381
00BAP Memorabilia Toronto Fall Expo Ruby-381
00Pacific-148
Copper-148
Gold-148
Ice Blue-148
Premiere Date-148
00Upper Deck-65
Exclusives Tier 1-65
Exclusives Tier 2-65
00Upper Deck Victory-89
00Upper Deck Vintage-134
01BAP Signature Series-37
Autographs-37
Autographs Gold-37
01Pacific-141
Extreme LTD-141
Hobby LTD-141
Premiere Date-141
Retail LTD-141
01Pacific Arena Exclusives-141
01Parkhurst-181
01UD Stanley Cup Champs-65
01Upper Deck-292
Exclusives-292
01Upper Deck Victory-133
Gold-133
01Upper Deck Vintage-96
01Czech Stadion-233
02BAP Memorabilia Stanley Cup Champions-SCC-14
02BAP Sig Series Auto Buybacks 1998-196
02BAP Sig Series Auto Buybacks 2001-37
02BAP Ultimate Mem Dynasty Jerseys-19
02BAP Ultimate Mem Dynasty Emblems-19
02BAP Ultimate Mem Dynasty Numbers-19
02Pacific Complete-438
Red-438
02Topps Total-167
02Upper Deck-67
Exclusives-67
Victory National Pride-NP45
03ITG Action-259
03Pacific-118
Blue-118
Red-118
03Pacific Complete-355
Red-355
03Parkhurst Original Six Detroit-11
03Upper Deck-311
Canadian Exclusives-311
HG-311
UD Exclusives-311
03Upper Deck MVP-150
Gold Script-150
Silver Script-150
Canadian Exclusives-150
04UD All-World-62
Gold-62
04Swedish Alfabilder Alfa Stars-16
04Swedish Alfabilder Autographs-120
04Swedish Alfabilder Limited Autographs-120
04Swedish Alfabilder Proof Parallels-16
04Swedish Elitset-224
Dominators-6
Gold-224
Signatures Series B-17
04Swedish Pure Skills-55
Parallel-55
05Parkhurst-176
Facsimile Auto Parallel-176
05The Cup Master Pressplate Rookie Update-252
05Upper Deck-70
HG Glossy-70
Notable Numbers-N-TH
05Upper Deck MVP-143
Gold-143
Platinum-143
05Upper Deck Rookie Update-252
Inspirations Patch Rookies-252
05Upper Deck Toronto Fall Expo-70
06Beehive Matted Materials-MMTH
06Beehive Remarkable Matted Materials-MMTH
06Beehive Signature Scrapbook-SSTH
06Black Diamond-30
Black-30
Gold-30
Ruby-30
Jerseys-JTH
Jerseys Black-JTH
Jerseys Gold-JTH
Jerseys Ruby-JTH
06Flair Showcase-42
Parallel-42
Stitches-SSTH
06Fleer-70
Tiffany-70
Fabricology-FTH
06Hot Prospects Hot Materials -HMTH
06Hot Prospects Hot Materials Red Hot-HMTH
06Hot Prospects Hot Materials White Hot-HMTH
06Hot Prospects Hotagraphs-HHO
06O-Pee-Chee-174
Rainbow-174
06Panini Stickers-264
06SP Authentic Sign of the Times Triples-ST3LHZ
06SP Game Used Authentic Fabrics-AFTH
06SP Game Used Authentic Fabrics Parallel-AFTH
06SP Game Used Authentic Fabrics Patches-AFTH
06SP Game Used Authentic Fabrics Dual-AF2HZ
06SP Game Used Authentic Fabrics Dual Patches-AF2HZ
06SP Game Used Authentic Fabrics Eights-AF8SWE
06SP Game Used Authentic Fabrics Eights Patches-AF8SWE
06SP Game Used Inked Sweaters-ISHO
06SP Game Used Inked Sweaters Patches-ISHO
06SP Game Used Inked Sweaters Dual-IS2ZH
06SP Game Used Inked Sweaters Dual Patches-IS2ZH
06SP Game Used Letter Marks-LMTH
06SP Game Used SIGnificance-STH
06SPx Winning Materials-WMHO
06SPx Winning Materials Spectrum-WMHO
06The Cup Autographed NHL Shields Duals-DASLH
06UD Artifacts Tundra Tandems-TTDH
06UD Artifacts Tundra Tandems Black-TTDH
06UD Artifacts Tundra Tandems Blue-TTDH
06UD Artifacts Tundra Tandems Gold-TTDH
06UD Artifacts Tundra Tandems Platinum-TTDH
06UD Artifacts Tundra Tandems Red-TTDH
06UD Artifacts Tundra Tandems Dual Patches Red-TTDH
06Ultra-69
Gold Medallion-69
Ice Medallion-69
06Upper Deck-70
Exclusives Parallel-70
High Gloss Parallel-70
Game Jerseys-J2TH
Game Patches-P2TH
Masterpieces-70
06Upper Deck MVP-102
Gold Script-102
Super Script-102
06Upper Deck Ovation-119
06Upper Deck Victory-74
06Upper Deck Victory Black-74
06Upper Deck Victory Gold-74
07Upper Deck Ovation-30
07Upper Deck Victory-99
Black-99
Gold-99

Holocek, Jiri
01Czech DS Legends-L1

Holopainen, Eero
66Finnish Jaakiekkosarja-170
70Finnish Jaakiekko-174
71Finnish Suomi Stickers-100
72Finnish Jaakiekko-143
73Finnish Jaakiekko-109

Holopainen, Paavo
71Finnish Suomi Stickers-300

Holowatiuk, Bill
92Cornell Big Red-15
93Cornell Big Red-13

Holowaty, Kelly
03Ohio State Buckeyes-8

Holsan, Jiri
97Czech APS Extraliga-214
98Czech OFS-403
99Czech OFS-164
00Czech DS Extraliga-141
00Czech OFS-123

Holscher, Henrik
94German DEL-313
95German DEL-305
96German DEL-333
03German DEL-54

Holse, Brian
98Danish Hockey League-78

Holsinger, Robert
00Amarillo Rattlers-10

Holsinger, Scott
92Quebec Pee-Wee Tournament-1235
93Quebec Pee-Wee Tournament-1246

Holst, Anders
99Danish Hockey League-122

Holst, Rasmus
98Danish Hockey League-110
99Danish Hockey League-123

Holt, Barton
92Saskatchewan JHL-133

Holt, Chris
05Hot Prospects-175
En Fuego-175
Red Hot-175
White Hot-175
05SP Authentic-233
Limited-233
05SP Game Used-164
Gold-164
05SPx-200
Spectrum-200
05The Cup Masterpiece Pressplates (Ice)-157
05The Cup Master Pressplate Rookie Update-160
05The Cup Masterpiece Pressplates SPA-233
05The Cup Masterpiece Pressplates SP GU-164
05The Cup Masterpiece Pressplates (SPx)-200
05The Cup Masterpiece Pressplates Trilogy-283
05Ultra-232
Gold-232
Ice-232
05Upper Deck Ice-157
05Upper Deck Rookie Update-160
05Upper Deck Trilogy-283

Holt, Randy
77O-Pee-Chee NHL-34
77Topps-34
78Canucks Royal Bank-11
78O-Pee-Chee-341
79O-Pee-Chee-4
79Topps-4
80Flames Postcards-5
80Pepsi-Cola Caps-4
81Capitals Team Issue-7
81O-Pee-Chee-41
82Capitals Team Issue-10
82Post Cereal-20
83Flyers J.C. Penney-11
83O-Pee-Chee-220

Holt, Todd
907th Inn. Sketch WHL-48
917th Inn. Sketch WHL-192
94Kansas City Blades-18

Holtari, Jukka
80Finnish Mallasjuoma-86

Holtby, Braden
06Saskatoon Blades-10

Holtby, Greg
83Saskatoon Blades-5
84Saskatoon Blades Stickers-7

Holtet, Marius
06Iowa Stars-12

Holton, Eric
96Arizona Icecats-7

Holtz, Don
02Arizona Icecats-8
03Arizona Icecats-9
04Arizona Icecats-6

Holub, Jan
02Czech OFS Plus-151
03Czech OFS Plus-111
04Czech OFS-68
06Czech OFS-88

Holum, Dave
93St. Cloud State Huskies-9
95Roanoke Express-4

Holunga, Shane
91Air Canada SJHL-C45
91Air Canada SJHL All-Stars-20

Holway, Albert
24C144 Champ's Cigarettes-32
24V145-2-56

Holy, Karel
81Swedish Semic Hockey VM Stickers-66

Holy, Martin
97Czech APS Extraliga-9
99Czech OFS-105
00Czech OFS-299
02Czech OFS Plus-135

Holy, Robert
94Czech APS Extraliga-23
99Czech Score Blue 2000-138
99Czech Score Red Ice 2000-138

Holzapfel, Cody
02Red Deer Rebels-6

Holzapfel, Riley
04Moose Jaw Warriors-17
05ITG Heroes/Prosp Toronto Expo Parallel -420
05Moose Jaw Warriors-11
05ITG Heroes and Prospects-420
Team Orr-TO12

Holzaphel, Rily
06Moose Jaw Warriors-16

Holzer, David
89Lethbridge Hurricanes-9

Holzer, Martin
94German First League-295
95German DEL-346
99German Bundesliga 2-275

Holzer, Matthias
93Swiss HNL-149
95Swiss HNL-22
96Swiss HNL-21
98Swiss Power Play Stickers-205
99Swiss Panini Stickers-146
00Swiss Panini Stickers-188
00Swiss Slapshot Mini-Cards-LT14
01Swiss HNL-206
02Swiss HNL-301
04Swiss Lausanne HC Postcards-16

Holzinger, Brian
91Upper Deck Czech World Juniors-72
95Be A Player-161
Signatures-S161
Signatures Die Cuts-S161
95Bowman-165
All-Foil-165
95Canada Games NHL POGS-39
95Donruss-298
95Emotion-17
generationNext-1
95Finest-67
Refractors-67
95Leaf-250
Studio Rookies-14
95Metal-177
95Panini Stickers-14
95Parkhurst International-27
Emerald Ice-27
95Pinnacle-205
Artist's Proofs-205
Rink Collection-205
95Playoff One on One-126
95Score-310
Black Ice Artist's Proofs-310
Black Ice-310
95Select Certified-110
Mirror Gold-110
Future-6
95SkyBox Impact-190
NHL On Fox-15
95SP-14
95Stadium Club-194
Members Only Master Set-194
95Summit-168
Artist's Proofs-168
Ice-168
95Topps-24
OPC Inserts-24
95Ultra-19
95Ultra-341
Gold Medallion-19
95Upper Deck-88
Electric Ice-88
Electric Ice Gold-88
95Zenith-126
Rookie Roll Call-5
95Classic-74
Autographs-9
Ice Breakers-BK18
Ice Breakers Die Cuts-BK18
95Classic Five-Sport *-159
Phone Cards $3-3
Strive For Five-HK11
96Black Diamond-118
Gold-118
96Collector's Choice-24
96Collector's Choice-342
96Donruss-226
Press Proofs-226
96Leaf-212
Press Proofs-212
96Score-266
Artist's Proofs-266
Dealer's Choice Artist's Proofs-266
Special Artist's Proofs-266
Golden Blades-266
96SP-18
Holoview Collection-HC19
96Upper Deck-16
96Assets *-14
A Cut Above-CA4
Hot Prints-14
96Classic Signings *-77
Blue-77
Die-Cuts-77
Freshly Inked-FS23
Red-77
96Visions *-90
97Be A Player-34
Autographs-34
Autographs Die-Cuts-34
Autographs Prismatic Die-Cuts-34
97Collector's Choice-25
Star Quest-SQ14
97Donruss-74
Press Proofs Silver-74
Press Proofs Gold-74
97Donruss Limited-58
97Donruss Limited-184
Exposure-58
Exposure-184
97Donruss Preferred-93
Cut to the Chase-93
97Donruss Priority-69
Stamp of Approval-69
97Leaf-120
Fractal Matrix-120
Fractal Matrix Die Cuts-120
97Leaf International-120
Universal Ice-120
97Pacific-158
Copper-158
Emerald Green-158
Ice Blue-158
Red-158
Silver-158
97Pacific Dynagon-11
Copper-11
Dark Grey-11
Emerald Green-11
Ice Blue-11
Red-11
Silver-11
Tandems-32
97Pacific Omega-23
Copper-23
Dark Gray-23
Emerald Green-23
Gold-23
Ice Blue-23
97Paramount-20
Copper-20
Dark Grey-20
Emerald Green-20
Ice Blue-20
Red-20
Silver-20
97Pinnacle Certified-118
Red-118
Mirror Blue-118
Mirror Gold-118
Mirror Red-118
97Pinnacle Inside-163
97Pinnacle Tot Cert Platinum Blue-118
97Pinnacle Tot Certi Platinum Gold-118
97Pinnacle Totally Certified Platinum Red-118
97Pinnacle Tot Cert Mirror Platinum Gold-118
97Score-172
97Score Sabres-9
Platinum-9
Premier-9
97SP Authentic-16
Sign of the Times-BH
97Upper Deck-15
Smooth Grooves-SG49
97Upper Deck Ice-19
Parallel-19
Power Shift-19
98Aurora-18
98Be A Player-15
Press Release-15
98BAP Gold-15
98BAP Autographs-15
98BAP Autographs Gold-15
98BAP Tampa Bay All Star Game-15
98Black Diamond-9
Double Diamond-9
Triple Diamond-9
Quadruple Diamond-9
98Pacific-106
Ice Blue-106
Red-106
98Pacific Dynagon Ice-19
Blue-19
Red-19
98Pacific Omega-24
Red-24
Opening Day Issue-24
98Paramount-20

Copper-20
Emerald Green-20
Holo-Electric-20
Ice Blue-20
Silver-20
98UD Choice-21
98UD Choice Preview-21
98UD Choice Prime Choice Reserve-21
98UD Choice Reserve-21
98Upper Deck-47
Exclusives-47
Exclusives 1 of 1-47
Gold Reserve-47
98Upper Deck MVP-20
Gold Script-20
Silver Script-20
Super Script-20
99BAP Memorabilia-257
99BAP Memorabilia-381
Gold-257
Gold-381
Silver-257
Silver-381
99O-Pee-Chee-193
99O-Pee-Chee Chrome-193
99O-Pee-Chee Chrome Refractors-193
99Pacific-38
Copper-38
Emerald Green-38
Gold-38
Ice Blue-38
Premiere Date-38
Red-38
99Topps/OPC-193
99Topps/OPC Chrome-193
Refractors-193
99Upper Deck Victory-40
99Slovakian Challengers-22
00BAP Memorabilia-347
Emerald-347
Ruby-347
Sapphire-347
Promos-347
00BAP Mem Chicago Sportsfest Copper-347
00BAP Memorabilia Chicago Sportsfest Blue-347
00BAP Memorabilia Chicago Sportsfest Gold-347
00BAP Memorabilia Chicago Sportsfest Ruby-347
00BAP Memorabilia Chicago Sun-Times Ruby-347
00BAP Memorabilia Chicago Sun-Times Gold-347
00BAP Mem Chicago Sun-Times Sapphire-347
00BAP Mem Toronto Fall Expo Copper-347
00BAP Memorabilia Toronto Fall Expo Gold-347
00BAP Memorabilia Toronto Fall Expo Ruby-347
00BAP Signature Series-52
Emerald-52
Ruby-52
Sapphire-52
Autographs-21
Autographs Gold-21
00Pacific-372
Copper-372
Gold-372
Ice Blue-372
Premiere Date-372
00Paramount-220
Copper-220
Gold-220
Holo-Gold-220
Holo-Silver-220
Ice Blue-220
Premiere Date-220
00Upper Deck-387
Exclusives Tier 1-387
Exclusives Tier 2-387
01BAP Memorabilia-294
Emerald-294
Ruby-294
Sapphire-294
01O-Pee-Chee-202
01O-Pee-Chee Premier Parallel-202
01Pacific-350
Extreme LTD-350
Hobby LTD-350
Premiere Date-350
Retail LTD-350
01Pacific Adrenaline-172
Blue-172
Premiere Date-172
Red-172
Retail-172
01Pacific Arena Exclusives-350
01Topps-202
OPC Parallel-202
01Upper Deck-386
Exclusives-386
01Upper Deck Victory-317
Gold-317
02BAP Sig Series Auto Buybacks 1998-15
02BAP Sig Series Auto Buybacks 2000-21
03Pacific-272
Blue-272
Red-272
03Pacific Complete-260
Red-260
03Bowling Green Falcons-1

Holzmann, Georg
82Swedish Semic VM Stickers-120
89Swedish Semic World Champ Stickers-118
92Finnish Semic-186
93Swedish Semic World Champ Stickers-160
94German DEL-64
95German DEL-63
95Swedish World Championships Stickers-73
96German DEL-249

Homer, Jan
99Czech OFS-458
00Czech OFS-357
01Czech OFS-82
02Czech OFS Plus-28

Homer, Kenzie
99Peoria Rivermen-27
02Rockford Ice Hogs-4
03Rockford Ice Hogs-7

Hommel, Christian
02German DEL City Press-160
03German DEL-146
04German DEL-190
05German DEL-108

Homola, Craig
82Birmingham South Stars-13

Honegger, Doug
96Swiss HNL-120

Honegger, Jean-Noel
93Swiss HNL-379

Honegger, Roman
93Swiss HNL-467
95Swiss HNL-293
96Swiss HNL-174

Hongisto, Kalevi
78Finnish SM-Liiga-145

Honing, Dustin
04Williams Lake Timberwolves-9

Honkaheimo, Otto
04Finnish Cardset-113
Parallel-84
05Finnish Cardset-103
06Finnish Cardset-107
06Finnish Cardset-285
Signature Sensations-20

Honkanen, Antero
71Finnish Suomi Stickers-262

Honkanen, Jaakko
65Finnish Hellas-35
66Finnish Jaakiekkosarja-40
70Finnish Jaakiekko-190
71Finnish Suomi Stickers-84
72Finnish Jaakiekko-247
72Finnish Panda Toronto-37
73Finnish Jaakiekko-245

Honkanen, Jani
06Fort Wayne Komets-8

Honkanen, Jouni
70Finnish Jaakiekko-366

Honkavaraa, Aarne
96Finnish SISU Redline-187

Honkonen, Mikko
95Finnish SISU-76
96Finnish SISU Redline-76
98Finnish Kerailysarja-156
99Danish Hockey League-74

Honneger, Doug
93Swiss HNL-40
95Finnish Semic World Championships-190

Honsberger, Olivier
95Swiss HNL-500
96Swiss HNL-422

Hontvet, Chad
00Lincoln Stars-14
01Lincoln Stars-13

Hood, Bruce
91Ultimate Original Six-86
French-86

Hood, Kyle
04Ohio State Buckeyes-18
05Ohio State Buckeyes-9
06Ohio State Buckeyes-21

Hood, Murray
89Hampton Roads Admirals-9A
89Hampton Roads Admirals-9H
90Hampton Roads Admirals-49
91Hampton Roads Admirals-5
98Hampton Roads Admirals 10th Anniversary-8

Hooey, Todd
82Oshawa Generals-10
84Moncton Golden Flames-19

Hooge, Clint
91Air Canada SJHL-D30
92Saskatchewan JHL-84

Hoogsteen, David
94Thunder Bay Flyers-11
99German EHC Straubing-11
01Rockford IceHogs-5

Hooper, Dale
96Dayton Bombers-9

Hooper, Nathan
04Mississauga Ice Dogs-22

Hooper, Tom
83Hall of Fame Postcards-M9
85Hall of Fame-173

Hoople, Ryan
95Lethbridge Hurricanes-9
96Lethbridge Hurricanes-7
97Bowman CHL-101
OPC-101
99Cincinnati Mighty Ducks-21
99Huntington Blizzard-15

Hooson, Bill
917th Inn. Sketch WHL-270

Hooton, Brock
03St. Cloud State Huskies-11
04St. Cloud State Huskies-15
05St. Cloud State Huskies-10
06St. Cloud State Huskies-15

Hoover, David
84Kingston Canadians-14

Hoover, Ron
89ProCards AHL-65
90ProCards AHL/IHL-126
91Upper Deck-287
French-287
92Peoria Rivermen-10
93Peoria Rivermen-13
95Peoria Rivermen-7

Hoover, Tim
82Sault Ste. Marie Greyhounds-13
83Sault Ste. Marie Greyhounds-12
84Sault Ste. Marie Greyhounds-10

Hopalainen, Eero
65Finnish Hellas-106

Hope, Jared
94Spokane Chiefs-14
95Spokane Chiefs-14

Hope, Joey
00Prince George Cougars-7
03Philadelphia Phantoms-10
04Philadelphia Phantoms-5
05Philadelphia Phantoms-11

Hopiavuori, Chris
97Owen Sound Platers-6
98Owen Sound Platers-5
99Owen Sound Platers-13

Hopiavuori, Ralph
72Cleveland Crusaders WHA-6

Hopkins, Dean
82Post Cereal-8
84Nova Scotia Oilers-20
85Nova Scotia Oilers-1
88Oilers Tenth Anniversary-135
88ProCards AHL-104
89Halifax Citadels-9
89ProCards AHL-164
90Halifax Citadels-10
90ProCards AHL/IHL-446
91ProCards-545

Hopkins, Dominic
99UK Guildford Flames-15
01UK Dundee Stars-12
02UK Dundee Stars-12

Hopkins, Larry
78Saginaw Gears-10
81Jets Postcards-7

Hopkins, Tom
89Peterborough Petes-115
897th Inn. Sketch OHL-115

Hoppe, Matthias
89Swedish Semic World Champ Stickers-105
94German DEL-435
95German DEL-386
96German DEL-293
98German DEL-224

Hoppe, Timmy
01Swiss HNL-455
02Swiss HNL-193

Hopper, Karl
01UK Hull Thunder-13
02UK Hull Thunder-14
05UK Hull Stingrays-10

Hopper, Rick
907th Inn. Sketch WHL-260
917th Inn. Sketch WHL-50

Hopps, Dana
93Quebec Pee-Wee Tournament-680

Hopson, John
05Maine Black Bears-9

Hopson, Keenan
04Maine Black Bears-10
05Maine Black Bears-10

Horacek, Jan
00Worcester Icecats-25
01Czech DS-31
01Hamilton Bulldogs-4
02Czech OFS Plus-336
06Czech HC Zlin Hame Postcards-3
06Czech OFS-225

Horacek, Jaroslav
96Czech APS Extraliga-11
97Czech APS Extraliga-297

Horacek, Tony
84Kelowna Wings-20
88ProCards AHL-139
90Bowman-104
Tiffany-104
90Flyers Postcards-9
90Pro Set-499
91Flyers J.C. Penney-11
91Pro Set-455
French-455
92Indianapolis Ice-14
93Indianapolis Ice-14
94Indianapolis Ice-9
96Cincinnati Cyclones-24

Horachek, Peter
88Flint Spirits-8
93Flint Generals-18
94Flint Generals-10
98Orlando Solar Bears-17
98Orlando Solar Bears II-22
01Trenton Titans-2-4

Horak, Gregor
93Swiss HNL-74
95Swiss HNL-361

Horak, Jakub
93Swiss HNL-113
95Swiss HNL-192
96Swiss HNL-84
98Swiss Power Play Stickers-206
99Swiss Panini Stickers-208
00Swiss Panini Stickers-225
01Swiss HNL-150
02Swiss HNL-39

Horak, Jody
04Minnesota Golden Gophers Women-7

Horak, Michal
96Czech APS Extraliga-260
97Czech APS Extraliga-237
98Czech OFS-338
99Czech Score Blue 2000-59
99Czech Score Red Ice 2000-59
03Czech OFS Plus-27
05Czech HC Vsetin-4
06Czech OFS-181

Horak, Robert
99Rouyn-Noranda Huskies-10
04Czech OFS-265

Horak, Roman
93Swedish Semic World Champ Stickers-96
94Czech APS Extraliga-113
95Czech APS Extraliga-373
95Finnish Semic World Championships-161
95Swedish World Championships Stickers-201
96Czech APS Extraliga-130
96Swedish Semic Wien-124
97Czech APS Extraliga-371
97Czech DS Stickers-68
98Czech DS-91
98Czech OFS-368
99Czech DS-49
99Czech OFS-307
99Czech OFS-514
All-Star Game Blue-514
All-Star Game Gold-514
All-Star Game Red-514
All-Star Game Silver-514
00Czech DS Extraliga-154
00Czech OFS-277
01Czech OFS-139

Horan, Brad
99Kingston Frontenacs-7
00Kingston Frontenacs-7
01Kingston Frontenacs-7
02Kingston Frontenacs-7

Horan, Brian
91ProCards-438
92Nashville Knights-17

Horava, Miloslav
82Swedish Semic VM Stickers-79
89Rangers Marine Midland Bank-6
90O-Pee-Chee-337
90Pro Set-198A
90Pro Set-198B
90Topps-337
Tiffany-337
90Upper Deck-13
French-13
91Swedish Semic Elitserien Stickers-203
92Swedish Semic Elitserien Stickers-226
93Swedish Semic Elitserien-198
94Czech APS Extraliga-254
95Czech APS Extraliga-127
97Czech DS Stickers-4
97Czech DS Stickers-119
98Czech OFS-269
Legends-2
99Czech DS-59
00Czech OFS-400
01Czech OFS Update-296
02Czech DS-50
02Czech DS-71
03Czech OFS Plus-221
04Czech OFS-53
05Swedish SHL Elitset-250
Gold-250
06Czech CP Cup Postcards-6
06Czech OFS Coaches-3
06Swedish SHL Elitset-245

Horava, Miroslav
83Swedish Semic VM Stickers-79
96Czech APS Extraliga-5
97Czech APS Extraliga-338

Horava, Petr
03Czech OFS Plus-233
04Czech OFS-54

Horbul, Doug
74NHL Action Stamps-300
74O-Pee-Chee NHL-317

Horcicka, Lubos
98Czech OFS-397
99Czech DS-156
99Czech OFS-533
00Czech DS Extraliga-133
00Czech OFS-109
00Czech OFS Star Emerald-30
00Czech OFS Star Pink-30
00Czech OFS Star Violet-30
02Czech OFS Plus-83
Checklists-C10
Trios-T17
03Czech OFS Plus-283
03Czech OFS Plus Insert B-B13
03Czech OFS Plus Insert P-P11

Horcoff, Shawn
00BAP Memorabilia-511
00SP Authentic-105
00SPx-138
00Titanium-118
Retail-118
00Titanium Draft Day Edition-118
00Titanium Draft Day Promos-118
00UD Reserve-95
00Upper Deck Ice-87
01BAP Signature Series-60
Autographs-60
Autographs Gold-60
01Pacific-158
Extreme LTD-158
Hobby LTD-158
Premiere Date-158
Retail LTD-158
01Pacific Arena Exclusives-158
02BAP Sig Series Auto Buybacks 2001-60
02Bowman YoungStars-153
Gold-153
Silver-153
Autographs-SH
Jerseys-SH
Patches-SH
Double Stuff-SH
Triple Stuff-SH
Sticks-SH
02NHL Power Play Stickers-30
02Oilers Postcards-4
02Pacific Complete-453
Red-453
03Bowman Future Fabrics-FF-SHO
03Bowman Future Fabric Patches-SHO
03Bowman Future Rivals-HH
03Bowman Future Rivals Patches-HH
03ITG Action-209
03Oilers Postcards-9
03O-Pee-Chee-46
03OPC Blue-46
03OPC Gold-46
03OPC Red-46
03Pacific Complete-301
Red-301
03Topps-46
Blue-46
Gold-46
Red-46
04Pacific-103
Blue-103
Red-103
04Swedish Elitset-259
Dominators-5
Gold-259
04Swedish Pure Skills-78
Parallel-78
05Be A Player Signatures-HF
05Be A Player Signatures Gold-HF
05Hot Prospects-39
En Fuego-39
Red Hot-39
White Hot-39
05Parkhurst-185
Facsimile Auto Parallel-185
True Colors-TCEDM
True Colors-TCEDM
True Colors-TCEDCA
True Colors-TCEDCA
05Upper Deck-79
HG Glossy-79
Jerseys Series II-J2SH
Majestic Materials-MMSH
05Upper Deck Toronto Fall Expo-79
05Swedish SHL Elitset-110
Gold-110
06Be A Player-114
Autographs-114
Signatures-HO
Signatures 25-126
Signatures Duals-DJS
Signatures Trios-TRSH
06Be A Player Portraits-46
06Black Diamond-33
Black-33
Gold-33
Ruby-33
Gemography-GSH
06Flair Showcase Inks-ISH
06Fleer-81
Tiffany-81
06Gatorade-25
06McDonald's Upper Deck Autographs-ASH
06O-Pee-Chee-204
Rainbow-204
Swatches-S-HO
06Panini Stickers-275
06SP Game Used Authentic Fabrics Fives-AP5SCP
06SP Game Used Authentic Fabrics Fives Patches-AP5SCP
06UD Artifacts Tundra Tandems-TTRS
06UD Artifacts Tundra Tandems Black-TTRS
06UD Artifacts Tundra Tandems Blue-TTRS
06UD Artifacts Tundra Tandems Gold-TTRS
06UD Artifacts Tundra Tandems Platinum-TTRS
06UD Artifacts Tundra Tandems Red-TTRS
06UD Artifacts Tundra Tandems Dual Patches Red-TTRS
06Ultra-81
Gold Medallion-81
Ice Medallion-81
06Upper Deck-330
Exclusives Parallel-330
High Gloss Parallel-330
Game Dated Moments-GD27
Masterpieces-330
Signature Sensations-SSST
06Upper Deck MVP-115
Gold Script-115
Super Script-115
Autographs-OALH
06Upper Deck Ovation-168
06Upper Deck Trilogy Ice Scripts-ISSH
06Upper Deck Trilogy Scripts-TSHO
06Upper Deck Victory-77
06Upper Deck Victory Black-77
06Upper Deck Victory Gold-77
07Upper Deck Ovation-83
07Upper Deck Victory-163
Black-163
Gold-163

Hordal, Craig
93Brandon Wheat Kings-2
94Prince Albert Raiders-9

Hordichuk, Darcy
00SP Authentic-134
00SPx-174
00Upper Deck Ice-106
01Parkhurst-258
01Parkhurst Beckett Promos-258
01Titanium Draft Day Edition-159
01Chicago Wolves-9
03ITG Action-220
03Panthers Team Issue-6
05Parkhurst-281
Facsimile Auto Parallel-281
06O-Pee-Chee-289
Rainbow-289

Hordler, Frank
03German Berlin Polar Bears Postcards-17
04German Berlin Polar Bears Postcards-15
04German DEL-69
05German DEL-30
06German DEL-19

Hordler, Jochen
94German First League-316

Hordy, Mike
81Indianapolis Checkers-9

Horeck, Pete
44Beehive Group II Photos-33
44Beehive Group II Photos-177

Horesovsky, Josef
69Swedish Hockey-29
70Finnish Jaakiekko-49
70Swedish Hockey-348
70Swedish Masterserien-79
70Swedish Masterserien-153
71Finnish Suomi Stickers-29
71Swedish Hockey-44
72Finnish Jaakiekko-10
72Finnish Hellas-82
72Finnish Panda Toronto-85
72Finnish Semic World Championship-23
72Swedish Stickers-22
72Swedish Stickers-47
72Swedish Semic World Championship-23
73Finnish Jaakiekko-51
73Swedish Stickers-28
74Finnish Jenkki-64
74Finnish Typotor-116
74Swedish Stickers-111
74Swedish Semic World Champ Stickers-54

Horisberger, Mirco
74Finnish Typotor-107

Horkko, Kari
72Finnish Jaakiekko-208
73Finnish Jaakiekko-279
78Finnish SM-Liiga-216
80Finnish Mallasjuoma-188

Horman, Barry
00Spokane Chiefs-9
01Spokane Chiefs-11
02Spokane Chiefs-8
03Everett Silvertips-11
04Swift Current Broncos-7

Horn, Alexander
94German DEL-424

Horn, Bill
91Michigan Falcons-4
92Anaheim Bullfrogs RHI-10
92Greensboro Monarchs-3
93Rochester Americans Kodak-12
94Greensboro Monarchs-14

Horna, Tomas
98Czech OFS-175
99Czech DS-161
99Czech OFS-165
00Czech DS Extraliga-140
00Czech OFS-122
01Czech OFS-170
02Czech OFS Plus-317
03Czech OFS Plus-220
03Czech OFS Plus Insert H-H15
04Czech OFS-55
05Czech HC Kladno-5
06Czech OFS-256

Hornak, Ernest
92Fort Worth Fire-8

Hornby, Greg
04Florida Everblades-18
05Idaho Steelheads-13

Horne, Buddy
52Juniors Blue Tint-119

Horne, Kyle
96UK Fife Flyers-16

Horne, Nathan
03Fresno Falcons-5

Horner, Kyle
01UK Fife Flyers-3

Horner, Red
320'Keefe Maple Leafs-2
33O-Pee-Chee V304A-10
33V129-1
33V252 Canadian Gum-31
33V288 Hamilton Gum-21
33V357 Ice Kings-16
34Beehive Group I Photos-326
34Sweet Caporal-46
36O-Pee-Chee V304D-122
37O-Pee-Chee V304E-134
37V356 Worldwide Gum-8
38Quaker Oats Photos-19
39O-Pee-Chee V301-1-10
83Hall of Fame-115
83Hall of Fame Postcards-H9
85Hall of Fame-115
02Maple Leafs Platinum Collection-52
04ITG Franchises Canadian-114
Autographs-RHO
04ITG Ultimate Memorabilia-70
Gold-70
Autographs-64
Autographs Gold-64
05ITG Ultimate Memorabilia Lumbergraphs-4
05ITG Ultimate Mem Leafs Forever Autos-2
05ITG Ultimate Mem Quad Paper Cuts Autos-6
06ITG Ultimate Memorabilia Lumbergraphs-13

Hornqvist, Patric
05Swedish SHL Elitset-167
06Swedish SHL Elitset-22

Hornseth, Richard
03Owen Sound Attack-10

Hornung, Blaire
91Air Canada SJHL-A7

Hornung, Brad
86Regina Pats-9

Hornung, Larry
71Blues Postcards-10
72O-Pee-Chee-317
73Quaker Oats WHA-26

Hornung, Todd
97Portland Winter Hawks-12
99Swift Current Broncos-7

Horny, Karel
96Czech APS Extraliga-112
97Czech APS Extraliga-116
97Czech DS Stickers-278
98Czech DS Stickers-59

Hornya, Robert
90ProCards AHL/IHL-165

Horras, Meghan
04Wisconsin Badgers Women-8

Horsky, Marek
05ITG Heroes/Prosp Toronto Expo Parallel -298
05ITG Heroes and Prospects-298
Autographs Series II-MHO

Horstad, Tor
57Swedish Alfabilder-116

Hortholary, Julien
93Quebec Pee-Wee Tournament-1650

Horton, Bill
72Cleveland Crusaders WHA-7

Horton, Nathan
01Oshawa Generals-1
02SPx Rookie Redemption-R218
03BAP Memorabilia-180
Emerald-180
Gold-180
Ruby-180
Sapphire-180
Draft Redemptions-3
Super Rookies-SR10
Super Rookies Gold-SR10
Super Rookies Silver-SR10
03BAP Ultimate Memorabilia Autographs-92
Gold-92
03BAP Ultimate Mem Auto Jerseys-92
03BAP Ultimate Mem Auto Emblems-92
03BAP Ultimate Mem Auto Numbers-92
03BAP Ultimate Mem Rookie Jersey Emblems-5
03BAP Ultimate Mem Rookie Jsy Emblem Gold-5
03BAP Ultimate Mem Rookie Jersey Numbers-5
03BAP Ultimate Mem Rookie Jsy Number Gold-5
03BAP Ultimate Memorabilia Triple Threads-29
03Beehive-213
Gold-213
Silver-213
Jumbo Variations-13
03Black Diamond-192
Black-192
Green-192
Red-192
03Bowman-111
Gold-111
Premier Performance-PP-NH
Premier Performance Patches-PP-NH
03Bowman Chrome-111
Refractors-111
Gold Refractors-111
Xfractors-111
03Crown Royale-118
Red-118
Retail-118
Jerseys-12
Patches-12
Royal Portraits-5
03eTopps-45
03ITG Action-617
03ITG Toronto Spring Expo Class of 2004-8
03ITG Used Signature Series-128
Autographs Gold-128
03ITG VIP Rookie Debut-19
03McDonald's Pacific-58
03O-Pee-Chee-335
03OPC Blue-335
03OPC Gold-335
03OPC Red-335
03Pacific-355
03Pacific Calder-166
03Pacific Complete-523
Red-523
03Pacific Exhibit-231
03Pacific Heads-Up-118
Hobby LTD-118
Retail LTD-118
Jerseys-13
Prime Prospects-9
Prime Prospects LTD-9
03Pacific Invincible-111
Blue-111
Red-111
Retail-111
03Pacific Luxury Suite-88
Gold-88
03Pacific Prism-157
03Pacific Quest for the Cup-118
Calder Contenders-9
03Pacific Supreme-118
03Pacific Supreme-118A
Blue-118
Red-118
Retail-118
03Panthers Team Issue-7
03Parkhurst Toronto Expo Rookie Preview-PRP-6
03Parkhurst Rookie-181
Calder Candidates-CMC-13
Calder Candidates Gold-CMC-13
Rookie Emblems-RE-5
Rookie Emblem Autographs-RE-NH
Rookie Emblems Gold-RE-5
Rookie Jerseys-RJ-5
Rookie Jersey Autographs-RJ-NH
Rookie Jerseys Gold-RJ-5
Rookie Numbers-RN-5
Rookie Number Autographs-RN-NH
Rookie Numbers Gold-RN-5
Teammates Gold-RT6
Teammates-RT6
03Private Stock Reserve-119
Blue-119
Red-119
Retail-119
Class Act-4
03SP Authentic-143
Limited-143
Signed Patches-NH
03SP Game Used-87
Gold-87
Rookie Exclusives-RE4
03SPx-228
Radiance-228
Spectrum-228
03Titanium-209
Patches-209
Right on Target-8
03Topps-335
Blue-335
Gold-335
Red-335
03Topps Pristine-119
03Topps Pristine-120
03Topps Pristine-121
Gold Refractor Die Cuts-119
Gold Refractor Die Cuts-120
Gold Refractor Die Cuts-121
Refractors-119
Refractors-120
Refractors-121
Mini-PM-NH
Press Plates Black-119
Press Plates Black-120
Press Plates Black-121
Press Plates Cyan-119
Press Plates Cyan-120
Press Plates Cyan-121
Press Plates Magenta-119
Press Plates Magenta-120
Press Plates Magenta-121
Press Plates Yellow-119
Press Plates Yellow-120
Press Plates Yellow-121
03Topps Traded Future Phenoms-FP-NH
03UD Honor Roll-188
03UD Premier Collection-113
NHL Shields-SH-NH
Signatures-PS-NH
Signatures Gold-PS-NH
Stars-ST-NH
Stars Patches-ST-NH
03Upper Deck-216
03Upper Deck-245
Canadian Exclusives-216
Canadian Exclusives-245
HG-216
HG-245
Rookie Threads-RT-9
03Upper Deck Classic Portraits-168
03Upper Deck Ice-126
Glass Parallel-126
03Upper Deck MVP-458
03Upper Deck Rookie Update-162
03Upper Deck Trilogy-176
Limited-176
03Upper Deck Victory-204
04Pacific-111
Blue-111
Red-111
04Pacific Montreal International-3
Gold-3
04Pacific Montreal International Gold-3
04Pacific Toronto Spring Expo-3
Gold-3
04SP Authentic-39
Limited-39
Octographs-OS-ROK
Sign of the Times-ST-HO
Sign of the Times-TS-LWH
Sign of the Times-TS-SHZ
Sign of the Times-QS-FSHZ
04Ultimate Collection Buybacks-70
04Ultimate Collection Signatures-US-NH
04Ultimate Collection Signature Logos-ULA-NH
04Ultimate Collection Signature Patches-SP-NH
04Upper Deck All-Star Promos-NH
04AHL Top Prospects-49
04San Antonio Rampage-14
05Be A Player Signatures-NH
05Be A Player Signatures Gold-NH
05Be A Player Triple Signatures-PAN
05Beehive Matted Materials-MMNH
05Beehive Signature Scrapbook-SSNH
05Hot Prospects-44
En Fuego-44
Red Hot-44
White Hot-44
05Panini Stickers-63
05Parkhurst-203
Facsimile Auto Parallel-203
05SP Authentic Prestigious Pairings-PPHB
05SP Game Used Authentic Fabrics-AF-NH
05SP Game Used Authentic Fabrics Autos-AAF-NH
05SP Game Used Authentic Fabrics Dual-WH
05SP Game Used Authentic Fabric Dual Auto-WH
05SP Game Used Authentic Fabrics Gold-AF-NH
05SP Game Used Authentic Fabrics Quad-HLBJ
05SP Game Used Authentic Patches-AP-NH
05SP Game Used Authentic Patches Quad -HLBJ
05SP Game Used Authentic Patch Autos-AAP-NH
05SP Game Used Authentic Patches Dual-WH
05SP Game Used Authentic Patch Dual Autos-WH
05SP Game Used Awesome Authentics-AA-NH
05SP Game Used SIGnificance Extra-WH
05SP Game Used SIGnificance Extra Gold-WH
05SP Game Used Significant Numbers-SN-NH
05SP Game Used Statscriptions-ST-NH
05SPx Winning Combos-WC-BH
05SPx Winning Combos-WC-WH
05SPx Winning Combos Autographs-AWC-WH
05SPx Winning Combos Gold-WC-BH
05SPx Winning Combos Gold-WC-WH
05SPx Winning Combos Spectrum-WC-BH
05SPx Winning Combos Spectrum-WC-WH
05SPx Winning Materials-WM-NH
05SPx Winning Materials Autographs-AWM-NH
05SPx Winning Materials Gold-WM-NH
05SPx Winning Materials Spectrum-WM-NH
05UD Artifacts Auto Facts-AF-NH
05UD Artifacts Auto Facts Blue-AF-NH
05UD Artifacts Auto Facts Copper-AF-NH
05UD Artifacts Auto Facts Pewter-AF-NH
05UD Artifacts Auto Facts Silver-AF-NH
05UD Artifacts Frozen Artifacts-FA-NH
05UD Artifacts Frozen Artifacts Autos-FA-NH
05UD Artifacts Frozen Artifacts Copper-FA-NH
05UD Artifacts Frozen Artifact Dual Auto-FAD-NH
05UD Artifact Frozen Artifact Dual Copper-FAD-NH
05UD Artifacts Frozen Artifacts Dual Gold-FAD-NH
05UD Artifact Frozen Artifact Dual Maroon-FAD-NH
05UD Artifacts Frozen Artifact Dual Pewter-FAD-NH
05UD Artifacts Frozen Artifact Dual Silver-FAD-NH
05UD Artifacts Frozen Artifacts Gold-FA-NH
05UD Artifacts Frozen Artifacts Maroon-FA-NH
05UD Artifacts Frozen Artifacts Patches-FP-NH
05UD Artifact Frozen Artifact Patch Autos-FP-NH
05UD Artifacts Frozen Art Patch Dual Auto-FGD-PR
05UD Artifact Frozen Artifact Patch Dual-FGD-PR
05UD Artifacts Frozen Art Patch Pewter-FP-NH
05UD Artifacts Frozen Art Patch Silver-FP-NH
05UD Artifacts Frozen Artifacts Pewter-FA-NH
05UD Artifacts Frozen Artifacts Silver-FA-NH
05UD Artifacts Remarkable Artifacts-RA-NH
05UD Artifacts Remarkable Artifacts Dual-RA-NH
05UD PowerPlay-50
Rainbow-50
05Ultimate Coll Ultimate Sigs Pairings-UPHO
05Ultra-91
Gold-91
Ice-91
05Upper Deck-84
HG Glossy-84
Jerseys-J-NH
Notable Numbers-N-NH
Ice Cool Threads-CTNH
Ice Cool Threads Autographs-ACTNH
Ice Cool Threads Glass-CTNH
Ice Cool Threads Patches-CTPNH
Ice Cool Threads Patch Autographs-CAPNH
Ice Fresh Ice Glass-FINH
05Upper Deck MVP-169
Gold-169
Platinum-169
05Upper Deck Rookie Update-42
05Upper Deck Trilogy Honorary Patches-HP-NH
05Upper Deck Tril Honorary Patch Script-HSP-NH
05Upper Deck Trilogy Honorary Swatches-HS-NH
05Upper Deck Tril Honorary Swatch Scripts-HSS-NH
05Upper Deck Trilogy Scripts-SFS-NH
05Upper Deck Toronto Fall Expo-84
05Upper Deck Victory-221
Black-221
Gold-221
Silver-221
06Be A Player Portraits-49
Signature Portraits-SPNH
06Black Diamond-36
Black-36
Gold-36
Ruby-36
Gemography-GNH
Jerseys-JNH
Jerseys Black-JNH
Jerseys Gold-JNH
Jerseys Ruby-JNH
Jerseys Black Autographs -JNH
06Flair Showcase Wave of the Future-WF16
06Fleer-84
Tiffany-84
06O-Pee-Chee-214
Rainbow-214
Autographs-A-NH
06Panini Stickers-53
06SP Game Used Authentic Fabrics-AFNH
06SP Game Used Authentic Fabrics Parallel-AFNH
06SP Game Used Authentic Fabrics Patches-AFNH
06SP Game Used Authentic Fabrics Dual-AF2BH
06SP Game Used Authentic Fabrics Dual Patches-AF2BH
06SP Game Used SIGnificance-SNH
06SPx SPxcitement-X43
06SPx SPxcitement Spectrum-X43
06SPx SPxcitement Autographs-X43
06UD Artifacts-56
Blue-56
Gold-56
Platinum-56
Radiance-56
Autographed Radiance Parallel-56
Red-56
Auto-Facts-AFNH
Auto-Facts Gold-AFNH
06Ultra-84
Gold Medallion-84
Ice Medallion-84
06Upper Deck Arena Giveaways-FLA2
06Upper Deck-84
Exclusives Parallel-84
High Gloss Parallel-84
Game Jerseys-J2NH
Game Patches-P2NH
Generations Duals-G2DH
Generations Patches Dual-G2PDH
Masterpieces-84
06Upper Deck MVP-123
Gold Script-123
Super Script-123
Jerseys-OJHL
Jerseys-OJSH
06Upper Deck Ovation-73
06Upper Deck Trilogy Honorary Scripted Patches-HSPNH
06Upper Deck Trilogy Honorary Scripted Swatches-HSSNH
06Upper Deck Victory-84
06Upper Deck Victory Black-84
06Upper Deck Victory Gold-84
06Upper Deck Victory Next In Line-NL23
07Upper Deck Ovation-81
07Upper Deck Victory-87
Black-87
Gold-87

Horton, Tim
44Beehive Group II Photos-408
45Quaker Oats Photos-23
52Parkhurst-58
53Parkhurst-13
54Parkhurst-31
54Parkhurst-90
55Parkhurst-3
Quaker Oats-3
57Parkhurst-T22
58Parkhurst-42
59Parkhurst-23
60Parkhurst-1
60Shirriff Coins-5
60York Photos-17
61Parkhurst-1
61Shirriff/Salada Coins-44
61York Yellow Backs-7
62Parkhurst-7
62Shirriff Coins-4
62York Iron-On Transfers-3
63Chex Photos-25
63Parkhurst-16
63Parkhurst-76
63Toronto Star-19
63York White Backs-1
64Beehive Group III Photos-165A
64Beehive Group III Photos-165B
64Coca-Cola Caps-94
64Topps-102
64Topps-105
64Toronto Star-17
65Coca-Cola-95
65Topps-79
66Maple Leafs Hockey Talks-5
66Topps-80
67Post Flip Books-3

67Topps-16
67Topps-127
67York Action Octagons-3
67York Action Octagons-21
67York Action Octagons-25
67York Action Octagons-31
68Maple Leafs White Border-4
68O-Pee-Chee-123
68O-Pee-Chee-201
Puck Stickers-18
68Post Marbles-12
68Shirriff Coins-172
68Topps-123
69Maple Leafs White Border Glossy-17
69O-Pee-Chee-182
69O-Pee-Chee-213
Four-in-One-1
69Topps-45
70Esso Power Players-183
70O-Pee-Chee-59
70Sargent Promotions Stamps-125
70Topps-59
71O-Pee-Chee-186
Posters-18
71Sargent Promotions Stamps-169
71Toronto Sun-218
72O-Pee-Chee-197
72Sabres Postcards-7
72Sargent Promotions Stamps-37
73O-Pee-Chee-189
73Sabres Postcards-3
83Hall of Fame-188
83Hall of Fame Postcards-J8
85Hall of Fame-188
90Oakville Horton-1
91Kraft-86
91Ultimate Original Six-37
91Ultimate Original Six-84
91Ultimate Original Six-97
French-37
French-84
French-97
92Hall of Fame Legends-24
92Parkhurst Parkie Reprints-PR16
93Parkhurst Parkie Reprints-PR34
93Parkhurst Parkie Reprints Case Inserts-3
93Sabres Noco-8
94Parkhurst Missing Link-127
94Parkhurst Tall Boys-131
94Parkhurst Tall Boys-135
95Parkhurst '66-67-103
Coins-103
99Upper Deck Century Legends-40
Century Collection-40
00Upper Deck Legends-122
Legendary Collection Bronze-122
Legendary Collection Gold-122
Legendary Collection Silver-122
01BAP Ultimate Mem All-Star History-16
01BAP Ultimate Mem Complete Package-2
01BAP Ultimate Mem Retro Teammates-8
01BAP Update Passing the Torch-PTT6
01Greats of the Game-30
01Parkhurst He Shoots-He Scores Points-3
01Parkhurst Heroes-H12
01Parkhurst Reprints-PR24
01Parkhurst Reprints-PR67
01Parkhurst Reprints-PR75
01Parkhurst Reprints-PR89
01Parkhurst Reprints-PR97
01Parkhurst Reprints-PR103
01Parkhurst Reprints-PR113
01Parkhurst Reprints-PR119
01Parkhurst Reprints-PR127
01Parkhurst Reprints-PR137
01Parkhurst Vintage Memorabilia-PV21
01SP Game Used Signs of Tradition-LCTH
01Topps Archives-76
01UD Stanley Cup Champs-25
01Upper Deck Legends-60
02BAP Memorabilia Mini Stanley Cups-2
02BAP NHL All-Star History-16
02BAP Ultimate Mem Blades of Steel-4
02BAP Ultimate Mem Complete Package-10
02BAP Ultimate Mem Paper Cuts Autos-27
02BAP Ultimate Mem Retro Teammates-8
02BAP Ultimate Mem Vintage Hat Tricks-4
02BAP Ultimate Mem Vintage Jerseys-37
02ITG Used Vintage Memorabilia-VM13
02ITG Used Vintage Memorabilia Gold-VM13
02Maple Leafs Platinum Collection-53
02Maple Leafs Platinum Collection-100
02Parkhurst Vintage Memorabilia-VM15
02Parkhurst Vintage Teammates-VT14
02Topps Heritage Reprint Relics-TH
02Topps Heritage Reprints-TH
03BAP Memorabilia Vintage Memorabilia-VM-3
03BAP Ultimate Memorabilia Cornerstones-4
03BAP Ultimate Mem Maple Leafs Forever-8
03BAP Ultimate Memorabilia Triple Threads-13
03BAP Ultimate Mem Vintage Blade of Steel-16
03BAP Ultimate Memorabilia Vintage Lumber-7
03Canada Post-13
03ITG Toronto Fall Expo Forever Rivals-FR8
03ITG Used Sig Series Vintage Mem -25
03ITG Used Sig Series Vintage Mem Gold-25
03ITG VIP Vintage Memorabilia-11
03Parkhurst Original Six Toronto-58
03Parkhurst Original Six Toronto-69
03Parkhurst Original Six Toronto-84
03Parkhurst Original Six Toronto-92
Inserts-T3
Memorabilia-TM24
Memorabilia-TM28
Memorabilia-TM40
Memorabilia-TM51
04ITG NHL AS FANtasy AS History Jerseys-SB16
04ITG Franchises Canadian-110
Double Memorabilia-DM14
Double Memorabilia Gold-DM14
Forever Rivals-FR9
Forever Rivals Gold-FR9
Memorabilia-SM23
Memorabilia Gold-SM23
Triple Memorabilia-TM6
Triple Memorabilia Gold-TM6
04ITG Franchises US East-348
04ITG Franchises US West-278
04ITG Ultimate Memorabilia-195
Gold-195
Blades of Steel-9
Complete Package-13
Cornerstones-3
Cornerstones Gold-3
Day In History-20
Day In History Gold-20
Maple Leafs Forever-7
Original Six-2
Paper Cuts-16
Paper Cuts Memorabilia-11
04UD Legends Classics Jersey Redemptions-JY10
04ITG Heroes and Prospects-123
04ITG Heroes/Prospects Toronto Expo '05-123
04ITG Heroes/Prospects Expo Heroes/Pros-123
05ITG Ultimate Memorabilia Level 1-93
05ITG Ultimate Memorabilia Level 2-93
05ITG Ultimate Memorabilia Level 3-93
05ITG Ultimate Memorabilia Level 4-93
05ITG Ultimate Memorabilia Level 5-93
05ITG Ultimate Mem Blades of Steel-8
05ITG Ultimate Mem Blades of Steel Gold-8
05ITG Ultimate Mem Complete Package-3
05ITG Ultimate Mem Complete Package Gold-3
05ITG Ultimate Mem Decades Jerseys-4
05ITG Ultimate Mem Decades Jerseys-6
05ITG Ultimate Mem Decades Jerseys Gold-4
05ITG Ultimate Mem Decades Jerseys Gold-6
05ITG Ultimate Mem Pass the Torch Jerseys-16
05ITG Ultimate Mem Passing Torch Jsy Gold-16
05ITG Ultimate Mem Raised to the Rafters-14
05ITG Ultimate Mem Raised Rafters Gold-14
05ITG Ultimate Mem Retro Teammate Jerseys-20
05ITG Ult Mem Retro Teammates Jersey Gold-20
05ITG Ultimate Mem 3 Star of the Game Jsy-5
05ITG Ult Mem 3 Star of the Game Jsy Gold-5
05ITG Ultimate Memorabilia Vintage Lumber-22
05ITG Ultimate Mem Vintage Lumber Gold-22
05ITG Heroes and Prospects He Shoots-He Scores Prizes-56
06ITG Ultimate Memorabilia-138
Artist Proof-138
Blades of Steel-30
Blades of Steel Gold-30
Complete Package-13
Complete Package Gold-13
Decades-2
Decades Gold-2
Double Memorabilia-11
Double Memorabilia Gold-11
Lumbergraphs-3
Passing The Torch-7
Passing The Torch Gold-7
Retro Teammates-5
Retro Teammates Gold-5
Road to the Cup-3
Road to the Cup Gold-3
Stick Rack-7
Stick Rack Gold-7
06The Cup Legendary Cuts-LCTH
06ITG Heroes and Prospects Heroes Memorabilia-HM18
06ITG Heroes and Prospects Heroes Memorabilia Gold-HM18
07Maple Leafs 1967 Commemorative-11

Horvath, Bronco

44Beehive Group II Photos-34
44Beehive Group II Photos-107
44Beehive Group II Photos-326
44Beehive Group II Photos-409
57Bruins Photos-9
57Topps-7
58Topps-35
59Topps-56
60NHL Ceramic Tiles-8
60Shirriff Coins-105
60Topps-54
Stamps-26
61Shirriff/Salada Coins-31
61Topps-40
62Topps-63
63Rochester Americans-16
64Beehive Group III Photos-166
94Parkhurst Missing Link-105
98Bruins Alumni-33
Autographs-33
03BAP Ultimate Mem Linemates Autos-9
04ITG Franchises US East-322
Autographs-A-BHV

Horvath, Jason

917th Inn. Sketch WHL-187

Horvath, Scott

02St. Michaels Majors-11
03Atlantic City Boardwalk Bullies-10
03Atlantic City Boardwalk Bullies RBI-22
04Atlantic City Boardwalk Bullies-6
04Atlantic City Boardwalk Bullies Kinko's-12
05Missouri River Otters-24
05Port Huron Flags-9

Horvath, Tony

75Hamilton Fincups-8

Horyna, Robert

90Newmarket Saints-7
96Czech APS Extraliga-266
97Czech APS Extraliga-221
98Czech DS Stickers-28
99Czech DS-44
99Czech OFS-7
99Czech OFS Goalie Die-Cuts-7

Hosek, Miroslav

94Czech APS Extraliga-259

Hospelt, Kai

04German Cologne Sharks Postcards-14
04German DEL Update-323A
05German DEL-206
06German DEL-123

Hospodar, Ed

80O-Pee-Chee-366
81O-Pee-Chee-233
82Whalers Junior Hartford Courant-7
83Whalers Junior Hartford Courant-6
85Flyers Postcards-13
86Flyers Postcards-11
87Sabres Blue Shield-12
87Sabres Wonder Bread/Hostess-11

Hospodar, Ladislav

94German First League-547

Hossa, Marcel

99UD Prospects-39
International Stars-IN10
00UD CHL Prospects-58
01BAP Memorabilia-324
Emerald-324
Ruby-324
Sapphire-324
01Parkhurst-320
01SPx-206
01Titanium Draft Day Edition-139
01UD Honor Roll-76
01UD Mask Collection-151
Gold-151
01UD Playmakers-123
01UD Premier Collection-99
01UD Top Shelf-130
01Upper Deck Ice-142
01Upper Deck MVP-225
01Upper Deck Victory-445
01Quebec Citadelles-27
02BAP First Edition-288
02BAP Signature Series All-Rookie-AR5
02BAP Signature Series Team Quads-TQ6
02BAP Ultimate Memorabilia Numerology-20
02Bowman YoungStars-110
Gold-110
Silver-110
Autographs-MH
Jerseys-MH
Patches-MH
Double Stuff-MH
Triple Stuff-MH
Rivals-NKMH
Rivals Patches-6
Sticks-MH
02O-Pee-Chee-296
02O-Pee-Chee Premier Blue Parallel-296
02O-Pee-Chee Premier Red Parallel-296
02O-Pee-Chee Factory Set-296
02Pacific Calder-76
Silver-76
Reflections-16
02Pacific Complete-556
Red-556
02Pacific Entry Draft-4
02Pacific Exclusive-90
Great Expectations-11
02Private Stock Reserve-52
Blue-52
Red-52
Retail-52
02SPx-114
02Stadium Club-111
Silver Decoy Cards-111
Proofs-111
02Topps-296
OPC Blue Parallel-296
OPC Red Parallel-296
Factory Set-296
02Topps Total-114
02UD Foundations-133
02Upper Deck-210
Exclusives-210
02Upper Deck MVP-207
Gold-207
Classics-207
Golden Classics-207
02Upper Deck Rookie Update-53
02Upper Deck Victory-115
Bronze-115
Gold-115
Silver-115
02Upper Deck Vintage-336
02Hamilton Bulldogs-26
03BAP Ultimate Mem Franch Present Future-21
03Beehive-105
Gold-105
Silver-105
Signatures-RF23
03Black Diamond-172
Black-172
Green-172
Red-172
03Canadiens Postcards-12
03Crown Royale Global Conquest-7
03ITG Action-354
Jerseys-M32
03McDonald's Pacific-27
Saturday Night Rivals-6
03O-Pee-Chee-80
03OPC Blue-80
03OPC Gold-80
03OPC Red-80
03Pacific-177
Blue-177
Red-177
03Pacific Exhibit-77
Blue Backs-77
Yellow Backs-77
03Pacific Invincible-49
Blue-49
Red-49
Retail-49
New Sensations-15
03Pacific Prism-56
Blue-56
Gold-56
Red-56
03Pacific Supreme-50
Blue-50
Red-50
Retail-50
03Parkhurst Original Six Montreal-15
Memorabilia-MM10
03Private Stock Reserve-53
Blue-53
Red-53
Retail-53
Rising Stock-10
03SP Authentic-46
Limited-46
03SP Game Used Authentic Fabrics-AFHA
03SP Game Used Authentic Fabrics-DFHH
03SP Game Used Authentic Fabrics-DFKH
03SP Game Used Authentic Fabrics-QKTHK
03SP Game Used Authentic Fabrics Gold-AFHA
03SP Game Used Authentic Fabrics Gold-DFHH
03SP Game Used Authentic Fabrics Gold-DFKH
03SP Game Used Authentic Fabrics Gold-QKTHK
03SP Game Used Authentic Patches-APMH
03SP Game Used Double Threads-DTKH
03SP Game Used Double Threads-DTSH
03SP Game Used Signers-SPSMH
03SP Game Used Team Threads-TTKTH
03SPx-53
Radiance-53
Spectrum-53
Big Futures-BF-MH
Big Futures Limited-BF-MH
VIP-VIP-KH
VIP Limited-VIP-KH
03Titanium-54
Hobby Jersey Number Parallels-54
Retail-54
Retail Jersey Number Parallels-54
03Topps-80
Blue-80
Gold-80
Red-80
03Topps C55-91
Minis-91
Minis American Back-91
Minis American Back Red-91
Minis Bazooka Back-91
Minis Brooklyn Back-91
Minis Hat Trick Back-91
Minis O Canada Back-91
Minis O Canada Back Red-91
Minis Stanley Cup Back-91
03UD Honor Roll-44
03UD Honor Roll-108
03UD Premier Collection Signatures-PS-MCH
03Upper Deck-101
Canadian Exclusives-101
HG-101
Shooting Stars-ST-MH
03Upper Deck Classic Portraits-51
Headliners-HH-HA
03Upper Deck Ice Authentics-IA-HA
03Upper Deck MVP-229
Gold Script-229
Silver Script-229
Canadian Exclusives-229
SportsNut-SN48
03Upper Deck Trilogy-51
Limited-51
03Upper Deck Victory-97
Bronze-97
Gold-97
Silver-97
04SP Authentic Buybacks-110
04SP Authentic Buybacks-111
04SP Authentic Rookie Review-RR-MH
04SP Authentic Sign of the Times-ST-MA
04SP Authentic Sign of the Times-DS-HH
04SP Authentic Sign of the Times-FS-MON
04UD All-World-70
Gold-70
Autographs-70
Dual Autographs-AD-MM
Quad Autographs-AQ-NAM
04Upper Deck-93
Canadian Exclusives-93
HG Glossy Gold-93
HG Glossy Silver-93
Jersey Autographs-GJA-HO
Jersey Autographs-GJA-HO/HS
04Swedish Pure Skills-80
Parallel-80
05Beehive Matted Materials-MMMH
05Beehive Matted Materials Remarkable-RMMH
05Beehive Signature Scrapbook-SSMH
05Black Diamond Gemography-G-HO
05Black Diamond Gemography Emerald-G-HO
05Black Diamond Gemography Gold-G-HO
05Black Diamond Gemography Onyx-G-HO
05Black Diamond Gemography Ruby-G-HO
05Parkhurst-332
Facsimile Auto Parallel-332
Signatures-HO
True Colors-TCNYR
True Colors-TCNYR
05SP Authentic Scripts to Success-SSMH
05SP Authentic Sign of the Times-HO
05SP Game Used Statscriptions-ST-HO
05SPx Winning Combos-WC-HH
05SPx Winning Combos-WC-HK
05SPx Winning Combos Autographs-AWC-MS
05SPx Winning Combos Gold-WC-HH
05SPx Winning Combos Gold-WC-HK
05SPx Winning Combos Spectrum-WC-HH
05SPx Winning Combos Spectrum-WC-HK
05UD Artifacts Auto Facts-AF-HO
05UD Artifacts Auto Facts Blue-AF-HO
05UD Artifacts Auto Facts Copper-AF-HO
05UD Artifacts Auto Facts Pewter-AF-HO
05UD Artifacts Auto Facts Silver-AF-HO
05UD Artifacts Frozen Artifacts-FA-HO
05UD Artifacts Frozen Artifacts Autos-FA-HO
05UD Artifacts Frozen Artifacts Copper-FA-HO
05UD Artifacts Frozen Artifacts Dual-FAD-HO
05UD Artifacts Frozen Artifact Dual Auto-FAD-HO
05UD Artifact Frozen Artifact Dual Copper-FAD-HO
05UD Artifacts Frozen Artifacts Dual Gold-FAD-HO
05UD Artifact Frozen Artifact Dual Maroon-FAD-HO
05UD Artifact Frozen Artifact Dual Pewter-FAD-HO
05UD Artifact Frozen Artifact Dual Silver-FAD-HO
05UD Artifacts Frozen Artifacts Gold-FA-HO
05UD Artifacts Frozen Artifacts Maroon-FA-HO
05UD Artifacts Frozen Artifacts Patches-FP-HO
05UD Artifact Frozen Artifact Patch Autos-FP-HO
05UD Artifacts Frozen Artifact Patch Dual-FPD-WG
05UD Artifacts Frozen Art Patch Dual Auto-FPD-WG
05UD Artifacts Frozen Art Patch Pewter-FP-HO
05UD Artifacts Frozen Art Patch Silver-FP-HO
05UD Artifacts Frozen Artifacts Pewter-FA-HO
05UD Artifacts Frozen Artifacts Silver-FA-HO
05UD Artifacts Remarkable Artifacts-RA-HS
05UD Artifacts Remarkable Artifacts Dual-RA-HS
05UD Toronto Fall Expo Priority Signings-PS-HS
05Ultimate Coll National Heroes Jersey-NHJHS
05Ultimate Coll National Heroes Patch-NHPHS
05Ultra-130
Gold-130
Ice-130
05Upper Deck-377
Big Playmakers-B-MAH
Jerseys-J-MAH
Jerseys Series II-J2HO
Notable Numbers-N-HO
Patches-P-MHO
Ice Fresh Ice-FIMH
Ice Fresh Ice Glass-FIMH
Ice Fresh Ice Glass Patches-FIPMH
05Upper Deck MVP-265
Gold-265
Platinum-265
05Upper Deck Trilogy Ice Scripts-IS-HS
06Flair Showcase Inks-IHO
06Flair Showcase Stitches-SSHO
06Fleer Fabricology-FMH
06Fleer Signing Day-SDHO
06Hot Prospects Hotagraphs-HMH
06SP Game Used SIGnificance-SHO
06UD Artifacts Tundra Tandems-TTHP
06UD Artifacts Tundra Tandems Black-TTHP
06UD Artifacts Tundra Tandems Blue-TTHP
06UD Artifacts Tundra Tandems Gold-TTHP
06UD Artifacts Tundra Tandems Platinum-TTHP
06UD Artifacts Tundra Tandems Red-TTHP
06UD Artifacts Tundra Tandems Dual Patches Red-TTHP
06Upper Deck Game Jerseys-JHO
06Upper Deck Game Patches-PHO
06Upper Deck Trilogy Scripts-TSMH

Hossa, Marian

93Quebec Pee-Wee Tournament-1554
97Donruss Elite-28
Aspirations-28
Status-28
97Donruss Preferred-162
Cut to the Chase-162
97Pacific Dynagon-NNO
Copper-NNO
Dark Grey-NNO
Emerald Green-NNO
Ice Blue-NNO
Red-NNO
Silver-NNO
97Paramount-125
Copper-125
Dark Grey-125
Emerald Green-125
Ice Blue-125
Red-125
Silver-125
97Pinnacle-17
Artist's Proofs-17
Rink Collection-17
Press Plates Back Black-17
Press Plates Back Cyan-17
Press Plates Back Magenta-17
Press Plates Back Yellow-17
Press Plates Front Black-17
Press Plates Front Cyan-17
Press Plates Front Magenta-17
Press Plates Front Yellow-17
97Upper Deck-326
97Portland Winter Hawks-4
98Be A Player-249
Press Release-249
98BAP Gold-249
98BAP Autographs-249
98BAP Autographs Gold-249
98Bowman's Best-107
Refractors-107
Atomic Refractors-107
Mirror Image Fusion-F13
Mirror Image Fusion Refractors-F13
Mirror Image Fusion Atomic Refractors-F13
98Finest Futures Finest-F16
98Finest Futures Finest Refractors-F16
98McDonald's Upper Deck-23
98OPC Chrome-104
Refractors-104
98Pacific Omega-164
Red-164
Opening Day Issue-164
98Revolution-99
Ice Shadow-99
Red-99
98Senators Team Issue-7
98SP Authentic Sign of the Times-MH
98SP Authentic Sign of the Times Gold-MH
98SPx Finite-58
98SPx Finite-140
Radiance-58
Radiance-140
Spectrum-58
Spectrum-140
98Topps-104
O-Pee-Chee-104
98UD Choice-142
Prime Choice Reserve-142
Reserve-142
98Upper Deck-6
Exclusives-6
Exclusives 1 of 1-6
Generation Next-GN2
Generation Next Quantum 1-GN2
Generation Next Quantum 2-GN2
Generation Next Quantum 3-GN2
Gold Reserve-6
98Bowman CHL-53
Golden Anniversary-53
OPC International-53
Scout's Choice-SC7
98Bowman Chrome CHL-53
Golden Anniversary-53
Golden Anniversary Refractors-53
OPC International-53
OPC International Refractors-53
Refractors-53
99Aurora-99
Striped-99
Premiere Date-99
Premiere Date Striped-99
99BAP Memorabilia-12
Gold-12
Silver-12
Selects Silver-SL15
Selects Gold-SL15
99BAP Millennium-170
Emerald-170
Ruby-170
Sapphire-170
Signatures-170
Signatures Gold-170
99Black Diamond-59
Diamond Cut-59
Final Cut-59
99Crown Royale-97
Limited Series-97
Premiere Date-97
Century 21-8
Ice Elite-18
Ice Elite Parallel-18
99Kraft Whiz Kid-2
99McDonald's Upper Deck-MCD20
99O-Pee-Chee-99
99O-Pee-Chee Autographs-TA8
99O-Pee-Chee Chrome-99
99O-Pee-Chee Chrome Refractors-99
99O-Pee-Chee Chrome Ice Futures-IF4
99O-Pee-Chee Chrome Ice Futures Refractor-IF4
99O-Pee-Chee Now Starring-NS2
99O-Pee-Chee Ice Futures-IF4
99Pacific-288
Copper-288
Emerald Green-288
Gold-288
Ice Blue-288
Premiere Date-288
Red-288
99Pacific Dynagon Ice-139
Blue-139
Copper-139
Gold-139
Premiere Date-139
Checkmates American-12
Checkmates American-27
Checkmates Canadian-27
99Pacific Omega-159
Copper-159
Gold-159
Ice Blue-159
Premiere Date-159
NHL Generations-7
5 Star Talents-17
5 Star Talents Parallel-17
99Pacific Prism-96
Holographic Blue-96
Holographic Gold-96
Holographic Mirror-96
Holographic Purple-96
Premiere Date-96
Clear Advantage-14
99Panini Stickers-114
99Paramount-162
Copper-162
Emerald-162
Gold-162
Holographic Emerald-162
Holographic Gold-162
Holographic Silver-162
Ice Blue-162
Premiere Date-162
Red-162
Silver-162
Ice Advantage-15
Ice Advantage Proofs-15
Toronto Fall Expo '99-162
99Revolution-102
Premiere Date-102
Red-102
Shadow Series-102
Showstoppers-24
Top of the Line-6
Copper-102
Gold-102
CSC Silver-102
99Senators Team Issue-8
99SP Authentic-60
Sign of the Times-MH
Sign of the Times Gold-MH
Tomorrow's Headliners-TH7
99SPx-107
Radiance-107
Spectrum-107
99Stadium Club-82
First Day Issue-82
One of a Kind-82
Printing Plates Black-82
Printing Plates Cyan-82
Printing Plates Magenta-82
Printing Plates Yellow-82
Capture the Action-CA5
Capture the Action Game View-CAG5
Chrome-30
Chrome Refractors-30
Chrome Oversized-14
Chrome Oversized Refractors-14
Co-Signers-CS2
Co-Signers-CS3
Lone Star Signatures-LS13
Souvenirs-SMH
99Topps Arena Giveaways-OTT-MH
99Topps/OPC-99
Autographs-TA8
Ice Futures-IF4
Now Starring-NS2
99Topps/OPC Chrome-99
Refractors-99
Ice Futures-IF4
Ice Futures Refractors-IF4
99Topps Gold Label Class 1-64
Black-64
Black One of One-64
One of One-64
Red-64
Red One of One-64
99Topps Gold Label Class 2-64
99Topps Gold Label Class 2 Black-64
99Topps Gold Label Class 2 Black 1 of 1-64
99Topps Gold Label Class 2 One of One-64
99Topps Gold Label Class 2 Red-64
99Topps Gold Label Class 2 Red One of One-64
99Topps Gold Label Class 3-64
99Topps Gold Label Class 3 Black-64
99Topps Gold Label Class 3 Black 1 of 1-64
99Topps Gold Label Class 3 One of One-64
99Topps Gold Label Class 3 Red-64
99Topps Gold Label Class 3 Red One of One-64
99Topps Gold Label Fresh Gold-FG16
99Topps Gold Label Fresh Gold Black-FG16
99Topps Gold Label Fresh Gold Black 1of1-FG16
99Topps Gold Label Fresh Gold One of One-FG16
99Topps Gold Label Fresh Gold Red-FG16
99Topps Gold Label Fresh Gold Red 1 of 1-FG16
99Topps Premier Plus-44
Parallel-44
The Next Ones-TNO2
99Topps Premiere Plus Promos-PP3
99Ultimate Victory-61
1/1-61
Parallel-61
Parallel 100-61
Smokin Guns-SG6
99Upper Deck-92
Exclusives-92
Exclusives 1 of 1-92
New Ice Age-N13
New Ice Age Quantum Gold-N13
New Ice Age Quantum Silver-N13
99Upper Deck Century Legends-73
Century Collection-73
99Upper Deck Gold Reserve-92
99Upper Deck HoloGrFx-41
Ausome-41
99Upper Deck MVP-144
Gold Script-144
Silver Script-144
Super Script-144
21st Century NHL-8
Game-Used Souvenirs-GU5
99Upper Deck MVP SC Edition-124
Gold Script-124
Silver Script-124
Super Script-124
Cup Contenders-CC7
99Upper Deck Ovation-39
Standing Ovation-39
99Upper Deck Retro-55
Gold-55
Platinum-55
99Upper Deck Victory-200
99Wayne Gretzky Hockey-116
99Quebec PeeWee Tournament Coll Souv-16
00Aurora-101
Pinstripes-101
Pinstripes Premiere Date-101
Premiere Date-101
Scouting Reports-15
00BAP Memorabilia-94
Emerald-94
Ruby-94
Sapphire-94
Promos-94
00BAP Mem Chicago Sportsfest Copper-94
00BAP Memorabilia Chicago Sportsfest Blue-94
00BAP Memorabilia Chicago Sportsfest Gold-94
00BAP Memorabilia Chicago Sportsfest Ruby-94
00BAP Memorabilia Chicago Sun-Times Ruby-94
00BAP Memorabilia Chicago Sun-Times Gold-94
00BAP Mem Chicago Sun-Times Sapphire-94
00BAP Mem Toronto Fall Expo Copper-94
00BAP Memorabilia Toronto Fall Expo Gold-94
00BAP Memorabilia Toronto Fall Expo Ruby-94
00BAP Parkhurst 2000-P98
00BAP Signature Series-237
Emerald-237
Ruby-237
Sapphire-237
Autographs-115
Autographs Gold-115
Franchise Players-F21
00BAP Ultimate Mem Game-Used Jerseys-GJ17
00BAP Ultimate Mem Game-Used Emblems-E15
00BAP Ultimate Mem Game-Used Numbers-N15
00BAP Ultimate Mem Game-Used Sticks-GS17
00Black Diamond-40
Gold-40
00Crown Royale-75
Ice Blue-75
Limited Series-75
Premiere Date-75
Red-75
00McDonald's Pacific-23
Blue-23
Checklists-5
00O-Pee-Chee-23
00O-Pee-Chee Parallel-23
00Pacific-278
Copper-278
Gold-278
Ice Blue-278
Premiere Date-278
2001: Ice Odyssey-16
Gold Crown Die Cuts-21
Reflections-14
00Pacific 2001: Ice Odyssey Anaheim Ntnl-16
00Paramount-172
Copper-172
Gold-172
Holo-Gold-172
Holo-Silver-172
Ice Blue-172
Premiere Date-172
Freeze Frame-24
00Private Stock-70
Gold-70
Premiere Date-70
Retail-70
Silver-70
PS-2001 Action-40
PS-2001 New Wave-16
00Revolution-103
Blue-103
Premiere Date-103
Red-103
HD NHL-23
00Senators Team Issue-8
00SP Authentic-62
00SP Game Used-42
00SPx-46
Spectrum-46
Highlight Heroes-HH9
00Stadium Club-103
00Titanium-65
Blue-65
Gold-65
Premiere Date-65
Red-65
Retail-65
All-Stars-7W
00Topps/OPC-23
Parallel-23
00Topps Chrome-22
OPC Refractors-22
Refractors-22
00Topps Gold Label Class 1-11
Gold-11
00Topps Gold Label Class 2-11
00Topps Gold Label Class 2 Gold-11
00Topps Gold Label Class 3-11
00Topps Gold Label Class 3 Gold-11
00Topps Gold Label New Generation-NG5
00Topps Gold Label New Generation 1 to 1-NG5
00Topps Heritage-68
Chrome Parallel-68
New Tradition-NT1
00Topps Premier Plus-23
Blue Ice-23
Aspirations-PA6
00Topps Stars-66
Blue-66
00UD Heroes-152
00UD Pros and Prospects-59
00UD Reserve-59
00Upper Deck-120
Exclusives Tier 1-120
Exclusives Tier 2-120
All-Star Class-A6
Fun-Damentals-F7
Rise to Prominence-RP5
00Upper Deck Ice-28
Immortals-28
Legends-28
Stars-28
00Upper Deck Legends-93
00Upper Deck Legends-95
Legendary Collection Bronze-93
Legendary Collection Bronze-95
Legendary Collection Gold-93
Legendary Collection Gold-95
Legendary Collection Silver-93
Legendary Collection Silver-95
00Upper Deck MVP-125
First Stars-125
Second Stars-125
Third Stars-125
00Upper Deck Victory-158
00Upper Deck Victory-159
00Upper Deck Victory-313
00Upper Deck Vintage-249
00Upper Deck Vintage-258
00Upper Deck Vintage-259
00Vanguard-69
High Voltage-24
High Voltage Gold-24
High Voltage Green-24
High Voltage Red-24
High Voltage Silver-24
Holographic Gold-69
Holographic Purple-69
Pacific Proofs-69
00Czech Stadion-123
01Atomic-69
Blue-69
Gold-69
Premiere Date-69
Red-69
Core Players-13
Power Play-25
01BAP Memorabilia-98
Emerald-98
Ruby-98
Sapphire-98
He Shoots-He Scores Prizes-23
01BAP Signature Series-20
Autographs-20
Autographs Gold-20
Jerseys-GJ-46
Jersey Autographs-GUMHO
Jersey and Stick Cards-GSJ-46
Emblems-GUE-45
Numbers-ITN-45
01BAP Update He Shoots-He Scores Points-6
01BAP Update He Shoots-He Scores Prizes-22
01Bowman YoungStars-45
Gold-45
Ice Cubed-45
01Crown Royale-101
Blue-101
Premiere Date-101
Red-101
Retail-101
Jewels of the Crown-23
01McDonald's Pacific-26
01O-Pee-Chee-29
01O-Pee-Chee Heritage Parallel-29
01O-Pee-Chee Heritage Parallel Limited-29
01O-Pee-Chee Premier Parallel-29
01Pacific-273
01Pacific-417
01Pacific-436
Extreme LTD-273
Gold-417
Gold-436
Hobby LTD-273
Premiere Date-273
Retail LTD-273
All-Stars-W6
Gold Crown Die-Cuts-15
Impact Zone-13
97-98 Subset-357
97-98 Subset Gold Parallel-357
01Pacific Adrenaline-134
Blue-134
Premiere Date-134
Red-134
Retail-134
01Pacific Arena Exclusives-273
01Pacific Arena Exclusives-417
01Pacific Arena Exclusives-436
01Pacific Heads-Up-69
Blue-69
Premiere Date-69
Red-69
Silver-69
Stat Masters-12
01Parkhurst-21
Gold-21
Silver-21
Jerseys-PJ57
Jersey and Stick-PSJ10
Sticks-PS52
Teammates-T16
01Private Stock-68
Gold-68
Premiere Date-68
Retail-68
Silver-68
01Private Stock Pacific Nights-68
01Senators Team Issue-10
01SP Authentic-57
Limited-57
Limited Gold-57
Sign of the Times-HO
Sign of the Times-HH
Sign of the Times-HT
Sign of the Times-PHG
01SP Game Used-36
Inked Sweaters-ISMH
Patches-PMH
Patches-CPHH
Patches-CPHL
Patches Signed-SPMH
Patches Signed-DSPHI
01SPx-44
01Sports Illustrated for Kids III-343
01Stadium Club-15
Award Winners-15
Master Photos-15
01Stadium Club Toronto Fall Expo-1
01Titanium-100
Hobby Parallel-100
Premiere Date-100
Retail-100
Retail Parallel-100
Double-Sided Jerseys-47
Double-Sided Jerseys-63
Double-Sided Patches-47
Double-Sided Patches-63
01Titanium Draft Day Edition-66
01Topps-29
Heritage Parallel-29
Heritage Parallel Limited-29
OPC Parallel-29
01Topps Chrome-29
Refractors-29
Black Border Refractors-29
01Topps Heritage-28
Refractors-28
01Topps Reserve-31
01UD Honor Roll Pucks-P-MH
01UD Honor Roll Pucks Gold-P-MH
01UD Honor Roll Sharp Skaters-SS5
01UD Mask Collection-68
Gold-68
01UD Playmakers-69
01UD Premier Collection-36
Signatures-HO
Signatures Black-HO
01UD Top Shelf-29
Jerseys-MH
Jersey Autographs-MH
01Upper Deck-122
Exclusives-122
Fantastic Finishers-FF7
Game Jerseys-NGMH
Game Jerseys-CHH
Patches-PMH
Tandems-T6
01Upper Deck Ice-32
01Upper Deck MVP-131
01Upper Deck Victory-242
01Upper Deck Victory-417
Gold-242
Gold-417
01Upper Deck Vintage-174
01Upper Deck Vintage-182
01Vanguard-69
Blue-69
Red-69
Memorabilia-45
One of Ones-69
Premiere Date-69
Proofs-69
Quebec Tournament Heroes-17
02McFarlane Hockey-210
02McFarlane Hockey-212
02Atomic-71
Blue-71
Gold-71
Red-71
Hobby Parallel-71
02BAP First Edition-75
02BAP First Edition-361
02BAP First Edition-418R

Jerseys-75
02BAP Memorabilia-83
02BAP Memorabilia-221
Emerald-83
Emerald-221
Ruby-83
Ruby-221
Sapphire-83
Sapphire-221
Franchise Players-FP-21
NHL All-Star Game-83
NHL All-Star Game-221
NHL All-Star Game Blue-83
NHL All-Star Game Blue-221
NHL All-Star Game Green-83
NHL All-Star Game Green-221
NHL All-Star Game Red-83
NHL All-Star Game Red-221
02BAP Memorabilia Toronto Fall Expo-83
02BAP Memorabilia Toronto Fall Expo-221
02BAP Signature Series-24
Autographs-24
Autograph Buybacks 1998-249
Autograph Buybacks 1999-170
Autograph Buybacks 2000-115
Autograph Buybacks 2001-20
Autographs Gold-24
Franchise Players-FJ21
Jerseys-SGJ48
Jersey Autographs-SGJ48
Team Quads-TQ20
02BAP Ultimate Memorabilia Jerseys-20
02BAP Ultimate Mem Jersey and Stick-26
02BAP Ultimate Memorabilia Nameplates-10
02Bowman YoungStars-20
Gold-20
Silver-20
02Crown Royale-67
Blue-67
Red-67
Retail-67
02eTopps-52
02ITG Used-53
02ITG Used-153
Franchise Players-F21
Franchise Players Autographs-F21
Franchise Players Gold-F21
Jerseys-GUJ48
Jersey Autographs-GUJ48
Jerseys Gold-GUJ48
Jersey and Stick-SJ48
Jersey and Stick Gold-SJ48
02McDonald's Pacific-29
02NHL Power Play Stickers-112
02O-Pee-Chee-127
02O-Pee-Chee Premier Blue Parallel-127
02O-Pee-Chee Premier Red Parallel-127
02O-Pee-Chee Factory Set-127
02Pacific-267
Blue-267
Red-267
02Pacific Calder-8
Silver-8
Chasing Glory-7
Hart Stoppers-7
02Pacific Complete-107
Red-107
02Pacific Exclusive-122
Jerseys-18
Jerseys Gold-18
02Pacific Heads-Up-87
Blue-87
Purple-87
Red-87
Quad Jerseys-19
Quad Jerseys Gold-19
02Pacific Quest for the Cup-71
Gold-71
Chasing the Cup-13
Jerseys-13
02Parkhurst-37
Bronze-37
Gold-37
Silver-37
Franchise Players-FP21
Teammates-TT11
02Parkhurst Retro-48
Minis-48
Franchise Players-RF21
He Shoots-He Scores Points-3
He Shoots-He Scores Prizes-18
Hopefuls-HH7
Hopefuls-RR2
Jerseys-RJ26
Jersey and Sticks-RSJ18
Memorabilia-RM4
02Private Stock Reserve-134
Red-134
Retail-134
Patches-134
02Senators Team Issue-7
02Senators Team Issue-11
02SP Authentic-63
Beckett Promos-63
02SP Game Used Authentic Fabrics-AFHO
02SP Game Used Authentic Fabrics-AFMH
02SP Game Used Authentic Fabrics Gold-AFHO
02SP Game Used Authentic Fabrics Gold-AFMH
02SP Game Used Authentic Fabrics Rainbow-AFHO
02SP Game Used Authentic Fabrics Rainbow-AFMH
02SPx-53
Spectrum Gold-53
Spectrum Silver-53
02Stadium Club-61
Silver Decoy Cards-61
Proofs-61
Passport-7
02Titanium-72
Blue-72
Red-72
Retail-72
Saturday Knights-6
02Topps-127
OPC Blue Parallel-127
OPC Red Parallel-127
Factory Set-127
02Topps Chrome-113
Black Border Refractors-113
Refractors-113
02Topps Heritage-73
Chrome Parallel-73
Great Skates-MHO
Great Skates Patches-MH
02Topps Total-10
02UD Artistic Impressions-62
Gold-62
02UD Artistic Impressions Beckett Promos-62
02UD Artistic Impressions Retrospectives-R62
02UD Artistic Impressions Retrospect Gold-R62
02UD Artistic Impress Retrospect Silver-R62
02UD Honor Roll-50
02UD Piece of History-63
02UD Premier Collection-39
02UD Top Shelf-62
Triple Jerseys-HTGHB
02Upper Deck-122
Exclusives-122
Blow-Ups-C28
Patch Card Logo-MH
02Upper Deck Classic Portraits-69
02Upper Deck MVP-127
Gold-127
Classics-127
Golden Classics-127
Overdrive-SO10
02Upper Deck Rookie Update-70
Jerseys-DHO
Jerseys Gold-DHO
02Upper Deck Victory-149
Bronze-149
Gold-149
Silver-149
National Pride-NP42
02Upper Deck Vintage-179
02Upper Deck Vintage-281
Green Backs-179
Tall Boys-T46
Tall Boys Gold-T46
02Vanguard-70
LTD-70
East Meets West-8
03BAP Memorabilia-47
Emerald-47
Gold-47
Ruby-47
Sapphire-47
Jerseys-GJ-20
Jersey Autographs-GJ-20
Stanley Cup Playoffs-SCP-9
03BAP Ultimate Memorabilia Autographs-61
Gold-61
03BAP Ultimate Mem Auto Jerseys-61
03BAP Ultimate Memorabilia Triple Threads-16
03Beehive-137
Variations-137
Gold-137
Silver-137
Jumbos-20
Jumbo Variations-20
Jerseys-JT33
Signatures-RF10
03Black Diamond-106
Black-106
Green-106
Red-106
Signature Gems-SG-22
Threads-DT-MH
Threads Green-DT-MH
Threads Red-DT-MH
Threads Black-DT-MH
03Bowman-18
Gold-18
03Bowman Chrome-18
Refractors-18
Gold Refractors-18
Xfractors-18
03Crown Royale-70
Blue-70
Retail-70
Lords of the Rink-15
03eTopps-30
03ITG Action-450
Jerseys-M160
Jerseys-M261
03ITG Used Signature Series-32
Gold-32
Autographs-MH
Autographs Gold-MH
Franchise-21
Franchise Autographs-21
Franchise Gold-21
Jerseys-23
Jerseys Gold-23
Jersey Autos-23
Jersey and Stick-23
Jersey and Stick Gold-23
Teammates-3
Teammates Gold-3
03McDonald's Pacific-36
Patches Silver-17
Patches Gold-17
Patches and Sticks-17
Saturday Night Rivals-6
03NHL Sticker Collection-95
03O-Pee-Chee-99
03OPC Blue-99
03OPC Gold-99
03OPC Red-99
03Pacific-238
Blue-238
Red-238
Main Attractions-10
03Pacific Calder-72
03Pacific Calder-153
Silver-72
03Pacific Complete-330
Red-330
03Pacific Exhibit-183
Blue Backs-183
Pursuing Prominence-9
03Pacific Heads-Up-69
Hobby LTD-69
Retail LTD-69
Fast Forwards-6
Fast Forwards LTD-6
03Pacific Invincible-69
Blue-69
Red-69
Retail-69
Afterburners-8
03Pacific Luxury Suite-43A
03Pacific Luxury Suite-43B
03Pacific Luxury Suite-43C
03Pacific Prism-133
Blue-133
Patches-133
Red-133
Retail-133
Paramount Prodigies-17
03Pacific Quest for the Cup-75
Blue-75
03Pacific Supreme-70
Blue-70
Red-70
Retail-70
03Pacific Toronto Fall Expo-5
03Parkhurst Rookie-20
Jerseys-GJ-28
Jerseys Gold-GJ-28
03Private Stock Reserve-186
Blue-186
Patches-186
Red-186
Retail-186
03Senators Postcards-12
03SP Authentic-62
Limited-62
10th Anniversary-SP16
10th Anniversary Limited-SP16
Breakout Seasons-B26
Breakout Seasons Limited-B26
Honors-H30
Honors Limited-H30
Sign of the Times-MHA
03SP Game Used-32
03SP Game Used-117
Gold-32
Gold-117
Authentic Fabrics-AFMH
Authentic Fabrics-DFHH
Authentic Fabrics-DFSH
Authentic Fabrics-QSAHL
Authentic Fabrics Gold-AFMH
Authentic Fabrics Gold-DFHH
Authentic Fabrics Gold-DFSH
Authentic Fabrics Gold-QSAHL
Limited Threads-LTMHO
Limited Threads Gold-LTMHO
Premium Patches-PPMH
Signers-SPSHA
Team Threads-TTSHL
Top Threads-SAHL
03SPx-67
03SPx-141
03SPx-157
Radiance-67
Radiance-141
Radiance-157
Spectrum-67
Spectrum-141
Spectrum-157
Fantasy Franchise-FF-EHJ
Fantasy Franchise-FF-HSL
Fantasy Franchise Limited-FF-EHJ
Fantasy Franchise Limited-FF-HSL
Origins-O-MH
Signature Threads-ST-MH
Style-SPX-HH
Style Limited-SPX-HH
Winning Materials-WM-MH
Winning Materials Limited-WM-MH
03Titanium-173
Hobby Jersey Number Parallels-173
Patches-173
Retail-173
Stat Masters-7
03Topps-99
03Topps-PP1
Blue-99
Gold-99
Red-99
Box Toppers-10
Topps/OPC Idols-II16
03Topps C55-10
Minis-10
Minis American Back-10
Minis American Back Red-10
Minis Bazooka Back-10
Minis Brooklyn Back-10
Minis Hat Trick Back-10
Minis O Canada Back-10
Minis O Canada Back Red-10
Minis Stanley Cup Back-10
Autographs-TA-MH
Relics-TRMH
03Topps Pristine-57
Gold Refractor Die Cuts-57
Refractors-57
Jersey Portions-PPJ-MHO
Jersey Portion Refractors-PPJ-MHO
Patches-PP-MHO
Patch Refractors-PP-MHO
Press Plates Black-57
Press Plates Cyan-57
Press Plates Magenta-57
Press Plates Yellow-57
03UD Honor Roll-60
03UD Honor Roll-102
Signature Class-SC11
03UD Premier Collection-39
NHL Shields-SH-MH
Signatures-PS-MAH
Signatures Gold-PS-MAH
Teammates-PT-OS
Teammates Patches-PT-OS
03Upper Deck-131
All-Star Class-AS-20
Big Playmakers-BP-MH
BuyBacks-99
BuyBacks-100
BuyBacks-101
BuyBacks-102
BuyBacks-103
BuyBacks-104
Canadian Exclusives-131
Franchise Fabrics-FF-MH
Gifted Greats-GG9
HG-131
Jerseys-UD-MH
Jersey Autographs-SJ-MH
Patches-PLG-MH
Patches-PNM-MH
Patches-PNR-MH
Team Essentials-TS-MH
Three Stars-TS2
03Upper Deck Classic Portraits-66
03Upper Deck Classic Portraits-112
03Upper Deck Classic Portraits-147
03Upper Deck Ice-63
Gold-63
Authentics-IA-MH
Breakers-IB-MH
Breaker Patches-IB-MH
Frozen Fabrics-FF-MH
Frozen Fabric Patches-FF-MH
Under Glass Autographs-UG-HA
03Upper Deck MVP-288
Gold Script-288
Silver Script-288
Canadian Exclusives-288
SportsNut-SN61
Talent-MT8
03Upper Deck Rookie Update-62
All-Star Lineup-AS4
Skills-SKMH
Super Stars-SSMH
03Upper Deck Trilogy-66
03Upper Deck Trilogy-116
Authentic Patches-AP9
Crest Variations-116
Limited-66
Limited-116
Limited Threads-LT25
Scripts-S2MH
Scripts Limited-S2MH
03Upper Deck Victory-130
Bronze-130
Gold-130
Silver-130
Freshman Flashback-FF30
Game Breakers-GB36
03Toronto Star-66
Foil-10
04Pacific-185
Blue-185
Red-185
Global Connection-7
04Pacific NHL All-Star Nets-1
Gold-1
04SP Authentic-61
04SP Authentic-131
Limited-61
Limited-131
Buybacks-112
Buybacks-113
Buybacks-114
Sign of the Times-DS-AH
Sign of the Times-DS-HH
Sign of the Times-QS-LKSN
Sign of the Times-FS-SEN
04UD All-World-71
Gold-71
Autographs-71
Dual Autographs-AD-MM
Quad Autographs-AQ-NAM
04UD Toronto Fall Expo Priority Signings-HO
04Ultimate Collection-75
Dual Logos-UL2-SH
Jerseys-UGJ-MH
Jerseys Gold-UGJ-MH
Patches-UP-MH
04Upper Deck-120
Big Playmakers-BP-HO
Canadian Exclusives-120
HG Glossy Gold-120
HG Glossy Silver-120
Jersey Autographs-GJA-HS
World's Best-WB22
World Cup Tribute-MH
World Cup Tribute-MGHOMI
04Swedish Pure Skills-77
Parallel-77
Professional Power-MH
05Be A Player-61
First Period-61
Second Period-61
Third Period-61
Overtime-61
Dual Signatures-HH
Dual Signatures-HR
Quad Signatures-OTWA
Signatures-MH
Signatures Gold-MH
Triple Signatures-BSH
Triple Signatures-HSN
05Beehive-6
05Beehive-245
Beige -6
Blue -6
Gold-6
Red -6
Matte-6
Matted Materials-MMHO
Matted Materials Remarkable-RMHO
Signature Scrapbook-SSHO
05Black Diamond-137
Emerald-137
Gold-137
Onyx-137
Ruby-137
05Hot Prospects-4
En Fuego-4
Red Hot-4
White Hot-4
05McDonalds Upper Deck-41
05Panini Stickers-8
05Parkhurst-20
Facsimile Auto Parallel-20
True Colors-TCATL
True Colors-TCATL
05SP Authentic-7
05SP Authentic-117
Limited-7
Limited-117
Octographs-OF
Sign of the Times Duals-DHK
Sign of the Times Triples-TKHL
05SP Game Used-6
Autographs-6
Gold-6
Authentic Fabrics-AF-HO
Authentic Fabrics Autographs-AAF-HO
Authentic Fabrics Dual-HK
Authentic Fabrics Dual Autographs-HK
Authentic Fabrics Gold-AF-HO
Authentic Fabrics Quad-KHLS
Authentic Patches Quad -KHLS
Authentic Fabrics Triple-SHA
Authentic Patches-AP-HO
Authentic Patches Autographs-AAP-HO
Authentic Patches Dual-HK
Authentic Patches Dual Autographs-HK
Authentic Patches Triple-SHA
SIGnificance-HO
SIGnificance Gold-S-HO
SIGnificance Extra-HK
SIGnificance Extra Gold-HK
Significant Numbers-SN-HO
05SPx-5
Spectrum-5
Winning Combos-WC-HH
Winning Combos-WC-MI
Winning Combos Autographs-AWC-HK
Winning Combos Gold-WC-HH
Winning Combos Gold-WC-MI
Winning Combos Spectrum-WC-HH
Winning Combos Spectrum-WC-MI
Winning Materials-WM-HO
Winning Materials Autographs-AWM-HO
Winning Materials Gold-WM-HO
Winning Materials Spectrum-WM-HO
Xcitement Superstars-XS-MH
Xcitement Superstars Gold-XS-MH
Xcitement Superstars Spectrum-XS-MH
05The Cup-4
Gold-4
Black Rainbow-4
Dual NHL Shields-DSHB
Dual NHL Shields Autographs-ADSKH
Emblems of Endorsement-EEHO
Honorable Numbers-HNHO
Limited Logos-LLMH
Masterpiece Pressplates-4
Noble Numbers Dual-DNNGH
Patch Variation-P4
Patch Variation Autographs-AP4
Property of-POMH
Scripted Numbers-SNTH
Scripted Numbers Dual-DSNKH
Scripted Numbers Dual-DSNSV
Scripted Swatches-SSHO
Signature Patches-SPMH
05UD Artifacts-70
05UD Artifacts-183
Blue-70
Blue-183
Gold-70
Gold-183
Green-70
Green-183
Pewter-70
Pewter-183
Red-70
Red-183
Auto Facts-AF-HS
Auto Facts Blue-AF-HS
Auto Facts Copper-AF-HS
Auto Facts Pewter-AF-HS
Auto Facts Silver-AF-HS
Gold Autographed-70
Gold Autographed-183
Remarkable Artifacts-RA-HO
Remarkable Artifacts Dual-RA-HO
Treasured Patches-TP-HO
Treasured Patches Autographed-TP-HO
Treasured Patches Dual-TPD-HO
Treasured Patches Dual Autographed-TPD-HO
Treasured Patches Pewter-TP-HO
Treasured Patches Silver-TP-HO
Treasured Swatches-TS-HO
Treasured Swatches Autographed-TS-HO
Treasured Swatches Blue-TS-HO
Treasured Swatches Copper-TS-HO
Treasured Swatches Dual-TSD-HO
Treasured Swatches Dual Autographed-TSD-HO
Treasured Swatches Dual Blue-TSD-HO
Treasured Swatches Dual Copper-TSD-HO
Treasured Swatches Dual Maroon-TSD-HO
Treasured Swatches Dual Pewter-TSD-HO
Treasured Swatches Dual Silver-TSD-HO
Treasured Swatches Maroon-TS-HO
Treasured Swatches Pewter-TS-HO
Treasured Swatches Silver-TS-HO
05UD PowerPlay-61
Rainbow-61
Power Marks-PMMH
05UD Toronto Fall Expo Priority Signings-PS-HO
05Ultimate Collection-5
Gold-5
Endorsed Emblems-EEHO
Jerseys Dual-DJKH
Marquee Attractions-MA5
Marquee Attractions Signatures-SMA5
National Heroes Jerseys-NHJHO
National Heroes Patches-NHPHO
Ultimate Achievements-UAHO
Ultimate Patches Dual-DPKH
Ultimate Signatures-USHO
Ultimate Signatures Pairings-UPKH
Ultimate Signatures Trios-UTKLH
05Ultra-11
Gold-11
Ice-11
Scoring Kings-SK23
Scoring Kings Jerseys-SKJ-HO
Scoring Kings Jersey Autographs-KAJ-HO
Scoring Kings Patches-SKP-HO
Scoring Kings Patch Autographs-KAP-HO
05Upper Deck-250
Big Playmakers-B-MHO
Goal Rush-GR11
Notable Numbers-N-MH
Patches-P-MH
Scrapbooks-HS21
Shooting Stars-S-MHO
05Upper Deck Hockey Showcase-HS31
05Upper Deck Showcase Promos-HS31
05Upper Deck Ice-7
Rainbow-7
Glacial Graphs-GGHO
05Upper Deck MVP-13
Gold-13
Platinum-13
05Upper Deck Rookie Update-5
05Upper Deck Trilogy-4
05Upper Deck Trilogy-147
Crystal-147
Honorary Patches-HP-HO
Honorary Patch Scripts-HSP-HO
Honorary Swatches-HS-HO
Honorary Swatch Scripts-HSS-HO
Ice Scripts-IS-HO
05Upper Deck Victory-137
05Upper Deck Victory-203
Black-137
Black-203
Gold-137
Gold-203
Silver-137
Silver-203
Blow-Ups-BU26
Game Breakers-GB29
05Swedish SHL Elitset-112
Gold-112
Playmakers-10
06Be A Player-113
Autographs-113
Profiles-PP16
Profiles Autographs-PP16
Signatures-MH
Signatures 10-124
Signatures 25-124
Signatures Duals-DKH
Signatures Trios-THKH
Up Close and Personal-UC30
Up Close and Personal Autographs-UC30
06Be A Player Portraits-7
Quadruple Signature Portraits-QHVHH
Signature Portraits-SPMH
06Beehive-97
Blue-97
Gold-97
Matte-97
Red Facsimile Signatures-97
Wood-97
06Black Diamond-88
Black-88
Gold-88
Ruby-88
Gemography-GMH
Jerseys-JMH
Jerseys Black-JMH
Jerseys Gold-JMH
Jerseys Ruby-JMH
Jerseys Black Autographs -JHO
06Flair Showcase-7
06Flair Showcase-104
06Flair Showcase-204
Parallel-7
Parallel-104
Parallel-204
Stitches-SSMH
06Fleer-12
Tiffany-12
Fabricology-FHO
Speed Machines-SM4
06Hot Prospects-5
Red Hot-5
White Hot-5
Hot Materials -HMMH
Hot Materials Red Hot-HMMH
Hot Materials White Hot-HMMH
06O-Pee-Chee-28
06O-Pee-Chee-606
Rainbow-28
Rainbow-606
Swatches-S-MH
06Panini Stickers-5
06SP Authentic-96
Limited-96
06SP Game Used-6
Gold-6
Rainbow-6
Authentic Fabrics Dual-AF2KH
Authentic Fabrics Dual Patches-AF2KH
Authentic Fabrics Triple-AF3ATL
Authentic Fabrics Triple Patches-AF3ATL
Authentic Fabrics Quads-AF4JHEG
Authentic Fabrics Quads Patches-AF4JHEG
06SPx-5
Spectrum-5
SPxcitement-X5
SPxcitement Spectrum-X5
SPxcitement Autographs-X5
Winning Materials-WMMH
Winning Materials Spectrum-WMMH
Winning Materials Autographs-WMMH
06The Cup Foundations-CQMH
06The Cup Foundations Patches-CQMH
06The Cup NHL Shields Duals-DSHKH
06UD Artifacts-96
06UD Artifacts-153
Blue-96
Blue-153
Gold-96
Gold-153
Platinum-96
Platinum-153
Radiance-96
Radiance-153
Autographed Radiance Parallel-96
Autographed Radiance Parallel-153
Red-96
Red-153
Treasured Patches Black-TSMH
Treasured Patches Blue-TSMH
Treasured Patches Gold-TSMH
Treasured Patches Platinum-TSMH
Treasured Patches Red-TSMH
Treasured Patches Autographed Black Tag
Parallel-TSMH
Treasured Swatches-TSMH
Treasured Swatches Black-TSMH
Treasured Swatches Blue-TSMH
Treasured Swatches Gold-TSMH
Treasured Swatches Platinum-TSMH
Treasured Swatches Red-TSMH
Treasured Swatches Autographed Black-TSMH
Tundra Tandems-TTHK
Tundra Tandems Black-TTHK
Tundra Tandems Blue-TTHK
Tundra Tandems Gold-TTHK
Tundra Tandems Platinum-TTHK
Tundra Tandems Red-TTHK
Tundra Tandems Dual Patches Red-TTHK
06UD Mini Jersey Collection-6
06UD Powerplay-5
Impact Rainbow-5
Power Marks-PMMH
Specialists-SMH
Specialists Patches-PMH
06Ultimate Collection Premium Patches-PS-MH
06Ultimate Collection Premium Swatches-PS-MH
06Ultra-10
Gold Medallion-10
Ice Medallion-10
06Upper Deck Arena Giveaways-ATL1
06Upper Deck-9
Exclusives Parallel-9
High Gloss Parallel-9
Game Jerseys-JMH
Game Patches-PMH
Generations Duals-G2HH
Generations Patches Dual-G2PHH
Masterpieces-9
Walmart Tins Oversize-9
06Upper Deck MVP-16
Gold Script-16
Super Script-16
International Icons-II3
Jerseys-OJHF
06Upper Deck Ovation-104
06Upper Deck Sweet Shot-5
Sweet Stitches-SSHO
Sweet Stitches Duals-SSHO
Sweet Stitches Triples-SSHO
06Upper Deck Trilogy-6
Combo Autographed Jerseys-CJHK
Combo Autographed Patches-CJHK
Honorary Scripted Patches-HSPMH
Honorary Scripted Swatches-HSSMH
Honorary Swatches-HSHO
06Upper Deck Victory-9
06Upper Deck Victory Black-9
06Upper Deck Victory Gold-9
06Upper Deck Victory GameBreakers-GB3
06Russian Sport Collection Olympic Stars-48
07Upper Deck Ovation-48
07Upper Deck Victory-77
Black-77
Gold-77
GameBreakers-GB29
Stars on Ice-SI27

Host, Charlie

96Denver University Pioneers-7

Hostak, Martin

90Flyers Postcards-10
90OPC Premier-44
90Pro Set-629
90Score Rookie/Traded-36T
90Upper Deck-542
French-542
91Bowman-233
91Stadium Club-337
91Upper Deck-473
French-473
91ProCards-285
92Swedish Semic Elitserien Stickers-236
93Swedish Semic Elitserien-206
94Finnish Jaa Kiekko-189
94Swedish Leaf-238
95Czech APS Extraliga-367
95Swedish Leaf-104
Face to Face-10
95Swedish Upper Deck-162
95Swedish World Championships Stickers-208
96Czech APS Extraliga-137
96Swedish Semic Wien-121
97Czech DS Stickers-70
97Swedish Collector's Choice-177
98Swedish UD Choice-145
99Swedish Upper Deck-147
00Swedish Upper Deck-132
SHL Signatures-MH
Top Playmakers-P6

Hostasek, Megan

06Ohio State Buckeyes Women-17

Hotham, Andrew

04Barrie Colts-23
04Erie Otters-12
05Erie Otters-15
06Erie Otters-17

Hotham, Greg

76Saginaw Gears-5
79Maple Leafs Postcards-12
83Penguins Heinz Photos-13
84Penguins Heinz Photos-12
88ProCards AHL-228
89ProCards AHL-118

Hotham, Scott

02Mississauga Ice Dogs-4
03Barrie Colts-11
04Barrie Colts-13

Hotz, Adrian

93Swiss HNL-480

Houck, Daniel

93Quebec Pee-Wee Tournament-1580

Houck, Paul

88ProCards IHL-20

Houda, Doug

85Medicine Hat Tigers-2
88Red Wings Little Caesars-9
89Red Wings Little Caesars-10
90O-Pee-Chee-410
90Score-11
Canadian-11
90ProCards AHL/IHL-479
91O-Pee-Chee-512
91Pro Set-81
French-81
91Score Canadian Bilingual-442
91Score Canadian English-442
91Topps-512
91Whalers Jr. 7-Eleven-15
92Whalers Dairymart-9
94Leaf-523
96Islander Postcards-6
97Be A Player-193
Autographs-193
Autographs Die-Cuts-193
Autographs Prismatic Die-Cuts-193
97Pacific Dynagon Best Kept Secrets-55
00Rochester Americans-10
02Rochester Americans-8
03Rochester Americans-1
04Rochester Americans-30

Houde, Eric

95Halifax Mooseheads-22
96Fredericton Canadiens-11
98Canadiens Team Issue-8
98Pacific-251
Ice Blue-251
Red-251
99Hamilton Bulldogs-5
00Chicago Wolves-10
00Utah Grizzlies-24
02German DEL City Press-285

Houde, Francois

93Quebec Pee-Wee Tournament-969

Houde, Marcel

51Bas Du Fleuve-41

Houde, Tommi

92Quebec Pee-Wee Tournament-770
93Quebec Pee-Wee Tournament-211

Houde-Brisson, Gabriel

03Drummondville Voltigeurs-8
04Chicoutimi Sagueneens-9
04Victoriaville Tigres-28

Houdek, Tomas

00Czech OFS-221
02Czech OFS Plus-84
03Czech OFS Plus-284

Hougen, Jim

82Medicine Hat Tigers-5

Hough, Mike

82Kitchener Rangers-20
83Fredericton Express-7
84Fredericton Express-12
85Fredericton Express-8
86Nordiques General Foods-11
86Nordiques McDonald's-11
86Nordiques Team Issue-10
86Fredericton Express-12
87Nordiques General Foods-15
87Nordiques Team Issue-13
87O-Pee-Chee Stickers-220
88Nordiques General Foods-18
88Nordiques Team Issue-35
88ProCards AHL-98
89Nordiques Team Issue-16
89Nordiques General Foods-13
89Nordiques Police-11
89O-Pee-Chee-266
90Bowman-174
Tiffany-174
90Nordiques Petro-Canada-11
90Nordiques Team Issue-11
90O-Pee-Chee-427
90Pro Set-247
90Pro Set-516
91Pro Set Platinum-217
91Bowman-144
91Nordiques Panini Team Stickers-9
91Nordiques Petro-Canada-10
91O-Pee-Chee-113
91Panini Stickers-254
91Parkhurst-150
French-150
91Pinnacle-194
French-194
91Pro Set-463
91Pro Set-582
French-463
French-582
91Score American-112
91Score Canadian Bilingual-112
91Score Canadian English-112
91Stadium Club-80
91Topps-113
91Upper Deck-562
French-562
92Bowman-178
92Durivage Panini-25
92Nordiques Petro-Canada-11
92O-Pee-Chee-392
92Panini Stickers-211
92Panini Stickers French-211
92Parkhurst-380
Emerald Ice-380
92Pinnacle-113
French-113
92Pro Set-154
92Pro Set-266
92Score-64
Canadian-64
92Stadium Club-434
92Topps-297
Gold-297G
92Ultra-175
93Donruss-122
93Durivage Score-45
93Leaf-247
93OPC Premier-482
Gold-482
93Pinnacle-402
Canadian-402
93PowerPlay-94
93Score-393
93Score-559
Gold-559
Canadian-393
Canadian-559
Canadian Gold-559
93Stadium Club-466
Members Only Master Set-466
First Day Issue-466
93Topps/OPC Premier-482
Gold-482
94Leaf-504
94OPC Premier-116
Special Effects-116
94Pinnacle-333
Artist's Proofs-333
Rink Collection-333
94Topps/OPC Premier-116
Special Effects-116
94Ultra-297
95Be A Player-122
Signatures-S122
Signatures Die Cuts-S122
96Pinnacle-76
Artist's Proofs-76
Foil-76
Premium Stock-76
Rink Collection-76
97Pacific Dynagon Best Kept Secrets-40
98Finest-83
No Protectors-83
No Protectors Refractors-83
Refractors-83
00Kitchener Rangers-14
04ITG Franchises Canadian-82
04ITG Franchises US East-351
Autographs-A-MHO

Houghton, Art

92Saskatchewan JHL-68

Houghton, Darren

91Air Canada SJHL-D13
92Saskatchewan JHL-79
01UK Hull Thunder-20

Houk, Rod

87Regina Pats-8
88Regina Pats-10
92Dayton Bombers-12

Houlder, Bill

87Capitals Kodak-34
88ProCards AHL-37
89Capitals Team Issue-7
90O-Pee-Chee-399
90Pro Set-417
90ProCards AHL/IHL-273
91ProCards-1
91Rochester Americans Postcards-11
92San Diego Gulls-11
93Donruss-8
93Leaf-315
93OPC Premier-403
Gold-403
93Parkhurst-272
Emerald Ice-272
93PowerPlay-4
93Score-639
Gold-639
Canadian-639
Canadian Gold-639
93Stadium Club-419
Members Only Master Set-419
First Day Issue-419
93Topps/OPC Premier-403
Gold-403
93Ultra-256
93Upper Deck-429
94Be A Player Signature Cards-43
94Lightning Postcards-11
94OPC Premier-92
Special Effects-92
94Pinnacle-206
Artist's Proofs-206
Rink Collection-206
94Topps/OPC Premier-92
Special Effects-92
94Ultra-4
94Ultra-362
94Upper Deck-183
Electric Ice-183
95Collector's Choice-243
Player's Club-243
Player's Club Platinum-243
95Lightning Team Issue-12
95Parkhurst International-464
Emerald Ice-464
95Upper Deck-475
Electric Ice-475
Electric Ice Gold-475
96Upper Deck-154
98OPC Chrome-46
Refractors-46
98Pacific-381
Ice Blue-381
Red-381
98Topps-46
O-Pee-Chee-46
99Pacific-372
Copper-372
Emerald Green-372
Gold-372

Ice Blue-372
Premiere Date-372
Red-372
00Upper Deck Vintage-207
01Upper Deck-331
Exclusives-331
03ITG Action-324

Houle, Adam
02Saskatoon Blades-10

Houle, Chris
02London Knights-22
03ECHL All-Stars-245

Houle, Daniel
01Quebec Remparts-14

Houle, Eric
93Amos Les Forestiers-9

Houle, Gerard
52Juniors Blue Tint-66

Houle, Jean-Francois
99Tallahassee Tiger Sharks-17
04Brampton Battalion-21
05Kingston Frontenacs-21

Houle, Kevin
86Sherbrooke Canadiens-20

Houle, Martin
02Cape Breton Screaming Eagles-2
03Cape Breton Screaming Eagles-31
04Cape Breton Screaming Eagles-1
04ITG Heroes and Prospects-91
Autographs-MH
04ITG Heroes/Prospects Toronto Expo '05-91
04ITG Heroes/Prospects Expo Heroes/Pros-91
06Be A Player-240
06Beehive-140
Matte-140
06Between The Pipes-37
Autographs-AMH
Emblems-GUE38
Emblems Gold-GUE38
Emblems Autographs-GUE38
Jerseys-GUJ38
Jerseys Gold-GUJ38
Jerseys Autographs-GUJ38
Numbers-GUN38
Numbers Gold-GUN38
Numbers Autographs-GUN38
Prospect Trios-PT04
Prospect Trios Gold-PT04
Shooting Gallery-SG07
Shooting Gallery Gold-SG07
06Hot Prospects-170
Red Hot-170
White Hot-170
06O-Pee-Chee-600
Rainbow-600
06SP Authentic-226
Limited-226
06The Cup Masterpiece Pressplates (Bee Hive)-140
06The Cup Masterpiece Pressplates (Marquee Rookies)-600
06The Cup Masterpiece Pressplates (SP Authentic)-226
06The Cup Masterpiece Pressplates (Ultimate Collection)-88
06UD Artifacts-252
06Ultimate Collection-88
06Upper Deck-481
Exclusives Parallel-481
High Gloss Parallel-481
Masterpieces-481
06Philadelphia Phantoms-9
06ITG Heroes and Prospects-32
Autographs-AMH
Complete AHL Logos-AHL10

Houle, Rejean
69Canadiens Postcards Color-11
70O-Pee-Chee-174
71Canadiens Postcards-8
71O-Pee-Chee-147
71Toronto Sun-151
72Canadiens Postcards-6
72Dimanche/Derniere Heure *-141
72O-Pee-Chee-210
72Sargent Promotions Stamps-125
74O-Pee-Chee WHA-41
74Team Canada L'Equipe WHA-9
75O-Pee-Chee WHA-84
76Canadiens Postcards-7
76O-Pee-Chee NHL-360
77Canadiens Postcards-8
77O-Pee-Chee NHL-241
77Topps-241
78Canadiens Postcards-8
78O-Pee-Chee-227
78Topps-227
79Canadiens Postcards-8
79O-Pee-Chee-34
79Topps-34
80Canadiens Postcards-8
80O-Pee-Chee-261
80Pepsi-Cola Caps-46
80Topps-261
81Canadiens Postcards-10
81O-Pee-Chee-183
81O-Pee-Chee Stickers-37
82Canadiens Postcards-9
82Canadiens Steinberg-7
82O-Pee-Chee-184
92Sport-Flash-10
92Sport-Flash Autographs-10
96Canadiens Postcards-12
02Canadiens AGF-NNO
03Parkhurst Original Six Montreal-34
Autographs-6
06Parkhurst-31
Autographs-31

Houle, Yvan
52Juniors Blue Tint-46

Hounsell, Samuel
04Victoriaville Tigres-18

House, Bobby
89Spokane Chiefs-11
907th Inn. Sketch WHL-190
917th Inn. Sketch WHL-208
91Star Pics-69
91Ultimate Draft-47
91Ultimate Draft French-47
92Brandon Wheat Kings-11
93Indianapolis Ice-13
94Indianapolis Ice-10
94Classic Pro Prospects-219
96Albany River Rats-7
97Albany River Rats-5
99St. John's Maple Leafs-10
00St. John's Maple Leafs-12
01St. John's Maple Leafs-11
02German DEL City Press-92
03German DEL-108
04German DEL-124
04German Hamburg Freezers Postcards-4

House, Matt
99Guelph Storm-22

House, Tanner
05Penticton Vees-6
06Penticton Vees-13

Houseman, Gary
03St. Cloud State Huskies-12
04St. Cloud State Huskies-16
05St. Cloud State Huskies-13
05St. Cloud State Huskies-16

Housley, Phil
82Sabres Milk Panels-11
83NHL Key Tags-10
83O-Pee-Chee-65
83O-Pee-Chee Stickers-238
83Puffy Stickers-12
83Topps Stickers-238
84O-Pee-Chee-23
84O-Pee-Chee Stickers-203
84O-Pee-Chee Stickers-204
84Sabres Blue Shield-9
84Topps-18
85O-Pee-Chee-63
85O-Pee-Chee Stickers-173
85Sabres Blue Shield-13
85Sabres Blue Shield Small-13
85Topps-63
86O-Pee-Chee-154
86O-Pee-Chee Stickers-47
86Sabres Blue Shield-15
86Sabres Blue Shield Small-15
86Topps-154
87O-Pee-Chee-33
87O-Pee-Chee Minis-17
87O-Pee-Chee Stickers-151
87Panini Stickers-24
87Sabres Blue Shield-13
87Sabres Wonder Bread/Hostess-12
87Topps-33
88O-Pee-Chee-119
88O-Pee-Chee Stickers-255
88Panini Stickers-220
88Sabres Blue Shield-11
88Sabres Wonder Bread/Hostess-11
88Topps-119
89O-Pee-Chee-59
89O-Pee-Chee Stickers-261
89Panini Stickers-205
89Sabres Blue Shield-7
89Sabres Campbell's-9
89Topps-59
89Swedish Semic World Champ Stickers-156
90Bowman-239
Tiffany-239
90Jets IGA-15
90Kraft-18
90Kraft-85
90O-Pee-Chee-89
90O-Pee-Chee-262
90OPC Premier-45
90Panini Stickers-21
90Pro Set-21A
90Pro Set-21B
90Pro Set-364
90Pro Set-562
90Score-145
Canadian-145
90Score Hottest/Rising Stars-63
90Score Rookie/Traded-3T
90Topps-89
90Topps-262
Tiffany-89
90Upper Deck-22
90Upper Deck-435
French-22
French-435
91Pro Set Platinum-137
91Bowman-197
91Jets Panini Team Stickers-13
91Jets Panini Team Stickers-H
91Jets IGA-14
91Kraft-33
91O-Pee-Chee-395
91OPC Premier-50
91Panini Stickers-65
91Parkhurst-205
French-205
91Pinnacle-4
French-4
91Pro Set-267
91Pro Set-295
French-267
French-295
Puck Candy-30
91Score American-271
91Score Canadian Bilingual-491
91Score Canadian English-491
91Stadium Club-65
91Topps-395
Team Scoring Leaders-11
91Upper Deck-106
91Upper Deck-624
French-106
French-624
91Finnish Semic World Champ Stickers-133
91Swedish Semic World Champ Stickers-133
92Bowman-20
92Bowman-208
92Humpty Dumpty II-8
92McDonald's Upper Deck-8
92O-Pee-Chee-298
92OPC Premier Star Performers-16
92Panini Stickers-61
92Panini Stickers French-61
92Parkhurst-208
Emerald Ice-208
92Pinnacle-70
French-70
92Pro Set-212
Gold Team Leaders-14
92Score-299
92Score-440
Canadian-299
Canadian-440
92Seasons Patches-59
92Stadium Club-14
92Topps-268
92Topps-456
Gold-268G
Gold-456G
92Ultra-241
92Upper Deck-24
92Upper Deck-276
92Upper Deck-628
92Finnish Semic-149
93Donruss-294
93Leaf-61
93McDonald's Upper Deck-6
93OPC Premier-36
93OPC Premier-503
Gold-36
Gold-503
Black Gold-4
93Panini Stickers-133
93Panini Stickers-196
93Parkhurst-174
Emerald Ice-174
93Pinnacle-351
Canadian-351
All-Stars-25
All-Stars Canadian-25
93PowerPlay-271
93PowerPlay-427
93Score-232
93Score-482
93Score-520
Gold-520
Canadian-232
Canadian-482
Canadian-520
Canadian Gold-520
93Stadium Club-104
Members Only Master Set-104
OPC-104
First Day Issue-104
First Day Issue OPC-104
All-Stars-9
All-Stars Members Only-9
All-Stars OPC-9
93Topps/OPC Premier-36
93Topps/OPC Premier-503
Gold-36
Gold-503
93Topps Premier Black Gold-19
93Ultra-100
93Ultra-409
All-Stars-18
93Upper Deck-525
SP-136
93Upper Deck Locker All-Stars-26
93Swedish Semic World Champ Stickers-174
94Be A Player-R78
94EA Sports-145
94Finest-91
Super Team Winners-91
Refractors-91
94Fleer-30
94Hockey Wit-101
94Leaf-450
94Leaf Limited-77
94OPC Premier-353
94OPC Premier-491
Special Effects-353
Special Effects-491
94Parkhurst-197
Gold-197
94Parkhurst SE-SE30
Gold-SE30
94Pinnacle-410
Artist's Proofs-410
Rink Collection-410
94Select-146
Gold-146
94SP-19
Die Cuts-19
94Topps/OPC Premier-347
94Topps/OPC Premier-353
94Topps/OPC Premier-491
Special Effects-353
Special Effects-491
94Ultra-269
94Upper Deck-169
Electric Ice-169
SP Inserts-SP102
SP Inserts Die Cuts-SP102
95Bashan Super Stickers-16
95Be A Player-72
Signatures-S72
Signatures Die Cuts-S72
95Canada Games NHL POGS-56
95Collector's Choice-212
Player's Club-212
Player's Club Platinum-212
95Donruss-74
95Emotion-22
95Finest-7
Refractors-7
95Hoyle Western Playing Cards-35
95Imperial Stickers-16
95Kraft-13
95Leaf-141
95Metal-19
95Panini Stickers-241
95Parkhurst International-30
Emerald Ice-30
95Playoff One on One-17
95Playoff One on One-129
95Score-45
Black Ice Artist's Proofs-45
Black Ice-45
95Select Certified-86
Mirror Gold-86
95SkyBox Impact-22
95SP-19
95Stadium Club Members Only-45
95Stadium Club-145
Members Only Master Set-145
95Summit-40
Artist's Proofs-40
Ice-40
95Topps-166
OPC Inserts-166
95Topps SuperSkills-66
Platinum-66
95Ultra-25
Gold Medallion-25
95Upper Deck-294
Electric Ice-294
Electric Ice Gold-294
Special Edition-SE13
Special Edition Gold-SE13
95Zenith-104
95Swedish Globe World Championships-106
95Swiss HNL-543
96Black Diamond-96
Gold-96
96Collector's Choice-150
96Donruss-201
Press Proofs-201
96Fleer-59
Norris-5
96Fleer Picks-22
96Leaf-65
Press Proofs-65
96Maggers-39
96Metal Universe-164
96Pinnacle-19
Artist's Proofs-19
Foil-19
Premium Stock-19
Rink Collection-19
96Playoff One on One-429
96Score-153
Artist's Proofs-153
Dealer's Choice Artist's Proofs-153
Special Artist's Proofs-153
Golden Blades-153
96SkyBox Impact-140
BladeRunners-7
NHL on Fox-10
96SP-167
96Summit-121
Artist's Proofs-121
Ice-121
Metal-121
Premium Stock-121
96Ultra-176
Gold Medallion-176
96Upper Deck-357
96Swedish Semic Wien-161
97Collector's Choice-275
97Donruss-150
Press Proofs Silver-150
Press Proofs Gold-150
97Pacific-259
Copper-259
Emerald Green-259
Ice Blue-259
Red-259
Silver-259
97Pacific Omega-238
Copper-238
Dark Gray-238
Emerald Green-238
Gold-238
Ice Blue-238
97Revolution-146
Copper-146
Emerald-146
Ice Blue-146
Silver-146
97SP Authentic-168
98Be A Player-167
Press Release-167
98BAP Gold-167
98BAP Autographs-167
98BAP Autographs Gold-167
98BAP AS Milestones-M16
98Pacific-96
Ice Blue-96
Red-96
98Pacific Dynagon Ice-26
Blue-26
Red-26
98UD Choice-220
Prime Choice Reserve-220
Reserve-220
98Upper Deck-233
Exclusives-233
Exclusives 1 of 1-233
Gold Reserve-233
98Upper Deck MVP-29
Gold Script-29
Silver Script-29
Super Script-29
99Aurora-22
Premiere Date-22
99BAP Memorabilia-218
Gold-218
Silver-218
99Pacific-56
Copper-56
Emerald Green-56
Gold-56
Ice Blue-56
Premiere Date-56
Red-56
99Pacific Omega-37
Copper-37
Gold-37
Ice Blue-37
Premiere Date-37
99Panini Stickers-193
99Panini Stickers-345
99Paramount-39
Copper-39
Emerald-39
Gold-39
Holographic Emerald-39
Holographic Gold-39
Holographic Silver-39
Ice Blue-39
Premiere Date-39
Red-39
Silver-39
99Revolution-24
Premiere Date-24
Red-24
Shadow Series-24
99SPx-23
Radiance-23
Spectrum-23
99Upper Deck-195
Exclusives-195
Exclusives 1 of 1-195
99Upper Deck Gold Reserve-195
99Upper Deck MVP-30
Gold Script-30
Silver Script-30
Super Script-30
99Upper Deck Victory-50
99Wayne Gretzky Hockey-30
00BAP Memorabilia-203
Emerald-203
Ruby-203
Sapphire-203
Promos-203
00BAP Mem Chicago Sportsfest Copper-203
00BAP Memorabilia Chicago Sportsfest Blue-203
00BAP Memorabilia Chicago Sportsfest Gold-203
00BAP Memorabilia Chicago Sportsfest Ruby-203
00BAP Memorabilia Chicago Sun-Times Ruby-203
00BAP Memorabilia Chicago Sun-Times Gold-203
00BAP Mem Chicago Sun-Times Sapphire-203
00BAP Mem Toronto Fall Expo Copper-203
00BAP Memorabilia Toronto Fall Expo Gold-203
00BAP Memorabilia Toronto Fall Expo Ruby-203
00BAP Parkhurst 2000-P132
00BAP Signature Series-240
Emerald-240
Ruby-240
Sapphire-240
Autographs-146
Autographs Gold-146
Department of Defense-DD16
00Crown Royale Game-Worn Jerseys-4
00Crown Royale Game-Worn Jersey Patches-4
00Crown Royale Premium-Sized Jerseys-4
00O-Pee-Chee-120
00O-Pee-Chee Parallel-120
00Pacific-65
Copper-65
Gold-65
Ice Blue-65
Premiere Date-65
00Panini Stickers-120
00Paramount-35
Copper-35
Gold-35
Holo-Gold-35
Holo-Silver-35
Ice Blue-35
Premiere Date-35
00Revolution-22
Blue-22
Premiere Date-22
Red-22
00Stadium Club-78
00Titanium Game Gear-1
00Titanium Game Gear-67
00Titanium Game Gear Patches-67
00Topps/OPC-120
Parallel-120
1000 Point Club-PC11
00Topps Chrome-93
OPC Refractors-93
Refractors-93
1000 Point Club Refractors-11
00Topps Stars Game Gear-GGPH
00Upper Deck-255
Exclusives Tier 1-255
Exclusives Tier 2-255
00Upper Deck MVP-33
First Stars-33
Second Stars-33
Third Stars-33
00Upper Deck Victory-38
00Upper Deck Vintage-55
01Atomic Jerseys-5
01Atomic Patches-5
01BAP Memorabilia-171
01BAP Memorabilia-347
Emerald-171
Emerald-347
Ruby-171
Ruby-347
Sapphire-171
Sapphire-347
01Pacific-60
Extreme LTD-60
Hobby LTD-60
Premiere Date-60
Retail LTD-60
01Pacific Arena Exclusives-60
01Titanium Draft Day Edition-23
02BAP All-Star Edition-30
Jerseys-30
Jerseys Gold-30
Jerseys Silver-30
02BAP Signature Series-48
Autographs-48
Autograph Buybacks 1998-167
Autograph Buybacks 2000-146
Autographs Gold-48
02O-Pee-Chee-262
02O-Pee-Chee Premier Blue Parallel-262
02O-Pee-Chee Premier Red Parallel-262
02O-Pee-Chee Factory Set-262
02Pacific-77
Blue-77
Red-77
02Pacific Complete-150
02Pacific Complete-236
Red-150
Red-236
02Parkhurst-135
Bronze-135
Gold-135
Silver-135
02Topps-262
OPC Blue Parallel-262
OPC Red Parallel-262
Factory Set-262
02Topps Total-166
02Upper Deck Victory-47
Bronze-47
Gold-47
Silver-47
03NHL Sticker Collection-177
03O-Pee-Chee-131
03OPC Blue-131
03OPC Gold-131
03OPC Red-131
03Topps-131
Blue-131
Gold-131
Red-131
03Upper Deck-182
Canadian Exclusives-182
HG-182
03Upper Deck MVP-399
Gold Script-399
Silver Script-399
Canadian Exclusives-399
04ITG Franchises Canadian-2
Autographs-PH2
Complete Jerseys-CJ8
Complete Jerseys Gold-CJ8
Double Memorabilia-DM21
Double Memorabilia Gold-DM21
Memorabilia-SM27
Memorabilia Gold-SM27
Original Sticks-OS13
Original Sticks Gold-OS13
Teammates-TM3
Teammates Gold-TM3
04ITG Franchises US East-345
Autographs-A-PH1
04ITG Ultimate Memorabilia Complete Logo-32
04ITG Ultimate Memorabilia Triple Threads-6
06ITG International Ice-134
Gold-134
Autographs-APHO

Houston, Ken
77O-Pee-Chee NHL-274
78Flames Majik Market-6
78O-Pee-Chee-348
79Flames Postcards-6
79Flames Team Issue-7
79O-Pee-Chee-310
80Flames Postcards-6
80O-Pee-Chee-303
80Pepsi-Cola Caps-5
81Flames Postcards-7
82Capitals Team Issue-11
82O-Pee-Chee-366
82O-Pee-Chee Stickers-221
82Post Cereal-3
82Topps Stickers-221
83O-Pee-Chee-371
83O-Pee-Chee Stickers-200
83Topps Stickers-200

Hoverberg, Sture
64Swedish Coralli ISHockey-140

Hovi, Sasu
00Finnish Cardset-328
02Finnish Cardset-26
03Finnish Cardset-141
04Finnish Cardset-293
06Czech OFS Goalies I-10

Hovinen, Niko
06Finnish Cardset-235
Between the Pipes-9

Hovinheimo, Jaakko
66Finnish Jaakiekkosarja-142

Hovland, Lon
98Fayetteville Force-10

Howald, Patrick
92Finnish Semic-216
93Swedish Semic World Champ Stickers-117
93Swiss HNL-100
95Swedish Globe World Championships-214
95Swedish World Championships Stickers-129
95Swiss HNL-98
96Swiss HNL-40
96Swiss HNL-521
96Swiss HNL-568
98Swiss Power Play Stickers-41
99Swiss Panini Stickers-41
00Swiss Panini Stickers-41
00Swiss Slapshot Mini-Cards-SCB9
01Swiss HNL-134
02Swiss HNL-49

Howard, Dean
06Oshawa Generals-6

Howard, Jim
04SP Authentic Rookie Redemptions-RR11
04Maine Black Bears-24
05Beehive-119
Beige -119
Blue -119
Gold-119
Red -119
Matte-119
Signature Scrapbook-SSJH
05Black Diamond-207
Emerald-207
Gold-207
Onyx-207
Ruby-207
05Hot Prospects-235
En Fuego-235
Hot Materials-HMJH
Red Hot-235
White Hot-235
05Parkhurst-625
Facsimile Auto Parallel-625
Signatures-JH
05SP Authentic-155
Limited-155
Prestigious Pairings-PPLH
Rarefied Rookies-RRJH
Rookie Authentics-RAJH
Sign of the Times Triples-TLOH
Sign of the Times Fives-TWLDH
05SP Game Used-150
Autographs-150
Gold-150
Auto Draft-AD-JH
Game Gear-GG-JH
Game Gear Autographs-AG-JH
Rookie Exclusives-JH
Rookie Exclusives Silver-RE-JH
Significant Numbers-SN-JH
05SPx-175
Spectrum-175
05The Cup-136
Autographed Rookie Patches Gold Rainbow-136
Black Rainbow Rookies-136
Masterpiece Pressplates (Artifacts)-211
Masterpiece Pressplates (Bee Hive)-119
Masterpiece Pressplates (Black Diamond)-207
Masterpiece Pressplates (Ice)-112
Masterpiece Pressplates (MVP)-420
Masterpiece Pressplates (Power Play)-166
Masterpiece Pressplates (Rookie Update)-208
Masterpiece Pressplates SPA Autos-155
Masterpiece Pressplates (SP Game Used)-150
Masterpiece Pressplates SPx Autos-175
Masterpiece Pressplates (Trilogy)-189
Masterpiece Pressplates Ult Coll Autos-114
Masterpiece Pressplates (Victory)-290
Masterpiece Pressplates Autographs-136
Platinum Rookies-136
05UD Artifacts-211
Gold-RED11
05UD PowerPlay-166
05UD Rookie Class-30
05Ultimate Collection-114
Autographed Patches-114
Ultimate Debut Threads Jerseys-DTJJH
Ultimate Debut Threads Patches-DTPJH
Ultimate Signatures-USJH
Ultimate Signatures Pairings-UPLH
05Ultra-270
Gold-270
Fresh Ink-FI-JI
Fresh Ink Blue-FI-JI
Ice-270
Rookie Uniformity Jerseys-RU-JH
Rookie Uniformity Jersey Autographs-ARU-JH
Rookie Uniformity Patches-RUP-JH
Rookie Uniformity Patch Autographs-ARP-JH
05Upper Deck-215
HG Glossy-215
Rookie Ink-RIJH
05Upper Deck Rookie Showcase-RS11
05Upper Deck Rookie Showcase Promos-RS11
05Upper Deck Rookie Threads-RTHO
05Upper Deck Rookie Threads Autographs-ARTHO
05Upper Deck Ice-112
Premieres Auto Patches-AIPJH
05Upper Deck MVP-420
Gold-420
Platinum-420
05Upper Deck Rookie Update-208
Inspirations Patch Rookies-208
05Upper Deck Trilogy-189
05Upper Deck Toronto Fall Expo-215
05Upper Deck Victory-290
Black-290
Gold-290
Silver-290
05AHL Top Prospects-19
06Be A Player Portraits First Exposures-FEJH
06Between The Pipes-22
Autographs-AJH
Emblems-GUE36
Emblems Gold-GUE36
Emblems Autographs-GUE36
Jerseys-GUJ36
Jerseys Gold-GUJ36
Jerseys Autographs-GUJ36
Numbers-GUN36
Numbers Gold-GUN36
Numbers Autographs-GUN36
Shooting Gallery-SG06
Shooting Gallery Gold-SG06
The Mask-M31
The Mask Gold-M31
The Mask Silver-M31
06Black Diamond Gemography-GJH
06AHL Top Prospects-12
06ITG Heroes and Prospects Complete AHL Logos-AHL06
06ITG Heroes and Prospects Jerseys-GUJ03
06ITG Heroes and Prospects Jerseys Gold-GUJ03
06ITG Heroes and Prospects Emblems-GUE03
06ITG Heroes and Prospects Emblems Gold-GUE03
06ITG Heroes and Prospects Numbers-GUN03
06ITG Heroes and Prospects Numbers Gold-GUN03
06ITG Heroes and Prospects Net Prospects-NPR03
06ITG Heroes and Prospects Net Prospects Gold-NPR03

Howard, Simon
99UK Guildford Flames-16
04UK Milton Keynes Lightning-17

Howard, Steve
02Macon Trax-14
04Huntsville Havoc-4

Howarth, Brent
03Kelowna Rockets-11
04Kelowna Rockets-24
05Kelowna Rockets-14

Howarth, Kyle
05Prince Albert Raiders-14

Howarth, Todd
92Thunder Bay Thunder Hawks-16
93Thunder Bay Senators-9
94Thunder Bay Senators-1
95Thunder Bay Senators-9
98Wichita Thunder-9
99Wichita Thunder-8

Howatt, Garry
74NHL Action Stamps-164
74O-Pee-Chee NHL-375
75O-Pee-Chee NHL-54
75Topps-54
76O-Pee-Chee NHL-206
76O-Pee-Chee NHL-389
76Topps-206
77O-Pee-Chee NHL-194
77Topps-194
78O-Pee-Chee-29
78Topps-29
79Islanders Transparencies-16
79O-Pee-Chee-205
79Topps-205
80O-Pee-Chee-386
82O-Pee-Chee-140
82O-Pee-Chee Stickers-133
82Post Cereal-7
82Topps Stickers-133
83O-Pee-Chee-229
02Fleer Throwbacks-84
Gold-84
Platinum-84
04ITG Franchises US East-377
Autographs-A-GHO

Howden, Brett
02Owen Sound Attack-2

Howe, Corey
92North Dakota Fighting Sioux-9

Howe, Gordie
44Beehive Group II Photos-178A
44Beehive Group II Photos-178B
48Exhibits Canadian-44
48Exhibits Canadian-53
51Parkhurst-66
52Parkhurst-88
52Royal Desserts-8
53Parkhurst-50
54Parkhurst-41
54Parkhurst-92
54Topps-8
56Adventure R749-63
561956 Adventure Gum-63
57Topps-42
58Topps-8
59Topps-48
59Topps-63
60Parkhurst-20
60Shirriff Coins-42
60Wonder Bread Labels-1
60Wonder Bread Premium Photos-1
61Parkhurst-20
61Shirriff/Salada Coins-66
62El Producto Discs-3
62Parkhurst-30
62Parkhurst-31
62Shirriff Coins-54
62York Iron-On Transfers-19
63Chex Photos-26
63Parkhurst-55
63Topps-31
63Topps-58
63Toronto Star-20
63York White Backs-45
64Beehive Group III Photos-77A
64Beehive Group III Photos-77B
64Coca-Cola Caps-44
64Coca-Cola Caps-45A
64Topps-89
64Toronto Star-18
65Coca-Cola-43
65Topps-108
65Topps-122
66Topps-109
66Topps-121
66Topps USA Test-23
67General Mills-2
67Post Cereal Box Backs-1
67Post Cereal Box Backs-2
67Topps-43
67Topps-131
68O-Pee-Chee-29
68O-Pee-Chee-203
Puck Stickers-22
68Shirriff Coins-44
68Topps-29
69Equitable Sports Hall of Fame-3
69O-Pee-Chee-61
69O-Pee-Chee-193A
69O-Pee-Chee-193B
69O-Pee-Chee-215
Four-in-One-14
Stamps-14
69Topps-61
70Colgate Stamps-47
70Dad's Cookies-57
70Esso Power Players-134
70O-Pee-Chee-29
70O-Pee-Chee-238
Deckle-18
70Red Wings Marathon-5
70Sargent Promotions Stamps-56
70Topps-29
Topps/OPC Sticker Stamps-13
71Mattel Mini-Records-5
71O-Pee-Chee-262
O-Pee-Chee/Topps Booklets-23
71Topps-70
71Toronto Sun-96
71Finnish Suomi Stickers-382
71Swedish Hockey-198
72Finnish Semic World Championship-190
72Swedish Semic World Championship-190
73O-Pee-Chee WHA Posters-13
73O-Pee-Chee WHA Posters-14
74O-Pee-Chee WHA-1
75Houston Aeros WHA-4
75O-Pee-Chee WHA-66
75O-Pee-Chee WHA-100
76O-Pee-Chee WHA-50
76O-Pee-Chee WHA-72
77O-Pee-Chee WHA-1
77Sportscasters-206
77Sportscasters-6309
77Finnish Sportscasters-70-1670
77Finnish Sportscasters-07-168
79O-Pee-Chee-175
79Topps-175
81Red Wings Oldtimers-22
82Neilson's Gretzky-10
83Hall of Fame-16
83Hall of Fame Postcards-B6
85Hall of Fame-16
88Esso All-Stars-18
89Sports Illustrated for Kids I-214
90Pro Set-654
90Pro Set-660
90Whalers Jr. 7-Eleven-14
91Parkhurst PHC-PHC1
91Parkhurst PHC French-PHC1
91Pro Set-344
French-344
91Finnish Semic World Champ Stickers-238
91Swedish Semic World Champ Stickers-238
92Gartlin USA Gordie Howe-1
92Hall of Fame Legends-9
92Upper Deck Gordie Howe Heroes-19
92Upper Deck Gordie Howe Heroes-20
92Upper Deck Gordie Howe Heroes-21
92Upper Deck Gordie Howe Heroes-22
92Upper Deck Gordie Howe Heroes-23
92Upper Deck Gordie Howe Heroes-24
92Upper Deck Gordie Howe Heroes-25
92Upper Deck Gordie Howe Heroes-26
92Upper Deck Gordie Howe Heroes-27
92Upper Deck Gordie Howe Heroes-NNO
92Upper Deck Sheets-3
92Upper Deck Sheets-4
93Parkhurst Cherry's Playoff Heroes-D17
93Parkhurst Parkie Reprints-PR33
93Parkhurst Parkie Reprints-PR42
93Parkhurst Parkie Reprints-PR51
93Parkhurst Parkie Reprints-PR60
93Parkhurst Parkie Reprints Case Inserts-1
93Parkhurst Parkie Reprints Case Inserts-7
93Upper Deck Locker All-Stars-42
93Upper Deck Locker All-Stars-AU
94Hockey Wit-9
94Parkhurst Missing Link-43
94Parkhurst Missing Link-145
94Parkhurst Missing Link-160
94Parkhurst Missing Link-162
94Parkhurst Missing Link-171
Autographs-1
94Parkhurst Tall Boys-46
94Parkhurst Tall Boys-144
94Parkhurst Tall Boys-154
94Parkhurst Tall Boys-171
94Parkhurst Tall Boys-177
Autographs-A5
95SLU Timeless Legends *-4
95Parkhurst '66-67 Promos-5
95Parkhurst '66-67-42
95Parkhurst '66-67-126
95Parkhurst '66-67-142
95Parkhurst '66-67-PR42
95Parkhurst '66-67-MHA1
95Parkhurst '66-67-MHA2
95Parkhurst '66-67-MHA3
95Parkhurst '66-67-MHA4
95Parkhurst '66-67-MHA5
95Parkhurst '66-67-MRH1
95Parkhurst '66-67-MRH2
95Parkhurst '66-67-MRH3
95Parkhurst '66-67-MRH4
95Parkhurst '66-67-MRH5
Coins-42
Coins-GH1
Coins-GH2
Coins-GH3
Coins-GH4
Coins-GH5
95Zeller's Masters of Hockey Signed-3
96SLU Canadian Timeless Legends-4
97Donruss Elite Back to the Future-8
97Donruss Elite Back to the Future Autos-8
97Highland Mint Legends Mint-Cards-1
97Highland Mint Legends Mint-Cards-2
97SP Authentic Mark of a Legend-M1
97SP Authentic Tradition-T1
98BAP AS Legend Gordie Howe-GH1
98BAP AS Legend Gordie Howe-GH2
98McDonalds Upper Deck Gretzkys Teammates-T2
98OPC Chrome Blast From the Past-7
98OPC Chrome Blast From Past Refractors-7
98Topps Blast From The Past-7
98Topps Blast From The Past Autographs-7
99Black Diamond A Piece of History-GH
99Black Diamond A Piece of History Double-GH
99Black Diamond A Piece of History Triple-GH
99Black Diamond Gordie Howe Gallery-GH1
99Black Diamond Gordie Howe Gallery-GH2
99Black Diamond Gordie Howe Gallery-GH3
99Black Diamond Gordie Howe Gallery-GH4
99Black Diamond Gordie Howe Gallery-GH5
99Black Diamond Gordie Howe Gallery-GH6
99Black Diamond Gordie Howe Gallery-GH7
99Black Diamond Gordie Howe Gallery-GH8
99Black Diamond Gordie Howe Gallery-GH9
99Black Diamond Gordie Howe Gallery-GH10
99SP Authentic Jersey Redemption-JGH
99SP Authentic Legendary Heroes-LH3
99SP Authentic Sign of the Times-HG
99SP Authentic Sign of the Times Gold-HG
99Upper Deck 500 Goal Club-500GH
99Upper Deck 500 Goal Club-500GH
99Upper Deck Century Legends-3
Century Collection-3
All Century Team-AC2
Century Artifacts-C7
Epic Signatures-GH
Epic Signatures 100-GH

Essence of the Game-E4
99Upper Deck Ovation Center Stage-CS6
99Upper Deck Ovation Center Stage-CS7
99Upper Deck Ovation Center Stage-CS8
99Upper Deck Ovation Center Stage-CS9
99Upper Deck Ovation Center Stage-CS10
99Upper Deck Ovation Center Stage-CS16
99Upper Deck Ovation Center Stage-CS17
99Upper Deck Ovation Center Stage-CS18
99Upper Deck Ovation Center Stage-CS19
99Upper Deck Ovation Center Stage-CS21
99Upper Deck Ovation Center Stage-CS26
99Upper Deck Ovation Center Stage-CS27
99Upper Deck Ovation Center Stage-CS28
99Upper Deck Ovation Center Stage-CS29
99Upper Deck Ovation Center Stage-CS30
99Upper Deck Ovation Super Signatures-SS2
99Upper Deck Ovation Super Signatures-SSG2
99Upper Deck Ovation Super Signatures-SSR2
99Upper Deck Ovation Super Signatures-SSRC
99Upper Deck PowerDeck-19
Auxiliary-19
Auxiliary 1 of 1-19
Time Capsule-T6
Time Capsule Auxiliary-T6
Time Capsule Auxiliary 1 of 1-T6
00BAP Ultimate Mem Gordie Howe No. 9-9-1
00BAP Ultimate Mem Gordie Howe No. 9-9-2
00BAP Ultimate Mem Gordie Howe No. 9-9-3
00BAP Ultimate Mem Gordie Howe No.9 Autos-9-1
00BAP Ultimate Mem Gordie Howe No.9 Autos-9-2
00BAP Ultimate Mem Gordie Howe No.9 Autos-9-3
00BAP Ultimate Mem Howe Retrospect Jersey-HL1
00BAP Ultimate Mem Howe Retrospect Jersey-HL2
00BAP Ultimate Mem Howe Retrospect Jersey-HL3
00BAP Ultimate Mem Howe Retrospect Jersey-HL4
00BAP Ultimate Mem Howe Retrospect Jersey-HL5
00BAP Ultimate Mem Howe Retrospect Jersey-HL6
00BAP Ultimate Mem Howe Retrospect Jersey-HL7
00BAP Ultimate Mem Howe Retro Jersey Auto-GH1
00BAP Ultimate Mem Howe Retro Jersey Auto-GH2
00BAP Ultimate Mem Howe Retro Jersey Auto-GH3
00BAP Ultimate Mem Howe Retro Jersey Auto-GH4
00BAP Ultimate Mem Howe Retro Jersey Auto-GH5
00BAP Ultimate Mem Howe Retro Jersey Auto-GH6
00BAP Ultimate Mem Howe Retro Jersey Auto-GH7
00BAP Ultimate Memorabilia NHL Records-R9
00BAP Ultimate Memorabilia Retro-Active-RA1
00BAP Ultimate Memorabilia Retro-Active-RA6
00BAP Ultimate Memorabilia Retro-Active-RA9
00SP Authentic Power Skaters-P3
00SP Authentic Sign of the Times-GH
00SP Authentic Sign of the Times-H/G
00SP Authentic Sign of the Times-HOG
00SP Game Used Patch Cards-P-GH
00SP Game Used Tools of the Game-GH
00SP Game Used Tools of the Game Excl-GH
00SP Game Used Tools of the Game Combos-C-HG
00SP Game Used Tools of the Game Combos-C-SH
00SP Game Used Tools of the Game Combos-C-YH
00Topps Heritage Arena Relics-DSA-GH
00Topps Heritage Arena Relics-HAA-GH
00Topps Heritage Autographs-HA-GH
00Topps Heritage Autoprotos-8
00UD Heroes-125
Game-Used Twigs-T-GH
Game-Used Twigs Gold-C-HY
Signs of Greatness-GH
00UD Reserve Buyback Autographs-118
00UD Reserve Buyback Autographs-119
00UD Reserve Buyback Autographs-120
00UD Reserve Buyback Autographs-121
00UD Reserve Buyback Autographs-122
00UD Reserve Buyback Autographs-123
00UD Reserve Buyback Autographs-124
00UD Reserve Buyback Autographs-125
00UD Reserve Buyback Autographs-126
00UD Reserve Buyback Autographs-127
00Upper Deck Legends-41
00Upper Deck Legends-47
Legendary Collection Bronze-41
Legendary Collection Bronze-47
Legendary Collection Gold-41
Legendary Collection Gold-47
Legendary Collection Silver-41
Legendary Collection Silver-47
Enshrined Stars-ES2
Epic Signatures-GH
Essence of the Game-EG8
Legendary Game Jerseys-JGH
Playoff Heroes-PH9
Supreme Milestones-SM2
01BAP Memorabilia 500 Goal Scorers-GS2
01BAP Sig Series 500 Goal Scorers-1
01BAP Sig Series 500 Goal Scorers Autos-1
01BAP Signature Series Vintage Autographs-VA-3
01BAP Signature Series Vintage Autographs-VA-4
01BAP Ultimate Mem All-Star History-20
01BAP Ultimate Memorabilia Autographs-19
01BAP Ultimate Mem Autographs Gold-19
01BAP Ultimate Memorabilia Cornerstones-4
01BAP Ultimate Memorabilia Decades-7
01BAP Ultimate Memorabilia Emblem Attic-7
01BAP Ultimate Mem 500 Goal Scorers-2
01BAP Ultimate Mem 500 Goal Scorers Autos-19
01BAP Ultimate Mem 500 Goal Jerseys/Stick-2
01BAP Ultimate Mem 500 Goal Emblems-2
01BAP Ultimate Memorabilia Gloves Are Off-2
01BAP Ultimate Memorabilia Name Plates-19
01BAP Ultimate Memorabilia Name Plates-33
01BAP Ultimate Mem Production Line-1
01BAP Ultimate Mem Production Line-4
01BAP Ultimate Mem Production Line-5
01BAP Ultimate Mem Prototypical Players-13
01BAP Ultimate Mem Prototypical Players-14
01BAP Ultimate Mem Prototypical Players-15
01BAP Ultimate Mem Retired Numbers-12
01BAP Ultimate Memorabilia Retro Trophies-2
01BAP Ultimate Mem Retro Teammates-3
01BAP Ultimate Mem Stanley Cup Winners-28
01BAP Update Rocket's Rivals-RR-1
01BAP Update Tough Customers-TC32
01Greats of the Game-1
Retro Collection-1
Autographs-1
Sticks-4
01Parkhurst Autographs-PA12
01Parkhurst Autographs-PA26
01Parkhurst Autographs-PA36
01Parkhurst 500 Goal Scorers-PGS2
01Parkhurst He Shoots-He Scores Points-18
01Parkhurst He Shoots-He Scores Prizes-35
01Parkhurst Heroes-H2
01Parkhurst Reprints-PR1
01Parkhurst Reprints-PR12
01Parkhurst Reprints-PR30
01Parkhurst Reprints-PR58
01Parkhurst Reprints-PR71
01Parkhurst Reprints-PR76
01Parkhurst Reprints-PR140
01Parkhurst Vintage Memorabilia-PV13
01Parkhurst Vintage Memorabilia-PV14
01Parkhurst Vintage Memorabilia-PV15
01SP Authentic-99
Limited-99
Limited Gold-99
Buybacks-8
Buybacks-10
Sign of the Times-GH
Sign of the Times-GO
Sign of the Times-HY
Sign of the Times-HGY
01SP Game Used Authentic Fabric-AFGH
01SP Game Used Authentic Fabric-HGBL
01SP Game Used Authentic Fabric Gold-AFGH
01SP Game Used Inked Sweaters-SGH
01SP Game Used Inked Sweaters-DSHG
01SP Game Used Inked Sweaters-DSYH
01SPx Signs of Xcellence-GH
01UD Challenge 4 the Cup All-Time Lineup-AT3
01UD Honor Roll-3
01UD Honor Roll-33
Original Six-OS3
01UD Premier Collection-19
Dual Jerseys-DHG
Dual Jerseys Black-DHG
Jerseys-GGH
Jerseys Black-G-GH
Signatures-GH
Signatures Black-GH
01UD Stanley Cup Champs-6
Sticks-S-GH
01Upper Deck Legends-15
01Upper Deck Legends-26
01Upper Deck Legends-91
01Upper Deck Legends-99
Epic Signatures-GH
Fiorentino Collection-FCGH
Jerseys-TTGH
Jerseys Platinum-TTGH
Sticks-PHGH
Sticks-PHMH
01Upper Deck Victory-391
01Upper Deck Victory-392
01Upper Deck Victory-393
01Upper Deck Victory-394
01Upper Deck Victory-395
01Upper Deck Victory-396
01Upper Deck Victory-397
01Upper Deck Victory-398
01Upper Deck Victory-399
01Upper Deck Victory-400
01Upper Deck Victory-401
01Upper Deck Victory-402
01Upper Deck Victory-403
01Upper Deck Victory-404
01Upper Deck Victory-405
01Upper Deck Victory-406
01Upper Deck Victory-407
01Upper Deck Victory-408
01Upper Deck Victory-409
01Upper Deck Victory-410
01Upper Deck Victory-411
01Upper Deck Victory-412
01Upper Deck Victory-413
01Upper Deck Victory-414
01Upper Deck Victory-415
01Upper Deck Victory-416
01Upper Deck Victory-417
01Upper Deck Victory-418
01Upper Deck Victory-419
01Upper Deck Victory-420
01Upper Deck Victory-421
01Upper Deck Victory-422
01Upper Deck Victory-423
01Upper Deck Victory-424
01Upper Deck Victory-425
01Upper Deck Victory-426
01Upper Deck Victory-427
01Upper Deck Victory-428
01Upper Deck Victory-429
01Upper Deck Victory-430
01Upper Deck Victory-431
01Upper Deck Victory-432
01Upper Deck Victory-433
01Upper Deck Victory-434
01Upper Deck Victory-435
01Upper Deck Victory-436
01Upper Deck Victory-437
01Upper Deck Victory-438
01Upper Deck Victory-439
01Upper Deck Victory-440
01Upper Deck Vintage Jerseys-SDGH
01Upper Deck Vintage Next In Line-NLHY
02BAP NHL All-Star History-20
02SP Authentic Sign of the Times-GH
02SP Authentic Sign of the Times-GW
02SP Authentic Sign of the Times-YH
02SP Authentic Sign of the Times-GHO
02SP Game Used-51
Signature Style-GH
02SPx-89
Spectrum Gold-89
Spectrum Silver-89
02UD Artistic Impressions-36
Gold-36
02UD Artistic Impressions Beckett Promos-36
02UD Artistic Impress Common Ground-CG9
02UD Artistic Impress Common Ground Gold-CG9
02UD Artistic Impressions Flashbacks-UD11
02UD Artistic Impressions Flashbacks Gold-UD11
02UD Artistic Impressions Great Depiction-GD9
02UD Artistic Impress Great Depiction Gold-GD9
02UD Artistic Impressions Retrospectives-R36
02UD Artistic Impressions Retrospect Gold-R36
02UD Artistic Impress Retrospect Auto-R36
02UD Artistic Impress Retrospect Silver-R36
02UD Chicago National Spokesmen-N10
02Upper Deck Collectors Club-NHL2
02UD Foundations-23
02UD Foundations-36
02UD Foundations-38
02UD Foundations-102
02UD Foundations-104
1000 Point Club-HO
Signs of Greatness-SGGH
02UD Honor Roll Signature Class-GH
02UD Piece of History-19
02UD Piece of History-112
02UD Piece of History-113
02UD Piece of History-114
Hockey Beginnings-HB4
Marks of Distinction-GH
Simply the Best-SB5
02UD Premier Collection-58A
Signatures Bronze-SGH
Signatures Gold-SGH
Signatures Silver-SGH
02UD Top Shelf Hardware Heroes-HHGLJ
02UD Top Shelf Milestones Jerseys-MGHLY
02UD Top Shelf Signatures-GH
02Upper Deck-187
Exclusives-187
Gifted Greats-GG9
Number Crunchers-NC4
Shooting Stars-SS6
Classic Portraits Mini-Busts-26
Classic Portraits Mini-Busts-27
Classic Portraits Mini-Busts-28
Classic Portraits Mini-Busts-29
Classic Portraits Mini-Busts-30
Classic Portraits Mini-Busts-31
Classic Portraits Mini-Busts-32
Classic Portraits Mini-Busts-33
Classic Portraits Mini-Busts-34
Classic Portraits Mini-Busts-35
MVP Prosign-GH
02Upper Deck National Convention *-N10
02Upper Deck Rookie Update-50
02Upper Deck Rookie Update-75
02Upper Deck Rookie Update-101
02Upper Deck Rookie Update-168
Autographs-GH
02Upper Deck USHL Gordie Howe-1
02Upper Deck Vintage Tall Boys-T66
02Upper Deck Vintage Tall Boys-T67
02Upper Deck Vintage Tall Boys-T68
02Upper Deck Vintage Tall Boys-T69
02Upper Deck Vintage Tall Boys-T70
02Upper Deck Vintage Tall Boys Gold-T66
02Upper Deck Vintage Tall Boys Gold-T67
02Upper Deck Vintage Tall Boys Gold-T68
02Upper Deck Vintage Tall Boys Gold-T69
02Upper Deck Vintage Tall Boys Gold-T70
02UD SuperStars *-81
Gold-81
Spokesmen-UD13
Spokesmen-UD28
Spokesmen Black-UD13
Spokesmen Black-UD28
Spokesmen Gold-UD13
Spokesmen Gold-UD28
03Beehive-69
Variations-69
Gold-69
Silver-69
Jumbos-11
Jumbo Variations-11
Signatures-RF5
Sticks Beige Border-BE29
Sticks Red Border-RE21
03Black Diamond Signature Gems-SG-13
03Canada Post-2
03SP Authentic Honors-H4
03SP Authentic Honors-H5
03SP Authentic Honors-H6
03SP Authentic Honors Limited-H4
03SP Authentic Honors Limited-H5
03SP Authentic Honors Limited-H6
03SP Authentic Sign of the Times-MH
03SP Authentic Sign of the Times-GMM
03SP Authentic Special Cuts-PROD
03SP Game Used Authentic Fabrics-DFHG
03SP Game Used Authentic Fabrics-DFYH
03SP Game Used Authentic Fabrics-QLGHL
03SP Game Used Authentic Fabrics Gold-DFHG
03SP Game Used Authentic Fabrics Gold-DFYH
03SP Game Used Authentic Fabrics Gold-QLGHL
03SP Game Used Limited Threads-LTMH
03SP Game Used Limited Threads Gold-LTMH
03SP Game Used Signers-SPSGH
03SP Game Used Team Threads-TTLGH
03SP Game Used Top Threads-LGHL
03SPx-102
Radiance-102
Spectrum-102
Fantasy Franchise-FF-HYZ
Fantasy Franchise-FF-LGH
Fantasy Franchise Limited-FF-HYZ
Fantasy Franchise Limited-FF-LGH
Style-SPX-HN
Style-SPX-HT
Style Limited-SPX-HN
Style Limited-SPX-HT
03UD Honor Roll Signature Class-SC12
03UD Premier Collection Legends-PL-MH
03UD Premier Collection Legends Patches-PL-MH
03UD Premier Collection Signatures-PS-MH
03UD Premier Collection Signatures Gold-PS-MH
03UD Toronto Fall Expo Priority Signings-GH
03Upper Deck BuyBacks-31
03Upper Deck BuyBacks-32
03Upper Deck BuyBacks-33
03Upper Deck BuyBacks-34
03Upper Deck BuyBacks-35
03Upper Deck BuyBacks-36
03Upper Deck Mr. Hockey-GH1
03Upper Deck Mr. Hockey-GH2
03Upper Deck Mr. Hockey-GH3
03Upper Deck Mr. Hockey-GH4
03Upper Deck Mr. Hockey-GH5
03Upper Deck Mr. Hockey-GH6
03Upper Deck Mr. Hockey-GH7
03Upper Deck Mr. Hockey-GH8
03Upper Deck Mr. Hockey-GH9
03Upper Deck Mr. Hockey-GH10
03Upper Deck Mr. Hockey-GH11
03Upper Deck Mr. Hockey-GH12
03Upper Deck Mr. Hockey-GH13
03Upper Deck Mr. Hockey-GH14
03Upper Deck Mr. Hockey-GH15
03Upper Deck Mr. Hockey-GH16
03Upper Deck Mr. Hockey-GH17
03Upper Deck Mr. Hockey-GH18
03Upper Deck Mr. Hockey-GH19
03Upper Deck Mr. Hockey-GH20
03Upper Deck Mr. Hockey-GH21
03Upper Deck Mr. Hockey-GH22
03Upper Deck Mr. Hockey-GH23
03Upper Deck Mr. Hockey-GH24
03Upper Deck Mr. Hockey-GH25
03Upper Deck Mr. Hockey-GH26
03Upper Deck Mr. Hockey-GH27
03Upper Deck Mr. Hockey-GH28
03Upper Deck Mr. Hockey-GH29
03Upper Deck Mr. Hockey-GH30
03Upper Deck Superstar Spotlight-SS15
03Upper Deck Classic Portraits-113
03Upper Deck Classic Portraits-137
Premium Portraits-PP-MH
03Upper Deck Ice Under Glass Autographs-UG-MH
03Upper Deck MVP ProSign-PS-GH
03Upper Deck Rookie Update-162
Top Draws-TD5
03Upper Deck Trilogy-32
03Upper Deck Trilogy-139
Crest Variations-139
Limited-32
Limited-139
Scripts-S3GH
Scripts-S3MH
Scripts-CSGH
Scripts-CSMH
Scripts-CSMH2
Scripts-CSMH3
Scripts-CSMH4
Scripts Limited-S3GH
Scripts Limited-S3MH
Scripts Red-S3MH
03Upper Deck Victory Freshman Flashback-FF50
04Upper Deck Sportsfest *-SF15
04Upper Deck National Convention *-TN14
04SP Authentic Buybacks-61
04SP Authentic Octographs-OS-ART
04SP Authentic Sign of the Times-ST-GH
04SP Authentic Sign of the Times-DS-HG
04SP Authentic Sign of the Times-DS-NH
04SP Authentic Sign of the Times-SS-ALS
04SP Authentic Sign of the Times-SS-ORG
04SP Authentic Sign of the Times-SS-RLW
04SP Game Used Hawaii Conference Patch-PPA6
04UD All-World-92
Autographs-92
04UD Legendary Signatures-40
AKA Autographs-AKA-GH
Autographs-GH
HOF Inks-HOF-GH
04UD Legends Classics-27
04UD Legends Classics-56
04UD Legends Classics-57
04UD Legends Classics-81
Gold-27
Gold-56
Gold-57
Gold-81
Platinum-27
Platinum-56
Platinum-57
Platinum-81
Silver-27
Silver-56
Silver-57
Silver-81
Jersey Redemptions-JY19
Signature Moments-M2
Signatures-CS2
Signatures-DC14
Signatures-TC7
Signatures-TC13
Signatures-QC2
Signatures-QC6
04Ultimate Collection-15
Buybacks-11
Buybacks-12
Buybacks-13
Jerseys-UGJ-GH
Jerseys Gold-UGJ-GH
Jersey Autographs-UGJA-GH
Patch Autographs-UPA-GHCN
Patch Autographs-UPA-WGGH
Signatures-US-GH
04Upper Deck-180
04Upper Deck-192
1997 Game Jerseys-GH
Big Playmakers-BP-GH
Canadian Exclusives-180
Canadian Exclusives-192
HG Glossy Gold-180
HG Glossy Gold-192
HG Glossy Silver-180
HG Glossy Silver-192
Jersey Autographs-GJA-GH
NHL's Best-NB-GH
Swatch of Six-SS-GH
Three Stars-AS14
04Upper Deck All-Star Promos-GH
04Upper Deck Sportsfest *-SF15
05Be A Player Dual Signatures-HO
05Be A Player Signatures-HO
05Be A Player Signatures Gold-HO
05Be A Player Triple Signatures-HGT
05Beehive-235
PhotoGraphs-PGGH
Signature Scrapbook-SSGH
05Black Diamond-185
Emerald-185
Gold-185
Onyx-185
Ruby-185
Gemography-G-GH
Gemography Emerald-G-GH
Gemography Gold-G-GH
Gemography Onyx-G-GH
Gemography Ruby-G-GH
05NHL Legends Medallions-9
05Parkhurst-500
Facsimile Auto Parallel-500
05SP Authentic-38
Limited-38
Exquisite Endorsements-EEGH
Immortal Inks-IIGH
Marks of Distinction-MDGH
Octographs-OH
Prestigious Pairings-PPHG
Six Star Signatures-SSHF
05SP Game Used Authentic Fabrics Dual-GH
05SP Game Used Authentic Fabric Dual Auto-GH
05SP Game Used Authentic Patches Dual-GH
05SP Game Used Authentic Patch Dual Autos-GH
05SP Game Used Game Gear-GG-GH1
05SP Game Used Game Gear-GG-GH2
05SP Game Used Game Gear Autographs-AG-GH1
05SP Game Used Signature Sticks-SS-GH1
05SP Game Used Signature Sticks-SS-GH2
05SP Game Used SIGnificance-GH
05SP Game Used SIGnificance Gold-S-GH
05SP Game Used SIGnificance Extra-GH
05SP Game Used SIGnificance Extra Gold-GH
05SP Game Used Significant Numbers-SN-GH
05SPx-103
Spectrum-103
Xcitement Legends-XL-GH
Xcitement Legends Gold-XL-GH
Xcitement Legends Spectrum-XL-GH
05The Cup-39
Gold-39
Black Rainbow-39
Hardware Heroes-HHGH1
Hardware Heroes-HHGH2
Masterpiece Pressplates-39
Patch Variation-P39
Patch Variation Autographs-AP39
Property of-POGH
Scripted Numbers-SNHH
Stanley Cup Titlists-TGH
05UD Artifacts-112
Blue-112
Gold-112
Green-112
Pewter-112
Red-112
Auto Facts Blue-AF-GH
Auto Facts Copper-AF-GH
Auto Facts Pewter-AF-GH
Auto Facts Silver-AF-GH
Gold Autographed-112
05UD Powerplay Power Marks-PMGH
05UD Toronto Fall Expo Priority Signings-PS-GH
05Ultimate Collection-34
Gold-34
Jerseys-JGH
Jerseys Dual-DJHY
Ultimate Achievements-UAGH
Ultimate Patches-PGH
Ultimate Patches Dual-DPHY
Ultimate Signatures-USGH
Ultimate Signatures Foursomes-UFGHLH
Ultimate Signatures Pairings-UPHG
05Upper Deck All-Time Greatest-21
05Upper Deck All-Time Greatest-70
05Upper Deck Notable Numbers-N-GH
05Upper Deck Hawaii Trade Conference Signature Supremacy *-SSP14
05Upper Deck Ice Glacial Graphs-GGGH
05Upper Deck MVP Monumental Moments-MM2
05Upper Deck Trilogy-109
Crystal-109
Crystal Autographs-109
Ice Scripts-IS-GH
Legendary Scripts-LEG-GH
Personal Scripts-PER-GH
05Upper Deck Victory-76
Black-76
Gold-76
Silver-76
Blow-Ups-BU13
06Beehive-204
5 X 7 Black and White-204
5 X 7 Dark Wood-204
PhotoGraphs-PGGH
Signature Scrapbook-SSGH
06Black Diamond-156B
Gold-156B
Ruby-156B
Gemography-GGH
06Flair Showcase-229
06Flair Showcase-281
Parallel-229
Parallel-281
Hot Numbers-HN17
Hot Numbers Parallel-HN17
06Parkhurst-144
06Parkhurst-179
Autographs-144
Autographs-179
Autographs Dual-DAHL
06SP Authentic-64
06SP Authentic-114
Limited-64
Limited-114
Sign of the Times-STGH
Sign of the Times Duals-STHO
Sign of the Times Triples-ST3LGH
Sign of the Times Quads-ST4LOGH
06SP Game Used-34
Gold-34
Rainbow-34
Authentic Fabrics Eights-AF8HOF
Authentic Fabrics Eights Patches-AF8HOF
Autographs-34
Inked Sweaters-ISGH
Inked Sweaters Dual-IS2HH2
Inked Sweaters Dual Patches-IS2HH2
Legendary Fabrics-LFGH
Legendary Fabrics Autographs-LFGH
Letter Marks-LMHO
SIGnificance-SGH
06SPx-34
06SPx-126
Spectrum-34
Spectrum-126
SPxcitement-X33
SPxcitement Spectrum-X33
SPxcitement Autographs-X33
06The Cup-29
Autographed Foundations-CQGH
Autographed Foundations Patches-CQGH
Autographed Patches-29
Black Rainbow-29
Foundations-CQGH
Foundations Patches-CQGH
Enshrinements-EGH
Gold-29
Gold Patches-29
Honorable Numbers-HNGH
Jerseys-29
Limited Logos-LLGH
Masterpiece Pressplates-29
Property of-POGH
Scripted Swatches Duals-DSGH
Signature Patches-SPGH
Stanley Cup Signatures-CSGH
06UD Artifacts-143
Blue-143
Gold-143
Platinum-143
Radiance-143
Autographed Radiance Parallel-143
Red-143
Auto-Facts-AFHO
Auto-Facts Gold-AFHO
06UD Mini Jersey Collection-39
Jerseys-GH
Jersey Variations-GH
Jersey Variations-GH
Jersey Autographs-GH
06UD Toronto Fall Expo Priority Signings -PSGH
06Ultimate Collection-25
Jerseys Triple-UJ3-GHL
Patches Triple-UJ3-GHL
Signatures-US-GH
Ultimate Achievements-UA-GH
06Upper Deck Signatures-SGH
06Upper Deck Sweet Shot-41
Signature Shots/Saves-SSGH
Signature Shots/Saves Ice Signings-SSIGH
Signature Shots/Saves Sticks-SSSGH
Signature Sticks-STGH
06Upper Deck Trilogy Frozen In Time-FT6
06Upper Deck Trilogy Honorary Scripted Swatches-HSSGH
06Upper Deck Trilogy Honorary Swatches-HSGH
06Upper Deck Trilogy Ice Scripts-IGH
06Upper Deck Trilogy Legendary Scripts-LSGH
06Upper Deck Trilogy Scripts-S1GH
06Upper Deck Trilogy Scripts-S2GH
06Upper Deck Trilogy Scripts-TSGH
07Upper Deck Goudey Sport Royalty Autographs-GH
07Upper Deck Goudey Sport Royalty-GH

Howe, Mark

73O-Pee-Chee WHA Posters-14
74O-Pee-Chee WHA-1
74Team Canada L'Equipe WHA-10
75Houston Aeros WHA-6
75O-Pee-Chee WHA-7
76O-Pee-Chee WHA-95
77O-Pee-Chee WHA-25
77Sportscasters-6309
77Finnish Sportscasters-70-1670
79O-Pee-Chee-216
79Topps-216
80O-Pee-Chee-91
80O-Pee-Chee-160
80Topps-91
80Topps-160
81O-Pee-Chee-128
81O-Pee-Chee Stickers-62
81O-Pee-Chee Stickers-145
81Post Standups-11
81Topps-E82
82McDonald's Stickers-31
82O-Pee-Chee-252
82O-Pee-Chee Stickers-131
82Post Cereal-7
82Topps Stickers-131
83Flyers J.C. Penney-12
83NHL Key Tags-92
83O-Pee-Chee-267
83O-Pee-Chee Stickers-171
83O-Pee-Chee Stickers-195
83O-Pee-Chee Stickers-196
83Puffy Stickers-8
83Topps Stickers-171
83Topps Stickers-195
83Topps Stickers-196
84O-Pee-Chee-161
84O-Pee-Chee Stickers-109
84Topps-118
85Flyers Postcards-14
85O-Pee-Chee-35
85O-Pee-Chee Stickers-93
85 7-Eleven Credit Cards-14
85Topps-35
86Flyers Postcards-12
86O-Pee-Chee-123
86O-Pee-Chee Stickers-116
86O-Pee-Chee Stickers-184
86O-Pee-Chee Stickers-246
86Topps-123
86Topps Sticker Inserts-6
87Flyers Postcards-9
87O-Pee-Che-54
87O-Pee-Chee Minis-18
87O-Pee-Chee Stickers-100
87O-Pee-Chee Stickers-112
87O-Pee-Chee Stickers-176
87Panini Stickers-124
87Topps-54
87Topps Sticker Inserts-3
88Esso All-Stars-19
88Flyers Postcards-3
88O-Pee-Chee-6
88O-Pee-Chee Stickers-104
88O-Pee-Chee Stickers-124
88Panini Stickers-316
88Topps-6
89Flyers Postcards-12
89O-Pee-Chee-191
89O-Pee-Chee Stickers-109
89Panini Stickers-300
89Topps-191
89Swedish Semic World Champ Stickers-160
90Flyers Postcards-11
90Kraft-19
90O-Pee-Chee-185
90Panini Stickers-122
90Pro Set-217
90Score-220
Canadian-220
90Score Hottest/Rising Stars-92
90Topps-185
Tiffany-185
90Upper Deck-261
French-261
91Flyers J.C. Penney-12
91O-Pee-Chee-466
91Parkhurst-130
French-130
91Pinnacle-297
91Pinnacle-418
French-297
French-418
91Pro Set-182
French-182
91Score American-252
91Score Canadian Bilingual-472
91Score Canadian English-472
91Topps-466
91Finnish Semic World Champ Stickers-134
91Swedish Semic World Champ Stickers-134
92Panini Stickers-191
92Panini Stickers French-191
92Parkhurst-279
Emerald Ice-279
92Pinnacle-244
92Pinnacle-322
French-244
French-322
92Score-217
Canadian-217
92Ultra-285
92Upper Deck-530
93Leaf-259
93OPC Premier-157
Gold-157
93Pinnacle-235
93Pinnacle-254
Canadian-235
Canadian-254
93PowerPlay-329
93Score-91
Canadian-91
93Stadium Club-112
Members Only Master Set-112
OPC-112
First Day Issue-112
First Day Issue OPC-112
93Topps/OPC Premier-157
Gold-157
94Pinnacle-295
Artist's Proofs-295
Rink Collection-295
94Upper Deck NHLPA/Be A Player-25
02UD Foundations-26
02UD Foundations-37
02UD Foundations-73
Canadian Heroes-CMH
Canadian Heroes Gold-CMH
Canadian Heroes Silver-C-MH
Classic Greats-GMH
Classic Greats Gold-GMH
Classic Greats Silver-G-MH
Defense First-DMH
Defense First Gold-DMH
Defense First Silver-D-MH
Power Stations-SMH
Power Stations Gold-SMH
Power Stations Silver-S-MH
03SP Authentic Sign of the Times-GMM
04ITG Franchises Update Original Sticks-UOS7
04ITG Franchises Upd Original Sticks Gold-UOS7
04ITG Franchises US East-355
04ITG Franchises US East-424
Autographs-A-MH
04ITG Franchises US West-216
04ITG Ultimate Memorabilia Autographs-34
04ITG Ultimate Mem Autographs Gold-34
04UD Legendary Signatures-56
Autographs-MH
Rearguard Retrospectives-BMMH
05ITG Heroes/Prosp Toronto Expo Parallel -200
05ITG Ultimate Mem Cornerstones Jerseys-10
05ITG Ultimate Mem Cornerst Jerseys Gold-10
05ITG Ultimate Mem Sticks and Jerseys-17
05ITG Ultimate Mem Stick and Jerseys Gold-17
05ITG Heroes and Prospects-200
Autographs Series II-MH
Hero Memorabilia-HM-56
06ITG International Ice-76
Gold-76
Autographs-AMH

Howe, Marty

73O-Pee-Chee WHA Posters-14
74O-Pee-Chee WHA-1
74Team Canada L'Equipe WHA-11
75Houston Aeros WHA-6
75O-Pee-Chee WHA-15
76O-Pee-Chee WHA-15
77O-Pee-Chee WHA-65
77Sportscasters-6309
77Finnish Sportscasters-70-1670
79O-Pee-Chee-46
79Topps-46
83O-Pee-Chee-139
83O-Pee-Chee Stickers-54
83Topps Stickers-54
83Whalers Junior Hartford Courant-7
84O-Pee-Chee-71
84Topps-55
99Chicago Wolves-24
03SP Authentic Sign of the Times-GMM

Howe, Mike

04Minnesota Golden Gophers-12
05Minnesota Golden Gophers-13
06Minnesota Golden Gophers-11

Howe, Syd

33O-Pee-Chee V304A-24
33V357 Ice Kings-72
34Beehive Group I Photos-104
35Diamond Matchbooks Tan 1-29
37V356 Worldwide Gum-75
39O-Pee-Chee V301-1-72
83Hall of Fame-174
83Hall of Fame Postcards-M10
85Hall of Fame-174
04ITG Franchises US East-436
04ITG Franchises US West-297
04ITG Ultimate Memorabilia-135
Gold-135
Motown Heroes-4
05The Cup Legendary Cuts-LCSH
06ITG Ultimate Memorabilia Sensational Sens Autos-4

Howell, Harry

44Beehive Group II Photos-327
53Parkhurst-57
54Parkhurst-70
54Topps-3
57Topps-51
58Topps-60
59Topps-20
59Topps-54
60NHL Ceramic Tiles-9
60Shirriff Coins-86
60Topps-49
Stamps-27
61Shirriff/Salada Coins-89
61Topps-51
62Topps-46
Hockey Bucks-11
63Topps-48
64Beehive Group III Photos-134
64Coca-Cola Caps-74
64Topps-83
64Toronto Star-19
65Coca-Cola-75
65Topps-22
66Topps-90
66Topps USA Test-18
67General Mills-3
67Post Cereal Box Backs-3
67Post Cereal Box Backs-4
67Topps-84
67Topps-119
67Topps-121
68Bauer Ads-13
68O-Pee-Chee-69
68Shirriff Coins-103
68Topps-69
69O-Pee-Chee-79
69Topps-79
70Dad's Cookies-58
70Esso Power Players-93
70O-Pee-Chee-72
Deckle-37
70Sargent Promotions Stamps-134
70Topps-72
71O-Pee-Chee-153
71Sargent Promotions Stamps-71
71Toronto Sun-117
72O-Pee-Chee-193
72Sargent Promotions Stamps-90
81TCMA-6
83Hall of Fame-83
83Hall of Fame Postcards-F7
85Hall of Fame-83
90Upper Deck-511
French-511
91Kraft-73
91Ultimate Original Six-23
French-23
92Parkhurst Parkie Reprints-PR15
93Parkhurst Parkie Reprints Case Inserts-6
94Parkhurst Missing Link-96
94Parkhurst Tall Boys-92
95Parkhurst '66-67-80
Coins-80
01Greats of the Game-58
Autographs-58
01Topps Archives-4
01Topps Heritage Autographs-AHH
01Topps Heritage Salute-S4
02Parkhurst Reprints-183
02Topps Rookie Reprints-7
02Topps Rookie Reprint Autographs-7
03Parkhurst Original Six New York-45
03Parkhurst Original Six New York-77
03Parkhurst Original Six New York-86
03Parkhurst Original Six New York-92
Autographs-10
04ITG Franchises US East-392
Autographs-A-HH
04ITG Franchises US West-265
04ITG Ultimate Memorabilia-29
Gold-29
Autographs-31
Autographs Gold-31
05ITG Heroes/Prosp Toronto Expo Parallel -4
05ITG Heroes and Prospects-4
Autographs-A-HH
06Parkhurst-32
06Parkhurst-219
Autographs-32
Autographs-219

Howes, Scott

06Drummondville Voltigeurs-21

Howse, Don

76Nova Scotia Voyageurs-7
77Nova Scotia Voyageurs-10

Howse, Jason

91British Columbia JHL-124

Howse, Jon

01Peterborough Petes-8
02Peterborough Petes-8

Howson, Scott

82Indianapolis Checkers-10
84Springfield Indians-9

Hoyda, Dave

79Jets Postcards-9
79O-Pee-Chee-338
80O-Pee-Chee-332
81O-Pee-Chee-366

Hoyden, Riku

71Finnish Suomi Stickers-362

Hoyem, Dag

92Norwegian Elite Series-159

Hoyer, Scott

04Kelowna Rockets-19

Hoyle, Jimmy

28V128-2 Paulin's Candy-88

Hoyt, Chase

99Arizona Icecats-11

Hrabal, Josef

03Czech OFS Plus-361
04Czech OFS-249
05Czech HC Vsetin-5
06Czech HC Vsetin Postcards-3
06Czech OFS-182

Hrabec, Rob

99OCN Blizzard-2

Hrachovina, Petr

99Czech Score Blue 2000-131
99Czech Score Red Ice 2000-131

Hradecky, Jiri

99Czech OFS-77

Hradecky, Tomas

99Czech OFS-464
99Czech Score Blue 2000-126
99Czech Score Blue 2000-129
99Czech Score Red Ice 2000-126
99Czech Score Red Ice 2000-129
03Czech OFS Plus-374

Hranac, Jan

97Czech APS Extraliga-203
99Czech Score Blue 2000-90
99Czech Score Red Ice 2000-90
00Czech OFS-143
01Czech OFS-110
02Czech OFS Plus-194
03Czech OFS Plus-91
06Czech OFS-134

Hrazdira, Michal

04Czech OFS-368

Hrazdira, Richard

96Czech APS Extraliga-168
97Czech APS Extraliga-78
98Czech DS Stickers-88
98Czech OFS-274
99Czech DS-1
Goalies-G1
99Czech OFS-545
00Czech DS Extraliga-50
00Czech OFS-350
00Czech OFS Star Emerald-6
00Czech OFS Star Pink-6
00Czech OFS Star Violet-6

Hrbacek, Marcel

99Czech Score Blue 2000-164
99Czech Score Red Ice 2000-164

Hrbaty, Jan

69Swedish Hockey-30
70Finnish Jaakiekko-50
70Swedish Hockey-359
70Swedish Masterserien-11
74Swedish Stickers-120
94Czech APS Extraliga-292
95Czech APS Extraliga-175
96Czech APS Extraliga-310

Hrbek, Petr

92Finnish Semic-132
92Classic-39
Gold-39
93Classic Pro Prospects-67
94German DEL-381
95Finnish Semic World Championships-163
95Swedish Globe World Championships-160
96Czech APS Extraliga-180
97Czech APS Extraliga-90
97Czech DS Extraliga-47
97Czech DS Stickers-51
98Czech DS-45
98Czech DS Stickers-97
98Czech OFS-257
99Czech OFS-265
99Czech DS-124
99Czech OFS-44
00Czech DS Extraliga-118
00Czech OFS-105
00Czech OFS-313
02Czech OFS Plus-318

Hrdel, Zbynek

02Rimouski Oceanic-6
03Rimouski Oceanic-10
03Rimouski Oceanic Sheets-5
04Rimouski Oceanic-14
06Springfield Falcons-21

Hrdina, Jan

95Seattle Thunderbirds-11
96Cleveland Lumberjacks-12
96Cleveland Lumberjacks Multi-Ad-14
98Crown Royale-109
Limited Series-109
98Pacific Dynagon Ice-150
Blue-150
Red-150
Rookies-6

98Pacific Omega-200
Red-200
Opening Day Issue-200
98SP Authentic-106
Power Shift-106
98Upper Deck-345
Exclusives-345
Exclusives 1 of 1-345
Gold Reserve-345
99BAP Memorabilia-247
Gold-247
Silver-247
99BAP Millennium-195
Emerald-195
Ruby-195
Sapphire-195
Signatures-195
Signatures Gold-195
99Kraft Whiz Kid-3
99O-Pee-Chee-179
99O-Pee-Chee Chrome-179
99O-Pee-Chee Chrome Refractors-179
99Pacific-337
Copper-337
Emerald Green-337
Gold-337
Ice Blue-337
Premiere Date-337
Red-337
99Pacific Omega-187
Copper-187
Gold-187
Ice Blue-187
Premiere Date-187
99Paramount-188
Copper-188
Emerald-188
Gold-188
Holographic Emerald-188
Holographic Gold-188
Holographic Silver-188
Ice Blue-188
Premiere Date-188
Red-188
Silver-188
99Revolution-117
Premiere Date-117
Red-117
Shadow Series-117
99SPx-122
Radiance-122
Spectrum-122
99Stadium Club-129
First Day Issue-129
One of a Kind-129
Printing Plates Black-129
Printing Plates Cyan-129
Printing Plates Magenta-129
Printing Plates Yellow-129
Capture the Action-CA10
Capture the Action Game View-CAG10
99Topps Arena Giveaways-PIT-JH
99Topps/OPC-179
99Topps/OPC Chrome-179
Refractors-179
99Topps Gold Label Fresh Gold-FG17
99Topps Gold Label Fresh Gold Black-FG17
99Topps Gold Label Fresh Gold Black 1of1-FG17
99Topps Gold Label Fresh Gold One of One-FG17
99Topps Gold Label Fresh Gold Red-FG17
99Topps Gold Label Fresh Gold Red 1 of 1-FG17
99Upper Deck-106
Exclusives-106
Exclusives 1 of 1-106
99Upper Deck Gold Reserve-106
99Upper Deck MVP-169
Gold Script-169
Silver Script-169
Super Script-169
ProSign-JHR
99Upper Deck Victory-238
99Upper Deck Victory-354
99Wayne Gretzky Hockey-139
99Czech OFS-22
99Czech OFS Jagr Team Embossed-22
00Aurora-115
Premiere Date-115
00BAP Memorabilia-216
Emerald-216
Ruby-216
Sapphire-216
Promos-216
00BAP Mem Chicago Sportsfest Copper-216
00BAP Memorabilia Chicago Sportsfest Blue-216
00BAP Memorabilia Chicago Sportsfest Gold-216
00BAP Memorabilia Chicago Sportsfest Ruby-216
00BAP Memorabilia Chicago Sun-Times Ruby-216
00BAP Memorabilia Chicago Sun-Times Gold-216
00BAP Mem Chicago Sun-Times Sapphire-216
00BAP Mem Toronto Fall Expo Copper-216
00BAP Memorabilia Toronto Fall Expo Gold-216
00BAP Memorabilia Toronto Fall Expo Ruby-216
00BAP Parkhurst 2000-P18
00BAP Signature Series-25
Emerald-25
Ruby-25
Sapphire-25
00O-Pee-Chee-208
00O-Pee-Chee Parallel-208
00Pacific-327
Copper-327
Gold-327
Ice Blue-327
Premiere Date-327
00Paramount-197
Copper-197
Gold-197
Holo-Gold-197
Holo-Silver-197
Ice Blue-197
Premiere Date-197
00Private Stock-79
Gold-79
Premiere Date-79
Retail-79
Silver-79
PS-2001 Action-46
00Revolution-117
Blue-117
Premiere Date-117
Red-117
00Titanium Game Gear-132
00Titanium Game Gear Patches-132
00Titanium Draft Day Edition-81
Patches-81
00Topps/OPC-208
Parallel-208
00Topps Chrome-137
OPC Refractors-137
Refractors-137
00Upper Deck-140
Exclusives Tier 1-140
Exclusives Tier 2-140
00Upper Deck MVP-142
First Stars-142
Second Stars-142
Third Stars-142
00Upper Deck Victory-187
00Upper Deck Vintage-289
00Vanguard-79
Holographic Gold-79
Holographic Purple-79
Pacific Proofs-79
00Czech OFS-394
01Atomic Jerseys-44
01Atomic Patches-44
01BAP Memorabilia-139
Emerald-139
Ruby-139
Sapphire-139
01BAP Signature Series-23
Autographs-23
Autographs Gold-23
01O-Pee-Chee-201
01O-Pee-Chee Premier Parallel-201
01Pacific-311
Extreme LTD-311
Hobby LTD-311
Premiere Date-311
Retail LTD-311
Jerseys-26
01Pacific Adrenaline-152
Blue-152
Premiere Date-152
Red-152
Retail-152
01Pacific Arena Exclusives-311
01Pacific Heads-Up Quad Jerseys-17
01Private Stock Game Gear-76
01Private Stock Game Gear Patches-76
01Titanium Double-Sided Jerseys-31
01Titanium Double-Sided Jerseys-35
01Titanium Double-Sided Patches-35
01Topps-201
OPC Parallel-201
01Upper Deck-369
Exclusives-369
01Upper Deck MVP-151
01Upper Deck Victory-279
Gold-279
01Vanguard Memorabilia-24
02BAP First Edition-95
02BAP First Edition-388
Jerseys-95
02BAP Memorabilia-76
Emerald-76
Ruby-76
Sapphire-76
NHL All-Star Game-76
NHL All-Star Game Blue-76
NHL All-Star Game Green-76
NHL All-Star Game Red-76
02BAP Memorabilia Toronto Fall Expo-76
02BAP Signature Series-114
Autographs-114
Autograph Buybacks 1999-195
Autograph Buybacks 2001-23
Autographs Gold-114
02O-Pee-Chee-246
02O-Pee-Chee Premier Blue Parallel-246
02O-Pee-Chee Premier Red Parallel-246
02O-Pee-Chee Factory Set-246
02Pacific-308
Blue-308
Red-308
02Pacific Complete-294
Red-294
02Parkhurst-142
Bronze-142
Gold-142
Silver-142
02Parkhurst Retro-76
Minis-76
02Topps-246
OPC Blue Parallel-246
OPC Red Parallel-246
Factory Set-246
02Topps Total-351
02Upper Deck-387
Exclusives-387
02Upper Deck Beckett UD Promos-387
02Upper Deck MVP-147
Gold-147
Classics-147
Golden Classics-147
02Upper Deck Victory-174
Bronze-174
Gold-174
Silver-174
02Upper Deck Vintage-204
02Upper Deck Vintage-314
02Czech DS-24
02Czech DS-52
02Czech DS-66
02Czech Stadion Olympics-334
03Beehive-151
Gold-151
Silver-151
03Black Diamond-48
Black-48
Green-48
Red-48
03Coyotes Postcards-8
03NHL Sticker Collection-113
03Pacific-263
Blue-263
Red-263
03Pacific Complete-310
Red-310
03Topps Traded-TT49
Blue-TT49
Gold-TT49
Red-TT49
03Upper Deck-147
Canadian Exclusives-147
HG-147
03Upper Deck MVP-325
Gold Script-325
Silver Script-325
Canadian Exclusives-325
04Czech OFS-332
Stars II-2
04Czech Zuma-21
05Parkhurst-139
Facsimile Auto Parallel-139
05Upper Deck MVP-118
Gold-118
Platinum-118
06Czech OFS Jagr Team-15
06Czech NHL ELH Postcards-3
06Finnish Cardset-207

Hrdina, Jaroslav

82Swedish Semic VM Stickers-97

Hrdina, Jiri

83Swedish Semic VM Stickers-97
88Flames Postcards-15
89O-Pee-Chee Stickers-60
89O-Pee-Chee Stickers-97
90Flames IGA/McGavin's-5
90O-Pee-Chee-234
90Panini Stickers-182
90Pro Set-421
90Topps-234
Tiffany-234
90Upper Deck-292
French-292
91Bowman-82
91Flames Panini Team Stickers-3
91O-Pee-Chee-213
91Pro Set-461
French-461
91Score Canadian Bilingual-418
91Score Canadian English-418
91Stadium Club-36
91Topps-213
92Stadium Club-158
92Topps-272
Gold-272G
98Czech OFS Legends-13
00Czech OFS-416

Hrebejk, Stepan

01Czech OFS-138
02Czech OFS Plus-173
03Czech OFS Plus-258
04Czech OFS-392
05Czech HC Ceski Budejovice-4
06Czech OFS-4

Hreben, Vratislav

99Czech Score Blue 2000-55
99Czech Score Red Ice 2000-55

Hrechkosy, Dave

74NHL Action Stamps-59
75O-Pee-Chee NHL-156
75O-Pee-Chee NHL-316
75Topps-156
75Topps-316
76O-Pee-Chee NHL-364

Hreuss, Michael

94German DEL-304
95German DEL-283
96German DEL-89
03Czech OFS Plus-366

Hriczov, Nick

97New Mexico Scorpions-15
98Bakersfield Condors-9

Hrina, Slavomir

01Czech OFS-60
02Czech OFS Plus-29

Hrivnak, Jim

89ProCards AHL-93
90Capitals Postcards-7
90Capitals Smokey-7
90O-Pee-Chee-9
90Pro Set-646
90Score-386
Canadian-386
90Topps-9
Tiffany-9
90ProCards AHL/IHL-216
91Bowman-305
91Capitals Kodak-10
91O-Pee-Chee-487
91Pro Set-509
French-509
91Stadium Club-264
91Topps-487
91Upper Deck-343
French-343
91ProCards-549
92Bowman-372
92Capitals Kodak-10
92Parkhurst-430
Emerald Ice-430
92Stadium Club-325
92Topps-18
Gold-18G
92Ultra-435
92Upper Deck-151
93Leaf-312
93Pinnacle-407
Canadian-407
93PowerPlay-428
93Score-201
93Score-563
Gold-563
Canadian-201
Canadian-563
Canadian Gold-563
93Stadium Club-421
Members Only Master Set-421
First Day Issue-421
93Ultra-410
94Milwaukee Admirals-10
00Finnish Cardset-102
01UK Manchester Storm Retro-15

Hrkac, Tony

87Blues Kodak-13
87Blues Team Issue-11
88Blues Kodak-10
88Blues Team Issue-11
88O-Pee-Chee-129
88O-Pee-Chee Minis-15
88O-Pee-Chee Stickers-19
88O-Pee-Chee Stickers-36
88O-Pee-Chee Stickers-129
88Panini Stickers-106
88Topps-129
89Nordiques Team Issue-17
89O-Pee-Chee-64
89O-Pee-Chee Stickers-25
89Panini Stickers-119
89Topps-64
90Bowman-172
Tiffany-172
90Nordiques Petro-Canada-12
90Nordiques Team Issue-12
90Panini Stickers-146
90Pro Set-248
90Score-256
Canadian-256
90Upper Deck-184
French-184
91Pro Set Platinum-105
91Bowman-141
91Nordiques Panini Team Stickers-10
91O-Pee-Chee-241
91OPC Premier-40
91Pro Set-205
French-205
91Score American-122
91Score Canadian Bilingual-122
91Score Canadian Bilingual-555
91Score Canadian English-122
91Score Canadian English-555
91Score Rookie/Traded-5T
91Sharks Sports Action-11
91Stadium Club-136
91Topps-241
91Upper Deck-56
French-56
92Score-407
Canadian-407
92Topps-524
Gold-524G
92Indianapolis Ice-15
92North Dakota Fighting Sioux-34
93Donruss-292
93Leaf-329
93Parkhurst-448
Emerald Ice-448
93Ultra-411
94Milwaukee Admirals-11
95Milwaukee Admirals-8
95Milwaukee Admirals Postcards-11
96Milwaukee Admirals-9
96Collector's Edge Ice-161
Prism-161
96Collector's Edge Ice Promos-PR6
98Pacific-210
Ice Blue-210
Red-210
99Upper Deck MVP SC Edition-5
Gold Script-5
Silver Script-5
Super Script-5
00BAP Signature Series-218
Emerald-218
Ruby-218
Sapphire-218
Autographs-178
Autographs Gold-178
01Pacific-5
Extreme LTD-5
Hobby LTD-5
Premiere Date-5
Retail LTD-5
01Pacific Arena Exclusives-5
01Parkhurst-360
01UD Mask Collection-6
Gold-6
02BAP First Edition-283
02BAP Sig Series Auto Buybacks 2000-178
02Pacific-15
Blue-15
Red-15
02Pacific Complete-245
Red-245
02Thrashers Postcards-6
02Topps Total-43
03ITG Action-97
03NHL Sticker Collection-8
03Milwaukee Admirals-8
03Milwaukee Admirals Postcards-11
04Milwaukee Admirals-29

Hromas, Karel

03Czech OFS Plus-168
04Everett Silvertips-8
05Everett Silvertips-13
06Czech OFS-81

Hronek, Lukas

01Czech OFS-1
01Czech OFS H Inserts-H1
02Czech DS-43
02Czech DS-64
02Czech DS-80
02Czech OFS Plus-237
Checklists-C5
02Czech OFS Plus Masks-M9
02Czech OFS Plus Trios-T13
03Czech OFS Plus-176
03Czech OFS Plus Insert H-H23
03Czech OFS Plus MS Praha-SE39
04Czech OFS-10
Goals-Against Leaders-10
Save Percentage Leaders-13
06Czech OFS-296

Hrooshkin, Dalen

99Muskegon Fury-29
00Louisiana Ice Gators-8

Hrstka, Ivo

94Czech APS Extraliga-20

Hrstka, Michael

04German Cologne Sharks Postcards-15

Hrubes, Milos

96Czech APS Extraliga-100
97Czech APS Extraliga-106
97Czech DS Extraliga-22
97Czech DS Stickers-271
98Czech DS Stickers-51

Hrubes, Roman

99Czech Score Blue 2000-2
99Czech Score Red Ice 2000-2

Hrudey, Kelly

81Indianapolis Checkers-10
82Indianapolis Checkers-11
83Islanders Team Issue-6
85Islanders News-26
85O-Pee-Chee-122
85O-Pee-Chee Stickers-79
85Topps-122
86Islanders Team Issue-18
86O-Pee-Chee-27
86O-Pee-Chee Stickers-212
86Topps-27
87O-Pee-Chee-119
87O-Pee-Chee Stickers-242
87Panini Stickers-90
87Topps-119
88Kings Postcards-6
88O-Pee-Chee-155
88O-Pee-Chee Stickers-109
88Panini Stickers-283
88Topps-155
89Kings Smokey-16
89O-Pee-Chee-166
89O-Pee-Chee-305
89O-Pee-Chee Stickers-149
89Panini Stickers-89
89Topps-166
90Bowman-144
Tiffany-144
90Kings Smokey-17
90O-Pee-Chee-103
90Panini Stickers-246
90Pro Set-119
90Score-115
Canadian-115
90Score Hottest/Rising Stars-55
90Topps-103
Tiffany-103
90Upper Deck-231
French-231
91Pro Set Platinum-54
91Bowman-183
91Kings Upper Deck Season Ticket-NNO
91O-Pee-Chee-195
91Panini Stickers-81
91Parkhurst-71
French-71
91Pinnacle-39
French-39
91Pro Set-102
French-102
Platinum PC-PC6
91Score American-231
91Score Canadian Bilingual-451
91Score Canadian English-451
91Stadium Club-120
91Topps-195
91Upper Deck-262
French-262
92Bowman-42
92Kraft-33
92O-Pee-Chee-44
92Panini Stickers-63
92Panini Stickers French-63
92Parkhurst-66
Emerald Ice-66
92Pinnacle-19
French-19
92Pro Set-70
92Score-155
Canadian-155
92Seasons Patches-12
92Stadium Club-391
92Topps-29
Gold-29G
92Ultra-84
92Upper Deck-270
93Donruss-161
93Kraft-55
93Leaf-39
93OPC Premier-471
Gold-471
93Panini Stickers-210
93Parkhurst-97
Emerald Ice-97
93Pinnacle-252
Canadian-252
93PowerPlay-117
93Score-140
Canadian-140
93Stadium Club-54
Members Only Master Set-54
OPC-54
First Day Issue-54
First Day Issue OPC-54
93Topps/OPC Premier-471
Gold-471
93Ultra-131
93Upper Deck-216
SP-71
94Be A Player 99 All-Stars-G13
94Be A Player Signature Cards-140
94Canada Games NHL POGS-282
94Donruss-207
94EA Sports-66
94Flair-80
94Fleer-95
94Hockey Wit-93
94Kraft-42
94Leaf-189
94OPC Premier-462
Special Effects-462
94Parkhurst SE-SE81
Gold-SE81
94Pinnacle-292
Artist's Proofs-292
Rink Collection-292
Masks-MA3
94Score-145
Gold-145
Platinum-145
94Select-34
Gold-34
94Stadium Club-208
Members Only Master Set-208
First Day Issue-208
Super Team Winner Cards-208
94Topps/OPC Premier-462
Special Effects-462
94Ultra-99
94Upper Deck-432
Electric Ice-432
95Bashan Super Stickers-61
95Canada Games NHL POGS-143
95Collector's Choice-147
Player's Club-147
Player's Club Platinum-147
95Donruss-215
95Imperial Stickers-61
95Kraft-36
95Panini Stickers-276
95Parkhurst International-103
Emerald Ice-103
95Pinnacle-122
Artist's Proofs-122
Rink Collection-122
95Playoff One on One-270
95Post Upper Deck-19
95Score-198
Black Ice Artist's Proofs-198
Black Ice-198
95Select Certified-65
Mirror Gold-65
95Stadium Club-8
Members Only Master Set-8
95Summit-55
Artist's Proofs-55
Ice-55
95Topps SuperSkills-87
Platinum-87
95Ultra-75
Gold Medallion-75
95Upper Deck-145
Electric Ice-145
Electric Ice Gold-145
95Zenith-55
96Be A Player-45
Autographs-45
Autographs Silver-45
96Black Diamond-62
Gold-62
96Donruss-209
Press Proofs-209
96Donruss Canadian Ice-36
Gold Press Proofs-36
Red Press Proofs-36
96Donruss Elite-60
Die Cut Stars-60
96Leaf-109
Press Proofs-109
96Leaf Preferred-39
Press Proofs-39
96Maggers-40
96Metal Universe-136
96Pinnacle-120
Artist's Proofs-120
Foil-120
Premium Stock-120
Rink Collection-120
Masks-10
Masks Die Cuts-10
96Pinnacle Fantasy-NNO1
96Pinnacle Fantasy-NNO2
96Pinnacle Fantasy-NNO3
96Playoff One on One-367
96Score-68
Artist's Proofs-68
Dealer's Choice Artist's Proofs-68
Special Artist's Proofs-68
Golden Blades-68
96Select Certified-87
Artist's Proofs-87
Blue-87
Mirror Blue-87
Mirror Gold-87
Mirror Red-87
Red-87
96SP-141
96Summit-126
Artist's Proofs-126
Ice-126
Metal-126
Premium Stock-126
96Ultra-150
Gold Medallion-150
96Upper Deck-330
96Zenith-57
Artist's Proofs-57
97Donruss-92
Press Proofs Silver-92
Press Proofs Gold-92
Limited Fabric of the Game-27
97Donruss Priority-85
Stamp of Approval-85
97Pacific-337
Copper-337
Emerald Green-337
Ice Blue-337
Red-337
Silver-337
97Pinnacle Inside Stand Up Guys-10A/B
97Pinnacle Inside Stand Up Guys-10C/D
97Pinnacle Inside Stand Up Guys Promos-10A/B
97Pinnacle Inside Stand Up Guys Promos-10C/D
97Score-50
Artist's Proofs-50
Golden Blades-50
97Sharks Fleer All-Star Sheet-2
98NHL Aces Playing Cards-19
98Pacific-382
Ice Blue-382
Red-382
01Saskatoon Blades-16
06Parkhurst-35
Autographs-35

Hruska, David

95Red Deer Rebels-7
96Czech APS Extraliga-234
99Czech OFS-314
00Czech DS Extraliga-130
00Czech OFS-175
01Czech OFS Update-288
01Czech OFS-158
02Czech DS-39
02Czech OFS Plus-238
03Czech OFS Plus-177
03Czech OFS Plus Insert H-H25
04Czech HC Slavia Praha Postcards-16
04Czech OFS-163
Goals Leaders-14
05Czech HC Slavia Praha-8
06Czech HC Slavia Praha Postcards-9
06Czech OFS-297

Hruska, Milan

03P.E.I. Rocket-8

Hruska, Ondrej

01Czech HC Vsetin-6
06Czech HC Liberec Postcards-2
06Czech OFS-89

Hruska, Radim

03Czech OFS Plus-29
05Czech HC Vsetin-7

Hrycuik, Jim

74Capitals White Borders-11
74NHL Action Stamps-322

Hrycuik, Tony

92British Columbia JHL-144

Hrycun, Kelly

96Alaska Gold Kings-7
97Bakersfield Fog-5
98Bakersfield Condors-10

Hrynewich, Steve

83Ottawa 67's-13
84Ottawa 67's-12

Hryniuk, Brett

92North Dakota Fighting Sioux-10

Hrytsak, Rob

91Johnstown Chiefs-15

Hsin, Cheng

79Panini Stickers-359

Huard, Bill

89Nashville Knights-9
90ProCards AHL/IHL-566
91ProCards-414
93Parkhurst-414
Emerald Ice-414
93Senators Kraft Sheets-10
93Upper Deck-485
94Senators Team Issue-15
96Stars Postcards-11
97Be A Player-31
Autographs-31
Autographs Die-Cuts-31
Autographs Prismatic Die-Cuts-31

Huard, Sebastien

93Quebec Pee-Wee Tournament-209

Huard, Stephane

917th Inn. Sketch QMJHL-16

Hub, Jaroslav

94Czech APS Extraliga-191
95Czech APS Extraliga-45
96Czech APS Extraliga-324
97Czech APS Extraliga-304
97Czech DS Extraliga-39
97Czech DS Stickers-162
98Czech DS Stickers-118
98Czech OFS-72
99Czech DS-53
99Czech OFS-288

Hubacek, Jiri

99Czech OFS-327

Hubacek, Petr

98Czech OFS-127
99Czech DS-178
99Czech OFS-422
00BAP Memorabilia-454
Emerald-454
Ruby-454
Sapphire-454
00BAP Signature Series-257
Emerald-257
Ruby-257
Sapphire-257
Autographs-248
Autographs Gold-248
00SP Authentic-117
00SPx-168
00Stadium Club-255
00Topps Chrome-246
Blue-246
Red-246
OPC Refractors-246
OPC Refractors Blue-246
OPC Refractors Red-246
Refractors-246
Refractors Blue-246
Refractors Red-246
00Topps Heritage-74
Chrome Parallel-74
00Topps Premier Plus-133
Blue Ice-133
00Topps Stars-102
Blue-102
00UD Pros and Prospects-118
00UD Reserve-110
00Upper Deck-420
Exclusives Tier 1-420
Exclusives Tier 2-420
00Upper Deck Vintage-390
01BAP Memorabilia-185
Emerald-185
Ruby-185
Sapphire-185
02Czech OFS Plus-30
03Czech OFS Plus-5
04Czech OFS-226
05Czech HC Vitkovice-3
06Czech CP Cup Postcards-7
06Czech IIHF World Championship Postcards-9
06Czech LG Hockey Games Postcards-4
06Czech OFS-48
Brothers-4
Goals Leaders-12
Points Leaders-11

Hubacek, Radek

04Czech OFS-393
04Czech OFS-394
06Czech OFS-309
Brothers-4

Hubacek, Vladimir

01Czech OFS-85

Hubalek, Roman

91Knoxville Cherokees-14

Hubbard, Bill

93Omaha Lancers-10

Hubbauer, Matt

00UD CHL Prospects-61
02Regina Pats-4
03Atlantic City Boardwalk Bullies-11
04Atlantic City Boardwalk Bullies Kinko's-17

Huber, John

75Roanoke Valley Rebels-9

Huber, Paul

94German First League-268

Huber, Phil

87Kamloops Blazers-9
88Kamloops Blazers-13
89Kamloops Blazers-10
90Richmond Renegades-4
907th Inn. Sketch Memorial Cup-6
91ProCards-458
92Richmond Renegades-7
95Signature Rookies-38
Signatures-38
98German DEL-7
99German DEL-322

Huber, Willie

79O-Pee-Chee-17
79Red Wings Postcards-7
79Topps-17
80O-Pee-Chee-173
80Topps-173
81O-Pee-Chee-89
81O-Pee-Chee Stickers-126
81Topps-W89
82O-Pee-Chee-85
82O-Pee-Chee Stickers-185
82Post Cereal-5
82Topps Stickers-185
83NHL Key Tags-31
83O-Pee-Chee-246
83O-Pee-Chee Stickers-139
83Puffy Stickers-21
83Topps Stickers-139
87Canucks Shell Oil-9
87O-Pee-Chee-93
87O-Pee-Chee Stickers-31
87Panini Stickers-109
87Topps-93

Hubick, Greg

75Maple Leafs Postcards-11

Hubinette, Per-Arne

67Swedish Hockey-10
67Swedish Hockey-140
69Swedish Hockey-152
70Swedish Hockey-5
71Swedish Hockey-79
72Swedish Stickers-54

Hubinette, Torbjorn

67Swedish Hockey-119
69Swedish Hockey-133
70Swedish Hockey-92
71Swedish Hockey-184

Hubl, Jaroslav

02Czech OFS Plus-352
06Czech OFS-135
Team Cards-5

Hubl, Viktor

98Czech OFS-267
99Czech OFS-148
00Czech DS Extraliga-117
00Czech OFS-95
01Czech OFS-7
01Czech OFS-7
02Czech OFS Plus-343
03Czech OFS Plus-90
04Czech OFS-94
05Czech HC Ceski Budejovice-5
06Czech HC Ceske Budejovice Postcards-2
06Czech OFS-5

Hubloo, Willie

02Bossier-Shreveport Mudbugs-11

Huck, Fran

69Swedish Hockey-356
70Esso Power Players-6
70Swedish Masterserien-25
70Swedish Masterserien-34
70Swedish Masterserien-95
70Swedish Masterserien-187
72Blues White Border-6
73Topps-63
74Minnesota Fighting Saints WHA-13
74O-Pee-Chee WHA-28
75O-Pee-Chee WHA-121

Huckle, Jeff

91Air Canada SJHL-C24

Hucko, Patrik

94Czech APS Extraliga-189
96Czech APS Extraliga-56
97Czech APS Extraliga-322
97Czech DS Stickers-233
98Czech DS Stickers-271
98Czech OFS-20
99German DEL-263
00Finnish Cardset-136
01Czech OFS-115
02Czech OFS Plus-31
03Czech OFS Plus-318
05Swedish SHL Elitset-208
Gold-208

Hucul, Fred

44Beehive Group II Photos-108
51Parkhurst-45
52Parkhurst-26
53Parkhurst-71

Huczkowski, Hans

93Swedish Semic Elitserien-259
95Swedish Upper Deck 1st Division Stars-DS4
99Swedish Upper Deck-148
00Swedish Upper Deck-131
02Swedish SHL-65
Parallel-65
03Swedish Elite-86
Silver-86
04Swedish Elitset-78
Gold-78

Huczkowski, Miika

05Finnish Cardset -241
06Finnish Cardset-68

Hudacek, Vladimir

94Czech APS Extraliga-252
95Czech APS Extraliga-294
97Czech APS Extraliga-220
97Czech DS Extraliga-13
98Czech DS Stickers-27
98Czech OFS-286
99Czech DS-2
99Czech OFS-8
99Czech OFS-490
99Czech OFS-551
99Czech OFS-NNO
All-Star Game Blue-490
All-Star Game Gold-490
All-Star Game Red-490
All-Star Game Silver-490
99Czech OFS Goalie Die-Cuts-8
00Czech DS Extraliga-49
Goalies-G5
Valuable Players-VP1
00Czech OFS-349
00Czech OFS Star Emerald-4
00Czech OFS Star Pink-4
00Czech OFS Star Violet-4
01Czech DS-2
01Czech OFS Gold Inserts-G6
02Czech OFS Plus-174
02Czech OFS Plus All-Star Game-H7
02Czech OFS Plus Masks-M14
02Czech OFS Plus Trios-T1
02Czech OFS Plus Duos-D19
03Czech OFS Plus-259
03Czech OFS Plus Insert B-B9
03Czech OFS Plus Insert P-P13
04Russian Legion-13

Huddy, Charlie

81Oilers West Edmonton Mall-5
82Oilers Red Rooster-22
83NHL Key Tags-40
83Oilers McDonald's-9
83O-Pee-Chee-30
83O-Pee-Chee Stickers-96
83Topps Stickers-96
83Vachon-27
84Oilers Red Rooster-22
84Oilers Team Issue-8
84O-Pee-Chee-244
84O-Pee-Chee Stickers-258
847-Eleven Discs-17
85Oilers Red Rooster-22
85O-Pee-Chee-187
85O-Pee-Chee Stickers-216
86Oilers Red Rooster-22
86Oilers Team Issue-22
86O-Pee-Chee-211
86O-Pee-Chee Stickers-69
87Oilers Team Issue-22
87O-Pee-Chee-207
87O-Pee-Chee Stickers-87
87Panini Stickers-260
88Oilers Tenth Anniversary-45
88Oilers Team Issue-10
88O-Pee-Chee-218
88O-Pee-Chee Stickers-221
88Panini Stickers-53
89Kraft-12
89Oilers Team Issue-10
89O-Pee-Chee-158
89O-Pee-Chee Stickers-220
89Panini Stickers-82
89Topps-158
90Oilers IGA-8
90O-Pee-Chee-344
90Panini Stickers-221
90Pro Set-85
90Score-199
Canadian-199
90Topps-344
Tiffany-344
90Upper Deck-341
French-341
91Bowman-103
91Oilers Panini Team Stickers-7
91OPC Premier-125
91Panini Stickers-129
91Parkhurst-298
French-298
91Pinnacle-225
French-225
91Pro Set-400
French-400
91Score Canadian Bilingual-247

91Score Canadian Bilingual-570
91Score Canadian English-247
91Score Canadian English-570
91Score Rookie/Traded-20T
91Stadium Club-203
91Upper Deck-569
  French-569
92Pinnacle-143
  French-143
92Score-92
  Canadian-92
92Stadium Club-372
92Topps-279
  Gold-279G
92Ultra-308
93OPC Premier-219
  Gold-219
93Pinnacle-296
  Canadian-296
93PowerPlay-361
93Score-90
  Canadian-90
93Stadium Club-308
  Members Only Master Set-308
  First Day Issue-308
93Topps/OPC Premier-219
  Gold-219
93Ultra-344
94Be A Player 99 All-Stars-G11
94Pinnacle-178
  Artist's Proofs-178
  Rink Collection-178
96Rochester Americans-11
04ITG Franchises Canadian-29
  Autographs-CHU

Hudec, Michal
03Czech OFS Plus-41
05Czech HC Ceski Budejovice-6
06Czech HC Ceske Budejovice Postcards-3
06Czech OFS-6

Hudec, Stanislav
00Chicoutimi Sagueneens-10
  Signed-10
01Chicoutimi Sagueneens-5
04Czech OFS-227
05Czech HC Vitkovice-4
06Czech OFS-49
  All Stars-8
  Defenders-3

Hudgin, Daniel
99Hull Olympiques-9
  Signed-9
01Moncton Wildcats-5
02Moncton Wildcats-19

Hudler, Jiri
00Czech DS Extraliga-23
00Czech OFS-340
01Czech National Team Postcards-5
01Czech OFS-74
01Czech OFS Red Inserts-RE21D
02Czech DS-41
02Czech DS-62
02Czech OFS Plus-67
02Czech OFS Plus All-Star Game-H8
02Czech OFS Plus Trios-T20
02Czech OFS Plus Duos-D1
03BAP Memorabilia-195
  Emerald-195
  Gold-195
  Ruby-195
  Sapphire-195
  Super Rookies-SR15
  Super Rookies Gold-SR15
  Super Rookies Silver-SR15
03BAP Ultimate Memorabilia Autographs-98
  Gold-98
03Beehive-212
  Gold-212
  Silver-212
  Jumbo Variations-12
03Black Diamond-155
  Black-155
  Green-155
  Red-155
03Bowman-114
  Gold-114
03Bowman Chrome-114
  Refractors-114
  Gold Refractors-114
  Xfractors-114
03Crown Royale-116
  Red-116
  Retail-116
  Royal Portraits-4
03ITG Action-621
03ITG Toronto Spring Expo Class of 2004-5
03ITG Used Signature Series-139
  Autographs Gold-139
03ITG VIP Rookie Debut-44
03O-Pee-Chee-332
03OPC Blue-332
03OPC Gold-332
03OPC Red-332
03Pacific-364
03Pacific Calder-115
  Silver-115
03Pacific Complete-594
  Red-594
03Pacific Heads-Up-114
  Hobby LTD-114
  Retail LTD-114
  Prime Prospects-8
  Prime Prospects LTD-8
03Pacific Luxury Suite-87
  Gold-87
03Pacific Prism-156
03Pacific Quest for the Cup-115
  Calder Contenders-8
03Pacific Supreme-117
03Pacific Supreme-117A
  Blue-117
  Red-117
  Retail-117
03Parkhurst Original Six Detroit-22
03Parkhurst Rookie-158
03Private Stock Reserve-118
  Blue-118
  Red-118
  Retail-118
03SP Authentic-154
  Limited-154
  Signed Patches-JH
03SP Game Used-51
  Gold-51
  Rookie Exclusives-RE5
03SPx-221
  Radiance-221
  Spectrum-221
03Titanium-117
  Hobby Jersey Number Parallels-117
  Retail-117
  Retail Jersey Number Parallels-117
03Topps-332
  Blue-332
  Gold-332
  Red-332
03Topps C55-152
  Minis-152
  Minis American Back-152
  Minis American Back Red-152
  Minis Bazooka Back-152
  Minis Brooklyn Back-152
  Minis Hat Trick Back-152
  Minis O Canada Back-152
  Minis O Canada Back Red-152
  Minis Stanley Cup Back-152
03Topps Pristine-140
03Topps Pristine-141
03Topps Pristine-142
  Gold Refractor Die Cuts-140
  Gold Refractor Die Cuts-141
  Gold Refractor Die Cuts-142
  Refractors-140
  Refractors-141
  Refractors-142
  Mini-PM-JHU
  Press Plates Black-140
  Press Plates Black-141
  Press Plates Black-142
  Press Plates Cyan-140
  Press Plates Cyan-141
  Press Plates Cyan-142
  Press Plates Magenta-140
  Press Plates Magenta-141
  Press Plates Magenta-142
  Press Plates Yellow-140
  Press Plates Yellow-141
  Press Plates Yellow-142
03UD Honor Roll-181
03UD Premier Collection-115
  NHL Shields-SH-JH
  Signatures-PS-JH
  Signatures Gold-PS-JH
  Stars-ST-JH
03Upper Deck-203
  Canadian Exclusives-203
  HG-203
03Upper Deck Ice-98
  Glass Parallel-98
03Upper Deck MVP-449
03Upper Deck Rookie Update-152
03Upper Deck Trilogy-142
  Limited-142
03Czech OFS Plus All-Star Game-H42
03Czech OFS Plus Insert S-S9
03Czech OFS Plus MS Praha-SE30
03Czech National Team Postcards-6
03Russian Hockey League-239
03Russian World Championship Stars-25
03AHL Top Prospects-12
03Grand Rapids Griffins-7
03Grand Rapids Griffins-25
03Pacific AHL Prospects-24
  Gold-24
  Destined for Greatness-6
04Pacific NHL All-Star FANtasy-4
04Pacific NHL All-Star FANtasy Gold-4
04Czech OFS-364
  Stars II-4
04ITG Heroes and Prospects-191
  Autographs-U-JH
04ITG Heroes/Prospects Toronto Expo '05-191
05ITG Heroes/Prosp Toronto Expo Parallel -267
05AHL All-Stars-14
05ITG Heroes and Prospects-267
  Autographs Series II-JHU
06O-Pee-Chee-189
  Rainbow-189
06Czech OFS Jagr Team-23
06ITG Heroes and Prospects-160
  AHL All-Star Jerseys-AJ03
  AHL All-Star Jerseys Gold-AJ03
  AHL All-Star Emblems-AE03
  AHL All-Star Emblems Gold-AE03
  AHL All-Star Numbers-AN03
  AHL All-Star Numbers Gold-AN03
  AHL Shooting Stars-AS04
  Autographs-AJH
  Complete AHL Logos-AHL11
  Jerseys-GUJ65
  Emblems-GUE65
  Numbers-GUN65
  Update Autographs-AJH

Hudon, Gil
83Springfield Indians-1

Hudson, Dave
72O-Pee-Chee-211
73O-Pee-Chee-234
74NHL Action Stamps-297
74O-Pee-Chee NHL-335
75O-Pee-Chee NHL-122
75Topps-122
76O-Pee-Chee NHL-299
76Rockies Coke Cans-11
76Rockies Puck Bucks-10
77O-Pee-Chee NHL-343
77Rockies Coke Cans-9
78O-Pee-Chee-299

Hudson, Gordie
50Quebec Citadelles-10
51Laval Dairy Subset-117
52St. Lawrence Sales-46

Hudson, Jeff
95Neepewa Natives-3

Hudson, Mike
85Sudbury Wolves-15
86Sudbury Wolves-15
88Blackhawks Coke-6
89Blackhawks Coke-17
90Blackhawks Coke-17
90O-Pee-Chee-424
90Pro Set-431
91Blackhawks Coke-10
91Bowman-399
91O-Pee-Chee-495
91Parkhurst-260
  French-260
91Pinnacle-38
  French-38
91Pro Set-369
  French-369
91Score Canadian Bilingual-389
91Score Canadian English-389
91Stadium Club-22
91Topps-495
92Blackhawks Coke-7
92Bowman-73
92Oilers Team Issue-7
92O-Pee-Chee-331
92Pinnacle-134
  French-134
92Score-156
  Canadian-156
92Stadium Club-182
92Topps-172
  Gold-172G
92Ultra-37
93Score-659
  Gold-659
  Canadian-659
  Canadian Gold-659
94Be A Player-R31
94Penguins Foodland-8
96Coyotes Coca-Cola-9
98German DEL-241

Hudson, Rob
84Ottawa 67's-13

Huebscher, Andre
05German DEL-226

Hueguenin, Rene
72Finnish Semic World Championship-154
72Swedish Semic World Championship-154

Huet, Cristobal
98Swiss Power Play Stickers-153
99Swiss Panini Stickers-153
00Swiss Panini Stickers-198
00Swiss Slapshot Mini-Cards-HCL1
01Swiss HNL-27
02BAP Memorabilia-324
02BAP Ultimate Memorabilia-73
02Pacific Calder-123
  Silver-123
02Pacific Complete-593
  Red-593
02Parkhurst Retro-248
  Minis-248
02SP Authentic-217
02SPx-185
02UD Premier Collection-95
  Gold-95
02Upper Deck Rookie Update-122
02Swiss HNL-493
02Manchester Monarchs-23
03BAP Memorabilia-109
  Emerald-109
  Gold-109
  Ruby-109
  Sapphire-109
03O-Pee-Chee-328
03OPC Blue-328
03OPC Gold-328
03OPC Red-328
03Pacific-156
  Blue-156
  Red-156
03Pacific Complete-435
  Red-435
03Pacific Heads-Up-47
  Hobby LTD-47
  Retail LTD-47
03Titanium-47
  Hobby Jersey Number Parallels-47
  Retail-47
  Retail Jersey Number Parallels-47
03Topps-328
  Blue-328
  Gold-328
  Red-328
03Upper Deck-336
  Canadian Exclusives-336
  HG-336
  UD Exclusives-336
03Upper Deck MVP-206
  Gold Script-206
  Silver Script-206
  Canadian Exclusives-206
03Upper Deck Victory-88
  Bronze-88
  Gold-88
  Silver-88
  Freshman Flashback-FF24
04Pacific-122
  Blue-122
  Red-122
04German Adler Mannheim Eagles Postcards-18
04German DEL-19
  Superstars-SU03
05ITG Heroes/Prosp Toronto Expo Parallel -429
05Canadiens Team Issue-9
05ITG Ultimate Memorabilia Double Autos-17
05ITG Ultimate Mem Double Autos Gold-17
05ITG Ultimate Mem Future Stars Autos-9
05ITG Ultimate Mem Future Star Autos Gold-9
05ITG Ultimate Memorabilia Triple Autos-3
05ITG Ultimate Memorabilia Triple Autos-13
05ITG Ultimate Mem Triple Autos Gold-3
05ITG Ultimate Mem Triple Autos Gold-13
05Parkhurst-261
  Facsimile Auto Parallel-261
05ITG Heroes and Prospects-429
  Autographs Update-A-CHT
06Be A Player-112
  Autographs-112
  Signatures-CR
  Signatures 10-123
  Signatures 25-123
  Signatures Duals-DHK
  Signatures Trios-THHK
  Unmasked Warriors-UM5
  Unmasked Warriors Autographs-UM5
  Up Close and Personal-UC11
  Up Close and Personal Autographs-UC11
06Be A Player Portraits-56
06Beehive-48
  Blue-48
  Matte-48
  Red Facsimile Signatures-48
  Wood-48
  Signature Scrapbook-SSHU
06Between The Pipes-59
  Aspiring-AS02
  Aspiring Gold-AS02
  Autographs-ACH
  Complete Jersey-CJ10
  Complete Jersey Gold-CJ10
  Double Jerseys-DJ05
  Double Jerseys Gold-DJ05
  Emblems-GUE46
  Emblems Gold-GUE46
  Emblems Autographs-GUE46
  Jerseys-GUJ46
  Jerseys Gold-GUJ46
  Jerseys Autographs-GUJ46
  Numbers-GUN46
  Numbers Gold-GUN46
  Numbers Autographs-GUN46
  Playing For Your Country-PC09
  Playing For Your Country Gold-PC09
  Prospect Trios-PT15
  Prospect Trios Gold-PT15
  Shooting Gallery-SG01
  Shooting Gallery Gold-SG01
  Stick and Jersey-SJ15
  Stick and Jersey Gold-SJ15
  Stick and Jersey Autographs-SJ15
  Stick Work-SW04
  Stick Work Gold-SW04
  The Mask-M14
  The Mask Gold-M14
  The Mask Silver-M14
  The Mask Game-Used-MGU08
  The Mask Game-Used Gold-MGU08
06Black Diamond-109
  Black-109
  Gold-109
  Ruby-109
06Canadiens Postcards-2
06Flair Showcase-56
  Parallel-56
  Hot Gloves-HG16
  Inks-ICH
06Fleer-102
  Tiffany-102
  Netminders-N13
06Gatorade-36
06Hot Prospects-52
  Red Hot-52
  White Hot-52
  Hotagraphs-HHU
06ITG International Ice-38
  Gold-38
  Autographs-ACH
  Goaltending Glory-GG13
  Goaltending Glory Gold-GG13
  Stick and Jersey-SJ28
  Stick and Jersey Gold-SJ28
06ITG Ultimate Memorabilia-33
  Artist Proof-33
  Autos-41
  Autos Gold-41
  Cornerstones-10
  Cornerstones Gold-10
  Decades-3
  Decades Gold-3
  Going For Gold-6
  Going For Gold Gold-6
  Jerseys Autos-15
  Jerseys Autos Gold-15
  Stick Rack-4
  Stick Rack Gold-4
06McDonald's Upper Deck Hot Gloves-HG5
06O-Pee-Chee-262
06O-Pee-Chee-610
  Rainbow-262
  Rainbow-610
  Autographs-A-CH
06Panini Stickers-72
06SP Authentic-50
  Limited-50
  Sign of the Times Duals-STHA
06SP Game Used-52
  Gold-52
  Rainbow-52
  Authentic Fabrics Dual-AF2AH
  Authentic Fabrics Dual Patches-AF2AH
  Authentic Fabrics Fives-AF5GAA
  Authentic Fabrics Fives Patches-AF5GAA
  Autographs-52
  Inked Sweaters-ISHU
  Inked Sweaters Patches-ISHU
  Inked Sweaters Dual-IS2HA
  Inked Sweaters Dual Patches-IS2HA
  Letter Marks-LMCH
  SIGnificance-SCH
06SPx-52
  Spectrum-52
  SPxcitement-X56
  SPxcitement Spectrum-X56
  SPxcitement Autographs-X56
  Winning Materials-WMCH
  Winning Materials Spectrum-WMCH
  Winning Materials Autographs-WMCH
06The Cup Autographed NHL Shields Duals-DASHA
06The Cup Signature Patches-SPCH
06UD Artifacts-48
06UD Artifacts-155
  Blue-48
  Blue-155
  Gold-48
  Gold-155
  Platinum-48
  Platinum-155
  Radiance-48
  Radiance-155
  Red-48
  Red-155
06UD Powerplay-53
  Impact Rainbow-53
  Goal Robbers-GR14
06Ultra-103
  Gold Medallion-103
  Ice Medallion-103
06Upper Deck-101
  Exclusives Parallel-101
  High Gloss Parallel-101
  Game Dated Moments-GD41
  Game Jerseys-J2CH
  Game Patches-P2CH
  Hometown Heroes-HH45
  Masterpieces-101
  Walmart Tins Oversize-101
06Upper Deck MVP-151
  Gold Script-151
  Super Script-151
  Last Line of Defense-LL5
06Upper Deck Ovation-76
06Upper Deck Sweet Shot-56
  Signature Shots/Saves-SSHU
  Signature Shots/Saves Sticks-SSSCH
  Signature Sticks-STCH
  Sweet Stitches-SSCH
  Sweet Stitches Duals-SSCH
  Sweet Stitches Triples-SSCH
06Upper Deck Trilogy-52
  Scripts-S2CH
06Upper Deck Victory-108
06Upper Deck Victory Black-108
06Upper Deck Victory Gold-108
06ITG Heroes and Prospects-17
  Autographs-ACH
  Jerseys-GUJ59
  Jerseys Gold-GUJ59
  Emblems-GUE59
  Emblems Gold-GUE59
  Numbers-GUN59
  Numbers Gold-GUN59
  Net Prospects-NPR05
  Net Prospects Gold-NPR05
07Upper Deck Ovation-22
07Upper Deck Victory-47
  Black-47
  Gold-47
  Stars on Ice-SI15

Huettl, Dave
92Northern Michigan Wildcats-12

Huffman, Kerry
87Flyers Postcards-11
88Flyers Postcards-5
88Panini Stickers-317
89Flyers Postcards-13
90Flyers Postcards-12
90O-Pee-Chee-516
91Flyers J.C. Penney-13
91Parkhurst-349
  French-349
92Nordiques Petro-Canada-12
92OPC Premier-48
92Parkhurst-382
  Emerald Ice-382
92Pro Set-136
92Score-239
  Canadian-239
92Stadium Club-381
92Topps-387
  Gold-387G
92Ultra-386
92Upper Deck-444
93Leaf-291
93OPC Premier-43
  Gold-43
93Score-182
  Canadian-182
93Stadium Club-33
  Members Only Master Set-33
  OPC-33
  First Day Issue-33
  First Day Issue OPC-33
93Topps/OPC Premier-43
  Gold-43
93Ultra-402
94Be A Player Signature Cards-83
94Senators Team Issue-16
94Stadium Club-127
  Members Only Master Set-127
  First Day Issue-127
  Super Team Winner Cards-127
95Senators Team Issue-13
95Topps-131
  OPC Inserts-131
96Las Vegas Thunder-9
97Grand Rapids Griffins-8
98Grand Rapids Griffins-10

Hugentobler, Roger
95Swiss HNL-317

Huggett, Andrew
01Kalamazoo K-Wings-1

Hughes, Bobby
04Kingston Frontenacs-10
05ITG Heroes/Prosp Toronto Expo Parallel -295
05Kingston Frontenacs-13
05ITG Heroes and Prospects-295
  Autographs Series II-JD
  Team Cherry-TC9
06Kingston Frontenacs-10
06ITG Heroes and Prospects-95
  Autographs-ABH

Hughes, Brendon
93Quebec Pee-Wee Tournament-641

Hughes, Brent
69O-Pee-Chee-144
70Sargent Promotions Stamps-147
71O-Pee-Chee-205
71Sargent Promotions Stamps-147
71Toronto Sun-198
72Blues White Border-7
72O-Pee-Chee-234
72Sargent Promotions Stamps-155
73O-Pee-Chee-184
73Red Wings McCarthy Postcards-9
74NHL Action Stamps-301
74Topps-73
76O-Pee-Chee WHA-34
76San Diego Mariners WHA-4
87Moncton Hawks-12
88ProCards AHL-184
89Jets Safeway-17
89ProCards AHL-31
90Upper Deck-333
  French-333
90Moncton Hawks-11
90ProCards AHL/IHL-244
91Baltimore Skipjacks-2
91ProCards-561
94Leaf-218
94Pinnacle-510
  Artist's Proofs-510
  Rink Collection-510
94Stadium Club-234
  Members Only Master Set-234
  First Day Issue-234
  Super Team Winner Cards-234
94Ultra-255
96Islander Postcards-7
97Pacific Dynagon Best Kept Secrets-56
99Austin Ice Bats-11
00Austin Ice Bats-23
01Austin Ice Bats-20
02Austin Ice Bats-19
03Austin Ice Bats-6
06Colorado EaglesÂ -12

Hughes, Chuck E.
92Birmingham Bulls-7
93Birmingham Bulls-7

Hughes, Dan
03UK Sheffield Steelers Stickers-15

Hughes, Don
67Swedish Hockey-270

Hughes, Frank
75Houston Aeros WHA-8
76O-Pee-Chee WHA-81
76Phoenix Roadrunners WHA-8

Hughes, Howie
68O-Pee-Chee-158
69O-Pee-Chee-142
70Sargent Promotions Stamps-80

Hughes, Jack
23V128-1 Paulin's Candy-3
24Crescent Selkirks-2
25Dominion Chocolates-92
28V128-2 Paulin's Candy-66

Hughes, Jason
917th Inn. Sketch OHL-273
93Kitchener Rangers-5
94Kitchener Rangers-6

Hughes, Jim
03Manchester Monarchs-23
05Manchester Monarchs-23

Hughes, John
74Phoenix Roadrunners WHA Pins-6
75O-Pee-Chee WHA-45
75Stingers Kahn's-5
76O-Pee-Chee WHA-106
76Stingers Kahn's-3
79Canucks Royal Bank-10
80Pepsi-Cola Caps-27
88Oilers Tenth Anniversary-116
04ITG Heroes and Prospects-218
04ITG Heroes/Prospects Toronto Expo '05-218

Hughes, John OHL
04Belleville Bulls-9
04ITG Heroes and Prospects-218
04ITG Heroes and Prospects Toronto Fall Expo '05-218
05Belleville Bulls-14
06Brampton Battalion-21

Hughes, Marty
01Roanoke Express-11

Hughes, Pat
36John Player & Son's Player's Cigarettes-31
76Nova Scotia Voyageurs-8
77Nova Scotia Voyageurs-11
78Canadiens Postcards-9
79O-Pee-Chee-65
79Topps-65
80O-Pee-Chee-347
81Oilers Red Rooster-16
82Oilers Red Rooster-16
82O-Pee-Chee-109
82Post Cereal-6
83NHL Key Tags-39
83Oilers McDonald's-15
83O-Pee-Chee-31
83O-Pee-Chee-213
83O-Pee-Chee Stickers-327
83O-Pee-Chee Stickers-328
83Topps Stickers-327
83Topps Stickers-328
83Vachon-28
84Oilers Red Rooster-16
84Oilers Team Issue-9
84O-Pee-Chee-245
847-Eleven Discs-18
85O-Pee-Chee Stickers-229
85Sabres Blue Shield-14
85Sabres Blue Shield Small-14
88Oilers Tenth Anniversary-24

Hughes, Peter
86Sudbury Wolves-17
87Sudbury Wolves-17

Hughes, Ryan
91Upper Deck Czech World Juniors-47
92Cornell Big Red-16
93Classic-69
94Classic Autographs-NNO
94Classic Pro Prospects-74

Hughes, Sean
01Fort Worth Brahmas-9
02Fort Worth Brahmas-6

Hughson, Luke
04Swift Current Broncos-8

Huhtala, Jorma
72Finnish Jaakiekko-304
78Finnish SM-Liiga-59
80Finnish Mallasjuoma-37

Huhtala, Tommi
05Finnish Cardset -220
06Finnish Cardset-231
06Finnish Ilves Team Set-7

Huhtanen, Tuomas
06Finnish Porin Assat Pelaajakortit-17

Huikari, Juha
71Finnish Suomi Stickers-301
80Finnish Mallasjuoma-100
82Swedish Semic VM Stickers-33
83Swedish Semic VM Stickers-33

Huikuri, Juha
78Finnish SM-Liiga-142

Huizenga, Kenny
97Anchorage Aces-3

Hukalo, David
03Kalamazoo Wings-15
04Fort Wayne Komets-6
05Fort Wayne Komets Choice-4
05Fort Wayne Komets Sprint-10
06Fort Wayne Komets-9

Hukkanen, Veijo
72Finnish Jaakiekko-280

Hulak, Dan
97Swift Current Broncos-7
98Swift Current Broncos-22
99Swift Current Broncos-8

Hulak, Derek
06Regina Pats-8
06Saskatoon Blades-11

Hulbig, Joe
97Pacific Dynagon Best Kept Secrets-38
99Providence Bruins-13
00Pacific-36
  Copper-36
  Gold-36
  Ice Blue-36
  Premiere Date-36
01Providence Bruins-13
02Albany River Rats-11
02Albany River Rats AAP-14
03Albany River Rats-15
03Albany River Rats Kinko's-14

Hulett, Dean
91Lake Superior State Lakers-12
92Lake Superior State Lakers-13
93Phoenix Roadrunners-10
93Classic-70
94Classic Autographs-NNO
94Classic Pro Prospects-142
95Louisiana Ice Gators-7
95Louisiana Ice Gators Playoffs-8
97Mississippi Sea Wolves-11

Hulit, Chris
03Oshawa Generals-17
04Ottawa 67's-21
05Ottawa 67's-16

Hulkkonen, Antti
99Finnish Cardset-59
01Finnish Cardset-326
02Finnish Cardset-175
03Finnish Cardset-161
04Finnish Cardset-174
  Parallel-128
05Finnish Cardset -155
06Swedish SHL Elitset-147

Hull, Bart
97Idaho Steelheads-21

Hull, Bobby
44Beehive Group II Photos-109A
44Beehive Group II Photos-109B
58Topps-66
59Topps-47
60Shirriff Coins-63
60Topps-58
  Stamps-28
60Wonder Bread Labels-2
60Wonder Bread Premium Photos-2
61Shirriff/Salada Coins-25
61Topps-29
62Shirriff Coins-47
62Shirriff Coins-57
62Topps-33
  Hockey Bucks-12
63Chex Photos-27
63Topps-33
63Toronto Star-21
64Beehive Group III Photos-41A
64Beehive Group III Photos-41B
64Beehive Group III Photos-41C
64Beehive Group III Photos-41D
64Beehive Group III Photos-41E
64Beehive Group III Photos-41F
64Coca-Cola Caps-25
64Topps-20
64Topps-107
64Toronto Star-20
65Coca-Cola-26
65Topps-59
66Topps-64
66Topps-112
66Topps-125
66Topps USA Test-40
67Topps-113
67Topps-124
68O-Pee-Chee-16
68O-Pee-Chee-204
  Puck Stickers-3
68Shirriff Coins-17
68Topps-16
69O-Pee-Chee-70
69O-Pee-Chee-216
  Four-in-One-9
  Stamps-15
69Topps-70
70Blackhawks Postcards-3
70Dad's Cookies-59
70Esso Power Players-116
70O-Pee-Chee-15
70O-Pee-Chee-235
  Deckle-30
70Sargent Promotions Stamps-43
70Topps-15
  Topps/OPC Sticker Stamps-14
71Bazooka-4
71O-Pee-Chee-50
71O-Pee-Chee-261
  O-Pee-Chee/Topps Booklets-1
  Posters-9
71Sargent Promotions Stamps-34
71Topps-1
71Topps-50
71Toronto Sun-66
71Finnish Suomi Stickers-383
71Swedish Hockey-200
72Kellogg's Iron-On Transfers-4
72O-Pee-Chee-228
72O-Pee-Chee-272
72O-Pee-Chee-336
727-Eleven Slurpee Cups WHA-11
72Topps-61
72Topps-126
72Finnish Semic World Championship-228
72Swedish Stickers-118
72Swedish Semic World Championship-228
73O-Pee-Chee WHA Posters-16
73Quaker Oats WHA-50
74O-Pee-Chee WHA-50
75O-Pee-Chee WHA-1
75O-Pee-Chee WHA-65
76O-Pee-Chee WHA-3
76O-Pee-Chee WHA-5
76O-Pee-Chee WHA-65
76O-Pee-Chee WHA-100
77O-Pee-Chee WHA-50
77Sportscasters-520
77Sportscasters-5003
77Sportscasters-5523
77Finnish Sportscasters-57-1358
77Finnish Sportscasters-58-1381
77Finnish Sportscasters-08-181
79Jets Postcards-10
79O-Pee-Chee-185
79Topps-185
81Philip Morris-NNO
81Topps Thirst Break-50
81Topps Thirst Break-51
81Topps Thirst Break-52
85Hall of Fame-242
88Esso All-Stars-20
90SLU Kenner Club Pieces *-15A
91Ultimate Original Six-57
91Ultimate Original Six-77
91Ultimate Original Six-82
91Ultimate Original Six-88
91Ultimate Original Six-89
91Ultimate Original Six-90
91Ultimate Original Six-91
91Ultimate Original Six-92
91Ultimate Original Six-96
91Ultimate Original Six-NNO
  French-57
  French-77
  French-82
  French-88
  French-89
  French-90
  French-91
  French-92
  French-96
  French-NNO
  Box Bottoms-2
91Finnish Semic World Champ Stickers-239
91Swedish Semic World Champ Stickers-239
92Future Trends '76 Canada Cup-107
92Future Trends '76 Canada Cup-110
92Future Trends '76 Canada Cup-139
92Future Trends '76 Canada Cup-142
92Future Trends '76 Canada Cup-178
92Sports Illustrated for Kids II-211
93Action Packed Prototypes-1
93Action Packed Prototypes-2
93American Licorice Sour Punch Caps-P
93Upper Deck Locker All-Stars-43
93Zeller's Masters of Hockey-5
93Zeller's Masters of Hockey Signed-5
94Parkhurst Tall Boys-25
94Parkhurst Tall Boys-136
  Autographs-A3
  Mail-Ins-AS5
  Mail-Ins-TW2
  Mail-Ins-TW6
94Los Angeles Blades RHI-18
94Signature Rookies Tetrad Titans *-122
94Signature Rookies Tetrad Titans Sigs-122
95SLU Timeless Legends *-5
95Parkhurst '66-67-21
95Parkhurst '66-67-124
95Parkhurst '66-67-129
95Parkhurst '66-67-130
95Parkhurst '66-67-141
  Coins-21
96SLU Canadian Timeless Legends-5
97Donruss Elite Back to the Future-6
97Donruss Elite Back to the Future Autos-6
97Highland Mint Mint-Cards Topps-11
97Highland Mint Mint-Cards Topps-12
97SP Authentic Mark of a Legend-M5
97SP Authentic Tradition-T5
98Blackhawks Legends-3
98OPC Chrome Blast From the Past-9
98OPC Chrome Blast From Past Refractors-9
98Topps Blast From The Past-9
98Topps Blast From The Past Autographs-9
98Upper Deck Game Jerseys-GJ3
98Upper Deck Game Jerseys-GJA1
98Arizona Icecats-12
99BAP Memorabilia AS Retail-R1
99BAP Memorabilia AS Retail Autographs-R1
99SP Authentic Legendary Heroes-LH5
99SP Authentic Sign of the Times-BH
99SP Authentic Sign of the Times Gold-BH
99Upper Deck 500 Goal Club-500BH
99Upper Deck 500 Goal Club-500BH
99Upper Deck Century Legends-8
  Century Collection-8
  All Century Team-AC3
  Epic Signatures-BH
  Epic Signatures 100-BH
  Essence of the Game-E7
99Upper Deck Retro-86
  Gold-86
  Platinum-86
  Inkredible-BOH
  Inkredible Level 2-BOH
00SP Authentic BuyBacks-12
00SP Authentic Power Skaters-P2
00SP Authentic Sign of the Times-BH
00SP Authentic Sign of the Times-H/H
00UD Heroes-122
  Game-Used Twigs-T-BH
  Game-Used Twigs Gold-C-HB
  Signs of Greatness-BH
00Upper Deck Legends-25
00Upper Deck Legends-117
  Legendary Collection Bronze-25
  Legendary Collection Bronze-117
  Legendary Collection Gold-25
  Legendary Collection Gold-117
  Legendary Collection Silver-25
  Legendary Collection Silver-117
  Enshrined Stars-ES4
  Epic Signatures-BHU
  Playoff Heroes-PH10
  Supreme Milestones-SM3
01BAP Memorabilia 500 Goal Scorers-GS28
01BAP Signature Series 500 Goal Scorers-8
01BAP Sig Series 500 Goal Scorers Autos-8
01BAP Signature Series Vintage Autographs-VA-7
01BAP Signature Series Vintage Autographs-VA-8
01BAP Ultimate Mem All-Star History-14
01BAP Ultimate Memorabilia Autographs-23
01BAP Ultimate Mem Autographs Gold-23
01BAP Ultimate Memorabilia Bloodlines-6
01BAP Ultimate Memorabilia Cornerstones-3
01BAP Ultimate Memorabilia Decades-11
01BAP Ultimate Memorabilia Emblem Attic-8
01BAP Ultimate Mem 500 Goal Scorers-4
01BAP Ultimate Mem 500 Goal Scorers Autos-1
01BAP Ultimate Mem 500 Goal Jerseys/Stick-4
01BAP Ultimate Mem 500 Goal Emblems-4
01BAP Ultimate Mem Prototypical Players-10
01BAP Ultimate Mem Prototypical Players-11
01BAP Ultimate Mem Prototypical Players-12
01BAP Ultimate Mem Retired Numbers-13
01BAP Ultimate Mem Retro Teammates-7
01BAP Update Passing the Torch-PTT2
01Fleer Legacy-2
01Fleer Legacy-12
  Ultimate-2
  Ultimate-12
  Memorabilia-14
  Memorabilia Autographs-3
01Greats of the Game-7
  Retro Collection-4
  Autographs-7
  Sticks-5
01Parkhurst 500 Goal Scorers-PGS1
01Parkhurst He Shoots-He Scores Points-4
01Parkhurst He Shoots-He Scores Prizes-38
01Parkhurst Heroes-H13
01Topps Archives-78
  Autographs-30
01UD Challenge 4 the Cup All-Time Lineup-AT1
01UD Honor Roll-1
01UD Honor Roll-31
  Original Six-OS2
01UD Premier Collection Jerseys-GBH
01UD Premier Collection Jerseys Black-G-BH
01UD Premier Collection Signatures-BH
01UD Premier Collection Signatures Black-BH
01UD Stanley Cup Champs-4
01Upper Deck Legends-11
01Upper Deck Legends-90
  Epic Signatures-BH
  Fiorentino Collection-FCBH
  Jerseys-TTBH
  Jerseys-TTHM
  Jerseys Platinum-TTBH
  Jerseys Platinum-TTHM
  Sticks-PHBH
  Sticks-PHHU
02BAP NHL All-Star History-14
02BAP Ultimate Memorabilia All-Star MVP-2
02BAP Ultimate Memorabilia All-Star MVP-3
02BAP Ultimate Memorabilia Emblem Attic-15
02BAP Ultimate Mem Playoff Scorers-18
02BAP Ultimate Mem Retro Teammates-3
02BAP Ultimate Memorabilia Retro Trophies-13
02BAP Ultimate Memorabilia Retro Trophies-19
02BAP Ultimate Mem Scoring Leaders-26
02BAP Ultimate Mem Scoring Leaders-29
02BAP Ultimate Mem Scoring Leaders-31
02BAP Ultimate Mem Vintage Jerseys-7
02BAP Ultimate Mem Vintage Jersey Autos-12
02Fleer Throwbacks-34
  Gold-34
  Platinum-34
  Autographs-13
  Stickwork-10
02Parkhurst Vintage Memorabilia-VM3
02Parkhurst Vintage Teammates-VT1
02Parkhurst Retro Nicknames-RN4
03BAP Ultimate Memorabilia Emblem Attic-17
03BAP Ultimate Mem Emblem Attic Gold-17
03BAP Ultimate Memorabilia Great Moments-2
03BAP Ultimate Memorabilia Linemates-5
03BAP Ultimate Mem Raised to the Rafters-12
03BAP Ultimate Mem Vintage Jerseys-38
03BAP Ultimate Mem Vintage Jerseys Gold-38
03Canada Post-11

Autographs-11
03ITG Used Signature Series-112B
Gold-119
Vintage Memorabilia-6
Vintage Memorabilia Gold-6
03ITG VIP Collages-27
03ITG VIP Collage Autographs-27
03ITG VIP MVP-8
03ITG VIP Vintage Memorabilia-21
03Pacific Exhibit-216
03Parkhurst Original Six Chicago-43
03Parkhurst Original Six Chicago-66
03Parkhurst Original Six Chicago-86
03Parkhurst Original Six Chicago-91
03Parkhurst Original Six Chicago-95
Autographs-7
Inserts-C2
Inserts-C6
Inserts-C12
Memorabilia-CM25
Memorabilia-CM31
Memorabilia-CM38
Memorabilia-CM52
03Parkhurst Orig Six He Shoots/Scores-21
03Parkhurst Orig Six He Shoots/Scores-21A
03Czech Stadion-646
04ITG NHL AS FANtasy AS History Jerseys-SB14
04ITG Franchises Canadian-135
Autographs-BH2
04ITG Franchises He Shoots/Scores Prizes-18
04ITG Franchises US East-352
04ITG Franchises US West-159
Autographs-A-BH1
Barn Burners-WBB8
Barn Burners Gold-WBB8
Double Memorabilia-WDM12
Double Memorabilia Autographs-WDMBH
Double Memorabilia Gold-WDM12
Forever Rivals-WFR5
Forever Rivals Gold-WFR5
Memorabilia-WSM17
Memorabilia Autographs-WSMBH
Memorabilia Gold-WSM17
Teammates-WTM2
Teammates Gold-WTM2
Trophy Winners-WTW3
Trophy Winners Gold-WTW3
04ITG Ultimate Memorabilia-10
04ITG Ultimate Memorabilia-48
Gold-10
Gold-48
Art Ross Trophy-3
Autographs-24
Autographs-27
Autographs Gold-24
Autographs Gold-27
Changing the Game-5
Complete Package-1
Cornerstones-2
Cornerstones Gold-2
Country of Origin-3
Country of Origin Gold-3
Day In History-18
Day In History-24
Day In History-26
Day In History-28
Day In History Gold-18
Day In History Gold-24
Day In History Gold-26
Day In History Gold-28
Emblem Attic-3
Emblem Attic Gold-3
Hart Trophy-6
Jersey Autographs-11
Jersey Autographs Gold-11
Jersey and Sticks-11
Jersey and Sticks Gold-11
Nicknames-28
Original Six-2
Original Six-14
Raised to the Rafters-7
Retro Teammates-3
Stick Autographs-14
Stick Autographs Gold-14
Vintage Lumber-6
04Pacific WHA Autographs-1
04SP Authentic Buybacks-15
04SP Authentic Sign of the Times-QS-HRBG
04SP Authentic Sign of the Times-QS-MHCL
04SP Authentic Sign of the Times-SS-ORG
04SP Authentic Sign of the Times-SS-RLW
04UD Legendary Signatures-9
AKA Autographs-AKA-BH
Autographs-BH
04UD Legends Classics-8
04UD Legends Classics-66
04UD Legends Classics-83
Gold-8
Gold-66
Gold-83
Platinum-8
Platinum-66
Platinum-83
Silver-8
Silver-66
Silver-83
Signature Moments-M50
Signatures-CS48
Signatures-DC3
Signatures-DC14
Signatures-QC3
04Ultimate Collection Jerseys-UGJ-BH
04Ultimate Collection Jerseys Gold-UGJ-BH
04Ultimate Collection Jersey Autographs-UGJA-BH
04Ultimate Collection Signatures-US-BH
04ITG Heroes and Prospects-140
Autographs-BH
04ITG Heroes/Prospects Toronto Expo '05-140
04ITG Heroes/Prospects Expo Heroes/Pros-140
05ITG Heroes/Prosp Toronto Expo Parallel -2
05Beehive PhotoGraphs-PGBH
05ITG Ultimate Memorabilia Level 1-12
05ITG Ultimate Memorabilia Level 2-12
05ITG Ultimate Memorabilia Level 3-12
05ITG Ultimate Memorabilia Level 4-12
05ITG Ultimate Memorabilia Level 5-12
05ITG Ultimate Mem Complete Jersey-24
05ITG Ultimate Mem Complete Jersey Gold-24
05ITG Ultimate Mem Complete Package-1
05ITG Ultimate Mem Complete Package Gold-1
05ITG Ultimate Mem Cornerstones Jerseys-1
05ITG Ultimate Mem Cornerst Jerseys Gold-1
05ITG Ultimate Mem Double Mem-20
05ITG Ultimate Mem Double Mem Autos-17
05ITG Ultimate Mem Double Mem Autos Gold-17
05ITG Ultimate Mem Double Mem Gold-20
05ITG Ultimate Memorabilia Emblem Attic-17
05ITG Ultimate Mem Emblem Attic Gold-17
05ITG Ultimate Memorabilia Emblems-11
05ITG Ultimate Memorabilia Emblems Gold-11
05ITG Ultimate Memorabilia In The Numbers-7
05ITG Ultimate Mem In The Numbers Gold-7
05ITG Ultimate Mem Jersey and Emblem-19
05ITG Ultimate Memorabilia Jersey Autos-11
05ITG Ultimate Mem Jersey Autos Gold-11
05ITG Ultimate Mem Jersey Emblems Gold-19
05ITG Ultimate Memorabilia Jerseys-4
05ITG Ultimate Memorabilia Jerseys Gold-4
05ITG Ultimate Mem Pass the Torch Jerseys-12
05ITG Ultimate Mem Passing Torch Jsy Gold-12
05ITG Ultimate Mem Raised to the Rafters-19
05ITG Ultimate Mem Raised Rafters Gold-19
05ITG Ultimate Mem Record Breaker Jerseys-2
05ITG Ultimate Mem Record Breaker Jerseys-7
05ITG Ultimate Mem RecBreak Jerseys Gold-2
05ITG Ultimate Mem RecBreak Jerseys Gold-7
05ITG Ultimate Mem Retro Teammate Jerseys-27
05ITG Ult Mem Retro Teammates Jersey Gold-27
05ITG Ultimate Mem Seams Unbelievable-13
05ITG Ultimate Mem Seam Unbelievable Gold-13
05ITG Ultimate Memorabilia Sextuple Autos-4
05ITG Ultimate Mem 3 Star of the Game Jsy-6
05ITG Ult Mem 3 Star of the Game Jsy Gold-6
05ITG Ultimate Memorabilia Trifecta Autos-1
05ITG Ultimate Mem Trifecta Autos Gold-1
05ITG Ultimate Memorabilia Triple Autos-1
05ITG Ultimate Mem Triple Autos Gold-1
05ITG Ultimate Mem Triple Threads Jerseys-6
05ITG Ultimate Mem Triple Thread Jsy Gold-6
05ITG Ultimate Memorabilia Ultimate Autos-31
05ITG Ultimate Mem Ultimate Autos Gold-31
05ITG Ultimate Memorabilia Vintage Lumber-16
05ITG Ultimate Mem Vintage Lumber Gold-16
05NHL Legends Medallions-6
05SP Authentic Exquisite Endorsements-EEBH
05SP Authentic Prestigious Pairings-PPHE
05SP Authentic Prestigious Pairings-PPHH
05SP Authentic Six Star Signatures-SSHF
05SP Game Used Game Gear-GG-BH2
05SP Game Used Game Gear Autographs-AG-BH2
05SP Game Used Signature Sticks-SS-BH1
05SP Game Used Signature Sticks-SS-BH2
05SP Game Used Statscriptions-ST-BH
05SPx-92
Spectrum-92
Xcitement Legends-XL-BH
Xcitement Legends Gold-XL-BH
Xcitement Legends Spectrum-XL-BH
05The Cup-26
Gold-26
Black Rainbow-26
Emblems of Endorsement-EEBH
Hardware Heroes-HHBH
Honorable Numbers-HNBH
Limited Logos-LLBH
Masterpiece Pressplates-26
Noble Numbers-NNHM
Noble Numbers Dual-DNNHS
Patch Variation-P26
Patch Variation Autographs-AP26
Property of-POBH
Scripted Numbers-SNHH
Scripted Numbers-SNHM
Scripted Swatches-SSBH
Stanley Cup Titlists-TBH
05Ultimate Coll Ultimate Achievements-UABH
05Ultimate Coll Ultimate Sigs Foursomes-UFGHLH
05Ultimate Coll Ultimate Sigs Pairings-UPHE
05Upper Deck Trilogy Legendary Scripts-LEG-BH
05Upper Deck Trilogy Personal Scripts-PER-BH
05ITG Heroes and Prospects-2
Aspiring-ASP16
Autographs-A-BOH
Future Teammates-FT12
He Shoots-He Scores Prizes-14
Hero Memorabilia-HM-18
Hero Memorabilia Dual-HDM-15
06Beehive-217
5 X 7 Black and White-217
06ITG International Ice-2
06ITG International Ice-117
Gold-2
Gold-117
Autographs-ABH
Autographs-ABH2
Best of the Best-BB12
Best of the Best Gold-BB12
Canadian Dream Team-DT01
Canadian Dream Team Gold-DT01
Greatest Moments-GM04
Greatest Moments-GM06
Greatest Moments Gold-GM04
Greatest Moments Gold-GM06
Hockey Passport-HP04
Hockey Passport Gold-HP04
International Rivals-IR06
Teammates-IT11
Teammates Gold-IT11
06ITG Ultimate Memorabilia-18
Artist Proof-18
Autos-16
Autos Gold-16
Bloodlines-7
Bloodlines Gold-7
Bloodlines Autos-6
Bloodlines Autos Gold-6
Boys Will Be Boys-23
Boys Will Be Boys Gold-23
Complete Package-3
Complete Package Gold-3
Cornerstones-4
Cornerstones Gold-4
Decades-1
Decades Gold-1
Double Memorabilia-8
Double Memorabilia Gold-8
Jerseys-18
Jerseys Gold-18
Jerseys and Emblems-15
Jerseys and Emblems Gold-15
Passing The Torch-12
Passing The Torch Gold-12
Raised to the Rafters-12
Raised to the Rafters Gold-12
Retro Teammates-7
Retro Teammates Gold-7
Stick Rack-12
Stick Rack Gold-12
Triple Thread Jerseys-7
Triple Thread Jerseys Gold-7
06Parkhurst-36
Autographs-36
Autographs Dual-DAHE
Autographs Dual-DAHP
06SP Authentic Sign of the Times-STBH
06SP Authentic Sign of the Times Quads-ST4EHSW
06SP Game Used Inked Sweaters Dual-IS2HH2
06SP Game Used Inked Sweaters Dual Patches-IS2HH2
06The Cup-19
Autographed Patches-19
Black Rainbow-19
Gold-19
Gold Patches-19
Jerseys-19
Masterpiece Pressplates-19
Stanley Cup Signatures-CSBH
06Ultimate Collection-16
Autographed Jerseys-AJ-BH
Signatures-US-BH
Ultimate Achievements-UA-BH
06Upper Deck Sweet Shot-25
Signature Shots/Saves-SSBH
Signature Shots/Saves Sticks-SSSBH
Signature Sticks-STBH
06Upper Deck Trilogy Ice Scripts-ISBH
06ITG Heroes and Prospects Heroes Memorabilia-HM13
06ITG Heroes and Prospects Heroes Memorabilia Gold-HM13

Hull, Brett

84Minnesota-Duluth Bulldogs-2
85Minnesota-Duluth Bulldogs-28
86Moncton Golden Flames-20
87Blues Team Issue-12
87Flames Red Rooster-8
88Blues Kodak-11
88Blues Team Issue-12
880-Pee-Chee-66
880-Pee-Chee Minis-16
880-Pee-Chee Stickers-16
880-Pee-Chee Stickers-81
880-Pee-Chee Stickers-127
880-Pee-Chee Stickers-210
88Panini Stickers-107
88Topps-66
89Blues Kodak-16
890-Pee-Chee-186
890-Pee-Chee Box Bottoms-F
890-Pee-Chee Stickers-22
89Panini Stickers-117
89Sports Illustrated for Kids I-193
89Topps-186
89Topps Box Bottoms-F
89Swedish Semic World Champ Stickers-167
90SLU Kenner Club Pieces *-15A
90Blues Kodak-10
90Bowman-24
Tiffany-24
90Bowman Hat Tricks-1
Tiffany-1
90Kraft-20
90Kraft-67
900-Pee-Chee-4
900-Pee-Chee-77
900-Pee-Chee-195
900-Pee-Chee-513
90OPC Premier-47
90Panini Stickers-262
90Panini Stickers-333
90Pro Set-1A
90Pro Set-263
90Pro Set-342
90Pro Set-378
90Pro Set-395
90Pro Set Player of the Month-P3
90Score-300
90Score-317
90Score-346
90Score-351
90Score-366
Canadian-300
Canadian-317
Canadian-346
Canadian-351
Canadian-366
90Score Hottest/Rising Stars-100
90Topps-4
90Topps-77
90Topps-195
Tiffany-4
Tiffany-77
Tiffany-195
Team Scoring Leaders-2
Team Scoring Leaders Tiffany-2
90Upper Deck-154
90Upper Deck-203
90Upper Deck-312
90Upper Deck-474
90Upper Deck-546
French-154
French-203
French-312
French-474
French-546
90Upper Deck Holograms-4
90Upper Deck Holograms-6
90UMD Hull Collection-1
90UMD Hull Collection-2
90UMD Hull Collection-3
90UMD Hull Collection-4
90UMD Hull Collection-5
90UMD Hull Collection-6
90UMD Hull Collection-7
90UMD Hull Collection-8
90UMD Hull Collection-9
90UMD Hull Collection-10
90UMD Hull Collection-11
90UMD Hull Collection-12
91Pro Set Platinum-109
91Pro Set Platinum-282
91Blues Postcards-10
91Bowman-367
91Bowman-375
91Gillette-14
91Kraft-66
91McDonald's Upper Deck-13
91McDonald's Upper Deck-H4
910-Pee-Chee-190
910-Pee-Chee-259
910-Pee-Chee-303
910-Pee-Chee-403
910-Pee-Chee-516
91OPC Premier-49
91Panini Stickers-25
91Panini Stickers-325
91Parkhurst-157
91Parkhurst-219
91Parkhurst-432
91Parkhurst-474
French-157
French-219
French-432
French-474
PHC-PHC6
PHC French-PHC6
91Pinnacle-200
91Pinnacle-356
91Pinnacle-376
French-200
French-356
French-376
B-B12
B French-B12
91Pro Set-215
91Pro Set-290
91Pro Set-320
91Pro Set-326
French-215
French-290
French-320
French-326
CC-CC6
CC French-CC6
Awards Special-AC6
NHL Sponsor Awards-AC18
Platinum PC-PC5
Puck Candy-24
St. Louis Midwest-4
91Score National-2
91Score Ntnl Candy Wholesalers Convention-2
91Score Fanfest-2
91Score American-1
91Score American-337
91Score American-347
91Score American-371
91Score American-404
91Score American-412
91Score American-428
91Score Canadian Bilingual-1
91Score Canadian Bilingual-261
91Score Canadian Bilingual-294
91Score Canadian Bilingual-302
91Score Canadian Bilingual-318
91Score Canadian Bilingual-367
91Score Canadian Bilingual-377
91Score Canadian English-1
91Score Canadian English-261
91Score Canadian English-294
91Score Canadian English-302
91Score Canadian English-318
91Score Canadian English-367
91Score Canadian English-377
91Score Hot Cards-3
91Score Kellogg's-21
91Stadium Club Charter Member-48
91Stadium Club Charter Member-49
91Stadium Club Members Only-45
91Stadium Club-67
91Topps-190
91Topps-259
91Topps-303
91Topps-403
91Topps-516
Topps/Bowman Preview Sheet-9
Team Scoring Leaders-20
91Upper Deck-7
91Upper Deck-33
91Upper Deck-45
91Upper Deck-464
91Upper Deck-622
91Upper Deck-SP1
French-33
French-45
French-464
French-622
Award Winner Holograms-AW3
Box Bottoms-2
Brett Hull Heroes-1
Brett Hull Heroes-2
Brett Hull Heroes-3
Brett Hull Heroes-4
Brett Hull Heroes-5
Brett Hull Heroes-6
Brett Hull Heroes-7
Brett Hull Heroes-8
Brett Hull Heroes-9
Brett Hull Heroes-AU1
Brett Hull Heroes-NNO
Brett Hull Heroes French-1
Brett Hull Heroes French-2
Brett Hull Heroes French-3
Brett Hull Heroes French-4
Brett Hull Heroes French-5
Brett Hull Heroes French-6
Brett Hull Heroes French-7
Brett Hull Heroes French-8
Brett Hull Heroes French-9
Brett Hull Heroes French-AU1
91Finnish Semic World Champ Stickers-144
91Swedish Semic World Champ Stickers-144
92Blues UD Best of the Blues-12
92Blues UD Best of the Blues-NNO
92Bowman-186
92Bowman-209
92High-5 Previews-P3
92Humpty Dumpty II-9
92Kraft-41
92McDonald's Upper Deck-H2
920-Pee-Chee-87
920-Pee-Chee-124
25th Anniv. Inserts-21
92OPC Premier Star Performers-21
92Panini Stickers-16
92Panini Stickers-289
92Panini Stickers French-16
92Panini Stickers French-289
92Parkhurst-153
92Parkhurst-459
Emerald Ice-153
Emerald Ice-459
92Pinnacle-100
92Pinnacle-257
French-100
French-257
Team Pinnacle-6
Team French-6
92Pro Set-156
92Pro Set-245
Gold Team Leaders-8
92Score-350
92Score-411
92Score-435
92Score-442
92Score-500
Canadian-350
Canadian-411
Canadian-435
Canadian-442
Canadian-500
92Seasons Patches-13
92Sports Illustrated for Kids II-638
92Stadium Club-1
92Stadium Club-258
92Topps-2
92Topps-260
92Topps-340
Gold-2G
Gold-260G
Gold-340G
92Ultra-186
All-Stars-12
92Upper Deck-29
92Upper Deck-423
92Upper Deck-620
All-World Team-W2
Gordie Howe Selects-G7
92Finnish Semic-156
93SLU Hockey Canadian-3
93SLU Hockey American-4
93Donruss-286
Elite Inserts-5
Special Print-U
93Kenner Starting Lineup Cards-4
93Kraft-35
93Leaf-255
Gold All-Stars-3
Studio Signature-8
93McDonald's Upper Deck-7
93OPC Premier-425
Gold-425
Black Gold-22
93Panini Stickers-N
93Parkhurst-180
Emerald Ice-180
East/West Stars-W7
USA/Canada Gold-G4
93Pinnacle-200
Canadian-200
All-Stars-34
All-Stars Canadian-34
Captains-20
Captains Canadian-20
Nifty Fifty-10
Team Pinnacle-6
93PowerPlay-211
Point Leaders-4
Slapshot Artists-4
93Score-335
Canadian-335
Dream Team-18
Dynamic Duos U.S.-4
Franchise-18
93Seasons Patches-6
93Stadium Club-65
Members Only Master Set-65
OPC-65
First Day Issue-65
First Day Issue OPC-65
All-Stars-4
All-Stars Members Only-4
All-Stars OPC-4
Finest-3
Finest Members Only-3
Master Photos-9
Master Photos Winners-9
93Topps/OPC Premier-425
Gold-425
93Topps Premier Black Gold-21
93Topps Premier Black Gold-B
93Ultra-117
Red Light Specials-4
Scoring Kings-3
93Upper Deck-160
93Upper Deck-232
Gretzky's Great Ones-GG3
Next In Line-NL2
NHL's Best-HB3
Silver Skates-R5
Silver Skates Gold-R5
SP-137
93Upper Deck Locker All-Stars-27
93Swedish Semic World Champ Stickers-185
93Fax Pax World of Sport*-26
94SLU Hockey American-6
94Action Packed Mammoth-MM2
94Be A Player-R48
99 All-Stars-G10
94Canada Games NHL POGS-203
94Donruss Dominators-8
94EA Sports-125
94Finest-42
Super Team Winners-42
Refractors-42
Bowman's Best-B15
Bowman's Best Refractors-B15
Division's Clear Cut-15
94Flair-153
Hot Numbers-4
94Fleer-187
Slapshot Artists-2
94Hockey Wit-97
94Kenner Starting Lineup Cards-7
94Kraft-6
94Leaf-16
Gold Stars-4
94Leaf Limited-2
Gold-2
94McDonald's Upper Deck-McD13
94NHLPA Phone Cards-2
94OPC Premier-417
94OPC Premier-465
Special Effects-417
Special Effects-465
94Parkhurst-309
Gold-309
Crash the Game Green-20
Crash the Game Blue-20
Crash the Game Gold-20
Crash the Game Red-20
Vintage-V35
94Parkhurst SE-SE154
Gold-SE154
94Pinnacle-450
Artist's Proofs-450
Rink Collection-450
Boomers-BR9
Team Pinnacle-TP11
Team Dufex Parallel-TP11
94Score-100
Gold-100
Platinum-100
Dream Team-DT22
Franchise-TF20
90 Plus Club-11
94Select-97
Gold-97
First Line-FL12
94SP-100
Die Cuts-100
Premier-29
Premier Die-Cuts-29
94Stadium Club Members Only-6
94Stadium Club-100
Members Only Master Set-100
First Day Issue-100
Dynasty and Destiny-3
Dynasty and Destiny Members Only-3
Finest Inserts-2
Finest Inserts Members Only-2
Super Team Winner Cards-100
94Topps/OPC Premier-417
94Topps/OPC Premier-465
Special Effects-417
Special Effects-465
94Topps Finest Inserts-2
94Topps/OPC Premier The Go To Guy-3
94Topps Finest Bronze-8
94Ultra-183
All-Stars-11
Red Light Specials-5
94Upper Deck-229
94Upper Deck-333
94Upper Deck-569
Electric Ice-229
Electric Ice-333
Electric Ice-569
Predictor Canadian-C17
94Upper Deck Predictor Canadian Exch Gold-C17
94Upper Deck Predictor Retail-R2
94Upper Deck Predictor Retail-R32
94Upper Deck Predictor Retail-R57
94Upper Deck Predictor Retail Exchange-R2
94Upper Deck Predictor Retail Exchange-R32
94Upper Deck Predictor Retail Exchange-R57
94Upper Deck SP Inserts-SP66
94Upper Deck SP Inserts Die Cuts-SP66
94Upper Deck NHLPA/Be A Player-8
94Finnish Jaa Kiekko-123
94Finnish Jaa Kiekko-347
94Swedish Olympics Lillehammer*-323
95SLU Hockey American-10
95Bashan Super Stickers-101
Die-Cut-11
95Be A Player-1
Signatures-S1
Signatures Die Cuts-S1
Lethal Lines-LL3
95Bowman-43
All-Foil-43
95Canada Games NHL POGS-7
95Canada Games NHL POGS-23
95Canada Games NHL POGS-236
95Collector's Choice-214
95Collector's Choice-364
Player's Club-214
Player's Club-364
Player's Club Platinum-214
Player's Club Platinum-364
Crash The Game-C5A
Crash The Game-C5B
Crash The Game-C5C
Crash The Game Gold-C5A
Crash The Game Gold-C5B
Crash The Game Gold-C5C
Crash the Game Silver Redeemed-C5
Crash the Game Silver Bonus-C5
Crash the Game Gold Redeemed-C5
Crash the Game Gold Bonus-C5
95Donruss-68
Dominators-6
Marksmen-7
Pro Pointers-6
95Donruss Elite-7
Die Cut Stars-7
Die Cut Uncut-7
Cutting Edge-12
95Emotion-148
Xcited-8
95Finest-10
95Finest-184
Refractors-10
Refractors-184
95Hoyle Western Playing Cards-36
95Imperial Stickers-101
Die Cut Superstars-11
95Kellogg's Donruss-5
95Kellogg's Donruss-6
95Kenner Starting Lineup Cards-11
95Kraft-66
95Leaf-209
Fire On Ice-9
Gold Stars-6
95Leaf Limited-28
Stars of the Game-10
95McDonald's Pinnacle-MCD-6
95Metal-125
Heavy Metal-5
International Steel-8
95NHL Aces Playing Cards-11D
95NHL Cool Trade-15
95NHL Cool Trade-RP15
95Panini Stickers-194
95Parkhurst International-172
Emerald Ice-172
Crown Collection Silver Series 1-10
Crown Collection Gold Series 1-10
NHL All-Stars-2
Parkie's Trophy Picks-PP54
95Pinnacle-15
Artist's Proofs-15
Rink Collection-15
Clear Shots-2
First Strike-12
95Pinnacle FANtasy-24
95Playoff One on One-89
95Playoff One on One-195
95Playoff One on One-307
95Pro Magnets-12
95Score-235
Black Ice Artist's Proofs-235
Black Ice-235
Border Battle-6
Dream Team-9
Lamplighters-11
95Select Certified-4
Mirror Gold-4
Gold Team-6
95SkyBox Impact-141
Ice Quake-2
95SP-121
Stars/Etoiles-E24
Stars/Etoiles Gold-E24
95Stadium Club Members Only-37
95Stadium Club-183
Members Only Master Set-183
Power Streak-PS9
Power Streak Members Only Master Set-PS9
95Summit-13
Artist's Proofs-13
Ice-13
GM's Choice-17
Mad Hatters-2
95Topps-10
95Topps-372
OPC Inserts-10
OPC Inserts-372
Hidden Gems-10HG
Marquee Men Power Boosters-10
Mystery Finest-M7
Mystery Finest Refractors-M7
Profiles-PF19
Rink Leaders-4RL
95Topps SuperSkills-48
Platinum-48
95Ultra-139
95Ultra-386
Gold Medallion-139
Extra Attackers-8
Red Light Specials-3
Red Light Specials Gold Medallion-3
95Upper Deck-233
95Upper Deck-251
95Upper Deck-486
Electric Ice-233
Electric Ice-251
Electric Ice-486
Electric Ice Gold-233
Electric Ice Gold-251
Electric Ice Gold-486
95Upper Deck All-Star Game Predictors-3
Redemption Winners-3
95Upper Deck Freeze Frame-F15
95Upper Deck Freeze Frame Jumbo-F15
95Upper Deck NHL All-Stars-AS3
95Upper Deck NHL All-Stars Jumbo-AS3
95Upper Deck Predictor Retail-R5
95Upper Deck Predictor Retail Exchange-R5
95Upper Deck Special Edition-SE157
95Upper Deck Special Edition Gold-SE157
95Zenith-1
Z-Team-15
95Finnish Semic World Championships-113
95Swedish Globe World Championships-115
95Swedish World Championships Stickers-299
96Be A Player Biscuit In The Basket-14
96Black Diamond-170
Gold-170
96Blues Dispatch 30th Anniversary-2
96Collector's Choice-223
96Collector's Choice-329
MVP-UD29
MVP Gold-UD29
Stick'Ums-S2
96Donruss-197
Press Proofs-197
Elite Inserts-4
Elite Inserts Gold-4
Go Top Shelf-6
96Donruss Canadian Ice-65
Gold Press Proofs-65
Red Press Proofs-65
96Donruss Elite-4
Die Cut Stars-4
Perspective-9
96Duracell All-Cherry Team-DC5
96Duracell L'Equipe Beliveau-JB5
96Flair-81
Blue Ice-81
Center Ice Spotlight-4
96Fleer-97
Art Ross-7
Picks Dream Lines-10
Picks Fabulous 50-19
Picks Fantasy Force-6
96Hockey Greats Coins-10
Gold-10
96Kraft Upper Deck-11
96Leaf-45
Press Proofs-45
96Leaf Leather And Laces Promos-P3
96Leaf Leather And Laces-3
96Leaf Sweaters Away-12
96Leaf Sweaters Home-12
96Leaf Limited-24
Gold-24
Stubble-15
96Leaf Preferred-106
Press Proofs-106
Steel Power-9
Vanity Plates-5
Vanity Plates Gold-5
96Maggers-41
96McDonald's Pinnacle-24
96Metal Universe-132
Lethal Weapons-7
Lethal Weapons Super Power-7
96NHL Aces Playing Cards-22
96NHL Pro Stamps-12
96Pinnacle-128
Artist's Proofs-128
Foil-128
Premium Stock-128
Rink Collection-128
By The Numbers-6
By The Numbers-P16
By The Numbers Premium-6
Team Pinnacle-6
96Pinnacle Fantasy-FC16
96Pinnacle Mint-14
Bronze-14
Gold-14
Silver-14
Coins Brass-14
Coins Solid Gold-14
Coins Gold Plated-14
Coins Nickel-14
Coins Silver-14
96Playoff One on One-427
96Score Samples-19
96Score-19
Artist's Proofs-19
Dealer's Choice Artist's Proofs-19
Special Artist's Proofs-19
Golden Blades-19
Sudden Death-4
Superstitions-11
96Select Certified-19
Artist's Proofs-19
Blue-19
Mirror Blue-19
Mirror Gold-19
Mirror Red-19
Red-19
Cornerstones-6
96SkyBox Impact-113
BladeRunners-8
96SP-136
Game Film-GF4
SPx Force-2
96SPx-40
Gold-40
Holoview Heroes-HH8
96Stadium Club Members Only-3
96Summit-35
Artist's Proofs-35
Ice-35
Metal-35
Premium Stock-35
High Voltage-16
High Voltage Mirage-16
96Team Out-31
96Topps Picks-29
Fantasy Team-FT12
OPC Inserts-29
Top Shelf-TS10
96Ultra-146
Gold Medallion-146
Mr. Momentum-4
96Upper Deck-324
Game Jerseys-GJ2
Generation Next-X6
Hart Hopefuls Bronze-HH13
Hart Hopefuls Gold-HH13
Hart Hopefuls Silver-HH13
Superstar Showdown-SS15B
96Upper Deck Ice-115
Parallel-115
96Zenith-67
Artist's Proofs-67
Z-Team-7
96Swedish Semic Wien-164
97Headliners Hockey-9
97Be A Player-15
Autographs-15
Autographs Die-Cuts-15
Autographs Prismatic Die-Cuts-15
One Timers-6
Take A Number-13
97Beehive-6
Golden Portraits-6
Team-14
Team Gold-14
97Black Diamond-19
Double Diamond-19
Triple Diamond-19
Quadruple Diamond-19
Premium Cut-PC18
Premium Cut Double Diamond-PC18
Premium Cut Quadruple Diamond Horiz-PC18
Premium Cut Triple Diamond-PC18
Premium Cut Quadruple Diamond Verticals-PC18
97Collector's Choice-224
Crash the Game-C26A
Crash the Game-C26B
Crash the Game-C26C
Crash the Game Exchange-CR26
Star Quest-SQ76
Stick'Ums-S26
97Crown Royale-117
Emerald Green-117
Ice Blue-117
Silver-117
Blades of Steel Die-Cuts-18
Hat Tricks Die-Cuts-16
Lamplighters Cel-Fusion Die-Cuts-18
97Donruss-71
Press Proofs Silver-71
Press Proofs Gold-71
Line 2 Line-18
Line 2 Line Die Cut-18
Red Alert-5
97Donruss Canadian Ice-17
Dominion Series-17
Provincial Series-17
Stanley Cup Scrapbook-6
97Donruss Elite-12
Aspirations-12
Status-12
Back to the Future-6
Back to the Future Autographs-6
97Donruss Limited-20
97Donruss Limited-51
97Donruss Limited-185
Exposure-20
Exposure-51
Exposure-185
Fabric of the Game-28
Fabric of the Game-38
97Donruss Preferred-15
97Donruss Preferred-193
Cut to the Chase-15
Cut to the Chase-193
Line of the Times-3C
97Donruss Preferred Line of Times Promos-3C
97Donruss Priority-9
Stamp of Approval-9
Direct Deposit-23
Postcards-28
Postcards Opening Day Issues-9
Stamps-28
Stamps Bronze-28
Stamps Gold-28
Stamps Silver-28
97Esso Olympic Hockey Heroes-27
97Esso Olympic Hockey Heroes French-27
97Flames Collector's Photos-16
97Highland Mint Mint-Cards Topps-13
97Highland Mint Mint-Cards Topps-14
97Highland Mint Mint-Coins-4
97Katch-129
97Katch-163
Gold-129
Gold-163
Silver-129
Silver-163
97Kraft-22
97Leaf-11
97Leaf-178
Fractal Matrix-11
Fractal Matrix-178
Fractal Matrix Die Cuts-11
Fractal Matrix Die Cuts-178
Banner Season-11
97Leaf International-11
Universal Ice-11
97McDonald's Upper Deck-16
97Pacific-16
Copper-16
Emerald Green-16
Ice Blue-16
Red-16
Silver-16
Card-Supials-18
Card-Supials Minis-18
Gold Crown Die-Cuts-19
Slap Shots Die-Cuts-9C
Team Checklists-21
97Pacific Dynagon-107
97Pacific Dynagon-143
Copper-107
Copper-143
Dark Grey-107
Dark Grey-143
Emerald Green-107
Emerald Green-143
Ice Blue-107
Ice Blue-143
Red-107
Red-143
Silver-107
Silver-143
Best Kept Secrets-81
Dynamic Duos-14B
Tandems-8
Tandems-18
97Pacific Invincible-120
Copper-120
Emerald Green-120

Ice Blue-120
Red-120
Silver-120
Attack Zone-21
Feature Performers-31
NHL Regime-169
Off The Glass-18
97Pacific Omega-194
Copper-194
Dark Gray-194
Emerald Green-194
Gold-194
Ice Blue-194
Game Face-17
97Panini Stickers-168
97Paramount-159
Copper-159
Dark Grey-159
Emerald Green-159
Ice Blue-159
Red-159
Silver-159
Big Numbers Die-Cuts-18
Photoengravings-18
97Pinnacle-35
Artist's Proofs-35
Rink Collection-35
Epix Game Emerald-18
Epix Game Orange-18
Epix Game Purple-18
Epix Moment Emerald-18
Epix Moment Orange-18
Epix Moment Purple-18
Epix Play Emerald-18
Epix Play Orange-18
Epix Play Purple-18
Epix Season Emerald-18
Epix Season Orange-18
Epix Season Purple-18
Press Plates Back Black-35
Press Plates Back Cyan-35
Press Plates Back Magenta-35
Press Plates Back Yellow-35
Press Plates Front Black-35
Press Plates Front Cyan-35
Press Plates Front Magenta-35
Press Plates Front Yellow-35
97Pinnacle Certified-70
Red-70
Mirror Blue-70
Mirror Gold-70
Mirror Red-70
Team-19
Gold Team Promo-19
Gold Team-19
97Pinnacle Inside-12
Coach's Collection-12
Executive Collection-12
Track-19
Cans-23
Cans Gold-23
97Pinnacle Mint-23
Bronze-23
Gold Team-23
Silver Team-23
Coins Brass-23
Coins Brass Proofs-23
Coins Gold Plated-23
Coins Gold Plated Proofs-23
Coins Nickel Silver-23
Coins Nickel Silver Proofs-23
Coins Solid Gold-23
Coins Solid Silver-23
Minternational-3
Minternational Coins-3
97Pinnacle Power Pack Blow-Ups-8
97Pinnacle Tot Cert Platinum Blue-70
97Pinnacle Tot Cert Platinum Gold-70
97Pinnacle Totally Certified Platinum Red-70
97Pinnacle Tot Cert Mirror Platinum Gold-70
97Post Pinnacle-11
97Revolution-121
Copper-121
Emerald-121
Ice Blue-121
Silver-121
Team Checklist Laser Cuts-21
97Score-81
Artist's Proofs-81
Golden Blades-81
97Score Blues-1
Platinum-1
Premier-1
97SP Authentic-138
Icons-I2
Icons Die-Cuts-I2
Icons Embossed-I2
Sign of the Times-BH
Tradition-T5
97SPx-43
Bronze-43
Gold-43
Silver-43
Steel-43
Dimension-SPX20
Grand Finale-43
97Studio-11
Press Proofs Silver-11
Press Proofs Gold-11
Hard Hats-20
Portraits-11
Silhouettes-8
Silhouettes 8x10-8
97Upper Deck-141
Blow-Ups 3 x 5-1-8
Game Dated Moments-141
Sixth Sense Masters-SS4
Sixth Sense Wizards-SS4
Smooth Grooves-SG16
The Specialists-16
The Specialists Level 2 Die Cuts-16
Three Star Selects-9C
97Upper Deck Crash the All-Star Game-3
97Upper Deck Crash the All-Star Game-AR3
97Upper Deck Diamond Vision-25
Signature Moves-25
97Upper Deck Ice-66
Parallel-66
Champions-IC16
Champions 2 Die Cuts-IC16
Lethal Lines-L8C
Lethal Lines 2-L8C
Power Shift-66
97Zenith-25
Z-Gold-25
Z-Silver-25
97Zenith 5 x 7-48
Gold Impulse-48
Silver Impulse-48
97Zenith Chasing The Cup-7
98Headliners Hockey XL-2
98Aurora-55
98Be A Player-189
Press Release-189
98BAP Gold-189
98BAP Autographs-189
98BAP Autographs Gold-189
98BAP AS Game Used Stick Cards-S11
98BAP AS Game Used Jersey Cards-AS12
98BAP AS Milestones-M6
98BAP Playoff Game Used Jerseys-G18
98BAP Playoff Practice Used Jerseys-P1
98Black Diamond-25
Double Diamond-25
Triple Diamond-25
Quadruple Diamond-25
Myriad-M16
Myriad 2-M16
Winning Formula Gold-WF26
Winning Formula Platinum-WF26
98Bowman's Best-10
Refractors-10
Atomic Refractors-10
98Crown Royale-38
Limited Series-38
Master Performers-7
Pillars of the Game-10
Pivotal Players-6
98Donruss Elite Promos-2
98Finest-19
No Protectors-19
No Protectors Refractors-19
Refractors-19
98Katch-162
98McDonalds Upper Deck Gretzkys Teammates-T5
98OPC Chrome-30
Refractors-30
Blast From the Past-6
Blast From the Past Refractors-6
98Pacific-16
Ice Blue-16
Red-16
Gold Crown Die-Cuts-30
Team Checklists-22
Timelines-17
98Pacific Dynagon Ice-56
Blue-56
Red-56
Forward Thinking-7
98Pacific Omega-70
Red-70
Opening Day Issue-70
EO Portraits-7
EO Portraits 1 of 1-7
Online-12
Planet Ice-9
Planet Ice Parallel-9
98Panini Photocards-34
98Panini Stickers-152
98Paramount-64
Copper-64
Emerald Green-64
Holo-Electric-64
Ice Blue-64
Silver-64
98Revolution-41
Ice Shadow-41
Red-41
Chalk Talk Laser-Cuts-6
Showstoppers-14
98SP Authentic-24
Power Shift-24
Authentics-12
Sign of the Times-BH
Sign of the Times Gold-BH
Snapshots-SS4
Stat Masters-S2
98SPx Finite-97
Radiance-97
Spectrum-97
98SPx Top Prospects-19
Radiance-19
Spectrum-19
Highlight Heroes-H12
Lasting Impressions-L16
Premier Stars-PS25
98Topps-30
O-Pee-Chee-30
Blast From The Past-6
98Topps Gold Label Class 1-92
Black-92
Black One of One-92
One of One-92
Red-92
Red One of One-92
98Topps Gold Label Class 2-92
98Topps Gold Label Class 2 Black-92
98Topps Gold Label Class 2 Black 1 of 1-92
98Topps Gold Label Class 2 One of One-92
98Topps Gold Label Class 2 Red-92
98Topps Gold Label Class 2 Red One of One-92
98Topps Gold Label Class 3-92
98Topps Gold Label Class 3 Black-92
98Topps Gold Label Class 3 Black 1 of 1-92
98Topps Gold Label Class 3 One of One-92
98Topps Gold Label Class 3 Red-92
98Topps Gold Label Class 3 Red One of One-92
98UD Choice-183
Mini Bobbing Head-BH4
98UD Choice Preview-183
98UD Choice Prime Choice Reserve-183
98UD Choice Reserve-183
98UD Choice StarQuest Blue-SQ22
98UD Choice StarQuest Gold-SQ22
98UD Choice StarQuest Green-SQ22
98UD Choice StarQuest Red-SQ22
98UD3-35
98UD3-95
98UD3-155
Die-Cuts-35
Die-Cuts-95
Die-Cuts-155
98Upper Deck-76
Exclusives-76
Exclusives 1 of 1-76
Fantastic Finishers-FF7
Fantastic Finishers Quantum 1-FF7
Fantastic Finishers Quantum 2-FF7
Fantastic Finishers Quantum 3-FF7
Profiles-P2
Profiles Quantum 1-P2
Profiles Quantum 2-P2
Profiles Quantum 3-P2
Gold Reserve-76
98Upper Deck MVP-59
Gold Script-59
Silver Script-59
Super Script-59
Game Souvenirs-BH
Special Forces-F1
98Slovakian Eurotel-6
99SLU Hockey One On One-1
99Aurora-44
Striped-44
Premiere Date-44
Premiere Date Striped-44
99BAP Memorabilia-45
Gold-45
Silver-45
Jersey Cards-J12
Jersey Emblems-E12
Jersey Numbers-I12
Jersey and Stick Cards-S12
AS Heritage Ruby-H12
AS Heritage Sapphire-H12
AS Heritage Emerald-H12
99BAP Update Double AS Jersey Cards-D16
99BAP Update Teammates Jersey Cards-TM4
99BAP Update Teammates Jersey Cards-TM46
99BAP Update Teammates Jersey Cards-TM47
99BAP Millennium-82
Emerald-82
Ruby-82
Sapphire-82
Signatures-82
Signatures Gold-82
Jerseys-J21
Jersey Autographs-J21
Jersey and Stick Cards-JS21
Jersey Emblems-E21
Jersey Numbers-N21
Pearson-P7
Pearson Autographs-P7
Players of the Decade-D8
Players of the Decade Autographs-D8
99Black Diamond-30
Diamond Cut-30
Final Cut-30
A Piece of History-BH
A Piece of History Double-BH
A Piece of History Triple-BH
Myriad-M5
99Crown Royale-44
Limited Series-44
Premiere Date-44
Ice Elite-10
Ice Elite Parallel-10
99Kraft Overtime Winners-1
99Kraft Stanley Cup Moments-3
99McDonald's Upper Deck-MCD7
99McDonald's Upper Deck-MCD7R
Signatures-BH
99O-Pee-Chee-138
99O-Pee-Chee Chrome-138
99O-Pee-Chee Chrome Refractors-138
99Pacific-120
Copper-120
Emerald Green-120
Gold-120
Ice Blue-120
Premiere Date-120
Red-120
Gold Crown Die-Cuts-14
Past and Present-10
99Pacific Dynagon Ice-65
Blue-65
Copper-65
Gold-65
Premiere Date-65
Checkmates American-8
Checkmates American-23
Checkmates Canadian-23
99Pacific Omega-72
Copper-72
Gold-72
Ice Blue-72
Premiere Date-72
Cup Contenders-6
99Pacific Prism-44
Holographic Blue-44
Holographic Gold-44
Holographic Mirror-44
Holographic Purple-44
Premiere Date-44
Clear Advantage-7
99Panini Stickers-225
99Panini Stickers-332
99Paramount-72
Copper-72
Emerald-72
Gold-72
Holographic Emerald-72
Holographic Gold-72
Holographic Silver-72
Ice Blue-72
Premiere Date-72
Red-72
Silver-72
Personal Best-13
Toronto Fall Expo '99-72
99Revolution-45
Premiere Date-45
Red-45
Shadow Series-45
NHL Icons-8
Showstoppers-13
Top of the Line-26
Copper-45
Gold-45
CSC Silver-45
99SP Authentic-28
Buyback Signatures-21
Buyback Signatures-22
Buyback Signatures-23
Buyback Signatures-24
Buyback Signatures-25
Buyback Signatures-26
Buyback Signatures-27
Buyback Signatures-28
Jersey Redemption-JBH
Sign of the Times-BHU
Sign of the Times Gold-BHU
Supreme Skill-SS4
99SPx-48
Radiance-48
Spectrum-48
Prolifics-P3
SPXcitement-X10
SPXtreme-XT12
Starscape-S1
Winning Materials-WM6
Winning Materials-WM-A2
99Stadium Club-31
First Day Issue-31
One of a Kind-31
Printing Plates Black-31
Printing Plates Cyan-31
Printing Plates Magenta-31
Printing Plates Yellow-31
Capture the Action-CA28
Capture the Action Game View-CAG28
Chrome-21
Chrome Refractors-21
99Stars Postcards-8
99Topps/OPC-138
99Topps/OPC Chrome-138
Refractors-138
99Topps Gold Label Class 1-53
Black-53
Black One of One-53
One of One-53
Red-53
Red One of One-53
99Topps Gold Label Class 2-53
99Topps Gold Label Class 2 Black-53
99Topps Gold Label Class 2 Black 1 of 1-53
99Topps Gold Label Class 2 One of One-53
99Topps Gold Label Class 2 Red-53
99Topps Gold Label Class 2 Red One of One-53
99Topps Gold Label Class 3-53
99Topps Gold Label Class 3 Black-53
99Topps Gold Label Class 3 Black 1 of 1-53
99Topps Gold Label Class 3 One of One-53
99Topps Gold Label Class 3 Red-53
99Topps Gold Label Class 3 Red One of One-53
99Topps Gold Label Quest for the Cup-QC9
99Topps Gold Label Quest for the Cup One of One -QC9
99Topps Gold Label Quest 4 the Cup Black-QC9
99Topps Gold Label Quest for the Cup Black One of One -QC9
99Topps Gold Label Quest for the Cup Red-QC9
99Topps Gold Label Quest for the Cup Red One of One -QC9
99Topps Premier Plus-9
Parallel-9
99Ultimate Victory-28
1/1-28
Parallel-28
Parallel 100-28
Smokin Guns-SG11
The Victors-V2
99Upper Deck-43
99Upper Deck-144
Exclusives-43
Exclusives-144
Exclusives 1 of 1-43
Exclusives 1 of 1-144
500 Goal Club-500BHU
500 Goal Club-500BHU
Crunch Time-CT8
Crunch Time Quantum Gold-CT8
Crunch Time Quantum Silver-CT8
Fantastic Finishers-FF1
Fantastic Finishers Quantum Gold-FF1
Fantastic Finishers Quantum Silver-FF1
Game Jerseys-BH
Game Jerseys-BHS
Game Jersey Patch-BHP
Headed for the Hall-HOF6
Headed for the Hall Quantum Gold-HOF6
Headed for the Hall Quantum Silver-HOF6
NHL Scrapbook-SB9
NHL Scrapbook Quantum Gold-SB9
NHL Scrapbook Quantum Silver-SB9
PowerDeck Inserts-PD6
Sixth Sense-SS3
Sixth Sense Quantum Gold-SS3
Sixth Sense Quantum Silver-SS3
99Upper Deck Century Legends-62
Century Collection-62
Epic Signatures-BRH
Epic Signatures 100-BRH
Essence of the Game-E7
99Upper Deck Gold Reserve-43
99Upper Deck Gold Reserve-144
Game-Used Souvenirs-GRBH
UD Authentics-BH
99Upper Deck HoloGrFx-18
Ausome-18
Pure Skill-PS7
Pure Skill Ausome-PS7
UD Authentics-BH
99Upper Deck MVP-60
Gold Script-60
Silver Script-60
Super Script-60
Game-Used Souvenirs-GU3
Hands of Gold-H2
ProSign-BH
99Upper Deck MVP SC Edition-57
Gold Script-57
Gold Script-219
Silver Script-57
Silver Script-219
Super Script-57
Super Script-219
Game-Used Souvenirs-GUBH
Great Combinations-GCHM
Great Combinations Parallel-GCHM
ProSign-BH
Stanley Cup Talent-SC6
99Upper Deck Ovation-21
Standing Ovation-21
A Piece Of History-BHP
A Piece Of History-BHS
Superstar Theater-ST3
99Upper Deck PowerDeck-9
Auxiliary-9
Auxiliary 1 of 1-9
Time Capsule-T7
Time Capsule Auxiliary-T7
Time Capsule Auxiliary 1 of 1-T7
99Upper Deck Retro-25
Gold-25
Platinum-25
Inkredible-BRH
Inkredible Level 2-BRH
99Upper Deck Victory-85
99Upper Deck Victory-87
99Upper Deck Victory-322
99Wayne Gretzky Hockey-54
Elements of the Game-EG6
Signs of Greatness-BH
Tools of Greatness-TGBH
00Aurora-44
Pinstripes-44
Pinstripes Premiere Date-44
Premiere Date-44
Championship Fever-8
Championship Fever Copper-8
Championship Fever Platinum Blue-8
Championship Fever Silver-8
Scouting Reports-7
Styrotechs-5A
00BAP Memorabilia-106
Emerald-106
Ruby-106
Sapphire-106
Promos-106
Jersey Cards-J30
Jersey Emblems-E30
Jersey Numbers-N30
Jersey and Stick Cards-JS30
Patent Power Jerseys-PP5
00BAP Mem Chicago Sportsfest Copper-106
00BAP Memorabilia Chicago Sportsfest Blue-106
00BAP Memorabilia Chicago Sportsfest Gold-106
00BAP Memorabilia Chicago Sportsfest Ruby-106
00BAP Memorabilia Chicago Sun-Times Ruby-106
00BAP Memorabilia Chicago Sun-Times Gold-106
00BAP Mem Chicago Sun-Times Sapphire-106
00BAP Mem Toronto Fall Expo Copper-106
00BAP Memorabilia Toronto Fall Expo Gold-106
00BAP Memorabilia Toronto Fall Expo Ruby-106
00BAP Mem Update Heritage Jersey Cards-H8
00BAP Mem Update Heritage Jersey Gold-H8
00BAP Memorabilia Update Teammates-TM15
00BAP Memorabilia Update Teammates Gold-TM15
00BAP Parkhurst 2000-P100
00BAP Signature Series-71
Emerald-71
Ruby-71
Sapphire-71
He Shoots-He Scores Points-7
He Shoots-He Scores Prizes-29
Jersey Cards-J21
Jersey and Stick Cards-GSJ21
Jersey Cards Autographs-J21
Jersey Emblems-E21
Jersey Numbers-IN21
00BAP Ultimate Memorabilia Active Eight-AE3
00BAP Ultimate Mem Game-Used Jerseys-GJ21
00BAP Ultimate Mem Game-Used Emblems-E19
00BAP Ultimate Mem Game-Used Numbers-N19
00BAP Ultimate Mem Game-Used Sticks-GS21
00BAP Ultimate Memorabilia Hart Trophy-H10
00BAP Ultimate Mem Journey Jerseys-JJ9
00BAP Ultimate Mem Journey Emblems-JE9
00BAP Ultimate Mem Journey Numbers-JI9
00BAP Ultimate Memorabilia Teammates-TM24
00BAP Ultimate Memorabilia Teammates-TM25
00BAP Ultimate Memorabilia Teammates-TM28
00BAP Ultimate Memorabilia Teammates-TM32
00Black Diamond-18
Gold-18
00Crown Royale-35
Ice Blue-35
Limited Series-35
Premiere Date-35
Red-35
Game-Worn Jerseys-8
Game-Worn Jersey Patches-8
Premium-Sized Game-Worn Jerseys-8
Jewels of the Crown-11
Now Playing-7
00McDonald's Pacific-11
Blue-11
00O-Pee-Chee-59
00O-Pee-Chee-330
00O-Pee-Chee Parallel-59
00O-Pee-Chee Parallel-330
00Pacific-131
Copper-131
Gold-131
Ice Blue-131
Premiere Date-131
Gold Crown Die Cuts-11
Reflections-7
00Panini Stickers-148
00Paramount-75
Copper-75
Gold-75
Holo-Gold-75
Holo-Silver-75
Ice Blue-75
Premiere Date-75
Epic Scope-8
Freeze Frame-12
Hall of Fame Bound-5
Hall of Fame Bound Canvas Proofs-5
Hall of Fame Bound Proofs-5
00Private Stock-31
Gold-31
Premiere Date-31
Retail-31
Silver-31
Artist's Canvas-9
Artist's Canvas Proofs-9
Extreme Action-7
PS-2001 Action-17
PS-2001 Stars-9
00Revolution-46
Blue-46
Premiere Date-46
Red-46
HD NHL-13
Ice Immortals-8
NHL Icons-9
Stat Masters-4
00SP Authentic-30
BuyBacks-31
BuyBacks-32
BuyBacks-33
BuyBacks-34
BuyBacks-35
BuyBacks-36
Sign of the Times-H/H
Sign of the Times-HLY
Significant Stars-ST2
00SP Game Used-19
Patch Cards-P-BH
Tools of the Game-BH
Tools of the Game Exclusives-BH
Tools of the Game Combos-C-HB
Tools of the Game Autographed Bronze-A-BR
Tools of the Game Autographed Silver-A-BR
Tools of the Game Autographed Gold-A-BR
00SPx-19
Spectrum-19
Highlight Heroes-HH6
Prolifics-P3
Winning Materials-BH
Winning Materials Autographs-SBH
00Stadium Club-94
Beam Team-BT7
00Stars Postcards-8
00Titanium-28
Blue-28
Gold-28
Premiere Date-28
Red-28
Retail-28
All-Stars-6NA
Game Gear-15
Game Gear-84
Game Gear-154
Game Gear Patches-84
00Titanium Draft Day Edition-30
00Topps/OPC-59
00Topps/OPC-330
Parallel-59
Parallel-330
Combos-TC9
Combos Jumbos-TC9
NHL Draft-D13
1000 Point Club-PC12
00Topps Chrome-47
OPC Refractors-47
Refractors-47
Combos-TC9
Combos Refractors-TC9
1000 Point Club Refractors-12
00Topps Gold Label Class 1-5
Gold-5
00Topps Gold Label Class 2-5
00Topps Gold Label Class 2 Gold-5
00Topps Gold Label Class 3-5
00Topps Gold Label Class 3 Gold-5
00Topps Gold Label Bullion-B2
00Topps Gold Label Bullion One to One-B2
00Topps Gold Label Golden Greats-GG6
00Topps Gold Label Golden Greats 1 to 1-GG6
00Topps Heritage-14
Chrome Parallel-14
Heroes-HH14
00Topps Premier Plus-56
Blue Ice-56
Trophy Tribute-TT11
World Premier-WP19
00Topps Stars-14
00Topps Stars-131
Blue-14
Blue-131
All-Star Authority-ASA2
00UD Heroes-37
Timeless Moments-TM4
00UD Pros and Prospects-28
NHL Passion-NP2
00UD Reserve-28
Power Portfolios-PP2
00Upper Deck-284
Exclusives Tier 1-284
Exclusives Tier 2-284
Dignitaries-D4
e-Cards-EC2
e-Card Prizes-ABH
e-Card Prizes-EBH
e-Card Prizes-SEBH
Fantastic Finishers-FF4
Frozen in Time-FT3
Game Jersey Autographs-HBH
Game Jersey Autographs Exclusives-EBH
Game Jersey Combos-DGH
Game Jersey Doubles-DBH
Game Jersey Patches-BHP
Game Jersey Patch Autographs Exclusives-BHP
Lord Stanley's Heroes-L3
Triple Threat-TT4
00Upper Deck Ice-14
Immortals-14
Legends-14
Stars-14
Clear Cut Autographs-BH
Game Jerseys-JCBH
00Upper Deck Legends-30
00Upper Deck Legends-37
Legendary Collection Bronze-30
Legendary Collection Bronze-37
Legendary Collection Gold-30
Legendary Collection Gold-37
Legendary Collection Silver-30
Legendary Collection Silver-37
Epic Signatures-BH
Legendary Game Jerseys-JBH
Playoff Heroes-PH8
Supreme Milestones-SM6
00Upper Deck MVP-57
First Stars-57
Second Stars-57
Talent-M6
Third Stars-57
00Upper Deck Victory-72
00Upper Deck Victory-247
00Upper Deck Victory-297
00Upper Deck Vintage-114
00Vanguard-34
High Voltage-11
High Voltage Gold-11
High Voltage Green-11
High Voltage Red-11
High Voltage Silver-11
Holographic Gold-34
Holographic Purple-34
In Focus-7
Pacific Proofs-34
Press East/West-5
00Czech Stadion-94
01McFarlane Hockey-70
01McFarlane Hockey-71
01Atomic-37
Blue-37
Gold-37
Premiere Date-37
Red-37
Statosphere-13
01BAP Memorabilia-92
01BAP Memorabilia-378
Emerald-92
Emerald-378
Ruby-92
Ruby-378
Sapphire-92
Sapphire-378
All-Star Jerseys-ASJ50
All-Star Emblems-ASE50
All-Star Numbers-ASN50
All-Star Teammates-AST46
500 Goal Scorers-GS8
01BAP Signature Series Certified 100-C51
01BAP Signature Series Certified 50-C51
01BAP Signature Series Certified 1 of 1's-C51
01BAP Signature Series 500 Goal Scorers-24
01BAP Ultimate Memorabilia Active Eight-5
01BAP Ultimate Mem All-Star History-40
01BAP Ultimate Memorabilia Bloodlines-6
01BAP Ultimate Memorabilia Dynamic Duos-4
01BAP Ultimate Mem 500 Goal Scorers-14
01BAP Ultimate Mem 500 Goal Jerseys/Stick-14
01BAP Ultimate Mem 500 Goal Emblems-14
01BAP Ultimate Mem Journey Jerseys-11
01BAP Ultimate Mem Journey Emblems-11
01BAP Ultimate Mem Prototypical Players-15
01BAP Ultimate Mem Scoring Leaders-9
01BAP Ultimate Mem Scoring Leaders-10
01BAP Ultimate Mem Scoring Leaders-11
01BAP Update Heritage-H13
01Bowman YoungStars-2
Gold-2
Ice Cubed-2
01Crown Royale-53
Blue-53
Premiere Date-53
Red-53
Retail-53
All-Star Honors-8
01McDonald's Pacific-9
Hockey Greats-3
Jersey Patches Silver-6
Jersey Patches Gold-6
01O-Pee-Chee-86
01O-Pee-Chee-86U
01O-Pee-Chee Heritage Parallel-86
01O-Pee-Chee Heritage Parallel Limited-86
01O-Pee-Chee Premier Parallel-86
01Pacific-126
01Pacific-428
Extreme LTD-126
Gold-428
Hobby LTD-126
Premiere Date-126
Retail LTD-126
All-Stars-NA6
01Pacific Adrenaline-66
Blue-66
Premiere Date-66
Red-66
Retail-66
Jerseys-15
Playmakers-4
World Beaters-5
01Pacific Arena Exclusives-126
01Pacific Arena Exclusives-428
01Pacific Heads-Up-30
Blue-30
Premiere Date-30
Red-30
Silver-30
Rink Immortals-4
Stat Masters-5
01Parkhurst-67
Gold-67
Silver-67
500 Goal Scorers-PGS8
Heroes-H13
Milestones-M20U
Milestones-M46
Sticks-PS59
Waving the Flag-26
01Private Stock-34
Gold-34
Premiere Date-34
Retail-34
Silver-34
Game Gear-43
01Private Stock Pacific Nights-34
01Private Stock PS-2002-28
01SP Authentic-26
01SP Authentic-100
Limited-26
Limited-100
Limited Gold-26
Limited Gold-100
01SP Game Used-19
01SPx-172
Hockey Treasures-HTBH
Hockey Treasures-HTHU
01Sports Illustrated for Kids III-277
01Stadium Club-105
Award Winners-105
Master Photos-105
01Titanium-50
Hobby Parallel-50
Premiere Date-50
Retail-50
Retail Parallel-50
01Titanium Draft Day Edition-38
01Topps-86
01Topps-86U
Heritage Parallel-86
Heritage Parallel Limited-86
OPC Parallel-86
Game-Worn Jersey-JBH
Shot Masters-SM3
01Topps Chrome-86
Refractors-86
Black Border Refractors-86
01Topps Heritage-162
01Topps Reserve-99
01UD Challenge for the Cup Century Men-CM9
01UD Challenge for the Cup Future Famers-FF3
01UD Honor Roll Jerseys-J-BH
01UD Honor Roll Jerseys Gold-J-BH
01UD Honor Roll Playoff Matchups-HS-HT
01UD Honor Roll Playoff Matchups Gold-HS-HT
01UD Mask Collection-34
Gold-34
Gloves-GGBH
01UD Playmakers-34
01UD Premier Collection-22
Dual Jerseys-DGH
Dual Jerseys Black-DGH
01UD Stanley Cup Champs-47
Jerseys-T-BH
Pieces of Glory-G-BH
Sticks-S-BH
01UD Top Shelf-21
Jerseys-BH
Sticks-SBH
Sticks Gold-SBH
01Upper Deck-62
01Upper Deck-213
Exclusives-62
Exclusives-213
Crunch Timers-CT5
Shooting Stars-SS5
01Upper Deck Ice-14
01Upper Deck Ice-95
Jerseys-J-BH
01Upper Deck MVP-66
Souvenirs-S-BH
Souvenirs Gold-S-BH
Watch-MW4
01Upper Deck Victory-110
01Upper Deck Victory-409
Gold-110
Gold-409
01Vanguard-36
Blue-36
Red-36
Memorabilia-46
One of Ones-36
Premiere Date-36
Proofs-36
Quebec Tournament Heroes-1
01Czech Stadion-239
02Atomic-37
Blue-37
Gold-37
Red-37
Hobby Parallel-37
Jerseys-7
Jerseys Gold-7
Patches-7
National Pride-U4
02BAP All-Star Edition-31
Jerseys-31
Jerseys Gold-31
Jerseys Silver-31
02BAP First Edition-190
02BAP First Edition-335
02BAP Memorabilia-41
Emerald-41
Ruby-41
Sapphire-41
All-Star Jerseys-ASJ-19
All-Star Emblems-ASE-6
All-Star Numbers-ASN-6
NHL All-Star Game-41
NHL All-Star Game Blue-41
NHL All-Star Game Green-41
NHL All-Star Game Red-41
Stanley Cup Champions-SCC-15
Teammates-TM-3
02BAP Memorabilia Toronto Fall Expo-41
02BAP NHL All-Star History-40
02BAP Sig Series Auto Buybacks 1998-189
02BAP Sig Series Auto Buybacks 1999-82
02BAP Signature Series Team Quads-TQ13
02BAP Signature Series Triple Memorabilia-TM7
02BAP Ultimate Memorabilia Active Eight-4
02BAP Ultimate Memorabilia All-Star MVP-4
02BAP Ultimate Memorabilia Dynamic Duos-5
02BAP Ultimate Mem Dynasty Jerseys-2
02BAP Ultimate Mem Dynasty Emblems-2
02BAP Ultimate Mem Dynasty Numbers-2
02BAP Ultimate Memorabilia Emblems-14
02BAP Ultimate Memorabilia Gloves Are Off-19
02BAP Ultimate Memorabilia Hat Tricks-13
02BAP Ultimate Memorabilia Jerseys-7
02BAP Ultimate Mem Jersey and Stick-5
02BAP Ultimate Mem Journey Jerseys-4
02BAP Ultimate Mem Journey Emblems-4
02BAP Ultimate Mem Lifetime Achievers-11
02BAP Ultimate Memorabilia Numbers-23
02BAP Ultimate Memorabilia Numerology-12
02BAP Ultimate Mem Playoff Scorers-3
02BAP Ultimate Mem Playoff Scorers-15
02BAP Ultimate Memorabilia Retro Trophies-19
02Bowman YoungStars-38
Gold-38
Silver-38
02Crown Royale-33
Blue-33
Red-33
Retail-33
02eTopps-32
02ITG Used-19
02ITG Used-119
Emblems-E32
Teammates-T20
Teammates Gold-T20
Triple Memorabilia-TM19
Triple Memorabilia Gold-TM19
02McDonald's Pacific Atomic-3
02O-Pee-Chee-92
02O-Pee-Chee Premier Blue Parallel-92
02O-Pee-Chee Premier Red Parallel-92
02O-Pee-Chee Factory Set-92
02Pacific-129
Blue-129
Red-129
02Pacific Calder-37
Silver-37
Hardware Heroes-4
02Pacific Complete-311
Red-311
02Pacific Exclusive-63
Etched in Stone-5
02Pacific Heads-Up-43
Blue-43
Purple-43
Red-43
Quad Jerseys-12
Quad Jerseys-29
Quad Jerseys Gold-12
Quad Jerseys Gold-29
Stat Masters-8
02Pacific Quest for the Cup-33
Gold-33
Raising the Cup-6
02Parkhurst-70
Bronze-70
Gold-70
Silver-70
College Ranks-CR8
College Ranks Jerseys-CRM8
Heroes-NH11
Patented Power-PP10
02Parkhurst Retro-55
Minis-55
Jerseys-RJ5
Jersey and Sticks-RSJ5
Memorabilia-RM30
Nicknames-RN23
02Private Stock Reserve-36
Blue-36
Red-36
Retail-36
02SP Authentic-32
02SP Authentic-97
Beckett Promos-32
02SP Game Used-57
Authentic Fabrics-AFBH
Authentic Fabrics-AFHU
Authentic Fabrics-CFSH
Authentic Fabrics Gold-AFBH
Authentic Fabrics Gold-AFHU
Authentic Fabrics Gold-CFSH
Authentic Fabrics Rainbow-AFBH
Authentic Fabrics Rainbow-AFHU
Authentic Fabrics Rainbow-CFSH
Piece of History-PHBH
Piece of History Gold-PHBH
Piece of History Rainbow-PHBH
Tools of the Game-BH
02SPx-29
02SPx-132
Spectrum Gold-29
Spectrum Silver-29
02Stadium Club-100
Silver Decoy Cards-100
Proofs-100
World Stage-WS7
02Titanium-36
Blue-36
Red-36
Retail-36
Jerseys-25
Jerseys Retail-25
Patches-25
02Topps-92
OPC Blue Parallel-92
OPC Red Parallel-92
Topps/OPC Hometown Heroes-HHU7
Factory Set-92
Factory Set Hometown Heroes-HHU7
02Topps Chrome-58

Black Border Refractors-58
Refractors-58
02Topps Heritage-11
Chrome Parallel-11
02Topps Total-258
Topps-TT10
02UD Foundations-82
02UD Honor Roll-27
02UD Piece of History-35
02UD Piece of History-99
Awards Collection-AC11
02UD Top Shelf Milestones Jerseys-MMHYR
02UD Top Shelf Shooting Stars-SHBH
02UD Top Shelf Sweet Sweaters-SWBH
02UD Top Shelf Triple Jerseys-HTSHR
02Upper Deck-68
02Upper Deck-192
Exclusives-68
Exclusives-192
Good Old Days-GOBH
Reaching Fifty-50BH
Reaching Fifty Gold-50BH
Classic Portraits Etched in Time-ET7
02Upper Deck MVP-66
Gold-66
Classics-66
Golden Classics-66
02Upper Deck Rookie Update-36
02Upper Deck Victory-78
Bronze-78
Gold-78
Silver-78
02Upper Deck Vintage-96
Green Backs-96
02Vanguard-36
LTD-36
Jerseys-18
Jerseys Gold-18
03McFarlane Hockey Red Wings-10
03McFarlane Hockey 3-Inch Duals-10
03BAP Memorabilia-17
Emerald-17
Gold-17
Ruby-17
Sapphire-17
Jersey and Stick-SJ-31
Jerseys-GJ-40
Jersey Autographs-GJ-40
03BAP Ultimate Memorabilia Autographs-142
Gold-142
03BAP Ultimate Mem Auto Jerseys-142
03BAP Ultimate Mem Auto Emblems-142
03BAP Ultimate Mem Auto Sticks-142
03BAP Ultimate Memorabilia Active Eight-3
03BAP Ultimate Memorabilia Active Eight-8
03BAP Ultimate Mem Always An All-Star-4
03BAP Ultimate Mem Always An AS Gold-4
03BAP Ultimate Mem Complete Jersey-4
03BAP Ultimate Mem Complete Jersey Gold-4
03BAP Ultimate Memorabilia Dynamic Duos-9
03BAP Ultimate Memorabilia Gloves Are Off-2
03BAP Ultimate Memorabilia Hat Tricks-14
03BAP Ultimate Memorabilia Heroes-7
03BAP Ultimate Mem Heroes Autos-4
03BAP Ultimate Mem Hometown Heroes-11
03BAP Ultimate Mem Hometown Heroes Gold-11
03BAP Ultimate Memorabilia Jerseys-17
03BAP Ultimate Memorabilia Jerseys Gold-17
03BAP Ultimate Mem Jersey and Emblems-5
03BAP Ultimate Mem Jersey and Emblem Gold-5
03BAP Ultimate Mem Jersey and Numbers-5
03BAP Ultimate Mem Jersey and Number Gold-5
03BAP Ultimate Mem Journey Jerseys-7
03BAP Ultimate Mem Journey Jerseys Gold-7
03BAP Ultimate Mem Journey Emblems-7
03BAP Ultimate Mem Journey Emblems Gold-7
03BAP Ultimate Mem Lifetime Achievers-6
03BAP Ultimate Memorabilia Linemates-9
03BAP Ultimate Mem Linemates Autos-12
03BAP Ultimate Mem Retro-Active Trophies-14
03BAP Ultimate Memorabilia Triple Threads-16
03Beehive-71
Gold-71
Silver-71
Sticks Beige Border-BE31
Sticks Red Border-RE2
03Black Diamond-64
Black-64
Green-64
Red-64
03Bowman-16
Gold-16
03Bowman Chrome-16
Refractors-16
Gold Refractors-16
Xfractors-16
03ITG Action-226
Highlight Reel-HR9
Jerseys-M188
Jerseys-M208
Jerseys-M226
03ITG Toronto Fall Expo Jerseys-FE20
03ITG Used Signature Series-94
Gold-94
Autographs-BHU
Autographs Gold-BHU
Jerseys-5
Jerseys Gold-5
Jersey Autos-5
Retrospectives-3A
Retrospectives-3B
Retrospectives-3C
Retrospectives-3D
Retrospectives-3E
Retrospectives-3F
Retrospectives Gold-3A
Retrospectives Gold-3B
Retrospectives Gold-3C
Retrospectives Gold-3D
Retrospectives Gold-3E
Retrospectives Gold-3F
Teammates-4
Teammates Gold-4
03ITG VIP Collages-12
03ITG VIP Collage Autographs-12
03ITG VIP Jerseys-18
03ITG VIP Jersey Autographs-18
03McDonald's Pacific Etched in Time-3
03NHL Sticker Collection-214
03O-Pee-Chee-270
03O-Pee-Chee-289
03OPC Blue-270
03OPC Blue-289
03OPC Gold-270
03OPC Gold-289
03OPC Red-270
03OPC Red-289
03Pacific-119
Blue-119
Red-119
Milestones-5
View from the Crease-6
03Pacific Calder-37
Silver-37
03Pacific Complete-104
Red-104
03Pacific Exhibit-168
03Pacific Exhibit-216
Blue Backs-168
History Makers-4
03Pacific Heads-Up-36
Hobby LTD-36
Retail LTD-36
Rink Immortals-5
Rink Immortals LTD-5
03Pacific Invincible-33
Blue-33
Red-33
Retail-33
Top Line-5
03Pacific Luxury Suite-33A
03Pacific Luxury Suite-33B
03Pacific Luxury Suite-33C
03Pacific Prism-37
Blue-37
Gold-37
Red-37
03Pacific Quest for the Cup-37
Blue-37
Raising the Cup-8
03Pacific Supreme-33
Blue-33
Red-33
Retail-33
Generations-5
Jerseys-11
Team-4
03Parkhurst Orig Six Boston Mem -BM44
03Parkhurst Orig Six Chicago Mem -CM44
03Parkhurst Original Six Detroit-12
Memorabilia-DM11
Memorabilia-DM19
Memorabilia-DM44
Memorabilia-DM51
03Parkhurst Orig Six He Shoots/Scores-28
03Parkhurst Orig Six He Shoots/Scores-28A
03Parkhurst Orig Six Montreal Mem-MM44
03Parkhurst Orig Six New York Mem-NM44
03Parkhurst Original Six Shooters-OSM4
03Parkhurst Orig Six Toronto Mem-TM44
03Parkhurst Rookie-49
Jerseys-GJ-38
Jersey Autographs-GUJ-BH
Jerseys Gold-GJ-38
Retro Rookies-RR-7
Retro Rookie Autographs-RR-BH
Retro Rookies Gold-RR-7
03Private Stock Reserve-165
Blue-165
Patches-165
Red-165
Retail-165
Moments in Time-7
03Serious NHL Starz-3
03SP Authentic 10th Anniversary-SP10
03SP Authentic 10th Anniversary Limited-SP10
03SP Game Used Authentic Fabrics-DFHY
03SP Game Used Authentic Fabrics-DFZH
03SP Game Used Authentic Fabrics-QYBHH
03SP Game Used Authentic Fabrics Gold-DFHY
03SP Game Used Authentic Fabrics Gold-DFZH
03SP Game Used Authentic Fabrics Gold-QYBHH
03SP Game Used Top Threads-YZHH
03SPx Fantasy Franchise-FF-HYS
03SPx Fantasy Franchise Limited-FF-HYS
03SPx Hall Pass-HP-BH
03SPx Hall Pass Limited-HP-BH
03Titanium-197
Patches-197
Stat Masters-6
03Topps-270
03Topps-289
Blue-270
Blue-289
Gold-270
Gold-289
Red-270
Red-289
Lost Rookies-BH
03Topps C55-70
Minis-70
Minis American Back-70
Minis American Back Red-70
Minis Bazooka Back-70
Minis Brooklyn Back-70
Minis Hat Trick Back-70
Minis O Canada Back-70
Minis O Canada Back Red-70
Minis Stanley Cup Back-70
Relics-TRBH
03Topps Pristine-70
Gold Refractor Die Cuts-70
Refractors-70
Press Plates Black-70
Press Plates Cyan-70
Press Plates Magenta-70
Press Plates Yellow-70
03UD Premier Collection-20
Stars-ST-BH
Stars Patches-ST-BH
Teammates-PT-DR2
Teammates Patches-PT-DR2
03Upper Deck-66
Canadian Exclusives-66
HG-66
Jerseys-UD-BH
Memorable Matchups-MM-HH
Patches-SP4
Classic Portraits Classic Colors-CC-BH
Classic Portraits Hockey Royalty-YHS
03Upper Deck Ice-29
Gold-29
Breakers-IB-BH
Breaker Patches-IB-BH
Clear Cut Winners-CC-BH
03Upper Deck MVP-143
Gold Script-143
Silver Script-143
Canadian Exclusives-143
Lethal Lineups-LL6
Souvenirs-S21
SportsNut-SN33
Threads-TC4
Winning Formula-WF6
03Upper Deck Rookie Update-31
All-Star Lineup-AS10
Skills-SKBH
Super Stars-SSBH
03Upper Deck Victory-63
Bronze-63
Gold-63
Silver-63
Freshman Flashback-FF18
Game Breakers-GB37
03Toronto Star-30
Foil-19
04ITG NHL AS FANtasy AS History Jerseys-SB40
04Pacific-93
Blue-93
Red-93
Global Connection-6
Philadelphia-5
04SP Authentic-68
04SP Authentic-137
04Ultimate Collection-33
Patches-UP-BH
04Upper Deck-135
Big Playmakers-BP-BH
Canadian Exclusives-135
HG Glossy Gold-135
HG Glossy Silver-135
World Cup Tribute-BH
World Cup Tribute-KTDWBH
05ITG Heroes/Prosp Toronto Expo Parallel -21
05ITG Heroes/Prosp Toronto Expo Parallel -346
05Be A Player-67
First Period-67
Second Period-67
Third Period-67
Overtime-67
Class Action-CA19
05Beehive-208
05Black Diamond-109
Emerald-109
Gold-109
Onyx-109
Ruby-109
Jerseys-J-BH
Jerseys Ruby-J-BH
Jersey Duals-DJ-BH
Jersey Triples-TJ-BH
Jersey Quads-QJ-BH
05ITG Ultimate Memorabilia Level 1-14
05ITG Ultimate Memorabilia Level 2-14
05ITG Ultimate Memorabilia Level 3-14
05ITG Ultimate Memorabilia Level 4-14
05ITG Ultimate Memorabilia Level 5-14
05ITG Ultimate Mem Complete Jersey-12
05ITG Ultimate Mem Complete Jersey Gold-12
05ITG Ultimate Mem Double Mem-7
05ITG Ultimate Mem Double Mem Gold-7
05ITG Ultimate Memorabilia Emblems-12
05ITG Ultimate Memorabilia Emblems Gold-12
05ITG Ultimate Memorabilia Gloves Are Off-10
05ITG Ultimate Mem Gloves Are Off Gold-10
05ITG Ultimate Memorabilia In The Numbers-8
05ITG Ultimate Mem In The Numbers Gold-8
05ITG Ultimate Mem Jersey and Emblem-18
05ITG Ultimate Memorabilia Jersey Autos-12
05ITG Ultimate Mem Jersey Autos Gold-12
05ITG Ultimate Mem Jersey Emblems Gold-18
05ITG Ultimate Memorabilia Jerseys-5
05ITG Ultimate Memorabilia Jerseys Gold-5
05ITG Ultimate Mem Pass the Torch Jerseys-12
05ITG Ultimate Mem Passing Torch Jsy Gold-12
05ITG Ultimate Mem Record Breaker Jerseys-9
05ITG Ultimate Mem RecBreak Jerseys Gold-9
05ITG Ultimate Memorabilia Triple Autos-20
05ITG Ultimate Mem Triple Autos Gold-20
05ITG Ultimate Memorabilia Ultimate Autos-30
05ITG Ultimate Mem Ultimate Autos Gold-30
05SP Authentic Prestigious Pairings-PPHH
05SP Game Used Authentic Fabrics Dual-DH
05SP Game Used Authentic Fabrics Triple-HND
05SP Game Used Authentic Patches Dual-DH
05SP Game Used Authentic Patches Triple-HND
05SPx-70
Spectrum-70
Winning Combos-WC-HD
Winning Combos-WC-HJ
Winning Combos Gold-WC-HJ
Winning Combos Spectrum-WC-HJ
Winning Materials-WM-BH
Winning Materials Gold-WM-BH
Winning Materials Spectrum-WM-BH
Xcitement Superstars-XS-BH
Xcitement Superstars Gold-XS-BH
Xcitement Superstars Spectrum-XS-BH
05UD Artifacts-77
05UD Artifacts-187
Blue-77
Blue-187
Gold-77
Gold-187
Green-77
Green-187
Pewter-77
Pewter-187
Red-77
Red-187
Frozen Artifacts-FA-BH
Frozen Artifacts Autographed-FA-BH
Frozen Artifacts Copper-FA-BH
Frozen Artifacts Dual-FAD-BH
Frozen Artifacts Dual Autographed-FAD-BH
Frozen Artifacts Dual Copper-FAD-BH
Frozen Artifacts Dual Gold-FAD-BH
Frozen Artifacts Dual Maroon-FAD-BH
Frozen Artifacts Dual Pewter-FAD-BH
Frozen Artifacts Dual Silver-FAD-BH
Frozen Artifacts Gold-FA-BH
Frozen Artifacts Maroon-FA-BH
Frozen Artifacts Patches-FP-BH
Frozen Artifacts Patches Autographed-FP-BH
Frozen Artifacts Patches Dual-FGD-DC
Frozen Artifacts Patches Dual Autos-FGD-DC
Frozen Artifacts Patches Pewter-FP-BH
Frozen Artifacts Patches Silver-FP-BH
Frozen Artifacts Pewter-FA-BH
Frozen Artifacts Silver-FA-BH
Gold Autographed-77
Gold Autographed-187
05UD PowerPlay-67
Rainbow-67
Specialists-TSBH
Specialists Patches-SPBH
05Upper Deck-144
Big Playmakers-B-BH
HG Glossy-144
Jerseys-J-BHU
Patches-P-BH
Scrapbooks-HS16
Shooting Stars-S-BH
MVP Monumental Moments-MM3
05Upper Deck Trilogy-149
Crystal-149
05Upper Deck Toronto Fall Expo-144
05Upper Deck Victory-148
Black-148
Gold-148
Silver-148
Blow-Ups-BU30
Game Breakers-GB34
Stars on Ice-SI34
05ITG Heroes and Prospects-21
05ITG Heroes and Prospects-346
AHL Grads-AG-2
AHL Grads Gold-AG-2
Autographs-A-BRH
Autographs-DA-HH
Autographs Series II-BRH2
He Shoots-He Scores Prizes-14
He Shoots-He Scores Prizes-59
Hero Memorabilia-HM-13
Hero Memorabilia Dual-HDM-2
National Pride-NPR-18
Spectrum-STM-04
Spectrum Gold-STM-04
06ITG International Ice-7
06ITG International Ice-36
Gold-7
Gold-36
Autographs-ABHU
Autographs-ABHU2
Complete Jersey-CJ14
Complete Jersey Gold-CJ14
Cornerstones-IC06
Cornerstones Gold-IC06
Emblem Autographs-GUE01
Emblem Autographs Gold-GUE01
Emblems-GUE01
Emblems Gold-GUE01
Hockey Passport-HP09
Hockey Passport Gold-HP09
International Rivals-IR16
International Rivals Gold-IR16
Jersey Autographs-GUJ01
Jersey Autographs Gold-GUJ01
Jerseys-GUJ01
Jerseys Gold-GUJ01
My Country My Team-MC4
My Country My Team Gold-MC4
Numbers-GUN01
Numbers Autographs-GUN01
Numbers Autographs Gold-GUN01
Numbers Gold-GUN01
Quad Patch-QP02
Quad Patch Gold-QP02
Stick and Jersey-SJ15
Stick and Jersey Gold-SJ15
Teammates-IT13
Teammates Gold-IT13
06ITG Ultimate Memorabilia-21
Artist Proof-21
Autos-17
Autos Gold-17
Bloodlines-7
Bloodlines Gold-7
Bloodlines Autos-6
Bloodlines Autos Gold-6
Bowman Factor-15
Bowman Factor Gold-15
Bowman Factor Autos-13
Bowman Factor Autos Gold-13
Boys Will Be Boys-1
Boys Will Be Boys Gold-1
Double Memorabilia-14
Double Memorabilia Gold-14
Double Memorabilia Autos-11
Double Memorabilia Autos Gold-11
Emblems-12
Emblems Gold-12
Gloves Are Off-3
Gloves Are Off Gold-3
Going For Gold-4
Going For Gold Gold-4
Jerseys-3
Jerseys Gold-3
Jerseys Autos-24
Jerseys Autos Gold-24
Journey Emblem-14
Journey Emblem Gold-14
Journey Jersey-14
Journey Jersey Gold-14
Passing The Torch-12
Passing The Torch Gold-12
Raised to the Rafters-9
Raised to the Rafters Gold-9
Retro Teammates-25
Retro Teammates Gold-25
Retrospective-4
Retrospective Gold-4
Road to the Cup-10
Road to the Cup Gold-10
Sensational Season-11
Sensational Season Gold-11
Stick Rack-5
Stick Rack Gold-5
Sticks Autos-20
Sticks Autos Gold-20
Triple Thread Jerseys-15
Triple Thread Jerseys Gold-15
06Stars Team Postcards-27

Hull, Dennis

64Beehive Group III Photos-42
65Coca-Cola-27
65Topps-64
66Topps-113
66Topps USA Test-1
67Topps-56
68Blackhawks Team Issue-1
68O-Pee-Chee-153
68Shirriff Coins-27
68Shirriff Coins-28
69O-Pee-Chee-71
69Topps-71
70Blackhawks Postcards-4
70Colgate Stamps-32
70Dad's Cookies-60
70Esso Power Players-117
70O-Pee-Chee-14
70Post Shooters-6
70Sargent Promotions Stamps-36
70Topps-14
71Letraset Action Replays-16
71O-Pee-Chee-85
71Sargent Promotions Stamps-46
71Topps-85
71Toronto Sun-67
72O-Pee-Chee-52
Team Canada-15
72Sargent Promotions Stamps-67
72Topps-164
73O-Pee-Chee-171
73Topps-60
74Lipton Soup-17
74Nabisco Sugar Daddy-12
74NHL Action Stamps-73
74O-Pee-Chee NHL-150
74Topps-150
75Nabisco Sugar Daddy-12
75O-Pee-Chee NHL-254
75Topps-254
76O-Pee-Chee NHL-195
76Topps-195
76Topps Glossy Inserts-16
77O-Pee-Chee NHL-225
77Sportscasters-2724
77Topps-225
91Future Trends Canada '72-89
91Future Trends Canada '72 French-89
94Parkhurst Tall Boys-39
95Parkhurst '66-67-37
Coins-37
99BAP Memorabilia AS Retail-R2
99BAP Memorabilia AS Retail Autographs-R2
01BAP Ultimate Memorabilia Bloodlines-6
01Parkhurst Autographs-PA55
01Topps Archives-25
Arena Seats-ASDH
Autographs-14
02BAP Ultimate Mem Vintage Jerseys-9
02Parkhurst Vintage Teammates-VT1
03BAP Ultimate Mem Vintage Jerseys-20
03BAP Ultimate Mem Vintage Jerseys Gold-20
03Parkhurst Original Six Chicago-46
Memorabilia-CM26
Memorabilia-CM58
04ITG Franchises US West-160
Autographs-A-DH
Memorabilia-WSM25
Memorabilia Autographs-WSMDH
Memorabilia Gold-WSM25
Teammates-WTM9
Teammates Gold-WTM9
04ITG Ultimate Memorabilia Original Six-4
04ITG Ultimate Mem Retro Teammates-3
04UD Legendary Signatures-26
Autographs-DH
Summit Stars-CDN6
Summit Stars Autographs-CDN-DH
05ITG Ultimate Mem Pass the Torch Jerseys-12
05ITG Ultimate Mem Passing Torch Jsy Gold-12
06ITG Ultimate Memorabilia Bloodlines-7
06ITG Ultimate Memorabilia Bloodlines Gold-7

Hull, Jody

89Panini Stickers-230
89Whalers Junior Milk-9
90OPC Premier-46
90Pro Set-490
90Upper Deck-322
French-322
91Score Canadian Bilingual-524
91Score Canadian English-524
91Stadium Club-100
91ProCards-201
92Parkhurst-119
Emerald Ice-119
92Senators Team Issue-6
92Upper Deck-539
93Leaf-157
93OPC Premier-212
Gold-212
93Panini Stickers-115
93Parkhurst-76
Emerald Ice-76
93Score-320
Canadian-320
93Stadium Club-344
Members Only Master Set-344
First Day Issue-344
93Topps/OPC Premier-212
Gold-212
93Upper Deck-112
93Upper Deck-510
94OPC Premier-427
Special Effects-427
94Parkhurst-89
Gold-89
94Stadium Club-199
Members Only Master Set-199
First Day Issue-199
Super Team Winner Cards-199
94Topps/OPC Premier-427
Special Effects-427
94Upper Deck-176
Electric Ice-176
95Be A Player-110
Signatures-S110
Signatures Die Cuts-S110
95Finest-109
Refractors-109
95Metal-59
95Panini Stickers-74
95Parkhurst International-353
Emerald Ice-353
95Pro Magnets-86
95SP-57
95Topps-134
OPC Inserts-134
95Ultra-241
95Upper Deck-50
Electric Ice-50
Electric Ice Gold-50
Special Edition-SE123
Special Edition Gold-SE123
96Collector's Choice-107
96NHL Pro Stamps-86
97Pacific Dynagon Best Kept Secrets-41
99Pacific-303
Copper-303
Emerald Green-303
Gold-303
Ice Blue-303
Premiere Date-303
Red-303
99Upper Deck-16
Exclusives-16
Exclusives 1 of 1-16
99Upper Deck Gold Reserve-16
99Upper Deck MVP-3
Gold Script-3
Silver Script-3
Super Script-3
99Upper Deck Victory-12
00Pacific-297
Copper-297
Gold-297
Ice Blue-297
Premiere Date-297
00Upper Deck-359
Exclusives Tier 1-359
Exclusives Tier 2-359
02NHL Power Play Stickers-121
02Pacific Complete-296
Red-296
02Senators Team Issue-8
02Senators Team Issue-10
03Senators Postcards-11
03Upper Deck MVP-304
Gold Script-304
Silver Script-304
Canadian Exclusives-304
03Binghamton Senators-8

Hull, Jon

93Quebec Pee-Wee Tournament-587

Hull, Jonathan

05Erie Otters-22

Hull, Mike

06Lincoln Stars Traded-5T
06Lincoln Stars Upper DeckÂ Signature Series -15

Hulse, Cale

917th Inn. Sketch WHL-43
92Classic-21
Gold-21
92Classic Four-Sport *-170
Gold-170
Autographs-170A
94Leaf-481
94OPC Premier-407
Special Effects-407
94Topps/OPC Premier-407
Special Effects-407
94Classic Pro Prospects-222
95Upper Deck-437
Electric Ice-437
Electric Ice Gold-437
96Collector's Choice-36
96Pinnacle-242
Artist's Proofs-242
Foil-242
Premium Stock-242
Rink Collection-242
97Be A Player-60
Autographs-60
Autographs Die-Cuts-60
Autographs Prismatic Die-Cuts-60
97Flames Collector's Photos-17
97Pacific Dynagon Best Kept Secrets-12
98OPC Chrome-32
Refractors-32
98Pacific-119
Ice Blue-119
Red-119
98Topps-32
O-Pee-Chee-32
99Ultimate Victory-14
1/1-14
Parallel-14
Parallel 100-14
00Upper Deck NHLPA-PA49
01O-Pee-Chee-115
01O-Pee-Chee Premier Parallel-115
01Topps-115
OPC Parallel-115
02Pacific Complete-51
Red-51
02Upper Deck-346
Exclusives-346
02Upper Deck Beckett UD Promos-346
03Coyotes Postcards-9

Hulst, Kent

89ProCards AHL-109
90Newmarket Saints-8
90ProCards AHL/IHL-149
91ProCards-380
93Portland Pirates-12
94Portland Pirates-10
95Portland Pirates-12
96Portland Pirates-10
96Portland Pirates Shop N' Save-5
97Portland Pirates-13
98Portland Pirates-9
99Portland Pirates-10
00Portland Pirates-1

Hult, Johan

99Swedish Upper Deck-99
00Swedish Upper Deck-100
02Swedish SHL-42
Parallel-42

Hultberg, John

94Dubuque Fighting Saints-14
95Slapshot-107
96Barrie Colts-10
97Barrie Colts-10
98San Antonio Iguanas-2

Hultgren, Herman

02Kalamazoo Wings-6

Hultgren, Kelly

93St. Cloud State Huskies-10
97Pensacola Ice Pilots-22
98Pensacola Ice Pilots-24
99Quad-City Mallards-15

Hultin, Bo

56Swedish Alfabilder-77

Hulton, Jim

86Kitchener Rangers-19
87Kitchener Rangers-20
00Belleville Bulls-27
01Belleville Bulls-11

Hulva, Jakub

01Czech OFS Update-318
02Czech OFS Plus-50
03Czech OFS Plus-6
04Czech OFS-228
05Czech HC Vitkovice-5

Hume, Fred

83Hall of Fame Postcards-A8
85Hall of Fame-233

Humeniuk, Scott

91ProCards-97
98Baton Rouge Kingfish-8

Humenny, Layne

92Saskatchewan JHL-58

Humes, Justin

93Quebec Pee-Wee Tournament-145

Huml, Dusan

94Czech APS Extraliga-152

Huml, Ivan

00SPx Rookie Redemption-RR3
00Providence Bruins-13
01BAP Memorabilia-367
Emerald-367
Ruby-367
Sapphire-367
01Parkhurst-304
01SP Authentic-136
Limited-136
Limited Gold-136
01SPx-198
01UD Challenge for the Cup-97
01UD Honor Roll-65
01UD Mask Collection-136
Gold-136
01UD Playmakers-105
01UD Premier Collection-90
01UD Top Shelf-123
01Upper Deck-416
Exclusives-416
01Upper Deck Ice-128
01Providence Bruins-15
02BAP Ultimate Mem Calder Candidates-6
02Bowman YoungStars-142
Gold-142
Silver-142
02Crown Royale Rookie Royalty-4
02ITG Used Calder Jerseys-C19
02ITG Used Calder Jerseys Gold-C19
02O-Pee-Chee-286
02O-Pee-Chee Premier Blue Parallel-286
02O-Pee-Chee Premier Red Parallel-286
02O-Pee-Chee Factory Set-286
02Pacific Calder-55
Silver-55
Reflections-2
02Pacific Complete-587
Red-587
02Pacific Exclusive Destined-4
02Pacific Exclusive Great Expectations-3
02Private Stock Reserve Class Act-3
02SP Authentic-109
02Titanium Right on Target-2
02Topps-286
OPC Blue Parallel-286
OPC Red Parallel-286
Factory Set-286
02Vanguard Prime Prospects-3
03ITG Action-35
Jerseys-M33
03O-Pee-Chee-177
03OPC Blue-177
03OPC Gold-177
03OPC Red-177
03Pacific Complete-25
Red-25
03Parkhurst Original Six Boston-15
Memorabilia-BM8
03Topps-177
Blue-177
Gold-177
Red-177
03Upper Deck MVP-35
Gold Script-35
Silver Script-35
Canadian Exclusives-35
03Providence Bruins-8
05Czech HC Kladno-6
06Finnish Cardset-341

Humphrey, Todd

91Michigan Falcons-15
93Flint Generals-20
94Flint Generals-11

Humphries, John

83Kingston Canadians-21

Hungle, Casey

91British Columbia JHL-61
92British Columbia JHL-96
95Tallahassee Tiger Sharks-16
98Fayetteville Force-7
98Tacoma Sabercats-10
99Tupelo T-Rex-14
00Fort Worth Brahmas-8

Hunkes, Jiri

02Czech OFS Plus-85
03Czech OFS Plus-285
04Czech OFS-316
05Czech HC Trinec-4
06Czech CP Cup Postcards-8
06Czech LG Hockey Games Postcards-5
06Finnish Cardset-284

Hunt, Brian

89ProCards AHL-38

Hunt, Curtis

84Prince Albert Raiders Stickers-14
87Flint Spirits-7
89ProCards IHL-186
90ProCards AHL/IHL-516
91ProCards-336
92St. John's Maple Leafs-8
93St. John's Maple Leafs-11
95Houston Aeros-9
97Grand Rapids Griffins-22
98Grand Rapids Griffins-21
99Grand Rapids Griffins-10

Hunt, Garet

04Vancouver Giants-17
05Vancouver Giants-11

Hunt, Gordy

97Toledo Storm-5

Hunt, Greg

91British Columbia JHL-83
92British Columbia JHL-173

Hunt, Jeff

99Ottawa 67's-25
00Ottawa 67's-25
01Ottawa 67's-25
02Ottawa 67's-23

Hunt, Nathan

02UK Hull Thunder-7

Hunt, Rick

84Nanaimo Clippers-10

Hunt, Roger

93Wichita Thunder-9

Hunter, Andria

94Classic Women of Hockey-W17

Hunter, Bill

74Team Canada L'Equipe WHA-12

Hunter, Brian

93Michigan Tech Huskies-10

Hunter, Christopher

93Quebec Pee-Wee Tournament-1424

Hunter, Cole

03OCN Blizzard-8
04Brandon Wheat Kings-8
05Brandon Wheat Kings-11

Hunter, Dale

80Nordiques Postcards-15
80Pepsi-Cola Caps-69
81Nordiques Postcards-9
81O-Pee-Chee-277
82Nordiques Postcards-10
82O-Pee-Chee-285
82O-Pee-Chee Stickers-26
82Post Cereal-16
82Topps Stickers-26
83Esso-10
83NHL Key Tags-111
83Nordiques Postcards-13
83O-Pee-Chee-293
83Vachon-66
84Kellogg's Accordion Discs-6
84Kellogg's Accordion Discs Singles-18
84Nordiques Postcards-12
84O-Pee-Chee-281
84O-Pee-Chee Stickers-179
85Nordiques General Foods-13
85Nordiques McDonald's-10
85Nordiques Placemats-3
85Nordiques Placemats-6
85Nordiques Provigo-12
85Nordiques Team Issue-11
85O-Pee-Chee-179
85O-Pee-Chee Stickers-151
86Kraft Drawings-27
86Nordiques General Foods-12
86Nordiques McDonald's-12
86Nordiques Team Issue-11
86Nordiques Yum-Yum-5
86O-Pee-Chee-192
86O-Pee-Chee Stickers-32
86Topps-192
87Capitals Kodak-32
87Capitals Team Issue-10
87O-Pee-Chee-245
87Panini Stickers-168
88Capitals Borderless-9
88Capitals Smokey-9
88O-Pee-Chee-70
88O-Pee-Chee Stickers-73
88Panini Stickers-372
88Topps-70
89Capitals Kodak-32
89Capitals Team Issue-8
89O-Pee-Chee-76
89Panini Stickers-346
89Topps-76
90Bowman-71
Tiffany-71
90Capitals Kodak-7
90Capitals Postcards-8
90Capitals Smokey-8
90O-Pee-Chee-129
90Panini Stickers-168
90Pro Set-312
90Score-44
Canadian-44
90Topps-129
Tiffany-129
90Upper Deck-219
French-219
91Pro Set Platinum-245
91Bowman-303
91Capitals Junior 5x7-11
91Capitals Kodak-11
91O-Pee-Chee-229
91Panini Stickers-203
91Parkhurst-195
French-195
91Pinnacle-40
French-40
91Pro Set-506
French-506
91Score American-56
91Score American-306
91Score Canadian Bilingual-56
91Score Canadian Bilingual-336
91Score Canadian English-56
91Score Canadian English-336
91Stadium Club-164
91Topps-229
91Upper Deck-209
French-209
92Bowman-303
92Capitals Kodak-11
92O-Pee-Chee-18
92OPC Premier Star Performers-2
92Panini Stickers-165
92Panini Stickers French-165
92Parkhurst Cherry Picks-CP7
92Parkhurst Cherry Picks Sheet-1
92Pinnacle-104
92Pinnacle-237
French-104
French-237
92Pro Set-202
92Score-231
Canadian-231
Sharpshooters-4
Sharpshooters Canadian-4
92Stadium Club-40
92Topps-464
Gold-464G
92Ultra-232
92Upper Deck-131
93Donruss-370
93Leaf-118
93Panini Stickers-26
93Parkhurst Cherry's Playoff Heroes-D6
93Pinnacle-13
Canadian-13
93PowerPlay-262
93Score-40
Canadian-40
93Ultra-135
94Canada Games NHL POGS-244
94Donruss-149
94Flair-199
94Fleer-235
94Leaf-183
94OPC Premier-506
Special Effects-506
94Parkhurst-254
Gold-254
94Pinnacle-85
Artist's Proofs-85
Rink Collection-85
94Score-143
Gold-143
Platinum-143
94Select-33
Gold-33
94SP-127
Die Cuts-127
94Stadium Club-134
Members Only Master Set-134
First Day Issue-134
Super Team Winner Cards-134
94Topps/OPC Premier-506
Special Effects-506
94Ultra-234
94Upper Deck-68
Electric Ice-68
95Be A Player-213
Signatures-S213
Signatures Die Cuts-S213
95Capitals Team Issue-9
95Collector's Choice-155
Player's Club-155
Player's Club Platinum-155
95Donruss-12
95Emotion-188
95Leaf-215
95Panini Stickers-135
95Parkhurst International-223
Emerald Ice-223
95Pinnacle-21
Artist's Proofs-21
Rink Collection-21
95Playoff One on One-322
95Pro Magnets-33
95Score-107
Black Ice Artist's Proofs-107
Black Ice-107
95SkyBox Impact-177

95SP-159
95Summit-5
Artist's Proofs-5
Ice-5
95Topps-177
OPC Inserts-177
95Ultra-175
Gold Medallion-175
95Upper Deck-442
Electric Ice-442
Electric Ice Gold-442
95Zenith Gifted Grinders-12
96Black Diamond-82
Gold-82
96Collector's Choice-288
96Donruss-199
Press Proofs-199
96Duracell All-Cherry Team-DC20
96Flair-99
Blue Ice-99
96Leaf-56
Press Proofs-56
96NHL Pro Stamps-33
96Score-110
Artist's Proofs-110
Dealer's Choice Artist's Proofs-110
Special Artist's Proofs-110
Golden Blades-110
96Upper Deck-178
97Collector's Choice-271
97Crown Royale-139
Emerald Green-139
Ice Blue-139
Silver-139
97Donruss-195
Press Proofs Silver-195
Press Proofs Gold-195
97Pacific-129
Copper-129
Emerald Green-129
Ice Blue-129
Red-129
Silver-129
97Pacific Invincible-146
Copper-146
Emerald Green-146
Ice Blue-146
Red-146
Silver-146
97Pacific Omega-239
Copper-239
Dark Gray-239
Emerald Green-239
Gold-239
Ice Blue-239
97Panini Stickers-115
97Paramount-194
Copper-194
Dark Grey-194
Emerald Green-194
Ice Blue-194
Red-194
Silver-194
97Revolution-147
Copper-147
Emerald-147
Ice Blue-147
Silver-147
97Score-201
97Upper Deck-175
97Sudbury Wolves Anniversary-10
98BAP AS Milestones-M17
98Capitals Kids and Cops-4
98OPC Chrome-58
Refractors-58
98Pacific-442
Ice Blue-442
Red-442
98Topps-58
O-Pee-Chee-58
98Upper Deck-383
Exclusives-383
Exclusives 1 of 1-383
Gold Reserve-383
99Pacific-107
Copper-107
Emerald Green-107
Gold-107
Ice Blue-107
Premiere Date-107
Red-107
00London Knights-1
00London Knights-U5
01Fleer Legacy-63
Ultimate-63
01Greats of the Game-18
Autographs-18
01Topps Archives-9
01London Knights-28
02Fleer Throwbacks-8
Gold-8
Platinum-8
Autographs-4
Scraps-8
Tie Downs-8
Squaring Off-6
Squaring Off Memorabilia-6
Stickwork-2
02UD Foundations-77
02UD Foundations-97
02London Knights-27
03London Knights-13
04ITG Franchises Canadian-79
Autographs-DHU2
04ITG Franchises US East-445
Autographs-A-DHU1
04London Knights-23
05ITG Tough Customers-DH
Autographs-DH
Famous Battles Autographs-HN
Stickwork-DH
05London Knights-22
06Parkhurst-40
06Parkhurst-216
06Parkhurst-231
Autographs-40
Autographs-216
Autographs-231
06London Knights-24

Hunter, Dave

79Oilers Postcards-12
79O-Pee-Chee-387
80O-Pee-Chee-293
80Pepsi-Cola Caps-28
81Oilers Red Rooster-12
81O-Pee-Chee-115
82Oilers Red Rooster-12
82O-Pee-Chee-110
82O-Pee-Chee Stickers-102
82Post Cereal-6
82Topps Stickers-102
83Oilers Dollars-H16
83Oilers McDonald's-8
83O-Pee-Chee-32
83O-Pee-Chee Stickers-154
83Topps Stickers-154
83Vachon-29
84Oilers Red Rooster-12
84Oilers Team Issue-10
84O-Pee-Chee-246
85Oilers Red Rooster-12
86Oilers Red Rooster-12
86Oilers Team Issue-12
87Panini Stickers-268
87Penguins Kodak-12
88Jets Police-10
88Oilers Tenth Anniversary-40
88Oilers Team Issue-11
88O-Pee-Chee-62
88O-Pee-Chee Stickers-235
88Panini Stickers-339
88Topps-62
04ITG Franchises Canadian-30
Autographs-DVH

Hunter, Dylan

01London Knights-11
02London Knights-8
03London Knights-21
04London Knights-15
04ITG Heroes and Prospects-203
04ITG Heroes/Prospects Toronto Expo '05-203
05ITG Heroes/Prosp Toronto Expo Parallel -285
05London Knights-2
05OHL Bell All-Star Classic-28
05ITG Heroes and Prospects-285
Autographs Series II-DHU
Memorial Cup-MC-3
06Rochester Americans-7

Hunter, Eric

03Prince George Cougars-16

Hunter, J.J.

98Kelowna Rockets-10
99Kelowna Rockets-2
00Prince Albert Raiders-8
01Columbus Cottonmouths-6
02Columbus Cottonmouths-7
02ECHL All-Star Southern-46
06Manitoba Moose-12

Hunter, Jim

83North Bay Centennials-11

Hunter, Logan

00London Knights-20
00London Knights-U4
01London Knights-12
02London Knights-3
03London Knights-14
05Port Huron Flags-13

Hunter, Luke

01Swift Current Broncos-14
02Swift Current Broncos-8
03Swift Current Broncos-6
04Swift Current Broncos-9
05Swift Current Broncos-11

Hunter, Mark

81Canadiens Postcards-11
82Canadiens Postcards-10
82Canadiens Steinberg-6
82O-Pee-Chee-185
82Post Cereal-10
83Canadiens Postcards-11
83Vachon-46
84Canadiens Postcards-10
85O-Pee-Chee Stickers-137
86O-Pee-Chee-57
86O-Pee-Chee Stickers-181
86Topps-57
87Blues Kodak-14
87O-Pee-Chee-50
87O-Pee-Chee Stickers-21
87Panini Stickers-313
87Topps-50
88Flames Postcards-11
88O-Pee-Chee-187
88O-Pee-Chee Stickers-14
88Panini Stickers-108
88Topps-187
90Flames IGA/McGavin's-6
90Pro Set-422
90Score Rookie/Traded-77T
91Bowman-9
91Flames Panini Team Stickers-4
91O-Pee-Chee-109
91Pinnacle-253
French-253
91Pro Set-390
French-390
91Score American-156
91Score American-306
91Score Canadian Bilingual-156
91Score Canadian Bilingual-336
91Score Canadian English-156
91Score Canadian English-336
91Stadium Club-15
91Topps-109
91Upper Deck-479
French-479
91Whalers Jr. 7-Eleven-16
92Score-194
Canadian-194
92Stadium Club-396
92Topps-36
Gold-36G
95Slapshot-355
95Sarnia Sting-25
96St. John's Maple Leafs-17
00London Knights-1
00London Knights-U2
04ITG Franchises Canadian-10
04ITG Franchises US West-284
Autographs-A-MHU
05SP Authentic Prestigious Pairings-PPPH

Hunter, Tim

85Flames Red Rooster-8
86Flames Red Rooster-7
87Flames Red Rooster-9
87Panini Stickers-216
88Flames Postcards-14
90Flames IGA/McGavin's-7
90O-Pee-Chee-434
90Pro Set-423
91Flames Panini Team Stickers-5
91Flames IGA-5
91Pinnacle-375
French-375
91Pro Set-366
French-366
91Score Canadian Bilingual-537
91Score Canadian English-537
91Upper Deck-221
French-221
92Nordiques Petro-Canada-13
92Score-403
Canadian-403
94Canucks Program Inserts-11
95Canucks Building the Dream Art-4
97Flames Collector's Photos-20
97Pacific Dynagon Best Kept Secrets-85
02Fleer Throwbacks-53
Gold-53
Platinum-53

Hunter, Todd

90 7th Inn. Sketch OHL-285
91 7th Inn. Sketch OHL-182
94Raleigh Icecaps-7

Hunter, Trent

98Prince George Cougars-10
99Prince George Cougars-17
01BAP Memorabilia-369
Emerald-369
Ruby-369
Sapphire-369
01Parkhurst-340
01UD Top Shelf-139
02BAP Memorabilia Future of the Game-FG-11
02SPx-117
02Stadium Club-119
Silver Decoy Cards-119
Proofs-119
02UD Foundations-137
02UD Piece of History-140
02Upper Deck-213
Exclusives-213
02Upper Deck MVP-209
Gold-209
Classics-209
Golden Classics-209
02Upper Deck Vintage-341
02AHL Top Prospects-21
03BAP Ultimate Mem Calder Candidates-6
03BAP Ultimate Mem Calder Candidates Gold-6
03BAP Ultimate Mem Rookie Jersey Emblems-25
03BAP Ultimate Mem Rookie Jsy Emblem Gold-25
03BAP Ultimate Mem Rookie Jersey Numbers-25
03BAP Ultimate Mem Rookie Jsy Number Gold-25
03BAP Ultimate Memorabilia Triple Threads-30
03ITG Action-379
03Pacific Calder-66
Silver-66
Reflections-6
03Pacific Complete-512
Red-512
03Pacific Heads-Up-63
Hobby LTD-63
Retail LTD-63
03Pacific Quest for the Cup-67
Blue-67
Calder Contenders-14
03Parkhurst Rookie Rookie Emblems-RE-32
03Parkhurst Rookie Rookie Emblems Gold-RE-32
03Parkhurst Rookie Rookie Jerseys-RJ-32
03Parkhurst Rookie Rookie Jerseys Gold-RJ-32
03Parkhurst Rookie Rookie Numbers-RN-32
03Parkhurst Rookie Rookie Numbers Gold-RN-32
03Titanium-65
Hobby Jersey Number Parallels-65
Retail-65
Retail Jersey Number Parallels-65
03Topps Traded-TT51
Blue-TT51
Gold-TT51
Red-TT51
03Upper Deck Ice-57
Gold-57
03Upper Deck Rookie Update-56
YoungStars-YS4
03Pacific AHL Prospect Destined Greatness-4
04Pacific-167
Blue-167
Red-167
04SP Authentic Buybacks-195
04SP Authentic Buybacks-196
04SP Authentic Sign of the Times-ST-TH
04SP Authentic Sign of the Times-DS-PH
04UD All-World-72
Gold-72
Autographs-72
Quad Autographs-AQ-YFW
04Upper Deck-113
Canadian Exclusives-113
HG Glossy Gold-113
HG Glossy Silver-113
YoungStars-YS-TH
04ITG Heroes and Prospects Emblems-30
04ITG Heroes and Prospects Emblems Gold-30
04ITG Heroes/Prospects He Shoots/Scores-22
04ITG Heroes and Prospects Jerseys-30
04ITG Heroes and Prospects Jerseys Gold-30
04ITG Heroes and Prospects Numbers-30
04ITG Heroes and Prospects Numbers Gold-30
05Be A Player-57
First Period-57
Second Period-57
Third Period-57
Overtime-57
Signatures-TR
Signatures Gold-TR
05Panini Stickers-99
05Parkhurst-306
Facsimile Auto Parallel-306
True Colors-TCNYI
True Colors-TCNYI
05SP Authentic Prestigious Pairings-PPPH
05SP Authentic Sign of the Times-TH
05SP Game Used Authentic Fabrics-AF-HU
05SP Game Used Authentic Fabrics Autos-AAF-HU
05SP Game Used Authentic Fabrics Dual-HS
05SP Game Used Authentic Fabric Dual Auto-HS
05SP Game Used Authentic Fabrics Gold-AF-HU
05SP Game Used Authentic Fabrics Quad-SDYH
05SP Game Used Authentic Patches Quad -SDYH
05SP Game Used Authentic Patches-AP-HU
05SP Game Used Authentic Patch Autos-AAP-HU
05SP Game Used Authentic Patches Dual-HS
05SP Game Used Authentic Patch Dual Autos-HS
05SP Game Used Authentic Patches Triple-HRR
05SP Game Used Auto Draft-AD-TH
05SP Game Used Game Gear-GG-TH
05SP Game Used Game Gear Autographs-AG-TH
05SP Game Used Signature Sticks-SS-TH
05SP Game Used SIGnificance-TH
05SP Game Used SIGnificance Gold-S-TH
05SP Game Used SIGnificance Extra-HP
05SP Game Used SIGnificance Extra Gold-HP
05SP Game Used Statscriptions-ST-TH
05The Cup Master Pressplate Rookie Update-247
05UD Artifacts Auto Facts-AF-TH
05UD Artifacts Auto Facts Blue-AF-TH
05UD Artifacts Auto Facts Copper-AF-TH
05UD Artifacts Auto Facts Pewter-AF-TH
05UD Artifacts Auto Facts Silver-AF-TH
05UD Toronto Fall Expo Priority Signings-PS-TH
05Ultra-125
Gold-125
Ice-125
05Upper Deck-119
Big Playmakers-B-TH
HG Glossy-119
Jerseys Series II-J2TH
Ice Glacial Graphs-GGTH
Ice Glacial Graphs Labels-GGTH
05Upper Deck MVP-250
Gold-250
Platinum-250
ProSign-P-TH
05Upper Deck Rookie Update-247
05Upper Deck Trilogy Scripts-SFS-TH
05Upper Deck Toronto Fall Expo-119
05Upper Deck Victory-125
Black-125
Gold-125
Silver-125
06Be A Player-111
Autographs-111
Signatures-HU
Signatures 25-122
Signatures Duals-DSH
06Fleer-125
Tiffany-125
06Hot Prospects Hotagraphs-HTH
06O-Pee-Chee-310
Rainbow-310
06Panini Stickers-96
06UD Artifacts Tundra Tandems-TTNY
06UD Artifacts Tundra Tandems Black-TTNY
06UD Artifacts Tundra Tandems Blue-TTNY
06UD Artifacts Tundra Tandems Gold-TTNY
06UD Artifacts Tundra Tandems Platinum-TTNY
06UD Artifacts Tundra Tandems Red-TTNY
06UD Artifacts Tundra Tandems Dual Patches Red-TTNY
06Ultra-124
Gold Medallion-124
Ice Medallion-124
06Upper Deck Arena Giveaways-NYI4
06Upper Deck-127
Exclusives Parallel-127
High Gloss Parallel-127
Masterpieces-127
06Upper Deck MVP-185
Gold Script-185
Super Script-185
Jerseys-OJHM
06Upper Deck Victory-128
06Upper Deck Victory Black-128
06Upper Deck Victory Gold-128

Hunwick, Matt

03Michigan Wolverines-29
04Michigan Wolverines-12

Hunziker, Adrian

99Swiss Panini Stickers-131

Huohvanainen, Henri

05Finnish Cardset -81
06Finnish Cardset-88

Huokko, Jan

92Swedish Semic Elitserien Stickers-160
93Swedish Semic Elitserien-130
94Swedish Leaf-6
95Swedish Leaf-65
95Swedish Upper Deck-99
Ticket to North America-NA14
98Swedish UD Choice-118
99Swedish Upper Deck-104
00Swedish Upper Deck-108
01Finnish Cardset-328
03Swedish Elite-261
Silver-261
04Swedish Elitset-271
Gold-271
05Swedish SHL Elitset-124
Gold-124
Series Two Signatures-25

Huot, Pierre-Luc

05Chicoutimi Sagueneens-14

Huotari, Harri

72Finnish Jaakiekko-305

Huotari, Jari

71Finnish Suomi Stickers-342
72Finnish Jaakiekko-323

Huppe, Curtis

95Medicine Hat Tigers-8
96Medicine Hat Tigers-8
97Lethbridge Hurricanes-7
98Tri-City Americans-20
99Bowman CHL-87
Gold-87
OPC International-87
02South Carolina Stingrays-10
02South Carolina Stingrays RBI-213
03South Carolina Stingrays-327

Huppe, Francois

93Swiss HNL-33
95Swiss HNL-485
99Swiss Panini Stickers-338

Hurajt, Radovan

04Slovakian Poprad Team Set-4

Huras, Larry

95Swiss HNL-30
99Swiss Panini Stickers-3
01Swiss HNL-1

Hurbanek, Joachim

74Finnish Jenkki-111
74Finnish Typotor-59
04German Berlin Eisbarens 50th Anniv-50

Hurbanek, Kay

04German Berlin Polar Bears Postcards-16
05German SC Bietigheim-Bissingen Steelers-21

Hurd, Kelly

90Michigan Tech Huskies-8
90Michigan Tech Huskies-9
90Michigan Tech Huskies-29
91ProCards-253
93Fort Wayne Komets-8
96Mississippi Sea Wolves-8
97Mississippi Sea Wolves-6
98ECHL All-Star Southern Conference-3
99Mississippi Sea Wolves Kelly Cup-19
99UHL All-Stars West-1T
00Fort Wayne Komets-7
00Fort Wayne Komets Shoe Carnival-7

Hurd, Paul

00Kelowna Rockets-23

Hurlbut, Jason

93Quebec Pee-Wee Tournament-491
96Sudbury Wolves-10

Hurlbut, Mike

89ProCards IHL-35
90ProCards AHL/IHL-12
91ProCards-196
92Upper Deck-448
92Binghamton Rangers-2
93Classic Pro Prospects-138
95Minnesota Moose-9
96Collector's Edge Ice-167
Prism-167
97Rochester Americans-4-1
98Rochester Americans-6
00Rochester Americans-11

Hurley, Craig

81Saskatoon Blades-17

Hurley, Darren

90 7th Inn. Sketch OHL-9
91 7th Inn. Sketch OHL-117
00UK Sekonda Superleague-45
03UK Basingstoke Bison-11

Hurley, Mark

95Tri-City Americans-12

Hurley, Mike

95Tri-City Americans-13
98Bowman CHL-54
Golden Anniversary-54
OPC International-54
98Bowman Chrome CHL-54
Golden Anniversary-54
Golden Anniversary Refractors-54
OPC International-54
OPC International Refractors-54
Refractors-54
02Trenton Titans-B-6

Hurme, Heikki

70Finnish Jaakiekko-138
71Finnish Suomi Stickers-225

Hurme, Jani

96Finnish SISU Redline At The Gala-4
96Finnish SISU Redline Keeping It Green-2
96Finnish SISU Redline Rookie Energy-1
96Finnish SISU Redline Silver Signatures-1
97Indianapolis Ice-9
98Cincinnati Cyclones-7
98Cincinnati Cyclones 2-20
98Detroit Vipers-18
99Finnish Cardset Aces High-C-A
99Grand Rapids Griffins-11
00BAP Memorabilia-179
Emerald-179
Ruby-179
Sapphire-179
Promos-179
00BAP Mem Chicago Sportsfest Copper-179
00BAP Memorabilia Chicago Sportsfest Blue-179
00BAP Memorabilia Chicago Sportsfest Gold-179
00BAP Memorabilia Chicago Sportsfest Ruby-179
00BAP Memorabilia Chicago Sun-Times Ruby-179
00BAP Memorabilia Chicago Sun-Times Gold-179
00BAP Mem Chicago Sun-Times Sapphire-179
00BAP Mem Toronto Fall Expo Copper-179
00BAP Memorabilia Toronto Fall Expo Gold-179
00BAP Memorabilia Toronto Fall Expo Ruby-179
00BAP Parkhurst 2000-P229
00BAP Signature Series-286
Emerald-286
Ruby-286
Sapphire-286
Autographs-227
Autographs Gold-227
00Black Diamond-82
Gold-82
00Crown Royale-135
21st Century Rookies-18
00Pacific-279
Copper-279
Gold-279
Ice Blue-279
Premiere Date-279
00Paramount-173
Copper-173
Gold-173
Holo-Gold-173
Holo-Silver-173
Ice Blue-173
Premiere Date-173
00Private Stock-133
Gold-133
Premiere Date-133
Retail-133
Silver-133
00Senators Team Issue-9
00SP Authentic-116
Sign of the Times-JH
00SP Game Used-76
00SPx-106
Spectrum-106
00Stadium Club-258
00Titanium-135
Retail-135
00Titanium Draft Day Edition-135
00Titanium Draft Day Promos-135
00Topps Gold Label Class 1-111
Gold-111
00Topps Gold Label Class 2-111
00Topps Gold Label Class 2 Gold-111
00Topps Gold Label Class 3-111
00Topps Gold Label Class 3 Gold-111
00Topps Heritage-90
Chrome Parallel-90
00Topps Premier Plus-124
Blue Ice-124
00Topps Stars-116
Blue-116
00UD Heroes-172
00UD Pros and Prospects-117
00UD Reserve-106
00Upper Deck-223
Exclusives Tier 1-223
Exclusives Tier 2-223
00Upper Deck Vintage-387
00Vanguard-136
Pacific Proofs-136
01BAP Memorabilia-144
Emerald-144
Ruby-144
Sapphire-144
01BAP Signature Series-109
Autographs-109
Autographs Gold-109
01Between the Pipes-22
He Shoots-He Saves Prizes-39
01Pacific-274
Extreme LTD-274
Hobby LTD-274
Premiere Date-274
Retail LTD-274
01Pacific Arena Exclusives-274
01Parkhurst-166
Teammates-T25
Waving the Flag-14
01Senators Team Issue-11
01SP Game Used Patches-PJH
01SP Game Used Patches-CPHB
01SP Game Used Patches-CPHH
01Stadium Club New Regime-NR9
01Upper Deck Game Jerseys-GJJH
01Upper Deck Game Jerseys-NGJH
01Upper Deck Game Jerseys-CHH
01Upper Deck Victory-252
Gold-252
01Finnish Cardset Haltmeisters-3
01Finnish Cardset Salt Lake City-1
02BAP First Edition-265
02BAP Memorabilia-52
Emerald-52
Ruby-52
Sapphire-52
NHL All-Star Game-52
NHL All-Star Game Blue-52
NHL All-Star Game Green-52
NHL All-Star Game Red-52
02BAP Memorabilia Toronto Fall Expo-52
02BAP Sig Series Auto Buybacks 2000-227
02BAP Sig Series Auto Buybacks 2001-109
02Between the Pipes-10
Gold-10
Silver-10
Blockers-2
Emblems-12
Jerseys-12
Numbers-12
Stick and Jerseys-12
02Pacific-268
Blue-268
Red-268
02Pacific Complete-424
Red-424
02UD Mask Collection-37
02UD Mask Collection-38
02UD Mask Collection Beckett Promos-37
02UD Mask Collection Beckett Promos-38
02Upper Deck Victory National Pride-NP25
02Finnish Cardset-176
02Finnish Cardset Dynamic Duos-8
03BAP Memorabilia-122
Emerald-122
Gold-122
Ruby-122
Sapphire-122
Deep in the Crease-D1
Tandems-T-9
03ITG Action-239
Homeboys-HB9
03Pacific-143
Blue-143
Red-143
03Upper Deck MVP-189
Gold Script-189
Silver Script-189
Canadian Exclusives-189
05Upper Deck Jerseys-J-JH
06Finnish Cardset-332
Between the Pipes-22

Hurme, Markku

94Finnish SISU-293
95Finnish SISU-11
96Finnish SISU Redline-9
98Finnish Keraliysarja-41
99Finnish Cardset-27
00Finnish Cardset-260
01Finnish Cardset-188
02Finnish Cardset-27
03Finnish Cardset-8
05Finnish Cardset -182
06Finnish Cardset-6

Hurras, Larry

98Swiss Power Play Stickers-3
00Swiss Panini Stickers-269

Hurst, Ronnie

44Beehive Group II Photos-410
51Laval Dairy Subset-119

Hurtaj, Lubomir

02Czech OFS Plus-356
04Czech OFS-44
05Czech HC Karlovy Vary-5

Hurtig, Lars

85Swedish Panini Stickers-171
86Swedish Panini Stickers-183
87Swedish Panini Stickers-185
89Swedish Semic Elitserien Stickers-158
90Swedish Semic Elitserien Stickers-238
91Swedish Semic Elitserien Stickers-168
92Swedish Semic Elitserien Stickers-194
93Swedish Semic Elitserien-164
94Swedish Leaf-90
Top Guns-3
95Swedish Leaf-251
95Swedish Upper Deck-131
96German DEL-153

Hurtubise, Mark

01Quebec Remparts-6
02Quebec Remparts-5
02Val d'Or Foreurs-5
03Val d'Or Foreurs-5

Husak, Phil

00Tacoma Sabercats-19

Husby, Roar

92Norwegian Elite Series-114

Huschto, Dieter

74Finnish Jenkki-114

Huscroft, Jamie

88Devils Caretta-12
88ProCards AHL-348
89ProCards AHL-217
90ProCards AHL/IHL-577
91ProCards-424
95Collector's Choice-126
Player's Club-126
Player's Club Platinum-126
97Be A Player-88
Autographs-88
Autographs Die-Cuts-88
Autographs Prismatic Die-Cuts-88
97Pacific Invincible NHL Regime-185
99BAP Millennium-244
Emerald-244
Ruby-244
Sapphire-244
Signatures-244
Signatures Gold-244
99Portland Pirates-11
02BAP Sig Series Auto Buybacks 1999-244
02Spokane Chiefs-27

Huselius, Kristian

97Swedish Collector's Choice-60
Crash the Game Exchange-C22
Crash the Game Redemption-R22
98Swedish UD Choice-98
99Swedish Upper Deck-77
Hands of Gold-15
SHL Signatures-7
Snapshots-15
00SPx Rookie Redemption-RR13
00Swedish Upper Deck-71
00Swedish Upper Deck-193
SHL Excellence-S3
SHL Signatures-KH
01Atomic-110
Premiere Date-110
01Atomic Toronto Fall Expo-110
01BAP Memorabilia-393
Emerald-393
Ruby-393
Sapphire-393
01BAP Signature Series-212
Autographs-212
Autographs Gold-212
He Shoots-He Scores Prizes-26
Jerseys-GJ-95
01Bowman YoungStars-152
Gold-152
Ice Cubed-152
Autographs-KH
Relics-JKH
Relics-SKH
Relics-DSKH
Rivals-R11
01Crown Royale-162
Crowning Achievement-5
Rookie Royalty-10
01O-Pee-Chee-335
01Pacific-456
01Pacific Adrenaline-210
Blue-210
Premiere Date-210
Red-210
Retail-210
Rookie Report-9
01Pacific Heads-Up-107
01Pacific High Voltage-5
01Parkhurst-261
Waving the Flag-20
01Parkhurst Beckett Promos-261
01Private Stock-123
Gold-123
Premiere Date-123
Retail-123
Silver-123
01Private Stock Pacific Nights-123
01Private Stock PS-2002-97
01SP Authentic-177
Limited-177
Limited Gold-177
01SP Game Used-79
01SPx-106
01Stadium Club-132
Award Winners-132
Master Photos-132
01Titanium-161
Retail-161
Rookie Team-6
Three-Star Selections-26
01Titanium Draft Day Edition-132
01Topps-335
01Topps Chrome-153
Refractors-153
Black Border Refractors-153
01Topps Heritage-146
01Topps Reserve-113
01UD Challenge for the Cup-108
01UD Honor Roll-73
01UD Mask Collection-147
Gold-147
01UD Playmakers-120
01UD Premier Collection-111
01UD Top Shelf-71
01Upper Deck-426
Exclusives-426
01Upper Deck Ice-55
01Upper Deck MVP-224
01Upper Deck Victory-444
01Upper Deck Vintage-281
01Vanguard-114
Blue-114
Red-114
One of Ones-114
Premiere Date-114
Prime Prospects-7
Proofs-114
02Atomic-45
Blue-45
Gold-45
Red-45
Cold Fusion-14
Hobby Parallel-45
02BAP First Edition-32
02BAP First Edition-383
02BAP First Edition-384
Jerseys-32
02BAP Memorabilia-27
Emerald-27
Ruby-27
Sapphire-27
Future of the Game-FG-14
NHL All-Star Game-27
NHL All-Star Game Blue-27
NHL All-Star Game Green-27
NHL All-Star Game Red-27
02BAP Memorabilia Toronto Fall Expo-27
02BAP Signature Series-106
Autographs-106
Autograph Buybacks 2001-212
Autographs Gold-106
Team Quads-TQ5
02BAP Ultimate Memorabilia Numerology-25
02Bowman YoungStars-143
Gold-143
Silver-143
02Crown Royale-42
Blue-42
Red-42
Retail-42
Dual Patches-11
02ITG Used-33
02ITG Used-133
02O-Pee-Chee-86
02O-Pee-Chee Premier Blue Parallel-86
02O-Pee-Chee Premier Red Parallel-86
02O-Pee-Chee Factory Set-86
02Pacific-154
Blue-154
Red-154
Shining Moments-6
02Pacific Calder Collection AS Fantasy-5
02Pacific Calder Collection All-Star Fantasy Gold-5
02Pacific Complete-316
Red-316
02Pacific Exclusive-76
Destined-7
Great Expectations-8
Jerseys-10
Jerseys Gold-10
02Pacific Heads-Up-52
Blue-52
Purple-52
Red-52
Quad Jerseys-36
Quad Jerseys Gold-36
02Pacific Toronto Spring Expo Rookie Coll-7
02Parkhurst-75
Bronze-75
Gold-75
Silver-75
02Parkhurst Retro-144
Minis-144
02Private Stock Reserve-42
Blue-42
Red-42
Retail-42
02SP Authentic-118
02SP Game Used Signature Style-KH
02SPx-35
Spectrum Gold-35
Spectrum Silver-35
02Stadium Club-72
Silver Decoy Cards-72
Proofs-72
YoungStars Relics-S7
YoungStars Relics-DS3
02Titanium-45
Blue-45
Red-45
Retail-45
Jerseys-32
Jerseys Retail-32
Patches-32
02Topps-86
OPC Blue Parallel-86
OPC Red Parallel-86
Own The Game-OTG13
Factory Set-86
02Topps Chrome-54
Black Border Refractors-54
Refractors-54
02Topps Total-320
02UD Artistic Impressions-41
Gold-41
02UD Artistic Impressions Beckett Promos-41
02UD Artistic Impressions Retrospectives-R41
02UD Artistic Impressions Retrospect Gold-R41
02UD Artistic Impress Retrospect Silver-R41
02Upper Deck Collectors Club-NHL19
02UD Honor Roll-33
02UD Piece of History-42
02UD Top Shelf-37
02Upper Deck-77
Exclusives-77
02Upper Deck Classic Portraits-44
02Upper Deck MVP-77
Gold-77
Classics-77
Golden Classics-77
Prosign-KH
02Upper Deck Rookie Update-44
02Upper Deck Victory-88
Bronze-88
Gold-88
Silver-88
02Upper Deck Vintage-114
02Upper Deck Vintage-315
Green Backs-114
02Vanguard-44
LTD-44
Jerseys-21
Jerseys Gold-21
03BAP Memorabilia-45
Emerald-45
Gold-45
Ruby-45
Sapphire-45
03Bowman-93
Gold-93
Future Fabrics-FF-KH
Future Fabric Patches-KH
Future Rivals-HG
Future Rivals Patches-HG
03Bowman Chrome-93
Refractors-93
Gold Refractors-93
Xfractors-93
03eTopps-7
03ITG Action-281
Jerseys-M110
03NHL Sticker Collection-47
03O-Pee-Chee-247
03OPC Blue-247
03OPC Gold-247
03OPC Red-247
03Pacific-144
Blue-144
Red-144
03Pacific Complete-62
Red-62
03Pacific Exhibit-63
Blue Backs-63
Yellow Backs-63
03Panthers Team Issue-8
03Topps-247
Blue-247
Gold-247
Red-247
Signs of Youth-KH
C55 Autographs-TA-KH
03Topps Pristine-81
Gold Refractor Die Cuts-81
Refractors-81
Patches-PP-KH
Patch Refractors-PP-KH
Popular Demand Relics-PD-KH
Popular Demand Relic Refractors-PD-KH
Press Plates Black-81
Press Plates Cyan-81
Press Plates Magenta-81
Press Plates Yellow-81
03Upper Deck-82
Canadian Exclusives-82
HG-82
03Upper Deck MVP-179
Gold Script-179
Silver Script-179
Canadian Exclusives-179
03Toronto Star-40
04Pacific-112
Blue-112
Red-112
04Upper Deck-75
Canadian Exclusives-75
HG Glossy Gold-75
HG Glossy Silver-75
04Swedish Alfabilder Alfa Stars-23
04Swedish Alfabilder Autographs-127
04Swedish Alfabilder Limited Autographs-127
04Swedish Alfabilder Proof Parallels-23
04Swedish Elitset-210
Dominators-2
Gold-210
05Panini Stickers-65
05Parkhurst-69

Facsimile Auto Parallel-69
05SP Authentic Sign of the Times-KH
05SP Game Used Auto Draft-AD-KH
05SP Game Used Statscriptions-ST-KH
05Upper Deck Notable Numbers-N-KH
05Upper Deck Victory-88
Black-88
Gold-88
Silver-88
06Gatorade-8
06O-Pee-Chee-74
Rainbow-74
06Panini Stickers-204
06Ultra-31
Gold Medallion-31
Ice Medallion-31
06Upper Deck-33
Exclusives Parallel-33
High Gloss Parallel-33
Masterpieces-33
06Upper Deck MVP-49
Gold Script-49
Super Script-49
06Upper Deck Victory-33
06Upper Deck Victory Black-33
06Upper Deck Victory Gold-33

Husgen, Jamie
87Moncton Hawks-13
88ProCards AHL-179

Huska, Ryan
93Kamloops Blazers-9
94Kamloops Blazers-21
95Indianapolis Ice-9
95Slapshot Memorial Cup-10
97Indianapolis Ice-10
04Kelowna Rockets-18

Huskins, Kent
01Norfolk Admirals-11
02Norfolk Admirals-12
03San Antonio Rampage-6
04Manitoba Moose-4
05Portland Pirates-18
06Portland Pirates-22
07Upper Deck Victory-233
Black-233
Gold-233

Huss, Anders
83Swedish Semic Elitserien-73
84Swedish Semic Elitserien-60
85Swedish Panini Stickers-66
86Swedish Panini Stickers-46
87Swedish Panini Stickers-61
89Swedish Semic Elitserien Stickers-37
90Swedish Semic Elitserien Stickers-187
91Swedish Semic Elitserien Stickers-39
92Swedish Semic Elitserien Stickers-69
93Swedish Semic Elitserien-45
94Swedish Leaf-61
Studio Signatures-2
95Swedish Upper Deck 1st Division Stars-DS1
96Swedish Brynas Tigers-22
97Swedish Collector's Choice-30
97Swedish Collector's Choice-205
Crash the Game Exchange-C18
Crash the Game Redemption-R18
Stick'Ums-S12
98Swedish UD Choice-47
00Swedish Upper Deck-177
Top Draws-T11

Hussey, Marc
907th Inn. Sketch WHL-146
917th Inn. Sketch WHL-278
92Classic-18
Gold-18
92Classic Four-Sport *-167
Gold-167
94St. John's Maple Leafs-13
95Saint John Flames-9
96Saint John Flames-8
97Indianapolis Ice-11
97Milwaukee Admirals-9
99UK London Knights-8
00German DEL-143
02UK Nottingham Panthers-3

Hussey, Matt
02Wilkes-Barre Scranton Penguins-7
03ITG VIP Rookie Debut-141
03Parkhurst Rookie-72
03UD Premier Collection-100
03Upper Deck Rookie Update-182
03Wilkes-Barre Scranton Penguins-11
04Wilkes-Barre Scranton Penguins-22
05WBS Penguins-13

Huston, Ron
74NHL Action Stamps-58
75Phoenix Roadrunners WHA-11
76O-Pee-Chee WHA-36
76Phoenix Roadrunners WHA-9

Huston, Sam
06Westside Warriors-21

Hutchings, Alex
06Barrie Colts-8

Hutchings, Greg
88Brandon Wheat Kings-24
89Brandon Wheat Kings-15
90Brandon Wheat Kings-11
907th Inn. Sketch WHL-228

Hutchings, John
81Oshawa Generals-10
82Oshawa Generals-20
83Oshawa Generals-5

Hutchings, S.
75HCA Steel City Vacuum-4

Hutchings, Steve
91Arizona Icecats-12
92Arizona Icecats-10
93Arizona Icecats-8
94Arizona Icecats-3

Hutchings, Ted
88Lethbridge Hurricanes-11

Hutchins, Grace
04Wisconsin Badgers Women-9

Hutchins, Jeff
03Mississippi Sea Wolves-5
05UK Coventry Blaze-11

Hutchinson, Andrew
00Michigan State Spartans-9
02Milwaukee Admirals-6
03Beehive-239
Gold-239
Silver-239
03ITG VIP Rookie Debut-47
03Pacific Complete-561
Red-561
03Parkhurst Rookie-63
03SP Authentic-91
Limited-91
03Topps Traded-TT121
Blue-TT121
Gold-TT121
Red-TT121
03UD Honor Roll-147
03Upper Deck-449
Canadian Exclusives-449
HG-449
UD Exclusives-449
03Upper Deck Rookie Update-112
03Milwaukee Admirals-9
03Milwaukee Admirals Postcards-12
03Pacific AHL Prospects-58
Gold-58
04AHL All-Stars-19
04Milwaukee Admirals-19
04ITG Heroes and Prospects Emblems-36
04ITG Heroes and Prospects Emblems Gold-36
04ITG Heroes and Prospects Jerseys-36
04ITG Heroes and Prospects Jerseys Gold-36
04ITG Heroes and Prospects Numbers-36
04ITG Heroes and Prospects Numbers Gold-36
05ITG Heroes/Prosp Toronto Expo Parallel -68
05ITG Heroes and Prospects-68
Autographs-A-AHU
06Hurricanes Postcards-13

Hutchinson, Dave
74NHL Action Stamps-117
75O-Pee-Chee NHL-390
76O-Pee-Chee NHL-346
76O-Pee-Chee NHL-386
77O-Pee-Chee NHL-380
78O-Pee-Chee-289
79O-Pee-Chee-302
80O-Pee-Chee-78
80Topps-78

Hutchinson, James
03UK Basingstoke Bison-4

Hutchinson, Troy
907th Inn. Sketch OHL-286
917th Inn. Sketch OHL-280

Hutchison, Dave
73Vancouver Blazers-12
78Maple Leafs Postcards-9
79Maple Leafs Postcards-13
80Blackhawks Postcards-3
81Blackhawks Borderless Postcards-10
81Blackhawks Brown Background-3
82Post Cereal-4

Hutson, Rob
99Muskegon Fury-34
00Muskegon Fury-24

Hutt, Malcolm
00Belleville Bulls-6
01Belleville Bulls-12
02Belleville Bulls-8
03Alaska Aces-6
03Peoria Rivermen-15
04Tulsa Oilers-11

Huttl, Karl
94German First League-232

Hutton, Bouse
83Hall of Fame Postcards-G9
85Hall of Fame-100

Hutton, Dwaine
83Saskatoon Blades-7
84Kelowna Wings-13
87Flint Spirits-8

Hutyra, Marian
95Slovakian-Quebec Pee-Wee Tournament-8

Hutyra, Peter
95Slovakian-Quebec Pee-Wee Tournament-9

Huura, Ilkka
71Finnish Suomi Stickers-343
72Finnish Jaakiekko-324

Huura, Pasi
91Finnish Semic World Champ Stickers-10
91Finnish Jyvas-Hyva Stickers-48
91Swedish Semic World Champ Stickers-10
92Finnish Jyvas-Hyva Stickers-132
93Finnish Jyvas-Hyva Stickers-236
93Finnish SISU-191
93Swedish Semic World Champ Stickers-51
94Finnish SISU-297
95Finnish SISU-34

Huusko, Anders
91Swedish Semic Elitserien Stickers-77
92Swedish Semic Elitserien Stickers-88
93Swedish Semic Elitserien-62
94Swedish Leaf-26
95Swedish Leaf-194
Face to Face-3
95Swedish Upper Deck-45
95Swedish Globe World Championships-49
97Swedish Collector's Choice-96
Crash the Game Exchange-C24
Crash the Game Redemption-R24
98Swedish UD Choice-112
99German DEL-111
00German DEL-37
02Swedish SHL-40
Parallel-40
03Swedish Elite-197
Silver-197
04Swedish Elitset-55
Gold-55
04Swedish HV71 Postcards-8
05Swedish SHL Elitset-57
Gold-57
Series One Signatures-9

Huusko, Erik
91Swedish Semic Elitserien Stickers-76
92Swedish Semic Elitserien Stickers-87
93Swedish Semic Elitserien-61
94Swedish Leaf-14
95Swedish Leaf-32
Face to Face-3
95Swedish Upper Deck-44
95Swedish Globe World Championships-45
95Swedish World Championships Stickers-150
98Swedish UD Choice-113

Huxley, Adam
01Saskatoon Blades-7
02Saskatoon Blades-17
04Las Vegas Wranglers-8
06Stockton Thunder-20

Huxley, Chris
06Sioux Falls Stampede -17

Huyber, Todd
93Fort Worth Fire-6
93Huntington Blizzard-13

Hwodeky, Rick
98Barrie Colts-10

Hyacinthe, Seneque
98Val d'Or Foreurs-19
00Val d'Or Foreurs-24
Signed-24

Hyatt, Brad
88ProCards AHL-196

Hyatt, Troy
907th Inn. Sketch WHL-17
917th Inn. Sketch WHL-130
93Seattle Thunderbirds-8

Hybler, Zbynek
01Swiss HNL-465

Hyde, Matthew
00Baie-Comeau Drakkar-15
Signed-15
01Baie-Comeau Drakkar-13

Hyduke, John
85Minnesota-Duluth Bulldogs-26

Hyka, Tomas
94Czech APS Extraliga-272

Hylak, Alexandr
03Czech OFS Plus-311
04Czech OFS-118

Hyland, Harry
10C56-10
10Sweet Caporal Postcards-30
11C55-30
12C57-19
83Hall of Fame-157
83Hall of Fame Postcards-L7
85Hall of Fame-157

Hyman, Adam
06UK Guildford Flames-20

Hyman, Dion
03Laredo Bucks-11
06Bloomington PrairieThunder-11

Hymovitz, David
97Indianapolis Ice-12
98IHL All-Star Eastern Conference-5
98Indianapolis Ice-22
99Lowell Lock Monsters-10
00Lowell Lock Monsters-12
01Grand Rapids Griffins-9
03Binghamton Senators-9
03Binghamton Senators Postcards-6
04Richmond Riverdogs-10
05Danbury Trashers-25
06Binghamton Senators 5th Anniversary-14

Hynd, Jason
91Air Canada SJHL-B23

Hynek, Pavel
00Czech OFS-289

Hynes, Dave
98Bruins Alumni-28
Autographs-28

Hynes, Gord
83Medicine Hat Tigers-18
85Medicine Hat Tigers-17
86Moncton Golden Flames-22
90Alberta International Team Canada-5
91Alberta International Team Canada-9
91Parkhurst-235
French-235
92Flyers J.C. Penney-14
92Flyers Upper Deck Sheets-8
92O-Pee-Chee-8
92Score-483
Canadian-483
Canadian Olympians-5
92Stadium Club-49
93Cincinnati Cyclones-10
95German DEL-387
96German DEL-295
98German DEL-233
99German DEL-2
00German DEL-1
Star Attractions-S2
01German Upper Deck-26

Hynes, Mark
04Fort Worth Brahmas-7A
04Fort Worth Brahmas-7B

Hynes, Shane
05Portland Pirates-23
06Augusta Lynx-5

Hynes, Wayne
85Medicine Hat Tigers-14
94German DEL-427
95German DEL-396
96German DEL-305
98German DEL-207
99German DEL-329
00German DEL-5
01German Upper Deck-170
02German Adler Mannheim Eagles Postcards-17
02German DEL City Press-242
Top Stars-GT9
03German DEL-109
04German DEL-125
04German DEL Update-316
04German Hannover Scorpions Postcards-12

Hynnes, Chris
93Thunder Bay Senators-4
95Thunder Bay Senators-10
95Signature Rookies-41
Signatures-41
96South Carolina Stingrays-33
98ECHL All-Star Southern Conference-19
99German DEL-93

Hynning, Fredrik
04Swedish Elitset-222
Gold-222
05Swedish Lulea Hockey Postcards-13
05Swedish SHL Elitset-90
Gold-90
06Swedish SHL Elitset-89

Hyokki, Kari
73Finnish Jaakiekko-271

Hyrsky, Dave
87Brockville Braves-15
88Brockville Braves-14

Hyrsky, Timo
70Finnish Jaakiekko-346

Hysing, Mats
67Swedish Hockey-11
67Swedish Hockey-187
69Swedish Hockey-187
69Swedish Hockey-243
70Swedish Hockey-140
70Swedish Masterserien-60
70Swedish Masterserien-110
71Swedish Hockey-232
72Swedish Stickers-219
73Swedish Stickers-67
74Swedish Stickers-169

Hytonen, Juha-Pekka
00Finnish Cardset-174
01Finnish Cardset-65
04Finnish Cardset-251
05Finnish Cardset -68
06Finnish Cardset-77

Hytti, Jari
72Finnish Jaakiekko-325
80Finnish Mallasjuoma-183

Hytti, Timo
72Finnish Jaakiekko-281

Hyttinen, Kimmo
93Finnish SISU-85
94Finnish SISU-115
94Finnish SISU-355

Hyun, Martin
04German DEL Update-335
04German Krefeld Penguins Postcards-9

Hyvari, Pauli
65Finnish Hellas-88

Hyvari, Pentti
65Finnish Hellas-93

Hyvarinen, Andy
04Guelph Storm-9
05Guelph Storm-B-03

Hyvarinen, Eero
04Finnish Cardset-255

Hyvarinen, Jari
98Finnish Keräilysarja-180
99Finnish Cardset-287
01Finnish Cardset-299

Hyvonen, Hannes
95Finnish SISU-131
96Finnish SISU Redline-141
98Finnish Keräilysarja-19
99Finnish Cardset-13
99Finnish Cardset-175
00Finnish Cardset-19
01BAP Memorabilia-426
Emerald-426
Ruby-426
Sapphire-426
01Parkhurst-343
01UD Mask Collection-165
Gold-165
01Finnish Cardset-19
01Cleveland Barons-8
02Upper Deck MVP-215
Gold-215
Classics-215
Golden Classics-215
02Finnish Cardset-177
03Swedish Elite-182
Enforcers-EF1
Silver-182
04Finnish Cardset-233
Stars of the Game-2
04Swedish Elitset-41
Gold-41
Signatures-15
04Swedish Pure Skills-116
Parallel-116

Hyvonen, Seppo
72Finnish Jaakiekko-173

Hyytiainen, Penti
66Finnish Jaakiekkosarja-164
69Swedish Hockey-315
70Swedish Hockey-221

Iafrate, Al
83Belleville Bulls-20
84Maple Leafs Postcards-11
85Maple Leafs Postcards-14
85O-Pee-Chee-210
85O-Pee-Chee Stickers-13
86Maple Leafs Postcards-11
86O-Pee-Chee-26
86O-Pee-Chee Stickers-148
86Topps-26
87Maple Leafs PLAY-19
87Maple Leafs Postcards-9
87Maple Leafs Postcards Oversized-9
87O-Pee-Chee-238
87O-Pee-Chee Stickers-160
87Panini Stickers-325
88Maple Leafs PLAY-19
88O-Pee-Chee-71
88O-Pee-Chee Stickers-180
88Panini Stickers-118
88Topps-71
89O-Pee-Chee-79
89O-Pee-Chee Stickers-178
89Panini Stickers-140
89Topps-79
89Swedish Semic World Champ Stickers-162
90Bowman-153
Tiffany-153
90Capitals Kodak-8
90Capitals Postcards-9
90Kraft-21
90Maple Leafs Postcards-7
90O-Pee-Chee-91
90OPC Premier-48
90Panini Stickers-290
90Pro Set-281
90Pro Set-354
90Score-195
90Score-334
Canadian-195
Canadian-334
90Score Hottest/Rising Stars-85
90Topps-91
Tiffany-91
90Upper Deck-157
90Upper Deck-539
French-157
French-539
91Pro Set Platinum-130
91Bowman-300
91Capitals Junior 5x7-12
91Capitals Kodak-12
91Maple Leafs Panini Team Stickers-9
91Maple Leafs Panini Team Stickers-G
91O-Pee-Chee-148
91Panini Stickers-208
91Parkhurst-194
French-194
91Pinnacle-207
French-207
91Pro Set-250
French-250
91Score American-209
91Score Canadian Bilingual-209
91Score Canadian English-209
91Stadium Club-372
91Topps-148
91Upper Deck-318
French-318
91Finnish Semic World Champ Stickers-135
91Swedish Semic World Champ Stickers-135
92Bowman-251
92Capitals Kodak-12
92O-Pee-Chee-341
92Panini Stickers-168
92Panini Stickers French-168
92Parkhurst-203
Emerald Ice-203
92Pinnacle Canadian Promo Panels-1
92Pinnacle-66
92Pinnacle-233
French-66
French-233
92Pro Set-205
92Score-11
Canadian-11
92Seasons Patches-67
92Stadium Club-302
92Topps-133
Gold-133G
92Ultra-233
92Upper Deck-54
93Donruss-371
93Donruss-402
Special Print-Y
93Kraft-12
93Leaf-141
93McDonald's Upper Deck-16
93OPC Premier-45
93OPC Premier-174
Gold-45
Gold-174
93Panini Stickers-32
93Parkhurst-217
Emerald Ice-217
93Pinnacle-189
Canadian-189
All-Stars-19
All-Stars-47
All-Stars Canadian-19
All-Stars Canadian-47
Team Pinnacle-9
Team Canadian-9
93PowerPlay-263
Slapshot Artists-5
93Score-188
93Score-450
Canadian-188
Canadian-450
Dream Team-9
93Stadium Club-80
93Stadium Club-455
Members Only Master Set-80
Members Only Master Set-455
OPC-80
First Day Issue-80
First Day Issue-455
First Day Issue OPC-80
All-Stars-3
All-Stars Members Only-3
All-Stars OPC-3
93Topps/OPC Premier-45
93Topps/OPC Premier-174
Gold-45
Gold-174
93Ultra-11
All-Stars-8
Speed Merchants-5
93Upper Deck-183
SP-170
93Upper Deck Locker All-Stars-37
93Swedish Semic World Champ Stickers-173
94Canada Games NHL POGS-36
94Donruss-205
94EA Sports-152
94EA Sports-190
94Flair-10
94Fleer-12
Slapshot Artists-3
94Hockey Wit-74
94Kraft-7
94Leaf-212
94OPC Premier-20
94OPC Premier-453
Special Effects-20
Special Effects-453
94Parkhurst-15
Gold-15
SE Vintage-22
94Pinnacle I Hobby Samples-BR1
94Pinnacle-39
Artist's Proofs-39
Rink Collection-39
Boomers-BR1
94Score-168
Gold-168
Platinum-168
94Select-80
Gold-80
94Stadium Club Members Only-31
94Stadium Club-202
Members Only Master Set-202
First Day Issue-202
Super Team Winner Cards-202
94Topps/OPC Premier-20
94Topps/OPC Premier-453
Special Effects-20
Special Effects-453
94Ultra-256
Speed Merchants-4
94Upper Deck-82
Electric Ice-82
SP Inserts-SP94
SP Inserts Die Cuts-SP94
94Upper Deck NHLPA/Be A Player-26
95Collector's Choice-195
Player's Club-195
Player's Club Platinum-195
95Emotion-7
95Panini Stickers-12
95Score-237
Black Ice Artist's Proofs-237
Black Ice-237
95SkyBox Impact-8
96Be A Player-19
Autographs-19
Autographs Silver-19
96Metal Universe-137
96Topps Picks-117
OPC Inserts-117
96Ultra-151
Gold Medallion-151
96Upper Deck-331
97Collector's Choice-223
97Pacific-177
Copper-177
Emerald Green-177
Ice Blue-177
Red-177
Silver-177
97Sharks Fleer All-Star Sheet-3
97Upper Deck-357
02Fleer Throwbacks-75
Gold-75
Platinum-75
04ITG Franchises US East-446
Autographs-A-IA
04UD Legendary Signatures-1
AKA Autographs-AKA-AI
Autographs-AI
04UD Legends Classics-1
Gold-1
Platinum-1
Silver-1
Signature Moments-M46
Signatures-CS44
05UD Artifacts-124
Blue-124
Gold-124
Green-124
Pewter-124
Red-124
Gold Autographed-124

Ianiero, Andrew
98Kingston Frontenacs-8
99Kingston Frontenacs-8
00Kingston Frontenacs-8
01Kingston Frontenacs-8
02Augusta Lynx-66
02ECHL All-Star Northern-24
03Bakersfield Condors-6
03ECHL All-Stars-271
05Bakersfield Condors-17
06Bakersfield Condors-9

Iannazzo, Dave
00Sioux Falls Stampede-10
04St. Cloud State Huskies-17

Iannetta, Matt
01London Knights-9

Iannone, Pat
00Kootenay Ice-11

Iaquinta, Aldo
97New Mexico Scorpions-26
97New Mexico Scorpions II-11

Ibelherr, Franz-Xavier
94German First League-205

Ibragimov, Rinat
04Russian Under-18 Team-6

Idalski, Brian
95Madison Monsters-13
96Madison Monsters-18
97Columbus Cottonmouths-5
98Columbus Cottonmouths-5
99Columbus Cottonmouths-20

Idema, Dan
02Medicine Hat Tigers-10
04South Surrey Eagles-9
04Surrey Eagles-8
04Saginaw Spirit-15
04Surrey Eagles-8

Iggulden, Mike
05Cleveland Barons-11

Iginla, Jarome
93Kamloops Blazers-10
94Parkhurst SE-SE260
Gold-SE260
94Select-165
Gold-165
94SP-181
94Kamloops Blazers-2
95Donruss Elite World Juniors-15
95SP-170
95Kamloops Blazers-1
95Classic-11
95Slapshot Memorial Cup-9
95Classic Five-Sport *-132
Autographs-132
96Be A Player Link to History-1A
96Be A Player Link to History Autographs-1A
96Be A Player Link to History Auto Silver-1A
96Black Diamond-164
Gold-164
Run for the Cup-RC19
96Collector's Choice-349
96Donruss Canadian Ice-124
Gold Press Proofs-124
Red Press Proofs-124
O Canada-4
96Donruss Elite-131
Die Cut Stars-131
Aspirations-19
96Flair-103
Blue Ice-103
96Hockey Greats Coins-23
Gold-23
96Kraft Upper Deck-49
96Leaf Limited Rookies-2
96Leaf Limited Rookies Gold-2
96Leaf Preferred-118
Press Proofs-118
96Metal Universe-182
96Pinnacle Mint-29
Bronze-29
Gold-29
Silver-29
Coins Brass-29
Coins Solid Gold-29
Coins Gold Plated-29
Coins Nickel-29
Coins Silver-29
96Select Certified-93
Artist's Proofs-93
Blue-93
Mirror Blue-93
Mirror Gold-93
Mirror Red-93
Red-93
96SP-23
SPx Force-4
SPx Force-5
SPx Force Autographs-4
96Ultra-24
Gold Medallion-24
Rookies-10
96Upper Deck-181
Generation Next-X21
Power Performers-P19
96Upper Deck Ice-78
Parallel-78
96Zenith-119
Artist's Proofs-119
96All-Sport PPF *-177
96All Sport PPF Gold *-177
97Black Diamond-132
Double Diamond-132
Triple Diamond-132
Quadruple Diamond-132
97Collector's Choice-34
97Collector's Choice-315
Crash the Game-C29A
Crash the Game-C29B
Crash the Game-C29C
Crash the Game Exchange-CR29
Star Quest-SQ12
Stick'Ums-S12
97Crown Royale-19
Emerald Green-19
Ice Blue-19
Silver-19
97Donruss-14
97Donruss-226
Press Proofs Silver-14
Press Proofs Silver-226
Press Proofs Gold-14
Press Proofs Gold-226
Line 2 Line-17
Line 2 Line Die Cut-17
97Donruss Canadian Ice-12
Dominion Series-12
Provincial Series-12
National Pride-13
97Donruss Elite-13
97Donruss Elite-121
Aspirations-13
Aspirations-121
Status-13
Status-121
Craftsmen-17
Master Craftsmen-17
97Donruss Limited-43
97Donruss Limited-114
97Donruss Limited-177
Exposure-43
Exposure-114
Exposure-177
Fabric of the Game-61
97Donruss Preferred-17
97Donruss Preferred-166
Cut to the Chase-17
Cut to the Chase-166
Line of the Times-7A
97Donruss Preferred Line of Times Promos-7A
97Donruss Priority-31
97Donruss Priority-191
Stamp of Approval-31
Stamp of Approval-191
Direct Deposit-9
Postcards-20
Postcards Opening Day Issues-19
Stamps-20
Stamps Bronze-20
Stamps Gold-20
Stamps Silver-20
97Katch-21
Gold-21
Silver-21
97Leaf-14
97Leaf-180
Fractal Matrix-14
Fractal Matrix-180
Fractal Matrix Die Cuts-14
Fractal Matrix Die Cuts-180
Banner Season-20
97Leaf International-14
Universal Ice-14
97McDonald's Upper Deck-12
97NHL Aces Playing Cards-17
97Pacific-12
Copper-12
Emerald Green-12
Ice Blue-12
Red-12
Silver-12
Card-Supials-3
Card-Supials Minis-3
Cramer's Choice-3
Gold Crown Die-Cuts-5
Team Checklists-4
97Pacific Dynagon-17
97Pacific Dynagon-137
Copper-17
Copper-137
Dark Grey-17
Dark Grey-137
Emerald Green-17
Emerald Green-137
Ice Blue-17
Ice Blue-137
Red-17
Red-137
Silver-17
Silver-137
Best Kept Secrets-13
Dynamic Duos-4B
Tandems-3
Tandems-23
97Pacific Invincible-19
Copper-19
Emerald Green-19
Ice Blue-19
Red-19
Silver-19
Attack Zone-4
Feature Performers-5
NHL Regime-29
Off The Glass-4
97Pacific Omega-30
Copper-30
Dark Gray-30
Emerald Green-30
Gold-30
Ice Blue-30
97Panini Stickers-194
97Panini Stickers-252
97Paramount-30
Copper-30
Dark Grey-30
Emerald Green-30
Ice Blue-30
Red-30
Silver-30
Canadian Greats-3
97Pinnacle-31
Artist's Proofs-31
Rink Collection-31
Press Plates Back Black-31
Press Plates Back Cyan-31
Press Plates Back Magenta-31
Press Plates Back Yellow-31
Press Plates Front Black-31
Press Plates Front Cyan-31
Press Plates Front Magenta-31
Press Plates Front Yellow-31
97Pinnacle Certified-55
Red-55
Mirror Blue-55
Mirror Gold-55
Mirror Red-55
97Pinnacle Inside-17
Coach's Collection-17
Executive Collection-17
Track-28
97Pinnacle Mint-9
Bronze-9
Gold Team-9
Silver Team-9
Coins Brass-9
Coins Brass Proofs-9
Coins Gold Plated-9
Coins Gold Plated Proofs-9
Coins Nickel Silver-9
Coins Nickel Silver Proofs-9
Coins Solid Gold-9
Coins Solid Silver-9
97Pinnacle Power Pack Blow-Ups-15
97Pinnacle Tot Cert Platinum Blue-55
97Pinnacle Tot Certi Platinum Gold-55
97Pinnacle Totally Certified Platinum Red-55
97Pinnacle Tot Cert Mirror Platinum Gold-55
97Revolution-18
Copper-18
Emerald-18
Ice Blue-18
Silver-18
97Score-123
Artist's Proofs-123
Golden Blades-123
Check It-7
97SP Authentic-20
Sign of the Times-JI
97SPx-7
Bronze-7
Gold-7
Silver-7
Steel-7
DuoView-4
DuoView Autographs-4
Grand Finale-7
97Studio-12
Press Proofs Silver-12
Press Proofs Gold-12
Hard Hats-12
Portraits-12
Portraits-NNOB
Silhouettes-24
Silhouettes 8x10-24
97Upper Deck-24
Game Jerseys-GJ4
Smooth Grooves-SG12
The Specialists-24
The Specialists Level 2 Die Cuts-24
97Upper Deck Ice-20
Parallel-20
Lethal Lines-L5C
Lethal Lines 2-L5C
Power Shift-20
97Zenith-1
Z-Gold-1
Z-Silver-1
97Zenith 5 x 7-20
Gold Impulse-20
Silver Impulse-20
98Aurora-25
98Be A Player-18
Press Release-18
98BAP Gold-18
98BAP Autographs-18
98BAP Autographs Gold-18
98BAP Tampa Bay All Star Game-18
98Black Diamond-12
Double Diamond-12
Triple Diamond-12
Quadruple Diamond-12
98Bowman's Best-65
Refractors-65
Atomic Refractors-65
98Crown Royale-19
Limited Series-19
98Finest-111
No Protectors-111
No Protectors Refractors-111
Refractors-111
98Katch-21
98OPC Chrome-52
Refractors-52
98Pacific-120
Ice Blue-120
Red-120
98Pacific Dynagon Ice-27
Blue-27
Red-27
98Pacific Omega-33
Red-33
Opening Day Issue-33
98Panini Stickers-181
98Paramount-28
Copper-28
Emerald Green-28
Holo-Electric-28
Ice Blue-28
Silver-28
98Revolution-20
Ice Shadow-20
Red-20
98SP Authentic-13
Power Shift-13
98Topps-52
O-Pee-Chee-52
Ice Age 2000-I3
98Topps Gold Label Class 1-35
Black-35
Black One of One-35
One of One-35
Red-35
Red One of One-35
98Topps Gold Label Class 2-35
98Topps Gold Label Class 2 Black-35
98Topps Gold Label Class 2 Black 1 of 1-35
98Topps Gold Label Class 2 One of One-35
98Topps Gold Label Class 2 Red-35
98Topps Gold Label Class 2 Red One of One-35
98Topps Gold Label Class 3-35
98Topps Gold Label Class 3 Black-35
98Topps Gold Label Class 3 Black 1 of 1-35
98Topps Gold Label Class 3 One of One-35
98Topps Gold Label Class 3 Red-35
98Topps Gold Label Class 3 Red One of One-35
98UD Choice-35
98UD Choice Preview-35
98UD Choice Prime Choice Reserve-35
98UD Choice Reserve-35
98Upper Deck-55
Exclusives-55
Exclusives 1 of 1-55
Gold Reserve-55
98Upper Deck MVP-34
Gold Script-34
Silver Script-34
Super Script-34
ProSign-JI
99Aurora-23
Striped-23
Premiere Date-23
Premiere Date Striped-23
99BAP Memorabilia-212
Gold-212
Silver-212
99BAP Millennium-39
Emerald-39
Ruby-39
Sapphire-39
Signatures-39
Signatures Gold-39
99Crown Royale-23
Limited Series-23
Premiere Date-23
99McDonald's Upper Deck-MCD5
99McDonald's Upper Deck-MCD5R

99O-Pee-Chee-74
99O-Pee-Chee Chrome-74
99O-Pee-Chee Chrome Refractors-74
99Pacific-57
Copper-57
Emerald Green-57
Gold-57
Ice Blue-57
Premiere Date-57
Red-57
Center Ice-4
Center Ice Proofs-4
Team Leaders-5
99Pacific Dynagon Ice-36
Blue-36
Copper-36
Gold-36
Premiere Date-36
99Pacific Omega-38
Copper-38
Gold-38
Ice Blue-38
Premiere Date-38
99Pacific Prism-24
Holographic Blue-24
Holographic Gold-24
Holographic Mirror-24
Holographic Purple-24
Premiere Date-24
99Panini Stickers-190
99Paramount-40
Copper-40
Emerald-40
Gold-40
Holographic Emerald-40
Holographic Gold-40
Holographic Silver-40
Ice Blue-40
Premiere Date-40
Red-40
Silver-40
Ice Advantage-4
Ice Advantage Proofs-4
Ice Alliance-5
99Revolution-25
Premiere Date-25
Red-25
Shadow Series-25
Ornaments-5
Top of the Line-23
Copper-25
Gold-25
CSC Silver-25
99SPx-24
Radiance-24
Spectrum-24
99Stadium Club-21
First Day Issue-21
One of a Kind-21
Printing Plates Black-21
Printing Plates Cyan-21
Printing Plates Magenta-21
Printing Plates Yellow-21
99Topps/OPC-74
99Topps/OPC Chrome-74
Refractors-74
99Topps Gold Label Class 1-74
Black-74
Black One of One-74
One of One-74
Red-74
Red One of One-74
99Topps Gold Label Class 2-74
99Topps Gold Label Class 2 Black-74
99Topps Gold Label Class 2 Black 1 of 1-74
99Topps Gold Label Class 2 One of One-74
99Topps Gold Label Class 2 Red-74
99Topps Gold Label Class 2 Red One of One-74
99Topps Gold Label Class 3-74
99Topps Gold Label Class 3 Black-74
99Topps Gold Label Class 3 Black 1 of 1-74
99Topps Gold Label Class 3 One of One-74
99Topps Gold Label Class 3 Red-74
99Topps Gold Label Class 3 Red One of One-74
99Upper Deck-28
Exclusives-28
Exclusives 1 of 1-28
99Upper Deck Gold Reserve-28
99Upper Deck MVP-32
Gold Script-32
Silver Script-32
Super Script-32
99Upper Deck MVP SC Edition-33
Gold Script-33
Silver Script-33
Super Script-33
99Upper Deck Retro-12
Gold-12
Platinum-12
99Upper Deck Victory-46
00Aurora-24
Premiere Date-24
00BAP Memorabilia-278
Emerald-278
Ruby-278
Sapphire-278
Promos-278
00BAP Mem Chicago Sportsfest Copper-278
00BAP Memorabilia Chicago Sportsfest Blue-278
00BAP Memorabilia Chicago Sportsfest Gold-278
00BAP Memorabilia Chicago Sportsfest Ruby-278
00BAP Memorabilia Chicago Sun-Times Ruby-278
00BAP Memorabilia Chicago Sun-Times Gold-278
00BAP Mem Chicago Sun-Times Sapphire-278
00BAP Mem Toronto Fall Expo Copper-278
00BAP Memorabilia Toronto Fall Expo Gold-278
00BAP Memorabilia Toronto Fall Expo Ruby-278
00BAP Parkhurst 2000-P62
00BAP Signature Series-18
Emerald-18
Ruby-18
Sapphire-18
Autographs-186
Autographs Gold-186
Franchise Players-F5
00Crown Royale-18
Ice Blue-18
Limited Series-18
Premiere Date-18
Red-18
Game-Worn Jersey Redemptions-2
00O-Pee-Chee-15
00O-Pee-Chee Parallel-15
00Pacific-66
Copper-66
Gold-66
Ice Blue-66
Premiere Date-66
2001: Ice Odyssey-4
00Pacific 2001: Ice Odyssey Anaheim Ntnl-4
00Panini Stickers-117
00Paramount-36
Copper-36
Gold-36
Holo-Gold-36
Holo-Silver-36
Ice Blue-36
Premiere Date-36
Jersey and Patches-1
00Private Stock Game Gear-11
00Private Stock Game Gear Patches-11
00Revolution-23
Blue-23
Premiere Date-23
Red-23
Game-Worn Jerseys-3
Game-Worn Jersey Patches-3
HD NHL-6
00SP Authentic-15
00Stadium Club-52
00Titanium-11
Blue-11
Gold-11
Premiere Date-11
Red-11
Retail-11
Game Gear-68
Game Gear Patches-68
00Topps/OPC-15
Parallel-15
00Topps Chrome-15
OPC Refractors-15
Refractors-15
00Topps Gold Label Class 1-31
Gold-31
00Topps Gold Label Class 2-31
00Topps Gold Label Class 2 Gold-31
00Topps Gold Label Class 3-31
00Topps Gold Label Class 3 Gold-31
00Topps Heritage-70
Chrome Parallel-70
00Topps Premier Plus-48
Blue Ice-48
Game-Used Memorabilia-GPJI
Game-Used Memorabilia-GPJIRF
00Topps Stars-74
Blue-74
00UD Reserve-12
00Upper Deck-254
Exclusives Tier 1-254
Exclusives Tier 2-254
00Upper Deck MVP-31
First Stars-31
Second Stars-31
Third Stars-31
00Upper Deck Victory-37
00Upper Deck Vintage-60
00Vanguard-16
Holographic Gold-16
Holographic Purple-16
Pacific Proofs-16
01Atomic-13
Blue-13
Gold-13
Premiere Date-13
Red-13
Power Play-5
Team Nucleus-2
01BAP Memorabilia-275
Emerald-275
Ruby-275
Sapphire-275
Country of Origin-CO47
01BAP Signature Series-5
Autographs-5
Autographs Gold-5
Franchise Jerseys-FP-5
He Shoots-He Scores Points-13
He Shoots-He Scores Prizes-9
Jerseys-GJ-9
Jersey Autographs-GUJI
Jersey and Stick Cards-GSJ-9
Emblems-GUE-11
Numbers-ITN-11
Teammates-TM-5
01BAP Ultimate Memorabilia Autographs-16
01BAP Ultimate Mem Autographs Gold-16
01BAP Ultimate Mem Complete Package-3
01BAP Ultimate Memorabilia Dynamic Duos-9
01BAP Ultimate Memorabilia Gloves Are Off-23
01BAP Ultimate Memorabilia Name Plates-18
01BAP Ultimate Mem Scoring Leaders-21
01BAP Update He Shoots-He Scores Prizes-5
01Bowman YoungStars-7
Gold-7
Ice Cubed-7
01Crown Royale-20
Blue-20
Premiere Date-20
Red-20
Retail-20
Crowning Achievement-11
Jewels of the Crown-3
Triple Threads-9
01McDonald's Pacific-3
Hometown Pride-4
Jersey Patches Silver-1
Jersey Patches Gold-1
01O-Pee-Chee-106
01O-Pee-Chee Heritage Parallel-106
01O-Pee-Chee Heritage Parallel Limited-106
01O-Pee-Chee Premier Parallel-106
01Pacific-61
01Pacific-405
Extreme LTD-61
Gold-405
Hobby LTD-61
Premiere Date-61
Retail LTD-61
01Pacific Adrenaline-25
Blue-25
Premiere Date-25
Red-25
Retail-25
Jerseys-5
01Pacific Arena Exclusives-61
01Pacific Arena Exclusives-405
01Pacific Heads-Up-12
Blue-12
Premiere Date-12
Red-12
Silver-12
Quad Jerseys-5
01Parkhurst-5
Gold-5
Silver-5
He Shoots-He Scores Prizes-3
01Private Stock-11
Gold-11
Premiere Date-11
Retail-11
Silver-11
Game Gear-15
Game Gear Patches-15
01Private Stock Pacific Nights-11
01Private Stock PS-2002-10
01SP Authentic-11
Limited-11
Limited Gold-11
Sign of the Times-JI
Sign of the Times-IH
01SP Game Used Authentic Fabric-AFJI
01SP Game Used Authentic Fabric-DFIS
01SP Game Used Authentic Fabric Gold-AFJI
01SP Game Used Inked Sweaters-ISJI
01SP Game Used Inked Sweaters-DSIG
01SP Game Used Patches-PJI
01SP Game Used Patches-CPAI
01SP Game Used Patches Signed-SPJI
01SP Game Used Patches Signed-DSPHI
01SPx-8
Hockey Treasures-HTJI
Hockey Treasures Autographed-STJI
01Sports Illustrated for Kids III-178
01Stadium Club-31
Award Winners-31
Master Photos-31
Souvenirs-JI
01Titanium-18
Hobby Parallel-18
Premiere Date-18
Retail-18
Retail Parallel-18
All-Stars-2
Double-Sided Jerseys-7
Saturday Knights-3
Three-Star Selections-12
01Titanium Draft Day Edition-15
01Topps-106
Heritage Parallel-106
Heritage Parallel Limited-106
OPC Parallel-106
01Topps Chrome-106
Refractors-106
Black Border Refractors-106
01Topps Heritage-40
Refractors-40
Jerseys-JJI
01Topps Reserve-38
Emblems-JI
Jerseys-JI
Name Plates-JI
Numbers-JI
Patches-JI
01UD Challenge for the Cup-9
Jersey Autographs-FPJI
01UD Honor Roll Pucks-P-JI
01UD Honor Roll Pucks Gold-P-JI
01UD Mask Collection-13
Gold-13
Double Patches-DPJI
Jerseys-J-JI
Jersey and Patch-JPJI
01UD Playmakers-16
Combo Jerseys-CJJI
Combo Jerseys Gold-CJJI
Jerseys-J-JI
Jerseys Gold-J-JI
Practice Jerseys-PJJI
Practice Jerseys Gold-PJJI
01UD Premier Collection-8
Dual Jerseys-DKI
Dual Jerseys Black-DKI
Jerseys-BJI
Jerseys Black-B-JI
Signatures-JI
Signatures Black-JI
01UD Top Shelf-5
Jerseys-JI
Jersey Autographs-JI
01Upper Deck-25
Exclusives-25
Game Jerseys-NGJI
01Upper Deck Ice-5
01Upper Deck MVP-25
Morning Skate Jerseys-J-JA
Morning Skate Jerseys-J-JI
Morning Skate Jersey Autographs-SJ-JA
Morning Skate Jersey Autographs-SJ-JI
01Upper Deck Victory-49
Gold-49
01Upper Deck Vintage-37
01Upper Deck Vintage-42
01Upper Deck Vintage-43
01Vanguard-12
Blue-12
Red-12
East Meets West-9
Memorabilia-4
One of Ones-12
Premiere Date-12
Proofs-12
V-Team-11
02McFarlane Hockey-110
02McFarlane Hockey-112
02Atomic-13
Blue-13
Gold-13
Red-13
Cold Fusion-5
Hobby Parallel-13
National Pride-C2
Power Converters-4
Super Colliders-3
02BAP All-Star Edition-32
Jerseys-32
Jerseys Gold-32
Jerseys Silver-32
02BAP First Edition-142
02BAP First Edition-313
02BAP First Edition-345
02BAP First Edition-371
02BAP First Edition-372
02BAP First Edition-387
02BAP First Edition-413R
Debut Jerseys-9
He Shoots-He Score Points-13
He Shoots-He Scores Prizes-4
Jerseys-142
Scoring Leaders-4
02BAP Memorabilia-117
02BAP Memorabilia-205
02BAP Memorabilia-239
Emerald-117
Emerald-205
Emerald-239
Ruby-117
Ruby-205
Ruby-239
Sapphire-117
Sapphire-205
Sapphire-239
All-Star Jerseys-ASJ-20
All-Star Emblems-ASE-7
All-Star Numbers-ASN-7
All-Star Teammmates-AST-28
Franchise Players-FP-5
He Shoots-He Scores Prizes-25
NHL All-Star Game-117
NHL All-Star Game-205
NHL All-Star Game-239
NHL All-Star Game Blue-117
NHL All-Star Game Blue-205
NHL All-Star Game Blue-239
NHL All-Star Game Green-117
NHL All-Star Game Green-205
NHL All-Star Game Green-239
NHL All-Star Game Red-117
NHL All-Star Game Red-205
NHL All-Star Game Red-239
Teammates-TM-20
02BAP Memorabilia Toronto Fall Expo-117
02BAP Memorabilia Toronto Fall Expo-205
02BAP Memorabilia Toronto Fall Expo-239
02BAP Signature Series-40
Autographs-40
Autograph Buybacks 1998-18
Autograph Buybacks 1999-39
Autograph Buybacks 2000-186
Autograph Buybacks 2001-5
Autographs Gold-40
Famous Scraps-FS5
Franchise Players-FJ5
Golf-GS42
Jerseys-SGJ5
Jersey Autographs-SGJ5
02BAP Ultimate Memorabilia Autographs-19
02BAP Ultimate Mem Autographs Gold-19
02BAP Ultimate Mem Blades of Steel-10
02BAP Ultimate Memorabilia Gloves Are Off-16
02BAP Ultimate Memorabilia Hat Tricks-11
02BAP Ultimate Memorabilia Jerseys-2
02BAP Ultimate Memorabilia Numerology-17
02BAP Ultimate Memorabilia Retro Trophies-13
02BAP Ultimate Mem Scoring Leaders-2
02Between the Pipes Nightmares-GN6
02Bowman Toronto Spring Expo-5
02Bowman YoungStars-40
Gold-40
Silver-40
02Crown Royale-14
Blue-14
Red-14
Retail-14
Lords of the Rink-5
02eTopps-1
02ITG Used-9
02ITG Used-109
Franchise Players-F5
Franchise Players Autographs-F5
Franchise Players Gold-F5
Jerseys-GUJ5
Jersey Autographs-GUJ5
Jerseys Gold-GUJ5
Emblems-E5
Jersey and Stick-SJ5
Jersey and Stick Gold-SJ5
Triple Memorabilia-TM4
Triple Memorabilia Gold-TM4
02McDonald's Pacific-5
Clear Advantage-3
Salt Lake Gold-8
02NHL Power Play Stickers-1
02O-Pee-Chee-12
02O-Pee-Chee-328
02O-Pee-Chee Jumbos-2
02O-Pee-Chee Premier Blue Parallel-12
02O-Pee-Chee Premier Blue Parallel-328
02O-Pee-Chee Premier Red Parallel-12
02O-Pee-Chee Premier Red Parallel-328
02O-Pee-Chee Factory Set-12
02O-Pee-Chee Factory Set-328
02O-Pee-Chee Factory Set Hometown Heroes-HHC1
02Pacific-54
Blue-54
Red-54
Impact Zone-4
Lamplighters-4
Main Attractions-4
Maximum Impact-11
02Pacific Calder-12
Silver-12
02Pacific Complete-10
Red-10
02Pacific Exclusive-23
Maximum Overdrive-5
02Pacific Heads-Up-16
Blue-16
Purple-16
Red-16
Bobble Heads-5
Etched in Time-4
Inside the Numbers-5
Stat Masters-5
02Pacific Quest for the Cup-12
Gold-12
02Parkhurst-97
Bronze-97
Gold-97
Silver-97
Franchise Players-FP5
Hardware-A2
Hardware-H2
Hardware-P2
Heroes-NH3
He Shoots-He Scores Points-18
He Shoots-He Scores Prizes-17
Jerseys-GJ44
Stick and Jerseys-SJ44
02Parkhurst Retro-2
Minis-2
Franchise Players-RF5
He Shoots-He Scores Prizes-25
02Private Stock Reserve-106
Red-106
Retail-106
Patches-106
02SP Authentic-12
02SP Authentic-93
Beckett Promos-12
Sign of the Times-JI
Sign of the Times-CI
Sign of the Times-HCI
Super Premiums-SPJI
02SP Game Used-7
Authentic Fabrics-AFJI
Authentic Fabrics Gold-AFJI
Authentic Fabrics Rainbow-AFJI
First Rounder Patches-JI
Piece of History-PHJI
Piece of History Gold-PHJI
Piece of History Rainbow-PHJI
Signature Style-JI
02SPx-10
Spectrum Gold-10
Spectrum Silver-10
Smooth Skaters-JI
Smooth Skaters Gold-JI
Smooth Skaters Silver-JI
Xtreme Talents-JI
Xtreme Talents Gold-JI
Xtreme Talents Silver-JI
02Stadium Club-2
Silver Decoy Cards-2
Proofs-2
Beam Team-BT4
Lone Star Signatures Blue-LSJI
Lone Star Signatures Red-LSJI
02Titanium-15
Blue-15
Red-15
Retail-15
Saturday Knights-1
02Topps-12
02Topps-328
OPC Blue Parallel-12
OPC Blue Parallel-328
OPC Red Parallel-12
OPC Red Parallel-328
Coast to Coast-CC3
Topps/OPC Hometown Heroes-HHC1
Own The Game-OTG1
Own The Game-OTG6
Factory Set-12
Factory Set-328
02Topps Chrome-12
Black Border Refractors-12
Refractors-12
e-Topps Decoy Cards-1
02Topps Heritage-2
02Topps Heritage-101
02Topps Heritage-108
02Topps Heritage-109
02Topps Heritage-119
Chrome Parallel-2
USA Test Parallel-2
02Topps Total-130
Award Winners-AW1
Production-TP1
Team Checklists-TTC4
Topps-TT1
02UD Artistic Impressions-13
Gold-13
Artist's Touch-ATJI
Artist's Touch Gold-ATJI
02UD Artistic Impressions Beckett Promos-13
02UD Artistic Impressions Retrospectives-R13
02UD Artistic Impressions Retrospect Gold-R13
02UD Artistic Impress Retrospect Auto-R13
02UD Artistic Impress Retrospect Silver-R13
02UD Honor Roll-10
Students of the Game-SG4
Team Warriors-TW2
02UD Mask Collection-16
02UD Mask Collection Beckett Promos-16
02UD Mask Collection Instant Offense-IOJI
02UD Mask Collection Patches-PGJI
02UD Piece of History-17
Awards Collection-AC4
Marks of Distinction-JI
02UD Premier Collection-9
Jerseys Bronze-JI
Jerseys Gold-JI
Jerseys Silver-JI
Patches-PJI
Signatures Bronze-SJI
Signatures Bronze-ASJI
Signatures Gold-SJI
Signatures Gold-ASJI
Signatures Silver-SJI
Signatures Silver-ASJI
02UD Top Shelf-12
Clutch Performers-CPJI
Dual Player Jerseys-RIW
Dual Player Jerseys-STIS
Signatures-JI
Triple Jerseys-HTKYI
Triple Jerseys-HTSIG
02Upper Deck-183
02Upper Deck-269
Exclusives-183
Exclusives-269
02Upper Deck Beckett UD Promos-269
02Upper Deck Difference Makers-JI
02Upper Deck Fan Favorites-JI
02Upper Deck Letters of Note-LNJI
02Upper Deck Letters of Note Gold-LNJI
02Upper Deck Pinpoint Accuracy-PAJI
02Upper Deck Reaching Fifty-50JI
02Upper Deck Reaching Fifty Gold-50JI
02Upper Deck Shooting Stars-SS2
02Upper Deck Sizzling Scorers-SS3
02Upper Deck Specialists-SRB
02Upper Deck Classic Portraits-14
Hockey Royalty-KSI
Hockey Royalty-SIT
Hockey Royalty Limited-KSI
Hockey Royalty Limited-SIT
Mini-Busts-44
Mini-Busts-45
Mini-Busts-46
Mini-Busts-47
Mini-Busts-48
Mini-Busts-49
Mini-Busts-50
Mini-Busts-51
Pillars of Strength-PS2
Stitches-CJI
Stitches Limited-CJI
02Upper Deck MVP-29
Gold-29
Classics-29
Golden Classics-29
Highlight Nights-HN3
Overdrive-SO3
Skate Around Jerseys-SAJI
Vital Forces-VF4
02Upper Deck Pearson Awards-2
02Upper Deck Rookie Update-17
02Upper Deck Rookie Update-111
02Upper Deck Rookie Update-152C
02Upper Deck Rookie Update-167
Autographs-JI
Jerseys-DJI
Jerseys Gold-DJI
02Upper Deck Victory-31
Bronze-31
Gold-31
Silver-31
National Pride-NP3
02Upper Deck Vintage-39
02Upper Deck Vintage-265
02Upper Deck Vintage-306
02Upper Deck Vintage-308
02Upper Deck Vintage-309
Jerseys-SOJI
Jerseys Gold-SO-JI
Tall Boys-T10
Tall Boys Gold-T10
02Vanguard-15
LTD-15
East Meets West-2
02UD SuperStars *-41
Gold-41
03McFarlane Hockey 3-Inch Duals-60
03BAP Memorabilia-33
Emerald-33
Gold-33
Ruby-33
Sapphire-33
Gloves-GUG15
He Shoots-He Scores Prizes-27
Jersey and Stick-SJ-3
Jerseys-GJ-3
Jersey Autographs-GJ-3
Practice Jerseys-PMP16
03BAP Ultimate Memorabilia Autographs-80
Gold-80
03BAP Ultimate Mem Blades of Steel-5
03BAP Ultimate Mem Complete Package-5
03BAP Ultimate Mem Complete Package Gold-5
03BAP Ultimate Memorabilia Emblems-7
03BAP Ultimate Memorabilia Emblems Gold-7
03BAP Ultimate Mem Franch Present Future-5
03BAP Ultimate Memorabilia Gloves Are Off-5
03BAP Ultimate Memorabilia Hat Tricks-11
03BAP Ultimate Memorabilia Heroes-3
03BAP Ultimate Mem Hometown Heroes-14
03BAP Ultimate Mem Hometown Heroes Gold-14
03BAP Ultimate Memorabilia Jerseys-25
03BAP Ultimate Memorabilia Jerseys Gold-25
03BAP Ultimate Mem Jersey and Emblems-14
03BAP Ultimate Mem Jersey and Emblem Gold-14
03BAP Ultimate Mem Jersey and Numbers-14
03BAP Ultimate Mem Jersey and Number Gold-14
03BAP Ultimate Mem Jersey and Stick-6
03BAP Ultimate Mem Jersey and Stick Gold-6
03BAP Ultimate Memorabilia Numbers-20
03BAP Ultimate Memorabilia Numbers Gold-20
03BAP Ultimate Mem Redemption Cards-4
03BAP Ultimate Mem Retro-Active Trophies-1
03Beehive-31
Variations-31
Gold-31
Silver-31
Jumbo Jerseys-BH5
Jerseys-JT29
Signatures-RF9
Sticks Beige Border-BE1
03Black Diamond-124
Black-124
Green-124
Red-124
Signature Gems-SG-28
03Bowman-80
Gold-80
Future Rivals-CI
Future Rivals Patches-CI
Goal to Goal-SI
03Bowman Chrome-80
Refractors-80
Gold Refractors-80
Xfractors-80
03Crown Royale-13
Blue-13
Retail-13
03eTopps-37
03ITG Action-38
Homeboys-HB5
Jerseys-M161
Jerseys-M245
03ITG Used Signature Series-53
Gold-53
Autographs-JI
Autographs Gold-JI
Franchise-5
Franchise Autographs-5
Franchise Gold-5
International Experience-6
International Experience Autographs-6
International Experience Emblems Gold-6
International Experience Emblems-6
International Experience Gold-6
Jerseys-12
Jerseys Gold-12
Jersey Autos-12
Emblems-16
Emblems Gold-16
Jersey and Stick-12
Jersey and Stick Gold-12
Oh Canada-16
Oh Canada Gold-16
Oh Canada Emblems-16
Oh Canada Emblems Gold-16
Triple Memorabilia-16
Triple Memorabilia Gold-16
03ITG VIP Jerseys-26
03ITG VIP Jersey Autographs-26
03McDonald's Pacific-7
Hockey Roots Checklists-4
Patches Silver-4
Patches Gold-4
Patches and Sticks-4
Saturday Night Rivals-1
03NHL Sticker Collection-164
03O-Pee-Chee-150
03OPC Blue-150
03OPC Gold-150
03OPC Red-150
03Pacific-50
Blue-50
Red-50
Maximum Impact-2
03Pacific Calder-13
03Pacific Calder-144
Silver-13
03Pacific Complete-219
Red-219
03Pacific Exhibit-157
Blue Backs-157
03Pacific Heads-Up-14
Hobby LTD-14
Retail LTD-14
03Pacific Invincible-13
Blue-13
Red-13
Retail-13
Featured Performers-5
03Pacific Luxury Suite-3A
03Pacific Luxury Suite-3B
03Pacific Luxury Suite-3C
03Pacific Luxury Suite-3D
03Pacific Prism-107
Blue-107
Patches-107
Red-107
Retail-107
03Pacific Quest for the Cup-15
Blue-15
Jerseys-3
03Pacific Supreme-13
Blue-13
Red-13
Retail-13
Jerseys-6
03Pacific Toronto Fall Expo-2
03Parkhurst Rookie-36
Jerseys-GJ-32
Jerseys Gold-GJ-32
Jersey and Sticks-SJ-9
Jersey and Sticks Gold-SJ-9
Teammates Gold-RT18
Teammates-RT18
03Private Stock Reserve-150
Blue-150
Patches-150
Red-150
Retail-150
03SP Authentic-12
Limited-12
Breakout Seasons-B19
Breakout Seasons Limited-B19
Sign of the Times-JI
Sign of the Times-IM
03SP Game Used-8
03SP Game Used-100
Gold-8
Gold-100
Authentic Fabrics-AFJI
Authentic Fabrics Gold-AFJI
Authentic Patches-APJI
Signers-SPSJI
03SPx-13
03SPx-118
Radiance-13
Radiance-118
Spectrum-13
Spectrum-118
Origins-O-JI
Signature Threads-ST-JI
Winning Materials-WM-JI
Winning Materials Limited-WM-JI
03Titanium-146
Hobby Jersey Number Parallels-146
Patches-146
Retail-146
03Topps-150
Blue-150
Gold-150
Red-150
Box Toppers-14
First Round Fabrics-JI
First Round Fabrics-BGJI
Topps/OPC Idols-CI8
03Topps All-Star Block Party-3
03Topps C55-3
Minis-3
Minis American Back-3
Minis American Back Red-3
Minis Bazooka Back-3
Minis Brooklyn Back-3
Minis Hat Trick Back-3
Minis O Canada Back-3
Minis O Canada Back Red-3
Minis Stanley Cup Back-3
Relics-TRJI
03Topps Pristine-71
Gold Refractor Die Cuts-71
Refractors-71
Patches-PP-JI
Patch Refractors-PP-JI
Popular Demand Relics-PD-JI
Popular Demand Relic Refractors-PD-JI
Press Plates Black-71
Press Plates Cyan-71
Press Plates Magenta-71
Press Plates Yellow-71
Stick Portions-PPS-JI
Stick Portion Refractors-PPS-JI
03Topps Traded Franchise Fabrics-FF-JI
03UD Honor Roll-10
Grade A Jerseys-GAJI
Signature Class-SC13
03UD Premier Collection-9
NHL Shields-SH-JI
Signatures-PS-JI
Signatures Gold-PS-JI
Stars-ST-JI
Stars Patches-ST-JI
03UD Toronto Fall Expo Priority Signings-JI
03Upper Deck-29
BuyBacks-110
BuyBacks-111
BuyBacks-112
Canadian Exclusives-29
Franchise Fabrics-FF-JI
HG-29
Jerseys-GJ-JI
Jersey Autographs-SJ-JI
NHL Best-NB-JI
Patches-SP6
Three Stars-TS13
03Upper Deck Classic Portraits-12
03Upper Deck Classic Portraits-148
03Upper Deck Ice-13
Gold-13
Authentics-IA-JI
03Upper Deck MVP-65
Gold Script-65
Silver Script-65
Canadian Exclusives-65
Souvenirs-S26
SportsNut-SN15
03Upper Deck Rookie Update-12
Super Stars-SSJI
03Upper Deck Trilogy-12
Limited-12
Limited Threads-LT4
03Upper Deck Victory-27
Bronze-27
Gold-27
Silver-27
Freshman Flashback-FF8
Game Breakers-GB47
03Toronto Star-17
Foil-18
04Pacific-40
Blue-40
Red-40
Cramer's Choice-3
04SP Authentic-14
04SP Authentic-103
Limited-14
Limited-103
Buybacks-71
Buybacks-72
Octographs-OS-CAP
Octographs-OS-ART
Octographs-OS-CUP
Rookie Review-RR-IG
Sign of the Times-ST-JI
Sign of the Times-DS-IR
Sign of the Times-TS-IKN
Sign of the Times-TS-ILN
Sign of the Times-QS-HINS
Sign of the Times-QS-IKHL
Sign of the Times-SS-CAN
Sign of the Times-SS-CNP
04UD All-World-98
04UD Toronto Fall Expo Pride of Canada-16
04UD Toronto Fall Expo Priority Signings-JI
04Ultimate Collection-6
04Ultimate Collection-62
Buybacks-21
Buybacks-22
Buybacks-23
Buybacks-24
Buybacks-25
Dual Logos-UL2-IK
Dual Logos-UL2-IL
Dual Logos-UL2-IS
Jerseys-UGJ-JI
Jerseys Gold-UGJ-JI
Jersey Autographs-UGJA-JI
Patch Autographs-UPA-JI
Patch Autographs-UPA-JIVL
Signatures-US-JI
Signature Logos-ULA-JI
Signature Patches-SP-JI
04Upper Deck-26
1997 Game Jerseys-JI
Big Playmakers-BP-JI
Canadian Exclusives-26
Clutch Performers-CP1
Hardware Heroes-AW6
Hardware Heroes-AW11
HG Glossy Gold-26
HG Glossy Silver-26
Jersey Autographs-GJA-JI
Three Stars-AS5
World's Best-WB2
World Cup Tribute-JI
World Cup Tribute-JSMLJI
05Be A Player-12
First Period-12
Second Period-12
Third Period-12
Overtime-12
Class Action-CA5
Dual Signatures-IM
Dual Signatures-LI
Outtakes-OT8
Quad Signatures-IMPL
Quad Signatures-ITLB
Quad Signatures-SSIR
Signatures-IG
Signatures Gold-IG
Triple Signatures-IBM
Triple Signatures-NKI
Triple Signatures-SIS
05Beehive-14
05Beehive-248
Beige -14
Blue -14
Gold-14
Red -14
Matte-14
PhotoGraphs-PGJI
Signature Scrapbook-SSJI
05Black Diamond-171
Emerald-171
Gold-171
Onyx-171
Ruby-171
Gemography-G-JI
Gemography Emerald-G-JI
Gemography Gold-G-JI
Gemography Onyx-G-JI
Gemography Ruby-G-JI
Jerseys-J-JI
Jerseys Ruby-J-JI
Jersey Duals-DJ-JI
Jersey Triples-TJ-JI
Jersey Quads-QJ-JI
05Hot Prospects-14
En Fuego-14
Red Hot-14
White Hot-14
05McDonalds Upper Deck-23
Autographs-MA5
Chasing the Cup-CC3
CHL Graduates-CG2
Jerseys-MJ11
Patches-MP11
Top Scorers-TS11
05Panini Stickers-199
05Parkhurst-67
05Parkhurst-505
05Parkhurst-574
05Parkhurst-675
Facsimile Auto Parallel-67
Facsimile Auto Parallel-505
Facsimile Auto Parallel-574
Facsimile Auto Parallel-675
Signatures-JI
True Colors-TCCGY
True Colors-TCCGY
True Colors-TCEDCA
True Colors-TCEDCA
05SP Authentic-16
05SP Authentic-110
Limited-16
Limited-110
Chirography-SPJI
Exquisite Endorsements-EEJI
Marks of Distinction-MDJI
Octographs-OF
Prestigious Pairings-PPIS
Sign of the Times-JI
Sign of the Times Triples-TIPN
Sign of the Times Fives-ISNKN
05SP Game Used-15
Autographs-15
Gold-15
Authentic Fabrics-AF-JI
Authentic Fabrics Autographs-AAF-JI
Authentic Fabrics Dual-IK
Authentic Fabrics Dual-IS
Authentic Fabrics Dual Autographs-IS
Authentic Fabrics Gold-AF-JI
Authentic Fabrics Quad-IAKL
Authentic Patches Quad -IAKL
Authentic Fabrics Triple-BIS
Authentic Fabrics Triple-INK
Authentic Fabrics Triple-ISL
Authentic Fabrics Triple-SFI
Authentic Fabrics Triple-SNI
Authentic Patches-AP-JI

Authentic Patches Autographs-AAP-JI
Authentic Patches Dual-IK
Authentic Patches Dual-IS
Authentic Patches Dual Autographs-IS
Authentic Patches Triple-BIS
Authentic Patches Triple-INK
Authentic Patches Triple-ISL
Authentic Patches Triple-SFI
Authentic Patches Triple-SNI
Auto Draft-AD-JI
Awesome Authentics-AA-JI
Awesome Authentics Gold-DA-JI
By the Letter-LM-JI
Game Gear-GG-JI
Game Gear Autographs-AG-JI
SIGnificance-JI
SIGnificance Gold-S-JI
SIGnificance Extra-IH
SIGnificance Extra Gold-IH
Significant Numbers-SN-JI
Statscriptions-ST-JI
05SPx-12
Spectrum-12
Winning Combos-WC-KI
Winning Combos Gold-WC-KI
Winning Combos Spectrum-WC-KI
Winning Materials-WM-JI
Winning Materials Autographs-AWM-JI
Winning Materials Gold-WM-JI
Winning Materials Spectrum-WM-JI
Xcitement Superstars-XS-JI
Xcitement Superstars Gold-XS-JI
Xcitement Superstars Spectrum-XS-JI
05The Cup-17
Gold-17
Black Rainbow-17
Dual NHL Shields-DSIK
Dual NHL Shields-DSIL
Dual NHL Shields-DSIN
Emblems of Endorsement-EEJI
Hardware Heroes-HHJI1
Hardware Heroes-HHJI2
Hardware Heroes-HHJI3
Hardware Heroes-HHJI4
Honorable Numbers-HNJI
Limited Logos-LLJI
Masterpiece Pressplates-17
Masterpiece Pressplates Rookie Upd Auto-259
Noble Numbers-NNIG
Noble Numbers-NNSI
Noble Numbers Dual-DNNHI
Patch Variation-P17
Patch Variation Autographs-AP17
Property of-POJI
Scripted Numbers-SNSI
Scripted Numbers Dual-DSNIK
Scripted Numbers Dual-DSNIN
Scripted Swatches-SSJI
Signature Patches-SPJI
05UD Artifacts-15
05UD Artifacts-156
Blue-15
Blue-156
Gold-15
Gold-156
Green-15
Green-156
Pewter-15
Pewter-156
Red-15
Red-156
Auto Facts-AF-JI
Auto Facts Blue-AF-JI
Auto Facts Copper-AF-JI
Auto Facts Pewter-AF-JI
Auto Facts Silver-AF-JI
Gold Autographed-15
Gold Autographed-156
Remarkable Artifacts-RA-JI
Remarkable Artifacts Dual-RA-JI
Treasured Patches-TP-JI
Treasured Patches Autographed-TP-JI
Treasured Patches Dual-TPD-JI
Treasured Patches Dual Autographed-TPD-JI
Treasured Patches Pewter-TP-JI
Treasured Patches Silver-TP-JI
Treasured Swatches-TS-JI
Treasured Swatches Autographed-TS-JI
Treasured Swatches Blue-TS-JI
Treasured Swatches Copper-TS-JI
Treasured Swatches Dual-TSD-JI
Treasured Swatches Dual Autographed-TSD-JI
Treasured Swatches Dual Blue-TSD-JI
Treasured Swatches Dual Copper-TSD-JI
Treasured Swatches Dual Maroon-TSD-JI
Treasured Swatches Dual Pewter-TSD-JI
Treasured Swatches Dual Silver-TSD-JI
Treasured Swatches Maroon-TS-JI
Treasured Swatches Pewter-TS-JI
Treasured Swatches Silver-TS-JI
05UD PowerPlay-14
05UD PowerPlay-95
Rainbow-14
Power Marks-PMJI
Specialists-TSJI
Specialists Patches-SPJI
05UD Toronto Fall Expo Priority Signings-PS-JI
05Ultimate Collection-15
Gold-15
Endorsed Emblems-EEJI
Jerseys-JJI
Jerseys Dual-DJPI
Marquee Attractions-MA11
Marquee Attractions Signatures-SMA11
National Heroes Jerseys-NHJJI
National Heroes Patches-NHPJI
Premium Patches-PPJI
Premium Swatches-PSJI
Ultimate Achievements-UAJI
Ultimate Patches-PJI
Ultimate Patches Dual-DPPI
Ultimate Signatures-USJI
Ultimate Signatures Foursomes-UFINNL
Ultimate Signatures Logos-SLJI
Ultimate Signatures Pairings-UPIN
Ultimate Signatures Trios-UTILN
05Ultra-31
Gold-31
Difference Makers-DM11
Difference Makers Jerseys-DMJ-JI
Difference Makers Jersey Autographs-DAJ-JI
Difference Makers Patches-DMP-JI
Difference Makers Patch Autographs-DAP-JI
Fresh Ink-FI-JI
Fresh Ink Blue-FI-JI
Ice-31
Scoring Kings-SK5
Scoring Kings Jerseys-SKJ-JI
Scoring Kings Jersey Autographs-KAJ-JI
Scoring Kings Patches-SKP-JI
Scoring Kings Patch Autographs-KAP-JI
05Upper Deck-25
05Upper Deck-200
05Upper Deck All-Time Greatest-9
05Upper Deck All-Time Greatest-65
05Upper Deck Big Playmakers-B-JI
05Upper Deck Goal Celebrations-GC4
05Upper Deck Goal Rush-GR13
05Upper Deck HG Glossy-25
05Upper Deck HG Glossy-200
05Upper Deck Hometown Heroes-HH4
05Upper Deck Jerseys-J-JI
05Upper Deck Jerseys Series II-J2JI
05Upper Deck Majestic Materials-MMJI
05Upper Deck NHL Generations-DIN
05Upper Deck NHL Generations-TSIR
05Upper Deck Notable Numbers-N-JI
05Upper Deck Patches-P-JI
05Upper Deck Playoff Performers-PP1
05Upper Deck Playoff Performers-PP5
05Upper Deck Scrapbooks-HS12
05Upper Deck Shooting Stars-S-JI
05Upper Deck Ice-14
Rainbow-14
Frozen Fabrics-FFJI
Frozen Fabrics Autographs-AFFJI
Frozen Fabrics Glass-FFJI
Frozen Fabrics Patches-FFPJI
Frozen Fabrics Patch Autographs-FAPJI
Glacial Graphs-GGJI
Signature Swatches-SSJI
05Upper Deck MVP-56
05Upper Deck MVP-440
Gold-56
Gold-440
Platinum-56
Platinum-440
ProSign-P-JI
Rising to the Occasion-RO4
05Upper Deck Rookie Update-13
05Upper Deck Rookie Update-259
05Upper Deck Trilogy-15
05Upper Deck Trilogy-98
Crystal-98
Crystal Autographs-98
Honorary Patches-HP-JI
Honorary Patch Scripts-HSP-JI
Honorary Swatches-HS-JI
Honorary Swatch Scripts-HSS-JI
Ice Scripts-IS-JI
Scripts-SSS-JI
05Upper Deck Toronto Fall Expo-25
05Upper Deck Toronto Fall Expo-200
05Upper Deck Victory-27
Black-27
Gold-27
Silver-27
Blow-Ups-BU6
Stars on Ice-SI7
05Czech Stadion-684
06Be A Player-110
Autographs-110
Profiles-PP23
Profiles Autographs-PP23
Signatures-JI
Signatures 10-121
Signatures 25-121
Signatures Duals-DIH
Signatures Duals-DIP
Signatures Trios-TIPT
Signatures Foursomes-FIBRC
Up Close and Personal-UC21
Up Close and Personal Autographs-UC21
06Be A Player Portraits-16
Dual Signature Portraits-DSIT
Quadruple Signature Portraits-QKIHN
Sensational Six-SSCDN
Signature Portraits-SPJI
Timeless Tens-TTCAN
Triple Signature Portraits-TCGY
06Beehive-85
06Beehive-222
Blue-85
Gold-85
Matte-85
Red Facsimile Signatures-85
Wood-85
5 X 7 Black and White-85
Matted Materials-MMJI
PhotoGraphs-PGJI
Remarkable Matted Materials-MMJi
Signature Scrapbook-SSJI
06Black Diamond-151B
Black-149B
Gold-151B
Ruby-151B
Gemography-GJI
06Flair Showcase-16
06Flair Showcase-174
06Flair Showcase-211
06Flair Showcase-274
Parallel-16
Parallel-174
Parallel-211
Parallel-274
Hot Numbers-HN5
Hot Numbers Parallel-HN5
Inks-IJI
Stitches-SSJI
06Fleer-29
Tiffany-29
Signing Day-SDJI
Total 0-03
06Gatorade-3
06Hot Prospects-15
Red Hot-15
White Hot-15
Hot Materials -HMIG
Hot Materials Red Hot-HMIG
Hot Materials White Hot-HMIG
Hotagraphs-HIG
06McDonald's Upper Deck-5
06McDonald's Upper Deck-53
Autographs-AJI
Clear Cut Winners-CC2
Jerseys-JJI
Patches-PJI
06NHL POG-16
06O-Pee-Chee-82
Rainbow-82
Autographs-A-JI
Swatches-S-JI
06Panini Stickers-196
06SP Authentic-87
06SP Authentic-118
Chirography-JI
Limited-87
Limited-118
Sign of the Times-STJI
Sign of the Times Duals-STIT
Sign of the Times Triples-ST3ITK
Sign of the Times Quads-ST4IKPT
06SP Game Used-13
Gold-13
Rainbow-13
Authentic Fabrics-AFJI
Authentic Fabrics Parallel-AFJI
Authentic Fabrics Patches-AFJI
Authentic Fabrics Dual-AF2IK
Authentic Fabrics Dual Patches-AF2IK
Authentic Fabrics Triple-AF3CGY
Authentic Fabrics Triple Patches-AF3CGY
Authentic Fabrics Quads-AF4IDCH
Authentic Fabrics Quads Patches-AF4IDCH
Authentic Fabrics Sixes-AF6MRT
Authentic Fabrics Sixes Patches-AF6MRT
Authentic Fabrics Sevens-AF7ART
Authentic Fabrics Sevens-AF7LBP
Authentic Fabrics Sevens Patches-AF7ART
Authentic Fabrics Sevens Patches-AF7LBP
Authentic Fabrics Eights-AF8CAN
Authentic Fabrics Eights Patches-AF8CAN
Autographs-13
Inked Sweaters-ISJI
Inked Sweaters Patches-ISJI
Inked Sweaters Dual-IS2IT
Inked Sweaters Dual Patches-IS2IT
Letter Marks-LMJI
06SPx-14
06SPx-103
Spectrum-14
Spectrum-103
SPxcitement-X15
SPxcitement Spectrum-X15
SPxcitement Autographs-X15
Winning Materials-WMJI
Winning Materials Spectrum-WMJI
Winning Materials Autographs-WMJI
06Sunkist-4
06The Cup-14
Autographed Foundations-CQJI
Autographed Foundations Patches-CQJI
Autographed NHL Shields Duals-DASIL
Autographed NHL Shields Duals-DASIP
Autographed NHL Shields Duals-DASIT
Autographed Patches-14
Black Rainbow-14
Foundations-CQJI
Foundations Patches-CQJI
Enshrinements-EJI
Gold-14
Gold Patches-14
Honorable Numbers-HNJI
Jerseys-14
Limited Logos-LLJI
Masterpiece Pressplates-14
NHL Shields Duals-DSHIB
Scripted Swatches-SSJI
Scripted Swatches Duals-DSTI
Signature Patches-SPJI
06UD Artifacts-84
06UD Artifacts-158
Blue-84
Blue-158
Gold-84
Gold-158
Platinum-84
Platinum-158
Radiance-84
Radiance-158
Autographed Radiance Parallel-84
Autographed Radiance Parallel-158
Red-84
Red-158
Auto-Facts-AFJI
Auto-Facts Gold-AFJI
Frozen Artifacts-FAJI
Frozen Artifacts Black-FAJI
Frozen Artifacts Blue-FAJI
Frozen Artifacts Gold-FAJI
Frozen Artifacts Platinum-FAJI
Frozen Artifacts Red-FAJI
Frozen Artifacts Autographed Black-FAJI
Frozen Artifacts Patches Black-FAJI
Frozen Artifacts Patches Blue-FAJI
Frozen Artifacts Patches Gold-FAJI
Frozen Artifacts Patches Platinum-FAJI
Frozen Artifacts Patches Red-FAJI
Frozen Artifacts Patches Autographed Black Tag Parallel-FAJI
Tundra Tandems-TTIT
Tundra Tandems Black-TTIT
Tundra Tandems Blue-TTIT
Tundra Tandems Gold-TTIT
Tundra Tandems Platinum-TTIT
Tundra Tandems Red-TTIT
Tundra Tandems Dual Patches Red-TTIT
06UD Mini Jersey Collection-16
06UD Powerplay-15
Impact Rainbow-15
In Action-IA1
Power Marks-PMJI
Specialists-SJI
Specialists Patches-PJI
06Ultimate Collection-11
Autographed Jerseys-AJ-JI
Autographed Patches-AJ-JI
Jerseys-UJ-JI
Jerseys Dual-UJ2-KI
Patches-UJ-JI
Patches Dual-UJ2-KI
Signatures-US-JI
Ultimate Achievements-UA-JI
Ultimate Signatures Logos-SL-JI
06Ultra-29
Gold Medallion-29
Ice Medallion-29
Action-UA2
Difference Makers-DM5
Fresh Ink-IJI
Scoring Kings-SK10
06Upper Deck Arena Giveaways-CGY1
06Upper Deck-28
Exclusives Parallel-28
High Gloss Parallel-28
All World-AW7
Game Dated Moments-GD37
Game Jerseys-JJI
Game Patches-PJI
Generations Duals-G2IL
Generations Triples-G3IML
Generations Patches Dual-G2PIL
Generations Patches Triple-G3PIML
Goal Rush-GR8
Masterpieces-28
Signatures-SJI
Walmart Tins Oversize-28
06Upper Deck MVP-45
Gold Script-45
Super Script-45
Autographs-OANI
Clutch Performers-CP5
Gotta Have Hart-HH14
Jerseys-OJIS
06Upper Deck Ovation-157
06Upper Deck Sweet Shot-19
Signature Shots/Saves-SSJI
Signature Shots/Saves Ice Signings-SSIJI
Signature Shots/Saves Sticks-SSSJI
Signature Sticks-STJI
Sweet Stitches-SSJI
Sweet Stitches Duals-SSJI
Sweet Stitches Triples-SSJI
06Upper Deck Trilogy-15
Combo Autographed Jerseys-CJIT
Combo Autographed Patches-CJIT
Combo Clearcut Autographs-C3IKP
Honorary Scripted Patches-HSPJI
Honorary Scripted Swatches-HSSJI
Honorary Swatches-HSJI
Ice Scripts-ISJI
Scripts-S2JI
Scripts-S3JI
Scripts-TSJI
06Upper Deck Victory-29
06Upper Deck Victory Black-29
06Upper Deck Victory Gold-29
06Upper Deck Victory GameBreakers-GB5
06Upper Deck Victory Oversize Cards-JI
06Russian Sport Collection Olympic Stars-35
07Upper Deck Ovation-43
3x5s-XL21
Autographed 3x5s-XLAJI
07Upper Deck Victory-151
Black-151
Gold-151
EA Sports Face-Off-F01
GameBreakers-GB38
Oversize Cards-OS35
Stars on Ice-SI39

Ignatius, Olli
80Finnish Mallasjuoma-8

Ignatjev, Victor
92Kansas City Blades-5
93Kansas City Blades-3
93Classic Pro Prospects-128
94Central Hockey League-60
97Long Beach Ice Dogs-8
99German DEL-33
01Russian Hockey League-54

Ignatov, Nikolai
00Russian Hockey League-327
03Russian Metallurg Magnitogorsk-5

Ignatushin, Igor
05Russian Hockey League RHL-11

Ignatz, Michael
93Quebec Pee-Wee Tournament-490

Ihalainen, Veikko
70Finnish Jaakiekko-228
71Finnish Suomi Stickers-243
73Finnish Jaakiekko-308

Ihnacak, Miroslav
87Panini Stickers-336
88ProCards AHL-14
89Halifax Citadels-10
89ProCards AHL-155
90Halifax Citadels-11
90ProCards AHL/IHL-463
04Slovakian Poprad Team Set-20

Ihnacak, Peter
82Swedish Semic VM Stickers-96
83O-Pee-Chee Stickers-32
83Puffy Stickers-3
83Topps Stickers-32
85O-Pee-Chee Stickers-19
86Maple Leafs Postcards-12
87Maple Leafs PLAY-24
87Maple Leafs Postcards-10
87Maple Leafs Postcards Oversized-10
87Panini Stickers-334
89ProCards AHL-120
94German DEL-240
95German DEL-234
96German DEL-85
98German DEL-268
99German DEL-49

Iivonen, Seppo
66Finnish Jaakiekkosarja-139

Ikola, Seppo
65Finnish Hellas-58

Ikola, Willard
04Michigan Wolverines TK Legacy-1950B
04Michigan Wolverines TK Legacy-H3
04Michigan Wolverines TK Legacy-HL9
04Michigan Wolverines TK Legacy-VH2

Ikonen, Jouko
71Finnish Suomi Stickers-322

Ikonen, Juha
93Finnish Jyvas-Hyva Stickers-203
94Finnish SISU-16
95Finnish SISU-93
96Finnish SISU Redline-89
98Finnish Kerailysarja-18
Leijonat-22
Off Duty-1
99Finnish Cardset-169
99Swedish Upper Deck-79
00Swedish Upper Deck-69
02Finnish Cardset-180
02Swedish SHL-117
Parallel-117

Ikonen, Markku
93Finnish SISU-156
94Finnish SISU-110
95Finnish SISU-62

Ilijow, Troy
03Greenville Grrrowl-10

Ilitch, Mike
91Pro Set NHL Sponsor Awards-AC22

Ilkka, Mikko
01Finnish Cardset-199

Illikainen, Darin
84Minnesota-Duluth Bulldogs-15
85Minnesota-Duluth Bulldogs-8

Ilmivalta, Pekka
93Finnish SISU-281

Ilvasky, Slavomir
94Finnish Jaa Kiekko-206

Ilvonen, Harri
06Finnish Cardset-321

Ilyin, Roman
91O-Pee-Chee Inserts-34R

Imbeau, Jean
917th Inn. Sketch QMJHL-67

Imbeault, Alexandre
03Quebec Remparts-12
04Victoriaville Tigres-8
05Victoriaville Tigres-12
06Chicoutimi Sagueneens-11

Imber, Shaun
907th Inn. Sketch OHL-159
917th Inn. Sketch OHL-323
917th Inn. Sketch Memorial Cup-19

Imdahl, Thomas
94German DEL-359
95German DEL-231

Imes, Chris
91Upper Deck Czech World Juniors-75
92Maine Black Bears-5
92Maine Black Bears-19
93PowerPlay-506
93Stadium Club Team USA-10
93Stadium Club Team USA Members Only-10
93Topps Premier Team USA-11
93Ultra-486
96Collector's Edge Ice-168
Prism-168

Imhauser, Peter
86Swedish Panini Stickers-149
87Swedish Panini Stickers-155
90Swedish Semic Elitserien Stickers-133

Imhof, Slaven
95Swiss HNL-329
96Swiss HNL-305

Imlach, Punch
51Laval Dairy QSHL-37
52St. Lawrence Sales-54
59Parkhurst-15
60Shirriff Coins-20
61Shirriff/Salada Coins-57
61York Yellow Backs-38
62Shirriff Coins-15
63Chex Photos-28
63Parkhurst-19
63Parkhurst-79
64Topps-45
65Topps-11
66Maple Leafs Hockey Talks-10
66Topps-11
66Topps USA Test-11
69Maple Leafs White Border Glossy-40
71Sabres Postcards-69
79Maple Leafs Postcards-14
85Hall of Fame-243
92Hall of Fame Legends-25
02Parkhurst Reprints-237
04Ultimate Collection Ultimate Cuts-UC-PI
05ITG Ultimate Memorabilia Builders Autos-6
06ITG Ultimate Memorabilia-118
Artist Proof-118

Immonen, Jarkko
01Finnish Cardset-376
02Finnish Cardset-181
03Finnish Cardset-81
04Finnish Cardset-87
04Finnish Cardset Signatures-20
04Finnish Cardset Stars of the Game-3
04Swedish Pure Skills-124
Parallel-124
05Finnish Cardset -73
Finnish Cardset Magicmakers-12
05Hartford Wolf Pack-12
06Be A Player-224
06Be A Player Portraits-116
06Beehive-137
Matte-137
06Black Diamond-152A
Black-152A
Gold-152A
Ruby-152A
06Flair Showcase-66
Parallel-66
06Fleer-206
Tiffany-206
06Hot Prospects-123
Red Hot-123
White Hot-123
Hot Materials -HMJI
Hot Materials Red Hot-HMJI
Hot Materials White Hot-HMJI
Hotagraphs-HJI
06O-Pee-Chee-526
Rainbow-526
06SP Authentic-190
Limited-190
06SP Game Used-135
Gold-135
Rainbow-135
Autographs-135
Inked Sweaters-ISIM
Inked Sweaters Patches-ISIM
Rookie Exclusives Autographs-REJI
06SPx-175
Spectrum-175
06The Cup-144
Autographed Rookie Masterpiece Pressplates-144
Gold Rainbow Autographed Rookie Patches-144
Masterpiece Pressplates (Artifacts)-223
Masterpiece Pressplates (Be A Player Portraits)-116
Masterpiece Pressplates (Bee Hive)-137
Masterpiece Pressplates (Black Diamond)-152
Masterpiece Pressplates (Marquee Rookies)-526
Masterpiece Pressplates (MVP)-338
Masterpiece Pressplates (Power Play)-116
Masterpiece Pressplates (SP Authentic Autographs)-190
Masterpiece Pressplates (SP Game Used)-135
Masterpiece Pressplates (SPx Autographs)-175
Masterpiece Pressplates (Sweet Beginnings)-139
Masterpiece Pressplates (Trilogy)-136
Masterpiece Pressplates (Ultimate Collection)-84
Masterpiece Pressplates (Victory)-223
Rookies Black-144
Rookies Platinum-144
06UD Artifacts-223
Blue-223
Gold-223
Radiance-223
Red-223
06UD Mini Jersey Collection-117
06UD Powerplay-116
Impact Rainbow-116
06Ultimate Collection-84
Ultimate Debut Threads Jerseys-DJ-JI
Ultimate Debut Threads Jerseys Autographs-DJ-JI
Ultimate Debut Threads Patches-DJ-JI
Ultimate Debut Threads Patches Autographs-DJ-JI
06Ultra-217
Gold Medallion-217
Ice Medallion-217
06Upper Deck-230
Exclusives Parallel-230
High Gloss Parallel-230
Masterpieces-230
Rookie Materials-RMJI
Rookie Materials Patches-RMJI
06Upper Deck MVP-338
Gold Script-338
Super Script-338
06Upper Deck Ovation-184
06Upper Deck Sweet Shot-139
Rookie Jerseys Autographs-139
06Upper Deck Trilogy-136
Honorary Swatches-HSIM
06Upper Deck Victory-223
06Upper Deck Victory Black-223
06Upper Deck Victory Gold-223
06Finnish Cardset-142
Signature Sensations-26
06Hartford Wolf Pack-13
06ITG Heroes and Prospects Jerseys-GUJ17
06ITG Heroes and Prospects Jerseys Gold-GUJ17
06ITG Heroes and Prospects Emblems-GUE17
06ITG Heroes and Prospects Emblems Gold-GUE17
06ITG Heroes and Prospects Numbers-GUN17
06ITG Heroes and Prospects Numbers Gold-GUN17
07Upper Deck Rookie Class -21

Immonen, Jarkko A.
05Finnish Cardset -311

Immonen, Jorma
72Finnish Jaakiekko-101
73Finnish Jaakiekko-129
78Finnish SM-Liiga-27
80Finnish Mallasjuoma-11

Immonen, Martti
71Finnish Suomi Stickers-151
72Finnish Jaakiekko-102
80Finnish Mallasjuoma-136

Immonen, Santeri
95Finnish SISU-44
98Finnish Kerailysarja-258
99Finnish Cardset-148
00UK Sekonda Superleague-112

Immonen, Tuomas
04Finnish Cardset-220
05Finnish Cardset -26

Immonen, Ville
98Finnish Kerailysarja-204
99Finnish Cardset-117
00Finnish Cardset-83
01Finnish Cardset-329
02Finnish Cardset-28
03Finnish Cardset-133

Immonen, Waltteri
91Finnish Jyvas-Hyva Stickers-24
92Finnish Jyvas-Hyva Stickers-54
93Finnish Jyvas-Hyva Stickers-110
93Finnish SISU-8
93Finnish SISU Autographs-8
93Swedish Semic World Champ Stickers-52
94Finnish SISU-24
94Finnish Jaa Kiekko-19
95Finnish SISU-46
Double Trouble-2
95Finnish SISU Limited-11
95Finnish Semic World Championships-7
95Swedish World Championships Stickers-170
96Finnish SISU Redline-45
At The Gala-3
98Finnish Kerailysarja-99

Imoo, Dusty
88Lethbridge Hurricanes-12
89Lethbridge Hurricanes-10
907th Inn. Sketch WHL-183
91ProCards-258

Imperatori, Paolo
95Swiss HNL-204
96Swiss HNL-374
00Swiss Panini Stickers-20
00Swiss Slapshot Mini-Cards-HCAP14
01Swiss HNL-227
02Swiss HNL-61

Impola, Kalle
72Finnish Jaakiekko-282

Infanger, Karl
97Wheeling Nailers-12
97Wheeling Nailers Photo Pack-12
98ECHL All-Star Northern Conference-20
99Mississippi Sea Wolves Kelly Cup-5

Ing, Peter
90Maple Leafs Postcards-8
90OPC Premier-49
90Pro Set-639
90Score-414
Canadian-414
90Score Rookie/Traded-11T
90Upper Deck-432
French-432
91Pro Set Platinum-41
91Bowman-157
91Maple Leafs Panini Team Stickers-10
91Oilers IGA-6
91Oilers Team Issue-7
91O-Pee-Chee-145
91OPC Premier-33
91Panini Stickers-99
91Pro Set-222
91Pro Set-388
French-222
French-388
91Score American-55
91Score Canadian Bilingual-55
91Score Canadian Bilingual-612
91Score Canadian English-55
91Score Canadian English-612
91Score Rookie/Traded-62T
91Score Young Superstars-12
91Stadium Club-352
91Topps-145
91Upper Deck-118
French-118
92Stadium Club-347
92Topps-423
Gold-423G
93Las Vegas Thunder-14
95Fort Wayne Komets-9

Ingarfield, Earl
44Beehive Group II Photos-328A
44Beehive Group II Photos-328B
58Topps-18
59Topps-10
60NHL Ceramic Tiles-27
60Shirriff Coins-92
61Shirriff/Salada Coins-82
61Topps-49
62Topps-51
Hockey Bucks-13
63Topps-55
64Beehive Group III Photos-135
64Coca-Cola Caps-80
64Topps-65
65Coca-Cola-81
66Topps-30
68Bauer Ads-14
68O-Pee-Chee-102
68Shirriff Coins-136
68Topps-102
69O-Pee-Chee-87
Four-in-One-9
69Topps-87
70Dad's Cookies-61
70Esso Power Players-97
70O-Pee-Chee-191
70Sargent Promotions Stamps-132
70Topps/OPC Sticker Stamps-15
72Finnish Semic World Championship-177
72Swedish Semic World Championship-177
94Parkhurst Tall Boys-91
95Parkhurst '66-67-87
Coins-87

Ingier, Per-Erik
74Finnish Typotor-76

Inglis, Bill
70O-Pee-Chee-130
70Sargent Promotions Stamps-27
70Topps-130
79Rochester Americans-7
02Fort Worth Brahmas-19

Ingman, Jan
83Swedish Semic Elitserien-115
84Swedish Semic Elitserien-115
85Swedish Panini Stickers-103
86Swedish Panini Stickers-99
89Swedish Semic Elitserien Stickers-87
90Swedish Semic Elitserien Stickers-264

Ingraham, Cal
92Maine Black Bears-16
92Maine Black Bears-34
93Maine Black Bears-53
95Tallahassee Tiger Sharks-12
98Idaho Steelheads-9
99Idaho Steelheads-1
00Idaho Steelheads-8
00Idaho Steelheads-22
01Idaho Steelheads-7

Ingram, Geoff
89Peterborough Petes-117
897th Inn. Sketch OHL-117

Ingram, Jim
91British Columbia JHL-56

Ingram, Ronald
44Beehive Group II Photos-179
63Parkhurst-54
63York White Backs-54
64Beehive Group III Photos-78
69Seattle Totems-10
94Parkhurst Missing Link-33

Ingvarsson, Ulf
70Swedish Hockey-205
71Swedish Hockey-286
72Swedish Stickers-71

Ingvordsen, Thomas
98Danish Hockey League-114

Inhacak, Miroslav
85Maple Leafs Postcards-15

Inhacak, Peter
82Maple Leafs Postcards-18
83Maple Leafs Postcards-11
83O-Pee-Chee-334
83Vachon-90
84Maple Leafs Postcards-12
85Maple Leafs Postcards-16

Inkinen, Mikko
95Finnish SISU-270
96Finnish SISU Redline-67
01UK Dundee Stars-8
02UK Dundee Stars-8

Inkpen, Dave
76O-Pee-Chee WHA-83
76Stingers Kahn's-2
79O-Pee-Chee-321

Inman, David
01Notre Dame Fighting Irish-2
02Charlotte Checkers-84

Innanen, Derek
92Western Michigan Broncos-13
93Western Michigan Broncos-16
96Mississippi Sea Wolves-9
98Amarillo Rattlers-7

Innerwinkler, Thomas
04Finnish Cardset-283

Innes, Judson
89Portland Winter Hawks-11

Inness, Gary
74Penguins Postcards-8
75O-Pee-Chee NHL-227
75Topps-227
76O-Pee-Chee NHL-331
77O-Pee-Chee WHA-18
79Capitals Team Issue-8
79O-Pee-Chee-358

Innoncentin, Giancarlo
93Quebec Pee-Wee Tournament-480

Insam, Adolf
82Swedish Semic VM Stickers-132
83Swedish Semic VM Stickers-132

Insana, Jon
00Michigan State Spartans-10
02Florida Everblades-21
03Florida Everblades-10
03Florida Everblades RBI Sports-165
05Muskegon Fury-7

Intranuovo, Ralph
907th Inn. Sketch OHL-160
917th Inn. Sketch OHL-332
917th Inn. Sketch Memorial Cup-20
92Classic-27
Gold-27
92Classic Four-Sport *-176
Gold-176
93Upper Deck-253
93Sault Ste. Marie Greyhound Memorial Cup-19
94Cape Breton Oilers-10
94Classic Pro Prospects-186
95Leaf-35
95Score-294
Black Ice Artist's Proofs-294
Black Ice-294
96Donruss-232
Press Proofs-232
96Leaf Gold Rookies-5
96Pinnacle-237
Artist's Proofs-237
Foil-237
Premium Stock-237
Rink Collection-237
96Score-263
Artist's Proofs-263
Dealer's Choice Artist's Proofs-263
Special Artist's Proofs-263
Golden Blades-263
96Summit-175
Artist's Proofs-175
Ice-175
Metal-175
Premium Stock-175
96Upper Deck-182
96Collector's Edge Ice-33
Prism-33
97Manitoba Moose-A1
98Manitoba Moose-C5
99German Adler Mannheim Eagles Postcards-10
99German DEL-10
00German DEL-158
01German Upper Deck-68
04German DEL-172
05German DEL-170

Intwert, Dean
89Portland Winter Hawks-12
907th Inn. Sketch WHL-326
917th Inn. Sketch WHL-333

Ioannou, Michael
93Quebec Pee-Wee Tournament-1422

Ioannou, Yianni
93Niagara Falls Thunder-8
95Classic-82

Iob, Tony
907th Inn. Sketch OHL-60
917th Inn. Sketch OHL-325
917th Inn. Sketch Memorial Cup-22
92Rochester Americans Kodak-11

Ion, Mickey
12C61 Lacrosse-12
83Hall of Fame Postcards-A9
85Hall of Fame-9

Iorianni, Matt
01London Knights-20
02London Knights-26

Iovio, Emilio
92Finnish Semic-255
95Swedish World Championships Stickers-86
96German DEL-224

Irbe, Arturs
89Russian National Team-8
90O-Pee-Chee-501
Red Army-7R
91Pro Set Platinum-270
91Pinnacle-323
French-323
91Upper Deck-532
French-532
91Finnish Semic World Champ Stickers-77
91Russian Tri-Globe Irbe-16
91Russian Tri-Globe Irbe-17
91Russian Tri-Globe Irbe-18
91Russian Tri-Globe Irbe-19
91Russian Tri-Globe Irbe-20
91Swedish Semic World Champ Stickers-77
91Kansas City Blades-5
91Star Pics-37
92Parkhurst-396
Emerald Ice-396
92Score-457
Canadian-457
92Stadium Club-131
92Topps-25
Gold-25G
92Ultra-401
Imports-5
92Russian Stars Red Ace-13
92Russian Tri-Globe From Russia With Puck-23
92Russian Tri-Globe From Russia With Puck-24
93Donruss-311
93Leaf-199
93OPC Premier-110
93OPC Premier-442
Gold-110
Gold-442
93Parkhurst-451
Emerald Ice-451
93Pinnacle-86
Canadian-86
93PowerPlay-221
Rising Stars-1
93Score-377
Canadian-377
93Stadium Club-4
Members Only Master Set-4
OPC-4
First Day Issue-4
First Day Issue OPC-4
93Topps/OPC Premier-110
93Topps/OPC Premier-442
Gold-110
Gold-442
93Ultra-145
93Upper Deck-125
93Classic Pro Prospects-117
94SLU Hockey American-7
94Canada Games NHL POGS-294
94Donruss-7
Dominators-7
Masked Marvels-4
94EA Sports-120
94Finest-104
Super Team Winners-104
Refractors-104
Division's Clear Cut-16
94Flair-166
94Fleer-197
Franchise Futures-4
Netminders-4
94Kenner Starting Lineup Cards-8
94Kraft-43
94Leaf-175
Limited Inserts-21
94Leaf Limited-74
94OPC Premier-260
Special Effects-260
94Parkhurst Vintage-V79
94Parkhurst SE-SE162
Gold-SE162
Euro-Stars-ES17
94Pinnacle-121
Artist's Proofs-121
Rink Collection-121
Goaltending Greats-GT9
94Score-10
Gold-10
Platinum-10
Franchise-TF21
94Select-37
Gold-37
94SP-105
Die Cuts-105
94Stadium Club Members Only-17
94Stadium Club-190
Members Only Master Set-190
First Day Issue-190
Dynasty and Destiny-1
Dynasty and Destiny Members Only-1
Super Team Winner Cards-190
94Topps/OPC Premier-260
Special Effects-260
94Ultra-195
Global Greats-3
Premier Pad Men-2
94Upper Deck-116
Electric Ice-116
SP Inserts-SP71
SP Inserts Die Cuts-SP71

95SLU Hockey Canadian-8
95Bashan Super Stickers-108
95Be A Player-23
Signatures-S23
Signatures Die Cuts-S23
95Canada Games NHL POGS-233
95Collector's Choice-64
Player's Club-64
Player's Club Platinum-64
95Donruss-239
95Emotion-156
95Hoyle Western Playing Cards-37
95Imperial Stickers-108
95Kenner Starting Lineup Cards-12
95Kraft-38
95Leaf-267
95Metal-130
95Panini Stickers-287
95Parkhurst International-188
95Parkhurst International-251
Emerald Ice-188
Emerald Ice-251
All-Stars-1
Goal Patrol-10
95Pinnacle FANtasy-7
95Playoff One on One-84
95Playoff One on One-191
95Playoff One on One-302
95Pro Magnets-119
95Pro Magnets Iron Curtain Insert-3
95Score-189
Black Ice Artist's Proofs-189
Black Ice-189
95Select Certified-91
Mirror Gold-91
95SkyBox Impact-148
95Stadium Club-58
Members Only Master Set-58
95Summit-84
Artist's Proofs-84
Ice-84
95Topps-296
OPC Inserts-296
95Ultra-146
Gold Medallion-146
95Upper Deck-403
Electric Ice-403
Electric Ice Gold-403
Special Edition-SE162
Special Edition Gold-SE162
95Zenith-81
96NHL Pro Stamps-119
96Playoff One on One-345
96Stars Postcards-12
96Summit-110
Artist's Proofs-110
Ice-110
Metal-110
Premium Stock-110
96Upper Deck-248
96Zenith-60
Artist's Proofs-60
97Pacific-188
Copper-188
Emerald Green-188
Ice Blue-188
Red-188
Silver-188
97Pinnacle-74
Artist's Proofs-74
Rink Collection-74
Press Plates Back Black-74
Press Plates Back Cyan-74
Press Plates Back Magenta-74
Press Plates Back Yellow-74
Press Plates Front Black-74
Press Plates Front Cyan-74
Press Plates Front Magenta-74
Press Plates Front Yellow-74
97Pinnacle Inside-61
Coach's Collection-61
Executive Collection-61
97Score-7
Artist's Proofs-7
Golden Blades-7
97Score Canucks-12
Platinum-12
Premier-12
97Upper Deck-377
98Be A Player-172
Press Release-172
98BAP Gold-172
98BAP Autographs-172
98BAP Autographs Gold-172
98Crown Royale-23
Limited Series-23
98Hurricanes Team Issue-1
98NHL Aces Playing Cards-25
98Pacific-427
Ice Blue-427
Red-427
98Pacific Dynagon Ice-33
Blue-33
Red-33
98Pacific Omega-42
Red-42
Opening Day Issue-42
98Panini Stickers-218
98Paramount-235
Copper-235
Emerald Green-235
Holo-Electric-235
Ice Blue-235
Silver-235
98Revolution-24
Ice Shadow-24
Red-24
All-Star Die Cuts-11
99Aurora-26
Striped-26
Premiere Date-26
Premiere Date Striped-26
Glove Unlimited-4
99BAP Memorabilia-4
Gold-4
Silver-4
99BAP Millennium-50
Emerald-50
Ruby-50
Sapphire-50
Signatures-50
Signatures Gold-50
Goalie Memorabilia-G8
99Black Diamond-19
Diamond Cut-19
Final Cut-19
99Crown Royale-27
Limited Series-27
Premiere Date-27
International Glory-4
International Glory Parallel-4
99O-Pee-Chee-107
99O-Pee-Chee Chrome-107
99O-Pee-Chee Chrome Refractors-107
99Pacific-72
Copper-72
Emerald Green-72
Gold-72
Ice Blue-72
Premiere Date-72
Red-72
In the Cage Net-Fusions-4
Team Leaders-6
99Pacific Dynagon Ice-41
Blue-41
Copper-41
Gold-41
Premiere Date-41
99Pacific Omega-45
Copper-45
Gold-45
Ice Blue-45
Premiere Date-45
99Pacific Prism-29
Holographic Blue-29
Holographic Gold-29
Holographic Mirror-29
Holographic Purple-29
Premiere Date-29
99Paramount-46
Copper-46
Emerald-46
Gold-46
Holographic Emerald-46
Holographic Gold-46
Holographic Silver-46
Ice Blue-46
Premiere Date-46
Red-46
Silver-46
Glove Side Net Fusions-4
99Revolution-28
Premiere Date-28
Red-28
Shadow Series-28
Copper-28
Gold-28
CSC Silver-28
99SP Authentic-17
99SPx-28
Radiance-28
Spectrum-28
99Stadium Club-67
First Day Issue-67
One of a Kind-67
Printing Plates Black-67
Printing Plates Cyan-67
Printing Plates Magenta-67
Printing Plates Yellow-67
99Topps/OPC-107
99Topps/OPC Chrome-107
Refractors-107
99Topps Gold Label Class 1-46
Black-46
Black One of One-46
One of One-46
Red-46
Red One of One-46
99Topps Gold Label Class 2-46
99Topps Gold Label Class 2 Black-46
99Topps Gold Label Class 2 Black 1 of 1-46
99Topps Gold Label Class 2 One of One-46
99Topps Gold Label Class 2 Red-46
99Topps Gold Label Class 2 Red One of One-46
99Topps Gold Label Class 3-46
99Topps Gold Label Class 3 Black-46
99Topps Gold Label Class 3 Black 1 of 1-46
99Topps Gold Label Class 3 One of One-46
99Topps Gold Label Class 3 Red-46
99Topps Gold Label Class 3 Red One of One-46
99Topps Premier Plus-55
Parallel-55
99Upper Deck-31
Exclusives-31
Exclusives 1 of 1-31
99Upper Deck Gold Reserve-31
99Upper Deck MVP-37
Gold Script-37
Silver Script-37
Super Script-37
Draw Your Own Trading Card-W7
99Upper Deck MVP SC Edition-38
Gold Script-38
Silver Script-38
Super Script-38
99Upper Deck Victory-56
99Upper Deck Victory-379
99Wayne Gretzky Hockey-38
Signs of Greatness-AI
Tools of Greatness-TGAI
00SLU Hockey-110
00Aurora-29
Premiere Date-29
00BAP Memorabilia-255
Emerald-255
Ruby-255
Sapphire-255
Promos-255
00BAP Mem Chicago Sportsfest Copper-255
00BAP Memorabilia Chicago Sportsfest Blue-255
00BAP Memorabilia Chicago Sportsfest Gold-255
00BAP Memorabilia Chicago Sportsfest Ruby-255
00BAP Memorabilia Chicago Sun-Times Ruby-255
00BAP Memorabilia Chicago Sun-Times Gold-255
00BAP Mem Chicago Sun-Times Sapphire-255
00BAP Mem Toronto Fall Expo Copper-255
00BAP Memorabilia Toronto Fall Expo Gold-255
00BAP Memorabilia Toronto Fall Expo Ruby-255
00BAP Parkhurst 2000-P8
00BAP Signature Series-238
Emerald-238
Ruby-238
Sapphire-238
Autographs-126
Autographs Gold-126
He Shoots-He Scores Prizes-15
00BAP Ultimate Mem Game-Used Jerseys-GJ13
00BAP Ultimate Mem Game-Used Emblems-E11
00BAP Ultimate Mem Game-Used Numbers-N11
00BAP Ultimate Mem Game-Used Sticks-GS13
00BAP Ultimate Memorabilia Goalie Sticks-G6
00Crown Royale-21
Ice Blue-21
Limited Series-21
Premiere Date-21
Red-21
00O-Pee-Chee-82
00O-Pee-Chee Parallel-82
00Pacific-83
Copper-83
Gold-83
Ice Blue-83
Premiere Date-83
00Panini Stickers-29
00Paramount-43
Copper-43
Gold-43
Holo-Gold-43
Holo-Silver-43
Ice Blue-43
Premiere Date-43
Glove Side Net Fusions-5
Glove Side Net Fusions Platinum-5
00Private Stock-17
Gold-17
Premiere Date-17
Retail-17
Silver-17
00Revolution-27
Blue-27
Premiere Date-27
Red-27
00SP Game Used-10
00SPx-11
Spectrum-11
00Stadium Club-65
00Titanium-15
Blue-15
Gold-15
Premiere Date-15
Red-15
Retail-15
00Topps/OPC-82
Parallel-82
Own the Game-OTG15
00Topps Chrome-65
OPC Refractors-65
Refractors-65
00Topps Gold Label Class 1-20
Gold-20
00Topps Gold Label Class 2-20
00Topps Gold Label Class 2 Gold-20
00Topps Gold Label Class 3-20
00Topps Gold Label Class 3 Gold-20
00Topps Gold Label Behind the Mask-BTM9
00Topps Gold Label Behind the Mask 1 to 1-BTM9
00Topps Heritage-63
Chrome Parallel-63
00Topps Premier Plus-18
Blue Ice-18
00Topps Stars-88
Blue-88
00UD Heroes-21
00UD Pros and Prospects-18
00Upper Deck-34
Exclusives Tier 1-34
Exclusives Tier 2-34
00Upper Deck Legends-23
00Upper Deck Legends-24
Legendary Collection Bronze-23
Legendary Collection Bronze-24
Legendary Collection Gold-23
Legendary Collection Gold-24
Legendary Collection Silver-23
Legendary Collection Silver-24
00Upper Deck MVP-35
First Stars-35
Game-Used Souvenirs-GSAI
Second Stars-35
Super Game-Used Souvenirs-GSAI
Third Stars-35
00Upper Deck Victory-44
00Upper Deck Vintage-69
00Upper Deck Vintage-73
00Upper Deck Vintage-74
Great Gloves-GG5
00Vanguard-20
Holographic Gold-20
Holographic Purple-20
Pacific Proofs-20
00Czech Stadion-110
01Atomic-17
Blue-17
Gold-17
Premiere Date-17
Red-17
Team Nucleus-3
01BAP Memorabilia-34
Emerald-34
Ruby-34
Sapphire-34
All-Star Jerseys-ASJ46
All-Star Emblems-ASE46
All-Star Numbers-ASN46
All-Star Teammates-AST28
Goalies Jerseys-GJ4
Stanley Cup Playoffs-SC4
01BAP Signature Series-129
Autographs-129
Autographs Gold-129
Jerseys-GJ-96
01Between the Pipes-16
01Between the Pipes-99
All-Star Jerseys-ASJ2
Goalie Gear-GG14
He Shoots-He Saves Prizes-22
Jerseys-GJ4
Jersey and Stick Cards-GSJ4
01Crown Royale-26
Blue-26
Premiere Date-26
Red-26
Retail-26
01O-Pee-Chee-73
01O-Pee-Chee Heritage Parallel-73
01O-Pee-Chee Heritage Parallel Limited-73
01O-Pee-Chee Premier Parallel-73
01Pacific-74
Extreme LTD-74
Hobby LTD-74
Premiere Date-74
Retail LTD-74
01Pacific Adrenaline-34
Blue-34
Premiere Date-34
Red-34
Retail-34
Creased Lightning-2
Power Play-7
01Pacific Arena Exclusives-74
01Pacific Heads-Up-16
Blue-16
Premiere Date-16
Red-16
Silver-16
01Parkhurst-136
Jerseys-PJ53
Teammates-T18
01Private Stock-15
Gold-15
Premiere Date-15
Retail-15
Silver-15
01Private Stock Pacific Nights-15
01SP Authentic Buybacks-1
01SP Authentic Sign of the Times-AI
01SPx-10
01Stadium Club-73
Award Winners-73
Master Photos-73
01Titanium-25
Hobby Parallel-25
Premiere Date-25
Retail-25
Retail Parallel-25
Double-Sided Jerseys-44
Double-Sided Jerseys-61
Double-Sided Patches-44
Double-Sided Patches-61
01Topps-73
Heritage Parallel-73
Heritage Parallel Limited-73
OPC Parallel-73
Own The Game-OTG25
01Topps Chrome-73
Refractors-73
Black Border Refractors-73
01Topps Heritage-45
01Topps Heritage-127
Refractors-45
01Topps Reserve-83
01UD Challenge for the Cup-13
Backstops-BB2
01UD Mask Collection-106
01UD Mask Collection-174
Gold-106
Gold-174
01UD Playmakers-19
01UD Premier Collection-9
Signatures-AI
Signatures Black-AI
01UD Top Shelf-83
01Upper Deck-32
Exclusives-32
01Upper Deck Ice-6
01Upper Deck MVP-30
Goalie Sticks-G-AI
Masked Men-MM12
01Upper Deck Victory-59
01Upper Deck Victory-65
Gold-59
Gold-65
01Upper Deck Vintage-45
01Upper Deck Vintage-52
01Vanguard-16
Blue-16
Red-16
One of Ones-16
Premiere Date-16
Proofs-16
02Atomic-17
Blue-17
Gold-17
Red-17
Denied-3
Hobby Parallel-17
02BAP All-Star Edition-33
Jerseys-33
Jerseys Gold-33
Jerseys Silver-33
02BAP First Edition-117
Jerseys-117
02BAP Memorabilia-13
Emerald-13
Ruby-13
Sapphire-13
All-Star Jerseys-ASJ-21
NHL All-Star Game-13
NHL All-Star Game Blue-13
NHL All-Star Game Green-13
NHL All-Star Game Red-13
Stanley Cup Playoffs-SC-26
02BAP Memorabilia Toronto Fall Expo-13
02BAP Signature Series-143
Autographs-143
Autograph Buybacks 1998-172
Autograph Buybacks 1999-50
Autograph Buybacks 2001-129
Autographs Gold-143
Golf-GS14
02BAP Ultimate Memorabilia Number Ones-1
02Between the Pipes-26
02Between the Pipes-126
Gold-26
Silver-26
All-Star Stick and Jersey-15
Behind the Mask-9
Emblems-1
Goalie Autographs-9
He Shoots-He Saves Points-5
He Shoots-He Saves Prizes-17
Jerseys-1
Numbers-1
Stick and Jerseys-1
02Crown Royale-18
Blue-18
Red-18
Retail-18
02Hurricanes Postcards-4
02O-Pee-Chee-254
02O-Pee-Chee Premier Blue Parallel-254
02O-Pee-Chee Premier Red Parallel-254
02O-Pee-Chee Factory Set-254
02Pacific-67
Blue-67
Red-67
Jerseys-6
Jerseys Holo-Silver-6
02Pacific Complete-549
Red-549
02Pacific Exclusive-29
Advantage-3
02Pacific Heads-Up-21
Blue-21
Purple-21
Red-21
Quad Jerseys-6
Quad Jerseys Gold-6
Showstoppers-4
02Parkhurst-5
Bronze-5
Gold-5
Silver-5
02Parkhurst Retro-148
Minis-148
02Private Stock Reserve-17
Blue-17
Red-17
Retail-17
InCrease Security-3
02SP Authentic-14
Beckett Promos-14
02SPx-13
Spectrum Gold-13
Spectrum Silver-13
02Stadium Club-64
Silver Decoy Cards-64
Proofs-64
02Titanium Jerseys-9
02Titanium Jerseys Retail-9
02Titanium Patches-9
02Topps-254
OPC Blue Parallel-254
OPC Red Parallel-254
Factory Set-254
02Topps Chrome-137
Black Border Refractors-137
Refractors-137
02Topps Total-83
02UD Artistic Impressions-14
Gold-14
02UD Artistic Impressions Beckett Promos-14
02UD Artistic Impressions Retrospectives-R14
02UD Artistic Impressions Retrospect Gold-R14
02UD Artistic Impress Retrospect Silver-R14
02UD Honor Roll-12
02UD Mask Collection-17
02UD Mask Collection-18
02UD Mask Collection Beckett Promos-17
02UD Mask Collection Beckett Promos-18
02UD Piece of History-14
02UD Top Shelf-16
02Upper Deck Super Saviors-SA3
02Upper Deck Classic Portraits-16
02Upper Deck MVP-36
Gold-36
Classics-36
Golden Classics-36
02Upper Deck Victory-42
Bronze-42
Gold-42
Silver-42
02Upper Deck Vintage-52
02Upper Deck Vintage-266
Green Backs-52
Tall Boys-T11
Tall Boys Gold-T11
02Czech Stadion Cup Finals-488
03Pacific-64
Blue-64
Red-64
03Pacific Complete-473
Red-473
03Pacific Exhibit-28
Blue Backs-28
Yellow Backs-28
03Pacific Prism-21
Blue-21
Gold-21
Red-21
03Russian World Championship Stars-23

Ircandia, Len
77Kalamazoo Wings-4

Iredale, John
94Finnish Jaa Kiekko-328

Ireland, Greg
98Dayton Bombers-20
98Dayton Bombers EBK-15
03Grand Rapids Griffins-23

Ireland, Randy
79Rochester Americans-8

Irgl, Zbynek
98Czech OFS-128
99Czech DS-182
99Czech OFS-224
99Czech OFS-515
All-Star Game Blue-515
All-Star Game Gold-515
All-Star Game Red-515
All-Star Game Silver-515
00Czech DS Extraliga-164
01Czech OFS Update-317
02Czech OFS Plus-52
03Czech OFS Plus-8
04Czech OFS-229
Goals Leaders-13
05Czech HC Vitkovice-6
06Czech CP Cup Postcards-10
06Czech IIHF World Championship Postcards-10
06Czech LG Hockey Games Postcards-6
06Czech OFS-51
Stars-25

Irmen, Danny
01Lincoln Stars-14
02Lincoln Stars-7
02Lincoln Stars-37
02Lincoln Stars-45
03Minnesota Golden Gophers-16
04Minnesota Golden Gophers-13
05Minnesota Golden Gophers-14

Ironstone, Joe
24V145-2-1

Irsag, Jake
95Slapshot-44

Irvin Jr., Dick
97Pinnacle Hockey Night in Canada-6
99CBC Hockey Night in Canada-1
04Upper Deck-202
06Parkhurst-41
Autographs-41
Autographs Dual-DAIM
06Upper Deck Sweet Shot Signature Shots/Saves-SSDI

Irvin, Dick
24Anonymous NHL-138
32O'Keefe Maple Leafs-20
60Topps-60
Stamps-29
83Hall of Fame Postcards-G10
85Hall of Fame-101
03BAP Ultimate Memorabilia Paper Cuts-45
04ITG Franchises Update-459
05ITG Ultimate Memorabilia Builders Autos-2
06ITG Ultimate Memorabilia Builders Autos-7
06Parkhurst Autographs Dual-DAIM

Irvine, Jack
51Laval Dairy QSHL-78
52St. Lawrence Sales-31

Irvine, Kurt
02UK Coventry Blaze-12
03UK Coventry Blaze History-2
04UK Milton Keynes Lightning-7

Irvine, Marty
94German First League-57

Irvine, Ted
68O-Pee-Chee-39
68Shirriff Coins-51
68Topps-39
69O-Pee-Chee-103
69Topps-103
70Esso Power Players-197
70O-Pee-Chee-65
70Sargent Promotions Stamps-114
70Topps-65
71O-Pee-Chee-74
71Sargent Promotions Stamps-126
71Toronto Sun-175
72O-Pee-Chee-212
72Sargent Promotions Stamps-152
73O-Pee-Chee-248
74NHL Action Stamps-195
74O-Pee-Chee NHL-264
74Topps-264
75O-Pee-Chee NHL-244
75Topps-244
76O-Pee-Chee NHL-347

Irving, Berg
28V128-2 Paulin's Candy-62

Irving, Joel
98Johnstown Chiefs-18
99ECHL All-Star Northern Conference-15
99Johnstown Chiefs-13
01South Carolina Stingrays-10
02South Carolina Stingrays-11
02South Carolina Stingrays RBI-214
03UK Sheffield Steelers-15
03UK Sheffield Steelers Stickers-13
04Odessa Jackalopes-10
05Bakersfield Condors-22

Irving, Kirk
04Camrose Kodiaks-2

Irving, Leland
04Everett Silvertips-18
05ITG Heroes/Prosp Toronto Expo Parallel -326
05Everett Silvertips-14
05ITG Heroes and Prospects-326
Autographs Series II-LI
He Shoots-He Scores Prizes-49
Team Orr-TO13
06Between The Pipes-35
06Between The Pipes-111
Aspiring-AS04
Aspiring Gold-AS04
Autographs-ALI2
Autographs-ALI
Double Memorabilia-DM09
Double Memorabilia Gold-DM09
Emblems-GUE41
Emblems Gold-GUE41
Emblems Autographs-GUE41
Gloves-GG11
Gloves Gold-GG11
Jerseys-GUJ41
Jerseys Gold-GUJ41
Jerseys Autographs-GUJ41
Numbers-GUN41
Numbers Gold-GUN41
Numbers Autographs-GUN41
Prospect Trios-PT05
Prospect Trios-PT06
Prospect Trios-PT09
Prospect Trios Gold-PT05
Prospect Trios Gold-PT06
Prospect Trios Gold-PT09
Stick and Jersey-SJ16
Stick and Jersey Gold-SJ16
Stick and Jersey Autographs-SJ16
06ITG Heroes and Prospects-112
Autographs-ALI
Complete Jerseys-CJ03
Complete Jerseys Gold-CJ03
Jerseys-GUJ38
Jerseys Gold-GUJ38
Emblems-GUE38
Emblems Gold-GUE38
Numbers-GUN38
Numbers Gold-GUN38
Net Prospects-NPR01
Net Prospects Gold-NPR01
Sticks and Jerseys-SJ07
Sticks and Jerseys Gold-SJ07
Triple Memorabilia-TM05
Triple Memorabilia Gold-TM05
07ITG Going For Gold World Juniors-2
Autographs-2
Emblems-GUE2
Jerseys-GUJ2
Numbers-GUN2

Irving, Stu
76Saginaw Gears-6
78Saginaw Gears-9

Irwin, Craig
04Arizona Icecats-7

Irwin, Doug
94German DEL-326
95German DEL-312

Irwin, Glen
75Houston Aeros WHA-9

Irwin, Ivan
54Topps-44
94Parkhurst Missing Link-107

Irwin, Jack
23V128-1 Paulin's Candy-22

Irwin, Joel
92British Columbia JHL-62
99Greensboro Generals-19
05Stockton Thunder-7

Irwin, Richard
96Guelph Storm-17

Isabelle, Simon
93Quebec Pee-Wee Tournament-1107

Isakov, Evgeni
02Russian Hockey League-172

Isaksson, Esa
65Finnish Hellas-25
66Finnish Jaakiekkosarja-10
69Swedish Hockey-367
70Finnish Jaakiekko-105
71Finnish Suomi Stickers-61
71Finnish Suomi Stickers-113
71Swedish Hockey-65
72Finnish Panda Toronto-96
72Finnish Semic World Championship-78
72Swedish Semic World Championship-78
73Finnish Jaakiekko-309
74Finnish Typotor-20

Isaksson, Magnus
05Swedish Lulea Hockey Postcards-22
05Swedish SHL Elitset-239
Gold-239

Isaksson, Ulf
82Swedish Semic VM Stickers-14
83Swedish Semic Elitserien-17
84Swedish Semic Elitserien-15

Isbister, Brad
93Portland Winter Hawks-12
95Classic-21
96Upper Deck Ice-125
97Be A Player-226
Autographs-226
Autographs Die-Cuts-226
Autographs Prismatic Die-Cuts-226
97Black Diamond-24
Double Diamond-24
Triple Diamond-24
Quadruple Diamond-24
97Collector's Choice-305
97Crown Royale-103
Emerald Green-103
Ice Blue-103
Silver-103
97Donruss Elite-46
Aspirations-46
Status-46
97Donruss Preferred-154
Cut to the Chase-154
97Donruss Priority-176
Stamp of Approval-176
97Katch-110
Gold-110
Silver-110
97Leaf-162
Fractal Matrix-162
Fractal Matrix Die Cuts-162
97Paramount-140
Copper-140
Dark Grey-140
Emerald Green-140
Ice Blue-140
Red-140
Silver-140
97Pinnacle-20
Artist's Proofs-20
Rink Collection-20
Press Plates Back Black-20
Press Plates Back Cyan-20
Press Plates Back Magenta-20
Press Plates Back Yellow-20
Press Plates Front Black-20
Press Plates Front Cyan-20
Press Plates Front Magenta-20
Press Plates Front Yellow-20
Certified Rookie Redemption-I
Certified Rookie Redemption Gold-I
Certified Rookie Redemption Mirror Gold-I
97Score-72
Artist's Proofs-72
Golden Blades-72
97SP Authentic-189
97Upper Deck-340
97Zenith Rookie Reign-7
97Bowman CHL-92
OPC-92
98Aurora-144
98Be A Player-109
Press Release-109
98BAP Gold-109
98BAP Autographs-109
98BAP Autographs Gold-109
98BAP Tampa Bay All Star Game-109
98OPC Chrome-169
Refractors-169
98Pacific-339
Ice Blue-339
Red-339
98Pacific Dynagon Ice-142
Blue-142
Red-142
98Paramount-181
Copper-181
Emerald Green-181
Holo-Electric-181
Ice Blue-181
Silver-181
98SPx Finite-65
98SPx Finite-146
Radiance-65
Radiance-146
Spectrum-65
Spectrum-146
98Topps-169
O-Pee-Chee-169
98UD Choice-161
98UD Choice Preview-161
98UD Choice Prime Choice Reserve-161
98UD Choice Reserve-161
98UD3-26
98UD3-86
98UD3-146
Die-Cuts-26
Die-Cuts-86
Die-Cuts-146
98Upper Deck-152
Exclusives-152
Exclusives 1 of 1-152
Generation Next-GN11
Generation Next Quantum 1-GN11
Generation Next Quantum 2-GN11
Generation Next Quantum 3-GN11
Gold Reserve-152
98Upper Deck MVP-159
Gold Script-159
Silver Script-159
Super Script-159
99Crown Royale-86
Limited Series-86
Premiere Date-86
99Pacific Omega-141
Copper-141
Gold-141
Ice Blue-141
Premiere Date-141
99Pacific Prism-87
Holographic Blue-87
Holographic Gold-87
Holographic Mirror-87
Holographic Purple-87
Premiere Date-87
99Panini Stickers-96
99Upper Deck Victory-182
00Aurora-89
Premiere Date-89
00BAP Memorabilia-102
Emerald-102
Ruby-102
Sapphire-102
Promos-102
00BAP Mem Chicago Sportsfest Copper-102
00BAP Memorabilia Chicago Sportsfest Blue-102
00BAP Memorabilia Chicago Sportsfest Gold-102
00BAP Memorabilia Chicago Sportsfest Ruby-102
00BAP Memorabilia Chicago Sun-Times Ruby-102
00BAP Memorabilia Chicago Sun-Times Gold-102
00BAP Mem Chicago Sun-Times Sapphire-102
00BAP Mem Toronto Fall Expo Copper-102
00BAP Memorabilia Toronto Fall Expo Gold-102
00BAP Memorabilia Toronto Fall Expo Ruby-102
00BAP Parkhurst 2000-P200
00BAP Signature Series-47
Emerald-47
Ruby-47
Sapphire-47
00Crown Royale-67
Ice Blue-67
Limited Series-67
Premiere Date-67
Red-67
00O-Pee-Chee-97
00O-Pee-Chee Parallel-97
00Pacific-250
Copper-250
Gold-250
Ice Blue-250
Premiere Date-250
00Panini Stickers-53
00Paramount-154
Copper-154
Gold-154
Holo-Gold-154
Holo-Silver-154
Ice Blue-154
Premiere Date-154
00Revolution-92
Blue-92
Premiere Date-92
Red-92
00SP Authentic-59
00Stadium Club-20
00Topps/OPC-97
Parallel-97
00Topps Chrome-77
OPC Refractors-77
Refractors-77
00Topps Gold Label Class 1-83
Gold-83
00Topps Gold Label Class 2-83
00Topps Gold Label Class 2 Gold-83
00Topps Gold Label Class 3-83
00Topps Gold Label Class 3 Gold-83
00Topps Heritage-127
00UD Pros and Prospects-54
00Upper Deck-337
Exclusives Tier 1-337
Exclusives Tier 2-337
00Upper Deck Victory-148
00Upper Deck Vintage-225
01BAP Memorabilia-250
Emerald-250
Ruby-250
Sapphire-250
01BAP Signature Series-81
Autographs-81
Autographs Gold-81
01O-Pee-Chee-77
01O-Pee-Chee Heritage Parallel-77
01O-Pee-Chee Heritage Parallel Limited-77
01O-Pee-Chee Premier Parallel-77
01Pacific-249
Extreme LTD-249
Hobby LTD-249
Premiere Date-249
Retail LTD-249
01Pacific Adrenaline-120
Blue-120
Premiere Date-120
Red-120
Retail-120
01Pacific Arena Exclusives-249
01Parkhurst-40
Gold-40
Silver-40
01Stadium Club-99
Award Winners-99
Master Photos-99
01Topps-77
Heritage Parallel-77
Heritage Parallel Limited-77
OPC Parallel-77
01Topps Heritage-98
Refractors-98
01Upper Deck-110
Exclusives-110
01Upper Deck Victory-225
Gold-225
01Upper Deck Vintage-163
02BAP Memorabilia-397
02BAP Sig Series Auto Buybacks 1998-109
02BAP Sig Series Auto Buybacks 2001-81
02BAP Signature Series Golf-GS12
02O-Pee-Chee-35
02O-Pee-Chee Premier Blue Parallel-35
02O-Pee-Chee Premier Red Parallel-35
02O-Pee-Chee Factory Set-35
02Pacific-237
Blue-237
Red-237
02Pacific Complete-8
Red-8
02Pacific Exclusive-107
02Parkhurst-193
Bronze-193
Gold-193
Silver-193
02Topps-35
OPC Blue Parallel-35
OPC Red Parallel-35
Factory Set-35
02Topps Total-29
02Upper Deck-356
Exclusives-356
02Upper Deck Beckett UD Promos-356
03ITG Action-213
03NHL Sticker Collection-74
03Oilers Postcards-10
03Pacific-133
Blue-133
Red-133
03Pacific Complete-115
Red-115
03Upper Deck-316
Canadian Exclusives-316
HG-316
UD Exclusives-316
03Upper Deck MVP-167
Gold Script-167
Silver Script-167
Canadian Exclusives-167
05Bruins Boston Globe-16
05Upper Deck MVP-37
Gold-37
Platinum-37
06Hartford Wolf Pack-12

Isbister, Matt
06Moose Jaw Warriors-10

Isen, Corey
95Slapshot-178
99San Angelo Outlaws-5

Iserhoff, Neil
91Oshawa Generals-8
91Oshawa Generals Sheet-26
917th Inn. Sketch OHL-156
92Oshawa Generals Sheet-26

Isfeld, Dale
95Neepewa Natives-14

Isherwood, Mark

06Medicine Hat Tigers-12
Iskrzycki, Bartlomiej
93Quebec Pee-Wee Tournament-1515
Iso-Eskeli, Juhani
66Finnish Jaakiekkosarja-84
Isomaki, Sakari
66Finnish Jaakiekkosarja-29
Isosalo, Samu
99UD Prospects-19
00Finnish Cardset-309
01Finnish Cardset-92
Isotalo, Jarkko
94Finnish SISU-284
Isotalus, Petri
00Finnish Cardset-60
Israel, Aaron
92Harvard Crimson-15
94Johnstown Chiefs-11
94Classic-119
Gold-119
Israel, Jamie
89Kitchener Rangers-20
90Kitchener Rangers-18
907th Inn. Sketch OHL-234
907th Inn. Sketch Memorial Cup-34
Israelson, Larry
75O-Pee-Chee WHA-46
Issel, Jason
93Prince Albert Raiders-12
94Prince Albert Raiders-10
95Prince Albert Raiders-9
96Prince Albert Raiders-9
Issel, Kim
84Prince Albert Raiders Stickers-15
88Oilers Tenth Anniversary-155
88ProCards AHL-86
89ProCards AHL-145
90Score-409
Canadian-409
Issila, Hannu
82Swedish Semic VM Stickers-27
Italiano, Jim
75HCA Steel City Vacuum-5
Itamies, Iiro
95Finnish SISU-82
96Finnish SISU Redline-82
96Finnish SISU Redline Promos-7
98Finnish Kerailysarja-206
Ito, Kengo
03Charlotte Checkers-71
Iuliano, Jerry
83Sault Ste. Marie Greyhounds-13
Ivan, Marek
96Lethbridge Hurricanes-8
97Moose Jaw Warriors-7
98Peoria Rivermen-15
99Czech OFS-454
00Czech DS Extraliga-165
00Czech OFS-255
01Czech OFS-11
02Czech OFS Plus-86
03Czech OFS Plus-286
04UK Nottingham Panthers-8
Ivan, Tommy
60Shirriff Coins-80
70Blackhawks Postcards-5
83Hall of Fame-158
83Hall of Fame Postcards-L8
85Hall of Fame-158
92Hall of Fame Legends-35
94Parkhurst Missing Link-42
04ITG Ultimate Mem Chitown Immortals-5
05ITG Ultimate Mem Quad Paper Cuts Autos-2
06ITG Ultimate Memorabilia-142
Artist Proof-142
Ivanans, Raitis
97Flint Generals-9
02Rockford Ice Hogs-3
03Milwaukee Admirals-16
03Milwaukee Admirals Postcards-13
04Hamilton Bulldogs-12
05Canadiens Team Issue-10
05Hot Prospects-246
En Fuego-246
Hot Materials-HMRI
Red Hot-246
White Hot-246
05SP Authentic-165
Limited-165
Sign of the Times-RA
05SP Game Used-158
Autographs-158
Gold-158
Rookie Exclusives-RI
Rookie Exclusives Silver-RE-RI
05SPx-140
Spectrum-140
05The Cup Masterpiece Pressplates (Ice)-155
05The Cup Master Pressplate Rookie Update-148
05The Cup Masterpiece Pressplate SPA Auto-165
05The Cup Masterpiece Pressplate SP GU-158
05The Cup Masterpiece Pressplates (SPx)-140
05The Cup Masterpiece Pressplates (SPx)-140
05Ultra-225
Gold-225
Fresh Ink-FI-RI
Fresh Ink Blue-FI-RI
Ice-225
Rookie Uniformity Jerseys-RU-RI
Rookie Uniformity Jersey Autographs-ARU-RI
Rookie Uniformity Patches-RUP-RI
Rookie Uniformity Patch Autographs-ARP-RI
05Upper Deck Rookie Ink-RIRI
05Upper Deck Rookie Threads-RTRI
05Upper Deck Rookie Threads Autographs-ARTRI
05Upper Deck Ice-155
Premieres Auto Patches-AIPRI
05Upper Deck Rookie Update-148
05Hamilton Bulldogs-10
06Fleer Signing Day-SDRI
Ivankovic, Frank
95Slapshot-156
Ivankovic, Vjeran
93Swiss HNL-173
95Swiss HNL-44
96Swiss HNL-191
98Swiss Power Play Stickers-20
99Swiss Panini Stickers-193
00Swiss Panini Stickers-259
00Swiss Slapshot Mini-Cards-EVZ11
01Swiss EV Zug Postcards-19
01Swiss HNL-183
02Swiss HNL-157
Ivannikov, Valeri
95Finnish Semic World Championships-122
95Swedish World Championships Stickers-26
99Russian Hockey League-65
99Russian Stars of Hockey-14
Ivanov, Alexei
03Russian Under-18 Team-3
04St. Michael's Majors-16
Ivanov, Denis
96Guelph Storm-5
99Russian Hockey League-36
00Bakersfield Condors-11
Ivanov, Mikhail
99Russian Dynamo Moscow-15
00Russian Dynamo Moscow-14
00Russian Dynamo Moscow Blue-White-4
01Russian Dynamo Moscow Mentos-5
02Russian SL-21
02Russian Transfert-24
Ivany, Ron
98German DEL-225
Ivarsson, Anders
86Swedish Panini Stickers-50
Ivarsson, Lars
84Swedish Semic Elitserien-54
85Swedish Panini Stickers-50
86Swedish Panini Stickers-33
87Swedish Panini Stickers-49
89Swedish Semic Elitserien Stickers-99
90Swedish Semic Elitserien Stickers-104
91Swedish Semic Elitserien Stickers-108
92Swedish Semic Elitserien Stickers-136
93Swedish Semic Elitserien-250
94Swedish Leaf-23
95Swedish Leaf-128
95Swedish Upper Deck-187
Ivarsson, Pierre
90Swedish Semic Elitserien Stickers-159
91Swedish Semic Elitserien Stickers-263
92Swedish Semic Elitserien Stickers-277
Ivashkin, Alexei
99Russian Hockey League-64
Ivaska, Dave
98Pensacola Ice Pilots-12
Ivicic, Martin
03Czech OFS Plus All-Star Game-H14
04Czech OFS Czech/Slovak-31
04Slovakian Skalica Team Set-25
Ivicic, Peter
04Slovakian Skalica Team Set-23
Jaakkola, Jarmo
71Finnish Suomi Stickers-280
Jaako, Kari
85Swedish Panini Stickers-164
86Swedish Panini Stickers-186
87Swedish Panini Stickers-184
89Swedish Semic Elitserien Stickers-162
90Swedish Semic Elitserien Stickers-43
91Swedish Semic Elitserien Stickers-291
Jaakola, Topi
04Finnish Cardset-259
05Finnish Cardset -91
06Finnish Cardset-271
Jaaskelainen, Jari
01Finnish Cardset-274
03Finnish Cardset-80
04Finnish Cardset-252
05Finnish Cardset -70
06Finnish Cardset-79
Jaaskelainen, Joonas
94Finnish SISU-226
95Finnish SISU-290
96Finnish SISU Redline-88
98Finnish Kerailysarja-23
Leijonat-25
99Finnish Cardset-17
00Finnish Cardset-10
01Finnish Cardset-318
01Finnish Cardset Dueling Aces-1
02Finnish Cardset-186
03Swedish Elite-207
Silver-207
Jaaskelainen, Juha
91Finnish Jyvas-Hyva Stickers-37
05Finnish Cardset -253
Jaaskelainen, Teemu
01Finnish Cardset-235
04Finnish Cardset-229
06Finnish Cardset-224
06Finnish Ilves Team Set-8
Jaaskelainen, Tuomo
00Finnish Cardset-292
01Finnish Cardset-64
03Finnish Cardset-78
Jablonic, Don
93Minnesota-Duluth Bulldogs-14
97Wheeling Nailers-3
97Wheeling Nailers Photo Pack-3
Jablonski, Jeff
91Nashville Knights-10
92Toledo Storm-16
92Toledo Storm Team Issue-14
95Roanoke Express-13
96Roanoke Express-15
01UK Manchester Storm Retro-19
Jablonski, Pat
88ProCards IHL-93
89Blues Kodak-1
89ProCards IHL-3
90ProCards AHL/IHL-97
91Blues Postcards-11
91O-Pee-Chee-246
91OPC Premier-29
91Pinnacle-331
French-331
91Score American-329
91Score Canadian Bilingual-359
91Score Canadian English-359
91Topps-246
91Upper Deck-107
French-107
92Bowman-66
92Lightning Sheraton-17
92O-Pee-Chee-311
92OPC Premier-95
92Parkhurst-404
Emerald Ice-404
92Pro Set-178
92Stadium Club-231
92Topps-396
Gold-396G
92Ultra-202
92Upper Deck-458
93OPC Premier-186
Gold-186
93Parkhurst-192
Emerald Ice-192
93Pinnacle Masks-5
93PowerPlay-444
93Score-349
Canadian-349
93Topps/OPC Premier-186
Gold-186
93Ultra-125
94Leaf-446
94Signature Rookies Tetrad *-106
Signatures-106
95Parkhurst International-386
Emerald Ice-386
96Be A Player-99
Autographs-99
Autographs Silver-99
96Canadiens Postcards-13
97Cleveland Lumberjacks-14
98Chicago Wolves-9
98IHL All-Star Western Conference-4
Jacico, Rastislav
93Quebec Pee-Wee Tournament-1721
Jacina, Greg
99Owen Sound Platers-16
00Owen Sound Attack-8
00UD CHL Prospects-43
01Mississauga Ice Dogs-20
01Owen Sound Attack-8
02Mississauga Ice Dogs-18
03Augusta Lynx-43
03ECHL All-Stars-272
04San Antonio Rampage-22
05Beehive-165
Matte-165
05Hot Prospects-134
En Fuego-134
Red Hot-134
White Hot-134
05SP Authentic-234
Limited-234
05SP Game Used-212
05SPx-261
05The Cup Masterpiece Pressplate Artifact-281
05The Cup Masterpiece Pressplate Bee Hive-165
05The Cup Masterpiece Pressplates (Ice)-196
05The Cup Master Pressplate Rookie Update-135
05The Cup Masterpiece Pressplates SPA-234
05The Cup Masterpiece Pressplates SP GU-212
05The Cup Masterpiece Pressplates (SPx)-261
05The Cup Masterpiece Pressplates Trilogy-260
05The Cup Masterpiece Pressplate Ult Coll-206
05UD Artifacts-281
05Ultimate Collection-206
Gold-206
05Upper Deck-479
05Upper Deck Ice-196
05Upper Deck Rookie Update-135
05Upper Deck Trilogy-260
06Rochester Americans-8
Jack, Adrian
04Penticton Vees-20
Jack, Justin
98Kelowna Rockets-11
Jack, Rob
84Nanaimo Clippers-11
Jackman, Barret
97Regina Pats-8
98SP Authentic-117
Power Shift-117
Sign of the Times-BJ
Sign of the Times Gold-BJ
98Upper Deck-394
Exclusives-394
Exclusives 1 of 1-394
Gold Reserve-394
99Black Diamond-100
Diamond Cut-100
Final Cut-100
99SPx-179
Radiance-179
Spectrum-179
99Upper Deck-312
Exclusives-312
Exclusives 1 of 1-312
99Upper Deck Gold Reserve-312
99Upper Deck MVP SC Edition-209
Gold Script-209
Silver Script-209
Super Script-209
Game-Used Souvenirs-GUBJ
ProSign-BJ
99Bowman CHL-38
Gold-38
OPC International-38
Autographs-BA3
Autographs Gold-BA3
Autographs Silver-BA3
01Worcester Icecats-9
02BAP Signature Series All-Rookie-AR9
02Blues Team Issue-8
02Bowman YoungStars-127
Gold-127
Silver-127
Autographs-BJ
Jerseys-BJ
Patches-BJ
Double Stuff-BJ
Triple Stuff-BJ
Rivals-BJDS
Rivals Patches-9
Sticks-BJ
02Pacific Calder-91
Silver-91
Reflections-19
02Pacific Complete-525
Red-525
02Pacific Exclusive-142
Great Expectations-15
02Parkhurst Retro Hopefuls-CH7
02Private Stock Reserve-83
Blue-83
Red-83
Retail-83
Class Act-10
Moments in Time-7
02Titanium Right on Target-18
02Vanguard Prime Prospects-20
03BAP Memorabilia-11
Emerald-11
Gold-11
Ruby-11
Sapphire-11
Future of the Game-FG-8
03BAP Ultimate Memorabilia Autographs-29
Gold-29
03BAP Ultimate Mem Auto Jerseys-29
03BAP Ultimate Mem Franch Present Future-25
03Black Diamond-171
Black-171
Green-171
Red-171
03Blues Team Set-10
03Bowman-6
Gold-6
Future Fabrics-FF-BJ
Future Fabric Patches-BJ
Future Rivals-JF
Future Rivals Patches-JF
03Bowman Chrome-6
Refractors-6
Gold Refractors-6
Xfractors-6
03Crown Royale Jerseys-21
03Crown Royale Patches-21
03ITG Action-506
Jerseys-M34
Trophy Winners-TW4
03ITG Used Signature Series Autographs-BJ
03ITG Used Sig Series Autographs Gold-BJ
03ITG Used Sig Series Intl Experience-8
03ITG Used Sig Ser Intl Experience Autos-8
03ITG Used Sig Ser Intl Exper Emblem Gold-8
03ITG Used Sig Ser Intl Experience Emblem-8
03ITG Used Sig Ser Intl Experience Gold-8
03ITG VIP Making the Bigs-6
03ITG VIP Sophomores-3
03McDonald's Pacific-42
03O-Pee-Chee-48
03OPC Blue-48
03OPC Gold-48
03OPC Red-48
03Pacific-282
Blue-282
Red-282
03Pacific Complete-191
Red-191
03Pacific Exhibit-189
Blue Backs-189
Pursuing Prominence-11
03Pacific Heads-Up-80
Hobby LTD-80
Retail LTD-80
Jerseys-23
03Pacific Invincible-80
Blue-80
Red-80
Retail-80
New Sensations-19
03Pacific Luxury Suite-45A
03Pacific Luxury Suite-45B
03Pacific Prism-83
Blue-83
Gold-83
Red-83
Paramount Prodigies-19
03Pacific Supreme-81
Blue-81
Red-81
Retail-81
Generations-9
03Parkhurst Rookie Road to the NHL-RNJ-7
03Parkhurst Rookie Road to the NHL Gold-RTN-7
03Parkhurst Rookie Road to the NHL Emblem-RTNE-7
03Parkhurst Rookie Road NHL Emblem Gold-RTNE-7
03Private Stock Reserve Rising Stock-12
03SPx Big Futures-BF-BJ
03SPx Big Futures Limited-BF-BJ
03Titanium-178
Hobby Jersey Number Parallels-178
Retail-178
Right on Target-14
03Topps-48
Blue-48
Gold-48
Red-48
03Topps C55-37
Minis-37
Minis American Back-37
Minis American Back Red-37
Minis Bazooka Back-37
Minis Brooklyn Back-37
Minis Hat Trick Back-37
Minis O Canada Back-37
Minis O Canada Back Red-37
Minis Stanley Cup Back-37
Award Winners-4
03Topps Traded Future Phenoms-FP-BJ
03Upper Deck-167
Canadian Exclusives-167
HG-167
03Upper Deck MVP-366
Gold Script-366
Silver Script-366
Canadian Exclusives-366
03Upper Deck Victory-169
Bronze-169
Gold-169
Silver-169
03Toronto Star-78
03Worcester Ice Cats 10th Anniversary-4
04Pacific-219
Blue-219
Red-219
04Upper Deck-153
Canadian Exclusives-153
HG Glossy Gold-153
HG Glossy Silver-153
04Missouri River Otters-28
05Be A Player Signatures-BJ
05Be A Player Signatures Gold-BJ
05Blues Team Set-8
05Hot Prospects-86
En Fuego-86
Red Hot-86
White Hot-86
05Panini Stickers-335
05Parkhurst-424
Facsimile Auto Parallel-424
True Colors-TCSTL
True Colors-TCSTL
05SP Authentic-86
Limited-86
05The Cup Master Pressplate Rookie Update-246
05Ultra-169
Gold-169
Ice-169
05Upper Deck-165
Big Playmakers-B-BJ
HG Glossy-165
Jerseys Series II-J2BJ
05Upper Deck MVP-332
Gold-332
Platinum-332
05Upper Deck Rookie Update-86
05Upper Deck Rookie Update-246
Inspirations Patch Rookies-246
05Upper Deck Toronto Fall Expo-165
05Upper Deck Victory-172
Black-172
Gold-172
Silver-172
06Black Diamond Jerseys-JBJ
06Black Diamond Jerseys Black-JBJ
06Black Diamond Jerseys Gold-JBJ
06Black Diamond Jerseys Ruby-JBJ
06Fleer Fabricology-FBJ
06O-Pee-Chee-423
Rainbow-423
06Panini Stickers-344
06SP Game Used Authentic Fabrics Sevens-AF7CAL
06SP Game Used Authentic Fabrics Sevens Patches-AF7CAL
06Upper Deck Arena Giveaways-STL2
06Upper Deck-169
Exclusives Parallel-169
High Gloss Parallel-169
Game Jerseys-JBA
Game Patches-PBA
Masterpieces-169
Victory-174
Victory Black-174
Victory Gold-174
07Upper Deck Ovation-59
07Upper Deck Victory-116
Black-116
Gold-116
Jackman, Jason
94Guelph Storm-13
95Slapshot-101
95Guelph Storm-4
96Guelph Storm-20
96Guelph Storm Premier Collection-6
97Guelph Storm-25
02Bakersfield Condors-9
03Bakersfield Condors-7
Jackman, Richard
95Slapshot-374
95Sault Ste. Marie Greyhounds-9
96Upper Deck Ice-133
96Sault Ste. Marie Greyhounds-7
96Sault Ste. Marie Greyhounds-8
96Sault Ste. Marie Greyhounds Autographed-7
96Sault Ste. Marie Greyhounds Autographed-8
96Coll Edge Future Legends Auto Hot Pick-3
96All Sport PPF *-174
96All Sport PPF Gold *-174
96Visions Signings *-65
Autographs-65A
Autographs Silver-65A
97Bowman CHL-36
OPC-36
97Players Club *-60
98Michigan K-Wings-14
98Bowman CHL-5
Golden Anniversary-5
OPC International-5
98Bowman Chrome CHL-5
Golden Anniversary-5
Golden Anniversary Refractors-5
OPC International-5
OPC International Refractors-5
Refractors-5
98Autographed Collection Autographs *-11
98Autographed Collection Sports City USA-SC10
99BAP Millennium Calder Candidate Ruby-C50
99BAP Millennium Calder Candidate Emerald-C50
99BAP Millennium Calder Cand Sapphire-C50
99Pacific Omega-79
Copper-79
Gold-79
Ice Blue-79
Premiere Date-79
99Michigan K-Wings-20
00BAP Memorabilia-487
Emerald-487
Ruby-487
Sapphire-487
00O-Pee-Chee-310
00O-Pee-Chee Parallel-310
00Private Stock-116
Gold-116
Premiere Date-116
Retail-116
Silver-116
00Stars Postcards-9
00Topps/OPC-310
Parallel-310
00Topps Chrome-205
OPC Refractors-205
Refractors-205
00Utah Grizzlies-30
01BAP Signature Series-208
Autographs-208
Autographs Gold-208
01Parkhurst-223
02BAP Sig Series Auto Buybacks 2001-208
02Maple Leafs Platinum Collection-23
02NHL Power Play Stickers-142
02Pacific Complete-461
Red-461
03Parkhurst Original Six Toronto-17
04Pacific-211
Blue-211
Red-211
05Parkhurst-387
Facsimile Auto Parallel-387
Jackman, Tim
02Syracuse Crunch-10
02Syracuse Crunch Sheets-17
03Beehive-243
Gold-243
Silver-243
03ITG Action-650
03ITG VIP Rookie Debut-89
03Pacific Calder-112
Silver-112
03Parkhurst Rookie-102
03Topps Traded-TT104
Blue-TT104
Gold-TT104
Red-TT104
03UD Premier Collection-62
03Upper Deck Rookie Update-111
03Pacific AHL Prospects-84
Gold-84
03Syracuse Crunch-11
04Syracuse Crunch-10
06Manchester Monarchs-21
Jackman, Alton
00OCN Blizzard-7
01OCN Blizzard-10
02OCN Blizzard-9
Jackson, Art
34Beehive Group I Photos-327
35O-Pee-Chee V304C-88
39O-Pee-Chee V301-1-93
Jackson, C.J.
99Dolphins NCL-9
03Portland Winter Hawks-10
Jackson, Dallas
02OCN Blizzard-5
03OCN Blizzard-9
Jackson, Dane
92Hamilton Canucks-11
94Score-216
Gold-216
Platinum-216
94Classic Pro Prospects-127
95Rochester Americans-6
96Rochester Americans-19
97Rochester Americans-1-1
00Rochester Americans-12
01Manchester Monarchs-1B
02Manchester Monarchs-9
Jackson, Dean
03Elmira Jackals-8
06Richmond Renegades-8
Jackson, Don
79Panini Stickers-212
82Oilers Red Rooster-29
83Oilers McDonald's-7
83O-Pee-Chee-33
83Vachon-30
84Oilers Red Rooster-29
84Oilers Team Issue-11
84O-Pee-Chee-247
85Oilers Red Rooster-29
88Oilers Tenth Anniversary-76
90Knoxville Cherokees-103
91Nordiques Petro-Canada-11
92Nordiques Petro-Canada-14
95Central Hockey League-90
96Kansas City Blades-22
01Senators Team Issue-12
02Senators Team Issue-29
03Senators Postcards-26
Jackson, Harold
35Diamond Matchbooks Tan 4-6
36O-Pee-Chee V304D-112
76Old Timers-8
05ITG Ultimate Mem Leafs Forever Autos-9
Jackson, Harvey
32O'Keefe Maple Leafs-11
33O-Pee-Chee V304A-33
33V129-6
33V252 Canadian Gum-32
33V288 Hamilton Gum-29
34Beehive Group I Photos-328
34Sweet Caporal-47
36O-Pee-Chee V304D-124
36Triumph Postcards-2
37O-Pee-Chee V304E-139
37V356 Worldwide Gum-51
38Quaker Oats Photos-20
39O-Pee-Chee V301-1-20
55Parkhurst-22
Quaker Oats-22
83Hall of Fame Postcards-M11
85Hall of Fame-175
91Pro Set-338
French-338
02BAP Ultimate Mem Paper Cuts Autos-19
02Maple Leafs Platinum Collection-54
02Parkhurst Reprints-203
03BAP Ultimate Memorabilia Linemates-11
03BAP Ultimate Mem Linemates Autos-4
03BAP Ultimate Memorabilia Paper Cuts-31
03BAP Ultimate Mem Vintage Blade of Steel-10
04ITG Franchises Update Linemates-ULI1
04ITG Franchises Update Linemates Gold-ULI1
04ITG Ultimate Memorabilia-13
Gold-13
Blades of Steel-11
Maple Leafs Forever-10
Paper Cuts Memorabilia-23
06ITG Ultimate Memorabilia Blades of Steel-3
06ITG Ultimate Memorabilia Blades of Steel Gold-3
06ITG Ultimate Memorabilia Maple Leafs Forever Autos-7
Jackson, Jeff
83Brantford Alexanders-14
84Maple Leafs Postcards-13
86Maple Leafs Postcards-13
87Nordiques General Foods-16
87Nordiques Team Issue-20
88Nordiques General Foods-19
88Nordiques Team Issue-18
88O-Pee-Chee-219
88O-Pee-Chee Stickers-190
89Nordiques Team Issue-18
89Nordiques General Foods-14
89Nordiques Police-12
89O-Pee-Chee Stickers-184
90Nordiques Petro-Canada-32
90Nordiques Team Issue-13
90O-Pee-Chee-249
90Topps-249
Tiffany-249
90Upper Deck-291
French-291
90Halifax Citadels-12
90ProCards AHL/IHL-459
91Lake Superior State Lakers-13
91ProCards-365
92Lake Superior State Lakers-14
01Guelph Storm-25
01Guelph Storm Memorial Cup-25
02Guelph Storm-26
Jackson, Jeremy
01Lethbridge Hurricanes-21
01Vancouver Giants-14
Jackson, Jim
82Ottawa 67's-9
83O-Pee-Chee-84
83O-Pee-Chee Stickers-146
83Topps Stickers-146
83Ottawa 67's-14
84O-Pee-Chee-225
84Ottawa 67's-14
88ProCards AHL-250
89ProCards AHL-279
03Gwinnett Gladiators-17
03Gwinnett Gladiators RBI Sports-203
04Gwinnett Gladiators-16
Jackson, Joshua
92Disney Mighty Ducks Movie-3
Jackson, Mark
03Fresno Falcons-6
Jackson, Mike
90Newmarket Saints-9
90ProCards AHL/IHL-169
93Memphis RiverKings-5
94Central Hockey League-48
95Central Hockey League-27
97Austin Ice Bats-8
99Memphis RiverKings All-Time-3
Jackson, Paul
93Wichita Thunder-10
94UK Sheffield Steelers-3
94Central Hockey League-80
98San Antonio Iguanas-4
Jackson, Paul A.
66Columbus Checkers-8
Jackson, Scott
05ITG Heroes/Prosp Toronto Expo Parallel -177
05ITG Heroes and Prospects-177
Autographs-A-SJ
Jackson, Stan
23V145-1-27
24C144 Champ's Cigarettes-33
24V145-2-60
Jackson, Steve
00Michigan State Spartans-11
Jackson, Tyler
93Quebec Pee-Wee Tournament-1230
Jackson, Walter
33V252 Canadian Gum-33
34Diamond Matchbooks Silver-31
Jacob, Guy
79Montreal Juniors-9
81Oshawa Generals-21
88Flint Spirits-9
Jacob, Ricky
97Central Texas Stampede-6
98San Antonio Iguanas-15
99San Antonio Iguanas-12
Jacobs, Ian
99Ottawa 67's-7
03Port Huron Beacons-14
Jacobs, Tim
76O-Pee-Chee NHL-370
Jacobsen, Anders
87Swedish Panini Stickers-253
Jacobsen, Fredrik
92Norwegian Elite Series-69
Jacobsen, Grant
01Regina Pats-10
02Kamloops Blazers-10
02Regina Pats-1
03Kamloops Blazers-6
Jacobsen, Lars
92Norwegian Elite Series-71
Jacobsen, Michael
00Belleville Bulls-5
01Owen Sound Attack-9
Jacobsen, Rasmus
98Danish Hockey League-117
99Danish Hockey League-32
Jacobsen, Tommy
99Norwegian National Team-4
99Norwegian National Team-5
Jacobsen, Tor Anders
92Norwegian Elite Series-103
Jacobson, Chris
97Portland Winter Hawks-16
Jacobson, David
02Kelowna Rockets-13
Jacobson, Garnet
95Prince Albert Raiders-10
96Prince Albert Raiders-10
99San Antonio Iguanas-11
Jacobson, Lee
02Fort Worth Brahmas-7
Jacobson, Ole
65Swedish Coralli ISHockey-171
Jacobson, Tommy
95Finnish Semic World Championships-179
95Swedish Leaf-193
Jacobsson, Bertil
69Swedish Hockey-244
70Swedish Hockey-141
71Swedish Hockey-233
Jacobsson, Curt
69Swedish Hockey-280
70Swedish Hockey-188
Jacobsson, Lars-Erik
71Swedish Hockey-267
Jacobsson, Leif
69Swedish Hockey-281
70Swedish Hockey-189
Jacobsson, Mats
84Swedish Semic Elitserien-36
Jacobsson, Orjan
92Swedish Semic Elitserien Stickers-251
Jacobsson, Peter
89Swedish Semic Elitserien Stickers-249
90Swedish Semic Elitserien Stickers-158
91Swedish Semic Elitserien Stickers-262
92Swedish Semic Elitserien Stickers-283
93Swedish Semic Elitserien-248
94Swedish Leaf-117
Jacobsson, Sven-Ake
71Swedish Hockey-213
72Swedish Stickers-190
74Swedish Stickers-224
Jacoby, Jake
93Waterloo Black Hawks-12
Jacques, Alexandre
97Toledo Storm-4
97Bowman CHL-80
OPC-80
99Cincinnati Mighty Ducks-18
03Toledo Storm-8
Jacques, Daniel
97Guelph Storm-3
Jacques, Dominic
93Quebec Pee-Wee Tournament-238
Jacques, Jean-Francois
01Baie-Comeau Drakkar-24
02Baie Comeau Drakkar-24
03Baie Comeau Drakkar-24
03Baie Comeau Drakkar-27
04Baie-Comeau Drakkar-7
05ITG Heroes/Prosp Toronto Expo Parallel -255
05Black Diamond-243
05Hot Prospects-131
En Fuego-131
Red Hot-131
White Hot-131
05Parkhurst-629
Facsimile Auto Parallel-629
05SP Authentic-261
Limited-261
05SP Game Used-211
05SPx-259
05The Cup Masterpiece Pressplate Artifact-278
05The Cup Master Pressplate Black Diamond-243
05The Cup Masterpiece Pressplates (Ice)-268
05The Cup Master Pressplate Rookie Update-133
05The Cup Masterpiece Pressplates SPA-261
05The Cup Masterpiece Pressplates SP GU-211
05The Cup Masterpiece Pressplates (SPx)-259
05The Cup Masterpiece Pressplates Trilogy-257
05The Cup Masterpiece Pressplate Ult Coll-205
05UD Artifacts-278
05Ultimate Collection-205
Gold-205
05Upper Deck Ice-268
05Upper Deck Rookie Update-133
05Upper Deck Trilogy-257
05AHL Top Prospects-20
05Extreme Top Prospects Signature Edition-S5
05Hamilton Bulldogs-11
05ITG Heroes and Prospects-255
Autographs Series II-JFJ
Jacques, Matt
00Lethbridge Hurricanes-9
Jacques, Real
52Bas Du Fleuve-7
Jacques, Steve
90ProCards AHL/IHL-358
Jadamzik, R.
95German DEL-339
Jadeland, Nicklas
06Swedish SHL Elitset-233
Jaegar, Brett
04Fresno Falcons-7
Jaeger, Brett
01Vancouver Giants-15
02Saskatoon Blades-22
05ITG Heroes/Prosp Toronto Expo Parallel -355
05Fresno Falcons-9
05ITG Heroes and Prospects-355
Autographs Series II-BJG
Jaeggi, Tom
93Swiss HNL-318
Jaffray, Jason
98Kootenay Ice-15
00Kootenay Ice-17
02ECHL All-Star Northern-25
02Roanoke Express-16
02Roanoke Express RBI Sports-196
03ECHL All-Stars-246
03Wheeling Nailers-86
05Manitoba Moose-10
06Manitoba Moose-10
Jagenstedt, Thomas
84Swedish Semic Elitserien-143
85Swedish Panini Stickers-20
Jager, Christoph
93Quebec Pee-Wee Tournament-1766
Jager, Florian
94German First League-230
Jager, Jesper
00Swedish Upper Deck-19
03Swedish Elite-268
Silver-268
04Swedish Elitset-123
Gold-123
Jager, Rolf
69Swedish Hockey-208
70Swedish Hockey-200
71Swedish Hockey-287
87Swedish Panini Stickers-25
Jaggli, Thomas
93Swiss HNL-394
96Swiss HNL-345
Jago, Dale
99German Bundesliga 2-14
01UK Manchester Storm Retro-1
Jagow, Jared
06Regina Pats-9
Jagr, Jaromir
90OPC Premier-50
90Penguins Foodland-11
90Pro Set-632
90Pro Set-632B
90Score-428
Canadian-428
90Score Rookie/Traded-70T
90Upper Deck-356
French-356
91Pro Set Platinum-92
91Bowman-95
91Gillette-34
91Kraft-3
91O-Pee-Chee-9
91O-Pee-Chee-40
91OPC Premier-24
91Panini Stickers-275
91Panini Stickers-344
91Parkhurst-132
91Parkhurst-461
French-132
91Penguins Coke/Elby's-68
91Penguins Foodland-11
91Penguins Foodland Coupon Stickers-7
91Pinnacle-53
French-53
91Pro Set-183
91Pro Set-319
French-183
91Score American-98
91Score American-351
91Score Canadian Bilingual-98
91Score Canadian Bilingual-381
91Score Canadian English-98
91Score Canadian English-381
91Score Hot Cards-8
91Score Young Superstars-38
91Stadium Club-343
91Topps-9
91Topps-40
91Upper Deck-20
91Upper Deck-42
91Upper Deck-256
91Upper Deck-617
French-20
French-42
French-256
French-617
Euro-Stars-6
Euro-Stars French-6
91Finnish Semic World Champ Stickers-225
91Swedish Semic World Champ Stickers-225
91Star Pics-70
92Bowman-231
92Bowman-302
92Humpty Dumpty II-10
92Kraft-42
92McDonald's Upper Deck-20
92O-Pee-Chee-102
92Panini Stickers-282
92Panini Stickers-294
92Panini Stickers-S
92Panini Stickers French-282
92Panini Stickers French-294
92Panini Stickers French-S
92Parkhurst-135
92Parkhurst-220
92Parkhurst-465
Emerald Ice-135
Emerald Ice-220
Emerald Ice-465
92Penguins Coke/Clark-8
92Penguins Foodland-3
92Penguins Foodland Coupon Stickers-3
92Pinnacle-275
French-275
Team 2000-15
Team 2000 French-15
Team Pinnacle-6
Team French-6
92Pro Set-141
92Score-113
92Score-494
Canadian-113

  Canadian-494
  Young Superstars-4
92Seasons Patches-35
92Sports Illustrated for Kids II-117
92Sports Illustrated for Kids II-765
92Stadium Club-498
92Topps-24
  Gold-24G
92Ultra-164
  All-Stars-6
  Imports-6
92Upper Deck-16
92Upper Deck-28
92Upper Deck-622
  All-World Team-W3
  Euro-Stars-E14
  World Junior Grads-WG6
92Finnish Semic-135
93SLU Hockey Canadian-4
93SLU Hockey American-5
93Donruss-270
  Ice Kings-3
93Kenner Starting Lineup Cards-5
93Kraft-13
93Leaf-346
93McDonald's Upper Deck-17
93OPC Premier-105
93OPC Premier-325
  Gold-105
  Gold-325
  Black Gold-19
93Panini Stickers-82
93Parkhurst-154
  Emerald Ice-154
93Penguins Foodland-23
93Pinnacle-195
  Canadian-195
  All-Stars-20
  All-Stars Canadian-20
  Team Pinnacle-6
  Team Canadian-6
  Team 2001-12
  Team 2001 Canadian-12
93PowerPlay-189
  Global Greats-3
  Point Leaders-5
93Score-50
  Canadian-50
  International Stars-9
  International Stars Canadian-9
93Seasons Patches-7
93Stadium Club-98
  Members Only Master Set-98
  OPC-98
  First Day Issue-98
  First Day Issue OPC-98
  All-Stars-4
  All-Stars Members Only-4
  All-Stars OPC-4
93Topps/OPC Premier-105
93Topps/OPC Premier-325
  Gold-105
  Gold-325
93Ultra-65
  Red Light Specials-5
93Upper Deck-139
  Future Heroes-33
  Silver Skates-R8
  Silver Skates Gold-R8
  SP-121
93Upper Deck Locker All-Stars-3
94SLU Hockey American-8
94Action Packed Big Picture Promos-BP3
94Be A Player-R63
94Canada Games NHL POGS-184
94Donruss-159
  Dominators-4
94EA Sports-107
94Finest-33
  Super Team Winners-33
  Refractors-33
  Bowman's Best-B20
  Bowman's Best Refractors-B20
  Ring Leaders-15
94Fleer-163
  Slapshot Artists-4
94Hockey Wit-107
94Kenner Starting Lineup Cards-9
94Kraft-8
94Leaf-151
  Gold Stars-15
94Leaf Limited-86
  Gold-6
94McDonald's Upper Deck-McD10
94OPC Premier-460
  Special Effects-460
94Parkhurst-174
94Parkhurst-314
  Gold-174
  Gold-314
  SE Euro-Stars-ES20
  SE Vintage-42
94Penguins Foodland-23
94Pinnacle-98
  Artist's Proofs-98
  Rink Collection-98
  Gamers-GR5
  Team Pinnacle-TP11
  Team Dufex Parallel-TP11
94Score-135
  Gold-135
  Platinum-135
  90 Plus Club-9
94Select-60
  Gold-60
94SP-89
  Die Cuts-89
  Premier-26
  Premier Die-Cuts-26
94Stadium Club Members Only-44
94Stadium Club-68
  Members Only Master Set-68
  First Day Issue-68
  Super Team Winner Cards-68
94Topps/OPC Premier-460
  Special Effects-460
94Topps Finest Bronze-1
94Ultra-164
  Global Greats-4
94Upper Deck-93
94Upper Deck-544
  Electric Ice-93
  Electric Ice-544
  Predictor Canadian-C24
94Upper Deck Predictor Canadian Exch Gold-C24
94Upper Deck Predictor Hobby-H24
94Upper Deck Predictor Hobby Exch Gold-H24
94Upper Deck Predictor Hobby Exch Silver-H24
94Upper Deck Predictor Retail-R18
94Upper Deck Predictor Retail-R29
94Upper Deck Predictor Retail-R39
94Upper Deck Predictor Retail Exchange-R18
94Upper Deck Predictor Retail Exchange-R29
94Upper Deck Predictor Retail Exchange-R39
94Upper Deck SP Inserts-SP60
94Upper Deck SP Inserts Die Cuts-SP60
94Czech APS Extraliga-68
94Finnish Jaa Kiekko-183
94Finnish Jaa Kiekko-351
94German First League-561
95Bashan Super Stickers-96
  Die-Cut-23
95Be A Player Lethal Lines-LL12
95Bowman-57
  All-Foil-57
  Bowman's Best-BB7
  Bowman's Best Refractors-BB7
95Canada Games NHL POGS-11
95Canada Games NHL POGS-216
95Collector's Choice-127
95Collector's Choice-378
95Collector's Choice-389
  Player's Club-127
  Player's Club-378
  Player's Club-389
  Player's Club Platinum-127
  Player's Club Platinum-378
  Player's Club Platinum-389
  Crash The Game-C7A
  Crash The Game-C7B
  Crash The Game-C7C
  Crash The Game Gold-C7A
  Crash The Game Gold-C7B
  Crash The Game Gold-C7C
  Crash the Game Silver Redeemed-C7
  Crash the Game Silver Bonus-C7
  Crash the Game Gold Redeemed-C7
  Crash the Game Gold Bonus-C7
95Donruss-142
  Dominators-2
  Elite Inserts-10
  Marksmen-5
95Donruss Elite-35
  Die Cut Stars-35
  Die Cut Uncut-35
  Cutting Edge-6
95Emotion-137
  Xcited-9
95Finest-70
95Finest-185
  Refractors-70
  Refractors-185
95Hoyle Eastern Playing Cards-32
95Imperial Stickers-96
  Die Cut Superstars-23
95Kraft-42
95Kraft-78
95Leaf-71
  Freeze Frame-4
  Gold Stars-5
  Road To The Cup-3
95Leaf Limited-73
  Stars of the Game-8
95McDonald's Pinnacle-MCD-1
95Metal-117
  Heavy Metal-6
  International Steel-9
95NHL Aces Playing Cards-12D
95NHL Cool Trade-20
95NHL Cool Trade-RP20
95NHL/NHLPA Playing Cards-NNO
95Panini Stickers-63
95Panini Stickers-150
95Parkhurst International-165
95Parkhurst International-244
  Emerald Ice-165
  Emerald Ice-244
  All-Stars-5
  Crown Collection Silver Series 2-1
  Crown Collection Gold Series 2-1
  NHL All-Stars-2
  Parkie's Trophy Picks-PP7
  Parkie's Trophy Picks-PP14
  Trophy Winners-2
95Penguins Foodland-5
95Pinnacle-11
  Artist's Proofs-11
  Rink Collection-11
  Clear Shots-11
  Global Gold-2
  Roaring 20s-13
95Playoff One on One-78
95Playoff One on One-185
95Playoff One on One-297
95Pro Magnets-92
95Score-1
  Black Ice Artist's Proofs-1
  Black Ice-1
  Border Battle-14
  Dream Team-8
  Lamplighters-12
95Select Certified-38
  Mirror Gold-38
  Gold Team-4
95SkyBox Impact-131
  Countdown to Impact-2
  Ice Quake-1
95SP-114
  Holoviews-FX18
  Holoviews Special FX-FX18
  Stars/Etoiles-E23
  Stars/Etoiles Gold-E23
95Stadium Club Members Only-5
95Stadium Club-70
  Members Only Master Set-70
  Generation TSC-GT3
  Generation TSC Members Only Master Set-GT3
95Summit-17
  Artist's Proofs-17
  Ice-17
  GM's Choice-11
  Mad Hatters-10
95Topps-200
95Topps-374
  OPC Inserts-200
  OPC Inserts-374
  Marquee Men Power Boosters-374
  Mystery Finest-M8
  Mystery Finest Refractors-M8
  Power Lines-5PL
  Profiles-PF4
  Young Stars-YS15
95Topps SuperSkills-20
  Platinum-20
95Ultra-123
95Ultra-387
  Gold Medallion-123
  Extra Attackers-9
  Red Light Specials-4
  Red Light Specials Gold Medallion-4
  Ultraview-4
  Ultraview Hot Pack-4
95Upper Deck-465
  Electric Ice-465
  Electric Ice Gold-465
95Upper Deck All-Star Game Predictors-17
  Redemption Winners-17
95Upper Deck Freeze Frame-F4
95Upper Deck Freeze Frame Jumbo-F4
95Upper Deck NHL All-Stars-AS3
95Upper Deck NHL All-Stars Jumbo-AS3
95Upper Deck Predictor Hobby-H2
95Upper Deck Predictor Hobby Exchange-H2
95Upper Deck Predictor Retail-R3
95Upper Deck Predictor Retail-R22
95Upper Deck Predictor Retail-R38
95Upper Deck Predictor Retail-R46
95Upper Deck Predictor Retail Exchange-R3
95Upper Deck Predictor Retail Exchange-R22
95Upper Deck Predictor Retail Exchange-R38
95Upper Deck Predictor Retail Exchange-R46
95Upper Deck Special Edition-SE153
95Upper Deck Special Edition Gold-SE153
95Zenith-3
  Z-Team-11
95Czech APS Extraliga-384
95Finnish Semic World Championships-158
95Swedish Globe World Championships-157
95Swedish World Championships Stickers-297
95Signature Rook Auto-Phonex Jagr-JJ1
95Signature Rook Auto-Phonex Jagr-JJ2
95Signature Rook Auto-Phonex Jagr-JJ3
95Signature Rook Auto-Phonex Jagr-JJ4
95Signature Rook Auto-Phonex Jagr-JJ5
95Signature Rookies Tetrad SR Force *-F8
96Headliners Hockey-7A
96Headliners Hockey-7B
96Be A Player Biscuit In The Basket-9
96Black Diamond-75
  Gold-75
  Run for the Cup-RC5
96Collector's Choice-211
96Collector's Choice-294
96Collector's Choice-328
  MVP-UD43
  MVP Gold-UD43
  Stick'Ums-S8
  Crash the Game-C6A
  Crash the Game-C6B
  Crash the Game-C6C
  Crash the Game Gold-C6A
  Crash the Game Gold-C6B
  Crash the Game Gold-C6C
  Crash the Game Exchange-CR6
  Crash the Game Exchange Gold-CR6
96Donruss-43
  Press Proofs-43
  Dominators-4
  Go Top Shelf-5
96Donruss Canadian Ice-1
  Gold Press Proofs-1
  Red Press Proofs-1
96Donruss Elite-8
  Die Cut Stars-8
  Perspective-8
96Flair-77
  Blue Ice-77
  Center Ice Spotlight-5
96Fleer-86
96Fleer-137
96Fleer-138
96Fleer-139
96Fleer-141
96Fleer-142
  Art Ross-8
  Pearson-5
  Picks Dream Lines-6
  Picks Fabulous 50-20
  Picks Fantasy Force-5
96Hockey Greats Coins-11
  Gold-11
96Kraft Upper Deck-32
96Kraft Upper Deck-57
96Leaf-106
  Press Proofs-106
96Leaf Leather And Laces Promos-P5
96Leaf Leather And Laces-5
96Leaf The Best Of ...-1
96Leaf Limited-11
  Gold-11
96Leaf Preferred-22
  Press Proofs-22
  Steel-37
  Steel Gold-37
  Steel Power-8
96Maggers-42
96McDonald's Pinnacle-23
96Metal Universe-127
  Ice Carvings-6
  Ice Carvings Super Power-6
  Lethal Weapons-8
  Lethal Weapons Super Power-8
96NHL Aces Playing Cards-23
96NHL Pro Stamps-92
96Penguins Tribune-Review-7
96Pinnacle-102
  Artist's Proofs-102
  Foil-102
  Premium Stock-102
  Rink Collection-102
  By The Numbers-8
  By The Numbers Premium-8
  Team Pinnacle-6
96Pinnacle Fantasy-FC7
96Pinnacle Mint-4
  Bronze-4
  Gold-4
  Silver-4
  Coins Brass-4
  Coins Solid Gold-4
  Coins Gold Plated-4
  Coins Nickel-4
  Coins Silver-4
96Playoff One on One-433
96Score-29
  Artist's Proofs-29
  Dealer's Choice Artist's Proofs-29
  Special Artist's Proofs-29
  Golden Blades-29
  Dream Team-7
  Sudden Death-9
96Select Certified-43
  Artist's Proofs-43
  Blue-43
  Mirror Blue-43
  Mirror Gold-43
  Mirror Red-43
  Red-43
  Cornerstones-3
96SkyBox Impact-101
  Countdown to Impact-4
  VersaTeam-5
96SP-126
  SPx Force-2
  SPx Force-5
  SPx Force Autographs-2
96SPx-38
  Gold-38
96Stadium Club Members Only-25
96Summit-85
  Artist's Proofs-85
  Ice-85
  Metal-85
  Premium Stock-85
  High Voltage-15
  High Voltage Mirage-15
  Untouchables-2
96Team Out-32
96Topps Picks-1
  Fantasy Team-FT14
  OPC Inserts-1
  Top Shelf-TS6
96Ultra-141
  Gold Medallion-141
  Clear the Ice-4
  Mr. Momentum-5
96Upper Deck-320
  Game Jerseys-GJ4
  Generation Next-X17
  Hart Hopefuls Bronze-HH18
  Hart Hopefuls Gold-HH18
  Hart Hopefuls Silver-HH18
  Lord Stanley's Heroes Finals-LS4
  Lord Stanley's Heroes Quarterfinals-LS4
  Lord Stanley's Heroes Semifinals-LS4
  Superstar Showdown-SS13B
96Upper Deck Ice-101
  Parallel-101
  Stanley Cup Foundation-S7
  Stanley Cup Foundation Dynasty-S7
96Zenith-74
  Artist's Proofs-74
  Champion Salute-6
  Champion Salute Diamond-6
96Swedish Semic Wien-125
97SLU Hockey One on One-2
97SLU Hockey Canadian-9
97Headliners Hockey-10
97SLU Hockey American-10
97NHL Pro Zone-20
97Be A Player One Timers-7
97Be A Player Take A Number-20
97Beehive-7
  Golden Portraits-7
  Team-10
  Team Gold-10
97Black Diamond-72
  Double Diamond-72
  Triple Diamond-72
  Quadruple Diamond-72
  Premium Cut-PC20
  Premium Cut Double Diamond-PC20
  Premium Cut Quadruple Diamond Horiz-PC20
  Premium Cut Triple Diamond-PC20
  Premium Cut Quadruple Diamond Verticals-PC20
97Collector's Choice-205
97Collector's Choice-314
  Crash the Game-C28A
  Crash the Game-C28B
  Crash the Game-C28C
  Crash the Game Exchange-CR28
  Star Quest-SQ89
  Stick'Ums-S15
97Crown Royale-110
  Emerald Green-110
  Ice Blue-110
  Silver-110
  Blades of Steel Die-Cuts-17
  Cramer's Choice Jumbos-9
  Cramer's Choice Jumbos Gold-9
  Cramer's Choice Jumbos Signed-9
  Hat Tricks Die-Cuts-15
  Lamplighters Cel-Fusion Die-Cuts-17
97Donruss-188
  Press Proofs Silver-188
  Press Proofs Gold-188
  Elite Inserts-2
  Line 2 Line-16
  Line 2 Line Die Cut-16
97Donruss Canadian Ice-8
  Dominion Series-8
  Provincial Series-8
  Stanley Cup Scrapbook-9
97Donruss Elite-11
97Donruss Elite-125
  Aspirations-11
  Aspirations-125
  Status-11
  Status-125
  Back to the Future-4
  Back to the Future Autographs-4
  Craftsmen-25
  Master Craftsmen-25
  Prime Numbers-6A
  Prime Numbers-6B
  Prime Numbers-6C
  Prime Numbers Die-Cuts-6A
  Prime Numbers Die-Cuts-6B
  Prime Numbers Die-Cuts-6C
97Donruss Limited-8
97Donruss Limited-55
  Exposure-8
  Exposure-55
  Fabric of the Game-14
97Donruss Preferred-125
97Donruss Preferred-192
  Cut to the Chase-125
  Cut to the Chase-192
  Line of the Times-1C
97Donruss Preferred Line of Times Promos-1C
97Donruss Preferred Precious Metals-10
97Donruss Priority-18
  Stamp of Approval-18
  Direct Deposit-4
  Postcards-4
  Postcards Opening Day Issues-16
  Stamps-4
  Stamps Bronze-4
  Stamps Gold-4
  Stamps Silver-4
97Esso Olympic Hockey Heroes-52
97Esso Olympic Hockey Heroes French-52
97Gatorade Stickers-5
97Highland Mint Mint-Cards Pinnacle/Score-5
97Highland Mint Mint-Cards Pinnacle/Score-6
97Highland Mint Mint-Coins-5
97Jell-O Juniors To Pros-9
97Katch-118
97Katch-162
  Gold-118
  Gold-162
  Silver-118
  Silver-162
97Kenner Starting Lineup Cards-10
97Kraft-10
97Leaf-10
97Leaf-177
  Fractal Matrix-10
  Fractal Matrix-177
  Fractal Matrix Die Cuts-10
  Fractal Matrix Die Cuts-177
  Banner Season-4
  Fire On Ice-3
97Leaf International-10
  Universal Ice-10
97McDonald's Upper Deck-20
97NHL Aces Playing Cards-36
97Pacific-68
  Copper-68
  Emerald Green-68
  Ice Blue-68
  Red-68
  Silver-68
  Cramer's Choice-10
  Gold Crown Die-Cuts-18
  Slap Shots Die-Cuts-8C
  Team Checklists-20
97Pacific Dynagon-102
97Pacific Dynagon-142
  Copper-102
  Copper-142
  Dark Grey-102
  Dark Grey-142
  Emerald Green-102
  Emerald Green-142
  Ice Blue-102
  Ice Blue-142
  Red-102
  Red-142
  Silver-102
  Silver-142
  Best Kept Secrets-77
  Dynamic Duos-13A
  Kings of the NHL-9
  Tandems-5
  Tandems-22
97Pacific Invincible-113
  Copper-113
  Emerald Green-113
  Ice Blue-113
  Red-113
  Silver-113
  Attack Zone-20
  Feature Performers-28
  NHL Regime-160
  NHL Regime-220
  Off The Glass-17
97Pacific Omega-186
  Copper-186
  Dark Gray-186
  Emerald Green-186
  Gold-186
  Ice Blue-186
  Game Face-16
  Silks-10
  Stick Handle Laser Cuts-17
97Panini Stickers-47
97Paramount-150
  Copper-150
  Dark Grey-150
  Emerald Green-150
  Ice Blue-150
  Red-150
  Silver-150
  Big Numbers Die-Cuts-17
  Photoengravings-17
97Penguins USPS Lineup Cards-NNO
97Pinnacle-30
97Pinnacle-193
  Artist's Proofs-30
  Rink Collection-30
  Epix Game Emerald-20
  Epix Game Orange-20
  Epix Game Purple-20
  Epix Moment Emerald-20
  Epix Moment Orange-20
  Epix Moment Purple-20
  Epix Play Emerald-20
  Epix Play Orange-20
  Epix Play Purple-20
  Epix Season Emerald-20
  Epix Season Orange-20
  Epix Season Purple-20
  Press Plates Back Black-30
  Press Plates Back Black-193
  Press Plates Back Cyan-30
  Press Plates Back Cyan-193
  Press Plates Back Magenta-30
  Press Plates Back Magenta-193
  Press Plates Back Yellow-30
  Press Plates Back Yellow-193
  Press Plates Front Black-30
  Press Plates Front Black-193
  Press Plates Front Cyan-30
  Press Plates Front Cyan-193
  Press Plates Front Magenta-30
  Press Plates Front Magenta-193
  Press Plates Front Yellow-30
  Press Plates Front Yellow-193
  Team Pinnacle-6
  Team Mirror-6
  Team Parallel-6
  Team Parallel Mirror-6
97Pinnacle Certified-35
  Red-35
  Mirror Blue-35
  Mirror Gold-35
  Mirror Red-35
  Team-14
  Gold Team Promo-14
  Gold Team-14
97Pinnacle Inside-6
  Coach's Collection-6
  Executive Collection-6
  Track-10
  Cans-2
  Cans Gold-2
97Pinnacle Mint-22
  Bronze-22
  Gold Team-22
  Silver Team-22
  Coins Brass-22
  Coins Brass Proofs-22
  Coins Gold Plated-22
  Coins Gold Plated Proofs-22
  Coins Nickel Silver-22
  Coins Nickel Silver Proofs-22
  Coins Solid Gold-22
  Coins Solid Silver-22
97Pinnacle Power Pack Blow-Ups-11
97Pinnacle Tot Cert Platinum Blue-35
97Pinnacle Tot Certi Platinum Gold-35
97Pinnacle Totally Certified Platinum Red-35
97Pinnacle Tot Cert Mirror Platinum Gold-35
97Post Pinnacle-21
97Revolution-113
  Copper-113
  Emerald-113
  Ice Blue-113
  Silver-113
  1998 All-Star Game Die-Cuts-17
  NHL Icons-9
  Team Checklist Laser Cuts-20
97Score-82
97Score-PR82
  Artist's Proofs-82
  Golden Blades-82
  Check It-13
97Score Penguins-4
  Platinum-4
  Premier-4
97SP Authentic-125
  Icons-I8
  Icons Die-Cuts-I8
  Icons Embossed-I8
97SPx-42
  Bronze-42
  Gold-42
  Silver-42
  Steel-42
  DuoView-2
  DuoView Autographs-2
  Grand Finale-42
97Studio-5
  Press Proofs Silver-5
  Press Proofs Gold-5
  Hard Hats-19
  Portraits-5
  Silhouettes-22
  Silhouettes 8x10-22
97Upper Deck-342
  Blow-Ups 3 x 5-2-7
  Blow-Ups 5 x 7-2A
  Game Dated Moments-342
  Sixth Sense Masters-SS2
  Sixth Sense Wizards-SS2
  Smooth Grooves-SG38
  The Specialists-3
  The Specialists Level 2 Die Cuts-3
  Three Star Selects-5B
97Upper Deck Crash the All-Star Game-16
97Upper Deck Crash the All-Star Game-AR16
97Upper Deck Diamond Vision-3
  Signature Moves-3
  Defining Moments-DM4
97Upper Deck Ice-68
  Parallel-68
  Champions-IC18
  Champions 2 Die Cuts-IC18
  Lethal Lines-L2C
  Lethal Lines 2-L2C
  Power Shift-68
97Zenith-31
  Z-Gold-31
  Z-Silver-31
97Zenith 5 x 7-8
  Gold Impulse-8
  Silver Impulse-8
97Zenith Chasing The Cup-3
97Pinnacle Collector's Club Team Pinnacle-H9
98Headliners Hockey XL-3
98SLU Hockey Classic Doubles-4
98SLU Hockey-90
98Aurora-154
  Atomic Laser Cuts-16
  Championship Fever-40
  Championship Fever Copper-40
  Championship Fever Ice Blue-40
  Championship Fever Red-40
  Championship Fever Silver-40
  Cubes-15
  Front Line Copper-8
  Front Line Ice Blue-8
  Front Line Red-8
  Man Advantage-16
  NHL Command-10
98Be A Player-261
  Press Release-261
98BAP Gold-261
98BAP Autographs-261
98BAP Autographs Gold-261
98BAP AS Game Used Stick Cards-S17
98BAP AS Game Used Jersey Cards-AS18
98BAP Playoff Game Used Jerseys-G23
98BAP Playoff Highlights-H5
98BAP Playoff Practice Used Jerseys-P7
98Black Diamond-69
  Double Diamond-69
  Triple Diamond-69
  Quadruple Diamond-69
  Myriad-M18
  Myriad 2-M18
  Winning Formula Gold-WF25
  Winning Formula Platinum-WF25
98Bowman's Best-4
  Refractors-4
  Atomic Refractors-4
  Autographs-A2A
  Autographs-A2B
  Autographs Refractors-A2A
  Autographs Refractors-A2B
  Autographs Atomic Refractors-A2A
  Autographs Atomic Refractors-A2B
  Mirror Image Fusion-F3
  Mirror Image Fusion Refractors-F3
  Mirror Image Fusion Atomic Refractors-F3
  Scotty Bowman's Best-SB6
  Scotty Refractors-SB6
  Scotty Atomic Refractors-SB6
98Crown Royale-110
  Limited Series-110
  Cramer's Choice Jumbos-10
  Cramer's Choice Jumbos Dark Blue-10
  Cramer's Choice Jumbos Green-10
  Cramer's Choice Jumbos Red-10
  Cramer's Choice Jumbos Light Blue-10
  Cramer's Choice Jumbos Gold-10
  Cramer's Choice Jumbos Purple-10
  Living Legends-10
  Master Performers-17
  Pillars of the Game-21
98Donruss Elite Promos-17
98Finest-74
  No Protectors-74
  No Protectors Refractors-74
  Refractors-74
  Centurion-C13
  Centurion Refractors-C13
  Double Sided Mystery Finest-M1
  Double Sided Mystery Finest-M2
  Double Sided Mystery Finest-M3
  Double Sided Mystery Finest-M4
  Double Sided Mystery Refractors-M1
  Double Sided Mystery Refractors-M2
  Double Sided Mystery Refractors-M3
  Double Sided Mystery Refractors-M4
  Oversize-6
  Oversize Refractors-6
  Red Lighters-R1
  Red Lighters Refractors-R1
98Katch-161
98Kenner Starting Lineup Cards-14
98Kraft Fearless Forwards-4
98McDonald's Upper Deck-11
98OPC Chrome-111
  Refractors-111
  Season's Best-SB19
  Season's Best Refractors-SB19
98Pacific-68
  Ice Blue-68
  Red-68
  Cramer's Choice-9
  Dynagon Ice Inserts-16
  Titanium Ice-16
  Gold Crown Die-Cuts-29
  Team Checklists-21
  Timelines-16
  Trophy Winners-3
98Pacific Dynagon Ice-151
  Blue-151
  Red-151
  Adrenaline Rush Bronze-10
  Adrenaline Rush Ice Blue-10
  Adrenaline Rush Red-10
  Adrenaline Rush Silver-10
  Forward Thinking-16
  Preeminent Players-10
  Team Checklists-21
98Pacific Omega-195
  Red-195
  Opening Day Issue-195
  Championship Spotlight-9
  Championship Spotlight Green-9
  Championship Spotlight Red-9
  Championship Spotlight Gold-9
  EO Portraits-18
  EO Portraits 1 of 1-18
  Face to Face-3
  Online-30
  Planet Ice-27
  Planet Ice Parallel-27
  Prism-18
  Toronto Spring Expo-195
98Panini Photocards-35
98Panini Photocards-97
98Panini Stickers-4
98Panini Stickers-48
98Paramount-192
  Copper-192
  Emerald Green-192
  Holo-Electric-192
  Ice Blue-192
  Silver-192
  Hall of Fame Bound-9
  Hall of Fame Bound Proofs-9
  Special Delivery Die-Cuts-16
  Team Checklists Die-Cuts-21
98Revolution-118
  Ice Shadow-118
  Red-118
  All-Star Die Cuts-12
  Chalk Talk Laser-Cuts-16
  NHL Icons-10
  Showstoppers-31
  Three Pronged Attack-29
  Three Pronged Attack Parallel-29
98SP Authentic-70
  Power Shift-70
  Snapshots-SS5
  Stat Masters-S7
98SPx Finite-94
98SPx Finite-165
98SPx Finite-174
  Radiance-94
  Radiance-165
  Radiance-174
  Spectrum-94
  Spectrum-165
  Spectrum-174
98SPx Top Prospects-49
  Radiance-49
  Spectrum-49
  Highlight Heroes-H25
  Lasting Impressions-L18
  Premier Stars-PS11
  Winning Materials-JJ
98Topps-111
  O-Pee-Chee-111
  Autographs-A5
  Local Legends-L4
  Mystery Finest Bronze-M6
  Mystery Finest Bronze Refractors-M6
  Mystery Finest Gold-M6
  Mystery Finest Gold Refractors-M6
  Mystery Finest Silver-M6
  Mystery Finest Silver Refractors-M6
  Season's Best-SB19
98Topps Gold Label Class 1-5
  Black-5
  Black One of One-5
  One of One-5
  Red-5
  Red One of One-5
98Topps Gold Label Class 2-5
98Topps Gold Label Class 2 Black-5
98Topps Gold Label Class 2 Black 1 of 1-5
98Topps Gold Label Class 2 One of One-5
98Topps Gold Label Class 2 Red-5
98Topps Gold Label Class 2 Red One of One-5
98Topps Gold Label Class 3-5
98Topps Gold Label Class 3 Black-5
98Topps Gold Label Class 3 Black 1 of 1-5
98Topps Gold Label Class 3 One of One-5
98Topps Gold Label Class 3 Red-5
98Topps Gold Label Class 3 Red One of One-5
98Topps Gold Label Goal Race '99-GR5
98Topps Gold Label Goal Race '99 Black-GR5
98Topps Gold Label Goal '99 Black 1 of 1-GR5
98Topps Gold Label Goal Race 99 1 of 1-GR5
98Topps Gold Label Goal Race '99 Red-GR5
98Topps Gold Label GoalRace 99 Red 1 of 1-GR5
98UD Choice-168
98UD Choice-226
  Mini Bobbing Head-BH5
  Prime Choice Reserve-168
  Prime Choice Reserve-226
  Reserve-168
  Reserve-226
  StarQuest Blue-SQ16
  StarQuest Gold-SQ16
  StarQuest Green-SQ16
  StarQuest Red-SQ16
98UD3-32
98UD3-92
98UD3-152
  Die-Cuts-32
  Die-Cuts-92
  Die-Cuts-152
98Upper Deck-27
98Upper Deck-161
  Exclusives-27
  Exclusives-161
  Exclusives 1 of 1-27
  Exclusives 1 of 1-161
  Fantastic Finishers-FF4
  Fantastic Finishers Quantum 1-FF4
  Fantastic Finishers Quantum 2-FF4
  Fantastic Finishers Quantum 3-FF4
  Frozen In Time-FT29
  Frozen In Time Quantum 1-FT29
  Frozen In Time Quantum 2-FT29
  Frozen In Time Quantum 3-FT29
  Game Jerseys-GJ16
  Generation Next-GN22
  Generation Next-GN23
  Generation Next-GN24
  Generation Next Quantum 1-GN22
  Generation Next Quantum 1-GN23
  Generation Next Quantum 1-GN24
  Generation Next Quantum 2-GN22
  Generation Next Quantum 2-GN23
  Generation Next Quantum 2-GN24
  Generation Next Quantum 3-GN22
  Generation Next Quantum 3-GN23
  Generation Next Quantum 3-GN24
  Lord Stanley's Heroes-LS3
  Lord Stanley's Heroes Quantum 1-LS3
  Lord Stanley's Heroes Quantum 2-LS3
  Lord Stanley's Heroes Quantum 3-LS3
  Profiles-P10
  Profiles Quantum 1-P10
  Profiles Quantum 2-P10
  Profiles Quantum 3-P10
  Gold Reserve-27
  Gold Reserve-161
98Upper Deck MVP-163
  Gold Script-163
  Silver Script-163
  Super Script-163
  OT Heroes-OT3
  Power Game-PG10
  Special Forces-F11
98Czech OFS-247
  Olympic Winners-3
98Czech Bonaparte-2B
98Czech Bonaparte-3C
98Czech Bonaparte-5C
98Czech Bonaparte-6D
98Czech Bonaparte-HOKEJ
98Czech Bonaparte Tall-2
98Czech Pexeso-10
98Czech Pexeso-18
98Czech Spaghetti-1
98Slovakian Eurotel-7
99SLU Hockey 12" Figures-4
99SLU Hockey-6
99SLU Hockey Pro Action-20
99Aurora-116
  Striped-116
  Premiere Date-116
  Premiere Date Striped-116
  Canvas Creations-10
  Championship Fever-18
  Championship Fever Copper-18
  Championship Fever Ice Blue-18
  Championship Fever Silver-18
  Complete Players-10
  Complete Players Parallel-10
  Complete Players Retail-10
  Complete Players Retail Parallel-10
  Styrotechs-17
99BAP Memorabilia-147
  Gold-147
  Silver-147
  Jersey Cards-J18
  Jersey Emblems-E18
  Jersey Numbers-I18
  Jersey and Stick Cards-S18
  Selects Silver-SL3
  Selects Gold-SL3
99BAP Update Double AS Jersey Cards-D1
99BAP Update Teammates Jersey Cards-TM8
99BAP Update Teammates Jersey Cards-TM19
99BAP Update Teammates Jersey Cards-TM32
99BAP Millennium-194
99BAP Millennium-NNO
  Emerald-194
  Ruby-194
  Sapphire-194
  Signatures-194
  Signatures Gold-194
  Jerseys-J12
  Jersey and Stick Cards-JS12
  Jersey Emblems-E12
  Jersey Numbers-N12
  Pearson-P1
  Pearson Autographs-P1
  Players of the Decade-D5
  Players of the Decade Autographs-D5
99Black Diamond-68
  Diamond Cut-68
  Final Cut-68
  A Piece of History-JJ
  A Piece of History Double-JJ
  A Piece of History Triple-JJ
  Diamonation-D14
  Diamond Might-DM5
  Diamond Skills-DS7
  Myriad-M8
99Crown Royale-112
  Limited Series-112
  Premiere Date-112
  Card-Supials-18
  Card-Supials Minis-18
  Century 21-9
  Cramer's Choice Jumbos-10
  Cramer's Choice Jumbos Dark Blue-10
  Cramer's Choice Jumbos Gold-10
  Cramer's Choice Jumbos Green-10
  Cramer's Choice Jumbos Light Blue-10
  Cramer's Choice Jumbos Purple-10
  Cramer's Choice Jumbos Red-10
  International Glory-21
  International Glory Parallel-21
  Team Captain Die-Cuts-7
99Hasbro Starting Lineup Cards-6
99Jell-O Partners of Power-2
99Kraft Dinner-2
99Kraft Peanut Butter-5
99Kraft Overtime Winners-5
99McDonald's Upper Deck-MCD6
99McDonald's Upper Deck-MCD6R
  Game Jerseys-GJJJ
99O-Pee-Chee-5
99O-Pee-Chee-280A
99O-Pee-Chee-280B
99O-Pee-Chee-280C
99O-Pee-Chee-280D

99O-Pee-Chee-280E
99O-Pee-Chee All-Topps-AT13
99O-Pee-Chee Chrome-5
99O-Pee-Chee Chrome-280A
99O-Pee-Chee Chrome-280B
99O-Pee-Chee Chrome-280C
99O-Pee-Chee Chrome-280D
99O-Pee-Chee Chrome-280E
99O-Pee-Chee Chrome All Topps-AT13
99O-Pee-Chee Chrome All-Topps Refractors-AT13
99O-Pee-Chee Chrome Ice Masters-IM4
99O-Pee-Chee Chrome Ice Masters Refractor-IM4
99O-Pee-Chee Chrome Refractors-5
99O-Pee-Chee Chrome Refractors-280A
99O-Pee-Chee Chrome Refractors-280B
99O-Pee-Chee Chrome Refractors-280C
99O-Pee-Chee Chrome Refractors-280D
99O-Pee-Chee Chrome Refractors-280E
99O-Pee-Chee Chrome A-Men-AM1
99O-Pee-Chee Chrome A-Men Refractors-AM1
99O-Pee-Chee Chrome Fantastic Finishers-FF2
99OPC Chrome Fantastic Finishers Ref-FF2
99O-Pee-Chee Ice Masters-IM4
99O-Pee-Chee A-Men-AM1
99O-Pee-Chee Fantastic Finishers-FF2
99O-Pee-Chee Top of the World-TW17
99Oscar Mayer Lunchables-4
99Pacific-338
Copper-338
Emerald Green-338
Gold-338
Ice Blue-338
Premiere Date-338
Red-338
Center Ice-17
Center Ice Proofs-17
Cramer's Choice-9
Gold Crown Die-Cuts-31
Home and Away-10
Home and Away-20
Past and Present-19
Team Leaders-22
99Pacific Dynagon Ice-159
Blue-159
Copper-159
Gold-159
Premiere Date-159
2000 All-Star Preview-16
Checkmates American-13
Checkmates American-28
Checkmates Canadian-28
Lamplighter Net-Fusions-10
Lords of the Rink-10
99Pacific Omega-188
Copper-188
Gold-188
Ice Blue-188
Premiere Date-188
Cup Contenders-17
EO Portraits-16
EO Portraits 1/1-16
Game-Used Jerseys-9
NHL Generations-10
5 Star Talents-18
5 Star Talents Parallel-18
World All-Stars-6
99Pacific Prism-114
Holographic Blue-114
Holographic Gold-114
Holographic Mirror-114
Holographic Purple-114
Premiere Date-114
Clear Advantage-18
Dial-a-Stats-9
Sno-Globe Die-Cuts-19
99Panini Stickers-3
99Panini Stickers-131
99Panini Stickers-317
99Paramount-189
Copper-189
Emerald-189
Gold-189
Holographic Emerald-189
Holographic Gold-189
Holographic Silver-189
Ice Blue-189
Premiere Date-189
Red-189
Silver-189
Hall of Fame Bound-9
Hall of Fame Bound Proofs-9
Ice Advantage-17
Ice Advantage Proofs-17
Ice Alliance-22
Personal Best-31
Toronto Fall Expo '99-189
99Revolution-118
Premiere Date-118
Red-118
Shadow Series-118
Ice Sculptures-10
NHL Icons-17
Ornaments-16
Top of the Line-29
Copper-118
Gold-118
CSC Silver-118
99SP Authentic-68
Honor Roll-HR6
Special Forces-SF7
Supreme Skill-SS11
99SPx-120
Radiance-120
Spectrum-120
Highlight Heroes-HH4
Prolifics-P2
SPXcitement-X15
SPXtreme-XT11
Starscape-S2
Winning Materials-WM4
99Stadium Club-1
First Day Issue-1
One of a Kind-1
Printing Plates Black-1
Printing Plates Cyan-1
Printing Plates Magenta-1
Printing Plates Yellow-1
Capture the Action-CA26
Capture the Action Game View-CAG26
Chrome-1
Chrome Refractors-1
Chrome Oversized-1
Chrome Oversized Refractors-1
Co-Signers-CS4
Co-Signers-CS5
Co-Signers-CS6
Eyes of the Game-EG1
Eyes of the Game Refractors-EG1
Lone Star Signatures-LS1
Onyx Extreme-OE1
Onyx Extreme Die-Cut-OE1
99Topps/OPC-5
99Topps/OPC-280A
99Topps/OPC-280B
99Topps/OPC-280C
99Topps/OPC-280D
99Topps/OPC-280E
All-Topps-AT13
A-Men-AM1
Fantastic Finishers-FF2
Ice Masters-IM4
99Topps Stanley Cup Heroes-SC11
99Topps Stanley Cup Heroes Refractors-SC11
99Topps/OPC Top of the World-TW17
99Topps/OPC Chrome-5
99Topps/OPC Chrome-280A
99Topps/OPC Chrome-280B
99Topps/OPC Chrome-280C
99Topps/OPC Chrome-280D
99Topps/OPC Chrome-280E
Refractors-5
Refractors-280A
Refractors-280B
Refractors-280C
Refractors-280D
Refractors-280E
All-Topps-AT13
All-Topps Refractors-AT13
A-Men-AM1
A-Men Refractors-AM1
Fantastic Finishers-FF2
Fantastic Finishers Refractors-FF2
Ice Masters-IM4
Ice Masters Refractors-IM4
99Topps Gold Label Class 1-15
Black-15
Black One of One-15
One of One-15
Red-15
Red One of One-15
99Topps Gold Label Class 2-15
99Topps Gold Label Class 2 Black-15
99Topps Gold Label Class 2 Black 1 of 1-15
99Topps Gold Label Class 2 One of One-15
99Topps Gold Label Class 2 Red-15
99Topps Gold Label Class 2 Red One of One-15
99Topps Gold Label Class 3-15
99Topps Gold Label Class 3 Black-15
99Topps Gold Label Class 3 Black 1 of 1-15
99Topps Gold Label Class 3 One of One-15
99Topps Gold Label Class 3 Red-15
99Topps Gold Label Class 3 Red One of One-15
99Topps Gold Label Prime Gold-PG4
99Topps Gold Label Prime Gold One of One -PG4
99Topps Gold Label Prime Gold Black-PG4
99Topps Gold Label Prime Gold Black One of One -PG4
99Topps Gold Label Prime Gold Red-PG4
99Topps Gold Label Prime Gold Red One of One -PG4
99Topps Pearson Award-1
99Topps Premier Plus-34
Parallel-34
Club Signings-CS5
Club Signings-CSC3
Code Red-CR6
Feature Presentations-FP7
Premier Team-PT2
Premier Team Parallel-PT2
99Ultimate Victory-69
1/1-69
Parallel-69
Parallel 100-69
Frozen Fury-FF8
Smokin Guns-SG1
Stature-S11
The Victors-V4
UV Extra-UV1
99Upper Deck-104
99Upper Deck-138
Exclusives-104
Exclusives-138
Exclusives 1 of 1-104
Exclusives 1 of 1-138
All-Star Class-AS3
All-Star Class Quantum Gold-AS3
All-Star Class Quantum Silver-AS3
Crunch Time-CT9
Crunch Time Quantum Gold-CT9
Crunch Time Quantum Silver-CT9
Fantastic Finishers-FF4
Fantastic Finishers Quantum Gold-FF4
Fantastic Finishers Quantum Silver-FF4
Game Jerseys-JJ
Game Jerseys Series II-JJ
Game Jersey Patch-JJP
Game Jersey Patch 1 of 1-JJSP
Game Jersey Patch Series II-JJP
Game Jersey Patch Series II 1 of 1-JJ-P1
Headed for the Hall-HOF5
Headed for the Hall Quantum Gold-HOF5
Headed for the Hall Quantum Silver-HOF5
Ice Gallery-IG1
Ice Gallery Quantum Gold-IG1
Ice Gallery Quantum Silver-IG1
Marquee Attractions-MA4
Marquee Attractions Quantum Gold-MA4
Marquee Attractions Quantum Silver-MA4
New Ice Age-N1
New Ice Age Quantum Gold-N1
New Ice Age Quantum Silver-N1
NHL Scrapbook-SB4
NHL Scrapbook Quantum Gold-SB4
NHL Scrapbook Quantum Silver-SB4
PowerDeck Inserts-PD3
Sixth Sense-SS9
Sixth Sense Quantum Gold-SS9
Sixth Sense Quantum Silver-SS9
99Upper Deck Century Legends-37
99Upper Deck Century Legends-52
Century Collection-37
Century Collection-52
Essence of the Game-E3
99Upper Deck Gold Reserve-104
99Upper Deck Gold Reserve-138
99Upper Deck HoloGrFx-47
Ausome-47
Impact Zone-IZ2
Impact Zone Ausome-IZ2
Pure Skill-PS9
Pure Skill Ausome-PS9
99Upper Deck MVP-165
Gold Script-165
Silver Script-165
Super Script-165
21st Century NHL-6
90's Snapshots-S2
Draw Your Own Trading Card-W14
Game-Used Souvenirs-GU12
Hands of Gold-H9
Talent-MVP8
99Upper Deck MVP SC Edition-146
Gold Script-146
Silver Script-146
Super Script-146
Clutch Performers-CP9
Golden Memories-GM9
Great Combinations-GCJS
Great Combinations Parallel-GCJS
Playoff Heroes-PH9
Second Season Snipers-SS10
Stanley Cup Talent-SC14
99Upper Deck Ovation-46
99Upper Deck Ovation-81
Standing Ovation-46
Standing Ovation-81
A Piece Of History-JJ
Lead Performers-LP8
Superstar Theater-ST7
99Upper Deck PowerDeck-17
Auxiliary-17
Auxiliary 1 of 1-17
Time Capsule-T1
Time Capsule Auxiliary-T1
Time Capsule Auxiliary 1 of 1-T1
99Upper Deck Retro-64
Gold-64
Platinum-64
Distant Replay-DR3
Distant Replay Level 2-DR3
Turn of the Century-TC3
99Upper Deck Victory-234
99Upper Deck Victory-235
99Upper Deck Victory-315
99Upper Deck Victory-328
99Upper Deck Victory-331
99Upper Deck Victory-336
99Wayne Gretzky Hockey-136
Changing The Game-CG4
Elements of the Game-EG11
Great Heroes-GH1
Will to Win-W3
99Czech DS-GC
National Stars-NS3
Premium-P6
99Czech OFS-23
99Czech OFS Jagr Team Embossed-23
99Slovakian Challengers-27
00SLU Hockey One On One-20
00McFarlane Hockey-100
00SLU Hockey-120
00Aurora-116
Pinstripes-116
Pinstripes Premiere Date-116
Premiere Date-116
Canvas Creations-9
Championship Fever-19
Championship Fever Copper-19
Championship Fever Platinum Blue-19
Championship Fever Silver-19
Dual Game-Worn Jerseys-4
Styrotechs-9A
00BAP Memorabilia-1
Emerald-1
Ruby-1
Sapphire-1
Promos-1
Jersey Cards-J9
Jersey Emblems-E9
Jersey Numbers-N9
Jersey and Stick Cards-JS9
Patent Power Jerseys-PP3
00BAP Mem Chicago Sportsfest Copper-1
00BAP Memorabilia Chicago Sportsfest Blue-1
00BAP Memorabilia Chicago Sportsfest Gold-1
00BAP Memorabilia Chicago Sportsfest Ruby-1
00BAP Memorabilia Chicago Sun-Times Ruby-1
00BAP Memorabilia Chicago Sun-Times Gold-1
00BAP Mem Chicago Sun-Times Sapphire-1
00BAP Mem Toronto Fall Expo Copper-1
00BAP Memorabilia Toronto Fall Expo Gold-1
00BAP Memorabilia Toronto Fall Expo Ruby-1
00BAP Memorabilia Update Teammates-TM3
00BAP Memorabilia Update Teammates-TM20
00BAP Memorabilia Update Teammates Gold-TM3
00BAP Memorabilia Update Teammates Gold-TM20
00BAP Parkhurst 2000-P215
00BAP Signature Series-22
Emerald-22
Ruby-22
Sapphire-22
Franchise Players-F24
He Shoots-He Scores Points-8
He Shoots-He Scores Prizes-40
Jersey Cards-J12
Jersey and Stick Cards-GSJ12
Jersey Cards Autographs-J12
Jersey Emblems-E12
Jersey Numbers-IN12
00BAP Ultimate Memorabilia Active Eight-AE4
00BAP Ultimate Memorabilia Captain's C-C5
00BAP Ultimate Mem Dynasty Jerseys-D8
00BAP Ultimate Mem Dynasty Emblems-D8
00BAP Ultimate Mem Game-Used Jerseys-GJ12
00BAP Ultimate Mem Game-Used Emblems-E10
00BAP Ultimate Mem Game-Used Numbers-N10
00BAP Ultimate Mem Game-Used Sticks-GS12
00BAP Ultimate Memorabilia Hart Trophy-H2
00BAP Ultimate Mem Magnificent Ones-ML2
00BAP Ultimate Mem Magnificent Ones Autos-ML2
00BAP Ultimate Memorabilia Retro-Active-RA9
00BAP Ultimate Memorabilia Teammates-TM39
00Black Diamond-47
00Black Diamond-90
Gold-47
Gold-90
Diamonation-IG7
Diamond Might-FP9
Diamond Skills-IC6
Game Gear-SJA
Myriad-CC5
00Crown Royale-86
Ice Blue-86
Limited Series-86
Premiere Date-86
Red-86
Game-Worn Jersey Redemptions-9
Jewels of the Crown-21
Landmarks-8
Now Playing-14
00Kraft-1
00McDonald's Pacific-27
Blue-27
Dial-A-Stats-5
Game Jerseys-9
00O-Pee-Chee-1
00O-Pee-Chee Parallel-1
00Pacific-328
Copper-328
Gold-328
Ice Blue-328
Premiere Date-328
2001: Ice Odyssey-18
Cramer's Choice-9
Euro-Stars-6
Jerseys-13
Jersey Patches-13
Gold Crown Die Cuts-28
Reflections-17
00Pacific 2001: Ice Odyssey Anaheim Ntnl-18
00Panini Stickers-81
00Paramount-198
Copper-198
Gold-198
Holo-Gold-198
Holo-Silver-198
Ice Blue-198
Premiere Date-198
Epic Scope-17
Freeze Frame-28
Hall of Fame Bound-10
Hall of Fame Bound Canvas Proofs-10
Hall of Fame Bound Proofs-10
Sub Zero-8
Sub Zero Gold-8
Sub Zero Red-1
00Private Stock-80
Gold-80
Premiere Date-80
Retail-80
Silver-80
Artist's Canvas-18
Artist's Canvas Proofs-18
Extreme Action-18
Game Gear-89
Game Gear Patches-89
PS-2001 Action-47
PS-2001 Stars-22
Reserve-18
00Revolution-118
Blue-118
Premiere Date-118
Red-118
Ice Immortals-18
NHL Game Gear-9
NHL Icons-17
Stat Masters-9
00SP Authentic-70
Honor-SP7
Significant Stars-ST6
Special Forces-SF7
00SP Game Used-48
Patch Cards-D-JL
Patch Cards-P-JJ
Tools of the Game-JJ
Tools of the Game Exclusives-JJ
Tools of the Game Combos-C-LJ
00SPx-54
00SPx-90
Spectrum-54
Spectrum-90
Highlight Heroes-HH12
Prolifics-P7
SPXcitement-X10
SPXtreme-S7
Winning Materials-JJ
Winning Materials-WJJ
00Stadium Club-6
Beam Team-BT6
Capture the Action-CA1
Capture the Action Game View-1
Special Forces-SF8
00Titanium-75
Blue-75
Gold-75
Premiere Date-75
Red-75
Retail-75
Game Gear-133
Game Gear-152
Game Gear Patches-133
Three-Star Selections-17
00Titanium Draft Day Edition-82
00Topps/OPC-1
Parallel-1
Combos-TC10
Combos Jumbos-TC10
Game-Worn Sweaters-GWJJ
Hobby Masters-HM5
Own the Game-OTG1
00Topps Chrome-1
OPC Refractors-1
Refractors-1
Combos-TC10
Combos Refractors-TC10
Hobby Masters Refractors-HM5
Rocket's Flare-RF4
Rocket's Flare Refractors-RF4
00Topps Gold Label Class 1-14
Gold-14
00Topps Gold Label Class 2-14
00Topps Gold Label Class 2 Gold-14
00Topps Gold Label Class 3-14
00Topps Gold Label Class 3 Gold-14
00Topps Gold Label Golden Greats-GG3
00Topps Gold Label Golden Greats 1 to 1-GG3
00Topps Heritage-3
00Topps Heritage-221
00Topps Heritage-235
00Topps Heritage-245
Chrome Parallel-3
Heroes-HH2
00Topps Premier Plus-6
Blue Ice-6
Masters of the Break-MB1
Team-PT8
Team Blue Ice-PR8
Trophy Tribute-TT2
World Premier-WP20
00Topps Stars-21
00Topps Stars-132
Blue-21
Blue-132
All-Star Authority-ASA5
Walk of Fame-WF3
00UD Heroes-155
Game-Used Twigs-T-JJ
Game-Used Twigs Gold-C-LJ
NHL Leaders-L9
Second Season Heroes-SS10
Timeless Moments-TM9
Today's Snipers-TS5
00UD Pros and Prospects-68
Championship Rings-CR8
Game Jerseys-JJ
Game Jersey Exclusives-JJ
Great Skates-GS8
NHL Passion-NP7
ProMotion-PM9
00UD Reserve-68
Power Portfolios-PP6
Practice Session Jerseys-JJ
Practice Session Jerseys Autographs-JJ
The Big Ticket-BT9
00Upper Deck-138
Exclusives Tier 1-138
Exclusives Tier 2-138
All-Star Class-A9
Dignitaries-D9
Fantastic Finishers-FF9
Frozen in Time-FT7
Fun-Damentals-F8
Game Jerseys-JJ
Game Jerseys-JJ
Game Jersey Autographs Exclusives-EJJ
Game Jersey Combos-DJL
Game Jersey Doubles-DJJ
Game Jersey Patches-JJP
Game Jersey Patches-PJJ
Game Jersey Patch Autographs Exclusives-JJP
Game Jersey Patch Exclusives Series II-EJJ
Gate Attractions-GA10
Lord Stanley's Heroes-L9
Number Crunchers-NC7
Profiles-P8
Skilled Stars-SS17
Triple Threat-TT9
00Upper Deck Ice-32
Immortals-32
Legends-32
Stars-32
Champions-IC6
Cool Competitors-CC5
Gallery-IG7
Game Jerseys-JCJJ
Rink Favorites-FP9
00Upper Deck Legends-107
00Upper Deck Legends-108
Legendary Collection Bronze-107
Legendary Collection Bronze-108
Legendary Collection Gold-107
Legendary Collection Gold-108
Legendary Collection Silver-107
Legendary Collection Silver-108
Essence of the Game-EG2
Legendary Game Jerseys-JJJ
Playoff Heroes-PH3
00Upper Deck MVP-143
First Stars-143
Game-Used Souvenirs-GSJJ
Second Stars-143
Super Game-Used Souvenirs-GSJJ
Talent-M14
Third Stars-143
Top Draws-TD10
Top Playmakers-TP9
Valuable Commodities-VC9
00Upper Deck Victory-183
00Upper Deck Victory-184
00Upper Deck Victory-256
00Upper Deck Victory-318
00Upper Deck Vintage-286
00Upper Deck Vintage-295
00Upper Deck Vintage-296
All UD Team-UD9
Dynasty: A Piece of History-LJ
Dynasty: A Piece of History Gold-LJ
National Heroes-NH19
00Vanguard-80
Cosmic Force-9
High Voltage-29
High Voltage Gold-29
High Voltage Green-29
High Voltage Red-29
High Voltage Silver-29
Holographic Gold-80
Holographic Purple-80
In Focus-15
Pacific Proofs-80
Press East/West-18
00Czech DS Extraliga Best of the Best-BBJ1
00Czech DS Extraliga Best of the Best-BBJ2
00Czech DS Extraliga Best of the Best-BBJ2
00Czech DS Extraliga Team Jagr-JT12
00Czech DS Extraliga Team Jagr Parallel-JT8
00Czech OFS-384
00Czech OFS-417
00Czech Stadion-57
00Czech Stadion-83
00Czech Stadion-146
00Czech Stadion-162
01McFarlane Hockey-75
01McFarlane Hockey-76
01Atomic-98
Blue-98
Gold-98
Premiere Date-98
Red-98
Blast-10
Core Players-20
Jerseys-50
Patches-50
Power Play-36
Statosphere-20
Team Nucleus-15
01BAP Memorabilia-129
Emerald-129
Ruby-129
Sapphire-129
All-Star Jerseys-ASJ37
All-Star Emblems-ASE37
All-Star Numbers-ASN37
All-Star Jersey Doubles-DASJ20
All-Star Teammates-AST21
All-Star Teammates-AST32
All-Star Teammates-AST36
All-Star Teammates-AST47
Country of Origin-CO24
He Shoots-He Scores Prizes-2
Patented Power-PP1
01BAP Signature Series Certified 100-C53
01BAP Signature Series Certified 50-C53
01BAP Signature Series Certified 1 of 1's-C53
01BAP Signature Series Franchise Jerseys-FP-30
01BAP Sig Series He Shoots/Scores Points-14
01BAP Sig Series He Shoots/Scores Prizes-8
01BAP Signature Series Jerseys-GJ-53
01BAP Sig Series Jersey and Stick Cards-GSJ-53
01BAP Signature Series Emblems-GUE-43
01BAP Signature Series Numbers-ITN-43
01BAP Signature Series Teammates-TM-30
01BAP Ultimate Memorabilia Active Eight-4
01BAP Ultimate Mem All-Star History-43
01BAP Ultimate Memorabilia Captain's C-6
01BAP Ultimate Mem Dynamic Duos-2
01BAP Ultimate Memorabilia Emblems-14
01BAP Ultimate Memorabilia Jerseys-14
01BAP Ultimate Mem Jerseys and Sticks-14
01BAP Ultimate Mem Journey Jerseys-20
01BAP Ultimate Mem Journey Emblems-20
01BAP Ultimate Memorabilia Name Plates-27
01BAP Ultimate Mem Prototypical Players-13
01BAP Ultimate Memorabilia Retro Trophies-2
01BAP Ultimate Memorabilia Retro Trophies-3
01BAP Ultimate Mem Retro Teammates-11
01BAP Update Travel Plans-TP1
01Bowman YoungStars-4
Gold-4
Ice Cubed-4
01Crown Royale-142
Blue-142
Premiere Date-142
Red-142
Retail-142
Crowning Achievement-20
Jewels of the Crown-30
Legendary Heroes-10
Triple Threads-20
01eTopps-34
01McDonald's Pacific-42
Cosmic Force-6
Jersey Patches Silver-20
Jersey Patches Gold-20
01Nortel All-Star Game Sheets-1
01O-Pee-Chee-32
01O-Pee-Chee-320
01O-Pee-Chee-325
01O-Pee-Chee-32U
01O-Pee-Chee Heritage Parallel-32
01O-Pee-Chee Heritage Parallel Limited-32
01O-Pee-Chee Premier Parallel-32
01O-Pee-Chee Premier Parallel-320
01O-Pee-Chee Premier Parallel-325
01Pacific-312
01Pacific-439
Extreme LTD-312
Gold-439
Hobby LTD-312
Premiere Date-312
Retail LTD-312
Cramer's Choice-8
Jerseys-27
Gold Crown Die-Cuts-16
01Pacific Adrenaline-197
Blue-197
Premiere Date-197
Red-197
Retail-197
Blade Runners-10
Jerseys-50
World Beaters-20
01Pacific Arena Exclusives-312
01Pacific Arena Exclusives-439
01Pacific Heads-Up-98
Blue-98
Premiere Date-98
Red-98
Silver-98
HD NHL-10
Quad Jerseys-17
Rink Immortals-10
Stat Masters-20
01Parkhurst-34
Gold-34
Silver-34
He Shoots-He Scores Prizes-28
Milestones-M3
Milestones-M4
Milestones-M8
Milestones-M49
Sticks-PS58
Teammates-T27
World Class Jerseys-WCJ7
World Class Emblems-WCE7
World Class Numbers-WCN7
Waving the Flag-9
01Private Stock-98
Gold-98
Premiere Date-98
Retail-98
Silver-98
Game Gear-100
Game Gear Patches-100
01Private Stock Pacific Nights-98
01Private Stock PS-2002-75
01Private Stock Reserve-S20
01SP Authentic-90
01SP Authentic-110
Limited-90
Limited-110
Limited Gold-90
Limited Gold-110
01SP Game Used-58
Authentic Fabric-AFJJ
Authentic Fabric Gold-AFJJ
Patches-PJJ
Patches-CPJB
Patches-CPLJ
Tools of the Game-TJA
Tools of the Game-TJJ
Tools of the Game-CTLJ
01SPx-68
Hidden Treasures-DTBJ
01Sports Illustrated for Kids III-159
01Sports Illustrated for Kids III-265
01Stadium Club-109
Award Winners-109
Master Photos-109
Gallery-G16
Gallery Gold-G16
01Titanium-142
Hobby Parallel-142
Premiere Date-142
Retail-142
Retail Parallel-142
All-Stars-20
Double-Sided Jerseys-43
Double-Sided Patches-43
Three-Star Selections-20
01Titanium Draft Day Edition-100
01Topps-32
01Topps-32U
01Topps-320
01Topps-325
Heritage Parallel-32
Heritage Parallel Limited-32
OPC Parallel-32
OPC Parallel-320
OPC Parallel-325
Captain's Cloth-CC1
Captain's Cloth-CC2
Own The Game-OTG1
Shot Masters-SM5
01Topps Chrome-32
Refractors-32
Black Border Refractors-32
01Topps Heritage-113
01Topps Heritage-123
01Topps Heritage-137
01Topps Heritage-160
01Topps Reserve-74
01UD Challenge for the Cup-88
Century Men-CM7
Cornerstones-CR10
01UD Honor Roll-9
01UD Honor Roll-39
01UD Honor Roll-100
01UD Mask Collection-100
Gold-100
Double Patches-DPJJ
Jerseys-J-JJ
Jersey and Patch-JPJJ
01UD Playmakers-100
01UD Premier Collection-50
Dual Jerseys-DHJ
Dual Jerseys-DJB
Dual Jerseys Black-DHJ
Dual Jerseys Black-DJB
Jerseys-BJA
Jerseys-BJJ
Jerseys Black-B-JA
Jerseys Black-B-JJ
01UD Stanley Cup Champs-85
Jerseys-T-JJ
Pieces of Glory-G-JJ
Sticks-S-JJ
01UD Top Shelf-45
Jerseys-JJ
Patches-PJJ
Sticks-BFJ
01Upper Deck-178
01Upper Deck-226
01Upper Deck-404
Exclusives-178
Exclusives-226
Exclusives-404
Crunch Timers-CT14
Game Jerseys-AJJ
Game Jerseys-CLJ
Game Jerseys Series II-PFJJ
Patches-PJJ
Patches Series II-PLJJ
Pride of a Nation-PNJJ
Pride of a Nation-DPHJ
Pride of a Nation-TPHJL
Shooting Stars-SS19
01Upper Deck Ice-42
Combos-C-JJ
Combos Gold-G-JJ
First Rounders-F-JJ
01Upper Deck MVP-188
Morning Skate Jerseys-J-JJ
Souvenirs-S-JJ
Souvenirs Gold-S-JJ
Watch-MW3
01Upper Deck Pearson Awards-1
01Upper Deck Victory-278
01Upper Deck Victory-392
Gold-278
Gold-392
01Upper Deck Vintage-256
01Upper Deck Vintage-261
01Upper Deck Vintage-262
01Upper Deck Vintage-263
01Vanguard-99
Blue-99
Red-99
East Meets West-1
In Focus-10
Memorabilia-33
Memorabilia-42
One of Ones-99
Patches-33
Premiere Date-99
Proofs-99
V-Team-20
01Czech DS-36
Ice Heroes-IH2
Top Gallery-1
Top Gallery-2
01Czech National Team Postcards-6
01Czech Stadion-251
01Czech Stadion-252
02Atomic-99
Blue-99
Gold-99
Red-99
Cold Fusion-24
Hobby Parallel-99
Jerseys-24
Jerseys Gold-24
Patches-24
02BAP All-Star Edition-34
02BAP All-Star Edition-35
02BAP All-Star Edition-36
He Shoots-He Scores Points-12
He Shoots-He Score Prizes-8
Jerseys-34
Jerseys-35
Jerseys-36
Jerseys Gold-34
Jerseys Gold-35
Jerseys Gold-36
Jerseys Silver-34
Jerseys Silver-35
Jerseys Silver-36
02BAP First Edition-131
02BAP First Edition-310
02BAP First Edition-370
02BAP First Edition-399
02BAP First Edition-404R
Debut Jerseys-12
He Shoots-He Scores Prizes-28
Jerseys-131
Scoring Leaders-20
02BAP Memorabilia-34
02BAP Memorabilia-230
02BAP Memorabilia-237
Emerald-34
Emerald-230
Emerald-237
Ruby-34
Ruby-230
Ruby-237
Sapphire-34
Sapphire-230
Sapphire-237
All-Star Jerseys-ASJ-22
All-Star Emblems-ASE-8
All-Star Numbers-ASN-8
All-Star Starting Lineup-AS-11
All-Star Teammmates-AST-5
All-Star Teammmates-AST-11
All-Star Teammmates-AST-16
All-Star Teammates-AST-29
All-Star Triple Jerseys-ASTJ-6
Franchise Players-FP-30
He Shoots-He Scores Points-17
He Shoots-He Scores Prizes-4
Mini Stanley Cups-30
NHL All-Star Game-34
NHL All-Star Game-230
NHL All-Star Game-237
NHL All-Star Game Blue-34
NHL All-Star Game Blue-230
NHL All-Star Game Blue-237
NHL All-Star Game Green-34
NHL All-Star Game Green-230
NHL All-Star Game Green-237
NHL All-Star Game Red-34
NHL All-Star Game Red-230
NHL All-Star Game Red-237
Teammates-TM-11
02BAP Memorabilia Toronto Fall Expo-34
02BAP Memorabilia Toronto Fall Expo-230
02BAP Memorabilia Toronto Fall Expo-237
02BAP NHL All-Star History-43
02BAP Sig Series Auto Buybacks 1998-261
02BAP Sig Series Auto Buybacks 1999-194
02BAP Signature Series Complete Jersey-CJ5
02BAP Signature Series Franchise Players-FJ30
02BAP Signature Series Jerseys-SGJ7
02BAP Signature Series Jersey Autographs-SGJ7
02BAP Signature Series Team Quads-TQ9
02BAP Ultimate Memorabilia Dynamic Duos-9
02BAP Ultimate Memorabilia Emblems-8
02BAP Ultimate Mem 500 Goal Scorers-3
02BAP Ultimate Mem 500 Goal Jersey/Stick-3
02BAP Ultimate Mem 500 Goal Emblems-3
02BAP Ultimate Memorabilia Jerseys-12
02BAP Ultimate Mem Jersey and Stick-14
02BAP Ultimate Mem Journey Jerseys-3
02BAP Ultimate Mem Journey Emblems-3
02BAP Ultimate Mem Lifetime Achievers-6
02BAP Ultimate Mem Magnificent Ones-3
02BAP Ultimate Mem Magnificent Ones Autos-3
02BAP Ultimate Memorabilia Nameplates-1
02BAP Ultimate Memorabilia Numbers-6
02BAP Ultimate Mem Retro Teammates-6
02BAP Ultimate Memorabilia Retro Trophies-6
02BAP Ultimate Mem Scoring Leaders-4
02BAP Ultimate Mem Scoring Leaders-5
02BAP Ultimate Mem Scoring Leaders-6
02BAP Ultimate Mem Scoring Leaders-9
02Between the Pipes Nightmares-GN3
02Bowman YoungStars-11
Gold-11
Silver-11
02Capitals Team Issue-4
02Crown Royale-99
Blue-99
Red-99
Retail-99
Jerseys-25
Jerseys Gold-25
Lords of the Rink-20
Royal Portraits-10
02eTopps-5
02ITG Used-77
02ITG Used-177
Franchise Players-F30
Franchise Players Autographs-F30
Franchise Players Gold-F30
International Experience-IE2
International Experience Gold-IE2
Jerseys-GUJ7
Jersey Autographs-GUJ7
Jerseys Gold-GUJ7
Emblems-E7
Jersey and Stick-SJ7
Jersey and Stick Gold-SJ7
Teammates-T18
Teammates Gold-T18
02McDonald's Pacific-42
Atomic-6
Jersey Patches Silver-20
Jersey Patches Gold-20
02Nextel NHL All-Star Game-3
02O-Pee-Chee-5
02O-Pee-Chee-327
02O-Pee-Chee Premier Blue Parallel-5
02O-Pee-Chee Premier Blue Parallel-327
02O-Pee-Chee Premier Red Parallel-5
02O-Pee-Chee Premier Red Parallel-327
02O-Pee-Chee Factory Set-5
02O-Pee-Chee Factory Set-327
02Pacific-392
Blue-392
Red-392
Jerseys-50
Jerseys Holo-Silver-50
Lamplighters-14
Main Attractions-20
02Pacific Calder-52
Silver-52
Hardware Heroes-12
02Pacific Complete-101
Red-101
02Pacific Exclusive-172
Etched in Stone-10
Maximum Overdrive-20
02Pacific Heads-Up-124
Blue-124
Purple-124
Red-124
Etched in Time-15
Inside the Numbers-24
Quad Jerseys-32
Quad Jerseys Gold-32
Stat Masters-15
02Pacific Quest for the Cup-98
Gold-98
Jerseys-24
Raising the Cup-12
02Parkhurst-21
Bronze-21
Gold-21
Silver-21
Franchise Players-FP30
Hardware-A3
Hardware-H3
Hardware-P3
He Shoots-He Scores Points-13
He Shoots-He Scores Prizes-3
Jerseys-GJ4
Mario's Mates-MM3
Milestones-MS5
Patented Power-PP3
Stick and Jerseys-SJ4
Teammates-TT17
02Parkhurst Retro-3
Minis-3
Franchise Players-RF30
He Shoots-He Scores Points-13
He Shoots-He Scores Prizes-4
Hopefuls-HH8
Hopefuls-RR1
Jerseys-RJ14
Jersey and Sticks-RSJ27
Memorabilia-RM22
02Private Stock Reserve-149
Red-149
Retail-149
Elite-6
02SP Authentic-88
Beckett Promos-88
Super Premiums-SPJJ

Super Premiums-DPKJ
02SP Game Used-50
Authentic Fabrics-AFJJ
Authentic Fabrics-CFJB
Authentic Fabrics-CFJJ
Authentic Fabrics Gold-AFJJ
Authentic Fabrics Gold-CFJB
Authentic Fabrics Gold-CFJJ
Authentic Fabrics Rainbow-AFJJ
Authentic Fabrics Rainbow-CFJB
Authentic Fabrics Rainbow-CFJJ
First Rounder Patches-JJ
Piece of History-PHJG
Piece of History-PHJJ
Piece of History Gold-PHJG
Piece of History Gold-PHJJ
Piece of History Rainbow-PHJG
Piece of History Rainbow-PHJJ
Tools of the Game-JJ
02SPx-75
02SPx-100
02SPx-135
Spectrum Gold-75
Spectrum Gold-100
Spectrum Silver-75
Spectrum Silver-100
Smooth Skaters-JJ
Smooth Skaters Gold-JJ
Smooth Skaters Silver-JJ
Winning Materials-WMJA
Winning Materials-WMJJ
Winning Materials Gold-JA
Winning Materials Gold-JJ
Winning Materials Silver-JA
Winning Materials Silver-JJ
Xtreme Talents-JJ
Xtreme Talents Gold-JJ
Xtreme Talents Silver-JJ
02Stadium Club-5
Silver Decoy Cards-5
Proofs-5
World Stage-WS10
02Titanium-99
Blue-99
Red-99
Retail-99
Jerseys-74
Jerseys Retail-74
Patches-74
02Topps-5
02Topps-327
OPC Blue Parallel-5
OPC Blue Parallel-327
OPC Red Parallel-5
OPC Red Parallel-327
Own The Game-OTG5
Factory Set-5
Factory Set-327
02Topps Chrome All-Star Fantasy-4
02Topps Chrome-5
Black Border Refractors-5
Refractors-5
e-Topps Decoy Cards-5
02Topps Heritage-6
Chrome Parallel-6
USA Test Parallel-6
02Topps Total-101
Production-TP15
Team Checklists-TTC30
Topps-TT20
02UD Artistic Impressions-88
Gold-88
Artist's Touch-ATJJ
Artist's Touch Gold-ATJJ
02UD Artistic Impressions Beckett Promos-88
02UD Artistic Impressions Common Ground-CG2
02UD Artistic Impress Common Ground Gold-CG2
02UD Artistic Impressions Flashbacks-UD9
02UD Artistic Impressions Flashbacks Gold-UD9
02UD Artistic Impressions Performers-SSJJ
02UD Artistic Impressions Performers Gold-SSJJ
02UD Artistic Impressions Retrospectives-R88
02UD Artistic Impressions Retrospect Gold-R88
02UD Artistic Impress Retrospect Silver-R88
02Upper Deck Collectors Club-NHL8
02UD Honor Roll-70
Grade A Jerseys-GAJJ
Grade A Jerseys-TJKB
Students of the Game-SG30
02UD Mask Collection-87
02UD Mask Collection Beckett Promos-87
02UD Mask Collection Instant Offense-IOJJ
02UD Mask Collection Patches-PGJJ
02UD Piece of History-90
02UD Piece of History-102
Awards Collection-AC27
02UD Premier Collection-54
Jerseys Bronze-JG
Jerseys Bronze-JJ
Jerseys Bronze-JK
Jerseys Gold-JG
Jerseys Gold-JJ
Jerseys Gold-JK
Jerseys Silver-JG
Jerseys Silver-JJ
Jerseys Silver-JK
NHL Patches-JJ1
Patches-PJJ
02UD Top Shelf-88
All-Stars-ASJJ
Clutch Performers-CPJJ
Dual Player Jerseys-STBJ
Dual Player Jerseys-STJK
Goal Oriented-GOJJ
Hardware Heroes-HGSLJ
Hardware Heroes-HHGLJ
Shooting Stars-SHJJ
Sweet Sweaters-SWJJ
Triple Jerseys-HTJHS
Triple Jerseys-HTLJT
Triple Jerseys-TSJBK
02Upper Deck-193
02Upper Deck-419
Exclusives-193
Exclusives-419
02Upper Deck Beckett UD Promos-419
02Upper Deck Difference Makers-JJ
02Upper Deck Fan Favorites-JJ
02Upper Deck First Class-UDJJ
02Upper Deck First Class Gold-UDJJ
02Upper Deck Gifted Greats-GG14
02Upper Deck Patch Card Logo-JJ
02Upper Deck Patch Card Name Plate-JJ
02Upper Deck Patchwork-PWJJ
02Upper Deck Playbooks Series II-JK
02Upper Deck Reaching Fifty-50JJ
02Upper Deck Reaching Fifty Gold-50JJ
02Upper Deck Shooting Stars-SS14
02Upper Deck Classic Portraits-98
Genuine Greatness-GG7
Headliners-JB
Headliners Limited-JB
Hockey Royalty-JHL
Hockey Royalty-KGJ
Hockey Royalty Limited-JHL
Hockey Royalty Limited-KGJ
Mini-Busts-52
Mini-Busts-53
Mini-Busts-54
Mini-Busts-55
02Upper Deck MVP-184
Gold-184
Classics-184
Golden Classics-184
Skate Around Jerseys-SDJM
Skate Around Jerseys-STSMJ
Souvenirs-S-JJ
Vital Forces-VF14
02Upper Deck Rookie Update-98
02Upper Deck Rookie Update-109
02Upper Deck Rookie Update-158A
02Upper Deck Rookie Update-159C
Jerseys-DJJ
Jerseys-SJK
Jerseys Gold-DJJ
Jerseys Gold-SJK
02Upper Deck Victory-213
Bronze-213
Gold-213
Silver-213
National Pride-NP21
02Upper Deck Vintage-258
02Upper Deck Vintage-290
Jerseys-FSJJ
Jerseys-SOJJ
Jerseys Gold-FS-JJ
Jerseys Gold-SO-JJ
Tall Boys-T64
Tall Boys Gold-T64
02Vanguard-99
LTD-99
In Focus-10
Jerseys-50
Jerseys Gold-50
V-Team-12
02Czech DS-25
02Czech DS-46
02Czech DS-60
02Czech DS-89
02Czech DS-90
02Czech IQ Sports Blue-12
02Czech IQ Sports Yellow-1
02Czech IQ Sports Yellow-13
02Czech IQ Sports Yellow-14
02Czech Stadion Olympics-335
02UD SuperStars *-249
Gold-249
Legendary Leaders Triple Jersey-CJS
03BAP Memorabilia-34
03BAP Memorabilia-208
Emerald-34
Gold-34
Ruby-34
Sapphire-34
All-Star Emblems-ASE-8
All-Star Jerseys-ASJ-2
All-Star Jerseys-ASJ-12
All-Star Jerseys-ASJ-32
All-Star Numbers-ASN-8
All-Star Staring Lineup-5
All-Star Teammates-AST2
He Shoots-He Scores Prizes-23
Jersey and Stick-SJ-36
Jerseys-GJ-46
Jersey Autographs-GJ-46
Stanley Cup Playoffs-SCP-14
03BAP Ultimate Memorabilia Autographs-143
Gold-143
03BAP Ultimate Mem Auto Sticks-143
03BAP Ultimate Mem Always An All-Star-14
03BAP Ultimate Mem Always An AS Gold-14
03Beehive-198
Variations-198
Gold-198
Silver-198
Sticks Beige Border-BE35
Sticks Blue Border-BL17
03Black Diamond-108
Black-108
Green-108
Red-108
03Bowman-68
Gold-68
Goal to Goal-JH
03Bowman Chrome-68
Refractors-68
Gold Refractors-68
Xfractors-68
03Crown Royale-99
Blue-99
Retail-99
Global Conquest-2
Lords of the Rink-24
03eTopps-38
03ITG Action-535
Highlight Reel-HR8
Jerseys-M189
Jerseys-M209
Jerseys-M270
03ITG Toronto Fall Expo Jerseys-FE17
03ITG Used Signature Series-108
Gold-108
Autographs-JJ
Autographs Gold-JJ
International Experience-15
International Experience Autographs-15
International Experience Emblems Gold-15
International Experience Emblems-15
International Experience Gold-15
Jerseys-13
Jerseys Gold-13
Jersey Autos-13
Retrospectives-2A
Retrospectives-2B
Retrospectives-2C
Retrospectives-2D
Retrospectives-2E
Retrospectives-2F
Retrospectives Gold-2A
Retrospectives Gold-2B
Retrospectives Gold-2C
Retrospectives Gold-2D
Retrospectives Gold-2E
Retrospectives Gold-2F
03ITG VIP International Experience-9
03McDonald's Pacific-55
Etched in Time-6
03NHL Sticker Collection-144
03O-Pee-Chee-30
03O-Pee-Chee-302
03OPC Blue-30
03OPC Blue-302
03OPC Gold-30
03OPC Gold-302
03OPC Red-30
03OPC Red-302
03Pacific-345
Blue-345
Red-345
Cramer's Choice-10
Jerseys-40
Jerseys Gold-40
Main Attractions-16
Milestones-8
03Pacific Calder-67
03Pacific Calder-151
Silver-67
03Pacific Complete-238
Red-238
03Pacific Exhibit-199
Blue Backs-199
03Pacific Heads-Up-99
Hobby LTD-99
Retail LTD-99
03Pacific Invincible-99
Blue-99
Red-99
Retail-99
Featured Performers-30
Top Line-10
03Pacific Luxury Suite-50A
03Pacific Luxury Suite-50B
03Pacific Luxury Suite-50C
03Pacific Prism-150
Blue-150
Patches-150
Red-150
Retail-150
Stat Masters-10
03Pacific Quest for the Cup-69
Blue-69
Jerseys-13
03Pacific Supreme-99
Blue-99
Red-99
Retail-99
Jerseys-25
Team-10
03Parkhurst Orig Six Boston Mem -BM45
03Parkhurst Orig Six Chicago Mem -CM45
03Parkhurst Orig Six Detroit Mem-DM45
03Parkhurst Orig Six Montreal Mem-MM45
03Parkhurst Orig Six New York Mem-NM45
03Parkhurst Original Six Shooters-OSM5
03Parkhurst Orig Six Toronto Mem-TM45
03Parkhurst Rookie-29
Retro Rookies-RR-5
Retro Rookie Autographs-RR-JJ
Retro Rookies Gold-RR-5
03Private Stock Reserve-211
Blue-211
Patches-211
Red-211
Retail-211
03SP Authentic-88
Limited-88
10th Anniversary-SP7
10th Anniversary Limited-SP7
Breakout Seasons-B20
Breakout Seasons Limited-B20
03SP Game Used-50
Gold-50
Authentic Fabrics-AFJJ
Authentic Fabrics-DFJB
Authentic Fabrics Gold-AFJJ
Authentic Fabrics Gold-DFJB
Game Gear-GGJGR
Game Gear-GGJJ
Game Gear Combo-GCJJ
Limited Threads-LTJJ
Limited Threads Gold-LTJJ
Premium Patches-PPJJ
Signers-SPSJB
03SPx-98
Radiance-98
Spectrum-98
Fantasy Franchise-FF-EHJ
Fantasy Franchise Limited-FF-EHJ
Origins-O-JJ
Style-SPX-HH
Style Limited-SPX-HH
Winning Materials-WM-JG
Winning Materials-WM-JJ
Winning Materials Limited-WM-JG
Winning Materials Limited-WM-JJ
03Titanium-170
Hobby Jersey Number Parallels-170
Patches-170
Retail-170
03Topps-30
03Topps-302
03Topps-PP2
Blue-30
Blue-302
Gold-30
Gold-302
Red-30
Red-302
Box Toppers-4
First Round Fabrics-JJ
First Round Fabrics-JJJL
Topps/OPC Idols-II12
03Topps All-Star Block Party-2
03Topps C55-68
Minis-68
Minis American Back-68
Minis American Back Red-68
Minis Bazooka Back-68
Minis Brooklyn Back-68
Minis Hat Trick Back-68
Minis O Canada Back-68
Minis O Canada Back Red-68
Minis Stanley Cup Back-68
Relics-TRJJ
03Topps Pristine-90
Gold Refractor Die Cuts-90
Refractors-90
Popular Demand Relics-PD-JJ
Popular Demand Relic Refractors-PD-JJ
Press Plates Black-90
Press Plates Cyan-90
Press Plates Magenta-90
Press Plates Yellow-90
03Topps Traded-TT25
Blue-TT25
Gold-TT25
Red-TT25
03UD Honor Roll-88
03UD Honor Roll-119
03UD Premier Collection-35
03Upper Deck-440
500 Goal Club-500-JJ
500 Goal Club-500-JJA
All-Star Class-AS-30
Big Playmakers-BP-JJ
Canadian Exclusives-440
Franchise Fabrics-FF-JJ
HG-440
Highlight Heroes-HH-JJ
Highlight Heroes Jerseys-HH-JJ
Patches-LD10
Superstar Spotlight-SS10
Team Essentials-TS-JJ
Three Stars-TS5
UD Exclusives-440
03Upper Deck Classic Portraits-98
03Upper Deck Classic Portraits-142
Classic Colors-CC-JJ
Headliners-HH-JJ
03Upper Deck Ice-60
Gold-60
Breakers-IB-JJ
Breaker Patches-IB-JJ
Clear Cut Winners-CC-JJ
03Upper Deck MVP-424
Gold Script-424
Silver Script-424
Canadian Exclusives-424
Souvenirs-S6
SportsNut-SN90
Talent-MT13
Threads-TC7
03Upper Deck Rookie Update-58
Skills-SKJJ
03Upper Deck Trilogy-98
Authentic Patches-AP4
Limited-98
Limited Threads-LT1
03Upper Deck Victory-195
Bronze-195
Gold-195
Silver-195
Freshman Flashback-FF46
Game Breakers-GB18
03Czech Stadion-536
03Toronto Star-98
Foil-21
04ITG NHL AS FANtasy AS History Jerseys-SB43
04Pacific-175
Blue-175
Red-175
Milestones-3
Philadelphia-8
04SP Authentic-57
04SP Authentic-128
04UD All-World-29
04UD All-World-120
Gold-29
04Ultimate Collection-26
04Ultimate Collection-66
Jerseys-UGJ-JJ
Jerseys Gold-UGJ-JJ
Patches-UP-JJ
04Upper Deck-117
Big Playmakers-BP-JJ
Canadian Exclusives-117
HG Glossy Gold-117
HG Glossy Silver-117
Patches-GJPA-JJ
Patches-GJPL-JJ
Patches-GJPN-JJ
Swatch of Six-SS-JJ
Three Stars-AS10
World's Best-WB9
World Cup Tribute-JJ
World Cup Tribute-PEJJHE
04Czech NHL ELH Postcards-7
04Czech OFS-56
Checklist Cards-3
Jaromir Jagr-J01
Jaromir Jagr-J02
Jaromir Jagr-J03
Jaromir Jagr-J04
Jaromir Jagr-J05
Jaromir Jagr-J06
Stars-2
Stars-51
04Czech Zuma-18
04Czech Zuma Stars-Z1
04Czech World Championship Postcards-10
04Russian Legion-2
04National Trading Card Day *-T12
05Be A Player-58
First Period-58
Second Period-58
Third Period-58
Overtime-58
Outtakes-OT32
05Beehive-59
05Beehive-201
Beige -59
Blue -59
Gold-59
Red -59
Matte-59
05Black Diamond-178
Emerald-178
Gold-178
Onyx-178
Ruby-178
Jerseys-J-JJ
Jerseys Ruby-J-JJ
Jersey Duals-DJ-JJ
Jersey Triples-TJ-JJ
05Hot Prospects-65
En Fuego-65
Red Hot-65
White Hot-65
05McDonalds Upper Deck-36
05Panini Stickers-103
05Parkhurst-317
05Parkhurst-528
05Parkhurst-594
05Parkhurst-690
Facsimile Auto Parallel-317
Facsimile Auto Parallel-528
Facsimile Auto Parallel-594
Facsimile Auto Parallel-690
True Colors-TCNYR
True Colors-TCNYR
True Colors-TCNJNY
True Colors-TCNJNY
True Colors-TCNYNY
True Colors-TCNYNY
05SP Authentic-65
05SP Authentic-103
Limited-65
Limited-103
05SP Game Used-67
Gold-67
Authentic Fabrics-AF-JJ
Authentic Fabrics Gold-AF-JJ
Authentic Fabrics Triple-HJH
Authentic Fabrics Triple-NPJ
Authentic Patches-AP-JJ
Authentic Patches Triple-HJH
Authentic Patches Triple-NPJ
Awesome Authentics-AA-JJ
Awesome Authentics Gold-DA-JJ
Game Gear-GG-JJ
05SPx-57
Spectrum-57
Winning Combos-WC-JM
Winning Combos-WC-JY
Winning Combos-WC-LJ
Winning Combos Gold-WC-JM
Winning Combos Gold-WC-JY
Winning Combos Gold-WC-LJ
Winning Combos Spectrum-WC-JM
Winning Combos Spectrum-WC-JY
Winning Combos Spectrum-WC-LJ
Winning Materials-WM-JJ
Winning Materials Gold-WM-JJ
Winning Materials Spectrum-WM-JJ
Xcitement Superstars-XS-JJ
Xcitement Superstars Gold-XS-JJ
Xcitement Superstars Spectrum-XS-JJ
05The Cup-69
Gold-69
Black Rainbow-69
Dual NHL Shields-DSJL
Dual NHL Shields-DSLJ
Masterpiece Pressplates-69
Masterpiece Pressplates (Rookie Update)-234
Noble Numbers-NNJJ
Noble Numbers Dual-DNNJH
Noble Numbers Dual-DNNLJ
Patch Variation-P69
Property of-POJJ
05UD Artifacts-64
05UD Artifacts-179
Blue-64
Blue-179
Gold-64
Gold-179
Green-64
Green-179
Pewter-64
Pewter-179
Red-64
Red-179
Gold Autographed-64
Gold Autographed-179
Treasured Patches-TP-JJ
Treasured Patches Autographed-TP-JJ
Treasured Patches Dual-TPD-JJ
Treasured Patches Dual Autographed-TPD-JJ
Treasured Patches Pewter-TP-JJ
Treasured Patches Silver-TP-JJ
Treasured Swatches-TS-JJ
Treasured Swatches Autographed-TS-JJ
Treasured Swatches Blue-TS-JJ
Treasured Swatches Copper-TS-JJ
Treasured Swatches Dual-TSD-JJ
Treasured Swatches Dual Autographed-TSD-JJ
Treasured Swatches Dual Blue-TSD-JJ
Treasured Swatches Dual Copper-TSD-JJ
Treasured Swatches Dual Maroon-TSD-JJ
Treasured Swatches Dual Pewter-TSD-JJ
Treasured Swatches Dual Silver-TSD-JJ
Treasured Swatches Maroon-TS-JJ
Treasured Swatches Pewter-TS-JJ
Treasured Swatches Silver-TS-JJ
05UD PowerPlay-57
05UD PowerPlay-111
Rainbow-57
Specialists-TSJJ
Specialists Patches-SPJJ
05Ultimate Collection-59
Gold-59
Jerseys-JJJ
National Heroes Jerseys-NHJJJ
National Heroes Patches-NHPJJ
Premium Patches-PPJJ
Premium Swatches-PSJJ
Ultimate Patches-PJJ
05Ultra-129
Gold-129
Ice-129
Scoring Kings-SK15
Scoring Kings Jerseys-SKJ-JJ
Scoring Kings Patches-SKP-JJ
05Upper Deck-126
05Upper Deck All-Time Greatest-39
05Upper Deck All-Time Greatest-48
05Upper Deck Big Playmakers-B-JJ
05Upper Deck Destined for the Hall-DH5
05Upper Deck Goal Celebrations-GC3
05Upper Deck HG Glossy-126
05Upper Deck Hometown Heroes-HH8
05Upper Deck Hometown Heroes-HH17
05Upper Deck Jerseys Series II-J2JJ
05Upper Deck Majestic Materials-MMJJ
05Upper Deck NHL Generations-DJH
05Upper Deck Patches-P-JJ
05Upper Deck Scrapbooks-HS23
05Upper Deck Shooting Stars-S-JJ
05Upper Deck Ice-62
Rainbow-62
Cool Threads-CTJJ
Cool Threads Glass-CTJJ
Cool Threads Patches-CTPJJ
05Upper Deck MVP-256
Gold-256
Platinum-256
Materials-M-JJ
Materials Duals-D-LJ
Monumental Moments-MM6
Rising to the Occasion-RO11
05Upper Deck Rookie Update-63
05Upper Deck Rookie Update-234
Inspirations Patch Rookies-234
05Upper Deck Trilogy-55
05Upper Deck Trilogy-118
Crystal-118
Honorary Patches-HP-JJ
Honorary Swatches-HS-JJ
05Upper Deck Toronto Fall Expo-126
05Upper Deck Victory-130
Black-130
Gold-130
Silver-130
Blow-Ups-BU24
Game Breakers-GB28
05Czech World Champions Postcards-15
05Czech Kvarteto Bonaparte-5a
05Czech Kvarteto Bonaparte-HOKEJ
05Czech Pexeso Mini Blue Set-10
05Czech Pexeso Mini Red Set-1
05Czech Stadion-673
05ITG Heroes and Prospects He Shoots-He Scores Prizes-48
05ITG Heroes and Prospects He Shoots-He Scores Prizes-58
06Sports Illustrated for Kids *-24
06Be A Player Portraits-68
06Beehive-35
06Beehive-179
Blue-35
Gold-35
Matte-35
Red Facsimile Signatures-35
Wood-35
5 X 7 Black and White-35
5 X 7 Cherry Wood-35
Matted Materials-MMJJ
06Black Diamond-161B
Black-157B
Gold-161B
Ruby-161B
Jerseys-JJJ
Jerseys Black-JJJ
Jerseys Gold-JJJ
Jerseys Ruby-JJJ
06Flair Showcase-188
06Flair Showcase-247
06Flair Showcase-288
Parallel-188
Parallel-247
Parallel-288
Hot Numbers-HN29
Hot Numbers Parallel-HN29
Stitches-SSJJ
06Fleer-127
Oversized-127
Tiffany-127
Fabricology-FJJ
Hockey Headliners-HL21
Total 0-015
06Hot Prospects-63
Red Hot-63
White Hot-63
Hot Materials -HMJJ
Hot Materials Red Hot-HMJJ
Hot Materials White Hot-HMJJ
06ITG International Ice-15
06ITG International Ice-52
Gold-15
Gold-52
Autographs-AJJ
Autographs-AJJ2
Best of the Best-BB11
Best of the Best Gold-BB11
Complete Jersey-CJ13
Complete Jersey Gold-CJ13
Cornerstones-IC05
Cornerstones Gold-IC05
Emblem Autographs-GUE23
Emblem Autographs Gold-GUE23
Emblems-GUE23
Emblems Gold-GUE23
Hockey Passport-HP01
Hockey Passport Gold-HP01
International Rivals-IR15
International Rivals Gold-IR15
Jersey Autographs-GUJ23
Jersey Autographs Gold-GUJ23
Jerseys-GUJ23
Jerseys Gold-GUJ23
My Country My Team-MC2
My Country My Team Gold-MC2
Numbers-GUN23
Numbers Autographs-GUN23
Numbers Autographs Gold-GUN23
Numbers Gold-GUN23
Passing The Torch-PTT11
Passing The Torch-PTT16
Passing The Torch Gold-PTT11
Passing The Torch Gold-PTT16
Stick and Jersey-SJ16
Stick and Jersey Gold-SJ16
Triple Memorabilia-TM06
Triple Memorabilia Gold-TM06
06ITG Ultimate Memorabilia-73
Artist Proof-73
Autos-18
Autos Gold-18
Autos Dual-1
Autos Dual Gold-1
Autos Triple-7
Autos Triple Gold-7
Blades of Steel-10
Blades of Steel Gold-10
Bowman Factor-13
Bowman Factor Gold-13
Bowman Factor Autos-11
Bowman Factor Autos Gold-11
Complete Jersey-6
Complete Jersey Gold-6
Decades-1
Decades-4
Decades Gold-1
Decades Gold-4
Double Memorabilia Autos-4
Double Memorabilia Autos Gold-4
First Round Picks-4
First Round Picks Gold-4
Going For Gold-13
Going For Gold Gold-13
In The Numbers-13
In The Numbers Gold-13
Jerseys-14
Jerseys Gold-14
Jerseys and Emblems-17
Jerseys and Emblems Gold-17
Jerseys Autos-25
Jerseys Autos Gold-25
Journey Emblem-9
Journey Emblem Gold-9
Journey Jersey-9
Journey Jersey Gold-9
Passing The Torch-14
Passing The Torch Gold-14
Retro Teammates-21
Retro Teammates Gold-21
Retrospective-5
Retrospective Gold-5
Ring Leaders-4
Ring Leaders Gold-4
Road to the Cup-8
Road to the Cup Gold-8
Seams Unbelievable-9
Seams Unbelievable Gold-9
Trifecta Autos-3
Trifecta Autos Gold-3
Triple Thread Jerseys-16
Triple Thread Jerseys Gold-16
06McDonald's Upper Deck-29
Jerseys-JJJ
Patches-PJJ
06NHL POG-42
06O-Pee-Chee-338
06O-Pee-Chee-659
06O-Pee-Chee-690
Rainbow-338
Rainbow-659
Rainbow-690
Swatches-S-JJ
06Panini Stickers-100
06SP Authentic-36
06SP Authentic-119
Limited-36
Limited-119
06SP Game Used-66
Gold-66
Rainbow-66
Authentic Fabrics-AFJJ
Authentic Fabrics Parallel-AFJJ
Authentic Fabrics Patches-AFJJ
Authentic Fabrics Dual-AF2JL
Authentic Fabrics Dual-AF2SJ
Authentic Fabrics Dual Patches-AF2JL
Authentic Fabrics Dual Patches-AF2SJ
Authentic Fabrics Triple-AF3NYR
Authentic Fabrics Triple Patches-AF3NYR
Authentic Fabrics Quads-AF4JHEG
Authentic Fabrics Quads Patches-AF4JHEG
Authentic Fabrics Fives-AF550G
Authentic Fabrics Fives-AF5AST
Authentic Fabrics Fives-AP5PTS
Authentic Fabrics Fives Patches-AF550G
Authentic Fabrics Fives Patches-AF5AST
Authentic Fabrics Fives Patches-AP5PTS
Authentic Fabrics Sixes-AF6500
Authentic Fabrics Sixes Patches-AF6500
Authentic Fabrics Sevens-AF7ART
Authentic Fabrics Sevens-AF7LBP
Authentic Fabrics Sevens-AF7MVP
Authentic Fabrics Sevens Patches-AF7ART
Authentic Fabrics Sevens Patches-AF7LBP
Authentic Fabrics Sevens Patches-AF7MVP
By The Letter-BLJJ
06SPx-68
06SPx-115
Spectrum-68
Spectrum-115
SPxcitement-X66
SPxcitement Spectrum-X66
Winning Materials-WMJJ
Winning Materials Spectrum-WMJJ
06The Cup-59
Black Rainbow-59
Foundations-CQJJ
Foundations Patches-CQJJ
Gold-59
Gold Patches-59
Jerseys-59
Masterpiece Pressplates-59
NHL Shields Duals-DSHJB
NHL Shields Duals-DSHJS
06UD Artifacts-36
06UD Artifacts-183
Blue-36
Blue-183
Gold-36
Gold-183
Platinum-36
Platinum-183
Radiance-36
Radiance-183
Red-36
Red-183
Treasured Patches Black-TSJJ
Treasured Patches Blue-TSJJ
Treasured Patches Gold-TSJJ
Treasured Patches Platinum-TSJJ
Treasured Patches Red-TSJJ
Treasured Swatches-TSJJ
Treasured Swatches Black-TSJJ
Treasured Swatches Blue-TSJJ
Treasured Swatches Gold-TSJJ
Treasured Swatches Platinum-TSJJ
Treasured Swatches Red-TSJJ
Tundra Tandems-TTBJ
Tundra Tandems Black-TTBJ
Tundra Tandems Blue-TTBJ
Tundra Tandems Gold-TTBJ
Tundra Tandems Platinum-TTBJ
Tundra Tandems Red-TTBJ
Tundra Tandems Dual Patches Red-TTBJ
06UD Mini Jersey Collection-65
06UD Powerplay-65
Impact Rainbow-65
In Action-IA7
Specialists-SJJ
Specialists Patches-PJJ
06Ultimate Collection-40
Jerseys-UJ-JJ
Jerseys Dual-UJ2-JL
Patches-UJ-JJ
Patches Dual-UJ2-JL
Premium Patches-PS-JJ
Premium Swatches-PS-JJ
06Ultra-129
Gold Medallion-129
Ice Medallion-129
Action-UA18
Difference Makers-DM21
Scoring Kings-SK11
06Upper Deck Arena Giveaways-NYR1
06Upper Deck-128
06Upper Deck-200
Exclusives Parallel-128
Exclusives Parallel-200
High Gloss Parallel-128
High Gloss Parallel-200
All World-AW26
Award Winners-AW5
Award Winners Canadian Exclusive-OAW3
Century Marks-CM4
Game Dated Moments-GD6
Game Jerseys-JJJ
Game Patches-PJJ
Generations Duals-G2JO
Generations Patches Dual-G2PJO
Goal Rush-GR2
Masterpieces-128
Masterpieces-200
Walmart Tins Oversize-128
06Upper Deck MVP-191
Gold Script-191
Super Script-191
Clutch Performers-CP6
Gotta Have Hart-HH7
International Icons-II17
Jerseys-OJDR
Jerseys-OJJF
Jerseys-OJJS
06Upper Deck Ovation-82
06Upper Deck Sweet Shot-70
Sweet Stitches-SSJJ
Sweet Stitches Duals-SSJJ
Sweet Stitches Triples-SSJJ
06Upper Deck Trilogy-64
Frozen In Time-FT8
06Upper Deck Victory-130
06Upper Deck Victory Black-130
06Upper Deck Victory Gold-130
06Upper Deck Victory GameBreakers-GB30
06Upper Deck Victory Oversize Cards-JJ
06Czech OFS Jagr Team-21
06Russian Sport Collection Olympic Stars-33
06ITG Heroes and Prospects-8
Autographs-AJJ
Heroes Memorabilia-HM07
Heroes Memorabilia Gold-HM07
Triple Memorabilia-TM10
07Upper Deck Victory-26
Black-26
Gold-26
GameBreakers-GB46
Oversize Cards-OS8
Stars on Ice-SI16

Jagr, Jaroslav
98Czech OFS-394
98Czech OFS-469
99Swiss Panini Stickers-308

Jahma, Taisto
66Finnish Jaakiekkosarja-95

Jais, Joachim
94German First League-214

Jakes, Jiri
00Brandon Wheat Kings-23
01Brandon Wheat Kings-10
01UD Prospects-17
Jerseys-J-JJ
Jerseys Gold-J-JJ
02Czech DS-53
02Czech DS-74
03Czech OFS Plus-169

Jakes, Tomas
95Czech APS Extraliga-26
96Czech APS Extraliga-221
97Czech APS Extraliga-298
97Czech DS Stickers-20
98Czech DS Stickers-113
98Czech OFS-341
99Czech DS-186
99Czech OFS-465
99Czech OFS-516
All-Star Game Blue-516
All-Star Game Gold-516
All-Star Game Red-516
All-Star Game Silver-516
00Czech DS Extraliga-99
00Czech OFS-190
01Czech OFS-106
02Czech OFS Plus All-Star Game-H9

Jakiel, Steve
04Lincoln Stars-21
05Lincoln Stars-23

Jakobs, Jens
05Swedish SHL Elitset Rookies-8

Jakobsen, Jan
98Danish Hockey League-52

Jakobsen, Tommy
92Finnish Semic-33
92Norwegian Elite Series-105
92Norwegian Elite Series-183
93Swedish Semic World Champ Stickers-233
94Finnish Jaa Kiekko-256
95Swedish Upper Deck-38
95Swedish Globe World Championships-194
96German DEL-11
96Swedish Semic Wien-203
98German DEL-288
99German DEL-166
00German DEL-29
01German Upper Deck-8
02German DEL City Press-49
03German Deg Metro Stars-4
03German DEL-33
All-Stars-AS18
04German DEL-47
04German Dusseldorf Metro Stars Postcards-6
05German DEL-78
Defender-DF09

Jakobsson, Kurt
67Swedish Hockey-238
71Swedish Hockey-274
72Swedish Stickers-247

Jakobsson, Lars-Erik
69Swedish Hockey-282
70Swedish Hockey-181

Jakobsson, Leif
67Swedish Hockey-239
71Swedish Hockey-275
72Swedish Stickers-248

Jakobsson, Peter
97Swedish Collector's Choice-51
98Swedish UD Choice-88
99Swedish Upper Deck-155
00Swedish Upper Deck-137
01German Upper Deck-96
02German DEL City Press-113
03German DEL-128

Jakobsson, Sven-Ake
67Swedish Hockey-141
69Swedish Hockey-153
70Swedish Hockey-122

Jakobsson, Urban
87Swedish Panini Stickers-269

Jakonen, Matti
70Finnish Jaakiekko-139
71Finnish Suomi Stickers-188

Jakopin, John
98New Haven Beast-16
99BAP Memorabilia-60
Gold-60
Silver-60
99Pacific Omega-105
Copper-105
Gold-105
Ice Blue-105
Premiere Date-105
99Louisville Panthers-11
00Panthers Team Issue-18
00Upper Deck NHLPA-PA39
01BAP Signature Series-16
Autographs-16
Autographs Gold-16
02BAP Sig Series Auto Buybacks 2001-16
02Cleveland Barons-8
03Hartford Wolf Pack-9

Jaks, Pauli
91Upper Deck-663
French-663
91Upper Deck Czech World Juniors-24
93Phoenix Roadrunners-11
94Upper Deck-387
Electric Ice-387
94Classic Pro Prospects-80
94Classic Four-Sport *-155
Gold-155
Printers Proofs-155
95Swiss HNL-187

96Swiss HNL-78
96Swiss HNL-527
98Swiss Power Play Stickers-4
99Swiss Panini Stickers-4
99Swiss Panini Stickers-254
00Swiss Panini Stickers-6
00Swiss Slapshot Mini-Cards-HCAP1
01Swiss HNL-213
02Swiss HNL-54
04Russian Legion-39

Jaks, Peter
91Finnish Semic World Champ Stickers-197
91Swedish Semic World Champ Stickers-197
92Finnish Semic-206
93Swiss HNL-150
95Swiss HNL-205
96Swiss HNL-93
96Swiss HNL-540
98Swiss Power Play Stickers-240
98Swiss Power Play Stickers-256
99Swiss Panini Stickers-242
00Swiss Panini Stickers-282
00Swiss Slapshot Mini-Cards-ZSCL11
01Swiss HNL-17
02Swiss HNL-18

Jalasvaara, Janne
04Finnish Cardset-201
05Finnish Cardset -1
06Finnish Cardset-259

Jalava, Harri
95Finnish SISU-395

Jalava, Pekka
66Finnish Jaakiekkosarja-33

Jalava, Tuomas
95Finnish SISU-348

Jalbert, Craig
95Slapshot-198

Jalbert, Dean
86Sudbury Wolves-10

Jalbert, Dominic
06Chicoutimi Sagueneens-12

Jalbert, Sami
93Quebec Pee-Wee Tournament-1011

Jalkanen, Samuli
04Finnish Cardset-237
05Finnish Cardset -227
06Finnish Cardset-247

Jalo, Risto
80Finnish Mallasjuoma-31
83Swedish Semic VM Stickers-40
88Oilers Tenth Anniversary-39
91Finnish Jyvas-Hyva Stickers-14
93Finnish Jyvas-Hyva Stickers-88
93Finnish SISU-121
93Finnish SISU Autographs-121
94Finnish SISU-213
95Finnish SISU-24
95Finnish SISU-179
95Finnish SISU Limited-90
95Finnish SISU Spotlights-6
96Finnish SISU Redline-19

Jalonen, Ari
71Finnish Suomi Stickers-302

Jalonen, Hannu
78Finnish SM-Liiga-140
80Finnish Mallasjuoma-91

Jalonen, Jukka
93Finnish Jyvas-Hyva Stickers-73
00UK Sekonda Superleague-108
06Finnish Cardset Trophy Winners-1

Jalonen, Kari
70Finnish Jaakiekko-367
71Finnish Suomi Stickers-303
78Finnish SM-Liiga-152
80Finnish Mallasjuoma-98
82Swedish Semic VM Stickers-37
87Swedish Panini Stickers-223
88Oilers Tenth Anniversary-148
89Swedish Semic World Champ Stickers-42
93Finnish SISU-386

Jam, Heikki
65Finnish Hellas-136

Jamalainen, Jarmo
72Finnish Jaakiekko-326

James, Angela
94Classic Women of Hockey-W6
97Collector's Choice-276

James, Brad
90ProCards AHL/IHL-137

James, Connor
04Bakersfield Condors-7
05Hot Prospects-140
En Fuego-140
Red Hot-140
White Hot-140
05SP Authentic-266
Limited-266
05SPx-264
05The Cup Masterpiece Pressplates (Ice)-243
05The Cup Master Pressplate Rookie Update-144
05The Cup Masterpiece Pressplates SPA-266
05The Cup Masterpiece Pressplates (SPx)-264
05The Cup Masterpiece Pressplates Trilogy-268
05Upper Deck Ice-243
05Upper Deck Rookie Update-144
05Upper Deck Trilogy-268
05Manchester Monarchs-8
05Manchester Monarchs-37
06Wilkes-Barre Scranton Penguins-4
06Wilkes-Barre Scranton Penguins Jerseys-7
06ITG Heroes and Prospects-56
Autographs-ACJ

James, David
83Kingston Canadians-22
03UK Cardiff Devils-5

James, David (UK)
03UK Cardiff Devils-5

James, Gerry
44Beehive Group II Photos-411
57Parkhurst-T8
60Parkhurst-7
60Shirriff Coins-17
94Parkhurst Missing Link-117

James, Graham
907th Inn. Sketch WHL-66

James, Jason
93Quebec Pee-Wee Tournament-1662

James, Mike
81Ottawa 67's-8
82Ottawa 67's-10
83Ottawa 67's-15
92Richmond Renegades-8
99Ottawa 67's-8
02Windsor Spitfires-8
03Johnstown Chiefs-12
03Johnstown Chiefs RBI Sports-216
04Johnstown Chiefs-9
06Port Huron Flags-9
06Toledo Storm-14

James, Ryan
95North Iowa Huskies-16

James, Simon
06UK Guildford Flames-14

Jamieson, Dusty
95Quebec Pee-Wee Tournament-607
97Guelph Storm-23
99O-Pee-Chee-254
99O-Pee-Chee Chrome-254
99O-Pee-Chee Chrome Refractors-254
99Topps/OPC-254
99Topps/OPC Chrome-254
Refractors-254
99Bowman CHL-22
Gold-22
OPC International-22
Autographs-BA19
00Sarnia Sting-16
02Charlotte Checkers-85
03ECHL All-Stars-247

Jamieson, Kule
93Quebec Pee-Wee Tournament-1201

Jamieson, Leigh
03UK Belfast Giants-5
04UK U-20 Team-8

Jaminki, Tommi
04Finnish Cardset-235

Jamsa, Markus
01Finnish Cardset-306

Jamsanen, Mikael
99Finnish Cardset-216
00Finnish Cardset-248
01Finnish Cardset-11

Jamsen, Lasse
95Finnish SISU-268
96Finnish SISU Redline-64
98Finnish Kerailysarja-140
99Finnish Cardset-78
00Finnish Cardset-316
01Finnish Cardset-104
02Finnish Cardset-185
03Finnish Cardset-93
04Finnish Cardset-130
05Finnish Cardset -300

Jamsen, Lauri
70Finnish Jaakiekko-156
71Finnish Suomi Stickers-227
72Finnish Jaakiekko-210
73Finnish Jaakiekko-282

Jamtin, Andreas
03Swedish Elite-199
Silver-199
04Swedish Elitset-199
Gold-199
04Swedish HV71 Postcards-2
05Finnish Cardset -337
06Swedish SHL Elitset-202

Jan, Ivo
97Johnstown Chiefs-19
99German DEL-309
04German DEL-231
04German Krefeld Penguins Postcards-10
05German DEL-227

Janasak, Steve
81Swedish Semic Hockey VM Stickers-91
95Signature Rookies Miracle on Ice-15
95Signature Rookies Miracle on Ice-16
95Signature Rook Miracle on Ice Sigs-15
95Signature Rook Miracle on Ice Sigs-16
04UD Legendary Signatures Miracle Men-USA16
04UD Legendary Sigs Miracle Men Autos-USA-JA

Jancarik, Petr
94Czech APS Extraliga-29
95Czech APS Extraliga-318
96Czech APS Extraliga-52
97Czech APS Extraliga-319
97Czech DS Stickers-230
98Czech DS Stickers-272
98Czech OFS-151
98Czech OFS-455
99Czech DS-76
99Czech OFS-91
00Czech DS Extraliga-89
00Czech OFS-36
01Czech OFS-51
02Czech OFS Plus-87
03Czech OFS Plus-287
04Czech OFS Defence Points-15

Jancevski, Dan
00London Knights-18
00London Knights-U3
01Utah Grizzlies-29
02Utah Grizzlies-3
03Pacific AHL Prospects-93
Gold-93
04Hamilton Bulldogs-13
05Iowa Stars-3
06Fleer-225
Tiffany-225
06O-Pee-Chee-532
Rainbow-532
06The Cup Masterpiece Pressplates (Marquee Rookies)-532
06The Cup Masterpiece Pressplates (MVP)-329
06The Cup Masterpiece Pressplates (Trilogy)-122
06The Cup Masterpiece Pressplates (Victory)-214
06Ultra-205
Gold Medallion-205
Ice Medallion-205
06Upper Deck MVP-329
Gold Script-329
Super Script-329
06Upper Deck Trilogy-122
06Upper Deck Victory-214
06Upper Deck Victory Black-214
06Upper Deck Victory Gold-214
06Hamilton Bulldogs-15

Jancovic, Dalimir
02Slovakian Kvarteto-25

Jandac, Josef
06Czech OFS Coaches-4

Jandel, Michal
93Quebec Pee-Wee Tournament-1709

Jandura, Pavel
98Arizona Icecats-13
99Arizona Icecats-12
00Arizona Icecats-11
01Arizona Icecats-7

Janecek, Filip
99Czech Score Blue 2000-128
99Czech Score Red Ice 2000-128

Janecky, Otakar
89Swedish Semic World Champ Stickers-191
92Finnish Jyvas-Hyva Stickers-57
93Finnish Jyvas-Hyva Stickers-108
93Finnish SISU-26
93Finnish SISU-364
93Finnish SISU-364B
94Finnish SISU-91
94Finnish SISU-373
94Finnish SISU Fire On Ice-4
94Finnish Jaa Kiekko-188
94Swedish Olympics Lillehammer*-321
95Finnish SISU-53
95Finnish SISU-171
95Finnish SISU-371
95Finnish SISU Limited-14
95Finnish SISU Spotlights-1
95Swedish World Championships Stickers-205
96Finnish SISU Redline-185
Mighty Adversaries-7
98Finnish Kerailysarja-116
99Finnish Cardset-168
99Finnish Cardset-217
00Czech DS Extraliga-90
00Czech OFS-42
00Czech OFS Star Emerald-12
00Czech OFS Star Pink-12
00Czech OFS Star Violet-12
01Czech OFS-245
All Stars-33
01Czech OFS Red Inserts-RE12D
02Czech OFS Plus-216
02Czech OFS Plus All-Star Game-H28
02Finnish Cardset-29
03Czech OFS Plus-45
03Czech Pardubice Postcards-5

Janecyk, Bob
83Blackhawks Postcards-9
84Kings Smokey-9
85O-Pee-Chee-223
85O-Pee-Chee Stickers-239
86Kings 20th Anniversary Team Issue-10
86O-Pee-Chee-131
86O-Pee-Chee Stickers-91
86Topps-131

Janelle, Dan
51Bas Du Fleuve-42
52Bas Du Fleuve-9

Janelle, Roland
917th Inn. Sketch CHL Award Winners-29

Janes, Brandon
99Lethbridge Hurricanes-12
99UD Prospects-83

Jang, Abraham
93Quebec Pee-Wee Tournament-1453

Janicki, Trevor
93Northern Michigan Wildcats-15
98Amarillo Rattlers-8
99Corpus Christi IceRays-8

Janiga, Michal
99Czech Score Blue 2000-118
99Czech Score Red Ice 2000-118

Janik, Doug
02BAP Memorabilia-367
02Upper Deck Rookie Update-148
02Rochester Americans-9
03Rochester Americans-10
04Rochester Americans-7
06Lightning Postcards-8

Janikowski, Janusz
94German DEL-413
95German DEL-419

Janiszewski, Henryk
79Panini Stickers-120

Janka, Markus
00German DEL-240
01German Upper Deck-232
02German DEL City Press-175
04German DEL-232
04German Krefeld Penguins Postcards-11

Janke, Dieter
04German Berlin Eisbarens 50th Anniv-44

Jankovych, Vitezslav
99Czech Score Blue 2000-83
99Czech Score Red Ice 2000-83
02Czech OFS Plus-152
Trios-T5
Duos-D23
03Czech OFS Plus-222

Jankowski, Lou
44Beehive Group II Photos-110
54Parkhurst-79
54Topps-28

Janku, Pavel
94Czech APS Extraliga-193
95Czech APS Extraliga-40
95Czech APS Extraliga-380
95Czech APS Extraliga-387
96Czech APS Extraliga-43
96Swedish Semic Wien-118
97Czech APS Extraliga-64
97Czech DS Extraliga-106
97Czech DS Stickers-101
98Czech DS-28
98Czech DS Stickers-295
98Czech OFS-89
98Czech OFS-465
99Czech DS-22
99Czech OFS-134
99Czech OFS-412
00Czech DS Extraliga-72
00Czech OFS-227
01Czech OFS-54
01Czech OFS Red Inserts-RE22D
02Czech OFS Plus-88
03Czech OFS Plus-288
03Czech OFS Plus Insert G-G10
04Czech OFS-209
Assist Leaders-11

Jankus, Jon
04Maine Black Bears-18
05Maine Black Bears-11

Jannard, Olivier
06Drummondville Voltigeurs-11

Janney, Craig
88Bruins Sports Action-5
88Bruins Sports Action-23
88Bruins Postcards-5
88O-Pee-Chee Stickers-90
89Bruins Sports Action-11
89O-Pee-Chee-190
89O-Pee-Chee-298
89O-Pee-Chee Stickers-29
89O-Pee-Chee Stickers-35
89O-Pee-Chee Stickers-38
89O-Pee-Chee Stickers-175
89Panini Stickers-198
89Topps-190
89Swedish Semic World Champ Stickers-173
90Bowman-33
Tiffany-33
90Bruins Sports Action-13
90O-Pee-Chee-212
90Panini Stickers-14
90Pro Set-8
90Score-118
Canadian-118
90Score Hottest/Rising Stars-58
90Score Young Superstars-30
90Topps-212
Tiffany-212
90Upper Deck-234
French-234
91Pro Set Platinum-3
91Bowman-355
91Kraft-31
91O-Pee-Chee-41
91OPC Premier-93
91Panini Stickers-170
91Parkhurst-4
91Parkhurst-378
French-4
French-378
91Pinnacle-57
French-57
91Pro Set-2
French-2
91Score American-253
91Score Canadian Bilingual-473
91Score Canadian English-473
91Stadium Club-147
91Topps-41
91Upper Deck-128
91Upper Deck-512
French-128
French-512
91Finnish Semic World Champ Stickers-143
91Swedish Semic World Champ Stickers-143
92Bowman-14
92O-Pee-Chee-325
92Panini Stickers-22
92Panini Stickers French-22
92Parkhurst-154
Emerald Ice-154
92Pinnacle-196
French-196
92Pro Set-157
92Score-285
Canadian-285
USA Greats-11
92Stadium Club-41
92Topps-134
Gold-134G
92Ultra-187
92Upper Deck-125
92Finnish Semic-160
93Donruss-295
93Leaf-181
93OPC Premier-120
Gold-120
93Panini Stickers-157
93Parkhurst-443
Emerald Ice-443
93Pinnacle-130
Canadian-130
93PowerPlay-212
93Score-186
Canadian-186
Dynamic Duos U.S.-4
93Stadium Club-335
Members Only Master Set-335
First Day Issue-335
Master Photos-22
Master Photos Winners-22
93Topps/OPC Premier-120
Gold-120
93Ultra-134
93Upper Deck-225
93Upper Deck-303
93Upper Deck-323
SP-138
93Swedish Semic World Champ Stickers-186
94Be A Player-R52
94Canada Games NHL POGS-204
94Donruss-28
94EA Sports-123
94Flair-154
94Hockey Wit-4
94Kraft-18
94Leaf-52
94Leaf Limited-91
94OPC Premier-60
Special Effects-60
94Parkhurst-200
Gold-200
94Pinnacle-84
Artist's Proofs-84
Rink Collection-84
94Score-127
Gold-127
Platinum-127
94Select-139
Gold-139
94SP-109
Die Cuts-109
94Topps/OPC Premier-60
Special Effects-60
94Ultra-363
94Upper Deck-18
Electric Ice-18
Predictor Retail-R16
94Upper Deck Predictor Retail Exchange-R16
94Upper Deck SP Inserts-SP67
94Upper Deck SP Inserts Die Cuts-SP67
94Finnish Jaa Kiekko-119
95Bashan Super Stickers-105
95Bashan Super Stickers-106
95Be A Player-47
Signatures-S47
Signatures Die Cuts-S47
95Bowman-3
All-Foil-3
95Canada Games NHL POGS-226
95Collector's Choice-264
Player's Club-264
Player's Club Platinum-264
95Donruss-137
95Donruss Elite-33
Die Cut Stars-33
Die Cut Uncut-33
95Emotion-157
95Finest-4
Refractors-4
95Imperial Stickers-106
95Leaf-98
95Leaf Limited-13
95Metal-131
95NHL Aces Playing Cards-2H
95Panini Stickers-277
95Parkhurst International-455
Emerald Ice-455
95Pinnacle-37
Artist's Proofs-37
Rink Collection-37
95Playoff One on One-192
95Pro Magnets-120
95Score-15
Black Ice Artist's Proofs-15
Black Ice-15
95Select Certified-33
Mirror Gold-33
95SkyBox Impact-149
95Stadium Club-179
Members Only Master Set-179
95Summit-49
Artist's Proofs-49
Ice-49
95Topps-95
OPC Inserts-95
95Topps SuperSkills-13
Platinum-13
95Ultra-147
Gold Medallion-147
95Upper Deck-315
Electric Ice-315
Electric Ice Gold-315
Special Edition-SE73
Special Edition Gold-SE73
95Finnish Semic World Championships-107
95Swedish Globe World Championships-118
95Swedish World Championships Stickers-228
96Black Diamond-45
Gold-45
96Collector's Choice-207
96Coyotes Coca-Cola-10
96Donruss-154
Press Proofs-154
96Donruss Elite-104
Die Cut Stars-104
96Fleer Picks-60
96Leaf-36
Press Proofs-36
96Leaf Limited-51
Gold-51
96Leaf Preferred-35
Press Proofs-35
96Metal Universe-117
96NHL Pro Stamps-120
96Pinnacle-48
Artist's Proofs-48
Foil-48
Premium Stock-48
Rink Collection-48
96Playoff One on One-384
96Score-57
Artist's Proofs-57
Dealer's Choice Artist's Proofs-57
Special Artist's Proofs-57
Golden Blades-57
96Select Certified-60
96Select Certified-P60
Artist's Proofs-60
Artist's Proofs-60B
Blue-60
Mirror Blue-60
Mirror Gold-60
Mirror Red-60
Red-60
96Summit-64
Artist's Proofs-64
Ice-64
Metal-64
Premium Stock-64
96Ultra-131
Gold Medallion-131
96Upper Deck-127
96Zenith-49
Artist's Proofs-49
96Swedish Semic Wien-170
97Collector's Choice-201
97Coyotes Face-Off Luncheon -8
97Donruss-46
Press Proofs Silver-46
Press Proofs Gold-46
97Donruss Limited-67
Exposure-67
97Donruss Priority-154
Stamp of Approval-154
97Pacific-148
Copper-148
Emerald Green-148
Ice Blue-148
Red-148
Silver-148
97Panini Stickers-161
97Revolution-106
Copper-106
Emerald-106
Ice Blue-106
Silver-106
97Score-154
Artist's Proofs-154
Golden Blades-154
97SP Authentic-123
97Upper Deck-334
98Black Diamond-81
Double Diamond-81
Triple Diamond-81
Quadruple Diamond-81
98Bowman's Best-94
Refractors-94
Atomic Refractors-94
98Pacific-340
Ice Blue-340
Red-340
98Panini Stickers-145
98SP Authentic-80
Power Shift-80
98UD Choice-156
Prime Choice Reserve-156
Reserve-156
98Upper Deck-366
Exclusives-366
Exclusives 1 of 1-366
Gold Reserve-366

Janos, Branislav
93Swedish Semic Elitserien-43
95Slovakian APS National Team-20
97Czech APS Extraliga-72
97Czech DS Extraliga-109
98Czech DS-124
98Czech DS Stickers-300
98Czech OFS-391
99Czech DS-112
99Czech OFS-195
00Czech OFS-229
01Czech OFS-55
01Slovakian Kvarteto-3C
03Czech OFS Plus All-Star Game-H15

Janostin, Pat
85Minnesota-Duluth Bulldogs-30

Janosz, Bob
99Muskegon Fury-14

Janov, Martem
94German DEL-363

Jansen, Alexander
98German DEL-305

Jansen, Arve
92Norwegian Elite Series-238

Jansen, Klaus
94German First League-154

Jansky, Peter
04Czech OFS-388
06Czech OFS-136

Janssen, Brent
05Dutch Vadeko Flyers -6

Janssen, Cam
02Windsor Spitfires-116
04Albany River Rats-9
05Hot Prospects-149
En Fuego-149
Red Hot-149
White Hot-149
05SP Authentic-231
Limited-231
05SPx-273
05The Cup Masterpiece Pressplate Artifact-297
05The Cup Masterpiece Pressplates (Ice)-201
05The Cup Master Pressplate Rookie Update-155
05The Cup Masterpiece Pressplates SPA-231
05The Cup Masterpiece Pressplates (SPx)-273
05The Cup Masterpiece Pressplates Trilogy-278
05The Cup Masterpiece Pressplate Ult Coll-188
05UD Artifacts-297
05Ultimate Collection-188
Gold-188
05Upper Deck Ice-201
05Upper Deck Rookie Update-155
05Upper Deck Trilogy-278
05Albany River Rats-11
06Devils Team Set-10
06Upper Deck-370
Exclusives Parallel-370
High Gloss Parallel-370
Masterpieces-370

Janssens, Mark
86Regina Pats-10
87Regina Pats-9
89Rangers Marine Midland Bank-15
90Bowman-226
Tiffany-226
90O-Pee-Chee-391
90Panini Stickers-101
90Pro Set-199
90Score Rookie/Traded-33T
90Topps-391
Tiffany-391
90Upper Deck-298
French-298
91Bowman-67
91O-Pee-Chee-186
91Pro Set-158
French-158
91Score Canadian Bilingual-421
91Score Canadian English-421
91Stadium Club-113
91Topps-186
91Upper Deck-228
French-228
92OPC Premier-117
92Whalers Dairymart-10
93OPC Premier-133
Gold-133
93Panini Stickers-127
93Parkhurst-355
Emerald Ice-355
93Score-339
Canadian-339
93Stadium Club-180
Members Only Master Set-180
OPC-180
First Day Issue-180
First Day Issue OPC-180
93Topps/OPC Premier-133
Gold-133
93Upper Deck-198
93Whalers Coke-7
94Leaf-361
94Parkhurst SE-SE70
Gold-SE70
94Stadium Club-212
Members Only Master Set-212
First Day Issue-212
Super Team Winner Cards-212
94Upper Deck-35
Electric Ice-35
95Upper Deck-312
Electric Ice-312
Electric Ice Gold-312
95Whalers Bob's Stores-10
96Be A Player-199
Autographs-199
Autographs Silver-199
96Whalers Kid's Club-18
97Pacific Invincible NHL Regime-2
97Upper Deck-5
99Blackhawks Chicago Sun-Times-3
99O-Pee-Chee-55
99O-Pee-Chee Chrome-55
99O-Pee-Chee Chrome Refractors-55
99Topps/OPC-55
99Topps/OPC Chrome-55
Refractors-55
99Upper Deck Retro-16
Gold-16
Platinum-16
00Upper Deck NHLPA-PA20

Jansson, Bjorn
71Swedish Hockey-222

Jansson, Conny
83Swedish Semic Elitserien-216
84Swedish Semic Elitserien-241
85Swedish Panini Stickers-239
86Swedish Panini Stickers-263
87Swedish Panini Stickers-247
89Swedish Semic Elitserien Stickers-234
90Swedish Semic Elitserien Stickers-60
91Swedish Semic Elitserien Stickers-239

Jansson, Hakan
98Colorado Gold Kings Postcards-17

Jansson, Hans Erik
73Swedish Stickers-175

Jansson, Karl-Erik
56Swedish Alfabilder-105

Jansson, Kent
65Swedish Coralli ISHockey-212

Jansson, Kjell
71Swedish Hockey-396
72Swedish Stickers-269

Jansson, Lars
57Swedish Alfabilder-144
89Swedish Semic Elitserien Stickers-174
90Swedish Semic Elitserien Stickers-7
91Swedish Semic Elitserien Stickers-205
92Swedish Semic Elitserien Stickers-228
93Swedish Semic Elitserien-199
94Swedish Leaf-20
95Swedish Leaf-100
95Swedish Upper Deck-154
98Swedish UD Choice-171
99German DEL-219
00Swedish Upper Deck-154
02German DEL City Press-176
03Swedish Elite-251
Silver-251
04Swedish Elitset-95
Gold-95
04Swedish MoDo Postcards-17

Jansson, Lars-Erik
57Swedish Alfabilder-100

Jansson, Lars-Gunnar
87Swedish Panini Stickers-4
93Swedish Semic Elitserien-289

Jansson, Leif
64Swedish Coralli ISHockey-88

Jansson, Magnus
90Swedish Semic Elitserien Stickers-292
91Swedish Semic Elitserien Stickers-70
92Swedish Semic Elitserien Stickers-92
93Swedish Semic Elitserien-65
94Swedish Leaf-62
95Swedish Leaf-185
95Swedish Upper Deck-47

Jansson, Martin
99Swedish Upper Deck-111
04Swedish Elitset-262
Gold-262
05Swedish SHL Elitset-266
Gold-266
06Swedish SHL Elitset-125

Jansson, Matti
65Finnish Hellas-43
66Finnish Jaakiekkosarja-43
70Finnish Jaakiekko-192

Jansson, Pelle
56Swedish Alfabilder-81

Jansson, Ronny
83Swedish Semic Elitserien-11

Jansson, Stefan
83Swedish Semic Elitserien-85
86Swedish Panini Stickers-68
87Swedish Panini Stickers-73
89Swedish Semic Elitserien Stickers-11

Jantovsky, Jiri
95Czech APS Extraliga-332
96Czech APS Extraliga-159
97Czech APS Extraliga-256
97Czech DS Stickers-258
98Czech DS-54
98Czech DS Stickers-141
98Czech OFS-154
99Czech DS-84
99Czech OFS-351
99Czech OFS-389
00Czech OFS-342
03Czech OFS Plus-398
04Czech OFS-11

Jantti, Jyrkki
71Finnish Suomi Stickers-365

Jantti, Kimmo
71Finnish Suomi Stickers-366

Jantunen, Marko
91Finnish Jyvas-Hyva Stickers-50
92Finnish Jyvas-Hyva Stickers-100
93Finnish Jyvas-Hyva Stickers-324
93Finnish SISU-54
94Finnish SISU-154
94Finnish SISU-176
94Finnish SISU-364
94Finnish SISU-386
94Finnish SISU Fire On Ice-5
94Finnish Jaa Kiekko-32
94Swedish Leaf-214
Foreign Affairs-3
95Finnish SISU Limited-69
95Swedish Leaf-147
Face to Face-4
Mega-3
95Swedish Upper Deck-211
95Swedish World Championships Stickers-173
96Saint John Flames-9
97Swedish Collector's Choice-76
Select-UD4
98Finnish Kerailysarja Leijonat-23
98Swedish UD Choice-75
99Swedish Upper Deck-67
SHL Signatures-6
00Swedish Upper Deck-83
02Swedish SHL-28
Parallel-28
03Finnish Cardset-69
03Finnish Cardset Globetrotters-GR4
04Finnish Cardset-69
Parallel-52
04Swedish Pure Skills-119
Parallel-119
05Finnish Cardset -233
06Finnish Cardset-303

Jaques, Steve
91ProCards-385
93Las Vegas Thunder-15
95Houston Aeros-10

Jarant, Mark
04Peoria Rivermen-3

Jardemyr, Daniel
90Swedish Semic Elitserien Stickers-84
91Swedish Semic Elitserien Stickers-9
92Swedish Semic Elitserien Stickers-34
98Danish Hockey League-24

Jardine, Jules
93Lakeland Ice Warriors-17

Jardine, Matt
93Quebec Pee-Wee Tournament-510

Jardine, Nicholas
93Quebec Pee-Wee Tournament-1310

Jardine, Ryan
99Black Diamond-107
Diamond Cut-107
Final Cut-107
99SP Authentic-131
99Upper Deck-310
Exclusives-310
Exclusives 1 of 1-310
99Upper Deck Gold Reserve-310
99Upper Deck MVP SC Edition-198
Gold Script-198
Silver Script-198
Super Script-198
01BAP Memorabilia-402
Emerald-402
Ruby-402
Sapphire-402
01Utah Grizzlies-24
03San Antonio Rampage-12
04San Antonio Rampage-12
05German DEL-327
06Swedish SHL Elitset-258

Jares, Richard
03Czech OFS Plus-112
04Czech OFS-69
05Czech HC Znojmo-6
06Czech OFS-205

Jarina, Kamil
99Czech Score Blue 2000-26
99Czech Score Red Ice 2000-26
03Czech OFS Plus-332
04Czech OFS-95
06Czech OFS Goalies I-12
06Czech OFS Goalies II-11

Jarkko, Erkki
66Finnish Jaakiekkosarja-158

Jarkko, Martti
72Finnish Jaakiekko-261
73Finnish Jaakiekko-152
74Finnish Typotor-27
78Finnish SM-Liiga-15
78Finnish SM-Liiga-193
79Panini Stickers-171
80Finnish Mallasjuoma-189
05Finnish Tappara Legendat-6

Jarkowsky, Terry
93Waterloo Black Hawks-13

Jarn, Heikki
71Finnish Suomi Stickers-62
71Finnish Suomi Stickers-115
72Finnish Jaakiekko-103
72Finnish Panda Toronto-97
72Finnish Semic World Championship-77
72Swedish Semic World Championship-77

Jarnberg, Per
84Swedish Semic Elitserien-58

Jarolin, Rene
04Slovakian Skalica Team Set-10

Jaros, Mike
99Charlotte Checkers-16
01Missouri River Otters-21

Jaros, Petr
99Czech Score Blue 2000-51
99Czech Score Red Ice 2000-51
02Czech OFS Plus-239
03Czech OFS Plus-181
03Czech OFS Plus-399
04Czech OFS-179
06Czech OFS-257

Jaroslav, Walter
94German DEL-32

Jaroslavtsev, Viktor
73Swedish Stickers-119

Jarram, David
03Sault Ste. Marie Greyhounds-10
04Ottawa 67's-14
04Sault Ste. Marie Greyhounds-4
06London Knights-7

Jarram, John
00Mississauga Ice Dogs-13
05Fort Wayne Komets Choice-19
05Fort Wayne Komets Sprint-11

Jarrett, Blair
02Mississauga Ice Dogs-22
03Mississauga Ice Dogs-12
04Sault Ste. Marie Greyhounds-20

Jarrett, Cole
00UD CHL Prospects-37
01Plymouth Whalers-11
02Plymouth Whalers-1
02Plymouth Whalers-16
03Bridgeport Sound Tigers-3A
06O-Pee-Chee-516
Rainbow-516
06The Cup Masterpiece Pressplates (Marquee Rookies)-516
06The Cup Masterpiece Pressplates (Power Play)-117
06The Cup Masterpiece Pressplates (Victory)-313
06UD Powerplay-117
Impact Rainbow-117
06Upper Deck Victory-313
06German DEL-16

Jarrett, Darrell
99Halifax Mooseheads-12

Jarrett, Doug
64Beehive Group III Photos-43
65Coca-Cola-34
66Topps-111
67Topps-112
68Blackhawks Team Issue-2
68O-Pee-Chee-13
68Shirriff Coins-26
68Topps-13
69O-Pee-Chee-67
Four-in-One-6
69Topps-67
70Blackhawks Postcards-6
70Dad's Cookies-62
70Esso Power Players-112
70O-Pee-Chee-150
70Sargent Promotions Stamps-34
71O-Pee-Chee-208
71Sargent Promotions Stamps-41
71Toronto Sun-68
72O-Pee-Chee-97
72Sargent Promotions Stamps-58
73O-Pee-Chee-187
73Topps-76
74NHL Action Stamps-79
74O-Pee-Chee NHL-351
75O-Pee-Chee NHL-333
94Parkhurst Tall Boys-38
95Parkhurst '66-67-27
Coins-27

Jarrett, Gary
67Topps-44
68O-Pee-Chee-87
68Shirriff Coins-120
68Topps-87
69O-Pee-Chee-85
69Topps-85
70Colgate Stamps-49
70Dad's Cookies-63
70Esso Power Players-101
70O-Pee-Chee-75
70Sargent Promotions Stamps-140
70Topps-75
71O-Pee-Chee-93
71Sargent Promotions Stamps-138
71Topps-93
71Toronto Sun-49
72Cleveland Crusaders WHA-8
73Quaker Oats WHA-27
74O-Pee-Chee WHA-61
75O-Pee-Chee WHA-87

Jarrett, Patrick
00Mississauga Ice Dogs-14
00UD CHL Prospects-13
02Owen Sound Attack-6
03Owen Sound Attack-7
04Owen Sound Attack-22

05German DEL-308
06German DEL-20
Jarry, Pierre
72Maple Leafs Postcards-12
72O-Pee-Chee-237
72Sargent Promotions Stamps-208
73O-Pee-Chee-186
73Red Wings McCarthy Postcards-10
74NHL Action Stamps-102
74O-Pee-Chee NHL-171
74Topps-171
75O-Pee-Chee NHL-359A
75O-Pee-Chee NHL-359B
76O-Pee-Chee NHL-49
76Topps-49
77O-Pee-Chee NHL-106
77Topps-106
Jarvela, Pekka
89Swedish Semic Elitserien Stickers-203
91Finnish Jyvas-Hyva Stickers-20
93Finnish Jyvas-Hyva Stickers-62
Jarvenpaa, Hannu
86Jets Postcards-10
87Jets Postcards-10
88Jets Police-11
88Jets Postcards-12
89O-Pee-Chee-292
89O-Pee-Chee Stickers-145
91Finnish Semic World Champ Stickers-23
91Swedish Semic Elitserien Stickers-150
91Swedish Semic World Champ Stickers-23
92Finnish Jyvas-Hyva Stickers-66
93Finnish SISU-273
94Finnish SISU-23
94Finnish SISU Horoscopes-17
95Finnish SISU-181
Jarvenpaa, Juha
92Finnish Jyvas-Hyva Stickers-41
93Finnish Jyvas-Hyva Stickers-77
93Finnish SISU-122
94Finnish SISU-87
94Finnish SISU-251
95Finnish SISU-25
95Finnish SISU-245
95Finnish SISU Limited-107
96Finnish SISU Redline-39
98Finnish Keralysarja-96
Jarvenpaa, Jukka-Pekka
71Finnish Suomi Stickers-208
72Finnish Jaakiekko-157
73Finnish Jaakiekko-218
78Finnish SM-Liiga-100
Jarvenpaa, Pertti
72Finnish Jaakiekko-283
73Finnish Jaakiekko-219
78Finnish SM-Liiga-106
80Finnish Mallasjuoma-41
Jarvenpaa, Torsti
72Finnish Jaakiekko-262
Jarventie, Martti
94Finest-130
Super Team Winners-130
Refractors-130
94Finnish SISU-235
95Finnish SISU-32
96Finnish SISU Redline-98
98Finnish Keralysarja-84
99Finnish Cardset-47
00SPx Rookie Redemption-RR16
00Finnish Cardset-217
01Parkhurst-294
01Parkhurst Beckett Promos-294
01SP Authentic-155
Limited-155
Limited Gold-155
01UD Challenge for the Cup-114
01Upper Deck Ice-58
01Finnish Cardset-140
01Quebec Citadelles-8
02Finnish Cardset-31
03Finnish Cardset-61
04Finnish Cardset-68
Parallel-51
05Finnish Cardset -57
06Finnish Cardset-239
Jarvholm, Erik
67Swedish Hockey-256
69Swedish Hockey-301
70Swedish Hockey-201
71Swedish Hockey-288
72Swedish Stickers-69
Jarvi, Iiro
88Nordiques General Foods-20
88Nordiques Team Issue-19
89Nordiques Team Issue-19
89Nordiques General Foods-15
89Nordiques Police-13
89O-Pee-Chee-264
89O-Pee-Chee Stickers-7
89O-Pee-Chee Stickers-192
89Panini Stickers-329
90Nordiques Team Issue-14
90O-Pee-Chee-52
90Topps-52
Tiffany-52
90ProCards AHL/IHL-451
92Finnish Jyvas-Hyva Stickers-17
92Finnish Semic-13
93Finnish Jyvas-Hyva Stickers-19
93Finnish SISU-106
94Finnish SISU-31
94Finnish SISU-379
95Finnish SISU-213
95Finnish SISU Limited-45
95Finnish SISU Spotlights-4
96Finnish SISU Redline Sledgehammers-8
96German DEL-60
99Finnish Cardset Aces High-C-6
Jarvinen, Erkki
66Finnish Jaakiekkosarja-192
73Finnish Jaakiekko-179
Jarvinen, Jari
71Finnish Suomi Stickers-345
72Finnish Jaakiekko-329
78Finnish SM-Liiga-52
80Finnish Mallasjuoma-26
92Finnish Jyvas-Hyva Stickers-88
93Finnish Jyvas-Hyva Stickers-171
93Finnish SISU-164
Jarvinen, Jouko
66Finnish Jaakiekkosarja-122
Jarvinen, Jussi-Pekka
92Finnish Jyvas-Hyva Stickers-163
Jarvinen, Kari
71Finnish Jaakiekko-306
72Finnish Jaakiekko-346
78Finnish SM-Liiga-57
80Finnish Mallasjuoma-34
Jarvinen, Keijo
70Finnish Jaakiekko-141
71Finnish Suomi Stickers-130
72Finnish Jaakiekko-193
73Finnish Jaakiekko-153
Jarvinen, Matti
01Finnish Cardset-367
Jarvinen, Pauli
89Swedish Semic World Champ Stickers-46
90Swedish Semic Elitserien Stickers-237
91Finnish Semic World Champ Stickers-14
91Swedish Semic Elitserien Stickers-164
91Swedish Semic World Champ Stickers-14
92Finnish Jyvas-Hyva Stickers-160
93Finnish Jyvas-Hyva Stickers-289
93Finnish SISU-73
93Finnish SISU Autographs-73
93Swedish Semic World Champ Stickers-64
94Finnish SISU-75
94Finnish SISU Fire On Ice-7
94Finnish Jaa Kiekko-50
95Finnish SISU-318
95Finnish SISU Limited-78
Jarvinen, Rauno
72Finnish Jaakiekko-284
Jarvinen, Timo
70Finnish Jaakiekko-242
71Finnish Suomi Stickers-209
93Finnish SISU-209
99Finnish Cardset-313
Jarvinen, Turo
05Finnish Cardset -20
06Finnish Cardset-19
Jarvis, Blaine
03Salmon Arm Silverbacks-9
Jarvis, Chad
93Quebec Pee-Wee Tournament-193
Jarvis, Doug
75Canadiens Postcards-7
76Canadiens Postcards-8
76O-Pee-Chee NHL-217
76O-Pee-Chee NHL-313
76Topps-217
77Canadiens Postcards-9
77O-Pee-Chee NHL-139
77Topps-139
78Canadiens Postcards-10
78O-Pee-Chee-13
78Topps-13
79Canadiens Postcards-9
79O-Pee-Chee-112
79Topps-112
80Canadiens Postcards-9
80O-Pee-Chee-76
80Pepsi-Cola Caps-47
80Topps-76
81Canadiens Postcards-12
81O-Pee-Chee-184
81O-Pee-Chee Stickers-34
82Capitals Team Issue-12
82O-Pee-Chee-367
82O-Pee-Chee Stickers-40
82Post Cereal-10
82Topps Stickers-40
83NHL Key Tags-132
83O-Pee-Chee-372
83O-Pee-Chee Stickers-208
83Topps Stickers-208
84Capitals Pizza Hut-9
84O-Pee-Chee-200
84O-Pee-Chee Stickers-129
84O-Pee-Chee Stickers-234
84Topps-145
85Capitals Pizza Hut-8
85O-Pee-Chee-151
85O-Pee-Chee Stickers-109
85Topps-151
86O-Pee-Chee-28
86Topps-28
86Whalers Junior Thomas'-11
87O-Pee-Chee-95
87O-Pee-Chee Minis-19
87O-Pee-Chee Stickers-183
87O-Pee-Chee Stickers-207
87Panini Stickers-52
87Panini Stickers-38
87Topps-95
87Whalers Jr. Burger King/Pepsi-9
94Stars HockeyKaps-15
04Hamilton Bulldogs-14
06Parkhurst-135
Autographs-135
Jarvis, Wes
81Capitals Team Issue-8
82Birmingham South Stars-14
88ProCards AHL-230
89ProCards AHL-205
96Kitchener Rangers-14
97Bowman CHL-158
OPC-158
Autographs-38
99Bowman CHL-156
Gold-156
OPC International-156
00Charlotte Checkers-13
01Hartford Wolf Pack-10
03St. Francis Xavier X-Men-4
04St. Francis Xavier X-Men-8
Jas, Jan
92Quebec Pee-Wee Tournament-1737
00Indianapolis Ice-9
03Fort Worth Brahmas-8
04Fort Worth Brahmas-8A
04Fort Worth Brahmas-8B
05Roanoke Valley Vipers-8
Jas, Peter
97Central Texas Stampede-7
99Indianapolis Ice-8
00Indianapolis Ice-10
Jasecko, Stanislav
95Slovakian APS National Team-8
96Grand Rapids Griffins-8
99Czech OFS-180
00Czech DS Extraliga-77
00Czech OFS-10
01Finnish Cardset-370
01Slovakian Kvarteto-2D
01Slovakian Kvarteto-4A
03Czech OFS Plus-260
03Czech OFS Defence Points-4
06Czech OFS-52
Jaskari, Jaakko
65Finnish Hellas-117
66Finnish Jaakiekkosarja-48
Jaskierski, Mieczyslaw
73Finnish Jaakiekko-92
74Finnish Jenkki-97
74Finnish Typotor-87
79Panini Stickers-131
Jaskin, Alexei
94Czech APS Extraliga-148
95Czech APS Extraliga-5
96Czech APS Extraliga-219
97Czech APS Extraliga-34
97Czech DS Extraliga-59
97Czech DS Stickers-21
98Czech DS-87
98Czech DS Stickers-171
98Czech OFS-103
99Czech DS-139
99Czech OFS-439
00Czech OFS-328
02Czech OFS Plus-68
Trios-T20
03Czech OFS Plus-31
04Czech OFS-250
Defence Points-8
Jasko, Thomas
04Fresno Falcons-8
Jasmin-Riel, Danick
02Rimouski Oceanic-7
03Rimouski Oceanic-11
Jason, Thomas
93Quebec Pee-Wee Tournament-1168
Jasovsky, Richard
02Brandon Wheat Kings-8
03Brandon Wheat Kings-8
Jaspers, Jason
98Sudbury Wolves-13
99Sudbury Wolves-17
00SP Authentic-130
00SP Game Used-88
00SPx-124
Spectrum-124
00UD Pros and Prospects-130
00Upper Deck-211
Exclusives Tier 1-211
Exclusives Tier 2-211
00Upper Deck Vintage-397
00Sudbury Wolves-19
02Springfield Falcons-12
03ITG Action-478
03Springfield Falcons Postcards-11
04Springfield Falcons-15
05Springfield Falcons-12
06German DEL-148
Jattne, Bert
71Swedish Hockey-76
73Swedish Stickers-191
74Swedish Stickers-144
Jaufmann, Andrej
94German DEL-114
99German Bundesliga 2-51
Javanainen, Arto
70Finnish Jaakiekko-329
78Finnish SM-Liiga-228
80Finnish Mallasjuoma-202
81Swedish Semic Hockey VM Stickers-33
82Swedish Semic VM Stickers-38
83Swedish Semic VM Stickers-38
91Finnish Jyvas-Hyva Stickers-69
92Finnish Jyvas-Hyva Stickers-192
93Finnish Jyvas-Hyva Stickers-356
93Finnish SISU-218
93Finnish SISU-388
95Finnish SISU Limited-25
Javeblad, Tomas
85Swedish Panini Stickers-178
86Swedish Panini Stickers-111
87Swedish Panini Stickers-170
89Swedish Semic Elitserien Stickers-147
90Swedish Semic Elitserien Stickers-225
Javin, Miroslav
94Czech APS Extraliga-124
95Czech APS Extraliga-32
96Czech APS Extraliga-314
97Czech APS Extraliga-294
97Czech DS Stickers-157
98Czech DS Stickers-110
98Czech OFS-317
98Czech OFS-489
99Czech DS-46
99Czech OFS-289
00Czech DS Extraliga-148
00Czech OFS-267
01Czech OFS-233
02Czech OFS Plus All-Star Game-H10
04Slovakian Poprad Team Set-5
Javor, Aljosa
93Quebec Pee-Wee Tournament-1785
Jaworski, Jason
03Muskegon Fury-10
05Quad City Mallards-6
Jax, Fredrik
90Swedish Semic Elitserien Stickers-221
91Swedish Semic Elitserien Stickers-145
92Upper Deck-230
94Anaheim Bullfrogs RHI-8
94Flint Generals-12
94Classic Pro Prospects-133
Jax, Hans
69Swedish Hockey-118
70Swedish Hockey-75
71Swedish Hockey-165
72Swedish Stickers-159
73Swedish Stickers-54
74Swedish Stickers-225
86Swedish Panini Stickers-162
Jay, Bob
90ProCards AHL/IHL-550
91ProCards-252
93Parkhurst-361
Emerald Ice-361
93Upper Deck-470
93Phoenix Roadrunners-12
96Detroit Vipers-9
97Detroit Vipers-5
98Detroit Vipers-13
98Detroit Vipers Freschetta-3
98Nashville Knights-10
Jaycock, Randy
93Dallas Freeze-9
Jean, Eric
01Drummondville Voltigeurs-6
Jean, Frederick
93Quebec Pee-Wee Tournament-1335
Jean, Maxime
917th Inn. Sketch QMJHL-53
Jean, Yanick
96Mississippi Sea Wolves-10
97Mobile Mysticks-8
97Mobile Mysticks Kellogg's-9
98Mobile Mysticks-8
Jeannin, Sandy
93Swiss HNL-502
95Swiss HNL-45
96Swiss HNL-192
96Swiss HNL-541
98Swiss Power Play Stickers-64
98Swiss Power Play Stickers-257
99Swiss Panini Stickers-66
99Swiss Panini Stickers-268
00Swiss Panini Stickers-214
00Swiss Panini Stickers National Team-P27
00Swiss Slapshot Mini-Cards-HCL15
01Swiss HNL-43
02Swiss HNL-285
02Swiss HNL-483
Jebavy, Jiri
06Czech OFS-298
Jech, Ctibor
03Czech OFS Plus-393
06Czech OFS-90
Jedamzik, Rafael
94German DEL-83
99German Bundesliga 2-98
Jefferson, Tom
04Oshawa Generals-9
04Oshawa Generals Autographs-9
Jeffrey, Dustin
04Mississauga Ice Dogs-6
Jeffrey, Larry
44Beehive Group II Photos-180
62York Iron-On Transfers-33
63Parkhurst-48
63York White Backs-41
64Beehive Group III Photos-79A
64Beehive Group III Photos-79B
64Beehive Group III Photos-167
64Coca-Cola Caps-47
64Topps-49
64Toronto Star-21
65Maple Leafs White Border-9
65Topps-83
67Topps-21
68O-Pee-Chee-74
68Shirriff Coins-106
70O-Pee-Chee-28
70Topps-28
94Parkhurst Tall Boys-59
95Parkhurst '66-67-115
Coins-115
07Maple Leafs 1967 Commemorative-12
Autographs-ALJ1
Autographs-ALJ2
Jeffrey, Mike
87Moncton Hawks-14
88ProCards AHL-158
89Johnstown Chiefs-33
Jeffrey, Ryan
05Wisconsin Badgers-14
Jehner, Markus
94German First League-387
Jelen, Jiri
97Czech APS Extraliga-191
99Czech OFS-123
00Czech OFS-76
Jelenic, Lee
92Quebec Pee-Wee Tournament-1428
01Flint Generals-8
Jelinek, Jiri
98Czech OFS-167
04Czech OFS-57
04Czech OFS-333
Jelinek, Marian
99Czech OFS-17
99Czech OFS Jagr Team Embossed-17
05Czech Pexeso Mini Red Set-18
Jelinek, Michal
98Czech OFS-290
99Czech OFS-124
Jelinek, Tomas
91Finnish Semic World Champ Stickers-122
91Swedish Semic World Champ Stickers-122
92Upper Deck-497
92Finnish Semic-141
93Upper Deck-165
93Swedish Semic World Champ Stickers-103
94Czech APS Extraliga-261
94Finnish Jaa Kiekko-179
95Czech APS Extraliga-138
96Czech APS Extraliga-365
95Swedish Globe World Championships-153
96Czech APS Extraliga-297
97Czech APS Extraliga-183
97Czech DS Extraliga-54
97Czech DS Stickers-221
98Czech DS-103
98Czech DS Stickers-155
98Czech OFS-70
Jellen, Hubert
94German First League-132
Jellis, Brad
05Fresno Falcons-24
Jelmini, David
93Swiss HNL-91
95Swiss HNL-467
96Swiss HNL-156
Jenacek, Lubos
94Czech APS Extraliga-244
95Czech APS Extraliga-16
96Czech APS Extraliga-391
Jenacek, Martin
94Czech APS Extraliga-22
99Czech Score Blue 2000-152
99Czech Score Red Ice 2000-152
00Czech OFS-372
01Czech OFS-92
02Czech OFS Plus-32
03Czech OFS Plus-135
04Czech OFS-279
06Czech OFS-137
Jenish, Jesse
03Saginaw Spirit-9
Jenkins, Barry
95Swiss HNL-262
Jenkins, Craig
89Nashville Knights-10
Jenkins, Jon
83Oshawa Generals-15
94Knoxville Cherokees-10
Jenkins, Roger
34Beehive Group I Photos-160
34Diamond Matchbooks Silver-32
34Sweet Caporal-4
35Diamond Matchbooks Tan 1-30
35O-Pee-Chee V304C-92
Jenkins, Scott
907th Inn. Sketch OHL-211
Jenkins, Todd
89Nashville Knights-11
Jenks, A.J.
06Plymouth Whalers-11
Jenner, Leo
05Plymouth Whalers-B-10
06Plymouth Whalers-12
Jenner, Ryan
03Victoriaville Tigres-13
04Victoriaville Tigres-24
05Victoriaville Tigres-3
Jenni, Marcel
93Swiss HNL-101
95Swedish World Championships Stickers-130
95Swiss HNL-149
96Swiss HNL-167
96Swiss HNL-542
98Swiss Power Play Stickers-170
98Swiss Power Play Stickers-258
99Swiss Panini Stickers-171
99Swiss Panini Stickers-269
00Swedish Upper Deck-91
00Swiss Panini Stickers National Team-P17
02Swedish SHL-31
Parallel-31
02Swiss HNL-484
03Swedish Elite-42
Silver-42
04Swedish Elitset-44
Gold-44
Signatures Series A-13
Jennings, Adam
02Red Deer Rebels-26
04Vancouver Giants-24
06Donruss Elite Status Autographs Gold-103
06Donruss Elite-103
06Donruss Elite Status Autographs Black-103
06Donruss Elite Aspirations-103
06Donruss Elite Status Gold-103
Status-103
Turn of the Century Autographs-103
Jennings, Grant
83Saskatoon Blades-3
84Saskatoon Blades Stickers-8
89Whalers Junior Milk-10
90O-Pee-Chee-510
90Pro Set-106
90Score Rookie/Traded-31T
90Whalers Jr. 7-Eleven-15
91O-Pee-Chee-468
91Penguins Coke/Elby's-3
91Score Canadian Bilingual-531
91Score Canadian English-531
91Topps-468
92Penguins Coke/Clark-9
92Score-542
Canadian-542
93Parkhurst-427
Emerald Ice-427
93Penguins Foodland-2
94Be A Player Signature Cards-51
94Maple Leafs Kodak-16
94Maple Leafs Pin-up Posters-27
94Penguins Foodland-1
Jennings, Jason
92Western Michigan Broncos-14
93Johnstown Chiefs-10
94Johnstown Chiefs-12
94Classic Pro Prospects-238
95Vancouver VooDoo RHI-9
00UK Guildford Flames-11
Jennings, William
34Beehive Group I Photos-105
83Hall of Fame Postcards-K8
85Hall of Fame-142
90Upper Deck French-209
01Upper Deck Legends-49
Jenny, Dominik
95Swiss HNL-304
96Swiss HNL-476
Jensen, Al
81Capitals Team Issue-9
82Post Cereal-20
83NHL Key Tags-132
83O-Pee-Chee-373
83O-Pee-Chee Stickers-202
83Topps Stickers-202
84Capitals Pizza Hut-10
84O-Pee-Chee-201
84O-Pee-Chee Stickers-128
84O-Pee-Chee Stickers-232
84Topps-146
85Capitals Pizza Hut-9
86Capitals Police-12
86O-Pee-Chee-135
86O-Pee-Chee Stickers-252
86Topps-135
Jensen, Anders V.
98Danish Hockey League-28
99Danish Hockey League-175
Jensen, Brian
99Danish Hockey League-34
Jensen, Chris
88ProCards AHL-125
89ProCards AHL-339
90ProCards AHL/IHL-38
91ProCards-275
93Portland Pirates-14
94Portland Pirates-11
95Minnesota Moose-2
97Wheeling Nailers-2
97Wheeling Nailers Photo Pack-2
Jensen, Chris DEF.
93Fort Worth Fire-7
Jensen, Christian
05Waterloo Blackhawks-13
Jensen, Claus
98Danish Hockey League-185
99Danish Hockey League-72
Jensen, Cody
96Regina Pats-22
97Regina Pats-17
98Prince Albert Raiders-11
99Medicine Hat Tigers-11
Jensen, Dan
98Danish Hockey League-176
98Danish Hockey League-183
99Danish Hockey League-63
99Danish Hockey League-86
99Danish Hockey League-195
Jensen, Darren
86O-Pee-Chee Stickers-187
Jensen, David A
84Whalers Junior Wendy's-8
84Springfield Indians-5
86Capitals Kodak-13
86Capitals Police-13
87Capitals Team Issue-11
Jensen, David H
92Upper Deck-379
Jensen, Eric
93Michigan Tech Huskies-2
Jensen, Flemming
98Danish Hockey League-103
Jensen, Fredrik
02Swedish SHL-45
Parallel-45
Jensen, James
94Central Hockey League-11
94Dallas Freeze-11
Jensen, Jan
98Danish Hockey League-196
99Danish Hockey League-1
99Danish Hockey League-83
Jensen, Jim
97Mobile Mysticks-5
97Mobile Mysticks Kellogg's-6
98Oklahoma City Blazers-10
Jensen, Joakim
04Baie-Comeau Drakkar-8
05Baie-Comeau Drakkar-14
Jensen, Joe
00Sioux Falls Stampede-11
01Sioux Falls Stampede-6
03St. Cloud State Huskies-14
04St. Cloud State Huskies-18
05St. Cloud State Huskies-9
06St. Cloud State Huskies-17
Jensen, Johan Moller
98Danish Hockey League-56
Jensen, Kenneth
98Danish Hockey League-2
99Danish Hockey League-2
Jensen, Kim
98Danish Hockey League-194
Jensen, Mark
06Kotoks Oilers -8
Jensen, Rene
98Danish Hockey League-101
99Danish Hockey League-128
Jensen, Soren
98Danish Hockey League-11
98Danish Hockey League-143
99Danish Hockey League-159
Jensen, Steve
77O-Pee-Chee NHL-238
77Topps-238
78O-Pee-Chee-45
78Topps-45
79Panini Stickers-220
79O-Pee-Chee-292
80Kings Card Night-5
80O-Pee-Chee-294
81O-Pee-Chee-154
82Post Cereal-8
Jenson, Christian
95Vancouver VooDoo RHI-3
Jenson, Wade
81Victoria Cougars-8
Jentzmik, Felix
93Quebec Pee-Wee Tournament-1768
Jerabek, Vladimir
95Czech APS Extraliga-173
96Czech APS Extraliga-177
97Czech APS Extraliga-76
97Czech DS Stickers-13
97Czech DS Stickers-48
98Czech OFS-260
99Czech OFS-336
Jerant, Mark
03Hershey Bears-20
03Hershey Bears Patriot News-9
Jern, Arne
55Swedish Alfabilder-20
Jernberg, Tomas
83Swedish Semic Elitserien-206
84Swedish Semic Elitserien-225
86Swedish Panini Stickers-264
Jerofejev, Dmitrij
96Czech APS Extraliga-199
97Czech APS Extraliga-129
97Czech DS Extraliga-98
97Czech DS Stickers-193
98Czech DS Stickers-253
99Czech DS-171
99Czech OFS-225
99Czech OFS-413
00Czech DS Extraliga-161
00Czech OFS-243
Jerofejevs, Aleksanders
04Sioux Falls Stampede-2-3
Jerome, Darcy
907th Inn. Sketch WHL-163
Jerrard, Paul
89ProCards IHL-96
91ProCards-151
03Hershey Bears-25
03Hershey Bears Patriot News-29
04Hershey Bears Patriot News-13
05Iowa Stars-19
06Iowa Stars-26
Jerwa, Joe
34Beehive Group I Photos-232
35Diamond Matchbooks Tan 2-29
35Diamond Matchbooks Tan 3-26
Jesiolowski, David
917th Inn. Sketch WHL-274
93Lethbridge Hurricanes-5
93Spokane Chiefs-14
00Indianapolis Ice-11
01BC Icemen-12
Jeslovsky, Richard
94German First League-662
Jessee, Scott
78Saginaw Gears-11
Jessesen, Glenn
92Norwegian Elite Series-204
Jessey, Ivan
88Lethbridge Hurricanes-13
Jessiman, Brent
82Brandon Wheat Kings-16
83Brandon Wheat Kings-14
05ITG Heroes and Prospects-351
Autographs Series II-HJ
Jessiman, Hugh
05Hartford Wolf Pack-13
06Hartford Wolf Pack-12
06ITG Heroes and Prospects-159
Autographs-AHJ
Update Autographs-AHJ
Jestadt, Jeff
91Ferris State Bulldogs-16
92Ferris State Bulldogs-16
93Roanoke Express-10
94Roanoke Express-8
95Roanoke Express-1
Jestadt, Ryan
99Ohio State Buckeyes-9
Jesue, Patrick
93Quebec Pee-Wee Tournament-858
Jetter, Thomas
93Quebec Pee-Wee Tournament-1779
99German Bundesliga 2-115
03German DEL-55
Jez, Petr
99Czech OFS-536
03Czech OFS Plus-382
05Czech HC Plzen-4
06Czech HC Plzen Postcards-13
02Czech OFS-273
Jezo, Alexander
93Quebec Pee-Wee Tournament-1553
Jezzone, Adrian
93Swiss HNL-319
99Swiss Panini Stickers-345
Jickling, Mike
89Spokane Chiefs-12
907th Inn. Sketch WHL-191
917th Inn. Sketch WHL-7
917th Inn. Sketch Memorial Cup-89
94Tampa Bay Tritons RHI-3
98Florida Everblades-9
98Long Beach Ice Dogs-6
00Florida Everblades-4
02South Carolina Stingrays-12
02South Carolina Stingrays RBI-215
03South Carolina Stingrays-328
Jilek, Martin
94German First League-548
Jillson, Jeff
00SPx Rookie Redemption-RR25
01Atomic-123
Premiere Date-123
01Atomic Toronto Fall Expo-123
01BAP Memorabilia-306
Emerald-306
Ruby-306
Sapphire-306
01BAP Signature Series-245
Autographs-245
Autographs Gold-245
01Bowman YoungStars-135
Gold-135
Ice Cubed-135
01Crown Royale-177
Rookie Royalty-19
01O-Pee-Chee-344
01Pacific-461
01Pacific Adrenaline-223
Blue-223
Premiere Date-223
Red-223
Retail-223
Rookie Report-17
01Pacific Heads-Up-118
01Pacific High Voltage-9
01Parkhurst-272
01Parkhurst Beckett Promos-272
01Private Stock-137
Gold-137
Premiere Date-137
Retail-137
Silver-137
01Private Stock Pacific Nights-137
01Private Stock PS-2002-88
01SP Authentic-170
Limited-170
Limited Gold-170
01SP Game Used-95
01SPx-124
01Stadium Club-124
Award Winners-124
Master Photos-124
01Titanium-180
Retail-180
01Titanium Draft Day Edition-165
01Topps-344
01Topps Chrome-162
Refractors-162
Black Border Refractors-162
01Topps Heritage-141
01Topps Reserve-119
01UD Challenge for the Cup-130
01UD Honor Roll-86
01UD Mask Collection-166
Gold-166
01UD Playmakers-139
01UD Premier Collection-106
01UD Top Shelf-135
01Upper Deck-225
Exclusives-225
01Upper Deck Ice-67
01Upper Deck Vintage-295
01Vanguard-128
Blue-128
Red-128
One of Ones-128
Premiere Date-128
Prime Prospects-17
Proofs-128
01Cleveland Barons-9
02BAP First Edition-227
02O-Pee-Chee-278
02O-Pee-Chee Premier Blue Parallel-278
02O-Pee-Chee Premier Red Parallel-278
02O-Pee-Chee Factory Set-278
02Pacific-334
Blue-334
Red-334
02Pacific Calder Collection AS Fantasy-10
02Pacific Calder Collection All-Star Fantasy Gold-10
02Pacific Complete-73
Red-73
02Pacific Entry Draft-10
02Parkhurst-31
Bronze-31
Gold-31
Silver-31
02SP Authentic-130
02Topps-278
OPC Blue Parallel-278
OPC Red Parallel-278
Factory Set-278
02Topps Total-394
03Beehive-16
Gold-16
Silver-16
03Pacific Complete-266
Red-266
03Parkhurst Original Six Boston-4
03Topps Traded-TT84
Blue-TT84
Gold-TT84
Red-TT84
03Upper Deck-263
Canadian Exclusives-263
HG-263
UD Exclusives-263
03Upper Deck MVP-46
Gold Script-46
Silver Script-46
Canadian Exclusives-46
04Rochester Americans-8
05Upper Deck MVP-52
Gold-52
Platinum-52
Jindra, Josef
99Czech OFS-181
00Czech OFS-14
01Czech OFS-123
02Czech OFS Plus-175
03Czech OFS Plus-261
Jindra, T.J.
04Notre Dame Fighting Irish-12
Jindrich, Robert
95Czech APS Extraliga-251
96Czech APS Extraliga-296
97Czech APS Extraliga-176
97Czech DS Extraliga-52
97Czech DS Stickers-214
98Czech DS Stickers-151
98Czech OFS-36
96Kentucky Thoroughblades-16
00Kentucky Thoroughblades-11
02Swedish SHL-264
Parallel-264
03Czech OFS Plus-383
04Czech HC Plzen Postcards-7
04Czech OFS-143
05Czech HC Plzen-5
Jinman, Lee
93North Bay Centennials-14
94North Bay Centennials-17
95Slapshot-58
95Slapshot-223
95Classic-90
96Michigan K-Wings-12
99Houston Aeros-10
00Jackson Bandits-23
01UK Nottingham Panthers-24
02UK Nottingham Panthers-17
03Swedish Elite-274
Silver-274
Jira, Petr
00Czech OFS-103
01Czech OFS-159
Jiranek, Martin
92Classic-69
Gold-69
93Portland Pirates-14
94Classic Pro Prospects-169
96German DEL-327
98German DEL-253
99German DEL-29
00German DEL-189
All-Star Class-A1
01German Upper Deck-202
02German DEL City Press-265
03German DEL-202
03German Nuremberg Ice Tigers Postcards-12
04German DEL-89
04German Ingolstadt Panthers-11
05German DEL-149
06German DEL-161
Jirik, Jaroslav
69Swedish Hockey-31
70Swedish Masterserien-141
77Sportscasters-4403
77Finnish Sportscasters-45-1069
Jiroutek, Jiri
94German First League-249
94German First League-664
Jirus, Valdemar
01Czech OFS-112
02Czech OFS Plus-6
02Czech OFS Plus-113
04Czech OFS-70
Czech/Slovak-8
Defence Points-9
05Czech HC Liberec-5
06Czech HC Liberec Postcards-3
06Czech OFS-91
All Stars-9
Defenders-5
Jiskra, Jason
93St. Cloud State Huskies-11
Joanette, Kitoute
51Laval Dairy QSHL-75
Joanette, Rosario
43Parade Sportive *-57
52St. Lawrence Sales-20
Joanisse, Andre
02Drummondville Voltigeurs-4
03Drummondville Voltigeurs-9
04Drummondville Voltigeurs-12
05Drummondville Voltigeurs-9
Job, Gregory
93Quebec Pee-Wee Tournament-1750
Jobe, Trevor
88ProCards AHL-241
89Hampton Roads Admirals-10A
89Hampton Roads Admirals-10H
90ProCards AHL/IHL-161
91Richmond Renegades-10
91Richmond Renegades Set 2-7
92Nashville Knights-16
97Flint Generals EBK-8
98Baton Rouge Kingfish-9
99Adirondack IceHawks-13
99Knoxville Speed-6
Jobidon, Steve
93Quebec Pee-Wee Tournament-983
Jobin, Daniel
93Quebec Pee-Wee Tournament-267
Jobin, David
98Swiss Power Play Stickers-40
99Swiss Panini Stickers-31
99Swiss Panini Stickers-282
00Swiss Panini Stickers-31
00Swiss Slapshot Mini-Cards-SCB2
01Swiss HNL-79
02Swiss HNL-235
02Swiss HNL-254
Jobin, Frederick
98Long Beach Ice Dogs-7
99San Diego Gulls-4
00Quad-City Mallards-4
01Quad-City Mallards-9
Jobs, Kristoffer
01Swedish Brynas Tigers-8
02Swedish SHL-149
Parallel-149
Jocher, Markus
99German DEL-326
02German DEL City Press-196
04German DEL-107
05German DEL-87
06German DEL-175
German Forwards-GF7
Jodoin, Clement
90Halifax Citadels-13
91ProCards AHL/IHL-447
91ProCards-544
95Halifax Mooseheads-24
96Halifax Mooseheads I-24
96Halifax Mooseheads II-24
02Canadiens Postcards-30

Jodoin, Mark
93Western Michigan Broncos-17
Jodoin, Roger
51Bas Du Fleuve-55
52Bas Du Fleuve-48
Jodzio, Rick
75O-Pee-Chee WHA-99
76O-Pee-Chee WHA-113
77Rockies Coke Cans-10
Joe, Colin
04Kelowna Rockets-13
05Kelowna Rockets-15
Joelsson, Rolf
67Swedish Hockey-155
Joensuu, Jesse
04Finnish Cardset-193
04Finnish Cardset Signatures-39
05Finnish Cardset -346
06Finnish Cardset-175
Signature Sensations-33
06Finnish Porin Assat Pelaajakortit-18
Joenvaara, Juha
00Finnish Cardset-183
01Finnish Cardset-80
Joffe, Aaron
90Arizona Icecats-8
91Arizona Icecats-8
92Arizona Icecats-7
Johannesen, Glen
88ProCards IHL-14
Johanneson, Connie
23Crescent Selkirks-11
28V128-2 Paulin's Candy-68
Johannsen, James
94German First League-273
Johannson, Eric
98Tri-City Americans-9
99UD Prospects-37
Johannson, Jim
88Salt Lake Golden Eagles-17
89ProCards IHL-70
90ProCards AHL/IHL-396
Johansen, Mortan
74Finnish Typotor-77
Johansen, Per Reidar
92Norwegian Elite Series-165
Johansen, Reino
92Norwegian Elite Series-80
Johansen, Roy
92Norwegian Elite Series-11
93Swedish Semic World Champ Stickers-243
94Finnish Jaa Kiekko-264
Johansen, Stig
92Finnish Semic-47
92Norwegian Elite Series-17
Johansen, Thomas
99Danish Hockey League-215
Johansen, Tom
92Finnish Semic-45
92Norwegian Elite Series-7
94Finnish Jaa Kiekko-269
98Danish Hockey League-38
Johansen, Trevor
77Maple Leafs Postcards-7
78Maple Leafs Postcards-10
78O-Pee-Chee-320
79Rockies Team Issue-9
Johansson, Ake
57Swedish Alfabilder-106
67Swedish Hockey-202
Johansson, Anders
64Swedish Coralli ISHockey-36
65Swedish Coralli ISHockey-36
67Swedish Hockey-33
69Swedish Hockey-46
69Swedish Hockey-336
70Swedish Hockey-246
71Swedish Hockey-303
72Swedish Stickers-289
98Danish Hockey League-22
99Danish Hockey League-21
Johansson, Andreas
91Swedish Semic Elitserien Stickers-101
92Swedish Semic Elitserien Stickers-113
93Swedish Semic Elitserien-85
94Finnish Jaa Kiekko-70
94Swedish Leaf-51
96Be A Player-103
Autographs-103
Autographs Silver-103
96Swedish Semic Wien-64
96Collector's Edge Ice-94
Prism-94
97Donruss Limited-121
97Donruss Limited-159
Exposure-121
Exposure-159
97Donruss Priority-134
Stamp of Approval-134
97Panini Stickers-53
98Pacific Omega-165
Red-165
Opening Day Issue-165
98Senators Team Issue-8
99Pacific-289
Copper-289
Emerald Green-289
Gold-289
Ice Blue-289
Premiere Date-289
Red-289
00Pacific-67
Copper-67
Gold-67
Ice Blue-67
Premiere Date-67
00Swiss Panini Stickers-42
00Swiss Slapshot Mini-Cards-SCB10
02BAP First Edition-90
Jerseys-90
02Pacific Complete-434
Red-434
02Titanium-59
Blue-59
Red-59
Retail-59
02Vanguard-58
LTD-58
03ITG Action-395
03NHL Sticker Collection-253
03O-Pee-Chee-193
03OPC Blue-193
03OPC Gold-193
03OPC Red-193
03Pacific-189
Blue-189
Red-189
03Pacific Complete-127
Red-127
03Pacific Exhibit-81
Blue Backs-81
Yellow Backs-81
03Pacific Supreme-54
Blue-54
Red-54
Retail-54
03Private Stock Reserve-56
Blue-56
Red-56
Retail-56
03Topps-193
Blue-193
Gold-193
Red-193
03Upper Deck-349
Canadian Exclusives-349
HG-349
UD Exclusives-349
03Upper Deck MVP-237
Gold Script-237
Silver Script-237
Canadian Exclusives-237
04Swedish Alfabilder Alfa Stars-10
04Swedish Alfabilder Proof Parallels-10
Johansson, Arne
67Swedish Hockey-157
69Swedish Hockey-316
70Swedish Hockey-222
Johansson, Bjorn
56Swedish Alfabilder-75
65Swedish Coralli ISHockey-203
67Swedish Hockey-156
69Swedish Hockey-168
72Finnish Jaakiekko-47
72Finnish Hellas-29
72Swedish Stickers-5
72Swedish Stickers-214
73Finnish Jaakiekko-28
73Swedish Stickers-5
73Swedish Stickers-64
74Finnish Jenkki-26
74Swedish Stickers-170
74Swedish Semic World Champ Stickers-5
77Rochester Americans-14
Johansson, Calle
83Swedish Semic Elitserien-227
85Swedish Panini Stickers-30
86Swedish Panini Stickers-7
87Sabres Blue Shield-14
87Sabres Wonder Bread/Hostess-13
88O-Pee-Chee Stickers-134
88O-Pee-Chee Stickers-254
88Panini Stickers-221
88Sabres Blue Shield-12
88Sabres Wonder Bread/Hostess-12
89Capitals Kodak-6
89Capitals Team Issue-9
89O-Pee-Chee-16
89Topps-16
90Bowman-75
Tiffany-75
90Capitals Kodak-9
90Capitals Postcards-10
90Capitals Smokey-9
90O-Pee-Chee-164
90Pro Set-313
90Score-309A
Canadian-309A
90Topps-164
Tiffany-164
90Upper Deck-149
French-149
91Pro Set Platinum-243
91Bowman-294
91Capitals Junior 5x7-13
91Capitals Kodak-13
91O-Pee-Chee-126
91Panini Stickers-205
91Parkhurst-410
French-410
91Pinnacle-232
French-232
91Pro Set-248
French-248
91Score American-155
91Score Canadian Bilingual-155
91Score Canadian English-155
91Stadium Club-188
91Topps-126
91Upper Deck-316
French-316
91Finnish Semic World Champ Stickers-207
91Swedish Semic Elitserien Stickers-340
91Swedish Semic World Champ Stickers-207
92Bowman-275
92Capitals Kodak-13
92O-Pee-Chee-223
92Parkhurst-201
92Pinnacle-30
French-30
92Pro Set-203
92Score-209
Canadian-209
92Stadium Club-341
92Topps-498
Gold-498G
92Ultra-234
92Upper Deck-139
92Finnish Semic-57
92Swedish Semic Elitserien Stickers-341
93Donruss-372
93Leaf-153
93OPC Premier-278
Gold-278
93Panini Stickers-31
93Pinnacle-107
Canadian-107
93PowerPlay-465
93Score-76
Canadian-76
93Stadium Club-451
Members Only Master Set-451
First Day Issue-451
93Topps/OPC Premier-278
Gold-278
93Swedish Semic World Champ Stickers-25
94Donruss-243
94Leaf-242
94OPC Premier-59
Special Effects-59
94Parkhurst SE-SE197
Gold-SE197
94Pinnacle-305
Artist's Proofs-305
Rink Collection-305
94Topps/OPC Premier-59
Special Effects-59
94Ultra-235
95Bashan Super Stickers-132
95Be A Player-54
Signatures-S54
Signatures Die Cuts-S54
95Canada Games NHL POGS-285
95Capitals Team Issue-10
95Collector's Choice-130
Player's Club-130
Player's Club Platinum-130
95Donruss-309
95Emotion-189
95Imperial Stickers-132
95Leaf-298
95Panini Stickers-143
95Parkhurst International-218
Emerald Ice-218
95SkyBox Impact-178
95Topps-274
OPC Inserts-274
95Ultra-176
Gold Medallion-176
95Swedish Globe World Championships-8
96Metal Universe-165
96Pinnacle-85
Artist's Proofs-85
Foil-85
Premium Stock-85
Rink Collection-85
96Topps Picks-161
OPC Inserts-161
96Swedish Semic Wien-42
97Pacific Invincible NHL Regime-208
97Pacific Omega-240
Copper-240
Dark Gray-240
Emerald Green-240
Gold-240
Ice Blue-240
97Panini Stickers-113
97SP Authentic-167
97Upper Deck-383
98Aurora-196
98Be A Player-297
Press Release-297
98BAP Gold-297
98BAP Autographs-297
98BAP Autographs Gold-297
98Capitals Kids and Cops-5
98Pacific-6
Ice Blue-6
Red-6
98Pacific Dynagon Ice-195
Blue-195
Red-195
98Panini Stickers-107
98Paramount-245
Copper-245
Emerald Green-245
Holo-Electric-245
Ice Blue-245
Silver-245
98UD Choice-219
98UD Choice Preview-219
98UD Choice Prime Choice Reserve-219
98UD Choice Reserve-219
98Upper Deck-382
Exclusives-382
Exclusives 1 of 1-382
Gold Reserve-382
99BAP Memorabilia-173
Gold-173
Silver-173
99Pacific-441
Copper-441
Emerald Green-441
Gold-441
Ice Blue-441
Premiere Date-441
Red-441
99Panini Stickers-170
00BAP Memorabilia-166
Emerald-166
Ruby-166
Sapphire-166
Promos-166
00BAP Mem Chicago Sportsfest Copper-166
00BAP Memorabilia Chicago Sportsfest Blue-166
00BAP Memorabilia Chicago Sportsfest Gold-166
00BAP Memorabilia Chicago Sportsfest Ruby-166
00BAP Memorabilia Chicago Sun-Times Ruby-166
00BAP Memorabilia Chicago Sun-Times Gold-166
00BAP Mem Chicago Sun-Times Sapphire-166
00BAP Mem Toronto Fall Expo Copper-166
00BAP Memorabilia Toronto Fall Expo Gold-166
00BAP Memorabilia Toronto Fall Expo Ruby-166
00BAP Parkhurst 2000-P34
00BAP Signature Series-94
Emerald-94
Ruby-94
Sapphire-94
Autographs-193
Autographs Gold-193
00O-Pee-Chee-185
00O-Pee-Chee Parallel-185
00Pacific-423
Copper-423
Gold-423
Ice Blue-423
Premiere Date-423
00Panini Stickers-107
00Topps/OPC-185
Parallel-185
00Upper Deck-176
Exclusives Tier 1-176
Exclusives Tier 2-176
01BAP Memorabilia-204
Emerald-204
Ruby-204
Sapphire-204
01Upper Deck Victory-358
Gold-358
01Upper Deck Vintage-254
02BAP Sig Series Auto Buybacks 1998-297
02BAP Sig Series Auto Buybacks 2000-193
02Pacific-393
Blue-393
Red-393
02Topps Total-243
03ITG Action-522
Johansson, Carl-Johan
05Swedish SHL Elitset-282
Gold-282
06Swedish SHL Elitset-136
Johansson, Christer
69Swedish Hockey-207
72Swedish Stickers-205
74Swedish Stickers-226
Johansson, Daniel
92Upper Deck-599
92Swedish Semic Elitserien Stickers-252
93Swedish Semic Elitserien-220
94Swedish Leaf-104
95Swedish Leaf-230
95Swedish Upper Deck-80
95Swedish Globe World Championships-56
97Swedish Collector's Choice-88
98Swedish UD Choice-102
99Finnish Cardset-294
01Swedish Brynas Tigers-9
02Swedish SHL-146
Parallel-146
03Swedish Elite-2
Silver-2
04Swedish Elitset-2
Gold-2
05Swedish SHL Elitset-146
Gold-146
06Swedish SHL Elitset-2
Johansson, Eric
02Albany River Rats-9
02Albany River Rats AAP-15
03Albany River Rats-16
03Albany River Rats Kinko's-15
04Albany River Rats-10
05Swedish SHL Elitset-262
Gold-262
06Swedish SHL Elitset-121
Johansson, Erik
55Swedish Alfabilder-12
Johansson, Frederik
90Swedish Semic Elitserien Stickers-146
94Parkhurst SE-SE241
Gold-SE241
95Swedish Upper Deck-130
97Swedish Collector's Choice-130
Johansson, Fredrik
02Swedish SHL-50
Parallel-50
03Swedish Elite-73
Silver-73
06Swedish SHL Elitset-178
Johansson, Glenn
83Swedish Semic Elitserien-208
84Swedish Semic Elitserien-233
85Swedish Panini Stickers-230
86Swedish Panini Stickers-260
87Swedish Panini Stickers-242
Johansson, Goran
67Swedish Hockey-142
69Swedish Hockey-154
Johansson, Gunnar
72Swedish Stickers-44
73Swedish Stickers-187
74Swedish Stickers-227
Johansson, Hans
83Swedish Semic Elitserien-59
84Swedish Semic Elitserien-59
Johansson, Ingemar
64Swedish Coralli ISHockey-32
65Swedish Coralli ISHockey-32
Johansson, Jakob
98Black Diamond-114
Double Diamond-114
Triple Diamond-114
Quadruple Diamond-114
98SPx Top Prospects-84
Radiance-84
Spectrum-84
03Swedish Elite-151
Silver-151
04Swedish Elitset-6
Gold-6
Johansson, Jan
67Swedish Hockey-221
69Swedish Hockey-260
70Swedish Hockey-150
71Swedish Hockey-243
71Swedish Hockey-397
89Swedish Semic Elitserien Stickers-211
Johansson, Jan-Erik
56Swedish Alfabilder-96
Johansson, Jens
83Swedish Semic Elitserien-174
84Swedish Semic Elitserien-199
86Swedish Panini Stickers-202
87Swedish Panini Stickers-194
98Danish Hockey League-39
99Danish Hockey League-216
Johansson, Jonas
02Swedish SHL Next Generation-NG7
02Kamloops Blazers-13
03Swedish Elite-224
Silver-224
03Kamloops Blazers-7
04Portland Pirates-12
05Swedish Lulea Hockey Postcards-2
05Hershey Bears-10
06O-Pee-Chee-535
Rainbow-535
06SP Game Used-160
Gold-160
Rainbow-160
06SPx-154
Spectrum-154
06The Cup-98
Autographed Rookie Masterpiece Pressplates-98
Gold Rainbow Autographed Rookies-98
Masterpiece Pressplates (Marquee Rookies)-535
Masterpiece Pressplates (MVP)-341
Masterpiece Pressplates (SP Game Used)-160
Masterpiece Pressplates (SPx)-154
Masterpiece Pressplates (Trilogy)-160
Masterpiece Pressplates (Victory)-282
Rookies Black-98
Rookies Platinum-98
06Ultimate Collection Ultimate Debut Threads Jerseys-DJ-JJ
06Ultimate Collection Ultimate Debut Threads Jerseys Autographs-DJ-JJ
06Ultimate Collection Ultimate Debut Threads Patches-DJ-JJ
06Ultimate Collection Ultimate Debut Threads Patches Autographs-DJ-JJ
06Upper Deck MVP-341
Gold Script-341
Super Script-341
06Upper Deck Trilogy-160
06Upper Deck Victory-282
Johansson, Kari
66Finnish Jaakiekkosarja-59
69Swedish Hockey-368
70Finnish Jaakiekko-140
71Finnish Suomi Stickers-189
72Finnish Jaakiekko-227
73Finnish Jaakiekko-261
74Finnish Typotor-37
Johansson, Kenneth
85Swedish Panini Stickers-177
86Swedish Panini Stickers-112
87Swedish Panini Stickers-110
89Swedish Semic Elitserien Stickers-97
90Swedish Semic Elitserien Stickers-101
92Swedish Semic Elitserien Stickers-249
93Swedish Semic Elitserien-218
94Swedish Leaf-161
95Swedish Leaf-224
Johansson, Kent
89Swedish Semic Elitserien Stickers-66
Johansson, Kjell
67Swedish Hockey-48
73Swedish Stickers-159
Johansson, Kjell-Ake
84Swedish Semic Elitserien-174
85Swedish Panini Stickers-158
86Swedish Panini Stickers-171
Johansson, Kristofer
99Swedish Upper Deck-47
Johansson, Lars-Erik
71Swedish Hockey-313
73Swedish Stickers-151
74Swedish Stickers-228
Johansson, Lars-Goran
67Swedish Hockey-240
69Swedish Hockey-283
71Swedish Hockey-276
72Finnish Jaakiekko-53
72Swedish Stickers-249
Johansson, Lars-Henrik
55Swedish Alfabilder-19
Johansson, Leif
89Swedish Semic Elitserien Stickers-213
Johansson, Lennart
64Swedish Coralli ISHockey-20
64Swedish Coralli ISHockey-85
65Swedish Coralli ISHockey-20
65Swedish Coralli ISHockey-85
67Swedish Hockey-47
69Swedish Hockey-62
70Swedish Hockey-27
71Swedish Hockey-104
71Swedish Hockey-344
Johansson, Magnus
97Swedish Collector's Choice-73
98Swedish UD Choice-69
99Swedish Upper Deck-71
00Swedish Upper Deck-61
02Swedish SHL-273
Parallel-273
03Swedish Elite Jerseys-5
04Swedish Elitset-202
Gold-202
04Swedish Pure Skills-42
Parallel-42
05Swedish SHL Elitset-70
06Swedish SHL Elitset-70
Johansson, Martin
72Swedish Stickers-199
74Swedish Stickers-171
02Swedish SHL-242
Parallel-242
03Swedish Elite-250
Silver-250
04Swedish Elitset-94
Gold-94
Johansson, Mathias
95Swedish Upper Deck-69
97Swedish Collector's Choice-61
99Swedish Upper Deck Hands of Gold-8
00Swedish Upper Deck-86
02NHL Power Play Stickers-10
02Swedish SHL-32
Parallel-32
03ITG Action-465
03O-Pee-Chee-308
03OPC Blue-308
03OPC Gold-308
03OPC Red-308
03Pacific-273
Blue-273
Red-273
03Topps-308
Blue-308
Gold-308
Red-308
03Swedish Elite-185
Silver-185
04Swedish Elitset-139
04Swedish Elitset-188
Gold-139
Gold-188
High Expectations-4
Signatures Series B-6
05Swedish SHL Elitset-46
Gold-46
Icons-3
Series Two Signatures-8
06Swedish SHL Elitset-48
Performers-5
Johansson, Mattias
91Swedish Semic Elitserien Stickers-102
91Swedish Semic Elitserien Stickers-330
92Swedish Semic Elitserien Stickers-117
93Parkhurst-537
Emerald Ice-537
93Swedish Semic Elitserien-88
94Swedish Leaf-234
95Swedish Leaf-44
Goldies-5
98Swedish UD Choice-95
99Swedish Upper Deck-64
Johansson, Michael
99Finnish Cardset-100
Johansson, Mikael
83Swedish Semic Elitserien-218
85Swedish Panini Stickers-86
86Swedish Panini Stickers-78
87Swedish Panini Stickers-82
89Swedish Semic Elitserien Stickers-61
89Swedish Semic World Champ Stickers-22
90Swedish Semic Elitserien Stickers-293
91Finnish Semic World Champ Stickers-43
91Swedish Semic Elitserien Stickers-65
91Swedish Semic Elitserien Stickers-350
91Swedish Semic World Champ Stickers-43
92Finnish Semic-64
93Swedish Semic World Champ Stickers-31
93Swiss HNL-24
94Swedish Leaf-255
95Finnish Semic World Championships-68
95Swedish Leaf-119
95Swedish Globe World Championships-30
95Swiss HNL-23
95Swiss HNL-527
95Swiss HNL-539
96Swedish Semic Wien-65
96Swiss HNL-22
97Swedish Collector's Choice-42
Crash the Game Exchange-C2
Crash the Game Redemption-R2
98Swedish UD Choice-56
99Swedish Upper Deck-41
00Swedish Upper Deck-58
00Swedish Upper Deck-187
SHL Signatures-MJ
Top Playmakers-P3
02Swedish SHL-18
Dynamic Duos-2
Parallel-18
03Swedish Elite-22
03Swedish Elite-166
Silver-22
Silver-166
04Swedish Elitset-20
Gold-20
05Swedish SHL Elitset-185
Gold-185
06Swedish SHL Elitset-190
06Swedish SHL Elitset-235
Johansson, Nils
64Swedish Coralli ISHockey-10
64Swedish Coralli ISHockey-152
65Swedish Coralli ISHockey-10
65Swedish Coralli ISHockey-152
67Swedish Hockey-12
67Swedish Hockey-120
69Swedish Hockey-134
69Swedish Hockey-188
70Finnish Jaakiekko-27
70Swedish Hockey-278
70Swedish Masterserien-56
70Swedish Masterserien-60
70Swedish Masterserien-102
71Swedish Hockey-139
72Swedish Stickers-123
73Swedish Stickers-173
81Swedish Semic Hockey VM Stickers-113
Johansson, Olof
32Swedish Marabou-150
83Swedish Semic Elitserien-212
Johansson, Olsten
57Swedish Alfabilder-101
Johansson, Per
72Swedish Stickers-206
Johansson, Per-Johan
93Swedish Semic Elitserien-41
94Swedish Leaf-251
95Swedish Leaf-174
Johansson, Peter
89Swedish Semic Elitserien Stickers-24
90Swedish Semic Elitserien Stickers-94
02German DEL City Press-114
Johansson, Roger
86Swedish Panini Stickers-95
87Swedish Panini Stickers-105
90Flames IGA/McGavin's-8
90O-Pee-Chee-96
90Pro Set-424
90Score Rookie/Traded-91T
90Topps-96
Tiffany-96
91Bowman-257
91Flames Panini Team Stickers-6
91Flames Panini Team Stickers-G
91O-Pee-Chee-53
91Stadium Club-375
91Topps-53
91Swedish Semic Elitserien Stickers-139
92Flames IGA-19
92Parkhurst-263
Emerald Ice-263
92Ultra-268
93OPC Premier-253
Gold-253
93Stadium Club-133
Members Only Master Set-133
OPC-133
First Day Issue-133
First Day Issue OPC-133
93Topps/OPC Premier-253
Gold-253
93Swedish Semic Elitserien-131
93Swedish Semic World Champ Stickers-29
94Blackhawks Coke-8
94Finnish Jaa Kiekko-62
94Swedish Leaf-259
Gold Cards-21
Guest Special-6
95Finnish Semic World Championships-58
95Swedish Leaf-218
Champs-9
Face to Face-5
95Swedish Upper Deck-62
95Swedish Globe World Championships-22
96Swedish Semic Wien-54
96Swedish Semic Wien Coca-Cola Dream Team-6
97Swedish Collector's Choice-57
97Swedish Collector's Choice-206
97Swedish Collector's Choice-217
Crash the Game Exchange-C20
Crash the Game Redemption-R20
Select-UD7
98Swedish UD Choice-84
99Swedish Upper Deck-53
Lasting Impressions-4
00Swedish Upper Deck-82
SHL Signatures-RJ
Top Draws-T5
Johansson, Soren
73Swedish Stickers-225
74Swedish Stickers-230
83Swedish Semic Elitserien-225
Johansson, Sten
71Swedish Hockey-151
Johansson, Stig-Goran
64Swedish Coralli ISHockey-74
65Swedish Coralli ISHockey-74
67Swedish Hockey-13
67Swedish Hockey-188
69Swedish Hockey-189
69Swedish Hockey-245
70Finnish Jaakiekko-28
70Swedish Hockey-142
70Swedish Hockey-283
70Swedish Masterserien-37
70Swedish Masterserien-116
71Finnish Suomi Stickers-47
71Swedish Hockey-15
71Swedish Hockey-234
72Finnish Jaakiekko-48
72Finnish Hellas-31
72Finnish Panda Toronto-69
72Finnish Semic World Championship-47
72Swedish Stickers-13
72Swedish Stickers-221
72Swedish Semic World Championship-47
73Swedish Stickers-65
74Swedish Stickers-229
74Swedish Semic World Champ Stickers-21
Johansson, Sune
56Swedish Alfabilder-76
57Swedish Alfabilder-99
Johansson, Sven Tumba
55Swedish Alfabilder-2
64Swedish Coralli ISHockey-1
65Swedish Coralli ISHockey-1
65Swedish Coralli ISHockey-125
81Swedish Semic Hockey VM Stickers-124
91Finnish Semic World Champ Stickers-233
91Swedish Semic World Champ Stickers-233
95Swedish Globe World Championships-68
97Swedish Alfabilder Autographs-1
01Swedish Alfabilder-1
03Czech Stadion-648
04Swedish Alfabilder Alfa Stars-48
04Swedish Alfabilder Alfa Star Golden Ice-2
04Swedish Alfabilder Next In Line-3
04Swedish Alfabilder Proof Parallels-48
Johansson, Sven-Olov
64Swedish Coralli ISHockey-125
64Swedish Coralli ISHockey-149
65Swedish Coralli ISHockey-149
Johansson, Thomas
90Swedish Semic Elitserien Stickers-282
91Swedish Semic Elitserien Stickers-64
92Swedish Semic Elitserien Stickers-81
93Swedish Semic Elitserien-55
94Swedish Leaf-121
95Swedish Leaf-30
95Swedish Upper Deck-40
98Swedish UD Choice-52
99Swedish Upper Deck-38
Hands of Gold-5
Hands of Gold-7
00Finnish Cardset-280
02Swedish SHL-209
Parallel-209
03Swedish Elite-211
Hot Numbers-HN8
Silver-211
04Swedish Elitset Jerseys Series 2-TJ
04Swedish Pure Skills-43
Parallel-43
05Swedish SHL Elitset-71
Gold-71
Icons-4
Series One Jerseys-3
06Swedish SHL Elitset-161
Johansson, Torbjorn
95Swedish Leaf-243
Rookies-5
95Swedish Upper Deck-96
97Swedish Collector's Choice-102
98Swedish UD Choice-119
99Swedish Upper Deck-105
02German DEL City Press-115
03Russian Hockey League-63
Johansson, Tord
71Swedish Hockey-205
72Swedish Stickers-184
Johansson, Ulf
69Swedish Hockey-169
Johansson, Uno
85Swedish Panini Stickers-193
Johansson, Yngve
55Swedish Alfabilder-5
Johanssonn, Stisse
72Swedish Stickers-220
John, Bernie
917th Inn. Sketch OHL-249
91Sudbury Wolves-6
92Sudbury Wolves-8
98Port Huron Border Cats-11
99Indianapolis Ice-9
00Indianapolis Ice-12
01Indianapolis Ice-11
01Indianapolis Ice-12
02Indianapolis Ice-8
03Indianapolis Ice-12
John, Peter
93Quebec Pee-Wee Tournament-1691
96German DEL-37
98German DEL-180
99German DEL-74
Johner, Dustin
03ECHL Update RBI Sports-283
04Las Vegas Wranglers-5
Johns, Don
60Shirriff Coins-93
63Topps-64
64Beehive Group III Photos-136
64Coca-Cola Caps-76
65Quebec Aces-10
94Parkhurst Tall Boys-98
Johns, Steven
03Minnesota State Mavericks-9
Johnsen, Mads
98Danish Hockey League-136
99Danish Hockey League-153
Johnsen, Pal
99Norwegian National Team-14
Johnson Jr., Tom
94Guelph Storm-15
Johnson, Aaron
99Rimouski Oceanic-21
Signed-21
00Rimouski Oceanic-22
Signed-22
01Rimouski Oceanic-21
03Beehive-224
Gold-224
Silver-224
03ITG VIP Rookie Debut-72
03Pacific Complete-552
Red-552
03Parkhurst Rookie-62
03SP Authentic-118
Limited-118
03SP Game Used-127
03Topps Traded-TT103
Blue-TT103
Gold-TT103
Red-TT103
03Upper Deck Rookie Update-128
03Pacific AHL Prospects-85
Gold-85
03Quebec Remparts Memorial Cup-7
03Syracuse Crunch-16
03Waterloo Blackhawks-12
04Syracuse Crunch-16
05Syracuse Crunch-24
Johnson, Adam
00Lethbridge Hurricanes-10
Johnson, Al
44Beehive Group II Photos-181
61Parkhurst-22
61Shirriff/Salada Coins-72
84Nanaimo Clippers-12
Johnson, Anders
92Quebec Pee-Wee Tournament-1516
97Dubuque Fighting Saints-17
00Connecticut Huskies-9
Johnson, Andy
95Slapshot-323
Johnson, Antony
93UK Humberside Hawks-12
94Finnish Jaa Kiekko-322
94UK Humberside Hawks-12
99UK Hull Thunder-8
01UK Hull Thunder-10
Johnson, Ben
97Spokane Chiefs-16
05UK Guildford Flames-4
06UK Guildford Flames-4
Johnson, Bill
52St. Lawrence Sales-60
54UK A and BC Chewing Gum-74
Johnson, Bob
72Blues White Border-8
74NHL Action Stamps-230
74Penguins Postcards-9
81Red Wings Oldtimers-1
85Flames Red Rooster-9
86Flames Red Rooster-8
90Penguins Foodland-7
90Pro Set-674
Johnson, Brent
94Owen Sound Platers-24
95Slapshot-281
95Owen Sound Platers-27
95Owen Sound Platers-29
96Owen Sound Platers-5
98Upper Deck-358
Exclusives-358
Exclusives 1 of 1-358
Gold Reserve-358
99Pacific-367
Copper-367
Emerald Green-367
Gold-367
Ice Blue-367
Premiere Date-367
Red-367
00BAP Memorabilia-439
Emerald-439
Ruby-439
Sapphire-439
00BAP Parkhurst 2000-P190
00BAP Signature Series-295
Emerald-295
Ruby-295
Sapphire-295
00Crown Royale-139
21st Century Rookies-21
00Private Stock-140
Gold-140
Premiere Date-140
Retail-140
Silver-140
PS-2001 Rookies-19
00Stadium Club-236
00Titanium-141
Retail-141
Three-Star Selections-26
00Titanium Draft Day Edition-141
00Titanium Draft Day Promos-141
00Topps Gold Label Class 1-88
Gold-88
00Topps Gold Label Class 2-88
00Topps Gold Label Class 2 Gold-88
00Topps Gold Label Class 3-88
00Topps Gold Label Class 3 Gold-88
00Topps Heritage-58
Chrome Parallel-58
00Topps Premier Plus-94
Blue Ice-94
00Topps Stars-149
Blue-149
00Vanguard-143
Pacific Proofs-143
01Atomic-81
Blue-81
Gold-81
Premiere Date-81
Red-81
01BAP Signature Series-21
Autographs-21
Autographs Gold-21
01BAP Ultimate Memorabilia Bloodlines-7
01Between the Pipes-46
Goalie Gear-GG25
Masks-28
Masks Silver-28
Masks Gold-28
01Bowman YoungStars-87
Gold-87
Ice Cubed-87
01Crown Royale-119
Blue-119
Premiere Date-119
Red-119
Retail-119
01Crown Royale Toronto Expo Rookie Coll-G6
01O-Pee-Chee-205
01O-Pee-Chee Premier Parallel-205
01Pacific-324
01Pacific-440
01Pacific-449
Extreme LTD-324
Gold-440
Hobby LTD-324
Premiere Date-324
Retail LTD-324
01Pacific Adrenaline-159
Blue-159
Premiere Date-159
Red-159
Retail-159
Creased Lightning-18
Power Play-30
01Pacific Arena Exclusives-324
01Pacific Arena Exclusives-440
01Parkhurst-57
Gold-57
Silver-57
01Private Stock-80
Gold-80
Premiere Date-80
Retail-80
Silver-80
01Private Stock Pacific Nights-80
01SP Game Used Authentic Fabric-AFBJ
01SP Game Used Authentic Fabric Gold-AFBJ
01SPx-191
01Stadium Club-89
Award Winners-89
Master Photos-89
New Regime-NR3
New Regime-NRABJ
01Titanium-116
Hobby Parallel-116
Premiere Date-116
Retail-116
Retail Parallel-116

01Topps-205
OPC Parallel-205
01Topps Heritage-58
Refractors-58
01Topps Reserve-94
01UD Challenge for the Cup-75
01UD Mask Collection-126
Gold-126
Double Patches-DPBJ
Dual Jerseys-PMMJ
Goalie Jerseys-SSBJ
Jerseys-J-BJ
Jersey and Patch-JPBJ
01UD Top Shelf-116
01Upper Deck-381
Exclusives-381
01Upper Deck Victory-302
Gold-302
01Vanguard-81
Blue-81
Red-81
One of Ones-81
Premiere Date-81
Prime Prospects-16
Proofs-81
01Worcester Icecats-29
02Atomic-82
Blue-82
Gold-82
Red-82
Denied-17
Hobby Parallel-82
02BAP First Edition-205
02BAP Memorabilia-42
Emerald-42
Ruby-42
Sapphire-42
NHL All-Star Game-42
NHL All-Star Game Blue-42
NHL All-Star Game Green-42
NHL All-Star Game Red-42
Stanley Cup Playoffs-SC-16
02BAP Memorabilia Toronto Fall Expo-42
02BAP Signature Series-139
Autographs-139
Autograph Buybacks 2001-21
Autographs Gold-139
Defensive Wall-DW7
Phenoms-YP8
02Between the Pipes-55
02Between the Pipes-145
Gold-55
Silver-55
Future Wave-12
Goalie Autographs-10
Masks II-26
Masks II Gold-26
Masks II Silver-26
Tandems-15
02Blues Team Issue-9
02Bowman YoungStars-93
Gold-93
Silver-93
02Crown Royale-81
Blue-81
Red-81
Retail-81
02O-Pee-Chee-122
02O-Pee-Chee Premier Blue Parallel-122
02O-Pee-Chee Premier Red Parallel-122
02O-Pee-Chee Factory Set-122
02Pacific-323
Blue-323
Red-323
02Pacific Complete-372
Red-372
02Pacific Exclusive-143
Advantage-13
02Pacific Heads-Up-103
Blue-103
Purple-103
Red-103
Showstoppers-17
02Pacific Quest for the Cup-82
Gold-82
Jerseys-18
02Pacific Toronto Fall Expo-10
Gold-10
02Parkhurst-29
Bronze-29
Gold-29
Silver-29
02Parkhurst Retro-189
Minis-189
02Private Stock Reserve-84
Blue-84
Red-84
Retail-84
InCrease Security-18
02SP Game Used Future Fabrics-FFBJ
02SP Game Used Future Fabrics Gold-FFBJ
02SP Game Used Future Fabrics Rainbow-FFBJ
02SPx-66
Spectrum Gold-66
Spectrum Silver-66
02Stadium Club-18
Silver Decoy Cards-18
Proofs-18
Puck Stops Here-PSH1
02Titanium-83
Blue-83
Red-83
Retail-83
02Topps-122
OPC Blue Parallel-122
OPC Red Parallel-122
Own The Game-OTG20
Factory Set-122
02Topps Chrome-78
Black Border Refractors-78
Refractors-78
02Topps Heritage-75
Chrome Parallel-75
02Topps Total-161
02UD Honor Roll-62
02UD Mask Collection-75
02UD Mask Collection-76
02UD Mask Collection-77
02UD Mask Collection-78
02UD Mask Collection-114
02UD Mask Collection Beckett Promos-75
02UD Mask Collection Beckett Promos-76
02UD Mask Collection Beckett Promos-77
02UD Mask Collection Beckett Promos-78
02UD Mask Collection Nation's Best-NDBJ
02UD Mask Collection Patches-PWBJ
02UD Piece of History-79
02UD Top Shelf-76
Stopper Jerseys-SSBJ
Triple Jerseys-TSDPJ
02Upper Deck-153
Exclusives-153
Saviors Jerseys-SVBJ
Super Saviors-SA13
02Upper Deck MVP-158
Gold-158
Classics-158
Golden Classics-158
02Upper Deck Victory-186
Bronze-186
Gold-186
Silver-186
02Upper Deck Vintage-224
02Upper Deck Vintage-286
Green Backs-224
03BAP Memorabilia-104
Emerald-104
Gold-104
Ruby-104
Sapphire-104
Deep in the Crease-D12
03Blues Team Set-11
03ITG Action-575
Jerseys-M35
03NHL Sticker Collection-280
03O-Pee-Chee-149
03OPC Blue-149
03OPC Gold-149
03OPC Red-149
03Pacific-283
Blue-283
Red-283
Jerseys-32
Jerseys Gold-32
03Pacific Complete-432
Red-432
03Pacific Invincible Jerseys-25
03Private Stock Reserve-84
Blue-84
Red-84
Retail-84
03Topps-149
Blue-149
Gold-149
Red-149
Topps/OPC Idols-UI18
03Topps Pristine-29
Gold Refractor Die Cuts-29
Refractors-29
Press Plates Black-29
Press Plates Cyan-29
Press Plates Magenta-29
Press Plates Yellow-29
03Topps Traded-TT76
Blue-TT76
Gold-TT76
Red-TT76
03Upper Deck-415
Canadian Exclusives-415
HG-415
UD Exclusives-415
03Upper Deck MVP-373
Gold Script-373
Silver Script-373
Canadian Exclusives-373
03Worcester Ice Cats 10th Anniversary-3
05Parkhurst-489
Facsimile Auto Parallel-489
06Fleer-198
Tiffany-198
06O-Pee-Chee-498
Rainbow-498
06Upper Deck MVP-296
Gold Script-296
Super Script-296

Johnson, Brian
85Minnesota-Duluth Bulldogs-18

Johnson, Brock
04Columbus Cottonmouths-17

Johnson, Chad HK
92North Dakota Fighting Sioux-12
93Fort Worth Fire-8

Johnson, Charlie
06Idaho Steelheads-7

Johnson, Chaz
01Rimouski Oceanic-1
01Val d'Or Foreurs-3
02Val d'Or Foreurs-23
03Val d'Or Foreurs-23
04Drummondville Voltigeurs-5
05Rockford Ice Hogs-7
06Rockford IceHogs-13

Johnson, Clint
95Minnesota Golden Gophers-16

Johnson, Colin
03South Carolina Stingrays-329

Johnson, Corey
92North Dakota Fighting Sioux-13

Johnson, Cory
917th Inn. Sketch OHL-227
95Muskegon Fury-6
96Grand Rapids Griffins-11
99Corpus Christi IceRays-9

Johnson, Craig
91Minnesota Golden Gophers-10
92Minnesota Golden Gophers-10
93PowerPlay-507
93Stadium Club Team USA-11
93Stadium Club Team USA Members Only-11
93Topps Premier Team USA-19
93Ultra-487
94Flair-155
94OPC Premier-369
Special Effects-369
94Topps/OPC Premier-369
Special Effects-369
94Upper Deck-253
Electric Ice-253
94Classic Pro Prospects Ice Ambassadors-IA14
94Classic Pro Prospects Intl Heroes-LP7
95Leaf-273
95Pinnacle-208
Artist's Proofs-208
Rink Collection-208
95Score-292
Black Ice Artist's Proofs-292
Black Ice-292
95SP-66B
95Upper Deck-139
Electric Ice-139
Electric Ice-308
Electric Ice Gold-139
96Collector's Choice-129
96Upper Deck-80
97Be A Player-100
Autographs-100
Autographs Die-Cuts-100
Autographs Prismatic Die-Cuts-100
97Pacific Dynagon Best Kept Secrets-46
98Pacific-236
Ice Blue-236
Red-236
99Pacific-191
Copper-191
Emerald Green-191
Gold-191
Ice Blue-191
Premiere Date-191
Red-191
00Upper Deck-84
Exclusives Tier 1-84
Exclusives Tier 2-84
00Upper Deck Vintage-170
02Kings Game Sheets-5
02Kings Game Sheets-6
02Pacific-167
Blue-167
Red-167
02Pacific Complete-380
Red-380
02Topps Total-42
04German DEL-126
04German Hamburg Freezers Postcards-5
05German DEL-67
06German DEL-44
Team Leaders-TL13

Johnson, Craig (Goalie)
92Windsor Spitfires-19

Johnson, Dan
70Canucks Royal Bank-8
70Esso Power Players-44
70Sargent Promotions Stamps-214
71O-Pee-Chee-95
71Sargent Promotions Stamps-210
71Toronto Sun-280
052005 Sacramento River Cats Multi-Ad-32

Johnson, Darcy
98CN Blizzard-6
99CN Blizzard-7
00CN Blizzard-6
01Colorado Gold Kings-11

Johnson, Darren
96Knoxville Cherokees-9

Johnson, Dion
91Air Canada SJHL-A11
92Saskatchewan JHL-121

Johnson, Doug
98BC Icemen-7
98BC Icemen II-5
01Odessa Jackalopes-12
02Austin Ice Bats-6
06Odessa Jackalopes-21

Johnson, Eric
93St. Cloud State Huskies-12

Johnson, Erik
97New Hampshire Wildcats-22
97New Hampshire Wildcats-23
00Sioux City Musketeers-14
06Minnesota Golden Gophers-12

Johnson, Erik (SC)
00Sioux City Musketeers-14

Johnson, Ernest
10C56-30
10Sweet Caporal Postcards-28
11C55-28
12C57-25
60Topps-4
Stamps-30
83Hall of Fame Postcards-A10
85Hall of Fame-10

Johnson, Gary
83Medicine Hat Tigers-4

Johnson, Greg
90Upper Deck-460
French-460
91UND Fighting Sioux Sports Collectors Card Set - 14
92North Dakota Fighting Sioux-11
93Donruss-94
93Leaf-370
93OPC Premier-457
Gold-457
93Parkhurst-270
Emerald Ice-270
93Pinnacle-453
Canadian-453
93PowerPlay-330
93Score-601
Gold-601
Canadian-601
Canadian Gold-601
93Stadium Club-367
Members Only Master Set-367
First Day Issue-367
93Topps/OPC Premier-457
Gold-457
93Ultra-306
Wave of the Future-7
93Upper Deck-452
93Classic Team Canada-TC1
94Donruss-150
94Leaf-355
94OPC Premier-257
Special Effects-257
94Parkhurst SE-SE48
Gold-SE48
94Pinnacle-511
Artist's Proofs-511
Rink Collection-511
94Score Team Canada-CT5
94Topps/OPC Premier-257
Special Effects-257
94Ultra-283
94Upper Deck-212
Electric Ice-212
94Swedish Olympics Lillehammer*-315
94Classic Pro Prospects-17
95Be A Player-73
Signatures-S73
Signatures Die Cuts-S73
95Parkhurst International-338
Emerald Ice-338
95Ultra-233
95Upper Deck-308
95Upper Deck-334
Electric Ice-334
Electric Ice Gold-334
96Collector's Choice-78
96Donruss-111
Press Proofs-111
96Fleer Picks-100
96Leaf-33
Press Proofs-33
96Pinnacle-140
Artist's Proofs-140
Foil-140
Premium Stock-140
Rink Collection-140
96Score-132
Artist's Proofs-132
Dealer's Choice Artist's Proofs-132
Special Artist's Proofs-132
Golden Blades-132
96Summit-49
Artist's Proofs-49
Ice-49
Metal-49
Premium Stock-49
96Upper Deck-254
97Collector's Choice-206
97Score Penguins-11
Platinum-11
Premier-11
97Upper Deck-134
98Be A Player-225
Press Release-225
98BAP Gold-225
98BAP Autographs-225
98BAP Autographs Gold-225
98Crown Royale-75
Limited Series-75
98Pacific-145
Ice Blue-145
Red-145
98Pacific Omega-129
Red-129
Opening Day Issue-129
98Predators Team Issue-12
98Upper Deck-306
Exclusives-306
Exclusives 1 of 1-306
Gold Reserve-306
98Upper Deck MVP-111
Gold Script-111
Silver Script-111
Super Script-111
99BAP Memorabilia-278
Gold-278
Silver-278
99BAP Millennium-141
Emerald-141
Ruby-141
Sapphire-141
Signatures-141
Signatures Gold-141
99Pacific-225
Copper-225
Emerald Green-225
Gold-225
Ice Blue-225
Premiere Date-225
Red-225
99Pacific Dynagon Ice-107
Blue-107
Copper-107
Gold-107
Premiere Date-107
99Paramount-125
Copper-125
Emerald-125
Gold-125
Holographic Emerald-125
Holographic Gold-125
Holographic Silver-125
Ice Blue-125
Premiere Date-125
Red-125
Silver-125
99Revolution-79
Premiere Date-79
Red-79
Shadow Series-79
99Stadium Club-24
First Day Issue-24
One of a Kind-24
Printing Plates Black-24
Printing Plates Cyan-24
Printing Plates Magenta-24
Printing Plates Yellow-24
99Upper Deck MVP SC Edition-102
Gold Script-102
Silver Script-102
Super Script-102
00BAP Memorabilia-338
Emerald-338
Ruby-338
Sapphire-338
Promos-338
00BAP Mem Chicago Sportsfest Copper-338
00BAP Memorabilia Chicago Sportsfest Blue-338
00BAP Memorabilia Chicago Sportsfest Gold-338
00BAP Memorabilia Chicago Sportsfest Ruby-338
00BAP Memorabilia Chicago Sun-Times Ruby-338
00BAP Memorabilia Chicago Sun-Times Gold-338
00BAP Mem Chicago Sun-Times Sapphire-338
00BAP Mem Toronto Fall Expo Copper-338
00BAP Memorabilia Toronto Fall Expo Gold-338
00BAP Memorabilia Toronto Fall Expo Ruby-338
00O-Pee-Chee-263B
00O-Pee-Chee Parallel-263B
00Pacific-222
Copper-222
Gold-222
Ice Blue-222
Premiere Date-222
00Panini Stickers-183
00Paramount-135
Copper-135
Gold-135
Holo-Gold-135
Holo-Silver-135
Ice Blue-135
Premiere Date-135
00Topps/OPC-263B
Parallel-263B
00Upper Deck-330
Exclusives Tier 1-330
Exclusives Tier 2-330
00Upper Deck Victory-129
00Upper Deck Vintage-198
01BAP Signature Series-17
Autographs-17
Autographs Gold-17
01Pacific-218
Extreme LTD-218
Hobby LTD-218
Premiere Date-218
Retail LTD-218
01Pacific Arena Exclusives-218
01Upper Deck-99
Exclusives-99
01Upper Deck Victory-200
Gold-200
01Upper Deck Vintage-145
02BAP First Edition-174
02BAP Sig Series Auto Buybacks 1998-225
02BAP Sig Series Auto Buybacks 1999-141
02BAP Sig Series Auto Buybacks 2001-17
02O-Pee-Chee-185
02O-Pee-Chee Premier Blue Parallel-185
02O-Pee-Chee Premier Red Parallel-185
02O-Pee-Chee Factory Set-185
02Pacific-211
Blue-211
Red-211
02Pacific Complete-342
Red-342
02Pacific Exclusive-99
02Predators Team Issue-3
02Private Stock Reserve-59
Blue-59
Red-59
Retail-59
02Topps-185
OPC Blue Parallel-185
OPC Red Parallel-185
Factory Set-185
02Topps Total-265
02UD Honor Roll-87
02Upper Deck Victory-121
Bronze-121
Gold-121
Silver-121
03Beehive-108
Gold-108
Silver-108
03ITG Action-302
03NHL Sticker Collection-254
03Pacific Complete-280
Red-280
03Upper Deck-107
Canadian Exclusives-107
HG-107
03Upper Deck MVP-243
Gold Script-243
Silver Script-243
Canadian Exclusives-243
05Panini Stickers-318
05Parkhurst-516
Facsimile Auto Parallel-516

Johnson, Gregg
03Boston University Terriers-3
05Binghamton Senators-19
05Binghamton Senators Quickway-19

Johnson, Ivan
30Rogers Peet Company *-29
33O-Pee-Chee V304A-39
33Sport Kings R338 *-30
33V129-33
34Beehive Group I Photos-279
34Sweet Caporal-42
35Diamond Matchbooks Tan 1-31
35Diamond Matchbooks Tan 2-30
35Diamond Matchbooks Tan 3-27
36Triumph Postcards-3
37V356 Worldwide Gum-21
69Equitable Sports Hall of Fame-4
83Hall of Fame Postcards-D5
85Hall of Fame-51
94Parkhurst Tall Boys Greats-11
02BAP Ultimate Mem Paper Cuts Autos-20
03Parkhurst Original Six New York-46
03Parkhurst Original Six New York-68
04ITG Franchises US East-366
04ITG Ultimate Memorabilia-32
Gold-32
Broadway Blueshirts-8

Johnson, Jack
07Upper Deck Ovation-80
07Upper Deck Victory-201
Black-201
Gold-201

Johnson, Jamie
03ECHL Update RBI Sports-141
03Louisiana Ice Gators-9
05Iowa Stars-17
06Augusta Lynx-6

Johnson, Jason
93Kitchener Rangers-23

Johnson, Jeff
90Pro Set-249

Johnson, Jeremy
93Quebec Pee-Wee Tournament-1234

Johnson, Jim (60s-70s)
61Sudbury Wolves-10
62Sudbury Wolves-12
68O-Pee-Chee-186
69O-Pee-Chee-97
69Topps-97
70Esso Power Players-213
70Sargent Promotions Stamps-153
71O-Pee-Chee-48
71Sargent Promotions Stamps-148
71Topps-48
71Toronto Sun-199
72Minnesota Fighting Saints Postcards WHA-9
74Minnesota Fighting Saints WHA-14

Johnson, Jim (80s)
84Minnesota-Duluth Bulldogs-20
86O-Pee-Chee-231
86O-Pee-Chee Stickers-128
86Penguins Kodak-12
87O-Pee-Chee-196
87O-Pee-Chee Stickers-172
87Panini Stickers-143
87Penguins Masks-5
87Penguins Kodak-13
87Topps-196
88O-Pee-Chee-148
88Panini Stickers-334
88Topps-148
89O-Pee-Chee-77
89Panini Stickers-320
89Penguins Foodland-2
89Topps-77
90O-Pee-Chee-98
90Pro Set-235
90Score-202
Canadian-202
90Topps-98
Tiffany-98
91O-Pee-Chee-426
91Parkhurst-303
French-303
91Pinnacle-235
French-235
91Pro Set-116
French-116
91Score American-52
91Score Canadian Bilingual-52
91Score Canadian English-52
91Topps-426
92Bowman-177
92Panini Stickers-94
92Panini Stickers French-94
92Pinnacle-137
French-137
92Pro Set-83
92Score-161
Canadian-161
92Stadium Club-75
92Topps-54
Gold-54G
92Ultra-95
92Finnish Semic-155
93OPC Premier-98
Gold-98
93Pinnacle-192
Canadian-192
93Score-144
Canadian-144
93Stadium Club-298
Members Only Master Set-298
First Day Issue-298
93Topps/OPC Premier-98
Gold-98
94Pinnacle-440
Artist's Proofs-440
Rink Collection-440
94Stars HockeyKaps-16
94Finnish Jaa Kiekko-110
95Capitals Team Issue-11
96Coyotes Coca-Cola-11
97Be A Player-104
Autographs-104
Autographs Die-Cuts-104
Autographs Prismatic Die-Cuts-104
97Pacific-174
Copper-174
Emerald Green-174
Ice Blue-174
Red-174
Silver-174

Johnson, Joe
97UK Guildford Flames-4
05Topps Luxury Box Divisions 6 Relics 25-6
05Topps Luxury Box Divisions 6 Relics 1-6
05Topps Luxury Box Divisions 6 Relics-6
05Topps Luxury Box Divisions 6 Relics 1-10
05Topps Luxury Box Divisions 6 Relics-10
05Topps Luxury Box Divisions 6 Relics 25-10

Johnson, John
89Niagara Falls Thunder-8
897th Inn. Sketch OHL-144
907th Inn. Sketch OHL-261
91Peterborough Petes-26
92Toledo Storm-13
93Quebec Pee-Wee Tournament-1319
93Wheeling Thunderbirds-11
99German Bundesliga 2-148

Johnson, Jonas
03Swedish Elite-177
Silver-177
04Swedish Elitset-33
Gold-33
04Swedish Pure Skills-23
Parallel-23
05Swedish SHL Elitset-35
Gold-35

Johnson, Josh
93Quebec Pee-Wee Tournament-855
04Minnesota-Duluth Bulldogs-11
07SPx Winning Materials 175 Blue-JJ
07Artifacts Divisional Artifacts Gold-JJ

Johnson, Justin
00Lincoln Stars-23
01Minnesota Golden Gophers-29
02Minnesota Golden Gophers-10
03Minnesota Golden Gophers-17
04Green Bay Gamblers-6
04Minnesota Golden Gophers-14

Johnson, Karl
91Air Canada SJHL-E9
92Saskatchewan JHL-17

Johnson, Keith
04Maine Black Bears-9
05Maine Black Bears-12

Johnson, Kenny
93UK Humberside Hawks-1
99Aurora-90
Premiere Date-90
99Upper Deck Gold Reserve-84

Johnson, Krista
04Minnesota Golden Gophers Women-6

Johnson, Lance
89Kamloops Blazers-11
907th Inn. Sketch WHL-288
907th Inn. Sketch Memorial Cup-7
917th Inn. Sketch WHL-83

Johnson, Marc
04Belleville Bulls-14

Johnson, Mark
79Panini Stickers-213
80USA Olympic Team Mini Pics-4
80O-Pee-Chee-69
80Topps-69
81Swedish Semic Hockey VM Stickers-100
82Whalers Junior Hartford Courant-8
83O-Pee-Chee-140
83O-Pee-Chee Stickers-254
83Puffy Stickers-17
83Topps Stickers-254
83Whalers Junior Hartford Courant-8
84O-Pee-Chee-72
84O-Pee-Chee Stickers-193
84Topps-56
84Whalers Junior Wendy's-9
85Devils Postcards-6
85O-Pee-Chee-44
85O-Pee-Chee Stickers-50
85Topps-44
86Devils Police-12
86O-Pee-Chee-112
86O-Pee-Chee Stickers-200
86Topps-112
87O-Pee-Chee-101
87O-Pee-Chee Stickers-64
87Panini Stickers-83
87Topps-101
88Devils Caretta-13
88O-Pee-Chee-45
88Topps-45
89Devils Caretta-12
89O-Pee-Chee-244
89Panini Stickers-260
89Swedish Semic World Champ Stickers-174
90O-Pee-Chee-178
90Panini Stickers-66
90Pro Set-168
90Topps-178
Tiffany-178
90Upper Deck-180
French-180
92Sports Illustrated for Kids II-666
95Madison Monsters-21
95Signature Rookies Miracle on Ice-17
95Signature Rookies Miracle on Ice-18
95Signature Rook Miracle on Ice Sigs-17
95Signature Rook Miracle on Ice Sigs-18
04UD Legendary Signatures AKA Autographs-AKA-MJ
04UD Legendary Signatures Miracle Men-USA5
04UD Legendary Signatures Miracle Men Autographs-USA-MJ
04Belleville Bulls-14
04Wisconsin Badgers Women-10

Johnson, Matt
93Peterborough Petes-22
94OPC Premier-339
Special Effects-339
94Pinnacle-496
Artist's Proofs-496
Rink Collection-496
94Topps/OPC Premier-339
Special Effects-339
94Upper Deck-203
Electric Ice-203
94Classic-65
Gold-65
Tri-Cards-T31
95Donruss-217
95Leaf-64
96Be A Player-215
Autographs-215
Autographs Silver-215
96Collector's Edge Future Legends-28
97Pacific-350
Copper-350
Emerald Green-350
Ice Blue-350
Red-350
Silver-350
98Upper Deck MVP-100
Gold Script-100
Silver Script-100
Super Script-100
99Paramount-12
Copper-12
Emerald-12
Gold-12
Holographic Emerald-12
Holographic Gold-12
Holographic Silver-12
Ice Blue-12
Premiere Date-12
Red-12
Silver-12
99Topps Arena Giveaways-ATL-MJ
00BAP Memorabilia Update Tough Materials-T23
00BAP Mem Update Tough Materials Gold-T23
00Topps Heritage-177
00Upper Deck NHLPA-PA44
01BAP Update Tough Customers-TC7
01BAP Update Tough Customers-TC22
01Pacific-196
Extreme LTD-196
Hobby LTD-196
Premiere Date-196
Retail LTD-196
01Pacific Arena Exclusives-196
01Arizona Icecats-8
02BAP Signature Series Famous Scraps-FS12
02Upper Deck-334
Exclusives-334
02Upper Deck Beckett UD Promos-334
02Arizona Icecats-9
03ITG Action-294
03Topps Own the Game-OTG18
03Upper Deck Tough Customers-TC-9
03Upper Deck MVP-216
Gold Script-216
Silver Script-216
Canadian Exclusives-216

Johnson, Michael
917th Inn. Sketch OHL-300
97Be A Player-218
Autographs-218
Autographs Die-Cuts-218
Autographs Prismatic Die-Cuts-218
One Timers-18
97Beehive-54
Authentic Autographs-54
Golden Portraits-54
97Black Diamond-118
Double Diamond-118
Triple Diamond-118
Quadruple Diamond-118
Premium Cut-PC27
Premium Cut Double Diamond-PC27
Premium Cut Quadruple Diamond Horiz-PC27
Premium Cut Triple Diamond-PC27
Premium Cut Quadruple Diamond Verticals-PC27
97Katch-166
Gold-166
Silver-166
97Pacific-335
Copper-335
Emerald Green-335
Ice Blue-335
Red-335
Silver-335
97Pacific Omega-221
Copper-221
Dark Gray-221
Emerald Green-221
Gold-221
Ice Blue-221
97SP Authentic-194
97Upper Deck Ice-48
Parallel-48
Power Shift-48
97Zenith-82
Z-Gold-82
Z-Silver-82
5 x 7 Gold Impulse-71
5 x 7 Silver Impulse-71
Rookie Reign-12
Z-Team-12
Z-Team Gold-12
98Aurora-181
98Be A Player-137
Press Release-137
98BAP Gold-137
98BAP Autographs-137
98BAP Autographs Gold-137
98BAP Tampa Bay All Star Game-137
98Bowman's Best-71
Refractors-71
Atomic Refractors-71
Performers-BP1
Performers Refractors-BP1
Performers Atomic Refractors-BP1
98Crown Royale-130
Limited Series-130
98Finest-37
No Protectors-37
No Protectors Refractors-37
Refractors-37
Centurion-C16
Centurion Refractors-C16
98Katch-142
98OPC Chrome-42
Refractors-42
Season's Best-SB7
Season's Best Refractors-SB7
98Pacific-413
Ice Blue-413
Red-413
98Pacific Dynagon Ice-179
Blue-179
Red-179
98Pacific Omega-227
Red-227
Opening Day Issue-227
98Panini Photocards-36
98Paramount-226
Copper-226
Emerald Green-226
Holo-Electric-226
Ice Blue-226
Silver-226
98Post-12
98Revolution-137
Ice Shadow-137
Red-137
98SP Authentic-81
Power Shift-81
98SPx Finite-81
98SPx Finite-122
Radiance-81
Radiance-122
Spectrum-81
Spectrum-122
98Topps-42
O-Pee-Chee-42
Ice Age 2000-I14
Season's Best-SB7
98Topps Gold Label Class 1-66
Black-66
Black One of One-66
One of One-66
Red-66
Red One of One-66
98Topps Gold Label Class 2-66
98Topps Gold Label Class 2 Black-66
98Topps Gold Label Class 2 Black 1 of 1-66
98Topps Gold Label Class 2 One of One-66
98Topps Gold Label Class 2 Red-66
98Topps Gold Label Class 2 Red One of One-66
98Topps Gold Label Class 3-66
98Topps Gold Label Class 3 Black-66
98Topps Gold Label Class 3 Black 1 of 1-66
98Topps Gold Label Class 3 One of One-66
98Topps Gold Label Class 3 Red-66
98Topps Gold Label Class 3 Red One of One-66
98UD Choice-199
Prime Choice Reserve-199
Reserve-199
StarQuest Blue-SQ27
StarQuest Gold-SQ27
StarQuest Green-SQ27
StarQuest Red-SQ27
98UD3-23
98UD3-83
98UD3-143
Die-Cuts-23
Die-Cuts-83
Die-Cuts-143
98Upper Deck-187
Exclusives-187
Exclusives 1 of 1-187
Fantastic Finishers-FF27
Fantastic Finishers Quantum 1-FF27
Fantastic Finishers Quantum 2-FF27
Fantastic Finishers Quantum 3-FF27
Frozen In Time-FT18
Frozen In Time Quantum 1-FT18
Frozen In Time Quantum 2-FT18
Frozen In Time Quantum 3-FT18
Gold Reserve-187
98Upper Deck MVP-199
Gold Script-199
Silver Script-199
Super Script-199
ProSign-MJ
98German DEL-194
99Aurora-135
Premiere Date-135
99Black Diamond-81
Diamond Cut-81
Final Cut-81
99O-Pee-Chee-172
99O-Pee-Chee Chrome-172
99O-Pee-Chee Chrome Refractors-172
99O-Pee-Chee Now Starring-NS11
99Pacific-406
Copper-406
Emerald Green-406
Gold-406
Ice Blue-406
Premiere Date-406
Red-406
99Pacific Dynagon Ice-188
Blue-188
Copper-188
Gold-188
Premiere Date-188
99Paramount-224
Copper-224
Emerald-224
Gold-224
Holographic Emerald-224
Holographic Gold-224
Holographic Silver-224
Ice Blue-224
Premiere Date-224
Red-224
99Revolution-137
Premiere Date-137
Red-137
Shadow Series-137
Copper-137
Gold-137
CSC Silver-137
99SP Authentic Buyback Signatures-30
99SP Authentic Buyback Signatures-31
99Stadium Club-95
First Day Issue-95
One of a Kind-95
Printing Plates Black-95
Printing Plates Cyan-95
Printing Plates Magenta-95
Printing Plates Yellow-95
99Topps/OPC-172
Now Starring-NS11
99Topps/OPC Chrome-172
Refractors-172
99Upper Deck-294
Exclusives-294
Exclusives 1 of 1-294
99Upper Deck Gold Reserve-294
99Upper Deck MVP-202
Gold Script-202
Silver Script-202

Super Script-202
99Upper Deck Victory-288
99Wayne Gretzky Hockey-163
00Aurora-133
Premiere Date-133
00BAP Memorabilia-380
Emerald-380
Ruby-380
Sapphire-380
Promos-380
00BAP Mem Chicago Sportsfest Copper-380
00BAP Memorabilia Chicago Sportsfest Blue-380
00BAP Memorabilia Chicago Sportsfest Gold-380
00BAP Memorabilia Chicago Sportsfest Ruby-380
00BAP Memorabilia Chicago Sun-Times Ruby-380
00BAP Memorabilia Chicago Sun-Times Gold-380
00BAP Mem Chicago Sun-Times Sapphire-380
00BAP Mem Toronto Fall Expo Copper-380
00BAP Memorabilia Toronto Fall Expo Gold-380
00BAP Memorabilia Toronto Fall Expo Ruby-380
00BAP Signature Series-3
Emerald-3
Ruby-3
Sapphire-3
Autographs-33
Autographs Gold-33
00O-Pee-Chee-239
00O-Pee-Chee Parallel-239
00Pacific-373
Copper-373
Gold-373
Ice Blue-373
Premiere Date-373
00Panini Stickers-91
00Paramount-221
Copper-221
Gold-221
Holo-Gold-221
Holo-Silver-221
Ice Blue-221
Premiere Date-221
00Revolution-133
Blue-133
Premiere Date-133
Red-133
00Stadium Club-127
00Titanium-88
Blue-88
Gold-88
Premiere Date-88
Red-88
Retail-88
00Topps/OPC-239
Parallel-239
00Topps Chrome-149
OPC Refractors-149
Refractors-149
00Topps Heritage-151
00UD Reserve-79
00Upper Deck-156
Exclusives Tier 1-156
Exclusives Tier 2-156
00Upper Deck MVP-161
First Stars-161
ProSign-MJ
Second Stars-161
Third Stars-161
00Upper Deck Victory-211
00Upper Deck Vintage-323
00Vanguard-89
Holographic Gold-89
Holographic Purple-89
Pacific Proofs-89
01BAP Memorabilia-264
Emerald-264
Ruby-264
Sapphire-264
01BAP Signature Series-166
Autographs-166
Autographs Gold-166
01Coyotes Team Issue-8
01Pacific-304
Extreme LTD-304
Hobby LTD-304
Premiere Date-304
Retail LTD-304
01Pacific Arena Exclusives-304
01Upper Deck-137
Exclusives-137
01Upper Deck Victory-267
01Bossier-Shreveport Mudbugs-7
02BAP Sig Series Auto Buybacks 1998-137
02BAP Sig Series Auto Buybacks 2000-33
02BAP Sig Series Auto Buybacks 2001-166
02Coyotes Team Issue-7
02Pacific-296
Blue-296
Red-296
02Pacific Complete-376
Red-376
02Vanguard-78
LTD-78
03BAP Memorabilia-56
Emerald-56
Gold-56
Ruby-56
Sapphire-56
03Beehive-152
Gold-152
Silver-152
03Black Diamond-169
Black-169
Green-169
Red-169
03Bowman-48
Gold-48
03Bowman Chrome-48
Refractors-48
Gold Refractors-48
Xtractors-48
03Coyotes Postcards-10
03ITG Action-438
03O-Pee-Chee-15
03OPC Blue-15
03OPC Gold-15
03OPC Red-15
03Pacific-264
Blue-264
Red-264
03Pacific Complete-271
Red-271
03Pacific Exhibit-115
Blue Backs-115
Yellow Backs-115
03Pacific Prism-79
Blue-79
Gold-79
Red-79
03Pacific Supreme-77
Blue-77
Red-77
Retail-77
03Private Stock Reserve-79
Blue-79
Red-79
Retail-79
03SP Authentic-67
Limited-67
03SPx-76
Radiance-76
Spectrum-76
03Topps-15
Blue-15
Gold-15
Red-15
03Topps C55-26
Minis-26
Minis American Back-26
Minis American Back Red-26
Minis Bazooka Back-26
Minis Brooklyn Back-26
Minis Hat Trick Back-26
Minis O Canada Back-26
Minis O Canada Back Red-26
Minis Stanley Cup Back-26
03Topps Pristine-25
Gold Refractor Die Cuts-25
Refractors-25
Press Plates Black-25
Press Plates Cyan-25
Press Plates Magenta-25
Press Plates Yellow-25
03UD Honor Roll-66
03Upper Deck-393
Canadian Exclusives-393
HG-393
UD Exclusives-393
03Upper Deck Classic Portraits-74
03Upper Deck MVP-320
Gold Script-320
Silver Script-320
Canadian Exclusives-320
SportsNut-SN69
03Upper Deck Trilogy-74
Limited-74
03Upper Deck Victory-144
Bronze-144
Gold-144
Silver-144
05Upper Deck-148
HG Glossy-148
05Upper Deck MVP-297
Gold-297
Platinum-297
05Upper Deck Toronto Fall Expo-148
06Upper Deck Masterpieces-356

Johnson, Mike(MINORS)
92Ottawa 67's-12

Johnson, Minors
92Oklahoma City Blazers-9
93Oklahoma City Blazers-7
94Birmingham Bulls-11
98Oklahoma City Blazers-7
00Fort Worth Brahmas-9
01Fort Worth Brahmas-10

Johnson, Norm
57Bruins Photos-10
58Topps-17

Johnson, Patrick
92Quebec Pee-Wee Tournament-1229
93Quebec Pee-Wee Tournament-1248
06Lincoln Stars Traded-2T
06Lincoln Stars Upper DeckÂ Signature Series -16

Johnson, Patrick (PW)
93Quebec Pee-Wee Tournament-1248

Johnson, Paul
99Quad-City Mallards-10
00Quad-City Mallards-14

Johnson, Perry
96Regina Pats-6
97Spokane Chiefs-3
98Bowman CHL-44
Golden Anniversary-44
OPC International-44
98Bowman Chrome CHL-44
Golden Anniversary-44
Golden Anniversary Refractors-44
OPC International-44
OPC International Refractors-44
Refractors-44
00UK Sekonda Superleague-93

Johnson, Peter
93UK Humberside Hawks-NNO
94UK Humberside Hawks-NNO

Johnson, Red
51Laval Dairy Subset-110

Johnson, Ryan
96Carolina Monarchs-13
98UD3-2
98UD3-62
98UD3-122
Die-Cuts-2
Die-Cuts-62
Die-Cuts-122
98Upper Deck-15
98Upper Deck-283
Exclusives-15
Exclusives-283
Exclusives 1 of 1-15
Exclusives 1 of 1-283
Gold Reserve-15
Gold Reserve-283
98New Haven Beast-13
99BAP Millennium Calder Candidates Ruby-C4
99BAP Millennium Calder Candidate Emerald-C4
99BAP Millennium Calder Cand Sapphire-C4
00Pacific-374
Copper-374
Gold-374
Ice Blue-374
Premiere Date-374
01Upper Deck-307
Exclusives-307
03Blues Team Set-12
03Upper Deck MVP-370
Gold Script-370
Silver Script-370
Canadian Exclusives-370
04Missouri River Otters-8
05Blues Team Set-9

Johnson, Scott
91Hampton Roads Admirals-6
93Quebec Pee-Wee Tournament-545

Johnson, Scott (PW)
93Quebec Pee-Wee Tournament-545

Johnson, Shane
91Air Canada SJHL-E4
917th Inn. Sketch OHL-342
92British Columbia JHL-69
00UK Sekonda Superleague-29
01UK Belfast Giants-4
03UK Belfast Giants-6

Johnson, Shaun
93UK Humberside Hawks-8
94UK Humberside Hawks-8
02UK Coventry Blaze-10
03UK Coventry Blaze-8
03UK Coventry Blaze History-10

Johnson, Stephen
92Quebec Pee-Wee Tournament-350
93UK Humberside Hawks-10
94UK Humberside Hawks-10
98UK Kingston Hawks-10
01UK Hull Thunder-9

Johnson, Steve
00Lincoln Stars-25
01Lincoln Stars-25
02Lincoln Stars-25
03Lincoln Stars-25
04Lincoln Stars-24
05Lincoln Stars-24
06Lincoln Stars-25

Johnson, Swe
83Swedish Semic Elitserien-96
85Swedish Panini Stickers-85
86Swedish Panini Stickers-79
87Swedish Panini Stickers-81
89Swedish Semic Elitserien Stickers-69
90Swedish Semic Elitserien Stickers-289
92Swedish Semic Elitserien Stickers-42
94Swedish Leaf-283

Johnson, Terry
81Fredericton Express-14
82Fredericton Express-14
84O-Pee-Chee-186
86Maple Leafs Postcards-14

Johnson, Todd
907th Inn. Sketch WHL-148
917th Inn. Sketch WHL-79
92Quebec Pee-Wee Tournament-1130
99German Bundesliga 2-238

Johnson, Tom
44Beehive Group II Photos-35
44Beehive Group II Photos-252
45Quaker Oats Photos-84
48Exhibits Canadian-10
51Parkhurst-7
52Parkhurst-9
54Parkhurst-10
55Parkhurst-49
55Parkhurst-71
Quaker Oats-49
57Parkhurst-M6
58Parkhurst-7
58Parkhurst-10
59Parkhurst-10
60NHL Ceramic Tiles-26
60Parkhurst-44
60Shirriff Coins-25
60York Photos-18
61Parkhurst-42
61Shirriff/Salada Coins-106
61York Yellow Backs-11
62Parkhurst-50
62Shirriff Coins-36
63Topps-4
64Beehive Group III Photos-13
64Coca-Cola Caps-7
64Topps-101
64Toronto Star-22
70Bruins Postcards-21
83Hall of Fame Postcards-D6
85Hall of Fame-52
93Parkhurst Parkie Reprints-PR55
94Parkhurst Missing Link-79
94Parkhurst Missing Link-143
94Parkhurst Tall Boys-12
06Parkhurst-42
Autographs-42

Johnson, Tony
05Stockton Thunder-8

Johnson, Trevor
97Moose Jaw Warriors-8
98Hampton Roads Admirals-5
98Kootenay Ice-16
99Hampton Roads Admirals-9
00Kootenay Ice-13
01South Carolina Stingrays-11
02South Carolina Stingrays-13
02South Carolina Stingrays RBI-216
03Muskegon Fury-11
03South Carolina Stingrays-330
05Muskegon Fury-8
05South Carolina Stingrays-5

Johnson, Troy
92Northern Michigan Wildcats-13

Johnson, Tyler
01Moose Jaw Warriors-15
06Cardinals Upper Deck World Series Champions-10

Johnsson, Anders
84Swedish Semic Elitserien-84

Johnsson, Jonas
91Swedish Semic Elitserien Stickers-49
92Swedish Semic Elitserien Stickers-71
93Swedish Semic Elitserien-46
94Swedish Leaf-13
95Swedish Leaf-177
95Swedish Upper Deck-26
95Swedish Upper Deck-250
95Swedish World Championships Stickers-148
96German DEL-150
98Swedish UD Choice-82
99Swedish Upper Deck-85
SHL Signatures-8
00Swedish Upper Deck-74
Top Playmakers-P4
02Swedish SHL-120
Parallel-120
03Swedish Elite Signatures-6
05Swedish SHL Elitset Icons-5

Johnsson, Kim
95Swedish Leaf-266
95Swedish Upper Deck-134
97Swedish Collector's Choice-136
98Swedish UD Choice-150
99BAP Memorabilia-200
Gold-200
Silver-200
99BAP Millennium-158
Emerald-158
Ruby-158
Sapphire-158
Signatures-158
Signatures Gold-158
Calder Candidates Ruby-C40
Calder Candidates Emerald-C40
Calder Candidates Sapphire-C40
99Pacific Dynagon Ice-130
Blue-130
Copper-130
Gold-130
Premiere Date-130
99Pacific Omega-155
Copper-155
Gold-155
Ice Blue-155
Premiere Date-155
99Panini Stickers-102
99SP Authentic-110
99Topps Arena Giveaways-NYR-KJ
99Topps Premier Plus-93
Parallel-93
00BAP Memorabilia-322
Emerald-322
Ruby-322
Sapphire-322
Promos-322
00BAP Mem Chicago Sportsfest Copper-322
00BAP Memorabilia Chicago Sportsfest Blue-322
00BAP Memorabilia Chicago Sportsfest Gold-322
00BAP Memorabilia Chicago Sportsfest Ruby-322
00BAP Memorabilia Chicago Sun-Times Ruby-322
00BAP Memorabilia Chicago Sun-Times Gold-322
00BAP Mem Chicago Sun-Times Sapphire-322
00BAP Mem Toronto Fall Expo Copper-322
00BAP Memorabilia Toronto Fall Expo Gold-322
00BAP Memorabilia Toronto Fall Expo Ruby-322
00O-Pee-Chee-227
00O-Pee-Chee Parallel-227
00Pacific-263
Copper-263
Gold-263
Ice Blue-263
Premiere Date-263
00Topps/OPC-227
Parallel-227
01BAP Memorabilia-423
Emerald-423
Ruby-423
Sapphire-423
01Flyers Postcards-9
01Parkhurst-227
01Parkhurst-368
01Upper Deck Vintage-170
02BAP Sig Series Auto Buybacks 1999-158
02Flyers Postcards-2
02O-Pee-Chee-140
02O-Pee-Chee Premier Blue Parallel-140
02O-Pee-Chee Premier Red Parallel-140
02O-Pee-Chee Factory Set-140
02Pacific-281
Blue-281
Red-281
02Pacific Complete-395
Red-395
02Topps-140
OPC Blue Parallel-140
OPC Red Parallel-140
Factory Set-140
02Topps Total-35
02Upper Deck-375
Exclusives-375
02Upper Deck Beckett UD Promos-375
02Upper Deck Victory National Pride-NP48
02Upper Deck Vintage-183
03Flyers Postcards-10
03ITG Action-453
03NHL Sticker Collection-109
03O-Pee-Chee-77
03OPC Blue-77
03OPC Gold-77
03OPC Red-77
03Pacific-253
Blue-253
Red-253
03Pacific Complete-325
Red-325
03Topps-77
Blue-77
Gold-77
Red-77
03Upper Deck-388
Canadian Exclusives-388
HG-388
UD Exclusives-388
03Upper Deck MVP-310
Gold Script-310
Silver Script-310
Canadian Exclusives-310
04Swedish Alfabilder Alfa Stars-3
04Swedish Alfabilder Alfa Star Golden Ice-12
04Swedish Alfabilder Proof Parallels-3
05Flyers Team Issue-10
05Parkhurst-357
Facsimile Auto Parallel-357
05Ultra-145
Gold-145
Ice-145
05Upper Deck-141
HG Glossy-141
05Upper Deck MVP-283
Gold-283
Platinum-283
05Upper Deck Toronto Fall Expo-141
06O-Pee-Chee-255
Rainbow-255
06Upper Deck-348
Exclusives Parallel-348
High Gloss Parallel-348
Masterpieces-348
06Upper Deck MVP-149
Gold Script-149
Super Script-149
06Wild Crime Prevention-2
06Wild Postcards-2

Johnsson, Kjell
69Swedish Hockey-61
70Swedish Hockey-22
71Swedish Hockey-98
72Swedish Stickers-83

Johnsson, Pierre
93Swedish Semic Elitserien-222
94Swedish Leaf-128
95Swedish Leaf-117
95Swedish Upper Deck-172
05Swedish SHL Elitset-257
Gold-257
06Swedish SHL Elitset-251

Johnston, Bernhard
94German DEL-247
95German DEL-241

Johnston, Billy-Jay
92Oshawa Generals Sheet-14
93Oshawa Generals-19
94Sarnia Sting-18
95Slapshot-264
98Baton Rouge Kingfish-10

Johnston, Chris
917th Inn. Sketch WHL-201
92Brandon Wheat Kings-12
93Brandon Wheat Kings-12
95Dayton Bombers-29
98Oklahoma City Blazers-14
01Fort Worth Brahmas-11

Johnston, Denny
98Medicine Hat Tigers-13
99Medicine Hat Tigers-15
00Medicine Hat Tigers-11
02Saskatoon Blades-6

Johnston, Ed
44Beehive Group II Photos-36
63Topps-2
64Beehive Group III Photos-12
64Coca-Cola Caps-1
64Topps-21
65Topps-97
66Topps-99
66Topps USA Test-64
67Topps-96
68O-Pee-Chee-133
69O-Pee-Chee-200
70Bruins Postcards-2
70Bruins Team Issue-5
70Dad's Cookies-64
70Esso Power Players-55
70O-Pee-Chee-133
70Sargent Promotions Stamps-5
71Bruins Postcards-1
71Letraset Action Replays-17
71O-Pee-Chee-172
71Sargent Promotions Stamps-15
71Topps-4
71Toronto Sun-11
72O-Pee-Chee-261
72Sargent Promotions Stamps-20
72Topps-13
73Mac's Milk-10
73Maple Leafs Postcards-11
73O-Pee-Chee-23
73Topps-23
74NHL Action Stamps-246
74O-Pee-Chee NHL-265
75O-Pee-Chee NHL-185
75Topps-185
76O-Pee-Chee NHL-285
77O-Pee-Chee NHL-276
91Future Trends Canada '72-93
91Future Trends Canada '72 French-93
93Kraft-36
93Penguins Foodland-19
94Parkhurst Tall Boys-15
94Parkhurst Tall Boys-167
94Parkhurst Tall Boys-168
94Penguins Foodland-11
95Parkhurst '66-67-18
Coins-18
95Penguins Foodland-22
01Topps Archives-34

Johnston, George
34Beehive Group I Photos-58

Johnston, Glen
87Sault Ste. Marie Greyhounds-35

Johnston, Greg
85Moncton Golden Flames-19
87O-Pee-Chee-102
87Topps-102
88Bruins Postcards-6
90Newmarket Saints-10
90ProCards AHL/IHL-160
91ProCards-353
92Topps-413
Gold-413G
94German DEL-155
95German DEL-156
96German DEL-229
98German DEL-43
99German DEL-285
00German DEL-39
All-Star Class-A5

Johnston, Jay
907th Inn. Sketch OHL-225

Johnston, Jeff
00Kitchener Rangers-15

Johnston, Joel
93Quebec Pee-Wee Tournament-555

Johnston, Joey
71O-Pee-Chee-182
71Sargent Promotions Stamps-143
71Toronto Sun-50
72O-Pee-Chee-96
72Sargent Promotions Stamps-45
72Topps-48
73O-Pee-Chee-172
73Topps-143
74NHL Action Stamps-57
74O-Pee-Chee NHL-56
74O-Pee-Chee NHL-185
74Topps-56
74Topps-185
75O-Pee-Chee NHL-193
75Topps-193
76O-Pee-Chee NHL-325

Johnston, Karl
91ProCards-95

Johnston, Kurt
95Slapshot-125

Johnston, Larry
71Sargent Promotions Stamps-65A
72Sargent Promotions Stamps-82
73O-Pee-Chee-251
73Red Wings Team Issue-12
73Red Wings McCarthy Postcards-11
75O-Pee-Chee NHL-352
81Red Wings Oldtimers-5

Johnston, Marshall
71Sargent Promotions Stamps-141
71Toronto Sun-51
72O-Pee-Chee-171
72Sargent Promotions Stamps-44
73O-Pee-Chee-21
73Topps-21
74O-Pee-Chee NHL-189
74Topps-189
81Rockies Postcards-7

Johnston, Marty
98Bowman CHL-86
Golden Anniversary-86
OPC International-86
98Bowman Chrome CHL-86
Golden Anniversary-86
Golden Anniversary Refractors-86
OPC International-86
OPC International Refractors-86
Refractors-86
02ECHL All-Star Southern-47
02Florida Everblades-11
02Florida Everblades RBI-122
03Peoria Rivermen-17
04UK Edinburgh Capitals-5

Johnston, Mike
03Canucks Postcards-10

Johnston, Neil
94Prince Albert Raiders-11

Johnston, Randy
81Indianapolis Checkers-11
82Indianapolis Checkers-12

Johnston, Ryan
96Saskatoon Blades-12
97Saskatoon Blades-10
98Brandon Wheat Kings-9
99Idaho Steelheads-18
00Missouri River Otters-17

Johnston, Scot
93Memphis RiverKings-6

Johnston, Shaun
93Quebec Pee-Wee Tournament-589

Johnston, Tyler
92British Columbia JHL-15
01Atlantic City Boardwalk Bullies-12

Johnstone, Alex
93Quebec Pee-Wee Tournament-511
96Halifax Mooseheads I-9
96Halifax Mooseheads II-9
97Halifax Mooseheads I-6
97Halifax Mooseheads II-7
98Halifax Mooseheads-15
98Halifax Mooseheads Second Edition-6

Johnstone, Chris
93Niagara Falls Thunder-27
95Slapshot-205

Johnstone, Dillon
06Chilliwack Bruins-18

Johnstone, Donald
99Hull Olympiques-4
Signed-4

Johnstone, Ed
79O-Pee-Chee-179
79Topps-179
80O-Pee-Chee-277
81O-Pee-Chee-226
81O-Pee-Chee Stickers-169
81Topps-E99
82O-Pee-Chee-226
82O-Pee-Chee Stickers-139
82Post Cereal-13
82Topps Stickers-139
83NHL Key Tags-88
83O-Pee-Chee-124
84O-Pee-Chee-55
84Topps-43
89New Haven Nighthawks-5
93Johnstown Chiefs-20
94Johnstown Chiefs-22
98Cincinnati Mighty Ducks-5
99Cincinnati Mighty Ducks-20

Johnstone, Jeff
93Niagara Falls Thunder-10
95Slapshot-193
95Classic-89

Jokela, Antti
03Finnish Cardset-99
05Finnish Cardset -99

Jokela, Mikko
98Black Diamond-99
Double Diamond-99
Triple Diamond-99
Quadruple Diamond-99
98SPx Top Prospects-72
Radiance-72
Spectrum-72
99Finnish Cardset-306
00Finnish Cardset-77
01Finnish Cardset-112
01Albany River Rats-7
02Finnish Cardset-182
02Albany River Rats-16
02Albany River Rats AAP-16
03Manitoba Moose-5
04Finnish Cardset-33
Parallel-23
05Finnish Cardset -27
06Finnish Cardset-29

Jokiharju, Juha
91Finnish Jyvas-Hyva Stickers-34
92Finnish Jyvas-Hyva Stickers-68
93Finnish Jyvas-Hyva Stickers-107
93Finnish SISU-13
94Finnish SISU-169
94Finnish SISU-320
94Finnish SISU-383
95Swedish Leaf-154

Jokila, Janne
01Finnish Cardset-359
03ECHL Update RBI Sports-124
06Finnish Cardset-313

Jokila, Jarmo
05Finnish Cardset -335

Jokilahti, Jarmo
92Finnish Jyvas-Hyva Stickers-71
93Finnish Jyvas-Hyva Stickers-140
93Finnish SISU-140

Jokinen, Ari
80Finnish Mallasjuoma-28

Jokinen, Arto
78Finnish SM-Liiga-103
80Finnish Mallasjuoma-16
83Swedish Semic VM Stickers-50

Jokinen, Jari
71Finnish Suomi Stickers-363
72Finnish Jaakiekko-327

Jokinen, Jorma
70Finnish Jaakiekko-347

Jokinen, Juha
06Finnish Cardset-333

Jokinen, Jussi
01Finnish Cardset-290
02Finnish Cardset-183
Bound for Glory-2
Signatures-2
03Finnish Cardset-92
04SP Authentic Rookie Redemptions-RR10
04Finnish Cardset-97
04Finnish Cardset Signatures-22
05Beehive-129
Beige -129
Blue -129
Gold-129
Red -129
Matte-129
05Black Diamond-159
Emerald-159
Gold-159
Onyx-159
Ruby-159
05Hot Prospects-234
En Fuego-234
Hot Materials-HMJJ
Red Hot-234
White Hot-234
05Parkhurst-624
Facsimile Auto Parallel-624
Signatures-JJ
True Colors-TCDAL
True Colors-TCDAL
05SP Authentic-153
Limited-153
Rarefied Rookies-RRJJ
Rookie Authentics-RAJJ
Sign of the Times Fives-MMZTJ
05SP Game Used-154
Autographs-154
Gold-154
Auto Draft-AD-JJ
Rookie Exclusives-JJ
Rookie Exclusives Silver-RE-JJ
Significant Numbers-SN-JJ
05SPx-180
Spectrum-180
Xcitement Rookies-XR-JJ
Xcitement Rookies Gold-XR-JJ
Xcitement Rookies Spectrum-XR-JJ
05The Cup-112
Autographed Rookie Patches Gold Rainbow-112
Black Rainbow Rookies-112
Masterpiece Pressplates (Artifacts)-210
Masterpiece Pressplates (Bee Hive)-129
Masterpiece Pressplates (Black Diamond)-159
Masterpiece Pressplates (Ice)-127
Masterpiece Pressplates (MVP)-426
Masterpiece Pressplates (Power Play)-138
Masterpiece Pressplates (Rookie Update)-207
Masterpiece Pressplates SPA Autos-153
Masterpiece Pressplates (SP Game Used)-154
Masterpiece Pressplates SPx Autos-180
Masterpiece Pressplates (Trilogy)-188
Masterpiece Pressplates Ult Coll Autos-113
Masterpiece Pressplates (Victory)-297
Masterpiece Pressplates Autographs-112
Platinum Rookies-112
05UD Artifacts-210
Gold-RED10
05UD PowerPlay-138
05UD Rookie Class-8
05Ultimate Collection-113
Autographed Patches-113
Autographed Shields-113
Ultimate Debut Threads Jerseys-DTJJ
Ultimate Debut Threads Jerseys Autos-DAJJ
Ultimate Debut Threads Patches-DTPJJ
Ultimate Debut Threads Patches Autos-DAPJJ
05Ultra-215
Gold-215
Ice-215
Rookie Uniformity Jerseys-RU-JJ
Rookie Uniformity Jersey Autographs-ARU-JJ
Rookie Uniformity Patches-RUP-JJ
Rookie Uniformity Patch Autographs-ARP-JJ
05Upper Deck-459
Rookie Ink-RIJJ
05Upper Deck Rookie Showcase-RS10
05Upper Deck Rookie Showcase Promos-RS10
05Upper Deck Rookie Threads-RTJJ
05Upper Deck Rookie Threads Autographs-ARTJJ
05Upper Deck Ice-127
Cool Threads-CTJK
Cool Threads Autographs-ACTJK
Cool Threads Glass-CTJK
Cool Threads Patches-CTPJK
Cool Threads Patch Autographs-CAPJK
Fresh Ice-FIJJ
Fresh Ice Glass-FIJJ
Fresh Ice Glass Patches-FIPJJ
Premieres Auto Patches-AIPJJ
05Upper Deck MVP-426
Gold-426
Platinum-426
05Upper Deck Rookie Update-207
Inspirations Patch Rookies-207
05Upper Deck Trilogy-188
05Upper Deck Victory-297
Black-297
Gold-297
Silver-297
05Finnish Cardset -93
Finnish Cardset Magicmakers-13
06Be A Player Portraits First Exposures-FEJJ
06Be A Player Portraits Signature Portraits-SPJJ
06Black Diamond Gemography-GJJ
06Flair Showcase Wave of the Future-WF12
06Fleer-66
Tiffany-66
06O-Pee-Chee-157
06O-Pee-Chee-619
Rainbow-157
Rainbow-619
06SP Game Used Authentic Fabrics Dual-AF2LJ
06SP Game Used Authentic Fabrics Dual Patches-AF2LJ
06SP Game Used Authentic Fabrics Fives-AP5RPT
06SP Game Used Authentic Fabrics Fives Patches-AP5RPT
06SP Game Used Authentic Fabrics Eights-AF8FIN
06SP Game Used Authentic Fabrics Eights Patches-AF8FIN
06SP Game Used Letter Marks-LMJJ
06Stars Team Postcards-9
06Ultra-66
Gold Medallion-66
Ice Medallion-66
06Upper Deck Arena Giveaways-DAL2
06Upper Deck Arena Giveaways-DAL2
06Upper Deck-63
Exclusives Parallel-63
High Gloss Parallel-63
Game Jerseys-J2JJ
Game Patches-P2JJ
Masterpieces-63
Shootout Artists-SA1
06Upper Deck MVP-96
Gold Script-96
Super Script-96
Jerseys-OJPJ
06Upper Deck Ovation-118
06Upper Deck Victory-62
06Upper Deck Victory Black-62
06Upper Deck Victory Gold-62
06Upper Deck Victory Next In Line-NL19
06Russian Sport Collection Olympic Stars-22

Jokinen, Jyrki
93Finnish Jyvas-Hyva Stickers-143
93Finnish SISU-157
94Finnish SISU-130

Jokinen, Kari
70Finnish Jaakiekko-310

Jokinen, Olli
97Donruss Elite-72
Aspirations-72
Status-72
97Donruss Preferred-147
97Donruss Preferred-196
Cut to the Chase-147
Cut to the Chase-196
97Leaf-155
Fractal Matrix-155
Fractal Matrix Die Cuts-155
97Pacific Dynagon-NNO
Copper-NNO
Dark Grey-NNO
Emerald Green-NNO
Ice Blue-NNO
Red-NNO
Silver-NNO
97Paramount-90
Copper-90
Dark Grey-90
Emerald Green-90
Ice Blue-90
Red-90
Silver-90
97Pinnacle-4
Artist's Proofs-4
Rink Collection-4
Press Plates Back Black-4
Press Plates Back Cyan-4
Press Plates Back Magenta-4
Press Plates Back Yellow-4
Press Plates Front Black-4
Press Plates Front Cyan-4
Press Plates Front Magenta-4
Press Plates Front Yellow-4
Certified Rookie Redemption-F
Certified Rookie Redemption Gold-F
Certified Rookie Redemption Mirror Gold-F
97Score-65
Artist's Proofs-65
Golden Blades-65
97Upper Deck-288
97Upper Deck Ice-58
Parallel-58
Lethal Lines-L9A
Lethal Lines 2-L9A
Power Shift-58
98Black Diamond-42
Double Diamond-42
Triple Diamond-42
Quadruple Diamond-42
98Bowman's Best-101
Refractors-101
Atomic Refractors-101
Mirror Image Fusion-F6
Mirror Image Fusion Refractors-F6
Mirror Image Fusion Atomic Refractors-F6
98Finest Futures Finest-F18
98Finest Futures Finest Refractors-F18
98Pacific Omega-117
Red-117
Opening Day Issue-117
98Revolution-67
Ice Shadow-67
Red-67
98SP Authentic-100
Power Shift-100
98SPx Finite-139
Radiance-139
Spectrum-139
98Topps Gold Label Class 1-43
Black-43
Black One of One-43
One of One-43
Red-43
Red One of One-43
98Topps Gold Label Class 2-43
98Topps Gold Label Class 2 Black-43
98Topps Gold Label Class 2 Black 1 of 1-43
98Topps Gold Label Class 2 One of One-43
98Topps Gold Label Class 2 Red-43
98Topps Gold Label Class 2 Red One of One-43
98Topps Gold Label Class 3-43
98Topps Gold Label Class 3 Black-43
98Topps Gold Label Class 3 Black 1 of 1-43
98Topps Gold Label Class 3 One of One-43
98Topps Gold Label Class 3 Red-43
98Topps Gold Label Class 3 Red One of One-43
98UD Choice-275
Prime Choice Reserve-275
Reserve-275
98UD3-11
98UD3-71
98UD3-131
Die-Cuts-11
Die-Cuts-71
Die-Cuts-131
98Upper Deck-12
Exclusives-12
Exclusives 1 of 1-12
Generation Next-GN25
Generation Next Quantum 1-GN25
Generation Next Quantum 2-GN25
Generation Next Quantum 3-GN25
Gold Reserve-12
98Upper Deck MVP-95
Gold Script-95
Silver Script-95
Super Script-95
98Finnish Kerailysarja Leijonat-24
99BAP Memorabilia-115
Gold-115
Silver-115
99BAP Millennium-152
Emerald-152
Ruby-152
Sapphire-152
Signatures-152
Signatures Gold-152
99Pacific-192
Copper-192
Emerald Green-192
Gold-192
Ice Blue-192
Premiere Date-192
Red-192
99Pacific Dynagon Ice-124
Blue-124
Copper-124
Gold-124
Premiere Date-124
99Panini Stickers-88
99SPx-95
Radiance-95
Spectrum-95
99Stadium Club-162
First Day Issue-162
One of a Kind-162
Printing Plates Black-162
Printing Plates Cyan-162
Printing Plates Magenta-162
Printing Plates Yellow-162
99Topps Arena Giveaways-NYI-OJ
99Upper Deck-254
Exclusives-254
Exclusives 1 of 1-254
99Upper Deck Gold Reserve-254

99Upper Deck Retro Generation-G8C
99Upper Deck Retro Generation Level 2-G8C
99Upper Deck Victory-183
99Finnish Cardset-191
Aces High-D-7
Most Wanted-2
00BAP Memorabilia-11
00BAP Memorabilia-411
Emerald-11
Emerald-411
Ruby-11
Ruby-411
Sapphire-11
Sapphire-411
Promos-11
00BAP Mem Chicago Sportsfest Copper-11
00BAP Memorabilia Chicago Sportsfest Blue-11
00BAP Memorabilia Chicago Sportsfest Gold-11
00BAP Memorabilia Chicago Sportsfest Ruby-11
00BAP Memorabilia Chicago Sun-Times Ruby-11
00BAP Memorabilia Chicago Sun-Times Gold-11
00BAP Mem Chicago Sun-Times Sapphire-11
00BAP Mem Toronto Fall Expo Copper-11
00BAP Memorabilia Toronto Fall Expo Gold-11
00BAP Memorabilia Toronto Fall Expo Ruby-11
00Pacific-441
Copper-441
Gold-441
Ice Blue-441
Premiere Date-441
00Panini Stickers-58
00Panthers Team Issue-15
00Private Stock Game Gear-51
00Titanium Game Gear-18
00Topps Heritage-172
00Upper Deck-304
Exclusives Tier 1-304
Exclusives Tier 2-304
00Upper Deck Victory-149
00Finnish Cardset-116
01Upper Deck-305
Exclusives-305
01Upper Deck Victory-157
Gold-157
02BAP Sig Series Auto Buybacks 1999-152
02Bowman YoungStars-64
Gold-64
Silver-64
02eTopps-51
02O-Pee-Chee-168
02O-Pee-Chee Premier Blue Parallel-168
02O-Pee-Chee Premier Red Parallel-168
02O-Pee-Chee Factory Set-168
02Pacific Complete-476
Red-476
02Pacific Quest for the Cup-41
Gold-41
02Parkhurst-192
Bronze-192
Gold-192
Silver-192
02Parkhurst Retro-187
Minis-187
02SP Authentic-41
Beckett Promos-41
02Titanium-46
Blue-46
Red-46
Retail-46
02Topps-168
OPC Blue Parallel-168
OPC Red Parallel-168
Factory Set-168
02Topps Total-398
02Upper Deck-322
Exclusives-322
02Upper Deck Beckett UD Promos-322
02Upper Deck Rookie Update-43
02Upper Deck Vintage-109
02Vanguard-45
LTD-45
02Finnish Cardset-30
02Finnish Cardset Dynamic Duos-5
02Finnish Cardset Solid Gold Six-Pack-5
03BAP Memorabilia-62
Emerald-62
Gold-62
Ruby-62
Sapphire-62
03BAP Ultimate Memorabilia Autographs-40
Gold-40
03Beehive-85
Gold-85
Silver-85
03Black Diamond-57
Black-57
Green-57
Red-57
03Bowman-102
Gold-102
03Bowman Chrome-102
Refractors-102
Gold Refractors-102
Xfractors-102
03Crown Royale-44
Blue-44
Retail-44
03ITG Action-278
First Time All-Star-FT5
Jerseys-M132
03ITG Used Signature Series-15
Gold-15
Autographs-OJ
Autographs Gold-OJ
03NHL Sticker Collection-44
03O-Pee-Chee-28
03O-Pee-Chee-303
03OPC Blue-28
03OPC Blue-303
03OPC Gold-28
03OPC Gold-303
03OPC Red-28
03OPC Red-303
03Pacific-145
Blue-145
Red-145
03Pacific Calder-46
Silver-46
03Pacific Complete-26
Red-26
03Pacific Exhibit-64
Blue Backs-64
Yellow Backs-64
03Pacific Heads-Up-44
Hobby LTD-44
Retail LTD-44
03Pacific Invincible-42
Blue-42
Red-42
Retail-42
Featured Performers-13
03Pacific Prism-44
Blue-44
Gold-44
Red-44
03Pacific Quest for the Cup-47
Blue-47
03Pacific Supreme-42
Blue-42
Red-42
Retail-42
Jerseys-15
03Panthers Team Issue-9
03Private Stock Reserve-169
Blue-169
Patches-169
Red-169
Retail-169
03SP Authentic-37
Limited-37
03SPx-43
Radiance-43
Spectrum-43
Big Futures-BF-OJ
Big Futures Limited-BF-OJ
03Titanium-157
Hobby Jersey Number Parallels-157
Patches-157
Retail-157
03Topps-28
03Topps-303
Blue-28
Blue-303
Gold-28
Gold-303
Red-28
Red-303
Topps/OPC Idols-II10
03Topps C55-34
Minis-34
Minis American Back-34
Minis American Back Red-34
Minis Bazooka Back-34
Minis Brooklyn Back-34
Minis Hat Trick Back-34
Minis O Canada Back-34
Minis O Canada Back Red-34
Minis Stanley Cup Back-34
03Topps Pristine-48
Gold Refractor Die Cuts-48
Refractors-48
Press Plates Black-48
Press Plates Cyan-48
Press Plates Magenta-48
Press Plates Yellow-48
03UD Honor Roll-34
03UD Premier Collection Teammates-PT-FP
03UD Premier Collection Teammates Patches-PT-FP
03Upper Deck-325
Canadian Exclusives-325
HG-325
UD Exclusives-325
03Upper Deck Classic Portraits-39
03Upper Deck Classic Portraits-157
03Upper Deck Ice-37
Gold-37
03Upper Deck MVP-177
Gold Script-177
Silver Script-177
Canadian Exclusives-177
SportsNut-SN39
03Upper Deck Rookie Update-39
03Upper Deck Trilogy-39
Limited-39
03Upper Deck Victory-78
Bronze-78
Gold-78
Silver-78
Game Breakers-GB20
03Toronto Star-42
04Pacific-113
Blue-113
Red-113
04SP Authentic-41
04UD All-World-74
Gold-74
04Upper Deck World Cup Tribute-OJSKTS
05Be A Player-38
First Period-38
Second Period-38
Third Period-38
Overtime-38
05Beehive-40
Matte-40
Matted Materials-MMOJ
05Black Diamond-36
Emerald-36
Gold-36
Onyx-36
Ruby-36
Jerseys-J-OJ
Jerseys Ruby-J-OJ
Jersey Duals-DJ-OJ
Jersey Triples-TJ-OJ
Jersey Quads-QJ-OJ
05Hot Prospects-42
En Fuego-42
Red Hot-42
White Hot-42
05Panini Stickers-56
05Parkhurst-201
05Parkhurst-513
Facsimile Auto Parallel-201
Facsimile Auto Parallel-513
Signatures-OJ
True Colors-TCFLA
True Colors-TCFLA
True Colors-TCFLTB
True Colors-TCFLTB
05SP Authentic-44
Limited-44
05SP Game Used Authentic Fabrics Quad-HLBJ
05SP Game Used Authentic Patches Quad -HLBJ
05The Cup-48
Gold-48
Black Rainbow-48
Dual NHL Shields-DSKJ
Dual NHL Shields-DSRO
Dual NHL Shields Autographs-ADSKJ
Emblems of Endorsement-EEOJ
Limited Logos-LLOJ
Masterpiece Pressplates-48
Masterpiece Pressplates (Rookie Update)-218
Patch Variation-P48
Patch Variation Autographs-AP48
Scripted Numbers Dual-DSNKJ
Scripted Swatches-SSOJ
Signature Patches-SPOJ
05UD Artifacts-45
Blue-45
Gold-45
Green-45
Pewter-45
Red-45
Gold Autographed-45
05UD PowerPlay-40
Rainbow-40
Specialists-TSOJ
Specialists Patches-SPOJ
05Ultimate Collection-43
Gold-43
National Heroes Jerseys-NHJOJ
National Heroes Patches-NHPOJ
05Ultra-89
Gold-89
Ice-89
05Upper Deck-82
05Upper Deck All-Time Greatest-26
05Upper Deck Big Playmakers-B-OJ
05Upper Deck HG Glossy-82
05Upper Deck Jerseys-J-OJ
05Upper Deck NHL Generations-TSKJ
05Upper Deck MVP-167
Gold-167
Platinum-167
05Upper Deck Rookie Update-43
05Upper Deck Rookie Update-218
Inspirations Patch Rookies-218
05Upper Deck Toronto Fall Expo-82
05Upper Deck Victory-86
Black-86
Gold-86
Silver-86
Game Breakers-GB21
05Finnish Cardset -23
Finnish Cardset Magicmakers-3
06Be A Player-109
Autographs-109
Signatures-OJ
Signatures 10-119
Signatures 25-119
Signatures Trios-TJBM
Signatures Foursomes-FSKJL
06Be A Player Portraits-48
Dual Signature Portraits-DSJB
Quadruple Signature Portraits-QKKJP
Signature Portraits-SPOJ
06Beehive-59
Blue-59
Matte-59
Red Facsimile Signatures-59
Wood-59
06Black Diamond-35
Black-35
Gold-35
Ruby-35
06Flair Showcase-47
06Flair Showcase-130
06Flair Showcase-235
Parallel-47
Parallel-130
Parallel-235
Inks-IOJ
Stitches-SSOJ
06Fleer-86
Tiffany-86
Fabricology-FOJ
Total O-011
06Hot Prospects-45
Red Hot-45
White Hot-45
06O-Pee-Chee-223
06O-Pee-Chee-683
Rainbow-223
Rainbow-683
Autographs-A-OJ
Swatches-S-OJ
06Panini Stickers-54
06SP Authentic-59
Limited-59
06SP Game Used-45
Gold-45
Rainbow-45
Authentic Fabrics Fives-AF5GWG
Authentic Fabrics Fives Patches-AF5GWG
Authentic Fabrics Eights-AF8FIN
Authentic Fabrics Eights Patches-AF8FIN
Inked Sweaters Dual-IS2OJ
Inked Sweaters Dual Patches-IS2OJ
Letter Marks-LMOJ
06SPx-42
Spectrum-42
SPxcitement-X44
SPxcitement Spectrum-X44
Winning Materials-WMOJ
Winning Materials Spectrum-WMOJ
06The Cup NHL Shields Duals-DSHEO
06UD Artifacts-57
06UD Artifacts-172
Blue-57
Blue-172
Gold-57
Gold-172
Platinum-57
Platinum-172
Radiance-57
Radiance-172
Autographed Radiance Parallel-57
Autographed Radiance Parallel-172
Red-57
Red-172
Auto-Facts-AFOJ
Auto-Facts Gold-AFOJ
Tundra Tandems-TTOT
Tundra Tandems Black-TTOT
Tundra Tandems Blue-TTOT
Tundra Tandems Gold-TTOT
Tundra Tandems Platinum-TTOT
Tundra Tandems Red-TTOT
Tundra Tandems Dual Patches Red-TTOT
06UD Mini Jersey Collection-47
06UD Powerplay-43
Impact Rainbow-43
06Ultra-86
Gold Medallion-86
Ice Medallion-86
06Upper Deck Arena Giveaways-FLA4
06Upper Deck-332
Exclusives Parallel-332
High Gloss Parallel-332
All World-AW14
Game Jerseys-J2OJ
Game Patches-P2OJ
Generations Duals-G2JK
Generations Triples-G3KJK
Generations Patches Dual-G2PJK
Generations Patches Triple-G3PKJK
Masterpieces-332
06Upper Deck MVP-126
Gold Script-126
Super Script-126
International Icons-II10
Jerseys-OJBJ
Jerseys-OJLJ
06Upper Deck Ovation-169
06Upper Deck Sweet Shot-49
Sweet Stitches-SSOJ
Sweet Stitches Duals-SSOJ
Sweet Stitches Triples-SSOJ
06Upper Deck Trilogy-44
Combo Clearcut Autographs-C2LJ
Ice Scripts-ISOJ
06Upper Deck Victory-85
06Upper Deck Victory Black-85
06Upper Deck Victory Gold-85
06Upper Deck Victory GameBreakers-GB20
07Upper Deck Ovation-82
07Upper Deck Victory-91
Black-91
Gold-91
GameBreakers-GB33

Jokinen, Pentti
65Finnish Hellas-22

Jokinen, Petri
72Finnish Jaakiekko-345

Jokinen, Satu
99Finnish Cardset Aces High-S-Q

Jokiraita, Juha
05Finnish Cardset -304

Jolette, Frank
98Guelph Storm-21

Jolette, Jonathan
00Baie-Comeau Drakkar-20
Signed-20
03Shawinigan Cataractes-17
04Austin Ice Bats-15

Joliat, Aurel
23V145-1-14
24Anonymous NHL-8
24C144 Champ's Cigarettes-34
24V130 Maple Crispette-14
24V145-2-48
25Dominion Chocolates-119
27La Patrie-4
27La Presse Photos-2
33O-Pee-Chee V304B-50
33V252 Canadian Gum-34
33V288 Hamilton Gum-27
33V357 Ice Kings-3
33V357-2 Ice Kings Premiums-3
34Beehive Group I Photos-161
34Diamond Matchbooks Silver-33
34Sweet Caporal-5
35Diamond Matchbooks Tan 1-32
35Diamond Matchbooks Tan 2-31
35Diamond Matchbooks Tan 3-28
36Champion Postcards-8
36O-Pee-Chee V304D-129
37O-Pee-Chee V304E-152
37V356 Worldwide Gum-65
43Parade Sportive *-40
55Parkhurst-58
Quaker Oats-58
83Hall of Fame-53
83Hall of Fame Postcards-D7
85Hall of Fame-53
93O-Pee-Chee Canadiens Hockey Fest-21
93O-Pee-Chee Canadiens Hockey Fest-59
02BAP Ultimate Mem Blades of Steel-9
02BAP Ultimate Memorabilia Emblem Attic-25
02BAP Ultimate Memorabilia Gloves Are Off-4
02BAP Ultimate Mem Paper Cuts Autos-33
02BAP Ultimate Mem Storied Franchise-25
02BAP Ultimate Mem Vintage Hat Tricks-2
02BAP Ultimate Mem Vintage Jerseys-3
03BAP Memorabilia Vintage Memorabilia-VM-13
03BAP Ultimate Memorabilia Emblem Attic-13
03BAP Ultimate Mem Emblem Attic Gold-13
03BAP Ultimate Memorabilia Gloves Are Off-13
03BAP Ultimate Mem Hometown Heroes-19
03BAP Ultimate Mem Hometown Heroes Gold-19
03BAP Ultimate Memorabilia Paper Cuts-6
03BAP Ultimate Mem Vintage Blade of Steel-17
03BAP Ultimate Mem Vint Complete Jersey-4
03BAP Ultimate Mem Vint Comp Jersey Gold-4
03BAP Ultimate Mem Vintage Hat Tricks-6
03BAP Ultimate Mem Vintage Jerseys-1
03BAP Ultimate Mem Vintage Jerseys Gold-1
03ITG Used Sig Series Triple Mem-8
03ITG Used Sig Series Triple Mem Gold-8
03ITG Used Sig Series Vintage Mem -21
03ITG Used Sig Series Vintage Mem Gold-21
03ITG VIP MVP-4
03ITG VIP Vintage Memorabilia-4
03Parkhurst Orig Six Montreal Mem-MM22
03Parkhurst Orig Six Montreal Mem-MM56
04ITG Franchises Canadian-63
Double Memorabilia-DM6
Double Memorabilia Gold-DM6
Memorabilia-SM29
Memorabilia Gold-SM29
Teammates-TM1
Teammates Gold-TM1
Triple Memorabilia-TM5
Triple Memorabilia Gold-TM5
04ITG Ultimate Memorabilia-14
Gold-14
Blades of Steel-21
Complete Jerseys-7
Emblem Attic-8
Emblem Attic Gold-8
Jerseys-3
Jerseys Gold-3
Original Six-20
Paper Cuts-4
Paper Cuts Memorabilia-7
05ITG Ultimate Memorabilia Level 1-5
05ITG Ultimate Memorabilia Level 2-5
05ITG Ultimate Memorabilia Level 3-5
05ITG Ultimate Memorabilia Level 4-5
05ITG Ultimate Memorabilia Level 5-5
05ITG Ultimate Mem Blades of Steel-11
05ITG Ultimate Mem Blades of Steel Gold-11
05ITG Ultimate Memorabilia Emblem Attic-7
05ITG Ultimate Mem Emblem Attic Gold-7
05ITG Ultimate Memorabilia Gloves Are Off-20
05ITG Ultimate Mem Gloves Are Off Gold-20
05ITG Ultimate Mem Passing Torch Jsy Gold-13
05ITG Ultimate Mem Retro Teammate Jerseys-7
05ITG Ult Mem Retro Teammates Jersey Gold-7
05ITG Ultimate Mem 3 Star of the Game Jsy-1
05ITG Ult Mem 3 Star of the Game Jsy Gold-1
06ITG Ultimate Memorabilia-10
Artist Proof-10
Blades of Steel-2
Blades of Steel Gold-2
Bleu Blanc et Rouge Autos-7
Cornerstones-2
Cornerstones Gold-2
Double Memorabilia-13
Double Memorabilia Gold-13
Emblem Attic-8
Emblem Attic Gold-8
Lumbergraphs-8
Retro Teammates-1
Retro Teammates Gold-1

Jolin, Dominci
93Quebec Pee-Wee Tournament-974

Jolin, Nicolas
92Quebec Pee-Wee Tournament-149
93Quebec Pee-Wee Tournament-1097

Joly, Greg
74Capitals White Borders-12
74NHL Action Stamps-321
74O-Pee-Chee NHL-294
75O-Pee-Chee NHL-170
75Topps-170
76O-Pee-Chee NHL-52
76Topps-52
77O-Pee-Chee NHL-273
78O-Pee-Chee-148
78Topps-148
79O-Pee-Chee-311
79Red Wings Postcards-6
80O-Pee-Chee-270
82O-Pee-Chee-86
82Post Cereal-5

Joly, Mario
99Hull Olympiques-13
Signed-13
00Hull Olympiques-12
Signed-12
01Quebec Remparts-18
04Tulsa Oilers-12

Jomphe, Daniel
84Chicoutimi Sagueneens-14

Jomphe, Jean-Francois
907th Inn. Sketch QMJHL-108
93San Diego Gulls-11
94Classic Pro Prospects-123
96Collector's Choice-8
96Ducks Team Issue-19
96Upper Deck-3
97Pacific Invincible NHL Regime-3
99German DEL-143
00German DEL-13
02German DEL City Press-138
03German DEL All-Stars-AS16

Jonak, Jiri
94Czech APS Extraliga-144
96Czech APS Extraliga-193
97Czech APS Extraliga-127
97Czech DS Extraliga-96
97Czech DS Stickers-190
98Czech DS Stickers-251

Jonas, Oliver
02German Berlin Polar Bears Postcards-13
02German DEL City Press-32
03German Berlin Polar Bears Postcards-18
03German DEL-67
04German Berlin Polar Bears Postcards-17
04German DEL-70
05German DEL-207

Jonas, Sebastian
05German DEL-171

Jonasson, Antero
67Swedish Hockey-222

Jonasson, Vincent
95Brandon Wheat Kings-10
04Austin Ice Bats-20

Jonathan, Stan
77O-Pee-Chee NHL-270
78O-Pee-Chee-181
78Topps-181
79O-Pee-Chee-263
79Topps-263
80O-Pee-Chee-113
80Topps-113
81O-Pee-Chee-13
82Post Cereal-1
83Penguins Heinz Photos-14
03Parkhurst Orig Six Boston Autos-8
04UD Legendary Signatures-77
Autographs-SJ
Linemates-SJDMTO
05ITG Tough Customers-SJ
Autographs-SJ
Jerseys-SJ
Stickwork-SJ

Joncas, Pierre-Alexandre
05Rimouski Oceanic-15
06Rimouski Oceanic-8

Jones, Blair
02Red Deer Rebels-11
03Red Deer Rebels-15
04Moose Jaw Warriors-10
05ITG Heroes/Prosp Toronto Expo Parallel -169
05Moose Jaw Warriors-12
05ITG Heroes and Prospects-169
Autographs-A-BJ
06Beehive-153
Matte-153
06Hot Prospects-178
Red Hot-178
White Hot-178
06O-Pee-Chee-590
Rainbow-590
06SP Authentic-216
Limited-216
06Springfield Falcons-6
06The Cup-159
Autographed Rookie Masterpiece Pressplates-159
Gold Rainbow Autographed Rookie Patches-159
Masterpiece Pressplates (Bee Hive)-153
Masterpiece Pressplates (Marquee Rookies)-590
Masterpiece Pressplates (SP Authentic)-216
Masterpiece Pressplates (Sweet Beginnings)-154
Masterpiece Pressplates (Ultimate Collection)-94
Rookies Black-159
Rookies Platinum-159
06Ultimate Collection-94
06Upper Deck-489
Exclusives Parallel-489
High Gloss Parallel-489
Masterpieces-489
06Upper Deck Sweet Shot-154
Rookie Jerseys Autographs-154
06AHL Top Prospects-41

Jones, Bob
87Sault Ste. Marie Greyhounds-5
89Sault Ste. Marie Greyhounds-18
90ProCards AHL/IHL-301
91ProCards-251
93Muskegon Fury-3
00St. Michaels Majors-18
01St. Michaels Majors-27
02St. Michaels Majors-26
03St. Michael's Majors-25
04Sudbury Wolves-24
05Sudbury Wolves-23
06Sudbury Wolves-26

Jones, Bobby
99Brampton Battalion-29
06Topps Big Game Picture Perfect Jerseys and Shorts Autographs-BJ

Jones, Brad
87Sault Ste. Marie Greyhounds-7
88Jets Postcards-13
89ProCards AHL-42
90Kings Smokey-21
91Bowman-181
91Flyers J.C. Penney-14
91O-Pee-Chee-478
91OPC Premier-115
91Parkhurst-127
French-127
91Pro Set-456
French-456
91Score Canadian Bilingual-603
91Score Canadian English-603
91Score Rookie/Traded-53T
91Stadium Club-368
91Topps-478
91Upper Deck-304
French-304
92Stadium Club-141
92Topps-299
Gold-299G
95Binghamton Rangers-9
96German DEL-67
98BC Icemen-18
98BC Icemen II-20
01BC Icemen-13

Jones, Casey
897th Inn. Sketch OHL-174

Jones, Chris
91British Columbia JHL-62
92British Columbia JHL-105

Jones, Corey
89Victoria Cougars-12
907th Inn. Sketch WHL-103
917th Inn. Sketch WHL-26

Jones, Daryl
92Saskatchewan JHL-153

Jones, Doug
85Kitchener Rangers-24
86Kitchener Rangers-23
87Kitchener Rangers-22
94Flint Generals-13
06Cedar Rapids RoughRiders-9

Jones, Doug (USHL)
06Cedar Rapids RoughRiders-9

Jones, Evan
03Halifax Mooseheads-5

Jones, FWD
99Guelph Storm-16

Jones, Harald
72Finnish Semic World Championship-159
72Swedish Semic World Championship-159

Jones, Jim
10C56-19

Jones, Jimmy
77Maple Leafs Postcards-8
78Maple Leafs Postcards-11
78O-Pee-Chee-288
79Maple Leafs Postcards-15
79O-Pee-Chee-288
05Topps Style Fan Favorites Autographs-JJ2

Jones, Keith
92Capitals Kodak-14
92OPC Premier-14
92Parkhurst-427
Emerald Ice-427
92Ultra-436
92Upper Deck-533
92Classic-96
Gold-96
93OPC Premier-96
Gold-96
93Parkhurst-495
Emerald Ice-495
93PowerPlay-466
93Score-417
Canadian-417
93Stadium Club-234
Members Only Master Set-234
OPC-234
First Day Issue-234
First Day Issue OPC-234
93Topps/OPC Premier-96
Gold-96
93Ultra-446
93Upper Deck-377
93Classic Pro Prospects-43
94Be A Player Signature Cards-131
94Leaf-506
94Pinnacle-378
Artist's Proofs-378
Rink Collection-378
94Upper Deck-411
Electric Ice-411
95Canada Games NHL POGS-282
95Capitals Team Issue-12
95Collector's Choice-166
Player's Club-166
Player's Club Platinum-166
95Donruss-282
95Leaf-105
95Metal-160
95Panini Stickers-140
95Parkhurst International-217
Emerald Ice-217
95Pinnacle-27
Artist's Proofs-27
Rink Collection-27
95Playoff One on One-323
95Score-95
Black Ice Artist's Proofs-95
Black Ice-95
95Stadium Club-88
Members Only Master Set-88
95Topps-73
OPC Inserts-73
95Upper Deck-451
Electric Ice-451
Electric Ice Gold-451
Special Edition-SE85
Special Edition Gold-SE85
96Be A Player-194
Autographs-194
Autographs Silver-194
96Black Diamond-39
Gold-39
96Collector's Choice-285
96Pinnacle-93
Artist's Proofs-93
Foil-93
Premium Stock-93
Rink Collection-93
96Playoff One on One-423
96Score-225
Artist's Proofs-225
Dealer's Choice Artist's Proofs-225
Special Artist's Proofs-225
Golden Blades-225
97Collector's Choice-59
97Donruss Limited-18
Exposure-18
97Pacific-291
Copper-291
Emerald Green-291
Ice Blue-291
Red-291
Silver-291
97Score-250
97Score Avalanche-9
Platinum-9
Premier-9
98Pacific Omega-175
Red-175
Opening Day Issue-175
98Upper Deck MVP-150
Gold Script-150
Silver Script-150
Super Script-150
99BAP Memorabilia-223
Gold-223
Silver-223
99BAP Millennium-187
Emerald-187
Ruby-187
Sapphire-187
Signatures-187
Signatures Gold-187
99Pacific-304
Copper-304
Emerald Green-304
Gold-304
Ice Blue-304
Premiere Date-304
Red-304
99Paramount-170
Copper-170
Emerald-170
Gold-170
Holographic Emerald-170
Holographic Gold-170
Holographic Silver-170
Ice Blue-170
Premiere Date-170
Red-170
Silver-170
99Upper Deck MVP-151
Gold Script-151
Silver Script-151
Super Script-151
99Upper Deck Victory-218
00BAP Memorabilia-340
Emerald-340
Ruby-340
Sapphire-340
Promos-340
00BAP Mem Chicago Sportsfest Copper-340
00BAP Memorabilia Chicago Sportsfest Blue-340
00BAP Memorabilia Chicago Sportsfest Gold-340
00BAP Memorabilia Chicago Sportsfest Ruby-340
00BAP Memorabilia Chicago Sun-Times Ruby-340
00BAP Memorabilia Chicago Sun-Times Gold-340
00BAP Mem Chicago Sun-Times Sapphire-340
00BAP Mem Toronto Fall Expo Copper-340
00BAP Memorabilia Toronto Fall Expo Gold-340
00BAP Memorabilia Toronto Fall Expo Ruby-340
00Pacific-298
Copper-298
Gold-298
Ice Blue-298
Premiere Date-298
00Upper Deck Vintage-269
02BAP Sig Series Auto Buybacks 1999-187

Jones, Landon
03Regina Pats-5
04Prince Albert Raiders-6

Jones, Matt
03North Dakota Fighting Sioux-8
04North Dakota Fighting Sioux-11
05Beehive-152
Matte-152
05Hot Prospects-160
En Fuego-160
Red Hot-160
White Hot-160
05SP Authentic-242
Limited-242
05SP Game Used-229
05SPx-278
05The Cup Masterpiece Pressplate Artifact-312
05The Cup Masterpiece Pressplate Bee Hive-152
05The Cup Masterpiece Pressplates (Ice)-215
05The Cup Master Pressplate Rookie Update-167
05The Cup Masterpiece Pressplates SPA-242
05The Cup Masterpiece Pressplates SP GU-229
05The Cup Masterpiece Pressplates (SPx)-278
05The Cup Masterpiece Pressplates Trilogy-291
05The Cup Masterpiece Pressplate Ult Coll-219
05UD Artifacts-312
05Ultimate Collection-219
Gold-219
05Upper Deck Ice-215
05Upper Deck Rookie Update-167
05Upper Deck Trilogy-291
05AHL Top Prospects-21
06ITG Heroes and Prospects-70
Autographs-AMJ

Jones, Mike
03Alaska Aces-7

Jones, Nick
95Roanoke Express-19

Jones, Randy
03ITG VIP Rookie Debut-132
03Parkhurst Rookie-130
03Upper Deck Rookie Update-130
03Philadelphia Phantoms-22
04Pacific-293
Blue-293
Red-293
04Philadelphia Phantoms-6
05Philadelphia Phantoms-12
06Flyers Postcards-3
06O-Pee-Chee-360
Rainbow-360

Jones, Ron
75O-Pee-Chee NHL-247
75Topps-247
89Windsor Spitfires-7

Jones, Ron (NHL)
75O-Pee-Chee NHL-247
75Topps-247

Jones, Ryan
92Quebec Pee-Wee Tournament-1178
93Quebec Pee-Wee Tournament-611

Jones, Sebastian
04German DEL-191

Jones, Simon
98Spokane Chiefs-12

Jones, Steve
95Slapshot-329
99Sioux City Musketeers-10

Jones, Steve (OHL)
95Slapshot-329

Jones, Steve (USHL)
99Sioux City Musketeers-10

Jones, Todd
92North Dakota Fighting Sioux-14

Jones, Ty
95Spokane Chiefs-7
96Spokane Chiefs-6
97Black Diamond-52
Double Diamond-52
Triple Diamond-52
Quadruple Diamond-52
97Spokane Chiefs-9
97Bowman CHL-142
OPC-142
Autographs-22
98Pacific Dynagon Ice-43
Blue-43
Red-43
98UD Choice-303
Prime Choice Reserve-303
Reserve-303
98Upper Deck-242
Exclusives-242
Exclusives 1 of 1-242
Generation Next-GN14
Generation Next Quantum 1-GN14
Generation Next Quantum 2-GN14
Generation Next Quantum 3-GN14
Gold Reserve-242
98Spokane Chiefs-13
99BAP Memorabilia-172
Gold-172
Silver-172
99Pacific-99
Copper-99
Emerald Green-99
Gold-99
Ice Blue-99
Premiere Date-99
Red-99
99SPx-34
Radiance-34
Spectrum-34
99Upper Deck-36
Exclusives-36
Exclusives 1 of 1-36
New Ice Age-N5
New Ice Age Quantum Gold-N5
New Ice Age Quantum Silver-N5
99Upper Deck Gold Reserve-36
99Upper Deck MVP-45
Gold Script-45
Silver Script-45
Super Script-45
99Upper Deck Victory-68
99Cleveland Lumberjacks-10
99Florida Everblades-16
01Norfolk Admirals-22

Jones-Parry, Shon
97Portland Winter Hawks-17
99Prince George Cougars-13

Jonfeldt, Johan
04Swedish Elitset-23
Gold-23

Joninen, Juha
98Finnish Kerailysarja-241

Jonses, Gunnar
57Swedish Alfabilder-87

Jonsson, Fredrik
97Swedish Collector's Choice-107

Jonsson, Haldor
56Swedish Alfabilder-58

Jonsson, Hans
83Swedish Semic Elitserien-237
91Swedish Semic Elitserien Stickers-210
92Swedish Semic Elitserien Stickers-231
93Swedish Semic Elitserien-201
94Swedish Leaf-44
95Swedish Leaf-102
95Swedish Upper Deck-156
97Swedish Collector's Choice-153
98Swedish UD Choice-170
99Pacific Omega-189
Copper-189
Gold-189
Ice Blue-189
Premiere Date-189
99Topps Premier Plus-92
Parallel-92
02Upper Deck MVP-150
Gold-150
Classics-150
Golden Classics-150
04Swedish Elitset-238
Gold-238
04Swedish MoDo Postcards-13
05Swedish SHL Elitset-93
06Swedish SHL Elitset-104

Jonsson, Jonas
90Swedish Semic Elitserien Stickers-121
91Swedish Semic Elitserien Stickers-124

Jonsson, Jorgen
92Swedish Semic Elitserien Stickers-272
93Swedish Semic Elitserien-236
94Swedish Leaf-69
Gold Cards-10
Top Guns-5
95Finnish Semic World Championships-66
95Swedish Leaf-215
95Swedish Upper Deck-72
Ticket to North America-NA9
95Swedish Globe World Championships-38
95Signature Rookies-46
Signatures-46
97Swedish Collector's Choice-64
Crash the Game Exchange-C21
Crash the Game Redemption-R21
Select-UD6
Stick'Ums-S4
98Swedish UD Choice-99
99Black Diamond-55
Diamond Cut-55
Final Cut-55
99Pacific Dynagon Ice-125
Blue-125
Copper-125
Gold-125
Premiere Date-125
99Pacific Omega-142
Copper-142
Gold-142
Ice Blue-142
Premiere Date-142

99Panini Stickers-87
99SP Authentic-109
99SPx-93
Radiance-93
Spectrum-93
99Stadium Club-176
First Day Issue-176
One of a Kind-176
Printing Plates Black-176
Printing Plates Cyan-176
Printing Plates Magenta-176
Printing Plates Yellow-176
99Topps Premier Plus-112
Parallel-112
99Ultimate Victory-102
1/1-102
Parallel-102
Parallel 100-102
99Upper Deck HoloGrFx-35
Ausome-35
99Wayne Gretzky Hockey-104
00BAP Memorabilia-225
Emerald-225
Ruby-225
Sapphire-225
Promos-225
00BAP Mem Chicago Sportsfest Copper-225
00BAP Memorabilia Chicago Sportsfest Blue-225
00BAP Memorabilia Chicago Sportsfest Gold-225
00BAP Memorabilia Chicago Sportsfest Ruby-225
00BAP Memorabilia Chicago Sun-Times Ruby-225
00BAP Memorabilia Chicago Sun-Times Gold-225
00BAP Mem Chicago Sun-Times Sapphire-225
00BAP Mem Toronto Fall Expo Copper-225
00BAP Memorabilia Toronto Fall Expo Gold-225
00BAP Memorabilia Toronto Fall Expo Ruby-225
00Pacific-431
Copper-431
Gold-431
Ice Blue-431
Premiere Date-431
00Swedish Upper Deck-90
00Swedish Upper Deck-191
SHL Excellence-S2
SHL Signatures-JJ
Top Playmakers-P5
02Swedish SHL-136
02Swedish SHL-174
Dynamic Duos-3
Parallel-136
Parallel-174
Sharpshooters-SS2
Signatures-5
Team Captains-3
03Swedish Elite-186
Hot Numbers-HN5
Signatures II-4
Silver-186
Stars of the Game-3
04Swedish Alfabilder Alfa Stars-27
04Swedish Alfabilder Alfa Star Golden Ice-9
04Swedish Alfabilder Proof Parallels-27
04Swedish Elitset-189
Gold-189
Limited Signatures-2
Signatures Series B-5
04Swedish Pure Skills-32
Parallel-32
05Swedish SHL Elitset-187
Icons-2
Playmakers-5
Series Two Jerseys-GWJJ
Series Two Signatures-31
06Swedish SHL Elitset-50
Playmakers-5

Jonsson, Kenny
92Upper Deck-596
92Swedish Semic Elitserien Stickers-253
93Parkhurst-535
Emerald Ice-535
93Swedish Semic Elitserien-223
93Swedish Semic Elitserien-304
93Classic-135
93Classic Four-Sport *-195
Gold-195
94Be A Player-R154
94Finest-5
94Finest-56
Super Team Winners-5
Super Team Winners-56
Refractors-5
Refractors-56
Bowman's Best-R18
Bowman's Best Refractors-R18
94Flair-182
94Fleer-216
94Leaf-472
94Leaf Limited-115
94Maple Leafs Kodak-17
94Maple Leafs Pin-up Posters-7
94OPC Premier-329
Special Effects-329
94Parkhurst SE-SE173
Gold-SE173
94Pinnacle-264
94Pinnacle-476
Artist's Proofs-264
Artist's Proofs-476
Rink Collection-264
Rink Collection-476
Rookie Team Pinnacle-4
94Score Top Rookie Redemption-6
94Select-172
Gold-172
Youth Explosion-YE4
94SP Premier-7
94SP Premier Die-Cuts-7
94Topps/OPC Premier-329
Special Effects-329
94Ultra-377
94Upper Deck-238
94Upper Deck-530
94Upper Deck-560
Electric Ice-238
Electric Ice-530
Electric Ice-560
Predictor Canadian-C11
94Upper Deck Predictor Canadian Exch Gold-C11
94Upper Deck Predictor Cdn Exch Silver-C11
94Upper Deck SP Inserts-SP168
94Upper Deck SP Inserts Die Cuts-SP168
94Swedish Leaf Gold Cards-11
94St. John's Maple Leafs-14
94Classic-25
Gold-25
ROY Sweepstakes-R8
Tri-Cards-T67
95Be A Player-180
Signatures-S180
Signatures Die Cuts-S180
95Bowman-86
All-Foil-86
95Canada Games NHL POGS-31
95Canada Games NHL POGS-267
95Collector's Choice-137
95Collector's Choice-373
Player's Club-137
Player's Club-373
Player's Club Platinum-137
Player's Club Platinum-373
95Donruss-115
95Donruss Elite-4
Die Cut Stars-4
Die Cut Uncut-4
95Emotion-172
95Finest-29
Refractors-29
95Leaf-24
95Leaf Limited-88
95McDonald's Pinnacle-MCD-36
95Metal-144
95Panini Stickers-208
95Panini Stickers-306
95Parkhurst International-203
Emerald Ice-203
95Pinnacle-130
Artist's Proofs-130
Rink Collection-130
95Playoff One on One-203
95Pro Magnets-78
95Score-30
Black Ice Artist's Proofs-30
Black Ice-30
95SkyBox Impact-162
NHL On Fox-13
95SP-147
95Stadium Club-107
Members Only Master Set-107
95Topps-211
OPC Inserts-211
New To The Game-9NG
95Ultra-161
Gold Medallion-161
95Upper Deck-463
Electric Ice-463
Electric Ice Gold-463
Special Edition-SE81
Special Edition Gold-SE81
95Finnish Semic World Championships-59
95Swedish Upper Deck-240
95Swedish Globe World Championships-15
95Images-59
Gold-59
Autographs-59A
96Black Diamond-73
Gold-73
96Collector's Choice-159
96Donruss-74
Press Proofs-74
96Donruss Elite-117
Die Cut Stars-117
96Fleer-65
96Fleer Picks-92
96Islander Postcards-8
96Leaf-60
Press Proofs-60
96Leaf Preferred-28
Press Proofs-28
96Metal Universe-93
96NHL Pro Stamps-78
96Pinnacle-91
Artist's Proofs-91
Foil-91
Premium Stock-91
Rink Collection-91
96Score-168
Artist's Proofs-168
Dealer's Choice Artist's Proofs-168
Special Artist's Proofs-168
Golden Blades-168
96SkyBox Impact-76
96SP-93
96Ultra-102
Gold Medallion-102
96Upper Deck-101
96Swedish Semic Wien-53
96Collector's Edge Ice Crucibles-C4
97Black Diamond-10
Double Diamond-10
Triple Diamond-10
Quadruple Diamond-10
97Collector's Choice-159
97Esso Olympic Hockey Heroes-46
97Esso Olympic Hockey Heroes French-46
97Katch-88
Gold-88
Silver-88
97Pacific Invincible NHL Regime-116
97Panini Stickers-76
97SP Authentic-95
97Upper Deck-312
98Be A Player-87
Press Release-87
98BAP Gold-87
98BAP Autographs-87
98BAP Autographs Gold-87
98BAP Tampa Bay All Star Game-87
98Pacific-282
Ice Blue-282
Red-282
98Pacific Omega-146
Red-146
Opening Day Issue-146
98Panini Stickers-77
98Paramount-143
Copper-143
Emerald Green-143
Holo-Electric-143
Ice Blue-143
Silver-143
98Revolution-87
Ice Shadow-87
Red-87
98Topps Gold Label Class 1-27
Black-27
Black One of One-27
One of One-27
Red-27
Red One of One-27
98Topps Gold Label Class 2-27
98Topps Gold Label Class 2 Black-27
98Topps Gold Label Class 2 Black 1 of 1-27
98Topps Gold Label Class 2 One of One-27
98Topps Gold Label Class 2 Red-27
98Topps Gold Label Class 2 Red One of One-27
98Topps Gold Label Class 3-27
98Topps Gold Label Class 3 Black-27
98Topps Gold Label Class 3 Black 1 of 1-27
98Topps Gold Label Class 3 One of One-27
98Topps Gold Label Class 3 Red-27
98Topps Gold Label Class 3 Red One of One-27
98UD Choice-125
98UD Choice Preview-125
98UD Choice Prime Choice Reserve-125
98UD Choice Reserve-125
98Upper Deck-318
Exclusives-318
Exclusives 1 of 1-318
Gold Reserve-318
98Upper Deck MVP-130
Gold Script-130
Silver Script-130
Super Script-130
99Aurora-90
Premiere Date-90
99BAP Memorabilia-232
Gold-232
Silver-232
99BAP Millennium-156
Emerald-156
Ruby-156
Sapphire-156
Signatures-156
Signatures Gold-156
99Crown Royale-87
Limited Series-87
Premiere Date-87
99O-Pee-Chee-113
99O-Pee-Chee Chrome-113
99O-Pee-Chee Chrome Refractors-113
99O-Pee-Chee Now Starring-NS4
99Pacific-255
Copper-255
Emerald Green-255
Gold-255
Ice Blue-255
Premiere Date-255
Red-255
99Pacific Dynagon Ice-126
Blue-126
Copper-126
Gold-126
Premiere Date-126
99Panini Stickers-92
99Paramount-142
Copper-142
Emerald-142
Gold-142
Holographic Emerald-142
Holographic Gold-142
Holographic Silver-142
Ice Blue-142
Premiere Date-142
Red-142
Silver-142
99Revolution-91
Premiere Date-91
Red-91
Shadow Series-91
99SP Authentic-54
99SPx-94
Radiance-94
Spectrum-94
99Stadium Club-11
First Day Issue-11
One of a Kind-11
Printing Plates Black-11
Printing Plates Cyan-11
Printing Plates Magenta-11
Printing Plates Yellow-11
99Topps/OPC-113
Now Starring-NS4
99Topps/OPC Chrome-113
Refractors-113
99Topps Gold Label Class 1-50
Black-50
Black One of One-50
One of One-50
Red-50
Red One of One-50
99Topps Gold Label Class 2-50
99Topps Gold Label Class 2 Black-50
99Topps Gold Label Class 2 Black 1 of 1-50
99Topps Gold Label Class 2 One of One-50
99Topps Gold Label Class 2 Red-50
99Topps Gold Label Class 2 Red One of One-50
99Topps Gold Label Class 3-50
99Topps Gold Label Class 3 Black-50
99Topps Gold Label Class 3 Black 1 of 1-50
99Topps Gold Label Class 3 One of One-50
99Topps Gold Label Class 3 Red-50
99Topps Gold Label Class 3 Red One of One-50
99Topps Premier Plus-33
Parallel-33
99Ultimate Victory-55
1/1-55
Parallel-55
Parallel 100-55
99Upper Deck-84
Exclusives-84
Exclusives 1 of 1-84
99Upper Deck Gold Reserve-84
99Upper Deck MVP-129
Gold Script-129
Silver Script-129
Super Script-129
99Upper Deck MVP SC Edition-114
Gold Script-114
Silver Script-114
Super Script-114
99Upper Deck Victory-179
99Wayne Gretzky Hockey-107
00BAP Memorabilia-150
Emerald-150
Ruby-150
Sapphire-150
Promos-150
00BAP Mem Chicago Sportsfest Copper-150
00BAP Memorabilia Chicago Sportsfest Blue-150
00BAP Memorabilia Chicago Sportsfest Gold-150
00BAP Memorabilia Chicago Sportsfest Ruby-150
00BAP Memorabilia Chicago Sun-Times Ruby-150
00BAP Memorabilia Chicago Sun-Times Gold-150
00BAP Mem Chicago Sun-Times Sapphire-150
00BAP Mem Toronto Fall Expo Copper-150
00BAP Memorabilia Toronto Fall Expo Gold-150
00BAP Memorabilia Toronto Fall Expo Ruby-150
00BAP Parkhurst 2000-P149
00BAP Signature Series-133
Emerald-133
Ruby-133
Sapphire-133
Autographs-79
Autographs Gold-79
Department of Defense-DD9
Jersey Cards-J18
Jersey and Stick Cards-GSJ18
Jersey Cards Autographs-J18
Jersey Emblems-E18
Jersey Numbers-IN18
00O-Pee-Chee-101
00O-Pee-Chee Parallel-101
00Pacific-442
Copper-442
Gold-442
Ice Blue-442
Premiere Date-442
00Panini Stickers-57
00SPx Winning Materials-KJ
00Stadium Club-39
Souvenirs-SCS5
00Titanium Game Gear-110
00Titanium Game Gear Patches-110
00Titanium Draft Day Edition-62
Patches-62
00Topps/OPC-101
Parallel-101
00Topps Chrome-79
OPC Refractors-79
Refractors-79
00UD Heroes Signs of Greatness-KJ
00Upper Deck-112
Exclusives Tier 1-112
Exclusives Tier 2-112
00Upper Deck MVP-111
First Stars-111
Second Stars-111
Third Stars-111
00Upper Deck Victory-145
00Upper Deck Vintage-231
00Upper Deck Vintage-233
01BAP Memorabilia-183
Emerald-183
Ruby-183
Sapphire-183
01BAP Signature Series Jerseys-GJ-42
01BAP Signature Series Jersey Autographs-GUKJ
01BAP Sig Series Jersey and Stick Cards-GSJ-42
01BAP Signature Series Teammates-TM-20
01Pacific-250
Extreme LTD-250
Hobby LTD-250
Premiere Date-250
Retail LTD-250
01Pacific Arena Exclusives-250
01Pacific Heads-Up Quad Jerseys-4
01Parkhurst-129
Sticks-PS50
01Private Stock Game Gear-63
01Private Stock Game Gear Patches-63
01Topps Reserve Emblems-KJ
01Topps Reserve Jerseys-KJ
01Topps Reserve Name Plates-KJ
01Topps Reserve Numbers-KJ
01Topps Reserve Patches-KJ
01Upper Deck-112
Exclusives-112
01Upper Deck MVP-121
01Upper Deck Victory-227
Gold-227
02BAP First Edition-97
Jerseys-97
02BAP Sig Series Auto Buybacks 1998-87
02BAP Sig Series Auto Buybacks 1999-156
02BAP Sig Series Auto Buybacks 2000-79
02BAP Signature Series Golf-GS47
02O-Pee-Chee-59
02O-Pee-Chee Premier Blue Parallel-59
02O-Pee-Chee Premier Red Parallel-59
02O-Pee-Chee Factory Set-59
02Pacific-238
Blue-238
Red-238
02Pacific Complete-161
Red-161
02Topps-59
OPC Blue Parallel-59
OPC Red Parallel-59
Factory Set-59
02Topps Total-74
03ITG Action-376
03NHL Sticker Collection-78
03O-Pee-Chee-275
03OPC Blue-275
03OPC Gold-275
03OPC Red-275
03Pacific Complete-82
Red-82
03Topps-275
Blue-275
Gold-275
Red-275
04Swedish Alfabilder Alfa Stars-4
04Swedish Alfabilder Proof Parallels-4
05Upper Deck MVP Materials-M-KJ

Jonsson, Kjell
64Swedish Coralli ISHockey-82
64Swedish Coralli ISHockey-102
65Swedish Coralli ISHockey-82
65Swedish Coralli ISHockey-102
67Swedish Hockey-289
69Swedish Hockey-337

Jonsson, Lars
00Swedish Upper Deck-110
00Swedish Upper Deck-216
02Swedish SHL Dynamic Duos-4
02Swedish SHL Signatures Series II-22
03Swedish Elite-58
Silver-58
04Swedish Elitset-281
Gold-281
05Swedish SHL Elitset-194
Gold-194
06Hot Prospects-172
Red Hot-172
White Hot-172
06O-Pee-Chee-571
Rainbow-571
06SP Authentic-223
Limited-223
06SP Game Used-138
Gold-138
Rainbow-138
06SPx-210
Spectrum-210
06The Cup Masterpiece Pressplates (Marquee Rookies)-571
06The Cup Masterpiece Pressplates (SP Authentic)-223
06The Cup Masterpiece Pressplates (SP Game Used)-138
06The Cup Masterpiece Pressplates (Victory)-323
06Upper Deck-482
Exclusives Parallel-482
High Gloss Parallel-482
Masterpieces-482
Victory-323
06Philadelphia Phantoms-5

Jonsson, Lennart
83Swedish Semic Elitserien-156
85Swedish Panini Stickers-207

Jonsson, Ove
67Swedish Hockey-223
69Swedish Hockey-261

Jonsson, Pierre
96German DEL-94

Jonsson, Robin
03Swedish Elite-179
Silver-179
04Swedish Elitset-181
Gold-181
05Swedish SHL Elitset-39
Gold-39
Star Potential-7
06Swedish SHL Elitset-42

Jonsson, Roger
97Swedish Collector's Choice-194
99Swedish Upper Deck-191

Jonsson, Stefan
83Swedish Semic Elitserien-204
84Swedish Semic Elitserien-227
85Swedish Panini Stickers-228
86Swedish Panini Stickers-256
87Swedish Panini Stickers-240
89Swedish Semic Elitserien Stickers-225
90Swedish Semic Elitserien Stickers-54
91Swedish Semic Elitserien Stickers-229
92Swedish Semic Elitserien Stickers-185
93Swedish Semic Elitserien-155
94Swedish Leaf-162
95Swedish Leaf-79
95Swedish Upper Deck-121
97Swedish Collector's Choice-123
98Swedish UD Choice-134

Jonsson, Tomas
81Swedish Semic Hockey VM Stickers-2
82O-Pee-Chee-202
82Post Cereal-12
83Islanders Team Issue-7
83NHL Key Tags-78
83O-Pee-Chee-9
83O-Pee-Chee Stickers-87
83Topps Stickers-87
83Swedish Semic Elitserien-181
84Islanders News-16
84O-Pee-Chee-128
85Islanders News-20
85O-Pee-Chee-154
85O-Pee-Chee Stickers-78
85Topps-154
86Islanders Team Issue-30
86O-Pee-Chee-78
86O-Pee-Chee Stickers-214
86Topps-78
87O-Pee-Chee-190
87Panini Stickers-92
87Topps-190
88Oilers Tenth Anniversary-149
88Oilers Team Issue-12
88O-Pee-Chee-108
88Topps-108
89Swedish Semic Elitserien Stickers-124
89Swedish Semic World Champ Stickers-5
90Swedish Semic Elitserien Stickers-202
91Finnish Semic World Champ Stickers-32
91Swedish Semic Elitserien Stickers-131
91Swedish Semic Elitserien Stickers-342
91Swedish Semic World Champ Stickers-32
92Swedish Semic Elitserien Stickers-153
93Swedish Semic Elitserien-124
93Swedish Semic World Champ Stickers-5
94Finnish Jaa Kiekko-54
94Swedish Leaf-100
Gold Cards-23
95Swedish Leaf-62
95Swedish Leaf-303
Champs-1
Face to Face-15
Mega-5
95Swedish Upper Deck-95
95Swedish Upper Deck-227
95Swedish Upper Deck-255
95Swedish Globe World Championships-14
95Swedish World Championships Stickers-141
96Swedish Semic Wien-47
96Swedish Semic Wien Coca-Cola Dream Team-3
97Swedish Collector's Choice-101
97Swedish Collector's Choice-201
Select-UD11
04Swedish Alfabilder Alfa Stars-42
04Swedish Alfabilder Alfa Star Golden Ice-6
04Swedish Alfabilder Autographs-110
04Swedish Alfabilder Limited Autographs-110
04Swedish Alfabilder Proof Parallels-42

Jooris, Mark
95German DEL-357
96German DEL-217
04German Berlin Eisbarens 50th Anniv-19

Jordan, Ric
72Whalers New England WHA-9

Jorde, Manfred
94German DEL-185

Jorde, Ryan
99Lethbridge Hurricanes-13
01Moose Jaw Warriors-1
02Rochester Americans-10
03Rochester Americans-11
04Rochester Americans-9
05Fort Wayne Komets Choice-24
05Fort Wayne Komets Sprint-12

Jorg, Fabian
05German DEL-66

Jorg, Thomas
03German Deg Metro Stars-5
04German DEL Update-291
04German Dusseldorf Metro Stars Postcards-7
06German DEL-43

Jorgensen, Christian
99Danish Hockey League-38

Jorgensen, Mike
98Las Vegas Coyotes RHI-7

Jorgensen, Reid
02Kamloops Blazers-6
03Kamloops Blazers-22
04Kamloops Blazers-3
05Kamloops Blazers-24
06Kamloops Blazers-11

Jorgenson, Ken
82Medicine Hat Tigers-6

Jorgenson, Kevin
87Portland Winter Hawks-13
88Portland Winter Hawks-13
89Portland Winter Hawks-13

Jorgenson, Len
88Kamloops Blazers-14

Jorgenson, Lynn
78Saginaw Gears-12

Jormakka, Tuomo
78Finnish SM-Liiga-161
80Finnish Mallasjuoma-153

Jorris, Mark
98Swiss Power Play Stickers-324

Jortikka, Ari
78Finnish SM-Liiga-99

Jortikka, Hannu
73Finnish Jaakiekko-280
78Finnish SM-Liiga-200
80Finnish Mallasjuoma-177
92Finnish Jyvas-Hyva Stickers-18
93Swiss HNL-58
94Swedish Leaf-302

Jorundson, Wes
93Quebec Pee-Wee Tournament-1228

Jory, Kurt
05Brandon Wheat Kings-12
06Moose Jaw Warriors-23

Josefowicz, Mike
01Macon Whoopee-11

Josefsen, Bjorge
99Norwegian National Team-21

Josefsson, Daniel
02Swedish SHL-181
Parallel-181

Josefsson, Ola
89Swedish Semic Elitserien Stickers-71
90Swedish Semic Elitserien Stickers-287
91Swedish Semic Elitserien Stickers-68
92Swedish Semic Elitserien Stickers-95
93Swedish Semic Elitserien-67
94Swedish Leaf-74
95Swedish Leaf-187
95Swedish Upper Deck-49

Joseph, Anthony
90Moncton Hawks-12

Joseph, Chris
88Oilers Tenth Anniversary-2
88Oilers Team Issue-13
88O-Pee-Chee Stickers-218
89O-Pee-Chee Stickers-225
89ProCards AHL-131
90Oilers IGA-9
90Pro Set-443
90Upper Deck-323
French-323
91Bowman-108
91Oilers Panini Team Stickers-8
91Oilers Team Issue-8
91O-Pee-Chee-432
91Score Canadian Bilingual-415
91Score Canadian English-415
91Stadium Club-362
91Topps-432
91Upper Deck-436
French-436
92Oilers IGA-11
92Oilers Team Issue-8
92O-Pee-Chee-203
93Donruss-492
93Lightning Season in Review-19
93OPC Premier-87
Gold-87
93PowerPlay-445
93Score-576
Gold-576
Canadian-576
Canadian Gold-576
93Topps/OPC Premier-87
Gold-87
94Canada Games NHL POGS-228
94Donruss-253
94Leaf-158
94OPC Premier-374
Special Effects-374
94Parkhurst SE-SE168
Gold-SE168
94Penguins Foodland-17
94Pinnacle-156
Artist's Proofs-156
Rink Collection-156
94Score-98
Gold-98
Platinum-98
94Stadium Club-224
Members Only Master Set-224
First Day Issue-224
Super Team Winner Cards-224
94Topps/OPC Premier-374
Special Effects-374
94Ultra-207
94Upper Deck-185
Electric Ice-185
95Be A Player-98
Signatures-S98
Signatures Die Cuts-S98
95Donruss-64
95Parkhurst International-433
Emerald Ice-433
95Penguins Foodland-19
95Topps-93
OPC Inserts-93
95Upper Deck-449
Electric Ice-449
Electric Ice Gold-449
96Canucks Postcards-32
97Pacific Invincible NHL Regime-202
98Cincinnati Cyclones-9
98Cincinnati Cyclones 2-15
00BAP Memorabilia-173
Emerald-173
Ruby-173
Sapphire-173
Promos-173
00BAP Mem Chicago Sportsfest Copper-173
00BAP Memorabilia Chicago Sportsfest Blue-173
00BAP Memorabilia Chicago Sportsfest Gold-173
00BAP Memorabilia Chicago Sportsfest Ruby-173
00BAP Memorabilia Chicago Sun-Times Ruby-173
00BAP Memorabilia Chicago Sun-Times Gold-173
00BAP Mem Chicago Sun-Times Sapphire-173
00BAP Mem Toronto Fall Expo Copper-173
00BAP Memorabilia Toronto Fall Expo Gold-173
00BAP Memorabilia Toronto Fall Expo Ruby-173
01Finnish Cardset-355
02German DEL City Press-243
03German DEL-6
03German Mannheim Eagles Postcards-20
04German Adler Mannheim Eagles Postcards-19
04German DEL-12

Joseph, Curtis
89Blues Kodak-31
89ProCards IHL-7
90Blues Kodak-11
90O-Pee-Chee-171
90OPC Premier-51
90Panini Stickers-272
90Pro Set-638
90Score-151
Canadian-151
90Score Young Superstars-15
90Topps-171
Tiffany-171
90Upper Deck-175
French-175
91Pro Set Platinum-225
91Blues Postcards-12
91O-Pee-Chee-417
91OPC Premier-165
91Panini Stickers-22
91Parkhurst-152
French-152
91Pinnacle-105
French-105
91Pro Set-473
French-473
91Score American-296
91Score Canadian Bilingual-516
91Score Canadian English-516
91Score Young Superstars-19
91Topps-417
91Upper Deck-139
French-139
91Air Canada SJHL-A49
92Blues UD Best of the Blues-9
92Bowman-368
92Kraft-31
92O-Pee-Chee-339
92Panini Stickers-15
92Panini Stickers French-15
92Parkhurst-155
92Parkhurst-503
Emerald Ice-155
Emerald Ice-503
92Pinnacle-54
92Pinnacle-264
French-54
French-264
92Pro Set-164
92Score-262
Canadian-262
Young Superstars-17
92Seasons Patches-14
92Stadium Club-327
92Topps-237
Gold-237G
92Ultra-188
92Upper Deck-186
93Donruss-296
93Leaf-2
Painted Warriors-2
93OPC Premier-222
93OPC Premier-272
Gold-222
Gold-272
93Panini Stickers-166
93Parkhurst-175
Emerald Ice-175
93Pinnacle-15
Canadian-15
93PowerPlay-213
Gamebreakers-4
Netminders-4
93Score-116
Canadian-116
93Stadium Club-162
Members Only Master Set-162
OPC-162
First Day Issue-162
First Day Issue OPC-162
93Topps/OPC Premier-222
93Topps/OPC Premier-272
Gold-222
Gold-272
93Topps Premier Black Gold-18
93Ultra-172
93Upper Deck-157
SP-139
94Be A Player-R71
94Be A Player-R101
94Be A Player-R174
Signature Cards-109
94Canada Games NHL POGS-293
94Donruss-287
Masked Marvels-5
94EA Sports-126
94Finest-29
Super Team Winners-29
Refractors-29
94Flair-156
94Fleer-188
Netminders-5
94Hockey Wit-35
94Kraft-44
94Kraft Goalie Masks-3
94Leaf-208
Crease Patrol-3
Gold Stars-7
94Leaf Limited-95
94OPC Premier-340
Special Effects-340
94Parkhurst-199
Gold-199
Vintage-V17
94Pinnacle I Hobby Samples-6
94Pinnacle-6
Artist's Proofs-6
Rink Collection-6
Goaltending Greats-GT13
Masks-MA10
Team Pinnacle-TP2
Team Dufex Parallel-TP2
94Score-181
Gold-181
Platinum-181
94Select-121
Gold-121
94SP-102
Die Cuts-102
94Stadium Club Members Only-22
94Stadium Club-142
Members Only Master Set-142
First Day Issue-142
Super Teams-20
Super Teams Members Only Master Set-20
Super Team Winner Cards-142
94Topps/OPC Premier-340
Special Effects-340
94Ultra-184
Premier Pad Men-3
94Upper Deck-91
Electric Ice-91
Predictor Hobby-H33
94Upper Deck Predictor Hobby Exch Gold-H33
94Upper Deck SP Inserts-SP68
94Upper Deck SP Inserts Die Cuts-SP68
95Collector's Choice-291
Player's Club-291
Player's Club Platinum-291
95Donruss-135
95Donruss Elite-59
Die Cut Stars-59
Die Cut Uncut-59
95Emotion-62
95Hoyle Western Playing Cards-38
95Leaf-281
95Panini Stickers-265
95Parkhurst International-350
Emerald Ice-350
95Score-251
Black Ice Artist's Proofs-251
Black Ice-251
95Select Certified-84
Mirror Gold-84
95SkyBox Impact-60
95SP-54
95Stadium Club Members Only-29
95Topps-215
OPC Inserts-215
95Ultra-140
Gold Medallion-140
Premier Pad Men-6
Premier Pad Men Gold Medallion-6
95Upper Deck-296
Electric Ice-296
Electric Ice Gold-296
96Be A Player-206
Autographs-206
Autographs Silver-206
Stacking the Pads-14
96Black Diamond-158
Gold-158
Run for the Cup-RC17
96Collector's Choice-90
96Collector's Choice-317
Jumbos-2
96Donruss-110
Press Proofs-110
Between the Pipes-8
96Donruss Canadian Ice-116
Gold Press Proofs-116
Red Press Proofs-116
96Donruss Elite-92
Die Cut Stars-92
96Duracell All-Cherry Team-DC4
96Flair-33
Blue Ice-33
Hot Gloves-5
96Fleer-37
96Frosted Flakes Masks-2
96Leaf-28
Press Proofs-28
Shut Down-5
96Leaf Limited-90
Gold-90
96Leaf Preferred Masked Marauders-10
96Leaf Preferred Vanity Plates-13
96Leaf Preferred Vanity Plates Gold-13
96McDonald's Pinnacle-40
96Metal Universe-53
96Oilers Postcards-31
96Pinnacle-164
Artist's Proofs-164
Foil-164
Premium Stock-164
Rink Collection-164
96Post Upper Deck-9
96Score-90
Artist's Proofs-90
Dealer's Choice Artist's Proofs-90
Special Artist's Proofs-90
Golden Blades-90
Net Worth-7
Sudden Death-6
96Select Certified-66
Artist's Proofs-66
Blue-66
Mirror Blue-66
Mirror Gold-66
Mirror Red-66
Red-66
Freezers-7
96SkyBox Impact-42
96SP-54
96Summit-150
Artist's Proofs-150
Ice-150
Metal-150
Premium Stock-150
In The Crease-5
In The Crease Premium Stock-5
96Topps Picks-83
OPC Inserts-83
96Ultra-59
Gold Medallion-59
96Upper Deck-256
Generation Next-X27
96Upper Deck Ice-21
Parallel-21
96Zenith-112
Artist's Proofs-112
96Collector's Edge Future Legends-29
96Collector's Edge Ice Livin' Large-L6
97Be A Player Stacking the Pads-7
97Beehive-12
Golden Portraits-12
97Black Diamond-126
Double Diamond-126
Triple Diamond-126
Quadruple Diamond-126
97Collector's Choice-89
Star Quest-SQ31
Stick'Ums-S6
World Domination-W19
97Crown Royale-53
Emerald Green-53
Ice Blue-53
Silver-53
Freeze Out Die-Cuts-8
97Donruss-43
Press Proofs Silver-43
Press Proofs Gold-43
Between The Pipes-8
97Donruss Canadian Ice-20
Dominion Series-20
Provincial Series-20
National Pride-27
Stanley Cup Scrapbook-2
97Donruss Elite-19
Aspirations-19
Status-19
Craftsmen-29
Master Craftsmen-29
97Donruss Limited-81
97Donruss Limited-103
97Donruss Limited-174
Exposure-81
Exposure-103
Exposure-174
Fabric of the Game-23
97Donruss Preferred-84
Cut to the Chase-84
Color Guard-3
Color Guard Promos-3
97Donruss Priority-123
Stamp of Approval-123
Postmaster General-4
Postmaster Generals Promos-4
97Esso Olympic Hockey Heroes-18
97Esso Olympic Hockey Heroes French-18
97Katch-57
Gold-57
Silver-57
97Kraft Team Canada-6
97Leaf-16
Fractal Matrix-16
Fractal Matrix Die Cuts-16
Pipe Dreams-4
97Leaf International-16
Universal Ice-16
97McDonald's Team Canada Coins-3
97McDonald's Upper Deck-27

Salt Lake Gold-1
02O-Pee-Chee-212
02O-Pee-Chee-212U
02O-Pee-Chee Jumbos-23
02O-Pee-Chee Premier Blue Parallel-212
02O-Pee-Chee Premier Red Parallel-212
02O-Pee-Chee Factory Set-212
02O-Pee-Chee Factory Set Hometown Heroes-HHC20
02Pacific-361
Blue-361
Red-361
Maximum Impact-8
02Pacific Calder-38
Silver-38
02Pacific Complete-379
Red-379
02Pacific Exclusive-64
Advantage-7
02Pacific Heads-Up-44
Blue-44
Purple-44
Red-44
Quad Jerseys-26
Quad Jerseys-28
Quad Jerseys Gold-26
Quad Jerseys Gold-28
Showstoppers-9
02Pacific Quest for the Cup-34
Gold-34
Chasing the Cup-6
02Pacific Toronto Fall Expo-1
Gold-1
02Parkhurst-106
Bronze-106
Gold-106
Silver-106
College Ranks-CR14
College Ranks Jerseys-CRM14
Hardware-V1
02Parkhurst Retro-146
Minis-146
02Private Stock Reserve-118
Red-118
Retail-118
InCrease Security-8
02SP Authentic-33
Beckett Promos-33
Sign of the Times-CJ
02SP Game Used-19
Piece of History-PHCJ
Piece of History Gold-PHCJ
Piece of History Rainbow-PHCJ
Signature Style-CJ
02SPx-30
02SPx-88
Spectrum Gold-30
Spectrum Gold-88
Spectrum Silver-30
Spectrum Silver-88
Winning Materials-WMCJ
Winning Materials Gold-CJ
Winning Materials Silver-CJ
02Stadium Club-101
Silver Decoy Cards-101
Proofs-101
02Titanium-37
Blue-37
Red-37
Retail-37
Masked Marauders-3
02Topps-212
02Topps-212U
OPC Blue Parallel-212
OPC Red Parallel-212
Topps/OPC Hometown Heroes-HHC20
Factory Set-212
02Topps Chrome-119
Black Border Refractors-119
Refractors-119
Chromographs-CGCJ
Chromograph Refractors-CGCJ
02Topps Heritage-157
02Topps Total-391
Topps-TT12
02UD Artistic Impressions-34
Gold-34
Artist's Touch-ATCJ
Artist's Touch Gold-ATCJ
02UD Artistic Impressions Beckett Promos-34
02UD Artistic Impressions Retrospectives-R34
02UD Artistic Impressions Retrospect Gold-R34
02UD Artistic Impressions Retrospect Auto-R34
02UD Artistic Impressions Retrospect Silver-R34
02UD Honor Roll-28
Students of the Game-SG12
02UD Mask Collection-30
02UD Mask Collection-31
02UD Mask Collection-32
02UD Mask Collection-33
02UD Mask Collection-93
02UD Mask Collection Beckett Promos-30
02UD Mask Collection Beckett Promos-31
02UD Mask Collection Beckett Promos-32
02UD Mask Collection Beckett Promos-33
02UD Mask Collection Career Wins-CWCJ
02UD Mask Collection Great Gloves-GGCJ
02UD Mask Collection Mini Masks-CJ
02UD Mask Collection Mini Masks Autos-CJ
02UD Mask Collection Nation's Best-NJBT
02UD Mask Collection Patches-PWCJ
02UD Mask Collection Super Stoppers-SSCJ
02UD Mask Collection View from the Cage-VCJ
02UD Piece of History-36
02UD Premier Collection-22
Jerseys Bronze-CJ
Jerseys Bronze-FJ
Jerseys Gold-CJ
Jerseys Gold-FJ
Jerseys Silver-CJ
Jerseys Silver-FJ
Patches-PCJ
02UD Top Shelf-84
Clutch Performers-CPCJ
Milestones Jerseys-MRBRJ
Stopper Jerseys-SSCJ
Sweet Sweaters-SWCJ
02Upper Deck-64
Exclusives-64
Blow-Ups-C14
Good Old Days-GOCJ
Last Line of Defense-LL4
Playbooks-PL13
02Upper Deck Classic Portraits-38
Mini-Busts-5
Mini-Busts-6
Mini-Busts-7
Mini-Busts-8
Mini-Busts-9
Mini-Busts-10
Mini-Busts-11
Mini-Busts-12
02Upper Deck MVP-65
Gold-65
Classics-65
Golden Classics-65
Prosign-CJ
02Upper Deck Rookie Update-37
Autographs-CJ
02Upper Deck Victory National Pride-NP13
02Upper Deck Vintage-94
Green Backs-94
Tall Boys-T27
Tall Boys Gold-T27
02Vanguard-37
LTD-37
Jerseys-19
Jerseys Gold-19
Stonewallers-3
V-Team-3
02UD SuperStars *-83
Gold-83
03McFarlane Hockey Red Wings-10
03BAP Memorabilia-111
Emerald-111
Gold-111
Ruby-111
Sapphire-111
Deep in the Crease-D8
He Shoots-He Scores Prizes-24
Jerseys-GJ-23
Practice Jerseys-PMP1
03BAP Ultimate Memorabilia Autographs-30
Gold-30
03BAP Ultimate Mem Auto Jerseys-30
03BAP Ultimate Memorabilia Active Eight-2
03BAP Ultimate Mem Complete Package-9
03BAP Ultimate Mem Complete Package Gold-9
03BAP Ultimate Mem Jersey and Emblems-8
03BAP Ultimate Mem Jersey and Emblem Gold-8
03BAP Ultimate Mem Jersey and Numbers-8
03BAP Ultimate Mem Jersey and Number Gold-8
03BAP Ultimate Memorabilia Nameplates-5
03BAP Ultimate Mem Nameplates Gold-5
03BAP Ultimate Memorabilia Triple Threads-3
03Beehive Sticks Beige Border-BE14
03Black Diamond Signature Gems-SG-14
03Duracell-3
03ITG Action-219
Oh Canada-OC11
03ITG Used Signature Series-98
Gold-98
Autographs-CJ
Autographs Gold-CJ
International Experience-5
International Experience Autographs-5
International Experience Emblems Gold-5
International Experience Emblems-5
International Experience Gold-5
Oh Canada-1
Oh Canada Gold-1
Oh Canada Emblems-1
Oh Canada Emblems Gold-1
Retrospectives-6A
Retrospectives-6B
Retrospectives-6C
Retrospectives-6D
Retrospectives-6E
Retrospectives-6F
Retrospectives Gold-6A
Retrospectives Gold-6B
Retrospectives Gold-6C
Retrospectives Gold-6D
Retrospectives Gold-6E
Retrospectives Gold-6F
03McDonald's Pacific-18
Net Fusions-2
03NHL Sticker Collection-220
03O-Pee-Chee-130
03OPC Blue-130
03OPC Gold-130
03OPC Red-130
03Pacific-120
Blue-120
Red-120
In the Crease-5
03Pacific Calder-38
Silver-38
03Pacific Complete-438
Red-438
03Pacific Invincible Jerseys-12
03Pacific Prism-38
Blue-38
Gold-38
Red-38
Crease Police-4
03Pacific Quest for the Cup-38
Blue-38
03Parkhurst Original Six Detroit-13
03Parkhurst Orig Six He Shoots/Scores-1
03Parkhurst Orig Six He Shoots/Scores-1A
03Parkhurst Orig Six He Shoots/Scores-25
03Parkhurst Orig Six He Shoots/Scores-25A
03Parkhurst Original Six Toronto-42
Memorabilia-TM32
03Parkhurst Rookie-51
Jerseys-GJ-35
Jersey Autographs-GUJ-CJ
Jerseys Gold-GJ-35
Retro Rookies-RR-13
Retro Rookies Gold-RR-13
03SP Authentic Sign of the Times-SG
03SP Game Used Game Gear-GGCJ
03SP Game Used Signers-SPSCJ
03Titanium-37
Hobby Jersey Number Parallels-37
Retail-37
Retail Jersey Number Parallels-37
03Topps-130
03Topps-PP3
Blue-130
Gold-130
Red-130
Lost Rookies-CJ
03Topps C55-109
Minis-109
Minis American Back-109
Minis American Back Red-109
Minis Bazooka Back-109
Minis Brooklyn Back-109
Minis Hat Trick Back-109
Minis O Canada Back-109
Minis O Canada Back Red-109
Minis Stanley Cup Back-109
03Topps Pristine-79
Gold Refractor Die Cuts-79
Refractors-79
Press Plates Black-79
Press Plates Cyan-79
Press Plates Magenta-79
Press Plates Yellow-79
Stick Portions-PPS-CJ
Stick Portion Refractors-PPS-CJ
03UD Honor Roll Signature Class-SC14
03UD Premier Collection NHL Shields-SH-CJ
03UD Premier Collection Signatures-PS-CJ
03UD Premier Collection Signatures Gold-PS-CJ
03UD Toronto Fall Expo Priority Signings-CJ
03Upper Deck BuyBacks-105
03Upper Deck BuyBacks-106
03Upper Deck BuyBacks-107
03Upper Deck BuyBacks-108
03Upper Deck BuyBacks-109
03Upper Deck Jersey Autographs-SJ-CJ
03Upper Deck Classic Portraits Classic Colors-CC-CJ
03Upper Deck MVP-159
Gold Script-159
Silver Script-159
Canadian Exclusives-159
ProSign-PS-CJ
03Upper Deck Trilogy Scripts-S2CJ
03Upper Deck Trilogy Scripts Limited-S2CJ
03Upper Deck Trilogy Scripts Red-S2CJ
03Upper Deck Victory-70
Bronze-70
Gold-70
Silver-70
04Pacific-94
Blue-94
Red-94
04Ultimate Collection Dual Logos-UL2-HJ
04Ultimate Collection Jerseys-UGJ-CJ
04Ultimate Collection Jerseys Gold-UGJ-CJ
04Ultimate Collection Patches-UP-CJ
04Upper Deck-67
Canadian Exclusives-67
HG Glossy Gold-67
HG Glossy Silver-67
05Be A Player-34
First Period-34
Second Period-34
Third Period-34
Overtime-34
05Beehive-69
05Beehive-207
Beige -69
Blue -69
Gold-69
Red -69
Matte-69
Matted Materials-MMCJ
05Black Diamond-95
Emerald-95
Gold-95
Onyx-95
Ruby-95
Jerseys-J-CJ
Jerseys Ruby-J-CJ
Jersey Duals-DJ-CJ
Jersey Triples-TJ-CJ
Jersey Quads-QJ-CJ
05Hot Prospects-75
En Fuego-75
Red Hot-75
White Hot-75
05McDonalds Upper Deck Goalie Factory-GF14
05McDonalds Upper Deck Goalie Gear-MG12
05Panini Stickers-322
05Parkhurst-367
Facsimile Auto Parallel-367
True Colors-TCPHX
True Colors-TCPHX
05SP Authentic-78
05SP Authentic-125
Limited-78
Limited-125
05SP Game Used-77
Gold-77
Authentic Fabrics-AF-CJ
Authentic Fabrics Gold-AF-CJ
Authentic Patches-AP-CJ
Awesome Authentics-AA-CJ
05SPx-71
Spectrum-71
Winning Combos-WC-HJ
Winning Combos Gold-WC-HJ
Winning Combos Spectrum-WC-HJ
Winning Materials-WM-CJ
Winning Materials Gold-WM-CJ
Winning Materials Spectrum-WM-CJ
05The Cup-81
Gold-81
Black Rainbow-81
Dual NHL Shields-DSJD
Masterpiece Pressplates-81
Masterpiece Pressplates (Rookie Update)-227
Noble Numbers-NNFJ
Patch Variation-P81
05UD Artifacts Treasured Patches-TP-CJ
05UD Artifacts Treasured Patch Autos-TP-CJ
05UD Artifacts Treasured Patches Dual-TPD-CJ
05UD Artifacts Treasured Patch Dual Autos-TPD-CJ
05UD Artifacts Treasured Patches Pewter-TP-CJ
05UD Artifacts Treasured Patches Silver-TP-CJ
05UD Artifacts Treasured Swatches-TS-CJ
05UD Artifacts Treasured Swatch Autos-TS-CJ
05UD Artifacts Treasured Swatches Blue-TS-CJ
05UD Artifacts Treasured Swatches Copper-TS-CJ
05UD Artifacts Treasured Swatches Dual-TSD-CJ
05UD Artifacts Treasured Swatch Dual Auto-TSD-CJ
05UD Artifacts Treasured Swatch Dual Blue-TSD-CJ
05UD Artifact Treasure Swatch Dual Copper-TSD-CJ
05UD Artifact Treasure Swatch Dual Maroon-TSD-CJ
05UD Artifact Treasure Swatch Dual Pewter-TSD-CJ
05UD Artifact TreasuredSwatch Dual Silver-TSD-CJ
05UD Artifacts Treasured Swatches Maroon-TS-CJ
05UD Artifacts Treasured Swatches Pewter-TS-CJ
05UD Artifacts Treasured Swatches Silver-TS-CJ
05Ultimate Collection-69
Gold-69
Jerseys Dual-DJJL
Ultimate Patches Dual-DPJL
05Ultra-147
Gold-147
Ice-147
05Upper Deck-392
Big Playmakers-B-CJ
Jerseys-J-CJ
Patches-P-CJ
05Upper Deck Hockey Showcase-HS22
05Upper Deck Showcase Promos-HS22
05Upper Deck Ice-75
Rainbow-75
05Upper Deck MVP-294
Gold-294
Platinum-294
05Upper Deck Rookie Update-75
05Upper Deck Rookie Update-227
Inspirations Patch Rookies-227
05Upper Deck Trilogy-69
Honorary Patches-HP-CJ
Honorary Patch Scripts-HSP-CJ
Honorary Swatches-HS-CJ
Honorary Swatch Scripts-HSS-CJ
05Upper Deck Victory-75
05Upper Deck Victory-238
Black-75
Black-238
Gold-75
Gold-238
Silver-75
Silver-238
06Be A Player-4
Autographs-4
Signatures-CJ
06Be A Player Portraits-79
06Between The Pipes Complete Jersey-CJ18
06Between The Pipes Complete Jersey Gold-CJ18
06Between The Pipes Emblems-GUE62
06Between The Pipes Emblems Gold-GUE62
06Between The Pipes Gloves-GG12
06Between The Pipes Gloves Gold-GG12
06Between The Pipes Jerseys-GUJ62
06Between The Pipes Jerseys Gold-GUJ62
06Between The Pipes Numbers-GUN62
06Between The Pipes Numbers Gold-GUN62
06Between The Pipes Pads-GP09
06Between The Pipes Pads Gold-GP09
06Between The Pipes Playing For Your Country-PC25
06Between The Pipes Playing For Your Country Gold-PC25
06Between The Pipes The Mask-M26
06Between The Pipes The Mask Gold-M26
06Between The Pipes The Mask Silver-M26
06Black Diamond-63
Black-63
Gold-63
Ruby-63
Jerseys-JCJ
Jerseys Black-JCJ
Jerseys Gold-JCJ
Jerseys Ruby-JCJ
06Flair Showcase-79
06Flair Showcase-155
Parallel-79
Parallel-155
Hot Gloves-HG23
06Fleer-149
Tiffany-149
Netminders-N20
06Hot Prospects-76
Red Hot-76
White Hot-76
Hot Materials -HMCJ
Hot Materials Red Hot-HMCJ
Hot Materials White Hot-HMCJ
06NHL POG-2
06O-Pee-Chee-373
06O-Pee-Chee-664
Rainbow-373
Rainbow-664
06Panini Stickers-318
06SP Authentic-27
Limited-27
06SP Game Used-79
Gold-79
Rainbow-79
Authentic Fabrics-AFCJ
Authentic Fabrics Parallel-AFCJ
Authentic Fabrics Patches-AFCJ
Authentic Fabrics Triple-AF3PHX
Authentic Fabrics Triple Patches-AF3PHX
Authentic Fabrics Quads-AF4BJTW
Authentic Fabrics Quads Patches-AF4BJTW
Authentic Fabrics Sixes-AF6WIN
Authentic Fabrics Sixes Patches-AF6WIN
06SPx-79
Spectrum-79
Winning Materials-WMCJ
Winning Materials Spectrum-WMCJ
06The Cup Foundations-CQCJ
06The Cup Foundations Patches-CQCJ
06The Cup NHL Shields Duals-DSHDJ
06The Cup NHL Shields Duals-DSHEC
06The Cup NHL Shields Duals-DSHJJ
06The Cup NHL Shields Duals-DSHJN
06UD Artifacts-25
Blue-25
Gold-25
Platinum-25
Radiance-25
Red-25
Treasured Patches Black-TSCJ
Treasured Patches Blue-TSCJ
Treasured Patches Gold-TSCJ
Treasured Patches Platinum-TSCJ
Treasured Patches Red-TSCJ
Treasured Swatches-TSCJ
Treasured Swatches Black-TSCJ
Treasured Swatches Blue-TSCJ
Treasured Swatches Gold-TSCJ
Treasured Swatches Platinum-TSCJ
Treasured Swatches Red-TSCJ
Tundra Tandems-TTCE
Tundra Tandems Black-TTCE
Tundra Tandems Blue-TTCE
Tundra Tandems Gold-TTCE
Tundra Tandems Platinum-TTCE
Tundra Tandems Red-TTCE
Tundra Tandems Dual Patches Red-TTCE
06UD Mini Jersey Collection-79
06UD Powerplay-77
Impact Rainbow-77
06Ultimate Collection Premium Patches-PS-CJ
06Ultimate Collection Premium Swatches-PS-CJ
06Ultra-149
Gold Medallion-149
Ice Medallion-149
06Upper Deck Arena Giveaways-PHX6
06Upper Deck-397
Exclusives Parallel-397
High Gloss Parallel-397
Game Jerseys-JCJ
Game Patches-PCJ
Masterpieces-397
06Upper Deck MVP-225
Gold Script-225
Super Script-225
Jerseys-OJJC
Last Line of Defense-LL18
06Upper Deck Ovation-189
06Upper Deck Sweet Shot-81
06Upper Deck Trilogy-76
06Upper Deck Victory-152
06Upper Deck Victory Black-152
06Upper Deck Victory Gold-152
07Upper Deck Victory-195
Black-195
Gold-195

Joseph, Fabian
82Victoria Cougars-10
83Victoria Cougars-12
88ProCards AHL-92
89ProCards AHL-137
91Alberta International Team Canada-10
92Score Canadian Olympians-8
93Alberta International Team Canada-7
93OPC Premier Team Canada-7
93PowerPlay-484
93Ultra-464
94Score Team Canada-CT10
94Milwaukee Admirals-12
95Milwaukee Admirals-9
95Milwaukee Admirals Postcards-5
96Milwaukee Admirals-10
96Collector's Edge Ice-162
Prism-162
97Milwaukee Admirals-24

Joseph, Shane
03Minnesota State Mavericks-10
04Cleveland Barons-13
05Cleveland Barons-12

Joseph, Tony
89ProCards AHL-48
90ProCards AHL/IHL-243
91ProCards-155

Joseph, Yann
93Quebec Pee-Wee Tournament-411
01New Mexico Scorpions-8
02Trenton Titans-A-4

Josephson, Mike
91British Columbia JHL-75
91British Columbia JHL-166
93Kamloops Blazers-11
95Lethbridge Hurricanes-10
96Lethbridge Hurricanes-9
98Baton Rouge Kingfish-11

Joslin, Derek
04Ottawa 67's-18
05ITG Heroes/Prosp Toronto Expo Parallel -288
05OHL Bell All-Star Classic-8
05Ottawa 67's-18
05ITG Heroes and Prospects-288
Autographs Series II-DJ
06Ottawa 67s-15

Joss, Eddie
51Laval Dairy Subset-120

Joss, Terry
95Slapshot-407

Jossa, Greg
93Quebec Pee-Wee Tournament-1409

Jost, Mike
93Quebec Pee-Wee Tournament-899

Jostne, Tom
92Norwegian Elite Series-236

Jotkus, Pete
37V356 Worldwide Gum-104

Joubert, Jacques
95Peoria Rivermen-8
96Milwaukee Admirals-11
99Danish Hockey League-16

Joudrey, Andrew
03Wisconsin Badgers-15
04Wisconsin Badgers-23
05Wisconsin Badgers-15

Joudrey, Kirk
93Quebec Pee-Wee Tournament-1182

Jouhkimainen, Miika
05Finnish Cardset -194
06Finnish Cardset-201

Joutsenvuori, Timo
71Finnish Suomi Stickers-364

Jovanovski, Ed
92Sports Illustrated for Kids II-540
93Windsor Spitfires-1
94Finest-149
Super Team Winners-149
Refractors-149
94Leaf Limited World Juniors Canada-5
94Parkhurst SE-SE207
Gold-SE207
94Pinnacle-524
Artist's Proofs-524
Rink Collection-524
94SP-140
Die Cuts-140
94Topps Finest Bronze-21
94Upper Deck-496
Electric Ice-496
94Windsor Spitfires-14
94Classic-1
Gold-1
CHL All-Stars-C6
Draft Day-5
Draft Day-6
Draft Day-7
Picks-CP11
ROY Sweepstakes-R9
Tri-Cards-T25
94Classic Pro Prospects-203
94Assets *-8
94Assets *-33
Die Cuts-DC9
Phone Cards One Minute/$2-10
94Classic Four-Sport *-115A
94Classic Four-Sport *-115B
Gold-115A
Gold-115B
Autographs-115A
BCs-BC17
High Voltage-HV4
Phone Cards-4
Printers Proofs-115A
Printers Proofs-115B
95Be A Player-178
Signatures-S178
Signatures Die Cuts-S178
95Bowman-100
All-Foil-100
Bowman's Best-BB19
Bowman's Best Refractors-BB19
95Collector's Choice-399
95Donruss Canadian World Junior Team-6
95Donruss Elite-68
Die Cut Stars-68
Die Cut Uncut-68
Rookies-11
95Emotion generationNext-9
95Finest-176
Refractors-176
95Metal-178
95Parkhurst International-536
Emerald Ice-536
Parkie's Trophy Picks-PP42
95Select Certified-137
Mirror Gold-137
Future-10
95SkyBox Impact-201
95SP-58
95Stadium Club-196
Members Only Master Set-196
Generation TSC-GT9
Generation TSC Members Only Master Set-GT9
95Summit-171
Artist's Proofs-171
Ice-171
95Topps-354
OPC Inserts-354
Canadian World Juniors-22CJ
SuperSkills Super Rookies-SR1
95Ultra-342
Extra Attackers-10
95Upper Deck-501
Electric Ice-501
Electric Ice Gold-501
Predictor Hobby-H24
Predictor Hobby Exchange-H24
95Zenith-121
Rookie Roll Call-7
95Classic-98
Autographs-10
CHL All-Stars-AS9
Ice Breakers-BK19
Ice Breakers Die Cuts-BK19
95Images-15
Gold-15
Clear Excitement-CE17
95Images Four-Sport *-94
Classic Performances-CP19
95Assets Gold *-10
95Assets Gold Phone Cards $2 *-10
95Classic Five-Sport *-138
Autographs-138
Strive For Five-HK13
96Black Diamond-18
Gold-18
Run for the Cup-RC15
96Collector's Choice-105
96Collector's Choice-318
96Collector's Choice-340
MVP-UD34
MVP Gold-UD34
96Donruss Dominators-10
96Donruss Hit List-3
96Donruss Rated Rookies-7
96Donruss Canadian Ice-35
Gold Press Proofs-35
Red Press Proofs-35
96Donruss Elite-82
Die Cut Stars-82
Aspirations-6
96Flair-37
Blue Ice-37
Hot Numbers-5
96Fleer-39
Rookie Sensations-6
96Fleer Picks-98
Fabulous 50-21
Jagged Edge-13
96Kraft Upper Deck-55
96Leaf-208
Press Proofs-208
Fire On Ice-13
96Leaf Leather And Laces Promos-P19
96Leaf Leather And Laces-19
96Leaf Limited-14
Gold-14
96Leaf Limited Bash the Boards Promos-P7
96Leaf Limited Bash The Boards-7
96Leaf Limited Bash The Boards Ltd Ed-7
96Leaf Preferred-68
Press Proofs-68
Vanity Plates-8
Vanity Plates Gold-8
96Maggers-43
96McDonald's Pinnacle-6
96Metal Universe-59
Cool Steel-5
Cool Steel Super Power-5
96NHL Aces Playing Cards-24
96Pinnacle-204
Artist's Proofs-204
Foil-204
Premium Stock-204
Rink Collection-204
By The Numbers-4
By The Numbers Premium-4
Team Pinnacle-7
96Post Upper Deck-10
96Score-239
Artist's Proofs-239
Dealer's Choice Artist's Proofs-239
Special Artist's Proofs-239
Check It-12
Golden Blades-239
96Select Certified-30
Artist's Proofs-30
Blue-30
Mirror Blue-30
Mirror Gold-30
Mirror Red-30
Red-30
96SkyBox Impact-45
Countdown to Impact-5
NHL on Fox-11
96SP-60
Game Film-GF14
96Stadium Club Members Only-47
96Summit-163
Artist's Proofs-163
Ice-163
Metal-163
Premium Stock-163
96Team Out-85
96Topps Picks Fantasy Team-FT8
96Topps Picks Ice D-ID5
96Topps Picks Rookie Stars-RS11
96Topps Picks Rookie Stars OPC-RS11
96Ultra-65
Gold Medallion-65
Power-7
Power Blue Line-5
96Upper Deck-66
96Upper Deck-362
Generation Next-X11
Power Performers-P8
Superstar Showdown-SS3B
96Upper Deck Ice-88
Parallel-88
Stanley Cup Foundation-S3
Stanley Cup Foundation Dynasty-S3
96Zenith-45
Artist's Proofs-45
96All-Sport PPF *-71
96All Sport PPF Gold *-71
96Assets *-17
Hot Prints-17
96Classic Signings *-75
Blue-75
Die-Cuts-75
Red-75
96Clear Assets *-58
96Visions *-92
96Visions Signings *-75
Autographs-75A
Autographs Silver-75A
97Be A Player-21
Autographs-21
Autographs Die-Cuts-21
Autographs Prismatic Die-Cuts-21
97Black Diamond-141
Double Diamond-141
Triple Diamond-141
Quadruple Diamond-141
97Collector's Choice-101
97Crown Royale-57
Emerald Green-57
Ice Blue-57
Silver-57
97Donruss-144
Press Proofs Silver-144
Press Proofs Gold-144
97Donruss Canadian Ice-14
Dominion Series-14
Provincial Series-14
97Donruss Elite-33
Aspirations-33
Status-33
97Donruss Limited-5
97Donruss Limited-37
Exposure-5
Exposure-37
97Donruss Preferred-19
Cut to the Chase-19
97Donruss Priority-27
Stamp of Approval-27
97Katch-61
Gold-61
Silver-61
97Leaf-17
Fractal Matrix-17
Fractal Matrix Die Cuts-17
97Leaf International-17
Universal Ice-17
97Pacific Dynagon-53
Copper-53
Dark Grey-53
Emerald Green-53
Ice Blue-53
Red-53
Silver-53
Tandems-49
97Pacific Invincible-60
Copper-60
Emerald Green-60
Ice Blue-60
Red-60
Silver-60
NHL Regime-85
97Pacific Omega-99
Copper-99
Dark Gray-99
Emerald Green-99
Gold-99
Ice Blue-99
97Paramount-80
Copper-80
Dark Grey-80
Emerald Green-80
Ice Blue-80
Red-80
Silver-80
97Pinnacle-113
Press Plates Back Black-113
Press Plates Back Cyan-113
Press Plates Back Magenta-113
Press Plates Back Yellow-113
Press Plates Front Black-113
Press Plates Front Cyan-113
Press Plates Front Magenta-113
Press Plates Front Yellow-113
97Pinnacle Certified-48
Red-48
Mirror Blue-48
Mirror Gold-48
Mirror Red-48
97Pinnacle Inside-86
Coach's Collection-86
Executive Collection-86
97Pinnacle Tot Cert Platinum Blue-48
97Pinnacle Tot Certi Platinum Gold-48
97Pinnacle Totally Certified Platinum Red-48
97Pinnacle Tot Cert Mirror Platinum Gold-48
97Revolution-60
Copper-60
Emerald-60
Ice Blue-60
Silver-60
97Score-235
97SP Authentic-65
97SPx-21
Bronze-21
Gold-21
Silver-21
Steel-21
Grand Finale-21
97Studio-39
Press Proofs Silver-39
Press Proofs Gold-39
97Upper Deck-284
97Upper Deck-389
Smooth Grooves-SG15
97Upper Deck Ice-26
Parallel-26
Power Shift-26
98Aurora-80
98Black Diamond Double Diamond-37
98Black Diamond Triple Diamond-37
98Black Diamond Quadruple Diamond-37
98Crown Royale-58
Limited Series-58
98Katch-61
98OPC Chrome-177
Refractors-177
98Pacific-222
Ice Blue-222
Red-222
98Pacific Dynagon Ice-81
Blue-81
Red-81
98Panini Stickers-61
98Paramount-96
Copper-96
Emerald Green-96
Holo-Electric-96
Ice Blue-96
Silver-96
98SP Authentic-37
Power Shift-37
Sign of the Times-EJ
Sign of the Times Gold-EJ
98SPx Finite-39
Radiance-39
Spectrum-39
98Topps-177
O-Pee-Chee-177
98UD Choice-91
98UD Choice Preview-91
98UD Choice Prime Choice Reserve-91
98UD Choice Reserve-91
98Upper Deck-101
Exclusives-101
Exclusives 1 of 1-101
Gold Reserve-101
98Upper Deck MVP-206
Gold Script-206
Silver Script-206
Super Script-206
99BAP Memorabilia-93
Gold-93
Silver-93
99BAP Millennium-234
Emerald-234
Ruby-234
Sapphire-234
Signatures-234
Signatures Gold-234
99O-Pee-Chee-35
99O-Pee-Chee Chrome-35
99O-Pee-Chee Chrome Refractors-35
99Pacific-424
Copper-424
Emerald Green-424
Gold-424
Ice Blue-424
Premiere Date-424
Red-424
99Panini Stickers-315
99Paramount-234
Copper-234
Emerald-234
Gold-234
Holographic Emerald-234
Holographic Gold-234
Holographic Silver-234
Ice Blue-234
Premiere Date-234
Red-234
Silver-234
99SPx-153
Radiance-153
Spectrum-153
99Topps Arena Giveaways-VAN-EJ
99Topps/OPC-35
99Topps/OPC Chrome-35
Refractors-35
99Upper Deck MVP-209
Gold Script-209
Silver Script-209
Super Script-209
99Upper Deck Victory-298
00BAP Memorabilia-28
Emerald-28
Ruby-28
Sapphire-28
Promos-28
00BAP Mem Chicago Sportsfest Copper-28
00BAP Memorabilia Chicago Sportsfest Blue-28
00BAP Memorabilia Chicago Sportsfest Gold-28
00BAP Memorabilia Chicago Sportsfest Ruby-28
00BAP Memorabilia Chicago Sun-Times Ruby-28
00BAP Memorabilia Chicago Sun-Times Gold-28
00BAP Mem Chicago Sun-Times Sapphire-28
00BAP Mem Toronto Fall Expo Copper-28
00BAP Memorabilia Toronto Fall Expo Gold-28
00BAP Memorabilia Toronto Fall Expo Ruby-28
00BAP Parkhurst 2000-P141
00BAP Signature Series-122
Emerald-122
Ruby-122
Sapphire-122
00O-Pee-Chee-206
00O-Pee-Chee Parallel-206
00Pacific-408
Copper-408
Gold-408
Ice Blue-408
Premiere Date-408
00Paramount-238
Copper-238
Gold-238
Holo-Gold-238
Holo-Silver-238
Ice Blue-238
Premiere Date-238
00Stadium Club-14
00Topps/OPC-206
Parallel-206
00Upper Deck-171
Exclusives Tier 1-171
Exclusives Tier 2-171
00Upper Deck MVP-173
First Stars-173
Second Stars-173
Third Stars-173
00Upper Deck Victory-231
01BAP Memorabilia-31
Emerald-31
Ruby-31
Sapphire-31
Country of Origin-CO57
01BAP Signature Series-199
Autographs-199
Autographs Gold-199
01BAP Update Heritage-H17
01Canucks Postcards-6
01O-Pee-Chee-40
01O-Pee-Chee Heritage Parallel-40
01O-Pee-Chee Heritage Parallel Limited-40
01O-Pee-Chee Premier Parallel-40
01Pacific-382
Extreme LTD-382
Hobby LTD-382
Premiere Date-382
Retail LTD-382
01Pacific Arena Exclusives-382
01Parkhurst-94
Gold-94
Silver-94
01Topps-40
Heritage Parallel-40
Heritage Parallel Limited-40
OPC Parallel-40
01Topps Chrome-40
Refractors-40
Black Border Refractors-40
01UD Mask Collection-96
Gold-96
01Upper Deck-400
Exclusives-400
01Upper Deck MVP-183
01Upper Deck Victory-342
01Upper Deck Victory-428
Gold-342
Gold-428
02BAP All-Star Edition-38
Jerseys-38
Jerseys Gold-38
Jerseys Silver-38
02BAP First Edition-88
02BAP First Edition-411R
Jerseys-88
02BAP Memorabilia-95
02BAP Memorabilia-238
Emerald-95
Emerald-238
Ruby-95
Ruby-238
Sapphire-95
Sapphire-238
All-Star Jerseys-ASJ-24
NHL All-Star Game-95
NHL All-Star Game-238
NHL All-Star Game Blue-95
NHL All-Star Game Blue-238
NHL All-Star Game Green-95
NHL All-Star Game Green-238

NHL All-Star Game Red-95
NHL All-Star Game Red-238
Teammates-TM-19
02BAP Memorabilia Toronto Fall Expo-95
02BAP Memorabilia Toronto Fall Expo-238
02BAP Signature Series-29
Autographs-29
Autograph Buybacks 1999-234
Autograph Buybacks 2001-199
Autographs Gold-29
Defensive Wall-DW10
Golf-GS36
02BAP Ultimate Memorabilia First Overall-4
02Canucks Team Issue-6
02McDonald's Pacific Salt Lake Gold-3
02NHL Power Play Stickers-161
02O-Pee-Chee-111
02O-Pee-Chee Premier Blue Parallel-111
02O-Pee-Chee Premier Red Parallel-111
02O-Pee-Chee Factory Set-111
02O-Pee-Chee Factory Set Hometown Heroes-HHC2
02Pacific-378
Blue-378
Red-378
02Pacific Complete-216
Red-216
02Pacific Exclusive-167
02Parkhurst-46
Bronze-46
Gold-46
Silver-46
Hardware-N4
02Parkhurst Retro-128
Minis-128
Hopefuls-NH6
02SP Authentic-86
Beckett Promos-86
Super Premiums-SPEJ
02Topps-111
OPC Blue Parallel-111
OPC Red Parallel-111
Topps/OPC Hometown Heroes-HHC2
Factory Set-111
02Topps Chrome-71
Black Border Refractors-71
Refractors-71
02Topps Total-125
02Upper Deck-416
Exclusives-416
All-Star Jerseys-ASEJ
All-Star Performers-ASEJ
02Upper Deck Beckett UD Promos-416
02Upper Deck Number Crunchers-NC13
02Upper Deck Rookie Update-151B
02Upper Deck Rookie Update-161C
02Upper Deck Victory-210
Bronze-210
Gold-210
Silver-210
02Upper Deck Vintage-248
03BAP Memorabilia-25
Emerald-25
Gold-25
Ruby-25
Sapphire-25
Practice Jerseys-PMP3
Stanley Cup Playoffs-SCP-4
03BAP Ultimate Memorabilia Autographs-68
Gold-68
03BAP Ultimate Mem Auto Jerseys-68
03Beehive-192
Gold-192
Silver-192
Sticks Beige Border-BE18
03Black Diamond-35
Black-35
Green-35
Red-35
Threads-DT-EJ
Threads Green-DT-EJ
Threads Red-DT-EJ
Threads Black-DT-EJ
03Canucks Postcards-11
03Canucks Sav-on-Foods-16
03Canucks Sav-on-Foods-21
03eTopps-35
03ITG Action-598
Jerseys-M36
03ITG Used Signature Series-52
Gold-52
Autographs-EJ
Autographs Gold-EJ
International Experience-12
International Experience Autographs-12
International Experience Emblems Gold-12
International Experience Emblems-12
International Experience Gold-12
Oh Canada-3
Oh Canada Gold-3
Oh Canada Emblems-3
Oh Canada Emblems Gold-3
03McDonald's Pacific-52
03NHL Sticker Collection-298
03O-Pee-Chee-127
03OPC Blue-127
03OPC Gold-127
03OPC Red-127
03Pacific-330
Blue-330
Red-330
03Pacific Complete-298
Red-298
03Pacific Exhibit-141
Blue Backs-141
Yellow Backs-141
03Pacific Prism-95
Blue-95
Gold-95
Red-95
03Private Stock Reserve-97
Blue-97
Red-97
Retail-97
03SP Authentic-84
Limited-84
03SP Game Used Authentic Fabrics-DFBJ
03SP Game Used Authentic Fabrics-QNBJM
03SP Game Used Authentic Fabrics Gold-DFBJ
03SP Game Used Authentic Fabrics Gold-QNBJM
03SP Game Used Team Threads-TTNBJ
03SP Game Used Top Threads-NBJM
03SPx-97
Radiance-97
Spectrum-97
Fantasy Franchise-FF-SBJ
Fantasy Franchise Limited-FF-SBJ
Style-SPX-JB
Style Limited-SPX-JB
03Topps-127
Blue-127
Gold-127
Red-127
03Topps C55-55
Minis-55
Minis American Back-55
Minis American Back Red-55
Minis Bazooka Back-55
Minis Brooklyn Back-55
Minis Hat Trick Back-55
Minis O Canada Back-55
Minis O Canada Back Red-55
Minis Stanley Cup Back-55
03UD Honor Roll-84
03UD Premier Collection-55
03Upper Deck-187
Canadian Exclusives-187
HG-187
Jerseys-UD-EJ
03Upper Deck Classic Portraits-97
03Upper Deck Ice-85
Gold-85
03Upper Deck MVP-411
Gold Script-411
Silver Script-411
Canadian Exclusives-411
SportsNut-SN88
03Upper Deck Rookie Update-85
03Upper Deck Trilogy-97
Limited-97
03Upper Deck Victory-189
Bronze-189
Gold-189
Silver-189
03Czech Stadion-542
03Toronto Star-95
04Pacific-255
Blue-255
Red-255
04SP Authentic-87
Limited-87
Buybacks-50
Buybacks-51
Buybacks-52
Buybacks-53
Buybacks-54
Buybacks-55
Rookie Review-RR-EJ
Sign of the Times-ST-EJ
Sign of the Times-DS-NJ
Sign of the Times-TS-LPJ
Sign of the Times-QS-VANC
Sign of the Times-FS-VAN
Sign of the Times-SS-CNP
Sign of the Times-SS-DEE
04UD Toronto Fall Expo Pride of Canada-8
04Ultimate Collection Patch Autographs-UPA-EJ
04Ultimate Collection Signature-US-EJ
04Ultimate Collection Signature Logos-ULA-EJ
04Ultimate Collection Signature Patches-SP-EJ
04Upper Deck-171
Canadian Exclusives-171
HG Glossy Gold-171
HG Glossy Silver-171
School of Hard Knocks-SHK6
World Cup Tribute-SNEJ
World Cup Tribute-EBEJWR
05Be A Player-89
First Period-89
Second Period-89
Third Period-89
Overtime-89
Outtakes-OT49
05Black Diamond-80
Emerald-80
Gold-80
Onyx-80
Ruby-80
Jerseys-J-EJ
Jerseys Ruby-J-EJ
Jersey Duals-DJ-EJ
Jersey Triples-TJ-EJ
Jersey Quads-QJ-EJ
05McDonalds Upper Deck-21
05Panini Stickers-357
05Parkhurst-473
05Parkhurst-584
Facsimile Auto Parallel-473
Facsimile Auto Parallel-584
True Colors-TCVAN
True Colors-TCVAN
05SP Game Used Authentic Fabrics Quad-KBJL
05SP Game Used Authentic Patches Quad -KBJL
05SP Game Used By the Letter-LM-EJ
05SP Game Used SIGnificance-EJ
05SP Game Used SIGnificance Gold-S-EJ
05SP Game Used Significant Numbers-SN-EJ
05SPx-100
Spectrum-100
Winning Combos-WC-VA
Winning Combos Autographs-AWC-JM
Winning Combos Gold-WC-VA
Winning Combos Spectrum-WC-VA
Winning Materials-WM-EJ
Winning Materials Gold-WM-EJ
Winning Materials Spectrum-WM-EJ
Xcitement Superstars-XS-EJ
Xcitement Superstars Gold-XS-EJ
Xcitement Superstars Spectrum-XS-EJ
05The Cup-99
Gold-99
Black Rainbow-99
Masterpiece Pressplates-99
Masterpiece Pressplates (Rookie Update)-203
Noble Numbers-NNMJ
Noble Numbers Dual-DNNBJ
Patch Variation-P99
Patch Variation Autographs-AP99
05UD Artifacts-97
05UD Artifacts-199
Blue-97
Blue-199
Gold-97
Gold-199
Green-97
Green-199
Pewter-97
Pewter-199
Red-97
Red-199
Gold Autographed-97
Gold Autographed-199
Remarkable Artifacts-RA-EJ
Remarkable Artifacts Dual-RA-EJ
05UD Powerplay Power Marks-PMEJ
05UD Powerplay Specialists-TSEJ
05UD Powerplay Specialists Patches-SPEJ
05Ultimate Collection-89
Gold-89
05Ultra-192
Gold-192
Fresh Ink-FI-EJ
Fresh Ink Blue-FI-EJ
Ice-192
05Upper Deck-185
Big Playmakers-B-EJ
HG Glossy-185
Jerseys-J-EJ
Jerseys Series II-J2EJ
Majestic Materials-MMEJ
Notable Numbers-N-EJ
Patches-P-EJ
School of Hard Knocks-HK6
05Upper Deck Ice-98
Rainbow-98
05Upper Deck MVP-380
Gold-380
Platinum-380
Materials Duals-D-JF
Materials Triples-T-VAN
05Upper Deck Rookie Update-203
Inspirations Patch Rookies-203
05Upper Deck Trilogy-89
05Upper Deck Trilogy-170
Crystal-170
Honorary Patches-HP-EJ
Honorary Swatches-HS-EJ
05Upper Deck Toronto Fall Expo-185
05Upper Deck Victory-192
Black-192
Gold-192
Silver-192
Blow-Ups-BU42
Stars on Ice-SI45
06Be A Player Portraits Signature Portraits-SPEJ
06Beehive-24
Blue-24
Matte-24
Red Facsimile Signatures-24
Wood-24
06Black Diamond-65
Black-65
Gold-65
Ruby-65
06Flair Showcase-97
06Flair Showcase-168
Parallel-97
Parallel-168
06Fleer-153
Tiffany-153
06McDonald's Upper Deck-48
06O-Pee-Chee-379
Rainbow-379
06Panini Stickers-316
06SP Game Used Authentic Fabrics-AFEJ
06SP Game Used Authentic Fabrics Parallel-AFEJ
06SP Game Used Authentic Fabrics Patches-AFEJ
06SP Game Used Authentic Fabrics Quads-AF4BPJM
06SP Game Used Authentic Fabrics Quads Patches-AF4BPJM
06The Cup NHL Shields Duals-DSHJJ
06UD Artifacts Tundra Tandems-TTCE
06UD Artifacts Tundra Tandems Black-TTCE
06UD Artifacts Tundra Tandems Blue-TTCE
06UD Artifacts Tundra Tandems Gold-TTCE
06UD Artifacts Tundra Tandems Platinum-TTCE
06UD Artifacts Tundra Tandems Red-TTCE
06UD Artifacts Tundra Tandems Dual Patches Red-TTCE
06UD Powerplay Specialists-SEJ
06UD Powerplay Specialists Patches-PEJ
06Ultra-152
Gold Medallion-152
Ice Medallion-152
Uniformity-UEJ
Uniformity Patches-UPEJ
06Upper Deck Arena Giveaways-PHX3
06Upper Deck-398
Exclusives Parallel-398
High Gloss Parallel-398
Game Jerseys-JEJ
Game Patches-PEJ
Masterpieces-398
Signature Sensations-SSEJ
06Upper Deck MVP-223
Gold Script-223
Super Script-223
Jerseys-OJJL
Jerseys-OJNJ
06Upper Deck Ovation-49
06Upper Deck Victory-194
06Upper Deck Victory-266
06Upper Deck Victory Black-194
06Upper Deck Victory Gold-194
07Upper Deck Victory-198
Black-198
Gold-198

Joyal, Dan
00OCN Blizzard-22

Joyal, Eddie
63York White Backs-48
64Beehive Group III Photos-80A
64Beehive Group III Photos-80B
64Beehive Group III Photos-168
64Coca-Cola Caps-54
65Topps-85
68O-Pee-Chee-40
68Shirriff Coins-55
68Topps-40
69O-Pee-Chee-108
Four-in-One-5
Stamps-16
69Topps-108
70Esso Power Players-156
70O-Pee-Chee-39
Deckle-3
70Sargent Promotions Stamps-67
70Topps-39
Topps/OPC Sticker Stamps-16
71O-Pee-Chee-23
71Sargent Promotions Stamps-74
71Topps-23
71Toronto Sun-118
72Finnish Semic World Championship-205
72Swedish Semic World Championship-205
75O-Pee-Chee WHA-36

Joyal, Eric
907th Inn. Sketch QMJHL-192
917th Inn. Sketch QMJHL-64
01Sorel Royaux-9

Joyal, Maxime
04Quebec Remparts-9
06Saint Johns Sea Dogs-20

Joyce, Bob
88Bruins Sports Action-6
88Bruins Sports Action-23
88Bruins Postcards-7
88O-Pee-Chee-2
88Topps-2
89Bruins Sports Action-12
89Capitals Kodak-27
89O-Pee-Chee-73
89O-Pee-Chee Stickers-4
89O-Pee-Chee Stickers-31
89Panini Stickers-199
89Topps-73
90Score-291
Canadian-291
90ProCards AHL/IHL-206
91Moncton Hawks-12
91ProCards-172
92North Dakota Fighting Sioux-35
93Las Vegas Thunder-16
94Las Vegas Thunder-8
98German DEL-82
99German DEL-332

Joyce, Duane
89ProCards IHL-126
90ProCards AHL/IHL-105
91Kansas City Blades-3
91ProCards-523
92Kansas City Blades-3
93Kansas City Blades-1
94Kansas City Blades-1
95Cincinnati Cyclones-10
96Cincinnati Cyclones-3

Joyce, Graham
52Juniors Blue Tint-120

Joyce, Joe
94Arizona Icecats-18
95Arizona Icecats-19

Joyce, John
94Birmingham Bulls-12
95Birmingham Bulls-17

Jozsa, Jason
06Las Vegas Wranglers-8

Jubenville, Jeff
907th Inn. Sketch WHL-3
917th Inn. Sketch WHL-123
93Tacoma Rockets-14
97Bakersfield Fog-6

Jubinville, Lee
03Camrose Kodiaks-17
04Camrose Kodiaks-6

Juchem, Peter
94German First League-529

Juckes, Gordon W
44Beehive Group II Photos-329
74Team Canada L'Equipe WHA-13
83Hall of Fame Postcards-K9
85Hall of Fame-143

Jucknischke, Andre
94German First League-555

Judd, Jaye
03Salmon Arm Silverbacks-10

Judson, Rick
92Toledo Storm-20
92Toledo Storm Team Issue-10
93Toledo Storm-22
94Anaheim Bullfrogs RHI-9
94Toledo Storm-10
95Anaheim Bullfrogs RHI-10
95Toledo Storm-12
96Anaheim Bullfrogs RHI-10
96Toledo Storm-20
97Toledo Storm-16
00Fort Wayne Komets-8
00Fort Wayne Komets Shoe Carnival-4
03Toledo Storm-9
06Toledo Storm-24

Judy, Tim
98Sioux City Musketeers-8
99Sioux City Musketeers-11
00Sioux City Musketeers-13

Judza, Bill
45Quaker Oats Photos-24A
45Quaker Oats Photos-24B
45Quaker Oats Photos-60C

Juhlin, Karl-Gerhard
57Swedish Alfabilder-95

Juhlin, Patrik
89Swedish Semic Elitserien Stickers-250
90Swedish Semic Elitserien Stickers-171
91Swedish Semic Elitserien Stickers-266
92Swedish Semic Elitserien Stickers-286
93Swedish Semic Elitserien-252
93Swedish Semic World Champ Stickers-11
94Finest-6
Super Team Winners-6
Refractors-6
94Flair-128
94Fleer-155
94OPC Premier-378
Special Effects-378
94Parkhurst SE-SE133
Gold-SE133
94Topps/OPC Premier-378
Special Effects-378
94Ultra-344
94Upper Deck-246
94Upper Deck-553
Electric Ice-246
Electric Ice-553
SP Inserts-SP148
SP Inserts Die Cuts-SP148
94Finnish Jaa Kiekko-68
94Swedish Leaf-222
Gold Cards-18
Guest Special-8
94Classic-80
Gold-80
ROY Sweepstakes-R10
Tri-Cards-T49
94Signature Rookies Gold Standard *-86
95Be A Player-119
Signatures-S119
Signatures Die Cuts-S119
95Collector's Choice-236
Player's Club-236
Player's Club Platinum-236
95Donruss-60
95Leaf-44
95Parkhurst International-160
Emerald Ice-160
95Finnish Semic World Championships-76
95Swedish Upper Deck-244
95Swedish Globe World Championships-31
95Signature Rookies Future Flash-FF3
95Signature Rookies Future Flash Sigs-FF3
95Signature Rookies Tetrad Autobilia *-43
96Swedish Semic Wien-62
98Finnish Keräilysarja-117
99Finnish Cardset-66
Aces High-D-8
00Swiss Panini Stickers-43
00Swiss Slapshot Mini-Cards-SCB11
01Swiss HNL-89
02Swiss HNL-80
02Swiss HNL-498

Jukosky, Kyle
05Belleville Bulls-4

Julian, Jason
917th Inn. Sketch OHL-335
92Oshawa Generals Sheet-10

Julien, Bruno
93Quebec Pee-Wee Tournament-284

Julien, Claude
83Fredericton Express-16
84Fredericton Express-8
85Fredericton Express-15
88ProCards AHL-105
89Halifax Citadels-11
89ProCards AHL-165
90Kansas City Blades-12
90ProCards AHL/IHL-587
91Moncton Hawks-13
91ProCards-171
00Hamilton Bulldogs-25
00QMJHL All-Star Program Inserts-22
01Hamilton Bulldogs-23
03Canadiens Postcards-13
06Devils Team Set-29

Julien, Marc-Andre
06Chicoutimi Sagueneens-13

Julien, Mathieu
92Quebec Pee-Wee Tournament-255
93Quebec Pee-Wee Tournament-352

Julien, Pierre
93Quebec Pee-Wee Tournament-445

Julien, Stephane
907th Inn. Sketch QMJHL-93
917th Inn. Sketch QMJHL-112
93Sherbrooke Faucons-16
96Pensacola Ice Pilots-2
99German Bundesliga 2-189
01Swiss HNL-466
02Swiss HNL-440
03German DEL-203
03German Nuremberg Ice Tigers Postcards-13
04German Cologne Sharks Postcards-16
04German DEL-213
All-Stars-AS3
05German DEL-208
All-Star Jerseys-AS05
Defender-DF10
Defender Promos-DF10
06German DEL-124
All-Star Jerseys-AS9

Julka, Chris
03Wisconsin Badgers-16

Julkunen, Olli
05Finnish Cardset -298
06Finnish Cardset-126

Juneau, Joe
91Alberta International Team Canada-11
91Parkhurst-234
French-234
92Bowman-292
92Bruins Postcards-3
92O-Pee-Chee-189
92OPC Premier-101
92Panini Stickers-L
92Panini Stickers French-L
92Parkhurst-2
Emerald Ice-2
92Pinnacle-221
French-221
Team 2000-19
Team 2000 French-19
92Pro Set-219
92Score-453
Canadian-453
Canadian Olympians-2
Young Superstars-22
92Seasons Patches-18
92Stadium Club-297
92Topps-365
Gold-365G
92Ultra-4
92Ultra-448
92Upper Deck-354
92Upper Deck-399
92Upper Deck-455
Ameri/Can Holograms-1
Calder Candidates-CC9
Gordie Howe Selects-G11
93Donruss-26
93Donruss-394
93Donruss-504
93Durivage Score-27
93Kraft-14
93Leaf-218
Gold Rookies-2
93OPC Premier-125
93OPC Premier-299
Gold-125
Gold-299
93Panini Stickers-143
93Panini Stickers-A
93Parkhurst-241
93Parkhurst-280
Emerald Ice-241
Emerald Ice-280
93Pinnacle I Samples-3
93Pinnacle-5
Canadian-5
Team 2001-4
Team 2001 Canadian-4
93PowerPlay-19
Point Leaders-6
Second Year Stars-2
93Score-330
Canadian-330
93Seasons Patches-8
93Stadium Club-202
Members Only Master Set-202
OPC-202
First Day Issue-202
First Day Issue OPC-202
93Topps/OPC Premier-125
93Topps/OPC Premier-299
Gold-125
Gold-299
93Topps Premier Black Gold-12
93Ultra-49
93Upper Deck-282
93Upper Deck-343
Future Heroes-35
NHL's Best-HB10
SP-9
93Upper Deck Locker All-Stars-53
94Be A Player-R85
94Be A Player-R100
94Canada Games NHL POGS-245
94Donruss-258
94EA Sports-10
94Finest-93
Super Team Winners-93
Refractors-93
94Flair-200
94Fleer-236
Franchise Futures-5
94Kraft-19
94Leaf-62
Fire on Ice-7
Limited Inserts-25
94Leaf Limited-38
94OPC Premier-100
Special Effects-100
94Parkhurst Crash the Game Green-25
94Parkhurst Crash the Game Blue-25
94Parkhurst Crash the Game Gold-25
94Parkhurst Crash the Game Red-25
94Parkhurst SE-SE198
Gold-SE198
Vintage-17
94Pinnacle I Hobby Samples-7
94Pinnacle-7
Artist's Proofs-7
Rink Collection-7
94Score-124
Gold-124
Platinum-124
Franchise-TF25
94Select-86
Gold-86
94SP-126
Die Cuts-126
94Topps/OPC Premier-100
Special Effects-100
94Ultra-388
94Upper Deck-88
Electric Ice-88
Predictor Retail-R15
94Upper Deck Predictor Retail Exchange-R15
94Upper Deck SP Inserts-SP175
94Upper Deck SP Inserts Die Cuts-SP175
94Upper Deck NHLPA/Be A Player-27
94Classic Pro Prospects Autographs-AU4
94Classic Pro Prospects Jumbos-PP11
95Bashan Super Stickers-129
Die-Cut-8
95Be A Player-58
Signatures-S58
Signatures Die Cuts-S58
95Bowman-39
All-Foil-39
95Canada Games NHL POGS-283
95Capitals Team Issue-13
95Collector's Choice-118
Player's Club-118
Player's Club Platinum-118
95Donruss-136
95Donruss Elite-104
Die Cut Stars-104
Die Cut Uncut-104
95Emotion-190
95Finest-124
Refractors-124
95Hoyle Eastern Playing Cards-33
95Imperial Stickers-129
Die Cut Superstars-8
95Kraft-5
95Leaf-188
95Leaf Limited-98
95Metal-161
95Panini Stickers-138
95Parkhurst International-221
Emerald Ice-221
95Playoff One on One-105
95Post Upper Deck-7
95Pro Magnets-34
95Score-256
Black Ice Artist's Proofs-256
Black Ice-256
95Select Certified-80
Mirror Gold-80
95SkyBox Impact-179
95SP-158
95Stadium Club-187
Members Only Master Set-187
95Summit-139
Artist's Proofs-139
Ice-139
95Topps-216
OPC Inserts-216
Home Grown Canada-HGC25
95Topps SuperSkills-25
Platinum-25
95Ultra-323
95Upper Deck-25
Electric Ice-25
Electric Ice Gold-25
Predictor Retail-R17
Predictor Retail Exchange-R17
Special Edition-SE86
Special Edition Gold-SE86
95Zenith-96
96Black Diamond-90
Gold-90
96Collector's Choice-277
96Collector's Choice-334
96Donruss-151
Press Proofs-151
96Donruss Canadian Ice-38
Gold Press Proofs-38
Red Press Proofs-38
96Donruss Elite-90
Die Cut Stars-90
96Fleer-118
96Fleer Picks-108
96Leaf-21
Press Proofs-21
96Leaf Preferred-49
Press Proofs-49
96Maggers-44
96Metal Universe-166
96NHL Aces Playing Cards-25
96NHL Pro Stamps-34
96Pinnacle-160
Artist's Proofs-160
Foil-160
Premium Stock-160
Rink Collection-160
96Score-144
Artist's Proofs-144
Dealer's Choice Artist's Proofs-144
Special Artist's Proofs-144
Golden Blades-144
96SkyBox Impact-141
96SP-166
Holoview Collection-HC17
96Summit-7
Artist's Proofs-7
Ice-7
Metal-7
Premium Stock-7
96Team Out-44
96Ultra-177
Gold Medallion-177
96Upper Deck-176
Generation Next-X40
96Zenith-27
Artist's Proofs-27
96Swedish Semic Wien-92
97Be A Player-184
Autographs-184
Autographs Die-Cuts-184
Autographs Prismatic Die-Cuts-184
97Collector's Choice-268
97Crown Royale-140
Emerald Green-140
Ice Blue-140
Silver-140
97Donruss-95
Press Proofs Silver-95
Press Proofs Gold-95
97Donruss Elite-41
Aspirations-41
Status-41
97Donruss Limited-61
Exposure-61
97Donruss Preferred-13
Cut to the Chase-13
97Donruss Priority-137
Stamp of Approval-137
97Katch-152
Gold-152
Silver-152
97Leaf-53
Fractal Matrix-53
Fractal Matrix Die Cuts-53
97Leaf International-53
Universal Ice-53
97Pacific-155
Copper-155
Emerald Green-155
Ice Blue-155
Red-155
Silver-155
Slap Shots Die-Cuts-12A
97Pacific Dynagon-131
Copper-131
Dark Grey-131
Emerald Green-131
Ice Blue-131
Red-131
Silver-131
Tandems-57
97Pacific Invincible-147
Copper-147
Emerald Green-147
Ice Blue-147
Red-147
Silver-147
97Pacific Omega-241
Copper-241
Dark Gray-241
Emerald Green-241
Gold-241
Ice Blue-241
97Paramount-195
Copper-195
Dark Grey-195
Emerald Green-195
Ice Blue-195
Red-195
Silver-195
97Pinnacle-107
Press Plates Back Black-107
Press Plates Back Cyan-107
Press Plates Back Magenta-107
Press Plates Back Yellow-107
Press Plates Front Black-107
Press Plates Front Cyan-107
Press Plates Front Magenta-107
Press Plates Front Yellow-107
97Pinnacle Certified-63
Red-63
Mirror Blue-63
Mirror Gold-63
Mirror Red-63
97Pinnacle Inside-151
97Pinnacle Tot Cert Platinum Blue-63
97Pinnacle Tot Certi Platinum Gold-63
97Pinnacle Totally Certified Platinum Red-63
97Pinnacle Tot Cert Mirror Platinum Gold-63
97Revolution-148
Copper-148
Emerald-148
Ice Blue-148
Silver-148
97Score-140
Artist's Proofs-140
Golden Blades-140
97SP Authentic-163
97SPx-49
Bronze-49
Gold-49
Silver-49
Steel-49
Grand Finale-49
97Studio-68
Press Proofs Silver-68
Press Proofs Gold-68
97Upper Deck-176
Three Star Selects-18C
98Aurora-197
98Be A Player-147
Press Release-147
98BAP Gold-147
98BAP Autographs-147
98BAP Autographs Gold-147
98BAP Tampa Bay All Star Game-147
98Bowman's Best-93
Refractors-93
Atomic Refractors-93
98Crown Royale-142
Limited Series-142
98Finest-78
No Protectors-78
No Protectors Refractors-78
Refractors-78
98Katch-152
98OPC Chrome-151
Refractors-151
98Pacific-90
Ice Blue-90
Red-90
98Pacific Dynagon Ice-196
Blue-196
Red-196
98Pacific Omega-247
Red-247
Opening Day Issue-247
98Panini Photocards-38
98Paramount-246
Copper-246
Emerald Green-246
Holo-Electric-246
Ice Blue-246
Silver-246
98Revolution-147
Ice Shadow-147
Red-147
98SP Authentic-89
Power Shift-89
Sign of the Times-JJ
Sign of the Times Gold-JJ
98Topps-151
O-Pee-Chee-151
98Topps Gold Label Class 1-40
Black-40
Black One of One-40
One of One-40
Red-40
Red One of One-40
98Topps Gold Label Class 2-40
98Topps Gold Label Class 2 Black-40
98Topps Gold Label Class 2 Black 1 of 1-40
98Topps Gold Label Class 2 One of One-40
98Topps Gold Label Class 2 Red-40
98Topps Gold Label Class 2 Red One of One-40
98Topps Gold Label Class 3-40
98Topps Gold Label Class 3 Black-40
98Topps Gold Label Class 3 Black 1 of 1-40
98Topps Gold Label Class 3 One of One-40
98Topps Gold Label Class 3 Red-40
98Topps Gold Label Class 3 Red One of One-40
98UD Choice-214
Prime Choice Reserve-214
Reserve-214
98Upper Deck-203
Exclusives-203
Exclusives 1 of 1-203
Gold Reserve-203
98Upper Deck MVP-216
Gold Script-216
Silver Script-216
Super Script-216
99Aurora-17
Premiere Date-17
99Crown Royale-98
Limited Series-98
Premiere Date-98
99Pacific-39
Copper-39
Emerald Green-39
Gold-39
Ice Blue-39
Premiere Date-39
Red-39
99Senators Team Issue-9
99Upper Deck MVP-22
Gold Script-22
Silver Script-22
Super Script-22
Draw Your Own Trading Card-W21
99Upper Deck Victory-38
99Wayne Gretzky Hockey-118
99Quebec PeeWee Tournament Coll Souv-5
00Aurora-111
Premiere Date-111
00O-Pee-Chee-33
00O-Pee-Chee Parallel-33
00Pacific-280
Copper-280
Gold-280
Ice Blue-280
Premiere Date-280
00Stadium Club-217
00Topps/OPC-33
Parallel-33
00Upper Deck-361
Exclusives Tier 1-361
Exclusives Tier 2-361
00Upper Deck Vintage-280
01Canadiens Postcards-11
01Pacific-305
Extreme LTD-305
Hobby LTD-305
Premiere Date-305
Retail LTD-305
01Pacific Adrenaline-96
Blue-96
Premiere Date-96
Red-96
Retail-96
01Pacific Arena Exclusives-305
01Parkhurst-207
01Private Stock PS-2002-41
02BAP Sig Series Auto Buybacks 1998-147
02Canadiens Postcards-24
02NHL Power Play Stickers-53
02Pacific-197
Blue-197
Red-197
02Pacific Complete-164
Red-164
02Parkhurst Retro-176
Minis-176
02Upper Deck Victory-114
Bronze-114
Gold-114
Silver-114
03Canadiens Postcards-14
03ITG Action-311
03Pacific Complete-78
Red-78
03Parkhurst Original Six Montreal-16
03Upper Deck MVP-227
Gold Script-227
Silver Script-227
Canadian Exclusives-227

Jung, Alexander
00German Berlin Polar Bears Postcards-12
00German DEL-60
02German DEL City Press-50
03German Deg Metro Stars-6
03German DEL-34
04German DEL-48
04German Dusseldorf Metro Stars Postcards-8
05German DEL-61
05German DEL-282
Goalies-G07
06German DEL-2

Jung, Florian
03German Deg Metro Stars-7
04German DEL-60
04German Dusseldorf Metro Stars Postcards-9
05German DEL-60

Jung, Kenny
02Barrie Colts-15

Jungwirth, Andrew
00Lethbridge Hurricanes-11

Jungwirth, Thomas
94German DEL-130
95German DEL-128

Junker, Steve
89Spokane Chiefs-13
907th Inn. Sketch WHL-193
91Upper Deck Czech World Juniors-57
917th Inn. Sketch WHL-9
917th Inn. Sketch Memorial Cup-80
93Donruss-202
93Leaf-402
93Parkhurst-394
Emerald Ice-394
93Ultra-367
93Upper Deck-241
94Classic Pro Prospects-193
98German DEL-75
99German Adler Mannheim Eagles Postcards-8
99German DEL-9
00German DEL-4
01German Upper Deck-179
02German Adler Mannheim Eagles Postcards-16
02German DEL City Press-244
03German Mannheim Eagles Postcards-19

Junkin, Dale
907th Inn. Sketch OHL-62
917th Inn. Sketch OHL-199
93Detroit Jr. Red Wings-9
93Niagara Falls Thunder-12
99UK Sheffield Steelers-7
01Fresno Falcons-7
03Rockford Ice Hogs-8

Junkin, Joe
75Roanoke Valley Rebels-6
Junkins, Matt
99Kingston Frontenacs-9
00London Knights-26
01London Knights-16
Junkka, Jonas
01Finnish Cardset-198
Junnila, Jyri
06Finnish Cardset-101
Junno, Juha
92Finnish Jyvas-Hyva Stickers-86
Juntunen, Eero
71Finnish Suomi Stickers-226
72Finnish Jaakiekko-209
73Finnish Jaakiekko-281
Juntunen, Henrik
05Finnish Cardset -224
06Finnish Cardset-290
Juojarvi, Tero
71Finnish Suomi Stickers-344
72Finnish Jaakiekko-328
Juppo, Janne
01Finnish Cardset-216
Jurak, Milan
96Czech APS Extraliga-284
Juran, Paul
96Arizona Icecats-8
Jurcina, Milan
00Halifax Mooseheads-7
01Halifax Mooseheads-3
02Halifax Mooseheads-4
03Providence Bruins-9
04SP Authentic Rookie Redemptions-RR36
04Providence Bruins-12
05Beehive-176
Matte-176
Signature Scrapbook-SSMJ
05Black Diamond-216
05Bruins Boston Globe-6
05Hot Prospects-222
En Fuego-222
Hot Materials-HMMJ
Red Hot-222
White Hot-222
05Parkhurst-607
Facsimile Auto Parallel-607
Signatures-MJ
True Colors-TCBOS
True Colors-TCBOS
05SP Authentic-137
Limited-137
Rarefied Rookies-RRMJ
05SP Game Used-156
Autographs-156
Gold-156
Auto Draft-AD-MJ
Rookie Exclusives-MJ
Rookie Exclusives Silver-RE-MJ
Significant Numbers-SN-MJ
05SPx-186
Spectrum-186
Xcitement Rookies-XR-MJ
Xcitement Rookies Gold-XR-MJ
Xcitement Rookies Spectrum-XR-MJ
05The Cup-141
Autographed Rookie Patches Gold Rainbow-141
Black Rainbow Rookies-141
Masterpiece Pressplates (Artifacts)-248
Masterpiece Pressplates (Bee Hive)-176
Masterpiece Pressplates (Black Diamond)-216
Masterpiece Pressplates (Ice)-146
Masterpiece Pressplates (MVP)-436
Masterpiece Pressplates (Rookie Update)-198
Masterpiece Pressplates SPA Autos-137
Masterpiece Pressplates (SP Game Used)-156
Masterpiece Pressplates SPx Autos-186
Masterpiece Pressplates (Trilogy)-176
Masterpiece Pressplates Ult Coll Autos-103
Masterpiece Pressplates Autographs-141
Noble Numbers-NNJJ
Platinum Rookies-141
05UD Artifacts-248
05Ultimate Collection-103
Autographed Patches-103
Autographed Shields-103
Ultimate Debut Threads Jerseys-DTJMJ
Ultimate Debut Threads Jerseys Autos-DAJMJ
Ultimate Debut Threads Patches-DTPMJ
Ultimate Debut Threads Patches Autos-DAPMJ
05Ultra-206
Gold-206
Ice-206
Rookie Uniformity Jerseys-RU-MJ
Rookie Uniformity Jersey Autographs-ARU-MJ
Rookie Uniformity Patches-RUP-MJ
Rookie Uniformity Patch Autographs-ARP-MJ
05Upper Deck-464
Rookie Ink-RIMJ
Rookie Threads-RTMJ
Rookie Threads Autographs-ARTMJ
05Upper Deck Ice-146
Fresh Ice-FIMJ
Fresh Ice Glass-FIMJ
Fresh Ice Glass Patches-FIPMJ
Premieres Auto Patches-AIPMJ
05Upper Deck MVP-436
Gold-436
Platinum-436
05Upper Deck Rookie Update-198
Inspirations Patch Rookies-198
05Upper Deck Trilogy-176
06Be A Player Portraits Dual Signature Portraits-DSCJ
06Be A Player Portraits First Exposures-FEMJ
06Be A Player Portraits Signature Portraits-SPMJ
06Black Diamond Jerseys-JMJ
06Black Diamond Jerseys Black-JMJ
06Black Diamond Jerseys Gold-JMJ
06Black Diamond Jerseys Ruby-JMJ
06Fleer Signing Day-SDMJ
06O-Pee-Chee-49
Rainbow-49
06UD Artifacts Tundra Tandems-TTZM
06UD Artifacts Tundra Tandems Black-TTZM
06UD Artifacts Tundra Tandems Blue-TTZM
06UD Artifacts Tundra Tandems Gold-TTZM
06UD Artifacts Tundra Tandems Platinum-TTZM
06UD Artifacts Tundra Tandems Red-TTZM
06UD Artifacts Tundra Tandems Dual Patches Red-TTZM
06Upper Deck Game Jerseys-J2MJ
06Upper Deck Game Patches-P2MJ
06Upper Deck MVP Jerseys-OJMJ
Jurco, Tomas
04Slovakian Poprad Team Set-11
Jurdic, Tomas
05Czech HC Trinec-5
Jurecka, Martin
03Czech OFS Plus-347
Jurecka, Petr
97Czech APS Extraliga-130
98Czech DS Stickers-254
98Czech OFS-352
99Czech DS-174
99Czech OFS-226
00Czech OFS-245
01Czech OFS-38
01Czech OFS-282
02Czech OFS Plus-53
03Czech OFS Plus-348
05Czech HC Vitkovice-7
06Czech OFS-53
Juri, Pietro
01Swiss HNL-434
Jurik, Juraj
94Czech APS Extraliga-197
95Czech APS Extraliga-121
96Czech APS Extraliga-107
97Czech APS Extraliga-115
97Czech DS Extraliga-26
97Czech DS Stickers-280
98Czech DS Stickers-57
06Czech OFS Coaches-5
Jurik, Milan
06Prince Albert Raiders-13
Jurinyi, Ludovit
04Slovakian Poprad Team Set-23
Jursinov, Vladimir
69Russian National Team Postcards-18
69Swedish Hockey-5
73Finnish Jaakiekko-217
79Russian National Team-3
84Russian National Team-22
87Russian National Team-24
90O-Pee-Chee-494
92Finnish Jyvas-Hyva Stickers-171
93Finnish Jyvas-Hyva Stickers-313
93Finnish SISU-28
93Finnish SISU-373
94Finnish SISU-398
95Finnish SISU-385
95Finnish SISU-396
99Swiss Panini Stickers-103
00Swiss Panini Stickers-149
01Swiss HNL-50
02Swiss HNL-33
Jurtaj, Lubomir
03Czech OFS Plus-381
Juselius, Heikki
65Finnish Hellas-92
66Finnish Jaakiekkosarja-102
72Finnish Jaakiekko-174
Jussila, Timo
65Finnish Hellas-48
65Finnish Hellas-156
Just, Peter
94German First League-659
Just, Sandro
93Swiss HNL-468
Justra, Jan
98Danish Hockey League-158
Jutila, Timo
80Finnish Mallasjuoma-160
89Swedish Semic Elitserien Stickers-152
90Swedish Semic Elitserien Stickers-226
91Finnish Semic World Champ Stickers-5
91Swedish Semic Elitserien Stickers-154
91Swedish Semic World Champ Stickers-5
92Finnish Jyvas-Hyva Stickers-161
93Finnish Jyvas-Hyva Stickers-285
93Finnish SISU-63
93Finnish SISU-368
93Finnish SISU Promos-NNO
93Swedish Semic World Champ Stickers-53
94Finnish SISU-59
94Finnish SISU-162
94Finnish SISU Fire On Ice-6
94Finnish Jaa Kiekko-5
95Finnish Jaa Kiekko Lehti Ad Cards-8
95Finnish SISU-180
95Finnish SISU-312
Double Trouble-8
Gold Cards-6
95Finnish SISU Limited-73
95Finnish Karjala World Champ Labels-3
95Finnish Semic World Championships-5
95Finnish Semic World Championships-202
95Swedish Globe World Championships-130
95Swedish World Championships Stickers-166
96Finnish SISU Redline-177
96Swedish Semic Wien-5
All-Stars-AS2
96Swiss HNL-31
98Finnish Kerailysarja-210
90's Top 12-10
Leijonat-6
99Finnish Cardset Aces High-H-4
02Finnish Cardset-184
05Finnish Tappara Legendat-15
Jutras, Claude
907th Inn. Sketch QMJHL-11
917th Inn. Sketch QMJHL-213
917th Inn. Sketch Memorial Cup-65
94Cape Breton Oilers-11
98Long Beach Ice Dogs-8
00UK Sekonda Superleague-78
Juutilainen, Mikko
99Finnish Cardset-298
00Finnish Cardset-75
Juzda, Bill
34Beehive Group I Photos-280
44Beehive Group II Photos-412
48Exhibits Canadian-31
51Parkhurst-77
Jylha, Juhani
65Finnish Hellas-26
69Swedish Hockey-369
70Finnish Jaakiekko-106
70Swedish Masterserien-84
71Finnish Suomi Stickers-114
73Finnish Jaakiekko-310
74Finnish Typotor-21
Jylhasaari, Tapio
70Finnish Jaakiekko-330
Jyrkkio, Juha
78Finnish SM-Liiga-75
80Finnish Mallasjuoma-206
Kaarela, Jari
72Finnish Jaakiekko-307
Kaario, Matti
78Finnish SM-Liiga-112
80Finnish Mallasjuoma-69
Kaarna, Ilkka
80Finnish Mallasjuoma-137
Kaartinen, Sami
98Finnish Kerailysarja-196
99Finnish Cardset-312
00Finnish Cardset-84
03Finnish Cardset-132
05Finnish Cardset -85
06Finnish Cardset-91
Kabanov, Gyori
00Russian Hockey League-80
Kabanov, Vitali
99Russian Hockey League-217
Kabat, Kurt
92Hampton Roads Admirals-8
Kabayama, Matt
82Medicine Hat Tigers-7
83Medicine Hat Tigers-17
Kaberg, Emil
05Swedish SHL Elitset-190
06Swedish SHL Elitset-188
Kaberle Sr., Frantisek
79Panini Stickers-80
81Swedish Semic Hockey VM Stickers-58
98Czech OFS-420
02Czech DS-63
Kaberle, Frantisek
93Upper Deck-261
94Czech APS Extraliga-51
95Czech APS Extraliga-361
95Swedish Leaf-272
95Swedish Upper Deck-155
Ticket to North America-NA18
95Swedish World Championships Stickers-190
96Swedish Semic Wien-106
97Czech APS Extraliga-345
97Swedish Collector's Choice-152
98Swedish UD Choice-172
99BAP Millennium Calder Candidates Ruby-C33
99BAP Millennium Calder Candidate Emerald-C33
99BAP Millennium Calder Cand Sapphire-C33
99Pacific Omega-115
Copper-115
Gold-115
Ice Blue-115
Premiere Date-115
99Pacific Prism-67
Holographic Blue-67
Holographic Gold-67
Holographic Mirror-67
Holographic Purple-67
Premiere Date-67
99Panini Stickers-254
99Panini Stickers-357
99Paramount-259
99Topps Arena Giveaways-LA-FK
99Upper Deck Arena Giveaways-LK1
99Czech DS National Stars-NS10
99Czech OFS-24
99Czech OFS Jagr Team Embossed-24
00BAP Memorabilia-35
Emerald-35
Ruby-35
Sapphire-35
Promos-35
00BAP Mem Chicago Sportsfest Copper-35
00BAP Memorabilia Chicago Sportsfest Blue-35
00BAP Memorabilia Chicago Sportsfest Gold-35
00BAP Memorabilia Chicago Sportsfest Ruby-35
00BAP Memorabilia Chicago Sun-Times Ruby-35
00BAP Memorabilia Chicago Sun-Times Gold-35
00BAP Mem Chicago Sun-Times Sapphire-35
00BAP Mem Toronto Fall Expo Copper-35
00BAP Memorabilia Toronto Fall Expo Gold-35
00BAP Memorabilia Toronto Fall Expo Ruby-35
00BAP Signature Series-107
Emerald-107
Ruby-107
Sapphire-107
Autographs-69
Autographs Gold-69
00Upper Deck-240
Exclusives Tier 1-240
Exclusives Tier 2-240
00Czech OFS-381
01Upper Deck Victory-22
Gold-22
01Czech Stadion-250
02BAP Memorabilia-59
Emerald-59
Ruby-59
Sapphire-59
NHL All-Star Game-59
NHL All-Star Game Blue-59
NHL All-Star Game Green-59
NHL All-Star Game Red-59
02BAP Memorabilia Toronto Fall Expo-59
02BAP Sig Series Auto Buybacks 2000-69
02Pacific-16
Blue-16
Red-16
02Pacific Complete-344
Red-344
02Thrashers Postcards-7
02Topps Total-50
02Upper Deck-254
Exclusives-254
02Upper Deck Beckett UD Promos-254
02Upper Deck MVP-7
Gold-7
Classics-7
Golden Classics-7
02Upper Deck Vintage-14
02Czech DS-14
02Czech DS-49
02Czech DS-92
02Czech IQ Sports Blue-13
03ITG Action-24
03NHL Sticker Collection-6
03O-Pee-Chee-44
03OPC Blue-44
03OPC Gold-44
03OPC Red-44
03Pacific Complete-131
Red-131
03Thrashers Postcards-6
03Titanium-4
Hobby Jersey Number Parallels-4
Retail-4
Retail Jersey Number Parallels-4
03Topps-44
Blue-44
Gold-44
Red-44
03Upper Deck-256
Canadian Exclusives-256
HG-256
UD Exclusives-256
03Upper Deck MVP-22
Gold Script-22
Silver Script-22
Canadian Exclusives-22
03Czech National Team Postcards-7
04Czech OFS-331
04Czech OFS-NNO
Stars II-1
04Czech Zuma-20
04Czech World Championship Postcards-11
04Swedish MoDo Postcards-12
05Parkhurst-93
Facsimile Auto Parallel-93
05Czech World Champions Postcards-1
06Hurricanes Postcards-14
06Panini Stickers-47
06Upper Deck MVP-60
Gold Script-60
Super Script-60
Kaberle, Tomas
95Czech APS Extraliga-80
96Czech APS Extraliga-81
97Czech APS Extraliga-199
97Czech DS Stickers-136
98Be A Player-287
Press Release-287
98BAP Gold-287
98BAP Autographs-287
98BAP Autographs Gold-287
98Black Diamond-82
Double Diamond-82
Triple Diamond-82
Quadruple Diamond-82
98Crown Royale Rookie Class-9
98Pacific Dynagon Ice-181
Blue-181
Red-181
Rookies-9
98Pacific Omega-233
Red-233
Opening Day Issue-233
98Revolution-139
Ice Shadow-139
Red-139
98SP Authentic-110
Power Shift-110
98SPx Top Prospects-56
Radiance-56
Spectrum-56
98Upper Deck-375
Exclusives-375
Exclusives 1 of 1-375
Gold Reserve-375
98Upper Deck MVP-197
Gold Script-197
Silver Script-197
Super Script-197
98Czech DS Stickers-231
99BAP Millennium-230
Emerald-230
Ruby-230
Sapphire-230
Signatures-230
Signatures Gold-230
99Kraft Whiz Kid-4
99Maple Leafs Pizza Pizza-3
99O-Pee-Chee-209
99O-Pee-Chee Chrome-209
99O-Pee-Chee Chrome Refractors-209
99Pacific-408
Copper-408
Emerald Green-408
Gold-408
Ice Blue-408
Premiere Date-408
Red-408
99Pacific Omega-226
Copper-226
Gold-226
Ice Blue-226
Premiere Date-226
99SPx-147
Radiance-147
Spectrum-147
99Topps Arena Giveaways-TOR-TK
99Topps/OPC-209
99Topps/OPC Chrome-209
Refractors-209
99Upper Deck-125
Exclusives-125
Exclusives 1 of 1-125
99Upper Deck Gold Reserve-125
99Upper Deck MVP-203
Gold Script-203
Silver Script-203
Super Script-203
ProSign-TK
99Upper Deck Victory-285
99Czech OFS-25
99Czech OFS Jagr Team Embossed-25
00BAP Memorabilia-254
Emerald-254
Ruby-254
Sapphire-254
Promos-254
00BAP Mem Chicago Sportsfest Copper-254
00BAP Memorabilia Chicago Sportsfest Blue-254
00BAP Memorabilia Chicago Sportsfest Gold-254
00BAP Memorabilia Chicago Sportsfest Ruby-254
00BAP Memorabilia Chicago Sun-Times Ruby-254
00BAP Memorabilia Chicago Sun-Times Gold-254
00BAP Mem Chicago Sun-Times Sapphire-254
00BAP Mem Toronto Fall Expo Copper-254
00BAP Memorabilia Toronto Fall Expo Gold-254
00BAP Memorabilia Toronto Fall Expo Ruby-254
00O-Pee-Chee-179
00O-Pee-Chee Parallel-179
00Pacific-393
Copper-393
Gold-393
Ice Blue-393
Premiere Date-393
00Paramount-231
Copper-231
Gold-231
Holo-Gold-231
Holo-Silver-231
Ice Blue-231
Premiere Date-231
00Topps/OPC-179
Parallel-179
00Upper Deck-395
Exclusives Tier 1-395
Exclusives Tier 2-395
00Czech OFS-380
01BAP Memorabilia-105
Emerald-105
Ruby-105
Sapphire-105
Country of Origin-CO43
01BAP Signature Series-50
Autographs-50
Autographs Gold-50
Department of Defense-DD-9
01O-Pee-Chee-119
01O-Pee-Chee Premier Parallel-119
01Pacific Adrenaline-182
Blue-182
Premiere Date-182
Red-182
Retail-182
01Parkhurst-88
Gold-88
Silver-88
Teammates-T7
Teammates-T27
01Topps-119
OPC Parallel-119
01Upper Deck-393
Exclusives-393
01Upper Deck Victory-330
Gold-330
01Czech DS-5
Best of the Best-BB2
01Czech OFS-167
01Czech OFS Red Inserts-RE4D
01Czech Stadion-221
02BAP All-Star Edition-39
Jerseys-39
Jerseys Gold-39
Jerseys Silver-39
02BAP First Edition-19
Jerseys-19
02BAP Sig Series Auto Buybacks 1998-287
02BAP Sig Series Auto Buybacks 1999-230
02BAP Sig Series Auto Buybacks 2001-50
02BAP Signature Series Defensive Wall-DW2
02Maple Leafs Platinum Collection-9
02Maple Leafs Team Issue-6
02NHL Power Play Stickers-139
02Pacific-362
Blue-362
Red-362
02Pacific Complete-208
Red-208
02Parkhurst Retro-134
Minis-134
Hopefuls-NH7
02Topps Total-140
02Upper Deck-411
Exclusives-411
02Upper Deck Beckett UD Promos-411
02Upper Deck Victory-199
Bronze-199
Gold-199
Silver-199
02Upper Deck Vintage-234
02Czech DS-50
02Czech DS-64
02Czech DS-96
02Czech Stadion Olympics-336
03ITG Action-580
Jerseys-M37
03NHL Sticker Collection-138
03O-Pee-Chee-224
03OPC Blue-224
03OPC Gold-224
03OPC Red-224
03Pacific-318
Blue-318
Red-318
03Pacific Complete-51
Red-51
03Parkhurst Original Six Toronto-14
Memorabilia-TM6
Memorabilia-TM18
03Topps-224
Blue-224
Gold-224
Red-224
03Topps C55-65
Minis-65
Minis American Back-65
Minis American Back Red-65
Minis Bazooka Back-65
Minis Brooklyn Back-65
Minis Hat Trick Back-65
Minis O Canada Back-65
Minis O Canada Back Red-65
Minis Stanley Cup Back-65
03Upper Deck-426
Canadian Exclusives-426
HG-426
UD Exclusives-426
03Upper Deck MVP-393
Gold Script-393
Silver Script-393
Canadian Exclusives-393
03Toronto Star-94
04Upper Deck World's Best-WB10
04Czech OFS-58
Stars-1
04Czech Zuma-19
05Panini Stickers-173
05Parkhurst-451
Facsimile Auto Parallel-451
05Upper Deck-181
HG Glossy-181
05Upper Deck MVP-358
Gold-358
Platinum-358
05Upper Deck Toronto Fall Expo-181
05Czech World Champions Postcards-19
05Czech Kvarteto Bonaparte-3a
05Czech Pexeso Mini Blue Set-5
05Czech Pexeso Mini Red Set-27
06Fleer-186
Tiffany-186
06Gatorade-67
06O-Pee-Chee-458
Rainbow-458
06Panini Stickers-165
06Ultra-186
Gold Medallion-186
Ice Medallion-186
06Upper Deck-185
Exclusives Parallel-185
High Gloss Parallel-185
Masterpieces-185
06Upper Deck MVP-272
Gold Script-272
Super Script-272
06Czech IIHF World Championship Postcards-11
06Czech OFS Jagr Team-17
06Russian Sport Collection Olympic Stars-29
07Upper Deck Victory-56
Black-56
Gold-56
Stars on Ice-SI49
Kabotoff, Scott
03ECHL Update RBI Sports-285
Kabrt, Pavel
96Czech APS Extraliga-161
97Czech APS Extraliga-259
98Czech DS Stickers-142
98Czech OFS-157
99Czech OFS-361
00Czech OFS-51
02Czech OFS Plus-153
Kachowski, Mark
84Kamloops Blazers-12
85Kamloops Blazers-9
87Penguins Kodak-14
89ProCards IHL-159
90ProCards AHL/IHL-378
Kachur, Eddie
71Johnstown Jets Acme-8
94Parkhurst Missing Link-37
Kachur, John
97Red Deer Rebels-7
98Wichita Thunder-10
99Wichita Thunder-9
Kachur, Trent
86Regina Pats-12
87Regina Pats-10
Kacik, Tadeusz
73Finnish Jaakiekko-93
74Finnish Jenkki-98
74Finnish Typotor-88
Kacir, Marian
93Owen Sound Platers-6
93Owen Sound Platers-12
97Czech APS Extraliga-335
98Czech DS-72
98Czech OFS-254
98Czech OFS-268
98Czech OFS-433
99German DEL-350
03Czech OFS Plus-94
Kaczowka, David
01Greenville Grrrowl-18
02Greenville Grrrowl-8
04Peoria Rivermen-18
Kadatskiy, Evgeny
02Peterborough Petes-11
Kadeikin, Airat
98Russian Hockey League-79
99Russian Hockey League-101
99Russian Stars Postcards-9
Kadera, Roman
93Upper Deck-267
94Czech APS Extraliga-135
95Czech APS Extraliga-234
95Czech APS Extraliga-377
96Czech APS Extraliga-16
97Czech APS Extraliga-334
97Czech DS Extraliga-117
97Czech DS Stickers-120
98Czech DS-120
98Czech DS Stickers-277
98Czech OFS-189
98Czech OFS-436
99Czech OFS-196
99Czech OFS-421
00Czech DS Extraliga-163
00Czech OFS-254
01Czech OFS-37
02Czech OFS Plus-54
Trios-T19
Duos-D7
03Czech OFS Plus-9
03Czech OFS Plus-333
03Czech OFS Plus Insert C-C11
03Czech OFS Plus Insert G-G6
03Czech OFS Plus Insert H-H3
03Czech OFS Plus Insert S-S10
Kadeykin, Anton
03Sarnia Sting-11
Kadlec, Arnold
81Swedish Semic Hockey VM Stickers-59
82Swedish Semic VM Stickers-82
83Swedish Semic VM Stickers-82
Kadlec, Drahomir
89Swedish Semic World Champ Stickers-187
92Finnish Jyvas-Hyva Stickers-9
93Swedish Semic World Champ Stickers-92
94Finnish Jaa Kiekko-170
94German DEL-176
95Finnish Semic World Championships-144
95German DEL-172
95Swedish World Championships Stickers-189
96Czech APS Extraliga-344
96German DEL-115
97Czech APS Extraliga-80
98Czech DS-68
98Czech OFS-315
Kadlec, Petr
95Czech APS Extraliga-349
96Czech APS Extraliga-6
97Czech APS Extraliga-155
97Czech DS Stickers-117
98Czech DS-69
98Czech DS Stickers-193
98Czech OFS-214
99Czech OFS-45
99Czech OFS-378
00Czech DS Extraliga-111
00Czech OFS-85
00Czech OFS-403
01Czech DS-6
01Czech OFS-3
All Stars-34
02Czech DS-6
02Czech OFS Plus-240
02Czech OFS Plus All-Star Game-H29
02Czech OFS Plus Trios-T13
03Czech OFS Plus-192
03Czech OFS Plus All-Star Game-H27
03Czech OFS Plus MS Praha-SE25
04Czech HC Slavia Praha Postcards-4
04Czech OFS-164
Defence Points-10
05Czech HC Slavia Praha-9
06Czech OFS-299
Defenders-11
Kadow, Harald
72Finnish Hellas-48
Kadri, Nazem
06Kitchener Rangers-10
Kaebel, Butch
90Knoxville Cherokees-110
92Birmingham Bulls-5
93Birmingham Bulls-5
93Peoria Rivermen-14
96Peoria Rivermen-10
96Peoria Rivermen Photo Album-10
97Peoria Rivermen-10
98Huntington Blizzard-19
99Huntington Blizzard-16
00Trenton Titans-17
03Tulsa Oilers-20
04Tulsa Oilers-13
Kaebel, Karson
92Northern Michigan Wildcats-14
93Northern Michigan Wildcats-16
94Dayton Bombers-7
96Peoria Rivermen-11
96Peoria Rivermen Photo Album-11
98Huntington Blizzard-7
99Odessa Jackalopes-9
Kaebel, Klage
93Omaha Lancers-11
04Tulsa Oilers-14
Kaese, Trent
87Flint Spirits-9
Kagaikin, Sergei
99Russian Hockey League-182
Kahelin, Timo
92Finnish Jyvas-Hyva Stickers-139
93Finnish Jyvas-Hyva Stickers-255
93Finnish SISU-284
Kahiluoto, Tommi
96Finnish SISU Redline-31
Kahkonen, Toni
06Finnish Cardset-194
Kahnberg, Magnus
00Swedish Upper Deck-66
02Swedish SHL-115
Parallel-115
03Swedish Elite-28
Silver-28
04Swedish Alfabilder Alfa Stars-9
04Swedish Alfabilder Proof Parallels-9
04Swedish Elitset-27
Dominators-1
Gold-27
05Swedish SHL Elitset-27
Gold-27
Series Two Signatures-6
06Swedish SHL Elitset-32
Kahonen, Jyrki
70Finnish Jaakiekko-314
Kaigorodov, Alexei
02Russian Hockey League-200
02Russian Young Lions-8
03Russian World Championship Team 2003-24
05Russian Hockey League RHL-3
06Black Diamond-194
Black-194
Gold-194
Ruby-194
06O-Pee-Chee-562
06O-Pee-Chee-616
Rainbow-562
Rainbow-616
06SP Game Used-137
Gold-137
Rainbow-137
06SPx-187
Spectrum-187
06The Cup Masterpiece Pressplates (Marquee Rookies)-562
06The Cup Masterpiece Pressplates (MVP)-305
06The Cup Masterpiece Pressplates (SP Game Used)-137
06The Cup Masterpiece Pressplates (Trilogy)-139
06The Cup Masterpiece Pressplates (Victory)-306
06UD Artifacts-251
06Ultra-244
06Ultra-246
Gold Medallion-244
Ice Medallion-244
06Upper Deck-478
Exclusives Parallel-478
High Gloss Parallel-478
Masterpieces-478
Rookie Game Dated Moments-RGD18
06Upper Deck MVP-305
Gold Script-305
Super Script-305
06Upper Deck Trilogy-139
06Upper Deck Victory-306
07Upper Deck Rookie Class -23
Kaijomaa, Kalle
04Finnish Cardset-288
05Finnish Cardset -129
06Finnish Cardset-308
Kaikkonen, Ari
70Finnish Jaakiekko-368
71Finnish Suomi Stickers-304
Kaiman, Tom
93Quebec Pee-Wee Tournament-892
01Michigan Tech Huskies-13
Kaip, Rylan
04North Dakota Fighting Sioux-12
Kaipainen, Matti
93Finnish SISU-124
94Finnish SISU-69
95Finnish SISU-236
96Finnish SISU Redline-34
98Finnish Kerailysarja-89
99Finnish Cardset-291
00Finnish Cardset-65
01Finnish Cardset-95
02Finnish Cardset-187
05Finnish Cardset -352
Kaiponen, Lasse
71Finnish Suomi Stickers-323
Kaiser, Vern
44Beehive Group II Photos-253
45Quaker Oats Photos-85
51Buffalo Bison-11
Kaistakari, Jarmo
80Finnish Mallasjuoma-132
Kaitala, Risto
65Finnish Hellas-17
66Finnish Jaakiekkosarja-8
Kaiton, Chuck
93Quebec Pee-Wee Tournament-819
Kaivola, Antti
72Finnish Jaakiekko-285
Kajer, Milos
94Czech APS Extraliga-69
95Czech APS Extraliga-90
Kajki, Milan
79Panini Stickers-77
Kajula, Timo
70Finnish Jaakiekko-369
Kajzer, Tomasz
93Quebec Pee-Wee Tournament-1508
Kajzerek, Marian
70Swedish Masterserien-196
Kakko, Erik
91Finnish Jyvas-Hyva Stickers-54
92Finnish Jyvas-Hyva Stickers-144
93Finnish Jyvas-Hyva Stickers-316
93Finnish SISU-33
94Finnish SISU-269
95Finnish SISU-21
96Finnish SISU Redline-16
98Finnish Kerailysarja-54
99Swiss Panini Stickers-135
00Swiss Panini Stickers-179
00Swiss Slapshot Mini-Cards-LT6
02Finnish Cardset-32
02Swedish SHL-276
Parallel-276
03Swedish Elite-26
Silver-26
04Finnish Cardset-127
04Finnish Cardset Signatures-25
05Finnish Cardset -295
06Finnish Cardset-124
Kakoske, Bryce
06Westside Warriors-20
Kalata, Andre
93Quebec Pee-Wee Tournament-1180
Kalawsky, Craig
86Regina Pats-13
87Regina Pats-11
Kaleniecki, Brandon
02Michigan Wolverines-29
03Michigan Wolverines-17
04Michigan Wolverines-3
Kales, Craig
82North Bay Centennials-11
83Kingston Canadians-20
Kaleta, Alex
34Beehive Group I Photos-59
44Beehive Group II Photos-330
Kaleta, Patrick
02Peterborough Petes-17
04Peterborough Petes Postcards-6
04Peterborough Petes Postcards-14
06Rochester Americans-9
07Upper Deck Victory-219
Black-219
Gold-219
Kalin, Rainer
01Swiss HNL-363
02Swiss HNL-176
Kalinin, Dimitri
99BAP Memorabilia-321
Gold-321
Silver-321
99Pacific Omega-29
Copper-29
Gold-29
Ice Blue-29
Premiere Date-29
00BAP Memorabilia-323
Emerald-323
Ruby-323
Sapphire-323
Promos-323
00BAP Mem Chicago Sportsfest Copper-323
00BAP Memorabilia Chicago Sportsfest Blue-323
00BAP Memorabilia Chicago Sportsfest Gold-323
00BAP Memorabilia Chicago Sportsfest Ruby-323
00BAP Memorabilia Chicago Sun-Times Ruby-323
00BAP Memorabilia Chicago Sun-Times Gold-323
00BAP Mem Chicago Sun-Times Sapphire-323
00BAP Mem Toronto Fall Expo Copper-323
00BAP Memorabilia Toronto Fall Expo Gold-323
00BAP Memorabilia Toronto Fall Expo Ruby-323
00BAP Signature Series-259
Emerald-259
Ruby-259
Sapphire-259
Autographs-7
Autographs Gold-7
00Crown Royale-113
00O-Pee-Chee-318
00O-Pee-Chee Parallel-318
00Private Stock-105
Gold-105
Premiere Date-105
Retail-105
Silver-105
PS-2001 Rookies-3
00Stadium Club-240
00Topps/OPC-318
Parallel-318
00Topps Chrome-213
OPC Refractors-213
Refractors-213
00Topps Premier Plus-89
Blue Ice-89
00Upper Deck-24
Exclusives Tier 1-24
Exclusives Tier 2-24
00Upper Deck MVP-188
First Stars-188
Second Stars-188
Third Stars-188
00Vanguard-105
Pacific Proofs-105
01BAP Memorabilia-111
Emerald-111
Ruby-111
Sapphire-111
01Parkhurst-230
01Upper Deck Victory-45
Gold-45
02BAP First Edition-203
02BAP Sig Series Auto Buybacks 2000-7
02Pacific Complete-387
Red-387
02Sabres Team Issue-7
02Topps Total-81
02Russian World Championships-14
03ITG Action-27
03O-Pee-Chee-166
03OPC Blue-166
03OPC Gold-166
03OPC Red-166
03Pacific Complete-356
Red-356
03Topps-166
Blue-166
Gold-166
Red-166
03Russian World Championship Team 2003-9
04Russian Back to Russia-22
04Russian World Championship Team-23
Kall, Per-Erik
69Swedish Hockey-209
Kalla, Jaroslav
98Czech OFS-370
99Czech OFS-135
00Czech OFS-179
03Czech OFS Plus-223
04Czech OFS-59
05Czech HC Kladno-7
06Czech HC Kladno Postcards-3
06Czech OFS-258
Kallarsson, Kaj
03Lincoln Stars-3
Kallarsson, Tom
98Finnish Kerailysarja-57
99Finnish Cardset-33
06Finnish Cardset-183
Kallay, Ian
90Fort Saskatchewan Traders-8
Kallio, Jorma
66Finnish Jaakiekkosarja-194
70Finnish Jaakiekko-126
71Finnish Suomi Stickers-176
72Finnish Jaakiekko-124
72Finnish Panda Toronto-24
73Finnish Jaakiekko-180
74Finnish Typotor-8
78Finnish SM-Liiga-177
Kallio, Markku
94Finnish SISU-311
Kallio, Tapio
72Finnish Jaakiekko-263
78Finnish SM-Liiga-195
Kallio, Tomi
95Collector's Choice-334
Player's Club-334
Player's Club Platinum-334
95Finnish SISU-335
Drafted Dozen-5
96Finnish SISU Redline-146
98Finnish Kerailysarja-242
99Finnish Cardset-139
99Finnish Cardset-192
00BAP Memorabilia-457
Emerald-457

Ruby-457
Sapphire-457
00BAP Parkhurst 2000-P242
00BAP Signature Series-291
Emerald-291
Ruby-291
Sapphire-291
Autographs-221
Autographs Gold-221
00Crown Royale-110
21st Century Rookies-1
00Titanium-103
Retail-103
00Titanium Draft Day Edition-103
00Titanium Draft Day Promos-103
00Topps Heritage-148
00Vanguard Pacific Proofs-103
00Finnish Cardset-236
00Finnish Cardset Master Blasters-8
01BAP Memorabilia-107
Emerald-107
Ruby-107
Sapphire-107
01BAP Signature Series-65
Autographs-65
Autographs Gold-65
01Pacific-19
Extreme LTD-19
Hobby LTD-19
Premiere Date-19
Retail LTD-19
01Pacific Adrenaline-9
Blue-9
Premiere Date-9
Red-9
Retail-9
01Pacific Arena Exclusives-19
01Parkhurst-220
01Titanium Draft Day Edition-6
01Topps Heritage-81
Refractors-81
01Upper Deck Victory-17
Gold-17
01Upper Deck Vintage-11
01Upper Deck Vintage-17
01Finnish Cardset-170
01Finnish Cardset Salt Lake City-10
02BAP Sig Series Auto Buybacks 2001-65
02O-Pee-Chee-181
02O-Pee-Chee Premier Blue Parallel-181
02O-Pee-Chee Premier Red Parallel-181
02O-Pee-Chee Factory Set-181
02Pacific-17
Blue-17
Red-17
02Pacific Complete-33
Red-33
02Pacific Exclusive-7
Jerseys-1
Jerseys Gold-1
02Pacific Heads-Up Quad Jerseys-2
02Pacific Heads-Up Quad Jerseys-33
02Pacific Heads-Up Quad Jerseys Gold-2
02Pacific Heads-Up Quad Jerseys Gold-33
02Titanium Jerseys-51
02Titanium Jerseys Retail-51
02Topps-181
OPC Blue Parallel-181
OPC Red Parallel-181
Factory Set-181
02Topps Total-298
02Upper Deck-8
Exclusives-8
02Vanguard Jerseys-34
02Vanguard Jerseys Gold-34
02Finnish Cardset-33
02Finnish Cardset Dynamic Duos-7
03Swedish Elite-178
Global Impact-GI3
Silver-178
04Swedish Elitset-144
04Swedish Elitset-179
Dominators-7
Gold-144
Gold-179
Signatures Series A-15
04Swedish Pure Skills-24
Parallel-24
05Swedish SHL Elitset-36
Gold-36
Series Two Signatures-7
Teammates-4
06Swedish SHL Elitset-39
Performers-4

Kalliomaki, Tuomas
93Finnish Jyvas-Hyva Stickers-172
93Finnish SISU-171
95Finnish SISU-350

Kallioniemi, Riku
95Finnish SISU-303
96Finnish SISU Redline-97
98Finnish Kerailysarja-188
99Finnish Cardset-108
00Finnish Cardset-202
01Finnish Cardset-109

Kallionpaa, Martti
65Finnish Hellas-64

Kallur, Anders
79Islanders Transparencies-6
80O-Pee-Chee-156
80Topps-156
81O-Pee-Chee-204
81O-Pee-Chee Stickers-162
81Topps-E90
82O-Pee-Chee-203
82O-Pee-Chee Stickers-57
82Post Cereal-12
82Topps Stickers-57
84Islanders News-9
85Islanders News-8
97Swedish Alfabilder Autographs-11
00Upper Deck Vintage Dynasty: A Piece of History-BK
00Upper Deck Vintage Dynasty: A Piece of History Gold-BK
01Swedish Alfabilder-11
04Swedish Alfabilder Alfa Stars-50
04Swedish Alfabilder Proof Parallels-50

Kalmikov, Konstantin
92Quebec Pee-Wee Tournament-1463
96Sudbury Wolves-11
96Sudbury Wolves Police-13
97Sudbury Wolves Police-5
99St. John's Maple Leafs-11
00St. John's Maple Leafs-10
01Louisiana Ice Gators-10
03Louisiana Ice Gators-10
04UK Nottingham Panthers-9

Kalmokoski, Ari
71Finnish Suomi Stickers-305

Kalous, Jiri
99Czech OFS-380

Kalser, Claudio
93Swiss HNL-304

Kalt, Dieter
93Swedish Semic World Champ Stickers-279
94Finnish Jaa Kiekko-241
95Austrian National Team-10
95Finnish Semic World Championships-186
95Swedish World Championships Stickers-267
96German DEL-178
96Swedish Semic Wien-217
00German DEL-141
02Swedish SHL-177
Parallel-177
Sharpshooters-SS3
Signatures Series II-25
03Swedish Elite-44
Silver-44
04Swedish Elitset-46
04Swedish Elitset-143
Gold-46
Gold-143

Kalteva, Mikko
04Finnish Cardset-239
05Finnish Cardset -228
06Finnish Cardset-54

Kalteva, Petri
93Finnish Jyvas-Hyva Stickers-295
93Finnish SISU-61
94Finnish SISU-296
95Finnish SISU-316

Kaltiainen, Matti
05Finnish Cardset -176
06Finnish Cardset-344
Between the Pipes-23
06Finnish Porin Assat Pelaajakortit-1

Kalto, Kari
98Finnish Kerailysarja-38
99Finnish Cardset-25
00Finnish Cardset-249
01Finnish Cardset-12
05Finnish Cardset -187
06Finnish Cardset-12

Kaltygen, Sergei
00Victoriaville Tigres-14
Signed-14

Kalus, Petr
05Regina Pats-8
06Providence Bruins-7
06ITG Heroes and Prospects-171
Autographs-APKA
Jerseys-GUJ62
Emblems-GUE62
Numbers-GUN62
Update Autographs-APKA
07Upper Deck Ovation-47
07Upper Deck Victory-207
Black-207
Gold-207

Kaluza, Peter
94German First League-402

Kaluzny, Mike
02OCN Blizzard-16

Kalwinski, Nick
93Quebec Pee-Wee Tournament-1321

Kalyuzhni, Alexei
98Russian Hockey League-152
99Russian Dynamo Moscow-22
00Russian Hockey League-106
02Russian Hockey League-179

Kamaev, Igor
02Russian Hockey League-83

Kamaletdinov, Rustem
99Russian Hockey League-154
00Russian Hockey League-279
02Russian Hockey League-226

Kamarainen, Jouko
78Finnish SM-Liiga-147
80Finnish Mallasjuoma-104

Kambeitz, Jim
83Medicine Hat Tigers-20

Kamber, Michel
95Swiss HNL-139
98Swiss Power Play Stickers-231
01Swiss HNL-262
02Swiss HNL-310
04Swiss Lausanne HC Postcards-20

Kamber, Oliver
99Swiss Panini Stickers-322
01Swiss HNL-274
02Swiss EV Zug Postcards-23
02Swiss HNL-232

Kamel, Noel
92Saskatchewan JHL-73

Kamenev, Vasili
95Signature Rookies Future Flash-FF5
95Signature Rook Future Flash Sigs-FF5

Kamensky, Valeri
87Russian National Team-7
89Russian National Team-9
89Swedish Semic World Champ Stickers-91
90O-Pee-Chee Red Army-4R
91Gillette-30
91Nordiques Petro-Canada-12
91O-Pee-Chee-513
91Parkhurst-362
French-362
91Pinnacle-340
French-340
91Score Rookie/Traded-76T
91Topps-513
91Upper Deck-273
91Upper Deck-SP1
French-273
91Finnish Semic World Champ Stickers-88
91Russian Stars Red Ace-6
91Russian Tri-Globe Kamensky-1
91Russian Tri-Globe Kamensky-2
91Russian Tri-Globe Kamensky-3
91Russian Tri-Globe Kamensky-4
91Russian Tri-Globe Kamensky-5
91Swedish Semic World Champ Stickers-88
92Bowman-432
92Humpty Dumpty I-12
92Nordiques Petro-Canada-15
92O-Pee-Chee-266
92Panini Stickers-295
92Panini Stickers-R
92Panini Stickers French-295
92Panini Stickers French-R
92Parkhurst-230
92Parkhurst-377
Emerald Ice-230
Emerald Ice-377
92Pinnacle-64
French-64
92Pro Set-148
92Score-360
Canadian-360
Young Superstars-24
92Stadium Club-344
92Topps-53
Gold-53G
92Upper Deck-27
Euro-Stars-E20
92Finnish Semic-112
92Russian Tri-Globe From Russia With Puck-11
92Russian Tri-Globe From Russia With Puck-12
93Donruss-277
93Leaf-207
93OPC Premier-85
Gold-85
93Panini Stickers-72
93Parkhurst-438
Emerald Ice-438
93Pinnacle-244
Canadian-244
93PowerPlay-199
93Score-326
Canadian-326
93Stadium Club-237
Members Only Master Set-237
OPC-237
First Day Issue-237
First Day Issue OPC-237
93Topps/OPC Premier-85
Gold-85
93Ultra-84
93Upper Deck-118
94Be A Player Signature Cards-158
94Canada Games NHL POGS-195
94Donruss-116
94Flair-147
94Fleer-177
94Leaf-117
94Nordiques Burger King-10
94OPC Premier-32
Special Effects-32
94Parkhurst-190
Gold-190
94Pinnacle-343
Artist's Proofs-343
Rink Collection-343
94Select-144
Gold-144
94Topps/OPC Premier-32
Special Effects-32
94Ultra-357
94Upper Deck-355
Electric Ice-355
94Finnish Jaa Kiekko-157
95Bashan Super Stickers-31
95Canada Games NHL POGS-74
95Collector's Choice-221
Player's Club-221
Player's Club Platinum-221
95Donruss-236
95Donruss Elite-22
Die Cut Stars-22
Die Cut Uncut-22
95Emotion-37
95Finest-164
Refractors-164
95Imperial Stickers-31
95Metal-33
95Panini Stickers-248
95Parkhurst International-48
Emerald Ice-48
95Playoff One on One-243
95Score-268
Black Ice Artist's Proofs-268
Black Ice-268
95Select Certified-105
Mirror Gold-105
95SkyBox Impact-36
95Stadium Club-161
Members Only Master Set-161
95Summit-6
Artist's Proofs-6
Ice-6
95Ultra-221
95Upper Deck-489
Electric Ice-489
Electric Ice Gold-489
95Finnish Semic World Championships-131
95Swedish Globe World Championships-179
95Swedish World Championships Stickers-36
95Swiss HNL-542
96Avalanche Photo Pucks-4
96Be A Player-33
Autographs-33
Autographs Silver-33
96Collector's Choice-62
96Collector's Choice Blow-Ups-62
96Donruss-14
Press Proofs-14
96Donruss Canadian Ice-32
Gold Press Proofs-32
Red Press Proofs-32
96Donruss Elite-118
Die Cut Stars-118
96Fleer-21
Art Ross-9
Picks Dream Lines-9
Picks Fabulous 50-22
96Leaf-170
Press Proofs-170
96Leaf Limited-81
Gold-81
96Leaf Preferred-53
Press Proofs-53
Steel-59
Steel Gold-59
96Maggers-45
96Metal Universe-33
96Pinnacle-47
Artist's Proofs-47
Foil-47
Premium Stock-47
Rink Collection-47
96Playoff One on One-420
96Score-157
Artist's Proofs-157
Dealer's Choice Artist's Proofs-157
Special Artist's Proofs-157
Golden Blades-157
96Select Certified-67
Artist's Proofs-67
Blue-67
Mirror Blue-67
Mirror Gold-67
Mirror Red-67
Red-67
96SkyBox Impact-23
BladeRunners-9
96Summit-59
Artist's Proofs-59
Ice-59
Metal-59
Premium Stock-59
96Topps Picks-39
OPC Inserts-39
96Ultra-36
Gold Medallion-36
96Upper Deck-241
Generation Next-X20
96Zenith-8
Artist's Proofs-8
96Swedish Semic Wien-149
97Collector's Choice-58
97Crown Royale-34
Emerald Green-34
Ice Blue-34
Silver-34
97Donruss-132
Press Proofs Silver-132
Press Proofs Gold-132
97Donruss Canadian Ice-82
Dominion Series-82
Provincial Series-82
97Donruss Elite-44
Aspirations-44
Status-44
97Donruss Limited-47
97Donruss Limited-111
Exposure-47
Exposure-111
97Donruss Priority-87
Stamp of Approval-87
97Pacific-213
Copper-213
Emerald Green-213
Ice Blue-213
Red-213
Silver-213
97Pacific Dynagon-30
Copper-30
Dark Grey-30
Emerald Green-30
Ice Blue-30
Red-30
Silver-30
Tandems-42
97Pacific Invincible-35
Copper-35
Emerald Green-35
Ice Blue-35
Red-35
Silver-35
97Pacific Omega-57
Copper-57
Dark Gray-57
Emerald Green-57
Gold-57
Ice Blue-57
97Panini Stickers-203
97Paramount-50
Copper-50
Dark Grey-50
Emerald Green-50
Ice Blue-50
Red-50
Silver-50
97Pinnacle-186
Press Plates Back Black-186
Press Plates Back Cyan-186
Press Plates Back Magenta-186
Press Plates Back Yellow-186
Press Plates Front Black-186
Press Plates Front Cyan-186
Press Plates Front Magenta-186
Press Plates Front Yellow-186
97Pinnacle Certified-67
Red-67
Mirror Blue-67
Mirror Gold-67
Mirror Red-67
97Pinnacle Inside-114
97Pinnacle Tot Cert Platinum Blue-67
97Pinnacle Tot Certi Platinum Gold-67
97Pinnacle Totally Certified Platinum Red-67
97Pinnacle Tot Cert Mirror Platinum Gold-67
97Revolution-33
Copper-33
Emerald-33
Ice Blue-33
Silver-33
97Score-186
97Score Avalanche-7
Platinum-7
Premier-7
97SP Authentic-39
97Upper Deck-254
98Aurora-47
98Be A Player-186
Press Release-186
98BAP Gold-186
98BAP Autographs-186
98BAP Autographs Gold-186
98Bowman's Best-89
Refractors-89
Atomic Refractors-89
98Finest-43
No Protectors-43
No Protectors Refractors-43
Refractors-43
98Katch-42
98OPC Chrome-39
Refractors-39
98Pacific-160
Ice Blue-160
Red-160
98Pacific Dynagon Ice-49
Blue-49
Red-49
98Panini Stickers-188
98Paramount-56
Copper-56
Emerald Green-56
Holo-Electric-56
Ice Blue-56
Silver-56
98SPx Finite-23
Radiance-23
Spectrum-23
98Topps-39
O-Pee-Chee-39
98UD Choice-58
Prime Choice Reserve-58
Reserve-58
98Upper Deck-249
Exclusives-249
Exclusives 1 of 1-249
Gold Reserve-249
99BAP Millennium-165
Emerald-165
Ruby-165
Sapphire-165
Signatures-165
Signatures Gold-165
99Pacific-108
Copper-108
Emerald Green-108
Gold-108
Ice Blue-108
Premiere Date-108
Red-108
99Pacific Dynagon Ice-131
Blue-131
Copper-131
Gold-131
Premiere Date-131
99Paramount-151
Copper-151
Emerald-151
Gold-151
Holographic Emerald-151
Holographic Gold-151
Holographic Silver-151
Ice Blue-151
Premiere Date-151
Red-151
Silver-151
99Stadium Club-155
First Day Issue-155
One of a Kind-155
Printing Plates Black-155
Printing Plates Cyan-155
Printing Plates Magenta-155
Printing Plates Yellow-155
99Upper Deck-257
Exclusives-257
Exclusives 1 of 1-257
99Upper Deck Gold Reserve-257
99Upper Deck Victory-196
99Wayne Gretzky Hockey-111
99Russian Fetisov Tribute-6
00Pacific-264
Copper-264
Gold-264
Ice Blue-264
Premiere Date-264
00Panini Stickers-63
00Private Stock Game Gear-74
00Titanium Game Gear-35
00Upper Deck-347
Exclusives Tier 1-347
Exclusives Tier 2-347
00Czech Stadion-112
01BAP Memorabilia-496
Emerald-496
Ruby-496
Sapphire-496
01Pacific-260
Extreme LTD-260
Hobby LTD-260
Premiere Date-260
Retail LTD-260
01Pacific Arena Exclusives-260
01Stars Postcards-9
01Upper Deck-289
Exclusives-289
02BAP Sig Series Auto Buybacks 1998-186
02BAP Sig Series Auto Buybacks 1999-165
03Russian Hockey League-166

Kamentsev, Pavel
98Russian Hockey League-41

Kames, Jaroslav
94Czech APS Extraliga-181
95Czech APS Extraliga-29
95Czech APS Extraliga-356
96Czech APS Extraliga-27
97Czech APS Extraliga-53
97Czech DS Extraliga-102
97Czech DS Stickers-94
98Czech DS-24
98Czech DS Stickers-287
98Czech OFS-18
99German DEL-61
00Czech DS Extraliga-13
Goalies-G2
00Czech OFS-320
00Czech OFS Star Emerald-1
00Czech OFS Star Pink-1
00Czech OFS Star Violet-1
01Russian Ultimate Line-4
04Czech OFS-119
05Czech HC Vitkovice-8
06Czech OFS Jagr Team-2

Kames, Jiri
98Czech OFS-404
99Czech DS-166
99Czech OFS-328
00Czech OFS-119
01Czech OFS-269

Kames, Vladimir
94German First League-556

Kamienski, Kurt
00Connecticut Huskies-10

Kaminski, Bernhard
95German DEL-35

Kaminski, Darcy
89Lethbridge Hurricanes-11
90Hampton Roads Admirals-47
91Hampton Roads Admirals-20
92Nashville Knights-22
94Central Hockey League-114

Kaminski, Ian
92Russian Stars Red Ace-33

Kaminski, Kevin
86Saskatoon Blades Photos-11
88Saskatoon Blades-23
89Nordiques Team Issue-20
89Nordiques General Foods-16
89Halifax Citadels-12
89ProCards AHL-170
90Nordiques Team Issue-15
90ProCards AHL/IHL-448
90ProCards AHL/IHL-544
93Donruss-505
93Parkhurst-493
Emerald Ice-493
93Portland Pirates-21
94Portland Pirates-12
94Classic Enforcers-E8
95Capitals Team Issue-14
96Be A Player-86
Autographs-86
Autographs Silver-86
97Portland Pirates-14
98Las Vegas Thunder-10
01Cincinnati Mighty Ducks-27
02Fleer Throwbacks-27
Gold-27
Platinum-27
Autographs-10
04Missouri River Otters-13
05Missouri River Otters-2

Kaminsky, Andrew
97Brandon Wheat Kings-13
98Brandon Wheat Kings-12

Kaminsky, Max
34Beehive Group I Photos-198
35Diamond Matchbooks Tan 1-33

Kaminsky, Yan
92Upper Deck-333
92Upper Deck-344
93Donruss-456
93Jets Readers Club-11
93Jets Ruffles-13
93Classic-88
94Leaf-173
94OPC Premier-399
Special Effects-399
94Pinnacle-263
Artist's Proofs-263
Rink Collection-263
94Score-221
Gold-221
Platinum-221
94Topps/OPC Premier-399
Special Effects-399
94Classic Pro Prospects-185

Kamman, Markus
94German First League-503

Kammerer, Axel
89Swedish Semic World Champ Stickers-123
92Finnish Semic-183
94German DEL-193
95German DEL-328
96German DEL-106
99German Bundesliga 2-28

Kammerloher, Bastian
94German First League-177

Kampersal, Jeffery
92Richmond Renegades-9

Kampf, Radek
96Czech APS Extraliga-299
97Czech DS Stickers-226

Kampfer, Steve
04Sioux City Musketeers-10

Kampman, Bingo
34Beehive Group I Photos-329
38Quaker Oats Photos-21
39O-Pee-Chee V301-1-3
40O-Pee-Chee V301-2-109

Kamppuri, Hannu
78Finnish SM-Liiga-1
78Finnish SM-Liiga-65
80Finnish Mallasjuoma-168
82Finnish Skopbank-4
82Swedish Semic VM Stickers-26
83Swedish Semic VM Stickers-26
84Devils Postcards-33
05Finnish Tappara Legendat-16

Kamsek, Luka
93Quebec Pee-Wee Tournament-1803

Kamula, Pete
52Juniors Blue Tint-19

Kana, Jan
06Czech OFS-318
Brothers-2

Kana, Tomas
06Czech OFS-54
Brothers-2

Kanaryekin, Leonid
98Russian Hockey League-28
00Russian Hockey League-45
03Russian National Team-31

Kane, Boyd
96Regina Pats-12
97Regina Pats-3
98Charlotte Checkers-9
98Hartford Wolf Pack-11
99Charlotte Checkers-21
00Charlotte Checkers-5
00Hartford Wolf Pack-14
01Hartford Wolf Pack-11
02Springfield Falcons-13
03BAP Ultimate Mem Rookie Jersey Emblems-29
03BAP Ultimate Mem Rookie Jsy Emblem Gold-29
03BAP Ultimate Mem Rookie Jersey Numbers-29
03BAP Ultimate Mem Rookie Jsy Number Gold-29
03ITG VIP Rookie Debut-45
03Parkhurst Rookie-133
03SP Authentic-93
Limited-93
03SPx-200
Radiance-200
Spectrum-200
03Topps Traded-TT161
Blue-TT161
Gold-TT161
Red-TT161
03Upper Deck-447
Canadian Exclusives-447
HG-447
UD Exclusives-447
03Philadelphia Phantoms-4
04Philadelphia Phantoms-7
05Hershey Bears-11
06ITG Heroes and Prospects Calder Cup Champions-CC10

Kane, Dan
84Moncton Golden Flames-7
03Bowling Green Falcons-12

Kane, Patrick
06London Knights-2
06ITG Heroes and Prospects-175
Autographs-APKN
Quad Emblems-QE13

Kane, Shaun
93Raleigh Icecaps-8

Kanerva, Petteri
78Finnish SM-Liiga-109
80Finnish Mallasjuoma-71

Kanervo, Kari
92Finnish Jyvas-Hyva Stickers-175

Kang, Matthew
04Owen Sound Attack-7
05Owen Sound Attack-13
06Kingston Frontenacs-7

Kangas, Antti
00Finnish Cardset-293
01Finnish Cardset-72

Kangas, Pasi
95Finnish SISU-266
99Finnish Cardset-276

Kangas, Vesa
89Swedish Semic Elitserien Stickers-161

Kangasalusta, Pekka
95Finnish SISU-231
96Finnish SISU Redline-30
98Finnish Kerailysarja-78
99Finnish Cardset-46
99Finnish Cardset-223
00Finnish Cardset-295
01Finnish Cardset-353

Kangasmaki, Aki
06Chilliwack Bruins-15

Kangasniemi, Miska
94Finest-134
Super Team Winners-134
Refractors-134
95Finnish SISU-60
98Finnish Kerailysarja-208
99Finnish Cardset-119
00Finnish Cardset-86
01Finnish Cardset-122
03Finnish Cardset-146
04Swedish Elitset-227
Gold-227
04Swedish Malmo Red Hawks-2
06Finnish Cardset-249

Kanigan, Justin
00Saskatoon Blades-19

Kanka, Michal
98Czech OFS-174
99Czech OFS-329

Kankaanpera, Ari
74Finnish Typotor-9
78Finnish SM-Liiga-50

Kankaanpera, Markus
98Finnish Kerailysarja-126
99Finnish Cardset-70
00Finnish Cardset-46
00Finnish Cardset Next Generation-8
01Finnish Cardset-218
04Finnish Cardset-240
05Finnish Cardset -53
06Finnish Cardset-55
Enforcers-8

Kankaanpera, Mikko
01Finnish Cardset-360

Kankaanpera, Risto
78Finnish SM-Liiga-56

Kanko, Petr
01Kitchener Rangers-6
02Kitchener Rangers Postcards-2
03Kitchener Rangers-13
03Kitchener Rangers Memorial Cup-11
04Manchester Monarchs-18
04Manchester Monarchs Tobacco-18
05Black Diamond-248
05Hot Prospects-137
En Fuego-137
Red Hot-137
White Hot-137
05SP Authentic-264
Limited-264
05SP Game Used-216
05SPx-266
05The Cup Masterpiece Pressplate Artifact-285
05The Cup Master Pressplate Black Diamond-248
05The Cup Masterpiece Pressplates (Ice)-241
05The Cup Master Pressplate Rookie Update-141
05The Cup Masterpiece Pressplates SPA-264
05The Cup Masterpiece Pressplates SP GU-216
05The Cup Masterpiece Pressplates (SPx)-266
05The Cup Masterpiece Pressplates Trilogy-264
05The Cup Masterpiece Pressplate Ult Coll-210
05UD Artifacts-285
05Ultimate Collection-210
Gold-210
05Upper Deck Ice-241
05Upper Deck Rookie Update-141
05Upper Deck Trilogy-264
05Manchester Monarchs-9
05Manchester Monarchs-38
06Manchester Monarchs-18

Kankovsky, Petr
94Czech APS Extraliga-192
95Czech APS Extraliga-188
96Czech APS Extraliga-323
97Czech DS Stickers-165
99Czech DS-189
99Czech OFS-466
00Czech OFS-316

Kankovsky, Roman
94Czech APS Extraliga-190
95Czech APS Extraliga-178
96Czech APS Extraliga-313
97Czech DS Stickers-154

Kannegiesser, Sheldon
71O-Pee-Chee-190
71Penguins Postcards-9
71Toronto Sun-219
74NHL Action Stamps-114
74O-Pee-Chee NHL-338
75O-Pee-Chee NHL-69
75Topps-69
76O-Pee-Chee NHL-335
78O-Pee-Chee-310

Kannewurf, Frank
94German DEL-37
95German DEL-30
99German Bundesliga 2-202

Kannisto, Mika
94Finnish SISU-294
95Finnish SISU-221
96Finnish SISU Redline-24
98Finnish Kerailysarja-61
99Finnish Cardset-341

Kantee, Kevin
04Finnish Cardset-64
Parallel-47
05Finnish Cardset -54
06Finnish Cardset-56

Kantor, Robert
95Czech APS Extraliga-207
97Czech APS Extraliga-336
98Czech DS Stickers-273
98Czech OFS-387
98Czech OFS-475
99Czech DS-56
99Czech OFS-352
99Czech OFS-407
00Czech OFS-164
01Finnish Cardset-197
02Finnish Cardset-188
03Russian Hockey League-55
03Russian Hockey League-235
04Finnish Cardset-155
Parallel-115
05Czech HC Pardubice-5
06Czech Super Six Postcards-6

Kaonpaa, Esko
65Finnish Hellas-129
66Finnish Jaakiekkosarja-149
71Finnish Suomi Stickers-177
72Finnish Jaakiekko-125
72Finnish Panda Toronto-25

Kapanen, Hannu
71Finnish Suomi Stickers-281
73Finnish Jaakiekko-196
78Finnish SM-Liiga-34
93Finnish Jyvas-Hyva Stickers-163
95Finnish SISU-389

Kapanen, Jari
73Finnish Jaakiekko-283
78Finnish SM-Liiga-80
80Finnish Mallasjuoma-14

Kapanen, Kimmo
93Finnish SISU-162
94Finnish SISU-229
95Finnish SISU-2
98Finnish Kerailysarja-141
Mad Masks-7
99Finnish Cardset-233
Puck Stoppers-6
00Finnish Cardset-22
01German Upper Deck-112
Jersey Cards-KK-J
02Finnish Cardset-34
02Swedish SHL-261
02Swedish SHL-293
Masks-8
Parallel-261
Parallel-293
03Swedish Elite-122
Jerseys-1
Masks-4
Masks II-2
Signatures II-7
Silver-122
Zero Hero-9
04Swedish Elitset-121
Gold-121
In The Crease-10
Jerseys Series 1-2
Signatures Series A-10
05Finnish Cardset -254
Finnish Cardset Super Snatchers-9
06Finnish Cardset-81
Between the Pipes-12
Signature Sensations-15
Superior Snatchers-3
Superior Snatchers Gold-3
Superior Snatchers Silver-3

Kapanen, Niko
98Finnish Kerailysarja-71
99Finnish Cardset-41
99Finnish Cardset-173
00SPx Rookie Redemption-RR10
00Finnish Cardset-120
00Finnish Cardset-340
01BAP Memorabilia-348
Emerald-348
Ruby-348
Sapphire-348
01BAP Signature Series-232
Autographs-232
Autographs Gold-232
01Bowman YoungStars-143
Gold-143
Ice Cubed-143
01Crown Royale-156
01O-Pee-Chee-354
01Parkhurst-287
01Parkhurst Beckett Promos-287
01Private Stock-119
Gold-119
Premiere Date-119
Retail-119
Silver-119
01Private Stock Pacific Nights-119
01SP Authentic-144
Limited-144
Limited Gold-144
01SP Game Used-74
01SPx-103
01Stadium Club-140
Award Winners-140
Master Photos-140
01Stars Postcards-10
01Stars Team Issue-4
01Titanium-155
Retail-155
01Titanium Draft Day Edition-124
01Topps-354
01Topps Chrome-172
Refractors-172
Black Border Refractors-172
01Topps Heritage-139
01Topps Reserve-111
01UD Challenge for the Cup-104
01UD Honor Roll-70
01UD Playmakers-114
01UD Premier Collection-94
01UD Top Shelf-70
01Upper Deck-421
Exclusives-421
01Upper Deck Ice-52
01Upper Deck Vintage-280
01Vanguard-108
Blue-108
Red-108
One of Ones-108
Premiere Date-108
Proofs-108
01Finnish Cardset-171
02BAP Signature Series Jerseys-SGJ60
02BAP Signature Series Jersey Autographs-SGJ60
02BAP Ultimate Mem Calder Candidates-2
02Bowman YoungStars-149
Gold-149
Silver-149
Autographs-NK
Jerseys-NK
Patches-NK
Double Stuff-NK
Triple Stuff-NK
Rivals-NKMH
Rivals Patches-6
Sticks-NK
02ITG Used Calder Jerseys-C15
02ITG Used Calder Jerseys Gold-C15
02Pacific Calder-66
Silver-66
02Pacific Complete-503
Red-503
02Parkhurst Retro-75
Minis-75
Hopefuls-CH4
02Stars Postcards-14
02Finnish Cardset-35
02Finnish Cardset Dynamic Duos-9
02Finnish Cardset Solid Gold Six-Pack-6
03BAP Ultimate Memorabilia Autographs-76
Gold-76
03Bowman-43
Gold-43
Future Fabrics-FF-NK
Future Fabric Patches-NK
Future Rivals-AK
Future Rivals-KD
Future Rivals Patches-AK
Future Rivals Patches-KD
Goal to Goal-KN
03Bowman Chrome-43
Refractors-43
Gold Refractors-43
Xfractors-43
03eTopps-6
03ITG Action-114
Jerseys-M38
03ITG Used Signature Series-27
Gold-27
Autographs-NK
Autographs Gold-NK
03O-Pee-Chee-25
03OPC Blue-25
03OPC Gold-25
03OPC Red-25
03Pacific Complete-393
Red-393
03Private Stock Reserve-29
Blue-29
Red-29
Retail-29
03Stars Postcards-10
03Topps-25

Blue-25
Gold-25
Red-25
Own the Game-OTG10
03Topps C55-93
Minis-93
Minis American Back-93
Minis American Back Red-93
Minis Bazooka Back-93
Minis Brooklyn Back-93
Minis Hat Trick Back-93
Minis O Canada Back-93
Minis O Canada Back Red-93
Minis Stanley Cup Back-93
03Upper Deck-63
Canadian Exclusives-63
HG-63
03Upper Deck MVP-135
Gold Script-135
Silver Script-135
Canadian Exclusives-135
04UD All-World-86
Gold-86
04Upper Deck-58
Canadian Exclusives-58
HG Glossy Gold-58
HG Glossy Silver-58
04Swiss EV Zug Postcards-2
05Parkhurst-157
Facsimile Auto Parallel-157
05Upper Deck-64
HG Glossy-64
Notable Numbers-N-NIK
05Upper Deck Toronto Fall Expo-64
05Upper Deck Victory-215
Black-215
Gold-215
Silver-215
06O-Pee-Chee-32
Rainbow-32
06Upper Deck-260
Exclusives Parallel-260
High Gloss Parallel-260
Masterpieces-260
06Upper Deck MVP-17
Gold Script-17
Super Script-17

Kapanen, Sami

91Upper Deck-674
French-674
91Upper Deck Czech World Juniors-37
92Finnish Jyvas-Hyva Stickers-102
93Finnish Jyvas-Hyva Stickers-174
93Finnish SISU-179
94Finnish SISU-163
94Finnish SISU-209
94Finnish SISU Fire On Ice-8
94Finnish SISU Magic Numbers-5
94Finnish SISU Specials-5
94Finnish Jaa Kiekko-39
95Parkhurst International-516
Emerald Ice-516
95Finnish Beckett Ad Cards-5
95Finnish SISU-12
Drafted Dozen-6
Gold Cards-13
95Finnish SISU Limited-72
Signed and Sealed-1
95Finnish Karjala World Champ Labels-4
95Finnish Kellogg's-6
95Finnish Semic World Championships-24
95Finnish Semic World Championships-231
95Swedish World Championships Stickers-183
96Be A Player-145
Autographs-145
Autographs Silver-145
96Whalers Kid's Club-16
96Swedish Semic Wien-19
97Black Diamond-147
Double Diamond-147
Triple Diamond-147
Quadruple Diamond-147
97Donruss Priority-73
Stamp of Approval-73
97Hurricanes Team Issue-13
97Pacific-192
Copper-192
Emerald Green-192
Ice Blue-192
Red-192
Silver-192
97Pacific Omega-41
Copper-41
Dark Gray-41
Emerald Green-41
Gold-41
Ice Blue-41
97Panini Stickers-25
97Revolution-23
Copper-23
Emerald-23
Ice Blue-23
Silver-23
97SP Authentic-27
97Upper Deck-239
97Zenith-69
Z-Gold-69
Z-Silver-69
98Aurora-33
98Be A Player-24
Press Release-24
98BAP Gold-24
98BAP Autographs-24
98BAP Autographs Gold-24
98BAP Tampa Bay All Star Game-24
98Black Diamond-17
Double Diamond-17
Triple Diamond-17
Quadruple Diamond-17
98Bowman's Best-97
Refractors-97
Atomic Refractors-97
98Crown Royale-24
Limited Series-24
98Finest-130
No Protectors-130
No Protectors Refractors-130
Refractors-130
98Hurricanes Team Issue-16
98Katch-30
98OPC Chrome-178
Refractors-178
98Pacific-134
Ice Blue-134
Red-134
98Pacific Dynagon Ice-34
Blue-34
Red-34
98Pacific Omega-43
Red-43
Opening Day Issue-43
98Panini Stickers-29
98Paramount-37
Copper-37
Emerald Green-37
Holo-Electric-37
Ice Blue-37
Silver-37
98SP Authentic-16
Power Shift-16
98SPx Finite-16
Radiance-16
Spectrum-16
98Topps-178
O-Pee-Chee-178
98Topps Gold Label Class 1-36
Black-36
Black One of One-36
One of One-36
Red-36
Red One of One-36
98Topps Gold Label Class 2-36
98Topps Gold Label Class 2 Black-36
98Topps Gold Label Class 2 Black 1 of 1-36
98Topps Gold Label Class 2 One of One-36
98Topps Gold Label Class 2 Red-36
98Topps Gold Label Class 2 Red One of One-36
98Topps Gold Label Class 3-36
98Topps Gold Label Class 3 Black-36
98Topps Gold Label Class 3 Black 1 of 1-36
98Topps Gold Label Class 3 One of One-36
98Topps Gold Label Class 3 Red-36
98Topps Gold Label Class 3 Red One of One-36
98UD Choice-40
Prime Choice Reserve-40
Reserve-40
98Upper Deck-57
Exclusives-57
Exclusives 1 of 1-57
Gold Reserve-57
98Upper Deck MVP-38
Gold Script-38
Silver Script-38
Super Script-38
98Finnish Kerailysarja 90's Top 12-7
98Finnish Kerailysarja Leijonat-26
99Aurora-27
Premiere Date-27
99BAP Memorabilia-55
Gold-55
Silver-55
99BAP Millennium-49
Emerald-49
Ruby-49
Sapphire-49
Signatures-49
Signatures Gold-49
99Black Diamond-20
Diamond Cut-20
Final Cut-20
99Crown Royale-28
Limited Series-28
Premiere Date-28
99O-Pee-Chee-69
99O-Pee-Chee Chrome-69
99O-Pee-Chee Chrome Refractors-69
99Pacific-73
Copper-73
Emerald Green-73
Gold-73
Ice Blue-73
Premiere Date-73
Red-73
99Pacific Dynagon Ice-42
Blue-42
Copper-42
Gold-42
Premiere Date-42
99Pacific Omega-46
Copper-46
Gold-46
Ice Blue-46
Premiere Date-46
99Pacific Prism-30
Holographic Blue-30
Holographic Gold-30
Holographic Mirror-30
Holographic Purple-30
Premiere Date-30
99Panini Stickers-43
99Paramount-47
Copper-47
Emerald-47
Gold-47
Holographic Emerald-47
Holographic Gold-47
Holographic Silver-47
Ice Blue-47
Premiere Date-47
Red-47
Silver-47
99Revolution-29
Premiere Date-29
Red-29
Shadow Series-29
99SP Authentic-18
99SPx-30
Radiance-30
Spectrum-30
99Stadium Club-134
First Day Issue-134
One of a Kind-134
Printing Plates Black-134
Printing Plates Cyan-134
Printing Plates Magenta-134
Printing Plates Yellow-134
99Topps/OPC-69
99Topps/OPC Chrome-69
Refractors-69
99Topps Gold Label Class 1-67
Black-67
Black One of One-67
One of One-67
Red-67
Red One of One-67
99Topps Gold Label Class 2-67
99Topps Gold Label Class 2 Black-67
99Topps Gold Label Class 2 Black 1 of 1-67
99Topps Gold Label Class 2 One of One-67
99Topps Gold Label Class 2 Red-67
99Topps Gold Label Class 2 Red One of One-67
99Topps Gold Label Class 3-67
99Topps Gold Label Class 3 Black-67
99Topps Gold Label Class 3 Black 1 of 1-67
99Topps Gold Label Class 3 One of One-67
99Topps Gold Label Class 3 Red-67
99Topps Gold Label Class 3 Red One of One-67
99Ultimate Victory-18
1/1-18
Parallel-18
Parallel 100-18
99Upper Deck-32
Exclusives-32
Exclusives 1 of 1-32
99Upper Deck Gold Reserve-32
99Upper Deck HoloGrFx-10
Ausome-10
99Upper Deck MVP-39
Gold Script-39
Silver Script-39
Super Script-39
ProSign-SK
99Upper Deck MVP SC Edition-39
Gold Script-39
Silver Script-39
Super Script-39
99Upper Deck Retro-15
Gold-15
Platinum-15
99Upper Deck Victory-54
99Wayne Gretzky Hockey-34
99Finnish Cardset Aces High-D-10
00Aurora-30
Premiere Date-30
00BAP Memorabilia-176
Emerald-176
Ruby-176
Sapphire-176
Promos-176
00BAP Mem Chicago Sportsfest Copper-176
00BAP Memorabilia Chicago Sportsfest Blue-176
00BAP Memorabilia Chicago Sportsfest Gold-176
00BAP Memorabilia Chicago Sportsfest Ruby-176
00BAP Memorabilia Chicago Sun-Times Ruby-176
00BAP Memorabilia Chicago Sun-Times Gold-176
00BAP Mem Chicago Sun-Times Sapphire-176
00BAP Mem Toronto Fall Expo Copper-176
00BAP Memorabilia Toronto Fall Expo Gold-176
00BAP Memorabilia Toronto Fall Expo Ruby-176
00BAP Parkhurst 2000-P137
00BAP Signature Series-225
Emerald-225
Ruby-225
Sapphire-225
00Crown Royale-22
Ice Blue-22
Limited Series-22
Premiere Date-22
Red-22
00O-Pee-Chee-38
00O-Pee-Chee Parallel-38
00Pacific-84
00Pacific-433
Copper-84
Copper-433
Gold-84
Gold-433
Ice Blue-84
Ice Blue-433
Premiere Date-84
Premiere Date-433
00Panini Stickers-25
00Paramount-44
Copper-44
Gold-44
Holo-Gold-44
Holo-Silver-44
Ice Blue-44
Premiere Date-44
00Private Stock-18
Gold-18
Premiere Date-18
Retail-18
Silver-18
PS-2001 New Wave-4
00Revolution-28
Blue-28
Premiere Date-28
Red-28
00Stadium Club-200
00Titanium Game Gear-3
00Topps/OPC-38
Parallel-38
00Topps Chrome-31
OPC Refractors-31
Refractors-31
00Topps Heritage-144
00UD Reserve-17
00Upper Deck-32
Exclusives Tier 1-32
Exclusives Tier 2-32
00Upper Deck MVP-40
First Stars-40
Second Stars-40
Third Stars-40
00Upper Deck Victory-43
00Upper Deck Vintage-67
00Vanguard-21
Holographic Gold-21
Holographic Purple-21
Pacific Proofs-21
00Finnish Cardset-358
01BAP Memorabilia Country of Origin-CO42
01BAP Signature Series Certified 100-C41
01BAP Signature Series Certified 50-C41
01BAP Signature Series Certified 1 of 1's-C41
01BAP Signature Series Autographs-LSK
01BAP Signature Series Autographs Gold-LSK
01BAP Signature Series Franchise Jerseys-FP-6
01BAP Sig Series He Shoots/Scores Prizes-22
01BAP Signature Series Jerseys-GJ-97
01BAP Signature Series Teammates-TM-6
01BAP Update He Shoots-He Scores Prizes-20
01Bowman YoungStars-62
Gold-62
Ice Cubed-62
01Crown Royale-27
Blue-27
Premiere Date-27
Red-27
Retail-27
01O-Pee-Chee-138
01O-Pee-Chee Premier Parallel-138
01Pacific-75
Extreme LTD-75
Hobby LTD-75
Premiere Date-75
Retail LTD-75
01Pacific Adrenaline-35
Blue-35
Premiere Date-35
Red-35
Retail-35
01Pacific Arena Exclusives-75
01Parkhurst-184
Teammates-T25
Waving the Flag-16
01Private Stock PS-2002-12
01SPx-163
01Titanium-26
Hobby Parallel-26
Premiere Date-26
Retail-26
Retail Parallel-26
All-Stars-3
01Topps-138
OPC Parallel-138
01Topps Chrome-112
Refractors-112
Black Border Refractors-112
01UD Mask Collection-15
Gold-15
Gloves-GGSK
01UD Playmakers-18
01Upper Deck-36
Exclusives-36
01Upper Deck MVP-34
01Upper Deck Victory-62
Gold-62
01Upper Deck Vintage-49
01Upper Deck Vintage-52
01Finnish Cardset-172
01Finnish Cardset Salt Lake City-12
02Atomic Power Converters-6
02BAP All-Star Edition-40
Jerseys-40
Jerseys Gold-40
Jerseys Silver-40
02BAP First Edition-30
Jerseys-30
02BAP Memorabilia-98
02BAP Memorabilia-400
Emerald-98
Ruby-98
Sapphire-98
NHL All-Star Game-98
NHL All-Star Game Blue-98
NHL All-Star Game Green-98
NHL All-Star Game Red-98
02BAP Memorabilia Toronto Fall Expo-98
02BAP Sig Series Auto Buybacks 1998-24
02BAP Sig Series Auto Buybacks 1999-49
02BAP Sig Series Auto Buybacks 2001-LSK
02BAP Signature Series Golf-GS82
02O-Pee-Chee-68
02O-Pee-Chee Premier Blue Parallel-68
02O-Pee-Chee Premier Red Parallel-68
02O-Pee-Chee Factory Set-68
02Pacific-68
Blue-68
Red-68
02Pacific Complete-6
Red-6
02Pacific Exclusive-30
02Pacific Heads-Up-22
Blue-22
Purple-22
Red-22
02Pacific Quest for the Cup-76
Gold-76
02Parkhurst-131
Bronze-131
Gold-131
Silver-131
Jerseys-GJ30
Stick and Jerseys-SJ30
02Parkhurst Retro-29
Minis-29
02Topps-68
OPC Blue Parallel-68
OPC Red Parallel-68
Factory Set-68
02Topps Chrome-46
Black Border Refractors-46
Refractors-46
02Topps Total-333
02UD Top Shelf-17
02Upper Deck-32
Exclusives-32
All-Star Jerseys-ASSK
All-Star Performers-ASSK
02Upper Deck MVP-31
Gold-31
Classics-31
Golden Classics-31
Overdrive-SO4
02Upper Deck Victory-36
Bronze-36
Gold-36
Silver-36
National Pride-NP22
02Upper Deck Vintage-44
Green Backs-44
02Finnish Cardset-36
02Finnish Cardset Dynamic Duos-3
02Finnish Cardset Solid Gold-4
03Flyers Postcards-11
03ITG Action-410
Jerseys-M39
03NHL Sticker Collection-36
03O-Pee-Chee-32
03OPC Blue-32
03OPC Gold-32
03OPC Red-32
03Pacific Complete-289
Red-289
03Topps-32
Blue-32
Gold-32
Red-32
03Upper Deck MVP-312
Gold Script-312
Silver Script-312
Canadian Exclusives-312
05Flyers Team Issue-11
05Parkhurst-356
Facsimile Auto Parallel-356
05Ultra-146
Gold-146
Ice-146
05Upper Deck-142
HG Glossy-142
Jerseys-J-SKA
Jerseys Series II-J2SK
Patches-P-SKP
05Upper Deck MVP-284
Gold-284
Platinum-284
05Upper Deck Toronto Fall Expo-142
06Flair Showcase Stitches-SSSK
06Fleer Fabricology-FSK
06Fleer Speed Machines-SM19
06Flyers Postcards-13
06O-Pee-Chee-364
Rainbow-364
06SP Game Used Authentic Fabrics Dual-AF2KG
06SP Game Used Authentic Fabrics Dual Patches-AF2KG
06UD Artifacts Tundra Tandems-TTSJ
06UD Artifacts Tundra Tandems Black-TTSJ
06UD Artifacts Tundra Tandems Blue-TTSJ
06UD Artifacts Tundra Tandems Gold-TTSJ
06UD Artifacts Tundra Tandems Platinum-TTSJ
06UD Artifacts Tundra Tandems Red-TTSJ
06UD Artifacts Tundra Tandems Dual Patches Red-TTSJ
06Upper Deck-148
Exclusives Parallel-148
High Gloss Parallel-148
Masterpieces-148

Kapitanchuk, Jeff

98Windsor Spitfires-5

Kapkaikin, Konstantin

91O-Pee-Chee Inserts-51R

Kapotocny, Daniel

00Czech OFS-244

Kappeler, Xavier

95Swiss HNL-468

Kapulovsky, Vladimir

05Russian Hockey League RHL-C3

Kapus, Richard

93Upper Deck-265
00Czech DS Extraliga-71
00Czech OFS-226
03Czech OFS Plus All-Star Game-H21

Kapusta, Tomas

89ProCards AHL-147
90ProCards AHL/IHL-235
91ProCards-231
93Finnish Jyvas-Hyva Stickers-48
93Finnish SISU-250
93Finnish SISU-361
93Swedish Semic World Champ Stickers-99
94Finnish SISU-225
94Finnish SISU Fire On Ice-9
95Finnish SISU-357
95Finnish SISU-372
95Finnish SISU Limited-87
95Swedish World Championships Stickers-210
96Czech APS Extraliga-227
97Czech APS Extraliga-41
97Czech DS Extraliga-61
97Czech DS Stickers-33
98Czech DS Stickers-178
98Czech OFS-281
98Finnish Kerailysarja-25
99Muskegon Fury-16
03Czech OFS Plus-389

Kapustin, Sergei

74Russian National Team-5
74Swedish Stickers-63
79Panini Stickers-153
79Russian National Team-17
80USSR Olympic Team Mini Pics-4
82Swedish Semic VM Stickers-71
83Swedish Semic VM Stickers-71
84Russian National Team-7
92Future Trends '76 Canada Cup-144

Kapynen, Tero

78Finnish SM-Liiga-196

Karabin, Ladislav

93Donruss-472
93Parkhurst-426
Emerald Ice-426
93Upper Deck-467
93Cleveland Lumberjacks-18
93Cleveland Lumberjacks Postcards-14
94Cleveland Lumberjacks-20
94Cleveland Lumberjacks Postcards-20
94Classic Pro Prospects-108
95Rochester Americans-7
00German DEL-208
01German Upper Deck-219
02German DEL City Press-286
04German DEL-268
05German DEL-172
All-Star Jerseys-AS06

Karafiat, Martin

02St. Michaels Majors-3

Karaga, Vadim

03London Knights-11

Karakas, Kraig

93Minnesota-Duluth Bulldogs-15

Karakas, Mike

34Beehive Group I Photos-60
35Diamond Matchbooks Tan 3-29
35Diamond Matchbooks Tan 4-7
35Diamond Matchbooks Tan 5-7
36O-Pee-Chee V304D-107
37Diamond Matchbooks Tan 6-7
37V356 Worldwide Gum-123
39O-Pee-Chee V301-1-47
43Parade Sportive *-58
43Parade Sportive *-59
04ITG Franchises Update-461

Karalahti, Jere

93Finnish SISU-86
93Finnish SISU-395
94Finest-126
Super Team Winners-126
Refractors-126
94Parkhurst SE-SE216
Gold-SE216
94Finnish SISU-2
94Finnish SISU Junior-4
95Finnish SISU-206
95Finnish Semic World Championships-237
96Finnish SISU Redline-4
98Finnish Kerailysarja-36
Leijonat-7
99Upper Deck MVP SC Edition-88
Gold Script-88
Silver Script-88
Super Script-88
99Finnish Cardset-182
99Finnish Cardset-220
Blazing Patriots-2
Par Avion-4
00BAP Memorabilia-248
Emerald-248
Ruby-248
Sapphire-248
Promos-248
00BAP Mem Chicago Sportsfest Copper-248
00BAP Memorabilia Chicago Sportsfest Blue-248
00BAP Memorabilia Chicago Sportsfest Gold-248
00BAP Memorabilia Chicago Sportsfest Ruby-248
00BAP Memorabilia Chicago Sun-Times Ruby-248
00BAP Memorabilia Chicago Sun-Times Gold-248
00BAP Mem Chicago Sun-Times Sapphire-248
00BAP Mem Toronto Fall Expo Copper-248
00BAP Memorabilia Toronto Fall Expo Gold-248
00BAP Memorabilia Toronto Fall Expo Ruby-248
00BAP Signature Series-27
Emerald-27
Ruby-27
Sapphire-27
Autographs-22
Autographs Gold-22
00Upper Deck-308
Exclusives Tier 1-308
Exclusives Tier 2-308
00Upper Deck Victory-110
00Finnish Cardset-232
02Finnish Cardset-189
03Finnish Cardset-17
03Finnish Cardset Globetrotters-GR5
04Finnish Cardset-16
04Finnish Cardset Signatures-5
04Swedish Pure Skills-102
Parallel-102
05Finnish Cardset -190
06Finnish Cardset-15
Enforcers-12

Karalis, Tom

85Fredericton Express-21
86Fredericton Express-13
87Flint Spirits-10
89ProCards IHL-117
90ProCards AHL/IHL-549
91ProCards-176
92Tulsa Oilers-7

Karam, Jake

92Cornell Big Red-17
93Cornell Big Red-14

Karamnov, Vitali

92Parkhurst-387
Emerald Ice-387
92Pinnacle-398
French-398
92Upper Deck-341
92Upper Deck-510
93Donruss-287
93Leaf-408
93OPC Premier-292
Gold-292
93Parkhurst-444
Emerald Ice-444
93PowerPlay-429
93Stadium Club-478
Members Only Master Set-478
First Day Issue-478
93Topps/OPC Premier-292
Gold-292
93Ultra-412
93Upper Deck-338
96German DEL-259
98German DEL-37
01Russian Hockey League-64

Karapuu, Mika

93Finnish SISU-44
93Finnish SISU-44B
96Finnish SISU Redline-121
96Finnish SISU Redline Promos-9

Karasch, Rick

02Arizona Icecats-10
03Arizona Icecats-10

Karasek, Ryan

94Dubuque Fighting Saints-15

Karasiewicz, Trevor

03Port Huron Beacons-15

Karatchun, Viktor

99German DEL-312

Karaulchuk, Alex

03Erie Otters-12

Karcher, Carl

94Ducks Carl's Jr.-27

Karel, Helmut

95Swedish World Championships Stickers-265

Karelius, Pertti

65Finnish Hellas-11
66Finnish Jaakiekkosarja-80

Karestal, Lars

67Swedish Hockey-203

Karetin, Sergei

04Russian Under-18 Team-14

Karg, Steffen

92Quebec Pee-Wee Tournament-1690
98German DEL-220
02German DEL City Press-287
04German DEL Update-302
04German Ingolstadt Panthers-12
05German DEL-328

Karger, Reinhard

70Finnish Jaakiekko-87
70Swedish Hockey-377
70Swedish Masterserien-173
74Finnish Typotor-60

Karhunen, Pekka

70Finnish Jaakiekko-311

Kari, Esa

70Finnish Jaakiekko-193

Kari, Harri

78Finnish SM-Liiga-199

Kariya, Martin

03Bridgeport Sound Tigers-8A
04ITG Heroes and Prospects-16
Autographs-MK
04ITG Heroes/Prospects Toronto Expo '05-16
04ITG Heroes/Prospects Expo Heroes/Pros-16
06Finnish Cardset-193

Kariya, Paul

91Upper Deck Czech World Juniors-50
91British Columbia JHL-84
91British Columbia JHL-86
91British Columbia JHL-91
91British Columbia JHL-93
91British Columbia JHL-168
92Sports Illustrated for Kids II-377
92Sports Illustrated for Kids II-792
92Upper Deck-586
92Upper Deck-SP3
92Maine Black Bears-20
93Alberta International Team Canada-8
93OPC Premier Team Canada-17
93PowerPlay-485
93Ultra-465
93Upper Deck Program of Excellence-E10
93Maine Black Bears-37
93Maine Black Bears-41
93Maine Black Bears-60
93Maine Black Bears-61
93Classic-4
93Classic-113
Crash Numbered-N2
Promos-NNO
Team Canada-TC2
Top Ten-DP4
93Classic Four-Sport *-188
Gold-188
LPs-LP25
94Be A Player Magazine-1
94Be A Player-R103
94Be A Player-R126
94Be A Player-R151
Signature Cards-151
Up Close and Personal-UC9
94Ducks Carl's Jr.-10
94Finest-7
Super Team Winners-7
Refractors-7
Bowman's Best-R1
Bowman's Best-X21
Bowman's Best Refractors-R1
Bowman's Best Refractors-X21
94Flair-4
94Fleer-3
Rookie Sensations-5
94Leaf-455
Limited Inserts-27
Phenoms-5
94Leaf Limited-107
Gold-5
94McDonald's Upper Deck-McD32
94NHLPA Phone Cards-3
94OPC Premier-405
Special Effects-405
94Parkhurst SE-SE8
Gold-SE8
Vintage-1
94Pinnacle-265
94Pinnacle-480
Artist's Proofs-265
Artist's Proofs-480
Rink Collection-265
Rink Collection-480
Rookie Team Pinnacle-9
94Score Team Canada-CT1
94Score Top Rookie Redemption-1
94Select-173
Gold-173
Youth Explosion-YE5
94SP-1
Die Cuts-1
Premier-1
Premier Die-Cuts-1
94Topps/OPC Premier-405
Special Effects-405
94Topps Finest Bronze-9
94Ultra Prospects-3
94Upper Deck-235
94Upper Deck-527
Electric Ice-235
Electric Ice-527
Predictor Canadian-C2
94Upper Deck Predictor Canadian Exch Gold-C2
94Upper Deck Predictor Cdn Exch Silver-C2
94Upper Deck Predictor Hobby-H14
94Upper Deck Predictor Hobby Exch Gold-H14
94Upper Deck Predictor Hobby Exch Silver-H14
94Upper Deck SP Inserts-SP91
94Upper Deck SP Inserts Die Cuts-SP91
94Finnish Jaa Kiekko-104
94Classic Pro Prospects-18
Ice Ambassadors-IA3
International Heroes-LP15
94Images *-106
95Upper Deck World Junior Alumni-5
95Bashan Super Stickers-2
Die-Cut-12
95Be A Player Lethal Lines-LL10
95Bowman-90
All-Foil-90
Bowman's Best-BB15
Bowman's Best Refractors-BB15
95Canada Games NHL POGS-32
95Collector's Choice-159
95Collector's Choice-363
95Collector's Choice-370
Player's Club-159
Player's Club-363
Player's Club-370
Player's Club Platinum-159
Player's Club Platinum-363
Player's Club Platinum-370
Crash The Game-C10A
Crash The Game-C10B
Crash The Game-C10C
Crash The Game Gold-C10A
Crash The Game Gold-C10B
Crash The Game Gold-C10C
Crash the Game Silver Redeemed-C10
Crash the Game Silver Bonus-C10
Crash the Game Gold Redeemed-C10
Crash the Game Gold Bonus-C10
95Donruss-57
Dominators-6
Elite Inserts-6
Pro Pointers-19
Rookie Team-3
95Donruss Elite-31
Die Cut Stars-31
Die Cut Uncut-31
Cutting Edge-5
95Emotion-3
Xcited-15
95Finest-165
95Finest-189
Refractors-165
Refractors-189
95Hoyle Western Playing Cards-39
95Imperial Stickers-2
Die Cut Superstars-12
95Kraft-55
95Leaf-304
Fire On Ice-11
Studio Rookies-3
95Leaf Limited-9
Stars of the Game-5
95McDonald's Pinnacle-MCD-11
95Metal-2
Heavy Metal-7
95NHL Aces Playing Cards-7H
95NHL Cool Trade-8
95NHL Cool Trade-RP8
95Panini Stickers-227
95Panini Stickers-300
95Parkhurst International-3
Emerald Ice-3
Crown Collection Silver Series 1-4
Crown Collection Gold Series 1-4
Crown Collection Silver Series 2-4
Crown Collection Gold Series 2-4
Parkie's Trophy Picks-PP15
Parkie's Trophy Picks-PP46
95Pinnacle-2
Artist's Proofs-2
Rink Collection-2
Clear Shots-3
Roaring 20s-2
95Pinnacle FANtasy-26
95Playoff One on One-2
95Playoff One on One-114
95Playoff One on One-223
95Post Upper Deck-20
95Pro Magnets-43
95Score-125
Black Ice Artist's Proofs-125
Black Ice-125
Dream Team-7
Golden Blades-9
95Select Certified Promos-13
95Select Certified-13
Mirror Gold-13
Future-3
95SkyBox Impact-3
95SkyBox Impact-230
Countdown to Impact-7
95SP-1
Holoviews-FX2
Holoviews Special FX-FX2
Stars/Etoiles-E1
Stars/Etoiles Gold-E1
95Stadium Club Members Only-46
95Stadium Club-174
Members Only Master Set-174
Generation TSC-GT1
Generation TSC Members Only Master Set-GT1
Nemeses-N9
Nemeses Members Only Master Set-N9
95Summit-2
Artist's Proofs-2
Ice-2
GM's Choice-19
95Topps-7
95Topps-217
OPC Inserts-7
OPC Inserts-217
Home Grown Canada-HGC7
Marquee Men Power Boosters-7
Mystery Finest-M13
Mystery Finest Refractors-M13
New To The Game-5NG
Young Stars-YS1
95Topps SuperSkills-16
Platinum-16
95Ultra-3
95Ultra-388
Gold Medallion-3
All-Rookies-5
All-Rookie Gold Medallion-5
Extra Attackers-11
High Speed-11
95Upper Deck-206
95Upper Deck-245
Electric Ice-206
Electric Ice-245
Electric Ice Gold-206
Electric Ice Gold-245
95Upper Deck All-Star Game Predictors-6
Redemption Winners-6
95Upper Deck Freeze Frame-F9
95Upper Deck Freeze Frame Jumbo-F9
95Upper Deck NHL All-Stars-AS14
95Upper Deck NHL All-Stars Jumbo-AS14
95Upper Deck Predictor Retail-R43
95Upper Deck Predictor Retail Exchange-R43
95Upper Deck Special Edition-SE1
95Upper Deck Special Edition Gold-SE1
95Zenith-17
Z-Team-14
95Finnish Semic World Championships-86
95Finnish Semic World Championships-206
95Swedish Globe World Championships-91
95Swedish World Championships Stickers-23
96SLU Hockey Canadian-5
96SLU Hockey American-8
96Be A Player Biscuit In The Basket-20
96Be A Player Link to History-6B
96Be A Player Link to History Autographs-6B
96Be A Player Link to History Auto Silver-6B
96Black Diamond-175
Gold-175
Run for the Cup-RC8
96Collector's Choice-1
96Collector's Choice-289
96Collector's Choice-309
MVP-UD10
MVP Gold-UD10
Stick'Ums-S14
Crash the Game-C24A
Crash the Game-C24B
Crash the Game-C24C
Crash the Game Gold-C24A
Crash the Game Gold-C24B
Crash the Game Gold-C24C
Crash the Game Exchange-CR24
Crash the Game Exchange Gold-CR24
96Donruss-142
Press Proofs-142
Dominators-8
Go Top Shelf-8
96Donruss Canadian Ice-3
Gold Press Proofs-3
Red Press Proofs-3
O Canada-2
96Donruss Elite-1
Die Cut Stars-1
Status-5
96Ducks Team Issue-22
96Duracell L'Equipe Beliveau-JB20
96Flair-2
Blue Ice-2
Center Ice Spotlight-6
96Fleer-2
96Fleer-141
Art Ross-10
Pearson-6
96Fleer Picks-6
Dream Lines-5
Fabulous 50-23
Jagged Edge-6
96Hockey Greats Coins-12
Gold-12
96Kenner Starting Lineup Cards-8
96Kraft Upper Deck-29
96Kraft Upper Deck-33
96Kraft Upper Deck-43
96Leaf-176
Press Proofs-176
Fire On Ice-4
Sweaters Away-5
Sweaters Home-5
96Leaf Limited-17
Gold-17
96Leaf Preferred-7
Press Proofs-7
Steel-34
Steel Gold-34
Steel Power-11
96Maggers-46
96McDonald's Pinnacle-29
96Metal Universe-2
Ice Carvings-7
Ice Carvings Super Power-7
Lethal Weapons-9
Lethal Weapons Super Power-9
96NHL Aces Playing Cards-26
96NHL Pro Stamps-43
96Pinnacle-184
Artist's Proofs-184
Foil-184
Premium Stock-184
Rink Collection-184
Team Pinnacle-5
Trophies-2
96Pinnacle Mint-5
Bronze-5
Gold-5
Silver-5
Coins Brass-5
Coins Solid Gold-5
Coins Gold Plated-5
Coins Nickel-5
Coins Silver-5
96Playoff One on One-353
96Post Upper Deck-11
96Score-8
Artist's Proofs-8
Dealer's Choice Artist's Proofs-8
Special Artist's Proofs-8
Golden Blades-8
Dream Team-2
Sudden Death-13
96Select Certified-14
Artist's Proofs-14
Blue-14
Mirror Blue-14
Mirror Gold-14

Mirror Red-14
Red-14
Cornerstones-11
96SkyBox Impact-2
Countdown to Impact-6
VersaTeam-6
96SP-1
Clearcut Winner-CW5
Game Film-GF9
96SPx-1
Gold-1
96Stadium Club Members Only-2
96Summit-116
Artist's Proofs-116
Ice-116
Metal-116
Premium Stock-116
High Voltage-3
High Voltage Mirage-3
Untouchables-7
96Team Out-1
96Topps Picks Fantasy Team-FT11
96Topps Picks Top Shelf-TS4
96Ultra-2
Gold Medallion-2
Power-8
Power Red Line-3
96Upper Deck-1
96Upper Deck Blow-Ups-4
96Upper Deck Generation Next-X1
96Upper Deck Hart Hopefuls Bronze-HH9
96Upper Deck Hart Hopefuls Gold-HH9
96Upper Deck Hart Hopefuls Silver-HH9
96Upper Deck Lord Stanley's Heroes Finals-LS12
96Upper Deck Lord Stanleys Heroes Qfinals-LS12
96Upper Deck Lord Stanleys Heroes Semis-LS12
96Upper Deck Superstar Showdown-SS1B
96Upper Deck Ice-76
Parallel-76
Stanley Cup Foundation-S6
Stanley Cup Foundation Dynasty-S6
96Zenith-90
Artist's Proofs-90
Z-Team-2
96Swedish Semic Wien-94
97SLU Hockey One on One-3
97Headliners Hockey-11
97NHL Pro Zone-30
97Be A Player One Timers-5
97Beehive-31
Golden Portraits-31
Team-1
Team Gold-1
97Black Diamond-14
Double Diamond-14
Triple Diamond-14
Quadruple Diamond-14
Premium Cut-PC26
Premium Cut Double Diamond-PC26
Premium Cut Quadruple Diamond Horiz-PC26
Premium Cut Triple Diamond-PC26
Premium Cut Quadruple Diamond Verticals-PC26
97Collector's Choice-9
97Collector's Choice-318
Crash the Game-C9A
Crash the Game-C9B
Crash the Game-C9C
Crash the Game Exchange-CR9
Star Quest-SQ85
Stick'Ums-S9
World Domination-W5
97Crown Royale-2
Emerald Green-2
Ice Blue-2
Silver-2
Blades of Steel Die-Cuts-1
Cramer's Choice Jumbos-1
Cramer's Choice Jumbos Gold-1
Cramer's Choice Jumbos Signed-1
Hat Tricks Die-Cuts-1
Lamplighters Cel-Fusion Die-Cuts-1
97Donruss-7
Press Proofs Silver-7
Press Proofs Gold-7
Elite Inserts-4
Line 2 Line-20
Line 2 Line Die Cut-20
97Donruss Canadian Ice-2
Dominion Series-2
Provincial Series-2
National Pride-3
Stanley Cup Scrapbook-20
97Donruss Elite-7
97Donruss Elite-136
Aspirations-7
Aspirations-136
Status-7
Status-136
Craftsmen-22
Master Craftsmen-22
Prime Numbers-5A
Prime Numbers-5B
Prime Numbers-5C
Prime Numbers Die-Cuts-5A
Prime Numbers Die-Cuts-5B
Prime Numbers Die-Cuts-5C
97Donruss Limited-35
97Donruss Limited-56
97Donruss Limited-114
Exposure-35
Exposure-56
Exposure-114
Fabric of the Game-10
Fabric of the Game-40
97Donruss Preferred-10
97Donruss Preferred-183
Cut to the Chase-10
Cut to the Chase-183
Line of the Times-4C
97Donruss Preferred Line of Times Promos-4C
97Donruss Preferred Precious Metals-8
97Donruss Priority-13
97Donruss Priority-204
Stamp of Approval-13
Stamp of Approval-204
Direct Deposit-14
Postcards-13
Postcards Opening Day Issues-12
Stamps-13
Stamps Bronze-13
Stamps Gold-13
Stamps Silver-13
97Esso Olympic Hockey Heroes-9
97Esso Olympic Hockey Heroes French-9
97Highland Mint Mint-Cards Pinnacle/Score-7
97Highland Mint Mint-Cards Pinnacle/Score-8
97Jell-O Juniors To Pros-2
97Katch-2
97Katch-159
Gold-2
Gold-159
Silver-2
Silver-159
97Kraft-5
97Kraft 3-D World's Best-8
97Kraft Team Canada-7
97Leaf-6
97Leaf-173
Fractal Matrix-6
Fractal Matrix-173
Fractal Matrix Die Cuts-6
Fractal Matrix Die Cuts-173
Banner Season-1
Fire On Ice-16
97Leaf International-6
Universal Ice-6
97McDonald's Team Canada Coins-7
97McDonald's Upper Deck-9
Game Film-6
97NHL Aces Playing Cards-14
97Pacific-9
Copper-9
Emerald Green-9
Ice Blue-9
Red-9
Silver-9
Card-Supials-1
Card-Supials Minis-1
Cramer's Choice-1
Gold Crown Die-Cuts-1
Slap Shots Die-Cuts-1A
97Pacific Dynagon-3
97Pacific Dynagon-135
Copper-3
Copper-135
Dark Grey-3
Dark Grey-135
Emerald Green-3
Emerald Green-135
Ice Blue-3
Ice Blue-135
Red-3
Red-135
Silver-3
Silver-135
Best Kept Secrets-2
Best Kept Secrets-103
Dynamic Duos-1A
Kings of the NHL-1
Tandems-2
Tandems-24
97Pacific Invincible-3
Copper-3
Emerald Green-3
Ice Blue-3
Red-3
Silver-3
Attack Zone-1
Feature Performers-1
NHL Regime-4
NHL Regime-215
Off The Glass-1
97Pacific Omega-3
Copper-3
Dark Gray-3
Emerald Green-3
Gold-3
Ice Blue-3
Game Face-1
Silks-1
Stick Handle Laser Cuts-1
Team Leaders-1
97Panini Stickers-121
97Panini Stickers-183
97Paramount-2
Copper-2
Dark Grey-2
Emerald Green-2
Ice Blue-2
Red-2
Silver-2
Big Numbers Die-Cuts-1
Canadian Greats-1
Photoengravings-1
97Pinnacle-53
97Pinnacle-NNO
Artist's Proofs-53
Rink Collection-53
Epix Game Emerald-19
Epix Game Orange-19
Epix Game Purple-19
Epix Moment Emerald-19
Epix Moment Orange-19
Epix Moment Purple-19
Epix Play Emerald-19
Epix Play Orange-19
Epix Play Purple-19
Epix Season Emerald-19
Epix Season Orange-19
Epix Season Purple-19
Press Plates Back Black-53
Press Plates Back Cyan-53
Press Plates Back Magenta-53
Press Plates Back Yellow-53
Press Plates Front Black-53
Press Plates Front Cyan-53
Press Plates Front Magenta-53
Press Plates Front Yellow-53
Team Pinnacle-4
Team Mirror-4
Team Parallel-4
Team Parallel Mirror-4
97Pinnacle Certified-34
Red-34
Mirror Blue-34
Mirror Gold-34
Mirror Red-34
Team-9
Gold Team Promo-9
Gold Team-9
97Pinnacle Inside-10
Coach's Collection-10
Executive Collection-10
Track-4
Cans-15
Cans Gold-15
Promos-10
97Pinnacle Mint-2
Bronze-2
Gold Team-2
Silver Team-2
Coins Brass-2
Coins Brass Proofs-2
Coins Gold Plated-2
Coins Gold Plated Proofs-2
Coins Nickel Silver-2
Coins Nickel Silver Proofs-2
Coins Solid Gold-2
Coins Solid Silver-2
97Pinnacle Power Pack Blow-Ups-2
97Pinnacle Power Pack Blow-Ups-P2
97Pinnacle Tot Cert Platinum Blue-34
97Pinnacle Tot Certi Platinum Gold-34
97Pinnacle Totally Certified Platinum Red-34
97Pinnacle Tot Cert Mirror Platinum Gold-34
97Post Pinnacle-7
97Revolution-2
Copper-2
Emerald-2
Ice Blue-2
Silver-2
NHL Icons-1
Team Checklist Laser Cuts-1
97Score-84
97Score-260
97Score-270
97Score-PR84
Artist's Proofs-84
Golden Blades-84
97Score Mighty Ducks-1
Platinum-1
Premier-1
97SP Authentic-6
Icons-I11
Icons Die-Cuts-I11
Icons Embossed-I11
97SPx-1
Bronze-1
Gold-1
Silver-1
Steel-1
Dimension-SPX19
Grand Finale-1
97Studio-4
Press Proofs Silver-4
Press Proofs Gold-4
Hard Hats-3
Portraits-4
Silhouettes-5
Silhouettes 8x10-5
97Upper Deck-211
Blow-Ups 3 x 5-2-1
Blow-Ups 5 x 7-1C
Game Dated Moments-211
Sixth Sense Masters-SS9
Sixth Sense Wizards-SS9
Smooth Grooves-SG9
The Specialists-9
The Specialists Level 2 Die Cuts-9
Three Star Selects-3C
97Upper Deck Crash the All-Star Game-2
97Upper Deck Crash the All-Star Game-AR2
97Upper Deck Diamond Vision-6
Signature Moves-6
97Upper Deck Ice-85
Parallel-85
Champions-IC9
Champions 2 Die Cuts-IC9
Lethal Lines-L1A
Lethal Lines 2-L1A
Power Shift-85
97Zenith-15
Z-Gold-15
Z-Silver-15
97Zenith 5 x 7-45
Gold Impulse-45
Silver Impulse-45
97Zenith Z-Team-6
97Zenith Z-Team 5x7-6
97Zenith Z-Team Gold-6
97Pinnacle Collector's Club Team Pinnacle-H4
98Headliners Hockey XL-4
98SLU Hockey-100
98Aurora-3
Atomic Laser Cuts-1
Championship Fever-1
Championship Fever Copper-1
Championship Fever Ice Blue-1
Championship Fever Red-1
Championship Fever Silver-1
Cubes-1
Man Advantage-1
98Be A Player-2
Press Release-2
98BAP Gold-2
98BAP Autographs-2
98BAP Autographs Gold-2
98BAP AS Game Used Stick Cards-S7
98BAP AS Game Used Jersey Cards-AS7
98BAP Playoff Game Used Jerseys-G12
98BAP Playoff Game Used Jersey Autographs-G12
98BAP Playoff Practice Used Jerseys-P18
98BAP Tampa Bay All Star Game-2
98Black Diamond-1
Double Diamond-1
Triple Diamond-1
Quadruple Diamond-1
Myriad-M3
Myriad 2-M3
Winning Formula Gold-WF1
Winning Formula Platinum-WF1
98Bowman's Best-2
Refractors-2
Atomic Refractors-2
Mirror Image Fusion-F2
Mirror Image Fusion Refractors-F2
Mirror Image Fusion Atomic Refractors-F2
Scotty Bowman's Best-SB9
Scotty Refractors-SB9
Scotty Atomic Refractors-SB9
98Crown Royale-3
Limited Series-3
Cramer's Choice Jumbos-1
Cramer's Choice Jumbos Dark Blue-1
Cramer's Choice Jumbos Green-1
Cramer's Choice Jumbos Red-1
Cramer's Choice Jumbos Light Blue-1
Cramer's Choice Jumbos Gold-1
Cramer's Choice Jumbos Purple-1
Living Legends-1
Master Performers-1
Pivotal Players-1
98Donruss Elite Promos-18
98Ducks Power Play-ANA1
98Finest-100
No Protectors-100
No Protectors Refractors-100
Refractors-100
Centurion-C10
Centurion Refractors-C10
Double Sided Mystery Finest-M11
Double Sided Mystery Finest-M12
Double Sided Mystery Finest-M13
Double Sided Mystery Finest-M14
Double Sided Mystery Refractors-M11
Double Sided Mystery Refractors-M12
Double Sided Mystery Refractors-M13
Double Sided Mystery Refractors-M14
Red Lighters-R3
Red Lighters Refractors-R3
98Jell-O Spoons-5
98Katch-158
98Kenner Starting Lineup Cards-15
98Kraft Fearless Forwards-5
98McDonald's Upper Deck-8
98NHL Game Day Promotion-ANA1
98OPC Chrome-53
Refractors-53
98Pacific-9
Ice Blue-9
Red-9
Dynagon Ice Inserts-1
Titanium Ice-1
Gold Crown Die-Cuts-1
Team Checklists-1
98Pacific Dynagon Ice-3
Blue-3
Red-3
Adrenaline Rush Bronze-1
Adrenaline Rush Ice Blue-1
Adrenaline Rush Red-1
Adrenaline Rush Silver-1
Forward Thinking-1
Preeminent Players-1
Team Checklists-1
Montreal Spring Expo '99-3
98Pacific Omega-4
Red-4
Opening Day Issue-4
Championship Spotlight-1
Championship Spotlight Green-1
Championship Spotlight Red-1
Championship Spotlight Gold-1
EO Portraits-1
EO Portraits 1 of 1-1
Face to Face-2
Online-1
Planet Ice-28
Planet Ice Parallel-28
Prism-1
98Panini Photocards-39
98Panini Stickers-170
98Paramount-3
Copper-3
Emerald Green-3
Holo-Electric-3
Ice Blue-3
Silver-3
Ice Galaxy-1
Ice Galaxy Gold-1
Ice Galaxy Silver-1
Special Delivery Die-Cuts-1
98Revolution-2
Ice Shadow-2
Red-2
All-Star Die Cuts-13
Chalk Talk Laser-Cuts-1
NHL Icons-1
Showstoppers-1
Three Pronged Attack-21
Three Pronged Attack Parallel-21
98SP Authentic-1
Power Shift-1
Snapshots-SS8
Stat Masters-S16
98SPx Finite-116
98SPx Finite-153
98SPx Finite-179
Radiance-116
Radiance-153
Radiance-179
Spectrum-116
Spectrum-153
Spectrum-179
98SPx Top Prospects-1
Radiance-1
Spectrum-1
Highlight Heroes-H1
Lasting Impressions-L3
Premier Stars-PS18
98Topps-53
O-Pee-Chee-53
Ice Age 2000-I1
98Topps Gold Label Class 1-51
Black-51
Black One of One-51
One of One-51
Red-51
Red One of One-51
98Topps Gold Label Class 2-51
98Topps Gold Label Class 2 Black-51
98Topps Gold Label Class 2 Black 1 of 1-51
98Topps Gold Label Class 2 One of One-51
98Topps Gold Label Class 2 Red-51
98Topps Gold Label Class 2 Red One of One-51
98Topps Gold Label Class 3-51
98Topps Gold Label Class 3 Black-51
98Topps Gold Label Class 3 Black 1 of 1-51
98Topps Gold Label Class 3 One of One-51
98Topps Gold Label Class 3 Red-51
98Topps Gold Label Class 3 Red One of One-51
98Topps Gold Label Goal Race '99-GR4
98Topps Gold Label Goal Race '99 Black-GR4
98Topps Gold Label Goal '99 Black 1 of 1-GR4
98Topps Gold Label Goal Race 99 1 of 1-GR4
98Topps Gold Label Goal Race '99 Red-GR4
98Topps Gold Label GoalRace 99 Red 1 of 1-GR4
98UD Choice-4
98UD Choice-224
98UD Choice-240
Mini Bobbing Head-BH11
Prime Choice Reserve-4
Prime Choice Reserve-224
Prime Choice Reserve-240
Reserve-4
Reserve-224
Reserve-240
StarQuest Blue-SQ25
StarQuest Gold-SQ25
StarQuest Green-SQ25
StarQuest Red-SQ25
98UD3-34
98UD3-94
98UD3-154
Die-Cuts-34
Die-Cuts-94
Die-Cuts-154
98Upper Deck-17
98Upper Deck-31
Exclusives-17
Exclusives-31
Exclusives 1 of 1-17
Exclusives 1 of 1-31
Fantastic Finishers-FF8
Fantastic Finishers Quantum 1-FF8
Fantastic Finishers Quantum 2-FF8
Fantastic Finishers Quantum 3-FF8
Frozen In Time-FT6
Frozen In Time Quantum 1-FT6
Frozen In Time Quantum 2-FT6
Frozen In Time Quantum 3-FT6
Generation Next-GN19
Generation Next-GN20
Generation Next-GN21
Generation Next Quantum 1-GN19
Generation Next Quantum 1-GN20
Generation Next Quantum 1-GN21
Generation Next Quantum 2-GN19
Generation Next Quantum 2-GN20
Generation Next Quantum 2-GN21
Generation Next Quantum 3-GN19
Generation Next Quantum 3-GN20
Generation Next Quantum 3-GN21
Lord Stanley's Heroes-LS17
Lord Stanley's Heroes Quantum 1-LS17
Lord Stanley's Heroes Quantum 2-LS17
Lord Stanley's Heroes Quantum 3-LS17
Profiles-P21
Profiles Quantum 1-P21
Profiles Quantum 2-P21
Profiles Quantum 3-P21
Gold Reserve-17
Gold Reserve-31
98Upper Deck MVP-1
Gold Script-1
Silver Script-1
Super Script-1
OT Heroes-OT9
Snipers-S6
Special Forces-F6
99SLU Hockey-8
99SLU Hockey Pro Action-30
99Aurora-2
Striped-2
Premiere Date-2
Premiere Date Striped-2
Canvas Creations-1
Championship Fever-1
Championship Fever Copper-1
Championship Fever Ice Blue-1
Championship Fever Silver-1
Complete Players-1
Complete Players Parallel-1
Complete Players Retail-1
Complete Players Retail Parallel-1
Styrotechs-1
99BAP Memorabilia-117
Gold-117
Silver-117
Jersey Cards-J7
Jersey Emblems-E7
Jersey Numbers-I7
Jersey and Stick Cards-S7
Selects Silver-SL8
Selects Gold-SL8
99BAP Update Double AS Jersey Cards-D5
99BAP Update Teammates Jersey Cards-TM10
99BAP Update Teammates Jersey Cards-TM12
99BAP Update Teammates Jersey Cards-TM26
99BAP Update Teammates Jersey Cards-TM45
99BAP Millennium-1
Emerald-1
Ruby-1
Sapphire-1
Signatures-1
Signatures Gold-1
Jerseys-J16
Jersey Autographs-J16
Jersey and Stick Cards-JS16
Jersey Emblems-E16
Jersey Numbers-N16
99Black Diamond-1
Diamond Cut-1
Final Cut-1
A Piece of History-PK
A Piece of History Double-PK
A Piece of History Triple-PK
Diamonation-D1
Diamond Skills-DS2
Myriad-M10
99Crown Royal-2
Limited Series-2
Premiere Date-2
Card-Supials-1
Card-Supials Minis-1
Century 21-1
Cramer's Choice Jumbos-1
Cramer's Choice Jumbos Dark Blue-1
Cramer's Choice Jumbos Gold-1
Cramer's Choice Jumbos Green-1
Cramer's Choice Jumbos Light Blue-1
Cramer's Choice Jumbos Purple-1
Cramer's Choice Jumbos Red-1
Ice Elite-1
Ice Elite Parallel-1
Team Captain Die-Cuts-1
99Hasbro Starting Lineup Cards-8
99Jell-O Partners of Power-11
99Kraft Dinner-4
99Kraft Peanut Butter-6
99McDonald's Upper Deck-MCD1
99McDonald's Upper Deck-MCD1R
99O-Pee-Chee-3
99O-Pee-Chee-281A
99O-Pee-Chee-281B
99O-Pee-Chee-281C
99O-Pee-Chee-281D
99O-Pee-Chee-281E
99O-Pee-Chee All-Topps-AT8
99O-Pee-Chee Chrome-3
99O-Pee-Chee Chrome-281A
99O-Pee-Chee Chrome-281B
99O-Pee-Chee Chrome-281C
99O-Pee-Chee Chrome-281D
99O-Pee-Chee Chrome-281E
99O-Pee-Chee Chrome All Topps-AT8
99O-Pee-Chee Chrome All-Topps Refractors-AT8
99O-Pee-Chee Chrome Ice Masters-IM13
99O-Pee-Chee Chrome Ice Masters Refractor-IM13
99O-Pee-Chee Chrome Refractors-3
99O-Pee-Chee Chrome Refractors-281A
99O-Pee-Chee Chrome Refractors-281B
99O-Pee-Chee Chrome Refractors-281C
99O-Pee-Chee Chrome Refractors-281D
99O-Pee-Chee Chrome Refractors-281E
99O-Pee-Chee Chrome A-Men-AM3
99O-Pee-Chee Chrome A-Men Refractors-AM3
99O-Pee-Chee Ice Masters-IM13
99O-Pee-Chee A-Men-AM3
99O-Pee-Chee Top of the World-TW13
99Oscar Mayer Lunchables-6
99Pacific-8
Copper-8
Emerald Green-8
Gold-8
Ice Blue-8
Premiere Date-8
Red-8
Center Ice-1
Center Ice Proofs-1
Cramer's Choice-1
Gold Crown Die-Cuts-1
Home and Away-1
Home and Away-11
Past and Present-1
Team Leaders-1
99Pacific Dynagon Ice-10
Blue-10
Copper-10
Gold-10
Premiere Date-10
2000 All-Star Preview-1
Checkmates American-1
Checkmates American-16
Checkmates Canadian-16
Lamplighter Net-Fusions-1
Lords of the Rink-1
99Pacific Omega-3
Copper-3
Gold-3
Ice Blue-3
Premiere Date-3
Cup Contenders-1
EO Portraits-1
EO Portraits 1/1-1
NHL Generations-1
North American All-Stars-1
5 Star Talents-13
5 Star Talents Parallel-13
99Pacific Prism-2
Holographic Blue-2
Holographic Gold-2
Holographic Mirror-2
Holographic Purple-2
Premiere Date-2
Clear Advantage-1
Dial-a-Stats-1
Sno-Globe Die-Cuts-1
99Panini Stickers-175
99Panini Stickers-321
99Paramount-3
Copper-3
Emerald-3
Gold-3
Holographic Emerald-3
Holographic Gold-3
Holographic Silver-3
Ice Blue-3
Premiere Date-3
Red-3
Silver-3
Hall of Fame Bound-1
Hall of Fame Bound Proofs-1
Ice Advantage-1
Ice Advantage Proofs-1
Ice Alliance-1
Personal Best-1
Toronto Fall Expo '99-3
99Revolution-2
Premiere Date-2
Red-2
Shadow Series-2
Ice Sculptures-1
Ornaments-1
Showstoppers-1
Top of the Line-1
Copper-2
Gold-2
CSC Silver-2
99SP Authentic-1
Honor Roll-HR1
Special Forces-SF1
Supreme Skill-SS1
99SPx-4
Radiance-4
Spectrum-4
Spectrum-154
Highlight Heroes-HH6
Prolifics-P1
SPXcitement-X16
SPXtreme-XT10
Starscape-S6
99Stadium Club-4
First Day Issue-4
One of a Kind-4
Printing Plates Black-4
Printing Plates Cyan-4
Printing Plates Magenta-4
Printing Plates Yellow-4
Capture the Action-CA11
Capture the Action Game View-CAG11
Chrome-4
Chrome Refractors-4
Chrome Oversized-3
Chrome Oversized Refractors-3
Eyes of the Game-EG3
Eyes of the Game Refractors-EG3
Onyx Extreme-OE5
Onyx Extreme Die-Cut-OE5
99Topps/OPC-3
99Topps/OPC-281A
99Topps/OPC-281B
99Topps/OPC-281C
99Topps/OPC-281D
99Topps/OPC-281E
All-Topps-AT8
A-Men-AM3
Ice Masters-IM13
Top of the World-TW13
99Topps/OPC Chrome-3
99Topps/OPC Chrome-281A
99Topps/OPC Chrome-281B
99Topps/OPC Chrome-281C
99Topps/OPC Chrome-281D
99Topps/OPC Chrome-281E
Refractors-3
Refractors-281A
Refractors-281B
Refractors-281C
Refractors-281D
Refractors-281E
All-Topps-AT8
All-Topps Refractors-AT8
A-Men-AM3
A-Men Refractors-AM3
Ice Masters-IM13
Ice Masters Refractors-IM13
99Topps Gold Label Class 1-13
Black-13
Black One of One-13
One of One-13
Red-13
Red One of One-13
99Topps Gold Label Class 2-13
99Topps Gold Label Class 2 Black-13
99Topps Gold Label Class 2 Black 1 of 1-13
99Topps Gold Label Class 2 One of One-13
99Topps Gold Label Class 2 Red-13
99Topps Gold Label Class 2 Red One of One-13
99Topps Gold Label Class 3-13
99Topps Gold Label Class 3 Black-13
99Topps Gold Label Class 3 Black 1 of 1-13
99Topps Gold Label Class 3 One of One-13
99Topps Gold Label Class 3 Red-13
99Topps Gold Label Class 3 Red One of One-13
99Topps Gold Label Prime Gold-PG2
99Topps Gold Label Prime Gold One of One -PG2
99Topps Gold Label Prime Gold Black-PG2
99Topps Gold Label Prime Gold Black One of One -PG2
99Topps Gold Label Prime Gold Red-PG2
99Topps Gold Label Prime Gold Red One of One -PG2
99Topps Premier Plus-40
Parallel-40
Feature Presentations-FP5
Premier Team-PT1
Premier Team Parallel-PT1
99Ultimate Victory-1
1/1-1
Parallel-1
Parallel 100-1
Frozen Fury-FF2
Smokin Guns-SG2
Stature-S1
UV Extra-UV5
99Upper Deck-11
99Upper Deck-139
Exclusives-11
Exclusives-139
Exclusives 1 of 1-11
Exclusives 1 of 1-139
All-Star Class-AS4
All-Star Class Quantum Gold-AS4
All-Star Class Quantum Silver-AS4
Crunch Time-CT29
Crunch Time Quantum Gold-CT29
Crunch Time Quantum Silver-CT29
Fantastic Finishers-FF13
Fantastic Finishers Quantum Gold-FF13
Fantastic Finishers Quantum Silver-FF13
Game Jerseys Series II-PK
Game Jersey Patch Series II-PKP
Game Jersey Patch Series II 1 of 1-PK-P1
Ice Gallery-IG2
Ice Gallery Quantum Gold-IG2
Ice Gallery Quantum Silver-IG2
Marquee Attractions-MA2
Marquee Attractions Quantum Gold-MA2
Marquee Attractions Quantum Silver-MA2
New Ice Age-N2
New Ice Age Quantum Gold-N2
New Ice Age Quantum Silver-N2
NHL Scrapbook-SB5
NHL Scrapbook Quantum Gold-SB5
NHL Scrapbook Quantum Silver-SB5
PowerDeck Inserts-PD2
Sixth Sense-SS1
Sixth Sense Quantum Gold-SS1
Sixth Sense Quantum Silver-SS1
99Upper Deck Century Legends-54
Century Collection-54
Essence of the Game-E1
99Upper Deck Gold Reserve-11
99Upper Deck Gold Reserve-139
Game-Used Souvenirs-GRPK
99Upper Deck HoloGrFx-2
Ausome-2
Impact Zone-IZ5
Impact Zone Ausome-IZ5
Pure Skill-PS1
Pure Skill Ausome-PS1
99Upper Deck MVP-4
Gold Script-4
Silver Script-4
Super Script-4
21st Century NHL-3
Draw Your Own Trading Card-W12
Game-Used Souvenirs-GU1
Game-Used Souvenirs-GU15
Hands of Gold-H8
Talent-MVP2
99Upper Deck MVP SC Edition-2
Gold Script-2
Silver Script-2
Super Script-2
Clutch Performers-CP1
Golden Memories-GM1
Great Combinations-GCKS
Great Combinations Parallel-GCKS
Playoff Heroes-PH1
Stanley Cup Talent-SC1
99Upper Deck Ovation-1
99Upper Deck Ovation-84
Standing Ovation-1
Standing Ovation-84
A Piece Of History-PK
Lead Performers-LP3
Superstar Theater-ST1
99Upper Deck PowerDeck-1
Auxiliary-1
Auxiliary 1 of 1-1
Time Capsule-T2
Time Capsule Auxiliary-T2
Time Capsule Auxiliary 1 of 1-T2
99Upper Deck Retro-1
Gold-1
Platinum-1
Distant Replay-DR4
Distant Replay Level 2-DR4
Generation-G7C
Generation Level 2-G7C
Turn of the Century-TC4
99Upper Deck Victory-1
99Upper Deck Victory-2
99Upper Deck Victory-316
99Upper Deck Victory-333
99Upper Deck Victory-338
99Wayne Gretzky Hockey-1
Changing The Game-CG3
Great Heroes-GH2
Tools of Greatness-TGPK
Will to Win-W1
99Slovakian Challengers-16
00SLU Hockey One On One-30
00McFarlane Hockey-40
00Aurora-2
Pinstripes-2
Pinstripes Premiere Date-2
Premiere Date-2
Canvas Creations-1
Championship Fever-1
Championship Fever Copper-1
Championship Fever Platinum Blue-1
Championship Fever Silver-1
Scouting Reports-1
Styrotechs-1A
00BAP Memorabilia-88
Emerald-88
Ruby-88
Sapphire-88
Promos-88
Jersey Cards-J31
Jersey Emblems-E31
Jersey Numbers-N31
Jersey and Stick Cards-JS31
Patent Power Jerseys-PP2
00BAP Mem Chicago Sportsfest Copper-88
00BAP Memorabilia Chicago Sportsfest Blue-88
00BAP Memorabilia Chicago Sportsfest Gold-88
00BAP Memorabilia Chicago Sportsfest Ruby-88
00BAP Memorabilia Chicago Sun-Times Ruby-88
00BAP Memorabilia Chicago Sun-Times Gold-88
00BAP Mem Chicago Sun-Times Sapphire-88
00BAP Mem Toronto Fall Expo Copper-88
00BAP Memorabilia Toronto Fall Expo Gold-88
00BAP Memorabilia Toronto Fall Expo Ruby-88
00BAP Memorabilia Update Teammates-TM23
00BAP Memorabilia Update Teammates-TM26
00BAP Memorabilia Update Teammates Gold-TM23
00BAP Memorabilia Update Teammates Gold-TM26
00BAP Parkhurst 2000-P151
00BAP Signature Series-192
Emerald-192
Ruby-192
Sapphire-192
Autographs-169
Autographs Gold-169
Franchise Players-F1
He Shoots-He Scores Points-10
He Shoots-He Scores Prizes-21
Jersey Cards-J16
Jersey and Stick Cards-GSJ16
Jersey Cards Autographs-J16
Jersey Emblems-E16
Jersey Numbers-IN16
00BAP Ultimate Memorabilia Autographs-16
Gold-16
00BAP Ultimate Memorabilia Captain's C-C6
00BAP Ultimate Mem Game-Used Jerseys-GJ16
00BAP Ultimate Mem Game-Used Emblems-E14
00BAP Ultimate Mem Game-Used Numbers-N14
00BAP Ultimate Mem Game-Used Sticks-GS16
00BAP Ultimate Memorabilia Retro-Active-RA7
00BAP Ultimate Memorabilia Teammates-TM21
00BAP Ultimate Memorabilia Teammates-TM23
00Black Diamond-1
00Black Diamond-85
Gold-1
Gold-85
Diamonation-IG1
Myriad-CC1
00Crown Royale-2
Ice Blue-2
Limited Series-2
Premiere Date-2
Red-2
Jewels of the Crown-1
Landmarks-1
Now Playing-1
00Kraft-8
00McDonald's Pacific-1
Blue-1
Dial-A-Stats-1
00O-Pee-Chee-3
00O-Pee-Chee Parallel-3
00Pacific-5
Copper-5
Gold-5
Ice Blue-5
Premiere Date-5
2001: Ice Odyssey-1
Cramer's Choice-1
Gold Crown Die Cuts-1
North American Stars-1
Reflections-1
00Pacific 2001: Ice Odyssey Anaheim Ntnl-1
00Panini Stickers-109
00Paramount-5
Copper-5
Gold-5
Holo-Gold-5
Holo-Silver-5
Ice Blue-5
Premiere Date-5
Epic Scope-1
Freeze Frame-1
Hall of Fame Bound-1
Hall of Fame Bound Canvas Proofs-1
Hall of Fame Bound Proofs-1
Sub Zero-1
Sub Zero Gold-1
Sub Zero Red-8
00Private Stock-2
Gold-2
Premiere Date-2
Retail-2
Silver-2
Artist's Canvas-1
Artist's Canvas Proofs-1
Extreme Action-1
PS-2001 Action-1
PS-2001 Stars-1
Reserve-1
00Revolution-2
Blue-2
Premiere Date-2
Red-2
HD NHL-1
Ice Immortals-1
NHL Icons-1
Stat Masters-21
00SP Authentic-1
Honor-SP1
Parents' Scrapbook-PS1
00SP Game Used-1
Patch Cards-D-KG
Patch Cards-P-PK
Tools of the Game-PK
Tools of the Game Exclusives-PK
Tools of the Game Combos-C-KS
00SPx-1
00SPx-81
Spectrum-1
Spectrum-81
Highlight Heroes-HH1
SPXtreme-S1
Winning Materials-PK
Winning Materials-WKA
00Stadium Club-51
Beam Team-BT1
Special Forces-SF3
00Titanium-1
Blue-1
Gold-1
Premiere Date-1
Red-1
Retail-1
All-Stars-1NA
Three-Star Selections-11
00Topps/OPC-3
Parallel-3
Combos-TC2
Combos Jumbos-TC2
Hobby Masters-HM7
Own the Game-OTG4
00Topps Chrome-3
OPC Refractors-3
Refractors-3
Combos-TC2
Combos Refractors-TC2
Hobby Masters Refractors-HM7
Rocket's Flare-RF2
Rocket's Flare Refractors-RF2
00Topps Gold Label Class 1-39
Gold-39
00Topps Gold Label Class 2-39
00Topps Gold Label Class 2 Gold-39
00Topps Gold Label Class 3-39
00Topps Gold Label Class 3 Gold-39
00Topps Gold Label Golden Greats-GG2
00Topps Gold Label Golden Greats 1 to 1-GG2
00Topps Heritage-8
00Topps Heritage-218
00Topps Heritage-235
Chrome Parallel-8
Heroes-HH20
00Topps Premier Plus-10
Blue Ice-10
Masters of the Break-MB7
Team-PT1
Team Blue Ice-PR1

Trophy Tribute-TT5
World Premier-WP9
00Topps Stars-5
00Topps Stars-134
Blue-5
Blue-134
Walk of Fame-WF2
00UD Heroes-139
Game-Used Twigs-T-PK
Game-Used Twigs Gold-C-KS
NHL Leaders-L1
Player Idols-PI4
Today's Snipers-TS1
00UD Pros and Prospects-1
Game Jerseys-PK
Game Jersey Exclusives-PK
Great Skates-GS1
00UD Reserve-1
On-Ice Success-OS1
The Big Ticket-BT1
00Upper Deck-1
Exclusives Tier 1-1
Exclusives Tier 2-1
Dignitaries-D1
Fantastic Finishers-FF1
Fun-Damentals-F1
Game Jerseys-PK
Game Jerseys-PK
Game Jersey Autographs Exclusives-EPK
Game Jersey Combos-DSK
Game Jersey Patches-PKP
Game Jersey Patches-PPK
Game Jersey Patch Autographs Exclusives-PKP
Game Jersey Patch Exclusives Series II-EPK
Gate Attractions-GA1
Rise to Prominence-RP1
Skilled Stars-SS1
Triple Threat-TT1
00Upper Deck Ice-1
Immortals-1
Legends-1
Stars-1
Cool Competitors-CC1
Game Jerseys-JCPK
Rink Favorites-FP1
00Upper Deck Legends-1
00Upper Deck Legends-3
Legendary Collection Bronze-1
Legendary Collection Bronze-3
Legendary Collection Gold-1
Legendary Collection Gold-3
Legendary Collection Silver-1
Legendary Collection Silver-3
Essence of the Game-EG1
Legendary Game Jerseys-JPK
00Upper Deck MVP-4
First Stars-4
Game-Used Souvenirs-GSPK
Second Stars-4
Super Game-Used Souvenirs-GSPK
Talent-M1
Third Stars-4
Top Playmakers-TP1
Valuable Commodities-VC1
00Upper Deck Victory-1
00Upper Deck Victory-8
00Upper Deck Victory-242
00Upper Deck Victory-282
00Upper Deck Vintage-9
00Upper Deck Vintage-11
00Upper Deck Vintage-12
All UD Team-UD5
National Heroes-NH1
Star Tandems-S1A
00Vanguard-2
Cosmic Force-1
High Voltage-1
High Voltage Gold-1
High Voltage Green-1
High Voltage Red-1
High Voltage Silver-1
Holographic Gold-2
Holographic Purple-2
In Focus-1
Pacific Proofs-2
Press East/West-1
01McFarlane Hockey Inserts-35
01Atomic-1
Blue-1
Gold-1
Premiere Date-1
Red-1
Blast-1
Core Players-1
Power Play-1
01BAP Memorabilia-196
Emerald-196
Ruby-196
Sapphire-196
All-Star Jerseys-ASJ2
All-Star Emblems-ASE2
All-Star Numbers-ASN2
All-Star Jersey Doubles-DASJ1
All-Star Starting Lineup-S10
All-Star Teammates-AST2
All-Star Teammates-AST10
All-Star Teammates-AST31
All-Star Teammates-AST44
All-Star Teammates-AST48
Country of Origin-CO4
He Shoots-He Scores Points-13
Patented Power-PP5
01BAP Signature Series Certified 100-C33
01BAP Signature Series Certified 50-C33
01BAP Signature Series Certified 1 of 1's-C33
01BAP Signature Series Autographs-LPK
01BAP Signature Series Autographs Gold-LPK
01BAP Signature Series Franchise Jerseys-FP-1
01BAP Sig Series He Shoots/Scores Points-15
01BAP Sig Series He Shoots/Scores Prizes-7
01BAP Sig Series International Medals-IG-5
01BAP Signature Series Jerseys-GJ-1
01BAP Signature Series Jersey Autographs-GUPK
01BAP Sig Series Jersey and Stick Cards-GSJ-1
01BAP Signature Series Emblems-GUE-1
01BAP Signature Series Numbers-ITN-1
01BAP Signature Series Teammates-TM-1
01BAP Ultimate Memorabilia Active Eight-1
01BAP Ultimate Mem All-Star History-47
01BAP Ultimate Memorabilia Autographs-7
01BAP Ultimate Mem Autographs Gold-7
01BAP Ultimate Memorabilia Bloodlines-8
01BAP Ultimate Memorabilia Captain's C-7
01BAP Ultimate Memorabilia Dynamic Duos-7
01BAP Ultimate Memorabilia Emblems-1
01BAP Ultimate Memorabilia Jerseys-1
01BAP Ultimate Mem Jerseys and Sticks-1
01BAP Ultimate Memorabilia Numbers-1
01BAP Ultimate Memorabilia Name Plates-3
01BAP Ultimate Mem Prototypical Players-11
01BAP Ultimate Memorabilia Retro Trophies-7
01BAP Update He Shoots-He Scores Prizes-6
01Bowman YoungStars-20
Gold-20
Ice Cubed-20
01Crown Royale-4
Blue-4
Premiere Date-4
Red-4
Retail-4
All-Star Honors-1
Jewels of the Crown-1
Legendary Heroes-1
Triple Threads-1
01eTopps-2
01McDonald's Pacific-1
Hometown Pride-2
01Nortel All-Star Game Sheets-7
01O-Pee-Chee-28
01O-Pee-Chee Heritage Parallel-28
01O-Pee-Chee Heritage Parallel Limited-28
01O-Pee-Chee Premier Parallel-28
01O-Pee-Chee Jumbos-4
01Pacific-6
01Pacific-401
Extreme LTD-6
Gold-401
Hobby LTD-6
Premiere Date-6
Retail LTD-6
All-Stars-NA1
Cramer's Choice-1
Gold Crown Die-Cuts-1
Impact Zone-1
01Pacific Adrenaline-3
Blue-3
Premiere Date-3
Red-3
Retail-3
Blade Runners-1
World Beaters-1
01Pacific Arena Exclusives-6
01Pacific Arena Exclusives-401
01Pacific Heads-Up-1
Blue-1
Premiere Date-1
Red-1
Silver-1
All-Star Net-5
HD NHL-1
Rink Immortals-1
Stat Masters-1
01Parkhurst-1
Gold-1
Silver-1
He Shoots-He Scores Points-16
He Shoots-He Scores Prizes-1
Heroes-H6
Jerseys-PJ24
Jersey and Stick-PSJ4
Sticks-PS24
Waving the Flag-4
01Private Stock-2
Gold-2
Premiere Date-2
Retail-2
Silver-2
Game Gear-2
Game Gear Patches-2
01Private Stock Pacific Nights-2
01Private Stock PS-2002-1
01Private Stock Reserve-S1
01SP Authentic-2
01SP Authentic-91
Limited-2
Limited-91
Limited Gold-2
Limited Gold-91
Jerseys-NNPK
01SP Game Used-1
Authentic Fabric-AFKA
Authentic Fabric-AFPK
Authentic Fabric-DFPK
Authentic Fabric Gold-AFKA
Authentic Fabric Gold-AFPK
Patches-PPK
Patches-CPGK
Patches-CPKS
Patches-CPSK
Patches-TPKYB
01SPx-1
01SPx-71
01Stadium Club-4
Award Winners-4
Master Photos-4
Gallery-G20
Gallery Gold-G20
NHL Passport-NHLP17
Perennials-P7
Souvenirs-PK
01Titanium-3
Hobby Parallel-3
Premiere Date-3
Retail-3
Retail Parallel-3
Double-Sided Jerseys-1
Double-Sided Patches-1
Saturday Knights-1
Three-Star Selections-11
01Titanium Draft Day Edition-2
01Topps-28
Heritage Parallel-28
Heritage Parallel Limited-28
OPC Parallel-28
Captain's Cloth-CC1
Captain's Cloth-CC3
Game-Worn Jersey-JPK
Shot Masters-SM10
01Topps Chrome-28
Refractors-28
Black Border Refractors-28
01Topps Heritage-54
Refractors-54
Captain's Cloth-CCPK
01Topps Reserve-18
Emblems-PK
Jerseys-PK
Name Plates-PK
Numbers-PK
Patches-PK
01UD Challenge for the Cup-1
Cornerstones-CR1
01UD Honor Roll-13
01UD Honor Roll-43
Honor Society-HS-HK
Honor Society Gold-HS-HK
Jerseys-J-PK
Sharp Skaters-SS1
Student of the Game-SG1
01UD Mask Collection-1
Gold-1
Double Patches-DPPK
Jerseys-J-PK
Jersey and Patch-JPPK
01UD Playmakers-3
Combo Jerseys-CJPK
Combo Jerseys Gold-CJPK
01UD Premier Collection-1
Dual Jerseys-DGK
Dual Jerseys-DKI
Dual Jerseys-DKS
Dual Jerseys-DLK
Dual Jerseys Black-DGK
Dual Jerseys Black-DKI
Dual Jerseys Black-DKS
Dual Jerseys Black-DLK
Jerseys-BPK
Jerseys-SPK
Jerseys Black-B-PK
Jerseys Black-S-PK
01UD Top Shelf-1
Jerseys-PK
Sticks-SPK
Sticks-KSF
Sticks Gold-SPK
Sticks Gold-KSF
01Upper Deck-1
Exclusives-1
Franchise Cornerstones-FC1
Game Jerseys-CKS
Game Jerseys Series II-PFPK
Game Jerseys Series II-SSPK
Gate Attractions-GA10
Leaders of the Pack-LP1
Patches-PPK
Patches Series II-PLPK
Patches Series II-PNPK
Pride of a Nation-DPLK
Shooting Stars-SS1
Skilled Stars-SS1
01Upper Deck Ice-1
Combos-C-PK
Combos Gold-G-PK
First Rounders-F-PK
01Upper Deck MVP-2
Talent-MT8
01Upper Deck Victory-9
Gold-9
01Upper Deck Vintage-3
01Upper Deck Vintage-8
01Upper Deck Vintage-9
Next In Line-NLLK
01Vanguard-2
Blue-2
Red-2
East Meets West-6
Memorabilia-1
Memorabilia-2
One of Ones-2
Premiere Date-2
Proofs-2
01Czech Stadion-240
02McFarlane Hockey Team Canada-10
02Atomic-2
Blue-2
Gold-2
Red-2
Cold Fusion-1
Hobby Parallel-2
National Pride-C1
02BAP All-Star Edition-41
02BAP All-Star Edition-42
02BAP All-Star Edition-43
He Shoots-He Score Prizes-10
Jerseys-41
Jerseys-42
Jerseys-43
Jerseys Gold-41
Jerseys Gold-42
Jerseys Gold-43
Jerseys Silver-41
Jerseys Silver-42
Jerseys Silver-43
02BAP First Edition-155
02BAP First Edition-316
02BAP First Edition-341
02BAP First Edition-408R
Debut Jerseys-16
He Shoots-He Score Points-14
He Shoots-He Scores Prizes-8
Jerseys-155
Scoring Leaders-1
02BAP Memorabilia-179
02BAP Memorabilia-201
Emerald-179
Emerald-201
Ruby-179
Ruby-201
Sapphire-179
Sapphire-201
All-Star Jerseys-ASJ-25
All-Star Emblems-ASE-10
All-Star Numbers-ASN-10
All-Star Teammmates-AST-6
All-Star Teammmates-AST-25
All-Star Triple Jerseys-ASTJ-7
Franchise Players-FP-1
He Shoots-He Scores Points-9
He Shoots-He Scores Prizes-12
NHL All-Star Game-179
NHL All-Star Game-201
NHL All-Star Game Blue-179
NHL All-Star Game Blue-201
NHL All-Star Game Green-179
NHL All-Star Game Green-201
NHL All-Star Game Red-179
NHL All-Star Game Red-201
02BAP Memorabilia Toronto Fall Expo-179
02BAP Memorabilia Toronto Fall Expo-201
02BAP NHL All-Star History-47
02BAP Signature Series-101
Autographs-101
Autograph Buybacks 1998-2
Autograph Buybacks 1999-1
Autograph Buybacks 2000-169
Autograph Buybacks 2001-LPK
Autographs Gold-101
Complete Jersey-CJ4
Franchise Players-FJ1
Golf-GS70
Jerseys-SGJ9
Jersey Autographs-SGJ9
Team Quads-TQ19
02BAP Ultimate Memorabilia Captains-1
02BAP Ultimate Memorabilia Dynamic Duos-6
02BAP Ultimate Memorabilia Emblems-12
02BAP Ultimate Memorabilia Jerseys-29
02BAP Ultimate Mem Jersey and Stick-18
02BAP Ultimate Mem Magnificent Ones-6
02BAP Ultimate Mem Magnificent Ones Autos-6
02BAP Ultimate Memorabilia Nameplates-20
02BAP Ultimate Memorabilia Numbers-22
02BAP Ultimate Memorabilia Numerology-11
02BAP Ultimate Memorabilia Retro Trophies-5
02Bowman YoungStars-7
Gold-7
Silver-7
02Crown Royale-2
Blue-2
Red-2
Retail-2
Lords of the Rink-1
Royal Portraits-1
02Ducks Team Issue-3
02eTopps-25
02ITG Used-2
02ITG Used-102
Franchise Players-F1
Franchise Players Autographs-F1
Franchise Players Gold-F1
Jerseys-GUJ9
Jersey Autographs-GUJ9
Jerseys Gold-GUJ9
Emblems-E9
Jersey and Stick-SJ9
Jersey and Stick Gold-SJ9
02McDonald's Pacific-1
Atomic-1
Salt Lake Gold-7
02O-Pee-Chee-8
02O-Pee-Chee Jumbos-11
02O-Pee-Chee Premier Blue Parallel-8
02O-Pee-Chee Premier Red Parallel-8
02O-Pee-Chee Factory Set-8
02Pacific-4
Blue-4
Red-4
Impact Zone-1
Main Attractions-1
02Pacific Calder-30
Silver-30
02Pacific Complete-108
Red-108
02Pacific Exclusive-2
Etched in Stone-1
Maximum Overdrive-1
02Pacific Heads-Up-2
Blue-2
Purple-2
Red-2
Etched in Time-1
Stat Masters-1
02Pacific Quest for the Cup-2
Gold-2
Chasing the Cup-1
02Parkhurst-57
Bronze-57
Gold-57
Silver-57
College Ranks-CR9
College Ranks Jerseys-CRM9
Franchise Players-FP1
He Shoots-He Scores Points-14
He Shoots-He Scores Prizes-5
Jerseys-GJ36
Mario's Mates-MM9
Patented Power-PP4
Stick and Jerseys-SJ36
02Parkhurst Retro-87
Minis-87
Franchise Players-RF1
He Shoots-He Scores Points-14
He Shoots-He Scores Prizes-12
Jerseys-RJ18
Jersey and Sticks-RSJ12
Memorabilia-RM27
02Private Stock Reserve-2
Blue-2
Red-2
Retail-2
02SP Authentic-2
02SP Authentic-91
Beckett Promos-2
Super Premiums-SPPK
02SP Game Used-1
Authentic Fabrics-AFKA
Authentic Fabrics-AFPK
Authentic Fabrics-CFLK
Authentic Fabrics Gold-AFKA
Authentic Fabrics Gold-AFPK
Authentic Fabrics Gold-CFLK
Authentic Fabrics Rainbow-AFKA
Authentic Fabrics Rainbow-AFPK
Authentic Fabrics Rainbow-CFLK
First Rounder Patches-PK
Piece of History-PHKA
Piece of History-PHPK
Piece of History Gold-PHKA
Piece of History Gold-PHPK
Piece of History Rainbow-PHKA
Piece of History Rainbow-PHPK
02SPx-1
02SPx-76
Spectrum Gold-1
Spectrum Gold-76
Spectrum Silver-1
Spectrum Silver-76
Smooth Skaters-PK
Smooth Skaters Gold-PK
Smooth Skaters Silver-PK
Winning Materials-WMKA
Winning Materials-WMPK
Winning Materials Gold-KA
Winning Materials Gold-PK
Winning Materials Silver-KA
Winning Materials Silver-PK
Xtreme Talents-PK
Xtreme Talents Gold-PK
Xtreme Talents Silver-PK
02Stadium Club-57
Silver Decoy Cards-57
Proofs-57
Beam Team-BT15
Passport-8
02Titanium-2
Blue-2
Red-2
Retail-2
02Topps-8
OPC Blue Parallel-8
OPC Red Parallel-8
Captain's Cloth-CC4
Captain's Cloth-CC7
Captain's Cloth-CC12
Coast to Coast-CC8
Topps/OPC Hometown Heroes-HHU5
Factory Set-8
Factory Set Hometown Heroes-HHU5
02Topps Chrome All-Star Fantasy-1
02Topps Chrome-8
Black Border Refractors-8
Refractors-8
02Topps Heritage-37
Chrome Parallel-37
02Topps Total-9
Team Checklists-TTC14
Topps-TT13
02UD Artistic Impressions-2
Gold-2
Artist's Touch-ATPK
Artist's Touch Gold-ATPK
02UD Artistic Impressions Beckett Promos-2
02UD Artistic Impressions Retrospectives-R2
02UD Artistic Impressions Retrospect Gold-R2
02UD Artistic Impress Retrospect Silver-R2
02Upper Deck Collectors Club-NHL12
02UD Honor Roll-1
02UD Honor Roll-71
Grade A Jerseys-GAPK
Students of the Game-SG1
02UD Mask Collection-2
02UD Mask Collection Beckett Promos-2
02UD Mask Collection Instant Offense-IOPK
02UD Mask Collection Patches-PGPK
02UD Piece of History-1
Awards Collection-AC1
Patches-PHPK
Stellar Stitches-SSPK
02UD Premier Collection-1
Jerseys Bronze-PK
Jerseys Bronze-KG
Jerseys Gold-PK
Jerseys Gold-KG
Jerseys Silver-PK
Jerseys Silver-KG
NHL Patches-PK1
Patches-PPK
02UD Top Shelf-3
All-Stars-ASPK
Clutch Performers-CPPK
Dual Player Jerseys-RKG
Goal Oriented-GOPK
Hardware Heroes-HGKSD
Shooting Stars-SHPK
Sweet Sweaters-SWPK
Triple Jerseys-HTKGF
Triple Jerseys-HTKYI
02Upper Deck-4
02Upper Deck-181
Exclusives-4
Exclusives-181
All-Star Jerseys-ASPK
All-Star Performers-ASPK
Blow-Ups-C1
Difference Makers-PK
Fan Favorites-PK
First Class-UDPK
First Class Gold-UDPK
Gifted Greats-GG1
Letters of Note-LNPK
Letters of Note Gold-LNPK
Patch Card Name Plate-PK
Patch Card Numbers-PK
Patchwork-PWPK
Pinpoint Accuracy-PAPK
Playbooks-PL1
Playbooks Series II-KG
Reaching Fifty-50PK
Reaching Fifty Gold-50PK
Shooting Stars-SS1
02Upper Deck Classic Portraits-2
Etched in Time-ET1
Genuine Greatness-GG1
Headliners-KF
Headliners Limited-KF
Hockey Royalty-KFG
Hockey Royalty-KSI
Hockey Royalty Limited-KFG
Hockey Royalty Limited-KSI
Mini-Busts-101
Mini-Busts-102
Mini-Busts-103
Mini-Busts-104
Starring Cast-CPK
Starring Cast Limited-CPK
02Upper Deck MVP-6
Gold-6
Classics-6
Golden Classics-6
Overdrive-SO1
Skate Around Jerseys-SAPK
Vital Forces-VF1
02Upper Deck Rookie Update-1
02Upper Deck Rookie Update-110
02Upper Deck Rookie Update-157A
Jerseys-DPK
Jerseys Gold-DPK
02Upper Deck Victory-2
Bronze-2
Gold-2
Silver-2
National Pride-NP2
02Upper Deck Vintage-2
02Upper Deck Vintage-261
Jerseys-SOPK
Jerseys Gold-SO-PK
Tall Boys-T1
Tall Boys Gold-T1
02Vanguard-2
LTD-2
In Focus-1
02UD SuperStars *-6
Gold-6
City All-Stars Dual Jersey-GAPK
City All-Stars Triple Jersey-DPE
03Avalanche Team Issue-10
03BAP Memorabilia-68
Emerald-68
Gold-68
Ruby-68
Sapphire-68
All-Star Complete Jerseys-ASCJ2
All-Star Emblems-ASE-2
All-Star Jerseys-ASJ-5
All-Star Jerseys-ASJ-24
All-Star Numbers-ASN-2
All-Star Teammates-AST4
Brush with Greatness-4
Brush with Greatness Contest Cards-4
He Shoots-He Scores Points-16
He Shoots-He Scores Prizes-4
Jerseys-GJ-49
Practice Jerseys-PMP10
Stanley Cup Playoffs-SCP-17
Stanley Cup Playoffs-SCP-29
03BAP Ultimate Mem Always An All-Star-6
03BAP Ultimate Mem Always An AS Gold-6
03BAP Ultimate Mem Complete Jersey-7
03BAP Ultimate Mem Complete Jersey Gold-7
03BAP Ultimate Memorabilia Dynamic Duos-5
03BAP Ultimate Memorabilia Emblems-20
03BAP Ultimate Memorabilia Emblems Gold-20
03BAP Ultimate Memorabilia Jerseys-1
03BAP Ultimate Memorabilia Jerseys Gold-1
03BAP Ultimate Mem Journey Jerseys-2
03BAP Ultimate Mem Journey Jerseys Gold-2
03BAP Ultimate Mem Journey Emblems-2
03BAP Ultimate Mem Journey Emblems Gold-2
03BAP Ultimate Memorabilia Nameplates-7
03BAP Ultimate Mem Nameplates Gold-7
03BAP Ultimate Memorabilia Numbers-1
03BAP Ultimate Memorabilia Numbers Gold-1
03BAP Ultimate Mem Perennial Power Jersey-9
03BAP Ult Mem Perenn Powerhouse Jsy Stick-9
03BAP Ultimate Mem Perennial Power Emblem-9
03BAP Ultimate Memorabilia Triple Threads-19
03Beehive-54
Gold-54
Silver-54
Jerseys-JT32
03Black Diamond-177
Black-177
Green-177
Red-177
Threads-DT-PK
Threads Green-DT-PK
Threads Red-DT-PK
Threads Black-DT-PK
03Bowman-9
Gold-9
03Bowman Chrome-9
Refractors-9
Gold Refractors-9
Xfractors-9
03Crown Royale-25
Blue-25
Retail-25
Lords of the Rink-7
03eTopps-19
03ITG Action-108
Jerseys-M190
Jerseys-M210
Oh Canada-OC5
03ITG Used Sig Series Intl Experience-11
03ITG Used Sig Ser Intl Exper Emblem Gold-11
03ITG Used Sig Ser Intl Experience Emblem-11
03ITG Used Sig Ser Intl Experience Gold-11
03ITG Used Signature Series Emblems-3
03ITG Used Signature Series Emblems Gold-3
03ITG Used Sig Series Jersey and Stick-18
03ITG Used Sig Ser Jersey and Stick Gold-18
03ITG Used Signature Series Oh Canada-10
03ITG Used Sig Series Oh Canada Gold-10
03ITG Used Sig Series Oh Canada Emblems-10
03ITG Used Sig Ser Oh Canada Emblems Gold-10
03ITG Used Sig Series Retrospectives-7A
03ITG Used Sig Series Retrospectives-7B
03ITG Used Sig Series Retrospectives-7C
03ITG Used Sig Series Retrospectives-7D
03ITG Used Sig Series Retrospectives-7E
03ITG Used Sig Series Retrospectives-7F
03ITG Used Sig Series Retrospectives Gold-7A
03ITG Used Sig Series Retrospectives Gold-7B
03ITG Used Sig Series Retrospectives Gold-7C
03ITG Used Sig Series Retrospectives Gold-7D
03ITG Used Sig Series Retrospectives Gold-7E
03ITG Used Sig Series Retrospectives Gold-7F
03ITG Used Signature Series Teammates-1
03ITG Used Sig Series Teammates Gold-1
03ITG VIP Collages-5
03Kraft-3
03McDonald's Pacific-12
Hockey Roots Checklists-2
Patches Silver-1
Patches Gold-1
Patches and Sticks-1
03NHL Sticker Collection-153
03O-Pee-Chee-10
03O-Pee-Chee-292
03O-Pee-Chee-296
03OPC Blue-10
03OPC Blue-292
03OPC Blue-296
03OPC Gold-10
03OPC Gold-292
03OPC Gold-296
03OPC Red-10
03OPC Red-292
03OPC Red-296
03Pacific-5
Blue-5
Red-5
Jerseys-1
Jerseys Gold-1
Main Attractions-1
View from the Crease-1
03Pacific Atlantic City National-6
03Pacific Calder-24
Silver-24
03Pacific Complete-314
Red-314
03Pacific Exhibit-161
03Pacific Exhibit-223
Blue Backs-161
History Makers-1
03Pacific Heads-Up-25
Hobby LTD-25
Retail LTD-25
03Pacific Invincible-23
Blue-23
Red-23
Retail-23
Afterburners-2
Top Line-3
03Pacific Luxury Suite-29A
03Pacific Luxury Suite-29B
03Pacific Luxury Suite-29C
03Pacific Luxury Suite-30A
03Pacific Luxury Suite-30B
03Pacific Luxury Suite-30C
03Pacific Prism-101
Blue-101
Patches-101
Red-101
Retail-101
Stat Masters-1
03Pacific Quest for the Cup-25
Blue-25
Chasing the Cup-4
03Pacific Supreme-23
Blue-23
Red-23
Retail-23
Jerseys-9
03Parkhurst Orig Six Boston Mem -BM49
03Parkhurst Orig Six Chicago Mem -CM49
03Parkhurst Orig Six Detroit Mem-DM49
03Parkhurst Orig Six Montreal Mem-MM49
03Parkhurst Orig Six New York Mem-NM49
03Parkhurst Original Six Shooters-OSM9
03Parkhurst Orig Six Toronto Mem-TM49
03Parkhurst Rookie-32
Jerseys-GJ-26
Jerseys Gold-GJ-26
Jersey and Sticks-SJ-13
Jersey and Sticks Gold-SJ-13
Retro Rookies-RR-15
Retro Rookies Gold-RR-15
03Private Stock Reserve-156
Blue-156
Patches-156
Red-156
Retail-156
Moments in Time-4
03SP Authentic-21
Limited-21
Breakout Seasons-B18
Breakout Seasons Limited-B18
Foundations-F3
Foundations Limited-F3
03SP Game Used-13
03SP Game Used-118
Gold-13
Gold-118
Authentic Fabrics-DFKF
Authentic Fabrics-DFKS
Authentic Fabrics-QFSKS
Authentic Fabrics Gold-DFKF
Authentic Fabrics Gold-DFKS
Authentic Fabrics Gold-QFSKS
Double Threads-DTKS
Double Threads-DTPK
Limited Threads-LTPK
Limited Threads Gold-LTPK
Premium Patches-PPPK
Team Threads-TTFSK
Top Threads-FSKS
03SPx-25
03SPx-124
03SPx-140
Radiance-25
Radiance-124
Radiance-140
Spectrum-25
Spectrum-124
Spectrum-140
Fantasy Franchise-FF-KSF
Fantasy Franchise-FF-KTH
Fantasy Franchise Limited-FF-KSF
Fantasy Franchise Limited-FF-KTH
VIP-VIP-SK
VIP Limited-VIP-SK
Winning Materials-WM-PK
Winning Materials Limited-WM-PK
03Titanium-195
Patches-195
03Topps-10
03Topps-292
03Topps-296
Blue-10
Blue-292
Blue-296
Gold-10
Gold-292
Gold-296
Red-10
Red-292
Red-296
Box Toppers-3
Topps/OPC Idols-CI19
03Topps C55-99
Minis-99
Minis American Back-99
Minis American Back Red-99
Minis Bazooka Back-99
Minis Brooklyn Back-99
Minis Hat Trick Back-99
Minis O Canada Back-99
Minis O Canada Back Red-99
Minis Stanley Cup Back-99
Relics-TRPK
03Topps Pristine-16
Gold Refractor Die Cuts-16
Refractors-16
Popular Demand Relics-PD-PK
Popular Demand Relic Refractors-PD-PK
Press Plates Black-16
Press Plates Cyan-16
Press Plates Magenta-16
Press Plates Yellow-16
03Topps Traded-TT82
Blue-TT82
Gold-TT82
Red-TT82
03UD Honor Roll-19
03UD Honor Roll-124
Grade A Jerseys-TCOL
03UD Premier Collection-15
Stars-ST-PK
Stars Patches-ST-PK
Teammates-PT-CA2
Teammates Patches-PT-CA2
03Upper Deck-49
All-Star Class-AS-4
Canadian Exclusives-49
Franchise Fabrics-FF-PK
HG-49
Magic Moments-MM-5
Memorable Matchups-MM-FK
Patches-SP1
Team Essentials-TP-PK
Three Stars-TS1
03Upper Deck Classic Portraits-22
03Upper Deck Classic Portraits-108
Classic Colors-CC-PK
Headliners-HH-PK
Hockey Royalty-FSK
03Upper Deck Ice-20
Gold-20
Breakers-IB-PK
Breaker Patches-IB-PK
Frozen Fabrics-FF-PK
Frozen Fabric Patches-FF-PK
03Upper Deck MVP-105
Gold Script-105
Silver Script-105
Canadian Exclusives-105
Souvenirs-S9
SportsNut-SN2
Winning Formula-WF9
03Upper Deck Rookie Update-20
Skills-SKPK
03Upper Deck Trilogy-22
Limited-22
03Upper Deck Victory-1
Bronze-1
Gold-1
Silver-1
Freshman Flashback-FF1
Game Breakers-GB2
03Czech Stadion-616
04ITG NHL AS FANtasy AS History Jerseys-SB47
04Pacific-68
Blue-68
Red-68
Global Connection-4
04SP Authentic-105
04Ultimate Collection Dual Logos-UL2-KS
04Ultimate Collection Jerseys-UGJ-PK
04Ultimate Collection Jerseys Gold-UGJ-PK
04Ultimate Collection Patches-UP-PK
04Upper Deck-46
Canadian Exclusives-46
HG Glossy Gold-46
HG Glossy Silver-46
Patches-GJPA-PK
Patches-GJPL-PK
Patches-GJPN-PK
05Be A Player Dual Signatures-PA
05Be A Player Signatures-PK
05Be A Player Signatures Gold-PK
05Be A Player Triple Signatures-AVS
05Be A Player Triple Signatures-NKI
05Beehive-50
05Beehive-196
Beige -50
Blue -50
Gold-50
Red -50
Matte-50
05Black Diamond-131
Emerald-131
Gold-131
Onyx-131
Ruby-131
Jerseys-J-PK
Jerseys Ruby-J-PK
Jersey Duals-DJ-PK
Jersey Triples-TJ-PK
Jersey Quads-QJ-PK
05Hot Prospects-55
En Fuego-55
Red Hot-55
White Hot-55
05Panini Stickers-307
05Parkhurst-268
05Parkhurst-687
Facsimile Auto Parallel-268
Facsimile Auto Parallel-687
True Colors-TCNSH
True Colors-TCNSH
05SP Authentic-55
05SP Authentic-112
Limited-55
Limited-112
05SP Game Used-55
Gold-55
Authentic Fabrics-AF-PK
Authentic Fabrics Dual-KV
Authentic Fabrics Gold-AF-PK
Authentic Fabrics Quad-KLHV
Authentic Patches Quad -KLHV
Authentic Fabrics Triple-VKL
Authentic Patches-AP-PK
Authentic Patches Dual-KV
Authentic Patches Triple-VKL
Awesome Authentics-AA-PK
Game Gear-GG-PK
05SPx-47
Spectrum-47
Winning Combos Gold-WC-VK
Winning Materials Gold-WM-PK
Winning Materials Spectrum-WM-PK
05The Cup-61
Gold-61
Black Rainbow-61
Dual NHL Shields-DSKS
Dual NHL Shields-DSKV
Masterpiece Pressplates-61
Noble Numbers-NNMK
Noble Numbers Dual-DNNKS
Noble Numbers Dual-DNNKV
Patch Variation-P61
Property of-POPK
05UD Artifacts Frozen Artifacts-FA-PK
05UD Artifacts Frozen Artifacts Autos-FA-PK
05UD Artifacts Frozen Artifacts Copper-FA-PK
05UD Artifacts Frozen Artifacts Dual-FAD-PK
05UD Artifacts Frozen Artifact Dual Auto-FAD-PK
05UD Artifact Frozen Artifact Dual Copper-FAD-PK
05UD Artifacts Frozen Artifacts Dual Gold-FAD-PK
05UD Artifact Frozen Artifact Dual Maroon-FAD-PK
05UD Artifact Frozen Artifact Dual Pewter-FAD-PK
05UD Artifact Frozen Artifact Dual Silver-FAD-PK
05UD Artifacts Frozen Artifacts Gold-FA-PK
05UD Artifacts Frozen Artifacts Maroon-FA-PK
05UD Artifacts Frozen Artifacts Patches-FP-PK
05UD Artifact Frozen Artifact Patch Autos-FP-PK
05UD Artifacts Frozen Artifact Patch Dual-FPD-PK
05UD Artifacts Frozen Art Patch Dual Auto-FPD-PK
05UD Artifacts Frozen Art Patch Pewter-FP-PK
05UD Artifacts Frozen Art Patch Silver-FP-PK
05UD Artifacts Frozen Artifacts Pewter-FA-PK
05UD Artifacts Frozen Artifacts Silver-FA-PK
05UD Powerplay Specialists-TSPK
05UD Powerplay Specialists Patches-SPPK
05Ultimate Collection-53
Gold-53
Jerseys-JPK
Jerseys Dual-DJKV
Premium Patches-PPPK
Ultimate Patches-PPK
Ultimate Patches Dual-DPKV
05Ultra-111
Gold-111
Ice-111
Scoring Kings-SK35
Scoring Kings Jerseys-SKJ-PK
Scoring Kings Patches-SKP-PK
05Upper Deck-355
05Upper Deck All-Time Greatest-2
05Upper Deck All-Time Greatest-69
05Upper Deck Big Playmakers-B-PK
05Upper Deck Hometown Heroes-HH20
05Upper Deck Jerseys-J-PK
05Upper Deck Jerseys Series II-J2PK
05Upper Deck Majestic Materials-MMPK
05Upper Deck Patches-P-PK
05Upper Deck Scrapbooks-HS8
05Upper Deck Shooting Stars-S-PK
05Upper Deck Hockey Showcase-HS11
05Upper Deck Showcase Promos-HS11
05Upper Deck Ice-54
Rainbow-54
Frozen Fabrics-FFPK
Frozen Fabrics Glass-FFPK
Frozen Fabrics Patches-FFPPK
05Upper Deck MVP-221
Gold-221
Platinum-221
Materials Triples-T-SKF
05Upper Deck Rookie Update-54
05Upper Deck Trilogy-49
05Upper Deck Trilogy-104
Crystal-104
Honorary Patches-HP-PK
Honorary Patch Scripts-HSP-PK
Honorary Swatches-HS-PK
Honorary Swatch Scripts-HSS-PK
05Upper Deck Victory-51
05Upper Deck Victory-226
Black-51
Black-226
Gold-51
Gold-226
Silver-51
Silver-226
Blow-Ups-BU10
Game Breakers-GB12
06Be A Player Portraits-60
Dual Signature Portraits-DSKV
Quadruple Signature Portraits-QKIHN
Signature Portraits-SPPK
06Beehive-44
06Beehive-187
Blue-44
Gold-44
Matte-44
Red Facsimile Signatures-44
Wood-44
5 X 7 Black and White-44
5 X 7 Dark Wood-44

Matted Materials-MMPK
06Black Diamond-140
Black-140
Gold-140
Ruby-140
Jerseys-JPK
Jerseys Black-JPK
Jerseys Gold-JPK
Jerseys Ruby-JPK
06Flair Showcase-57
06Flair Showcase-138
06Flair Showcase-242
06Flair Showcase-286
Parallel-57
Parallel-138
Parallel-242
Parallel-286
06Fleer-109
Tiffany-109
Speed Machines-SM16
Total 0-013
06Hot Prospects-55
Red Hot-55
White Hot-55
06McDonald's Upper Deck-26
Jerseys-JPK
Patches-PPK
06NHL POG-26
06O-Pee-Chee-290
06O-Pee-Chee-657
06O-Pee-Chee-688
Rainbow-290
Rainbow-657
Rainbow-688
Swatches-S-PK
06Panini Stickers-304
06SP Authentic-46
06SP Authentic-145
Limited-46
Limited-145
06SP Game Used-57
Gold-57
Rainbow-57
Authentic Fabrics-AFPK
Authentic Fabrics Parallel-AFPK
Authentic Fabrics Patches-AFPK
Authentic Fabrics Dual-AF2KV
Authentic Fabrics Dual Patches-AF2KV
Authentic Fabrics Triple-AF3NAS
Authentic Fabrics Triple Patches-AF3NAS
Authentic Fabrics Quads-AF4SKGN
Authentic Fabrics Quads Patches-AF4SKGN
Authentic Fabrics Sixes-AF6BYN
Authentic Fabrics Sixes Patches-AF6BYN
Authentic Fabrics Eights-AF8CAN
Authentic Fabrics Eights Patches-AF8CAN
By The Letter-BLPK
06SPx-56
06SPx-114
Spectrum-56
Spectrum-114
SPxcitement-X58
SPxcitement Spectrum-X58
Winning Materials-WMPK
Winning Materials Spectrum-WMPK
06The Cup-50
Black Rainbow-50
Foundations-CQPK
Foundations Patches-CQPK
Gold-50
Gold Patches-50
Jerseys-50
Masterpiece Pressplates-50
NHL Shields Duals-DSHKR
NHL Shields Duals-DSHKS
NHL Shields Duals-DSHSK
NHL Shields Duals-DSHVK
06UD Artifacts-45
06UD Artifacts-177
Blue-45
Blue-177
Gold-45
Gold-177
Platinum-45
Platinum-177
Radiance-45
Radiance-177
Red-45
Red-177
Treasured Patches Black-TSPK
Treasured Patches Blue-TSPK
Treasured Patches Gold-TSPK
Treasured Patches Platinum-TSPK
Treasured Patches Red-TSPK
Treasured Swatches-TSPK
Treasured Swatches Black-TSPK
Treasured Swatches Blue-TSPK
Treasured Swatches Gold-TSPK
Treasured Swatches Platinum-TSPK
Treasured Swatches Red-TSPK
Tundra Tandems-TTKA
Tundra Tandems Black-TTKA
Tundra Tandems Blue-TTKA
Tundra Tandems Gold-TTKA
Tundra Tandems Platinum-TTKA
Tundra Tandems Red-TTKA
Tundra Tandems Dual Patches Red-TTKA
06UD Mini Jersey Collection-58
06UD Powerplay-57
Impact Rainbow-57
Specialists-SPK
Specialists Patches-PPK
06Ultimate Collection-36
Jerseys-UJ-PK
Jerseys Dual-UJ2-KA
Patches-UJ-PK
Patches Dual-UJ2-KA
06Ultra-112
Gold Medallion-112
Ice Medallion-112
Action-UA15
Scoring Kings-SK23
06Upper Deck Arena Giveaways-NSH4
06Upper Deck-359
Exclusives Parallel-359
High Gloss Parallel-359
All World-AW18
Game Jerseys-J2PK
Game Patches-P2PK
Masterpieces-359
Oversized Wal-Mart Exclusives-359
Shootout Artists-SA5
06Upper Deck MVP-162
Gold Script-162
Super Script-162
Jerseys-OJKW
Jerseys-OJKZ
06Upper Deck Ovation-176
06Upper Deck Sweet Shot-60
Sweet Stitches-SSPK
Sweet Stitches Duals-SSPK
Sweet Stitches Triples-SSPK
06Upper Deck Trilogy-56
06Upper Deck Victory-109
06Upper Deck Victory Black-109
06Upper Deck Victory Gold-109
06Upper Deck Victory GameBreakers-GB26
06Upper Deck Victory Oversize Cards-PK
07Upper Deck Ovation-74
07Upper Deck Victory-106
Black-106
Gold-106
GameBreakers-GB15
Oversize Cards-OS28

Kariya, Steve
99BAP Memorabilia-211
Gold-211
Silver-211
99BAP Millennium-241
Emerald-241
Ruby-241
Sapphire-241
Signatures-241
Signatures Gold-241
Calder Candidates Ruby-C15
Calder Candidates Emerald-C15
Calder Candidates Sapphire-C15
99Black Diamond-85
Diamond Cut-85
Final Cut-85
Diamonation-D16
99Crown Royale-136
Limited Series-136
Premiere Date-136
Prospects Parallel-136
Card-Supials-20
Card-Supials Minis-20
Ice Elite-25
Ice Elite Parallel-25
99O-Pee-Chee Chrome-290
99O-Pee-Chee Chrome Refractors-290
99Pacific Dynagon Ice-1
Blue-1
Copper-1
Gold-1
Premiere Date-1
Checkmates American-1
Checkmates American-16
Checkmates Canadian-1
99Pacific Omega-233
Copper-233
Gold-233
Ice Blue-233
Premiere Date-233
NHL Generations-1
5 Star Talents-6
5 Star Talents Parallel-6
99Pacific Prism-140
Holographic Blue-140
Holographic Gold-140
Holographic Mirror-140
Holographic Purple-140
Premiere Date-140
Ice Prospects-9
99Panini Stickers-313
99Panini Stickers-356
99Paramount-269
99SP Authentic-119
Special Forces-SF10
Tomorrow's Headliners-TH10
99SPx-154
Radiance-154
SPXcitement-X11
99Stadium Club-197
First Day Issue-197
One of a Kind-197
Printing Plates Black-197
Printing Plates Cyan-197
Printing Plates Magenta-197
Printing Plates Yellow-197
Chrome-47
Chrome Refractors-47
Chrome Oversized-19
Chrome Oversized Refractors-19
99Topps Arena Giveaways-VAN-SK
99Topps/OPC Chrome-290
Refractors-290
99Topps Gold Label Class 1-100
Black-100
Black One of One-100
One of One-100
Red-100
Red One of One-100
99Topps Gold Label Class 2-100
99Topps Gold Label Class 2 Black-100
99Topps Gold Label Class 2 Black 1 of 1-100
99Topps Gold Label Class 2 One of One-100
99Topps Gold Label Class 2 Red-100
99Topps Gold Label Class 2 Red One of One-100
99Topps Gold Label Class 3-100
99Topps Gold Label Class 3 Black-100
99Topps Gold Label Class 3 Black 1 of 1-100
99Topps Gold Label Class 3 One of One-100
99Topps Gold Label Class 3 Red-100
99Topps Gold Label Class 3 Red One of One-100
99Topps Gold Label Fresh Gold-FG18
99Topps Gold Label Fresh Gold Black-FG18
99Topps Gold Label Fresh Gold Black 1of1-FG18
99Topps Gold Label Fresh Gold One of One-FG18
99Topps Gold Label Fresh Gold Red-FG18
99Topps Gold Label Fresh Gold Red 1 of 1-FG18
99Topps Premier Plus-118
Parallel-118
Premier Rookies-PR8
Premier Rookies Parallel-PR8
The Next Ones-TNO5
99Ultimate Victory-104
1/1-104
Parallel-104
Parallel 100-104
Frozen Fury-FF4
Smokin Guns-SG4
99Upper Deck-297
Exclusives-297
Exclusives 1 of 1-297
All-Star Class-AS13
All-Star Class Quantum Gold-AS13
All-Star Class Quantum Silver-AS13
Ice Gallery-IG9
Ice Gallery Quantum Gold-IG9
Ice Gallery Quantum Silver-IG9
NHL Scrapbook-SB14
NHL Scrapbook Quantum Gold-SB14
NHL Scrapbook Quantum Silver-SB14
Sixth Sense-SS11
Sixth Sense Quantum Gold-SS11
Sixth Sense Quantum Silver-SS11
99Upper Deck Arena Giveaways-VC1
99Upper Deck Gold Reserve-297
99Upper Deck HoloGrFx-58
Ausome-58
99Upper Deck MVP SC Edition-181
Gold Script-181
Silver Script-181
Super Script-181
Cup Contenders-CC10
99Upper Deck Ovation-57
99Upper Deck Ovation-82
Standing Ovation-57
Standing Ovation-82
A Piece Of History-SK
Lead Performers-LP10
99Upper Deck Victory-363
99Wayne Gretzky Hockey-171
00Aurora-143
Premiere Date-143
00BAP Memorabilia-86
Emerald-86
Ruby-86
Sapphire-86
Promos-86
00BAP Mem Chicago Sportsfest Copper-86
00BAP Memorabilia Chicago Sportsfest Blue-86
00BAP Memorabilia Chicago Sportsfest Gold-86
00BAP Memorabilia Chicago Sportsfest Ruby-86
00BAP Memorabilia Chicago Sun-Times Ruby-86
00BAP Memorabilia Chicago Sun-Times Gold-86
00BAP Mem Chicago Sun-Times Sapphire-86
00BAP Mem Toronto Fall Expo Copper-86
00BAP Memorabilia Toronto Fall Expo Gold-86
00BAP Memorabilia Toronto Fall Expo Ruby-86
00BAP Parkhurst 2000-P53
00BAP Signature Series-131
Emerald-131
Ruby-131
Sapphire-131
Autographs-58
Autographs Gold-58
00Pacific-409
Copper-409
Gold-409
Ice Blue-409
Premiere Date-409
00Paramount-239
Copper-239
Gold-239
Holo-Gold-239
Holo-Silver-239
Ice Blue-239
Premiere Date-239
00Private Stock-95
Gold-95
Premiere Date-95
Retail-95
Silver-95
PS-2001 Action-57
PS-2001 New Wave-25
00Revolution-143
Blue-143
Premiere Date-143
Red-143
00Upper Deck Victory-242
01BAP Ultimate Memorabilia Bloodlines-8
01Manitoba Moose-12
02BAP Sig Series Auto Buybacks 1999-241
02BAP Sig Series Auto Buybacks 2000-58
02Pacific Complete-81
Red-81
02Manitoba Moose-6
03Albany River Rats-17
03Albany River Rats Kinko's-16
04Finnish Cardset-56
Parallel-42
04Swedish Pure Skills-114
Parallel-114
05Finnish Cardset -184
Finnish Cardset Magicmakers-7
06Swedish SHL Elitset-181

Karjala, Pekka
78Finnish SM-Liiga-135

Karjalainen, Kyosti
87Swedish Panini Stickers-57
89Swedish Semic Elitserien Stickers-40
90ProCards AHL/IHL-350
91Parkhurst-295
French-295
91Upper Deck-606
French-606
91ProCards-398
92Upper Deck-111
Euro-Stars-E6
92Swedish Semic Elitserien Stickers-193
93Swedish Semic Elitserien-159
94Swedish Leaf-261
95Swedish Leaf-105
95Swedish Upper Deck-163
97Swedish Collector's Choice-173
97Swedish Collector's Choice-219
98German DEL-277
99German DEL-154
00Swedish Upper Deck-52

Karjalainen, Petri
78Finnish SM-Liiga-176
80Finnish Mallasjuoma-169

Karjalainen, Sami
95Finnish SISU-238
99Finnish Cardset-48
00Finnish Cardset-37
01Finnish Cardset-150

Karjalainen, Tuomo
01Finnish Cardset-135
03Finnish Cardset-156
04Finnish Cardset-168
Parallel-124
05Finnish Cardset -152
Finnish Cardset Super Snatchers-16

Karjalainen, Vesa
92Finnish Jyvas-Hyva Stickers-90
94Finnish SISU-291
95Finnish SISU-145
95Finnish SISU Limited-96
00Czech DS Extraliga-47
00Czech OFS-150

Karkkainen, Pentti
66Finnish Jaakiekkosarja-133

Karl, Steffen
93Quebec Pee-Wee Tournament-1772

Karlander, Al
70Esso Power Players-139
70Sargent Promotions Stamps-58
71Toronto Sun-97
73Red Wings Team Issue-13
76O-Pee-Chee WHA-104

Karlander, Kevin
00Louisiana Ice Gators-9

Karlander, Kory
91Air Canada SJHL-D4
91Air Canada SJHL All-Stars-15
91Air Canada SJHL All-Stars-47
92Northern Michigan Wildcats-15
93Northern Michigan Wildcats-17
98Detroit Vipers-10
98Peoria Rivermen-16
00UK Sekonda Superleague-175
01UK Belfast Giants-27
03Grand Rapids Griffins-26
05Kalamazoo Wings-18

Karlberg, Mikael
91Swedish Semic Elitserien Stickers-274
92Swedish Semic Elitserien Stickers-293
93Swedish Semic Elitserien-21
95Swedish Leaf-237
95Swedish Upper Deck-104
98Swedish UD Choice-132
99Swedish Upper Deck-118
00Swedish Upper Deck-118
02Swedish SHL-197
Parallel-197

Karlen, Rainer
99Swiss Panini Stickers-357
01Swiss HNL-342
02Swiss HNL-155

Karlin, Mattias
98UD Choice-290
Prime Choice Reserve-290
Reserve-290
98Swedish UD Choice-215
99Swedish Upper Deck-184
00Providence Bruins-18
01Providence Bruins-18

Karlsson, Anders
84Swedish Semic Elitserien-133

Karlsson, Andreas
93Swedish Semic Elitserien-141
94Swedish Leaf-226
Rookie Rockets-9
95Swedish Leaf-67
95Swedish Upper Deck-110
97Swedish Collector's Choice-105
98Swedish UD Choice-124
99BAP Memorabilia-308
Gold-308
Silver-308
99Crown Royale-7
Limited Series-7
Premiere Date-7
Prospects Parallel-7
99Upper Deck Gold Reserve-337
00BAP Memorabilia-447
Emerald-447
Ruby-447
Sapphire-447
00Panini Stickers-7
00Upper Deck-215
Exclusives Tier 1-215
Exclusives Tier 2-215
00Upper Deck MVP-185
First Stars-185
Second Stars-185
Third Stars-185
00Upper Deck Victory-273
02Chicago Wolves-13
04Swedish Elitset-198
Gold-198
04Swedish Pure Skills-38
Parallel-38
05Swedish SHL Elitset-58
Gold-58
06Lightning Postcards-10
06Swedish SHL Elitset-62
Playmakers-7

Karlsson, Arne
73Swedish Stickers-3

Karlsson, Bengt Ake
71Swedish Hockey-336
72Swedish Stickers-105
72Swedish Stickers-223
74Swedish Stickers-232

Karlsson, Bengt-Goran
64Swedish Coralli ISHockey-95
67Swedish Hockey-158
69Swedish Hockey-317
70Swedish Hockey-223
72Finnish Semic World Championship-65
72Swedish Stickers-250
72Swedish Semic World Championship-65
74Swedish Stickers-231

Karlsson, Berny
57Swedish Alfabilder-139
65Swedish Coralli ISHockey-95
67Swedish Hockey-290
69Swedish Hockey-170
70Swedish Hockey-191
72Swedish Stickers-251

Karlsson, Bert-Olav
90Swedish Semic Elitserien Stickers-68
98Swedish UD Choice-146

Karlsson, Bertil
57Swedish Alfabilder-141
64Swedish Coralli ISHockey-5
64Swedish Coralli ISHockey-113
65Swedish Coralli ISHockey-5
65Swedish Coralli ISHockey-113
67Swedish Hockey-173
69Swedish Hockey-63
69Swedish Hockey-80
71Swedish Hockey-277

Karlsson, Christer
71Swedish Hockey-226

Karlsson, FWD
84Swedish Semic Elitserien-189

Karlsson, Gabriel
99Swedish Upper Deck-98
00Finnish Cardset-227
02Swedish SHL-256
Parallel-256
03Swedish Elite-118
Silver-118
04Swedish Elitset-118
Gold-118
05Swedish SHL Elitset-129
Gold-129

Karlsson, Hans
64Swedish Coralli ISHockey-73

Karlsson, Ingvar
87Swedish Panini Stickers-67

Karlsson, Jacob
89Swedish Semic Elitserien Stickers-84
90Swedish Semic Elitserien Stickers-257
91Swedish Semic Elitserien Stickers-88
92Upper Deck-229
92Swedish Semic Elitserien Stickers-108
93Swedish Semic Elitserien-81
95Swedish Leaf-291
97Swedish Collector's Choice-185
98Swedish UD Choice-184
99German DEL-237

Karlsson, Jakob
89Swedish Semic Elitserien Stickers-84
90Swedish Semic Elitserien Stickers-257
91Swedish Semic Elitserien Stickers-88
92Upper Deck-229
92Swedish Semic Elitserien Stickers-108
93Swedish Semic Elitserien-81
95Swedish Leaf-291
97Swedish Collector's Choice-185
98Swedish UD Choice-184
99German DEL-237
02German DEL City Press-116
04Swedish Elitset-205
Gold-205

Karlsson, Jan
72Swedish Stickers-268
83Swedish Semic Elitserien-155
85Swedish Panini Stickers-206
89Swedish Semic Elitserien Stickers-248
89Swedish Semic Elitserien Stickers-266
90Swedish Semic Elitserien Stickers-155
91Swedish Semic Elitserien Stickers-260

Karlsson, Jan-Ake
71Swedish Hockey-325
71Swedish Hockey-398
72Swedish Stickers-141

Karlsson, Jens
02Swedish SHL-116
Next Generation-NG9
Parallel-116
03Swedish Elite-33
Silver-33
04Swedish Elitset-34
Gold-34
05Swedish SHL Elitset-200
Gold-200
06German DEL-110

Karlsson, Lars
83Swedish Semic Elitserien-128
84Swedish Semic Elitserien-31
84Swedish Semic Elitserien-118
85Swedish Panini Stickers-29
86Swedish Panini Stickers-6
87Swedish Panini Stickers-29
89Swedish Semic Elitserien Stickers-94
90Swedish Semic Elitserien Stickers-265
91Swedish Semic Elitserien Stickers-30
91Swedish Semic Elitserien Stickers-93
92Swedish Semic Elitserien Stickers-52
92Swedish Semic Elitserien Stickers-121
93Swedish Semic Elitserien-27
93Swedish Semic Elitserien-94
94Swedish Leaf-231
95Swedish Leaf-168

Karlsson, Marcus
91Swedish Semic Elitserien Stickers-326
95German DEL-75
95Swedish Leaf-277
Rookies-8
95Swedish Upper Deck-158
97Swedish Collector's Choice-155
00Swedish Upper Deck-169
00Swedish Upper Deck-220

Karlsson, Martin
72Swedish Stickers-207
73Swedish Stickers-26
74Swedish Stickers-233
96German DEL-269

Karlsson, Mattias
04Swedish Elitset-148
Gold-148

Karlsson, Nils-Erik
69Swedish Hockey-171

Karlsson, Ove
83Swedish Semic Elitserien-235

Karlsson, Pentti
72Finnish Jaakiekko-83
73Finnish Jaakiekko-130
78Finnish SM-Liiga-134

Karlsson, Per
73Swedish Stickers-41

Karlsson, Peter
92Swedish Semic Elitserien Stickers-282
93Swedish Semic Elitserien-247

Karlsson, Ragnar
99Swedish Upper Deck-128
03Swedish Elite-217
Silver-217
05Swedish Lulea Hockey Postcards-15
05Swedish SHL Elitset-236
Gold-236
06Swedish SHL Elitset-91

Karlsson, Rauno
70Finnish Jaakiekko-295

Karlsson, Reine
83Swedish Semic Elitserien-215
84Swedish Semic Elitserien-240
85Swedish Panini Stickers-238
86Swedish Panini Stickers-265
87Swedish Panini Stickers-249

Karlsson, Robert
98Swedish UD Choice-23

Karlsson, Roger
92Swedish Semic Elitserien Stickers-58

Karlsson, Rolf
67Swedish Hockey-204
71Swedish Hockey-326

Karlsson, Ronnie
92Swedish Semic Elitserien Stickers-28

Karlsson, Sebastian
05Swedish SHL Elitset-178
Gold-178
06Swedish SHL Elitset-156

Karlsson, Stefan
67Swedish Hockey-49
69Swedish Hockey-64
69Swedish Hockey-190
70Finnish Jaakiekko-29
70Swedish Hockey-28
70Swedish Hockey-284
70Swedish Masterserien-45
70Swedish Masterserien-118
71Finnish Suomi Stickers-48
71Swedish Hockey-16
71Swedish Hockey-105
72Finnish Jaakiekko-49
72Finnish Hellas-32
72Finnish Panda Toronto-70
72Finnish Semic World Championship-51
72Swedish Stickers-14
72Swedish Stickers-94
72Swedish Semic World Championship-51
73Finnish Jaakiekko-29
73Swedish Stickers-19
73Swedish Stickers-167
74Finnish Jenkki-27
74Finnish Typotor-97
74Swedish Stickers-234
74Swedish Semic World Champ Stickers-14
84Swedish Semic Elitserien-242

Karlsson, Torgny
86Swedish Panini Stickers-135

Karlsson, Torsten
67Swedish Hockey-174

Karlstad, Jon Magne
92Norwegian Elite Series-14
92Norwegian Elite Series-182
93Swedish Semic World Champ Stickers-235

Karlstrom, G.
98Danish Hockey League-46

Karlstrom, Per-Agne
57Swedish Alfabilder-90
64Swedish Coralli ISHockey-46

Karmanos, Jason
92Harvard Crimson-16
93Donruss Team USA-10
93Pinnacle-494
Canadian-494

Karny, Tomas
03Czech OFS Plus-317

Karouk, Kenneth
94German DEL-174

Karp, Herman
71Rochester Americans-9

Karpa, Dave
91Ferris State Bulldogs-17
92Nordiques Petro-Canada-16
92Parkhurst-151
Emerald Ice-151
92Upper Deck-517
92Ferris State Bulldogs-17
92Classic-68
Gold-68
93OPC Premier-408
Gold-408
93Parkhurst-165
Emerald Ice-165
93PowerPlay-421
93Score-611
Gold-611
Canadian-611
Canadian Gold-611
93Stadium Club-296
Members Only Master Set-296
First Day Issue-296
93Topps/OPC Premier-408
Gold-408
93Ultra-97
Prospects-3
93Upper Deck-375
94OPC Premier-202
Special Effects-202
94Parkhurst SE-SE145
Gold-SE145
94Topps/OPC Premier-202
Special Effects-202
94Upper Deck-41
Electric Ice-41
95Collector's Choice-192
Player's Club-192
Player's Club Platinum-192
95Ducks Team Issue-2
95Parkhurst International-273
Emerald Ice-273
95Upper Deck-119
Electric Ice-119
Electric Ice Gold-119
96Be A Player-41
Autographs-41
Autographs Silver-41
96Ducks Team Issue-17
97Pacific Dynagon Best Kept Secrets-3
97Score Mighty Ducks-19
Platinum-19
Premier-19
97Upper Deck-217
98Hurricanes Team Issue-19
98Pacific-57
Ice Blue-57
Red-57
99Cincinnati Cyclones-10
00Pacific-85
Copper-85
Gold-85
Ice Blue-85
Premiere Date-85
00Upper Deck NHLPA-PA16
01Pacific-76
Extreme LTD-76
Hobby LTD-76
Premiere Date-76
Retail LTD-76
01Pacific Arena Exclusives-76
02Rangers Team Issue-6
02Hartford Wolf Pack-11
03Russian Hockey League-274

Karpen, Mark
90Kansas City Blades-17
93Muskegon Fury-8
94Central Hockey League-115
98Wichita Thunder-11
99Wichita Thunder-10
00Knoxville Speed-22
00Wichita Thunder-13

Karpenko, Igor
96Las Vegas Thunder-10
00Russian Hockey League-112
00Russian Hockey League-113
01Russian Hockey League-67
02Russian Ultimate Line-7

Karpf, Andy
00Swiss Panini Stickers-306

Karpov, Sergei
04Russian World Junior Team-12

Karpov, Valeri
93Classic-90
94Ducks Carl's Jr.-11
94Fleer-4
94Leaf-486
Phenoms-10
94Leaf Limited-51
94OPC Premier-284
Special Effects-284
94Parkhurst SE-SE6
Gold-SE6
Vintage-6
94Pinnacle-486
Artist's Proofs-486
Rink Collection-486
Rookie Team Pinnacle-11
94Select-183
Gold-183
94Topps/OPC Premier-284
Special Effects-284
94Upper Deck-256
94Upper Deck-570
Electric Ice-256
Electric Ice-570
Predictor Canadian-C6
94Upper Deck Predictor Canadian Exch Gold-C6
94Upper Deck Predictor Cdn Exch Silver-C6
94Upper Deck SP Inserts-SP92
94Upper Deck SP Inserts Die Cuts-SP92
94Classic-43
Gold-43
ROY Sweepstakes-R11
Tri-Cards-T1
Pro Prospects Ice Ambassadors-IA20
94Signature Rookies Gold Standard *-87
Signatures-GS7
94Signature Rookies Tetrad *-107
Signatures-107
95Be A Player-205
Signatures-S205
Signatures Die Cuts-S205
95Collector's Choice-211
Player's Club-211
Player's Club Platinum-211
95Donruss-191
95Leaf-80
95Parkhurst International-277
Emerald Ice-277
95Score-170
Black Ice Artist's Proofs-170
Black Ice-170
95Topps-137
OPC Inserts-137
95Upper Deck-378
Electric Ice-378
Electric Ice Gold-378
Special Edition-SE93
Special Edition Gold-SE93
98Russian Hockey League-8
99Russian Hockey League-1
99Russian Metallurg Magnetogorsk-43
99Russian Stars of Hockey-9
00Russian Hockey League-159
01Russian Dynamo Moscow-10
02Russian Hockey League-153
02Russian SL-9
02Russian World Championships-15

Karpov, Vladimir
04Russian Moscow Dynamo-14

Karpovtsev, Alexander
91O-Pee-Chee Inserts-35R
92Upper Deck-351
92Russian Stars Red Ace-10
93Donruss-212
93OPC Premier-358
Gold-358
93Parkhurst-269
Emerald Ice-269
93Pinnacle-437
Canadian-437
93PowerPlay-391
93Score-591
Gold-591
Canadian-591
Canadian Gold-591
93Stadium Club-291
Members Only Master Set-291
First Day Issue-291
93Topps/OPC Premier-358
Gold-358
93Ultra-372
93Upper Deck-484
SP-100
93Swedish Semic World Champ Stickers-133
93Classic-89
94Donruss-327
94Leaf-118
94OPC Premier-255
94O-Pee-Chee Finest Inserts-4
94OPC Premier Special Effects-255
94Parkhurst SE-SE114
Gold-SE114
94Pinnacle-364
Artist's Proofs-364
Rink Collection-364
94Topps/OPC Premier-255
Special Effects-255
94Upper Deck-288
Electric Ice-288
94Finnish Jaa Kiekko-138
94Classic All-Rookie Team-AR6
94Classic Pro Prospects-19
95Canada Games NHL POGS-188
95Parkhurst International-142
Emerald Ice-142
95Upper Deck-288
Electric Ice-288
Electric Ice Gold-288
96Be A Player-118
Autographs-118
Autographs Silver-118
97Collector's Choice-169
97Pacific-223
Copper-223
Emerald Green-223
Ice Blue-223
Red-223
Silver-223
97Panini Stickers-90
97Score Rangers-8
Platinum-8
Premier-8
99BAP Memorabilia-109
Gold-109
Silver-109
99Maple Leafs Pizza Pizza-9
99Maple Leafs Pizza Pizza-15
99O-Pee-Chee Chrome Positive Performers-PP1
99OPC Chrome Pos Performers Ref-PP1
99O-Pee-Chee Positive Performers-PP1
99Pacific-409
Copper-409
Emerald Green-409
Gold-409
Ice Blue-409
Premiere Date-409
Red-409
99Panini Stickers-155
99Panini Stickers-329
99Stadium Club-79
First Day Issue-79
One of a Kind-79
Printing Plates Black-79
Printing Plates Cyan-79
Printing Plates Magenta-79
Printing Plates Yellow-79
99Topps/OPC Positive Performers-PP1
99Topps/OPC Chrome Positive Performers-PP1
99Topps/OPC Chrome Positive PerformersRef-PP1
99Upper Deck MVP SC Edition-180
Gold Script-180
Silver Script-180
Super Script-180
00BAP Memorabilia-213
00BAP Memorabilia-449
Emerald-213
Emerald-449
Ruby-213
Ruby-449
Sapphire-213
Sapphire-449
Promos-213
00BAP Mem Chicago Sportsfest Copper-213
00BAP Memorabilia Chicago Sportsfest Blue-213
00BAP Memorabilia Chicago Sportsfest Gold-213
00BAP Memorabilia Chicago Sportsfest Ruby-213
00BAP Memorabilia Chicago Sun-Times Ruby-213
00BAP Memorabilia Chicago Sun-Times Gold-213
00BAP Mem Chicago Sun-Times Sapphire-213
00BAP Mem Toronto Fall Expo Copper-213
00BAP Memorabilia Toronto Fall Expo Gold-213
00BAP Memorabilia Toronto Fall Expo Ruby-213
00Pacific-394
Copper-394
Gold-394
Ice Blue-394
Premiere Date-394
00Russian Dynamo Moscow-30
00Russian Hockey League-321
02Upper Deck-283
Exclusives-283
02Upper Deck Beckett UD Promos-283
03Blackhawks Postcards-8
03ITG Action-143
03Pacific Complete-253
Red-253
03Parkhurst Original Six Chicago-13
03Upper Deck-287
Canadian Exclusives-287
HG-287
UD Exclusives-287
03Upper Deck MVP-97
Gold Script-97
Silver Script-97
Canadian Exclusives-97
04Russian Back to Russia-23

Karppinen, Veikko
06Finnish Cardset-277

Karpuk, Ken
95German DEL-222
98Amarillo Rattlers-19

Karrbrandt, Thomas
83Swedish Semic Elitserien-230

Karrenbauer, Bernd
70Finnish Jaakiekko-88
70Swedish Hockey-369
70Swedish Masterserien-176
74Finnish Jenkki-105
04German Berlin Eisbarens 50th Anniv-36

Karrer, Guillaume
00Chicoutimi Sagueneens-20
Signed-20

Kars, Marcel
97Barrie Colts-11

Karsums, Martins
03Moncton Wildcats-7
04Moncton Wildcats-19
05Moncton Wildcats-13
06Providence Bruins-8

Kartio, Dave
74Sioux City Musketeers-7

Kartsalo, Vesa
66Finnish Jaakiekkosarja-208

Kartsev, Denis
98Russian Hockey League-153
99Russian Dynamo Moscow-18
00Russian Dynamo Moscow-27
03Russian Hockey League-56
04Russian Moscow Dynamo-15

Karttunen, Johannes
65Finnish Hellas-66
66Finnish Jaakiekkosarja-28

Karvonen, Jorma
72Finnish Jaakiekko-286

Karvonen, Pekka
72Finnish Jaakiekko-287

Kasatonov, Alexei
82Swedish Semic VM Stickers-57
83Swedish Semic VM Stickers-57
84Russian National Team-8
87Russian National Team-8
89Russian National Team-10
89Swedish Semic World Champ Stickers-81
90Devils Team Issue-13
90O-Pee-Chee-358
90Panini Stickers-335
90Pro Set-169
90Score-209
Canadian-209
90Topps-358
Tiffany-358
90Upper Deck-286
French-286
91Pro Set Platinum-198
91Bowman-276
91O-Pee-Chee-439
91Panini Stickers-216
91Parkhurst-319
French-319
91Pinnacle-255
French-255
91Score American-194
91Score Canadian Bilingual-194
91Score Canadian English-194
91Stadium Club-282
91Topps-439
91Upper Deck-185
French-185
91Finnish Semic World Champ Stickers-214
91Russian Stars Red Ace-7
91Russian Sports Unite Hearts-4
91Russian Stars in NHL-4
91Swedish Semic World Champ Stickers-214
92Bowman-323
92O-Pee-Chee-353
92Panini Stickers-180
92Panini Stickers French-180
92Pinnacle-289
French-289
92Pro Set-101
92Score-394
Canadian-394
92Stadium Club-406
92Topps-152
Gold-152G
92Ultra-340
92Upper Deck-96
92Finnish Semic-101
93Donruss-5
93Leaf-381
93OPC Premier-492
Gold-492
93Parkhurst-276
Emerald Ice-276
93Pinnacle-359
Canadian-359
93PowerPlay-5
93Score-61
93Score-528
Gold-528
Canadian-61
Canadian-528
Canadian Gold-528
93Stadium Club-332
Members Only Master Set-332
First Day Issue-332
93Topps/OPC Premier-492
Gold-492
93Ultra-257
93Upper Deck-474
94Canada Games NHL POGS-37
94EA Sports-1
94Leaf-473
94OPC Premier-159
Special Effects-159
94Parkhurst-195
Gold-195
94Parkhurst SE-SE9
Gold-SE9
94Pinnacle-398
Artist's Proofs-398
Rink Collection-398

94Score-183
Gold-183
Platinum-183
94Stadium Club Members Only-9
94Topps/OPC Premier-159
Special Effects-159
94Ultra-257
94Upper Deck-208
Electric Ice-208
94Finnish Jaa Kiekko-143
95Canada Games NHL POGS-37
95Collector's Choice-115
Player's Club-115
Player's Club Platinum-115
95Parkhurst International-15
Emerald Ice-15
95Playoff One on One-6
95Upper Deck-69
Electric Ice Gold-69
95Swedish Globe World Championships-237
99Russian Stars of Hockey-35
06ITG International Ice-156
Gold-156
Autographs-AAK

Kaser, Roland
99Swiss Panini Stickers-42
99Swiss Panini Stickers-294
00Swiss Panini Stickers-44
01Swiss HNL-228
02Swiss HNL-441

Kashuba, Keith
93Quebec Pee-Wee Tournament-794

Kasik, Jan
99Czech Score Blue 2000-100
99Czech Score Red Ice 2000-100

Kasik, Jaroslav
04Czech OFS-322

Kasik, Martin
01Cape Breton Screaming Eagles-8
03Victoriaville Tigers-14

Kasik, Petr
95Czech APS Extraliga-81
96Czech APS Extraliga-76
97Czech DS Stickers-138
03Czech OFS Plus-234
04Czech OFS-327

Kasjajev, Alexander
74Swedish Stickers-51

Kasjyanchuk, Konstantin
03Russian Hockey League-72

Kaski, Jari
73Finnish Jaakiekko-246

Kaski, Matti
65Finnish Hellas-145

Kaski, Olli
92Finnish Jyvas-Hyva Stickers-196
93Finnish Jyvas-Hyva Stickers-345
93Finnish SISU-212
94Finnish SISU-365
94Swedish Leaf-171
Foreign Affairs-8
95Finnish SISU-353
Double Trouble-3
95Finnish SISU Limited-20
95Finnish Semic World Championships-32
96German DEL-154
98German DEL-85
99Finnish Cardset-339

Kaski, Pekka
78Finnish SM-Liiga-79

Kaskinen, Aki
99Finnish Cardset-299

Kasowski, Peter
92Dayton Bombers-13
94Los Angeles Blades RHI-9
97UK Guildford Flames-10
99UK Guildford Flames-18

Kaspar, Lukas
03Czech OFS Plus-95
04Ottawa 67's-1
05Cleveland Barons-13
05Extreme Top Prospects Signature Edition-S19

Kasparaitis, Darius
91Upper Deck-650
French-650
91Upper Deck Czech World Juniors-11
92OPC Premier-103
92Parkhurst-102
92Parkhurst-215
Emerald Ice-102
Emerald Ice-215
92Pinnacle-407
French-407
92Ultra-344
92Upper Deck-335
92Upper Deck-554
92Upper Deck-563
92Upper Deck-623
Calder Candidates-CC13
Euro-Rookies-ER7
92Russian Stars Red Ace-11
92Russian Stars Red Ace-1
92Classic-4
Gold-4
LPs-LP4
92Classic Four-Sport *-154
Gold-154
93Donruss-203
93Leaf-101
Gold Rookies-13
93OPC Premier-112
93OPC Premier-443
Gold-112
Gold-443
93Parkhurst-122
Emerald Ice-122
93Pinnacle-84
Canadian-84
93PowerPlay-149
Second Year Stars-3
93Score-124
Canadian-124
International Stars-17
International Stars Canadian-17
93Stadium Club-101
Members Only Master Set-101
OPC-101
First Day Issue-101
First Day Issue OPC-101
93Topps/OPC Premier-112
93Topps/OPC Premier-443
Gold-112
Gold-443
93Ultra-160
93Upper Deck-173
SP-91
93Swedish Semic World Champ Stickers-146
94Be A Player-R148
Signature Cards-142
94Canada Games NHL POGS-161
94Donruss-252
94EA Sports-80
94Fleer-122
94Leaf-27
94OPC Premier-211
Special Effects-211
94Panini Stickers-52
94Parkhurst-133
Gold-133
SE Vintage-27
94Pinnacle-26
Artist's Proofs-26
Rink Collection-26
94Score Samples-C13
94Score-11
Gold-11
Platinum-11
Check It-CI3
94Stadium Club Super Teams-14
94Stadium Club Super Team MemberOnly Set-14
94Topps/OPC Premier-211
Special Effects-211
94Ultra-129
94Upper Deck-298
Electric Ice-298
SP Inserts-SP46
SP Inserts Die Cuts-SP46
95Collector's Choice-2
Player's Club-2
Player's Club Platinum-2
95Leaf-235
95Panini Stickers-96
95Parkhurst International-402
Emerald Ice-402
95Score-40
Black Ice Artist's Proofs-40
Black Ice-40
95Upper Deck-447
Electric Ice-447
Electric Ice Gold-447
96Black Diamond-61
Gold-61
96Collector's Choice-162
96SP-129
96Team Out-59
96Upper Deck-293
97Be A Player-159
Autographs-159
Autographs Die-Cuts-159
Autographs Prismatic Die-Cuts-159
97Collector's Choice-211
97Pacific-61
Copper-61
Emerald Green-61
Ice Blue-61
Red-61
Silver-61
97Panini Stickers-46
97Paramount-151
Copper-151
Dark Grey-151
Emerald Green-151
Ice Blue-151
Red-151
Silver-151
97Penguins USPS Lineup Cards-NNO
97Score-162
97Score Penguins-10
Platinum-10
Premier-10
97Upper Deck-136
97Upper Deck-391
98Aurora-155
98Be A Player-113
Press Release-113
98BAP Gold-113
98BAP Autographs-113
98BAP Autographs Gold-113
98BAP Tampa Bay All Star Game-113
98Finest-25
No Protectors-25
No Protectors Refractors-25
Refractors-25
98Katch-120
98Pacific-354
Ice Blue-354
Red-354
98Panini Stickers-50
98Paramount-193
Copper-193
Emerald Green-193
Holo-Electric-193
Ice Blue-193
Silver-193
98Upper Deck-160
Exclusives-160
Exclusives 1 of 1-160
Game Jerseys-GJ22
Gold Reserve-160
99BAP Memorabilia-127
Gold-127
Silver-127
99O-Pee-Chee-98
99O-Pee-Chee Chrome-98
99O-Pee-Chee Chrome Refractors-98
99Pacific-339
Copper-339
Emerald Green-339
Gold-339
Ice Blue-339
Premiere Date-339
Red-339
99Panini Stickers-135
99Topps/OPC-98
99Topps/OPC Chrome-98
Refractors-98
99Upper Deck MVP SC Edition-152
Gold Script-152
Silver Script-152
Super Script-152
99Russian Fetisov Tribute-29
00BAP Memorabilia-334
Emerald-334
Ruby-334
Sapphire-334
Promos-334
00BAP Mem Chicago Sportsfest Copper-334
00BAP Memorabilia Chicago Sportsfest Blue-334
00BAP Memorabilia Chicago Sportsfest Gold-334
00BAP Memorabilia Chicago Sportsfest Ruby-334
00BAP Memorabilia Chicago Sun-Times Ruby-334
00BAP Memorabilia Chicago Sun-Times Gold-334
00BAP Mem Chicago Sun-Times Sapphire-334
00BAP Mem Toronto Fall Expo Copper-334
00BAP Memorabilia Toronto Fall Expo Gold-334
00BAP Memorabilia Toronto Fall Expo Ruby-334
00BAP Signature Series-61
Emerald-61
Ruby-61
Sapphire-61
Autographs-112
Autographs Gold-112
00O-Pee-Chee-104
00O-Pee-Chee Parallel-104
00Pacific-329
Copper-329
Gold-329
Ice Blue-329
Premiere Date-329
00Panini Stickers-86
00Titanium Game Gear-134
00Titanium Game Gear Patches-134
00Titanium Draft Day Edition-83
Patches-83
00Topps/OPC-104
Parallel-104
00Upper Deck-372
Exclusives Tier 1-372
Exclusives Tier 2-372
00Upper Deck Vintage-295
01BAP Memorabilia-460
Emerald-460
Ruby-460
Sapphire-460
01BAP Sig Series Department of Defense-DD-11
01BAP Sig Series International Medals-IB-3
01O-Pee-Chee-221
01O-Pee-Chee Premier Parallel-221
01Pacific-313
Extreme LTD-313
Hobby LTD-313
Premiere Date-313
Retail LTD-313
01Pacific Arena Exclusives-313
01Pacific Heads-Up Quad Jerseys-17
01Pacific Heads-Up Quad Jerseys-29
01Parkhurst-373
Waving the Flag-32
01SPx-168
01Topps-221
OPC Parallel-221
01Upper Deck-371
Exclusives-371
01Upper Deck Victory-288
Gold-288
01Vanguard Memorabilia-25
01Vanguard Patches-25
01Czech Stadion-234
02BAP First Edition-245
02BAP First Edition-381
02BAP Memorabilia-267
Emerald-267
Ruby-267
Sapphire-267
NHL All-Star Game-267
NHL All-Star Game Blue-267
NHL All-Star Game Green-267
NHL All-Star Game Red-267
02BAP Memorabilia Toronto Fall Expo-267
02BAP Sig Series Auto Buybacks 1998-113
02BAP Sig Series Auto Buybacks 2000-112
02BAP Signature Series Defensive Wall-DW4
02BAP Signature Series Golf-GS26
02ITG Used International Experience-IE23
02ITG Used International Experience Gold-IE23
02Pacific-92
Blue-92
Red-92
02Pacific Complete-390
Red-390
02Parkhurst-105
Bronze-105
Gold-105
Silver-105
02Parkhurst Retro-192
Minis-192
02Rangers Team Issue-7
02Stadium Club-109
Silver Decoy Cards-109
Proofs-109
02Topps Heritage-161
02Topps Total-169
02Upper Deck-361
Exclusives-361
02Upper Deck Beckett UD Promos-361
02Russian Olympic Team-9
03ITG Action-341
Jerseys-M40
03NHL Sticker Collection-89
03O-Pee-Chee-279
03OPC Blue-279
03OPC Gold-279
03OPC Red-279
03Parkhurst Original Six New York-15
Memorabilia-NM9
03Rangers Team Issue-8
03Topps-279
Blue-279
Gold-279
Red-279
04Russian Back to Russia-28
05Panini Stickers-106
05Parkhurst-330
Facsimile Auto Parallel-330
05Upper Deck-127
HG Glossy-127
05Upper Deck MVP-257
Gold-257
Platinum-257
05Upper Deck Toronto Fall Expo-127
06O-Pee-Chee-330
Rainbow-330
06Panini Stickers-108
06Upper Deck-133
Exclusives Parallel-133
High Gloss Parallel-133
Masterpieces-133
06Russian Sport Collection Olympic Stars-6
06Russian Torino Olympic Team-21
06Hartford Wolf Pack-10

Kasparek, Milan
97Czech APS Extraliga-218

Kasparik, Pavel
99Czech OFS-106
00Czech DS Extraliga-132
00Czech OFS-177
01Czech OFS-10
02Czech OFS Plus-7
03Czech OFS Plus-114
04Czech HC Sparta Praha Postcards-8
04Czech OFS-188
06Czech OFS-226

Kasper, Kris
04Peoria Rivermen-13

Kasper, Lee
93Phoenix Cobras RHI-2
06Cubs Team Issue-8

Kasper, Oliver
94German DEL-352

Kasper, Peter
95Austrian National Team-11
95Swedish World Championships Stickers-260
99Florida Everblades-5

Kasper, Steve
81O-Pee-Chee-4
81O-Pee-Chee Stickers-51
81Topps-E68
82O-Pee-Chee-12
82O-Pee-Chee Stickers-81
82O-Pee-Chee Stickers-253
82Post Cereal-1
82Topps Stickers-81
82Topps Stickers-253
83Bruins Team Issue-7
83O-Pee-Chee-50
83O-Pee-Chee Stickers-53
83Topps Stickers-53
84Bruins Postcards-7
85O-Pee-Chee-79
85Topps-79
86O-Pee-Chee-97
86O-Pee-Chee Stickers-40
86Topps-97
87O-Pee-Chee-162
87O-Pee-Chee Stickers-668
87Panini Stickers-15
87Topps-162
88Bruins Sports Action-7
88Bruins Postcards-8
88Kings Postcards-14
88O-Pee-Chee-176
88O-Pee-Chee Stickers-27
88Panini Stickers-210
88Topps-176
89Kings Smokey-5
89O-Pee-Chee-194
89O-Pee-Chee Stickers-152
89Panini Stickers-92
89Topps-194
90Bowman-147
Tiffany-147
90Kings Smokey-7
90O-Pee-Chee-269
90Panini Stickers-238
90Pro Set-120
90Score-247
Canadian-247
90Topps-153
Tiffany-153
90Upper Deck-140
French-140
91Bowman-187
91Flyers J.C. Penney-15
91O-Pee-Chee-302
91OPC Premier-85
91Panini Stickers-88
91Pro Set-449
French-449
91Score American-256
91Score Canadian Bilingual-574
91Score Canadian English-574
91Score Rookie/Traded-24T
91Stadium Club-139
91Topps-302
91Upper Deck-576
French-576
92Bowman-33
92Durivage Panini-4
92Flyers Upper Deck Sheets-12
92Lightning Sheraton-18
92Parkhurst-403
Emerald Ice-403
92Score-306
Canadian-306
92Stadium Club-71
92Topps-150
Gold-150G
93OPC Premier-73
Gold-73
93Stadium Club-122
Members Only Master Set-122
OPC-122
First Day Issue-122
First Day Issue OPC-122
93Topps/OPC Premier-73
Gold-73

Kasperczyk, Jedrzej
89Swedish Semic World Champ Stickers-139
92Finnish Semic-286
94German DEL-156
95German DEL-157
96German DEL-212
99German Bundesliga 2-252

Kassa, Peter
93Quebec Pee-Wee Tournament-1718

Kassian, Matt
03Vancouver Giants-18
04Vancouver Giants-15
05ITG Heroes/Prosp Toronto Expo Parallel -175
05Kamloops Blazers-16
05ITG Heroes and Prospects-175
Autographs-A-MKA
06Kamloops Blazers-12

Kastak, Kamil
92Finnish Semic-133
92Swedish Semic Elitserien Stickers-143
93Finnish SISU-193
93Swedish Semic World Champ Stickers-107
94Finnish Jaa Kiekko-175
95Swedish Globe World Championships-162
95Swedish World Championships Stickers-199
96Czech APS Extraliga-178
97Czech DS Stickers-55

Kastelic, Ed
84Moncton Golden Flames-23
87Capitals Kodak-29
87Capitals Team Issue-12
89Whalers Junior Milk-11
90O-Pee-Chee-404
90Pro Set-450
90Whalers Jr. 7-Eleven-16
91Whalers Jr. 7-Eleven-17
92Phoenix Roadrunners-9

Kastelic, Joe
52Juniors Blue Tint-31

Kastner, Milan
94Czech APS Extraliga-91
95Czech APS Extraliga-327
97Czech DS Stickers-264
99Czech DS-190
99Czech OFS-467

Kastner, Thomas
04German Weiden Blue Devils-13

Kasutin, Ivan
04Russian Under-18 Team-10

Kasyanov, Rinat
99Russian Hockey League-52
99Russian Hockey League-255

Kaszap, Thierry
01Drummondville Voltigeurs-5

Kaszycki, Mike
78O-Pee-Chee-171
78Topps-171
79Islanders Transparencies-7
79O-Pee-Chee-87
79Topps-87
80O-Pee-Chee-371

Katainen, Pentti
65Finnish Hellas-60

Katalina, Stefan
03Oklahoma City Blazers-11

Katavisto, Ari
99Finnish Cardset-214

Katcher, Jeff
96Brandon Wheat Kings-13
98Tri-City Americans-5

Katelnikoff, Tracey
86Saskatoon Blades Photos-12
88Saskatoon Blades-18

Kathan, Klaus
94German First League-360
98German DEL-298
98German DEL-326
99German DEL-261
99German DEL-380
00German DEL-126
01German Upper Deck-126
02German Adler Mannheim Eagles Postcards-6
02German DEL City Press-245
Top Stars-GT10
03German DEL-7
03German Mannheim Eagles Postcards-18
04German DEL-49
04German Dusseldorf Metro Stars Postcards-10
05German DEL-68
05German DEL-296
06German DEL-45

Kathan, Peter
94German DEL-173

Katic, Mark
06Sarnia Sting-11

Katsuras, Sam
93Quebec Pee-Wee Tournament-566

Katz, Alex
93Quebec Pee-Wee Tournament-716

Katz, Florian
02German Berlin Polar Bears Postcards-14

Katzburg, Andrew
04New Mexico Scorpions-13

Katzur, Gunther
04German Berlin Eisbarens 50th Anniv-64

Kaufman, Evan
04Minnesota Golden Gophers-15

Kaufman, Jeff
98Owen Sound Platers-7

Kaufman, Mark
98Swiss Power Play Stickers-318
02Kalamazoo Wings-24

Kaufmann, Andrej
04German DEL-269

Kaufmann, Beat
72Finnish Semic World Championship-156
72Swedish Semic World Championship-156

Kaufmann, Evan
05Minnesota Golden Gophers-15
06Minnesota Golden Gophers-13

Kauhanen, Heikki
71Finnish Suomi Stickers-244
73Finnish Jaakiekko-311

Kauhanen, Ilpo
907th Inn. Sketch OHL-35
91Cornwall Royals-13
917th Inn. Sketch OHL-19
94Finnish SISU-278
95Finnish SISU-108
Ghost Goalies-10
96Finnish SISU Redline-122
96Finnish SISU Redline Foil Parallels-122
96Finnish SISU Redline Mighty Adversaries-3
99German Bundesliga 2-30
01German Upper Deck-127
02German DEL City Press-139
03German DEL-129
04German DEL-152
04German Hannover Scorpions Postcards-13
05German DEL-361
Goalies-G08

Kauhanen, Timo
95Finnish SISU-298

Kauk, Bryan
04Kamloops Blazers-2
05Brandon Wheat Kings-13

Kaukokari, Mauri
70Finnish Jaakiekko-108
72Finnish Jaakiekko-84
72Finnish Panda Toronto-4
73Finnish Jaakiekko-131

Kaukokari, Mikko
99Finnish Cardset-210
00Finnish Cardset-12

Kaukorari, Mauri
71Finnish Suomi Stickers-116

Kaulas, Ethan
04Arizona Icecats-20

Kaunonen, Arto
71Finnish Suomi Stickers-190
72Finnish Jaakiekko-228
73Finnish Jaakiekko-262
78Finnish SM-Liiga-206

Kaupinsalo, Kari
78Finnish SM-Liiga-154
80Finnish Mallasjuoma-125

Kauppila, Jari
73Finnish Jaakiekko-284
92Finnish Jyvas-Hyva Stickers-147
93Finnish Jyvas-Hyva Stickers-268
94Finnish SISU-230
95Finnish SISU-26
96Finnish SISU Redline-21
98Finnish Keraillysarja-110
99Finnish Cardset-63
99Finnish Cardset-170
00Finnish Cardset-137
02Finnish Cardset-37
03Finnish Cardset-121
04Finnish Cardset-182
Parallel-135
05Finnish Cardset -161
06Swedish SHL Elitset-199

Kauppila, Kari
72Finnish Jaakiekko-211
78Finnish SM-Liiga-210
80Finnish Mallasjuoma-184

Kauppila, Matti
73Finnish Jaakiekko-285

Kauppinen, Marko
98Finnish Keraillysarja-128
99Finnish Cardset-261
00Finnish Cardset-40
01Finnish Cardset-351
02Finnish Cardset-190
03Finnish Cardset-158
04Swedish Elitset-253
Gold-253
05Finnish Cardset -317
06Finnish Cardset-145

Kauppinen, Mika
98Finnish Keraillysarja-201
99Finnish Cardset-311
00Finnish Cardset-208
01Finnish Cardset-116
02Finnish Cardset-191
03Finnish Cardset-135
04Finnish Cardset-144
Parallel-108

Kautonen, Veli-Pekka
92Finnish Jyvas-Hyva Stickers-166
93Finnish Jyvas-Hyva Stickers-299
93Finnish SISU-98
94Finnish SISU-265
95Finnish SISU-198
96German DEL-266
98German DEL-33
99Finnish Cardset-293
00Finnish Cardset-257

Kautto, Matti
65Finnish Hellas-103

Kautz, Joe
02Michigan Wolverines-17
03Michigan Wolverines-12

Kauvosaari, Jarkko
04Finnish Cardset-268
05Finnish Cardset -107
06Finnish Cardset-116

Kauzala, Mike
93Quebec Pee-Wee Tournament-804

Kavanagh, Chris
98BC Icemen-14
98BC Icemen II-17

Kavanagh, Mike
03Oshawa Generals-22

Kavanagh, Pat
99Syracuse Crunch-23
00SPx Rookie Redemption-RR29
00Kansas City Blades-17
01BAP Memorabilia-332
Emerald-332
Ruby-332
Sapphire-332
01SPx-131
01UD Top Shelf-66
01UD Top Shelf-66B
01Upper Deck-209
Exclusives-209
01Upper Deck Ice-71
01Manitoba Moose-13
02Manitoba Moose-23
03Manitoba Moose-11
04Binghamton Senators-7
04Binghamton Senators Hess-5
05Philadelphia Phantoms-13

Kavanaugh, Mike
04Oshawa Generals-16
04Oshawa Generals Autographs-16

Kavulic, Ondrej
98Czech OFS-346
99Czech OFS-58

Kay, A.
28V128-2 Paulin's Candy-55

Kaye, Michael
04Lethbridge Hurricanes-12
05Lethbridge Hurricanes-10

Kaykho, Arttu
00UK Sekonda Superleague-113

Kayser, Steve
84Ottawa 67's-15

Kazak, Dustin
97Lethbridge Hurricanes-8
99Lethbridge Hurricanes-14
00Prince Albert Raiders-9

Kazakov, Alexander
98Russian Hockey League-60

Kazarian, Bryan
98Owen Sound Platers-22
99Black Diamond-113
Diamond Cut-113
Final Cut-113
99Upper Deck-335
Exclusives-335
Exclusives 1 of 1-335
99Upper Deck Gold Reserve-335
99Upper Deck MVP SC Edition-208
Gold Script-208
Silver Script-208
Super Script-208
99Owen Sound Platers-20
00Owen Sound Attack-9

Kazatkjin, Yevgeny
73Swedish Stickers-110

Kazda, Richard
96Barrie Colts-11

Kazionov, Dmitri
02Russian Young Lions-1
03Russian Hockey League-112
03Russian SL-20
04Russian World Junior Team-19

Kazuik, Garnet
84Brandon Wheat Kings-1

Kea, Ed
75O-Pee-Chee NHL-383
76O-Pee-Chee NHL-361
77O-Pee-Chee NHL-301
78Flames Majik Market-19
78O-Pee-Chee-277
79O-Pee-Chee-390
81O-Pee-Chee-294
81Topps-W118
82Post Cereal-17

Kealty, Jeff
93Classic-104
95Donruss Elite World Juniors-28
98Milwaukee Admirals-8
98Milwaukee Admirals Postcards-6

Kean, Jason
04Fort Wayne Komets-7
04Fort Wayne Komets Shoe Carnival-6
05Fort Wayne Komets Choice-18

Kean, Mitch
94Huntington Blizzard-15

Keane, Mike
88Canadiens Postcards-14
89Canadiens Kraft-11
89Canadiens Postcards-15
90Canadiens Postcards-17
90O-Pee-Chee-325
90Pro Set-521
90Score Rookie/Traded-102T
90Topps-325
Tiffany-325
90Upper Deck-382
French-382
91Pro Set Platinum-191
91Bowman-334
91Canadiens Panini Team Stickers-13
91Canadiens Postcards-14
91O-Pee-Chee-434
91Panini Stickers-190
91Parkhurst-311
French-311
91Pinnacle-265
French-265
91Pro Set-121
French-121
91Score American-360
91Score Canadian Bilingual-251
91Score Canadian English-251
91Stadium Club-236
91Topps-434
92Bowman-290
92Canadiens Postcards-14
92Humpty Dumpty I-13
92O-Pee-Chee-274
92Parkhurst-318
Emerald Ice-318
92Pinnacle-164
French-164
92Score-179
Canadian-179
92Stadium Club-349
92Topps-478
Gold-478G
92Ultra-106
92Upper Deck-164
93Canadiens Molson-7
93Canadiens Postcards-12
93Donruss-451
93Leaf-279
93OPC Premier-139
Gold-139
93Pinnacle-339
Canadian-339
93PowerPlay-129
93Score-170
Canadian-170
93Stadium Club-92
Members Only Master Set-92
OPC-92
First Day Issue-92
First Day Issue OPC-92
93Topps/OPC Premier-139
Gold-139
93Ultra-196
94Canada Games NHL POGS-135
94Canadiens Postcards-13
94Donruss-134
94Hockey Wit-63
94OPC Premier-497
Special Effects-497
94Pinnacle-151
Artist's Proofs-151
Rink Collection-151
94Score-187
Gold-187
Platinum-187
94Stadium Club-18
Members Only Master Set-18
First Day Issue-18
Super Team Winner Cards-18
94Topps/OPC Premier-497
Special Effects-497
94Ultra-110
95Be A Player-103
Signatures-S103
Signatures Die Cuts-S103
95Canada Games NHL POGS-149
95Canadiens Postcards-7
95Collector's Choice-153
Player's Club-153
Player's Club Platinum-153
95Panini Stickers-40
95Pinnacle-83
Artist's Proofs-83
Rink Collection-83
95Score-266
Black Ice Artist's Proofs-266
Black Ice-266
95Stadium Club-43
Members Only Master Set-43
95Topps-281
OPC Inserts-281
95Upper Deck-388
Electric Ice-388
Electric Ice-446
Electric Ice Gold-388
Electric Ice Gold-446
97Be A Player-101
Autographs-101
Autographs Die-Cuts-101
Autographs Prismatic Die-Cuts-101
97Collector's Choice-63
97Pacific-239
Copper-239
Emerald Green-239
Ice Blue-239
Red-239
Silver-239
97Score Rangers-3
Platinum-3
Premier-3
97Upper Deck-315
98Be A Player-42
Press Release-42
98BAP Gold-42
98BAP Autographs-42
98BAP Autographs Gold-42
98BAP Tampa Bay All Star Game-42
98Pacific-178
Ice Blue-178
Red-178
98SPx Finite-27
Radiance-27
Spectrum-27
98Upper Deck-77
Exclusives-77
Exclusives 1 of 1-77
Gold Reserve-77
99Pacific-121
Copper-121
Emerald Green-121
Gold-121
Ice Blue-121
Premiere Date-121
Red-121
99Stars Postcards-9
99Upper Deck MVP SC Edition-62
Gold Script-62
Silver Script-62
Super Script-62
00O-Pee-Chee-256B
00O-Pee-Chee Parallel-256B
00Pacific-132
Copper-132
Gold-132
Ice Blue-132
Premiere Date-132
00Stars Postcards-10
00Titanium Game Gear-85
00Titanium Game Gear Patches-85
00Topps/OPC-256B
Parallel-256B
00Topps Chrome-156
OPC Refractors-156
Refractors-156
00Upper Deck-57
Exclusives Tier 1-57
Exclusives Tier 2-57
01BAP Memorabilia-476
Emerald-476
Ruby-476
Sapphire-476
01Pacific Heads-Up Quad Jerseys-24
01UD Stanley Cup Champs-45
02Avalanche Postcards-1
02BAP Sig Series Auto Buybacks 1998-42
02BAP Signature Series Golf-GS59
02Pacific Complete-194
Red-194
03Canucks Postcards-12
03Canucks Sav-on-Foods-3
03ITG Action-162
05Manitoba Moose-12
06Manitoba Moose-8

Keans, Doug
78Saginaw Gears-13
84Bruins Postcards-8
84O-Pee-Chee-5
84Topps-4
85O-Pee-Chee-133
85Topps-133
86O-Pee-Chee-22
86Topps-22
87O-Pee-Chee-147
87O-Pee-Chee Stickers-139
87Panini Stickers-4
87Topps-147
88ProCards AHL-38

Kearns, Bracken
06Milwaukee Admirals -7

Kearns, Dennis
71Canucks Royal Bank-13
71O-Pee-Chee-231
71Toronto Sun-281
72Canucks Royal Bank-8
72Sargent Promotions Stamps-224
73Canucks Royal Bank-7
73O-Pee-Chee-162
73Topps-173
74Canucks Royal Bank-8
74NHL Action Stamps-288
74O-Pee-Chee NHL-366
75Canucks Royal Bank-9
75O-Pee-Chee NHL-188
75Topps-188
76Canucks Royal Bank-7
76O-Pee-Chee NHL-338
76O-Pee-Chee NHL-395
77Canucks Canada Dry Cans-6
77Canucks Royal Bank-9
77O-Pee-Chee NHL-175
77Topps-175
78Canucks Royal Bank-12
78O-Pee-Chee-191
78Topps-191
79Panini Stickers-58
79Canucks Royal Bank-11
79O-Pee-Chee-76
79Topps-76
80Canucks Silverwood Dairies-11
80Canucks Team Issue-11
80O-Pee-Chee-392
80Pepsi-Cola Caps-109
81O-Pee-Chee-337
81O-Pee-Chee Stickers-249
04ITG Franchises Canadian-122
Autographs-DK

Kearns, John
03Chicago Steel-14

Kearns, Justin
98BC Icemen-8
98BC Icemen II-7
00Rockford IceHogs-10
01Columbus Cottonmouths-7
01Indianapolis Ice-13
02Indianapolis Ice-9

Kearns, Richard
99Brampton Battalion-23

Keating, Jack
34Beehive Group I Photos-106
36Providence Reds-4
39O-Pee-Chee V301-1-67

Keating, Mike
75Hamilton Fincups-9

Keats, Duke
23V128-1 Paulin's Candy-45
83Hall of Fame Postcards-D8
85Hall of Fame-54
92Hall of Fame Legends-20

Keczmer, Dan
90ProCards AHL/IHL-114
91O-Pee-Chee Inserts-3S
91Whalers Jr. 7-Eleven-18
93Donruss-406
93OPC Premier-461
Gold-461
93Parkhurst-82
Emerald Ice-82
93Pinnacle-218
Canadian-218
93PowerPlay-304
93Stadium Club First Day Issue-311
93Topps/OPC Premier-461
Gold-461
93Upper Deck-249
94Stadium Club-262
Members Only Master Set-262
First Day Issue-262
Super Team Winner Cards-262
95Upper Deck-410
Electric Ice-410
Electric Ice Gold-410
96Michigan K-Wings-1
99Panini Stickers-267
99Milwaukee Admirals Keebler-9

Keefe, Adam
00Sudbury Wolves-18
01Kitchener Rangers-17
03Kitchener Rangers-14
03Kitchener Rangers Memorial Cup-12
04Kitchener Rangers-20
06Manitoba Moose-17

Keefe, Jerry
00UK Sekonda Superleague-176
01UK Belfast Giants-29
01Atlantic City Boardwalk Bullies-13

Keefe, Sheldon
94Quebec Pee-Wee Tournament-1717
98Barrie Colts-13
99Black Diamond-96
Diamond Cut-96
Final Cut-96
99O-Pee-Chee-264
99O-Pee-Chee Chrome-264
99O-Pee-Chee Chrome Refractors-264
99SP Authentic-123
99Topps/OPC-264
99Topps/OPC Chrome-264
Refractors-264
99Ultimate Victory-107
1/1-107
Parallel-107

Parallel 100-107
99Upper Deck-309
Exclusives-309
Exclusives 1 of 1-309
99Upper Deck Gold Reserve-309
99Upper Deck MVP SC Edition-195
Gold Script-195
Silver Script-195
Super Script-195
99Upper Deck Ovation-64
Standing Ovation-64
99Upper Deck Victory-361
99Bowman CHL-14
99Bowman CHL-125
Gold-14
Gold-125
OPC International-14
OPC International-125
Autographs-BA34
Autographs Gold-BA34
Autographs Silver-BA34
99UD Prospects-3
00BAP Memorabilia-495
Emerald-495
Ruby-495
Sapphire-495
00Crown Royale-141
00SPx-130
Spectrum-130
00Topps Heritage-135
00Vanguard-146
Pacific Proofs-146
01BAP Memorabilia-297
Emerald-297
Ruby-297
Sapphire-297
01O-Pee-Chee-274
01O-Pee-Chee Premier Parallel-274
01Topps-274
OPC Parallel-274
01Upper Deck Ice-120
02O-Pee-Chee-264
02O-Pee-Chee Premier Blue Parallel-264
02O-Pee-Chee Premier Red Parallel-264
02O-Pee-Chee Factory Set-264
02Pacific Complete-413
Red-413
02Topps-264
OPC Blue Parallel-264
OPC Red Parallel-264
Factory Set-264
02Topps Total-65
02Upper Deck Victory-191
Bronze-191
Gold-191
Silver-191
03ITG Action-578
03Lightning Team Issue-28
03Hershey Bears-16
03Hershey Bears Patriot News-10

Keeling, Butch
33O-Pee-Chee V304A-36
33V129-30
33V357 Ice Kings-20
34Beehive Group I Photos-281
34Diamond Matchbooks Silver-34
35Diamond Matchbooks Tan 1-34
35Diamond Matchbooks Tan 2-32
35Diamond Matchbooks Tan 3-30
37V356 Worldwide Gum-15

Keenan, Cory
87Kitchener Rangers-11
88Kitchener Rangers-11
89Kitchener Rangers-12
897th Inn. Sketch OHL-179
907th Inn. Sketch Memorial Cup-40
95Signature Rookies Auto-Phonex-20
95Signature Rook Auto-Phonex Phone Cards-20

Keenan, Larry
61Parkhurst-13
61Shirriff/Salada Coins-55
61York Yellow Backs-32
68O-Pee-Chee-115
68Shirriff Coins-155
68Topps-115
70Esso Power Players-90
70O-Pee-Chee-104
70Topps-104
71Sargent Promotions Stamps-31
71Toronto Sun-29

Keenan, Mike
85Flyers Postcards-15
86Flyers Postcards-13
87Flyers Postcards-3
88Blackhawks Coke-7
89Blackhawks Coke-25
90Blackhawks Coke-25
91Blackhawks Coke-11
04Ultimate Collection-53
04Upper Deck-201
Canadian Exclusives-201
HG Glossy Gold-201
HG Glossy Silver-201
06Parkhurst-43
Autographs-43

Keene, Jerod
03Arizona Icecats-11

Keetley, Matt
04Medicine Hat Tigers-10
05Medicine Hat Tigers-13
06Medicine Hat Tigers-13

Kehle, Markus
94German DEL-79
95German DEL-298

Kehle, Toni
72Finnish Semic World Championship-93
72Swedish Semic World Championship-93

Kehler, Drew
96Kamloops Blazers-13
97Regina Pats-14

Kehler, J.D.
98Brandon Wheat Kings-10
99Brandon Wheat Kings-12
00Brandon Wheat Kings-15

Kehler, Joff
00Spokane Chiefs-10
01Spokane Chiefs-12
02Spokane Chiefs-9

Kehoe, Jim
01Sudbury Wolves-7
01Sudbury Wolves Police-6
03Owen Sound Attack-17
04St. Francis Xavier X-Men-9

Kehoe, Rick
72Maple Leafs Postcards-13
72O-Pee-Chee-277
72Sargent Promotions Stamps-209
73Mac's Milk-11
73Maple Leafs Postcards-12
73Maple Leafs Postcards-13
73Maple Leafs Postcards-14
73O-Pee-Chee-60
73Topps-179
74NHL Action Stamps-231
74O-Pee-Chee NHL-81
74Penguins Postcards-10
74Topps-81
75O-Pee-Chee NHL-39
75Topps-39
76O-Pee-Chee NHL-124
76Topps-124
77O-Pee-Chee NHL-33
77Penguins Puck Bucks-17
77Topps-33
78O-Pee-Chee-213
78Topps-213
79O-Pee-Chee-109
79Topps-109
80O-Pee-Chee-18
80O-Pee-Chee-117
80Topps-18
80Topps-117
81O-Pee-Chee-254
81O-Pee-Chee-260
81O-Pee-Chee-267
81O-Pee-Chee Stickers-182
81O-Pee-Chee Stickers-261
81Topps-17
81Topps-60
81Topps-E128
82O-Pee-Chee-271
82O-Pee-Chee Stickers-143
82Post Cereal-15
82Topps Stickers-143
83NHL Key Tags-104
83O-Pee-Chee-274
83O-Pee-Chee-282
83O-Pee-Chee Stickers-11
83O-Pee-Chee Stickers-231
83O-Pee-Chee Stickers-232
83Penguins Heinz Photos-15
83Puffy Stickers-8
83Topps Stickers-11
83Topps Stickers-231
83Topps Stickers-232
84Kellogg's Accordion Discs-5A
84Kellogg's Accordion Discs Singles-19
84O-Pee-Chee-177
84O-Pee-Chee Stickers-117
84Penguins Heinz Photos-13
847-Eleven Discs-40
84Topps-125
93Penguins Foodland-6
95Penguins Foodland-11
01Greats of the Game-87
Autographs-87
04ITG Franchises US West-269
Autographs-A-RKE

Kehrer, Glen
90Hampton Roads Admirals-48

Kehrig, Ryan
00Saskatoon Blades-23

Keichinger, Chris
98Kelowna Rockets-12

Keijser, Kjell
67Swedish Hockey-64
71Swedish Hockey-354

Keiler, Andreas
94German First League-538

Keiller, Ian
917th Inn. Sketch OHL-104

Keiller, Jimmy
37V356 Worldwide Gum-120

Keily, Darren
96Barrie Colts-12
97Barrie Colts-12
98Barrie Colts-24
99Sudbury Wolves-3
00Sudbury Wolves-3
01Sudbury Wolves-8
01Sudbury Wolves Police-3

Keimann, Dan
98Florida Everblades-20

Keimu, Pekka
70Swedish Hockey-301

Keinanen, Jani
98Finnish Kerailysarja-63
99Finnish Cardset-297
00Finnish Cardset-73
01Finnish Cardset-103
02Finnish Cardset-192
04Finnish Cardset-40
Parallel-29
05Finnish Cardset -34
06Finnish Cardset-216

Keinonen, Heikki
66Finnish Jaakiekkosarja-176
70Finnish Jaakiekko-243
71Finnish Suomi Stickers-210

Keinonen, Heimo
70Finnish Jaakiekko-244
71Finnish Suomi Stickers-211
72Finnish Jaakiekko-158
73Finnish Jaakiekko-220

Keinonen, Matti
65Finnish Hellas-23
66Finnish Jaakiekkosarja-26
69Swedish Hockey-370
70Finnish Jaakiekko-61
70Finnish Jaakiekko-229
70Swedish Hockey-302
70Swedish Masterserien-165
71Finnish Suomi Stickers-152
72Finnish Jaakiekko-62
72Finnish Jaakiekko-104
72Finnish Semic World Championship-91
72Swedish Stickers-35
72Swedish Semic World Championship-91
73Finnish Jaakiekko-64
73Finnish Jaakiekko-197
73Swedish Stickers-37
77Finnish Sportscasters-40-937
92Finnish Jyvas-Hyva Stickers-120

Keith, Cam
06Peoria Rivermen-6

Keith, Duncan
03Kelowna Rockets Memorial Cup-9
03Norfolk Admirals-11
04SP Authentic Rookie Redemptions-RR33
04Norfolk Admirals-9
04ITG Heroes and Prospects-3
Autographs-DK
04ITG Heroes/Prospects Toronto Expo '05-3
04ITG Heroes/Prospects Expo Heroes/Pros-3
05Beehive Signature Scrapbook-SSDK
05Black Diamond-155
Emerald-155
Gold-155
Onyx-155
Ruby-155
05Hot Prospects-195
Autographed Patch Variation-195
Autographed Patch Variation Gold-195
Hot Materials-HMDK
Red Hot-195
05Parkhurst Signatures-DK
05SP Authentic-147
Limited-147
Sign of the Times-DK
05SP Game Used-114
Autographs-114
Gold-114
Auto Draft-AD-DK
Rookie Exclusives-DK
Rookie Exclusives Silver-RE-DK
05SPx-133
Spectrum-133
Xcitement Rookies-XR-DK
Xcitement Rookies Gold-XR-DK
Xcitement Rookies Spectrum-XR-DK
05The Cup-186
Black Rainbow Rookies-186
Masterpiece Pressplates (Artifacts)-259
Masterpiece Pressplates (Black Diamond)-155
Masterpiece Pressplates (Ice)-148
Masterpiece Pressplates (MVP)-435
Masterpiece Pressplates (Rookie Update)-253
Masterpiece Pressplates SPA Autos-147
Masterpiece Pressplates (SP Game Used)-114
Masterpiece Pressplates (SPx)-133
Masterpiece Pressplates (SPx)-133
Masterpiece Pressplates (Trilogy)-240
Masterpiece Pressplates Ult Coll-141
Masterpiece Pressplates Autographs-186
Platinum Rookies-186
05UD Artifacts-259
05Ultimate Collection-141
Gold-141
05Ultra-211
Gold-211
Ice-211
Rookie Uniformity Jerseys-RU-DK
Rookie Uniformity Jersey Autographs-ARU-DK
Rookie Uniformity Patches-RUP-DK
Rookie Uniformity Patch Autographs-ARP-DK
05Upper Deck-230
HG Glossy-230
Rookie Threads-RTDK
Rookie Threads Autographs-ARTDK
05Upper Deck Ice-148
Premieres Auto Patches-AIPDK
05Upper Deck MVP-435
Gold-435
Platinum-435
05Upper Deck Rookie Update-253
Inspirations Patch Rookies-253
05Upper Deck Trilogy-240
05Upper Deck Toronto Fall Expo-230
06Be A Player-108
Autographs-108
Signatures-DK
Signatures 25-118
Signatures Duals-DCH
06Black Diamond Jerseys-JDK
06Black Diamond Jerseys Black-JDK
06Black Diamond Jerseys Gold-JDK
06Black Diamond Jerseys Ruby-JDK
06Blackhawks Postcards-13
06Flair Showcase Inks-IDK
06Hot Prospects Hotagraphs-HDK
06O-Pee-Chee-118
Rainbow-118
Swatches-S-DK
06SP Game Used SIGnificance-SDK
06Ultra-47
Gold Medallion-47
Ice Medallion-47
06Upper Deck-44
Exclusives Parallel-44
High Gloss Parallel-44
Game Jerseys-JDK
Game Patches-PDK
Masterpieces-44
06Upper Deck MVP-66
Gold Script-66
Super Script-66
Autographs-OABK
07Upper Deck Ovation-39
07Upper Deck Victory-121
Black-121
Gold-121

Keith, Matt
99Spokane Chiefs-11
00Spokane Chiefs-11
01Spokane Chiefs-13
02Red Deer Rebels-19
03ITG VIP Rookie Debut-126
03Parkhurst Rookie-100
03Topps Traded-TT96
Blue-TT96
Gold-TT96
Red-TT96
03Upper Deck Rookie Update-201
03Norfolk Admirals-12
04Pacific-274
Blue-274
Red-274
04Norfolk Admirals-10
05Norfolk Admirals-16
06Portland Pirates-16

Keitl, Michael
94German First League-274

Kekalainen, Janne
93Finnish SISU-174
94Finnish SISU-21
95Finnish SISU-278
95Finnish SISU Limited-71
96Finnish SISU Redline-79
98Finnish Kerailysarja-154

Kekalainen, Jarmo
91Upper Deck-108
French-108
Euro-Stars-1
Euro-Stars French-1
91Finnish Jyvas-Hyva Stickers-33
92Finnish Jyvas-Hyva Stickers-158
92Finnish Semic-22
93Parkhurst-410
Emerald Ice-410
93Senators Kraft Sheets-11
93Swedish Semic World Champ Stickers-65
94Finnish SISU-366
94Finnish Jaa Kiekko-26
94Swedish Leaf-229
Foreign Affairs-7
94Classic Pro Prospects-198

Kekalainen, Saku
05Finnish Cardset -84

Kelfer, Mike
89ProCards AHL-246
90Kansas City Blades-16
90ProCards AHL/IHL-592

Kelham, A.J.
917th Inn. Sketch WHL-237
01UK Nottingham Panthers-22
02UK London Knights-8
03UK Coventry Blaze History-5

Kell, Trevor
03London Knights-8
04London Knights-5
05London Knights-3
06Sarnia Sting-2

Kelland, Chris
93UK Sheffield Steelers-11
94Finnish Jaa Kiekko-316
94UK Sheffield Steelers-22
95UK Sheffield Steelers-10
97UK Sheffield Steelers-12
00UK Sheffield Steelers Centurions-7

Kellar, Becky
04Canadian Womens World Championship Team-11
06ITG Going For Gold-4
06ITG Going For Gold Samples-4
06ITG Going For Gold Autographs-AK
06ITG Going For Gold Jerseys-GUJ4

Kelleher, Chris
00Wilkes-Barre Scranton Penguins-9
01BAP Memorabilia-440
Emerald-440
Ruby-440
Sapphire-440
01UD Mask Collection-137
Gold-137
01Providence Bruins-5
02Upper Deck MVP-195
Gold-195
Classics-195
Golden Classics-195
02Providence Bruins-3
03German DEL-186
04Wilkes-Barre Scranton Penguins-4
05WBS Penguins-14
06Swedish SHL Elitset-204

Kelleher, Tim
03Tulsa Oilers-8

Keller, Aaron
93Kamloops Blazers-12
94Kamloops Blazers-16
95Kamloops Blazers-22
95Slapshot Memorial Cup-7

Keller, Andreas
93Swiss HNL-102
95Swiss HNL-99
96Swiss HNL-333
98Swiss Power Play Stickers-145
00Swiss Panini Stickers-160
00Swiss Slapshot Mini-Cards-EHCK10
01Swiss HNL-66
02Swiss HNL-272

Keller, Bruce
94German First League-608

Keller, Florian
94German DEL-386
95German DEL-374
96German DEL-174
99German Bundesliga 2-24
02German Berlin Polar Bears Postcards-15
02German DEL City Press-33
03German Berlin Polar Bears Postcards-19
03German DEL-68
04German Berlin Polar Bears Postcards-18
04German DEL-71
05German DEL-150
06German DEL-99

Keller, Hans
72Finnish Semic World Championship-143
72Swedish Semic World Championship-143

Keller, John
84Kitchener Rangers-24

Keller, Justin
00Spokane Chiefs-12
01Saskatoon Blades-8
03Kelowna Rockets-12
03Kelowna Rockets-12
04Kelowna Rockets-3
04Kelowna Rockets-3
05Kelowna Rockets-16
05Kelowna Rockets-16
05ITG Heroes and Prospects Oh Canada-OC-16
05ITG Heroes and Prospects Oh Canada-OC-16
05ITG Heroes and Prospects Oh Canada Gold-OC-16
05ITG Heroes and Prospects Oh Canada Gold-OC-16
06Springfield Falcons-12
06Springfield Falcons-12

Keller, Markus
93Swiss HNL-356

Keller, Mathias
93Swiss HNL-450
95Swiss HNL-173
96Swiss HNL-306
99Swiss Panini Stickers-352

Keller, Olivier
93Swiss HNL-41
95Swiss HNL-67
96Swiss HNL-211
98Swiss Power Play Stickers-86
99Swiss Panini Stickers-158
99Swiss Panini Stickers-256
00Swiss Panini Stickers-203
00Swiss Panini Stickers National Team-P5
00Swiss Slapshot Mini-Cards-HCL5
01Swiss HNL-30
02Swiss HNL-25
02Swiss HNL-485

Keller, Pirmin
95Swiss HNL-454
96Swiss HNL-444

Keller, Roger
93Swiss HNL-451
95Swiss HNL-330

Keller, Ronny
93Quebec Pee-Wee Tournament-1629
96Swiss HNL-307
99Swiss Panini Stickers-230
00Swiss Panini Stickers-152
01Swiss HNL-58
02Swiss HNL-292

Keller, Ryan
91British Columbia JHL-57
92British Columbia JHL-213
01Saskatoon Blades-9
02Saskatoon Blades-23
03Saskatoon Blades-23
04Saskatoon Blades-14
05Muskegon Fury-9

Keller, Tylor
04Columbus Cottonmouths-8

Kellerman, Tyson
03Kitchener Rangers-15
04St. Francis Xavier X-Men-10

Kellett, Kevin
95Prince Albert Raiders-11
96Prince Albert Raiders-11
97Prince Albert Raiders-10
98Prince Albert Raiders-12
99Johnstown Chiefs-25
99Tallahassee Tiger Sharks-1

Kelley, Robert
93Memphis RiverKings-7

Kellgren, Christer
83Swedish Semic Elitserien-232

Kelln, Travis
907th Inn. Sketch WHL-21

Kello, Michal
02Czech OFS Plus-304

Kellogg, Allen
52Juniors Blue Tint-24

Kellogg, Bob
93Indianapolis Ice-15
94Indianapolis Ice-11
94Classic Pro Prospects-63

Kellogg, Christopher
93Quebec Pee-Wee Tournament-887

Kelly, Bob
70Esso Power Players-206
71O-Pee-Chee-203
71Sargent Promotions Stamps-157
71Toronto Sun-200
71Rochester Americans-10
72Flyers Mighty Milk-6
72Sargent Promotions Stamps-163
73Flyers Linnett-8
73O-Pee-Chee-253
74NHL Action Stamps-200
74NHL Action Stamps-223
74O-Pee-Chee NHL-380
74Penguins Postcards-11
75Flyers Canada Dry Cans-9
75O-Pee-Chee NHL-184
75Topps-184
76O-Pee-Chee NHL-219
76Topps-219
77O-Pee-Chee NHL-178
77Topps-178
78O-Pee-Chee-71
78Topps-71
79O-Pee-Chee-14
79Topps-14
81O-Pee-Chee-349
81O-Pee-Chee Stickers-195
81Topps-E119
92Parkhurst-477
Emerald Ice-477
04ITG Franchises US East-429
Autographs-A-BK
05Georgia Legends-28

Kelly, Brent
99Guelph Storm-17
03Johnstown Chiefs-19
03Johnstown Chiefs RBI Sports-217
04Johnstown Chiefs-10

Kelly, Brock
89Nashville Knights-12
91Nashville Knights-16

Kelly, Bud
05Belleville Bulls-11

Kelly, Chris
99O-Pee-Chee-270
99O-Pee-Chee Chrome-270
99O-Pee-Chee Chrome Refractors-270
99Topps/OPC-270
99Topps/OPC Chrome-270
Refractors-270
99Bowman CHL-8
Gold-8
OPC International-8
Autographs-BA28
Autographs Gold-BA28
Autographs Silver-BA28
00London Knights-24
00London Knights-U1
00UD CHL Prospects-35
01Grand Rapids Griffins-14
03Binghamton Senators-10
03Binghamton Senators Postcards-1
03Pacific AHL Prospects-7
Gold-7
04Binghamton Senators-8
04Binghamton Senators Hess-1
06Gatorade-60
06O-Pee-Chee-354
Rainbow-354
06Senators Postcards-7
06Binghamton Senators 5th Anniversary-15

Kelly, Chuck
67Columbus Checkers-7

Kelly, Dan
06Kitchener Rangers-24

Kelly, Diarmuid
99Kelowna Rockets-9
00Red Deer Rebels-9
Signed-9
01Red Deer Rebels-9
02Red Deer Rebels-20

Kelly, J. Bob
73Blues White Border-10
74O-Pee-Chee NHL-143
74Topps-143
75O-Pee-Chee NHL-263
75Topps-263
76O-Pee-Chee NHL-261
76Topps-261
77O-Pee-Chee NHL-14
77Topps-14
78O-Pee-Chee-189
78Topps-189
79O-Pee-Chee-306

Kelly, Jason
97Charlotte Checkers-10

Kelly, John P.
82Post Cereal-8
06Parkhurst-44
Autographs-44

Kelly, Justin
97Spokane Chiefs-15
00Saskatoon Blades-27
01Saskatoon Blades-10
03ECHL All-Stars-273
03Las Vegas Wranglers-8
05Johnstown Chiefs-12

Kelly, Kendel
92British Columbia JHL-2

Kelly, Kyle
06Victoriaville Tigres-20

Kelly, Mark
97Toledo Storm-29

Kelly, Matt
03Belleville Bulls-3
04Belleville Bulls-17
05OHL Bell All-Star Classic-39

Kelly, Pat
77Rockies Coke Cans-11

Kelly, Paul
88ProCards AHL-217
89ProCards AHL-3
93Muskegon Fury-10
94Muskegon Fury-13
95Muskegon Fury-7
98Topeka Scarecrows-20
99Topeka Scarecrows-20
01Bakersfield Condors-21
02Bakersfield Condors-21
03Bakersfield Condors-4

Kelly, Peter
34Beehive Group I Photos-107

Kelly, Red
44Beehive Group II Photos-182
44Beehive Group II Photos-413A
44Beehive Group II Photos-413B
51Parkhurst-55
52Parkhurst-67
52Royal Desserts-7
53Parkhurst-40
54Parkhurst-42
54Parkhurst-91
54Topps-5
57Topps-48
58Topps-61
59Topps-65
60Parkhurst-9
60Shirriff Coins-4
60York Photos-19
61Parkhurst-9
61Shirriff/Salada Coins-49
61York Yellow Backs-21
62Parkhurst-5
62Shirriff Coins-9
62York Iron-On Transfers-20
63Chex Photos-29
63Maple Leafs Team Issue-11
63Parkhurst-3
63Parkhurst-63
63Toronto Star-22
63York White Backs-12
64Beehive Group III Photos-169
64Coca-Cola Caps-93
64Topps-44
65Coca-Cola-93
65Maple Leafs White Border-11
65Topps-15
66Topps-79
66Topps USA Test-42
71Penguins Postcards-10
73Maple Leafs Postcards-15
74O-Pee-Chee NHL-76
74Topps-76
83Hall of Fame-55
83Hall of Fame Postcards-D9
85Hall of Fame-55
90Upper Deck-502
French-502
91Kraft-81
91Ultimate Original Six-38
91Ultimate Original Six-79
French-38
French-79
92Parkhurst Parkie Reprints-PR10
93Parkhurst Parkie Reprints-PR58
94Parkhurst Missing Link-52
94Parkhurst Missing Link-142
94Parkhurst Tall Boys-127
94Parkhurst Tall Boys-165
94Zeller's Masters of Hockey-3
94Zeller's Masters of Hockey Signed-3
95Parkhurst '66-67-109
Coins-109
99BAP Memorabilia AS Retail-R11
99BAP Memorabilia AS Retail Autographs-R11
99Upper Deck Century Legends-22
Century Collection-22
99Upper Deck Retro-98
Gold-98
Platinum-98
00Topps Heritage Autographs-HA-RK
00Topps Heritage Autoproofs-5
01BAP Signature Series Vintage Autographs-VA-12
01BAP Ultimate Mem Stanley Cup Winners-4
01Fleer Legacy-38
Ultimate-38
01Greats of the Game-78
Autographs-78
01Parkhurst Autographs-PA40
01Parkhurst Reprints-PR17
01Parkhurst Reprints-PR31
01Parkhurst Reprints-PR53
01Parkhurst Reprints-PR54
01Parkhurst Reprints-PR60
01Parkhurst Reprints-PR93
01Parkhurst Reprints-PR109
01Parkhurst Reprints-PR144
01Parkhurst Reprints-PR149
01Topps Archives-72
01Upper Deck Legends-19
02BAP Ultimate Memorabilia Emblem Attic-26
02BAP Ultimate Memorabilia Numerology-7
02BAP Ultimate Mem Retro Teammates-8
02BAP Ultimate Mem Vintage Jerseys-31
02BAP Ultimate Mem Vintage Jersey Autos-6
02ITG Used Vintage Memorabilia-VM8
02ITG Used Vintage Memorabilia Gold-VM8
02Maple Leafs Platinum Collection-55
02Maple Leafs Platinum Collection-76
Autographs-76
02Parkhurst Vintage Teammates-VT14
02Parkhurst Retro Nicknames-RN11
02Topps Heritage Reprint Autographs-RK
02Topps Heritage Reprint Relics-RK
02Topps Heritage Reprints-RK
03BAP Ultimate Memorabilia Cornerstones-4
03BAP Ultimate Mem Hometown Heroes-10
03BAP Ultimate Mem Hometown Heroes Gold-10
03BAP Ultimate Mem Vintage Jerseys-30
03BAP Ultimate Mem Vintage Jerseys Gold-30
03Canada Post-17
03ITG Used Signature Series-114
Gold-114
Autographs-RK
Autographs Gold-RK
Vintage Memorabilia-10
Vintage Memorabilia Autographs-10
Vintage Memorabilia Gold-10
03Parkhurst Original Six Detroit-42
03Parkhurst Original Six Detroit-63
03Parkhurst Original Six Detroit-78
03Parkhurst Original Six Detroit-84
Autographs-OS-RK
Inserts-D-8
Inserts-D-12
03Parkhurst Original Six Toronto-52
03Parkhurst Original Six Toronto-85
Autographs-5
Inserts-T8
Memorabilia-TM29
Memorabilia-TM52
04ITG Franchises Canadian-87
Forever Rivals-FR2
Forever Rivals Gold-FR2
04ITG Franchises Update Teammates-UTM3
04ITG Franchises Update Teammates Gold-UTM3
04ITG Franchises US West-204
Autographs-A-RK
04ITG Ultimate Memorabilia-81
04ITG Ultimate Memorabilia-91
Gold-81
Gold-91
Autographs-65
Autographs Gold-65
Jerseys-7
Jerseys Gold-7
Jersey Autographs-36
Jersey Autographs Gold-36
Original Six-17
04UD Legends Classics-46
04UD Legends Classics-90
Gold-46
Gold-90
Platinum-46
Platinum-90
Silver-46
Silver-90
Jersey Redemptions-JY12
Signature Moments-M4
Signatures-CS4
Signatures-TC13
04ITG Heroes and Prospects-148
Autographs-RKE
04ITG Heroes/Prospects Toronto Expo '05-148
04ITG Heroes/Prospects Expo Heroes/Pros-148
05ITG Heroes/Prosp Toronto Expo Parallel -7
05Beehive-238
05ITG Ultimate Memorabilia Level 1-83
05ITG Ultimate Memorabilia Level 2-83
05ITG Ultimate Memorabilia Level 3-83
05ITG Ultimate Memorabilia Level 4-83
05ITG Ultimate Memorabilia Level 5-83
05ITG Ultimate Mem Retro Teammate Jerseys-20
05ITG Ult Mem Retro Teammates Jersey Gold-20
05ITG Ultimate Memorabilia Stick Autos-11
05ITG Ultimate Mem Stick Autos Gold-11
05ITG Ultimate Mem Sticks and Jerseys-14
05ITG Ultimate Mem Stick and Jerseys Gold-14
05ITG Ultimate Mem 3 Star of the Game Jsy-6
05ITG Ult Mem 3 Star of the Game Jsy Gold-6
05ITG Ultimate Memorabilia Ultimate Autos-29
05ITG Ultimate Mem Ultimate Autos Gold-29
05ITG Ultimate Memorabilia Vintage Lumber-9
05ITG Ultimate Mem Vintage Lumber Gold-9
05SP Authentic Sign of the Times Fives-SMSMK
05SP Authentic Six Star Signatures-SSTO
05SPx Xcitement Legends-XL-RK
05SPx Xcitement Legends Gold-XL-RK
05SPx Xcitement Legends Spectrum-XL-RK
05UD Artifacts-125
Blue-125
Gold-125
Green-125
Pewter-125
Red-125
Gold Autographed-125
05ITG Heroes and Prospects-7
Autographs-A-RK
Hero Memorabilia-HM-39
06ITG Ultimate Memorabilia-120
Artist Proof-120
Boys Will Be Boys-22
Boys Will Be Boys Gold-22
Ring Leaders-12
Ring Leaders Gold-12
Road to the Cup-1
Road to the Cup Gold-1
Stick Rack-7
Stick Rack-11
Stick Rack Gold-7
Stick Rack Gold-11
06Parkhurst-45
06Parkhurst-178
Autographs-45
Autographs-178
Autographs Dual-DALK
06SP Authentic Sign of the Times Triples-ST3BEK
06The Cup-32
Black Rainbow-32
Gold-32
Masterpiece Pressplates-32
Stanley Cup Signatures-CSKE
Stanley Cup Signatures-CSRK
Stanley Cup Titlists-TRK
06Upper Deck Sweet Shot Signature Shots/Saves Ice Signings-SSIRK
06ITG Heroes and Prospects Heroes Memorabilia-HM16
06ITG Heroes and Prospects Heroes Memorabilia Gold-HM16
07Maple Leafs 1967 Commemorative-13
Autographs-ARK1
Autographs-ARK2

Kelly, Regan
05UK Sheffield Steelers Supplementary-6
Gold-6
Silver-6
05Danbury Trashers-10

Kelly, Regis
34Beehive Group I Photos-330
35O-Pee-Chee V304C-87
36Champion Postcards-7
37O-Pee-Chee V304E-145
37V356 Worldwide Gum-86
38Quaker Oats Photos-22
39O-Pee-Chee V301-1-9

Kelly, Richard
92Quebec Pee-Wee Tournament-1858
00Kelowna Rockets-25
01Kelowna Rockets-7
02Kelowna Rockets-6
03Saskatoon Blades-10
03St. Michael's Majors-16

Kelly, Ron
06Westside Warriors-14

Kelly, Ryan
04Lincoln Stars Update-37

Kelly, Steve
93Prince Albert Raiders-13
94Prince Albert Raiders-12
95Prince Albert Raiders-12
95Classic-6
CHL All-Stars-AS6
Ice Breakers-BK6
Ice Breakers Die Cuts-BK6
95Images-39
Gold-39
Platinum Premier Draft Choice-PD3
95Classic Five-Sport *-128
Autographs-128
Strive For Five-HK4
96Metal Universe-183
96Oilers Postcards-10
97Donruss-216
Press Proofs Silver-216
Press Proofs Gold-216
Rated Rookies-8
Medallist-8
97Donruss Canadian Ice-130
Dominion Series-130
Provincial Series-130
97Donruss Limited-107
Exposure-107
97Pinnacle Inside-117
97Upper Deck-188
99Albany River Rats-15
00BAP Memorabilia-37
Emerald-37
Ruby-37
Sapphire-37
Promos-37
00BAP Mem Chicago Sportsfest Copper-37
00BAP Memorabilia Chicago Sportsfest Blue-37
00BAP Memorabilia Chicago Sportsfest Gold-37
00BAP Memorabilia Chicago Sportsfest Ruby-37
00BAP Memorabilia Chicago Sun-Times Ruby-37
00BAP Memorabilia Chicago Sun-Times Gold-37
00BAP Mem Chicago Sun-Times Sapphire-37
00BAP Mem Toronto Fall Expo Copper-37
00BAP Memorabilia Toronto Fall Expo Gold-37
00BAP Memorabilia Toronto Fall Expo Ruby-37
00Devils Team Issue-10
01Manchester Monarchs-12B
02Manchester Monarchs-10
03Manchester Monarchs-8
03Manchester Monarchs Team Issue-8
03Pacific AHL Prospects-50
Gold-50
04German Adler Mannheim Eagles Postcards-20
04German DEL-13
05German DEL-249
05German DEL-320
06German DEL-56

Kelman, Scott
97Seattle Thunderbirds-12
98SP Authentic-125
Power Shift-125
Sign of the Times-SK
Sign of the Times Gold-SK
98Upper Deck-402
Exclusives-402
Exclusives 1 of 1-402
Gold Reserve-402
99Upper Deck-325
Exclusives-325
Exclusives 1 of 1-325
99Upper Deck Gold Reserve-325
99Upper Deck MVP SC Ed Game-Used Souvenir-GUSK
99Upper Deck MVP SC Edition ProSign-SK
99Bowman CHL-9
Gold-9
OPC International-9
Autographs-BA29
Autographs Gold-BA29
Autographs Silver-BA29
Scout's Choice-SC2
03Augusta Lynx-44
06Albany River Rats-14

Kelman, Todd
92British Columbia JHL-198
00UK Sekonda Superleague-24
01UK Belfast Giants-19
03UK Belfast Giants-7

Kelner, Curtis
05Calgary Hitmen-7

Kelner, Roman
98Czech OFS-360
99Czech OFS-423
04Slovakian Skalica Team Set-13

Kelsey, Scot
94Central Hockey League-81
94San Antonio Iguanas-9
95Central Hockey League-28
99Memphis RiverKings All-Time-16

Kemp, Chad
05Bossier-Shreveport Mudbugs-7

Kemp, Dylan
95Prince Albert Raiders-13
96Prince Albert Raiders-12
97Saskatoon Blades-11

Kemp, John
82Kingston Canadians-13

Kemp, Kevin
76Saginaw Gears-7

Kemp, Nick
04Sioux City Musketeers-11

Kemp, T.J.
05Reading Royals-7

Kemper, Andreas
94German First League-406

Kemper, Andrew
917th Inn. Sketch WHL-128
93Saskatoon Blades-13

Kemper, Kai
94German First League-442

Kempf, Markus
94German DEL-116
95German DEL-117
99German Bundesliga 2-258

Kempffer, Mick
96Charlotte Checkers-8
97Columbus Cottonmouths-6
98Columbus Cottonmouths-6
99Columbus Cottonmouths-3
00Columbus Cottonmouths-4
04Columbus Cottonmouths-2

Kemppainen, Hannu
78Finnish SM-Liiga-166
80Finnish Mallasjuoma-120

Kemppainen, Joonas
06Finnish Cardset-354
06Finnish Porin Assat Pelaajakortit-25

Kemppainen, Pasi
94Finnish SISU-310
95Finnish SISU-282

Kemppi, Miikka
94Finnish SISU-271
95Finnish SISU-118

Kemppinen, Jyri
71Finnish Suomi Stickers-324

Kenady, Chris
95Classic-75
Autographs-11
95Classic Five-Sport *-139
Autographs-139
99Hartford Wolf Pack-13
00SPx-104
Spectrum-104
00Hartford Wolf Pack-15
02Fresno Falcons-3
03Las Vegas Wranglers-9
03Las Vegas Wranglers RBI-231

Kendall, Bobby
92Quebec Pee-Wee Tournament-1761
93Quebec Pee-Wee Tournament-172

Kendall, Carl
12C57-35

Kendall, Colin
92Quebec Pee-Wee Tournament-1758
03Bossier-Shreveport Mudbugs-9

Kendall, Jason
93Cornell Big Red-15

Kendall, William

34Beehive Group I Photos-331
34Diamond Matchbooks Silver-35
35Diamond Matchbooks Tan 1-35
35Diamond Matchbooks Tan 2-33

Kenepp, Justin
92Quebec Pee-Wee Tournament-1407
93Quebec Pee-Wee Tournament-765

Kenig, Kasper
01Finnish Cardset-33
05Finnish Cardset -262
06Finnish Cardset-87

Kenig, Max
01Finnish Cardset-193
05Finnish Cardset -83

Kennedy, Bob
49All-Star Photos-10
88Flint Spirits-10
89Johnstown Chiefs-24
07Topps Distinguished Service Cuts-BK

Kennedy, Courtney
98Minnesota Golden Gophers Women-10

Kennedy, Craig
00UD CHL Prospects-30
02Windsor Spitfires-13

Kennedy, Dean
82Brandon Wheat Kings-3
83NHL Key Tags-51
86Kings 20th Anniversary Team Issue-11
87Panini Stickers-276
88Kings Postcards-20
89Sabres Blue Shield-8
89Sabres Campbell's-10
90Bowman-248
Tiffany-248
90Pro Set-22
90Sabres Blue Shield-10
90Sabres Campbell's-11
90Score-299
Canadian-299
90Upper Deck-380
French-380
91Jets IGA-15
91O-Pee-Chee-388
91Score Canadian Bilingual-431
91Score Canadian English-431
91Topps-388
92Pinnacle-239
French-239
92Score-211
Canadian-211
93Jets Readers Club-12
93Jets Ruffles-14
93Kraft-37
93Pinnacle-178
Canadian-178
93Score-366
Canadian-366
94Leaf-500

Kennedy, DEF
02Chicago Steel-12

Kennedy, Forbes
44Beehive Group II Photos-111
44Beehive Group II Photos-183
57Topps-50
58Topps-11
59Topps-52
63Topps-19
64Beehive Group III Photos-14
64Coca-Cola Caps-10
64Toronto Star-23
65Coca-Cola-8
68O-Pee-Chee-97
68Shirriff Coins-132
68Topps-97
94Parkhurst Missing Link-35
94Parkhurst Tall Boys-16

Kennedy, Jack
93Quebec Pee-Wee Tournament-1292

Kennedy, Joey
92British Columbia JHL-89

Kennedy, Jordan
02Sault Ste. Marie Greyhounds-22

Kennedy, Matt
06Guelph Storm-6

Kennedy, Mike
917th Inn. Sketch WHL-131
94Fleer-54
94Stars Postcards-12
94Upper Deck-326
Electric Ice-326
94Classic Pro Prospects-79
95Collector's Choice-205
Player's Club-205
Player's Club Platinum-205
95Donruss-192
95Leaf-7
95Panini Stickers-171
95Topps-27
OPC Inserts-27
New To The Game-7NG
95Ultra-39
Gold Medallion-39
95Images-73
Gold-73
96Stars Postcards-13
96Collector's Edge Ice-140
Crucibles-C14
Prism-140
97St. John's Maple Leafs-13
99German DEL-336
00German DEL-237
01German Upper Deck-183
02German DEL City Press-246
03German Mannheim Eagles Postcards-17

Kennedy, Peter
02Minnesota Golden Gophers-11
03Minnesota Golden Gophers-18
04Minnesota Golden Gophers-16
05Minnesota Golden Gophers-16
06New Mexico Scorpions-19

Kennedy, Roger
04Halifax Mooseheads-23
05Halifax Mooseheads-2
06Halifax Mooseheads-3

Kennedy, Ron
77Kalamazoo Wings-5
95German DEL-123
96German DEL-22
04German Ingolstadt Panthers-13

Kennedy, Shannon
98Minnesota Golden Gophers Women-11

Kennedy, Sheldon
89ProCards AHL-320
90O-Pee-Chee-520
91O-Pee-Chee-317
91Red Wings Little Caesars-9
91Topps-317
91Upper Deck-408
French-408
91ProCards-134
92Topps-368
Gold-368G
93Leaf-246
93OPC Premier-221
Gold-221
93Score-361
Canadian-361
93Topps/OPC Premier-221
Gold-221
94OPC Premier-408
Special Effects-408
94Topps/OPC Premier-408
Special Effects-408
94Upper Deck-437
Electric Ice-437
97Collector's Choice-21
97Donruss Press Proofs Silver-36
97Donruss Press Proofs Gold-36
97NHL Aces Playing Cards-23
97Pacific Invincible NHL Regime-13

Kennedy, Ted
44Beehive Group II Photos-414
45Quaker Oats Photos-25A
45Quaker Oats Photos-25B
45Quaker Oats Photos-25C
45Quaker Oats Photos-25D
45Quaker Oats Photos-25E
45Quaker Oats Photos-25F
48Exhibits Canadian-32
51Parkhurst-86
52Parkhurst-44
53Parkhurst-7
54Parkhurst-29
54Parkhurst-96
54Parkhurst-99
55Parkhurst-29
Quaker Oats-29
64Beehive Group III Photos-170
83Hall of Fame Postcards-E9
85Hall of Fame-69
94Parkhurst Missing Link-116
00Topps Heritage Arena Relics-OSA-TK
01BAP Ultimate Mem All-Star History-3
01BAP Ultimate Memorabilia Gloves Are Off-7
01BAP Ultimate Mem Stanley Cup Winners-21
02BAP NHL All-Star History-3
02BAP Ultimate Memorabilia Gloves Are Off-11
02BAP Ultimate Memorabilia Great Moments-1
02Maple Leafs Platinum Collection-56
02Maple Leafs Platinum Collection-103
02Parkhurst Reprints-172
02Parkhurst Reprints-176
02Parkhurst Reprints-192
02Parkhurst Vintage Memorabilia-VM19
03BAP Ultimate Memorabilia Autographs-154
Gold-154
03BAP Ultimate Mem Linemates Autos-11
03BAP Ultimate Mem Maple Leafs Forever-14
03ITG Toronto Fall Expo Forever Rivals-FR9
03ITG Used Signature Series-119
Autographs-TK
Autographs Gold-TK
Vintage Memorabilia-8
Vintage Memorabilia Autographs-8
Vintage Memorabilia Gold-8
03ITG VIP MVP-6
03Parkhurst Original Six Toronto-38
03Parkhurst Original Six Toronto-74
Autographs-6
Inserts-T5
Inserts-T7
Memorabilia-TM22
Memorabilia-TM38
04ITG NHL AS FANtasy AS History Jerseys-SB3
04ITG Franchises Canadian-88
Autographs-TK
04ITG Ultimate Memorabilia-35
Gold-35
Autographs-67
Autographs Gold-67
Cornerstones-7
Cornerstones Gold-7
Nicknames-14
Nickname Autographs-4
Original Six-9
05ITG Heroes/Prosp Toronto Expo Parallel -193
05ITG Ultimate Memorabilia Level 1-90
05ITG Ultimate Memorabilia Level 2-90
05ITG Ultimate Memorabilia Level 3-90
05ITG Ultimate Memorabilia Level 4-90
05ITG Ultimate Memorabilia Level 5-90
05ITG Ultimate Mem Decades Jerseys-6
05ITG Ultimate Mem Decades Jerseys Gold-6
05ITG Ultimate Memorabilia Double Autos-7
05ITG Ultimate Mem Double Autos Gold-7
05ITG Ultimate Mem Double Mem Autos-7
05ITG Ultimate Mem Double Mem Autos Gold-7
05ITG Ultimate Mem 3 Star of the Game Jsy-2
05ITG Ult Mem 3 Star of the Game Jsy Gold-2
05ITG Ultimate Memorabilia Triple Autos-5
05ITG Ultimate Mem Triple Autos Gold-5
05ITG Ultimate Memorabilia Ultimate Autos-28
05ITG Ultimate Mem Ultimate Autos Gold-28
05ITG Heroes and Prospects-193
Autographs Series II-TKE
06ITG Ultimate Memorabilia-134
Artist Proof-134
Autos Triple-9
Autos Triple Gold-9
Cornerstones-3
Cornerstones Gold-3
Decades-2
Decades Gold-2

Kennedy, Tim
04Sioux City Musketeers-12

Kennedy, Troy
85Kamloops Blazers-10
88Brandon Wheat Kings-9
95UK Guildford Flames-12

Kennedy, Tyler
02Sault Ste. Marie Greyhounds-9
03Sault Ste. Marie Greyhounds-11
04Sault Ste. Marie Greyhounds-11
05ITG Heroes/Prosp Toronto Expo Parallel -284
05OHL Bell All-Star Classic-29
05ITG Heroes and Prospects-284
Autographs Series II-TK
06Wilkes-Barre Scranton Penguins-21
06Wilkes-Barre Scranton Penguins Jerseys-11
06ITG Heroes and Prospects National Pride-NP09
06ITG Heroes and Prospects National Pride Gold-NP09

Kenney, Jay
96Charlotte Checkers-9
97Charlotte Checkers-13
98Peoria Rivermen-8

Kenney, Nick
95Cincinnati Cyclones-21
97Cincinnati Cyclones-23
98Cincinnati Cyclones-24
98Cincinnati Cyclones 2-28
99Cincinnati Cyclones-23
00Cincinnati Cyclones-25

Kennholt, Kenneth
89Swedish Semic Elitserien Stickers-56
90Swedish Semic Elitserien Stickers-277
91Finnish Semic World Champ Stickers-37
91Swedish Semic Elitserien Stickers-58
91Swedish Semic Elitserien Stickers-344
91Swedish Semic World Champ Stickers-37
92Swedish Semic Elitserien Stickers-79
93Swedish Semic Elitserien-101
93Swedish Semic World Champ Stickers-3
94Swedish Leaf-5
95Swedish Leaf-50
Champs-14
Face to Face-6
95Swedish Upper Deck-79
97Swedish Collector's Choice-37

Kennish, Ian
92Harvard Crimson-17

Kenny, Brad
03UK Belfast Giants-8

Kenny, Brendan
92British Columbia JHL-65
93Western Michigan Broncos-18
98Amarillo Rattlers-9

Kenny, Grant
03Yarmouth Mariners-12

Kenny, Rob
92Binghamton Rangers-8
94Binghamton Rangers-7
97Long Beach Ice Dogs-9

Kenny, Shane
93Owen Sound Platers-13
94Owen Sound Platers-2
95Slapshot-283
95Owen Sound Platers-8
95Owen Sound Platers-33
95Classic-42
95Classic-93
95Signature Rookies Auto-Phonex-21
95Signature Rook Auto-Phonex Phone Cards-21
95Classic Five-Sport *-158
Autographs-158
96Sarnia Sting-11
98Rochester Americans-24
04Fort Wayne Komets-8
04Fort Wayne Komets Shoe Carnival-7

Kent, Brian
92Oshawa Generals Sheet-23

Kent, Derrick
00Halifax Mooseheads-8
01Halifax Mooseheads-10
02Halifax Mooseheads-10
03Gatineau Olympiques-12

Kent, Reg
71Johnstown Jets Acme-9
72Johnstown Jets-15

Kentel, Tyson
98Medicine Hat Tigers-14

Kenyon, Chris
98Baton Rouge Kingfish-25

Kenyon, Cyndy
04Wisconsin Badgers Women-11

Kenyon, Jason
06Austin Ice Bats-17

Keogan, Murray
74O-Pee-Chee WHA-44
74Phoenix Roadrunners WHA Pins-7
75Phoenix Roadrunners WHA-12

Keon, Dave
44Beehive Group II Photos-415
60Wonder Bread Labels-3
60Wonder Bread Premium Photos-3
60York Photos-20
61Parkhurst-5
61Shirriff/Salada Coins-58
61York Yellow Backs-4
62El Producto Discs-4
62Parkhurst-15
62Shirriff Coins-12
62Shirriff Coins-52
62Shirriff Coins-55
62York Iron-On Transfers-9
63Chex Photos-30
63Maple Leafs Team Issue-12
63Maple Leafs Team Issue-13
63Parkhurst-75
63Toronto Star-23
63York White Backs-6
64Beehive Group III Photos-171A
64Beehive Group III Photos-171B
64Coca-Cola Caps-99
64Topps-94
64Toronto Star-24
65Coca-Cola-99
65Coca-Cola Booklets-B
65Maple Leafs White Border-12
65Topps-17
66Maple Leafs Hockey Talks-3
66Topps-78
66Topps USA Test-30
67Post Flip Books-6
67Topps-11
67York Action Octagons-4
67York Action Octagons-13
67York Action Octagons-19
68O-Pee-Chee-198
Puck Stickers-19
68Post Marbles-13
68Shirriff Coins-169
68Topps-128
69Maple Leafs White Border Glossy-18
69Maple Leafs White Border Glossy-19
69Maple Leafs White Border Matte-2
69O-Pee-Chee-51
Four-in-One-11
Stamps-17
69Topps-51
70Dad's Cookies-65
70Esso Power Players-27
70O-Pee-Chee-219
Deckle-47
70Sargent Promotions Stamps-208
70Topps/OPC Sticker Stamps-17
71Bazooka-11
71Letraset Action Replays-1
71Maple Leafs Postcards-8
71O-Pee-Chee-80
71O-Pee-Chee-259
O-Pee-Chee/Topps Booklets-16
Posters-3
71Sargent Promotions Stamps-206
71Topps-80
71Toronto Sun-261
72Maple Leafs Postcards-14
72Maple Leafs Postcards-15
72O-Pee-Chee-108
72O-Pee-Chee-209
72Sargent Promotions Stamps-206
72Topps-88
72Finnish Semic World Championship-164
72Swedish Semic World Championship-164
73Maple Leafs Postcards-16
73O-Pee-Chee-150
73Topps-85
74Lipton Soup-50
74Maple Leafs Postcards-10
74Maple Leafs Postcards-11
74NHL Action Stamps-256
74O-Pee-Chee NHL-151
74Topps-151
75O-Pee-Chee WHA-97
76O-Pee-Chee WHA-52
79O-Pee-Chee-279
80O-Pee-Chee-272
81O-Pee-Chee-129
81Topps-E83
82Post Cereal-7
85Hall of Fame-255
91Ultimate Original Six-39
French-39
92Parkhurst Parkie Reprints-PR21
92Parkhurst Promo Sheets-2
93Parkhurst Parkie Reprints-PR67
94Parkhurst Missing Link Future Stars-FS2
94Parkhurst Tall Boys-111
Autographs-A6
94Zeller's Masters of Hockey-4
94Zeller's Masters of Hockey Signed-4
95Parkhurst '66-67-100
Coins-100
99BAP Memorabilia AS Canadian Hobby-CH2
99BAP Memorabilia AS Cdn Hobby Autos-CH2
04ITG Franchises Update-469
04ITG Franchises Update-496
Autographs-DKN1
Autographs-DKN2
Original Sticks-UOS2
Original Sticks Autographs-UOSDK
Original Sticks Gold-UOS2
Teammates-UTM3
Teammates Gold-UTM3
Trophy Winners-UTW3
Trophy Winners Gold-UTW3
04UD Legends Classics Jersey Redemptions-JY14
05ITG Heroes/Prosp Toronto Expo Parallel -14
05ITG Ultimate Memorabilia Level 1-23
05ITG Ultimate Memorabilia Level 2-23
05ITG Ultimate Memorabilia Level 3-23
05ITG Ultimate Memorabilia Level 4-23
05ITG Ultimate Memorabilia Level 5-23
05ITG Ultimate Mem Complete Jersey-23
05ITG Ultimate Mem Complete Jersey Gold-23
05ITG Ultimate Mem Cornerstones Jerseys-5
05ITG Ultimate Mem Cornerst Jerseys Gold-5
05ITG Ultimate Mem Decades Jerseys-6
05ITG Ultimate Mem Decades Jerseys Gold-6
05ITG Ultimate Memorabilia Double Autos-7
05ITG Ultimate Mem Double Autos Gold-7
05ITG Ultimate Mem Double Mem-13
05ITG Ultimate Mem Double Mem Autos-7
05ITG Ultimate Mem Double Mem Autos Gold-7
05ITG Ultimate Mem Double Mem Gold-13
05ITG Ultimate Memorabilia Emblem Attic-15
05ITG Ultimate Mem Emblem Attic Gold-15
05ITG Ultimate Memorabilia Emblems-6
05ITG Ultimate Memorabilia Emblems Gold-6
05ITG Ultimate Memorabilia In The Numbers-1
05ITG Ultimate Mem In The Numbers Gold-1
05ITG Ultimate Mem Jersey and Emblem-27
05ITG Ultimate Memorabilia Jersey Autos-13
05ITG Ultimate Mem Jersey Autos Gold-13
05ITG Ultimate Mem Jersey Emblems Gold-27
05ITG Ultimate Memorabilia Jerseys-10
05ITG Ultimate Mem Jerseys Gold-10
05ITG Ultimate Mem Pass the Torch Jerseys-19
05ITG Ultimate Mem Passing Torch Jsy Gold-19
05ITG Ultimate Memorabilia R.O.Y. Autos-12
05ITG Ultimate Mem R.O.Y. Autos Gold-12
05ITG Ultimate Memorabilia R.O.Y. Emblems-1
05ITG Ultimate Mem R.O.Y. Emblems Gold-1
05ITG Ultimate Memorabilia R.O.Y. Jerseys-1
05ITG Ultimate Mem R.O.Y. Jerseys Gold-1
05ITG Ultimate Memorabilia R.O.Y. Numbers-1
05ITG Ultimate Mem R.O.Y. Numbers Gold-1
05ITG Ultimate Memorabilia Stick Autos-12
05ITG Ultimate Mem Stick Autos Gold-12
05ITG Ultimate Mem 3 Star of the Game Jsy-7
05ITG Ult Mem 3 Star of the Game Jsy Gold-7
05ITG Ultimate Memorabilia Trifecta Autos-2
05ITG Ultimate Mem Trifecta Autos Gold-2
05ITG Ultimate Memorabilia Triple Autos-5
05ITG Ultimate Mem Triple Autos Gold-5
05ITG Ultimate Mem Triple Threads Jerseys-7
05ITG Ultimate Mem Triple Thread Jsy Gold-7
05ITG Ultimate Memorabilia Ultimate Autos-27
05ITG Ultimate Mem Ultimate Autos Gold-27
05ITG Ultimate Mem Ult Hero Double Jersey-4
05ITG Ult Mem Ult Hero Double Jsy Gold-4
05ITG Ultimate Mem Ult Hero Single Jersey-4
05ITG Ult Mem Ult Hero Single Jersey Gold-4
05ITG Ultimate Mem Ult Hero Triple Jersey-4
05ITG Ult Mem Ult Hero Triple Jersey Gold-4
05ITG Ultimate Memorabilia Vintage Lumber-19
05ITG Ultimate Mem Vintage Lumber Gold-19
05ITG Heroes and Prospects-14
Aspiring-ASP3
Autographs-A-DK
Future Teammates-FT7
Hero Memorabilia-HM-41
Hero Memorabilia Dual-HDM-13
06ITG Ultimate Memorabilia-37
Artist Proof-37
Autos-19
Autos Gold-19
Autos Triple-9
Autos Triple Gold-9
Blades of Steel-6
Blades of Steel Gold-6
Boys Will Be Boys-10
Boys Will Be Boys Gold-10
Captain-C-3
Captain-C Gold-3
Complete Jersey-12
Complete Jersey Gold-12
Cornerstones-3
Cornerstones Gold-3
Decades-2
Decades Gold-2
Double Memorabilia-12
Double Memorabilia Gold-12
In The Numbers-12
In The Numbers Gold-12
Jerseys-21
Jerseys Gold-21
Jerseys and Emblems-13
Jerseys and Emblems Gold-13
Jerseys Autos-26
Jerseys Autos Gold-26
Journey Emblem-3
Journey Emblem Gold-3
Journey Jersey-3
Journey Jersey Gold-3
Legendary Captains-2
Legendary Captains Gold-2
Passing The Torch-2
Passing The Torch Gold-2
R.O.Y. Autos-18
R.O.Y. Autos Gold-18
R.O.Y. Emblems-18
R.O.Y. Emblems Gold-18
R.O.Y. Jerseys-18
R.O.Y. Jerseys Gold-18
R.O.Y. Numbers-18
R.O.Y. Numbers Gold-18
Retro Teammates-5
Retro Teammates Gold-5
Ring Leaders-9
Ring Leaders Gold-9
Road to the Cup-3
Road to the Cup Gold-3
Seams Unbelievable-4
Seams Unbelievable Gold-4
Stick Rack-3
Stick Rack-9
Stick Rack Gold-3
Stick Rack Gold-9
Sticks and Jerseys-2
Sticks and Jerseys Gold-2
Sticks Autos-13
Sticks Autos Gold-13
Triple Thread Jerseys-7
Triple Thread Jerseys Gold-7
06ITG Heroes and Prospects Heroes Memorabilia-HM10
06ITG Heroes and Prospects Heroes Memorabilia Gold-HM10
07Maple Leafs 1967 Commemorative-14
Sticks-SDK

Kepl, Richard
06Czech OFS-274

Kerasiotis, Lee
93Quebec Pee-Wee Tournament-1452

Kerch, Alexander
90O-Pee-Chee-474
94Classic Pro Prospects-176
99German DEL-300
00German DEL-202
01German Upper Deck-25
Gate Attractions-GA2

Kerch, Kerry
82Kitchener Rangers-6

Keremidschieff, Gary
84Nanaimo Clippers-13

Kerestes, Jaroslav
99Columbus Cottonmouths-19
00Columbus Cottonmouths-5
01Columbus Cottonmouths-8
03New Mexico Scorpions-10
03Odessa Jackalopes-12

Keresztes, Otto
94German DEL-347
99German Bundesliga 2-236

Kerluke, Dan
01Fresno Falcons-8
01Idaho Steelheads-8
05Maine Black Bears-30

Kerman, Kalle
03Finnish Cardset-134
04Finnish Cardset-143
Parallel-107
05Swedish SHL Elitset-263
Gold-263
Teammates-10
06Swedish SHL Elitset-221

Kern, Josh
97Dubuque Fighting Saints-8
02Peoria Rivermen-21
02Peoria Rivermen RBI Sports-161

Kerr, Alan
84Springfield Indians-8
85Islanders News-9
86Islanders Team Issue-1
88O-Pee-Chee-63
88O-Pee-Chee Stickers-106
88Panini Stickers-288
88Topps-63
89Islanders Team Issue-10
89Panini Stickers-275
90Bowman-118
Tiffany-118
90O-Pee-Chee-50
90Panini Stickers-89
90Pro Set-184
90Score-307A
Canadian-307A
90Topps-50
Tiffany-50
90Upper Deck-388
French-388
91Parkhurst-273
French-273
91Pro Set-376
French-376
91Score Canadian Bilingual-571
91Score Canadian English-571

Kerr, Albert
10Sweet Caporal Postcards-10
11C55-10
12C57-33

Kerr, Allen
907th Inn. Sketch Memorial Cup-58

Kerr, Brian
00Sioux City Musketeers-15

Kerr, Chris
91British Columbia JHL-81
91British Columbia JHL-128
93Quebec Pee-Wee Tournament-546
95Slapshot-421

Kerr, Dave
33O-Pee-Chee V304B-59
33V252 Canadian Gum-35
33V357 Ice Kings-19
34Beehive Group I Photos-282
34Sweet Caporal-43
35Diamond Matchbooks Tan 2-34
35Diamond Matchbooks Tan 3-31
37V356 Worldwide Gum-53
39O-Pee-Chee V301-1-37
40O-Pee-Chee V301-2-139
03BAP Ultimate Memorabilia Paper Cuts-41
05ITG Ultimate Mem Marvelous Maroons Auto-6
06ITG Ultimate Memorabilia Marvelous Maroons Autos-3

Kerr, Kevin
83North Bay Centennials-12
88ProCards AHL-252
90Cincinnati Cyclones-32
90ProCards AHL/IHL-282
91Cincinnati Cyclones-10
92Anaheim Bullfrogs RHI-5
92Birmingham Bulls-15
93Anaheim Bullfrogs RHI-7
93Birmingham Bulls-15
93Flint Generals-13
94Flint Generals-12
95Flint Generals-2
96Flint Generals-11
97Flint Generals-10
97Flint Generals EBK-11
98Mobile Mysticks-4
98Quad-City Mallards-12
98UHL All-Stars-19
99Quad-City Mallards-21
99UHL All-Stars West-19T

Kerr, Randy
91Air Canada SJHL-C7

Kerr, Reg
79Blackhawks Postcards-8
79O-Pee-Chee-67
79Topps-67
80O-Pee-Chee-377
81Blackhawks Borderless Postcards-11
81O-Pee-Chee-58
81O-Pee-Chee Stickers-118
81Topps-W70
82O-Pee-Chee-67
82O-Pee-Chee Stickers-176
82Post Cereal-4
82Topps Stickers-176
83Moncton Alpines-11
88Oilers Tenth Anniversary-75
94Arizona Icecats-21

Kerr, Ryan
05Lethbridge Hurricanes-11

Kerr, Scott
83Kitchener Rangers-14

Kerr, Stuart
01Spokane Chiefs-14
02Red Deer Rebels-17
03Red Deer Rebels-17
04Moose Jaw Warriors-16

Kerr, Tim
81O-Pee-Chee-251
82O-Pee-Chee-253
82Post Cereal-14
83Flyers J.C. Penney-13
84O-Pee-Chee-162
84O-Pee-Chee-364
84O-Pee-Chee Stickers-105
84O-Pee-Chee Stickers-106
847-Eleven Discs-37
84Topps-119
85Flyers Postcards-16
85O-Pee-Chee-91
85O-Pee-Chee-260
85O-Pee-Chee Box Bottoms-H
85O-Pee-Chee Stickers-96
857-Eleven Credit Cards-14
85Topps-91
85Topps Box Bottoms-H
86Flyers Postcards-14
86O-Pee-Chee-134
86O-Pee-Chee-261
86O-Pee-Chee Box Bottoms-G
86O-Pee-Chee Stickers-240
86Topps-134
86Topps Box Bottoms-G
87Flyers Postcards-15
87O-Pee-Chee-144
87O-Pee-Chee Box Bottoms-B
87O-Pee-Chee Minis-20
87O-Pee-Chee Stickers-103
87Panini Stickers-128
87Topps-144
87Topps Box Bottoms-B
87Topps Sticker Inserts-10
88Esso All-Stars-21
88Flyers Postcards-10
88Panini Stickers-321
89Flyers Postcards-14
89O-Pee-Chee-72
89O-Pee-Chee Box Bottoms-G
89O-Pee-Chee Stickers-110
89O-Pee-Chee Stickers-216
89Panini Stickers-294
89Panini Stickers-377
89Topps-72
89Topps Box Bottoms-G
90Flyers Postcards-13
90O-Pee-Chee-210
90Panini Stickers-120
90Pro Set-218
90Score-177
Canadian-177
90Score Hottest/Rising Stars-77
90Topps-210
Tiffany-210
90Upper Deck-247
90Upper Deck-304
French-247
French-304
91Pro Set Platinum-80
91O-Pee-Chee-164
91OPC Premier-83
91Panini Stickers-226
91Pinnacle-52
French-52
91Pro Set-180
91Pro Set-446
French-180
French-446
91Score American-108
91Score Canadian Bilingual-108
91Score Canadian Bilingual-565
91Score Canadian English-108
91Score Canadian English-565
91Score Rookie/Traded-15T
91Stadium Club-130
91Topps-164
92OPC Premier-127
92Pinnacle-368
French-368
92Score-93
Canadian-93
92Topps-351
Gold-351G
92Ultra-74
92Whalers Dairymart-11
93Flyers Lineup Sheets-19
01Topps Archives-22
02UD Foundations-75
04ITG Franchises US East-430
Autographs-A-TKR

Kerrigan, Steve
92Dayton Bombers-14
93Dayton Bombers-26

Kerrivan, Brad
93Quebec Pee-Wee Tournament-187

Kersey, Jade
91British Columbia JHL-44
92British Columbia JHL-99

Kerth, Werner
93Swedish Semic World Champ Stickers-280
94Finnish Jaa Kiekko-243
95Austrian National Team-12
95Swedish World Championships Stickers-266
96Swedish Semic Wien-218

Kertudo, Gael
95Swiss HNL-501
96Swiss HNL-423

Kesa, Dan
90Prince Albert Raiders-6
907th Inn. Sketch WHL-271
91Prince Albert Raiders-6
917th Inn. Sketch WHL-247
92Hamilton Canucks-12
93PowerPlay-460
94Classic Pro Prospects-116
96Detroit Vipers-10
97Detroit Vipers-3
99Pacific-340
Copper-340
Emerald Green-340
Gold-340
Ice Blue-340
Premiere Date-340
Red-340
00Manitoba Moose-13

Kesa, Teemu
99Finnish Cardset-247
01Finnish Cardset-297
04Albany River Rats-11
05Albany River Rats-12
06Finnish Porin Assat Pelaajakortit-29

Kesalainen, Erkki
73Finnish Jaakiekko-181

Keserich, Ian
04Ohio State Buckeyes-16
05Ohio State Buckeyes-16

Keski-Kungas, Stefan
04German Weiden Blue Devils-14

Keskinen, Esa
89Swedish Semic World Champ Stickers-48
91Finnish Semic World Champ Stickers-19
91Finnish Jyvas-Hyva Stickers-62
91Swedish Semic World Champ Stickers-19
92Finnish Jyvas-Hyva Stickers-176
92Finnish Semic-24
93Finnish Jyvas-Hyva Stickers-318
93Finnish SISU-40
93Finnish SISU-360
93Finnish SISU-370
93Finnish SISU-370B
93Finnish SISU-372
93Finnish SISU-372B
94Finnish SISU-156
94Finnish SISU-164
94Finnish SISU-367
94Finnish SISU Fire On Ice-10
94Finnish SISU Specials-7
94Finnish Jaa Kiekko-41
94Swedish Leaf-177
Foreign Affairs-2
95Finnish SISU Gold Cards-14
95Finnish SISU Limited-8
95Finnish Karjala World Champ Labels-5
95Finnish Semic World Championships-9
95Swedish Leaf-56
95Swedish Leaf-306
Champs-7
Mega-6
95Swedish Upper Deck-89
95Swedish Upper Deck-225
95Swedish Globe World Championships-144
95Swedish World Championships Stickers-172
96Swedish Semic Wien-9
97Swedish Collector's Choice-94
97Swedish Collector's Choice-222
Crash the Game Exchange-C25
Crash the Game Redemption-R25
98Finnish Keraílysarja Leijonat-27
98Swedish UD Choice-108
Day in the Life-5
99Finnish Cardset-332
02Finnish Cardset-194

Keskinen, Jere
93Finnish SISU-18

Kesler, Ryan
98Quebec Pee Wee Tournament-157
02Ohio State Buckeyes-20
03BAP Memorabilia Draft Redemptions-23
03BAP Ultimate Mem Rookie Jersey Emblems-31
03BAP Ultimate Mem Rookie Jsy Emblem Gold-31
03BAP Ultimate Mem Rookie Jersey Numbers-31
03BAP Ultimate Mem Rookie Jsy Number Gold-31
03Beehive-217
Gold-217
Silver-217
03ITG Action-638
03ITG Used Signature Series-172
Gold-172
03ITG VIP Rookie Debut-66
03Pacific-368
03Pacific Calder-137
Silver-137
03Pacific Complete-509
Red-509
03Pacific Luxury Suite-78
Gold-78
03Pacific Quest for the Cup-137
03Parkhurst Rookie-137
Rookie Emblems-RE-47
Rookie Emblems Gold-RE-47
Rookie Jerseys-RJ-47
Rookie Jerseys Gold-RJ-47
Rookie Numbers-RN-47
Rookie Numbers Gold-RN-47
03SP Authentic-111
Limited-111
03SP Game Used-125
03SPx-232
03Titanium-138
Hobby Jersey Number Parallels-138
Retail-138
Retail Jersey Number Parallels-138
03Topps Traded-TT141
Blue-TT141
Gold-TT141
Red-TT141
03UD Premier Collection-93
03Upper Deck-454
Canadian Exclusives-454
HG-454
UD Exclusives-454
03Upper Deck Classic Portraits-192
03Upper Deck Ice-118
Glass Parallel-118
03Upper Deck Rookie Update-153
03Upper Deck Trilogy-184
03AHL Top Prospects-13
03Manitoba Moose-17
04SP Authentic Sign of the Times-QS-BBLK
04SP Authentic Sign of the Times-QS-VANC
04SP Authentic Sign of the Times-FS-VAN
04AHL All-Stars-21
04AHL Top Prospects-32
04Manitoba Moose-16
04ITG Heroes and Prospects-43
Autographs-RK
Combos-11
He Shoots-He Scores Prizes-33
04ITG Heroes/Prospects Toronto Expo '05-43
04ITG Heroes/Prospects Expo Heroes/Pros-43
05ITG Heroes/Prosp Toronto Expo Parallel -64
05Be A Player Signatures-RK
05Be A Player Signatures Gold-RK
05Black Diamond Gemography-G-RK
05Black Diamond Gemography Emerald-G-RK
05Black Diamond Gemography Gold-G-RK
05Black Diamond Gemography Onyx-G-RK
05Black Diamond Gemography Ruby-G-RK
05Parkhurst-479
Facsimile Auto Parallel-479
05SP Authentic Scripts to Success-SSRK
05SP Authentic Sign of the Times-RK
05SP Game Used Authentic Fabrics Quad-KBJL
05SP Game Used Authentic Patches Quad -KBJL
05SP Game Used Auto Draft-AD-RK
05SP Game Used Statscriptions-ST-RK
05UD Artifacts Auto Facts-AF-RK
05UD Artifacts Auto Facts Blue-AF-RK
05UD Artifacts Auto Facts Copper-AF-RK
05UD Artifacts Auto Facts Pewter-AF-RK
05UD Artifacts Auto Facts Silver-AF-RK
05UD Artifacts Remarkable Artifacts-RA-RK
05UD Artifacts Remarkable Artifacts Dual-RA-RK
05UD Powerplay Power Marks-PMRK
05Ultra-196
Gold-196
Fresh Ink-FI-RK
Fresh Ink Blue-FI-RK
Ice-196
05Upper Deck-432
Ice Fresh Ice-FIRK
Ice Fresh Ice Glass-FIRK
Ice Fresh Ice Glass Patches-FIPRK
Ice Glacial Graphs-GGRK
Ice Glacial Graphs Labels-GGRK
MVP Materials-M-RK
MVP ProSign-P-RK
Trilogy Scripts-SFS-RK
05ITG Heroes and Prospects-64
Autographs-A-RKS
He Shoots-He Scores Prizes-39
Jerseys-GUJ-10
Jerseys Gold-GUJ-10
Emblems-GUE-10
Emblems Gold-GUE-10
Numbers-GUN-10
Numbers Gold-GUN-10
06Canucks Postcards-9
06Flair Showcase Inks-IKE
06Flair Showcase Wave of the Future-WF41
06Fleer-194
Tiffany-194
06Gatorade-87
06O-Pee-Chee-472
Rainbow-472
06Ultra-193
Gold Medallion-193
Ice Medallion-193
06Upper Deck-194
Exclusives Parallel-194
High Gloss Parallel-194
Game Jerseys-J2RK
Game Patches-P2RK
Masterpieces-194
Signatures-SRK
06Upper Deck MVP-286
Gold Script-286
Super Script-286
Jerseys-OJBK
06Upper Deck Victory Next In Line-NL46

Kessel, Phil
05Minnesota Golden Gophers-17
06Be A Player-202
Autographs-202
Profiles-PP10
Profiles Autographs-PP10
Signatures 10-202
Signatures 25-202
Signatures Duals-DBK
Signatures Trios-TBKS
Signatures Foursomes-FSSLK
06Be A Player Portraits-109
06Beehive-105
Blue-105
Gold-105
Matte-105
Red Facsimile Signatures-105
Wood-105
5 X 7 Black and White-105
5 X 7 Dark Wood-105
06Black Diamond-202
Black-202
Gold-202
Ruby-202
06Flair Showcase-303
06Hot Prospects-141
Red Hot-141
White Hot-141
Hot Materials -HMPK
Hot Materials Red Hot-HMPK
Hot Materials White Hot-HMPK
Hotagraphs-HPK
06ITG International Ice-110
Gold-110
Autographs-APK
06ITG Ultimate Memorabilia-117
Artist Proof-117
Autos Dual-5
Autos Dual Gold-5
Complete Jersey-24
Complete Jersey Gold-24
Future Star-10
Future Star Gold-10
Future Star Autos-1
Future Star Autos Gold-1
Future Star Patches Autos-1
Future Star Patches Autos Gold-1
R.O.Y. Autos-3
R.O.Y. Autos Gold-3
R.O.Y. Emblems-3
R.O.Y. Emblems Gold-3
R.O.Y. Jerseys-3
R.O.Y. Jerseys Gold-3
R.O.Y. Numbers-3
R.O.Y. Numbers Gold-3
06O-Pee-Chee-543
06O-Pee-Chee-623
Rainbow-543
Rainbow-623
Autographs-A-PK
06SP Authentic-163
Limited-163
Sign of the Times-STPK
Sign of the Times Duals-STKB
Sign of the Times Duals-STNK
Sign of the Times Triples-ST3BBK
Sign of the Times Quads-ST4MKSL
06SP Game Used-106
Gold-106
Rainbow-106
Autographs-106
Letter Marks-LMPK
Rookie Exclusives Autographs-REPK
06SPx-189
Spectrum-189
06The Cup-170
Autographed Foundations-CQKE

Autographed Foundations Patches-CQKE
Autographed NHL Shields Duals-DASKB
Autographed NHL Shields Duals-DASKL
Autographed NHL Shields Duals-DASMK
Autographed NHL Shields Duals-DASSK
Autographed Rookie Masterpiece Pressplates-170
Foundations-CQKE
Foundations Patches-CQKE
Enshrinements-EPK
Gold Rainbow Autographed Rookie Patches-170
Honorable Numbers-HNPK
Limited Logos-LLPK
Masterpiece Pressplates (Be A Player Portraits)-109
Masterpiece Pressplates (Bee Hive)-105
Masterpiece Pressplates (Marquee Rookies)-543
Masterpiece Pressplates (MVP)-299
Masterpiece Pressplates (SP Authentic Autographs)-163
Masterpiece Pressplates (SP Game Used)-106
Masterpiece Pressplates (SPx Autographs)-189
Masterpiece Pressplates (Sweet Beginnings)-104
Masterpiece Pressplates (Trilogy)-105
Masterpiece Pressplates (Ultimate Collection Autographs)-104
Masterpiece Pressplates (Victory)-289
NHL Shields Duals-DSHKO
NHL Shields Duals-DSHPA
NHL Shields Duals-DSHPY
Property of-POKE
Rookies Black-170
Rookies Platinum-170
Scripted Swatches-SSPK
Signature Patches-SPPK
06UD Artifacts-233
06UD Mini Jersey Collection-103
06Ultimate Collection-104
Autographed Jerseys-AJ-PK
Autographed Patches-AJ-PK
Jerseys Triple-UJ3-ENK
Patches Triple-UJ3-ENK
Rookies Autographed NHL Shields-104
Rookies Autographed Patches-104
Signatures-US-PK
Ultimate Debut Threads Jerseys-DJ-PK
Ultimate Debut Threads Jerseys Autographs-DJ-PK
Ultimate Debut Threads Patches-DJ-PK
Ultimate Debut Threads Patches Autographs-DJ-PK
06Ultra-250
Gold Medallion-250
Ice Medallion-250
06Upper Deck-204
06Upper Deck-250
Exclusives Parallel-204
Exclusives Parallel-250
High Gloss Parallel-204
High Gloss Parallel-250
Masterpieces-204
Masterpieces-250
Rookie Game Dated Moments-RGD2
Rookie Headliners-RH22
Rookie Materials-RMPK
Rookie Materials Patches-RMPK
Signatures-SPK
06Upper Deck MVP-299
Gold Script-299
Super Script-299
06Upper Deck Ovation-154
06Upper Deck Sweet Shot-104
Rookie Jerseys Autographs-104
Signature Shots/Saves-SSPK
Signature Shots/Saves Ice Signings-SSIPK
Signature Shots/Saves Sticks-SSSPK
Signature Sticks-STPK
06Upper Deck Trilogy-105
06Upper Deck Victory-289
06ITG Heroes and Prospects-136
Autographs-APK
Class of 2006-CL02
Complete Jerseys-CJ06
Complete Jerseys Gold-CJ06
Jerseys-GUJ61
Jerseys Gold-GUJ61
Emblems-GUE61
Emblems Gold-GUE61
Numbers-GUN61
Numbers Gold-GUN61
Quad Emblems-QE16
07Upper Deck All-Star Game Redemptions-AS2
07Upper Deck Rookie Class -4
07Upper Deck Rookie Class C-Card Insert-CC2
07Upper Deck Victory-66
Black-66
Gold-66
Stars on Ice-SI6

Kessell, Rick
72Sargent Promotions Stamps-177

Kesselring, Casey
92Saskatchewan JHL-111
98ECHL All-Star Northern Conference-17
01Greensboro Generals-10
01Macon Whoopee-20

Kessler, Dino
92Finnish Semic-204
93Swiss HNL-114
95Swedish World Championships Stickers-121
95Swiss HNL-163
95Swiss HNL-518
95Swiss HNL-530
96Swiss HNL-58
98Swiss Power Play Stickers-207
98Swiss Power Play Stickers-259
99Swiss Panini Stickers-209
00Swiss Panini Stickers-251
00Swiss Slapshot Mini-Cards-EVZ5
02Swiss HNL-340

Kessler, Roman
93Swiss HNL-380

Kesti, Jari
00Finnish Cardset-146

Ketola, Juha-Pekka
01Sherbrooke Castors-4
04Finnish Cardset-317

Ketola, Simo
80Finnish Mallasjuoma-211

Ketola, Stefan
91Swedish Semic Elitserien Stickers-75
92Swedish Semic Elitserien Stickers-320
93Swedish Semic Elitserien-285
94Swedish Leaf-269
95Swedish Leaf-24
95Swedish Upper Deck-29
00Swiss Panini Stickers-321
01Swiss HNL-354
01UK Manchester Storm Retro-18
02Swiss HNL-396

Ketola, Toni
71Finnish Suomi Stickers-367

Ketola, Veli-Pekka
65Finnish Hellas-38
66Finnish Jaakiekkosarja-51
69Swedish Hockey-371
70Finnish Jaakiekko-62
70Finnish Jaakiekko-175
70Swedish Hockey-303
70Swedish Masterserien-158
71Finnish Suomi Stickers-63
71Finnish Suomi Stickers-85
71Swedish Hockey-66
72Finnish Jaakiekko-63
72Finnish Jaakiekko-248
72Finnish Hellas-2
72Finnish Panda Toronto-38
72Finnish Panda Toronto-98
72Finnish Semic World Championship-79
72Swedish Stickers-36
72Swedish Semic World Championship-79
73Finnish Jaakiekko-65
73Finnish Jaakiekko-247
74Finnish Jenkki-6
74Finnish Typotor-45
74Swedish Stickers-108
74Swedish Semic World Champ Stickers-83
75O-Pee-Chee WHA-15
76O-Pee-Chee WHA-88
77Finnish Sportscasters-17-397
78Finnish SM-Liiga-13
78Finnish SM-Liiga-233
80Finnish Mallasjuoma-209
81Rockies Postcards-8
82Swedish Semic VM Stickers-162
91Finnish Semic World Champ Stickers-230
91Swedish Semic World Champ Stickers-230
93Finnish Jyvas-Hyva Stickers-343
93Finnish SISU-207
94Finnish SISU-400
95Finnish SISU-387
96Finnish SISU Redline-196
96Swedish Semic Wien Hockey Legends-HL13

Ketter, Kerry
72Flames Postcards-6

Ketterer, Markus
91Upper Deck-23
French-23
91Finnish Semic World Champ Stickers-2
91Finnish Jyvas-Hyva Stickers-19
91Swedish Semic World Champ Stickers-2
92Finnish Jyvas-Hyva Stickers-53
92Finnish Semic-3
93Swedish Semic World Champ Stickers-45
93Rochester Americans Kodak-13
93Classic-39
94Finnish Jaa Kiekko-4
94Swedish Olympics Lillehammer*-301
94Classic Pro Prospects-167
95Finnish Semic World Championships-47
95Swedish Leaf-211
95Swedish Upper Deck-56
95Swedish Upper Deck-224
95Swedish Globe World Championships-127
96Swedish Semic Wien-32
Super Goalies-SG8
98Finnish Kerailysarja-97
Leijonat-1
Mad Masks-5
02Finnish Cardset-38

Kettles, Kyle
99Medicine Hat Tigers-24
99Medicine Hat Tigers-31
00Medicine Hat Tigers-12
01Moose Jaw Warriors-21
02Louisiana Ice Gators-9
04Louisiana Ice Gators-9

Kettner, Tommy
94German First League-355

Kettunen, Pertti
70Finnish Jaakiekko-312

Kettunen, Seppo
72Finnish Jaakiekko-288
73Finnish Jaakiekko-221

Keup, Ben
04Idaho Steelheads-8

Kewin, Shea
05Ottawa 67's-5
06Oshawa Generals-12

Keyes, Erin
04Ohio State Buckeyes Women-16

Keyes, Richard
02Kalamazoo Wings-19

Keyes, Tim
95Slapshot-256

Keys, Erin
06Ohio State Buckeyes Women-12

Khabibulin, Nikolai
91Upper Deck-652
French-652
91Upper Deck Czech World Juniors-13
93Swedish Semic World Champ Stickers-129
94Finest-27
Super Team Winners-27
Refractors-27
94Fleer-242
94Upper Deck-420
Electric Ice-420
94Finnish Jaa Kiekko-135
94Signature Rookies Gold Standard *-88
94Signature Rookies Tetrad *-108
Signatures-108
95Be A Player-176
Signatures-S176
Signatures Die Cuts-S176
95Bowman-89
All-Foil-89
95Collector's Choice-75
Player's Club-75
Player's Club Platinum-75
95Donruss-185
95Emotion-193
95Finest-63
Refractors-63
95Jets Readers Club-4
95Jets Team Issue-10
95Leaf-27
95Metal-162
95Panini Stickers-221
95Parkhurst International-230
Emerald Ice-230
95Pinnacle-118
Artist's Proofs-118
Rink Collection-118
95Score-142
Black Ice Artist's Proofs-142
Black Ice-142
95SkyBox Impact-181
95Stadium Club-157
Members Only Master Set-157
95Topps-48
OPC Inserts-48
95Ultra-180
95Ultra-372
Gold Medallion-180
95Upper Deck-85
Electric Ice-85
Electric Ice Gold-85
95Images-42
Gold-42
96Be A Player Stacking the Pads-7
96Black Diamond-36
Gold-36
96Collector's Choice-204
96Coyotes Coca-Cola-12
96Coyotes Coca-Cola-13
96Donruss-172
Press Proofs-172
Between the Pipes-9
Dominators-2
96Donruss Canadian Ice-95
Gold Press Proofs-95
Red Press Proofs-95
96Donruss Elite-49
Die Cut Stars-49
Painted Warriors-9
Painted Warriors Promos-P9
96Flair-71
Blue Ice-71
96Fleer-90
96Fleer Picks-86
96Leaf-63
Press Proofs-63
Shut Down-9
The Best Of ...-6
96Leaf Limited-60
Gold-60
96Leaf Preferred-10
Press Proofs-10
Steel-30
Steel Gold-30
Masked Marauders-9
96Metal Universe-118
96Pinnacle-161
Artist's Proofs-161
Foil-161
Premium Stock-161
Rink Collection-161
Masks-7
Masks Die Cuts-7
96Score-105
Artist's Proofs-105
Dealer's Choice Artist's Proofs-105
Special Artist's Proofs-105
Golden Blades-105
Net Worth-18
Sudden Death-15
96Select Certified-17
Artist's Proofs-17
Blue-17
Mirror Blue-17
Mirror Gold-17
Mirror Red-17
Red-17
Freezers-14
96SkyBox Impact-105
96SP-120
96Summit-41
Artist's Proofs-41
Ice-41
Metal-41
Premium Stock-41
In The Crease-12
In The Crease Premium Stock-12
96Team Out-65
96Ultra-132
Gold Medallion-132
96Upper Deck-126
96Zenith-40
Artist's Proofs-40
96Swedish Semic Wien-129
96Collector's Edge Ice-70
Crucibles-C12
Prism-70
97Be A Player-13
Autographs-13
Autographs Die-Cuts-13
Autographs Prismatic Die-Cuts-13
Stacking the Pads-13
97Black Diamond-53
Double Diamond-53
Triple Diamond-53
Quadruple Diamond-53
97Collector's Choice-193
Star Quest-SQ35
97Coyotes Face-Off Luncheon -10
97Crown Royale-104
Emerald Green-104
Ice Blue-104
Silver-104
Freeze Out Die-Cuts-15
97Donruss-120
Press Proofs Silver-120
Press Proofs Gold-120
97Donruss Canadian Ice-75
Dominion Series-75
Provincial Series-75
97Donruss Limited-124
Exposure-124
Fabric of the Game-30
97Donruss Preferred-101
Cut to the Chase-101
97Donruss Priority-36
Stamp of Approval-36
97Esso Olympic Hockey Heroes-40
97Esso Olympic Hockey Heroes French-40
97Katch-111
Gold-111
Silver-111
97Leaf-62
Fractal Matrix-62
Fractal Matrix Die Cuts-62
Pipe Dreams-13
97Leaf International-62
Universal Ice-62
97Pacific-6
Copper-6
Emerald Green-6
Ice Blue-6
Red-6
Silver-6
In The Cage Laser Cuts-16
97Pacific Dynagon-96
Copper-96
Dark Grey-96
Emerald Green-96
Ice Blue-96
Red-96
Silver-96
Stonewallers-17
Tandems-64
97Pacific Invincible-107
Copper-107
Emerald Green-107
Ice Blue-107
Red-107
Silver-107
NHL Regime-153
97Pacific Omega-174
Copper-174
Dark Gray-174
Emerald Green-174
Gold-174
Ice Blue-174
97Panini Stickers-155
97Paramount-141
Copper-141
Dark Grey-141
Emerald Green-141
Ice Blue-141
Red-141
Silver-141
Glove Side Laser Cuts-16
97Pinnacle-94
Artist's Proofs-94
Rink Collection-94
Press Plates Back Black-94
Press Plates Back Cyan-94
Press Plates Back Magenta-94
Press Plates Back Yellow-94
Press Plates Front Black-94
Press Plates Front Cyan-94
Press Plates Front Magenta-94
Press Plates Front Yellow-94
Masks-9
Masks Die Cuts-9
Masks Jumbos-9
97Pinnacle Masks Promos-9
97Pinnacle Tins-6
97Pinnacle Certified-16
Red-16
Mirror Blue-16
Mirror Gold-16
Mirror Red-16
97Pinnacle Inside-44
Coach's Collection-44
Executive Collection-44
Stand Up Guys-9A/B
Stand Up Guys-9C/D
Stand Up Guys Promos-9A/B
Stand Up Guys Promos-9C/D
Stoppers-16
97Pinnacle Tot Cert Platinum Blue-16
97Pinnacle Tot Certi Platinum Gold-16
97Pinnacle Totally Certified Platinum Red-16
97Pinnacle Tot Cert Mirror Platinum Gold-16
97Revolution-107
Copper-107
Emerald-107
Ice Blue-107
Silver-107
Return to Sender Die-Cuts-15
97Score-10
Artist's Proofs-10
Golden Blades-10
Net Worth-9
97SP Authentic-120
Sign of the Times-NK
97Studio-63
Press Proofs Silver-63
Press Proofs Gold-63
97Upper Deck-129
97Zenith-76
Z-Gold-76
Z-Silver-76
98SLU Hockey Extended-104
98Aurora-145
98Be A Player-108
Press Release-108
98BAP Gold-108
98BAP Autographs-108
98BAP Autographs Gold-108
98BAP Tampa Bay All Star Game-108
98Bowman's Best-23
Refractors-23
Atomic Refractors-23
98Crown Royale-103
Limited Series-103
98Finest-15
No Protectors-15
No Protectors Refractors-15
Refractors-15
98Katch-109
98Kenner Starting Lineup Cards-17
98NHL Aces Playing Cards-36
98OPC Chrome-115
Refractors-115
98Pacific-341
Ice Blue-341
Red-341
98Pacific Dynagon Ice-143
Blue-143
Red-143
98Pacific Omega-184
Red-184
Opening Day Issue-184
Online-28
98Panini Photocards-40
98Panini Stickers-147
98Paramount-182
Copper-182
Emerald Green-182
Holo-Electric-182
Ice Blue-182
Silver-182
Glove Side Laser Cuts-15
98Revolution-110
Ice Shadow-110
Red-110
All-Star Die Cuts-14
Showstoppers-28
Three Pronged Attack-18
Three Pronged Attack Parallel-18
98SP Authentic-67
Power Shift-67
98SPx Finite-66
Radiance-66
Spectrum-66
98Topps-115
O-Pee-Chee-115
Ice Age 2000-I15
98Topps Gold Label Class 1-70
Black-70
Black One of One-70
One of One-70
Red-70
Red One of One-70
98Topps Gold Label Class 2-70
98Topps Gold Label Class 2 Black-70
98Topps Gold Label Class 2 Black 1 of 1-70
98Topps Gold Label Class 2 One of One-70
98Topps Gold Label Class 2 Red-70
98Topps Gold Label Class 2 Red One of One-70
98Topps Gold Label Class 3-70
98Topps Gold Label Class 3 Black-70
98Topps Gold Label Class 3 Black 1 of 1-70
98Topps Gold Label Class 3 One of One-70
98Topps Gold Label Class 3 Red-70
98Topps Gold Label Class 3 Red One of One-70
98UD Choice-162
Prime Choice Reserve-162
Reserve-162
98Upper Deck-157
Exclusives-157
Exclusives 1 of 1-157
Gold Reserve-157
98Upper Deck MVP-158
Gold Script-158
Silver Script-158
Super Script-158
99SLU Hockey-9
99Aurora-109
Premiere Date-109
Glove Unlimited-16
99BAP Memorabilia-100
Gold-100
Silver-100
99BAP Update Teammates Jersey Cards-TM20
99BAP Millennium-191
Emerald-191
Ruby-191
Sapphire-191
Signatures-191
Signatures Gold-191
99Crown Royale-108
Limited Series-108
Premiere Date-108
99Hasbro Starting Lineup Cards-9
99O-Pee-Chee-47
99O-Pee-Chee Chrome-47
99O-Pee-Chee Chrome Refractors-47
99O-Pee-Chee Chrome Postmasters-PM3
99O-Pee-Chee Chrome Postmasters Refractor-PM3
99O-Pee-Chee Post Masters-PM3
99O-Pee-Chee Top of the World-TW8
99Pacific-321
Copper-321
Emerald Green-321
Gold-321
Ice Blue-321
Premiere Date-321
Red-321
In the Cage Net-Fusions-15
99Pacific Dynagon Ice-152
Blue-152
Copper-152
Gold-152
Premiere Date-152
99Pacific Omega-182
Copper-182
Gold-182
Ice Blue-182
Premiere Date-182
99Pacific Prism-108
Holographic Blue-108
Holographic Gold-108
Holographic Mirror-108
Holographic Purple-108
Premiere Date-108
99Paramount-179
Copper-179
Emerald-179
Gold-179
Holographic Emerald-179
Holographic Gold-179
Holographic Silver-179
Ice Blue-179
Premiere Date-179
Red-179
Silver-179
Glove Side Net Fusions-16
99Revolution-111
Premiere Date-111
Red-111
Shadow Series-111
Copper-111
Gold-111
CSC Silver-111
99SPx-118
Radiance-118
Spectrum-118
99Stadium Club-120
First Day Issue-120
One of a Kind-120
Printing Plates Black-120
Printing Plates Cyan-120
Printing Plates Magenta-120
Printing Plates Yellow-120
99Topps/OPC-47
Postmasters-PM3
Top of the World-TW8
99Topps/OPC Chrome-47
Refractors-47
Postmasters-PM3
Postmasters Refractors-PM3
99Upper Deck-271
Exclusives-271
Exclusives 1 of 1-271
Ultimate Defense-UD8
Ultimate Defense Quantum Gold-UD8
Ultimate Defense Quantum Silver-UD8
99Upper Deck Gold Reserve-271
99Upper Deck MVP-161
Gold Script-161
Silver Script-161
Super Script-161
Draw Your Own Trading Card-W26
Last Line-LL10
99Upper Deck Retro-62
Gold-62
Platinum-62
99Upper Deck Victory-225
99Upper Deck Victory-380
99Wayne Gretzky Hockey Signs of Greatness-NK
99Wayne Gretzky Hockey Tools of Greatness-TGNK
00BAP Memorabilia Jersey Cards-J21
00BAP Memorabilia Jersey Emblems-E21
00BAP Memorabilia Jersey Numbers-N21
00BAP Memorabilia Jersey and Stick Cards-JS21
00BAP Memorabilia Update Teammates-TM33
00BAP Memorabilia Update Teammates-TM38
00BAP Memorabilia Update Teammates Gold-TM33
00BAP Memorabilia Update Teammates Gold-TM38
00BAP Signature Series-221
Emerald-221
Ruby-221
Sapphire-221
Autographs-209
Autographs Gold-209
00BAP Ultimate Memorabilia Autographs-31
Gold-31
00BAP Ultimate Memorabilia Goalie Sticks-G23
00BAP Ultimate Memorabilia Teammates-TM10
00Pacific-317
Copper-317
Gold-317
Ice Blue-317
Premiere Date-317
00Private Stock-75
Gold-75
Premiere Date-75
Retail-75
Silver-75
00Revolution-113
Blue-113
Premiere Date-113
Red-113
NHL Game Gear-8
00Titanium Game Gear-126
00Titanium Game Gear Patches-126
01Atomic-88
Blue-88
Gold-88
Premiere Date-88
Red-88
01BAP Memorabilia-304
Emerald-304
Ruby-304
Sapphire-304
All-Star Jerseys-ASJ39
All-Star Emblems-ASE39
All-Star Numbers-ASN39
All-Star Teammates-AST28
All-Star Teammates-AST40
Country of Origin-CO44
01BAP Sig Series International Medals-IB-1
01BAP Signature Series Jerseys-GJ-72
01BAP Signature Series Teammates-TM-27
01BAP Ultimate Mem Legend Terry Sawchuk-5
01BAP Ultimate Memorabilia Name Plates-12
01BAP Update Travel Plans-TP14
01Between the Pipes-63
All-Star Jerseys-ASJ15
He Shoots-He Saves Points-4
He Shoots-He Saves Prizes-13
Jerseys-GJ32
Jersey and Stick Cards-GSJ30
Masks-40
Masks Silver-40
Masks Gold-40
01Bowman YoungStars-19
Gold-19
Ice Cubed-19
01Crown Royale-127
Blue-127
Premiere Date-127
Red-127
Retail-127
01Pacific-351
Extreme LTD-351
Hobby LTD-351
Premiere Date-351
Retail LTD-351
01Pacific Adrenaline-173
Blue-173
Premiere Date-173
Red-173
Retail-173
Jerseys-44
Power Play-33
01Pacific Arena Exclusives-351
01Pacific Heads-Up-86
Blue-86
Premiere Date-86
Red-86
Silver-86
01Parkhurst-241
Waving the Flag-31
01Private Stock PS-2002-67
01SP Authentic-81
Limited-81
Limited Gold-81
01SPx-193
01Sports Illustrated for Kids III-150
01Titanium-125
Hobby Parallel-125
Premiere Date-125
Retail-125
Retail Parallel-125
All-Stars-18
Three-Star Selections-9
01Topps Chrome-136
Refractors-136
Black Border Refractors-136
01UD Challenge for the Cup-81
01UD Mask Collection-127
01UD Mask Collection-188
Gold-127
Gold-188
01UD Playmakers-90
01UD Top Shelf-118
01Upper Deck-157
Exclusives-157
01Upper Deck Ice-121
01Upper Deck MVP-171
Goalie Sticks-G-NK
01Upper Deck Victory-324
Gold-324
01Upper Deck Vintage-229
01Upper Deck Vintage-234
01Vanguard Stonewallers-18
02Atomic-89
Blue-89
Gold-89
Red-89
Denied-19
Hobby Parallel-89
02BAP All-Star Edition-44
He Shoots-He Score Prizes-11
Jerseys-44
Jerseys Gold-44
Jerseys Silver-44
02BAP First Edition-80
02BAP First Edition-367
Jerseys-80
02BAP Memorabilia-40
02BAP Memorabilia-227
Emerald-40
Emerald-227
Ruby-40
Ruby-227
Sapphire-40
Sapphire-227
All-Star Jerseys-ASJ-26
Franchise Players-FP-27
NHL All-Star Game-40
NHL All-Star Game-227
NHL All-Star Game Blue-40
NHL All-Star Game Blue-227
NHL All-Star Game Green-40
NHL All-Star Game Green-227
NHL All-Star Game Red-40
NHL All-Star Game Red-227
02BAP Memorabilia Toronto Fall Expo-40
02BAP Memorabilia Toronto Fall Expo-227
02BAP Signature Series-118
Autographs-118
Autograph Buybacks 1998-108
Autograph Buybacks 1999-191
Autograph Buybacks 2000-209
Autographs Gold-118
02Between the Pipes-47
02Between the Pipes-147
Gold-47
Silver-47
All-Star Stick and Jersey-11
Behind the Mask-6
Blockers-15
Complete Package-CP10
Double Memorabilia-14
Emblems-22
Goalie Autographs-12
He Shoots-He Saves Points-13
He Shoots-He Saves Prizes-13
Jerseys-22
Masks II-27
Masks II Gold-27
Masks II Silver-27
Numbers-22
Pads-10
Stick and Jerseys-22
Trappers-GT7
02Bowman YoungStars-74
Gold-74
Silver-74
02Crown Royale-87
Blue-87
Red-87
Retail-87
Dual Patches-20
Coats of Armor-9
02ITG Used-59
02ITG Used-159
Franchise Players-F27
Franchise Players Autographs-F27
Franchise Players Gold-F27
International Experience-IE28
International Experience Gold-IE28
02Lightning Team Issue-5
02O-Pee-Chee-135
02O-Pee-Chee Premier Blue Parallel-135
02O-Pee-Chee Premier Red Parallel-135
02O-Pee-Chee Factory Set-135
02Pacific-348
Blue-348
Red-348
02Pacific Complete-447
Red-447
02Pacific Exclusive-155
02Pacific Heads-Up-111
Blue-111
Purple-111
Red-111
Inside the Numbers-20
Quad Jerseys-25
Quad Jerseys-30
Quad Jerseys Gold-25
Quad Jerseys Gold-30
Showstoppers-19
02Pacific Quest for the Cup-88
Gold-88
02Pacific Toronto Fall Expo-5
Gold-5
02Parkhurst-39
Bronze-39
Gold-39
Silver-39
Franchise Players-FP27
02Parkhurst Retro-155
Minis-155
Hopefuls-VH8
Memorabilia-RM21
02Private Stock Reserve-143
Red-143
Retail-143
Patches-143
02SP Authentic-80
Beckett Promos-80
Sign of the Times-NK
Sign of the Times-KN
02SP Game Used Signature Style-NK
02SPx-67
Spectrum Gold-67
Spectrum Silver-67
02Stadium Club-93
Silver Decoy Cards-93
Proofs-93
Puck Stops Here-PSH8
02Titanium-89
Blue-89
Red-89
Retail-89
Jerseys-64
Jerseys Retail-64
Patches-64
Masked Marauders-6
02Topps-135
OPC Blue Parallel-135
OPC Red Parallel-135
Factory Set-135
02Topps Chrome-85
Black Border Refractors-85
Refractors-85
02Topps Heritage-29
Chrome Parallel-29
02Topps Total-303
Team Checklists-TTC27
02UD Artistic Impressions-80
Gold-80
02UD Artistic Impressions Beckett Promos-80
02UD Artistic Impressions Retrospectives-R80
02UD Artistic Impressions Retrospect Gold-R80
02UD Artistic Impress Retrospect Silver-R80
02UD Honor Roll-63
Signature Class-NK
02UD Mask Collection-79
02UD Mask Collection-80
02UD Mask Collection-81
02UD Mask Collection-106
02UD Mask Collection Beckett Promos-79
02UD Mask Collection Beckett Promos-80
02UD Mask Collection Beckett Promos-81
02UD Mask Collection Mini Masks-NK
02UD Mask Collection Mini Masks Autos-NK
02UD Piece of History-80
02UD Premier Collection-49A
Signatures Bronze-SNK
Signatures Gold-SNK
Signatures Silver-SNK
02UD Top Shelf-81
02Upper Deck-158
Exclusives-158
Last Line of Defense-LL12
02Upper Deck Classic Portraits-89
02Upper Deck MVP-165
Gold-165
Classics-165
Golden Classics-165
02Upper Deck Rookie Update-90
02Upper Deck Victory-193
Bronze-193
Gold-193
Silver-193
National Pride-NP38
02Upper Deck Vintage-230
02Upper Deck Vintage-287
02Upper Deck Vintage-319
Green Backs-230
Tall Boys-T59
Tall Boys Gold-T59
02Vanguard-88
LTD-88
Jerseys-42
Jerseys Gold-42
Stonewallers-11
02Russian Olympic Faces-1
02Russian Olympic Faces-2
02Russian Olympic Team-7
03McFarlane Hockey-20
03McFarlane Hockey-22
03BAP Memorabilia-148
Emerald-148
Gold-148
Ruby-148
Sapphire-148
All-Star Staring Lineup-1
Masks III-12
Masks III Gold-12
Masks III Silver-12
Masks III Autographs-M-NK
Masks III Memorabilia-12
03BAP Ultimate Memorabilia Autographs-59
Gold-59
03BAP Ultimate Mem Auto Jerseys-59
03BAP Ultimate Mem Complete Package-3
03BAP Ultimate Mem Complete Package Gold-3
03BAP Ultimate Mem Franch Present Future-27
03BAP Ultimate Mem Jersey and Stick-14
03BAP Ultimate Mem Jersey and Stick Gold-14
03BAP Ultimate Memorabilia Triple Threads-3
03Beehive-174
Variations-174
Gold-174
Silver-174
03Black Diamond-21
Black-21
Green-21
Red-21
03Bowman-88
Gold-88
03Bowman Chrome-88
Refractors-88
Gold Refractors-88
Xfractors-88
03Crown Royale-88
Blue-88
Retail-88
Gauntlet of Glory-18
03ITG Action-558
Homeboys-HB8
Jerseys-M133
03ITG Used Signature Series-45
Gold-45
Autographs-NKH
Autographs Gold-NKH
Goalie Gear-5
Goalie Gear Autographs-5
Goalie Gear Gold-5
International Experience-21
International Experience Autographs-21
International Experience Emblems Gold-21
International Experience Emblems-21
International Experience Gold-21
Jerseys-31
Jerseys Gold-31
Jersey Autos-31
Emblems-26
Emblems Gold-26
Jersey and Stick-31
Jersey and Stick Gold-31
03Lightning Team Issue-31
03NHL Sticker Collection-130
03O-Pee-Chee-21
03OPC Blue-21
03OPC Gold-21
03OPC Red-21
03Pacific-307
Blue-307
Red-307
03Pacific Calder-89
Silver-89
03Pacific Complete-411
Red-411
03Pacific Exhibit-192
03Pacific Exhibit-215
Blue Backs-192
03Pacific Heads-Up-86
Hobby LTD-86
Retail LTD-86
Stonewallers-10
Stonewallers LTD-10
03Pacific Invincible-86
Blue-86
Red-86
Retail-86
Freeze Frame-21
Jerseys-29
03Pacific Luxury Suite-17A
03Pacific Luxury Suite-17B
03Pacific Luxury Suite-17C
03Pacific Luxury Suite-17D
03Pacific Luxury Suite-47A
03Pacific Luxury Suite-47B
03Pacific Luxury Suite-47C
03Pacific Prism-141
Blue-141
Patches-141
Red-141
Retail-141
03Pacific Quest for the Cup-91
Blue-91
Jerseys-17
03Pacific Supreme-87
Blue-87
Red-87
Retail-87
03Parkhurst Rookie-17
03Private Stock Reserve-199
Blue-199
Patches-199
Red-199
Retail-199
Increase Security-15
03SP Authentic-78
Limited-78
03SP Game Used-43
03SP Game Used-111
Gold-43
Gold-111
Authentic Fabrics-DFVN
Authentic Fabrics Gold-DFVN
Double Threads-DTLK
03SPx-87
Radiance-87
Spectrum-87
03Titanium-181
Hobby Jersey Number Parallels-181
Patches-181
Retail-181
Masked Marauders-9
03Topps-21
Blue-21
Gold-21
Red-21
03Topps C55-69
Minis-69
Minis American Back-69
Minis American Back Red-69
Minis Bazooka Back-69
Minis Brooklyn Back-69
Minis Hat Trick Back-69
Minis O Canada Back-69

Minis O Canada Back Red-69
Minis Stanley Cup Back-69
Relics-TRNK
03Topps Pristine-64
Gold Refractor Die Cuts-64
Refractors-64
Mini-PM-NK
Popular Demand Relics-PD-NK
Popular Demand Relic Refractors-PD-NK
Press Plates Black-64
Press Plates Cyan-64
Press Plates Magenta-64
Press Plates Yellow-64
03UD Honor Roll-78
03UD Premier Collection-50
Teammates-PT-TL
Teammates Patches-PT-TL
03Upper Deck-422
Canadian Exclusives-422
HG-422
UD Exclusives-422
03Upper Deck All-Star Promos-AS11
03Upper Deck Classic Portraits-89
03Upper Deck Ice-79
Gold-79
03Upper Deck MVP-386
Gold Script-386
Silver Script-386
Canadian Exclusives-386
Masked Men-MM3
SportsNut-SN78
03Upper Deck Rookie Update-78
Skills-SKNK
Top Draws-TD14
03Upper Deck Trilogy-89
Limited-89
03Upper Deck Victory-174
Bronze-174
Gold-174
Silver-174
Game Breakers-GB14
03Toronto Star-83
04Pacific-237
Blue-237
Red-237
In The Crease-9
04SP Authentic-80
04SP Authentic-144
Limited-80
Limited-144
Buybacks-160
Buybacks-161
Octographs-OS-CUP
Sign of the Times-ST-NK
Sign of the Times-DS-KL
Sign of the Times-DS-NK
Sign of the Times-TS-KLL
Sign of the Times-QS-LRLK
04UD All-World-27
Gold-27
Autographs-27
Dual Autographs-AD-LK
Five Autographs-AF-GOL
Five Autographs-AF-YGN
04Ultimate Collection Dual Logos-UL2-KL
04Ultimate Collection Jerseys-UGJ-NK
04Ultimate Collection Jerseys Gold-UGJ-NK
04Ultimate Collection Jersey Autographs-UGJA-NK
04Ultimate Collection Patches-UP-NK
04Ultimate Collection Patch Autographs-UPA-NK
04Ultimate Collection Signatures-US-NK
04Ultimate Collection Signature Logos-ULA-NK
04Ultimate Collection Signature Patches-SP-NK
04Upper Deck-161
Canadian Exclusives-161
Clutch Performers-CP6
HG Glossy Gold-161
HG Glossy Silver-161
04Russian Back to Russia-24
05Be A Player-81
First Period-81
Second Period-81
Third Period-81
Overtime-81
05Beehive-19
05Beehive-250
Beige -19
Blue -19
Gold-19
Red -19
Matte-19
Matted Materials-MMNK
Matted Materials Remarkable-RMNK
Signature Scrapbook-SSNK
05Black Diamond-147
Emerald-147
Gold-147
Onyx-147
Ruby-147
Gemography-G-NK
Gemography Emerald-G-NK
Gemography Gold-G-NK
Gemography Onyx-G-NK
Gemography Ruby-G-NK
05Hot Prospects-21
En Fuego-21
Red Hot-21
White Hot-21
05McDonalds Upper Deck Goalie Factory-GF10
05Panini Stickers-212
05Parkhurst-106
05Parkhurst-677
Facsimile Auto Parallel-106
Facsimile Auto Parallel-677
True Colors-TCCHI
True Colors-TCCHI
True Colors-TCCHDE
True Colors-TCCHDE
05SP Authentic-21
05SP Authentic-108
Limited-21
Limited-108
Prestigious Pairings-PPKN
Sign of the Times Triples-TKRB
05SP Game Used-20
Gold-20
Authentic Fabrics-AF-NK
Authentic Fabrics Dual-KK
Authentic Fabrics Gold-AF-NK
Authentic Patches-AP-NK
Authentic Patches Dual-KK
Auto Draft-AD-NK
Awesome Authentics-AA-NK
Significant Numbers-SN-NK
05SPx-18
Spectrum-18
Winning Combos-WC-KR
Winning Combos Gold-WC-KR
Winning Combos Spectrum-WC-KR
Winning Materials-WM-NK
Winning Materials Gold-WM-NK
Winning Materials Spectrum-WM-NK
05The Cup-24
Gold-24
Black Rainbow-24
Masterpiece Pressplates-24
Noble Numbers Dual-DNNNK
Patch Variation-P24
Property of-PONK
05UD Artifacts Treasured Patches-TP-NK
05UD Artifacts Treasured Patch Autos-TP-NK
05UD Artifacts Treasured Patches Dual-TPD-NK
05UD Artifacts Treasured Patch Dual Autos-TPD-NK
05UD Artifacts Treasured Patches Pewter-TP-NK
05UD Artifacts Treasured Patches Silver-TP-NK
05UD Artifacts Treasured Swatches-TS-NK
05UD Artifacts Treasured Swatch Autos-TS-NK
05UD Artifacts Treasured Swatches Blue-TS-NK
05UD Artifacts Treasured Swatches Copper-TS-NK
05UD Artifacts Treasured Swatches Dual-TSD-NK
05UD Artifacts Treasured Swatch Dual Auto-TSD-NK
05UD Artifacts Treasured Swatch Dual Blue-TSD-NK
05UD Artifact Treasure Swatch Dual Copper-TSD-NK
05UD Artifact Treasure Swatch Dual Maroon-TSD-NK
05UD Artifact Treasure Swatch Dual Pewter-TSD-NK
05UD Artifact TreasuredSwatch Dual Silver-TSD-NK
05UD Artifacts Treasured Swatches Maroon-TS-NK
05UD Artifacts Treasured Swatches Pewter-TS-NK
05UD Artifacts Treasured Swatches Silver-TS-NK
05UD PowerPlay-80
05UD PowerPlay-117
05UD PowerPlay-132
Rainbow-80
Power Marks-PMNK
05Ultimate Collection-19
Gold-19
Marquee Attractions-MA13
Ultimate Achievements-UANK
Ultimate Signatures-USNK
Ultimate Signatures Pairings-UPKN
05Ultra-47
Gold-47
Ice-47
05Upper Deck-286
Big Playmakers-B-NK
Hometown Heroes-HH22
Jerseys-J-NK
Jerseys Series II-J2NK
Notable Numbers-N-NK
Patches-P-NK
Scrapbooks-HS14
05Upper Deck Hockey Showcase-HS33
05Upper Deck Showcase Promos-HS33
05Upper Deck Ice-20
Rainbow-20
Frozen Fabrics-FFNK
Frozen Fabrics Patches-FFPNK
Frozen Fabrics Patch Autographs-FAPNK
05Upper Deck MVP-85
Gold-85
Platinum-85
Materials Triples-T-LKF
05Upper Deck Rookie Update-20
05Upper Deck Trilogy-20
Honorary Patches-HP-NK
Honorary Patch Scripts-HSP-NK
Honorary Swatches-HS-NK
Honorary Swatch Scripts-HSS-NK
05Upper Deck Victory-176
05Upper Deck Victory-210
Black-176
Black-210
Gold-176
Gold-210
Silver-176
Silver-210
Blow-Ups-BU37
Stars on Ice-SI40
05Czech Stadion-683
06Be A Player-107
Autographs-107
Signatures-NK
Signatures 10-117
Signatures Duals-DKR
Signatures Trios-TRKS
Up Close and Personal-UC39
Up Close and Personal Autographs-UC39
06Be A Player Portraits-24
Dual Signature Portraits-DSNT
Signature Portraits-SPNK
Timeless Tens-TTNET
06Beehive-79
Blue-79
Gold-79
Matte-79
Red Facsimile Signatures-79
Wood-79
06Between The Pipes The Mask-M19
06Between The Pipes The Mask Gold-M19
06Between The Pipes The Mask Silver-M19
06Black Diamond-20
Black-20
Gold-20
Ruby-20
Jerseys-JNK
Jerseys Black-JNK
Jerseys Gold-JNK
Jerseys Ruby-JNK
Jerseys Black Autographs -JNK
06Blackhawks Postcards-14
06Flair Showcase-24
06Flair Showcase-117
06Flair Showcase-217
Parallel-24
Parallel-117
Parallel-217
Hot Gloves-HG7
Hot Numbers-HN8
Hot Numbers Parallel-HN8
06Fleer-45
Tiffany-45
Netminders-N7
06Hot Prospects-23
Red Hot-23
White Hot-23
06McDonald's Upper Deck-9
06NHL POG-40
06O-Pee-Chee-106
06O-Pee-Chee-677
Rainbow-106
Rainbow-677
06Panini Stickers-208
06SP Authentic-81
Limited-81
Sign of the Times Duals-STHK
06SP Game Used-21
Gold-21
Rainbow-21
Authentic Fabrics Dual-AF2HK
Authentic Fabrics Dual Patches-AF2HK
Authentic Fabrics Triple-AF3CHI
Authentic Fabrics Triple Patches-AF3CHI
Authentic Fabrics Eights-AF8RUS
Authentic Fabrics Eights Patches-AF8RUS
Autographs-21
06SPx-19
Spectrum-19
SPxcitement-X19
SPxcitement Spectrum-X19
SPxcitement Autographs-X19
06The Cup Limited Logos-LLNK
06UD Artifacts-79
06UD Artifacts-160
Blue-79
Blue-160
Gold-79
Gold-160
Platinum-79
Platinum-160
Radiance-79
Radiance-160
Red-79
Red-160
Treasured Patches Black-TSNK
Treasured Patches Blue-TSNK
Treasured Patches Gold-TSNK
Treasured Patches Platinum-TSNK
Treasured Patches Red-TSNK
Treasured Swatches-TSNK
Treasured Swatches Black-TSNK
Treasured Swatches Blue-TSNK
Treasured Swatches Gold-TSNK
Treasured Swatches Platinum-TSNK
Treasured Swatches Red-TSNK
Tundra Tandems-TTKH
Tundra Tandems-TTRK
Tundra Tandems Black-TTKH
Tundra Tandems Black-TTRK
Tundra Tandems Blue-TTKH
Tundra Tandems Blue-TTRK
Tundra Tandems Gold-TTKH
Tundra Tandems Gold-TTRK
Tundra Tandems Platinum-TTKH
Tundra Tandems Platinum-TTRK
Tundra Tandems Red-TTKH
Tundra Tandems Red-TTRK
Tundra Tandems Dual Patches Red-TTKH
Tundra Tandems Dual Patches Red-TTRK
06UD Mini Jersey Collection-22
06UD Powerplay-23
Impact Rainbow-23
06Ultra-42
Gold Medallion-42
Ice Medallion-42
06Upper Deck Arena Giveaways-CHI6
06Upper Deck-45
Exclusives Parallel-45
High Gloss Parallel-45
Game Jerseys-JNK
Game Patches-PNK
Masterpieces-45
Signatures-SNK
Signature Sensations-SSNK
06Upper Deck MVP-61
Gold Script-61
Super Script-61
Last Line of Defense-LL10
06Upper Deck Ovation-10
06Upper Deck Sweet Shot-23
06Upper Deck Trilogy-22
Combo Clearcut Autographs-C2CK
Honorary Scripted Patches-HSPNK
Honorary Scripted Swatches-HSSNK
06Upper Deck Victory-42
06Upper Deck Victory Black-42
06Upper Deck Victory Gold-42
06Upper Deck Victory GameBreakers-GB9
06Upper Deck Victory Oversize Cards-NK
07Upper Deck Ovation-91
07Upper Deck Victory-118
Black-118
Gold-118

Khaidarov, Ravil

91O-Pee-Chee Inserts-36R
91Russian Stars Red Ace-8
92Upper Deck-347
92Finnish Semic-118
94Finnish Jaa Kiekko-162
94German First League-79
99German Bundesliga 2-113
03German DEL-56

Khaidarov, Remir

98Russian Hockey League-84
99Russian Hockey League-80
00Russian Hockey League-32

Khairetdinov, Renat

00Russian Hockey League-16
01Russian Hockey League-11
01Russian Hockey League-83
03Russian Hockey League-248

Khalizov, Svatoslav

89Russian National Team-11
94German First League-142
99Russian Stars Postcards-10

Khanarski, Pavel

00Russian Hockey League-50

Kharin, Sergei

90Jets IGA-16
90Moncton Hawks-13
90ProCards AHL/IHL-261
91Score American-394
91Score Canadian Bilingual-284
91Score Canadian English-284
91Upper Deck-381
French-381
91ProCards-540
92Cincinnati Cyclones-13
93Dayton Bombers-14
95Dayton Bombers-9
95Dayton Bombers-P2
98Muskegon Fury-21
99Muskegon Fury-1
00Muskegon Fury-9

Kharitonov, Alexander

98Russian Hockey League-156
99Russian Dynamo Moscow-13
99Russian Stars of Hockey-16
99Russian Fetisov Tribute-21
00BAP Memorabilia-416
Emerald-416
Ruby-416
Sapphire-416
00BAP Signature Series-272
Emerald-272
Ruby-272
Sapphire-272
Autographs-234
Autographs Gold-234
00Black Diamond-131
00Private Stock-145
Gold-145
Premiere Date-145
Retail-145
Silver-145
PS-2001 Rookies-22
00SP Authentic-123
00SP Game Used-83
00Titanium-144
Retail-144
00Titanium Draft Day Edition-144
00Titanium Draft Day Promos-144
00Topps Gold Label Class 1-113
Gold-113
00Topps Gold Label Class 2-113
00Topps Gold Label Class 2 Gold-113
00Topps Gold Label Class 3-113
00Topps Gold Label Class 3 Gold-113
00Topps Heritage-95
Chrome Parallel-95
00Topps Premier Plus-114
Blue Ice-114
00UD Pros and Prospects-123
00UD Reserve-114
00Upper Deck-437
Exclusives Tier 1-437
Exclusives Tier 2-437
00Russian Champions-4
01BAP Memorabilia-165
Emerald-165
Ruby-165
Sapphire-165
01Pacific-352
Extreme LTD-352
Hobby LTD-352
Premiere Date-352
Retail LTD-352
01Pacific Arena Exclusives-352
01Russian Hockey League-82
02BAP Sig Series Auto Buybacks 2000-234
02Russian Hockey League-250
03Russian Hockey League-36
04Russian Moscow Dynamo-32
06Russian Torino Olympic Team-13

Kharlamov, Alexander

91Future Trends Canada '72-100
92Russian Stars Red Ace-12
92Russian Stars Red Ace-17
93Parkhurst-529
Emerald Ice-529
93Pinnacle-504
Canadian-504
93Classic-105
94Score-213
Gold-213
Platinum-213
94Classic-13
Gold-13
94Classic Four-Sport *-129
Gold-129
Printers Proofs-129
95Portland Pirates-13
95Images Four-Sport *-106
96Portland Pirates-22
96Collector's Edge Ice-56
Prism-56
97Hampton Roads Admirals-9
98Hampton Roads Admirals-8
99Tacoma Sabercats-8
00Russian Dynamo Moscow-17
00Russian Hockey League-319
05ITG Ultimate Mem Pass the Torch Jerseys-3
05ITG Ultimate Mem Passing Torch Jsy Gold-3

Kharlamov, Valeri

69Russian National Team Postcards-15
69Swedish Hockey-1
70Finnish Jaakiekko-3
70Russian National Team Postcards-17
70Swedish Hockey-322
70Swedish Masterserien-21
70Swedish Masterserien-30
70Swedish Masterserien-125
71Finnish Suomi Stickers-3
71Swedish Hockey-34
72Finnish Jaakiekko-24
72Finnish Hellas-76
72Finnish Panda Toronto-50
72Finnish Semic World Championship-17
72Swedish Stickers-30
72Swedish Stickers-50
72Swedish Semic World Championship-17
73Finnish Jaakiekko-4
73Russian National Team-8
73Russian National Team-9
73Swedish Stickers-87
74Finnish Jenkki-45
74Finnish Typotor-67
74Russian National Team-6
74Swedish Stickers-5
74Swedish Semic World Champ Stickers-34
77Finnish Sportscasters-26-673
79Panini Stickers-151
79Russian National Team-15
81Swedish Semic Hockey VM Stickers-50
91Future Trends Canada '72-58
91Future Trends Canada '72-100
91Future Trends Canada '72 French-58
91Future Trends Canada '72 French-100
91Finnish Semic World Champ Stickers-244
91Swedish Semic World Champ Stickers-244
92Future Trends '76 Canada Cup-108
95Swedish Globe World Championships-241
99Russian Stars of Hockey-34
02BAP Ultimate Memorabilia-100
Emblems-30
Jerseys-39
Numbers-20
Numerology-19
Vintage Jerseys-39
02Parkhurst-250
Bronze-250
Gold-250
Silver-250
Heroes-NH1
Vintage Teammates-VT15
03BAP Ultimate Memorabilia Heroes-1
03BAP Ultimate Mem Vintage Jerseys-35
03BAP Ultimate Mem Vintage Jerseys Gold-35
03Czech Stadion-551
04ITG Ultimate Memorabilia-198
Gold-198
Country of Origin-6
Country of Origin Gold-6
05ITG Ultimate Memorabilia Level 1-98
05ITG Ultimate Memorabilia Level 2-98
05ITG Ultimate Memorabilia Level 3-98
05ITG Ultimate Memorabilia Level 4-98
05ITG Ultimate Memorabilia Level 5-98
05ITG Ultimate Mem Pass the Torch Jerseys-3
05ITG Ultimate Mem Retro Teammate Jerseys-30
05ITG Ult Mem Retro Teammates Jersey Gold-30
05ITG Ultimate Mem Seams Unbelievable-18
05ITG Ultimate Mem Seam Unbelievable Gold-18
05ITG Heroes and Prospects Hero Mem-HM-27
06ITG International Ice-61
Gold-61
Best of the Best-BB05
Best of the Best Gold-BB05
Cornerstones-IC02
Cornerstones-IC07
Cornerstones Gold-IC02
Cornerstones Gold-IC07
Emblems-GUE05
Emblems Gold-GUE05
Hockey Passport-HP03
Hockey Passport Gold-HP03
International Rivals-IR04
International Rivals Gold-IR04
Jerseys-GUJ05
Jerseys Gold-GUJ05
Numbers-GUN05
Numbers Gold-GUN05
Passing The Torch-PTT12
Passing The Torch Gold-PTT12
Teammates-IT19
Teammates Gold-IT19
Triple Memorabilia-TM03
Triple Memorabilia Gold-TM03
06ITG Ultimate Memorabilia-146
Artist Proof-146
Cornerstones-1
Cornerstones Gold-1
Going For Gold-24
Going For Gold Gold-24
Passing The Torch-17
Passing The Torch Gold-17
Retro Teammates-11
Retro Teammates Gold-11

Khasanov, Rinat

98Russian Hockey League-101
01Russian Hockey League-173
02Russian Hockey League-260
03Russian Hockey League-122

Khasanshin, Ruslan

04Russian RHL-15

Khatsei, Evgeni

03Russian Avangard Omsk-19

Khatsej, Igor

99Russian Stars Postcards-11

Khavanov, Alexander

92Birmingham Bulls-9
93Birmingham Bulls-9
99Russian Dynamo Moscow-7
99Russian Stars of Hockey-4
00BAP Memorabilia-455
Emerald-455
Ruby-455
Sapphire-455
00SP Authentic-161
00SPx-185
00Topps Stars-104
Blue-104
00UD Reserve-113
00Upper Deck Ice-122
00Russian Champions-1
02BAP First Edition-292
02Blues Team Issue-10
02Pacific Complete-287
Red-287
02Topps Total-133
02Upper Deck-401
Exclusives-401
02Upper Deck Beckett UD Promos-401
03Blues Team Set-13
03ITG Action-570
03Pacific Complete-83
Red-83
03Upper Deck MVP-365
Gold Script-365
Silver Script-365
Canadian Exclusives-365
03Russian World Championship Stars-29
03Russian World Championship Team 2003-22
05Parkhurst-464
Facsimile Auto Parallel-464

Khlistov, Denis

00Russian Hockey League-144
01Russian Hockey League-107

Khlopotnov, Denis

96Upper Deck Ice-141
98Muskegon Fury-22
99Russian Hockey League-156
00Russian Hockey League-324
01Russian Hockey League-131
03Russian Hockey League-90

Khmylev, Oleg

00Russian Hockey League-166
02Russian Hockey League-270
04Russian Super League All-Stars-23

Khmylev, Yuri

87Russian National Team-9
89Russian National Team-12
89Swedish Semic World Champ Stickers-94
91O-Pee-Chee Inserts-16R
92Parkhurst-255
Emerald Ice-255
92Sabres Blue Shield-9
92Sabres Jubilee Foods-6
92Ultra-260
92Upper Deck-504
92Russian Stars Red Ace-13
93Donruss-36
93Leaf-211
93OPC Premier-389
Gold-389
93Panini Stickers-106
93Pinnacle-201
Canadian-201
93PowerPlay-30
93Score-302
Canadian-302
93Stadium Club-241
Members Only Master Set-241
OPC-241
First Day Issue-241
First Day Issue OPC-241
93Topps/OPC Premier-389
Gold-389
93Ultra-173
94Canada Games NHL POGS-53
94Donruss-324
94Fleer-22
94Leaf-297
94OPC Premier-14
Special Effects-14
94Parkhurst-22
Gold-22
94Pinnacle-69
Artist's Proofs-69
Rink Collection-69
94Topps/OPC Premier-14
Special Effects-14
94Ultra-264
94Upper Deck-368
Electric Ice-368
SP Inserts-SP98
SP Inserts Die Cuts-SP98
95Be A Player-4
Signatures-S4
Signatures Die Cuts-S4
95Canada Games NHL POGS-45
95Collector's Choice-23
Player's Club-23
Player's Club Platinum-23
95Donruss-18
95Panini Stickers-17
95Parkhurst International-23
Emerald Ice-23
95Playoff One on One-231
95Pro Magnets-108
95Score-61
Black Ice Artist's Proofs-61
Black Ice-61
95Topps-371
OPC Inserts-371
95Upper Deck-27
Electric Ice-27
Electric Ice Gold-27
96Donruss-185
Press Proofs-185
96NHL Pro Stamps-108
96Playoff One on One-414
96Score-199
Artist's Proofs-199
Dealer's Choice Artist's Proofs-199
Special Artist's Proofs-199
Golden Blades-199

Kholomeyev, Alex

92Fort Worth Fire-9
94Central Hockey League-24
97Fort Worth Brahmas-8
99Corpus Christi IceRays-10
99Fort Worth Brahmas-8

Khomitsky, Vadim

02Russian Hockey League-107
03Russian Hockey League-213
03Russian SL-35

Khomutov, Andrei

82Swedish Semic VM Stickers-68
83Swedish Semic VM Stickers-68
84Russian National Team-9
87Russian National Team-10
89Russian National Team-13
89Swedish Semic World Champ Stickers-93
90O-Pee-Chee Red Army-3R
91Finnish Semic World Champ Stickers-99
91Swedish Semic World Champ Stickers-99
93Swedish Semic World Champ Stickers-148
93Swiss HNL-48
94Finnish Jaa Kiekko-154
95Finnish Semic World Championships-139
95Swedish Globe World Championships-178
95Swedish World Championships Stickers-50
95Swiss HNL-74
95Swiss HNL-513
96Swedish Semic Wien-152
96Swiss HNL-218

Khomutov, Dmitri

99Russian Hockey League-110
02Russian Hockey League-30

Khomutov, Ivan

03London Knights-5
04Albany River Rats-12
05Albany River Rats-13

Khramchenko, Dmitri

00Russian Hockey League-83

Khristich, Dimitri

89Capitals Team Issue-10
90Capitals Kodak-10
90O-Pee-Chee Red Army-16R
90Upper Deck-537
French-537
91Pro Set Platinum-242
91Bowman-307
91Capitals Junior 5x7-14
91Capitals Kodak-14
91O-Pee-Chee-78
91OPC Premier-176
91Parkhurst-189
French-189
91Pinnacle-162
French-162
91Pro Set-260
French-260
91Score American-175
91Score Canadian Bilingual-175
91Score Canadian English-175
91Score Young Superstars-6
91Stadium Club-359
91Topps-78
91Upper Deck-157
French-157
92Bowman-427
92Capitals Kodak-15
92O-Pee-Chee-286
92Panini Stickers-N
92Panini Stickers French-N
92Parkhurst-428
Emerald Ice-428
92Pinnacle-146
French-146
Team 2000-25
Team 2000 French-25
92Pro Set-208
92Score-33
Canadian-33
Sharpshooters-27
Sharpshooters Canadian-27
Young Superstars-15
92Stadium Club-86
92Topps-470
Gold-470G
92Ultra-235
Imports-7
92Upper Deck-219
92Russian Stars Red Ace-3
93Donruss-373
93Leaf-168
93OPC Premier-210
Gold-210
93Panini Stickers-28
93Parkhurst-220
Emerald Ice-220
93Pinnacle-44
Canadian-44
Team 2001-23
Team 2001 Canadian-23
93PowerPlay-264
93Score-80
Canadian-80
International Stars-20
International Stars Canadian-20
93Stadium Club-277
Members Only Master Set-277
First Day Issue-277
93Topps/OPC Premier-210
Gold-210
93Ultra-59
93Upper Deck-135
SP-171
94Canada Games NHL POGS-246
94Donruss-264
94EA Sports-154
94Flair-201
94Fleer-237
94Leaf-190
94OPC Premier-534
Special Effects-534
94Parkhurst-252
Gold-252
94Pinnacle-59
Artist's Proofs-59
Rink Collection-59
94Score-118
Gold-118
Platinum-118
94Select-104
Gold-104
94SP-130
Die Cuts-130
94Stadium Club-12
Members Only Master Set-12
First Day Issue-12
Super Team Winner Cards-12
94Topps/OPC Premier-534
Special Effects-534
94Ultra-236
94Upper Deck-76
Electric Ice-76
SP Inserts-SP87
SP Inserts Die Cuts-SP87
95Bashan Super Stickers-60
95Be A Player-36
Signatures-S36
Signatures Die Cuts-S36
95Bowman-61
All-Foil-61
95Canada Games NHL POGS-133
95Collector's Choice-183
Player's Club-183
Player's Club Platinum-183
95Donruss-265
95Emotion-82
95Finest-166
Refractors-166
95Hoyle Eastern Playing Cards-34
95Imperial Stickers-60
95Leaf-139
95Metal-72
95Panini Stickers-268
95Parkhurst International-108
Emerald Ice-108
95Score-151
Black Ice Artist's Proofs-151
Black Ice-151
95SkyBox Impact-80
95SP-67
95Stadium Club-68
Members Only Master Set-68
95Summit-153
Artist's Proofs-153
Ice-153
95Topps-248
OPC Inserts-248
95Ultra-250
95Upper Deck-287
Electric Ice-287
Electric Ice Gold-287
96Black Diamond-108
Gold-108
96Collector's Choice-123
96Collector's Choice-320
96Donruss-56
Press Proofs-56
96Donruss Canadian Ice-105
Gold Press Proofs-105
Red Press Proofs-105
96Donruss Elite-70
Die Cut Stars-70
96Flair-46
Blue Ice-46
96Fleer-50
96Fleer Picks-134
96Leaf-168
Press Proofs-168
96Leaf Preferred-79
Press Proofs-79
96Metal Universe-75
96Pinnacle-190
Artist's Proofs-190
Foil-190
Premium Stock-190
Rink Collection-190
96Score-122
Artist's Proofs-122
Dealer's Choice Artist's Proofs-122
Special Artist's Proofs-122
Golden Blades-122
96Select Certified-46
Artist's Proofs-46
Blue-46
Mirror Blue-46
Mirror Gold-46
Mirror Red-46
Red-46
96SkyBox Impact-58
96Summit-27
Artist's Proofs-27
Ice-27
Metal-27
Premium Stock-27
96Ultra-79
Gold Medallion-79
96Upper Deck-76
96Zenith-88
Artist's Proofs-88
97Be A Player-61
Autographs-61
Autographs Die-Cuts-61
Autographs Prismatic Die-Cuts-61
97Collector's Choice-119
Crash the Game-C17A
Crash the Game-C17B
Crash the Game-C17C
Crash the Game Exchange-CR17
Star Quest-SQ27
97Donruss-89
Press Proofs Silver-89
Press Proofs Gold-89
97Donruss Canadian Ice-58
Dominion Series-58
Provincial Series-58
97Donruss Limited-73
Exposure-73
97Donruss Preferred-92
Cut to the Chase-92
97Donruss Priority-39
Stamp of Approval-39
97Katch-11
Gold-11
Silver-11
97Leaf-29
Fractal Matrix-29
Fractal Matrix Die Cuts-29
97Leaf International-29
Universal Ice-29
97NHL Aces Playing Cards-4
97Pacific-219
Copper-219
Emerald Green-219
Ice Blue-219
Red-219
Silver-219
97Pacific Dynagon-60
Copper-60
Dark Grey-60
Emerald Green-60
Ice Blue-60
Red-60
Silver-60
Tandems-36
97Pacific Invincible-68
Copper-68
Emerald Green-68
Ice Blue-68
Red-68
Silver-68
97Pacific Omega-17
Copper-17
Dark Gray-7
Dark Gray-17
Emerald Green-17
Gold-17
Ice Blue-17
97Panini Stickers-226
97Paramount-14
Copper-14
Dark Grey-14
Emerald Green-14
Ice Blue-14
Red-14
Silver-14
97Pinnacle-179
Press Plates Back Black-179
Press Plates Back Cyan-179
Press Plates Back Magenta-179
Press Plates Back Yellow-179
Press Plates Front Black-179
Press Plates Front Cyan-179
Press Plates Front Magenta-179
Press Plates Front Yellow-179
97Pinnacle Certified-126
Red-126
Mirror Blue-126
Mirror Gold-126
Mirror Red-126
97Pinnacle Inside-124
97Pinnacle Tot Cert Platinum Blue-126
97Pinnacle Tot Cert Platinum Gold-126
97Pinnacle Totally Certified Platinum Red-126
97Pinnacle Tot Cert Mirror Platinum Gold-126
97Revolution-10
Copper-10
Emerald-10
Ice Blue-10
Silver-10
97Score-111
Artist's Proofs-111
Golden Blades-111
97Score Bruins-5
Platinum-5
Premier-5
97SP Authentic-12
97Studio-80
Press Proofs Silver-80
Press Proofs Gold-80
97Upper Deck-80
98Aurora-13
98Be A Player-11
Press Release-11
98BAP Gold-11
98BAP Autographs-11
98BAP Autographs Gold-11
98BAP Tampa Bay All Star Game-11
98Crown Royale-9
Limited Series-9
98Finest-117
No Protectors-117
No Protectors Refractors-117
Refractors-117
98Katch-9
98OPC Chrome-164
Refractors-164
98Pacific-83
Ice Blue-83
Red-83
98Pacific Dynagon Ice-11
Blue-11
Red-11
98Pacific Omega-16
Red-16
Opening Day Issue-16
98Panini Stickers-8
98Paramount-15
Copper-15
Emerald Green-15
Holo-Electric-15
Ice Blue-15
Silver-15
98Revolution-10
Ice Shadow-10
Red-10
98Topps-164
O-Pee-Chee-164
98Topps Gold Label Class 1-23
Black-23
Black One of One-23
One of One-23
Red-23
Red One of One-23
98Topps Gold Label Class 2-23
98Topps Gold Label Class 2 Black-23
98Topps Gold Label Class 2 Black 1 of 1-23
98Topps Gold Label Class 2 One of One-23
98Topps Gold Label Class 2 Red-23
98Topps Gold Label Class 2 Red One of One-23
98Topps Gold Label Class 3-23
98Topps Gold Label Class 3 Black-23
98Topps Gold Label Class 3 Black 1 of 1-23
98Topps Gold Label Class 3 One of One-23
98Topps Gold Label Class 3 Red-23
98Topps Gold Label Class 3 Red One of One-23
98UD Choice-12
Prime Choice Reserve-12
Reserve-12
98Upper Deck MVP-16
Gold Script-16
Silver Script-16
Super Script-16
99Maple Leafs Pizza Pizza-1
99O-Pee-Chee-68
99O-Pee-Chee Chrome-68
99O-Pee-Chee Chrome Refractors-68
99Pacific-25
Copper-25
Emerald Green-25
Gold-25
Ice Blue-25
Premiere Date-25
Red-25
99Pacific Omega-227
Copper-227
Gold-227
Ice Blue-227
Premiere Date-227
99Pacific Prism-138
Holographic Blue-138
Holographic Gold-138
Holographic Mirror-138

Holographic Purple-138
Premiere Date-138
99Panini Stickers-159
99Panini Stickers-330
99Paramount-22
Copper-22
Emerald-22
Gold-22
Holographic Emerald-22
Holographic Gold-22
Holographic Silver-22
Ice Blue-22
Premiere Date-22
Red-22
Silver-22
99Topps/OPC-68
99Topps/OPC Chrome-68
Refractors-68
99Wayne Gretzky Hockey-164
00BAP Parkhurst 2000-P227
00BAP Signature Series-53
Emerald-53
Ruby-53
Sapphire-53
Autographs-31
Autographs Gold-31
00Pacific-395
Copper-395
Gold-395
Ice Blue-395
Premiere Date-395
01BAP Signature Series-147
Autographs-147
Autographs Gold-147
01Pacific-394
Extreme LTD-394
Hobby LTD-394
Premiere Date-394
Retail LTD-394
01Pacific Arena Exclusives-394
01Upper Deck-408
Exclusives-408
02BAP First Edition-213
02BAP Sig Series Auto Buybacks 1998-11
02BAP Sig Series Auto Buybacks 2000-31
02BAP Sig Series Auto Buybacks 2001-147
02Pacific-394
Blue-394
Red-394
02Topps Total-20

Khudobin, Anton
04Russian Under-18 Team-20
05Saskatoon Blades-10

Khudyakov, Denis
02Windsor Spitfires-28
04Russian World Junior Team-22

Kiang, Hsi
79Panini Stickers-358

Kiansten, Jussi
72Finnish Jaakiekko-264

Kibermanis, Chris
93Red Deer Rebels-9
95Red Deer Rebels-8

Kidd, Ian
89ProCards IHL-182
90ProCards AHL/IHL-323
91ProCards-601
93Cincinnati Cyclones-11

Kidd, Josh
04Erie Otters-16
05Erie Otters-16
06Erie Otters-15

Kidd, Trevor
88Brandon Wheat Kings-21
89Brandon Wheat Kings-1
90Score-438
Canadian-438
90Upper Deck-463
French-463
90Brandon Wheat Kings-15
907th Inn. Sketch WHL-226
91Alberta International Team Canada-12
91O-Pee-Chee-312
91Score American-381
91Score Canadian Bilingual-271
91Score Canadian English-271
91Topps-312
91Upper Deck-449
91Upper Deck-684
French-449
French-684
91Upper Deck Czech World Juniors-58
917th Inn. Sketch Memorial Cup-74
92Score Canadian Olympians-12
92Topps-280
Gold-280G
92Upper Deck-134
92Upper Deck-385
92Salt Lake Golden Eagles-11
93Leaf-385
93PowerPlay-305
93Score-660
Gold-560
Gold-660
Canadian-660
Canadian Gold-660
93Ultra-281
93Upper Deck-399
94Be A Player Signature Cards-167
94Canada Games NHL POGS-275
94Donruss-4
94Flair-25
94Fleer-31
94Kraft-45
94Leaf-322
94OPC Premier-413
94O-Pee-Chee Finest Inserts-5
94OPC Premier Special Effects-413
94Parkhurst-288
Gold-288
94Parkhurst SE-SE24
Gold-SE24
94Pinnacle-365
Artist's Proofs-365
Rink Collection-365
Masks-MA7
94Score-259
Gold-259
Platinum-259
94SP-21
Die Cuts-21
94Stadium Club-106
Members Only Master Set-106
First Day Issue-106
Super Team Winner Cards-106
94Topps/OPC Premier-413
Special Effects-413
94Ultra-30
94Upper Deck-395
Electric Ice-395
SP Inserts-SP12
SP Inserts Die Cuts-SP12
95Upper Deck World Junior Alumni-10
95Bashan Super Stickers-17
95Canada Games NHL POGS-60
95Collector's Choice-69
Player's Club-69
Player's Club Platinum-69
95Donruss-31
Between The Pipes-4
Dominators-8
Pro Pointers-16
95Emotion-23
95Imperial Stickers-17
95Kraft-24
95Leaf-83
95Leaf Limited-31
95Metal-20
95Panini Stickers-243
95Parkhurst International-35
Emerald Ice-35
Goal Patrol-8
95Pinnacle-151
Artist's Proofs-151
Rink Collection-151
95Playoff One on One-233
95Pro Magnets-47
95Score Promos-19
95Score-19
Black Ice Artist's Proofs-19
Black Ice-19
95Select Certified-40
Mirror Gold-40
95SkyBox Impact-23
Deflectors-10
95SP-21
95Stadium Club-72
Members Only Master Set-72
95Summit-138
Artist's Proofs-138
Ice-138
95Topps-154
OPC Inserts-154
Canadian Gold-4CG
Home Grown Canada-HGC13
95Topps SuperSkills-82
Platinum-82
95Ultra-26
Gold Medallion-26
Rising Stars-4
Rising Stars Gold Medallion-4
95Upper Deck-143
95Upper Deck-229
Electric Ice-143
Electric Ice-229
Electric Ice Gold-143
Electric Ice Gold-229
Special Edition-SE15
Special Edition Gold-SE15
95Zenith-67
96Be A Player-127
Autographs-127
Autographs Silver-127
96Collector's Choice-34
96Collector's Choice-312
96Donruss-160
Press Proofs-160
96Donruss Canadian Ice-37
Gold Press Proofs-37
Red Press Proofs-37
96Donruss Elite-45
Die Cut Stars-45
96Flair-13
Blue Ice-13
96Fleer-13
96Leaf-67
Press Proofs-67
96Leaf Limited-25
Gold-25
96Leaf Preferred-116
Press Proofs-116
96Maggers-47
96McDonald's Pinnacle-34
96Metal Universe-20
96NHL Pro Stamps-47
96Pinnacle-174
Artist's Proofs-174
Foil-174
Premium Stock-174
Rink Collection-174
96Score-58
Artist's Proofs-58
Dealer's Choice Artist's Proofs-58
Special Artist's Proofs-58
Golden Blades-58
96Select Certified-21
Artist's Proofs-21
Blue-21
Mirror Blue-21
Mirror Gold-21
Mirror Red-21
Red-21
96SkyBox Impact-14
96SP-21
96Summit-36
Artist's Proofs-36
Ice-36
Metal-36
Premium Stock-36
96Team Out-73
96Ultra-25
Gold Medallion-25
96Upper Deck-25
96Zenith-11
Artist's Proofs-11
96Collector's Edge Ice Crucibles-C21
97Collector's Choice-37
97Crown Royale-24
Emerald Green-24
Ice Blue-24
Silver-24
97Donruss-59
Press Proofs Silver-59
Press Proofs Gold-59
97Donruss Canadian Ice-60
Dominion Series-60
Provincial Series-60
97Donruss Elite-107
Aspirations-107
Status-107
97Donruss Limited-10
Exposure-10
97Donruss Preferred-73
Cut to the Chase-73
97Donruss Priority-98
Stamp of Approval-98
97Flames Collector's Photos-3
97Hurricanes Team Issue-14
97Leaf-126
Fractal Matrix-126
Fractal Matrix Die Cuts-126
97Leaf International-126
Universal Ice-126
97Pacific-133
Copper-133
Emerald Green-133
Ice Blue-133
Red-133
Silver-133
In The Cage Laser Cuts-3
97Pacific Dynagon-18
Copper-18
Dark Grey-18
Emerald Green-18
Ice Blue-18
Red-18
Silver-18
Stonewallers-4
Tandems-23
97Pacific Invincible-20
Copper-20
Emerald Green-20
Ice Blue-20
Red-20
Silver-20
97Pacific Omega-42
Copper-42
Dark Gray-42
Emerald Green-42
Gold-42
Ice Blue-42
97Paramount-35
Copper-35
Dark Grey-35
Emerald Green-35
Ice Blue-35
Red-35
Silver-35
Glove Side Laser Cuts-3
97Pinnacle-60
Artist's Proofs-60
Rink Collection-60
Press Plates Back Black-60
Press Plates Back Cyan-60
Press Plates Back Magenta-60
Press Plates Back Yellow-60
Press Plates Front Black-60
Press Plates Front Cyan-60
Press Plates Front Magenta-60
Press Plates Front Yellow-60
97Pinnacle Certified-21
Red-21
Mirror Blue-21
Mirror Gold-21
Mirror Red-21
97Pinnacle Inside-87
Coach's Collection-87
Executive Collection-87
Stand Up Guys-8A/B
Stand Up Guys-8C/D
Stand Up Guys Promos-8A/B
Stand Up Guys Promos-8C/D
97Pinnacle Tot Cert Platinum Blue-21
97Pinnacle Tot Certi Platinum Gold-21
97Pinnacle Totally Certified Platinum Red-21
97Pinnacle Tot Cert Mirror Platinum Gold-21
97Revolution-24
Copper-24
Emerald-24
Ice Blue-24
Silver-24
97Score-37
Artist's Proofs-37
Golden Blades-37
Net Worth-3
97Studio-61
Press Proofs Silver-61
Press Proofs Gold-61
97Upper Deck-23
98SLU Hockey Extended-103
98Aurora-34
98Be A Player-22
Press Release-22
98BAP Gold-22
98BAP Autographs-22
98BAP Autographs Gold-22
98BAP Tampa Bay All Star Game-22
98Bowman's Best-30
Refractors-30
Atomic Refractors-30
98Crown Royale-25
Limited Series-25
98Finest-85
No Protectors-85
No Protectors Refractors-85
Refractors-85
Promos-PP4
98Hurricanes Team Issue-20
98Kenner Starting Lineup Cards-16
98NHL Aces Playing Cards-48
98OPC Chrome-66
Refractors-66
98Pacific-135
Ice Blue-135
Red-135
98Pacific Dynagon Ice-35
Blue-35
Red-35
98Pacific Omega-44
Red-44
Opening Day Issue-44
98Panini Stickers-24
98Paramount-38
Copper-38
Emerald Green-38
Holo-Electric-38
Ice Blue-38
Silver-38
Glove Side Laser Cuts-4
98Revolution-25
Ice Shadow-25
Red-25
98SPx Finite-15
Radiance-15
Spectrum-15
98Topps-66
O-Pee-Chee-66
98UD Choice-42
Prime Choice Reserve-42
Reserve-42
98Upper Deck-58
Exclusives-58
Exclusives 1 of 1-58
Gold Reserve-58
98Upper Deck MVP-36
Gold Script-36
Silver Script-36
Super Script-36
99Black Diamond-43
Diamond Cut-43
Final Cut-43
99Crown Royale-60
Limited Series-60
Premiere Date-60
99Pacific-74
Copper-74
Emerald Green-74
Gold-74
Ice Blue-74
Premiere Date-74
Red-74
99Pacific Dynagon Ice-89
Blue-89
Copper-89
Gold-89
Premiere Date-89
99Pacific Prism-61
Holographic Blue-61
Holographic Gold-61
Holographic Mirror-61
Holographic Purple-61
Premiere Date-61
99SP Authentic-38
99SPx-72
Radiance-72
Spectrum-72
99Upper Deck-230
Exclusives-230
Exclusives 1 of 1-230
99Upper Deck Gold Reserve-230
99Upper Deck Victory-127
99Wayne Gretzky Hockey-75
00Aurora-61
Premiere Date-61
00BAP Memorabilia-48
Emerald-48
Ruby-48
Sapphire-48
Promos-48
00BAP Mem Chicago Sportsfest Copper-48
00BAP Memorabilia Chicago Sportsfest Blue-48
00BAP Memorabilia Chicago Sportsfest Gold-48
00BAP Memorabilia Chicago Sportsfest Ruby-48
00BAP Memorabilia Chicago Sun-Times Ruby-48
00BAP Memorabilia Chicago Sun-Times Gold-48
00BAP Mem Chicago Sun-Times Sapphire-48
00BAP Mem Toronto Fall Expo Copper-48
00BAP Memorabilia Toronto Fall Expo Gold-48
00BAP Memorabilia Toronto Fall Expo Ruby-48
00BAP Parkhurst 2000-P138
00BAP Signature Series-23
Emerald-23
Ruby-23
Sapphire-23
00Black Diamond-27
Gold-27
00O-Pee-Chee-207
00O-Pee-Chee Parallel-207
00Pacific-178
Copper-178
Gold-178
Ice Blue-178
Premiere Date-178
00Panthers Team Issue-29
00Paramount-104
Copper-104
Gold-104
Holo-Gold-104
Holo-Silver-104
Ice Blue-104
Premiere Date-104
00Private Stock-43
Gold-43
Premiere Date-43
Retail-43
Silver-43
00Revolution-62
Blue-62
Premiere Date-62
Red-62
00SP Game Used-28
00SPx-29
Spectrum-29
00Stadium Club-166
00Titanium-40
Blue-40
Gold-40
Premiere Date-40
Red-40
Retail-40
00Topps/OPC-207
Parallel-207
00Topps Chrome-136
OPC Refractors-136
Refractors-136
00UD Heroes-52
00Upper Deck-77
Exclusives Tier 1-77
Exclusives Tier 2-77
00Upper Deck MVP-82
First Stars-82
Second Stars-82
Third Stars-82
00Upper Deck Victory-107
00Upper Deck Vintage-155
00Upper Deck Vintage-161
Great Gloves-GG10
01BAP Memorabilia Goalies Jerseys-GJ10
01BAP Signature Series-185
Autographs-185
Autographs Gold-185
01Between the Pipes-62
Double Memorabilia-DM8
Goalie Gear-GG16
Jerseys-GJ21
Jersey and Stick Cards-GSJ20
Tandems-GT4
01O-Pee-Chee-243
01O-Pee-Chee Premier Parallel-243
01Pacific-171
Extreme LTD-171
Hobby LTD-171
Premiere Date-171
Retail LTD-171
01Pacific Adrenaline-81
Blue-81
Premiere Date-81
Red-81
Retail-81
Power Play-16
01Pacific Arena Exclusives-171
01Topps-243
OPC Parallel-243
02BAP First Edition-130
Jerseys-130
02BAP Sig Series Auto Buybacks 1998-22
02BAP Sig Series Auto Buybacks 2001-185
02BAP Signature Series Golf-GS99
02Between the Pipes-46
Gold-46
Silver-46
Blockers-17
Double Memorabilia-16
Jerseys-39
Tandems-14
02Crown Royale-91
Blue-91
Red-91
Retail-91
02Maple Leafs Platinum Collection-10
02Maple Leafs Team Issue-7
02NHL Power Play Stickers-133
02Pacific-155
Blue-155
Red-155
02Pacific Complete-263
Red-263
02UD Mask Collection-82
02UD Mask Collection-83
02UD Mask Collection Beckett Promos-82
02UD Mask Collection Beckett Promos-83
02Upper Deck-407
Exclusives-407
02Upper Deck Beckett UD Promos-407
03BAP Memorabilia-168
Emerald-168
Gold-168
Ruby-168
Sapphire-168
Deep in the Crease-D9
Tandems-T-10
03ITG Action-510
03Pacific-319
Blue-319
Red-319
03Pacific Complete-430
Red-430
03Parkhurst Original Six Toronto-29
Memorabilia-TM13
03Upper Deck MVP-406
Gold Script-406
Silver Script-406
Canadian Exclusives-406
05German DEL-130
Goalies-G06
06German DEL All-Star Jerseys-AS10

Kidney, Kyle
01Quad-City Mallards-10
02Pee Dee Pride RBI-139
03Florence Pride-151

Kieca, Mariusz
92Finnish Semic-268

Kienass, Torsten
92Finnish Semic-179
94Finnish Jaa Kiekko-274
94German DEL-84
95German DEL-79
95German DEL-436
95Swedish World Championships Stickers-55
96German DEL-322
99German DEL-348
99German DEL-368
00German DEL-45
01German Upper Deck-51
02German DEL City Press-51
05German DEL-44
06German DEL-34
Team Leaders-TL4

Kiene, Chris
89ProCards AHL-221
90ProCards AHL/IHL-575
91Moncton Hawks-14
91ProCards-165

Kieras, Mindraugas
04UK Edinburgh Capitals-2

Kiereck, Matt
92Sudbury Wolves-14

Kiesman, Michael
98Prince George Cougars-11
00Johnstown Chiefs-16
03Fresno Falcons-7
04Fresno Falcons-9

Kiessling, George
93Quebec Pee-Wee Tournament-617

Kiessling, Udo
79Panini Stickers-100
82Swedish Semic VM Stickers-105
83Swedish Semic VM Stickers-105
89Swedish Semic World Champ Stickers-107
91Finnish Semic World Champ Stickers-157
91Swedish Semic World Champ Stickers-157
94German DEL-268
95German DEL-248

Kihlstrom, Christer
71Swedish Hockey-337
72Swedish Stickers-148

Kihlstrom, Mats
83Swedish Semic Elitserien-200
84Swedish Semic Elitserien-52
85Swedish Panini Stickers-51
86Swedish Panini Stickers-249
87Swedish Panini Stickers-236
89Swedish Semic Elitserien Stickers-220
89Swedish Semic World Champ Stickers-7
90Swedish Semic Elitserien Stickers-53
91Swedish Semic Elitserien Stickers-228

Kiilholma, Juha
03Finnish Cardset-181
04Finnish Cardset-200
Parallel-147
05Finnish Cardset -174

Kiili, Lasse
65Finnish Hellas-1
69Swedish Hockey-372
70Finnish Jaakiekko-157
71Finnish Suomi Stickers-228
72Finnish Jaakiekko-212
73Finnish Jaakiekko-198
74Finnish Typotor-31

Kiimalainen, Markku
78Finnish SM-Liiga-7
78Finnish SM-Liiga-144
80Finnish Mallasjuoma-99
81Swedish Semic Hockey VM Stickers-27
82Finnish Skopbank-5
82Swedish Semic VM Stickers-40

Kiiski, Tommi
92Finnish Jyvas-Hyva Stickers-39

Kiiskinen, Tuomas
05Finnish Cardset -80
06Finnish Cardset-90
Signature Sensations-16

Kiiskinen, Ville
00Finnish Cardset-323

Kikesch, Jeff
97Louisville Riverfrogs-14

Kilbourne, B.J.
99Mobile Mysticks-11
02Trenton Titans-A-5

Kilburg, Brian
02Tri-City Stormfront-3

Kilchor, Martin
99Swiss Panini Stickers-29

Kilduff, David
91British Columbia JHL-87
92British Columbia JHL-135

Kiley, Chris
93RPI Engineers-12

Kiley, Ryan
03Cape Fear Fire Antz-4

Kilger, Chad
93Kingston Frontenacs-17
94Classic Draft Prospects-DP3
95Bashan Super Stickers-3
95Be A Player-167
Signatures-S167
Signatures Die Cuts-S167
95Bowman-137
All-Foil-137
Bowman's Best-BB25
Bowman's Best Refractors-BB25
95Donruss-379
Rated Rookies-7
95Donruss Elite-55
Die Cut Stars-55
Die Cut Uncut-55
Rookies-9
95Emotion generatioNext-10
95Finest-81
Refractors-81
95Imperial Stickers-3
95Leaf Limited-34
Rookie Phenoms-3
95Metal-179
95Parkhurst International-255
95Parkhurst International-500
Emerald Ice-255
Emerald Ice-500
95Select Certified-116
Mirror Gold-116
95SkyBox Impact-188
NHL On Fox-18
95SP-163
95Stadium Club-202
Members Only Master Set-202
95Summit-179
Artist's Proofs-179
Ice-179
95Topps-301
OPC Inserts-301
SuperSkills Super Rookies-SR5
95Ultra-343
95Upper Deck-262
Electric Ice-262
Electric Ice Gold-262
95Zenith-139
Rookie Roll Call-12
95Classic-4
95Classic-86
CHL All-Stars-AS10
Ice Breakers-BK4
Ice Breakers Die Cuts-BK4
95Images-84
Gold-84
Platinum Premier Draft Choice-PD7
95Classic Five-Sport *-143
Strive For Five-HK9
96Collector's Choice-200
96Collector's Choice-337
96Coyotes Coca-Cola-14
96Donruss-236
Press Proofs-236
96Leaf-203
Press Proofs-203
96Score-255
Artist's Proofs-255
Dealer's Choice Artist's Proofs-255
Special Artist's Proofs-255
Golden Blades-255
96Summit-155
Artist's Proofs-155
Ice-155
Metal-155
Premium Stock-155
96Topps Picks-151
OPC Inserts-151
96Upper Deck-130
97Coyotes Face-Off Luncheon -11
97Donruss-175
Press Proofs Silver-175
Press Proofs Gold-175
97Donruss Limited-73
Exposure-73
97Leaf-137
Fractal Matrix-137
Fractal Matrix Die Cuts-137
97Leaf International-137
Universal Ice-137
97Upper Deck-130
97Springfield Falcons-12
98Pacific-146
Ice Blue-146
Red-146
98Upper Deck-244
Exclusives-244
Exclusives 1 of 1-244
Gold Reserve-244
99Pacific-157
Copper-157
Emerald Green-157
Gold-157
Ice Blue-157
Premiere Date-157
Red-157
00Canadiens Postcards-12
01Canadiens Postcards-12
01Pacific-208
Extreme LTD-208
Hobby LTD-208
Premiere Date-208
Retail LTD-208
01Pacific Arena Exclusives-208
01Upper Deck-325
Exclusives-325
01Upper Deck Victory-190
Gold-190
02Canadiens Postcards-8
02NHL Power Play Stickers-49
02Pacific Complete-195
Red-195
02Upper Deck-338
Exclusives-338
02Upper Deck Beckett UD Promos-338
03Canadiens Postcards-15
03ITG Action-318
03Parkhurst Original Six Montreal-17
Memorabilia-MM9
05Parkhurst-457
Facsimile Auto Parallel-457
06Gatorade-72
06O-Pee-Chee-468
Rainbow-468

Kilgour, Ben
03Louisiana Ice Gators-11

Killam, Ryan
93Quebec Pee-Wee Tournament-1611

Killeen, Patrick
06Brampton Battalion-2

Killen, Frank
93UK Humberside Hawks-20

Killewald, Erica
98Minnesota Golden Gophers Women-12

Killi, Lasse
66Finnish Jaakiekkosarja-74

Killing, Geoff
04Belleville Bulls-8
05Belleville Bulls-12
06Belleville Bulls-16

Kilpatrick, Gary
69Seattle Totems-7

Kilpatrick, Gen.J.R.
83Hall of Fame-116
83Hall of Fame Postcards-H10
85Hall of Fame-116

Kilpelainen, Eero
04Peterborough Petes Postcards-5
06Finnish Cardset-345
Between the Pipes-24
06Finnish Porin Assat Pelaajakortit-2

Kilpio, Raimo
65Finnish Hellas-79
66Finnish Jaakiekkosarja-15
70Finnish Jaakiekko-194
71Finnish Suomi Stickers-86
72Finnish Jaakiekko-249
72Finnish Panda Toronto-39
73Finnish Jaakiekko-248
74Finnish Typotor-46
96Finnish SISU Redline-189

Kilrea, Brian
81Ottawa 67's-9
82Ottawa 67's-11
83Ottawa 67's-16
85Islanders News-30
907th Inn. Sketch OHL-100
917th Inn. Sketch OHL-309
92Ottawa 67's-13
99Ottawa 67's-26
00Ottawa 67's-24
00Ottawa 67's-27
01Ottawa 67's-24
02Ottawa 67's-24
03Ottawa 67's-NNO

Kilrea, Hec
24Anonymous NHL-19
24Anonymous NHL-20
33V129-17
33V357 Ice Kings-64
34Beehive Group I Photos-108
34Beehive Group I Photos-332
35O-Pee-Chee V304C-86
37V356 Worldwide Gum-24
39O-Pee-Chee V301-1-71

Kilrea, Ken
34Beehive Group I Photos-109

Kilrea, Wally
33O-Pee-Chee V304B-63
33V357 Ice Kings-53
34Beehive Group I Photos-110

Kim, Alex
93Quebec Pee-Wee Tournament-1243
99Des Moines Buccaneers-14
02Reading Royals-31
02Reading Royals RBI Sports-176
06Bakersfield Condors-10

Kim, Han-Sung
03Greenville Grrrowl-11

Kim, Matthew
93Quebec Pee-Wee Tournament-1262

Kim, Ryan
03Chicago Steel-13

Kimble, Darin
88Nordiques General Foods-21
88Nordiques Team Issue-36
88ProCards AHL-110
89Nordiques Team Issue-21
89Nordiques General Foods-17
89Nordiques Police-14
90Nordiques Petro-Canada-13
90Nordiques Team Issue-16
90O-Pee-Chee-437
90Pro Set-517
91Blues Postcards-13
91Bowman-381
91Nordiques Panini Team Stickers-11
91O-Pee-Chee-156
91Parkhurst-377
French-377
91Score Canadian Bilingual-526
91Score Canadian English-526
91Stadium Club-278
91Topps-156
92Stadium Club-486
92Topps-511
Gold-511G
93Blackhawks Coke-24
94Blackhawks Coke-9
99Peoria Rivermen-23
00Missouri River Otters-11
01Missouri River Otters-18
02Fleer Throwbacks-58
Gold-58
Platinum-58

Kimento, Jeremiah
93Quebec Pee-Wee Tournament-1320
01Notre Dame Fighting Irish-1

Kimker, Andreas
94German First League-328

Kimmalainen, Markku
77Finnish Sportscasters-90-2150

Kimura, Kevin
92British Columbia JHL-32

Kinaschuk, Brett
91Air Canada SJHL-D5
92Saskatchewan JHL-30

Kinaschuk, Kent
92Saskatchewan JHL-36

Kinasewich, Ryan
99Medicine Hat Tigers-19
00Medicine Hat Tigers-13
04Reading Royals-13

Kinateder, Christan
04German Weiden Blue Devils-15

Kincaid, Cameron
95Slapshot-428

Kinch, Matt
98Calgary Hitmen-1
98Calgary Hitmen Autographs-1
99Calgary Hitmen-12
99Calgary Hitmen Autographs-12
00Calgary Hitmen-15
01Hartford Wolf Pack-12
02Hartford Wolf Pack-12
03Hartford Wolf Pack-10
05German DEL-339
06German DEL-176

Kinch, Rob
92Saskatchewan JHL-44

Kinder, Sjur
92Norwegian Elite Series-178

Kinding, Bjorn
93Swiss HNL-109

Kindl, Jakub
03Czech OFS Plus-379
04Kitchener Rangers-12
05ITG Heroes/Prosp Toronto Expo Parallel -130
05Kitchener Rangers-14
05ITG Heroes and Prospects-130
Autographs-A-JK
06Kitchener Rangers-1

Kindler, Beat
93Swiss HNL-413
95Swiss HNL-239
96Swiss HNL-251
98Swiss Power Play Stickers-333
99Swiss Panini Stickers-327
00Swiss Panini Stickers-309
01Swiss HNL-259
02Swiss HNL-84

Kindrachuk, Orest
73Flyers Linnett-9
74NHL Action Stamps-212
74O-Pee-Chee NHL-334
75Flyers Canada Dry Cans-10
75O-Pee-Chee NHL-389
76O-Pee-Chee NHL-233
76Topps-233
77O-Pee-Chee NHL-26
77Topps-26
78O-Pee-Chee-114
78Topps-114
79O-Pee-Chee-218
79Topps-218
80O-Pee-Chee-292
92Parkhurst-476
Emerald Ice-476
04ITG Franchises US East-421
Autographs-A-OK

Kindred, Garrett
06Fayetteville FireAntz-6

Kindret, Ryan
03Vernon Vipers-8

Kinell, Bengt
85Swedish Panini Stickers-191

King, Archie
75Hamilton Fincups-10

King, Colt
99Guelph Storm-15
00UD CHL Prospects-41
01UD Prospects-14
Autographs-A-CK
Jersey Autographs-S-CK
Jerseys-J-CK
Jerseys-C-KW
Jerseys Gold-J-CK
Jerseys Gold-C-KW
02Saginaw Spirit-1
03Sarnia Sting-12
06Port Huron Flags-23

King, D.J.
01Lethbridge Hurricanes-13
04Worcester IceCats-13
05Peoria Rivermen-12
06Black Diamond-165A
Black-165A
Gold-165A
Ruby-165A
06Hot Prospects-177
Red Hot-177
White Hot-177
06O-Pee-Chee-550
Rainbow-550
06SP Game Used-152
Gold-152
Rainbow-152
06SPx-159
Spectrum-159
06The Cup-106
Autographed Rookie Masterpiece Pressplates-106
Gold Rainbow Autographed Rookies-106
Masterpiece Pressplates (Black Diamond)-165
Masterpiece Pressplates (Marquee Rookies)-550
Masterpiece Pressplates (MVP)-319
Masterpiece Pressplates (SP Game Used)-152
Masterpiece Pressplates (SPx)-159
Masterpiece Pressplates (Trilogy)-152
Masterpiece Pressplates (Victory)-296
Rookies Black-106
Rookies Platinum-106
06Ultimate Collection Ultimate Debut Threads Jerseys-DJ-DK
06Ultimate Collection Ultimate Debut Threads Jerseys Autographs-DJ-DK
06Ultimate Collection Ultimate Debut Threads Patches-DJ-DK
06Ultimate Collection Ultimate Debut Threads Patches Autographs-DJ-DK
06Upper Deck-243
Exclusives Parallel-243
High Gloss Parallel-243
Masterpieces-243
Rookie Materials-RMDK
Rookie Materials Patches-RMDK
06Upper Deck MVP-319
Gold Script-319
Super Script-319
06Upper Deck Trilogy-152
06Upper Deck Victory-296
06Peoria Rivermen-7

King, Dave
89Swedish Semic World Champ Stickers-52
90Alberta International Team Canada-21
91Alberta International Team Canada-13
92Flames IGA-26
92Finnish Semic-74
93Kraft-38

King, Derek
84Sault Ste. Marie Greyhounds-11
88Panini Stickers-289
89O-Pee-Chee-6
89O-Pee-Chee Stickers-116
89Panini Stickers-271
89Topps-6
89ProCards AHL-250
90O-Pee-Chee-128
90Pro Set-185
90Score Rookie/Traded-86T
90Topps-128
Tiffany-128
90Upper Deck-407
French-407
91Pro Set Platinum-201
91Pro Set Platinum-286
91Bowman-220
91O-Pee-Chee-455
91Panini Stickers-247
91Parkhurst-108
French-108
91Pinnacle-107
French-107
91Pro Set-146
French-146
91Score American-167
91Score Canadian Bilingual-167
91Score Canadian English-167
91Stadium Club-82
91Topps-455
91Upper Deck-382
French-382
92Bowman-188
92O-Pee-Chee-79
92Panini Stickers-199
92Panini Stickers French-199

92Parkhurst-100
Emerald Ice-100
92Pinnacle-17
French-17
92Pro Set-110
92Score-255
Canadian-255
Sharpshooters-15
Sharpshooters Canadian-15
92Stadium Club-82
92Topps-431
Gold-431G
92Ultra-128
92Upper Deck-191
93Donruss-204
93Leaf-119
93OPC Premier-176
Gold-176
93Panini Stickers-58
93Parkhurst-119
Emerald Ice-119
93Pinnacle-128
Canadian-128
93PowerPlay-150
93Score-48
Canadian-48
Dynamic Duos Canadian-9
93Stadium Club-215
Members Only Master Set-215
OPC-215
First Day Issue-215
First Day Issue OPC-215
93Topps/OPC Premier-176
Gold-176
93Ultra-176
93Upper Deck-417
94Be A Player Signature Cards-6
94Canada Games NHL POGS-157
94Donruss-30
94Flair-103
94Fleer-123
94Hockey Wit-28
94Leaf-188
94OPC Premier-304
Special Effects-304
94Parkhurst-132
Gold-132
94Pinnacle-302
Artist's Proofs-302
Rink Collection-302
94Select-9
Gold-9
94Stadium Club-108
Members Only Master Set-108
First Day Issue-108
Super Team Winner Cards-108
94Topps/OPC Premier-304
Special Effects-304
94Ultra-325
94Upper Deck-59
Electric Ice-59
95Bashan Super Stickers-76
95Canada Games NHL POGS-172
95Donruss-300
95Imperial Stickers-76
95Imperial Stickers-77
95Leaf-261
95Panini Stickers-92
95Parkhurst International-132
Emerald Ice-132
95Score-238
Black Ice Artist's Proofs-238
Black Ice-238
95Stadium Club-81
Members Only Master Set-81
95Topps-202
OPC Inserts-202
96Islander Postcards-9
96SP-95
96Upper Deck Ice-40
Parallel-40
97Be A Player-40
Autographs-40
Autographs Die-Cuts-40
Autographs Prismatic Die-Cuts-40
97Collector's Choice-112
97Donruss-69
Press Proofs Silver-69
Press Proofs Gold-69
97Pacific Invincible-24
Copper-24
Emerald Green-24
Ice Blue-24
Red-24
Silver-24
NHL Regime-37
97Panini Stickers-23
97Paramount-181
Copper-181
Dark Grey-181
Emerald Green-181
Ice Blue-181
Red-181
Silver-181
97Score Maple Leafs-18
Platinum-18
Premier-18
98Be A Player-135
Press Release-135
98BAP Gold-135
98BAP Autographs-135
98BAP Autographs Gold-135
98BAP Tampa Bay All Star Game-135
98OPC Chrome-84
Refractors-84
98Pacific-414
Ice Blue-414
Red-414
98Paramount-228
Copper-228
Emerald Green-228
Holo-Electric-228
Ice Blue-228
Silver-228
98Topps-84
O-Pee-Chee-84
98Upper Deck-373
Exclusives-373
Exclusives 1 of 1-373
Gold Reserve-373
99BAP Memorabilia-124
Gold-124
Silver-124
99Pacific-410
Copper-410
Emerald Green-410
Gold-410
Ice Blue-410
Premiere Date-410
Red-410
99Paramount-226
Copper-226
Emerald-226
Gold-226
Holographic Emerald-226
Holographic Gold-226
Holographic Silver-226
Ice Blue-226
Premiere Date-226
Red-226
99Revolution-139
Premiere Date-139
Red-139
Shadow Series-139
Copper-139
Gold-139
CSC Silver-139
99Upper Deck Victory-291
99Grand Rapids Griffins-12
00Grand Rapids Griffins-11
01German Upper Deck-184
02BAP Sig Series Auto Buybacks 1998-135
02Grand Rapids Griffins-15
03Parkhurst Original Six Detroit-29
03Grand Rapids Griffins-8

King, Derek E.
96UK Fife Flyers-4
97UK Fife Flyers-4
01UK Fife Flyers-2

King, Dwight
05Lethbridge Hurricanes-12

King, Frank
44Beehive Group II Photos-254
51Laval Dairy QSHL-10

King, Goal
90Hampton Roads Admirals-41
90ProCards AHL/IHL-492
92Stadium Club-269
92Toledo Storm-8
92Toledo Storm Team Issue-8
03German DEL-147

King, Grant
99UK Guildford Flames-19
00UK Guildford Flames-12
01UK Guildford Flames-12
01UK Guildford Flames-30
02UK Guildford Flames-11
02UK Guildford Flames-26

King, Jacob
03Sault Ste. Marie Greyhounds-12
04Sault Ste. Marie Greyhounds-16

King, Jason
99Halifax Mooseheads-8
00Halifax Mooseheads-9
01Halifax Mooseheads-9
02BAP Memorabilia-308
02BAP Ultimate Memorabilia-55
02SP Authentic-218
02Upper Deck Rookie Update-143
02Manitoba Moose-12
03Beehive-190
Variations-190
Gold-190
Silver-190
03Canucks Postcards-13
03Canucks Sav-on-Foods-13
03Canucks Sav-on-Foods-20
03Crown Royale-97
Blue-97
Retail-97
03Pacific Calder-98
Silver-98
03Pacific Complete-585
Red-585
03Pacific Heads-Up-96
Hobby LTD-96
Retail LTD-96
Prime Prospects-20
Prime Prospects LTD-20
03Pacific Quest for the Cup-98
Blue-98
Calder Contenders-20
03SP Authentic-85
Limited-85
03Titanium-95
Hobby Jersey Number Parallels-95
Retail-95
Retail Jersey Number Parallels-95
Right on Target-16
03Topps Traded-TT63
Blue-TT63
Gold-TT63
Red-TT63
03Upper Deck-437
Canadian Exclusives-437
HG-437
UD Exclusives-437
03Upper Deck Ice-86
Gold-86
Breakers-IB-JK
Breaker Patches-IB-JK
Frozen Fabrics-FF-JK
Frozen Fabric Patches-FF-JK
03Upper Deck Rookie Update-87
03Pacific AHL Prospect Destined Greatness-8
04AHL All-Stars-21
04AHL Top Prospects-31
04Manitoba Moose-14
04ITG Heroes and Prospects-181
04ITG Heroes/Prospects Toronto Expo '05-181
05Hot Prospects Hot Materials-HMKI
05Upper Deck MVP-381
Gold-381
Platinum-381
06Ultra Uniformity-UJK
06Ultra Uniformity Patches-UPJK
06Swedish SHL Elitset-270

King, Justin
06Texas Tornados-7

King, Kevin
89Sault Ste. Marie Greyhounds-12
907th Inn. Sketch OHL-70
907th Inn. Sketch OHL-161
917th Inn. Sketch OHL-228

King, Kris
88Red Wings Little Caesars-11
89Rangers Marine Midland Bank-12
90O-Pee-Chee-526
90Pro Set-491
90Score Rookie/Traded-76T
90Upper Deck-440
French-440
91Bowman-59
91O-Pee-Chee-498
91Parkhurst-337
French-337
91Pinnacle-362
French-362
91Pro Set-445
French-445
91Score American-363
91Score Canadian Bilingual-402
91Score Canadian English-402
91Stadium Club-26
91Topps-498
91Upper Deck-330
French-330
92Bowman-380
92O-Pee-Chee-86
92Parkhurst-442
Emerald Ice-442
92Pinnacle-168
92Pinnacle-253
French-168
French-253
92Score-181
Canadian-181
92Stadium Club-187
92Topps-509
Gold-509G
92Upper Deck-78
93Donruss-379
93Jets Ruffles-15
93Leaf-253
93Parkhurst-478B
Emerald Ice-478B
93Pinnacle-316
Canadian-316
93Score-362
Canadian-362
93Upper Deck-14
94Be A Player Signature Cards-15
94Leaf-395
94Parkhurst-269
Gold-269
94Stadium Club-124
Members Only Master Set-124
First Day Issue-124
Super Team Winner Cards-124
94Upper Deck-308
Electric Ice-308
95Collector's Choice-215
Player's Club-215
Player's Club Platinum-215
95Jets Readers Club-5
95Jets Team Issue-11
95Parkhurst International-502
Emerald Ice-502
95Upper Deck-141
Electric Ice-141
Electric Ice Gold-141
96Coyotes Coca-Cola-15
96Coyotes Coca-Cola-16
96Kraft Upper Deck-35
96Pinnacle Trophies-7
97Be A Player-108
Autographs-108
Autographs Die-Cuts-108
Autographs Prismatic Die-Cuts-108
97Pacific-90
Copper-90
Emerald Green-90
Ice Blue-90
Red-90
Silver-90
98Be A Player-288
Press Release-288
98BAP Gold-288
98BAP Autographs-288
98BAP Autographs Gold-288
98OPC Chrome-160
Refractors-160
98Pacific-415
Ice Blue-415
Red-415
98Topps-160
O-Pee-Chee-160
02BAP Sig Series Auto Buybacks 1998-288
02Fleer Throwbacks-9
Gold-9
Platinum-9

King, Larry
91Pro Set Platinum-292

King, Mike
83Kingston Canadians-9

King, Randy
04Everett Silvertips-17

King, Scott
93Sault Ste. Marie Greyhounds-5
05German DEL-6

King, Scott BU
97New Orleans Brass-19
99Mississippi Sea Wolves-15
00Charlotte Checkers-3
02German DEL City Press-161
04German DEL-233
All-Stars-AS19
04German Krefeld Penguins Postcards-12
06German DEL-162
New Arrivals-NA4

King, Steve
82Oshawa Generals-13
83Kingston Canadians-19

King, Steven
91ProCards-199
92Parkhurst-347
Emerald Ice-347
92Ultra-355
92Upper Deck-575
92Binghamton Rangers-13
93Donruss-1
93Leaf-410
93OPC Premier-303
Gold-303
93Parkhurst-1
Emerald Ice-1
93Pinnacle-345
Canadian-345
93PowerPlay-6
93Score-382
93Score-514
Gold-514
Canadian-382
Canadian-514
Canadian Gold-514
93Stadium Club-377
Members Only Master Set-377
First Day Issue-377
93Topps/OPC Premier-303
Gold-303
93Ultra-258
93Upper Deck-24
93Classic-136
93Classic Pro Prospects-60
93Classic Pro Prospects-74
Prototypes-PR1
93Classic Four-Sport *-237
94Ducks Carl's Jr.-12
94OPC Premier-220
Special Effects-220
94Topps/OPC Premier-220
Special Effects-220

King, Steven E.
96UK Fife Flyers-9
97UK Fife Flyers-11
97Cincinnati Cyclones-9
01UK Fife Flyers-5

King, TC
69Swedish Hockey-357

King, Wayne
74NHL Action Stamps-56

Kinghan, Rob
907th Inn. Sketch OHL-36
917th Inn. Sketch OHL-29

Kinghorn, Ron
91ProCards-433

Kingsbury, Gina
04Canadian Womens World Championship Team-12
06ITG Going For Gold-15
06ITG Going For Gold Samples-15
06ITG Going For Gold Autographs-AKI
06ITG Going For Gold Jerseys-GUJ15

Kingston, George
95German DEL-428

Kinisky, Al
907th Inn. Sketch WHL-4
917th Inn. Sketch WHL-339
92British Columbia JHL-178

Kink, Georg
94German First League-285

Kink, Markus
04German DEL-14
05German DEL-250

Kinkel, Bill
01Kitchener Rangers-19
02Kingston Frontenacs-8

Kinnear, Geordie
907th Inn. Sketch OHL-363
91Peterborough Petes-24
917th Inn. Sketch OHL-132
96Albany River Rats-8
97Albany River Rats-6
98Albany River Rats-10
01Albany River Rats-27
02Albany River Rats-28
03Albany River Rats-30

Kinney, Bonnie
95Slapshot Memorial Cup-17

Kinney, Donnie
94Kamloops Blazers-7
95Kamloops Blazers-15
96Kamloops Blazers-14
97Bowman CHL-91
OPC-91
98Kamloops Blazers-15
99Bowman CHL-110
Gold-110
OPC International-110

Kinney, Ken
95Vancouver VooDoo RHI-18

Kinniburgh, Todd
89Portland Winter Hawks-14

Kinnunen, Jorma
70Finnish Jaakiekko-370

Kinnunen, Kari
65Finnish Hellas-63
70Finnish Jaakiekko-176
71Finnish Suomi Stickers-101
72Finnish Jaakiekko-144
73Finnish Jaakiekko-110

Kinnunen, Mikko
01Finnish Cardset-330

Kinnunen, Veli-Pekka
80Finnish Mallasjuoma-52

Kinos, Lauri
00Peoria Rivermen-5
02Peoria Rivermen-4

Kinzel, Dieter
83Swedish Semic VM Stickers-162

Kiopini, Serge
90Montreal-Bourassa AAA-13

Kipp, Damon
05Salmon Arm Silverbacks-10

Kipp, Reed
03Vernon Vipers-9
04Vernon Vipers-18

Kiprusoff, Jarmo
70Finnish Jaakiekko-296

Kiprusoff, Marko
91Upper Deck-671
French-671
91Upper Deck Czech World Juniors-34
93Finnish Jyvas-Hyva Stickers-321
93Finnish SISU-35
94Finnish SISU-7
94Finnish SISU-161
94Finnish SISU NHL Draft-2
94Finnish Jaa Kiekko-18
95Bowman-109
All-Foil-109
95Donruss-351
95Parkhurst International-268
Emerald Ice-268
95Stadium Club-141
Members Only Master Set-141
95Finnish Beckett Ad Cards-6
95Finnish SISU-163
95Finnish SISU-200
Gold Cards-7
95Finnish SISU Limited-5
95Finnish Karjala World Champ Labels-6
95Finnish Kellogg's-2
95Finnish Semic World Championships-2
95Swedish Globe World Championships-131
95Swedish World Championships Stickers-169
96Leaf-233
Press Proofs-233
96Pinnacle-234
Artist's Proofs-234
Foil-234
Premium Stock-234
Rink Collection-234
96Upper Deck-188
96Swedish Semic Wien-2
All-Stars-AS3
97Swedish Collector's Choice-135
Crash the Game Exchange-C13
Crash the Game Redemption-R13
98Finnish Keralysarja-230
Leijonat-8
Off Duty-11
99Finnish Cardset-133
99Finnish Cardset-183
Aces High-D-4
00Swiss Panini Stickers-153
00Swiss Slapshot Mini-Cards-EHCK3
01Parkhurst-252
01Parkhurst Beckett Promos-252
01Finnish Cardset-160
02Finnish Cardset-39
02Swiss HNL-293
04Finnish Cardset-169
04Finnish Cardset Signatures-34
05Finnish Cardset -153
06Finnish Cardset-157

Kiprusoff, Miikka
94Finest-125
Super Team Winners-125
Refractors-125
95Finnish SISU-122
Drafted Dozen-8
97Swedish Collector's Choice-1
Stick'Ums-S1
98Finnish Keralysarja-228
99Finnish Cardset-178
Blazing Patriots-1
Par Avion-8
99AHL All-Stars-5
99Kentucky Thoroughblades-17
00BAP Memorabilia-506
00Kentucky Thoroughblades-12
01BAP Memorabilia-201
Emerald-201
Ruby-201
Sapphire-201
01BAP Signature Series-221
Autographs-221
Autographs Gold-221
01Between the Pipes-20
Future Wave-FW7
He Shoots-He Saves Prizes-32
Jerseys-GJ41
Masks-39
Masks Silver-39
Masks Gold-39
Tandems-GT1
01O-Pee-Chee-275
01O-Pee-Chee Premier Parallel-275
01Pacific-337
Extreme LTD-337
Hobby LTD-337
Premiere Date-337
Retail LTD-337
01Pacific Adrenaline-165
Blue-165
Premiere Date-165
Red-165
Retail-165
Power Play-31
Rookie Report-18
01Pacific Arena Exclusives-337
01Parkhurst-293
Waving the Flag-15
01Parkhurst Beckett Promos-293
01Private Stock-109
Gold-109
Premiere Date-109
Retail-109
Silver-109
01Private Stock Pacific Nights-109
01Private Stock PS-2002-89
01SPx-123
01Stadium Club-115
Award Winners-115
Master Photos-115
01Topps-275
OPC Parallel-275
01Topps Chrome-141
Refractors-141
Black Border Refractors-141
01Upper Deck Victory-386
Gold-386
01Finnish Cardset-158
01Finnish Cardset Haltmeisters-2
01Finnish Cardset Salt Lake City-2
02BAP First Edition-241
02BAP Sig Series Auto Buybacks 2001-221
02Between the Pipes-13
Gold-13
Silver-13
Emblems-2
Future Wave-1
Jerseys-2
Masks II-25
Masks II Gold-25
Masks II Silver-25
Numbers-2
Stick and Jerseys-2
Tandems-4
02Pacific Calder-94
Silver-94
02Pacific Complete-273
Red-273
02Pacific Heads-Up Quad Jerseys-24
02Pacific Heads-Up Quad Jerseys Gold-24
02Parkhurst-40
Bronze-40
Gold-40
Silver-40
02Titanium Jerseys-61
02Titanium Jerseys Retail-61
02Titanium Patches-61
02UD Mask Collection-72
02UD Mask Collection-74
02UD Mask Collection Beckett Promos-72
02UD Mask Collection Beckett Promos-74
02Upper Deck Vintage-320
02Finnish Cardset-40
03BAP Memorabilia-144
03BAP Memorabilia-232
Emerald-144
Gold-144
Ruby-144
Sapphire-144
03ITG Action-674
03O-Pee-Chee-62
03OPC Blue-62
03OPC Gold-62
03OPC Red-62
03Pacific-295
Blue-295
Red-295
Jerseys-34
Jerseys Gold-34
03Pacific Calder-14
Silver-14
03Pacific Complete-434
Red-434
03Pacific Invincible Jerseys-27
03Pacific Quest for the Cup-16
Blue-16
03Parkhurst Rookie-15
03Titanium-17
Hobby Jersey Number Parallels-17
Retail-17
Retail Jersey Number Parallels-17
03Topps-62
Blue-62
Gold-62
Red-62
03Topps Traded-TT4
Blue-TT4
Gold-TT4
Red-TT4
03Upper Deck MVP-356
Gold Script-356
Silver Script-356
Canadian Exclusives-356
03Upper Deck Rookie Update-13
04Pacific-41
Blue-41
Red-41
In The Crease-2
04SP Authentic-16
04UD All-World-77
Gold-77
04Ultimate Collection-7
04Ultimate Collection-68
Dual Logos-UL2-IK
04Upper Deck-30
Canadian Exclusives-30
HG Glossy Gold-30
HG Glossy Silver-30
World Cup Tribute-MK
World Cup Tribute-KLMK
04Swedish Elitset-277
Dominators-3
Gold-277
Masks-8
04Swedish Pure Skills-89
Parallel-89
Signatures-15
Signatures Limited-4
The Wall-MK
05Be A Player-13
First Period-13
Second Period-13
Third Period-13
Overtime-13
Class Action-CA14
Outtakes-OT9
World Cup Salute-WCS13
05Beehive-15
05Beehive-249
Beige -15
Blue -15
Gold-15
Red -15
Matte-15
Matted Materials-MMMK
05Black Diamond-91
Emerald-91
Gold-91
Onyx-91
Ruby-91
05Hot Prospects-15
En Fuego-15
Red Hot-15
White Hot-15
05McDonalds Upper Deck-5
Goalie Factory-GF5
05Panini Stickers-200
05Parkhurst-73
Facsimile Auto Parallel-73
True Colors-TCCGY
True Colors-TCCGY
True Colors-TCEDCA
True Colors-TCEDCA
05SP Authentic-17
Limited-17
05SP Game Used-16
Gold-16
Authentic Fabrics Dual-IK
Authentic Fabrics Dual-KK
Authentic Fabrics Quad-IAKL
Authentic Patches Quad -IAKL
Authentic Fabrics Triple-KRT
Authentic Fabrics Triple-NKL
Authentic Patches Dual-IK
Authentic Patches Dual-KK
Authentic Patches Triple-KRT
Authentic Patches Triple-NKL
Awesome Authentics-AA-MK
05SPx-13
Spectrum-13
Winning Combos-WC-KI
Winning Combos-WC-KN
Winning Combos Gold-WC-KI
Winning Combos Spectrum-WC-KI
Winning Materials-WM-KF
05The Cup-19
Gold-19
Black Rainbow-19
Dual NHL Shields-DSIK
Dual NHL Shields-DSKJ
Dual NHL Shields Autographs-ADSKJ
Emblems of Endorsement-EEMK
Honorable Numbers-HNMK
Limited Logos-LLMK
Masterpiece Pressplates-19
Masterpiece Pressplates Rookie Upd Auto-258
Noble Numbers-NNKL
Patch Variation-P19
Patch Variation Autographs-AP19
Scripted Numbers-SNKL
Scripted Numbers Dual-DSNIK
Scripted Numbers Dual-DSNKL
Scripted Swatches-SSMK
Signature Patches-SPMK
05UD Artifacts-16
Blue-16
Gold-16
Green-16
Pewter-16
Red-16
Gold Autographed-16
05UD PowerPlay-16
Rainbow-16
05Ultimate Collection-16
Gold-16
05Ultra-30
Gold-30
Ice-30
05Upper Deck-30
HG Glossy-30
Jerseys-J-MK
Jerseys Series II-J2MK
Patches-P-MKF
05Upper Deck Ice-15
Rainbow-15
Frozen Fabrics-FFMK
Frozen Fabrics Glass-FFMK
Frozen Fabrics Patches-FFPMK
05Upper Deck Rookie Update-16
05Upper Deck Rookie Update-258
05Upper Deck Trilogy-17
05Upper Deck Trilogy-99
Crystal-99
Honorary Patches-HP-MK
Honorary Swatches-HS-MK
Honorary Swatch Scripts-HSS-MK
05Upper Deck Toronto Fall Expo-30
05Upper Deck Victory-30
Black-30
Gold-30
Silver-30
Blow-Ups-BU7
Stars on Ice-SI8
05Czech Stadion-685
05Swedish SHL Elitset-131
Gold-131
Stoppers-12
06Be A Player Portraits-17
Quadruple Signature Portraits-QKKJP
Signature Portraits-SPMK
Timeless Tens-TTNET
Triple Signature Portraits-TCGY
06Beehive-86
06Beehive-224
Blue-86
Gold-86
Matte-86
Red Facsimile Signatures-86
Wood-86
5 X 7 Black and White-86
5 X 7 Dark Wood-86
06Between The Pipes The Mask-M03
06Between The Pipes The Mask Gold-M03
06Between The Pipes The Mask Silver-M03
06Between The Pipes The Mask Game-Used-MGU09
06Between The Pipes The Mask Game-Used Gold-MGU09
06Black Diamond-129
Black-129
Black-150B
Gold-129
Ruby-129
Gemography-GMK
Jerseys-JMK
Jerseys Black-JMK
Jerseys Gold-JMK
Jerseys Ruby-JMK
Jerseys Black Autographs -JKI
06Flair Showcase-17
06Flair Showcase-175
06Flair Showcase-212
06Flair Showcase-275
Parallel-17
Parallel-175
Parallel-212
Parallel-275
Hot Gloves-HG5
Hot Numbers-HN4
Hot Numbers Parallel-HN4
Inks-IKI
Stitches-SSMK
06Fleer-30
Oversized-30
Tiffany-30
Fabricology-FMK
Hockey Headliners-HL20
Netminders-N5
Signing Day-SDKI
06Gatorade-1
06Hot Prospects-18
Red Hot-18
White Hot-18
06ITG International Ice Cornerstones-IC04
06ITG International Ice Cornerstones Gold-IC04
06ITG International Ice Goaltending Glory-GG22
06ITG International Ice Goaltending Glory Gold-GG22
06ITG International Ice Passing The Torch-PTT6
06ITG International Ice Passing The Torch Gold-PTT6
06McDonald's Upper Deck-6
Autographs-AMK
Hardware Heroes-HH6
Hot Gloves-HG4
Jerseys-JMK
Patches-PMK
06O-Pee-Chee-71
06O-Pee-Chee-609
06O-Pee-Chee-675
Rainbow-71
Rainbow-609
Rainbow-675
06Panini Stickers-197
06SP Authentic-85
06SP Authentic-139
Limited-85
Limited-139
Sign of the Times Triples-ST3ITK
Sign of the Times Quads-ST4IKPT
06SP Game Used-14
Gold-14
Rainbow-14
Authentic Fabrics Dual-AF2IK
Authentic Fabrics Dual Patches-AF2IK
Authentic Fabrics Triple-AF3CGY
Authentic Fabrics Triple Patches-AF3CGY
Authentic Fabrics Fives-AF5GAA
Authentic Fabrics Fives Patches-AF5GAA
Authentic Fabrics Sixes-AF6JEN
Authentic Fabrics Sixes Patches-AF6JEN
Authentic Fabrics Sevens-AF7VEZ
Authentic Fabrics Sevens Patches-AF7VEZ
Authentic Fabrics Eights-AF8FIN
Authentic Fabrics Eights Patches-AF8FIN
By The Letter-BLMK
06SPx-15
Spectrum-15
SPxcitement-X16
SPxcitement Spectrum-X16
06Sunkist-10
06The Cup-15
Black Rainbow-15
Gold-15
Gold Patches-15
Jerseys-15
Masterpiece Pressplates-15
06UD Artifacts-85
06UD Artifacts-157
Blue-85
Blue-157
Gold-85
Gold-157
Platinum-85
Platinum-157
Radiance-85
Radiance-157
Autographed Radiance Parallel-85
Autographed Radiance Parallel-157
Red-85
Red-157
Auto-Facts-AFMK
Auto-Facts Gold-AFMK
Frozen Artifacts-FAMK
Frozen Artifacts Black-FAMK
Frozen Artifacts Blue-FAMK
Frozen Artifacts Gold-FAMK
Frozen Artifacts Platinum-FAMK
Frozen Artifacts Red-FAMK
Frozen Artifacts Autographed Black-FAMK
Frozen Artifacts Patches Black-FAMK
Frozen Artifacts Patches Blue-FAMK
Frozen Artifacts Patches Gold-FAMK
Frozen Artifacts Patches Platinum-FAMK
Frozen Artifacts Patches Red-FAMK
Frozen Artifacts Patches Autographed Black Tag Parallel-FAMK
Tundra Tandems-TTKP
Tundra Tandems Black-TTKP
Tundra Tandems Blue-TTKP
Tundra Tandems Gold-TTKP
Tundra Tandems Platinum-TTKP
Tundra Tandems Red-TTKP
Tundra Tandems Dual Patches Red-TTKP
06UD Mini Jersey Collection-14
06UD Powerplay-14
Impact Rainbow-14
Goal Robbers-GR4
Specialists-SMK
Specialists Patches-PMK
06Ultimate Collection-10
Autographed Jerseys-AJ-MK
Autographed Patches-AJ-MK
Jerseys Dual-UJ2-KI
Patches Dual-UJ2-KI
Premium Patches-PS-MK
Premium Swatches-PS-MK
Ultimate Achievements-UA-MK
06Ultra-28
Gold Medallion-28
Ice Medallion-28
Difference Makers-DM6
Uniformity-UMK
Uniformity Patches-UPMM
Uniformity Autographed Jerseys-UAMK
06Upper Deck Arena Giveaways-CGY6
06Upper Deck-282
06Upper Deck-449
Exclusives Parallel-282
Exclusives Parallel-449
High Gloss Parallel-282
High Gloss Parallel-449
All World-AW22
Award Winners-AW2
Award Winners Canadian Exclusive-OAW8
Award Winners Canadian Exclusive-OAW9
Game Dated Moments-GD5
Game Jerseys-JMK
Game Patches-PMK
Generations Duals-G2KL
Generations Triples-G3KTL
Generations Patches Dual-G2PKL
Generations Patches Triple-G3PKTL
Hometown Heroes-HH32
Masterpieces-282
Masterpieces-449
Oversized Wal-Mart Exclusives-282
Signature Sensations-SSMK
Statistical Leaders-SL6
Zero Men-ZM4
06Upper Deck MVP-41
Gold Script-41
Super Script-41
Autographs-OAKL
Gotta Have Hart-HH17
Jerseys-OJKL
Last Line of Defense-LL2
06Upper Deck Ovation-8
06Upper Deck Sweet Shot-20
Signature Shots/Saves-SSMK
Signature Shots/Saves Ice Signings-SSIMK
Signature Shots/Saves Sticks-SSSMK
Signature Sticks-STMK
Sweet Stitches-SSMK
Sweet Stitches Duals-SSMK
Sweet Stitches Triples-SSMK
06Upper Deck Trilogy-14
Combo Autographed Jerseys-CJKL
Combo Autographed Patches-CJKL
Combo Clearcut Autographs-C2KN
Combo Clearcut Autographs-C3IKP
Honorary Scripted Patches-HSPMK
Honorary Scripted Swatches-HSSMK
Honorary Swatches-HSMK
Ice Scripts-ISMI
Scripts-S2MK
Scripts-S3MK
Scripts-TSMK
06Upper Deck Victory-28
06Upper Deck Victory Black-28
06Upper Deck Victory Gold-28
06Upper Deck Victory GameBreakers-GB6
06Upper Deck Victory Oversize Cards-MK
07Upper Deck Victory-145
Black-145
Gold-145
GameBreakers-GB47
Oversize Cards-OS34
Stars on Ice-SI34

Kirby, Mike
89Regina Pats-10

Kirby, Travis
92Saskatchewan JHL-141

Kirbyson, Kevyn
05Vernon Vipers-13

Kirchhoff, Ryan
99Des Moines Buccaneers-18

Kiriakou, Lou
84Moncton Golden Flames-9

Kiriakou, Thomas
05Ottawa 67's-6
06Ottawa 67s-3

Kirik, Vladimir
98Russian Hockey League-166

Kirilenko, Dmitri
99Russian Hockey League-152
01Russian Hockey League-104
02Russian Hockey League-236

Kirk, Bobby
34Beehive Group I Photos-283

Kirk, Darren
95Neepewa Natives-4
96OCN Blizzard-16

Kirk, Gavin
73Quaker Oats WHA-5
75O-Pee-Chee WHA-103
76O-Pee-Chee WHA-99

Kirkpatrick, Bob
34Beehive Group I Photos-284

Kirkpatrick, Dave
92British Columbia JHL-5

Kirkwood, Brad
96UK Guildford Flames-16

Kirnan, Nicole
93Quebec Pee-Wee Tournament-669

Kirsch, Martin
94German First League-126

Kirsch, Rob
93North Bay Centennials-24

Kirton, Douglas
94German First League-340
98German DEL-149
99German DEL-87

Kirton, Mark
79Maple Leafs Postcards-16
80Maple Leafs Postcards-16
81O-Pee-Chee-90
81Topps-W90
82O-Pee-Chee-87
82Post Cereal-5
83Canucks Team Issue-10
83O-Pee-Chee-352
83Vachon-109
85Fredericton Express-19
86Fredericton Express-14
88ProCards AHL-227

Kirton, Scott
92British Columbia JHL-237
92North Dakota Fighting Sioux-15
96Charlotte Checkers-10
97Wheeling Nailers-8

97Wheeling Nailers Photo Pack-8
01UK Dundee Stars-18
02UK Dundee Stars-18
03Greenville Grrrowl-12
Kirveskoski, Veikko
73Finnish Jaakiekko-222
Kirwan, Jeff
95Swift Current Broncos-7
96Swift Current Broncos-20
97Swift Current Broncos-19
Kirwin, Andrew
93Quebec Pee-Wee Tournament-486
Kiseleev, Sergei
00Russian Hockey League-111
01Russian Hockey League-19
Kiser, Nate
01Plymouth Whalers-12
02Plymouth Whalers-2
03ECHL All-Stars-248
05South Carolina Stingrays-14
Kish, Andor
93Quebec Pee-Wee Tournament-735
Kish, Larry
02Columbus Cottonmouths-21
Kisil, John
93Michigan Tech Huskies-17
Kisilivich, Brent
82Medicine Hat Tigers-8
83Medicine Hat Tigers-5
Kisio, Kelly
84O-Pee-Chee-56
84O-Pee-Chee Stickers-40
85O-Pee-Chee-101
85Topps-101
86O-Pee-Chee-116
86O-Pee-Chee Stickers-163
86Topps-116
87O-Pee-Chee-76
87O-Pee-Chee Stickers-28
87Panini Stickers-115
87Topps-76
88O-Pee-Chee-143
88O-Pee-Chee Stickers-239
88Panini Stickers-307
88Topps-143
89O-Pee-Chee-171
89Panini Stickers-287
89Rangers Marine Midland Bank-11
89Topps-171
90O-Pee-Chee-239
90Panini Stickers-94
90Pro Set-200
90Score-37
Canadian-37
90Topps-239
Tiffany-239
90Upper Deck-296
French-296
91Pro Set Platinum-104
91Bowman-72
91O-Pee-Chee-335
91OPC Premier-69
91Panini Stickers-291
91Parkhurst-165
French-165
91Pinnacle-231
French-231
91Pro Set-168
91Pro Set-479
French-168
French-479
Puck Candy-26
91Score American-288
91Score Canadian Bilingual-553
91Score Canadian English-553
91Score Rookie/Traded-3T
91Sharks Sports Action-12
91Stadium Club-186
91Topps-335
91Upper Deck-515
French-515
92Bowman-166
92O-Pee-Chee-232
92Panini Stickers-124
92Panini Stickers French-124
92Parkhurst-166
Emerald Ice-166
92Pinnacle-362
French-362
92Pro Set-167
92Score-57
Canadian-57
92Stadium Club-454
92Topps-331
Gold-331G
92Ultra-196
93Donruss-55
93Leaf-208
93OPC Premier-455
Gold-455
93Panini Stickers-256
93Parkhurst-33
Emerald Ice-33
93Pinnacle-395
Canadian-395
All-Stars-30
All-Stars Canadian-30
93PowerPlay-37
93Score-27
93Score-556
Gold-556
Canadian-27
Canadian-556
Canadian Gold-556
93Stadium Club-30
Members Only Master Set-30
OPC-30
First Day Issue-30
First Day Issue OPC-30
All-Stars-10
All-Stars Members Only-10
All-Stars OPC-10
93Topps/OPC Premier-455
Gold-455
93Ultra-155
93Ultra-282
93Upper Deck-304
93Upper Deck Locker All-Stars-28
94Canada Games NHL POGS-55
94EA Sports-117
94Leaf-493
94Pinnacle-306
Artist's Proofs-306
Rink Collection-306
95Collector's Choice-193
Player's Club-193
Player's Club Platinum-193
04ITG Franchises US West-299
Autographs-A-KK
05Calgary Hitmen-24
06Parkhurst-47
06Parkhurst-199
Autographs-47
Autographs-199
Kisskeys, Rick
03Minnesota State Mavericks-11
Kister, Ed
85London Knights-11
86Kitchener Rangers-11
Kitchen, Bill
83Nova Scotia Voyageurs-2
Kitchen, Mike
76Rockies Coke Cans-12
77O-Pee-Chee NHL-267
77Rockies Coke Cans-12
78O-Pee-Chee-338
79Rockies Team Issue-10
81O-Pee-Chee-339
81Rockies Postcards-9
82Post Cereal-11
83Devils Postcards-11
83NHL Key Tags-77
Kitchen, Robert
93Quebec Pee-Wee Tournament-542
Kitchen, Ryan
02Sault Ste. Marie Greyhounds-19
03Oshawa Generals-24
04Guelph Storm-15
Kitchener, Craig
80Oshawa Generals-3
Kitching, Gary
91Ferris State Bulldogs-18
92Ferris State Bulldogs-18
Kitteringham, Craig
88ProCards AHL-135
Kitts, Mark
00Prince George Cougars-19
01Moose Jaw Warriors-17
Kiuru, Esko
66Finnish Jaakiekkosarja-141
Kiuru, Jussi
93Finnish SISU-201
93Finnish SISU-201B
94Finnish SISU-283
95Finnish SISU-105
Kivela, Antero
77Finnish Sportscasters-90-2148
78Finnish SM-Liiga-19
78Finnish SM-Liiga-219
79Panini Stickers-163
80Finnish Mallasjuoma-199
Kivela, Keijo
78Finnish SM-Liiga-54
Kivela, Kimo
65Finnish Hellas-74
67Swedish Hockey-241
Kivela, Pasi
92Finnish Jyvas-Hyva Stickers-32
Kivela, Teppo
91Finnish Semic World Champ Stickers-15
91Finnish Jyvas-Hyva Stickers-8
91Swedish Semic World Champ Stickers-15
92Finnish Jyvas-Hyva Stickers-6
93Finnish Jyvas-Hyva Stickers-23
93Finnish SISU-95
94Finnish SISU-210
94Finnish SISU-375
94Finnish SISU Horoscopes-10
95Finnish SISU-155
95Finnish SISU Limited-23
96Finnish SISU Redline-155
96Swedish Brynas Tigers-10
97Swedish Collector's Choice-24
98Swedish UD Choice-45
Kivell, Drew
99Sudbury Wolves-19
00Sudbury Wolves-21
01Kingston Frontenacs-9
02Kingston Frontenacs-9
04Lakehead University Thunderwolves-20
Kivell, Rob
83Victoria Cougars-13
84Victoria Cougars-12
85Moncton Golden Flames-10
Kivenmaki, Marko
98Finnish Kerailysarja-270
99Finnish Cardset-152
00Finnish Cardset-305
03Finnish Cardset-178
04Finnish Cardset-195
Parallel-144
05Finnish Cardset -170
06Finnish Cardset-176
Signature Sensations-34
06Finnish Porin Assat Pelaajakortit-19
Kivi, Karri
93Finnish Jyvas-Hyva Stickers-346
93Finnish SISU-215
94Finnish SISU-134
95Finnish SISU-352
Double Trouble-3
95Swedish World Championships Stickers-165
96Finnish SISU Redline-153
97Swedish Collector's Choice-2
00Finnish Cardset-54
Kiviaho, Tommy
93Finnish Jyvas-Hyva Stickers-257
93Finnish SISU-293
94Finnish SISU-338
94Finnish SISU Horoscopes-16
95Finnish SISU-36
96Finnish SISU Redline-8
98Finnish Kerailysarja-24
99Finnish Cardset-15
Kiviharju, Jani
98Finnish Kerailysarja-244
99Finnish Cardset-136
00Finnish Cardset-99
01Finnish Cardset-364
02Finnish Cardset-195
Kivila, Pasi
93Finnish Jyvas-Hyva Stickers-58
93Finnish SISU-248
94Finnish SISU-83
Kivinen, Teemu
93Finnish SISU-60
Kivon, Martin
03Czech OFS Plus-86
04Czech OFS-26
Kiyaga, Arthur
03Victoriaville Tigres-15
04Victoriaville Tigres-14
06Fort Wayne Komets-10
Kizito, Andrew
05Kingston Frontenacs-10
06Kingston Frontenacs-20
Kjaer, Lars Erik
92Norwegian Elite Series-163
Kjaergaard, Christian
99Danish Hockey League-60
Kjeldsberg, Christian
92Norwegian Elite Series-53
Kjellberg, Patric
89Swedish Semic Elitserien Stickers-25
90Swedish Semic Elitserien Stickers-91
91Swedish Semic Elitserien Stickers-20
92Canadiens Postcards-15
92OPC Premier-29
92Upper Deck-498
92Fredericton Canadiens-13
93Swedish Semic Elitserien-117
93Swedish Semic World Champ Stickers-42
93Classic Pro Prospects-21
94Finnish Jaa Kiekko-78
94Swedish Leaf-16
Gold Cards-17
Top Guns-9
95Swedish Leaf-190
Champs-2
95Swedish Upper Deck-53
97Swedish Collector's Choice-46
Crash the Game Exchange-C1
Crash the Game Redemption-R1
98Pacific Dynagon Ice-103
Blue-103
Red-103
98Predators Team Issue-13
99Pacific-226
Copper-226
Emerald Green-226
Gold-226
Ice Blue-226
Premiere Date-226
Red-226
99Pacific Omega-127
Copper-127
Gold-127
Ice Blue-127
Premiere Date-127
99Panini Stickers-264
99Upper Deck MVP SC Edition-103
Gold Script-103
Silver Script-103
Super Script-103
00Aurora-77
Premiere Date-77
00BAP Memorabilia-301
Emerald-301
Ruby-301
Sapphire-301
Promos-301
00BAP Mem Chicago Sportsfest Copper-301
00BAP Memorabilia Chicago Sportsfest Blue-301
00BAP Memorabilia Chicago Sportsfest Gold-301
00BAP Memorabilia Chicago Sportsfest Ruby-301
00BAP Memorabilia Chicago Sun-Times Ruby-301
00BAP Memorabilia Chicago Sun-Times Gold-301
00BAP Mem Chicago Sun-Times Sapphire-301
00BAP Mem Toronto Fall Expo Copper-301
00BAP Memorabilia Toronto Fall Expo Gold-301
00BAP Memorabilia Toronto Fall Expo Ruby-301
00Crown Royale Game-Worn Jerseys-16
00Crown Royale Game-Worn Jersey Patches-16
00Crown Royale Premium-Sized Jerseys-16
00O-Pee-Chee-261A
00O-Pee-Chee Parallel-261A
00Pacific-440
Copper-440
Gold-440
Ice Blue-440
Premiere Date-440
00Panini Stickers-180
00Stadium Club-149
00Titanium Game Gear-103
00Titanium Game Gear Patches-103
00Titanium Draft Day Edition-54
Patches-54
00Topps/OPC-261A
Parallel-261A
00Topps Chrome-157
OPC Refractors-157
Refractors-157
00Upper Deck-326
Exclusives Tier 1-326
Exclusives Tier 2-326
00Upper Deck MVP-102
First Stars-102
Second Stars-102
Third Stars-102
00Upper Deck Victory-132
00Upper Deck Vintage-204
01O-Pee-Chee-148
01O-Pee-Chee Premier Parallel-148
01Pacific-219
Extreme LTD-219
Hobby LTD-219
Premiere Date-219
Retail LTD-219
01Pacific Adrenaline-105
Blue-105
Premiere Date-105
Red-105
Retail-105
Jerseys-23
01Pacific Arena Exclusives-219
01Parkhurst-180
01Topps-148
OPC Parallel-148
01Upper Deck-328
Exclusives-328
01Upper Deck MVP-109
01Upper Deck Victory-198
Gold-198
01Upper Deck Vintage-144
02Pacific Complete-200
Red-200
Kjenstad, Olaf
91 7th Inn. Sketch WHL-313
93Seattle Thunderbirds-10
94Birmingham Bulls-14
95Birmingham Bulls-20
96Knoxville Cherokees-21
97Columbus Cottonmouths-7
98Cincinnati Cyclones-10
98Cincinnati Cyclones 2-22
99Columbus Cottonmouths-24
99San Diego Gulls-5
00Asheville Smoke-7
01Columbus Cottonmouths-9
02Greensboro Generals RBI-12
Kjernisted, Glen
04Thetford Mines Prolab-16
Kjogx, Thomas
98Danish Hockey League-20
99Danish Hockey League-20
Klaar, Manfred
94German First League-365
Klaers, John
94Central Hockey League-82
94San Antonio Iguanas-10
Klann, Zechariah
00Sioux City Musketeers-16
Klapac, Filip
96Czech APS Extraliga-95
Klapac, Jan
69Swedish Hockey-32
72Finnish Jaakiekko-11
72Finnish Hellas-88
73Finnish Jaakiekko-52
74Finnish Jenkki-74
Klapac, Jiri
74Swedish Semic World Champ Stickers-62
Klapkowski, Gary
04Saginaw Spirit-9
Klapstein, Terry
89Victoria Cougars-13
Klaren, Nick
02Tri-City Stormfront-4
Klasen, Linus
04Lincoln Stars-23
Klasnick, Rob
93Omaha Lancers-12
Klasons, George
77Kalamazoo Wings-1
Klassen, Chad
01Spokane Chiefs-15
02Spokane Chiefs-10
04Spokane Chiefs Magnets-4
05Saskatoon Blades-11
Klassen, Hayley
06Ohio State Buckeyes Women-7
Klassen, Jason
91Prince Albert Raiders-7
91 7th Inn. Sketch WHL-248
Klassen, Ralph
76O-Pee-Chee NHL-282
77O-Pee-Chee NHL-372
78O-Pee-Chee-346
Klassen, Sam
06Saskatoon Blades-12
Klassen, Todd
90 7th Inn. Sketch WHL-111
91 7th Inn. Sketch WHL-295
Klatt, Bill
72Minnesota Fighting Saints Postcards WHA-10
Klatt, David
98Kamloops Blazers-16
Klatt, Trent
91Parkhurst-452
French-452
91Minnesota Golden Gophers-11
92Parkhurst-317
Emerald Ice-317
92Pro Set-229
92Score-482
Canadian-482
92Upper Deck-62
92Classic-89
Gold-89
93Donruss-82
93Leaf-14
93OPC Premier-523
Gold-523
93Parkhurst-48
Emerald Ice-48
93PowerPlay-62
93Topps/OPC Premier-523
Gold-523
93Ultra-157
Prospects-4
93Upper Deck-152
94Canada Games NHL POGS-143
94Donruss-37
94Leaf-316
94OPC Premier-46
Special Effects-46
94Parkhurst SE-SE43
Gold-SE43
94Pinnacle-442
Artist's Proofs-442
Rink Collection-442
94SP-29
Die Cuts-29
94Stadium Club Super Teams-6
94Stadium Club Super Team MemberOnly Set-6
94Stars HockeyKaps-17
94Stars Postcards-13
94Topps/OPC Premier-46
Special Effects-46
94Ultra-53
94Upper Deck-374
Electric Ice-374
95Canada Games NHL POGS-88
95Collector's Choice-36
Player's Club-36
Player's Club Platinum-36
95Donruss-330
95Leaf-57
95Panini Stickers-172
95Pinnacle-193
Artist's Proofs-193
Rink Collection-193
95Topps-106
OPC Inserts-106
95Upper Deck-162
Electric Ice-162
Electric Ice Gold-162
96Be A Player-157
Autographs-157
Autographs Silver-157
96Flyers Postcards-11
97Collector's Choice-191
97Pacific-251
Copper-251
Emerald Green-251
Ice Blue-251
Red-251
Silver-251
97Pacific Omega-166
Copper-166
Dark Gray-166
Emerald Green-166
Gold-166
Ice Blue-166
97Score Flyers-8
Platinum-8
Premier-8
97Upper Deck-120
98Pacific-327
Ice Blue-327
Red-327
98Paramount-175
Copper-175
Emerald Green-175
Holo-Electric-175
Ice Blue-175
Silver-175
99Syracuse Crunch-10
00Pacific-410
Copper-410
Gold-410
Ice Blue-410
Premiere Date-410
00Upper Deck-172
Exclusives Tier 1-172
Exclusives Tier 2-172
01Upper Deck-402
Exclusives-402
02BAP Signature Series Golf-GS98
02Canucks Team Issue-7
02NHL Power Play Stickers-149
02Pacific Complete-355
Red-355
03Pacific-331
Blue-331
Red-331
03Pacific Complete-163
Red-163
03Topps Traded-TT43
Blue-TT43
Gold-TT43
Red-TT43
04Pacific-123
Blue-123
Red-123
05Be A Player Signatures-KA
05Be A Player Signatures Gold-KA
05Upper Deck-89
HG Glossy-89
05Upper Deck Toronto Fall Expo-89
Klau, Steffen
94German First League-412
Klauda, Radek
96Czech APS Extraliga-210
Klaus, Martin
03Czech OFS Plus-388
Klay, Reto
02Swiss HNL-469
Klears, John
92Norwegian Elite Series-237
Klebnikov, Alexander
00Russian Dynamo Moscow-31
Kleckers, Christoph
94German First League-551
99German Bundesliga 2-133
Kledrowetz, Juraj
03Czech OFS Plus All-Star Game-H8
04Czech OFS Czech/Slovak-32
Klee, Ken
93Portland Pirates-6
93Classic Pro Prospects-82
94Portland Pirates-13
95Be A Player-162
Signatures-S162
Signatures Die Cuts-S162
95Bowman-163
All-Foil-163
95Capitals Team Issue-15
95Upper Deck-128
Electric Ice-128
Electric Ice Gold-128
97Be A Player-91
Autographs-91
Autographs Die-Cuts-91
Autographs Prismatic Die-Cuts-91
97Pacific Invincible NHL Regime-209
97Upper Deck-386
98Be A Player-149
Press Release-149
98BAP Gold-149
98BAP Autographs-149
98BAP Autographs Gold-149
98BAP Tampa Bay All Star Game-149
99Pacific-442
Copper-442
Emerald Green-442
Gold-442
Ice Blue-442
Premiere Date-442
Red-442
00BAP Memorabilia-376
Emerald-376
Ruby-376
Sapphire-376
Promos-376
00BAP Mem Chicago Sportsfest Copper-376
00BAP Memorabilia Chicago Sportsfest Blue-376
00BAP Memorabilia Chicago Sportsfest Gold-376
00BAP Memorabilia Chicago Sportsfest Ruby-376
00BAP Memorabilia Chicago Sun-Times Ruby-376
00BAP Memorabilia Chicago Sun-Times Gold-376
00BAP Mem Chicago Sun-Times Sapphire-376
00BAP Mem Toronto Fall Expo Copper-376
00BAP Memorabilia Toronto Fall Expo Gold-376
00BAP Memorabilia Toronto Fall Expo Ruby-376
00Pacific-424
Copper-424
Gold-424
Ice Blue-424
Premiere Date-424
01O-Pee-Chee-250
01O-Pee-Chee Premier Parallel-250
01Topps-250
OPC Parallel-250
02BAP Sig Series Auto Buybacks 1998-149
02Upper Deck-422
Exclusives-422
02Upper Deck Beckett UD Promos-422
03ITG Action-530
03Pacific Complete-328
Red-328
03Parkhurst Original Six Toronto-10
03Upper Deck-429
Canadian Exclusives-429
HG-429
UD Exclusives-429
05Parkhurst Facsimile Auto Parallel-463
06Upper Deck-184
HG Glossy-184
06Upper Deck MVP-361
Gold-361
Platinum-361
06Upper Deck Toronto Fall Expo-184
06Avalanche Team Postcards-7
Kleeb, Ivo
95Swiss HNL-112
98Swiss Power Play Stickers-129
Klein, Jim
34Beehive Group I Photos-234
34Diamond Matchbooks Silver-36
Klein, Kevin
00St. Michaels Majors-19
01St. Michaels Majors-7
02St. Michaels Majors-6
03Guelph Storm-5
04Milwaukee Admirals-23
04ITG Heroes and Prospects-86
Autographs-KKL
04ITG Heroes/Prospects Toronto Expo '05-86
04ITG Heroes/Prospects Expo Heroes/Pros-86
05Black Diamond-257
06Hot Prospects-145
En Fuego-145
Red Hot-145
White Hot-145
05SP Authentic-248
Limited-248
05SP Game Used-220
05SPx-271
05The Cup Masterpiece Pressplate Artifact-294
05The Cup Master Pressplate Black Diamond-257
05The Cup Masterpiece Pressplates (Ice)-220
05The Cup Master Pressplate Rookie Update-152
05The Cup Masterpiece Pressplates SP GU-220
05The Cup Masterpiece Pressplates SPA-248
05The Cup Masterpiece Pressplates (SPx)-271
05The Cup Masterpiece Pressplates Trilogy-275
05The Cup Masterpiece Pressplate Ult Coll-213
05UD Artifacts-294
05Ultimate Collection-213
Gold-213
05Upper Deck Ice-220
05Upper Deck Rookie Update-152
05Upper Deck Trilogy-275
05Milwaukee Admirals Choice-8
05Milwaukee Admirals Pepsi-10
06Milwaukee Admirals -8
Klein, Lloyd
35Diamond Matchbooks Tan 1-36
35Diamond Matchbooks Tan 2-35
35Diamond Matchbooks Tan 3-32
Kleinendorst, Kurt
00Devils Team Issue-27
Kleinendorst, Scot
85Whalers Junior Wendy's-8
86Whalers Junior Thomas'-12
87Whalers Jr. Burger King/Pepsi-10
88Whalers Junior Ground Round-8
89Capitals Kodak-29
89Capitals Team Issue-11
Kleininger, Oliver
94German First League-227
Kleisinger, Curtis
91Air Canada SJHL-B16
Klejna, Michal
06Brampton Battalion-23
Klema, David
03Boston University Terriers-20
Klemm, Jon
89Spokane Chiefs-14
90 7th Inn. Sketch WHL-197
91ProCards-534
91 7th Inn. Sketch Memorial Cup-71
91 7th Inn. Sketch Memorial Cup-77
94Nordiques Burger King-11
95SkyBox Impact-194
95Upper Deck-93
Electric Ice-93
Electric Ice Gold-93
Special Edition-SE20
Special Edition Gold-SE20
96Be A Player-144
Autographs-144
Autographs Silver-144
97Pacific Dynagon Best Kept Secrets-25
98Avalanche Team Issue-5
98OPC Chrome-113
Refractors-113
98Topps-113
O-Pee-Chee-113
99Avalanche Team Issue-12
00Stadium Club-144
00Titanium Game Gear-75
00Titanium Game Gear Patches-75
00Upper Deck Vintage-89
01BAP Memorabilia Stanley Cup Champions-CA12
01Pacific Heads-Up Quad Jerseys-9
01UD Stanley Cup Champs-43
01Upper Deck-272
Exclusives-272
02Pacific-78
Blue-78
Red-78
02Pacific Complete-331
Red-331
02Topps Total-47
02Upper Deck-37
Exclusives-37
03ITG Action-147
03Parkhurst Original Six Chicago-9
03Stars Postcards-11
03Upper Deck-286
Canadian Exclusives-286
HG-286
UD Exclusives-286
05Parkhurst-153
Facsimile Auto Parallel-153
06Stars Team Postcards-10
Klempa, Martin
04UK EIHL All-Stars-7
05UK Coventry Blaze-1
Klenner, Sebastian
94German DEL-405
99German DEL-307
00German DEL-22
02German DEL City Press-117
03German DEL-99
04German DEL-108
05German DEL-88
Klepis, Jakub
02BAP Memorabilia Draft Redemptions-16
02Czech OFS Plus-241
03Czech OFS Plus-182
03Czech OFS Plus Insert M-M6
03Czech OFS Plus MS Praha-SE45
04AHL Top Prospects-42
04Portland Pirates-24
04ITG Heroes and Prospects-188
04ITG Heroes/Prospects Toronto Expo '05-188
05Beehive-144
Beige -144
Blue -144
Gold-144
Red -144
Matte-144
05Black Diamond-292
05Hot Prospects-272
En Fuego-272
Hot Materials-HMJK
Red Hot-272
White Hot-272
05Parkhurst True Colors-TCWAS
05Parkhurst True Colors-TCWAS
05SP Authentic-220
Limited-220
05SP Game Used-179
Autographs-179
Gold-179
05SPx-243
Spectrum-243
05The Cup-146
Autographed Rookie Patches Gold Rainbow-146
Black Rainbow Rookies-146
Masterpiece Pressplates (Artifacts)-341
Masterpiece Pressplates (Bee Hive)-144
Masterpiece Pressplates (Black Diamond)-292
Masterpiece Pressplates (Ice)-179
Masterpiece Pressplates (Rookie Update)-236
Masterpiece Pressplates SPA Autos-220
Masterpiece Pressplates (SP Game Used)-179
Masterpiece Pressplates SPx Autos-243
Masterpiece Pressplates (Trilogy)-317
Masterpiece Pressplates Ult Coll-183
Masterpiece Pressplates (Victory)-265
Masterpiece Pressplates Autographs-146
Platinum Rookies-146
05UD Artifacts-341
05Ultimate Collection-183
Gold-183
Ultimate Debut Threads Jerseys-DTJJK
Ultimate Debut Threads Patches-DTPJK
05Upper Deck-473
05Upper Deck Ice-179
Premieres Auto Patches-AIPJK
05Upper Deck Rookie Update-236
Inspirations Patch Rookies-236
05Upper Deck Trilogy-317
05Upper Deck Victory-265
Black-265
Gold-265
Silver-265
05Hershey Bears-12
06Be A Player Portraits First Exposures-FEJK
06Black Diamond Jerseys-JJK
06Black Diamond Jerseys Black-JJK
06Black Diamond Jerseys Gold-JJK
06Black Diamond Jerseys Ruby-JJK
06Upper Deck Game Jerseys-J2JK
06Upper Deck Game Patches-P2JK
Klesla, Rostislav
98Sioux City Musketeers-9
99Brampton Battalion-9
99UD Prospects-22
00BAP Signature Series-420
Emerald-420
Ruby-420
Sapphire-420
00BAP Signature Series-285
Emerald-285
Ruby-285
Sapphire-285
Autographs-247
Autographs Gold-247
00Black Diamond-116
00Private Stock-113
Gold-113
Premiere Date-113
Retail-113
Silver-113
00SP Authentic-101
Sign of the Times-RK
00SP Game Used-66
00SPx-158
00Stadium Club-248
00Titanium Draft Day Edition-157
00Titanium Draft Day Promos-157
00Topps Chrome-245
Blue-245
Red-245
OPC Refractors-245
OPC Refractors Blue-245
OPC Refractors Red-245
Refractors-245
Refractors Blue-245
Refractors Red-245
00Topps Gold Label Class 1-110
Gold-110
00Topps Gold Label Class 2-110
00Topps Gold Label Class 2 Gold-110
00Topps Gold Label Class 3-110
00Topps Gold Label Class 3 Gold-110
00Topps Heritage-76
Chrome Parallel-76
00Topps Premier Plus-119
Blue Ice-119
Rookies-PR3
Rookies Blue Ice-PR3
00Topps Stars-108
Blue-108
Progression-P7
00UD Heroes-162
00UD Pros and Prospects-101
00UD Reserve-92
00Upper Deck-228
Exclusives Tier 1-228
Exclusives Tier 2-228
00Upper Deck Ice-86
00Upper Deck Vintage-371
00Vanguard-114
Pacific Proofs-114
00Brampton Battalion-9
00Brampton Battalion-28
01Atomic Rookie Reaction-4
01BAP Memorabilia-210
Emerald-210
Ruby-210
Sapphire-210
01BAP Signature Series-8
Autographs-8
Autographs Gold-8
Department of Defense-DD-12
Franchise Jerseys-FP-9
Jerseys-GJ-2
Jersey Autographs-GURK
Jersey and Stick Cards-GSJ-2
01Blue Jackets Donatos Pizza-9
01Bowman YoungStars-139
Gold-139
Ice Cubed-139
01Crown Royale-43
Blue-43
Premiere Date-43
Red-43
Retail-43
Crowning Achievement-4
Rookie Royalty-7
01O-Pee-Chee-271
01O-Pee-Chee Premier Parallel-271
01Pacific-113
Extreme LTD-113
Hobby LTD-113
Premiere Date-113
Retail LTD-113
01Pacific Adrenaline-53
Blue-53
Premiere Date-53
Red-53
Retail-53
Rookie Report-7
01Pacific Arena Exclusives-113
01Parkhurst-260
01Parkhurst Beckett Promos-260
01Private Stock-103
Gold-103
Premiere Date-103
Retail-103
Silver-103
Moments in Time-4
01Private Stock Pacific Nights-103
01Private Stock PS-2002-96
01SP Authentic Buybacks-30
01SP Authentic Sign of the Times-RK
01SPx-171
Hidden Treasures-TTKBL
01Stadium Club-112
Award Winners-112
Master Photos-112
01Titanium-40
Hobby Parallel-40
Premiere Date-40
Retail-40
Retail Parallel-40
01Titanium Draft Day Edition-30
01Titanium Draft Day Edition-120
01Topps-271
OPC Parallel-271
01Topps Chrome-138
Refractors-138
Black Border Refractors-138
01UD Honor Roll-28
01UD Honor Roll-58
01UD Mask Collection-27
Gold-27
Double Patches-DPRK
Jerseys-J-RK
Jersey and Patch-JPRK
01UD Playmakers-30
01UD Premier Collection-16
Signatures-RK
Signatures Black-RK
01UD Top Shelf-13
01Upper Deck-54
Exclusives-54
01Upper Deck MVP-54
01Upper Deck Victory-371
Gold-371
01Upper Deck Vintage-75
01Upper Deck Vintage-78
01Vanguard-29
Blue-29
Red-29
One of Ones-29
Premiere Date-29
Prime Prospects-4
Proofs-29
01Czech Stadion-237
01UD Prospects Autographs-A-RK
02BAP First Edition-20
02BAP First Edition-332
02BAP First Edition-349
02BAP First Edition-423H
Jerseys-20
02BAP Memorabilia-106
02BAP Memorabilia-209
Emerald-106
Emerald-209
Ruby-106
Ruby-209
Sapphire-106
Sapphire-209
Franchise Players-FP-9
Future of the Game-FG-19
NHL All-Star Game-106
NHL All-Star Game-209
NHL All-Star Game Blue-106
NHL All-Star Game Blue-209
NHL All-Star Game Green-106
NHL All-Star Game Green-209
NHL All-Star Game Red-106
NHL All-Star Game Red-209
02BAP Memorabilia Toronto Fall Expo-106
02BAP Memorabilia Toronto Fall Expo-209
02BAP Signature Series-71
Autographs-71
Autograph Buybacks 2000-247
Autograph Buybacks 2001-8
Autographs Gold-71
02Bowman YoungStars-108
Gold-108
Silver-108
Autographs-RK
Jerseys-RK
Patches-RK
Double Stuff-RK
Triple Stuff-RK
Rivals-RKAV
Rivals Patches-7
Sticks-RK
02Crown Royale Dual Patches-7
02ITG Used-18
02ITG Used-118
Franchise Players-F9
Franchise Players Autographs-F9
Franchise Players Gold-F9
02O-Pee-Chee-21
02O-Pee-Chee Premier Blue Parallel-21
02O-Pee-Chee Premier Red Parallel-21
02O-Pee-Chee Factory Set-21
02Pacific-100
Blue-100
Red-100
02Pacific Complete-40
Red-40
02Pacific Exclusive-51
02Pacific Heads-Up-35
Blue-35
Purple-35
Red-35
Quad Jerseys-10
Quad Jerseys Gold-10
02Pacific Toronto Spring Expo Rookie Coll-5
02Parkhurst-62
Bronze-62
Gold-62
Silver-62
Franchise Players-FP9
Jerseys-GJ20
Stick and Jerseys-SJ20
02Parkhurst Retro-115
Minis-115
02SP Authentic-27
02SP Authentic-114
Beckett Promos-27
02SP Game Used First Rounder Patches-RK
02SP Game Used Future Fabrics-FFRK
02SP Game Used Future Fabrics Gold-FFRK
02SP Game Used Future Fabrics Rainbow-FFRK
02SPx-21
Spectrum Gold-21
Spectrum Silver-21
02Stadium Club-84
Silver Decoy Cards-84
Proofs-84
Lone Star Signatures Blue-LSRK
Lone Star Signatures Red-LSRK
02Titanium Jerseys-19
02Titanium Jerseys Retail-19
02Titanium Patches-19
02Topps-21
OPC Blue Parallel-21
OPC Red Parallel-21
Factory Set-21
02Topps Chrome-21
Black Border Refractors-21
Refractors-21
02Topps Heritage-41
Chrome Parallel-41
02Topps Total-8
Signatures-RK
02UD Artistic Impressions-27
Gold-27
02UD Artistic Impressions Beckett Promos-27

02UD Artistic Impressions Retrospectives-R27
02UD Artistic Impressions Retrospect Gold-R27
02UD Artistic Impress Retrospect Silver-R27
02UD Piece of History-22
02UD Top Shelf Dual Player Jerseys-RLK
02UD Top Shelf Signatures-RK
02UD Top Shelf Sweet Sweaters-SWRK
02Upper Deck-49
Exclusives-49
Bright Futures-RK
Hot Spots-HSRK
On the Rise-ORRK
02Upper Deck Classic Portraits-30
Hockey Royalty-KTK
Hockey Royalty Limited-KTK
Stitches-CRS
Stitches Limited-CRS
02Upper Deck MVP-55
Gold-55
Classics-55
Golden Classics-55
Skate Around Jerseys-SDBK
Skate Around Jerseys-STWKT
Souvenirs-S-RK
02Upper Deck Victory-61
Bronze-61
Gold-61
Silver-61
02Upper Deck Vintage-73
02Upper Deck Vintage-269
Green Backs-73
Jerseys-HSRK
Jerseys Gold-HS-RK
Tall Boys-T21
Tall Boys Gold-T21
02Vanguard Jerseys-14
02Vanguard Jerseys Gold-14
02Czech DS-15
03BAP Ultimate Memorabilia Autographs-74
Gold-74
03ITG Action-130
Jerseys-M41
03ITG Used Signature Series-8
Gold-8
Autographs-RK1
Autographs Gold-RK
03O-Pee-Chee-236
03OPC Blue-236
03OPC Gold-236
03OPC Red-236
03Pacific-93
Blue-93
Red-93
03Pacific Complete-42
Red-42
03Private Stock Reserve-161
Blue-161
Red-161
Retail-161
03Topps-236
Blue-236
Gold-236
Red-236
03Topps C55-128
Minis-128
Minis American Back-128
Minis American Back Red-128
Minis Bazooka Back-128
Minis Brooklyn Back-128
Minis Hat Trick Back-128
Minis O Canada Back-128
Minis O Canada Back Red-128
Minis Stanley Cup Back-128
03Upper Deck-56
Canadian Exclusives-56
HG-56
03Upper Deck MVP-123
Gold Script-123
Silver Script-123
Canadian Exclusives-123
03Toronto Star-16
04Upper Deck-51
Canadian Exclusives-51
HG Glossy Gold-51
HG Glossy Silver-51
04Czech OFS-251
Checklist Cards-12
Stars-34
04Czech Zuma-9
05Parkhurst-146
Facsimile Auto Parallel-146
05SP Game Used Game Gear-GG-RK
05The Cup Master Pressplate Rookie Update-241
05Ultra-64
Gold-64
Ice-64
05Upper Deck Big Playmakers-B-RK
05Upper Deck Notable Numbers-N-RK
05Upper Deck Rookie Update-241
Inspirations Patch Rookies-241
05Upper Deck Victory-55
Black-55
Gold-55
Silver-55
06Black Diamond Jerseys-JRK
06Black Diamond Jerseys Black-JRK
06Black Diamond Jerseys Gold-JRK
06Black Diamond Jerseys Ruby-JRK
06Black Diamond Jerseys Black Autographs -JRK
06Fleer Fabricology-FRK
06Hot Prospects Hotagraphs-HRK
06O-Pee-Chee-141
Rainbow-141
Swatches-S-RK
06Panini Stickers-237
06SP Game Used SIGnificance-SRK
06UD Artifacts Auto-Facts-AFRK
06UD Artifacts Auto-Facts Gold-AFRK
06Ultra-59
Gold Medallion-59
Ice Medallion-59
06Upper Deck-307
Exclusives Parallel-307
High Gloss Parallel-307
Masterpieces-307
06Upper Deck MVP-82
Gold Script-82
Super Script-82
06Czech OFS Jagr Team-9

Kletke, Daniel
00Austin Ice Bats-7
03Huntsville Channel Cats-10

Kletzel, Chad
97Lethbridge Hurricanes-9

Kletzel, Dean
93Brandon Wheat Kings-16
94Brandon Wheat Kings-8
95Brandon Wheat Kings-11
95Slapshot Memorial Cup-39

Kletzel, Derek
907th Inn. Sketch WHL-161
917th Inn. Sketch WHL-283

Kletzien, Heidi
04Wisconsin Badgers Women-12

Klevakin, Dmitri
94Parkhurst SE-SE232
Gold-SE232
94SP-166
Die Cuts-166
94Upper Deck-515
Electric Ice-515
98Russian Hockey League-93
99Russian Hockey League-218
00Russian Hockey League-283
02Russian Hockey League-11

Klie, Jamie
04Saginaw Spirit-12
05Saginaw Spirit-12

Kliemann, Matthias
94German DEL-392
95German DEL-415

Klima, Petr
86O-Pee-Chee-98
86O-Pee-Chee Stickers-129
86O-Pee-Chee Stickers-162
86Topps-98
87O-Pee-Chee-26
87O-Pee-Chee Stickers-104
87Panini Stickers-246
87Red Wings Little Caesars-16
87Topps-26
88O-Pee-Chee-28
88O-Pee-Chee Stickers-251
88Panini Stickers-44
88Red Wings Little Caesars-12
88Topps-28
89Oilers Team Issue-11
90Bowman-197
Tiffany-197
90Oilers IGA-10
90O-Pee-Chee-85
90Panini Stickers-228
90Pro Set-86
90Score-232
Canadian-232
90Topps-85
Tiffany-85
90Upper Deck-282
French-282
91Pro Set Platinum-37
91Bowman-96
91Bowman-104
91Oilers Panini Team Stickers-9
91Oilers IGA-7
91Oilers Team Issue-9
91O-Pee-Chee-193
91OPC Premier-61
91Panini Stickers-126
91Parkhurst-280
91Parkhurst-458
French-280
91Pinnacle-159
French-159
91Pro Set-72
French-72
91Score American-136
91Score Canadian Bilingual-136
91Score Canadian English-136
91Score Kellogg's-17
91Stadium Club-61
91Topps-193
91Upper Deck-111
French-111
91Finnish Semic World Champ Stickers-220
91Swedish Semic World Champ Stickers-220
92Bowman-135
92Oilers IGA-10
92Panini Stickers-105
92Panini Stickers French-105
92Parkhurst-54
Emerald Ice-54
92Pinnacle-344
French-344
92Score-383
Canadian-383
Sharpshooters-24
Sharpshooters Canadian-24
92Stadium Club-368
92Topps-26
Gold-26G
92Ultra-59
Imports-8
92Upper Deck-551
93Donruss-317
93Leaf-321
93Lightning Season in Review-20
93Panini Stickers-234
93Parkhurst-195
Emerald Ice-195
93Pinnacle-349
Canadian-349
93PowerPlay-232
93Score-242
93Score-518
Gold-518
Canadian-242
Canadian-518
Canadian Gold-518
93Ultra-425
93Upper Deck-291
93Upper Deck-526
SP-152
93Swedish Semic World Champ Stickers-104
94Be A Player Signature Cards-155
94Canada Games NHL POGS-224
94Donruss-249
94EA Sports-47
94Flair-174
94Fleer-208
94Leaf-171
94Lightning Photo Album-18
94OPC Premier-318
Special Effects-318
94Parkhurst-219
Gold-219
94Pinnacle-311
Artist's Proofs-311
Rink Collection-311
94SP-110
Die Cuts-110
94Stadium Club-136
Members Only Master Set-136
First Day Issue-136
Super Teams-22
Super Teams Members Only Master Set-22
Super Team Winner Cards-136
94Topps/OPC Premier-318
Special Effects-318
94Ultra-208
94Upper Deck-86
Electric Ice-86
94German First League-663
95Bowman-22
All-Foil-22
95Canada Games NHL POGS-251
95Collector's Choice-134
Player's Club-134
Player's Club Platinum-134
95Donruss-110
95Emotion-165
95Finest-112
Refractors-112
95Hoyle Eastern Playing Cards-35
95Leaf-321
95Lightning Team Issue-13
95Metal-138
95Panini Stickers-130
95Parkhurst International-197
Emerald Ice-197
95Playoff One on One-311
95Score-65
Black Ice Artist's Proofs-65
Black Ice-65
95SkyBox Impact-156
95SP-136
95Stadium Club-185
Members Only Master Set-185
95Summit-141
Artist's Proofs-141
Ice-141
95Topps-238
OPC Inserts-238
95Ultra-153
Gold Medallion-153
95Upper Deck-118
Electric Ice-118
Electric Ice Gold-118
Special Edition-SE167
Special Edition Gold-SE167
96Collector's Choice-246
96Donruss-196
Press Proofs-196
96Leaf-39
Press Proofs-39
96Maggers-48
96Metal Universe-76
96Oilers Postcards-85
96Pinnacle-79
Artist's Proofs-79
Foil-79
Premium Stock-79
Rink Collection-79
96Playoff One on One-404
96Score-202
Artist's Proofs-202
Dealer's Choice Artist's Proofs-202
Special Artist's Proofs-202
Golden Blades-202
96Upper Deck-156
96Cleveland Lumberjacks-13
97Pacific-347
Copper-347
Emerald Green-347
Ice Blue-347
Red-347
Silver-347
97Panini Stickers-217
01Czech OFS-165
01Czech OFS Red Inserts-RE8D
02Czech OFS Plus-195
Trios-T7

Klima, Tomas
98Danish Hockey League-57

Klimak, Lukas
06Czech OFS-66

Klimenko, Gleb
02Russian Hockey League-5

Klimenta, Tomas
04Czech OFS-338
06Czech OFS-92

Klimentiev, Sergei
94Signature Rookies Tetrad *-109
Signatures-109
95Rochester Americans-8
96Rochester Americans-2
96Collector's Edge Ice-64
Prism-64
97Rochester Americans-5-2
98Milwaukee Admirals-3
99Russian Hockey League-129
00Russian Hockey League-272
01Russian Hockey League-103
04Russian Super League All-Stars-19

Klimes, Michal
98Czech OFS-412
99Czech OFS-182
01Czech OFS-122

Klimes, Tomas
01Czech OFS-265
02Czech OFS Plus-370

Klimov, Konstantin
73Swedish Stickers-116
74Swedish Stickers-62

Klimovich, Sergei
92Upper Deck-339
92Russian Stars Red Ace-14
92Russian Stars Red Ace-30
92Classic-46
Gold-46
92Classic Four-Sport *-187
Gold-187
93Upper Deck-275
94Indianapolis Ice-12
95Indianapolis Ice-10
96Collector's Edge Ice-135
Prism-135
97Las Vegas Thunder-18
99German DEL-167
00Russian Dynamo Moscow-16
00Russian Hockey League-318

Klimt, Tomas
93Upper Deck-263
95Czech APS Extraliga-256
96Czech APS Extraliga-304
97Czech APS Extraliga-240
97Czech DS Extraliga-18
97Czech DS Stickers-220
98Czech DS Stickers-37
98Czech OFS-335
99Czech Score Blue 2000-92
99Czech Score Red Ice 2000-92
00Czech OFS-127
01Czech OFS-175
03Czech OFS Plus-226
03Czech OFS Plus Insert M-M8
04Czech OFS-60

Kline, Chad
01Western Michigan Broncos-5

Kline, Chris
93Quebec Pee-Wee Tournament-1187

Klinga, Vladimir
04Slovakian Poprad Team Set-2

Klinge, Manuel
04German DEL Update-326
04German DEL Update-326A
05German DEL-199

Klinkhammer, Rob
04Lethbridge Hurricanes-17

Klippenstein, Wade
95Alaska Gold Kings-8
01Prince Albert Raiders-11

Klisiak, Waldemar
95Czech APS Extraliga-312

Kljna, Michal
05Brampton Battalion-22

Kloboucek, Jan
92British Columbia JHL-222
98Czech OFS-64
99Czech OFS-78
00Czech OFS-89
01Czech OFS-10
02Czech OFS Plus-196
03Czech OFS Plus-96
04Czech OFS-96

Kloboucek, Jiri
92Cornell Big Red-18
93Cornell Big Red-16
97Czech APS Extraliga-216

Klochkov, Vladislav
96Saskatoon Blades-13
97Lethbridge Hurricanes-10

Klockare, Stefan
90Swedish Semic Elitserien Stickers-183
91Swedish Semic Elitserien Stickers-38
92Upper Deck-224
92Swedish Semic Elitserien Stickers-56
93Swedish Semic Elitserien-32
94Swedish Leaf-73
95Swedish Leaf-16
95Swedish Upper Deck-24
96Swedish Brynas Tigers-8
97Swedish Collector's Choice-20
00Swedish Upper Deck-167

Kloepzig, Steve
86Portland Winter Hawks-10
87Kamloops Blazers-10

Kloiber, Ralph
74Sioux City Musketeers-8

Klostreich, Page
92North Dakota Fighting Sioux-16

Kloti, Marco
93Swiss HNL-12
95Swiss HNL-9
96Swiss HNL-9
98Swiss Power Play Stickers-108
99Swiss Panini Stickers-109
00Swiss Panini Stickers-154
00Swiss Slapshot Mini-Cards-EHCK4
02Swiss HNL-111

Klotz, Garrett
05Red Deer Rebels-7
06Saskatoon Blades-13

Kloucek, Tomas
99Hartford Wolf Pack-14
00BAP Memorabilia-519
00SP Authentic-154
00Topps Heritage-81
Chrome Parallel-81
00Hartford Wolf Pack-16
01BAP Signature Series-100
Autographs-100
Autographs Gold-100
01O-Pee-Chee-284
01O-Pee-Chee Premier Parallel-284
01Stadium Club Souvenirs-TK
01Stadium Club Souvenirs-TKMM
01Topps-284
OPC Parallel-284
Reserve Emblems-TK
Reserve Jerseys-TK
Reserve Name Plates-TK
Reserve Numbers-TK
Reserve Patches-TK
01Upper Deck Victory-239
Gold-239
02BAP Sig Series Auto Buybacks 2001-100
02Milwaukee Admirals-1
02Milwaukee Admirals Postcards-9
03Thrashers Postcards-7
04Czech HC Slavia Praha Postcards-5
04Czech OFS-165
04Czech OFS-375
Stars-21
05Chicago Wolves-8
06Syracuse Crunch-15

Kloz, Vojtech
02Chicago Steel-13
06Czech OFS-29

Klubertanz, Kyle
04Wisconsin Badgers-14
05Wisconsin Badgers-16

Kluczkowski, Steve
897th Inn. Sketch OHL-54

Kluge, Rainer
99German DEL-411

Klugel, Gerhard
04German Berlin Eisbarens 50th Anniv-51

Kluin, Torsten
94German First League-627

Klukay, Joe
44Beehive Group II Photos-38
44Beehive Group II Photos-416
45Quaker Oats Photos-26A
45Quaker Oats Photos-26B
48Exhibits Canadian-33
51Parkhurst-74
52Parkhurst-75
53Parkhurst-94
54Parkhurst-54
55Parkhurst-6
Quaker Oats-6
76Old Timers-9
81Red Wings Oldtimers-18

Kluzak, Gord
83Bruins Team Issue-8
83NHL Key Tags-2
83O-Pee-Chee-51
83O-Pee-Chee Stickers-185
83Topps Stickers-185
84Bruins Postcards-9
84O-Pee-Chee-6
84O-Pee-Chee Stickers-186
84Topps-5
85O-Pee-Chee-167
86O-Pee-Chee-54
86Topps-54
88Bruins Sports Action-8
88Bruins Postcards-9
88O-Pee-Chee-23
88O-Pee-Chee Stickers-25
88Panini Stickers-205
88Topps-23
89Bruins Sports Action Update-4
90O-Pee-Chee-495
90Pro Set-383
90Score-367
Canadian-367

Klyazmin, Sergei
00Halifax Mooseheads-10
01Halifax Mooseheads-5
04Hershey Bears Patriot News-14

Klyn, Brad
92British Columbia JHL-161

Klynck, Beryl
52Juniors Blue Tint-123

Klyne, Lawrence
92British Columbia JHL-91

Klyshin, Sergei
00Russian Hockey League-109

Kmit, Jaroslav
03Czech OFS Plus All-Star Game-H11
04Czech OFS Czech/Slovak-33

Knackstedt, Jordan
05Red Deer Rebels-8
06Moose Jaw Warriors-14

Knapp, Dan
02Ohio State Buckeyes-20
03Ohio State Buckeyes-9
04Ohio State Buckeyes-9
05Ohio State Buckeyes-10

Knaub, Sean
92Quebec Pee-Wee Tournament-1453
93Quebec Pee-Wee Tournament-781

Knauft, Lorne
93Flint Generals-15
94Brantford Smoke-5
96Flint Generals-12
97Flint Generals-11
97Flint Generals EBK-5
98Flint Generals-17
01Flint Generals-9

Knebl, Marek
04Swift Current Broncos-10

Knecht, Daniel
93Swiss HNL-25
95Swiss HNL-408

Knecht, Marco
93Swiss HNL-13
95Swiss HNL-399
96Swiss HNL-10
98Swiss Power Play Stickers-132
02Swiss HNL-198

Knechtel, Kyle
05Mississauga Ice Dogs-17
05Owen Sound Attack-24

Knesaurek, Rob
88Sudbury Wolves-23
89Sudbury Wolves-25

Knezevic, Gorazd
93Quebec Pee-Wee Tournament-1787

Knibbs, Kalvin
907th Inn. Sketch WHL-26

Knick, Andy
95Arizona Icecats-11
96Arizona Icecats-9

Knickle, Rick
86Sherbrooke Canadiens-21
89ProCards IHL-26
90ProCards AHL/IHL-515
91ProCards-320
92San Diego Gulls-13
93Score-466
Canadian-466
93Phoenix Roadrunners-13
93Classic Pro Prospects-121
BCs-BC12
96Milwaukee Admirals-12
96Collector's Edge Ice-122
Prism-122
The Wall-TW3

Knight, Brad
91British Columbia JHL-29

Knight, Chris
93Quebec Pee-Wee Tournament-602

Knight, Curtis
91Air Canada SJHL-A17
92Saskatchewan JHL-40

Knight, Darryl
96Sarnia Sting-12
98Guelph Storm-17
99Kingston Frontenacs-10

Knight, Jason
91Saskatoon Blades-9
917th Inn. Sketch WHL-337

Knight, Jeff
907th Inn. Sketch WHL-44
91Air Canada SJHL-C39
91Air Canada SJHL All-Stars-38

Knight, Justin
93Quebec Pee-Wee Tournament-882

Knight, Keith
82Kingston Canadians-15

Knight, Michael
01Belleville Bulls-13
02Belleville Bulls-9
03Belleville Bulls-10
03Plymouth Whalers-16

Knight, Terry
83Medicine Hat Tigers-7

Knights, Michael
97UK Kingston Hawks Stickers-4
99UK Basingstoke Bison-20

Knipscheer, Fred
93Parkhurst-18
Emerald Ice-18
94Leaf-331
94Pinnacle-249
Artist's Proofs-249
Rink Collection-249
94Score-220
Gold-220
Platinum-220
94Stadium Club-17
Members Only Master Set-17
First Day Issue-17
Super Team Winner Cards-17
94Classic Autographs-NNO
94Classic Tri-Cards-T4
94Classic Pro Prospects-60
95Playoff One on One-227
98Cincinnati Cyclones-11
98Cincinnati Cyclones 2-4

Knobel, Markus
93Swiss HNL-294

Knoblauch, Kris
96Red Deer Rebels-20
04Austin Ice Bats-5
06Prince Albert Raiders-26

Knobloch, Thomas
94German DEL-401
95German DEL-420
99German Bundesliga 2-302

Knoff, Alexander
94German First League-447

Knold, Martin
99Swedish Upper Deck-121
02Swedish SHL-47
Parallel-47
03Swedish Elite-69
Silver-69
04German DEL-173
04Swedish Elitset-62
Gold-62
05German DEL-173
Defender-DF11

Knold, Per Christian
92Finnish Semic-48
92Norwegian Elite Series-87

Knop, Matt
93Quebec Pee-Wee Tournament-888

Knopf, Karl
93Swiss HNL-344
95Swiss HNL-400
96Swiss HNL-346
01Swiss HNL-345
02Swiss HNL-417

Knopfli, Martin
95Swiss HNL-331

Knopp, Ben
99Upper Deck Sobey's Memorial Cup-9
99UD Prospects-29
00UD CHL Prospects-57
03Syracuse Crunch-6

Knopp, Kevin
95South Carolina Stingrays-20
96South Carolina Stingrays-28
00Idaho Steelheads-9
02Lexington Men O'War-25

Knorr, Derek
91Air Canada SJHL-D15
95Flint Generals-18
98BC Icemen-13
98BC Icemen II-15

Knott, Christian
94German First League-343

Knowles, Daryl
01St. Michaels Majors-20
02St. Michaels Majors-22
03Mississauga Ice Dogs-13

Knox, Blake
907th Inn. Sketch WHL-49
917th Inn. Sketch WHL-139
98Las Vegas Coyotes RHI-5
00UK Sekonda Superleague-46

Knox, Cameron
92British Columbia JHL-145

Knox, Jason
89Victoria Cougars-14
90Saskatoon Blades-7
907th Inn. Sketch WHL-248
917th Inn. Sketch WHL-155
95Oklahoma Coyotes RHI-11
95Vancouver VooDoo RHI-6
01Colorado Gold Kings-12

Knox, Kim
98New Hampshire Wildcats-7

Knox, Paul
52Juniors Blue Tint-143

Knox, Ryan
02Pee Dee Pride RBI-141

Knox, Seymour
93Action Packed HOF Induction-7

Knuble, Mike
91Michigan Wolverines-8
93Michigan Wolverines-11
95Adirondack Red Wings-11
97Be A Player-43
Autographs-43
Autographs Die-Cuts-43
Autographs Prismatic Die-Cuts-43
97Donruss-225
Press Proofs Silver-225
Press Proofs Gold-225
97Donruss Limited-2
97Donruss Limited-17
Exposure-2
Exposure-17
97Pinnacle Inside-172
97Score Red Wings-20
Platinum-20
Premier-20
97SP Authentic-180
97Upper Deck-187
97Upper Deck Ice-39
Parallel-39
Power Shift-39
98Pacific-194
Ice Blue-194
Red-194
98Upper Deck-325
Exclusives-325
Exclusives 1 of 1-325
Gold Reserve-325
98Upper Deck MVP-136
Gold Script-136
Silver Script-136
Super Script-136
99Pacific-271
Copper-271
Emerald Green-271
Gold-271
Ice Blue-271
Premiere Date-271
Red-271
00Pacific-37
Copper-37
Gold-37
Ice Blue-37
Premiere Date-37
01Pacific-32
Extreme LTD-32
Hobby LTD-32
Premiere Date-32
Retail LTD-32
01Pacific Arena Exclusives-32
01Upper Deck Victory-31
Gold-31
02Pacific Complete-184
Red-184
03Bruins Team Issue-3
03ITG Action-63
03O-Pee-Chee-136
03OPC Blue-136
03OPC Gold-136
03OPC Red-136
03Pacific-27
Blue-27
Red-27
03Pacific Complete-186
Red-186
03Pacific Exhibit-13
Blue Backs-13
Yellow Backs-13
03Pacific Heads-Up-7
Hobby LTD-7
Retail LTD-7
03Pacific Prism-10
Blue-10
Gold-10
Red-10
03Pacific Quest for the Cup-7
Blue-7
03Parkhurst Original Six Boston-16
Memorabilia-BM13
03Private Stock Reserve-9
Blue-9
Red-9
Retail-9
03Titanium-8
Hobby Jersey Number Parallels-8
Retail-8
Retail Jersey Number Parallels-8
03Topps-136
Blue-136
Gold-136
Red-136
03Topps Pristine-37
Gold Refractor Die Cuts-37
Refractors-37
Press Plates Black-37
Press Plates Cyan-37
Press Plates Magenta-37
Press Plates Yellow-37
03Upper Deck-19
Canadian Exclusives-19
HG-19
03Upper Deck MVP-33
Gold Script-33
Silver Script-33
Canadian Exclusives-33
04Pacific-21
Blue-21
Red-21
04Swedish Elitset-211
Gold-211
04Swedish Pure Skills-47
Parallel-47
05Be A Player Signatures-ME
05Be A Player Signatures Gold-ME
05Flyers Team Issue-12
05Panini Stickers-136
05Parkhurst-353
Facsimile Auto Parallel-353
05Upper Deck-391
05Upper Deck MVP-285
Gold-285
Platinum-285
05Swedish SHL Elitset-78
06Be A Player-106
Autographs-106
Signatures-KN
Signatures 25-116
06Flyers Postcards-11
06O-Pee-Chee-362
Rainbow-362
06Panini Stickers-131
06Upper Deck-144
Exclusives Parallel-144
High Gloss Parallel-144
Masterpieces-144
06Upper Deck MVP-218
Gold Script-218
Super Script-218
06Upper Deck Ovation-86
07Upper Deck Victory-30
Black-30
Gold-30

Knudsen, Kasper Haslund
98Danish Hockey League-62
99Danish Hockey League-101

Knudsen, Nicolaus
03Saskatoon Blades-8
04Saskatoon Blades-1

Knudsen, Tim
01Kalamazoo K-Wings-17
03Missouri River Otters-22

Knupp, Chris
93Quebec Pee-Wee Tournament-714

Knupp, Kevin B
93Quebec Pee-Wee Tournament-1278

Knutsen, Espen
92Finnish Semic-40
92Norwegian Elite Series-16
92Norwegian Elite Series-181
92Norwegian Elite Series-194
92Norwegian Elite Series-200
93Swedish Semic World Champ Stickers-241
94Finnish Jaa Kiekko-261
94Swedish Leaf-264
Foreign Affairs-1
95Swedish Leaf-35
Face to Face-13
95Swedish Upper Deck-51
Ticket to North America-NA6
95Swedish Globe World Championships-198
95Swedish Globe World Championships-252
95Swedish World Championships Stickers-248
96Swedish Semic Wien-206
97Black Diamond-81
Double Diamond-81
Triple Diamond-81
Quadruple Diamond-81
97Donruss Elite-106
97Donruss Elite-144
Aspirations-106
Aspirations-144
Status-106
Status-144
97Donruss Preferred-161
Cut to the Chase-161
97Donruss Priority-172
Stamp of Approval-172
Direct Deposit-26
97Katch-3
Gold-3
Silver-3
97Pacific Dynagon-NNO
Copper-NNO
Dark Grey-NNO
Emerald Green-NNO
Ice Blue-NNO
Red-NNO
Silver-NNO
97Paramount-3
Copper-3
Dark Grey-3
Emerald Green-3
Ice Blue-3
Red-3
Silver-3
97Pinnacle-1
Artist's Proofs-1
Rink Collection-1
Press Plates Back Black-1
Press Plates Back Cyan-1
Press Plates Back Magenta-1
Press Plates Back Yellow-1
Press Plates Front Black-1
Press Plates Front Cyan-1
Press Plates Front Magenta-1
Press Plates Front Yellow-1
Certified Rookie Redemption-K
Certified Rookie Redemption Gold-K
Certified Rookie Redemption Mirror Gold-K
97Score-66
Artist's Proofs-66
Golden Blades-66
97Score Mighty Ducks-20
Platinum-20
Premier-20
97SP Authentic-169
97Upper Deck-216
97Upper Deck Ice-44
Parallel-44
Power Shift-44
98Swedish UD Choice-64
99Swedish Upper Deck-49
SHL Signatures-4
Snapshots-5
00BAP Parkhurst 2000-P198
00Panini Stickers-142
00Topps Heritage-159
00Upper Deck-50
Exclusives Tier 1-50
Exclusives Tier 2-50
01BAP Memorabilia-258
Emerald-258
Ruby-258
Sapphire-258
01BAP Signature Series-181
Autographs-181
Autographs Gold-181
01Blue Jackets Donatos Pizza-8
01O-Pee-Chee-70
01O-Pee-Chee Heritage Parallel-70
01O-Pee-Chee Heritage Parallel Limited-70
01O-Pee-Chee Premier Parallel-70
01Pacific-114
Extreme LTD-114
Hobby LTD-114
Premiere Date-114
Retail LTD-114
01Pacific Adrenaline-54
Blue-54
Premiere Date-54
Red-54
Retail-54
01Pacific Arena Exclusives-114
01Parkhurst-193
01Private Stock-26
Gold-26
Premiere Date-26
Retail-26
Silver-26
01Private Stock Pacific Nights-26
01Stadium Club-97
Award Winners-97
Master Photos-97
01Topps-70
Heritage Parallel-70
Heritage Parallel Limited-70
OPC Parallel-70
01Topps Chrome-70
Refractors-70
Black Border Refractors-70
01Topps Heritage-19
Refractors-19
01UD Challenge for the Cup-21
01UD Mask Collection Double Patches-DPEK
01UD Mask Collection Jerseys-J-EK
01UD Mask Collection Jersey and Patch-JPEK
01UD Top Shelf-89
01Upper Deck-53
Exclusives-53
01Upper Deck MVP-52
01Upper Deck Victory-101
Gold-101
01Upper Deck Vintage-73
01Upper Deck Vintage-78
02Atomic-29
Blue-29
Gold-29
Red-29
Hobby Parallel-29
02BAP First Edition-225
02BAP Signature Series-59
Autographs-59
Autograph Buybacks 2001-181
Autographs Gold-59
Phenoms-YP12
02O-Pee-Chee-175
02O-Pee-Chee Premier Blue Parallel-175
02O-Pee-Chee Premier Red Parallel-175
02O-Pee-Chee Factory Set-175
02Pacific-101
Blue-101
Red-101
02Pacific Complete-126
Red-126
02Pacific Exclusive-52
02Parkhurst-173
Bronze-173
Gold-173
Silver-173
02Parkhurst Retro-149
Minis-149
02Private Stock Reserve-31
Blue-31
Red-31
Retail-31
02SP Game Used Piece of History-PHEK
02SP Game Used Piece of History Gold-PHEK
02SP Game Used Piece of History Rainbow-PHEK
02Topps-175
OPC Blue Parallel-175
OPC Red Parallel-175
Factory Set-175
02Topps Chrome-102
Black Border Refractors-102
Refractors-102
02Topps Total-349
02UD Artistic Impressions-26
Gold-26
02UD Artistic Impressions Beckett Promos-26
02UD Artistic Impressions Retrospectives-R26
02UD Artistic Impressions Retrospect Gold-R26
02UD Artistic Impress Retrospect Silver-R26
02UD Piece of History-21
02UD Top Shelf-25
Shooting Stars-SHEK
02Upper Deck-53
Exclusives-53
02Upper Deck Classic Portraits-29
Hockey Royalty-KTK
Hockey Royalty Limited-KTK
02Upper Deck MVP-56
Gold-56
Classics-56
Golden Classics-56
Skate Around Jerseys-SAEK
02Upper Deck Victory-59
Bronze-59
Gold-59
Silver-59
02Upper Deck Vintage-79
Tall Boys-T20
Tall Boys Gold-T20
03ITG Action-199
03O-Pee-Chee-264
03OPC Blue-264
03OPC Gold-264

03OPC Red-264
03Pacific Complete-255
Red-255
03Topps-264
Blue-264
Gold-264
Red-264
03Upper Deck-301
Canadian Exclusives-301
HG-301
UD Exclusives-301
04Swedish Djurgardens Postcards-3
04Swedish Elitset-167
Dominators-7
Gold-167
04Swedish Pure Skills-13
Parallel-13

Knutson, Patrick
00Sioux City Musketeers-17
01Lincoln Stars-15

Knutsson, Knut
57Swedish Alfabilder-88
64Swedish Coralli ISHockey-60
65Swedish Coralli ISHockey-60

Knuude, Mike
83Belleville Bulls-6
84Belleville Bulls-6

Knyazev, Igor
99Russian Hockey League-140
00Russian Hockey League-274
02Lowell Lock Monsters-1
03Springfield Falcons Postcards-6
04ITG Heroes and Prospects-6
04ITG Heroes/Prospects Toronto Expo '05-6
04ITG Heroes/Prospects Expo Heroes/Pros-6

Knyazev, Igor A.
98Danish Hockey League-207
99Danish Hockey League-137

Koalska, Matt
00Minnesota Golden Gophers-8
01Minnesota Golden Gophers-22
02Minnesota Golden Gophers-22
03Minnesota Golden Gophers-19
06Fleer-227
Tiffany-227
06O-Pee-Chee-513
Rainbow-513
06SPx-198
Spectrum-198
06The Cup Masterpiece Pressplates (Artifacts)-212
06The Cup Masterpiece Pressplates (Marquee Rookies)-513
06The Cup Masterpiece Pressplates (MVP)-347
06The Cup Masterpiece Pressplates (Power Play)-115
06The Cup Masterpiece Pressplates (Trilogy)-131
06The Cup Masterpiece Pressplates (Victory)-230
06UD Artifacts-212
Blue-212
Gold-212
Platinum-212
Radiance-212
Red-212
06UD Powerplay-115
Impact Rainbow-115
06Upper Deck-229
Exclusives Parallel-229
High Gloss Parallel-229
Masterpieces-229
06Upper Deck MVP-347
Gold Script-347
Super Script-347
06Upper Deck Trilogy-131
06Upper Deck Victory-230
06Upper Deck Victory Black-230
06Upper Deck Victory Gold-230

Kobach, Reto
98Swiss Power Play Stickers-208
99Swiss Panini Stickers-210
00Swiss Panini Stickers-253
01Swiss EV Zug Postcards-14
01Swiss HNL-172
02Swiss HNL-184

Kobasew, Chuck
01BAP Memorabilia Draft Redemptions-14
01SPx Rookie Redemption-R5
01Kelowna Rockets-8
02Atomic-104
Blue-104
Gold-104
Red-104
Hobby Parallel-104
02BAP All-Star Edition-135
Gold-135
Silver-135
02BAP First Edition-437H
02BAP Memorabilia-278
Emerald-278
Ruby-278
Sapphire-278
NHL All-Star Game-278
NHL All-Star Game Blue-278
NHL All-Star Game Green-278
NHL All-Star Game Red-278
02BAP Memorabilia Toronto Fall Expo-278
02BAP Signature Series-185
Autographs-185
Autographs Gold-185
Jerseys-SGJ58
Jersey Autographs-SGJ58
02BAP Ultimate Memorabilia-8
Autographs-5
Autographs Gold-5
Calder Candidates-17
02Bowman YoungStars-160
Gold-160
Silver-160
02Crown Royale-106
Blue-106
Purple-106
Red-106
Retail-106
Rookie Royalty-5
02eTopps-45
02ITG Used-88
Calder Jerseys-C5
Calder Jerseys Gold-C5
02NHL Power Play Stickers-21
02O-Pee-Chee-339
02O-Pee-Chee Premier Blue Parallel-339
02O-Pee-Chee Premier Red Parallel-339
02O-Pee-Chee Factory Set-339
02Pacific-403
02Pacific Calder-107
Silver-107
02Pacific Complete-573
Red-573
02Pacific Exclusive-195
Blue-195
Gold-195
02Pacific Heads-Up-129
02Pacific Quest for the Cup-108
Gold-108
02Parkhurst-208
Bronze-208
Gold-208
Silver-208
Hardware-C1
Jerseys-GJ56
02Parkhurst Retro-208
Minis-208
02Private Stock Reserve-155
Blue-155
Red-155
Retail-155
Class Act-4
Moments in Time-1
02SP Authentic-183
Signed Patches-PCK
02SP Game Used-70
02SPx-148
02Stadium Club-125
Silver Decoy Cards-125
Proofs-125
02Titanium-108
Blue-108
Red-108
Retail-108
Right on Target-3
02Topps-339
OPC Blue Parallel-339
OPC Red Parallel-339
Factory Set-339
02Topps Chrome-174
Black Border Refractors-174
Refractors-174
02Topps Heritage-141
02Topps Total-410
02UD Artistic Impressions-116
Gold-116
Common Ground-CG15
Common Ground Gold-CG15
02UD Foundations-146
02UD Honor Roll-147
02UD Mask Collection-158
02UD Piece of History-125
02UD Premier Collection-79
Gold-79
Signatures Bronze-SCK
Signatures Gold-SCK
Signatures Silver-SCK
02UD Top Shelf-125
02Upper Deck-228
Exclusives-228
02Upper Deck Classic Portraits-105
02Upper Deck Rookie Update-167
Autographs-CK
02Vanguard-106
LTD-106
Prime Prospects-5
03BAP Memorabilia-91
Emerald-91
Gold-91
Ruby-91
Sapphire-91
03BAP Ultimate Memorabilia Autographs-11
Gold-11
03Beehive Signatures-RF13
03Bowman-31
Gold-31
03Bowman Chrome-31
Refractors-31
Gold Refractors-31
Xfractors-31
03Crown Royale-14
Blue-14
Retail-14
03ITG Action-59
Jerseys-M42
03ITG Used Signature Series-42
Gold-42
Autographs-CK
Autographs Gold-CK
03McDonald's Pacific-8
03Pacific-51
Blue-51
Red-51
03Pacific Calder-15
Silver-15
03Pacific Calder Collection NHL All-Star Block Party Gold-2
03Pacific Complete-558
Red-558
03Pacific Invincible New Sensations-6
03Pacific Supreme-14
Blue-14
Red-14
Retail-14
03Private Stock Reserve-16
Blue-16
Red-16
Retail-16
Rising Stock-4
03SP Authentic Sign of the Times-CK
03Topps Traded-TT33
Blue-TT33
Gold-TT33
Red-TT33
03UD Honor Roll Signature Class-SC29
03Upper Deck-32
Canadian Exclusives-32
HG-32
03Upper Deck All-Star Promos-AS4
03Upper Deck Ice Authentics-IA-CK
03Upper Deck MVP-73
Gold Script-73
Silver Script-73
Canadian Exclusives-73
03Czech Stadion-562
04SP Authentic Octographs-OS-CUP
04SP Authentic Sign of the Times-QS-IKHL
04UD Toronto Fall Expo Priority Signings-CK
04Upper Deck-29
Canadian Exclusives-29
HG Glossy Gold-29
HG Glossy Silver-29
Jersey Autographs-GJA-CK
04AHL All-Stars-22
04AHL Top Prospects-25
04Lowell Lock Monsters-11
04Lowell Lock Monsters Photo Album-11
05ITG Heroes/Prosp Toronto Expo Parallel -95
05Panini Stickers-208
05Parkhurst-72
Facsimile Auto Parallel-72
Signatures-CK
True Colors-TCCGY
True Colors-TCCGY
True Colors-TCEDCA
True Colors-TCEDCA
05UD Powerplay Power Marks-PMCK
05Ultra-36
Gold-36
Ice-36
05Upper Deck-275
Jerseys-J-CK
Notable Numbers-N-CK
Patches-P-CK
05Upper Deck MVP-62
Gold-62
Platinum-62
05Upper Deck Trilogy Scripts-SFS-CK
05ITG Heroes and Prospects-95
Autographs-A-CK
Jerseys-GUJ-18
Jerseys Gold-GUJ-18
Emblems-GUE-18
Emblems Gold-GUE-18
Numbers-GUN-18
Numbers Gold-GUN-18
06Be A Player-105
Autographs-105
Signatures-CH
Signatures 25-115
06Black Diamond-14
Black-14
Gold-14
Ruby-14
Gemography-GCK
Jerseys-JCK
Jerseys Black-JCK
Jerseys Gold-JCK
Jerseys Ruby-JCK
Jerseys Black Autographs -JCK
06Flair Showcase Inks-IKO
06Fleer-33
Tiffany-33
Signing Day-SDCK
06Gatorade-7
06Hot Prospects Hotagraphs-HKO
06O-Pee-Chee-81
Rainbow-81
Swatches-S-CK
06SP Game Used Authentic Fabrics Dual-AF2TK
06SP Game Used Authentic Fabrics Dual Patches-AF2TK
06SP Game Used Letter Marks-LMCK
06SP Game Used SIGnificance-SCK
06UD Artifacts Auto-Facts-AFCK
06UD Artifacts Auto-Facts Gold-AFCK
06UD Artifacts Frozen Artifacts-FACK
06UD Artifacts Frozen Artifacts Black-FACK
06UD Artifacts Frozen Artifacts Blue-FACK
06UD Artifacts Frozen Artifacts Gold-FACK
06UD Artifacts Frozen Artifacts Platinum-FACK
06UD Artifacts Frozen Artifacts Red-FACK
06UD Artifacts Frozen Artifacts Autographed Black-FACK
06UD Artifacts Frozen Artifacts Patches Black-FACK
06UD Artifacts Frozen Artifacts Patches Blue-FACK
06UD Artifacts Frozen Artifacts Patches Gold-FACK
06UD Artifacts Frozen Artifacts Patches Platinum-FACK
06UD Artifacts Frozen Artifacts Patches Red-FACK
06UD Artifacts Frozen Artifacts Patches Autographed Black Tag Parallel-FACK
06Ultra-30
Gold Medallion-30
Ice Medallion-30
Fresh Ink-ICK
06Upper Deck Arena Giveaways-CGY3
06Upper Deck-34
Exclusives Parallel-34
High Gloss Parallel-34
Game Jerseys-J2CK
Game Patches-P2CK
Masterpieces-34
06Upper Deck MVP-48
Gold Script-48
Super Script-48
Autographs-OAPK
Jerseys-OJCJ
06Upper Deck Ovation-109
06Upper Deck Trilogy Honorary Scripted Patches-HSPCK
06Upper Deck Trilogy Honorary Scripted Swatches-HSSCK
06Upper Deck Trilogy Ice Scripts-ISCK
06Upper Deck Trilogy Scripts-TSCK
06Upper Deck Victory-32
06Upper Deck Victory Black-32
06Upper Deck Victory Gold-32

Kobel, Peter
93Swiss HNL-174
96Swiss HNL-193
98Swiss Power Play Stickers-67
99Swiss Panini Stickers-116

Koberle, Walter
72Finnish Semic World Championship-115
72Swedish Semic World Championship-115
79Panini Stickers-111
94German First League-498
03German Deg Metro Stars-8
04German Dusseldorf Metro Stars Postcards-11

Kobezda, Jan
98ECHL All-Star Southern Conference-17
99Missouri River Otters-11
99Missouri River Otters Sheet-9

Kobrc, Roman
92British Columbia JHL-233

Kobzev, Igor
74Swedish Stickers-69

Kocak, Peter
04Slovakian Skalica Team Set-12

Kocar, Jaroslav
99Czech Score Blue 2000-57
99Czech Score Red Ice 2000-57

Koch, Geoff
93Quebec Pee-Wee Tournament-601

Koch, Paul
95Toledo Storm-4
96Toledo Storm-5
98Chicago Wolves-21
98Chicago Wolves Turner Cup-4

Koch, Thomas
04Swedish Elitset-219
Gold-219
05Swedish Lulea Hockey Postcards-7
05Swedish SHL Elitset-87
Gold-87
06Swedish SHL Elitset-87

Kochan, Dieter
92British Columbia JHL-64
93Northern Michigan Wildcats-18
97Louisville Riverfrogs-21
98BC Icemen-17
98BC Icemen II-19
99UHL All-Stars East-16T
00BAP Memorabilia-234
Emerald-234
Ruby-234
Sapphire-234
Promos-234
00BAP Mem Chicago Sportsfest Copper-234
00BAP Memorabilia Chicago Sportsfest Blue-234
00BAP Memorabilia Chicago Sportsfest Gold-234
00BAP Memorabilia Chicago Sportsfest Ruby-234
00BAP Memorabilia Chicago Sun-Times Ruby-234
00BAP Memorabilia Chicago Sun-Times Gold-234
00BAP Mem Chicago Sun-Times Sapphire-234
00BAP Mem Toronto Fall Expo Copper-234
00BAP Memorabilia Toronto Fall Expo Gold-234
00BAP Memorabilia Toronto Fall Expo Ruby-234
00Black Diamond-84
Gold-84
00Pacific-375
Copper-375
Gold-375
Ice Blue-375
Premiere Date-375
00Revolution-134
Blue-134
Premiere Date-134
Red-134
00SPx-118
Spectrum-118
00Titanium-145
Retail-145
00Titanium Draft Day Edition-145
00Titanium Draft Day Promos-145
00Upper Deck-227
Exclusives Tier 1-227
Exclusives Tier 2-227
01Between the Pipes-69
02Between the Pipes-48
Gold-48
Silver-48
02Pacific-349
Blue-349
Red-349
03Bridgeport Sound Tigers-5A
05Portland Pirates-11

Kochegarov, Alexei
99Russian Hockey League-162
01Russian Hockey League-144

Kochin, Vladimir
98Russian Hockey League-146
00Russian Hockey League-382

Kochta, Jiri
70Finnish Jaakiekko-51
70Swedish Hockey-360
70Swedish Masterserien-155
71Finnish Suomi Stickers-30
71Swedish Hockey-54
72Finnish Jaakiekko-12
72Finnish Hellas-87
72Finnish Semic World Championship-28
72Swedish Semic World Championship-28
73Finnish Jaakiekko-53
73Swedish Stickers-32
74Finnish Jenkki-75
74Finnish Typotor-117
74Swedish Stickers-110
74Swedish Semic World Champ Stickers-58
94German DEL-390
95German DEL-406
98German DEL-19

Koci, David
00Prince George Cougars-4
01Wilkes-Barre Scranton Penguins-3
03Wilkes-Barre Scranton Penguins-12
04Wilkes-Barre Scranton Penguins-3
05WBS Penguins-15
06Norfolk Admirals-2

Koci, Vaclav
02Czech OFS Plus-154
03Czech OFS Plus-115
03Czech OFS Plus-262
06Czech OFS-93

Kocian, Aaron
93Quebec Pee-Wee Tournament-624

Kock, Enrico
94German First League-45

Kock, Jan
73Swedish Stickers-240
74Swedish Stickers-172
83Swedish Semic Elitserien-55
84Swedish Semic Elitserien-55

Kockare, Heimo
65Swedish Coralli ISHockey-182

Kocur, Joe
83Saskatoon Blades-22
87Panini Stickers-251
87Red Wings Little Caesars-17
88Red Wings Little Caesars-13
89Panini Stickers-67
89Red Wings Little Caesars-11
90O-Pee-Chee-55
90Panini Stickers-211
90Pro Set-73
90Score-201
Canadian-201
90Topps-55
Tiffany-55
90Upper Deck-411
French-411
91Bowman-69
91O-Pee-Chee-427
91Pinnacle-240
French-240
91Score American-92
91Score Canadian Bilingual-92
91Score Canadian English-92
91Stadium Club-365
91Topps-427
92Bowman-80
92O-Pee-Chee-169
92Pinnacle-152
French-152
92Score-24
Canadian-24
92Stadium Club-417
92Topps-128
Gold-128G
93OPC Premier-512
Gold-512
93Parkhurst-401
Emerald Ice-401
93Pinnacle-184
Canadian-184
93Score-270
Canadian-270
93Topps/OPC Premier-512
Gold-512
94Pinnacle-243
Artist's Proofs-243
Rink Collection-243
94Stadium Club-73
Members Only Master Set-73
First Day Issue-73
Super Team Winner Cards-73
94Upper Deck-479
Electric Ice-479
95Upper Deck-314
Electric Ice-314
Electric Ice Gold-314
96Red Wings Detroit News/Free Press-1
97Be A Player-153
Autographs-153
Autographs Die-Cuts-153
Autographs Prismatic Die-Cuts-153
97Pacific Invincible NHL Regime-70
98Pacific-195
Ice Blue-195
Red-195
98Pacific Omega-80
Red-80
Opening Day Issue-80
99Upper Deck MVP Draw Your Own-W1
01Fleer Legacy-47
Ultimate-47
02Fleer Throwbacks-65
Gold-65
Platinum-65
Autographs-21
Scraps-4
Tie Downs-4
Squaring Off-1
Squaring Off Memorabilia-1
04ITG Franchises US West-225
Autographs-A-JKO
05ITG Tough Customers-JK
Autographs-JK
06Parkhurst-49
06Parkhurst-228
06Parkhurst-238
Autographs-49
Autographs-228
Autographs-238
Autographs Dual-DAPK

Kocur, Kory
86Saskatoon Blades Photos-13
88Saskatoon Blades-24
90Score-384
Canadian-384
90ProCards AHL/IHL-483
91ProCards-255

Kodman, Neil
04Lethbridge Hurricanes-16

Koehler, Gary
98Florida Everblades-10

Koehler, Greg
98New Haven Beast-19
99Cincinnati Cyclones-11
00Cincinnati Cyclones-6
02Parkhurst-239
Bronze-239
Gold-239
Silver-239
02SP Authentic-149
02SPx-165
02UD Honor Roll-118
02UD Mask Collection-129
02UD Top Shelf-116
02Upper Deck-212
Exclusives-212
02Milwaukee Admirals-15
03Elmira Jackals-9
04Lincoln Stars-10

Koehler, J.J.
04Lincoln Stars-10

Koenig, Holger
04German Weiden Blue Devils-16

Koenig, Trevor
98Dayton Bombers-7
98Dayton Bombers EBK-14
00San Diego Gulls-5
04Atlantic City Boardwalk Bullies-15
06UK Coventry Blaze-15

Kofler, Andreas
93Quebec Pee-Wee Tournament-1536

Kofler, Manuel
99German Bundesliga 2-222
00German DEL-112
01German Upper Deck-252
02German DEL City Press-93
04German DEL-31
05German DEL-7
06German DEL-7
German Forwards-GF5

Kogut, Derek
93Quebec Pee-Wee Tournament-173

Kohanskey, Matt
03Cape Fear Fire Antz-5

Koharski, Don
90Pro Set-691

Kohl, Peter
99German DEL-395

Kohler, Becrich
05Czech HC Vitkovice-9
06Czech OFS-55

Kohler, Jerome
01Swiss HNL-416
02Swiss HNL-173

Kohler, Sebastien
99Swiss Panini Stickers-303
01Swiss HNL-402

Kohler, Swen
01Swiss HNL-355

Kohler, Willy
93Swiss HNL-278
95Swiss HNL-383

Kohli, Marcel
93Swiss HNL-464
95Swiss HNL-289
96Swiss HNL-274

Kohmann, Christian
94German DEL-345
95German DEL-320
96German DEL-346
00German DEL-199
01German Upper Deck-220
02German DEL City Press-289
03German DEL-91
04German DEL-109
05German DEL-89

Kohn, Bill
95Minnesota Golden Gophers-17
96Minnesota Golden Gophers-15
97Minnesota Golden Gophers-9
98Minnesota Golden Gophers-9

Kohn, Dustin
03Calgary Hitmen-10
04Calgary Hitmen-8
05ITG Heroes/Prosp Toronto Expo Parallel -166
05Brandon Wheat Kings-14
05ITG Heroes and Prospects-166
Autographs-A-DKO
Oh Canada-OC-15
Oh Canada Gold-OC-15
06ITG Heroes and Prospects-188
Autographs-ADK
Update Autographs-ADK

Kohn, Ladislav
94Parkhurst SE-SE211
Gold-SE211
94Upper Deck-509
Electric Ice-509
95Bowman-122
All-Foil-122
95Saint John Flames-10
96Fleer-128
Calder Candidates-5
96SkyBox Impact-151
96Saint John Flames-10
97Saint John Flames-12
99BAP Millennium-8
Emerald-8
Ruby-8
Sapphire-8
Signatures-8
Signatures Gold-8
Calder Candidates Ruby-C13
Calder Candidates Emerald-C13
Calder Candidates Sapphire-C13
99Pacific-451
99Pacific Omega-8
Copper-8
Gold-8
Ice Blue-8
Premiere Date-8
99Topps Arena Giveaways-ANA-LK
99Upper Deck Arena Giveaways-AM1
99Upper Deck MVP SC Edition-7
Gold Script-7
Silver Script-7
Super Script-7
00O-Pee-Chee-260A
00O-Pee-Chee Parallel-260A
00Pacific-6
Copper-6
Gold-6
Ice Blue-6
Premiere Date-6
00Topps/OPC-260A
Parallel-260A
00Upper Deck-5
Exclusives Tier 1-5
Exclusives Tier 2-5
00Upper Deck Victory-2
01Upper Deck Victory-23
Gold-23
02BAP Sig Series Auto Buybacks 1999-8
03Finnish Cardset-11
04Finnish Cardset-11
04Finnish Cardset Signatures-2
04Swedish Pure Skills-98
Parallel-98
05Finnish Cardset -6
06Finnish Cardset-8

Koho, Ville
01Finnish Cardset-334
04Finnish Cardset-289
05Finnish Cardset -130
06Finnish Cardset-138

Kohtala, Luke
03Wisconsin Badgers-17
04Wisconsin Badgers-26

Kohut, Jozef
03UK Guildford Flames-13
04UK Guildford Flames-14
05UK Guildford Flames-18
06UK Guildford Flames-19

Kohvakka, Teemu
93Finnish SISU-153
95Finnish Semic World Championships-239

Koikkalainen, Jaakko
66Finnish Jaakiekkosarja-143
70Finnish Jaakiekko-259

Koistinen, Keijo
65Finnish Hellas-39

Koistinen, Matti
06Finnish Cardset-320

Koistinen, Ville
01Finnish Cardset-233
04Finnish Cardset-48
Parallel-35
05Finnish Cardset -42
06Finnish Cardset-42
Signature Sensations-7
06Milwaukee Admirals -9

Koivisto, Arto
04Finnish Cardset-244
05Finnish Cardset -236
06Finnish Cardset-61

Koivisto, Keijo
80Finnish Mallasjuoma-73

Koivisto, Rami
93Finnish Jyvas-Hyva Stickers-119
93Finnish SISU-15
93Finnish SISU Promos-NNO
94Finnish SISU-102

Koivisto, Tom
93Finnish SISU-34
94Finnish SISU-292
95Finnish SISU-217
96Finnish SISU Redline-17
98Finnish Kerailysarja-55
Off Duty-3
99Finnish Cardset-263
00Finnish Cardset-41
01Finnish Cardset-253
02Atomic-131
02BAP All-Star Edition-130
Gold-130
Silver-130
02BAP Memorabilia-290
Emerald-290
Ruby-290
Sapphire-290
NHL All-Star Game-290
NHL All-Star Game Blue-290
NHL All-Star Game Green-290
NHL All-Star Game Red-290
02BAP Memorabilia Toronto Fall Expo-290
02BAP Ultimate Memorabilia-20
02Blues Team Issue-11
02Bowman YoungStars-145
Gold-145
Silver-145
02Crown Royale-134
Blue-134
Purple-134
Red-134
Retail-134
02ITG Used-86
02Parkhurst-220
Bronze-220
Gold-220
Silver-220
02Private Stock Reserve-180
Blue-180
Red-180
Retail-180
02SP Authentic-157
02SP Game Used-91
02Titanium-134
Blue-134
Red-134
Retail-134
02Topps Chrome-164
Black Border Refractors-164
Refractors-164
02Topps Heritage-148
02Topps Total-419
02UD Honor Roll-125
02UD Mask Collection-135
02UD Top Shelf-118
02Upper Deck-451
Exclusives-451
02Upper Deck Classic Portraits-127
02Vanguard-131
LTD-131
02Finnish Cardset-41
03Worcester Ice Cats-9
04Swedish Elitset-170
Gold-170
04Swedish Pure Skills-16
Parallel-16
05Swedish SHL Elitset-23
Gold-23
06Swedish SHL Elitset-27

Koivisto, Toni
00Finnish Cardset-189
01Finnish Cardset-90
02Finnish Cardset-196
03Finnish Cardset-107
04Finnish Cardset-120
Parallel-89
05Finnish Cardset -221
06Finnish Cardset-48
06Finnish Ilves Team Set-9

Koivu, Eerikki
05Finnish Cardset -243
06Finnish Cardset-71

Koivu, Jukka
73Finnish Jaakiekko-287

Koivu, Mikko
00Finnish Cardset-222
00Finnish Cardset Next Generation-1
01BAP Memorabilia Draft Redemptions-6
01Finnish Cardset-142
01Finnish Cardset-NNO
02Finnish Cardset-197
Bound for Glory-3
02Finnish Cardset Dynamic Duos-1
02Finnish Cardset Signatures-3
03Finnish Cardset-162
03Finnish Cardset Vintage 1983-VI1
04AHL All-Stars-23
04AHL All-Stars-47
04AHL Top Prospects-23
04Houston Aeros-10
04ITG Heroes and Prospects-186
Autographs-U-MKO
04ITG Heroes/Prospects Toronto Expo '05-186
04ITG Heroes/Prosp Toronto Expo Parallel -78
05Beehive-145
Beige -145
Blue -145
Gold-145
Red -145
Matte-145
Signature Scrapbook-SSMK
05Black Diamond-252
05Hot Prospects-242
En Fuego-242
Hot Materials-HMMK
Red Hot-242
White Hot-242
05Parkhurst-634
Facsimile Auto Parallel-634
Signatures-KO
True Colors-TCMIN
True Colors-TCMIN
05SP Authentic-193
Limited-193
Exquisite Endorsements-EEMK
Rarefied Rookies-RRMK
05SP Game Used-170
Autographs-170
Gold-170
05SPx-232
Spectrum-232
05The Cup-121
Autographed Rookie Patches Gold Rainbow-121
Black Rainbow Rookies-121
Dual NHL Shields-DSGK
Dual NHL Shields Autographs-ADSGK
Masterpiece Pressplates (Artifacts)-287
Masterpiece Pressplates (Bee Hive)-145
Masterpiece Pressplates (Black Diamond)-252
Masterpiece Pressplates (Ice)-116
Masterpiece Pressplates Rookie Upd Auto-267
Masterpiece Pressplates SPA Autos-193
Masterpiece Pressplates (SP Game Used)-170
Masterpiece Pressplates SPx Autos-232
Masterpiece Pressplates (Trilogy)-269
Masterpiece Pressplates Ult Coll-186
Masterpiece Pressplates (Victory)-300
Masterpiece Pressplates Autographs-121
Platinum Rookies-121
05UD Artifacts-287
05UD Rookie Class-36
05Ultimate Collection-186
Gold-186
Marquee Attractions-MA25
Ultimate Debut Threads Jerseys-DTJMK
Ultimate Debut Threads Patches-DTPMK
05Upper Deck-450
Rookie Ink-RIMK
05Upper Deck Ice-116
Premieres Auto Patches-AIPMK
05Upper Deck Rookie Update-267
05Upper Deck Trilogy-269
05Upper Deck Victory-300
Black-300
Gold-300
Silver-300
05ITG Heroes and Prospects-78
Autographs-A-MK
Complete Jerseys-CJ-17
Complete Jerseys Gold-CJ-17
Complete Logos-AHL-1
Future Teammates-FT1
He Shoots-He Scores Prizes-30
Jerseys-GUJ-7
Jerseys Gold-GUJ-07
Emblems-GUE-7
Emblems Gold-GUE-07
Numbers-GUN-7
Numbers Gold-GUN-07
Nameplates-N-7
Nameplates Gold-N-07
National Pride-NPR-8
06Be A Player Portraits Dual Signature Portraits-DSKK
06Be A Player Portraits First Exposures-FEMK
06Be A Player Portraits Signature Portraits-SPKO
06Black Diamond-108
Black-108
Gold-108
Ruby-108
06Flair Showcase Wave of the Future-WF20
06Fleer-100
Tiffany-100
Signing Day-SDMK
06O-Pee-Chee-251
06O-Pee-Chee-636
Rainbow-251
Rainbow-636
Autographs-A-KO
06SP Game Used Inked Sweaters-ISKO
06SP Game Used Inked Sweaters Patches-ISKO
06SP Game Used SIGnificance-SKO
06Ultra Uniformity-UKO
06Ultra Uniformity Patches-UPKO
06Ultra Uniformity Autographed Jerseys-UAKO
06Upper Deck-347
Exclusives Parallel-347
High Gloss Parallel-347
Generations Duals-G2JK
Generations Triples-G3KJK
Generations Patches Dual-G2PJK
Generations Patches Triple-G3PKJK
Masterpieces-347
Shootout Artists-SA7
06Upper Deck MVP-144
Gold Script-144
Super Script-144
Jerseys-OJKR
06Upper Deck Ovation-171
06Upper Deck Trilogy Combo Clearcut Autographs-C2KK
06Upper Deck Trilogy Ice Scripts-ISMK
06Upper Deck Victory-101
06Upper Deck Victory Black-101
06Upper Deck Victory Gold-101
06Upper Deck Victory Next In Line-NL28
06Wild Crime Prevention-7
06Wild Postcards-7
07Upper Deck Ovation-78
07Upper Deck Victory-141
Black-141
Gold-141

Koivu, Saku
92Upper Deck-617
92Finnish Jyvas-Hyva Stickers-177
93Parkhurst-521
Emerald Ice-521
93Upper Deck-569
93Finnish Jyvas-Hyva Stickers-323
93Finnish SISU-41
93Finnish SISU-389
93Finnish SISU Autographs-41
93Classic-40
93Classic Four-Sport *-202
Gold-202
94Finnish SISU-211
94Finnish SISU-NNO2
94Finnish SISU Fire On Ice-11
94Finnish SISU Junior-1
94Finnish SISU Specials-10
94Finnish Jaa Kiekko-27
94Classic-95
Gold-95
Tri-Cards-T34
Pro Prospects Ice Ambassadors-IA15
95Bashan Super Stickers-65
95Be A Player-174
Signatures-S174
Signatures Die Cuts-S174
Lethal Lines-LL5
95Bowman-148
All-Foil-148
Bowman's Best-BB17
Bowman's Best Refractors-BB17
95Canadiens Postcards-8
95Canadiens Sheets-4
95Collector's Choice-397
95Donruss-283
Rated Rookies-1
95Donruss Elite-67
Die Cut Stars-67
Die Cut Uncut-67
Rookies-8
95Emotion generatioNext-7
95Finest-85
Refractors-85
95Imperial Stickers-65
95Leaf Limited-118
Rookie Phenoms-9
95McDonald's Pinnacle-MCD-39
95Metal-180
International Steel-10
Winners-2
95NHL Cool Trade-13
95NHL Cool Trade-RP13
95Parkhurst International-263
95Parkhurst International-505
95Parkhurst International-NNO4
95Parkhurst International-NNO6
Emerald Ice-263
Emerald Ice-505
Crown Collection Silver Series 1-15
Crown Collection Gold Series 1-15
Parkie's Trophy Picks-PP39
95Playoff One on One-164
95Select Certified-117
Mirror Gold-117
Future-5
95SkyBox Impact-206
95SP-73
95Stadium Club-203
Members Only Master Set-203
95Summit-186
Artist's Proofs-186
Ice-186
95Topps-306
OPC Inserts-306
SuperSkills Super Rookies-SR11
95Ultra-344
Extra Attackers-12
95Upper Deck-259
Electric Ice-259
Electric Ice Gold-259
Predictor Hobby-H22
Predictor Hobby Exchange-H22
95Zenith-144
Rookie Roll Call-1
95Finnish Beckett Ad Cards-1
95Finnish Jaa Kiekko Lehti Ad Cards-3
95Finnish SISU-165
95Finnish SISU-199
95Finnish SISU-400
95Finnish SISU-NNOA
95Finnish SISU-NNOB
95Finnish SISU-NNO
95Finnish SISU-NNO
Gold Cards-15
95Finnish SISU Limited-6
95Finnish SISU Specials-3
95Finnish Karjala World Champ Labels-7
95Finnish Kellogg's-5
95Finnish Semic World Championships-11
95Finnish Semic World Championships-205
95Finnish Semic World Championships-219
95Finnish Semic World Championships-220
95Finnish Semic World Championships-221
95Finnish Semic World Championships-222
95Finnish Semic World Championships-223
95Finnish Semic World Championships-224
95Swedish Globe World Championships-139
95Swedish World Championships Stickers-174
96Be A Player Biscuit In The Basket-22

96Black Diamond-178
Gold-178
Run for the Cup-RC2
96Canadiens Postcards-14
96Canadiens Sheets-9
96Collector's Choice-134
96Collector's Choice-321
MVP-UD38
MVP Gold-UD38
Crash the Game-C15A
Crash the Game-C15B
Crash the Game-C15C
Crash the Game Gold-C15A
Crash the Game Gold-C15B
Crash the Game Gold-C15C
Crash the Game Exchange-CR15
Crash the Game Exchange Gold-CR15
96Collector's Choice Blow-Ups Bi-Way-4
96Donruss Dominators-10
96Donruss Hit List-19
96Donruss Rated Rookies-6
96Donruss Canadian Ice-40
Gold Press Proofs-40
Red Press Proofs-40
96Donruss Elite-80
Die Cut Stars-80
Aspirations-5
96Duracell L'Equipe Beliveau-JB10
96Flair-48
Blue Ice-48
Hot Numbers-6
96Fleer-54
96Fleer-136
Rookie Sensations-7
96Fleer Picks-76
Jagged Edge-7
96Kraft Upper Deck-5
96Kraft Upper Deck-66
96Leaf-204
Press Proofs-204
96Leaf Leather And Laces Promos-P20
96Leaf Leather And Laces-20
96Leaf Sweaters Away-15
96Leaf Sweaters Home-15
96Leaf Limited-10
Gold-10
96Leaf Preferred-45
Press Proofs-45
Steel-5
Steel Gold-5
96Maggers-49
96McDonald's Pinnacle-5
96Metal Universe-80
96Pinnacle-202
Artist's Proofs-202
Foil-202
Premium Stock-202
Rink Collection-202
Team Pinnacle-10
96Pinnacle Mint-9
Bronze-9
Gold-9
Silver-9
Coins Brass-9
Coins Solid Gold-9
Coins Gold Plated-9
Coins Nickel-9
Coins Silver-9
96Playoff One on One-388
96Score Samples-238
96Score-238
Artist's Proofs-238
Dealer's Choice Artist's Proofs-238
Special Artist's Proofs-238
Check It-11
Golden Blades-238
96Select Certified-64
Artist's Proofs-64
Blue-64
Mirror Blue-64
Mirror Gold-64
Mirror Red-64
Red-64
Cornerstones-8
96SkyBox Impact-62
96SkyBox Impact-169
NHL on Fox-13
96SP-79
Clearcut Winner-CW2
Holoview Collection-HC15
96SPx-21
96SPx-GF1
Gold-21
96Stadium Club Members Only-46
96Summit-152
Artist's Proofs-152
Ice-152
Metal-152
Premium Stock-152
High Voltage-14
High Voltage Mirage-14
96Team Out-26
96Topps Picks Rookie Stars-RS5
96Topps Picks Rookie Stars OPC-RS5
96Ultra-87
Gold Medallion-87
96Upper Deck-82
Generation Next-X16
Hart Hopefuls Bronze-HH5
Hart Hopefuls Gold-HH5
Hart Hopefuls Silver-HH5
Lord Stanley's Heroes Finals-LS20
Lord Stanley's Heroes Quarterfinals-LS20
Lord Stanley's Heroes Semifinals-LS20
Superstar Showdown-SS14B
96Upper Deck Ice-89
Parallel-89
Stanley Cup Foundation-S4
Stanley Cup Foundation Dynasty-S4
96Zenith-58
Artist's Proofs-58
Assailants-5
96Swedish Semic Wien-11
96Swedish Semic Wien-37
96Swedish Semic Wien-237
96Swedish Semic Wien-238
96Swedish Semic Wien-239
96Swedish Semic Wien-240
96Swedish Semic Wien-NNO
All-Stars-AS5
97Be A Player-3
97Be A Player-P3
Autographs-3
Autographs Die-Cuts-3
Autographs Prismatic Die-Cuts-3
One Timers-14
97Beehive-13
Golden Portraits-13
Team-13
Team Gold-13
97Black Diamond-46
Double Diamond-46
Triple Diamond-46
Quadruple Diamond-46
97Canadiens Postcards-10
97Collector's Choice-129
Crash the Game-C11A
Crash the Game-C11B
Crash the Game-C11C
Crash the Game Exchange-CR11
Star Quest-SQ47
Stick'Ums-S5
97Crown Royale-69
Emerald Green-69
Ice Blue-69
Silver-69
Blades of Steel Die-Cuts-12
Lamplighters Cel-Fusion Die-Cuts-10
97Donruss-53
Press Proofs Silver-53
Press Proofs Gold-53
97Donruss Canadian Ice-19
Dominion Series-19
Provincial Series-19
97Donruss Elite-20
Aspirations-20
Status-20
97Donruss Limited-9
97Donruss Limited-34
97Donruss Limited-165
Exposure-9
Exposure-34
Fabric of the Game-8
97Donruss Preferred-11
Cut to the Chase-11
97Donruss Priority-14
97Donruss Priority-210
Stamp of Approval-14
Stamp of Approval-210
Direct Deposit-21
Postcards-27
Postcards Opening Day Issues-27
Stamps-27
Stamps Bronze-27
Stamps Gold-27
Stamps Silver-27
97Esso Olympic Hockey Heroes-48
97Esso Olympic Hockey Heroes French-48
97Gatorade Stickers-2
97Jell-O Juniors To Pros-10
97Katch-75
Gold-75
Silver-75
97Kraft-11
97Kraft 3-D World's Best-4
97Leaf-19
Fractal Matrix-19
Fractal Matrix Die Cuts-19
Banner Season-15
97Leaf International-19
Universal Ice-19
97McDonald's Upper Deck-4
Game Film-8
97NHL Aces Playing Cards-49
97Pacific-272
Copper-272
Emerald Green-272
Ice Blue-272
Red-272
Silver-272
97Pacific Dynagon-63
Copper-63
Dark Grey-63
Emerald Green-63
Ice Blue-63
Red-63
Silver-63
Tandems-14
97Pacific Invincible-71
Copper-71
Emerald Green-71
Ice Blue-71
Red-71
Silver-71
Feature Performers-18
Off The Glass-11
97Pacific Omega-118
Copper-118
Dark Gray-118
Emerald Green-118
Gold-118
Gold-247
Ice Blue-118
Game Face-10
Stick Handle Laser Cuts-10
97Panini Stickers-28
97Paramount-95
Copper-95
Dark Grey-95
Emerald Green-95
Ice Blue-95
Red-95
Silver-95
Photoengravings-12
97Pinnacle-26
Artist's Proofs-26
Rink Collection-26
Epix Game Emerald-10
Epix Game Orange-10
Epix Game Purple-10
Epix Moment Emerald-10
Epix Moment Orange-10
Epix Moment Purple-10
Epix Play Emerald-10
Epix Play Orange-10
Epix Play Purple-10
Epix Season Emerald-10
Epix Season Orange-10
Epix Season Purple-10
Press Plates Back Black-26
Press Plates Back Cyan-26
Press Plates Back Magenta-26
Press Plates Back Yellow-26
Press Plates Front Black-26
Press Plates Front Cyan-26
Press Plates Front Magenta-26
Press Plates Front Yellow-26
Team Pinnacle-7
Team Mirror-7
Team Parallel-7
Team Parallel Mirror-7
97Pinnacle Certified-44
Red-44
Mirror Blue-44
Mirror Gold-44
Mirror Red-44
Team-18
Gold Team Promo-18
Gold Team-18
97Pinnacle Inside-13
Coach's Collection-13
Executive Collection-13
Track-16
Cans-3
Cans Gold-3
97Pinnacle Mint-15
Bronze-15
Gold Team-15
Silver Team-15
Coins Brass-15
Coins Brass Proofs-15
Coins Gold Plated-15
Coins Gold Plated Proofs-15
Coins Nickel Silver-15
Coins Nickel Silver Proofs-15
Coins Solid Gold-15
Coins Solid Silver-15
97Pinnacle Power Pack Blow-Ups-10
97Pinnacle Tot Cert Platinum Blue-44
97Pinnacle Tot Certi Platinum Gold-44
97Pinnacle Totally Certified Platinum Red-44
97Pinnacle Tot Cert Mirror Platinum Gold-44
97Post Pinnacle-18
97Revolution-71
Copper-71
Emerald-71
Ice Blue-71
Silver-71
1998 All-Star Game Die-Cuts-12
Team Checklist Laser Cuts-13
97Score-94
Artist's Proofs-94
Golden Blades-94
97Score Canadiens-7
Platinum-7
Premier-7
97SP Authentic-80
Icons-I31
Icons Die-Cuts-I31
Icons Embossed-I31
97SPx-24
Bronze-24
Gold-24
Silver-24
Steel-24
Grand Finale-24
97Studio-19
Press Proofs Silver-19
Press Proofs Gold-19
Hard Hats-15
Portraits-19
97Upper Deck-293
Game Jerseys-GJ9
Sixth Sense Masters-SS15
Sixth Sense Wizards-SS15
Smooth Grooves-SG18
Three Star Selects-8B
97Upper Deck Ice-78
Parallel-78
Champions-IC4
Champions 2 Die Cuts-IC4
Lethal Lines-L9B
Lethal Lines 2-L9B
Power Shift-78
97Zenith-26
Z-Gold-26
Z-Silver-26
97Zenith 5 x 7-37
Gold Impulse-37
Silver Impulse-37
97Zenith Chasing The Cup-13
98Aurora-94
Championship Fever-24
Championship Fever Copper-24
Championship Fever Ice Blue-24
Championship Fever Red-24
Championship Fever Silver-24
98Be A Player-218
Press Release-218
98BAP Gold-218
98BAP Autographs-218
98BAP Autographs Gold-218
98Black Diamond-46
Double Diamond-46
Triple Diamond-46
Quadruple Diamond-46
Myriad-M22
Myriad 2-M22
98Bowman's Best-44
Refractors-44
Atomic Refractors-44
98Canadiens Team Issue-9
98Crown Royale-70
Limited Series-70
Master Performers-12
Pillars of the Game-15
Pivotal Players-13
98Donruss Elite Promos-3
98Finest-45
No Protectors-45
No Protectors Refractors-45
Refractors-45
Centurion-C4
Centurion Refractors-C4
98Katch-75
98McDonald's Upper Deck-4
98OPC Chrome-76
Refractors-76
98Pacific-252
Ice Blue-252
Red-252
Dynagon Ice Inserts-11
Titanium Ice-11
Gold Crown Die-Cuts-17
Team Checklists-13
98Pacific Dynagon Ice-96
Blue-96
Red-96
Forward Thinking-12
Team Checklists-13
98Pacific Omega-123
Red-123
Opening Day Issue-123
Face to Face-7
Online-18
98Panini Photocards-41
98Panini Photocards-103
98Panini Stickers-32
98Paramount-113
Copper-113
Emerald Green-113
Holo-Electric-113
Ice Blue-113
Silver-113
Special Delivery Die-Cuts-10
Team Checklists Die-Cuts-13
98Revolution-74
Ice Shadow-74
Red-74
Showstoppers-20
98SP Authentic-41
Power Shift-41
98SPx Finite-115
Radiance-115
Spectrum-115
98SPx Top Prospects-33
Radiance-33
Spectrum-33
Highlight Heroes-H16
Lasting Impressions-L22
98Topps-76
O-Pee-Chee-76
Ice Age 2000-I9
Mystery Finest Bronze-M18
Mystery Finest Bronze Refractors-M18
Mystery Finest Gold-M18
Mystery Finest Gold Refractors-M18
Mystery Finest Silver-M18
Mystery Finest Silver Refractors-M18
98Topps Gold Label Class 1-17
Black-17
Black One of One-17
One of One-17
Red-17
Red One of One-17
98Topps Gold Label Class 2-17
98Topps Gold Label Class 2 Black-17
98Topps Gold Label Class 2 Black 1 of 1-17
98Topps Gold Label Class 2 One of One-17
98Topps Gold Label Class 2 Red-17
98Topps Gold Label Class 2 Red One of One-17
98Topps Gold Label Class 3-17
98Topps Gold Label Class 3 Black-17
98Topps Gold Label Class 3 Black 1 of 1-17
98Topps Gold Label Class 3 One of One-17
98Topps Gold Label Class 3 Red-17
98Topps Gold Label Class 3 Red One of One-17
98UD Choice-105
Mini Bobbing Head-BH28
98UD Choice Preview-105
98UD Choice Prime Choice Reserve-105
98UD Choice Reserve-105
98UD Choice StarQuest Blue-SQ8
98UD Choice StarQuest Gold-SQ8
98UD Choice StarQuest Green-SQ8
98UD Choice StarQuest Red-SQ8
98UD3-43
98UD3-103
98UD3-163
Die-Cuts-43
Die-Cuts-103
Die-Cuts-163
98Upper Deck-28
98Upper Deck-290
Exclusives-28
Exclusives-290
Exclusives 1 of 1-28
Exclusives 1 of 1-290
Frozen In Time-FT12
Frozen In Time Quantum 1-FT12
Frozen In Time Quantum 2-FT12
Frozen In Time Quantum 3-FT12
Lord Stanley's Heroes-LS18
Lord Stanley's Heroes Quantum 1-LS18
Lord Stanley's Heroes Quantum 2-LS18
Lord Stanley's Heroes Quantum 3-LS18
Profiles-P19
Profiles Quantum 1-P19
Profiles Quantum 2-P19
Profiles Quantum 3-P19
Gold Reserve-28
Gold Reserve-290
98Upper Deck MVP-104
Gold Script-104
Silver Script-104
Super Script-104
98Finnish Kerailysarja 90's Top 12-11
98Finnish Kerailysarja Dream Team-6
98Slovakian Eurotel-8
99Aurora-75
Striped-75
Premiere Date-75
Premiere Date Striped-75
99BAP Memorabilia-185
Gold-185
Silver-185
Jersey Cards-J26
Jersey Emblems-E26
Jersey Numbers-I26
Jersey and Stick Cards-S26
99BAP Millennium Prototypes-5
99BAP Millennium-128
Emerald-128
Ruby-128
Sapphire-128
Signatures-128
Signatures Gold-128
Jerseys-J4
Jersey and Stick Cards-JS4
Jersey Emblems-E4
Jersey Numbers-N4
99Black Diamond-48
Diamond Cut-48
Final Cut-48
99Crown Royale-70
Limited Series-70
Premiere Date-70
International Glory-13
International Glory Parallel-13
99Kraft Dinner-5
99McDonald's Upper Deck-MCD14
99McDonald's Upper Deck-MCD14R
Signatures-SK
99O-Pee-Chee-90
99O-Pee-Chee Chrome-90
99O-Pee-Chee Chrome Refractors-90
99O-Pee-Chee Top of the World-TW2
99Oscar Mayer Lunchables-7
99Pacific-205
Copper-205
Emerald Green-205
Gold-205
Ice Blue-205
Premiere Date-205
Red-205
Team Leaders-14
99Pacific Dynagon Ice-102
Blue-102
Copper-102
Gold-102
Premiere Date-102
99Pacific Omega-119
Copper-119
Gold-119
Ice Blue-119
Premiere Date-119
99Pacific Prism-72
Holographic Blue-72
Holographic Gold-72
Holographic Mirror-72
Holographic Purple-72
Premiere Date-72
99Panini Stickers-65
99Paramount-117
Copper-117
Emerald-117
Gold-117
Holographic Emerald-117
Holographic Gold-117
Holographic Silver-117
Ice Blue-117
Premiere Date-117
Red-117
Silver-117
Personal Best-20
Toronto Fall Expo '99-117
99Revolution-75
Premiere Date-75
Red-75
Shadow Series-75
Copper-75
Gold-75
CSC Silver-75
99SP Authentic-43
99SPx-78
Radiance-78
Spectrum-78
99Stadium Club-17
First Day Issue-17
One of a Kind-17
Printing Plates Black-17
Printing Plates Cyan-17
Printing Plates Magenta-17
Printing Plates Yellow-17
Chrome-16
Chrome Refractors-16
99Topps/OPC-90
Top of the World-TW2
99Topps/OPC Chrome-90
Refractors-90
99Topps Gold Label Class 1-7
Black-7
Black One of One-7
One of One-7
Red-7
Red One of One-7
99Topps Gold Label Class 2-7
99Topps Gold Label Class 2 Black-7
99Topps Gold Label Class 2 Black 1 of 1-7
99Topps Gold Label Class 2 One of One-7
99Topps Gold Label Class 2 Red-7
99Topps Gold Label Class 2 Red One of One-7
99Topps Gold Label Class 3-7
99Topps Gold Label Class 3 Black-7
99Topps Gold Label Class 3 Black 1 of 1-7
99Topps Gold Label Class 3 One of One-7
99Topps Gold Label Class 3 Red-7
99Topps Gold Label Class 3 Red One of One-7
99Topps Premier Plus-60
Parallel-60
99Topps Premiere Plus Promos-PP4
99Ultimate Victory-44
1/1-44
Parallel-44
Parallel 100-44
99Upper Deck-67
99Upper Deck-157
Exclusives-67
Exclusives-157
Exclusives 1 of 1-67
Exclusives 1 of 1-157
99Upper Deck Gold Reserve-67
99Upper Deck Gold Reserve-157
99Upper Deck MVP-100
Gold Script-100
Silver Script-100
Super Script-100
99Upper Deck MVP SC Edition-91
Gold Script-91
Silver Script-91
Super Script-91
99Upper Deck Retro-41
Gold-41
Platinum-41
99Upper Deck Victory-142
99Upper Deck Victory-143
99Wayne Gretzky Hockey-85
99Finnish Cardset-193
Aces High-H-K
Blazing Patriots-5
Most Wanted-6
00SLU Hockey-140
00Aurora-72
Premiere Date-72
Dual Game-Worn Jerseys-1
Game-Worn Jerseys-5
Game-Worn Jersey Patches-5
00BAP Memorabilia-151
Emerald-151
Ruby-151
Sapphire-151
Promos-151
00BAP Mem Chicago Sportsfest Copper-151
00BAP Memorabilia Chicago Sportsfest Blue-151
00BAP Memorabilia Chicago Sportsfest Gold-151
00BAP Memorabilia Chicago Sportsfest Ruby-151
00BAP Memorabilia Chicago Sun-Times Ruby-151
00BAP Memorabilia Chicago Sun-Times Gold-151
00BAP Mem Chicago Sun-Times Sapphire-151
00BAP Mem Toronto Fall Expo Copper-151
00BAP Memorabilia Toronto Fall Expo Gold-151
00BAP Memorabilia Toronto Fall Expo Ruby-151
00BAP Parkhurst 2000-P124
00BAP Signature Series-91
Emerald-91
Ruby-91
Sapphire-91
Autographs-163
Autographs Gold-163
Franchise Players-F16
Jersey Cards-J4
Jersey and Stick Cards-GSJ4
Jersey Cards Autographs-J4
Jersey Emblems-E4
Jersey Numbers-IN4
00BAP Ultimate Memorabilia Autographs-4
Gold-4
00BAP Ultimate Memorabilia Captain's C-C4
00BAP Ultimate Mem Game-Used Jerseys-GJ48
00BAP Ultimate Mem Game-Used Sticks-GS48
00Black Diamond-31
Gold-31
00Canadiens Postcards-27
00Crown Royale-55
Ice Blue-55
Limited Series-55
Premiere Date-55
Red-55
00McDonald's Pacific-19
Blue-19
Checklists-4
00O-Pee-Chee-89
00O-Pee-Chee Parallel-89
00Pacific-209
00Pacific-439
Copper-209
Copper-439
Gold-209
Gold-439
Ice Blue-209
Ice Blue-439
Premiere Date-209
Premiere Date-439
00Panini Stickers-39
00Paramount-126
Copper-126
Gold-126
Holo-Gold-126
Holo-Silver-126
Ice Blue-126
Premiere Date-126
Freeze Frame-20
Jersey and Patches-6
00Private Stock-51
Gold-51
Premiere Date-51
Retail-51
Silver-51
Game Gear-57
Game Gear Patches-57
PS-2001 Action-28
PS-2001 Stars-16
Reserve-12
00Revolution-76
Blue-76
Premiere Date-76
Red-76
Game-Worn Jerseys-6
Game-Worn Jersey Patches-6
HD NHL-19
00SPx-35
Spectrum-35
00Stadium Club-188
00Titanium-47
Blue-47
Gold-47
Premiere Date-47
Red-47
Retail-47
00Topps/OPC-89
Parallel-89
00Topps Chrome-71
OPC Refractors-71
Refractors-71
00Topps Gold Label Class 1-48
Gold-48
00Topps Gold Label Class 2-48
00Topps Gold Label Class 2 Gold-48
00Topps Gold Label Class 3-48
00Topps Gold Label Class 3 Gold-48
00Topps Heritage-39
Chrome Parallel-39
Arena Relics-OSA-SK
Original Six Relics-OSJ-SK
Original Six Relics-OSJ
00Topps Premier Plus-83
Blue Ice-83
00Topps Stars-69
Blue-69
00UD Heroes-62
00UD Reserve-46
00Upper Deck-319
Exclusives Tier 1-319
Exclusives Tier 2-319
00Upper Deck Legends-63
Legendary Collection Bronze-63
Legendary Collection Gold-63
Legendary Collection Silver-63
00Upper Deck MVP-94
First Stars-94
Second Stars-94
Third Stars-94
00Upper Deck Victory-117
00Upper Deck Victory-118
00Upper Deck Victory-307
00Upper Deck Vintage-186
00Upper Deck Vintage-196
00Upper Deck Vintage-197
National Heroes-NH13
00Vanguard-51
Holographic Gold-51
Holographic Purple-51
Pacific Proofs-51
00Czech Stadion-84
00Finnish Cardset-356
00Finnish Cardset-NNO
01Atomic-51
Blue-51
Gold-51
Premiere Date-51
Red-51
Core Players-9
Jerseys-33
Patches-33
Power Play-19
01BAP Memorabilia-286
Emerald-286
Ruby-286
Sapphire-286
He Shoots-He Scores Points-5
He Shoots-He Scores Prizes-36
01BAP Signature Series Certified 100-C40
01BAP Signature Series Certified 50-C40
01BAP Signature Series Certified 1 of 1's-C40
01BAP Sig Series He Shoots/Scores Prizes-25
01BAP Signature Series Jerseys-GJ-32
01BAP Sig Series Jersey and Stick Cards-GSJ-32
01BAP Ultimate Memorabilia Les Canadiens-9
01BAP Update Passing the Torch-PTT4
01Bowman YoungStars-95
Gold-95
Ice Cubed-95
01Canadiens Postcards-13
01Crown Royale Jewels of the Crown-17
01Crown Royale Triple Threads-12
01McDonald's Pacific-21
Jersey Patches Silver-12
Jersey Patches Gold-12
01O-Pee-Chee-66
01O-Pee-Chee Heritage Parallel-66
01O-Pee-Chee Heritage Parallel Limited-66
01O-Pee-Chee Premier Parallel-66
01Pacific-209
Extreme LTD-209
Hobby LTD-209
Premiere Date-209
Retail LTD-209
Adrenaline Jerseys-22
01Pacific Arena Exclusives-209
01Pacific Heads-Up-50
Blue-50
Premiere Date-50
Red-50
Silver-50
01Parkhurst-143
He Shoots-He Scores Prizes-19
Jerseys-PJ37
01Private Stock Game Gear-54
01Private Stock Game Gear Patches-54
01SP Game Used Authentic Fabric-AFSK
01SP Game Used Authentic Fabric Gold-AFSK
01SPx-34
01Stadium Club-12
Award Winners-12
Master Photos-12
Gallery-G35
Gallery Gold-G35
NHL Passport-NHLP7
Souvenirs-SK
Souvenirs-JHSK
01Topps-66
Heritage Parallel-66
Heritage Parallel Limited-66
OPC Parallel-66
Captain's Cloth-CC2
01Topps Chrome-66
Refractors-66
Black Border Refractors-66
01Topps Heritage-21
Refractors-21
Captain's Cloth-CCSK
01Topps Reserve-36
Emblems-SK
Jerseys-SK
Name Plates-SK
Numbers-SK
Patches-SK
01UD Honor Roll Pucks-P-SK
01UD Honor Roll Pucks Gold-P-SK
01UD Mask Collection Double Patches-DPSK
01UD Mask Collection Jerseys-J-SK
01UD Mask Collection Jersey and Patch-JPSK
01UD Premier Collection Jerseys-BSK
01UD Premier Collection Jerseys Black-B-SK
01UD Top Shelf-23
01Upper Deck-90
Exclusives-90
Pride of a Nation-PNSK
Pride of a Nation-DPSK
01Upper Deck MVP-97
01Upper Deck Victory-185
Gold-185
01Upper Deck Vintage-131
01Upper Deck Vintage-138
01Upper Deck Vintage-139
01Vanguard Memorabilia-15
01Czech Stadion-244
02McFarlane Hockey Toys-R-Us-20
02McFarlane Hockey-220
02Atomic-55
Blue-55
Gold-55
Red-55
Cold Fusion-15
Hobby Parallel-55
02BAP All-Star Edition-45
Jerseys-45
Jerseys Gold-45
Jerseys Silver-45
02BAP First Edition-92
He Shoots-He Score Points-3
He Shoots-He Score Prizes-13
Jerseys-92
02BAP Memorabilia-181
Emerald-181
Ruby-181
Sapphire-181
All-Star Jerseys-ASJ-27
NHL All-Star Game-181
NHL All-Star Game Blue-181
NHL All-Star Game Green-181
NHL All-Star Game Red-181
Stanley Cup Playoffs-SC-23
Teammates-TM-12
02BAP Memorabilia Toronto Fall Expo-181
02BAP Signature Series-130
Autographs-130
Autograph Buybacks 1998-218
Autograph Buybacks 1999-128
Autograph Buybacks 2000-163
Autographs Gold-130
Jerseys-SGJ49
Jersey Autographs-SGJ49
Team Quads-TQ6
02BAP Ultimate Memorabilia Autographs-25
02BAP Ultimate Mem Autographs Gold-25
02BAP Ultimate Memorabilia Captains-4
02BAP Ultimate Memorabilia Dynamic Duos-8
02BAP Ultimate Memorabilia Emblems-27
02BAP Ultimate Memorabilia Jerseys-33
02BAP Ultimate Mem Jersey and Stick-25
02BAP Ultimate Memorabilia Numbers-13
02BAP Ultimate Memorabilia Retro Trophies-4
02Bowman YoungStars-13
Gold-13
Silver-13
02Canadiens Postcards-2
02Crown Royale-51
Blue-51
Red-51
Retail-51
Lords of the Rink-13
02eTopps-14
02ITG Used-40
02ITG Used-140
International Experience-IE14
International Experience Gold-IE14
Jerseys-GUJ49
Jersey Autographs-GUJ49
Jerseys Gold-GUJ49
Emblems-E36
Jersey and Stick-SJ49
Jersey and Stick Gold-SJ49
Teammates-T6
Teammates Gold-T6
02McDonald's Pacific-21
Cup Contenders Die-Cuts-4
02NHL Power Play Stickers-47
02O-Pee-Chee-27
02O-Pee-Chee Jumbos-13
02O-Pee-Chee Premier Blue Parallel-27
02O-Pee-Chee Premier Red Parallel-27
02O-Pee-Chee Factory Set-27
02O-Pee-Chee Factory Set Hometown Heroes-HHC8
02Pacific-198
Blue-198
Red-198
Impact Zone-7
02Pacific Calder-42
Silver-42
02Pacific Complete-9
Red-9
02Pacific Exclusive-91
Maximum Overdrive-11
02Pacific Heads-Up-64
Blue-64
Purple-64
Red-64
Bobble Heads-6
Quad Jerseys-15
Quad Jerseys Gold-15
02Pacific Quest for the Cup-50
Gold-50
02Parkhurst-48
Bronze-48
Gold-48
Silver-48
Jerseys-GJ7
Stick and Jerseys-SJ7
Teammates-TT7
02Parkhurst Retro-181
Minis-181
Jerseys-RJ35
Memorabilia-RM25
02Private Stock Reserve-53
Blue-53
Red-53
Retail-53
02SP Authentic-48
Beckett Promos-48
Super Premiums-DPTK
02SP Game Used-26
Authentic Fabrics-AFSK
Authentic Fabrics-CFTK
Authentic Fabrics Gold-AFSK
Authentic Fabrics Gold-CFTK
Authentic Fabrics Rainbow-AFSK
Authentic Fabrics Rainbow-CFTK
First Rounder Patches-SK
Piece of History-PHKU
Piece of History-PHSK
Piece of History Gold-PHKU
Piece of History Gold-PHSK
Piece of History Rainbow-PHKU
Piece of History Rainbow-PHSK
02SPx-41
Spectrum Gold-41
Spectrum Silver-41
Xtreme Talents-SK
Xtreme Talents Gold-SK
Xtreme Talents Silver-SK
02Stadium Club-41
Silver Decoy Cards-41
Proofs-41
Passport-1
02Titanium-55
Blue-55
Red-55
Retail-55
02Topps-27
OPC Blue Parallel-27
OPC Red Parallel-27
Captain's Cloth-CC5
Captain's Cloth-CC7
Captain's Cloth-CC14
Topps/OPC Hometown Heroes-HHC8
Factory Set-27
02Topps Chrome-27
Black Border Refractors-27
Refractors-27
02Topps Heritage-36
Chrome Parallel-36
02Topps Total-395
Award Winners-AW9
02UD Artistic Impressions-47
Gold-47
02UD Artistic Impressions Beckett Promos-47
02UD Artistic Impressions Common Ground-CG8
02UD Artistic Impress Common Ground Gold-CG8
02UD Artistic Impressions Retrospectives-R47
02UD Artistic Impressions Retrospect Gold-R47
02UD Artistic Impress Retrospect Silver-R47
02UD Honor Roll-39
02UD Honor Roll-86
Grade A Jerseys-GASK
Students of the Game-SG17
Team Warriors-TW8
02UD Mask Collection-47
02UD Mask Collection Beckett Promos-47
02UD Mask Collection Instant Offense-IOSK
02UD Piece of History-49
02UD Premier Collection-30
Jerseys Bronze-SK
Jerseys Bronze-TK
Jerseys Gold-SK
Jerseys Gold-TK
Jerseys Silver-SK
Jerseys Silver-TK
Patches-PSK
02UD Top Shelf-46
Shooting Stars-SHSK
Sweet Sweaters-SWSK
02Upper Deck-96
Exclusives-96
Blow-Ups-C22
Fan Favorites-SK
Letters of Note-LNSK
Letters of Note Gold-LNSK
Patch Card Logo-SK
Patchwork-PWSK
Playbooks Series II-KT
02Upper Deck Classic Portraits-51
Headliners-TK
Headliners Limited-TK
02Upper Deck MVP-99
Gold-99
Classics-99
Golden Classics-99
02Upper Deck Rookie Update-52
Jerseys-DSK
Jerseys Gold-DSK
02Upper Deck Victory-110
Bronze-110
Gold-110
Silver-110
02Upper Deck Vintage-132
02Upper Deck Vintage-276
Green Backs-132
Tall Boys-T36
Tall Boys Gold-T36
02Vanguard-55
LTD-55
02Finnish Cardset-198
02Finnish Cardset Dynamic Duos-1
02Finnish Cardset Solid Gold-5
03McFarlane Hockey 3-Inch Duals-60
03BAP Memorabilia-80
Emerald-80
Gold-80
Ruby-80
Sapphire-80
Jerseys-GJ-22
03BAP Ultimate Memorabilia Autographs-50
Gold-50
03BAP Ultimate Mem Auto Jerseys-50
03BAP Ultimate Mem Complete Jersey-20
03BAP Ultimate Mem Complete Jersey Gold-20
03BAP Ultimate Memorabilia Dynamic Duos-1

03BAP Ultimate Memorabilia Emblems-26
03BAP Ultimate Memorabilia Emblems Gold-26
03BAP Ultimate Memorabilia Jerseys-40
03BAP Ultimate Memorabilia Jerseys Gold-40
03BAP Ultimate Memorabilia Numbers-29
03BAP Ultimate Memorabilia Numbers Gold-29
03BAP Ultimate Memorabilia Triple Threads-18
03Beehive-107
Variations-107
Gold-107
Silver-107
Jerseys-JT28
03Black Diamond-91
Black-91
Green-91
Red-91
03Bowman-94
Gold-94
03Bowman Chrome-94
Refractors-94
Gold Refractors-94
Xfractors-94
03Canadiens Postcards-16
03Crown Royale-54
Blue-54
Retail-54
Global Conquest-3
Jerseys-13
Patches-13
03eTopps-26
03ITG Action-391
Homeboys-HB9
Jerseys-M162
03ITG Toronto Fall Expo Forever Rivals-FR1
03ITG Toronto Fall Expo Jerseys-FE4
03ITG Used Signature Series-58
Gold-58
Autographs-SK
Autographs Gold-SK
International Experience-17
International Experience Autographs-17
International Experience Autographs Gold-17
International Experience Emblems-17
International Experience Gold-17
Jersey and Stick-17
Jersey and Stick Gold-17
03ITG VIP Jerseys-28
03McDonald's Pacific-28
Patches Silver-14
Patches Gold-14
Patches and Sticks-14
Saturday Night Rivals-4
03NHL Sticker Collection-56
03O-Pee-Chee-210
03OPC Blue-210
03OPC Gold-210
03OPC Red-210
03Pacific-178
Blue-178
Red-178
Jerseys-20
Jerseys Gold-20
Main Attractions-8
03Pacific Calder-54
Silver-54
03Pacific Complete-287
Red-287
03Pacific Exhibit-174
Blue Backs-174
03Pacific Heads-Up-52
Hobby LTD-52
Retail LTD-52
03Pacific Invincible-50
Blue-50
Red-50
Retail-50
03Pacific Luxury Suite-38A
03Pacific Luxury Suite-38B
03Pacific Luxury Suite-38C
03Pacific Montreal International-1
03Pacific Prism-123
Blue-123
Patches-123
Red-123
Retail-123
03Pacific Quest for the Cup-55
Blue-55
03Pacific Supreme-51
Blue-51
Red-51
Retail-51
03Parkhurst Orig Six He Shoots/Scores-8
03Parkhurst Orig Six He Shoots/Scores-8A
03Parkhurst Original Six Montreal-18
03Parkhurst Original Six Montreal-71
Inserts-M15
Memorabilia-MM5
Memorabilia-MM13
Memorabilia-MM52
03Parkhurst Rookie Teammates Gold-RT20
03Parkhurst Rookie Teammates-RT20
03Private Stock Reserve-173
Blue-173
Patches-173
Red-173
Retail-173
03SP Authentic-48
Limited-48
Breakout Seasons-B30
Breakout Seasons Limited-B30
Foundations-F10
Foundations Limited-F10
Honors-H27
Honors Limited-H27
Sign of the Times-SK
Sign of the Times-TK
03SP Game Used-25
Gold-25
Authentic Fabrics-AFSK
Authentic Fabrics-DFKH
Authentic Fabrics-DFLK
Authentic Fabrics-DFTK
Authentic Fabrics-QKTHK
Authentic Fabrics Gold-AFSK
Authentic Fabrics Gold-DFKH
Authentic Fabrics Gold-DFLK
Authentic Fabrics Gold-DFTK
Authentic Fabrics Gold-QKTHK
Double Threads-DTKH
Team Threads-TTKTH
03SPx-51
03SPx-134
03SPx-182
Radiance-51
Radiance-134
Radiance-182
Spectrum-51
Spectrum-134
Spectrum-182
Signature Threads-ST-SK
VIP-VIP-KH
VIP Limited-VIP-KH
03Titanium-161
Hobby Jersey Number Parallels-161
Retail-161
03Topps-210
Blue-210
Gold-210
Red-210
Box Toppers-24
Topps/OPC Idols-II19
03Topps C55-111
Minis-111
Minis American Back-111
Minis American Back Red-111
Minis Bazooka Back-111
Minis Brooklyn Back-111
Minis Hat Trick Back-111
Minis O Canada Back-111
Minis O Canada Back Red-111
Minis Stanley Cup Back-111
Relics-TRSK
03Topps Pristine-52
Gold Refractor Die Cuts-52
Refractors-52
Jersey Portions-PPJ-SK
Jersey Portion Refractors-PPJ-SK
Patches-PP-SK
Patch Refractors-PP-SK
Press Plates Black-52
Press Plates Cyan-52
Press Plates Magenta-52
Press Plates Yellow-52
03UD Honor Roll-45
03UD Honor Roll-125
Signature Class-SC15
03UD Premier Collection-29
NHL Shields-SH-SK
Signatures-PS-SK
Signatures Gold-PS-SK
Teammates-PT-MC
Teammates Patches-PT-MC
03Upper Deck-99
All-Star Class-AS-15
Big Playmakers-BP-SK
BuyBacks-113
BuyBacks-114
BuyBacks-115
BuyBacks-116
BuyBacks-117
BuyBacks-118
BuyBacks-119
BuyBacks-120
BuyBacks-121
BuyBacks-122
Canadian Exclusives-99
HG-99
Jerseys-GJ-SK
Jersey Autographs-SJ-SK
03Upper Deck Classic Portraits-50
Classic Stitches-CS-SK
Hockey Royalty-KTH
03Upper Deck Ice-47
Gold-47
Authentics-IA-SK
03Upper Deck MVP-221
Gold Script-221
Silver Script-221
Canadian Exclusives-221
SportsNut-SN47
03Upper Deck Rookie Update-47
03Upper Deck Rookie Update-155
03Upper Deck Rookie Update-160
Skills-SKSK
Super Stars-SSSK
03Upper Deck Trilogy-50
Limited-50
03Upper Deck Victory-95
Bronze-95
Gold-95
Silver-95
Game Breakers-GB46
03Toronto Star-49
Foil-17
04Pacific-137
Blue-137
Red-137
04SP Authentic-48
04SP Authentic-120
Limited-120
Buybacks-175
Octographs-OS-CAP
Sign of the Times-ST-SK
Sign of the Times-TS-RKR
Sign of the Times-SS-FIN
04UD All-World-19
04UD All-World-118
Gold-19
Dual Autographs-AD-KK
Triple Autographs-AT-KHK
04Ultimate Collection Buybacks-85
04Ultimate Collection Buybacks-86
04Ultimate Collection Dual Logos-UL2-KT
04Ultimate Collection Jerseys-UGJ-SK
04Ultimate Collection Jerseys Gold-UGJ-SK
04Ultimate Collection Jersey Autographs-UGJA-SK
04Ultimate Collection Patches-UP-SK
04Ultimate Collection Patch Autographs-UPA-SK
04Ultimate Collection Signatures-US-SK
04Ultimate Collection Signature Logos-ULA-SK
04Ultimate Collection Signature Patches-SP-SK
04Upper Deck-91
1997 Game Jerseys-SK
Canadian Exclusives-91
Heritage Classic-CC-SK
HG Glossy Gold-91
HG Glossy Silver-91
Swatch of Six-SS-SK
World's Best-WB12
World Cup Tribute-SK
World Cup Tribute-OJSKTS
04Finnish Cardset-306
04Finnish Cardset Saku Koivu Golden Sigs-1
04Finnish Cardset Saku Koivu Golden Sigs-2
04Finnish Cardset Saku Koivu Golden Sigs-3
04Finnish Cardset Tribute to Koivu-1
04Finnish Cardset Tribute to Koivu-2
04Finnish Cardset Tribute to Koivu-3
04Swedish Pure Skills-141
Parallel-141
Professional Power-SK
05Be A Player-46
First Period-46
Second Period-46
Third Period-46
Overtime-46
Outtakes-OT27
05Beehive-51
05Beehive-194
Beige -46
Blue -46
Gold-46
Red -46
Matte-46
Matted Materials-MMSK
05Black Diamond-136
Emerald-136
Gold-136
Onyx-136
Ruby-136
Jerseys-J-SK
Jerseys Ruby-J-SK
Jersey Duals-DJ-SK
Jersey Triples-TJ-SK
Jersey Quads-QJ-SK
05Canadiens Team Issue-11
05Hot Prospects-52
En Fuego-52
Red Hot-52
White Hot-52
05McDonalds Upper Deck-10
Jerseys-MJ8
Patches-MP8
05Panini Stickers-70
05Parkhurst-249
05Parkhurst-515
05Parkhurst-686
Facsimile Auto Parallel-249
Facsimile Auto Parallel-515
Facsimile Auto Parallel-686
True Colors-TCMTL
True Colors-TCMTL
True Colors-TCMOBO
True Colors-TCMOBO
True Colors-TCTOMO
True Colors-TCTOMO
05SP Authentic-52
Limited-52
Exquisite Endorsements-EESK
Marks of Distinction-MDSK
Prestigious Pairings-PPGS
Sign of the Times Duals-DKP
Sign of the Times Quads-QTRRK
05SP Game Used-54
Autographs-54
Gold-54
Authentic Fabrics-AF-SK
Authentic Fabrics Dual Autographs-KT
Authentic Fabrics Gold-AF-SK
Authentic Patches Quad -TRRK
Authentic Fabrics Triple-KSK
Authentic Patches-AP-SK
Authentic Patches Dual-KT
Authentic Patches Dual Autographs-KT
Authentic Patches Triple-KSK
Auto Draft-AD-SK
Awesome Authentics-AA-SK
Game Gear-GG-SK
Game Gear Autographs-AG-SK
05SPx-43
Spectrum-43
Winning Combos-WC-HK
Winning Combos-WC-LK
Winning Combos-WC-RK
Winning Combos Autographs-AWC-LK
Winning Combos Autographs-AWC-MS
Winning Combos Gold-WC-HK
Winning Combos Gold-WC-LK
Winning Combos Gold-WC-RK
Winning Combos Spectrum-WC-HK
Winning Combos Spectrum-WC-LK
Winning Combos Spectrum-WC-RK
Winning Materials-WM-SK
Winning Materials Gold-WM-SK
Winning Materials Spectrum-WM-SK
Xcitement Superstars-XS-SK
Xcitement Superstars Gold-XS-SK
Xcitement Superstars Spectrum-XS-SK
05The Cup-53
Gold-53
Black Rainbow-53
Dual NHL Shields-DSKT
Dual NHL Shields-DSPK
Dual NHL Shields Autographs-ADSKT
Dual NHL Shields Autographs-ADSPK
Emblems of Endorsement-EESK
Hardware Heroes-HHSK
Honorable Numbers-HNSK
Limited Logos-LLSK
Masterpiece Pressplates-53
Masterpiece Pressplates Rookie Upd Auto-267
Noble Numbers-NNKA
Noble Numbers-NNPK
Noble Numbers Dual-DNNFI
Noble Numbers Dual-DNNKT
Patch Variation-P53
Patch Variation Autographs-AP53
Property of-POSK
Scripted Numbers Dual-DSNKJ
Scripted Swatches-SSSK
Signature Patches-SPSK
05UD Artifacts-54
05UD Artifacts-173
Blue-54
Blue-173
Gold-54
Gold-173
Green-54
Green-173
Pewter-54
Pewter-173
Red-54
Red-173
Auto Facts-AF-SK
Auto Facts Blue-AF-SK
Auto Facts Copper-AF-SK
Auto Facts Pewter-AF-SK
Auto Facts Silver-AF-SK
Gold Autographed-54
Gold Autographed-173
Remarkable Artifacts-RA-SK
Remarkable Artifacts Dual-RA-SK
Treasured Patches-TP-SK
Treasured Patches Autographed-TP-SK
Treasured Patches Dual-TPD-SK
Treasured Patches Dual Autographed-TPD-SK
Treasured Patches Pewter-TP-SK
Treasured Patches Silver-TP-SK
Treasured Swatches-TS-SK
Treasured Swatches Autographed-TS-SK
Treasured Swatches Blue-TS-SK
Treasured Swatches Copper-TS-SK
Treasured Swatches Dual-TSD-SK
Treasured Swatches Dual Autographed-TSD-SK
Treasured Swatches Dual Blue-TSD-SK
Treasured Swatches Dual Copper-TSD-SK
Treasured Swatches Dual Maroon-TSD-SK
Treasured Swatches Dual Pewter-TSD-SK
Treasured Swatches Dual Silver-TSD-SK
Treasured Swatches Maroon-TS-SK
Treasured Swatches Pewter-TS-SK
Treasured Swatches Silver-TS-SK
05Ultimate Collection-50
Gold-50
Endorsed Emblems-EESK
Jerseys-JSK
Jerseys Dual-DJKP
Jerseys Triple-TJKTP
Marquee Attractions-MA27
Marquee Attractions Signatures-SMA27
National Heroes Patches-NHPSK
Premium Swatches-PSSK
Ultimate Achievements-UASK
Ultimate Patches-PSK
Ultimate Patches Dual-DPKP
Ultimate Patches Triple-TPKTP
Ultimate Signatures-USSK
Ultimate Signatures Logos-SLSK
Ultimate Signatures Pairings-UPKP
05Ultra-104
Gold-104
Fresh Ink-FI-SK
Fresh Ink Blue-FI-SK
Ice-104
05Upper Deck-98
Big Playmakers-B-SK
HG Glossy-98
Hometown Heroes-HH7
Jerseys-J-SK
Majestic Materials-MMSK
NHL Generations-TLKR
NHL Generations-TSKJ
Notable Numbers-N-SK
Patches-P-SK
05Upper Deck Ice-50
Rainbow-50
Frozen Fabrics-FFSK
Frozen Fabrics Autographs-AFFSK
Frozen Fabrics Glass-FFSK
Frozen Fabrics Patches-FFPSK
Frozen Fabrics Patch Autographs-FAPSK
Signature Swatches-SSSK
05Upper Deck MVP-200
Gold-200
Platinum-200
05Upper Deck Rookie Update-50
05Upper Deck Rookie Update-267
05Upper Deck Trilogy-48
05Upper Deck Trilogy-116
Crystal-116
Crystal Autographs-116
Honorary Patches-HP-SK
Honorary Patch Scripts-HSP-SK
Honorary Swatches-HS-SK
Honorary Swatch Scripts-HSS-SK
Ice Scripts-IS-SK
05Upper Deck Toronto Fall Expo-98
05Upper Deck Victory-103
Black-103
Gold-103
Silver-103
Blow-Ups-BU20
Game Breakers-GB25
05Finnish Cardset -156
Finnish Cardset Magicmakers-16
06Be A Player-104
Autographs-104
Profiles-PP7
Profiles Autographs-PP7
Signatures-KO
Signatures 10-113
Signatures 25-113
Signatures Duals-DHK
Signatures Duals-DSK
Signatures Trios-TKRL
Signatures Foursomes-FSKJL
Up Close and Personal-UC51
Up Close and Personal Autographs-UC51
06Be A Player Portraits-58
Dual Signature Portraits-DSKK
Quadruple Signature Portraits-QKKJP
Sensational Six-SSSJM
Signature Portraits-SPSK
06Beehive-47
06Beehive-191
Blue-47
Gold-47
Matte-47
Red Facsimile Signatures-47
Wood-47
5 X 7 Black and White-47
Matted Materials-MMSK
Remarkable Matted Materials-MMSK
06Black Diamond-138
Black-138
Gold-138
Ruby-138
06Flair Showcase-53
06Flair Showcase-186
06Flair Showcase-239
06Flair Showcase-284
Parallel-53
Parallel-186
Parallel-239
Parallel-284
Hot Numbers-HN26
Hot Numbers Parallel-HN26
06Fleer-103
Oversized-103
Tiffany-103
Total O-012
06Gatorade-31
06Hot Prospects-51
Red Hot-51
White Hot-51
Hot Materials -HMSK
Hot Materials Red Hot-HMSK
Hot Materials White Hot-HMSK
06McDonald's Upper Deck-23
06McDonald's Upper Deck-51
Autographs-ASK
Clear Cut Winners-CC5
Jerseys-JSK
Patches-PSK
06NHL POG-50
06O-Pee-Chee-274
06O-Pee-Chee-656
06O-Pee-Chee-686
Rainbow-274
Rainbow-656
Rainbow-686
06Panini Stickers-64
06SP Authentic-48
06SP Authentic-153
Limited-48
Limited-153
Sign of the Times-STSK
Sign of the Times Duals-STDS
Sign of the Times Triples-ST3RKH
06SP Game Used-55
Gold-55
Rainbow-55
Authentic Fabrics-AFSK
Authentic Fabrics Parallel-AFSK
Authentic Fabrics Patches-AFSK
Authentic Fabrics Dual-AF2KR
Authentic Fabrics Dual Patches-AF2KR
Authentic Fabrics Triple-AF3MTL
Authentic Fabrics Triple Patches-AF3MTL
Authentic Fabrics Sixes-AF6MAS
Authentic Fabrics Sixes Patches-AF6MAS
Authentic Fabrics Eights-AF8FIN
Authentic Fabrics Eights Patches-AF8FIN
Autographs-55
By The Letter-BLSK
Inked Sweaters-ISSK
Inked Sweaters Patches-ISSK
Inked Sweaters Dual-IS2KR
Inked Sweaters Dual Patches-IS2KR
Letter Marks-LMSK
06SPx-53
Spectrum-53
SPxcitement-X55
SPxcitement Spectrum-X55
SPxcitement Autographs-X55
Winning Materials-WMSK
Winning Materials Spectrum-WMSK
Winning Materials Autographs-WMSK
06The Cup-44
Autographed Foundations-CQSK
Autographed Foundations Patches-CQSK
Autographed NHL Shields Duals-DASKR
Autographed Patches-44
Black Rainbow-44
Foundations-CQSK
Foundations Patches-CQSK
Gold-44
Gold Patches-44
Honorable Numbers-HNSK
Jerseys-44
Limited Logos-LLSK
Masterpiece Pressplates-44
NHL Shields Duals-DSHKK
Scripted Swatches-SSSK
Signature Patches-SPSK
06UD Artifacts-47
06UD Artifacts-175
Blue-47
Blue-175
Gold-47
Gold-175
Platinum-47
Platinum-175
Radiance-47
Radiance-175
Autographed Radiance Parallel-47
Autographed Radiance Parallel-175
Red-47
Red-175
Frozen Artifacts-FASK
Frozen Artifacts Black-FASK
Frozen Artifacts Blue-FASK
Frozen Artifacts Gold-FASK
Frozen Artifacts Platinum-FASK
Frozen Artifacts Red-FASK
Frozen Artifacts Autographed Black-FASK
Frozen Artifacts Patches Black-FASK
Frozen Artifacts Patches Blue-FASK
Frozen Artifacts Patches Gold-FASK
Frozen Artifacts Patches Platinum-FASK
Frozen Artifacts Patches Red-FASK
Frozen Artifacts Patches Autographed Black Tag Parallel-FASK
Treasured Patches Black-TSSK
Treasured Patches Blue-TSSK
Treasured Patches Gold-TSSK
Treasured Patches Platinum-TSSK
Treasured Patches Red-TSSK
Treasured Patches Autographed Black Tag Parallel-TSSK
Treasured Swatches-TSSK
Treasured Swatches Black-TSSK
Treasured Swatches Blue-TSSK
Treasured Swatches Gold-TSSK
Treasured Swatches Platinum-TSSK
Treasured Swatches Red-TSSK
Treasured Swatches Autographed Black-TSSK
Tundra Tandems-TTKK
Tundra Tandems Black-TTKK
Tundra Tandems Blue-TTKK
Tundra Tandems Gold-TTKK
Tundra Tandems Red-TTKK
Tundra Tandems Dual Patches Red-TTKK
06UD Mini Jersey Collection-54
06UD Powerplay-52
Impact Rainbow-52
In Action-IA5
Power Marks-PMSK
06Ultimate Collection-32
Signatures-US-SK
Ultimate Achievements-UA-SK
Ultimate Signatures Logos-SL-SK
06Ultra-102
Gold Medallion-102
Ice Medallion-102
Action-UA14
Difference Makers-DM18
Fresh Ink-ISK
Scoring Kings-SK27
Uniformity-USK
Uniformity Patches-UPSK
Uniformity Autographed Jerseys-UASK
06Upper Deck-100
Exclusives Parallel-100
High Gloss Parallel-100
All World-AW16
Game Jerseys-J2KO
Game Patches-P2KO
Generations Duals-G2KD
Generations Triples-G3KJK
Generations Patches Dual-G2PKD
Generations Patches Triple-G3PKJK
Masterpieces-100
Walmart Tins Oversize-100
06Upper Deck MVP-152
Gold Script-152
Super Script-152
International Icons-II12
Jerseys-OJKS
Jerseys-OJSK
06Upper Deck Ovation-173
06Upper Deck Sweet Shot-55
Signature Shots/Saves Sticks-SSSSK
Signature Sticks-STSK
Sweet Stitches-SSSK
Sweet Stitches Duals-SSSK
Sweet Stitches Triples-SSSK
06Upper Deck Trilogy-51
Combo Autographed Jerseys-CJKR
Combo Autographed Patches-CJKR
Combo Clearcut Autographs-C2KK
Honorary Scripted Patches-HSPSK
Honorary Scripted Swatches-HSSSK
Honorary Swatches-HSSK
Ice Scripts-ISSK
Scripts-S3SK
06Upper Deck Victory-103
06Upper Deck Victory Black-103
06Upper Deck Victory Gold-103
06Upper Deck Victory GameBreakers-GB23
06Upper Deck Victory Oversize Cards-SK
06Russian Sport Collection Olympic Stars-23
07Upper Deck Victory-53
Black-53
Gold-53
GameBreakers-GB4
Oversize Cards-OS15
Stars on Ice-SI18

Koivula, Ville
99Finnish Cardset-292

Koivulahti, Pertti
70Finnish Jaakiekko-209
71Finnish Suomi Stickers-131
72Finnish Jaakiekko-194
73Finnish Jaakiekko-154
77Finnish Sportscasters-76-1801
78Finnish SM-Liiga-17
78Finnish SM-Liiga-190
80Finnish Mallasjuoma-166
81Swedish Semic Hockey VM Stickers-35
82Finnish Skopbank-6
05Finnish Tappara Legendat-27

Koivunen, Hannu
66Finnish Jaakiekkosarja-85
70Finnish Jaakiekko-158
71Finnish Suomi Stickers-229

Koivunen, Jarmo
70Finnish Jaakiekko-159
71Finnish Suomi Stickers-230
72Finnish Jaakiekko-85
73Finnish Jaakiekko-132

Koivunen, Karo
06Finnish Cardset-299

Koivunen, Keijo
72Finnish Jaakiekko-145

Koivunen, Matti
65Finnish Hellas-24
70Finnish Jaakiekko-297

Koivunen, Petro
92Finnish Jyvas-Hyva Stickers-119
93Finnish Jyvas-Hyva Stickers-202
93Finnish SISU-277
94Finnish SISU-66
94Finnish SISU Fire On Ice-12
95Finnish SISU-89
95Finnish SISU Limited-60
98Finnish Kerailysarja-152

Koivunen, Toni
92Finnish Jyvas-Hyva Stickers-152
93Finnish Jyvas-Hyva Stickers-263
93Finnish SISU-300
95Finnish SISU-267
96Finnish SISU Redline-68
98Finnish Kerailysarja-132
99Finnish Cardset-74
00Finnish Cardset-127
01Finnish Cardset-321
02Finnish Cardset-199
02Swedish SHL-270
Parallel-270
03Swedish Elite-276
Silver-276
04Finnish Cardset-135
Parallel-100
05Finnish Cardset -297
06Finnish Cardset-132

Koivunoro, Mikko
94Finnish SISU-266
95Finnish SISU-88
96Finnish SISU Redline-92
00UK Sekonda Superleague-79
01UK Guildford Flames-20
03UK Nottingham Panthers-10

Kojevnikov, Alexandre
03Quebec Remparts-13

Kojola, Heikki
72Finnish Jaakiekko-86

Kokanas, Angelo
95Neepewa Natives-12

Kokela, Ilpo
74Finnish Typotor-13

Kokko, Petri
94Finest-127
Super Team Winners-127
Refractors-127
94Finnish SISU-19
95Finnish SISU-31
96Finnish SISU Redline-29
00Finnish Cardset-203
01Finnish Cardset-111
03Finnish Cardset-130
04Finnish Cardset-140
Parallel-104
05Finnish Cardset -128
06Swedish SHL Elitset-280

Kokko, Sami
92Finnish Jyvas-Hyva Stickers-112

Kokkola, Jari
70Finnish Jaakiekko-348

Kokkonen, Olli
72Finnish Jaakiekko-213

Kokkonen, Timo
70Finnish Jaakiekko-298
71Finnish Suomi Stickers-191
72Finnish Jaakiekko-229
73Finnish Jaakiekko-263

Kokorev, Dmitri
99Russian Dynamo Moscow-12
00Russian Dynamo Moscow-33
02Russian Hockey League-86

Kokrment, Jindrich
81Swedish Semic Hockey VM Stickers-69
82Swedish Semic VM Stickers-90
83Swedish Semic VM Stickers-90

Kolacek, Kamil
94Czech APS Extraliga-226
99Czech Score Blue 2000-29
99Czech Score Red Ice 2000-29

Kolacek, Richard
99Czech Score Blue 2000-17
99Czech Score Red Ice 2000-17

Kolacz, Miroslaw
93Quebec Pee-Wee Tournament-1511

Kolanos, Krystofer
00SPx Rookie Redemption-RR23
01Atomic-121
Premiere Date-121
01Atomic Toronto Fall Expo-121
01BAP Memorabilia-365
Emerald-365
Ruby-365
Sapphire-365
01BAP Signature Series-243
Autographs-243
Autographs Gold-243
01Bowman YoungStars-148
Gold-148
Ice Cubed-148
01Coyotes Team Issue-9
01Crown Royale-174
Crowning Achievement-9
Rookie Royalty-15
01O-Pee-Chee-334
01Pacific-460
01Pacific Adrenaline-221
Blue-221
Premiere Date-221
Red-221
Retail-221
Rookie Report-14
01Pacific Heads-Up-116
01Pacific High Voltage-8
01Parkhurst-266
01Parkhurst Beckett Promos-266
01Private Stock-136
Gold-136
Premiere Date-136
Retail-136
Silver-136
Moments in Time-9
01Private Stock Pacific Nights-136
01Private Stock PS-2002-101
01Private Stock Reserve-R8
01SP Authentic-179
Limited-179
Limited Gold-179
01SP Game Used-94
01SPx-151
01SPx-151
Rookie Treasures-RTKK
01Titanium-176
Retail-176
Double-Sided Jerseys-71
Double-Sided Patches-71
Rookie Team-10
Three-Star Selections-30
01Titanium Draft Day Edition-74
01Titanium Draft Day Edition-160
01Topps-334
01Topps Chrome-152
Refractors-152
Black Border Refractors-152
01Topps Heritage-150
01Topps Reserve-109
01UD Challenge for the Cup-128
01UD Honor Roll-99
01UD Mask Collection-162
Gold-162
01UD Playmakers-136
01UD Premier Collection-114
01UD Top Shelf-73
01Upper Deck-228
Exclusives-228
01Upper Deck Ice-65
01Upper Deck MVP-231
01Upper Deck Victory-451
01Upper Deck Vintage-294
01Vanguard-126
Blue-126
Red-126
One of Ones-126
Premiere Date-126
Prime Prospects-15
Proofs-126
02BAP First Edition-287
02BAP Memorabilia-78
Emerald-78
Ruby-78
Sapphire-78
NHL All-Star Game-78
NHL All-Star Game Blue-78
NHL All-Star Game Green-78
NHL All-Star Game Red-78
02BAP Memorabilia Toronto Fall Expo-78
02BAP Signature Series-97
Autographs-97
Autographs Gold-97
02Coyotes Team Issue-17
02O-Pee-Chee-208
02O-Pee-Chee Premier Blue Parallel-208
02O-Pee-Chee Premier Red Parallel-208
02O-Pee-Chee Factory Set-208
02Pacific-297
Blue-297
Red-297
Shining Moments-10
02Pacific Calder Collection AS Fantasy-9
02Pacific Calder Collection All-Star Fantasy Gold-9
02Pacific Complete-27
Red-27
02Pacific Entry Draft-9
02Pacific Exclusive-134
Great Expectations-14
02Pacific Heads-Up-96
Blue-96
Purple-96
Red-96
Head First-13
Quad Jerseys-21
Quad Jerseys-35
Quad Jerseys Gold-21
Quad Jerseys Gold-35
02Pacific Toronto Spring Expo Rookie Coll-10
02Parkhurst-61
Bronze-61
Gold-61
Silver-61
02SP Game Used First Rounder Patches-KK
02Stadium Club-58
Silver Decoy Cards-58
Proofs-58
02Topps-208
OPC Blue Parallel-208
OPC Red Parallel-208
Signs of the Future-KK
Factory Set-208
02Topps Chrome-117
Black Border Refractors-117
Refractors-117
02Topps Heritage-92
Chrome Parallel-92
Autographs-KK
Autographs Black-KK
Autographs Red-KK
02Topps Total-210
Signatures-KK
02UD Top Shelf Dual Player Jerseys-RYK
02UD Top Shelf Dual Player Jerseys-STKB
02UD Top Shelf Shooting Stars-SHKK
02Upper Deck On the Rise-ORKK
02Upper Deck Classic Portraits Headliners-LK
02Upper Deck Classic Portraits Headliners Limited-LK
02Upper Deck Classic Portraits Stitches-CKK
02Upper Deck Classic Portraits Stitches Limited-CKK
02Upper Deck Victory-162
Bronze-162
Gold-162
Silver-162
02Vanguard Jerseys-35
02Vanguard Jerseys Gold-35
03Coyotes Postcards-11
03ITG Action-456
03Pacific Complete-213
Red-213
04Finnish Cardset-8
04German DEL Superstars-SU20

Kolar, Jan
99Czech OFS-362
00Czech OFS-54
02Czech OFS Plus-217
03Czech OFS Plus-60
04Czech OFS-120
05Czech HC Pardubice-6
06Czech HC Pardubice Postcards-7
06Czech OFS-116
06Czech OFS-316

Kolaric, Bostjan
93Quebec Pee-Wee Tournament-1806

Kolarik, Chad
04Michigan Wolverines-6

Kolarik, Jan
06Victoriaville Tigres-8

Kolarik, Michal
01Czech OFS-127

Kolarik, Pavel
97Czech APS Extraliga-153
98Czech DS Stickers-191
98Czech OFS-212
99Czech DS-117
99Czech OFS-384
00SPx-153
00Upper Deck Ice-108
00Providence Bruins-8
01Upper Deck Victory-363
Gold-363
01Czech DS-33
01Providence Bruins-9
02Czech OFS Plus-242
03Czech OFS Plus-183
04Czech HC Slavia Praha Postcards-15
04Czech OFS-166
05Czech HC Slavia Praha-10
06Czech HC Slavia Praha Postcards-10

Kolarik, Tyler
94Quebec Int. Pee-Wees-41
05Syracuse Crunch-8

Kolarz, Michael
04Kingston Frontenacs-11
05Kingston Frontenacs-16
06Kingston Frontenacs-15

Kolbe, Jim
70Swedish Masterserien-174
92Arizona Icecats-18

Kolda Sr., Ladislav
83Swedish Semic VM Stickers-83
94German First League-506

Kolda, Ladislav
01Owen Sound Attack-10
02Owen Sound Attack-17

Koleda, Marian
93Quebec Pee-Wee Tournament-1716

Koledaev, Alexei
98Russian Hockey League-94
99Russian Hockey League-219
00Russian Hockey League-189

Koleff, Jim
93Swiss HNL-59
95Swiss HNL-157
96Swiss HNL-52
98Swiss Power Play Stickers-152
99Swiss Panini Stickers-152
00Swiss Panini Stickers-197
02Swiss HNL-67

Kolehmainen, Janne
05Finnish Cardset -313
06Finnish Cardset-143

Kolehmainen, Pasi
95Finnish SISU-273

Kolehmainen, Rainer
65Finnish Hellas-133

Kolek, Vladimir
96Czech APS Extraliga-2

Kolenda, Mike
91Ferris State Bulldogs-19
92Ferris State Bulldogs-19
95Toledo Storm-18
96Toledo Storm-27
97Toledo Storm-18

Kolesar, Mark
917th Inn. Sketch WHL-212
92Brandon Wheat Kings-13
93Brandon Wheat Kings-14
94St. John's Maple Leafs-15
95Bowman-142
All-Foil-142
95St. John's Maple Leafs-13
96Upper Deck-190
96St. John's Maple Leafs-18
96Collector's Edge Ice-86
Prism-86
99German DEL-203
00UK Sekonda Superleague-80
01UK London Knights-12
02UK London Knights-7

Koleski, Matt
95Alaska Gold Kings-9

Kolesnik, Vitaly
05ITG Heroes/Prosp Toronto Expo Parallel -274
05Black Diamond-228
05Hot Prospects-120
En Fuego-120
Red Hot-120
White Hot-120
05SP Authentic-258
Limited-258
05SP Game Used-203
05SPx-254
05The Cup Masterpiece Pressplate Artifact-265
05The Cup Master Pressplate Black Diamond-228
05The Cup Masterpiece Pressplate (Ice)-227
05The Cup Master Pressplate Rookie Update-122
05The Cup Masterpiece Pressplate SPA-258
05The Cup Masterpiece Pressplate SP GU-203
05The Cup Masterpiece Pressplates (SPx)-254
05The Cup Masterpiece Pressplate Trilogy-242
05The Cup Masterpiece Pressplate Ult Coll-200
05UD Artifacts-265
05Ultimate Collection-200
Gold-200
05Upper Deck Ice-227

05Upper Deck Rookie Update-122
05Upper Deck Trilogy-242
05AHL All-Stars-15
05AHL Top Prospects-22
05ITG Heroes and Prospects-274
Autographs Series II-VK

Kolewaski, Tony
00Saskatoon Blades-29

Kolito, Ronald
93Quebec Pee-Wee Tournament-1759

Kolkka, Vaino
66Finnish Jaakiekkosarja-195
70Finnish Jaakiekko-63
70Finnish Jaakiekko-109
70Swedish Hockey-304
70Swedish Masterserien-163
71Finnish Suomi Stickers-117
72Finnish Jaakiekko-87
72Finnish Panda Toronto-5
73Finnish Jaakiekko-133

Kolkunov, Alexei
95SP-182
02Russian Hockey League-99

Kollar, Tomas
03Swedish Elite-163
Silver-163
04Swedish Elitset-17
Gold-17
High Expectations-2
05Swedish SHL Elitset-276
Gold-276

Kolle, Olaf-Bjorn
94German First League-649

Koller, Toni
93Swiss HNL-112
95Swiss HNL-346

Kolliker, Jakob
93Swiss HNL-186
95Swiss HNL-344
96Swiss HNL-317
96Swiss HNL-525
98Swiss Power Play Stickers-127

Kollmeder, Volker
94German First League-42

Kolloch, Markus
94German First League-451

Kolnik, Juraj
99Rimouski Oceanic-22
Signed-22
99Bowman CHL-58
Gold-58
OPC International-58
00BAP Memorabilia-518
00Black Diamond-72
Gold-72
00Upper Deck-207
Exclusives Tier 1-207
Exclusives Tier 2-207
00Upper Deck Ice-52
Immortals-52
Legends-52
Stars-52
00Upper Deck MVP-217
First Stars-217
Second Stars-217
Third Stars-217
00Lowell Lock Monsters-13
00QMJHL All-Star Program Inserts-42
01BAP Memorabilia-160
Emerald-160
Ruby-160
Sapphire-160
01UD Top Shelf-105
01Upper Deck Victory-380
Gold-380
02O-Pee-Chee-289
02O-Pee-Chee Premier Blue Parallel-289
02O-Pee-Chee Premier Red Parallel-289
02O-Pee-Chee Factory Set-289
02Topps-289
OPC Blue Parallel-289
OPC Red Parallel-289
Factory Set-289
04Pacific-114
Blue-114
Red-114
04San Antonio Rampage-15
05Parkhurst-216
Facsimile Auto Parallel-216
05Upper Deck-332
06O-Pee-Chee-216
Rainbow-216

Kolnik, Lubomir
91Finnish Semic World Champ Stickers-119
91Swedish Semic World Champ Stickers-119
92Finnish Semic-143
94Finnish Jaa Kiekko-203
95Finnish SISU-291
95Finnish SISU-373
95Slovakian APS National Team-21
96Swedish Semic Wien-232
01Slovakian Kvarteto-4B
01Slovakian Kvarteto-5C
03Czech OFS Plus All-Star Game-H12

Kolodziejczyk, Marcin
93Quebec Pee-Wee Tournament-1510

Kolomatis, David
06Owen Sound Attack-6

Kolosov, Sergei
06Cedar Rapids RoughRiders-10

Kolozsy, Tony
93Omaha Lancers-13

Kolstad, Dean
89ProCards IHL-94
91O-Pee-Chee Inserts-4S
91Kansas City Blades-19
91ProCards-518
92Kansas City Blades-20
94Minnesota Moose-6
97Central Texas Stampede-8

Koltsov, Kirill
00Russian Hockey League-228
01Russian Hockey League-81
01Russian Young Lions-5
02Russian Future Stars-8
02Russian Hockey League-127
02Russian Hockey League-190
03Manitoba Moose-22
03Pacific AHL Prospects-54
Gold-54
04ITG Heroes and Prospects-35
04ITG Heroes/Prospects Toronto Expo '05-35
04ITG Heroes/Prospects Expo Heroes/Pros-35
05Russian Hockey League RHL-36

Koltsov, Konstantin
98Russian Hockey League-136
99Russian Hockey League-269
02BAP Memorabilia-354
02BAP Ultimate Memorabilia-67
02SP Authentic-215
02SPx-193
02UD Premier Collection-98
Gold-98
02Wilkes-Barre Scranton Penguins-20
03Beehive-155
Gold-155
Silver-155
03ITG Action-477
03Pacific Complete-517
Red-517
03Topps Traded-TT57
Blue-TT57
Gold-TT57
Red-TT57
03Upper Deck-401
Canadian Exclusives-401
HG-401
UD Exclusives-401
04Russian Back to Russia-3
05Parkhurst-392
Facsimile Auto Parallel-392
05Upper Deck MVP-312
Gold-312
Platinum-312
05WBS Penguins-16

Kolu, Tomi-Pekka
99Finnish Cardset-101

Kolusz, Marcin
03Vancouver Giants-9
06Czech OFS-158

Kolzig, Olaf
90Score-392
Canadian-392
91O-Pee-Chee-290
91Topps-290
91Baltimore Skipjacks-6
91Hampton Roads Admirals-7
91ProCards-550
92Rochester Americans Dunkin' Donuts-9
92Rochester Americans Kodak-12
93OPC Premier-291
Gold-291
93Stadium Club-438
Members Only Master Set-438
First Day Issue-438
93Topps/OPC Premier-291
Gold-291
93Ultra-447
93Upper Deck-326
93Portland Pirates-23
94Upper Deck-486
Electric Ice-486
95Capitals Team Issue-16
95Donruss-254
95Parkhurst International-220
Emerald Ice-220
95Pinnacle-134
Artist's Proofs-134
Rink Collection-134
95Stadium Club-217
Members Only Master Set-217
95Upper Deck-103
Electric Ice-103
Electric Ice Gold-103
96Be A Player-78
Autographs-78
Autographs Silver-78
96Summit-48
Artist's Proofs-48
Ice-48
Metal-48
Premium Stock-48
96Upper Deck-354
97Crown Royale-141
Emerald Green-141
Ice Blue-141
Silver-141
Freeze Out Die-Cuts-20
97Donruss Priority-35
Stamp of Approval-35
97Pacific Invincible NHL Regime-210
97Pacific Omega-242
Copper-242
Dark Gray-242
Emerald Green-242
Gold-242
Ice Blue-242
97Paramount-196
Copper-196
Dark Grey-196
Emerald Green-196
Ice Blue-196
Red-196
Silver-196
97Pinnacle-89
Artist's Proofs-89
Rink Collection-89
Press Plates Back Black-89
Press Plates Back Cyan-89
Press Plates Back Magenta-89
Press Plates Back Yellow-89
Press Plates Front Black-89
Press Plates Front Cyan-89
Press Plates Front Magenta-89
Press Plates Front Yellow-89
Inside Stand Up Guys-7A/B
Inside Stand Up Guys-7C/D
Inside Stand Up Guys Promos-7A/B
Inside Stand Up Guys Promos-7C/D
97Revolution-149
Copper-149
Emerald-149
Ice Blue-149
Silver-149
Return to Sender Die-Cuts-20
97Score-25
Artist's Proofs-25
Golden Blades-25
97Zenith-59
Z-Gold-59
Z-Silver-59
97Zenith 5 x 7-30
Gold Impulse-30
Silver Impulse-30
98SLU Hockey Extended-105
98Aurora-198
Championship Fever-50
Championship Fever Copper-50
Championship Fever Ice Blue-50
Championship Fever Red-50
Championship Fever Silver-50
Cubes-20
98Black Diamond-89
Double Diamond-89
Triple Diamond-89
Quadruple Diamond-89
98Bowman's Best-59
Refractors-59
Atomic Refractors-59
98Capitals Kids and Cops-1
98Crown Royale-143
Limited Series-143
Pivotal Players-25
98Finest-126
No Protectors-126
No Protectors Refractors-126
Refractors-126
98Katch-155
98Kenner Starting Lineup Cards-18
98Lunchables Goalie Greats Rounds-4
98Lunchables Goalie Greats Squares-4
98NHL Aces Playing Cards-1
98OPC Chrome-193
Refractors-193
98Pacific-37
Ice Blue-37
Red-37
Dynagon Ice Inserts-20
Titanium Ice-20
Gold Crown Die-Cuts-36
Team Checklists-27
98Pacific Dynagon Ice-197
Blue-197
Red-197
Watchmen-10
98Pacific Omega-248
Red-248
Opening Day Issue-248
98Panini Photocards-42
98Panini Stickers-108
98Paramount-247
Copper-247
Emerald Green-247
Holo-Electric-247
Ice Blue-247
Silver-247
Glove Side Laser Cuts-20
98Revolution-148
Ice Shadow-148
Red-148
Three Pronged Attack-20
Three Pronged Attack Parallel-20
98SP Authentic-87
Power Shift-87
98SPx Finite-88
Radiance-88
Spectrum-88
98Topps-193
O-Pee-Chee-193
Mystery Finest Bronze-M2
Mystery Finest Bronze Refractors-M2
Mystery Finest Gold-M2
Mystery Finest Gold Refractors-M2
Mystery Finest Silver-M2
Mystery Finest Silver Refractors-M2
98Topps Gold Label Class 1-63
Black-63
Black One of One-63
One of One-63
Red-63
Red One of One-63
98Topps Gold Label Class 2-63
98Topps Gold Label Class 2 Black-63
98Topps Gold Label Class 2 Black 1 of 1-63
98Topps Gold Label Class 2 One of One-63
98Topps Gold Label Class 2 Red-63
98Topps Gold Label Class 2 Red One of One-63
98Topps Gold Label Class 3-63
98Topps Gold Label Class 3 Black-63
98Topps Gold Label Class 3 Black 1 of 1-63
98Topps Gold Label Class 3 One of One-63
98Topps Gold Label Class 3 Red-63
98Topps Gold Label Class 3 Red One of One-63
98UD Choice-215
98UD Choice Preview-215
98UD Choice Prime Choice Reserve-215
98UD Choice Reserve-215
98Upper Deck-205
Exclusives-205
Exclusives 1 of 1-205
Gold Reserve-205
98Upper Deck MVP-210
Gold Script-210
Silver Script-210
Super Script-210
98Hampton Roads Admirals 10th Anniversary-9
99SLU Hockey One On One-3
99SLU Hockey-10
99SLU Hockey Pro Action Deluxe-30
99Aurora-149
Premiere Date-149
Glove Unlimited-20
99BAP Memorabilia-54
Gold-54
Silver-54
99BAP Update Teammates Jersey Cards-TM32
99BAP Millennium Prototypes-8
99BAP Millennium-246
Emerald-246
Ruby-246
Sapphire-246
Signatures-246
Signatures Gold-246
99Black Diamond-88
Diamond Cut-88
Final Cut-88
99Crown Royale-143
Limited Series-143
Premiere Date-143
99Hasbro Starting Lineup Cards-10
99O-Pee-Chee-132
99O-Pee-Chee Chrome-132
99O-Pee-Chee Chrome Refractors-132
99O-Pee-Chee Top of the World-TW19
99Pacific-443
Copper-443
Emerald Green-443
Gold-443
Ice Blue-443
Premiere Date-443
Red-443
In the Cage Net-Fusions-20
99Pacific Dynagon Ice-202
Blue-202
Copper-202
Gold-202
Premiere Date-202
99Pacific Omega-243
Copper-243
Gold-243
Ice Blue-243
Premiere Date-243
World All-Stars-10
99Pacific Prism-148
Holographic Blue-148
Holographic Gold-148
Holographic Mirror-148
Holographic Purple-148
Premiere Date-148
99Paramount-245
Copper-245
Emerald-245
Gold-245
Holographic Emerald-245
Holographic Gold-245
Holographic Silver-245
Ice Blue-245
Premiere Date-245
Red-245
Silver-245
Glove Side Net Fusions-20
99Revolution-149
Premiere Date-149
Red-149
Shadow Series-149
99SP Authentic-88
99SPx-161
Radiance-161
Spectrum-161
99Stadium Club-19
First Day Issue-19
One of a Kind-19
Printing Plates Black-19
Printing Plates Cyan-19
Printing Plates Magenta-19
Printing Plates Yellow-19
Goalie Cam-GC4
99Topps/OPC-132
Top of the World-TW19
99Topps/OPC Chrome-132
Refractors-132
99Topps Premier Plus-36
Parallel-36
99Ultimate Victory-88
1/1-88
Parallel-88
Parallel 100-88
99Upper Deck-301
Exclusives-301
Exclusives 1 of 1-301
99Upper Deck Gold Reserve-301
99Upper Deck HoloGrFx-60
Ausome-60
99Upper Deck MVP-217
Gold Script-217
Silver Script-217
Super Script-217
99Upper Deck MVP SC Edition-189
Gold Script-189
Silver Script-189
Super Script-189
99Upper Deck Ovation-60
Standing Ovation-60
99Upper Deck Victory-309
99Upper Deck Victory-384
99Wayne Gretzky Hockey-176
00SLU Hockey One On One-30
00SLU Hockey One On One-40
00Aurora-148
Pinstripes-148
Pinstripes Premiere Date-148
Premiere Date-148
Autographs-148
00BAP Memorabilia-80
Emerald-80
Ruby-80
Sapphire-80
Promos-80
Georges Vezina-V1
Jersey Cards-J10
Jersey Emblems-E10
Jersey Numbers-N10
Jersey and Stick Cards-JS10
00BAP Mem Chicago Sportsfest Copper-80
00BAP Memorabilia Chicago Sportsfest Blue-80
00BAP Memorabilia Chicago Sportsfest Gold-80
00BAP Memorabilia Chicago Sportsfest Ruby-80
00BAP Memorabilia Chicago Sun-Times Ruby-80
00BAP Memorabilia Chicago Sun-Times Gold-80
00BAP Mem Chicago Sun-Times Sapphire-80
00BAP Mem Toronto Fall Expo Copper-80
00BAP Memorabilia Toronto Fall Expo Gold-80
00BAP Memorabilia Toronto Fall Expo Ruby-80
00BAP Parkhurst 2000-P93
00BAP Signature Series-12
Emerald-12
Ruby-12
Sapphire-12
Autographs-125
Autographs Gold-125
Franchise Players-F30
He Shoots-He Scores Prizes-14
00BAP Ultimate Memorabilia Autographs-5
Gold-5
00BAP Ultimate Mem Game-Used Jerseys-GJ43
00BAP Ultimate Mem Game-Used Emblems-E35
00BAP Ultimate Mem Game-Used Numbers-N35
00BAP Ultimate Mem Game-Used Sticks-GS43
00BAP Ultimate Memorabilia Goalie Sticks-G30
00BAP Ultimate Mem Plante Jersey Cards-PJ12
00BAP Ultimate Mem Plante Skate Cards-PS12
00Black Diamond-59
Gold-59
Game Gear-LOK
00Crown Royale-107
Ice Blue-107
Limited Series-107
Premiere Date-107
Red-107
00McDonald's Pacific-36
Blue-36
00O-Pee-Chee-8
00O-Pee-Chee Parallel-8
00Pacific-425
Copper-425
Gold-425
Ice Blue-425
Premiere Date-425
Euro-Stars-10
Jerseys-15
Jersey Patches-15
Gold Crown Die Cuts-36
00Paramount-246
Copper-246
Gold-246
Holo-Gold-246
Holo-Silver-246
Ice Blue-246
Premiere Date-246
Freeze Frame-36
Jersey and Patches-10
Glove Side Net Fusions-20
Glove Side Net Fusions Platinum-20
00Private Stock-99
Gold-99
Premiere Date-99
Retail-99
Silver-99
Game Gear-104
PS-2001 Action-60
00Revolution-148
Blue-148
Premiere Date-148
Red-148
HD NHL-36
Ice Immortals-20
NHL Icons-20
Stat Masters-20
00SP Authentic-89
Super Stoppers-SS7
00SP Game Used-59
00SPx-70
Spectrum-70
00Stadium Club-129
Capture the Action-CA6
Capture the Action Game View-6
Glove Save-GS7
00Titanium-99
Blue-99
Gold-99
Premiere Date-99
Red-99
Retail-99
Game Gear-150
Game Gear Patches-150
Three-Star Selections-10
00Topps/OPC-8
Parallel-8
Own the Game-OTG13
00Topps Chrome-8
OPC Refractors-6
Refractors-8
00Topps Gold Label Class 1-4
Gold-4
00Topps Gold Label Class 2-4
00Topps Gold Label Class 2 Gold-4
00Topps Gold Label Class 3-4
00Topps Gold Label Class 3 Gold-4
00Topps Gold Label Behind the Mask-BTM7
00Topps Gold Label Behind the Mask 1 to 1-BTM7
00Topps Heritage-5
00Topps Heritage-226
00Topps Heritage-244
Chrome Parallel-5
00Topps Premier Plus-16
Blue Ice-16
Masters of the Break-MB16
00Topps Stars-20
Blue-20
00UD Heroes-117
00UD Pros and Prospects-88
00UD Reserve-88
Gold Strike-GS10
00Upper Deck-408
Exclusives Tier 1-408
Exclusives Tier 2-408
Profiles-P10
Skilled Stars-SS20
Triple Threat-TT10
UD Flashback-UD8
00Upper Deck Ice-40
Immortals-40
Legends-40
Stars-40
00Upper Deck Legends-131
00Upper Deck Legends-132
Legendary Collection Bronze-131
Legendary Collection Bronze-132
Legendary Collection Gold-131
Legendary Collection Gold-132
Legendary Collection Silver-131
Legendary Collection Silver-132
00Upper Deck MVP-181
First Stars-181
Masked Men-MM10
Second Stars-181
Third Stars-181
00Upper Deck Victory-233
00Upper Deck Victory-239
00Upper Deck Victory-330
00Upper Deck Vintage-360
00Upper Deck Vintage-369
00Upper Deck Vintage-370
Great Gloves-GG20
00Vanguard-99
Holographic Gold-99
Holographic Purple-99
Pacific Proofs-99
00Czech Stadion-66
01Atomic-99
Blue-99
Gold-99
Premiere Date-99
Red-99
01BAP Memorabilia-67
Emerald-67
Ruby-67
Sapphire-67
All-Star Teammates-AST18
Goalies Jerseys-GJ19
He Shoots-He Scores Prizes-15
Stanley Cup Playoffs-SC6
01BAP Signature Series Certified 100-C30
01BAP Signature Series Certified 50-C30
01BAP Signature Series Certified 1 of 1's-C30
01BAP Signature Series Autographs-LOK
01BAP Signature Series Autographs Gold-LOK
01BAP Signature Series Jerseys-GJ-66
01BAP Signature Series Jersey Autographs-GUOK
01BAP Sig Series Jersey and Stick Cards-GSJ-66
01BAP Signature Series Emblems-GUE-31
01BAP Signature Series Numbers-ITN-31
01BAP Ultimate Mem Legend Terry Sawchuk-16
01Between the Pipes-21
01Between the Pipes-105
01Between the Pipes-110
All-Star Jerseys-ASJ6
Double Memorabilia-DM4
Goalie Gear-GG9
He Shoots-He Saves Points-5
He Shoots-He Saves Prizes-17
Jerseys-GJ19
Emblems-GUE7
Jersey and Stick Cards-GSJ18
Masks-30
Masks Silver-30
Masks Gold-30
Trophy Winners-TW5
01Bowman YoungStars-57
Gold-57
Ice Cubed-57
01Crown Royale-143
Blue-143
Premiere Date-143
Red-143
Retail-143
01O-Pee-Chee-7
01O-Pee-Chee Heritage Parallel-7
01O-Pee-Chee Heritage Parallel Limited-7
01O-Pee-Chee Premier Parallel-7
01Pacific-395
Extreme LTD-395
Hobby LTD-395
Premiere Date-395
Retail LTD-395
Steel Curtain-20
01Pacific Adrenaline-198
Blue-198
Premiere Date-198
Red-198
Retail-198
Power Play-36
01Pacific Arena Exclusives-395
01Pacific Heads-Up-99
Blue-99
Premiere Date-99
Red-99
Silver-99
Showstoppers-20
01Parkhurst-60
Gold-60
Silver-60
Jerseys-PJ60
Jersey and Stick-PSJ11
Sticks-PS39
Teammates-T6
World Class Jerseys-WCJ3
World Class Emblems-WCE3
World Class Numbers-WCN3
01Private Stock-99
Gold-99
Premiere Date-99
Retail-99
Silver-99
01Private Stock Pacific Nights-99
01SP Authentic-89
Limited-89
Limited Gold-89
Buybacks-22
Sign of the Times-OK
01SP Game Used-59
Inked Sweaters-ISOK
Inked Sweaters-DSKB
Patches-POK
Patches-CPKB
Patches-CPKR
Patches Signed-SPOK
Patches Signed-DSPBK
Patches Signed-DSPKB
Patches Signed-DSPKBO
Tools of the Game-TOK
Tools of the Game-CTKB
Tools of the Game-CTKT
Tools of the Game-TTKCH
Tools of the Game-TTRBK
01SPx-70
01Stadium Club-37
Award Winners-37
Master Photos-37
Gallery-G10
Gallery Gold-G10
Lone Star Signatures-LS2
01Titanium-143
Hobby Parallel-143
Premiere Date-143
Retail-143
Retail Parallel-143
01Topps-7
Heritage Parallel-7
Heritage Parallel Limited-7
OPC Parallel-7
Own The Game-OTG24
01Topps Chrome-7
Refractors-7
Black Border Refractors-7
01Topps Heritage-5
Refractors-5
Autographs-AOK
01Topps Reserve-93
01UD Challenge for the Cup-89
Backstops-BB10
01UD Mask Collection-130
01UD Mask Collection-190
Gold-130
Gold-190
Goalie Pads-GPOK
Sticks-SSOK
01UD Playmakers-99
01UD Premier Collection Jerseys-BOK
01UD Premier Collection Jerseys Black-B-OK
01UD Premier Collection Signatures-OK
01UD Premier Collection Signatures Black-OK
01UD Top Shelf-121
01Upper Deck-174
Exclusives-174
Game Jerseys-GJOK
Goalies in Action-GL9
Last Line of Defense-LL10
01Upper Deck Ice-126
01Upper Deck MVP-187
Goalie Sticks-G-OK
Masked Men-MM6
01Upper Deck Victory-349
01Upper Deck Victory-355
01Upper Deck Victory-407
Gold-349
Gold-355
Gold-407
01Upper Deck Vintage-257
01Upper Deck Vintage-259
01Upper Deck Vintage-260
01Vanguard-100
Blue-100
Red-100
Memorabilia-35
One of Ones-100
Premiere Date-100
Proofs-100
Stonewallers-20
02McFarlane Hockey-20
02McFarlane Hockey-22
02Atomic-100
Blue-100
Gold-100
Red-100
Hobby Parallel-100
02BAP All-Star Edition-46
Jerseys-46
Jerseys Gold-46
Jerseys Silver-46
02BAP First Edition-94
02BAP First Edition-336
02BAP First Edition-403R
Jerseys-94
02BAP Memorabilia-94
Emerald-94
Ruby-94
Sapphire-94
NHL All-Star Game-94
NHL All-Star Game Blue-94
NHL All-Star Game Green-94
NHL All-Star Game Red-94
02BAP Memorabilia Toronto Fall Expo-94
02BAP Signature Series-120
Autographs-120
Autograph Buybacks 1999-246
Autograph Buybacks 2000-125
Autograph Buybacks 2001-LOK
Autographs Gold-120
Defensive Wall-DW9
Golf-GS65
Team Quads-TQ9
02BAP Ultimate Memorabilia Cup Duels-18
02Between the Pipes-3
02Between the Pipes-150
Gold-3
Silver-3
All-Star Stick and Jersey-7
Behind the Mask-16
Blockers-11
Double Memorabilia-6
Emblems-23
Goalie Autographs-13
He Shoots-He Saves Points-14
He Shoots-He Saves Prizes-3
Jerseys-23
Masks II-30
Masks II Gold-30
Masks II Silver-30
Nightmares-GN9
Numbers-23
Stick and Jerseys-23
Tandems-20
Trappers-GT9
02Bowman YoungStars-36
Gold-36
Silver-36
02Capitals Team Issue-5
02Crown Royale-100
Blue-100
Red-100
Retail-100
Dual Patches-23
02ITG Used-78
02ITG Used-178
International Experience-IE9
International Experience Gold-IE9
Teammates-T18
Teammates Gold-T18
02O-Pee-Chee-156
02O-Pee-Chee Premier Blue Parallel-156
02O-Pee-Chee Premier Red Parallel-156
02O-Pee-Chee Factory Set-156
02Pacific-395
Blue-395
Red-395
02Pacific Complete-486
Red-486
02Pacific Exclusive-173
Jerseys-25
Jerseys Gold-25
02Pacific Heads-Up-125
Blue-125
Purple-125
Red-125
02Pacific Quest for the Cup-99
Gold-99
Jerseys-25
02Parkhurst-50
Bronze-50
Gold-50
Silver-50
Hardware-V9
Teammates-TT17
02Parkhurst Retro-127
Minis-127
Nicknames-RN27
02Private Stock Reserve-99
Blue-99
Red-99
Retail-99
02SP Authentic-89
Beckett Promos-89
Super Premiums-SPOK
Super Premiums-DPKJ
02SP Game Used-49
Authentic Fabrics-AFOK
Authentic Fabrics Gold-AFOK
Authentic Fabrics Rainbow-AFOK
First Rounder Patches-OK
Tools of the Game-OK
02SPx-74
Spectrum Gold-74
Spectrum Silver-74
Winning Materials-WMKO
Winning Materials Gold-KO
Winning Materials Silver-KO
Xtreme Talents-OK
Xtreme Talents Gold-OK
Xtreme Talents Silver-OK
02Stadium Club-36
Silver Decoy Cards-36
Proofs-36
02Titanium Jerseys-75
02Titanium Jerseys Retail-75
02Titanium Patches-75
02Topps-156
OPC Blue Parallel-156
OPC Red Parallel-156
Factory Set-156
02Topps Chrome-95
Black Border Refractors-95
Refractors-95
02Topps Heritage-70
Chrome Parallel-70
02Topps Total-237
02UD Artistic Impressions-90
Gold-90
Artist's Touch-ATOK
Artist's Touch Gold-ATOK
02UD Artistic Impressions Beckett Promos-90
02UD Artistic Impressions Retrospectives-R90
02UD Artistic Impressions Retrospect Gold-R90
02UD Artistic Impress Retrospect Silver-R90
02UD Honor Roll-69
Grade A Jerseys-GAOK
Grade A Jerseys-TJKB
02UD Mask Collection-87
02UD Mask Collection-88
02UD Mask Collection-89
02UD Mask Collection-90
02UD Mask Collection-107
02UD Mask Collection Beckett Promos-87
02UD Mask Collection Beckett Promos-88
02UD Mask Collection Beckett Promos-89
02UD Mask Collection Beckett Promos-90
02UD Mask Collection Career Wins-CWOK
02UD Mask Collection Great Gloves-GGOK
02UD Mask Collection Masked Marvels-MMOK
02UD Mask Collection Patches-PWOK
02UD Mask Collection Super Stoppers-SSOK
02UD Mask Collection View from the Cage-VOK
02UD Piece of History-88
Awards Collection-AC28
02UD Premier Collection-55
Jerseys Bronze-OK
Jerseys Bronze-JK
Jerseys Gold-OK
Jerseys Gold-JK
Jerseys Silver-OK
Jerseys Silver-JK
Patches-POK
02UD Top Shelf-90
Dual Player Jerseys-STGK
Dual Player Jerseys-STJK
Dual Player Jerseys-STKB
Dual Player Jerseys-STKF
Dual Player Jerseys-STKT
Dual Player Jerseys-STKW
Dual Player Jerseys-STLD
Dual Player Jerseys-STMA
Dual Player Jerseys-STMM
Dual Player Jerseys-STNL
Dual Player Jerseys-STPD
Dual Player Jerseys-STSA
Dual Player Jerseys-STSH
Dual Player Jerseys-STSM
Dual Player Jerseys-STSN
Dual Player Jerseys-STST
Dual Player Jerseys-STTD
Dual Player Jerseys-STTG
Dual Player Jerseys-STYH
Dual Player Jerseys-STYS
Hardware Heroes-HHBRK
Stopper Jerseys-SSOK
Sweet Sweaters-SWOK
Triple Jerseys-TSJBK
02Upper Deck-173
Exclusives-173
Blow-Ups-C42
Goaltender Threads-OK
Goaltender Threads Gold-OK
Last Line of Defense-LL14
Patch Card Numbers-OK
Playbooks Series II-JK
Saviors Jerseys-SVOK
Super Saviors-SA14
02Upper Deck Classic Portraits-100
Hockey Royalty-HBK
Hockey Royalty Limited-HBK
Pillars of Strength-PS10
02Upper Deck MVP-186
Gold-186
Classics-186
Golden Classics-186
Masked Men-MM7
Skate Around Jerseys-SAOK
Skate Around Jerseys-SDKC
02Upper Deck Rookie Update-99
Jerseys-DOK
Jerseys-SJK
Jerseys Gold-DOK
Jerseys Gold-SJK
02Upper Deck Victory-218
Bronze-218
Gold-218
Silver-218
National Pride-NP30
02Upper Deck Vintage-256
02Upper Deck Vintage-290
Green Backs-256
Jerseys-EEOK
Jerseys Gold-EE-OK
Tall Boys-T65
Tall Boys Gold-T65
02Vanguard-100
LTD-100
03BAP Memorabilia-149
Emerald-149
Gold-149
Ruby-149
Sapphire-149
Gloves-GUG4
Masks III-11
Masks III Gold-11
Masks III Silver-11
Masks III Autographs-M-OK
Masks III Memorabilia-11
03BAP Ultimate Memorabilia Autographs-13
Gold-13
03BAP Ultimate Mem Auto Jerseys-13
03BAP Ultimate Mem Franch Present Future-30
03BAP Ultimate Memorabilia Triple Threads-6
03Beehive-199
Gold-199
Silver-199
Sticks Beige Border-BE20
Sticks Blue Border-BL12
03Black Diamond-15
Black-15
Green-15
Red-15
03Bowman-56
Gold-56
03Bowman Chrome-56
Refractors-56
Gold Refractors-56
Xfractors-56
03Crown Royale-100
Blue-100
Retail-100
Global Conquest-4
03Duracell-9
03ITG Action-553
Jerseys-M134
Jerseys-M236
03ITG Used Signature Series-64
Gold-64
Autographs-OK
Autographs Gold-OK
Franchise-30
Franchise Autographs-30
Franchise Gold-30
Goalie Gear-11
Goalie Gear Autographs-11
Goalie Gear Gold-11
Jerseys-32
Jerseys Gold-32
Jersey Autos-32
Jersey and Stick-32
Jersey and Stick Gold-32
Triple Memorabilia-17
Triple Memorabilia Gold-17
03ITG VIP Netminders-7
03NHL Sticker Collection-150
03O-Pee-Chee-202
03OPC Blue-202
03OPC Gold-202
03OPC Red-202
03Pacific-346
Blue-346
Red-346
03Pacific Calder-161
03Pacific Complete-421
Red-421
03Pacific Exhibit-200

Blue Backs-200
03Pacific Invincible-100
Blue-100
Red-100
Retail-100
Freeze Frame-24
Jerseys-32
03Pacific Luxury Suite-23A
03Pacific Luxury Suite-23B
03Pacific Luxury Suite-23C
03Pacific Luxury Suite-23D
03Pacific Prism-100
Blue-100
Gold-100
Red-100
03Pacific Supreme-100
Blue-100
Red-100
Retail-100
03Parkhurst Rookie-52
03Private Stock Reserve-100
Blue-100
Red-100
Retail-100
03SP Authentic-89
Limited-89
03SP Game Used Game Gear-GGOK
03SPx-99
Radiance-99
Spectrum-99
03Titanium-190
Hobby Jersey Number Parallels-190
Patches-190
Retail-190
03Topps-202
Blue-202
Gold-202
Red-202
03Topps C55-78
Minis-78
Minis American Back-78
Minis American Back Red-78
Minis Bazooka Back-78
Minis Brooklyn Back-78
Minis Hat Trick Back-78
Minis O Canada Back-78
Minis O Canada Back Red-78
Minis Stanley Cup Back-78
03Topps Pristine-34
Gold Refractor Die Cuts-34
Refractors-34
Mini-PM-OK
Press Plates Black-34
Press Plates Cyan-34
Press Plates Magenta-34
Press Plates Yellow-34
03UD Honor Roll-89
03UD Premier Collection-59
03Upper Deck-198
Canadian Exclusives-198
HG-198
03Upper Deck Classic Portraits-100
03Upper Deck Ice-90
Gold-90
03Upper Deck MVP-435
Gold Script-435
Silver Script-435
Canadian Exclusives-435
Souvenirs-S7
SportsNut-SN89
03Upper Deck Rookie Update-90
03Upper Deck Trilogy-100
Limited-100
03Upper Deck Victory-200
Bronze-200
Gold-200
Silver-200
03Toronto Star-99
04Pacific-264
Blue-264
Red-264
04SP Authentic-90
04SP Authentic-150
04Ultimate Collection-42
04Ultimate Collection-72
04Upper Deck-178
Canadian Exclusives-178
HG Glossy Gold-178
HG Glossy Silver-178
World's Best-WB15
World Cup Tribute-OK
World Cup Tribute-JHOK
04German Berlin Polar Bears Postcards-19
04German DEL Global Players-GP1
04German DEL Superstars-SU06
05Be A Player-90
First Period-90
Second Period-90
Third Period-90
Overtime-90
Outtakes-OT50
Signatures-OK
Signatures Gold-OK
05Beehive-90
05Beehive-220
Beige -90
Blue -90
Gold-90
Red -90
Matte-90
05Black Diamond-126
Emerald-126
Gold-126
Onyx-126
Ruby-126
05Hot Prospects-100
En Fuego-100
Red Hot-100
White Hot-100
05McDonalds Upper Deck-15
Goalie Gear-MG5
05Panini Stickers-176
05Parkhurst-485
Facsimile Auto Parallel-485
Signatures-OK
True Colors-TCWAS
True Colors-TCWAS
05SP Authentic-100
05SP Authentic-129
Limited-100
Limited-129
Chirography-SPOK
Octographs-OG
Sign of the Times Duals-DKO
05SP Game Used-99
Autographs-99
Gold-99
Authentic Fabrics-AF-OK
Authentic Fabrics Autographs-AAF-OK
Authentic Fabrics Gold-AF-OK
Authentic Patches-AP-OK
Authentic Patches Autographs-AAP-OK
Awesome Authentics-AA-OK
Awesome Authentics Gold-DA-OK
Endorsed Equipment-EE-OK
Game Gear-GG-OK
Game Gear Autographs-AG-OK
Signature Sticks-SS-OK
SIGnificance-OK
SIGnificance Gold-S-OK
Statscriptions-ST-OK
05SPx-90
Spectrum-90
Winning Materials-WM-OK
Winning Materials Autographs-AWM-OK
Winning Materials Gold-WM-OK
Winning Materials Spectrum-WM-OK
Xcitement Superstars-XS-OK
Xcitement Superstars Gold-XS-OK
Xcitement Superstars Spectrum-XS-OK
05The Cup-100
Gold-100
Black Rainbow-100
Emblems of Endorsement-EEOK
Honorable Numbers-HNOK
Limited Logos-LLOK
Masterpiece Pressplates-100
Patch Variation-P100
Patch Variation Autographs-AP100
Scripted Swatches-SSOK
Signature Patches-SPOK
05UD Artifacts-100
05UD Artifacts-200
Blue-100
Blue-200
Gold-100
Gold-200
Green-100
Green-200
Pewter-100
Pewter-200
Red-100
Red-200
Gold Autographed-100
Gold Autographed-200
Remarkable Artifacts-RA-OK
Remarkable Artifacts Dual-RA-OK
05UD PowerPlay-90
Rainbow-90
Specialists-TSOK
Specialists Patches-SPOK
05Ultimate Collection-90
Gold-90
Endorsed Emblems-EEOK
Marquee Attractions-MA50
Marquee Attractions Signatures-SMA50
National Heroes Jerseys-NHJOK
National Heroes Patches-NHPOK
05Ultra-197
Gold-197
Ice-197
05Upper Deck-193
05Upper Deck All-Time Greatest-59
05Upper Deck Big Playmakers-B-OK
05Upper Deck HG Glossy-193
05Upper Deck Hometown Heroes-HH28
05Upper Deck Jerseys-J-OK
05Upper Deck Jerseys Series II-J2OK
05Upper Deck Majestic Materials-MMOK
05Upper Deck Notable Numbers-N-MO
05Upper Deck Patches-P-OK
05Upper Deck Ice-100
Rainbow-100
05Upper Deck MVP-384
Gold-384
Platinum-384
ProSign-P-OK
05Upper Deck Rookie Update-100
05Upper Deck Trilogy-90
05Upper Deck Trilogy-155
Crystal-155
Honorary Patches-HP-OK
Honorary Patch Scripts-HSP-OK
Honorary Swatches-HS-OK
Honorary Swatch Scripts-HSS-OK
05Upper Deck Toronto Fall Expo-193
05Upper Deck Victory-196
Black-196
Gold-196
Silver-196
05German DEL-281
DEB-Jerseys-TR03
06Be A Player-103
Autographs-103
Signatures-OK
Signatures 10-112
Signatures Trios-TOKC
Signatures Foursomes-FLTKG
Up Close and Personal-UC40
Up Close and Personal Autographs-UC40
06Be A Player Portraits-100
Dual Signature Portraits-DSOK
Signature Portraits-SPOK
06Beehive-2
Matte-2
06Black Diamond-84
Black-84
Gold-84
Ruby-84
06Flair Showcase-100
06Flair Showcase-170
06Flair Showcase-270
Parallel-100
Parallel-170
Parallel-270
Hot Gloves-HG30
Inks-IOK
06Fleer-196
Tiffany-196
Fabricology-FOK
Netminders-N24
06Hot Prospects-99
Red Hot-99
White Hot-99
Hot Materials -HMOK
Hot Materials Red Hot-HMOK
Hot Materials White Hot-HMOK
06O-Pee-Chee-487
Rainbow-487
06Panini Stickers-175
06SP Authentic-2
Limited-2
06SP Game Used-100
Gold-100
Rainbow-100
Authentic Fabrics-AFOK
Authentic Fabrics Parallel-AFOK
Authentic Fabrics Patches-AFOK
Authentic Fabrics Dual-AF2KO
Authentic Fabrics Dual Patches-AF2KO
Authentic Fabrics Triple-AF3WAS
Authentic Fabrics Triple Patches-AF3WAS
Authentic Fabrics Sevens-
AF7VEZ
Authentic Fabrics Sevens Patches-AF7VEZ
By The Letter-BLOK
06SPx-99
Spectrum-99
SPxcitement-X100
SPxcitement Spectrum-X100
Winning Materials-WMOK
Winning Materials Spectrum-WMOK
06The Cup Foundations-CQOK
06The Cup Foundations Patches-CQOK
06The Cup NHL Shields Duals-DSHKZ
06UD Artifacts-2
Blue-2
Gold-2
Platinum-2
Radiance-2
Red-2
Treasured Patches Black-TSOK
Treasured Patches Blue-TSOK
Treasured Patches Gold-TSOK
Treasured Patches Platinum-TSOK
Treasured Patches Red-TSOK
Treasured Swatches-TSOK
Treasured Swatches Black-TSOK
Treasured Swatches Blue-TSOK
Treasured Swatches Gold-TSOK
Treasured Swatches Platinum-TSOK
Treasured Swatches Red-TSOK
Tundra Tandems-TTKO
Tundra Tandems Black-TTKO
Tundra Tandems Blue-TTKO
Tundra Tandems Gold-TTKO
Tundra Tandems Platinum-TTKO
Tundra Tandems Red-TTKO
Tundra Tandems Dual Patches Red-TTKO
06UD Mini Jersey Collection-99
06UD Powerplay-100
Impact Rainbow-100
Specialists-SOK
Specialists Patches-POK
06Ultimate Collection Premium Patches-PS-OK
06Ultimate Collection Premium Swatches-PS-OK
06Ultra-195
Gold Medallion-195
Ice Medallion-195
Fresh Ink-IOK
06Upper Deck Arena Giveaways-WSH6
06Upper Deck-443
Exclusives Parallel-443
High Gloss Parallel-443
Award Winners Canadian Exclusive-OAW11
Game Jerseys-J2OK
Game Patches-P2OK
Masterpieces-443
06Upper Deck MVP-293
Gold Script-293
Super Script-293
International Icons-II25
Jerseys-OJKD
Jerseys-OJLK
Last Line of Defense-LL14
06Upper Deck Ovation-99
06Upper Deck Sweet Shot Sweet Stitches-SSOK
06Upper Deck Sweet Shot Sweet Stitches Duals-SSOK
06Upper Deck Sweet Shot Sweet Stitches Triples-SSOK
06Upper Deck Trilogy-100
Honorary Swatches-HSOK
06Upper Deck Victory-200
06Upper Deck Victory Black-200
06Upper Deck Victory Gold-200
07Upper Deck Ovation-1
07Upper Deck Victory-92
Black-92
Gold-92

Koma, Jaroslav
06Czech HC Pardubice Postcards-8
06Czech OFS-117

Komadoski, Neil
73O-Pee-Chee-16
73Topps-16
74NHL Action Stamps-112
74O-Pee-Chee NHL-358
75O-Pee-Chee NHL-238
75Topps-238
76O-Pee-Chee NHL-284
77O-Pee-Chee NHL-344
78O-Pee-Chee-382
01Notre Dame Fighting Irish-6
02Notre Dame Fighting Irish-12
03Notre Dame Fighting Irish-9
04Binghamton Senators-9
06Binghamton Senators-12

Komar, Eliot
96Arizona Icecats-10

Komarek, Lukas
04Slovakian Skalica Team Set-27

Komarniski, Zenith
95Upper Deck-516
Electric Ice-516
Electric Ice Gold-516
95Tri-City Americans-14
97Spokane Chiefs-5
97Bowman CHL-85
OPC-85
98UD Choice-263
Prime Choice Reserve-263
Reserve-263
98Bowman CHL-46
Golden Anniversary-46
OPC International-46
98Bowman Chrome CHL-46
Golden Anniversary-46
Golden Anniversary Refractors-46
OPC International-46
OPC International Refractors-46
Refractors-46
99Pacific Omega-238
Copper-238
Gold-238
Ice Blue-238
Premiere Date-238
99Syracuse Crunch-4
00O-Pee-Chee-291
00O-Pee-Chee Parallel-291
00Topps/OPC-291
Parallel-291
00Topps Chrome-186
OPC Refractors-186
Refractors-186
00Kansas City Blades-4
01Manitoba Moose-14
02Manitoba Moose-3
03Syracuse Crunch-5
04Syracuse Crunch-5

Komarov, Alexei
99Russian Hockey League-31
02Utah Grizzlies-22
04Russian Moscow Dynamo-16

Komarov, Leo
05Finnish Cardset -351
06Finnish Cardset-302
Playmakers Rookies-12
Playmakers Rookies Gold-12
Playmakers Rookies Silver-12

Komarov, Pavel
95Binghamton Rangers-10
99Russian Hockey League-257
00Russian Hockey League-141

Komarov, Sergei
00Russian Hockey League-247

Komisarek, Mike
96Quebec Pee-Wee Tournament-899
01BAP Memorabilia Draft Redemptions-7
02BAP Memorabilia-304
02BAP Ultimate Memorabilia-34
02Pacific Calder-127
Silver-127
02Pacific Complete-570
Red-570
02Pacific Quest for the Cup-127
Gold-127
02Parkhurst Retro-239
Minis-239
02SP Authentic-204
02SPx-186
02Upper Deck Classic Portraits-136
02Upper Deck Rookie Update-121
02AHL Top Prospects-22
02Hamilton Bulldogs-24
03BAP Memorabilia-57
Emerald-57
Gold-57
Ruby-57
Sapphire-57
Future of the Game-FG-10
03Black Diamond-49
Black-49
Green-49
Red-49
03Canadiens Postcards-17
03ITG Action-387
03Parkhurst Original Six Montreal-29
Memorabilia-MM57
03SP Game Used Authentic Fabrics-QKTHK
03SP Game Used Authentic Fabrics Gold-QKTHK
03SPx-52
03SPx-165
Radiance-52
Radiance-165
Spectrum-52
Spectrum-165
03UD Honor Roll-96
03Upper Deck-102
Canadian Exclusives-102
HG-102
Jerseys-UD-MK
03Upper Deck Classic Portraits-53
03Upper Deck MVP-232
Gold Script-232
Silver Script-232
Canadian Exclusives-232
03Upper Deck Victory-99
Bronze-99
Gold-99
Silver-99
Freshman Flashback-FF26
03AHL Top Prospects-14
05Canadiens Team Issue-12
05Upper Deck MVP-209
Gold-209
Platinum-209
06Black Diamond Jerseys-JMI
06Black Diamond Jerseys Black-JMI
06Black Diamond Jerseys Gold-JMI
06Black Diamond Jerseys Ruby-JMI
06Canadiens Postcards-10
06Fleer Fabricology-FKO
06Gatorade-45
06O-Pee-Chee-267
Rainbow-267
06Upper Deck Game Jerseys-JMI
06Upper Deck Game Patches-PMI

Komissarov, Oleg
99Russian Hockey League-204
00Russian Hockey League-365

Komma, Michael
94German DEL-61
95German DEL-61
99German DEL-291
03German Deg Metro Stars-9

Komonosky, Ward
84Prince Albert Raiders Stickers-16

Kompon, Jamie
90Cincinnati Cyclones-35

Kompon, Mike
05Reading Royals-8

Komsi, Antti
66Finnish Jaakiekkosarja-209

Konder, Peter
03UK Guildford Flames-16
04UK Guildford Flames-18

Kondrashkin, Sergei
93Parkhurst-532
Emerald Ice-532
93Pinnacle-511
Canadian-511

Kondratiev, Maxim
02SPx Rookie Redemption-R211
02Russian Hockey League-56
02Russian Hockey League-189
03BAP Memorabilia-197
Emerald-197
Gold-197
Ruby-197
Sapphire-197
03Beehive-235
Gold-235
Silver-235
03Black Diamond-153
Black-153
Green-153
Red-153
03Bowman-117
Gold-117
03Bowman Chrome-117
Refractors-117
Gold Refractors-117
Xfractors-117
03ITG Action-623
03ITG VIP Rookie Debut-38
03Pacific Complete-534
Red-534
03Pacific Luxury Suite-77
Gold-77
03Pacific Supreme-138
Blue-138
Red-138
Retail-138
03Parkhurst Original Six Toronto-5
03Parkhurst Rookie-172
03Private Stock Reserve-138
Blue-138
Red-138
Retail-138
03SP Authentic-110
Limited-110
03SP Game Used-80
Gold-80
03Titanium-137
Hobby Jersey Number Parallels-137
Retail-137
Retail Jersey Number Parallels-137
03Topps Pristine-161
03Topps Pristine-162
03Topps Pristine-163
Gold Refractor Die Cuts-161
Gold Refractor Die Cuts-162
Gold Refractor Die Cuts-163
Refractors-161
Refractors-162
Refractors-163
Press Plates Black-161
Press Plates Black-162
Press Plates Black-163
Press Plates Cyan-161
Press Plates Cyan-162
Press Plates Cyan-163
Press Plates Magenta-161
Press Plates Magenta-162
Press Plates Magenta-163
Press Plates Yellow-161
Press Plates Yellow-162
Press Plates Yellow-163
03UD Honor Roll-141
03Upper Deck-243
Canadian Exclusives-243
HG-243
03Upper Deck Classic Portraits-182
03Upper Deck Ice-102
Glass Parallel-102
03Upper Deck MVP-459
03Upper Deck Trilogy-169
Limited-169
03Russian National Team-33
04Russian Back to Russia-20
04Russian World Championship Team-4

Konecny, Cory
05Kitchener Rangers-25

Konecny, Jan
99Czech Score Blue 2000-142
99Czech Score Red Ice 2000-142

Konecny, Kamil
96Czech APS Extraliga-97
97Czech APS Extraliga-314
98Czech OFS-177
99Czech OFS-403
99Czech OFS-416
00Czech OFS-237

Konecny, Michal
95Czech APS Extraliga-210

Konecny, Rastislav
06Saskatoon Blades-14

Koniger, Stefan
94German DEL-225

Konigsson, Christopher
05Swedish SHL Elitset-240

Konik, Brad
92Harvard Crimson-18
96Providence Bruins-27

Konik, George
72Minnesota Fighting Saints Postcards WHA-11
72Finnish Semic World Championship-132
72Swedish Semic World Championship-132

Konjuchov, Dimitri
94German First League-647

Konkel, Bryan
01Michigan Tech Huskies-14

Konkov, Sergei
03Russian Hockey League-256

Konopasek, Stanislav
97Czech APS Extraliga-380

Konopka, Zenon
95Quebec Pee-Wee Tournament-552
99Ottawa 67's-9
00Ottawa 67's-12
01Ottawa 67's-14
02ECHL All-Star Northern-26
02ECHL Update-U-12
04Cincinnati Mighty Ducks-11
05Black Diamond-212
05Hot Prospects-102
En Fuego-102
Red Hot-102
White Hot-102
05SP Authentic-222
Limited-222
05SP Game Used-191
05SPx-216
Spectrum-216
05The Cup Masterpiece Pressplate Artifact-244
05The Cup Master Pressplate Black Diamond-212
05The Cup Master Pressplate (Ice)-187
05The Cup Master Pressplate Rookie Update-103
05The Cup Masterpiece Pressplates SPA-222
05The Cup Masterpiece Pressplates SP GU-191
05The Cup Masterpiece Pressplates (SPx)-216
05The Cup Masterpiece Pressplates Trilogy-222
05The Cup Masterpiece Pressplate Ult Coll-134
05UD Artifacts-244
05Ultimate Collection-134
Gold-134
05Upper Deck Ice-187
05Upper Deck Rookie Update-103
05Upper Deck Trilogy-222
06Portland Pirates-3

Konovalenko, Viktor
70Finnish Jaakiekko-5
70Russian National Team Postcards-1
70Swedish Hockey-231
70Swedish Hockey-232
70Swedish Hockey-233
70Swedish Hockey-234
70Swedish Hockey-235
70Swedish Hockey-236
70Swedish Hockey-237
70Swedish Hockey-238
70Swedish Hockey-239
70Swedish Hockey-240
70Swedish Hockey-241
70Swedish Hockey-242
70Swedish Hockey-313
70Swedish Masterserien-130
71Finnish Suomi Stickers-4
71Swedish Hockey-26
72Finnish Panda Toronto-51
72Finnish Semic World Championship-1
72Swedish Semic World Championship-1
74Swedish Semic World Champ Stickers-50

Konowalchuk, Steve
907th Inn. Sketch WHL-312
91Upper Deck Czech World Juniors-73
917th Inn. Sketch WHL-30
91Classic-46
91Star Pics-9
91Ultimate Draft-41
91Ultimate Draft French-41
91Classic Four-Sport *-46
Autographs-46A
92Capitals Kodak-16
92OPC Premier-15
92Parkhurst-202
Emerald Ice-202
92Ultra-437
92Upper Deck-418
93Parkhurst-223
Emerald Ice-223
93Score-458
Canadian-458
93Stadium Club-481
Members Only Master Set-481
First Day Issue-481
93Upper Deck-28
93Classic Pro Prospects-102
94Leaf-423
94OPC Premier-273
Special Effects-273
94Parkhurst SE-SE192
Gold-SE192
94Pinnacle-348
Artist's Proofs-348
Rink Collection-348
94Topps/OPC Premier-273
Special Effects-273
94Ultra-389
94Upper Deck-214
Electric Ice-214
95Canada Games NHL POGS-279
95Capitals Team Issue-17
95Collector's Choice-318
Player's Club-318
Player's Club Platinum-318
95Donruss-296
95Leaf-323
95Panini Stickers-137
95Parkhurst International-493
Emerald Ice-493
95SP-160
95Ultra-324
96Be A Player-173
Autographs-173
Autographs Silver-173
96Collector's Choice-281
96Pinnacle-131
Artist's Proofs-131
Foil-131
Premium Stock-131
Rink Collection-131
96Score-135
Artist's Proofs-135
Dealer's Choice Artist's Proofs-135
Special Artist's Proofs-135
Golden Blades-135
96Upper Deck-179
97Collector's Choice-274
97Pacific-69
Copper-69
Emerald Green-69
Ice Blue-69
Red-69
Silver-69
97Pacific Dynagon-132
Copper-132
Dark Grey-132
Emerald Green-132
Ice Blue-132
Red-132
Silver-132
Tandems-58
97Pacific Invincible-148
Copper-148
Emerald Green-148
Ice Blue-148
Red-148
Silver-148
97Paramount-197
Copper-197
Dark Grey-197
Emerald Green-197
Ice Blue-197
Red-197
Silver-197
97Score-220
97Upper Deck-174
98Be A Player-148
Press Release-148
98BAP Gold-148
98BAP Autographs-148
98BAP Autographs Gold-148
98BAP Tampa Bay All Star Game-148
98Capitals Kids and Cops-6
98Pacific-443
Ice Blue-443
Red-443
98Paramount-248
Copper-248
Emerald Green-248
Holo-Electric-248
Ice Blue-248
Silver-248
99BAP Memorabilia-283
Gold-283
Silver-283
99O-Pee-Chee-77
99O-Pee-Chee Chrome-77
99O-Pee-Chee Chrome Refractors-77
99Pacific-444
Copper-444
Emerald Green-444
Gold-444
Ice Blue-444
Premiere Date-444
Red-444
99Pacific Omega-244
Copper-244
Gold-244
Ice Blue-244
Premiere Date-244
99Paramount-246
Copper-246
Emerald-246
Gold-246
Holographic Emerald-246
Holographic Gold-246
Holographic Silver-246
Ice Blue-246
Premiere Date-246
Red-246
Silver-246
99Stadium Club Promos-PP2
99Stadium Club-26
First Day Issue-26
One of a Kind-26
Printing Plates Black-26
Printing Plates Cyan-26
Printing Plates Magenta-26
Printing Plates Yellow-26
99Topps/OPC-77
99Topps/OPC Chrome-77
Refractors-77
99Ultimate Victory-89
1/1-89
Parallel-89
Parallel 100-89
00BAP Memorabilia-315
Emerald-315
Ruby-315
Sapphire-315
Promos-315
00BAP Mem Chicago Sportsfest Copper-315
00BAP Memorabilia Chicago Sportsfest Blue-315
00BAP Memorabilia Chicago Sportsfest Gold-315
00BAP Memorabilia Chicago Sportsfest Ruby-315
00BAP Memorabilia Chicago Sun-Times Ruby-315
00BAP Memorabilia Chicago Sun-Times Gold-315
00BAP Mem Chicago Sun-Times Sapphire-315
00BAP Mem Toronto Fall Expo Copper-315
00BAP Memorabilia Toronto Fall Expo Gold-315
00BAP Memorabilia Toronto Fall Expo Ruby-315
00BAP Signature Series-227
Emerald-227
Ruby-227
Sapphire-227
Autographs-13
Autographs Gold-13
00O-Pee-Chee-176
00O-Pee-Chee Parallel-176
00Pacific-426
Copper-426
Gold-426
Ice Blue-426
Premiere Date-426
00Paramount-247
Copper-247
Gold-247
Holo-Gold-247
Holo-Silver-247
Ice Blue-247
Premiere Date-247
00Titanium Game Gear-50
00Topps/OPC-176
Parallel-176
00Upper Deck-404
Exclusives Tier 1-404
Exclusives Tier 2-404
00Upper Deck Vintage-363
01BAP Memorabilia-189
Emerald-189
Ruby-189
Sapphire-189
01O-Pee-Chee-203
01O-Pee-Chee Premier Parallel-203
01Pacific-396
Extreme LTD-396
Hobby LTD-396
Premiere Date-396
Retail LTD-396
01Pacific Adrenaline-199
Blue-199
Premiere Date-199
Red-199
Retail-199
01Pacific Arena Exclusives-396
01Topps-203
OPC Parallel-203
01Upper Deck-406
Exclusives-406
01Upper Deck Victory-352
Gold-352
01Upper Deck Vintage-252
01Upper Deck Vintage-260
02BAP Sig Series Auto Buybacks 1998-148
02BAP Sig Series Auto Buybacks 2000-13
02BAP Signature Series Golf-GS88
02Capitals Team Issue-6
02Pacific-396
Blue-396
Red-396
02SP Game Used Piece of History-PHKO
02SP Game Used Piece of History Gold-PHKO
02SP Game Used Piece of History Rainbow-PHKO
02Topps Total-188
02UD Honor Roll-100
02Upper Deck-176
Exclusives-176
Classic Portraits Hockey Royalty-KGJ
Classic Portraits Hockey Royalty Limited-KGJ
02Upper Deck MVP-188
Gold-188
Classics-188
Golden Classics-188
02Upper Deck Victory-215
Bronze-215
Gold-215
Silver-215
02Upper Deck Vintage-253
Jerseys-HSSK
Jerseys Gold-HS-SK
03Avalanche Team Issue-11
03ITG Action-581
03NHL Sticker Collection-149
03O-Pee-Chee-107
03OPC Blue-107
03OPC Gold-107
03OPC Red-107
03Pacific Complete-383
Red-383
03Topps-107
Blue-107
Gold-107
Red-107
03Topps Traded-TT23
Blue-TT23
Gold-TT23
Red-TT23
03Upper Deck-197
03Upper Deck-290
Canadian Exclusives-197
Canadian Exclusives-290
HG-197
HG-290
UD Exclusives-290
03Upper Deck MVP-432
Gold Script-432
Silver Script-432
Canadian Exclusives-432
05Panini Stickers-234
05Parkhurst-133
Facsimile Auto Parallel-133
05Upper Deck-48
HG Glossy-48
Jerseys-J-SKO
06Upper Deck MVP-102
Gold-102
Platinum-102
Materials-M-SK
05Upper Deck Toronto Fall Expo-48
06Panini Stickers-226
06Upper Deck Game Jerseys-J2SK
06Upper Deck Game Patches-P2SK

Konroyd, Steve
80Oshawa Generals-9
81Flames Postcards-8
82O-Pee-Chee-48
83O-Pee-Chee-85
83Vachon-9
84O-Pee-Chee-226
85Flames Red Rooster-10
86Islanders Team Issue-28
87O-Pee-Chee-153
87Topps-153
88O-Pee-Chee-171
88O-Pee-Chee Stickers-110
88Panini Stickers-284
88Topps-171
89Blackhawks Coke-21
89O-Pee-Chee-220
90Blackhawks Coke-21
90Pro Set-52
90Score-29
Canadian-29
91Pro Set Platinum-177
91Blackhawks Coke-12
91O-Pee-Chee-366
91Parkhurst-287
French-287
91Pinnacle-180
French-180
91Score American-189
91Score Canadian Bilingual-189
91Score Canadian English-189
91Topps-366
91Whalers Jr. 7-Eleven-19
92Bowman-16
92O-Pee-Chee-238
92Parkhurst-299
Emerald Ice-299
92Pinnacle-352
French-352
92Pro Set-62
92Score-172
Canadian-172
92Stadium Club-236
92Topps-411
Gold-411G
92Ultra-300
92Whalers Dairymart-12
93Score-219
Canadian-219
94OPC Premier-394
Special Effects-394
94Pinnacle-339
Artist's Proofs-339
Rink Collection-339
94Topps/OPC Premier-394
Special Effects-394

Kons, Arndt
94German First League-507

Kons, Benedikt
94German First League-510

Konsorada, Tim
00Brandon Wheat Kings-17
01Brandon Wheat Kings-17
02Brandon Wheat Kings-15
03Brandon Wheat Kings-9
04Brandon Wheat Kings-15
05Syracuse Crunch-20

Konstantinov, Evgeny
01BAP Memorabilia-391
Emerald-391
Ruby-391
Sapphire-391
01Parkhurst-345
01UD Top Shelf-140
02UD Mask Collection-81
02UD Mask Collection Beckett Promos-81
02Upper Deck-221
Exclusives-221
02Springfield Falcons-14
03Pensacola Ice Pilots-348
05Russian Hockey League RHL-55

Konstantinov, Vladimir
87Russian National Team-11
89Russian National Team-14
89Swedish Semic World Champ Stickers-86
90O-Pee-Chee Red Army-21R
91Pro Set Platinum-254
91OPC Premier-118A
91OPC Premier-118B
91OPC Premier-155
91Parkhurst-46
French-46
91Pinnacle-311
French-311
91Pro Set-533
French-533
91Score Canadian Bilingual-659
91Score Canadian English-659
91Score Rookie/Traded-109T
91Upper Deck-594
French-594
91Finnish Semic World Champ Stickers-81
91Russian Stars Red Ace-9
91Russian Sports Unite Hearts-5
91Russian Stars in NHL-5
91Swedish Semic World Champ Stickers-81
92Bowman-326
92O-Pee-Chee-267
92Parkhurst-283
Emerald Ice-283
92Pinnacle-76
French-76
92Pro Set-44
92Score-31
92Score-503
Canadian-31
Canadian-503
Young Superstars-23
92Stadium Club-418
92Topps-14
92Topps-165
Gold-14G
Gold-165G
92Ultra-49
92Upper Deck-267
92Upper Deck-357
All-Rookie Team-AR5
All-Rookie Team-AR7
All-World Team-W5
Euro-Stars-E10

92Finnish Semic-108
93Leaf-237
93OPC Premier-108
Gold-108
93Parkhurst-325
Emerald Ice-325
93Pinnacle-264
Canadian-264
93PowerPlay-73
93Score-20
Canadian-20
93Stadium Club-333
Members Only Master Set-333
First Day Issue-333
93Topps/OPC Premier-108
Gold-108
93Ultra-150
93Upper Deck-366
94Canada Games NHL POGS-94
94Flair-49
94Fleer-60
94Leaf-391
94OPC Premier-448
Special Effects-448
94Parkhurst SE-SE53
Gold-SE53
94Pinnacle-116
Artist's Proofs-116
Rink Collection-116
94Score-96
Gold-96
Platinum-96
94Stadium Club-159
Members Only Master Set-159
First Day Issue-159
Super Team Winner Cards-159
94Topps/OPC Premier-448
Special Effects-448
94Ultra-61
94Upper Deck-189
Electric Ice-189
94German First League-624
95Be A Player-216
Signatures-S216
Signatures Die Cuts-S216
95Emotion-54
95Leaf-283
95Metal-46
95Parkhurst International-69
Emerald Ice-69
95Pinnacle-129
Artist's Proofs-129
Rink Collection-129
95Playoff One on One-145
95Score-176
Black Ice Artist's Proofs-176
Black Ice-176
95SkyBox Impact-53
95Ultra-46
Gold Medallion-46
95Upper Deck-190
Electric Ice-190
Electric Ice Gold-190
96Black Diamond-16
Gold-16
96Collector's Choice-82
96Collector's Choice-302
96Collector's Choice-316
96Donruss-83
Press Proofs-83
96Fleer-31
96Fleer-143
Norris-6
96Leaf-110
Press Proofs-110
96Metal Universe-46
Cool Steel-6
Cool Steel Super Power-6
96Pinnacle-65
Artist's Proofs-65
Foil-65
Premium Stock-65
Rink Collection-65
96Score-84
Artist's Proofs-84
Dealer's Choice Artist's Proofs-84
Special Artist's Proofs-84
Golden Blades-84
96SkyBox Impact-35
NHL on Fox-12
96SP-53
96Summit-63
Artist's Proofs-63
Ice-63
Metal-63
Premium Stock-63
96Topps Picks-169
OPC Inserts-169
96Ultra-51
Gold Medallion-51
Power-9
Power Blue Line-6
96Upper Deck-52
Power Performers-P12
97Collector's Choice-82
Star Quest-SQ33
97Donruss-65
Press Proofs Silver-65
Press Proofs Gold-65
97NHL Aces Playing Cards-52
97Pacific-189
Copper-189
Emerald Green-189
Ice Blue-189
Red-189
Silver-189
Card-Supials-7
Card-Supials Minis-7
97Pacific Dynagon-42
Copper-42
Dark Grey-42
Emerald Green-42
Ice Blue-42
Red-42
Silver-42
Dynamic Duos-7B
Tandems-26
97Pacific Invincible-47
Copper-47
Emerald Green-47
Ice Blue-47
Red-47
Silver-47
Feature Performers-13
97Panini Stickers-147
97Pinnacle Inside-126
97Score-228
97Score Red Wings-9
Platinum-9
Premier-9
97Upper Deck-63
97Upper Deck-203
Game Dated Moments-63
04ITG Franchises US West-209
04ITG Ultimate Memorabilia-137
Gold-137

Konsti, Kalle
03UK London Racers-5

Kontilla, Mikko
93Finnish SISU-20

Kontio, Esa
70Finnish Jaakiekko-371

Kontiola, Petri
04Finnish Cardset-161
04Finnish Cardset Signatures-32
05Finnish Cardset -145
06Finnish Cardset-152
Signature Sensations-28

Kontny, Josef
94German DEL-152
95German DEL-147

Kontos, Chris
87Penguins Kodak-15
89ProCards AHL-14
90ProCards AHL/IHL-359
91Alberta International Team Canada-14
92Lightning Sheraton-19
92OPC Premier-123
92Parkhurst-176
Emerald Ice-176
92Stadium Club Members Only-45
92Ultra-412
92Upper Deck-502
93Alberta International Team Canada-9
93Leaf-160
93OPC Premier-215
Gold-215
Team Canada-14
93Panini Stickers-213
93Parkhurst-197
Emerald Ice-197
93Pinnacle-8
Canadian-8
93PowerPlay-233
93Score-113
Canadian-113
93Topps/OPC Premier-215
Gold-215
93Ultra-162
93Upper Deck-54
94EA Sports-131
94Score Team Canada-CT6
95Cincinnati Cyclones-11

Kontsek, Roman
94Finnish Jaa Kiekko-204
96Czech APS Extraliga-64
97Czech APS Extraliga-337
97Czech DS Extraliga-112
98Czech DS Stickers-280
99Czech OFS-290
00Czech OFS-281
01Slovakian Kvarteto-4D

Konttila, Mikko
93Finnish SISU-19
94Finnish SISU-111
94Finnish SISU-350
95Finnish SISU-280
98Finnish Kerailysarja-159
99Swedish Upper Deck-51
00Finnish Cardset-350
01Finnish Cardset-152

Konttinen, Tero
04Finnish Cardset-241
05Finnish Cardset -231
06Finnish Porin Assat Pelaajakortit-8

Kontto, Pertti
65Finnish Hellas-71

Koopman, Kevin
907th Inn. Sketch WHL-257
917th Inn. Sketch WHL-188

Koopmans, Brad
91British Columbia JHL-70

Koopmans, Leo
79Panini Stickers-282

Koopmans, Logan
01Lethbridge Hurricanes-14
06Toledo Storm-13

Kopat, Vladimir
98Russian Hockey League-145
99Russian Hockey League-191
00Russian Hockey League-381

Kopatz, Wilhelm
04German Berlin Eisbarens 50th Anniv-43

Kopczynski, Adam
73Finnish Jaakiekko-94
74Finnish Jenkki-99
74Finnish Typotor-89

Kopec, Dan
90Brandon Wheat Kings-12
907th Inn. Sketch WHL-227
917th Inn. Sketch WHL-204

Kopeck, Mervin
95Central Hockey League-45

Kopecky, Jan
98Czech OFS-223
99Czech DS-123
99Czech OFS-46
99Czech OFS-471
99Czech OFS-498
All-Star Game Blue-498
All-Star Game Gold-498
All-Star Game Red-498
All-Star Game Silver-498
00Czech OFS-96
01Czech OFS-195
02Czech OFS Plus-136
Duos-D25

Kopecky, Ludvik
94German First League-188

Kopecky, Milan
02Czech OFS Plus-362
03Czech OFS Plus-184
04Czech OFS-167
05Czech HC Ceski Budejovice-7
06Czech OFS-138

Kopecky, Tomas
00Lethbridge Hurricanes-12
00UD CHL Prospects-71
01Lethbridge Hurricanes-6
02AHL Top Prospects-23
02Grand Rapids Griffins-16
03Grand Rapids Griffins-9
04ITG Heroes and Prospects-18
Autographs-TK
Combos-7
Complete Emblems-19
Emblems-52
Emblems Gold-52
He Shoots-He Scores Prizes-15
Jersey Autographs-52
Jerseys-52
Jerseys Gold-52
Numbers-52
Numbers Gold-52
04ITG Heroes/Prospects Toronto Expo '05-18
04ITG Heroes/Prospects Expo Heroes/Pros-18
06Be A Player Portraits-106
06Beehive-117
Blue-117
Matte-117
Red Facsimile Signatures-117
Wood-117
06Black Diamond-156A
Black-156A
Gold-156A
Ruby-156A
06Flair Showcase-39
06Flair Showcase-125
Parallel-39
Parallel-125
06Fleer-212
Tiffany-212
06Hot Prospects-112
Red Hot-112
White Hot-112
Hotagraphs-HTK
06O-Pee-Chee-528
06O-Pee-Chee-639
Rainbow-528
Rainbow-639
06SP Authentic-177
Limited-177
06SP Game Used-114
Gold-114
Rainbow-114
Rookie Exclusives Autographs-RETK
06SPx-176
Spectrum-176
06The Cup-126
Autographed Rookie Masterpiece Pressplates-126
Gold Rainbow Autographed Rookie Patches-126
Masterpiece Pressplates (Artifacts)-225
Masterpiece Pressplates (Be A Player Portraits)-106
Masterpiece Pressplates (Bee Hive)-117
Masterpiece Pressplates (Black Diamond)-156
Masterpiece Pressplates (Marquee Rookies)-528
Masterpiece Pressplates (MVP)-356
Masterpiece Pressplates (Power Play)-105
Masterpiece Pressplates (SP Authentic Autographs)-177
Masterpiece Pressplates (SP Game Used)-114
Masterpiece Pressplates (SPx Autographs)-176
Masterpiece Pressplates (Sweet Beginnings)-121
Masterpiece Pressplates (Trilogy)-112
Masterpiece Pressplates (Ultimate Collection)-73
Masterpiece Pressplates (Victory)-201
Rookies Black-126
Rookies Platinum-126
06UD Artifacts-225
Blue-225
Gold-225
Platinum-225
Radiance-225
Red-225
06UD Mini Jersey Collection-105
06UD Powerplay-105
Impact Rainbow-105
06Ultimate Collection-73
Ultimate Debut Threads Jerseys-DJ-TK
Ultimate Debut Threads Jerseys Autographs-DJ-TK
Ultimate Debut Threads Patches-DJ-TK
Ultimate Debut Threads Patches Autographs-DJ-TK
06Ultra-206
Gold Medallion-206
Ice Medallion-206
06Upper Deck-211
Exclusives Parallel-211
High Gloss Parallel-211
Masterpieces-211
Rookie Game Dated Moments-RGD7
Rookie Headliners-RH17
Rookie Materials-RMTK
Rookie Materials Patches-RMTK
06Upper Deck MVP-356
Gold Script-356
Super Script-356
06Upper Deck Ovation-69
06Upper Deck Sweet Shot-121
Rookie Jerseys Autographs-121
06Upper Deck Trilogy-112
06Upper Deck Victory-201
06Upper Deck Victory Black-201
06Upper Deck Victory Gold-201
06ITG Heroes and Prospects-38
Autographs-ATK
07Upper Deck Rookie Class -32

Kopf, Bernhard
94German First League-167

Kopf, Ernst
92Upper Deck-372
92Finnish Semic-181
93Swedish Semic World Champ Stickers-161
94Finnish Jaa Kiekko-284
94German DEL-98
95Finnish Semic World Championships-168
95Swedish World Championships Stickers-71
96German DEL-283

Kopfler, Manuel
04German Augsburg Panthers Postcards-16

Kopitar, Anze
05Swedish SHL Elitset-275
Gold-275
Series Two Signatures-24
06Be A Player-213
06Be A Player Portraits-115
06Beehive-125
Blue-125
Gold-125
Matte-125
Red Facsimile Signatures-125
Wood-125
06Black Diamond-200
Black-200
Gold-200
Ruby-200
06Flair Showcase-314
06Hot Prospects-117
Red Hot-117
White Hot-117
Hot Materials -HMAK
Hot Materials Red Hot-HMAK
Hot Materials White Hot-HMAK
Hotagraphs-HAK
06ITG Ultimate Memorabilia First Round Picks-10
06ITG Ultimate Memorabilia First Round Picks Gold-10
06ITG Ultimate Memorabilia Future Star-7
06ITG Ultimate Memorabilia Future Star Gold-7
06ITG Ultimate Memorabilia Future Star Autos-21
06ITG Ultimate Memorabilia Future Star Autos Gold-21
06ITG Ultimate Memorabilia Future Star Patches Autos-21
06ITG Ultimate Memorabilia Future Star Patches Autos Gold-21
06ITG Ultimate Memorabilia R.O.Y. Autos-1
06ITG Ultimate Memorabilia R.O.Y. Autos Gold-1
06ITG Ultimate Memorabilia R.O.Y. Emblems-1
06ITG Ultimate Memorabilia R.O.Y. Emblems Gold-1
06ITG Ultimate Memorabilia R.O.Y. Jerseys-1
06ITG Ultimate Memorabilia R.O.Y. Jerseys Gold-1
06ITG Ultimate Memorabilia R.O.Y. Numbers-1
06ITG Ultimate Memorabilia R.O.Y. Numbers Gold-1
06ITG Ultimate Memorabilia Triple Thread Jerseys-14
06ITG Ultimate Memorabilia Triple Thread Jerseys Gold-14
06O-Pee-Chee-539
06O-Pee-Chee-636
Rainbow-539
Rainbow-636
06SP Authentic-184
Chirography-AK
Limited-184
Sign of the Times Duals-STFK
06SP Game Used-122
Gold-122
Rainbow-122
Autographs-122
Rookie Exclusives Autographs-REAK
06SPx-179
Spectrum-179
06The Cup-173
Autographed Foundations-CQAK
Autographed Foundations Patches-CQAK
Autographed NHL Shields Duals-DASBK
Autographed NHL Shields Duals-DASFK
Autographed NHL Shields Duals-DASKO
Autographed Rookie Masterpiece Pressplates-173
Foundations-CQAK
Foundations Patches-CQAK
Enshrinements-EAK
Gold Rainbow Autographed Rookie Patches-173
Honorable Numbers-HNAK
Limited Logos-LLAK
Masterpiece Pressplates (Be A Player Portraits)-115
Masterpiece Pressplates (Bee Hive)-125
Masterpiece Pressplates (Marquee Rookies)-539
Masterpiece Pressplates (MVP)-306
Masterpiece Pressplates (SP Authentic Autographs)-184
Masterpiece Pressplates (SP Game Used)-122
Masterpiece Pressplates (SPx Autographs)-179
Masterpiece Pressplates (Sweet Beginnings)-130
Masterpiece Pressplates (Trilogy)-118
Masterpiece Pressplates (Ultimate Collection Autographs)-114
Masterpiece Pressplates (Victory)-285
NHL Shields Duals-DSHJA
NHL Shields Duals-DSHKC
NHL Shields Duals-DSHPA
Property of-POAK
Rookies Black-173
Rookies Platinum-173
Signature Patches-SPAK
06UD Artifacts-244
06UD Mini Jersey Collection-109
06Ultimate Collection-114
Rookies Autographed NHL Shields-114
Rookies Autographed Patches-114
Signatures-US-AK
Ultimate Debut Threads Jerseys-DJ-AK
Ultimate Debut Threads Jerseys Autographs-DJ-AK
Ultimate Debut Threads Patches-DJ-AK
Ultimate Debut Threads Patches Autographs-DJ-AK
06Ultra-233
Gold Medallion-233
Ice Medallion-233
06Upper Deck-216
Exclusives Parallel-216
High Gloss Parallel-216
Masterpieces-216
Rookie Game Dated Moments-RGD12
Rookie Headliners-RH25
Rookie Materials-RMKO
Rookie Materials Patches-RMKO
06Upper Deck MVP-306
Gold Script-306
Super Script-306
06Upper Deck Sweet Shot-130
Rookie Jerseys Autographs-130
Signature Shots/Saves-SSAK
Signature Shots/Saves Sticks-SSSAK
06Upper Deck Trilogy-118
06Upper Deck Victory-285
06ITG Heroes and Prospects-131
Autographs-AAK
Quad Emblems-QE16
07Upper Deck Ovation-26
07Upper Deck Rookie Class -14
07Upper Deck Rookie Class C-Card Insert-CC4
07Upper Deck Victory-192
Black-192
Gold-192
GameBreakers-GB32

Kopitz, Lasse
01German Upper Deck-268
02German DEL City Press-162
03German DEL-204
03German Nuremberg Ice Tigers Postcards-14
04German DEL-250
04German Nuremburg Ice Tigers Postcards-9
05German DEL-209
05German DEL-287
06German DEL-125

Koponen, Tero
05Finnish Cardset -251

Koponen, Ville-Matti
05Finnish Cardset -122
06Finnish Cardset-131

Kopot, Artem
91Upper Deck Czech World Juniors-9

Kopp, John
04Penticton Vees-19
05Penticton Vees-7

Koppchen, Patrick
02German DEL City Press-94
03German DEL-111
04German DEL-153
04German Hannover Scorpions Postcards-14
05German DEL-131

Koppel, Marco
95Swiss HNL-174
96Swiss HNL-438

Kopriva, Bretislav
94Czech APS Extraliga-300
95Czech APS Extraliga-124

Kopriva, Miroslav
04Czech OFS-329
06Hot Prospects-165
Red Hot-165
White Hot-165
06O-Pee-Chee-534
Rainbow-534
06SP Authentic-237
Limited-237
06SP Game Used-124
Gold-124
Rainbow-124
06SPx-153
Spectrum-153
06The Cup-164
Autographed Rookie Masterpiece Pressplates-164
Gold Rainbow Autographed Rookie Patches-164
Masterpiece Pressplates (Artifacts)-230
Masterpiece Pressplates (Marquee Rookies)-534
Masterpiece Pressplates (MVP)-349
Masterpiece Pressplates (Power Play)-109
Masterpiece Pressplates (SP Authentic)-237
Masterpiece Pressplates (SP Game Used)-124
Masterpiece Pressplates (SPx)-153
Masterpiece Pressplates (Trilogy)-120
Masterpiece Pressplates (Victory)-229
Rookies Black-164
Rookies Platinum-164
06UD Artifacts-230
Blue-230
Gold-230
Platinum-230
Radiance-230
Red-230
06UD Powerplay-109
Impact Rainbow-109
06Ultimate Collection Ultimate Debut Threads Jerseys-DJ-MK
06Ultimate Collection Ultimate Debut Threads Jerseys Autographs-DJ-MK
06Ultimate Collection Ultimate Debut Threads Patches-DJ-MK
06Ultimate Collection Ultimate Debut Threads Patches Autographs-DJ-MK
06Ultra-210
Gold Medallion-210
Ice Medallion-210
06Upper Deck-219
Exclusives Parallel-219
High Gloss Parallel-219
Masterpieces-219
06Upper Deck MVP-349
Gold Script-349
Super Script-349
06Upper Deck Trilogy-120
06Upper Deck Victory-229
06Upper Deck Victory Black-229
06Upper Deck Victory Gold-229

Koprivica, Braden
00Arizona Icecats-12
01Arizona Icecats-9
02Arizona Icecats-11

Kopta, Petr
94German DEL-425
95German DEL-112
96German DEL-55

Koptin, Nikolai
00Russian Hockey League-345

Korab, Jerry
71Toronto Sun-69
72O-Pee-Chee-285
73Canucks Royal Bank-8
73O-Pee-Chee-203
74Nabisco Sugar Daddy-16
74NHL Action Stamps-43
74O-Pee-Chee NHL-354
74Sabres Postcards-11
75O-Pee-Chee NHL-192
75Topps-192
76O-Pee-Chee NHL-27
76Sabres Glasses-1
76Topps-27
77O-Pee-Chee NHL-128
77Topps-128
78O-Pee-Chee-231
78Topps-231
79O-Pee-Chee-74
79Sabres Bells-3
79Sabres Milk Panels-3
79Topps-74
80Kings Card Night-6
80O-Pee-Chee-300
81O-Pee-Chee-145
81O-Pee-Chee Stickers-240
81Topps-W97
82Post Cereal-8
83NHL Key Tags-50
83O-Pee-Chee Stickers-297
83Topps Stickers-297

Korb, Manfred
94German First League-208

Korbela, Jaroslav
82Swedish Semic VM Stickers-95
83Swedish Semic VM Stickers-95

Korber, Daniel
94German DEL-279
95German DEL-275
96German DEL-171
98German DEL-17
99Alexandria Warthogs-7

Korber, Hannes
99German DEL-30

Korchinkski, Larry
83Saskatoon Blades-16

Kordic, Dan
907th Inn. Sketch WHL-40
91Flyers J.C. Penney-16
91Pinnacle-338
French-338
91Pro Set-553
French-553
96Flyers Postcards-12
97Be A Player-158
Autographs-158
Autographs Die-Cuts-158
Autographs Prismatic Die-Cuts-158
97Pacific Invincible NHL Regime-142

Kordic, John
85Canadiens Postcards-14
86Canadiens Postcards-8
87Canadiens Postcards-11
87Canadiens Vachon Stickers-57
87Canadiens Vachon Stickers-58
90O-Pee-Chee-401
90Pro Set-536
91Nordiques Petro-Canada-13
91Pro Set-468
French-468

Koreis, Jakub
02Czech OFS Plus-357
03Guelph Storm-22
06Czech OFS Jagr Team-5

Korenko, Joel
93Brandon Wheat Kings-11
94Brandon Wheat Kings-9

Koreshkov, Alexander
98Russian Hockey League-17
99Russian Hockey League-14
99Russian Hockey League-NNO
99Russian Metallurg Magnetogorsk-45
02Russian Hockey League-76

Koreshkov, Evgeni
98Russian Hockey League-4
98Russian Hockey League-128
99Russian Hockey League-13
99Russian Hockey League-NNO
99Russian Metallurg Magnetogorsk-44
04Russian Super League All-Stars-28

Koreshkov, Igor
99Russian Hockey League-NNO

Korhon, Lubomir
99Czech OFS-209
00Czech OFS-368
01Czech OFS-239
02Czech OFS Plus All-Star Game-H11
03Czech OFS Plus-128
04Czech OFS-136
05Czech HC Pardubice-7
06Czech OFS-159

Korhonen, Aki
98Finnish Kerailysarja-150
99Finnish Cardset-209

Korhonen, Erkki
78Finnish SM-Liiga-84
80Finnish Mallasjuoma-60

Korhonen, Jari
03Finnish Cardset-75
04Finnish Cardset-83
Parallel-63
06Finnish Cardset-5

Korhonen, Juha
71Finnish Suomi Stickers-368

Korhonen, Markus
95Finnish SISU-136
98Finnish Kerailysarja-75
00Finnish Cardset-52
00Finnish Cardset Masquerade-6
01Finnish Cardset-279
02Finnish Cardset-42
03Swedish Elite-145
Global Impact-GI1
Silver-145
04Russian Legion-34
04Swedish Elitset-1
Gold-1
In The Crease-1
Jerseys Series 1-1
05Swedish SHL Elitset-145
Gold-145
06Finnish Cardset-281
Between the Pipes-16
06Swedish SHL Elitset Goal Patrol-2

Korhonen, Matti
66Finnish Jaakiekkosarja-106

Korhonen, Risto
06Finnish Cardset-211

Korhonen, Ville
05Finnish Cardset -219
06Finnish Cardset-47
06Finnish Ilves Team Set-10

Korinek, Jakub
04Czech OFS-345

Korinek, Petr
93Finnish Jyvas-Hyva Stickers-233
93Finnish SISU-205
94Finnish SISU-244
94Finnish SISU Fire On Ice-13
95Finnish SISU-78
95Finnish SISU-374
95Finnish SISU Limited-68
96Czech APS Extraliga-301
97Czech DS Stickers-225
97Swedish Collector's Choice-181
98Czech DS-59
98Czech OFS-43
98Czech OFS-464
99Czech DS-95
99Czech OFS-125
99Czech OFS-477
00Czech DS Extraliga-32
00Czech OFS-68
00Czech OFS Star Emerald-17
00Czech OFS Star Pink-17
00Czech OFS Star Violet-17
01Czech OFS Red Inserts-RE20D
03Czech OFS Plus All-Star Game-H17

Korjakoff, Pekka
65Finnish Hellas-51

Korkeamaki, Jorma
70Finnish Jaakiekko-331

Korkeavuori, Olli
04Finnish Cardset-276
05Finnish Cardset -113
06Finnish Cardset-121

Kormanyos, Nick
06Fayetteville FireAntz-7

Kormunda, Pavel
99Czech Score Blue 2000-148
99Czech Score Red Ice 2000-148

Korn, Jim
79Red Wings Postcards-8
81O-Pee-Chee-91
81O-Pee-Chee Stickers-127
81Topps-W91
82Maple Leafs Postcards-19
82O-Pee-Chee-323
83Maple Leafs Postcards-12
83O-Pee-Chee-335
83Vachon-91
84Maple Leafs Postcards-14
84O-Pee-Chee-304
84O-Pee-Chee Stickers-17
85Maple Leafs Postcards-17
86Sabres Blue Shield-16
86Sabres Blue Shield Small-16
88Devils Caretta-14
89Devils Caretta-13
89Panini Stickers-261
90O-Pee-Chee-450

Korneev, Konstantin
02Russian Hockey League-203
03Russian Hockey League-159
04Russian World Junior Team-1

Korneev, Vladislav
00Russian Hockey League-285

Korney, Mike
75O-Pee-Chee NHL-342

Korobkin, Sergei
98Russian Hockey League-51

Korobolin, Alexander
99Hartford Wolf Pack-15
00Russian Hockey League-226
01Russian Hockey League-101

Korobov, Maxim
01Russian Hockey League-20

Korol, Dave
88ProCards AHL-13
89ProCards IHL-121
90ProCards AHL/IHL-309
91ProCards-328

Korol, Kevin
98Kelowna Rockets-13
99Kelowna Rockets-27
01Regina Pats-11

Korolev, Andrei
95Swedish Leaf-295
95Swedish Upper Deck-197
99Russian Hockey League-251

Korolev, Evgeny
95Slapshot-325
99Pacific Omega-146
Copper-146
Gold-146
Ice Blue-146
Premiere Date-146
99Lowell Lock Monsters-19
00Louisville Panthers-19
03Russian Hockey League-202

Korolev, Igor
91O-Pee-Chee Inserts-37R
92OPC Premier-53
92Parkhurst-158
Emerald Ice-158
92Pinnacle-417
French-417
92Ultra-395
92Upper Deck-338
92Upper Deck-581
Calder Candidates-CC2
Euro-Rookies-ER3
92Russian Stars Red Ace-15
92Russian Stars Red Ace-10
93Donruss-297
93Leaf-96
93OPC Premier-409
Gold-409
93Parkhurst-446
Emerald Ice-446
93PowerPlay-214
93Score-271
Canadian-271
93Stadium Club-119
Members Only Master Set-119
OPC-119
First Day Issue-119
First Day Issue OPC-119
93Topps/OPC Premier-409
Gold-409
93Ultra-185
93Upper Deck-353
93Swedish Semic World Champ Stickers-145
94Donruss-239
94Leaf-90
94Parkhurst SE-SE156
Gold-SE156
94Stadium Club-46
Members Only Master Set-46
First Day Issue-46
Super Team Winner Cards-46
94Upper Deck-184
94Upper Deck-344
Electric Ice-184
Electric Ice-344
94Finnish Jaa Kiekko-161
95Be A Player-135
Signatures-S135
Signatures Die Cuts-S135
95Bowman-9
All-Foil-9
95Canada Games NHL POGS-291
95Collector's Choice-257
Player's Club-257
Player's Club Platinum-257
95Donruss-352
95Finest-84
Refractors-84
95Jets Readers Club-6
95Jets Team Issue-12
95Leaf-48
95Leaf Limited-32
95Metal-163
95Panini Stickers-215
95Parkhurst International-227
Emerald Ice-227
95Playoff One on One-327
95SP-168
95Stadium Club-131
Members Only Master Set-131
95Summit-28
Artist's Proofs-28
Ice-28
95Topps-146
OPC Inserts-146
95Ultra-327
95Upper Deck-299
Electric Ice-299
Electric Ice Gold-299
Special Edition-SE90
Special Edition Gold-SE90
95Zenith-63
96Collector's Choice-202
96Coyotes Coca-Cola-17
96Playoff One on One-407
96Swedish Semic Wien-145
96Michigan K-Wings-8
97Pacific Omega-222
Copper-222
Dark Gray-222
Emerald Green-222
Gold-222
Ice Blue-222
97Panini Stickers-159
97Revolution-135
Copper-135
Emerald-135
Ice Blue-135
Silver-135
98Aurora-183
98Be A Player-289
Press Release-289
98BAP Gold-289
98BAP Autographs-289
98BAP Autographs Gold-289
98Finest-47
No Protectors-47
No Protectors Refractors-47
Refractors-47
98Pacific-416
Ice Blue-416
Red-416
98Pacific Dynagon Ice-182
Blue-182
Red-182
98Pacific Omega-229
Red-229
Opening Day Issue-229
98Panini Stickers-163
98Paramount-229
Copper-229
Emerald Green-229
Holo-Electric-229
Ice Blue-229
Silver-229
99BAP Memorabilia-207
Gold-207
Silver-207
99BAP Millennium-231
Emerald-231
Ruby-231
Sapphire-231
Signatures-231
Signatures Gold-231
99Maple Leafs Pizza Pizza-16
99Pacific-411
Copper-411
Emerald Green-411
Gold-411
Ice Blue-411
Premiere Date-411
Red-411
99Paramount-227
Copper-227
Emerald-227
Gold-227
Holographic Emerald-227
Holographic Gold-227
Holographic Silver-227
Ice Blue-227
Premiere Date-227
Red-227
Silver-227
99Ultimate Victory-83
1/1-83
Parallel-83
Parallel 100-83
00O-Pee-Chee-267B
00O-Pee-Chee Parallel-267B
00Pacific-396
Copper-396
Gold-396
Ice Blue-396
Premiere Date-396
00Panini Stickers-99
00Stadium Club-136
00Topps/OPC-267B
Parallel-267B
00Upper Deck-393
Exclusives Tier 1-393
Exclusives Tier 2-393
01Upper Deck-268
Exclusives-268
02BAP Sig Series Auto Buybacks 1998-289
02BAP Sig Series Auto Buybacks 1999-231
02Pacific Complete-369
Red-369
02Topps Total-389
03Blackhawks Postcards-9
03Parkhurst Original Six Chicago-10
04Russian Back to Russia-7

Korolev, Sergei
02Russian Hockey League-256
02Russian Transfert-13
03Russian Hockey League-158
03Russian National Team-13
04Russian RHL-20

Korolkov, Vladimir
01Russian Dynamo Moscow-18

Koroll, Cliff
70Esso Power Players-124
70O-Pee-Chee-147
70Sargent Promotions Stamps-37
71O-Pee-Chee-209
71Sargent Promotions Stamps-35
71Toronto Sun-70
72O-Pee-Chee-222
72Sargent Promotions Stamps-59
73O-Pee-Chee-28
73Topps-28
74NHL Action Stamps-77
74O-Pee-Chee NHL-35
74Topps-35
75O-Pee-Chee NHL-139
75Topps-139
76O-Pee-Chee NHL-242
76O-Pee-Chee NHL-382
76Topps-242
77Coca-Cola-12
77O-Pee-Chee NHL-146
77Topps-146
78O-Pee-Chee-239
78Topps-239
79Blackhawks Postcards-9
79O-Pee-Chee-102
79Topps-102
80Blackhawks Postcards-4
81Blackhawks Borderless Postcards-12
81Blackhawks Brown Background-4
83Blackhawks Postcards-10
85Blackhawks Team Issue-3
04ITG Franchises Update Autographs-CK
04ITG Franchises US West-176

Korolyuk, Alexander
94Parkhurst SE-SE228
Gold-SE228
94SP-165
Die Cuts-165
94Upper Deck-517
Electric Ice-517
95SP-179
97Kentucky Thoroughblades-9
98Pacific-383
Ice Blue-383
Red-383
98Kentucky Thoroughblades-13
99BAP Millennium-215
Emerald-215
Ruby-215
Sapphire-215
Signatures-215
Signatures Gold-215
99O-Pee-Chee-235
99O-Pee-Chee Chrome-235
99O-Pee-Chee Chrome Refractors-235
99Pacific-373
Copper-373
Emerald Green-373
Gold-373
Ice Blue-373
Premiere Date-373
Red-373
99Pacific Omega-207
Copper-207
Gold-207
Ice Blue-207
Premiere Date-207
99Paramount-205
Copper-205
Emerald-205
Gold-205
Holographic Emerald-205
Holographic Gold-205
Holographic Silver-205
Ice Blue-205
Premiere Date-205
Red-205
Silver-205
99Topps/OPC-235
99Topps/OPC Chrome-235
Refractors-235
99Topps Gold Label Class 1-82
Black-82

Black One of One-82
One of One-82
Red-82
Red One of One-82
99Topps Gold Label Class 2-82
99Topps Gold Label Class 2 Black-82
99Topps Gold Label Class 2 Black 1 of 1-82
99Topps Gold Label Class 2 One of One-82
99Topps Gold Label Class 2 Red-82
99Topps Gold Label Class 2 Red One of One-82
99Topps Gold Label Class 3-82
99Topps Gold Label Class 3 Black-82
99Topps Gold Label Class 3 Black 1 of 1-82
99Topps Gold Label Class 3 One of One-82
99Topps Gold Label Class 3 Red-82
99Topps Gold Label Class 3 Red One of One-82
99Upper Deck MVP SC Edition-158
Gold Script-158
Silver Script-158
Super Script-158
99Russian Fetisov Tribute-1
00O-Pee-Chee-268A
00O-Pee-Chee Parallel-268A
00Pacific-359
Copper-359
Gold-359
Ice Blue-359
Premiere Date-359
00Panini Stickers-205
00Stadium Club-108
00Topps/OPC-268A
Parallel-268A
00Upper Deck Vintage-303
01Upper Deck-148
Exclusives-148
01Upper Deck Victory-301
Gold-301
02BAP Sig Series Auto Buybacks 1999-215
02Russian Transfert-4
03Sharks Postcards-8
03Upper Deck-406
Canadian Exclusives-406
HG-406
UD Exclusives-406
04Pacific-229
Blue-229
Red-229
05Russian Hockey League RHL-14
06Russian Torino Olympic Team-10

Koronov, Evgeny
03Russian Hockey League-93

Korotkov, Konstantin
91Upper Deck-654
French-654
91Upper Deck Czech World Juniors-15
92Classic-56
Gold-56

Korotkov, Viktor
73Swedish Stickers-111

Korotvicka, Jan
02Czech OFS Plus-320
04Czech OFS-267

Korovkin, Nikita
00Kamloops Blazers-11
02Kamloops Blazers-14

Korpela, Harri
01Finnish Cardset-285

Korpela, Kimmo
72Finnish Jaakiekko-265

Korpf, Heinrich
94German First League-125

Korpi, Kiira
05Finnish Tappara Legendat-7
05Finnish Tappara Legendat-14
05Finnish Tappara Legendat-21
05Finnish Tappara Legendat-28

Korpi, Rauno
99Swiss Panini Stickers-202
05Finnish Tappara Legendat-32

Korpikari, Oskar
04Finnish Cardset-92
Parallel-68
05Finnish Cardset -88
06Finnish Cardset-93

Korpikoski, Lauri
04Finnish Cardset-180
04Finnish Cardset Signatures-36
05Finnish Cardset -160
06Finnish Cardset-163
06Hartford Wolf Pack-15

Korpinen, Riku
04P.E.I. Rocket-18

Korpisalo, Jari
92Finnish Jyvas-Hyva Stickers-202
93Finnish Jyvas-Hyva Stickers-357
93Finnish SISU-223
93Finnish SISU Autographs-223
93Swedish Semic World Champ Stickers-66
94Finnish SISU-217
94Finnish SISU-378
94Finnish SISU Fire On Ice-14
94Finnish SISU Magic Numbers-8
94Finnish SISU Specials-2
94Finnish Jaa Kiekko-42
95Finnish SISU-154
95Finnish SISU Limited-22
95Finnish SISU Spotlights-2
95Finnish Semic World Championships-18
96Finnish SISU Redline-161
96Finnish SISU Redline-184
Mighty Adversaries-8
98Finnish Kerailysarja Leijonat-28
98German DEL-80
99German DEL-324
00Finnish Cardset-226
01Finnish Cardset-151
01Finnish Cardset Dueling Aces-8
02Finnish Cardset-43
03Finnish Cardset-176
04Finnish Cardset-192
Parallel-142

Korsch, Roland
01Swiss HNL-456
02Swiss HNL-435

Korsunov, Vladimir
00Russian Hockey League-265
01Russian Hockey League-77

Kortelainen, Mika
92Finnish Jyvas-Hyva Stickers-10
93Finnish SISU-104
94Finnish SISU-105
95Finnish SISU-8
95Finnish SISU Limited-43
96Finnish SISU Redline-13
Mighty Adversaries-4
96Finnish SISU Redline Promos-1
98Finnish Kerailysarja-46
99Finnish Cardset-229
00Finnish Cardset-21
01Finnish Cardset-205
02Finnish Cardset-44

Kortelainen, Tuomo
03Finnish Cardset-73

Kortesoja, Jarkko
95Finnish SISU-69

Korthuis, Matt
05Dutch Vadeko Flyers -7

Kortko, Roger
81Saskatoon Blades-11
84Springfield Indians-22
85Islanders News-10
86Islanders Team Issue-27
88ProCards AHL-56

Korvulahti, Pertti
79Panini Stickers-174

Kos, Kyle
96Red Deer Rebels-6
97Red Deer Rebels-8
97Bowman CHL-156
OPC-156
Autographs-36
98Red Deer Rebels-7
99Detroit Vipers-11

Kos, Milrod
06Westside Warriors-22

Kosak, George
98Pensacola Ice Pilots-19

Kosc, Branislav
93Quebec Pee-Wee Tournament-1551

Koshechkin, Vasili
03Russian Hockey League-128

Kosick, Mark
02German Berlin Polar Bears Postcards-16
03Wheeling Nailers-87
04German DEL Update-325B
04Wheeling Nailers SGA-1

Koskela, Ilpo
66Finnish Jaakiekkosarja-109
69Swedish Hockey-373
70Finnish Jaakiekko-64
70Finnish Jaakiekko-177
70Swedish Hockey-295
70Swedish Masterserien-83
71Finnish Suomi Stickers-64
71Finnish Suomi Stickers-102
71Swedish Hockey-61
72Finnish Jaakiekko-146
72Finnish Panda Toronto-99
72Finnish Semic World Championship-72
72Swedish Semic World Championship-72
73Finnish Jaakiekko-66
73Finnish Jaakiekko-111
74Swedish Semic World Champ Stickers-100
77Finnish Sportscasters-52-1243
91Finnish Semic World Champ Stickers-227
91Swedish Semic World Champ Stickers-227
96Finnish SISU Redline-193

Koskela, Pekka
78Finnish SM-Liiga-102

Koskela, Pentti
71Finnish Suomi Stickers-178
72Finnish Jaakiekko-126
72Finnish Panda Toronto-26

Koskela, Terho
89Swedish Semic Elitserien Stickers-275
90Swedish Semic Elitserien Stickers-42
91Swedish Semic Elitserien Stickers-292
92Swedish Semic Elitserien Stickers-313
93Swedish Semic Elitserien-279
94Swedish Leaf-58
Studio Signatures-12
98Abilene Aviators-16

Koskela, Timo
00Finnish Cardset-158
01Finnish Cardset-43
06Finnish Cardset-264

Koskenkorva, Kimmo
00Finnish Cardset-181
01Finnish Cardset-78
02Finnish Cardset-45
04Finnish Cardset-295
05Finnish Cardset -308
06Finnish Cardset-139

Koski, Corey
98Kelowna Rockets-14

Koski, Kris
93Quebec Pee-Wee Tournament-718
00Michigan State Spartans-12

Koski, Petri
92Finnish Jyvas-Hyva Stickers-150
93Finnish Jyvas-Hyva Stickers-261
93Finnish SISU-286

Koskilahti, Jukka
73Finnish Jaakiekko-286
78Finnish SM-Liiga-214

Koskimaki, Tapani
66Finnish Jaakiekkosarja-6
70Finnish Jaakiekko-230
71Finnish Suomi Stickers-245
74Finnish Typotor-22
78Finnish SM-Liiga-160

Koskimies, Heikki
65Finnish Hellas-155

Koskinen, Hannu
77Finnish Sportscasters-86-2064
78Finnish SM-Liiga-120
80Finnish Mallasjuoma-88
81Swedish Semic Hockey VM Stickers-30
82Finnish Skopbank-7
82Swedish Semic VM Stickers-44

Koskinen, Kalle
93Finnish SISU-6
93Finnish SISU-142
94Finnish SISU-39
94Finnish SISU Junior-5
95Finnish SISU-58
96Finnish SISU Redline-56
98Finnish Kerailysarja-124
99Finnish Cardset-71
00Finnish Cardset-312
01Finnish Cardset-309
02Swedish SHL-263
Parallel-263
03Swedish Elite-125
Silver-125
04Swedish Elitset-125
Gold-125
05Swedish SHL Elitset-134
Gold-134
06Swedish SHL Elitset-278

Koskinen, Kari
70Finnish Jaakiekko-332

Koskinen, Matti
66Finnish Jaakiekkosarja-118
71Finnish Suomi Stickers-282
73Finnish Jaakiekko-199

Koskinen, Petri
04Finnish Cardset-279
06Finnish Cardset-311

Koskinen, Tapio
70Finnish Jaakiekko-195
71Finnish Suomi Stickers-87
72Finnish Jaakiekko-250
72Finnish Panda Toronto-40
73Finnish Jaakiekko-249
74Finnish Jenkki-7
74Finnish Typotor-47
78Finnish SM-Liiga-230
80Finnish Mallasjuoma-205

Koslow, Patrick
02German DEL City Press-12
05German DEL-45

Koslowski, Thorsten
94German DEL-218

Kosmachev, Dmitry
02Russian Hockey League-111
03Russian Under-18 Team-18
04Russian World Junior Team-16

Kosobud, John
96Mississippi Sea Wolves-11
97Mississippi Sea Wolves-4
99Mississippi Sea Wolves-13
99Mississippi Sea Wolves Kelly Cup-11

Kosonen, Lauri
70Finnish Jaakiekko-313
72Finnish Jaakiekko-330

Koss, Dustin
94Thunder Bay Flyers-12

Kossig, Markus
94German First League-299

Kossman, Hans
93Swiss HNL-381
96Swiss HNL-495

Kostadine, Jason
00Hull Olympiques-13
Signed-13
01Hull Olympiques-14
02Quebec Remparts-10
03Quebec Remparts Memorial Cup-8
05Stockton Thunder-9
06Augusta Lynx-7

Kostal, Jan
99Czech OFS-136
00Czech OFS-181
01Czech OFS-199
02Czech OFS Plus-281
03Czech OFS Plus-72
04Czech OFS-27
05Czech HC Karlovy Vary-6
06Czech OFS-30

Kostelnak, David
99Czech Score Blue 2000-104
99Czech Score Red Ice 2000-104

Kosti, Rick
84Minnesota-Duluth Bulldogs-16
85Moncton Golden Flames-15

Kostiainen, Jouni
71Finnish Suomi Stickers-325

Kostic, Dejan
93Swedish Semic Elitserien-262

Kostichkin, Pavel
90O-Pee-Chee Red Army-20R
91O-Pee-Chee Inserts-17R
93Classic Pro Prospects-137
98Danish Hockey League-37
99Danish Hockey League-214

Kostin, Valeri
74Swedish Stickers-41

Kostitsyn, Andrei
03BAP Memorabilia Draft Redemptions-10
03Russian Hockey League-253
04Hamilton Bulldogs-15
05ITG Heroes/Prosp Toronto Expo Parallel -231
05Beehive-99
Matte-99
05Black Diamond-255
05Hot Prospects-244
En Fuego-244
Hot Materials-HMAK
Red Hot-244
White Hot-244
05Parkhurst-638
Facsimile Auto Parallel-638
Signatures-AK
05SP Authentic-213
05SP Game Used-219
05SPx-234
Spectrum-234
05The Cup-143
Autographed Rookie Patches Gold Rainbow-143
Black Rainbow Rookies-143
Masterpiece Pressplates (Artifacts)-292
Masterpiece Pressplates (Bee Hive)-99
Masterpiece Pressplates (Black Diamond)-255
Masterpiece Pressplates (Ice)-214
Masterpiece Pressplates Rookie Upd Auto-269
Masterpiece Pressplates SPA Autos-213
Masterpiece Pressplates (SP Game Used)-219
Masterpiece Pressplates SPx Autos-234
Masterpiece Pressplates (Trilogy)-272
Masterpiece Pressplates Ult Coll-170
Masterpiece Pressplates Autographs-143
Platinum Rookies-143
05UD Artifacts-292
05UD Rookie Class-48
05Ultimate Collection-170
Gold-170
Ultimate Debut Threads Jerseys-DTJAK
05Upper Deck-482
05Upper Deck Ice-214
05Upper Deck Rookie Update-269
05Upper Deck Trilogy-272
05Hamilton Bulldogs-12
05ITG Heroes and Prospects-231
05ITG Heroes and Prospects-290
Autographs Series II-AK
Autographs Series II-SKO
06Be A Player Portraits First Exposures-FEAK
06Black Diamond Jerseys-JKO
06Black Diamond Jerseys Black-JKO
06Black Diamond Jerseys Gold-JKO
06Black Diamond Jerseys Ruby-JKO
06SP Game Used Letter Marks-LMAK
06SP Game Used SIGnificance-SAK
06UD Artifacts Auto-Facts-AFAK
06UD Artifacts Auto-Facts Gold-AFAK
06UD Toronto Fall Expo Priority Signings -PSAK
06Upper Deck Game Jerseys-JKS
06Upper Deck Game Patches-PKS
06Upper Deck MVP Autographs-OARK
06Upper Deck Trilogy Ice Scripts-ISAK
06Hamilton Bulldogs-16

Kostitsyn, Sergei
05London Knights-7
06London Knights-13
06ITG Heroes and Prospects-120
Autographs-ASK

Kostka, Robert
94Czech APS Extraliga-30
95Czech APS Extraliga-134
96Czech APS Extraliga-12
97Czech APS Extraliga-150
97Czech DS Stickers-115
98Czech DS Stickers-189
98Czech OFS-211

Kostka, Vladimir
74Swedish Stickers-114

Kostli, Peter
93Swiss HNL-452

Kostner, Erwin
82Swedish Semic VM Stickers-125
83Swedish Semic VM Stickers-125
92Finnish Semic-245

Kostolny, Milan
94Detroit Jr. Red Wings-20
95Slapshot-228
95Slapshot Memorial Cup-94

Kostopoulos, Tom
00Wilkes-Barre Scranton Penguins-10
01BAP Memorabilia-331
Emerald-331
Ruby-331
Sapphire-331
01Parkhurst-342
01SPx-214
01UD Playmakers-138
01UD Premier Collection-79
01Wilkes-Barre Scranton Penguins-16
02Wilkes-Barre Scranton Penguins-21
03Wilkes-Barre Scranton Penguins-13
04Manchester Monarchs-22
04Manchester Monarchs Tobacco-22
05Manchester Monarchs-39
06O-Pee-Chee-238
Rainbow-238

Kostovic, Dario
01Swiss HNL-67
02Swiss HNL-122

Kosttstorfer, Rainer
02German DEL City Press-288

Kostuch, Jeff
917th Inn. Sketch OHL-41
93Owen Sound Platers-14
94Owen Sound Platers-10
95Hampton Roads Admirals-18
95Classic-93
96Louisville Riverfrogs-10
97Louisville Riverfrogs-8
99Rockford IceHogs-10

Kostuchenko, Malcolm
91Air Canada SJHL All-Stars-10

Kostur, Matus
02Columbus Cottonmouths-8
03Albany River Rats-18
03Albany River Rats Kinko's-17
03Columbus Cottonmouths-30
03ECHL Update RBI Sports-114

Kosturik, Mark
94German DEL-65
95German DEL-64
95German DEL-435
96German DEL-216
98German DEL-185
99German DEL-226
00German DEL-92

Kostynski, Doug
85Moncton Golden Flames-8
86Moncton Golden Flames-4

Kostyrev, Artjom
04German DEL Update-345
06German DEL-35

Kosyl, Walery
70Swedish Masterserien-198
73Finnish Jaakiekko-95
74Finnish Jenkki-100

Kot, Justin
03Oklahoma City Blazers-12

Kotala, Lumir
94Czech APS Extraliga-136

Kotalik, Ales
97Czech APS Extraliga-288
98Czech OFS-414
99Czech OFS-280
00SPx Rookie Redemption-RR4
00Czech DS Extraliga-83
00Czech OFS-19
01BAP Memorabilia-361
Emerald-361
Ruby-361
Sapphire-361
01Parkhurst-306
01SPx-199
01Titanium Draft Day Edition-111
01UD Honor Roll-66
01UD Premier Collection-54
01Upper Deck Ice-46
01Czech DS-57
01Czech OFS All Stars-35
02O-Pee-Chee-297
02O-Pee-Chee Premier Blue Parallel-297
02O-Pee-Chee Premier Red Parallel-297
02O-Pee-Chee Factory Set-297
02Pacific-43
Blue-43
Red-43
02Pacific Calder-57
Silver-57
Reflections-3
02Pacific Complete-546
Red-546
02Pacific Quest 4 the Cup CalderContender-2
02Topps-297
OPC Blue Parallel-297
OPC Red Parallel-297
Factory Set-297
02Upper Deck Vintage-349
03BAP Memorabilia-4
Emerald-4
Gold-4
Ruby-4
Sapphire-4
03Beehive-22
Gold-22
Silver-22
03Black Diamond-42
Black-42
Green-42
Red-42
03Bowman-22
Gold-22
03Bowman Chrome-22
Refractors-22
Gold Refractors-22
Xfractors-22
03ITG Action-3
03O-Pee-Chee-24
03OPC Blue-24
03OPC Gold-24
03OPC Red-24
03Pacific-41
Blue-41
Red-41
03Pacific Calder Contenders Entry Draft-2
03Pacific Complete-302
Red-302
03Pacific Exhibit-20
Blue Backs-20
Yellow Backs-20
03Pacific Heads-Up Jerseys-4
03Pacific Invincible New Sensations-4
03Pacific Luxury Suite-27A
03Pacific Luxury Suite-27B
03Pacific Prism Rookie Revolution-2
03Pacific Quest for the Cup-12
Blue-12
03Pacific Supreme-11
Blue-11
Red-11
Retail-11
03Private Stock Reserve-13
Blue-13
Red-13
Retail-13
Rising Stock-2
03SP Game Used Limited Threads-LTAK
03SP Game Used Limited Threads Gold-LTAK
03SPx Big Futures-BF-AK
03SPx Big Futures Limited-BF-AK
03Topps-24
Blue-24
Gold-24
Red-24
Own the Game-OTG9
03Topps Pristine-38
Gold Refractor Die Cuts-38
Refractors-38
Press Plates Black-38
Press Plates Cyan-38
Press Plates Magenta-38
Press Plates Yellow-38
03UD Honor Roll-103
03Upper Deck-22
Canadian Exclusives-22
HG-22
03Upper Deck MVP-53
Gold Script-53
Silver Script-53
Canadian Exclusives-53
03Upper Deck Victory-21
Bronze-21
Gold-21
Silver-21
04Czech NHL ELH Postcards-8
04Czech OFS-71
Stars-48
04Czech Zuma-30
05Parkhurst-50
Facsimile Auto Parallel-50
05Upper Deck-269
06Fleer-25
Tiffany-25
06O-Pee-Chee-61
Rainbow-61
06Panini Stickers-31
06Ultra-24
Gold Medallion-24
Ice Medallion-24
06Upper Deck-273
Exclusives Parallel-273
High Gloss Parallel-273
Masterpieces-273
06Upper Deck MVP-33
Gold Script-33
Super Script-33
06Upper Deck Ovation-7
06Upper Deck Victory-26
06Upper Deck Victory Black-26
06Upper Deck Victory Gold-26
06Czech OFS Jagr Team-16

Kotasek, Martin
94Czech APS Extraliga-200
95Czech APS Extraliga-48
96Czech APS Extraliga-46
97Czech APS Extraliga-140
98Czech DS-107
98Czech DS Stickers-260
98Czech OFS-123
99Czech DS-12
99Czech OFS-210
00Czech OFS-367
02Czech OFS Plus-319

Kotaska, Ivo
02Czech OFS Plus-176
06Czech OFS-206

Kotatko, Jan
02Czech OFS Plus-340

Kotewa, Nathan
98Sioux City Musketeers-10

Kothmayr, Markus
94German First League-283

Kothmayr, Peter
94German First League-270

Kotkaniemi, Mikael
93Finnish Jyvas-Hyva Stickers-349
93Finnish SISU-231
94Finnish SISU-125
95Finnish SISU-159

Kotkas, Pentti
65Finnish Hellas-141

Kotlov, Yevgeny
73Swedish Stickers-130

Kotomkin, Alexander
74Swedish Stickers-82

Kotonski, Andrzej
92Finnish Semic-282

Kotrla, Jindrich
95Czech APS Extraliga-163
96Czech APS Extraliga-185
98Czech OFS-11
99Czech DS-67
99Czech OFS-339
00Czech OFS-149
01Czech OFS-157
02Czech OFS Plus-197
02Czech National Team Postcards-5
03Czech National Team Postcards-8
04Czech HC Sparta Praha Postcards-9
04Czech OFS-189
04Czech OFS-389
05Czech HC Ceski Budejovice-8
06Czech HC Ceske Budejovice Postcards-4
06Czech OFS-8

Kotschnew, Dmitri
01German Upper Deck-113
02German DEL City Press-163
03German DEL-148
04German DEL-174
05German DEL-175
05German DEL-373
06German DEL-111

Kotsopoulos, Chris
82O-Pee-Chee-124
82O-Pee-Chee Stickers-132
82Post Cereal-7
82Topps Stickers-132
82Whalers Junior Hartford Courant-9
83NHL Key Tags-46
83Whalers Junior Hartford Courant-9
84O-Pee-Chee-73
84Whalers Junior Wendy's-10
85Maple Leafs Postcards-18
86Maple Leafs Postcards-15
87Maple Leafs PLAY-16
87Maple Leafs Postcards-11
87Maple Leafs Postcards Oversized-11
87O-Pee-Chee-244
88Maple Leafs PLAY-16
89O-Pee-Chee-279
89O-Pee-Chee Stickers-180
89ProCards AHL-309

Kotsopoulos, Evan
01Guelph Storm-17
04Kingston Frontenacs-1

Kotsopoulos, Tommy
93Quebec Pee-Wee Tournament-1406
93Quebec Pee-Wee Tournament-1426
98Sudbury Wolves-10
99Sudbury Wolves-19B
00Sudbury Wolves-22
04Odessa Jackalopes-11

Kottstorfer, Rainer
04German DEL-243
04German Krefeld Penguins Postcards-13
05German DEL-228
06German DEL-135

Kotyk, Seamus
94Quebec Pee-Wee Tournament-565
99Ottawa 67's-23
99Bowman CHL-142
Gold-142
OPC International-142
00Ottawa 67's-20
01Cleveland Barons-10
02Cleveland Barons-9
03BAP Memorabilia-248
03ITG Used Signature Series-170
Gold-170
03ITG VIP Rookie Debut-64
03Parkhurst Rookie-83
03SP Authentic-119
Limited-119
03UD Honor Roll-138
03Upper Deck-459
Canadian Exclusives-459
HG-459
UD Exclusives-459
03Upper Deck Rookie Update-110
03Cleveland Barons-12
03Pacific AHL Prospects-21
Gold-21
04Milwaukee Admirals-6

Kotyk, Travis
03OCN Blizzard-10

Kotyluk, Kevin
02Fort Wayne Komets-8
03Fort Wayne Komets-9
03Fort Wayne Komets 2003 Champions-19
03Fort Wayne Komets Shoe Carnival-7
04Kalamazoo Wings-21
05Bakersfield Condors-2

Kouba, Ladislav
00Red Deer Rebels-10
Signed-10
01Red Deer Rebels-10
02Red Deer Rebels-18
03Springfield Falcons Postcards-22
04New Mexico Scorpions-6
04New Mexico Scorpions-21

Koudelka, Martin
96Czech APS Extraliga-160
98Czech DS Stickers-143
98Czech OFS-379
99Czech OFS-363
00Czech OFS-50

Koukal, Petr
02Czech OFS Plus-218
03Czech OFS Plus-51
03Czech Pardubice Postcards-6
04Czech OFS-121
06Czech HC Pardubice Postcards-9
06Czech OFS-118

Koulikov, Alexander
93UK Humberside Hawks-23

Koulikov, Slava
97UK Kingston Hawks Stickers-14
99UK Hull Thunder-17
01UK Dundee Stars-16
02UK Dundee Stars-16
05UK Hull Stingrays-19

Kounovsky, Petr
99Czech OFS-330

Kourilin, Evgeny
98Anchorage Aces-18

Kourula, Aarre-Kari
80Finnish Mallasjuoma-48

Kout, Martin
93Swiss HNL-14
95Swiss HNL-35
96Swiss HNL-181
98Swiss Power Play Stickers-232
99Swiss Panini Stickers-231
00Swiss Panini Stickers-272
01Swiss HNL-4
02Swiss HNL-13

Koutsky, Vladislav
04Czech OFS-210
06Czech HC Pardubice Postcards-10
06Czech OFS-119

Koutuaniemi, Jouni
80Finnish Mallasjuoma-102

Kovacavic, Jure
95Slapshot-267

Kovacik, Miroslav
04Czech OFS-280

Kovacs, Bill
89Sudbury Wolves-3
907th Inn. Sketch OHL-385
90Sudbury Wolves-14
917th Inn. Sketch OHL-348
92Raleigh Icecaps-4
93Birmingham Bulls Birmingham News-11

Kovacs, Frank
87Regina Pats-13
88Regina Pats-11
89Regina Pats-9
907th Inn. Sketch WHL-179
917th Inn. Sketch WHL-232
92Dayton Bombers-15
94German DEL-348
95Saint John Flames-11
97UK Sheffield Steelers-6

Kovacs, John
907th Inn. Sketch QMJHL-74
917th Inn. Sketch QMJHL-240

Kovalchuk, Ilya
99Russian Hockey League-141
00SPx Rookie Redemption-RR2
00Russian Hockey League-127
00Russian Hockey League-296
01Atomic-104
Premiere Date-104
Rookie Reaction-2
01Atomic Toronto Fall Expo-104
01BAP Memorabilia-372
Emerald-372
Ruby-372
Sapphire-372
Draft Redemptions-1
01BAP Signature Series-207
Autographs-207
Autographs Gold-207
Franchise Jerseys-FP-2
He Shoots-He Scores Points-16
He Shoots-He Scores Prizes-5
International Medals-IB-7
Jerseys-GJ-45
Jersey Autographs-GUIK
Jersey and Stick Cards-GSJ-45
Emblems-GUE-2
Numbers-ITN-2
Teammates-TM-2
01BAP Ultimate Memorabilia Dynamic Duos-13
01BAP Ultimate Memorabilia Emblems-4
01BAP Ultimate Memorabilia Jerseys-4
01BAP Ultimate Mem Jerseys and Sticks-4
01BAP Ultimate Memorabilia Numbers-3
01BAP Ultimate Memorabilia Name Plates-22
01BAP Update He Shoots-He Scores Prizes-1
01Bowman YoungStars-159
Gold-159
Ice Cubed-159
Autographs-IK
Relics-JIK
Relics-SIK
Relics-DSIK
Rivals-R5
01Crown Royale-147
Crowning Achievement-2
Rookie Royalty-2
01eTopps-31
01O-Pee-Chee-331
01Pacific-454
01Pacific Adrenaline-203
Blue-203
Premiere Date-203
Red-203
Retail-203
Rookie Report-3
01Pacific Heads-Up-103
01Pacific High Voltage-2
01Parkhurst-295
He Shoots-He Scores Prizes-18
01Parkhurst Beckett Promos-295
01Private Stock-113
Gold-113
Premiere Date-113
Retail-113
Silver-113
Game Gear-6
Moments in Time-2
01Private Stock Pacific Nights-113
01Private Stock PS-2002-94
01Private Stock Reserve-R2
01SP Authentic-175
Limited-175
Limited Gold-175
Sign of the Times-IK
Sign of the Times-BKK
01SP Game Used-66
01SPx-148
01SPx-148
Rookie Treasures-RTIK
01Sports Illustrated for Kids III-384
01Stadium Club-121
Award Winners-121
Master Photos-121
Lone Star Signatures-LS7
01Titanium-147
Retail-147
Double-Sided Jerseys-23
Double-Sided Jerseys-39
Rookie Team-2
Three-Star Selections-22
01Titanium Draft Day Edition-7
01Titanium Draft Day Edition-105
01Titanium Draft Day Edition-1AU
01Topps-331
01Topps Chrome-149
Refractors-149
Black Border Refractors-149
01Topps Heritage-138
Autographs-AIK
01Topps Reserve-115
01UD Challenge for the Cup-95
Cornerstones-CR2
01UD Honor Roll-100
01UD Mask Collection-132
Gold-132
01UD Playmakers-104
01UD Premier Collection-109
Jerseys-BIK
Jerseys Black-B-IK
Signatures-IK
Signatures Black-IK
01UD Top Shelf-68
01Upper Deck-211
01Upper Deck-242
Exclusives-211
Exclusives-242
01Upper Deck Ice-44
01Upper Deck MVP-221
01Upper Deck Victory-441
01Upper Deck Vintage-275
01Vanguard-103
Blue-103
Red-103
Memorabilia-42
One of Ones-103
Premiere Date-103
Prime Prospects-2
Proofs-103
01Russian Young Lions-1
02McFarlane Hockey-120
02McFarlane Hockey-122
02McFarlane Hockey-124
02Atomic-5
Blue-5
Gold-5
Red-5
Cold Fusion-3
Hobby Parallel-5
Power Converters-2
Super Colliders-1
02BAP All-Star Edition-102
Gold-102
Silver-102
02BAP First Edition-134
02BAP First Edition-318
02BAP First Edition-342
02BAP First Edition-383
02BAP First Edition-384
02BAP First Edition-424H
Debut Jerseys-14
He Shoots-He Score Points-5
He Shoots-He Scores Prizes-16
Jerseys-134
02BAP Memorabilia-65
02BAP Memorabilia-202
Emerald-65
Emerald-202
Ruby-65
Ruby-202
Sapphire-65
Sapphire-202
Franchise Players-FP-2
Future of the Game-FG-3
He Shoots-He Scores Points-16
He Shoots-He Scores Prizes-5
NHL All-Star Game-65
NHL All-Star Game-202
NHL All-Star Game Blue-65
NHL All-Star Game Blue-202
NHL All-Star Game Green-65
NHL All-Star Game Green-202
NHL All-Star Game Red-65
NHL All-Star Game Red-202
02BAP Memorabilia Toronto Fall Expo-65
02BAP Memorabilia Toronto Fall Expo-202
02BAP Signature Series-39
Autographs-39
Autograph Buybacks 2001-207
Autographs Gold-39
Famous Scraps-FS7
Jerseys-SGJ10
Jersey Autographs-SGJ10
Team Quads-TQ12
02BAP Ultimate Memorabilia Dynamic Duos-3
02BAP Ultimate Memorabilia Emblems-28
02BAP Ultimate Memorabilia First Overall-6
02BAP Ultimate Memorabilia Jerseys-11
02BAP Ultimate Mem Jersey and Stick-8
02BAP Ultimate Memorabilia Nameplates-11
02BAP Ultimate Memorabilia Numbers-4
02BAP Ultimate Memorabilia Numerology-19
02Between the Pipes Nightmares-GN1
02Bowman Toronto Spring Expo-1
02Bowman Toronto Spring Expo-1B
02Bowman YoungStars-165
Gold-165
Silver-165
02Crown Royale-5
Blue-5
Red-5
Retail-5
Jerseys-2
Jerseys Gold-2
Dual Patches-1
Lords of the Rink-3
Royal Portraits-2
02eTopps-10
02ITG Used-5
02ITG Used-105
Franchise Players-F2
Franchise Players Autographs-F2
Franchise Players Gold-F2
Jerseys-GUJ10
Jersey Autographs-GUJ10
Jerseys Gold-GUJ10
Emblems-E10
Jersey and Stick-SJ10
Jersey and Stick Gold-SJ10
Teammates-T7
Teammates Gold-T7
02McDonald's Pacific-3
Clear Advantage-2
Jersey Patches Silver-2
Jersey Patches Gold-2
02O-Pee-Chee-11
02O-Pee-Chee Premier Blue Parallel-11
02O-Pee-Chee Premier Red Parallel-11
02O-Pee-Chee Factory Set-11
02Pacific-18
Blue-18
Red-18
Cramer's Choice-2
Impact Zone-2
Jerseys-NNO
Lamplighters-2
Main Attractions-2
Maximum Impact-9
Shining Moments-2
02Pacific Calder Collection AS Fantasy-2
02Pacific Calder Collection All-Star Fantasy Gold-2
02Pacific Calder-2
Silver-2
02Pacific Chicago National *-1
02Pacific Complete-105
Red-105
02Pacific Entry Draft-1
02Pacific Exclusive-8
Destined-3
Great Expectations-2
Maximum Overdrive-3
02Pacific Heads-Up-6
Blue-6
Purple-6
Red-6
Bobble Heads-7
Etched in Time-2
Head First-2
Inside the Numbers-3
Quad Jerseys-2
Quad Jerseys-35
Quad Jerseys Gold-2
Quad Jerseys Gold-35
Stat Masters-3
02Pacific Quest for the Cup-5
Gold-5
Chasing the Cup-3
02Pacific Toronto Spring Expo Rookie Coll-2
02Parkhurst-24
Bronze-24
Gold-24
Silver-24
Franchise Players-FP2
Heroes-NH1

He Shoots-He Scores Points-19
He Shoots-He Scores Prizes-6
Jerseys-GJ19
Patented Power-PP9
Stick and Jerseys-SJ19
Teammates-TT9
02Parkhurst Retro-54
Minis-54
He Shoots-He Scores Points-15
He Shoots-He Scores Prizes-5
Hopefuls-RR6
Jerseys-RJ37
Jersey and Sticks-RSJ25
Memorabilia-RM11
02Private Stock Reserve-103
Red-103
Retail-103
Elite-1
Patches-103
02SP Authentic-5
02SP Authentic-108
Beckett Promos-5
Sign of the Times-KA
Sign of the Times-KH
02SP Game Used-2
Authentic Fabrics-AFIK
Authentic Fabrics-AFKK
Authentic Fabrics Gold-AFIK
Authentic Fabrics Gold-AFKK
Authentic Fabrics Rainbow-AFIK
Authentic Fabrics Rainbow-AFKK
First Rounder Patches-IK
Future Fabrics-FFIK
Future Fabrics-FFKO
Future Fabrics Gold-FFIK
Future Fabrics Gold-FFKO
Future Fabrics Rainbow-FFIK
Future Fabrics Rainbow-FFKO
Piece of History-PHKK
Piece of History Gold-PHKK
Piece of History Rainbow-PHKK
Signature Style-IK
02SPx-3
Spectrum Gold-3
Spectrum Silver-3
Winning Materials-WMIK
Winning Materials Gold-IK
Winning Materials Silver-IK
02Stadium Club-10
Silver Decoy Cards-10
Proofs-10
Lone Star Signatures Blue-LSIL
Lone Star Signatures Red-LSIL
World Stage-WS8
YoungStars Relics-S1
YoungStars Relics-DS1
YoungStars Relics-APIK
02Thrashers Postcards-8
02Titanium-5
Blue-5
Red-5
Retail-5
Jerseys-3
Jerseys Retail-3
Patches-3
Shadows-1
02Topps-11
OPC Blue Parallel-11
OPC Red Parallel-11
Coast to Coast-CC6
Topps/OPC Hometown Heroes-HHU17
Own The Game-OTG12
Signs of the Future-IK
Factory Set-11
Factory Set Hometown Heroes-HHU17
02Topps Chrome All-Star Fantasy-6
02Topps Chrome-11
Black Border Refractors-11
Refractors-11
02Topps Heritage-79
Chrome Parallel-79
USA Test Parallel-79
02Topps Total-335
Team Checklists-TTC1
Topps-TT7
02UD Artistic Impressions-4
Gold-4
Artist's Touch-ATIK
Artist's Touch Gold-ATIK
02UD Artistic Impressions Beckett Promos-4
02UD Artistic Impressions Great Depiction-GD5
02UD Artistic Impress Great Depiction Gld-GD5
02UD Artistic Impressions Retrospectives-R4
02UD Artistic Impressions Retrospect Gold-R4
02UD Artistic Impress Retrospect Auto-R4
02UD Artistic Impress Retrospect Silver-R4
02Upper Deck Collectors Club-NHL18
02UD Honor Roll-3
02UD Mask Collection-6
02UD Mask Collection Beckett Promos-6
02UD Mask Collection Patches-PGIK
02UD Piece of History-3
02UD Premier Collection-2
Jerseys Bronze-IK
Jerseys Gold-IK
Jerseys Silver-IK
Patches-PIK
Signatures Bronze-SIK
Signatures Gold-SIK
Signatures Silver-SIK
02UD Top Shelf-4
Clutch Performers-CPIK
Dual Player Jerseys-RBK
Goal Oriented-GOIK
02Upper Deck-7
Exclusives-7
Blow-Ups-C2
Difference Makers-IK
Game Jersey Autographs-IK
Game Jersey Series II-GJIK
Hot Spots-HSIK
On the Rise-ORIK
Patch Card Logo-IK
Sizzling Scorers-SS1
02Upper Deck Classic Portraits-5
Hockey Royalty-KFB
Hockey Royalty Limited-KFB
Mini-Busts-36
Mini-Busts-37
Mini-Busts-38
Mini-Busts-39
Mini-Busts-40
Mini-Busts-41
Mini-Busts-42
Mini-Busts-43
Pillars of Strength-PS1
02Upper Deck MVP-10
Gold-10
Classics-10
Golden Classics-10
Highlight Nights-HN1
Overdrive-SO2
Vital Forces-VF2
02Upper Deck Rookie Update-6
02Upper Deck Rookie Update-114
Autographs-IK
Jerseys-DIK
Jerseys-SKH
Jerseys Gold-DIK
Jerseys Gold-SKH
02Upper Deck Victory-10
Bronze-10
Gold-10
Silver-10
National Pride-NP31
02Upper Deck Vintage-13
02Upper Deck Vintage-262
02Upper Deck Vintage-315
Green Backs-13
Tall Boys-T4
Tall Boys Gold-T4
02Vanguard-6
LTD-6
East Meets West-1
In Focus-2
Jerseys-3
Jerseys Gold-3
V-Team-7
02Russian Olympic Team-4
02UD SuperStars *-22
02UD SuperStars *-253
Gold-22
Gold-253
03BAP Memorabilia-31
Emerald-31
Gold-31
Ruby-31
Sapphire-31
Brush with Greatness-17
Brush with Greatness Contest Cards-17
Jersey and Stick-SJ-23
Jerseys-GJ-32
Jersey Autographs-GJ-32
03BAP Ultimate Memorabilia Autographs-145
Gold-145
03BAP Ultimate Mem Auto Jerseys-145
03BAP Ultimate Mem Auto Emblems-145
03BAP Ultimate Mem Auto Sticks-145
03BAP Ultimate Mem Complete Jersey-19
03BAP Ultimate Mem Complete Jersey Gold-19
03BAP Ultimate Memorabilia Dynamic Duos-7
03BAP Ultimate Memorabilia Emblems-6
03BAP Ultimate Memorabilia Emblems Gold-6
03BAP Ultimate Mem Franch Present Future-2
03BAP Ultimate Memorabilia Heroes-1
03BAP Ultimate Memorabilia Jerseys-9
03BAP Ultimate Memorabilia Jerseys Gold-9
03BAP Ultimate Mem Jersey and Emblems-13
03BAP Ultimate Mem Jersey and Emblem Gold-13
03BAP Ultimate Mem Jersey and Numbers-13
03BAP Ultimate Mem Jersey and Number Gold-13
03BAP Ultimate Memorabilia Numbers-7
03BAP Ultimate Memorabilia Numbers Gold-7
03BAP Ultimate Mem Redemption Cards-4
03BAP Ultimate Mem Seams Unbelievable-7
03BAP Ultimate Memorabilia Triple Threads-17
03Beehive-12
Variations-12
Gold-12
Silver-12
Jumbos-3
Jumbo Variations-3
Jerseys-JT9
Sticks Beige Border-BE33
Sticks Red Border-RE13
03Black Diamond-51
Black-51
Green-51
Red-51
Signature Gems-SG-12
Threads-DT-IK
Threads Green-DT-IK
Threads Red-DT-IK
Threads Black-DT-IK
03Bowman-17
Gold-17
Future Rivals-LK
Future Rivals Patches-LK
Goal to Goal-TK
03Bowman Chrome-17
Refractors-17
Gold Refractors-17
Xfractors-17
03Crown Royale-4
Blue-4
Retail-4
Global Conquest-6
Jerseys-2
Patches-2
Lords of the Rink-2
03ITG Action-34
Jerseys-M191
Jerseys-M211
03ITG Toronto Fall Expo Jerseys-FE18
03ITG Used Signature Series-96
Gold-96
Autographs-IK
Autographs Gold-IK
Franchise-2
Franchise Autographs-2
Franchise Gold-2
Jerseys-11
Jerseys Gold-11
Jersey Autos-11
Emblems-22
Emblems Gold-22
Jersey and Stick-11
Jersey and Stick Gold-11
03ITG VIP Brightest Stars-4
03ITG VIP Collages-10
03ITG VIP Collage Autographs-10
03ITG VIP Jerseys-16
03ITG VIP Jersey Autographs-16
03ITG VIP Jersey and Emblems-11
03ITG VIP Jersey and Numbers-11
03McDonald's Pacific-3
Patches Silver-6
Patches Gold-6
Patches and Sticks-6
03NHL Sticker Collection-4
03O-Pee-Chee-190
03OPC Blue-190
03OPC Gold-190
03OPC Red-190
03Pacific-16
Blue-16
Red-16
Jerseys-4
Jerseys Gold-4
Main Attractions-2
03Pacific Atlantic City National-2
03Pacific Calder-4
03Pacific Calder-142
Silver-4
03Pacific Complete-367
Red-367
03Pacific Exhibit-154
03Pacific Exhibit-219
Blue Backs-154
Pursuing Prominence-2
03Pacific Heads-Up-4
Hobby LTD-4
Retail LTD-4
Fast Forwards-2
Fast Forwards LTD-2
In Focus-2
In Focus LTD-2
Jerseys-2
Mini Sweaters-2
03Pacific Invincible-5
Blue-5
Red-5
Retail-5
Afterburners-1
New Sensations-3
03Pacific Luxury Suite-2A
03Pacific Luxury Suite-2B
03Pacific Luxury Suite-2C
03Pacific Luxury Suite-2D
03Pacific Luxury Suite-25A
03Pacific Luxury Suite-25B
03Pacific Luxury Suite-25C
03Pacific Prism-103
Blue-103
Patches-103
Red-103
Retail-103
Paramount Prodigies-4
03Pacific Quest for the Cup-4
Blue-4
Chasing the Cup-2
Jerseys-1
03Pacific Supreme-5
Blue-5
Red-5
Retail-5
Jerseys-2
03Parkhurst Rookie-19
Emblems-GUE-9
Emblem Autographs-GUE-IK
Emblems Gold-GUE-9
High Expectations-HE-1
High Expectations Gold-HE-1
Jerseys-GJ-2
Jerseys Gold-GJ-2
03Private Stock Reserve-143
Blue-143
Patches-143
Red-143
Retail-143
Rising Stock-1
03SP Authentic-5
Limited-5
Breakout Seasons-B25
Breakout Seasons Limited-B25
Sign of the Times-IK
03SP Game Used-4
03SP Game Used-103
Gold-4
Gold-103
Authentic Fabrics-DFHK
Authentic Fabrics Gold-DFHK
Authentic Patches-APIK
Limited Threads-LTIK
Limited Threads Gold-LTIK
Team Threads-TTKHK
03SPx-5
03SPx-145
03SPx-173
Radiance-5
Radiance-145
Radiance-173
Spectrum-5
Spectrum-145
Spectrum-173
Big Futures-BF-IK
Big Futures Limited-BF-IK
Fantasy Franchise-FF-KFB
Fantasy Franchise Limited-FF-KFB
Signature Threads-ST-IK
03Thrashers Postcards-9
03Titanium-191
Patches-191
Highlight Reels-1
Stat Masters-2
03Topps-190
Blue-190
Gold-190
Red-190
First Overall Fabrics-IL
First Overall Fabrics-JTIK
First Overall Fabrics-RNIK
Topps/OPC Idols-II14
Signs of Youth-IK
03Topps C55-17
03Topps C55-17B
Minis-17
Minis American Back-17
Minis American Back Red-17
Minis Bazooka Back-17
Minis Brooklyn Back-17
Minis Hat Trick Back-17
Minis O Canada Back-17
Minis O Canada Back Red-17
Minis Stanley Cup Back-17
Autographs-TA-IK
Relics-TRIK
03Topps Pristine-35
Gold Refractor Die Cuts-35
Refractors-35
Jersey Portions-PPJ-IK
Jersey Portion Refractors-PPJ-IK
Patches-PP-IK
Patch Refractors-PP-IK
Press Plates Black-35
Press Plates Cyan-35
Press Plates Magenta-35
Press Plates Yellow-35
03Topps Traded Franchise Fabrics-FF-IK
03UD Honor Roll-4
03UD Honor Roll-94
Signature Class-SC16
03UD Premier Collection-4
NHL Shields-SH-IK
Signatures-PS-IK
Signatures Gold-PS-IK
Stars-ST-IK
Stars Patches-ST-IK
03UD Toronto Fall Expo Priority Signings-IK
03Upper Deck-254
All-Star Class-AS-2
Big Playmakers-BP-IK
BuyBacks-123
BuyBacks-124
BuyBacks-125
Canadian Exclusives-254
HG-254
Jerseys-GJ-IK
Jerseys-UD-IK
NHL Best-NB-IK
UD Exclusives-254
03Upper Deck Classic Portraits-5
03Upper Deck Ice-5
Gold-5
Authentics-IA-IK
Breakers-IB-IK
Breaker Patches-IB-IK
Under Glass Autographs-UG-IK
03Upper Deck MVP-17
Gold Script-17
Silver Script-17
Canadian Exclusives-17
SportsNut-SN5
Talent-MT12
03Upper Deck Rookie Update-5
All-Star Lineup-AS2
Top Draws-TD11
03Upper Deck Trilogy-5
03Upper Deck Trilogy-115
Crest Variations-115
Limited-5
Limited-115
Scripts-S2IK
Scripts Limited-S2IK
Scripts Red-S2IK
03Upper Deck Victory-7
Bronze-7
Gold-7
Silver-7
Freshman Flashback-FF3
Game Breakers-GB3
03Russian World Championship Stars-30
03Russian World Championship Team 2003-23
03Russian World Championships Preview-5
03Toronto Star-5
Foil-26
04ITG NHL AS FANtasy AS History Jerseys-SB54
04Pacific-11
Blue-11
Red-11
All-Stars-1
Cramer's Choice-1
Global Connection-1
Gold Crown Die-Cuts-1
04Pacific NHL Draft All-Star Nets-1
04Pacific National Convention-1
04SP Authentic-5
04SP Authentic-101
Limited-5
Limited-101
Buybacks-67
Buybacks-68
Buybacks-69
Rookie Review-RR-IK
Sign of the Times-ST-IK
Sign of the Times-DS-KN
Sign of the Times-DS-LK
Sign of the Times-TS-HLK
Sign of the Times-TS-IKN
Sign of the Times-QS-LKSN
Sign of the Times-QS-NHKS
Sign of the Times-FS-SES
04UD All-World-26
Gold-26
Autographs-26
Quad Autographs-AQ-RUS
Five Autographs-AF-YGN
Six Autographs-AS-RUS
04Ultimate Collection-3
04Ultimate Collection-73
Buybacks-16
Buybacks-17
Buybacks-18
Buybacks-19
Patches-UP-IK
Patch Autographs-UPA-IKRN
Signatures-US-IK
04Upper Deck-8
Big Playmakers-BP-IK
Canadian Exclusives-8
Hardware Heroes-AW6
HG Glossy Gold-8
HG Glossy Silver-8
Jersey Autographs-GJA-IK
Jersey Autographs-GJA-IL/PB
World's Best-WB18
World Cup Tribute-IK
World Cup Tribute-IKAK
World Cup Tribute-PDMAIK
04Russian Back to Russia-8
04Russian World Championship Team-17
05ITG Heroes/Prosp Toronto Expo Parallel -198
05Be A Player-3
First Period-3
Second Period-3
Third Period-3
Overtime-3
Class Action-CA3
Outtakes-OT4
05Beehive-4
05Beehive-244
Beige -4
Blue -4
Gold-4
Red -4
Matte-4
Matted Materials-MMIK
Matted Materials Remarkable-RMIK
05Black Diamond-169
Emerald-169
Gold-169
Onyx-169
Ruby-169
Gemography-G-IK
Gemography Emerald-G-IK
Gemography Gold-G-IK
Gemography Onyx-G-IK
Gemography Ruby-G-IK
05Hot Prospects-5
En Fuego-5
Red Hot-5
White Hot-5
05ITG Ultimate Memorabilia Level 1-51
05ITG Ultimate Memorabilia Level 2-51
05ITG Ultimate Memorabilia Level 3-51
05ITG Ultimate Memorabilia Level 4-51
05ITG Ultimate Memorabilia Level 5-51
05ITG Ultimate Mem Complete Jersey-26
05ITG Ultimate Mem Complete Jersey Gold-26
05ITG Ultimate Memorabilia Double Autos-19
05ITG Ultimate Mem Double Autos Gold-19
05ITG Ultimate Memorabilia Jersey Autos-14
05ITG Ultimate Mem Jersey Autos Gold-14
05ITG Ultimate Memorabilia Sextuple Autos-3
05ITG Ultimate Memorabilia Stick Autos-13
05ITG Ultimate Mem Stick Autos Gold-13
05ITG Ultimate Mem Sticks and Jerseys-3
05ITG Ultimate Mem Stick and Jerseys Gold-3
05ITG Ultimate Memorabilia Triple Autos-7
05ITG Ultimate Memorabilia Triple Autos-18
05ITG Ultimate Mem Triple Autos Gold-7
05ITG Ultimate Mem Triple Autos Gold-18
05McDonalds Upper Deck-42
Chasing the Cup-CC8
Top Scorers-TS13
05Panini Stickers-7
05Parkhurst-18
05Parkhurst-672
Facsimile Auto Parallel-18
Facsimile Auto Parallel-672
True Colors-TCATL
True Colors-TCATL
05SP Authentic-5
05SP Authentic-106
Limited-5
Limited-106
Chirography-SPIK
Exquisite Endorsements-EEIK
Marks of Distinction-MDIK
Octographs-OF
Prestigious Pairings-PPLK
Sign of the Times Duals-DHK
Sign of the Times Triples-TKHL
Sign of the Times Fives-ISNKN
05SP Game Used-4
Autographs-4
Gold-4
Authentic Fabrics-AF-IK
Authentic Fabrics Autographs-AAF-IK
Authentic Fabrics Dual-HK
Authentic Fabrics Dual Autographs-HK
Authentic Fabrics Gold-AF-IK
Authentic Fabrics Quad-KHLS
Authentic Patches Quad -KHLS
Authentic Fabrics Triple-DKF
Authentic Fabrics Triple-INK
Authentic Fabrics Triple-KNS
Authentic Patches-AP-IK
Authentic Patches Autographs-AAP-IK
Authentic Patches Dual-HK
Authentic Patches Dual Autographs-HK
Authentic Patches Triple-DKF
Authentic Patches Triple-INK
Authentic Patches Triple-KNS
Awesome Authentics-AA-IK
Awesome Authentics Gold-DA-IK
By the Letter-LM-IK
Game Gear-GG-IK
Game Gear Autographs-AG-IK
SIGnificance-IK
SIGnificance Gold-S-IK
SIGnificance Extra-HK
SIGnificance Extra Gold-HK
Significant Numbers-SN-IK
05SPx-3
Spectrum-3
Winning Combos-WC-MI
Winning Combos Autographs-AWC-HK
Winning Combos Gold-WC-MI
Winning Combos Spectrum-WC-MI
Winning Materials-WM-IK
Winning Materials Autographs-AWM-IK
Winning Materials Gold-WM-IK
Winning Materials Spectrum-WM-IK
Xcitement Superstars-XS-IK
Xcitement Superstars Gold-XS-IK
Xcitement Superstars Spectrum-XS-IK
05The Cup-3
Gold-3
Black Rainbow-3
Dual NHL Shields-DSKD
Dual NHL Shields-DSKO
Dual NHL Shields Autographs-ADSKH
Dual NHL Shields Autographs-ADSKO
Dual NHL Shields Autographs-ADSLK
Emblems of Endorsement-EEIK
Hardware Heroes-HHIK
Honorable Numbers-HNIK
Limited Logos-LLIK
Masterpiece Pressplates-3
Masterpiece Pressplates Rookie Upd Auto-275
Noble Numbers-NNKC
Patch Variation-P3
Patch Variation Autographs-AP3
Property of-POIK
Scripted Numbers-SNKC
Scripted Numbers Dual-DSNKH
Scripted Numbers Dual-DSNKO
Scripted Swatches-SSIK
Signature Patches-SPIK
05UD Artifacts-5
05UD Artifacts-152
Blue-5
Blue-152
Gold-5
Gold-152
Green-5
Green-152
Pewter-5
Pewter-152
Red-5
Red-152
Auto Facts-AF-IK
Auto Facts Blue-AF-IK
Auto Facts Copper-AF-IK
Auto Facts Pewter-AF-IK
Auto Facts Silver-AF-IK
Gold Autographed-5
Gold Autographed-152
Remarkable Artifacts-RA-IK
Remarkable Artifacts Dual-RA-IK
Treasured Patches-TP-IK
Treasured Patches Autographed-TP-IK
Treasured Patches Dual-TPD-IK
Treasured Patches Dual Autographed-TPD-IK
Treasured Patches Pewter-TP-IK
Treasured Patches Silver-TP-IK
Treasured Swatches-TS-IK
Treasured Swatches Autographed-TS-IK
Treasured Swatches Blue-TS-IK
Treasured Swatches Copper-TS-IK
Treasured Swatches Dual-TSD-IK
Treasured Swatches Dual Autographed-TSD-IK
Treasured Swatches Dual Blue-TSD-IK
Treasured Swatches Dual Copper-TSD-IK
Treasured Swatches Dual Maroon-TSD-IK
Treasured Swatches Dual Pewter-TSD-IK
Treasured Swatches Dual Silver-TSD-IK
Treasured Swatches Maroon-TS-IK
Treasured Swatches Pewter-TS-IK
Treasured Swatches Silver-TS-IK
05UD PowerPlay-5
05UD PowerPlay-105
Rainbow-5
Power Marks-PMIK
05Ultimate Collection-4
Gold-4
Endorsed Emblems-EEIK
Jerseys-JIK
Jerseys Dual-DJKH
Marquee Attractions-MA4
Marquee Attractions Signatures-SMA4
National Heroes Jerseys-NHJIK
National Heroes Patches-NHPIK
Premium Patches-PPIK
Premium Swatches-PSIK
Ultimate Achievements-UAIK
Ultimate Patches-PIK
Ultimate Patches Dual-DPKH
Ultimate Signatures-USIK
Ultimate Signatures Logos-SLIK
Ultimate Signatures Pairings-UPKH
Ultimate Signatures Trios-UTKLH
05Ultra-9
Gold-9
Fresh Ink-FI-IK
Fresh Ink Blue-FI-IK
Ice-9
Scoring Kings-SK20
Scoring Kings Jerseys-SKJ-IK
Scoring Kings Jersey Autographs-KAJ-IK
Scoring Kings Patches-SKP-IK
Scoring Kings Patch Autographs-KAP-IK
05Upper Deck-7
05Upper Deck All-Time Greatest-3
05Upper Deck Big Playmakers-B-IK
05Upper Deck Goal Celebrations-GC1
05Upper Deck Goal Rush-GR8
05Upper Deck HG Glossy-7
05Upper Deck Hometown Heroes-HH9
05Upper Deck Jerseys Series II-J2IK
05Upper Deck Majestic Materials-MMIK
05Upper Deck NHL Generations-DKZ
05Upper Deck NHL Generations-TFKA
05Upper Deck Notable Numbers-N-IK
05Upper Deck Patches-P-IK
05Upper Deck Scrapbooks-HS1
05Upper Deck Shooting Stars-S-IK
05Upper Deck Ice-5
Rainbow-5
Frozen Fabrics-FFIK
Frozen Fabrics Autographs-AFFIK
Frozen Fabrics Glass-FFIK
Frozen Fabrics Patches-FFPIK
Frozen Fabrics Patch Autographs-FAPIK
Glacial Graphs-GGIK
Signature Swatches-SSIK
05Upper Deck MVP-26
Gold-26
Platinum-26
Rising to the Occasion-RO14
05Upper Deck Rookie Update-4
05Upper Deck Rookie Update-275
05Upper Deck Trilogy-5
05Upper Deck Trilogy-94
Crystal-94
Crystal Autographs-94
Honorary Patches-HP-IK
Honorary Patch Scripts-HSP-IK
Honorary Swatches-HS-IK
Honorary Swatch Scripts-HSS-IK
Ice Scripts-IS-IK
Scripts-SSS-IK
05Upper Deck Toronto Fall Expo-7
05Upper Deck Victory-8
Black-8
Gold-8
Silver-8
Blow-Ups-BU3
Game Breakers-GB3
Stars on Ice-SI3
05ITG Heroes and Prospects-198
Autographs Series II-IK
Autographs Series II-HK
Hero Memorabilia-HM-46
National Pride-NPR-31
Spectrum-STM-02
Spectrum Gold-STM-02
06Be A Player Portraits-5
06Beehive-95
06Beehive-232
Blue-95
Gold-95
Matte-95
Red Facsimile Signatures-95
Wood-95
5 X 7 Black and White-95
5 X 7 Dark Wood-95
Matted Materials-MMIK
Remarkable Matted Materials-MMIK
06Black Diamond-148B
Black-148B
Gold-148B
Ruby-148B
Jerseys-JIK
Jerseys Black-JIK
Jerseys Gold-JIK
Jerseys Ruby-JIK
Jerseys Black Autographs -JIK
06Flair Showcase-6
06Flair Showcase-172
06Flair Showcase-205
06Flair Showcase-272
Parallel-6
Parallel-172
Parallel-205
Parallel-272
Inks-IIK
Wave of the Future-WF3
06Fleer-10
Tiffany-10
Fabricology-FIK
Hockey Headliners-HL8
Speed Machines-SM3
Total 0-01
06Hot Prospects-4
Red Hot-4
White Hot-4
Hot Materials -HMIK
Hot Materials Red Hot-HMIK
Hot Materials White Hot-HMIK
Hotagraphs-HIK
06ITG International Ice-145
Gold-145
Autographs-AIK
Emblem Autographs-GUE40
Emblem Autographs Gold-GUE40
Emblems-GUE40
Emblems Gold-GUE40
Jersey Autographs-GUJ40
Jersey Autographs Gold-GUJ40
Jerseys-GUJ40
Jerseys Gold-GUJ40
Numbers-GUN40
Numbers Autographs-GUN40
Numbers Autographs Gold-GUN40
Numbers Gold-GUN40
Passing The Torch-PTT12
Passing The Torch Gold-PTT12
Quad Patch-QP06
Quad Patch Gold-QP06
06ITG Ultimate Memorabilia-90
Artist Proof-90
Autos-42
Autos Gold-42
Autos Dual-11
Autos Dual Gold-11
Autos Triple-7
Autos Triple Gold-7
Complete Jersey-25
Complete Jersey Gold-25
Double Memorabilia Autos-8
Double Memorabilia Autos Gold-8
First Round Picks-3
First Round Picks Gold-3
Going For Gold-11
Going For Gold Gold-11
Jerseys and Emblems-14
Jerseys and Emblems Gold-14
Jerseys Autos-27
Jerseys Autos Gold-27
Passing The Torch-18
Passing The Torch Gold-18
Triple Thread Jerseys-1
Triple Thread Jerseys Gold-1
06McDonald's Upper Deck-2
Autographs-AIK
Jerseys-JIK
Patches-PIK
06O-Pee-Chee-22
06O-Pee-Chee-605
06O-Pee-Chee-672
Rainbow-22
Rainbow-605
Rainbow-672
Autographs-A-IK
06Panini Stickers-6
06SP Authentic-98
06SP Authentic-117
Limited-98
Limited-117
Sign of the Times Duals-STKL
06SP Game Used-4
Gold-4
Rainbow-4
Authentic Fabrics-AFIK
Authentic Fabrics Parallel-AFIK
Authentic Fabrics Patches-AFIK
Authentic Fabrics Dual-AF2KH
Authentic Fabrics Dual Patches-AF2KH
Authentic Fabrics Triple-AF3ATL
Authentic Fabrics Triple Patches-AF3ATL
Authentic Fabrics Fives-AF51ST
Authentic Fabrics Fives-AF550G
Authentic Fabrics Fives Patches-AF51ST
Authentic Fabrics Fives Patches-AF550G
Authentic Fabrics Sixes-AF6MRT
Authentic Fabrics Sixes Patches-AF6MRT
Authentic Fabrics Eights-AF8RUS
Authentic Fabrics Eights Patches-AF8RUS
Autographs-4
Inked Sweaters-ISIK
Inked Sweaters Patches-ISIK
Inked Sweaters Dual-IS2KL
Inked Sweaters Dual-IS2OK
Inked Sweaters Dual Patches-IS2KL
Inked Sweaters Dual Patches-IS2OK
Letter Marks-LMIK
SIGnificance-SIK
06SPx-6
06SPx-102
Spectrum-6
Spectrum-102
SPxcitement-X3
SPxcitement Spectrum-X3
SPxcitement Autographs-X3
Winning Materials-WMIK
Winning Materials Spectrum-WMIK
Winning Materials Autographs-WMIK
06The Cup-4
Autographed Foundations-CQIK
Autographed Foundations Patches-CQIK
Autographed NHL Shields Duals-DASIA
Autographed NHL Shields Duals-DASIK
Autographed Patches-4
Black Rainbow-4
Foundations-CQIK
Foundations Patches-CQIK
Enshrinements-EIK
Gold-4
Gold Patches-4
Honorable Numbers-HNIK
Jerseys-4
Limited Logos-LLIK
Masterpiece Pressplates-4
NHL Shields Duals-DSHKH
Scripted Swatches-SSIK
Scripted Swatches Duals-DSKL
Signature Patches-SPIK
06UD Artifacts-95
06UD Artifacts-152
Blue-95
Blue-152
Gold-95
Gold-152
Platinum-95
Platinum-152
Radiance-95
Radiance-152
Autographed Radiance Parallel-95
Autographed Radiance Parallel-152
Red-95
Red-152
Auto-Facts-AFIK
Auto-Facts Gold-AFIK
Treasured Patches Black-TSIK
Treasured Patches Blue-TSIK
Treasured Patches Gold-TSIK
Treasured Patches Platinum-TSIK
Treasured Patches Red-TSIK
Treasured Patches Autographed Black Tag Parallel-TSIK
Treasured Swatches-TSIK
Treasured Swatches Black-TSIK
Treasured Swatches Blue-TSIK
Treasured Swatches Gold-TSIK
Treasured Swatches Platinum-TSIK
Treasured Swatches Red-TSIK
Treasured Swatches Autographed Black-TSIK
Tundra Tandems-TTHK
Tundra Tandems-TTKL
Tundra Tandems Black-TTHK
Tundra Tandems Black-TTKL
Tundra Tandems Blue-TTHK
Tundra Tandems Blue-TTKL
Tundra Tandems Gold-TTHK
Tundra Tandems Gold-TTKL
Tundra Tandems Platinum-TTHK
Tundra Tandems Platinum-TTKL
Tundra Tandems Red-TTHK
Tundra Tandems Red-TTKL
Tundra Tandems Dual Patches Red-TTHK
Tundra Tandems Dual Patches Red-TTKL
06UD Mini Jersey Collection-4
Jerseys-IK
Jersey Variations-IK
Jersey Autographs-IK
06UD Powerplay-4
Impact Rainbow-4
Specialists-SIK
Specialists Patches-PIK
06Ultimate Collection-2
Autographed Jerseys-AJ-IK
Autographed Patches-AJ-IK
Jerseys-UJ-IK
Jerseys Triple-UJ3-OMK
Patches-UJ-IK
Patches Triple-UJ3-OMK
Premium Patches-PS-IK
Premium Swatches-PS-IK
Signatures-US-IK
Ultimate Achievements-UA-IK
Ultimate Signatures Logos-SL-IK
06Ultra-11
Gold Medallion-11
Ice Medallion-11
Difference Makers-DM2
Scoring Kings-SK9
06Upper Deck Arena Giveaways-ATL4
06Upper Deck-258
Exclusives Parallel-258
High Gloss Parallel-258
All-Time Greatest-ATG2
All World-AW21
Game Dated Moments-GD20
Game Jerseys-JIK
Game Patches-PIK
Generations Triples-G3SKO
Generations Patches Triple-G3PSKO
Goal Rush-GR4
Masterpieces-258
Oversized Wal-Mart Exclusives-258
06Upper Deck Entry Draft-DR5
06Upper Deck MVP-11
Gold Script-11
Super Script-11
Clutch Performers-CP18
Gotta Have Hart-HH19
International Icons-II2
Jerseys-OJOK
06Upper Deck Ovation-53
06Upper Deck Sweet Shot-4
Signature Shots/Saves-SSIK
Signature Shots/Saves Ice Signings-SSIIK
Signature Shots/Saves Sticks-SSSIK
Signature Sticks-STIK
Sweet Stitches-SSIK
Sweet Stitches Duals-SSIK
Sweet Stitches Triples-SSIK
06Upper Deck Trilogy-4
Combo Autographed Jerseys-CJHK
Combo Autographed Patches-CJHK
Honorary Scripted Patches-HSPIK
Honorary Scripted Swatches-HSSIK
Honorary Swatches-HSIK
Scripts-S1IK
Scripts-S2IK
Scripts-S3IK
06Upper Deck Victory-7
06Upper Deck Victory Black-7
06Upper Deck Victory Gold-7
06Upper Deck Victory GameBreakers-GB2
06Upper Deck Victory Next In Line-NL4
06Upper Deck Victory Oversize Cards-IK
06Russian Sport Collection Olympic Stars-8
06Russian Torino Olympic Team-11
06ITG Heroes and Prospects Triple Memorabilia-TM03
06ITG Heroes and Prospects Triple Memorabilia Gold-TM03
07Upper Deck Victory-79
Black-79
Gold-79
GameBreakers-GB9
Oversize Cards-OS22
Stars on Ice-SI17

Kovalenko, Andrei

91O-Pee-Chee Inserts-18R
92Nordiques Petro-Canada-17
92OPC Premier-93
92Parkhurst-150
92Parkhurst-223
Emerald Ice-150
Emerald Ice-223
92Pinnacle-395
French-395
92Ultra-387
Imports-9
92Upper Deck-567
Calder Candidates-CC17
Euro-Rookies-ER14
Gordie Howe Selects-G19
92Finnish Semic-117
92Russian Stars Red Ace-16
92Russian Stars Red Ace-34
93Donruss-278
93Leaf-122
Gold Rookies-6
93OPC Premier-124
93OPC Premier-198
Gold-124
Gold-198
93Panini Stickers-71
93Parkhurst-167
Emerald Ice-167
93Pinnacle-171
Canadian-171
93PowerPlay-200
93Score-174
Canadian-174
93Stadium Club-77
Members Only Master Set-77
OPC-77
First Day Issue-77
First Day Issue OPC-77
93Topps/OPC Premier-124
93Topps/OPC Premier-198
Gold-124
Gold-198
93Topps Premier Black Gold-17
93Ultra-144
93Upper Deck-85
94Canada Games NHL POGS-196
94Donruss-6
94Fleer-178
94Leaf-71
94Nordiques Burger King-12
94OPC Premier-97
Special Effects-97

94Pinnacle-128
Artist's Proofs-128
Rink Collection-128
94Score-39
Gold-39
Platinum-39
94Topps/OPC Premier-97
Special Effects-97
94Ultra-175
94Upper Deck-272
Electric Ice-272
95Be A Player-118
Signatures-S118
Signatures Die Cuts-S118
95Canada Games NHL POGS-75
95Collector's Choice-54
Player's Club-54
Player's Club Platinum-54
95Donruss-374
95Leaf-130
95Parkhurst International-51
95Parkhurst International-382
Emerald Ice-51
Emerald Ice-382
95Playoff One on One-138
95Score-253
Black Ice Artist's Proofs-253
Black Ice-253
95Upper Deck-446
95Finnish Semic World Championships-133
95Swedish Globe World Championships-176
95Swedish World Championships Stickers-42
96Black Diamond-51
Gold-51
96Collector's Choice-137
96Maggers-50
96Metal Universe-54
96Oilers Postcards-51
96Pinnacle-152
Artist's Proofs-152
Foil-152
Premium Stock-152
Rink Collection-152
96Score-196
Artist's Proofs-196
Dealer's Choice Artist's Proofs-196
Special Artist's Proofs-196
Golden Blades-196
96SP-58
96Swedish Semic Wien-144
97Collector's Choice-90
97Katch-58
Gold-58
Silver-58
97Pacific-51
Copper-51
Emerald Green-51
Ice Blue-51
Red-51
Silver-51
97Panini Stickers-209
97Paramount-76
Copper-76
Dark Grey-76
Emerald Green-76
Ice Blue-76
Red-76
Silver-76
97Pinnacle Certified-106
Red-106
Mirror Blue-106
Mirror Gold-106
Mirror Red-106
97Pinnacle Inside-177
97Pinnacle Tot Cert Platinum Blue-106
97Pinnacle Tot Cert Platinum Gold-106
97Pinnacle Totally Certified Platinum Red-106
97Pinnacle Tot Cert Mirror Platinum Gold-106
97Score-178
98Be A Player-202
Press Release-202
98BAP Gold-202
98BAP Autographs-202
98BAP Autographs Gold-202
98Panini Stickers-194
98Revolution-55
Ice Shadow-55
Red-55
99Pacific-75
Copper-75
Emerald Green-75
Gold-75
Ice Blue-75
Premiere Date-75
Red-75
99Panini Stickers-46
99Ultimate Victory-17
1/1-17
Parallel-17
Parallel 100-17
00Pacific-86
Copper-86
Gold-86
Ice Blue-86
Premiere Date-86
00Panini Stickers-28
00Upper Deck-246
Exclusives Tier 1-246
Exclusives Tier 2-246
00Upper Deck Vintage-30
01Pacific-33
Extreme LTD-33
Hobby LTD-33
Premiere Date-33
Retail LTD-33
01Pacific Arena Exclusives-33
01Russian Lightnings-8
02BAP Sig Series Auto Buybacks 1998-202
02Russian Hockey League-232
02Russian World Championships-16
03Russian National Team-15
03Russian Postcards-3
04Russian RHL-2

Kovalev, Alexei
91Upper Deck-655
French-655
91Upper Deck Czech World Juniors-16
91Star Pics-48
92OPC Premier-126
92Parkhurst-109
92Parkhurst-225
Emerald Ice-109
Emerald Ice-225
92Pinnacle-403
French-403
92Ultra-137
Imports-10
92Upper Deck-573
92Upper Deck-633
Calder Candidates-CC11
Euro-Rookies-ER10
Gordie Howe Selects-G13
World Junior Grads-WG9
92Russian Stars Red Ace-17
92Russian Stars Red Ace-8
93Donruss-220
93Leaf-147
93OPC Premier-187
Gold-187
93Parkhurst-130
93Parkhurst-238
Emerald Ice-130
Emerald Ice-238
93Pinnacle-76
Canadian-76
Team 2001-7
Team 2001 Canadian-7
93PowerPlay-159
93Score-203
Canadian-203
International Stars-19
International Stars Canadian-19
93Stadium Club-129
Members Only Master Set-129
OPC-129
First Day Issue-129
First Day Issue OPC-129
93Topps/OPC Premier-187
Gold-187
93Ultra-115
93Upper Deck-27
Hat Tricks-HT7
NHL's Best-HB6
SP-101
93Upper Deck Locker All-Stars-54
93Classic-137
93Classic Pro Prospects-10
93Classic Pro Prospects-74
BCs-BC1
LPs-LP2
94Canada Games NHL POGS-163
94Donruss-268
94Flair-112
Scoring Power-4
94Fleer-133
94Leaf-92
94Leaf Limited-59
94McDonald's Upper Deck-McD38
94OPC Premier-185
Special Effects-185
94Parkhurst-142
Gold-142
Vintage-V24
SE Euro-Stars-ES18
94Pinnacle-107
Artist's Proofs-107
Rink Collection-107
World Edition-WE12
94Select-66
Gold-66
94SP-76
Die Cuts-76
94Topps/OPC Premier-185
Special Effects-185
94Ultra-331
94Upper Deck-207
94Upper Deck-567
Electric Ice-207
Electric Ice-567
SP Inserts-SP49
SP Inserts Die Cuts-SP49
94Classic Pro Prospects-52
Autographs-AU5
95Bashan Super Stickers-81
95Be A Player-182
Signatures-S182
Signatures Die Cuts-S182
Lethal Lines-LL15
95Canada Games NHL POGS-184
95Collector's Choice-234
Player's Club-234
Player's Club Platinum-234
95Donruss-216
95Emotion-113
95Imperial Stickers-81
95Leaf-203
95Leaf Limited-48
95Metal-95
Winners-3
95Panini Stickers-106
95Parkhurst International-139
Emerald Ice-139
95Playoff One on One-67
95Score-79
Black Ice Artist's Proofs-79
Black Ice-79
95Select Certified-88
Mirror Gold-88
95SkyBox Impact-109
95SP-99
95Stadium Club-218
Members Only Master Set-218
95Summit-97
Artist's Proofs-97
Ice-97
95Topps-90
OPC Inserts-90
Young Stars-YS9
95Ultra-275
95Upper Deck-132
Electric Ice-132
Electric Ice Gold-132
Special Edition-SE56
Special Edition Gold-SE56
95Swedish Globe World Championships-177
96Black Diamond-27
Gold-27
96Collector's Choice-176
96Donruss-176
Press Proofs-176
96Donruss Canadian Ice-41
Gold Press Proofs-41
Red Press Proofs-41
96Fleer-69
96Leaf-135
Press Proofs-135
96Leaf Preferred-96
Press Proofs-96
96Metal Universe-97
96Pinnacle-45
Artist's Proofs-45
Foil-45
Premium Stock-45
Rink Collection-45
96Score-61
Artist's Proofs-61
Dealer's Choice Artist's Proofs-61
Special Artist's Proofs-61
Golden Blades-61
96SkyBox Impact-80
96SP-104
Holoview Collection-HC7
96Summit-82
Artist's Proofs-82
Ice-82
Metal-82
Premium Stock-82
96Topps Picks-79
OPC Inserts-79
96Ultra-107
Gold Medallion-107
96Upper Deck-103
97Pacific-119
Copper-119
Emerald Green-119
Ice Blue-119
Red-119
Silver-119
97Pacific Dynagon-79
Copper-79
Dark Grey-79
Emerald Green-79
Ice Blue-79
Red-79
Silver-79
Tandems-72
97Pacific Invincible-87
Copper-87
Emerald Green-87
Ice Blue-87
Red-87
Silver-87
97Panini Stickers-85
97Paramount-116
Copper-116
Dark Grey-116
Emerald Green-116
Ice Blue-116
Red-116
Silver-116
97Pinnacle-120
Press Plates Back Black-120
Press Plates Back Cyan-120
Press Plates Back Magenta-120
Press Plates Back Yellow-120
Press Plates Front Black-120
Press Plates Front Cyan-120
Press Plates Front Magenta-120
Press Plates Front Yellow-120
97Score-156
Artist's Proofs-156
Golden Blades-156
97Score Rangers-7
Platinum-7
Premier-7
97SP Authentic-102
97Upper Deck-319
98Aurora-123
98Be A Player-92
Press Release-92
98BAP Gold-92
98BAP Autographs-92
98BAP Autographs Gold-92
98BAP Tampa Bay All Star Game-92
98Finest-113
No Protectors-113
No Protectors Refractors-113
Refractors-113
98Pacific-294
Ice Blue-294
Red-294
98Pacific Dynagon Ice-122
Blue-122
Red-122
98Pacific Omega-196
Red-196
Opening Day Issue-196
98Panini Stickers-84
98Paramount-153
Copper-153
Emerald Green-153
Holo-Electric-153
Ice Blue-153
Silver-153
98Revolution-119
Ice Shadow-119
Red-119
99Aurora-117
Premiere Date-117
99BAP Memorabilia-71
Gold-71
Silver-71
99BAP Millennium-197
Emerald-197
Ruby-197
Sapphire-197
Signatures-197
Signatures Gold-197
99Black Diamond-70
Diamond Cut-70
Final Cut-70
99Crown Royale-113
Limited Series-113
Premiere Date-113
99O-Pee-Chee-66
99O-Pee-Chee Chrome-66
99O-Pee-Chee Chrome Refractors-66
99Pacific-341
Copper-341
Emerald Green-341
Gold-341
Ice Blue-341
Premiere Date-341
Red-341
99Pacific Dynagon Ice-160
Blue-160
Copper-160
Gold-160
Premiere Date-160
99Pacific Omega-190
Copper-190
Gold-190
Ice Blue-190
Premiere Date-190
99Pacific Prism-115
Holographic Blue-115
Holographic Gold-115
Holographic Mirror-115
Holographic Purple-115
Premiere Date-115
99Panini Stickers-134
99Paramount-190
Copper-190
Emerald-190
Gold-190
Holographic Emerald-190
Holographic Gold-190
Holographic Silver-190
Ice Blue-190
Premiere Date-190
Red-190
Silver-190
99Revolution-119
Premiere Date-119
Red-119
Shadow Series-119
99SP Authentic-69
99SPx-124
Radiance-124
Spectrum-124
99Stadium Club-22
First Day Issue-22
One of a Kind-22
Printing Plates Black-22
Printing Plates Cyan-22
Printing Plates Magenta-22
Printing Plates Yellow-22
99Topps/OPC-66
99Topps/OPC Chrome-66
Refractors-66
99Topps Gold Label Class 1-80
Black-80
Black One of One-80
One of One-80
Red-80
Red One of One-80
99Topps Gold Label Class 2-80
99Topps Gold Label Class 2 Black-80
99Topps Gold Label Class 2 Black 1 of 1-80
99Topps Gold Label Class 2 One of One-80
99Topps Gold Label Class 2 Red-80
99Topps Gold Label Class 2 Red One of One-80
99Topps Gold Label Class 3-80
99Topps Gold Label Class 3 Black-80
99Topps Gold Label Class 3 Black 1 of 1-80
99Topps Gold Label Class 3 One of One-80
99Topps Gold Label Class 3 Red-80
99Topps Gold Label Class 3 Red One of One-80
99Upper Deck-275
Exclusives-275
Exclusives 1 of 1-275
99Upper Deck Gold Reserve-275
99Upper Deck MVP-170
Gold Script-170
Silver Script-170
Super Script-170
99Upper Deck MVP SC Edition-147
Gold Script-147
Silver Script-147
Super Script-147
99Upper Deck Ovation-47
Standing Ovation-47
99Upper Deck Victory-241
99Wayne Gretzky Hockey-140
99Russian Stars of Hockey-30
00Aurora-117
Premiere Date-117
00BAP Memorabilia-77
Emerald-77
Ruby-77
Sapphire-77
Promos-77
00BAP Mem Chicago Sportsfest Copper-77
00BAP Memorabilia Chicago Sportsfest Blue-77
00BAP Memorabilia Chicago Sportsfest Gold-77
00BAP Memorabilia Chicago Sportsfest Ruby-77
00BAP Memorabilia Chicago Sun-Times Ruby-77
00BAP Memorabilia Chicago Sun-Times Gold-77
00BAP Mem Chicago Sun-Times Sapphire-77
00BAP Mem Toronto Fall Expo Copper-77
00BAP Memorabilia Toronto Fall Expo Gold-77
00BAP Memorabilia Toronto Fall Expo Ruby-77
00BAP Parkhurst 2000-P84
00BAP Signature Series-24
Emerald-24
Ruby-24
Sapphire-24
00O-Pee-Chee-31
00O-Pee-Chee Parallel-31
00Pacific-330
Copper-330
Gold-330
Ice Blue-330
Premiere Date-330
00Panini Stickers-84
00Paramount-199
Copper-199
Gold-199
Holo-Gold-199
Holo-Silver-199
Ice Blue-199
Premiere Date-199
00Revolution-119
Blue-119
Premiere Date-119
Red-119
00SP Authentic-71
00Stadium Club-46
00Titanium-76
Blue-76
Gold-76
Premiere Date-76
Red-76
Retail-76
Game Gear-135
Game Gear-155
Game Gear Patches-135
00Titanium Draft Day Edition-84
Patches-84
00Topps/OPC-31
Parallel-31
00Topps Chrome-29
OPC Refractors-29
Refractors-29
00Topps Gold Label Class 1-45
Gold-45
00Topps Gold Label Class 2-45
00Topps Gold Label Class 2 Gold-45
00Topps Gold Label Class 3-45
00Topps Gold Label Class 3 Gold-45
00Topps Heritage-123
00Topps Premier Plus-46
Blue Ice-46
00Topps Stars-70
Blue-70
00UD Heroes-95
00UD Pros and Prospects-70
00Upper Deck-368
Exclusives Tier 1-368
Exclusives Tier 2-368
00Upper Deck MVP-141
First Stars-141
Second Stars-141
Third Stars-141
00Upper Deck Victory-190
00Upper Deck Vintage-291
01Atomic-78
Blue-78
Gold-78
Premiere Date-78
Red-78
Statosphere-17
Team Nucleus-11
01BAP Memorabilia-168
Emerald-168
Ruby-168
Sapphire-168
All-Star Jerseys-ASJ13
All-Star Emblems-ASE13
All-Star Numbers-ASN13
All-Star Teammates-AST6
Country of Origin-CO33
01BAP Sig Series International Medals-IB-8
01Bowman YoungStars-56
Gold-56
Ice Cubed-56
01Crown Royale-115
Blue-115
Premiere Date-115
Red-115
Retail-115
Triple Threads-17
01O-Pee-Chee-95
01O-Pee-Chee Heritage Parallel-95
01O-Pee-Chee Heritage Parallel Limited-95
01O-Pee-Chee Premier Parallel-95
01Pacific-314
Extreme LTD-314
Hobby LTD-314
Premiere Date-314
Retail LTD-314
All-Stars-W8
01Pacific Adrenaline-153
Blue-153
Premiere Date-153
Red-153
Retail-153
Jerseys-35
World Beaters-15
01Pacific Arena Exclusives-314
01Pacific Heads-Up-77
Blue-77
Premiere Date-77
Red-77
Silver-77
Quad Jerseys-18
Quad Jerseys-29
01Parkhurst-17
Gold-17
Silver-17
01Private Stock-77
Gold-77
Premiere Date-77
Retail-77
Silver-77
Game Gear-77
Game Gear Patches-77
01Private Stock Pacific Nights-77
01SP Authentic-69
Limited-69
Limited Gold-69
Sign of the Times-AK
Sign of the Times-BKK
01SP Game Used-45
Authentic Fabric-AFAK
Authentic Fabric-DFLK
Authentic Fabric-TFLKL
Authentic Fabric Gold-AFAK
Inked Sweaters-ISAK
Inked Sweaters-DSLK
01SPx-51
01Sports Illustrated for Kids III-66
01Stadium Club-35
Award Winners-35
Master Photos-35
NHL Passport-NHLP6
01Titanium-112
Hobby Parallel-112
Premiere Date-112
Retail-112
Retail Parallel-112
Double-Sided Jerseys-36
01Topps-95
Heritage Parallel-95
Heritage Parallel Limited-95
OPC Parallel-95
Own The Game-OTG5
Shot Masters-SM14
Stars of the Game-SG8
01Topps Chrome-95
Refractors-95
Black Border Refractors-95
01Topps Heritage-52
Refractors-52
01Topps Reserve-42
Emblems-AK
Jerseys-AK
Name Plates-AK
Numbers-AK
Patches-AK
01UD Challenge for the Cup-67
01UD Honor Roll Pucks-P-AK
01UD Honor Roll Pucks Gold-P-AK
01UD Mask Collection-78
Gold-78
01UD Playmakers-78
01UD Premier Collection Signatures-AK
01UD Premier Collection Signatures Black-AK
01UD Top Shelf-33
01Upper Deck-139
Exclusives-139
Game Jerseys Series II-PFAK
Gate Attractions-GA6
Pride of a Nation-TPFKK
Shooting Stars-SS13
01Upper Deck Ice-114
01Upper Deck MVP-154
01Upper Deck Victory-281
01Upper Deck Victory-416
Gold-281
Gold-416
01Upper Deck Vintage-200
01Upper Deck Vintage-207
01Upper Deck Vintage-208
01Vanguard Memorabilia-25
01Vanguard Memorabilia-39
01Vanguard Patches-25
01Vanguard Patches-39
01Czech Stadion-256
02BAP All-Star Edition-47
Jerseys-47
Jerseys Gold-47
Jerseys Silver-47
02BAP First Edition-199
Scoring Leaders-15
02BAP Memorabilia-46
02BAP Memorabilia-315
Emerald-46
Ruby-46
Sapphire-46
All-Star Jerseys-ASJ-28
NHL All-Star Game-46
NHL All-Star Game Blue-46
NHL All-Star Game Green-46
NHL All-Star Game Red-46
Teammates-TM-15
02BAP Memorabilia Toronto Fall Expo-46
02BAP Signature Series-10
Autographs-10
Autograph Buybacks 1998-92
Autograph Buybacks 1999-197
Autographs Gold-10
Jerseys-SGJ69
Jersey Autographs-SGJ69
Team Quads-TQ8
02Bowman YoungStars-49
Gold-49
Silver-49
02Crown Royale-77
Blue-77
Red-77
Retail-77
Dual Patches-18
02ITG Used Teammates-T1
02ITG Used Teammates Gold-T1
02O-Pee-Chee-147
02O-Pee-Chee Premier Blue Parallel-147
02O-Pee-Chee Premier Red Parallel-147
02O-Pee-Chee Factory Set-147
02Pacific-309
Blue-309
Red-309
02Pacific Calder-45
Silver-45
02Pacific Complete-3
Red-3
02Pacific Exclusive-137
Jerseys-20
Jerseys Gold-20
02Pacific Heads-Up-99
Blue-99
Purple-99
Red-99
02Pacific Quest for the Cup-65
Gold-65
02Parkhurst-2
Bronze-2
Gold-2
Silver-2
Teammates-TT14
02Parkhurst Retro-4
Minis-4
02Private Stock Reserve-80
Blue-80
Red-80
Retail-80
02SP Authentic-72
Beckett Promos-72
02SP Game Used Authentic Fabrics-AFKO
02SP Game Used Authentic Fabrics-AFKV
02SP Game Used Authentic Fabrics Gold-AFKO
02SP Game Used Authentic Fabrics Gold-AFKV
02SP Game Used Authentic Fabrics Rainbow-AFKO
02SP Game Used Authentic Fabrics Rainbow-AFKV
02SP Game Used First Rounder Patches-AK
02SP Game Used Tools of the Game-AK
02SPx-60
Spectrum Gold-60
Spectrum Silver-60
02Stadium Club-35
Silver Decoy Cards-35
Proofs-35
World Stage-WS15
02Titanium-81
Blue-81
Red-81
Retail-81
02Topps-147
OPC Blue Parallel-147
OPC Red Parallel-147
Factory Set-147
02Topps Chrome-89
Black Border Refractors-89
Refractors-89
02Topps Heritage-95
Chrome Parallel-95
Great Skates-AK
Great Skates Patches-AK
02Topps Total-162
02UD Artistic Impressions-70
Gold-70
02UD Artistic Impressions Beckett Promos-70
02UD Artistic Impressions Retrospectives-R70
02UD Artistic Impressions Retrospect Gold-R70
02UD Artistic Impressions Retrospect Silver-R70
02UD Honor Roll-57
02UD Piece of History-71
Exquisite Combos-ECLK
02UD Premier Collection-35
Jerseys Bronze-AK
Jerseys Gold-AK
Jerseys Silver-AK
02UD Top Shelf-72
Signatures-AK
02Upper Deck-140
Exclusives-140
Patchwork-PWAK
Playbooks Series II-LK
02Upper Deck Classic Portraits-78
02Upper Deck MVP-145
Gold-145
Classics-145
Golden Classics-145
Overdrive-SO12
Skate Around Jerseys-SDKR
Skate Around Jerseys-STKFS
Souvenirs-S-AK
02Upper Deck Rookie Update-64
02Upper Deck Victory-173
Bronze-173
Gold-173
Silver-173
National Pride-NP37
02Upper Deck Vintage-206
02Upper Deck Vintage-284
Green Backs-206
02Vanguard-80
LTD-80
02Russian Olympic Team-6
02UD SuperStars City ASTriple Jersey *-JKA
03BAP Memorabilia-5
Emerald-5
Gold-5
Ruby-5
Sapphire-5
All-Star Emblems-ASE-7
All-Star Jerseys-ASJ-9
All-Star Numbers-ASN-7
All-Star Starting Lineup-6
03BAP Ultimate Memorabilia Autographs-1
Gold-1
03Beehive-127
Gold-127
Silver-127
03Black Diamond-43
Black-43
Green-43
Red-43
03Bowman-40
Gold-40
03Bowman Chrome-40
Refractors-40
Gold Refractors-40
Xfractors-40
03Crown Royale-67
Blue-67
Retail-67
03ITG Action-303
03ITG Used Signature Series-18
Gold-18
Autographs-AK1
Autographs-AK2
Autographs Gold-AK1
Autographs Gold-AK2
Jerseys-1
Jerseys Gold-1
Jersey Autos-1
Jersey and Stick-1
Jersey and Stick Gold-1
Teammates-10
Teammates Gold-10
03NHL Sticker Collection-114
03O-Pee-Chee-50
03OPC Blue-50
03OPC Gold-50
03OPC Red-50
03Pacific-225
Blue-225
Red-225
03Pacific Calder-55
Silver-55
03Pacific Complete-281
Red-281
03Pacific Exhibit-99
Blue Backs-99
Yellow Backs-99
03Pacific Heads-Up-65
Hobby LTD-65
Retail LTD-65
03Pacific Invincible-65
Blue-65
Red-65
Retail-65
03Pacific Prism-70
Blue-70
Gold-70
Red-70
03Pacific Quest for the Cup-70
Blue-70
03Pacific Supreme-66
Blue-66
Red-66
Retail-66
03Parkhurst Orig Six He Shoots/Scores-24
03Parkhurst Orig Six He Shoots/Scores-24A
03Parkhurst Original Six New York-2
Inserts-N15
Memorabilia-NM56
Memorabilia-NM57
03Parkhurst Rookie-23
03Private Stock Reserve-69
Blue-69
Red-69
Retail-69
03Rangers Team Issue-9
03SP Game Used Team Threads-TTBLK
03SPx-65
Radiance-65
Spectrum-65
Fantasy Franchise-FF-BLK
Fantasy Franchise Limited-FF-BLK
03Topps-50
Blue-50
Gold-50
Red-50
Topps/OPC Idols-II2
03Topps C55-51
Minis-51
Minis American Back-51
Minis American Back Red-51
Minis Bazooka Back-51
Minis Brooklyn Back-51
Minis Hat Trick Back-51
Minis O Canada Back-51
Minis O Canada Back Red-51
Minis Stanley Cup Back-51
03Topps Pristine-89
Gold Refractor Die Cuts-89
Refractors-89
Press Plates Black-89
Press Plates Cyan-89
Press Plates Magenta-89
Press Plates Yellow-89
03Topps Traded-TT83
Blue-TT83
Gold-TT83
Red-TT83
03UD Honor Roll-54
Grade A Jerseys-TNYR
03Upper Deck-124
Canadian Exclusives-124
HG-124
Jerseys-GJ-AK
03Upper Deck Classic Portraits-62
Hockey Royalty-BLC
03Upper Deck MVP-276
Gold Script-276
Silver Script-276
Canadian Exclusives-276
Souvenirs-S18
SportsNut-SN59
03Upper Deck Trilogy-62
Limited-62
03Upper Deck Victory-121
Bronze-121
Gold-121
Silver-121
Freshman Flashback-FF28
Game Breakers-GB21
03Toronto Star-58
04Pacific-138
Blue-138
Red-138
04UD All-World-24
Gold-24
04Upper Deck World Cup Tribute-AK
04Upper Deck World Cup Tribute-IKAK
04Upper Deck World Cup Tribute-AKAYSS
04Russian Back to Russia-35
05Beehive Matted Materials-MMAK
05Canadiens Team Issue-13
05Panini Stickers-71
05Parkhurst-251
Facsimile Auto Parallel-251
True Colors-TCMTL
True Colors-TCMTL
True Colors-TCTOMO
True Colors-TCTOMO
05SP Game Used By the Letter-LM-AK
05SP Game Used Game Gear-GG-AK
05UD Powerplay Specialists-TSAKO
05UD Powerplay Specialists Patches-SPAK
05Ultimate Coll National Heroes Jersey-NHJAK
05Ultimate Coll National Heroes Patch-NHPAK
05Upper Deck-350
Jerseys-J-AK
Jerseys Series II-J2AK
05Upper Deck MVP-204
Gold-204
Platinum-204
05Upper Deck Victory-225
Black-225
Gold-225
06Be A Player-102
Autographs-102
Signatures-AK
Signatures 10-110
Signatures Duals-DKS
Signatures Trios-THHK
Signatures Foursomes-FOFKF
06Beehive-50
Matte-50
06Black Diamond-45
Black-45
Gold-45
Ruby-45
Jerseys-JAK
Jerseys Black-JAK
Jerseys Gold-JAK
Jerseys Ruby-JAK
06Canadiens Postcards-11
06Flair Showcase Stitches-SSAK
06Fleer-104
Tiffany-104
Fabricology-FAK
Speed Machines-SM15
06Gatorade-38
06O-Pee-Chee-270
Rainbow-270
06Panini Stickers-65
06SP Game Used-56
Gold-56
Rainbow-56
Authentic Fabrics Eights-AF8RUS
Authentic Fabrics Eights Patches-AF8RUS
06SPx-51
06SPx-113
Spectrum-51
Spectrum-113
06Sunkist-1
06The Cup NHL Shields Duals-DSHKK
06UD Artifacts-50
Blue-50
Gold-50
Radiance-50
Red-50
Treasured Patches Platinum-TSAK
Treasured Patches Red-TSAK
Treasured Swatches-TSAK
Treasured Swatches Black-TSAK
Treasured Swatches Blue-TSAK
Treasured Swatches Red-TSAK
Tundra Tandems-TTAS
Tundra Tandems-TTKK
Tundra Tandems Black-TTAS
Tundra Tandems Black-TTKK
Tundra Tandems Blue-TTAS
Tundra Tandems Blue-TTKK
Tundra Tandems Gold-TTAS
Tundra Tandems Gold-TTKK
Tundra Tandems Red-TTAS
Tundra Tandems Red-TTKK
Tundra Tandems Dual Patches Red-TTAS
Tundra Tandems Dual Patches Red-TTKK
06UD Powerplay-54
Impact Rainbow-54
Specialists-SAK
Specialists Patches-PAK
06Ultimate Collection Premium Patches-PS-AK
06Ultimate Collection Premium Swatches-PS-AK
06Ultra-104
Gold Medallion-104
Ice Medallion-104
06Upper Deck-102
Exclusives Parallel-102
High Gloss Parallel-102
Game Jerseys-JAK
Game Patches-PAK
Generations Duals-G2FK
Masterpieces-102
06Upper Deck MVP-157
Gold Script-157
Super Script-157
Jerseys-OJDK
06Upper Deck Ovation-127
06Upper Deck Trilogy-54
06Upper Deck Victory-104
06Upper Deck Victory Black-104
06Upper Deck Victory Gold-104
06Upper Deck Victory GameBreakers-GB24
06Russian Sport Collection Olympic Stars-7
06Russian Torino Olympic Team-9
07Upper Deck Ovation-76
07Upper Deck Victory-48
Black-48
Gold-48

Kovalev, Andrei
91Finnish Semic World Champ Stickers-93
91Swedish Semic World Champ Stickers-93
94German DEL-423
95Swiss HNL-121
96German DEL-81
98German DEL-225
99German DEL-130
00German DEL-207
Profiles-P9
01German Upper Deck-221

Kovalyov, Andrei
91O-Pee-Chee Inserts-38R

Kovanen, Tommi
96Finnish SISU Redline-70
99Finnish Cardset-295
03Finnish Cardset-74
04Finnish Cardset-81
Parallel-62
05Finnish Cardset -64

Kovar, Robin
01Vancouver Giants-16
04Czech OFS-252
06Czech HC Zlin Hame Postcards-4
06Czech OFS-227

Kovarik, Jiri
94German First League-450

Kovarik, Martin
94Czech APS Extraliga-143
95Czech APS Extraliga-247

Koverko, Trevor
04Owen Sound Attack-19
05Owen Sound Attack-5
06Oshawa Generals-15

Kovin, V.
80USSR Olympic Team Mini Pics-5

Kowal, Jack
96Louisville Riverfrogs-19
97Louisville Riverfrogs-18
00Sioux City Musketeers-18

Kowal, Joe
79Rochester Americans-9

Kowal, Tom
93Omaha Lancers-14
02Tri-City Stormfront-24

Kowalchuch, Peter
52Juniors Blue Tint-173

Kowalchuk, Kevin
83Saskatoon Blades-13
84Saskatoon Blades Stickers-9

Kowalchuk, Sheldon
88Brandon Wheat Kings-13

Kowalczyk, Pavel
94Czech APS Extraliga-185

95Czech APS Extraliga-34
96Czech APS Extraliga-35
97Czech APS Extraliga-55
97Czech DS Extraliga-103
97Czech DS Stickers-96
98Czech DS-105
98Czech DS Stickers-288
98Czech OFS-117
99Czech DS-173
99Czech OFS-424
03Czech OFS Plus-19
03Czech OFS Plus All-Star Game-H13
04Czech OFS-253
Defence Points-14

Kowalek, Eric
03Arizona Icecats-12
04Arizona Icecats-8

Kowalski, Craig
04Florida Everblades-22
05Florida Everblades-13

Kowalski, Ed
99San Angelo Outlaws-6
00Muskegon Fury-6

Kowalski, Jason
99Owen Sound Platers-25
02OCN Blizzard-15

Kowalski, Rafal
93Quebec Pee-Wee Tournament-1517

Kowalski, Scott
91British Columbia JHL-53

Kowalsky, Rick
89Sault Ste. Marie Greyhounds-14
907th Inn. Sketch OHL-162
917th Inn. Sketch OHL-330
917th Inn. Sketch Memorial Cup-11
93Sault Ste. Marie Greyhound Memorial Cup-13
94Hampton Roads Admirals-13
94Classic Pro Prospects-136
95Hampton Roads Admirals-10
96Hampton Roads Admirals-HRA16
97Hampton Roads Admirals-10
98Hampton Roads Admirals 10th Anniversary-14
98Portland Pirates-10
99Hampton Roads Admirals-10
00UK Sekonda Superleague-61
01Roanoke Express-12
02Roanoke Express-17
02Roanoke Express RBI Sports-197
03Roanoke Express-312

Kozack, Kelly
83Brandon Wheat Kings-5

Kozak, Don
74NHL Action Stamps-124
74O-Pee-Chee NHL-98
74O-Pee-Chee NHL-111
74Topps-98
74Topps-111
75O-Pee-Chee NHL-276
75Topps-276
76O-Pee-Chee NHL-185
76Topps-185
77O-Pee-Chee NHL-316
79O-Pee-Chee-342

Kozak, George
96Pensacola Ice Pilots-23
97Pensacola Ice Pilots-23

Kozak, Phil
03Saginaw Spirit-10

Kozak, Rick
02Brandon Wheat Kings-16
03Kamloops Blazers-13

Kozak, Todd
91Air Canada SJHL-C23
92Saskatchewan JHL-90

Kozakowski, Jeff
93Waterloo Black Hawks-14
99Mobile Mysticks-13
02Muskegon Fury-12

Kozar, Randy
75Roanoke Valley Rebels-3

Kozek, Andrew
04South Surrey Eagles-10
04South Surrey Eagles-11
04Surrey Eagles-9a
04Surrey Eagles-9b
04Surrey Eagles-9

Kozel, Brent
93Quebec Pee-Wee Tournament-1331

Kozhevnikov, Alexander
04Russian World Junior Team-14

Kozhevnikov, Mikhail
04German DEL Update-315
04German Hannover Scorpions Postcards-15

Kozic, Zoran
03UK London Racers-6

Kozier, David
03UK Manchester Phoenix-9

Kozin, Valentin
74Swedish Stickers-44

Koziol, Soren
98Danish Hockey League-217
99Danish Hockey League-135

Koziol, Wolfgang
94German First League-106

Kozitsyn, Artem
02Val d'Or Foreurs-7
03Val d'Or Foreurs-8

Kozjevnikov, Aleksandr
82Swedish Semic VM Stickers-73
83Swedish Semic VM Stickers-73
89Swedish Semic Elitserien Stickers-17

Kozlov, Andrei
94Erie Panthers-11

Kozlov, Slava
91Parkhurst-266
French-266
91Upper Deck-5
91Upper Deck-462
French-5
French-462
91Finnish Semic World Champ Stickers-98
91Russian Sports Unite Hearts-2
91Swedish Semic World Champ Stickers-98
92Bowman-300
92O-Pee-Chee-235
92OPC Premier-71
92Parkhurst-40
Emerald Ice-40
92Pinnacle-230
French-230
Team 2000-13
Team 2000 French-13
92Pro Set-225
92Score-473
Canadian-473
Young Superstars-32
92Stadium Club-62
92Topps-35
Gold-35G
92Ultra-50
92Upper Deck-294
World Junior Grads-WG2
92Finnish Semic-111
92Russian Stars Red Ace-18
92Russian Tri-Globe From Russia With Puck-13
92Russian Tri-Globe From Russia With Puck-14
93Donruss-91
93Leaf-303
93OPC Premier-494
Gold-494
93Parkhurst-57
Emerald Ice-57
93PowerPlay-331
Rising Stars-2
93Score-421
Canadian-421
93Stadium Club-388
Members Only Master Set-388
First Day Issue-388
93Topps/OPC Premier-494
Gold-494
93Ultra-174
93Upper Deck-495
93Classic Pro Prospects-135
94Canada Games NHL POGS-88
94Donruss-180
94Flair-50
94Fleer-61
94Leaf-236
94Leaf Limited-55
94OPC Premier-145
Special Effects-145
94Parkhurst-66
Gold-66
Vintage-V48
94Pinnacle-92
Artist's Proofs-92
Rink Collection-92
94Score-70
Gold-70
Platinum-70
94Select-103
Gold-103
94SP-35
Die Cuts-35
94Stadium Club-97
Members Only Master Set-97
First Day Issue-97
Super Team Winner Cards-97
94Topps/OPC Premier-145
Special Effects-145
94Ultra-284
94Upper Deck-373
Electric Ice-373
SP Inserts-SP23
SP Inserts Die Cuts-SP23
94Finnish Jaa Kiekko-152
94Classic Pro Prospects-214
Jumbos-PP17
95Be A Player-99
Signatures-S99
Signatures Die Cuts-S99
95Bowman-77
All-Foil-77
95Canada Games NHL POGS-97
95Collector's Choice-32
Player's Club-32
Player's Club Platinum-32
95Donruss-134
95Donruss Elite-87
Die Cut Stars-87
Die Cut Uncut-87
95Emotion-55
95Finest-83
Refractors-83
95Leaf-210
Road To The Cup-8
95Metal-47
95Panini Stickers-180
95Parkhurst International-65
Emerald Ice-65
95Pinnacle-128
Artist's Proofs-128
Rink Collection-128
95Playoff One on One-254
95Score-165
Black Ice Artist's Proofs-165
Black Ice-165
95SkyBox Impact-54
95SP-49
95Stadium Club-84
Members Only Master Set-84
95Summit-83
Artist's Proofs-83
Ice-83
95Topps-322
OPC Inserts-322
Power Lines-8PL
95Ultra-47
Gold Medallion-47
95Upper Deck-154
Electric Ice-154
Electric Ice Gold-154
Special Edition-SE117
Special Edition Gold-SE117
95Finnish Semic World Championships-137
95Swedish World Championships Stickers-45
96Black Diamond-113
Gold-113
96Collector's Choice-81
Crash the Game-C18A
Crash the Game-C18B
Crash the Game-C18C
Crash the Game Gold-C18A
Crash the Game Gold-C18B
Crash the Game Gold-C18C
Crash the Game Exchange-CR18
Crash the Game Exchange Gold-CR18
96Donruss-19
Press Proofs-19
96Donruss Canadian Ice-71
Gold Press Proofs-71
Red Press Proofs-71
96Donruss Elite-81
Die Cut Stars-81
96Fleer-32
96Leaf-196
Press Proofs-196
96Leaf Limited-88
Gold-88
96Leaf Preferred Steel-38
96Leaf Preferred Steel Gold-38
96Maggers-51
96Metal Universe-47
96Pinnacle-129
Artist's Proofs-129
Foil-129
Premium Stock-129
Rink Collection-129
96Score-158
Artist's Proofs-158
Dealer's Choice Artist's Proofs-158
Special Artist's Proofs-158
Golden Blades-158
96SkyBox Impact-36
96SP-49
96Summit-84
Artist's Proofs-84
Ice-84
Metal-84
Premium Stock-84
96Team Out-8
96Topps Picks-67
OPC Inserts-67
96Ultra-52
Gold Medallion-52
96Upper Deck-251
96Zenith-22
Artist's Proofs-22
96Swedish Semic Wien-146
96Collector's Edge Ice Crucibles-C17
97Be A Player-97
Autographs-97
Autographs Die-Cuts-97
Autographs Prismatic Die-Cuts-97
97Black Diamond-129
Double Diamond-129
Triple Diamond-129
Quadruple Diamond-129
97Collector's Choice-85
Star Quest-SQ13
97Crown Royale-46
Emerald Green-46
Ice Blue-46
Silver-46
97Donruss-119
Press Proofs Silver-119
Press Proofs Gold-119
Canadian Ice Stanley Cup Scrapbook-25
97Donruss Elite-25
Aspirations-25
Status-25
97Donruss Preferred-134
Cut to the Chase-134
97Donruss Priority-130
Stamp of Approval-130
97Katch-50
Gold-50
Silver-50
97Leaf-31
Fractal Matrix-31
Fractal Matrix Die Cuts-31
97Leaf International-31
Universal Ice-31
97Pacific-267
Copper-267
Emerald Green-267
Ice Blue-267
Red-267
Silver-267
97Pacific Invincible-48
Copper-48
Emerald Green-48
Ice Blue-48
Red-48
Silver-48
97Pacific Omega-81
Copper-81
Dark Gray-81
Emerald Green-81
Gold-81
Ice Blue-81
97Panini Stickers-153
97Paramount-66
Copper-66
Dark Grey-66
Emerald Green-66
Ice Blue-66
Red-66
Silver-66
97Pinnacle-117
Press Plates Back Black-117
Press Plates Back Cyan-117
Press Plates Back Magenta-117
Press Plates Back Yellow-117
Press Plates Front Black-117
Press Plates Front Cyan-117
Press Plates Front Magenta-117
Press Plates Front Yellow-117
97Pinnacle Inside-116
97Score-209
97Score Red Wings-7
Platinum-7
Premier-7
97SP Authentic-50
97Upper Deck-271
Blow-Ups 3 x 5-2-5
Blow-Ups 5 x 7-5C
Game Dated Moments-271
98Be A Player-49
Press Release-49
98BAP Tampa Bay All Star Game-49
98Pacific Dynagon Ice-63
98Panini Stickers-132
98Paramount-76
Copper-76
Emerald Green-76
Holo-Electric-76
Ice Blue-76
Silver-76
98UD Choice Preview-78
98Upper Deck Gold Reserve-264
99BAP Memorabilia-290
Gold-290
Silver-290
99O-Pee-Chee-213
99O-Pee-Chee Chrome-213
99O-Pee-Chee Chrome Refractors-213
99Pacific-140
Copper-140
Emerald Green-140
Gold-140
Ice Blue-140
Premiere Date-140
Red-140
99Pacific Dynagon Ice-74
Blue-74
Copper-74
Gold-74
Premiere Date-74
99Panini Stickers-236
99Paramount-81
Copper-81
Emerald-81
Gold-81
Holographic Emerald-81
Holographic Gold-81
Holographic Silver-81
Ice Blue-81
Premiere Date-81
Red-81
99Revolution-52
Premiere Date-52
Red-52
Shadow Series-52
99Topps/OPC-213
99Topps/OPC Chrome-213
Refractors-213
99Upper Deck-53
Exclusives-53
Exclusives 1 of 1-53
99Upper Deck Gold Reserve-53
99Upper Deck MVP-76
Gold Script-76
Silver Script-76
Super Script-76
99Upper Deck Victory-101
99Russian Stars of Hockey-32
99Russian Fetisov Tribute-27
00BAP Memorabilia-4
Emerald-4
Ruby-4
Sapphire-4
Promos-4
00BAP Mem Chicago Sportsfest Copper-4
00BAP Memorabilia Chicago Sportsfest Blue-4
00BAP Memorabilia Chicago Sportsfest Gold-4
00BAP Memorabilia Chicago Sportsfest Ruby-4
00BAP Memorabilia Chicago Sun-Times Ruby-4
00BAP Memorabilia Chicago Sun-Times Gold-4
00BAP Mem Chicago Sun-Times Sapphire-4
00BAP Mem Toronto Fall Expo Copper-4
00BAP Memorabilia Toronto Fall Expo Gold-4
00BAP Memorabilia Toronto Fall Expo Ruby-4
00BAP Memorabilia Update Teammates-TM17
00BAP Memorabilia Update Teammates-TM35
00BAP Memorabilia Update Teammates Gold-TM17
00BAP Memorabilia Update Teammates Gold-TM35
00BAP Ultimate Mem Dynasty Jerseys-D19
00BAP Ultimate Mem Dynasty Emblems-D19
00BAP Ultimate Memorabilia Teammates-TM2
00O-Pee-Chee-231
00O-Pee-Chee Parallel-231
00Pacific-149
Copper-149
Gold-149
Ice Blue-149
Premiere Date-149
00Panini Stickers-154
00Topps/OPC-231
Parallel-231
00Upper Deck-292
Exclusives Tier 1-292
Exclusives Tier 2-292
00Upper Deck Victory-86
00Upper Deck Vintage-135
01O-Pee-Chee-228
01O-Pee-Chee Premier Parallel-228
01Pacific-142
Extreme LTD-142
Hobby LTD-142
Premiere Date-142
Retail LTD-142
01Pacific Adrenaline-23
Blue-23
Premiere Date-23
Red-23
Retail-23
01Pacific Arena Exclusives-142
01Parkhurst-226
01Topps-228
OPC Parallel-228
01Topps Heritage-187
01UD Mask Collection Double Patches-DPKO
01UD Mask Collection Jerseys-J-KO
01UD Mask Collection Jersey and Patch-JPKO
01UD Stanley Cup Champs-60
01Upper Deck-252
Exclusives-252
01Upper Deck Victory-126
Gold-126
02BAP Memorabilia-243
Emerald-243
Ruby-243
Sapphire-243
NHL All-Star Game-243
NHL All-Star Game Blue-243
NHL All-Star Game Green-243
NHL All-Star Game Red-243
02BAP Memorabilia Toronto Fall Expo-243
02BAP Sig Series Auto Buybacks 1998-49
02BAP Ultimate Mem Dynasty Jerseys-20
02BAP Ultimate Mem Dynasty Emblems-20
02BAP Ultimate Mem Dynasty Numbers-20
02Pacific-44
Blue-44
Red-44
02Pacific Complete-127
Red-127
02Thrashers Postcards-9
02Topps Total-233
02Upper Deck-252
Exclusives-252
02Upper Deck Beckett UD Promos-252
03BAP Memorabilia-98
Emerald-98
Gold-98
Ruby-98
Sapphire-98
03Beehive-10
Gold-10
Silver-10
03ITG Action-99
Jerseys-M43
03O-Pee-Chee-196
03OPC Blue-196
03OPC Gold-196
03OPC Red-196
03Pacific-17
Blue-17
Red-17
03Pacific Complete-373
Red-373
03Pacific Exhibit-10
Blue Backs-10
Yellow Backs-10
03Pacific Prism-6
Blue-6
Gold-6
Red-6
03Pacific Quest for the Cup-5
Blue-5
03Private Stock Reserve-6
Blue-6
Red-6
Retail-6
03Thrashers Postcards-8
03Titanium-5
Hobby Jersey Number Parallels-5
Retail-5
Retail Jersey Number Parallels-5
03Topps-196
Blue-196
Gold-196
Red-196
03Topps C55-71
Minis-71
Minis American Back-71
Minis American Back Red-71
Minis Bazooka Back-71
Minis Brooklyn Back-71
Minis Hat Trick Back-71
Minis O Canada Back-71
Minis O Canada Back Red-71
Minis Stanley Cup Back-71
03Topps Pristine-2
Gold Refractor Die Cuts-2
Refractors-2
Press Plates Black-2
Press Plates Cyan-2
Press Plates Magenta-2
Press Plates Yellow-2
03Upper Deck-9
Canadian Exclusives-9
HG-9
04Pacific-12
Blue-12
Red-12
04Russian Back to Russia-5
05Panini Stickers-17
05Parkhurst-21
Facsimile Auto Parallel-21
05Upper Deck-254
05Upper Deck MVP-24
Gold-24
Platinum-24
06Be A Player-101
Autographs-101
Signatures-KZ
Signatures 25-109
Signatures Duals-DKH
Signatures Trios-THKH
06Black Diamond-4
Black-4
Gold-4
Ruby-4
06Fleer-14
Tiffany-14
06O-Pee-Chee-33
Rainbow-33
06Panini Stickers-7
06Ultra-12
Gold Medallion-12
Ice Medallion-12
06Upper Deck Arena Giveaways-ATL2
06Upper Deck-10
Exclusives Parallel-10
High Gloss Parallel-10
Masterpieces-10
Shootout Artists-SA10
06Upper Deck MVP-13
Gold Script-13
Super Script-13
06Upper Deck Ovation-3
06Upper Deck Victory-11
06Upper Deck Victory Black-11
06Upper Deck Victory Gold-11
07Upper Deck Victory-75
Black-75
Gold-75

Kozlov, Viktor
92Upper Deck-613
92Classic-61
92Classic-62
Gold-61
Gold-62
92Classic Four-Sport *-225
Gold-225
BCs-BC12
93Swedish Semic World Champ Stickers-140
93Classic-6
Top Ten-DP6
93Classic Pro Prospects-93
BCs-BC9
LPs-LP4
93Classic C3 *-24
93Classic Four-Sport *-190
Gold-190
94Be A Player-R158
Signature Cards-153A
Signature Cards-153B
94Finest-46
Super Team Winners-46
Refractors-46
94Leaf-451
Phenoms-8
94Leaf Limited-21
94McDonald's Upper Deck-McD33
94Parkhurst SE-SE159
Gold-SE159
Vintage-43
94Pinnacle-477
94Pinnacle-481
Artist's Proofs-477
Artist's Proofs-481
Rink Collection-477
Rink Collection-481
Rookie Team Pinnacle-5
94Score Top Rookie Redemption-10
94Select-174
Gold-174
Youth Explosion-YE6
94SP Premier-3
94SP Premier Die-Cuts-3
94Ultra-366
Prospects-4
94Upper Deck-265
Electric Ice-265
Predictor Canadian-C3
94Upper Deck Predictor Canadian Exch Gold-C3
94Upper Deck Predictor Cdn Exch Silver-C3
94Upper Deck SP Inserts-SP162
94Upper Deck SP Inserts Die Cuts-SP162
94Classic-113
Gold-113
ROY Sweepstakes-R12
Tri-Cards-T61
Pro Prospects Ice Ambassadors-IA17
95Bowman-159
All-Foil-159
95Canada Games NHL POGS-229
95Collector's Choice-252
Player's Club-252
Player's Club Platinum-252
95Donruss-171
95Leaf-73
95Leaf Limited-77
95Panini Stickers-279
95Parkhurst International-187
95Parkhurst International-515
Emerald Ice-187
Emerald Ice-515
95Pinnacle-99
Artist's Proofs-99
Rink Collection-99
Global Gold-16
95Score-114
Black Ice Artist's Proofs-114
Black Ice-114
95Stadium Club-137
Members Only Master Set-137
95Summit-142
Artist's Proofs-142
Ice-142
95Topps-357
OPC Inserts-357
95Upper Deck-92
Electric Ice-92
Electric Ice Gold-92
95Kansas City Blades-21
96Collector's Choice-237
96Upper Deck-152
96Swedish Semic Wien-147
96Collector's Edge Ice-145
Crucibles-C10
Prism-145
96Collector's Edge Ice Promos-PR4
97Collector's Choice-217
97Crown Royale-58
Emerald Green-58
Ice Blue-58
Silver-58
97Donruss Limited-91
Exposure-91
97Pacific-125
Copper-125
Emerald Green-125
Ice Blue-125
Red-125
Silver-125
97Pacific Dynagon-113
Copper-113
Dark Grey-113
Emerald Green-113
Ice Blue-113
Red-113
Silver-113
Tandems-64
97Panini Stickers-231
97Paramount-166
Copper-166
Dark Grey-166
Emerald Green-166
Ice Blue-166
Red-166
Silver-166
97Score-223
97SP Authentic-70
97Upper Deck-359
98Aurora-63
98Aurora-81
98Be A Player-60
Press Release-60
98BAP Gold-49
98BAP Gold-60
98BAP Autographs-49
98BAP Autographs-60
98BAP Autographs Gold-49
98BAP Autographs Gold-60
98BAP Tampa Bay All Star Game-60
98Crown Royale-59
Limited Series-59
98Finest-94
No Protectors-94
No Protectors Refractors-94
Refractors-94
98OPC Chrome-83
Refractors-83
98Pacific-196
98Pacific-223
Ice Blue-196
Ice Blue-223
Red-196
Red-223
98Pacific Dynagon Ice-63
98Pacific Dynagon Ice-82
Blue-63
Blue-82
Red-63
Red-82
98Pacific Omega-103
Red-103
Opening Day Issue-103
98Panini Stickers-62
98Paramount-97
Copper-97
Emerald Green-97
Holo-Electric-97
Ice Blue-97
Silver-97
98Revolution-62
Ice Shadow-62
Red-62
98Topps-83
O-Pee-Chee-83
98UD Choice-78
Prime Choice Reserve-78
Reserve-78
98Upper Deck-98
98Upper Deck-264
Exclusives-98
Exclusives-264
Exclusives 1 of 1-98
Exclusives 1 of 1-264
Gold Reserve-98
99Aurora-63
Premiere Date-63
99BAP Memorabilia-5
Gold-5
Silver-5
99BAP Millennium-110
Emerald-110
Ruby-110
Sapphire-110
Signatures-110
Signatures Gold-110
99Pacific-173
Copper-173
Emerald Green-173
Gold-173
Ice Blue-173
Premiere Date-173
Red-173
99Pacific Dynagon Ice-90
Blue-90
Copper-90
Gold-90
Premiere Date-90
99Pacific Omega-98
Copper-98
Gold-98
Ice Blue-98
Premiere Date-98
World All-Stars-5
99Pacific Prism-62
Holographic Blue-62
Holographic Gold-62
Holographic Mirror-62
Holographic Purple-62
Premiere Date-62
99Panini Stickers-60
99Paramount-100
Copper-100
Emerald-100
Gold-100
Holographic Emerald-100
Holographic Gold-100
Holographic Silver-100
Ice Blue-100
Premiere Date-100
Red-100
Silver-100
99Revolution-64
Premiere Date-64
Red-64
Shadow Series-64
99SP Authentic-39
99SPx-71
Radiance-71
Spectrum-71
99Topps Gold Label Class 1-84
Black-84
Black One of One-84
One of One-84
Red-84
Red One of One-84
99Topps Gold Label Class 2-84
99Topps Gold Label Class 2 Black-84
99Topps Gold Label Class 2 Black 1 of 1-84
99Topps Gold Label Class 2 One of One-84
99Topps Gold Label Class 2 Red-84
99Topps Gold Label Class 2 Red One of One-84
99Topps Gold Label Class 3-84
99Topps Gold Label Class 3 Black-84
99Topps Gold Label Class 3 Black 1 of 1-84
99Topps Gold Label Class 3 One of One-84
99Topps Gold Label Class 3 Red-84
99Topps Gold Label Class 3 Red One of One-84
99Ultimate Victory-40
1/1-40
Parallel-40
Parallel 100-40
99Upper Deck-232
Exclusives-232
Exclusives 1 of 1-232
99Upper Deck Gold Reserve-232
99Upper Deck MVP-86
Gold Script-86
Silver Script-86
Super Script-86
99Upper Deck MVP SC Edition-78
Gold Script-78
Silver Script-78
Super Script-78
Great Combinations-GCBK
Great Combinations Parallel-GCBK
99Upper Deck Victory-123
99Wayne Gretzky Hockey-76
99Russian Fetisov Tribute-4
00Aurora-62
Premiere Date-62
00BAP Memorabilia-171
Emerald-171
Ruby-171
Sapphire-171
Promos-171
00BAP Mem Chicago Sportsfest Copper-171
00BAP Memorabilia Chicago Sportsfest Blue-171
00BAP Memorabilia Chicago Sportsfest Gold-171
00BAP Memorabilia Chicago Sportsfest Ruby-171
00BAP Memorabilia Chicago Sun-Times Ruby-171
00BAP Memorabilia Chicago Sun-Times Gold-171
00BAP Mem Chicago Sun-Times Sapphire-171
00BAP Mem Toronto Fall Expo Copper-171
00BAP Memorabilia Toronto Fall Expo Gold-171
00BAP Memorabilia Toronto Fall Expo Ruby-171
00BAP Parkhurst 2000-P143
00BAP Signature Series-178
Emerald-178
Ruby-178
Sapphire-178
Autographs-26
Autographs Gold-26
00O-Pee-Chee-138
00O-Pee-Chee Parallel-138
00Pacific-179
Copper-179
Gold-179
Ice Blue-179
Premiere Date-179
00Panini Stickers-33
00Panthers Team Issue-25
00Paramount-105
Copper-105
Gold-105
Holo-Gold-105
Holo-Silver-105
Ice Blue-105
Premiere Date-105
00Private Stock-44
Gold-44
Premiere Date-44
Retail-44
Silver-44
00Revolution-63
Blue-63
Premiere Date-63
Red-63
00SPx-30
Spectrum-30
00Stadium Club-63
00Topps/OPC-138
Parallel-138
00Topps Chrome-103
OPC Refractors-103
Refractors-103
00UD Heroes-53
00UD Pros and Prospects-38
00Upper Deck-305
Exclusives Tier 1-305
Exclusives Tier 2-305
00Upper Deck Legends-56
Legendary Collection Bronze-56
Legendary Collection Gold-56
Legendary Collection Silver-56
00Upper Deck MVP-83
First Stars-83
Second Stars-83
Third Stars-83
00Upper Deck Victory-104
00Upper Deck Vintage-152
00Vanguard-46
Holographic Gold-46
Holographic Purple-46
Pacific Proofs-46
01BAP Memorabilia-259
Emerald-259
Ruby-259
Sapphire-259
All-Star Jerseys-ASJ30
All-Star Emblems-ASE30
All-Star Numbers-ASN30
All-Star Teammates-AST14
01Crown Royale-64
Blue-64
Premiere Date-64
Red-64
Retail-64
01O-Pee-Chee-135
01O-Pee-Chee Premier Parallel-135
01Pacific-172
Extreme LTD-172
Hobby LTD-172
Premiere Date-172
Retail LTD-172
01Pacific Adrenaline-82
Blue-82
Premiere Date-82
Red-82
Retail-82
01Pacific Arena Exclusives-172
01Parkhurst-171
Jerseys-PJ45
Teammates-T10
01Titanium-60
Hobby Parallel-60
Premiere Date-60
Retail-60
Retail Parallel-60
01Topps-135
OPC Parallel-135
01UD Mask Collection-39
Gold-39
01Upper Deck-303
Exclusives-303
Pride of a Nation-PNVK
Pride of a Nation-DPFK
Pride of a Nation-TPFKK
01Upper Deck MVP-79
01Upper Deck Victory-148
Gold-148
01Upper Deck Vintage-107
01Upper Deck Vintage-113
02BAP First Edition-168
02BAP Sig Series Auto Buybacks 1998-60
02BAP Sig Series Auto Buybacks 1999-110
02BAP Sig Series Auto Buybacks 2000-26
02O-Pee-Chee-132
02O-Pee-Chee Premier Blue Parallel-132
02O-Pee-Chee Premier Red Parallel-132
02O-Pee-Chee Factory Set-132
02Pacific Complete-248
Red-248
02Topps-132
OPC Blue Parallel-132
OPC Red Parallel-132
Factory Set-132
02Topps Total-135
02Upper Deck-320
Exclusives-320
02Upper Deck Beckett UD Promos-320
02Upper Deck Classic Portraits-43
02Upper Deck MVP-79
Gold-79
Classics-79
Golden Classics-79
02Upper Deck Vintage-107
02Upper Deck Vintage-273
03ITG Action-255
03O-Pee-Chee-85
03OPC Blue-85
03OPC Gold-85
03OPC Red-85
03Pacific-146
Blue-146
Red-146
03Pacific Complete-181
Red-181
03Panthers Team Issue-10
03Private Stock Reserve-42
Blue-42
Red-42
Retail-42
03SP Game Used Team Threads-TTKHK
03Titanium-43
Hobby Jersey Number Parallels-43
Retail-43
Retail Jersey Number Parallels-43
03Topps-85
Blue-85
Gold-85
Red-85
03Upper Deck-81
Canadian Exclusives-81
HG-81
03Upper Deck MVP-16
03Upper Deck MVP-178
Gold Script-16
Gold Script-178
Silver Script-16
Silver Script-178
Canadian Exclusives-16
Canadian Exclusives-178
03Upper Deck Victory-79
Bronze-79
Gold-79
Silver-79
04Russian Back to Russia-17
05Devils Team Issue-17
05Parkhurst-293
Facsimile Auto Parallel-293
True Colors-TCNJD
True Colors-TCNJD
05SP Game Used Authentic Fabrics Quad-BEGK
05SP Game Used Authentic Patches Quad -BEGK
05Ultimate Coll National Heroes Jersey-NHJVK
05Ultimate Coll National Heroes Patch-NHPVK
05Upper Deck-365
Jerseys-J-VK
Jerseys Series II-J2VK
05Upper Deck MVP-238
Gold-238
Platinum-238
Materials-M-VK
06O-Pee-Chee-321
Rainbow-321
06Russian Torino Olympic Team-15
07Upper Deck Victory-17
Black-17
Gold-17

Kozlowski, Adam
93Quebec Pee-Wee Tournament-840

Koznev, Alexei
99Russian Hockey League-222
99Russian Stars of Hockey-22
00Russian Hockey League-377
02Russian Hockey League-152
02Russian World Championships-10

Kozoriz, John
00UD CHL Prospects-15
01Mississauga Ice Dogs-11
04Odessa Jackalopes-12
05Odessa Jackalopes-11
06Odessa Jackalopes-11

Kozrev, Andrei
00Russian Hockey League-385

Kozuch, Stanislav
04Slovakian Poprad Team Set-3

Kozurok, Chico
61Sudbury Wolves-11
62Sudbury Wolves-13

Kozyrev, Andrei
98Indianapolis Ice-12
03Russian Hockey League-69

Kracik, Jaroslav
02Czech OFS Plus-324
04Czech HC Plzen Postcards-8
04Czech OFS-145
05Czech HC Plzen-6
06Czech LG Hockey Games Postcards-7
Kradolfer, Roland
95Swiss HNL-219
96Swiss HNL-324
01Swiss HNL-445
02Swiss HNL-211
Kraemer, Chris
907th Inn. Sketch OHL-163
917th Inn. Sketch OHL-78
Kraemer, Greg
93Kingston Frontenacs-18
Kraft, Brian
94Anchorage Aces-7
Kraft, Milan
97Czech APS Extraliga-190
98Prince Albert Raiders-13
99Black Diamond-102
Diamond Cut-102
Final Cut-102
99SP Authentic-125
99Ultimate Victory-110
1/1-110
Parallel-110
Parallel 100-110
99Upper Deck-326
Exclusives-326
Exclusives 1 of 1-326
99Upper Deck Gold Reserve-326
99Upper Deck MVP SC Edition-197
Gold Script-197
Silver Script-197
Super Script-197
Game-Used Souvenirs-GUMK
Game-Used Souvenirs-SGMK
ProSign-MK
99Upper Deck Ovation-72
Standing Ovation-72
99Bowman CHL-88
Gold-88
OPC International-88
99UD Prospects-26
International Stars-IN6
00BAP Memorabilia-415
Emerald-415
Ruby-415
Sapphire-415
00BAP Parkhurst 2000-P170
00BAP Signature Series-282
Emerald-282
Ruby-282
Sapphire-282
Autographs-244
Autographs Gold-244
00Black Diamond-106
00Crown Royale-138
21st Century Rookies-20
00SP Authentic BuyBacks-94
00SP Authentic Sign of the Times-MK
00SP Authentic Sign of the Times-L/K
00SPx-145
00Stadium Club-228
00Titanium-140
Retail-140
00Titanium Draft Day Edition-85
00Titanium Draft Day Edition-140
Patches-85
00Titanium Draft Day Promos-140
00Topps Gold Label Autographs-GLA-MK
00Topps Heritage-43
Chrome Parallel-43
00Topps Premier Plus-98
Blue Ice-98
Private Signings-PSMK
00Topps Stars-146
Blue-146
00UD Heroes-94
00UD Reserve-69
00Upper Deck-213
00Upper Deck-371
Exclusives Tier 1-213
Exclusives Tier 1-371
Exclusives Tier 2-213
Exclusives Tier 2-371
Triple Threat-TT9
00Upper Deck Vintage-290
00Vanguard-142
Pacific Proofs-142
01BAP Memorabilia-44
Emerald-44
Ruby-44
Sapphire-44
01BAP Signature Series-167
Autographs-167
Autographs Gold-167
Teammates-TM-24
01O-Pee-Chee-283
01O-Pee-Chee Premier Parallel-283
01Pacific Adrenaline Jerseys-36
01Pacific Heads-Up Quad Jerseys-27
01Parkhurst-54
Gold-54
Silver-54
Jerseys-PJ52
Teammates-T2
01Private Stock Game Gear-78
01Private Stock Game Gear Patches-78
01SP Authentic Sign of the Times-MK
01Stadium Club-120
Award Winners-120
Master Photos-120
01Topps-283
OPC Parallel-283
01Upper Deck Ice Autographs-MK
02BAP First Edition-45
Jerseys-45
02BAP Memorabilia-18
Emerald-18
Ruby-18
Sapphire-18
NHL All-Star Game-18
NHL All-Star Game Blue-18
NHL All-Star Game Green-18
NHL All-Star Game Red-18
02BAP Memorabilia Toronto Fall Expo-18
02BAP Sig Series Auto Buybacks 2001-167
02Pacific-310
Blue-310
Red-310
02Pacific Complete-479
Red-479
02SP Authentic Sign of the Times-MK
02SP Game Used Signature Style-MK
02Czech DS-61
02Czech DS-75
02Wilkes-Barre Scranton Penguins-8
03ITG Action-454
03Pacific Complete-79
Red-79
04Pacific-212
Blue-212
Red-212
04Czech OFS-146
04Czech OFS-379
Stars-17
04Czech World Championship Postcards-12
05Black Diamond-69
Emerald-69
Gold-69
Onyx-69
Ruby-69
05Upper Deck Victory-154
Black-154
Gold-154
Silver-154
05Russian Hockey League RHL-21
06Czech OFS-31
Stars-5
06Czech NHL ELH Postcards-4
Kraft, Ryan
94Minnesota Golden Gophers-17
95Minnesota Golden Gophers-18
96Minnesota Golden Gophers-16
97Minnesota Golden Gophers-5
98ECHL All-Star Northern Conference-15
99ECHL All-Star Northern Conference-20
00Kentucky Thoroughblades-13
00Kentucky Thoroughblades-SP1
01Cleveland Barons-11
02BAP Memorabilia-363
02Upper Deck Rookie Update-140
02Cleveland Barons-10
03Bridgeport Sound Tigers-1B
05German DEL-195
Kraft, Stian
92Norwegian Elite Series-169
92Norwegian Elite Series-216
Kraft, Thomas
92British Columbia JHL-34
Kraftcheck, Steve
44Beehive Group II Photos-331
44Beehive Group II Photos-417
51Parkhurst-92
52Parkhurst-23
58Parkhurst-37
Krahn, Brent
99Calgary Hitmen-13
99Calgary Hitmen Autographs-13
99UD Prospects-42
00Calgary Hitmen-16
00UD CHL Prospects-49
Autographs-A-BK
Game Jersey Autographs-S-BK
Game Jerseys-BK
Game Jerseys-B-B
Game Jerseys-L-K
01UD Prospects Autographs-A-BK
02Calgary Hitmen-25
03BAP Memorabilia-198
Emerald-198
Gold-198
Ruby-198
Sapphire-198
Super Rookies-SR20
Super Rookies Gold-SR20
Super Rookies Silver-SR20
03Crown Royale-105
Red-106
Retail-105
Retail-106
03ITG Action-624
03ITG Used Signature Series-159
Gold-159
03ITG VIP Rookie Debut-43
03Pacific Calder-105
Silver-105
03Pacific Complete-478
03Pacific Complete-572
Red-478
Red-572
03Pacific Heads-Up-104
Hobby LTD-104
Retail LTD-104
03Pacific Luxury Suite-83
Gold-83
03Pacific Quest for the Cup-104
03Pacific Supreme-107
Blue-109
Red-109
Retail-107
03Parkhurst Rookie-113
03Private Stock Reserve-107
Blue-107
Red-107
Retail-107
03SP Authentic-94
Limited-94
03Titanium-105
Hobby Jersey Number Parallels-105
Retail-105
Retail Jersey Number Parallels-105
03Upper Deck-446
Canadian Exclusives-446
HG-446
UD Exclusives-446
03Las Vegas Wranglers-10
03Las Vegas Wranglers RBI-232
03Lowell Lock Monsters-5
04AHL Top Prospects-26
04Lowell Lock Monsters-12
04Lowell Lock Monsters Photo Album-12
05ITG Heroes/Prosp Toronto Expo Parallel -229
05ITG Heroes and Prospects-229
Autographs Series II-BK
Complete Logos-AHL-17
He Shoots-He Scores Prizes-22
Jerseys-GUJ-88
Jerseys Gold-GUJ-88
Emblems-GUE-88
Emblems Gold-GUE-88
Numbers-GUN-88
Numbers Gold-GUN-88
Measuring Up-MU8
Measuring Up Gold-MU8
Net Prospects-NP-12
Net Prospects Dual-NPD6
Net Prospects Dual Gold-NPD6
Net Prospects Gold-NP-12
06Between The Pipes-4
Autographs-ABK
Emblems-GUE43
Emblems Gold-GUE43
Emblems Autographs-GUE43
Jerseys-GUJ43
Jerseys Gold-GUJ43
Jerseys Autographs-GUJ43
Numbers-GUN43
Numbers Gold-GUN43
Numbers Autographs-GUN43
Kraiger, Jens
93Quebec Pee-Wee Tournament-1527
Kraiger, Yogi
51Laval Dairy QSHL-9
51Laval Dairy Subset-9
52St. Lawrence Sales-48
Krainz, Martin
93Swedish Semic World Champ Stickers-274
94Finnish Jaa Kiekko-235
95Austrian National Team-13
95Swedish World Championships Stickers-264
Krajcovic, Lubos
95Waterloo Blackhawks -10
98Muskegon Fury-4
99Indianapolis Ice-10
00Indianapolis Ice-13
Krajicek, Jan
94Czech APS Extraliga-188
95Czech APS Extraliga-37
96Czech APS Extraliga-34
97Czech APS Extraliga-56
97Czech DS Stickers-98
98Czech DS Stickers-289
98Czech OFS-67
99Czech DS-116
99Czech OFS-47
04UK Edinburgh Capitals-1
06UK Nottingham Panthers-5
Krajicek, Lukas
01BAP Memorabilia-435
Emerald-435
Ruby-435
Sapphire-435
Draft Redemptions-24
01Parkhurst-317
01UD Mask Collection-148
Gold-148
01UD Premier Collection-102
01Czech OFS-121
01Peterborough Petes-20
01UD Prospects-18
Jerseys-J-LK
Jerseys-C-KP
Jerseys Gold-J-LK
Jerseys Gold-C-KP
02BAP First Edition-257
02BAP First Edition-425R
02O-Pee-Chee-284
02O-Pee-Chee Premier Blue Parallel-284
02O-Pee-Chee Premier Red Parallel-284
02O-Pee-Chee Factory Set-284
02SPx-112
02Topps-284
OPC Blue Parallel-284
OPC Red Parallel-284
Factory Set-284
02UD Foundations-131
02Upper Deck-206
Exclusives-206
02Upper Deck MVP-203
Gold-203
Classics-203
Golden Classics-203
02Upper Deck Vintage-334
02Czech DS-51
02Czech DS-72
02Czech OFS Plus-282
02Peterborough Petes-24
03Czech OFS Plus-73
03AHL Top Prospects-15
03Pacific AHL Prospects-74
Gold-74
03San Antonio Rampage-3
04Pacific-284
Blue-284
Red-284
04Czech OFS-39
04San Antonio Rampage-2
05Parkhurst-213
Facsimile Auto Parallel-213
05Upper Deck-333
05Czech HC Karlovy Vary-7
06Canucks Postcards-10
06Gatorade-85
06O-Pee-Chee-482
Rainbow-482
06Upper Deck-441
Exclusives Parallel-441
High Gloss Parallel-441
Masterpieces-441
06Czech IIHF World Championship Postcards-12
06Czech LG Hockey Games Postcards-8
06Czech OFS Jagr Team-7
Krajnc, Gregor
92Pee Dee Pride RBI-140
Krajov, Vitali
74Swedish Stickers-89
Krake, Paul
92Oklahoma City Blazers-10
94Central Hockey League-49
95Central Hockey League-78
Krake, Skip
67Topps-93
68O-Pee-Chee-3
68O-Pee-Chee-43
68Shirriff Coins-60
68Topps-3
68Topps-43
69O-Pee-Chee-141
70Dad's Cookies-66
70Esso Power Players-82
70O-Pee-Chee-126
70Sargent Promotions Stamps-24
70Topps-126
72Cleveland Crusaders WHA-9
Krakivsky, Sean
94German First League-468
Krakiwsky, Sean
85Minnesota-Duluth Bulldogs-32
Kral, Richard
94Czech APS Extraliga-43
95Czech APS Extraliga-236
96Czech APS Extraliga-60
97Czech APS Extraliga-327
97Czech DS Extraliga-111
97Czech DS Stickers-241
98Czech DS-118
98Czech DS Stickers-274
98Czech OFS-389
98Czech OFS-435
99Czech DS-105
99Czech OFS-197
00Czech DS Extraliga-67
00Czech OFS-223
00Czech OFS Star Emerald-24
00Czech OFS Star Pink-24
00Czech OFS Star Violet-24
01Czech National Team Postcards-7
01Czech OFS-66
01Czech OFS Red Inserts-RE23D
02Czech DS-8
02Czech OFS Plus-89
02Czech OFS Plus All-Star Game-H12
02Czech OFS Plus Trios-T16
02Czech OFS Plus Duos-D8
03Czech OFS Plus-289
03Czech OFS Plus All-Star Game-H34
03Czech OFS Plus Insert C-C10
03Czech OFS Plus Insert G-G8
03Czech OFS Plus Insert H-H9
03Czech OFS Plus Insert S-S1
03Czech OFS Plus MS Praha-SE48
04Czech OFS-211
05Czech HC Hame Zlin-7
06Czech OFS-275
Stars-10
Kral, Vaclav
97Czech APS Extraliga-287
98Czech OFS-206
98Czech OFS-460
99Czech DS-35
99Czech OFS-261
99Czech OFS-282
99Czech OFS-499
All-Star Game Blue-499
All-Star Game Gold-499
All-Star Game Red-499
All-Star Game Silver-499
00Czech DS Extraliga-78
00Czech OFS-15
00Czech OFS Star Emerald-13
00Czech OFS Star Pink-13
00Czech OFS Star Violet-13
02Czech OFS Plus-262
Kralik, Jiri
81Swedish Semic Hockey VM Stickers-55
82Swedish Semic VM Stickers-76
83Swedish Semic VM Stickers-76
98Czech OFS-318
01Czech DS Legends-L2
Krall, Jon
03Wisconsin Badgers-18
04Las Vegas Wranglers-2
Krall, Justin
96Peoria Rivermen-12
96Peoria Rivermen Photo Album-12
97Peoria Rivermen-13
98Dayton Bombers-8
98Dayton Bombers EBK-10
Kramer, Mike
04Lincoln Stars-15
05Lincoln Stars-17
05Lincoln Stars Update Traded-11T
06Lincoln Stars-15
06Lincoln Stars Traded-13T
06Lincoln Stars Upper DeckÂ Signature Series -17
Kramer, Rene
05German DEL-34
Kramer, Ted
91Michigan Wolverines-9
92Phoenix Roadrunners-11
Kramny, Tomas
94Czech APS Extraliga-121
95Czech APS Extraliga-297
96Czech APS Extraliga-197
97Czech APS Extraliga-108
98Czech DS Stickers-53
99Czech Score Blue 2000-141
99Czech Score Red Ice 2000-141
Kramskoy, Vladimir
93Swedish Semic Elitserien-271
00Russian Hockey League-51
02Russian Hockey League-112
Kranwinkel, Markus
94German DEL-226
94German DEL-236
Krapf, Andy
93Swiss HNL-345
95Swiss HNL-409
96Swiss HNL-347
98Swiss Power Play Stickers-334
Kraske, Wolgang
04German Berlin Eisbarens 50th Anniv-15
Krasny, Tomas
95Czech APS Extraliga-216
96Czech APS Extraliga-182
97Czech APS Extraliga-93
97Czech DS Stickers-53
Krasotkin, Dmitri
95Swedish World Championships Stickers-29
98Russian Hockey League-36
99Russian Stars of Hockey-7
00Russian Hockey League-220
02Russian Hockey League-229
04Russian Super League All-Stars-3
Kratena, Ivo
03Regina Pats-12
Kratena, Ondrej
95Upper Deck-540
Electric Ice-540
Electric Ice Gold-540
95Czech APS Extraliga-119
96Czech APS Extraliga-233
97Czech APS Extraliga-40
97Czech APS Extraliga-366
97Czech APS Extraliga-374
97Czech DS Extraliga-63
97Czech DS Stickers-31
98Czech DS-80
98Czech DS Stickers-18
98Czech DS Stickers-179
98Czech OFS-109
98Czech OFS-431
98Czech OFS-490
99Czech DS-150
99Czech OFS-107
00Czech DS Extraliga-10
00Czech OFS-305
01Czech OFS Red Inserts-RE19D
02Czech DS-32
02Czech OFS Plus-8
03Czech OFS Plus-156
03Czech OFS Plus All-Star Game-H32
03Czech OFS Plus Insert C-C9
03Czech OFS Plus Insert M-M13
03Czech OFS Plus MS Praha-SE6
04Czech HC Sparta Praha Postcards-10
04Czech OFS-326
05Czech HC Sparta Praha-7
06Czech HC Sparta Praha Postcards-11
06Czech OFS-80
Goals Leaders-13
Kratky, Petr
95Czech APS Extraliga-157
96Czech APS Extraliga-176
99Czech DS-61
99Czech OFS-149
05Dutch Vadeko Flyers -8
Kratochvil, Jiri
99Czech OFS-541
Kratofil, A.J.
98Sioux City Musketeers-11
99Sioux City Musketeers-12
Kratoska, Ales
96Czech APS Extraliga-208
97Czech APS Extraliga-145
97Czech DS Stickers-205
98Czech DS-108
98Czech OFS-357
99Finnish Cardset-342
00Finnish Cardset-198
02Czech OFS Plus-263
02Czech OFS Plus-348
03Czech OFS Plus-202
04Czech OFS-168
05Czech HC Ceski Budejovice-9
Kratschmar, Jiri
93Quebec Pee-Wee Tournament-1765
Kratt, Oliver
94German First League-75
Krattli, Claudio
93Swiss HNL-305
95Swiss HNL-429
Kratz, Michael
94German DEL-353
Kratzmeir, Christian
94German First League-244
Kraus, Andreas
94German First League-253
Kraus, Jakub
98Czech OFS-339
99Czech Score Blue 2000-60
99Czech Score Red Ice 2000-60
01Czech OFS-187
02Czech OFS Plus-283
03Czech OFS Plus-70
04Czech OFS-41
06Czech OFS-183
Kraus, Johannes
94German First League-353
Kraus, Kevin
06Kamloops Blazers-13
Kraus, Peter
94German First League-528
Kraus, Richard
92British Columbia JHL-186
Kraus, Tim
03Vancouver Giants-21
04Vancouver Giants-20
05Vancouver Giants-12
Krause, Frank
04German Berlin Eisbarens 50th Anniv-68
Krause, Sean
91British Columbia JHL-60
Krause, Sebastian
93Quebec Pee-Wee Tournament-1767
Krauss, Daryl
91Air Canada SJHL-B43
92Saskatchewan JHL-144
Krauss, Rob
90Cincinnati Cyclones-33
92Birmingham Bulls-16
93Birmingham Bulls-16
Kravchuk, Igor
90O-Pee-Chee Red Army-11R
91O-Pee-Chee Inserts-19R
91Parkhurst-257
91Parkhurst-461
French-257
91Finnish Semic World Champ Stickers-82
91Russian Stars Red Ace-10
91Swedish Semic World Champ Stickers-82
92Blackhawks Coke-11
92Bowman-408
92Oilers Team Issue-9
92O-Pee-Chee-161
92Panini Stickers-297
92Panini Stickers-A
92Panini Stickers French-297
92Panini Stickers French-A
92Parkhurst-35
92Parkhurst-291
Emerald Ice-35
Emerald Ice-291
92Pinnacle-225
French-225
92Pro Set-35
92Score-454
Canadian-454
92Seasons Patches-69
92Stadium Club-7
92Topps-200
Gold-200G
92Ultra-38
92Upper Deck-239
92Upper Deck-367
Euro-Stars-E7
92Finnish Semic-103
92Russian Tri-Globe From Russia With Puck-17
92Russian Tri-Globe From Russia With Puck-18
93Donruss-116
93Leaf-163
93OPC Premier-495
Gold-495
93Parkhurst-65
Emerald Ice-65
93Pinnacle-36
Canadian-36
93PowerPlay-81
93Score-309
Canadian-309
93Stadium Club-204
Members Only Master Set-204
OPC-204
First Day Issue-204
First Day Issue OPC-204
93Topps/OPC Premier-495
Gold-495
93Ultra-80
93Upper Deck-174
94Canada Games NHL POGS-367
94Donruss-259
94EA Sports-44
94Flair-58
94Fleer-70
94Leaf-244
94OPC Premier-172
Special Effects-172
94Parkhurst SE-SE58
Gold-SE58
94Pinnacle-96
Artist's Proofs-96
Rink Collection-96
94Score-33
Gold-33
Platinum-33
94Topps/OPC Premier-172
Special Effects-172
94Ultra-72
94Upper Deck-463
Electric Ice-463
95Canada Games NHL POGS-109
95Emotion-63
95Panini Stickers-264
95Parkhurst International-74
Emerald Ice-74
95Playoff One on One-148
95SkyBox Impact-61
95Ultra-54
Gold Medallion-54
95Upper Deck-146
Electric Ice-146
Electric Ice Gold-146
95Swedish Globe World Championships-167
96Be A Player-3
Autographs-3
Autographs Silver-3
96Playoff One on One-372
96Swedish Semic Wien-132
97Pacific Invincible NHL Regime-170
97Pacific Omega-155
Copper-155
Dark Gray-155
Emerald Green-155
Gold-155
Ice Blue-155
97Panini Stickers-165
97Paramount-126
Copper-126
Dark Grey-126
Emerald Green-126
Ice Blue-126
Red-126
Silver-126
98Aurora-130
98Crown Royale-93
Limited Series-93
98OPC Chrome-36
Refractors-36
98Pacific-310
Ice Blue-310
Red-310
98Pacific Dynagon Ice-127
Blue-127
Red-127
98Panini Stickers-46
98Paramount-163
Copper-163
Emerald Green-163
Holo-Electric-163
Ice Blue-163
Silver-163
98Senators Team Issue-9
98Topps-36
O-Pee-Chee-36
98Upper Deck-330
Exclusives-330
Exclusives 1 of 1-330
Gold Reserve-330
99BAP Memorabilia-40
Gold-40
Silver-40
99Pacific-290
Copper-290
Emerald Green-290
Gold-290
Ice Blue-290
Premiere Date-290
Red-290
99Panini Stickers-118
99Senators Team Issue-10
00BAP Memorabilia-330
Emerald-330
Ruby-330
Sapphire-330
Promos-330
00BAP Mem Chicago Sportsfest Copper-330
00BAP Memorabilia Chicago Sportsfest Blue-330
00BAP Memorabilia Chicago Sportsfest Gold-330
00BAP Memorabilia Chicago Sportsfest Ruby-330
00BAP Memorabilia Chicago Sun-Times Ruby-330
00BAP Memorabilia Chicago Sun-Times Gold-330
00BAP Memorabilia Chicago Sun-Times Sapphire-330
00BAP Mem Toronto Fall Expo Copper-330
00BAP Memorabilia Toronto Fall Expo Gold-330
00BAP Memorabilia Toronto Fall Expo Ruby-330
00Panini Stickers-68
01Upper Deck-257
Exclusives-257
02Upper Deck MVP-30
Gold-30
Classics-30
Golden Classics-30
Kravets, Mikhail
91Kansas City Blades-13
91ProCards-505
92Upper Deck-542
92Kansas City Blades-16
92Classic-106
Gold-106
93Kansas City Blades-15
95Milwaukee Admirals Postcards-19
96Louisiana Ice Gators II-6
97Louisiana Ice Gators-17
99Mississippi Sea Wolves-22
99Mississippi Sea Wolves Kelly Cup-20
Krawinkel, Markus
95German DEL-221
96German DEL-71
Krayer, Jim
96Johnstown Chiefs-8
Krayer, Paul
89Nashville Knights-13
Krayev, Maxim
00Russian Hockey League-217
Krayzel, Ludek
95Czech APS Extraliga-311
96Czech APS Extraliga-205
98Czech OFS-356
99Czech DS-175
99Czech OFS-227
99Czech OFS-478
99Czech OFS-517
All-Star Game Blue-517
All-Star Game Gold-517
All-Star Game Red-517
All-Star Game Silver-517
00Finnish Cardset-207
01Czech OFS-36
02Czech OFS Plus-55
03Czech OFS Plus-11
04Czech OFS-366
Krayzel, Martin
03Baie Comeau Drakkar-5
04Czech OFS-230
Krebs, Thomas
94German First League-397
Krecek, Karel
98Danish Hockey League-54
Kreiss, Harold
82Swedish Semic VM Stickers-106
83Swedish Semic VM Stickers-106
89Swedish Semic World Champ Stickers-109
91Finnish Semic World Champ Stickers-156
91Swedish Semic World Champ Stickers-156
92Finnish Semic-173
94German DEL-274
95German DEL-266
96German DEL-160
Krejci, David
04Gatineau Olympiques-15
05ITG Heroes/Prosp Toronto Expo Parallel -140
05Extreme Top Prospects Signature Edition-S6
05Gatineau Olympiques-8
05ITG Heroes and Prospects-140
Autographs-A-DKR
06AHL Top Prospects-36
06Providence Bruins-9
07Upper Deck Victory-228
Black-228
Gold-228
Krejci, Lukas
96Slovakian Quebec Pee-Wee Tournament-13
Krejcir, Tomas
94German First League-102
Krekula, Fredrik
97Swedish Collector's Choice-14
98Swedish UD Choice-13
99Swedish Upper Deck-13
06Swedish SHL Elitset-269
Krelove, Michael
01Guelph Storm-9
01Guelph Storm Memorial Cup-9
02Sault Ste. Marie Greyhounds-5
05Roanoke Valley Vipers-4
Krenrich, Rob
93Quebec Pee-Wee Tournament-671
Krentz, Dale
88ProCards AHL-15
89ProCards AHL-319
94German DEL-281
95German DEL-372
Krenzelok, Lukas
01Czech OFS-283
02Czech OFS Plus-312
03Czech OFS Plus-12
04Czech OFS-231
05Czech HC Vitkovice-10
06Czech OFS-263
Krepelka, Paul
91Hampton Roads Admirals-8
92Hampton Roads Admirals-2
Kreps, Kamil
03Brampton Batallion-9
03Brampton Batallion-NNO
04San Antonio Rampage-18
06Hot Prospects-195
06Rochester Americans-10
Kress, Jamie
92Oshawa Generals Sheet-2
Kress, Jon
00Prince Albert Raiders-10
01Prince Albert Raiders-10
02Prince Albert Raiders-12
Kress, Mark
03Everett Silvertips-7
04Everett Silvertips-11
05Everett Silvertips-15
Kress, Michael
95Swiss HNL-10
96Swiss HNL-11
98Swiss Power Play Stickers-59
99Swiss Panini Stickers-67
00Swiss Panini Stickers-107
01Swiss HNL-105
02Swiss HNL-251
04Swiss Davos Postcards-18
Krestan, Radek
01Czech OFS-238
01Czech OFS-270
02Czech OFS Plus-305
Krestanovich, Derek
00Kamloops Blazers-12
01Moose Jaw Warriors-7
04Fresno Falcons-10
05Fresno Falcons-10
Krestanovich, Jordan
94Quebec Pee-Wee Tournament-1169
98Calgary Hitmen-9
98Calgary Hitmen Autographs-9
99Calgary Hitmen-14
99Calgary Hitmen Autographs-14
00SP Authentic-131
00SP Game Used-89
00SPx-126
Spectrum-126
00UD Heroes-178
00UD Pros and Prospects-131
00UD Reserve-117
00Upper Deck-440
Exclusives Tier 1-440
Exclusives Tier 2-440
00Upper Deck Vintage-398
01Calgary Hitmen-17
01Hershey Bears-12
02SPx-107
02Upper Deck-201
Exclusives-201
02Upper Deck Vintage-326
02Hershey Bears-11
03Hershey Bears-7
03Hershey Bears Patriot News-11
05Swedish SHL Elitset-260
Gold-260
Kretchine, Vladimir
93Windsor Spitfires-17
93Classic-41
93Classic Four-Sport *-220
Gold-220
94Windsor Spitfires-19
95Slapshot-422
01Russian Hockey League-125
Kretinsky, Ales
99Czech Score Blue 2000-102
99Czech Score Red Ice 2000-102
02Czech OFS Plus-109
03Czech OFS Plus-243
04Czech OFS-306
05Czech HC Znojmo-7
06Czech OFS All Stars-22
Kretschmer, Horst
79Panini Stickers-102
83Swedish Semic VM Stickers-120
Kreus, Nick
93Quebec Pee-Wee Tournament-653
Kreuser, Jeff
98Kansas City Blades-28
99Kansas City Blades Supercuts-24
Kreutzer, Christopher
94German DEL-85
95German DEL-80
Kreutzer, Daniel
98German DEL-57
99German DEL-183
00German DEL-122
Star Attractions-S4
01German Upper Deck-253
02German DEL City Press-52
Top Stars-GT8
03German Deg Metro Stars-10
03German DEL-35
04German DEL-81
04German Dusseldorf Metro Stars Postcards-12
05German DEL-69
05German DEL-293
Star Attack-ST03
06German DEL-46
06German DEL-188
German Forwards-GF4
Kreutzer, Kevin
98Charlotte Checkers-10
99San Angelo Outlaws-7
Kreuzmann, Jaroslav
94Czech APS Extraliga-160
95Czech APS Extraliga-261
99Czech Score Blue 2000-68
99Czech Score Red Ice 2000-68
Krikunov, Ilya
03Russian Hockey League-103
04Russian World Junior Team-8
Krikunov, Vladimir
04Russian Moscow Dynamo-36
Krinner, Anton
91Finnish Semic World Champ Stickers-171
91Swedish Semic World Champ Stickers-171
94German DEL-16
95German DEL-144
96German DEL-244
99German Bundesliga 2-79
Krisak, Patrik
93Upper Deck-266
Krisay, Wes
00Arizona Icecats-13
01Arizona Icecats-10
02Arizona Icecats-12
Krischuk, Jason
06Las Vegas Wranglers-9
Krisko, Dan
907th Inn. Sketch OHL-262
917th Inn. Sketch OHL-216
Krisky, Dave
04Williams Lake Timberwolves-10
04Williams Lake Timberwolves-23
Kriss, Aaron
95Tallahassee Tiger Sharks-4
98Dayton Bombers-9
98Dayton Bombers EBK-2
Kristan, Robert
06Swedish SHL Elitset-145
Kristek, Jaroslav
98Tri-City Americans-7
99Black Diamond-111
Diamond Cut-111
Final Cut-111
99SP Authentic-127
99Upper Deck-323
Exclusives-323
Exclusives 1 of 1-323
99Upper Deck Gold Reserve-323
99Upper Deck MVP SC Edition-201
Gold Script-201
Silver Script-201
Super Script-201
99UD Prospects-44
International Stars-IN9
00Rochester Americans-13
02Rochester Americans-11
03Czech OFS Plus-263
03Czech OFS Plus Insert M-M25
04Czech OFS-281
06Czech HC Zlin Hame Postcards-5
06Czech OFS-228
Kristek, Marek
93Quebec Pee-Wee Tournament-1552
Kristensen, Kasper
98Danish Hockey League-15
99Danish Hockey League-156
Kristensen, Tore
92Norwegian Elite Series-129
Kristiansen, Erik
87Swedish Panini Stickers-41
92Finnish Semic-38
92Norwegian Elite Series-27

93Swedish Semic World Champ Stickers-238
94Finnish Jaa Kiekko-262
94Swedish Olympics Lillehammer*-312

Kristiansen, Kent Inge
92Norwegian Elite Series-220

Kristiansen, Ketil
92Norwegian Elite Series-234

Kristiansen, Martin
98Danish Hockey League-168
99Danish Hockey League-52

Kristiansen, Pal
92Norwegian Elite Series-15
94Finnish Jaa Kiekko-257

Kristiansen, Rasmus
99Danish Hockey League-104

Kristiansen, Thomas
92Norwegian Elite Series-152

Kristin, Miroslav
96Slovakian Quebec Pee-Wee Tournament-14

Kristoffersson, Marcus
98Swedish UD Choice-111
00Finnish Cardset-225
01Utah Grizzlies-16
02Utah Grizzlies-20
03Swedish Elite-167
Silver-167
04Swedish Djurgardens Postcards-4
04Swedish Elitset-21
Gold-21
05Swedish SHL Elitset-169
Autographed Jerseys-GWAMK
Gold-169
06Swedish SHL Elitset-273

Kristoffersson, Sven
56Swedish Alfabilder-93

Krivchenkov, Alexei
95Hampton Roads Admirals-13
96Hampton Roads Admirals-HRA15
97Cleveland Lumberjacks-15
97Cleveland Lumberjacks Postcards-19
00Russian Hockey League-375

Krivokhija, Yuri
93Anaheim Bullfrogs RHI-8
97Johnstown Chiefs-29
01Anchorage Aces-5

Krivokrasov, Sergei
91Upper Deck-658
French-658
91Upper Deck Czech World Juniors-19
92OPC Premier-9
92Parkhurst-36
Emerald Ice-36
92Pinnacle-410
French-410
92Ultra-276
92Upper Deck-582
Euro-Rookies-ER5
92Russian Tri-Globe From Russia With Puck-9
92Russian Tri-Globe From Russia With Puck-10
92Indianapolis Ice-16
92Classic-42
Gold-42
92Classic Four-Sport *-183
Gold-183
93Donruss-74
93Leaf-434
93Pinnacle-419
Canadian-419
93PowerPlay-51
93Score-464
Canadian-464
93Ultra-112
93Indianapolis Ice-17
93Classic-138
93Classic Pro Prospects-38
93Classic Four-Sport *-238
Gold-238
94Blackhawks Coke-10
94Donruss-91
94Fleer-41
94Leaf-238
94OPC Premier-513
Special Effects-513
94Parkhurst SE-SE37
Gold-SE37
Vintage-19
94Pinnacle Rookie Team Pinnacle-12
94Topps/OPC Premier-513
Special Effects-513
94Upper Deck-80
Electric Ice-80
94Indianapolis Ice-13
94Classic Pro Prospects-220
95Be A Player-187
Signatures-S187
Signatures Die Cuts-S187
95Blackhawks Coke-9
95Canada Games NHL POGS-65
95Collector's Choice-96
Player's Club-96
Player's Club Platinum-96
95Donruss-203
95Emotion-29
95Leaf-32
Studio Rookies-18
95Panini Stickers-161
95Parkhurst International-314
Emerald Ice-314
95Pinnacle-154
Artist's Proofs-154
Rink Collection-154
95Score-62
Black Ice Artist's Proofs-62
Black Ice-62
95SkyBox Impact-29
NHL On Fox-6
95Topps New To The Game-16NG
95Ultra-33
Gold Medallion-33
95Upper Deck-11
Electric Ice-11
Electric Ice Gold-11
97Pacific-134
Copper-134
Emerald Green-134
Ice Blue-134
Red-134
Silver-134
97Panini Stickers-135
97Paramount-45
Copper-45
Dark Grey-45
Emerald Green-45
Ice Blue-45
Red-45
Silver-45
97SP Authentic-34
97Upper Deck-37
98Aurora-102
98Be A Player-223
Press Release-223
98BAP Gold-223
98BAP Autographs-223
98BAP Autographs Gold-223
98Black Diamond-48
Double Diamond-48
Triple Diamond-48
Quadruple Diamond-48
98Crown Royale-76
Limited Series-76
98OPC Chrome-211
Refractors-211
98Pacific-147
Ice Blue-147
Red-147
98Pacific Dynagon Ice-104
Blue-104
Red-104
98Pacific Omega-130
Red-130
Opening Day Issue-130
98Panini Stickers-138
98Paramount-124
Copper-124
Emerald Green-124
Holo-Electric-124
Ice Blue-124
Silver-124
98Predators Team Issue-14
98Revolution-79
Ice Shadow-79
Red-79
All-Star Die Cuts-15
98SP Authentic-45
Power Shift-45
98Topps-211
O-Pee-Chee-211
98Upper Deck-302
Exclusives-302
Exclusives 1 of 1-302
Gold Reserve-302
98Upper Deck MVP-114
Gold Script-114
Silver Script-114
Super Script-114
99Aurora-79
Premiere Date-79
99BAP Memorabilia-53
99BAP Memorabilia-372
Gold-53
Gold-372
Silver-53
Silver-372
99BAP Millennium-140
Emerald-140
Ruby-140
Sapphire-140
Signatures-140
Signatures Gold-140
99Crown Royale-75
Limited Series-75
Premiere Date-75
99O-Pee-Chee-189
99O-Pee-Chee Chrome-189
99O-Pee-Chee Chrome Refractors-189
99Pacific-227
Copper-227
Emerald Green-227
Gold-227
Ice Blue-227
Premiere Date-227
Red-227
99Pacific Dynagon Ice-108
Blue-108
Copper-108
Gold-108
Premiere Date-108
99Panini Stickers-270
99Paramount-126
Copper-126
Emerald-126
Gold-126
Holographic Emerald-126
Holographic Gold-126
Holographic Silver-126
Ice Blue-126
Premiere Date-126
Red-126
Silver-126
99Revolution-80
Premiere Date-80
Red-80
Shadow Series-80
99Stadium Club-46
First Day Issue-46
One of a Kind-46
Printing Plates Black-46
Printing Plates Cyan-46
Printing Plates Magenta-46
Printing Plates Yellow-46
99Topps/OPC-189
99Topps/OPC Chrome-189
Refractors-189
99Ultimate Victory-48
1/1-48
Parallel-48
Parallel 100-48
99Upper Deck-75
Exclusives-75
Exclusives 1 of 1-75
99Upper Deck Gold Reserve-75
99Upper Deck MVP-109
Gold Script-109
Silver Script-109
Super Script-109
99Upper Deck Victory-157
99Wayne Gretzky Hockey-91
00BAP Memorabilia-271
Emerald-271
Ruby-271
Sapphire-271
Promos-271
00BAP Mem Chicago Sportsfest Copper-271
00BAP Memorabilia Chicago Sportsfest Blue-271
00BAP Memorabilia Chicago Sportsfest Gold-271
00BAP Memorabilia Chicago Sportsfest Ruby-271
00BAP Memorabilia Chicago Sun-Times Ruby-271
00BAP Memorabilia Chicago Sun-Times Gold-271
00BAP Mem Chicago Sun-Times Sapphire-271
00BAP Mem Toronto Fall Expo Copper-271
00BAP Memorabilia Toronto Fall Expo Gold-271
00BAP Memorabilia Toronto Fall Expo Ruby-271
00O-Pee-Chee-154
00O-Pee-Chee Parallel-154
00Pacific-68
Copper-68
Gold-68
Ice Blue-68
Premiere Date-68
00Panini Stickers-173
00Paramount-119
Copper-119
Gold-119
Holo-Gold-119
Holo-Silver-119
Ice Blue-119
Premiere Date-119
00Private Stock-49
Gold-49
Premiere Date-49
Retail-49
Silver-49
00Stadium Club-203
00Topps/OPC-154
Parallel-154
00Topps Chrome-240
OPC Refractors-240
Refractors-240
00Upper Deck-315
Exclusives Tier 1-315
Exclusives Tier 2-315
00Upper Deck Vintage-180
00Upper Deck Vintage-185
00Vanguard-50
Holographic Gold-50
Holographic Purple-50
Pacific Proofs-50
01BAP Memorabilia-260
Emerald-260
Ruby-260
Sapphire-260
01BAP Signature Series-40
Autographs-40
Autographs Gold-40
02BAP Sig Series Auto Buybacks 1998-223
02BAP Sig Series Auto Buybacks 1999-140
02BAP Sig Series Auto Buybacks 2001-40
02Russian Transfert-31
03Russian Avangard Omsk-7
03Russian National Team-36

Krivolapov, Viktor
73Swedish Stickers-109

Krivomaz, Evgeny
99Rockford IceHogs-11
00Rockford IceHogs-11

Krivomazov, Roman
99Russian Hockey League-232

Krivonozhkin, Maxim
03Russian Hockey League-240
03Russian Young Lions-6

Kriz, David
99Czech OFS-297

Kriz, Ondrej
93Dayton Bombers-6
98Czech OFS-38
99Czech DS-168
99Czech OFS-166
00Czech DS Extraliga-142
00Czech OFS-114
01Czech OFS-174

Kriz, Pavel
95Saskatoon Blades-10
95Signature Rookies Auto-Phonex-22
95Signature Rook Auto-Phonex Phone Cards-22
96Czech APS Extraliga-150
97Czech APS Extraliga-258
97Czech DS Stickers-250
98Czech DS-51
98Czech OFS-150

Krizan, Karol
03Czech OFS Plus All-Star Game-H7
05Swedish SHL Elitset-241
Catchers-9
Catchers Gold-9
Gold-241
06Swedish SHL Elitset-102
Goal Patrol-14
In The Crease-8

Krizek, Pavel
99Czech OFS-534

Krocak, Jiri
95Czech APS Extraliga-277
96Czech APS Extraliga-126
97Czech APS Extraliga-8
98Czech OFS-398
99Czech DS-159
99Czech OFS-167

Krog, Jason
96New Hampshire Wildcats-25
97New Hampshire Wildcats-15
98New Hampshire Wildcats-4
99BAP Memorabilia-346
Gold-346
Silver-346
99SP Authentic-108
99Lowell Lock Monsters-16
00BAP Memorabilia-392
Emerald-392
Ruby-392
Sapphire-392
Promos-392
00BAP Mem Chicago Sportsfest Copper-392
00BAP Memorabilia Chicago Sportsfest Blue-392
00BAP Memorabilia Chicago Sportsfest Gold-392
00BAP Memorabilia Chicago Sportsfest Ruby-392
00BAP Memorabilia Chicago Sun-Times Ruby-392
00BAP Memorabilia Chicago Sun-Times Gold-392
00BAP Mem Chicago Sun-Times Sapphire-392
00BAP Mem Toronto Fall Expo Copper-392
00BAP Memorabilia Toronto Fall Expo Gold-392
00BAP Memorabilia Toronto Fall Expo Ruby-392
00O-Pee-Chee-294
00O-Pee-Chee Parallel-294
00Pacific-251
Copper-251
Gold-251
Ice Blue-251
Premiere Date-251
Autographs-251
00Paramount-155
Copper-155
Gold-155
Holo-Gold-155
Holo-Silver-155
Ice Blue-155
Premiere Date-155
00Topps/OPC-294
Parallel-294
00Topps Chrome-189
OPC Refractors-189
Refractors-189
00Upper Deck MVP-198
First Stars-198
Second Stars-198
Third Stars-198
00Upper Deck Victory-265
00Lowell Lock Monsters-18
01Upper Deck Victory-220
Gold-220
02Pacific Complete-415
Red-415
02Cincinnati Mighty Ducks-B-13
03ITG Action-39
03Pacific Complete-14
Red-14
03Upper Deck-4
Canadian Exclusives-4
HG-4
03Upper Deck MVP-1
Gold Script-1
Silver Script-1
Canadian Exclusives-1

Krol, Joe
34Beehive Group I Photos-236

Krolak, Curt
92Fort Worth Fire-10

Kroll, Johann
05Ohio State Buckeyes-20
06Ohio State Buckeyes-9

Kromm, Bobby
81Red Wings Oldtimers-7

Kromm, Richard
84O-Pee-Chee-227
85Flames Red Rooster-11
85O-Pee-Chee-222
86Islanders Team Issue-26
86O-Pee-Chee-229
87Panini Stickers-103
88ProCards AHL-318
89Swedish Semic Elitserien Stickers-136
89ProCards AHL/IHL-498
91ProCards-465
93Cincinnati Cyclones-26
94Carolina Monarchs-14
98Muskegon Fury-10
98Muskegon Fury-12
99Muskegon Fury-25
00Muskegon Fury-20
01Calgary Hitmen-12
01Calgary Hitmen Autographed-12
02Calgary Hitmen-9

Kromp, Wolfgang
94Finnish Jaa Kiekko-249
95Swedish World Championships Stickers-270

Kron, Robert
89Swedish Semic World Champ Stickers-199
90Canucks Mohawk-11
90OPC Premier-52
90Pro Set-642
90Score Rookie/Traded-65T
90Upper Deck-528
French-528
91Pro Set Platinum-122
91Bowman-320
91Canucks Panini Team Stickers-10
91Canucks Autograph Cards-9
91Canucks Team Issue 8x10-9
91O-Pee-Chee-52
91Panini Stickers-47
91Parkhurst PHC-PHC4
91Parkhurst PHC French-PHC4
91Pro Set-239
French-239
91Score Canadian Bilingual-257
91Score Canadian English-257
91Stadium Club-240
91Topps-52
91Upper Deck-225
French-225
Euro-Stars-8
Euro-Stars French-8
92Bowman-413
92Canucks Road Trip Art-9
92O-Pee-Chee-2
92Panini Stickers-33
92Panini Stickers French-33
92Stadium Club-155
92Topps-80
Gold-80G
92Upper Deck-69
92Finnish Semic-139
93Donruss-143
93Leaf-171
93Parkhurst-90
Emerald Ice-90
93Pinnacle-421
Canadian-421
93PowerPlay-351
93Score-428
Canadian-428
93Upper Deck-359
SP-61
93Whalers Coke-8
94Be A Player Signature Cards-66
94Canada Games NHL POGS-114
94Donruss-114
94Leaf-101
94OPC Premier-296
Special Effects-296
94Parkhurst SE-SE76
Gold-SE76
94Pinnacle-336
Artist's Proofs-336
Rink Collection-336
94Stadium Club-146
Members Only Master Set-146
First Day Issue-146
Super Team Winner Cards-146
94Topps/OPC Premier-296
Special Effects-296
94Ultra-90
94Upper Deck-408
Electric Ice-408
94Finnish Jaa Kiekko-181
95Collector's Choice-298
Player's Club-298
Player's Club Platinum-298
95Donruss-231
95Leaf-257
95Parkhurst International-92
Emerald Ice-92
95Pinnacle-85
Artist's Proofs-85
Rink Collection-85
95Score-154
Black Ice Artist's Proofs-154
Black Ice-154
95Topps-161
OPC Inserts-161
95Upper Deck-400
Electric Ice-400
Electric Ice Gold-400
95Whalers Bob's Stores-11
96Leaf-57
Press Proofs-57
96Pinnacle-132
Artist's Proofs-132
Foil-132
Premium Stock-132
Rink Collection-132
96Score-195
Artist's Proofs-195
Dealer's Choice Artist's Proofs-195
Special Artist's Proofs-195
Golden Blades-195
96Whalers Kid's Club-10
97Be A Player-140
Autographs-140
Autographs Die-Cuts-140
Autographs Prismatic Die-Cuts-140
97Hurricanes Team Issue-15
97Pacific-114
Copper-114
Emerald Green-114
Ice Blue-114
Red-114
Silver-114
97Panini Stickers-19
98Aurora-35
98Be A Player-25
Press Release-25
98BAP Gold-25
98BAP Autographs-25
98BAP Autographs Gold-25
98BAP Tampa Bay All Star Game-25
98Finest-97
No Protectors-97
No Protectors Refractors-97
Refractors-97
98Pacific-136
Ice Blue-136
Red-136
98Pacific Dynagon Ice-36
Blue-36
Red-36
98Panini Stickers-27
98Paramount-39
Copper-39
Emerald Green-39
Holo-Electric-39
Ice Blue-39
Silver-39
99Pacific-76
Copper-76
Emerald Green-76
Gold-76
Ice Blue-76
Premiere Date-76
Red-76
99Panini Stickers-45
00Pacific-87
Copper-87
Gold-87
Ice Blue-87
Premiere Date-87
00Topps Chrome-225
OPC Refractors-225
Refractors-225
00Upper Deck-282
Exclusives Tier 1-282
Exclusives Tier 2-282
01Blue Jackets Donatos Pizza-4
02BAP Sig Series Auto Buybacks 1998-25

Kronick, Dan
05St. Cloud State Huskies-16
06St. Cloud State Huskies-18

Kronwall, Niklas
99Swedish Upper Deck-37
00Swedish Upper Deck-45
SHL Signatures-NK
02Swedish SHL-157
Parallel-157
03BAP Ultimate Mem Rookie Jersey Emblems-22
03BAP Ultimate Mem Rookie Jsy Emblem Gold-22
03BAP Ultimate Mem Rookie Jersey Numbers-22
03BAP Ultimate Mem Rookie Jsy Number Gold-22
03Beehive-203
Gold-203
Silver-203
03ITG Action-646
03ITG Used Signature Series-155
Gold-155
03ITG VIP Rookie Debut-79
03Pacific-365
03Pacific Calder-116
Silver-116
03Pacific Complete-578
Red-578
03Parkhurst Rookie-132
Rookie Emblems-RE-38
Rookie Emblems Gold-RE-38
Rookie Jerseys-RJ-38
Rookie Jerseys Gold-RJ-38
Rookie Numbers-RN-38
Rookie Numbers Gold-RN-38
03SP Authentic-159
03Titanium-118
Hobby Jersey Number Parallels-118
Retail-118
Retail Jersey Number Parallels-118
03Topps Traded-TT107
Blue-TT107
Gold-TT107
Red-TT107
03UD Premier Collection-60
03Upper Deck Rookie Update-91
03Upper Deck Trilogy-188
03Swedish Elite-14
Signatures II-8
Silver-14
03AHL Top Prospects-16
03Grand Rapids Griffins-10
03Pacific AHL Prospects-25
Gold-25
04AHL All-Stars-24
04AHL Top Prospects-14
05ITG Heroes/Prosp Toronto Expo Parallel -99
05ITG Heroes and Prospects-99
Shooting Stars-AS-8

Kronwall, Staffan
03Swedish Elite-157
Silver-157
04Swedish Djurgardens Postcards-5
04Swedish Elitset-13
Gold-13
05ITG Heroes/Prosp Toronto Expo Parallel -381
05Beehive-162
Matte-162
05Black Diamond-287
05Hot Prospects-177
En Fuego-177
Red Hot-177
White Hot-177
05Parkhurst-459
Facsimile Auto Parallel-459
05SP Authentic-246
Limited-246
05SP Game Used-185
Gold-185
05SPx-217
Spectrum-217
05The Cup Masterpiece Pressplate Artifact-334
05The Cup Masterpiece Pressplate Bee Hive-162
05The Cup Masterpiece Pressplate Black Diamond-287
05The Cup Masterpiece Pressplates (Ice)-183
05The Cup Master Pressplate Rookie Update-185
05The Cup Masterpiece Pressplates SPA-246
05The Cup Masterpiece Pressplates SP GU-185
05The Cup Masterpiece Pressplates (SPx)-217
05The Cup Masterpiece Pressplates Trilogy-311
05The Cup Masterpiece Pressplate Ult Coll-176
05UD Artifacts-334
05Ultimate Collection-176
Gold-176
05Upper Deck-466
05Upper Deck Ice-183
05Upper Deck Rookie Update-185
05Upper Deck Trilogy-311
05AHL Top Prospects-23
05ITG Heroes and Prospects-381
Autographs Update-A-SK
06Toronto Marlies-15
06ITG Heroes and Prospects-163
Autographs-ASKR
Jerseys-GUJ23
Jerseys Gold-GUJ23
Emblems-GUE23
Emblems Gold-GUE23
Numbers-GUN23
Numbers Gold-GUN23

Kroon, Hans
05Dutch Vadeko Flyers -9

Kroon, Jan-Olov
67Swedish Hockey-103
69Swedish Hockey-119
70Swedish Hockey-10
71Swedish Hockey-85
72Swedish Stickers-61
73Swedish Stickers-199
74Swedish Stickers-235

Kroon, Paul
05Dutch Vadeko Flyers -10

Kroon, Ulf
67Swedish Hockey-121

Krooshoop, Mike
93Kamloops Blazers-13

Kropac, Radoslav
00Finnish Cardset-290
01Czech OFS-241
01Czech OFS Red Inserts-RE14D
02Czech OFS Plus-155
Duos-D22
03Czech OFS Plus-116
03Czech OFS Plus Insert G-G3
03Czech OFS Plus Insert S-S8
05Czech HC Vitkovice-11
06Czech OFS-57

Kropec, Denis
93Quebec Pee-Wee Tournament-1807

Kropf, Barret
91Air Canada SJHL-A31

Kropf, Martin
95German DEL-380

Kroseberg, Gunnar
95Madison Monsters-14

Krotak, Arne
03Czech OFS Plus All-Star Game-H6
04Czech OFS Czech/Slovak-34

Kroupa, Vlastimil
93Donruss-315
93Leaf-439
93Parkhurst-266
Emerald Ice-266
93Ultra-414
93Upper Deck-437
SP-144
93Kansas City Blades-17
94Donruss-277
94Leaf-265
94Leaf Limited-64
94OPC Premier-113
Special Effects-113
94Parkhurst SE-SE167
Gold-SE167
94Pinnacle-242
Artist's Proofs-242
Rink Collection-242
94Topps/OPC Premier-113
Special Effects-113
94Ultra-196
94Upper Deck-453
Electric Ice-453
94Kansas City Blades-19
94Classic Pro Prospects-4
97Devils Team Issue-7
97Czech APS Extraliga-353
98Kansas City Blades-15
99German DEL-343
00Czech DS Extraliga-4
00Czech OFS-294
01Czech OFS-156
02Czech OFS Plus-198
Duos-D20
03Czech OFS Plus-97
04Czech OFS-97
06Czech OFS-185

Krovopuskov, Alexei
99ECHL All-Star Northern Conference-1
99Greensboro Generals-15
00Russian Hockey League-195
00Muskegon Fury-23
01Russian Hockey League-154

Krstev, Angel
99Czech OFS-48
99Lethbridge Hurricanes-15
00Czech DS Extraliga-113
00Czech OFS-87
02Czech OFS Plus-156
Trios-T5
Duos-D23
03Czech OFS Plus-117
03Czech OFS Plus-334
04Czech OFS-337
05Czech HC Liberec-6
06Czech HC Liberec Postcards-4
06Czech OFS-94
Defenders-13

Krstic, Alex
01Swiss HNL-392

Kruchinin, Andrei
00Russian Hockey League-169
01Russian Hockey League-127

Kruchkowski, Corey
92British Columbia JHL-191

Krueckl, Tim
04Fort Wayne Komets Shoe Carnival-8
04Kalamazoo Wings-15

Krueger, Justin
05Penticton Vees-8

Krueger, Ralph
99Swiss Panini Stickers-250
02Swiss HNL-228

Krueger, Shawn
917th Inn. Sketch OHL-276

Krug, Jason
91Air Canada SJHL-E32
92Saskatchewan JHL-101

Kruger, Martin
71Swedish Hockey-345

Kruger, Patrick
00Swiss Panini Stickers-87
00Swiss Slapshot Mini-Cards-EHCC8
01Swiss HNL-247

Kruger, Raphael
94German DEL-372
95German DEL-365
98Swiss Power Play Stickers-250

Kruger, Trevor
89Hampton Roads Admirals-11A
89Hampton Roads Admirals-11H

Kruhlak, Rob
92Northern Michigan Wildcats-16

Krulis, Jan
94Czech APS Extraliga-74
95Czech APS Extraliga-82
96Czech APS Extraliga-77
97Czech APS Extraliga-197
97Czech DS Extraliga-90
97Czech DS Stickers-133
98Czech DS Stickers-229
98Czech DS-158
99Czech OFS-331
99Czech OFS-500
All-Star Game Blue-500
All-Star Game Gold-500
All-Star Game Red-500
All-Star Game Silver-500
00Czech DS Extraliga-135
00Czech OFS-112
01Czech OFS-184
All Stars-36
03Czech OFS Plus-227
04UK Nottingham Panthers-10

Krull, Harald
82Swedish Semic VM Stickers-108

Krull, Johan
04Ohio State Buckeyes-16

Kruminsch, Juris
94German First League-400

Krumpschmid, Norm
94Muskegon Fury-11

Krupa, Michal
93Quebec Pee-Wee Tournament-1550

Krupp, Uwe
86Sabres Blue Shield-17
86Sabres Blue Shield Small-17
87Sabres Blue Shield-15
87Sabres Wonder Bread/Hostess-14
88O-Pee-Chee-220
88Sabres Blue Shield-13
88Sabres Wonder Bread/Hostess-13
89Panini Stickers-216
89Sabres Blue Shield-9
89Sabres Campbell's-11
90O-Pee-Chee-390
90Panini Stickers-22
90Pro Set-23
90Sabres Blue Shield-11
90Sabres Campbell's-12
90Score-169
Canadian-169
90Topps-390
Tiffany-390
90Upper Deck-187
French-187
91Pro Set Platinum-202
91Bowman-26
91O-Pee-Chee-155
91OPC Premier-140
91Panini Stickers-305
91Parkhurst-109
French-109
91Pinnacle-19
French-19
91Pro Set-20
91Pro Set-301
91Pro Set-436
French-20
French-301
French-436
91Score American-84
91Score Canadian Bilingual-84
91Score Canadian English-84
91Score Rookie/Traded-104T
91Stadium Club-62
91Topps-155
91Upper Deck-102
91Upper Deck-540
French-102
French-540
91Finnish Semic World Champ Stickers-162
91Swedish Semic World Champ Stickers-162
92Bowman-349
92O-Pee-Chee-173
92Panini Stickers-202
92Panini Stickers French-202
92Parkhurst-101
92Parkhurst-453
Emerald Ice-101
Emerald Ice-453
92Pinnacle-86
92Pinnacle-240
French-86
French-240
92Pro Set-109
92Score-77
Canadian-77
92Stadium Club-177
92Topps-158
Gold-158G
92Ultra-129
92Upper Deck-187
93Donruss-205
93Leaf-57
93OPC Premier-3
Gold-3
93Parkhurst-388
Emerald Ice-388
93Pinnacle-259
Canadian-259
93PowerPlay-151
93Score-87
Canadian-87
International Stars-11
International Stars Canadian-11
93Stadium Club-138
Members Only Master Set-138
OPC-138
First Day Issue-138
First Day Issue OPC-138
93Topps/OPC Premier-3
Gold-3
93Swedish Semic World Champ Stickers-168
94Be A Player Signature Cards-163
94Canada Games NHL POGS-201
94Fleer-179
94Leaf-422
94Nordiques Burger King-13
94Pinnacle-382
Artist's Proofs-382
Rink Collection-382
94Stadium Club-172
Members Only Master Set-172
First Day Issue-172
Super Team Winner Cards-172
94Ultra-358
94Upper Deck-310
Electric Ice-310
95Canada Games NHL POGS-79
95Collector's Choice-80
Player's Club-80
Player's Club Platinum-80
95Donruss-49
95Emotion-38
95Leaf-266
95Panini Stickers-252
95Parkhurst International-50
Emerald Ice-50
95Pinnacle-46
Artist's Proofs-46
Rink Collection-46
Global Gold-8
95Score-108
Black Ice Artist's Proofs-108
Black Ice-108
95German DEL-444
96Be A Player-87
Autographs-87
Autographs Silver-87
96Collector's Choice-56
96Donruss-114
Press Proofs-114
96Leaf-49
Press Proofs-49
96Metal Universe-34
96Pinnacle-24
Artist's Proofs-24
Foil-24
Premium Stock-24
Rink Collection-24
96Score-175
Artist's Proofs-175
Dealer's Choice Artist's Proofs-175
Special Artist's Proofs-175
Golden Blades-175
96SkyBox Impact-24
96Summit-38
Artist's Proofs-38
Ice-38
Metal-38
Premium Stock-38
96Topps Picks-163
OPC Inserts-163
96Upper Deck-39
97Kraft-13
97Pacific-265
Copper-265
Emerald Green-265
Ice Blue-265
Red-265
Silver-265
Invincible NHL Regime-53
97Pacific Omega-58
Copper-58
Dark Gray-58
Emerald Green-58
Gold-58
Ice Blue-58
97Panini Stickers-200
97Score Avalanche-15
Platinum-15
Premier-15
98OPC Chrome-11
Refractors-11
98Pacific-161
Ice Blue-161
Red-161
98Pacific Dynagon Ice-64
Blue-64
Red-64
98Panini Stickers-187
98Topps-11
O-Pee-Chee-11
98Upper Deck-269
Exclusives-269
Exclusives 1 of 1-269
Gold Reserve-269
06German DEL-189

Kruppke, Gord
89ProCards AHL-312
90ProCards AHL/IHL-469
91ProCards-138

93Score-467
Canadian-467
95Houston Aeros-11
Kruse, Eric
92Michigan State Spartans-13
93Michigan State Spartans-11
Kruse, Paul
88Kamloops Blazers-15
89Kamloops Blazers-12
90ProCards AHL/IHL-621
907th Inn. Sketch Memorial Cup-8
91ProCards-581
92Salt Lake Golden Eagles-12
92Classic-115
Gold-115
94Leaf-352
95Canada Games NHL POGS-53
95Leaf-251
95Panini Stickers-235
95Pinnacle-66
Artist's Proofs-66
Rink Collection-66
95Playoff One on One-130
95Topps-51
OPC Inserts-51
96Islander Postcards-10
97Be A Player-42
Autographs-42
Autographs Die-Cuts-42
Autographs Prismatic Die-Cuts-42
97Pacific Invincible NHL Regime-117
00Chicago Wolves-11
01UK Sheffield Steelers-10
Krushel, Rod
91Air Canada SJHL-A12
91Air Canada SJHL All-Stars-33
Krushelnyski, Mike
79Montreal Juniors-10
83Bruins Team Issue-9
83NHL Key Tags-5
83O-Pee-Chee-52
83O-Pee-Chee Stickers-43
83Topps Stickers-43
84Oilers Red Rooster-26
84Oilers Team Issue-12
84O-Pee-Chee-248
84O-Pee-Chee Stickers-188
84Topps-6
85Oilers Red Rooster-26
85O-Pee-Chee-49
85O-Pee-Chee Stickers-223
85Topps-49
86Kraft Drawings-28
86Oilers Red Rooster-26
86Oilers Team Issue-26
86O-Pee-Chee-193
86O-Pee-Chee Stickers-74
86Topps-193
87Oilers Team Issue-26
87O-Pee-Chee-202
87O-Pee-Chee Stickers-90
87Panini Stickers-266
88Kings Postcards-11
88Kings Smokey-14
88Oilers Tenth Anniversary-79
88O-Pee-Chee-221
88O-Pee-Chee Stickers-226
89Kings Smokey-12
89O-Pee-Chee-104
89O-Pee-Chee Stickers-153
89Panini Stickers-94
89Topps-104
90Bowman-145
Tiffany-145
90Maple Leafs Postcards-9
90O-Pee-Chee-167
90Panini Stickers-245
90Pro Set-121A
90Pro Set-121B
90Pro Set-537
90Score-227
Canadian-227
90Score Rookie/Traded-47T
90Topps-167
Tiffany-167
90Upper Deck-394
French-394
91Pro Set Platinum-119
91Bowman-166
91Maple Leafs PLAY-19
91O-Pee-Chee-324
91OPC Premier-189
91Panini Stickers-97
91Pinnacle-269
French-269
91Pro Set-233
French-233
91Score American-33
91Score Canadian Bilingual-33
91Score Canadian English-33
91Stadium Club-54
91Topps-324
91Upper Deck-320
French-320
92Bowman-2
92Durivage Panini-5
92Maple Leafs Kodak-26
92O-Pee-Chee-335
92Panini Stickers-78
92Panini Stickers French-78
92Parkhurst-411
Emerald Ice-411
92Score-283
Canadian-283
92Stadium Club-487
92Topps-450
Gold-450G
92Ultra-421
92Upper Deck-87
93Durivage Score-31
93Maple Leafs Score Black's-23
93OPC Premier-169
Gold-169
93Panini Stickers-229
93Pinnacle-328
Canadian-328
93Score-367
Canadian-367
93Stadium Club-306
Members Only Master Set-306
First Day Issue-306
93Topps/OPC Premier-169
Gold-169
94Be A Player Signature Cards-177
94Leaf-438
04ITG Franchises Canadian-31
Autographs-MKR
05SP Game Used Heritage Classic-HC-MK
05SP Game Used Heritage Classic Autos-HCA-MK
05SP Game Used Heritage Classic Patches-HCP-MK
05SP GameUsed Heritage Classic Patch Auto-HAP-MK
06Parkhurst-104
Autographs-104
06UD Artifacts-146
Blue-146
Gold-146
Platinum-146
Radiance-146
Red-146
Tundra Tandems-TTAK
Tundra Tandems Black-TTAK
Tundra Tandems Blue-TTAK
Tundra Tandems Gold-TTAK
Tundra Tandems Platinum-TTAK
Tundra Tandems Red-TTAK
Tundra Tandems Dual Patches Red-TTAK
Krutov, Alexei
02Russian Hockey League-1
03Russian Hockey League-98
Krutov, Vladimir
81Swedish Semic Hockey VM Stickers-45
82Swedish Semic VM Stickers-62
83Swedish Semic VM Stickers-62
84Russian National Team-10
87Russian National Team-12
89Canucks Mohawk-7
89Kraft-40
89Russian National Team-15
89Swedish Semic World Champ Stickers-89
90O-Pee-Chee-380
90Panini Stickers-304
90Panini Stickers-337
90Pro Set-296
90Score-273
Canadian-273
90Topps-380
Tiffany-380
90Upper Deck-77
French-77
95Swedish Globe World Championships-240
99Russian Fetisov Tribute-15
03BAP Ultimate Memorabilia Linemates-12
05ITG Ultimate Mem Pass the Torch Jerseys-3
05ITG Ultimate Mem Passing Torch Jsy Gold-3
05ITG Ultimate Memorabilia Stick Autos-14
05ITG Ultimate Mem Stick Autos Gold-14
05ITG Ultimate Memorabilia Triple Autos-4
05ITG Ultimate Mem Triple Autos Gold-4
05ITG Ultimate Memorabilia Ultimate Autos-25
05ITG Ultimate Mem Ultimate Autos Gold-25
06ITG International Ice-95
Gold-95
Autographs-AVK
Emblems-GUE03
Emblems Gold-GUE03
International Rivals-IR11
International Rivals Gold-IR11
Jerseys-GUJ03
Jerseys Gold-GUJ03
Numbers-GUN03
Numbers Gold-GUN03
Stick and Jersey-SJ23
Stick and Jersey Gold-SJ23
Teammates-IT17
Teammates Gold-IT17
Triple Memorabilia-TM07
Triple Memorabilia Gold-TM07
Kruzich, Gary
88Flint Spirits-11
03Bowling Green Falcons-13
Kryazhev, Oleg
98Russian Hockey League-43
99Russian Hockey League-172
Krygier, Bryan
92Nashville Knights-20
Krygier, Todd
88ProCards AHL-63
89Whalers Junior Milk-12
89ProCards AHL-294
90Bowman-251
Tiffany-251
90O-Pee-Chee-260
90Panini Stickers-35
90Pro Set-107
90Score-237
Canadian-237
90Topps-260
Tiffany-260
90Upper Deck-417
French-417
90Whalers Jr. 7-Eleven-17
91Bowman-2
91Capitals Junior 5x7-15
91Capitals Kodak-15
91O-Pee-Chee-449
91Panini Stickers-317
91Parkhurst-408
French-408
91Pinnacle-242
91Pinnacle-394
French-242
French-394
91Pro Set-83
French-83
91Score American-97
91Score Canadian Bilingual-97
91Score Canadian Bilingual-637
91Score Canadian English-97
91Score Canadian English-637
91Score Rookie/Traded-87T
91Stadium Club-45
91Topps-449
91Upper Deck-215
91Upper Deck-582
French-215
French-582
92Capitals Kodak-17
92Pinnacle-204
French-204
92Pro Set-270
92Score-98
Canadian-98
92Stadium Club-474
92Topps-502
Gold-502G
92Ultra-438
93OPC Premier-188
Gold-188
93PowerPlay-467
93Score-357
Canadian-357
93Stadium Club-337
Members Only Master Set-337
First Day Issue-337
93Topps/OPC Premier-188
Gold-188
93Ultra-448
93Upper Deck-207
94Ducks Carl's Jr.-13
94Parkhurst-258
Gold-258
94Pinnacle-455
Artist's Proofs-455
Rink Collection-455
94Stadium Club-256
Members Only Master Set-256
First Day Issue-256
Super Team Winner Cards-256
94Upper Deck-477
Electric Ice-477
95Be A Player-93
Signatures-S93
Signatures Die Cuts-S93
95Collector's Choice-241
Player's Club-241
Player's Club Platinum-241
95Donruss-335
95Finest-114
Refractors-114
95Metal-3
95Panini Stickers-226
95Parkhurst International-276
Emerald Ice-276
95Pinnacle-183
Artist's Proofs-183
Rink Collection-183
95Playoff One on One-224
95SkyBox Impact-4
95Stadium Club-19
Members Only Master Set-19
95Topps-163
OPC Inserts-163
95Ultra-201
95Upper Deck-9
Electric Ice-9
Electric Ice Gold-9
96Donruss-202
Press Proofs-202
96Leaf-70
Press Proofs-70
96Playoff One on One-363
96Score-203
Artist's Proofs-203
Dealer's Choice Artist's Proofs-203
Special Artist's Proofs-203
Golden Blades-203
97Pacific-318
Copper-318
Emerald Green-318
Ice Blue-318
Red-318
Silver-318
98Orlando Solar Bears II-15
Krykov, Valeri
92Finnish Jyvas-Hyva Stickers-16
93Finnish Jyvas-Hyva Stickers-18
93Finnish SISU-260
94Finnish SISU-260
94Finnish SISU Horoscopes-11
95Finnish SISU-115
96Finnish SISU Redline-134
96Finnish SISU Redline Promos-10
98Finnish Kerailysarja-217
99Finnish Cardset-123
00Finnish Cardset-129
01Finnish Cardset-7
02Finnish Cardset-46
02Swedish SHL-269
Parallel-269
03Swedish Elite-129
Silver-129
04Swedish Elitset-129
Gold-129
05Swedish SHL Elitset-287
Gold-287
Teammates-12
Krylov, Gennady
73Swedish Stickers-115
Krymusa, Tim
98Spokane Chiefs-14
99Spokane Chiefs-12
00Spokane Chiefs-13
01Spokane Chiefs-16
02Spokane Chiefs-11
Krys, Mark
91Johnstown Chiefs-4
93Rochester Americans Kodak-14
96Syracuse Crunch-5
98German DEL-77
Krysanov, Anton
05Russian Hockey League RHL-4
Kryskow, Dave
74Capitals White Borders-13
74NHL Action Stamps-320
74NHL Action Stamps Update-10
74O-Pee-Chee NHL-62
74Topps-62
75O-Pee-Chee NHL-158
75Topps-158
Kryway, Cam
01Colorado Gold Kings-13
Krywulak, Jason
907th Inn. Sketch WHL-27
917th Inn. Sketch WHL-178
Kryznowski, Ed
44Beehive Group II Photos-39
51Parkhurst-33
52Parkhurst-29
Kuba, Filip
96Czech APS Extraliga-300
96Carolina Monarchs-15
98Kentucky Thoroughblades-14
99BAP Millennium-109
Emerald-109
Ruby-109
Sapphire-109
Signatures-109
Signatures Gold-109
Calder Candidates Ruby-C19
Calder Candidates Emerald-C19
Calder Candidates Sapphire-C19
99Pacific Omega-105
Copper-105
Gold-105
Ice Blue-105
Premiere Date-105
99Upper Deck MVP SC Edition-82
Gold Script-82
Silver Script-82
Super Script-82
00Crown Royale-128
00Private Stock-126
Gold-126
Premiere Date-126
Retail-126
Silver-126
00Titanium-127
Retail-127
00Titanium Draft Day Edition-127
00Titanium Draft Day Promos-127
00Topps Chrome-236
OPC Refractors-236
Refractors-236
00Vanguard-128
Pacific Proofs-128
01Pacific-197
Extreme LTD-197
Hobby LTD-197
Premiere Date-197
Retail LTD-197
01Pacific Arena Exclusives-197
01Titanium Double-Sided Jerseys-70
01Titanium Double-Sided Patches-70
01Titanium Draft Day Edition-46
01Upper Deck-316
Exclusives-316
02BAP Memorabilia-199
Emerald-199
Ruby-199
Sapphire-199
NHL All-Star Game-199
NHL All-Star Game Blue-199
NHL All-Star Game Green-199
NHL All-Star Game Red-199
02BAP Memorabilia Toronto Fall Expo-199
02BAP Sig Series Auto Buybacks 1999-109
02O-Pee-Chee-118
02O-Pee-Chee Premier Blue Parallel-118
02O-Pee-Chee Premier Red Parallel-118
02O-Pee-Chee Factory Set-118
02Pacific-184
Blue-184
Red-184
02Pacific Complete-75
Red-75
02Pacific Heads-Up Quad Jerseys-14
02Pacific Heads-Up Quad Jerseys Gold-14
02Topps-118
OPC Blue Parallel-118
OPC Red Parallel-118
Factory Set-118
02Topps Total-198
02Upper Deck-90
Exclusives-90
02Upper Deck Victory-106
Bronze-106
Gold-106
Silver-106
02Upper Deck Vintage-128
02Czech DS-16
03ITG Action-231
03Pacific-166
Blue-166
Red-166
Jerseys-19
Jerseys Gold-19
03Pacific Complete-153
Red-153
03Pacific Exhibit-73
Blue Backs-73
Yellow Backs-73
03Private Stock Reserve-172
Blue-172
Patches-172
Red-172
Retail-172
03Upper Deck-341
Canadian Exclusives-341
HG-341
UD Exclusives-341
03Upper Deck MVP-213
Gold Script-213
Silver Script-213
Canadian Exclusives-213
03Wild Law Enforcement Cards-4
04Pacific-133
Blue-133
Red-133
04Upper Deck-89
Canadian Exclusives-89
HG Glossy Gold-89
HG Glossy Silver-89
05Black Diamond-44
Emerald-44
Gold-44
Onyx-44
Ruby-44
05Parkhurst-243
Facsimile Auto Parallel-243
05Ultra-102
Gold-102
Ice-102
05Upper Deck-95
HG Glossy-95
05Upper Deck MVP-192
Gold-192
Platinum-192
05Upper Deck Toronto Fall Expo-95
05Wild Crime Prevention-4
06Lightning Postcards-11
06O-Pee-Chee-441
Rainbow-441
06Panini Stickers-154
06Upper Deck-424
Exclusives Parallel-424
High Gloss Parallel-424
Masterpieces-424
06Upper Deck MVP-265
Gold Script-265
Super Script-265
Kubacki, Jeff
93Quebec Pee-Wee Tournament-1181
Kubaliak, Martin
02Medicine Hat Tigers-11
Kubalik, Tomas
06Czech HC Plzen Postcards-15
Kubel, Rasmus
98Danish Hockey League-195
99Danish Hockey League-82
Kubena, Petr
96Czech APS Extraliga-28
99Czech OFS-546
99Czech Score Blue 2000-14
99Czech Score Red Ice 2000-14
Kubenko, Viktor
04Slovakian Poprad Team Set-28
Kubes, Ondrej
02Czech OFS Plus-358
03Czech OFS Plus-203
Kubiak, Ralf
94German First League-477
Kubicek, Michal
94Czech APS Extraliga-101
95Czech APS Extraliga-62
Kubina, Pavel
95Czech APS Extraliga-298
98Bowman's Best-133
Refractors-133
Atomic Refractors-133
98Pacific Omega-224
Red-224
Opening Day Issue-224
98Upper Deck-368
Exclusives-368
Exclusives 1 of 1-368
Gold Reserve-368
98Czech Pexeso Series Two-2
98Czech Pexeso Series Two-18
99BAP Memorabilia-31
Gold-31
Silver-31
99BAP Millennium-221
Emerald-221
Ruby-221
Sapphire-221
Signatures-221
Signatures Gold-221
99Pacific-391
Copper-391
Emerald Green-391
Gold-391
Ice Blue-391
Premiere Date-391
Red-391
99Panini Stickers-146
99Paramount-218
Copper-218
Emerald-218
Gold-218
Holographic Emerald-218
Holographic Gold-218
Holographic Silver-218
Ice Blue-218
Premiere Date-218
Red-218
Silver-218
99SPx-141
Radiance-141
Spectrum-141
99Stadium Club-131
First Day Issue-131
One of a Kind-131
Printing Plates Black-131
Printing Plates Cyan-131
Printing Plates Magenta-131
Printing Plates Yellow-131
99Upper Deck MVP-194
Gold Script-194
Silver Script-194
Super Script-194
99Upper Deck Victory-275
99Czech OFS-26
99Czech OFS Jagr Team Embossed-26
00BAP Memorabilia-116
Emerald-116
Ruby-116
Sapphire-116
Promos-116
00BAP Mem Chicago Sportsfest Copper-116
00BAP Memorabilia Chicago Sportsfest Blue-116
00BAP Memorabilia Chicago Sportsfest Gold-116
00BAP Memorabilia Chicago Sportsfest Ruby-116
00BAP Memorabilia Chicago Sun-Times Ruby-116
00BAP Memorabilia Chicago Sun-Times Gold-116
00BAP Mem Chicago Sun-Times Sapphire-116
00BAP Mem Toronto Fall Expo Copper-116
00BAP Memorabilia Toronto Fall Expo Gold-116
00BAP Memorabilia Toronto Fall Expo Ruby-116
00BAP Parkhurst 2000-P48
00BAP Signature Series-231
Emerald-231
Ruby-231
Sapphire-231
Autographs-54
Autographs Gold-54
00O-Pee-Chee-269A
00O-Pee-Chee Parallel-269A
00Pacific-376
Copper-376
Gold-376
Ice Blue-376
Premiere Date-376
00Panini Stickers-92
00Stadium Club-64
00Topps/OPC-269A
Parallel-269A
00Topps Stars-78
Blue-78
00Upper Deck-388
Exclusives Tier 1-388
Exclusives Tier 2-388
00Upper Deck Victory-214
00Czech DS Extraliga Team Jagr-JT6
00Czech OFS-383
01O-Pee-Chee-189
01O-Pee-Chee Premier Parallel-189
01Pacific-353
Extreme LTD-353
Hobby LTD-353
Premiere Date-353
Retail LTD-353
01Pacific Arena Exclusives-353
01Parkhurst-113
01Topps-189
OPC Parallel-189
01Upper Deck Victory-320
Gold-320
01Upper Deck Vintage-232
02BAP Memorabilia-70
Emerald-70
Ruby-70
Sapphire-70
NHL All-Star Game-70
NHL All-Star Game Blue-70
NHL All-Star Game Green-70
NHL All-Star Game Red-70
02BAP Memorabilia Toronto Fall Expo-70
02BAP Sig Series Auto Buybacks 1999-221
02Lightning Team Issue-6
02O-Pee-Chee-247
02O-Pee-Chee Premier Blue Parallel-247
02O-Pee-Chee Premier Red Parallel-247
02O-Pee-Chee Factory Set-247
02Pacific-350
Blue-350
Red-350
02Pacific Complete-239
Red-239
02Topps-247
OPC Blue Parallel-247
OPC Red Parallel-247
Factory Set-247
02Topps Total-249
02Upper Deck-157
Exclusives-157
02Upper Deck Victory-197
Bronze-197
Gold-197
Silver-197
02Upper Deck Vintage-229
02Upper Deck Vintage-287
02Czech DS-17
02Czech Stadion Olympics-339
03Lightning Team Issue-7
03NHL Sticker Collection-128
03O-Pee-Chee-91
03OPC Blue-91
03OPC Gold-91
03OPC Red-91
03Pacific Complete-84
Red-84
03Topps-91
Blue-91
Gold-91
Red-91
03Upper Deck-174
Canadian Exclusives-174
HG-174
03Upper Deck MVP-383
Gold Script-383
Silver Script-383
Canadian Exclusives-383
04Pacific-238
Blue-238
Red-238
04Upper Deck-159
Canadian Exclusives-159
HG Glossy Gold-159
HG Glossy Silver-159
04Czech OFS-365
Stars-32
Stars II-16
04Czech Zuma-27
05Panini Stickers-161
05Parkhurst-438
Facsimile Auto Parallel-438
05Ultra-178
Gold-178
Ice-178
05Upper Deck-175
HG Glossy-175
05Upper Deck MVP-348
Gold-348
Platinum-348
05Upper Deck Toronto Fall Expo-175
05Czech World Champions Postcards-9
05Czech Kvarteto Bonaparte-2c
05Czech Pexeso Mini Blue Set-13
05Czech Pexeso Mini Red Set-19
05Czech Stadion-686
06Gatorade-75
06Panini Stickers-162
06Czech NHL ELH Postcards-5
Kubincak, Vojtech
98Czech OFS-15
99Czech OFS-150
00Czech DS Extraliga-45
00Czech OFS-147
01Czech OFS-153
02Czech OFS Plus-157
03Czech OFS Plus-98
04Czech OFS-98
06Czech OFS-139
Kubis, Milan
98Czech DS Stickers-63
98Czech OFS-325
Kubis, Pavel
06Czech HC Zlin Hame Postcards-6
06Czech OFS-229
Kubos, Petr
96Czech APS Extraliga-222
98Prince George Cougars-12
99Czech OFS-59
00Czech OFS-329
01Czech OFS-59
02Czech OFS Plus-69
Trios-T21
03Czech OFS Plus-30
04Czech OFS-404
04Russian Legion-30
06Czech OFS-58
Kubus, Vladimir
04Cape Breton Screaming Eagles-10
05Cape Breton Screaming Eagles-9
Kucera, Frank
89Swedish Semic World Champ Stickers-184
90OPC Premier-53
90Pro Set-599
90ProCards AHL/IHL-411
91Blackhawks Coke-13
91Bowman-404
91Score Canadian Bilingual-390
91Score Canadian English-390
91Upper Deck-468
French-468
91ProCards-495
92Bowman-7
92Parkhurst-269
Emerald Ice-269
92Score-346
Canadian-346
92Stadium Club-438
92Topps-520
Gold-520G
92Ultra-277
92Finnish Semic-128
93Blackhawks Coke-4
93Donruss-439
93Score-372
Canadian-372
93Stadium Club-442
Members Only Master Set-442
First Day Issue-442
94Leaf-392
94Pinnacle-210
Artist's Proofs-210
Rink Collection-210
94Stadium Club-49
Members Only Master Set-49
First Day Issue-49
Super Team Winner Cards-49
94Czech APS Extraliga-79
94Finnish Jaa Kiekko-169
95Be A Player-33
Signatures-S33
Signatures Die Cuts-S33
95Canada Games NHL POGS-129
95Collector's Choice-304
Player's Club-304
Player's Club Platinum-304
95Emotion-75
95Leaf-50
95Panini Stickers-34
95Playoff One on One-264
95Topps-84
OPC Inserts-84
95Ultra-67
Gold Medallion-67
95Whalers Bob's Stores-12
95Finnish Semic World Championships-146
97Czech APS Extraliga-6
97Czech APS Extraliga-350
97Czech DS Extraliga-80
98Czech DS-10
98Czech DS Stickers-211
98Czech OFS-134
98Czech OFS-234
98Czech OFS-448
Olympic Winners-4
98Czech Bonaparte-5B
98Czech DS-143
National Stars-NS6
99Czech OFS-108
99Czech OFS-262
99Czech OFS-496
All-Star Game Blue-496
All-Star Game Gold-496
All-Star Game Red-496
All-Star Game Silver-496
00Upper Deck NHLPA-PA26
00Czech DS Extraliga Valuable Players-VP2
00Czech DS Extraliga World Champions-WCH5
00Czech OFS-401
01Czech National Team Postcards-8
01Czech OFS Red Inserts-RE10D
02Czech DS-5
02Czech OFS Plus-243
Trios-T12
Duos-D5
02Czech IQ Sports Blue-14
02Czech IQ Sports Blue-15
02Czech IQ Sports Yellow-16
03Czech OFS Plus-185
03Czech OFS Plus All-Star Game-H30
04Czech OFS-169
Kucera, Jiri
89Swedish Semic World Champ Stickers-195
91Finnish Jyvas-Hyva Stickers-57
93Finnish SISU-72
93Swedish Semic World Champ Stickers-98
94Czech APS Extraliga-140
94Finnish SISU-14
94Finnish Jaa Kiekko-190
94Swedish Leaf-187
Foreign Affairs-5
95Czech APS Extraliga-78
95Czech APS Extraliga-364
95Finnish SISU Limited-76
95Finnish Semic World Championships-150
95Swedish Leaf-83
95Swedish Upper Deck-126
95Swedish Globe World Championships-161
95Swedish World Championships Stickers-200
96Czech APS Extraliga-302
96Swedish Semic Wien-117
97Czech DS Stickers-16
97Czech DS Stickers-219
98Czech Pexeso-17
98Swedish UD Choice-148
99Swedish Upper Deck-150
Lasting Impressions-8
00Swedish Upper Deck-126
02Czech OFS Plus-137
Kucera, Josef
01Czech OFS-126
Gold Inserts-G8
02Czech OFS Plus-177
03Czech OFS Plus-264
03Czech OFS Plus Checklists-11
03Czech OFS Plus Checklists-13
03Czech OFS Plus Insert H-H1
03Czech OFS Plus MS Praha-SE43
05Czech HC Vsetin-8
06Czech OFS-326
06Czech OFS-328
Kucera, Marcel
99Czech Score Blue 2000-61
99Czech Score Red Ice 2000-61
01Czech OFS-192
01Czech OFS H Inserts-H2
02Czech OFS Plus-284
02Czech OFS Plus Masks-M18
Kucera, Martin
04Slovakian Skalica Team Set-1
Kucera, Radek
99Czech Score Blue 2000-146
99Czech Score Red Ice 2000-146
Kucera, Robert
97Czech APS Extraliga-167
98Czech OFS-73
Kucharcik, Tomas
94Czech APS Extraliga-153
95Czech APS Extraliga-253
95Czech APS Extraliga-350
95Czech APS Extraliga-381
96Czech APS Extraliga-14
97Czech APS Extraliga-162
97Czech DS Extraliga-79
97Czech DS Stickers-124
98Czech DS-76
98Czech DS Stickers-199
98Czech OFS-218
98Czech OFS-463
98Czech Pexeso Series Two-5
99Czech DS-120
99Czech OFS-263
99Czech OFS-385
00Finnish Cardset-348
01Finnish Cardset-224
02Czech DS-13
02Czech National Team Postcards-6
02Finnish Cardset-200
03Finnish Cardset-39
04Czech OFS-296
Kucharczyk, Radim
99Czech OFS-60
01Czech OFS-73
02Czech OFS Plus-70
Trios-T21
04Czech OFS-317
04Czech OFS-380
06Czech OFS-207
Kucharzj, Jevgenij
74Swedish Stickers-65
Kucheran, Bob
80Oshawa Generals-5
Kuchler, Jiri
97Czech APS Extraliga-212
99Czech Score Blue 2000-5
99Czech Score Red Ice 2000-5
06Czech OFS-259
Kuchma, Bill
84Ottawa 67's-16
Kuchyna, Petr
94Czech APS Extraliga-170
94Czech APS Extraliga-273
95Czech APS Extraliga-359
96Czech APS Extraliga-29
96Swedish Semic Wien-110
97Czech APS Extraliga-57
97Czech DS Extraliga-104
97Czech DS Stickers-95
98Czech DS-67
98Czech DS Stickers-290
98Czech OFS-314
99Finnish Cardset-145
00Finnish Cardset-271
04Czech OFS-12
Kucirek, Zdenek
99Czech Score Blue 2000-154
99Czech Score Red Ice 2000-154
Kucko, Andrej
96Slovakian Quebec Pee-Wee Tournament-15
Kuckrec, Richard
01Czech OFS-263
Kucny, Jiri
06Czech HC Vsetin Postcards-4
06Czech OFS-184
Kucsulain, Mike
99Louisiana Ice Gators-5
00Louisiana Ice Gators-7
Kuda, Petr
94Czech APS Extraliga-50
95Czech APS Extraliga-83
Kudashov, Alexei
93Donruss-345
93Parkhurst-260
Emerald Ice-260
93Pinnacle-445
Canadian-445
93Score-623
Gold-623
Canadian-623
Canadian Gold-623
93Upper Deck-427
SP-159
93St. John's Maple Leafs-12
93Classic-42
94Donruss-84
94Leaf-181
94Maple Leafs Gangsters-10
94OPC Premier-78
Special Effects-78
94Parkhurst SE-SE180
Gold-SE180
94Topps/OPC Premier-78
Special Effects-78
94St. John's Maple Leafs-16
94Classic Pro Prospects-106
96German DEL-284
96Collector's Edge Ice-23
Prism-23
98Russian Hockey League-55
99Russian Dynamo Moscow-18
99Russian Stars of Hockey-3
00Russian Dynamo Moscow-22
00Russian Dynamo Moscow Blue-White-2
01Russian Dynamo Moscow-7
01Russian Lightnings-3
03Russian Hockey League-41
03Russian SL-27
04Russian Moscow Dynamo-17
Kudelka, David
99Czech OFS-468
04Bakersfield Condors-8
06Bakersfield Condors-7
Kudelka, Tomas
04Czech OFS-266
05Lethbridge Hurricanes-14
Kudelski, Bob
88ProCards AHL-206
89Kings Smokey-20
90Kings Smokey-20
90O-Pee-Chee-46
90Panini Stickers-232
90Pro Set-122
90Score-305A
Canadian-305A
90Topps-46
Tiffany-46
90Upper Deck-433
French-433
91Pro Set Platinum-181
91Bowman-189
91O-Pee-Chee-61
91OPC Premier-178
91Panini Stickers-87
91Parkhurst-299
French-299
91Pinnacle-113
French-113
91Pro Set-99
French-99
91Score American-154
91Score Canadian Bilingual-154
91Score Canadian English-154
91Stadium Club-40
91Topps-61

91Upper Deck-301
French-301
92Bowman-12
92O-Pee-Chee-326
92Panini Stickers-69
92Panini Stickers French-69
92Parkhurst-357
Emerald Ice-357
92Pinnacle-84
French-84
92Score-221
Canadian-221
92Stadium Club-149
92Topps-145
Gold-145G
93Donruss-232
93Donruss-434
93Leaf-48
93OPC Premier-40
Gold-40
93Panini Stickers-114
93Parkhurst-408
Emerald Ice-408
93Pinnacle-38
Canadian-38
93PowerPlay-170
93PowerPlay-348
93Score-257
93Score-549
Gold-549
Canadian-257
Canadian-549
Canadian Gold-549
93Senators Kraft Sheets-12
93Stadium Club-120
Members Only Master Set-120
OPC-120
First Day Issue-120
First Day Issue OPC-120
93Topps/OPC Premier-40
Gold-40
93Ultra-85
93Upper Deck-17
SP-110
94Canada Games NHL POGS-105
94Donruss-227
94EA Sports-95
94Flair-64
94Fleer-79
94Leaf-314
94OPC Premier-245
Special Effects-245
94Parkhurst-83
Gold-83
SE Vintage-35
94Pinnacle-284
Artist's Proofs-284
Rink Collection-284
94Score-28
Gold-28
Platinum-28
94Select-55
Gold-55
94SP-46
Die Cuts-46
94Stadium Club Members Only-43
94Topps/OPC Premier-245
Special Effects-245
94Topps Finest Inserts-23
94Ultra-80
94Upper Deck-376
Electric Ice-376
SP Inserts-SP29
SP Inserts Die Cuts-SP29
95Collector's Choice-226
Player's Club-226
Player's Club Platinum-226
95Hoyle Eastern Playing Cards-36
95Playoff One on One-260
95Pro Magnets-87
95Upper Deck-138
Electric Ice-138
Electric Ice Gold-138
96NHL Pro Stamps-87

Kudermetov, Eduard
98Russian Hockey League-122
99Russian Hockey League-79
00Russian Hockey League-33
03Russian Hockey League-86

Kudinov, Andrei
94Binghamton Rangers-8
95Binghamton Rangers-11
98Russian Hockey League-35
99Russian Hockey League-26
99Russian Metallurg Magnetogorsk-40
00Russian Hockey League-241
02Russian Hockey League-20

Kudrna, Jan
02Czech OFS Plus-329
03Czech OFS Plus-290
03Czech OFS Plus-363

Kudrna, Jaroslav
95Czech APS Extraliga-333
97Czech APS Extraliga-260
97Czech DS Extraliga-73
98Czech DS-56
98Czech DS Stickers-138
98Czech OFS-158
99Czech DS-80
99Czech OFS-92
00Czech DS Extraliga-93
00Czech OFS-45
01Czech OFS-256
02Czech OFS Plus-344
03Czech OFS Plus-52
03Czech Pardubice Postcards-7
04Czech HC Plzen Postcards-9
04Czech OFS-377
05Czech HC Trinec-6
06Czech LG Hockey Games Postcards-9
06Czech OFS-161
Goals Leaders-4
Points Leaders-5

Kudrna, Jiri
99Czech Score Blue 2000-114
99Czech Score Red Ice 2000-114
02Czech OFS Plus-158

Kudrna, Ladislav
95Czech APS Extraliga-147
96Czech APS Extraliga-4
97Czech APS Extraliga-339
99Czech DS-183
99Czech OFS-9
99Czech OFS Goalie Die-Cuts-9
00Czech DS Extraliga-98
00Czech OFS-188
01Czech OFS-111
01Czech OFS H Inserts-H10

Kudrna, Petr
98Brandon Wheat Kings-11
99Lethbridge Hurricanes-16

Kudroc, Kristian
99Black Diamond-108
Diamond Cut-108
Final Cut-108
99SP Authentic-126
99Upper Deck-313
Exclusives-313
Exclusives 1 of 1-313
99Upper Deck Gold Reserve-313
99Upper Deck MVP SC Edition-199
Gold Script-199
Silver Script-199
Super Script-199
99Quebec Remparts-21
Signed-21
00BAP Memorabilia-515
01BAP Memorabilia-202
Emerald-202
Ruby-202
Sapphire-202
01BAP Signature Series-85
Autographs-85
Autographs Gold-85
01O-Pee-Chee-314
01O-Pee-Chee Premier Parallel-314
01Pacific-354
Extreme LTD-354
Hobby LTD-354
Premiere Date-354
Retail LTD-354
01Pacific Arena Exclusives-354
01Topps-314
OPC Parallel-314
02BAP Sig Series Auto Buybacks 2001-85
02O-Pee-Chee-288
02O-Pee-Chee Premier Blue Parallel-288
02O-Pee-Chee Premier Red Parallel-288
02O-Pee-Chee Factory Set-288
02Topps-288
OPC Blue Parallel-288
OPC Red Parallel-288
Factory Set-288
02Springfield Falcons-15
03San Antonio Rampage-21
05Finnish Cardset -306
06Finnish Cardset-227
Enforcers-2
06Finnish Ilves Team Set-11

Kuehner, Kyle
04South Surrey Eagles-12
04Surrey Eagles-10
04Surrey Eagles-10

Kuenzi, Werner
72Finnish Semic World Championship-146
72Swedish Semic World Championship-146

Kufflick, Jerome
95Saskatoon Blades-11

Kuhl, Marcus
79Panini Stickers-113
82Swedish Semic VM Stickers-110
83Swedish Semic VM Stickers-110
94German DEL-272
95German DEL-263

Kuhn, Bernd
72Finnish Hellas-55
72Finnish Semic World Championship-110
72Swedish Semic World Championship-110

Kuhn, Florian
96German DEL-116

Kuhn, Jon
93Quebec Pee-Wee Tournament-790

Kuhn, Tyler
91Air Canada SJHL-D45
91Air Canada SJHL All-Stars-17
92Saskatchewan JHL-19

Kuhnekath, Ulrik
94German First League-432

Kuhnel, Matthias
94German First League-617

Kuhnhackl, Erich
79Panini Stickers-103
82Swedish Semic VM Stickers-112
83Swedish Semic VM Stickers-112
98German DEL-340

Kuhnhauser, Bernd
94German DEL-87
95German DEL-92
95German DEL-428
96German DEL-280
98German DEL-303
99German DEL-250
99German DEL-376
00German DEL-47
01German Upper Deck-52
02German DEL City Press-53
04German DEL-50
04German Dusseldorf Metro Stars Postcards-13

Kuhnhauser, Bobo
03German Deg Metro Stars-11

Kuhnke, Harald
83Swedish Semic VM Stickers-159
94German DEL-135
95German DEL-137
04German Berlin Eisbarens 50th Anniv-67

Kuhta, Kimmo
98Finnish Keralysarja-39
99Finnish Cardset-23
00Finnish Cardset-139
01Finnish Cardset-20
02Finnish Cardset-47
03Finnish Cardset-22
04Finnish Cardset-21
Parallel-14
06Finnish Cardset-200

Kuhtinov, Roman
00Russian Hockey League-185

Kuiper, Nick
04Norfolk Admirals-11
05Norfolk Admirals-17
06Augusta Lynx-8

Kuiri, Tapio
70Finnish Jaakiekko-372

Kuisma, Ilpo
70Finnish Jaakiekko-210
71Finnish Suomi Stickers-132
72Finnish Jaakiekko-195
73Finnish Jaakiekko-67
73Finnish Jaakiekko-155

Kuisma, Jarmo
72Finnish Jaakiekko-266

Kuismanen, Pertti
66Finnish Jaakiekkosarja-77
70Finnish Jaakiekko-160

Kuivalainen, Pasi
92Finnish Jyvas-Hyva Stickers-87
93Finnish Jyvas-Hyva Stickers-164
93Finnish SISU-161
94Finnish SISU-1
94Finnish SISU Magic Numbers-1
94Finnish SISU NHL Phenoms-9
94Finnish Jaa Kiekko-2
95Finnish SISU-272
Ghost Goalies-9
95Finnish SISU Limited-64
95Finnish Semic World Championships-1
96Finnish SISU Redline-69
At The Gala-5
96Finnish SISU Redline Foil Parallels-69
96Finnish SISU Redline Mighty Adversaries-5
96Finnish SISU Redline Promos-6
96Finnish SISU Redline Silver Signatures-2
98Finnish Keralysarja-251
Mad Masks-12
Off Duty-12
99Finnish Cardset-244
Puck Stoppers-3
00Finnish Cardset-193
01Finnish Cardset-97
01Finnish Cardset Haltmeisters-12
02Finnish Cardset-48

Kujala, Petri
93Finnish SISU-144
93Finnish SISU-183B
95Finnish SISU-269
05German DEL-46

Kuk, Dustin
93Quebec Pee-Wee Tournament-1301
00Peoria Rivermen-10
01Peoria Rivermen-11

Kukacka, Zbynek
917th Inn. Sketch OHL-306
94Czech APS Extraliga-82
95Czech APS Extraliga-285
97Czech APS Extraliga-230
98Czech DS Stickers-39
98German DEL-76

Kukhtinov, Roman
98Russian Hockey League-97
99Russian Hockey League-211

Kuki, Arto
94Finnish SISU NHL Draft-4
95Finnish SISU-295
96Finnish SISU Redline Rookie Energy-7
99Finnish Cardset-212
01Finnish Cardset-132
02Finnish Cardset-201
03Finnish Cardset-154
04Finnish Cardset-245
05Finnish Cardset -239
06Finnish Cardset-243

Kukko, Jouko
80Finnish Mallasjuoma-141

Kukkola, Ilpo
78Finnish SM-Liiga-133

Kukkonen, Lasse
00Finnish Cardset-180
01Finnish Cardset-73
02Finnish Cardset-202
03Black Diamond-164
Black-164
Green-164
Red-164
03Blackhawks Postcards-10
03Bowman-138
Gold-138
03Bowman Chrome-138
Refractors-138
Gold Refractors-138
Xfractors-138
03ITG VIP Rookie Debut-8
03Pacific Complete-539
Red-539
03Parkhurst Original Six Chicago-22
03Parkhurst Rookie-107
03Private Stock Reserve-109
Blue-109
Red-109
Retail-109
03SP Game Used-55
Gold-55
03SPx-193
Radiance-193
Spectrum-193
03Topps Traded-TT94
Blue-TT94
Gold-TT94
Red-TT94
03Upper Deck-207
Canadian Exclusives-207
HG-207
03Upper Deck Trilogy-145
Limited-145
03Finnish Cardset D-Day-DD3
03Norfolk Admirals-13
04Finnish Cardset-93
Parallel-69
05Finnish Cardset -89
06Blackhawks Postcards-20
06Finnish Cardset Signature Sensations-18
06Finnish Cardset Trophy Winners-5

Kukowski, Betsey
98Minnesota Golden Gophers Women-13

Kukuk, Philip
94German DEL-20

Kukulies, Sven
99German DEL-396

Kukulka, Bobby
06Port Huron Flags-5

Kukulowicz, Adolph
52Juniors Blue Tint-78

Kukumberg, Roman
03Czech OFS Plus All-Star Game-H5
04Czech OFS Czech/Slovak-35

Kulabuchov, Vadim
94Czech APS Extraliga-270
95German DEL-426

Kulagin, Boris
73Russian National Team-23
74Russian National Team-7
74Swedish Stickers-66

Kulak, Stu
81Victoria Cougars-9
82Victoria Cougars-11
83Fredericton Express-23
86Canucks Team Issue-7
86Oilers Red Rooster-8
86Oilers Team Issue-8
87Nordiques General Foods-17
87Nordiques Team Issue-12
88Oilers Tenth Anniversary-44
88ProCards AHL-176
89ProCards AHL-33
90Kansas City Blades-9
90ProCards AHL/IHL-586
94Central Hockey League-83
94San Antonio Iguanas-11
98Phoenix Mustangs-7
99Austin Ice Bats-17

Kulemin, Nikolai
04Russian Under-18 Team-9
05Russian Hockey League RHL-40

Kuleshov, Mikhail
01Hershey Bears-13
02Hershey Bears-12
03ITG Used Signature Series-200
Gold-200
03ITG VIP Rookie Debut-125
03Parkhurst Rookie-97
03Topps Traded-TT100
Blue-TT100
Gold-TT100
Red-TT100
03Upper Deck Rookie Update-200
03Hershey Bears-11
03Hershey Bears Patriot News-12
04Pacific-276
Blue-276
Red-276

Kulhanek, Colby
06Chilliwack Bruins-16

Kulhoranta, Kai
71Finnish Suomi Stickers-326

Kulich, Vladimir
95Slovakian-Quebec Pee-Wee Tournament-12

Kulikov, Alexander
74Swedish Stickers-84

Kulikov, Dmitri
99Russian Hockey League-108
01Russian Hockey League-167

Kulikov, Vladimir
99Russian Hockey League-143

Kullman, Arnie
98Hershey Bears-37

Kullman, Ed
44Beehive Group II Photos-332
51Parkhurst-101
52Parkhurst-18
53Parkhurst-61
02Parkhurst Reprints-162

Kulmala, Arto
94Finnish SISU-78
95Finnish SISU-114
96Finnish SISU Redline-128
98Finnish Keralysarja Off Duty-10

Kulonen, Jouni
00Finnish Cardset-176
01Finnish Cardset-68

Kulonen, Timo
92Finnish Jyvas-Hyva Stickers-122
93Finnish Jyvas-Hyva Stickers-226
93Finnish SISU-189
94Finnish SISU-237
95Finnish SISU-139

Kultakuusi, Mauri
78Finnish SM-Liiga-93

Kultanen, Jarno
94Finnish SISU-228
95Finnish SISU-73
98Finnish Keralysarja-33
99Finnish Cardset-21
00BAP Memorabilia-408
Emerald-408
Ruby-408
Sapphire-408
00BAP Signature Series-145
Emerald-145
Ruby-145
Sapphire-145
Autographs-201
Autographs Gold-201
00SP Authentic-136
00SPx-176
00Stadium Club-260
00Topps Stars-119
Blue-119
00UD Pros and Prospects-95
00Upper Deck Ice-109
00Finnish Cardset-15
02BAP Sig Series Auto Buybacks 2000-201
02Finnish Cardset-49
03Finnish Cardset-18
04Finnish Cardset-17
04Finnish Cardset Signatures-6
04Swedish Pure Skills-103
Parallel-103
05Swedish SHL Elitset-258
Gold-258
06Swedish SHL Elitset-118

Kulyash, Denis
05Russian Hockey League RHL-1

Kulzer, Thomas
94German First League-36

Kumala, Arto
98Finnish Keralysarja-221
99Finnish Cardset-124

Kummer, Wolfgang
93Swedish Semic World Champ Stickers-164
94German DEL-96
95German DEL-97
96German DEL-131
98German DEL-312
99German DEL-258

Kummu, Ryan
01Greensboro Generals-6

Kumpel, Mark
84Fredericton Express-19
85Nordiques General Foods-14
85Nordiques McDonald's-11
85Nordiques Provigo-13
85Nordiques Team Issue-12
86Nordiques General Foods-13
86Nordiques McDonald's-13
89Jets Safeway-18
90Jets IGA-17
90O-Pee-Chee-444
91Jets Panini Team Stickers-14
91Moncton Hawks-15
91ProCards-184
98Portland Pirates-19
99Portland Pirates-12

Kumpula, Ari
98Finnish Keralysarja-98
99Finnish Cardset-234

Kumstat, Pavel
96Czech APS Extraliga-200
97Czech APS Extraliga-131
97Czech DS Stickers-191
98Czech DS Stickers-250
99Czech DS-185
99Czech OFS-469
00Czech DS Extraliga-101
00Czech OFS-192
01Czech OFS-105
02Czech OFS Plus-110
03Czech OFS Plus-13
04Czech OFS-232

Kumstat, Petr
00Czech OFS-208
02Czech OFS Plus-111
03Czech OFS Plus-74
04Czech OFS-28
05Czech HC Karlovy Vary-8
06Czech OFS-32
Team Cards-2

Kuna, Martin
01Baie-Comeau Drakkar-9

Kunast, Christian
94German DEL-265
95German DEL-243
96German DEL-114
98German DEL-84
99German DEL-337
00German DEL-173
01German Upper Deck-185
Goalies in Action-G8
Jersey Cards-CK-J
02German DEL City Press-95
Top Stars-GT6
03German DEL-110
04German DEL-151
04German Hannover Scorpions Postcards-16
05German DEL-132

Kunce, Daniel
94German DEL-183
95German DEL-175
96German DEL-133
98German DEL-266
99German DEL-41
00German DEL-196
01German Upper Deck-159
02German DEL City Press-221
03German DEL-187
04German DEL-234
04German Krefeld Penguins Postcards-14
05German DEL-229

Kunce, Georg
95German DEL-174

Kunce, Gerhard
95German DEL-433

Kung, Andreas
03Swiss EV Zug Postcards-14

Kungle, Jeff
91Air Canada SJHL-B41
91Air Canada SJHL All-Stars-1
96Peoria Rivermen-13
96Peoria Rivermen Photo Album-14
97Austin Ice Bats-9
99Austin Ice Bats-8
00Austin Ice Bats-8
02Austin Ice Bats-20

Kunitz, Chris
03BAP Ultimate Memorabilia Autographs-90
Gold-90
03ITG Action-659
03ITG Used Signature Series-142
Autographs Gold-142
03ITG VIP Rookie Debut-108
03Pacific Calder-101
Silver-101
03Pacific Complete-588
Red-588
03Parkhurst Rookie-173
03Topps Traded-TT115
Blue-TT115
Gold-TT115
Red-TT115
03Upper Deck Rookie Update-134
03Cincinnati Mighty Ducks-B8
03Pacific AHL Prospects-17
Gold-17
04Pacific-271
Blue-271
Red-271
04Cincinnati Mighty Ducks-14
04ITG Heroes and Prospects-40
Autographs-CK
Emblems-41
Emblems Gold-41
Jersey Autographs-41
Jerseys-41
Jerseys Gold-41
Numbers-41
Numbers Gold-41
04ITG Heroes/Prospects Toronto Expo '05-40
04ITG Heroes/Prospects Expo Heroes/Pros-40
05Beehive Signature Scrapbook-SSCK
05Parkhurst-6
Facsimile Auto Parallel-6
05Ultra Fresh Ink-FI-CK
05Ultra Fresh Ink Blue-FI-CK
05Upper Deck-247
06Be A Player-100
Autographs-100
Signatures-CK
Signatures 25-108
Signatures Duals-DMK
06Flair Showcase Inks-ICK
06Hot Prospects Hotagraphs-HCK
06O-Pee-Chee-6
Rainbow-6
Autographs-A-CK
06Panini Stickers-192
06UD Powerplay Power Marks-PMCK
06Upper Deck-253
Exclusives Parallel-253
High Gloss Parallel-253
Masterpieces-253
Signature Sensations-SSCK
06Upper Deck MVP-6
Gold Script-6
Super Script-6
Autographs-OAMK
06Upper Deck Trilogy Scripts-TSKU
07Upper Deck Victory-170
Black-170
Gold-170

Kuntar, Les
92Fredericton Canadiens-14
93Fredericton Canadiens-13
93Classic Pro Prospects-72
94Parkhurst-114
Gold-114
96Collector's Edge Ice The Wall-TW9

Kuntos, Jiri
94Czech APS Extraliga-7
95Czech APS Extraliga-106
96Czech APS Extraliga-54
97Czech APS Extraliga-321
97Czech DS Stickers-228
98Czech DS-116
98Czech DS Stickers-269
98Czech OFS-180
99Czech DS-101
99Czech OFS-198
99Czech OFS-518
All-Star Game Blue-518
All-Star Game Gold-518
All-Star Game Red-518
All-Star Game Silver-518
00Czech DS Extraliga-66
00Czech OFS-216
02Czech OFS Plus-199
03Czech OFS Plus-178

Kuntz, Al
51Laval Dairy Subset-108
52St. Lawrence Sales-66

Kuntz, Dean
88Saskatoon Blades-4

Kuntz, Mark
85Medicine Hat Tigers-3
88Lethbridge Hurricanes-14
91Richmond Renegades-12
91Richmond Renegades Set 2-17
92Richmond Renegades-10
00Fresno Falcons-28
01Fresno Falcons-25

Kunzi, Andre
93Swiss HNL-115
95Swiss HNL-164
96Swiss HNL-59
98Swiss Power Play Stickers-209
99Swiss Panini Stickers-211
00Swiss Panini Stickers-252
00Swiss Slapshot Mini-Cards-EVZ6
01Swiss EV Zug Postcards-13
01Swiss HNL-173

Kunzi, Thomas
93Swiss HNL-116
95Swiss HNL-165
96Swiss HNL-60
98Swiss Power Play Stickers-210
99Swiss Panini Stickers-10
00Swiss Panini Stickers-11
00Swiss Slapshot Mini-Cards-HCAP5
01Swiss HNL-198
02Swiss HNL-326

Kuokkanen, Jouni
96Seattle Thunderbirds-13
97Seattle Thunderbirds-11
04Lakehead University Thunderwolves-11

Kuokkanen, Juha
00Finnish Cardset-319
01Finnish Cardset-323
02Finnish Cardset-203
03Finnish Cardset-127
04Finnish Cardset-282

Kuokkanen, Martti
65Finnish Hellas-57
71Finnish Suomi Stickers-283
73Finnish Jaakiekko-200

Kuoppala, Ismo
94Finnish SISU-354
95Finnish SISU-87
96Finnish SISU Redline-52
98Finnish Keralysarja-166
99Finnish Cardset-82
00Finnish Cardset-187
04Finnish Cardset-51
Parallel-38
06Finnish Cardset-185

Kuosmanen, Pentti
70Finnish Jaakiekko-349

Kupaks, Arturs
94Greensboro Monarchs-13
96Toledo Storm-18
98ECHL All-Star Northern Conference-12
00Idaho Steelheads-10
01New Mexico Scorpions-15
02New Mexico Scorpions-7
03New Mexico Scorpions-12
04Austin Ice Bats-19

Kupari, Marko
93Finnish SISU-155

Kuparinen, Matti
04Finnish Cardset-316
05Finnish Cardset -169
06Finnish Cardset-177
06Finnish Porin Assat Pelaajakortit-20

Kuparinen, Mikko
98Finnish Keralysarja-60
99Finnish Cardset Par Avion-6
00Johnstown Chiefs-17
02Finnish Cardset-50
03Swedish Elite-146
Silver-146
04Swedish Elitset-147
Gold-147
05Swedish SHL Elitset-3
Gold-3
06Finnish Cardset-237

Kupka, Tomas
94Czech APS Extraliga-266
95Czech APS Extraliga-143
96Czech APS Extraliga-18
97Czech APS Extraliga-165
97Czech DS Stickers-128
98Czech DS Stickers-202
98Czech OFS-172
99Czech DS-165
99Czech OFS-168
00UK Sekonda Superleague-119

Kupreenkov, Alexei
99Russian Hockey League-210

Kups, Derek
99Fort Worth Brahmas-9
01Bossier-Shreveport Mudbugs-8

Kurashov, Konstantin
90O-Pee-Chee-469
91O-Pee-Chee Inserts-52R

Kurawski, Mark
89ProCards IHL-52

Kurceba, Paul
03Red Deer Rebels-3
05Kootenay Ice-11

Kurina, Tomas
93Quebec Pee-Wee Tournament-1545

Kuriplach, Kamil
99Columbus Cottonmouths-2
01Asheville Smoke-11
03Wheeling Nailers-88

Kuris, Marcel
97Peoria Rivermen-20
98Bakersfield Condors-11

Kurjenniemi, Janne
95Finnish SISU-66

Kurk, Kevin
05Fort Wayne Komets Choice-16

Kurka, Tomas
02BAP Memorabilia-368
02BAP Ultimate Memorabilia-98
02Pacific Complete-548
Red-548
02SP Authentic-219
02Upper Deck Rookie Update-130
02Lowell Lock Monsters-13
03ITG Action-104
03O-Pee-Chee-324
03OPC Blue-324
03OPC Gold-324
03OPC Red-324
03Topps-324
Blue-324
Gold-324
Red-324
03Lowell Lock Monsters-23
03Lowell Lock Monsters Photo Album-7
04Czech OFS-99
Stars-5
05Finnish Cardset -263
06Finnish Cardset-234
06Finnish Ilves Team Set-12

Kurkinen, Risto
90Swedish Semic Elitserien Stickers-111
91Finnish Semic World Champ Stickers-16
91Swedish Semic Elitserien Stickers-116
91Swedish Semic World Champ Stickers-16
92Finnish Jyvas-Hyva Stickers-85
93Finnish Jyvas-Hyva Stickers-139
93Finnish SISU-158
94Finnish SISU-325
94Finnish SISU Fire On Ice-15
95Finnish SISU Limited-51

Kurmann, Danny
95Swiss HNL-NNO

Kurochkin, Nikolai
98Russian Hockey League-95
00Russian Hockey League-187

Kurochkin, Vyacheslav
99Russian Hockey League-228
99Russian Stars Postcards-12

Kuronen, Juho
05Finnish Cardset -256

Kurowski, Marek
94German First League-324

Kurri, Jari
77Finnish Sportscasters-77-1848
78Finnish SM-Liiga-76
80Pepsi-Cola Caps-29
81Oilers Red Rooster-17
81O-Pee-Chee-107
81O-Pee-Chee Stickers-11
81O-Pee-Chee Stickers-211
81Topps-18
82Oilers Red Rooster-17
82O-Pee-Chee-111
82O-Pee-Chee Stickers-108
82O-Pee-Chee Stickers-109
82Post Cereal-6
82Topps Stickers-108
82Topps Stickers-109
83NHL Key Tags-40
83Oilers McDonald's-5
83O-Pee-Chee-34
83O-Pee-Chee Stickers-104
83Puffy Stickers-5
83Topps Stickers-104
83Vachon-31
84Kellogg's Accordion Discs-1
84Kellogg's Accordion Discs Singles-20
84Oilers Red Rooster-17
84Oilers Team Issue-13
84O-Pee-Chee-215
84O-Pee-Chee-249
84O-Pee-Chee Stickers-249
84O-Pee-Chee Stickers-250
847-Eleven Discs-19
84Topps-52
84Topps-161
85Oilers Red Rooster-17
85O-Pee-Chee-155
85O-Pee-Chee-261
85O-Pee-Chee Stickers-121
85O-Pee-Chee Stickers-201
85O-Pee-Chee Stickers-231
857-Eleven Credit Cards-6
85Topps-155
85Topps Sticker Inserts-3
86Kraft Drawings-29
86Oilers Red Rooster-17
86Oilers Team Issue-17
86O-Pee-Chee-108
86O-Pee-Chee-258
86O-Pee-Chee Box Bottoms-H
86O-Pee-Chee Stickers-73
86O-Pee-Chee Stickers-118
86O-Pee-Chee Stickers-185
86Topps-108
86Topps Box Bottoms-H
86Topps Sticker Inserts-10
87Oilers Team Issue-17
87O-Pee-Chee-148
87O-Pee-Chee Minis-21
87O-Pee-Chee Stickers-82
87O-Pee-Chee Stickers-117
87Panini Stickers-262
87Topps-148
87Topps Sticker Inserts-4
88Esso All-Stars-22
88Oilers Tenth Anniversary-41
88Oilers Team Issue-14
88O-Pee-Chee-147
88O-Pee-Chee Stickers-227
88Panini Stickers-59
88Topps-147
89Kraft-13
89Kraft All-Stars Stickers-5
89Oilers Team Issue-12
89O-Pee-Chee-43
89O-Pee-Chee Box Bottoms-I
89O-Pee-Chee Stickers-221
89Panini Stickers-73
89Panini Stickers-181
89Topps-43
89Topps Box Bottoms-I
89Finnish Pelimiehen-2
90Bowman-191
Tiffany-191
90Bowman Hat Tricks-19
Tiffany-19
90Kraft-68
90O-Pee-Chee-5
90O-Pee-Chee-108
90Panini Stickers-222
90Pro Set-87A
90Pro Set-87B
90Pro Set-348A
90Pro Set-348B
90Score-158
90Score-348
Canadian-158
Canadian-348
90Topps-5
90Topps-108
Tiffany-5
Tiffany-108
90Upper Deck-146
French-146
91Pro Set Platinum-48
91Kraft-67
91O-Pee-Chee-295
91OPC Premier-111
91Parkhurst-72
91Parkhurst-210
91Parkhurst-223
French-72
French-210
French-223
91Pinnacle-48
French-48
91Pro Set-93
French-93
91Score Canadian Bilingual-600
91Score Canadian English-600
91Score Rookie/Traded-50T
91Topps-295
91Upper Deck-24
91Upper Deck-366
French-24
French-366
91Finnish Semic World Champ Stickers-18
91Swedish Semic World Champ Stickers-18
92Bowman-94
92Jofa/Koho-2
92O-Pee-Chee-205
92Panini Stickers-66
92Panini Stickers French-66
92Parkhurst-67
92Parkhurst-445
Emerald Ice-67
Emerald Ice-445
92Pinnacle-60
French-60
92Pro Set-68
92Score-398
Canadian-398
92Stadium Club Members Only-46
92Stadium Club-138
92Topps-51
Gold-51G
92Ultra-85
Imports-11
92Upper Deck-218
World Junior Grads-WG4
92Finnish Semic-17
93Donruss-151
93Leaf-240
93McDonald's Upper Deck-8
93OPC Premier-206
Gold-206
93Panini Stickers-202
93Parkhurst-365
Emerald Ice-365
93Pinnacle-75
Canadian-75
All-Stars-35
All-Stars Canadian-35
93PowerPlay-118
Global Greats-4
93Score-100
93Score-446
Canadian-100
Canadian-446
Dynamic Duos U.S.-7
International Stars-7
International Stars Canadian-7
93Stadium Club-400
Members Only Master Set-400
First Day Issue-400
All-Stars-12
All-Stars Members Only-12
All-Stars OPC-12
Master Photos-14
Master Photos Winners-14
93Topps/OPC Premier-206
Gold-206
93Ultra-165
93Upper Deck-332
93Upper Deck Locker All-Stars-29
93Swedish Semic World Champ Stickers-67
93Classic-121
94Be A Player-R25
99 All-Stars-G16
94Canada Games NHL POGS-127
94Donruss-93
94Finest-81
Super Team Winners-81
Refractors-81
Ring Leaders-3
94Flair-81
94Fleer-96
94Hockey Wit-89
94Leaf-104
94Leaf Limited-105
94OPC Premier-25
Special Effects-25

94Parkhurst-104
Gold-104
SE Euro-Stars-ES9
SE Vintage-24
94Pinnacle-35
Artist's Proofs-35
Rink Collection-35
World Edition-WE7
94Post Box Backs-14
94Score-114
Gold-114
Platinum-114
94Select-71
Gold-71
94SP-57
Die Cuts-57
94Topps/OPC Premier-25
Special Effects-25
94Ultra-100
Global Greats-5
94Upper Deck-293
94Upper Deck-559
Electric Ice-293
Electric Ice-559
SP Inserts-SP37
SP Inserts Die Cuts-SP37
94Finnish SISU-207
94Finnish SISU Guest Specials-2
94Finnish Jaa Kiekko-24
94Finnish Jaa Kiekko-346
95Be A Player-201
Signatures-S201
Signatures Die Cuts-S201
95Canada Games NHL POGS-134
95Collector's Choice-16
Player's Club-16
Player's Club Platinum-16
95Donruss-133
95Emotion-83
95Hoyle Western Playing Cards-41
95Leaf-122
95Panini Stickers-270
95Parkhurst International-102
95Parkhurst International-239
Emerald Ice-102
Emerald Ice-239
95Pinnacle-22
Artist's Proofs-22
Rink Collection-22
Global Gold-4
95Playoff One on One-271
95Pro Magnets-68
95Score-115
Black Ice Artist's Proofs-115
Black Ice-115
95Select Certified-35
Mirror Gold-35
95SkyBox Impact-81
95Stadium Club-151
Members Only Master Set-151
95Summit-32
Artist's Proofs-32
Ice-32
95Topps-239
OPC Inserts-239
95Ultra-251
95Upper Deck-372
Electric Ice-372
Electric Ice Gold-372
Special Edition-SE41
Special Edition Gold-SE41
95Zenith-50
95Finnish Jaa Kiekko Lehti Ad Cards-2
95Finnish SISU Limited-16
Signed and Sealed-7
95Finnish SISU Specials-4
95Finnish Semic World Championships-17
95Finnish Semic World Championships-204
95Swedish Globe World Championships-137
95Swedish World Championships Stickers-293
96Headliners Hockey-8
96Collector's Choice-173
96Donruss Canadian Ice-49
Gold Press Proofs-49
Red Press Proofs-49
96Donruss Elite-85
Die Cut Stars-85
96Ducks Team Issue-23
96Metal Universe-3
96NHL Pro Stamps-68
96Playoff One on One-412
96Select Certified-86
Artist's Proofs-86
Blue-86
Mirror Blue-86
Mirror Gold-86
Mirror Red-86
Red-86
96SP-3
96Summit-47
Artist's Proofs-47
Ice-47
Metal-47
Premium Stock-47
96Topps Picks 500 Club-FC3
96Ultra-3
Gold Medallion-3
96Upper Deck-212
Generation Next-X24
96Swedish Semic Wien-24
Nordic Stars-NS4
97Headliners Hockey-12
97Be A Player-7
Autographs-7
Autographs Die-Cuts-7
Autographs Prismatic Die-Cuts-7
97Collector's Choice-10
97Crown Royale-35
Emerald Green-35
Ice Blue-35
Silver-35
97Pacific Slap Shots Die-Cuts-1B
97Pacific Omega-59
Copper-59
Dark Gray-59
Emerald Green-59
Gold-59
Ice Blue-59
97Panini Stickers-189
97Paramount-51
Copper-51
Dark Grey-51
Emerald Green-51
Ice Blue-51
Red-51
Silver-51
97Pinnacle Inside-113
97Revolution-34
Copper-34
Emerald-34
Ice Blue-34
Silver-34
97Score Avalanche-5
Platinum-5
Premier-5
97SP Authentic-42
98McDonalds Upper Deck Gretzkys Teammates-T9
98Pacific-162
Ice Blue-162
Red-162
98Upper Deck Frozen In Time-FT8
98Upper Deck Frozen In Time Quantum 1-FT8
98Upper Deck Frozen In Time Quantum 2-FT8
98Upper Deck Frozen In Time Quantum 3-FT8
98Finnish Kerailysarja Dream Team-1
98Slovakian Eurotel-9
99Upper Deck Century Legends-48
Century Collection-48
99Upper Deck Retro-108
Gold-108
Platinum-108
Generation-G8A
Generation Level 2-G8A
99Finnish Cardset Aces High-J1
99Finnish Valio World Championships-2
99Russian Fetisov Tribute-26
00Upper Deck 500 Goal Club-500JK
00Upper Deck 500 Goal Club-500JK
00Upper Deck Legends-50
Legendary Collection Bronze-50
Legendary Collection Gold-50
Legendary Collection Silver-50
Epic Signatures-JK
Legendary Game Jerseys-JJK
01BAP Memorabilia 500 Goal Scorers-GS11
01BAP Signature Series 500 Goal Scorers-12
01BAP Sig Series 500 Goal Scorers Autos-12
01BAP Signature Series Vintage Autographs-VA-29
01BAP Ultimate Mem 500 Goal Scorers-19
01BAP Ultimate Mem 500 Goal Scorers Autos-9
01BAP Ultimate Mem 500 Goal Jerseys/Stick-19
01BAP Ultimate Mem 500 Goal Emblems-19
01BAP Ultimate Mem Playoff Records-7
01BAP Ultimate Mem Playoff Records-8
01BAP Ultimate Memorabilia Retro Trophies-7
01BAP Ultimate Mem Retro Teammates-13
01BAP Ultimate Mem Scoring Leaders-5
01BAP Ultimate Mem Stanley Cup Winners-16
01Fleer Legacy-8
01Fleer Legacy-57
Ultimate-8
Ultimate-57
In the Corners-2
01Greats of the Game-86
Autographs-86
01Parkhurst Autographs-PA32
01Parkhurst 500 Goal Scorers-PGS11
01Parkhurst Sticks-PS66
01SP Authentic Jerseys-NNJK
01UD Stanley Cup Champs-11
01Upper Deck Legends-23
01Upper Deck Legends-97
Sticks-PHJK
01Finnish Cardset-NNO
02BAP Memorabilia Mini Stanley Cups-25
02Parkhurst Vintage Memorabilia-VM6
02UD Foundations 1000 Point Club-KU
02UD Foundations 1000 Point Club-KU2
02UD Foundations Signs of Greatness-SGJK
02UD Piece of History Heroes Jerseys-HHJK
02UD Piece of History Mark of Distinction-JK
02Finnish Cardset-51
03BAP Ultimate Memorabilia Heroes-15
03BAP Ultimate Mem Hometown Heroes-17
03BAP Ultimate Mem Hometown Heroes Gold-17
03SP Authentic Sign of the Times-JK
03SP Authentic Sign of the Times-GK
03SP Authentic Sign of the Times-GKF
03Upper Deck Trilogy-129
Authentic Patches-AP30
Crest Variations-129
Limited-129
Scripts-S3JK
Scripts Limited-S3JK
Scripts Red-S3JK
04ITG Franchises Canadian-27
Autographs-JK
Complete Jerseys-CJ10
Complete Jerseys Gold-CJ10
Double Memorabilia-DM18
Double Memorabilia Autographs-DM18
Double Memorabilia Gold-DM18
Forever Rivals-FR6
Forever Rivals Gold-FR6
Memorabilia-SM24
Memorabilia Autographs-SM24
Memorabilia Gold-SM24
Original Sticks-OS15
Original Sticks Gold-OS15
Teammates-TM2
Teammates Gold-TM2
04ITG Franchises He Shoots/Scores Prizes-3
04ITG Franchises Update-451
04ITG Franchises US West-240
Complete Jerseys-WCJ2
Complete Jerseys Gold-WCJ2
Double Memorabilia-WDM9
Double Memorabilia Gold-WDM9
Memorabilia-WSM13
Memorabilia Gold-WSM13
Original Sticks-WOS5
Original Sticks Gold-WOS5
04ITG Ultimate Memorabilia-140
04ITG Ultimate Memorabilia-142
Gold-140
Gold-142
Complete Logo-13
Country of Origin-5
Country of Origin Gold-5
Day In History-21
Day In History Gold-21
Jersey Autographs-10
Jersey Autographs Gold-10
Raised to the Rafters-10
Retro Teammates-8
Stick Autographs-32
Stick Autographs Gold-32
Triple Threads-9
04MasterCard Priceless Moments-4
04SP Authentic Buybacks-70
04SP Authentic Rookie Review-RR-JK
04SP Authentic Sign of the Times-ST-KU
04SP Authentic Sign of the Times-TS-GKF
04SP Authentic Sign of the Times-SS-AWS
04SP Authentic Sign of the Times-SS-FIN
04SP Authentic Sign of the Times-SS-RLW
04UD All-World-16
04UD All-World-110B
Gold-16
Autographs-16
Autographs-108
Dual Autographs-AD-KK
Dual Autographs-AD-KL
Triple Autographs-AT-KHK
Triple Autographs-AT-KSN
Quad Autographs-AQ-ALS
Five Autographs-AF-AST
04UD Legendary Signatures-46
Autographs-JK
Linemates-GAWGJK
04UD Legends Classics-30
04UD Legends Classics-67
Gold-30
Gold-67
Platinum-30
Platinum-67
Silver-30
Silver-67
Signature Moments-M26
Signature Moments-M56
Signatures-CS26
Signatures-TC11
Signatures-QC2
04Ultimate Collection Buybacks-20
04Ultimate Collection Jerseys-UGJ-JK
04Ultimate Collection Jerseys Gold-UGJ-JK
04Ultimate Collection Jersey Autographs-UGJA-JK
04Ultimate Collection Patch Autographs-UPA-JK
04Ultimate Collection Patch Autographs-UPA-WGJK
04Ultimate Collection Signatures-US-JK
04Ultimate Collection Signature Logos-ULA-JK
04Ultimate Collection Signature Patches-SP-JK
04Upper Deck Heritage Classic-CC-JK
05Beehive-229
05ITG Ultimate Memorabilia Level 1-53
05ITG Ultimate Memorabilia Level 2-53
05ITG Ultimate Memorabilia Level 3-53
05ITG Ultimate Memorabilia Level 4-53
05ITG Ultimate Memorabilia Level 5-53
05ITG Ultimate Mem Cornerstones Jerseys-7
05ITG Ultimate Mem Cornerst Jerseys Gold-7
05ITG Ultimate Mem Jersey and Emblem-1
05ITG Ultimate Mem Jersey Emblems Gold-1
05ITG Ultimate Memorabilia Jerseys-19
05ITG Ultimate Memorabilia Jerseys Gold-19
05ITG Ultimate Mem Record Breaker Jerseys-9
05ITG Ultimate Mem RecBreak Jerseys Gold-9
05ITG Ultimate Mem Retro Teammate Jerseys-6
05ITG Ult Mem Retro Teammates Jersey Gold-6
05ITG Ultimate Mem Sticks and Jerseys-13
05ITG Ultimate Mem Stick and Jerseys Gold-13
05ITG Ultimate Mem 3 Star of the Game Jsy-17
05ITG Ult Mem 3 Star of the Game Jsy Gold-17
05SP Authentic Exquisite Endorsements-EEJK
05SP Authentic Prestigious Pairings-PPFK
05SP Game Used Authentic Fabrics Dual-GK
05SP Game Used Authentic Fabrics Quad-GMCF
05SP Game Used Authentic Fabrics Triple-KSK
05SP Game Used Authentic Patches Dual-GK
05SP Game Used Authentic Patches Triple-KGM
05SP Game Used Authentic Patches Triple-KSK
05SP Game Used Auto Draft-AD-JK
05SP Game Used Game Gear Autographs-AG-JK
05SP Game Used Significant Numbers-SN-JK
05SPx-106
Spectrum-106
Winning Combos-WC-BK
Winning Combos Gold-WC-BK
Winning Combos Spectrum-WC-BK
Xcitement Legends-XL-JK
Xcitement Legends Gold-XL-JK
Xcitement Legends Spectrum-XL-JK
05The Cup Property of-POJK
05UD Artifacts-126
Blue-126
Gold-126
Green-126
Pewter-126
Red-126
Auto Facts-AF-JK
Auto Facts Blue-AF-JK
Auto Facts Copper-AF-JK
Auto Facts Pewter-AF-JK
Auto Facts Silver-AF-JK
Frozen Artifacts-FA-JK
Frozen Artifacts Autographed-FA-JK
Frozen Artifacts Copper-FA-JK
Frozen Artifacts Dual-FAD-JK
Frozen Artifacts Dual Autographed-FAD-JK
Frozen Artifacts Dual Copper-FAD-JK
Frozen Artifacts Dual Gold-FAD-JK
Frozen Artifacts Dual Maroon-FAD-JK
Frozen Artifacts Dual Pewter-FAD-JK
Frozen Artifacts Dual Silver-FAD-JK
Frozen Artifacts Gold-FA-JK
Frozen Artifacts Maroon-FA-JK
Frozen Artifacts Patches-FP-JK
Frozen Artifacts Patches Autographed-FP-JK
Frozen Artifacts Patches Dual-FPD-JK
Frozen Artifacts Patches Dual Autos-FPD-JK
Frozen Artifacts Patches Pewter-FP-JK
Frozen Artifacts Patches Silver-FP-JK
Frozen Artifacts Pewter-FA-JK
Frozen Artifacts Silver-FA-JK
Gold Autographed-126
Remarkable Artifacts-RA-JK
Remarkable Artifacts Dual-RA-JK
05Upper Deck All-Time Greatest-24
05Upper Deck Big Playmakers-B-JK
05Upper Deck NHL Generations-DKS
05Upper Deck Notable Numbers-N-JK
05Upper Deck Patches-P-JK
05Upper Deck Ice Signature Swatches-SSJK
05Upper Deck Trilogy-160
Crystal-160
Legendary Scripts-LEG-JK
06ITG International Ice-32
06ITG International Ice-58
06ITG International Ice-81
Gold-32
Gold-58
Gold-81
Autographs-AJK
Autographs-AJK2
Autographs-AJK3
Complete Jersey-CJ18
Complete Jersey Gold-CJ18
Cornerstones-IC04
Cornerstones Gold-IC04
Emblem Autographs-GUE29
Emblem Autographs Gold-GUE29
Emblems-GUE29
Emblems Gold-GUE29
Hockey Passport-HP07
Hockey Passport Gold-HP07
International Rivals-IR09
International Rivals Gold-IR09
Jersey Autographs-GUJ29
Jersey Autographs Gold-GUJ29
Jerseys-GUJ29
Jerseys Gold-GUJ29
My Country My Team-MC18
My Country My Team Gold-MC18
Numbers-GUN29
Numbers Autographs-GUN29
Numbers Autographs Gold-GUN29
Numbers Gold-GUN29
Stick and Jersey-SJ18
Stick and Jersey Gold-SJ18
06ITG Ultimate Memorabilia-72
Artist Proof-72
Autos-20
Autos Gold-20
Cornerstones-8
Cornerstones Gold-8
Going For Gold-12
Going For Gold Gold-12
Jerseys Autos-28
Jerseys Autos Gold-28
Retro Teammates-16
Retro Teammates Gold-16
Ring Leaders-11
Ring Leaders Gold-11
Road to the Cup-7
Road to the Cup Gold-7
Stick Rack-26
Stick Rack Gold-26
Sticks Autos-6
Sticks Autos Gold-6
06Parkhurst-51
Autographs-51
06SP Authentic Sign of the Times-STJK
06The Cup-35
Autographed Foundations-CQJK
Autographed Foundations Patches-CQJK
Autographed NHL Shields Duals-DASGK
Autographed Patches-35
Black Rainbow-35
Foundations-CQJK
Foundations Patches-CQJK
Enshrinements-EJK
Gold-35
Gold Patches-35
Hardware Heroes Patches-HHJK
Honorable Numbers-HNJK
Jerseys-35
Limited Logos-LLJK
Masterpiece Pressplates-35
Scripted Swatches-SSJK
Scripted Swatches Duals-DSKF
Signature Patches-SPJK
Stanley Cup Signatures-CSJK
Stanley Cup Titlists Patches-TJK
06Ultimate Collection-28
Autographed Jerseys-AJ-JK
Autographed Patches-AJ-JK
Jerseys-UJ-JK
Jerseys Dual-UJ2-KS
Patches-UJ-JK
Patches Dual-UJ2-KS
Signatures-US-JK
Ultimate Achievements-UA-JK
06Upper Deck Sweet Shot-46
Signature Shots/Saves Ice Signings-SSIJK
Signature Shots/Saves Sticks-SSSJK
Signature Sticks-STJK
06ITG Heroes and Prospects Triple Memorabilia-TM01
06ITG Heroes and Prospects Triple Memorabilia Gold-TM01

Kurt, Gary
71O-Pee-Chee-181
72O-Pee-Chee-306
75O-Pee-Chee WHA-126
75Phoenix Roadrunners WHA-13
76O-Pee-Chee WHA-102
76Phoenix Roadrunners WHA-10

Kurtenbach, Orland
44Beehive Group II Photos-40
61Shirriff/Salada Coins-14
61Topps-15
61Union Oil WHL-11
63Topps-20
64Beehive Group III Photos-15
64Beehive Group III Photos-137
64Beehive Group III Photos-172
64Coca-Cola Caps-4
64Topps-18
64Toronto Star-25
65Coca-Cola-105
65Maple Leafs White Border-13
65Topps-20
66Topps-25
66Topps USA Test-25
67Topps-87
68O-Pee-Chee-170
68Shirriff Coins-100
69O-Pee-Chee-188
70Canucks Royal Bank-9
70Colgate Stamps-23
70Dad's Cookies-67
70Esso Power Players-53
70O-Pee-Chee-117
Deckle-45
70Post Shooters-7
70Sargent Promotions Stamps-212
70Topps-117
71Bazooka-13
71Canucks Royal Bank-6
71Letraset Action Replays-7
71O-Pee-Chee-42
O-Pee-Chee/Topps Booklets-20
Posters-12
71Sargent Promotions Stamps-216
71Topps-42
71Toronto Sun-282
72Canucks Royal Bank-9
72O-Pee-Chee-141
72O-Pee-Chee-149
Player Crests-22
72Sargent Promotions Stamps-215
72Topps-46
72Finnish Semic World Championship-209
72Swedish Semic World Championship-209
73Canucks Royal Bank-9
73Mac's Milk-12
73O-Pee-Chee-4
73Topps-157
91Ultimate Original Six-24
French-24
94Parkhurst Tall Boys-7
95Parkhurst '66-67-90
Coins-90

Kurtenbach, Terry
94UK Guildford Flames-3
95UK Guildford Flames-4
95UK Guildford Flames-26
96UK Guildford Flames-4
97UK Guildford Flames-5
04UK Guildford Flames-30

Kurtz, Brett
94Los Angeles Blades RHI-10

Kurtz, Justin
93Brandon Wheat Kings-6
94Parkhurst SE-SE262
Gold-SE262
94Brandon Wheat Kings-10
95Brandon Wheat Kings-12
95Signature Rookies Auto-Phonex-23
95Signature Rook Auto-Phonex Phone Cards-23
95Slapshot Memorial Cup-32
96Brandon Wheat Kings-22
97Las Vegas Thunder-22
97Bowman CHL-111
OPC-111
99Manitoba Moose-13
00Manitoba Moose-14
01BAP Signature Series-205
Autographs-205
Autographs Gold-205
01UD Honor Roll-89
01UD Premier Collection-85
01Manitoba Moose-15
02BAP Sig Series Auto Buybacks 2001-205
02Manitoba Moose-21
03German DEL-188
04German DEL-235
04German Krefeld Penguins Postcards-15

Kurvers, Tom
84Canadiens Postcards-11
85Canadiens Placemats-2
85Canadiens Placemats-7
85Canadiens Postcards-15
85Canadiens Provigo-7
85O-Pee-Chee-219
85O-Pee-Chee Stickers-129
86O-Pee-Chee Stickers-10
86Sabres Blue Shield-18
86Sabres Blue Shield Small-18
88Devils Caretta-15
88O-Pee-Chee-222
89O-Pee-Chee-9
89O-Pee-Chee Stickers-84
89Panini Stickers-252
89Topps-9
90Canucks Mohawk-12
90Maple Leafs Postcards-10
90O-Pee-Chee-11
90Panini Stickers-287
90Pro Set-282
90Score-142
Canadian-142
90Topps-11
Tiffany-11
90Upper Deck-160
French-160
91Bowman-319
91Maple Leafs Panini Team Stickers-11
91OPC Premier-98
91Panini Stickers-43
91Parkhurst-112
French-112
91Pinnacle-7
French-7
91Pro Set-244
91Pro Set-428
French-244
French-428
91Score American-174
91Score Canadian Bilingual-174
91Score Canadian Bilingual-568
91Score Canadian English-174
91Score Canadian English-568
91Score Rookie/Traded-18T
92Bowman-259
92O-Pee-Chee-202
92Pinnacle-324
'French-324
92Score-232
Canadian-232
92Stadium Club-409
92Topps-118
Gold-118G
92Upper Deck-292
93OPC Premier-279
Gold-279
93Parkhurst-392
Emerald Ice-392
93PowerPlay-384
93Stadium Club-279
Members Only Master Set-279
First Day Issue-279
93Topps/OPC Premier-279
Gold-279
93Ultra-368
93Upper Deck-381
94Ducks Carl's Jr.-14
94Fleer-5
94Leaf-449
94Parkhurst SE-SE4
Gold-SE4
94Pinnacle-380
Artist's Proofs-380
Rink Collection-380
94Upper Deck-123
Electric Ice-123
95Stadium Club Members Only-24
04Minnesota-Duluth Bulldogs-28

Kurvinen, Mikko
00Finnish Cardset-135
01Finnish Cardset-18
04Finnish Cardset-212
05Finnish Cardset -14
06Swedish SHL Elitset-253

Kurylowski, Zbysek
93Swiss HNL-306

Kurzawski, Mark
88ProCards IHL-100

Kus, Petr
99Czech Score Blue 2000-84
99Czech Score Red Ice 2000-84
00Czech DS Extraliga-26
00Czech OFS-58

Kush, Nathan
93Quebec Pee-Wee Tournament-763

Kushner, Dale
85Medicine Hat Tigers-12
89ProCards AHL-243
90Flyers Postcards-14
90OPC Premier-54
90ProCards AHL/IHL-28
91Bowman-247
91O-Pee-Chee-415
91Score Canadian Bilingual-512
91Score Canadian English-512
91Stadium Club-349
91Topps-415
91Upper Deck-429
French-429
91ProCards-268
94Saint John Flames-11

Kuskin, Viktor
71Swedish Hockey-30
72Finnish Semic World Championship-4
72Swedish Semic World Championship-4

Kuster, Henry
95Bowman Draft Prospects-P21
95Medicine Hat Tigers-9
95Classic-63
Autographs-12
CHL All-Stars-AS3
96Medicine Hat Tigers-9
96Visions Signings *-73
Autographs-73A
Autographs Silver-73A
97Medicine Hat Tigers-11
99San Antonio Iguanas-8
06Austin Ice Bats-18

Kustra, Damon
89Saskatoon Blades-3

Kuta, Boguslav
94German First League-521

Kutlak, Zdenek
98Czech OFS-416
99Czech OFS-183
00Providence Bruins-5
01BAP Memorabilia-344
Emerald-344
Ruby-344
Sapphire-344
01Parkhurst-305
01SP Game Used-67
01SPx-95
01UD Top Shelf-48
01UD Top Shelf-48B
01Upper Deck-182
Exclusives-182
01Upper Deck Ice-45
01Upper Deck MVP-191
01Upper Deck Victory-363
Gold-363
01Upper Deck Vintage-277
01Providence Bruins-7
02Providence Bruins-6
03Providence Bruins-10
04Czech OFS-45
05Czech HC Ceski Budejovice-10
06Czech CP Cup Postcards-11
06Czech IIHF World Championship Postcards-13
06Czech LG Hockey Games Postcards-10
06Czech OFS-9

Kutny, Vladimir
02Quebec Remparts-6
03Quebec Remparts Memorial Cup-9
03Val d'Or Foreurs-7

Kutyavin, Sergei
00Russian Hockey League-355
01Russian Hockey League-88

Kuukauppi, Urpo
73Finnish Jaakiekko-201

Kuukka, Mikko
03Red Deer Rebels-5
05Finnish Cardset -216
06Finnish Cardset-225
06Finnish Ilves Team Set-13

Kuuluvainen, Timo
05Finnish Cardset -86

Kuusela, Kristian
04Finnish Cardset-315
05Finnish Cardset -167
06Finnish Cardset-174
Signature Sensations-32
06Finnish Porin Assat Pelaajakortit-15

Kuusinen, Pentti
66Finnish Jaakiekkosarja-181

Kuusisaari, Juha
95Finnish SISU-346

Kuusisto, Jarmo
80Finnish Mallasjuoma-114
89Swedish Semic World Champ Stickers-36
91Finnish Jyvas-Hyva Stickers-47
92Finnish Jyvas-Hyva Stickers-128
93Finnish Jyvas-Hyva Stickers-230
93Finnish SISU-186
94Finnish SISU-5
94Finnish SISU Magic Numbers-3
95Finnish SISU-169
95Finnish SISU-182
95Finnish SISU Limited-30
95Finnish SISU Specials-5
98Danish Hockey League-180
98Finnish Kerailysarja 90's Top 12-8
99Danish Hockey League-53
02Finnish Cardset-52

Kuusisto, Matti
01Finnish Cardset-184
05Finnish Cardset -258
06Finnish Cardset-83

Kuusisto, Osmo
70Finnish Jaakiekko-178

Kuusisto, Pekka
65Finnish Hellas-65
66Finnish Jaakiekkosarja-20
70Finnish Jaakiekko-127
71Finnish Suomi Stickers-179
72Finnish Jaakiekko-127
72Finnish Panda Toronto-27
73Finnish Jaakiekko-68
73Finnish Jaakiekko-182

Kuusisto, Riku
92Finnish Jyvas-Hyva Stickers-113
93Finnish SISU-274

Kuusisto, Teemu
04Finnish Cardset-247
05Finnish Cardset -62

Kuusisto, Veikko
66Finnish Jaakiekkosarja-113

Kuvaldin, Alexander
98Russian Hockey League-154
99Russian Dynamo Moscow-17
99Russian Stars of Hockey-19
00Russian Dynamo Moscow-15
01Russian Dynamo Moscow-11
03Russian Hockey League-33
03Russian SL-22

Kuveko, Evgeni
98Russian Hockey League-61
99Russian Stars Postcards-13

Kuwabara, Ryan
897th Inn. Sketch OHL-55
907th Inn. Sketch OHL-85
917th Inn. Sketch OHL-303
92Fredericton Canadiens-15
93Fredericton Canadiens-14

Kuzela, Milan
72Finnish Jaakiekko-13
72Finnish Hellas-96
72Finnish Panda Toronto-86
73Finnish Jaakiekko-54
74Finnish Jenkki-76
74Swedish Stickers-12

Kuzkin, Viktor
69Russian National Team Postcards-4
69Swedish Hockey-6
71Finnish Suomi Stickers-5
72Finnish Jaakiekko-26
72Finnish Hellas-64
72Finnish Panda Toronto-52
73Russian National Team-25
73Swedish Stickers-100
74Russian National Team-8
74Swedish Semic World Champ Stickers-45
91Future Trends Canada '72-41

Kuzmenko, Denis
99Russian Hockey League-192
01Russian Hockey League-21
03Russian Hockey League-227

Kuzmin, Andrei
00Russian Dynamo Moscow-13
00Russian Hockey League-72
00Russian Hockey League-314

Kuzmin, Anton
03Russian Avangard Omsk-24

Kuzmin, Boris
98Russian Hockey League-96
00Russian Hockey League-68

Kuzmin, Oleg
00Russian Hockey League-75
00Knoxville Speed-26

Kuzmin, Valeri
74Swedish Stickers-53

Kuzminsky, Alexander
91Upper Deck-656
French-656
91Upper Deck Czech World Juniors-17
99German DEL-272
00German DEL-106
02German DEL City Press-290

Kuznetsov, Juri
90O-Pee-Chee-489
93Swedish Semic Elitserien-5
94Finnish SISU-316
95Finnish SISU-3
98Finnish Kerailysarja-187
99Finnish Cardset-305
99Russian Hockey League-22
00Finnish Cardset-322
00Russian Hockey League-107
00Russian Hockey League-273
01Finnish Cardset-110
01Russian Hockey League-129
01Russian Hockey League-132
02Finnish Cardset-53
02Russian Hockey League-133
02Russian Hockey League-149
03Russian Hockey League-204
03Russian Hockey League-206

Kuznetsov, Maxim
94Select-157
Gold-157
95Signature Rookies Future Flash-FF7
95Signature Rook Future Flash Sigs-FF7
95Signature Rookies Tetrad SR Force *-F9
99Cincinnati Mighty Ducks-28
00BAP Memorabilia-460
Emerald-460
Ruby-460
Sapphire-460
00Upper Deck NHLPA-PA32
01BAP Memorabilia-115
Emerald-115
Ruby-115
Sapphire-115
01Titanium Draft Day Edition-127
01Upper Deck Victory-369
Gold-369
03Upper Deck MVP-198
Gold Script-198
Silver Script-198
Canadian Exclusives-198
04Russian Back to Russia-12
04Russian Moscow Dynamo-18

Kuznetsov, Viktor
74Swedish Stickers-54

Kuznik, Greg
95Seattle Thunderbirds-13
96Seattle Thunderbirds-22
97Seattle Thunderbirds-19
98Florida Everblades-11
98Bowman CHL-47
Golden Anniversary-47
OPC International-47
98Bowman Chrome CHL-47
Golden Anniversary-47
Golden Anniversary Refractors-47
OPC International-47
OPC International Refractors-47
Refractors-47
99Cincinnati Cyclones-12
99Florida Everblades-3
00SPx-154
00Cincinnati Cyclones-3
02Lowell Lock Monsters-16

Kuzyk, Cam
03Colorado Eagles-10
03Tulsa Oilers-9

Kvalevog, Toby
93Donruss Team USA-11
93Pinnacle-480
Canadian-480
93Upper Deck-555

Kvapil, Marek
04Saginaw Spirit-2
05Springfield Falcons-14
06Springfield Falcons-16

Kvartalnov, Andrei
91O-Pee-Chee Inserts-53R
93Swiss HNL-307
95Swiss HNL-279
95Swiss HNL-526

Kvartalnov, Dmitri
89Russian National Team-16
91ProCards-313
92Bruins Postcards-4
92OPC Premier-6
92Parkhurst-7
92Parkhurst-222
Emerald Ice-7
Emerald Ice-222
92Pinnacle-405
French-405
92Ultra-252
Imports-12
92Upper Deck-455
92Upper Deck-561
92Russian Stars Red Ace-18
92Russian Stars Red Ace-9
92Classic-93
92Classic-120
Gold-93
Gold-120
LPs-LP6
92Classic Four-Sport *-222
Gold-222
BCs-BC10
93Donruss-27
93Leaf-143
93OPC Premier-197
Gold-197
93Panini Stickers-7
93Parkhurst-287
Emerald Ice-287
93Pinnacle-161
Canadian-161
93PowerPlay-20
Second Year Stars-4
93Score-187
Canadian-187
93Topps/OPC Premier-197
Gold-197
93Ultra-82
93Upper Deck-19
93Upper Deck Locker All-Stars-55
93Classic Pro Prospects-32
93Classic Pro Prospects-AU1
BCs-BC17
94EA Sports-195
95Swiss HNL-206
96Swiss HNL-94
96Swiss HNL-583
99German Adler Mannheim Eagles Postcards-9
01Russian Lightnings-6
04Russian Super League All-Stars-30

Kvasha, Oleg
92Quebec Pee-Wee Tournament-1778
98Be A Player-210
Press Release-210
98BAP Gold-210
98BAP Autographs-210
98BAP Autographs Gold-210
98Bowman's Best-126
Refractors-126
Atomic Refractors-126
98Crown Royale-60
Limited Series-60
98Pacific Dynagon Ice-83
Blue-83
Red-83
98Pacific Omega-108
Red-108
Opening Day Issue-108
98Panini Photocards-43
98SP Authentic-98
Power Shift-98
98Topps Gold Label Class 1-25
Black-25
Black One of One-25
One of One-25
Red-25
Red One of One-25
98Topps Gold Label Class 2-25
98Topps Gold Label Class 2 Black-25
98Topps Gold Label Class 2 Black 1 of 1-25
98Topps Gold Label Class 2 One of One-25
98Topps Gold Label Class 2 Red-25
98Topps Gold Label Class 2 Red One of One-25
98Topps Gold Label Class 3-25
98Topps Gold Label Class 3 Black-25
98Topps Gold Label Class 3 Black 1 of 1-25
98Topps Gold Label Class 3 One of One-25
98Topps Gold Label Class 3 Red-25
98Topps Gold Label Class 3 Red One of One-25
98Upper Deck-416
Exclusives-416
Exclusives 1 of 1-416
Generation Next-GN24
Generation Next Quantum 1-GN24
Generation Next Quantum 2-GN24
Generation Next Quantum 3-GN24
Gold Reserve-416
98Upper Deck MVP-92
Gold Script-92
Silver Script-92
Super Script-92
99BAP Memorabilia-11
Gold-11
Silver-11
99BAP Millennium-108
Emerald-108
Ruby-108
Sapphire-108
Signatures-108
Signatures Gold-108
99O-Pee-Chee-200
99O-Pee-Chee Chrome-200
99O-Pee-Chee Chrome Refractors-200
99Pacific-174
Copper-174
Emerald Green-174
Gold-174
Ice Blue-174
Premiere Date-174

Red-174
99Panini Stickers-63
99Paramount-101
Copper-101
Emerald-101
Gold-101
Holographic Emerald-101
Holographic Gold-101
Holographic Silver-101
Ice Blue-101
Premiere Date-101
Red-101
Silver-101
99SPx-70
Radiance-70
Spectrum-70
99Topps Arena Giveaways-FLO-OK
99Topps/OPC-200
99Topps/OPC Chrome-200
Refractors-200
99Upper Deck-231
Exclusives-231
Exclusives 1 of 1-231
99Upper Deck Gold Reserve-231
99Upper Deck MVP-89
Gold Script-89
Silver Script-89
Super Script-89
99Upper Deck Victory-124
99Quebec PeeWee Tournament Coll Souv-12
00BAP Memorabilia-402
Emerald-402
Ruby-402
Sapphire-402
00Pacific-180
Copper-180
Gold-180
Ice Blue-180
Premiere Date-180
00Upper Deck-341
Exclusives Tier 1-341
Exclusives Tier 2-341
00Upper Deck Victory-105
01Upper Deck Victory-228
Gold-228
02BAP Sig Series Auto Buybacks 1998-210
02BAP Sig Series Auto Buybacks 1999-108
02Pacific Complete-326
Red-326
02Topps Total-296
02Upper Deck-357
Exclusives-357
02Upper Deck Beckett UD Promos-357
02Upper Deck Vintage-159
03ITG Action-400
03Pacific Complete-145
Red-145
03Private Stock Reserve-64
Blue-64
Red-64
Retail-64
03Upper Deck-364
Canadian Exclusives-364
HG-364
UD Exclusives-364
04Pacific-168
Blue-168
Red-168
04Upper Deck-108
Canadian Exclusives-108
HG Glossy Gold-108
HG Glossy Silver-108
04Russian Back to Russia-25
05Parkhurst Facsimile Auto Parallel-311

Kverka, Jaromir
94Czech APS Extraliga-89
95Czech APS Extraliga-191
97Czech APS Extraliga-10
98Czech DS-29
98Czech DS Stickers-218
98Czech OFS-88
99Czech DS-23
99Czech OFS-137
00Czech DS Extraliga-127
00Czech OFS-172
01Czech OFS-190
All Stars-19
02Czech OFS Plus-285
03UK Basingstoke Bison-12

Kvetan, Branislav
01Louisiana Ice Gators-11
02Louisiana Ice Gators-10
03Tulsa Oilers-10
04Czech OFS-297
05Roanoke Valley Vipers-9

Kveton, David
05Czech HC Vsetin-9
06Czech OFS-185
06Gatineau Olympiques-26

Kveton, Lukas
03Czech OFS Plus-265
06Czech OFS-10

Kvietok, Martin
93Quebec Pee-Wee Tournament-1710

Kwas, Chris
97Regina Pats-21

Kwasigroch, Piotr
89Swedish Semic World Champ Stickers-148
94German DEL-164
95German DEL-163
96German DEL-237

Kwasniewski, Ken
93RPI Engineers-13

Kwiatkowski, Darren
87Regina Pats-14

Kwiatkowski, Jason
90Prince Albert Raiders-7
907th Inn. Sketch WHL-276
91Prince Albert Raiders-8
917th Inn. Sketch WHL-245
92Tacoma Rockets-11

Kwiatkowski, Joel
97Bowman CHL-84
OPC-84
98Cincinnati Mighty Ducks-14
98Bowman CHL-45
Golden Anniversary-45
OPC International-45
98Bowman Chrome CHL-45
Golden Anniversary-45
Golden Anniversary Refractors-45
OPC International-45
OPC International Refractors-45
Refractors-45
99Cincinnati Mighty Ducks-7

00Grand Rapids Griffins-12
01BAP Memorabilia-429
Emerald-429
Ruby-429
Sapphire-429
01SP Authentic-164
Limited-164
Limited Gold-164
01SPx-145
01SPx-145
Rookie Treasures-RTJK
01UD Top Shelf-60
01UD Top Shelf-60B
01Upper Deck-200
Exclusives-200
01Upper Deck MVP-209
01Upper Deck Victory-382
Gold-382
01Grand Rapids Griffins-21
02NHL Power Play Stickers-120
02Pacific Calder-99
Silver-99
02Pacific Complete-529
Red-529
02Senators Team Issue-20
03Pacific Complete-391
Red-391
04San Antonio Rampage-6

Kwong, Larry
51Laval Dairy QSHL-73
52St. Lawrence Sales-19

Kyha, Tuomo
99Finnish Cardset-146
00Finnish Cardset-106

Kyhos, Vladimir
95Czech APS Extraliga-149
96Czech APS Extraliga-166

Kyle, Doug
83Saskatoon Blades-20

Kyle, Gus
44Beehive Group II Photos-333

Kyle, Scott
75HCA Steel City Vacuum-6

Kyle, Walt
51Parkhurst-21
93Seattle Thunderbirds-11
99Hamilton Bulldogs-4

Kyle, William
51Laval Dairy QSHL-39

Kyllastinen, Hannu
65Finnish Hellas-59

Kyllonen, Marku
91Finnish Jyvas-Hyva Stickers-40
98Danish Hockey League-104
99Danish Hockey League-119

Kyllonen, Pekka
70Finnish Jaakiekko-373

Kyndl, Roman
96Slovakian Quebec Pee-Wee Tournament-16

Kyntola, Jorma
65Finnish Hellas-53

Kyntola, Timo
70Finnish Jaakiekko-179
71Finnish Suomi Stickers-103
72Finnish Jaakiekko-147
73Finnish Jaakiekko-112

Kypreos, Nick
83North Bay Centennials-13
89Capitals Team Issue-12
90Bowman-67
Tiffany-67
90Capitals Kodak-11
90Capitals Postcards-11
90Capitals Smokey-10
90O-Pee-Chee-440
90Pro Set-551
91Bowman-301
91Capitals Junior 5x7-16
91Capitals Kodak-16
91O-Pee-Chee-511
91Panini Stickers-204
91Parkhurst-411
French-411
91Pro Set-513
French-513
91Score Canadian Bilingual-432
91Score Canadian English-432
91Stadium Club-307
91Topps-511
92Parkhurst-297
Emerald Ice-297
92Topps-193
Gold-193G
92Ultra-301
92Upper Deck-447
92Whalers Dairymart-13
93Donruss-140
93Leaf-414
93Pinnacle-83
Canadian-83
93PowerPlay-105
93Score-404
Canadian-404
93Upper Deck-11
94Be A Player-R21
Signature Cards-54
94Leaf-406
94Pinnacle-408
Artist's Proofs-408
Rink Collection-408
94Stadium Club-154
Members Only Master Set-154
First Day Issue-154
Super Team Winner Cards-154
95Upper Deck-493
Electric Ice-493
Electric Ice Gold-493
97Be A Player-128
Autographs-128
Autographs Die-Cuts-128
Autographs Prismatic Die-Cuts-128
02Fleer Throwbacks-50
Gold-50
Platinum-50

Kypreyenkov, Alexei
00Russian Hockey League-140

Kyres, Teddy
00Victoriaville Tigres-4
Signed-4
01Moncton Wildcats-13

Kyro, Roger
92Upper Deck-226
93Swedish Semic Elitserien-12
95Swedish Leaf-173

95Swedish Upper Deck-27
96Swedish Brynas Tigers-18
97Swedish Collector's Choice-26
98Swedish UD Choice-40
99Swedish Upper Deck-24
00Swedish Upper Deck-38
01Swedish Brynas Tigers-10
02Swedish SHL-7
Parallel-7
03Swedish Elite-8
Silver-8
04Swedish Elitset-8
04Swedish Elitset-140
Gold-8
Gold-140

Kyrzakos, Jeff
05Owen Sound Attack-12

Kysela, Daniel
94Czech APS Extraliga-118
96Czech APS Extraliga-195
99Czech OFS-228
01Czech OFS Update-287
01Czech OFS Update-290

Kysela, Robert
94Czech APS Extraliga-220
95Czech APS Extraliga-170
96Czech APS Extraliga-179
97Czech APS Extraliga-88
97Czech DS Extraliga-8
97Czech DS Stickers-44
98Czech DS-48
98Czech DS Stickers-94
98Czech OFS-264
99Czech DS-64
99Czech OFS-151
00Czech DS Extraliga-48
00Czech OFS-151
01Czech OFS-172
03Czech OFS Plus-228
04Czech OFS-330

Kyselev, Andrei
00Russian Hockey League-10

Kyte, Jeremy
02Macon Trax-8
03Greenville Grrrowl-13

Kyte, Jim
82Jets Postcards-10
83Jets Postcards-10
83Vachon-128
84Jets Police-10
85Jets Police-9
86Jets Postcards-11
87Jets Postcards-11
87O-Pee-Chee-226
87Panini Stickers-362
88Jets Police-12
88Jets Postcards-14
88O-Pee-Chee Stickers-145
89O-Pee-Chee-295
89O-Pee-Chee Stickers-140
90ProCards AHL/IHL-374
91Flames IGA-6
91Pinnacle-398
French-398
91Pro Set-612
French-612
91Score Canadian Bilingual-547
91Score Canadian English-547
93Las Vegas Thunder-17
94Las Vegas Thunder-9
94Classic Enforcers-E9
96Kansas City Blades-13
04ITG Franchises Canadian-146
Autographs-JKY

L'Hebreux, Maxime
93Quebec Pee-Wee Tournament-1024

L'Henry, Fabrice
94French National Team-17
98German DEL-138

L'Heureux, Conrad
51Laval Dairy Lac St. Jean-28
52Bas Du Fleuve-59

L'Heureux, Wilf
23V128-1 Paulin's Candy-17

L'Italien, Eric
99Rouyn-Noranda Huskies-11
03Quebec Remparts-18

Laakkio, Seppo
70Finnish Jaakiekko-280
71Finnish Suomi Stickers-153
72Finnish Jaakiekko-105
73Finnish Jaakiekko-202

Laakkonen, Janne
02Finnish Cardset-204
03Finnish Cardset-40
04Finnish Cardset-41
Parallel-30
06Finnish Cardset-204

Laakso, Aki
72Finnish Jaakiekko-331

Laakso, Teemu
06Finnish Cardset-14

Laaksonen, Antti
96Denver University Pioneers-6
97Providence Bruins-8
98Black Diamond Triple Diamond-102
98Pacific Dynagon Ice-12
Blue-12
Red-12
98Upper Deck-223
Exclusives-223
Exclusives 1 of 1-223
Gold Reserve-223
98Providence Bruins-12
99Providence Bruins-14
00BAP Memorabilia-317
Emerald-317
Ruby-317
Sapphire-317
Promos-317
00BAP Mem Chicago Sportsfest Copper-317
00BAP Memorabilia Chicago Sportsfest Blue-317
00BAP Memorabilia Chicago Sportsfest Gold-317
00BAP Memorabilia Chicago Sportsfest Ruby-317
00BAP Memorabilia Chicago Sun-Times Ruby-317
00BAP Memorabilia Chicago Sun-Times Gold-317
00BAP Mem Chicago Sun-Times Sapphire-317
00BAP Mem Toronto Fall Expo Copper-317
00BAP Memorabilia Toronto Fall Expo Gold-317
00BAP Memorabilia Toronto Fall Expo Ruby-317
00Panini Stickers-174
01BAP Signature Series-160
Autographs-160
Autographs Gold-160

01Pacific-198
Extreme LTD-198
Hobby LTD-198
Premiere Date-198
Retail LTD-198
01Pacific Arena Exclusives-198
01Upper Deck Victory-180
Gold-180
01Upper Deck Vintage-128
01Finnish Cardset-169
02BAP Sig Series Auto Buybacks 2001-160
02Pacific-185
Blue-185
Red-185
02Pacific Complete-425
Red-425
02Topps Total-393
02Upper Deck MVP-93
Gold-93
Classics-93
Golden Classics-93
02Finnish Cardset-205
03ITG Action-270
03NHL Sticker Collection-248
03Pacific-167
Blue-167
Red-167
03Pacific Complete-178
Red-178
03Upper Deck-338
Canadian Exclusives-338
HG-338
UD Exclusives-338
04Pacific-134
Blue-134
Red-134
05Parkhurst-127
Facsimile Auto Parallel-127
05Upper Deck-297
05Upper Deck MVP-108
Gold-108
Platinum-108
06O-Pee-Chee-129
Rainbow-129
06Upper Deck-304
Exclusives Parallel-304
High Gloss Parallel-304
Masterpieces-304

Laaksonen, Ilkka
73Finnish Jaakiekko-288

Laaksonen, Mika
94Finnish SISU-137
95Finnish SISU-71
96Finnish SISU Redline-73
98Finnish Keraillysarja-257
99Finnish Cardset-282
00Finnish Cardset-20
01Finnish Cardset-85

Laaksonen, Mikko
95Finnish SISU-347

Laaksonen, Tom
92Finnish Jyvas-Hyva Stickers-117
95Finnish SISU-208
98Finnish Keraillysarja-42
99Finnish Cardset-24

Laamanen, Jukka
95Finnish SISU-263
96Finnish SISU Redline-57
01Finnish Cardset-371
02Finnish Cardset-206

Laamanen, Jukka-Pekka
03Finnish Cardset-48
04Finnish Cardset-221
05Finnish Cardset-204
06Finnish Cardset-274

Laan, John
94Brantford Smoke-15
95Central Hockey League-63

Laapas, Jorma
65Finnish Hellas-3

Laapas, Marru
95Finnish SISU-327
96Finnish SISU Redline-140

Laatikainen, Arto
98Black Diamond-102
Quadruple Diamond-102
98SPx Top Prospects-70
Radiance-70
Spectrum-70
99Finnish Cardset-12
00Finnish Cardset-124
01Finnish Cardset-6
02Finnish Cardset-54
03Finnish Cardset-6
04Finnish Cardset-4
Parallel-4
05Finnish Cardset-3
06Finnish Cardset-3

Labadie, Michel
52Juniors Blue Tint-70
62Quebec Aces-14

Labanski, Greg
95Slapshot-227

Labarbera, Jason
93Quebec Pee-Wee Tournament-1227
97Portland Winter Hawks-21
98Bowman CHL-140
Golden Anniversary-140
OPC International-140
Autographs Blue-A2
Autographs Gold-A2
Autographs Silver-A2
98Bowman Chrome CHL-140
Golden Anniversary-140
Golden Anniversary Refractors-140
OPC International-140
OPC International Refractors-140
Refractors-140
00BAP Memorabilia-453
Emerald-453
Ruby-453
Sapphire-453
00SP Game Used-74
00SPx-165
00Topps Stars-124
Blue-124
00UD Pros and Prospects-115
00UD Reserve-105
00Upper Deck-417
Exclusives Tier 1-417
Exclusives Tier 2-417
00Charlotte Checkers-1
00Hartford Wolf Pack-17
01Between the Pipes-55
01Hartford Wolf Pack-13

02Between the Pipes-86
Gold-86
Silver-86
02UD Mask Collection-56
02UD Mask Collection Beckett Promos-56
02Hartford Wolf Pack-13
03BAP Memorabilia Deep in the Crease-D5
03Pacific Complete-457
Red-457
03Parkhurst Original Six New York-26
03Hartford Wolf Pack-11
03Pacific AHL Prospects-33
Gold-33
04AHL All-Stars-25
04AHL Top Prospects-19
04Hartford Wolf Pack-10
05ITG Heroes/Prosp Toronto Expo Parallel -56
05ITG Ultimate Mem Future Stars Autos-16
05ITG Ultimate Mem Future Star Autos Gold-16
05ITG Ultimate Mem Future Stars Jerseys-17
05ITG Ultimate Mem Future Stars Jerseys Gold-17
05ITG Ultimate Mem Future Stars Mem Autos-16
05ITG Ultimate Mem Fut Star Mem Auto Gold-16
05ITG Ultimate Memorabilia R.O.Y. Autos-10
05ITG Ultimate Mem R.O.Y. Autos Gold-10
05Parkhurst-230
Facsimile Auto Parallel-230
Signatures-JL
05Upper Deck-338
05ITG Heroes and Prospects-56
Autographs-A-JLB
Complete Logos-AHL-9
He Shoots-He Scores Prizes-29
Jerseys-GUJ-20
Jerseys Gold-GUJ-20
Emblems-GUE-20
Emblems Gold-GUE-20
Numbers-GUN-20
Numbers Gold-GUN-20
Measuring Up-MU2
Measuring Up Gold-MU2
Nameplates-N-23
Nameplates Gold-N-23
Net Prospects-NP-10
Net Prospects Dual-NPD2
Net Prospects Dual Gold-NPD2
Net Prospects Gold-NP-10
Shooting Stars-AS-1
06Between The Pipes-19
Autographs-AJLB
Prospect Trios-PT14
Prospect Trios Gold-PT14
Stick and Jersey-SJ17
Stick and Jersey Gold-SJ17
06Ultra Fresh Ink-JL
06Upper Deck Trilogy Scripts-TSJL
06Manchester Monarchs-7

Labarre, Jean-Francois
03Lubbock Cotton Kings-11
06Fort Wayne Komets-11

Labatte, Neil
78Blues Postcards-14

Labayle, Stephane
93Quebec Pee-Wee Tournament-1649

Labbe, Carl
93Quebec Pee-Wee Tournament-261

Labbe, Danny
93Quebec Pee-Wee Tournament-274

Labbe, Jean-Francois
907th Inn. Sketch QMJHL-88
917th Inn. Sketch QMJHL-122
93Thunder Bay Senators-1
98Hartford Wolf Pack-12
99Hartford Wolf Pack-16
00BAP Memorabilia-226
Emerald-226
Ruby-226
Sapphire-226
Promos-226
00BAP Mem Chicago Sportsfest Copper-226
00BAP Memorabilia Chicago Sportsfest Blue-226
00BAP Memorabilia Chicago Sportsfest Gold-226
00BAP Memorabilia Chicago Sportsfest Ruby-226
00BAP Memorabilia Chicago Sun-Times Ruby-226
00BAP Memorabilia Chicago Sun-Times Gold-226
00BAP Mem Chicago Sun-Times Sapphire-226
00BAP Mem Toronto Fall Expo Copper-226
00BAP Memorabilia Toronto Fall Expo Gold-226
00BAP Memorabilia Toronto Fall Expo Ruby-226
00Syracuse Crunch-2
01Between the Pipes-159
01Syracuse Crunch-1
02Between the Pipes-64
Gold-64
Silver-64
02Pacific Complete-404
Red-404
02UD Mask Collection-24
02UD Mask Collection-25
02UD Mask Collection Beckett Promos-24
02UD Mask Collection Beckett Promos-25
03Russian Hockey League-121
03Russian SL-7
03St. Georges de Beauce Garaga-10
04German Augsburg Panthers Postcards-17
05German DEL-269
Goalies-G09
06German DEL-163

Labbe, Kevin
99Medicine Hat Tigers-7

Labelle, Eric
01Austin Ice Bats-6
02Columbia Inferno-103
03Columbia Inferno-105

Labelle, Jonathan
00Hull Olympiques-11
Signed-11
01Hull Olympiques-12
02Cape Breton Screaming Eagles-14

Labelle, Marc
91ProCards-87
92Thunder Bay Thunder Hawks-8
93Cincinnati Cyclones-12
95Cincinnati Cyclones-12
97Cincinnati Cyclones-10
98El Paso Buzzards-18

Labelle, Marc-Andre
06Moncton Wildcats-17

Labelle, Olivier
02Hull Olympiques-12
03Gatineau Olympiques-13
03Hull Olympiques Memorial Cup-8
04Gatineau Olympiques-11
06Syracuse Crunch-25

Labelle, Serge

917th Inn. Sketch QMJHL-20

Labenski, Greg
98Bowman CHL-6
Golden Anniversary-6
OPC International-6
98Bowman Chrome CHL-6
Golden Anniversary-6
Golden Anniversary Refractors-6
OPC International-6
OPC International Refractors-6
Refractors-6
99Bowman CHL-138
Gold-138
OPC International-138
01Louisiana Ice Gators-12
04Cleveland Barons-14
04Kalamazoo Wings-9
05Kalamazoo Wings-17

Labenski, John
93Lakeland Ice Warriors-18

Laberge, Gilles
84Chicoutimi Sagueneens-15

Laberge, Jonathan
05Saint John's Sea Dogs-12
06Saint Johns Sea Dogs-9

Laberge, Steve
93Quebec Pee-Wee Tournament-383

Labine, Leo
44Beehive Group II Photos-41
44Beehive Group II Photos-184
52Parkhurst-81
53Parkhurst-93
54Parkhurst-61
54Topps-19
55Bruins Photos-8
57Bruins Photos-11
57Topps-9
58Bruins Photos-7
58Topps-4
59Topps-7
60Shirriff Coins-117
60Topps-13
61Parkhurst-33
61Shirriff/Salada Coins-64
61Union Oil WHL-3
62Parkhurst-26
91Ultimate Original Six-50
French-50
93Parkhurst Parkie Reprints Case Inserts-10
94Parkhurst Missing Link-4

Labonte, Alexandre
05Saint John's Sea Dogs-4
06Saint Johns Sea Dogs-14

Labonte, Charline
96Quebec Pee-Wee Tournament-1288
99UD Prospects-54
Signatures of Tradition-CL
04Canadian Womens World Championship Team-13
06ITG Going For Gold-1
06ITG Going For Gold Samples-1
06ITG Going For Gold Autographs-AL
06ITG Going For Gold Jerseys-GUJ1

Labonte, Doris
00Rimouski Oceanic-25
Signed-25

Laborte, Benoit
95Finnish Semic World Championships-198

Labossiere, Barrett
96OCN Blizzard-10
97OCN Blizzard-9
98OCN Blizzard-9

Labossiere, Gaston
51Laval Dairy Lac St. Jean-51

Labossiere, Gord
44Beehive Group II Photos-334
61Sudbury Wolves-12
62Sudbury Wolves-14
64Beehive Group III Photos-138
65Quebec Aces-11
68O-Pee-Chee-38
68Shirriff Coins-54
68Topps-38
69O-Pee-Chee-109
69Topps-109
70Esso Power Players-152
70O-Pee-Chee-38
70Topps-38
72O-Pee-Chee-303
75Houston Aeros WHA-10
75O-Pee-Chee WHA-89

Labraaten, Dan
70Swedish Hockey-76
71Swedish Hockey-17
71Swedish Hockey-166
72Finnish Semic World Championship-67
72Swedish Stickers-161
72Swedish Semic World Championship-67
73Swedish Stickers-55
74Swedish Stickers-236
74Swedish Semic World Champ Stickers-23
77O-Pee-Chee WHA-57
79O-Pee-Chee-92
79Red Wings Postcards-9
79Topps-92
80O-Pee-Chee-217
80Topps-217
81Flames Postcards-9
81O-Pee-Chee-42
83Swedish Semic Elitserien-142
84Swedish Semic Elitserien-163
85Swedish Panini Stickers-125
85Swedish Panini Stickers-126
85Swedish Panini Stickers-147
86Swedish Panini Stickers-150
87Swedish Panini Stickers-162

Labraaten, Jan
93Swedish Semic Elitserien-317
95Collector's Choice-353
Player's Club-353
Player's Club Platinum-353
95Signature Rookies Auto-Phonex-24
95Signature Rook Auto-Phonex Phone Cards-24
95Signature Rookies Tetrad Autobilia *-44

Labraaten, Leif
71Swedish Hockey-152
72Swedish Stickers-129

Labraaten, Ulf
83Swedish Semic Elitserien-239

Labranche, Emmanuel
93Drummondville Voltigeurs-9
97Flint Generals EBK-19

Labre, Brent
00Mississauga Ice Dogs-15

Labre, Yvon

73O-Pee-Chee-247
74Capitals White Borders-14
74O-Pee-Chee NHL-345
75O-Pee-Chee NHL-61
75Topps-61
76O-Pee-Chee NHL-161
76O-Pee-Chee NHL-396
76Topps-161
77O-Pee-Chee NHL-31
77Topps-31
78O-Pee-Chee-324
79Capitals Team Issue-9
79O-Pee-Chee-343
04ITG Franchises US East-443
Autographs-A-YL

Labrecque, Dave
93Quebec Pee-Wee Tournament-1033

Labrecque, Guillaume
02Hull Olympiques-10
03Gatineau Olympiques-14
03Hull Olympiques Memorial Cup-9
04Gatineau Olympiques-18
05Gatineau Olympiques-3
05Shawinigan Cataractes-21

Labrecque, Patrick
907th Inn. Sketch QMJHL-215
91ProCards-532
94Fredericton Canadiens-15
94Wheeling Thunderbirds-16
95Upper Deck-379
Electric Ice-379
Electric Ice Gold-379
95Fredericton Canadiens-15
96Leaf-224
Press Proofs-224
96Pinnacle-246
Artist's Proofs-246
Foil-246
Premium Stock-246
Rink Collection-246
96Summit-177
Artist's Proofs-177
Ice-177
Premium Stock-177
01Sorel Royaux-10
02Russian Hockey League-269
02Russian Ultimate Line-9

Labrie, Guy
51Laval Dairy QSHL-47
52Bas Du Fleuve-16
52St. Lawrence Sales-74

Labrier, Bob
84Kamloops Blazers-13
85Kamloops Blazers-11

Labrosse, Claude
62Quebec Aces-15

LaBrosse, Dwight
01Guelph Storm-24
01Guelph Storm Memorial Cup-24
02Kingston Frontenacs-10

Labzov, Leonid
98Russian Hockey League-81
99Russian Hockey League-102
02Russian Hockey League-272

Lacasse, Benoit
92Quebec Pee-Wee Tournament-782
93Quebec Pee-Wee Tournament-1043

Lacasse, Loic
03Baie Comeau Drakkar-16
04Baie-Comeau Drakkar-10
05Baie-Comeau Drakkar-20
05Drummondville Voltigeurs-31
06Oshawa Generals-22
06Quebec Remparts-11

Lacasse, Philippe
99Hull Olympiques-16
Signed-16
00Hull Olympiques-15
Signed-15
01Hull Olympiques-16

LaCasse, Rene
63Quebec Aces-17
64Quebec Aces-11

Laceby, Michael
92Quebec Pee-Wee Tournament-351
93Quebec Pee-Wee Tournament-482

Lach, Elmer
34Beehive Group I Photos-162
40O-Pee-Chee V301-2-125
43Parade Sportive *-60
43Parade Sportive *-77
44Beehive Group II Photos-255
45Quaker Oats Photos-86A
45Quaker Oats Photos-86B
45Quaker Oats Photos-86C
45Quaker Oats Photos-86D
48Exhibits Canadian-11
48Exhibits Canadian-60
51Parkhurst-1
52Parkhurst-6
53Parkhurst-30
53Parkhurst-31
83Hall of Fame-129
83Hall of Fame Postcards-I9
85Hall of Fame-129
91Pro Set-337
French-337
93O-Pee-Chee Canadiens Hockey Fest-34
93Parkhurst Parkie Reprints-PR36
94Parkhurst Tall Boys Greats-4
01BAP Memorabilia Rocket's Mates-RM7
01BAP Signature Series Vintage Autographs-VA-15
01Parkhurst Autographs-PA8
01Parkhurst Reprints-PR78
02Parkhurst Reprints-235
03BAP Ultimate Memorabilia Linemates-10
03BAP Ultimate Mem Linemates Autos-2
03BAP Ultimate Mem Vintage Blade of Steel-9
03Parkhurst Original Six Montreal-37
03Parkhurst Original Six Montreal-64
03Parkhurst Original Six Montreal-83
Autographs-7
Inserts-M12
04ITG Franchises Canadian-61
Autographs-EL
04ITG Franchises Update Linemates-ULI2
04ITG Franchises Update Linemates Gold-ULI2
04ITG Ultimate Memorabilia-78
Gold-78
Autographs-57
Autographs Gold-57
Blades of Steel-6
Day In History-13
Day In History-40
Day In History Gold-13

Day In History Gold-40
04ITG Heroes and Prospects-160
Autographs-EL
04ITG Heroes/Prospects Toronto Expo '05-160
04ITG Heroes/Prospects Expo Heroes/Pros-160
05ITG Ultimate Memorabilia Level 1-32
05ITG Ultimate Memorabilia Level 2-32
05ITG Ultimate Memorabilia Level 3-32
05ITG Ultimate Memorabilia Level 4-32
05ITG Ultimate Memorabilia Level 5-32
05ITG Ultimate Mem Blades of Steel-5
05ITG Ultimate Mem Blades of Steel Gold-5
05ITG Ultimate Memorabilia Double Autos-16
05ITG Ultimate Mem Double Autos Gold-16
05ITG Ultimate Mem Record Breaker Jerseys-3
05ITG Ultimate Mem RecBreak Jerseys Gold-3
05ITG Ultimate Memorabilia Ultimate Autos-24
05ITG Ultimate Mem Ultimate Autos Gold-24
06ITG Ultimate Memorabilia Blades of Steel-1
06ITG Ultimate Memorabilia Blades of Steel Gold-1
06ITG Ultimate Memorabilia Retro Teammates-17
06ITG Ultimate Memorabilia Retro Teammates Gold-17
06Parkhurst-52
Autographs-52
Autographs Dual-DABL
06The Cup Hardware Heroes-HHEL
06The Cup Stanley Cup Signatures-CSLE
06The Cup Stanley Cup Titlists-TEL
06ITG Heroes and Prospects-1
Autographs-AEL

Lachaine, Dominic
02Val d'Or Foreurs-21
03Val d'Or Foreurs-3

LaChaine, Martin
97Macon Whoopee-8
97Macon Whoopee Autographs-8

LaChaine, Matthew
05PEI Rocket-23
06PEI Rocket-19

Lachance, Alexandre
92Quebec Pee-Wee Tournament-786
93Quebec Pee-Wee Tournament-1042

Lachance, Bernard
93Quebec Pee-Wee Tournament-950

Lachance, Bob
93Donruss Team USA-12
93Pinnacle-495
Canadian-495
93Upper Deck-564
98Indianapolis Ice-18
02German DEL City Press-96

Lachance, Bryan
00Bakersfield Condors-12

Lachance, Claude
93Quebec Pee-Wee Tournament-279

Lachance, David
93Quebec Pee-Wee Tournament-255

Lachance, Dominic
92Quebec Pee-Wee Tournament-1273
93Quebec Pee-Wee Tournament-1378

Lachance, Gerard
51Bas Du Fleuve-34
52Bas Du Fleuve-15

Lachance, Jean-Vincent
01Chicoutimi Sagueneens-19

Lachance, Jimmy
88Richelieu Riverains-14

Lachance, John
93Quebec Pee-Wee Tournament-143

Lachance, Jonathan
01Baie-Comeau Drakkar-3

Lachance, Kevin
00Quebec Remparts-22
Signed-22
01Quebec Remparts-22
02Quebec Remparts-20
03Quebec Remparts Memorial Cup-10

Lachance, Louis-Phillipe
03Quebec Remparts-14
04P.E.I. Rocket-30
05PEI Rocket-3
06Rimouski Oceanic-18

Lachance, Marcel
77Granby Vics-12

Lachance, Marco
92Quebec Pee-Wee Tournament-1248
93Quebec Pee-Wee Tournament-363

Lachance, Mathieu
92Quebec Pee-Wee Tournament-575
93Quebec Pee-Wee Tournament-400

Lachance, Michel
93Quebec Pee-Wee Tournament-1044

Lachance, Patrice
93Quebec Pee-Wee Tournament-1067

Lachance, Patrick
93Quebec Pee-Wee Tournament-995

Lachance, Scott
91Parkhurst-326
French-326
91Upper Deck-692
French-692
91Upper Deck Czech World Juniors-79
91Arena Draft Picks-3
91Arena Draft Picks French-3
91Arena Draft Picks-32
91Arena Draft Picks French-32
91Arena Draft Picks Autographs-3
91Arena Draft Picks Autographs French-3
91Classic-4
91Star Pics-24
91Ultimate Draft-4
91Ultimate Draft-56
91Ultimate Draft-60
91Ultimate Draft-81
91Ultimate Draft French-4
91Classic Four-Sport *-4
Autographs-4A
92Bowman-438
92O-Pee-Chee-390
92OPC Premier-79
92Panini Stickers-Q
92Panini Stickers French-Q
92Parkhurst-105
Emerald Ice-105
92Pinnacle-223
92Pinnacle-244
French-223
French-244
Team 2000-6
Team 2000 French-6
92Pro Set-234
92Score-449
Canadian-449
Young Superstars-12

92Seasons Patches-52
92Stadium Club-201
92Topps-366
Gold-366G
92Ultra-130
92Upper Deck-360
92Upper Deck-398
92Upper Deck-409
92Upper Deck-571
Ameri/Can Holograms-4
Calder Candidates-CC16
93Donruss-206
93Leaf-139
93OPC Premier-257
Gold-257
93Panini Stickers-63
93Parkhurst-120
Emerald Ice-120
93Pinnacle-62
Canadian-62
Team 2001-21
Team 2001 Canadian-21
93PowerPlay-152
93Score-103
Canadian-103
93Stadium Club-465
Members Only Master Set-465
First Day Issue-465
Master Photos-16
Master Photos Winners-16
93Topps Premier Promo Sheet-257
93Topps/OPC Premier-257
Gold-257
93Ultra-369
93Upper Deck-320
SP-92
94Be A Player-R44
Signature Cards-82
94Donruss-41
94Fleer-124
94Leaf-372
94OPC Premier-66
Special Effects-66
94Parkhurst-140
Gold-140
94Pinnacle-193
Artist's Proofs-193
Rink Collection-193
94Score-195
Gold-195
Platinum-195
94Topps/OPC Premier-66
Special Effects-66
94Ultra-326
94Upper Deck-412
Electric Ice-412
95Donruss-353
95Hoyle Eastern Playing Cards-37
95Leaf-202
95Panini Stickers-97
95Pinnacle-167
Artist's Proofs-167
Rink Collection-167
95Playoff One on One-281
95Score-177
Black Ice Artist's Proofs-177
Black Ice-177
95SkyBox Impact-101
95Ultra-94
Gold Medallion-94
95Upper Deck-390
Electric Ice-390
Electric Ice Gold-390
96Be A Player-27
Autographs-27
Autographs Silver-27
96Flair-55
Blue Ice-55
96Islander Postcards-12
97Donruss-142
Press Proofs Silver-142
Press Proofs Gold-142
97Donruss Limited-166
Exposure-166
97Donruss Preferred-143
Cut to the Chase-143
97Leaf-95
Fractal Matrix-95
Fractal Matrix Die Cuts-95
97Leaf International-95
Universal Ice-95
97Pacific-85
Copper-85
Emerald Green-85
Ice Blue-85
Red-85
Silver-85
97Score-259
98Be A Player-84
Press Release-84
98BAP Gold-84
98BAP Autographs-84
98BAP Autographs Gold-84
98BAP Tampa Bay All Star Game-84
99Panini Stickers-69
99Upper Deck-241
Exclusives-241
Exclusives 1 of 1-241
99Upper Deck Gold Reserve-241
99Upper Deck Victory-152
00Upper Deck NHLPA-PA86
01Canucks Postcards-7
01O-Pee-Chee-254
01O-Pee-Chee Premier Parallel-254
01Topps-254
OPC Parallel-254
02BAP Sig Series Auto Buybacks 1998-84
03ITG Action-164
03NHL Sticker Collection-198
03Pacific Complete-431
Red-431

Lachapelle, Bryan
03Greenville Grrrowl-14

Lachapelle, Eric
03St. Jean Mission-14

Lacher, Blaine
91Lake Superior State Lakers-14
92Lake Superior State Lakers-15
94Finest-95
Super Team Winners-95
Refractors-95
Bowman's Best-R3
Bowman's Best Refractors-R3
94Fleer-13
Rookie Sensations-6
94SP-7
Die Cuts-7
Premier-8
Premier Die-Cuts-8
94Upper Deck-495
94Upper Deck-539
Electric Ice-495
Electric Ice-539
SP Inserts-SP95
SP Inserts Die Cuts-SP95
94Classic-35
Gold-35
ROY Sweepstakes-R13
Tri-Cards-T4
95Canada Games NHL POGS-38
95Collector's Choice-22
Player's Club-22
Player's Club Platinum-22
95Donruss-123
Between The Pipes-1
Rookie Team-5
95Emotion-8
95Kraft-19
95Leaf-3
Studio Rookies-5
95Leaf Limited-41
95Metal-7
95Panini Stickers-13
95Panini Stickers-302
95Parkhurst International-14
Emerald Ice-14
95Pinnacle-147
Artist's Proofs-147
Rink Collection-147
Masks-1
95Playoff One on One-7
95Playoff One on One-119
95Pro Magnets-17
95Score-17
Black Ice Artist's Proofs-17
Black Ice-17
95SkyBox Impact Promo Panel-1
95SkyBox Impact-9
95SkyBox Impact-232
95SkyBox Impact-NNO
95SkyBox Impact-NNO
Deflectors-5
95Stadium Club Members Only-50
95Stadium Club-104
Members Only Master Set-104
95Summit-127
Artist's Proofs-127
Ice-127
95Topps-23
OPC Inserts-23
New To The Game-15NG
95Ultra-10
Gold Medallion-10
All-Rookies-6
All-Rookie Gold Medallion-6
Premier Pad Men-7
Premier Pad Men Gold Medallion-7
95Upper Deck-385
Electric Ice-385
Electric Ice Gold-385
Predictor Hobby-H15
Predictor Hobby Exchange-H15
Special Edition-SE7
Special Edition Gold-SE7
95Zenith-78
95Images-9
Gold-9
Autographs-9A'
Clear Excitement-CE9
95Assets Gold *-6
95Assets Gold Phone Cards $2 *-6
96NHL Pro Stamps-17

Lackey, Carl
70Swedish Masterserien-17
04Green Bay Gamblers-7

Lackey, Jerry
70Swedish Masterserien-182

Lackey, Miroslav
69Swedish Hockey-33
70Finnish Jaakiekko-52
70Swedish Hockey-346
70Swedish Masterserien-142

LAckner, Andrew
06Bloomington PrairieThunder-12

Laco, Marek
95Slovakian-Quebec Pee-Wee Tournament-13

Lacombe, Frank
72Nordiques Postcards-14
73Nordiques Team Issue-15
76Nordiques Postcards-15

Lacombe, Kevin
02Drummondville Voltigeurs-8
03Drummondville Voltigeurs-10

Lacombe, Normand
85Sabres Blue Shield-15
85Sabres Blue Shield Small-15
86Sabres Blue Shield-19
86Sabres Blue Shield Small-19
87Oilers Team Issue-19
88Oilers Tenth Anniversary-81
88Oilers Team Issue-15
89Oilers Team Issue-13
89Panini Stickers-84
90Flyers Postcards-15
90Pro Set-500
90Score Rookie/Traded-99T
91Bowman-248
91O-Pee-Chee-357
91Score Canadian Bilingual-394
91Score Canadian English-394
91Stadium Club-363
91Topps-357

Lacombe, Patrick
917th Inn. Sketch QMJHL-87

LaCosta, Dan
02Owen Sound Attack-24
03Owen Sound Attack-23
04Owen Sound Attack-17
05ITG Heroes/Prosp Toronto Expo Parallel -287
05OHL Bell All-Star Classic-16
05ITG Heroes and Prospects-287
Autographs Series II-DL
Oh Canada-OC-17
Oh Canada Gold-OC-17
06Between The Pipes Prospect Trios-PT08
06Between The Pipes Prospect Trios Gold-PT08
06Syracuse Crunch-21

Lacoste, Yvon
65Quebec Aces-12

Lacour, Robin
93Detroit Jr. Red Wings-5
94Kitchener Rangers Update-32
95Slapshot-36
96Sudbury Wolves-12
96Sudbury Wolves Police-14

Lacoursiere, Joseph
51Laval Dairy Lac St. Jean-16
52Bas Du Fleuve-4

Lacouture, Dan
94Select-154
Gold-154
95Classic-64
99BAP Memorabilia-70
Gold-70
Silver-70
99Hamilton Bulldogs-9
00Private Stock-118
Gold-118
Premiere Date-118
Retail-118
Silver-118
01Upper Deck MVP-214
02Pacific Complete-275
Red-275
03Parkhurst Original Six New York-12
03Rangers Team Issue-10
05Bruins Boston Globe-23
06Devils Team Set-11

LaCouture, Dave
92Maine Black Bears-9
92Maine Black Bears-24

Lacroix, Alphonse
24Anonymous NHL-5
24Anonymous NHL-11

Lacroix, Andre
68O-Pee-Chee-184
68Shirriff Coins-128
69O-Pee-Chee-98
Four-in-One-10
Stamps-18
69Topps-98
70Colgate Stamps-29
70Dad's Cookies-68
70Esso Power Players-204
70Flyers Postcards-7
70O-Pee-Chee-84
70Sargent Promotions Stamps-154
70Topps-84
Topps/OPC Sticker Stamps-18
71O-Pee-Chee-33
71Sargent Promotions Stamps-39
71Topps-33
71Toronto Sun-201
727-Eleven Slurpee Cups WHA-12
73O-Pee-Chee WHA Posters-10
73Quaker Oats WHA-6
74O-Pee-Chee WHA-60
74San Diego Mariners WHA-1
75O-Pee-Chee WHA-10
75O-Pee-Chee WHA-64
76O-Pee-Chee WHA-70
76O-Pee-Chee WHA-80
77O-Pee-Chee WHA-30
79O-Pee-Chee-107
79Topps-107
04ITG Franchises Update Autographs-ALX
04Pacific WHA Autographs-2
06ITG International Ice-106
Gold-106
Autographs-AAL

Lacroix, Daniel
89ProCards IHL-31
90ProCards AHL/IHL-7
91ProCards-194
92Binghamton Rangers-19
92Classic-58
Gold-58
93Leaf-351
94Upper Deck-283
Electric Ice-283
94Classic Enforcers-E2
94Classic Pro Prospects-69
95Binghamton Rangers-12
96Be A Player-135
Autographs-135
Autographs Silver-135
96Flyers Postcards-13
97Pacific Dynagon Best Kept Secrets-70
97Pacific Invincible NHL Regime-143
97Score Flyers-20
Platinum-20
Premier-20
99Chicago Wolves-22
00UK Sekonda Superleague-197
01Atlantic City Boardwalk Bullies-14

Lacroix, Eric
92St. John's Maple Leafs-9
92Classic-58
92Classic-77
Gold-58
Gold-77
93St. John's Maple Leafs-13
94Be A Player Signature Cards-13
94Fleer-97
94Parkhurst-234
Gold-234
94Upper Deck-352
Electric Ice-352
94Classic Pro Prospects-164
95Canada Games NHL POGS-142
95Collector's Choice-276
Player's Club-276
Player's Club Platinum-276
95Parkhurst International-107
Emerald Ice-107
95Pinnacle-82
Artist's Proofs-82
Rink Collection-82
95Topps-32
OPC Inserts-32
95Ultra-252
95Upper Deck-122
Electric Ice-122
Electric Ice Gold-122
96Upper Deck-244
97Pacific-161
Copper-161
Emerald Green-161
Ice Blue-161
Red-161
Silver-161
97Score Avalanche-13
Platinum-13
Premier-13
98Be A Player-38
Press Release-38
98BAP Gold-38
98BAP Autographs-38
98BAP Autographs Gold-38
98BAP Tampa Bay All Star Game-38
98Pacific-163
Ice Blue-163
Red-163
98Upper Deck-71
Exclusives-71
Exclusives 1 of 1-71
Gold Reserve-71
00Stadium Club-109
02BAP Sig Series Auto Buybacks 1998-38

Lacroix, Martin
92Classic-78
Gold-78
92Classic Four-Sport *-200
01Sorel Royaux-11

Lacroix, Maxime
04Quebec Remparts-4
05Quebec Remparts-9
05Quebec Remparts Signature Series-9
06Quebec Remparts-17
06ITG Heroes and Prospects Memorial Cup Champions-MC10

Lacroix, Philip
02Baie Comeau Drakkar-16

Lacroix, Pierre
80Nordiques Postcards-16
80Pepsi-Cola Caps-70
81Nordiques Postcards-10
81O-Pee-Chee-278
82O-Pee-Chee-286
83NHL Key Tags-44
83O-Pee-Chee Stickers-261
83Topps Stickers-261
83Whalers Junior Hartford Courant-10

Lacroix, Renald
51Laval Dairy Subset-116
52St. Lawrence Sales-29

Lacroix, Simon
94Thunder Bay Flyers-13

Lacroix, Sylvain
93Quebec Pee-Wee Tournament-1352

Laczko, Guido
93Swiss HNL-504
95Swiss HNL-332
96Swiss HNL-308

Ladd, Andrew
03Calgary Hitmen-11
04ITG Top Prospects Spring Expo-12
04Calgary Hitmen-9
04ITG Heroes and Prospects-53
Autographs-AL
Top Prospects-12
04ITG Heroes/Prospects Toronto Expo '05-53
04ITG Heroes/Prospects Expo Heroes/Pros-53
05ITG Heroes/Prosp Toronto Expo Parallel -379
05Beehive-156
Matte-156
05Black Diamond-221
05Hot Prospects-226
En Fuego-226
Hot Materials-HMAL
Red Hot-226
White Hot-226
05Parkhurst-615
Facsimile Auto Parallel-615
Signatures-AL
True Colors-TCCAR
True Colors-TCCAR
05SP Authentic-216
Limited-216
05SP Game Used-197
05SPx-224
Spectrum-224
05The Cup-148
Autographed Rookie Patches Gold Rainbow-148
Black Rainbow Rookies-148
Masterpiece Pressplates (Artifacts)-256
Masterpiece Pressplates (Bee Hive)-156
Masterpiece Pressplates (Black Diamond)-221
Masterpiece Pressplates (Ice)-217
Masterpiece Pressplates Rookie Upd Auto-261
Masterpiece Pressplates SPA Autos-216
Masterpiece Pressplates (SP Game Used)-197
Masterpiece Pressplates SPx Autos-224
Masterpiece Pressplates (Trilogy)-233
Masterpiece Pressplates Ult Coll-180
Masterpiece Pressplates Autographs-148
Platinum Rookies-148
05UD Artifacts-256
05UD Rookie Class-23
05Ultimate Collection-180
Gold-180
Ultimate Debut Threads Jerseys-DTJAL
Ultimate Debut Threads Patches-DTPAL
05Upper Deck Ice-217
05Upper Deck Rookie Update-261
05Upper Deck Trilogy-233
05ITG Heroes and Prospects-379
Autographs Series II-AL
Jerseys-GUJ-107
Jerseys Gold-GUJ-107
Emblems-GUE-92
Emblems Gold-GUE-92
Numbers-GUN-92
Numbers Gold-GUN-92
06Be A Player-99
Autographs-99
Signatures-AL
Signatures 25-107
Portraits First Exposures-FEAL
Portraits Signature Portraits-SPAL
06Black Diamond Gemography-GAL
06Black Diamond Jerseys-JLA
06Black Diamond Jerseys Black-JLA
06Black Diamond Jerseys Gold-JLA
06Black Diamond Jerseys Ruby-JLA
06Flair Showcase Inks-IAL
06Fleer-42
Tiffany-42
06Hurricanes Postcards-15
06O-Pee-Chee-92
Rainbow-92
06SP Game Used Letter Marks-LMAL
06SP Game Used SIGnificance-SAL
06UD Toronto Fall Expo Priority Signings -PSAL
06Ultra-36
Gold Medallion-36
Ice Medallion-36
Fresh Ink-IAL
06Upper Deck Arena Giveaways-CAR5
06Upper Deck-288
Exclusives Parallel-288
High Gloss Parallel-288
Game Jerseys-JLA
Game Patches-PLA
Masterpieces-288
06Upper Deck MVP-55
Gold Script-55
Super Script-55
Autographs-OACL
Jerseys-OJHL
Jerseys-OJLF
06Upper Deck Trilogy Ice Scripts-ISAL
06Upper Deck Trilogy Scripts-TSAL
06ITG Heroes and Prospects Quad Emblems-QE09
06ITG Heroes and Prospects Quad Emblems Gold-QE09

Ladobruk, Kyle
99Kamloops Blazers-12
00Kamloops Blazers-13
01Regina Pats-12
02Regina Pats-13

Ladouceur, Denis
02Bakersfield Condors-10
03Bakersfield Condors-24
04UK London Racers-5
04UK London Racers Playoffs-9

Ladouceur, Randy
84O-Pee-Chee-60
85O-Pee-Chee-216
87Whalers Jr. Burger King/Pepsi-11
88Whalers Junior Ground Round-9
89Whalers Junior Milk-13
90O-Pee-Chee-162
90Panini Stickers-41
90Pro Set-108
90Topps-162
Tiffany-162
90Upper Deck-151
French-151
90Whalers Jr. 7-Eleven-18
91Bowman-5
91Parkhurst-289
French-289
91Pinnacle-224
French-224
91Pro Set-396
91Pro Set-573
French-396
French-573
91Score American-436
91Score Canadian Bilingual-407
91Score Canadian English-407
91Whalers Jr. 7-Eleven-20
92Bowman-107
92O-Pee-Chee-299
92Pinnacle-291
French-291
92Score-61
Canadian-61
92Stadium Club-156
92Topps-344
Gold-344G
92Whalers Dairymart-14
93OPC Premier-469
Gold-469
93Pinnacle-389
Canadian-389
93Score-553
Gold-553
Canadian-553
Canadian Gold-553
93Stadium Club-271
Members Only Master Set-271
First Day Issue-271
93Topps/OPC Premier-469
Gold-469
94Canada Games NHL POGS-365
94Ducks Carl's Jr.-15
94EA Sports-2
94Parkhurst SE-SE3
Gold-SE3
94Stadium Club-69
Members Only Master Set-69
First Day Issue-69
Super Team Winner Cards-69
95Be A Player-37
Signatures-S37
Signatures Die Cuts-S37
95Parkhurst International-7
Emerald Ice-7

LaFayette, Justin
91ProCards-493

LaFayette, Nathan
907th Inn. Sketch OHL-25
907th Inn. Sketch OHL-63
91Cornwall Royals-18
917th Inn. Sketch OHL-14
917th Inn. Sketch CHL Award Winners-3
917th Inn. Sketch Memorial Cup-114
91Star Pics-56
91Ultimate Draft-46
91Ultimate Draft French-46
92Upper Deck-588
93Peoria Rivermen-15
93Classic-22
94Canada Games NHL POGS-340
94Canucks Program Inserts-12
94Donruss-156
94Flair-190
94Leaf-216
94OPC Premier-18
94O-Pee-Chee Finest Inserts-22
94OPC Premier Special Effects-18
94Parkhurst-247
Gold-247
SE Vintage-44
94Pinnacle-453
Artist's Proofs-453
Rink Collection-453
94Topps/OPC Premier-18
Special Effects-18
94Ultra-225
94Upper Deck-448
Electric Ice-448
94Classic Pro Prospects-195
95Images-40
Gold-40
99Upper Deck Victory-137
99Lowell Lock Monsters-4

Laferriere, Rick
81Rockies Postcards-10

Laferriere, Sebastien
04Rimouski Oceanic-15
05Rimouski Oceanic-9

Lafferty, Sean
93Quebec Pee-Wee Tournament-805

Laflamme, Brian
93Quebec Pee-Wee Tournament-443

Laflamme, Christian
93Upper Deck Program of Excellence-E6
95Classic-40
95Images-87
Gold-87
95Classic Five-Sport *-145
Autographs-145
97Pacific Omega-52
Copper-52
Dark Gray-52
Emerald Green-52
Gold-52
Ice Blue-52
97Upper Deck-185
98Be A Player-32
Press Release-32
98BAP Gold-32
98BAP Autographs-32
98BAP Autographs Gold-32
98BAP Tampa Bay All Star Game-32
98Blackhawks Chicago Sun-Times-4
98Pacific-148
Ice Blue-148
Red-148
98Upper Deck-64
Exclusives-64
Exclusives 1 of 1-64
Gold Reserve-64
99Ultimate Victory-36
1/1-36
Parallel-36
Parallel 100-36
00Canadiens Postcards-14
00Upper Deck Vintage-194
01Worcester Icecats-23
02BAP Sig Series Auto Buybacks 1998-32
02Blues Team Issue-12
02Worcester IceCats-16
03Blues Team Set-14
04German DEL-193
05German DEL-270

Laflamme, Daniel
907th Inn. Sketch QMJHL-103
917th Inn. Sketch QMJHL-183
03St. Georges de Beauce Garaga-11
04St Georges de Beauce Garaga-13

Laflamme, Dominic
92Quebec Pee-Wee Tournament-671
93Quebec Pee-Wee Tournament-1117

Laflamme, Eric
92Quebec Pee-Wee Tournament-150
93Quebec Pee-Wee Tournament-312

LaFleche, Miguel
99Ohio State Buckeyes-10
00Ohio State Buckeyes-9
01Ohio State Buckeyes-8
02Ohio State Buckeyes-7

Lafleur, Antoine
05PEI Rocket-24
06PEI Rocket-4

LaFleur, Brian
93Minnesota Golden Gophers-15
94Minnesota Golden Gophers-18
95Minnesota Golden Gophers-19
96Minnesota Golden Gophers-17
97Pensacola Ice Pilots-11
98Quad-City Mallards-13
98UHL All-Stars-18
99Quad-City Mallards-19
01Anchorage Aces-6

Lafleur, Guy
70Canadiens Pins-6
71Canadiens Postcards-9
71Colgate Heads-5
71O-Pee-Chee-148
Posters-13
71Toronto Sun-152
72Canadiens Postcards-7
72Canadiens Great West Life Prints-5
72Dimanche/Derniere Heure *-142
72Dimanche/Derniere Heure *-143
72O-Pee-Chee-59
72Topps-79
73Canadiens Postcards-7
73O-Pee-Chee-72
73Topps-72
74Canadiens Postcards-8
74NHL Action Stamps-152
74O-Pee-Chee NHL-232
74Topps-232
75Canadiens Postcards-8
75Heroes Stand-Ups-9
75O-Pee-Chee NHL-126
75O-Pee-Chee NHL-208
75O-Pee-Chee NHL-290
75O-Pee-Chee NHL-322
75Topps-126
75Topps-208
75Topps-290
75Topps-322
76Canadiens Postcards-9
76O-Pee-Chee NHL-1
76O-Pee-Chee NHL-2
76O-Pee-Chee NHL-3
76O-Pee-Chee NHL-5
76O-Pee-Chee NHL-163
76O-Pee-Chee NHL-388
76Topps-1
76Topps-2
76Topps-3
76Topps-5
76Topps-163
76Topps Glossy Inserts-11
77Canadiens Postcards-10
77O-Pee-Chee NHL-1
77O-Pee-Chee NHL-2
77O-Pee-Chee NHL-3
77O-Pee-Chee NHL-7
77O-Pee-Chee NHL-200
77O-Pee-Chee NHL-214
77O-Pee-Chee NHL-216
77O-Pee-Chee NHL-218
77Sportscasters-3807
77Sportscasters-5118
77Topps-1
77Topps-2
77Topps-3
77Topps-7
77Topps-200
77Topps-214
77Topps-216
77Topps-218
77Topps/O-Pee-Chee Glossy-7
Square-7
77Finnish Sportscasters-38-895
77Finnish Sportscasters-57-1356
78Canadiens Postcards-11
78O-Pee-Chee-3
78O-Pee-Chee-63
78O-Pee-Chee-64
78O-Pee-Chee-65
78O-Pee-Chee-69
78O-Pee-Chee-90
78O-Pee-Chee-326
78Topps-3
78Topps-63
78Topps-64
78Topps-65
78Topps-69
78Topps-90
79Canadiens Postcards-10
79O-Pee-Chee-1
79O-Pee-Chee-2
79O-Pee-Chee-3
79O-Pee-Chee-7
79O-Pee-Chee-200
79Topps-1
79Topps-2
79Topps-3
79Topps-7
79Topps-200
80Canadiens Postcards-10
80O-Pee-Chee-10
80O-Pee-Chee-82
80O-Pee-Chee-162
80O-Pee-Chee-163
80O-Pee-Chee-216
80O-Pee-Chee Super-10
80Topps-10
80Topps-82
80Topps-162
80Topps-163
80Topps-216
81Canadiens Postcards-13
81O-Pee-Chee-177
81O-Pee-Chee-195
81O-Pee-Chee Stickers-29
81O-Pee-Chee Stickers-41
81Topps-19
82Canadiens Postcards-11
82Canadiens Steinberg-8
82McDonald's Stickers-8
82Neilson's Gretzky-31
82O-Pee-Chee-186
82O-Pee-Chee-187
82O-Pee-Chee Stickers-28
82O-Pee-Chee Stickers-29
82Post Cereal-10
82Topps Stickers-28
82Topps Stickers-29
83Canadiens Postcards-12
83NHL Key Tags-65
83O-Pee-Chee-183
83O-Pee-Chee-189
83O-Pee-Chee Stickers-2
83O-Pee-Chee Stickers-58
83O-Pee-Chee Stickers-59
83Puffy Stickers-4
83Topps Stickers-2
83Topps Stickers-58
83Topps Stickers-59
83Vachon-47
84Canadiens Postcards-12
84Kellogg's Accordion Discs-3B
84Kellogg's Accordion Discs Singles-21
84O-Pee-Chee-264
84O-Pee-Chee-360
84O-Pee-Chee Stickers-149
84O-Pee-Chee Stickers-150
84Topps-81
88Esso All-Stars-23
89Kraft-31
89Nordiques Team Issue-22
89Nordiques General Foods-18
89Nordiques Police-15
89O-Pee-Chee-189
89O-Pee-Chee Stickers-245
89Topps-189
90Kraft-22
90Nordiques Petro-Canada-14
90O-Pee-Chee-142
90OPC Premier-55
90Panini Stickers-145
90Pro Set-250
90Score-290
Canadian-290
90Score Hottest/Rising Stars-96
90Topps-142
Tiffany-142
90Upper Deck-162
French-162
91Kraft-66
91Nordiques Panini Team Stickers-12
91Nordiques Panini Team Stickers-C
91Nordiques Panini Team Stickers-D
91Nordiques Panini Team Stickers-G
91O-Pee-Chee-1
91O-Pee-Chee-2
91O-Pee-Chee-3
91Pro Set-317
French-317
91Score American-401
91Score American-402
91Score American-403
91Score Canadian Bilingual-291
91Score Canadian Bilingual-292
91Score Canadian Bilingual-293
91Score Canadian English-291
91Score Canadian English-292
91Score Canadian English-293
91Topps-1
91Topps-2
91Topps-3
91Upper Deck-219
91Upper Deck-638
French-219
French-638
93American Licorice Sour Punch Caps-2
93O-Pee-Chee Canadiens Hockey Fest-17
93O-Pee-Chee Canadiens Hockey Fest-57
93Titrex Guy Lafleur Insert-1
94Titrex Guy Lafleur-1
94Titrex Guy Lafleur-2
94Titrex Guy Lafleur-3
94Titrex Guy Lafleur-4
94Titrex Guy Lafleur-5
94Titrex Guy Lafleur-6
94Titrex Guy Lafleur-7
94Titrex Guy Lafleur-8
94Titrex Guy Lafleur-9
94Titrex Guy Lafleur-10
94Titrex Guy Lafleur-11
94Titrex Guy Lafleur-12
94Titrex Guy Lafleur-13
94Titrex Guy Lafleur-14
94Titrex Guy Lafleur-15
94Titrex Guy Lafleur-16
94Titrex Guy Lafleur-17
94Titrex Guy Lafleur-18
94Titrex Guy Lafleur-19
94Titrex Guy Lafleur-20
94Titrex Guy Lafleur-21
94Titrex Guy Lafleur-22
94Titrex Guy Lafleur-23
94Titrex Guy Lafleur-24
96Swedish Semic Wien Hockey Legends-HL2
99BAP Millennium Pearson-P12
99BAP Millennium Pearson Autographs-P12
99Topps Stanley Cup Heroes-SC3
99Topps Stanley Cup Heroes Refractors-SC3
99Topps Stanley Cup Heroes Autographs-SCA3
99Upper Deck 500 Goal Club-500GL
99Upper Deck 500 Goal Club-500GL
99Upper Deck Century Legends-11
Century Collection-11
00UD Heroes-129
Signs of Greatness-GL
00Upper Deck Legends-67
00Upper Deck Legends-73
Legendary Collection Bronze-67
Legendary Collection Bronze-73
Legendary Collection Gold-67
Legendary Collection Gold-73
Legendary Collection Silver-67
Legendary Collection Silver-73
Enshrined Stars-ES7
Epic Signatures-GL
Essence of the Game-EG1
01BAP Memorabilia 500 Goal Scorers-GS15
01BAP Signature Series 500 Goal Scorers-6
01BAP Sig Series 500 Goal Scorers Autos-6
01BAP Signature Series Vintage Autographs-VA-40
01BAP Ultimate Mem All-Star History-28
01BAP Ultimate Memorabilia Autographs-21
01BAP Ultimate Mem Autographs Gold-21
01BAP Ultimate Mem Complete Package-5
01BAP Ultimate Memorabilia Cornerstones-2
01BAP Ultimate Memorabilia Decades-15
01BAP Ultimate Mem Dynasty Jerseys-6
01BAP Ultimate Mem Dynasty Emblems-6
01BAP Ultimate Mem Dynasty Numbers-6
01BAP Ultimate Memorabilia Emblem Attic-9
01BAP Ultimate Mem 500 Goal Scorers-6
01BAP Ultimate Mem 500 Goal Scorers Autos-8
01BAP Ultimate Mem 500 Goal Jerseys/Stick-6
01BAP Ultimate Mem 500 Goal Emblems-6
01BAP Ultimate Memorabilia Gloves Are Off-10
01BAP Ultimate Memorabilia Les Canadiens-15
01BAP Ultimate Mem Retired Numbers-14
01BAP Ultimate Memorabilia Retro Trophies-17
01BAP Ultimate Memorabilia Retro Trophies-20
01BAP Ultimate Mem Retro Teammates-10
01BAP Ultimate Mem Stanley Cup Winners-17
01BAP Update Passing the Torch-PTT4
01Fleer Legacy-3
01Fleer Legacy-13
Ultimate-3
Ultimate-13
In the Corners-3
Memorabilia-4
Memorabilia-15
Memorabilia Autographs-4
01Greats of the Game-8
Retro Collection-5
Autographs-8
Board Certified-2
Jerseys-4
Patches Gold-4
01Parkhurst Autographs-PA28
01Parkhurst 500 Goal Scorers-PGS15
01Parkhurst Heroes-H6
01Parkhurst Sticks-PS64
01Topps Archives-28
Arena Seats-ASGLA
Autographs-11
01UD Stanley Cup Champs-15
Jerseys-T-GL
Pieces of Glory-G-GL
Sticks-S-GL
01Upper Deck Game Jerseys-AGL
01Upper Deck Legends-34
01Upper Deck Legends-95
Epic Signatures-GL
Fiorentino Collection-FCGL
Jerseys-TTFL
Jerseys-TTGL
Jerseys-TTLA
Jerseys-TTLF
Jerseys-TTGU
Jerseys-TTGY
Jerseys-TTSL
Jerseys Platinum-TTFL
Jerseys Platinum-TTGL
Jerseys Platinum-TTGU
Jerseys Platinum-TTGY
Jerseys Platinum-TTLA
Jerseys Platinum-TTLF
Jerseys Platinum-TTSL
Sticks-PHGL
01Upper Deck Vintage Jerseys-SDGL
01Upper Deck Vintage Next In Line-NLLK
01Upper Deck Vintage Sweaters of Honor-SHGL
02BAP Memorabilia-246
Emerald-246
Ruby-246
Sapphire-246
Mini Stanley Cups-16
NHL All-Star Game-246
NHL All-Star Game Blue-246
NHL All-Star Game Green-246
NHL All-Star Game Red-246
02BAP Memorabilia Toronto Fall Expo-246
02BAP NHL All-Star History-28
02BAP Ultimate Mem Complete Package-3
02BAP Ultimate Memorabilia Conn Smythe-9
02BAP Ultimate Memorabilia Emblem Attic-12
02BAP Ultimate Memorabilia Gloves Are Off-5
02BAP Ultimate Memorabilia Numerology-14
02BAP Ultimate Mem Retro Teammates-4
02BAP Ultimate Mem Scoring Leaders-16
02BAP Ultimate Mem Scoring Leaders-17
02BAP Ultimate Mem Scoring Leaders-18
02BAP Ultimate Mem Seams Unbelievable-5
02BAP Ultimate Mem Storied Franchise-11
02BAP Ultimate Mem Vintage Hat Tricks-5

02BAP Ultimate Mem Vintage Jerseys-18
02BAP Ultimate Mem Vintage Jersey Autos-7
02Parkhurst Heroes-NH7
02Parkhurst Vintage Memorabilia-VM9
02Parkhurst Vintage Teammates-VT9
02UD Foundations-51
02UD Foundations-64
02UD Foundations-78
02UD Foundations-115
1000 Point Club-GL
1000 Point Club-LA
1000 Point Club-LA1
1000 Point Club-LA2
1000 Point Club-LA3
1000 Point Club Gold-GL
1000 Point Club Gold-LA
1000 Point Club Silver-GL
1000 Point Club Silver-LA
Canadian Heroes-CGL
Canadian Heroes Gold-CGL
Canadian Heroes Silver-C-GL
Classic Greats-GGL
Classic Greats Gold-GGL
Classic Greats Silver-G-GL
Signs of Greatness-SGGL
02UD Piece of History Historical Swatches-HSGL
02UD Piece of History Mark of Distinction-GL
03BAP Ultimate Memorabilia Autographs-161
Gold-161
03BAP Ultimate Memorabilia Cornerstones-3
03BAP Ultimate Memorabilia Heroes-5
03BAP Ultimate Mem Heroes Autos-2
03BAP Ultimate Memorabilia Linemates-8
03BAP Ultimate Mem Retro-Active Trophies-20
03BAP Ultimate Mem Vint Complete Package-7
03BAP Ultimate Mem Vint Comp Package Gold-7
03Beehive-102
Variations-102
Gold-102
Silver-102
Jumbos-16
Jumbo Variations-16
Sticks Beige Border-BE39
03Canada Post-14
Autographs-14
03ITG Toronto Fall Expo Forever Rivals-FR4
03ITG Used Signature Series-118
Gold-118
Autographs-GL
Autographs Gold-GL
Vintage Memorabilia-14
Vintage Memorabilia Autographs-14
Vintage Memorabilia Gold-14
03ITG VIP MVP-23
03Pacific Exhibit-219
03Pacific Quest for the Cup Eternal Champ-1
03Parkhurst Orig Six He Shoots/Scores-11
03Parkhurst Orig Six He Shoots/Scores-11A
03Parkhurst Original Six Montreal-42
03Parkhurst Original Six Montreal-70
03Parkhurst Original Six Montreal-88
03Parkhurst Original Six Montreal-93
03Parkhurst Original Six Montreal-94
Autographs-8
Inserts-M7
Inserts-M16
Memorabilia-MM18
Memorabilia-MM26
Memorabilia-MM33
Memorabilia-MM39
Memorabilia-MM56
03Parkhurst Original Six New York-48
Autographs-11
03Parkhurst Rookie High Expectations-HE-5
03Parkhurst Rookie High Expectations Gold-HE-5
03SP Authentic Honors-H16
03SP Authentic Honors Limited-H16
03SP Authentic Sign of the Times-GL
03SP Game Used Authentic Fabrics-DFLK
03SP Game Used Authentic Fabrics-DFSG
03SP Game Used Authentic Fabrics-QLGHL
03SP Game Used Authentic Fabrics Gold-DFLK
03SP Game Used Authentic Fabrics Gold-DFSG
03SP Game Used Authentic Fabrics Gold-QLGHL
03SP Game Used Limited Threads-LTGL
03SP Game Used Limited Threads Gold-LTGL
03SP Game Used Premium Patches-PPGL
03SP Game Used Top Threads-LGHL
03SPx-113
Radiance-113
Spectrum-113
03UD Premier Collection Legends-PL-GL
03UD Premier Collection Legends Patches-PL-GL
03UD Premier Collection Signatures-PS-GL
03UD Premier Collection Signatures Gold-PS-GL
03Upper Deck-472
Canadian Exclusives-472
HG-472
UD Exclusives-472
03Upper Deck Trilogy-53
03Upper Deck Trilogy-130
Authentic Patches-AP28
Authentic Patches-AP38
Crest Variations-130
Limited-53
Limited-130
Scripts-S3GL
Scripts-CSGL
Scripts-CSGL2
Scripts Limited-S3GL
Scripts Red-S3GL
03Czech Stadion-611
04ITG NHL AS FANtasy AS History Jerseys-SB28
04ITG Franchises Canadian-48
Autographs-GL
Double Memorabilia-DM10
Double Memorabilia Autographs-DM10
Double Memorabilia Gold-DM10
Forever Rivals-FR4
Forever Rivals Gold-FR4
Memorabilia-SM13
Memorabilia Autographs-SM13
Memorabilia Gold-SM13
Original Sticks-OS3
Original Sticks Autographs-OS3
Original Sticks Gold-OS3
Triple Memorabilia-TM3
Triple Memorabilia Autographs-TM3
Triple Memorabilia Gold-TM3
Trophy Winners-TW1
Trophy Winners Gold-TW1
04ITG Franchises He Shoots/Scores Prizes-9
04ITG Franchises Update-490
Linemates-ULI4
Linemates Gold-ULI4
04ITG Ultimate Memorabilia-44
04ITG Ultimate Memorabilia-171
04ITG Ultimate Memorabilia-183
Gold-44
Gold-171
Gold-183
Art Ross Trophy-8
Complete Package-3
Conn Smythe Trophy-8
Cornerstones-4
Cornerstones Gold-4
Country of Origin-20
Country of Origin Gold-20
Day In History-45
Day In History-48
Day In History Gold-45
Day In History Gold-48
Hart Trophy-5
Jersey Autographs-8
Jersey Autographs Gold-8
Jersey and Sticks-14
Jersey and Sticks Gold-14
Nicknames-29
Nickname Autographs-8
Original Six-1
Retro Teammates-9
Stick Autographs-18
Stick Autographs Gold-18
Triple Threads-12
04SP Authentic Octographs-OS-ART
04SP Authentic Sign of the Times-ST-GL
04SP Authentic Sign of the Times-FS-MON
04SP Authentic Sign of the Times-SS-ALS
04SP Authentic Sign of the Times-SS-ORG
04UD Legendary Signatures-42
AKA Autographs-AKA-GL
Autographs-GL
Linemates-SCPMGL
04UD Legends Classics-29
04UD Legends Classics-75
04UD Legends Classics-87
Gold-29
Gold-75
Gold-87
Platinum-29
Platinum-75
Platinum-87
Silver-29
Silver-75
Silver-87
Jersey Redemptions-JY25
Signature Moments-M29
Signatures-CS29
Signatures-DC2
Signatures-DC13
Signatures-TC14
Signatures-TC15
Signatures-QC2
04Ultimate Collection Buybacks-14
04Ultimate Collection Buybacks-15
04Ultimate Collection Jerseys-UGJ-GL
04Ultimate Collection Jerseys Gold-UGJ-GL
04Ultimate Collection Jersey Autographs-UGJA-GL
04Upper Deck Heritage Classic-CC-LU
04ITG Heroes and Prospects-143
Autographs-GL
04ITG Heroes/Prospects Toronto Expo '05-143
04ITG Heroes/Prospects Expo Heroes/Pros-143
05ITG Heroes/Prosp Toronto Expo Parallel -26
05ITG Heroes/Prosp Toronto Expo Parallel -339
05Beehive-230
Matted Materials-MMGL
Matted Materials Remarkable-RMGL
PhotoGraphs-PGGL
Signature Scrapbook-SSGL
05Black Diamond Jerseys-J-GL
05Black Diamond Jerseys Ruby-J-GL
05Black Diamond Jersey Duals-DJ-GL
05Black Diamond Jersey Triples-TJ-GL
05Black Diamond Jersey Quads-QJ-GL
05ITG Ultimate Memorabilia Level 1-46
05ITG Ultimate Memorabilia Level 2-46
05ITG Ultimate Memorabilia Level 3-46
05ITG Ultimate Memorabilia Level 4-46
05ITG Ultimate Memorabilia Level 5-46
05ITG Ultimate Mem Complete Package-8
05ITG Ultimate Mem Complete Package Gold-8
05ITG Ultimate Mem Cornerstones Jerseys-9
05ITG Ultimate Mem Cornerst Jerseys Gold-9
05ITG Ultimate Mem Decades Jerseys-3
05ITG Ultimate Mem Decades Jerseys Gold-3
05ITG Ultimate Mem Double Mem-5
05ITG Ultimate Mem Double Mem Autos-20
05ITG Ultimate Mem Double Mem Autos Gold-20
05ITG Ultimate Mem Double Mem Gold-5
05ITG Ultimate Mem First Overall Jerseys-2
05ITG Ultimate Mem 1st Overall Jsy Gold-2
05ITG Ultimate Mem First Rounders Jerseys-1
05ITG Ultimate Mem First Rounders Jerseys-4
05ITG Ultimate Mem 1st Round Jersey Gold-1
05ITG Ultimate Mem 1st Round Jersey Gold-4
05ITG Ultimate Mem Jersey and Emblem-2
05ITG Ultimate Memorabilia Jersey Autos-15
05ITG Ultimate Mem Jersey Autos Gold-15
05ITG Ultimate Mem Jersey Emblems Gold-2
05ITG Ultimate Memorabilia Jerseys-16
05ITG Ultimate Memorabilia Jerseys Gold-16
05ITG Ultimate Mem Pass the Torch Jerseys-13
05ITG Ultimate Mem Passing Torch Jsy Gold-13
05ITG Ultimate Mem Record Breaker Jerseys-8
05ITG Ultimate Mem RecBreak Jerseys Gold-8
05ITG Ultimate Mem Retro Teammate Jerseys-13
05ITG Ultimate Mem Retro Teammate Jerseys-16
05ITG Ult Mem Retro Teammates Jersey Gold-13
05ITG Ult Mem Retro Teammates Jersey Gold-16
05ITG Ultimate Memorabilia Sextuple Autos-5
05ITG Ultimate Memorabilia Stick Autos-15
05ITG Ultimate Mem Stick Autos Gold-15
05ITG Ultimate Mem Sticks and Jerseys-11
05ITG Ultimate Mem Stick and Jerseys Gold-11
05ITG Ultimate Mem 3 Star of the Game Jsy-11
05ITG Ult Mem 3 Star of the Game Jsy Gold-11
05ITG Ultimate Memorabilia Triple Autos-8
05ITG Ultimate Mem Triple Autos Gold-8
05ITG Ultimate Mem Triple Threads Jerseys-10
05ITG Ultimate Mem Triple Thread Jsy Gold-10
05ITG Ultimate Memorabilia Ultimate Autos-23
05ITG Ultimate Mem Ultimate Autos Gold-23
05NHL Legends Medallions-7
05SP Authentic Exquisite Endorsements-EELF
05SP Authentic Immortal Inks-IIGL
05SP Authentic Marks of Distinction-MDGL
05SP Authentic Octographs-OH
05SP Authentic Prestigious Pairings-PPGS
05SP Authentic Sign of the Times Fives-LRMMG
05SP Authentic Six Star Signatures-SSHF
05SP Authentic Six Star Signatures-SSMO
05SP Game Used Authentic Fabric Dual Auto-LD
05SP Game Used Authentic Patches Dual-LD
05SP Game Used Authentic Patch Dual Autos-LD
05SP Game Used Auto Draft-AD-GU
05SP Game Used Game Gear-GG-GL
05SP Game Used Game Gear Autographs-AG-GL
05SP Game Used Oldtimer's Challenge-OC-GL
05SP Game Used Oldtimer's Challenge Autos-OCA-GL
05SP Game Used Oldtimer's Challenge Patch-OCP-GL
05SP Game Used Oldtime Chall Patch Autoa-OAP-GL
05SP Game Used Statscriptions-ST-GL
05SPx-105
Spectrum-105
Winning Combos-WC-LK
Winning Combos Autographs-AWC-LK
Winning Combos Gold-WC-LK
Winning Combos Spectrum-WC-LK
Winning Materials-WM-GL
Winning Materials Gold-WM-GL
Winning Materials Spectrum-WM-GL
Xcitement Legends-XL-GL
Xcitement Legends Gold-XL-GL
Xcitement Legends Spectrum-XL-GL
05The Cup-57
Gold-57
Black Rainbow-57
Emblems of Endorsement-EEGL
Hardware Heroes-HHGL1
Hardware Heroes-HHGL2
Hardware Heroes-HHGL3
Honorable Numbers-HNGL
Limited Logos-LLLF
Masterpiece Pressplates-57
Noble Numbers Dual-DNNLB
Patch Variation-P57
Patch Variation Autographs-AP57
Scripted Numbers Dual-DSNLS
Scripted Swatches-SSGL
Signature Patches-SPGL
Stanley Cup Titlists-TGL
05UD Artifacts-127
Blue-127
Gold-127
Green-127
Pewter-127
Red-127
Gold Autographed-127
05Ultimate Collection Endorsed Emblems-EEGL
05Ultimate Coll Ultimate Achievements-UALA
05Ultimate Coll Ultimate Sigs Foursomes-UFGHLH
05Ultimate Coll Ultimate Sigs Trios-UTLBR
05Upper Deck All-Time Greatest-76
05Upper Deck Jerseys-J-GL
05Upper Deck NHL Generations-TLKR
05Upper Deck Patches-P-GL
05Upper Deck Trilogy-163
Crystal-163
Legendary Scripts-LEG-GL
Personal Scripts-PER-GL
Scripts-SSS-GL
05ITG Heroes and Prospects-26
05ITG Heroes and Prospects-339
Aspiring-ASP13
Autographs-A-GLF
Autographs Series II-GLF2
CHL Grads-CG-8
CHL Grads Gold-CG-8
He Shoots-He Scores Prizes-2
Hero Memorabilia-HM-20
Hero Memorabilia Dual-HDM-12
Spectrum-STM-05
Spectrum Gold-STM-05
06Beehive-192
5 X 7 Black and White-192
PhotoGraphs-PGGL
06ITG International Ice-63
06ITG International Ice-121
Gold-63
Gold-121
Autographs-AGL
Autographs-AGL2
International Rivals-IR10
International Rivals Gold-IR10
Stick and Jersey-SJ20
Stick and Jersey Gold-SJ20
Teammates-IT05
Teammates Gold-IT05
06ITG Ultimate Memorabilia-60
Artist Proof-60
Autos-21
Autos Gold-21
Bowman Factor-4
Bowman Factor Gold-4
Bowman Factor Autos-4
Bowman Factor Autos Gold-4
Boys Will Be Boys-3
Boys Will Be Boys Gold-3
Complete Package-14
Complete Package Gold-14
Cornerstones-2
Cornerstones Gold-2
Decades-1
Decades-3
Decades Gold-1
Decades Gold-3
Double Memorabilia-23
Double Memorabilia Gold-23
Double Memorabilia Autos-3
Double Memorabilia Autos Gold-3
First Round Picks-11
First Round Picks Gold-11
Jerseys-20
Jerseys Gold-20
Jerseys Autos-29
Jerseys Autos Gold-29
Passing The Torch-1
Passing The Torch Gold-1
Retro Teammates-12
Retro Teammates Gold-12
Ring Leaders-10
Ring Leaders Gold-10
Road to the Cup-5
Road to the Cup Gold-5
Stick Rack-1
Stick Rack Gold-1
Sticks Autos-5
Sticks Autos Gold-5
Triple Thread Jerseys-2
Triple Thread Jerseys Gold-2
06O-Pee-Chee Swatches-S-GL
06Parkhurst-55
Autographs-55
Autographs Dual-DALL
06SP Authentic Sign of the Times Duals-STLR
06SP Authentic Sign of the Times Duals-STMC
06SP Authentic Sign of the Times Triples-ST3LRS
06SP Authentic Sign of the Times Quads-ST4BLSR
06SP Game Used Authentic Fabrics Eights-AF8HOF
06SP Game Used Authentic Fabrics Eights Patches-AF8HOF
06SP Game Used Inked Sweaters Dual-IS2CL
06SP Game Used Inked Sweaters Dual Patches-IS2CL
06SP Game Used Legendary Fabrics-LFGL
06SP Game Used Legendary Fabrics Autographs-LFGL
06SPx-129
Spectrum-129
SPxcitement-X54
SPxcitement Spectrum-X54
SPxcitement Autographs-X54
06The Cup-46
Autographed Foundations-CQGL
Autographed Foundations Patches-CQGL
Autographed Patches-46
Black Rainbow-46
Foundations-CQGL
Foundations Patches-CQGL
Gold-46
Gold Patches-46
Honorable Numbers-HNLA
Jerseys-46
Limited Logos-LLGL
Masterpiece Pressplates-46
Scripted Swatches-SSGL
Scripted Swatches Duals-DSLR
Signature Patches-SPGL
Stanley Cup Signatures-CSGL
06UD Artifacts-118
Blue-118
Gold-118
Platinum-118
Radiance-118
Autographed Radiance Parallel-118
Red-118
Auto-Facts-AFGL
Auto-Facts Gold-AFGL
Tundra Tandems-TTGP
Tundra Tandems-TTLB
Tundra Tandems-TTLS
Tundra Tandems Black-TTGP
Tundra Tandems Black-TTLB
Tundra Tandems Black-TTLS
Tundra Tandems Blue-TTGP
Tundra Tandems Blue-TTLB
Tundra Tandems Blue-TTLS
Tundra Tandems Gold-TTGP
Tundra Tandems Gold-TTLB
Tundra Tandems Gold-TTLS
Tundra Tandems Platinum-TTGP
Tundra Tandems Platinum-TTLB
Tundra Tandems Platinum-TTLS
Tundra Tandems Red-TTGP
Tundra Tandems Red-TTLB
Tundra Tandems Red-TTLS
Tundra Tandems Dual Patches Red-TTGP
Tundra Tandems Dual Patches Red-TTLB
Tundra Tandems Dual Patches Red-TTLS
06Ultimate Collection Autographed Jerseys-AJ-GL
06Ultimate Collection Autographed Patches-AJ-GL
06Ultimate Collection Jerseys-UJ-GL
06Ultimate Collection Jerseys Triple-UJ3-LRS
06Ultimate Collection Patches-UJ-GL
06Ultimate Collection Patches Triple-UJ3-LRS
06Ultimate Collection Ultimate Achievements-UA-GL
06Upper Deck All-Time Greatest-ATG25
06Upper Deck Sweet Shot-58
Signature Shots/Saves Sticks-SSSLA
Signature Sticks-STGL
Sweet Stitches-SSGL
Sweet Stitches Duals-SSGL
Sweet Stitches Triples-SSGL
06Upper Deck Trilogy Combo Autographed Jerseys-CJCL
06Upper Deck Trilogy Combo Autographed Patches-CJCL
06Upper Deck Trilogy Combo Clearcut Autographs-C3BLS
06Upper Deck Trilogy Frozen In Time-FT7
06Upper Deck Trilogy Honorary Scripted Patches-HSPGL
06Upper Deck Trilogy Honorary Scripted Swatches-HSSGL
06Upper Deck Trilogy Honorary Swatches-HSGL
06Upper Deck Trilogy Ice Scripts-ISGL
06Upper Deck Trilogy Legendary Scripts-LSGL
06Upper Deck Trilogy Scripts-S1GL
06Upper Deck Trilogy Scripts-S2GL
06ITG Heroes and Prospects-13
Autographs-AGLF

Lafleur, Marc

94Thunder Bay Flyers-14

Lafleur, Patrick

92Quebec Pee-Wee Tournament-850
95Halifax Mooseheads-3

Lafleur, Stephen

98Owen Sound Platers-18

Lafoley, Grayson

92Ottawa 67's-14

Lafontaine, Nicolas

05Chicoutimi Sagueneens-28

LaFontaine, Pat

84O-Pee-Chee-129
84O-Pee-Chee-392
84Topps-96
85Islanders News-11
85O-Pee-Chee-137
85O-Pee-Chee Stickers-74
85Topps-137
86Islanders Team Issue-23
86O-Pee-Chee-2
86O-Pee-Chee Stickers-206
86Topps-2
87O-Pee-Chee-173
87O-Pee-Chee Minis-22
87O-Pee-Chee Stickers-243
87Panini Stickers-98
87Topps-173
88Frito-Lay Stickers-14
88O-Pee-Chee-123
88O-Pee-Chee Box Bottoms-C
88O-Pee-Chee Stickers-111
88Panini Stickers-290
88Topps-123
88Topps Box Bottoms-C
89Islanders Team Issue-11
89O-Pee-Chee-60
89O-Pee-Chee Stickers-119
89Panini Stickers-264
89Sports Illustrated for Kids I-96
89Topps-60
89Swedish Semic World Champ Stickers-164
90Bowman-123
Tiffany-123
90Bowman Hat Tricks-9
Tiffany-9
90Kraft-23
90Kraft-86
90O-Pee-Chee-184
90O-Pee-Chee-315
90OPC Premier-56
90Panini Stickers-81
90Pro Set-186
90Pro Set-372
90Score-250
Canadian-250
90Score Hottest/Rising Stars-95
90Topps-184
90Topps-315
Tiffany-184
Team Scoring Leaders-10
Team Scoring Leaders Tiffany-10
90Upper Deck-246
90Upper Deck-306
90Upper Deck-479
French-246
French-306
French-479
91Pro Set Platinum-157
91Bowman-222
91Gillette-23
91Kraft-25
91McDonald's Upper Deck-6
91O-Pee-Chee-80
91OPC Premier-64
91Panini Stickers-243
91Parkhurst-16
French-16
91Pinnacle-25
French-25
91Pro Set-149
91Pro Set-308
91Pro Set-358
French-149
French-308
French-358
Player of the Month-P5
91Sabres Blue Shield-9
91Sabres Pepsi/Campbell's-9
91Score American-260
91Score American-332
91Score Canadian Bilingual-362
91Score Canadian Bilingual-480
91Score Canadian English-362
91Score Canadian English-480
91Score Rookie/Traded-100T
91Score Kellogg's-15
91Stadium Club-123
91Topps-80
Topps/Bowman Preview Sheet-7
Team Scoring Leaders-12
91Upper Deck-253
91Upper Deck-556
French-253
French-556
91Finnish Semic World Champ Stickers-138
91Swedish Semic World Champ Stickers-138
92Bowman-142
92Humpty Dumpty II-11
92O-Pee-Chee-285
92OPC Premier Star Performers-17
92Panini Stickers-246
92Panini Stickers French-246
92Parkhurst-12
Emerald Ice-12
92Pinnacle-7
92Pinnacle-254
French-7
French-254
92Pro Set-13
92Sabres Blue Shield-10
92Sabres Jubilee Foods-7
92Score Canadian Promo Sheets-1
92Score Canadian Promo Sheets-2
92Score-6
92Score-420
Canadian-6
Canadian-420
Sharpshooters-8
Sharpshooters Canadian-8
USA Greats-1
92Seasons Patches-42
92Stadium Club-95
92Topps-345
Gold-345G
92Ultra-16
92Upper Deck-165
92Upper Deck-456
Gordie Howe Selects-G3
92Finnish Semic-159
93SLU Hockey Canadian-5
93SLU Hockey American-6
93Donruss-37
Ice Kings-2
93Kenner Starting Lineup Cards-6
93Kraft-39
93Leaf-12
Gold All-Stars-1
Studio Signature-3
93McDonald's Upper Deck-18
93OPC Premier-171
93OPC Premier-490
Gold-171
Gold-490
Black Gold-14
93Panini Stickers-101
93Panini Stickers-137
93Parkhurst-289
Emerald Ice-289
East/West Stars-E8
93Pinnacle II Samples-300
93Pinnacle-300
Canadian-300
All-Stars-11
All-Stars Canadian-11
Captains-3
Captains Canadian-3
Nifty Fifty-12
93PowerPlay-31
Point Leaders-7
93Sabres Noco-9
93Score-345
Canadian-345
Dream Team-13
Dynamic Duos U.S.-2
Franchise-2
93Stadium Club-20
93Stadium Club-460
Members Only Master Set-20
Members Only Master Set-460
OPC-20
First Day Issue-20
First Day Issue-460
First Day Issue OPC-20
All-Stars-5
All-Stars Members Only-5
All-Stars OPC-5
Master Photos-1
Master Photos Winners-1
93Topps/OPC Premier-171
93Topps/OPC Premier-490
Gold-171
Gold-490
93Topps Premier Black Gold-24
93Ultra-219
All-Stars-4
Premier Pivots-3
Scoring Kings-1
Speed Merchants-6
93Upper Deck-137
93Upper Deck-221
93Upper Deck-287
Hat Tricks-HT10
SP-17
93Upper Deck Locker All-Stars-4
93Swedish Semic World Champ Stickers-183
94SLU Hockey American-9
94Be A Player-R79
94Be A Player-R132
Signature Cards-63
94Canada Games NHL POGS-50
94Donruss-300
94EA Sports-15
94Finest-70
Super Team Winners-70
Refractors-70
94Flair-19
Center Spotlight-5
94Fleer-23
94Hockey Wit-105
94Kenner Starting Lineup Cards-10
94Kraft-10
94Leaf-278
Gold Stars-14
94Leaf Limited-63
94OPC Premier-180
Special Effects-180
94Parkhurst-310
Gold-310
Crash the Game Green-3
Crash the Game Blue-3
Crash the Game Gold-3
Crash the Game Red-3
Vintage-V73
94Parkhurst SE-SE18
Gold-SE18
94Pinnacle-350
Artist's Proofs-350
Rink Collection-350
Gamers-GR2
94Score Samples-2
94Score-2
Gold-2
Platinum-2
Franchise-TF3
94Select-57
Gold-57
94SP-12
Die Cuts-12
94Topps/OPC Premier-180
Special Effects-180
The Go To Guy-6
94Ultra-24
Premier Pivots-5
Speed Merchants-5
94Upper Deck-17
Electric Ice-17
Ice Gallery-IG14
Predictor Retail-R17
Predictor Retail-R22
Predictor Retail-R47
Predictor Retail-R55
94Upper Deck Predictor Retail Exchange-R17
94Upper Deck Predictor Retail Exchange-R22
94Upper Deck Predictor Retail Exchange-R47
94Upper Deck Predictor Retail Exchange-R55
94Upper Deck SP Inserts-SP99
94Upper Deck SP Inserts Die Cuts-SP99
94Upper Deck NHLPA/Be A Player-28
94Finnish Jaa Kiekko-120
94Finnish Jaa Kiekko-359
94Swedish Olympics Lillehammer*-325
95Bashan Super Stickers-11
Die-Cut-3
95Bowman-29
All-Foil-29
95Canada Games NHL POGS-42
95Collector's Choice-157
Player's Club-157
Player's Club Platinum-157
Crash The Game-C27A
Crash The Game-C27B
Crash The Game-C27C
Crash The Game Gold-C27A
Crash The Game Gold-C27B
Crash The Game Gold-C27C
Crash the Game Silver Redeemed-C27
Crash the Game Silver Bonus-C27
Crash the Game Gold Redeemed-C27
Crash the Game Gold Bonus-C27
95Donruss-172
Pro Pointers-2
95Donruss Elite-75
Die Cut Stars-75
Die Cut Uncut-75
95Emotion-18
95Finest-40
95Finest-130
Refractors-40
Refractors-130
95Hoyle Eastern Playing Cards-38
95Imperial Stickers-11
Die Cut Superstars-3
95Leaf-140
95Leaf Limited-113
95Metal-16
International Steel-11
95NHL Aces Playing Cards-5S
95Panini Stickers-15
95Parkhurst International-20
Emerald Ice-20
Parkie's Trophy Picks-PP49
95Pinnacle-54
Artist's Proofs-54
Rink Collection-54
95Playoff One on One-13
95Playoff One on One-127
95Pro Magnets-109
95Score-201
Black Ice Artist's Proofs-201
Black Ice-201
Border Battle-7
Golden Blades-8
95Select Certified-18
Mirror Gold-18
95SkyBox Impact-17
95SP-12
Stars/Etoiles-E5
Stars/Etoiles Gold-E5
95Stadium Club-164
Members Only Master Set-164
95Summit-34
Artist's Proofs-34
Ice-34
95Topps-13
95Topps-250
OPC Inserts-13
OPC Inserts-250
Home Grown USA-HGA4
Marquee Men Power Boosters-13
Power Lines-6PL
Rink Leaders-5RL
95Topps SuperSkills-5
Platinum-5
95Ultra-20
95Ultra-389
Gold Medallion-20
95Upper Deck-386
Electric Ice-386
Electric Ice Gold-386
Predictor Retail-R19
Predictor Retail-R29
Predictor Retail Exchange-R19
Predictor Retail Exchange-R29
Special Edition-SE10
Special Edition Gold-SE10
95Zenith-85
95Finnish Semic World Championships-114
95Swedish Globe World Championships-116
96SLU Hockey American-9
96Be A Player Link to History-8B
96Be A Player Link to History Autographs-8B
96Be A Player Link to History Auto Silver-8B
96Collector's Choice-23
96Collector's Choice-311
MVP-UD40
MVP Gold-UD40
Stick'Ums-S21
96Collector's Choice Blow-Ups-23
96Donruss-113
Press Proofs-113
96Donruss Canadian Ice-11
Gold Press Proofs-11
Red Press Proofs-11
96Donruss Elite-101
Die Cut Stars-101
Perspective-10
96Flair-9
Blue Ice-9
96Fleer-11
Art Ross-11
96Fleer Picks-38
Dream Lines-10
96Kenner Starting Lineup Cards-9
96Kraft Upper Deck-34
96Leaf-44
Press Proofs-44
96Leaf Limited-59
Gold-59
96Leaf Preferred-11
Press Proofs-11
Steel-22
Steel Gold-22
96Metal Universe-15
Ice Carvings-8
Ice Carvings Super Power-8
96NHL Aces Playing Cards-27
96NHL Pro Stamps-109
96Pinnacle-27
Artist's Proofs-27
Foil-27
Premium Stock-27
Rink Collection-27
96Score-139
Artist's Proofs-139
Dealer's Choice Artist's Proofs-139
Special Artist's Proofs-139
Golden Blades-139
96Select Certified-9
Artist's Proofs-9
Blue-9
Mirror Blue-9
Mirror Gold-9
Mirror Red-9
Red-9
96SkyBox Impact-11
BladeRunners-10
96SP-15
Holoview Collection-HC8
Game Film-GF18
96SPx-18
Gold-18
96Summit-127
Artist's Proofs-127
Ice-127
Metal-127
Premium Stock-127
96Ultra-17
Gold Medallion-17
Mr. Momentum-6
96Upper Deck-15
Superstar Showdown-SS17B
96Zenith-83
Artist's Proofs-83
Assailants-9
96Swedish Semic Wien-165
97Headliners Hockey-13
97Be A Player One Timers-15
97Beehive-43
Golden Portraits-43
Team-18
Team Gold-18
97Black Diamond-133
Double Diamond-133
Triple Diamond-133
Quadruple Diamond-133
Premium Cut-PC22
Premium Cut Double Diamond-PC22
Premium Cut Quadruple Diamond Horiz-PC22
Premium Cut Triple Diamond-PC22
Premium Cut Quadruple Diamond Verticals-PC22
97Collector's Choice-31
97Crown Royale-85
Emerald Green-85
Ice Blue-85
Silver-85
Lamplighters Cel-Fusion Die-Cuts-12
97Donruss-133
Press Proofs Silver-133
Press Proofs Gold-133
97Donruss Canadian Ice-69
Dominion Series-69
Provincial Series-69
97Donruss Elite-111
97Donruss Elite-146
Aspirations-111
Aspirations-146
Status-111
Status-146
97Donruss Limited-111
Exposure-111
97Donruss Preferred-58
Cut to the Chase-58
97Donruss Priority-160
Stamp of Approval-160
97Highland Mint Mint-Cards Pinnacle/Score-9
97Highland Mint Mint-Cards Pinnacle/Score-10
97Katch-93
Gold-93
Silver-93
97Leaf-34
Fractal Matrix-34
Fractal Matrix Die Cuts-34
97Leaf International-34
Universal Ice-34
97Pacific Omega-146
Copper-146
Dark Gray-146
Emerald Green-146
Gold-146
Ice Blue-146
Stick Handle Laser Cuts-14
97Paramount-117
Copper-117
Dark Grey-117
Emerald Green-117
Ice Blue-117
Red-117
Silver-117
97Pinnacle-69
Artist's Proofs-69
Rink Collection-69
Press Plates Back Black-69
Press Plates Back Cyan-69
Press Plates Back Magenta-69
Press Plates Back Yellow-69
Press Plates Front Black-69
Press Plates Front Cyan-69
Press Plates Front Magenta-69
Press Plates Front Yellow-69
97Pinnacle Certified-80
Red-80
Mirror Blue-80
Mirror Gold-80
Mirror Red-80
97Pinnacle Inside-39
Coach's Collection-39
Executive Collection-39
97Pinnacle Tot Cert Platinum Blue-80
97Pinnacle Tot Cert Platinum Gold-80
97Pinnacle Totally Certified Platinum Red-80
97Pinnacle Tot Cert Mirror Platinum Gold-80
97Revolution-88
Copper-88
Emerald-88
Ice Blue-88
Silver-88
97Score-104
Artist's Proofs-104
Golden Blades-104
97Score Rangers-10
Platinum-10
Premier-10
97SP Authentic-98
Icons-I1
Icons Die-Cuts-I1
Icons Embossed-I1
97SPx-5
Bronze-5
Gold-5
Silver-5
Steel-5
Grand Finale-5
97Studio-50
Press Proofs Silver-50
Press Proofs Gold-50
97Upper Deck-318
97Upper Deck Ice-72
Parallel-72
Power Shift-72
97Zenith-44
Z-Gold-44
Z-Silver-44
97Zenith 5 x 7-26
Gold Impulse-26
Silver Impulse-26
97Zenith Chasing The Cup-14
98Pacific-295
Ice Blue-295
Red-295
Timelines-12
98Paramount-154
Copper-154
Emerald Green-154
Holo-Electric-154
Ice Blue-154
Silver-154
98SPx Finite-56
Radiance-56
Spectrum-56
98UD Choice-130
Prime Choice Reserve-130
Reserve-130
98Upper Deck-133
Exclusives-133
Exclusives 1 of 1-133
Gold Reserve-133
98Slovakian Eurotel-10
00Upper Deck Legends-15
Legendary Collection Bronze-15
Legendary Collection Gold-15
Legendary Collection Silver-15

Epic Signatures-PL
Legendary Game Jerseys-JPL
00Upper Deck Vintage Dynasty: A Piece of History-LL
00Upper Deck Vintage Dynasty: A Piece of History Gold-LL
01Topps Archives-79
02Topps Rookie Reprints-1
02Topps Rookie Reprint Autographs-1
04ITG Franchises Update Double Mem-UDM1
04ITG Franchises Update Double Mem Gold-UDM1
04ITG Franchises US East-339
04ITG Franchises US East-376
Autographs-A-PL1
Autographs-A-PL2
Barn Burners-EBB9
Barn Burners Gold-EBB9
Forever Rivals-EFR4
Forever Rivals Gold-EFR4
Memorabilia-ESM33
Memorabilia Autographs-ESM-PL
Memorabilia Gold-ESM33
04ITG Ultimate Memorabilia-114
Gold-114
Autographs-47
Autographs Gold-47
Jersey Autographs-7
Jersey Autographs Gold-7
Stick Autographs-20
Stick Autographs Gold-20
05ITG Heroes/Prosp Toronto Expo Parallel -28
05ITG Ultimate Memorabilia Level 1-75
05ITG Ultimate Memorabilia Level 2-75
05ITG Ultimate Memorabilia Level 3-75
05ITG Ultimate Memorabilia Level 4-75
05ITG Ultimate Memorabilia Level 5-75
05ITG Ultimate Mem Double Mem Autos-13
05ITG Ultimate Mem Double Mem Autos Gold-13
05ITG Ultimate Memorabilia Emblems-10
05ITG Ultimate Memorabilia Emblems Gold-10
05ITG Ultimate Memorabilia In The Numbers-6
05ITG Ultimate Mem In The Numbers Gold-6
05ITG Ultimate Mem Jersey and Emblem-20
05ITG Ultimate Mem Jersey Emblems Gold-20
05ITG Ultimate Memorabilia Jerseys-27
05ITG Ultimate Memorabilia Jerseys Gold-27
05ITG Ultimate Mem Pass the Torch Jerseys-20
05ITG Ultimate Mem Passing Torch Jsy Gold-20
05ITG Ultimate Mem Raised to the Rafters-7
05ITG Ultimate Mem Raised Rafters Gold-7
05ITG Ultimate Mem Seams Unbelievable-16
05ITG Ultimate Mem Seam Unbelievable Gold-16
05ITG Ultimate Mem Sticks and Jerseys-12
05ITG Ultimate Mem Stick and Jerseys Gold-12
05ITG Ultimate Memorabilia Triple Autos-16
05ITG Ultimate Mem Triple Autos Gold-16
05ITG Ultimate Memorabilia Ultimate Autos-22
05ITG Ultimate Mem Ultimate Autos Gold-22
05ITG Heroes and Prospects-28
Aspiring-ASP8
Autographs-A-PLF
Future Teammates-FT9
Hero Memorabilia-HM-7
National Pride-NPR-21
06ITG International Ice-6
06ITG International Ice-45
06ITG International Ice-51
Gold-6
Gold-45
Gold-51
Autographs-APL
Autographs-APL2
Autographs-APL3
Cornerstones-IC06
Cornerstones Gold-IC06
Emblem Autographs-GUE28
Emblem Autographs Gold-GUE28
Emblems-GUE28
Emblems Gold-GUE28
International Rivals-IR12
International Rivals-IR14
International Rivals Gold-IR12
International Rivals Gold-IR14
Jersey Autographs-GUJ28
Jersey Autographs Gold-GUJ28
Jerseys-GUJ28
Jerseys Gold-GUJ28
My Country My Team-MC5
My Country My Team Gold-MC5
Numbers-GUN28
Numbers Autographs-GUN28
Numbers Autographs Gold-GUN28
Numbers Gold-GUN28
Quad Patch-QP02
Quad Patch Gold-QP02
Teammates-IT14
Teammates Gold-IT14
06ITG Ultimate Memorabilia-109
Artist Proof-109
Autos-22
Autos Gold-22
Emblems-13
Emblems Gold-13
First Round Picks-16
First Round Picks Gold-16
Gloves Are Off-16
Gloves Are Off Gold-16
Jerseys Autos-30
Jerseys Autos Gold-30
Raised to the Rafters-1
Raised to the Rafters Gold-1
Sticks Autos-12
Sticks Autos Gold-12
06Parkhurst-143
06Parkhurst-224
Autographs-143
Autographs-224
Autographs Dual-DALS
06The Cup Enshrinements-EPL
06The Cup Honorable Numbers-HNPL
06The Cup Limited Logos-LLPL
06The Cup Scripted Swatches-SSPL

Lafontaine, Tommy
03Victoriaville Tigers-16
04Victoriaville Tigres-11

Laforce, Ernest
43Parade Sportive *-61

LaForest, Bob
82North Bay Centennials-12

Laforest, Magella
51Bas Du Fleuve-30

LaForest, Mark
82North Bay Centennials-13
87Flyers Postcards-30
88Flyers Postcards-25
89ProCards AHL-124
90Upper Deck-81
French-81
90ProCards AHL/IHL-13
91ProCards-208
94Milwaukee Admirals-13
95Milwaukee Admirals-10
95Milwaukee Admirals Postcards-18
96Collector's Edge Ice-163
Prism-163

Laforge, Alain
86Kingston Canadians-28
88Niagara Falls Thunder-21
89Sudbury Wolves-7
907th Inn. Sketch OHL-386
90Sudbury Wolves-19

Laforge, Bill
80Oshawa Generals-17
88Niagara Falls Thunder-22

Laforge, Claude
58Topps-33
59Topps-64
62Parkhurst-24
68Shirriff Coins-133

Laforge, Marc
84Kingston Canadians-16
85Kingston Canadians-16
86Kingston Canadians-16
88ProCards AHL-49
90ProCards AHL/IHL-233
91ProCards-216
94Cape Breton Oilers-12
97Anchorage Aces-10
98San Antonio Iguanas-10
99San Antonio Iguanas-16
00Indianapolis Ice-14

Lafoy, Mike
82Kingston Canadians-20

Laframboise, Peter
72O-Pee-Chee-263
72Sargent Promotions Stamps-53
73O-Pee-Chee-244
74Capitals White Borders-15
74NHL Action Stamps-317
74O-Pee-Chee NHL-166
74Topps-166
75O-Pee-Chee NHL-364

Lafrance, Darryl
91Oshawa Generals-14
91Oshawa Generals Sheet-13
917th Inn. Sketch OHL-157
92Oshawa Generals Sheet-17
93Oshawa Generals-14
95Flint Generals-15
95Classic-91
97New Orleans Brass-2

Lafrance, Eric
907th Inn. Sketch QMJHL-183
917th Inn. Sketch QMJHL-170

Lafrance, Goalie
99Hull Olympiques-22
Signed-22
00Hull Olympiques-21
Signed-21
01Hull Olympiques-21
02Hull Olympiques-21
03Hull Olympiques Memorial Cup-10

Lafrance, Leo
27La Patrie-3

Lafrance, Marc
93Quebec Pee-Wee Tournament-469

Lafrance, Toby
04Victoriaville Tigres-29
05Victoriaville Tigres-7
06Victoriaville Tigres-24

Lafreniere, Chris
907th Inn. Sketch WHL-195
917th Inn. Sketch Memorial Cup-75

Lafreniere, Colin
02Prince Albert Raiders-13
03Prince Albert Raiders-6

Lafreniere, Gary
99OCN Blizzard-6

Lafreniere, Jason
83Brantford Alexanders-6
85Nordiques McDonald's-12
85Nordiques Team Issue-13
86Nordiques General Foods-14
86Nordiques Team Issue-12
87Nordiques General Foods-18
87Nordiques Team Issue-6
87O-Pee-Chee Stickers-130
87O-Pee-Chee Stickers-219
87Panini Stickers-171
88O-Pee-Chee-223
88O-Pee-Chee Stickers-185
89ProCards IHL-25
90Alberta International Team Canada-14
92Atlanta Knights-8
93Parkhurst-466
Emerald Ice-466
96Michigan K-Wings-5
98German DEL-182
02UK Guildford Flames-9
02UK Guildford Flames-21

Lafreniere, Marc
90Rayside-Balfour Jr. Canadians-10
91Rayside-Balfour Jr. Canadians-8

Lafreniere, Patrick
99Hull Olympiques-21
Signed-21

Lafreniere, Real
51Bas Du Fleuve-26
52Bas Du Fleuve-63

Lafreniere, Roger
61Hamilton Red Wings-10

Lagace, Jean-Guy
74NHL Action Stamps Update-15
74O-Pee-Chee NHL-299
74Penguins Postcards-12
75O-Pee-Chee NHL-141
75Topps-141

Lagace-Daigle, Simon
99UD Prospects-62

Laganas, Chris
91Greensboro Monarchs-7
92Oklahoma City Blazers-11
93Oklahoma City Blazers-8
94Central Hockey League-61
94Oklahoma City Blazers-7

Laginski, Al
89Rayside-Balfour Jr. Canadians-12

Lagola, Philip
93Quebec Pee-Wee Tournament-723

LaGrand, Scott
92Classic-79
Gold-79
92Classic Four-Sport *-201
Gold-201

Lahache, Hunter
02Reading Royals-15

Lahaye, Lester
52Juniors Blue Tint-45

Lahde, Kyosti
72Finnish Jaakiekko-176

Lahey, Matt
04Ottawa 67's-23
05Ottawa 67's-19
06Ottawa 67s-4

Lahey, Matthew
95Slapshot-326
96Sault Ste. Marie Greyhounds-9
96Sault Ste. Marie Greyhounds Autographed-9
97Guelph Storm-15

Lahey, Pat
82Sault Ste. Marie Greyhounds-14
83Sault Ste. Marie Greyhounds-14

Lahn, Stefan
94German First League-87
95German DEL-290
96German DEL-317

Lahnalampi, Derek
94North Bay Centennials-3

Lahteenmaki, Ari
78Finnish SM-Liiga-42
80Finnish Mallasjuoma-20

Lahtela, Pekka
66Finnish Jaakiekkosarja-65
70Finnish Jaakiekko-161
71Finnish Suomi Stickers-231
72Finnish Jaakiekko-214

Lahti, Janne
01Finnish Cardset-228
03Finnish Cardset-41
04Finnish Cardset-227
05Finnish Cardset -36
06Finnish Cardset-217

Lahti, Miika
05Finnish Cardset -252
06Finnish Cardset-252
Playmakers Rookies-10
Playmakers Rookies Gold-10
Playmakers Rookies Silver-10
Signature Sensations-13

Lahti, Pekka
66Finnish Jaakiekkosarja-27

Lahtinen, Jouni
95Finnish SISU-239
96Finnish SISU Redline-37

Lahtinen, Juhani
65Finnish Hellas-125
66Finnish Jaakiekkosarja-201
70Finnish Jaakiekko-128

Lahtinen, Timo
66Finnish Jaakiekkosarja-200
70Finnish Jaakiekko-129
71Finnish Suomi Stickers-154
72Finnish Jaakiekko-106
73Finnish Jaakiekko-203
83Swedish Semic Elitserien-219
84Swedish Semic Elitserien-243
91Swedish Semic Elitserien Stickers-309
92Swedish Semic Elitserien Stickers-331
93Swedish Semic Elitserien-296
98German DEL-108

Laich, Brooks
03BAP Memorabilia-227
03ITG VIP Rookie Debut-116
03Parkhurst Rookie-118
03Upper Deck Rookie Update-197
03AHL Top Prospects-17
03Binghamton Senators-11
03Binghamton Senators Postcards-7
04Portland Pirates-14
05Parkhurst-483
Facsimile Auto Parallel-483
05Hershey Bears-25
06Upper Deck-195
Exclusives Parallel-195
High Gloss Parallel-195
Masterpieces-195
06ITG Heroes and Prospects Calder Cup Champions-CC05

Laidlaw, Ken
66Columbus Checkers-9

Laidlaw, Tom
81O-Pee-Chee-234
82O-Pee-Chee-227
82Post Cereal-13
83O-Pee-Chee-247
84O-Pee-Chee-144
86O-Pee-Chee-147
86O-Pee-Chee Stickers-223
86Topps-147
88Kings Postcards-19
88Kings Smokey-15
88O-Pee-Chee-37
88Panini Stickers-71
88Topps-37
89Kings Smokey-23
89O-Pee-Chee-34
89Topps-34
90Kings Smokey-12
90O-Pee-Chee-524
90Pro Set-123
90Score-69
Canadian-69
90Upper Deck-119
French-119

Laiho, Jari
73Finnish Jaakiekko-312
78Finnish SM-Liiga-172
80Finnish Mallasjuoma-130

Laine, Antti
71Finnish Suomi Stickers-246

Laine, Ari
71Finnish Suomi Stickers-369

Laine, Arto
70Finnish Jaakiekko-231
71Finnish Suomi Stickers-247
72Finnish Jaakiekko-347
73Finnish Jaakiekko-313
80Finnish Mallasjuoma-50

Laine, Erkki
82Swedish Semic VM Stickers-43
83Swedish Semic VM Stickers-43
84Swedish Semic Elitserien-110
85Swedish Panini Stickers-104
86Swedish Panini Stickers-98
87Swedish Panini Stickers-100
89Swedish Semic World Champ Stickers-45
91Finnish Jyvas-Hyva Stickers-51
93Finnish SISU-291
93Finnish SISU-297

Laine, Harri
80Finnish Mallasjuoma-77

Laine, Heikki
05Finnish Cardset -200
06Finnish Cardset-24

Laine, Ismo
72Finnish Jaakiekko-332

Laine, Juhani
71Finnish Suomi Stickers-284
73Finnish Jaakiekko-204

Laine, Mika
71Finnish Suomi Stickers-346

Laine, Mikko
04Finnish Cardset-217
05Finnish Cardset -208
06Finnish Cardset-192

Laine, Pekka
78Finnish SM-Liiga-125
80Finnish Mallasjuoma-79

Laine, Sami
95Finnish SISU-212
96Finnish SISU Redline-7
98Odessa Jackalopes-9
99Odessa Jackalopes-6

Laine, Teemu
01Finnish Cardset-56
03Finnish Cardset-70
04Finnish Cardset-166
Parallel-122
05Finnish Cardset -150
06Finnish Cardset-156

Laine, Tommi
06Finnish Cardset-338

Laing, Joel
00Wilkes-Barre Scranton Penguins-11
02UK Sheffield Steelers-10
04UK Thommo's Top 10-6

Laing, Quintin
98Kelowna Rockets-15
00Jackson Bandits-21
01Norfolk Admirals-18
02Norfolk Admirals-13
03ITG VIP Rookie Debut-128
03Parkhurst Rookie-96
03Upper Deck Rookie Update-203
03Norfolk Admirals-14
04Norfolk Admirals-12
05Norfolk Admirals-19

Lainio, Kari
71Finnish Suomi Stickers-370

Lainsbury, Clayton
04Northern Michigan Wildcats-10

Laird, Justin
04Tulsa Oilers-15

Laird, Rob
89Capitals Kodak-xx
90ProCards AHL/IHL-217
91ProCards-571
95Phoenix Roadrunners-23
99Fort Wayne Komets Points Leaders-10
99Fort Wayne Komets Penalty Leaders-5

Laise, Vince
05Maine Black Bears-13

Laitila, Janne
00Finnish Cardset-107

Laitinen, Ilkka
99Finnish Cardset-252

Laitinen, Jarno
06Finnish Ilves Team Set-14

Laitinen, Kari
89Swedish Semic World Champ Stickers-43
92Finnish Jyvas-Hyva Stickers-5

Laitinen, Miro
00Finnish Cardset-331
01Finnish Cardset-125

Laitinen, Veli-Pekka
99Finnish Cardset-95
00Finnish Cardset-70
01Finnish Cardset-311
02Finnish Cardset-55
02Swedish SHL-148
Parallel-148
03Swedish Elite-5
Silver-5
04Finnish Cardset-34
Parallel-24
05Finnish Cardset -28
06Finnish Cardset-30

Laitre, Martin
907th Inn. Sketch QMJHL-254
99Hamilton Bulldogs-11
00Hamilton Bulldogs-16

Laituri, Timo
92Norwegian Elite Series-98

Lajeunesse, Bruno
907th Inn. Sketch QMJHL-132

Lajeunesse, Martin
907th Inn. Sketch QMJHL-242
917th Inn. Sketch QMJHL-126

Lajeunesse, Oliver
05Chicoutimi Sagueneens-21

Lajeunesse, Serge
70Esso Power Players-131
71O-Pee-Chee-136

Lajeunesse, Simon
93Quebec Pee-Wee Tournament-272
99O-Pee-Chee-258
99O-Pee-Chee Chrome-258
99O-Pee-Chee Chrome Refractors-258
99Topps/OPC-258
99Topps/OPC Chrome-258
Refractors-258
99Bowman CHL-39
Gold-39
OPC International-39
Autographs-BA2
Autographs Gold-BA2
Autographs Silver-BA2
00Val d'Or Foreurs-13
Signed-13
01Between the Pipes-160
02Between the Pipes-99
Gold-99
Silver-99
Jerseys-48
02Peoria Rivermen-2
03BAP Memorabilia Deep in the Crease-D14
03San Antonio Rampage-20
04Fresno Falcons-11

Lajoie, Claude
84Chicoutimi Sagueneens-16

Lajoie, Erik
02Val d'Or Foreurs-10
03Val d'Or Foreurs-11
04Baie-Comeau Drakkar-5

Lajoie, Serge
86Kamloops Blazers-9
94German First League-379

Lake, Allan
86Kitchener Rangers-16
87Kitchener Rangers-28

Lake, Eric
06Lincoln Stars-5
06Lincoln Stars Upper DeckÂ Signature Series -18

Lake, Fred
10C56-27
10Sweet Caporal Postcards-9
11C55-9
12C57-31

Lake, Ryan
01UK Hull Thunder-12
02UK Hull Thunder-13
03UK Sheffield Steelers-16
03UK Sheffield Steelers Stickers-4
05UK Hull Stingrays-17

Lake, Troy
00Roanoke Express-4
01Roanoke Express-13

Laker, Cam
93Quebec Pee-Wee Tournament-1616

Lakhmatov, Vitaly
99Swiss Panini Stickers-21
00Swiss Panini Stickers-21
01Swiss HNL-229
02Swiss HNL-202

Lakos, Andre
98Barrie Colts-2
99Albany River Rats-16
00Albany River Rats-12
01Albany River Rats-6
04Syracuse Crunch-15

Lakosil, Vlastimil
97Czech APS Extraliga-316
98Czech OFS-384
99Czech DS-99
Goalies-G8
99Czech OFS-10
99Czech OFS Goalie Die-Cuts-10
00Czech DS Extraliga-62
Goalies-G6
00Czech OFS-213
00Czech OFS Star Emerald-23
00Czech OFS Star Pink-23
00Czech OFS Star Violet-23
01Czech OFS-47
Gold Inserts-G4
02Czech OFS Plus-90
Trios-T16
Duos-D9
03Czech OFS Plus-291
03Czech OFS Plus Checklists-14
03Czech OFS Plus Insert B-B6
03Czech OFS Plus Insert P-P7
03Czech OFS Plus MS Praha-SE34
04Czech OFS-212
Team Cards-10

Lakovic, Greg
97Toledo Storm-3
98Huntsville Channel Cats-10

Lakovic, Sasha
94Central Hockey League-99
95Las Vegas Thunder-4
97Albany River Rats-7
98Devils Team Issue-14
99Albany River Rats-17
01Bakersfield Condors-13

Lakso, Bob
88ProCards IHL-1
89ProCards IHL-125
90ProCards AHL/IHL-542
91ProCards-257

Laksola, Pekka
91Finnish Jyvas-Hyva Stickers-60
92Finnish Jyvas-Hyva Stickers-167
93Finnish Jyvas-Hyva Stickers-290
93Finnish SISU-66
94Finnish SISU-64
94Finnish SISU-377
95Finnish SISU-111
95Finnish SISU-183
Double Trouble-8
95Finnish SISU Limited-74
95Finnish Semic World Championships-33
96German DEL-254

Laksola, Reijo
73Finnish Jaakiekko-223
78Finnish SM-Liiga-24
80Finnish Mallasjuoma-24

Lala, Jiri
81Swedish Semic Hockey VM Stickers-70
82Swedish Semic VM Stickers-89
83Swedish Semic VM Stickers-89
89Swedish Semic World Champ Stickers-198
91Finnish Semic World Champ Stickers-114
91Swedish Semic World Champ Stickers-114
94German DEL-113
95German DEL-115
98Czech OFS Legends-16
01Czech DS Legends-L12

Lalancette, Jacques
51Laval Dairy Lac St. Jean-24
52Bas Du Fleuve-33

Lalande, Francis
93Quebec Pee-Wee Tournament-906

Lalande, Hec
52Juniors Blue Tint-170
57Topps-31
94Parkhurst Missing Link-38

Lalande, Kevin
04Belleville Bulls-10
05ITG Heroes/Prosp Toronto Expo Parallel -123
05Belleville Bulls-17
05OHL Bell All-Star Classic-1
05ITG Heroes and Prospects-123
Autographs-A-KLA
06Between The Pipes-32
Autographs-AKLA
Prospect Trios-PT05
Prospect Trios-PT10
Prospect Trios Gold-PT05
Prospect Trios Gold-PT10
06Belleville Bulls-21
06ITG Heroes and Prospects Jerseys-GUJ37
06ITG Heroes and Prospects Jerseys Gold-GUJ37
06ITG Heroes and Prospects Emblems-GUE37
06ITG Heroes and Prospects Emblems Gold-GUE37
06ITG Heroes and Prospects Numbers-GUN37
06ITG Heroes and Prospects Numbers Gold-GUN37

Laliberte, David
03P.E.I. Rocket-9
04P.E.I. Rocket-5
05PEI Rocket-11
06PEI Rocket-1

Laliberte, Gaetan
51Bas Du Fleuve-18

Laliberte, Hugues
907th Inn. Sketch QMJHL-213
917th Inn. Sketch QMJHL-26

Laliberte, John
03Boston University Terriers-4
06Milwaukee Admirals -10

Laliberte, Olivier
04Gatineau Olympiques-5
05Gatineau Olympiques-2
06Gatineau Olympiques-2

Laliberte, Spike
51Laval Dairy QSHL-59

Lalime, Patrick
917th Inn. Sketch QMJHL-71
94Hampton Roads Admirals-3
95Cleveland Lumberjacks-16
95Cleveland Lumberjacks Postcards-15
96Be A Player Link to History-10A
96Be A Player Link to History Autographs-10A
96Be A Player Link to History Auto Silver-10A
96Be A Player Stacking the Pads-1
96Black Diamond-168
Gold-168
96Donruss Elite-133
Die Cut Stars-133
96Flair-121
Blue Ice-121
Hot Gloves-6
96Select Certified-108
Artist's Proofs-108
Blue-108
Mirror Blue-108
Mirror Gold-108
Mirror Red-108
Red-108
96Ultra-142
Gold Medallion-142
96Upper Deck Ice-54
Parallel-54
96Cleveland Lumberjacks Multi-Ad-15
97SLU Hockey American-11
97Collector's Choice-208
Star Quest-SQ40
97Donruss-76
Press Proofs Silver-76
Press Proofs Gold-76
Canadian Ice Les Gardiens-9
97Donruss Canadian Ice Les Gardiens Promo-9
97Donruss Limited-142
97Donruss Limited-159
Exposure-142
Exposure-159
97Kenner Starting Lineup Cards-11
97Leaf-111
Fractal Matrix-111
Fractal Matrix Die Cuts-111
97Leaf International-111
Universal Ice-111
97Pacific-40
Copper-40
Emerald Green-40
Ice Blue-40
Red-40
Silver-40
In The Cage Laser Cuts-17
97Pacific Dynagon-103
97Pacific Dynagon-142
Copper-103
Copper-142
Dark Grey-103
Dark Grey-142
Emerald Green-103
Emerald Green-142
Ice Blue-103
Ice Blue-142
Red-103
Red-142
Silver-103
Silver-142
Best Kept Secrets-78
Dynamic Duos-13B
Stonewallers-18
Tandems-9
Tandems-22
97Pacific Invincible-114
Copper-114
Emerald Green-114
Ice Blue-114
Red-114
Silver-114
Feature Performers-29
NHL Regime-161
97Panini Stickers-246
97Pinnacle Certified-23
Red-23
Mirror Blue-23
Mirror Gold-23
Mirror Red-23
97Pinnacle Inside-67
Coach's Collection-67
Executive Collection-67
Stand Up Guys-6A/B
Stand Up Guys-6C/D
Stand Up Guys Promos-6A/B
Stand Up Guys Promos-6C/D
97Pinnacle Tot Cert Platinum Blue-23
97Pinnacle Tot Certi Platinum Gold-23
97Pinnacle Totally Certified Platinum Red-23
97Pinnacle Tot Cert Mirror Platinum Gold-23
97Score-40
Artist's Proofs-40
Golden Blades-40
97Score Penguins-3
Platinum-3
Premier-3
97Upper Deck-133
Game Dated Moments-133
Smooth Grooves-SG40
Three Star Selects-12A
98Hampton Roads Admirals 10th Anniversary-16
98Kansas City Blades-22
99Pacific Dynagon Ice-140
Blue-140
Copper-140
Gold-140
Premiere Date-140
99Pacific Omega-160
Copper-160
Gold-160
Ice Blue-160
Premiere Date-160
99Senators Team Issue-11
99SP Authentic-61
00BAP Memorabilia-273
Emerald-273
Ruby-273
Sapphire-273
Promos-273
00BAP Mem Chicago Sportsfest Copper-273
00BAP Memorabilia Chicago Sportsfest Blue-273
00BAP Memorabilia Chicago Sportsfest Gold-273
00BAP Memorabilia Chicago Sportsfest Ruby-273
00BAP Memorabilia Chicago Sun-Times Ruby-273
00BAP Memorabilia Chicago Sun-Times Gold-273
00BAP Mem Chicago Sun-Times Sapphire-273
00BAP Mem Toronto Fall Expo Copper-273
00BAP Memorabilia Toronto Fall Expo Gold-273
00BAP Memorabilia Toronto Fall Expo Ruby-273
00BAP Parkhurst 2000-P43
00BAP Signature Series-78
Emerald-78
Ruby-78
Sapphire-78
Autographs-30
Autographs Gold-30
00BAP Ultimate Memorabilia Goalie Sticks-G21
00Crown Royale-76
Ice Blue-76
Limited Series-76
Premiere Date-76
Red-76
00O-Pee-Chee-265B
00O-Pee-Chee Parallel-265B
00Pacific-281
Copper-281
Gold-281
Ice Blue-281
Premiere Date-281
00Paramount-174
Copper-174
Gold-174
Holo-Gold-174
Holo-Silver-174
Ice Blue-174
Premiere Date-174
00Revolution-104
Blue-104
Premiere Date-104
Red-104
00Senators Team Issue-10
00SP Authentic-63
00Stadium Club-125
00Titanium-66
Blue-66
Gold-66
Premiere Date-66
Red-66
Retail-66
00Topps/OPC-265B
Parallel-265B
00Topps Chrome-158
OPC Refractors-158
Refractors-158
00UD Heroes-85
00UD Reserve-60
00Upper Deck-123
Exclusives Tier 1-123
Exclusives Tier 2-123
00Upper Deck MVP-123
First Stars-123
Second Stars-123
Third Stars-123
00Upper Deck Vintage-252
00Upper Deck Vintage-258
00Upper Deck Vintage-259
00Czech Stadion-121
01Atomic-70
Blue-70
Gold-70
Premiere Date-70
Red-70
01BAP Memorabilia-27
Emerald-27
Ruby-27
Sapphire-27
01BAP Signature Series-104
Autographs-104
Autographs Gold-104
Jerseys-GJ-76
Teammates-TM-21
01BAP Update He Shoots-He Scores Prizes-7
01Between the Pipes-43
01Between the Pipes-104
Future Wave-FW3
Goalie Gear-GG26
He Shoots-He Saves Prizes-14
Jersey and Stick Cards-GSJ32
Masks-23
Masks Silver-23
Masks Gold-23
01Bowman YoungStars-71
Gold-71
Ice Cubed-71
01Crown Royale-102
Blue-102
Premiere Date-102
Red-102
Retail-102
01McDonald's Pacific-27
01O-Pee-Chee-133
01O-Pee-Chee Premier Parallel-133
01Pacific-275
Extreme LTD-275
Hobby LTD-275
Premiere Date-275
Retail LTD-275
Impact Zone-14
Steel Curtain-14
01Pacific Adrenaline-135
Blue-135
Premiere Date-135
Red-135
Retail-135
Creased Lightning-14
Power Play-25
01Pacific Arena Exclusives-275
01Pacific Heads-Up-70
Blue-70
Premiere Date-70
Red-70
Silver-70
Showstoppers-15
01Pacific Montreal International-7
01Parkhurst-83
Gold-83
Silver-83
01Private Stock-69
Gold-69
Premiere Date-69
Retail-69
Silver-69
01Private Stock Pacific Nights-69
01Senators Team Issue-13
01SPx-186
01Stadium Club-59
Award Winners-59
Master Photos-59
01Titanium-101
Hobby Parallel-101
Premiere Date-101
Retail-101
Retail Parallel-101
Double-Sided Jerseys-48
Double-Sided Jerseys-64
Double-Sided Patches-48
Double-Sided Patches-64
01Titanium Draft Day Edition-67
01Topps-133
OPC Parallel-133
Own The Game-OTG26
01Topps Chrome-133
Refractors-133
Black Border Refractors-133
01Topps Heritage-83
Refractors-83
01Topps Reserve-57
01UD Mask Collection-121
Gold-121
01Upper Deck-124
Exclusives-124
Goalies in Action-GL8
01Upper Deck MVP-133
Masked Men-MM9
01Upper Deck Victory-241
01Upper Deck Victory-248
Gold-241
Gold-248
01Upper Deck Vintage-179
01Vanguard-70
Blue-70
Red-70
One of Ones-70
Premiere Date-70
Proofs-70
Stonewallers-14
02Atomic-72
Blue-72
Gold-72
Red-72
Denied-14
Hobby Parallel-72
02BAP First Edition-121
Jerseys-121
02BAP Memorabilia-155
Emerald-155
Ruby-155
Sapphire-155
NHL All-Star Game-155
NHL All-Star Game Blue-155
NHL All-Star Game Green-155
NHL All-Star Game Red-155
Stanley Cup Playoffs-SC-2
02BAP Memorabilia Toronto Fall Expo-155
02BAP Signature Series-35
Autographs-35
Autograph Buybacks 2000-30
Autograph Buybacks 2001-104
Autographs Gold-35
Defensive Wall-DW8
Team Quads-TQ20
02Between the Pipes-7
02Between the Pipes-141
Gold-7
Silver-7
Behind the Mask-8
Blockers-12
Emblems-24
Goalie Autographs-14
He Shoots-He Saves Points-6
He Shoots-He Saves Prizes-10
Jerseys-24
Masks II-20
Masks II Gold-20
Masks II Silver-20
Numbers-24
Stick and Jerseys-24
Tandems-5
02Bowman YoungStars-76
Gold-76
Silver-76
02Crown Royale-68
Blue-68
Red-68
Retail-68
Coats of Armor-8
02McDonald's Pacific-30
Glove Side Net-Fusions-5
02NHL Power Play Stickers-118
02O-Pee-Chee-61
02O-Pee-Chee Premier Blue Parallel-61
02O-Pee-Chee Premier Red Parallel-61
02O-Pee-Chee Factory Set-61
02O-Pee-Chee Factory Set Hometown Heroes-HHC11
02Pacific-269
Blue-269
Red-269
02Pacific Complete-473
Red-473
02Pacific Exclusive-123
02Pacific Heads-Up-88
Blue-88
Purple-88
Red-88
Quad Jerseys-19
Quad Jerseys Gold-19
Showstoppers-15
02Pacific Les Gardiens-7
Gold-7
02Pacific Quest for the Cup-72
Gold-72

02Pacific Toronto Fall Expo-4
Gold-4
02Parkhurst-8
Bronze-8
Gold-8
Silver-8
Hardware-V6
02Parkhurst Retro-138
Minis-138
Hopefuls-VH4
02Private Stock Reserve-73
Blue-73
Red-73
Retail-73
02Senators Team Issue-9
02Senators Team Issue-25
02SP Authentic-64
Beckett Promos-64
02SPx-52
Spectrum Gold-52
Spectrum Silver-52
02Stadium Club-70
Silver Decoy Cards-70
Proofs-70
Lone Star Signatures Blue-LSPL
Lone Star Signatures Red-LSPL
02Titanium-73
Blue-73
Red-73
Retail-73
Jerseys-48
Jerseys Retail-48
Patches-48
02Topps-61
OPC Blue Parallel-61
OPC Red Parallel-61
Topps/OPC Hometown Heroes-HHC11
Factory Set-61
02Topps Chrome-43
Black Border Refractors-43
Refractors-43
02Topps Heritage-59
Chrome Parallel-59
Crease Piece-PL
Crease Piece Patches-PL
02Topps Total-358
02UD Mask Collection-58
02UD Mask Collection-59
02UD Mask Collection-113
02UD Mask Collection Beckett Promos-58
02UD Mask Collection Beckett Promos-59
02UD Piece of History-62
02UD Top Shelf-61
02Upper Deck-121
Exclusives-121
Super Saviors-SA10
02Upper Deck MVP-126
Gold-126
Classics-126
Golden Classics-126
02Upper Deck Rookie Update-71
02Upper Deck Victory-147
Bronze-147
Gold-147
Silver-147
02Upper Deck Vintage-176
02Upper Deck Vintage-281
Green Backs-176
02Vanguard-71
LTD-71
Jerseys-32
Jerseys Gold-32
Stonewallers-9
03McFarlane Hockey-220
03McFarlane Hockey-222
03BAP Memorabilia-152
Emerald-152
Gold-152
Ruby-152
Sapphire-152
Gloves-GUG5
Tandems-T-2
03BAP Ultimate Memorabilia Autographs-24
Gold-24
03BAP Ultimate Mem Auto Jerseys-24
03Beehive-138
Gold-138
Silver-138
Jerseys-JT18
03Black Diamond-143
Black-143
Green-143
Red-143
03Bowman-70
Gold-70
Future Rivals-LT
Future Rivals Patches-LT
03Bowman Chrome-70
Refractors-70
Gold Refractors-70
Xfractors-70
03Crown Royale-71
Blue-71
Retail-71
Gauntlet of Glory-14
03Duracell-2
03eTopps-12
03ITG Action-430
First Time All-Star-FT7
Jerseys-M135
Jerseys-M230
03ITG Used Signature Series-49
Gold-49
Autographs-PL
Autographs Gold-PL
Goalie Gear-26
Goalie Gear Autographs-26
Goalie Gear Gold-26
03ITG VIP Netminders-8
03McDonald's Pacific-37
Patches Silver-18
Patches Gold-18
Patches and Sticks-18
Saturday Night Rivals-5
03NHL Sticker Collection-100
03O-Pee-Chee-12
03O-Pee-Chee-295
03OPC Blue-12
03OPC Blue-295
03OPC Gold-12
03OPC Gold-295
03OPC Red-12
03OPC Red-295
03Pacific-239
Blue-239
Red-239
In the Crease-8
03Pacific Complete-440
Red-440
03Pacific Exhibit-184
03Pacific Exhibit-210
Blue Backs-184
Standing on Tradition-9
03Pacific Heads-Up-70
Hobby LTD-70
Retail LTD-70
Stonewallers-9
Stonewallers LTD-9
03Pacific Invincible-70
Blue-70
Red-70
Retail-70
Freeze Frame-16
Jerseys-21
03Pacific Luxury Suite-43A
03Pacific Luxury Suite-43B
03Pacific Luxury Suite-43C
03Pacific Prism Crease Police-7
03Pacific Quest for the Cup-76
Blue-76
03Pacific Supreme-71
Blue-71
Red-71
Retail-71
Standing Guard-10
03Parkhurst Rookie Records-RRE-7
03Parkhurst Rookie Records Gold-RRE-7
03Private Stock Reserve-187
Blue-187
Patches-187
Red-187
Retail-187
Increase Security-11
03Senators Postcards-24
03SP Authentic-63
Limited-63
03SP Game Used-31
Gold-31
Authentic Fabrics-QSAHL
Authentic Fabrics Gold-QSAHL
Authentic Patches-APPL
Game Gear-GGPL
Team Threads-TTSHL
Top Threads-SAHL
03SPx-66
Radiance-66
Spectrum-66
Fantasy Franchise-FF-HSL
Fantasy Franchise Limited-FF-HSL
03Titanium-174
Hobby Jersey Number Parallels-174
Patches-174
Retail-174
Masked Marauders-8
03Topps-12
03Topps-295
Blue-12
Blue-295
Gold-12
Gold-295
Red-12
Red-295
Topps/OPC Idols-CI11
Own the Game-OTG12
03Topps C55-6
Minis-6
Minis American Back-6
Minis American Back Red-6
Minis Bazooka Back-6
Minis Brooklyn Back-6
Minis Hat Trick Back-6
Minis O Canada Back-6
Minis O Canada Back Red-6
Minis Stanley Cup Back-6
Relics-TRPL
03Topps Pristine-23
Gold Refractor Die Cuts-23
Refractors-23
Jersey Portions-PPJ-PL
Jersey Portion Refractors-PPJ-PL
Mini-PM-PL
Patches-PP-PL
Patch Refractors-PP-PL
Press Plates Black-23
Press Plates Cyan-23
Press Plates Magenta-23
Press Plates Yellow-23
03UD Honor Roll-61
03UD Premier Collection-40
03Upper Deck-137
Canadian Exclusives-137
HG-137
Patches-SV8
Super Saviors-SS-PL
03Upper Deck Classic Portraits-69
03Upper Deck Ice-61
Gold-61
03Upper Deck MVP-302
Gold Script-302
Silver Script-302
Canadian Exclusives-302
Masked Men-MM6
SportsNut-SN60
03Upper Deck Rookie Update-63
Skills-SKPL
Super Stars-SSPL
03Upper Deck Trilogy-69
Limited-69
Limited Threads-LT20
03Upper Deck Victory-135
Bronze-135
Gold-135
Silver-135
03Toronto Star-68
04Pacific-186
Blue-186
Red-186
04Upper Deck-155
Canadian Exclusives-155
HG Glossy Gold-155
HG Glossy Silver-155
05Black Diamond-74
Emerald-74
Gold-74
Onyx-74
Ruby-74
Jerseys-J-PL
Jerseys Ruby-J-PL
Jersey Duals-DJ-PL
Jersey Triples-TJ-PL
Jersey Quads-QJ-PL
05Blues Team Set-10
05Panini Stickers-337
05Parkhurst-427
Facsimile Auto Parallel-427
True Colors-TCSTL
True Colors-TCSTL
05UD Powerplay Specialists-TSPL
05UD Powerplay Specialists Patches-SPPL
05Ultra-165
Gold-165
Ice-165
05Upper Deck-166
Big Playmakers-B-PL
HG Glossy-166
Notable Numbers-N-PLA
Patches-P-PL
05Upper Deck MVP-333
Gold-333
Platinum-333
Materials-M-PL
05Upper Deck Trilogy-77
05Upper Deck Toronto Fall Expo-166
05Upper Deck Victory-170
Black-170
Gold-170
Silver-170
05Peoria Rivermen-22
06Fleer Fabricology-FPL
06Ultra Uniformity-UPL
06Ultra Uniformity Patches-UPPL
06Norfolk Admirals-1

Lalonde, Bobby
71Canucks Royal Bank-1
71Toronto Sun-283
72Canucks Royal Bank-10
72O-Pee-Chee-217
73Canucks Royal Bank-10
73O-Pee-Chee-179
73Topps-189
74Canucks Royal Bank-9
74O-Pee-Chee NHL-392
75Canucks Royal Bank-10
75O-Pee-Chee NHL-246
75Topps-246
76Canucks Royal Bank-8
76O-Pee-Chee NHL-278
77O-Pee-Chee NHL-313
78Flames Majik Market-7
78O-Pee-Chee-285
79O-Pee-Chee-326
80O-Pee-Chee-265

Lalonde, Christian
91Michigan Falcons-1
92Anaheim Bullfrogs RHI-15
93Anaheim Bullfrogs RHI-9

Lalonde, Edouard
10C56-36
10Sweet Caporal Postcards-42
11C55-42
12C57-44
12C61 Lacrosse-11
23V128-1 Paulin's Candy-38
24V130 Maple Crispette-27
25Dominion Chocolates-95
27La Patrie-17
55Parkhurst-55
Quaker Oats-55
60Topps-48
Stamps-31
83Hall of Fame Postcards-E10
85Hall of Fame-70
99Upper Deck Century Legends-32
Century Collection-32
02ITG Used Vintage Memorabilia-VM1
02ITG Used Vintage Memorabilia Gold-VM1
02Parkhurst Reprints-208
03BAP Memorabilia Vintage Memorabilia-VM-8
03BAP Ultimate Memorabilia Paper Cuts-50
03Parkhurst Original Six Montreal-77
Memorabilia-MM21
04ITG Franchises Canadian Memorabilia-SM26
04ITG Franchises Canadian Mem Gold-SM26
04ITG Franchises Update-478
04ITG Ultimate Memorabilia-66
Gold-66
Original Six-12
Paper Cuts Memorabilia-5
05ITG Ultimate Memorabilia Level 1-74
05ITG Ultimate Memorabilia Level 2-74
05ITG Ultimate Memorabilia Level 3-74
05ITG Ultimate Memorabilia Level 4-74
05ITG Ultimate Memorabilia Level 5-74
05ITG Ultimate Mem Record Breaker Jerseys-1
05ITG Ultimate Mem RecBreak Jerseys Gold-1
06ITG Ultimate Memorabilia-107
Artist Proof-107

Lalonde, Gregg
94Sudbury Wolves Police-20
95Slapshot-384
95Sudbury Wolves-9
95Sudbury Wolves Police-11

Lalonde, Guy
51Bas Du Fleuve-16

Lalonde, Herve
52Juniors Blue Tint-38

Lalonde, Jacob
04Sault Ste. Marie Greyhounds-23

Lalonde, Mike
05Stockton Thunder-10
06Stockton Thunder-7

Lalonde, Pierre-Francois
917th Inn. Sketch QMJHL-205

Lalonde, Rob
06Reading Royals-1

Lalonde, Robert
72Sargent Promotions Stamps-221

Lalonde, Ron
74NHL Action Stamps-221
74NHL Action Stamps Update-42
74Penguins Postcards-13
75O-Pee-Chee NHL-152
75Topps-152
76O-Pee-Chee NHL-339
77O-Pee-Chee NHL-378
78O-Pee-Chee-371

Lalonde, Shawn
06Belleville Bulls-17

Lalonde, Todd
85Sudbury Wolves-7
86Sudbury Wolves-2
87Sudbury Wolves-4
88Sudbury Wolves-24
95Slapshot-405
97Sudbury Wolves Anniversary-11
00Fort Worth Brahmas-10
01Fort Worth Brahmas-13

Lalonde-McNicoll, Cedric
05Shawinigan Cataractes-15

Lalor, Mike
83Nova Scotia Voyageurs-12
85Canadiens Postcards-16
85Canadiens Provigo-8
86Canadiens Postcards-9
86Kraft Drawings-30
87Canadiens Postcards-12
87Canadiens Vachon Stickers-22
87Canadiens Vachon Stickers-59
87Canadiens Vachon Stickers-60
88Blues Kodak-12
88Canadiens Postcards-15
89Blues Kodak-26
90Capitals Kodak-12
90Capitals Postcards-12
90Capitals Smokey-11
90O-Pee-Chee-341
90OPC Premier-57
90Panini Stickers-267
90Pro Set-264
90Pro Set-552
90Score-67
Canadian-67
90Score Rookie/Traded-98T
90Topps-341
Tiffany-341
90Upper Deck-40
French-40
91Capitals Junior 5x7-17
91O-Pee-Chee-483
91Parkhurst-427
French-427
91Pro Set-255
French-255
91Score American-249
91Score Canadian Bilingual-469
91Score Canadian English-469
91Topps-483
92Bowman-319
92Pinnacle-123
French-123
92Pro Set-268
92Score-363
Canadian-363
92Stadium Club-190
92Topps-140
Gold-140G
93Donruss-306
93Kraft-40
93Leaf-399
94Stars Postcards-14
96Stars Postcards-14

Laluk, Laird
95Saskatoon Blades-12
96Saskatoon Blades-14

Laluk, Scott
92Brandon Wheat Kings-14
93Brandon Wheat Kings-4
94Brandon Wheat Kings-11
95Slapshot Memorial Cup-29

Lamande, Etienne
93Quebec Pee-Wee Tournament-1655

Lamarche, Alexandre
02Baie Comeau Drakkar-3
03Baie Comeau Drakkar-8
04Chicoutimi Sagueneens-1

Lamarche, Martin
917th Inn. Sketch QMJHL-90
95PEI Senators-10
96Saint John Flames-11
98Fort Worth Brahmas-16
99Fort Worth Brahmas-10
01Thetford Mines Coyotes-24

Lamarre, Sandy
97El Paso Buzzards-16
98El Paso Buzzards-17
01Kalamazoo K-Wings-20

Lamb, Bryce
06Prince Albert Raiders-22

Lamb, Garth
89Nashville Knights-14

Lamb, Jeff
88ProCards AHL-150
89ProCards IHL-110

Lamb, Joe
33O-Pee-Chee V304A-2
33V357 Ice Kings-41
34Beehive Group I Photos-237
34Diamond Matchbooks Silver-37
34Sweet Caporal-6
35Diamond Matchbooks Tan 1-37
37V356 Worldwide Gum-37
38Bruins Garden Magazine Supplement-4

Lamb, Kirk
01Trenton Titans-1-4

Lamb, Kyle
03Regina Pats-10
03Sudbury Wolves-12
04Vancouver Giants-19
05Mississauga Ice Dogs-9
05Owen Sound Attack-4
05Vancouver Giants-13
06Mississauga Ice Dogs-21

Lamb, Mark
82Medicine Hat Tigers-9
83Medicine Hat Tigers-8
84Moncton Golden Flames-6
85Moncton Golden Flames-7
88Oilers Tenth Anniversary-61
88Oilers Team Issue-16
88ProCards AHL-89
89Oilers Team Issue-14
90Oilers IGA-11
90O-Pee-Chee-25
90Pro Set-88
90Score-308C
Canadian-308C
90Topps-25
Tiffany-25
91Oilers Panini Team Stickers-10
91Oilers IGA-8
91Oilers Team Issue-10
91Score Canadian Bilingual-652
91Score Canadian English-652
92O-Pee-Chee-322
92Parkhurst-116
Emerald Ice-116
92Pinnacle-374
French-374
92Score-514
Canadian-514
92Senators Team Issue-7
92Topps-230
Gold-230G
93Donruss-230
93Flyers Lineup Sheets-20
93Leaf-308
93OPC Premier-271
Gold-271
93Panini Stickers-117
93Pinnacle-323
Canadian-323
Captains-16
Captains Canadian-16
93PowerPlay-171
93Score-407
Canadian-407
93Senators Kraft Sheets-13
93Stadium Club-172
Members Only Master Set-172
OPC-172
First Day Issue-172
First Day Issue OPC-172
93Topps/OPC Premier-271
Gold-271
94Canada Games NHL POGS-178
94Leaf-337
94Pinnacle-163
Artist's Proofs-163
Rink Collection-163
94Stadium Club-206
Members Only Master Set-206
First Day Issue-206
Super Team Winner Cards-206
95Houston Aeros-12
99Houston Aeros-4

Lamberg, Antti-Pekka
01Finnish Cardset-196
04Finnish Cardset-277

Lambert, Dale
98UK Kingston Hawks-1

Lambert, Dan
907th Inn. Sketch OHL-164
91Pinnacle-346
French-346
91Upper Deck-592
French-592
92Bowman-356
92O-Pee-Chee-357
92Topps-364
Gold-364G
92Upper Deck-251
93Finnish Jyvas-Hyva Stickers-26
93Finnish SISU-87
96Collector's Edge Future Legends-30
97Long Beach Ice Dogs-10
98Long Beach Ice Dogs-9
99German DEL-110
00German DEL-149
01German Upper Deck-160
02German DEL City Press-222
03German DEL-112
04German DEL-154
04German Hannover Scorpions Postcards-17
05German DEL-133
06German DEL-83

Lambert, Denny
89Sault Ste. Marie Greyhounds-8
91ProCards-324
917th Inn. Sketch Memorial Cup-17
92San Diego Gulls-14
93San Diego Gulls-12
95Bowman-98
All-Foil-98
95Topps-286
OPC Inserts-286
95Ultra-4
Gold Medallion-4
96Be A Player-68
Autographs-68
Autographs Silver-68
96Senators Pizza Hut-11
97Pacific Invincible NHL Regime-134
98Aurora-103
98Pacific-311
Ice Blue-311
Red-311
98Pacific Omega-131
Red-131
Opening Day Issue-131
98Paramount-125
Copper-125
Emerald Green-125
Holo-Electric-125
Ice Blue-125
Silver-125
98Predators Team Issue-15
99Pacific-228
Copper-228
Emerald Green-228
Gold-228
Ice Blue-228
Premiere Date-228
Red-228
00Pacific-20
Copper-20
Gold-20
Ice Blue-20
Premiere Date-20
00Upper Deck Vintage-23
01BAP Update Tough Customers-TC23
01BAP Update Tough Customers-TC33
03Sault Ste. Marie Greyhounds-25

Lambert, Judd
92British Columbia JHL-42
97Albany River Rats-8

Lambert, Lane
81Saskatoon Blades-19
84O-Pee-Chee-60
87Nordiques General Foods-19
87Nordiques Team Issue-5
87Red Wings Little Caesars-18
88Nordiques General Foods-22
88Nordiques Team Issue-20
88O-Pee-Chee-224
88O-Pee-Chee Stickers-183
88Panini Stickers-356
93Swiss HNL-503
95Swiss HNL-362
96Cleveland Lumberjacks-14
96Cleveland Lumberjacks Multi-Ad-16
97Cleveland Lumberjacks-16
97Cleveland Lumberjacks Postcards-14
98Cleveland Lumberjacks-12
99Houston Aeros-7
06Milwaukee Admirals -23

Lambert, Michael
03P.E.I. Rocket-10
04Hamilton Bulldogs-16
05Hamilton Bulldogs-13
06Hamilton Bulldogs-17

Lambert, Ross
83Moncton Alpines-13
84Nova Scotia Oilers-23

Lambert, Sylvio
51Laval Dairy Lac St. Jean-21

Lambert, Vincent
03Cape Breton Screaming Eagles-28
04Cape Breton Screaming Eagles-11
05Saint John's Sea Dogs-22

Lambert, Yves
917th Inn. Sketch QMJHL-272

Lambert, Yvon
72Dimanche/Derniere Heure *-144
73Canadiens Postcards-8
74Canadiens Postcards-9
74NHL Action Stamps-147
74O-Pee-Chee NHL-342
75Canadiens Postcards-9
75O-Pee-Chee NHL-17
75Topps-17
76Canadiens Postcards-10
76O-Pee-Chee NHL-232
76Topps-232
77Canadiens Postcards-11
77O-Pee-Chee NHL-151
77Topps-151
78Canadiens Postcards-12
78O-Pee-Chee-147
78Topps-147
79Canadiens Postcards-11
79O-Pee-Chee-24
79Topps-24
80Canadiens Postcards-11
80O-Pee-Chee-246
80Pepsi-Cola Caps-48
80Topps-246
81O-Pee-Chee-185
81O-Pee-Chee Stickers-35
81Sabres Milk Panels-16
82O-Pee-Chee-27
82O-Pee-Chee Stickers-125
82Post Cereal-2
82Topps Stickers-125

Lamberty, Ralf
94German First League-603

Lambros, James
92Michigan State Spartans-14

Lamby, Dick
79Panini Stickers-208

LaMere, Ryan
03St. Cloud State Huskies-15

Lamey, Rob
96UK Guildford Flames-2
99UK Guildford Flames-20
00UK Guildford Flames-13
06UK Guildford Flames-5

Lamia, Nick
98Danish Hockey League-53

Lamich, Martin
97Czech APS Extraliga-142
98Czech OFS-125
99Czech DS-177
99Czech OFS-425

Laming, Andrew
917th Inn. Sketch WHL-65

Lamirande, Charles
51Laval Dairy Lac St. Jean-31

Lamirande, Gaston
51Laval Dairy Lac St. Jean-39

Lamirande, J.P.
51Laval Dairy QSHL-31
52St. Lawrence Sales-95

Lamirande, Maurice
51Bas Du Fleuve-38
52Bas Du Fleuve-5

Lammassaari, Petri
05Finnish Cardset -286
06Finnish Cardset-114
Playmakers Rookies-7
Playmakers Rookies Gold-7
Playmakers Rookies Silver-7
Signature Sensations-21

Lamme, Natalie
04Minnesota Golden Gophers Women-5

Lammens, Hank
88ProCards AHL-320
89ProCards AHL-233
92Alberta International Team Canada-10
93Parkhurst-409
Emerald Ice-409
94Swedish Olympics Lillehammer*-317

Lammers, Jason
98Idaho Steelheads-10

Lammers, John
03Lethbridge Hurricanes-2
04Lethbridge Hurricanes-8
05Everett Silvertips-16
06Iowa Stars-13

Lamminger, Daniel
93Swiss HNL-279
96Swiss HNL-486

Lamonde, Jean Paul
56Quebec Aces-8

Lamontagne, Guy
93Quebec Pee-Wee Tournament-421

Lamontagne, Richard
93Quebec Pee-Wee Tournament-1061

Lamoreux, Leo
34Beehive Group I Photos-163
43Parade Sportive *-11

Lamoriello, Lou
88Devils Caretta-16
89Devils Caretta-14
90Devils Team Issue-14
96Devils Team Issue-NNO
97Devils Team Issue-31
98Devils Team Issue-15
99Devils Team Issue-29
00Devils Team Issue-29
01Devils Team Issue-10
02Devils Team Issue-25
03Devils Team Issue-41
05Devils Team Issue-6
06Devils Team Set-28

Lamothe, Carl
907th Inn. Sketch QMJHL-255
917th Inn. Sketch QMJHL-148

Lamothe, Marc
917th Inn. Sketch OHL-240
93Kingston Frontenacs-2
94Fredericton Canadiens-16
95Fredericton Canadiens-16
97Indianapolis Ice-13
98Indianapolis Ice-14
99BAP Memorabilia-399
Gold-399
Silver-399
99Pacific Omega-58
Copper-58
Gold-58
Ice Blue-58
Premiere Date-58
99Cleveland Lumberjacks-11
00Syracuse Crunch-1
01Hamilton Bulldogs-20
02Between the Pipes-87
Gold-87
Silver-87
02Grand Rapids Griffins-17
03BAP Memorabilia Deep in the Crease-D8
03Parkhurst Original Six Detroit-24
03Grand Rapids Griffins-11
03Pacific AHL Prospects-26
Gold-26
04Russian Legion-31

Lamoureux, Denis
96Johnstown Chiefs-9

Lamoureux, Guillaume
98Val d'Or Foreurs-3

Lamoureux, Mitch
80Oshawa Generals-15
81Oshawa Generals-6
92San Diego Gulls-15
96Providence Bruins-22
98Hershey Bears-1
98Hershey Bears-20

Lamoureux, Patrick
917th Inn. Sketch QMJHL-51

Lamoureux, Philippe
01Lincoln Stars-16
02Lincoln Stars-1
02Lincoln Stars-40
03Lincoln Stars-1
03Lincoln Stars Update-39
03Lincoln Stars Update-43
03Lincoln Stars Update-44
04North Dakota Fighting Sioux-13

Lamoureux, Pierre-Paul
05Red Deer Rebels-9

Lamoureux, Robert
72Finnish Jaakiekko-215
73Finnish Jaakiekko-289

Lampainen, Matti
65Finnish Hellas-80

Lampe, Eric
03Chicago Steel-12

Lampert, Reinhard
93Swedish Semic World Champ Stickers-287
94Finnish Jaa Kiekko-247

Lampinen, Juha
92Finnish Jyvas-Hyva Stickers-42
93Finnish Jyvas-Hyva Stickers-85
93Finnish SISU-113
94Finnish SISU-54
95Finnish SISU-232
96German DEL-95

Lampman, Bryce
02Hartford Wolf Pack-14
03ITG VIP Rookie Debut-135
03Parkhurst Rookie-73
03UD Premier Collection-87
03Upper Deck Rookie Update-181
03Hartford Wolf Pack-12
04Pacific-292
Blue-292
Red-292
04Hartford Wolf Pack-11
05Hartford Wolf Pack-14
06Hartford Wolf Pack-4

Lampman, Josh
93Waterloo Black Hawks-15

Lampman, Mike
72Blues White Border-9
73Blues White Border-11
76O-Pee-Chee NHL-375
77O-Pee-Chee NHL-396

Lamprecht, Pascal
96Swiss HNL-409
01Swiss HNL-446
02Swiss HNL-188

Lampron, Patrick
917th Inn. Sketch QMJHL-98

Lamy, Jonathan
92Quebec Pee-Wee Tournament-905
93Quebec Pee-Wee Tournament-147

Landegren, Dan
71Swedish Hockey-235
72Swedish Stickers-222
73Swedish Stickers-75
74Swedish Stickers-237

Landeskog, Tony
84Swedish Semic Elitserien-130

Landgren, Reine
89Swedish Semic Elitserien Stickers-232
90Swedish Semic Elitserien Stickers-64
91Swedish Semic Elitserien Stickers-242

Landini, Mark
94Wheeling Thunderbirds-23

Landman, Erik
01Fort Wayne Komets-10

Landman, Jacco
05Dutch Vadeko Flyers -11

Landmesser, Derek
98Thunder Bay Thunder Cats-14
99Rockford IceHogs-12
03Memphis RiverKings-9
04Memphis RiverKings-6

Landoli, Nicky
94UK Guildford Flames-17

Landolt, Patrick
01Swiss HNL-393

Landolt, Shaun
01Moose Jaw Warriors-20
03Calgary Hitmen-12
04Calgary Hitmen-10

Landon, Bruce
72Whalers New England WHA-10
76O-Pee-Chee WHA-48

Landon, Larry
83Nova Scotia Voyageurs-23

Landry, Alexandre
93Quebec Pee-Wee Tournament-125

Landry, Andre
99Shawinigan Cataractes-21
Signed-21

Landry, Christian
05Baie-Comeau Drakkar-8

Landry, Eric
93Guelph Storm-10
95Slapshot-318
96Roanoke Express-3
97Saint John Flames-13
99Indianapolis Ice-11
99Kentucky Thoroughblades-18
00Canadiens Postcards-15
00SP Authentic-148
00SPx-180
00Titanium-129
Retail-129
00Titanium Draft Day Edition-129
00Titanium Draft Day Promos-129
00Upper Deck Ice-91
00Austin Ice Bats-9
01Quebec Citadelles-3
02Utah Grizzlies-28
04Swiss Lausanne HC Postcards-23

Landry, Jerome
93Quebec Pee-Wee Tournament-4

Landry, John
82Kingston Canadians-17
84Sudbury Wolves-11

Landry, Jordan
93Quebec Pee-Wee Tournament-1232
95Kamloops Blazers-27
98Tri-City Americans-15
02Fresno Falcons-10
03Fresno Falcons-8

Landry, Roger
52Juniors Blue Tint-160

Landry, Roland
52Bas Du Fleuve-8

Landry, Sean
93Quebec Pee-Wee Tournament-21

Landry, Trent
97Dubuque Fighting Saints-14
00Connecticut Huskies-11

Landstrom, Kjell
71Swedish Hockey-236
72Swedish Stickers-223
73Swedish Stickers-76
74Swedish Stickers-238

Lane, Chris
95Spokane Chiefs-4
96Spokane Chiefs-4

Lane, Gordie
77O-Pee-Chee NHL-287
78Capitals Team Issue-6
78O-Pee-Chee-284
79O-Pee-Chee-325
80O-Pee-Chee-323
81O-Pee-Chee-212
83O-Pee-Chee-10
84Islanders News-17
85Islanders News-21
85O-Pee-Chee Stickers-77

Lane, Jesse
99Des Moines Buccaneers-8
01Hull Olympiques-15

Lane, Mitch
93Michigan Tech Huskies-22

Lang, Arne Kuben
56Swedish Alfabilder-88

Lang, Bill
907th Inn. Sketch OHL-310
917th Inn. Sketch OHL-60
93North Bay Centennials-9
01Bossier-Shreveport Mudbugs-9

Lang, Chad
91Peterborough Petes-22
917th Inn. Sketch OHL-129
93Peterborough Petes-15
93Classic Four-Sport *-214
Gold-214
95Classic-94
98Huntington Blizzard-3
98Peoria Rivermen-23
01Bossier-Shreveport Mudbugs-10

Lang, Glen
95Central Hockey League-64

Lang, Jared
00OCN Blizzard-5
02OCN Blizzard-10
03OCN Blizzard-11

Lang, Jason
93Quebec Pee-Wee Tournament-1461

Lang, Jeff
06Stockton Thunder-4

Lang, Karel
82Swedish Semic VM Stickers-77
83Swedish Semic VM Stickers-77
94German DEL-225
95German DEL-219
96German DEL-69
98German DEL-25
99German DEL-125
00German DEL-154

Lang, Kjell
69Swedish Hockey-86

Lang, Lubomir
94German First League-587

Lang, Lukas
04German DEL Update-340
04German Nuremburg Ice Tigers Postcards-10
05German DEL-268

Lang, Robert
92OPC Premier-47
92Parkhurst-64
92Parkhurst-227
Emerald Ice-64
Emerald Ice-227
92Pinnacle-411
French-411
92Upper Deck-552
Euro-Rookies-ER4
92Phoenix Roadrunners-12
93Score-456
Canadian-456
93Ultra-188
93Classic Pro Prospects-46
94Be A Player Signature Cards-174
94Leaf-429
94OPC Premier-218
Special Effects-218
94Parkhurst-286
Gold-286
94Parkhurst SE-SE78

Gold-SE78
94Pinnacle-413
Artist's Proofs-413
Rink Collection-413
94Topps/OPC Premier-218
Special Effects-218
94Ultra-101
94Upper Deck-175
Electric Ice-175
94Czech APS Extraliga-222
94Finnish Jaa Kiekko-186
95Collector's Choice-175
Player's Club-175
Player's Club Platinum-175
95Parkhurst International-101
Emerald Ice-101
95Topps-186
OPC Inserts-186
95Upper Deck-281
Electric Ice-281
Electric Ice Gold-281
95Swedish Globe World Championships-155
97Be A Player-14
Autographs-14
Autographs Die-Cuts-14
Autographs Prismatic Die-Cuts-14
97Czech APS Extraliga-355
97Czech DS Stickers-17
97Czech DS Stickers-73
98Be A Player-263
Press Release-263
98BAP Gold-263
98BAP Autographs-263
98BAP Autographs Gold-263
98Pacific-355
Ice Blue-355
Red-355
98Pacific Omega-197
Red-197
Opening Day Issue-197
98Czech DS Stickers-17
98Czech OFS-238
Olympic Winners-19
98Czech Bonaparte-1C
98Czech Pexeso-3
98Czech Spaghetti-5
98Slovakian Eurotel-12
99Crown Royale-114
Limited Series-114
Premiere Date-114
99Pacific-342
Copper-342
Emerald Green-342
Gold-342
Ice Blue-342
Premiere Date-342
Red-342
99Panini Stickers-133
99Upper Deck MVP SC Edition-150
Gold Script-150
Silver Script-150
Super Script-150
00BAP Memorabilia-382
Emerald-382
Ruby-382
Sapphire-382
Promos-382
00BAP Mem Chicago Sportsfest Copper-382
00BAP Memorabilia Chicago Sportsfest Blue-382
00BAP Memorabilia Chicago Sportsfest Gold-382
00BAP Memorabilia Chicago Sportsfest Ruby-382
00BAP Memorabilia Chicago Sun-Times Ruby-382
00BAP Memorabilia Chicago Sun-Times Gold-382
00BAP Mem Chicago Sun-Times Sapphire-382
00BAP Mem Toronto Fall Expo Copper-382
00BAP Memorabilia Toronto Fall Expo Gold-382
00BAP Memorabilia Toronto Fall Expo Ruby-382
00BAP Parkhurst 2000-P201
00BAP Signature Series-207
Emerald-207
Ruby-207
Sapphire-207
Autographs-65
Autographs Gold-65
00O-Pee-Chee-224
00O-Pee-Chee Parallel-224
00Pacific-331
Copper-331
Gold-331
Ice Blue-331
Premiere Date-331
00Panini Stickers-85
00Paramount-200
Copper-200
Gold-200
Holo-Gold-200
Holo-Silver-200
Ice Blue-200
Premiere Date-200
00Stadium Club-104
00Titanium Game Gear-136
00Titanium Game Gear Patches-136
00Topps/OPC-224
Parallel-224
00Upper Deck-139
Exclusives Tier 1-139
Exclusives Tier 2-139
00Upper Deck Victory-186
00Upper Deck Vintage-292
00Czech Stadion-69
01BAP Memorabilia-103
Emerald-103
Ruby-103
Sapphire-103
01Bowman YoungStars-99
Gold-99
Ice Cubed-99
01Crown Royale-116
Blue-116
Premiere Date-116
Red-116
Retail-116
01O-Pee-Chee-78
01O-Pee-Chee Heritage Parallel-78
01O-Pee-Chee Heritage Parallel Limited-78
01O-Pee-Chee Premier Parallel-78
01Pacific-315
Extreme LTD-315
Hobby LTD-315
Premiere Date-315
Retail LTD-315
01Pacific Adrenaline-154
Blue-154
Premiere Date-154
Red-154
Retail-154
Jerseys-37
01Pacific Arena Exclusives-315
01Private Stock PS-2002-58
01SP Game Used Authentic Fabric-AFRL
01SP Game Used Authentic Fabric-TFLKL
01SP Game Used Authentic Fabric Gold-AFRL
01SPx-54
01Sports Illustrated for Kids III-371
01Titanium-113
Hobby Parallel-113
Premiere Date-113
Retail-113
Retail Parallel-113
01Titanium Draft Day Edition-79
01Topps-78
Heritage Parallel-78
Heritage Parallel Limited-78
OPC Parallel-78
01Topps Chrome-78
Refractors-78
Black Border Refractors-78
01Topps Heritage-89
Refractors-89
Jerseys-JRL
01Topps Reserve Emblems-RL
01Topps Reserve Jerseys-RL
01Topps Reserve Name Plates-RL
01Topps Reserve Numbers-RL
01Topps Reserve Patches-RL
01Upper Deck-140
Exclusives-140
Pride of a Nation-TPHJL
01Upper Deck MVP-153
01Upper Deck Victory-282
Gold-282
01Upper Deck Vintage-203
01Vanguard Memorabilia-26
02Atomic Jerseys-25
02Atomic Jerseys Gold-25
02Atomic Patches-25
02BAP Memorabilia-172
02BAP Memorabilia-264
Emerald-172
Emerald-264
Ruby-172
Ruby-264
Sapphire-172
Sapphire-264
NHL All-Star Game-172
NHL All-Star Game-264
NHL All-Star Game Blue-172
NHL All-Star Game Blue-264
NHL All-Star Game Green-172
NHL All-Star Game Green-264
NHL All-Star Game Red-172
NHL All-Star Game Red-264
02BAP Memorabilia Toronto Fall Expo-172
02BAP Memorabilia Toronto Fall Expo-264
02BAP Signature Series-30
Autographs-30
Autograph Buybacks 1998-263
Autographs Gold-30
Golf-GS77
02Capitals Team Issue-7
02O-Pee-Chee-182
02O-Pee-Chee-182U
02O-Pee-Chee Premier Blue Parallel-182
02O-Pee-Chee Premier Red Parallel-182
02O-Pee-Chee Factory Set-182
02Pacific-311
Blue-311
Red-311
02Pacific Complete-306
Red-306
02Pacific Exclusive-174
02Pacific Heads-Up Quad Jerseys-22
02Pacific Heads-Up Quad Jerseys Gold-22
02Parkhurst-185
Bronze-185
Gold-185
Silver-185
02Parkhurst Retro-186
Minis-186
02Private Stock Reserve-150
Red-150
Retail-150
Patches-150
02Topps-182
02Topps-182U
OPC Blue Parallel-182
OPC Red Parallel-182
Factory Set-182
02Topps Chrome-105
Black Border Refractors-105
Refractors-105
02Topps Heritage-175
02Topps Total-216
02UD Top Shelf Goal Oriented-GORL
02UD Top Shelf Shooting Stars-SHRL
02Upper Deck-420
Exclusives-420
02Upper Deck Beckett UD Promos-420
02Upper Deck Specialists-SRL
02Upper Deck Classic Portraits Hockey Royalty-JHL
02Upper Deck Classic Portraits Hockey Royalty-LLN
02Upper Deck Classic Portraits Hockey Royalty Limited-JHL
02Upper Deck Classic Portraits Hockey Royalty Limited-LLN
02Upper Deck MVP-187
Gold-187
Classics-187
Golden Classics-187
02Upper Deck Victory National Pride-NP20
02Upper Deck Vintage-260
Green Backs-260
02Czech IQ Sports Blue-16
02Czech IQ Sports Yellow-17
02Czech Stadion Olympics-338
03Beehive-196
Gold-196
Silver-196
03ITG Action-569
03ITG Action-663
03NHL Sticker Collection-145
03O-Pee-Chee-47
03OPC Blue-47
03OPC Gold-47
03OPC Red-47
03Pacific-347
Blue-347
Red-347
03Pacific Calder-39
Silver-39
03Pacific Complete-65
Red-65
03Pacific Heads-Up-100
Hobby LTD-100
Retail LTD-100
03Pacific Quest for the Cup-39
Blue-39
03Parkhurst Rookie-33
03Private Stock Reserve-212
Blue-212
Patches-212
Red-212
Retail-212
03Titanium-100
Hobby Jersey Number Parallels-100
Retail-100
Retail Jersey Number Parallels-100
03Topps-47
Blue-47
Gold-47
Red-47
03Topps Traded-TT14
Blue-TT14
Gold-TT14
Red-TT14
03Upper Deck-193
Canadian Exclusives-193
HG-193
03Upper Deck MVP-425
Gold Script-425
Silver Script-425
Canadian Exclusives-425
04Pacific-95
Blue-95
Red-95
All-Stars-7
04Upper Deck-65
Canadian Exclusives-65
HG Glossy Gold-65
HG Glossy Silver-65
05Be A Player Signatures-LA
05Be A Player Signatures Gold-LA
05Panini Stickers-263
05Parkhurst-175
Facsimile Auto Parallel-175
True Colors-TCDET
True Colors-TCDET
05SP Game Used Authentic Fabrics Triple-SEL
05SP Game Used Authentic Patches Triple-SEL
05UD Powerplay Specialists-TSRL
05UD Powerplay Specialists Patches-SPRL
05Upper Deck-68
HG Glossy-68
05Upper Deck MVP-141
Gold-141
Platinum-141
Materials-M-RL
05Upper Deck Toronto Fall Expo-68
05Upper Deck Victory-72
Black-72
Gold-72
Silver-72
Stars on Ice-SI22
05Czech Kvarteto Bonaparte-8b
05Czech Pexeso Mini Blue Set-17
06Flair Showcase Stitches-SSRL
06Fleer-74
Tiffany-74
Fabricology-FRL
06O-Pee-Chee-176
Rainbow-176
Swatches-S-RL
06Panini Stickers-261
06The Cup NHL Shields Duals-DSHRW
06Upper Deck-74
Exclusives Parallel-74
High Gloss Parallel-74
Masterpieces-74
06Upper Deck MVP-107
Gold Script-107
Super Script-107
Jerseys-OJLS

Lang, Ryan
06Augusta Lynx-9

Langager, Jay
98Swift Current Broncos-16
99Swift Current Broncos-9
00Swift Current Broncos-11
01Greenville Grrrowl-9
02Johnstown Chiefs-8
03Johnstown Chiefs-7
03Johnstown Chiefs RBI Sports-218

Langager, Shane
88Saskatoon Blades-9
89Saskatoon Blades-9

Langauer, Michael
907th Inn. Sketch QMJHL-139

Langbacka, Jan
92Finnish Jyvas-Hyva Stickers-108
93Finnish Jyvas-Hyva Stickers-198
93Finnish SISU-266
94Finnish SISU-26

Langdon, Darren
92Dayton Bombers-16
93Anaheim Bullfrogs RHI-10
94Binghamton Rangers-9
95Bowman-92
All-Foil-92
95Donruss-224
95Leaf-262
95Metal-181
95Parkhurst International-528
Emerald Ice-528
95SkyBox Impact-212
95Topps-116
OPC Inserts-116
95Ultra-102
95Ultra-345
Gold Medallion-102
96Be A Player-9
Autographs-9
Autographs Silver-9
98OPC Chrome-172
Refractors-172
98Pacific-296
Ice Blue-296
Red-296
98Topps-172
O-Pee-Chee-172
00BAP Memorabilia-360
Emerald-360
Ruby-360
Sapphire-360
Promos-360
00BAP Mem Chicago Sportsfest Copper-360
00BAP Memorabilia Chicago Sportsfest Blue-360
00BAP Memorabilia Chicago Sportsfest Gold-360
00BAP Memorabilia Chicago Sportsfest Ruby-360
00BAP Memorabilia Chicago Sun-Times Ruby-360
00BAP Memorabilia Chicago Sun-Times Gold-360
00BAP Mem Chicago Sun-Times Sapphire-360
00BAP Mem Toronto Fall Expo Copper-360
00BAP Memorabilia Toronto Fall Expo Gold-360
00BAP Memorabilia Toronto Fall Expo Ruby-360
00Topps Heritage-165
00Upper Deck NHLPA-PA17
01BAP Update Tough Customers-TC10
01BAP Update Tough Customers-TC20
01Pacific-406
Gold-406
01Pacific Arena Exclusives-406
03Canadiens Postcards-18
03Parkhurst Original Six Montreal-28
03Topps Tough Materials-DL
03Topps Tough Materials-PWDL
05Devils Team Issue-20

Langdon, Kyle
93Quebec Pee-Wee Tournament-874

Langdon, Mark
02Barrie Colts-12
03Barrie Colts-12
04Barrie Colts 10th Anniversary-16
04Richmond Riverdogs-12

Langdon, Sean
01Kingston Frontenacs-10
03Sudbury Wolves-13

Langdon, Steve
77Rochester Americans-15

Langdone, Ashley
00San Diego Gulls-6
04Bakersfield Condors-9

Lange, Carsten
94German First League-499

Lange, Jason
04Lakehead University Thunderwolves-6

Lange, Lennart
64Swedish Coralli ISHockey-56
65Swedish Coralli ISHockey-56
67Swedish Hockey-104
71Swedish Hockey-355

Lange, Patrick
94German DEL-195
95German DEL-309

Langelier-Parent, Maxime
05Gatineau Olympiques-19

Langelle, Pete
34Beehive Group I Photos-333
39O-Pee-Chee V301-1-7
40O-Pee-Chee V301-2-117

Langen, Mike
907th Inn. Sketch WHL-270
91Air Canada SJHL-A13

Langenbrunner, Jamie
93Donruss Team USA-13
93Pinnacle-496
Canadian-496
93Upper Deck-566
93Peterborough Petes-20
94Finest-120
Super Team Winners-120
Refractors-120
94Leaf Limited World Juniors USA-7
94Parkhurst SE-SE248
Gold-SE248
94Score Gold-211
94SP-194
94Classic-24
Gold-24
Tri-Cards-T16
95Summit-170
Artist's Proofs-170
Ice-170
95Ultra-346
95Upper Deck-503
Electric Ice-503
Electric Ice Gold-503
95Zenith-129
95Classic-94
95Images-48
Gold-48
Autographs-48A
96Be A Player Link to History-6A
96Be A Player Link to History Autographs-6A
96Be A Player Link to History Auto Silver-6A
96Black Diamond-126
Gold-126
96Collector's Choice-74
96Donruss-218
Press Proofs-218
96Donruss Canadian Ice-137
Gold Press Proofs-137
Red Press Proofs-137
96Donruss Elite-144
Die Cut Stars-144
Aspirations-21
96Flair-105
Blue Ice-105
96Fleer-129
Calder Candidates-6
96Leaf-225
Press Proofs-225
Limited Rookies-8
Limited Rookies Gold-8
96Leaf Preferred-144
Press Proofs-144
96Metal Universe-184
96Pinnacle-247
Artist's Proofs-247
Foil-247
Premium Stock-247
Rink Collection-247
96Score-254
Artist's Proofs-254
Dealer's Choice Artist's Proofs-254
Special Artist's Proofs-254
Golden Blades-254
96Select Certified-115
Artist's Proofs-115
Blue-115
Mirror Blue-115
Mirror Gold-115
Mirror Red-115
Red-115
96SkyBox Impact-152
96SP-46
96Stars Postcards-15
96Summit-192
Artist's Proofs-192
Ice-192
Metal-192
Premium Stock-192
96Ultra-43
Gold Medallion-43
Rookies-11
96Upper Deck-48
96Upper Deck Ice-15
Parallel-15
96Zenith-139
Artist's Proofs-139
96Collector's Edge Ice-141
Platinum Club-6
Prism-141
97Collector's Choice-69
97Donruss-97
Press Proofs Silver-97
Press Proofs Gold-97
97Donruss Canadian Ice-103
Dominion Series-103
Provincial Series-103
97Donruss Limited-167
Exposure-167
97Donruss Preferred-20
Cut to the Chase-20
97Donruss Priority-79
Stamp of Approval-79
97Leaf-46
Fractal Matrix-46
Fractal Matrix Die Cuts-46
97Leaf International-46
Universal Ice-46
97Pacific-110
Copper-110
Emerald Green-110
Ice Blue-110
Red-110
Silver-110
97Pacific Dynagon-36
Copper-36
Dark Grey-36
Emerald Green-36
Ice Blue-36
Red-36
Silver-36
Tandems-32
97Pacific Invincible-40
Copper-40
Emerald Green-40
Ice Blue-40
Red-40
Silver-40
97Pacific Omega-70
Copper-70
Dark Gray-70
Emerald Green-70
Gold-70
Ice Blue-70
97Paramount-58
Copper-58
Dark Grey-58
Emerald Green-58
Ice Blue-58
Red-58
Silver-58
97Pinnacle Inside-100
97Revolution-41
Copper-41
Emerald-41
Ice Blue-41
Silver-41
97Score-211
97SP Authentic-47
Sign of the Times-JLA
97Upper Deck-260
97Zenith-61
Z-Gold-61
Z-Silver-61
97Zenith 5 x 7-51
Gold Impulse-51
Silver Impulse-51
98Aurora-56
98Crown Royale-39
Limited Series-39
98OPC Chrome-7
Refractors-7
98Pacific-15
Ice Blue-15
Red-15
98Pacific Dynagon Ice-57
Blue-57
Red-57
98Pacific Omega-71
Red-71
Opening Day Issue-71
98Paramount-65
Copper-65
Emerald Green-65
Holo-Electric-65
Ice Blue-65
Silver-65
98Revolution-42
Ice Shadow-42
Red-42
98Topps-7
O-Pee-Chee-7
98UD Choice-61
98UD Choice Preview-61
98UD Choice Prime Choice Reserve-61
98UD Choice Reserve-61
98Upper Deck-81
Exclusives-81
Exclusives 1 of 1-81
Gold Reserve-81
99Aurora-45
Premiere Date-45
99BAP Memorabilia-256
Gold-256
Silver-256
99BAP Millennium-75
Emerald-75
Ruby-75
Sapphire-75
Signatures-75
Signatures Gold-75
99O-Pee-Chee-60
99O-Pee-Chee Chrome-60
99O-Pee-Chee Chrome Refractors-60
99O-Pee-Chee Now Starring-NS10
99Pacific-122
Copper-122
Emerald Green-122
Gold-122
Ice Blue-122
Premiere Date-122
Red-122
99Pacific Dynagon Ice-66
Blue-66
Copper-66
Gold-66
Premiere Date-66
99Panini Stickers-228
99Paramount-73
Copper-73
Emerald-73
Gold-73
Holographic Emerald-73
Holographic Gold-73
Holographic Silver-73
Ice Blue-73
Premiere Date-73
Red-73
Silver-73
99Revolution-46
Premiere Date-46
Red-46
Shadow Series-46
99SPx-52
Radiance-52
Spectrum-52
99Stars Postcards-10
99Topps/OPC-60
Now Starring-NS10
99Topps/OPC Chrome-60
Refractors-60
99Upper Deck-45
Exclusives-45
Exclusives 1 of 1-45
99Upper Deck Arena Giveaways-DS2
99Upper Deck Gold Reserve-45
99Upper Deck MVP-64
Gold Script-64
Silver Script-64
Super Script-64
99Upper Deck Victory-90
99Wayne Gretzky Hockey-56
00BAP Memorabilia-156
Emerald-156
Ruby-156
Sapphire-156
Promos-156
00BAP Mem Chicago Sportsfest Copper-156,
00BAP Memorabilia Chicago Sportsfest Blue-156
00BAP Memorabilia Chicago Sportsfest Gold-156
00BAP Memorabilia Chicago Sportsfest Ruby-156
00BAP Memorabilia Chicago Sun-Times Ruby-156
00BAP Memorabilia Chicago Sun-Times Gold-156
00BAP Mem Chicago Sun-Times Sapphire-156
00BAP Mem Toronto Fall Expo Copper-156
00BAP Memorabilia Toronto Fall Expo Gold-156
00BAP Memorabilia Toronto Fall Expo Ruby-156
00BAP Parkhurst 2000-P188
00Crown Royale Game-Worn Jerseys-9
00Crown Royale Game-Worn Jersey Patches-9
00Crown Royale Premium-Sized Jerseys-9
00O-Pee-Chee-118
00O-Pee-Chee Parallel-118
00Pacific-133
Copper-133
Gold-133
Ice Blue-133
Premiere Date-133
00Panini Stickers-149
00Paramount-76
Copper-76
Gold-76
Holo-Gold-76
Holo-Silver-76
Ice Blue-76
Premiere Date-76
00Private Stock Game Gear-37
00Private Stock Game Gear Patches-37
00Revolution Game-Worn Jerseys-5
00Revolution Game-Worn Jersey Patches-5
00Stadium Club-130
00Stars Postcards-11
00Titanium Game Gear-86
00Titanium Game Gear Patches-86
00Titanium Draft Day Edition-31
Patches-31
00Topps/OPC-118
Parallel-118
00Topps Chrome-91
OPC Refractors-91
Refractors-91
00Upper Deck-286
Exclusives Tier 1-286
Exclusives Tier 2-286
00Upper Deck MVP-60
First Stars-60
Second Stars-60
Third Stars-60
00Upper Deck Victory-75
00Upper Deck Vintage-116
00Vanguard Dual Game-Worn Jerseys-15
00Vanguard Dual Game-Worn Patches-15
01BAP Memorabilia-114
01BAP Memorabilia-465
Emerald-114
Emerald-465
Ruby-114
Ruby-465
Sapphire-114
Sapphire-465
01O-Pee-Chee-208
01O-Pee-Chee Premier Parallel-208
01Pacific-127
Extreme LTD-127
Hobby LTD-127
Premiere Date-127
Retail LTD-127
Jerseys-11
01Pacific Arena Exclusives-127
01Parkhurst-385
01Private Stock Game Gear-36
01Private Stock Game Gear Patches-36
01Stars Postcards-11
01Titanium Double-Sided Jerseys-16
01Titanium Double-Sided Patches-16
01Titanium Draft Day Edition-54
01Topps-208
OPC Parallel-208
01UD Stanley Cup Champs-52
01Upper Deck-58
Exclusives-58
01Upper Deck Victory-116
Gold-116
01Vanguard Memorabilia-12
01Vanguard Patches-12
02BAP Memorabilia-28
Emerald-28
Ruby-28
Sapphire-28
NHL All-Star Game-28
NHL All-Star Game Blue-28
NHL All-Star Game Green-28
NHL All-Star Game Red-28
02BAP Memorabilia Toronto Fall Expo-28
02BAP Sig Series Auto Buybacks 1999-75
02Devils Team Issue-12
02O-Pee-Chee-170
02O-Pee-Chee Premier Blue Parallel-170
02O-Pee-Chee Premier Red Parallel-170
02O-Pee-Chee Factory Set-170
02Pacific-224
Blue-224
Red-224
Jerseys-30
Jerseys Holo-Silver-30
02Pacific Complete-450
Red-450
02Pacific Quest for the Cup-59
Gold-59
02Topps-170
OPC Blue Parallel-170
OPC Red Parallel-170
Factory Set-170
02Topps Total-75
02Upper Deck-104
Exclusives-104
02Vanguard-62
LTD-62
03BAP Memorabilia-32
Emerald-32
Gold-32
Ruby-32
Sapphire-32
Stanley Cup Champions-SCC-2
Stanley Cup Playoffs-SCP-24
03Beehive-111
Gold-111
Silver-111
03Black Diamond-123
Black-123
Green-123
Red-123
03Devils Team Issue-15
03eTopps-8
03ITG Action-301
Jerseys-M111
03NHL Sticker Collection-67
03O-Pee-Chee-248
03OPC Blue-248
03OPC Gold-248
03OPC Red-248
03Pacific-201
Blue-201
Red-201
03Pacific Complete-217
Red-217
03Pacific Exhibit-87
Blue Backs-87
Yellow Backs-87
03Pacific Heads-Up-60
Hobby LTD-60
Retail LTD-60
03Pacific Invincible-58
Blue-58
Red-58
Retail-58
03Pacific Prism-62
Blue-62
Gold-62
Red-62
03Pacific Supreme-60
Blue-60
Red-60
Retail-60
03Private Stock Reserve-61
Blue-61
Red-61
Retail-61
03SPx-59
Radiance-59
Spectrum-59
03Topps-248
Blue-248
Gold-248
Red-248
Topps/OPC Idols-UI20
03Topps C55-125
Minis-125
Minis American Back-125
Minis American Back Red-125
Minis Bazooka Back-125
Minis Brooklyn Back-125
Minis Hat Trick Back-125
Minis O Canada Back-125
Minis O Canada Back Red-125
Minis Stanley Cup Back-125
03Upper Deck-359
Big Playmakers-BP-JL
Canadian Exclusives-359
HG-359
UD Exclusives-359
03Upper Deck Classic Portraits-57
03Upper Deck MVP-248
Gold Script-248
Silver Script-248
Canadian Exclusives-248
SportsNut-SN51
03Upper Deck Trilogy-57
Limited-57
03Upper Deck Victory-108
Bronze-108
Gold-108
Silver-108
03Czech Stadion-606
03Toronto Star-55
04Pacific-159
Blue-159
Red-159
04German DEL Superstars-SU12
04German Ingolstadt Panthers-14
05Devils Team Issue-21
05Panini Stickers-84
05Parkhurst-288
Facsimile Auto Parallel-288
05Upper Deck-367
05Upper Deck MVP-239
Gold-239
Platinum-239
05Upper Deck Victory-229
Black-229
Gold-229
Silver-229
06Devils Team Set-12
06O-Pee-Chee-299
Rainbow-299
06Panini Stickers-82
06Upper Deck-118
Exclusives Parallel-118
High Gloss Parallel-118
Masterpieces-118
06Upper Deck MVP-179
Gold Script-179
Super Script-179

Langer, Christian
93Swiss HNL-372
95Swiss HNL-89
96Swiss HNL-32
98Swiss Power Play Stickers-181
99German DEL-80
99German DEL-374
00Swiss Panini Stickers-81
00Swiss Slapshot Mini-Cards-EHCC3

Langevin, Chris
85Sabres Blue Shield-16
85Sabres Blue Shield Small-16

Langevin, Dave
79Islanders Transparencies-8
80O-Pee-Chee-188
80Topps-188
81O-Pee-Chee-213
82O-Pee-Chee-204
82Post Cereal-12
83Islanders Team Issue-8
83NHL Key Tags-80
83O-Pee-Chee-11
83O-Pee-Chee Stickers-83
83Topps Stickers-83
84Islanders News-18
85Islanders News-22
85North Stars 7-Eleven-11
85North Stars Postcards-15
86O-Pee-Chee-218
97Idaho Steelheads-22
00Upper Deck Vintage Dynasty: A Piece of History-LL
00Upper Deck Vintage Dynasty: A Piece of History Gold-LL

Langevin, Jean
93Quebec Pee-Wee Tournament-282

Langevin, Pascal
93Quebec Pee-Wee Tournament-200

Langfeld, Josh
01BAP Memorabilia-430
Emerald-430
Ruby-430
Sapphire-430
01Parkhurst-332
01UD Mask Collection-158
Gold-158
01Grand Rapids Griffins-13
02Upper Deck-217
Exclusives-217
03Binghamton Senators-12
03Binghamton Senators Postcards-2
04Binghamton Senators-10
04Binghamton Senators Hess-10
05Bruins Boston Globe-22
05Parkhurst-48
Facsimile Auto Parallel-48
06Binghamton Senators 5th Anniversary-16

Langhammer, Jakub
02Spokane Chiefs-12
06Czech HC Sparta Praha Postcards-9
06Czech OFS-79

Langill, Eric
93Quebec Pee-Wee Tournament-20

Langille, Derek
90Newmarket Saints-13
90ProCards AHL/IHL-153
91Moncton Hawks-16
91ProCards-173

Langille, Matt
93Quebec Pee-Wee Tournament-696

Langis, Owen
03Camrose Kodiaks-10

Langkow, Daymond
93Upper Deck Program of Excellence-E7
94Lightning Postcards-12
94Tri-City Americans-6
94Classic Draft Prospects-DP4
95Collector's Choice-402
95Donruss-324
Elite World Juniors-16
95Leaf Limited-45
95Metal-182
95Parkhurst International-270
Emerald Ice-270
95Select Certified-124
Mirror Gold-124
95SkyBox Impact-222
95SP-139
95Upper Deck-270
95Upper Deck-526
Electric Ice-270
Electric Ice-526
Electric Ice Gold-270
Electric Ice Gold-526
95Zenith-143
95Tri-City Americans-15
95Tri-City Americans-30
95Classic-5
CHL All-Stars-AS4
Ice Breakers-BK5
Ice Breakers Die Cuts-BK5
95Images-83
Gold-83
Clear Excitement-CE12
Platinum Premier Draft Choice-PD6
95Signature Rookies-22
Auto-Phonex Prodigies-P2
Signatures-22
95Classic Five-Sport *-147
Strive For Five-HK8
95Signature Rookies Tetrad Autobilia *-45
95Signature Rookies Tetrad SR Force *-F4
96Black Diamond-46
Gold-46
96Collector's Choice-346
96Donruss Canadian Ice-135
Gold Press Proofs-135
Red Press Proofs-135
96Donruss Elite-134
Die Cut Stars-134
Aspirations-13
96Fleer-130
Calder Candidates-7
96Leaf-232
Press Proofs-232
96Leaf Preferred-140
Press Proofs-140
96Metal Universe-185
96Pinnacle-240
Artist's Proofs-240

Foil-240
Premium Stock-240
Rink Collection-240
96Select Certified-117
Artist's Proofs-117
Blue-117
Mirror Blue-117
Mirror Gold-117
Mirror Red-117
Red-117
96SkyBox Impact-153
96SP-146
96Summit-186
Artist's Proofs-186
Ice-186
Metal-186
Premium Stock-186
96Ultra-158
Gold Medallion-158
96Upper Deck-340
Generation Next-X30
96Zenith-141
Artist's Proofs-141
96Classic Signings Freshly Inked *-FS26
97Be A Player-176
Autographs-176
Autographs Die-Cuts-176
Autographs Prismatic Die-Cuts-176
97Collector's Choice-243
97Donruss-18
Press Proofs Silver-18
Press Proofs Gold-18
97Donruss Canadian Ice-70
Dominion Series-70
Provincial Series-70
National Pride-21
97Donruss Elite-36
Aspirations-36
Status-36
97Donruss Limited-31
97Donruss Limited-133
97Donruss Limited-192
Exposure-31
Exposure-133
Exposure-192
Fabric of the Game-48
97Donruss Preferred-23
Cut to the Chase-23
97Donruss Priority-21
Stamp of Approval-21
97Katch-136
Gold-136
Silver-136
97Leaf-103
Fractal Matrix-103
Fractal Matrix Die Cuts-103
97Leaf International-103
Universal Ice-103
97Pacific Dynagon-119
Copper-119
Dark Grey-119
Emerald Green-119
Ice Blue-119
Red-119
Silver-119
Tandems-65
97Pacific Invincible-133
Copper-133
Emerald Green-133
Ice Blue-133
Red-133
Silver-133
97Pacific Omega-210
Copper-210
Dark Gray-210
Emerald Green-210
Gold-210
Ice Blue-210
97Paramount-174
Copper-174
Dark Grey-174
Emerald Green-174
Ice Blue-174
Red-174
Silver-174
97Pinnacle-112
Press Plates Back Black-112
Press Plates Back Cyan-112
Press Plates Back Magenta-112
Press Plates Back Yellow-112
Press Plates Front Black-112
Press Plates Front Cyan-112
Press Plates Front Magenta-112
Press Plates Front Yellow-112
97Pinnacle Inside-99
97Score-167
97SP Authentic-145
97Studio-48
Press Proofs Silver-48
Press Proofs Gold-48
Hard Hats-6
97Upper Deck-158
Smooth Grooves-SG32
Three Star Selects-15C
97Upper Deck Ice-15
Parallel-15
Power Shift-15
98Be A Player-129
Press Release-129
98BAP Gold-129
98BAP Autographs-129
98BAP Autographs Gold-129
98BAP Tampa Bay All Star Game-129
98OPC Chrome-72
Refractors-72
98Pacific-400
Ice Blue-400
Red-400
98Topps-72
O-Pee-Chee-72
98UD Choice-192
Prime Choice Reserve-192
Reserve-192
99Pacific-305
Copper-305
Emerald Green-305
Gold-305
Ice Blue-305
Premiere Date-305
Red-305
99Pacific Omega-170
Copper-170
Gold-170
Ice Blue-170
Premiere Date-170
99Paramount-171

Copper-171
Emerald-171
Gold-171
Holographic Emerald-171
Holographic Gold-171
Holographic Silver-171
Ice Blue-171
Premiere Date-171
Red-171
Silver-171
99Upper Deck Arena Giveaways-PF2
99Upper Deck MVP SC Edition-136
Gold Script-136
Silver Script-136
Super Script-136
00BAP Memorabilia-324
Emerald-324
Ruby-324
Sapphire-324
Promos-324
00BAP Mem Chicago Sportsfest Copper-324
00BAP Memorabilia Chicago Sportsfest Blue-324
00BAP Memorabilia Chicago Sportsfest Gold-324
00BAP Memorabilia Chicago Sportsfest Ruby-324
00BAP Memorabilia Chicago Sun-Times Ruby-324
00BAP Memorabilia Chicago Sun-Times Gold-324
00BAP Mem Chicago Sun-Times Sapphire-324
00BAP Mem Toronto Fall Expo Copper-324
00BAP Memorabilia Toronto Fall Expo Gold-324
00BAP Memorabilia Toronto Fall Expo Ruby-324
00BAP Parkhurst 2000-P175
00BAP Signature Series-175
Emerald-175
Ruby-175
Sapphire-175
00O-Pee-Chee-98
00O-Pee-Chee Parallel-98
00Pacific-299
Copper-299
Gold-299
Ice Blue-299
Premiere Date-299
Jerseys-11
Jersey Patches-11
00Panini Stickers-77
00Paramount-181
Copper-181
Gold-181
Holo-Gold-181
Holo-Silver-181
Ice Blue-181
Premiere Date-181
00Private Stock Game Gear-82
00Private Stock Game Gear Patches-82
00Topps/OPC-98
Parallel-98
00Upper Deck-355
Exclusives Tier 1-355
Exclusives Tier 2-355
00Upper Deck Victory-173
00Upper Deck Vintage-262
01Atomic-76
Blue-76
Gold-76
Premiere Date-76
Red-76
01BAP Signature Series-142
Autographs-142
Autographs Gold-142
01Coyotes Team Issue-10
01Pacific-288
Extreme LTD-288
Hobby LTD-288
Premiere Date-288
Retail LTD-288
01Pacific Adrenaline-149
Blue-149
Premiere Date-149
Red-149
Retail-149
Jerseys-34
01Pacific Arena Exclusives-288
01Private Stock-76
Gold-76
Premiere Date-76
Retail-76
Silver-76
01Private Stock Pacific Nights-76
01Titanium-109
Hobby Parallel-109
Premiere Date-109
Retail-109
Retail Parallel-109
Double-Sided Jerseys-71
Double-Sided Patches-71
01Titanium Draft Day Edition-75
01Upper Deck-362
Exclusives-362
01Upper Deck Victory-255
Gold-255
01Vanguard-77
Blue-77
Red-77
One of Ones-77
Premiere Date-77
Proofs-77
02Atomic Jerseys-18
02Atomic Jerseys Gold-18
02Atomic Patches-18
02BAP First Edition-274
02BAP Memorabilia-48
Emerald-48
Ruby-48
Sapphire-48
NHL All-Star Game-48
NHL All-Star Game Blue-48
NHL All-Star Game Green-48
NHL All-Star Game Red-48
02BAP Memorabilia Toronto Fall Expo-48
02BAP Signature Series-96
Autographs-96
Autograph Buybacks 1998-129
Autograph Buybacks 2001-142
Autographs Gold-96
02Coyotes Team Issue-6
02O-Pee-Chee-244
02O-Pee-Chee Premier Blue Parallel-244
02O-Pee-Chee Premier Red Parallel-244
02O-Pee-Chee Factory Set-244
02Pacific-298
Blue-298
Red-298
Jerseys-41
Jerseys Holo-Silver-41
02Pacific Complete-22
Red-22

02Pacific Exclusive-135
02Pacific Heads-Up-97
Blue-97
Purple-97
Red-97
Quad Jerseys-21
Quad Jerseys Gold-21
02Parkhurst-157
Bronze-157
Gold-157
Silver-157
02Parkhurst Retro-64
Minis-64
02Private Stock Reserve-137
Red-137
Retail-137
Patches-137
02Topps-244
OPC Blue Parallel-244
OPC Red Parallel-244
Factory Set-244
02Topps Total-182
02Upper Deck-381
Exclusives-381
02Upper Deck Beckett UD Promos-381
02Upper Deck Victory-167
Bronze-167
Gold-167
Silver-167
02Upper Deck Vintage-196
03BAP Memorabilia-22
Emerald-22
Gold-22
Ruby-22
Sapphire-22
03BAP Ultimate Memorabilia Autographs-70
Gold-70
03Bowman-33
Gold-33
03Bowman Chrome-33
Refractors-33
Gold Refractors-33
Xfractors-33
03Coyotes Postcards-12
03eTopps-34
03ITG Action-483
03ITG Used Signature Series-89
Gold-89
Autographs-DLA
Autographs Gold-DLA
03NHL Sticker Collection-266
03O-Pee-Chee-11
03OPC Blue-11
03OPC Gold-11
03OPC Red-11
03Pacific-265
Blue-265
Red-265
03Pacific Complete-218
Red-218
03Pacific Exhibit-116
Blue Backs-116
Yellow Backs-116
03Pacific Invincible-77
Blue-77
Red-77
Retail-77
03Private Stock Reserve-80
Blue-80
Red-80
Retail-80
03Topps-11
Blue-11
Gold-11
Red-11
03Topps Pristine-92
Gold Refractor Die Cuts-92
Refractors-92
Press Plates Black-92
Press Plates Cyan-92
Press Plates Magenta-92
Press Plates Yellow-92
03Upper Deck-148
Canadian Exclusives-148
HG-148
03Upper Deck MVP-323
Gold Script-323
Silver Script-323
Canadian Exclusives-323
04Pacific-202
Blue-202
Red-202
05Be A Player Signatures-LW
05Be A Player Signatures Gold-LW
05Panini Stickers-203
05Parkhurst-68
Facsimile Auto Parallel-68
05Upper Deck-274
Notable Numbers-N-DLW
05Upper Deck MVP-67
Gold-67
Platinum-67
05Upper Deck Rookie Update-15
06Black Diamond-13
Black-13
Gold-13
Ruby-13
06Fleer-31
Tiffany-31
06Gatorade-5
06O-Pee-Chee-78
Rainbow-78
06Panini Stickers-203
06Ultra-32
Gold Medallion-32
Ice Medallion-32
06Upper Deck Arena Giveaways-CGY5
06Upper Deck-280
Exclusives Parallel-280
High Gloss Parallel-280
Masterpieces-280
06Upper Deck MVP-50
Gold Script-50
Super Script-50
06Upper Deck Ovation-58
06Upper Deck Victory-31
06Upper Deck Victory Black-31
06Upper Deck Victory Gold-31
07Upper Deck Ovation-42
07Upper Deck Victory-146
Black-146
Gold-146

Langkow, Scott

93Portland Winter Hawks-13
96Springfield Falcons-35
96Collector's Edge Ice-71

Prism-71
97Springfield Falcons-13
99BAP Memorabilia-368
Gold-368
Silver-368
99Pacific-332
Copper-332
Emerald Green-332
Gold-332
Ice Blue-332
Premiere Date-332
Red-332
99Upper Deck Victory-15
01Kalamazoo K-Wings-18
02Finnish Cardset-207
02Finnish Cardset-298
03Finnish Cardset-169
04Finnish Cardset-185
Parallel-138
Stars of the Game-4
04Swedish Pure Skills-143
Parallel-143
05Finnish Cardset -279
06Swedish SHL Elitset-192

Langlais, Alain

89New Haven Nighthawks-6

Langlais, Chad

06Lincoln Stars-3
06Lincoln Stars Traded-8T
06Lincoln Stars Traded-15T
06Lincoln Stars Upper DeckÂ Signature Series -19

Langley, Eric

93Quebec Pee-Wee Tournament-659

Langlois, Albert

44Beehive Group II Photos-256
44Beehive Group II Photos-335
58Parkhurst-5
59Parkhurst-45
60Parkhurst-39
60Shirriff Coins-24
60Topps Stamps-32
60York Photos-21
61Parkhurst-37
61Shirriff/Salada Coins-94
61Topps-46
62Topps-47
Hockey Bucks-14
63Topps-49
64Beehive Group III Photos-81
64Coca-Cola Caps-38
64Topps-13
65Coca-Cola-2
65Topps-33
94Parkhurst Tall Boys-52

Langlois, Alexandre

93Quebec Pee-Wee Tournament-311

Langlois, Benoit

92Quebec Pee-Wee Tournament-84
93Quebec Pee-Wee Tournament-1110

Langlois, Charlie

24Anonymous NHL-76
24V130 Maple Crispette-26
24V145-2-17
27La Patrie-12
27La Presse Photos-14

Langlois, Jim

60NHL Ceramic Tiles-11

Langlois, Jocelyn

907th Inn. Sketch QMJHL-79
917th Inn. Sketch QMJHL-40
97Macon Whoopee-6
97Macon Whoopee Autographs-6
00Rockford IceHogs-12

Langlois, Louis C

24C144 Champ's Cigarettes-35

Langlois, Luc

92Quebec Pee-Wee Tournament-529
93Quebec Pee-Wee Tournament-1129

Langlois, Mirko

93Sherbrooke Faucons-21

Langlois, Patrick

92Fredericton Canadiens-16
93Fredericton Canadiens-15
94Fredericton Canadiens-17
95Fredericton Canadiens-17
96Fredericton Canadiens-26

Langlois, Peter

84Kitchener Rangers-9

Langner, Paul

72Finnish Hellas-47
72Finnish Semic World Championship-111
72Swedish Semic World Championship-111

Langstrom, Juhani

71Finnish Suomi Stickers-286

Langtry, Jack

25Dominion Chocolates-86

Langway, Rod

78Canadiens Postcards-13
79Canadiens Postcards-12
80Canadiens Postcards-12
80O-Pee-Chee-344
80Pepsi-Cola Caps-49
81Canadiens Postcards-14
81O-Pee-Chee-186
81O-Pee-Chee Stickers-39
82Capitals Team Issue-13
82McDonald's Stickers-32
82O-Pee-Chee-368
82O-Pee-Chee Stickers-34
82Post Cereal-10
82Topps Stickers-34
83NHL Key Tags-127
83O-Pee-Chee-207
83O-Pee-Chee-365
83O-Pee-Chee-374
83O-Pee-Chee Stickers-201
83O-Pee-Chee Stickers-313
83Puffy Stickers-19
83Topps Stickers-201
83Topps Stickers-313
84Capitals Pizza Hut-11
84O-Pee-Chee-202
84O-Pee-Chee-210
84O-Pee-Chee-377
84O-Pee-Chee Stickers-125
84O-Pee-Chee Stickers-126
84O-Pee-Chee Stickers-230
847-Eleven Discs-54
84Topps-147
84Topps-156
85Capitals Pizza Hut-10
85O-Pee-Chee-8
85O-Pee-Chee Stickers-105
85O-Pee-Chee Stickers-113

857-Eleven Credit Cards-20
85Topps-8
85Topps Sticker Inserts-10
86Capitals Kodak-14
86Capitals Police-14
86O-Pee-Chee-164
86O-Pee-Chee Stickers-249
86Topps-164
87Capitals Kodak-5
87Capitals Team Issue-13
87O-Pee-Chee-108
87O-Pee-Chee Stickers-236
87Panini Stickers-178
87Topps-108
88Capitals Borderless-10
88Capitals Smokey-10
88Esso All-Stars-24
88O-Pee-Chee-192
88O-Pee-Chee Stickers-69
88Panini Stickers-366
88Topps-192
89Capitals Kodak-5
89Capitals Team Issue-13
89O-Pee-Chee-55
89O-Pee-Chee Stickers-77
89Panini Stickers-350
89Topps-55
89Swedish Semic World Champ Stickers-159
90Capitals Kodak-13
90Capitals Postcards-13
90Capitals Smokey-12
90Kraft-24
90O-Pee-Chee-353
90Pro Set-314
90Score-20
Canadian-20
90Score Hottest/Rising Stars-11
90Topps-353
Tiffany-353
90Upper Deck-57
90Upper Deck-309
French-57
French-309
91Capitals Junior 5x7-18
91Capitals Kodak-17
91O-Pee-Chee-105
91Panini Stickers-209
91Parkhurst-197
French-197
91Pinnacle-195
French-195
91Pro Set-259
91Pro Set-587
French-259
French-587
91Score American-228
91Score Canadian Bilingual-228
91Score Canadian English-228
91Stadium Club-225
91Topps-105
91Upper Deck-314
French-314
92Bowman-279
92Capitals Kodak-18
92O-Pee-Chee-347
92Panini Stickers-169
92Panini Stickers French-169
92Parkhurst-433
Emerald Ice-433
92Pinnacle-131
French-131
92Score-143
Canadian-143
92Stadium Club-215
92Topps-46
Gold-46G
93Score-145
Canadian-145
94Hockey Wit-26
96Swedish Semic Wien Hockey Legends-HL8
96Richmond Renegades-12
97Providence Bruins-24
01Greats of the Game Autographs-NNO
01Upper Deck Legends-67
02Fleer Throwbacks-16
Gold-16
Platinum-16
02UD Foundations-55
02UD Foundations-99
04ITG Franchises Update-477
04ITG Franchises US East-447
Autographs-A-RLN
04UD Legendary Signatures Autographs-LY
05SP Game Used Heritage Classic-HC-RL
05SP Game Used Heritage Classic Autos-HCA-RL
05SP Game Used Heritage Classic Patches-HCP-RL
05SP GameUsed Heritage Classic Patch Auto-HAP-RL
06ITG International Ice-114
Gold-114
Autographs-ARLW
06Parkhurst-59
06Parkhurst-215
Autographs-59
Autographs-215
06UD Artifacts Auto-Facts-AFRL
06UD Artifacts Auto-Facts Gold-AFRL
06UD Artifacts Tundra Tandems-TTCL
06UD Artifacts Tundra Tandems Black-TTCL
06UD Artifacts Tundra Tandems Blue-TTCL
06UD Artifacts Tundra Tandems Gold-TTCL
06UD Artifacts Tundra Tandems Platinum-TTCL
06UD Artifacts Tundra Tandems Red-TTCL
06UD Artifacts Tundra Tandems Dual Patches Red-TTCL

Langwieder, Stefan

05German DEL-362

Lanicek, Michal

99Czech Score Blue 2000-72
99Czech Score Red Ice 2000-72

Laniel, Fabien

03P.E.I. Rocket-12
04P.E.I. Rocket-29

Laniel, Jonathan

06Erie Otters-22

Laniel, Marc

88ProCards AHL-328
89ProCards AHL-227
90ProCards AHL/IHL-567
92Norwegian Elite Series-125
93Fredericton Canadiens-16
95Houston Aeros-13
96Cincinnati Cyclones-26
98German DEL-214
99German DEL-197

00German DEL-169
01UK Sheffield Steelers-11
02UK Sheffield Steelers-11

Lanier, Jonas

01German Upper Deck-243
02German DEL City Press-223
04German DEL Update-314
04German Hannover Scorpions Postcards-18
05German DEL-334

Lanigan, Gerry

94Detroit Jr. Red Wings-8
95Slapshot-18
95Barrie Colts-15
95Slapshot Memorial Cup-82
97Barrie Colts-13

Lanigan, Shane

96Regina Pats-3
97Regina Pats-18

Laniuk, Corey

98Phoenix Mustangs-13
01Flint Generals-10

Lank, Jeff

91Prince Albert Raiders-9
917th Inn. Sketch WHL-256
93Prince Albert Raiders-14
94Prince Albert Raiders-13

Lankshear, Mike

92Quebec Pee-Wee Tournament-11
95Slapshot-102
95Guelph Storm-16
96Guelph Storm-24
96Guelph Storm Premier Collection-8
03UK Manchester Phoenix-5

Lannon, Ryan

96Quebec Pee-Wee Tournament-1106
05AHL Top Prospects-24
05WBS Penguins-17
06Wilkes-Barre Scranton Penguins-17
06Wilkes-Barre Scranton Penguins Jerseys-6

Lanochkin, Vitaly

03Baie Comeau Drakkar-13
04Baie-Comeau Drakkar-24

Lanoie, Laurent

02Drummondville Voltigeurs-10

Lanteigne, Eric

89Rayside-Balfour Jr. Canadians-13

Lanthier, Jean-Marc

80Quebec Remparts-8
83Fredericton Express-5
85Canucks Team Issue-12
85Fredericton Express-13
86Fredericton Express-15
88ProCards AHL-155
89ProCards AHL-220

Lanthier, Michael

01Chicoutimi Sagueneens-15

Lantz, Kent

86Swedish Panini Stickers-212
89Swedish Semic Elitserien Stickers-188
90Swedish Semic Elitserien Stickers-16
91Swedish Semic Elitserien Stickers-217

Lanyon, Ted

72Johnstown Jets-8

Lanz, Frtiz

95Swiss HNL-316

Lanz, Rick

80Canucks Silverwood Dairies-12
80Canucks Team Issue-12
80Pepsi-Cola Caps-110
80Oshawa Generals-24
81Canucks Team Issue-12
81O-Pee-Chee-338
82Canucks Team Issue-11
82O-Pee-Chee-348
83Canucks Team Issue-11
83NHL Key Tags-121
83O-Pee-Chee-353
83O-Pee-Chee Stickers-280
83Topps Stickers-280
83Vachon-110
84Canucks Team Issue-12
84O-Pee-Chee-321
84O-Pee-Chee Stickers-276
85Canucks Team Issue-12
85O-Pee-Chee-197
86Canucks Team Issue-13
86O-Pee-Chee-179
86Topps-179
87Maple Leafs PLAY-11
87Maple Leafs Postcards-12
87Maple Leafs Postcards Oversized-12
87O-Pee-Chee-239
87O-Pee-Chee Stickers-157
88Maple Leafs PLAY-9
88O-Pee-Chee-225
88O-Pee-Chee Stickers-176
92Atlanta Knights-5

Lanzinger, Gunter

95Austrian National Team-14
95Swedish World Championships Stickers-271

Lapacek, Stanislav

98Czech OFS-406

Lapaire, Jean-Chalres

01Swiss HNL-417

Lapenkov, Evgeny

01Russian Hockey League-145

Lapensee, Bruno

86Kitchener Rangers-25

Laperriere, Daniel

92OPC Premier-39
92Upper Deck-525
92Peoria Rivermen-11
92Classic-57
92Classic-75
Gold-57
Gold-75
92Classic Four-Sport *-199
Gold-199
93Donruss-485
93OPC Premier-526
Gold-526
93Topps/OPC Premier-526
Gold-526
93Peoria Rivermen-16
94Donruss-187
94Leaf-156
94Score-219
Gold-219
Platinum-219
94Stadium Club-243
Members Only Master Set-243
First Day Issue-243
Super Team Winner Cards-243
94Classic Pro Prospects-184

96Portland Pirates-24
98German DEL-206
99German DEL-198
00German Berlin Polar Bears Postcards-13
00German DEL-70
01German Berlin Polar Bears Postcards-9
01German Upper Deck-35

Laperriere, Gilles

52Juniors Blue Tint-67

Laperriere, Ian

907th Inn. Sketch QMJHL-14
917th Inn. Sketch QMJHL-281
917th Inn. Sketch Memorial Cup-56
92Classic-57
Gold-57
93Drummondville Voltigeurs-10
94Fleer-189
94Leaf-464
94OPC Premier-307
Special Effects-307
94SP Premier-14
94SP Premier Die-Cuts-14
94Topps/OPC Premier-307
Special Effects-307
94Upper Deck-306
Electric Ice-306
94Classic-69
Gold-69
Tri-Cards-T58
95Canada Games NHL POGS-33
95Canada Games NHL POGS-235
95Collector's Choice-19
Player's Club-19
Player's Club Platinum-19
95Donruss-5
95Emotion-149
95Leaf-99
Studio Rookies-10
95Leaf Limited-53
95Panini Stickers-155
95Panini Stickers-190
95Panini Stickers-305
95Parkhurst International-176
95Parkhurst International-408
Emerald Ice-176
Emerald Ice-408
95Pinnacle-127
Artist's Proofs-127
Rink Collection-127
95Playoff One on One-308
95Score-72
Black Ice Artist's Proofs-72
Black Ice-72
95SkyBox Impact-142
NHL On Fox-7
95Topps-347
OPC Inserts-347
New To The Game-20NG
95Ultra-141
Gold Medallion-141
All-Rookies-7
All-Rookie Gold Medallion-7
95Upper Deck-32
Electric Ice-32
Electric Ice Gold-32
Special Edition-SE69
Special Edition Gold-SE69
95Images-7
Gold-7
Clear Excitement-CE7
Platinum Prospects-PR3
96Black Diamond-10
Gold-10
96Playoff One on One-403
96Upper Deck Ice-30
Parallel-30
96Collector's Edge Ice Crucibles-C2
97Be A Player-189
Autographs-189
Autographs Die-Cuts-189
Autographs Prismatic Die-Cuts-189
97Collector's Choice-120
97Pacific Dynagon Best Kept Secrets-47
97Upper Deck-83
98Be A Player-65
Press Release-65
98BAP Gold-65
98BAP Autographs-65
98BAP Autographs Gold-65
98BAP Tampa Bay All Star Game-65
98Pacific-237
Ice Blue-237
Red-237
98Upper Deck-108
Exclusives-108
Exclusives 1 of 1-108
Gold Reserve-108
99Wayne Gretzky Hockey-79
00BAP Memorabilia Update Tough Materials-T26
00BAP Mem Update Tough Materials Gold-T26
00Topps Gold Label Class 1-93
Gold-93
00Topps Gold Label Class 2-93
00Topps Gold Label Class 2 Gold-93
00Topps Gold Label Class 3-93
00Topps Gold Label Class 3 Gold-93
00Upper Deck-313
Exclusives Tier 1-313
Exclusives Tier 2-313
01BAP Update Tough Customers-TC3
01BAP Update Tough Customers-TC28
01Upper Deck-81
Exclusives-81
01Upper Deck Victory-169
Gold-169
02BAP Sig Series Auto Buybacks 1998-65
02BAP Signature Series Famous Scraps-FS3
02Kings Game Sheets-13
02Kings Game Sheets-14
02O-Pee-Chee-209
02O-Pee-Chee Premier Blue Parallel-209
02O-Pee-Chee Premier Red Parallel-209
02O-Pee-Chee Factory Set-209
02Pacific-168
Blue-168
Red-168
02Topps-209
OPC Blue Parallel-209
OPC Red Parallel-209
Factory Set-209
02Topps Total-14
02Upper Deck-80
Exclusives-80
03ITG Action-234
03Pacific Complete-97
Red-97

03Upper Deck-89
Canadian Exclusives-89
HG-89
03Upper Deck MVP-196
Gold Script-196
Silver Script-196
Canadian Exclusives-196
05Be A Player Signatures-IL
05Be A Player Signatures Gold-IL
05Parkhurst-126
Facsimile Auto Parallel-126
Signatures-IL
05SP Authentic Sign of the Times-IL
05SP Game Used Statscriptions-ST-IL
05Ultra Fresh Ink-FI-IL
05Ultra Fresh Ink Blue-FI-IL
05Upper Deck-294
Notable Numbers-N-IL
06Avalanche Team Postcards-8
06O-Pee-Chee-128
Rainbow-128
06Panini Stickers-228
06Upper Deck-305
Exclusives Parallel-305
High Gloss Parallel-305
Masterpieces-305

Laperriere, Jacques

44Beehive Group II Photos-257
63Chex Photos-31
63Parkhurst-27
63Parkhurst-86
63York White Backs-34
64Beehive Group III Photos-109
64Canadiens Postcards-10
64Coca-Cola Caps-56
64Topps-53
64Toronto Star-26
65Canadiens Steinberg Glasses-5
65Coca-Cola-56
65Coca-Cola Booklets-C
65Topps-3
66Topps-67
66Topps-122
67Canadiens IGA-2
67Post Cereal Box Backs-5
67Post Cereal Box Backs-6
67Post Flip Books-4
67Topps-7
67York Action Octagons-5
67York Action Octagons-11
67York Action Octagons-18
68Canadiens IGA-2
68Canadiens Postcards BW-8
68O-Pee-Chee-58
68Post Marbles-14
68Shirriff Coins-78
68Topps-58
69Canadiens Postcards Color-12
69O-Pee-Chee-3
Four-in-One-2
69Topps-3
70Canadiens Pins-7
70Dad's Cookies-69
70Esso Power Players-2
70O-Pee-Chee-52
70O-Pee-Chee-245
Deckle-20
70Post Shooters-8
70Sargent Promotions Stamps-97
70Topps-52
Topps/OPC Sticker Stamps-19
71Canadiens Postcards-10
71Letraset Action Replays-2
71O-Pee-Chee-144
71Sargent Promotions Stamps-108
71Toronto Sun-153
72Canadiens Postcards-11
72Dimanche/Derniere Heure *-145
72Dimanche/Derniere Heure *-146
72O-Pee-Chee-205
Player Crests-11
72Sargent Promotions Stamps-121
72Finnish Semic World Championship-225
72Swedish Stickers-112
72Swedish Semic World Championship-225
73Canadiens Postcards-9
73O-Pee-Chee-40
73Topps-137
74Canadiens Postcards-10
74NHL Action Stamps-154
74O-Pee-Chee NHL-202
74Topps-202
81Canadiens Postcards-15
82Canadiens Postcards-12
83Canadiens Postcards-14
84Canadiens Postcards-15
84Canadiens Postcards-13
85Hall of Fame-260
86Canadiens Postcards-10
87Canadiens Postcards-13
87Canadiens Vachon Stickers-8
87Canadiens Vachon Stickers-11
88Canadiens Postcards-16
88Esso All-Stars-25
89Canadiens Postcards-16
90Canadiens Postcards-18
91Canadiens Postcards-15
92Sport-Flash-1
92Sport-Flash Autographs-1
93O-Pee-Chee Canadiens Hockey Fest-15
93O-Pee-Chee Canadiens Hockey Fest-36
94Parkhurst Tall Boys-72
94Parkhurst Tall Boys-140
94Parkhurst Tall Boys-149
94Parkhurst Tall Boys-161
Mail-Ins-AS3
95Parkhurst '66-67 Promos-3
95Parkhurst '66-67-65
95Parkhurst '66-67-122
95Parkhurst '66-67-128
95Parkhurst '66-67-PR128
Coins-65
95Zeller's Masters of Hockey Signed-4
96Canadiens Postcards-15
01BAP Ultimate Mem Stanley Cup Winners-12
01Parkhurst Autographs-PA46
02BAP Ultimate Mem Storied Franchise-15
02Parkhurst Reprints-287
03ITG Used Signature Series Norris Trophy-13
03ITG Used Sig Series Norris Trophy Gold-13
03Parkhurst Original Six Montreal-36
Autographs-9
03Parkhurst Rookie ROYalty-VR-12
03Parkhurst Rookie ROYalty Gold-VR-12
04ITG Franchises Canadian-62
Autographs-JL

Memorabilia-SM25
Memorabilia Gold-SM25
04ITG Ultimate Memorabilia-73
Gold-73
Jersey Autographs-23
Jersey Autographs Gold-23
Norris Trophy-4
Retro Teammates-15
Triple Threads-1
05Devils Team Issue-4
06Devils Team Set-30

Lapeyre, Jody
95Tri-City Americans-16
98Tri-City Americans-22

Lapierre, Eric
92Quebec Pee-Wee Tournament-174
93Quebec Pee-Wee Tournament-310

Lapierre, Mathieu
92Quebec Pee-Wee Tournament-232
93Quebec Pee-Wee Tournament-246

Lapierre, Maxim
03P.E.I. Rocket-13
04P.E.I. Rocket-14
05Beehive-98
Matte-98
05Black Diamond-256
05Hot Prospects-204
Autographed Patch Variation-204
Hot Materials-HMML
Red Hot-204
05Parkhurst-637
Facsimile Auto Parallel-637
Signatures-ML
05SP Authentic-200
05SP Game Used-217
05SPx-233
Spectrum-233
05The Cup-129
Autographed Rookie Patches Gold Rainbow-129
Black Rainbow Rookies-129
Masterpiece Pressplates (Artifacts)-290
Masterpiece Pressplates (Bee Hive)-98
Masterpiece Pressplates (Black Diamond)-256
Masterpiece Pressplates (Ice)-199
Masterpiece Pressplates (Rookie Update)-214
Masterpiece Pressplates SPA Autos-200
Masterpiece Pressplates (SP Game Used)-217
Masterpiece Pressplates SPx Autos-233
Masterpiece Pressplates (Trilogy)-271
Masterpiece Pressplates Ult Coll-191
Masterpiece Pressplates Autographs-129
Platinum Rookies-129
05UD Artifacts-290
05Ultimate Collection-191
Gold-191
Ultimate Debut Threads Jerseys-DTJML
05Upper Deck-474
05Upper Deck Ice-199
05Upper Deck Rookie Update-214
Inspirations Patch Rookies-214
05Upper Deck Trilogy-271
05Hamilton Bulldogs-14
06Hamilton Bulldogs-18

Lapin, Evgeni
00Russian Hockey League-186
01Russian Dynamo Moscow-8
01Russian Dynamo Moscow Mentos-2
03Russian Hockey League-197

Lapin, Mikhail
92Western Michigan Broncos-15
93Western Michigan Broncos-19

Lapin, Misha
93Western Michigan Broncos-19

Lapinkoski, Marko
92Finnish Jyvas-Hyva Stickers-169

LaPlante, Alain
99Muskegon Fury-21

Laplante, Darryl
95Classic-49
98Upper Deck-9
Exclusives-9
Exclusives 1 of 1-9
Gold Reserve-9
99BAP Memorabilia-264
Gold-264
Silver-264
99Upper Deck Arena Giveaways-DR2
99Cincinnati Mighty Ducks-14
00O-Pee-Chee-316
00O-Pee-Chee Parallel-316
00Pacific-150
Copper-150
Gold-150
Ice Blue-150
Premiere Date-150
00Topps/OPC-316
Parallel-316
00Topps Chrome-211
OPC Refractors-211
Refractors-211
00Upper Deck-316
Exclusives Tier 1-316
Exclusives Tier 2-316
00Cleveland Lumberjacks-15
03Reading Royals-21

Laplante, Eric
96Halifax Mooseheads I-10
96Halifax Mooseheads II-10
97Halifax Mooseheads I-7
98Quebec Remparts-10
Signed-10
99Quebec Remparts-6
Signed-6
00Kentucky Thoroughblades-14
01Cleveland Barons-12
02Cleveland Barons-11

Laplante, Nicolas
04Victoriaville Tigres-27

Laplante, Richard
01Swiss HNL-356

LaPlante, Sebastien
93Greensboro Monarchs-7
95Central Hockey League-99
01Calgary Hitmen-13
01Calgary Hitmen Autographed-13
02Roanoke Express-1
02Roanoke Express RBI Sports-198

Laplante, Steve
917th Inn. Sketch QMJHL-58

Lapointe Sr., Guy
51Bas Du Fleuve-11

Lapointe, Carl
93Swiss HNL-269

Lapointe, Claude
89Halifax Citadels-13
89ProCards AHL-166
90Nordiques Petro-Canada-33
90Halifax Citadels-14
90ProCards AHL/IHL-445
91Pro Set Platinum-267
91Nordiques Petro-Canada-14
91O-Pee-Chee-431
91Parkhurst-370
French-370
91Pinnacle-313
French-313
91Pro Set-556
French-556
91Topps-431
91Upper Deck-488
French-488
92Bowman-421
92Durivage Panini-6
92Nordiques Petro-Canada-18
92O-Pee-Chee-320
92Panini Stickers-213
92Panini Stickers French-213
92Pinnacle-141
French-141
92Pro Set-151
Rookie Goal Leaders-12
92Score-219
Canadian-219
92Stadium Club-93
92Topps-94
Gold-94G
92Ultra-176
92Upper Deck-147
93Donruss-285
93Durivage Score-24
93Leaf-64
93OPC Premier-251
Gold-251
93Parkhurst-437
Emerald Ice-437
93Pinnacle-294
Canadian-294
93PowerPlay-422
93Score-352
Canadian-352
93Topps/OPC Premier-251
Gold-251
93Ultra-403
94Leaf-304
94Nordiques Burger King-14
94Pinnacle-231
Artist's Proofs-231
Rink Collection-231
94Score-194
Gold-194
Platinum-194
96Be A Player-200
Autographs-200
Autographs Silver-200
96Islander Postcards-11
97Pacific Invincible NHL Regime-118
97Upper Deck-311
98OPC Chrome-167
Refractors-167
98Topps-167
O-Pee-Chee-167
99O-Pee-Chee-210
99O-Pee-Chee Chrome-210
99O-Pee-Chee Chrome Refractors-210
99Pacific-256
Copper-256
Emerald Green-256
Gold-256
Ice Blue-256
Premiere Date-256
Red-256
99Paramount-143
Copper-143
Emerald-143
Gold-143
Holographic Emerald-143
Holographic Gold-143
Holographic Silver-143
Ice Blue-143
Premiere Date-143
Red-143
Silver-143
99Topps/OPC-210
99Topps/OPC Chrome-210
Refractors-210
99Upper Deck MVP-128
Gold Script-128
Silver Script-128
Super Script-128
99Upper Deck Victory-186
99Wayne Gretzky Hockey-106
00O-Pee-Chee-91
00O-Pee-Chee Parallel-91
00Pacific-252
Copper-252
Gold-252
Ice Blue-252
Premiere Date-252
00Paramount-156
Copper-156
Gold-156
Holo-Gold-156
Holo-Silver-156
Ice Blue-156
Premiere Date-156
00Private Stock Game Gear-70
00Private Stock Game Gear Patches-70
00Stadium Club-198
00Titanium Draft Day Edition-63
Patches-63
00Topps/OPC-91
Parallel-91
00Topps Chrome-73
OPC Refractors-73
Refractors-73
00Topps Heritage-209
00Upper Deck-113
Exclusives Tier 1-113
Exclusives Tier 2-113
00Upper Deck MVP-115
First Stars-115
Second Stars-115
Third Stars-115
00Upper Deck Victory-146
00Upper Deck Vintage-228
00Vanguard Dual Game-Worn Jerseys-20
00Vanguard Dual Game-Worn Patches-20
01O-Pee-Chee-150
01O-Pee-Chee Premier Parallel-150
01Pacific-251
Extreme LTD-251
Hobby LTD-251
Premiere Date-251
Retail LTD-251
01Pacific Arena Exclusives-251
01Topps-150
OPC Parallel-150
01Upper Deck-342
Exclusives-342
01Vanguard Memorabilia-36
02Pacific Complete-384
Red-384
02Topps Total-150
03Flyers Postcards-12
03ITG Action-459

Lapointe, Danny
03Prince George Cougars-18

Lapointe, Guy
69Canadiens Postcards Color-13
70Canadiens Pins-8
70Esso Power Players-5
70O-Pee-Chee-177
70Sargent Promotions Stamps-105
71Canadiens Postcards-11
71O-Pee-Chee-145
71Sargent Promotions Stamps-98
71Toronto Sun-154
72Canadiens Postcards-9
72Dimanche/Derniere Heure *-147
72Dimanche/Derniere Heure *-148
72O-Pee-Chee-86
Team Canada-16
72Sargent Promotions Stamps-113
72Topps-57
73Canadiens Postcards-10
73Mac's Milk-13
73O-Pee-Chee-114
73Topps-170
74Canadiens Postcards-11
74Lipton Soup-16
74NHL Action Stamps-150
74O-Pee-Chee NHL-70
74Topps-70
75Canadiens Postcards-10
75O-Pee-Chee NHL-198
75O-Pee-Chee NHL-293
75Topps-198
75Topps-293
76Canadiens Postcards-11
76O-Pee-Chee NHL-223
76Topps-223
76Topps Glossy Inserts-17
77Canadiens Postcards-12
77Coca-Cola-13
77O-Pee-Chee NHL-60
77Topps-60
78Canadiens Postcards-14
78O-Pee-Chee-260
78Topps-260
79Canadiens Postcards-13
79O-Pee-Chee-135
79Topps-135
80Canadiens Postcards-13
80O-Pee-Chee-201
80Pepsi-Cola Caps-50
80Topps-201
81Canadiens Postcards-16
82O-Pee-Chee-305
82Post Cereal-17
84Nordiques Postcards-13
87Nordiques General Foods-31
88Esso All-Stars-26
88Nordiques General Foods-6
89Nordiques Team Issue-23
91Future Trends Canada '72-92
91Future Trends Canada '72 French-92
92Future Trends '76 Canada Cup-171
93Action Packed HOF Induction-2
01BAP Ultimate Mem Dynasty Jerseys-7
01BAP Ultimate Mem Dynasty Emblems-7
01BAP Ultimate Mem Dynasty Numbers-7
01BAP Ultimate Memorabilia Les Canadiens-17
01BAP Ultimate Mem Retro Teammates-9
01BAP Ultimate Mem Stanley Cup Winners-15
01Greats of the Game-20
Autographs-20
01Parkhurst Autographs-PA58
01Topps Archives-10
Arena Seats-ASGL
01Topps Chrome Reprints-7
01Topps Chrome Reprint Refractors-7
01Topps Chrome Reprint Autographs-7
01Upper Deck Legends-40
01Upper Deck Vintage Sweaters of Honor-SHLA
02BAP Memorabilia Mini Stanley Cups-17
02BAP Ultimate Mem Storied Franchise-12
03Parkhurst Original Six Montreal-47
Memorabilia-MM59
04ITG Franchises Canadian-60
Autographs-GLP
Memorabilia-SM10
Memorabilia Autographs-SM10
Memorabilia Gold-SM10
Original Sticks-OS5
Original Sticks Autographs-OS5
Original Sticks Gold-OS4
Teammates-TM7
Teammates Gold-TM7
04ITG Ultimate Memorabilia-150
Gold-150
Autographs-5
Autographs Gold-5
Jersey Autographs-6
Jersey Autographs Gold-6
Original Six-11
Stick Autographs-9
Stick Autographs Gold-9
Triple Threads-1
04UD Legendary Signatures-43
Autographs-LA
04ITG Heroes and Prospects-163
Autographs-GLA
Hero Memorabilia-24
04ITG Heroes/Prospects Toronto Expo '05-163
05Beehive PhotoGraphs-PGLA
05SP Authentic Exquisite Endorsements-EEGL
05SP Authentic Six Star Signatures-SSMO
05SPx-132
05The Cup-58
Gold-58
Black Rainbow-58
Masterpiece Pressplates-58
Patch Variation-P58
Patch Variation Autographs-AP58
05ITG Heroes and Prospects Hero Mem-HM-51
06ITG International Ice-119
Gold-119
Autographs-AGLP
06ITG Ultimate Memorabilia-61
Artist Proof-61
Boys Will Be Boys-15
Boys Will Be Boys Gold-15
Stick Rack-10
Stick Rack Gold-10
06SP Game Used Authentic Fabrics Dual-AF2RL
06SP Game Used Authentic Fabrics Dual Patches-AF2RL
06UD Artifacts-119
Blue-119
Gold-119
Radiance-119
Red-119

Lapointe, Herve
907th Inn. Sketch QMJHL-107
917th Inn. Sketch QMJHL-179

Lapointe, Jimmy
92Quebec Pee-Wee Tournament-695
93Quebec Pee-Wee Tournament-295

Lapointe, Kevin
93Quebec Pee-Wee Tournament-1013
05Muskegon Fury-10

Lapointe, Martin
90Upper Deck-467
French-467
907th Inn. Sketch QMJHL-25
907th Inn. Sketch Memorial Cup-61
91Gillette-20
91Parkhurst-267
French-267
91Pinnacle-355
French-355
91Pro Set-532
French-532
91Red Wings Little Caesars-10
91Score Canadian Bilingual-655
91Score Canadian English-655
91Score Rookie/Traded-105T
91Upper Deck-63
91Upper Deck-66
91Upper Deck-685
French-63
French-66
French-685
91Upper Deck Czech World Juniors-59
917th Inn. Sketch Memorial Cup-102
91Arena Draft Picks-8
91Arena Draft Picks French-8
91Arena Draft Picks Autographs-8
91Arena Draft Picks Autographs French-8
91Classic-9
91Star Pics-5
91Ultimate Draft-9
91Ultimate Draft-65
91Classic Four-Sport *-9
92Pinnacle-365
French-365
92Pro Set-226
92Score-409
Canadian-409
92Upper Deck-405
92Upper Deck-584
93Durivage Score-6
93Leaf-336
93OPC Premier Gold-263
93Parkhurst-63
Emerald Ice-63
93PowerPlay-332
93Topps/OPC Premier Gold-263G
93Upper Deck-257
94Be A Player Signature Cards-133
94Leaf-201
94Parkhurst-70
Gold-70
94Pinnacle-449
Artist's Proofs-449
Rink Collection-449
94Stadium Club-151
Members Only Master Set-151
First Day Issue-151
Super Team Winner Cards-151
94Ultra-285
94Upper Deck-406
Electric Ice-406
94Classic Pro Prospects-173
95Upper Deck World Junior Alumni-11
95Parkhurst International-340
Emerald Ice-340
95Upper Deck-200
Electric Ice-200
Electric Ice Gold-200
96Be A Player-128
Autographs-128
Autographs Silver-128
96Black Diamond-13
Gold-13
96Collector's Edge Ice-4
Prism-4
QuantumMotion-9
97Collector's Choice-86
97Pacific-241
Copper-241
Emerald Green-241
Ice Blue-241
Red-241
Silver-241
97Score Red Wings-10
Platinum-10
Premier-10
97Upper Deck-58
98Be A Player-198
Press Release-198
98BAP Gold-198
98BAP Autographs-198
98BAP Autographs Gold-198
98Katch-54
98Pacific-197
Ice Blue-197
Red-197
98Pacific Omega-81
Red-81
Opening Day Issue-81
98Upper Deck-86
Exclusives-86
Exclusives 1 of 1-86
Gold Reserve-86
99BAP Memorabilia-235
Gold-235
Silver-235
99Pacific-141
Copper-141
Emerald Green-141
Gold-141
Ice Blue-141
Premiere Date-141
Red-141
99Upper Deck MVP SC Edition-68
Gold Script-68
Silver Script-68
Super Script-68
99Russian Fetisov Tribute-38
00BAP Memorabilia-361
Emerald-361
Ruby-361
Sapphire-361
Promos-361
00BAP Mem Chicago Sportsfest Copper-361
00BAP Memorabilia Chicago Sportsfest Blue-361
00BAP Memorabilia Chicago Sportsfest Gold-361
00BAP Memorabilia Chicago Sportsfest Ruby-361
00BAP Memorabilia Chicago Sun-Times Ruby-361
00BAP Memorabilia Chicago Sun-Times Gold-361
00BAP Mem Chicago Sun-Times Sapphire-361
00BAP Mem Toronto Fall Expo Copper-361
00BAP Memorabilia Toronto Fall Expo Gold-361
00BAP Memorabilia Toronto Fall Expo Ruby-361
00BAP Parkhurst 2000-P153
00BAP Signature Series-31
Emerald-31
Ruby-31
Sapphire-31
Autographs-62
Autographs Gold-62
00O-Pee-Chee-243
00O-Pee-Chee Parallel-243
00Pacific-151
Copper-151
Gold-151
Ice Blue-151
Premiere Date-151
00Paramount-86
Copper-86
Gold-86
Holo-Gold-86
Holo-Silver-86
Ice Blue-86
Premiere Date-86
00Topps/OPC-243
Parallel-243
00Topps Heritage-122
00Topps Stars Game Gear-GGML
00UD Heroes-43
00Upper Deck-290
Exclusives Tier 1-290
Exclusives Tier 2-290
00Upper Deck Victory-91
01BAP Memorabilia-319
Emerald-319
Ruby-319
Sapphire-319
01BAP Signature Series Certified 100-C26
01BAP Signature Series Certified 50-C26
01BAP Signature Series Certified 1 of 1's-C26
01BAP Signature Series Autographs-LML
01BAP Signature Series Autographs Gold-LML
01O-Pee-Chee-181
01O-Pee-Chee Premier Parallel-181
01Pacific-143
Extreme LTD-143
Hobby LTD-143
Premiere Date-143
Retail LTD-143
01Pacific Adrenaline-14
Blue-14
Premiere Date-14
Red-14
Retail-14
01Pacific Arena Exclusives-143
01Parkhurst-90
Gold-90
Silver-90
01Topps-181
OPC Parallel-181
01Topps Heritage-169
01UD Honor Roll Tough Customers-TC1
01Upper Deck-245
Exclusives-245
02BAP First Edition-230
02BAP Sig Series Auto Buybacks 1998-198
02BAP Sig Series Auto Buybacks 2001-LML
02BAP Ultimate Mem Dynasty Jerseys-12
02BAP Ultimate Mem Dynasty Emblems-12
02BAP Ultimate Mem Dynasty Numbers-12
02O-Pee-Chee-219
02O-Pee-Chee Premier Blue Parallel-219
02O-Pee-Chee Premier Red Parallel-219
02O-Pee-Chee Factory Set-219
02Pacific-29
Blue-29
Red-29
02Pacific Complete-135
Red-135
02Parkhurst-34
Bronze-34
Gold-34
Silver-34
02Parkhurst Retro-133
Minis-133
02Topps-219
OPC Blue Parallel-219
OPC Red Parallel-219
Factory Set-219
02Topps Total-308
02Upper Deck-13
Exclusives-13
02Upper Deck MVP-16
Gold-16
Classics-16
Golden Classics-16
02Upper Deck Victory-21
Bronze-21
Gold-21
Silver-21
02Upper Deck Vintage-20
02Augusta Lynx-67
03Bruins Team Issue-4
03ITG Action-28
03NHL Sticker Collection-13
03Pacific Complete-292
Red-292
03Parkhurst Original Six Boston-20
Memorabilia-BM3
03Parkhurst Original Six Detroit Inserts-D-18
03Upper Deck MVP-45
Gold Script-45
Silver Script-45
Canadian Exclusives-45
05Be A Player Signatures-ML
05Be A Player Signatures Gold-ML
05Black Diamond-8
Emerald-8
Gold-8
Onyx-8
Ruby-8
05Panini Stickers-222
05Parkhurst-104
Facsimile Auto Parallel-104
05Upper Deck-288
05Upper Deck MVP-92
Gold-92
Platinum-92
06Blackhawks Postcards-4
06O-Pee-Chee-109
Rainbow-109
06Panini Stickers-216
06Upper Deck-297
Exclusives Parallel-297
High Gloss Parallel-297
Masterpieces-297

Lapointe, Maxime
93Swiss HNL-430
95Swiss HNL-249
96Swiss HNL-398
98Swiss Power Play Stickers-322
99Swiss Panini Stickers-328
01Swiss HNL-335
02Swiss HNL-460

Lapointe, Normand
75O-Pee-Chee WHA-85

Lapointe, Rick
76O-Pee-Chee NHL-48
76Topps-48
77O-Pee-Chee NHL-152
77Topps-152A
77Topps-152B
78O-Pee-Chee-322
79O-Pee-Chee-121
79Topps-121
81O-Pee-Chee-295
81O-Pee-Chee Stickers-134
81Topps-W119
82Nordiques Postcards-11
82Post Cereal-17
83Nordiques Postcards-14
83O-Pee-Chee-294
83Fredericton Express-8
84Kings Smokey-19

Lapointe, Rodney
87Sudbury Wolves-7

Lapointe, Ron
79Montreal Juniors-11
88Nordiques General Foods-6
88Nordiques Team Issue-2
89ProCards IHL-189

Lapointe, Steve
907th Inn. Sketch QMJHL-208

Lapointe, Sylvain
917th Inn. Sketch QMJHL-216
93Wheeling Thunderbirds-17

Laporte, Alexandre
95Atlanta Knights-12
99Tallahassee Tiger Sharks-9

Laporte, Benoit
92Finnish Semic-235
98Swiss Power Play Stickers-335
99Swiss Panini Stickers-326
04German Augsburg Panthers Postcards-18

Laporte, Roger
88Richelieu Riverains-15

Laporte, Yves
51Laval Dairy Lac St. Jean-56

Lappalainen, Harri
70Finnish Jaakiekko-211

Lappalainen, Joni
04Finnish Cardset-224
05Finnish Cardset -31
06Finnish Cardset-35

Lappin, Chris
92Greensboro Monarchs-18

Lappin, Mike
92Raleigh Icecaps-37
92Classic-76
Gold-76

Lappin, Peter
88Salt Lake Golden Eagles-4
89ProCards IHL-84
90Score-403
Canadian-403
90Upper Deck-235
French-235
90ProCards AHL/IHL-109
91O-Pee-Chee Inserts-5S
91Kansas City Blades-10
91ProCards-522

Laprade, Edgar
43Parade Sportive *-63
44Beehive Group II Photos-336
51Parkhurst-96
52Parkhurst-100
52Royal Desserts-3
54Topps-56
93Action Packed HOF Induction-1
04ITG Franchises US East-381
06Parkhurst-60
Autographs-60

Laprise, Pierre-Luc
01Cape Breton Screaming Eagles-3
02Val d'Or Foreurs-2

Laprise, Sebastien
98Val d'Or Foreurs-15
00Chicoutimi Sagueneens-7
Signed-7
00Halifax Mooseheads-11
02Drummondville Voltigeurs-13

Lapsjenkov, Gennadi
74Swedish Stickers-37

Laramee, Craig
93Quebec Pee-Wee Tournament-818

Laraque, Georges
95Classic-28
99BAP Millennium-100
Emerald-100
Ruby-100
Sapphire-100
Signatures-100
Signatures Gold-100
99Pacific-158
Copper-158
Emerald Green-158
Gold-158
Ice Blue-158
Premiere Date-158
Red-158
99Topps Arena Giveaways-EDM-GL
99Upper Deck Gold Reserve-341
00Pacific-168
Copper-168
Gold-168
Ice Blue-168
Premiere Date-168
00Topps Heritage-161
00Upper Deck-301
Exclusives Tier 1-301
Exclusives Tier 2-301
00Upper Deck Vintage-148
01BAP Update Tough Customers-TC16
01BAP Update Tough Customers-TC24
01BAP Update Tough Customers-TC29
01Pacific-159
01Pacific-411
Extreme LTD-159
Gold-411
Hobby LTD-159
Premiere Date-159
Retail LTD-159
01Pacific Arena Exclusives-159
01Pacific Arena Exclusives-411
01Upper Deck Victory-144
Gold-144
02BAP Sig Series Auto Buybacks 1999-100
02BAP Signature Series Famous Scraps-FS11
02BAP Signature Series Team Quads-TQ17
02Oilers Postcards-12
02O-Pee-Chee-200
02O-Pee-Chee Premier Blue Parallel-200
02O-Pee-Chee Premier Red Parallel-200
02O-Pee-Chee Factory Set-200
02Pacific-144
Blue-144
Red-144
02Topps-200
OPC Blue Parallel-200
OPC Red Parallel-200
Factory Set-200
02Topps Total-337
02Upper Deck-317
Exclusives-317
02Upper Deck Beckett UD Promos-317
02Upper Deck Number Crunchers-NC6
02Upper Deck Vintage-103
02Upper Deck Vintage-272
03BAP Memorabilia Stanley Cup Playoffs-SCP-8
03Black Diamond-127
Black-127
Green-127
Red-127
03Crown Royale-40
Blue-40
Retail-40
03ITG Action-232
Jerseys-M44
03McDonald's Pacific-22
03Oilers Postcards-11
03O-Pee-Chee-16
03O-Pee-Chee-288
03OPC Blue-16
03OPC Blue-288
03OPC Gold-16
03OPC Gold-288
03OPC Red-16
03OPC Red-288
03Pacific-134
Blue-134
Red-134
03Pacific Exhibit-59
Blue Backs-59
Yellow Backs-59
03Private Stock Reserve-37
Blue-37
Red-37
Retail-37
03Topps-16
03Topps-288
Blue-16
Blue-288
Gold-16
Gold-288
Red-16
Red-288
Signs of Toughness-GL
Tough Materials-GL
Tough Materials-GLSP
Tough Materials Signed-GL
C55 Relics-TRGL
03Upper Deck-79
Canadian Exclusives-79
Fan Favorites-FF4
HG-79
Tough Customers-TC-12
03Upper Deck MVP-169
Gold Script-169
Silver Script-169
Canadian Exclusives-169
04SP Authentic Sign of the Times-ST-GE
04SP Authentic Sign of the Times-DS-LW
05Panini Stickers-275
05Parkhurst-199
Facsimile Auto Parallel-199
05SP Authentic Sign of the Times-GL
05SP Game Used Auto Draft-AD-GL
05SPx Winning Combos-WC-WL
05SPx Winning Combos Autographs-AWC-WL
05SPx Winning Combos Gold-WC-WL
05SPx Winning Combos Spectrum-WC-WL
05UD Artifacts Auto Facts-AF-GL
05UD Artifacts Auto Facts Blue-AF-GL
05UD Artifacts Auto Facts Copper-AF-GL
05UD Artifacts Auto Facts Pewter-AF-GL
05UD Artifacts Auto Facts Silver-AF-GL
05Upper Deck-322
Jerseys-J-GUL
Notable Numbers-N-GL
05Upper Deck MVP-159
Gold-159
Platinum-159
05Upper Deck Victory-82
Black-82
Gold-82
Silver-82
06Be A Player-98
Autographs-98
Signatures-GL
Signatures Duals-DPL
06Black Diamond Gemography-GGL
06Fleer Signing Day-SDGL
06O-Pee-Chee-380
Rainbow-380
06UD Powerplay Last Man Standing-LM5
06Upper Deck-402
Exclusives Parallel-402
High Gloss Parallel-402
Game Jerseys-JGL
Game Patches-PGL
Masterpieces-402

Laraque, Jules-Edy
99Halifax Mooseheads-17
00Halifax Mooseheads-12

Larche, Roger
907th Inn. Sketch QMJHL-15
917th Inn. Sketch QMJHL-293
917th Inn. Sketch Memorial Cup-67
92Greensboro Monarchs-10
93Roanoke Express-11

Lardner, Tab
01Austin Ice Bats-7
02Austin Ice Bats-7
03Austin Ice Bats-7

Larin, Daniel
92Oklahoma City Blazers-12
93Phoenix Cobras RHI-11
96German DEL-242
98Oklahoma City Blazers-20

Larionov, Igor
83Swedish Semic VM Stickers-74
84Russian National Team-11
87Russian National Team-13
89Canucks Mohawk-8
89Kraft-41
89Russian National Team-17
89Swedish Semic World Champ Stickers-90
90Bowman-63
Tiffany-63
90Canucks Mohawk-13
90Kraft-25
90O-Pee-Chee-359
90Panini Stickers-294
90Panini Stickers-336
90Pro Set-297
90Score-123
Canadian-123
90Topps-359
Tiffany-359
90Upper Deck-128
French-128
91Pro Set Platinum-126
91Bowman-326
91Canucks Panini Team Stickers-11
91Canucks Autograph Cards-10
91Canucks Molson-4
91Canucks Team Issue 8x10-10
91O-Pee-Chee-480
91Panini Stickers-42
91Parkhurst-406
French-406
91Pinnacle-293
French-293
91Pro Set-246
French-246
91Score American-168
91Score Canadian Bilingual-168
91Score Canadian English-168
91Stadium Club-150
91Topps-480
91Upper Deck-298
French-298
Euro-Stars-18
Euro-Stars French-18
91Finnish Semic World Champ Stickers-217
91Russian Stars Red Ace-11
91Russian Sports Unite Hearts-6
91Russian Stars in NHL-6
91Swedish Semic World Champ Stickers-217
92Bowman-350
92O-Pee-Chee-159
92Panini Stickers-32
92Panini Stickers French-32
92Score-58
Canadian-58
Sharpshooters-13
Sharpshooters Canadian-13
92Stadium Club-299
92Topps-512
Gold-512G
92Russian Tri-Globe From Russia With Puck-1
92Russian Tri-Globe From Russia With Puck-2
93Donruss-305
93Leaf-391
93Parkhurst-185
Emerald Ice-185
93Pinnacle-367
Canadian-367
93PowerPlay-436
93Score-535
Gold-535
Canadian-535
Canadian Gold-535
Dynamic Duos U.S.-8
93Ultra-415
94Canada Games NHL POGS-216
94Donruss-106
94Leaf-311
94Leaf Limited-47
94OPC Premier-170
Special Effects-170
94Parkhurst Vintage-V88
94Parkhurst SE-SE164
Gold-SE164
94Pinnacle-74
Artist's Proofs-74
Rink Collection-74
94Score-61
Gold-61
Platinum-61
94Select-40
Gold-40
94Topps/OPC Premier-170
Special Effects-170
94Ultra-197
94Upper Deck-65
Electric Ice-65
94Finnish Jaa Kiekko-156
95Be A Player-206
Signatures-S206
Signatures Die Cuts-S206
95Canada Games NHL POGS-222
95Collector's Choice-239
Player's Club-239
Player's Club Platinum-239
95Finest-57
Refractors-57
95Hoyle Western Playing Cards-42
95Leaf-318
95Parkhurst International-184

95Parkhurst International-336
Emerald Ice-184
Emerald Ice-336
95Pinnacle-81
Artist's Proofs-81
Rink Collection-81
95Playoff One on One-85
95Score-254
Black Ice Artist's Proofs-254
Black Ice-254
95Summit-76
Artist's Proofs-76
Ice-76
95Ultra-234
95Upper Deck-213
95Upper Deck-349
Electric Ice-213
Electric Ice-349
Electric Ice Gold-213
Electric Ice Gold-349
95Swedish Globe World Championships-239
95Swedish World Championships Stickers-283
96Collector's Choice-83
96Donruss-167
Press Proofs-167
96Donruss Canadian Ice-117
Gold Press Proofs-117
Red Press Proofs-117
96Donruss Elite-50
Die Cut Stars-50
96Fleer Picks-110
96Leaf-104
Press Proofs-104
96Leaf Preferred-75
Press Proofs-75
96Maggers-52
96Pinnacle-74
Artist's Proofs-74
Foil-74
Premium Stock-74
Rink Collection-74
96Playoff One on One-346
96Score-178
Artist's Proofs-178
Dealer's Choice Artist's Proofs-178
Special Artist's Proofs-178
Golden Blades-178
96Select Certified-62
Artist's Proofs-62
Blue-62
Mirror Blue-62
Mirror Gold-62
Mirror Red-62
Red-62
96Summit-40
Artist's Proofs-40
Ice-40
Metal-40
Premium Stock-40
96Upper Deck-51
96Zenith-96
Artist's Proofs-96
97Donruss Limited-178
Exposure-178
97Donruss Priority-90
Stamp of Approval-90
97Pacific-49
Copper-49
Emerald Green-49
Ice Blue-49
Red-49
Silver-49
97Pacific Omega-82
Copper-82
Dark Gray-82
Emerald Green-82
Gold-82
Ice Blue-82
97Panini Stickers-152
97Pinnacle-129
Press Plates Back Black-129
Press Plates Back Cyan-129
Press Plates Back Magenta-129
Press Plates Back Yellow-129
Press Plates Front Black-129
Press Plates Front Cyan-129
Press Plates Front Magenta-129
Press Plates Front Yellow-129
97Pinnacle Inside-146
97Score Red Wings-5
Platinum-5
Premier-5
97SP Authentic-54
97Upper Deck Ice Lethal Lines-L6B
97Upper Deck Ice Lethal Lines 2-L6B
98Aurora-64
98Be A Player-199
Press Release-199
98BAP Gold-199
98BAP Autographs-199
98BAP Autographs Gold-199
98Pacific-198
Ice Blue-198
Red-198
98Pacific Omega-82
Red-82
Opening Day Issue-82
98Panini Stickers-131
98Paramount-77
Copper-77
Emerald Green-77
Holo-Electric-77
Ice Blue-77
Silver-77
98UD Choice-71
98UD Choice Preview-71
98UD Choice Prime Choice Reserve-71
98UD Choice Reserve-71
98Upper Deck-261
Exclusives-261
Exclusives 1 of 1-261
Gold Reserve-261
99BAP Memorabilia-138
Gold-138
Silver-138
99Pacific-142
Copper-142
Emerald Green-142
Gold-142
Ice Blue-142
Premiere Date-142
Red-142
99Pacific Omega-82
Copper-82
Gold-82
Ice Blue-82
Premiere Date-82
99Panini Stickers-230
99Paramount-82
Copper-82
Emerald-82
Gold-82
Holographic Emerald-82
Holographic Gold-82
Holographic Silver-82
Ice Blue-82
Premiere Date-82
Red-82
Silver-82
99SPx-59
Radiance-59
Spectrum-59
99Upper Deck-52
Exclusives-52
Exclusives 1 of 1-52
99Upper Deck Gold Reserve-52
99Upper Deck MVP-74
Gold Script-74
Silver Script-74
Super Script-74
ProSign-IL
99Upper Deck Victory-102
99Russian Fetisov Tribute-37
00BAP Memorabilia-328
00BAP Memorabilia-490
Emerald-328
Emerald-490
Ruby-328
Ruby-490
Sapphire-328
Sapphire-490
Promos-328
00BAP Mem Chicago Sportsfest Copper-328
00BAP Memorabilia Chicago Sportsfest Blue-328
00BAP Memorabilia Chicago Sportsfest Gold-328
00BAP Memorabilia Chicago Sportsfest Ruby-328
00BAP Memorabilia Chicago Sun-Times Ruby-328
00BAP Memorabilia Chicago Sun-Times Gold-328
00BAP Mem Chicago Sun-Times Sapphire-328
00BAP Mem Toronto Fall Expo Copper-328
00BAP Memorabilia Toronto Fall Expo Gold-328
00BAP Memorabilia Toronto Fall Expo Ruby-328
00BAP Parkhurst 2000-P204
00BAP Signature Series-146
Emerald-146
Ruby-146
Sapphire-146
Autographs-212
Autographs Gold-212
00O-Pee-Chee-257A
00O-Pee-Chee Parallel-257A
00Pacific-152
Copper-152
Gold-152
Ice Blue-152
Premiere Date-152
00Panini Stickers-155
00SPx-137
00Stadium Club-226
00Topps/OPC-257A
Parallel-257A
00Upper Deck-302
Exclusives Tier 1-302
Exclusives Tier 2-302
00Upper Deck Vintage-153
01BAP Signature Series-183
Autographs-183
Autographs Gold-183
01Pacific-144
Extreme LTD-144
Hobby LTD-144
Premiere Date-144
Retail LTD-144
01Pacific Arena Exclusives-144
01Parkhurst-151
01Upper Deck-291
Exclusives-291
02BAP Signature Series-169
Autographs-169
Autograph Buybacks 1998-199
Autograph Buybacks 2000-212
Autograph Buybacks 2001-183
Autographs Gold-169
02BAP Ultimate Mem Dynasty Jerseys-6
02BAP Ultimate Mem Dynasty Emblems-6
02BAP Ultimate Mem Dynasty Numbers-6
02BAP Ultimate Mem Global Dominators-5
02Pacific-130
Blue-130
Red-130
02Pacific Complete-339
Red-339
02Parkhurst-196
Bronze-196
Gold-196
Silver-196
02Parkhurst Retro-121
Minis-121
02Topps Total-278
02Upper Deck-65
Exclusives-65
03BAP Ultimate Memorabilia Linemates-12
03Devils Team Issue-8
03ITG Action-235
Jerseys-M45
03Pacific-121
Blue-121
Red-121
03Pacific Complete-464
Red-464
03Parkhurst Orig Six Detroit Mem-DM12
03Topps Traded-TT48
Blue-TT48
Gold-TT48
Red-TT48
03Upper Deck-363
Canadian Exclusives-363
HG-363
UD Exclusives-363
03Upper Deck MVP-149
Gold Script-149
Silver Script-149
Canadian Exclusives-149
04UD All-World-87
04UD All-World-110C
Gold-87
Autographs-87
Autographs-119
Triple Autographs-AT-LTZ
Quad Autographs-AQ-RUS
Five Autographs-AF-AST
05UD Artifacts-128
Blue-128
Gold-128
Green-128
Pewter-128
Red-128
Gold Autographed-128
06ITG International Ice-93
Gold-93
Autographs-AIL
International Rivals-IR15
International Rivals Gold-IR15
Passing The Torch-PTT15
Passing The Torch Gold-PTT15
Stick and Jersey-SJ22
Stick and Jersey Gold-SJ22
Teammates-IT17
Teammates Gold-IT17
Triple Memorabilia-TM07
Triple Memorabilia Gold-TM07
06ITG Ultimate Memorabilia-69
Artist Proof-69
Retro Teammates-24
Retro Teammates Gold-24

Larivee, Francis
95Bowman Draft Prospects-P22
97St. John's Maple Leafs-14
99Greensboro Generals-21

Larivee, Paul
51Laval Dairy QSHL-79
52St. Lawrence Sales-33

Lariviere, Christian
907th Inn. Sketch QMJHL-221
91Johnstown Chiefs-13
917th Inn. Sketch CHL Award Winners-28
93Fredericton Canadiens-17

Lariviere, Garry
75Phoenix Roadrunners WHA-14
76Phoenix Roadrunners WHA-11
77O-Pee-Chee WHA-26
79O-Pee-Chee-291
80Nordiques Postcards-17
80Pepsi-Cola Caps-71
81Oilers Red Rooster-6
81Oilers West Edmonton Mall-6
81O-Pee-Chee-116
82Oilers Red Rooster-6
82O-Pee-Chee-116
82Post Cereal-6
88Oilers Tenth Anniversary-84

Lariviere, Jacques
99Rimouski Oceanic-17
Signed-17
00St. John's Maple Leafs-14
01Memphis RiverKings-9
01St. John's Maple Leafs-12

Lariviere, Jean Paul
80Quebec Remparts-9

Larkin, Bryan
84Saskatoon Blades Stickers-10
86Saskatoon Blades Photos-14

Larkin, Huey
80Sault Ste. Marie Greyhounds-9
81Sault Ste. Marie Greyhounds-15
82Sault Ste. Marie Greyhounds-15

Larkin, Jim
92Birmingham Bulls-2
93Birmingham Bulls-2
93Birmingham Bulls Birmingham News-12
94Birmingham Bulls-16

Larkin, Mike
96Hampton Roads Admirals-HRA2
97Hampton Roads Admirals-11

Larkin, Wayne
60Cleveland Barons-10

Larman, Drew
03Sarnia Sting-13
04London Knights-16
05ITG Heroes and Prospects Memorial Cup-MC-11
06Hot Prospects-159
Red Hot-159
White Hot-159
06O-Pee-Chee-585
Rainbow-585
06Rochester Americans-11
06SP Authentic-241
Limited-241
06SP Game Used Rookie Exclusives Autographs-REDL
06The Cup-97
Autographed Rookie Masterpiece Pressplates-97
Gold Rainbow Autographed Rookies-97
Masterpiece Pressplates (Marquee Rookies)-585
Masterpiece Pressplates (SP Authentic)-241
Rookies Black-97
Rookies Platinum-97
06Upper Deck-471
Exclusives Parallel-471
High Gloss Parallel-471
Masterpieces-471

Larmer, Jeff
83Devils Postcards-12
83NHL Key Tags-73
83O-Pee-Chee-230
83O-Pee-Chee Stickers-186
83Topps Stickers-186
84O-Pee-Chee-36
85Nova Scotia Oilers-2
91ProCards-613

Larmer, Steve
82Blackhawks Postcards-10
83Blackhawks Postcards-11
83NHL Key Tags-27
83O-Pee-Chee-105
83O-Pee-Chee-206
83O-Pee-Chee Stickers-108
83O-Pee-Chee Stickers-312
83Puffy Stickers-17
83Topps Stickers-108
83Topps Stickers-312
84O-Pee-Chee-37
84O-Pee-Chee Stickers-29
84Topps-30
85Blackhawks Team Issue-1
85O-Pee-Chee-132
85O-Pee-Chee Stickers-28
85Topps-132
86Blackhawks Coke-6
86O-Pee-Chee-139
86O-Pee-Chee Stickers-157
86Topps-139
87Blackhawks Coke-6
87O-Pee-Chee-59
87O-Pee-Chee Stickers-81
87Panini Stickers-226
87Topps-59
88Blackhawks Coke-8
88O-Pee-Chee-154
88O-Pee-Chee Minis-17
88O-Pee-Chee Stickers-12
88Panini Stickers-26
88Topps-154
89Blackhawks Coke-3
89O-Pee-Chee-179
89O-Pee-Chee Box Bottoms-J
89O-Pee-Chee Stickers-17
89Panini Stickers-43
89Sports Illustrated for Kids I-254
89Topps-179
89Topps Box Bottoms-J
90Blackhawks Coke-3
90Bowman-5
Tiffany-5
90Kraft-26
90O-Pee-Chee-56
90OPC Premier-58
90Panini Stickers-194
90Pro Set-53A
90Pro Set-53B
90Pro Set-345
90Score-135
Canadian-135
90Score Hottest/Rising Stars-61
90Topps-56
Tiffany-56
Team Scoring Leaders-1
Team Scoring Leaders Tiffany-1
90Upper Deck-242
90Upper Deck-499
French-242
French-499
91Pro Set Platinum-28
91Pro Set Platinum-287
91Blackhawks Coke-14
91Bowman-395
91Bowman-405
91Kraft-69
91McDonald's Upper Deck-15
91O-Pee-Chee-75
91OPC Premier-60
91OPC Premier-135
91Panini Stickers-8
91Parkhurst-34
91Parkhurst-457
French-34
91Pinnacle-29
91Pinnacle-357
French-29
French-357
91Pro Set-49
91Pro Set-279
French-49
French-279
Awards Special-AC13
91Score American-140
91Score Canadian Bilingual-140
91Score Canadian English-140
91Stadium Club-270
91Topps-75
Team Scoring Leaders-21
91Upper Deck-15
91Upper Deck-257
French-15
French-257
91Finnish Semic World Champ Stickers-73
91Swedish Semic World Champ Stickers-73
92Blackhawks Coke-9
92Bowman-61
92O-Pee-Chee-32
92Panini Stickers-5
92Panini Stickers French-5
92Parkhurst-30
Emerald Ice-30
92Pinnacle-74
French-74
92Pro Set-31
92Score-266
Canadian-266
92Seasons Patches-2
92Stadium Club-54
92Topps-497
Gold-497G
92Ultra-39
92Upper Deck-4
92Upper Deck-135
Gordie Howe Selects-G6
92Finnish Semic-91
93Donruss-461
93OPC Premier-240
Gold-240
93Panini Stickers-146
93Parkhurst-404B
Emerald Ice-404B
93Pinnacle-356
Canadian-356
93PowerPlay-52
93PowerPlay-392
93Score Samples-3
93Score-3
93Score-525
Gold-525
Canadian-3
Canadian-525
Canadian Gold-525
Dream Team-22
93Stadium Club-236
93Stadium Club-398
Members Only Master Set-236
Members Only Master Set-398
OPC-236
First Day Issue-236
First Day Issue-398
First Day Issue OPC-236
93Topps/OPC Premier-240
Gold-240
93Ultra-129
93Ultra-373
93Upper Deck-172
93Upper Deck-471
Hat Tricks-HT14
NHLPA/Roots-22
94Be A Player-R169
99 All-Stars-G12
Signature Cards-146
94Canada Games NHL POGS-164
94Donruss-231
94EA Sports-29
94Finest-63
Super Team Winners-63
Refractors-63
94Flair-113
94Fleer-134
94Hockey Wit-43
94Leaf-270
94OPC Premier-418
94OPC Premier-532
Special Effects-418
Special Effects-532
94Parkhurst-146
Gold-146
94Pinnacle-88
Artist's Proofs-88
Rink Collection-88
94Score-40
Gold-40
Platinum-40
94Select-112
Gold-112
94Stadium Club-242
Members Only Master Set-242
First Day Issue-242
Super Teams-15
Super Teams Members Only Master Set-15
Super Team Winner Cards-242
94Topps/OPC Premier-418
94Topps/OPC Premier-532
Special Effects-418
Special Effects-532
94Ultra-138
94Upper Deck-40
Electric Ice-40
94Finnish Jaa Kiekko-90
95Collector's Choice-154
Player's Club-154
Player's Club Platinum-154
95Donruss-2
95Emotion-114
95Leaf-178
95Panini Stickers-107
95Score-211
Black Ice Artist's Proofs-211
Black Ice-211
95Topps Hidden Gems-7HG
95Ultra-103
Gold Medallion-103
95Finnish Semic World Championships-100
98Blackhawks Legends-4
01Greats of the Game-24
Autographs-24
02UD Foundations-16
02UD Foundations-69
Signs of Greatness-SGSL
03Parkhurst Original Six Chicago-38
03Parkhurst Original Six Chicago-100
Autographs-8
04UD Legendary Signatures-79
Autographs-SL
Linemates-SLDEMG
06ITG International Ice-112
Gold-112
Autographs-ASL

Larner, Don
96Las Vegas Thunder-11
96Toledo Storm-32

Larnerd, John F
93Quebec Pee-Wee Tournament-1581

Larney, Rob
97UK Guildford Flames-2

Laroche, Benoit
93Quebec Pee-Wee Tournament-907

Laroche, Christian
03Gatineau Olympiques-15
03Victoriaville Tigers-17

Laroche, Gilles
51Bas Du Fleuve-8
92Quebec Pee-Wee Tournament-521

Laroche, Jasmyn
93Quebec Pee-Wee Tournament-273

Laroche, Jean-Francois
917th Inn. Sketch QMJHL-161

Laroche, Marc-Andre
05Rimouski Oceanic-23
06Rimouski Oceanic-12

Laroche, Martin
98Baton Rouge Kingfish-12

Larochelle, Allan
83Saskatoon Blades-23

Larochelle, Claude
78Saginaw Gears-14

Larochelle, Claude (AHL)
50Quebec Citadelles-11

Larochelle, Dany
917th Inn. Sketch QMJHL-81
93Sherbrooke Faucons-5

Larochelle, Eric
01Guelph Storm Memorial Cup-5
02Guelph Storm-8
03Sudbury Wolves-14

Larochelle, Martin
917th Inn. Sketch QMJHL-137

Larochelle, R.J.
05Swift Current Broncos-7
06Swift Current Broncos-5

Larochelle, Tommy
93Quebec Pee-Wee Tournament-453

Larochelle, Wildor
24Anonymous NHL-7
24Anonymous NHL-7
27La Patrie-7
27La Presse Photos-11
33O-Pee-Chee V304A-21
33V288 Hamilton Gum-14
33V357 Ice Kings-28
34Diamond Matchbooks Silver-38
34Sweet Caporal-7
35Diamond Matchbooks Tan 1-38
35Diamond Matchbooks Tan 2-36
35Diamond Matchbooks Tan 3-33
35Diamond Matchbooks Tan 4-8
37V356 Worldwide Gum-34

Larocque, Andre
80Quebec Remparts-10

Larocque, Denis
88ProCards AHL-219
89ProCards IHL-33
90Moncton Hawks-14
90ProCards AHL/IHL-257
92Dayton Bombers-17

Larocque, Ian
01Austin Ice Bats-5

Larocque, Jean-Sebastien
98Guelph Storm-5

Larocque, Mario
92Quebec Pee-Wee Tournament-571
95Bowman Draft Prospects-P23
98Cleveland Lumberjacks-13
99Pacific-400
Copper-400
Emerald Green-400
Gold-400
Ice Blue-400
Premiere Date-400
Red-400
99Detroit Vipers-3
03Wheeling Nailers-89
05Danbury Trashers-16
06Fort Wayne Komets-12

Larocque, Michel
72Dimanche/Derniere Heure *-149
73Canadiens Postcards-11
74Canadiens Postcards-12
74NHL Action Stamps-149
74O-Pee-Chee NHL-297
75Canadiens Postcards-11
75O-Pee-Chee NHL-362
76Canadiens Postcards-12
76O-Pee-Chee NHL-6
76O-Pee-Chee NHL-79
76Topps-6
76Topps-79
77Canadiens Postcards-13
77O-Pee-Chee NHL-6
77O-Pee-Chee NHL-177
77Topps-6
77Topps-177
78Canadiens Postcards-15
78O-Pee-Chee-158
78Topps-158
79Canadiens Postcards-14
79O-Pee-Chee-296
80Canadiens Postcards-14
81Maple Leafs Postcards-8
81O-Pee-Chee-319
81O-Pee-Chee Stickers-105
81O-Pee-Chee Stickers-259
82Maple Leafs Postcards-20
82Maple Leafs Postcards-21
82O-Pee-Chee-324
82O-Pee-Chee Stickers-77
82Post Cereal-18
82Topps Stickers-77
99Baie-Comeau Drakkar-27
01Pacific-87
Extreme LTD-87
Hobby LTD-87
Premiere Date-87
Retail LTD-87
01Pacific Arena Exclusives-87
01SPx-125
01UD Top Shelf-49
01UD Top Shelf-49B
01Upper Deck-183
Exclusives-183
01Upper Deck MVP-193
01Upper Deck Victory-366
Gold-366
01Upper Deck Vintage Sweaters of Honor-SHML

Larocque, Stephane
917th Inn. Sketch QMJHL-259
93Sherbrooke Faucons-13
96Fort Worth Fire-4
97Fort Worth Brahmas-9
98Fort Worth Brahmas-13
99Fort Worth Brahmas-11
01Sorel Royaux-12

Laroruk, Cam
84Kelowna Wings-19

Larose, Benoit
907th Inn. Sketch QMJHL-59
917th Inn. Sketch QMJHL-247
917th Inn. Sketch CHL Award Winners-23

Larose, Chad
01Plymouth Whalers-6
01Plymouth Whalers-30
02Plymouth Whalers-7
02Plymouth Whalers-19
03Florida Everblades-11
03Florida Everblades RBI Sports-166
04Lowell Lock Monsters-13
04Lowell Lock Monsters Photo Album-13
05ITG Heroes/Prosp Toronto Expo Parallel -243
05Hot Prospects-112
En Fuego-112
Red Hot-112
White Hot-112
05SP Authentic-256
Limited-256
05SP Game Used-198
05SPx-250
05The Cup Masterpiece Pressplate Artifact-257
05The Cup Masterpiece Pressplates (Ice)-240
05The Cup Master Pressplate Rookie Update-114
05The Cup Masterpiece Pressplates SPA-256
05The Cup Masterpiece Pressplates SP GU-198
05The Cup Masterpiece Pressplates (SPx)-250
05The Cup Masterpiece Pressplates Trilogy-234
05The Cup Masterpiece Pressplate Ult Coll-198
05UD Artifacts-257
05Ultimate Collection-198
Gold-198
05Upper Deck Ice-240
05Upper Deck Rookie Update-114
05Upper Deck Trilogy-234
05ITG Heroes and Prospects-243
Autographs Series II-CLR
06Hurricanes Postcards-16
06O-Pee-Chee-91
Rainbow-91

Larose, Claude
64Beehive Group III Photos-110A
64Beehive Group III Photos-110B
64Canadiens Postcards-11
64Coca-Cola Caps-62
65Coca-Cola-62
65Topps-75
66Canadiens IGA-5
66Topps-10
67Canadiens IGA-11
67Topps-4
68O-Pee-Chee-51
68Shirriff Coins-69
68Topps-51
69Canadiens Postcards Color-14
69O-Pee-Chee-194
Four-in-One-12
69Topps-126
70Esso Power Players-10
70O-Pee-Chee-56
70Sargent Promotions Stamps-101
70Topps-56
71Canadiens Postcards-12
71O-Pee-Chee-146
71Sargent Promotions Stamps-106
71Toronto Sun-155
72Canadiens Postcards-10
72Dimanche/Derniere Heure *-150
72Dimanche/Derniere Heure *-151
72O-Pee-Chee-231
72Sargent Promotions Stamps-122
72Finnish Semic World Championship-199
72Swedish Semic World Championship-199
73Canadiens Postcards-12
74Canadiens Postcards-13
74NHL Action Stamps-157
74NHL Action Stamps Update-32
74O-Pee-Chee NHL-124
74Topps-124
75O-Pee-Chee NHL-112
75Stingers Kahn's-6
75Topps-112
76O-Pee-Chee NHL-310
76Stingers Kahn's-4
77O-Pee-Chee NHL-167
77O-Pee-Chee WHA-43
77Topps-167
88ProCards AHL-60
88ProCards AHL-282
94Parkhurst Tall Boys-71
95Parkhurst '66-67-69
Coins-69

Larose, Cory
00Jackson Bandits-10
02Hartford Wolf Pack-15
03ITG VIP Rookie Debut-122
03Parkhurst Rookie-77
03Topps Traded-TT146
Blue-TT146
Gold-TT146
Red-TT146
03UD Premier Collection-120
03Upper Deck Rookie Update-198
03Hartford Wolf Pack-13
04Chicago Wolves-17

Larose, Guy
87Moncton Hawks-15
88ProCards AHL-182
89ProCards AHL-29
90Jets IGA-18
90Moncton Hawks-15
90ProCards AHL/IHL-259
91Parkhurst-399
French-399
91ProCards-195
92Bowman-281
92Maple Leafs Kodak-27
92O-Pee-Chee-269
92OPC Premier-128
92Stadium Club-237
92Topps-477
Gold-47G
92Upper Deck-527
98Chicago Wolves-17
99Chicago Wolves-11
00Chicago Wolves-12
01Augusta Lynx-7

Larose, Paul
72Nordiques Postcards-15
73Nordiques Team Issue-16

Larose, Ray
64Quebec Aces-12
69Seattle Totems-12

Larouche, Dave
95Central Hockey League-65

Larouche, Mike
83North Bay Centennials-14
84Ottawa 67's-17

Larouche, Pierre
74Penguins Postcards-14
75O-Pee-Chee NHL-305
75Topps-305
76O-Pee-Chee NHL-1
76O-Pee-Chee NHL-5
76O-Pee-Chee NHL-199
76O-Pee-Chee NHL-392
76Topps-1
76Topps-5
76Topps-199
77Canadiens Postcards-14
77O-Pee-Chee NHL-102
77Penguins Puck Bucks-10
77Topps-102
78Canadiens Postcards-16
78O-Pee-Chee-35
78Topps-35
79Canadiens Postcards-15
79O-Pee-Chee-233
79Topps-233
80Canadiens Postcards-15
80O-Pee-Chee-151
80O-Pee-Chee-216
80Pepsi-Cola Caps-51
80Topps-151
80Topps-216
81O-Pee-Chee-187
81O-Pee-Chee Stickers-38
82O-Pee-Chee-125
82O-Pee-Chee Stickers-127
82Post Cereal-7
82Topps Stickers-127
82Whalers Junior Hartford Courant-10
83NHL Key Tags-48
83Puffy Stickers-13
84O-Pee-Chee-145
84O-Pee-Chee-363
84O-Pee-Chee Stickers-103
84Topps-108
85O-Pee-Chee-54
85O-Pee-Chee Stickers-85
85Topps-54
87Panini Stickers-116
01Topps Archives-40
Arena Seats-ASPL
04ITG Franchises US West-277
Autographs-A-PLA
06Parkhurst-61
Autographs-61

Larouche, Steve
907th Inn. Sketch QMJHL-30
91ProCards-83
917th Inn. Sketch Memorial Cup-29
92Fredericton Canadiens-17
93Atlanta Knights-6
93Classic Pro Prospects-78
94Classic Pro Prospects-160
95Donruss-39
95Emotion-125
95Leaf-94
95Panini Stickers-55
95Pinnacle-209
Artist's Proofs-209
Rink Collection-209
95Playoff One on One-179
95Pro Magnets-114
95Score-302
Black Ice Artist's Proofs-302
Black Ice-302
95Topps-38
OPC Inserts-38
95Ultra-112
Gold Medallion-112
95Upper Deck-89
Electric Ice-89
Electric Ice Gold-89
95Binghamton Rangers-13
95Images-31
Gold-31
96NHL Pro Stamps-114
98Chicago Wolves-13
98Chicago Wolves Turner Cup-10
99Chicago Wolves-7
00Chicago Wolves-13
01German Berlin Polar Bears Postcards-10
01German Upper Deck-36
02German DEL City Press-266
03German DEL-205
03German Nuremberg Ice Tigers Postcards-15
04Finnish Cardset-115
Parallel-86

Larouche, Ugo
93Quebec Pee-Wee Tournament-74

Larranaga, Felipe
99Des Moines Buccaneers-2

Larrivee, Christian
00Chicoutimi Sagueneens-11
Signed-11
01Chicoutimi Sagueneens-6
03Columbus Cottonmouths-26
03ECHL Update RBI Sports-115
04Hamilton Bulldogs-17

Larrivee, Jacques
93Amos Les Forestiers-10

Larsen, Bo
98Danish Hockey League-216
99Danish Hockey League-29

Larsen, Brad
94Parkhurst SE-SE269
Gold-SE269
94Select-164
Gold-164
94SP-187
Die Cuts-187
95Donruss Elite World Juniors-17
95Upper Deck-534
Electric Ice-534
Electric Ice Gold-534
95Swift Current Broncos-8
95Classic-45
95Signature Rookies Auto-Phonex-25
95Signature Rook Auto-Phonex Phone Cards-25
96Upper Deck Ice-134
96Swift Current Broncos-17
97Collector's Choice-308
97Bowman CHL-116
OPC-116
98Hershey Bears-10
00Hershey Bears-7
01Avalanche Team Issue-7
01BAP Signature Series-210
Autographs-210
Autographs Gold-210
01Upper Deck MVP-199
02BAP Sig Series Auto Buybacks 2001-210
03Thrashers Postcards-10
03Hershey Bears Patriot News-13
04Chicago Wolves-2

Larsen, Greg
83North Bay Centennials-15

Larsen, Jonas
92Norwegian Elite Series-229

Larsen, Rico
98Danish Hockey League-59
99Danish Hockey League-57

Larsen, Roar
92Norwegian Elite Series-66

Larsen, Sjur Rakstad
92Norwegian Elite Series-221

Larsen, Tommy
92Norwegian Elite Series-28

Larsh, Jeff
02Sault Ste. Marie Greyhounds-13
03Sault Ste. Marie Greyhounds-13
04Sault Ste. Marie Greyhounds-14

Larson, Brett
93Minnesota-Duluth Bulldogs-16
95Madison Monsters-15
99San Diego Gulls-6
00San Diego Gulls-7

Larson, Dave
92Minnesota Golden Gophers-6
93Minnesota Golden Gophers-16
94Minnesota Golden Gophers-19
95Minnesota Golden Gophers-20
96Quad-City Mallards-5
97Mobile Mysticks-9
97Mobile Mysticks Kellogg's-5

Larson, Dean
96Anchorage Aces-4
97Anchorage Aces-11
98Anchorage Aces-21
99Anchorage Aces-17
01Anchorage Aces-7

Larson, Garrett
03St. Cloud State Huskies-16
05Colorado Eagles-10

Larson, Jon
92North Dakota Fighting Sioux-17
93Knoxville Cherokees-6
94Roanoke Express-6
95Roanoke Express-18

Larson, Justin
06Sudbury Wolves-13

Larson, Norman
34Beehive Group I Photos-238
40O-Pee-Chee V301-2-127

Larson, Reed
78O-Pee-Chee-226
78Topps-226
79O-Pee-Chee-213
79Red Wings Postcards-11
79Topps-213

800-Pee-Chee-43
80Topps-43
810-Pee-Chee-92
810-Pee-Chee Stickers-124
81Topps-W92
820-Pee-Chee-88
820-Pee-Chee-89
820-Pee-Chee Stickers-180
82Post Cereal-5
82Topps Stickers-180
83NHL Key Tags-34
830-Pee-Chee-125
830-Pee-Chee Stickers-134
83Puffy Stickers-18
83Topps Stickers-134
84Kellogg's Accordion Discs-2
84Kellogg's Accordion Discs Singles-22
840-Pee-Chee-58
840-Pee-Chee Stickers-36
84Topps-44
850-Pee-Chee-55
850-Pee-Chee Stickers-33
85Topps-55
860-Pee-Chee-110
860-Pee-Chee Stickers-39
86Topps-110
870-Pee-Chee-131
870-Pee-Chee Stickers-142
87Panini Stickers-7
87Topps-131
88Bruins Sports Action-9
88Oilers Tenth Anniversary-56
880-Pee-Chee-145
88Topps-145
03Parkhurst Original Six Detroit-43
03Parkhurst Original Six Detroit-79
Autographs-OS-RL
04ITG Franchises US West-208
Autographs-A-RLA
06Parkhurst-63
06Parkhurst-181
Autographs-63
Autographs-181
Autographs Dual-DAOL

Larsson, Bengt
55Swedish Alfabilder-7
67Swedish Hockey-34
67Swedish Hockey-35

Larsson, Bjorn
64Swedish Corall ISHockey-3
64Swedish Corall ISHockey-43
65Swedish Corall ISHockey-3
65Swedish Corall ISHockey-43
65Swedish Corall ISHockey-187
69Swedish Hockey-47

Larsson, Bo
83Swedish Semic Elitserien-76
84Swedish Semic Elitserien-122

Larsson, Carl-Erik
84Swedish Semic Elitserien-168
86Swedish Panini Stickers-158
87Swedish Panini Stickers-164
90Swedish Semic Elitserien Stickers-143

Larsson, Curt
65Swedish Corall ISHockey-175
67Swedish Hockey-189
69Swedish Hockey-246
70Swedish Hockey-130
71Swedish Hockey-223
72Finnish Hellas-39
72Swedish Stickers-212
73Finnish Jaakiekko-30
73Swedish Stickers-59
74Swedish Stickers-19
74Swedish Stickers-145
74Swedish Semic World Champ Stickers-24

Larsson, Daniel
06Swedish SHL Elitset-158

Larsson, Ivar
64Swedish Corall ISHockey-151
65Swedish Corall ISHockey-151
67Swedish Hockey-122
69Swedish Hockey-135
70Swedish Hockey-84
71Swedish Hockey-176
72Swedish Stickers-166
74Swedish Stickers-146

Larsson, Jan
84Swedish Semic Elitserien-65
86Swedish Panini Stickers-52
87Swedish Panini Stickers-63
89Swedish Semic Elitserien Stickers-41
90Swedish Semic Elitserien Stickers-188
91Swedish Semic Elitserien Stickers-41
92Swedish Semic Elitserien Stickers-66
93Swedish Semic World Champ Stickers-16
93Swiss HNL-103
95Finnish Semic World Championships-73
95Swedish Leaf-274
Champs-8
95Swedish Upper Deck-165
97Swedish Collector's Choice-32
Crash the Game Exchange-C19
Crash the Game Redemption-R19
98Swedish UD Choice-44
99Swedish Upper Deck-28
Hands of Gold-3
Hands of Gold-5
00Swedish Upper Deck-43
SHL Signatures-JL
Top Playmakers-P2
01Swedish Brynas Tigers-11
02Swedish SHL-10
Parallel-10
Team Captains-1

Larsson, Jorgen
87Swedish Panini Stickers-254

Larsson, Kjell
64Swedish Corall ISHockey-76
65Swedish Corall ISHockey-76
67Swedish Hockey-159
85Swedish Panini Stickers-220
92Finnish Semic-218
95Swiss HNL-56

Larsson, Lars-Erik
67Swedish Hockey-160
71Swedish Hockey-322

Larsson, Mas-Ake
56Swedish Alfabilder-89

Larsson, Nisse
67Swedish Hockey-50

Larsson, Olle
56Swedish Alfabilder-59

Larsson, Ove
71Swedish Hockey-251
72Swedish Stickers-233
73Swedish Stickers-241
74Swedish Stickers-239

Larsson, Peter
86Swedish Panini Stickers-268
87Swedish Panini Stickers-246
89Swedish Semic Elitserien Stickers-235
90Swedish Semic Elitserien Stickers-189
91Swedish Semic Elitserien Stickers-43
92Swedish Semic Elitserien Stickers-72
93Swedish Semic Elitserien-47
94Swedish Leaf-193
Playmakers-5
95Swedish Leaf-23
95Swedish Upper Deck-34
98Finnish Kerailysarja-90
99Finnish Cardset-162
99German DEL-159
00German DEL-179
02Finnish Cardset-56
02Swedish SHL-142
02Swedish SHL-258
Parallel-142
Parallel-258
Sharpshooters-SS6
03Swedish Elite-120
Silver-120
04Swedish Elitset-120
Gold-120

Larsson, Robert
86Swedish Panini Stickers-226
89Swedish Semic Elitserien Stickers-195

Larsson, Rolf
65Swedish Corall ISHockey-116
67Swedish Hockey-175
69Swedish Hockey-172
71Swedish Hockey-252

Larsson, Stefan
83Swedish Semic Elitserien-229
87Swedish Panini Stickers-156
89Swedish Semic Elitserien Stickers-273
90Swedish Semic Elitserien Stickers-34
91Swedish Semic Elitserien Stickers-282
92Swedish Semic Elitserien Stickers-308
93Swedish Semic Elitserien-275
93Swedish Semic World Champ Stickers-7
94Swedish Leaf-34
95Swedish Leaf-139
Face to Face-4
95Swedish Upper Deck-208
95Swedish Globe World Championships-25
95Swedish World Championships Stickers-142
97Swedish Collector's Choice-74
98Swedish UD Choice-72
99Swedish Upper Deck-73

Larsson, Stig
67Swedish Hockey-65
69Swedish Hockey-98
70Swedish Hockey-55
71Swedish Hockey-126
72Finnish Jaakiekko-50
72Finnish Hellas-34
72Swedish Stickers-110
73Swedish Stickers-212
74Swedish Stickers-240

Larsson, Tore
69Swedish Hockey-173

Larsson, Ulf
67Swedish Hockey-257
69Swedish Hockey-302
70Swedish Hockey-206
71Swedish Hockey-293

Larsson, Urban
83Swedish Semic Elitserien-109

Larsson, Vilgot
57Swedish Alfabilder-89
64Swedish Corall ISHockey-48

Lartama, Mika
93Finnish Jyvas-Hyva Stickers-49
93Finnish SISU-249
95Finnish SISU Limited-85

Larter, Brad
00Kitchener Rangers-16
01Moncton Wildcats-12
03Yarmouth Mariners-13

Larter, Tyler
84Sault Ste. Marie Greyhounds-12
87Sault Ste. Marie Greyhounds-4
88ProCards AHL-32
89ProCards AHL-94
90ProCards AHL/IHL-207
91Moncton Hawks-17
91ProCards-181

LaRue, Rob
98Minnesota Golden Gophers-7

Larway, Don
75Houston Aeros WHA-11
770-Pee-Chee WHA-48

Lasak, Jan
93Quebec Pee-Wee Tournament-1717
99ECHL All-Star Northern Conference-12
99Hampton Roads Admirals-11
00Milwaukee Admirals Keebler-8
00Milwaukee Admirals Postcards-8
01Parkhurst-341
01UD Top Shelf-138
01Milwaukee Admirals-15
02BAP Memorabilia-60
Emerald-60
Ruby-60
Sapphire-60
NHL All-Star Game-60
NHL All-Star Game Blue-60
NHL All-Star Game Green-60
NHL All-Star Game Red-60
02BAP Memorabilia Toronto Fall Expo-60
02BAP Signature Series All-Rookie-AR7
02Between the Pipes-92
Gold-92
Silver-92
02Pacific Calder-77
Silver-77
02Pacific Complete-530
Red-530
02SPx-115
02UD Foundations-135
02UD Mask Collection-48
02UD Mask Collection-49
02UD Mask Collection Beckett Promos-48
02UD Mask Collection Beckett Promos-49
02UD Piece of History-138
02Upper Deck MVP-208
Gold-208
Classics-208
Golden Classics-208
02Upper Deck Vintage-339
02Slovakian Kvarteto-4
02Milwaukee Admirals-10
02Milwaukee Admirals Postcards-10
03BAP Memorabilia Deep in the Crease-D6
03Russian Hockey League-71
03Russian World Championship Stars-3
04Czech OFS-133
Stars-14
Team Cards-6
05Czech HC Pardubice-8
06Czech HC Pardubice Postcards-11
06Czech OFS-120
Goalies I-11
Goalies II-13
Team Cards-6
06Czech Super Six Postcards-7

Lascala, Frank
90Richmond Renegades-15
92Dallas Freeze-11
93Dallas Freeze-10
94Central Hockey League-12
94Dallas Freeze-12
96German DEL-220
96St. Louis Vipers RHI-1

Lascek, Stanislav
04Chicoutimi Sagueneens-17
05ITG Heroes/Prosp Toronto Expo Parallel -305
05Chicoutimi Sagueneens-2
05Extreme Top Prospects Signature Edition-S21
05ITG Heroes and Prospects-305
Autographs Series II-SL

Lashmett, Jordan
98Sioux City Musketeers-12

Lashoff, Brian
06Barrie Colts-4

Lashoff, Matt
03Kitchener Rangers-16
04Kitchener Rangers-18
04ITG Heroes and Prospects-93
Autographs-ML
04ITG Heroes/Prospects Toronto Expo '05-93
04ITG Heroes/Prospects Expo Heroes/Pros-93
05ITG Heroes/Prosp Toronto Expo Parallel -117
05Kitchener Rangers-4
05OHL Bell All-Star Classic-5
05ITG Heroes and Prospects-117
Autographs-A-MLF
06Be A Player-228
06Beehive-104
Matte-104
06Flair Showcase-304
06Hot Prospects-145
Red Hot-145
White Hot-145
060-Pee-Chee-573
Rainbow-573
06SP Authentic-165
Limited-165
06SP Game Used-107
Gold-107
Rainbow-107
Autographs-107
06SPx-212
Spectrum-212
06The Cup-113
Autographed Rookie Masterpiece Pressplates-113
Gold Rainbow Autographed Rookie Patches-113
Masterpiece Pressplates (Bee Hive)-104
Masterpiece Pressplates (Marquee Rookies)-573
Masterpiece Pressplates (SP Authentic Autographs)-165
Masterpiece Pressplates (SP Game Used)-107
Masterpiece Pressplates (Sweet Beginnings)-107
Masterpiece Pressplates (Ultimate Collection Autographs)-103
Masterpiece Pressplates (Victory)-320
NHL Shields Duals-DSHSL
Rookies Black-113
Rookies Platinum-113
06UD Artifacts-269
06Ultimate Collection-103
Rookies Autographed NHL Shields-103
Rookies Autographed Patches-103
Ultimate Debut Threads Jerseys-DJ-ML
Ultimate Debut Threads Jerseys Autographs-DJ-ML
Ultimate Debut Threads Patches-DJ-ML
Ultimate Debut Threads Patches Autographs-DJ-ML
06Upper Deck-453
Exclusives Parallel-453
High Gloss Parallel-453
Masterpieces-453
Rookie Headliners-RH14
06Upper Deck Sweet Shot-107
Rookie Jerseys Autographs-107
06Upper Deck Victory-320
06AHL Top Prospects-37
06Providence Bruins-10
07Upper Deck Rookie Class -29

Laskoski, Gary
83NHL Key Tags-56
830-Pee-Chee-156
830-Pee-Chee Stickers-296
83Topps Stickers-296

Lassas, Ake
57Swedish Alfabilder-92

Lassila, Hannu
81Swedish Semic Hockey VM Stickers-20

Lassila, Teemu
03Finnish Cardset-155
04Finnish Cardset-167
Parallel-123
Stars of the Game-5
04Swedish Pure Skills-139
Parallel-139
05Finnish Cardset Super Snatchers-17
05Swedish SHL Elitset-158
Catchers-2
Catchers Gold-2
Gold-158
06Swedish SHL Elitset-159
Goal Patrol-3
In The Crease-2

Lassu, Dion
98Kootenay Ice-5
01Greensboro Generals-14

Laszkiewicz, Leszek
98German DEL-261
02Czech OFS Plus-56

Latal, Jaromir
92Norwegian Elite Series-6
92Norwegian Elite Series-193
94Czech APS Extraliga-5
95Czech APS Extraliga-103
96Czech APS Extraliga-7
97Czech DS Stickers-114

Latal, Jiri
89ProCards AHL-344
90Flyers Postcards-16
90OPC Premier-59
90Pro Set-501
90Upper Deck-410
French-410
91Flyers J.C. Penney-17
910-Pee-Chee-444
91Pro Set-454
French-454
91Score Canadian Bilingual-540
91Score Canadian English-540
91Topps-444
91Upper Deck-404
French-404
95Czech APS Extraliga-104
96Czech APS Extraliga-263
98Czech OFS-326

Latal, Martin
06PEI Rocket-12

Latendresse, Guillaume
03Drummondville Voltigeurs-11
04Drummondville Voltigeurs-1
05ITG Heroes/Prosp Toronto Expo Parallel -151
05Drummondville Voltigeurs-1
05Extreme Top Prospects Signature Edition-S3
05ITG Heroes and Prospects-151
Aspiring-ASP13
Autographs-A-GL
Autographs-DA-LL
Complete Jerseys-CJ-21
Complete Jerseys Gold-CJ-21
Complete Logos-CHL-2
He Shoots-He Scores Prizes-2
He Shoots-He Scores Prizes-31
Jerseys-GUJ-28
Jerseys Gold-GUJ-28
Emblems-GUE-28
Emblems Gold-GUE-28
Numbers-GUN-28
Numbers Gold-GUN-28
Making the Bigs-MTB-13
Spectrum-STM-05
Spectrum Gold-STM-05
06Be A Player-231
Autographs-231
Profiles-PP24
Profiles Autographs-PP24
Signatures 10-231
Signatures 25-231
Signatures Trios-TKRL
Signatures Foursomes-FSSLK
06Be A Player Portraits-112
06Beehive-130
Blue-130
Gold-130
Matte-130
Red Facsimile Signatures-130
Wood-130
06Black Diamond-203
Black-203
Gold-203
Ruby-203
06Canadiens Postcards-12
06Flair Showcase-316
06Gatorade-41
06Hot Prospects-119
Red Hot-119
White Hot-119
Hot Materials -HMGL
Hot Materials Red Hot-HMGL
Hot Materials White Hot-HMGL
Hotagraphs-HGL
060-Pee-Chee-544
060-Pee-Chee-622
Rainbow-544
Rainbow-622
06SP Authentic-186
Limited-186
Sign of the Times Duals-STRL
Sign of the Times Quads-ST4MKSL
06SP Game Used-126
Gold-126
Rainbow-126
Autographs-126
Letter Marks-LMGL
Rookie Exclusives Autographs-REGL
SIGnificance-SGL
06SPx-190
Spectrum-190
06The Cup-138
Autographed NHL Shields Duals-DASKL
Autographed NHL Shields Duals-DASLP
Autographed NHL Shields Duals-DASMC
Autographed NHL Shields Duals-DASRL
Autographed Rookie Masterpiece Pressplates-138
Enshrinements-EGL
Gold Rainbow Autographed Rookie Patches-138
Honorable Numbers-HNGL
Masterpiece Pressplates (Be A Player Portraits)-112
Masterpiece Pressplates (Bee Hive)-130
Masterpiece Pressplates (Marquee Rookies)-544
Masterpiece Pressplates (MVP)-300
Masterpiece Pressplates (SP Authentic Autographs)-186
Masterpiece Pressplates (SP Game Used)-126
Masterpiece Pressplates (SPx Autographs)-190
Masterpiece Pressplates (Sweet Beginnings)-133
Masterpiece Pressplates (Trilogy)-123
Masterpiece Pressplates (Ultimate Collection Autographs)-116
Masterpiece Pressplates (Victory)-290
NHL Shields Duals-DSHLP
Rookies Black-138
Rookies Platinum-138
Signature Patches-SPLA
06UD Artifacts-246
06UD Mini Jersey Collection-112
06Ultimate Collection-116
Rookies Autographed NHL Shields-116
Rookies Autographed Patches-116
Signatures-US-GL
Ultimate Debut Threads Jerseys-DJ-GL
Ultimate Debut Threads Jerseys Autographs-DJ-GL
Ultimate Debut Threads Patches-DJ-GL
Ultimate Debut Threads Patches Autographs-DJ-GL
06Ultra-249
06Ultra-250
Gold Medallion-249
Ice Medallion-249
06Upper Deck-221
Exclusives Parallel-221
High Gloss Parallel-221
Masterpieces-221
Rookie Game Dated Moments-RGD13
Rookie Headliners-RH24
Rookie Materials-RMGL
Rookie Materials Patches-RMGL
Signatures-SGL
06Upper Deck MVP-300
Gold Script-300
Super Script-300
06Upper Deck Ovation-172
06Upper Deck Sweet Shot-134
Rookie Jerseys Autographs-134
Signature Shots/Saves-SSGL
Signature Shots/Saves Sticks-SSSGL
06Upper Deck Trilogy-123
06Upper Deck Victory-290
06ITG Heroes and Prospects-126
06ITG Heroes and Prospects-149
Triple Memorabilia-TM06
Triple Memorabilia Gold-TM06
07Upper Deck Ovation-23
3x5s-XL13
Autographed 3x5s-XLAGL
07Upper Deck Rookie Class -5
07Upper Deck Victory-49
Black-49
Gold-49

Latendresse, Mike
92Maine Black Bears-21
93Maine Black Bears-42
94Toledo Storm-11
95Birmingham Bulls-10
97Wheeling Nailers-11
97Wheeling Nailers Photo Pack-11

Latendresse, Olivier
02Val d'Or Foreurs-13
03Val d'Or Foreurs-14
05ITG Heroes/Prosp Toronto Expo Parallel -301
05ITG Heroes and Prospects-301
Autographs Series II-OL
06ITG Heroes and Prospects National Pride-NP07
06ITG Heroes and Prospects National Pride Gold-NP07

Later, Steven
02Saskatoon Blades-5
03Brandon Wheat Kings-15
03Prince George Cougars-20
04Brandon Wheat Kings-6

Laterreur, Yan
917th Inn. Sketch QMJHL-261

Latorre, T.J.
01Ohio State Buckeyes-9

Latos, Jim
84Saskatoon Blades Stickers-11
86Portland Winter Hawks-11
89ProCards IHL-30
90Kansas City Blades-20
90ProCards AHL/IHL-585
93Wichita Thunder-11
94Central Hockey League-116
95Louisiana Ice Gators-8
95Louisiana Ice Gators Playoffs-9
96Louisiana Ice Gators II-7

Latouche, Dominic
93Quebec Pee-Wee Tournament-265

Latour, Yannick
99Quad-City Mallards-2
00Knoxville Speed-15

Latta, David
83Kitchener Rangers-19
84Kitchener Rangers-23
85Kitchener Rangers-22
86Kitchener Rangers-22
87Nordiques General Foods-20
87Nordiques Team Issue-22
88Nordiques General Foods-23
88Nordiques Team Issue-21
89Nordiques Team Issue-24
89Nordiques General Foods-19
89Nordiques Police-16
90Nordiques Team Issue-17
90Halifax Citadels-15
90ProCards AHL/IHL-461
91ProCards-376
92Cincinnati Cyclones-14
97Anchorage Aces-12

Latta, Ken
80Sault Ste. Marie Greyhounds-21
81Sault Ste. Marie Greyhounds-16
83Pinebridge Bucks-7

Lattery, Dana
04Las Vegas Wranglers-9

Latti, Petri
93Finnish SISU-204
93Finnish SISU-204B
94Finnish SISU-356
95Finnish SISU-100
96Finnish SISU Redline-104
99Finnish Cardset-89
00Finnish Cardset-66
01Finnish Cardset-93
02Finnish Cardset-65

Latto, Gordon
96UK Fife Flyers-13
97UK Fife Flyers-13

Latulippe, Charles
93Quebec Pee-Wee Tournament-1021

Latulippe, Francois
92Quebec Pee-Wee Tournament-171
93Quebec Pee-Wee Tournament-1108

Latulippe, Jay
06Odessa Jackalopes-12

Latulippe, Martin
93Drummondville Voltigeurs-5

Latvala, Jan
93Finnish SISU-138
94Finnish SISU-29
95Finnish SISU-262
96Finnish SISU Redline-60
98Finnish Kerailysarja-122
99Finnish Cardset-97
00Finnish Cardset-195
01Finnish Cardset-99
02Finnish Cardset-208
03Finnish Cardset-60
04Finnish Cardset-66
Parallel-49
05Finnish Cardset -229
06Finnish Cardset-57

Lauber, Bernhard
93Swiss HNL-453
95Swiss HNL-333
96Swiss HNL-252

Lauber, Matthias
98Swiss Power Play Stickers-351
99Swiss Panini Stickers-345
00Swiss Panini Stickers-223
01Swiss HNL-122
02Swiss HNL-139

Lauderdale, Phil
04Ohio State Buckeyes-20
05Ohio State Buckeyes-19
06Ohio State Buckeyes-15

Lauer, Brad
86Islanders Team Issue-6
880-Pee-Chee-226
900-Pee-Chee-217
90Topps-217
Tiffany-217
90ProCards AHL/IHL-501
91Blackhawks Coke-15
91Pro Set-375
French-375
91Stadium Club-142
91ProCards-490
92Indianapolis Ice-17
94Cleveland Lumberjacks-9
94Cleveland Lumberjacks Postcards-9
95Cleveland Lumberjacks-17
95Cleveland Lumberjacks Postcards-16
96Cleveland Lumberjacks-15
96Cleveland Lumberjacks Multi-Ad-17
97Cleveland Lumberjacks-17
97Cleveland Lumberjacks Postcards-21
99Utah Grizzlies-25
00Utah Grizzlies-4
01UK Sheffield Steelers-12

Laufman, Ken
52St. Lawrence Sales-56

Laughlin, Craig
81Canadiens Postcards-17
82Capitals Team Issue-14
82Post Cereal-10
830-Pee-Chee-375
84Capitals Pizza Hut-12
840-Pee-Chee-203
85Capitals Pizza Hut-11
850-Pee-Chee-190
86Capitals Kodak-15
86Capitals Police-15
860-Pee-Chee-35
860-Pee-Chee Stickers-253
86Topps-35
87Capitals Kodak-18
87Capitals Team Issue-14
870-Pee-Chee-161
87Panini Stickers-182
87Topps-161
88Maple Leafs PLAY-18
890-Pee-Chee-275
890-Pee-Chee Stickers-171

Laughlin, Dan
95Madison Monsters-10

Laughton, Mike
67Seals Team Issue-15
690-Pee-Chee-148
700-Pee-Chee-74
70Sargent Promotions Stamps-136
70Topps-74
74San Diego Mariners WHA-2

Laukkanen, Janne
91Upper Deck-22
French-22
92Finnish Jyvas-Hyva Stickers-21
92Finnish Semic-7
93Finnish Jyvas-Hyva Stickers-46
93Finnish SISU-239
93Finnish SISU-367
93Finnish SISU Autographs-239
93Finnish SISU Promos-NNO
93Swedish Semic World Champ Stickers-54
93Classic-43
93Classic Four-Sport *-259
Gold-259
94Finest-8
Super Team Winners-8
Refractors-8
94Flair-148
94Leaf-447
94Nordiques Burger King-15
94OPC Premier-411
Special Effects-411
94Parkhurst SE-SE142
Gold-SE142
94Pinnacle-485
Artist's Proofs-485
Rink Collection-485
Rookie Team Pinnacle-3
94Select-181
Gold-181
Youth Explosion-YE3
94Topps/OPC Premier-411
Special Effects-411
94Ultra-359
94Upper Deck-251
94Upper Deck-565
Electric Ice-251
Electric Ice-565
SP Inserts-SP157
SP Inserts Die Cuts-SP157
94Finnish Jaa Kiekko-17
94Classic-102
Gold-102
95Leaf-46
95Parkhurst International-52
Emerald Ice-52
95Upper Deck-123
Electric Ice-123
Electric Ice Gold-123
95Finnish SISU Limited-83
Leaf Gallery-2
95Finnish Semic World Championships-12
95Swedish Globe World Championships-134
95Images-63
Gold-63
96Collector's Choice-187
96Senators Pizza Hut-12
96Upper Deck-116
96Swedish Semic Wien-29
96Collector's Edge Ice-28
Prism-28
97Be A Player-90
Autographs-90
Autographs Die-Cuts-90
Autographs Prismatic Die-Cuts-90
97Pacific Invincible NHL Regime-135
97Panini Stickers-40
98OPC Chrome-153
Refractors-153
98Pacific-312
Ice Blue-312
Red-312
98Panini Stickers-45
98Senators Team Issue-10
98Topps-153
O-Pee-Chee-153
98Upper Deck-141
Exclusives-141
Exclusives 1 of 1-141
Gold Reserve-141
98Finnish Kerailysarja 90's Top 12-3
98Finnish Kerailysarja Leijonat-9
98Slovakian Eurotel-11
99Panini Stickers-109
99Senators Team Issue-12
99Finnish Cardset Aces High-C-4
00BAP Memorabilia-141
Emerald-141
Ruby-141
Sapphire-141
Promos-141
00BAP Mem Chicago Sportsfest Copper-141
00BAP Memorabilia Chicago Sportsfest Blue-141
00BAP Memorabilia Chicago Sportsfest Gold-141
00BAP Memorabilia Chicago Sportsfest Ruby-141
00BAP Memorabilia Chicago Sun-Times Ruby-141
00BAP Memorabilia Chicago Sun-Times Gold-141
00BAP Mem Chicago Sun-Times Sapphire-141
00BAP Mem Toronto Fall Expo Copper-141
00BAP Memorabilia Toronto Fall Expo Gold-141
00BAP Memorabilia Toronto Fall Expo Ruby-141
000-Pee-Chee-267A
000-Pee-Chee Parallel-267A
00Pacific-332
Copper-332
Gold-332
Ice Blue-332
Premiere Date-332
00Topps/OPC-267A
Parallel-267A
00Upper Deck Vintage-293
00Finnish Cardset-354
01BAP Signature Series-48
Autographs-48
Autographs Gold-48
01Parkhurst-163
01Upper Deck Victory-285
Gold-285
02BAP Sig Series Auto Buybacks 2001-48
02Topps Total-165
02Finnish Cardset-209
02Hartford Wolf Pack-16

Laukkanen, Jari
92Finnish Jyvas-Hyva Stickers-97
93Finnish Jyvas-Hyva Stickers-17
93Finnish SISU-100
94Finnish SISU-84
95Finnish SISU-9
96Finnish SISU Redline-10
00Finnish Cardset-59
01Finnish Cardset-79
02Finnish Cardset-210

Laukkanen, Jarmo
70Finnish Jaakiekko-281

Laukkanen, Pekka
70Finnish Jaakiekko-350

Laukkanen, Tuomo
80Finnish Mallasjuoma-149

Laurence, Don
790-Pee-Chee-369
81Indianapolis Checkers-12
82Indianapolis Checkers-13

Laurendeau, Dave
93Quebec Pee-Wee Tournament-126

Lauridsen, Michael
99Danish Hockey League-186

Laurie, Rob
92Anaheim Bullfrogs RHI-9
93Anaheim Bullfrogs RHI-11
93Johnstown Chiefs-16
94Anaheim Bullfrogs RHI-10
94Johnstown Chiefs-13
95Anaheim Bullfrogs RHI-12
95Toledo Storm-1
96Anaheim Bullfrogs RHI-3
97Fort Worth Brahmas-10
98Flint Generals-18
99Austin Ice Bats-15
00Fort Worth Brahmas-11
01El Paso Buzzards-14
02El Paso Buzzards-6

Laurila, Harri
91Finnish Jyvas-Hyva Stickers-29
92Finnish Jyvas-Hyva Stickers-72
93Finnish Jyvas-Hyva Stickers-135
93Finnish SISU-146
93Swedish Semic World Champ Stickers-55
94Finnish SISU-170
94Finnish SISU-326
94Finnish Jaa Kiekko-13
95Finnish SISU-151
95Finnish SISU-184
95Finnish SISU Limited-47
95Finnish Semic World Championships-36
96Finnish SISU Redline-125
99Finnish Cardset-237

Laurila, Henri
00Finnish Cardset-310
01Finnish Cardset-312
04Finnish Cardset-230

Laurila, Marty
93Waterloo Black Hawks-16

Laurila, Tim
01Michigan Tech Huskies-15
03Oklahoma City Blazers-13

Laurin, Don
88Brandon Wheat Kings-15

Laurin, Patrick
03Baie Comeau Drakkar-17

Laurin, Steve
90ProCards AHL/IHL-555

Laurin, Todd
98Amarillo Rattlers-10

Laursen, Gorm
92Norwegian Elite Series-164

Laus, Paul
88Niagara Falls Thunder-17
89Niagara Falls Thunder-9
897th Inn. Sketch OHL-142
90Knoxville Cherokees-102
90ProCards AHL/IHL-534
91ProCards-293
92Cleveland Lumberjacks-3
93OPC Premier-402
Gold-402
93Panthers Team Issue-4
93Stadium Club-292
Members Only Master Set-292
First Day Issue-292
93Topps/OPC Premier-402
Gold-402
94Donruss-201
95Canada Games NHL POGS-121
95Playoff One on One-41
96Be A Player-192
Autographs-192
Autographs Silver-192
97Pacific Dynagon Best Kept Secrets-42
97Revolution-61
Copper-61
Emerald-61
Ice Blue-61
Silver-61
97Upper Deck-75
98Aurora-82
98Pacific-224
Ice Blue-224
Red-224
98Pacific Dynagon Ice-84
Blue-84
Red-84
98Pacific Omega-104
Red-104
Opening Day Issue-104
98Paramount-98
Copper-98
Emerald Green-98
Holo-Electric-98
Ice Blue-98
Silver-98
99BAP Millennium-117
Emerald-117
Ruby-117
Sapphire-117
Signatures-117
Signatures Gold-117
99Pacific-175
Copper-175
Emerald Green-175
Gold-175
Ice Blue-175
Premiere Date-175
Red-175
00BAP Memorabilia-55
Emerald-55
Ruby-55
Sapphire-55
Promos-55
00BAP Mem Chicago Sportsfest Copper-55
00BAP Memorabilia Chicago Sportsfest Blue-55
00BAP Memorabilia Chicago Sportsfest Gold-55
00BAP Memorabilia Chicago Sportsfest Ruby-55
00BAP Memorabilia Chicago Sun-Times Ruby-55
00BAP Memorabilia Chicago Sun-Times Gold-55
00BAP Mem Chicago Sun-Times Sapphire-55
00BAP Mem Toronto Fall Expo Copper-55
00BAP Memorabilia Toronto Fall Expo Gold-55
00BAP Memorabilia Toronto Fall Expo Ruby-55
00BAP Memorabilia Update Teammates-TM8
00BAP Memorabilia Update Teammates Gold-TM8
00BAP Memorabilia Update Tough Materials-T5
00BAP Mem Update Tough Materials Gold-T5
00BAP Ultimate Memorabilia Teammates-TM19
00Pacific-181
Copper-181
Gold-181
Ice Blue-181
Premiere Date-181
00Panthers Team Issue-9
01BAP Update Tough Customers-TC7
01BAP Update Tough Customers-TC26
01BAP Update Tough Customers-TC29
02BAP Sig Series Auto Buybacks 1999-117
02Topps Total-352

Lautenschlager, Beat
93Swiss HNL-187
96Swiss HNL-472
01Swiss HNL-461
02Swiss HNL-196

Laux, James
93Quebec Pee-Wee Tournament-1578
04Wheeling Nailers Riesbeck's-12

Lauze, Philippe
00Rimouski Oceanic-1
Signed-1
01Rimouski Oceanic-2
02Rimouski Oceanic-8
03Rimouski Oceanic-12
03Rimouski Oceanic Sheets-2

Lauzon, Marc
93Quebec Pee-Wee Tournament-140
01BC Icemen-14

Lauzon, Ryan
93Quebec Pee-Wee Tournament-194
99Hull Olympiques-18
Signed-18
02Augusta Lynx-68

Lauzon, Serge
84Chicoutimi Sagueneens-17

Lavack, Brian
96Madison Monsters-19

Lavalee, Charlie
83Moncton Alpines-27

Lavallee, Guillaume
01Shawinigan Cataractes-16
02Halifax Mooseheads-2
03Rimouski Oceanic-13
03Rimouski Oceanic Sheets-4

Lavallee, Jordan
02Quebec Remparts-8
03Quebec Remparts Memorial Cup-11
03Quebec Remparts-15
04Quebec Remparts-2
05Quebec Remparts-13
05Quebec Remparts Signature Series-13
06ITG Heroes and Prospects Memorial Cup Champions-MC04

Lavallee, Kevin
80Flames Postcards-8
80Pepsi-Cola Caps-6
81Flames Postcards-10
810-Pee-Chee-43

82O-Pee-Chee-49
82O-Pee-Chee Stickers-220
82Post Cereal-3
82Topps Stickers-220
83O-Pee-Chee-157
84O-Pee-Chee-183
86Penguins Kodak-13
94German DEL-100
95German DEL-142
06German DEL-8
Lavallee, Martin
907th Inn. Sketch QMJHL-24
907th Inn. Sketch QMJHL-184
917th Inn. Sketch QMJHL-168
917th Inn. Sketch Memorial Cup-27
Lavallee, Richard
79Montreal Juniors-12
Lavallere, Sebastein
907th Inn. Sketch QMJHL-185
LaVarre, Mark
83North Bay Centennials-16
85Nova Scotia Oilers-8
87Blackhawks Coke-7
88ProCards AHL-68
Lave, Rob
93North Bay Centennials-3
Lavell, Mike
95Slapshot-274
Lavender, Brian
71Blues Postcards-11
72O-Pee-Chee-270
73Red Wings Team Issue-14
LaVerde, Vincent
05Waterloo Blackhawks-14
Laverdiere, Justin
03Quebec Remparts-16
Lavergne, Dan
98Odessa Jackalopes-11
Lavergne, Martin
93Quebec Pee-Wee Tournament-133
Lavigne, Eric
907th Inn. Sketch QMJHL-150
917th Inn. Sketch QMJHL-214
91Arena Draft Picks-19
91Arena Draft Picks French-19
91Arena Draft Picks Autographs-19
91Arena Draft Picks Autographs French-19
91Classic-22
91Star Pics-42
91Ultimate Draft-21
91Ultimate Draft French-21
91Classic Four-Sport *-22
Autographs-22A
93Phoenix Roadrunners-15
94Los Angeles Blades RHI-16
94Classic Pro Prospects-191
95PEI Senators-11
96Rochester Americans-22
97Rochester Americans-4-5
98Cleveland Lumberjacks-14
99Cleveland Lumberjacks-12
00UK Nottingham Panthers-25
00UK Sekonda Superleague-129
00Sherbrooke Castors-4
Signed-4
01UK Hull Thunder-22
02UK Hull Thunder-24
03Thetford Mines Prolab-10
04Thetford Mines Prolab-12
Lavinsh, Rodrigo
94Raleigh Icecaps-8
95Tallahassee Tiger Sharks-1
99Finnish Cardset-251
02Russian Transfert-29
03Russian World Championship Stars-34
05Swedish SHL Elitset-150
06Swedish SHL Elitset-5
Laviolette, Jack
10C56-21
10Sweet Caporal Postcards-45
11C55-45
12C57-46
12C61 Lacrosse-35
27La Patrie-19
83Hall of Fame-159
83Hall of Fame Postcards-L9
85Hall of Fame-159
Laviolette, Kerry
83Saskatoon Blades-9
Laviolette, Peter
89ProCards IHL-43
90ProCards AHL/IHL-16
91ProCards-197
93PowerPlay-508
93Stadium Club Team USA-12
93Stadium Club Team USA Members Only-12
93Topps Premier Team USA-3
93Ultra-488
96Providence Bruins-6
97Wheeling Nailers-25
97Wheeling Nailers Photo Pack-25
98Providence Bruins-1
06Hurricanes Postcards-17
Laviolette, Ted
90Montreal-Bourassa AAA-14
01Kalamazoo K-Wings-21
Lavis, Simon
04UK Guildford Flames-15
Lavitt, Sam
51Buffalo Bison-12
Lavkainen, Pekka
71Finnish Suomi Stickers-263
Lavkainen, Pentti
71Finnish Suomi Stickers-264
LaVoie, Danny
99Bowman CHL-63
Gold-63
OPC International-63
04Thetford Mines Prolab-4
Lavoie, Daryl
92Windsor Spitfires-13
93Windsor Spitfires-5
00UK Nottingham Panthers-9
00UK Sekonda Superleague-130
01UK Hull Thunder-21
Lavoie, Dominic
88ProCards IHL-74
89Blues Kodak-38
89ProCards IHL-20
90Bowman-26
Tiffany-26
90Score-416
Canadian-416
90ProCards AHL/IHL-95
92Ultra-145
93Leaf-415
93Parkhurst-366
Emerald Ice-366
93Upper Deck-444
93Phoenix Roadrunners-16
99German DEL-228
00German DEL-94
01German Upper Deck-97
Lavoie, Donald
93Quebec Pee-Wee Tournament-389
Lavoie, Etienne
907th Inn. Sketch QMJHL-230
917th Inn. Sketch QMJHL-127
Lavoie, Henrick
04Drummondville Voltigeurs-6
Lavoie, Julien
01Moncton Wildcats-22
Lavoie, Mathieu
06Quebec Remparts-26
Lavoie, Pascal
92Quebec Pee-Wee Tournament-869
93Quebec Pee-Wee Tournament-526
Lavoie, Paul
52Bas Du Fleuve-43
99Baie-Comeau Drakkar-13
Lavoie, Roberto
80Quebec Remparts-11
93Swiss HNL-288
Lavoie, Sansdrick
06Victoriaville Tigres-9
Lavoie, Simon
92Quebec Pee-Wee Tournament-805
93Quebec Pee-Wee Tournament-961
Lavoie, Yannick
93Amos Les Forestiers-11
Lavrantiev, Dimitri
98Danish Hockey League-106
99Danish Hockey League-118
Law, Brian
91British Columbia JHL-151
Law, Cam
99Knoxville Speed-7
Law, Jeremy
04Huntsville Havoc-8
Law, Kirby
93Saskatoon Blades-14
95Lethbridge Hurricanes-11
96Lethbridge Hurricanes-10
97Brandon Wheat Kings-14
98Orlando Solar Bears II-16
99Louisville Panthers-15
01BAP Memorabilia-433
Emerald-433
Ruby-433
Sapphire-433
01SPx-146
01SPx-146
Rookie Treasures-RTKL
01UD Top Shelf-61
01UD Top Shelf-61B
01Upper Deck-202
Exclusives-202
01Upper Deck MVP-210
02Philadelphia Phantoms-5
03Pacific AHL Prospects-63
Gold-63
03Philadelphia Phantoms-12
04Houston Aeros-11
05AHL All-Stars-16
05Philadelphia Phantoms All-Decade Team-9
06ITG Heroes and Prospects AHL Shooting Stars-AS11
Lawless, Paul
83O-Pee-Chee-141
85Whalers Junior Wendy's-9
86Whalers Junior Thomas'-13
87Panini Stickers-48
87Whalers Jr. Burger King/Pepsi-12
93Cincinnati Cyclones-13
95Cincinnati Cyclones-13
96Cincinnati Cyclones-13
96Collector's Edge Ice-112
Prism-112
97Austin Ice Bats-22
Lawmaster, Jason
99ECHL All-Star Northern Conference-13
99Peoria Rivermen-20
00Peoria Rivermen-17
01Peoria Rivermen-22
02Peoria Rivermen-20
02Peoria Rivermen Photo Pack-6
02Peoria Rivermen RBI Sports-162
03Muskegon Fury-12
05Muskegon Fury-11
Lawrence, Brett
91Knoxville Cherokees-18
Lawrence, Chris
03Sault Ste. Marie Greyhounds-14
04Sault Ste. Marie Greyhounds-8
05Mississauga Ice Dogs-24
06Mississauga Ice Dogs-5
Lawrence, Dave
04Arizona Icecats-9
Lawrence, David
03UK Sheffield Steelers-17
03UK Sheffield Steelers Stickers-6
04UK Sheffield Steelers-2
04UK U-20 Team-1
Lawrence, Derek
92British Columbia JHL-220
Lawrence, Doug
95Central Hockey League-46
Lawrence, Mark
88Niagara Falls Thunder-5
89Niagara Falls Thunder-10
897th Inn. Sketch OHL-131
907th Inn. Sketch OHL-108
917th Inn. Sketch OHL-40
94Upper Deck-260
Electric Ice-260
94Classic Pro Prospects-172
95Leaf-59
96Michigan K-Wings-18
99Pacific-257
Copper-257
Emerald Green-257
Gold-257
Ice Blue-257
Premiere Date-257
Red-257
99Upper Deck-252
Exclusives-252
Exclusives 1 of 1-252
99Upper Deck Gold Reserve-252
00Chicago Wolves-14
01Kalamazoo K-Wings-15
02Kalamazoo Wings-17
Lawrence, Nathan
04Waterloo Blackhawks-4
Lawrence, Peter
93Quebec Pee-Wee Tournament-512
Lawrence, Robbie
03Ottawa 67's-12
04Ottawa 67's-6
05Ottawa 67's-7
Lawrence, Tony
04Bakersfield Condors-10
Lawson, Charlie
98Abilene Aviators-8
Lawson, Dan
06Lincoln Stars Traded-6T
06Lincoln Stars Upper DeckÂ Signature Series -20
Lawson, Danny
70Esso Power Players-179
71Sabres Postcards-78
71Toronto Sun-30
72Philadelphia Blazers-1
727-Eleven Slurpee Cups WHA-13
73Quaker Oats WHA-48
74O-Pee-Chee WHA-25
75O-Pee-Chee WHA-86
76O-Pee-Chee WHA-8
Lawson, Eddie
63Rochester Americans-17
Lawson, Eric
02Kalamazoo Wings-4
Lawson, Harry
01Western Michigan Broncos-9
Lawson, Jeff
91Air Canada SJHL-E40
92Saskatchewan JHL-124
Lawson, Karl
96Flint Generals-24
Lawson, Lucas
03ECHL Update RBI Sports-60
03Hartford Wolf Pack-14
05Finnish Cardset -250
Lawson, Tom
00Knoxville Speed-5
02Fort Wayne Komets-9
02Fort Wayne Komets Shoe Carnival-5
03Fort Wayne Komets 2003 Champions-5
03Fort Wayne Komets 2003 Champions-7
03Fort Wayne Komets 2003 Champions-16
03Hershey Bears-22
03Hershey Bears Patriot News-14
04Hershey Bears Patriot News-15
04ITG Heroes and Prospects-49
Autographs-TL
04ITG Heroes/Prospects Toronto Expo '05-49
04ITG Heroes/Prospects Expo Heroes/Pros-49
Lawson, Tyler
02Barrie Colts-16
Lawton, Brian
83North Stars Postcards-11
84North Stars Postcards-12
85North Stars Postcards-16
86North Stars Postcards-17
87North Stars Postcards-18
87O-Pee-Chee-145
87Panini Stickers-300
87Topps-145
88O-Pee-Chee-20
88O-Pee-Chee Stickers-198
88Panini Stickers-94
88Topps-20
89Bruins Sports Action Update-5
89Nordiques Team Issue-25
89O-Pee-Chee-91
89Topps-91
89Swedish Semic World Champ Stickers-172
90ProCards AHL/IHL-355
91Parkhurst-167
French-167
91Pro Set-482
French-482
91Score Canadian Bilingual-648
91Score Canadian English-648
91Score Rookie/Traded-98T
91Sharks Sports Action-13
91Upper Deck-572
French-572
92Bowman-254
92O-Pee-Chee-276
92Panini Stickers-132
92Panini Stickers French-132
92Parkhurst-163
Emerald Ice-163
92Pinnacle-71
French-71
92Pro Set-173
92Score-343
Canadian-343
92Stadium Club-171
92Topps-435
Gold-435G
92Ultra-197
92Kansas City Blades-7
Lawton, Danny
73Vancouver Blazers-13
Laxdal, Derek
83Brandon Wheat Kings-19
84Brandon Wheat Kings-11
85Brandon Wheat Kings-11
88Maple Leafs PLAY-21
89O-Pee-Chee-169
89O-Pee-Chee Stickers-181
89Topps-169
89ProCards AHL-108
90ProCards AHL/IHL-494
91ProCards-466
92Alberta International Team Canada-11
94Roanoke Express-16
99UK Sheffield Steelers-8
01Odessa Jackalopes-13
02Odessa Jackalopes-21
05Idaho Steelheads-25
06Idaho Steelheads-24
Laxton, Daniel
79Montreal Juniors-13
Laxton, Francois
79Montreal Juniors-14
Laxton, Matt
93Quebec Pee-Wee Tournament-1403
Lay, Mike
82Medicine Hat Tigers-10
83Medicine Hat Tigers-21
94German DEL-269
95German DEL-401
96German DEL-309
Laycock, Rick
94German First League-86
95German DEL-18
Laycock, Travis
90Prince Albert Raiders-8
907th Inn. Sketch WHL-272
91Prince Albert Raiders-10
917th Inn. Sketch WHL-255
Laycoe, Hal
43Parade Sportive *-65
44Beehive Group II Photos-42
44Beehive Group II Photos-258
45Quaker Oats Photos-88A
45Quaker Oats Photos-88B
48Exhibits Canadian-12
51Parkhurst-25
52Parkhurst-71
53Parkhurst-87
54Parkhurst-52
54Topps-38
55Bruins Photos-9
Layden, Ryley
98Tri-City Americans-11
00Lethbridge Hurricanes-13
01Lethbridge Hurricanes-12
Laylin, Cory
91Minnesota Golden Gophers-12
99German Bundesliga 2-209
00San Diego Gulls-8
01German Upper Deck-114
02German DEL City Press-77
Layton, Ian
907th Inn. Sketch WHL-154
Layzell, Brad
93RPI Engineers-14
94Fredericton Canadiens-18
96Milwaukee Admirals-13
Lazar, Cheyne
98San Antonio Iguanas-17
Lazarenko, Alexei
99Russian Hockey League-29
00Russian Hockey League-2
Lazarev, Evgeny
98Hershey Bears-1
98Hershey Bears-6
00Hershey Bears-8
01Hershey Bears-14
04Wheeling Nailers Riesbeck's-10
Lazaro, Jeff
90ProCards AHL/IHL-124
91Bowman-352
91Bruins Sports Action-9
91O-Pee-Chee-380
91Pro Set-13
French-13
91Score Canadian Bilingual-445
91Score Canadian English-445
91Stadium Club-397
91Topps-380
91Upper Deck-364
French-364
91ProCards-65
92Panini Stickers-139
92Panini Stickers French-139
92Topps-224
Gold-224G
93PowerPlay-509
93Stadium Club Team USA-13
93Stadium Club Team USA Members Only-13
93Topps Premier Team USA-21
93Ultra-489
94Finnish Jaa Kiekko-131
95Finnish Semic World Championships-119
95German DEL-329
95Swedish World Championships Stickers-230
96German DEL-107
97New Orleans Brass-1
99ECHL All-Star Southern Conference-9
Lazaruk, Kris
05Kootenay Ice-12
Lazerev, Pavel
99Danish Hockey League-133
Lazo, Miroslav
03Czech OFS Plus-235
Leach, Brenn
82Victoria Cougars-12
83Victoria Cougars-14
Leach, Jamie
88Niagara Falls Thunder-12
89ProCards IHL-143
90O-Pee-Chee-377
90OPC Premier-60
90Score-420
Canadian-420
90Topps-377
Tiffany-377
91O-Pee-Chee-492
91Penguins Coke/Elby's-20
91Stadium Club-296
91Topps-492
91Upper Deck-447
French-447
92Bowman-320
92Stadium Club-329
92Topps-362
Gold-362G
92Upper Deck-168
93OPC Premier Gold-528
93Topps/OPC Premier Gold-528G
93Cincinnati Cyclones-14
95Rochester Americans-9
00UK Nottingham Panthers-19
00UK Sekonda Superleague-136
Leach, Jay
91ProCards-116
01Devils Team Issue-11
02Augusta Lynx-69
03Trenton Titans-361
05Hot Prospects-105
En Fuego-105
Red Hot-105
White Hot-105
05The Cup Masterpiece Pressplates (Ice)-188
05The Cup Master Pressplate Rookie Update-105
05Upper Deck Ice-188
05Upper Deck Rookie Update-105
05Providence Bruins-7
06Providence Bruins-11
Leach, Reggie
70Bruins Postcards-9
71Bruins Postcards-19
71O-Pee-Chee-175
71Toronto Sun-12
72O-Pee-Chee-51
72Sargent Promotions Stamps-54
72Topps-17
73O-Pee-Chee-84
73Topps-84
74NHL Action Stamps-201
74O-Pee-Chee NHL-95
74Topps-95
75Flyers Canada Dry Cans-11
75Heroes Stand-Ups-22
75O-Pee-Chee NHL-166
75O-Pee-Chee NHL-325
75Topps-166
75Topps-325
76O-Pee-Chee NHL-1
76O-Pee-Chee NHL-65
76O-Pee-Chee NHL-110
76O-Pee-Chee NHL-215
76O-Pee-Chee NHL-391
76Topps-1
76Topps-65
76Topps-110
76Topps-215
76Topps Glossy Inserts-21
77O-Pee-Chee NHL-185
77Topps-185
77Topps/O-Pee-Chee Glossy-8
Square-8
78O-Pee-Chee-165
78Topps-165
79O-Pee-Chee-95
79Topps-95
80O-Pee-Chee-70
80O-Pee-Chee-249
80Topps-70
80Topps-249
81O-Pee-Chee-243
81O-Pee-Chee Stickers-181
81Topps-E106
82O-Pee-Chee-90
82Post Cereal-14
83O-Pee-Chee Stickers-9
83Topps Stickers-9
92Future Trends '76 Canada Cup-172
92Parkhurst-471
Emerald Ice-471
93Parkhurst Cherry's Playoff Heroes-D19
01BAP Ultimate Mem Dynasty Jerseys-8
01BAP Ultimate Mem Dynasty Emblems-8
01BAP Ultimate Mem Dynasty Numbers-8
01BAP Ultimate Mem Playoff Records-6
01Greats of the Game-35
Autographs-35
01Parkhurst Autographs-PA54
01Topps Archives-43
01Upper Deck Legends-70
02BAP Ultimate Memorabilia All-Star MVP-20
02BAP Ultimate Memorabilia Conn Smythe-8
02Topps Stanley Cup Heroes-RL
02Topps Stanley Cup Heroes Autographs-RL
04ITG Franchises US East-416
Autographs-A-RL
Barn Burners-EBB5
Barn Burners Gold-EBB5
Double Memorabilia-EDM17
Double Memorabilia Gold-EDM17
Memorabilia-ESM4
Memorabilia Gold-ESM4
Original Sticks-EOS7
Original Sticks Gold-EOS7
Teammates-ETM6
Teammates Gold-ETM6
Trophy Winners-ETW6
Trophy Winners Gold-ETW6
04ITG Franchises US West-157
04ITG Ultimate Mem Broad St Bullie Jersey-6
04ITG Ult Mem Broad St Bullie Jersey Auto-6
04ITG Ultimate Mem Broad St Bullie Emblem-6
04ITG Ult Mem Broad St Bullie Emblem Auto-6
04ITG Ultimate Mem Broad St Bullie Number-6
04ITG Ult Mem Broad St Bullie Number Auto-6
04ITG Ultimate Memorabilia Day In History-2
04ITG Ultimate Mem Day In History Gold-2
04ITG Ultimate Mem Retro Teammates-11
04SP Authentic Buybacks-164
04SP Authentic Sign of the Times-TS-CLR
04SP Authentic Sign of the Times-QS-MHCL
04UD Legendary Signatures-68
Autographs-RL
Linemates-BBBCRL
04UD Legends Classics-47
Gold-47
Platinum-47
Silver-47
Jersey Redemptions-JY31
Signature Moments-M12
Signature Moments-M55
Signatures-CS12
Signatures-TC6
05Beehive Signature Scrapbook-SSRL
05ITG Ultimate Mem Record Breaker Jerseys-1
05ITG Ult Mem RecBreak Jerseys Gold-1
05ITG Ultimate Mem 3 Star of the Game Jsy-15
05ITG Ult Mem 3 Star of the Game Jsy Gold-15
05SP Game Used Statscriptions-ST-RL
05SPx Xcitement Legends-XL-RL
05SPx Xcitement Legends Gold-XL-RL
05SPx Xcitement Legends Spectrum-XL-RL
05UD Artifacts-129
Blue-129
Gold-129
Green-129
Pewter-129
Red-129
Gold Autographed-129
06ITG Ultimate Memorabilia Road to the Cup-9
06ITG Ultimate Memorabilia Road to the Cup Gold-9
06ITG Ultimate Memorabilia Stick Rack-15
06ITG Ultimate Memorabilia Stick Rack Gold-15
06Parkhurst-64
Autographs-64
Autographs Dual-DACL
06SP Authentic Sign of the Times Duals-STLG
06SP Game Used Letter Marks-LMRL
06SP Game Used SIGnificance-SLE
06The Cup Stanley Cup Signatures-CSRL
06UD Artifacts-120
Blue-120
Gold-120
Platinum-120
Radiance-120
Autographed Radiance Parallel-120
Red-120
Auto-Facts-AFLE
Auto-Facts Gold-AFLE
06Upper Deck Trilogy Combo Clearcut Autographs-C3CLP
06Upper Deck Trilogy Legendary Scripts-LSRL
06Upper Deck Trilogy Scripts-TSRL
Leach, Simon
98UK Kingston Hawks-21
Leach, Stephen
86Capitals Police-16
88Capitals Borderless-11
88Capitals Smokey-11
89Capitals Kodak-21
89Capitals Team Issue-14
89O-Pee-Chee-67
89O-Pee-Chee Stickers-79
89Panini Stickers-349
89Topps-67
90Capitals Kodak-14
90Capitals Postcards-14
90Capitals Smokey-13
90O-Pee-Chee-235
90Panini Stickers-166
90Pro Set-315
90Score-279
Canadian-279
90Topps-235
Tiffany-235
91Pro Set Platinum-151
91Bowman-306
91Bruins Sports Action-10
91O-Pee-Chee-100
91OPC Premier-12
91Panini Stickers-211
91Parkhurst-6
French-6
91Pinnacle-46
French-46
91Pro Set-253
91Pro Set-346
French-253
French-346
91Score Canadian Bilingual-576
91Score Canadian English-576
91Score Rookie/Traded-26T
91Stadium Club-226
91Topps-100
92Bowman-298
92Bruins Postcards-5
92O-Pee-Chee-112
92Parkhurst-241
Emerald Ice-241
92Pinnacle-73
French-73
92Pro Set-6
92Score-54
Canadian-54
92Stadium Club-68
92Topps-16
Gold-16G
92Ultra-5
92Upper Deck-61
93Donruss-28
93Leaf-3
93OPC Premier-507
Gold-507
93Panini Stickers-5
93Parkhurst-285
Emerald Ice-285
93Pinnacle-73
Canadian-73
93PowerPlay-21
93Score-88
Canadian-88
93Stadium Club-187
Members Only Master Set-187
OPC-187
First Day Issue-187
First Day Issue OPC-187
93Topps/OPC Premier-507
Gold-507
93Ultra-268
94Leaf-420
94OPC Premier-268
Special Effects-268
94Pinnacle-298
Artist's Proofs-298
Rink Collection-298
94Score-79
Gold-79
Platinum-79
94Topps/OPC Premier-268
Special Effects-268
94Upper Deck-342
Electric Ice-342
95Be A Player-109
Signatures-S109
Signatures Die Cuts-S109
95Parkhurst International-284
Emerald Ice-284
96Leaf-153
Electric Ice-453
Electric Ice Gold-453
96Upper Deck-142
97Hurricanes Team Issue-16
97Pacific Invincible NHL Regime-171
97Paramount-36
Copper-36
Dark Grey-36
Emerald Green-36
Ice Blue-36
Red-36
Silver-36
98OPC Chrome-28
Refractors-28
98Topps-28
O-Pee-Chee-28
00Pacific-333
Copper-333
Gold-333
Ice Blue-333
Premiere Date-333
Leadbeater, Larry
92Quebec Pee-Wee Tournament-919
93Quebec Pee-Wee Tournament-579
Leader, Al
83Hall of Fame Postcards-M12
85Hall of Fame-176
Leahy, Greg
87Portland Winter Hawks-14
88Portland Winter Hawks-14
89Portland Winter Hawks-15
90Saskatoon Blades-11
907th Inn. Sketch WHL-75
Leahy, Patrick
01Trenton Titans-2-5
02Providence Bruins-19
03BAP Ultimate Mem Rookie Jersey Emblems-39
03BAP Ultimate Mem Rookie Jsy Emblem Gold-39
03BAP Ultimate Mem Rookie Jersey Numbers-39
03BAP Ultimate Mem Rookie Jsy Number Gold-39
03ITG VIP Rookie Debut-76
03Pacific Complete-581
Red-581
03Pacific Heads-Up-103
Hobby LTD-103
Retail LTD-103
03Parkhurst Original Six Boston-6
03Parkhurst Rookie-143
Rookie Emblems-RE-49
Rookie Emblems Gold-RE-49
Rookie Jerseys-RJ-49
Rookie Jerseys Gold-RJ-49
Rookie Numbers-RN-49
Rookie Numbers Gold-RN-49
03Topps Traded-TT155
Blue-TT155
Gold-TT155
Red-TT155
03Upper Deck Rookie Update-107
03Pacific AHL Prospects-67
Gold-67
03Providence Bruins-11
04Providence Bruins-13
06Milwaukee Admirals -11
Leary, Denis
94Be A Player-R141
Leasa, Ryan
04Austin Ice Bats-4
Leask, Patrick
05Saint John's Sea Dogs-17
Leask, Rob
907th Inn. Sketch OHL-212
91Oshawa Generals-9
917th Inn. Sketch OHL-166
93Johnstown Chiefs-19
94Johnstown Chiefs-14
96German DEL-31
98German DEL-177
99German DEL-52
00German Berlin Polar Bears Postcards-14
01German Berlin Polar Bears Postcards-11
02German Berlin Polar Bears Postcards-17
02German DEL City Press-34
03German Berlin Polar Bears Postcards-20
03German DEL-69
04German Berlin Polar Bears Postcards-26
04German DEL-72
05German DEL-31
06German DEL-283
Leavins, Bobby
96Brandon Wheat Kings-24
97Brandon Wheat Kings-15
98Spokane Chiefs-15
Leavins, Jim
90Swedish Semic Elitserien Stickers-252
Leavitt, Alex
03Swift Current Broncos-7
04Everett Silvertips-3
Leavitt, Jeff
02Windsor Spitfires-23
04Belleville Bulls-5
05Belleville Bulls-20
06Belleville Bulls-8
Leavold, Brady
04Swift Current Broncos-11
06Swift Current Broncos-14
Lebda, Brett
96Quebec Pee-Wee Tournament-166
01Notre Dame Fighting Irish-7
02Notre Dame Fighting Irish-13
03Notre Dame Fighting Irish-7
05Beehive-180
Matte-180
05Black Diamond-238
05Hot Prospects-199
Autographed Patch Variation-199
Autographed Patch Variation Gold-199
Red Hot-199
05Parkhurst-183
Facsimile Auto Parallel-183
Signatures-BL
05SP Authentic-156
Limited-156
Sign of the Times-BL
05SP Game Used-105
Autographs-105
Gold-105
Rookie Exclusives-BL
Rookie Exclusives Silver-RE-BL
05SPx-148
Spectrum-148
05The Cup-181
Black Rainbow Rookies-181
Masterpiece Pressplates (Artifacts)-273
Masterpiece Pressplates (Bee Hive)-180
Masterpiece Pressplates (Black Diamond)-238
Masterpiece Pressplates (Ice)-150
Masterpiece Pressplates (Rookie Update)-129
Masterpiece Pressplates SPA Autos-156
Masterpiece Pressplates (SP Game Used)-105
Masterpiece Pressplates (SPx)-148
Masterpiece Pressplates (SPx)-148
Masterpiece Pressplates (Trilogy)-191
Masterpiece Pressplates Ult Coll-147
Masterpiece Pressplates Autographs-181
Platinum Rookies-181
05UD Artifacts-273
05Ultimate Collection-147
Gold-147
05Ultra-216
Gold-216
Fresh Ink-FI-BL
Fresh Ink Blue-FI-BL
Ice-216
Rookie Uniformity Jerseys-RU-BL
Rookie Uniformity Jersey Autographs-ARU-BL
Rookie Uniformity Patches-RUP-BL
Rookie Uniformity Patch Autographs-ARP-BL
05Upper Deck-237
HG Glossy-237
Rookie Threads-RTBL
Rookie Threads Autographs-ARTBL
05Upper Deck Ice-150
Premieres Auto Patches-AIPBL
05Upper Deck Rookie Update-129
05Upper Deck Trilogy-191
05Upper Deck Toronto Fall Expo-237
06O-Pee-Chee-188
Rainbow-188
06UD Artifacts Auto-Facts-AFBL
06UD Artifacts Auto-Facts Gold-AFBL
06Upper Deck Signatures-SBL
Lebeau, Patrick
90ProCards AHL/IHL-73
91Score American-390
91Score Canadian Bilingual-280
91Score Canadian English-280
91Stadium Club-373
91Upper Deck-453
91Upper Deck-644
French-453
French-644
91ProCards-72
92Salt Lake Golden Eagles-13
93Upper Deck-499
93Cincinnati Cyclones-15
93Classic Pro Prospects-28
95Swiss HNL-46
96Swiss HNL-194
99Swiss Panini Stickers-23
03German DEL-100
04German DEL-110
05German DEL-90
All-Star Jerseys-AS08
Star Attack-ST04
06German DEL-57
Lebeau, Stephan
88ProCards AHL-281
89Canadiens Kraft-12
89Canadiens Postcards-17
90Bowman-53
Tiffany-53
90Canadiens Postcards-19
90O-Pee-Chee-388
90Pro Set-152
90Score-262
Canadian-262
90Topps-388
Tiffany-388
90Upper Deck-51
French-51
91Pro Set Platinum-190
91Bowman-333
91Canadiens Panini Team Stickers-14
91Canadiens Postcards-16
91Kraft-26
91O-Pee-Chee-135
91Panini Stickers-191
91Parkhurst-87
French-87
91Pinnacle-139
French-139
91Pro Set-120
French-120
91Score American-274
91Score Canadian Bilingual-494
91Score Canadian English-494
91Score Young Superstars-7
91Stadium Club-283
91Topps-135
91Upper Deck-261
91Upper Deck-644
French-261
French-644
92Bowman-346
92Canadiens Postcards-16
92Durivage Panini-7
92O-Pee-Chee-293
92Panini Stickers-151
92Panini Stickers French-151
92Parkhurst-82
Emerald Ice-82
92Pinnacle-341
French-341
92Score-246
Canadian-246
92Stadium Club-431
92Topps-69
Gold-69G
92Ultra-329
92Upper Deck-213
93Canadiens Postcards-13
93Donruss-175
93Durivage Score-14
93Leaf-190
93O-Pee-Chee Canadiens Hockey Fest-7
93OPC Premier-462
Gold-462
93Panini Stickers-16
93Parkhurst-374
Emerald Ice-374
93Pinnacle-136
Canadian-136
93PowerPlay-130
93Score-72
Canadian-72
93Stadium Club-343
Members Only Master Set-343
First Day Issue-343
93Topps/OPC Premier-462
Gold-462
93Ultra-241
93Upper Deck-402
SP-78
94Canada Games NHL POGS-32
94Donruss-234
94Ducks Carl's Jr.-16
94EA Sports-209
94Leaf-162
94OPC Premier-63
Special Effects-63
94Parkhurst-2
Gold-2
Crash the Game Green-1
Crash the Game Blue-1
Crash the Game Gold-1
Crash the Game Red-1
SE Vintage-11
94Pinnacle-67
Artist's Proofs-67
Rink Collection-67
94Score-128
Gold-128
Platinum-128
94Select-65
Gold-65
94SP-3
Die Cuts-3
94Topps/OPC Premier-63
Special Effects-63
94Ultra-5
94Upper Deck-53
Electric Ice-53
SP Inserts-SP2
SP Inserts Die Cuts-SP2

95Ultra-5
Gold Medallion-5
95Swiss HNL-150
96Swiss HNL-169
96Swiss HNL-573
98Swiss Power Play Stickers-306
99Swiss Panini Stickers-22
00Swiss Panini Stickers-22
00Swiss Slapshot Mini-Cards-HCAP15
05Victoriaville Tigres-22

Lebedev, Gennady
900-Pee-Chee-508

Lebedev, Yuri
73Finnish Jaakiekko-6
73Russian National Team-15
73Swedish Stickers-94
74Russian National Team-9
74Swedish Stickers-60
74Swedish Semic World Champ Stickers-40
79Panini Stickers-156
79Russian National Team-18
81Swedish Semic Hockey VM Stickers-47
82Swedish Semic VM Stickers-74
91Future Trends Canada '72-37
91Future Trends Canada '72 French-37

Lebel, Bobby
96Rimouski Oceanic-13

Lebel, Layne
90Michigan Tech Huskies-10
91Michigan Tech Huskies-7
93Michigan Tech Huskies-15
94Central Hockey League-50

Lebel, Pascal
05PEI Rocket-27

Lebel, Robert
83Hall of Fame-117
83Hall of Fame Postcards-H11
85Hall of Fame-117

Leblanc, Andre
93Quebec Pee-Wee Tournament-1208

LeBlanc, Bill
51Bas Du Fleuve-31
51Laval Dairy QSHL-7
52Bas Du Fleuve-13

Leblanc, Carl
907th Inn. Sketch QMJHL-66
917th Inn. Sketch QMJHL-29
93Knoxville Cherokees-7
94Knoxville Cherokees-15
95South Carolina Stingrays-16
96Quad-City Mallards-10
97Quad-City Mallards-12
98Quad-City Mallards-4
99Colorado Gold Kings Taco Bell-16
99Colorado Gold Kings Wendy's-8

LeBlanc, Dan
897th Inn. Sketch OHL-43

Leblanc, Dennis
907th Inn. Sketch QMJHL-224
04Thetford Mines Prolab-23

LeBlanc, Derek
03Brandon Wheat Kings-23
04Brandon Wheat Kings-19
05Calgary Hitmen-8

Leblanc, Devon
05Red Deer Rebels-10

Leblanc, Francois
907th Inn. Sketch QMJHL-45

Leblanc, Gregoire
93Quebec Pee-Wee Tournament-438

LeBlanc, J.P.
72Los Angeles Sharks WHA-7
73Quaker Oats WHA-42
740-Pee-Chee WHA-36
760-Pee-Chee NHL-326
770-Pee-Chee NHL-133
77Topps-133

Leblanc, Jacques
907th Inn. Sketch QMJHL-211

LeBlanc, Jason
93Quebec Pee-Wee Tournament-698

LeBlanc, Jean
86Fredericton Express-16

Leblanc, Jeff
98Quebec Remparts-11
Signed-11

LeBlanc, John
88Oilers Team Issue-17
89ProCards AHL-149
91Moncton Hawks-18
91ProCards-169
92Bowman-419
920-Pee-Chee-287
92Stadium Club-388
92Topps-88
Gold-88G

Leblanc, Louis-Etienne
04Chicoutimi Sagueneens-12
05Chicoutimi Sagueneens-17

LeBlanc, Mario
97Dubuque Fighting Saints-5

LeBlanc, Michel
92Finnish Semic-222
95Finnish Semic World Championships-197

Leblanc, Mike
89Rayside-Balfour Jr. Canadians-14

Leblanc, Pierre-Andre
00Baie-Comeau Drakkar-3
Signed-3

Leblanc, Ray
83Kitchener Rangers-30
87Flint Spirits-11
89ProCards IHL-67
90ProCards AHL/IHL-553
91Parkhurst-255
French-255
91ProCards-502
92Score-486
Canadian-486
92Upper Deck-381
92Indianapolis Ice-18
93Cincinnati Cyclones-16
97Flint Generals-12
98Chicago Wolves Turner Cup-3
99Jacksonville Lizard Kings-6

Leblanc, Robin
99Baie-Comeau Drakkar-14
00Baie-Comeau Drakkar-7
Signed-7
00UD CHL Prospects-76
01Baie-Comeau Drakkar-6
01UD Prospects-15
Jerseys-J-RL
Jerseys Gold-J-RL
02Baie Comeau Drakkar-8
03Baie Comeau Drakkar-10

Lebler, Brian
04Penticton Vees-6
05Penticton Vees-9

Leblond-Letourneau, Pierre-Luc
03Baie Comeau Drakkar-19
04Baie-Comeau Drakkar-19

Lebold, Dan
96Kitchener Rangers-15
99Kitchener Rangers-10
00Kitchener Rangers-17

LeBoutillier, Pete
93Red Deer Rebels-10
93Red Deer Rebels-11
97Score Mighty Ducks-17
Platinum-17
Premier-17
98Cincinnati Mighty Ducks-25
99Cincinnati Mighty Ducks-16
00Lowell Lock Monsters-11
01UK Sheffield Steelers-13

Lebrasseur, Pascal
907th Inn. Sketch QMJHL-17
917th Inn. Sketch QMJHL-76

Lebreau, Jean
907th Inn. Sketch QMJHL-267

LeBreton, Shayne
98Odessa Jackalopes-13

Lebrun, Al
61Topps-61
62Topps-50

Lebrun, J.C.
51Laval Dairy Subset-94

Lebrun, Olivier
93Quebec Pee-Wee Tournament-90

LeBrun, Sean
89ProCards AHL-247
90ProCards AHL/IHL-495
91ProCards-474
92Richmond Renegades-11

Lebsack, Greg
83Saskatoon Blades-18

Lecavalier, Vincent
94Quebec Int. Pee-Wees-11
94Quebec Pee-Wee Tournament-11
96Rimouski Oceanic-14
96Rimouski Oceanic Quebec Police-13
97Black Diamond-150
Double Diamond-150
Triple Diamond-150
Quadruple Diamond-150
97Upper Deck-412
97Zenith-95
Z-Gold-95
Z-Silver-95
97Zenith 5 x 7-75
Gold Impulse-75
Silver Impulse-75
97Rimouski Oceanic-4
97Bowman CHL-69
OPC-69
98Be A Player-279
Press Release-279
98BAP Gold-279
98BAP Autographs-279
98BAP Autographs Gold-279
98Black Diamond-80
Double Diamond-80
Triple Diamond-80
Quadruple Diamond-80
Myriad-M1
Myriad 2-M1
Winning Formula Gold-WF5
Winning Formula Platinum-WF5
98Bowman's Best-109
Refractors-109
Atomic Refractors-109
Mirror Image Fusion-F5
Mirror Image Fusion Refractors-F5
Mirror Image Fusion Atomic Refractors-F5
Performers-BP10
Performers Refractors-BP10
Performers Atomic Refractors-BP10
98Crown Royale-124
Limited Series-124
Pivotal Players-21
Rookie Class-8
98Finest Futures Finest-F3
98Finest Futures Finest Refractors-F3
98OPC Chrome-224
Refractors-224
98Pacific Dynagon Ice-173
Blue-173
Red-173
Forward Thinking-17
Rookies-8
Team Checklists-24
98Pacific Omega-219
Red-219
Opening Day Issue-219
Online-31
Planet Ice-3
Planet Ice Parallel-3
98Panini Photocards-44
98Revolution-133
Ice Shadow-133
Red-133
Chalk Talk Laser-Cuts-17
Showstoppers-32
98SP Authentic-109
Power Shift-109
Sign of the Times-VL
Sign of the Times Gold-VL
Snapshots-SS18
Stat Masters-S27
98SPx Top Prospects-53
Radiance-53
Spectrum-53
Highlight Heroes-H26
Lasting Impressions-L1
Premier Stars-PS12
98Topps-224
O-Pee-Chee-224
98Topps Gold Label Class 1-61
Black-61
Black One of One-61
One of One-61
Red-61
Red One of One-61
98Topps Gold Label Class 2-61
98Topps Gold Label Class 2 Black-61
98Topps Gold Label Class 2 Black 1 of 1-61
98Topps Gold Label Class 2 One of One-61
98Topps Gold Label Class 2 Red-61
98Topps Gold Label Class 2 Red One of One-61
98Topps Gold Label Class 3-61
98Topps Gold Label Class 3 Black-61
98Topps Gold Label Class 3 Black 1 of 1-61
98Topps Gold Label Class 3 One of One-61
98Topps Gold Label Class 3 Red-61
98Topps Gold Label Class 3 Red One of One-61
98UD Choice-259
Prime Choice Reserve-259
Reserve-259
98Upper Deck-414
Exclusives-414
Exclusives 1 of 1-414
Game Jerseys-GJ2
Game Jerseys-GJA3
Generation Next-GN3
Generation Next Quantum 1-GN3
Generation Next Quantum 2-GN3
Generation Next Quantum 3-GN3
Profiles-P16
Profiles Quantum 1-P16
Profiles Quantum 2-P16
Profiles Quantum 3-P16
Gold Reserve-414
98Upper Deck MVP-187
Gold Script-187
Silver Script-187
Super Script-187
Game Souvenirs-VL
Game Souvenirs-VLA
Power Game-PG5
ProSign-VL
Snipers-S1
Special Forces-F3
98Bowman CHL-103
98Bowman CHL-128
Golden Anniversary-103
Golden Anniversary-128
OPC International-103
OPC International-128
Autographs Blue-A10
Autographs Gold-A10
Autographs Silver-A10
Scout's Choice-SC12
98Bowman Chrome CHL-103
98Bowman Chrome CHL-128
Golden Anniversary-103
Golden Anniversary-128
Golden Anniversary Refractors-103
Golden Anniversary Refractors-128
OPC International-103
OPC International-128
OPC International Refractors-103
OPC International Refractors-128
Refractors-103
Refractors-128
99Aurora-131
Striped-131
Premiere Date-131
Premiere Date Striped-131
99BAP Memorabilia-116
Gold-116
Silver-116
Selects Silver-SL20
Selects Gold-SL20
99BAP Millennium-220
Emerald-220
Ruby-220
Sapphire-220
Signatures-220
Signatures Gold-220
99Black Diamond-78
Diamond Cut-78
Final Cut-78
99Crown Royale-129
Limited Series-129
Premiere Date-129
Century 21-10
Ice Elite-23
Ice Elite Parallel-23
99O-Pee-Chee-147
99O-Pee-Chee Autographs-TA9
99O-Pee-Chee Chrome-147
99O-Pee-Chee Chrome Refractors-147
99O-Pee-Chee Now Starring-NS13
99Pacific-392
Copper-392
Emerald Green-392
Gold-392
Ice Blue-392
Premiere Date-392
Red-392
Gold Crown Die-Cuts-32
Team Leaders-25
99Pacific Dynagon Ice-181
Blue-181
Copper-181
Gold-181
Premiere Date-181
99Pacific Omega-216
Copper-216
Gold-216
Ice Blue-216
Premiere Date-216
EO Portraits-17
EO Portraits 1/1-17
NHL Generations-9
5 Star Talents-23
5 Star Talents Parallel-23
99Pacific Prism-132
Holographic Blue-132
Holographic Gold-132
Holographic Mirror-132
Holographic Purple-132
Premiere Date-132
Clear Advantage-19
99Panini Stickers-148
99Paramount-219
Copper-219
Emerald-219
Gold-219
Holographic Emerald-219
Holographic Gold-219
Holographic Silver-219
Ice Blue-219
Premiere Date-219
Red-219
Silver-219
Ice Alliance-25
Personal Best-33
Toronto Fall Expo '99-219
99Revolution-133
Premiere Date-133
Red-133
Shadow Series-133
Ornaments-17
Showstoppers-32
Copper-133
Gold-133
CSC Silver-133
99SP Authentic-78
Tomorrow's Headliners-TH9
99SPx-137
Radiance-137
Spectrum-137
Prolifics-P8
99Stadium Club-23
First Day Issue-23
One of a Kind-23
Printing Plates Black-23
Printing Plates Cyan-23
Printing Plates Magenta-23
Printing Plates Yellow-23
Capture the Action-CA9
Capture the Action Game View-CAG9
Chrome-19
Chrome Refractors-19
99Topps Arena Giveaways-TB-VL
99Topps/OPC-147
Autographs-TA9
Now Starring-NS13
99Topps/OPC Chrome-147
Refractors-147
99Topps Gold Label Class 1-66
Black-66
Black One of One-66
One of One-66
Red-66
Red One of One-66
99Topps Gold Label Class 2-66
99Topps Gold Label Class 2 Black-66
99Topps Gold Label Class 2 Black 1 of 1-66
99Topps Gold Label Class 2 One of One-66
99Topps Gold Label Class 2 Red-66
99Topps Gold Label Class 2 Red One of One-66
99Topps Gold Label Class 3-66
99Topps Gold Label Class 3 Black-66
99Topps Gold Label Class 3 Black 1 of 1-66
99Topps Gold Label Class 3 One of One-66
99Topps Gold Label Class 3 Red-66
99Topps Gold Label Class 3 Red One of One-66
99Topps Gold Label Fresh Gold-FG20
99Topps Gold Label Fresh Gold Black-FG20
99Topps Gold Label Fresh Gold Black 1of1-FG20
99Topps Gold Label Fresh Gold One of One-FG20
99Topps Gold Label Fresh Gold Red-FG20
99Topps Gold Label Fresh Gold Red 1 of 1-FG20
99Topps Premier Plus-19
Parallel-19
The Next Ones-TNO1
99Ultimate Victory-79
1/1-79
Parallel-79
Parallel 100-79
99Upper Deck-117
Exclusives-117
Exclusives 1 of 1-117
Crunch Time-CT1
Crunch Time Quantum Gold-CT1
Crunch Time Quantum Silver-CT1
Marquee Attractions-MA11
Marquee Attractions Quantum Gold-MA11
Marquee Attractions Quantum Silver-MA11
New Ice Age-N9
New Ice Age Quantum Gold-N9
New Ice Age Quantum Silver-N9
Sixth Sense-SS18
Sixth Sense Quantum Gold-SS18
Sixth Sense Quantum Silver-SS18
99Upper Deck Century Legends-72
Century Collection-72
99Upper Deck Gold Reserve-117
99Upper Deck HoloGrFx-54
Ausome-54
99Upper Deck MVP-190
Gold Script-190
Silver Script-190
Super Script-190
21st Century NHL-5
99Upper Deck MVP SC Edition-167
Gold Script-167
Silver Script-167
Super Script-167
Cup Contenders-CC9
Great Combinations-GCLS
Great Combinations Parallel-GCLS
99Upper Deck Ovation-53
Standing Ovation-53
99Upper Deck Retro-72
Gold-72
Platinum-72
Generation-G5C
Generation Level 2-G5C
Inkredible-VL
Inkredible Level 2-VL
Turn of the Century-TC1
99Upper Deck Victory-269
99Upper Deck Victory-270
99Wayne Gretzky Hockey-156
99Quebec PeeWee Tournament Coll Souv-22
00SLU Hockey-150
00Aurora-134
Premiere Date-134
Scouting Reports-18
00BAP Memorabilia-209
Emerald-209
Ruby-209
Sapphire-209
Promos-209
00BAP Mem Chicago Sportsfest Copper-209
00BAP Memorabilia Chicago Sportsfest Blue-209
00BAP Memorabilia Chicago Sportsfest Gold-209
00BAP Memorabilia Chicago Sportsfest Ruby-209
00BAP Memorabilia Chicago Sun-Times Ruby-209
00BAP Memorabilia Chicago Sun-Times Gold-209
00BAP Mem Chicago Sun-Times Sapphire-209
00BAP Mem Toronto Fall Expo Copper-209
00BAP Memorabilia Toronto Fall Expo Gold-209
00BAP Memorabilia Toronto Fall Expo Ruby-209
00BAP Parkhurst 2000-P21
00BAP Signature Series-212
Emerald-212
Ruby-212
Sapphire-212
Autographs-116
Autographs Gold-116
Franchise Players-F27
He Shoots-He Scores Prizes-9
00BAP Ultimate Memorabilia Autographs-21
Gold-21
00BAP Ultimate Mem Game-Used Jerseys-GJ14
00BAP Ultimate Mem Game-Used Emblems-E12
00BAP Ultimate Mem Game-Used Numbers-N12
00BAP Ultimate Mem Game-Used Sticks-GS14
00Black Diamond-53
Gold-53
Diamonation-IG8
00Crown Royale-96
Ice Blue-96
Limited Series-96
Premiere Date-96
Red-96
Jewels of the Crown-23
Now Playing-16
00Kraft-18
00McDonald's Pacific-30
Blue-30
Gold Crown Die Cuts-6
00O-Pee-Chee-26
00O-Pee-Chee Parallel-26
00Pacific-377
Copper-377
Gold-377
Ice Blue-377
Premiere Date-377
2001: Ice Odyssey-19
Autographs-377
Gold Crown Die Cuts-32
Reflections-18
00Pacific 2001: Ice Odyssey Anaheim Ntnl-19
00Panini Stickers-88
00Paramount-222
Copper-222
Gold-222
Holo-Gold-222
Holo-Silver-222
Ice Blue-222
Premiere Date-222
Epic Scope-18
Freeze Frame-33
00Private Stock-91
Gold-91
Premiere Date-91
Retail-91
Silver-91
Artist's Canvas-19
Artist's Canvas Proofs-19
Extreme Action-19
Game Gear-93
PS-2001 Action-54
PS-2001 New Wave-23
Reserve-19
00Revolution-135
Blue-135
Premiere Date-135
Red-135
HD NHL-32
00SP Authentic-80
Parents' Scrapbook-PS7
00SP Game Used-54
00SPx-63
Spectrum-63
SPXcitement-X13
00Stadium Club-37
Beam Team-BT11
Capture the Action-CA14
Capture the Action Game View-14
00Titanium-89
Blue-89
Gold-89
Premiere Date-89
Red-89
Retail-89
Three-Star Selections-19
00Titanium Draft Day Edition-93
00Topps/OPC-26
Parallel-26
Combos-TC7
Combos Jumbos-TC7
NHL Draft-D1
00Topps Chrome-25
OPC Refractors-25
Refractors-25
Combos-TC7
Combos Refractors-TC7
00Topps Gold Label Class 1-69
Gold-69
00Topps Gold Label Class 2-69
00Topps Gold Label Class 2 Gold-69
00Topps Gold Label Class 3-69
00Topps Gold Label Class 3 Gold-69
00Topps Gold Label New Generation-NG2
00Topps Gold Label New Generation 1 to 1-NG2
00Topps Heritage-4
Chrome Parallel-4
New Tradition-NT4
00Topps Premier Plus-72
Blue Ice-72
Aspirations-PA2
World Premier-WP13
00Topps Stars-1
00Topps Stars-140
Blue-1
Blue-140
Autographs-AVL
Progression-P1
00UD Heroes-157
Player Idols-PI5
00UD Pros and Prospects-79
00UD Reserve-77
The Big Ticket-BT10
00Upper Deck-386
Exclusives Tier 1-386
Exclusives Tier 2-386
Rise to Prominence-RP8
Skilled Stars-SS18
00Upper Deck Ice-36
Immortals-36
Legends-36
Stars-36
Gallery-IG8
00Upper Deck Legends-118
00Upper Deck Legends-119
Legendary Collection Bronze-118
Legendary Collection Bronze-119
Legendary Collection Gold-118
Legendary Collection Gold-119
Legendary Collection Silver-118
Legendary Collection Silver-119
00Upper Deck MVP-163
First Stars-163
Second Stars-163
Third Stars-163
00Upper Deck Victory-208
00Upper Deck Victory-209
00Upper Deck Victory-325
00Upper Deck Vintage-322
00Upper Deck Vintage-332
00Upper Deck Vintage-333
00Vanguard-90
High Voltage-31
High Voltage Gold-31
High Voltage Green-31
High Voltage Red-31
High Voltage Silver-31
Holographic Gold-90
Holographic Purple-90
In Focus-16
Pacific Proofs-90
Press East/West-19
01Atomic-89
Blue-89
Gold-89
Premiere Date-89
Red-89
Core Players-18
Power Play-31
01BAP Memorabilia-85
Emerald-85
Ruby-85
Sapphire-85
He Shoots-He Scores Points-14
He Shoots-He Scores Prizes-21
01BAP Signature Series Certified 100-C49
01BAP Signature Series Certified 50-C49
01BAP Signature Series Certified 1 of 1's-C49
01BAP Signature Series Autographs-LVL
01BAP Signature Series Autographs Gold-LVL
01BAP Signature Series Franchise Jerseys-FP-27
01BAP Signature Series Jerseys-GJ-59
01BAP Signature Series Jersey Autographs-GUVL
01BAP Sig Series Jersey and Stick Cards-GSJ-59
01BAP Signature Series Emblems-GUE-50
01BAP Signature Series Numbers-ITN-50
01BAP Signature Series Teammates-TM-27
01BAP Update He Shoots-He Scores Prizes-17
01Bowman YoungStars-68
Gold-68
Ice Cubed-68
01Crown Royale-128
Blue-128
Premiere Date-128
Red-128
Retail-128
01eTopps-29
01McDonald's Pacific-37
Hometown Pride-7
Jersey Patches Silver-17
Jersey Patches Gold-17
01O-Pee-Chee-44
01O-Pee-Chee Heritage Parallel-44
01O-Pee-Chee Heritage Parallel Limited-44
01O-Pee-Chee Premier Parallel-44
01Pacific-355
01Pacific-422
Extreme LTD-355
Gold-422
Hobby LTD-355
Premiere Date-355
Retail LTD-355
Top Draft Picks-3
01Pacific Top Draft Picks Draft Day Promo-3
01Pacific Adrenaline-174
Blue-174
Premiere Date-174
Red-174
Retail-174
Jerseys-45
01Pacific Arena Exclusives-355
01Pacific Arena Exclusives-422
01Pacific Heads-Up-87
Blue-87
Premiere Date-87
Red-87
Silver-87
Quad Jerseys-27
Stat Masters-17
01Pacific Montreal International-9
01Parkhurst-87
Gold-87
Silver-87
Heroes-H1
Jerseys-PJ3
Jersey and Stick-PSJ12
Sticks-PS3
01Private Stock-88
Gold-88
Premiere Date-88
Retail-88
Silver-88
Game Gear-93
Game Gear Patches-93
01Private Stock Pacific Nights-88
01Private Stock PS-2002-68
01Private Stock Reserve-S18
01SP Authentic-80
Limited-80
Limited Gold-80
Sign of the Times-VL
Sign of the Times-TL
01SP Game Used-52
Inked Sweaters-ISVL
01SPx-63
01SPx-79
01Stadium Club-14
Award Winners-14
Master Photos-14
Gallery-G39
Gallery Gold-G39
01Titanium-126
Hobby Parallel-126
Premiere Date-126
Retail-126
Retail Parallel-126
Double-Sided Jerseys-40
Double-Sided Patches-40
01Titanium Draft Day Edition-88
01Topps-44
Heritage Parallel-44
Heritage Parallel Limited-44
OPC Parallel-44
Autographs-AVL
Captain's Cloth-CC1
Captain's Cloth-CC3
Game-Worn Jersey-JVL
Jumbo Jersey Autographs-JJA-VL
01Topps Chrome-44
Refractors-44
Black Border Refractors-44
01Topps Heritage-55
Refractors-55
Autographs-AVL
Captain's Cloth-CCVL
01Topps Reserve-21
Emblems-VL
Jerseys-VL
Name Plates-VL
Numbers-VL
Patches-VL
01UD Challenge for the Cup-79
01UD Honor Roll Pucks-P-VL
01UD Honor Roll Pucks Gold-P-VL
01UD Mask Collection-89
Gold-89
01UD Playmakers-88
01UD Top Shelf-40
Jerseys-VL
Jersey Autographs-VL
01Upper Deck-387
Exclusives-387
Franchise Cornerstones-FC5
Game Jerseys-NGVL
Skilled Stars-SS18
Tandems-T10
01Upper Deck Ice-39
01Upper Deck MVP-169
Souvenirs-C-VL
Souvenirs Gold-C-VL
01Upper Deck Victory-315
01Upper Deck Victory-440
Gold-315
Gold-440
01Upper Deck Vintage-228
01Upper Deck Vintage-234
01Vanguard-89
Blue-89
Red-89
Memorabilia-30
One of Ones-89
Premiere Date-89
Proofs-89
Quebec Tournament Heroes-19
02Atomic-90
Blue-90
Gold-90
Red-90
Hobby Parallel-90
02BAP First Edition-43
02BAP First Edition-419H
Jerseys-43
02BAP Memorabilia-187
Emerald-187
Ruby-187
Sapphire-187
NHL All-Star Game-187
NHL All-Star Game Blue-187
NHL All-Star Game Green-187
NHL All-Star Game Red-187
02BAP Memorabilia Toronto Fall Expo-187
02BAP Signature Series-137
Autographs-137
Autograph Buybacks 1998-279
Autograph Buybacks 1999-220
Autograph Buybacks 2000-116
Autograph Buybacks 2001-LVL
Autographs Gold-137
Franchise Players-FJ27
Jerseys-SGJ70
Jersey Autographs-SGJ70
02BAP Ultimate Memorabilia First Overall-15
02BAP Ultimate Memorabilia Jerseys-40
02BAP Ultimate Memorabilia Numerology-6
02Bowman YoungStars-22
Gold-22
Silver-22
02Crown Royale-88
Blue-88
Red-88
Retail-88
Lords of the Rink-18
02ITG Used-70
02ITG Used-170
02Lightning Team Issue-7
02O-Pee-Chee-14
02O-Pee-Chee Premier Blue Parallel-14
02O-Pee-Chee Premier Red Parallel-14
02O-Pee-Chee Factory Set-14
02Pacific-351
Blue-351
Red-351
02Pacific Calder-49
Silver-49
02Pacific Complete-16
Red-16
02Pacific Exclusive-156
02Pacific Heads-Up-112
Blue-112
Purple-112
Red-112
Head First-14
02Pacific Quest for the Cup-89
Gold-89
02Parkhurst-77
Bronze-77
Gold-77
Silver-77
02Parkhurst Retro-172
Minis-172
Franchise Players-RF27
Jerseys-RJ39
02Private Stock Reserve-91
Blue-91
Red-91
Retail-91
02SP Authentic-81
Beckett Promos-81
02SP Game Used-45
First Rounder Patches-VL
02SPx-68
Spectrum Gold-68
Spectrum Silver-68
02Stadium Club-26
Silver Decoy Cards-26
Proofs-26
Passport-9
02Titanium-90
Blue-90
Red-90
Retail-90
02Topps-14
OPC Blue Parallel-14
OPC Red Parallel-14
Factory Set-14
02Topps Chrome-14
Black Border Refractors-14
Refractors-14
02Topps Heritage-69
Chrome Parallel-69
02Topps Total-5
02UD Artistic Impressions-81
Gold-81
02UD Artistic Impressions Beckett Promos-81
02UD Artistic Impressions Retrospectives-R81
02UD Artistic Impressions Retrospect Gold-R81
02UD Artistic Impress Retrospect Silver-R81
02UD Honor Roll-64
02UD Honor Roll-97
Students of the Game-SG28
02UD Piece of History-81
02UD Premier Collection-48A
02UD Top Shelf-80
02Upper Deck-160
Exclusives-160
Blow-Ups-C37
Patch Card Name Plate-VL
02Upper Deck Classic Portraits-90
02Upper Deck MVP-166
Gold-166
Classics-166
Golden Classics-166
02Upper Deck Victory-195
Bronze-195
Gold-195
Silver-195
02Upper Deck Vintage-226
02Upper Deck Vintage-287
Green Backs-226
Tall Boys-T58
Tall Boys Gold-T58
02Vanguard-89
LTD-89
East Meets West-7
03McFarlane Hockey-30
03McFarlane Hockey-32
03BAP Memorabilia-97
Emerald-97
Gold-97
Ruby-97
Sapphire-97
Stanley Cup Playoffs-SCP-23
03BAP Ultimate Memorabilia Autographs-12
Gold-12
03BAP Ultimate Mem Auto Jerseys-12
03BAP Ultimate Mem Auto Emblems-12
03BAP Ultimate Memorabilia Emblems-30
03BAP Ultimate Memorabilia Emblems Gold-30
03BAP Ultimate Mem Franch Present Future-27
03BAP Ultimate Memorabilia Heroes-18
03BAP Ultimate Mem Heroes Autos-8
03BAP Ultimate Memorabilia Jerseys-32
03BAP Ultimate Memorabilia Jerseys Gold-32
03BAP Ultimate Mem Jersey and Stick-16
03BAP Ultimate Mem Jersey and Stick Gold-16
03BAP Ultimate Memorabilia Numbers-25
03BAP Ultimate Memorabilia Numbers Gold-25
03BAP Ultimate Mem Ultimate Captains-5
03Beehive-175
Variations-175
Gold-175
Silver-175
Jumbo Jerseys-BH18
Jerseys-JT6
Sticks Beige Border-BE42
03Black Diamond-4
Black-4
Green-4
Red-4
03Bowman-4
Gold-4
Future Rivals-LK
Future Rivals Patches-LK
03Bowman Chrome-4
Refractors-4
Gold Refractors-4
Xfractors-4
03Crown Royale-89
Blue-89
Retail-89
Jerseys-22
Patches-22
Lords of the Rink-20
03ITG Action-593
First Time All-Star-FT6
Jerseys-M136
Jerseys-M267
03ITG Toronto Fall Expo Jerseys-FE2
03ITG Used Signature Series-30
Gold-30
Autographs-VL
Autographs Gold-VL
Franchise-27
Franchise Autographs-27
Franchise Gold-27
Jerseys-45
Jerseys Gold-45
Jersey Autos-45
Emblems-32
Emblems Gold-32
Jersey and Stick-45
Jersey and Stick Gold-45
03Kraft-5
03Lightning Team Issue-10
03McDonald's Pacific-44
Canadian Pride-6
Hockey Roots Checklists-6
Patches Silver-21
Patches Gold-21
Patches and Sticks-21
03NHL Sticker Collection-124
03O-Pee-Chee-192
03OPC Blue-192
03OPC Gold-192
03OPC Red-192
03Pacific-308
Blue-308
Red-308
Jerseys-35
Jerseys Gold-35
03Pacific Calder-90
03Pacific Calder-157
Silver-90
03Pacific Complete-231
Red-231
03Pacific Exhibit-193
Blue Backs-193
Pursuing Prominence-12
03Pacific Heads-Up-87
Hobby LTD-87
Retail LTD-87
03Pacific Invincible-87
Blue-87
Red-87
Retail-87
Featured Performers-27

03Pacific Luxury Suite-18A
03Pacific Luxury Suite-18B
03Pacific Luxury Suite-18C
03Pacific Luxury Suite-18D
03Pacific Luxury Suite-47A
03Pacific Luxury Suite-47B
03Pacific Luxury Suite-47C
03Pacific Prism-142
Blue-142
Patches-142
Red-142
Retail-142
Paramount Prodigies-20
03Pacific Quest for the Cup-92
Blue-92
03Pacific Supreme-88
Blue-88
Red-88
Retail-88
Jerseys-22
03Parkhurst Rookie-13
High Expectations-HE-13
High Expectations Gold-HE-13
Jerseys-GJ-37
Jerseys Gold-GJ-37
Jersey and Sticks-SJ-23
Jersey and Sticks Gold-SJ-23
03Private Stock Reserve-200
Blue-200
Patches-200
Red-200
Retail-200
03SP Authentic-79
Limited-79
Breakout Seasons-B14
Breakout Seasons Limited-B14
03SP Game Used-44
Gold-44
Authentic Fabrics-DFVN
Authentic Fabrics Gold-DFVN
Authentic Patches-APVL
Double Threads-DTLK
Double Threads-DTLS
Limited Threads-LTVL
Limited Threads Gold-LTVL
03SPx-89
03SPx-136
Radiance-89
Radiance-136
Spectrum-89
Spectrum-136
VIP-VIP-LS
VIP Limited-VIP-LS
03Titanium-182
Hobby Jersey Number Parallels-182
Patches-182
Retail-182
03Topps-192
Blue-192
Gold-192
Red-192
First Overall Fabrics-VL
First Overall Fabrics-JTVL
First Overall Fabrics-VLEL
Topps/OPC Idols-CI15
03Topps C55-20
Minis-20
Minis American Back-20
Minis American Back Red-20
Minis Bazooka Back-20
Minis Brooklyn Back-20
Minis Hat Trick Back-20
Minis O Canada Back-20
Minis O Canada Back Red-20
Minis Stanley Cup Back-20
Relics-TRVL
03Topps Pristine-30
Gold Refractor Die Cuts-30
Refractors-30
Patches-PP-VL
Patch Refractors-PP-VL
Press Plates Black-30
Press Plates Cyan-30
Press Plates Magenta-30
Press Plates Yellow-30
03Topps Traded Franchise Fabrics-FF-VL
03UD Honor Roll-79
03UD Honor Roll-104
Grade A Jerseys-GAVL
03UD Premier Collection Stars-ST-VL
03UD Premier Collection Stars Patches-ST-VL
03UD Premier Collection Teammates-PT-TL
03UD Premier Collection Teammates Patches-PT-TL
03Upper Deck-171
All-Star Class-AS-26
Canadian Exclusives-171
Franchise Fabrics-FF-VL
HG-171
NHL Best-NB-VL
Patches-SP8
Team Essentials-TP-VL
03Upper Deck Classic Portraits-87
03Upper Deck Classic Portraits-151
03Upper Deck Ice-78
Gold-78
Breakers-IB-VL
Breaker Patches-IB-VL
03Upper Deck MVP-377
Gold Script-377
Silver Script-377
Canadian Exclusives-377
SportsNut-SN79
03Upper Deck Rookie Update-79
Skills-SKVL
Super Stars-SSVL
03Upper Deck Trilogy-87
Limited-87
03Upper Deck Victory-171
Bronze-171
Gold-171
Silver-171
Freshman Flashback-FF42
Game Breakers-GB19
03Toronto Star-84
04Pacific-239
Blue-239
Red-239
04Pacific National Convention-6
04SP Authentic-82
04SP Authentic-143
Limited-82
Buybacks-197
Octographs-OS-CUP
Sign of the Times-ST-VL
Sign of the Times-DS-LL
Sign of the Times-QS-LRLK
Sign of the Times-QS-TPLS
04UD All-World-28
Gold-28
Autographs-28
Dual Autographs-AD-LK
Five Autographs-AF-YGN
Six Autographs-AS-RUS
04UD Toronto Fall Expo Pride of Canada-17
04Ultimate Collection-37
04Ultimate Collection-64
Dual Logos-UL2-IL
Dual Logos-UL2-KL
Dual Logos-UL2-LL
Jerseys-UGJ-VL
Jerseys Gold-UGJ-VL
Jersey Autographs-UGJA-VL
Patches-UP-VL
Patch Autographs-UPA-VL
Patch Autographs-UPA-JIVL
Signatures-US-VL
Signature Logos-ULA-VL
Signature Patches-SP-VL
04Upper Deck-156
Canadian Exclusives-156
HG Glossy Gold-156
HG Glossy Silver-156
Three Stars-AS8
World Cup Tribute-VL
World Cup Tribute-MSVLBR
04Russian Legion-24
04Rimouski Oceanic Season Ticket-4
05Be A Player-80
First Period-80
Second Period-80
Third Period-80
Overtime-80
Dual Signatures-LL
Dual Signatures-VR
Outtakes-OT44
Signatures-VL
Signatures Gold-VL
Triple Signatures-TBL
Triple Signatures-TLP
World Cup Salute-WCS2
05Beehive-81
05Beehive-215
Beige -81
Blue -81
Gold-81
Red -81
Matte-81
05Black Diamond-142
Emerald-142
Gold-142
Onyx-142
Ruby-142
05Hot Prospects-88
En Fuego-88
Red Hot-88
White Hot-88
05Lightning Team Issue-4
05McDonalds Upper Deck-4
CHL Graduates-CG4
05Panini Stickers-151
05Parkhurst-433
05Parkhurst-503
05Parkhurst-575
05Parkhurst-697
Facsimile Auto Parallel-433
Facsimile Auto Parallel-503
Facsimile Auto Parallel-575
Facsimile Auto Parallel-697
True Colors-TCTBL
True Colors-TCTBL
True Colors-TCFLTB
True Colors-TCFLTB
05SP Authentic-89
05SP Authentic-127
Limited-89
Limited-127
Chirography-SPVL
Exquisite Endorsements-EEVL
Marks of Distinction-MDVL
Prestigious Pairings-PPLR
Sign of the Times-VL
Sign of the Times Duals-DSL
Sign of the Times Triples-TSLR
05SP Game Used-88
Autographs-88
Gold-88
Authentic Fabrics-AF-VL
Authentic Fabrics Autographs-AAF-VL
Authentic Fabrics Dual-LS
Authentic Fabrics Dual Autographs-LS
Authentic Fabrics Gold-AF-VL
Authentic Fabrics Quad-BLSR
Authentic Patches Quad -BLSR
Authentic Patches-AP-VL
Authentic Patches Autographs-AAP-VL
Authentic Patches Dual-LS
Authentic Patches Dual Autographs-LS
Auto Draft-AD-VL
Awesome Authentics-AA-VL
Awesome Authentics Gold-DA-VL
SIGnificance-VL
SIGnificance Gold-S-VL
Significant Numbers-SN-VL
Statscriptions-ST-VL
05SPx-80
Spectrum-80
Winning Combos-WC-SL
Winning Combos-WC-TB
Winning Combos Autographs-AWC-RL
Winning Combos Autographs-AWC-SL
Winning Combos Gold-WC-SL
Winning Combos Gold-WC-TB
Winning Combos Spectrum-WC-SL
Winning Combos Spectrum-WC-TB
Winning Materials-WM-VL
Winning Materials Autographs-AWM-VL
Winning Materials Gold-WM-VL
Winning Materials Spectrum-WM-VL
Xcitement Superstars-XS-VL
Xcitement Superstars Gold-XS-VL
Xcitement Superstars Spectrum-XS-VL
05The Cup-90
Gold-90
Black Rainbow-90
Dual NHL Shields Autographs-ADSLL
Emblems of Endorsement-EEVL
Honorable Numbers-HNVL
Limited Logos-LLVL
Masterpiece Pressplates-90
Masterpiece Pressplates (Rookie Update)-245
Noble Numbers-NNBL
Noble Numbers Dual-DNNLL
Noble Numbers Dual-DNNLR
Patch Variation-P90
Patch Variation Autographs-AP90
Scripted Numbers-SNJV
Scripted Numbers-SNLB
Scripted Numbers Dual-DSNPL
Scripted Swatches-SSVL
Signature Patches-SPVL
Stanley Cup Titlists-TVL
05UD Artifacts-92
05UD Artifacts-194
Blue-92
Blue-194
Gold-92
Gold-194
Green-92
Green-194
Pewter-92
Pewter-194
Red-92
Red-194
Auto Facts-AF-VL
Auto Facts Blue-AF-VL
Auto Facts Copper-AF-VL
Auto Facts Pewter-AF-VL
Auto Facts Silver-AF-VL
Gold Autographed-92
Gold Autographed-194
Remarkable Artifacts-RA-VL
Remarkable Artifacts Dual-RA-VL
Treasured Patches-TP-VL
Treasured Patches Autographed-TP-VL
Treasured Patches Dual-TPD-VL
Treasured Patches Dual Autographed-TPD-VL
Treasured Patches Pewter-TP-VL
Treasured Patches Silver-TP-VL
Treasured Swatches-TS-VL
Treasured Swatches Autographed-TS-VL
Treasured Swatches Blue-TS-VL
Treasured Swatches Copper-TS-VL
Treasured Swatches Dual-TSD-VL
Treasured Swatches Dual Autographed-TSD-VL
Treasured Swatches Dual Blue-TSD-VL
Treasured Swatches Dual Copper-TSD-VL
Treasured Swatches Dual Maroon-TSD-VL
Treasured Swatches Dual Pewter-TSD-VL
Treasured Swatches Dual Silver-TSD-VL
Treasured Swatches Maroon-TS-VL
Treasured Swatches Pewter-TS-VL
Treasured Swatches Silver-TS-VL
05UD Powerplay Specialists-TSVL
05UD Powerplay Specialists Patches-SPVL
05Ultimate Collection-81
Gold-81
Jerseys-JVL
Jerseys Dual-DJSL
Jerseys Triple-TJLVR
Marquee Attractions-MA43
National Heroes Jerseys-NHJVL
National Heroes Patches-NHPVL
Premium Patches-PPVL
Premium Swatches-PSVL
Ultimate Achievements-UAVL
Ultimate Patches-PVL
Ultimate Patches Dual-DPSL
Ultimate Patches Triple-TPLVR
Ultimate Signatures-USVL
Ultimate Signatures Logos-SLVL
Ultimate Signatures Pairings-UPSL
Ultimate Signatures Trios-UTLLR
05Ultra-173
Gold-173
Fresh Ink-FI-VL
Fresh Ink Blue-FI-VL
Ice-173
Scoring Kings-SK39
Scoring Kings-SKJ-VL
Scoring Kings Jersey Autographs-KAJ-VL
Scoring Kings Patches-SKP-VL
Scoring Kings Patch Autographs-KAP-VL
05Upper Deck-416
05Upper Deck All-Time Greatest-54
05Upper Deck Big Playmakers-B-VL
05Upper Deck Jerseys-J-VL
05Upper Deck Jerseys Series II-J2VL
05Upper Deck Majestic Materials-MMVL
05Upper Deck NHL Generations-DML
05Upper Deck Notable Numbers-N-VL
05Upper Deck Patches-P-VL
05Upper Deck Shooting Stars-S-VL
05Upper Deck Ice-89
Rainbow-89
Frozen Fabrics-FFVL
Frozen Fabrics Autographs-AFFVL
Frozen Fabrics Glass-FFVL
Frozen Fabrics Patches-FFPVL
Frozen Fabrics Patch Autographs-FAPVL
Signature Swatches-SSVL
05Upper Deck MVP-350
Gold-350
Platinum-350
05Upper Deck Rookie Update-87
05Upper Deck Rookie Update-245
Inspirations Patch Rookies-245
05Upper Deck Trilogy-83
05Upper Deck Trilogy-127
Crystal-127
Crystal Autographs-127
Honorary Patches-HP-VL
Honorary Patch Scripts-HSP-VL
Honorary Swatches-HS-VL
Honorary Swatch Scripts-HSS-VL
Ice Scripts-IS-VL
05Upper Deck Victory-174
Black-174
Gold-174
Silver-174
Blow-Ups-BU36
Game Breakers-GB41
05Czech Stadion-687
06Be A Player-97
Autographs-97
Profiles-PP1
Profiles Autographs-PP1
Signatures-VL
Signatures 10-105
Signatures 25-105
Signatures Duals-DLS
Signatures Trios-TLRS
Signatures Foursomes-FSLST
Up Close and Personal-UC58
Up Close and Personal Autographs-UC58
06Be A Player Portraits-90
06Beehive-9
06Beehive-166
Blue-9
Gold-9
Matte-9
Red Facsimile Signatures-9
Wood-9
5 X 7 Black and White-9
5 X 7 Dark Wood-9
PhotoGraphs-PGVL
06Black Diamond-145
Black-145
Black-164B
Gold-145
Ruby-145
06Flair Showcase-87
06Flair Showcase-195
06Flair Showcase-262
06Flair Showcase-296
Parallel-87
Parallel-195
Parallel-262
Parallel-296
Hot Numbers-HN36
Hot Numbers Parallel-HN36
Inks-IVL
06Fleer-172
Tiffany-172
Signing Day-SDVL
06Hot Prospects-87
Red Hot-87
White Hot-87
Hotagraphs-HVL
06ITG Ultimate Memorabilia Autos-70
06ITG Ultimate Memorabilia Autos Gold-70
06ITG Ultimate Memorabilia Complete Jersey-21
06ITG Ultimate Memorabilia Complete Jersey Gold-21
06ITG Ultimate Memorabilia First Round Picks-23
06ITG Ultimate Memorabilia First Round Picks Gold-23
06ITG Ultimate Memorabilia Going For Gold-28
06ITG Ultimate Memorabilia Going For Gold Gold-28
06ITG Ultimate Memorabilia Jerseys-27
06ITG Ultimate Memorabilia Jerseys Gold-27
06ITG Ultimate Memorabilia Jerseys and Emblems-21
06ITG Ultimate Memorabilia Jerseys and Emblems Gold-21
06ITG Ultimate Memorabilia Jerseys Autos-67
06ITG Ultimate Memorabilia Jerseys Autos Gold-67
06ITG Ultimate Memorabilia Sticks and Jerseys-12
06ITG Ultimate Memorabilia Sticks and Jerseys Gold-12
06ITG Ultimate Memorabilia Sticks Autos-32
06ITG Ultimate Memorabilia Sticks Autos Gold-32
06Lightning Postcards-12
06McDonald's Upper Deck-43
Autographs-AVL
Jerseys-JVL
Patches-PVL
06NHL POG-17
06O-Pee-Chee-453
06O-Pee-Chee-697
Rainbow-453
Rainbow-697
Swatches-S-VL
06Panini Stickers-149
06SP Authentic-10
06SP Authentic-159
Limited-10
Limited-159
Sign of the Times Duals-STLT
06SP Game Used-89
Gold-89
Rainbow-89
Authentic Fabrics-AFVL
Authentic Fabrics Parallel-AFVL
Authentic Fabrics Patches-AFVL
Authentic Fabrics Dual-AF2LR
Authentic Fabrics Dual Patches-AF2LR
Authentic Fabrics Triple-AF3TBL
Authentic Fabrics Triple Patches-AF3TBL
Authentic Fabrics Quads-AF4LMSB
Authentic Fabrics Quads Patches-AF4LMSB
Authentic Fabrics Eights-AF8CAN
Authentic Fabrics Eights Patches-AF8CAN
By The Letter-BLVL
Inked Sweaters-ISVL
Inked Sweaters Patches-ISVL
06SPx-90
Spectrum-90
SPxcitement-X88
SPxcitement Spectrum-X88
SPxcitement Autographs-X88
Winning Materials-WMVL
Winning Materials Spectrum-WMVL
Winning Materials Autographs-WMVL
06Sunkist-8
06The Cup-81
Autographed Foundations-CQVL
Autographed Foundations Patches-CQVL
Autographed NHL Shields Duals-DASIL
Autographed NHL Shields Duals-DASSL
Autographed Patches-81
Black Rainbow-81
Foundations-CQVL
Foundations Patches-CQVL
Enshrinements-EVL
Gold-81
Gold Patches-81
Honorable Numbers-HNVL
Jerseys-81
Limited Logos-LLVL
Masterpiece Pressplates-81
NHL Shields Duals-DSHLR
Scripted Swatches-SSVL
Scripted Swatches Duals-DSLS
Signature Patches-SPVL
Stanley Cup Signatures-CSVL
06UD Artifacts-12
06UD Artifacts-197
Blue-12
Blue-197
Gold-12
Gold-197
Platinum-12
Platinum-197
Radiance-12
Radiance-197
Autographed Radiance Parallel-12
Autographed Radiance Parallel-197
Red-12
Red-197
Tundra Tandems-TTLR
Tundra Tandems Black-TTLR
Tundra Tandems Blue-TTLR
Tundra Tandems Gold-TTLR
Tundra Tandems Platinum-TTLR
Tundra Tandems Red-TTLR
Tundra Tandems Dual Patches Red-TTLR
06UD Mini Jersey Collection-87
06UD Powerplay-90
Impact Rainbow-90
06Ultimate Collection-54
Autographed Jerseys-AJ-VL
Autographed Patches-AJ-VL
Jerseys-UJ-VL
Jerseys Dual-UJ2-LS
Patches-UJ-VL
Patches Dual-UJ2-LS
Signatures-US-VL
Ultimate Achievements-UA-VL
Ultimate Signatures Logos-SL-VL
06Ultra-176
Gold Medallion-176
Ice Medallion-176
Action-UA27
Difference Makers-DM30
Scoring Kings-SK30
06Upper Deck Arena Giveaways-TBL4
06Upper Deck-422
Exclusives Parallel-422
High Gloss Parallel-422
Game Jerseys-JVL
Game Patches-PVL
Generations Triples-G3LTS
Generations Patches Triple-G3PLTS
Hometown Heroes-HH47
Masterpieces-422
Oversized Wal-Mart Exclusives-422
Shootout Artists-SA12
Signatures-SVL
06Upper Deck MVP-264
Gold Script-264
Super Script-264
International Icons-II21
Jerseys-OJEV
Jerseys-OJLJ
06Upper Deck Ovation-93
06Upper Deck Sweet Shot-91
Signature Shots/Saves-SSVL
Signature Shots/Saves Sticks-SSSVL
Sweet Stitches-SSVL
Sweet Stitches Duals-SSVL
Sweet Stitches Triples-SSVL
06Upper Deck Trilogy-89
Combo Clearcut Autographs-C2LS
Honorary Scripted Patches-HSPVL
Honorary Scripted Swatches-HSSVL
Honorary Swatches-HSVL
Ice Scripts-ISVL
Scripts-S1VL
Scripts-S3VL
06Upper Deck Victory-178
06Upper Deck Victory Black-178
06Upper Deck Victory Gold-178
06Upper Deck Victory GameBreakers-GB46
06Upper Deck Victory Oversize Cards-VL
06Russian Sport Collection Olympic Stars-36
07Sports Illustrated for Kids *-166
07Upper Deck Ovation-57
3x5s-XL6
07Upper Deck Victory-72
Black-72
Gold-72
GameBreakers-GB20
Oversize Cards-OS19
Stars on Ice-SI37

Lechenne, Vincent

93Swiss HNL-151
95Swiss HNL-100
96Swiss HNL-41
01Swiss HNL-295
02Swiss HNL-372

Lechl, Jurgen

94German DEL-329
95German DEL-302
96German DEL-330

Lechner, Alexander

93Quebec Pee-Wee Tournament-1532

Lechtaler, Christian

91Swedish Semic Elitserien Stickers-298
98Swedish UD Choice-24
00Swedish Upper Deck-20

Lecklin, Kimmo

93Finnish SISU-30
94Finnish SISU-47
98Swedish UD Choice-83
99Finnish Cardset-327

Leclair, Alain

90Rayside-Balfour Jr. Canadians-11

LeClair, Corey

00Brampton Battalion-8
02Guelph Storm-10

Leclair, Jackie

44Beehive Group II Photos-259
51Laval Dairy QSHL-12
51Laval Dairy Subset-98
52St. Lawrence Sales-57
55Parkhurst-36
Quaker Oats-36
94Parkhurst Missing Link-83

LeClair, John

91Pro Set Platinum-259
91Bowman-344
91Canadiens Postcards-17
91O-Pee-Chee-209
91OPC Premier-105
91OPC Premier-186
91Parkhurst-84
French-84
91Pinnacle-322
French-322
91Pro Set-545
French-545
91Score American-313
91Score Canadian Bilingual-343
91Score Canadian English-343
91Topps-209
91Upper Deck-345
French-345
92Bowman-8
92Canadiens Postcards-17
92O-Pee-Chee-386
92Parkhurst-326
Emerald Ice-326
92Sports Illustrated for Kids II-657
92Stadium Club-181
92Topps-500
Gold-500G
92Ultra-330
92Upper Deck-55
93Canadiens Postcards-14
93Donruss-176
93Leaf-98
93OPC Premier-181
Gold-181
93Parkhurst-107
Emerald Ice-107
93Pinnacle-112
Canadian-112
93Score-318
Canadian-318
93Stadium Club-95
Members Only Master Set-95
OPC-95
First Day Issue-95
First Day Issue OPC-95
93Topps/OPC Premier-181
Gold-181
93Ultra-215
93Upper Deck-167
SP-79
94Canada Games NHL POGS-136
94Canadiens Postcards-14
94Donruss-98
94Fleer-156
94Leaf-5
94OPC Premier-117
Special Effects-117
94Parkhurst-111
Gold-111
94Pinnacle-272
Artist's Proofs-272
Rink Collection-272
94SP-85
Die Cuts-85
94Topps/OPC Premier-117
Special Effects-117
94Ultra-111
94Upper Deck-330
Electric Ice-330
94Classic Pro Prospects-54
95Bashan Super Stickers-92
95Be A Player-130
Signatures-S130
Signatures Die Cuts-S130
95Bowman-63
All-Foil-63
95Canada Games NHL POGS-10
95Canada Games NHL POGS-206
95Collector's Choice-261
95Collector's Choice-376
Player's Club-261
Player's Club-376
Player's Club Platinum-261
Player's Club Platinum-376
Crash The Game-C23A
Crash The Game-C23B
Crash The Game-C23C
Crash The Game Gold-C23A
Crash The Game Gold-C23B
Crash The Game Gold-C23C
Crash the Game Silver Redeemed-C23
Crash the Game Silver Bonus-C23
Crash the Game Gold Redeemed-C23
Crash the Game Gold Bonus-C23
95Donruss-114
Dominators-2
95Donruss Elite-56
Die Cut Stars-56
Die Cut Uncut-56
95Emotion-132
95Finest-60
95Finest-179
Refractors-60
Refractors-179
95Hoyle Eastern Playing Cards-39
95Imperial Stickers-92
95Kraft-46
95Leaf-95
95Leaf Limited-85
95McDonald's Pinnacle-MCD-20
95Metal-111
Iron Warriors-5
95NHL Aces Playing Cards-12S
95Panini Stickers-116
95Parkhurst International-157
Emerald Ice-157
95Pinnacle-51
Artist's Proofs-51
Rink Collection-51
Roaring 20s-16
95Playoff One on One-293
95Pro Magnets-53
95Score-9
Black Ice Artist's Proofs-9
Black Ice-9
95Select Certified-44
Mirror Gold-44
95SkyBox Impact-126
95SkyBox Impact-244
95SP-108
95Stadium Club-77
Members Only Master Set-77
Power Streak-PS6
Power Streak Members Only Master Set-PS6
95Summit-75
Artist's Proofs-75
Ice-75
Mad Hatters-3
95Topps-65
OPC Inserts-65
Home Grown USA-HGA9
Power Lines-1PL
95Topps SuperSkills-42
Platinum-42
95Ultra-118
Gold Medallion-118
Crease Crashers-5
Red Light Specials-5
Red Light Specials Gold Medallion-5
95Upper Deck-7
95Upper Deck-247
Electric Ice-7
Electric Ice-247
Electric Ice Gold-7
Electric Ice Gold-247
95Upper Deck All-Star Game Predictors-24
Redemption Winners-24
95Upper Deck NHL All-Stars-AS14
95Upper Deck NHL All-Stars Jumbo-AS14
95Upper Deck Special Edition-SE63
95Upper Deck Special Edition Gold-SE63
95Zenith-59
Gifted Grinders-7
96SLU Hockey Canadian-6
96SLU Hockey American-10
96Be A Player Biscuit In The Basket-17
96Black Diamond-110
Gold-110
96Collector's Choice-190
96Collector's Choice-326
MVP-UD8
MVP Gold-UD8
Crash the Game-C12A
Crash the Game-C12B
Crash the Game-C12C
Crash the Game Gold-C12A
Crash the Game Gold-C12B
Crash the Game Gold-C12C
Crash the Game Exchange-CR12
Crash the Game Exchange Gold-CR12
96Donruss-36
Press Proofs-36
Hit List-13
96Donruss Canadian Ice-100
Gold Press Proofs-100
Red Press Proofs-100
96Donruss Elite-57
Die Cut Stars-57
96Flair-69
Blue Ice-69
96Fleer Promo Sheet-1
96Fleer Promo Sheet-2
96Fleer-81
96Fleer-142
Art Ross-12
96Fleer Picks-30
Dream Lines-7
Fabulous 50-24
Fantasy Force-1
96Flyers Postcards-14
96Kenner Starting Lineup Cards-10
96Kraft Upper Deck-57
96Leaf-83
Press Proofs-83
96Leaf Limited-15
Gold-15
96Leaf Preferred-105
Press Proofs-105
Steel-39
Steel Gold-39
96Maggers-53
96McDonald's Pinnacle-4
96Metal Universe-113
Lethal Weapons-10
Lethal Weapons Super Power-10
96NHL Pro Stamps-53
96Pinnacle-49
Artist's Proofs-49
Foil-49
Premium Stock-49
Rink Collection-49
96Score-161
Artist's Proofs-161
Dealer's Choice Artist's Proofs-161
Special Artist's Proofs-161
Golden Blades-161
96Select Certified-33
Artist's Proofs-33
Blue-33
Mirror Blue-33
Mirror Gold-33
Mirror Red-33
Red-33
96SkyBox Impact-96
96SkyBox Impact-S1
96SkyBox Impact-NNO
BladeRunners-11
96SP-112
Game Film-GF17
96SPx-34
Gold-34
96Stadium Club Members Only-43
96Summit-6
Artist's Proofs-6
Ice-6
Metal-6
Premium Stock-6
96Team Out-3
96Topps Picks Top Shelf-TS1
96Ultra-125
96Ultra-S125
Gold Medallion-125
Clear the Ice-5
96Upper Deck-118
96Upper Deck-368
Power Performers-P3
96Upper Deck Ice-98
Parallel-98
Stanley Cup Foundation-S10
Stanley Cup Foundation Dynasty-S10
96Zenith-17
Artist's Proofs-17
Assailants-10
97Be A Player-250
Autographs-250
Autographs Die-Cuts-250
Autographs Prismatic Die-Cuts-250
One Timers-9
97Beehive-5
Golden Portraits-5
Team-12
Team Gold-12
97Black Diamond-65
Double Diamond-65
Triple Diamond-65
Quadruple Diamond-65
Premium Cut-PC6
Premium Cut Double Diamond-PC6
Premium Cut Quadruple Diamond Horiz-PC6
Premium Cut Triple Diamond-PC6
Premium Cut Quadruple Diamond Verticals-PC6
97Collector's Choice-182
Star Quest-SQ52
97Crown Royale-98
Emerald Green-98
Ice Blue-98
Silver-98
Hat Tricks Die-Cuts-12
Lamplighters Cel-Fusion Die-Cuts-13
97Donruss-29
97Donruss-229
Press Proofs Silver-29
Press Proofs Silver-229
Press Proofs Gold-29
Press Proofs Gold-229
Red Alert-7
97Donruss Canadian Ice-93
Dominion Series-93
Provincial Series-93
Stanley Cup Scrapbook-29
97Donruss Elite-71
Aspirations-71
Status-71
97Donruss Limited-15
97Donruss Limited-90
97Donruss Limited-94
97Donruss Limited-168
Exposure-15
Exposure-90
Exposure-94
Exposure-168
Fabric of the Game-63
97Donruss Preferred-76
Cut to the Chase-76
Line of the Times-3A
97Donruss Preferred Line of Times Promos-3A
97Donruss Priority-132
97Donruss Priority-205
Stamp of Approval-132
Stamp of Approval-205
Direct Deposit-28
Postcards-21
Postcards Opening Day Issues-26
Stamps-21
Stamps Bronze-21
Stamps Gold-21
Stamps Silver-21
97Esso Olympic Hockey Heroes-25
97Esso Olympic Hockey Heroes French-25
97Flyers Phone Cards-3
97Katch-106
Gold-106
Silver-106
97Kraft-23
97Leaf-100
Fractal Matrix-100
Fractal Matrix Die Cuts-100
Banner Season-7
97Leaf International-100
Universal Ice-100
97NHL Aces Playing Cards-30
97Pacific-10
Copper-10
Emerald Green-10
Ice Blue-10
Red-10
Silver-10
Card-Supials-14
Card-Supials Minis-14
Slap Shots Die-Cuts-6C
97Pacific Dynagon-90
97Pacific Dynagon-141
Copper-90
Copper-141
Dark Grey-90
Dark Grey-141
Emerald Green-90
Emerald Green-141
Ice Blue-90
Ice Blue-141
Red-90
Red-141
Silver-90
Silver-141
Best Kept Secrets-71
Tandems-15
Tandems-20
97Pacific Invincible-101
Copper-101
Emerald Green-101
Ice Blue-101
Red-101
Silver-101
Attack Zone-17
Feature Performers-24
NHL Regime-144
97Pacific Omega-167
Copper-167
Dark Gray-167
Emerald Green-167
Gold-167
Ice Blue-167
Game Face-12
Stick Handle Laser Cuts-15
97Panini Stickers-98
97Panini Stickers-125
97Paramount-133
Copper-133
Dark Grey-133
Emerald Green-133
Ice Blue-133
Red-133
Silver-133
Photoengravings-14
97Pinnacle-57
97Pinnacle-196
Artist's Proofs-57
Rink Collection-57
Epix Game Emerald-23
Epix Game Orange-23
Epix Game Purple-23
Epix Moment Emerald-23
Epix Moment Orange-23
Epix Moment Purple-23
Epix Play Emerald-23
Epix Play Orange-23
Epix Play Purple-23
Epix Season Emerald-23
Epix Season Orange-23
Epix Season Purple-23
Press Plates Back Black-57
Press Plates Back Black-196
Press Plates Back Cyan-57
Press Plates Back Cyan-196
Press Plates Back Magenta-57
Press Plates Back Magenta-196
Press Plates Back Yellow-57
Press Plates Back Yellow-196
Press Plates Front Black-57
Press Plates Front Black-196
Press Plates Front Cyan-57
Press Plates Front Cyan-196
Press Plates Front Magenta-57
Press Plates Front Magenta-196
Press Plates Front Yellow-57
Press Plates Front Yellow-196
Team Pinnacle-8
Team Mirror-8
Team Parallel-8
Team Parallel Mirror-8
97Pinnacle Certified-119
Red-119
Mirror Blue-119
Mirror Gold-119
Mirror Red-119
Team-20
Gold Team Promo-20

Gold Team-20
97Pinnacle Inside-58
Coach's Collection-58
Executive Collection-58
Track-25
Cans-6
Cans Gold-6
97Pinnacle Mint-20
Bronze-20
Gold Team-20
Silver Team-20
Coins Brass-20
Coins Brass Proofs-20
Coins Gold Plated-20
Coins Gold Plated Proofs-20
Coins Nickel Silver-20
Coins Nickel Silver Proofs-20
Coins Solid Gold-20
Coins Solid Silver-20
97Pinnacle Power Pack Blow-Ups-23
97Pinnacle Tot Certi Platinum Blue-119
97Pinnacle Tot Certi Platinum Gold-119
97Pinnacle Totally Certified Platinum Red-119
97Pinnacle Tot Cert Mirror Platinum Gold-119
97Revolution-102
Copper-102
Emerald-102
Ice Blue-102
Silver-102
1996 All-Star Game Die-Cuts-15
97Score-108
Artist's Proofs-108
Golden Blades-108
Check It-5
97Score Flyers-4
Platinum-4
Premier-4
97SP Authentic-114
Icons-I17
Icons Die-Cuts-I17
Icons Embossed-I17
97SPx-38
Bronze-38
Gold-38
Silver-38
Steel-38
Grand Finale-38
97Studio-22
Press Proofs Silver-22
Press Proofs Gold-22
Portraits-25
Silhouettes-15
Silhouettes 8x10-15
97Upper Deck-123
Smooth Grooves-SG50
The Specialists-20
The Specialists Level 2 Die Cuts-20
Three Star Selects-9B
97Upper Deck Crash the All-Star Game-15
97Upper Deck Crash the All-Star Game-AR15
97Upper Deck Ice-75
Parallel-75
Lethal Lines-L8A
Lethal Lines 2-L8A
Power Shift-75
97Zenith-8
Z-Gold-8
Z-Silver-8
97Zenith 5 x 7-47
Gold Impulse-47
Silver Impulse-47
97Zenith Chasing The Cup-8
97Zenith Z-Team-7
97Zenith Z-Team 5x7-7
97Zenith Z-Team Gold-7
98SLU Hockey Classic Doubles-5
98SLU Hockey One on One-6
98Aurora-140
Atomic Laser Cuts-14
Championship Fever-35
Championship Fever Copper-35
Championship Fever Ice Blue-35
Championship Fever Red-35
Championship Fever Silver-35
Cubes-13
Man Advantage-14
98Be A Player-250
Press Release-250
98BAP Gold-250
98BAP Autographs-250
98BAP Autographs Gold-250
98BAP AS Game Used Stick Cards-S20
98BAP AS Game Used Jersey Cards-AS22
98BAP Playoff Game Used Jerseys-G5
98BAP Playoff Game Used Jersey Autographs-G5
98BAP Playoff Practice Used Jerseys-P13
98Black Diamond-63
Double Diamond-63
Triple Diamond-63
Quadruple Diamond-63
Myriad-M24
Myriad 2-M24
Winning Formula Gold-WF22
Winning Formula Platinum-WF22
98Bowman's Best-7
Refractors-7
Atomic Refractors-7
Mirror Image Fusion-F1
Mirror Image Fusion Refractors-F1
Mirror Image Fusion Atomic Refractors-F1
98Crown Royale-99
Limited Series-99
Master Performers-15
Pillars of the Game-17
Pivotal Players-18
98Donruss Elite Promos-1
98Finest-51
No Protectors-51
No Protectors Refractors-51
Refractors-51
Double Sided Mystery Finest-M41
Double Sided Mystery Finest-M45
Double Sided Mystery Finest-M46
Double Sided Mystery Finest-M47
Double Sided Mystery Refractors-M41
Double Sided Mystery Refractors-M45
Double Sided Mystery Refractors-M46
Double Sided Mystery Refractors-M47
Red Lighters-R16
Red Lighters Refractors-R16
98Katch-105
98Kraft Fearless Forwards-6
98OPC Chrome-60
Refractors-60
Season's Best-SB16
Season's Best-SB28
Season's Best Refractors-SB16
Season's Best Refractors-SB28
98Pacific-51
Ice Blue-51
Red-51
Dynagon Ice Inserts-14
Titanium Ice-14
Gold Crown Die-Cuts-24
Timelines-13
98Pacific Dynagon Ice-137
Blue-137
Red-137
Forward Thinking-14
98Pacific Omega-176
Red-176
Opening Day Issue-176
EO Portraits-15
EO Portraits 1 of 1-15
Face to Face-9
Online-25
Planet Ice-15
Planet Ice Parallel-15
Prism-15
98Panini Photocards-45
98Panini Stickers-88
98Paramount-176
Copper-176
Emerald Green-176
Holo-Electric-176
Ice Blue-176
Silver-176
Special Delivery Die-Cuts-13
98Revolution-105
Ice Shadow-105
Red-105
All-Star Die Cuts-16
Chalk Talk Laser-Cuts-13
Showstoppers-25
Three Pronged Attack-28
Three Pronged Attack Parallel-28
98SP Authentic-63
Power Shift-63
Snapshots-SS11
Stat Masters-S9
98SPx Finite-60
98SPx Finite-102
98SPx Finite-164
Radiance-60
Radiance-102
Radiance-164
Spectrum-60
Spectrum-102
Spectrum-164
98SPx Top Prospects-44
Radiance-44
Spectrum-44
Highlight Heroes-H22
Lasting Impressions-L24
Premier Stars-PS9
Winning Materials-JL
98Topps-60
O-Pee-Chee-60
Autographs-A3
Mystery Finest Bronze-M10
Mystery Finest Bronze Refractors-M10
Mystery Finest Gold-M10
Mystery Finest Gold Refractors-M10
Mystery Finest Silver-M10
Mystery Finest Silver Refractors-M10
Season's Best-SB16
Season's Best-SB28
98Topps Gold Label Class 1-86
Black-86
Black One of One-86
One of One-86
Red-86
Red One of One-86
98Topps Gold Label Class 2-86
98Topps Gold Label Class 2 Black-86
98Topps Gold Label Class 2 Black 1 of 1-86
98Topps Gold Label Class 2 One of One-86
98Topps Gold Label Class 2 Red-86
98Topps Gold Label Class 2 Red One of One-86
98Topps Gold Label Class 3-86
98Topps Gold Label Class 3 Black-86
98Topps Gold Label Class 3 Black 1 of 1-86
98Topps Gold Label Class 3 One of One-86
98Topps Gold Label Class 3 Red-86
98Topps Gold Label Class 3 Red One of One-86
98Topps Gold Label Goal Race '99-GR2
98Topps Gold Label Goal Race '99 Black-GR2
98Topps Gold Label Goal '99 Black 1 of 1-GR2
98Topps Gold Label Goal Race 99 1 of 1-GR2
98Topps Gold Label Goal Race '99 Red-GR2
98Topps Gold Label GoalRace 99 Red 1 of 1-GR2
98UD Choice-153
98UD Choice-235
Blow-Ups-3
Mini Bobbing Head-BH6
98UD Choice Preview-153
98UD Choice Prime Choice Reserve-153
98UD Choice Prime Choice Reserve-235
98UD Choice Reserve-153
98UD Choice Reserve-235
98UD Choice StarQuest Blue-SQ15
98UD Choice StarQuest Gold-SQ15
98UD Choice StarQuest Green-SQ15
98UD Choice StarQuest Red-SQ15
98UD3-56
98UD3-116
98UD3-176
Die-Cuts-56
Die-Cuts-116
Die-Cuts-176
98Upper Deck-143
Exclusives-143
Exclusives 1 of 1-143
Fantastic Finishers-FF25
Fantastic Finishers Quantum 1-FF25
Fantastic Finishers Quantum 2-FF25
Fantastic Finishers Quantum 3-FF25
Frozen In Time-FT27
Frozen In Time Quantum 1-FT27
Frozen In Time Quantum 2-FT27
Frozen In Time Quantum 3-FT27
Lord Stanley's Heroes-LS25
Lord Stanley's Heroes Quantum 1-LS25
Lord Stanley's Heroes Quantum 2-LS25
Lord Stanley's Heroes Quantum 3-LS25
Profiles-P25
Profiles Quantum 1-P25
Profiles Quantum 2-P25
Profiles Quantum 3-P25
Gold Reserve-143
98Upper Deck MVP-148
Gold Script-148
Silver Script-148
Super Script-148
Game Souvenirs-JL
OT Heroes-OT14
Power Game-PG6
98Slovakian Eurotel-13
99Aurora-105
Striped-105
Premiere Date-105
Premiere Date Striped-105
Canvas Creations-8
Championship Fever-16
Championship Fever Copper-16
Championship Fever Ice Blue-16
Championship Fever Silver-16
Complete Players-8
Complete Players Parallel-8
Complete Players Retail-8
Complete Players Retail Parallel-8
Styrotechs-14
99BAP Memorabilia-73
Gold-73
Silver-73
Jersey Cards-J22
Jersey Emblems-E22
Jersey Numbers-I22
Jersey and Stick Cards-S22
AS Heritage Ruby-H2
AS Heritage Sapphire-H2
AS Heritage Emerald-H2
99BAP Update Double AS Jersey Cards-D14
99BAP Update Teammates Jersey Cards-TM7
99BAP Update Teammates Jersey Cards-TM15
99BAP Update Teammates Jersey Cards-TM18
99BAP Update Teammates Jersey Cards-TM49
99BAP Millennium-179
Emerald-179
Ruby-179
Sapphire-179
Signatures-179
Signatures Gold-179
Jerseys-J7
Jersey Autographs-J7
Jersey and Stick Cards-JS7
Jersey Emblems-E7
Jersey Numbers-N7
99Black Diamond-64
Diamond Cut-64
Final Cut-64
A Piece of History-JL
A Piece of History Double-JL
A Piece of History Triple-JL
Diamond Might-DM4
99Crown Royale-102
Limited Series-102
Premiere Date-102
Gold Crown Die-Cuts Jumbos-6
Ice Elite-19
Ice Elite Parallel-19
99Jell-O Pudding Super Skills-3
99McDonald's Upper Deck Signatures-JL
99O-Pee-Chee-19
99O-Pee-Chee All-Topps-AT7
99O-Pee-Chee Autographs-TA1
99O-Pee-Chee Chrome-19
99O-Pee-Chee Chrome All Topps-AT7
99O-Pee-Chee Chrome All-Topps Refractors-AT7
99O-Pee-Chee Chrome Ice Masters-IM5
99O-Pee-Chee Chrome Ice Masters Refractor-IM5
99O-Pee-Chee Chrome Refractors-19
99O-Pee-Chee Chrome Fantastic Finishers-FF5
99OPC Chrome Fantastic Finishers Ref-FF5
99O-Pee-Chee Chrome Positive Performers-PP2
99OPC Chrome Pos Performers Ref-PP2
99O-Pee-Chee Ice Masters-IM5
99O-Pee-Chee Fantastic Finishers-FF5
99O-Pee-Chee Positive Performers-PP2
99O-Pee-Chee Top of the World-TW10
99Pacific-306
Copper-306
Emerald Green-306
Gold-306
Ice Blue-306
Premiere Date-306
Red-306
Gold Crown Die-Cuts-25
Home and Away-8
Home and Away-18
Past and Present-16
99Pacific Dynagon Ice-147
Blue-147
Copper-147
Gold-147
Premiere Date-147
2000 All-Star Preview-14
Checkmates American-12
Checkmates American-27
Checkmates Canadian-12
Lamplighter Net-Fusions-8
99Pacific Omega-171
Copper-171
Gold-171
Ice Blue-171
Premiere Date-171
Cup Contenders-15
Game-Used Jerseys-6
NHL Generations-8
5 Star Talents-8
5 Star Talents Parallel-8
99Pacific Prism-102
Holographic Blue-102
Holographic Gold-102
Holographic Mirror-102
Holographic Purple-102
Premiere Date-102
Clear Advantage-15
Sno-Globe Die-Cuts-15
99Panini Stickers-125
99Panini Stickers-325
99Paramount-172
Copper-172
Emerald-172
Gold-172
Holographic Emerald-172
Holographic Gold-172
Holographic Silver-172
Ice Blue-172
Premiere Date-172
Red-172
Silver-172
Personal Best-25
99Revolution-108
Premiere Date-108
Red-108
Shadow Series-108
NHL Icons-13
Ornaments-14
Showstoppers-26
Top of the Line-7
Copper-108
Gold-108
CSC Silver-108
99SP Authentic-64
Buyback Signatures-39
Buyback Signatures-40
Buyback Signatures-41
Buyback Signatures-42
Sign of the Times-JL
Sign of the Times Gold-JL
Supreme Skill-SS9
99SPx-110
Radiance-110
Spectrum-110
Prolifics-P12
SPXcitement-X19
SPXtreme-XT17
99Stadium Club-65
First Day Issue-65
One of a Kind-65
Printing Plates Black-65
Printing Plates Cyan-65
Printing Plates Magenta-65
Printing Plates Yellow-65
Chrome-25
Chrome Refractors-25
Co-Signers-CS6
Co-Signers-CS8
Co-Signers-CS9
Lone Star Signatures-LS10
Onyx Extreme-OE9
Onyx Extreme Die-Cut-OE9
Souvenirs-SJL
99Topps/OPC-19
All-Topps-AT7
Fantastic Finishers-FF5
Ice Masters-IM5
Positive Performers-PP2
Top of the World-TW10
99Topps/OPC Chrome-19
Refractors-19
All-Topps-AT7
All-Topps Refractors-AT7
Fantastic Finishers-FF5
Fantastic Finishers Refractors-FF5
Ice Masters-IM5
Ice Masters Refractors-IM5
Positive Performers-PP2
Positive Performers Refractors-PP2
99Topps Gold Label Class 1-25
Black-25
Black One of One-25
One of One-25
Red-25
Red One of One-25
99Topps Gold Label Class 2-25
99Topps Gold Label Class 2 Black-25
99Topps Gold Label Class 2 Black 1 of 1-25
99Topps Gold Label Class 2 One of One-25
99Topps Gold Label Class 2 Red-25
99Topps Gold Label Class 2 Red One of One-25
99Topps Gold Label Class 3-25
99Topps Gold Label Class 3 Black-25
99Topps Gold Label Class 3 Black 1 of 1-25
99Topps Gold Label Class 3 One of One-25
99Topps Gold Label Class 3 Red-25
99Topps Gold Label Class 3 Red One of One-25
99Topps Gold Label Prime Gold-PG8
99Topps Gold Label Prime Gold One of One -PG8
99Topps Gold Label Prime Gold Black-PG8
99Topps Gold Label Prime Gold Black One of One -PG8
99Topps Gold Label Prime Gold Red-PG8
99Topps Gold Label Prime Gold Red One of One -PG8
99Topps Premier Plus-13
Parallel-13
99Ultimate Victory-65
1/1-65
Parallel-65
Parallel 100-65
99Upper Deck-158
99Upper Deck-269
Exclusives-158
Exclusives-269
Exclusives 1 of 1-158
Exclusives 1 of 1-269
All-Star Class-AS8
All-Star Class Quantum Gold-AS8
All-Star Class Quantum Silver-AS8
Crunch Time-CT22
Crunch Time Quantum Gold-CT22
Crunch Time Quantum Silver-CT22
Fantastic Finishers-FF2
Fantastic Finishers Quantum Gold-FF2
Fantastic Finishers Quantum Silver-FF2
Game Jerseys-JL
Game Jerseys Series II-JL
Game Jersey Patch-JLP
Game Jersey Patch Series II-JLP
Game Jersey Patch Series II 1 of 1-JL-P1
NHL Scrapbook-SB13
NHL Scrapbook Quantum Gold-SB13
NHL Scrapbook Quantum Silver-SB13
99Upper Deck Century Legends-67
Century Collection-67
99Upper Deck Gold Reserve-158
99Upper Deck Gold Reserve-269
99Upper Deck HoloGrFx-44
Ausome-44
99Upper Deck MVP-148
Gold Script-148
Silver Script-148
Super Script-148
99Upper Deck MVP SC Edition-132
Gold Script-132
Silver Script-132
Super Script-132
Clutch Performers-CP8
Game-Used Souvenirs-GUJC
Great Combinations-GCLL
Great Combinations Parallel-GCLL
Second Season Snipers-SS8
Stanley Cup Talent-SC13
99Upper Deck Ovation-42
Standing Ovation-42
Lead Performers-LP6
99Upper Deck Retro-58
Gold-58
Platinum-58
99Upper Deck Victory-211
99Upper Deck Victory-330
99Wayne Gretzky Hockey-123
Will to Win-W8
99Slovakian Challengers-29
00SP Authentic Autographed Replica Jersey-3
00Aurora-107
Pinstripes-107
Pinstripes Premiere Date-107
Premiere Date-107
Canvas Creations-8
Championship Fever-18
Championship Fever-NNO
Championship Fever Copper-18
Championship Fever Copper-NNO
Championship Fever Platinum Blue-18
Championship Fever Platinum Blue-NNO
Championship Fever Silver-18
Championship Fever Silver-NNO
Scouting Reports-17
Styrotechs-8A
00BAP Memorabilia-111
Emerald-111
Ruby-111
Sapphire-111
Promos-111
Jersey Cards-J32
Jersey Emblems-E32
Jersey Numbers-N32
Jersey and Stick Cards-JS32
Patent Power Jerseys-PP6
00BAP Mem Chicago Sportsfest Copper-111
00BAP Memorabilia Chicago Sportsfest Blue-111
00BAP Memorabilia Chicago Sportsfest Gold-111
00BAP Memorabilia Chicago Sportsfest Ruby-111
00BAP Memorabilia Chicago Sun-Times Ruby-111
00BAP Memorabilia Chicago Sun-Times Gold-111
00BAP Mem Chicago Sun-Times Sapphire-111
00BAP Mem Toronto Fall Expo Copper-111
00BAP Memorabilia Toronto Fall Expo Gold-111
00BAP Memorabilia Toronto Fall Expo Ruby-111
00BAP Parkhurst 2000-P69
00BAP Signature Series-184
Emerald-184
Ruby-184
Sapphire-184
Autographs-87
Autographs Gold-87
Franchise Players-F22
Jersey Cards-J7
Jersey and Stick Cards-GSJ7
Jersey Cards Autographs-J7
Jersey Emblems-E7
Jersey Numbers-IN7
00BAP Ultimate Memorabilia Autographs-7
Gold-7
00BAP Ultimate Mem Game-Used Jerseys-GJ7
00BAP Ultimate Mem Game-Used Emblems-E5
00BAP Ultimate Mem Game-Used Numbers-N5
00BAP Ultimate Mem Game-Used Sticks-GS7
00BAP Ultimate Memorabilia Teammates-TM29
00Black Diamond-43
Gold-43
Diamonation-IG6
Diamond Might-FP8
Diamond Skills-IC5
00Crown Royale-80
Ice Blue-80
Limited Series-80
Premiere Date-80
Red-80
Game-Worn Jerseys-20
Game-Worn Jersey Patches-20
Premium-Sized Game-Worn Jerseys-20
Jewels of the Crown-19
Now Playing-13
00Kraft-10
00McDonald's Pacific-25
Blue-25
00O-Pee-Chee-7
00O-Pee-Chee Parallel-7
00Pacific-300
Copper-300
Gold-300
Ice Blue-300
Premiere Date-300
Autographs-300
Gold Crown Die Cuts-23
North American Stars-9
Reflections-15
00Panini Stickers-74
00Paramount-182
Copper-182
Gold-182
Holo-Gold-182
Holo-Silver-182
Ice Blue-182
Premiere Date-182
Epic Scope-16
Freeze Frame-26
Hall of Fame Bound-9
Hall of Fame Bound Canvas Proofs-9
Hall of Fame Bound Proofs-9
00Private Stock-73
Gold-73
Premiere Date-73
Retail-73
Silver-73
Artist's Canvas-16
Artist's Canvas Proofs-16
Extreme Action-15
Game Gear-83
Game Gear Patches-83
PS-2001 Action-42
PS-2001 Stars-19
Reserve-16
00Revolution-109
Blue-109
Premiere Date-109
Red-109
HD NHL-25
Ice Immortals-15
NHL Icons-16
Stat Masters-8
00SP Authentic-64
BuyBacks-83
BuyBacks-84
BuyBacks-85
BuyBacks-86
BuyBacks-87
BuyBacks-88
BuyBacks-89
BuyBacks-90
Parents' Scrapbook-PS6
Sign of the Times-JL
Sign of the Times-LMB
Special Forces-SF5
00SP Game Used-45
Patch Cards-P-JL
Tools of the Game-JL
Tools of the Game Exclusives-JL
Tools of the Game Combos-C-LB
Tools of the Game Autographed Bronze-A-JL
Tools of the Game Autographed Silver-A-JL
Tools of the Game Autographed Gold-A-JL
00SPx-51
00SPx-75
00SPx-89
Spectrum-51
Spectrum-75
Spectrum-89
Prolifics-P6
SPXtreme-S6
Winning Materials-JL
Winning Materials-WLE
Winning Materials Autographs-SJL
00Stadium Club-36
Capture the Action-CA8
Capture the Action Game View-8
Special Forces-SF9
00Titanium-70
Blue-70
Gold-70
Premiere Date-70
Red-70
Retail-70
Game Gear-42
Game Gear-122
Game Gear Patches-122
00Titanium Draft Day Edition-73
Patches-73
00Topps/OPC-7
Parallel-7
Autographs-AJL
Combos-TC3
Combos Jumbos-TC3
00Topps Chrome-7
OPC Refractors-7
Refractors-7
Combos-TC3
Combos Refractors-TC3
Rocket's Flare-RF3
Rocket's Flare Refractors-RF3
00Topps Gold Label Class 1-56
Gold-56
00Topps Gold Label Class 2-56
00Topps Gold Label Class 2 Gold-56
00Topps Gold Label Class 3-56
00Topps Gold Label Class 3 Gold-56
00Topps Gold Label Game-Worn Jerseys-GLJ-JL
00Topps Gold Label Golden Greats-GG4
00Topps Gold Label Golden Greats 1 to 1-GG4
00Topps Heritage-30
Chrome Parallel-30
Heroes-HH13
00Topps Premier Plus-54
Blue Ice-54
Club Signings-CS-3
Club Signings-CSC-2
Team-PT3
Team Blue Ice-PR3
World Premier-WP10
00Topps Stars-9
Blue-9
All-Star Authority-ASA11
Walk of Fame-WF9
00UD Heroes-153
Game-Used Twigs-T-JL
Game-Used Twigs Gold-C-FL
NHL Leaders-L7
Second Season Heroes-SS9
Signs of Greatness-JL
Today's Snipers-TS4
00UD Pros and Prospects-62
Game Jersey Autograph Exclusives-S-JL
Game Jersey Autographs-S-JL
Great Skates-GS7
NHL Passion-NP5
ProMotion-PM8
00UD Reserve-62
Buyback Autographs-104
Buyback Autographs-105
Buyback Autographs-106
Buyback Autographs-107
Buyback Autographs-108
Buyback Autographs-109
Buyback Autographs-110
Buyback Autographs-111
Buyback Autographs-112
Practice Session Jerseys-JL
Practice Session Jerseys Autographs-JL
The Big Ticket-BT8
00Upper Deck-126
Exclusives Tier 1-126
Exclusives Tier 2-126
e-Cards-EC5
e-Card Prizes-AJL
e-Card Prizes-EJL
e-Card Prizes-SEJL
Fantastic Finishers-FF7
Game Jerseys-JL
Game Jersey Autographs-HJL
Game Jersey Autographs Exclusives-EJL
Game Jersey Autographs Exclusives-ESJL
Game Jersey Combos-DLC
Game Jersey Patches-JLP
Game Jersey Patches-PJL
Game Jersey Patch Autographs Exclusives-JLP
Game Jersey Patch Autographs Exclusives-PSJL
Game Jersey Patch Exclusives Series II-EJL
Gate Attractions-GA9
Number Crunchers-NC3
Profiles-P7
Skilled Stars-SS15
Triple Threat-TT4
UD Flashback-UD6
00Upper Deck Ice-30
Immortals-30
Legends-30
Stars-30
Champions-IC5
Gallery-IG6
Game Jerseys-JCJL
Rink Favorites-FP8
00Upper Deck Legends-100
00Upper Deck Legends-101
Legendary Collection Bronze-100
Legendary Collection Bronze-101
Legendary Collection Gold-100
Legendary Collection Gold-101
Legendary Collection Silver-100
Legendary Collection Silver-101
Epic Signatures-JL
Legendary Game Jerseys-JJL
00Upper Deck MVP-124
First Stars-124
Game-Used Souvenirs-GSJL
Second Stars-124
Super Game-Used Souvenirs-GSJL
Talent-M13
Third Stars-124
Top Draws-TD8
00Upper Deck Victory-166
00Upper Deck Victory-167
00Upper Deck Victory-253
00Upper Deck Victory-314
00Upper Deck Vintage-260
00Upper Deck Vintage-271
00Upper Deck Vintage-272
All UD Team-UD6
National Heroes-NH17
Star Tandems-S5A
00Vanguard-73
High Voltage-25
High Voltage Gold-25
High Voltage Green-25
High Voltage Red-25
High Voltage Silver-25
Holographic Gold-73
Holographic Purple-73
In Focus-14
Pacific Proofs-73
01McFarlane Hockey-40
01Atomic-72
Blue-72
Gold-72
Premiere Date-72
Red-72
Core Players-14
Power Play-26
01BAP Memorabilia-266
Emerald-266
Ruby-266
Sapphire-266
All-Star Jersey Doubles-DASJ24
All-Star Teammates-AST33
Country of Origin-CO58
01BAP Signature Series Certified 100-C17
01BAP Signature Series Certified 50-C17
01BAP Signature Series Certified 1 of 1's-C17
01BAP Signature Series Autographs-LJL
01BAP Signature Series Autographs Gold-LJL
01BAP Signature Series Franchise Jerseys-FP-22
01BAP Sig Series He Shoots/Scores Points-4
01BAP Sig Series He Shoots/Scores Prizes-18
01BAP Sig Series International Medals-IS-5
01BAP Signature Series Jerseys-GJ-49
01BAP Signature Series Jersey Autographs-GUJL
01BAP Sig Series Jersey and Stick Cards-GSJ-49
01BAP Signature Series Emblems-GUE-48
01BAP Signature Series Numbers-ITN-48
01BAP Signature Series Teammates-TM-23
01BAP Ultimate Memorabilia Autographs-12
01BAP Ultimate Mem Autographs Gold-12
01BAP Ultimate Memorabilia Dynamic Duos-2
01BAP Ultimate Memorabilia Gloves Are Off-20
01BAP Ultimate Memorabilia Jerseys-3
01BAP Ultimate Mem Jerseys and Sticks-3
01BAP Ultimate Memorabilia Emblems-3
01BAP Ultimate Memorabilia Numbers-2
01BAP Ultimate Memorabilia Name Plates-32
01Bowman YoungStars-65
Gold-65
Ice Cubed-65
01Crown Royale-107
Blue-107
Premiere Date-107
Red-107
Retail-107
01eTopps-9
01Flyers Postcards-11
01McDonald's Pacific-29
01O-Pee-Chee-42
01O-Pee-Chee Heritage Parallel-42
01O-Pee-Chee Heritage Parallel Limited-42
01O-Pee-Chee Premier Parallel-42
01Pacific-289
Extreme LTD-289
Hobby LTD-289
Premiere Date-289
Retail LTD-289
01Pacific Adrenaline-140
Blue-140
Premiere Date-140
Red-140
Retail-140
Jerseys-32
World Beaters-14
01Pacific Arena Exclusives-289
01Pacific Heads-Up-72
Blue-72
Premiere Date-72
Red-72
Silver-72
Quad Jerseys-15
01Parkhurst-95
Gold-95
Silver-95
He Shoots-He Scores Prizes-14
Jerseys-PJ22
Jersey and Stick-PSJ18
Sticks-PS22
Teammates-T13
Waving the Flag-27
01Private Stock-72
Gold-72
Premiere Date-72
Retail-72
Silver-72
Game Gear-71
Game Gear Patches-71
01Private Stock Pacific Nights-72
01Private Stock PS-2002-54
01Private Stock Reserve-S13
01SP Authentic-61
01SP Authentic-104
Limited-61
Limited-104
Limited Gold-61
Limited Gold-104
Buybacks-11
Buybacks-12
Jerseys-NNJL
Sign of the Times-JL
Sign of the Times-LR
01SP Game Used-38
Authentic Fabric-AFJL
Authentic Fabric-DFLB
Authentic Fabric-DFPL
Authentic Fabric-TFLRP
Authentic Fabric Gold-AFJL
Inked Sweaters-SJL
Inked Sweaters-ISJL
Inked Sweaters-DSLG
Inked Sweaters-DSLK
Patches-PJL
Patches-CPHL
Patches-CPLP
Patches-TPSLS
Patches Signed-SPJL
Patches Signed-DSPBL
Tools of the Game-TLE
Tools of the Game-CTLJ
Tools of the Game-TTFSL
Tools of the Game Signed-STJL
Tools of the Game Signed-STLE
Tools of the Game Signed-SCLT
01SPx-49
01SPx-88
Hockey Treasures-HTJL
Hockey Treasures-HTLE
Hockey Treasures Autographed-STJL
Hockey Treasures Autographed-STLE
Signs of Xcellence-JL
01Stadium Club-84
Award Winners-84
Master Photos-84
Gallery-G18
Gallery Gold-G18
NHL Passport-NHLP15
Perennials-P6
01Titanium-105
Hobby Parallel-105
Premiere Date-105
Retail-105
Retail Parallel-105
Double-Sided Jerseys-50
Double-Sided Jerseys-51
Double-Sided Patches-50
Double-Sided Patches-51
01Titanium Draft Day Edition-71
01Topps-42
Heritage Parallel-42
Heritage Parallel Limited-42
OPC Parallel-42
Shot Masters-SM15
01Topps Chrome-42
Refractors-42
Black Border Refractors-42
01Topps Heritage-10
Refractors-10
Jerseys-JL
01Topps Reserve-32
Emblems-JL
Jerseys-JL
Name Plates-JL
Numbers-JL
Patches-JL
01UD Challenge for the Cup-61
Jerseys-FPJL
Jerseys-UCLB
Jersey Autographs-UCLG
01UD Honor Roll-97
Jerseys-J-JL
Jerseys Gold-J-JL
01UD Mask Collection-71
Gold-71
01UD Playmakers-71
Combo Jerseys-CJJL
Combo Jerseys Gold-CJJL
Practice Jerseys-PJJL
Practice Jerseys Gold-PJJL
01UD Premier Collection-38
Jerseys-BJL
Jerseys Black-B-JL
Signatures-JL
Signatures Black-JL
01UD Stanley Cup Champs-66
01UD Top Shelf-112
Jerseys-JL
Jersey Autographs-JL
Sticks-SJL
Sticks Gold-SJL
01Upper Deck-220
01Upper Deck-356
01Upper Deck-410
Exclusives-220
Exclusives-356
Exclusives-410
Fantastic Finishers-FF5
Franchise Cornerstones-FC14
Game Jerseys Series II-FJJL
Game Jerseys Series II-PFJL
Game Jersey Autographs-SJL
Game Jersey Autographs-SJJL
Gate Attractions-GA4
Patches-PJL
Patches Series II-PNJL
Patches Series II-NAJL
Pride of a Nation-DPLM
Shooting Stars-SS12
Skilled Stars-SS19
Tandems-T7
01Upper Deck Ice-112
Combos-C-JL
Combos Gold-G-JL
Jerseys-J-JL
01Upper Deck MVP-140
Morning Skate Jerseys-J-JL
Morning Skate Jerseys-J-JO
Morning Skate Jersey Autographs-SJ-JL
Souvenirs-S-JL
Souvenirs Gold-S-JL
Talent-MT12
01Upper Deck Victory-254
01Upper Deck Victory-399
Gold-254
Gold-399
01Upper Deck Vintage-186
01Upper Deck Vintage-191
01Vanguard-73
Blue-73
Red-73
One of Ones-73
Premiere Date-73
Proofs-73
01Czech Stadion-324
02Atomic Jerseys-17
02Atomic Jerseys Gold-17
02Atomic Patches-17
02BAP All-Star Edition-48
He Shoots-He Scores Prizes-12
Jerseys-48
Jerseys Gold-48
Jerseys Silver-48
02BAP First Edition-51
Jerseys-51

02BAP Memorabilia-112
02BAP Memorabilia-250
Emerald-112
Emerald-250
Ruby-112
Ruby-250
Sapphire-112
Sapphire-250
All-Star Jerseys-ASJ-29
All-Star Triple Jerseys-ASTJ-8
Mini Stanley Cups-31
NHL All-Star Game-112
NHL All-Star Game-250
NHL All-Star Game Blue-112
NHL All-Star Game Blue-250
NHL All-Star Game Green-112
NHL All-Star Game Green-250
NHL All-Star Game Red-112
NHL All-Star Game Red-250
02BAP Memorabilia Toronto Fall Expo-112
02BAP Memorabilia Toronto Fall Expo-250
02BAP Signature Series-113
Autographs-113
Autograph Buybacks 1998-250
Autograph Buybacks 1999-179
Autograph Buybacks 2000-87
Autograph Buybacks 2001-LJL
Autographs Gold-113
Jerseys-SGJ26
Jersey Autographs-SGJ26
Team Quads-TQ3
02BAP Ultimate Memorabilia Emblems-24
02BAP Ultimate Memorabilia Hat Tricks-2
02BAP Ultimate Memorabilia Jerseys-18
02BAP Ultimate Memorabilia Numbers-12
02BAP Ultimate Mem Storied Franchise-6
02Bowman YoungStars-9
Gold-9
Silver-9
02Crown Royale-71
Blue-71
Red-71
Retail-71
02Flyers Postcards-4
02ITG Used-56
02ITG Used-156
Jerseys-GUJ26
Jersey Autographs-GUJ26
Jerseys Gold-GUJ26
Emblems-E26
Jersey and Stick-SJ26
Jersey and Stick Gold-SJ26
Teammates-T15
Teammates Gold-T15
Triple Memorabilia-TM6
Triple Memorabilia Gold-TM6
02O-Pee-Chee-7
02O-Pee-Chee Premier Blue Parallel-7
02O-Pee-Chee Premier Red Parallel-7
02O-Pee-Chee Factory Set-7
02Pacific-282
Blue-282
Red-282
02Pacific Complete-129
Red-129
02Pacific Exclusive-127
02Pacific Heads-Up-91
Blue-91
Purple-91
Red-91
02Parkhurst-66
Bronze-66
Gold-66
Silver-66
He Shoots-He Scores Prizes-23
Jerseys-GJ8
Stick and Jerseys-SJ8
Teammates-TT2
02Parkhurst Retro-109
Minis-109
Jerseys-RJ25
02Private Stock Reserve-74
Blue-74
Red-74
Retail-74
02SP Authentic-68
Beckett Promos-68
Sign of the Times-JL
Sign of the Times-GL
Sign of the Times-LW
02SP Game Used Authentic Fabrics-AFJL
02SP Game Used Authentic Fabrics-CFTL
02SP Game Used Authentic Fabrics Gold-AFJL
02SP Game Used Authentic Fabrics Gold-CFTL
02SP Game Used Authentic Fabrics Rainbow-AFJL
02SP Game Used Authentic Fabrics Rainbow-CFTL
02SP Game Used Piece of History-PHJL
02SP Game Used Piece of History Gold-PHJL
02SP Game Used Piece of History Rainbow-PHJL
02SP Game Used Signature Style-JL
02SP Game Used Tools of the Game-JL
02SPx-96
Spectrum Gold-96
Spectrum Silver-96
Winning Materials-WMLE
Winning Materials Gold-LE
Winning Materials Silver-LE
Xtreme Talents-JL
Xtreme Talents Gold-JL
Xtreme Talents Silver-JL
02Stadium Club-77
Silver Decoy Cards-77
Proofs-77
02Titanium Jerseys-52
02Titanium Jerseys Retail-52
02Topps-7
OPC Blue Parallel-7
OPC Red Parallel-7
Captain's Cloth-CC2
Topps/OPC Hometown Heroes-HHU11
Factory Set-7
Factory Set Hometown Heroes-HHU11
02Topps Chrome-7
Black Border Refractors-7
Refractors-7
02Topps Heritage-76
Chrome Parallel-76
02Topps Total-228
Team Checklists-TTC22
02UD Artistic Impressions-64
Gold-64
02UD Artistic Impressions Beckett Promos-64
02UD Artistic Impressions Performers-SSJL
02UD Artistic Impressions Performers Gold-SSJL
02UD Artistic Impressions Retrospectives-R64
02UD Artistic Impressions Retrospect Gold-R64
02UD Artistic Impress Retrospect Silver-R64
02UD Honor Roll-53
Signature Class-JL
Team Warriors-TW11
02UD Mask Collection-63
02UD Mask Collection Beckett Promos-63
02UD Premier Collection-41
Signatures Bronze-SJL
Signatures Gold-SJL
Signatures Silver-SJL
02UD Top Shelf-65
Milestones Jerseys-MLNLA
Signatures-JL
Triple Jerseys-HTLRR
Triple Jerseys-TSLGC
02Upper Deck-376
Exclusives-376
02Upper Deck Beckett UD Promos-376
02Upper Deck Game Jersey Autographs-JL
02Upper Deck Game Jersey Series II-GJJL
02Upper Deck Patchwork-PWJL
02Upper Deck Playbooks Series II-LW
02Upper Deck Reaching Fifty-50JL
02Upper Deck Reaching Fifty Gold-50JL
02Upper Deck Classic Portraits-71
Hockey Royalty-LRR
Hockey Royalty Limited-LRR
02Upper Deck MVP-133
Gold-133
Classics-133
Golden Classics-133
Skate Around Jerseys-SAJL
Skate Around Jerseys-SDDL
Skate Around Jerseys-SDLC
Skate Around Jerseys-SDLP
Skate Around Jerseys-STLPR
02Upper Deck Rookie Update-73
02Upper Deck Rookie Update-149C
02Upper Deck Rookie Update-150C
02Upper Deck Rookie Update-152A
02Upper Deck Rookie Update-159A
02Upper Deck Rookie Update-160A
Autographs-JL
02Upper Deck Victory-158
Bronze-158
Gold-158
Silver-158
02Upper Deck Vintage-188
Green Backs-188
Jerseys-SOJL
Jerseys Gold-SO-JL
02Vanguard-74
LTD-74
East Meets West-5
Jerseys-33
Jerseys Gold-33
02UD SuperStars City AS Dual Jersey-JLDS
03BAP Memorabilia-43
Emerald-43
Gold-43
Ruby-43
Sapphire-43
All-Star Emblems-ASE-18
All-Star Jerseys-ASJ-33
All-Star Numbers-ASN-18
Jersey and Stick-SJ-18
03BAP Ultimate Memorabilia Autographs-65
Gold-65
03BAP Ultimate Mem Auto Jerseys-65
03BAP Ultimate Mem Auto Emblems-65
03BAP Ultimate Mem Franch Present Future-22
03BAP Ultimate Memorabilia Gloves Are Off-10
03BAP Ultimate Memorabilia Hat Tricks-18
03BAP Ultimate Memorabilia Jerseys-30
03BAP Ultimate Memorabilia Jerseys Gold-30
03BAP Ultimate Memorabilia Linemates-2
03BAP Ultimate Mem Linemates Autos-8
03BAP Ultimate Memorabilia Triple Threads-25
03Beehive-140
Gold-140
Silver-140
Sticks Blue Border-BL7
03Black Diamond-68
Black-68
Green-68
Red-68
Signature Gems-SG-16
03Flyers Postcards-13
03ITG Action-433
Jerseys-M163
Jerseys-M224
03ITG Used Signature Series-61
Gold-61
Autographs-JL
Autographs Gold-JL
Game-Day Jerseys-9
Game-Day Jerseys Gold-9
Jerseys-18
Jerseys Gold-18
Jersey Autos-18
Emblems-36
Emblems Gold-36
Teammates-2
Teammates Gold-2
03NHL Sticker Collection-104
03O-Pee-Chee-167
03OPC Blue-167
03OPC Gold-167
03OPC Red-167
03Pacific-254
Blue-254
Red-254
Main Attractions-11
03Pacific Atlantic City National-1
03Pacific Complete-169
Red-169
03Pacific Exhibit-185
Blue Backs-185
03Pacific Invincible-74
Blue-74
Red-74
Retail-74
03Pacific Prism-76
Blue-76
Gold-76
Red-76
03Pacific Supreme-74
Blue-74
Red-74
Retail-74
03Parkhurst Original Six Montreal-32
Memorabilia-MM55
03Private Stock Reserve-76
Blue-76
Red-76
Retail-76
03SP Authentic Sign of the Times-JLC
03SP Game Used Authentic Fabrics-QARGL
03SP Game Used Authentic Fabrics Gold-QARGL
03SP Game Used Team Threads-TTARL
03SP Game Used Top Threads-ARGL
03SPx-70
Radiance-70
Spectrum-70
Fantasy Franchise-FF-LRA
Fantasy Franchise Limited-FF-LRA
Signature Threads-ST-JL
03Titanium-202
Patches-202
03Topps-167
Blue-167
Gold-167
Red-167
Topps/OPC Idols-UI11
Pristine Patches-PP-JL
Pristine Patch Refractors-PP-JL
Pristine Popular Demand Relics-PD-JL
Pristine Popular Demand Relic Refractor-PD-JL
Pristine Stick Portions-PPS-JL
Pristine Stick Portion Refractors-PPS-JL
03UD Honor Roll-62
Signature Class-SC17
03Upper Deck-386
BuyBacks-52
BuyBacks-53
BuyBacks-54
Canadian Exclusives-386
HG-386
UD Exclusives-386
03Upper Deck Classic Portraits-72
Hockey Royalty-RLA
03Upper Deck MVP-313
Gold Script-313
Silver Script-313
Canadian Exclusives-313
Lethal Lineups-LL2
Souvenirs-S10
SportsNut-SN66
03Upper Deck Rookie Update Super Stars-SSJL
03Upper Deck Rookie Update Top Draws-TD16
03Upper Deck Trilogy-72
Authentic Patches-AP26
Limited-72
Scripts-S2JL
Scripts Limited-S2JL
03Upper Deck Victory-141
Bronze-141
Gold-141
Silver-141
Freshman Flashback-FF33
Game Breakers-GB26
03Toronto Star-70
04Pacific-195
Blue-195
Red-195
Philadelphia-11
04SP Authentic-135
04UD Toronto Fall Expo Priority Signings-JL
04Ultimate Collection Dual Logos-UL2-LP
04Upper Deck Jersey Autographs-GJA-JL
05Black Diamond-108
Emerald-108
Gold-108
Onyx-108
Ruby-108
05Panini Stickers-148
05Parkhurst-386
Facsimile Auto Parallel-386
True Colors-TCPIT
True Colors-TCPIT
True Colors-TCPHPI
True Colors-TCPHPI
05SP Game Used-78
Gold-78
Authentic Fabrics Quad-TRGL
Authentic Patches Quad -PRLL
Authentic Patches Quad -TRGL
Awesome Authentics-AA-JL
Awesome Authentics Gold-DA-JL
05SPx Winning Combos-WC-LF
05SPx Winning Combos Gold-WC-LF
05SPx Winning Combos Gold-WC-LL
05SPx Winning Combos Spectrum-WC-LF
05SPx Winning Combos Spectrum-WC-LL
05SPx Winning Materials-WM-JL
05SPx Winning Materials Gold-WM-JL
05SPx Winning Materials Spectrum-WM-JL
05The Cup Master Pressplate Rookie Update-239
05UD PowerPlay-66
Rainbow-66
Specialists-TSJL
Specialists Patches-SPJL
05UD Toronto Fall Expo Priority Signings-PS-JL
05Ultra-157
Gold-157
Ice-157
05Upper Deck-399
Big Playmakers-B-JL
Patches-P-JLE
Shooting Stars-S-JL
05Upper Deck Hockey Showcase-HS38
05Upper Deck Showcase Promos-HS38
05Upper Deck MVP-310
Gold-310
Platinum-310
Materials-M-JL
05Upper Deck Trilogy Honorary Patches-HP-JL
05Upper Deck Tril Honorary Patch Script-HSP-JL
05Upper Deck Trilogy Honorary Swatches-HS-JL
05Upper Deck Tril Honorary Swatch Scripts-HSS-JL
05Upper Deck Trilogy Scripts-SCS-JL
05Upper Deck Victory-143
05Upper Deck Victory-241
Black-143
Black-241
Gold-143
Gold-241
Silver-143
Silver-241
Stars on Ice-SI33
06Be A Player Portraits Signature Portraits-SPLE
06Fleer-159
Tiffany-159
06O-Pee-Chee-403
Rainbow-403
06Panini Stickers-141
06SP Game Used By The Letter-BLLC
06The Cup NHL Shields Duals-DSHRL
06UD Artifacts Tundra Tandems-TTLM
06UD Artifacts Tundra Tandems Black-TTLM
06UD Artifacts Tundra Tandems Blue-TTLM
06UD Artifacts Tundra Tandems Gold-TTLM
06UD Artifacts Tundra Tandems Platinum-TTLM
06UD Artifacts Tundra Tandems Red-TTLM
06UD Artifacts Tundra Tandems Dual Patches Red-TTLM
06Ultra-159
Gold Medallion-159
Ice Medallion-159
06Upper Deck-157
Exclusives Parallel-157
High Gloss Parallel-157
Masterpieces-157
06Upper Deck MVP-236
Gold Script-236
Super Script-236
Jerseys-OJSL
06Upper Deck Ovation-89

Leclair, Nelson
67Columbus Checkers-9

Leclair, Steve
93Quebec Pee-Wee Tournament-930

Leclaire, Pascal
96Quebec Pee-Wee Tournament-328
98Halifax Mooseheads-2
98Halifax Mooseheads Second Edition-22
99Halifax Mooseheads-2
99UD Prospects-88
00Halifax Mooseheads-13
00UD CHL Prospects-79
00UD CHL Prospects-90
Autographs-A-PL
CHL Class-CC9
Destination the Show-D6
Great Desire-GD6
Supremacy-CS10
01BAP Memorabilia Draft Redemptions-8
01UD Prospects Autographs-A-PL
02BAP First Edition-432H
02BAP Memorabilia-350
02BAP Ultimate Memorabilia-43
02Between the Pipes-108
Gold-108
Silver-108
02Crown Royale-108
Blue-108
Purple-108
Red-108
Retail-108
02Pacific Calder-111
Silver-111
Reflections-7
02Pacific Complete-576
Red-576
02Pacific Quest for the Cup-112
Gold-112
Calder Contenders-5
02Parkhurst-215
Bronze-215
Gold-215
Silver-215
02Parkhurst Retro-206
Minis-206
02SP Authentic-185
02SPx-176
02Titanium-110
Blue-110
Red-110
Retail-110
02UD Artistic Impressions-96
Gold-96
Common Ground-CG1
Common Ground-CG22
Common Ground Gold-CG1
Common Ground Gold-CG22
Retrospectives-R96
Retrospectives Gold-R96
Retrospectives Signed-R96
Retrospectives Silver-R96
02UD Foundations-165
02UD Honor Roll-111
02UD Mask Collection-113
02UD Premier Collection-74
Gold-74
Jerseys Bronze-PL
Jerseys Bronze-PA
Jerseys Gold-PL
Jerseys Gold-PA
Jerseys Silver-PL
Jerseys Silver-PA
02Upper Deck Classic Portraits-132
02Upper Deck Rookie Update-170
02Vanguard-108
LTD-108
02AHL Top Prospects-24
02Syracuse Crunch-2
02Syracuse Crunch Sheets-15
03BAP Memorabilia-150
Emerald-150
Gold-150
Ruby-150
Sapphire-150
03ITG Action-115
03Pacific-94
Blue-94
Red-94
03Pacific Calder Contenders Entry Draft-5
03Pacific Complete-426
Red-426
03Pacific Montreal Olympic Stadium Show-2
Gold-2
03SP Authentic Sign of the Times-PL
03SP Authentic Sign of the Times-NL
03SP Game Used Authentic Fabrics-DFBP
03SP Game Used Authentic Fabrics Gold-DFBP
03SPx Big Futures-BF-PL
03SPx Big Futures Limited-BF-PL
03Topps Traded-TT74
Blue-TT74
Gold-TT74
Red-TT74
03Upper Deck-53
Canadian Exclusives-53
HG-53
Rookie Update Top Draws-TD12
Trilogy Scripts-S1PL
Trilogy Scripts Limited-S1PL
Trilogy Scripts Red-S1PL
03AHL Top Prospects-18
03Pacific AHL Prospects-86
Gold-86
Autographs-6
Crease Lightning-8
03Syracuse Crunch-20
04Syracuse Crunch-20
04ITG Heroes and Prospects-7
Autographs-PL
Combos-9
He Shoots-He Scores Prizes-14
Net Prospects-26
Net Prospects Gold-26
04ITG Heroes/Prospects Toronto Expo '05-7
04ITG Heroes/Prospects Expo Heroes/Pros-7
05ITG Heroes/Prosp Toronto Expo Parallel -89
05Parkhurst-148
Facsimile Auto Parallel-148
05SP Authentic Scripts to Success-SSPL
05SP Authentic Sign of the Times-PL
05SP Game Used Statscriptions-ST-PL
05UD Powerplay Specialists-TSLC
05UD Powerplay Specialists Patches-SPLC
05Upper Deck-300
Notable Numbers-N-PLE
05Upper Deck Victory-59
Black-59
Gold-59
Silver-59
05ITG Heroes and Prospects-89
Autographs-A-PL
Complete Logos-AHL-4
He Shoots-He Scores Prizes-26
Jerseys-GUJ-12
Jerseys Gold-GUJ-12
Emblems-GUE-12
Emblems Gold-GUE-12
Numbers-GUN-12
Numbers Gold-GUN-12
Net Prospects-NP-6
Net Prospects Dual-NPD5
Net Prospects Dual Gold-NPD5
Net Prospects Gold-NP-06
06Be A Player Portraits-32
06Beehive-72
06Beehive-212
Blue-72
Matte-72
Red Facsimile Signatures-72
Wood-72
06Between The Pipes-72
Autographs-APL
Emblems-GUE39
Emblems Gold-GUE39
Emblems Autographs-GUE39
Jerseys-GUJ39
Jerseys Gold-GUJ39
Jerseys Autographs-GUJ39
Numbers-GUN39
Numbers Gold-GUN39
Numbers Autographs-GUN39
Prospect Trios-PT02
Prospect Trios Gold-PT02
06Black Diamond-24
Black-24
Gold-24
Ruby-24
06Flair Showcase Hot Gloves-HG21
06Fleer-59
Tiffany-59
06Hot Prospects-31
Red Hot-31
White Hot-31
06O-Pee-Chee-149
06O-Pee-Chee-634
Rainbow-149
Rainbow-634
Swatches-S-PL
06Panini Stickers-238
06SP Authentic-73
Limited-73
06SP Game Used-30
Gold-30
Rainbow-30
Authentic Fabrics-AFPL
Authentic Fabrics Parallel-AFPL
Authentic Fabrics Patches-AFPL
Authentic Fabrics Dual-AF2LC
Authentic Fabrics Dual Patches-AF2LC
Authentic Fabrics Triple-AF3CLB
Authentic Fabrics Triple Patches-AF3CLB
06The Cup NHL Shields Duals-DSHNL
06UD Artifacts Tundra Tandems-TTPT
06UD Artifacts Tundra Tandems Black-TTPT
06UD Artifacts Tundra Tandems Blue-TTPT
06UD Artifacts Tundra Tandems Gold-TTPT
06UD Artifacts Tundra Tandems Platinum-TTPT
06UD Artifacts Tundra Tandems Red-TTPT
06UD Artifacts Tundra Tandems Dual Patches Red-TTPT
06UD Powerplay-31
Impact Rainbow-31
06Ultimate Collection Jerseys Dual-UJ2-NL
06Ultimate Collection Patches Dual-UJ2-NL
06Ultimate Collection Premium Patches-PS-PL
06Ultimate Collection Premium Swatches-PS-PL
06Upper Deck Arena Giveaways-CLB2
06Upper Deck-56
Exclusives Parallel-56
High Gloss Parallel-56
Masterpieces-56
06Upper Deck MVP-84
Gold Script-84
Super Script-84
06Upper Deck Ovation-115
06Upper Deck Sweet Shot-33
Sweet Stitches-SSPL
Sweet Stitches Duals-SSPL
Sweet Stitches Triples-SSPL
06Upper Deck Trilogy-28
06Upper Deck Victory-59
06Upper Deck Victory Black-59
06Upper Deck Victory Gold-59
06ITG Heroes and Prospects Making The Bigs-MTB06
06ITG Heroes and Prospects Making The Bigs Gold-MTB06
07Upper Deck Ovation-35
07Upper Deck Victory-128
Black-128
Gold-128

Leclerc, Francis
93Quebec Pee-Wee Tournament-1397

Leclerc, Jean
52Juniors Blue Tint-43

Leclerc, Justin
05Lethbridge Hurricanes-15
06Between The Pipes-29
Autographs-AJL

Leclerc, Marc-Andre
00OCN Blizzard-2
01OCN Blizzard-26

LeClerc, Martin-Benoit
93Quebec Pee-Wee Tournament-7

Leclerc, Mathieu
99Rouyn-Noranda Huskies-12
00Rouyn-Noranda Huskies-12
Signed-12

LeClerc, Mike
95Brandon Wheat Kings-13
95Classic-47
95Slapshot Memorial Cup-38
97Upper Deck-181
98Bowman's Best-117
Refractors-117
Atomic Refractors-117
Mirror Image Fusion-F2
Mirror Image Fusion Refractors-F2
Mirror Image Fusion Atomic Refractors-F2
98Upper Deck-213
Exclusives-213
Exclusives 1 of 1-213
Gold Reserve-213
98Cincinnati Mighty Ducks-8
99BAP Memorabilia-170
Gold-170
Silver-170
99Pacific Prism-3
Holographic Blue-3
Holographic Gold-3
Holographic Mirror-3
Holographic Purple-3
Premiere Date-3
99Upper Deck Arena Giveaways-AM2
99Upper Deck MVP SC Edition-6
Gold Script-6
Silver Script-6
Super Script-6
99Cincinnati Mighty Ducks-22
00Titanium Game Gear-53
00Titanium Game Gear Patches-53
00Titanium Draft Day Edition-2
Patches-2
00Upper Deck-4
Exclusives Tier 1-4
Exclusives Tier 2-4
00Upper Deck Vintage-7
01BAP Signature Series-73
Autographs-73
Autographs Gold-73
01O-Pee-Chee-199
01O-Pee-Chee Premier Parallel-199
01Pacific-7
Extreme LTD-7
Hobby LTD-7
Premiere Date-7
Retail LTD-7
97-98 Subset-352
97-98 Subset Gold Parallel-352
01Pacific Arena Exclusives-7
01Pacific Heads-Up Quad Jerseys-1
01Private Stock Game Gear-3
01Private Stock Game Gear Patches-3
01Topps-199
OPC Parallel-199
01Upper Deck-3
Exclusives-3
01Upper Deck MVP-5
01Upper Deck Victory-7
Gold-7
01Upper Deck Vintage-6
01Upper Deck Vintage-9
02BAP Memorabilia-82
Emerald-82
Ruby-82
Sapphire-82
NHL All-Star Game-82
NHL All-Star Game Blue-82
NHL All-Star Game Green-82
NHL All-Star Game Red-82
02BAP Memorabilia Toronto Fall Expo-82
02BAP Sig Series Auto Buybacks 2001-73
02O-Pee-Chee-62
02O-Pee-Chee Premier Blue Parallel-62
02O-Pee-Chee Premier Red Parallel-62
02O-Pee-Chee Factory Set-62
02Pacific-5
Blue-5
Red-5
02Pacific Complete-93
Red-93
02Titanium Jerseys-1
02Titanium Jerseys Retail-1
02Titanium Patches-1
02Topps-62
OPC Blue Parallel-62
OPC Red Parallel-62
Factory Set-62
02Topps Total-25
02Upper Deck Classic Portraits-3
02Upper Deck MVP-1
Gold-1
Classics-1
Golden Classics-1
02Upper Deck Victory-7
Bronze-7
Gold-7
Silver-7
02Upper Deck Vintage-4
02Upper Deck Vintage-261
03ITG Action-64
03NHL Sticker Collection-156
03Pacific-6
Blue-6
Red-6
03Pacific Complete-75
Red-75
03Pacific Exhibit-2
Blue Backs-2
Yellow Backs-2
03Upper Deck-248
Canadian Exclusives-248
HG-248
UD Exclusives-248
05Parkhurst-83
Facsimile Auto Parallel-83

Leclerc, Paul
51Laval Dairy QSHL-80
52St. Lawrence Sales-18

Leclerc, Renald
76O-Pee-Chee WHA-28

Leclerc, Roland
52Juniors Blue Tint-79

Lecompte, Eric
917th Inn. Sketch QMJHL-217
93Quebec Pee-Wee Tournament-227
93Classic-23
93Classic Four-Sport *-205
Gold-205
94Classic-41
Gold-41
Tri-Cards-T13
95Indianapolis Ice-11
96Collector's Edge Future Legends-31
96Collector's Edge Ice-136
Prism-136
97Indianapolis Ice-14
98Cincinnati Mighty Ducks-10
02Swiss HNL-471

Lecompte, Francois
79Montreal Juniors-15

Lecompte, Vincent
93Quebec Pee-Wee Tournament-988

Lecours, Danny
81Milwaukee Admirals-10

Lecuyer, Doug
80Blackhawks White Border-7
81O-Pee-Chee-367

Lecuyer, Steve
03Indianapolis Ice-13

Ledaire, Colin
02Quebec Remparts-3

Leddy, Josh
02Tri-City Stormfront-11

Ledermann, Jorg
95Swiss HNL-502
96Swiss HNL-424
98Swiss Power Play Stickers-334
99Swiss Panini Stickers-329

Ledgard, Tom
04UK Milton Keynes Lightning-20

Ledin, Per
98Swedish UD Choice-30
02Swedish SHL-63
Parallel-63
03Swedish Elite-87
Silver-87
04Swedish Elitset-79
Gold-79
04Swedish Pure Skills-54
Parallel-54
05Swedish SHL Elitset-191
Gold-191
06Swedish SHL Elitset-51

Ledlin, Frederik
94German DEL-291

Ledock, Rene
94German DEL-140

Leduc, Albert
24Anonymous NHL-6
27La Patrie-10
27La Presse Photos-10
33O-Pee-Chee V304A-46
33V129-27
55Parkhurst-61
Quaker Oats-61
02Parkhurst Reprints-209

Leduc, Bob
72O-Pee-Chee-322
73O-Pee-Chee WHA Posters-9

Leduc, Mike
91British Columbia JHL-69

Leduc, Nicolas
05PEI Rocket-17

Leduc, Raymond
51Bas Du Fleuve-5
52Bas Du Fleuve-60

Leduc, Rich
75O-Pee-Chee WHA-113
76O-Pee-Chee WHA-41
77O-Pee-Chee WHA-13
79O-Pee-Chee-283
80Nordiques Postcards-18
80O-Pee-Chee-122
80Pepsi-Cola Caps-72
80Topps-122

Ledyard, Grant
86Kings 20th Anniversary Team Issue-12
87Panini Stickers-273
88Capitals Borderless-12
88Capitals Smokey-12
89Sabres Blue Shield-10
89Sabres Campbell's-12
90O-Pee-Chee-406
90Pro Set-24
90Sabres Blue Shield-12
90Sabres Campbell's-13
90Score-233
Canadian-233
91Bowman-40
91O-Pee-Chee-386
91Parkhurst-241
French-241
91Sabres Blue Shield-10
91Sabres Pepsi/Campbell's-10
91Score American-362
91Score Canadian Bilingual-401
91Score Canadian English-401
91Stadium Club-169
91Topps-386
92Bowman-27
92O-Pee-Chee-393
92Panini Stickers-244
92Panini Stickers French-244
92Pinnacle-205
French-205
92Sabres Blue Shield-11
92Score-358
Canadian-358
92Stadium Club-79
92Topps-321
Gold-321G
93Donruss-89
93Leaf-394
93Parkhurst-321
Emerald Ice-321
93Pinnacle-413
Canadian-413
93PowerPlay-325
93Score-568
Gold-568
Canadian-568
Canadian Gold-568
93Ultra-299
94Canada Games NHL POGS-84
94Donruss-312
94Flair-42
94Leaf-263
94OPC Premier-98
Special Effects-98
94Pinnacle-204
Artist's Proofs-204
Rink Collection-204
94Stars HockeyKaps-18
94Stars Postcards-15
94Topps/OPC Premier-98
Special Effects-98
94Ultra-54
95Be A Player-104
Signatures-S104
Signatures Die Cuts-S104
95Canada Games NHL POGS-90
95Panini Stickers-176
95Playoff One on One-141
95Topps-157
OPC Inserts-157
95Ultra-40
Gold Medallion-40
96Stars Postcards-16
97Pacific-345
Copper-345
Emerald Green-345
Ice Blue-345
Red-345
Silver-345
97Score Canucks-15
Platinum-15
Premier-15
98Pacific-84
Ice Blue-84
Red-84
00Pacific-282
Copper-282
Gold-282
Ice Blue-282
Premiere Date-282

Lee, Bill
52Juniors Blue Tint-144
06Greats of the Game Nickname Greats-BL
06Greats of the Game Nickname Greats Auto-BL

Lee, Brian
03Erie Otters-13
04Erie Otters-13
04Lincoln Stars Update-31
05Norfolk Admirals-4

Lee, Casey
04Kootenay Ice-13
05Kootenay Ice-13

Lee, Chris
04Florida Everblades-23
05Florida Everblades-19

Lee, John
93Quebec Pee-Wee Tournament-1279

Lee, Mark
03P.E.I. Rocket-11
06Hartford Wolf Pack-3

Lee, Mike
98Tri-City Americans-21
00Kootenay Ice-14
02Columbus Cottonmouths-9

Lee, Patrick
05Erie Otters-6
06Erie Otters-3

Lee, Peter
76Nova Scotia Voyageurs-9
78O-Pee-Chee-244
78Topps-244
79O-Pee-Chee-45
79Topps-45
80O-Pee-Chee-278
81O-Pee-Chee-258
81O-Pee-Chee Stickers-185
81Topps-E114
82Post Cereal-15
83NHL Key Tags-99
83Penguins Heinz Photos-16

Lee, Peter-John
04German Berlin Eisbarens 50th Anniv-61

Lee, Phil
94UK Solihul Barons-8
95UK Solihull Barons-8

Lee, Steve
77Kalamazoo Wings-11

Lee, Thomas
03Barrie Colts-1

Lee, Victor
02Russian Hockey League-8

Leeb, Brad
95Red Deer Rebels-9
96Red Deer Rebels-21
97Red Deer Rebels-9
98Red Deer Rebels-8
99Pacific Omega-240
Copper-240
Gold-240
Ice Blue-240
Premiere Date-240
99Syracuse Crunch-8
99Bowman CHL-89
Gold-89
OPC International-89
00Kansas City Blades-18
01Titanium-182
Retail-182
01Manitoba Moose-16
03Pacific Complete-568
Red-568
06Toronto Marlies-16

Leeb, Greg
94Spokane Chiefs-5
95Spokane Chiefs-15
96Spokane Chiefs-12
97Spokane Chiefs-14
97Bowman CHL-94
OPC-94
98Michigan K-Wings-8
98Bowman CHL-55
Golden Anniversary-55
OPC International-55
98Bowman Chrome CHL-55
Golden Anniversary-55
Golden Anniversary Refractors-55
OPC International-55
OPC International Refractors-55
Refractors-55
99Michigan K-Wings-13
00Utah Grizzlies-12
01Hamilton Bulldogs-9
02German DEL City Press-13
03German DEL-206
03German Nuremberg Ice Tigers Postcards-16
04German DEL-251
05German DEL-271
06German DEL-164
Team Leaders-TL6

Leef, Ron
99Fort Wayne Komets Points Leaders-14

Leefe, Erik

95Saskatoon Blades-13
Leek, Mikael
83Swedish Semic Elitserien-145
Leeman, Gary
81Regina Pats-12
82Regina Pats-14
83Canadian National Juniors-8
83Maple Leafs Postcards-13
83Regina Pats-14
84Maple Leafs Postcards-15
84O-Pee-Chee-305
85Maple Leafs Postcards-19
86Kraft Drawings-31
86Maple Leafs Postcards-16
87Maple Leafs PLAY-10
87Maple Leafs Postcards-13
87Maple Leafs Postcards Oversized-13
87O-Pee-Chee-240
87O-Pee-Chee Stickers-161
87Panini Stickers-331
88Maple Leafs PLAY-8
88O-Pee-Chee-11
88O-Pee-Chee Stickers-178
88Panini Stickers-125
88Topps-11
89Kraft-36
89O-Pee-Chee-22
89O-Pee-Chee Stickers-168
89Panini Stickers-133
89Topps-22
90Bowman-155
Tiffany-155
90Bowman Hat Tricks-10
Tiffany-10
90Kraft-27
90Maple Leafs Postcards-11
90O-Pee-Chee-135
90Panini Stickers-279
90Pro Set-283
90Score Promos-40
90Score-40
Canadian-40
90Score Hottest/Rising Stars-20
90Topps-135
Tiffany-135
Team Scoring Leaders-13
Team Scoring Leaders Tiffany-13
90Upper Deck-243
90Upper Deck-310
French-243
French-310
91Pro Set Platinum-115
91Pro Set Platinum-162
91Bowman-161
91Kraft-10
91Maple Leafs Panini Team Stickers-12
91Maple Leafs Panini Team Stickers-H
91Maple Leafs PLAY-21
91O-Pee-Chee-188
91OPC Premier-106
91OPC Premier-134
91Parkhurst-173
91Parkhurst-254
French-173
French-254
91Pinnacle-31
French-31
91Pro Set-231
French-231
91Score American-77
91Score Canadian Bilingual-77
91Score Canadian English-77
91Stadium Club-158
91Topps-188
91Upper Deck-272
91Upper Deck-528
French-272
French-528
92Bowman-192
92Flames IGA-3
92O-Pee-Chee-33
92Panini Stickers-41
92Panini Stickers French-41
92Parkhurst-323
Emerald Ice-323
92Pinnacle-184
French-184
92Score-171
Canadian-171
92Stadium Club-272
92Topps-85
Gold-85G
92Ultra-22
92Upper Deck-66
93Canadiens Postcards-15
93OPC Premier-397
Gold-397
93Score-147
Canadian-147
93Stadium Club-244
Members Only Master Set-244
OPC-244
First Day Issue-244
First Day Issue OPC-244
93Topps/OPC Premier-397
Gold-397
93Ultra-353
94Be A Player Signature Cards-73
98German DEL-188
Leeming, Bob
89Windsor Spitfires-8
Lees, Nick
01Barrie Colts-9
02Barrie Colts-8
03Saginaw Spirit-11
04Barrie Colts 10th Anniversary-18
Leetch, Brian
88O-Pee-Chee Stickers-189
88Panini Stickers-301
89O-Pee-Chee-136
89O-Pee-Chee-321
89O-Pee-Chee-326
89O-Pee-Chee Stickers-39
89O-Pee-Chee Stickers-91
89O-Pee-Chee Stickers-215
89O-Pee-Chee Stickers-240
89Panini Stickers-279
89Panini Stickers-378
89Rangers Marine Midland Bank-2
89Sports Illustrated for Kids I-116
89Topps-136
89Swedish Semic World Champ Stickers-161
90Bowman-215A
90Bowman-215B
Tiffany-215A
Tiffany-215B
90Kraft-28
90O-Pee-Chee-221
90OPC Premier-61
90Panini Stickers-95
90Pro Set-201
90Pro Set-373
90Score-225
Canadian-225
90Score Hottest/Rising Stars-93
90Score Young Superstars-2
90Topps-221
Tiffany-221
90Upper Deck-253
90Upper Deck-315
90Upper Deck-485
French-253
French-315
French-485
91Pro Set Platinum-79
91Pro Set Platinum-284
91Bowman-75
91Kraft-73
91McDonald's Upper Deck-12
91O-Pee-Chee-108
91O-Pee-Chee-215
91O-Pee-Chee-269
91OPC Premier-57
91OPC Premier-183
91Panini Stickers-284
91Parkhurst-119
91Parkhurst-438
91Parkhurst-464
91Parkhurst-471
French-119
French-438
French-464
French-471
PHC-PHC8
PHC French-PHC8
91Pinnacle-136
French-136
B-B3
B French-B3
91Pro Set-159
91Pro Set-309
French-159
French-309
91Score American-5
91Score American-333
91Score American-343
91Score Canadian Bilingual-5
91Score Canadian Bilingual-363
91Score Canadian Bilingual-373
91Score Canadian English-5
91Score Canadian English-363
91Score Canadian English-373
91Score Kellogg's-8
91Stadium Club Members Only-46
91Stadium Club-201
91Topps-108
91Topps-269
Team Scoring Leaders-4
91Upper Deck-35
91Upper Deck-153
91Upper Deck-610
91Upper Deck-612
French-35
French-153
French-610
French-612
91Finnish Semic World Champ Stickers-131
91Swedish Semic World Champ Stickers-131
92Bowman-149
92Bowman-232
92Humpty Dumpty I-14
92McDonald's Upper Deck-H4
92O-Pee-Chee-378
Trophy Winners-2
92Panini Stickers-239
92Panini Stickers French-239
92Parkhurst-110
92Parkhurst-467
Emerald Ice-110
Emerald Ice-467
92Pinnacle-15
French-15
Team Pinnacle-3
Team French-3
92Pro Set-112
Award Winners-CC4
92Score-375
92Score-416
92Score-491
92Score-522
Canadian-375
Canadian-416
Canadian-491
Canadian-522
USA Greats-8
92Seasons Patches-28
92Stadium Club-73
92Stadium Club-248
92Topps-261
92Topps-293
Gold-261G
Gold-293G
92Ultra-138
Award Winners-2
92Upper Deck-34
92Upper Deck-284
92Upper Deck-434
92Upper Deck-640
World Junior Grads-WG15
92Finnish Semic-150
93Donruss-221
93Leaf-70
93OPC Premier-25
93OPC Premier-505
Gold-25
Gold-505
93Panini Stickers-96
93Parkhurst-131
Emerald Ice-131
93Pinnacle II Samples-275
93Pinnacle-275
Canadian-275
Team Pinnacle-2
Team Canadian-2
93PowerPlay-160
Slapshot Artists-6
93Score-235
Canadian-235
Dream Team-6
Franchise-13
93Stadium Club-88
Members Only Master Set-88
OPC-88
First Day Issue-88
First Day Issue OPC-88
93Topps/OPC Premier-25
93Topps/OPC Premier-505
Gold-25
Gold-505
93Ultra-132
93Upper Deck-348
SP-102
93Upper Deck Locker All-Stars-5
93Swedish Semic World Champ Stickers-171
94SLU Hockey Canadian-5
94Hockey Canadian-5
94SLU Hockey American-10
94Be A Player-R46
94Be A Player-R149
Signature Cards-46
94Canada Games NHL POGS-170
94Canada Games NHL POGS-260
94Canada Games NHL POGS-327
94Canada Games NHL POGS-334
94Donruss-152
Dominators-2
94EA Sports-85
94Finest-49
Super Team Winners-49
Refractors-49
Bowman's Best-B12
Bowman's Best-X24
Bowman's Best Refractors-B12
Bowman's Best Refractors-X24
94Flair-114
Scoring Power-5
94Fleer-135
Headliners-5
94Hockey Wit-71
94Kenner Starting Lineup Cards-11
94Kraft-64
94Leaf-403
Gold Stars-6
94Leaf Limited-33
94McDonald's Upper Deck-McD6
94OPC Premier-37
94OPC Premier-450
94OPC Premier-485
94OPC Premier-500
Special Effects-37
Special Effects-450
Special Effects-485
Special Effects-500
94Parkhurst-151
Gold-151
Vintage-V15
94Pinnacle-155
Artist's Proofs-155
Rink Collection-155
Team Pinnacle-TP4
Team Dufex Parallel-TP4
World Edition-WE15
94Score-184
Gold-184
Platinum-184
Dream Team-DT4
94Select-24
Gold-24
First Line-FL3
94SP-74
Die Cuts-74
94Stadium Club Members Only-24
94Stadium Club-55
94Stadium Club-150
Members Only Master Set-55
Members Only Master Set-150
First Day Issue-55
First Day Issue-150
Finest Inserts-7
Finest Inserts Members Only-7
Super Teams-15
Super Teams Members Only Master Set-15
Super Team Winner Cards-55
Super Team Winner Cards-150
94Topps/OPC Premier-37
94Topps/OPC Premier-120
94Topps/OPC Premier-450
94Topps/OPC Premier-485
94Topps/OPC Premier-500
Special Effects-37
Special Effects-450
Special Effects-485
Special Effects-500
94Topps Finest Bronze-14
94Ultra-139
All-Stars-2
Award Winners-7
Speed Merchants-6
94Upper Deck-231
94Upper Deck-444
Electric Ice-231
Electric Ice-444
Predictor Canadian-C28
94Upper Deck Predictor Canadian Exch Gold-C28
94Upper Deck Predictor Hobby-H11
94Upper Deck Predictor Hobby Exch Gold-H11
94Upper Deck Predictor Hobby Exch Silver-H11
94Upper Deck Predictor Retail-R13
94Upper Deck Predictor Retail-R45
94Upper Deck Predictor Retail-R51
94Upper Deck Predictor Retail Exchange-R13
94Upper Deck Predictor Retail Exchange-R45
94Upper Deck Predictor Retail Exchange-R51
94Upper Deck SP Inserts-SP50
94Upper Deck SP Inserts Die Cuts-SP50
94Upper Deck NHLPA/Be A Player-9
94Finnish Jaa Kiekko-113
94Finnish Jaa Kiekko-339
94Signature Rookies Gold Standard Legends-L5
95Bashan Super Stickers-79
Die Cut-7
95Bowman-32
All-Foil-32
Bowman's Best-BB14
Bowman's Best Refractors-BB14
95Canada Games NHL POGS-186
95Collector's Choice-247
Player's Club-247
Player's Club Platinum-247
95Donruss-181
Dominators-3
Pro Pointers-5
95Donruss Elite-98
Die Cut Stars-98
Die Cut Uncut-98
95Emotion-115
Xcited-6
95Finest-41
95Finest-115
Refractors-41
Refractors-115
95Hoyle Eastern Playing Cards-41
95Imperial Stickers-79
Die Cut Superstars-7
95Leaf-93
Gold Stars-3
95Leaf Limited-90
95Metal-96
Heavy Metal-8
International Steel-12
95NHL Aces Playing Cards-6C
95Panini Stickers-110
95Parkhurst International-144
Emerald Ice-144
Crown Collection Silver Series 2-14
Crown Collection Gold Series 2-14
Parkie's Trophy Picks-PP21
95Pinnacle-133
Artist's Proofs-133
Rink Collection-133
First Strike-6
95Playoff One on One-68
95Playoff One on One-174
95Playoff One on One-283
95Pro Magnets-97
95Score-124
Black Ice Artist's Proofs-124
Black Ice-124
95Select Certified-27
Mirror Gold-27
95SkyBox Impact-110
95SP-94
Stars/Etoiles-E20
Stars/Etoiles Gold-E20
95Stadium Club Members Only-3
95Stadium Club-30
Members Only Master Set-30
Metalists-M8
Metalists Members Only Master Set-M8
Nemeses-N5
Nemeses Members Only Master Set-N5
95Summit-23
Artist's Proofs-23
Ice-23
GM's Choice-4
95Topps-75
OPC Inserts-75
Home Grown USA-HGA1
Mystery Finest-M16
Mystery Finest Refractors-M16
Profiles-PF2
95Topps SuperSkills-19
Platinum-19
95Ultra-104
95Ultra-390
Gold Medallion-104
Ultraview-5
Ultraview Hot Pack-5
95Upper Deck-236
95Upper Deck-487
Electric Ice-236
Electric Ice-487
Electric Ice Gold-236
Electric Ice Gold-487
95Upper Deck All-Star Game Predictors-25
Redemption Winners-25
95Upper Deck Freeze Frame-F18
95Upper Deck Freeze Frame Jumbo-F18
95Upper Deck NHL All-Stars-AS7
95Upper Deck NHL All-Stars Jumbo-AS7
95Upper Deck Predictor Hobby-H33
95Upper Deck Predictor Hobby Exchange-H33
95Upper Deck Predictor Retail-R18
95Upper Deck Predictor Retail Exchange-R18
95Upper Deck Special Edition-SE55
95Upper Deck Special Edition Gold-SE55
95Zenith-32
95Finnish Semic World Championships-105
95Swedish Globe World Championships-103
95Swedish World Championships Stickers-300
95Signature Rookies Cool Five-CF3
95Signature Rookies Cool Five Signatures-CF3
96SLU Hockey Canadian-7
96Headliners Hockey-9
96SLU Hockey American-11
96Be A Player-55
96Be A Player-P55
Autographs-55
Autographs Silver-55
96Black Diamond-12
Gold-12
96Collector's Choice-169
96Collector's Choice-303
96Collector's Choice-324
MVP-UD30
MVP Gold-UD30
Crash the Game-C27A
Crash the Game-C27B
Crash the Game-C27C
Crash the Game Gold-C27A
Crash the Game Gold-C27B
Crash the Game Gold-C27C
Crash the Game Exchange-CR27
Crash the Game Exchange Gold-CR27
96Donruss-13
Press Proofs-13
96Donruss Canadian Ice-108
Gold Press Proofs-108
Red Press Proofs-108
96Donruss Elite-125
Die Cut Stars-125
96Flair-60
Blue Ice-60
96Fleer-70
96Fleer-140
Norris-7
96Fleer Picks-12
Fabulous 50-25
Jagged Edge-17
96Kenner Starting Lineup Cards-11
96Kraft Upper Deck-1
96Leaf-165
Press Proofs-165
96Leaf Limited-82
Gold-82
96Leaf Preferred-42
Press Proofs-42
Steel-23
Steel Gold-23
96Maggers-54
96McDonald's Pinnacle-20
96Metal Universe-98
Ice Carvings-9
Ice Carvings Super Power-9
96NHL Aces Playing Cards-28
96NHL Pro Stamps-97
96Pinnacle-193
Artist's Proofs-193
Foil-193
Premium Stock-193
Rink Collection-193
96Score-179
Artist's Proofs-179
Dealer's Choice Artist's Proofs-179
Special Artist's Proofs-179
Golden Blades-179
96Select Certified-76
Artist's Proofs-76
Blue-76
Mirror Blue-76
Mirror Gold-76
Mirror Red-76
Red-76
96SkyBox Impact-81
NHL on Fox-14
96SP-101
96SPx-26
Gold-26
96Stadium Club Members Only-33
96Summit-96
Artist's Proofs-96
Ice-96
Metal-96
Premium Stock-96
96Team Out-78
96Topps Picks Fantasy Team-FT5
96Topps Picks Ice D-ID1
96Ultra-108
Gold Medallion-108
Power-10
Power Blue Line-7
96Upper Deck-300
Generation Next-X23
Superstar Showdown-SS7B
96Upper Deck Ice-43
Parallel-43
96Zenith-85
Artist's Proofs-85
96Swedish Semic Wien-160
97Headliners Hockey-14
97Beehive-28
Golden Portraits-28
97Black Diamond-33
Double Diamond-33
Triple Diamond-33
Quadruple Diamond-33
Premium Cut-PC10
Premium Cut Double Diamond-PC10
Premium Cut Quadruple Diamond Horiz-PC10
Premium Cut Triple Diamond-PC10
Premium Cut Quadruple Diamond Verticals-PC10
97Collector's Choice-162
Star Quest-SQ20
97Crown Royale-86
Emerald Green-86
Ice Blue-86
Silver-86
Blades of Steel Die-Cuts-15
97Donruss-156
97Donruss-230
Press Proofs Silver-156
Press Proofs Silver-230
Press Proofs Gold-156
Press Proofs Gold-230
Line 2 Line-3
Line 2 Line Die Cut-3
97Donruss Canadian Ice-88
Dominion Series-88
Provincial Series-88
97Donruss Elite-40
97Donruss Elite-116
Aspirations-40
Aspirations-116
Status-40
Status-116
Craftsmen-30
Master Craftsmen-30
97Donruss Limited-70
97Donruss Limited-179
97Donruss Limited-182
Exposure-70
Exposure-179
Exposure-182
Fabric of the Game-64
97Donruss Preferred-22
97Donruss Preferred-188
Cut to the Chase-22
Cut to the Chase-188
97Donruss Priority-74
Stamp of Approval-74
Postcards-22
Stamps-22
Stamps Bronze-22
Stamps Gold-22
Stamps Silver-22
97Esso Olympic Hockey Heroes-29
97Esso Olympic Hockey Heroes French-29
97Katch-94
Gold-94
Silver-94
97Leaf-117
Fractal Matrix-117
Fractal Matrix Die Cuts-117
Banner Season-17
97Leaf International-117
Universal Ice-117
97NHL Aces Playing Cards-26
97Pacific-2
Copper-2
Emerald Green-2
Ice Blue-2
Red-2
Silver-2
Slap Shots Die-Cuts-5C
97Pacific Dynagon-80
Copper-80
Dark Grey-80
Emerald Green-80
Ice Blue-80
Red-80
Silver-80
Best Kept Secrets-62
Best Kept Secrets-108
Tandems-19
97Pacific Invincible-88
Copper-88
Emerald Green-88
Ice Blue-88
Red-88
Silver-88
Attack Zone-15
NHL Regime-129
97Pacific Omega-147
Copper-147
Dark Gray-147
Emerald Green-147
Gold-147
Ice Blue-147
97Panini Stickers-84
97Panini Stickers-120
97Paramount-118
Copper-118
Dark Grey-118
Emerald Green-118
Ice Blue-118
Red-118
Silver-118
97Pinnacle-92
97Pinnacle-195
Artist's Proofs-92
Rink Collection-92
Press Plates Back Black-92
Press Plates Back Black-195
Press Plates Back Cyan-92
Press Plates Back Cyan-195
Press Plates Back Magenta-92
Press Plates Back Magenta-195
Press Plates Back Yellow-92
Press Plates Back Yellow-195
Press Plates Front Black-92
Press Plates Front Black-195
Press Plates Front Cyan-92
Press Plates Front Cyan-195
Press Plates Front Magenta-92
Press Plates Front Magenta-195
Press Plates Front Yellow-92
Press Plates Front Yellow-195
Team Pinnacle-3
Team Mirror-3
Team Parallel-3
Team Parallel Mirror-3
97Pinnacle Certified-36
Red-36
Mirror Blue-36
Mirror Gold-36
Mirror Red-36
Team-6
Gold Team Promo-6
Gold Team-6
97Pinnacle Inside-20
Coach's Collection-20
Executive Collection-20
97Pinnacle Mint-19
Bronze-19
Gold Team-19
Silver Team-19
Coins Brass-19
Coins Brass Proofs-19
Coins Gold Plated-19
Coins Gold Plated Proofs-19
Coins Nickel Silver-19
Coins Nickel Silver Proofs-19
Coins Solid Gold-19
Coins Solid Silver-19
97Pinnacle Tot Cert Platinum Blue-36
97Pinnacle Tot Cert Platinum Gold-36
97Pinnacle Totally Certified Platinum Red-36
97Pinnacle Tot Cert Mirror Platinum Gold-36
97Post Pinnacle-4
97Revolution-89
Copper-89
Emerald-89
Ice Blue-89
Silver-89
97Score-126
Artist's Proofs-126
Golden Blades-126
97Score Rangers-2
Platinum-2
Premier-2
97SP Authentic-100
Icons-I39
Icons Die-Cuts-I39
Icons Embossed-I39
97SPx-33
Bronze-33
Gold-33
Silver-33
Steel-33
Grand Finale-33
97Studio-86
Press Proofs Silver-86
Press Proofs Gold-86
Portraits-35
Silhouettes-23
Silhouettes 8x10-23
97Upper Deck-316
Game Dated Moments-316
Game Jerseys-GJ14
Sixth Sense Masters-SS5
Sixth Sense Wizards-SS5
Smooth Grooves-SG22
The Specialists-28
The Specialists Level 2 Die Cuts-28
Three Star Selects-4B
97Upper Deck Crash the All-Star Game-19
97Upper Deck Crash the All-Star Game-AR19
97Upper Deck Diamond Vision-12
Signature Moves-12
97Upper Deck Ice-76
Parallel-76
Lethal Lines-L10A
Lethal Lines 2-L10A
Power Shift-76
97Zenith-13
Z-Gold-13
Z-Silver-13
97Zenith 5 x 7-65
Gold Impulse-65
Silver Impulse-65
98SLU Hockey-110
98Aurora-124
98Be A Player-238
Press Release-238
98BAP Gold-238
98BAP Autographs-238
98BAP Autographs Gold-238
98BAP Playoff Highlights-H16
98Black Diamond-56
Double Diamond-56
Triple Diamond-56
Quadruple Diamond-56
98Bowman's Best-25
Refractors-25
Atomic Refractors-25
Mirror Image Fusion-F7
Mirror Image Fusion Refractors-F7
Mirror Image Fusion Atomic Refractors-F7
98Crown Royale-89
Limited Series-89
98Finest-137
No Protectors-137
No Protectors Refractors-137
Refractors-137
Promos-PP6
98Katch-93
98Kenner Starting Lineup Cards-19
98Kraft Peanut Butter-2
98McDonalds Upper Deck Gretzkys Teammates-T4
98NHL Game Day Promotion-NYR3
98OPC Chrome-75
Refractors-75
Board Members-B3
Board Members Refractors-B3
98Pacific-297
Ice Blue-297
Red-297
98Pacific Dynagon Ice-123
Blue-123
Red-123
98Pacific Omega-158
Red-158
Opening Day Issue-158
98Panini Photocards-46
98Panini Stickers-83
98Paramount-155
Copper-155
Emerald Green-155
Holo-Electric-155
Ice Blue-155
Silver-155
98Rangers Power Play-NYR3
98Revolution-94
Ice Shadow-94
Red-94
98SP Authentic-57
Power Shift-57
Snapshots-SS17
98SPx Finite-111
Radiance-111
Spectrum-111
98SPx Top Prospects-39
Radiance-39
Spectrum-39
Premier Stars-PS6
98Topps-75
O-Pee-Chee-75
Autographs-A9
Board Members-B3
98Topps Gold Label Class 1-85
Black-85
Black One of One-85
One of One-85
Red-85
Red One of One-85
98Topps Gold Label Class 2-85
98Topps Gold Label Class 2 Black-85
98Topps Gold Label Class 2 Black 1 of 1-85
98Topps Gold Label Class 2 One of One-85
98Topps Gold Label Class 2 Red-85
98Topps Gold Label Class 2 Red One of One-85
98Topps Gold Label Class 3-85
98Topps Gold Label Class 3 Black-85
98Topps Gold Label Class 3 Black 1 of 1-85
98Topps Gold Label Class 3 One of One-85
98Topps Gold Label Class 3 Red-85
98Topps Gold Label Class 3 Red One of One-85
98UD Choice-129
98UD Choice-238
Mini Bobbing Head-BH29
98UD Choice Preview-129
98UD Choice Prime Choice Reserve-129
98UD Choice Prime Choice Reserve-238
98UD Choice Reserve-129
98UD Choice Reserve-238
98UD Choice StarQuest Blue-SQ7
98UD Choice StarQuest Gold-SQ7
98UD Choice StarQuest Green-SQ7
98UD Choice StarQuest Red-SQ7
98Upper Deck-322
Exclusives-322
Exclusives 1 of 1-322
Lord Stanley's Heroes-LS13
Lord Stanley's Heroes Quantum 1-LS13
Lord Stanley's Heroes Quantum 2-LS13
Lord Stanley's Heroes Quantum 3-LS13
Gold Reserve-322
98Upper Deck MVP-133
Gold Script-133
Silver Script-133
Super Script-133
99Aurora-94
Striped-94
Premiere Date-94
Premiere Date Striped-94
99BAP Memorabilia-18
Gold-18
Silver-18
Jersey Cards-J16
Jersey Emblems-E16
Jersey Numbers-I16
Jersey and Stick Cards-S16
Selects Silver-SL10
Selects Gold-SL10
99BAP Update Double AS Jersey Cards-D17
99BAP Update Teammates Jersey Cards-TM6
99BAP Update Teammates Jersey Cards-TM21
99BAP Update Teammates Jersey Cards-TM50
99BAP Millennium-159
Emerald-159
Ruby-159
Sapphire-159
Signatures-159
Signatures Gold-159
Jerseys-J26
Jersey Autographs-J26
Jersey and Stick Cards-JS26
Jersey Emblems-E26
Jersey Numbers-N26
99Black Diamond-57
Diamond Cut-57
Final Cut-57
99Crown Royale-91
Limited Series-91
Premiere Date-91
99O-Pee-Chee-30
99O-Pee-Chee All-Topps-AT6
99O-Pee-Chee Chrome-30
99O-Pee-Chee Chrome All Topps-AT6
99O-Pee-Chee Chrome All-Topps Refractors-AT6
99O-Pee-Chee Chrome Ice Masters-IM10
99O-Pee-Chee Chrome Ice Masters Refractor-IM10
99O-Pee-Chee Chrome Refractors-30
99O-Pee-Chee Ice Masters-IM10
99Pacific-272
Copper-272
Emerald Green-272
Gold-272
Ice Blue-272
Premiere Date-272
Red-272
99Pacific Dynagon Ice-132
Blue-132
Copper-132
Gold-132
Premiere Date-132
99Pacific Omega-151
Copper-151
Gold-151
Ice Blue-151
Premiere Date-151
99Pacific Prism-91
Holographic Blue-91
Holographic Gold-91
Holographic Mirror-91
Holographic Purple-91
Premiere Date-91
99Panini Stickers-98
99Paramount-152
Copper-152
Emerald-152
Gold-152
Holographic Emerald-152
Holographic Gold-152
Holographic Silver-152
Ice Blue-152
Premiere Date-152
Red-152
Silver-152
Ice Alliance-18
99Revolution-97
Premiere Date-97
Red-97
Shadow Series-97
Copper-97
Gold-97
CSC Silver-97
99SP Authentic-58
99SPx-97
Radiance-97
Spectrum-97
99Stadium Club-12
First Day Issue-12
One of a Kind-12
Printing Plates Black-12
Printing Plates Cyan-12
Printing Plates Magenta-12
Printing Plates Yellow-12
Chrome-11
Chrome Refractors-11
99Topps/OPC-30
All-Topps-AT6
Ice Masters-IM10
99Topps Stanley Cup Heroes-SC15
99Topps Stanley Cup Heroes Refractors-SC15
99Topps/OPC Chrome-30
Refractors-30
All-Topps-AT6
All-Topps Refractors-AT6
Ice Masters-IM10
Ice Masters Refractors-IM10
99Topps Gold Label Class 1-29
Black-29
Black One of One-29
One of One-29
Red-29
Red One of One-29
99Topps Gold Label Class 2-29
99Topps Gold Label Class 2 Black-29
99Topps Gold Label Class 2 Black 1 of 1-29
99Topps Gold Label Class 2 One of One-29
99Topps Gold Label Class 2 Red-29
99Topps Gold Label Class 2 Red One of One-29
99Topps Gold Label Class 3-29
99Topps Gold Label Class 3 Black-29
99Topps Gold Label Class 3 Black 1 of 1-29
99Topps Gold Label Class 3 One of One-29
99Topps Gold Label Class 3 Red-29
99Topps Gold Label Class 3 Red One of One-29
99Topps Premier Plus-61
Parallel-61
Calling All Calders-CAC10
99Ultimate Victory-59
1/1-59
Parallel-59
Parallel 100-59
99Upper Deck-258
Exclusives-258
Exclusives 1 of 1-258
Headed for the Hall-HOF9
Headed for the Hall Quantum Gold-HOF9
Headed for the Hall Quantum Silver-HOF9
99Upper Deck Gold Reserve-258
UD Authentics-BL
99Upper Deck HoloGrFx-39
Ausome-39
99Upper Deck MVP-132
Gold Script-132
Silver Script-132
Super Script-132
99Upper Deck MVP SC Edition-120
Gold Script-120
Silver Script-120
Super Script-120
Great Combinations-GCGL
Great Combinations Parallel-GCGL
ProSign-BL
99Upper Deck Ovation-38
Standing Ovation-38
99Upper Deck Retro-51
Gold-51
Platinum-51
Generation-G1B
Generation Level 2-G1B
99Upper Deck Victory-187
99Upper Deck Victory-192
99Upper Deck Victory-345
99Wayne Gretzky Hockey-114
00Aurora-95
Premiere Date-95
00BAP Memorabilia-89
Emerald-89
Ruby-89
Sapphire-89
Promos-89
Jersey Cards-J38
Jersey Emblems-E38

Jersey Numbers-N38
Jersey and Stick Cards-JS38
00BAP Mem Chicago Sportsfest Copper-89
00BAP Memorabilia Chicago Sportsfest Blue-89
00BAP Memorabilia Chicago Sportsfest Gold-89
00BAP Memorabilia Chicago Sportsfest Ruby-89
00BAP Memorabilia Chicago Sun-Times Ruby-89
00BAP Memorabilia Chicago Sun-Times Gold-89
00BAP Mem Chicago Sun-Times Sapphire-89
00BAP Mem Toronto Fall Expo Copper-89
00BAP Memorabilia Toronto Fall Expo Gold-89
00BAP Memorabilia Toronto Fall Expo Ruby-89
00BAP Memorabilia Update Teammates-TM7
00BAP Memorabilia Update Teammates-TM40
00BAP Memorabilia Update Teammates Gold-TM7
00BAP Memorabilia Update Teammates Gold-TM40
00BAP Parkhurst 2000-P29
00BAP Signature Series-219
Emerald-219
Ruby-219
Sapphire-219
Autographs-188
Autographs Gold-188
Department of Defense-DD1
Franchise Players-F20
He Shoots-He Scores Prizes-30
Jersey Cards-J26
Jersey and Stick Cards-GSJ26
Jersey Cards Autographs-J26
Jersey Emblems-E26
Jersey Numbers-IN26
00BAP Ultimate Memorabilia Autographs-26
Gold-26
00BAP Ultimate Mem Game-Used Jerseys-GJ26
00BAP Ultimate Mem Game-Used Sticks-GS26
00BAP Ultimate Memorabilia Norris Trophy-N4
00BAP Ultimate Memorabilia Norris Trophy-N9
00Crown Royale-70
Ice Blue-70
Limited Series-70
Premiere Date-70
Red-70
00O-Pee-Chee-153
00O-Pee-Chee Parallel-153
00Pacific-265
Copper-265
Gold-265
Ice Blue-265
Premiere Date-265
00Panini Stickers-60
00Paramount-163
Copper-163
Gold-163
Holo-Gold-163
Holo-Silver-163
Ice Blue-163
Premiere Date-163
00Private Stock-65
Gold-65
Premiere Date-65
Retail-65
Silver-65
Game Gear-75
Game Gear-76
Game Gear Patches-75
PS-2001 Action-37
00Revolution-96
Blue-96
Premiere Date-96
Red-96
Game-Worn Jerseys-8
Game-Worn Jersey Patches-8
00SP Authentic-57
00SP Game Used Tools of the Game-BL
00SP Game Used Tools of the Game Excl-BL
00Stadium Club-194
00Titanium-61
Blue-61
Gold-61
Premiere Date-61
Red-61
Retail-61
Game Gear-36
Game Gear-114
Game Gear Patches-114
00Titanium Draft Day Edition-66
Patches-66
00Topps/OPC-153
Parallel-153
00Topps Chrome-109
OPC Refractors-109
Refractors-109
00Topps Gold Label Class 1-91
Gold-91
00Topps Gold Label Class 2-91
00Topps Gold Label Class 2 Gold-91
00Topps Gold Label Class 3-91
00Topps Gold Label Class 3 Gold-91
00Topps Gold Label Bullion-B9
00Topps Gold Label Bullion One to One-B9
00Topps Heritage-56
Chrome Parallel-56
00Topps Premier Plus Trophy Tribute-TT15
00Topps Stars-72
Blue-72
00UD Heroes-78
00UD Reserve-58
00Upper Deck-344
Exclusives Tier 1-344
Exclusives Tier 2-344
Dignitaries-D8
Game Jersey Combos-DYL
Ice Clear Cut Autographs-BL
00Upper Deck Legends-92
Legendary Collection Bronze-92
Legendary Collection Gold-92
Legendary Collection Silver-92
00Upper Deck MVP-117
First Stars-117
Second Stars-117
Third Stars-117
00Upper Deck Victory-154
00Upper Deck Vintage-236
00Vanguard-65
Holographic Gold-65
Holographic Purple-65
Pacific Proofs-65
00Czech Stadion-90
01Atomic-64
Blue-64
Gold-64
Premiere Date-64
Red-64
01BAP Memorabilia-290
Emerald-290
Ruby-290
Sapphire-290
All-Star Jerseys-ASJ22
All-Star Emblems-ASE22
All-Star Numbers-ASN22
All-Star Jersey Doubles-DASJ11
All-Star Teammates-AST4
All-Star Teammates-AST7
All-Star Teammates-AST38
Country of Origin-CO16
He Shoots-He Scores Prizes-37
01BAP Signature Series Certified 100-C5
01BAP Signature Series Certified 50-C5
01BAP Signature Series Certified 1 of 1's-C5
01BAP Signature Series Autographs-LBL
01BAP Signature Series Autographs Gold-LBL
01BAP Sig Series Department of Defense-DD-2
01BAP Signature Series Jerseys-GJ-39
01BAP Signature Series Jersey Autographs-GUBL
01BAP Sig Series Jersey and Stick Cards-GSJ-39
01BAP Signature Series Emblems-GUE-37
01BAP Signature Series Numbers-ITN-37
01BAP Ultimate Mem All-Star History-41
01BAP Ultimate Memorabilia Autographs-2
01BAP Ultimate Mem Autographs Gold-2
01BAP Ultimate Memorabilia Calder Trophy-13
01BAP Ultimate Memorabilia Captain's C-8
01BAP Ultimate Memorabilia Cornerstones-5
01BAP Ultimate Memorabilia Emblems-9
01BAP Ultimate Memorabilia Jerseys-9
01BAP Ultimate Mem Jerseys and Sticks-9
01BAP Ultimate Memorabilia Numbers-8
01BAP Ultimate Memorabilia Name Plates-16
01BAP Update Passing the Torch-PTT5
01Bowman YoungStars-55
Gold-55
Ice Cubed-55
01Crown Royale-95
Blue-95
Premiere Date-95
Red-95
Retail-95
01O-Pee-Chee-4
01O-Pee-Chee Heritage Parallel-4
01O-Pee-Chee Heritage Parallel Limited-4
01O-Pee-Chee Premier Parallel-4
01Pacific-261
01Pacific-435
Extreme LTD-261
Gold-435
Hobby LTD-261
Premiere Date-261
Retail LTD-261
01Pacific Adrenaline-126
Blue-126
Premiere Date-126
Red-126
Retail-126
01Pacific Arena Exclusives-261
01Pacific Arena Exclusives-435
01Pacific Heads-Up-64
Blue-64
Premiere Date-64
Red-64
Silver-64
Quad Jerseys-14
Quad Jerseys-22
01Parkhurst-28
Gold-28
Silver-28
Heroes-H7
Jerseys-PJ27
Milestones-M6
Sticks-PS27
Teammates-T3
Teammates-T24
Waving the Flag-24
01Private Stock-62
Gold-62
Premiere Date-62
Retail-62
Silver-62
01Private Stock Pacific Nights-62
01SPx Hidden Treasures-DTYL
01Sports Illustrated for Kids III-37
01Stadium Club-34
Award Winners-34
Master Photos-34
01Titanium-93
Hobby Parallel-93
Premiere Date-93
Retail-93
Retail Parallel-93
Double-Sided Jerseys-26
Double-Sided Jerseys-29
Double-Sided Patches-26
Double-Sided Patches-29
01Titanium Draft Day Edition-60
01Topps-4
Heritage Parallel-4
Heritage Parallel Limited-4
OPC Parallel-4
01Topps Chrome-4
Refractors-4
Black Border Refractors-4
01Topps Heritage-33
01Topps Heritage-126
Refractors-33
Jerseys-JBL
01Topps Reserve-44
Emblems-BL
Jerseys-BL
Name Plates-BL
Numbers-BL
Patches-BL
01UD Challenge for the Cup Jerseys-UCLL
01UD Honor Roll-17
01UD Honor Roll-47
Jerseys-J-BL
Jerseys Gold-J-BL
Pucks-P-BL
Pucks Gold-P-BL
01UD Playmakers-65
01UD Premier Collection Dual Jerseys-DLR
01UD Premier Collection Dual Jersey Black-DLR
01UD Stanley Cup Champs-82
Jerseys-T-BL
Pieces of Glory-G-BL
Sticks-S-BL
01UD Top Shelf-108
01Upper Deck-117
Exclusives-117
Pride of a Nation-TPAWL
01Upper Deck MVP-124
01Upper Deck Victory-233
01Upper Deck Victory-410
Gold-233
Gold-410
01Upper Deck Vintage-169
01Upper Deck Vintage-173
01Vanguard-63
Blue-63
Red-63
One of Ones-63
Premiere Date-63
Proofs-63
02Atomic National Pride-U5
02BAP All-Star Edition-49
02BAP All-Star Edition-50
He Shoots-He Scores Points-1
He Shoots-He Score Prizes-13
Jerseys-49
Jerseys-50
Jerseys Gold-49
Jerseys Gold-50
Jerseys Silver-49
Jerseys Silver-50
02BAP First Edition-3
02BAP First Edition-308
02BAP First Edition-427R
Jerseys-3
02BAP Memorabilia-24
Emerald-24
Ruby-24
Sapphire-24
All-Star Jerseys-ASJ-30
All-Star Emblems-ASE-11
All-Star Numbers-ASN-11
All-Star Triple Jerseys-ASTJ-9
Mini Stanley Cups-32
NHL All-Star Game-24
NHL All-Star Game Blue-24
NHL All-Star Game Green-24
NHL All-Star Game Red-24
Teammates-TM-7
02BAP Memorabilia Toronto Fall Expo-24
02BAP NHL All-Star History-41
02BAP Signature Series-177
Autographs-177
Autograph Buybacks 1998-238
Autograph Buybacks 1999-159
Autograph Buybacks 2000-188
Autograph Buybacks 2001-LBL
Autographs Gold-177
Defensive Wall-DW4
Golf-GS9
Jerseys-SGJ28
Jersey Autographs-SGJ28
Team Quads-TQ4
02BAP Ultimate Memorabilia Active Eight-7
02BAP Ultimate Memorabilia Autographs-17
02BAP Ultimate Mem Autographs Gold-17
02BAP Ultimate Memorabilia Conn Smythe-22
02BAP Ultimate Memorabilia Emblems-17
02BAP Ultimate Mem Lifetime Achievers-9
02BAP Ultimate Memorabilia Numbers-16
02BAP Ultimate Memorabilia Numerology-5
02BAP Ultimate Mem Playoff Scorers-9
02Bowman YoungStars-42
Gold-42
Silver-42
02Crown Royale Jerseys-13
02Crown Royale Jerseys Gold-13
02Crown Royale Dual Patches-16
02ITG Used-47
02ITG Used-147
International Experience-IE22
International Experience Gold-IE22
Jerseys-GUJ28
Jersey Autographs-GUJ28
Jerseys Gold-GUJ28
Emblems-E28
Jersey and Stick-SJ28
Jersey and Stick Gold-SJ28
Teammates-T11
Teammates Gold-T11
02O-Pee-Chee-57
02O-Pee-Chee Premier Blue Parallel-57
02O-Pee-Chee Premier Red Parallel-57
02O-Pee-Chee Factory Set-57
02Pacific-252
Blue-252
Red-252
02Pacific Calder-24
Silver-24
02Pacific Complete-428
Red-428
02Pacific Exclusive-115
02Pacific Heads-Up-81
Blue-81
Purple-81
Red-81
Quad Jerseys-29
Quad Jerseys Gold-29
02Parkhurst-82
Bronze-82
Gold-82
Silver-82
Hardware-N9
He Shoots-He Scores Prizes-28
Jerseys-GJ3
Stick and Jerseys-SJ3
Teammates-TT1
02Parkhurst Retro-96
Minis-96
02Private Stock Reserve-68
Blue-68
Red-68
Retail-68
02SP Authentic Super Premiums-SPBL
02SP Game Used Authentic Fabrics-AFBL
02SP Game Used Authentic Fabrics Gold-AFBL
02SP Game Used Authentic Fabrics Rainbow-AFBL
02SP Game Used First Rounder Patches-BLE
02SP Game Used Piece of History-PHBL
02SP Game Used Piece of History Gold-PHBL
02SP Game Used Piece of History Rainbow-PHBL
02SPx Milestones-MBL
02SPx Milestones Gold-BL
02SPx Milestones Silver-BL
02SPx Winning Materials-WMBL
02SPx Winning Materials Gold-BL
02SPx Winning Materials Silver-BL
02Stadium Club-87
Silver Decoy Cards-87
Proofs-87
Champions Fabric-FC8
Champions Patches-PC-8
02Topps-57
OPC Blue Parallel-57
OPC Red Parallel-57
Factory Set-57
02Topps Chrome-41
Black Border Refractors-41
Refractors-41
02Topps Heritage-89
Chrome Parallel-89
Calder Cloth-BL
Great Skates-BL
02Topps Total-64
02UD Artistic Impressions-60
Gold-60
02UD Artistic Impressions Beckett Promos-60
02UD Artistic Impressions Flashbacks-UD4
02UD Artistic Impressions Flashbacks Gold-UD4
02UD Artistic Impressions Retrospectives-R60
02UD Artistic Impressions Retrospect Gold-R60
02UD Artistic Impress Retrospect Silver-R60
02UD Honor Roll-90
02UD Piece of History-61
Awards Collection-AC19
Patches-PHBL
02UD Top Shelf Clutch Performers-CPBL
02UD Top Shelf Dual Player Jerseys-STBE
02UD Top Shelf Hardware Heroes-HYNLR
02UD Top Shelf Shooting Stars-SHBL
02Upper Deck-363
Exclusives-363
02Upper Deck Beckett UD Promos-363
02Upper Deck Difference Makers-BL
02Upper Deck Fan Favorites-BL
02Upper Deck Playbooks Series II-LL
02Upper Deck Specialists-SBL
02Upper Deck Classic Portraits-66
Hockey Royalty-LBL
Hockey Royalty Limited-LBL
02Upper Deck MVP-120
Gold-120
Classics-120
Golden Classics-120
02Upper Deck Rookie Update-68
02Upper Deck Rookie Update-154C
02Upper Deck Rookie Update-155B
02Upper Deck Rookie Update-162A
02Upper Deck Victory-141
Bronze-141
Gold-141
Silver-141
02Upper Deck Vintage-173
02Upper Deck Vintage-300
Green Backs-173
03BAP Memorabilia All-Star Emblems-ASE-9
03BAP Memorabilia All-Star Jerseys-ASJ-13
03BAP Memorabilia All-Star Jerseys-ASJ-25
03BAP Memorabilia All-Star Numbers-ASN-9
03BAP Memorabilia All-Star Staring Lineup-2
03BAP Memorabilia All-Star Teammates-AST5
03BAP Memorabilia All-Star Teammates-AST7
03BAP Memorabilia All-Star Teammates-AST10
03BAP Mem He Shoots-He Scores Prizes-29
03BAP Memorabilia Jerseys-GJ-28
03BAP Ultimate Memorabilia Autographs-139
Gold-139
03BAP Ultimate Mem Auto Jerseys-139
03BAP Ultimate Mem Auto Emblems-139
03BAP Ultimate Memorabilia Active Eight-7
03BAP Ultimate Mem Always An All-Star-3
03BAP Ultimate Mem Always An AS Gold-3
03BAP Ultimate Memorabilia Emblems-12
03BAP Ultimate Memorabilia Emblems Gold-12
03BAP Ultimate Mem Jersey and Emblems-6
03BAP Ultimate Mem Jersey and Emblem Gold-6
03BAP Ultimate Mem Jersey and Numbers-6
03BAP Ultimate Mem Jersey and Number Gold-6
03BAP Ultimate Mem Jersey and Stick-2
03BAP Ultimate Mem Jersey and Stick Gold-2
03BAP Ultimate Mem Journey Jerseys-5
03BAP Ultimate Mem Journey Jerseys Gold-5
03BAP Ultimate Mem Journey Emblems-5
03BAP Ultimate Mem Journey Emblems Gold-5
03BAP Ultimate Mem Lifetime Achievers-7
03BAP Ultimate Memorabilia Nameplates-11
03BAP Ultimate Mem Nameplates Gold-11
03BAP Ultimate Mem Retro Teammates-4
03BAP Ultimate Mem Retro-Active Trophies-11
03Beehive-129
Gold-129
Silver-129
03Bowman-2
Gold-2
03Bowman Chrome-2
Refractors-2
Gold Refractors-2
Xfractors-2
03eTopps-54
03ITG Action-344
03ITG Action-632
Jerseys-M164
03ITG Used Signature Series-55
Gold-55
Autographs-BL
Autographs Gold-BL
International Experience-28
International Experience Autographs-28
International Experience Emblems Gold-28
International Experience Emblems-28
International Experience Gold-28
Jersey and Stick-30
Jersey and Stick Gold-30
Norris Trophy-10
Norris Trophy Gold-10
Retrospectives-14A
Retrospectives-14B
Retrospectives-14C
Retrospectives-14D
Retrospectives-14E
Retrospectives-14F
Retrospectives Gold-14A
Retrospectives Gold-14B
Retrospectives Gold-14C
Retrospectives Gold-14D
Retrospectives Gold-14E
Retrospectives Gold-14F
Teammates-12
Teammates Gold-12
03NHL Sticker Collection-88
03O-Pee-Chee-60
03OPC Blue-60
03OPC Gold-60
03OPC Red-60
03Pacific-226
Blue-226
Red-226
03Pacific Complete-112
Red-112
03Pacific Luxury Suite-42A
03Pacific Luxury Suite-42B
03Pacific Luxury Suite-42C
03Pacific Prism-71
Blue-71
Gold-71
Red-71
03Parkhurst Original Six New York-18
03Parkhurst Original Six New York-62
03Parkhurst Original Six New York-72
03Parkhurst Original Six New York-93
03Parkhurst Original Six New York-99
Inserts-N12
Inserts-N14
Memorabilia-NM2
Memorabilia-NM13
03Parkhurst Rookie-4
Emblems-GUE-4
Emblem Autographs-GUE-BL
Emblems Gold-GUE-4
Jerseys-GJ-7
Jerseys Gold-GJ-7
Jersey and Sticks-SJ-8
Jersey and Sticks Gold-SJ-8
Records-RRE-5
Records Gold-RRE-5
Retro Rookies-RR-9
Retro Rookies Gold-RR-9
ROYalty-VR-8
ROYalty Autographs-VR-BL
ROYalty Gold-VR-8
03Private Stock Reserve-70
Blue-70
Red-70
Retail-70
03Rangers Team Issue-11
03SP Game Used Authentic Fabrics-DFLP
03SP Game Used Authentic Fabrics Gold-DFLP
03SP Game Used Limited Threads-LTBL
03SP Game Used Limited Threads Gold-LTBL
03SPx Origins-O-BL
03Titanium-68
Hobby Jersey Number Parallels-68
Retail-68
Retail Jersey Number Parallels-68
03Topps-60
Blue-60
Gold-60
Red-60
Box Toppers-7
Topps/OPC Idols-UI17
03Topps C55-2
Minis-2
Minis American Back-2
Minis American Back Red-2
Minis Bazooka Back-2
Minis Brooklyn Back-2
Minis Hat Trick Back-2
Minis O Canada Back-2
Minis O Canada Back Red-2
Minis Stanley Cup Back-2
03Topps Pristine-22
Gold Refractor Die Cuts-22
Refractors-22
Press Plates Black-22
Press Plates Cyan-22
Press Plates Magenta-22
Press Plates Yellow-22
03Topps Traded-TT30
Blue-TT30
Gold-TT30
Red-TT30
03Upper Deck-374
Canadian Exclusives-374
Franchise Fabrics-FF-BL
HG-374
Patches-LD8
UD Exclusives-374
Ice Breakers-IB-BL
Ice Breaker Patches-IB-BL
Ice Clear Cut Winners-CC-BL
Ice Icons-I-BL
Ice Icons Jerseys-I-BL
03Upper Deck Victory-127
Bronze-127
Gold-127
Silver-127
04ITG NHL AS FANtasy AS History Jerseys-SB41
04Pacific-245
Blue-245
Red-245
Philadelphia-16
04SP Authentic-148
Limited-148
Buybacks-16
Buybacks-17
Buybacks-18
Buybacks-19
Buybacks-20
Sign of the Times-ST-BL
Sign of the Times-DS-LB
Sign of the Times-TS-LPJ
Sign of the Times-SS-DEE
Sign of the Times-SS-USA
04Ultimate Collection Patches-UP-BL
04Ultimate Collection Signatures-US-BL
04Ultimate Collection Signature Logos-ULA-BL
04Ultimate Collection Signature Patches-SP-BL
04Upper Deck NHL's Best-NB-BL
04Upper Deck World Cup Tribute-BL
04Upper Deck World Cup Tribute-BLBR
04Upper Deck World Cup Tribute-CCRELDH
05ITG Heroes/Prosp Toronto Expo Parallel -25
05Beehive-10
Matte-10
05Black Diamond-78
Emerald-78
Gold-78
Onyx-78
Ruby-78
05Bruins Boston Globe-12
05Hot Prospects-8
En Fuego-8
Red Hot-8
White Hot-8
05ITG Ultimate Memorabilia Level 1-15
05ITG Ultimate Memorabilia Level 2-15
05ITG Ultimate Memorabilia Level 3-15
05ITG Ultimate Memorabilia Level 4-15
05ITG Ultimate Memorabilia Level 5-15
05ITG Ultimate Mem Complete Jersey-10
05ITG Ultimate Mem Complete Jersey Gold-10
05ITG Ultimate Mem Cornerstones Jerseys-6
05ITG Ultimate Mem Cornerst Jerseys Gold-6
05ITG Ultimate Memorabilia Double Autos-1
05ITG Ultimate Mem Double Autos Gold-1
05ITG Ultimate Mem Double Mem Autos-4
05ITG Ultimate Mem Double Mem Autos Gold-4
05ITG Ultimate Memorabilia Emblems-24
05ITG Ultimate Memorabilia Emblems Gold-24
05ITG Ultimate Mem First Rounders Jerseys-3
05ITG Ultimate Mem First Rounders Jerseys-8
05ITG Ultimate Mem 1st Round Jersey Gold-3
05ITG Ultimate Mem 1st Round Jersey Gold-8
05ITG Ultimate Memorabilia In The Numbers-16
05ITG Ultimate Mem In The Numbers Gold-16
05ITG Ultimate Mem Jersey and Emblem-6
05ITG Ultimate Memorabilia Jersey Autos-16
05ITG Ultimate Mem Jersey Autos Gold-16
05ITG Ultimate Mem Jersey Emblems Gold-6
05ITG Ultimate Memorabilia Jerseys-6
05ITG Ultimate Memorabilia Jerseys Gold-6
05ITG Ultimate Mem Pass the Torch Jerseys-16
05ITG Ultimate Mem Passing Torch Jsy Gold-16
05ITG Ultimate Memorabilia R.O.Y. Autos-1
05ITG Ultimate Mem R.O.Y. Autos Gold-1
05ITG Ultimate Memorabilia R.O.Y. Emblems-6
05ITG Ultimate Mem R.O.Y. Emblems Gold-6
05ITG Ultimate Memorabilia R.O.Y. Jerseys-6
05ITG Ultimate Mem R.O.Y. Jerseys Gold-6
05ITG Ultimate Memorabilia R.O.Y. Numbers-6
05ITG Ultimate Mem R.O.Y. Numbers Gold-6
05ITG Ultimate Mem Retro Teammate Jerseys-29
05ITG Ult Mem Retro Teammates Jersey Gold-29
05ITG Ultimate Mem Seams Unbelievable-19
05ITG Ultimate Mem Seam Unbelievable Gold-19
05ITG Ultimate Memorabilia Stick Autos-16
05ITG Ultimate Mem Stick Autos Gold-16
05ITG Ultimate Mem 3 Star of the Game Jsy-23
05ITG Ult Mem 3 Star of the Game Jsy Gold-23
05ITG Ultimate Memorabilia Triple Autos-16
05ITG Ultimate Mem Triple Autos Gold-16
05ITG Ultimate Memorabilia Ultimate Autos-21
05ITG Ultimate Mem Ultimate Autos Gold-21
05Panini Stickers-20
05Parkhurst-43
05Parkhurst-527
Facsimile Auto Parallel-43
Facsimile Auto Parallel-527
True Colors-TCBOS
True Colors-TCBOS
True Colors-TCMOBO
True Colors-TCMOBO
05SP Authentic-9
Limited-9
Marks of Distinction-MDBL
Sign of the Times Triples-TRBL
05SP Game Used-9
Autographs-9
Gold-9
Auto Draft-AD-BL
05SPx-95
Spectrum-95
Winning Combos-WC-BL
Winning Combos Gold-WC-BL
Winning Combos Spectrum-WC-BL
Winning Materials-WM-BL
Winning Materials Autographs-AWM-BL
Winning Materials Gold-WM-BL
Winning Materials Spectrum-WM-BL
Xcitement Superstars-XS-BL
Xcitement Superstars Gold-XS-BL
Xcitement Superstars Spectrum-XS-BL
05The Cup-12
Gold-12
Black Rainbow-12
Dual NHL Shields Autographs-ADSBL
Emblems of Endorsement-EEBL
Hardware Heroes-HHBL1
Hardware Heroes-HHBL2
Hardware Heroes-HHBL3
Honorable Numbers-HNBL
Masterpiece Pressplates-12
Masterpiece Pressplates (Rookie Update)-229
Patch Variation-P12
Patch Variation Autographs-AP12
Scripted Numbers-SNBL
Signature Patches-SPBL
Stanley Cup Titlists-TLE
05UD Artifacts Auto Facts-AF-BL
05UD Artifacts Auto Facts Blue-AF-BL
05UD Artifacts Auto Facts Copper-AF-BL
05UD Artifacts Auto Facts Pewter-AF-BL
05UD Artifacts Auto Facts Silver-AF-BL
05UD Artifacts Remarkable Artifacts-RA-BL
05UD Artifacts Remarkable Artifacts Dual-RA-BL
05UD Artifacts Treasured Patches-TP-BL
05UD Artifacts Treasured Patch Autos-TP-BL
05UD Artifacts Treasured Patches Dual-TPD-BL
05UD Artifacts Treasured Patch Dual Autos-TPD-BL
05UD Artifacts Treasured Patches Pewter-TP-BL
05UD Artifacts Treasured Patches Silver-TP-BL
05UD Artifacts Treasured Swatches-TS-BL
05UD Artifacts Treasured Swatch Autos-TS-BL
05UD Artifacts Treasured Swatches Blue-TS-BL
05UD Artifacts Treasured Swatches Copper-TS-BL
05UD Artifacts Treasured Swatches Dual-TSD-BL
05UD Artifacts Treasured Swatch Dual Auto-TSD-BL
05UD Artifacts Treasured Swatch Dual Blue-TSD-BL
05UD Artifact Treasure Swatch Dual Copper-TSD-BL
05UD Artifact Treasure Swatch Dual Maroon-TSD-BL
05UD Artifact Treasure Swatch Dual Pewter-TSD-BL
05UD Artifact TreasuredSwatch Dual Silver-TSD-BL
05UD Artifacts Treasured Swatches Maroon-TS-BL
05UD Artifacts Treasured Swatches Pewter-TS-BL
05UD Artifacts Treasured Swatches Silver-TS-BL
05UD PowerPlay-86
Rainbow-86
05Ultimate Collection-10
Gold-10
Endorsed Emblems-EEBL
Ultimate Signatures-USBL
05Ultra-19
Gold-19
Ice-19
05Upper Deck-257
05Upper Deck All-Time Greatest-40
05Upper Deck All-Time Greatest-80
05Upper Deck Jerseys Series II-J2BL
05Upper Deck Notable Numbers-N-BL
05Upper Deck Patches-P-BL
05Upper Deck Hockey Showcase-HS6
05Upper Deck Showcase Promos-HS6
05Upper Deck Ice-10
Rainbow-10
Signature Swatches-SSBL
05Upper Deck MVP-34
Gold-34
Platinum-34
05Upper Deck Rookie Update-8
05Upper Deck Rookie Update-229
Inspirations Patch Rookies-229
05Upper Deck Trilogy-11
Honorary Patches-HP-BL
Honorary Patch Scripts-HSP-BL
Honorary Swatches-HS-BL
Honorary Swatch Scripts-HSS-BL
05Upper Deck Victory-187
05Upper Deck Victory-205
Black-187
Black-205
Gold-187
Gold-205
Silver-187
Silver-205
Stars on Ice-SI42
05ITG Heroes and Prospects-25
Autographs-A-BL
He Shoots-He Scores Prizes-9
Hero Memorabilia-HM-14
Hero Memorabilia Dual-HDM-9
National Pride-NPR-20
06Be A Player Portraits Signature Portraits-SPBL
06Black Diamond Gemography-GBL
06Black Diamond Jerseys-JBL
06Black Diamond Jerseys Black-JBL
06Black Diamond Jerseys Gold-JBL
06Black Diamond Jerseys Ruby-JBL
06Black Diamond Jerseys Black Autographs -JBL
06Flair Showcase-108
06Flair Showcase-208
Parallel-108
Parallel-208
Inks-IBL
06Fleer Hockey Headliners-HL11
06Fleer Signing Day-SDBL
06ITG International Ice-82
Gold-82
Autographs-ABL
Best of the Best-BB02
Best of the Best Gold-BB02
Complete Jersey-CJ15
Complete Jersey Gold-CJ15
Cornerstones-IC06
Cornerstones Gold-IC06
Emblem Autographs-GUE27
Emblem Autographs Gold-GUE27
Emblems-GUE27
Emblems Gold-GUE27
Jersey Autographs-GUJ27
Jersey Autographs Gold-GUJ27
Jerseys-GUJ27
Jerseys Gold-GUJ27
Numbers-GUN27
Numbers Autographs-GUN27
Numbers Autographs Gold-GUN27
Numbers Gold-GUN27
Quad Patch-QP02
Quad Patch Gold-QP02
Stick and Jersey-SJ05
Stick and Jersey Gold-SJ05
Teammates-IT12
Teammates Gold-IT12
06ITG Ultimate Memorabilia-22
Artist Proof-22
Autos-43
Autos Gold-43
Captain-C-10
Captain-C Gold-10
Cornerstones-6
Cornerstones Gold-6
Decades-4
Decades Gold-4
First Round Picks-28
First Round Picks Gold-28
Going For Gold-5
Going For Gold Gold-5
Jerseys and Emblems-9
Jerseys and Emblems Gold-9
Jerseys Autos-31
Jerseys Autos Gold-31
Journey Emblem-8
Journey Emblem Gold-8
Journey Jersey-8
Journey Jersey Gold-8
R.O.Y. Autos-14
R.O.Y. Autos Gold-14
R.O.Y. Emblems-14
R.O.Y. Emblems Gold-14
R.O.Y. Jerseys-14
R.O.Y. Jerseys Gold-14
R.O.Y. Numbers-14
R.O.Y. Numbers Gold-14
Retro Teammates-23
Retro Teammates Gold-23
Stick Rack-27
Stick Rack Gold-27
Triple Thread Jerseys-6
Triple Thread Jerseys Gold-6
06SP Game Used Authentic Fabrics-AFBL
06SP Game Used Authentic Fabrics Parallel-AFBL
06SP Game Used Authentic Fabrics Patches-AFBL
06SPx Winning Materials-WMBL
06SPx Winning Materials Spectrum-WMBL
06UD Powerplay Specialists-SBL
06UD Powerplay Specialists Patches-PBL
06Ultra Fresh Ink-IBL
06Upper Deck Game Dated Moments-GD16
06Upper Deck Signature Sensations-SSBL
06Upper Deck Ovation-54
06Upper Deck Victory-14
06Upper Deck Victory Black-14
06Upper Deck Victory Gold-14
06ITG Heroes and Prospects-3
Autographs-ABL
Heroes Memorabilia-HM09
Heroes Memorabilia Gold-HM09

Lefebvre, Blair

04Minnesota-Duluth Bulldogs-12

Lefebvre, Darren

02Spokane Chiefs-13

Lefebvre, Fredrick

88Richelieu Riverains-16
907th Inn. Sketch QMJHL-194

Lefebvre, Guillaume

00Rouyn-Noranda Huskies-8
Signed-8
01BAP Memorabilia-425
Emerald-425
Ruby-425
Sapphire-425
01Parkhurst-338
01UD Mask Collection-161
Gold-161
02O-Pee-Chee-309
02O-Pee-Chee Premier Blue Parallel-309
02O-Pee-Chee Premier Red Parallel-309
02O-Pee-Chee Factory Set-309
02Topps-309
OPC Blue Parallel-309
OPC Red Parallel-309
Factory Set-309
02Upper Deck MVP-214
Gold-214
Classics-214
Golden Classics-214
02AHL Top Prospects-25
02Philadelphia Phantoms-10
03ITG Action-490
03Wilkes-Barre Scranton Penguins-14
04Wilkes-Barre Scranton Penguins-15
05WBS Penguins-18

Lefebvre, Guy

907th Inn. Sketch QMJHL-96

Lefebvre, Jean-Sebastien

917th Inn. Sketch QMJHL-144

Lefebvre, Marc

99Ottawa 67's-10
00Ottawa 67's-9
03UK Sheffield Steelers-18
03UK Sheffield Steelers Stickers-16
04UK Sheffield Steelers-9
05UK Coventry Blaze-19

Lefebvre, Martin

907th Inn. Sketch QMJHL-186

Lefebvre, Nicolas

907th Inn. Sketch QMJHL-84
907th Inn. Sketch QMJHL-248
917th Inn. Sketch QMJHL-266

Lefebvre, Normand

79Rochester Americans-10

LeFebvre, Patrice

90ProCards AHL/IHL-337
93Las Vegas Thunder-18
94Las Vegas Thunder-11
95Las Vegas Thunder-5
96Las Vegas Thunder-12
96Collector's Edge Ice-153
Prism-153
97Las Vegas Thunder-15
98IHL All-Star Western Conference-15
98Las Vegas Thunder-11
99German Adler Mannheim Eagles Postcards-7
99German DEL-8
00German DEL-84
All-Star Class-A2
04UK Thommo's Top 10-10

Lefebvre, Stephane

83Nova Scotia Voyageurs-4
93Guelph Storm-19

Lefebvre, Sylvain

88ProCards AHL-297
89Canadiens Kraft-13
89Canadiens Postcards-18
90Bowman-48
Tiffany-48
90Canadiens Postcards-20
90O-Pee-Chee-159
90Panini Stickers-59
90Pro Set-472
90Score-307C
Canadian-307C
90Topps-159
Tiffany-159
90Upper Deck-421
French-421
91Bowman-332
91Canadiens Panini Team Stickers-15
91Canadiens Postcards-18
91O-Pee-Chee-489
91Parkhurst-307
French-307
91Score Canadian Bilingual-245
91Score Canadian English-245
91Stadium Club-208
91Topps-489
91Upper Deck-171
French-171
92Bowman-307
92Maple Leafs Kodak-13
92O-Pee-Chee-303
92OPC Premier-108
92Parkhurst-416
Emerald Ice-416
92Score-405
Canadian-405
92Stadium Club-367
92Topps-341
Gold-341G
93Donruss-331
93Leaf-267
Maple Leafs Score Black's-12
93OPC Premier-331
Gold-331
93Pinnacle-317
Canadian-317
93PowerPlay-450
93Score-359
Canadian-359
93Stadium Club-48
Members Only Master Set-48
OPC-48
First Day Issue-48
First Day Issue OPC-48
93Topps/OPC Premier-331
Gold-331
93Ultra-430
94Be A Player-R66
Signature Cards-41
94Flair-149
94Fleer-180
94Leaf-507
94Nordiques Burger King-16
94OPC Premier-364
Special Effects-364
94Pinnacle-379
Artist's Proofs-379
Rink Collection-379
94Topps/OPC Premier-364
Special Effects-364
94Ultra-176
94Ultra-360
94Upper Deck-335
Electric Ice-335
95Donruss-288
95Leaf-292
95Parkhurst International-321
Emerald Ice-321
95Pinnacle-131
Artist's Proofs-131
Rink Collection-131
95Playoff One on One-26
95Score-192
Black Ice Artist's Proofs-192
Black Ice-192

95Topps-279
OPC Inserts-279
95Ultra-222
95Upper Deck-342
Electric Ice-342
Electric Ice Gold-342
96Be A Player-54
Autographs-54
Autographs Silver-54
96Donruss-81
Press Proofs-81
96Leaf-98
Press Proofs-98
96Score-226
Artist's Proofs-226
Dealer's Choice Artist's Proofs-226
Special Artist's Proofs-226
Golden Blades-226
96Summit-149
Artist's Proofs-149
Ice-149
Metal-149
Premium Stock-149
97Pacific Invincible NHL Regime-54
97Score Avalanche-16
Platinum-16
Premier-16
98Be A Player-184
Press Release-184
98BAP Gold-184
98BAP Autographs-184
98BAP Autographs Gold-184
99Pacific-109
Copper-109
Emerald Green-109
Gold-109
Ice Blue-109
Premiere Date-109
Red-109
00Paramount-164
Copper-164
Gold-164
Holo-Gold-164
Holo-Silver-164
Ice Blue-164
Premiere Date-164
00Titanium Game Gear-115
00Titanium Game Gear Patches-115
01Pacific-262
Extreme LTD-262
Hobby LTD-262
Premiere Date-262
Retail LTD-262
01Pacific Arena Exclusives-262
01Pacific Heads-Up Quad Jerseys-25
02BAP Sig Series Auto Buybacks 1998-184
02Rangers Team Issue-8

Leffler, Brett

05Regina Pats-9
06Regina Pats-10

Lefley, Bryan

72O-Pee-Chee-252
72Sargent Promotions Stamps-139
74NHL Action Stamps-299
76O-Pee-Chee NHL-159
76Rockies Coke Cans-13
76Rockies Puck Bucks-11
77O-Pee-Chee NHL-297
77Rockies Coke Cans-13
78O-Pee-Chee-370
95Swiss HNL-84

Lefley, Chuck

69Swedish Hockey-358
72Canadiens Postcards-11
72Dimanche/Derniere Heure *-152
72Dimanche/Derniere Heure *-153
73Canadiens Postcards-13
73O-Pee-Chee-44
73Topps-154
74Canadiens Postcards-14
74NHL Action Stamps-155
74NHL Action Stamps Update-33
74O-Pee-Chee NHL-178
74Topps-178
75O-Pee-Chee NHL-282
75Topps-282
76O-Pee-Chee NHL-63
76O-Pee-Chee NHL-393
76Topps-63
77O-Pee-Chee NHL-340
80O-Pee-Chee-395

Lefrancois, Gilbert

99Shawinigan Cataractes-15
Signed-15
00Shawinigan Cataractes-9
Signed-9

Lefrancois, Mathieu

93Quebec Pee-Wee Tournament-93

Lefreniere, Jason

87Nordiques Yum-Yum-6

Legace, Manny

907th Inn. Sketch OHL-263
917th Inn. Sketch OHL-217
92Upper Deck-585
93Alberta International Team Canada-10
93OPC Premier Team Canada-2
93Niagara Falls Thunder-25
93Classic-24
93Classic Four-Sport *-227
Gold-227
94Score Team Canada-CT20
94Classic Pro Prospects Ice Ambassadors-IA5
94Classic Pro Prospects Intl Heroes-LP16
95Upper Deck World Junior Alumni-2
96Springfield Falcons-30
96Collector's Edge Future Legends-9
96Collector's Edge Ice Platinum Club-3
97Las Vegas Thunder-2
98Crown Royale-63
Limited Series-63
Rookie Class-4
98Long Beach Ice Dogs-10
99Upper Deck-66
Exclusives-66
Exclusives 1 of 1-66
99Upper Deck Gold Reserve-66
99Upper Deck MVP-99
Gold Script-99
Silver Script-99
Super Script-99
99Manitoba Moose-1
00BAP Parkhurst 2000-P208
00Titanium-32
Blue-32
Gold-32
Premiere Date-32
Red-32
Retail-32
01BAP Memorabilia-132
Emerald-132
Ruby-132
Sapphire-132
01BAP Signature Series-10
Autographs-10
Autographs Gold-10
01Between the Pipes-28
Double Memorabilia-DM12
Goalie Gear-GG11
He Shoots-He Saves Prizes-28
Jerseys-GJ37
Jersey and Stick Cards-GSJ25
Masks-15
Masks Silver-15
Masks Gold-15
Tandems-GT9
01O-Pee-Chee-136
01O-Pee-Chee Premier Parallel-136
01Pacific-145
Extreme LTD-145
Hobby LTD-145
Premiere Date-145
Retail LTD-145
Steel Curtain-7
01Pacific Arena Exclusives-145
01Parkhurst-155
01Topps-136
OPC Parallel-136
01Upper Deck Victory-131
Gold-131
01Upper Deck Vintage-268
02BAP First Edition-85
Jerseys-85
02BAP Memorabilia Stanley Cup Champions-SCC-9
02BAP Signature Series-104
Autographs-104
Autograph Buybacks 2001-10
Autographs Gold-104
02BAP Ultimate Mem Dynasty Jerseys-11
02BAP Ultimate Mem Dynasty Emblems-11
02BAP Ultimate Mem Dynasty Numbers-11
02Between the Pipes-28
Gold-28
Silver-28
Double Memorabilia-12
02O-Pee-Chee-153
02O-Pee-Chee Premier Blue Parallel-153
02O-Pee-Chee Premier Red Parallel-153
02O-Pee-Chee Factory Set-153
02Pacific-131
Blue-131
Red-131
02Pacific Complete-109
Red-109
02Parkhurst Retro-116
Minis-116
02Topps-153
OPC Blue Parallel-153
OPC Red Parallel-153
Factory Set-153
Heritage Crease Piece-ML
Heritage Crease Piece Patches-ML
02Topps Total-129
02UD Mask Collection-30
02UD Mask Collection-31
02UD Mask Collection Beckett Promos-30
02UD Mask Collection Beckett Promos-31
02Upper Deck-313
Exclusives-313
02Upper Deck Beckett UD Promos-313
03BAP Memorabilia-134
Emerald-134
Gold-134
Ruby-134
Sapphire-134
Deep in the Crease-D8
Tandems-T-3
03ITG Action-261
Jerseys-M46
03Pacific-122
Blue-122
Red-122
03Pacific Complete-491
Red-491
03Parkhurst Original Six Detroit-18
Memorabilia-DM6
Memorabilia-DM59
03Topps Pristine Jersey Portions-PPJ-ML
03Topps Pristine Jersey Portion Refractor-PPJ-ML
03Topps Pristine Patches-PP-ML
03Topps Pristine Patch Refractors-PP-ML
03Upper Deck-73
Canadian Exclusives-73
HG-73
03Upper Deck MVP-158
Gold Script-158
Silver Script-158
Canadian Exclusives-158
03Upper Deck Victory-69
Bronze-69
Gold-69
Silver-69
04Pacific-96
Blue-96
Red-96
04SP Authentic-31
Limited-31
Sign of the Times-ST-LE
Sign of the Times-SS-CAN
05Black Diamond-85
Emerald-85
Gold-85
Onyx-85
Ruby-85
05Parkhurst-169
05Parkhurst-596
Facsimile Auto Parallel-169
Facsimile Auto Parallel-596
True Colors-TCDET
True Colors-TCDET
True Colors-TCCHDE
True Colors-TCCHDE
05SP Authentic Chirography-SPML
05SP Authentic Prestigious Pairings-PPLH
05SP Authentic Sign of the Times Duals-DLO
05SP Authentic Sign of the Times Triples-TLOH
05SP Game Used-38
Autographs-38
Gold-38
Authentic Fabrics-AF-LE
Authentic Fabrics Autographs-AAF-LE
Authentic Fabrics Gold-AF-LE
Authentic Fabrics Quad-YDSL
Authentic Patches Quad -YDSL
Authentic Patches-AP-LE
Authentic Patches Autographs-AAP-LE
Awesome Authentics-AA-ML
SIGnificance-ML
SIGnificance Gold-S-ML
05SPx Winning Combos-WC-ZL
05SPx Winning Combos Autographs-AWC-ZL
05SPx Winning Combos Gold-WC-ZL
05SPx Winning Combos Spectrum-WC-ZL
05SPx Winning Materials-WM-ML
05SPx Winning Materials Gold-WM-ML
05SPx Winning Materials Spectrum-WM-ML
05The Cup Emblems of Endorsement-EEML
05The Cup Limited Logos-LLML
05The Cup Noble Numbers-NNKL
05The Cup Scripted Numbers-SNKL
05UD Artifacts-36
Blue-36
Gold-36
Green-36
Pewter-36
Red-36
Auto Facts-AF-ML
Auto Facts Blue-AF-ML
Auto Facts Copper-AF-ML
Auto Facts Pewter-AF-ML
Auto Facts Silver-AF-ML
Gold Autographed-36
05Ultimate Collection Endorsed Emblems-EEML
05Ultimate Coll Ultimate Achievements-UAML
05Ultimate Collection Ultimate Signatures-USML
05Ultimate Coll Ultimate Sigs Pairings-UPLH
05Ultra-73
Gold-73
Ice-73
05Upper Deck-69
HG Glossy-69
Jerseys Series II-J2ML
Majestic Materials-MMLE
Notable Numbers-N-ML
05Upper Deck MVP-148
Gold-148
Platinum-148
05Upper Deck Trilogy-32
05Upper Deck Toronto Fall Expo-69
05Upper Deck Victory-216
Black-216
Gold-216
Silver-216
06Beehive-12
Matte-12
06Between The Pipes The Mask-M25
06Between The Pipes The Mask Gold-M25
06Between The Pipes The Mask Silver-M25
06Black Diamond-74
Black-74
Gold-74
Ruby-74
06Flair Showcase Inks-IML
06Flair Showcase Stitches-SSML
06Fleer-167
Tiffany-167
06Hot Prospects-81
Red Hot-81
White Hot-81
06NHL POG-3
06O-Pee-Chee-432
Rainbow-432
Swatches-S-ML
06Panini Stickers-347
06SP Authentic-15
Limited-15
06SP Game Used Authentic Fabrics Triple-AF3STL
06SP Game Used Authentic Fabrics Triple Patches-AF3STL
06SP Game Used Authentic Fabrics Fives-AF5GAA
06SP Game Used Authentic Fabrics Fives Patches-AF5GAA
06The Cup NHL Shields Duals-DSHLS
06UD Powerplay-87
Impact Rainbow-87
06Upper Deck Arena Giveaways-STL4
06Upper Deck-419
Exclusives Parallel-419
High Gloss Parallel-419
Game Jerseys-JML
Game Patches-PML
Masterpieces-419
06Upper Deck MVP-251
Gold Script-251
Super Script-251
Autographs-OALW
Last Line of Defense-LL25
06Upper Deck Sweet Shot Signature Sticks-STLE
06Upper Deck Trilogy-87
Combo Clearcut Autographs-C2LZ
Combo Clearcut Autographs-C3LDZ
Honorary Scripted Patches-HSPML
Honorary Scripted Swatches-HSSML
Honorary Swatches-HSLE
Scripts-TSML
06Upper Deck Victory-71
06Upper Deck Victory-274
06Upper Deck Victory Black-71
06Upper Deck Victory Gold-71
07Upper Deck Ovation-7
07Upper Deck Victory-112
Black-112
Gold-112

Legare, Martin

92Quebec Pee-Wee Tournament-478
93Quebec Pee-Wee Tournament-1078

Legault, Alexandre

907th Inn. Sketch QMJHL-7
917th Inn. Sketch QMJHL-193
917th Inn. Sketch Memorial Cup-51

Legault, Derek

93Quebec Pee-Wee Tournament-18

Legault, Eric

93Quebec Pee-Wee Tournament-95

Legault, Jason

04Victoriaville Tigres-10
05Victoriaville Tigres-2
06Victoriaville Tigres-13

Legault, Jay

93Quebec Pee-Wee Tournament-554
95Slapshot-239
97Bowman CHL-148
OPC-148
Autographs-28
98Bowman CHL-20
Golden Anniversary-20
OPC International-20
98Bowman Chrome CHL-20
Golden Anniversary-20
Golden Anniversary Refractors-20
OPC International-20
OPC International Refractors-20
Refractors-20
99Cincinnati Mighty Ducks-25
01Milwaukee Admirals-16
03Florida Everblades-12

Legault, Jeremie

96Madison Monsters-5

Legault, Marc

917th Inn. Sketch QMJHL-211

Legault, Olivier

03Lewiston Maineiacs-12
05Drummondville Voltigeurs-26

Legault, Paul

50Quebec Citadelles-13

Legault, Shawn

99Austin Ice Bats-2
99Austin Ice Bats-31
02Austin Ice Bats-8
03Austin Ice Bats-8
04New Mexico Scorpions-16

Legault, Tommy

05Rimouski Oceanic-30
06Rimouski Oceanic-23

Legein, Stefan

04Mississauga Ice Dogs-21
05Mississauga Ice Dogs-22
06Mississauga Ice Dogs-3

Leger, Bob

51Laval Dairy Subset-95
52Bas Du Fleuve-58
52St. Lawrence Sales-102

Leger, Dave

03Cape Fear Fire Antz-6

Leger, Germain

51Laval Dairy QSHL-26

Leger, Jim

00Wilkes-Barre Scranton Penguins-12
01Johnstown Chiefs-11
02Johnstown Chiefs-9
03Atlantic City Boardwalk Bullies-12
04Atlantic City Boardwalk Bullies Kinko's-22
04Idaho Steelheads-11

Leger, Roger

43Parade Sportive *-68
44Beehive Group II Photos-260
45Quaker Oats Photos-89A
45Quaker Oats Photos-89B
45Quaker Oats Photos-89C
52St. Lawrence Sales-9

Legg, Chris

03Austin Ice Bats-9

Legg, Mike

93Michigan Wolverines-12
00Idaho Steelheads-11
02Augusta Lynx-70

Legge, Barry

80Jets Postcards-10
80Pepsi-Cola Caps-129

Legge, Josh

00Owen Sound Attack-10
01Sudbury Wolves-9
01Sudbury Wolves Police-7
02Greenville Grrrowl-7
03Toledo Storm-4
04Missouri River Otters-19
05Odessa Jackalopes-12
06Odessa Jackalopes-13

Legge, Randy

76San Diego Mariners WHA-5

Leggett, Alan

91ProCards-315
92Raleigh Icecaps-5
92Raleigh Icecaps-30
93Raleigh Icecaps-9
95San Diego Barracudas RHI-6

Leggett, Casey

92Quebec Pee-Wee Tournament-655
97Rimouski Oceanic-55
99Quebec Remparts-22
Signed-22

Leggo, Tyler

01Sudbury Wolves-10
01Sudbury Wolves Police-15

Legris, Hector

52Bas Du Fleuve-39

Legue, Jeff

99Cornwall Colts-4
05South Carolina Stingrays-2

Legwand, David A

93Quebec Pee-Wee Tournament-1760
94Quebec Pee-Wee Tournament-888
97Black Diamond-35
Double Diamond-35
Triple Diamond-35
Quadruple Diamond-35
98Black Diamond-115
Double Diamond-115
Triple Diamond-115
Quadruple Diamond-115
98Bowman's Best-136
Refractors-136
Atomic Refractors-136
98Finest Futures Finest-F1
98Finest Futures Finest Refractors-F1
98OPC Chrome-234
Refractors-234
98SPx Top Prospects-88
Radiance-88
Spectrum-88
98Topps-234
O-Pee-Chee-234
98UD Choice-302
Prime Choice Reserve-302
Reserve-302
98Bowman CHL-14
98Bowman CHL-147
Golden Anniversary-14
Golden Anniversary-147
OPC International-14
OPC International-147
Autographs Blue-A11
Autographs Gold-A11
Autographs Silver-A11
98Bowman Chrome CHL-14
98Bowman Chrome CHL-147
Golden Anniversary-14
Golden Anniversary-147
Golden Anniversary Refractors-14
Golden Anniversary Refractors-147
OPC International-14
OPC International-147
OPC International Refractors-14
OPC International Refractors-147
Refractors-14
Refractors-147
99Aurora-80
Premiere Date-80
99BAP Memorabilia-236
Gold-236
Silver-236
99BAP Millennium-136
Emerald-136
Ruby-136
Sapphire-136
Signatures-136
Signatures Gold-136
Calder Candidates Ruby-C17
Calder Candidates Emerald-C17
Calder Candidates Sapphire-C17
99Black Diamond-49
Diamond Cut-49
Final Cut-49
Diamonation-D9
99Crown Royale-76
Limited Series-76
Premiere Date-76
Prospects Parallel-76
Ice Elite-15
Ice Elite Parallel-15
99McDonald's Upper Deck-MCD17
99O-Pee-Chee-248
99O-Pee-Chee Chrome-248
99O-Pee-Chee Chrome Refractors-248
99Pacific-229
Copper-229
Emerald Green-229
Gold-229
Ice Blue-229
Premiere Date-229
Red-229
Gold Crown Die-Cuts-20
99Pacific Dynagon Ice-109
Blue-109
Copper-109
Gold-109
Premiere Date-109
99Pacific Omega-130
Copper-130
Gold-130
Ice Blue-130
Premiere Date-130
NHL Generations-5
5 Star Talents-3
5 Star Talents Parallel-3
99Pacific Prism-76
Holographic Blue-76
Holographic Gold-76
Holographic Mirror-76
Holographic Purple-76
Premiere Date-76
Ice Prospects-4
99Panini Stickers-268
99Paramount-127
Copper-127
Emerald-127
Gold-127
Holographic Emerald-127
Holographic Gold-127
Holographic Silver-127
Ice Blue-127
Premiere Date-127
Red-127
Silver-127
99SP Authentic-46
Sign of the Times-DL
Sign of the Times Gold-DL
Tomorrow's Headliners-TH5
99SPx-82
99SPx-177
Radiance-82
Radiance-177
Spectrum-82
Spectrum-177
Prolifics-P15
SPXcitement-X5
SPXtreme-XT19
99Stadium Club-200
First Day Issue-200
One of a Kind-200
Printing Plates Black-200
Printing Plates Cyan-200
Printing Plates Magenta-200
Printing Plates Yellow-200
Chrome-50
Chrome Refractors-50
Chrome Oversized-20
Chrome Oversized Refractors-20
99Topps Arena Giveaways-NAS-DL
99Topps/OPC-248
99Topps/OPC Chrome-248
Refractors-248
99Topps Gold Label Class 1-86
Black-86
Black One of One-86
One of One-86
Red-86
Red One of One-86
99Topps Gold Label Class 2-86
99Topps Gold Label Class 2 Black-86
99Topps Gold Label Class 2 Black 1 of 1-86
99Topps Gold Label Class 2 One of One-86
99Topps Gold Label Class 2 Red-86
99Topps Gold Label Class 2 Red One of One-86
99Topps Gold Label Class 3-86
99Topps Gold Label Class 3 Black-86
99Topps Gold Label Class 3 Black 1 of 1-86
99Topps Gold Label Class 3 One of One-86
99Topps Gold Label Class 3 Red-86
99Topps Gold Label Class 3 Red One of One-86
99Topps Gold Label Fresh Gold-FG12
99Topps Gold Label Fresh Gold Black-FG12
99Topps Gold Label Fresh Gold Black 1of1-FG12
99Topps Gold Label Fresh Gold One of One-FG12
99Topps Gold Label Fresh Gold Red-FG12
99Topps Gold Label Fresh Gold Red 1 of 1-FG12
99Topps Premier Plus-135
Parallel-135
Game Pieces-GPDL
Premier Rookies-PR7
Premier Rookies Parallel-PR7
Signing Bonus-SB1
The Next Ones-TN06
99Ultimate Victory-47
1/1-47
Parallel-47
Parallel 100-47
99Upper Deck-73
99Upper Deck-160
Exclusives-73
Exclusives-160
Exclusives 1 of 1-73
Exclusives 1 of 1-160
Crunch Time-CT17
Crunch Time Quantum Gold-CT17
Crunch Time Quantum Silver-CT17
New Ice Age-N8
New Ice Age Quantum Gold-N8
New Ice Age Quantum Silver-N8
Sixth Sense-SS10
Sixth Sense Quantum Gold-SS10
Sixth Sense Quantum Silver-SS10
99Upper Deck Arena Giveaways-NP1
99Upper Deck Century Legends-77
Century Collection-77
99Upper Deck Gold Reserve-73
99Upper Deck Gold Reserve-160
UD Authentics-DL
99Upper Deck HoloGrFx-31
Ausome-31
UD Authentics-DL
99Upper Deck MVP-110
Gold Script-110
Silver Script-110
Super Script-110
21st Century NHL-1
Draft Report-DR5
99Upper Deck MVP SC Edition-97
Gold Script-97
Silver Script-97
Super Script-97
Cup Contenders-CC5
ProSign-DL
99Upper Deck Ovation-32
Standing Ovation-32
99Upper Deck PowerDeck-13
Auxiliary-13
Auxiliary 1 of 1-13
99Upper Deck Retro-43
Gold-43
Platinum-43
99Upper Deck Victory-154
99Upper Deck Victory-156
99Wayne Gretzky Hockey-90
Signs of Greatness-DL
99Quebec PeeWee Tournament Coll Souv-23
99Bowman CHL-147
Gold-147
OPC International-147
Scout's Choice-SC13
00Aurora-78
Pinstripes-78
Pinstripes Premiere Date-78
Premiere Date-78
Autographs-78
00BAP Memorabilia-263
Emerald-263
Ruby-263
Sapphire-263
Promos-263
00BAP Mem Chicago Sportsfest Copper-263
00BAP Memorabilia Chicago Sportsfest Blue-263
00BAP Memorabilia Chicago Sportsfest Gold-263
00BAP Memorabilia Chicago Sportsfest Ruby-263
00BAP Memorabilia Chicago Sun-Times Ruby-263
00BAP Memorabilia Chicago Sun-Times Gold-263
00BAP Mem Chicago Sun-Times Sapphire-263
00BAP Mem Toronto Fall Expo Copper-263
00BAP Memorabilia Toronto Fall Expo Gold-263
00BAP Memorabilia Toronto Fall Expo Ruby-263
00BAP Parkhurst 2000-P87
00BAP Signature Series-101
Emerald-101
Ruby-101
Sapphire-101
Autographs-6
Autographs Gold-6
Franchise Players-F17
00Black Diamond-32
Gold-32
00Crown Royale-60
Ice Blue-60
Limited Series-60
Premiere Date-60
Red-60
Game-Worn Jersey Redemptions-4
00McDonald's Pacific Gold Crown Die Cuts-3
00O-Pee-Chee-24
00O-Pee-Chee Parallel-24
00Pacific-223
Copper-223
Gold-223
Ice Blue-223
Premiere Date-223
Autographs-223
00Paramount-136
Copper-136
Gold-136
Holo-Gold-136
Holo-Silver-136
Ice Blue-136
Premiere Date-136
00Private Stock-55
Gold-55
Premiere Date-55
Retail-55
Silver-55
PS-2001 Action-30
PS-2001 New Wave-12
00Revolution-82
Blue-82
Premiere Date-82
Red-82
00SP Authentic-49
BuyBacks-54
BuyBacks-55
Sign of the Times-DL
00SP Game Used-35
Tools of the Game-DL
Tools of the Game Exclusives-DL
00SPx-36
Spectrum-36
00Stadium Club-32
00Titanium-51
Blue-51
Gold-51
Premiere Date-51
Red-51
Retail-51
Game Gear-104
Game Gear Patches-104
00Titanium Draft Day Edition-55
Patches-55
00Topps/OPC-24
Parallel-24
Game-Worn Sweaters-GWDL
00Topps Chrome-23
OPC Refractors-23
Refractors-23
00Topps Gold Label Class 1-78
Gold-78
00Topps Gold Label Class 2-78
00Topps Gold Label Class 2 Gold-78
00Topps Gold Label Class 3-78
00Topps Gold Label Class 3 Gold-78
00Topps Gold Label New Generation-NG10
00Topps Gold Label New Generation 1 to 1-NG10
00Topps Heritage-47
Chrome Parallel-47
00Topps Premier Plus-4
Blue Ice-4
Aspirations-PA9
00Topps Stars-27
Blue-27
Game Gear-GGDL
00UD Heroes-68
00UD Pros and Prospects-47
00UD Reserve-47
00Upper Deck-97
Exclusives Tier 1-97
Exclusives Tier 2-97
00Upper Deck Ice-23
Immortals-23
Legends-23
Stars-23
Game Jerseys-JCDL
00Upper Deck Legends-74
00Upper Deck Legends-75
Legendary Collection Bronze-74
Legendary Collection Bronze-75
Legendary Collection Gold-74
Legendary Collection Gold-75
Legendary Collection Silver-74
Legendary Collection Silver-75
00Upper Deck MVP-98
First Stars-98
ProSign-DL
Second Stars-98
Third Stars-98
00Upper Deck Victory-126
00Upper Deck Victory-128
00Upper Deck Victory-308
00Upper Deck Vintage-202
00Upper Deck Vintage-208
00Upper Deck Vintage-209
00Vanguard-54
Holographic Gold-54
Holographic Purple-54
Pacific Proofs-54
01Atomic-55
Blue-55
Gold-55
Premiere Date-55
Red-55
01BAP Memorabilia-128
Emerald-128
Ruby-128
Sapphire-128
01BAP Signature Series-28
Autographs-28
Autographs Gold-28
Franchise Jerseys-FP-17
01Bowman YoungStars-160
Gold-160
Ice Cubed-160
Autographs-DL
Relics-JDL
Relics-SDL
Relics-DSDL
Rivals-R8
01Crown Royale-81
Blue-81
Premiere Date-81
Red-81
Retail-81
01O-Pee-Chee-244
01O-Pee-Chee Premier Parallel-244
01Pacific-220
Extreme LTD-220
Hobby LTD-220
Premiere Date-220
Retail LTD-220
01Pacific Adrenaline-106
Blue-106
Premiere Date-106
Red-106
Retail-106
01Pacific Arena Exclusives-220
01Pacific Heads-Up-54
Blue-54
Premiere Date-54
Red-54
Silver-54
Breaking the Glass-13
Quad Jerseys-13
01Parkhurst-47
Gold-47
Silver-47
01Private Stock-53
Gold-53
Premiere Date-53
Retail-53
Silver-53
Game Gear Patches-58
01Private Stock Pacific Nights-53
01SP Authentic-45
01SP Authentic-113
Limited-45
Limited-113
Limited Gold-45
Limited Gold-113
01SPx-35
01Stadium Club-29
Award Winners-29
Master Photos-29
01Titanium-79
Hobby Parallel-79
Premiere Date-79
Retail-79
Retail Parallel-79
01Topps-244
OPC Parallel-244
01Topps Chrome-20
Refractors-20
Black Border Refractors-20
01Topps Heritage-20
Refractors-20
01UD Honor Roll Jerseys-J-DL
01UD Honor Roll Jerseys Gold-J-DL
01UD Mask Collection-53
Gold-53
01UD Playmakers-55
01UD Top Shelf-24
01Upper Deck-96
Exclusives-96
01Upper Deck MVP-104
01Upper Deck Victory-201
Gold-201
01Upper Deck Vintage-140
01Upper Deck Vintage-148
01Vanguard-54
Blue-54
Red-54
One of Ones-54
Premiere Date-54
Proofs-54
02BAP First Edition-106
Jerseys-106
02BAP Sig Series Auto Buybacks 1999-136
02BAP Sig Series Auto Buybacks 2001-28
02BAP Signature Series Franchise Players-FJ17
02BAP Signature Series Golf-GS30
02BAP Signature Series Phenoms-YP4
02Bowman YoungStars-96
Gold-96
Silver-96
02Crown Royale-54
Blue-54
Red-54
Retail-54
02O-Pee-Chee-25
02O-Pee-Chee Premier Blue Parallel-25
02O-Pee-Chee Premier Red Parallel-25
02O-Pee-Chee Factory Set-25
02Pacific-212
Blue-212
Red-212
02Pacific Exclusive-100
Jerseys-15
Jerseys Gold-15
02Pacific Heads-Up-69
Blue-69
Purple-69
Red-69
Quad Jerseys-16
Quad Jerseys Gold-16
02Pacific Quest for the Cup-54
Gold-54
02Parkhurst-74
Bronze-74
Gold-74
Silver-74
Teammates-TT10
02Parkhurst Retro-168
Minis-168
Franchise Players-RF17
02Private Stock Reserve-128
Red-128
Retail-128
Patches-128
02SP Authentic-51
Beckett Promos-51
02SP Game Used First Rounder Patches-DL
02SP Game Used Piece of History-PHDL
02SP Game Used Piece of History Gold-PHDL
02SP Game Used Piece of History Rainbow-PHDL
02SPx Winning Materials-WMDL
02SPx Winning Materials Gold-DL
02SPx Winning Materials Silver-DL
02Stadium Club-52
Silver Decoy Cards-52
Proofs-52
YoungStars Relics-S8
YoungStars Relics-DS2
02Titanium-60
Blue-60
Red-60
Retail-60
Jerseys-37
Jerseys Retail-37
Patches-37
02Topps-25
OPC Blue Parallel-25
OPC Red Parallel-25
Signs of the Future-DL
Factory Set-25
02Topps Chrome-25
Black Border Refractors-25
Refractors-25
02Topps Heritage-60
Chrome Parallel-60
02Topps Total-58
02UD Artistic Impressions-50
Gold-50
02UD Artistic Impressions Beckett Promos-50
02UD Artistic Impressions Retrospectives-R50
02UD Artistic Impressions Retrospect Gold-R50
02UD Artistic Impress Retrospect Silver-R50
02UD Honor Roll-42
02UD Premier Collection-32
02UD Top Shelf-49
Dual Player Jerseys-RNL
Dual Player Jerseys-STHL
02Upper Deck-343
Exclusives-343
02Upper Deck Beckett UD Promos-343
02Upper Deck Bright Futures-DL
02Upper Deck CHL Graduates-CGDL
02Upper Deck CHL Graduates Gold-CGDL
02Upper Deck Hot Spots-HSDL
02Upper Deck Classic Portraits Hockey Royalty-DLH
02Upper Deck Classic Portraits Hockey Royalty Limited-DLH
02Upper Deck Rookie Update-55
02Upper Deck Victory-118
Bronze-118
Gold-118
Silver-118
02Upper Deck Vintage-145
Green Backs-145
02Vanguard-59
LTD-59
03BAP Memorabilia-21
Emerald-21
Gold-21
Ruby-21
Sapphire-21
03BAP Ultimate Memorabilia Autographs-51
Gold-51
03BAP Ultimate Mem Franch Present Future-17
03Beehive-109
Gold-109
Silver-109
03Black Diamond-13
Black-13

Green-13
Red-13
03Bowman-87
Gold-87
03Bowman Chrome-87
Refractors-87
Gold Refractors-87
Xfractors-87
03ITG Action-343
Jerseys-M47
Jerseys-M257
03ITG Used Signature Series-70
Gold-70
Autographs-DL
Autographs Gold-DL
03NHL Sticker Collection-256
03O-Pee-Chee-78
03OPC Blue-78
03OPC Gold-78
03OPC Red-78
03Pacific-190
Blue-190
Red-190
03Pacific Complete-113
Red-113
03Pacific Exhibit-176
03Pacific Exhibit-209
Blue Backs-176
03Pacific Heads-Up-57
Hobby LTD-57
Retail LTD-57
03Pacific Invincible-52
Blue-52
Red-52
Retail-52
Featured Performers-17
03Pacific Prism-126
Blue-126
Patches-126
Red-126
Retail-126
Paramount Prodigies-15
03Pacific Supreme-55
Blue-55
Red-55
Retail-55
03Parkhurst Rookie Teammates Gold-RT13
03Parkhurst Rookie Teammates-RT13
03Private Stock Reserve-176
Blue-176
Patches-176
Red-176
Retail-176
03SP Authentic-49
Limited-49
03SPx-55
Radiance-55
Spectrum-55
03Titanium-58
Hobby Jersey Number Parallels-58
Retail-58
Retail Jersey Number Parallels-58
03Topps-78
Blue-78
Gold-78
Red-78
Topps/OPC Idols-UI16
03Topps C55-94
Minis-94
Minis American Back-94
Minis American Back Red-94
Minis Bazooka Back-94
Minis Brooklyn Back-94
Minis Hat Trick Back-94
Minis O Canada Back-94
Minis O Canada Back Red-94
Minis Stanley Cup Back-94
Relics-TRDL
03Topps Pristine-86
Gold Refractor Die Cuts-86
Refractors-86
Jersey Portions-PPJ-DL
Jersey Portion Refractors-PPJ-DL
Patches-PP-DL
Patch Refractors-PP-DL
Press Plates Black-86
Press Plates Cyan-86
Press Plates Magenta-86
Press Plates Yellow-86
03UD Honor Roll-46
03Upper Deck-106
Canadian Exclusives-106
HG-106
03Upper Deck Classic Portraits-54
03Upper Deck Ice-49
Gold-49
03Upper Deck MVP-235
Gold Script-235
Silver Script-235
Canadian Exclusives-235
03Upper Deck Trilogy-54
Limited-54
03Upper Deck Victory-102
Bronze-102
Gold-102
Silver-102
04Pacific-148
Blue-148
Red-148
04SP Authentic Rookie Review-RR-DL
04SP Authentic Sign of the Times-ST-DL
04SP Authentic Sign of the Times-SS-USA
04Upper Deck-97
Canadian Exclusives-97
HG Glossy Gold-97
HG Glossy Silver-97
05Be A Player Signatures-DL
05Be A Player Signatures Gold-DL
05Black Diamond-120
Emerald-120
Gold-120
Onyx-120
Ruby-120
05Hot Prospects Hot Materials-HMDL
05Panini Stickers-313
05Parkhurst-280
Facsimile Auto Parallel-280
True Colors-TCNSH
True Colors-TCNSH
05SP Game Used Authentic Fabrics Dual-HL
05SP Game Used Authentic Fabrics Quad-KLHV
05SP Game Used Authentic Patches Quad -KLHV
05SP Game Used Authentic Fabrics Triple-VKL
05SP Game Used Authentic Patches Dual-HL
05SP Game Used Authentic Patches Triple-VKL
05SP Game Used Awesome Authentics-AA-DL
05SP Game Used Awesome Authentics Gold-DA-DL
05SP Game Used Game Gear-GG-DL
05SP Game Used Game Gear Autographs-AG-DL
05SP Game Used Signature Sticks-SS-DL
05SP Game Used SIGnificance-DL
05SP Game Used SIGnificance Gold-S-DL
05SP Game Used Statscriptions-ST-DL
05SPx-49
Spectrum-49
05UD Artifacts Auto Facts-AF-DL
05UD Artifacts Auto Facts Blue-AF-DL
05UD Artifacts Auto Facts Copper-AF-DL
05UD Artifacts Auto Facts Pewter-AF-DL
05UD Artifacts Auto Facts Silver-AF-DL
05UD Artifacts Remarkable Artifacts-RA-DL
05UD Artifacts Remarkable Artifacts Dual-RA-DL
05Ultimate Collection Endorsed Emblems-EEDL
05Ultra-113
Gold-113
Ice-113
05Upper Deck-106
Big Playmakers-B-DL
HG Glossy-106
Jerseys-J-DL
Notable Numbers-N-DL
Patches-P-DL
05Upper Deck MVP-216
Gold-216
Platinum-216
05Upper Deck Trilogy Honorary Patches-HP-DL
05Upper Deck Trill Honorary Patch Script-HSP-DL
05Upper Deck Trilogy Honorary Swatches-HS-DL
05Upper Deck Trill Honorary Swatch Scripts-HSS-DL
05Upper Deck Toronto Fall Expo-106
05Upper Deck Victory-109
Black-109
Gold-109
Silver-109
06Be A Player-96
Autographs-96
Signatures-DL
Signatures 10-104
Signatures Duals-DNA
Signatures Trios-TFLS
06Flair Showcase Stitches-SSDL
06Fleer-112
Tiffany-112
Fabricology-FDL
06O-Pee-Chee-282
Rainbow-282
06Panini Stickers-309
06Ultra-111
Gold Medallion-111
Ice Medallion-111
Uniformity-UDL
Uniformity Patches-UPDL
06Upper Deck Arena Giveaways-NSH2
06Upper Deck-109
Exclusives Parallel-109
High Gloss Parallel-109
Masterpieces-109
Signatures-SDL
Victory-115
Victory Black-115
Victory Gold-115

Lehikoinen, Ari
80Finnish Mallasjuoma-139

Lehikoinen, Tero
92Finnish Jyvas-Hyva Stickers-79

Lehkonen, Ismo
80Finnish Mallasjuoma-55

Lehkonen, Timo
91Finnish Jyvas-Hyva Stickers-7
92Finnish Jyvas-Hyva Stickers-19
93Finnish SISU-375
94Finnish SISU-219

Lehman, Hugh
60Topps-38
Stamps-33
83Hall of Fame Postcards-N7
85Hall of Fame-202

Lehman, Jason
98Thunder Bay Thunder Cats-1

Lehman, Jody
01South Carolina Stingrays-12
02UK Coventry Blaze-2
03UK Coventry Blaze-9
03UK Coventry Blaze Calendars-7
03UK Coventry Blaze History-12
04UK Coventry Blaze-8
04UK Coventry Blaze Champions-1
04UK EIHL All-Stars-1
05UK Sheffield Steelers-1
Gold-1
Silver-1

Lehman, Scott
02St. Michaels Majors-10
03St. Michael's Majors-9
04St. Michael's Majors-10
05OHL Bell All-Star Classic-30

Lehmann, Michael
94German First League-222

Lehmann, Tommy
83Swedish Semic Elitserien-22
84Swedish Semic Elitserien-20
85Swedish Panini Stickers-19
90Swedish Semic Elitserien Stickers-89
91Swedish Semic Elitserien Stickers-18
92Swedish Semic Elitserien Stickers-239
94Swedish Leaf-72
95Swedish Leaf-159
95Swedish Upper Deck-15

Lehner, Bjorn
94German First League-250

Lehner, Josef
94German DEL-58
95German DEL-53
95Swedish World Championships Stickers-57
96German DEL-252
98German DEL-322
99German Bundesliga 2-278
06German DEL-177

Lehnigk, Peter
04German Berlin Eisbarens 50th Anniv-65

Lehoux, Guy
91ProCards-350
917th Inn. Sketch Memorial Cup-55
92St. John's Maple Leafs-10
93St. John's Maple Leafs-14
94St. John's Maple Leafs-17
95St. John's Maple Leafs-14
96St. John's Maple Leafs-19
98German DEL-215
99German DEL-200
01German Upper Deck-204
02German DEL City Press-267
03German DEL-207
03German Nuremberg Ice Tigers Postcards-17
04German DEL-236
04German Krefeld Penguins Postcards-16
05German DEL-188

Lehoux, Hugo
99Halifax Mooseheads-19
00Halifax Mooseheads-14
04Lakehead University Thunderwolves-13

Lehoux, Jason
93Quebec Pee-Wee Tournament-365
96Rimouski Oceanic Update-4
99Hull Olympiques-14
Signed-14
99Rouyn-Noranda Huskies-13
00Albany River Rats-13
01Albany River Rats-18
02Albany River Rats-12
02Albany River Rats AAP-17

Lehoux, Yanick
96Quebec Pee-Wee Tournament-333
99Baie-Comeau Drakkar-15
99UD Prospects-56
00Baie-Comeau Drakkar-12
Signed-12
00UD CHL Prospects-77
01Baie-Comeau Drakkar-10
02Manchester Monarchs-11
03Manchester Monarchs-9
03Manchester Monarchs Team Issue-9
03Pacific AHL Prospects-51
Gold-51
04AHL Top Prospects-27
04Manchester Monarchs-24
04Manchester Monarchs Tobacco-24
04ITG Heroes and Prospects-23
Autographs-YL
Complete Emblems-21
Emblems-48
Emblems Gold-48
He Shoots-He Scores Prizes-31
Jersey Autographs-48
Jerseys-48
Jerseys Gold-48
Numbers-48
Numbers Gold-48
04ITG Heroes/Prospects Toronto Expo '05-23
04ITG Heroes/Prospects Expo Heroes/Pros-23
05ITG Heroes/Prosp Toronto Expo Parallel -70
05Black Diamond-250
05Hot Prospects-136
En Fuego-136
Red Hot-136
White Hot-136
05SP Authentic-235
Limited-235
05SP Game Used-214
05SPx-263
05The Cup Masterpiece Pressplate Artifact-283
05The Cup Master Pressplate Black Diamond-250
05The Cup Masterpiece Pressplates (Ice)-204
05The Cup Master Pressplate Rookie Update-140
05The Cup Masterpiece Pressplates SPA-235
05The Cup Masterpiece Pressplates SP GU-214
05The Cup Masterpiece Pressplates (SPx)-263
05The Cup Masterpiece Pressplates Trilogy-265
05The Cup Masterpiece Pressplate Ult Coll-177
05UD Artifacts-283
05Ultimate Collection-177
Gold-177
05Upper Deck Ice-204
05Upper Deck Rookie Update-140
05Upper Deck Trilogy-265
05Manchester Monarchs-40
05ITG Heroes and Prospects-70
Autographs-A-YL

Lehr, Ryan
03Baie Comeau Drakkar-3
04Baie-Comeau Drakkar-20
05Baie-Comeau Drakkar-4
05Chicoutimi Sagueneens-24

Lehrke, Tyler
04Green Bay Gamblers-8

Lehtera, Jori
06Finnish Cardset-246

Lehtera, Tero
91Upper Deck Czech World Juniors-32
92Finnish Jyvas-Hyva Stickers-109
93Finnish Jyvas-Hyva Stickers-197
93Finnish SISU-272
94Finnish SISU-9
94Finnish SISU Fire On Ice-16
94Finnish SISU NHL Draft-6
94Swedish Leaf-200
Foreign Affairs-10
95Finnish SISU-257
Gold Cards-16
95Finnish SISU Limited-62
95Finnish Karjala World Champ Labels-8
95Finnish Semic World Championships-27
95Swedish World Championships Stickers-176
96Finnish SISU Redline-97
96Swedish Semic Wien-17
98Finnish Kerailysarja Leijonat-29
98Fort Wayne Komets-15
99Finnish Cardset-270
00Finnish Cardset-214
01Finnish Cardset-190
02Finnish Cardset-211
03Russian Hockey League-181

Lehti, Pertti
78Finnish SM-Liiga-220

Lehtinen, Arto
71Finnish Suomi Stickers-306

Lehtinen, Jere
92Upper Deck-615
92Finnish Jyvas-Hyva Stickers-107
92Classic-31
Gold-31
93Finnish Jyvas-Hyva Stickers-322
93Finnish SISU-47
94Finnish SISU-20
94Finnish SISU-155
94Finnish SISU-157
94Finnish Jaa Kiekko-29
94Classic-72
Gold-72
Tri-Cards-T16
Pro Prospects Ice Ambassadors-IA16
95Be A Player-175
Signatures-S175
Signatures Die Cuts-S175
95Bowman-150
All-Foil-150
95Donruss-332
95Finest-53
Refractors-53
95Leaf Limited-39
95Metal-183
International Steel-13
95Parkhurst International-265
95Parkhurst International-518
Emerald Ice-265
Emerald Ice-518
95SkyBox Impact-195
95SP-41
95Stadium Club-199
Members Only Master Set-199
95Summit-173
Artist's Proofs-173
Ice-173
95Ultra-347
95Upper Deck-398
Electric Ice-398
Electric Ice Gold-398
95Zenith-145
95Finnish Beckett Ad Cards-2
95Finnish SISU-164
Gold Cards-17
95Finnish SISU Limited-9
95Finnish SISU Specials-7
95Finnish Karjala World Champ Labels-9
95Finnish Semic World Championships-20
95Finnish Semic World Championships-232
96Black Diamond-87
Gold-87
96Collector's Choice-75
96Donruss Rated Rookies-4
96Donruss Canadian Ice-111
Gold Press Proofs-111
Red Press Proofs-111
96Donruss Elite-77
Die Cut Stars-77
Aspirations-10
96Fleer Picks-144
96Leaf-201
Press Proofs-201
96Leaf Limited-77
Gold-77
96Leaf Preferred-47
Press Proofs-47
Steel-63
Steel Gold-63
96Score-246
Artist's Proofs-246
Dealer's Choice Artist's Proofs-246
Special Artist's Proofs-246
Golden Blades-246
96Stars Postcards-17
96Stars Score Sheet-246
96Summit-153
Artist's Proofs-153
Ice-153
Metal-153
Premium Stock-153
96Topps Picks Rookie Stars-RS2
96Topps Picks Rookie Stars OPC-RS2
96Upper Deck-49
96Zenith-51
Artist's Proofs-51
96Swedish Semic Wien-20
96Swedish Semic Wien-37
All-Stars-AS4
97Be A Player-123
Autographs-123
Autographs Die-Cuts-123
Autographs Prismatic Die-Cuts-123
97Black Diamond-40
Double Diamond-40
Triple Diamond-40
Quadruple Diamond-40
97Collector's Choice-74
97Donruss-30
Press Proofs Silver-30
Press Proofs Gold-30
97Donruss Elite-68
Aspirations-68
Status-68
97Donruss Limited-135
Exposure-135
97Donruss Preferred-65
Cut to the Chase-65
97Donruss Priority-63
Stamp of Approval-63
97Katch-45
Gold-45
Silver-45
97Leaf-98
Fractal Matrix-98
Fractal Matrix Die Cuts-98
97Leaf International-98
Universal Ice-98
97NHL Aces Playing Cards-28
97Pacific Invincible NHL Regime-61
97Pacific Omega-71
Copper-71
Dark Gray-71
Emerald Green-71
Gold-71
Ice Blue-71
97Panini Stickers-145
97Paramount-59
Copper-59
Dark Grey-59
Emerald Green-59
Ice Blue-59
Red-59
Silver-59
97Pinnacle-118
Press Plates Back Black-118
Press Plates Back Cyan-118
Press Plates Back Magenta-118
Press Plates Back Yellow-118
Press Plates Front Black-118
Press Plates Front Cyan-118
Press Plates Front Magenta-118
Press Plates Front Yellow-118
97Pinnacle Inside-187
97Revolution-42
Copper-42
Emerald-42
Ice Blue-42
Silver-42
97Score-188
97SP Authentic-48
97Upper Deck-52
Smooth Grooves-SG26
Three Star Selects-8C
98Aurora-57
98Be A Player-44
Press Release-44
98BAP Gold-44
98BAP Autographs-44
98BAP Autographs Gold-44
98BAP Tampa Bay All Star Game-44
98Bowman's Best-76
Refractors-76
Atomic Refractors-76
98Crown Royale-40
Limited Series-40
98Katch-45
98Pacific-179
Ice Blue-179
Red-179
98Pacific Dynagon Ice-58
Blue-58
Red-58
98Pacific Omega-72
Red-72
Opening Day Issue-72
98Panini Stickers-120
98Panini Stickers-226
98Paramount-66
Copper-66
Emerald Green-66
Holo-Electric-66
Ice Blue-66
Silver-66
98Revolution-43
Ice Shadow-43
Red-43
98SP Authentic-27
Power Shift-27
98SPx Finite-28
Radiance-28
Spectrum-28
98UD Choice-68
Prime Choice Reserve-68
Reserve-68
98Upper Deck-258
Exclusives-258
Exclusives 1 of 1-258
Gold Reserve-258
98Upper Deck MVP-67
Gold Script-67
Silver Script-67
Super Script-67
98Finnish Kerailysarja 90's Top 12-1
98Finnish Kerailysarja Dream Team-5
99Aurora-46
Premiere Date-46
99BAP Memorabilia-48
Gold-48
Silver-48
99BAP Millennium-81
Emerald-81
Ruby-81
Sapphire-81
Signatures-81
Signatures Gold-81
99Crown Royale-45
Limited Series-45
Premiere Date-45
99O-Pee-Chee-226
99O-Pee-Chee Chrome-226
99O-Pee-Chee Chrome Refractors-226
99O-Pee-Chee Chrome Positive Performers-PP6
99OPC Chrome Pos Performers Ref-PP6
99O-Pee-Chee Positive Performers-PP6
99O-Pee-Chee Top of the World-TW3
99Pacific-123
Copper-123
Emerald Green-123
Gold-123
Ice Blue-123
Premiere Date-123
Red-123
99Pacific Dynagon Ice-67
Blue-67
Copper-67
Gold-67
Premiere Date-67
2000 All-Star Preview-10
99Pacific Omega-73
Copper-73
Gold-73
Ice Blue-73
Premiere Date-73
99Panini Stickers-7
99Paramount-74
Copper-74
Emerald-74
Gold-74
Holographic Emerald-74
Holographic Gold-74
Holographic Silver-74
Ice Blue-74
Premiere Date-74
Red-74
Silver-74
99Revolution-47
Premiere Date-47
Red-47
Shadow Series-47
99SPx-51
Radiance-51
Spectrum-51
99Stadium Club-148
First Day Issue-148
One of a Kind-148
Printing Plates Black-148
Printing Plates Cyan-148
Printing Plates Magenta-148
Printing Plates Yellow-148
99Stars Postcards-11
99Topps/OPC-226
Positive Performers-PP6
Top of the World-TW3
99Topps/OPC Chrome-226
Refractors-226
Positive Performers-PP6
Positive Performers Refractors-PP6
99Topps Premier Plus-75
Parallel-75
99Upper Deck-215
Exclusives-215
Exclusives 1 of 1-215
99Upper Deck Gold Reserve-215
99Upper Deck MVP-63
Gold Script-63
Silver Script-63
Super Script-63
99Upper Deck Victory-93
99Wayne Gretzky Hockey-59
99Finnish Cardset-NNO
Aces High-D-K
Jere Lehtinen Triple Threat-1
99Slovakian Challengers-26
00BAP Parkhurst 2000-P184
00BAP Signature Series-62
Emerald-62
Ruby-62
Sapphire-62
Autographs-123
Autographs Gold-123
00O-Pee-Chee-195
00O-Pee-Chee Parallel-195
00Pacific-134
00Pacific-435
Copper-134
Copper-435
Gold-134
Gold-435
Ice Blue-134
Ice Blue-435
Premiere Date-134
Premiere Date-435
00Paramount-77
Copper-77
Gold-77
Holo-Gold-77
Holo-Silver-77
Ice Blue-77
Premiere Date-77
00Private Stock Game Gear-38
00Private Stock Game Gear Patches-38
00Stars Postcards-12
00Titanium Game Gear-87
00Titanium Game Gear Patches-87
00Titanium Draft Day Edition-32
00Topps/OPC-195
Parallel-195
00Topps Chrome-129
OPC Refractors-129
Refractors-129
00UD Heroes-41
00Upper Deck-60
Exclusives Tier 1-60
Exclusives Tier 2-60
00Upper Deck Victory-79
00Upper Deck Vintage-113
00Vanguard Dual Game-Worn Jerseys-15
00Vanguard Dual Game-Worn Patches-15
00Finnish Cardset-357
01BAP Memorabilia-131
Emerald-131
Ruby-131
Sapphire-131
01Bowman YoungStars-91
Gold-91
Ice Cubed-91
01Crown Royale-47
Blue-47
Premiere Date-47
Red-47
Retail-47
01EA Sports-4
01O-Pee-Chee-114
01O-Pee-Chee Premier Parallel-114
01Pacific-128
Extreme LTD-128
Hobby LTD-128
Premiere Date-128
Retail LTD-128
01Pacific Arena Exclusives-128
01Pacific Heads-Up Quad Jerseys-24
01Stars Postcards-12
01Titanium-44
Hobby Parallel-44
Premiere Date-44
Retail-44
Retail Parallel-44
01Topps-114
OPC Parallel-114
01Topps Chrome-114
Refractors-114
Black Border Refractors-114
01UD Honor Roll Defense First-DF2
01UD Mask Collection-29
Gold-29
01UD Stanley Cup Champs-54
01Upper Deck-285
Exclusives-285
EA Sports Gold-4
01Upper Deck MVP-58
01Upper Deck Victory-119
Gold-119
01Upper Deck Vintage-84
01Vanguard Memorabilia-22
01Vanguard Patches-22
01Finnish Cardset Salt Lake City-9
02BAP Sig Series Auto Buybacks 1998-44
02BAP Sig Series Auto Buybacks 1999-81
02BAP Sig Series Auto Buybacks 2000-123
02Bowman YoungStars-80
Gold-80
Silver-80
02O-Pee-Chee-162
02O-Pee-Chee Premier Blue Parallel-162
02O-Pee-Chee Premier Red Parallel-162
02O-Pee-Chee Factory Set-162
02Pacific-113
Blue-113
Red-113
02Pacific Complete-117
Red-117
02Pacific Exclusive-56
02Pacific Heads-Up Quad Jerseys-33
02Pacific Heads-Up Quad Jerseys Gold-33
02Pacific Quest for the Cup-28
Gold-28
02Parkhurst-195
Bronze-195
Gold-195
Silver-195
02Parkhurst Retro-101
Minis-101
02Stars Postcards-5
02Topps-162
OPC Blue Parallel-162
OPC Red Parallel-162
Factory Set-162
02Topps Chrome-97
Black Border Refractors-97
Refractors-97
02Topps Total-138
02Upper Deck-60
Exclusives-60
Specialists-SJL
Classic Portraits Hockey Royalty-MML
Classic Portraits Hockey Royalty-SLN
Classic Portraits Hockey Royalty Limited-MML
Classic Portraits Hockey Royalty Limited-SLN
02Upper Deck MVP-58
Gold-58
Classics-58
Golden Classics-58
02Upper Deck Victory-67
Bronze-67
Gold-67
Silver-67
National Pride-NP24
02Upper Deck Vintage-84
02Finnish Cardset-212
03BAP Memorabilia-39
Emerald-39
Gold-39
Ruby-39
Sapphire-39
03Beehive-62
Gold-62
Silver-62
03ITG Action-142
03O-Pee-Chee-39
03OPC Blue-39
03OPC Gold-39
03OPC Red-39
03Pacific-106
Blue-106
Red-106
03Pacific Complete-118
Red-118
03Pacific Exhibit-48
Blue Backs-48
Yellow Backs-48
03Pacific Prism-35
Blue-35
Gold-35
Red-35
03Private Stock Reserve-30
Blue-30
Red-30
Retail-30
03Stars Postcards-12
03Titanium-34
Hobby Jersey Number Parallels-34
Retail-34
Retail Jersey Number Parallels-34
03Topps-39
Blue-39
Gold-39
Red-39
C55 Award Winners-14
03Upper Deck-61
Canadian Exclusives-61
HG-61
03Upper Deck MVP-130
Gold Script-130
Silver Script-130
Canadian Exclusives-130
03Upper Deck Victory-58
Bronze-58
Gold-58
Silver-58
04Pacific-85
Blue-85
Red-85
05Black Diamond-29
Emerald-29
Gold-29
Onyx-29
Ruby-29
05Panini Stickers-250
05Parkhurst-166
Facsimile Auto Parallel-166
05SP Game Used Authentic Fabrics Triple-DLP
05SP Game Used Authentic Patches Triple-DLP
05The Cup Master Pressplate Rookie Update-207
05Ultimate Coll National Heroes Jersey-NHJJL
05Ultimate Coll National Heroes Patch-NHPJL
05Ultra-72
Gold-72
Ice-72
05Upper Deck-307
Big Playmakers-B-JLU
Jerseys-J-JLE
Jerseys Series II-J2JE
NHL Generations-DLH
Notable Numbers-N-JEL
Patches-P-JEL
05Upper Deck MVP-133
Gold-133
Platinum-133
05Upper Deck Rookie Update-207
Inspirations Patch Rookies-207
05Upper Deck Victory-64
Black-64
Gold-64
Silver-64
06Be A Player-95
Autographs-95
Signatures-JE
Signatures 10-103
Signatures Duals-DTL
Signatures Trios-TTLO
Signatures Foursomes-FSKJL
06Beehive Matted Materials-MMLE
06Black Diamond-28
Black-28
Gold-28
Ruby-28
Jerseys-JLE
Jerseys Black-JLE
Jerseys Gold-JLE
Jerseys Ruby-JLE
06Flair Showcase-37
Parallel-37
Stitches-SSLE
06Fleer-67
Tiffany-67
Fabricology-FLE
06Hot Prospects Hot Materials -HMJL
06Hot Prospects Hot Materials Red Hot-HMJL
06Hot Prospects Hot Materials White Hot-HMJL
06O-Pee-Chee-168
Rainbow-168
Swatches-S-JL
06Panini Stickers-248
06SP Game Used Authentic Fabrics-AFJL
06SP Game Used Authentic Fabrics Parallel-AFJL
06SP Game Used Authentic Fabrics Patches-AFJL
06SP Game Used Authentic Fabrics Dual-AF2LJ
06SP Game Used Authentic Fabrics Dual Patches-AF2LJ
06SP Game Used Authentic Fabrics Sixes-AF6SEL
06SP Game Used Authentic Fabrics Sixes Patches-AF6SEL
06SP Game Used Authentic Fabrics Eights-AF8FIN
06SP Game Used Authentic Fabrics Eights Patches-AF8FIN
06Stars Team Postcards-11
06The Cup NHL Shields Duals-DSHLZ
06UD Powerplay Specialists-SJL
06UD Powerplay Specialists Patches-PJL
06Ultimate Collection Premium Patches-PS-JL
06Ultimate Collection Premium Swatches-PS-JL
06Ultra-68
Gold Medallion-68
Ice Medallion-68
Uniformity-UJL
Uniformity Patches-UPJL
06Upper Deck-65
Exclusives Parallel-65
High Gloss Parallel-65
Game Jerseys-JLE
Game Patches-PLE
Masterpieces-65
06Upper Deck MVP-98
Gold Script-98
Super Script-98
06Upper Deck Ovation-165
06Upper Deck Victory-65
06Upper Deck Victory Black-65
06Upper Deck Victory Gold-65
06Russian Sport Collection Olympic Stars-24

Lehtinen, Mika
94Finnish SISU-321
95Finnish SISU-325
96Finnish SISU Redline-136
98Finnish Kerailysarja-236
99Finnish Cardset-329
00Finnish Cardset-339
01Finnish Cardset-136
03Swedish Elite-104
Signatures-7
Silver-104
04Finnish Cardset-5
Parallel-5
05Finnish Cardset -327

Lehtinen, Rob
04Northern Michigan Wildcats-11

Lehtinen, Sami
99Finnish Cardset-92
Puck Stoppers-4
00Finnish Cardset-69
00Finnish Cardset Masquerade-3
01Finnish Cardset-324

Lehtio, Rauno
65Finnish Hellas-100
66Finnish Jaakiekkosarja-178
70Finnish Jaakiekko-245
71Finnish Suomi Stickers-212

Lehtio, Risto
65Finnish Hellas-101
66Finnish Jaakiekkosarja-186

Lehtivuori, Joonas
06Finnish Ilves Team Set-15

Lehto, Antti
80Finnish Mallasjuoma-58

Lehto, Joni
897th Inn. Sketch OHL-53
907th Inn. Sketch OHL-86
91ProCards-455
91Richmond Renegades-5
94Finnish SISU-343
95Finnish SISU-162
95Finnish SISU-299
Double Trouble-4
95Finnish SISU Limited-31
Signed and Sealed-5
95Finnish SISU Painkillers-3
96Finnish SISU Redline-176
Sledgehammers-9
96German DEL-66
96Swedish Semic Wien-33
98Finnish Kerailysarja Leijonat-10

Lehto, Kai
72Finnish Jaakiekko-308

Lehto, Markus
80Oshawa Generals-14
83Swedish Semic VM Stickers-32

Lehto, Mika
98Finnish Kerailysarja-252
99Finnish Cardset-336
00Finnish Cardset-168
01Finnish Cardset-61
02Finnish Cardset-213
02Finnish Cardset-300
03Finnish Cardset-142
04Finnish Cardset-150
Parallel-112
05Finnish Cardset -137
Finnish Cardset Super Snatchers-15
06Finnish Cardset-144
Between the Pipes-20
Signature Sensations-27
Superior Snatchers-4
Superior Snatchers Gold-4
Superior Snatchers Silver-4

Lehto, Petteri
80Finnish Mallasjuoma-197

Lehtolainen, Pekka
65Finnish Hellas-104
66Finnish Jaakiekkosarja-187

Lehtonen, Antero
72Finnish Jaakiekko-267
73Finnish Jaakiekko-156
77Finnish Sportscasters-54-1273
78Finnish SM-Liiga-14
78Finnish SM-Liiga-188
79Capitals Team Issue-10
80Finnish Mallasjuoma-176
81Swedish Semic Hockey VM Stickers-36

Lehtonen, Erkki
78Finnish SM-Liiga-187
80Finnish Mallasjuoma-164
05Finnish Tappara Legendat-11

Lehtonen, Kari
00Finnish Cardset-278
01Finnish Cardset-248
01Finnish Cardset-NNO
02BAP Memorabilia Draft Redemptions-2
02Finnish Cardset-147
02Finnish Cardset-214
Bound for Glory-4
02Finnish Cardset Dynamic Duos-2
02Finnish Cardset Kari Lehtonen Honors-1
02Finnish Cardset Kari Lehtonen Honors-2
02Finnish Cardset Kari Lehtonen Honors-3
02Finnish Cardset Kari Lehtonen Trophies-1
02Finnish Cardset Kari Lehtonen Trophies-2
02Finnish Cardset Kari Lehtonen Trophies-3

02Finnish Cardset Signatures-4
03BAP Memorabilia-236
03BAP Ultimate Memorabilia Autographs-122
Gold-122
03BAP Ultimate Mem Hometown Heroes-17
03BAP Ultimate Mem Hometown Heroes Gold-17
03BAP Ultimate Memorabilia Nameplates-26
03BAP Ultimate Mem Nameplates Gold-26
03BAP Ultimate Mem Rookie Jersey Emblems-1
03BAP Ultimate Mem Rookie Jsy Emblem Gold-1
03BAP Ultimate Mem Rookie Jersey Numbers-1
03BAP Ultimate Mem Rookie Jsy Number Gold-1
03ITG Action-626
03ITG Toronto Spring Expo Class of 2004-10
03ITG Used Signature Series-152
Gold-152
Gold-152A
Autographs-152A
Autographs Gold-152
Jerseys-51
Jerseys Gold-51
Jersey Autos-51
Emblems-41
Emblems Gold-41
03ITG VIP Rookie Debut-140
03Pacific Calder-102
Silver-102
03Pacific Complete-543
Red-543
03Parkhurst Toronto Expo Rookie Preview-PRP-19
03Parkhurst Rookie-193
Rookie Emblems-RE-23
Rookie Emblem Autographs-RE-KL
Rookie Emblems Gold-RE-23
Rookie Jerseys-RJ-23
Rookie Jersey Autographs-RJ-KL
Rookie Jerseys Gold-RJ-23
Rookie Numbers-RN-23
Rookie Number Autographs-RN-KL
Rookie Numbers Gold-RN-23
03Topps Traded-TT85
Blue-TT85
Gold-TT85
Red-TT85
03UD Premier Collection-98
03Upper Deck Rookie Update-176
03Finnish Cardset D-Day-DD4
03AHL Top Prospects-19
03Chicago Wolves-12
03Pacific AHL Prospects-13
Gold-13
Autographs-1
Crease Lightning-2
04Pacific-272
Blue-272
Red-272
04SP Authentic-6
Limited-6
Octographs-OS-GOA
Octographs-OS-ROK
Rookie Review-RR-KL
Sign of the Times-ST-KL
Sign of the Times-DS-KN
Sign of the Times-DS-RL
Sign of the Times-TS-HLK
Sign of the Times-TS-KLL
Sign of the Times-FS-GOL
Sign of the Times-FS-SES
Sign of the Times-SS-FIN
04Ultimate Collection Signatures-US-KL
04Ultimate Collection Signature Patches-SP-KL
04Upper Deck-12
Canadian Exclusives-12
HG Glossy Gold-12
HG Glossy Silver-12
World's Best-WB13
World Cup Tribute-KLMK
World Cup Tribute-KLJPTR
04AHL All-Stars-26
04AHL All-Stars-47
04AHL Top Prospects-7
04Chicago Wolves-1
04ITG Heroes and Prospects-24
Aspiring-4
Combos-1
Emblems-5
Emblems Gold-5
He Shoots-He Scores Prizes-1
He Shoots-He Scores Prizes-5
He Shoots-He Scores Prizes-9
Jersey Autographs-5
Jerseys-5
Jerseys Gold-5
National Pride-7
Net Prospects-1
Net Prospects Gold-1
Numbers-5
Numbers Gold-5
04ITG Heroes/Prospects Toronto Expo '05-24
04ITG Heroes/Prospects Expo Heroes/Pros-24
05ITG Heroes/Prosp Toronto Expo Parallel -62
05ITG Heroes/Prosp Toronto Expo Parallel -348
05Be A Player-5
First Period-5
Second Period-5
Third Period-5
Overtime-5
Dual Signatures-DK
Dual Signatures-RL
Quad Signatures-TLAL
Signatures-KL
Signatures Gold-KL
Triple Signatures-LLA
05Beehive-5
Matte-5
05Black Diamond-128
Emerald-128
Gold-128
Onyx-128
Ruby-128
05Hot Prospects-6
En Fuego-6
Red Hot-6
White Hot-6
05ITG Ultimate Mem First Rounders Jerseys-5
05ITG Ultimate Mem 1st Round Jersey Gold-5
05ITG Ultimate Memorabilia Triple Autos-3
05ITG Ultimate Mem Triple Autos Gold-3
05McDonalds Upper Deck Goalie Factory-GF12
05Panini Stickers-10
05Parkhurst-29
Facsimile Auto Parallel-29
True Colors-TCATL
True Colors-TCATL
05SP Authentic-6
Limited-6
Exquisite Endorsements-EEKL
Marks of Distinction-MDKL
Prestigious Pairings-PPLK
Scripts to Success-SSKL
Sign of the Times-KL
Sign of the Times Triples-TKHL
05SP Game Used-5
Autographs-5
Gold-5
Authentic Fabrics-AF-KL
Authentic Fabrics Autographs-AAF-KL
Authentic Fabrics Dual-LN
Authentic Fabrics Dual Autographs-LN
Authentic Fabrics Gold-AF-KL
Authentic Fabrics Quad-KHLS
Authentic Patches Quad -KHLS
Authentic Fabrics Triple-NKL
Authentic Fabrics Triple-RLA
Authentic Patches-AP-KL
Authentic Patches Autographs-AAP-KL
Authentic Patches Dual-LN
Authentic Patches Dual Autographs-LN
Authentic Patches Triple-NKL
Authentic Patches Triple-RLA
Significant Numbers-SN-KL
Statscriptions-ST-KL
05SPx-4
Spectrum-4
Winning Combos-WC-RL
Winning Combos Autographs-AWC-AK
Winning Combos Gold-WC-RL
Winning Combos Spectrum-WC-RL
Winning Materials-WM-KL
Winning Materials Gold-WM-KL
Winning Materials Spectrum-WM-KL
05The Cup-5
Gold-5
Black Rainbow-5
Dual NHL Shields Autographs-ADSLK
Emblems of Endorsement-EEKL
Honorable Numbers-HNKL
Masterpiece Pressplates-5
Patch Variation-P5
Patch Variation Autographs-AP5
Scripted Numbers Dual-DSNKL
Scripted Swatches-SSKL
05UD Artifacts-6
Blue-6
Gold-6
Green-6
Pewter-6
Red-6
Auto Facts-AF-KL
Auto Facts Blue-AF-KL
Auto Facts Copper-AF-KL
Auto Facts Pewter-AF-KL
Auto Facts Silver-AF-KL
Gold Autographed-6
Remarkable Artifacts-RA-KL
Remarkable Artifacts Dual-RA-KL
05UD PowerPlay-6
Rainbow-6
05Ultimate Collection-6
Gold-6
Endorsed Emblems-EEKL
Jerseys-JKL
Jerseys Dual-DJTL
Premium Patches-PPKL
Premium Swatches-PSKL
Ultimate Patches-PKL
Ultimate Patches Dual-DPTL
Ultimate Signatures-USKL
Ultimate Signatures Logos-SLKL
Ultimate Signatures Trios-UTKLH
05Ultra-8
Gold-8
Ice-8
05Upper Deck-9
HG Glossy-9
Jerseys-J-KL
Jerseys Series II-J2KL
Majestic Materials-MMKL
NHL Generations-TBLL
Notable Numbers-N-KL
Scrapbooks-HS4
05Upper Deck Ice-6
Rainbow-6
Fresh Ice-FIKL
Fresh Ice Glass-FIKL
Fresh Ice Glass Patches-FIPKL
05Upper Deck MVP-15
Gold-15
Platinum-15
05Upper Deck Rookie Update-6
05Upper Deck Trilogy-6
05Upper Deck Trilogy-131
Crystal-131
Honorary Patches-HP-KL
Honorary Patch Scripts-HSP-KL
Honorary Swatches-HS-KL
Honorary Swatch Scripts-HSS-KL
Scripts-SFS-KL
05Upper Deck Toronto Fall Expo-9
05Upper Deck Victory-9
Black-9
Gold-9
Silver-9
05ITG Heroes and Prospects-62
05ITG Heroes and Prospects-348
AHL Grads-AG-4
AHL Grads Gold-AG-4
Autograph Memorabilia-GA-04
Autograph Memorabilia Gold-GA-04
Autographs Series II-KL2
He Shoots-He Scores Prizes-3
He Shoots-He Scores Prizes-19
Jerseys-GUJ-97
Jerseys Gold-GUJ-97
Measuring Up-MU20
Measuring Up Gold-MU20
Nameplates-N-3
Nameplates Gold-N-03
National Pride-NPR-1
Net Prospects-NP-1
Net Prospects Dual-NPD7
Net Prospects Dual Gold-NPD7
Net Prospects Gold-NP-01
Shooting Stars-AS-7
Spectrum-STM-09
Spectrum Gold-STM-09
06Be A Player Portraits-6
Signature Portraits-SPKL
06Beehive-96
06Beehive-233
Blue-96
Gold-96
Matte-96
Red Facsimile Signatures-96
Wood-96
5 X 7 Black and White-96
PhotoGraphs-PGKL
06Between The Pipes-67
06Between The Pipes-110
Autographs-AKL2
Autographs-AKL
Complete Jersey-CJ12
Complete Jersey Gold-CJ12
Double Jerseys-DJ16
Double Jerseys Gold-DJ16
Emblems-GUE09
Emblems Gold-GUE09
Jerseys-GUJ09
Jerseys Gold-GUJ09
Numbers-GUN09
Numbers Gold-GUN09
Playing For Your Country-PC26
Playing For Your Country Gold-PC26
Prospect Trios-PT13
Prospect Trios Gold-PT13
Shooting Gallery-SG08
Shooting Gallery Gold-SG08
The Mask-M02
The Mask Gold-M02
The Mask Silver-M02
The Mask Game-Used-MGU10
The Mask Game-Used Gold-MGU10
06Black Diamond-127
Black-127
Gold-127
Ruby-127
Gemography-GKL
06Flair Showcase-8
06Flair Showcase-105
06Flair Showcase-203
Parallel-8
Parallel-105
Parallel-203
Hot Gloves-HG2
Hot Numbers-HN2
Hot Numbers Parallel-HN2
Inks-IKL
Wave of the Future-WF2
06Fleer-11
Tiffany-11
Fabricology-FKL
Netminders-N2
06Hot Prospects-6
Red Hot-6
White Hot-6
Hotagraphs-HKL
06ITG Ultimate Memorabilia-84
Artist Proof-84
Autos-44
Autos Gold-44
Autos Dual-11
Autos Dual Gold-11
First Round Picks-9
First Round Picks Gold-9
Jerseys Autos-32
Jerseys Autos Gold-32
06O-Pee-Chee-25
Rainbow-25
Swatches-S-KL
06Panini Stickers-9
06SP Authentic-97
06SP Authentic-128
Limited-97
Limited-128
Sign of the Times Duals-STKL
06SP Game Used-5
Gold-5
Rainbow-5
Authentic Fabrics Triple-AF3ATL
Authentic Fabrics Triple Patches-AF3ATL
Authentic Fabrics Eights-AF8FIN
Authentic Fabrics Eights Patches-AF8FIN
Autographs-5
By The Letter-BLKL
Inked Sweaters-ISKL
Inked Sweaters Patches-ISKL
Inked Sweaters Dual-IS2KL
Inked Sweaters Dual Patches-IS2KL
SIGnificance-SKL
06SPx-4
Spectrum-4
SPxcitement-X4
SPxcitement Spectrum-X4
SPxcitement Autographs-X4
Winning Materials-WMKL
Winning Materials Spectrum-WMKL
Winning Materials Autographs-WMKL
06The Cup-3
Autographed Foundations-CQKL
Autographed Foundations Patches-CQKL
Autographed NHL Shields Duals-DASIK
Autographed NHL Shields Duals-DASLT
Autographed Patches-3
Black Rainbow-3
Foundations-CQKL
Foundations Patches-CQKL
Enshrinements-EKL
Gold-3
Gold Patches-3
Honorable Numbers-HNKL
Jerseys-3
Limited Logos-LLKL
Masterpiece Pressplates-3
Property of-POKL
Scripted Swatches Duals-DSKL
Signature Patches-SPKL
06UD Artifacts-97
Blue-97
Gold-97
Platinum-97
Radiance-97
Red-97
Tundra Tandems-TTKL
Tundra Tandems Black-TTKL
Tundra Tandems Blue-TTKL
Tundra Tandems Gold-TTKL
Tundra Tandems Platinum-TTKL
Tundra Tandems Red-TTKL
Tundra Tandems Dual Patches Red-TTKL
06UD Mini Jersey Collection-5
06UD Powerplay-6
Impact Rainbow-6
Goal Robbers-GR2
Specialists-SKL
Specialists Patches-PKL
06Ultimate Collection-3
Autographed Jerseys-AJ-KL
Autographed Patches-AJ-KL
Jerseys-UJ-KL
Patches-UJ-KL
Premium Patches-PS-KL
Premium Swatches-PS-KL
Signatures-US-KL
Ultimate Signatures Logos-SL-KL
06Ultra-8
Gold Medallion-8
Ice Medallion-8
Action-UA1
06Upper Deck Arena Giveaways-ATL6
06Upper Deck-8
Exclusives Parallel-8
High Gloss Parallel-8
All World-AW5
Game Jerseys-J2KL
Game Patches-P2KL
Generations Duals-G2KL
Generations Triples-G3KTL
Generations Patches Dual-G2PKL
Generations Patches Triple-G3PKTL
Hometown Heroes-HH48
Masterpieces-8
Signature Sensations-SSKL
Walmart Tins Oversize-8
06Upper Deck MVP-14
Gold Script-14
Super Script-14
Jerseys-OJLK
Jerseys-OJWL
Last Line of Defense-LL11
06Upper Deck Ovation-103
06Upper Deck Sweet Shot-6
Signature Shots/Saves-SSKL
Signature Shots/Saves Ice Signings-SSIKL
Signature Shots/Saves Sticks-SSSKL
Signature Sticks-STKL
Sweet Stitches-SSKL
Sweet Stitches Duals-SSKL
Sweet Stitches Triples-SSKL
06Upper Deck Trilogy-5
Combo Autographed Jerseys-CJKL
Combo Autographed Patches-CJKL
Honorary Scripted Patches-HSPKL
Honorary Scripted Swatches-HSSKL
Honorary Swatches-HSKL
Scripts-S1KL
Scripts-TSKL
06Upper Deck Victory-8
06Upper Deck Victory Black-8
06Upper Deck Victory Gold-8
06Upper Deck Victory Next In Line-NL5
06Upper Deck Victory Oversize Cards-KL
06ITG Heroes and Prospects Quad Emblems-QE04
06ITG Heroes and Prospects Quad Emblems Gold-QE04
07Sports Illustrated for Kids *-133
07Upper Deck Ovation-98
07Upper Deck Victory-74
Black-74
Gold-74
GameBreakers-GB13
Oversize Cards-OS21

Lehtonen, Lauri
65Finnish Hellas-69
66Finnish Jaakiekkosarja-17

Lehtonen, Mikko
00Finnish Cardset-179
01Finnish Cardset-77
02Finnish Cardset-57
03Finnish Cardset-89
04Finnish Cardset-95
Parallel-71
05Finnish Cardset -269
06Black Diamond-168A
Black-168A
Gold-168A
Ruby-168A
06Hot Prospects-166
Red Hot-166
White Hot-166
06O-Pee-Chee-556
Rainbow-556
06SP Authentic-235
Limited-235
06SP Game Used-129
Gold-129
Rainbow-129
06SPx-162
Spectrum-162
06The Cup-100
Autographed Rookie Masterpiece Pressplates-100
Gold Rainbow Autographed Rookies-100
Masterpiece Pressplates (Black Diamond)-168
Masterpiece Pressplates (Marquee Rookies)-556
Masterpiece Pressplates (MVP)-321
Masterpiece Pressplates (SP Authentic)-235
Masterpiece Pressplates (SP Game Used)-129
Masterpiece Pressplates (SPx)-162
Masterpiece Pressplates (Trilogy)-125
Masterpiece Pressplates (Victory)-302
NHL Shields Duals-DSHAM
Rookies Black-100
Rookies Platinum-100
06Ultimate Collection Ultimate Debut Threads Jerseys-DJ-MI
06Ultimate Collection Ultimate Debut Threads Jerseys Autographs-DJ-MI
06Ultimate Collection Ultimate Debut Threads Patches-DJ-MI
06Ultimate Collection Ultimate Debut Threads Patches Autographs-DJ-MI
06Upper Deck-223
Exclusives Parallel-223
High Gloss Parallel-223
Masterpieces-223
Rookie Game Dated Moments-RGD15
06Upper Deck MVP-321
Gold Script-321
Super Script-321
06Upper Deck Trilogy-125
06Upper Deck Victory-302
06Finnish Cardset-10
06Finnish Cardset-96
Signature Sensations-1

Lehtonen, Mikko (BOS)
06Finnish Cardset-10

Lehtonen, Pertti
91Finnish Jyvas-Hyva Stickers-5
92Finnish Jyvas-Hyva Stickers-4
93Finnish Jyvas-Hyva Stickers-16
93Finnish SISU-91
94Finnish SISU-223
95Finnish SISU-185
95Finnish SISU-204
Double Trouble-5
95Finnish SISU Limited-38
96Finnish SISU Redline-5
98Finnish Kerailysarja 90's Top 12-2
02Finnish Cardset-58

Lehtonen, Pertti A.
78Finnish SM-Liiga-29
80Finnish Mallasjuoma-17
82Swedish Semic VM Stickers-30
83Swedish Semic VM Stickers-30

Lehtonen, Riku-Petteri
96Finnish SISU Redline-138
98Finnish Kerailysarja-12
99Finnish Cardset-10
01German Upper Deck-70

Lehtonen, Sami
93Finnish SISU-115
94Finnish SISU-168
94Finnish SISU-342
94Finnish SISU Horoscopes-19
95Finnish SISU-109
96Finnish SISU Redline-126

Lehtonen, Timo
70Finnish Jaakiekko-299

Lehtonen, Topi
00Finnish Cardset-188
01Finnish Cardset-86
04Finnish Cardset-126
Parallel-93
05Finnish Cardset -280

Lehtonen, Vesa
94Finnish SISU-306

Lehtoranta, Vesa
72Finnish Jaakiekko-196

Lehtorinne, Timo
71Finnish Suomi Stickers-248

Lehun, Jonathan
03Owen Sound Attack-14
04Owen Sound Attack-9
05Florida Everblades-1

Lehvonen, Henry
80Finnish Mallasjuoma-43

Leibel, Brian
87Regina Pats-15
88Regina Pats-12

Leibel, Cody
93Quebec Pee-Wee Tournament-478
96Barrie Colts-13
01Fort Worth Brahmas-12

Leibnitz, Jo Espen
92Norwegian Elite Series-225

Leibzig, David
93Swiss HNL-42
95Swiss HNL-496
98Swiss Power Play Stickers-321
01Swiss HNL-327

Leidborg, Gunnar
82Swedish Semic VM Stickers-3
83Swedish Semic Elitserien-1
84Swedish Semic Elitserien-1
85Swedish Panini Stickers-4
94German DEL-5
95German DEL-384
96Swiss HNL-151
98German DEL-291
99German DEL-313

Leidl, Mike
04Williams Lake Timberwolves-11

Leier, Dan
83Saskatoon Blades-6

Leighton, Michael
95Quebec Pee-Wee Tournament-608
98Windsor Spitfires-6
01Norfolk Admirals-13
02BAP Memorabilia-349
02BAP Ultimate Memorabilia-63
02Parkhurst Retro-215
Minis-215
02SP Authentic-171
02UD Artistic Impressions-101
Gold-101
02UD Honor Roll-134
02UD Mask Collection-155
02UD Premier Collection-90
Gold-90
02AHL Top Prospects-26
02Norfolk Admirals-14
03BAP Memorabilia-143
Emerald-143
Gold-143
Ruby-143
Sapphire-143
Deep in the Crease-D2
03Beehive-42
Gold-42
Silver-42
03Blackhawks Postcards-11
03ITG Action-159
03Pacific Complete-480
Red-480
03Pacific Heads-Up-21
03Pacific Heads-Up-22
Hobby LTD-21
Hobby LTD-22
Retail LTD-21
Retail LTD-22
03Parkhurst Original Six Chicago-24
03Topps Traded-TT36
Blue-TT36
Gold-TT36
Red-TT36
03Upper Deck-288
Canadian Exclusives-288
HG-288
UD Exclusives-288
03Upper Deck MVP-99
Gold Script-99
Silver Script-99
Canadian Exclusives-99
04Norfolk Admirals-13
05ITG Heroes/Prosp Toronto Expo Parallel -102
05ITG Heroes and Prospects-102
Autographs-A-MLN
06Between The Pipes-38
Autographs-AML
06Flyers Postcards-20

Leikko, Samu
66Finnish Jaakiekkosarja-30

Leimbeck, Matt
97Minnesota Golden Gophers-24
98Minnesota Golden Gophers-25
99Minnesota Golden Gophers-8
00Minnesota Golden Gophers-9

Leime, Eikke
79Montreal Juniors-16

Leimgruber, Boris
93Swiss HNL-505
95Swiss HNL-384
98Swiss Power Play Stickers-42
99Swiss Panini Stickers-43
00Swiss Panini Stickers-45
00Swiss Slapshot Mini-Cards-SCB13
01Swiss HNL-336
02Swiss HNL-130

Leimu, Pekka
66Finnish Jaakiekkosarja-190
69Swedish Hockey-374
70Finnish Jaakiekko-65
70Finnish Jaakiekko-130
70Swedish Masterserien-161
71Finnish Suomi Stickers-180
72Finnish Jaakiekko-128
72Finnish Panda Toronto-28
73Finnish Jaakiekko-183

Leinauer, Gerhard
98German DEL-NNO
99German DEL-398

Leinhos, Jamie
01Sorel Royaux-13

Leinhos, Justin
01Sorel Royaux-14

Leino, Ville
04Finnish Cardset-55
Parallel-41
05Finnish Cardset -212
06Finnish Cardset-38

Leinonen, Ari
72Finnish Jaakiekko-348

Leinonen, Marko
93Finnish SISU-137
95Finnish SISU-261
96Finnish SISU Redline-55
98Finnish Kerailysarja-119
Mad Masks-6
Off Duty-6

Leinonen, Mikko
72Finnish Jaakiekko-268
77Finnish Sportscasters-76-1821
79Panini Stickers-178
80Finnish Mallasjuoma-107
81Swedish Semic Hockey VM Stickers-28
82O-Pee-Chee-4
82Finnish Skopbank-8
82Swedish Semic VM Stickers-160
83NHL Key Tags-90
83O-Pee-Chee-248
05Finnish Tappara Legendat-5

Leinonen, Sami
94Finnish SISU-202
95Finnish SISU-141
99German Bundesliga 2-264

Leinonen, Tero
01Finnish Cardset-266
02Finnish Cardset-215
02Finnish Cardset-299
03Finnish Cardset-71
04Swedish Elitset-251
Gold-251
04Swedish Pure Skills-73
Parallel-73
05Swedish Lulea Hockey Postcards-26
05Swedish SHL Elitset Stoppers-10
06Swedish SHL Elitset-212

Leinonen, Timo
99Finnish Cardset-202
99Finnish Cardset-337

Leinonen, Tuomas
72Finnish Jaakiekko-269
06Finnish Cardset-270

Leinweber, Chris
03Binghamton Senators-13
03Johnstown Chiefs RBI Sports-219
04Johnstown Chiefs-11

Leinweber, Curtis
06Okotoks Oilers -9

Leirivaara, Juhani
66Finnish Jaakiekkosarja-130

Leiter, Bob
63Topps-14
64Beehive Group III Photos-16
64Coca-Cola Caps-18
64Topps-63
71Penguins Postcards-11
71Toronto Sun-220
72Flames Postcards-5
72O-Pee-Chee-218
72Sargent Promotions Stamps-9
73O-Pee-Chee-117
73Topps-117
74NHL Action Stamps-15
74O-Pee-Chee NHL-51
74Topps-51
75O-Pee-Chee NHL-191
75Topps-191
94Parkhurst Tall Boys-11

Leiter, Ken
84Springfield Indians-6
86Islanders Team Issue-19
87O-Pee-Chee Stickers-131
87Panini Stickers-93

Leitner, Florian
94German First League-352

Leitza, Brian
98Kansas City Blades-2
99Tacoma Sabercats-7

Lejcyk, Leszek
92Finnish Semic-266

Lejczyk, Leszek
89Swedish Semic World Champ Stickers-127

Lejeune, Antoine
92Quebec Pee-Wee Tournament-916
93Quebec Pee-Wee Tournament-141

Lekkerimaki, Sami
92Finnish Jyvas-Hyva Stickers-151
93Finnish Jyvas-Hyva Stickers-267
93Finnish SISU-292

Leknes, Geir
92Norwegian Elite Series-119

Lekovic, Boris
03Saskatoon Blades-3

Leksell, Sture
67Swedish Hockey-105

Leksola, Pekka
94Finnish Jaa Kiekko-16

Lekun, Mike
80Oshawa Generals-19
81Oshawa Generals-15

Lelacheur, Robert
88Saskatoon Blades-11
89Saskatoon Blades-11
90Saskatoon Blades-9
907th Inn. Sketch WHL-82

Lelievre, Mathieu
93Quebec Pee-Wee Tournament-1005

Lemaire, Ed
85Sudbury Wolves-17

Lemaire, Jacques
64Canadiens Postcards-12
67Canadiens IGA-25
67Topps-3
68Canadiens IGA-25
68Canadiens Postcards BW-9
68O-Pee-Chee-63
68Post Marbles-15
68Shirriff Coins-88
68Topps-63
69Canadiens Postcards Color-15
69O-Pee-Chee-8
69Topps-8
70Canadiens Pins-9
70Colgate Stamps-30
70Dad's Cookies-70
70Esso Power Players-17
70O-Pee-Chee-57
Deckle-19
70Post Shooters-9
70Sargent Promotions Stamps-103
70Topps-57
Topps/OPC Sticker Stamps-20
71Canadiens Postcards-13
71Letraset Action Replays-15
71O-Pee-Chee-71
71Sargent Promotions Stamps-105
71Topps-71
71Toronto Sun-156
72Canadiens Postcards-12
72Dimanche/Derniere Heure *-154
72Dimanche/Derniere Heure *-155
72O-Pee-Chee-77
72Sargent Promotions Stamps-115
72Topps-25
72Finnish Semic World Championship-208
72Swedish Semic World Championship-208
73Canadiens Postcards-14
73Mac's Milk-14
73O-Pee-Chee-56
73Topps-56
74Canadiens Postcards-15
74Lipton Soup-38
74NHL Action Stamps-145
74O-Pee-Chee NHL-24
74Topps-24
75Canadiens Postcards-12
75Heroes Stand-Ups-10
75O-Pee-Chee NHL-258
75Topps-258
76Canadiens Postcards-13
76O-Pee-Chee NHL-129
76Topps-129
77Canadiens Postcards-15
77O-Pee-Chee NHL-254
77Sportscasters-8119
77Topps-254
77Finnish Sportscasters-85-2035
78Canadiens Postcards-17
78O-Pee-Chee-180
78Topps-180
83Canadiens Postcards-13
84Canadiens Postcards-14
85Hall of Fame-245
93O-Pee-Chee Canadiens Hockey Fest-62
94Kraft-61
94Parkhurst Tall Boys Future Stars-FS1
96Devils Team Issue-NNO
97Devils Team Issue-28
01Greats of the Game-66
Autographs-66
01Topps Archives-65
Arena Seats-ASJL
Autographs-8
03Topps Stanley Cup Heroes-JL
03Topps Stanley Cup Heroes Autographs-JL
04ITG Franchises Canadian-56
Autographs-JLE
04ITG Ultimate Memorabilia-151
Gold-151
06Parkhurst-136
Autographs-136
Autographs Dual-DALL
06The Cup-49
Black Rainbow-49
Gold-49
Hardware Heroes-HHJL
Masterpiece Pressplates-49
Stanley Cup Signatures-CSJL
Stanley Cup Titlists-TJL

Lemaire, Mattews
02Rimouski Oceanic-9
03Rimouski Oceanic-14
03Rimouski Oceanic Sheets-1

Lemander, Hannu
65Finnish Hellas-85
66Finnish Jaakiekkosarja-90
72Finnish Jaakiekko-175

Lemanowicz, David
91British Columbia JHL-18
94Spokane Chiefs-25
95Spokane Chiefs-1
96Carolina Monarchs-16
04Memphis RiverKings-5

Lemanski, Casey
92British Columbia JHL-163

LeMarque, Eric
91Greensboro Monarchs-8
94French National Team-15
94Los Angeles Blades RHI-8

Lemay, Dave
907th Inn. Sketch OHL-37
91Cornwall Royals-5
917th Inn. Sketch OHL-5
93Owen Sound Platers-15
95Buffalo Stampedes RHI-37
00Fort Wayne Komets-9
00Fort Wayne Komets Shoe Carnival-11
01Bossier-Shreveport Mudbugs-11

Lemay, Jean-Simon
92Quebec Pee-Wee Tournament-774
96Halifax Mooseheads I-11
96Halifax Mooseheads II-11

Lemay, Justin
93Quebec Pee-Wee Tournament-1079

Lemay, Louis-Philip
00Sherbrooke Castors-12
Signed-12
01Sherbrooke Castors-14

Lemay, Marc
80Quebec Remparts-12

Lemay, Moe
81Ottawa 67's-10
82Canucks Team Issue-12
83Fredericton Express-12
84Canucks Team Issue-13
84O-Pee-Chee-322
85Canucks Team Issue-13
85O-Pee-Chee-173
85O-Pee-Chee Stickers-246
86Canucks Team Issue-8
86O-Pee-Chee-249
88Oilers Tenth Anniversary-43
94German First League-576
96German DEL-215

Lemay, Yanick
907th Inn. Sketch QMJHL-223
917th Inn. Sketch QMJHL-17

Lembke, Jeff
92North Dakota Fighting Sioux-18

Lemelin, Alexandre Dulac
03Baie Comeau Drakkar-25

Lemelin, Jacques
72Nordiques Postcards-16

Lemelin, Nicolas
93Quebec Pee-Wee Tournament-260

Lemelin, Rejean
78Flames Majik Market-1
80Flames Postcards-7
81Flames Postcards-11
81O-Pee-Chee-44
82O-Pee-Chee-50
83O-Pee-Chee-86
83O-Pee-Chee Stickers-266
83Topps Stickers-266
83Vachon-10
84O-Pee-Chee-228
84O-Pee-Chee Stickers-240
847-Eleven Discs-5
84Topps-25
85Flames Red Rooster-12
85O-Pee-Chee-95
85O-Pee-Chee Stickers-210
85Topps-95
86Flames Red Rooster-9
86Kraft Drawings-32
86O-Pee-Chee-102
86O-Pee-Chee Stickers-83
86Topps-102
87Panini Stickers-204
88Bruins Sports Action-10
88Bruins Postcards-10
88O-Pee-Chee-186
88O-Pee-Chee Minis-18
88O-Pee-Chee Stickers-24
88Panini Stickers-203
88Topps-186
89Bruins Sports Action-13
89Bruins Sports Action Update-12
89O-Pee-Chee-40
89Panini Stickers-195
89Topps-40
90Bowman-32
Tiffany-32
90Bruins Sports Action-14
90Bruins Sports Action-26
90O-Pee-Chee-343
90O-Pee-Chee-486
90Panini Stickers-13
90Pro Set-9
90Pro Set-382
90Score-159
90Score-365
Canadian-159
Canadian-365
90Topps-343
Tiffany-343
90Upper Deck-209
90Upper Deck-215
French-215
91Bowman-354
91O-Pee-Chee-497
91Panini Stickers-172
91Score American-127
91Score Canadian Bilingual-127
91Score Canadian English-127
91Stadium Club-23
91Topps-497
92Durivage Panini-48
98Bruins Alumni-1
Autographs-1
04ITG Franchises Canadian-3
Autographs-RLM
06Parkhurst-65

Lemelin, Roger
76Rockies Puck Bucks-12

Lemelin, Vincent
93Quebec Pee-Wee Tournament-1026

Lemerise, Jonathan
92Quebec Pee-Wee Tournament-801
93Quebec Pee-Wee Tournament-963

Lemieux, Alain
85Fredericton Express-7
86Nordiques McDonald's-14
99Jacksonville Lizard Kings-14

Lemieux, Andre
77Granby Vics-13

Lemieux, Bob
67Seals Team Issue-16
77Kalamazoo Wings-3

Lemieux, Carl
84Richelieu Riverains-8

Lemieux, Claude
85Canadiens Postcards-17
86Canadiens Postcards-11
86Kraft Drawings-33
87Canadiens Postcards-14
87Canadiens Vachon Stickers-31
87O-Pee-Chee-227
87O-Pee-Chee Stickers-19
87Panini Stickers-63
88Canadiens Postcards-17
88O-Pee-Chee-227
88O-Pee-Chee Stickers-43
88Panini Stickers-257
89Canadiens Kraft-14
89Canadiens Postcards-19
89O-Pee-Chee-234
89O-Pee-Chee Stickers-52
89Panini Stickers-240

90Devils Team Issue-15
90O-Pee-Chee-451
90OPC Premier-62
90Pro Set-153
90Pro Set-478
90Score-111
Canadian-111
90Score Rookie/Traded-9T
90Upper Deck-447
French-447
91Pro Set Platinum-196
91Bowman-271
91Bowman-277
91O-Pee-Chee-394
91Panini Stickers-224
91Parkhurst-101
French-101
91Pinnacle-70
French-70
91Pro Set-135
French-135
91Score American-22
91Score Canadian Bilingual-22
91Score Canadian English-22
91Stadium Club-18
91Topps-394
91Upper Deck-294
French-294
92Bowman-49
92Durivage Panini-14
92O-Pee-Chee-67
92Panini Stickers-172
92Panini Stickers French-172
92Parkhurst-89
Emerald Ice-89
92Pinnacle-259
92Pinnacle-284
French-259
French-284
92Pro Set-98
92Score-8
Canadian-8
92Sports Illustrated for Kids II-618
92Stadium Club-50
92Topps-43
Gold-43G
92Ultra-114
92Upper Deck-163
93Donruss-187
93Durivage Score-47
93Leaf-125
93OPC Premier-134
Gold-134
93Panini Stickers-35
93Parkhurst-110
Emerald Ice-110
93Pinnacle-251
Canadian-251
93PowerPlay-137
93Score-160
Canadian-160
93Stadium Club-39
Members Only Master Set-39
OPC-39
First Day Issue-39
First Day Issue OPC-39
93Topps/OPC Premier-134
Gold-134
93Ultra-5
93Upper Deck-296
93Upper Deck-391
SP-83
94Be A Player Signature Cards-27
94Canada Games NHL POGS-145
94Donruss-82
94EA Sports-77
94Fleer-113
94Leaf-185
94OPC Premier-204
Special Effects-204
94Parkhurst-129
Gold-129
Vintage-V59
94Pinnacle-287
Artist's Proofs-287
Rink Collection-287
94Score Check It-CI16
94Select-73
Gold-73
94Topps/OPC Premier-204
Special Effects-204
94Ultra-118
94Upper Deck-303
Electric Ice-303
95Bowman-13
All-Foil-13
95Collector's Choice-262
95Collector's Choice-392
Player's Club-262
Player's Club-392
Player's Club Platinum-262
Player's Club Platinum-392
Crash The Game-C28A
Crash The Game-C28B
Crash The Game-C28C
Crash The Game Gold-C28A
Crash The Game Gold-C28B
Crash The Game Gold-C28C
Crash the Game Silver Redeemed-C28
Crash the Game Silver Bonus-C28
Crash the Game Gold Redeemed-C28
Crash the Game Gold Bonus-C28
95Donruss-343
95Donruss Elite-44
Die Cut Stars-44
Die Cut Uncut-44
95Emotion-97
95Finest-47
Refractors-47
95Kraft-79
95Leaf-311
Road To The Cup-10
95Leaf Limited-27
95Metal-34
Iron Warriors-6
95NHL Aces Playing Cards-4H
95Panini Stickers-1
95Panini Stickers-2
95Panini Stickers-82
95Parkhurst International-319
Emerald Ice-319
95Pinnacle-119
Artist's Proofs-119
Rink Collection-119
First Strike-10
95Playoff One on One-244
95Pro Magnets-3
95Score-269
Black Ice Artist's Proofs-269
Black Ice-269
95Select Certified-99
Mirror Gold-99
Double Strike-19
Double Strike Gold-19
95SkyBox Impact-37
95SP-35
95Stadium Club-189
Members Only Master Set-189
Nemeses-N3
Nemeses Members Only Master Set-N3
95Summit-129
Artist's Proofs-129
Ice-129
95Topps-114
OPC Inserts-114
95Ultra-192
95Ultra-223
Gold Medallion-192
Crease Crashers-6
95Upper Deck-44
95Upper Deck-258
95Upper Deck-456
Electric Ice-44
Electric Ice-258
Electric Ice-456
Electric Ice Gold-44
Electric Ice Gold-258
Electric Ice Gold-456
Special Edition-SE50
Special Edition-SE108
Special Edition Gold-SE50
Special Edition Gold-SE108
95Zenith-116
Gifted Grinders-4
95Images Platinum Players-PL5
96Headliners Hockey-10
96Avalanche Photo Pucks-1
96Collector's Choice-57
MVP-UD6
MVP Gold-UD6
96Donruss-23
Press Proofs-23
Hit List-18
96Donruss Canadian Ice-115
Gold Press Proofs-115
Red Press Proofs-115
96Donruss Elite-110
Die Cut Stars-110
96Fleer-22
96Fleer-142
96Leaf-17
Press Proofs-17
96Leaf Limited-46
Gold-46
96Leaf Limited Bash the Boards Promos-P6
96Leaf Limited Bash The Boards-6
96Leaf Limited Bash The Boards Ltd Ed-6
96Leaf Preferred-24
Press Proofs-24
Steel-31
Steel Gold-31
96Maggers-55
96Metal Universe-35
96NHL Pro Stamps-3
96Pinnacle-113
Artist's Proofs-113
Foil-113
Premium Stock-113
Rink Collection-113
96Score-116
Artist's Proofs-116
Dealer's Choice Artist's Proofs-116
Special Artist's Proofs-116
Golden Blades-116
96Select Certified-53
Artist's Proofs-53
Blue-53
Mirror Blue-53
Mirror Gold-53
Mirror Red-53
Red-53
96SkyBox Impact-25
BladeRunners-12
96SP-39
96Summit-113
Artist's Proofs-113
Ice-113
Metal-113
Premium Stock-113
96Team Out-37
96Topps Picks-89
OPC Inserts-89
96Ultra-37
Gold Medallion-37
96Upper Deck-207
96Upper Deck-245
Power Performers-P17
96Zenith-102
Artist's Proofs-102
Champion Salute-10
Champion Salute Diamond-10
96Swedish Semic Wien-91
97Headliners Hockey-15
97Avalanche Pins-6
97Collector's Choice-62
97Crown Royale-36
Emerald Green-36
Ice Blue-36
Silver-36
97Donruss-88
Press Proofs Silver-88
Press Proofs Gold-88
Canadian Ice National Pride-25
97Donruss Limited-15
Exposure-15
97Donruss Preferred-126
Cut to the Chase-126
97Donruss Priority-127
Stamp of Approval-127
97Katch-39
Gold-39
Silver-39
97Pacific-3
Copper-3
Emerald Green-3
Ice Blue-3
Red-3
Silver-3
Slap Shots Die-Cuts-2C
97Pacific Dynagon-31
Copper-31
Dark Grey-31
Emerald Green-31
Ice Blue-31
Red-31
Silver-31
Dynamic Duos-5B
Tandems-25
97Pacific Invincible-36
Copper-36
Emerald Green-36
Ice Blue-36
Red-36
Silver-36
Attack Zone-5
Feature Performers-8
97Pacific Omega-60
Copper-60
Dark Gray-60
Emerald Green-60
Gold-60
Ice Blue-60
97Paramount-52
Copper-52
Dark Grey-52
Emerald Green-52
Ice Blue-52
Red-52
Silver-52
97Pinnacle-163
Press Plates Back Black-163
Press Plates Back Cyan-163
Press Plates Back Magenta-163
Press Plates Back Yellow-163
Press Plates Front Black-163
Press Plates Front Cyan-163
Press Plates Front Magenta-163
Press Plates Front Yellow-163
97Pinnacle Certified-129
Red-129
Mirror Blue-129
Mirror Gold-129
Mirror Red-129
97Pinnacle Inside-156
97Pinnacle Tot Certi Platinum Blue-129
97Pinnacle Tot Certi Platinum Gold-129
97Pinnacle Totally Certified Platinum Red-129
97Pinnacle Tot Cert Mirror Platinum Gold-129
97Revolution-35
Copper-35
Emerald-35
Ice Blue-35
Silver-35
97Score-158
Artist's Proofs-158
Golden Blades-158
97Score Avalanche-11
Platinum-11
Premier-11
97SP Authentic-38
97Studio-78
Press Proofs Silver-78
Press Proofs Gold-78
97Upper Deck-47
97Upper Deck-202
Game Dated Moments-47
97Zenith-57
Z-Gold-57
Z-Silver-57
97Zenith 5 x 7-36
Gold Impulse-36
Silver Impulse-36
98Aurora-48
98Avalanche Team Issue-6
98Kraft Fearless Forwards-7
98OPC Chrome-65
Refractors-65
98Pacific-164
Ice Blue-164
Red-164
98Pacific Dynagon Ice-50
Blue-50
Red-50
98Pacific Omega-61
Red-61
Opening Day Issue-61
98Panini Photocards-47
98Paramount-57
Copper-57
Emerald Green-57
Holo-Electric-57
Ice Blue-57
Silver-57
98Revolution-37
Ice Shadow-37
Red-37
98Topps-65
O-Pee-Chee-65
98UD Choice-55
98UD Choice Preview-55
98UD Choice Prime Choice Reserve-55
98UD Choice Reserve-55
98Upper Deck-73
Exclusives-73
Exclusives 1 of 1-73
Gold Reserve-73
99Aurora-40
Premiere Date-40
99BAP Memorabilia-208
Gold-208
Silver-208
99Crown Royale-82
Limited Series-82
Premiere Date-82
99Devils Team Issue-15
99Kraft Face Off Rivals-5
99Kraft Stanley Cup Moments-4
99Pacific-110
Copper-110
Emerald Green-110
Gold-110
Ice Blue-110
Premiere Date-110
Red-110
99Pacific Omega-137
Copper-137
Gold-137
Ice Blue-137
Premiere Date-137
99Pacific Prism-83
Holographic Blue-83
Holographic Gold-83
Holographic Mirror-83
Holographic Purple-83
Premiere Date-83
99Panini Stickers-80
99Paramount-65
Copper-65
Emerald-65
Gold-65
Holographic Emerald-65
Holographic Gold-65
Holographic Silver-65
Ice Blue-65
Premiere Date-65
Red-65
Silver-65
99Revolution-41
Premiere Date-41
Red-41
Shadow Series-41
99SP Authentic-50
99Topps Stanley Cup Heroes-SC13
99Topps Stanley Cup Heroes Refractors-SC13
99Upper Deck MVP SC Edition-106
Gold Script-106
Silver Script-106
Super Script-106
Second Season Snipers-SS6
99Upper Deck Victory-84
00SLU Hockey-160
00BAP Memorabilia-373
Emerald-373
Ruby-373
Sapphire-373
Promos-373
00BAP Mem Chicago Sportsfest Copper-373
00BAP Memorabilia Chicago Sportsfest Blue-373
00BAP Memorabilia Chicago Sportsfest Gold-373
00BAP Memorabilia Chicago Sportsfest Ruby-373
00BAP Memorabilia Chicago Sun-Times Ruby-373
00BAP Memorabilia Chicago Sun-Times Gold-373
00BAP Mem Chicago Sun-Times Sapphire-373
00BAP Mem Toronto Fall Expo Copper-373
00BAP Memorabilia Toronto Fall Expo Gold-373
00BAP Memorabilia Toronto Fall Expo Ruby-373
00BAP Parkhurst 2000-P181
00O-Pee-Chee-54
00O-Pee-Chee Parallel-54
00Pacific-236
Copper-236
Gold-236
Ice Blue-236
Premiere Date-236
00SPx-143
00Topps/OPC-54
Parallel-54
00Upper Deck MVP-104
First Stars-104
Second Stars-104
Third Stars-104
01BAP Signature Series-121
Autographs-121
Autographs Gold-121
01Bowman YoungStars-81
Gold-81
Ice Cubed-81
01Coyotes Team Issue-11
01Crown Royale-113
Blue-113
Premiere Date-113
Red-113
Retail-113
01O-Pee-Chee-238
01O-Pee-Chee Premier Parallel-238
01Pacific-306
Extreme LTD-306
Hobby LTD-306
Premiere Date-306
Retail LTD-306
01Pacific Adrenaline-150
Blue-150
Premiere Date-150
Red-150
Retail-150
01Pacific Arena Exclusives-306
01Stadium Club-28
Award Winners-28
Master Photos-28
01Titanium-110
Hobby Parallel-110
Premiere Date-110
Retail-110
Retail Parallel-110
01Topps-238
OPC Parallel-238
01Topps Chrome-33
Refractors-33
Black Border Refractors-33
01Topps Heritage-68
Refractors-68
01UD Challenge for the Cup-65
01UD Mask Collection-75
Gold-75
01UD Stanley Cup Champs-81
Pieces of Glory-G-CL
Sticks-S-CL
01Upper Deck Game Jerseys Series II-FJCL
02BAP Sig Series Auto Buybacks 2001-121
02BAP Ultimate Memorabilia Conn Smythe-23
02O-Pee-Chee-227
02O-Pee-Chee Premier Blue Parallel-227
02O-Pee-Chee Premier Red Parallel-227
02O-Pee-Chee Factory Set-227
02Pacific-299
Blue-299
Red-299
02SP Game Used Piece of History-PHCL
02SP Game Used Piece of History Gold-PHCL
02SP Game Used Piece of History Rainbow-PHCL
02Topps-227
OPC Blue Parallel-227
OPC Red Parallel-227
Factory Set-227
02Topps Total-90
02UD Piece of History Awards Collection-AC21
02UD Piece of History Threads-TTCL
02UD Top Shelf Clutch Performers-CPCL
02UD Top Shelf Dual Player Jerseys-STLD
02UD Top Shelf Sweet Sweaters-SWCL
02Upper Deck-378
Exclusives-378
02Upper Deck Beckett UD Promos-378
02Upper Deck Hot Spots-HSCL
02Upper Deck Classic Portraits Headliners-LK
02Upper Deck Classic Portraits Headliners Limited-LK
02Upper Deck Classic Portraits Hockey Royalty-BLB
02Upper Deck Classic Portraits Hockey Royalty Limited-BLB
02Upper Deck Vintage-198
Green Backs-198
03ITG Action-459
03Swiss EV Zug Postcards-28
06Parkhurst-115
Autographs-115

Lemieux, Francis

01Chicoutimi Sagueneens-18
04Chicoutimi Sagueneens-7
05Hamilton Bulldogs-15
06Hamilton Bulldogs-19

Lemieux, Jean

74NHL Action Stamps-13
75O-Pee-Chee NHL-367
76O-Pee-Chee NHL-272

Lemieux, Jocelyn

87Blues Kodak-15
87Panini Stickers-319
88ProCards AHL-291
89Canadiens Postcards-20
90Blackhawks Coke-12
90O-Pee-Chee-237
90Panini Stickers-190
90Pro Set-432
90Score Rookie/Traded-66T
90Topps-237
Tiffany-237
90Upper Deck-544
French-544
91Blackhawks Coke-16
91O-Pee-Chee-453
91Panini Stickers-20
91Parkhurst-256
French-256
91Score Canadian Bilingual-447
91Score Canadian English-447
91Stadium Club-356
91Topps-453
91Upper Deck-438
French-438
92Bowman-72
92Durivage Panini-15
92O-Pee-Chee-153
92Panini Stickers-8
92Panini Stickers French-8
92Parkhurst-275
Emerald Ice-275
92Score-309
Canadian-309
92Stadium Club-446
92Topps-300
Gold-300G
93Blackhawks Coke-21
93Donruss-440
93Durivage Score-43
93OPC Premier-295
Gold-295
93Panini Stickers-152
93Parkhurst-43
Emerald Ice-43
93Pinnacle-302
Canadian-302
93Score-420
Canadian-420
93Stadium Club-255
Members Only Master Set-255
First Day Issue-255
93Topps/OPC Premier-295
Gold-295
94Be A Player Signature Cards-129
94Canada Games NHL POGS-115
94Leaf-502
94OPC Premier-122
Special Effects-122
94Pinnacle-89
Artist's Proofs-89
Rink Collection-89
94Topps/OPC Premier-122
Special Effects-122
94Upper Deck-372
Electric Ice-372
95Collector's Choice-138
Player's Club-138
Player's Club Platinum-138
95Parkhurst International-393
Emerald Ice-393
95Pinnacle-62
Artist's Proofs-62
Rink Collection-62
95Whalers Bob's Stores-13
96Collector's Choice-42
97Coyotes Face-Off Luncheon -12
98Long Beach Ice Dogs-11

Lemieux, Mario

83Canadian National Juniors-9
85O-Pee-Chee-9
85O-Pee-Chee-262
85O-Pee-Chee Box Bottoms-I
85O-Pee-Chee Stickers-97
85O-Pee-Chee Stickers-199
857-Eleven Credit Cards-15
85Topps-9
85Topps Box Bottoms-I
86O-Pee-Chee-122
86O-Pee-Chee Box Bottoms-I
86O-Pee-Chee Stickers-120
86O-Pee-Chee Stickers-233
86Penguins Kodak-14
86Topps-122
86Topps Box Bottoms-I
86Topps Sticker Inserts-9
87O-Pee-Chee-15
87O-Pee-Chee Minis-23
87O-Pee-Chee Stickers-120
87O-Pee-Chee Stickers-170
87Panini Stickers-146
87Penguins Masks-6
87Penguins Kodak-16
87Pro-Sport All-Stars-5
87Topps-15
87Topps Sticker Inserts-11
88Esso All-Stars-27
88Frito-Lay Stickers-1
88O-Pee-Chee-1
88O-Pee-Chee Minis-19
88O-Pee-Chee Stickers-116
88O-Pee-Chee Stickers-204
88O-Pee-Chee Stickers-210
88O-Pee-Chee Stickers-211
88O-Pee-Chee Stickers-232
88Panini Stickers-340
88Panini Stickers-400
88Panini Stickers-401
88Topps-1
88Topps Sticker Inserts-2
89Action Packed Prototypes-2
89Action Packed Prototypes-3
89Kraft-55
89Kraft All-Stars Stickers-5
89O-Pee-Chee-1
89O-Pee-Chee-312
89O-Pee-Chee-319
89O-Pee-Chee-327
89O-Pee-Chee Box Bottoms-A
89O-Pee-Chee Stickers-55
89O-Pee-Chee Stickers-158
89O-Pee-Chee Stickers-199
89O-Pee-Chee Stickers-208
89O-Pee-Chee Stickers-238
89Panini Stickers-184
89Panini Stickers-309
89Panini Stickers-375
89Penguins Coke/Elby's-3
89Penguins Foodland-10
89Sports Illustrated for Kids I-1
89Topps-1
89Topps Box Bottoms-A
89Topps Sticker Inserts-3
89Swedish Semic World Champ Stickers-64
90SLU Kenner Club Pieces *-17
90Bowman-204
Tiffany-204
90Bowman Hat Tricks-2
Tiffany-2
90Kraft-29
90Kraft-87
90O-Pee-Chee-175
90O-Pee-Chee Box Bottoms-G
90OPC Premier-63
90Panini Stickers-136
90Panini Stickers-326
90Penguins Foodland-13
90Pro Set-236
90Pro Set-362
90Score-2
90Score-337
Canadian-2
Canadian-337
90Score Hottest/Rising Stars-34
90Topps-175
Tiffany-175
90Topps Box Bottoms-G
90Topps Team Scoring Leaders-17
90Topps Team Scoring Leaders Tiffany-17
90Upper Deck-59
90Upper Deck-144
90Upper Deck-305
French-59
French-144
French-305
91Pro Set Platinum-91
91Pro Set Platinum-144
91Bowman-87
91Bowman-425
91Gillette-33
91Kraft-1
91O-Pee-Chee-153
91O-Pee-Chee-523
91OPC Premier-114
91Panini Stickers-268
91Parkhurst-137
91Parkhurst-459
91Parkhurst-467
French-137
French-459
French-467
PHC-PHC7
PHC French-PHC7
91Penguins Men in Black-1
91Penguins Coke/Elby's-66
91Penguins Foodland-4
91Penguins Foodland Coupon Stickers-8
91Pinnacle-1
91Pinnacle-380
French-1
French-380
B-B5
B French-B5
91Pro Set-194
91Pro Set-318
91Pro Set-581
French-194
French-318
French-581
Player of the Month-P3
91Score American-200
91Score American-335
91Score American-425
91Score American-426
91Score Canadian Bilingual-200
91Score Canadian Bilingual-315
91Score Canadian Bilingual-316
91Score Canadian Bilingual-365
91Score Canadian English-200
91Score Canadian English-315
91Score Canadian English-316
91Score Canadian English-365
91Score Hot Cards-5
91Stadium Club Charter Member-50
91Stadium Club Members Only-47
91Stadium Club Members Only-48
91Stadium Club-174
91Topps-153
91Topps-523
Topps/Bowman Preview Sheet-1
91Upper Deck-47
91Upper Deck-156
91Upper Deck-611
French-45
French-47
French-156
French-611
Award Winner Holograms-AW9
92All World Mario Lemieux Promos-1A
92All World Mario Lemieux Promos-1B
92All World Mario Lemieux Promos-1C
92All World Mario Lemieux Promos-1D
92All World Mario Lemieux Promos-1E
92All World Mario Lemieux Promos-1F
92Bowman-189
92Bowman-233
92Bowman-440
92Clark Candy Mario Lemieux-1
92Clark Candy Mario Lemieux-2
92Clark Candy Mario Lemieux-3
92Durivage Panini-8
92High-5 Previews-P2
92Humpty Dumpty II-12
92Jofa/Koho-3
92Kellogg's Posters-1
92Kraft-43
92McDonald's Upper Deck-21
92O-Pee-Chee-220
92O-Pee-Chee-240
92O-Pee-Chee-292
25th Anniv. Inserts-18
92OPC Premier Star Performers-22
92Panini Stickers-220
92Panini Stickers-280
92Panini Stickers French-220
92Panini Stickers French-280
92Parkhurst-136
92Parkhurst-462
92Parkhurst-498
Emerald Ice-136
Emerald Ice-462
Emerald Ice-498
92Penguins Coke/Clark-10
92Penguins Foodland-1
92Penguins Foodland Coupon Stickers-4
92Pinnacle-300
French-300
92Pro Set-1
92Pro Set-139
92Score-390
92Score-413
92Score-433
92Score-448
92Score-519
Canadian-390
Canadian-413
Canadian-433
Canadian-448
Canadian-519
92Seasons Patches-34
92Sports Illustrated for Kids II-125
92Sports Illustrated for Kids II-453
92Stadium Club-94
92Stadium Club-251
92Topps-212
92Topps-265
92Topps-504
Gold-212G
Gold-265G
Gold-504G
92Ultra-165
All-Stars-4
Award Winners-5
92Upper Deck-26
92Upper Deck-433
92Upper Deck-436
92Upper Deck-454
Gordie Howe Selects-G9
World Junior Grads-WG11
92Finnish Semic-86
92Classic-66
92Classic-SP
92Classic-AU1
Gold-66
Gold Promo-NNO
Promos-2
93SLU Hockey Canadian-6
93SLU Hockey American-7
93Donruss-262
Elite Inserts-1
Ice Kings-7
Special Print-R
Special Print-NNO
93Kenner Starting Lineup Cards-7
93Kraft-43
93Kraft-56
93Kraft-71
93Leaf Chicago National-1
93Leaf-1
93Leaf-210
Gold All-Stars-1
Hat Trick Artists-1
Hat Trick Artists-4
Mario Lemieux-1
Mario Lemieux-2
Mario Lemieux-3
Mario Lemieux-4
Mario Lemieux-5
Mario Lemieux-6
Mario Lemieux-7
Mario Lemieux-8
Mario Lemieux-9
Mario Lemieux-10
93McDonald's Upper Deck-H1
93OPC Premier-37
93OPC Premier-91
93OPC Premier-185
93OPC Premier-220
Gold-37
Gold-91
Gold-185
Gold-220
Black Gold-18
93Panini Stickers-136
93Panini Stickers-H
93Parkhurst-425
Emerald Ice-425
Cherry's Playoff Heroes-D2
East/West Stars-E2
First Overall-F10
USA/Canada Gold-G2
93Penguins Foodland-1
93Pinnacle-221
93Pinnacle-230
93Pinnacle-310
Canadian-221
Canadian-230
Canadian-310
Captains-18
Captains Canadian-18
Nifty Fifty-4
Team Pinnacle-5
Team Canadian-5
93PowerPlay-190
Gamebreakers-5
Point Leaders-6
93Score-350
93Score-479
93Score-480
Canadian-350
Canadian-479
Canadian-480
Dream Team-10
Dynamic Duos Canadian-8
Franchise-16
93Seasons Patches-9
93Stadium Club-143
93Stadium Club-146
93Stadium Club-148
93Stadium Club-310
Members Only Master Set-143
Members Only Master Set-146
Members Only Master Set-148
Members Only Master Set-310
OPC-143
OPC-146
OPC-148
First Day Issue-143
First Day Issue-146
First Day Issue-148
First Day Issue-310
First Day Issue OPC-143
First Day Issue OPC-146
First Day Issue OPC-148
All-Stars-23
All-Stars Members Only-23
All-Stars OPC-23
Finest-10
Finest Members Only-10
93Topps/OPC Premier-37
93Topps/OPC Premier-91
93Topps/OPC Premier-185
93Topps/OPC Premier-220
Gold-37
Gold-91
Gold-185
Gold-220
93Topps Premier Black Gold-9
93Topps Premier Black Gold-A
93Topps Premier Finest-10
93Ultra-116
Award Winners-4
Premier Pivots-4
Red Light Specials-6
Scoring Kings-4
93Upper Deck-301
93Upper Deck-407
Award Winners-AW1
Gretzky's Great Ones-GG4
NHL's Best-HB7
Program of Excellence-E13
Silver Skates-H1
Silver Skates Gold-H1
SP-122
93Upper Deck Locker All-Stars-6
93Swedish Semic World Champ Stickers-198
94Hockey Canadian-6
94SLU Hockey Canadian-6
94SLU Hockey American-11
94Be A Player-R69
94Canada Games NHL POGS-185
94Donruss-5
Dominators-1
Elite Inserts-6
Ice Masters-5
94EA Sports-105
94EA Sports-189
94Flair-135
Center Spotlight-6
Hot Numbers-5
94Hockey Wit-66
94Kenner Starting Lineup Cards-12
94Leaf-1
Fire on Ice-9
Gold Stars-11
Limited Inserts-18
94Leaf Limited-1
Gold-1
94OPC Premier-250
Special Effects-250
94Parkhurst-296
Gold-296
Crash the Game Green-18
Crash the Game Blue-18
Crash the Game Gold-18
Crash the Game Red-18
Vintage-V6
94Pinnacle-170
Artist's Proofs-170
Rink Collection-170
Team Pinnacle-TP10
Team Dufex Parallel-TP10
World Edition-WE8
94Score Dream Team-DT15
94Score Franchise-TF18
94Stadium Club-60
Members Only Master Set-60
First Day Issue-60
Finest Inserts-1
Finest Inserts Members Only-1
Super Team Winner Cards-60
94Topps/OPC Premier-250
Special Effects-250
94Topps Finest Bronze-16
94Ultra-165
Scoring Kings-5
94Upper Deck-22
Electric Ice-22
SP Inserts-SP61
SP Inserts Die Cuts-SP61
95Bashan Super Stickers-97
Die-Cut-24
95Be A Player Lethal Lines-LL11
95Bowman-40
All-Foil-40
Bowman's Best-BB10
Bowman's Best Refractors-BB10
95Canada Games NHL POGS-2
95Canada Games NHL POGS-211
95Collector's Choice-256
Player's Club-256
Player's Club Platinum-256
Crash The Game-C25A
Crash The Game-C25B
Crash The Game-C25C
Crash The Game Gold-C25A
Crash The Game Gold-C25B
Crash The Game Gold-C25C
Crash the Game Silver Redeemed-C25
Crash the Game Silver Bonus-C25
Crash the Game Gold Redeemed-C25
Crash the Game Gold Bonus-C25
95Donruss-270
Dominators-1
Elite Inserts-9
Pro Pointers-14
95Donruss Elite-51
95Donruss Elite-80
Die Cut Stars-51
Die Cut Stars-66
Die Cut Stars-66U
Die Cut Uncut-51
Die Cut Uncut-66
Die Cut Uncut-66U
Cutting Edge-2
Lemieux/Lindros Series-1
Lemieux/Lindros Series-2
Lemieux/Lindros Series-3
Lemieux/Lindros Series-4
Lemieux/Lindros Series-5
Lemieux/Lindros Series-6
Lemieux/Lindros Series-7

95Emotion-138
Xcel-8
Xcited-10
95Finest-150
95Finest-190
Refractors-150
Refractors-190
95Imperial Stickers-97
Die Cut Superstars-24
95Kellogg's Donruss-1
95Kellogg's Donruss-2
95Kellogg's Donruss-3
95Kellogg's Donruss-4
95Kraft-8
95Leaf-1
95Leaf-NNO
Freeze Frame-7
Lemieux's Best-1
Lemieux's Best-2
Lemieux's Best-3
Lemieux's Best-4
Lemieux's Best-5
Lemieux's Best-6
Lemieux's Best-7
Lemieux's Best-8
Lemieux's Best-9
Lemieux's Best-10
95Leaf Limited-1
Stars of the Game-1
95McDonald's Pinnacle-MCD-15
95Metal-118
Heavy Metal-9
International Steel-14
95NHL Aces Playing Cards-12H
95NHL Cool Trade-4
95NHL Cool Trade-RP4
95Panini Stickers-59
95Parkhurst International-170
Emerald Ice-170
Crown Collection Silver Series 1-3
Crown Collection Gold Series 1-3
NHL All-Stars-1
Parkie's Trophy Picks-PP2
Parkie's Trophy Picks-PP11
95Penguins Foodland-23
95Pinnacle-192
Artist's Proofs-192
Rink Collection-192
Clear Shots-13
First Strike-13
95Pinnacle FANtasy-8
95Playoff One on One-79
95Playoff One on One-186
95Playoff One on One-298
95Pro Magnets-93
95Select Certified-1
Mirror Gold-1
Gold Team-3
95SkyBox Impact-132
Countdown to Impact-3
Ice Quake-7
95SP-113
Holoviews-FX17
Holoviews Special FX-FX17
Stars/Etoiles-E22
Stars/Etoiles Gold-E22
95Stadium Club-180
Members Only Master Set-180
Metalists-M2
Metalists Members Only Master Set-M2
Nemeses-N2
Nemeses Members Only Master Set-N2
95Summit-118
Artist's Proofs-118
Ice-118
GM's Choice-10
95Topps-100
OPC Inserts-100
Home Grown Canada-HGC30
Mystery Finest-M2
Mystery Finest Refractors-M2
Profiles-PF15
Rink Leaders-2RL
95Topps SuperSkills-1
Platinum-1
95Ultra-288
95Ultra-391
Extra Attackers-13
Ultraview-6
Ultraview Hot Pack-6
95Upper Deck-84
95Upper Deck-231
Electric Ice-84
Electric Ice-231
Electric Ice Gold-84
Electric Ice Gold-231
95Upper Deck All-Star Game Predictors-16
Redemption Winners-16
95Upper Deck Freeze Frame-F16
95Upper Deck Freeze Frame Jumbo-F16
95Upper Deck NHL All-Stars-AS5
95Upper Deck NHL All-Stars Jumbo-AS5
95Upper Deck Predictor Hobby-H4
95Upper Deck Predictor Hobby Exchange-H4
95Upper Deck Predictor Retail-R32
95Upper Deck Predictor Retail-R42
95Upper Deck Predictor Retail-R53
95Upper Deck Predictor Retail Exchange-R32
95Upper Deck Predictor Retail Exchange-R42
95Upper Deck Predictor Retail Exchange-R53
95Upper Deck Special Edition-SE152
95Upper Deck Special Edition Gold-SE152
95Zenith-108
Z-Team-3
95Finnish Semic World Championships-93
95Swedish Globe World Championships-87
95Swedish World Championships Stickers-277
96Headliners Hockey-11A
96Headliners Hockey-11B
96Be A Player-NNO
Biscuit In The Basket-2
Lemieux Die Cut-1
Lemieux Die Cut-2
96Black Diamond-166
Gold-166
Run for the Cup-RC3
96Collector's Choice-210
96Collector's Choice-293
96Collector's Choice-335
Stick'Ums-S7
Crash the Game-C5A
Crash the Game-C5B
Crash the Game-C5C
Crash the Game Gold-C5A
Crash the Game Gold-C5B
Crash the Game Gold-C5C
Crash the Game Exchange-CR5
Crash the Game Exchange Gold-CR5
96Donruss-131
Press Proofs-131
Dominators-4
Go Top Shelf-1
96Donruss Canadian Ice-31
Gold Press Proofs-31
Red Press Proofs-31
Mario Lemieux Scrapbook-1
Mario Lemieux Scrapbook-2
Mario Lemieux Scrapbook-3
Mario Lemieux Scrapbook-4
Mario Lemieux Scrapbook-5
Mario Lemieux Scrapbook-6
Mario Lemieux Scrapbook-7
Mario Lemieux Scrapbook-8
Mario Lemieux Scrapbook-9
Mario Lemieux Scrapbook-10
Mario Lemieux Scrapbook-11
Mario Lemieux Scrapbook-12
Mario Lemieux Scrapbook-13
Mario Lemieux Scrapbook-14
Mario Lemieux Scrapbook-15
Mario Lemieux Scrapbook-16
Mario Lemieux Scrapbook-17
Mario Lemieux Scrapbook-18
Mario Lemieux Scrapbook-19
Mario Lemieux Scrapbook-20
Mario Lemieux Scrapbook-21
Mario Lemieux Scrapbook-22
Mario Lemieux Scrapbook-23
Mario Lemieux Scrapbook-24
Mario Lemieux Scrapbook-25
Mario Lemieux Scrapbook-NNO1
Mario Lemieux Scrapbook-NNO2
O Canada-13
96Donruss Elite-109
Die Cut Stars-109
Hart to Hart-1
Hart to Hart-2
Hart to Hart-3
Hart to Hart-4
Hart to Hart-5
Hart to Hart-6
Hart to Hart-AU1
Hart to Hart-AU2
Hart to Hart-AU3
Hart to Hart-AU4
Hart to Hart-AU5
Hart to Hart-AU6
Hart to Hart-NNO
Perspective-4
96Flair-78
Blue Ice-78
Hot Numbers-7
Now And Then-2
96Fleer-87
96Fleer-137
96Fleer-138
96Fleer-139
96Fleer-141
Art Ross-13
Pearson-7
Picks Captain's Choice-3
Picks Dream Lines-1
Picks Fabulous 50-26
96Hockey Greats Coins-13
Gold-13
96Kraft Upper Deck-22
96Kraft Upper Deck-28
96Kraft Upper Deck-37
96Kraft Upper Deck-54
96Kraft Upper Deck-56
96Kraft Upper Deck-67
96Leaf-84
Press Proofs-84
Fire On Ice-1
Sweaters Away-1
Sweaters Home-1
96Leaf Limited-85
Gold-85
Stubble-7
96Leaf Preferred-113
Press Proofs-113
Steel Power-2
Vanity Plates-6
Vanity Plates Gold-6
96Maggers-56
96Maple Leafs Postcards-2
96McDonald's Pinnacle-21
96Metal Universe-128
Ice Carvings-10
Ice Carvings Super Power-10
Lethal Weapons-11
Lethal Weapons Super Power-11
96NHL Aces Playing Cards-29
96NHL Pro Stamps-93
96Penguins Tribune-Review-8
96Pinnacle-86
Artist's Proofs-86
Foil-86
Premium Stock-86
Rink Collection-86
Team Pinnacle-2
Trophies-1
96Pinnacle Fantasy-FC4
96Pinnacle Mint-1
Bronze-1
Gold-1
Silver-1
Coins Brass-1
Coins Solid Gold-1
Coins Gold Plated-1
Coins Nickel-1
Coins Silver-1
96Playoff One on One-436
96Score-6
Artist's Proofs-6
Dealer's Choice Artist's Proofs-6
Special Artist's Proofs-6
Golden Blades-6
Dream Team-6
Sudden Death-7
96Select Certified-10
Artist's Proofs-10
Blue-10
Mirror Blue-10
Mirror Gold-10
Mirror Red-10
Red-10
Cornerstones-2
96SkyBox Impact-102
Countdown to Impact-7
VersaTeam-7
96SP-125
Clearcut Winner-CW3
SPx Force-1
96SPx-37
Gold-37
Holoview Heroes-HH6
96Stadium Club Members Only-24
96Summit-32
Artist's Proofs-32
Ice-32
Metal-32
Premium Stock-32
High Voltage-8
High Voltage Mirage-8
Untouchables-1
96Team Out-17
96Topps Picks-3
500 Club-FC5
Fantasy Team-FT15
OPC Inserts-3
96Ultra-143
Gold Medallion-143
Power-11
Power Red Line-4
96Upper Deck-321
Game Jerseys-GJ6
Hart Hopefuls Bronze-HH16
Hart Hopefuls Gold-HH16
Hart Hopefuls Silver-HH16
Lord Stanley's Heroes Finals-LS3
Lord Stanley's Heroes Quarterfinals-LS3
Lord Stanley's Heroes Semifinals-LS3
Superstar Showdown-SS5B
96Upper Deck Ice-114
Parallel-114
Stanley Cup Foundation-S7
Stanley Cup Foundation Dynasty-S7
96Zenith-114
Artist's Proofs-114
Champion Salute-5
Champion Salute Diamond-5
96Swedish Semic Wien-85
97Headliners Hockey-16
97Highland Mint Mint-Cards Topps-15
97Highland Mint Mint-Cards Topps-16
97Highland Mint Mint-Coins-6
97Highland Mint Mint-Coins-7
97Highland Mint Mint-Coins-8
97Highland Mint Sandblast Mint-Cards-1
97Highland Mint Sandblast Mint-Cards-2
97Pinnacle Lemieux 600 Goals Commemorative -1
97Pinnacle Mario's Moments-1
97Pinnacle Mario's Moments-2
97Pinnacle Mario's Moments-3
97Pinnacle Mario's Moments-4
97Pinnacle Mario's Moments-5
97Pinnacle Mario's Moments-6
97Pinnacle Mario's Moments-7
97Pinnacle Mario's Moments-8
97Pinnacle Mario's Moments-9
97Pinnacle Mario's Moments-10
97Pinnacle Mario's Moments-11
97Pinnacle Mario's Moments-12
97Pinnacle Mario's Moments-13
97Pinnacle Mario's Moments-14
97Pinnacle Mario's Moments-15
97Pinnacle Mario's Moments-16
97Pinnacle Mario's Moments-17
97Pinnacle Mario's Moments-18
97Pinnacle Mario's Moments-NNO
98SLU Hockey 12" Figures-2
98BAP Playoff Legend Mario Lemieux-L1
98BAP Playoff Legend Mario Lemieux-L2
98BAP Playoff Legend Mario Lemieux-L3
98BAP Playoff Legend Mario Lemieux-L4
98McDonalds Upper Deck Gretzkys Teammates-T12
99BAP Millennium Pearson-P3
99BAP Millennium Pearson Autographs-P3
99Topps Stanley Cup Heroes-SC1
99Topps Stanley Cup Heroes Refractors-SC1
99Topps Stanley Cup Heroes Autographs-SCA1
99Topps Premier Plus Club Signings-CS6
99Topps Premier Plus Club Signings-CSC3
99Upper Deck Century Legends-4
Century Collection-4
All Century Team-AC7
Epic Signatures-ML
Epic Signatures 100-ML
Essence of the Game-E3
Jerseys of the Century-JC5
Jerseys of the Century-JCA2
99Upper Deck Retro-83
Gold-83
Platinum-83
Distant Replay-DR12
Distant Replay Level 2-DR12
Generation-G5B
Generation Level 2-G5B
Inkredible-ML
Inkredible Level 2-ML
Memento-RM3
Turn of the Century-TC13
00BAP Memorabilia-501
Mario Lemieux Legends-L1
Mario Lemieux Legends-L2
Mario Lemieux Legends-L3
Mario Lemieux Legends-L4
Mario Lemieux Legends-L5
Mario Lemieux Legends-L6
Mario Lemieux Legends-L7
Mario Lemieux Legends-L8
Mario Lemieux Legends-L9
Mario Lemieux Legends-L10
Mario Lemieux Legends Autographs-L1
Mario Lemieux Legends Autographs-L2
Mario Lemieux Legends Autographs-L3
Mario Lemieux Legends Autographs-L4
Mario Lemieux Legends Autographs-L5
Mario Lemieux Legends Autographs-L6
Mario Lemieux Legends Autographs-L7
Mario Lemieux Legends Autographs-L8
Mario Lemieux Legends Autographs-L9
Mario Lemieux Legends Autographs-L10
Patent Power Jerseys-PP1
Update Teammates-TM3
Update Teammates Gold-TM3
00BAP Parkhurst 2000-P166
00BAP Signature Series-75
Emerald-75
Ruby-75
Sapphire-75
He Shoots-He Scores Points-11
He Shoots-He Scores Prizes-39
Mario Lemieux Legend-LM1
Mario Lemieux Legend-LM2
Mario Lemieux Legend-LM3
Mario Lemieux Legend-LM4
Mario Lemieux Legend-LM5
Mario Lemieux Legend Autographs-LM1
Mario Lemieux Legend Autographs-LM2
Mario Lemieux Legend Autographs-LM3
Mario Lemieux Legend Autographs-LM4
Mario Lemieux Legend Autographs-LM5
Mario Lemieux Retrospective-R1
Mario Lemieux Retrospective-R2
Mario Lemieux Retrospective-R3
Mario Lemieux Retrospective-R4
Mario Lemieux Retrospective-R5
Mario Lemieux Retrospective-R6
Mario Lemieux Retrospective-R7
Mario Lemieux Retrospective-R8
Mario Lemieux Retrospective-R9
Mario Lemieux Retrospective-R10
Mario Lemieux Retrospective-R11
Mario Lemieux Retrospective-R12
Mario Lemieux Retrospective-R13
Mario Lemieux Retrospective-R14
Mario Lemieux Retrospective-R15
Mario Lemieux Retrospective-R16
Mario Lemieux Retrospective-R17
Mario Lemieux Retrospective-R18
Mario Lemieux Retrospective-R19
Mario Lemieux Retrospective-R20
00BAP Ultimate Memorabilia Autographs-11
Gold-11
00BAP Ultimate Memorabilia Active Eight-AE1
00BAP Ultimate Memorabilia Active Eight-AE3
00BAP Ultimate Memorabilia Active Eight-AE4
00BAP Ultimate Memorabilia Captain's C-C10
00BAP Ultimate Mem Dynasty Jerseys-D6
00BAP Ultimate Mem Dynasty Emblems-D6
00BAP Ultimate Memorabilia Hart Trophy-H5
00BAP Ultimate Memorabilia Hart Trophy-H8
00BAP Ultimate Memorabilia Hart Trophy-H13
00BAP Ultimate Mem Magnificent Ones-ML1
00BAP Ultimate Mem Magnificent Ones-ML2
00BAP Ultimate Mem Magnificent Ones-ML3
00BAP Ultimate Mem Magnificent Ones-ML4
00BAP Ultimate Mem Magnificent Ones-ML5
00BAP Ultimate Mem Magnificent Ones-ML6
00BAP Ultimate Mem Magnificent Ones-ML7
00BAP Ultimate Mem Magnificent Ones-ML8
00BAP Ultimate Mem Magnificent Ones-ML9
00BAP Ultimate Mem Magnificent Ones-ML10
00BAP Ultimate Mem Magnificent Ones Autos-ML1
00BAP Ultimate Mem Magnificent Ones Autos-ML2
00BAP Ultimate Mem Magnificent Ones Autos-ML3
00BAP Ultimate Mem Magnificent Ones Autos-ML4
00BAP Ultimate Mem Magnificent Ones Autos-ML5
00BAP Ultimate Mem Magnificent Ones Autos-ML6
00BAP Ultimate Mem Magnificent Ones Autos-ML7
00BAP Ultimate Mem Magnificent Ones Autos-ML8
00BAP Ultimate Mem Magnificent Ones Autos-ML9
00BAP Ultimate Mem Magnificent Ones Autos-ML10
00BAP Ultimate Memorabilia NHL Records-R7
00BAP Ultimate Memorabilia Retro-Active-RA3
00BAP Ultimate Memorabilia Retro-Active-RA6
00BAP Ultimate Memorabilia Teammates-TM39
00Black Diamond-107
00Crown Royale-87
Ice Blue-87
Limited Series-87
Premiere Date-87
Red-87
Jewels of the Crown-22
Landmarks-9
Now Playing-15
00Private Stock-152
Gold-152
Premiere Date-152
Retail-152
Silver-152
00SP Authentic-72
BuyBacks-92
BuyBacks-93
Honor-SP6
Sign of the Times-ML
Sign of the Times-L/K
Sign of the Times-HLY
Significant Stars-ST7
00SP Game Used-49
Patch Cards-D-JL
Patch Cards-P-ML
Tools of the Game-ML
Tools of the Game Exclusives-ML
Tools of the Game Combos-C-LG
Tools of the Game Combos-C-LJ
00SPx-144
Winning Materials-ML
Winning Materials Autographs-SML
00Titanium-77
Blue-77
Gold-77
Premiere Date-77
Red-77
Retail-77
All-Stars-9NA
Game Gear-44
Game Gear-151
Three-Star Selections-18
00Titanium Draft Day Edition-86
00Topps/OPC Combos-TC10
00Topps/OPC Combos Jumbos-TC10
00Topps/OPC Lemieux Reprints-1
00Topps/OPC Lemieux Reprints-2
00Topps/OPC Lemieux Reprints-3
00Topps/OPC Lemieux Reprints-4
00Topps/OPC Lemieux Reprints-5
00Topps/OPC Lemieux Reprints-6
00Topps/OPC Lemieux Reprints-7
00Topps/OPC Lemieux Reprints-8
00Topps/OPC Lemieux Reprints-9
00Topps/OPC Lemieux Reprints-10
00Topps/OPC Lemieux Reprints-11
00Topps/OPC Lemieux Reprints-12
00Topps/OPC Lemieux Reprints-13
00Topps/OPC Lemieux Reprints-14
00Topps/OPC Lemieux Reprints-15
00Topps/OPC Lemieux Reprints-16
00Topps/OPC Lemieux Reprints-17
00Topps/OPC Lemieux Reprints-18
00Topps/OPC Lemieux Reprints-19
00Topps/OPC Lemieux Reprints-20
00Topps/OPC Lemieux Reprints-21
00Topps/OPC Lemieux Reprints-22
00Topps/OPC Lemieux Reprints-23
00Topps/OPC Lemieux Reprints Autographs-1
00Topps/OPC Lemieux Reprints Autographs-2
00Topps/OPC Lemieux Reprints Autographs-3
00Topps/OPC Lemieux Reprints Autographs-4
00Topps/OPC Lemieux Reprints Autographs-5
00Topps/OPC Lemieux Reprints Autographs-6
00Topps/OPC Lemieux Reprints Autographs-7
00Topps/OPC Lemieux Reprints Autographs-8
00Topps/OPC Lemieux Reprints Autographs-9
00Topps/OPC Lemieux Reprints Autographs-10
00Topps/OPC Lemieux Reprints Autographs-11
00Topps/OPC Lemieux Reprints Autographs-12
00Topps/OPC Lemieux Reprints Autographs-13
00Topps/OPC Lemieux Reprints Autographs-14
00Topps/OPC Lemieux Reprints Autographs-15
00Topps/OPC Lemieux Reprints Autographs-16
00Topps/OPC Lemieux Reprints Autographs-17
00Topps/OPC Lemieux Reprints Autographs-18
00Topps/OPC Lemieux Reprints Autographs-19
00Topps/OPC Lemieux Reprints Autographs-20
00Topps/OPC Lemieux Reprints Autographs-21
00Topps/OPC Lemieux Reprints Autographs-22
00Topps/OPC Lemieux Reprints Autographs-23
00Topps Chrome Combos-TC10
00Topps Chrome Combos Refractors-TC10
00Topps Chrome Mario Lemieux Reprints-1
00Topps Chrome Mario Lemieux Reprints-2
00Topps Chrome Mario Lemieux Reprints-3
00Topps Chrome Mario Lemieux Reprints-4
00Topps Chrome Mario Lemieux Reprints-5
00Topps Chrome Mario Lemieux Reprints-6
00Topps Chrome Mario Lemieux Reprints-7
00Topps Chrome Mario Lemieux Reprints-8
00Topps Chrome Mario Lemieux Reprints-9
00Topps Chrome Mario Lemieux Reprints-10
00Topps Chrome Mario Lemieux Reprints-11
00Topps Chrome Mario Lemieux Reprints-12
00Topps Chrome Mario Lemieux Reprints-13
00Topps Chrome Mario Lemieux Reprints-14
00Topps Chrome Mario Lemieux Reprints-15
00Topps Chrome Mario Lemieux Reprints-16
00Topps Chrome Mario Lemieux Reprints-17
00Topps Chrome Mario Lemieux Reprints-18
00Topps Chrome Mario Lemieux Reprints-19
00Topps Chrome Mario Lemieux Reprints-20
00Topps Chrome Mario Lemieux Reprints-21
00Topps Chrome Mario Lemieux Reprints-22
00Topps Chrome Mario Lemieux Reprints-23
00Topps Chrome Lemieux Reprints Refr-1
00Topps Chrome Lemieux Reprints Refr-2
00Topps Chrome Lemieux Reprints Refr-3
00Topps Chrome Lemieux Reprints Refr-4
00Topps Chrome Lemieux Reprints Refr-5
00Topps Chrome Lemieux Reprints Refr-6
00Topps Chrome Lemieux Reprints Refr-7
00Topps Chrome Lemieux Reprints Refr-8
00Topps Chrome Lemieux Reprints Refr-9
00Topps Chrome Lemieux Reprints Refr-10
00Topps Chrome Lemieux Reprints Refr-11
00Topps Chrome Lemieux Reprints Refr-12
00Topps Chrome Lemieux Reprints Refr-13
00Topps Chrome Lemieux Reprints Refr-14
00Topps Chrome Lemieux Reprints Refr-15
00Topps Chrome Lemieux Reprints Refr-16
00Topps Chrome Lemieux Reprints Refr-17
00Topps Chrome Lemieux Reprints Refr-18
00Topps Chrome Lemieux Reprints Refr-19
00Topps Chrome Lemieux Reprints Refr-20
00Topps Chrome Lemieux Reprints Refr-21
00Topps Chrome Lemieux Reprints Refr-22
00Topps Chrome Lemieux Reprints Refr-23
00Topps Gold Label Class 1-37
Gold-37
00Topps Gold Label Class 2-37
00Topps Gold Label Class 2 Gold-37
00Topps Gold Label Class 3-37
00Topps Gold Label Class 3 Gold-37
00Topps Heritage-73
Chrome Parallel-73
00Topps Premier Plus-66
Blue Ice-66
00Topps Stars-100
Blue-100
Autographs-AML
Progression-P1
Progression-P2
Progression-P3
00UD Heroes-136
Game-Used Twigs-T-ML
Game-Used Twigs Gold-C-LJ
Player Idols-PI5
Signs of Greatness-ML
00UD Pros and Prospects-69
Great Skates-GS2
NHL Passion-NP8
00UD Reserve-70
Gold Strike-GS8
00Upper Deck 500 Goal Club-500ML
00Upper Deck 500 Goal Club-500ML
00Upper Deck Game Jersey Combos-DGL
00Upper Deck Game Jersey Combos-DJL
00Upper Deck Ice-75
00Upper Deck Legends-105
00Upper Deck Legends-108
Legendary Collection Bronze-105
Legendary Collection Bronze-108
Legendary Collection Gold-105
Legendary Collection Gold-108
Legendary Collection Silver-105
Legendary Collection Silver-108
Enshrined Stars-ES3
Epic Signatures-ML
Legendary Game Jerseys-JML
Supreme Milestones-SM11
00Upper Deck Vintage Dynasty: A Piece of History-LJ
00Upper Deck Vintage Dynasty: A Piece of History Gold-LJ
00Vanguard-151
00Czech Stadion-79
00Czech Stadion-147
00Czech Stadion-148
00Czech Stadion-162
01McFarlane Hockey-80
01McFarlane Hockey-81
01Atomic-79
Blue-79
Gold-79
Premiere Date-79
Red-79
Blast-9
Core Players-15
Jerseys-45
Power Play-27
Statosphere-18
Team Nucleus-11
01BAP Memorabilia-66
Emerald-66
Ruby-66
Sapphire-66
All-Star Jerseys-ASJ16
All-Star Emblems-ASE16
All-Star Numbers-ASN16
All-Star Jersey Doubles-DASJ22
All-Star Teammates-AST2
All-Star Teammates-AST12
Country of Origin-CO1
Country of Origin-CO48
500 Goal Scorers-GS9
He Shoots-He Scores Points-19
He Shoots-He Scores Prizes-14
Patented Power-PP2
Stanley Cup Playoffs-SC24
01BAP Signature Series Certified 100-C54
01BAP Signature Series Certified 50-C54
01BAP Signature Series Certified 1 of 1's-C54
01BAP Signature Series Autographs-XLML
01BAP Signature Series Autographs Gold-XLML
01BAP Signature Series 500 Goal Scorers-26
01BAP Signature Series 500 Goal Scorers-ML
01BAP Sig Series 500 Goal Scorers Autos-26
01BAP Signature Series Franchise Jerseys-FP-24
01BAP Sig Series He Shoots/Scores Points-18
01BAP Sig Series He Shoots/Scores Prizes-3
01BAP Sig Series International Medals-IG-6
01BAP Signature Series Jerseys-GJ-54
01BAP Signature Series Jersey Autographs-GUML
01BAP Sig Series Jersey and Stick Cards-GSJ-54
01BAP Signature Series Emblems-GUE-13
01BAP Signature Series Numbers-ITN-13
01BAP Signature Series Teammates-TM-24
01BAP Ultimate Memorabilia Active Eight-1
01BAP Ultimate Memorabilia Active Eight-4
01BAP Ultimate Memorabilia Active Eight-5
01BAP Ultimate Memorabilia Active Eight-8
01BAP Ultimate Mem All-Star History-37
01BAP Ultimate Memorabilia Autographs-28
01BAP Ultimate Mem Autographs Gold-28
01BAP Ultimate Memorabilia Calder Trophy-16
01BAP Ultimate Memorabilia Captain's C-9
01BAP Ultimate Memorabilia Dynamic Duos-12
01BAP Ultimate Memorabilia Emblems-10
01BAP Ultimate Mem 500 Goal Scorers-3
01BAP Ultimate Mem 500 Goal Scorers Autos-15
01BAP Ultimate Mem 500 Goal Jerseys/Stick-3
01BAP Ultimate Mem 500 Goal Emblems-3
01BAP Ultimate Memorabilia Gloves Are Off-3
01BAP Ultimate Memorabilia Jerseys-10
01BAP Ultimate Mem Jerseys and Sticks-10
01BAP Ultimate Memorabilia Made to Order-3
01BAP Ultimate Memorabilia Made to Order-4
01BAP Ultimate Memorabilia Made to Order-5
01BAP Ultimate Memorabilia Numbers-9
01BAP Ultimate Memorabilia Name Plates-2
01BAP Ultimate Mem Playoff Records-15
01BAP Ultimate Mem Prototypical Players-8
01BAP Ultimate Memorabilia Retro Trophies-4
01BAP Ultimate Memorabilia Retro Trophies-5
01BAP Ultimate Memorabilia Retro Trophies-16
01BAP Ultimate Memorabilia Retro Trophies-17
01BAP Ultimate Memorabilia Retro Trophies-19
01BAP Ultimate Mem Retro Teammates-11
01BAP Ultimate Mem Scoring Leaders-7
01BAP Ultimate Mem Scoring Leaders-8
01BAP Ultimate Mem Scoring Leaders-15
01Bowman YoungStars-3
Gold-3
Ice Cubed-3
01Crown Royale-117
Blue-117
Premiere Date-117
Red-117
Retail-117
All-Star Honors-17
Crowning Achievement-19
Jewels of the Crown-25
Legendary Heroes-8
Triple Threads-17
01EA Sports-1
01EA Sports-2
01eTopps-23
01Fleer Legacy-1
01Fleer Legacy-25
Ultimate-1
Ultimate-25
In the Corners-4
Memorabilia-5
Memorabilia-16
Memorabilia Autographs-5
01Greats of the Game-81
Retro Collection-12
Autographs-81
Board Certified-3
01McDonald's Pacific-31
Cosmic Force-2
Jersey Patches Silver-15
Jersey Patches Gold-15
01O-Pee-Chee-1
01O-Pee-Chee-326
01O-Pee-Chee-327
01O-Pee-Chee-328
01O-Pee-Chee-329
01O-Pee-Chee-330
01O-Pee-Chee Heritage Parallel-1
01O-Pee-Chee Heritage Parallel Limited-1
01O-Pee-Chee Premier Parallel-1
01O-Pee-Chee Premier Parallel-326
01O-Pee-Chee Premier Parallel-327
01O-Pee-Chee Premier Parallel-328
01O-Pee-Chee Premier Parallel-329
01O-Pee-Chee Premier Parallel-330
01O-Pee-Chee Jumbos-1
01Pacific-316
01Pacific-419
01Pacific-439
Extreme LTD-316
Gold-419
Gold-439
Hobby LTD-316
Premiere Date-316
Retail LTD-316
All-Stars-NA10
Cramer's Choice-9
Jerseys-28
Gold Crown Die-Cuts-17
97-98 Subset-66
97-98 Subset Gold Parallel-66
Top Draft Picks-10
01Pacific Top Draft Picks Draft Day Promo-10
01Pacific Adrenaline-155
Blue-155
Premiere Date-155
Red-155
Retail-155
Blade Runners-9
Jerseys-38
World Beaters-16
01Pacific Arena Exclusives-316
01Pacific Arena Exclusives-419
01Pacific Arena Exclusives-439
01Pacific Heads-Up-78
Blue-78
Premiere Date-78
Red-78
Silver-78
HD NHL-7
Quad Jerseys-17
Quad Jerseys-21
Rink Immortals-9
Stat Masters-14
01Pacific Montreal International-8
01Parkhurst-24
Gold-24
Silver-24
500 Goal Scorers-PGS9
He Shoots-He Scores Points-19
He Shoots-He Scores Prizes-8
Heroes-H14
Jerseys-PJ1
Milestones-M20
Milestones-M21U
Milestones-M36
Sticks-PS1
Teammates-T2
Teammates-T28
Waving the Flag-1
01Private Stock-78
Gold-78
Premiere Date-78
Retail-78
Silver-78
Game Gear-79
Game Gear Patches-79
01Private Stock Pacific Nights-78
01Private Stock PS-2002-59
01Private Stock Reserve-S15
01SP Authentic-68
01SP Authentic-106
Limited-68
Limited-106
Limited Gold-68
Limited Gold-106
Jerseys-NNML
01SP Game Used-43
Authentic Fabric-AFML
Authentic Fabric-DFLG
Authentic Fabric-DFLK
Authentic Fabric-TFLKL
Authentic Fabric-GYSL
Authentic Fabric-HGBL
Authentic Fabric Gold-AFML
Patches-PML
Patches-CPLJ
Patches-TPLGY
01SPx-52
01SPx-78
01SPx-89
Hidden Treasures-TTYLS
Hockey Treasures-HTML
01Stadium Club-18
Award Winners-18
Master Photos-18
Gallery-G21
Gallery Gold-G21
Heart and Soul-HS4
NHL Passport-NHLP18
Perennials-P9
01Titanium-114
Hobby Parallel-114
Premiere Date-114
Retail-114
Retail Parallel-114
Double-Sided Jerseys-32
Saturday Knights-18
Three-Star Selections-18
01Titanium Draft Day Edition-80
01Topps-1
01Topps-326
01Topps-327
01Topps-328
01Topps-329
01Topps-330
Heritage Parallel-1
Heritage Parallel Limited-1
OPC Parallel-1
OPC Parallel-326
OPC Parallel-327
OPC Parallel-328
OPC Parallel-329
OPC Parallel-330
Mario Lemieux Reprints-1
Mario Lemieux Reprints-2
Mario Lemieux Reprints-3
Mario Lemieux Reprints-4
Mario Lemieux Reprints-5
Mario Lemieux Reprints-6
Mario Lemieux Reprints-7
Mario Lemieux Reprints-8
Mario Lemieux Reprints-9
Mario Lemieux Reprints-10
Mario Returns Autographs-MR1
Mario Returns Autographs-MR2
Mario Returns Autographs-MR3
Mario Returns Autographs-MR4
Mario Returns Autographs-MR5
Shot Masters-SM1
Stars of the Game-SG1
01Topps Chrome-1
Refractors-1
Black Border Refractors-1
Mario Lemieux Reprints-1
Mario Lemieux Reprints-2
Mario Lemieux Reprints-3
Mario Lemieux Reprints-4
Mario Lemieux Reprints-5
Mario Lemieux Reprints-6
Mario Lemieux Reprints-7
Mario Lemieux Reprints-8
Mario Lemieux Reprints-9
Mario Lemieux Reprints-10
Mario Lemieux Reprint Refractors-1
Mario Lemieux Reprint Refractors-2
Mario Lemieux Reprint Refractors-3
Mario Lemieux Reprint Refractors-4
Mario Lemieux Reprint Refractors-5
Mario Lemieux Reprint Refractors-6
Mario Lemieux Reprint Refractors-7
Mario Lemieux Reprint Refractors-8
Mario Lemieux Reprint Refractors-9
Mario Lemieux Reprint Refractors-10
Mario Returns-MR1
Mario Returns-MR2
Mario Returns-MR3
Mario Returns-MR4
Mario Returns-MR5
Mario Returns Refractors-MR1
Mario Returns Refractors-MR2
Mario Returns Refractors-MR3
Mario Returns Refractors-MR4
Mario Returns Refractors-MR5
01Topps Heritage-1
01Topps Heritage-120
Refractors-1
01Topps Reserve-3
Emblems-ML
Jerseys-ML
Name Plates-ML
Numbers-ML
Patches-ML
01UD Challenge for the Cup-68
Century Men-CM8
Cornerstones-CR7
Jerseys-FPML
01UD Honor Roll-8
01UD Honor Roll-38
Jerseys-J-ML
Jerseys Gold-J-ML
Playoff Matchups-HS-LH
Playoff Matchups Gold-HS-LH
01UD Mask Collection-79
Gold-79
Double Patches-DPML
Jerseys-J-ML
Jersey and Patch-JPML
01UD Playmakers-79
Jerseys-J-ML
Jerseys Gold-J-ML
01UD Premier Collection-41
Dual Jerseys-DGL
Dual Jerseys-DLK
Dual Jerseys Black-DGL
Dual Jerseys Black-DLK
Jerseys-GML
Jerseys Black-G-ML
01UD Stanley Cup Champs-86
Jerseys-T-ML
Pieces of Glory-G-ML
Sticks-S-ML
01UD Top Shelf-34
Jerseys-ML
Sticks-SML
Sticks Gold-SML
01Upper Deck-138
Exclusives-138
Fantastic Finishers-FF4
Franchise Cornerstones-FC3
Game Jerseys-CLJ
Game Jerseys Series II-PFML
Gate Attractions-GA5
Leaders of the Pack-LP11
Patches-PML
Patches Series II-PLML
Patches Series II-PNML
Patches Series II-NAML
Pride of a Nation-PNML
Pride of a Nation-DPLK
Pride of a Nation-TPYRL
Shooting Stars-SS14
Skilled Stars-SS2
EA Sports Gold-1
EA Sports Gold-2
01Upper Deck Ice-36
Combos-C-ML
Combos Gold-G-ML
01Upper Deck MVP-150
Souvenirs-S-ML
Souvenirs Gold-S-ML
Talent-MT4
Valuable Commodities-VC5
Watch-MW1
01Upper Deck Pearson Awards-2
01Upper Deck Victory-280
01Upper Deck Victory-391
Gold-280
Gold-391
01Upper Deck Vintage-201
01Upper Deck Vintage-208
01Vanguard-80
Blue-80
Red-80
East Meets West-1
In Focus-8
Memorabilia-26
Memorabilia-44
One of Ones-80
Premiere Date-80
Proofs-80
Quebec Tournament Heroes-2
V-Team-17
02McFarlane Hockey Team Canada-20
02Atomic-80
Blue-80
Gold-80
Red-80
Cold Fusion-20
Hobby Parallel-80
Jerseys-19
Jerseys Gold-19
Patches-19
National Pride-C9
02BAP All-Star Edition-51
02BAP All-Star Edition-52
02BAP All-Star Edition-53
He Shoots-He Scores Points-19
He Shoots-He Score Prizes-14
Jerseys-51
Jerseys-52
Jerseys-53
Jerseys Gold-51
Jerseys Gold-52
Jerseys Gold-53
Jerseys Silver-51
Jerseys Silver-52
Jerseys Silver-53
02BAP First Edition-1
02BAP First Edition-160
02BAP First Edition-323
02BAP First Edition-364
02BAP First Edition-426R
He Shoots-He Score Points-20
He Shoots-He Scores Prizes-2
Jerseys-1
Jerseys-160
Magnificent Inserts-MI1
Magnificent Inserts-MI2
Magnificent Inserts-MI3
Magnificent Inserts-MI4
Magnificent Inserts-MI5
Magnificent Inserts-MI6
Magnificent Inserts-MI7
Magnificent Inserts-MI8

Magnificent Inserts-MI9
Magnificent Inserts-MI10
02BAP Memorabilia-157
02BAP Memorabilia-224
Emerald-157
Emerald-224
Ruby-157
Ruby-224
Sapphire-157
Sapphire-224
All-Star Jerseys-ASJ-31
All-Star Emblems-ASE-12
All-Star Numbers-ASN-12
All-Star Teammmates-AST-4
All-Star Teammmates-AST-22
All-Star Teammmates-AST-28
All-Star Triple Jerseys-ASTJ-10
Franchise Players-FP-24
He Shoots-He Scores Points-19
He Shoots-He Scores Prizes-2
Magnificent Inserts-MI1
Magnificent Inserts-MI2
Magnificent Inserts-MI3
Magnificent Inserts-MI4
Magnificent Inserts-MI5
Magnificent Inserts-MI6
Magnificent Inserts-MI7
Magnificent Inserts-MI8
Magnificent Inserts-MI9
Magnificent Inserts-MI10
Magnificent Inserts Autographs-MI1
Magnificent Inserts Autographs-MI2
Magnificent Inserts Autographs-MI3
Magnificent Inserts Autographs-MI4
Magnificent Inserts Autographs-MI5
Magnificent Inserts Autographs-MI6
Magnificent Inserts Autographs-MI7
Magnificent Inserts Autographs-MI8
Magnificent Inserts Autographs-MI9
Magnificent Inserts Autographs-MI10
Mini Stanley Cups-29
NHL All-Star Game-157
NHL All-Star Game-224
NHL All-Star Game Blue-157
NHL All-Star Game Blue-224
NHL All-Star Game Green-157
NHL All-Star Game Green-224
NHL All-Star Game Red-157
NHL All-Star Game Red-224
Teammates-TM-15
02BAP Memorabilia Toronto Fall Expo-157
02BAP Memorabilia Toronto Fall Expo-224
02BAP NHL All-Star History-37
02BAP Signature Series-135
Autographs-135
Autographs Gold-135
Complete Jersey-CJ1
Franchise Players-FJ24
Golf-GS49
Jerseys-SGJ1
Jersey Autographs-SGJ1
Magnificent Inserts-MI1
Magnificent Inserts-MI2
Magnificent Inserts-MI3
Magnificent Inserts-MI4
Magnificent Inserts-MI5
Magnificent Inserts-MI6
Magnificent Inserts-MI7
Magnificent Inserts-MI8
Magnificent Inserts-MI9
Magnificent Inserts-MI10
Magnificent Inserts Autographs-MI1
Magnificent Inserts Autographs-MI2
Magnificent Inserts Autographs-MI3
Magnificent Inserts Autographs-MI4
Magnificent Inserts Autographs-MI5
Magnificent Inserts Autographs-MI6
Magnificent Inserts Autographs-MI7
Magnificent Inserts Autographs-MI8
Magnificent Inserts Autographs-MI9
Magnificent Inserts Autographs-MI10
Team Quads-TQ8
Triple Memorabilia-TM1
02BAP Ultimate Memorabilia Active Eight-2
02BAP Ultimate Memorabilia Active Eight-7
02BAP Ultimate Memorabilia Active Eight-8
02BAP Ultimate Memorabilia All-Star MVP-11
02BAP Ultimate Memorabilia All-Star MVP-12
02BAP Ultimate Memorabilia All-Star MVP-13
02BAP Ultimate Memorabilia Autographs-16
02BAP Ultimate Mem Autographs Gold-16
02BAP Ultimate Mem Blades of Steel-8
02BAP Ultimate Memorabilia Captains-2
02BAP Ultimate Mem Complete Package-5
02BAP Ultimate Memorabilia Conn Smythe-19
02BAP Ultimate Memorabilia Conn Smythe-20
02BAP Ultimate Memorabilia Dynamic Duos-1
02BAP Ultimate Memorabilia Emblems-9
02BAP Ultimate Mem Global Dominators-1
02BAP Ultimate Memorabilia Gloves Are Off-2
02BAP Ultimate Memorabilia Great Moments-4
02BAP Ultimate Memorabilia Hat Tricks-10
02BAP Ultimate Memorabilia Jerseys-4
02BAP Ultimate Mem Jersey and Stick-15
02BAP Ultimate Mem Lifetime Achievers-14
02BAP Ultimate Mem Magnificent Inserts-1
02BAP Ultimate Mem Magnificent Inserts-2
02BAP Ultimate Mem Magnificent Inserts-3
02BAP Ultimate Mem Magnificent Inserts-4
02BAP Ultimate Mem Magnificent Inserts-5
02BAP Ultimate Mem Magnificent Inserts-6
02BAP Ultimate Mem Magnificent Inserts-7
02BAP Ultimate Mem Magnificent Inserts-8
02BAP Ultimate Mem Magnificent Inserts-9
02BAP Ultimate Mem Magnificent Inserts-10
02BAP Ultimate Mem Magnificent Autos-1
02BAP Ultimate Mem Magnificent Autos-2
02BAP Ultimate Mem Magnificent Autos-3
02BAP Ultimate Mem Magnificent Autos-4
02BAP Ultimate Mem Magnificent Autos-5
02BAP Ultimate Mem Magnificent Autos-6
02BAP Ultimate Mem Magnificent Autos-7
02BAP Ultimate Mem Magnificent Autos-8
02BAP Ultimate Mem Magnificent Autos-9
02BAP Ultimate Mem Magnificent Autos-10
02BAP Ultimate Mem Magnificent Ones-1
02BAP Ultimate Mem Magnificent Ones-2
02BAP Ultimate Mem Magnificent Ones-3
02BAP Ultimate Mem Magnificent Ones-4
02BAP Ultimate Mem Magnificent Ones-5
02BAP Ultimate Mem Magnificent Ones-6
02BAP Ultimate Mem Magnificent Ones-7
02BAP Ultimate Mem Magnificent Ones-8
02BAP Ultimate Mem Magnificent Ones-9
02BAP Ultimate Mem Magnificent Ones-10
02BAP Ultimate Mem Magnificent Ones Autos-1
02BAP Ultimate Mem Magnificent Ones Autos-2
02BAP Ultimate Mem Magnificent Ones Autos-3
02BAP Ultimate Mem Magnificent Ones Autos-4
02BAP Ultimate Mem Magnificent Ones Autos-5
02BAP Ultimate Mem Magnificent Ones Autos-6
02BAP Ultimate Mem Magnificent Ones Autos-7
02BAP Ultimate Mem Magnificent Ones Autos-8
02BAP Ultimate Mem Magnificent Ones Autos-9
02BAP Ultimate Mem Magnificent Ones Autos-10
02BAP Ultimate Memorabilia Nameplates-13
02BAP Ultimate Memorabilia Numbers-2
02BAP Ultimate Mem Playoff Scorers-10
02BAP Ultimate Mem Playoff Scorers-17
02BAP Ultimate Mem Retro Teammates-6
02BAP Ultimate Memorabilia Retro Trophies-1
02BAP Ultimate Memorabilia Retro Trophies-9
02BAP Ultimate Memorabilia Retro Trophies-12
02BAP Ultimate Memorabilia Retro Trophies-17
02BAP Ultimate Mem Scoring Leaders-3
02BAP Ultimate Mem Scoring Leaders-7
02BAP Ultimate Mem Scoring Leaders-8
02BAP Ultimate Mem Scoring Leaders-10
02BAP Ultimate Mem Scoring Leaders-11
02BAP Ultimate Mem Scoring Leaders-12
02BAP Ultimate Mem Scoring Leaders-13
02BAP Ultimate Mem Seams Unbelievable-1
02Between the Pipes Nightmares-GN2
02Bowman YoungStars-26
Gold-26
Silver-26
02Crown Royale-78
Blue-78
Red-78
Retail-78
Jerseys-16
Jerseys Gold-16
Dual Patches-17
Lords of the Rink-16
Royal Portraits-9
02eTopps-18
02Fleer Lemieux All-Star Fantasy-1
02ITG Used-62
02ITG Used-162
Franchise Players-F24
Franchise Players Autographs-F24
Franchise Players Gold-F24
International Experience-IE1
International Experience Gold-IE1
Jerseys-GUJ1
Jersey Autographs-GUJ1
Jerseys Gold-GUJ1
Emblems-E1
Jersey and Stick-SJ1
Jersey and Stick Gold-SJ1
Magnificent Inserts-MI1
Magnificent Inserts-MI2
Magnificent Inserts-MI3
Magnificent Inserts-MI4
Magnificent Inserts-MI5
Magnificent Inserts-MI6
Magnificent Inserts-MI7
Magnificent Inserts-MI8
Magnificent Inserts-MI9
Magnificent Inserts-MI10
Magnificent Inserts Autographs-MI1
Magnificent Inserts Autographs-MI2
Magnificent Inserts Autographs-MI3
Magnificent Inserts Autographs-MI4
Magnificent Inserts Autographs-MI5
Magnificent Inserts Autographs-MI6
Magnificent Inserts Autographs-MI7
Magnificent Inserts Autographs-MI8
Magnificent Inserts Autographs-MI9
Magnificent Inserts Autographs-MI10
Teammates-T1
Teammates Gold-T1
Triple Memorabilia-TM2
Triple Memorabilia Gold-TM2
02McDonald's Pacific-32
Jersey Patches Silver-14
Jersey Patches Gold-14
Salt Lake Gold-10
02O-Pee-Chee-2
02O-Pee-Chee Jumbos-19
02O-Pee-Chee Premier Blue Parallel-2
02O-Pee-Chee Premier Red Parallel-2
02O-Pee-Chee Factory Set-2
02Pacific-312
Blue-312
Red-312
Cramer's Choice-9
Impact Zone-9
Jerseys-42
Jerseys Holo-Silver-42
Lamplighters-11
Main Attractions-16
Maximum Impact-15
02Pacific Calder-27
Silver-27
Chasing Glory-8
Hardware Heroes-10
02Pacific Complete-303
Red-303
02Pacific Exclusive-138
Etched in Stone-9
Maximum Overdrive-16
02Pacific Heads-Up-100
Blue-100
Purple-100
Red-100
Etched in Time-13
Inside the Numbers-17
Quad Jerseys-28
Quad Jerseys Gold-28
Stat Masters-12
02Pacific Quest for the Cup-80
Gold-80
Jerseys-17
Raising the Cup-11
02Parkhurst-115
Bronze-115
Gold-115
Silver-115
Franchise Players-FP24
Hardware-A8
Hardware-H9
Hardware-P8
Heroes-NH5
Heroes-NH7
He Shoots-He Scores Points-20
He Shoots-He Scores Prizes-1
Jerseys-GJ1
Magnificent Inserts-MI1
Magnificent Inserts-MI2
Magnificent Inserts-MI3
Magnificent Inserts-MI4
Magnificent Inserts-MI5
Magnificent Inserts-MI6
Magnificent Inserts-MI7
Magnificent Inserts-MI8
Magnificent Inserts-MI9
Magnificent Inserts-MI10
Magnificent Inserts Autographs-MI1
Magnificent Inserts Autographs-MI2
Magnificent Inserts Autographs-MI3
Magnificent Inserts Autographs-MI4
Magnificent Inserts Autographs-MI5
Magnificent Inserts Autographs-MI6
Magnificent Inserts Autographs-MI7
Magnificent Inserts Autographs-MI8
Magnificent Inserts Autographs-MI9
Magnificent Inserts Autographs-MI10
Mario's Mates-MM1
Mario's Mates-MM2
Mario's Mates-MM3
Mario's Mates-MM4
Mario's Mates-MM5
Mario's Mates-MM6
Mario's Mates-MM7
Mario's Mates-MM8
Mario's Mates-MM9
Mario's Mates-MM10
Patented Power-PP1
Stick and Jerseys-SJ1
Teammates-TT14
02Parkhurst Retro-1
Minis-1
Back In Time-1
Back In Time-2
Back In Time-3
Back In Time-4
Back In Time-5
Back In Time-6
Back In Time-7
Back In Time-8
Back In Time-9
Back In Time-10
Back In Time-11
Back In Time-12
Back In Time-13
Back In Time-14
Back In Time-15
Back In Time Autographs-1
Back In Time Autographs-2
Back In Time Autographs-3
Back In Time Autographs-4
Back In Time Autographs-5
Back In Time Autographs-6
Back In Time Autographs-7
Back In Time Autographs-8
Back In Time Autographs-9
Back In Time Autographs-10
Back In Time Autographs-11
Back In Time Autographs-12
Back In Time Autographs-13
Back In Time Autographs-14
Back In Time Autographs-15
Franchise Players-RF24
He Shoots-He Scores Points-18
He Shoots-He Scores Prizes-2
Hopefuls-HH1
Jerseys-RJ15
Jersey and Sticks-RSJ11
Magnificent Inserts-MI1
Magnificent Inserts-MI2
Magnificent Inserts-MI3
Magnificent Inserts-MI4
Magnificent Inserts-MI5
Magnificent Inserts-MI6
Magnificent Inserts-MI7
Magnificent Inserts-MI8
Magnificent Inserts-MI9
Magnificent Inserts-MI10
Magnificent Inserts Autographs-MI1
Magnificent Inserts Autographs-MI2
Magnificent Inserts Autographs-MI3
Magnificent Inserts Autographs-MI4
Magnificent Inserts Autographs-MI5
Magnificent Inserts Autographs-MI6
Magnificent Inserts Autographs-MI7
Magnificent Inserts Autographs-MI8
Magnificent Inserts Autographs-MI9
Magnificent Inserts Autographs-MI10
Memorabilia-RM1
Memorabilia-RM8
Memorabilia-RM29
Nicknames-RN30
02Private Stock Reserve-138
Red-138
Retail-138
Elite-5
02SP Authentic-73
02SP Authentic-102
Beckett Promos-73
Super Premiums-SPML
Super Premiums-DPGL
Super Premiums-TPGLY
02SP Game Used-40
02SP Game Used-52
02SP Game Used-54
Authentic Fabrics-AFML
Authentic Fabrics-CFLK
Authentic Fabrics Gold-AFML
Authentic Fabrics Gold-CFLK
Authentic Fabrics Rainbow-AFML
Authentic Fabrics Rainbow-CFLK
First Rounder Patches-ML
Piece of History-PHML
Piece of History Gold-PHML
Piece of History Rainbow-PHML
02SPx-61
02SPx-97
02SPx-129
Spectrum Gold-61
Spectrum Gold-97
Spectrum Silver-61
Spectrum Silver-97
Milestones-MML
Milestones Gold-ML
Milestones Silver-ML
Smooth Skaters-ML
Smooth Skaters Gold-ML
Smooth Skaters Silver-ML
Winning Materials-WMML
Winning Materials Gold-ML
Winning Materials Silver-ML
02Stadium Club-6
Silver Decoy Cards-6
Proofs-6
Beam Team-BT2
02Titanium-82
Blue-82
Red-82
Retail-82
Jerseys-54
Jerseys Retail-54
Patches-54
Saturday Knights-7
02Topps-2
OPC Blue Parallel-2
OPC Red Parallel-2
Captain's Cloth-CC1
Captain's Cloth-CC6
Captain's Cloth-CC8
Coast to Coast-CC1
Topps/OPC Hometown Heroes-HHU3
Factory Set-2
Factory Set Hometown Heroes-HHU3
02Topps Chrome-2
Black Border Refractors-2
Refractors-2
02Topps Heritage-7
Chrome Parallel-7
USA Test Parallel-7
02Topps Total-96
Team Checklists-TTC24
Topps-TT18
02UD Artistic Impressions-72
Gold-72
Artist's Touch-ATML
Artist's Touch Gold-ATML
02UD Artistic Impressions Beckett Promos-72
02UD Artistic Impressions Common Ground-CG6
02UD Artistic Impress Common Ground Gold-CG6
02UD Artistic Impressions Flashbacks-UD3
02UD Artistic Impressions Flashbacks Gold-UD3
02UD Artistic Impressions Great Depiction-GD6
02UD Artistic Impress Great Depiction Gld-GD6
02UD Artistic Impressions Retrospectives-R72
02UD Artistic Impressions Retrospect Gold-R72
02UD Artistic Impress Retrospect Silver-R72
02Upper Deck Collectors Club-NHL5
02UD Foundations-159
02UD Honor Roll-58
02UD Honor Roll-94
Students of the Game-SG25
Team Warriors-TW12
02UD Mask Collection-70
02UD Mask Collection Beckett Promos-70
02UD Mask Collection Instant Offense-IOML
02UD Piece of History-72
02UD Piece of History-93
Awards Collection-AC22
Exquisite Combos-ECLK
02UD Premier Collection-43
Jerseys Bronze-ML
Jerseys Bronze-GL
Jerseys Gold-ML
Jerseys Gold-GL
Jerseys Silver-ML
Jerseys Silver-GL
NHL Patches-ML1
Patches-PML
02UD Top Shelf-71
Clutch Performers-CPML
Hardware Heroes-HGSLJ
Hardware Heroes-HHGLJ
Milestones Jerseys-MGHLY
Shooting Stars-SHML
Triple Jerseys-HTGLB
Triple Jerseys-HTLJT
02Upper Deck-141
02Upper Deck-191
Exclusives-141
Exclusives-191
Blow-Ups-C33
CHL Graduates-CGML
CHL Graduates Gold-CGML
Difference Makers-ML
First Class-UDML
First Class Gold-UDML
Gifted Greats-GG13
Letters of Note-LNML
Letters of Note Gold-LNML
Patch Card Logo-ML
Patch Card Name Plate-ML
Patch Card Numbers-ML
Patchwork-PWML
Pinpoint Accuracy-PAML
Playbooks Series II-LK
Reaching Fifty-50ML
Reaching Fifty Gold-50ML
Shooting Stars-SS12
02Upper Deck Classic Portraits-80
Etched in Time-ET13
Headliners-LM
Headliners Limited-LM
Hockey Royalty-GLS
Hockey Royalty-LLN
Hockey Royalty-LLT
Hockey Royalty Limited-GLS
Hockey Royalty Limited-LLN
Hockey Royalty Limited-LLT
Mini-Busts-81
Mini-Busts-82
Pillars of Strength-PS8
02Upper Deck MVP-148
Gold-148
Classics-148
Golden Classics-148
Highlight Nights-HN6
Vital Forces-VF12
02Upper Deck Rookie Update-79
02Upper Deck Rookie Update-105
Jerseys-DML
Jerseys Gold-DML
02Upper Deck Victory-172
Bronze-172
Gold-172
Silver-172
National Pride-NP11
02Upper Deck Vintage-202
02Upper Deck Vintage-284
02Upper Deck Vintage-303
Tall Boys-T52
Tall Boys Gold-T52
02Vanguard-81
LTD-81
East Meets West-3
In Focus-9
Jerseys-37
Jerseys Gold-37
V-Team-11
02UD SuperStars *-197
Gold-197
City All-Stars Dual Jersey-MLBG
Legendary Leaders Triple Jersey-RJM
Legendary Leaders Triple Jersey-TEM
03McFarlane Hockey 12-Inch Figures-10
03McFarlane Hockey 3-Inch Duals-40
03McFarlane Hockey-40
03McFarlane Hockey-42
03McFarlane Hockey-44
03BAP Memorabilia-48
Emerald-48
Gold-48
Ruby-48
Sapphire-48
All-Star Staring Lineup-4
Brush with Greatness-1
Brush with Greatness Contest Cards-1
Gloves-GUG12
He Shoots-He Scores Prizes-22
Jersey and Stick-SJ-35
Jerseys-GJ-45
Jersey Autographs-GJ-45
03BAP Ultimate Memorabilia Autographs-147
Gold-147
03BAP Ultimate Mem Auto Jerseys-147
03BAP Ultimate Mem Auto Emblems-147
03BAP Ultimate Mem Auto Sticks-147
03BAP Ultimate Memorabilia Active Eight-3
03BAP Ultimate Memorabilia Active Eight-5
03BAP Ultimate Memorabilia Active Eight-8
03BAP Ultimate Mem Always An All-Star-16
03BAP Ultimate Mem Always An AS Gold-16
03BAP Ultimate Mem Blades of Steel-1
03BAP Ultimate Memorabilia Career Year-8
03BAP Ultimate Mem Complete Jersey-2
03BAP Ultimate Mem Complete Jersey Gold-2
03BAP Ultimate Mem Complete Package-1
03BAP Ultimate Mem Complete Package Gold-1
03BAP Ultimate Memorabilia Dynamic Duos-3
03BAP Ultimate Memorabilia Emblems-14
03BAP Ultimate Memorabilia Emblems Gold-14
03BAP Ultimate Mem Franch Present Future-24
03BAP Ultimate Memorabilia Gloves Are Off-3
03BAP Ultimate Memorabilia Hat Tricks-8
03BAP Ultimate Memorabilia Heroes-5
03BAP Ultimate Memorabilia Heroes-17
03BAP Ultimate Memorabilia Heroes-19
03BAP Ultimate Mem Heroes Autos-2
03BAP Ultimate Mem Heroes Autos-9
03BAP Ultimate Mem Hometown Heroes-20
03BAP Ultimate Mem Hometown Heroes Gold-20
03BAP Ultimate Memorabilia Jerseys-4
03BAP Ultimate Memorabilia Jerseys Gold-4
03BAP Ultimate Mem Jersey and Emblems-22
03BAP Ultimate Mem Jersey and Emblem Gold-22
03BAP Ultimate Mem Jersey and Numbers-22
03BAP Ultimate Mem Jersey and Number Gold-22
03BAP Ultimate Mem Jersey and Stick-4
03BAP Ultimate Mem Jersey and Stick Gold-4
03BAP Ultimate Mem Lifetime Achievers-1
03BAP Ultimate Mem Magnificent Career-1
03BAP Ultimate Mem Magnificent Career-2
03BAP Ultimate Mem Magnificent Career-3
03BAP Ultimate Mem Magnificent Career-4
03BAP Ultimate Mem Magnificent Career-5
03BAP Ultimate Mem Magnificent Career-6
03BAP Ultimate Mem Magnificent Career-7
03BAP Ultimate Mem Magnificent Career-8
03BAP Ultimate Mem Magnificent Career-9
03BAP Ultimate Mem Magnificent Career-10
03BAP Ultimate Mem Magnif Career Autos-1
03BAP Ultimate Mem Magnif Career Autos-2
03BAP Ultimate Mem Magnif Career Autos-3
03BAP Ultimate Mem Magnif Career Autos-4
03BAP Ultimate Mem Magnif Career Autos-5
03BAP Ultimate Mem Magnif Career Autos-6
03BAP Ultimate Mem Magnif Career Autos-7
03BAP Ultimate Mem Magnif Career Autos-8
03BAP Ultimate Mem Magnif Career Autos-9
03BAP Ultimate Mem Magnificent Prospects-1
03BAP Ultimate Mem Magnificent Prospects-2
03BAP Ultimate Mem Magnificent Prospects-3
03BAP Ultimate Mem Magnificent Prospects-4
03BAP Ultimate Mem Magnificent Prospects-5
03BAP Ultimate Mem Magnificent Prospects-6
03BAP Ultimate Mem Magnificent Prospects-7
03BAP Ultimate Mem Magnificent Prospects-8
03BAP Ultimate Mem Magnificent Prospects-9
03BAP Ultimate Mem Magnificent Prospects-10
03BAP Ultimate Mem Magnif Prospect Autos-1
03BAP Ultimate Mem Magnif Prospect Autos-2
03BAP Ultimate Mem Magnif Prospect Autos-3
03BAP Ultimate Mem Magnif Prospect Autos-4
03BAP Ultimate Mem Magnif Prospect Autos-5
03BAP Ultimate Mem Magnif Prospect Autos-6
03BAP Ultimate Mem Magnif Prospect Autos-7
03BAP Ultimate Mem Magnif Prospect Autos-8
03BAP Ultimate Mem Magnif Prospect Autos-9
03BAP Ultimate Mem Magnif Prospect Autos-10
03BAP Ultimate Memorabilia Nameplates-13
03BAP Ultimate Mem Nameplates Gold-13
03BAP Ultimate Memorabilia Numbers-3
03BAP Ultimate Memorabilia Numbers Gold-3
03BAP Ultimate Mem Retro-Active Trophies-3
03BAP Ultimate Mem Retro-Active Trophies-5
03BAP Ultimate Mem Retro-Active Trophies-9
03BAP Ultimate Mem Retro-Active Trophies-20
03BAP Ultimate Mem Seams Unbelievable-1
03BAP Ultimate Memorabilia Triple Threads-16
03BAP Ultimate Mem Ultimate Captains-7
03BAP Ultimate Mem Ultimate Captains-8
03Beehive-158
Variations-158
Gold-158
Silver-158
Jumbos-22
Jumbo Jerseys-BH3
Jerseys-JT37
03Black Diamond-135
Black-135
Green-135
Red-135
Threads-DT-ML
Threads Green-DT-ML
Threads Red-DT-ML
Threads Black-DT-ML
03Bowman-66
Gold-66
03Bowman Chrome-66
Refractors-66
Gold Refractors-66
Xfractors-66
03Crown Royale-80
Blue-80
Retail-80
Global Conquest-1
Jerseys-20
Patches-20
Lords of the Rink-18
03eTopps-11
03ITG Action-445
Center of Attention-CA1
Highlight Reel-HR4
Homeboys-HB10
Jerseys-M192
Jerseys-M212
Jerseys-M237
Jerseys-M264
Oh Canada-OC1
03ITG Toronto Fall Expo Jerseys-FE24
03ITG Used Signature Series-110
Gold-110
Autographs-ML
Autographs Gold-ML
Franchise-24
Franchise Autographs-24
Franchise Gold-24
Game-Day Jerseys-4
Game-Day Jerseys Gold-4
International Experience-2
International Experience Autographs-2
International Experience Emblems Gold-2
International Experience Emblems-2
International Experience Gold-2
Jerseys-24
Jerseys Gold-24
Jersey Autos-24
Emblems-6
Emblems Gold-6
Jersey and Stick-24
Jersey and Stick Gold-24
Retrospectives-4A
Retrospectives-4B
Retrospectives-4C
Retrospectives-4D
Retrospectives-4E
Retrospectives-4F
Retrospectives Gold-4A
Retrospectives Gold-4B
Retrospectives Gold-4C
Retrospectives Gold-4D
Retrospectives Gold-4E
Retrospectives Gold-4F
Triple Memorabilia-20
Triple Memorabilia Gold-20
03ITG VIP Brightest Stars-1
03ITG VIP Collages-1
03ITG VIP Collage Autographs-1
03ITG VIP International Experience-1
03ITG VIP Jerseys-2
03ITG VIP Jersey Autographs-2
03ITG VIP Jersey and Emblems-2
03ITG VIP Jersey and Numbers-2
03ITG VIP Mighty Mario-1
03ITG VIP Mighty Mario-2
03ITG VIP Mighty Mario-3
03ITG VIP Mighty Mario-4
03ITG VIP Mighty Mario-5
03ITG VIP Mighty Mario-6
03ITG VIP Mighty Mario-7
03ITG VIP Mighty Mario-8
03ITG VIP Mighty Mario-9
03ITG VIP Mighty Mario-10
03ITG VIP MVP-25
03McDonald's Pacific-41
Etched in Time-5
Patches Silver-20
Patches Gold-20
Patches and Sticks-20
03NHL Sticker Collection-115
03O-Pee-Chee-100
03OPC Blue-100
03OPC Gold-100
03OPC Red-100
03Pacific-274
Blue-274
Red-274
Cramer's Choice-8
Jerseys-31
Jerseys Gold-31
Main Attractions-12
03Pacific Calder-81
03Pacific Calder-155
Silver-81
03Pacific Complete-140
Red-140
03Pacific Exhibit-188
03Pacific Exhibit-221
Blue Backs-188
History Makers-6
03Pacific Heads-Up-79
Hobby LTD-79
Retail LTD-79
Jerseys-22
Rink Immortals-9
Rink Immortals LTD-9
03Pacific Invincible-78
Blue-78
Red-78
Retail-78
Featured Performers-24
Top Line-8
03Pacific Luxury Suite-16A
03Pacific Luxury Suite-16B
03Pacific Luxury Suite-16C
03Pacific Prism-138
Blue-138
Patches-138
Red-138
Retail-138
Stat Masters-7
03Pacific Quest for the Cup-84
Blue-84
Connquest-6
Jerseys-16
Raising the Cup-15
03Pacific Supreme-79
Blue-79
Red-79
Retail-79
Generations-8
Jerseys-21
Team-7
03Parkhurst Orig Six Boston Mem -BM41
03Parkhurst Orig Six Chicago Mem -CM41
03Parkhurst Orig Six Detroit Mem-DM41
03Parkhurst Orig Six Montreal Mem-MM41
03Parkhurst Orig Six New York Mem-NM41
03Parkhurst Original Six Shooters-OSM1
03Parkhurst Orig Six Toronto Mem-TM41
03Parkhurst Rookie-11
Emblems-GUE-10
Emblem Autographs-GUE-ML
Emblems Gold-GUE-10
High Expectations-HE-4
High Expectations Gold-HE-4
Jerseys-GJ-1
Jersey Autographs-GUJ-ML
Jerseys Gold-GJ-1
Jersey and Sticks-SJ-1
Jersey and Sticks Gold-SJ-1
ROYalty-VR-9
ROYalty Autographs-VR-ML
ROYalty Gold-VR-9
Teammates Gold-RT1
Teammates-RT1
03Private Stock Reserve-194
Blue-194
Patches-194
Red-194
Retail-194
Moments in Time-9
03Serious NHL Starz-1
03SP Authentic-69
Limited-69
10th Anniversary-SP4
10th Anniversary Limited-SP4
Breakout Seasons-B29
Breakout Seasons Limited-B29
Honors-H17
Honors Limited-H17
03SP Game Used-37
03SP Game Used-105
Gold-37
Gold-105
Authentic Fabrics-AFML
Authentic Fabrics-DFLG
Authentic Fabrics-QLGHL
Authentic Fabrics Gold-AFML
Authentic Fabrics Gold-DFLG
Authentic Fabrics Gold-QLGHL
Authentic Patches-APML
Double Threads-DTLG
Premium Patches-PPML
Team Threads-TTLBF
Team Threads-TTLGH
Top Threads-LGHL
03SPx-78
03SPx-114
03SPx-144
03SPx-176
Radiance-78
Radiance-114
Radiance-144
Radiance-176
Spectrum-78
Spectrum-114
Spectrum-144
Spectrum-176
Fantasy Franchise-FF-LGH
Fantasy Franchise Limited-FF-LGH
Hall Pass-HP-ML
Hall Pass Limited-HP-ML
Origins-O-ML
Style-SPX-LH
Style Limited-SPX-LH
03Titanium-203
Patches-203
Highlight Reels-8
Stat Masters-8
03Topps-100
Blue-100
Gold-100
Red-100
Box Toppers-11
First Overall Fabrics-ML
First Overall Fabrics-MLMM
First Overall Fabrics-MLRN
Topps/OPC Idols-CI4
Lost Rookies-ML
03Topps C55-66
03Topps C55-66B
Minis-66
Minis American Back-66
Minis American Back Red-66
Minis Bazooka Back-66
Minis Brooklyn Back-66
Minis Hat Trick Back-66
Minis O Canada Back-66
Minis O Canada Back Red-66
Minis Stanley Cup Back-66
Relics-TRML
03Topps Pristine-26
Gold Refractor Die Cuts-26
Refractors-26
Popular Demand Relics-PD-ML
Popular Demand Relic Refractors-PD-ML
Press Plates Black-26
Press Plates Cyan-26
Press Plates Magenta-26
Press Plates Yellow-26
03Topps Traded Franchise Fabrics-FF-ML
03UD Honor Roll-68
03UD Honor Roll-130
Grade A Jerseys-GAML
03UD Premier Collection-45
Skills-SK-LT
Skills Patches-SK-LT
Super Stars-SS-ML
Super Stars Patches-SS-ML
Teammates-PT-PP
Teammates Patches-PT-PP
03Upper Deck-151
03Upper Deck-444
All-Star Class-AS-23
All-Star Lineup-AS4
Big Playmakers-BP-ML
Canadian Exclusives-151
Canadian Exclusives-444
Fan Favorites-FF9
Franchise Fabrics-FF-ML
Gifted Greats-GG4
HG-151
HG-444
Jerseys-GJ-ML
NHL Best-NB-ML
Patches-LD3
Patches-PLG-ML
Patches-PNM-ML
Patches-PNR-ML
Performers-PS13
Power Zone-PZ-9
Superstar Spotlight-SS9
Team Essentials-TL-ML
Team Essentials-TP-ML
Three Stars-TS12
UD Exclusives-444
03Upper Deck Classic Portraits-77
03Upper Deck Classic Portraits-103
03Upper Deck Classic Portraits-136
Genuine Greatness-GG-ML
Headliners-HH-ML
Hockey Royalty-LYG
Premium Portraits-PP-ML
03Upper Deck Ice-69
Gold-69
Breakers-IB-ML
Breaker Patches-IB-ML
Clear Cut Winners-CC-ML
Icons-I-ML
Icons Jerseys-I-ML
03Upper Deck MVP-333
Gold Script-333
Silver Script-333
Canadian Exclusives-333
SportsNut-SN71
Talent-MT1
03Upper Deck Rookie Update-69
Skills-SKML
Super Stars-SSML
03Upper Deck Trilogy-77
03Upper Deck Trilogy-112
Authentic Patches-AP8
Crest Variations-112
Limited-77
Limited-112
Limited Threads-LT3
03Upper Deck Victory-149
Bronze-149
Gold-149
Silver-149
Freshman Flashback-FF36
Game Breakers-GB30
03Toronto Star-74
Foil-1
04ITG NHL AS FANtasy AS History Jerseys-SB37
04ITG Franchises He Shoots/Scores Prizes-28
04ITG Franchises Update Memorabilia-USM2
04ITG Franchises Update Memorabilia Gold-USM2
04ITG Franchises Update Trophy Winners-UTW1
04ITG Franchises Update Trophy Win Gold-UTW1
04ITG Franchises US West-267
Autographs-A-MLE
Barn Burners-WBB1
Barn Burners Gold-WBB1
Complete Jerseys-WCJ7
Complete Jerseys Gold-WCJ7
Double Memorabilia-WDM10
Double Memorabilia Autographs-WDMML
Double Memorabilia Gold-WDM10
Memorabilia-WSM14
Memorabilia-WSM30
Memorabilia Autographs-WSMML1
Memorabilia Autographs-WSMML2
Memorabilia Gold-WSM14
Memorabilia Gold-WSM30
Original Sticks-WOS13
Original Sticks Autographs-WOSML
Original Sticks Gold-WOS13
Teammates-WTM5
Teammates Gold-WTM5
Triple Memorabilia Autographs-WTMML
Triple Memorabilia Gold-WTM8
Trophy Winners-WTW2
Trophy Winners Gold-WTW2
04ITG Ultimate Memorabilia-180
Gold-180
Archives 1st Edition-22
Archives 1st Edition-27
Archives 1st Edition-28
Archives 1st Edition-30
Archives 1st Edition-31
Archives 1st Edition-32
Art Ross Trophy-1
Autographs-54
Autographs Gold-54
Blades of Steel-13
Calder Trophy-1
Changing the Game-3
Complete Logo-14
Complete Logo-15
Complete Logo-16
Complete Package-4
Conn Smythe Trophy-4
Country of Origin-4
Country of Origin Gold-4
Day In History-32
Day In History-41
Day In History-50
Day In History Gold-32
Day In History Gold-41
Day In History Gold-50
Gloves are Off-4
Hart Trophy-1
Heroes Mario Lemieux-1
Heroes Mario Lemieux-2
Heroes Mario Lemieux-3
Heroes Mario Lemieux-4
Heroes Mario Lemieux-5
Heroes Mario Lemieux-6
Heroes Mario Lemieux-7
Heroes Mario Lemieux-8
Heroes Mario Lemieux-9
Heroes Mario Lemieux-10
Jerseys-6
Jerseys Gold-6
Jersey Autographs-31
Jersey Autographs Gold-31
Jersey and Sticks-13
Jersey and Sticks Gold-13
Nicknames-5
Nickname Autographs-2
Seams Unbelievable-1
Stick Autographs-8
Stick Autographs Gold-8
Triple Threads-11
04MasterCard Priceless Moments-6
04Pacific-213
Blue-213
Red-213
Cramer's Choice-8
Milestones-5
Philadelphia-13
04SP Authentic-72
04SP Authentic-138
04SP Game Used Hawaii Conference Patch-PP19
04UD All-World-101
04UD Toronto Fall Expo Pride of Canada-18
04Ultimate Collection-34
04Ultimate Collection-59
Dual Logos-UL2-GL
Dual Logos-UL2-RL
Dual Logos-UL2-TL
Jerseys-UGJ-ML
Jerseys Gold-UGJ-ML
Patches-UP-ML
04Upper Deck-138
04Upper Deck-189

Big Playmakers-BP-ML
Canadian Exclusives-138
Canadian Exclusives-189
Clutch Performers-CP7
HG Glossy Gold-138
HG Glossy Gold-189
HG Glossy Silver-138
HG Glossy Silver-189
NHL's Best-NB-ML
Patches-GJPA-ML
Patches-GJPL-ML
Patches-GJPN-ML
Three Stars-AS11
World's Best-WB5
World Cup Tribute-JSMLJI
04ITG Heroes and Prospects-172
Aspiring-1
Aspiring-2
Autographs-MLE
He Shoots-He Scores Prizes-4
Hero Memorabilia-14
04ITG Heroes/Prospects Toronto Expo '05-172
04ITG Heroes/Prospects Expo Heroes/Pros-172
05ITG Heroes/Prosp Toronto Expo Parallel -40
05ITG Heroes/Prosp Toronto Expo Parallel -196
05ITG Heroes/Prosp Toronto Expo Parallel -338
05Be A Player-72
First Period-72
Second Period-72
Third Period-72
Overtime-72
Class Action-CA20
Ice Icons-ICE2
Outtakes-OT40
05Beehive-71
05Beehive-209
Beige -71
Blue -71
Gold-71
Red -71
Matte-71
Matted Materials-MMML
05Black Diamond-181
Emerald-181
Gold-181
Onyx-181
Ruby-181
Jerseys-J-ML
Jerseys Ruby-J-ML
Jersey Duals-DJ-ML
Jersey Triples-TJ-ML
Jersey Quads-QJ-ML
05Hot Prospects-78
En Fuego-78
Red Hot-78
White Hot-78
05ITG Sidney Crosby Series Memorabilia-SCM1
05ITG Sidney Crosby Series Memorabilia-SCM2
05ITG Sidney Crosby Series Memorabilia-SCM3
05ITG Sidney Crosby Series Memorabilia-SCM4
05ITG Sidney Crosby Series Memorabilia-SCM5
05ITG Sidney Crosby Series Memorabilia-SCM6
05ITG Sidney Crosby Series Memorabilia-SCM7
05ITG Ultimate Memorabilia Level 1-67
05ITG Ultimate Memorabilia Level 2-67
05ITG Ultimate Memorabilia Level 3-67
05ITG Ultimate Memorabilia Level 4-67
05ITG Ultimate Memorabilia Level 5-67
05ITG Ultimate Mem Blades of Steel-2
05ITG Ultimate Mem Blades of Steel Gold-2
05ITG Ultimate Mem Complete Jersey-20
05ITG Ultimate Mem Complete Jersey Gold-20
05ITG Ultimate Mem Complete Package-18
05ITG Ultimate Mem Complete Package Gold-18
05ITG Ultimate Memorabilia Double Autos-8
05ITG Ultimate Memorabilia Double Autos-14
05ITG Ultimate Mem Double Autos Gold-8
05ITG Ultimate Mem Double Autos Gold-14
05ITG Ultimate Mem Double Mem-17
05ITG Ultimate Mem Double Mem Autos-8
05ITG Ultimate Mem Double Mem Autos Gold-8
05ITG Ultimate Mem Double Mem Gold-17
05ITG Ultimate Memorabilia Emblems-19
05ITG Ultimate Memorabilia Emblems Gold-19
05ITG Ultimate Mem First Overall Jerseys-5
05ITG Ultimate Mem 1st Overall Jsy Gold-5
05ITG Ultimate Mem First Rounders Jerseys-1
05ITG Ultimate Mem First Rounders Jerseys-2
05ITG Ultimate Mem First Rounders Jerseys-6
05ITG Ultimate Mem First Rounders Jerseys-9
05ITG Ultimate Mem 1st Round Jersey Gold-1
05ITG Ultimate Mem 1st Round Jersey Gold-2
05ITG Ultimate Mem 1st Round Jersey Gold-6
05ITG Ultimate Mem 1st Round Jersey Gold-9
05ITG Ultimate Memorabilia Gloves Are Off-3
05ITG Ultimate Mem Gloves Are Off Gold-3
05ITG Ultimate Memorabilia In The Numbers-25
05ITG Ultimate Mem In The Numbers Gold-25
05ITG Ultimate Mem Jersey and Emblem-12
05ITG Ultimate Memorabilia Jersey Autos-17
05ITG Ultimate Mem Jersey Autos Gold-17
05ITG Ultimate Mem Jersey Emblems Gold-12
05ITG Ultimate Memorabilia Jerseys-24
05ITG Ultimate Mem Jerseys Gold-24
05ITG Ultimate Mem Pass the Torch Jerseys-1
05ITG Ultimate Mem Passing Torch Jsy Gold-1
05ITG Ultimate Memorabilia R.O.Y. Autos-18
05ITG Ultimate Mem R.O.Y. Autos Gold-18
05ITG Ultimate Memorabilia R.O.Y. Emblems-5
05ITG Ultimate Mem R.O.Y. Emblems Gold-5
05ITG Ultimate Memorabilia R.O.Y. Jerseys-5
05ITG Ultimate Mem R.O.Y. Jerseys Gold-5
05ITG Ultimate Memorabilia R.O.Y. Numbers-5
05ITG Ultimate Mem R.O.Y. Numbers Gold-5
05ITG Ultimate Mem Raised to the Rafters-1
05ITG Ultimate Mem Raised Rafters Gold-1
05ITG Ultimate Mem Retro Teammate Jerseys-5
05ITG Ult Mem Retro Teammates Jersey Gold-5
05ITG Ultimate Mem Seams Unbelievable-1
05ITG Ultimate Mem Seam Unbelievable Gold-1
05ITG Ultimate Memorabilia Sextuple Autos-3
05ITG Ultimate Memorabilia Stick Autos-17
05ITG Ultimate Mem Stick Autos Gold-17
05ITG Ultimate Mem Sticks and Jerseys-1
05ITG Ultimate Mem Stick and Jerseys Gold-1
05ITG Ultimate Memorabilia Trifecta Autos-7
05ITG Ultimate Mem Trifecta Autos Gold-7
05ITG Ultimate Memorabilia Triple Autos-17
05ITG Ultimate Mem Triple Autos Gold-17
05ITG Ultimate Mem Triple Threads Jerseys-3
05ITG Ultimate Mem Triple Thread Jsy Gold-3
05ITG Ultimate Memorabilia Ultimate Autos-20
05ITG Ultimate Mem Ultimate Autos Gold-20
05ITG Ultimate Mem Ult Hero Double Jerseys-5
05ITG Ult Mem Ult Hero Double Jersey Gold-5
05ITG Ultimate Mem Ult Hero Single Jersey-5
05ITG Ult Mem Ult Hero Single Jersey Gold-5
05ITG Ultimate Mem Ult Hero Triple Jerseys-5
05ITG Ult Mem Ult Hero Triple Jersey Gold-5
05McDonalds Upper Deck-28
Jerseys-MJ1
Patches-MP1
Top Scorers-TS4
05Panini Stickers-140
05Parkhurst-390
05Parkhurst-590
Facsimile Auto Parallel-390
Facsimile Auto Parallel-590
True Colors-TCPIT
True Colors-TCPIT
True Colors-TCPHPI
True Colors-TCPHPI
05SP Authentic-79
05SP Authentic-101
Limited-79
Limited-101
05SP Game Used-79
Gold-79
Authentic Fabrics-AF-ML
Authentic Fabrics Gold-AF-ML
Authentic Fabrics Quad-MLYS
Authentic Patches Quad -MLYS
Authentic Patches Quad -PRLL
Authentic Fabrics Triple-GLY
Authentic Patches-AP-ML
Authentic Fabrics Dual-GL
Authentic Patches Triple-GLY
Awesome Authentics-AA-LX
By the Letter-LM-ML
Game Gear-GG-ML
05SPx-72
Spectrum-72
Winning Combos-WC-LF
Winning Combos-WC-LJ
Winning Combos Gold-WC-LF
Winning Combos Gold-WC-LJ
Winning Combos Spectrum-WC-LF
Winning Combos Spectrum-WC-LJ
Winning Materials-WM-LX
Winning Materials Gold-WM-LX
Winning Materials Spectrum-WM-LX
Xcitement Superstars-XS-ML
Xcitement Superstars Gold-XS-ML
Xcitement Superstars Spectrum-XS-ML
05The Cup-82
Gold-82
Black Rainbow-82
Dual NHL Shields-DSQL
Dual NHL Shields-DSLC
Dual NHL Shields-DSLJ
Masterpiece Pressplates-82
Noble Numbers Dual-DNNCL
Noble Numbers Dual-DNNGL
Noble Numbers Dual-DNNLJ
Noble Numbers Dual-DNNYL
Patch Variation-P82
05UD Artifacts-81
05UD Artifacts-189
Blue-81
Blue-189
Gold-81
Gold-189
Green-81
Green-189
Pewter-81
Pewter-189
Red-81
Red-189
Frozen Artifacts-FA-ML
Frozen Artifacts Autographed-FA-ML
Frozen Artifacts Copper-FA-ML
Frozen Artifacts Dual-FAD-ML
Frozen Artifacts Dual Autographed-FAD-ML
Frozen Artifacts Dual Copper-FAD-ML
Frozen Artifacts Dual Gold-FAD-ML
Frozen Artifacts Dual Maroon-FAD-ML
Frozen Artifacts Dual Pewter-FAD-ML
Frozen Artifacts Dual Silver-FAD-ML
Frozen Artifacts Gold-FA-ML
Frozen Artifacts Maroon-FA-ML
Frozen Artifacts Patches-FP-ML
Frozen Artifacts Patches Autographed-FP-ML
Frozen Artifacts Patches Dual-FPD-ML
Frozen Artifacts Patches Dual Autos-FPD-ML
Frozen Artifacts Patches Pewter-FP-ML
Frozen Artifacts Patches Silver-FP-ML
Frozen Artifacts Pewter-FA-ML
Frozen Artifacts Silver-FA-ML
Gold Autographed-81
Gold Autographed-189
Treasured Patches-TP-ML
Treasured Patches Autographed-TP-ML
Treasured Patches Dual-TPD-ML
Treasured Patches Dual Autographed-TPD-ML
Treasured Patches Pewter-TP-ML
Treasured Patches Silver-TP-ML
Treasured Swatches-TS-ML
Treasured Swatches Autographed-TS-ML
Treasured Swatches Blue-TS-ML
Treasured Swatches Copper-TS-ML
Treasured Swatches Dual-TSD-ML
Treasured Swatches Dual Autographed-TSD-ML
Treasured Swatches Dual Blue-TSD-ML
Treasured Swatches Dual Copper-TSD-ML
Treasured Swatches Dual Maroon-TSD-ML
Treasured Swatches Dual Pewter-TSD-ML
Treasured Swatches Dual Silver-TSD-ML
Treasured Swatches Maroon-TS-ML
Treasured Swatches Pewter-TS-ML
Treasured Swatches Silver-TS-ML
05UD PowerPlay-71
05UD PowerPlay-100
Rainbow-71
Specialists-TSML
Specialists Patches-SPML
05Ultimate Collection-71
Gold-71
Jerseys-JML
Jerseys Dual-DJLC
Jerseys Triple-TJGLC
Premium Patches-PPML
Premium Swatches-PSML
Ultimate Patches-PML
Ultimate Patches Dual-DPLC
05Ultra-154
Gold-154
Ice-154
Scoring Kings-SK1
Scoring Kings Jerseys-SKJ-ML
Scoring Kings Patches-SKP-ML
Super Six-SS1
Super Six Jerseys-SSJ-ML
Super Six Patches-SSP-ML
05Upper Deck-150
05Upper Deck All-Time Greatest-47
05Upper Deck All-Time Greatest-85
05Upper Deck Big Playmakers-B-ML
05Upper Deck Destined for the Hall-DH6
05Upper Deck Goal Rush-GR7
05Upper Deck HG Glossy-150
05Upper Deck Hometown Heroes-HH13
05Upper Deck Jerseys-J-ML
05Upper Deck Jerseys Series II-J2LX
05Upper Deck Majestic Materials-MMML
05Upper Deck NHL Generations-DGL
05Upper Deck Patches-P-ML
05Upper Deck Playoff Performers-PP7
05Upper Deck Scrapbooks-HS6
05Upper Deck Shooting Stars-S-ML
05Upper Deck Ice-76
Rainbow-76
Frozen Fabrics-FFML
Frozen Fabrics Glass-FFML
Frozen Fabrics Patches-FFPML
05Upper Deck MVP-306
05Upper Deck MVP-444
Gold-306
Gold-444
Platinum-306
Platinum-444
Materials Duals-D-LJ
Monumental Moments-MM5
Rising to the Occasion-RO2
05Upper Deck Rookie Update-76
05Upper Deck Trilogy-72
05Upper Deck Trilogy-123
Crystal-123
Honorary Patches-HP-ML
Honorary Swatches-HS-ML
05Upper Deck Toronto Fall Expo-150
05Upper Deck Victory-155
Black-155
Gold-155
Silver-155
Blow-Ups-BU31
Game Breakers-GB36
Stars on Ice-SI35
05Czech Stadion-679
05ITG Heroes and Prospects-40
05ITG Heroes and Prospects-196
05ITG Heroes and Prospects-338
Aspiring-ASP2
Aspiring-ASP19
Aspiring-ASP20
Autographs-A-ML
Autographs Series II-ML2
Autographs Series II-ML3
CHL Grads-CG-5
CHL Grads Gold-CG-5
Future Teammates-FT4
He Shoots-He Scores Prizes-1
He Shoots-He Scores Prizes-8
He Shoots-He Scores Prizes-11
He Shoots-He Scores Prizes-42
He Shoots-He Scores Prizes-52
Hero Memorabilia-HM-1
Hero Memorabilia Dual-HDM-14
Spectrum-STM-03
Spectrum Gold-STM-03
06Beehive-170
5 X 7 Black and White-170
5 X 7 Dark Wood-170
Matted Materials-MMML
PhotoGraphs-PGML
06Black Diamond-165B
Gold-165B
Ruby-165B
Gemography-GML
06Flair Showcase-256
06Flair Showcase-293
Parallel-256
Parallel-293
Hot Numbers-HN34
Hot Numbers Parallel-HN34
Inks-ILX
Stitches-SSLM
06Fleer Hockey Headliners-HL6
06Hot Prospects Hot Materials -HMML
06Hot Prospects Hot Materials Red Hot-HMML
06Hot Prospects Hot Materials White Hot-HMML
06Hot Prospects Hotagraphs-HML
06ITG International Ice-17
Gold-17
Autographs-AML
Best of the Best-BB06
Best of the Best Gold-BB06
Canadian Dream Team-DT08
Canadian Dream Team Gold-DT08
Complete Jersey-CJ07
Complete Jersey Gold-CJ07
Cornerstones-IC01
Cornerstones Gold-IC01
Double Memorabilia-DM06
Double Memorabilia Gold-DM06
Emblems-GUE19
Emblems Gold-GUE19
Greatest Moments-GM08
Greatest Moments Gold-GM08
Hockey Passport-HP10
Hockey Passport Gold-HP10
International Rivals-IR11
International Rivals Gold-IR11
Jerseys-GUJ19
Jerseys Gold-GUJ19
My Country My Team-MC15
My Country My Team Gold-MC15
Numbers-GUN19
Numbers Gold-GUN19
Passing The Torch-PTT10
Passing The Torch Gold-PTT10
Quad Patch-QP05
Quad Patch Gold-QP05
Stick and Jersey-SJ01
Stick and Jersey Gold-SJ01
Teammates-IT02
Teammates-IT09
Teammates Gold-IT02
Teammates Gold-IT09
Triple Memorabilia-TM05
Triple Memorabilia Gold-TM05
06ITG Phenoms Idols Gold-IDSC
06ITG Phenoms Idols Silver-IDSC
06ITG Phenoms Teammates Gold-TMSC
06ITG Phenoms Teammates Silver-TMSC
06ITG Ultimate Memorabilia-96
Artist Proof-96
Autos Dual-1
Autos Dual Gold-1
Autos Triple-8
Autos Triple Gold-8
Blades of Steel-24
Blades of Steel Gold-24
Bowman Factor-14
Bowman Factor Gold-14
Bowman Factor Autos-12
Bowman Factor Autos Gold-12
Boys Will Be Boys-7
Boys Will Be Boys Gold-7
Captain-C-2
Captain-C Gold-2
Complete Jersey-19
Complete Jersey Gold-19
Complete Package-8
Complete Package Gold-8
Double Memorabilia-24
Double Memorabilia Gold-24
Double Memorabilia Autos-4
Double Memorabilia Autos Gold-4
Emblems-8
Emblems Gold-8
First Round Picks-29
First Round Picks Gold-29
Gloves Are Off-14
Gloves Are Off Gold-14
Going For Gold-17
Going For Gold Gold-17
In The Numbers-4
In The Numbers Gold-4
Jerseys-16
Jerseys Gold-16
Jerseys and Emblems-11
Jerseys and Emblems Gold-11
Legendary Captains-5
Legendary Captains Gold-5
Passing The Torch-14
Passing The Torch Gold-14
Portrait in Courage-1
Portrait in Courage-2
Portrait in Courage-3
Portrait in Courage-4
Portrait in Courage-5
Portrait in Courage-6
Portrait in Courage-7
Portrait in Courage-8
Portrait in Courage-9
Portrait in Courage-10
Portrait in Courage-11
Portrait in Courage-12
Portrait in Courage-13
Portrait in Courage-14
Portrait in Courage-15
Portrait in Courage-16
Portrait in Courage-17
Portrait in Courage-18
Portrait in Courage-19
Portrait in Courage-20
Portrait in Courage Gold-1
Portrait in Courage Gold-2
Portrait in Courage Gold-3
Portrait in Courage Gold-4
Portrait in Courage Gold-5
Portrait in Courage Gold-6
Portrait in Courage Gold-7
Portrait in Courage Gold-8
Portrait in Courage Gold-9
Portrait in Courage Gold-10
Portrait in Courage Gold-11
Portrait in Courage Gold-12
Portrait in Courage Gold-13
Portrait in Courage Gold-14
Portrait in Courage Gold-15
Portrait in Courage Gold-16
Portrait in Courage Gold-17
Portrait in Courage Gold-18
Portrait in Courage Gold-19
Portrait in Courage Gold-20
R.O.Y. Autos-16
R.O.Y. Autos Gold-16
R.O.Y. Emblems-16
R.O.Y. Emblems Gold-16
R.O.Y. Jerseys-16
R.O.Y. Jerseys Gold-16
R.O.Y. Numbers-16
R.O.Y. Numbers Gold-16
Raised to the Rafters-11
Raised to the Rafters Gold-11
Retro Teammates-21
Retro Teammates Gold-21
Retrospective-2
Retrospective Gold-2
Ring Leaders-5
Ring Leaders Gold-5
Road to the Cup-8
Road to the Cup Gold-8
Sensational Season-2
Sensational Season Gold-2
Stick Rack-8
Stick Rack-16
Stick Rack Gold-8
Stick Rack Gold-16
Sticks and Jerseys-15
Sticks and Jerseys Gold-15
Trifecta Autos-2
Trifecta Autos Gold-2
Triple Thread Jerseys-3
Triple Thread Jerseys Gold-3
Ultimate Hero Single Jerseys-6
Ultimate Hero Single Jerseys Gold-6
Ultimate Hero Double Jerseys-6
Ultimate Hero Double Jerseys Gold-6
Ultimate Hero Triple Jerseys-6
Ultimate Hero Triple Jerseys Gold-6
06NHL POG-27
06O-Pee-Chee Swatches-S-LX
06Parkhurst-150
06Parkhurst-204
Autographs-150
Autographs-204
06SP Authentic-23
06SP Authentic-131
Limited-23
Limited-131
Sign of the Times-STML
Sign of the Times Duals-STGL
Sign of the Times Duals-STLM
Sign of the Times Triples-ST3LFM
Sign of the Times Triples-ST3LGH
Sign of the Times Quads-ST4LOGH
06SP Game Used-81
Gold-81
Rainbow-81
Authentic Fabrics Sixes-AF6MAS
Authentic Fabrics Sixes Patches-AF6MAS
Authentic Fabrics Sevens-AF7ART
Authentic Fabrics Sevens-AF7CON
Authentic Fabrics Sevens-AF7LBP
Authentic Fabrics Sevens Patches-AF7ART
Authentic Fabrics Sevens Patches-AF7CON
Authentic Fabrics Sevens Patches-AF7LBP
Authentic Fabrics Eights-AF8HOF
Authentic Fabrics Eights Patches-AF8HOF
By The Letter-BLML
Inked Sweaters-ISML
Inked Sweaters Patches-ISML
Inked Sweaters Dual-IS2GL
Inked Sweaters Dual Patches-IS2GL
Legendary Fabrics-LFML
Legendary Fabrics Autographs-LFML
06SPx-83
06SPx-135
Spectrum-83
Spectrum-135
SPxcitement-X79
SPxcitement Spectrum-X79
SPxcitement Autographs-X79
06The Cup-75
Autographed Foundations-CQML
Autographed Foundations Patches-CQML
Autographed NHL Shields Duals-DASGL
Autographed NHL Shields Duals-DASLR
Autographed Patches-75
Black Rainbow-75
Foundations-CQML
Foundations Patches-CQML
Enshrinements-EML
Gold-75
Gold Patches-75
Hardware Heroes Patches-HHML1
Hardware Heroes Patches-HHML2
Hardware Heroes Patches-HHML3
Hardware Heroes Patches-HHML4
Honorable Numbers-HNML
Jerseys-75
Limited Logos-LLML
Masterpiece Pressplates-75
Property of-POML
Scripted Swatches-SSML
Scripted Swatches Duals-DSGL
Scripted Swatches Duals-DSLM
Signature Patches-SPLX
Stanley Cup Signatures-CSML
Stanley Cup Titlists Patches-TML
06UD Artifacts-147
Blue-147
Gold-147
Platinum-147
Radiance-147
Autographed Radiance Parallel-147
Red-147
Auto-Facts-AFML
Auto-Facts Gold-AFML
Treasured Patches Black-TSML
Treasured Patches Blue-TSML
Treasured Patches Gold-TSML
Treasured Patches Platinum-TSML
Treasured Patches Red-TSML
Treasured Patches Autographed Black Tag Parallel-TSML
Treasured Swatches-TSML
Treasured Swatches Black-TSML
Treasured Swatches Blue-TSML
Treasured Swatches Gold-TSML
Treasured Swatches Platinum-TSML
Treasured Swatches Red-TSML
Treasured Swatches Autographed Black-TSML
Tundra Tandems-TTLC
Tundra Tandems Black-TTLC
Tundra Tandems Blue-TTLC
Tundra Tandems Gold-TTLC
Tundra Tandems Platinum-TTLC
Tundra Tandems Red-TTLC
Tundra Tandems Dual Patches Red-TTLC
06UD Powerplay Cup Celebrations-CC6
06Ultimate Collection-49
Autographed Jerseys-AJ-ML
Autographed Patches-AJ-ML
Jerseys-UJ-ML
Jerseys Dual-UJ2-GL
Jerseys Triple-UJ3-GHL
Patches-UJ-ML
Patches Dual-UJ2-GL
Patches Triple-UJ3-GHL
Signatures-US-ML
Ultimate Achievements-UA-ML
06Upper Deck All-Time Greatest-ATG18
06Upper Deck All-Time Greatest-ATG24
06Upper Deck Game Jerseys-J2LX
06Upper Deck Game Jerseys-J2LX
06Upper Deck Game Patches-PLX
06Upper Deck Game Patches-P2LX
06Upper Deck Generations Triples-G3GCL
06Upper Deck Generations Patches Triple-G3PGCL
06Upper Deck Signature Sensations-SSML
06Upper Deck MVP Autographs-OAGL
06Upper Deck MVP Clutch Performers-CP25
06Upper Deck MVP Gotta Have Hart-HH8
06Upper Deck MVP Jerseys-OJGL
06Upper Deck Sweet Shot-84
Signature Shots/Saves-SSML
Signature Shots/Saves Sticks-SSSML
Signature Sticks-STML
Sweet Stitches-SSML
Sweet Stitches Duals-SSML
Sweet Stitches Triples-SSML
06Upper Deck Trilogy Combo Autographed Jerseys-CJLG
06Upper Deck Trilogy Combo Autographed Patches-CJLG
06Upper Deck Trilogy Honorary Scripted Patches-HSPLE
06Upper Deck Trilogy Honorary Scripted Swatches-HSSLE
06Upper Deck Trilogy Honorary Swatches-HSML
06Upper Deck Trilogy Legendary Scripts-LSML
06Upper Deck Trilogy Scripts-S1ML
06Upper Deck Trilogy Scripts-S2ML
06ITG Heroes and Prospects-9
Autographs-AML
Double Memorabilia-DM02
Double Memorabilia Gold-DM02
Triple Memorabilia-TM04
Triple Memorabilia Gold-TM04

Lemieux, Real
68O-Pee-Chee-36
68Shirriff Coins-50
68Topps-36
69O-Pee-Chee-190
70Sargent Promotions Stamps-70
71O-Pee-Chee-154
71Sargent Promotions Stamps-72
71Toronto Sun-119
72Sargent Promotions Stamps-91
73O-Pee-Chee-122
73Topps-122
75O-Pee-Chee NHL-274
75Topps-274

Lemieux, Richard
72Canucks Royal Bank-11
72O-Pee-Chee-202
72Sargent Promotions Stamps-218
73Canucks Royal Bank-11
73O-Pee-Chee-53
73Topps-53
74NHL Action Stamps-298
74O-Pee-Chee NHL-114
74Topps-114
76O-Pee-Chee WHA-74

Lemire, Beau
96Arizona Icecats-11

Lemire, Bruno
99Hull Olympiques-5
Signed-5
00Hull Olympiques-5
Signed-5

Lemire, Rene
92Norwegian Elite Series-151

Lemm, Romano
02Swiss HNL-124

Lemmer, Michael
94German First League-614

Lemoine, Jean-Philippe
92Finnish Semic-223
93Swedish Semic World Champ Stickers-254
94Finnish Jaa Kiekko-213
94French National Team-16
95Swedish World Championships Stickers-101

Lemola, Olli
71Finnish Suomi Stickers-327

Lemonde, Bernie
50Quebec Citadelles-12
51Laval Dairy Subset-90
52Bas Du Fleuve-37

Lempiainen, Mikko
93Finnish Jyvas-Hyva Stickers-204
93Finnish SISU-271

Lempio, Joachim
83Swedish Semic VM Stickers-146
94German DEL-128
04German Berlin Eisbarens 50th Anniv-48

Len, Trevor
00OCN Blizzard-18
01OCN Blizzard-20
02OCN Blizzard-18

Lenardon, Tim
88ProCards AHL-347
91ProCards-149

Lenarduzzi, Mike
89Oshawa Generals-12
90 7th Inn. Sketch OHL-165
91 7th Inn. Sketch OHL-310
91 7th Inn. Sketch Memorial Cup-1
93Parkhurst-87
Emerald Ice-87
93Pinnacle-207
Canadian-207
93Ultra-72
Prospects-5
97Mobile Mysticks-18
97Mobile Mysticks Kellogg's-20

Lencucha, Mike
98Spokane Chiefs-16
99Spokane Chiefs-13

Lendick, Mathieu
98Val d'Or Foreurs-S2

Lendzyk, Taras
91Air Canada SJHL-B13
91Air Canada SJHL All-Stars-37
93Minnesota-Duluth Bulldogs-17
96South Carolina Stingrays-35
99Charlotte Checkers-9

Lener, Slavomir
92Flames IGA-28
96Czech APS Extraliga-119
96Czech APS Extraliga-335
97Czech APS Extraliga-1
97Czech APS Extraliga-341
98Czech OFS-226
98Czech Bonaparte-6C
98Czech Pexeso-21
00Panthers Team Issue-5

Lenes, Peter
04Sioux City Musketeers-13

LeNeveu, David
03AHL Top Prospects-20
03Pacific AHL Prospects-77
Gold-77
Autographs-4
Jerseys-5
03Springfield Falcons Postcards-24
04SP Authentic Rookie Redemptions-RR23
04AHL Top Prospects-55
04ITG Heroes and Prospects-27
Aspiring-16
Autographs-DL
Complete Emblems-20
Emblems-6
Emblems Gold-6
He Shoots-He Scores Prizes-26
Jersey Autographs-6
Jerseys-6
Jerseys Gold-6
Net Prospects-14
Net Prospects Gold-14
Numbers-6
Numbers Gold-6
04ITG Heroes/Prospects Toronto Expo '05-27
04ITG Heroes/Prospects Expo Heroes/Pros-27
05Beehive-125
Beige -125
Blue -125
Gold-125
Red -125
Matte-125
Signature Scrapbook-SSDL
05Black Diamond-154
Emerald-154
Gold-154
Onyx-154
Ruby-154
05Hot Prospects-260
En Fuego-260
Hot Materials-HMLE
Red Hot-260
White Hot-260
05Parkhurst Signatures-DL
05Parkhurst True Colors-TCPHX
05Parkhurst True Colors-TCPHX
05SP Authentic-179
Limited-179
Rarefied Rookies-RRDL
05SP Game Used-125
Autographs-125
Gold-125
Auto Draft-AD-DL
Rookie Exclusives-DL
Rookie Exclusives Silver-RE-DL
Significant Numbers-SN-DL
05SPx-145
Spectrum-145
Xcitement Rookies-XR-DL
Xcitement Rookies Gold-XR-DL
Xcitement Rookies Spectrum-XR-DL
05The Cup-118
Autographed Rookie Patches Gold Rainbow-118
Black Rainbow Rookies-118
Masterpiece Pressplates (Artifacts)-223
Masterpiece Pressplates (Bee Hive)-125
Masterpiece Pressplates (Black Diamond)-154
Masterpiece Pressplates (Ice)-141
Masterpiece Pressplates (MVP)-402
Masterpiece Pressplates (Power Play)-159
Masterpiece Pressplates (Power Play)-159
Masterpiece Pressplates (Rookie Update)-227
Masterpiece Pressplates SPA Autos-179
Masterpiece Pressplates (SP Game Used)-125
Masterpiece Pressplates (SPx)-145
Masterpiece Pressplates (SPx)-145
Masterpiece Pressplates (Trilogy)-209
Masterpiece Pressplates Ult Coll-163
Masterpiece Pressplates (Victory)-267
Masterpiece Pressplates Autographs-118
Platinum Rookies-118
05UD Artifacts-223
Gold-RED23
05UD PowerPlay-159
05Ultimate Collection-163
Gold-163
Jerseys Dual-DJJL
Ultimate Debut Threads Jerseys-DTJDL
Ultimate Debut Threads Jerseys Autos-DAJDL
Ultimate Debut Threads Patches-DTPDL
Ultimate Debut Threads Patches Autos-DAPDL
Ultimate Patches Dual-DPJL
05Ultra-239
Gold-239
Fresh Ink-FI-DL
Fresh Ink Blue-FI-DL
Ice-239
Rookie Uniformity Jerseys-RU-DL
Rookie Uniformity Jersey Autographs-ARU-DL
Rookie Uniformity Patches-RUP-DL
Rookie Uniformity Patch Autographs-ARP-DL
05Upper Deck-217
HG Glossy-217
Rookie Ink-RIDL
05Upper Deck Rookie Showcase-RS23
05Upper Deck Rookie Showcase Promos-RS23
05Upper Deck Rookie Threads-RTDL
05Upper Deck Rookie Threads Autographs-ARTDL
05Upper Deck Ice-141
Premieres Auto Patches-AIPDL
05Upper Deck MVP-402
Gold-402
Platinum-402
05Upper Deck Rookie Update-227
Inspirations Patch Rookies-227
05Upper Deck Trilogy-209
05Upper Deck Toronto Fall Expo-217
05Upper Deck Victory-267
Black-267
Gold-267
Silver-267
06Beehive Signature Scrapbook-SSDL
06Between The Pipes-12
Autographs-ADL
Emblems-GUE67
Emblems Gold-GUE67
Gloves-GG08
Gloves Gold-GG08
Jerseys-GUJ67
Jerseys Gold-GUJ67
Numbers-GUN67
Numbers Gold-GUN67
Prospect Trios-PT20
Prospect Trios Gold-PT20
06Flair Showcase Inks-IDL
06Hot Prospects Hotagraphs-HDL
06O-Pee-Chee-388
Rainbow-388
06Ultra Fresh Ink-IDL
06Upper Deck-154
Exclusives Parallel-154
High Gloss Parallel-154
Masterpieces-154
06Upper Deck MVP-229
Gold Script-229
Super Script-229
Autographs-OALS
06Upper Deck Trilogy Scripts-TSDL
06ITG Heroes and Prospects-52
Autographs-ADL

Lennartsson, Jonas
02Bakersfield Condors-11
03Bakersfield Condors-25
05UK Sheffield Steelers-15
Gold-15
Silver-15

Lenoski, Stephan
03Brandon Wheat Kings-3
04Brandon Wheat Kings-23
05Brandon Wheat Kings-15

Lensen, Brian
93Quebec Pee-Wee Tournament-1613

Lensky, Scott
93Quebec Pee-Wee Tournament-747

Lent, Nick
01Columbus Cottonmouths-10
03Reading Royals-12
03Reading Royals RBI Sports-293

Lenton, Ryan
01Michigan Tech Huskies-16

Lentowich, Alex
02Swift Current Broncos-9
03Swift Current Broncos-8

Lentz, Charlie
93Omaha Lancers-15

Lenyk, Terry
93Quebec Pee-Wee Tournament-1415

Leon, Matt
98Cincinnati Mighty Ducks-16

Leonard, Gerry
69Seattle Totems-5

Leonard, Roger
04Louisiana Ice Gators-10

Leonard, Sebastien
02Baie Comeau Drakkar-15

Leonard, Seth
99Kelowna Rockets-18
00Kelowna Rockets-17
01Kelowna Rockets-9
02Prince Albert Raiders-14
03Prince Albert Raiders-24
06Colorado EaglesÂ -13

Leong, Bo
69Swedish Hockey-303

Leonhardt, Bjorn
96German DEL-183
98German DEL-193
99German Adler Mannheim Eagles Postcards-18
99German DEL-17
01German Upper Deck-250

Leonov, Dmitri
93Spokane Chiefs-15
94Spokane Chiefs-21
95Spokane Chiefs-5
97Idaho Steelheads-17
98Idaho Steelheads-11
00Manitoba Moose-15

Leonov, Yuri
91O-Pee-Chee Inserts-39R
93Swiss HNL-152

Leontiev, Oleg
98Russian Hockey League-33
98Russian Hockey League-127
99Russian Hockey League-25
99Russian Metallurg Magnetogorsk-48

Leopold, Jordan
98Minnesota Golden Gophers-13
99Minnesota Golden Gophers-9
00Minnesota Golden Gophers-10
01Minnesota Golden Gophers-13
02Atomic-126
02BAP All-Star Edition-132
Gold-132
Silver-132
02BAP Memorabilia-283
Emerald-283
Ruby-283
Sapphire-283
NHL All-Star Game-283
NHL All-Star Game Blue-283
NHL All-Star Game Green-283
NHL All-Star Game Red-283
02BAP Memorabilia Toronto Fall Expo-283
02BAP Signature Series-195
All-Rookie-AR8
Autographs-195
Autographs Gold-195
Jerseys-SGJ59
Jersey Autographs-SGJ59
02BAP Ultimate Memorabilia-9
Autographs-7
Autographs Gold-7
Calder Candidates-14
02Bowman YoungStars-117
Gold-117
Silver-117
Autographs-JL
Jerseys-JL
Patches-JL
Double Stuff-JL
Triple Stuff-JL
Rivals-JLTP
Rivals Patches-13
Sticks-JL
02Crown Royale-107
Blue-107
Purple-107
Red-107
Retail-107
02ITG Used-97
Calder Jerseys-C9
Calder Jerseys Gold-C9
02Pacific Calder-108
Silver-108
Reflections-5
02Pacific Complete-544
Red-544
02Pacific Quest for the Cup-109
Gold-109
02Parkhurst-209
Bronze-209
Gold-209
Silver-209
Hardware-C5
Jerseys-GJ55
02Parkhurst Retro-209
Minis-209
02Private Stock Reserve-156
Blue-156
Red-156
Retail-156
02SP Authentic-196
Signed Patches-PJL
02SP Game Used-71
02SPx-168
02Titanium-109
Blue-109
Red-109
Retail-109
Right on Target-4
02Topps Chrome-160
Black Border Refractors-160
Refractors-160
02Topps Total-439
02UD Artistic Impressions-129
Gold-129
Common Ground-CG14
Common Ground Gold-CG14
02UD Honor Roll-105
02UD Mask Collection-173
02UD Premier Collection-47B
Gold-47
02UD Top Shelf-124
02Upper Deck-430
Exclusives-430
02Upper Deck Rookie Update-155A
02Upper Deck Rookie Update-155B
02Upper Deck Rookie Update-155C
02Vanguard-107
LTD-107
Prime Prospects-6
03Black Diamond-118
Black-118

Green-118
Red-118
03Bowman Future Fabrics-FF-JL
03Bowman Future Fabric Patches-JL
03eTopps-4
03ITG Action-48
Jerseys-M48
03O-Pee-Chee-208
03OPC Blue-208
03OPC Gold-208
03OPC Red-208
03Pacific-52
Blue-52
Red-52
03Pacific Calder Collection NHL All-Star Block Party Gold-3
03Pacific Complete-228
Red-228
03Pacific Invincible New Sensations-7
03Private Stock Reserve-17
Blue-17
Red-17
Retail-17
03SP Authentic Sign of the Times-JL
03SPx Big Futures-BF-JL
03SPx Big Futures Limited-BF-JL
03Titanium-18
Hobby Jersey Number Parallels-18
Retail-18
Retail Jersey Number Parallels-18
03Topps-208
Blue-208
Gold-208
Red-208
C55 Relics-TRJL
Traded Future Phenoms-FP-JL
03Upper Deck-31
Canadian Exclusives-31
HG-31
Shooting Stars-ST-JL
03Upper Deck All-Star Promos-S6
03Upper Deck All-Star Promos-AS13
03Upper Deck MVP-72
Gold Script-72
Silver Script-72
Canadian Exclusives-72
03Upper Deck Trilogy Scripts-S1JL
03Upper Deck Trilogy Scripts Limited-S1JL
03Upper Deck Trilogy Scripts Red-S1JL
03Upper Deck Victory-29
Bronze-29
Gold-29
Silver-29
Freshman Flashback-FF9
04ITG All-Star FANtasy Hail Minnesota-4
04Pacific-42
Blue-42
Red-42
04Upper Deck-28
Canadian Exclusives-28
HG Glossy Gold-28
HG Glossy Silver-28
05Be A Player Signatures-LE
05Be A Player Signatures Gold-LE
05Black Diamond-12
Emerald-12
Gold-12
Onyx-12
Ruby-12
05Panini Stickers-209
05Parkhurst-79
Facsimile Auto Parallel-79
True Colors-TCCGY
True Colors-TCCGY
05UD Artifacts-17
Blue-17
Gold-17
Green-17
Pewter-17
Red-17
Gold Autographed-17
05UD PowerPlay-15
Rainbow-15
Specialists-TSLE
Specialists Patches-SPLE
05Ultimate Coll National Heroes Jersey-NHJLE
05Ultimate Coll National Heroes Patch-NHPLE
05Ultra-35
Gold-35
Ice-35
05Upper Deck-26
Big Playmakers-B-JOL
HG Glossy-26
Jerseys Series II-J2LE
05Upper Deck Ice-16
Rainbow-16
Fresh Ice-FIJL
Fresh Ice Glass-FIJL
Fresh Ice Glass Patches-FIPJL
05Upper Deck MVP-57
Gold-57
Platinum-57
05Upper Deck Trilogy-16
05Upper Deck Toronto Fall Expo-26
05Upper Deck Victory-29
Black-29
Gold-29
Silver-29
06Avalanche Team Postcards-9
06Be A Player-94
Autographs-94
Signatures-LE
Signatures 25-101
06O-Pee-Chee Swatches-S-LE
06SP Game Used By The Letter-BLLE
06Upper Deck Game Jerseys-JJO
06Upper Deck Game Patches-PJO
06Upper Deck MVP Jerseys-OJJL
06Upper Deck Victory-239

Leopold, Michael
99German DEL-399

Leoppky, Mark
92Saskatchewan JHL-26

Lepage, Bertrand
52Bas Du Fleuve-42
52Juniors Blue Tint-69

Lepage, Jason
06Moncton Wildcats-6

Lepage, Martin
907th Inn. Sketch QMJHL-138
917th Inn. Sketch QMJHL-207
95Wheeling Thunderbirds-15
95Wheeling Thunderbirds Series II-9
96Wheeling Nailers-12
96Wheeling Nailers Photo Pack-19

Lepage, Patrick
01Rimouski Oceanic-19
02Baie Comeau Drakkar-14
03Salmon Arm Silverbacks-11

Lepage, Pierre
77Granby Vics-14

Lepage, Simon
03Baie Comeau Drakkar-15

Lepaus, Marko
70Finnish Jaakiekko-315
71Finnish Suomi Stickers-347

Lephart, Mike
02Philadelphia Phantoms-18
04Colorado Eagles-9

Lepine, Guillaume
04Chicoutimi Sagueneens-10
05Chicoutimi Sagueneens-20

Lepine, Hector
24Anonymous NHL-10

Lepine, Jos.
51Laval Dairy QSHL-46

Lepine, Pit
24Anonymous NHL-13
27La Patrie-5
27La Presse Photos-4
33O-Pee-Chee V304A-20
33V129-42
33V252 Canadian Gum-36
33V288 Hamilton Gum-23
33V357 Ice Kings-46
34Beehive Group I Photos-164
34Diamond Matchbooks Silver-39
34Sweet Caporal-8
35Diamond Matchbooks Tan 1-39
35Diamond Matchbooks Tan 2-37
35Diamond Matchbooks Tan 3-34
37O-Pee-Chee V304E-159
37V356 Worldwide Gum-78
05ITG Ultimate Mem Bleu Blanc Rouge Autos-14

Lepisto, Jussi
78Finnish SM-Liiga-70
80Finnish Mallasjuoma-62
84Swedish Semic Elitserien-151
85Swedish Panini Stickers-135

Lepisto, Sami
04Finnish Cardset-67
Parallel-50
05Finnish Cardset -230
Finnish Cardset Magicmakers-9
06Finnish Cardset-58
Signature Sensations-10

Lepler, P.J.
93St. Cloud State Huskies-13
96Richmond Renegades-13
97Louisville Riverfrogs-3

Lepp, Josh
01Kelowna Rockets-10
02Kelowna Rockets-1
03Kelowna Rockets Memorial Cup-10
04Moose Jaw Warriors-23

Lepp, Mike
93Quebec Pee-Wee Tournament-1442

Leppa, Henry
66Finnish Jaakiekkosarja-60
70Finnish Jaakiekko-180
71Finnish Suomi Stickers-104
72Finnish Jaakiekko-148
72Finnish Hellas-3
73Finnish Jaakiekko-69
73Finnish Jaakiekko-113
74Finnish Jenkki-8
74Finnish Typotor-14
74Finnish Typotor-50
74Swedish Stickers-100
74Swedish Semic World Champ Stickers-84
77Finnish Sportscasters-108-2573
78Finnish SM-Liiga-78
80Finnish Mallasjuoma-65

Leppanen, Antti
66Finnish Jaakiekkosarja-152
71Finnish Suomi Stickers-134
72Finnish Jaakiekko-197
73Finnish Jaakiekko-70
73Finnish Jaakiekko-157
74Finnish Jenkki-9
74Finnish Typotor-28
74Finnish Typotor-51
74Swedish Stickers-104
74Swedish Semic World Champ Stickers-97
77Finnish Sportscasters-16-364
05Finnish Tappara Legendat-1

Leppanen, Erkka
06Finnish Cardset-70

Leppanen, Janne
92Finnish Jyvas-Hyva Stickers-99

Leppanen, Jari
72Finnish Jaakiekko-309

Leppanen, Kalevi
65Finnish Hellas-10
66Finnish Jaakiekkosarja-83
70Finnish Jaakiekko-300

Leppanen, Reijo
70Finnish Jaakiekko-142
71Finnish Suomi Stickers-192
72Finnish Jaakiekko-230
73Finnish Jaakiekko-264
74Finnish Jenkki-10
74Finnish Typotor-38
77Finnish Sportscasters-83-1970
78Finnish SM-Liiga-212
80Finnish Mallasjuoma-185
81Swedish Semic Hockey VM Stickers-29
82Finnish Skopbank-9
82Swedish Semic VM Stickers-45
83Swedish Semic VM Stickers-45

Leppik, Heikki
71Finnish Suomi Stickers-285
73Finnish Jaakiekko-205

Leroux, David
01Shawinigan Cataractes-17
02Shawinigan Cataractes-13

Leroux, Francois
88Oilers Tenth Anniversary-147
90Score-393
Canadian-393
90ProCards AHL/IHL-239
91ProCards-215
92Oilers Team Issue-10
92Western Michigan Broncos-16
93Parkhurst-412
Emerald Ice-412
94Penguins Foodland-13
95Penguins Foodland-6
95Playoff One on One-81
96Be A Player-112
Autographs-112
Autographs Silver-112
97Pacific Invincible NHL Regime-162
97Macon Whoopee-15
97Macon Whoopee Autographs-15
99Asheville Smoke-8
01German Upper Deck-20
02Wilkes-Barre Scranton Penguins-19

Leroux, Jean-Yves
97Be A Player-45
Autographs-45
Autographs Die-Cuts-45
Autographs Prismatic Die-Cuts-45
97Donruss-211
Press Proofs Silver-211
Press Proofs Gold-211
97Donruss Preferred-157
Cut to the Chase-157
97Leaf-161
Fractal Matrix-161
Fractal Matrix Die Cuts-161
97Pinnacle Inside-186
97Upper Deck-249
98Aurora-42
98Pacific-149
Ice Blue-149
Red-149
98Paramount-49
Copper-49
Emerald Green-49
Holo-Electric-49
Ice Blue-49
Silver-49
98UD Choice-52
Prime Choice Reserve-52
Reserve-52
99Blackhawks Chicago Sun-Times-4
99Pacific-90
Copper-90
Emerald Green-90
Gold-90
Ice Blue-90
Premiere Date-90
Red-90
00Upper Deck-270
Exclusives Tier 1-270
Exclusives Tier 2-270
00Upper Deck Vintage-80
01Norfolk Admirals-8
03St. Georges de Beauce Garaga-12

Leroux, Jonah
00Brampton Battalion-15

Leroux, Kelly
96Johnstown Chiefs-10
97Johnstown Chiefs-20

LeRoux, Rod
96Seattle Thunderbirds-3
97Seattle Thunderbirds-3
98Kootenay Ice-8

Lesage, Marc
02Calgary Hitmen-15

Leschasin, Ryan
92Fort Worth Fire-11
93Fort Worth Fire-9
94Central Hockey League-13
94Dallas Freeze-13

Leschev, Albert
99Russian Stars Postcards-14
02Russian Hockey League-100
03Russian Hockey League-94

Leschyshyn, Curtis
86Saskatoon Blades Photos-15
88Nordiques General Foods-24
88Nordiques Team Issue-22
89Nordiques Team Issue-26
89Nordiques General Foods-20
89Nordiques Police-17
89Panini Stickers-334
90Nordiques Petro-Canada-15
90Nordiques Team Issue-18
90O-Pee-Chee-216
90Panini Stickers-150
90Pro Set-251
90Score-92
Canadian-92
90Score Hottest/Rising Stars-44
90Topps-216
Tiffany-216
90Upper Deck-295
French-295
91Bowman-142
91Nordiques Panini Team Stickers-13
91Nordiques Petro-Canada-15
91O-Pee-Chee-39
91Panini Stickers-256
91Parkhurst-367
French-367
91Pinnacle-258
French-258
91Pro Set-198
French-198
91Score American-58
91Score Canadian Bilingual-58
91Score Canadian English-58
91Stadium Club-156
91Topps-39
91Upper Deck-413
French-413
92Bowman-335
92Nordiques Petro-Canada-19
92O-Pee-Chee-306
92Panini Stickers-217
92Panini Stickers French-217
92Pinnacle-46
French-46
92Score-87
Canadian-87
92Stadium Club-413
92Topps-124
Gold-124G
93Donruss-273
93Leaf-305
93OPC Premier-487
Gold-487
93Parkhurst-436
Emerald Ice-436
93Pinnacle-49
Canadian-49
93PowerPlay-423
93Score-42
Canadian-42
93Stadium Club-336
Members Only Master Set-336
First Day Issue-336
93Topps/OPC Premier-487
Gold-487
93Ultra-404
93Upper Deck-133
94Canada Games NHL POGS-202
94EA Sports-110
94Leaf-548
94Nordiques Burger King-17
94OPC Premier-62
Special Effects-62
94Pinnacle-24
Artist's Proofs-24
Rink Collection-24
94Score-64
Gold-64
Platinum-64
94Topps/OPC Premier-62
Special Effects-62
95Be A Player-129
Signatures-S129
Signatures Die Cuts-S129
95Canada Games NHL POGS-80
95Collector's Choice-305
Player's Club-305
Player's Club Platinum-305
95Emotion-39
95Panini Stickers-253
95Playoff One on One-240
95Score-153
Black Ice Artist's Proofs-153
Black Ice-153
95SkyBox Impact-38
95Ultra-133
Gold Medallion-133
96Black Diamond-7
Gold-7
96Donruss-48
Press Proofs-48
96Leaf-126
Press Proofs-126
96Score-216
Artist's Proofs-216
Dealer's Choice Artist's Proofs-216
Special Artist's Proofs-216
Golden Blades-216
96Whalers Kid's Club-22
97Hurricanes Team Issue-17
97Pacific Invincible NHL Regime-38
97Upper Deck-35
98Hurricanes Team Issue-7
98Panini Stickers-26
99Pacific Omega-47
Copper-47
Gold-47
Ice Blue-47
Premiere Date-47
00Panini Stickers-172
00Topps Premier Plus-44
Blue Ice-44
00Upper Deck Vintage-177
01Senators Team Issue-14
02NHL Power Play Stickers-113
02Senators Team Issue-10
02Senators Team Issue-4
03Senators Postcards-5

Lesieur, Art
35Diamond Matchbooks Tan 2-38
35Diamond Matchbooks Tan 3-35
36Providence Reds-5
05ITG Ultimate Mem Bleu Blanc Rouge Autos-9

Leska, Petr
94Flint Generals-15
95Czech APS Extraliga-50
96Czech APS Extraliga-47
97Czech APS Extraliga-70
98Czech DS Stickers-303
98Czech OFS-31
99Czech DS-10
99Czech OFS-211
99Czech OFS-519
All-Star Game Blue-519
All-Star Game Gold-519
All-Star Game Red-519
All-Star Game Silver-519
00Czech DS Extraliga-60
00Czech OFS-365
01Czech OFS-91
All Stars-25
01Czech OFS Red Inserts-RE17D
02Czech DS-35
02Czech OFS Plus-9
02Czech OFS Plus All-Star Game-H13
02Czech OFS Plus Trios-T15
03Czech OFS Plus-136
03Czech OFS Plus MS Praha-SE15
04Czech OFS-283
Assist Leaders-2
Points Leaders-2
05Czech HC Hame Zlin-8
05Swedish SHL Elitset-278
Gold-278
06Czech HC Zlin Hame Postcards-7
06Czech OFS-230
Stars-7
Team Cards-13

Lesley, Bob
95Swiss HNL-158

Leslie, Alex
52Juniors Blue Tint-21

Leslie, Andrew
04Swift Current Broncos-12
05Moose Jaw Warriors-13
05Red Deer Rebels-11

Leslie, Boe
01Swiss HNL-418

Leslie, Glen
85London Knights-18

Leslie, Lance
94Thunder Bay Senators-14
96Kentucky Thoroughblades-11
96Louisville Riverfrogs-22
97Louisville Riverfrogs-22
98Wichita Thunder-12
99Wichita Thunder-11
00Lubbock Cotton Kings-10
00Wichita Thunder-14

Leslie, Laura
94Classic Women of Hockey-W11

Leslie, Lee J
90Prince Albert Raiders-9
907th Inn. Sketch WHL-275
91Prince Albert Raiders-11
917th Inn. Sketch WHL-243
92Peoria Rivermen-12
92Classic-26
Gold-26
92Classic Four-Sport *-175
93Kansas City Blades-10
94Kansas City Blades-12
95Peoria Rivermen-9

Leslie, Nate
01UK Dundee Stars-2
01UK London Knights-9
02UK Dundee Stars-2
02UK London Knights-5

Leslie, Reagan
00Brandon Wheat Kings-4
01Brandon Wheat Kings-12
02Brandon Wheat Kings-2
03Brandon Wheat Kings-13
05Bakersfield Condors-6
06Bakersfield Condors-24

Lessard, Alexandre
93Quebec Pee-Wee Tournament-128

Lessard, Benoit
03Val d'Or Foreurs-1

Lessard, Christian
92Quebec Pee-Wee Tournament-484
93Quebec Pee-Wee Tournament-1379

Lessard, Dannick
03St. Georges de Beauce Garaga-13

Lessard, David
917th Inn. Sketch QMJHL-288
92Quebec Pee-Wee Tournament-726
93Quebec Pee-Wee Tournament-924
97New Mexico Scorpions-17
03Thetford Mines Prolab-11
04St Georges de Beauce Garaga-9

Lessard, Francis
92Quebec Pee-Wee Tournament-1024
93Quebec Pee-Wee Tournament-1338
01BAP Memorabilia-420
Emerald-420
Ruby-420
Sapphire-420
01UD Mask Collection-135
Gold-135
02Thrashers Postcards-10
02Chicago Wolves-14
03Thrashers Postcards-11
05Chicago Wolves-9
06Hartford Wolf Pack-27

Lessard, Jerome
93Quebec Pee-Wee Tournament-1102

Lessard, Jim
91British Columbia JHL-43
91British Columbia JHL-169
94Dayton Bombers-6

Lessard, Jonathan
99Shawinigan Cataractes-1
Signed-1
00Shawinigan Cataractes-4
Signed-4
01Shawinigan Cataractes-5

Lessard, Junior
93Quebec Pee-Wee Tournament-396
94Quebec Pee-Wee Tournament-902
04Houston Aeros-12
04Minnesota-Duluth Bulldogs-29
04ITG Heroes and Prospects-200
04ITG Heroes/Prospects Toronto Expo '05-200
05ITG Heroes/Prosp Toronto Expo Parallel -271
05Beehive-171
Matte-171
05Black Diamond-234
05Hot Prospects-125
En Fuego-125
Red Hot-125
White Hot-125
05SP Authentic-241
Limited-241
05SP Game Used-177
Gold-177
05SPx-209
Spectrum-209
05The Cup Masterpiece Pressplate Artifact-271
05The Cup Masterpiece Pressplate Bee Hive-171
05The Cup Master Pressplate Black Diamond-234
05The Cup Masterpiece Pressplates (Ice)-194
05The Cup Master Pressplate Rookie Update-127
05The Cup Masterpiece Pressplates SPA-241
05The Cup Masterpiece Pressplates SP GU-177
05The Cup Masterpiece Pressplates (SPx)-209
05The Cup Masterpiece Pressplates Trilogy-250
05The Cup Masterpiece Pressplate Ult Coll-145
05UD Artifacts-271
05Ultimate Collection-145
Gold-145
05Upper Deck Ice-194
05Upper Deck Rookie Update-127
05Upper Deck Trilogy-250
05AHL All-Stars-17
05Iowa Stars-12
05ITG Heroes and Prospects-271
Autographs Series II-JL
06Iowa Stars-14

Lessard, Louis-Philippe
01Drummondville Voltigeurs-7
01Halifax Mooseheads-20

Lessard, Mario
76Saginaw Gears-8
79O-Pee-Chee-389
80Kings Card Night-7
81O-Pee-Chee-146
81O-Pee-Chee Stickers-238
81Topps-W98
82O-Pee-Chee-156
82O-Pee-Chee Stickers-236
82Post Cereal-8
82Topps Stickers-236

Lessard, Maxime
01Cape Breton Screaming Eagles-2
02Cape Breton Screaming Eagles-3

Lessard, Owen
90ProCards AHL/IHL-405
91ProCards-478
92Indianapolis Ice-19

Lessard, Paul
51Bas Du Fleuve-24

Lessard, Pierre-Luc
04Gatineau Olympiques-13
05Gatineau Olympiques-12
06PEI Rocket-8

Lessard, Pierre-Marc
06Moncton Wildcats-8

Lessard, Rick
84Ottawa 67's-19
88Salt Lake Golden Eagles-18
89ProCards IHL-196
90ProCards AHL/IHL-605
91Pro Set-560
French-560
91Upper Deck-520
French-520
91Kansas City Blades-2
91ProCards-519

Lessard, Stephane
80Quebec Remparts-13

Lessnick, Alexandre
93Quebec Pee-Wee Tournament-415

Lessor, Douglas
52Juniors Blue Tint-48

Lestander, Roland
69Swedish Hockey-174
72Swedish Stickers-196

Lester, Don
94Richmond Renegades-8
95Alaska Gold Kings-10
97Bakersfield Fog-7
98Colorado Gold Kings-9
98Colorado Gold Kings Postcards-19
99Colorado Gold Kings Taco Bell-6
99Colorado Gold Kings Wendy's-21

Lester, Joey
93Quebec Pee-Wee Tournament-558

Lesueur, Percy
10C56-2
10Sweet Caporal Postcards-16
11C55-16
12C57-27
83Hall of Fame-37
83Hall of Fame Postcards-C7
85Hall of Fame-37

Lesuk, Bill
71Toronto Sun-202
72Flyers Mighty Milk-7
72O-Pee-Chee-245
73O-Pee-Chee-205
74Capitals White Borders-16
76O-Pee-Chee WHA-121
78Jets Postcards-10
79Jets Postcards-11
79O-Pee-Chee-312

Leswick, Jack
34Diamond Matchbooks Silver-40

Leswick, Tony
44Beehive Group II Photos-185
44Beehive Group II Photos-337
51Parkhurst-59
52Parkhurst-65
52Royal Desserts-1
53Parkhurst-43
54Parkhurst-45
54Topps-45

Leszczynski, Matt
03Sault Ste. Marie Greyhounds-15
04Sault Ste. Marie Greyhounds-19

Letang, Alan
91Cornwall Royals-25
917th Inn. Sketch OHL-26
94Sarnia Sting-24
95Fredericton Canadiens-18
96Fredericton Canadiens-12
99BAP Memorabilia-356
Gold-356
Silver-356
99Pacific Omega-79
Copper-79
Gold-79
Ice Blue-79
Premiere Date-79
99Stars Postcards-12
99Topps Premier Plus-89
Parallel-89
00Upper Deck MVP-191
First Stars-191
Second Stars-191
Third Stars-191
00Utah Grizzlies-19
03Bridgeport Sound Tigers-4A
04German DEL-127
04German Hamburg Freezers Postcards-6
05German DEL-109
06German DEL-72
Team Leaders-TL5

Letang, Kristopher
05ITG Heroes/Prosp Toronto Expo Parallel -146
05ITG Heroes and Prospects-146
Autographs-A-KLT
Oh Canada-OC-6
Oh Canada Gold-OC-6
06Be A Player-244
06Be A Player Portraits-119
06Beehive-145
Matte-145
06Black Diamond-163A
Black-163A
Gold-163A
Ruby-163A
06Flair Showcase-324
06Hot Prospects-129
Red Hot-129
White Hot-129
Hot Materials -HMKL
Hot Materials Red Hot-HMKL
Hot Materials White Hot-HMKL
06O-Pee-Chee-547
06O-Pee-Chee-645
Rainbow-547
Rainbow-645
06SP Authentic-200
Limited-200
06SP Game Used-148
Gold-148
Rainbow-148
06SPx-182
Spectrum-182
06The Cup-151
Autographed Rookie Masterpiece Pressplates-151
Gold Rainbow Autographed Rookie Patches-151
Masterpiece Pressplates (Be A Player Portraits)-119
Masterpiece Pressplates (Bee Hive)-145
Masterpiece Pressplates (Black Diamond)-163
Masterpiece Pressplates (Marquee Rookies)-547
Masterpiece Pressplates (MVP)-309
Masterpiece Pressplates (SP Authentic Autographs)-200
Masterpiece Pressplates (SP Game Used)-148
Masterpiece Pressplates (SPx Autographs)-182
Masterpiece Pressplates (Sweet Beginnings)-148
Masterpiece Pressplates (Trilogy)-148
Masterpiece Pressplates (Ultimate Collection Autographs)-126
Masterpiece Pressplates (Victory)-293
NHL Shields Duals-DSHJK
Rookies Black-151
Rookies Platinum-151
06UD Mini Jersey Collection-116
06Ultimate Collection-126
Rookies Autographed NHL Shields-126
Rookies Autographed Patches-126
Ultimate Debut Threads Jerseys-DJ-KL
Ultimate Debut Threads Jerseys Autographs-DJ-KL
Ultimate Debut Threads Patches-DJ-KL
Ultimate Debut Threads Patches Autographs-DJ-KL
06Ultra-236
Gold Medallion-236
Ice Medallion-236
06Upper Deck-240
Exclusives Parallel-240
High Gloss Parallel-240
Masterpieces-240
Rookie Game Dated Moments-RGD23
Rookie Headliners-RH18
Rookie Materials-RMKL
Rookie Materials Patches-RMKL
06Upper Deck MVP-309
Gold Script-309
Super Script-309
06Upper Deck Sweet Shot-148
Rookie Jerseys Autographs-148
06Upper Deck Trilogy-148
06Upper Deck Victory-293
06ITG Heroes and Prospects-145
06ITG Heroes and Prospects-193
Autographs-AKL
Autographs-AKL2
07Upper Deck Rookie Class -34
07ITG Going For Gold World Juniors-5
Autographs-5
Emblems-GUE5
Jerseys-GUJ5
Numbers-GUN5

Letendre, Joe
97Macon Whoopee-7
97Macon Whoopee Autographs-7

Letendre, Luce
97Collector's Choice-290

Letizia, Mike
02Plymouth Whalers-11
05Plymouth Whalers-A-12
06Rockford IceHogs -14

Letourneau, Guillaume
05Rimouski Oceanic-24

Letourneau, Mathieu
92Quebec Pee-Wee Tournament-172
93Amos Les Forestiers-12

Letourneau, Ray
91ProCards-263

Letourneau, Sebastien
93Quebec Pee-Wee Tournament-461

Letov, Evgeni
00Russian Hockey League-349

Letowski, Trevor
94Sarnia Sting-13
95Slapshot-341
95Sarnia Sting-11
96Upper Deck Ice-121
96Sarnia Sting-13
96Sarnia Sting-14
97Springfield Falcons-14
97Bowman CHL-26
OPC-26
99BAP Memorabilia-160
Gold-160
Silver-160
99BAP Millennium-193
Emerald-193
Ruby-193
Sapphire-193
Signatures-193
Signatures Gold-193
Calder Candidates Ruby-C10
Calder Candidates Emerald-C10
Calder Candidates Sapphire-C10
99Pacific-462
99Pacific Omega-186
Copper-186
Gold-186
Ice Blue-186
Premiere Date-186
99SP Authentic-65
99Topps Arena Giveaways-PHO-TL
99Upper Deck-103
Exclusives-103
Exclusives 1 of 1-103
99Upper Deck Arena Giveaways-PC1
99Upper Deck Gold Reserve-103
99Upper Deck MVP-164
Gold Script-164
Silver Script-164
Super Script-164
99Upper Deck Victory-226
00BAP Memorabilia-201
Emerald-201
Ruby-201
Sapphire-201
Promos-201
00BAP Mem Chicago Sportsfest Copper-201
00BAP Memorabilia Chicago Sportsfest Blue-201
00BAP Memorabilia Chicago Sportsfest Gold-201
00BAP Memorabilia Chicago Sportsfest Ruby-201
00BAP Memorabilia Chicago Sun-Times Ruby-201
00BAP Memorabilia Chicago Sun-Times Gold-201
00BAP Mem Chicago Sun-Times Sapphire-201
00BAP Mem Toronto Fall Expo Copper-201
00BAP Memorabilia Toronto Fall Expo Gold-201
00BAP Memorabilia Toronto Fall Expo Ruby-201
00BAP Signature Series-111
Emerald-111
Ruby-111
Sapphire-111
Autographs-140
Autographs Gold-140
00O-Pee-Chee-190
00O-Pee-Chee Parallel-190
00Pacific-318
Copper-318
Gold-318
Ice Blue-318
Premiere Date-318
00Paramount-190
Copper-190
Gold-190
Holo-Gold-190
Holo-Silver-190
Ice Blue-190
Premiere Date-190
00Stadium Club-154
00Topps/OPC-190
Parallel-190
Own the Game-OTG26
00Topps Chrome-126
OPC Refractors-126
Refractors-126
00Topps Heritage-137
00Upper Deck-134
Exclusives Tier 1-134
Exclusives Tier 2-134
00Upper Deck MVP-140
First Stars-140
Second Stars-140
Third Stars-140
00Upper Deck Victory-179
00Upper Deck Vintage-277
01BAP Memorabilia-409
Emerald-409
Ruby-409
Sapphire-409
01O-Pee-Chee-191
01O-Pee-Chee Premier Parallel-191
01Parkhurst-366
01SP Authentic Sign of the Times-TRL
01SPx Signs of Xcellence-TL
01Topps-191
OPC Parallel-191
Reserve Emblems-TL
Reserve Jerseys-TL
Reserve Name Plates-TL
Reserve Numbers-TL
Reserve Patches-TL
01Upper Deck-367
Exclusives-367
01Upper Deck Victory-274
Gold-274
02BAP Sig Series Auto Buybacks 1999-193
02BAP Sig Series Auto Buybacks 2000-140
02NHL Power Play Stickers-159
02Pacific Complete-181
Red-181
02Topps Total-396
03Beehive-57
Gold-57
Silver-57
03Pacific Complete-351
Red-351
03Upper Deck-295
Canadian Exclusives-295
HG-295
UD Exclusives-295
04Pacific-76
Blue-76
Red-76
05Parkhurst-144
Facsimile Auto Parallel-144
05Upper Deck-303
05Upper Deck MVP-123
Gold-123
Platinum-123
06Hurricanes Postcards-18

Letsvheyev, Albert
00Russian Hockey League-251

Lettgen, Jorg
94German First League-93

Lettieri, Sal
03Odessa Jackalopes-13

Letts, Ryan
05Calgary Hitmen-9

Leuenberger, Lars
95Swiss HNL-101
98Swiss Power Play Stickers-43
99Swiss Panini Stickers-44
00Swiss Panini Stickers-137
00Swiss Slapshot Mini-Cards-HCFG9
01Swiss HNL-135
02Swiss HNL-274

Leuenberger, Marc
91Finnish Semic World Champ Stickers-187
91Swedish Semic World Champ Stickers-187
93Swiss HNL-49
95Swiss HNL-75
00Swiss Panini Stickers-32
01Swiss HNL-81
02Swiss HNL-76

Leuenberger, Olivier
93Swiss HNL-465

Leuenberger, Sven
91Finnish Semic World Champ Stickers-180
91Swedish Semic World Champ Stickers-180
92Finnish Semic-201
93Swedish Semic World Champ Stickers-115
93Swiss HNL-92
95Swedish World Championships Stickers-122
95Swiss HNL-90
96Swiss HNL-33
96Swiss HNL-533
98Swiss Power Play Stickers-32
99Swiss Panini Stickers-32
00Swiss Panini Stickers-33
00Swiss Slapshot Mini-Cards-SCB3
01Swiss HNL-80
02Swiss HNL-257

Leurs, Frank
70Flyers Postcards-3

Leuschner, Stefan
94German First League-327

Leuthner, Martin
94German First League-292

Leuthold, Ronnie
93Swiss HNL-175

Lev, Jakub
04Czech OFS-61
05Czech HC Kladno-8
06Czech HC Kladno Postcards-2
06Czech OFS-260

Levac, Frederic
96Rimouski Oceanic-15
96Rimouski Oceanic Quebec Police-14

Levac, Justin
05Brampton Battalion-15
06Brampton Battalion-17

Levanen, Marko
98Finnish Kerailysarja-153

Levasseur, Chris
87Moncton Hawks-16

Levasseur, Jean-Philippe
05ITG Heroes/Prosp Toronto Expo Parallel -144
05ITG Heroes and Prospects-144
Autographs-A-JPL
06Between The Pipes-27
Autographs-AJPL

99Crown Royale-50
Limited Series-50
Premiere Date-50
99Hasbro Starting Lineup Cards-11
99Kraft Peanut Butter-7
99O-Pee-Chee-25
99O-Pee-Chee All-Topps-AT5
99O-Pee-Chee Chrome-25
99O-Pee-Chee Chrome All Topps-AT5
99O-Pee-Chee Chrome All-Topps Refractors-AT5
99O-Pee-Chee Chrome Ice Masters-IM19
99O-Pee-Chee Chrome Ice Masters Refractor-IM19
99O-Pee-Chee Chrome Refractors-25
99O-Pee-Chee Ice Masters-IM19
99O-Pee-Chee Top of the World-TW6
99Pacific-143
Copper-143
Emerald Green-143
Gold-143
Ice Blue-143
Premiere Date-143
Red-143
99Pacific Dynagon Ice-75
Blue-75
Copper-75
Gold-75
Premiere Date-75
2000 All-Star Preview-7
99Pacific Omega-83
Copper-83
Gold-83
Ice Blue-83
Premiere Date-83
World All-Stars-3
99Pacific Prism-52
Holographic Blue-52
Holographic Gold-52
Holographic Mirror-52
Holographic Purple-52
Premiere Date-52
99Panini Stickers-233
99Panini Stickers-346
99Paramount-83
Copper-83
Emerald-83
Gold-83
Holographic Emerald-83
Holographic Gold-83
Holographic Silver-83
Ice Blue-83
Premiere Date-83
Red-83
Silver-83
99Revolution-53
Premiere Date-53
Red-53
Shadow Series-53
99SPx-58
Radiance-58
Spectrum-58
99Stadium Club-10
First Day Issue-10
One of a Kind-10
Printing Plates Black-10
Printing Plates Cyan-10
Printing Plates Magenta-10
Printing Plates Yellow-10
Capture the Action-CA20
Capture the Action Game View-CAG20
Chrome-10
Chrome Refractors-10
Onyx Extreme-OE7
Onyx Extreme Die-Cut-OE7
99Topps/OPC-25
All-Topps-AT5
Ice Masters-IM19
Top of the World-TW6
99Topps/OPC Chrome-25
Refractors-25
All-Topps-AT5
All-Topps Refractors-AT5
Ice Masters-IM19
Ice Masters Refractors-IM19
99Topps Gold Label Class 1-20
Black-20
Black One of One-20
One of One-20
Red-20
Red One of One-20
99Topps Gold Label Class 2-20
99Topps Gold Label Class 2 Black-20
99Topps Gold Label Class 2 Black 1 of 1-20
99Topps Gold Label Class 2 One of One-20
99Topps Gold Label Class 2 Red-20
99Topps Gold Label Class 2 Red One of One-20
99Topps Gold Label Class 3-20
99Topps Gold Label Class 3 Black-20
99Topps Gold Label Class 3 Black 1 of 1-20
99Topps Gold Label Class 3 One of One-20
99Topps Gold Label Class 3 Red-20
99Topps Gold Label Class 3 Red One of One-20
99Topps Gold Label Prime Gold-PG6
99Topps Gold Label Prime Gold One of One -PG6
99Topps Gold Label Prime Gold Black-PG6
99Topps Gold Label Prime Gold Black One of One -PG6
99Topps Gold Label,Prime Gold Red-PG6
99Topps Gold Label Prime Gold Red One of One -PG6
99Topps Premier Plus-47
Parallel-47
Game Pieces-GPNL
99Upper Deck-51
Exclusives-51
Exclusives 1 of 1-51
All-Star Class-AS15
All-Star Class Quantum Gold-AS15
All-Star Class Quantum Silver-AS15
99Upper Deck Gold Reserve-51
99Upper Deck MVP-72
Gold Script-72
Silver Script-72
Super Script-72
99Upper Deck Victory-103
99Upper Deck Victory-324
99Upper Deck Victory-342
99Wayne Gretzky Hockey-66
00Aurora-50
Premiere Date-50
00BAP Memorabilia-217
Emerald-217
Ruby-217
Sapphire-217
Promos-217
Jersey Cards-J17
Jersey Emblems-E17
Jersey Numbers-N17
Jersey and Stick Cards-JS17
00BAP Mem Chicago Sportsfest Copper-217
00BAP Memorabilia Chicago Sportsfest Blue-217
00BAP Memorabilia Chicago Sportsfest Gold-217
00BAP Memorabilia Chicago Sportsfest Ruby-217
00BAP Memorabilia Chicago Sun-Times Ruby-217
00BAP Memorabilia Chicago Sun-Times Gold-217
00BAP Mem Chicago Sun-Times Sapphire-217
00BAP Mem Toronto Fall Expo Copper-217
00BAP Memorabilia Toronto Fall Expo Gold-217
00BAP Memorabilia Toronto Fall Expo Ruby-217
00BAP Memorabilia Update Teammates-TM12
00BAP Memorabilia Update Teammates-TM17
00BAP Memorabilia Update Teammates Gold-TM12
00BAP Memorabilia Update Teammates Gold-TM17
00BAP Parkhurst 2000-P49
00BAP Signature Series-30
Emerald-30
Ruby-30
Sapphire-30
Autographs-52
Autographs Gold-52
Department of Defense-DD4
He Shoots-He Scores Prizes-27
Jersey Cards-J37
Jersey and Stick Cards-GSJ37
Jersey Cards Autographs-J37
Jersey Emblems-E37
Jersey Numbers-IN37
00BAP Ultimate Memorabilia Autographs-39
Gold-39
00BAP Ultimate Mem Dynasty Jerseys-D15
00BAP Ultimate Mem Dynasty Emblems-D15
00BAP Ultimate Mem Game-Used Jerseys-GJ50
00BAP Ultimate Mem Game-Used Sticks-GS50
00BAP Ultimate Memorabilia Teammates-TM6
00BAP Ultimate Memorabilia Teammates-TM7
00BAP Ultimate Memorabilia Teammates-TM8
00O-Pee-Chee-60
00O-Pee-Chee Parallel-60
00Pacific-153
00Pacific-436
Copper-153
Copper-436
Gold-153
Gold-436
Ice Blue-153
Ice Blue-436
Premiere Date-153
Premiere Date-436
00Panini Stickers-153
00Paramount-87
Copper-87
Gold-87
Holo-Gold-87
Holo-Silver-87
Ice Blue-87
Premiere Date-87
00Private Stock Game Gear-45
00Private Stock Game Gear Patches-45
00Revolution-52
Blue-52
Premiere Date-52
Red-52
NHL Game Gear-5
00SP Authentic-33
BuyBacks-26
BuyBacks-27
BuyBacks-28
BuyBacks-29
BuyBacks-30
Sign of the Times-NL
Sign of the Times-Y/L
00SP Game Used-24
Tools of the Game-NL
Tools of the Game Exclusives-NL
Tools of the Game Combos-C-OL
00SPx Winning Materials-NL
00Stadium Club-88
Special Forces-SF14
00Titanium-33
Blue-33
Gold-33
Premiere Date-33
Red-33
Retail-33
All-Stars-4W
00Titanium Draft Day Edition-38
00Topps/OPC-60
Parallel-60
00Topps Chrome-48
OPC Refractors-48
Refractors-48
00Topps Gold Label Class 1-86
Gold-86
00Topps Gold Label Class 2-86
00Topps Gold Label Class 2 Gold-86
00Topps Gold Label Class 3-86
00Topps Gold Label Class 3 Gold-86
00Topps Heritage-61
00Topps Heritage-223
00Topps Heritage-236
Chrome Parallel-61
00Topps Premier Plus-70
Blue Ice-70
World Premier-WP7
00Topps Stars-46
Blue-46
00UD Heroes-46
00Upper Deck-67
Exclusives Tier 1-67
Exclusives Tier 2-67
Game Jersey Autographs-HNL
Game Jersey Autographs Exclusives-ENL
00Upper Deck MVP-67
First Stars-67
Second Stars-67
Third Stars-67
00Upper Deck Victory-88
00Upper Deck Vintage-126
00Vanguard-38
Holographic Gold-38
Holographic Purple-38
Pacific Proofs-38
01BAP Memorabilia-93
Emerald-93
Ruby-93
Sapphire-93
All-Star Jerseys-ASJ7
All-Star Emblems-ASE7
All-Star Numbers-ASN7
All-Star Jersey Doubles-DASJ4
All-Star Starting Lineup-S2
All-Star Teammates-AST6
Country of Origin-CO31
01BAP Signature Series-156
Autographs-156
Autographs Gold-156
Department of Defense-DD-3
Jerseys-GJ-22
Jersey Autographs-GUNL
Jersey and Stick Cards-GSJ-22
Emblems-GUE-21
Numbers-ITN-21
01BAP Ultimate Memorabilia Emblems-21
01BAP Ultimate Memorabilia Jerseys-21
01BAP Ultimate Mem Jerseys and Sticks-21
01BAP Ultimate Memorabilia Numbers-21
01BAP Ultimate Memorabilia Name Plates-31
01BAP Ultimate Mem Prototypical Players-6
01BAP Ultimate Memorabilia Retro Trophies-18
01BAP Update He Shoots-He Scores Points-7
01BAP Update He Shoots-He Scores Prizes-19
01Bowman YoungStars-83
Gold-83
Ice Cubed-83
01Crown Royale-54
Blue-54
Premiere Date-54
Red-54
Retail-54
01Nortel All-Star Game Sheets-4
01O-Pee-Chee-22
01O-Pee-Chee-316
01O-Pee-Chee Heritage Parallel-22
01O-Pee-Chee Heritage Parallel Limited-22
01O-Pee-Chee Premier Parallel-22
01O-Pee-Chee Premier Parallel-316
01Pacific-146
01Pacific-429
Extreme LTD-146
Gold-429
Hobby LTD-146
Premiere Date-146
Retail LTD-146
01Pacific Adrenaline-67
Blue-67
Premiere Date-67
Red-67
Retail-67
01Pacific Arena Exclusives-146
01Pacific Arena Exclusives-429
01Pacific Heads-Up All-Star Net-6
01Parkhurst-41
Gold-41
Silver-41
Jerseys-PJ11
Sticks-PS11
Teammates-T1
Waving the Flag-18
01Private Stock-35
Gold-35
Premiere Date-35
Retail-35
Silver-35
01Private Stock Pacific Nights-35
01SPx Hidden Treasures-TTKBL
01Sports Illustrated for Kids III-96
01Stadium Club-81
Award Winners-81
Master Photos-81
Gallery-G28
Gallery Gold-G28
NHL Passport-NHLP2
01Stadium Club Toronto Fall Expo-4
01Titanium-51
Hobby Parallel-51
Premiere Date-51
Retail-51
Retail Parallel-51
All-Stars-9
01Topps-22
01Topps-316
Heritage Parallel-22
Heritage Parallel Limited-22
OPC Parallel-22
OPC Parallel-316
01Topps Chrome-22
Refractors-22
Black Border Refractors-22
01Topps Heritage-3
01Topps Heritage-112
01Topps Heritage-126
01Topps Heritage-134
Refractors-3
01Topps Reserve-39
01UD Challenge for the Cup-30
Jerseys-FPNL
01UD Honor Roll-16
01UD Honor Roll-46
Jerseys-J-NL
Jerseys Gold-J-NL
01UD Mask Collection Double Patches-DPNL
01UD Mask Collection Jerseys-J-NL
01UD Mask Collection Jersey and Patch-JPNL
01UD Premier Collection Dual Jerseys-DLH
01UD Premier Collection Dual Jersey Black-DLH
01UD Stanley Cup Champs-58
Pieces of Glory-G-NL
01UD Top Shelf-92
Sticks-SNL
Sticks-LOH
Sticks Gold-SNL
Sticks Gold-LOH
01Upper Deck-63
Exclusives-63
Game Jerseys Series II-DJYL
Pride of a Nation-TPFSL
01Upper Deck Ice-98
01Upper Deck Victory-124
01Upper Deck Victory-401
Gold-124
Gold-401
01Upper Deck Vintage-93
01Upper Deck Vintage-96
Next In Line-NLBL
01Vanguard East Meets West-10
01Vanguard Memorabilia-14
01Czech Stadion-222
02Atomic-39
Blue-39
Gold-39
Red-39
Hobby Parallel-39
Power Converters-7
02BAP All-Star Edition-54
02BAP All-Star Edition-55
He Shoots-He Scores Points-14
He Shoots-He Score Prizes-15
Jerseys-54
Jerseys-55
Jerseys Gold-54
Jerseys Gold-55
Jerseys Silver-54
Jerseys Silver-55
02BAP First Edition-158
02BAP First Edition-303
02BAP First Edition-382
02BAP First Edition-385
02BAP First Edition-396
Debut Jerseys-15
Jerseys-158
02BAP Memorabilia-194
Emerald-194
Ruby-194
Sapphire-194
All-Star Jerseys-ASJ-32
All-Star Emblems-ASE-13
All-Star Numbers-ASN-13
All-Star Starting Lineup-AS-8
All-Star Teammmates-AST-29
All-Star Triple Jerseys-ASTJ-11
He Shoots-He Scores Prizes-29
Mini Stanley Cups-36
NHL All-Star Game-194
NHL All-Star Game Blue-194
NHL All-Star Game Green-194
NHL All-Star Game Red-194
Stanley Cup Champions-SCC-8
Stanley Cup Playoffs-SC-32
02BAP Memorabilia Toronto Fall Expo-194
02BAP Signature Series-162
Autographs-162
Autograph Buybacks 1998-197
Autograph Buybacks 1999-87
Autograph Buybacks 2000-52
Autograph Buybacks 2001-156
Autographs Gold-162
Jerseys-SGJ25
Jersey Autographs-SGJ25
Team Quads-TQ13
02BAP Ultimate Memorabilia Conn Smythe-30
02BAP Ultimate Mem Dynasty Jerseys-15
02BAP Ultimate Mem Dynasty Emblems-15
02BAP Ultimate Mem Dynasty Numbers-15
02BAP Ultimate Memorabilia Emblems-18
02BAP Ultimate Memorabilia Jerseys-27
02BAP Ultimate Mem Jersey and Stick-13
02BAP Ultimate Mem Lifetime Achievers-2
02BAP Ultimate Memorabilia Nameplates-4
02BAP Ultimate Memorabilia Numbers-30
02BAP Ultimate Memorabilia Numerology-8
02BAP Ultimate Memorabilia Retro Trophies-11
02BAP Ultimate Memorabilia Retro Trophies-16
02Bowman YoungStars-1
Gold-1
Silver-1
02Crown Royale-35
Blue-35
Red-35
Retail-35
02eTopps-8
02ITG Used-27
02ITG Used-127
International Experience-IE5
International Experience Gold-IE5
Jerseys-GUJ25
Jersey Autographs-GUJ25
Jerseys Gold-GUJ25
Emblems-E25
Jersey and Stick-SJ25
Jersey and Stick Gold-SJ25
Teammates-T9
Teammates Gold-T9
Triple Memorabilia-TM5
Triple Memorabilia Gold-TM5
02Nextel NHL All-Star Game-4
02O-Pee-Chee-223
02O-Pee-Chee-324
02O-Pee-Chee Premier Blue Parallel-223
02O-Pee-Chee Premier Blue Parallel-324
02O-Pee-Chee Premier Red Parallel-223
02O-Pee-Chee Premier Red Parallel-324
02O-Pee-Chee Factory Set-223
02O-Pee-Chee Factory Set-324
02Pacific-132
Blue-132
Red-132
02Pacific Calder-20
Silver-20
Hardware Heroes-5
02Pacific Complete-1
Red-1
02Pacific Exclusive-65
Jerseys-8
Jerseys Gold-8
02Pacific Heads-Up-45
Blue-45
Purple-45
Red-45
Quad Jerseys-12
Quad Jerseys Gold-12
02Pacific Quest for the Cup-35
Gold-35
Jerseys-9
02Parkhurst-113
Bronze-113
Gold-113
Silver-113
Hardware-N1
He Shoots-He Scores Prizes-22
Jerseys-GJ39
Stick and Jerseys-SJ39
02Parkhurst Retro-61
Minis-61
He Shoots-He Scores Prizes-24
Hopefuls-HH5
Hopefuls-NH1
Jerseys-RJ32
Jersey and Sticks-RSJ22
Memorabilia-RM5
02Private Stock Reserve-119
Red-119
Retail-119
Patches-119
02SP Authentic-34
Beckett Promos-34
02SP Game Used Piece of History-PHLM
02SP Game Used Piece of History-PHNL
02SP Game Used Piece of History Gold-PHLM
02SP Game Used Piece of History Gold-PHNL
02SP Game Used Piece of History Rainbow-PHLM
02SP Game Used Piece of History Rainbow-PHNL
02SPx-28
Spectrum Gold-28
Spectrum Silver-28
Xtreme Talents-NL
Xtreme Talents Gold-NL
Xtreme Talents Silver-NL
02Stadium Club-3
Silver Decoy Cards-3
Proofs-3
World Stage-WS9
02Titanium-38
Blue-38
Red-38
Retail-38
02Topps-223
02Topps-324
OPC Blue Parallel-223
OPC Blue Parallel-324
OPC Red Parallel-223
OPC Red Parallel-324
Factory Set-223
Factory Set-324
02Topps Chrome-123
Black Border Refractors-123
Refractors-123
02Topps Heritage-1
02Topps Heritage-104
02Topps Heritage-113
02Topps Heritage-121
Chrome Parallel-1
02Topps Total-1
Award Winners-AW3
Topps-TT3
02UD Artistic Impressions-32
Gold-32
02UD Artistic Impressions Beckett Promos-32
02UD Artistic Impressions Common Ground-CG4
02UD Artistic Impressions Common Ground-CG18
02UD Artistic Impress Common Ground Gold-CG4
02UD Artistic Impress Common Ground Gold-CG18
02UD Artistic Impressions Retrospectives-R32
02UD Artistic Impressions Retrospect Gold-R32
02UD Artistic Impress Retrospect Silver-R32
02Upper Deck Collectors Club-NHL17
02UD Honor Roll-26
02UD Piece of History-34
Awards Collection-AC14
02UD Premier Collection-24
02UD Top Shelf Clutch Performers-CPNL
02UD Top Shelf Dual Player Jerseys-RLK
02UD Top Shelf Dual Player Jerseys-STFL
02UD Top Shelf Hardware Heroes-HPMBL
02UD Top Shelf Shooting Stars-SHNL
02Upper Deck-63
Exclusives-63
Blow-Ups-C15
Fan Favorites-NL
Patchwork-PWNL
Playbooks Series II-SL
02Upper Deck Classic Portraits-35
Headliners-LF
Headliners Limited-LF
Hockey Royalty-SNL
Hockey Royalty-SYL
Hockey Royalty Limited-SNL
Hockey Royalty Limited-SYL
02Upper Deck MVP-68
Gold-68
Classics-68
Golden Classics-68
02Upper Deck Rookie Update-38
02Upper Deck Rookie Update-154A
02Upper Deck Rookie Update-162B
02Upper Deck Victory National Pride-NP44
02Upper Deck Vintage-91
02Upper Deck Vintage-271
02Upper Deck Vintage-310
Green Backs-91
02Vanguard-38
LTD-38
03McFarlane Hockey-50
03McFarlane Hockey-52
03BAP Memorabilia-61
Emerald-61
Gold-61
Ruby-61
Sapphire-61
All-Star Emblems-ASE-3
All-Star Jerseys-ASJ-6
All-Star Jerseys-ASJ-19
All-Star Jerseys-ASJ-26
All-Star Numbers-ASN-3
All-Star Staring Lineup-8
All-Star Teammates-AST4
All-Star Teammates-AST9
Brush with Greatness-11
Brush with Greatness Contest Cards-11
He Shoots-He Scores Points-5
He Shoots-He Scores Prizes-5
Jersey and Stick-SJ-30
Jerseys-GJ-39
Jersey Autographs-GJ-39
03BAP Ultimate Memorabilia Autographs-152
Gold-152
03BAP Ultimate Mem Auto Jerseys-152
03BAP Ultimate Mem Auto Emblems-152
03BAP Ultimate Memorabilia Active Eight-4
03BAP Ultimate Mem Always An All-Star-9
03BAP Ultimate Mem Always An AS Gold-9
03BAP Ultimate Mem Complete Jersey-10
03BAP Ultimate Mem Complete Jersey Gold-10
03BAP Ultimate Memorabilia Emblems-19
03BAP Ultimate Memorabilia Emblems Gold-19
03BAP Ultimate Memorabilia Jerseys-29
03BAP Ultimate Memorabilia Jerseys Gold-29
03BAP Ultimate Mem Jersey and Emblems-29
03BAP Ultimate Mem Jersey and Emblem Gold-29
03BAP Ultimate Mem Jersey and Numbers-29
03BAP Ultimate Mem Jersey and Number Gold-29
03BAP Ultimate Memorabilia Nameplates-20
03BAP Ultimate Mem Nameplates Gold-20
03BAP Ultimate Memorabilia Numbers-23
03BAP Ultimate Memorabilia Numbers Gold-23
03BAP Ultimate Mem Retro-Active Trophies-10
03BAP Ultimate Memorabilia Triple Threads-11
03Beehive-72
Gold-72
Silver-72
03Black Diamond-126
Black-126
Green-126
Red-126
03Bowman-5
Gold-5
03Bowman Chrome-5
Refractors-5
Gold Refractors-5
Xtractors-5
03Crown Royale-36
Blue-36
Retail-36
03ITG Action-275
Jerseys-M193
Jerseys-M213
Trophy Winners-TW3
03ITG Toronto Fall Expo Jerseys-FE13
03ITG Used Signature Series-41
Gold-41
Autographs-NL
Autographs Gold-NL
International Experience-23
International Experience Autographs-23
International Experience Emblems Gold-23
International Experience Emblems-23
International Experience Gold-23
Jerseys-30
Jerseys Gold-30
Jersey Autos-30
Norris Trophy-1
Norris Trophy Gold-1
03ITG VIP Collages-23
03ITG VIP Collage Autographs-23
03ITG VIP International Experience-6
03ITG VIP Jerseys-8
03ITG VIP Jersey Autographs-8
03NHL Sticker Collection-218
03O-Pee-Chee-189
03O-Pee-Chee-297
03OPC Blue-189
03OPC Blue-297
03OPC Gold-189
03OPC Gold-297
03OPC Red-189
03OPC Red-297
03Pacific-123
Blue-123
Red-123
03Pacific Complete-290
Red-290
03Pacific Exhibit-54
Blue Backs-54
Yellow Backs-54
03Pacific Invincible-34
Blue-34
Red-34
Retail-34
03Pacific Luxury Suite-34A
03Pacific Luxury Suite-34B
03Pacific Quest for the Cup Connquest-3
03Pacific Quest 4 the Cup Raising the Cup-9
03Parkhurst Original Six Detroit-19
03Parkhurst Original Six Detroit-64
03Parkhurst Original Six Detroit-98
Inserts-D-13
Memorabilia-DM1
Memorabilia-DM14
03Parkhurst Orig Six He Shoots/Scores-29
03Parkhurst Orig Six He Shoots/Scores-29A
03Parkhurst Rookie-34
Jerseys-GJ-39
Jerseys Gold-GJ-39
03Private Stock Reserve-33
Blue-33
Red-33
Retail-33
03SP Authentic Breakout Seasons-B3
03SP Authentic Breakout Seasons Limited-B3
03SP Game Used Authentic Fabrics-DFHL
03SP Game Used Authentic Fabrics Gold-DFHL
03Titanium-198
Patches-198
03Topps-189
03Topps-297
Blue-189
Blue-297
Gold-189
Gold-297
Red-189
Red-297
Topps/OPC Idols-II13
03Topps C55-5
Minis-5
Minis American Back-5
Minis American Back Red-5
Minis Bazooka Back-5
Minis Brooklyn Back-5
Minis Hat Trick Back-5
Minis O Canada Back-5
Minis O Canada Back Red-5
Minis Stanley Cup Back-5
Award Winners-10
03Topps Pristine-12
Gold Refractor Die Cuts-12
Refractors-12
Press Plates Black-12
Press Plates Cyan-12
Press Plates Magenta-12
Press Plates Yellow-12
03Upper Deck-67
All-Star Class-AS-11
Canadian Exclusives-67
Franchise Fabrics-FF-NL
HG-67
NHL Best-NB-NL
Classic Portraits Hockey Royalty-PLB
Ice Breakers-IB-NL
Ice Breaker Patches-IB-NL
Ice Clear Cut Winners-CC-NL
03Upper Deck MVP-145
Gold Script-145
Silver Script-145
Canadian Exclusives-145
03Upper Deck Rookie Update AS Lineup-AS12
03Upper Deck Trilogy Authentic Patches-AP40
03Upper Deck Victory-65
Bronze-65
Gold-65
Silver-65
03Toronto Star-34
04Pacific-97
Blue-97
Red-97
All-Stars-8
Global Connection-6
04SP Authentic-112
04Ultimate Collection-77
Dual Logos-UL2-NR
Dual Logos-UL2-SL
04Upper Deck-61
Canadian Exclusives-61
HG Glossy Gold-61
HG Glossy Silver-61
NHL's Best-NB-NL
World's Best-WB26
World Cup Tribute-NL
World Cup Tribute-NLMO
World Cup Tribute-HZTSNL
04Swedish Alfabilder Alfa Stars-5
04Swedish Alfabilder Autographs-107
04Swedish Alfabilder Limited Autographs-107
04Swedish Alfabilder Next In Line-2
04Swedish Alfabilder Proof Parallels-5
05Be A Player-31
First Period-31
Second Period-31
Third Period-31
Overtime-31
Dual Signatures-DL
Dual Signatures-LP
Quad Signatures-GDEF
Signatures-NL
Signatures Gold-NL
Triple Signatures-LBP
Triple Signatures-SNL
05Beehive-34
Matte-34
05Black Diamond-96
Emerald-96
Gold-96
Onyx-96
Ruby-96
05Hot Prospects-37
En Fuego-37
Red Hot-37
White Hot-37
05Panini Stickers-261
05Parkhurst-170
Facsimile Auto Parallel-170
True Colors-TCDET
True Colors-TCDET
True Colors-TCCHDE
True Colors-TCCHDE
05SP Game Used Authentic Fabrics-AF-NL
05SP Game Used Authentic Fabrics Gold-AF-NL
05SP Game Used Authentic Fabrics Quad-LZDC
05SP Game Used Authentic Patches Quad -LZDC
05SP Game Used Authentic Patches-AP-NL
05SP Game Used Awesome Authentics-AA-NL
05SPx-31
Spectrum-31
Winning Combos-WC-RW
Winning Combos Gold-WC-RW
Winning Combos Spectrum-WC-RW
05UD PowerPlay-35
Rainbow-35
05Ultimate Collection-33
Gold-33
National Heroes Jerseys-NHJNL
National Heroes Patches-NHPNL
05Ultra-77
Gold-77
Ice-77
05Upper Deck-67
Big Playmakers-B-NL
HG Glossy-67
Jerseys Series II-J2NL
Majestic Materials-MMNL
Patches-P-NL
05Upper Deck Ice-34
Rainbow-34
05Upper Deck MVP-147
Gold-147
Platinum-147
05Upper Deck Rookie Update-37
05Upper Deck Trilogy Honorary Patches-HP-NL
05Upper Deck Tril Honorary Patch Script-HSP-NL
05Upper Deck Trilogy Honorary Swatches-HS-NL
05Upper Deck Tril Honorary Swatch Scripts-HSS-NL
05Upper Deck Toronto Fall Expo-67
05Upper Deck Victory-73
Black-73
Gold-73
Silver-73
Stars on Ice-SI20
06Sports Illustrated for Kids *-67
06Be A Player-93
Autographs-93
Profiles-PP14
Profiles Autographs-PP14
Signatures-NL
Signatures 10-100
Signatures 25-100
Signatures Duals-DFL
Signatures Foursomes-FFLNA
Up Close and Personal-UC38
Up Close and Personal Autographs-UC38
06Be A Player Portraits-41
Dual Signature Portraits-DSHL
Sensational Six-SSSTR
Signature Portraits-SPNL
06Beehive-67
06Beehive-206
Blue-67
Gold-67
Matte-67
Red Facsimile Signatures-67
Wood-67
5 X 7 Black and White-67
Matted Materials-MMNL
PhotoGraphs-PGNL
Remarkable Matted Materials-MMNL
06Black Diamond-136
Black-136
Gold-136
Ruby-136
06Fleer-72
Tiffany-72
06Hot Prospects-38
Red Hot-38
White Hot-38
Hot Materials -HMNL
Hot Materials Red Hot-HMNL
Hot Materials White Hot-HMNL
06ITG International Ice-68
Gold-68
Autographs-ANL
Best of the Best-BB09
Best of the Best Gold-BB09
Complete Jersey-CJ16
Complete Jersey Gold-CJ16
Cornerstones-IC03
Cornerstones Gold-IC03
Emblem Autographs-GUE06
Emblem Autographs Gold-GUE06
Emblems-GUE06
Emblems Gold-GUE06
Jersey Autographs-GUJ06
Jersey Autographs Gold-GUJ06
Jerseys-GUJ06
Jerseys Gold-GUJ06
Numbers-GUN06
Numbers Autographs-GUN06
Numbers Autographs Gold-GUN06
Numbers Gold-GUN06
Passing The Torch-PTT14
Passing The Torch Gold-PTT14
Stick and Jersey-SJ26
Stick and Jersey Gold-SJ26
Teammates-IT16
Teammates Gold-IT16
06ITG Ultimate Memorabilia-108
Artist Proof-108
Autos-45
Autos Gold-45
Autos Dual-6
Autos Dual Gold-6
Autos Triple-2
Autos Triple Gold-2
Complete Jersey-15
Complete Jersey Gold-15
Cornerstones-5
Cornerstones Gold-5
Decades-5
Decades Gold-5
Double Memorabilia Autos-10
Double Memorabilia Autos Gold-10
Going For Gold-20
Going For Gold Gold-20
Jerseys-23
Jerseys Gold-23
Jerseys and Emblems-18
Jerseys and Emblems Gold-18
Jerseys Autos-33
Jerseys Autos Gold-33
Passing The Torch-5
Passing The Torch Gold-5
Retro Teammates-25
Retro Teammates Gold-25
Road to the Cup-10
Road to the Cup Gold-10
Sticks Autos-11
Sticks Autos Gold-11
Trifecta Autos-1
Trifecta Autos Gold-1
Triple Thread Jerseys-6
Triple Thread Jerseys Gold-6
06McDonald's Upper Deck Hardware Heroes-HH3
06O-Pee-Chee-178
06O-Pee-Chee-651
06O-Pee-Chee-681
Rainbow-178
Rainbow-651
Rainbow-681
Autographs-A-NL
Swatches-S-NL
06Panini Stickers-259
06SP Authentic-68
06SP Authentic-142
Chirography-NL
Limited-68
Limited-142
Sign of the Times-STNL
Sign of the Times Duals-STLS
Sign of the Times Triples-ST3LHZ
06SP Game Used-38
Gold-38
Rainbow-38
Authentic Fabrics-AFNL
Authentic Fabrics Parallel-AFNL
Authentic Fabrics Patches-AFNL
Authentic Fabrics Triple-AF3DET
Authentic Fabrics Triple Patches-AF3DET
Authentic Fabrics Fives-AF5DPT
Authentic Fabrics Fives Patches-AF5DPT
Authentic Fabrics Sixes-AF6NOR
Authentic Fabrics Sixes Patches-AF6NOR
Authentic Fabrics Sevens-AF7CON
Authentic Fabrics Sevens Patches-AF7CON
Authentic Fabrics Eights-AF8SWE
Authentic Fabrics Eights Patches-AF8SWE
Autographs-38
By The Letter-BLNL
Inked Sweaters-ISNL
Inked Sweaters Patches-ISNL
Inked Sweaters Dual-IS2LS
Inked Sweaters Dual Patches-IS2LS
Letter Marks-LMNL
06SPx-35
Spectrum-35
SPxcitement-X36
SPxcitement Spectrum-X36
SPxcitement Autographs-X36
Winning Materials-WMNL
Winning Materials Spectrum-WMNL
Winning Materials Autographs-WMNL
06The Cup Autographed Foundations-CQNL
06The Cup Autographed Foundations Patches-CQNL
06The Cup Autographed NHL Shields Duals-DASHL
06The Cup Autographed NHL Shields Duals-DASLH
06The Cup Foundations-CQNL
06The Cup Foundations Patches-CQNL
06The Cup Enshrinements-ENL
06The Cup Hardware Heroes Patches-HHNL
06The Cup Honorable Numbers-HNNL
06The Cup Limited Logos-LLNL
06The Cup NHL Shields Duals-DSHDL
06The Cup NHL Shields Duals-DSHFL
06The Cup NHL Shields Duals-DSHLC
06The Cup Property of-PONL
06The Cup Scripted Swatches-SSNL
06The Cup Scripted Swatches Duals-DSZL
06The Cup Signature Patches-SPNL
06The Cup Stanley Cup Signatures-CSNL
06UD Artifacts-65
Blue-65
Gold-65
Platinum-65
Radiance-65
Red-65
Frozen Artifacts-FANL
Frozen Artifacts Black-FANL
Frozen Artifacts Blue-FANL
Frozen Artifacts Gold-FANL
Frozen Artifacts Platinum-FANL
Frozen Artifacts Red-FANL
Frozen Artifacts Patches Black-FANL
Frozen Artifacts Patches Blue-FANL
Frozen Artifacts Patches Gold-FANL
Frozen Artifacts Patches Platinum-FANL
Frozen Artifacts Patches Red-FANL
Tundra Tandems-TTNH
Tundra Tandems Black-TTNH
Tundra Tandems Blue-TTNH
Tundra Tandems Gold-TTNH
Tundra Tandems Platinum-TTNH
Tundra Tandems Red-TTNH
Tundra Tandems Dual Patches Red-TTNH
06UD Mini Jersey Collection-37

06UD Powerplay-37
Impact Rainbow-37
06Ultimate Collection-24
Autographed Jerseys-AJ-NL
Autographed Patches-AJ-NL
Jerseys-UJ-NL
Jerseys Dual-UJ2-HL
Jerseys Triple-UJ3-SFL
Patches-UJ-NL
Patches Dual-UJ2-HL
Patches Triple-UJ3-SFL
Signatures-US-NL
Ultimate Achievements-UA-NL
Ultimate Signatures Logos-SL-NL
06Ultra-71
Gold Medallion-71
Ice Medallion-71
06Upper Deck Arena Giveaways-DET5
06Upper Deck-324
Exclusives Parallel-324
High Gloss Parallel-324
All World-AW2
Award Winners-AW3
Award Winners Canadian Exclusive-OAW10
Game Jerseys-J2NL
Game Patches-P2NL
Generations Duals-G2LP
Generations Patches Dual-G2PLP
Hometown Heroes-HH49
Masterpieces-324
Oversized Wal-Mart Exclusives-324
06Upper Deck MVP-105
Gold Script-105
Super Script-105
Autographs-OALZ
International Icons-II8
Jerseys-OJLM
Jerseys-OJLZ
06Upper Deck Ovation-18
06Upper Deck Sweet Shot-38
Signature Shots/Saves-SSNL
Signature Shots/Saves Ice Signings-SSINL
Signature Shots/Saves Sticks-SSSNL
Signature Sticks-STNL
Sweet Stitches-SSNL
Sweet Stitches Duals-SSNL
Sweet Stitches Triples-SSNL
06Upper Deck Trilogy-37
Combo Autographed Jerseys-CJLZ
Combo Autographed Patches-CJLZ
Honorary Scripted Patches-HSPNL
Honorary Scripted Swatches-HSSNL
Scripts-S1NL
Scripts-S2NL
Scripts-S3NL
06Upper Deck Victory-72
06Upper Deck Victory Black-72
06Upper Deck Victory Gold-72
06Russian Sport Collection Olympic Stars-18
06ITG Heroes and Prospects Heroes Memorabilia-HM25
07Upper Deck Ovation-31
07Upper Deck Victory-101
Black-101
Gold-101
Stars on Ice-SI5

Lieb, Holger
94German First League-266

Liebel, Tyler
06Bakersfield Condors-18

Liebenow, Josh
04Huntsville Havoc-12

Liebert, Frank
94German First League-472

Liebsch, Ulrich
91Finnish Semic World Champ Stickers-168
91Swedish Semic World Champ Stickers-168
94German First League-141
95German DEL-69
99German Bundesliga 2-47

Liemgruber, Boris
96Swiss HNL-245

Lien, Pal Raab
92Norwegian Elite Series-84

Liesch, Thomas
93Swiss HNL-290
95Swiss HNL-416
96Swiss HNL-449
98Swiss Power Play Stickers-309

Lievers, Brett
93St. Cloud State Huskies-14
96Collector's Edge Future Legends-32
00Finnish Cardset-184
01Finnish Cardset-81
02Finnish Cardset-60
03Finnish Cardset-96

Liffiton, David
01Plymouth Whalers-23
02Plymouth Whalers-26
02Plymouth Whalers-27
03Plymouth Whalers-17
04Hartford Wolf Pack-13
05Hartford Wolf Pack-15
06Fleer-226
Tiffany-226
06O-Pee-Chee-527
Rainbow-527
06SPx-200
Spectrum-200
06The Cup Masterpiece Pressplates (Artifacts)-224
06The Cup Masterpiece Pressplates (Marquee Rookies)-527
06The Cup Masterpiece Pressplates (MVP)-330
06The Cup Masterpiece Pressplates (Trilogy)-137
06The Cup Masterpiece Pressplates (Victory)-316
06UD Artifacts-224
Blue-224
Gold-224
Platinum-224
Radiance-224
Red-224
06Upper Deck MVP-330
Gold Script-330
Super Script-330
06Upper Deck Ovation-133
06Upper Deck Trilogy-137
06Upper Deck Victory-316
06Hartford Wolf Pack-25

Lightbody, Quade
93Peterborough Petes-25
94Detroit Jr. Red Wings-3
95Slapshot-9
95Barrie Colts-16
95Slapshot Memorial Cup-77
02Kalamazoo Wings-5

03Bossier-Shreveport Mudbugs-10
05Bossier-Shreveport Mudbugs-8

Liikkanen, Jari
94Finnish SISU-218

Liimainen, Sami
04Chicago Steel-8

Liimatainen, Petri
89Swedish Semic Elitserien Stickers-6
90Swedish Semic Elitserien Stickers-80
91Swedish Semic Elitserien Stickers-5
92Swedish Semic Elitserien Stickers-32
93Swedish Semic Elitserien-175
94Swedish Leaf-19
96German DEL-77
98German DEL-20
99Swiss Panini Stickers-33
00German DEL-40
01German Upper Deck-139
02Swedish Malmo Red Hawks-17
02Swedish SHL-231
Parallel-231
03Swedish Elite-91
Hot Numbers-HN11
Signatures II-17
Silver-91
04Swedish Elitset-85
04Swedish Elitset-269
Gold-85
Gold-269
05Swedish SHL Elitset-122
Gold-122
Series One Signatures-3

Liitsola, Seppo
05Finnish Tappara Legendat-2

Likens, Jeff
03Wisconsin Badgers-20
04Wisconsin Badgers-10
05Wisconsin Badgers-18

Liksiutkin, Viktor
74Swedish Stickers-45

Liles, John-Michael
94Quebec Pee-Wee Tournament-246
00Michigan State Spartans-13
02SPx Rookie Redemption-R198
03Avalanche Team Issue-12
03BAP Memorabilia-203
03BAP Ultimate Memorabilia Autographs-97
Gold-97
03BAP Ultimate Mem Rookie Jersey Emblems-34
03BAP Ultimate Mem Rookie Jsy Emblem Gold-34
03BAP Ultimate Mem Rookie Jersey Numbers-34
03BAP Ultimate Mem Rookie Jsy Number Gold-34
03Black Diamond-160
Black-160
Green-160
Red-160
03Bowman-135
Gold-135
03Bowman Chrome-135
Refractors-135
Gold Refractors-135
Xfractors-135
03Crown Royale-110
Red-111
Retail-110
Retail-111
03ITG Action-631
03ITG Used Signature Series-158
Gold-158
03ITG VIP Rookie Debut-30
03Pacific Complete-510
Red-510
03Parkhurst Rookie-188
All-Rookie-ART-9
All-Rookie Autographs-ART-JL
All-Rookie Gold-ART-9
Rookie Emblems-RE-34
Rookie Emblem Autographs-RE-JLI
Rookie Emblems Gold-RE-34
Rookie Jerseys-RJ-34
Rookie Jersey Autographs-RJ-JLI
Rookie Jerseys Gold-RJ-34
Rookie Numbers-RN-34
Rookie Number Autographs-RN-JLI
Rookie Numbers Gold-RN-34
Teammates Gold-RT17
Teammates-RT17
03SP Authentic-102
Limited-102
03SP Game Used-58
Gold-58
03SPx-194
Radiance-194
Spectrum-194
03Topps C55-155
Minis-155
Minis American Back-155
Minis American Back Red-155
Minis Bazooka Back-155
Minis Brooklyn Back-155
Minis Hat Trick Back-155
Minis O Canada Back-155
Minis O Canada Back Red-155
Minis Stanley Cup Back-155
03Topps Pristine-170
03Topps Pristine-171
03Topps Pristine-172
Gold Refractor Die Cuts-170
Gold Refractor Die Cuts-171
Gold Refractor Die Cuts-172
Refractors-170
Refractors-171
Refractors-172
Press Plates Black-170
Press Plates Black-171
Press Plates Black-172
Press Plates Cyan-170
Press Plates Cyan-171
Press Plates Cyan-172
Press Plates Magenta-170
Press Plates Magenta-171
Press Plates Magenta-172
Press Plates Yellow-170
Press Plates Yellow-171
Press Plates Yellow-172
03Topps Traded-TT163
Blue-TT163
Gold-TT163
Red-TT163
03UD Honor Roll-135
03Upper Deck-212
Canadian Exclusives-212
HG-212
03Upper Deck Classic Portraits-184
03Upper Deck Ice-114

Glass Parallel-114
03Upper Deck MVP-465
03Upper Deck Rookie Update-193
03Upper Deck Trilogy-146
Limited-146
04Pacific-277
Blue-277
Red-277
04SP Authentic Sign of the Times-ST-ML
04SP Authentic Sign of the Times-QS-IKHL
04German DEL Superstars-SU15
05Be A Player Signatures-JM
05Be A Player Signatures Gold-JM
05Panini Stickers-228
05Parkhurst-123
Facsimile Auto Parallel-123
Signatures-LI
05SP Authentic Scripts to Success-SSJM
05SP Authentic Sign of the Times-JM
05SP Game Used Statscriptions-ST-JM
05Ultra-59
Gold-59
Ice-59
05Upper Deck-47
HG Glossy-47
Notable Numbers-N-JLI
05Upper Deck MVP-101
Gold-101
Platinum-101
ProSign-P-JL
05Upper Deck Toronto Fall Expo-47
06Be A Player-92
Autographs-92
Signatures-JL
Signatures 25-99
06Hot Prospects Hotagraphs-HJL
06O-Pee-Chee-125
Rainbow-125
Autographs-A-JL
06Panini Stickers-227
06Upper Deck Arena Giveaways-COL3
06Upper Deck-53
Exclusives Parallel-53
High Gloss Parallel-53
Masterpieces-53
06Upper Deck MVP-72
Gold Script-72
Super Script-72
Autographs-OARL
Jerseys-OJPL
06Upper Deck Trilogy Scripts-TSLI

Lilius, Jarmo
72Finnish Jaakiekko-310
80Finnish Mallasjuoma-35

Lilja, Andreas
95Swedish Leaf-259
99Swedish Upper Deck-154
00BAP Memorabilia-520
00Lowell Lock Monsters-2
01BAP Memorabilia-179
Emerald-179
Ruby-179
Sapphire-179
01BAP Signature Series-213
Autographs-213
Autographs Gold-213
01O-Pee-Chee-288
01O-Pee-Chee Premier Parallel-288
01Pacific-182
Extreme LTD-182
Hobby LTD-182
Premiere Date-182
Retail LTD-182
01Pacific Arena Exclusives-182
01Parkhurst-268
01Parkhurst Beckett Promos-268
01Topps-288
OPC Parallel-288
01Upper Deck Victory-374
Gold-374
02BAP Sig Series Auto Buybacks 2001-213
03ITG Action-266
04Swedish Elitset-252
Dominators-6
Gold-252
Limited Signatures-4
Signatures Series B-10
05Be A Player Signatures-AL
05Be A Player Signatures Gold-AL
06O-Pee-Chee-187
Rainbow-187

Lilja, Kalle
55Swedish Alfabilder-21

Lilja, Karl-Erik
64Swedish Coralli ISHockey-70
83Swedish Semic Elitserien-81
84Swedish Semic Elitserien-81
85Swedish Panini Stickers-72
86Swedish Panini Stickers-65
87Swedish Panini Stickers-71
89Swedish Semic Elitserien Stickers-58

Lilja, Tobias
97Swedish Collector's Choice-183

Lilja, Tomas
89Swedish Semic Elitserien Stickers-155
90Swedish Semic Elitserien Stickers-230
91Swedish Semic Elitserien Stickers-155
92Swedish Semic Elitserien Stickers-184
93Swedish Semic Elitserien-154
94Swedish Leaf-227

Liljequist, Urs
93Swiss HNL-388

Lillejord, Landon
00Prince Albert Raiders-11
01Prince Albert Raiders-12

Lilley, John
91Upper Deck Czech World Juniors-70
93PowerPlay-510
93Stadium Club Team USA-14
93Stadium Club Team USA Members Only-14
93Topps Premier Team USA-8
93Ultra-490
94Donruss-260
94Ducks Carl's Jr.-17
94Fleer-6
94Leaf-178
94OPC Premier-499
Special Effects-499
94Parkhurst-8
Gold-8
94Score-228
Gold-228
Platinum-228
94Select-191
Gold-191

94Stadium Club-139
Members Only Master Set-139
First Day Issue-139
Super Team Winner Cards-139
94Topps/OPC Premier-499
Special Effects-499
94Ultra-251
94Upper Deck-165
Electric Ice-165
94Finnish Jaa Kiekko-130
94Classic Autographs-NNO
95Finnish Semic World Championships-111
95Swedish World Championships Stickers-225
98German DEL-59
99German DEL-205

Lilley, Les
52Juniors Blue Tint-140

Lillie, Jeff
93Kitchener Rangers-25

Lillie, Shawn
90Richmond Renegades-8
91Knoxville Cherokees-12

Lilljebjorn, Ake
83Swedish Semic Elitserien-52
84Swedish Semic Elitserien-51
85Swedish Panini Stickers-48
86Swedish Panini Stickers-30
87Swedish Panini Stickers-5
89Swedish Semic Elitserien Stickers-2
90Swedish Semic Elitserien Stickers-27
91Swedish Semic Elitserien Stickers-277
92Swedish Semic Elitserien Stickers-150
93Swedish Semic Elitserien-123
94Swedish Leaf-102
Clean Sweepers-6
96German DEL-270
97Swedish Collector's Choice-100
02UK London Knights-2

Lilyholm, Len
72Minnesota Fighting Saints Postcards WHA-12
72Finnish Semic World Championship-125
72Swedish Semic World Championship-125

Limatainen, P.
95German DEL-226

Limoges, Renald
51Bas Du Fleuve-27
52Bas Du Fleuve-55

Limpright, Shawn
01Moose Jaw Warriors-12
02Roanoke Express-18
03ECHL All-Stars-249
03Roanoke Express-313
04Las Vegas Wranglers-14
05Las Vegas Wranglers-10
06Las Vegas Wranglers-10

Lincoln, Bill
97Hampton Roads Admirals-12

Lincourt, Maxime
03Quebec Remparts-17
04Quebec Remparts-5
05Rimouski Oceanic-12

Lind, Eric
92Quebec Pee-Wee Tournament-1834
01Greenville Grrrowl-3
02Greenville Grrrowl-18
05Danbury Trashers-3

Lind, Juha
93Finnish SISU-24
94Finnish SISU-49
94Finnish SISU-153
94Finnish SISU Horoscopes-1
95Finnish SISU-50
Limited Leaf Gallery-8
95Finnish Semic World Championships-235
96Finnish SISU Redline-186
97Donruss Preferred-164
Cut to the Chase-164
97Leaf-160
Fractal Matrix-160
Fractal Matrix Die Cuts-160
97Pacific Omega-72
Copper-72
Dark Gray-72
Emerald Green-72
Gold-72
Ice Blue-72
97Pinnacle-2
Artist's Proofs-2
Rink Collection-2
Press Plates Back Black-2
Press Plates Back Cyan-2
Press Plates Back Magenta-2
Press Plates Back Yellow-2
Press Plates Front Black-2
Press Plates Front Cyan-2
Press Plates Front Magenta-2
Press Plates Front Yellow-2
97Score-64
Artist's Proofs-64
Golden Blades-64
97Upper Deck-261
98Pacific-180
Ice Blue-180
Red-180
98Paramount-67
Copper-67
Emerald Green-67
Holo-Electric-67
Ice Blue-67
Silver-67
98UD Choice-64
Prime Choice Reserve-64
Reserve-64
98Finnish Keralysarja-118
Leijonat-30
99BAP Memorabilia-203
Gold-203
Silver-203
99Stars Postcards-13
99Finnish Cardset-194
Aces High-H-8
Par Avion-5
00BAP Memorabilia-63
Emerald-63
Ruby-63
Sapphire-63
Promos-63
00BAP Mem Chicago Sportsfest Copper-63
00BAP Memorabilia Chicago Sportsfest Blue-63
00BAP Memorabilia Chicago Sportsfest Gold-63
00BAP Memorabilia Chicago Sportsfest Ruby-63
00BAP Memorabilia Chicago Sun-Times Ruby-63
00BAP Memorabilia Chicago Sun-Times Gold-63
00BAP Mem Chicago Sun-Times Sapphire-63
00BAP Mem Toronto Fall Expo Copper-63

00BAP Memorabilia Toronto Fall Expo Gold-63
00BAP Memorabilia Toronto Fall Expo Ruby-63
00Canadiens Postcards-16
00Finnish Cardset-119
01Finnish Cardset-175
02Finnish Cardset-61
02Swedish SHL-97
Dynamic Duos-7
Parallel-97
Signatures-14
03Swedish Elite-264
Global Impact-GI11
Silver-264
04Finnish Cardset-74
Parallel-56

Lind, Lennart
67Swedish Hockey-51
67Swedish Hockey-224
69Swedish Hockey-65
69Swedish Hockey-262
70Swedish Hockey-29
71Swedish Hockey-106
73Swedish Stickers-168

Lind, Levi
05Regina Pats-10
06Regina Pats-11

Lind, Mats
67Swedish Hockey-143
69Swedish Hockey-155
70Swedish Hockey-123
72Finnish Jaakiekko-51
74Finnish Jenkki-28

Lind, Mikael
95Swedish Leaf-171
00Swedish Upper Deck-176
02Swedish SHL-109
Parallel-109
03Swedish Elite-155
Hot Numbers-HN10
Silver-155
04Swedish Elitset-154
Gold-154
Signatures-13
04Swedish Pure Skills-7
Parallel-7
05Swedish SHL Elitset-11
Gold-11
Playmakers-1
Teammates-1
06Swedish SHL Elitset-12
Playmakers-1

Lind, Percy
65Swedish Coralli ISHockey-69

Lind, Rune
64Swedish Coralli ISHockey-33
65Swedish Coralli ISHockey-33

Lindahl, Erik
67Swedish Hockey-205

Lindal, Kirby
90Richmond Renegades-9
91Richmond Renegades Set 2-3
92Raleigh Icecaps-6
92Raleigh Icecaps-32

Lindberg, Anders
72Swedish Stickers-200
87Swedish Panini Stickers-260
98Odessa Jackalopes-10

Lindberg, Bjorn
69Swedish Hockey-338
70Swedish Hockey-254
71Swedish Hockey-314
73Swedish Stickers-148

Lindberg, Bob
72Finnish Semic World Championship-136
72Swedish Semic World Championship-136

Lindberg, Chris
89ProCards AHL-290
90Alberta International Team Canada-15
91Alberta International Team Canada-15
91Parkhurst-251
French-251
92Flames IGA-21
92OPC Premier-4
92Parkhurst-27
Emerald Ice-27
92Score-485
Canadian-485
Canadian Olympians-6
92Stadium Club-407
92Topps-320
Gold-320G
92Ultra-269
92Upper Deck-97
93OPC Premier-76
Gold-76
93Parkhurst-440
Emerald Ice-440
93Stadium Club-84
Members Only Master Set-84
OPC-84
First Day Issue-84
First Day Issue OPC-84
93Topps/OPC Premier-76
Gold-76
93Ultra-62
93Ultra-405
93Upper Deck-196
94German DEL-235
95German DEL-232
96German DEL-83
98Swiss Power Play Stickers-192
02Swiss HNL-411

Lindberg, Erik
05Swedish Lulea Hockey Postcards-4
05Swedish SHL Elitset-230
Gold-230
06Swedish SHL Elitset-84

Lindberg, Goran
67Swedish Hockey-291
69Swedish Hockey-339
70Swedish Hockey-247

Lindberg, Hannu
66Finnish Jaakiekkosarja-111
70Finnish Jaakiekko-282

Lindberg, Hans
65Swedish Coralli ISHockey-88
67Swedish Hockey-14
67Swedish Hockey-52
69Swedish Hockey-66
70Finnish Jaakiekko-30
70Swedish Hockey-30
70Swedish Hockey-285
70Swedish Masterserien-120
71Finnish Suomi Stickers-49

71Swedish Hockey-18
71Swedish Hockey-107
72Finnish Panda Toronto-71
72Finnish Semic World Championship-57
72Swedish Stickers-15
72Swedish Stickers-91
72Swedish Semic World Championship-57
73Swedish Stickers-198
74Swedish Stickers-241
85Swedish Panini Stickers-165
86Swedish Panini Stickers-2

Lindberg, Hans-Ove
57Swedish Alfabilder-113

Lindberg, Jan
73Finnish Jaakiekko-114
84Swedish Semic Elitserien-144

Lindberg, Lasse
80Finnish Mallasjuoma-126

Lindberg, Mats
87Swedish Panini Stickers-268
89Swedish Semic Elitserien Stickers-23
90Swedish Semic Elitserien Stickers-93
91Swedish Semic Elitserien Stickers-19
92Swedish Semic Elitserien Stickers-40
94Swedish Leaf-60
95Swedish Leaf-157
95Swedish Upper Deck-14
97Swedish Collector's Choice-13
98Swedish UD Choice-16
99Swedish Upper Deck-16
Hands of Gold-1
00Swedish Upper Deck-10
00Swedish Upper Deck-209
SHL Signatures-ML
Top Playmakers-P1

Lindberg, Torbjorn
89Swedish Semic Elitserien Stickers-151
90Swedish Semic Elitserien Stickers-229
91Swedish Semic Elitserien Stickers-159
92Swedish Semic Elitserien Stickers-180
93Swedish Semic Elitserien-151
94Swedish Leaf-125
95Swedish Leaf-77
95Swedish Upper Deck-116
99Swedish Upper Deck-140
00Swedish Upper Deck-121

Lindbergh, Pelle
83Flyers J.C. Penney-14
83O-Pee-Chee-268
83O-Pee-Chee Stickers-197
83Topps Stickers-197
85Flyers Postcards-17
85O-Pee-Chee-110
85O-Pee-Chee Stickers-91
85O-Pee-Chee Stickers-193
85Topps-110
85Topps Sticker Inserts-6
85Swedish Panini Stickers-117
85Swedish Panini Stickers-118
95Swedish Globe World Championships-65
01Between the Pipes-115
04ITG Franchises He Shoots/Scores Prizes-50
04ITG Franchises Update Memorabilia-USM7
04ITG Franchises Update Memorabilia Gold-USM7
04ITG Franchises US East-422
Double Memorabilia-EDM19
Double Memorabilia Gold-EDM19
Goalie Gear-EGG5
Goalie Gear Gold-EGG5
Original Sticks-EOS8
Original Sticks Gold-EOS8
Trophy Winners-ETW10
Trophy Winners Gold-ETW10
04ITG Ultimate Memorabilia-58
Gold-58
Cornerstones-8
Cornerstones Gold-8
Country of Origin-1
Country of Origin Gold-1
Gloves are Off-7
Goalie Gear-15
Vezina Trophy-3
05ITG Ultimate Memorabilia Level 1-79
05ITG Ultimate Memorabilia Level 2-79
05ITG Ultimate Memorabilia Level 3-79
05ITG Ultimate Memorabilia Level 4-79
05ITG Ultimate Memorabilia Level 5-79
05ITG Ultimate Memorabilia Goalie Gear-16
05ITG Ultimate Mem Goalie Gear Gold-16
05ITG Ultimate Mem Pass the Torch Jerseys-15
05ITG Ultimate Mem Passing Torch Jsy Gold-15
05ITG Heroes and Prospects National Pride-NPR-22
06Between The Pipes-129
Aspiring-AS08
Aspiring Gold-AS08
Shooting Gallery-SG07
Shooting Gallery Gold-SG07
Stick Work-SW03
Stick Work Gold-SW03
06ITG International Ice-104
Gold-104
Goaltending Glory-GG07
Goaltending Glory Gold-GG07
06ITG Ultimate Memorabilia-114
Artist Proof-114
Paper Cuts Autos-13

Lindblom, Claes
83Swedish Semic Elitserien-189
84Swedish Semic Elitserien-212
86Swedish Panini Stickers-238
87Swedish Panini Stickers-224
89Swedish Semic Elitserien Stickers-256
90Swedish Semic Elitserien Stickers-164
91Swedish Semic Elitserien Stickers-269
92Swedish Semic Elitserien Stickers-295
93Swedish Semic Elitserien-260
94Swedish Leaf-83
95Swedish Leaf-130
95Swedish Upper Deck-199

Lindblom, Goran
82Swedish Semic VM Stickers-4
83Swedish Semic Elitserien-177
84Swedish Semic Elitserien-197
86Swedish Panini Stickers-221
87Swedish Panini Stickers-215

Lindblom, Ulf
84Swedish Semic Elitserien-202

Lindbom, Johan
94Swedish Leaf-235
95Swedish Leaf-55
95Swedish Upper Deck-88
Ticket to North America-NA12
97Hartford Wolf Pack-11
98Swedish UD Choice-114
99Swedish Upper Deck-102

SHL Signatures-10
00Swedish Upper Deck-101
00Swedish Upper Deck-197

Linde, Bertil
32Swedish Marabou-149

Lindegren, Pentti
65Finnish Hellas-140

Lindelof, Peter
02Swedish SHL-17
Parallel-17

Lindemann, Guido
96Swiss HNL-562

Lindemann, Sven
96Swiss HNL-557
98Swiss Power Play Stickers-116
98Swiss Power Play Stickers-280
99Swiss Panini Stickers-117
00Swiss Panini Stickers-161
00Swiss Slapshot Mini-Cards-EHCK11
01Swiss HNL-68
02Swiss HNL-41

Linden, Bjorn
95Swedish Leaf-288

Linden, Jamie
89Portland Winter Hawks-16
90Prince Albert Raiders-10
907th Inn. Sketch WHL-283
917th Inn. Sketch WHL-24
92Upper Deck-38
93Birmingham Bulls Birmingham News-23
93Cincinnati Cyclones-17
94Classic Pro Prospects-134
95Score Promos-313
95Score-313
Black Ice Artist's Proofs-313
Black Ice-313
96Grand Rapids Griffins-12

Linden, Trevor
88Canucks Mohawk-11
89Canucks Mohawk-10
89Kraft-42
89O-Pee-Chee-89
89O-Pee-Chee Stickers-40
89O-Pee-Chee Stickers-61
89O-Pee-Chee Stickers-112
89O-Pee-Chee Stickers-249
89Panini Stickers-148
89Topps-89
90Bowman-61
Tiffany-61
90Canucks Mohawk-15
90Canucks Molson-4
90Kraft-30
90O-Pee-Chee-225
90Panini Stickers-299
90Pro Set-299
90Score-32
Canadian-32
90Score Hottest/Rising Stars-16
90Score Young Superstars-19
90Topps-225
Tiffany-225
90Upper Deck-256
90Upper Deck-480
French-256
French-480
91Pro Set Platinum-124
91Pro Set Platinum-280
91Bowman-327
91Canucks Panini Team Stickers-13
91Canucks Panini Team Stickers-H
91Canucks Autograph Cards-12
91Canucks Molson-5
91Canucks Team Issue 8x10-12
91Gillette-5
91Kraft-30
91O-Pee-Chee-364
91OPC Premier-77
91Panini Stickers-36
91Parkhurst-179
French-179
91Pinnacle-2
French-2
91Pro Set-236
91Pro Set-294
91Pro Set-586
French-236
French-294
French-586
91Score American-8
91Score American-339
91Score Canadian Bilingual-8
91Score Canadian Bilingual-369
91Score Canadian English-8
91Score Canadian English-369
91Score Kellogg's-20
91Score Young Superstars-11
91Stadium Club-84
91Topps-364
Team Scoring Leaders-17
91Upper Deck-97
91Upper Deck-174
91Upper Deck-628
French-97
French-174
French-628
92Bowman-210
92Bowman-261
92Canucks Road Trip Art-11
92Humpty Dumpty II-13
92Kraft-44
92McDonald's Upper Deck-9
92O-Pee-Chee-120
92Panini Stickers-28
92Panini Stickers French-28
92Parkhurst-190
Emerald Ice-190
92Pinnacle-47
French-47
Team 2000-24
Team 2000 French-24
92Pro Set-197
Gold Team Leaders-12
92Score-305
92Score-438
Canadian-305
Canadian-438
Young Superstars-16
92Seasons Patches-30
92Stadium Club-80
92Topps-499
Gold-499G
92Ultra-222
92Upper Deck-38
92Upper Deck-158

World Junior Grads-WG14
93Donruss-354
93Kraft-41
93Kraft Recipes-4
93Kraft Recipes French-4
93Leaf-193
93OPC Premier-225
Gold-225
93Panini Stickers-172
93Parkhurst-215
Emerald Ice-215
93Pinnacle-43
Canadian-43
Captains-24
Captains Canadian-24
Team 2001-16
Team 2001 Canadian-16
93PowerPlay-251
93Score-117
Canadian-117
93Stadium Club-357
Members Only Master Set-357
First Day Issue-357
93Topps/OPC Premier-225
Gold-225
93Ultra-109
93Upper Deck-383
NHLPA/Roots-1
SP-164
94Be A Player-R53
94Be A Player-R139
94Canada Games NHL POGS-343
94Canucks Program Inserts-13
94Donruss-181
94Flair-191
94Fleer-225
94Hockey Wit-106
94Kraft-20
94Leaf-527
94Leaf Limited-112
94OPC Premier-75
Special Effects-75
94Parkhurst-241
Gold-241
SE Vintage-5
94Pinnacle-8
Artist's Proofs-8
Rink Collection-8
Northern Lights-NL18
94Select-11
Gold-11
94SP-122
Die Cuts-122
94Topps/OPC Premier-75
Special Effects-75
94Ultra-226
94Upper Deck-319
Electric Ice-319
SP Inserts-SP83
SP Inserts Die Cuts-SP83
95Bashan Super Stickers-125
95Be A Player-41
Signatures-S41
Signatures Die Cuts-S41
95Bowman-46
All-Foil-46
95Canada Games NHL POGS-271
95Canucks Building the Dream Art-16
95Collector's Choice-122
Player's Club-122
Player's Club Platinum-122
95Donruss-385
95Donruss Elite-45
Die Cut Stars-45
Die Cut Uncut-45
95Emotion-180
95Finest-144
Refractors-144
95Hoyle Western Playing Cards-44
95Imperial Stickers-125
95Kraft-12
95Leaf-161
95Leaf Limited-42
95Metal-151
95NHL Aces Playing Cards-5H
95Panini Stickers-288
95Parkhurst International-209
Emerald Ice-209
95Playoff One on One-208
95Post Upper Deck-14
95Pro Magnets-27
95Score-208
Black Ice Artist's Proofs-208
Black Ice-208
95Select Certified-87
Mirror Gold-87
Double Strike-11
Double Strike Gold-11
95SkyBox Impact-169
95SP-150
95Stadium Club-160
Members Only Master Set-160
95Stadium Club Master Photo Test-4
95Summit-102
Artist's Proofs-102
Ice-102
95Topps-12
95Topps-125
OPC Inserts-12
OPC Inserts-125
Home Grown Canada-HGC12
Marquee Men Power Boosters-12
95Topps SuperSkills-33
Platinum-33
95Ultra-169
Gold Medallion-169
Crease Crashers-7
95Upper Deck-33
Electric Ice-33
Electric Ice Gold-33
Special Edition-SE82
Special Edition Gold-SE82
95Zenith-87
Gifted Grinders-6
96Black Diamond-115
Gold-115
96Canucks Postcards-16
96Collector's Choice-268
96Collector's Choice-333
96Donruss-102
Press Proofs-102
Dominators-7
Hit List-11
96Donruss Canadian Ice-52
Gold Press Proofs-52
Red Press Proofs-52

96Donruss Elite-68
Die Cut Stars-68
96Duracell All-Cherry Team-DC11
96Duracell L'Equipe Beliveau-JB11
96Flair-95
Blue Ice-95
96Fleer-112
Picks Captain's Choice-9
Picks Fabulous 50-27
96Kraft Upper Deck-35
96Leaf-187
Press Proofs-187
96Leaf Leather And Laces Promos-P12
96Leaf Leather And Laces-12
96Leaf Limited-74
Gold-74
Stubble-18
96Leaf Preferred-59
Press Proofs-59
Steel-24
Steel Gold-24
96Maggers-57
96Metal Universe-157
96NHL Aces Playing Cards-30
96NHL Pro Stamps-27
96Pinnacle-111
Artist's Proofs-111
Foil-111
Premium Stock-111
Rink Collection-111
96Score-173
Artist's Proofs-173
Dealer's Choice Artist's Proofs-173
Special Artist's Proofs-173
Check It-10
Golden Blades-173
96Select Certified-42
Artist's Proofs-42
Blue-42
Mirror Blue-42
Mirror Gold-42
Mirror Red-42
Red-42
96SkyBox Impact-133
96Summit-134
Artist's Proofs-134
Ice-134
Metal-134
Premium Stock-134
96Topps Picks-45
OPC Inserts-45
96Ultra-168
Gold Medallion-168
96Upper Deck-169
Generation Next-X2
Power Performers-P16
96Upper Deck Ice-70
Parallel-70
96Zenith-95
Artist's Proofs-95
97Be A Player-9
Autographs-9
Autographs Die-Cuts-9
Autographs Prismatic Die-Cuts-9
97Beehive-40
Golden Portraits-40
97Collector's Choice-259
World Domination-W10
97Crown Royale-135
Emerald Green-135
Ice Blue-135
Silver-135
97Donruss-86
Press Proofs Silver-86
Press Proofs Gold-86
97Donruss Canadian Ice-32
Dominion Series-32
Provincial Series-32
National Pride-16
97Donruss Elite-89
Aspirations-89
Status-89
97Donruss Limited-19
Exposure-19
97Donruss Preferred-89
Cut to the Chase-89
97Donruss Priority-111
Stamp of Approval-111
97Esso Olympic Hockey Heroes-8
97Esso Olympic Hockey Heroes French-8
97Katch-146
Gold-146
Silver-146
97Kraft Team Canada-8
97Leaf-39
97Leaf-188
97Leaf-189
97Leaf-190
97Leaf-191
97Leaf-192
97Leaf-193
97Leaf-194
97Leaf-195
97Leaf-196
97Leaf-197
97Leaf-NNO
Fractal Matrix-39
Fractal Matrix-188
Fractal Matrix-189
Fractal Matrix-190
Fractal Matrix-191
Fractal Matrix-192
Fractal Matrix-193
Fractal Matrix-194
Fractal Matrix-195
Fractal Matrix-196
Fractal Matrix-197
Fractal Matrix Die Cuts-39
Fractal Matrix Die Cuts-188
Fractal Matrix Die Cuts-189
Fractal Matrix Die Cuts-190
Fractal Matrix Die Cuts-191
Fractal Matrix Die Cuts-192
Fractal Matrix Die Cuts-193
Fractal Matrix Die Cuts-194
Fractal Matrix Die Cuts-195
Fractal Matrix Die Cuts-196
Fractal Matrix Die Cuts-197
97Leaf International-39
Universal Ice-39
97McDonald's Team Canada Coins-1
97McDonald's Upper Deck-22
97NHL Aces Playing Cards-29
97Pacific-154
Copper-154
Emerald Green-154
Ice Blue-154
Red-154
Silver-154
Slap Shots Die-Cuts-11B
97Pacific Dynagon-127
Copper-127
Dark Grey-127
Emerald Green-127
Ice Blue-127
Red-127
Silver-127
Best Kept Secrets-110
Tandems-59
97Pacific Invincible-142
Copper-142
Emerald Green-142
Ice Blue-142
Red-142
Silver-142
97Pacific Omega-230
Copper-230
Dark Gray-230
Emerald Green-230
Gold-230
Ice Blue-230
97Panini Stickers-242
97Paramount-188
Copper-188
Dark Grey-188
Emerald Green-188
Ice Blue-188
Red-188
Silver-188
97Pinnacle-106
Press Plates Back Black-106
Press Plates Back Cyan-106
Press Plates Back Magenta-106
Press Plates Back Yellow-106
Press Plates Front Black-106
Press Plates Front Cyan-106
Press Plates Front Magenta-106
Press Plates Front Yellow-106
97Pinnacle Certified-104
Red-104
Mirror Blue-104
Mirror Gold-104
Mirror Red-104
97Pinnacle Inside-150
97Pinnacle Tot Certi Platinum Blue-104
97Pinnacle Tot Certi Platinum Gold-104
97Pinnacle Totally Certified Platinum Red-104
97Pinnacle Tot Cert Mirror Platinum Gold-104
97Revolution-141
Copper-141
Emerald-141
Ice Blue-141
Silver-141
97Score-144
Artist's Proofs-144
Golden Blades-144
97Score Canucks-4
Platinum-4
Premier-4
97SP Authentic-160
97Studio-101
Press Proofs Silver-101
Press Proofs Gold-101
97Upper Deck-169
Three Star Selects-17B
97Zenith-73
Z-Gold-73
Z-Silver-73
98Aurora-116
Championship Fever-28
Championship Fever Copper-28
Championship Fever Ice Blue-28
Championship Fever Red-28
Championship Fever Silver-28
98Be A Player-234
Press Release-234
98BAP Gold-234
98BAP Autographs-234
98BAP Autographs Gold-234
98Bowman's Best-100
Refractors-100
Atomic Refractors-100
98Crown Royale-83
Limited Series-83
Pivotal Players-15
98Finest-110
No Protectors-110
No Protectors Refractors-110
Refractors-110
98Islanders Power Play-NYI1
98Katch-89
98Katch-107
98OPC Chrome-117
Refractors-117
98Pacific-32
Ice Blue-32
Red-32
Gold Crown Die-Cuts-21
98Pacific Dynagon Ice-115
Blue-115
Red-115
Team Checklists-16
98Pacific Omega-147
Red-147
Opening Day Issue-147
98Panini Photocards-48
98Paramount-144
Copper-144
Emerald Green-144
Holo-Electric-144
Ice Blue-144
Silver-144
98Revolution-88
Ice Shadow-88
Red-88
98SP Authentic-51
Power Shift-51
98SPx Finite-50
Radiance-50
Spectrum-50
98Topps-117
O-Pee-Chee-117
98Topps Gold Label Class 1-42
Black-42
Black One of One-42
One of One-42
Red-42
Red One of One-42
98Topps Gold Label Class 2-42
98Topps Gold Label Class 2 Black-42
98Topps Gold Label Class 2 Black 1 of 1-42
98Topps Gold Label Class 2 One of One-42
98Topps Gold Label Class 2 Red-42
98Topps Gold Label Class 2 Red One of One-42
98Topps Gold Label Class 3-42
98Topps Gold Label Class 3 Black-42
98Topps Gold Label Class 3 Black 1 of 1-42
98Topps Gold Label Class 3 One of One-42
98Topps Gold Label Class 3 Red-42
98Topps Gold Label Class 3 Red One of One-42
98UD Choice-122
Prime Choice Reserve-122
Reserve-122
98Upper Deck-124
Exclusives-124
Exclusives 1 of 1-124
Gold Reserve-124
98Upper Deck MVP-131
Gold Script-131
Silver Script-131
Super Script-131
99BAP Memorabilia-194
Gold-194
Silver-194
99BAP Millennium-129
Emerald-129
Ruby-129
Sapphire-129
Signatures-129
Signatures Gold-129
99Crown Royale-71
Limited Series-71
Premiere Date-71
Ice Elite-14
Ice Elite Parallel-14
99O-Pee-Chee-71
99O-Pee-Chee Chrome-71
99O-Pee-Chee Chrome Refractors-71
99Pacific-258
Copper-258
Emerald Green-258
Gold-258
Ice Blue-258
Premiere Date-258
Red-258
Center Ice-13
Center Ice Proofs-13
99Pacific Dynagon Ice-103
Blue-103
Copper-103
Gold-103
Premiere Date-103
99Pacific Omega-120
Copper-120
Gold-120
Ice Blue-120
Premiere Date-120
99Pacific Prism-73
Holographic Blue-73
Holographic Gold-73
Holographic Mirror-73
Holographic Purple-73
Premiere Date-73
99Panini Stickers-66
99Paramount-118
Copper-118
Emerald-118
Gold-118
Holographic Emerald-118
Holographic Gold-118
Holographic Silver-118
Ice Blue-118
Premiere Date-118
Red-118
Silver-118
99SPx-80
Radiance-80
Spectrum-80
99Stadium Club-159
First Day Issue-159
One of a Kind-159
Printing Plates Black-159
Printing Plates Cyan-159
Printing Plates Magenta-159
Printing Plates Yellow-159
99Topps/OPC-71
99Topps/OPC Chrome-71
Refractors-71
99Topps Gold Label Class 1-63
Black-63
Black One of One-63
One of One-63
Red-63
Red One of One-63
99Topps Gold Label Class 2-63
99Topps Gold Label Class 2 Black-63
99Topps Gold Label Class 2 Black 1 of 1-63
99Topps Gold Label Class 2 One of One-63
99Topps Gold Label Class 2 Red-63
99Topps Gold Label Class 2 Red One of One-63
99Topps Gold Label Class 3-63
99Topps Gold Label Class 3 Black-63
99Topps Gold Label Class 3 Black 1 of 1-63
99Topps Gold Label Class 3 One of One-63
99Topps Gold Label Class 3 Red-63
99Topps Gold Label Class 3 Red One of One-63
99Upper Deck-71
Exclusives-71
Exclusives 1 of 1-71
99Upper Deck Gold Reserve-71
99Upper Deck MVP-106
Gold Script-106
Silver Script-106
Super Script-106
ProSign-TL
99Upper Deck Victory-146
99Wayne Gretzky Hockey-87
00Aurora-73
Premiere Date-73
00BAP Memorabilia-285
00BAP Memorabilia-"NNO
Emerald-285
Ruby-285
Sapphire-285
Promos-285
00BAP Mem Chicago Sportsfest Copper-285
00BAP Memorabilia Chicago Sportsfest Blue-285
00BAP Memorabilia Chicago Sportsfest Gold-285
00BAP Memorabilia Chicago Sportsfest Ruby-285
00BAP Memorabilia Chicago Sun-Times Ruby-285
00BAP Memorabilia Chicago Sun-Times Gold-285
00BAP Mem Chicago Sun-Times Sapphire-285
00BAP Mem Toronto Fall Expo Copper-285
00BAP Memorabilia Toronto Fall Expo Gold-285
00BAP Memorabilia Toronto Fall Expo Ruby-285
00BAP Mem Update Heritage Jersey Cards-H20
00BAP Mem Update Heritage Jersey Gold-H20
00BAP Parkhurst 2000-P30
00BAP Signature Series-213
Emerald-213
Ruby-213
Sapphire-213
Autographs-127
Autographs Gold-127
00Canadiens Postcards-17
00Kraft-26
00O-Pee-Chee-32
00O-Pee-Chee Parallel-32
00Pacific-210
Copper-210
Gold-210
Ice Blue-210
Premiere Date-210
00Panini Stickers-40
00Paramount-127
Copper-127
Gold-127
Holo-Gold-127
Holo-Silver-127
Ice Blue-127
Premiere Date-127
00Private Stock-52
Gold-52
Premiere Date-52
Retail-52
Silver-52
Extreme Action-11
Game Gear-59
00Revolution-77
Blue-77
Premiere Date-77
Red-77
00SP Authentic-48
00SP Game Used-33
00Stadium Club-55
00Titanium-48
Blue-48
Gold-48
Premiere Date-48
Red-48
Retail-48
Game Gear-27
Game Gear-28
00Topps/OPC-32
Parallel-32
00Upper Deck Vintage-196
00Vanguard-52
Holographic Gold-52
Holographic Purple-52
Pacific Proofs-52
01BAP Memorabilia-495
Emerald-495
Ruby-495
Sapphire-495
01BAP Signature Series-125
Autographs-125
Autographs Gold-125
01Canucks Postcards-8
01O-Pee-Chee-193
01O-Pee-Chee Premier Parallel-193
01Pacific-397
Extreme LTD-397
Hobby LTD-397
Premiere Date-397
Retail LTD-397
01Pacific Arena Exclusives-397
01Parkhurst-161
01Parkhurst-399
01SPx-196
01Topps-193
OPC Parallel-193
01UD Challenge for the Cup-85
01UD Mask Collection Double Patches-DPTL
01UD Mask Collection Jerseys-J-TL
01UD Mask Collection Jersey and Patch-JPTL
01UD Playmakers-96
01Upper Deck Ice-124
01Upper Deck Victory-357
Gold-357
02BAP First Edition-401R
02BAP Memorabilia-245
Emerald-245
Ruby-245
Sapphire-245
NHL All-Star Game-245
NHL All-Star Game Blue-245
NHL All-Star Game Green-245
NHL All-Star Game Red-245
02BAP Memorabilia Toronto Fall Expo-245
02BAP Signature Series-38
Autographs-38
Autograph Buybacks 1998-234
Autograph Buybacks 1999-129
Autograph Buybacks 2001-125
Autographs Gold-38
02BAP Ultimate Memorabilia Numerology-18
02Canucks Team Issue-8
02NHL Power Play Stickers-162
02O-Pee-Chee-180
02O-Pee-Chee Premier Blue Parallel-180
02O-Pee-Chee Premier Red Parallel-180
02O-Pee-Chee Factory Set-180
02Pacific-379
Blue-379
Red-379
02Pacific Complete-53
Red-53
02Parkhurst-183
Bronze-183
Gold-183
Silver-183
02SP Game Used First Rounder Patches-TL
02Topps-180
OPC Blue Parallel-180
OPC Red Parallel-180
Factory Set-180
02Topps Total-105
02Upper Deck-418
Exclusives-418
02Upper Deck Beckett UD Promos-418
02Upper Deck CHL Graduates-CGTL
02Upper Deck CHL Graduates Gold-CGTL
02Upper Deck Victory-207
Bronze-207
Gold-207
Silver-207
02Upper Deck Vintage-244
02Upper Deck Vintage-289
03McFarlane Hockey-230
03McFarlane Hockey-232
03Beehive-191
Gold-191
Silver-191
03Canucks Postcards-14
03Canucks Sav-on-Foods-1
03ITG Action-583
Jerseys-M49
03Kraft-4
03NHL Sticker Collection-294
03O-Pee-Chee-214
03OPC Blue-214
03OPC Gold-214
03OPC Red-214
03Pacific-332
Blue-332
Red-332
03Pacific Complete-151
Red-151
03Pacific Exhibit-142
Blue Backs-142
Yellow Backs-142
03Private Stock Reserve-98
Blue-98
Red-98
Retail-98
03Topps-214
Blue-214
Gold-214
Red-214
03UD Honor Roll Grade A Jerseys-TVAN
03Upper Deck-432
Canadian Exclusives-432
HG-432
UD Exclusives-432
03Upper Deck MVP-413
Gold Script-413
Silver Script-413
Canadian Exclusives-413
Lethal Lineups-LL4
03Upper Deck Victory-191
Bronze-191
Gold-191
Silver-191
04Pacific-256
Blue-256
Red-256
04SP Authentic-89
04Upper Deck-172
Canadian Exclusives-172
HG Glossy Gold-172
HG Glossy Silver-172
05Be A Player Dual Signatures-NL
05Be A Player Signatures-TL
05Be A Player Signatures Gold-TL
05Black Diamond-125
Emerald-125
Gold-125
Onyx-125
Ruby-125
05Panini Stickers-363
05Parkhurst-481
Facsimile Auto Parallel-481
True Colors-TCVAN
True Colors-TCVAN
05SP Authentic Prestigious Pairings-PPNL
05SP Authentic Sign of the Times-TL
05SP Game Used Authentic Fabrics Quad-KBJL
05SP Game Used Authentic Patches Quad -KBJL
05SP Game Used Authentic Fabrics Triple-ISL
05SP Game Used Authentic Fabrics Triple-MLR
05SP Game Used Authentic Patches Triple-ISL
05SP Game Used Authentic Patches Triple-MLR
05SP Game Used SIGnificance-TL
05SP Game Used SIGnificance Gold-S-TL
05SP Game Used Statscriptions-ST-TL
05UD Artifacts-99
Blue-99
Gold-99
Green-99
Pewter-99
Red-99
Auto Facts-AF-TL
Auto Facts Blue-AF-TL
Auto Facts Copper-AF-TL
Auto Facts Pewter-AF-TL
Auto Facts Silver-AF-TL
Gold Autographed-99
05UD Powerplay Specialists-TSTL
05UD Powerplay Specialists Patches-SPTL
05Ultra-194
Gold-194
Fresh Ink-FI-TL
Fresh Ink Blue-FI-TL
Ice-194
05Upper Deck-187
05Upper Deck All-Time Greatest-58
05Upper Deck HG Glossy-187
05Upper Deck Jerseys Series II-J2TL
05Upper Deck Notable Numbers-N-TL
05Upper Deck Ice Glacial Graphs-GGTL
05Upper Deck MVP-371
Gold-371
Platinum-371
Materials Duals-D-LC
Materials Triples-T-VAN
ProSign-P-TL
05Upper Deck Toronto Fall Expo-187
05Upper Deck Victory-195
Black-195
Gold-195
Silver-195
06Canucks Postcards-11
06Flair Showcase Stitches-SSTL
06Gatorade-86
06O-Pee-Chee-484
Rainbow-484
06The Cup NHL Shields Duals-DSHLL
06Upper Deck Arena Giveaways-VAN5
06Upper Deck-440
Exclusives Parallel-440
High Gloss Parallel-440
Game Jerseys-JTL
Game Patches-PTL
Masterpieces-440
Signature Sensations-SSTL
07Upper Deck Ovation-53
07Upper Deck Victory-136
Black-136
Gold-136

Lindenberg, Jesse
02Lincoln Stars-19
03Lincoln Stars-17

Lindenmann, M.
74Finnish Typotor-108

Lindenzweig, Volker
94German First League-385

Linder, Engelbert
95Austrian National Team-15
95Swedish World Championships Stickers-261

Linder, Olle
56Swedish Alfabilder-102

Linder, Patrik
55Swedish Alfabilder-24

Lindfors, Freddy
67Swedish Hockey-206
84Swedish Semic Elitserien-194
86Swedish Panini Stickers-164
87Swedish Panini Stickers-169
91Swedish Semic Elitserien Stickers-308
92Swedish Semic Elitserien Stickers-330

Lindfors, Sakari
89Swedish Semic World Champ Stickers-29
91Finnish Semic World Champ Stickers-3
91Finnish Jyvas-Hyva Stickers-1
91Swedish Semic World Champ Stickers-3
92Finnish Jyvas-Hyva Stickers-2
92Finnish Semic-4
93Finnish Jyvas-Hyva Stickers-14
93Finnish SISU-83
93Finnish SISU Autographs-83
93Swedish Semic World Champ Stickers-46
94Finnish SISU-35
94Finnish SISU NHL Phenoms-10
95Finnish SISU-202
Ghost Goalies-1
95Finnish SISU Limited-37
Leaf Gallery-9
96Finnish SISU Redline-2
96Finnish SISU Redline Foil Parallels-2
96Finnish SISU Redline Mighty Adversaries-8
96Swedish Semic Wien-35
00Finnish Cardset-253
01Finnish Cardset-14
01Finnish Cardset Haltmeisters-11
02Finnish Cardset-62

Lindgren, Fredrik
06Swedish SHL Elitset-264

Lindgren, Hakan
70Swedish Hockey-6
71Swedish Hockey-80
72Swedish Stickers-55
73Swedish Stickers-193
74Swedish Stickers-173

Lindgren, Jari
78Finnish SM-Liiga-194
80Finnish Mallasjuoma-171
82Swedish Semic VM Stickers-39
83Swedish Semic VM Stickers-39
84Swedish Semic Elitserien-183
85Swedish Panini Stickers-172
86Swedish Panini Stickers-181
87Swedish Panini Stickers-181

Lindgren, Joakim
93Swedish Semic Elitserien-24

Lindgren, Kakari
65Swedish Coralli ISHockey-179
67Swedish Hockey-66
72Swedish Stickers-234
73Swedish Stickers-235

Lindgren, Krister
67Swedish Hockey-271
72Swedish Stickers-280

Lindgren, Lars
78Canucks Royal Bank-14
79Panini Stickers-191
79Canucks Royal Bank-13
80Canucks Silverwood Dairies-13
80Canucks Team Issue-13
80O-Pee-Chee-177
80Pepsi-Cola Caps-111
80Topps-177
82Canucks Team Issue-13
82O-Pee-Chee-349
82Post Cereal-19
82Swedish Semic VM Stickers-144
83North Stars Postcards-13
83O-Pee-Chee-354
84Swedish Semic Elitserien-172
85Swedish Panini Stickers-162
86Swedish Panini Stickers-168
87Swedish Panini Stickers-175

Lindgren, Lennart
69Swedish Hockey-175

Lindgren, Mats
91Swedish Semic Elitserien Stickers-328
93Parkhurst-511
93Parkhurst-534
Emerald Ice-511
Emerald Ice-534
93Upper Deck-570
93Swedish Semic Elitserien-89
93Classic-139
93Classic Four-Sport *-198
Gold-198
94Swedish Leaf-63
94Swedish Leaf-NNO2
94Classic-108
Gold-108
Tri-Cards-T22
95Swedish Globe World Championships-63
95Swedish World Championships Stickers-153
96Flair-109
Blue Ice-109
96Oilers Postcards-14
97Be A Player-154
Autographs-154
Autographs Die-Cuts-154
Autographs Prismatic Die-Cuts-154
97Pacific-190
Copper-190
Emerald Green-190
Ice Blue-190
Red-190
Silver-190
97Panini Stickers-213
97Panini Stickers-251
97Upper Deck-68
98Pacific-212
Ice Blue-212
Red-212
98Panini Stickers-193
99BAP Memorabilia-205
Gold-205
Silver-205
99O-Pee-Chee-221
99O-Pee-Chee Chrome-221
99O-Pee-Chee Chrome Refractors-221
99Pacific-259
Copper-259
Emerald Green-259
Gold-259
Ice Blue-259
Premiere Date-259
Red-259
99Panini Stickers-90
99Paramount-144
Copper-144
Emerald-144
Gold-144
Holographic Emerald-144
Holographic Gold-144
Holographic Silver-144
Ice Blue-144
Premiere Date-144
Red-144
Silver-144
99Revolution-92
Premiere Date-92
Red-92
Shadow Series-92
99Stadium Club-42
First Day Issue-42
One of a Kind-42
Printing Plates Black-42
Printing Plates Cyan-42
Printing Plates Magenta-42
Printing Plates Yellow-42
99Topps/OPC-221
99Topps/OPC Chrome-221
Refractors-221
00BAP Memorabilia-125
Emerald-125
Ruby-125
Sapphire-125
Promos-125
00BAP Mem Chicago Sportsfest Copper-125
00BAP Memorabilia Chicago Sportsfest Blue-125
00BAP Memorabilia Chicago Sportsfest Gold-125
00BAP Memorabilia Chicago Sportsfest Ruby-125
00BAP Memorabilia Chicago Sun-Times Ruby-125
00BAP Memorabilia Chicago Sun-Times Gold-125
00BAP Mem Chicago Sun-Times Sapphire-125
00BAP Mem Toronto Fall Expo Copper-125
00BAP Memorabilia Toronto Fall Expo Gold-125
00BAP Memorabilia Toronto Fall Expo Ruby-125
00Panini Stickers-55
00Private Stock Game Gear-71
00Private Stock Game Gear Patches-71
01Crown Royale Triple Threads-14
01Titanium Draft Day Edition-56
01Vanguard Memorabilia-36
03Canucks Postcards-15

Lindgren, Niclas
84Swedish Semic Elitserien-236
85Swedish Panini Stickers-235
86Swedish Panini Stickers-262
87Swedish Panini Stickers-248

Lindgren, Perttu
05Finnish Cardset -218
06Finnish Cardset-45
Playmakers Rookies-1
Playmakers Rookies Gold-1
Playmakers Rookies Silver-1
Signature Sensations-8
Trophy Winners-2
06Finnish Ilves Team Set-16

Lindgren, Peter
84Swedish Semic Elitserien-128
85Swedish Panini Stickers-75

Lindgren, Terry
93Red Deer Rebels-12
95Red Deer Rebels-10
96Louisville Riverfrogs-8
97Louisville Riverfrogs-5
98ECHL All-Star Southern Conference-2
99Florida Everblades-13
00Florida Everblades-15
01Florida Everblades-5
02Florida Everblades-24
03Florida Everblades-13

Lindgren, Tommie
67Swedish Hockey-67
72Swedish Stickers-227
73Swedish Stickers-230

Lindgren, Tore
89Swedish Semic Elitserien Stickers-244
90Swedish Semic Elitserien Stickers-157
91Swedish Semic Elitserien Stickers-261

Lindgren, Viktor
06Swedish SHL Elitset-223

Lindh, Fredrik
92Swedish Semic Elitserien Stickers-355
94Swedish Leaf-201
99Odessa Jackalopes-4

Lindh, Mats
72Finnish Hellas-35
72Swedish Stickers-16
72Swedish Stickers-296
73Swedish Stickers-153
74Swedish Stickers-242
74Swedish Semic World Champ Stickers-25

Lindh, Patrik
89Swedish Semic Elitserien Stickers-238

Lindh, Rune
67Swedish Hockey-36

Lindholm, Christopher
03Swedish Elite-206
Silver-206

Lindholm, Jan
83Swedish Semic Elitserien-31
84Swedish Semic Elitserien-30
85Swedish Panini Stickers-28

Lindholm, Mikael
86Swedish Panini Stickers-51
89Kings Smokey-3
90ProCards AHL/IHL-351
91Swedish Semic Elitserien Stickers-40
92Swedish Semic Elitserien Stickers-73
95Swedish Leaf-248
95Swedish Upper Deck-124
98Swedish UD Choice-160
99Swedish Upper Deck-163

Lindholm, Ulf
65Finnish Hellas-139

Lindkvist, Gunnar
71Swedish Hockey-86

Lindkvist, Lennart
67Swedish Hockey-207

Lindlof, Joni
03Kelowna Rockets-13
04Finnish Cardset-225

Lindman, Martin
99German DEL-146
00German Berlin Polar Bears Postcards-15
00German DEL-72
01German Berlin Polar Bears Postcards-14
02Swedish SHL-262
Parallel-262
04Swedish Elitset-36
Gold-36
04Swedish Malmo Red Hawks-1
05German DEL-8
06Swedish SHL Elitset-8

Lindman, Mikael
86Swedish Panini Stickers-225
89Swedish Semic Elitserien Stickers-33
90Swedish Semic Elitserien Stickers-180
91Swedish Semic Elitserien Stickers-34
92Swedish Semic Elitserien Stickers-54
93Swedish Semic Elitserien-29
94Swedish Leaf-37
95Swedish Leaf-178
95Swedish Upper Deck-21
96Swedish Brynas Tigers-5
98Swedish UD Choice-106
99Swedish Upper Deck-91
00Swedish Upper Deck-96

Lindmark, Orjan
84Swedish Semic Elitserien-157
85Swedish Panini Stickers-139
86Swedish Panini Stickers-147
87Swedish Panini Stickers-153
89Swedish Semic Elitserien Stickers-130
90Swedish Semic Elitserien Stickers-208
91Swedish Semic Elitserien Stickers-136
92Swedish Semic Elitserien Stickers-159
93Swedish Semic Elitserien-129
94Swedish Leaf-124
95Swedish Leaf-64
95Swedish Upper Deck-98
98German DEL-52
99German DEL-193
01German Upper Deck-128
02German DEL City Press-177
03German DEL-157
05Swedish SHL Elitset-64
Series Two Signatures-15

Lindmark, Pekka
04Swedish Alfabilder Alfa Stars-54
04Swedish Alfabilder Alfa Star Golden Ice-5
04Swedish Alfabilder Proof Parallels-54

Lindmark, Peter
82Swedish Semic VM Stickers-1
83Swedish Semic VM Stickers-1
84Swedish Semic Elitserien-99
85Swedish Panini Stickers-91
85Swedish Panini Stickers-115
85Swedish Panini Stickers-116
86Swedish Panini Stickers-84
87Swedish Panini Stickers-89
89Swedish Semic World Champ Stickers-3
90Swedish Semic Elitserien Stickers-125
91Finnish Semic World Champ Stickers-27
91Swedish Semic Elitserien Stickers-176
91Swedish Semic Elitserien Stickers-337
91Swedish Semic World Champ Stickers-27
92Swedish Semic Elitserien Stickers-199
93Swedish Semic Elitserien-170
94Swedish Leaf-75
Clean Sweepers-1
95Swedish Leaf-257
Champs-4
97Swedish Alfabilder Autographs-18
01Swedish Alfabilder-18

Lindolf, Joni
02Kelowna Rockets-9
03Kelowna Rockets Memorial Cup-11

Lindquist, Magnus
02Swedish SHL-249
02Swedish SHL-292
Masks-7
Parallel-249
Parallel-292
03Swedish Elite-111
Silver-111
04Swedish Elitset-109
Gold-109
05Swedish SHL Elitset-118
Gold-118
06Swedish SHL Elitset Goal Patrol-17

Lindqvist, Fredrik
92Swedish Semic Elitserien Stickers-72
91Classic-44
91Ultimate Draft-39
91Classic Four-Sport *-44
Autographs-44A
92Swedish Semic Elitserien Stickers-97
93Swedish Semic Elitserien-70
94Swedish Leaf-86
95Swedish Leaf-189
Goldies-3
95Swedish Upper Deck Ticket North America-NA7
97Swedish Collector's Choice-45
98Bowman's Best-122
Refractors-122
Atomic Refractors-122
Mirror Image Fusion-F4
Mirror Image Fusion Refractors-F4
Mirror Image Fusion Atomic Refractors-F4
98Upper Deck-270
Exclusives-270
Exclusives 1 of 1-270
Gold Reserve-270
99Upper Deck MVP-83
Gold Script-83
Silver Script-83
Super Script-83
99Upper Deck Victory-115
99Swiss Panini Stickers-68
00Swedish Upper Deck-146
00Swedish Upper Deck-205
00Swedish Upper Deck-218
SHL Signatures-FL
Top Draws-T9
02Swedish SHL-164
Parallel-164
Signatures Series II-17
03Swedish Elite-21
Silver-21

Lindqvist, Kenneth
88Swedish Panini Stickers-258

Lindqvist, Magnus
97Swedish Collector's Choice-166

Lindqvist, Robin
06Swedish Lulea Hockey Postcards-19
06Swedish SHL Elitset Rookies-6
06Swedish SHL Elitset-94

Lindqvist, Roger
69Swedish Hockey-120
70Swedish Hockey-77
71Swedish Hockey-167
73Swedish Stickers-50

Lindqvist, Sten

57Swedish Alfabilder-126

Lindroos, Jari

91Finnish Jyvas-Hyva Stickers-26
92Finnish Jyvas-Hyva Stickers-74
93Finnish Jyvas-Hyva Stickers-137
93Finnish SISU-154
93Finnish SISU Promos-NNO
94Finnish SISU-25
94Finnish SISU-374
95Finnish SISU-186
95Finnish SISU-252
95Finnish SISU Limited-50
96Finnish SISU Redline-51
Mighty Adversaries-9
96Finnish SISU Redline Promos-4
98Finnish Kerailysarja 90's Top 12-6

Lindros, Brett

93Alberta International Team Canada-11
93OPC Premier Team Canada-1
93Pinnacle-NNO
93Pinnacle-NNO
93PowerPlay-486
93Ultra-466
93Kingston Frontenacs-23
94Be A Player-R153
94Finest-9
Super Team Winners-9
Refractors-9
Bowman's Best-R10
Bowman's Best Refractors-R10
94Flair-104
94Fleer-125
Rookie Sensations-7
94Leaf-445
Phenoms-2
94Leaf Limited-50
94McDonald's Upper Deck-McD34
94OPC Premier-384
94OPC Premier-514
Special Effects-384
Special Effects-514
94Parkhurst SE-SE109
Gold-SE109
Vintage-36
94Pinnacle-257
94Pinnacle-478
Artist's Proofs-257
Artist's Proofs-478
Rink Collection-257
Rink Collection-478
Rookie Team Pinnacle-11
94Score Team Canada-CT24
94Score Top Rookie Redemption-3
94Select-178
Gold-178
Youth Explosion-YE12
94SP-70
Die Cuts-70
Premier-10
Premier Die-Cuts-10
94Topps/OPC Premier-384
94Topps/OPC Premier-514
Special Effects-384
Special Effects-514
94Ultra-327
Prospects-5
94Upper Deck-240
94Upper Deck-537
94Upper Deck-551
Electric Ice-240
Electric Ice-537
Electric Ice-551
Predictor Canadian-C7
94Upper Deck Predictor Canadian Exch Gold-C7
94Upper Deck Predictor Cdn Exch Silver-C7
94Upper Deck SP Inserts-SP136
94Upper Deck SP Inserts Die Cuts-SP136
94Finnish Jaa Kiekko-106
94Classic Pro Prospects-204
International Heroes-LP17
95Canada Games NHL POGS-171
95Collector's Choice-129
Player's Club-129
Player's Club Platinum-129
95Donruss-174
95Emotion-105
95Leaf-15
95Leaf Limited-86
95McDonald's Pinnacle-MCD-33
95Panini Stickers-94
95Parkhurst International-133
Emerald Ice-133
95Pinnacle Full Contact-7
95Playoff One on One-63
95Playoff One on One-171
95Pro Magnets-56
95Score-14
Black Ice Artist's Proofs-14
Black Ice-14
Check It-3
95Select Certified-61
Mirror Gold-61
95SkyBox Impact-102
NHL On Fox-12
95Stadium Club-108
Members Only Master Set-108
95Summit-104
Artist's Proofs-104
Ice-104
95Topps-41
OPC Inserts-41
95Ultra-95
95Ultra-267
Gold Medallion-95
95Upper Deck-82
95Upper Deck-257
Electric Ice-82
Electric Ice-257
Electric Ice Gold-82
Electric Ice Gold-257
Special Edition-SE54
Special Edition Gold-SE54
95Zenith-84
95Finnish Semic World Championships-101
96NHL Pro Stamps-56

Lindros, Eric

89Oshawa Generals-31
89Oshawa Generals 7th Inning Sketch-1
897th Inn. Sketch OHL-1
897th Inn. Sketch OHL-188
897th Inn. Sketch OHL-195
897th Inn. Sketch OHL-196
90Score-330C
90Score-440A
90Score-440C
90Score-B1
90Score-B2
90Score-B3
90Score-B4
90Score-B5
Canadian-330C
Canadian-440A
Canadian-440C
Canadian-B1
Canadian-B2
Canadian-B3
Canadian-B4
Canadian-B5
90Score Rookie/Traded-88T
90Score Young Superstars-40
90Upper Deck-451
90Upper Deck-473
French-473
907th Inn. Sketch OHL-1
907th Inn. Sketch Memorial Cup-88
907th Inn. Sketch Memorial Cup-99
91Pinnacle-365
French-365
91Score American-354
91Score American-355
91Score American-356
91Score Canadian Bilingual-329
91Score Canadian Bilingual-330
91Score Canadian Bilingual-384
91Score Canadian Bilingual-385
91Score Canadian English-329
91Score Canadian English-330
91Score Canadian English-384
91Score Canadian English-385
91Score Eric Lindros-1
91Score Eric Lindros-2
91Score Eric Lindros-3
91Score Hot Cards-1
91Score Rookie/Traded-88T
91Score Young Superstars-30
91Upper Deck-7
91Upper Deck-9
French-7
French-9
91Oshawa Generals-21
91Oshawa Generals Sheet-15
917th Inn. Sketch CHL Award Winners-1
917th Inn. Sketch CHL Award Winners-8
917th Inn. Sketch CHL Award Winners-10
917th Inn. Sketch Memorial Cup-96
917th Inn. Sketch Memorial Cup-119
91Classic-1
91Classic Promos-1
91Classic Four-Sport *-1
92Bowman-442
92Flyers J.C. Penney-15
92Flyers Upper Deck Sheets-11
92Flyers Upper Deck Sheets-31
92Flyers Upper Deck Sheets-42
92Jofa/Koho-4
92OPC Premier-102
Top Rookies-1
92Panini Stickers-P
92Panini Stickers French-P
92Parkhurst-128
Emerald Ice-128
Cherry Picks-CP6
92Pinnacle American Promo Panel-1
92Pinnacle-88
92Pinnacle-236
French-88
French-236
Team 2000-1
Team 2000 French-1
Team Pinnacle-5
Team French-5
Eric Lindros-1
Eric Lindros-2
Eric Lindros-3
Eric Lindros-4
Eric Lindros-5
Eric Lindros-6
Eric Lindros-7
Eric Lindros-8
Eric Lindros-9
Eric Lindros-10
Eric Lindros-11
Eric Lindros-12
Eric Lindros-13
Eric Lindros-14
Eric Lindros-15
Eric Lindros-16
Eric Lindros-17
Eric Lindros-18
Eric Lindros-19
Eric Lindros-20
Eric Lindros-21
Eric Lindros-22
Eric Lindros-23
Eric Lindros-24
Eric Lindros-25
Eric Lindros-26
Eric Lindros-27
Eric Lindros-28
Eric Lindros-29
Eric Lindros-30
92Pro Set-236
92Score-432
92Score-550
92Score-NNO
Canadian-432
Canadian-550
Canadian Olympians-1
Young Superstars-1
92Seasons Patches-38
92Sports Illustrated for Kids II-135
92Sports Illustrated for Kids II-399
92Sports Illustrated for Kids II-623
92Sports Illustrated for Kids II-794
92Stadium Club Members Only-47
92Stadium Club-501
92Topps-529
Gold-529G
92Ultra-157
92Upper Deck-88
92Upper Deck-470
Calder Candidates-CC6
Gordie Howe Selects-G14
World Junior Grads-WG12
92Finnish Semic-88
93SLU Hockey Canadian-7
93SLU Hockey American-8
93Donruss-242
Elite Inserts-4
Ice Kings-9
Special Print-Q
93Flyers J.C. Penney-13
93Flyers Lineup Sheets-21
93Flyers Lineup Sheets-22
93Flyers Lineup Sheets-23
93Flyers Lineup Sheets-41
93Flyers Lineup Sheets-42
93Kenner Starting Lineup Cards-8
93Kraft-15
93Kraft-57
93Leaf-233
Gold Rookies-3
Hat Trick Artists-7
Studio Signature-10
93OPC Premier-121
93OPC Premier-310
Gold-121
Gold-310
Black Gold-12
93Panini Stickers-144
93Panini Stickers-E
93Parkhurst-236
93Parkhurst-416
Emerald Ice-236
Emerald Ice-416
Cherry's Playoff Heroes-D15
East/West Stars-E1
First Overall-F3
USA/Canada Gold-G3
93Pinnacle Power-1
93Pinnacle I Samples-4
93Pinnacle-1
93Pinnacle-AU2
93Pinnacle-NNO
93Pinnacle-NNO
93Pinnacle-NNO
Canadian-1
Canadian-AU2
Team Pinnacle-11
Team Canadian-11
Team 2001-1
Team 2001 Canadian-1
93PowerPlay-183
Gamebreakers-6
Second Year Stars-5
93Score Samples-1
93Score-1
93Score-NNO
Canadian-1
Canadian-NNO
Canadian Gold-NNO
Dream Team-12
Dynamic Duos U.S.-1
Franchise-15
93Seasons Patches-10
93Stadium Club-10
Members Only Master Set-10
OPC-10
First Day Issue-10
First Day Issue OPC-10
Master Photos-5
Master Photos Winners-5
93Topps/OPC Premier-121
93Topps/OPC Premier-310
Gold-121
Gold-310
93Topps Premier Black Gold-13
93Topps Premier Black Gold-B
93Topps Premier Finest-3
93Ultra-161
93Ultra-249
Premier Pivots-5
93Upper Deck-30
93Upper Deck-280
Future Heroes-31
NHL's Best-HB8
NHLPA/Roots-23
Program of Excellence-E12
Silver Skates-H3
Silver Skates Gold-H3
SP-116
93Upper Deck Locker All-Stars-56
93Swedish Semic World Champ Stickers-201
93Fax Pax World of Sport*-27
94Hockey Canadian-7
94SLU Hockey Canadian-7
94SLU Hockey American-12
94Be A Player-R106
94Be A Player-R178
Up Close and Personal-UC2
94Canada Games NHL POGS-358
94Donruss-137
Dominators-1
Elite Inserts-7
Ice Masters-6
94EA Sports-99
94Finest-38
Super Team Winners-38
Refractors-38
Bowman's Best-B16
Bowman's Best Refractors-B16
Division's Clear Cut-8
94Flair-129
Center Spotlight-7
Scoring Power-6
94Fleer-157
Headliners-6
94Hockey Wit-88
94Kenner Starting Lineup Cards-13
94Kraft-21
94Leaf-415
Fire on Ice-6
Gold Stars-11
Limited Inserts-17
94Leaf Limited-58
Gold-4
94McDonald's Upper Deck-McD9
94NHLPA Phone Cards-4
94OPC Premier-241
94OPC Premier-400
Special Effects-241
Special Effects-400
94Parkhurst-301
Gold-301
Crash the Game Green-17
Crash the Game Blue-17
Crash the Game Gold-17
Crash the Game Red-17
Vintage-V69
94Parkhurst SE-SE131
Gold-SE131
94Pinnacle I Hobby Samples-1
94Pinnacle-1
Artist's Proofs-1
Rink Collection-1
Boomers-BR16
Gamers-GR16
Team Pinnacle-TP8
Team Dufex Parallel-TP8
World Edition-WE14
94Post Box Backs-15
94Score Samples-1
94Score-1
Gold-1
Platinum-1
Check It-CI1
Dream Team-DT19
Franchise-TF17
90 Plus Club-12
94Select-100
Gold-100
First Line-FL5
94SP-84
Die Cuts-84
Premier-30
Premier Die-Cuts-30
94Stadium Club Members Only-28
94Stadium Club-88
94Stadium Club-203
Members Only Master Set-88
Members Only Master Set-203
First Day Issue-88
First Day Issue-203
Dynasty and Destiny-2
Dynasty and Destiny Members Only-2
Super Teams-17
Super Teams Members Only Master Set-17
Super Team Winner Cards-88
Super Team Winner Cards-203
94Topps/OPC Premier-241
94Topps/OPC Premier-400
Special Effects-241
Special Effects-400
94Topps Finest Inserts-12
94Topps/OPC Premier The Go To Guy-10
94Topps Finest Bronze-2
94Ultra-345
All-Stars-3
Power-5
Premier Pivots-6
Scoring Kings-6
94Upper Deck-98
Electric Ice-98
Predictor Canadian-C23
94Upper Deck Predictor Canadian Exch Gold-C23
94Upper Deck Predictor Hobby-H8
94Upper Deck Predictor Hobby-H23
94Upper Deck Predictor Hobby Exch Gold-H8
94Upper Deck Predictor Hobby Exch Gold-H23
94Upper Deck Predictor Hobby Exch Silver-H8
94Upper Deck Predictor Hobby Exch Silver-H23
94Upper Deck Predictor Retail-R9
94Upper Deck Predictor Retail-R28
94Upper Deck Predictor Retail Exchange-R9
94Upper Deck Predictor Retail Exchange-R28
94Upper Deck SP Inserts-SP149
94Upper Deck SP Inserts Die Cuts-SP149
94Upper Deck NHLPA/Be A Player-29
94Finnish Jaa Kiekko-88
94Finnish Jaa Kiekko-360
94Swedish Olympics Lillehammer*-314
95Bashan Super Stickers-90
Die-Cut-17
95Be A Player Lethal Lines-LL14
95Bowman-71
All-Foil-71
Bowman's Best-BB3
Bowman's Best Refractors-BB3
95Canada Games NHL POGS-9
95Canada Games NHL POGS-201
95Collector's Choice-57
95Collector's Choice-377
95Collector's Choice-388
Player's Club-57
Player's Club-377
Player's Club-388
Player's Club Platinum-57
Player's Club Platinum-377
Player's Club Platinum-388
Crash The Game-C4A
Crash The Game-C4B
Crash The Game-C4C
Crash The Game Gold-C4A
Crash The Game Gold-C4B
Crash The Game Gold-C4C
Crash the Game Silver Redeemed-C4
Crash the Game Silver Bonus-C4
Crash the Game Gold Redeemed-C4
Crash the Game Gold Bonus-C4
95Donruss-1
Dominators-1
Elite Inserts-8
Marksmen-3
Pro Pointers-13
95Donruss Elite-88
95Donruss Elite-110
Die Cut Stars-88
Die Cut Stars-88U
Die Cut Stars-110
Die Cut Uncut-88
Die Cut Uncut-88U
Die Cut Uncut-110
Cutting Edge-1
Lemieux/Lindros Series-1E
Lemieux/Lindros Series-2E
Lemieux/Lindros Series-3E
Lemieux/Lindros Series-4E
Lemieux/Lindros Series-5E
Lemieux/Lindros Series-6E
Lemieux/Lindros Series-7E
95Emotion-133
Ntense Power-4
Xcel-6
95Finest-1
95Finest-88
Refractors-1
Refractors-88
95Hoyle Eastern Playing Cards-1
95Imperial Stickers-90
Die Cut Superstars-17
95Kraft-41
95Kraft-72
95Leaf-82
Fire On Ice-2
Gold Stars-4
Road To The Cup-4
95Leaf Limited-99
Stars of the Game-2
95McDonald's Pinnacle-MCD-2
95Metal-112
Iron Warriors-7
Winners-4
95NHL Aces Playing Cards-1H
95NHL Cool Trade-9
95NHL Cool Trade-RP9
95Panini Stickers-113
95Panini Stickers-146
95Parkhurst International-154
Emerald Ice-154
Crown Collection Silver Series 1-1
Crown Collection Gold Series 1-1
Crown Collection Silver Series 2-11
Crown Collection Gold Series 2-11
Parkie's Trophy Picks-PP1
Parkie's Trophy Picks-PP10
Trophy Winners-1
95Pinnacle-9
Artist's Proofs-9
Rink Collection-9
Clear Shots-4
Roaring 20s-1
95Pinnacle FANtasy-27
95Playoff One on One-76
95Playoff One on One-182
95Playoff One on One-294
95Post Upper Deck-6
95Pro Magnets-54
95Score-150
Black Ice Artist's Proofs-150
Black Ice-150
Check It-1
Dream Team-3
Lamplighters-15
95Select Certified-15
Mirror Gold-15
Gold Team-1
95SkyBox Impact-127
Countdown to Impact-1
Ice Quake-4
95SP-106
Holoviews-FX16
Holoviews Special FX-FX16
Stars/Etoiles-E21
Stars/Etoiles Gold-E21
95Stadium Club Members Only-15
95Stadium Club-181
Members Only Master Set-181
Nemeses-N1
Nemeses Members Only Master Set-N1
Power Streak-PS2
Power Streak Members Only Master Set-PS2
95Summit-19
Artist's Proofs-19
Ice-19
GM's Choice-5
Mad Hatters-1
95Topps-1
95Topps-327
OPC Inserts-1
OPC Inserts-327
Home Grown Canada-HGC6
Marquee Men Power Boosters-1
Mystery Finest-M4
Mystery Finest Refractors-M4
Power Lines-1PL
Profiles-PF7
95Topps SuperSkills-40
Platinum-40
95Ultra-119
95Ultra-392
Gold Medallion-119
Crease Crashers-8
Premier Pivots-4
Premier Pivots Gold Medallion-4
Red Light Specials-6
Red Light Specials Gold Medallion-6
Ultraview-7
Ultraview Hot Pack-7
95Upper Deck-374
Electric Ice-374
Electric Ice Gold-374
95Upper Deck All-Star Game Predictors-18
Redemption Winners-18
95Upper Deck Freeze Frame-F3
95Upper Deck Freeze Frame Jumbo-F3
95Upper Deck NHL All-Stars-AS17
95Upper Deck NHL All-Stars Jumbo-AS17
95Upper Deck Predictor Hobby-H1
95Upper Deck Predictor Hobby Exchange-H1
95Upper Deck Predictor Retail-R2
95Upper Deck Predictor Retail-R21
95Upper Deck Predictor Retail-R33
95Upper Deck Predictor Retail-R52
95Upper Deck Predictor Retail Exchange-R2
95Upper Deck Predictor Retail Exchange-R21
95Upper Deck Predictor Retail Exchange-R33
95Upper Deck Predictor Retail Exchange-R52
95Upper Deck Special Edition-SE148
95Upper Deck Special Edition Gold-SE148
95Zenith-6
Z-Team-7
95Finnish Semic World Championships-94
95Swedish Globe World Championships-88
95Swedish Globe World Championships-262
95Swedish Globe World Championships-263
95Swedish Globe World Championships-264
95Swedish World Championships Stickers-278
96SLU Hockey Canadian-8
96SLU Hockey American-12
96Headliners Hockey-12A
96Headliners Hockey-12B
96Be A Player Biscuit In The Basket-3
96Be A Player Lindros Die Cut-1
96Be A Player Lindros Die Cut-2
96Be A Player Link to History-7B
96Be A Player Link to History Autographs-7B
96Be A Player Link to History Auto Silver-7B
96Black Diamond-157
Gold-157
Run for the Cup-RC20
96Collector's Choice-188
96Collector's Choice-291
96Collector's Choice-335
Stick'Ums-S9
Crash the Game-C28A
Crash the Game-C28B
Crash the Game-C28C
Crash the Game Gold-C28A
Crash the Game Gold-C28B
Crash the Game Gold-C28C
Crash the Game Exchange-CR28
Crash the Game Exchange Gold-CR28
96Donruss-137
Press Proofs-137
Dominators-5
Elite Inserts-9
Elite Inserts Gold-9
Go Top Shelf-9
Hit List-1
Hit List-P1
96Donruss Canadian Ice-7
Gold Press Proofs-7
Red Press Proofs-7
O Canada-11
96Donruss Elite-7
96Donruss Elite-149
Die Cut Stars-7
Die Cut Stars-149
Hart to Hart-*1
Hart to Hart-*2
Hart to Hart-*3
Hart to Hart-*4
Hart to Hart-*5
Hart to Hart-*6
Hart to Hart-1AU
Hart to Hart-2AU
Hart to Hart-3AU
Hart to Hart-4AU
Hart to Hart-5AU
Hart to Hart-6AU
Hart to Hart-NNO
Status-8
96Duracell All-Cherry Team-DC6
96Flair-70
Blue Ice-70
Hot Numbers-8
Now And Then-3
96Fleer-82
Art Ross-14
Pearson-8
96Fleer Picks-4
Captain's Choice-1
Dream Lines-1
Fabulous 50-28
96Flyers Postcards-15
96Hockey Greats Coins-14
Gold-14
96Kenner Starting Lineup Cards-12
96Kraft Upper Deck-23
96Kraft Upper Deck-37
96Kraft Upper Deck-58
96Kraft Upper Deck-68
96Leaf-148
96Leaf-240
Press Proofs-148
Press Proofs-240
Fire On Ice-8
96Leaf Leather And Laces Promos-P10
96Leaf Leather And Laces-10
96Leaf Sweaters Away-3
96Leaf Sweaters Home-3
96Leaf The Best Of ...-3
96Leaf Limited-47
96Leaf Limited-NNO
Gold-47
96Leaf Limited Bash the Boards Promos-P1
96Leaf Limited Bash The Boards-1
96Leaf Limited Bash The Boards Ltd Ed-1
96Leaf Limited Stubble-2
96Leaf Preferred-117
Press Proofs-117
Steel-18
Steel-77
Steel Gold-18
Steel Power-12
Vanity Plates-7
Vanity Plates Gold-7
96Maggers-58
96McDonald's Pinnacle-25
96Metal Universe-114
Cool Steel-7
Cool Steel Super Power-7
Lethal Weapons-12
Lethal Weapons Super Power-12
96NHL Aces Playing Cards-31
96NHL Pro Stamps-54
96Pinnacle-107
Artist's Proofs-107
Foil-107
Premium Stock-107
Rink Collection-107
By The Numbers-14
By The Numbers Premium-14
Team Pinnacle-3
96Pinnacle Fantasy-FC3
96Pinnacle Mint-3
96Pinnacle Mint-P3A
96Pinnacle Mint-P3B
Bronze-3
Gold-3
Silver-3
Coins Brass-3
Coins Solid Gold-3
Coins Gold Plated-3
Coins Nickel-3
Coins Silver-3
96Playoff One on One-439
96Post Upper Deck-12
96Score-7
Artist's Proofs-7
Dealer's Choice Artist's Proofs-7
Special Artist's Proofs-7
Check It-1
Golden Blades-7
Dream Team-1
96Select Certified-1
Artist's Proofs-1
Blue-1
Mirror Blue-1
Mirror Gold-1
Mirror Red-1
Red-1
Cornerstones-1
96SkyBox Impact-97
Countdown to Impact-8
VersaTeam-8
96SP-114
Game Film-GF6
SPx Force-1
96SPx-33
Gold-33
96Stadium Club Members Only-30
96Summit-117
Artist's Proofs-117
Ice-117
Metal-117
Premium Stock-117
High Voltage-9
High Voltage-P16
High Voltage Mirage-9
Untouchables-6
96Team Out-16
96Topps Picks Fantasy Team-FT22
96Topps Picks Top Shelf-TS3
96Ultra-126
Gold Medallion-126
Clear the Ice-6
Mr. Momentum-7
96Upper Deck-306
Game Jerseys-GJ8
Hart Hopefuls Bronze-HH3
Hart Hopefuls Gold-HH3
Hart Hopefuls Silver-HH3
Lord Stanley's Heroes Finals-LS13
Lord Stanley's Heroes Quarterfinals-LS13
Lord Stanley's Heroes Semifinals-LS13
Superstar Showdown-SS3A
96Upper Deck Ice-113
Parallel-113
Stanley Cup Foundation-S10
Stanley Cup Foundation Dynasty-S10
96Zenith-61
Artist's Proofs-61
Assailants-8
Z-Team-1
96Swedish Semic Wien-88
97SLU Hockey One on One-3
97SLU Hockey Canadian-10
97SLU Hockey American-12
97Headliners Hockey-17
97NHL Pro Zone-40
97Be A Player-1
Autographs-1
Autographs Die-Cuts-1
Autographs Prismatic Die-Cuts-1
One Timers-3
Take A Number-10
97Beehive-1
97Beehive-P1
Golden Portraits-1
Team-8
Team Gold-8
97Black Diamond-145
Double Diamond-145
Triple Diamond-145
Quadruple Diamond-145
Premium Cut-PC13
Premium Cut Double Diamond-PC13
Premium Cut Quadruple Diamond Horiz-PC13
Premium Cut Triple Diamond-PC13
Premium Cut Quadruple Diamond Verticals-PC13
97Collector's Choice-186
Crash the Game-C20A
Crash the Game-C20B
Crash the Game-C20C
Crash the Game Exchange-CR20
Star Quest-SQ88
Stick'Ums-S10
World Domination-W7
97Crown Royale-99
Emerald Green-99
Ice Blue-99
Silver-99
Blades of Steel Die-Cuts-16
Cramer's Choice Jumbos-8
Cramer's Choice Jumbos Gold-8
Cramer's Choice Jumbos Signed-8
Hat Tricks Die-Cuts-19
Lamplighters Cel-Fusion Die-Cuts-14
97Donruss-3
Press Proofs Silver-3
Press Proofs Gold-3
Elite Inserts-3
Line 2 Line-8
Line 2 Line Die Cut-8
97Donruss Canadian Ice-3
Dominion Series-3
Provincial Series-3
National Pride-8
Stanley Cup Scrapbook-32
97Donruss Elite-10
97Donruss Elite-119
Aspirations-10
Aspirations-119
Status-10
Status-119
Back to the Future-1
Back to the Future Autographs-1
Craftsmen-2
Master Craftsmen-2
Prime Numbers-4A
Prime Numbers-4B
Prime Numbers-4C
Prime Numbers Die-Cuts-4A
Prime Numbers Die-Cuts-4B
Prime Numbers Die-Cuts-4C
97Donruss Limited-30
97Donruss Limited-50
97Donruss Limited-183
97Donruss Limited-P183
Exposure-30
Exposure-50
Exposure-183
Fabric of the Game-37
Fabric of the Game-55
97Donruss Preferred-5
97Donruss Preferred-180
Cut to the Chase-5
Cut to the Chase-180
Line of the Times-2A
97Donruss Preferred Line of Times Promos-2A
97Donruss Preferred Precious Metals-7
97Donruss Priority-2
97Donruss Priority-188
97Donruss Priority-NNO
97Donruss Priority-NNO
97Donruss Priority-NNO
Stamp of Approval-2
Stamp of Approval-188
Direct Deposit-16
Postcards-8
Postcards Opening Day Issues-2
Stamps-8
Stamps Bronze-8
Stamps Gold-8
Stamps Silver-8
97Esso Olympic Hockey Heroes-6
97Esso Olympic Hockey Heroes French-6
97Flyers Phone Cards-4
97Gatorade Stickers-2
97Highland Mint Mint-Cards Topps-17
97Highland Mint Mint-Cards Topps-18
97Highland Mint Mint-Coins-9
97Highland Mint Mint-Coins-10
97Jell-O Junior To Pros-3
97Katch-107
97Katch-158
Gold-107
Gold-158
Silver-107
Silver-158
97Kenner Starting Lineup Cards-12
97Kraft-6
97Kraft Team Canada-3
97Leaf-1
97Leaf-168
Fractal Matrix-1
Fractal Matrix-168
Fractal Matrix Die Cuts-1
Fractal Matrix Die Cuts-168
Banner Season-2
Fire On Ice-2
Lindros Collection-1
Lindros Collection-2
Lindros Collection-3
Lindros Collection-4
Lindros Collection-5
97Leaf International-1
Universal Ice-1
97McDonald's Team Canada Coins-9
97McDonald's Upper Deck-8
Game Film-4
97NHL Aces Playing Cards-7
97Pacific-88
Copper-88
Emerald Green-88
Ice Blue-88
Red-88
Silver-88
Card-Supials-15
Card-Supials Minis-15
Cramer's Choice-9
Gold Crown Die-Cuts-17
Slap Shots Die-Cuts-6B
Team Checklists-18
97Pacific Dynagon-91
97Pacific Dynagon-141
Copper-91
Copper-141
Dark Grey-91
Dark Grey-141
Emerald Green-91
Emerald Green-141
Ice Blue-91
Ice Blue-141
Red-91
Red-141
Silver-91
Silver-141
Best Kept Secrets-72
Dynamic Duos-11A
Kings of the NHL-8
Tandems-1
Tandems-20
97Pacific Invincible-102
Copper-102
Emerald Green-102
Ice Blue-102
Red-102
Silver-102
Attack Zone-18
Feature Performers-25
NHL Regime-145
NHL Regime-219
Off The Glass-14
97Pacific Omega-168
97Pacific Omega-248
Copper-168
Copper-248
Dark Gray-168
Dark Gray-248
Emerald Green-168
Emerald Green-248
Gold-168
Gold-248
Ice Blue-168
Ice Blue-248
Game Face-13
Silks-9
Stick Handle Laser Cuts-16
Team Leaders-16
97Panini Stickers-92
97Paramount-134
Copper-134
Dark Grey-134
Emerald Green-134
Ice Blue-134
Red-134
Silver-134
Big Numbers Die-Cuts-15
Canadian Greats-11
Photoengravings-15
97Pinnacle-48
Artist's Proofs-48
Rink Collection-48
Epix Game Emerald-13
Epix Game Orange-13
Epix Game Purple-13
Epix Moment Emerald-13
Epix Moment Orange-13
Epix Moment Purple-13
Epix Play Emerald-13
Epix Play Orange-13
Epix Play Purple-13
Epix Season Emerald-13
Epix Season Orange-13
Epix Season Purple-13
Press Plates Back Black-48
Press Plates Back Cyan-48
Press Plates Back Magenta-48
Press Plates Back Yellow-48
Press Plates Front Black-48
Press Plates Front Cyan-48
Press Plates Front Magenta-48
Press Plates Front Yellow-48
Team Pinnacle-5
Team Mirror-5
Team Parallel-5
Team Parallel Mirror-5
97Pinnacle Certified-31
Red-31
Mirror Blue-31
Mirror Gold-31
Mirror Red-31
Team-8
Gold Team Promo-8
Gold Team-8
97Pinnacle Inside-4
Coach's Collection-4
Executive Collection-4
Track-3
Cans-10
Cans Gold-10
97Pinnacle Mint-1
Bronze-1
Gold Team-1
Silver Team-1
Coins Brass-1

Coins Brass Proofs-1
Coins Gold Plated-1
Coins Gold Plated Proofs-1
Coins Nickel Silver-1
Coins Nickel Silver Proofs-1
Coins Solid Gold-1
Coins Solid Silver-1
Minternational-1
Minternational Coins-1
97Pinnacle Power Pack Blow-Ups-1
97Pinnacle Tot Cert Platinum Blue-31
97Pinnacle Tot Certi Platinum Gold-31
97Pinnacle Totally Certified Platinum Red-31
97Pinnacle Tot Cert Mirror Platinum Gold-31
97Post Pinnacle-1
97Revolution-103
Copper-103
Emerald-103
Ice Blue-103
Silver-103
1998 All-Star Game Die-Cuts-16
NHL Icons-8
Team Checklist Laser Cuts-18
97Score-88
97Score-265
Artist's Proofs-88
Golden Blades-88
Check It-1
97Score Flyers-3
Platinum-3
Premier-3
97SP Authentic-111
Icons-I7
Icons Die-Cuts-I7
Icons Embossed-I7
97SPx-36
Bronze-36
Gold-36
Silver-36
Steel-36
Dimension-SPX4
Grand Finale-36
97Studio-3
97Studio-108
97Studio-P3
Press Proofs Silver-3
Press Proofs Silver-108
Press Proofs Gold-3
Press Proofs Gold-108
Hard Hats-2
Portraits-3
Silhouettes-2
Silhouettes 8x10-2
97Upper Deck-331
Blow-Ups 3 x 5-2-8
Blow-Ups 5 x 7-3B
Game Dated Moments-331
Sixth Sense Masters-SS17
Sixth Sense Wizards-SS17
Smooth Grooves-SG48
The Specialists-6
The Specialists Level 2 Die Cuts-6
Three Star Selects-1A
97Upper Deck Crash the All-Star Game-13
97Upper Deck Crash the All-Star Game-AR13
97Upper Deck Diamond Vision-22
Signature Moves-22
97Upper Deck Ice-88
Parallel-88
Champions-IC3
Champions 2 Die Cuts-IC3
Lethal Lines-L2B
Lethal Lines 2-L2B
Power Shift-88
97Zenith-6
Z-Gold-6
Z-Silver-6
97Zenith 5 x 7-2
Gold Impulse-2
Silver Impulse-2
97Zenith Chasing The Cup-4
97Zenith Z-Team-4
97Zenith Z-Team 5x7-4
97Zenith Z-Team Gold-4
97Pinnacle Collector's Club Team Pinnacle-H3
98SLU Hockey One on One-2
98Pinnacle Team Pinnacle Collector's Club-4
98Headliners Hockey XL-5
98SLU Hockey-120
98Aurora-141
Atomic Laser Cuts-15
Championship Fever-36
Championship Fever Copper-36
Championship Fever Ice Blue-36
Championship Fever Red-36
Championship Fever Silver-36
Cubes-14
Front Line Copper-7
Front Line Ice Blue-7
Front Line Red-7
Man Advantage-15
NHL Command-9
98Be A Player-100
Press Release-100
98BAP Gold-100
98BAP Autographs-100
98BAP Autographs Gold-100
98BAP AS Game Used Stick Cards-S1
98BAP AS Game Used Jersey Cards-AS1
98BAP Playoff Game Used Jerseys-G4
98BAP Playoff Game Used Jersey Autographs-G4
98BAP Playoff Practice Used Jerseys-P10
98BAP Tampa Bay All Star Game-100
98Black Diamond-62
Double Diamond-62
Triple Diamond-62
Quadruple Diamond-62
Myriad-M14
Myriad 2-M14
Winning Formula Gold-WF21
Winning Formula Platinum-WF21
98Bowman's Best-42
Refractors-42
Atomic Refractors-42
Mirror Image Fusion-F5
Mirror Image Fusion Refractors-F5
Mirror Image Fusion Atomic Refractors-F5
Scotty Bowman's Best-SB5
Scotty Refractors-SB5
Scotty Atomic Refractors-SB5
98Crown Royale-100
Limited Series-100
Cramer's Choice Jumbos-9
Cramer's Choice Jumbos Dark Blue-9
Cramer's Choice Jumbos Green-9
Cramer's Choice Jumbos Red-9
Cramer's Choice Jumbos Light Blue-9
Cramer's Choice Jumbos Gold-9
Cramer's Choice Jumbos Purple-9
Living Legends-9
Master Performers-16
Pillars of the Game-18
98Donruss Elite Promos-19
98Finest-149
No Protectors-149
No Protectors Refractors-149
Refractors-149
Double Sided Mystery Finest-M3
Double Sided Mystery Finest-M6
Double Sided Mystery Finest-M8
Double Sided Mystery Finest-M10
Double Sided Mystery Refractors-M3
Double Sided Mystery Refractors-M6
Double Sided Mystery Refractors-M8
Double Sided Mystery Refractors-M10
Oversize-7
Oversize Refractors-7
Red Lighters-R11
Red Lighters Refractors-R11
98Jell-O Spoons-6
98Katch-157
98Kenner Starting Lineup Cards-20
98McDonald's Upper Deck-10
98OPC Chrome-18
Refractors-18
98Pacific-88
Ice Blue-88
Red-88
Cramer's Choice-8
Dynagon Ice Inserts-15
Titanium Ice-15
Gold Crown Die-Cuts-25
Team Checklists-19
Timelines-14
98Pacific Dynagon Ice-138
Blue-138
Red-138
Adrenaline Rush Bronze-9
Adrenaline Rush Ice Blue-9
Adrenaline Rush Red-9
Adrenaline Rush Silver-9
Forward Thinking-15
Preeminent Players-9
Team Checklists-19
98Pacific Omega-177
Red-177
Opening Day Issue-177
Championship Spotlight-8
Championship Spotlight Green-8
Championship Spotlight Red-8
Championship Spotlight Gold-8
EO Portraits-16
EO Portraits 1 of 1-16
Face to Face-10
Online-26
Planet Ice-29
Planet Ice Parallel-29
Prism-16
Toronto Spring Expo-177
98Panini Photocards-49
98Panini Photocards-104
98Panini Stickers-94
98Paramount-177
Copper-177
Emerald Green-177
Holo-Electric-177
Ice Blue-177
Silver-177
Hall of Fame Bound-8
Hall of Fame Bound Proofs-8
Ice Galaxy-9
Ice Galaxy Gold-9
Ice Galaxy Silver-9
Special Delivery Die-Cuts-14
Team Checklists Die-Cuts-19
98Post-8
98Revolution-106
Ice Shadow-106
Red-106
All-Star Die Cuts-18
Chalk Talk Laser-Cuts-14
NHL Icons-9
Showstoppers-26
Three Pronged Attack-6
Three Pronged Attack Parallel-6
98SP Authentic-61
Power Shift-61
Snapshots-SS9
Stat Masters-S6
98SPx Finite-100
98SPx Finite-152
98SPx Finite-172
Radiance-100
Radiance-152
Radiance-172
Spectrum-100
Spectrum-152
Spectrum-172
98SPx Top Prospects-43
Radiance-43
Spectrum-43
Highlight Heroes-H21
Lasting Impressions-L14
Premier Stars-PS8
Winning Materials-EL
98Topps-18
O-Pee-Chee-18
Ice Age 2000-I10
Local Legends-L9
Mystery Finest Bronze-M9
Mystery Finest Bronze Refractors-M9
Mystery Finest Gold-M9
Mystery Finest Gold Refractors-M9
Mystery Finest Silver-M9
Mystery Finest Silver Refractors-M9
98Topps Gold Label Class 1-13
Black-13
Black One of One-13
One of One-13
Red-13
Red One of One-13
98Topps Gold Label Class 2-13
98Topps Gold Label Class 2 Black-13
98Topps Gold Label Class 2 Black 1 of 1-13
98Topps Gold Label Class 2 One of One-13
98Topps Gold Label Class 2 Red-13
98Topps Gold Label Class 2 Red One of One-13
98Topps Gold Label Class 3-13
98Topps Gold Label Class 3 Black-13
98Topps Gold Label Class 3 Black 1 of 1-13
98Topps Gold Label Class 3 One of One-13
98Topps Gold Label Class 3 Red-13
98Topps Gold Label Class 3 Red One of One-13
98Topps Gold Label Goal Race '99-GR1
98Topps Gold Label Goal Race '99 Black-GR1
98Topps Gold Label Goal '99 Black 1 of 1-GR1
98Topps Gold Label Goal Race 99 1 of 1-GR1
98Topps Gold Label Goal Race '99 Red-GR1
98Topps Gold Label GoalRace 99 Red 1 of 1-GR1
98UD Choice-152
98UD Choice-237
Mini Bobbing Head-BH8
Prime Choice Reserve-152
Prime Choice Reserve-237
Reserve-152
Reserve-237
StarQuest Blue-SQ28
StarQuest Gold-SQ28
StarQuest Green-SQ28
StarQuest Red-SQ28
98UD3-37
98UD3-97
98UD3-157
Die-Cuts-37
Die-Cuts-97
Die-Cuts-157
98Upper Deck-333
Exclusives-333
Exclusives 1 of 1-333
Fantastic Finishers-FF11
Fantastic Finishers Quantum 1-FF11
Fantastic Finishers Quantum 2-FF11
Fantastic Finishers Quantum 3-FF11
Frozen In Time-FT9
Frozen In Time Quantum 1-FT9
Frozen In Time Quantum 2-FT9
Frozen In Time Quantum 3-FT9
Generation Next-GN10
Generation Next-GN11
Generation Next-GN12
Generation Next Quantum 1-GN10
Generation Next Quantum 1-GN11
Generation Next Quantum 1-GN12
Generation Next Quantum 2-GN10
Generation Next Quantum 2-GN11
Generation Next Quantum 2-GN12
Generation Next Quantum 3-GN10
Generation Next Quantum 3-GN11
Generation Next Quantum 3-GN12
Lord Stanley's Heroes-LS16
Lord Stanley's Heroes Quantum 1-LS16
Lord Stanley's Heroes Quantum 2-LS16
Lord Stanley's Heroes Quantum 3-LS16
Profiles-P4
Profiles Quantum 1-P4
Profiles Quantum 2-P4
Profiles Quantum 3-P4
Gold Reserve-333
98Upper Deck MVP-147
Gold Script-147
Silver Script-147
Super Script-147
Game Souvenirs-EL
OT Heroes-OT10
Power Game-PG3
Snipers-S7
Special Forces-F5
98Slovakian Eurotel-14
99SLU Hockey-12
99SLU Hockey Pro Action-40
99Aurora-106
Striped-106
Premiere Date-106
Premiere Date Striped-106
Canvas Creations-9
Championship Fever-17
Championship Fever Copper-17
Championship Fever Ice Blue-17
Championship Fever Silver-17
Complete Players-9
Complete Players Parallel-9
Complete Players Retail-9
Complete Players Retail Parallel-9
Styrotechs-15
99BAP Memorabilia-167
Gold-167
Silver-167
Jersey Cards-J1
Jersey Emblems-E1
Jersey Numbers-I1
Jersey and Stick Cards-S1
Selects Silver-SL7
Selects Gold-SL7
99BAP Update Double AS Jersey Cards-D2
99BAP Update Teammates Jersey Cards-TM7
99BAP Update Teammates Jersey Cards-TM18
99BAP Update Teammates Jersey Cards-TM29
99BAP Update Teammates Jersey Cards-TM49
99BAP Millennium-178
Emerald-178
Ruby-178
Sapphire-178
Signatures-178
Signatures Gold-178
Jerseys-J18
Jersey Autographs-J18
Jersey and Stick Cards-JS18
Jersey Emblems-E18
Jersey Numbers-N18
Pearson-P4
Pearson Autographs-P4
Players of the Decade-D6
Players of the Decade Autographs-D6
99Black Diamond-62
Diamond Cut-62
Final Cut-62
A Piece of History-EL
A Piece of History Double-EL
A Piece of History Triple-EL
Diamonation-D12
Diamond Might-DM3
Diamond Skills-DS6
Myriad-M9
99Crown Royale-103
Limited Series-103
Premiere Date-103
Card-Supials-16
Card-Supials Minis-16
Cramer's Choice Jumbos-9
Cramer's Choice Jumbos Dark Blue-9
Cramer's Choice Jumbos Gold-9
Cramer's Choice Jumbos Green-9
Cramer's Choice Jumbos Light Blue-9
Cramer's Choice Jumbos Purple-9
Cramer's Choice Jumbos Red-9
International Glory-18
International Glory Parallel-18
Team Captain Die-Cuts-5
99Hasbro Starting Lineup Cards-12
99Jell-O Partners of Power-3
99Kraft Dinner-7
99McDonald's Upper Deck-MCD2
99McDonald's Upper Deck-MCD2R
Game Jerseys-GJEL
99O-Pee-Chee-7
99O-Pee-Chee-282A
99O-Pee-Chee-282B
99O-Pee-Chee-282C
99O-Pee-Chee-282D
99O-Pee-Chee-282E
99O-Pee-Chee All-Topps-AT10
99O-Pee-Chee Chrome-7
99O-Pee-Chee Chrome-282A
99O-Pee-Chee Chrome-282B
99O-Pee-Chee Chrome-282C
99O-Pee-Chee Chrome-282D
99O-Pee-Chee Chrome-282E
99O-Pee-Chee Chrome All Topps-AT10
99O-Pee-Chee Chrome All-Topps Refractors-AT10
99O-Pee-Chee Chrome Ice Masters-IM3
99O-Pee-Chee Chrome Ice Masters Refractor-IM3
99O-Pee-Chee Chrome Refractors-7
99O-Pee-Chee Chrome Refractors-282A
99O-Pee-Chee Chrome Refractors-282B
99O-Pee-Chee Chrome Refractors-282C
99O-Pee-Chee Chrome Refractors-282D
99O-Pee-Chee Chrome Refractors-282E
99O-Pee-Chee Chrome A-Men-AM6
99O-Pee-Chee Chrome A-Men Refractors-AM6
99O-Pee-Chee Chrome Positive Performers-PP3
99OPC Chrome Pos Performers Ref-PP3
99O-Pee-Chee Ice Masters-IM3
99O-Pee-Chee A-Men-AM6
99O-Pee-Chee Positive Performers-PP3
99Oscar Mayer Lunchables-8
99Pacific-307
Copper-307
Emerald Green-307
Gold-307
Ice Blue-307
Premiere Date-307
Red-307
Center Ice-16
Center Ice Proofs-16
Cramer's Choice-8
Gold Crown Die-Cuts-26
Home and Away-9
Home and Away-19
Past and Present-17
Team Leaders-20
99Pacific Dynagon Ice-148
Blue-148
Copper-148
Gold-148
Premiere Date-148
2000 All-Star Preview-15
Checkmates American-3
Checkmates American-18
Checkmates Canadian-3
Lamplighter Net-Fusions-9
Lords of the Rink-9
99Pacific Omega-172
Copper-172
Gold-172
Ice Blue-172
Premiere Date-172
EO Portraits-13
EO Portraits 1/1-13
Game-Used Jerseys-7
NHL Generations-9
5 Star Talents-9
5 Star Talents Parallel-9
99Pacific Prism-103
Holographic Blue-103
Holographic Gold-103
Holographic Mirror-103
Holographic Purple-103
Premiere Date-103
Clear Advantage-16
Dial-a-Stats-8
Sno-Globe Die-Cuts-16
99Panini Stickers-121
99Panini Stickers-323
99Paramount-173
Copper-173
Emerald-173
Gold-173
Holographic Emerald-173
Holographic Gold-173
Holographic Silver-173
Ice Blue-173
Premiere Date-173
Red-173
Silver-173
Hall of Fame Bound-8
Hall of Fame Bound Proofs-8
Ice Advantage-16
Ice Advantage Proofs-16
Ice Alliance-20
Personal Best-26
Toronto Fall Expo '99-173
99Revolution-107
Premiere Date-107
Red-107
Shadow Series-107
Ice Sculptures-9
NHL Icons-14
Ornaments-15
Top of the Line-18
Copper-107
Gold-107
CSC Silver-107
99SP Authentic-63
Honor Roll-HR5
Special Forces-SF8
99SPx-108
Radiance-108
Spectrum-108
Highlight Heroes-HH9
SPXcitement-X9
SPXtreme-XT9
Starscape-S5
Winning Materials-WM9
99Stadium Club-13
First Day Issue-13
One of a Kind-13
Printing Plates Black-13
Printing Plates Cyan-13
Printing Plates Magenta-13
Printing Plates Yellow-13
Capture the Action-CA13
Capture the Action Game View-CAG13
Chrome-12
Chrome Refractors-12
Chrome Oversized-8
Chrome Oversized Refractors-8
Eyes of the Game-EG6
Eyes of the Game Refractors-EG6
Onyx Extreme-OE4
Onyx Extreme Die-Cut-OE4
99Topps/OPC-7
99Topps/OPC-282A
99Topps/OPC-282B
99Topps/OPC-282C
99Topps/OPC-282D
99Topps/OPC-282E
All-Topps-AT10
A-Men-AM6
Ice Masters-IM3
Positive Performers-PP3
99Topps/OPC Chrome-7
99Topps/OPC Chrome-282A
99Topps/OPC Chrome-282B
99Topps/OPC Chrome-282C
99Topps/OPC Chrome-282D
99Topps/OPC Chrome-282E
Refractors-7
Refractors-282A
Refractors-282B
Refractors-282C
Refractors-282D
Refractors-282E
All-Topps-AT10
All-Topps Refractors-AT10
A-Men-AM6
A-Men Refractors-AM6
Ice Masters-IM3
Ice Masters Refractors-IM3
Positive Performers-PP3
Positive Performers Refractors-PP3
99Topps Gold Label Class 1-12
Black-12
Black One of One-12
One of One-12
Red-12
Red One of One-12
99Topps Gold Label Class 2-12
99Topps Gold Label Class 2 Black-12
99Topps Gold Label Class 2 Black 1 of 1-12
99Topps Gold Label Class 2 One of One-12
99Topps Gold Label Class 2 Red-12
99Topps Gold Label Class 2 Red One of One-12
99Topps Gold Label Class 3-12
99Topps Gold Label Class 3 Black-12
99Topps Gold Label Class 3 Black 1 of 1-12
99Topps Gold Label Class 3 One of One-12
99Topps Gold Label Class 3 Red-12
99Topps Gold Label Class 3 Red One of One-12
99Topps Gold Label Quest for the Cup-QC3
99Topps Gold Label Quest for the Cup One of One -QC3
99Topps Gold Label Quest 4 the Cup Black-QC3
99Topps Gold Label Quest for the Cup Black One of One -QC3
99Topps Gold Label Quest for the Cup Red-QC3
99Topps Gold Label Quest for the Cup Red One of One -QC3
99Topps Premier Plus-80
Parallel-80
Premier Team-PT3
Premier Team Parallel-PT3
99Ultimate Victory-64
1/1-64
Parallel-64
Parallel 100-64
Frozen Fury-FF1
Smokin Guns-SG10
Stature-S9
UV Extra-UV8
99Upper Deck-94
99Upper Deck-137
Exclusives-94
Exclusives-137
Exclusives 1 of 1-94
Exclusives 1 of 1-137
All-Star Class-AS12
All-Star Class Quantum Gold-AS12
All-Star Class Quantum Silver-AS12
Crunch Time-CT18
Crunch Time Quantum Gold-CT18
Crunch Time Quantum Silver-CT18
Fantastic Finishers-FF3
Fantastic Finishers Quantum Gold-FF3
Fantastic Finishers Quantum Silver-FF3
Game Jerseys-EL
Game Jersey Patch-ELP
Game Jersey Patch 1 of 1-ELSP
Headed for the Hall-HOF7
Headed for the Hall Quantum Gold-HOF7
Headed for the Hall Quantum Silver-HOF7
Ice Gallery-IG7
Ice Gallery Quantum Gold-IG7
Ice Gallery Quantum Silver-IG7
Marquee Attractions-MA3
Marquee Attractions Quantum Gold-MA3
Marquee Attractions Quantum Silver-MA3
NHL Scrapbook-SB10
NHL Scrapbook Quantum Gold-SB10
NHL Scrapbook Quantum Silver-SB10
Sixth Sense-SS4
Sixth Sense Quantum Gold-SS4
Sixth Sense Quantum Silver-SS4
99Upper Deck Century Legends-61
Century Collection-61
Essence of the Game-E4
99Upper Deck Gold Reserve-94
99Upper Deck Gold Reserve-137
Game-Used Souvenirs-GREL
99Upper Deck HoloGrFx-43
Ausome-43
Impact Zone-IZ3
Impact Zone Ausome-IZ3
Pure Skill-PS8
Pure Skill Ausome-PS8
99Upper Deck MVP-146
Gold Script-146
Silver Script-146
Super Script-146
90's Snapshots-S4
Game-Used Souvenirs-GU9
Game-Used Souvenirs-GU23
Hands of Gold-H7
Talent-MVP4
99Upper Deck MVP SC Edition-131
Gold Script-131
Silver Script-131
Super Script-131
Game-Used Souvenirs-GUEL
Golden Memories-GM8
Great Combinations-GCLL
Great Combinations Parallel-GCLL
Playoff Heroes-PH8
Second Season Snipers-SS7
Stanley Cup Talent-SC12
99Upper Deck Ovation-41
99Upper Deck Ovation-85
Standing Ovation-41
Standing Ovation-85
Lead Performers-LP15
Superstar Theater-ST6
99Upper Deck PowerDeck-16
Auxiliary-16
Auxiliary 1 of 1-16
99Upper Deck Retro-57
Gold-57
Platinum-57
99Upper Deck Victory-210
99Upper Deck Victory-212
99Wayne Gretzky Hockey-122
Changing The Game-CG2
Elements of the Game-EG7
Great Heroes-GH7
Tools of Greatness-TGEL
00McFarlane Hockey-110
00Aurora-108
Premiere Date-108
Game-Worn Jerseys-9
Game-Worn Jersey Patches-9
00BAP Memorabilia-224
Emerald-224
Ruby-224
Sapphire-224
Promos-224
Jersey Cards-J16
Jersey Emblems-E16
Jersey Numbers-N16
Jersey and Stick Cards-JS16
00BAP Mem Chicago Sportsfest Copper-224
00BAP Memorabilia Chicago Sportsfest Blue-224
00BAP Memorabilia Chicago Sportsfest Gold-224
00BAP Memorabilia Chicago Sportsfest Ruby-224
00BAP Memorabilia Chicago Sun-Times Ruby-224
00BAP Memorabilia Chicago Sun-Times Gold-224
00BAP Mem Chicago Sun-Times Sapphire-224
00BAP Mem Toronto Fall Expo Copper-224
00BAP Memorabilia Toronto Fall Expo Gold-224
00BAP Memorabilia Toronto Fall Expo Ruby-224
00BAP Signature Series-246
Emerald-246
Ruby-246
Sapphire-246
Autographs-208
Autographs Gold-208
00BAP Ultimate Memorabilia Autographs-18
Gold-18
00BAP Ultimate Memorabilia Active Eight-AE4
00BAP Ultimate Memorabilia Hart Trophy-H6
00Black Diamond Game Gear-GEL
00Crown Royale-81
Ice Blue-81
Limited Series-81
Premiere Date-81
Red-81
Jewels of the Crown-20
00McDonald's Pacific-26
Blue-26
Dial-A-Stats-4
Game Jerseys-8
00O-Pee-Chee-197
00O-Pee-Chee Parallel-197
00Pacific-301
Copper-301
Gold-301
Ice Blue-301
Premiere Date-301
Gold Crown Die Cuts-24
Reflections-16
00Panini Stickers-75
00Paramount-183
Copper-183
Gold-183
Holo-Gold-183
Holo-Silver-183
Ice Blue-183
Premiere Date-183
Game Used Sticks-15
00Private Stock-74
Gold-74
Premiere Date-74
Retail-74
Silver-74
Extreme Action-16
Game Gear-84
Game Gear-85
Game Gear Patches-84
PS-2001 Action-43
PS-2001 Stars-20
Reserve-17
00Revolution-110
Blue-110
Premiere Date-110
Red-110
00SP Game Used Tools of the Game-EL
00SP Game Used Tools of the Game Excl-EL
00Stadium Club-97
Beam Team-BT29
00Titanium-71
Blue-71
Gold-71
Premiere Date-71
Red-71
Retail-71
00Topps/OPC-197
Parallel-197
NHL Draft-D2
00Topps Chrome-131
OPC Refractors-131
Refractors-131
00Topps Stars-41
Blue-41
00Upper Deck Game Jersey Patches-ELP
00Upper Deck Game Jersey Patch Autos Excl-ELP
00Upper Deck Number Crunchers-NC4
00Upper Deck Legends-98
Legendary Collection Bronze-98
Legendary Collection Gold-98
Legendary Collection Silver-98
00Upper Deck MVP-137
First Stars-137
Game-Used Souvenirs-GSEL
Second Stars-137
Super Game-Used Souvenirs-GSEL
Talent-M12
Third Stars-137
Top Draws-TD7
Top Playmakers-TP8
Valuable Commodities-VC8
00Upper Deck Victory-168
00Upper Deck Victory-315
00Vanguard-74
Cosmic Force-8
Dual Game-Worn Jerseys-3
Dual Game-Worn Patches-3
High Voltage-26
High Voltage Gold-26
High Voltage Green-26
High Voltage Red-26
High Voltage Silver-26
Holographic Gold-74
Holographic Purple-74
Pacific Proofs-74
Press East/West-17
00Czech Stadion-68
01McFarlane Hockey-85
01McFarlane Hockey-86
01Atomic-65
Blue-65
Gold-65
Premiere Date-65
Red-65
Blast-8
Power Play-23
Team Nucleus-10
01BAP Memorabilia-315
Emerald-315
Ruby-315
Sapphire-315
All-Star Jerseys-ASJ47
All-Star Emblems-ASE47
All-Star Numbers-ASN47
All-Star Jersey Doubles-DASJ21
All-Star Teammates-AST25
All-Star Teammates-AST34
All-Star Teammates-AST39
All-Star Teammates-AST47
Country of Origin-CO2
01BAP Signature Series Certified 100-C14
01BAP Signature Series Certified 50-C14
01BAP Signature Series Certified 1 of 1's-C14
01BAP Signature Series Franchise Jerseys-FP-19
01BAP Sig Series He Shoots/Scores Points-5
01BAP Sig Series He Shoots/Scores Prizes-10
01BAP Sig Series International Medals-IG-7
01BAP Signature Series Jerseys-GJ-38
01BAP Sig Series Jersey and Stick Cards-GSJ-38
01BAP Signature Series Emblems-GUE-36
01BAP Signature Series Numbers-ITN-36
01BAP Signature Series Teammates-TM-19
01BAP Ultimate Mem All-Star History-46
01BAP Ultimate Mem Complete Package-6
01BAP Ultimate Memorabilia Dynamic Duos-13
01BAP Ultimate Memorabilia Emblems-18
01BAP Ultimate Memorabilia Gloves Are Off-11
01BAP Ultimate Memorabilia Jerseys-18
01BAP Ultimate Mem Jerseys and Sticks-18
01BAP Ultimate Memorabilia Numbers-20
01BAP Ultimate Memorabilia Name Plates-10
01BAP Update He Shoots-He Scores Prizes-11
01BAP Update Travel Plans-TP10
01Bowman YoungStars-36
Gold-36
Ice Cubed-36
01Crown Royale-96
Blue-96
Premiere Date-96
Red-96
Retail-96
All-Star Honors-15
Crowning Achievement-18
Jewels of the Crown-21
Legendary Heroes-6
Triple Threads-11
01eTopps-30
01Pacific-290
Extreme LTD-290
Hobby LTD-290
Premiere Date-290
Retail LTD-290
Top Draft Picks-5
01Pacific Top Draft Picks Draft Day Promo-5
01Pacific Adrenaline-127
Blue-127
Premiere Date-127
Red-127
Retail-127
Blade Runners-8
Jerseys-28
World Beaters-12
01Pacific Arena Exclusives-290
01Parkhurst-61
Gold-61
Silver-61
He Shoots-He Scores Prizes-31
Sticks-PS62
Teammates-T24
Waving the Flag-7
01Private Stock-63
Gold-63
Premiere Date-63
Retail-63
Silver-63
Game Gear-67
Game Gear Patches-67
01Private Stock Pacific Nights-63
01Private Stock PS-2002-48
01Private Stock Reserve-S11
01SP Authentic-55
Limited-55
Limited Gold-55
Jerseys-NNEL
01SP Game Used-34
01SPx-185
01Stadium Club-101
Award Winners-101
Master Photos-101
01Titanium-94
Hobby Parallel-94
Premiere Date-94
Retail-94
Retail Parallel-94
Double-Sided Jerseys-25
Double-Sided Jerseys-27
Double-Sided Patches-25
Double-Sided Patches-27
Saturday Knights-14
Three-Star Selections-16
01Titanium Draft Day Edition-61
01Topps Chrome-134
Refractors-134
Black Border Refractors-134
01Topps Heritage-179
01Topps Reserve-63
01UD Challenge for the Cup-59
Jerseys-FPEL
Jerseys-UCLL
01UD Honor Roll Jerseys-J-EL
01UD Honor Roll Jerseys-J-LI
01UD Honor Roll Jerseys Gold-J-EL
01UD Honor Roll Jerseys Gold-J-LI
01UD Mask Collection-65
Gold-65
01UD Playmakers-67
01UD Premier Collection-34
Jerseys-BEL
Jerseys Black-B-EL
01UD Top Shelf-28
01Upper Deck-118
01Upper Deck-346
Exclusives-118
Exclusives-346
01Upper Deck Ice-106
01Upper Deck MVP-127
Morning Skate Jerseys-J-EL
01Vanguard-64
Blue-64
Red-64
East Meets West-5
Memorabilia-19
Memorabilia-38
One of Ones-64
Patches-38
Premiere Date-64
Proofs-64
Quebec Tournament Heroes-10
V-Team-16
01Czech Stadion-236
02McFarlane Hockey Team Canada-10
02Atomic-68
Blue-68
Gold-68
Red-68
Cold Fusion-17
Hobby Parallel-68
Power Converters-14
Super Colliders-10
02BAP All-Star Edition-56
He Shoots-He Scores Points-2
He Shoots-He Score Prizes-16
Jerseys-56
Jerseys Gold-56
Jerseys Silver-56
02BAP First Edition-150
02BAP First Edition-325
02BAP First Edition-405R
Debut Jerseys-13
He Shoots-He Score Points-8
He Shoots-He Scores Prizes-18
Jerseys-150
Scoring Leaders-12
02BAP Memorabilia-85
02BAP Memorabilia-231
02BAP Memorabilia-236
Emerald-85
Emerald-231
Emerald-236
Ruby-85
Ruby-231
Ruby-236
Sapphire-85
Sapphire-231
Sapphire-236
All-Star Jerseys-ASJ-33
All-Star Emblems-ASE-14
All-Star Numbers-ASN-14
All-Star Teammmates-AST-12
All-Star Teammmates-AST-13
All-Star Teammmates-AST-20
All-Star Triple Jerseys-ASTJ-12
He Shoots-He Scores Points-15
He Shoots-He Scores Prizes-6
NHL All-Star Game-85
NHL All-Star Game-231
NHL All-Star Game-236
NHL All-Star Game Blue-85
NHL All-Star Game Blue-231
NHL All-Star Game Blue-236
NHL All-Star Game Green-85
NHL All-Star Game Green-231
NHL All-Star Game Green-236
NHL All-Star Game Red-85
NHL All-Star Game Red-231
NHL All-Star Game Red-236
Teammates-TM-6
02BAP Memorabilia Toronto Fall Expo-85
02BAP Memorabilia Toronto Fall Expo-231
02BAP Memorabilia Toronto Fall Expo-236
02BAP NHL All-Star History-46
02BAP Sig Series Auto Buybacks 1998-100
02BAP Sig Series Auto Buybacks 1999-178
02BAP Sig Series Auto Buybacks 2000-208
02BAP Signature Series Golf-GS38
02BAP Signature Series Jerseys-SGJ8
02BAP Signature Series Jersey Autographs-SGJ8
02BAP Signature Series Team Quads-TQ4
02BAP Signature Series Triple Memorabilia-TM5
02BAP Ultimate Mem Complete Package-2
02BAP Ultimate Memorabilia Dynamic Duos-7
02BAP Ultimate Memorabilia Emblems-25
02BAP Ultimate Memorabilia First Overall-5
02BAP Ultimate Memorabilia Gloves Are Off-12
02BAP Ultimate Memorabilia Hat Tricks-17
02BAP Ultimate Memorabilia Jerseys-10
02BAP Ultimate Mem Journey Jerseys-6
02BAP Ultimate Mem Journey Emblems-6
02BAP Ultimate Mem Lifetime Achievers-8
02BAP Ultimate Memorabilia Numbers-7
02BAP Ultimate Mem Playoff Scorers-6
02Between the Pipes Nightmares-GN9
02Bowman YoungStars-8
Gold-8
Silver-8
02Crown Royale-64
Blue-64
Red-64
Retail-64
Lords of the Rink-15
02eTopps-19
02ITG Used-48
02ITG Used-148
Jerseys-GUJ8
Jersey Autographs-GUJ8
Jerseys Gold-GUJ8
Emblems-E8
Jersey and Stick-SJ8
Jersey and Stick Gold-SJ8
Teammates-T4
Teammates Gold-T4
Triple Memorabilia-TM9

Triple Memorabilia Gold-TM9
02McDonald's Pacific-27
Jersey Patches Silver-11
Jersey Patches Gold-11
Salt Lake Gold-6
02O-Pee-Chee-17
02O-Pee-Chee Premier Blue Parallel-17
02O-Pee-Chee Premier Red Parallel-17
02O-Pee-Chee Factory Set-17
02Pacific-253
Blue-253
Red-253
Impact Zone-8
Lamplighters-10
Maximum Impact-14
02Pacific Calder-46
Silver-46
Hardware Heroes-8
02Pacific Chicago National *-7
02Pacific Complete-201
Red-201
02Pacific Exclusive-116
Etched in Stone-8
Jerseys-17
Jerseys Gold-17
02Pacific Heads-Up-82
Blue-82
Purple-82
Red-82
Bobble Heads-8
Etched in Time-12
Inside the Numbers-15
Quad Jerseys-18
Quad Jerseys Gold-18
Stat Masters-11
02Pacific Quest for the Cup-66
Gold-66
Chasing the Cup-11
02Parkhurst-58
Bronze-58
Gold-58
Silver-58
Hardware-A1
Hardware-H1
Hardware-P1
Heroes-NH6
He Shoots-He Scores Points-15
He Shoots-He Scores Prizes-4
Jerseys-GJ15
Mario's Mates-MM5
Patented Power-PP8
Stick and Jerseys-SJ15
Teammates-TT1
02Parkhurst Retro-9
Minis-9
He Shoots-He Scores Points-16
He Shoots-He Scores Prizes-6
Jerseys-RJ27
Jersey and Sticks-RSJ19
Nicknames-RN29
02Private Stock Reserve-133
Red-133
Retail-133
Patches-133
02SP Authentic-59
02SP Authentic-100
Beckett Promos-59
02SP Game Used-32
First Rounder Patches-EL
Piece of History-PHEL
Piece of History Gold-PHEL
Piece of History Rainbow-PHEL
02SPx-49
02SPx-145
Spectrum Gold-49
Spectrum Silver-49
Winning Materials-WMEL
Winning Materials Gold-EL
Winning Materials Silver-EL
02Stadium Club-17
Silver Decoy Cards-17
Proofs-17
Passport-3
02Titanium-69
Blue-69
Red-69
Retail-69
Jerseys-44
Jerseys Retail-44
Patches-45
02Topps-17
OPC Blue Parallel-17
OPC Red Parallel-17
First Round Fabric-EL
Factory Set-17
02Topps Chrome-17
Black Border Refractors-17
Refractors-17
First Round Fabric Patches-EL
02Topps Heritage-74
Chrome Parallel-74
02Topps Total-4
Topps-TT16
02UD Artistic Impressions-58
Gold-58
02UD Artistic Impressions Beckett Promos-58
02UD Artistic Impressions Retrospectives-R58
02UD Artistic Impressions Retrospect Gold-R58
02UD Artistic Impress Retrospect Silver-R58
02UD Honor Roll-47
Students of the Game-SG21
Team Warriors-TW10
02UD Mask Collection Instant Offense-IOEL
02UD Mask Collection Patches-PGEL
02UD Piece of History-58
02UD Piece of History-103
Exquisite Combos-ECLM
Patches-PHEL
02UD Premier Collection-36
Jerseys Bronze-EL
Jerseys Bronze-BL
Jerseys Gold-EL
Jerseys Gold-BL
Jerseys Silver-EL
Jerseys Silver-BL
Patches-PEL
02UD Top Shelf-59
Clutch Performers-CPEL
Milestones Jerseys-MLNLA
02Upper Deck-115
Exclusives-115
Blow-Ups-C26
CHL Graduates-CGEL
CHL Graduates Gold-CGEL
Number Crunchers-NC8
Playbooks Series II-LL
02Upper Deck Classic Portraits-64
Hockey Royalty-LBL
Hockey Royalty-LLT
Hockey Royalty Limited-LBL
Hockey Royalty Limited-LLT
Pillars of Strength-PS7
02Upper Deck MVP-119
Gold-119
Classics-119
Golden Classics-119
Highlight Nights-HN5
Skate Around Jerseys-SAEL
Skate Around Jerseys-SDFL
Skate Around Jerseys-SDLF
Skate Around Jerseys-SDNL
Skate Around Jerseys-STLNT
Vital Forces-VF10
02Upper Deck Rookie Update Jerseys-DEL
02Upper Deck Rookie Update Jerseys-SLB
02Upper Deck Rookie Update Jerseys Gold-DEL
02Upper Deck Rookie Update Jerseys Gold-SLB
02Upper Deck Victory-140
Bronze-140
Gold-140
Silver-140
National Pride-NP9
02Upper Deck Vintage-171
02Upper Deck Vintage-280
Green Backs-171
Jerseys-SOEL
Jerseys Gold-SO-EL
Tall Boys-T43
Tall Boys Gold-T43
02Vanguard-68
LTD-68
02UD SuperStars City AS Dual Jersey-MPEL
02UD SuperStars City ASTriple Jersey *-REA
03BAP Memorabilia-27
Emerald-27
Gold-27
Ruby-27
Sapphire-27
Gloves-GUG13
He Shoots/He Scores Prizes-28
Jersey and Stick-SJ-21
Jerseys-GJ-26
Jersey Autographs-GJ-26
Practice Jerseys-PMP9
03BAP Ultimate Memorabilia Autographs-149
Gold-149
03BAP Ultimate Mem Auto Jerseys-149
03BAP Ultimate Mem Auto Emblems-149
03BAP Ultimate Mem Always An All-Star-7
03BAP Ultimate Mem Always An AS Gold-7
03BAP Ultimate Mem Complete Package-8
03BAP Ultimate Mem Complete Package Gold-8
03BAP Ultimate Memorabilia Dynamic Duos-5
03BAP Ultimate Memorabilia Emblems-4
03BAP Ultimate Memorabilia Emblems Gold-4
03BAP Ultimate Memorabilia Gloves Are Off-8
03BAP Ultimate Memorabilia Hat Tricks-10
03BAP Ultimate Mem Hometown Heroes-13
03BAP Ultimate Mem Hometown Heroes Gold-13
03BAP Ultimate Memorabilia Jerseys-26
03BAP Ultimate Memorabilia Jerseys Gold-26
03BAP Ultimate Mem Jersey and Emblems-12
03BAP Ultimate Mem Jersey and Emblem Gold-12
03BAP Ultimate Mem Jersey and Numbers-12
03BAP Ultimate Mem Jersey and Number Gold-12
03BAP Ultimate Memorabilia Linemates-2
03BAP Ultimate Mem Linemates Autos-8
03BAP Ultimate Memorabilia Nameplates-15
03BAP Ultimate Mem Nameplates Gold-15
03BAP Ultimate Memorabilia Numbers-21
03BAP Ultimate Memorabilia Numbers Gold-21
03BAP Ultimate Memorabilia Triple Threads-20
03Beehive-131
Gold-131
Silver-131
Jerseys-JT16
Sticks Red Border-RE10
03Black Diamond-104
Black-104
Green-104
Red-104
Threads-DT-EL
Threads Green-DT-EL
Threads Red-DT-EL
Threads Black-DT-EL
03Crown Royale Jerseys-16
03Crown Royale Patches-16
03ITG Action-339
Homeboys-HB7
Jerseys-M165
03ITG Used Signature Series-107
Gold-107
Autographs-EL
Autographs Gold-EL
Franchise-19
Franchise Autographs-19
Franchise Gold-19
Jerseys-8
Jerseys Gold-8
Jersey Autos-8
Jersey and Stick-8
Jersey and Stick Gold-8
Oh Canada-9
Oh Canada Gold-9
Oh Canada Emblems-9
Oh Canada Emblems Gold-9
Teammates-10
Teammates Gold-10
Triple Memorabilia-18
Triple Memorabilia Gold-18
03McDonald's Pacific-33
03NHL Sticker Collection-85
03O-Pee-Chee-88
03OPC Blue-88
03OPC Gold-88
03OPC Red-88
03Pacific-227
Blue-227
Red-227
Jerseys-26
Jerseys Gold-26
Maximum Impact-6
03Pacific Calder-68
Silver-68
03Pacific Complete-137
Red-137
03Pacific Exhibit-181
Blue Backs-181
03Pacific Heads-Up-66
Hobby LTD-66
Retail LTD-66
03Pacific Invincible-66
Blue-66
Red-66
Retail-66
Featured Performers-20
03Pacific Luxury Suite-42A
03Pacific Luxury Suite-42B
03Pacific Luxury Suite-42C
03Pacific Prism-131
Blue-131
Patches-131
Red-131
Retail-131
03Pacific Quest for the Cup-71
Blue-71
03Pacific Supreme-67
Blue-67
Red-67
Retail-67
Jerseys-18
03Parkhurst Orig Six He Shoots/Scores-23
03Parkhurst Orig Six He Shoots/Scores-23A
03Parkhurst Original Six New York-20
Memorabilia-NM3
Memorabilia-NM14
Memorabilia-NM20
03Parkhurst Rookie-54
Jersey and Sticks-SJ-7
Jersey and Sticks Gold-SJ-7
Retro Rookies-RR-19
Retro Rookies Gold-RR-19
03Private Stock Reserve-183
Blue-183
Patches-183
Red-183
Retail-183
03Rangers Team Issue-12
03SP Authentic-58
Limited-58
Sign of the Times-EL
Sign of the Times-BL
03SP Game Used-29
Gold-29
Authentic Fabrics-AFEL
Authentic Fabrics Gold-AFEL
Authentic Patches-APEL
Signers-SPSEL
Team Threads-TTBLK
03SPx-64
Radiance-64
Spectrum-64
Fantasy Franchise-FF-BLK
Fantasy Franchise Limited-FF-BLK
Signature Threads-ST-EL
03Titanium-171
Hobby Jersey Number Parallels-171
Patches-171
Retail-171
03Topps-88
Blue-88
Gold-88
Red-88
First Overall Fabrics-EL
First Overall Fabrics-MSEL
First Overall Fabrics-VLEL
Pristine Jersey Portions-PPJ-EL
Pristine Jersey Portion Refractors-PPJ-EL
Pristine Patches-PP-EL
Pristine Patch Refractors-PP-EL
03UD Honor Roll-55
Grade A Jerseys-TNYR
Signature Class-SC18
03UD Premier Collection-37
NHL Shields-SH-EL
Signatures-PS-EL
Signatures Gold-PS-EL
Teammates-PT-NR
Teammates Patches-PT-NR
03Upper Deck-373
Canadian Exclusives-373
Gifted Greats-GG5
HG-373
Jerseys-GJ-EL
Jersey Autographs-SJ-EL
Memorable Matchups-MM-LS
Power Zone-PZ-10
UD Exclusives-373
03Upper Deck Classic Portraits-63
03Upper Deck Classic Portraits-106
03Upper Deck Classic Portraits-141
Classic Colors-CC-EL
Headliners-HH-EL
Hockey Royalty-BLC
03Upper Deck Ice-59
Gold-59
Under Glass Autographs-UG-EL
03Upper Deck MVP-279
Gold Script-279
Silver Script-279
Canadian Exclusives-279
Souvenirs-S25
SportsNut-SN57
03Upper Deck Rookie Update Skills-SKEL
03Upper Deck Trilogy-63
03Upper Deck Trilogy-117
Authentic Patches-AP34
Crest Variations-117
Limited-63
Limited-117
03Upper Deck Victory-123
Bronze-123
Gold-123
Silver-123
03Czech Stadion-541
03Toronto Star-60
04ITG NHL AS FANtasy AS History Jerseys-SB46
04Pacific-176
Blue-176
Red-176
Philadelphia-9
04SP Authentic-55
04Upper Deck-114
Canadian Exclusives-114
HG Glossy Gold-114
HG Glossy Silver-114
05ITG Heroes/Prosp Toronto Expo Parallel -197
05ITG Heroes/Prosp Toronto Expo Parallel -341
05Be A Player Signatures-EL
05Be A Player Signatures Gold-EL
05Be A Player Triple Signatures-PDL
05Beehive-85
05Beehive-218
Beige -85
Blue -85
Gold-85
Red -85
Matte-85
Matted Materials-MMEL
05Black Diamond-121
Emerald-121
Gold-121
Onyx-121
Ruby-121
05Hot Prospects-95
En Fuego-95
Red Hot-95
White Hot-95
05ITG Ultimate Memorabilia Level 1-33
05ITG Ultimate Memorabilia Level 2-33
05ITG Ultimate Memorabilia Level 3-33
05ITG Ultimate Memorabilia Level 4-33
05ITG Ultimate Memorabilia Level 5-33
05ITG Ultimate Mem Complete Jersey-9
05ITG Ultimate Mem Complete Jersey Gold-9
05ITG Ultimate Mem Complete Package-10
05ITG Ultimate Mem Complete Package Gold-10
05ITG Ultimate Mem Double Mem-2
05ITG Ultimate Mem Double Mem Gold-2
05ITG Ultimate Memorabilia Jersey Autos-18
05ITG Ultimate Mem Jersey Autos Gold-18
05ITG Ultimate Mem Seams Unbelievable-8
05ITG Ultimate Mem Seam Unbelievable Gold-8
05ITG Ultimate Memorabilia Sextuple Autos-3
05ITG Ultimate Memorabilia Stick Autos-18
05ITG Ultimate Mem Stick Autos Gold-18
05ITG Ultimate Mem Sticks and Jerseys-5
05ITG Ultimate Mem Stick and Jerseys Gold-5
05ITG Ultimate Memorabilia Ultimate Autos-19
05ITG Ultimate Mem Ultimate Autos Gold-19
05McDonalds Upper Deck-2
05Panini Stickers-165
05Parkhurst-456
Facsimile Auto Parallel-456
True Colors-TCTOR
True Colors-TCTOR
True Colors-TCOTTO
True Colors-TCOTTO
05SP Authentic-92
Limited-92
05SP Game Used-93
Gold-93
Authentic Fabrics Quad-DLBN
Authentic Patches Quad -DLBN
Authentic Fabrics Triple-NSL
Authentic Patches Triple-NSL
Awesome Authentics-AA-EL
05SPx-87
Spectrum-87
Winning Combos Gold-WC-LL
Winning Combos Gold-WC-LS
Winning Combos Spectrum-WC-LL
Winning Combos Spectrum-WC-LS
05The Cup-95
Gold-95
Black Rainbow-95
Dual NHL Shields-DSME
Masterpiece Pressplates-95
Noble Numbers Dual-DNNSL
Patch Variation-P95
05UD Artifacts Frozen Artifacts-FA-EL
05UD Artifacts Frozen Artifacts Autos-FA-EL
05UD Artifacts Frozen Artifacts Copper-FA-EL
05UD Artifacts Frozen Artifacts Dual-FAD-EL
05UD Artifacts Frozen Artifact Dual Auto-FAD-EL
05UD Artifact Frozen Artifact Dual Copper-FAD-EL
05UD Artifacts Frozen Artifact Dual Gold-FAD-EL
05UD Artifact Frozen Artifact Dual Maroon-FAD-EL
05UD Artifacts Frozen Artifact Dual Pewter-FAD-EL
05UD Artifacts Frozen Artifact Dual Silver-FAD-EL
05UD Artifacts Frozen Artifacts Gold-FA-EL
05UD Artifacts Frozen Artifacts Maroon-FA-EL
05UD Artifacts Frozen Artifacts Patches-FP-EL
05UD Artifact Frozen Artifact Patch Autos-FP-EL
05UD Artifact Frozen Artifact Patch Dual-FPD-EL
05UD Artifact Frozen Art Patch Dual Auto-FPD-EL
05UD Artifacts Frozen Art Patch Pewter-FP-EL
05UD Artifacts Frozen Art Patch Silver-FP-EL
05UD Artifacts Frozen Artifacts Pewter-FA-EL
05UD Artifacts Frozen Artifacts Silver-FA-EL
05Ultimate Collection-83
Gold-83
Jerseys-JEL
Jerseys Dual-DJAL
Jerseys Triple-TJSLA
Premium Patches-PPEL
Premium Swatches-PSEL
Ultimate Patches-PEL
Ultimate Patches Dual-DPAL
Ultimate Patches Triple-TPSLA
05Ultra-181
Gold-181
Ice-181
05Upper Deck-425
05Upper Deck All-Time Greatest-83
05Upper Deck Big Playmakers-B-EL
05Upper Deck Hometown Heroes-HH27
05Upper Deck Jerseys-J-EL
05Upper Deck Jerseys Series II-J2EL
05Upper Deck Majestic Materials-MMEL
05Upper Deck Notable Numbers-N-EL
05Upper Deck Patches-P-EL
05Upper Deck Shooting Stars-S-EL
05Upper Deck Hockey Showcase-HS32
05Upper Deck Showcase Promos-HS32
05Upper Deck Ice-92
Rainbow-92
05Upper Deck MVP-364
Gold-364
Platinum-364
05Upper Deck Rookie Update-95
05Upper Deck Trilogy-86
Honorary Patches-HP-EL
Honorary Patch Scripts-HSP-EL
Honorary Swatches-HS-EL
Honorary Swatch Scripts-HSS-EL
05Upper Deck Victory-246
Black-246
Gold-246
Silver-246
Stars on Ice-SI28
05ITG Heroes and Prospects-197
05ITG Heroes and Prospects-341
Autographs Series II-EL
Autographs Series II-EL2
Autographs Series II-LT2
Hero Memorabilia-HM-45
National Pride-NPR-27
06Be A Player Portraits-38
06Beehive-70
06Beehive-210
Blue-70
Gold-70
Matte-70
Red Facsimile Signatures-70
Wood-70
06Black Diamond-100
Black-100
Gold-100
Ruby-100
Jerseys-JEL
Jerseys Black-JEL
Jerseys Gold-JEL
Jerseys Ruby-JEL
06Flair Showcase-92
06Flair Showcase-166
Parallel-92
Parallel-166
Hot Numbers-HN39
Hot Numbers Parallel-HN39
Stitches-SSEL
06Fleer-65
Tiffany-65
Fabricology-FEL
06Hot Prospects-34
Red Hot-34
White Hot-34
06ITG International Ice Double Memorabilia-DM01
06ITG International Ice Double Memorabilia Gold-DM01
06ITG International Ice Emblem Autographs-GUE36
06ITG International Ice Emblem Autographs Gold-GUE36
06ITG International Ice Emblems-GUE36
06ITG International Ice Emblems Gold-GUE36
06ITG International Ice Jersey Autographs-GUJ36
06ITG International Ice Jersey Autographs Gold-GUJ36
06ITG International Ice Jerseys-GUJ36
06ITG International Ice Jerseys Gold-GUJ36
06ITG International Ice My Country My Team-MC21
06ITG International Ice My Country My Team Gold-MC21
06ITG International Ice Numbers-GUN36
06ITG International Ice Numbers Autographs-GUN36
06ITG International Ice Numbers Autographs Gold-GUN36
06ITG International Ice Numbers Gold-GUN36
06ITG International Ice Stick and Jersey-SJ10
06ITG International Ice Stick and Jersey Gold-SJ10
06ITG International Ice Teammates-IT08
06ITG International Ice Teammates Gold-IT08
06ITG Ultimate Memorabilia Gloves Are Off-10
06ITG Ultimate Memorabilia Gloves Are Off Gold-10
06ITG Ultimate Memorabilia Journey Emblem-7
06ITG Ultimate Memorabilia Journey Emblem Gold-7
06ITG Ultimate Memorabilia Journey Jersey-7
06ITG Ultimate Memorabilia Journey Jersey Gold-7
06ITG Ultimate Memorabilia Passing The Torch-19
06ITG Ultimate Memorabilia Passing The Torch Gold-19
06ITG Ultimate Memorabilia Triple Thread Jerseys-15
06ITG Ultimate Memorabilia Triple Thread Jerseys Gold-15
06NHL POG-34
06O-Pee-Chee-163
06O-Pee-Chee-649
Rainbow-163
Rainbow-649
06Panini Stickers-246
06SP Authentic-71
Limited-71
06SP Game Used-33
Gold-33
Rainbow-33
Authentic Fabrics Dual-AF2ML
Authentic Fabrics Dual Patches-AF2ML
Authentic Fabrics Triple-AF3DAL
Authentic Fabrics Triple Patches-AF3DAL
06SPx-29
06SPx-120
Spectrum-29
Spectrum-120
SPxcitement-X31
SPxcitement Spectrum-X31
06Stars Team Postcards-12
06The Cup Foundations-CQEL
06The Cup Foundations Patches-CQEL
06The Cup NHL Shields Duals-DSHEM
06The Cup NHL Shields Duals-DSHML
06The Cup Property of-POEL
06UD Artifacts-70
Blue-70
Gold-70
Platinum-70
Radiance-70
Red-70
Treasured Patches Black-TSEL
Treasured Patches Blue-TSEL
Treasured Patches Gold-TSEL
Treasured Patches Platinum-TSEL
Treasured Patches Red-TSEL
Treasured Swatches-TSEL
Treasured Swatches Black-TSEL
Treasured Swatches Blue-TSEL
Treasured Swatches Gold-TSEL
Treasured Swatches Platinum-TSEL
Treasured Swatches Red-TSEL
Tundra Tandems-TTML
Tundra Tandems Black-TTML
Tundra Tandems Blue-TTML
Tundra Tandems Gold-TTML
Tundra Tandems Platinum-TTML
Tundra Tandems Red-TTML
Tundra Tandems Dual Patches Red-TTML
06UD Mini Jersey Collection-32
06UD Powerplay-35
Impact Rainbow-35
06Ultimate Collection Jerseys-UJ-EL
06Ultimate Collection Jerseys Dual-UJ2-ML
06Ultimate Collection Patches-UJ-EL
06Ultimate Collection Patches Dual-UJ2-ML
06Ultimate Collection Premium Patches-PS-EL
06Ultimate Collection Premium Swatches-PS-EL
06Ultra-67
Gold Medallion-67
Ice Medallion-67
Uniformity-UEL
Uniformity Patches-UPEL
06Upper Deck Arena Giveaways-DAL5
06Upper Deck Arena Giveaways-DAL5
06Upper Deck-318
Exclusives Parallel-318
High Gloss Parallel-318
Game Jerseys-JEL
Game Patches-PEL
Masterpieces-318
Oversized Wal-Mart Exclusives-318
06Upper Deck MVP-95
Gold Script-95
Super Script-95
Gotta Have Hart-HH10
Jerseys-OJRL
06Upper Deck Sweet Shot-35
Sweet Stitches-SSEL
Sweet Stitches Duals-SSEL
Sweet Stitches Triples-SSEL
06Upper Deck Trilogy-34
06Upper Deck Victory-185
06Upper Deck Victory-244
06Upper Deck Victory Black-185
06Upper Deck Victory Gold-185
07Upper Deck All-Star Game Redemptions-AS3
07Upper Deck Victory-185
Black-185
Gold-185
07ITG Going For Gold World Juniors-23
Autographs-23

Lindsay, Bert

10Sweet Caporal Postcards-21
11C55-21
12C57-13

Lindsay, Bill

907th Inn. Sketch WHL-113
917th Inn. Sketch WHL-304
92Bowman-404
92Nordiques Petro-Canada-20
92OPC Premier-5
92Parkhurst-376
Emerald Ice-376
92Pro Set-239
92Score-463
Canadian-463
92Topps-373
Gold-373G
92Ultra-388
92Upper Deck-472
93OPC Premier-436
Gold-436
93Panthers Team Issue-5
93Parkhurst-350
Emerald Ice-350
93PowerPlay-95
93Stadium Club-253
Members Only Master Set-253
First Day Issue-253
93Topps/OPC Premier-436
Gold-436
94OPC Premier-522
Special Effects-522
94Stadium Club-222
Members Only Master Set-222
First Day Issue-222
Super Team Winner Cards-222
94Topps/OPC Premier-522
Special Effects-522
95Canada Games NHL POGS-117
95Collector's Choice-12
Player's Club-12
Player's Club Platinum-12
95Parkhurst International-356
Emerald Ice-356
95Topps-83
OPC Inserts-83
95Upper Deck-63
Electric Ice-63
Electric Ice Gold-63
96Be A Player-204
Autographs-204
Autographs Silver-204
96Black Diamond-11
Gold-11
96Collector's Choice-108
96Donruss-75
Press Proofs-75
96Leaf-66
Press Proofs-66
96Pinnacle-192
Artist's Proofs-192
Foil-192
Premium Stock-192
Rink Collection-192
96Score-223
Artist's Proofs-223
Dealer's Choice Artist's Proofs-223
Special Artist's Proofs-223
Golden Blades-223
96Upper Deck Ice-22
Parallel-22
97Collector's Choice-108
97Pacific Invincible NHL Regime-86
97Upper Deck-74
98Upper Deck-102
Exclusives-102
Exclusives 1 of 1-102
Gold Reserve-102
99Pacific-176
Copper-176
Emerald Green-176
Gold-176
Ice Blue-176
Premiere Date-176
Red-176
00Pacific-69
Copper-69
Gold-69
Ice Blue-69
Premiere Date-69
01BAP Memorabilia-422
Emerald-422
Ruby-422
Sapphire-422
02Canadiens Postcards-6
02NHL Power Play Stickers-59
03Pacific Complete-226
Red-226

Lindsay, Bob

87Brockville Braves-13
88Brockville Braves-10

Lindsay, Cody

06Ottawa 67's-5

Lindsay, Craig

99Memphis RiverKings All-Time-19

Lindsay, Evan

96Prince Albert Raiders-13
97Prince Albert Raiders-11
98Prince Albert Raiders-14
98Bowman CHL-61
Golden Anniversary-61
OPC International-61
98Bowman Chrome CHL-61
Golden Anniversary-61
Golden Anniversary Refractors-61
OPC International-61
OPC International Refractors-61
Refractors-61
00Asheville Smoke-24
02Roanoke Express-19
03UK London Racers-7

Lindsay, Jeff

90Knoxville Cherokees-105
91Michigan Falcons-10

Lindsay, Mark

05Fort Wayne Komets Choice-22
05Fort Wayne Komets Sprint-13
05Missouri River Otters-11

Lindsay, Ryan

93Oshawa Generals-25
95Slapshot-253
99Quad-City Mallards-7
99UHL All-Stars West-7T
00Quad-City Mallards-9

Lindsay, Scott

90Fort Saskatchewan Traders-9
917th Inn. Sketch WHL-322

Lindsay, Ted

44Beehive Group II Photos-112
44Beehive Group II Photos-186
48Exhibits Canadian-45
51Parkhurst-56
52Parkhurst-87
52Royal Desserts-5
53Parkhurst-52
54Parkhurst-46
54Topps-51
57Topps-21
58Topps-63
59Topps-6
64Beehive Group III Photos-82
64Coca-Cola Caps-48
64Topps-82
76Old Timers-10
83Hall of Fame-151
83Hall of Fame Postcards-L10
85Hall of Fame-151
91Kraft-70
91Ultimate Original Six-70
91Ultimate Original Six-94
French-70
French-94
92Hall of Fame Legends-19
92Parkhurst Parkie Reprints-PR31
92Zeller's Masters of Hockey-3
92Zeller's Masters of Hockey Signed-3
93Parkhurst Parkie Reprints-PR49
94Parkhurst Missing Link-44
94Parkhurst Missing Link-140
94Parkhurst Tall Boys-64
97Beehive-60
Golden Portraits-60
Golden Originals Autographs-60
99BAP Memorabilia AS Retail-R12
99BAP Memorabilia AS Retail Autographs-R12
99Upper Deck Century Legends-21
Century Collection-21
All Century Team-AC9
Epic Signatures-TL
Epic Signatures 100-TL
Essence of the Game-E8
99Upper Deck Retro-97
Gold-97
Platinum-97
Inkredible-TL
Inkredible Level 2-TL
00Topps Stanley Cup Heroes-SHTL
00Topps Stanley Cup Heroes Autographs-SHTL
00Topps Heritage Autographs-HA-TL
00Topps Heritage Autoproofs-51
00Upper Deck Legends-42
Legendary Collection Bronze-42
Legendary Collection Gold-42
Legendary Collection Silver-42
Enshrined Stars-ES15
Epic Signatures-TL
01BAP Signature Series Vintage Autographs-VA-9
01BAP Ultimate Mem All-Star History-9
01BAP Ultimate Memorabilia Autographs-26
01BAP Ultimate Mem Autographs Gold-26
01BAP Ultimate Memorabilia Cornerstones-4
01BAP Ultimate Memorabilia Decades-8
01BAP Ultimate Memorabilia Emblem Attic-10
01BAP Ultimate Mem Production Line-3
01BAP Ultimate Mem Production Line-4
01BAP Ultimate Mem Production Line-5
01BAP Ultimate Mem Retired Numbers-15
01BAP Ultimate Mem Retro Teammates-3
01BAP Ultimate Mem Stanley Cup Winners-26
01BAP Update Rocket's Rivals-RR-2
01BAP Update Tough Customers-TC31
01Fleer Legacy-35
Ultimate-35
01Greats of the Game-74
Autographs-74
01Parkhurst Autographs-PA39
01Parkhurst He Shoots-He Scores Points-5
01Parkhurst He Shoots-He Scores Prizes-37
01Parkhurst Heroes-H10
01Parkhurst Reprints-PR90
01Parkhurst Reprints-PR96
01Parkhurst Reprints-PR126
01Parkhurst Vintage Memorabilia-PV28
01Parkhurst Vintage Memorabilia-PV29
01UD Stanley Cup Champs-7
01Upper Deck Legends-17
Epic Signatures-TL
02BAP NHL All-Star History-9
02BAP Ultimate Memorabilia Emblem Attic-13
02BAP Ultimate Mem Seams Unbelievable-2
02BAP Ultimate Mem Vintage Jerseys-35
02BAP Ultimate Mem Vintage Jersey Autos-8
02Fleer Throwbacks-10
Gold-10
Platinum-10
Autographs-5
02UD Foundations Signs of Greatness-SGTL
03BAP Memorabilia Vintage Memorabilia-VM-10
03BAP Ultimate Memorabilia Autographs-159
Gold-159
03BAP Ultimate Memorabilia Cornerstones-7
03BAP Ultimate Mem Raised to the Rafters-8
03BAP Ultimate Mem Retro Teammates-3
03BAP Ultimate Mem Retro-Active Trophies-1
03BAP Ultimate Memorabilia Triple Threads-27
03BAP Ultimate Mem Vint Complete Jersey-9
03BAP Ultimate Mem Vint Comp Jersey Gold-9
03BAP Ultimate Mem Vintage Jerseys-15
03BAP Ultimate Mem Vintage Jerseys Gold-15
03ITG Used Signature Series-113
Gold-113
Autographs-TL
Autographs Gold-TL
Vintage Memorabilia-5
Vintage Memorabilia Autographs-5
Vintage Memorabilia Gold-5
03ITG VIP Collages-26
03ITG VIP Collage Autographs-26
03ITG VIP Vintage Memorabilia-9
03Parkhurst Original Six Chicago-56
Autographs-9
03Parkhurst Original Six Detroit-40
03Parkhurst Original Six Detroit-66
03Parkhurst Original Six Detroit-76
03Parkhurst Original Six Detroit-85
Autographs-OS-TL
Inserts-D-2
Inserts-D-5
Memorabilia-DM30
Memorabilia-DM40
Memorabilia-DM51
03Parkhurst Orig Six He Shoots/Scores-27
03Parkhurst Orig Six He Shoots/Scores-27A
03SP Authentic Special Cuts-PROD
03SPx-108
Radiance-108
Spectrum-108
03Upper Deck Trilogy-131
Crest Variations-131
Limited-131
Scripts-S3TL
Scripts-CSTL
Scripts-CSTL2
Scripts-CSTL3
Scripts-CSTL4
Scripts Limited-S3TL
Scripts Red-S3TL
04Canada Post-29
04Canada Post Autographs-5
04ITG NHL AS FANtasy AS History Jerseys-SB9
04ITG Franchises He Shoots/Scores Prizes-24
04ITG Franchises US West-203
Autographs-A-TL
Barn Burners-WBB7
Barn Burners Gold-WBB7
Forever Rivals-WFR3
Forever Rivals Gold-WFR3
Memorabilia-WSM3
Memorabilia Autographs-WSMTL
Memorabilia Gold-WSM3
Teammates-WTM1
Teammates Gold-WTM1
Trophy Winners-WTW4
Trophy Winners Gold-WTW4
04ITG Ultimate Memorabilia-7
04ITG Ultimate Memorabilia-11
Gold-7
Gold-11
Art Ross Trophy-7
Auto Threads-4
Autographs-68
Autographs Gold-68
Changing the Game-4
Cornerstones-1
Cornerstones Gold-1
Day In History-3
Day In History Gold-3
Jerseys-17
Jerseys Gold-17
Jersey Autographs-30
Jersey Autographs Gold-30
Nicknames-23
Nickname Autographs-7
Original Six-2
Original Six-9
Retro Teammates-6
04UD Legendary Signatures-82
Autographs-TL
04UD Legends Classics-51
Gold-51
Platinum-51
Silver-51
Signature Moments-M10
Signature Moments-M64
Signatures-CS10
Signatures-TC13
Signatures-QC3
04ITG Heroes and Prospects-147
Autographs-TLI
Hero Memorabilia-27
04ITG Heroes/Prospects Toronto Expo '05-147
04ITG Heroes/Prospects Expo Heroes/Pros-147
05ITG Heroes/Prosp Toronto Expo Parallel -38
05ITG Tough Customers-TL
Autographs-TL
05ITG Ultimate Memorabilia Level 1-91
05ITG Ultimate Memorabilia Level 2-91
05ITG Ultimate Memorabilia Level 3-91
05ITG Ultimate Memorabilia Level 4-91
05ITG Ultimate Memorabilia Level 5-91
05ITG Ultimate Mem Cornerstones Jerseys-4
05ITG Ultimate Mem Cornerst Jerseys Gold-4
05ITG Ultimate Mem Decades Jerseys-2
05ITG Ultimate Mem Decades Jerseys Gold-2
05ITG Ultimate Memorabilia Double Autos-10
05ITG Ultimate Mem Double Autos Gold-10
05ITG Ultimate Mem Double Mem Autos-6
05ITG Ultimate Mem Double Mem Autos Gold-6
05ITG Ultimate Mem Pass the Torch Jerseys-10
05ITG Ultimate Mem Passing Torch Jsy Gold-10
05ITG Ultimate Mem Record Breaker Jerseys-3
05ITG Ultimate Mem RecBreak Jerseys Gold-3
05ITG Ultimate Mem Retro Teammate Jerseys-4
05ITG Ult Mem Retro Teammates Jersey Gold-4
05ITG Ultimate Mem 3 Star of the Game Jsy-4
05ITG Ult Mem 3 Star of the Game Jsy Gold-4
05ITG Ultimate Memorabilia Triple Autos-20
05ITG Ultimate Mem Triple Autos Gold-20
05ITG Ultimate Memorabilia Ultimate Autos-18
05ITG Ultimate Mem Ultimate Autos Gold-18
05NHL Legends Medallions-8
05The Cup Stanley Cup Titlists-TTL
05Upper Deck Trilogy Legendary Scripts-LEG-TL
05ITG Heroes and Prospects-38
Autographs-A-TL
Hero Memorabilia-HM-38
06Beehive Signature Scrapbook-SSTL
06ITG Ultimate Memorabilia-135
Artist Proof-135
Autos-24
Autos Gold-24
Autos Dual-2
Autos Dual Gold-2
Cornerstones-5
Cornerstones Gold-5
Decades-1

Decades-5
Decades Gold-1
Decades Gold-5
Retro Teammates-3
Retro Teammates Gold-3
Road to the Cup-1
Road to the Cup Gold-1
Triple Thread Jerseys-8
Triple Thread Jerseys Gold-8
06Parkhurst-66
06Parkhurst-177
06Parkhurst-239
Autographs-66
Autographs-177
Autographs-239
Autographs Dual-DAHL
Autographs Dual-DALK
06SP Game Used Letter Marks-LMTL
06SP Game Used SIGnificance-STL
06SPx SPxcitement-X37
06SPx SPxcitement Spectrum-X37
06The Cup-31
Black Rainbow-31
Gold-31
Masterpiece Pressplates-31
Stanley Cup Signatures-CSTL
06UD Artifacts-121
Blue-121
Gold-121
Platinum-121
Radiance-121
Autographed Radiance Parallel-121
Red-121
Auto-Facts-AFTL
Auto-Facts Gold-AFTL
06Ultimate Collection Signatures-US-TL
06Upper Deck All-Time Greatest-ATG8
06Upper Deck Sweet Shot-42
Signature Shots/Saves Sticks-SSSTL
06Upper Deck Trilogy Legendary Scripts-LSTL
06Upper Deck Trilogy Scripts-TSTL

Lindskog, Lars
84Swedish Semic Elitserien-132

Lindstahl, Sam
84Swedish Semic Elitserien-220
85Swedish Panini Stickers-221
86Swedish Panini Stickers-246
87Swedish Panini Stickers-213
89Swedish Semic Elitserien Stickers-192
90Swedish Semic Elitserien Stickers-76
91Swedish Semic Elitserien Stickers-3
92Swedish Semic Elitserien Stickers-27
94Swedish Leaf-11
95Swedish Upper Deck 1st Division Stars-DS9

Lindstedt, Johan
90Swedish Semic Elitserien Stickers-294
91Swedish Semic Elitserien Stickers-74

Lindster, Thomas
85Swedish Panini Stickers-195
86Swedish Panini Stickers-132
87Swedish Panini Stickers-121

Lindstrom, Bertil
64Swedish Coralli ISHockey-90

Lindstrom, Billy
70Swedish Hockey-255

Lindstrom, Curt
95Finnish Karjala World Champ Labels-10

Lindstrom, Eje
57Swedish Alfabilder-73
65Swedish Coralli ISHockey-174

Lindstrom, Evert
71Swedish Hockey-315
72Swedish Stickers-297
73Swedish Stickers-150

Lindstrom, Joakim
02Swedish SHL-85
02Swedish SHL-246
Next Generation-NG6
Parallel-85
Parallel-246
03Swedish Elite-109
Rookies-9
Silver-109
04Swedish Elitset Future Stars-11
04Swedish MoDo Postcards-14
05Black Diamond-233
05Hot Prospects-122
En Fuego-122
Red Hot-122
White Hot-122
05SP Game Used-206
05SPx-256
05The Cup Masterpiece Pressplate Artifact-270
05The Cup Master Pressplate Black Diamond-233
05The Cup Master Pressplate Rookie Update-126
05The Cup Masterpiece Pressplates SP GU-206
05The Cup Masterpiece Pressplates (SPx)-256
05The Cup Masterpiece Pressplates Trilogy-246
05The Cup Masterpiece Pressplate Ult Coll-201
05UD Artifacts-270
05Ultimate Collection-201
Gold-201
05Upper Deck Rookie Update-126
05Upper Deck Trilogy-246
05Syracuse Crunch-22
06Syracuse Crunch-24

Lindstrom, Johan
96Swedish Brynas Tigers-23
99Swedish Upper Deck-33
02Swedish SHL-165
Parallel-165
03Swedish Elite-222
Silver-222
04Swedish Elitset-212
Gold-212
05Swedish SHL Elitset-226
06Swedish SHL Elitset-80

Lindstrom, Kaj
00Finnish Cardset-71
01Finnish Cardset-100
07Topps Allen and Ginter Mini A and G Back-44

Lindstrom, Orjan
71Swedish Hockey-253
72Swedish Stickers-235
73Swedish Stickers-236
74Swedish Stickers-244

Lindstrom, Roger
83Swedish Semic Elitserien-12
84Swedish Semic Elitserien-11
85Swedish Panini Stickers-12

Lindstrom, Sanny
01Quad-City Mallards-11
03Swedish Elite-270
Silver-270

04Swedish Elitset-124
Gold-124
05Swedish SHL Elitset-133
06Swedish SHL Elitset-277

Lindstrom, Seppo
69Swedish Hockey-375
70Finnish Jaakiekko-66
70Finnish Jaakiekko-143
70Swedish Hockey-296
70Swedish Masterserien-20
71Finnish Suomi Stickers-65
71Finnish Suomi Stickers-193
71Swedish Hockey-62
72Finnish Jaakiekko-231
72Finnish Panda Toronto-100
72Finnish Semic World Championship-73
72Swedish Semic World Championship-73
73Finnish Jaakiekko-71
73Finnish Jaakiekko-265
74Finnish Typotor-39
74Swedish Stickers-107
74Swedish Semic World Champ Stickers-77
77Finnish Sportscasters-83-1982

Lindstrom, Soren
64Swedish Coralli ISHockey-158
65Swedish Coralli ISHockey-158

Lindstrom, Sven Bertil
69Swedish Hockey-81
71Swedish Hockey-127
72Swedish Stickers-108
73Swedish Stickers-217

Lindstrom, Willy
71Swedish Hockey-316
72Swedish Stickers-298
73Swedish Stickers-22
73Swedish Stickers-149
74Swedish Stickers-243
74Swedish Semic World Champ Stickers-17
770-Pee-Chee WHA-39
78Jets Postcards-11
79Jets Postcards-12
790-Pee-Chee-368
80Jets Postcards-11
800-Pee-Chee-142
80Pepsi-Cola Caps-130
80Topps-142
81Jets Postcards-9
810-Pee-Chee-368
82Jets Postcards-12
820-Pee-Chee-384
820-Pee-Chee Stickers-209
82Post Cereal-21
82Topps Stickers-209
83Oilers McDonald's-17
830-Pee-Chee-35
830-Pee-Chee Stickers-91
83Topps Stickers-91
83Vachon-32
84Oilers Red Rooster-19
84Oilers Team Issue-14
840-Pee-Chee-250
840-Pee-Chee Stickers-260
850-Pee-Chee-217
850-Pee-Chee Stickers-226
860-Pee-Chee-232
860-Pee-Chee Stickers-227
86Penguins Kodak-15
87Swedish Panini Stickers-58
88Oilers Tenth Anniversary-23
89Swedish Semic Elitserien Stickers-39

Lineker, Craig
03Regina Pats-2
04Regina Pats-3
05Calgary Hitmen-10
06Chilliwack Bruins-7

Linesman, Ted
83Kingston Canadians-13
84Kingston Canadians-27
85Kingston Canadians-27
86Kingston Canadians-29

Linford, Dave
88Kamloops Blazers-16

Ling, David
93Kingston Frontenacs-16
95Saint John Flames-12
95Classic-86
96Fredericton Canadiens-13
96Collector's Edge Future Legends-10
96Collector's Edge Ice-77
Prism-77
97Score Canadiens-16
Platinum-16
Premier-16
98Kansas City Blades-12
99IHL All-Stars-15
99Kansas City Blades Supercuts-9
00Utah Grizzlies-25
01BAP Memorabilia-415
Emerald-415
Ruby-415
Sapphire-415
01Upper Deck Ice-135
01Syracuse Crunch-12
02Syracuse Crunch-11
02Syracuse Crunch Sheets-4
05Russian Hockey League RHL-32

Ling, Jamie
91Air Canada SJHL-A29
91Air Canada SJHL All-Stars-25
91Air Canada SJHL All-Stars-49
98Dayton Bombers-10
98Dayton Bombers EBK-5
98ECHL All-Star Northern Conference-3
99ECHL All-Star Northern Conference-11

Lingemann, Boris
95German DEL-90
96German DEL-288
99German Bundesliga 2-104
00German DEL-57
04German DEL-270

Lingemann, Max
05German DEL-329

Linglet, Charles
99Baie-Comeau Drakkar-16
00Baie-Comeau Drakkar-23
Signed-23
01Baie-Comeau Drakkar-21
02Baie Comeau Drakkar-22
03Alaska Aces-8
03ECHL All-Stars-274
06Peoria Rivermen-8

Lingley, Tyrone
93Quebec Pee-Wee Tournament-1460

Lingren, Steve
917th Inn. Sketch WHL-61

94Dayton Bombers-16
95Dayton Bombers-6
95Dayton Bombers-24
96Dayton Bombers-3
98Kentucky Thoroughblades-15
99Kansas City Blades Supercuts-10
00Kansas City Blades-12
02German DEL City Press-140
03Rochester Americans-12
04Rochester Americans-10

Linhart, Tomas
02London Knights-25
02Mississauga Ice Dogs-9
04Czech OFS-122
06Czech HC Pardubice Postcards-12
06Czech OFS-121

Liniger, Michael
98Swiss Power Play Stickers-146
99Swiss Panini Stickers-147
01Swiss HNL-230
02Swiss HNL-204

Link, Brad
98Wichita Thunder-13
99Wichita Thunder-12

Link, Tony
94Anchorage Aces-2

Link, Tracy
94Anchorage Aces-10

Linna, Kaj
95PEI Senators-12
95Classic-76
95Classic Five-Sport *-141
98Finnish Kerailysarja Leijonat-11

Linna, Troy
93Quebec Pee-Wee Tournament-1330
01El Paso Buzzards-15

Linnell, Derek
92Raleigh Icecaps-7
92Raleigh Icecaps-24
93Raleigh Icecaps-10
94Raleigh Icecaps-9
95Alaska Gold Kings-11

Linnik, Maxim
00Muskegon Fury-12
02Arkansas Riverblades-7

Linnonmaa, Harri
65Finnish Hellas-61
70Finnish Jaakiekko-67
70Finnish Jaakiekko-110
70Swedish Hockey-305
71Finnish Suomi Stickers-66
71Finnish Suomi Stickers-118
71Swedish Hockey-67
72Finnish Jaakiekko-64
72Finnish Jaakiekko-88
72Finnish Hellas-4
72Finnish Panda Toronto-6
72Finnish Panda Toronto-101
72Finnish Semic World Championship-80
72Swedish Semic World Championship-80
73Finnish Jaakiekko-134
74Swedish Stickers-36
74Swedish Semic World Champ Stickers-85
78Finnish SM-Liiga-36
80Finnish Mallasjuoma-10

Linse, Martin
83Swedish Semic Elitserien-93

Linseman, Ken
790-Pee-Chee-241
79Topps-241
800-Pee-Chee-24
80Topps-24
810-Pee-Chee-244
810-Pee-Chee Stickers-176
81Topps-E107
82Oilers Red Rooster-13
820-Pee-Chee-115
820-Pee-Chee Stickers-112
82Post Cereal-14
82Topps Stickers-112
83NHL Key Tags-39
83Oilers Dollars-H17
83Oilers McDonald's-1
830-Pee-Chee-36
830-Pee-Chee Stickers-102
83Puffy Stickers-6
83Topps Stickers-102
83Vachon-33
84Bruins Postcards-10
840-Pee-Chee-7
87Panini Stickers-16
88Bruins Sports Action-11
88Bruins Postcards-11
88Oilers Tenth Anniversary-47
880-Pee-Chee-118
88Panini Stickers-211
88Topps-118
89Bruins Sports Action-14
890-Pee-Chee-62
890-Pee-Chee Stickers-26
89Panini Stickers-190
89Topps-62
90Oilers IGA-12
900-Pee-Chee-345
90Panini Stickers-111
90Pro Set-219
90Pro Set-444
90Score-380
Canadian-380
90Score Rookie/Traded-95T
90Topps-345
Tiffany-345
91Bowman-105
91Oilers Panini Team Stickers-11
910-Pee-Chee-146
91Score American-359
91Score Canadian Bilingual-239
91Score Canadian Bilingual-622
91Score Canadian English-239
91Score Canadian English-622
91Stadium Club-295
91Topps-146
98Bruins Alumni-13
Autographs-13
01Topps Archives-75
Autographs-27
02Fleer Throwbacks-62
Gold-62
Platinum-62
04UD Legendary Signatures-97
Autographs-KL

Linseman, Mike
81Kingston Canadians-12

Linseman, Steve
83Brantford Alexanders-15

84Belleville Bulls-18

Linteau, Richard
80Quebec Remparts-15

Lintner, Richard
97Springfield Falcons-16
98Milwaukee Admirals-11
98Milwaukee Admirals Postcards-8
99BAP Memorabilia-343
Gold-343
Silver-343
99Pacific Omega-131
Copper-131
Gold-131
Ice Blue-131
Premiere Date-131
99Paramount-260
99Topps Premier Plus-94
Parallel-94
00Upper Deck Victory-269
02Slovakian Kvarteto-7
02Swedish SHL-141
Parallel-141
03Swedish Elite-160
Global Impact-GI2
Silver-160
06Swedish SHL Elitset-267

Liotti, Louis
04Sioux City Musketeers-14

Lipansky, Jan
03Czech OFS Plus-87
04Czech OFS-43

Lipensky, Ales
96Czech APS Extraliga-282

Lipiansky, Jan
97Czech APS Extraliga-238
98Czech DS Stickers-43
00Czech DS Extraliga-22
00Czech OFS-339
01Finnish Cardset-374
03Czech OFS Plus-87
04Czech OFS-43

Lipina, Petr
96Czech APS Extraliga-71
00Czech OFS-207

Lipka, Rastislav
00Spokane Chiefs-14
01Prince Albert Raiders-13
02Prince Albert Raiders-15

Lipkowski, Krzysztof
93Quebec Pee-Wee Tournament-1518

Lipovsky, Miroslav
04Russian Legion-18

Lipsett, Chris
92Clarkson Knights-9
96Roanoke Express-23
98Roanoke Express-22
99Kentucky Thoroughblades-19
00Kentucky Thoroughblades-15
01UK Sheffield Steelers-14
02German DEL City Press-164
03Alaska Aces-9

Lipsey, Daryl
00UK Sekonda Superleague-88
01UK Manchester Storm-19
01UK Manchester Storm Retro-6
02UK Manchester Storm-18

Liptrott, Peter
86Kingston Canadians-8
87Kingston Canadians-8
91Richmond Renegades Set 2-9
94Brantford Smoke-4
96Louisville Riverfrogs-4

LiPuma, Chris
88Kitchener Rangers-25
89Kitchener Rangers-25
90Kitchener Rangers-24
907th Inn. Sketch OHL-235
907th Inn. Sketch Memorial Cup-44
917th Inn. Sketch OHL-94
92Atlanta Knights-18
93Donruss-493
93Lightning Season in Review-21
93Pinnacle-208
Canadian-208
93PowerPlay-446
93Ultra-178
All-Rookies-4
93Atlanta Knights-17
93Classic Pro Prospects-118
94Ultra-372
94Atlanta Knights-20
94Classic Pro Prospects-20
95Atlanta Knights-13
96Kentucky Thoroughblades-12
98Chicago Wolves-8
99Chicago Wolves-20
00Chicago Wolves-15
02Orlando Seals-6

Lirette, Noel
66Columbus Checkers-10

Lisabeth, Travis
99Kingston Frontenacs-11
00Kingston Frontenacs-9
03Mississippi Sea Wolves-10

Liscak, Robert
92Quebec Pee-Wee Tournament-1720
03Augusta Lynx-45
03Providence Bruins-12
04Slovakian Skalica Team Set-16

Liscomb, Brett
05Ottawa 67's-25
06Ottawa 67s-6

Liscombe, Carl
34Beehive Group I Photos-112
390-Pee-Chee V301-1-74

Lisin, Enver
04Russian Hope-3
04Russian Under-18 Team-15
06Beehive-142
Blue-142
Matte-142
Red Facsimile Signatures-142
Wood-142
06Black Diamond-197
Black-197
Gold-197
Ruby-197
06Flair Showcase-321
06Hot Prospects-189
060-Pee-Chee-560
Rainbow-560
06SP Authentic-233
Limited-233
06SP Game Used-141

Gold-141
Rainbow-141
06The Cup Masterpiece Pressplates (Bee Hive)-142
06The Cup Masterpiece Pressplates (Marquee Rookies)-560
06The Cup Masterpiece Pressplates (MVP)-355
06The Cup Masterpiece Pressplates (SP Authentic)-233
06The Cup Masterpiece Pressplates (SP Game Used)-141
06The Cup Masterpiece Pressplates (Trilogy)-135
06The Cup Masterpiece Pressplates (Victory)-312
06UD Artifacts-253
06Ultra-245
06Ultra-247
Gold Medallion-245
Ice Medallion-245
06Upper Deck-484
Exclusives Parallel-484
High Gloss Parallel-484
Masterpieces-484
Rookie Headliners-RH3
Signatures-SEL
06Upper Deck MVP-355
Gold Script-355
Super Script-355
06Upper Deck Trilogy-135
06Upper Deck Victory-312
07Upper Deck Rookie Class -8

Liska, Jan
99Czech OFS-344

Liska, Jaroslav
95Czech APS Extraliga-52
96Czech APS Extraliga-238
97Czech APS Extraliga-265
98Czech OFS-409
99Czech OFS-176
00Czech OFS-2

Liska, Jozef
04Slovakian Skalica Team Set-19

Liske, Payton
04Owen Sound Attack-14
05Owen Sound Attack-20

Lisko, Craig
91Ferris State Bulldogs-20
92Ferris State Bulldogs-20

Lisko, Matti
70Finnish Jaakiekko-316
72Finnish Jaakiekko-333

Listwan, Darryn
91Air Canada SJHL-B32
91Air Canada SJHL-E14

Lisy, Peter
85Kitchener Rangers-20
86London Knights-18

Litke, Dane
92Manitoba Junior League-181
98Florida Everblades-12
99Florida Everblades-4

Litma, Lasse
72Finnish Jaakiekko-270
73Finnish Jaakiekko-158
77Finnish Sportscasters-84-2016
78Finnish SM-Liiga-9
78Finnish SM-Liiga-181
79Panini Stickers-169
80Finnish Mallasjuoma-159
81Swedish Semic Hockey VM Stickers-22
82Swedish Semic VM Stickers-35
83Swedish Semic VM Stickers-35
05Finnish Tappara Legendat-17

Little, Bryan
03Barrie Colts-10
04Barrie Colts-12
04Barrie Colts 10th Anniversary-2
04ITG Heroes and Prospects-60
Autographs-BL
04ITG Heroes/Prospects Toronto Expo '05-60
04ITG Heroes/Prospects Expo Heroes/Pros-60
05ITG Heroes/Prosp Toronto Expo Parallel -120
05OHL Bell All-Star Classic-31
05ITG Heroes and Prospects-120
Autographs-A-BLI
Complete Jerseys-CJ-12
Complete Jerseys Gold-CJ-12
Jerseys-GUJ-68
Jerseys Gold-GUJ-68
Emblems-GUE-68
Emblems Gold-GUE-68
Numbers-GUN-68
Numbers Gold-GUN-68
Nameplates-N-46
Nameplates Gold-N-46
Team Orr-T014
06ITG Ultimate Memorabilia Future Star-16
06ITG Ultimate Memorabilia Future Star Gold-16
06ITG Ultimate Memorabilia Future Star Autos-7
06ITG Ultimate Memorabilia Future Star Autos Gold-7
06ITG Ultimate Memorabilia Future Star Patches Autos-7
06ITG Ultimate Memorabilia Future Star Patches Autos Gold-7
06Barrie Colts-10
06ITG Heroes and Prospects-86
Autographs-ABLI
Class of 2006-CL08
Jerseys-GUJ43
Jerseys Gold-GUJ43
Emblems-GUE43
Emblems Gold-GUE43
Numbers-GUN43
Numbers Gold-GUN43
Quad Emblems-QE01
Quad Emblems Gold-QE01
07ITG Going For Gold World Juniors-17
Autographs-17
Emblems-GUE17
Jerseys-GUJ17
Numbers-GUN17

Little, Mike
93Portland Winter Hawks-14

Little, Neil
93RPI Engineers-15
94Classic-75
Gold-75
98Grand Rapids Griffins-11
01BAP Memorabilia-443
Emerald-443
Ruby-443
Sapphire-443
01Parkhurst-335
01UD Mask Collection-160
Gold-160
02BAP First Edition-300

02Between the Pipes-41
Gold-41
Silver-41
02Pacific-283
Blue-283
Red-283
02Upper Deck MVP-213
Gold-213
Classics-213
Golden Classics-213
02Philadelphia Phantoms-21
03Philadelphia Phantoms-16
04Philadelphia Phantoms-8
04ITG Heroes and Prospects Net Prospects-15
04ITG Heroes and Prosp Net Prospects Gold-15
05Finnish Cardset -175
05Philadelphia Phantoms All-Decade Team-6

Little, Richard
92Norwegian Elite Series-137

Littlejohn, Frank
05Missouri River Otters-17

Littman, David
89ProCards IHL-103
90ProCards AHL/IHL-269
91ProCards-19
91Rochester Americans Dunkin' Donuts-9
91Rochester Americans Kodak-15
91Rochester Americans Postcards-13
92Atlanta Knights-23
92Classic-104
Gold-104
93Ultra-237
All-Rookies-5
96Collector's Edge Ice-150
Prism-150
98Orlando Solar Bears-13
98Orlando Solar Bears II-1

Litvinenko, Alexei
99Russian Dynamo Moscow-4
00Russian Hockey League-214

Litzenberger, Ed
44Beehive Group II Photos-113
44Beehive Group II Photos-187
44Beehive Group II Photos-261
44Beehive Group II Photos-419
52St. Lawrence Sales-7
57Topps-26
58Topps-16
59Topps-61
60Shirriff Coins-62
60Topps-21
61Parkhurst-28
61Shirriff/Salada Coins-71
62Parkhurst-12
62Shirriff Coins-18
63Chex Photos-32
63Parkhurst-6
63Parkhurst-66
64Beehive Group III Photos-173
91Ultimate Original Six-58
French-58
93Parkhurst Parkie Reprints-PR66
94Parkhurst Missing Link-24
02Parkhurst Reprints-267
02Parkhurst Reprints-276
02Parkhurst Reprints-284
03Parkhurst Original Six Chicago-79
Autographs-10

Liukka, Simo
96Finnish SISU Redline-114

Liukonnen, Mikko
02Swiss HNL-436

Lius, Joni
92Finnish Jyvas-Hyva Stickers-84
93Finnish Jyvas-Hyva Stickers-142
93Finnish SISU-152
94Finnish SISU-17
95Finnish SISU-64
95Finnish SISU Limited-49
97Swedish Collector's Choice-77
98Finnish Kerailysarja-238
Leijonat-31
99Finnish Cardset-140
00Finnish Cardset-219
02Finnish Cardset-217
04Finnish Cardset-177
Parallel-131
05Finnish Cardset -332

Liut, Mike
800-Pee-Chee-31
80Topps-31
810-Pee-Chee-289
810-Pee-Chee-301
810-Pee-Chee Stickers-129
810-Pee-Chee Stickers-153
81Post Standups-13
81Topps-20
81Topps-W128
820-Pee-Chee-306
820-Pee-Chee Stickers-196
82Post Cereal-17
82Topps Stickers-196
830-Pee-Chee-309
830-Pee-Chee-316
830-Pee-Chee Stickers-129
83Puffy Stickers-14
83Topps Stickers-129
840-Pee-Chee-187
840-Pee-Chee Stickers-57
84Topps-132
850-Pee-Chee-88
850-Pee-Chee Stickers-169
857-Eleven Credit Cards-7
85Topps-88
85Whalers Junior Wendy's-10
860-Pee-Chee-133
860-Pee-Chee Stickers-52
86Topps-133
86Whalers Junior Thomas'-14
870-Pee-Chee-152
870-Pee-Chee Minis-24
870-Pee-Chee Stickers-121
870-Pee-Chee Stickers-209
87Panini Stickers-38
87Topps-152
87Topps Sticker Inserts-8
87Whalers Jr. Burger King/Pepsi-13
880-Pee-Chee-127
880-Pee-Chee Minis-20
880-Pee-Chee Stickers-263
88Panini Stickers-235
88Topps-127
88Whalers Junior Ground Round-10
89Capitals Kodak-1
890-Pee-Chee-97

890-Pee-Chee-317
890-Pee-Chee Stickers-267
89Sports Illustrated for Kids I-250
89Topps-97
89Whalers Junior Milk-14
90Bowman-66
Tiffany-66
90Capitals Kodak-15
90Capitals Postcards-15
90Capitals Smokey-14
90Kraft-31
900-Pee-Chee-44
90Panini Stickers-165
90Pro Set-316
90Score-68
90Score-354
Canadian-68
Canadian-354
90Score Hottest/Rising Stars-32
90Topps-44
Tiffany-44
90Upper Deck-127
French-127
91Bowman-290
91Capitals Junior 5x7-19
91Capitals Kodak-18
910-Pee-Chee-154
91Parkhurst-196
French-196
91Pinnacle-169
French-169
91Pro Set Platinum PC-PC16
91Score American-99
91Score Canadian Bilingual-99
91Score Canadian English-99
91Stadium Club-10
91Topps-154
91Upper Deck-259
French-259
92Blues UD Best of the Blues-4
92Score-368
Canadian-368
92Topps-307
Gold-307G
99BAP Millennium Pearson-P10
99BAP Millennium Pearson Autographs-P10
01Fleer Legacy-49
Ultimate-49
01Greats of the Game-83
Autographs-83
04ITG Franchises US East-356
04ITG Franchises US West-295
Autographs-A-ML
06Parkhurst-67
Autographs-67
Autographs Dual-DALD

Liv, Stefan
00Swedish Upper Deck-92
02Swedish SHL-178
02Swedish SHL-286
Masks-2
Netminders-NM3
Parallel-178
Parallel-286
02Swedish SHL Promos-TCC4
02Swedish SHL Signatures Series II-6
03Swedish Elite-189
Hot Numbers-HN1
Masks-2
Masks II-1
Signatures II-14
Silver-189
Zero Hero-6
04Swedish Alfabilder Alfa Stars-7
04Swedish Alfabilder Proof Parallels-7
04Swedish Elitset-47
Gold-47
In The Crease-5
Jerseys Series 2-SL
Masks-4
04Swedish Pure Skills-34
Parallel-34
05Swedish SHL Elitset-50
Catchers-5
Catchers Gold-5
Gold-50
Series One Jerseys-1
Series Two Signatures-12
Stoppers-7
06Beehive-118
Matte-118
06Between The Pipes-46
Autographs-ASL
06Hot Prospects-155
Red Hot-155
White Hot-155
060-Pee-Chee-588
Rainbow-588
06SP Authentic-244
Limited-244
06The Cup-127
Autographed Rookie Masterpiece Pressplates-127
Gold Rainbow Autographed Rookie Patches-127
Masterpiece Pressplates (Bee Hive)-118
Masterpiece Pressplates (Marquee Rookies)-588
Masterpiece Pressplates (SP Authentic)-244
Masterpiece Pressplates (Sweet Beginnings)-122
Masterpiece Pressplates (Ultimate Collection)-72
Rookies Black-127
Rookies Platinum-127
06Ultimate Collection-72
06Upper Deck-466
Exclusives Parallel-466
High Gloss Parallel-466
Masterpieces-466
06Upper Deck Sweet Shot-122
Rookie Jerseys Autographs-122
06Swedish SHL Elitset-53
Goal Patrol-8
In The Crease-5

Livernoche, Patrick
93Drummondville Voltigeurs-19

Livinenko, Alexei
01Russian Hockey League-78

Liwing, Jonas
05Swedish SHL Elitset-160
Gold-160
06Swedish SHL Elitset-16

Lizon, Erick
04Victoriaville Tigres-23
05Victoriaville Tigres-18
06Rockford IceHogs -15

Lizotte, David
92Quebec Pee-Wee Tournament-186
03Greenville Grrrowl-15

Ljungberg, Christer
91Swedish Semic Elitserien Stickers-248

Ljungberg, Thomas
85Swedish Panini Stickers-190
86Swedish Panini Stickers-124
87Swedish Panini Stickers-243
89Swedish Semic Elitserien Stickers-230
90Swedish Semic Elitserien Stickers-112
91Swedish Semic Elitserien Stickers-119
92Swedish Semic Elitserien Stickers-148
93Swedish Semic Elitserien-119
94Swedish Leaf-64

Ljungqvist, Daniel
02Swedish SHL-35
Parallel-35
03Swedish Elite-46
Silver-46
04Swedish Elitset-193
Gold-193
05Swedish SHL Elitset-52
05Swedish SHL Elitset-271
Gold-52
Gold-271

Ljusterang, Per
89Swedish Semic Elitserien Stickers-154
90Swedish Semic Elitserien Stickers-227
91Swedish Semic Elitserien Stickers-157
92Swedish Semic Elitserien Stickers-259
93Swedish Semic Elitserien-224

Llado, Roald
93Quebec Pee-Wee Tournament-779

Llano, Kirk
97Quad-City Mallards-6
98Colorado Gold Kings-10
98Colorado Gold Kings Postcards-21
98Las Vegas Coyotes RHI-8
99Topeka Scarecrows-9

Lloyd, Darryl
02Windsor Spitfires-22

Lloyd, Don
03Kootenay Ice-4
04Swift Current Broncos-13
05Swift Current Broncos-13

Lloyd, Jason
02Kamloops Blazers-7

Loach, Lonnie
88Flint Spirits-12
88ProCards IHL-101
89ProCards IHL-60
90ProCards AHL/IHL-538
91ProCards-120
92Parkhurst-305
Emerald Ice-305
92Ultra-146
92Ultra-309
92Upper Deck-466
92Classic-95
Gold-95
92Classic Four-Sport *-210
Gold-210
93PowerPlay-7
93San Diego Gulls-13
96Collector's Edge Ice-123
Prism-123
99Missouri River Otters-12
99Missouri River Otters Sheet-10
99UHL All-Stars West-5T
00Missouri River Otters-2
01Missouri River Otters-3
03Missouri River Otters-24

Loach, Mike
93Windsor Spitfires-11
95Slapshot-288
95Owen Sound Platers-26
95Owen Sound Platers-30
97Toledo Storm-25

Lobb, Aaron
00London Knights-4
01Guelph Storm-11
01Guelph Storm Memorial Cup-11
01UD Prospects-10
Jerseys-J-AL
Jerseys Gold-J-AL
02Guelph Storm-22
03Brampton Batallion-10
03Oshawa Generals-15

Lobsinger, Lucas
05Mississauga Ice Dogs-7
06Mississauga Ice Dogs-22

Locas, Jacques
43Parade Sportive *-70
43Parade Sportive *-71
45Quaker Oats Photos-90
48Exhibits Canadian-13
51Laval Dairy QSHL-95
51Laval Dairy Subset-57
52St. Lawrence Sales-81

Locas, WHA
750-Pee-Chee WHA-129
75Stingers Kahn's-7
76Stingers Kahn's-5

Lochead, Billy
74NHL Action Stamps-97
740-Pee-Chee NHL-318
750-Pee-Chee NHL-103
75Topps-103
760-Pee-Chee NHL-122
76Topps-122
770-Pee-Chee NHL-212
77Topps-212
780-Pee-Chee-122
78Topps-122
790-Pee-Chee-301
94German DEL-343
95German DEL-308
96German DEL-91

Locher, Thomas
93Swiss HNL-295

Lochi, Patrick
01UK Dundee Stars-14
02UK Dundee Stars-14

Locke, Chad
05PEI Rocket-21
06PEI Rocket-22

Locke, Corey
01Ottawa 67's-21
02Ottawa 67's-22
03Ottawa 67's-13
03Ottawa 67's-NNO
04Hamilton Bulldogs-18
04ITG Heroes and Prospects-64
Aspiring-15
Autographs-CL
Complete Emblems-4

Emblems-21
Emblems Gold-21
He Shoots-He Scores Prizes-19
Jersey Autographs-21
Jerseys-21
Jerseys Gold-21
Numbers-21
Numbers Gold-21
04ITG Heroes/Prospects Toronto Expo '05-64
04ITG Heroes/Prospects Expo Heroes/Pros-64
05ITG Heroes/Prosp Toronto Expo Parallel -91
05AHL All-Stars-18
05Hamilton Bulldogs-16
05ITG Heroes and Prospects-91
Autographs-A-CL
06Hamilton Bulldogs-20
06ITG Heroes and Prospects-71
Autographs-ACL
Jerseys-GUJ09
Jerseys Gold-GUJ09
Emblems-GUE09
Emblems Gold-GUE09
Numbers-GUN09
Numbers Gold-GUN09

Locke, Steve
88Niagara Falls Thunder-23

Locker, Derek
93Minnesota-Duluth Bulldogs-18

Lockett, Ken
74Canucks Royal Bank-11
74NHL Action Stamps-282
75Canucks Royal Bank-12
76San Diego Mariners WHA-6

Lockhart, Tommy
83Hall of Fame Postcards-C8
85Hall of Fame-38

Locking, Norm
35Diamond Matchbooks Tan 1-40
35Diamond Matchbooks Tan 2-41
35Diamond Matchbooks Tan 3-37

Lockridge, Tim
81Indianapolis Checkers-13
82Indianapolis Checkers-14

Lockwood, Joe
88ProCards IHL-32

Lococo, Mike
81Sault Ste. Marie Greyhounds-17
82Sault Ste. Marie Greyhounds-16
83Sault Ste. Marie Greyhounds-15

Lodberg, Kristian
98Danish Hockey League-7
99Danish Hockey League-10

Loder, Jeff
96Roanoke Express-7
99Saginaw Gears-3
99UHL All-Stars West-15T

Lodge, Erik
04Lakehead University Thunderwolves-4

Lodin, Hans
86Swedish Panini Stickers-203
87Swedish Panini Stickers-193
89Swedish Semic Elitserien Stickers-175
90Swedish Semic Elitserien Stickers-8
91Swedish Semic Elitserien Stickers-204
92Swedish Semic Elitserien Stickers-227
93Swedish Semic Elitserien-127
94Swedish Leaf-112
95Swedish Leaf-63
95Swedish Upper Deck-97
97Swedish Collector's Choice-103
98Swedish UD Choice-120
99German DEL-316
00German DEL-171
01German Upper Deck-186
02Swedish SHL-192
Parallel-192
03Swedish Elite-59
Silver-59

Loeding, Mark
01Atlantic City Boardwalk Bullies-15
02Atlantic City Boardwalk Bullies-12

Loen, Matt
95Madison Monsters-17
96Madison Monsters-12
02Rockford Ice Hogs-9

Loeppky, Mark
91Air Canada SJHL-E7

Loewen, Darcy
89ProCards AHL-269
90Sabres Campbell's-14
90ProCards AHL/IHL-284
91Upper Deck-421
French-421
91ProCards-4
91Rochester Americans Dunkin' Donuts-10
91Rochester Americans Kodak-16
92OPC Premier-7
92Parkhurst-355
Emerald Ice-355
92Senators Team Issue-8
93OPC Premier-184
Gold-184
93Parkhurst-407
Emerald Ice-407
93Senators Kraft Sheets-14
93Stadium Club-318
Members Only Master Set-318
First Day Issue-318
93Topps/OPC Premier-184
Gold-184
94Las Vegas Thunder-12
95Las Vegas Thunder-6
96Las Vegas Thunder-13
97Las Vegas Thunder-5
99Idaho Steelheads-15
00Idaho Steelheads-12

Loewen, Jamie
95Alaska Gold Kings-12

Lofberg, Christofer
05Swedish SHL Elitset-166
06Swedish SHL Elitset-21

Lofgren, Bengt
69Swedish Hockey-304

Lofgren, Borje
55Swedish Alfabilder-13

Lofqvist, William
67Swedish Hockey-176
69Swedish Hockey-69
70Swedish Hockey-18
71Finnish Suomi Stickers-51
71Swedish Hockey-3
71Swedish Hockey-96
72Swedish Stickers-81
73Finnish Jaakiekko-32
73Swedish Stickers-2
73Swedish Stickers-155
74Finnish Jenkki-30
74Swedish Stickers-147
74Swedish Semic World Champ Stickers-2

Lofroth, Shawn
96Alaska Gold Kings-8

Lofstedt, Borje
69Swedish Hockey-87

Lofstrom, Jonas
95Swedish Leaf-169
95Swedish Upper Deck-28
96Swedish Brynas Tigers-11

Lofstrom, Per
95Swedish Leaf-176
95Swedish Upper Deck-25
96Swedish Brynas Tigers-20
97Swedish Collector's Choice-22
98Swedish UD Choice-38
99Finnish Cardset-315
00Swedish Upper Deck-111
02Swedish SHL-193
Parallel-193

Lofthouse, Mark
78Capitals Team Issue-7
79Capitals Team Issue-11
80O-Pee-Chee-331
88ProCards AHL-132
89New Haven Nighthawks-7

Lofton, Lucas
04Hartford Wolf Pack-12

Loftus, Dave
99Arizona Icecats-13
00Arizona Icecats-14
01Arizona Icecats-11
02Arizona Icecats-13

Logan Sr., Jim
52Juniors Blue Tint-151

Logan, Bob
76Cubs TCMA 1938-23
87Sabres Wonder Bread/Hostess-16
88ProCards AHL-215

Logan, Dan
86Regina Pats-14
86Saskatoon Blades Photos-16

Logan, Dave
78O-Pee-Chee-343
80Canucks Silverwood Dairies-14
80Canucks Team Issue-14
80Pepsi-Cola Caps-112

Logan, Jim
98Dayton Bombers-11
00Fort Wayne Komets-10
00Fort Wayne Komets Shoe Carnival-12
01Fort Wayne Komets-11
01Fort Wayne Komets Shoe Carnival-15

Logan, Joe
03Vancouver Giants-8
05Saskatoon Blades-12
06Saskatoon Blades-15

Logan, Tim
87Regina Pats-16

Loges, Al
93Michigan Wolverines-13

Loginov, Albert
98Russian Hockey League-46
99Russian Hockey League-157

Loginov, Andrei
00Russian Hockey League-48
01Russian Hockey League-134

Loginov, Denis
03Russian Hockey League-257
03Russian Under-18 Team-17
03Russian World Championships Preview-3

Loginov, Vladimir
00Russian Hockey League-71
01Russian Hockey League-163
03Russian Hockey League-123

Lohko, Raimo
66Finnish Jaakiekkosarja-88

Lohko, Timo
96Finnish SISU Redline-113

Lohman, Lars
65Swedish Coralli ISHockey-190

Lohrei, David
98Fayetteville Force-1
02ECHL Update-U-13
02Reading Royals-3

Loi, Brad
84Richelieu Riverains-10

Loicq, Paul
83Hall of Fame-234
83Hall of Fame Postcards-F8
85Hall of Fame-234

Loikala, Jani-Matti
95Finnish SISU-249
99Finnish Cardset-304
01Finnish Cardset-267

Loikas, Juha-Pekka
04Finnish Cardset-226
05Finnish Cardset -35
06Finnish Cardset-37

Loikets, Chad
03Erie Otters-14
04Erie Otters-14
05Erie Otters-17
06Gatineau Olympiques-25

Loiselle, Claude
87Panini Stickers-85
88Devils Caretta-17
88Panini Stickers-273
89Nordiques Team Issue-27
89Nordiques General Foods-21
89Nordiques Police-18
90Bowman-175
Tiffany-175
90Nordiques Petro-Canada-16
90Nordiques Team Issue-19
90Panini Stickers-151
90Pro Set-252
90Score-207
Canadian-207
90Upper Deck-338
French-338
91Maple Leafs PLAY-22
91Nordiques Panini Team Stickers-14
91Pinnacle-296
French-296
91Pro Set-493
French-493
91Score Canadian Bilingual-532
91Score Canadian English-532
92Pinnacle-219
French-219
92Score-328
Canadian-328
92Topps-338
Gold-338G
93OPC Premier-328
Gold-328
93Topps/OPC Premier-328
Gold-328

Loiselle, Pierre
98Quebec Remparts-12
Signed-12

Loisette, Jean-Marie
56Quebec Aces-9

Lojek, Martin
03Brampton Batallion-11
04Brampton Battalion-8
06Rochester Americans-12
07Upper Deck Victory-215
Black-215
Gold-215

Lojkin, Alexei
95Fredericton Canadiens-19
96Fredericton Canadiens-14

Loksa, Michal
95Slovakian-Quebec Pee-Wee Tournament-14

Loktev, Konstantin
73Swedish Stickers-98

Lomakin, Andrei
89Swedish Semic World Champ Stickers-98
90O-Pee-Chee-472
91Pro Set Platinum-208
91Flyers J.C. Penney-18
91O-Pee-Chee Inserts-40R
91OPC Premier-178
91Parkhurst-131
French-131
91Pinnacle-305
French-305
91Score Canadian Bilingual-660
91Score Canadian English-660
91Score Rookie/Traded-110T
91Upper Deck-518
French-518
91Russian Stars Red Ace-12
91Star Pics-17
92Bowman-286
92Flyers J.C. Penney-16
92Flyers Upper Deck Sheets-19
92Flyers Upper Deck Sheets-43
92O-Pee-Chee-37
92Panini Stickers-193
92Panini Stickers French-193
92Pinnacle-162
French-162
92Score-129
Canadian-129
92Stadium Club-115
92Topps-380
Gold-380G
92Ultra-372
92Upper Deck-428
Euro-Stars-E17
92Finnish Semic-115
92Russian Tri-Globe From Russia With Puck-3
92Russian Tri-Globe From Russia With Puck-4
93Donruss-128
93Leaf-401
93OPC Premier-82
Gold-82
93Panini Stickers-52
93Panthers Team Issue-6
93Parkhurst-349
Emerald Ice-349
93Pinnacle-360
Canadian-360
93PowerPlay-96
93Score-529
Gold-529
Canadian-529
Canadian Gold-529
93Stadium Club-57
93Stadium Club-402
Members Only Master Set-57
Members Only Master Set-402
OPC-57
First Day Issue-57
First Day Issue-402
First Day Issue OPC-57
93Topps/OPC Premier-82
Gold-82
93Ultra-327
93Upper Deck-102
93Swedish Semic World Champ Stickers-143
94Canada Games NHL POGS-106
94Donruss-85
94EA Sports-52
94Leaf-302
94OPC Premier-177
Special Effects-177
94Parkhurst-84
Gold-84
94Pinnacle-337
Artist's Proofs-337
Rink Collection-337
94Topps/OPC Premier-177
Special Effects-177
94Ultra-81
94Upper Deck-471
Electric Ice-471
94Finnish Jaa Kiekko-160
95Swiss HNL-68
96German DEL-39

Lomanno, Luciano
03Halifax Mooseheads-23
04Halifax Mooseheads-18
05Halifax Mooseheads-5
06Halifax Mooseheads-5

Lomas, David
02Windsor Spitfires-4
05Kitchener Rangers-26

Lomas, Mike
06Brampton Battalion-20

Lombard, Dan
02ECHL All-Star Northern-27
03Florence Pride-152

Lombardi, Daniel
06Sarnia Sting-17

Lombardi, Matthew
00Victoriaville Tigres-3
Signed-3
02SPx Rookie Redemption-R194
03BAP Memorabilia-196
Emerald-196
Gold-196
Ruby-196
Sapphire-196
03BAP Ultimate Memorabilia Autographs-95
Gold-95
03BAP Ultimate Mem Auto Jerseys-95
03BAP Ultimate Mem Auto Emblems-95
03BAP Ultimate Mem Auto Numbers-95
03BAP Ultimate Mem Calder Candidates-9
03BAP Ultimate Mem Calder Candidates Gold-9
03BAP Ultimate Mem Franch Present Future-5
03BAP Ultimate Mem Rookie Jersey Emblems-10
03BAP Ultimate Mem Rookie Jsy Emblem Gold-10
03BAP Ultimate Mem Rookie Jersey Numbers-10
03BAP Ultimate Mem Rookie Jsy Number Gold-10
03BAP Ultimate Memorabilia Triple Threads-32
03Black Diamond-158
Black-158
Green-158
Red-158
03Bowman-127
Gold-127
03Bowman Chrome-127
Refractors-127
Gold Refractors-127
Xfractors-127
03Crown Royale-106
Red-107
Retail-106
Retail-107
Jerseys-5
Patches-5
03ITG Action-630
03ITG Toronto Spring Expo Class of 2004-2
03ITG Used Signature Series-130
Autographs Gold-130
03ITG VIP Rookie Debut-29
03Pacific-362
03Pacific Calder-164
03Pacific Complete-513
Red-513
03Pacific Exhibit-228
03Pacific Heads-Up-105
Hobby LTD-105
Retail LTD-105
Jerseys-6
Prime Prospects-4
Prime Prospects LTD-4
03Pacific Invincible-104
Blue-104
Red-104
Retail-104
03Pacific Luxury Suite-55
Gold-55
03Pacific Prism-153
03Pacific Quest for the Cup-105
Calder Contenders-3
03Pacific Supreme-108
Blue-107
Red-107
Retail-108
03Parkhurst Toronto Expo Rookie Preview-PRP-14
03Parkhurst Rookie-186
Calder Candidates-CMC-8
Calder Candidates Gold-CMC-8
Rookie Emblems-RE-35
Rookie Emblems Gold-RE-35
Rookie Jerseys-RJ-35
Rookie Jerseys Gold-RJ-35
Rookie Numbers-RN-35
Rookie Numbers Gold-RN-35
Teammates Gold-RT18
Teammates-RT18
03SP Authentic-107
Limited-107
03SP Game Used-54
Gold-54
03SPx-201
Radiance-201
Spectrum-201
03Titanium-208
Patches-208
03Topps Pristine-164
03Topps Pristine-165
03Topps Pristine-166
Gold Refractor Die Cuts-164
Gold Refractor Die Cuts-165
Gold Refractor Die Cuts-166
Refractors-164
Refractors-165
Refractors-166
Press Plates Black-164
Press Plates Black-165
Press Plates Black-166
Press Plates Cyan-164
Press Plates Cyan-165
Press Plates Cyan-166
Press Plates Magenta-164
Press Plates Magenta-165
Press Plates Magenta-166
Press Plates Yellow-164
Press Plates Yellow-165
Press Plates Yellow-166
03Topps Traded-TT91
Blue-TT91
Gold-TT91
Red-TT91
03UD Honor Roll-191
03Upper Deck-205
Canadian Exclusives-205
HG-205
03Upper Deck Ice-112
Glass Parallel-112
03Upper Deck MVP-446
03Upper Deck Rookie Update-192
YoungStars-YS14
03Upper Deck Trilogy-144
Limited-144
04Pacific-43
Blue-43
Red-43
04SP Authentic-15
Limited-15
Octographs-OS-CUP
Sign of the Times-ST-LO
05Parkhurst True Colors-TCCGY
05Parkhurst True Colors-TCCGY
05SP Game Used Authentic Fabrics Quad-IAKL
05SP Game Used Authentic Patches Quad -IAKL
05UD Toronto Fall Expo Priority Signings-PS-ML
05Ultra-33
Gold-33
Ice-33
05Upper Deck-277
Jerseys-J-MLO
Jerseys Series II-J2LO
Ice Cool Threads-CTML
Ice Cool Threads Glass-CTML
Ice Cool Threads Patches-CTPML
05Upper Deck MVP-68
Gold-68
Platinum-68
06Gatorade-6
06O-Pee-Chee-85
Rainbow-85
06Upper Deck MVP Jerseys-OJFM
07Upper Deck Ovation-94
07Upper Deck Victory-150
Black-150
Gold-150

Lombardi, Michael
04Barrie Colts-3
06Barrie Colts-25

Lombardo, Chris
93Quebec Pee-Wee Tournament-755

Lombardo, Joe
95Slapshot-389
95Sudbury Wolves-3
95Sudbury Wolves Police-12
96Sudbury Wolves Police-15

Lomow, Boyd
83Brandon Wheat Kings-13
84Brandon Wheat Kings-21

Lomow, Byron
83Brandon Wheat Kings-6
84Brandon Wheat Kings-3
85Brandon Wheat Kings-3
89ProCards IHL-141
90ProCards AHL/IHL-526

Loncan, Adam
98Prince George Cougars-13
05Odessa Jackalopes-14

Loney, Brian
94Classic Pro Prospects-217
95Parkhurst International-481
Emerald Ice-481
96Syracuse Crunch-17
99German DEL-160
01Greensboro Generals-8

Loney, Troy
83Penguins Coke-14
87Penguins Kodak-17
88Panini Stickers-341
89Panini Stickers-319
89Penguins Foodland-13B
90O-Pee-Chee-347
90Panini Stickers-138
90Pro Set-237
90Score-371
Canadian-371
90Topps-347
Tiffany-347
90Upper Deck-367
French-367
91Parkhurst-352
French-352
91Penguins Coke/Elby's-24
91Penguins Foodland-7
91Score Canadian Bilingual-522
91Score Canadian English-522
91Upper Deck-489
French-489
92Penguins Coke/Clark-11
92Penguins Foodland-8
92Penguins Foodland Coupon Stickers-5
92Score-348
Canadian-348
92Stadium Club-357
92Topps-397
Gold-397G
92Ultra-378
92Upper Deck-208
93Kraft-41
93OPC Premier-340
Gold-340
93Parkhurst-9
Emerald Ice-9
93Pinnacle-379
Canadian-379
Captains-1
Captains Canadian-1
93PowerPlay-8
93Score-547
Gold-547
Canadian-547
Canadian Gold-547
93Stadium Club-395
Members Only Master Set-395
First Day Issue-395
93Topps/OPC Premier-340
Gold-340
93Ultra-259
93Upper Deck-438
SP-2
94Be A Player Signature Cards-84
94EA Sports-4
94Leaf-435
94OPC Premier-363
Special Effects-363
94Parkhurst-5
Gold-5
94Pinnacle-396
Artist's Proofs-396
Rink Collection-396
94Score-67
Gold-67
Platinum-67
94Topps/OPC Premier-363
Special Effects-363
94Upper Deck-385
Electric Ice-385

Long, Andrew
92Quebec Pee-Wee Tournament-239
94Guelph Storm-26
95Slapshot-103
95Guelph Storm-7
96Guelph Storm-25
97Guelph Storm-18
98New Haven Beast-19
98Bowman CHL-17
Golden Anniversary-17
OPC International-17
98Bowman Chrome CHL-17
Golden Anniversary-17
Golden Anniversary Refractors-17
OPC International-17
OPC International Refractors-17
Refractors-17
99Louisville Panthers-27
01Florida Everblades-7
02Columbus Cottonmouths-11

Long, Barry
72O-Pee-Chee-288
75O-Pee-Chee WHA-69
75O-Pee-Chee WHA-90
76O-Pee-Chee WHA-7
78Jets Postcards-12
79Red Wings Postcards-10
80Jets Postcards-12
80O-Pee-Chee-258
80Pepsi-Cola Caps-131
80Topps-258
81O-Pee-Chee-369
81O-Pee-Chee Stickers-142
83Jets Postcards-11
84Jets Police-23
85Jets Police-23

Long, Bill
86London Knights-13

Long, Colin
05Kelowna Rockets-17
06Texas Tornados-10

Long, Eddie
99Fort Wayne Komets Points Leaders-3
99Fort Wayne Komets Penalty Leaders-10
01Fort Wayne Komets Shoe Carnival-12

Long, Eric
94Raleigh Icecaps-10
99Colorado Gold Kings Wendy's-3
02Arkansas Riverblades-8

Long, Joe
04Green Bay Gamblers-9

Long, Marc
98Sudbury Wolves-11
03UK London Racers-8

Long, Stan
51Buffalo Bison-13

Long, Ted
75Hamilton Fincups-11

Longauer, Michal
917th Inn. Sketch QMJHL-202

Longbroek, David
92British Columbia JHL-45

Longchamps, R.J.
93Quebec Pee-Wee Tournament-599

Longe, Benny
81Ottawa 67's-11

Longman, Gary
66Columbus Checkers-11

Longo, Chris
89Peterborough Petes-114
897th Inn. Sketch OHL-114
897th Inn. Sketch OHL-178
907th Inn. Sketch OHL-364
91Peterborough Petes-7
917th Inn. Sketch OHL-128
93Portland Pirates-17
94Portland Pirates-14
94Classic Pro Prospects-89
96Springfield Falcons-16
97Cleveland Lumberjacks-18
97Cleveland Lumberjacks Postcards-11
98Cleveland Lumberjacks-15
99Cleveland Lumberjacks-13
00Cleveland Lumberjacks-8

Longo, John
93Quebec Pee-Wee Tournament-1293
03Atlantic City Boardwalk Bullies-13
04Atlantic City Boardwalk Bullies Kinko's-16

Longo, Mike
90Rayside-Balfour Jr. Canadians-12
91Rayside-Balfour Jr. Canadians-9

Longobardi, Ciro
00Connecticut Huskies-12

Longstaff, David
97UK Sheffield Steelers-8
99UK Sheffield Steelers-9
00UK Sekonda Superleague-154
00UK Sheffield Steelers-14
00UK Sheffield Steelers Centurions-3
02UK Manchester Storm-12

Longstaff, Scott
91British Columbia JHL-2

Longtry, Doc
23V128-1 Paulin's Candy-57

Lonn, Anders
95Swedish Upper Deck 1st Division Stars-DS12
97Swedish Collector's Choice-116
98Swedish UD Choice-130
99Swedish Upper Deck-97

Lonn, Mats
64Swedish Coralli ISHockey-8
65Swedish Coralli ISHockey-8
67Swedish Hockey-144
69Swedish Hockey-156
70Swedish Hockey-124
71Swedish Hockey-214
72Swedish Stickers-191

Lonnberg, Harri
93Finnish SISU-225
94Finnish SISU-221
95Finnish SISU-308
Painkillers-4
98Finnish Kerailysarja-220

Lonsberry, Ross
67Topps-35
69O-Pee-Chee-104
69Topps-104
70Esso Power Players-151
70O-Pee-Chee-37
70Sargent Promotions Stamps-66
70Topps-37
71O-Pee-Chee-121
71Sargent Promotions Stamps-69
71Topps-121
71Toronto Sun-120
72O-Pee-Chee-166
72Sargent Promotions Stamps-166
72Topps-112
72Finnish Semic World Championship-206
72Swedish Semic World Championship-206
73Flyers Linnett-10
73O-Pee-Chee-36
73Topps-36
74NHL Action Stamps-199
74O-Pee-Chee NHL-144
74Topps-144
75Flyers Canada Dry Cans-12
75O-Pee-Chee NHL-110
75Topps-110
76O-Pee-Chee NHL-201
76Topps-201
77O-Pee-Chee NHL-257
77Topps-257
78O-Pee-Chee-186
78Topps-186
79O-Pee-Chee-58
79Topps-58
80O-Pee-Chee-388
81O-Pee-Chee-263

Lonsinger, Bryan
92Harvard Crimson-19

Loob, Hakan
82Swedish Semic VM Stickers-22
83Vachon-11
83Swedish Semic VM Stickers-22
84O-Pee-Chee-229
84O-Pee-Chee Stickers-242
85Flames Red Rooster-13
85O-Pee-Chee-184
86Flames Red Rooster-10
86Kraft Drawings-35
87Flames Red Rooster-10
87Flames Red Rooster-11
87O-Pee-Chee-208
87O-Pee-Chee Stickers-44
87Panini Stickers-214
88Flames Postcards-17
88O-Pee-Chee-110
88O-Pee-Chee Box Bottoms-O
88O-Pee-Chee Minis-21
88O-Pee-Chee Stickers-94
88O-Pee-Chee Stickers-118
88Panini Stickers-9
88Topps-110
88Topps Box Bottoms-O
88Topps Sticker Inserts-3
89Swedish Semic Elitserien Stickers-91
90Swedish Semic Elitserien Stickers-260
91Finnish Semic World Champ Stickers-38
91Swedish Semic Elitserien Stickers-92
91Swedish Semic Elitserien Stickers-315
91Swedish Semic Elitserien Stickers-318
91Swedish Semic Elitserien Stickers-325
91Swedish Semic Elitserien Stickers-347
91Swedish Semic World Champ Stickers-38
92Finnish Semic-61
92Swedish Semic Elitserien Stickers-111
92Swedish Semic Elitserien Stickers-337
92Swedish Semic Elitserien Stickers-340
92Swedish Semic Elitserien Stickers-346
93Swedish Semic Elitserien-84
93Swedish Semic Elitserien-303
93Swedish Semic World Champ Stickers-9
94Finnish Jaa Kiekko-64
94Swedish Leaf-39
Gold Cards-8
Playmakers-6
Top Guns-2
95Finnish Semic World Championships-75
95Swedish Leaf-1
95Swedish Leaf-305
Champs-3
Face to Face-5
Mega-9
95Swedish Upper Deck-64
95Swedish Upper Deck-223
95Swedish Upper Deck-252
95Swedish Globe World Championships-52
95Swedish Globe World Championships-246
97Swedish Alfabilder Autographs-17
01Swedish Alfabilder-17
04ITG Franchises Canadian-4
Forever Rivals-FR6
Forever Rivals Gold-FR6
Memorabilia-SM32
Memorabilia Gold-SM32
04ITG Franchises Update Autographs-HL
04ITG Franchises Update Complete Jerseys-UCJ3
04ITG Franchises Upd Complete Jersey Gold-UCJ3
04UD All-World-55
04UD All-World-116
Gold-55
Autographs-55
Autographs-116
Dual Autographs-AD-KL
Dual Autographs-AD-LS
Triple Autographs-AT-NLN
Triple Autographs-AT-SLN
Quad Autographs-AQ-ALS
Quad Autographs-AQ-OAS
04Swedish Alfabilder Alfa Stars-52
04Swedish Alfabilder Alfa Star Golden Ice-3
04Swedish Alfabilder Next In Line-5
04Swedish Alfabilder Proof Parallels-52
05SPx Xcitement Legends-XL-HL
05SPx Xcitement Legends Gold-XL-HL
05SPx Xcitement Legends Spectrum-XL-HL
05UD Artifacts-130
Blue-130
Gold-130
Green-130
Pewter-130
Red-130
Gold Autographed-130
06Parkhurst-154
Autographs-154

Loob, Jan
86Swedish Panini Stickers-267

Loob, Peter
83Swedish Semic Elitserien-205
84Fredericton Express-14
86Swedish Panini Stickers-261

Looby, Mike
03Sault Ste. Marie Greyhounds-17
05Kingston Frontenacs-19
06Rio Grande Valley Killer Bees-14

Loof, Mattias
92Swedish Semic Elitserien Stickers-171
93Swedish Semic Elitserien-140
94Swedish Leaf-247
95Swedish Leaf-293
95Swedish Upper Deck-198
97Swedish Collector's Choice-188
98Swedish UD Choice-188
99German DEL-222
00German DEL-90
01German Upper Deck-98
02German DEL City Press-118
03German DEL-130

Looney, Shelley
94Classic Women of Hockey-W34

Loong, Arne
64Swedish Coralli ISHockey-63
65Swedish Coralli ISHockey-126

Looser, Patrick
93Swiss HNL-481
95Swiss HNL-151
96Swiss HNL-287
99Swiss Panini Stickers-323
00Swiss Panini Stickers-300
01Swiss HNL-394

Loosli, Thomas
93Swiss HNL-253

Loov, Mats
83Swedish Semic Elitserien-146
84Swedish Semic Elitserien-166
85Swedish Panini Stickers-151
86Swedish Panini Stickers-129
87Swedish Panini Stickers-120
89Swedish Semic Elitserien Stickers-108
90Swedish Semic Elitserien Stickers-114
92Swedish Semic Elitserien Stickers-266
93Swedish Semic Elitserien-240
94Swedish Leaf-93
Top Guns-10
95Swedish Leaf-122
Face to Face-11
95Swedish Upper Deck-185

Lopatka, Geoff
92Cornell Big Red-19
93Cornell Big Red-17

Lopes, George
93Quebec Pee-Wee Tournament-1423

Loponen, Jouni
94Finnish SISU-286
95Finnish SISU-59
95Finnish SISU Limited-48
96Finnish SISU Redline-58
97Swedish Collector's Choice-86
98Finnish Kerailysarja-231
Leijonat-12
99Finnish Cardset-134
00Finnish Cardset-94
02Finnish Cardset-218
02Swedish SHL-37
Parallel-37
03Swedish Elite-49
Silver-49
04Swedish Elitset-50
Gold-50
05Finnish Cardset -270
06Finnish Cardset-97

Loppi, Matias
05Finnish Cardset -116
06Finnish Cardset-125

Lopponen, Jari
71Finnish Suomi Stickers-328

Lopresti, Pete
76O-Pee-Chee NHL-184
76Topps-184
77O-Pee-Chee NHL-13
77Topps-13
78O-Pee-Chee-230
78Topps-230
79Panini Stickers-206
79O-Pee-Chee-364
88Oilers Tenth Anniversary-122

LoPresti, Sam
34Beehive Group I Photos-64

Loprieno, Joe
04Chicago Steel-10

Loranger, Guy
02Thetford Mines Coyotes-12

Lord, Adam
92British Columbia JHL-160
98Amarillo Rattlers-11
99San Angelo Outlaws-8

Lord, Andrew
03Vernon Vipers-10

Lord, Lars-Erik
90Swedish Semic Elitserien Stickers-200

Lord, Philippe
92Quebec Pee-Wee Tournament-70
93Quebec Pee-Wee Tournament-293
96Rimouski Oceanic-17
96Rimouski Oceanic Quebec Police-16

Lorentz, Dave
89Peterborough Petes-109
897th Inn. Sketch OHL-109

Lorentz, Jim
70Esso Power Players-249
70O-Pee-Chee-209
70Sargent Promotions Stamps-192
71O-Pee-Chee-227
71Sargent Promotions Stamps-192
71Topps-13
71Toronto Sun-239
72O-Pee-Chee-116
72Sabres Postcards-8
72Sargent Promotions Stamps-36
72Topps-68
73O-Pee-Chee-75
73Sabres Bells-2
73Sabres Postcards-4
73Topps-171
74NHL Action Stamps-48
74O-Pee-Chee NHL-61
74Sabres Postcards-12
74Topps-61
75O-Pee-Chee NHL-28
75Sabres Linnett-4
75Topps-28
76O-Pee-Chee NHL-162
76Topps-162
77O-Pee-Chee NHL-58
77Topps-58
78O-Pee-Chee-161
78Topps-161
03South Carolina Stingrays-331
04Fresno Falcons-12

Lorentz, Tom
84Minnesota-Duluth Bulldogs-14
85Minnesota-Duluth Bulldogs-20

Lorenz, Danny
91ProCards-457
92Ultra-345
93Leaf-343
93Classic Pro Prospects-132
95Cincinnati Cyclones-14
96Milwaukee Admirals-14
96Collector's Edge Ice-113
Prism-113
97Milwaukee Admirals-10
98German DEL-244
00Tacoma Sabercats-8
01UK Nottingham Panthers-15
03New Mexico Scorpions-8

Lorenzi, Carlo
95Swedish World Championships Stickers-84

Lorenzo, Johnny
907th Inn. Sketch QMJHL-196
917th Inn. Sketch QMJHL-70

Lorer, Eduard
94German First League-537

Loretto, Chuck
94Central Hockey League-100
Lorimer, Bob
79Islanders Transparencies-10
79O-Pee-Chee-181
79Topps-181
80O-Pee-Chee-138
80Topps-138
81O-Pee-Chee-214
81Rockies Postcards-13
82O-Pee-Chee-142
82O-Pee-Chee Stickers-228
82Post Cereal-11
82Topps Stickers-228
83Devils Postcards-15
83NHL Key Tags-72
83O-Pee-Chee-232
84Devils Postcards-4
84O-Pee-Chee-114
Loring, Al
88ProCards AHL-208
Loring, Brad
90 7th Inn. Sketch WHL-119
91British Columbia JHL-145
92British Columbia JHL-36
Lorrain, Rod
34Beehive Group I Photos-165
37O-Pee-Chee V304E-176
38Quaker Oats Photos-23
39O-Pee-Chee V301-1-23
Lortscher, Arnold
01Swiss HNL-361
02Swiss HNL-413
Losch, Mike
94German DEL-49
95German DEL-43
04German Berlin Eisbarens 50th Anniv-2
Loschbrandt, Jan Petter
92Norwegian Elite Series-128
Loscheck, Volker
94German First League-457
Loschek, Jorg
94German First League-454
Lostedt, Patrik
05Finnish Cardset -192
06Finnish Cardset-198
Loth, Andreas
94German DEL-257
95German DEL-255
99German DEL-179
99German DEL-389
00German DEL-120
01German Upper Deck-129
02German DEL City Press-178
03German DEL-158
04German DEL-90
04German DEL Update-324A
04German Ingolstadt Panthers-29
Lotila, Petteri
99Finnish Cardset-286
01Finnish Cardset-89
03UK Manchester Phoenix-11
Lotila, Tenho
66Finnish Jaakiekkosarja-5
Lotjonen, Osmo
71Finnish Suomi Stickers-287
73Finnish Jaakiekko-206
Lotvonen, Kimmo
95Finnish SISU-301
96Finnish SISU Redline-96
98Finnish Kerailysarja-167
99Finnish Cardset-80
00Finnish Cardset-303
01Finnish Cardset-280
02Finnish Cardset-63
03Finnish Cardset-90
04Finnish Cardset-260
06Swedish SHL Elitset-279
Loubier, Yves
91 7th Inn. Sketch QMJHL-274
98Thetford Mines Coyotes-16
01Thetford Mines Coyotes-17
Loucks, Bob
89Lethbridge Hurricanes-12
90 7th Inn. Sketch WHL-137
90 7th Inn. Sketch WHL-149
91 7th Inn. Sketch WHL-359
95Tri-City Americans-17
00Medicine Hat Tigers-14
Loucks, Scott
90 7th Inn. Sketch WHL-296
91 7th Inn. Sketch WHL-87
93Kamloops Blazers-14
Louder, Greg
94Wheeling Thunderbirds-10
Louder, Mathieu
93Quebec Pee-Wee Tournament-971
Loughlean, Cody
04Oklahoma City Blazers-10
Loughlin, Clem
24Anonymous NHL-127
35Diamond Matchbooks Tan 4-10
Loughren, Kris
92Quebec Pee-Wee Tournament-921
93Quebec Pee-Wee Tournament-580
Louhi, Jyrki
98Finnish Kerailysarja-64
99Finnish Cardset-37
00Finnish Cardset-269
03Finnish Cardset-36
04Finnish Cardset-36
Parallel-26
05Finnish Cardset -29
06Finnish Cardset-241
Louhivaara, Ossi
04Finnish Cardset-253
05Finnish Cardset -71
06Finnish Cardset-80
Louis, Mark
03Brandon Wheat Kings-19
04Brandon Wheat Kings-22
05Brandon Wheat Kings-18
Louis-Seize, Eric
06Halifax Mooseheads-21
Loup, Thierry
93Swiss HNL-490
95Swiss HNL-440
96Swiss HNL-428
Loustel, Ron
81Saskatoon Blades-23
82Brandon Wheat Kings-22
Louttit, Eddie
52Juniors Blue Tint-11
Louttit, Paul
81Ottawa 67's-12
82Ottawa 67's-12
Louzek, Martin
99Czech OFS-432
Lovatsis, George
06Barrie Colts-23
Lovdahl, Anders
99Calgary Hitmen-15
99Calgary Hitmen Autographs-15
Lovdahl, Orjan
92Finnish Semic-39
92Norwegian Elite Series-60
95Swedish Globe World Championships-191
95Swedish World Championships Stickers-247
Love, Brad
91 7th Inn. Sketch OHL-198
Love, Brandon
93Quebec Pee-Wee Tournament-856
Love, Dominik
94UK Humberside Hawks-23
97UK Kingston Hawks Stickers-7
98UK Kingston Hawks-6
Love, Mitch
01Swift Current Broncos-15
02Swift Current Broncos-10
03Everett Silvertips-17
04Everett Silvertips-4
06Albany River Rats-15
Love, Tyler
96Saskatoon Blades-15
97OCN Blizzard-24
Loveday, Lowell
83Moncton Alpines-6
84Nova Scotia Oilers-4
Lovell, Greg
93Kingston Frontenacs-1
Lovell, Jamie
05Odessa Jackalopes-15
Lovell, John
91Cornwall Royals-6
91 7th Inn. Sketch OHL-25
93Guelph Storm-28
95Slapshot-305
96Owen Sound Platers-1
Lovell, Marc
03UK Manchester Phoenix-14
Lovell, Tim
93Maine Black Bears-52
98Tacoma Sabercats-11
99Providence Bruins-15
Loven, Fredrik
95Collector's Choice-351
Player's Club-351
Player's Club Platinum-351
95SP-188
Loverock, Andrew
06Mississauga Ice Dogs-23
Lovgren, Bengt
67Swedish Hockey-258
70Swedish Hockey-209
71Swedish Hockey-296
72Swedish Stickers-72
74Swedish Stickers-250
Lovgren, Kurt
57Swedish Alfabilder-122
Lovgren, Mikael
97Swedish Collector's Choice-128
98Swedish UD Choice-142
99Swedish Upper Deck-144
Lovsin, Dave
91Air Canada SJHL-D17
91Air Canada SJHL-D32
Lovsin, Ken
90ProCards AHL/IHL-195
91Baltimore Skipjacks-5
91ProCards-557
93Alberta International Team Canada-12
93OPC Premier Team Canada-4
93PowerPlay-487
93Ultra-467
94Score Team Canada-CT16
Low, Chris
93Brandon Wheat Kings-15
94Brandon Wheat Kings-12
99Alexandria Warthogs-8
Low, Reed
00SP Authentic-163
00SPx-187
00Titanium-142
Retail-142
00Titanium Draft Day Edition-142
00Titanium Draft Day Promos-142
00Topps Heritage-89
Chrome Parallel-89
00Upper Deck Ice-100
01BAP Signature Series-145
Autographs-145
Autographs Gold-145
01Pacific-325
01Pacific-420
Extreme LTD-325
Gold-420
Hobby LTD-325
Premiere Date-325
Retail LTD-325
01Pacific Arena Exclusives-325
01Pacific Arena Exclusives-420
02BAP Sig Series Auto Buybacks 2001-145
02Blues Team Issue-13
02Pacific-324
Blue-324
Red-324
02Pacific Complete-491
Red-491
02Upper Deck-398
Exclusives-398
02Upper Deck Beckett UD Promos-398
03Beehive-167
Gold-167
Silver-167
03Blues Team Set-15
03ITG Action-554
03O-Pee-Chee-184
03O-Pee-Chee-283
03OPC Blue-184
03OPC Blue-283
03OPC Gold-184
03OPC Gold-283
03OPC Red-184
03OPC Red-283
03Pacific Complete-368
Red-368
03Topps-184
03Topps-283
Blue-184
Blue-283
Gold-184
Gold-283
Red-184
Red-283
Own the Game-OTG17
Tough Materials-RL
Tough Materials-KSRL
03Upper Deck-168
Canadian Exclusives-168
HG-168
Tough Customers-TC-3
03Upper Deck MVP-371
Gold Script-371
Silver Script-371
Canadian Exclusives-371
03Worcester Ice Cats 10th Anniversary-20
06Norfolk Admirals-15
Low, Ron
72Maple Leafs Postcards-16
72O-Pee-Chee-258
74Capitals White Borders-17
74NHL Action Stamps-308
74O-Pee-Chee NHL-39
74Topps-39
75O-Pee-Chee NHL-25
75Topps-25
76O-Pee-Chee NHL-69
76Topps-69
77O-Pee-Chee NHL-305
78O-Pee-Chee-237
78Topps-237
79O-Pee-Chee-348
80O-Pee-Chee-333
80Pepsi-Cola Caps-30
81Oilers Red Rooster-30
81Oilers Red Rooster-30
82O-Pee-Chee-112
82O-Pee-Chee Stickers-107
82Topps Stickers-107
83Devils Postcards-16
83O-Pee-Chee-233
84Devils Postcards-30
84O-Pee-Chee-115
85Nova Scotia Oilers-25
88Oilers Tenth Anniversary-36
90Oilers IGA-13
91Oilers IGA-28
92Oilers IGA-28
99Houston Aeros-21
01Topps Archives-64
Low, Steven
93Sherbrooke Faucons-23
97Pensacola Ice Pilots-12
99San Diego Gulls-7
03St. Jean Mission-15
Lowe, Connor
00Prince Albert Raiders-12
Lowe, Darren
87Flint Spirits-12
88ProCards AHL-152
89ProCards IHL-45
90ProCards AHL/IHL-310
Lowe, Ed
03Elmira Jackals-10
Lowe, Jason
91British Columbia JHL-28
Lowe, Kevin
79Oilers Postcards-13
80Pepsi-Cola Caps-31
81Oilers Red Rooster-4
81O-Pee-Chee-117
82Oilers Red Rooster-4
82O-Pee-Chee-113
82O-Pee-Chee Stickers-96
82Post Cereal-6
82Topps Stickers-96
83NHL Key Tags-38
83Oilers McDonald's-13
83O-Pee-Chee-37
83O-Pee-Chee Stickers-101
83Topps Stickers-101
83Vachon-34
84Kellogg's Accordion Discs-3A
84Kellogg's Accordion Discs-3B
84Kellogg's Accordion Discs Singles-23
84Oilers Red Rooster-4
84Oilers Team Issue-15
84O-Pee-Chee-251
84O-Pee-Chee Stickers-253
84 7-Eleven Discs-20
85Oilers Red Rooster-4
85O-Pee-Chee-239
85O-Pee-Chee Stickers-219
86Kraft Drawings-36
86Oilers Red Rooster-4
86Oilers Team Issue-4
86O-Pee-Chee-197
86O-Pee-Chee Stickers-70
86Topps-197
87Oilers Team Issue-4
87O-Pee-Chee-200
87O-Pee-Chee Minis-25
87O-Pee-Chee Stickers-84
87Panini Stickers-257
88Oilers Tenth Anniversary-5
88Oilers Team Issue-18
88O-Pee-Chee-229
88O-Pee-Chee Stickers-219
88Panini Stickers-54
89Kraft-14
89Kraft All-Stars Stickers-6
89Oilers Team Issue-15
89O-Pee-Chee-227
89O-Pee-Chee Stickers-224
89Panini Stickers-79
89Panini Stickers-180
89Swedish Semic World Champ Stickers-62
90Bowman-198
Tiffany-198
90Oilers IGA-14
90O-Pee-Chee-307
90Panini Stickers-224
90Panini Stickers-330
90Pro Set-89
90Pro Set-339
90Pro Set-380
90Score-170
Canadian-170
90Score Hottest/Rising Stars-75
90Topps-307
Tiffany-307
90Upper Deck-262
French-262
91Pro Set Platinum-38
91Bowman-115
91Oilers Panini Team Stickers-12
91Oilers IGA-9
91Oilers Team Issue-11
91O-Pee-Chee-220
91Panini Stickers-131
91Parkhurst-51
French-51
91Pinnacle-188
91Pinnacle-371
French-188
French-371
91Pro Set-76
91Pro Set-572
French-76
French-572
91Score American-109
91Score Canadian Bilingual-109
91Score Canadian English-109
91Stadium Club-179
91Topps-220
91Upper Deck-186
French-186
92Bowman-99
92Durivage Panini-42
92O-Pee-Chee-302
92Panini Stickers-107
92Panini Stickers French-107
92Parkhurst-348
Emerald Ice-348
92Pinnacle-338
French-338
92Score-39
Canadian-39
92Stadium Club-385
92Topps-290
Gold-290G
92Ultra-60
92Ultra-356
93OPC Premier-464
Gold-464
93Panini Stickers-97
93Pinnacle-11
Canadian-11
All-Stars-3
All-Stars Canadian-3
93PowerPlay-393
93Score-112
Canadian-112
93Stadium Club-165
Members Only Master Set-165
OPC-165
First Day Issue-165
First Day Issue OPC-165
All-Stars-19
All-Stars Members Only-19
All-Stars OPC-19
93Topps/OPC Premier-464
Gold-464
93Ultra-375
94Canada Games NHL POGS-171
94Finest Ring Leaders-2
94Parkhurst SE-SE112
Gold-SE112
94Pinnacle-338
Artist's Proofs-338
Rink Collection-338
94Stadium Club-173
Members Only Master Set-173
First Day Issue-173
Super Team Winner Cards-173
94Upper Deck-393
Electric Ice-393
95Be A Player-40
Signatures-S40
Signatures Die Cuts-S40
95Pinnacle-89
Artist's Proofs-89
Rink Collection-89
95Score-248
Black Ice Artist's Proofs-248
Black Ice-248
95Upper Deck-414
Electric Ice-414
Electric Ice Gold-414
96Oilers Postcards-4
97Pacific Invincible NHL Regime-78
97Upper Deck-279
Lowe, Ross
44Beehive Group II Photos-262
45Quaker Oats Photos-91
51Parkhurst-18
Lowe, Steve
95Slapshot-174
95Sault Ste. Marie Greyhounds-10
95Classic-95
98Kansas City Blades-16
00Tacoma Sabercats-15
02Fresno Falcons-8
Lowery, Andrew
93Quebec Pee-Wee Tournament-513
Lowery, Ryan
06Lincoln Stars-16
Lowes, Bob
95Slapshot Memorial Cup-50
01Regina Pats-13
Lowes, Joe
94Brantford Smoke-25
Lowgren, Torgny
92Swedish Semic Elitserien Stickers-271
95Swedish Leaf-238
95Swedish Upper Deck-106
Lowrey, Fred
24C144 Champ's Cigarettes-36
24V130 Maple Crispette-28
24V145-2-36
Lowry, Dave
85Canucks Team Issue-15
86Canucks Team Issue-9
87Canucks Shell Oil-11
87Panini Stickers-353
88ProCards IHL-67
89Blues Kodak-10
90Blues Kodak-12
90Bowman-15
Tiffany-15
90O-Pee-Chee-370
90Pro Set-265
90Score Rookie/Traded-38T
90Topps-370
Tiffany-370
90Upper Deck-349
French-349
91Blues Postcards-14
91Bowman-373
91O-Pee-Chee-180
91Panini Stickers-32
91Parkhurst-376
French-376
91Pinnacle-276
French-276
91Score American-149
91Score Canadian Bilingual-149
91Score Canadian English-149
91Stadium Club-303
91Topps-180
92Bowman-370
92O-Pee-Chee-219
92Panini Stickers-21
92Panini Stickers French-21
92Score-109
Canadian-109
92Stadium Club-10
92Topps-42
Gold-42G
93Donruss-125
93Leaf-238
93OPC Premier-244
Gold-244
93Parkhurst-79
Emerald Ice-79
93Pinnacle-408
Canadian-408
Expansion-4
93PowerPlay-97
93Score-564
Gold-564
Canadian-564
Canadian Gold-564
93Stadium Club-121
93Stadium Club-379
Members Only Master Set-121
Members Only Master Set-379
OPC-121
First Day Issue-121
First Day Issue-379
First Day Issue OPC-121
93Topps Premier Promo Sheet-244
93Topps/OPC Premier-244
Gold-244
93Upper Deck-67
94Be A Player Signature Cards-102
94Canada Games NHL POGS-107
94Donruss-20
94Leaf-414
94OPC Premier-89
Special Effects-89
94Pinnacle-184
Artist's Proofs-184
Rink Collection-184
94Score-81
Gold-81
Platinum-81
94Topps/OPC Premier-89
Special Effects-89
94Ultra-82
94Upper Deck-291
Electric Ice-291
95Canada Games NHL POGS-118
95Collector's Choice-299
Player's Club-299
Player's Club Platinum-299
95Donruss-222
95Leaf-256
95Panini Stickers-73
95Pinnacle-199
Artist's Proofs-199
Rink Collection-199
95Playoff One on One-261
95Score-218
Black Ice Artist's Proofs-218
Black Ice-218
95Upper Deck-175
Electric Ice-175
Electric Ice Gold-175
96Donruss-174
Press Proofs-174
96Leaf-125
Press Proofs-125
96Pinnacle-81
Artist's Proofs-81
Foil-81
Premium Stock-81
Rink Collection-81
96Score-194
Artist's Proofs-194
Dealer's Choice Artist's Proofs-194
Special Artist's Proofs-194
Golden Blades-194
96Upper Deck-264
97Be A Player-183
Autographs-183
Autographs Die-Cuts-183
Autographs Prismatic Die-Cuts-183
97Pacific Invincible NHL Regime-87
99O-Pee-Chee-190
99O-Pee-Chee Chrome-190
99O-Pee-Chee Chrome Refractors-190
99Topps/OPC-190
99Topps/OPC Chrome-190
Refractors-190
01BAP Signature Series-89
Autographs-89
Autographs Gold-89
01Pacific-62
Extreme LTD-62
Hobby LTD-62
Premiere Date-62
Retail LTD-62
01Pacific Arena Exclusives-62
01Upper Deck-26
Exclusives-26
01Upper Deck Victory-53
Gold-53
02BAP Sig Series Auto Buybacks 2001-89
02Upper Deck Vintage-42
03Pacific Complete-63
Red-63
03Upper Deck MVP-70
Gold Script-70
Silver Script-70
Canadian Exclusives-70
05Calgary Hitmen-26
Lowry, Matt
06Medicine Hat Tigers-14
Loxam, Ryan
91British Columbia JHL-51
92British Columbia JHL-210
Loya, Cliff
04Wheeling Nailers Riesbeck's-6
Loyer, Pat
83Brandon Wheat Kings-7
84Brandon Wheat Kings-9
Loyns, Lynn
98Spokane Chiefs-17
99Spokane Chiefs-14
00Spokane Chiefs-15
01SPx Rookie Redemption-R25
01Cleveland Barons-13
02BAP All-Star Edition-109
Gold-109
Silver-109
02BAP Memorabilia-378
02BAP Signature Series-199
Autographs-199
Autographs Gold-199
02Crown Royale-136
Blue-136
Purple-136
Red-136
Retail-136
02ITG Used-100
02Pacific Calder-145
Silver-145
02Pacific Complete-512
Red-512
02Pacific Quest for the Cup-146
Gold-146
02SP Authentic-156
02SP Game Used-102
02SPx-170
02Titanium-136
Blue-136
Red-136
Retail-136
02Topps Total-430
02UD Honor Roll-163
02UD Top Shelf-117
02Upper Deck-449
Exclusives-449
02Vanguard-133
LTD-133
02Cleveland Barons-13
03Cleveland Barons-13
04Lowell Lock Monsters-14
04Lowell Lock Monsters Photo Album-14
Lozanov, Dejan
00Swiss Panini Stickers-155
01Swiss HNL-263
02Swiss HNL-126
Lozinik, Tim
99Anchorage Aces-8
Lozinski, Larry
81O-Pee-Chee-99
Lube, J.F.
98ECHL All-Star Southern Conference-15
Lubeigt, Benoit
93Quebec Pee-Wee Tournament-1658
Luber, Philippe
95Swiss HNL-47
96Swiss HNL-114
99Swiss Panini Stickers-346
00Swiss Panini Stickers-237
00Swiss Slapshot Mini-Cards-RJ12
01Swiss HNL-159
02Swiss HNL-315
Lubina, Ladislav
91Finnish Semic World Champ Stickers-121
91Swedish Semic World Champ Stickers-121
94Czech APS Extraliga-45
95Czech APS Extraliga-325
96Czech APS Extraliga-153
97Czech APS Extraliga-329
97Czech DS Extraliga-114
97Czech DS Stickers-253
98Czech DS-119
98Czech DS Stickers-275
98Czech OFS-185
99Czech DS-82
00Czech DS Extraliga-91
00Czech OFS-43
01Czech OFS-255
02Czech OFS Plus-219
02Czech OFS Plus All-Star Game-H30
02Czech OFS Plus Trios-T9
02Czech OFS Plus Duos-D11
03Czech OFS Plus-310
03Czech OFS Plus Insert M-M3
03Czech Pardubice Postcards-8
04Czech OFS-123
05Czech HC Pardubice-9
Lubiniecki, Daryl
81Saskatoon Blades-13
Lubitz, Pat
93Quebec Pee-Wee Tournament-600
Lucak, Josef
95Czech APS Extraliga-222
Lucas, Corey
02Macon Trax-6
04Fort Wayne Komets Shoe Carnival-9
Lucas, Tyrel
04Calgary Hitmen-11
Lucci, Mike
03Oklahoma City Blazers-14
Luce, Don
70Esso Power Players-136
71O-Pee-Chee-166
71Sabres Postcards-87
71Sargent Promotions Stamps-26
71Toronto Sun-31
72O-Pee-Chee-95
72Sabres Pepsi Pinback Buttons-2
72Sabres Postcards-9
72Sargent Promotions Stamps-33
72Topps-106
73O-Pee-Chee-38
73Sabres Postcards-5
73Topps-38
74NHL Action Stamps-52
74O-Pee-Chee NHL-79
74Sabres Postcards-13
74Topps-79
75O-Pee-Chee NHL-113
75Sabres Linnett-5
75Topps-113
76O-Pee-Chee NHL-94
76Topps-94
77O-Pee-Chee NHL-231
77Topps-231
78O-Pee-Chee-58
78Topps-58
79O-Pee-Chee-194
79Topps-194
80O-Pee-Chee-302
81Maple Leafs Postcards-9
81O-Pee-Chee-147
81Topps-W99
93Sabres Noco-10
04ITG Franchises US East-347
Autographs-A-DLU
Luce, Jonathan
98San Angelo Outlaws-26
Luce, Scott
87Sudbury Wolves-24
Luchinkin, Sergei
95Signature Rookies Club Promos-1
95Signature Rookies Future Flash-FF8
95Signature Rook Future Flash Sigs-FF8
95Signature Rookies Tetrad Autobilia *-46
99Russian Hockey League-38
02Russian Hockey League-103
Luchkin, Vladislav
00Russian Hockey League-379
Luchkow, Faron
90Fort Saskatchewan Traders-10
Lucia, Don
99Minnesota Golden Gophers-10
00Minnesota Golden Gophers-11
01Minnesota Golden Gophers-2
02Minnesota Golden Gophers-29
03Minnesota Golden Gophers-8
04Minnesota Golden Gophers-17
05Minnesota Golden Gophers-26
06Minnesota Golden Gophers-24
Lucia, Tony
06Minnesota Golden Gophers-14
Lucic, Milan
05Vancouver Giants-14
Lucier, Sebastien
00Chicoutimi Sagueneens-9
Signed-9
01Chicoutimi Sagueneens-2
Luciuk, Andrew
99Muskegon Fury-13
00Muskegon Fury-10
02Muskegon Fury-14
03Kalamazoo Wings-19
04Kalamazoo Wings-19
05UK Sheffield Steelers Supplementary-2
Gold-2
Silver-2
05Fort Wayne Komets Choice-7
Lucka, Martin
06Czech OFS-231
Luckner, Harald
82Swedish Semic VM Stickers-25
83Swedish Semic Elitserien-111
84Swedish Semic Elitserien-111
85Swedish Panini Stickers-99
86Swedish Panini Stickers-97
87Swedish Panini Stickers-99
91Swedish Semic Elitserien Stickers-305
92Swedish Semic Elitserien Stickers-327
Luckovitch, Jeff
00Sarnia Sting-17
Lucky, Jeff
99Spokane Chiefs-15
00Spokane Chiefs-16
01Spokane Chiefs-17
01UD Prospects-29
Jerseys-J-JL
Jerseys Gold-J-JL
02Spokane Chiefs-14
Lucyk, Carey
89ProCards IHL-133
90ProCards AHL/IHL-548
91ProCards-242
93Fort Wayne Komets-9
99Fort Wayne Komets Penalty Leaders-13
Lucyk, Luke
02Tri-City Stormfront-5
04Notre Dame Fighting Irish-9
Ludemann, Mirko
94Finnish Jaa Kiekko-275
94German DEL-205
95German DEL-200
96German DEL-434
95Swedish World Championships Stickers-53
96German DEL-342
96Swedish Semic Wien-194
98German DEL-96
98German DEL-315
99German DEL-106
00German DEL-132
Profiles-P7
01German Upper Deck-140
Skilled Stars-SS8
02German DEL City Press-198
Top Stars-GT5
03German DEL-172
04German Cologne Sharks Postcards-18
04German DEL-214
05German DEL-211
06German DEL-126
Ludke, Flavio
01Swiss HNL-51
02Swiss HNL-290
Ludvig, Jan
83Devils Postcards-17
84Devils Postcards-29
84O-Pee-Chee-116
84O-Pee-Chee Stickers-76
84Topps-88
86Devils Police-13
87Sabres Blue Shield-16
87Sabres Wonder Bread/Hostess-17
88Sabres Blue Shield-14
88Sabres Wonder Bread/Hostess-15
Ludvigsen, Henning
98Danish Hockey League-69
Ludvik, David
02Czech OFS Plus-112
03Czech OFS Plus-244
04Czech OFS-308
06Czech HC Plzen Postcards-3
Ludwar, Kane
00Saskatoon Blades-10
01Saskatoon Blades-19
Ludwig, Andreas
83Swedish Semic VM Stickers-152
94German First League-291
95German DEL-343
Ludwig, Craig
82Canadiens Postcards-13
82Canadiens Steinberg-9
83Canadiens Postcards-16
83O-Pee-Chee-190
83Vachon-48
84Canadiens Postcards-15
84O-Pee-Chee-265
84O-Pee-Chee Stickers-154
85Canadiens Postcards-18
85Canadiens Provigo-9
85O-Pee-Chee-192
85O-Pee-Chee Stickers-130
86Canadiens Postcards-12
86Kraft Drawings-37
86O-Pee-Chee-220
86O-Pee-Chee Stickers-14
87Canadiens Postcards-15
87Canadiens Vachon Stickers-33
87Canadiens Vachon Stickers-35
87Canadiens Vachon Stickers-80
87Canadiens Vachon Stickers-81
87Canadiens Vachon Stickers-85
87Panini Stickers-59
88Canadiens Postcards-18
88O-Pee-Chee-230
88O-Pee-Chee Stickers-48
88Panini Stickers-254
89Canadiens Kraft-15
89Canadiens Postcards-21
89Canadiens Provigo Figurines-17
89O-Pee-Chee-236
90O-Pee-Chee-412
90OPC Premier-64
90Pro Set-154
90Pro Set-484
90Score-165
Canadian-165
90Score Hottest/Rising Stars-74
90Score Rookie/Traded-8T
90Upper Deck-186
French-186
91Bowman-221
91O-Pee-Chee-150
91OPC Premier-80
91Panini Stickers-242
91Pinnacle-248
91Pinnacle-404
French-248
French-404
91Pro Set-155
91Pro Set-411
French-155
French-411
91Score American-13
91Score Canadian Bilingual-13
91Score Canadian Bilingual-561
91Score Canadian English-13
91Score Canadian English-561
91Score Rookie/Traded-11T
91Stadium Club-38
91Topps-150
92Pro Set-79
92Score-94
Canadian-94
92Stadium Club-354
92Topps-154
Gold-154G
92Ultra-320
93Leaf-432
93OPC Premier-191
Gold-191
93Pinnacle-303
Canadian-303
93Score-282
Canadian-282
93Stadium Club-173
Members Only Master Set-173
OPC-173
First Day Issue-173
First Day Issue OPC-173
93Topps/OPC Premier-191
Gold-191
94Leaf-424
94Pinnacle-233
Artist's Proofs-233
Rink Collection-233
94Stadium Club-214
Members Only Master Set-214
First Day Issue-214
Super Team Winner Cards-214
94Stars HockeyKaps-19
94Stars Postcards-16
94Ultra-280
95Be A Player-128
Signatures-S128
Signatures Die Cuts-S128
96Collector's Choice-76
96Stars Postcards-18
97Pacific Invincible NHL Regime-62
98Pacific-3
Ice Blue-3
Red-3
00Utah Grizzlies-20
04ITG Franchises US West-196
Autographs-A-CLU
06Stars Team Postcards-28
Ludzik, Ryan
05Erie Otters-19
06Erie Otters-24
Ludzik, Steve
82Blackhawks Postcards-11
83Blackhawks Postcards-12
83O-Pee-Chee-106
84O-Pee-Chee-38
85Blackhawks Team Issue-20
86Blackhawks Coke-7
87Blackhawks Coke-8
88ProCards IHL-102
89ProCards AHL-271
90ProCards AHL/IHL-276
91ProCards-15
91Rochester Americans Kodak-17
93Muskegon Fury-2
98Detroit Vipers-22
98IHL All-Star Eastern Conference-22
Luethi, Claude
01Swiss HNL-296
02Swiss HNL-183
Luger, Billie
03St. Cloud State Huskies-17
Luger, Mark
94Roanoke Express-17
Luhning, Warren
93Michigan Wolverines-14
97Score-69
Artist's Proofs-69
Golden Blades-69
98UD3-12
98UD3-72

98UD3-132
Die-Cuts-12
Die-Cuts-72
Die-Cuts-132
98Upper Deck-125
Exclusives-125
Exclusives 1 of 1-125
Gold Reserve-125
99Pacific-260
Copper-260
Emerald Green-260
Gold-260
Ice Blue-260
Premiere Date-260
Red-260
99Stars Postcards-14

Luhrmann, Scott
92Toledo Storm-3
92Toledo Storm Team Issue-3
95Toledo Storm-24
96Toledo Storm-NNO

Luik, Jaan
91Cincinnati Cyclones-11
91ProCards-37

Luik, Scott
89Oshawa Generals-34
89Oshawa Generals 7th Inning Sketch-21
897th Inn. Sketch OHL-21
907th Inn. Sketch OHL-341
907th Inn. Sketch Memorial Cup-93
91Cincinnati Cyclones-12

Lukac, Josef
96Czech APS Extraliga-51
04UK Coventry Blaze Champions-7

Lukac, Vincent
82Swedish Semic VM Stickers-100
83Swedish Semic VM Stickers-100
98Czech OFS Legends-19

Lukacevic, Ned
02Spokane Chiefs-15
04Spokane Chiefs Magnets-6
05Swift Current Broncos-22
06Manchester Monarchs-15
06Reading Royals-12

Lukacs, Rob
98Odessa Jackalopes-2

Lukasak, Jeff
92Quebec Pee-Wee Tournament-1856
02Muskegon Fury-15

Luker, Jason
93Quebec Pee-Wee Tournament-619

Lukes, Christian
94German DEL-301
95German DEL-268
96German DEL-162
98German DEL-239
99German DEL-4
99German DEL-384
01German Upper Deck-9
02German DEL City Press-14

Lukes, Frantisek
00St. Michaels Majors-20
01St. Michaels Majors-17
02St. Michaels Majors-16
03Springfield Falcons Postcards-16
04Idaho Steelheads-14
06Czech OFS-140

Lukes, Radek
99Czech Score Blue 2000-143
99Czech Score Red Ice 2000-143

Lukey, Chris
87Kingston Canadians-28
89Hampton Roads Admirals-12A
89Hampton Roads Admirals-12H

Lukin, Jarret
00Kamloops Blazers-14
03Kamloops Blazers-21
04Medicine Hat Tigers-11

Luknowsky, Jay
90Michigan Tech Huskies-12
95German DEL-233
96German DEL-84
99German Bundesliga 2-151

Lukowich, Brad
93Kamloops Blazers-15
94Kamloops Blazers-12
95Kamloops Blazers-6
95Slapshot Memorial Cup-19
96Michigan K-Wings-14
98IHL All-Star Eastern Conference-20
98Michigan K-Wings-15
99BAP Memorabilia-51
Gold-51
Silver-51
99BAP Millennium-80
Emerald-80
Ruby-80
Sapphire-80
Signatures-80
Signatures Gold-80
Calder Candidates Ruby-C39
Calder Candidates Emerald-C39
Calder Candidates Sapphire-C39
99Pacific-124
Copper-124
Emerald Green-124
Gold-124
Ice Blue-124
Premiere Date-124
Red-124
99Stars Postcards-15
99Topps Premier Plus-97
Parallel-97
99Upper Deck MVP SC Edition-63
Gold Script-63
Silver Script-63
Super Script-63
00Stars Postcards-13
00Upper Deck NHLPA-PA29
01Pacific-129
Extreme LTD-129
Hobby LTD-129
Premiere Date-129
Retail LTD-129
01Pacific Arena Exclusives-129
01Stars Postcards-13
02BAP Sig Series Auto Buybacks 1999-80
02Lightning Team Issue-8
02Pacific Complete-330
Red-330
03ITG Action-576
03Lightning Team Issue-33
04Fort Worth Brahmas-9
05Parkhurst Facsimile Auto Parallel-312
06Devils Team Set-13
06O-Pee-Chee-305
Rainbow-305

Lukowich, Morris
78Jets Postcards-13
79Jets Postcards-13
79O-Pee-Chee-202
79Topps-202
80Jets Postcards-13
80O-Pee-Chee-107
80O-Pee-Chee-227
80O-Pee-Chee Super-24
80Topps-107
80Topps-227
81Jets Postcards-10
81O-Pee-Chee-370
81O-Pee-Chee Stickers-138
81Post Standups-19
82Jets Postcards-13
82O-Pee-Chee-383
82O-Pee-Chee Stickers-205
82Post Cereal-21
82Topps Stickers-205
83Esso-11
83Jets Postcards-12
83NHL Key Tags-136
83O-Pee-Chee-386
83O-Pee-Chee Stickers-281
83Puffy Stickers-3
83Topps Stickers-281
83Vachon-129
84Jets Police-11
84O-Pee-Chee-340
85O-Pee-Chee-129
85Topps-129
86Kings 20th Anniversary Team Issue-13
04ITG Franchises Canadian-145
Autographs-MLU

Luksa, Chuck
76Nova Scotia Voyageurs-10
77Nova Scotia Voyageurs-12
79O-Pee-Chee-370

Lukscheider, Vladimir
94German First League-599

Lulin, Andrei
95Swedish Leaf-298
98Swedish UD Choice-183
99Swedish Upper Deck-186

Lumbard, Todd
82Regina Pats-2
83Regina Pats-2
84Springfield Indians-3

Lumby, Jeff
92Hamilton Canucks-13

Lumela, Pekka
80Finnish Mallasjuoma-82

Lumley, Dave
77Nova Scotia Voyageurs-13
79Oilers Postcards-14
80O-Pee-Chee-271
80Pepsi-Cola Caps-32
81Oilers Red Rooster-20
81Oilers West Edmonton Mall-7
82Oilers Red Rooster-20
82O-Pee-Chee-114
82O-Pee-Chee Stickers-101
82Post Cereal-6
82Topps Stickers-101
83Oilers McDonald's-22
83O-Pee-Chee-38
83Vachon-35
84Oilers Red Rooster-8
84Oilers Team Issue-16
84O-Pee-Chee-252
85Oilers Red Rooster-20
88Oilers Tenth Anniversary-35

Lumley, Harry
43Parade Sportive *-74
44Beehive Group II Photos-43
44Beehive Group II Photos-114
44Beehive Group II Photos-188
44Beehive Group II Photos-420
45Quaker Oats Photos-28
48Exhibits Canadian-46
51Parkhurst-47
52Parkhurst-59
53Parkhurst-1
54Parkhurst-16
54Parkhurst-91
54Parkhurst-92
54Parkhurst-93
55Parkhurst-1
55Parkhurst-70
55Parkhurst-73
55Parkhurst-74
55Parkhurst-76
Quaker Oats-1
Quaker Oats-70
Quaker Oats-73
Quaker Oats-76
83Hall of Fame-21
83Hall of Fame Postcards-B7
85Hall of Fame-21
91Ultimate Original Six-51
French-51
92Hall of Fame Legends-1
92Parkhurst Parkie Reprints-PR5
01Between the Pipes-125
01Between the Pipes-139
01Parkhurst Reprints-PR15
01Parkhurst Reprints-PR22
01Parkhurst Reprints-PR58
01Parkhurst Reprints-PR104
02BAP Ultimate Memorabilia Emblem Attic-16
02BAP Ultimate Mem Paper Cuts Autos-10
02BAP Ultimate Mem Vintage Jerseys-19
02Between the Pipes He Shoots/Saves Prize-21
02Between the Pipes Trappers-GT10
02Between the Pipes Vintage Memorabilia-2
02ITG Used Vintage Memorabilia-VM9
02ITG Used Vintage Memorabilia Gold-VM9
02Maple Leafs Platinum Collection-57
02Maple Leafs Platinum Collection-106
02Parkhurst Vintage Teammates-VT16
03BAP Ultimate Memorabilia Cornerstones-6
03BAP Ultimate Memorabilia Emblem Attic-7
03BAP Ultimate Mem Emblem Attic Gold-7
03BAP Ultimate Mem Maple Leafs Forever-9
03BAP Ultimate Memorabilia Triple Threads-8
03BAP Ultimate Mem Vintage Jerseys-11
03BAP Ultimate Mem Vintage Jerseys Gold-11
03BAP Ultimate Memorabilia Vintage Lumber-11
03ITG Used Signature Series Goalie Gear-35
03ITG Used Sig Series Goalie Gear Autos-35
03ITG Used Sig Series Goalie Gear Gold-35
03ITG VIP Vintage Memorabilia-16
03Parkhurst Original Six Chicago-51
Memorabilia-CM18
Memorabilia-CM29
Memorabilia-CM54
03Parkhurst Original Six Detroit-58
03Parkhurst Original Six Toronto-47
03Parkhurst Rookie Before the Mask-BTM-3
03Parkhurst Rookie Before the Mask Gold-BTM-3
03SP Authentic Special Cuts-HL
04ITG Franchises US West-217
Double Memorabilia-WDM2
Double Memorabilia Gold-WDM2
Forever Rivals-WFR3
Forever Rivals Gold-WFR3
Memorabilia-WSM4
Memorabilia Gold-WSM4
Original Sticks-WOS2
Original Sticks Gold-WOS2
Triple Memorabilia Gold-WTM2
04ITG Ultimate Memorabilia-33
04ITG Ultimate Memorabilia-76
Gold-33
Gold-76
Autographs-59
Autographs Gold-59
Chitown Immortals-6
Complete Jerseys-11
Goalie Gear-9
Jersey and Sticks-20
Jersey and Sticks Gold-20
Motown Heroes-9
Original Six-8
Original Six-10
Paper Cuts Memorabilia-20
Triple Threads-3
Vintage Lumber-1
05ITG Ultimate Mem Decades Jerseys-5
05ITG Ultimate Mem Decades Jerseys Gold-5
05ITG Ultimate Memorabilia Emblem Attic-16
05ITG Ultimate Mem Emblem Attic Gold-16
05ITG Ultimate Memorabilia Goalie Gear-10
05ITG Ultimate Mem Goalie Gear Gold-10
05ITG Ultimate Mem Motown Heroes Autos-5
05ITG Ultimate Mem Quad Paper Cuts Autos-3
05ITG Ultimate Mem Retro Teammate Jerseys-28
05ITG Ult Mem Retro Teammates Jersey Gold-28
05ITG Ultimate Memorabilia Vintage Lumber-17
05ITG Ultimate Mem Vintage Lumber Gold-17
06Between The Pipes Shooting Gallery-SG04
06Between The Pipes Shooting Gallery Gold-SG04
06ITG Ultimate Memorabilia Emblem Attic-6
06ITG Ultimate Memorabilia Emblem Attic Gold-6
06ITG Ultimate Memorabilia Stick Rack-19
06ITG Ultimate Memorabilia Stick Rack Gold-19

Lumme, Jyrki
88ProCards AHL-273
89Canadiens Postcards-22
90Canucks Mohawk-16
90Pro Set-300
90Score-132
Canadian-132
90Upper Deck-297
French-297
91Pro Set Platinum-237
91Bowman-321
91Canucks Panini Team Stickers-14
91Canucks Autograph Cards-13
91Canucks Team Issue 8x10-13
91O-Pee-Chee-419
91Parkhurst-180
French-180
91Pinnacle-237
French-237
91Pro Set-240
French-240
91Score American-242
91Score Canadian Bilingual-462
91Score Canadian English-462
91Stadium Club-154
91Topps-419
91Upper Deck-114
French-114
91Finnish Semic World Champ Stickers-202
91Swedish Semic World Champ Stickers-202
92Bowman-170
92Canucks Road Trip Art-12
92O-Pee-Chee-265
92Panini Stickers-36
92Panini Stickers French-36
92Parkhurst-191
Emerald Ice-191
92Pinnacle-65
French-65
92Pro Set-196
92Score-318
Canadian-318
Young Superstars-34
92Stadium Club-321
92Topps-510
Gold-510G
92Ultra-223
92Upper Deck-137
92Finnish Semic-6
93Donruss-347
93Leaf-231
93OPC Premier-475
Gold-475
93Panini Stickers-175
93Parkhurst-483
Emerald Ice-483
93Pinnacle-21
Canadian-21
93PowerPlay-252
93Score-134
Canadian-134
93Stadium Club-108
Members Only Master Set-108
OPC-108
First Day Issue-108
First Day Issue OPC-108
93Topps/OPC Premier-475
Gold-475
93Ultra-126
93Swedish Semic World Champ Stickers-56
94Canada Games NHL POGS-339
94Canucks Program Inserts-14
94Donruss-190
94EA Sports-139
94EA Sports-205
94Flair-192
94Fleer-226
94Leaf-287
94OPC Premier-442
Special Effects-442
94Parkhurst SE-SE190
Gold-SE190
Euro-Stars-ES8
94Pinnacle-86
Artist's Proofs-86
Rink Collection-86
94Score-35
Gold-35
Platinum-35
94Stadium Club-132
Members Only Master Set-132
First Day Issue-132
Super Team Winner Cards-132
94Topps/OPC Premier-442
Special Effects-442
94Ultra-227
94Upper Deck-148
Electric Ice-148
94Finnish SISU-360
94Finnish SISU Guest Specials-3
94Finnish Jaa Kiekko-8
95Be A Player-2
Signatures-S2
Signatures Die Cuts-S2
95Canada Games NHL POGS-277
95Canucks Building the Dream Art-6
95Donruss-109
95Leaf-328
95Parkhurst International-215
Emerald Ice-215
95Pinnacle-73
Artist's Proofs-73
Rink Collection-73
Global Gold-13
95Score-102
Black Ice Artist's Proofs-102
Black Ice-102
95Summit-164
Artist's Proofs-164
Ice-164
95Topps-204
OPC Inserts-204
95Upper Deck-356
Electric Ice-356
Electric Ice Gold-356
95Finnish SISU Limited-101
Leaf Gallery-1
95Finnish Semic World Championships-38
95Swedish Globe World Championships-129
96Canucks Postcards-21
96Collector's Choice-269
96Donruss-5
Press Proofs-5
96Fleer Picks-94
96Leaf-123
Press Proofs-123
96Pinnacle-185
Artist's Proofs-185
Foil-185
Premium Stock-185
Rink Collection-185
96Score-22
Artist's Proofs-22
Dealer's Choice Artist's Proofs-22
Special Artist's Proofs-22
Golden Blades-22
96SP-160
96Team Out-84
96Upper Deck-172
96Swedish Semic Wien-26
97Collector's Choice-262
97Pacific-232
Copper-232
Emerald Green-232
Ice Blue-232
Red-232
Silver-232
97Panini Stickers-244
97Score Canucks-8
Platinum-8
Premier-8
97Upper Deck-378
98Be A Player-259
Press Release-259
98BAP Gold-259
98BAP Autographs-259
98BAP Autographs Gold-259
98Pacific-428
Ice Blue-428
Red-428
98Pacific Omega-185
Red-185
Opening Day Issue-185
98Panini Stickers-222
98UD Choice-205
98UD Choice Preview-205
98UD Choice Prime Choice Reserve-205
98UD Choice Reserve-205
98Upper Deck-340
Exclusives-340
Exclusives 1 of 1-340
Gold Reserve-340
98Finnish Kerailysarja Dream Team-3
99BAP Memorabilia-260
Gold-260
Silver-260
99O-Pee-Chee-222
99O-Pee-Chee Chrome-222
99O-Pee-Chee Chrome Refractors-222
99Pacific-322
Copper-322
Emerald Green-322
Gold-322
Ice Blue-322
Premiere Date-322
Red-322
99Panini Stickers-279
99Paramount-180
Copper-180
Emerald-180
Gold-180
Holographic Emerald-180
Holographic Gold-180
Holographic Silver-180
Ice Blue-180
Premiere Date-180
Red-180
Silver-180
99Topps/OPC-222
99Topps/OPC Chrome-222
Refractors-222
99Upper Deck MVP SC Edition-143
Gold Script-143
Silver Script-143
Super Script-143
99Finnish Cardset Aces High-H-5
00BAP Memorabilia-280
Emerald-280
Ruby-280
Sapphire-280
Promos-280
00BAP Mem Chicago Sportsfest Copper-280
00BAP Memorabilia Chicago Sportsfest Blue-280
00BAP Memorabilia Chicago Sportsfest Gold-280
00BAP Memorabilia Chicago Sportsfest Ruby-280
00BAP Memorabilia Chicago Sun-Times Ruby-280
00BAP Memorabilia Chicago Sun-Times Gold-280
00BAP Mem Chicago Sun-Times Sapphire-280
00BAP Mem Toronto Fall Expo Copper-280
00BAP Memorabilia Toronto Fall Expo Gold-280
00BAP Memorabilia Toronto Fall Expo Ruby-280
00BAP Parkhurst 2000-P135
00BAP Signature Series-10
Emerald-10
Ruby-10
Sapphire-10
Autographs-104
Autographs Gold-104
00Crown Royale Game-Worn Jerseys-21
00Crown Royale Game-Worn Jersey Patches-21
00Crown Royale Premium-Sized Jerseys-21
00O-Pee-Chee-266A
00O-Pee-Chee Parallel-266A
00Pacific-319
Copper-319
Gold-319
Ice Blue-319
Premiere Date-319
00Panini Stickers-187
00Titanium Game Gear-127
00Titanium Game Gear Patches-127
00Titanium Draft Day Edition-77
Patches-77
00Topps/OPC-266A
Parallel-266A
00Upper Deck Vintage-279
00Finnish Cardset-353
01Atomic Jerseys-18
01Atomic Patches-18
01Pacific Jerseys-25
01Pacific Heads-Up Quad Jerseys-26
01Parkhurst-218
01Vanguard Memorabilia-22
01Vanguard Patches-22
01Finnish Cardset Salt Lake City-6
02BAP Sig Series Auto Buybacks 1998-259
02BAP Sig Series Auto Buybacks 2000-104
02Maple Leafs Platinum Collection-11
02NHL Power Play Stickers-141
02Pacific Complete-283
Red-283
02Pacific Heads-Up Quad Jerseys-33
02Pacific Heads-Up Quad Jerseys Gold-33
02Finnish Cardset-64
03Upper Deck MVP-404
Gold Script-404
Silver Script-404
Canadian Exclusives-404
05Finnish Cardset -214
06Finnish Cardset-41

Lund, Arne
57Swedish Alfabilder-131

Lund, Billy
93St. Cloud State Huskies-15

Lund, Hans Inge
65Swedish Coralli ISHockey-211

Lund, Jamie
91British Columbia JHL-142

Lund, Joe
51Cleveland Barons-20

Lund, Josh
05Salmon Arm Silverbacks-11

Lund, Larry
73Quaker Oats WHA-19
74O-Pee-Chee WHA-22
75Houston Aeros WHA-12
77O-Pee-Chee WHA-19

Lund, Mikkel Quistgaard
98Danish Hockey League-72

Lund, Pentti
44Beehive Group II Photos-44
44Beehive Group II Photos-339
51Parkhurst-31
52Parkhurst-83
02Parkhurst Reprints-155

Lund, Staffan
86Swedish Panini Stickers-100
87Swedish Panini Stickers-98

Lund, Stephen
05PEI Rocket-2
06PEI Rocket-5

Lund, Tom
70Finnish Jaakiekko-351
95North Iowa Huskies-17

Lund, Tom (Finn)
70Finnish Jaakiekko-351

Lundback, Patrik
86Swedish Panini Stickers-93
97Swedish Collector's Choice-95

Lundberg, Anders
69Swedish Hockey-82

Lundberg, Bengt
71Swedish Hockey-327
72Swedish Stickers-140

Lundberg, Christer
71Swedish Hockey-87
73Swedish Stickers-205
74Swedish Stickers-245

Lundberg, Emil
02Swedish SHL-66
Parallel-66
03Swedish Elite-231
Silver-231
04Swedish Elitset-76
Gold-76
05Swedish Lulea Hockey Postcards-11
05Swedish SHL Elitset-88
Gold-88
06Finnish Cardset-315
06Swedish SHL Elitset-88

Lundberg, Eric
06Augusta Lynx-10

Lundberg, Jerry
83Swedish Semic Elitserien-159

Lundberg, Joakim
92Swedish Semic Elitserien Stickers-82
94Swedish Leaf-213
95Swedish Leaf-188
95Swedish Upper Deck-41
98Swedish UD Choice-186
99Swedish Upper Deck-189
00Swedish Upper Deck-138
02Swedish Malmo Red Hawks-1
02Swedish SHL-229
Parallel-229
03Swedish Elite-89
Silver-89

Lundberg, Lars-Gunnar
72Swedish Stickers-208
74Swedish Stickers-246
96Swedish Semic Wien Hockey Legends-HL12

Lundberg, Niclas
91Swedish Semic Elitserien Stickers-275

Lundberg, Pertti
71Finnish Suomi Stickers-348

Lundbergh, Per
89Swedish Semic Elitserien Stickers-265

Lundbohm, Andy
99Kentucky Thoroughblades-20
00Kentucky Thoroughblades-16
01Cleveland Barons-14
03St. Cloud State Huskies-18

Lundbohm, Bryan
01Milwaukee Admirals-17
01Milwaukee Admirals Postcards-2
02Milwaukee Admirals-25
03Swiss HNL-427
03Milwaukee Admirals-28
03Milwaukee Admirals Postcards-14
04Fort Worth Brahmas-10
04Milwaukee Admirals-12

Lundbohm, David
04Florida Everblades-13
05Providence Bruins-8

Lunde, Dale
72Finnish Jaakiekko-334

Lunde, Lars Erik
92Norwegian Elite Series-116

Lunde, Len
44Beehive Group II Photos-115A
44Beehive Group II Photos-115B
44Beehive Group II Photos-189
58Topps-15
59Topps-22
60Parkhurst-35
60Shirriff Coins-54
61Parkhurst-24
62Parkhurst-35
64Beehive Group III Photos-44
70Esso Power Players-52
70O-Pee-Chee-230
72Finnish Jaakiekko-129

Lunde, Raymond
92Norwegian Elite Series-150

Lundell, Jan
98Finnish Kerailysarja-28
Mad Masks-2
00Finnish Cardset-264
05Finnish Cardset -10
Finnish Cardset Super Snatchers-1
06Finnish Cardset-13
Between the Pipes-4
Superior Snatchers-5
Superior Snatchers Gold-5
Superior Snatchers Silver-5

Lundell, Lars Ake
65Swedish Coralli ISHockey-184
67Swedish Hockey-68
69Swedish Hockey-99
70Swedish Hockey-56
71Swedish Hockey-119
72Swedish Stickers-103
73Swedish Stickers-222
74Swedish Stickers-174

Lundell, Per
89Swedish Semic Elitserien Stickers-127
90Swedish Semic Elitserien Stickers-204
91Swedish Semic Elitserien Stickers-83
92Swedish Semic Elitserien Stickers-107
93Swedish Semic Elitserien-79
94Swedish Leaf-4
95Swedish Leaf-220
95Swedish Upper Deck-59
96German DEL-191
98German DEL-264
99Swedish Upper Deck-106
02Swedish SHL-168
Parallel-168

Lunden, Hannu
70Finnish Jaakiekko-232
71Finnish Suomi Stickers-249
73Finnish Jaakiekko-290

Lunden, Martti
70Finnish Jaakiekko-333

Lunden, Tomas
84Swedish Semic Elitserien-131

Lundenes, Hakan
74Finnish Typotor-78

Lundgren, Assar
71Swedish Hockey-185
72Swedish Stickers-173

Lundgren, Tony
83Swedish Semic Elitserien-44
84Swedish Semic Elitserien-44

Lundh, Staffan
84Swedish Semic Elitserien-112
85Swedish Panini Stickers-110
89Swedish Semic Elitserien Stickers-86
90Swedish Semic Elitserien Stickers-267
91Swedish Semic Elitserien Stickers-96
92Swedish Semic Elitserien Stickers-114
95Swedish Upper Deck 1st Division Stars-DS20

Lundholm, Bengt
79Panini Stickers-197
81Jets Postcards-11
81Swedish Semic Hockey VM Stickers-13
82Jets Postcards-14
82O-Pee-Chee-385
82Post Cereal-21
82Swedish Semic VM Stickers-151
83Jets Postcards-13
83O-Pee-Chee-387
83Vachon-130
84Jets Police-12
84O-Pee-Chee-341

Lundholm, David
03North Dakota Fighting Sioux-28

Lundholm, Joakim
89Swedish Semic Elitserien Stickers-259

Lundin, Henrik
92Swedish Semic Elitserien Stickers-317
93Swedish Semic Elitserien-282
98Danish Hockey League-202
99Danish Hockey League-73

Lundin, Matt
04Maine Black Bears-23
05Maine Black Bears-15
06Sioux Falls Stampede -6

Lundin, Mike
04Maine Black Bears-1
05Maine Black Bears-16

Lundin, Thomas
83Swedish Semic Elitserien-226

Lundmark, Ake
56Swedish Alfabilder-62

Lundmark, Claes
95German DEL-48

Lundmark, Curt
69Swedish Hockey-318
70Swedish Hockey-217
72Swedish Stickers-275
85Swedish Panini Stickers-176
86Swedish Panini Stickers-110
87Swedish Panini Stickers-109
91Swedish Semic Elitserien Stickers-360

Lundmark, David
83Kingston Canadians-11

Lundmark, Erik
02Plymouth Whalers-25
03Plymouth Whalers-18
05Saginaw Spirit-13

Lundmark, Goran
69Swedish Hockey-83

Lundmark, Jamie
95Quebec Pee-Wee Tournament-1438
98SP Authentic-126
Power Shift-126
98Upper Deck-403
Exclusives-403
Exclusives 1 of 1-403
Gold Reserve-403
99Black Diamond-92
Diamond Cut-92
Final Cut-92
99O-Pee-Chee-252
99O-Pee-Chee Chrome-252
99O-Pee-Chee Chrome Refractors-252
99SPx-169
Radiance-169
Spectrum-169
99Topps/OPC-252
99Topps/OPC Chrome-252
Refractors-252
99Upper Deck-321
Exclusives-321
Exclusives 1 of 1-321
99Upper Deck Gold Reserve-321
99Upper Deck MVP SC Edition-211
Gold Script-211
Silver Script-211
Super Script-211
99Upper Deck Ovation-71
Standing Ovation-71
99Bowman CHL-32
99Bowman CHL-90
Gold-32
Gold-90
OPC International-32
OPC International-90
Autographs-BA9
Autographs Gold-BA9
Autographs Silver-BA9
Scout's Choice-SC10
99UD Prospects-27
CHL Class-C9
Destination the Show-DS5
Signatures of Tradition-JL
00UD CHL Prospects-66
Future Leaders-FL6
Game Jersey Autographs-S-JL
Game Jerseys-JL
Game Jerseys-L-B
Game Jerseys-L-K
Game Jerseys-S-L
01SPx Rookie Redemption-R20
01Hartford Wolf Pack-14
01UD Prospects Autographs-A-JL
02Bowman YoungStars-152
Gold-152
Silver-152
02Crown Royale Rookie Royalty-16
02Pacific Calder-84
Silver-84
02Pacific Complete-524
Red-524
02Pacific Exclusive-185
Blue-185
Gold-185
Destined-9
02Private Stock Reserve Moments in Time-6
02Stadium Club-112
Silver Decoy Cards-112
Proofs-112
02Titanium Right on Target-16
02Topps Heritage-168
02Topps Total-425
02UD Artistic Impressions Right Track-RTJL
02UD Artistic Impression Right Track Gold-RTJL
02Upper Deck Bright Futures-JL
02Vanguard Prime Prospects-17
03Bowman-23
Gold-23
Future Fabrics-FF-JLU
Future Fabric Patches-JLU
Future Rivals-WL
Future Rivals Patches-WL
03Bowman Chrome-23
Refractors-23
Gold Refractors-23
Xfractors-23
03ITG Action-334
03O-Pee-Chee-227
03OPC Blue-227
03OPC Gold-227
03OPC Red-227
03Pacific Complete-93
Red-93
03Parkhurst Original Six New York-7
Memorabilia-NM12
03Rangers Team Issue-13
03Topps-227
Blue-227
Gold-227
Red-227
First Round Fabrics-JL
First Round Fabrics-JJJL
Traded Future Phenoms-FP-JLU
03Upper Deck-129
Canadian Exclusives-129
HG-129
03Upper Deck MVP-285
Gold Script-285
Silver Script-285
Canadian Exclusives-285
04Hartford Wolf Pack-14
05Black Diamond-57
Emerald-57
Gold-57
Onyx-57
Ruby-57
05Parkhurst Facsimile Auto Parallel-381
05SP Authentic Scripts to Success-SSJL
05SP Authentic Sign of the Times-JL
05SP Game Used Statscriptions-ST-JL
05Ultra-149
Gold-149
Ice-149
05Upper Deck-124
Big Playmakers-B-JEL
HG Glossy-124
Notable Numbers-N-JAL
05Upper Deck Toronto Fall Expo-124
05Upper Deck Victory-131
Black-131
Gold-131
Silver-131
06Flair Showcase Stitches-SSLU
06Fleer Fabricology-FJL
06O-Pee-Chee-72
Rainbow-72
06Upper Deck-31
Exclusives Parallel-31
High Gloss Parallel-31
Game Jerseys-JLU
Game Patches-PLU
Masterpieces-31
06Upper Deck MVP-43
Gold Script-43
Super Script-43

Lundmark, Jason
05Colorado Eagles-11

Lundmark, Mats
72Swedish Stickers-76
74Swedish Stickers-175
86Swedish Panini Stickers-239

Lundmark, Peter
83Swedish Semic Elitserien-188
84Swedish Semic Elitserien-211
86Swedish Panini Stickers-236
89Swedish Semic Elitserien Stickers-138
90Swedish Semic Elitserien Stickers-211
92Swedish Semic Elitserien Stickers-261
93Swedish Semic Elitserien-229
94Swedish Leaf-221
95Swedish Leaf-283
95Swedish Upper Deck-178
99German Bundesliga 2-65

Lundqvist, Bernt
67Swedish Hockey-292

Lundqvist, Christer
86Swedish Panini Stickers-32

Lundqvist, Henrik
00Swedish Upper Deck-60
02Swedish SHL-111
Next Generation-NG5
Parallel-111
03Swedish Elite-170
Jerseys-4
Silver-170
Zero Hero-1
04SP Authentic Rookie Redemptions-RR20
04Swedish Alfabilder Alfa Stars-30
04Swedish Alfabilder Proof Parallels-30
04Swedish Elitset-169
Dominators-4
Gold-169
High Expectations-3
In The Crease-3
Jerseys Series 1-4
Masks-3
Signatures Series A-14
04Swedish Pure Skills-15
Parallel-15
The Wall-HL
05ITG Heroes/Prosp Toronto Expo Parallel -277
05ITG Heroes/Prosp Toronto Expo Parallel -378
05Beehive-126
Beige -126
Blue -126
Gold-126
Red -126
Matte-126
05Black Diamond-156
Emerald-156
Gold-156
Onyx-156
Ruby-156
05Hot Prospects-254
Hot Materials-HMHL
Red Hot-254
White Hot-254
05ITG Ultimate Memorabilia Level 1-48
05ITG Ultimate Memorabilia Level 2-48
05ITG Ultimate Memorabilia Level 3-48
05ITG Ultimate Memorabilia Level 4-48
05ITG Ultimate Memorabilia Level 5-48
05ITG Ultimate Mem Cornerstones Jerseys-6
05ITG Ultimate Mem Cornerst Jerseys Gold-6
05ITG Ultimate Memorabilia Double Autos-9
05ITG Ultimate Mem Double Autos Gold-9
05ITG Ultimate Mem Double Mem Autos-5
05ITG Ultimate Mem Double Mem Autos Gold-5
05ITG Ultimate Mem Future Stars Autos-2
05ITG Ultimate Mem Future Star Autos Gold-2
05ITG Ultimate Mem Future Stars Jerseys-2
05ITG Ultimate Mem Fut Stars Jerseys Gold-2
05ITG Ultimate Mem Future Stars Mem Autos-2
05ITG Ultimate Mem Fut Star Mem Auto Gold-2
05ITG Ultimate Memorabilia Jersey Autos-38
05ITG Ultimate Mem Jersey Autos Gold-38
05ITG Ultimate Memorabilia R.O.Y. Autos-8
05ITG Ultimate Mem R.O.Y. Autos Gold-8
05ITG Ultimate Memorabilia R.O.Y. Emblems-11
05ITG Ultimate Mem R.O.Y. Emblems Gold-11
05ITG Ultimate Memorabilia R.O.Y. Jerseys-11
05ITG Ultimate Mem R.O.Y. Jerseys Gold-11
05ITG Ultimate Memorabilia R.O.Y. Numbers-11
05ITG Ultimate Mem R.O.Y. Numbers Gold-11
05ITG Ultimate Memorabilia Sextuple Autos-2
05ITG Ultimate Memorabilia Triple Autos-13
05ITG Ultimate Memorabilia Triple Autos-15
05ITG Ultimate Mem Triple Autos Gold-13
05ITG Ultimate Mem Triple Autos Gold-15
05Panini Stickers-6

05Parkhurst-599
05Parkhurst-646
Facsimile Auto Parallel-599
Facsimile Auto Parallel-646
True Colors-TCNYR
True Colors-TCNYR
True Colors-TCNJNY
True Colors-TCNJNY
True Colors-TCNYNY
True Colors-TCNYNY
05SP Authentic-171
Limited-171
Exquisite Endorsements-EEHL
Prestigious Pairings-PPLM
Rarefied Rookies-RRHL
Rookie Authentics-RAHL
Sign of the Times Duals-DWL
Sign of the Times Fives-POCLS
Sign of the Times Fives-TWLDH
05SP Game Used-131
Autographs-131
Gold-131
Game Gear-GG-HL
Game Gear Autographs-AG-HL
Rookie Exclusives-HL
Rookie Exclusives Silver-RE-HL
Significant Numbers-SN-HL
05SPx-173
Spectrum-173
Xcitement Rookies-XR-HL
Xcitement Rookies Gold-XR-HL
Xcitement Rookies Spectrum-XR-HL
05The Cup-177
Autographed Rookie Patches Gold Rainbow-177
Black Rainbow Rookies-177
Dual NHL Shields-DSJL
Dual NHL Shields Autographs-ADSLP
Masterpiece Pressplates (Artifacts)-219
Masterpiece Pressplates (Bee Hive)-126
Masterpiece Pressplates (Black Diamond)-156
Masterpiece Pressplates (Ice)-137
Masterpiece Pressplates (MVP)-418
Masterpiece Pressplates (Power Play)-148
Masterpiece Pressplates (Power Play)-148
Masterpiece Pressplates Rookie Upd Auto-270
Masterpiece Pressplates SPA Autos-171
Masterpiece Pressplates (SP Game Used)-131
Masterpiece Pressplates SPx Autos-173
Masterpiece Pressplates (Trilogy)-202
Masterpiece Pressplates Ult Coll Autos-97
Masterpiece Pressplates (Victory)-288
Masterpiece Pressplates Autographs-177
Noble Numbers-NNLM
Platinum Rookies-177
Scripted Numbers-SNLM
Scripted Swatches-SSHL
Signature Patches-SPHL
05UD Artifacts-219
Gold-RED19
05UD PowerPlay-148
05UD Rookie Class-3
Commemorative Boxtoppers-CC-3
05Ultimate Collection-97
Autographed Patches-97
Autographed Shields-97
Jerseys-JHL
Jerseys Dual-DJML
Marquee Attractions-MA31
Marquee Attractions Signatures-SMA31
Premium Patches-PPHL
Premium Swatches-PSHL
Ultimate Debut Threads Jerseys-DTJHL
Ultimate Debut Threads Jerseys Autos-DAJHL
Ultimate Debut Threads Patches-DTPHL
Ultimate Debut Threads Patches Autos-DAPHL
Ultimate Patches-PHL
Ultimate Patches Dual-DPML
Ultimate Signatures-USHL
Ultimate Signatures Logos-SLHL
Ultimate Signatures Pairings-UPLM
Ultimate Signatures Pairings-UPLT
Ultimate Signatures Trios-UTLTD
05Ultra-269
Gold-269
Ice-269
Rookie Uniformity Jerseys-RU-HL
Rookie Uniformity Jersey Autographs-ARU-HL
Rookie Uniformity Patches-RUP-HL
Rookie Uniformity Patch Autographs-ARP-HL
05Upper Deck-216
HG Glossy-216
Majestic Materials-MMHL
Rookie Ink-RIHL
05Upper Deck Rookie Showcase-RS20
05Upper Deck Rookie Showcase Promos-RS20
05Upper Deck Rookie Threads-RTHL
05Upper Deck Rookie Threads Autographs-ARTHL
05Upper Deck Stars in the Making-SM6
05Upper Deck Ice-137
Cool Threads-CTHL
Cool Threads Autographs-ACTHL
Cool Threads Glass-CTHL
Cool Threads Patches-CTPHL
Cool Threads Patch Autographs-CAPHL
Premieres Auto Patches-AIPHL
05Upper Deck MVP-418
Gold-418
Platinum-418
05Upper Deck Rookie Update-270
05Upper Deck Trilogy-202
05Upper Deck Toronto Fall Expo-216
05Upper Deck Victory-288
Black-288
Gold-288
Silver-288
05Swedish SHL Elitset Series One Jerseys-4
05Swedish SHL Elitset Series 2 Signatures-30
05Swedish SHL Elitset Star Potential-6
05Swedish SHL Elitset Stoppers-4
05ITG Heroes and Prospects-277
05ITG Heroes and Prospects-378
Autograph Memorabilia-GA-10
Autograph Memorabilia Gold-GA-10
Autographs Series II-HL
Autographs Series II-HL2
Autographs Series II-LN
Autographs Series II-PL
Jerseys-GUJ-94
Jerseys Gold-GUJ-94
Measuring Up-MU9
Measuring Up Gold-MU9
06Be A Player-91
Autographs-91
Signatures-HL
Signatures 10-98
Signatures 25-98
Signatures Duals-DHM
Signatures Foursomes-FLTKG
Unmasked Warriors-UM6
Unmasked Warriors Autographs-UM6
Up Close and Personal-UC19
Up Close and Personal Autographs-UC19
06Be A Player Portraits-69
Dual Signature Portraits-DSLP
First Exposures-FEHL
Signature Portraits-SPHL
Timeless Tens-TTNET
06Beehive-37
06Beehive-181
Blue-37
Gold-37
Matte-37
Red Facsimile Signatures-37
Wood-37
5 X 7 Black and White-37
5 X 7 Dark Wood-37
06Between The Pipes-63
Aspiring-AS08
Aspiring Gold-AS08
Autographs-AHL
Double Jerseys-DJ08
Double Jerseys Gold-DJ08
Emblems-GUE03
Emblems Gold-GUE03
Emblems Autographs-GUE03
Jerseys-GUJ03
Jerseys Gold-GUJ03
Jerseys Autographs-GUJ03
Numbers-GUN03
Numbers Gold-GUN03
Numbers Autographs-GUN03
Playing For Your Country-PC13
Playing For Your Country Gold-PC13
Shooting Gallery-SG05
Shooting Gallery-SG08
Shooting Gallery Gold-SG05
Shooting Gallery Gold-SG08
Stick and Jersey-SJ19
Stick and Jersey Gold-SJ19
Stick and Jersey Autographs-SJ19
The Mask-M12
The Mask-M36
The Mask Gold-M12
The Mask Gold-M36
The Mask Silver-M12
The Mask Silver-M36
The Mask Game-Used-MGU11
The Mask Game-Used Gold-MGU11
06Black Diamond-115
Black-115
Gold-115
Ruby-115
06Flair Showcase-65
06Flair Showcase-144
06Flair Showcase-248
Parallel-65
Parallel-144
Parallel-248
Hot Gloves-HG20
Wave of the Future-WF27
06Fleer-128
Tiffany-128
Hockey Headliners-HL10
Netminders-N17
06Hot Prospects-65
Red Hot-65
White Hot-65
06ITG International Ice-18
Gold-18
Autographs-AHL
Complete Jersey-CJ11
Complete Jersey Gold-CJ11
Cornerstones-IC03
Cornerstones Gold-IC03
Goaltending Glory-GG05
Goaltending Glory Gold-GG05
Hockey Passport-HP11
Hockey Passport Gold-HP11
Stick and Jersey-SJ09
Stick and Jersey Gold-SJ09
Teammates-IT16
Teammates Gold-IT16
Triple Memorabilia-TM08
Triple Memorabilia Gold-TM08
06ITG Ultimate Memorabilia-64
Artist Proof-64
Autos-46
Autos Gold-46
Decades-8
Decades Gold-8
Going For Gold-9
Going For Gold Gold-9
Jerseys Autos-34
Jerseys Autos Gold-34
Stick Rack-14
Stick Rack Gold-14
Sticks Autos-10
Sticks Autos Gold-10
06McDonald's Upper Deck-30
Autographs-AHL
Hot Gloves-HG10
Rookie Review-RR3
06NHL POG-38
06O-Pee-Chee-323
Rainbow-323
06Panini Stickers-102
06SP Authentic-38
06SP Authentic-115
Limited-38
Limited-115
06SP Game Used-67
Gold-67
Rainbow-67
Authentic Fabrics-AFHL
Authentic Fabrics Parallel-AFHL
Authentic Fabrics Patches-AFHL
Authentic Fabrics Dual-AF2JL
Authentic Fabrics Dual Patches-AF2JL
Authentic Fabrics Triple-AF3NYR
Authentic Fabrics Triple Patches-AF3NYR
Authentic Fabrics Fives-AF5GAA
Authentic Fabrics Fives Patches-AF5GAA
Authentic Fabrics Eights-AF8SWE
Authentic Fabrics Eights Patches-AF8SWE
Inked Sweaters Dual-IS2LP
Inked Sweaters Dual Patches-IS2LP
06SPx-67
Spectrum-67
SPxcitement-X67
SPxcitement Spectrum-X67
Winning Materials-WMHL
Winning Materials Spectrum-WMHL
06The Cup-61
Autographed Foundations-CQHL
Autographed Foundations Patches-CQHL
Autographed NHL Shields Duals-DASLD
Autographed Patches-61
Black Rainbow-61
Foundations-CQHL
Foundations Patches-CQHL
Gold-61
Gold Patches-61
Honorable Numbers-HNHL
Jerseys-61
Limited Logos-LLHL
Masterpiece Pressplates-61
Scripted Swatches-SSHL
06UD Artifacts-37
06UD Artifacts-184
Blue-37
Blue-184
Gold-37
Gold-184
Platinum-37
Platinum-184
Radiance-37
Radiance-184
Red-37
Red-184
06UD Mini Jersey Collection-66
Jerseys-HL
Jersey Variations-HL
06UD Powerplay-66
Impact Rainbow-66
Goal Robbers-GR13
06UD Toronto Fall Expo Priority Signings -PSHL
06Ultimate Collection-42
Jerseys-UJ-HL
Jerseys Dual-UJ2-JL
Patches-UJ-HL
Patches Dual-UJ2-JL
Signatures-US-HL
06Ultra-127
Gold Medallion-127
Ice Medallion-127
Difference Makers-DM22
06Upper Deck Arena Giveaways-NYR4
06Upper Deck-377
Exclusives Parallel-377
High Gloss Parallel-377
Game Dated Moments-GD17
Game Jerseys-J2HL
Game Patches-P2HL
Hometown Heroes-HH36
Masterpieces-377
Oversized Wal-Mart Exclusives-377
Signatures-SHL
06Upper Deck MVP-196
Gold Script-196
Super Script-196
Jerseys-OJBL
Jerseys-OJLD
Last Line of Defense-LL3
06Upper Deck Ovation-131
06Upper Deck Sweet Shot-71
Sweet Stitches-SSHL
Sweet Stitches Duals-SSHL
Sweet Stitches Triples-SSHL
06Upper Deck Trilogy-65
06Upper Deck Victory-129
06Upper Deck Victory Black-129
06Upper Deck Victory Gold-129
06Upper Deck Victory GameBreakers-GB31
06Upper Deck Victory Next In Line-NL33
06Upper Deck Victory Oversize Cards-HL
06Russian Sport Collection Olympic Stars-19
06ITG Heroes and Prospects Quad Emblems-QE06
06ITG Heroes and Prospects Quad Emblems Gold-QE06
06ITG Heroes and Prospects Sticks and Jerseys-SJ14
06ITG Heroes and Prospects Sticks and Jerseys Gold-SJ14
07Upper Deck Victory-21
Black-21
Gold-21
EA Sports Face-Off-FO2
GameBreakers-GB49
Oversize Cards-OS6

Lundqvist, Jan
70Swedish Hockey-207
71Swedish Hockey-294

Lundqvist, Joel
02Swedish SHL-144
02Swedish SHL-280
Dynamic Duos-9
Next Generation-NG1
Parallel-144
Parallel-280
Signatures Series II-8
03Swedish Elite-30
Enforcers-EF5
Signatures-3
Silver-30
04Swedish Elitset-174
Gold-174
05Swedish SHL Elitset-30
Gold-30
Series Two Signatures-32
06Stars Team Postcards-13
06Swedish SHL Elitset-35
Playmakers-4
06AHL Top Prospects-18
06Iowa Stars-15
07Upper Deck Victory-237
Black-237
Gold-237

Lundqvist, Lars
64Swedish Coralli ISHockey-131
65Swedish Coralli ISHockey-131

Lundqvist, Per
71Swedish Hockey-186
74Swedish Stickers-247
81Swedish Semic Hockey VM Stickers-9

Lundqvist, Stefan
98Swedish UD Choice-42
99Swedish Upper Deck-26

Lundqvist, Sven-Erik
69Swedish Hockey-84

Lundrigan, Joe
72Maple Leafs Postcards-17
72Tulsa Oilers Milk Panels-1
74Capitals White Borders-18
74NHL Action Stamps-310
74O-Pee-Chee NHL-277

Lundstrom Jr., Per Anton
95Collector's Choice-346
Player's Club-346
Player's Club Platinum-346
95SP-187
95Upper Deck-562
Electric Ice-562
Electric Ice Gold-562
95Swedish Leaf-275
98Swedish UD Choice-18
99Swedish Upper Deck-8
00Swedish Upper Deck-2
02Swedish SHL-158
Parallel-158
04German DEL-271
06Swedish SHL Elitset-263

Lundstrom, Ake
69Swedish Hockey-264
70Swedish Hockey-159
71Swedish Hockey-256

Lundstrom, Arne
69Swedish Hockey-263
70Swedish Hockey-155
71Swedish Hockey-254
72Swedish Stickers-237
73Swedish Stickers-234
74Swedish Stickers-248

Lundstrom, Finn
69Swedish Hockey-176
70Swedish Hockey-156
71Swedish Hockey-255
73Swedish Stickers-238
74Swedish Stickers-249

Lundstrom, Fredrik
83Swedish Semic Elitserien-70
84Swedish Semic Elitserien-70

Lundstrom, Hans
69Swedish Hockey-85

Lundstrom, Jan
83Swedish Semic Elitserien-40
84Swedish Semic Elitserien-40
84Swedish Semic Elitserien-43

Lundstrom, Joakim
03Swedish Elite-1
Rookies-2
Silver-1
04Swedish Elitset Future Stars-9
04Swedish Elitset Signatures-12

Lundstrom, Jon
83Swedish Semic Elitserien-43
85Swedish Panini Stickers-40
86Swedish Panini Stickers-24

Lundstrom, Lars-Erik
93Swiss HNL-387

Lundstrom, Mats
83Swedish Semic Elitserien-183
83Swedish Semic Elitserien-194
84Swedish Semic Elitserien-217
86Swedish Panini Stickers-242
87Swedish Panini Stickers-221
89Swedish Semic Elitserien Stickers-205
90Swedish Semic Elitserien Stickers-38
91Swedish Semic Elitserien Stickers-289
93Swedish Semic Elitserien-214

Lundstrom, Per Anton
64Swedish Coralli ISHockey-145
65Swedish Coralli ISHockey-127
67Swedish Hockey-69
69Swedish Hockey-100
70Swedish Hockey-57
71Swedish Hockey-134
06Swedish SHL Elitset-263

Lundstrom, Tobias
99Swedish Upper Deck-168
00Swedish Upper Deck-150
SHL Signatures-TL
03Swedish Bjorkloven Umea-1

Lundstrom, Tord
64Swedish Coralli ISHockey-24
64Swedish Coralli ISHockey-78
65Swedish Coralli ISHockey-24
65Swedish Coralli ISHockey-78
67Swedish Hockey-15
67Swedish Hockey-53
69Swedish Hockey-67
69Swedish Hockey-191
70Finnish Jaakiekko-31
70Swedish Hockey-31
70Swedish Hockey-286
70Swedish Masterserien-40
70Swedish Masterserien-47
70Swedish Masterserien-59
70Swedish Masterserien-114
71Finnish Suomi Stickers-50
71Swedish Hockey-19
71Swedish Hockey-108
72Finnish Jaakiekko-52
72Finnish Hellas-30
72Finnish Panda Toronto-72
72Finnish Semic World Championship-58
72Swedish Stickers-17
72Swedish Stickers-88
72Swedish Semic World Championship-58
73Finnish Jaakiekko-31
73Swedish Stickers-14
73Swedish Stickers-162
74Finnish Jenkki-29
74Swedish Stickers-318
81Swedish Semic Hockey VM Stickers-117
87Swedish Panini Stickers-46
97Swedish Alfabilder Autographs-8
98Swedish UD Choice-206
98Swedish UD Choice-211
01Swedish Alfabilder-8

Lundstrom, Ulf
64Swedish Coralli ISHockey-162
65Swedish Coralli ISHockey-162
70Swedish Hockey-208
71Swedish Hockey-295
72Swedish Stickers-75

Lundvall, Lars-Erik
55Swedish Alfabilder-18
64Swedish Coralli ISHockey-15
64Swedish Coralli ISHockey-99
65Swedish Coralli ISHockey-15
65Swedish Coralli ISHockey-99
67Swedish Hockey-293
81Swedish Semic Hockey VM Stickers-123

Lundy, Pat
44Beehive Group II Photos-116

Lune, Kevin
88Brockville Braves-24
95Central Hockey League-47
95Wheeling Thunderbirds Series II-10
96Peoria Rivermen-14
96Peoria Rivermen Photo Album-15
98San Antonio Iguanas-11
98Topeka Scarecrows-17

Lunner, Stefan
83Swedish Semic Elitserien-124
84Swedish Semic Elitserien-147
85Swedish Panini Stickers-133

Luojola, Hannu
66Finnish Jaakiekkosarja-54
70Finnish Jaakiekko-144
71Finnish Suomi Stickers-67
71Finnish Suomi Stickers-194
71Swedish Hockey-63
72Finnish Jaakiekko-232
72Finnish Semic World Championship-74
72Swedish Semic World Championship-74
73Finnish Jaakiekko-266
78Finnish SM-Liiga-159

Luoma, Jari
84Swedish Semic Elitserien-221
87Swedish Panini Stickers-234
89Swedish Semic Elitserien Stickers-218
90Swedish Semic Elitserien Stickers-52

Luoma, Mikko
98Finnish Kerailysarja-121
99Finnish Cardset-273
00Finnish Cardset-330
01Finnish Cardset-123
02Finnish Cardset-219
03ITG VIP Rookie Debut-92
03Parkhurst Rookie-85
03SPx-239
03Upper Deck Rookie Update-119
03Finnish Cardset D-Day-DD5
04Swedish Malmo Red Hawks-13
04Swedish Pure Skills Signatures-9
05Swedish SHL Elitset-221
Gold-221
06Swedish SHL Elitset-69

Luomala, Marko
99Finnish Cardset-343
04Finnish Cardset-53
Parallel-39
05Finnish Cardset -45
06Finnish Cardset-291

Luongo, Chris
89ProCards IHL-107
90ProCards AHL/IHL-484
91ProCards-125
92OPC Premier-35
92Ultra-362
92Upper Deck-534
93Ultra-96
96Milwaukee Admirals-15
98German DEL-67
99German DEL-317
01German Upper Deck-203
02German DEL City Press-268
03German DEL-189

Luongo, Fabio
04Williams Lake Timberwolves-12

Luongo, Roberto
97Beehive-69
Authentic Autographs-69
Golden Portraits-69
97Black Diamond-131
Double Diamond-131
Triple Diamond-131
Quadruple Diamond-131
97Donruss Elite-51
Aspirations-51
Status-51
Back to the Future-7
Back to the Future Autographs-7
97Zenith-97
Z-Gold-97
Z-Silver-97
97Zenith 5 x 7-77
Gold Impulse-77
Silver Impulse-77
97Bowman CHL-42
97Bowman CHL-159
OPC-42
OPC-159
Autographs-39
Bowman's Best-18
Bowman's Best Atomic Refractors-18
Bowman's Best Refractor-18
98Black Diamond-92
Double Diamond-92
Triple Diamond-92
Quadruple Diamond-92
98SPx Top Prospects-62
Radiance-62
Spectrum-62
98UD Choice-258
Prime Choice Reserve-258
Reserve-258
98Upper Deck Game Jerseys-GJ5
98Val d'Or Foreurs-9
99BAP Memorabilia-307
Gold-307
Silver-307
99BAP Millennium Calder Candidates Ruby-C37
99BAP Millennium Calder Candidate Emerald-C37
99BAP Millennium Calder Cand Sapphire-C37
99Crown Royale-88
Limited Series-88
Premiere Date-88
Prospects Parallel-88
Card-Supials-15
Card-Supials Minis-15
Century 21-7
99O-Pee-Chee-250
99O-Pee-Chee Chrome-250
99O-Pee-Chee Chrome Refractors-250
99Pacific-459
99Pacific Omega-143
Copper-143
Gold-143
Ice Blue-143
Premiere Date-143
NHL Generations-4
5 Star Talents-5
5 Star Talents Parallel-5
99Pacific Prism-88
Holographic Blue-88
Holographic Gold-88
Holographic Mirror-88
Holographic Purple-88
Premiere Date-88
99SP Authentic-53
99SPx-176
Radiance-176
Spectrum-176
99Topps Arena Giveaways-NYI-RL
99Topps/OPC-250
99Topps/OPC Chrome-250
Refractors-250
99Topps Gold Label Class 1-94
Black-94
Black One of One-94
One of One-94
Red-94
Red One of One-94
99Topps Gold Label Class 2-94
99Topps Gold Label Class 2 Black-94
99Topps Gold Label Class 2 Black 1 of 1-94
99Topps Gold Label Class 2 One of One-94
99Topps Gold Label Class 2 Red-94
99Topps Gold Label Class 2 Red One of One-94
99Topps Gold Label Class 3-94
99Topps Gold Label Class 3 Black-94
99Topps Gold Label Class 3 Black 1 of 1-94
99Topps Gold Label Class 3 One of One-94
99Topps Gold Label Class 3 Red-94
99Topps Gold Label Class 3 Red One of One-94
99Topps Premier Plus-121
Parallel-121
99Upper Deck-163
Exclusives-163
Exclusives 1 of 1-163
99Upper Deck Arena Giveaways-NI1
99Upper Deck Gold Reserve-163
99Upper Deck MVP SC Edition-112
Gold Script-112
Silver Script-112
Super Script-112
99Upper Deck Victory-359
99Wayne Gretzky Hockey-108
99Bowman CHL-43
Gold-43
OPC International-43
Scout's Choice-SC21
00Aurora-63
Pinstripes-63
Pinstripes Premiere Date-63
Premiere Date-63
Dual Game-Worn Jerseys-2
Game-Worn Jerseys-4
Game-Worn Jersey Patches-4
Scouting Reports-12
00BAP Memorabilia-163
00BAP Memorabilia-463
Emerald-163
Emerald-463
Ruby-163
Ruby-463
Sapphire-163
Sapphire-463
Promos-163
00BAP Mem Chicago Sportsfest Copper-163
00BAP Memorabilia Chicago Sportsfest Blue-163
00BAP Memorabilia Chicago Sportsfest Gold-163
00BAP Memorabilia Chicago Sportsfest Ruby-163
00BAP Memorabilia Chicago Sun-Times Ruby-163
00BAP Memorabilia Chicago Sun-Times Gold-163
00BAP Mem Chicago Sun-Times Sapphire-163
00BAP Mem Toronto Fall Expo Copper-163
00BAP Memorabilia Toronto Fall Expo Gold-163
00BAP Memorabilia Toronto Fall Expo Ruby-163
00BAP Parkhurst 2000-P72
00BAP Parkhurst 2000-P244
00BAP Signature Series-278
Emerald-278
Ruby-278
Sapphire-278
Autographs-204
Autographs Gold-204
He Shoots-He Scores Prizes-4
00BAP Ultimate Mem Game-Used Jerseys-GJ41
00BAP Ultimate Mem Game-Used Emblems-E33
00BAP Ultimate Mem Game-Used Numbers-N33
00BAP Ultimate Mem Game-Used Sticks-GS41
00BAP Ultimate Memorabilia Goalie Sticks-G13
00BAP Ultimate Mem Plante Jersey Cards-PJ10
00BAP Ultimate Mem Plante Skate Cards-PS10
00Black Diamond Game Gear-LRL
00Crown Royale-123
21st Century Rookies-10
00O-Pee-Chee-271
00O-Pee-Chee Parallel-271
00Pacific-253
Copper-253
Gold-253
Ice Blue-253
Premiere Date-253
2001: Ice Odyssey-15
Gold Crown Die Cuts-20
00Pacific 2001: Ice Odyssey Anaheim Ntnl-15
00Panthers Team Issue-7
00Private Stock Game Gear-52
00Private Stock Game Gear Patches-52
00SP Game Used TOTG Auto Bronze-A-RL
00SP Game Used TOTG Auto Silver-A-RL
00SP Game Used Tool of the Game Auto Gold-A-RL
00SPx Winning Materials-WLU
00Stadium Club-220
00Titanium-120
Retail-120
00Titanium Draft Day Edition-120
00Titanium Draft Day Promos-120
00Topps/OPC-271
Parallel-271
00Topps Chrome-166
OPC Refractors-166
Refractors-166
00Topps Gold Label Class 1-63
Gold-63
00Topps Gold Label Class 2-63
00Topps Gold Label Class 2 Gold-63
00Topps Gold Label Class 3-63
00Topps Gold Label Class 3 Gold-63
00Topps Gold Label New Generation-NG9
00Topps Gold Label New Generation 1 to 1-NG9
00Topps Heritage-46
Chrome Parallel-46
00Topps Stars Progression-P4
00UD Heroes Signs of Greatness-RL
00UD Reserve-38
00Upper Deck-303
Exclusives Tier 1-303
Exclusives Tier 2-303
Game Jersey Autographs Canadian-CRL
Game Jersey Combos-DCL
MVP Excellence-ME1
MVP Game-Used Souvenirs-GSRL
MVP Mark of Excellence-SGJL
MVP ProSign-RL
MVP Super Game-Used Souvenirs-GSRL
00Upper Deck Vintage-158
00Upper Deck Vintage-160
00Vanguard-121
Pacific Proofs-121
01Atomic-46
Blue-46
Gold-46
Premiere Date-46
Red-46
01BAP Memorabilia-77
Emerald-77
Ruby-77
Sapphire-77
Goalies Jerseys-GJ10
He Shoots-He Scores Prizes-19
01BAP Signature Series-12
Autographs-12
Autographs Gold-12
Jerseys-GJ-29
Jersey Autographs-GURL
Jersey and Stick Cards-GSJ-29
Emblems-GUE-27
Numbers-ITN-27
Teammates-TM-13
01BAP Ultimate Mem Legend Terry Sawchuk-11
01BAP Update He Shoots-He Scores Prizes-28
01Between the Pipes-33
Double Memorabilia-DM11
Future Wave-FW4
Goalie Gear-GG10
He Shoots-He Saves Points-6
He Shoots-He Saves Prizes-40
Jerseys-GJ10
Jersey and Stick Cards-GSJ9
Masks-17
Masks Silver-17
Masks Gold-17
Tandems-GT4
01Bowman YoungStars-131
Gold-131
Ice Cubed-131
Autographs-RL
Relics-JRL
Relics-SRL
Relics-DSRL
Rivals-R1
01Crown Royale-65
Blue-65
Premiere Date-65
Red-65
Retail-65
01eTopps-14
01O-Pee-Chee-68
01O-Pee-Chee Heritage Parallel-68
01O-Pee-Chee Heritage Parallel Limited-68
01O-Pee-Chee Premier Parallel-68
01Pacific-173
01Pacific-431
Extreme LTD-173
Gold-431
Hobby LTD-173
Premiere Date-173
Retail LTD-173
Steel Curtain-9
01Pacific Adrenaline-83
Blue-83
Premiere Date-83
Red-83
Retail-83
Creased Lightning-8
Power Play-17
01Pacific Arena Exclusives-173
01Pacific Arena Exclusives-431
01Pacific Heads-Up-44
Blue-44
Premiere Date-44
Red-44
Silver-44
Breaking the Glass-11
Prime Picks-2
Showstoppers-9
01Pacific Montreal International-3
01Parkhurst-43
Gold-43
Silver-43
Jerseys-PJ35
Teammates-T10
Teammates-T20
01Private Stock-43
Gold-43
Premiere Date-43
Retail-43
Silver-43
01Private Stock Pacific Nights-43
01Private Stock PS-2002-35
01Private Stock Reserve-G6
01SP Authentic-37
Limited-37
Limited Gold-37
Sign of the Times-RL
Sign of the Times-BL
Sign of the Times-DL
01SPx-175
01Stadium Club-80
Award Winners-80
Master Photos-80
Gallery-G11
Gallery Gold-G11
New Regime-NR6
New Regime-NRARL
01Titanium-61
Hobby Parallel-61
Premiere Date-61
Retail-61
Retail Parallel-61
01Topps-68
Heritage Parallel-68
Heritage Parallel Limited-68
OPC Parallel-68
01Topps Chrome-68
Refractors-68
Black Border Refractors-68
01Topps Heritage-32
Refractors-32
01Topps Reserve-52
01UD Challenge for the Cup-35
01UD Honor Roll Jerseys-J-RL
01UD Honor Roll Jerseys Gold-J-RL
01UD Mask Collection-113
Gold-113
Goalie Jerseys-SSRL
01UD Playmakers-44
01UD Premier Collection-27
01UD Top Shelf-95
Goalie Gear-LPRL
01Upper Deck-75
Exclusives-75
Goalies in Action-GL10
Ice Autographs-RL
01Upper Deck MVP-82
01Upper Deck Victory-146
01Upper Deck Victory-154
Gold-146
Gold-154
01Upper Deck Vintage-111
01Upper Deck Vintage-113
01Vanguard-43
Blue-43
Red-43
One of Ones-43
Premiere Date-43
Proofs-43
Stonewallers-9
02Atomic-46
Blue-46
Gold-46
Red-46
Denied-8
Hobby Parallel-46
02BAP First Edition-89
02BAP First Edition-337
02BAP First Edition-353
02BAP First Edition-417H
Jerseys-89
02BAP Memorabilia-88
02BAP Memorabilia-213
Emerald-88
Emerald-213
Ruby-88
Ruby-213
Sapphire-88
Sapphire-213
Franchise Players-FP-13
Future of the Game-FG-4
He Shoots-He Scores Prizes-21
NHL All-Star Game-88
NHL All-Star Game-213
NHL All-Star Game Blue-88
NHL All-Star Game Blue-213
NHL All-Star Game Green-88
NHL All-Star Game Green-213
NHL All-Star Game Red-88
NHL All-Star Game Red-213
02BAP Memorabilia Toronto Fall Expo-88
02BAP Memorabilia Toronto Fall Expo-213
02BAP Signature Series-127
Autographs-127
Autograph Buybacks 2001-12
Autographs Gold-127
Franchise Players-FJ13
Phenoms-YP9
Team Quads-TQ5
02BAP Ultimate Mem Jersey and Stick-19
02BAP Ultimate Memorabilia Number Ones-6
02BAP Ultimate Memorabilia Numerology-4
02Between the Pipes-4
02Between the Pipes-133
Gold-4
Silver-4
Behind the Mask-4
Blockers-13
Emblems-26
Future Wave-3
Goalie Autographs-15
He Shoots-He Saves Points-15
He Shoots-He Saves Prizes-2
Inspirations-I4
Jerseys-26
Masks II-13
Masks II Gold-13
Masks II Silver-13
Numbers-26
Stick and Jerseys-26
02Bowman YoungStars-25
Gold-25
Silver-25
02Crown Royale-43
Blue-43
Red-43
Retail-43
Coats of Armor-4
02eTopps-36
02ITG Used-34
02ITG Used-134
Franchise Players-F13
Franchise Players Autographs-F13
Franchise Players Gold-F13
02McDonald's Pacific-17
02O-Pee-Chee-108
02O-Pee-Chee Premier Blue Parallel-108
02O-Pee-Chee Premier Red Parallel-108
02O-Pee-Chee Factory Set-108
02Pacific-156
Blue-156
Red-156
02Pacific Complete-128
Red-128
02Pacific Exclusive-77
Advantage-8
Jerseys-11
Jerseys Gold-11
02Pacific Heads-Up-53
Blue-53
Purple-53
Red-53
Quad Jerseys-25
Quad Jerseys Gold-25
Showstoppers-10
02Pacific Les Gardiens-4
Gold-4
02Pacific Quest for the Cup-42
Gold-42
02Pacific Toronto Fall Expo-5
Gold-5
02Parkhurst-47
Bronze-47
Gold-47
Silver-47
Franchise Players-FP13
Hardware-V8
02Parkhurst Retro-72
Minis-72
Franchise Players-RF13
He Shoots-He Scores Prizes-21
Jerseys-RJ19
02Private Stock Reserve-124
Red-124
Retail-124
InCrease Security-10
Patches-124
02SP Authentic-40
Beckett Promos-40
02SP Game Used-21
First Rounder Patches-RL

Tools of the Game-RL
02SPx-34
Spectrum Gold-34
Spectrum Silver-34
02Stadium Club-29
Silver Decoy Cards-29
Proofs-29
Puck Stops Here-PSH9
YoungStars Relics-S9
YoungStars Relics-DS3
02Titanium-47
Blue-47
Red-47
Retail-47
Jerseys-33
Jerseys Retail-33
Patches-33
02Topps-108
OPC Blue Parallel-108
OPC Red Parallel-108
Factory Set-108
02Topps Chrome-69
Black Border Refractors-69
Refractors-69
02Topps Heritage-8
Chrome Parallel-8
02Topps Total-54
Team Checklists-TTC12
02UD Artistic Impressions-40
Gold-40
02UD Artistic Impressions Beckett Promos-40
02UD Artistic Impressions Retrospectives-R40
02UD Artistic Impressions Retrospect Gold-R40
02UD Artistic Impress Retrospect Silver-R40
02UD Honor Roll-32
02UD Mask Collection-37
02UD Mask Collection-38
02UD Mask Collection Beckett Promos-37
02UD Mask Collection Beckett Promos-38
02UD Mask Collection Great Gloves-GGRL
02UD Mask Collection Masked Marvels-MMRL
02UD Mask Collection Nation's Best-NLBT
02UD Mask Collection Patches-PWRL
02UD Mask Collection View from the Cage-VRL
02UD Piece of History-41
02UD Premier Collection-40
02UD Top Shelf-36
Dual Player Jerseys-STBL
02Upper Deck-76
Exclusives-76
Blow-Ups-C18
Goaltender Threads-RL
Goaltender Threads Gold-RL
Last Line of Defense-LL6
02Upper Deck Classic Portraits-42
02Upper Deck MVP-76
Gold-76
Classics-76
Golden Classics-76
02Upper Deck Rookie Update-45
Jerseys-DRL
Jerseys Gold-DRL
02Upper Deck Victory-90
Bronze-90
Gold-90
Silver-90
02Upper Deck Vintage-111
02Upper Deck Vintage-273
Green Backs-111
Tall Boys-T30
Tall Boys Gold-T30
02Vanguard-46
LTD-46
Stonewallers-4
03BAP Memorabilia-157
Emerald-157
Gold-157
Ruby-157
Sapphire-157
Deep in the Crease-D14
Jersey and Stick-SJ-16
Jerseys-GJ-18
Jersey Autographs-GJ-18
Masks III-4
Masks III Gold-4
Masks III Silver-4
Masks III Autographs-M-RL
Masks III Memorabilia-4
Tandems-T-9
03BAP Ultimate Memorabilia Autographs-133
Gold-133
03BAP Ultimate Mem Auto Jerseys-133
03BAP Ultimate Mem Auto Emblems-133
03BAP Ultimate Memorabilia Emblems-25
03BAP Ultimate Memorabilia Emblems Gold-25
03BAP Ultimate Mem Franch Present Future-13
03BAP Ultimate Memorabilia Heroes-11
03BAP Ultimate Mem Heroes Autos-6
03BAP Ultimate Mem Hometown Heroes-2
03BAP Ultimate Mem Hometown Heroes Gold-2
03BAP Ultimate Memorabilia Jerseys-22
03BAP Ultimate Memorabilia Jerseys Gold-22
03BAP Ultimate Mem Jersey and Emblems-36
03BAP Ultimate Mem Jersey and Emblem Gold-36
03BAP Ultimate Mem Jersey and Numbers-36
03BAP Ultimate Mem Jersey and Number Gold-36
03BAP Ultimate Memorabilia Numbers-17
03BAP Ultimate Memorabilia Numbers Gold-17
03BAP Ultimate Memorabilia Triple Threads-5
03Beehive-86
Variations-86
Gold-86
Silver-86
Jumbos-13
Jumbo Jerseys-BH19
Jerseys-JT22
Signatures-RF14
03Black Diamond-103
Black-103
Green-103
Red-103
Threads-DT-RL
Threads Green-DT-RL
Threads Red-DT-RL
Threads Black-DT-RL
03Bowman-60
Gold-60
Future Rivals-ML
Future Rivals Patches-ML
03Bowman Chrome-60
Refractors-60
Gold Refractors-60
Xfractors-60
03Crown Royale-45
Blue-45
Retail-45
Gauntlet of Glory-10
03Duracell-7
03eTopps-24
03ITG Action-298
Homeboys-HB13
Jerseys-M166
Jerseys-M253
03ITG Toronto Fall Expo Jerseys-FE5
03ITG Used Signature Series-34
Gold-34
Autographs-RL
Autographs Gold-RL
Franchise-13
Franchise Autographs-13
Franchise Gold-13
Goalie Gear-2
Goalie Gear Autographs-2
Goalie Gear Gold-2
Jerseys-40
Jerseys Gold-40
Jersey Autos-40
Emblems-30
Emblems Gold-30
Jersey and Stick-40
Jersey and Stick Gold-40
Teammates-11
Teammates Gold-11
03ITG VIP Collages-24
03ITG VIP Collage Autographs-24
03ITG VIP Netminders-2
03McDonald's Pacific-25
Net Fusions-3
03NHL Sticker Collection-50
03O-Pee-Chee-153
03OPC Blue-153
03OPC Gold-153
03OPC Red-153
03Pacific-147
Blue-147
Red-147
03Pacific Calder-47
Silver-47
03Pacific Complete-417
Red-417
03Pacific Exhibit-171
Blue Backs-171
Standing on Tradition-6
03Pacific Heads-Up-45
Hobby LTD-45
Retail LTD-45
03Pacific Invincible-43
Blue-43
Red-43
Retail-43
Freeze Frame-8
03Pacific Luxury Suite-36A
03Pacific Luxury Suite-36B
03Pacific Prism-45
Blue-45
Gold-45
Red-45
03Pacific Quest for the Cup-48
Blue-48
03Pacific Supreme-43
Blue-43
Red-43
Retail-43
Standing Guard-7
03Panthers Team Issue-11
03Parkhurst Rookie-39
Jerseys-GJ-22
Jersey Autographs-GJJ-RL
Jerseys Gold-GJ-22
Jersey and Sticks-SJ-24
Jersey and Sticks Gold-SJ-24
Retro Rookies-RR-8
Retro Rookies Gold-RR-8
03Private Stock Reserve-43
Blue-43
Red-43
Retail-43
03SP Authentic-38
Limited-38
03SP Game Used-21
Gold-21
Authentic Fabrics-AFRL
Authentic Fabrics-DFBL
Authentic Fabrics Gold-AFRL
Authentic Fabrics Gold-DFBL
Double Threads-DTBL
Game Gear-GGRL
Game Gear Combo-GCRL
Limited Threads-LTRL
Limited Threads Gold-LTRL
Premium Patches-PPRL
Signers-SPSRL
03SPx-41
03SPx-185
Radiance-41
Radiance-185
Spectrum-41
Spectrum-185
Style-SPX-BG
Style Limited-SPX-BG
03Titanium-158
Hobby Jersey Number Parallels-158
Patches-158
Retail-158
03Topps-153
Blue-153
Gold-153
Red-153
Box Toppers-9
03Topps C55-29
Minis-29
Minis American Back-29
Minis American Back Red-29
Minis Bazooka Back-29
Minis Brooklyn Back-29
Minis Hat Trick Back-29
Minis O Canada Back-29
Minis O Canada Back Red-29
Minis Stanley Cup Back-29
Relics-TRRL
03Topps Pristine-14
Gold Refractor Die Cuts-14
Refractors-14
Jersey Portions-PPJ-RL
Jersey Portion Refractors-PPJ-RL
Mini-PM-RL
Patches-PP-RL
Patch Refractors-PP-RL
Press Plates Black-14
Press Plates Cyan-14
Press Plates Magenta-14
Press Plates Yellow-14
03Topps Traded Franchise Fabrics-FF-RL
03UD Honor Roll-35
03UD Premier Collection-25
NHL Shields-SH-RL
Signatures-PS-RL
Signatures Gold-PS-RL
Stars-ST-RL
Stars Patches-ST-RL
Teammates-PT-FP
Teammates Patches-PT-FP
03Upper Deck-85
Big Playmakers-BP-RL
Canadian Exclusives-85
Fan Favorites-FF3
Franchise Fabrics-FF-RL
HG-85
Patches-SV2
03Upper Deck Classic Portraits-42
03Upper Deck Ice-38
Gold-38
Authentics-IA-RL
Under Glass Autographs-UG-RL
03Upper Deck MVP-188
Gold Script-188
Silver Script-188
Canadian Exclusives-188
Masked Men-MM7
SportsNut-SN38
03Upper Deck Rookie Update-37
03Upper Deck Trilogy-42
Limited-42
03Upper Deck Victory-82
Bronze-82
Gold-82
Silver-82
Freshman Flashback-FF21
Game Breakers-GB24
03Russian World Championship Stars-16
03Toronto Star-41
Foil-16
04Pacific-115
Blue-115
Red-115
In The Crease-6
04SP Authentic-40
04SP Authentic-116
Limited-40
Limited-116
Buybacks-171
Buybacks-172
Buybacks-173
Octographs-OS-GOA
Rookie Review-RR-RL
Sign of the Times-ST-RL
Sign of the Times-DS-KL
Sign of the Times-DS-WL
Sign of the Times-TS-KLL
Sign of the Times-TS-LWH
Sign of the Times-TS-RLB
Sign of the Times-FS-SES
04UD Toronto Fall Expo Pride of Canada-2
04UD Toronto Fall Expo Priority Signings-RL
04Ultimate Collection-19
Buybacks-78
Buybacks-79
Buybacks-80
Buybacks-81
Buybacks-82
Buybacks-83
Buybacks-84
Dual Logos-UL2-LB
Patch Autographs-UPA-RL
Signatures-US-RL
Signature Logos-ULA-RL
Signature Patches-SP-RL
04Upper Deck-78
Canadian Exclusives-78
HG Glossy Gold-78
HG Glossy Silver-78
Jersey Autographs-GJA-RL
World Cup Tribute-RL
World Cup Tribute-MBRL
World Cup Tribute-MBRLJT
04Upper Deck Pearson Awards-3
05Be A Player-39
First Period-39
Second Period-39
Third Period-39
Overtime-39
Dual Signatures-FL
Dual Signatures-LW
Dual Signatures-RL
Dual Signatures-TL
Outtakes-OT24
Quad Signatures-BLTG
Quad Signatures-TLAL
Signatures-RL
Signatures Gold-RL
Triple Signatures-DRL
Triple Signatures-LLA
05Beehive-38
05Beehive-190
Beige-38
Blue-38
Gold-38
Red-38
Matte-38
Signature Scrapbook-SSLU
05Black Diamond-97
Emerald-97
Gold-97
Onyx-97
Ruby-97
Jerseys-J-RL
Jerseys Ruby-J-RL
Jersey Duals-DJ-RL
Jersey Triples-TJ-RL
Jersey Quads-QJ-RL
05Hot Prospects-43
En Fuego-43
Red Hot-43
White Hot-43
05McDonalds Upper Deck-19
Goalie Factory-GF2
Goalie Gear-MG3
05Panini Stickers-55
05Parkhurst-202
05Parkhurst-562
05Parkhurst-683
Facsimile Auto Parallel-202
Facsimile Auto Parallel-562
Facsimile Auto Parallel-683
True Colors-TCFLA
True Colors-TCFLA
True Colors-TCFLTB
True Colors-TCFLTB
05SP Authentic-43
Limited-43
Chirography-SPRL
Exquisite Endorsements-EERL
Marks of Distinction-MDRL
Sign of the Times-RL
Six Star Signatures-SSGO
05SP Game Used-44
Autographs-44
Gold-44
Authentic Fabrics-AF-RL
Authentic Fabrics Autographs-AAF-RL
Authentic Fabrics Gold-AF-RL
Authentic Fabrics Quad-HLBJ
Authentic Fabrics Quad-RBLT
Authentic Patches Quad-HLBJ
Authentic Patches Quad-RBLT
Authentic Patches-AP-RL
Authentic Patches Autographs-AAP-RL
Awesome Authentics-AA-RL
SIGnificance-RL
SIGnificance Gold-S-RL
SIGnificance Extra-BL
SIGnificance Extra Gold-BL
Significant Numbers-SN-RL
Statscriptions-ST-LU
05SPx-35
05SPx-121
Spectrum-35
Spectrum-121
Winning Combos-WC-FL
Winning Combos Autographs-AWC-BL
Winning Combos Gold-WC-FL
Winning Combos Spectrum-WC-FL
Winning Materials-WM-RL
Winning Materials Autographs-AWM-RL
Xcitement Superstars-XS-RL
Xcitement Superstars Gold-XS-RL
Xcitement Superstars Spectrum-XS-RL
05The Cup-47
Gold-47
Black Rainbow-47
Dual NHL Shields-DSLB
Dual NHL Shields-DSRO
Dual NHL Shields Autographs-ADSTL
Emblems of Endorsement-EERL
Honorable Numbers-HNRL
Limited Logos-LLRL
Masterpiece Pressplates-47
Noble Numbers-NNLA
Noble Numbers-NNLR
Patch Variation-P47
Patch Variation Autographs-AP47
Scripted Numbers-SNLA
Scripted Numbers-SNLR
Scripted Numbers Dual-DSNTL
Scripted Swatches-SSRL
Signature Patches-SPRL
05UD Artifacts-44
05UD Artifacts-169
Blue-44
Blue-169
Gold-44
Gold-169
Green-44
Green-169
Pewter-44
Pewter-169
Red-44
Red-169
Auto Facts-AF-RL
Auto Facts Blue-AF-RL
Auto Facts Copper-AF-RL
Auto Facts Pewter-AF-RL
Auto Facts Silver-AF-RL
Frozen Artifacts-FA-RL
Frozen Artifacts Autographed-FA-RL
Frozen Artifacts Copper-FA-RL
Frozen Artifacts Dual-FAD-RL
Frozen Artifacts Dual Autographed-FAD-RL
Frozen Artifacts Dual Copper-FAD-RL
Frozen Artifacts Dual Gold-FAD-RL
Frozen Artifacts Dual Maroon-FAD-RL
Frozen Artifacts Dual Pewter-FAD-RL
Frozen Artifacts Dual Silver-FAD-RL
Frozen Artifacts Gold-FA-RL
Frozen Artifacts Maroon-FA-RL
Frozen Artifacts Pewter-FA-RL
Frozen Artifacts Silver-FA-RL
Goalie Gear-FG-RL
Goalie Gear Autographed-FG-RL
Goalie Gear Dual-FGD-RL
Goalie Gear Dual Autographed-FGD-RL
Goalie Gear Pewter-FG-RL
Goalie Gear Silver-FG-RL
Gold Autographed-44
Gold Autographed-169
Remarkable Artifacts-RA-RL
Remarkable Artifacts Dual-RA-RL
05UD PowerPlay-39
Rainbow-39
05UD Toronto Fall Expo Priority Signings-PS-RL
05Ultimate Collection-42
Gold-42
Endorsed Emblems-EERL
Jerseys-JRL
Marquee Attractions-MA23
Marquee Attractions Signatures-SMA23
National Heroes Jerseys-NHJRL
National Heroes Patches-NHPRL
Premium Patches-PPRL
Premium Swatches-PSRL
Ultimate Achievements-UARL
Ultimate Patches-PRL
Ultimate Signatures-USRL
Ultimate Signatures Foursomes-UFRBGL
Ultimate Signatures Logos-SLRL
05Ultra-86
Gold-86
Fresh Ink-FI-RL
Fresh Ink Blue-FI-RL
Ice-86
05Upper Deck-80
05Upper Deck All-Time Greatest-25
05Upper Deck Big Playmakers-B-RL
05Upper Deck HG Glossy-80
05Upper Deck Jerseys-J-RLU
05Upper Deck Jerseys Series II-J2RL
05Upper Deck Majestic Materials-MMRL
05Upper Deck NHL Generations-TBLL
05Upper Deck NHL Generations-TRBL
05Upper Deck Notable Numbers-N-RL
05Upper Deck Patches-P-RL
05Upper Deck Ice-40
Rainbow-40
Cool Threads-CTRL
Cool Threads Autographs-ACTRL
Cool Threads Glass-CTRL
Cool Threads Patches-CTPRL
Cool Threads Patch Autographs-CAPRL
Glacial Graphs-GGRL
05Upper Deck MVP-165
Gold-165
Platinum-165
05Upper Deck Rookie Update-41
05Upper Deck Trilogy-40
05Upper Deck Trilogy-140
Crystal-140
Honorary Patches-HP-RL
Honorary Patch Scripts-HSP-RL
Honorary Swatches-HS-RL
Honorary Swatch Scripts-HSS-RL
Scripts-SCS-RL
05Upper Deck Toronto Fall Expo-80
05Upper Deck Victory-85
Black-85
Gold-85
Silver-85
Stars on Ice-SI23
06Sports Illustrated for Kids *-11
06Be A Player-90
Autographs-90
Signatures-RL
Signatures 10-97
Signatures 25-97
Signatures Duals-DLN
Signatures Trios-TLNM
Signatures Foursomes-FLTFR
Unmasked Warriors-UM10
Unmasked Warriors Autographs-UM10
Up Close and Personal-UC48
Up Close and Personal Autographs-UC48
06Be A Player Portraits-98
Dual Signature Portraits-DSLN
Sensational Six-SSGOL
Signature Portraits-SPRL
Timeless Tens-TTNET
Triple Signature Portraits-TLWF
06Beehive-4
06Beehive-162
Blue-4
Gold-4
Matte-4
Red Facsimile Signatures-4
Wood-4
5 X 7 Black and White-4
5 X 7 Dark Wood-4
Matted Materials-MMRL
PhotoGraphs-PGRL
Remarkable Matted Materials-MMRL
06Between The Pipes-75
06Between The Pipes-119
Aspiring-AS04
Aspiring Gold-AS04
Autographs-ARL
Autographs-ARL2
Complete Jersey-CJ14
Complete Jersey Gold-CJ14
Double Jerseys-DJ25
Double Jerseys-DJ29
Double Jerseys Gold-DJ25
Double Jerseys Gold-DJ29
Double Memorabilia-DM10
Double Memorabilia Gold-DM10
Emblems-GUE10
Emblems Gold-GUE10
Emblems Autographs-GUE10
Jerseys-GUJ10
Jerseys Gold-GUJ10
Jerseys Autographs-GUJ10
Numbers-GUN10
Numbers Gold-GUN10
Numbers Autographs-GUN10
Playing For Your Country-PC04
Playing For Your Country Gold-PC04
Stick and Jersey-SJ18
Stick and Jersey Gold-SJ18
Stick and Jersey Autographs-SJ18
Stick Work-SW01
Stick Work Gold-SW01
06Black Diamond-147
Black-147
Gold-147
Ruby-147
06Canucks Postcards-12
06Flair Showcase-45
06Flair Showcase-185
06Flair Showcase-234
06Flair Showcase-283
Parallel-46
Parallel-185
Parallel-234
Parallel-283
Hot Gloves-HG13
06Fleer-187
Tiffany-187
Netminders-N11
06Gatorade-77
06Hot Prospects-94
Red Hot-94
White Hot-94
Hot Materials -HMRL
Hot Materials Red Hot-HMRL
Hot Materials White Hot-HMRL
Hotagraphs-HRL
06ITG Ultimate Memorabilia-121
Artist Proof-121
Autos-47
Autos Gold-47
Autos Dual-12
Autos Dual Gold-12
Double Memorabilia Autos-12
Double Memorabilia Autos Gold-12
Emblems-26
Emblems Gold-26
First Round Picks-27
First Round Picks Gold-27
Jerseys Autos-35
Jerseys Autos Gold-35
Sticks and Jerseys-10
Sticks and Jerseys Gold-10
Sticks Autos-9
Sticks Autos Gold-9
Triple Thread Jerseys-4
Triple Thread Jerseys Gold-4
06McDonald's Upper Deck Autographs-ARL
06McDonald's Upper Deck Hot Gloves-HG7
06McDonald's Upper Deck Patches-PRL
06NHL POG-58
06O-Pee-Chee-471
Rainbow-471
Autographs-A-RL
06Panini Stickers-352
06SP Authentic-4
06SP Authentic-151
Limited-4
Limited-151
Sign of the Times Duals-STLB
Sign of the Times Triples-ST3NLM
Sign of the Times Quads-ST4RBLF
06SP Game Used-97
Gold-97
Rainbow-97
Authentic Fabrics-AFRL
Authentic Fabrics Parallel-AFRL
Authentic Fabrics Patches-AFRL
Authentic Fabrics Dual-AF2NL
Authentic Fabrics Dual Patches-AF2NL
Authentic Fabrics Quads-AF4RBTL
Authentic Fabrics Quads Patches-AF4RBTL
Authentic Fabrics Eights-AF8CAN
Authentic Fabrics Eights Patches-AF8CAN
Autographs-97
By The Letter-BLRL
Inked Sweaters Dual-IS2BL
Inked Sweaters Dual Patches-IS2BL
Letter Marks-LMLU
06SPx-96
06SPx-112
Spectrum-96
Spectrum-112
SPxcitement-X97
SPxcitement Spectrum-X97
SPxcitement Autographs-X97
Winning Materials-WMRL
Winning Materials Spectrum-WMRL
Winning Materials Autographs-WMRL
06The Cup-87
Autographed Foundations Patches-CQRL
Autographed NHL Shields Duals-DASLB
Autographed NHL Shields Duals-DASLN
Autographed Patches-87
Black Rainbow-87
Foundations-CQRL
Foundations Patches-CQRL
Enshrinements-ERL
Gold-87
Gold Patches-87
Honorable Numbers-HNRL
Jerseys-87
Limited Logos-LLRL
Masterpiece Pressplates-87
NHL Shields Duals-DSHLL
Scripted Swatches-SSRL
Scripted Swatches Duals-DSLN
Signature Patches-SPRL
06UD Artifacts-3
06UD Artifacts-171
Blue-3
Blue-171
Gold-3
Gold-171
Platinum-3
Platinum-171
Radiance-3
Radiance-171
Autographed Radiance Parallel-3
Autographed Radiance Parallel-171
Red-3
Red-171
Frozen Artifacts-FARL
Frozen Artifacts Black-FARL
Frozen Artifacts Blue-FARL
Frozen Artifacts Gold-FARL
Frozen Artifacts Platinum-FARL
Frozen Artifacts Red-FARL
Frozen Artifacts Autographed Black-FARL
Frozen Artifacts Patches Black-FARL
Frozen Artifacts Patches Blue-FARL
Frozen Artifacts Patches Gold-FARL
Frozen Artifacts Patches Platinum-FARL
Frozen Artifacts Patches Red-FARL
Frozen Artifacts Patches Autographed Black Tag Parallel-FARL
Tundra Tandems-TTLN
Tundra Tandems Black-TTLN
Tundra Tandems Blue-TTLN
Tundra Tandems Gold-TTLN
Tundra Tandems Platinum-TTLN
Tundra Tandems Red-TTLN
Tundra Tandems Dual Patches Red-TTLN
06UD Mini Jersey Collection-96
06UD Powerplay-96
Impact Rainbow-96
Goal Robbers-GR9
06Ultimate Collection-59
Jerseys-UJ-RL
Jerseys Dual-UJ2-LN
Jerseys Triple-UJ3-RBL
Patches-UJ-RL
Patches Dual-UJ2-LN
Patches Triple-UJ3-RBL
06Ultra-189
Gold Medallion-189
Ice Medallion-189
Action-UA12
Difference Makers-DM16
06Upper Deck Arena Giveaways-VAN3
06Upper Deck-436
Exclusives Parallel-436
High Gloss Parallel-436
Game Jerseys-J2RL
Game Patches-P2RL
Generations Duals-G2BL
Generations Patches Dual-G2PBL
Hometown Heroes-HH50
Masterpieces-436
Oversized Wal-Mart Exclusives-436
Signatures-SRL
Zero Men-ZM3
06Upper Deck MVP-282
Gold Script-282
Super Script-282
Autographs-OAKL
Jerseys-OJKL
Jerseys-OJRM
Last Line of Defense-LL7
06Upper Deck Ovation-71
06Upper Deck Sweet Shot-98
Sweet Stitches-SSRL
Sweet Stitches Duals-SSRL
Sweet Stitches Triples-SSRL
06Upper Deck Trilogy-95
Combo Autographed Jerseys-CJNL
Combo Autographed Patches-CJNL
Combo Clearcut Autographs-C2LJ
Honorary Scripted Patches-HSPRL
Honorary Scripted Swatches-HSSRL
Honorary Swatches-HSRL
Scripts-S1RL
Scripts-S3RL
06Upper Deck Victory-83
06Upper Deck Victory-279
06Upper Deck Victory Black-83
06Upper Deck Victory Gold-83
06Upper Deck Victory GameBreakers-GB19
06Upper Deck Victory Oversize Cards-RL
06ITG Heroes and Prospects Double Memorabilia-DM09
06ITG Heroes and Prospects Heroes Memorabilia-HM24
06ITG Heroes and Prospects Quad Emblems-QE14
06ITG Heroes and Prospects Triple Memorabilia-TM12
07Upper Deck Victory-131
Black-131
Gold-131
GameBreakers-GB6
Oversize Cards-OS31
Stars on Ice-SI1
07ITG Going For Gold World Juniors-24
Autographs-24
Emblems-GUE24
Jerseys-GUJ24

Luostarinen, Ari

98Finnish Keraily sarja-142
05Finnish Cardset -75

Luostarinen, Esko

05Finnish Tappara Legendat-26

Luostarinen, Timo

66Finnish Jaakiekkosarja-138

Luoto, Harry

70Finnish Jaakiekko-162

Luotonen, Tuomas

01Finnish Cardset-251

Luovi, Mikko

91Upper Deck Czech World Juniors-33
92Finnish Jyvas-Hyva Stickers-40
93Upper Deck-271
93Finnish Jyvas-Hyva Stickers-82
93Finnish SISU-120
94Finnish SISU-267
94Finnish SISU Horoscopes-14
95Finnish SISU-309
96Finnish SISU Redline-99
96Swedish Brynas Tigers-19
97Swedish Collector's Choice-28
98Swedish UD Choice-48
99Swedish Upper Deck-32
00Swedish Upper Deck-40
01Swedish Brynas Tigers-12
03Finnish Cardset-105
04Swedish Elitset-153
Gold-153

Lupandin, Andrei

92Quebec Pee-Wee Tournament-1456
95Brandon Wheat Kings-14
96Brandon Wheat Kings-16
97Brandon Wheat Kings-16
98Brandon Wheat Kings-13
99Idaho Steelheads-10
03Mississippi Sea Wolves-6
05Quad City Mallards-7
06Quad City Mallards-7

Lupaschuk, Ross

97Prince Albert Raiders-12
98SP Authentic-118
Power Shift-118
Sign of the Times-RL
Sign of the Times Gold-RL
98Upper Deck-395
Exclusives-395
Exclusives 1 of 1-395
Gold Reserve-395
98Prince Albert Raiders-15
99Bowman CHL-18
Gold-18
OPC International-18
Autographs-BA38
Autographs Gold-BA38
Autographs Silver-BA38
00Red Deer Rebels-11
Signed-11
01Wilkes-Barre Scranton Penguins-8
02Wilkes-Barre Scranton Penguins-6
03AHL Top Prospects-21
03Wilkes-Barre Scranton Penguins-15
04Wilkes-Barre Scranton Penguins-8
05Swedish SHL Elitset-256
Gold-256
06Swedish SHL Elitset-228

Lupien, Camille

51Laval Dairy Lac St. Jean-26

Lupien, Gilles

76Nova Scotia Voyageurs-11
77Canadiens Postcards-16
78Canadiens Postcards-18
79Canadiens Postcards-16
80O-Pee-Chee-298

Lupien, Steve

907th Inn. Sketch QMJHL-2
917th Inn. Sketch Memorial Cup-49

Lupul, Dale

05Bossier-Shreveport Mudbugs-9

Lupul, Gary

80Canucks Silverwood Dairies-15
80Canucks Team Issue-15
81Canucks Team Issue-13
81Fredericton Express-5
82O-Pee-Chee-354
82Post Cereal-19
82Fredericton Express-5
82Victoria Cougars-13
83Canucks Team Issue-12
83O-Pee-Chee-355
83Vachon-111
84Canucks Team Issue-15
84O-Pee-Chee-323
84 7-Eleven Discs-49
84Kelowna Wings-32
85Canucks Team Issue-16
85Fredericton Express-6

Lupul, Joffrey

00Medicine Hat Tigers-15
02BAP Memorabilia Draft Redemptions-7
02SPx Rookie Redemption-R214
02Medicine Hat Tigers-12
03BAP Memorabilia-184
Emerald-184
Gold-184
Ruby-184
Sapphire-184
Super Rookies-SR2
Super Rookies Gold-SR2
Super Rookies Silver-SR2
03BAP Ultimate Memorabilia Autographs-96
Gold-96
03BAP Ultimate Mem Auto Jerseys-96
03BAP Ultimate Mem Auto Emblems-96
03BAP Ultimate Mem Auto Numbers-96
03BAP Ultimate Mem Calder Candidates-12
03BAP Ultimate Mem Calder Candidates Gold-12
03BAP Ultimate Mem Franch Present Future-1
03BAP Ultimate Mem Magnificent Prospects-7
03BAP Ultimate Mem Magnif Prospect Autos-7
03BAP Ultimate Mem Rookie Jersey Emblems-35
03BAP Ultimate Mem Rookie Jsy Emblem Gold-35
03BAP Ultimate Mem Rookie Jersey Numbers-35
03BAP Ultimate Mem Rookie Jsy Number Gold-35
03Beehive-201
Gold-201
Silver-201
Jumbo Variations-1
03Black Diamond-189
Black-189
Green-189
Red-189
03Bowman-112
Gold-112
Premier Performance-PP-JL
Premier Performance Patches-PP-JL
03Bowman Chrome-112
Refractors-112
Gold Refractors-112
Xfractors-112
03Crown Royale-102
Red-102
Retail-102
Royal Portraits-1
03eTopps-46
03ITG Action-618
03ITG Toronto Spring Expo Class of 2004-3
03ITG Used Signature Series-179
Gold-179
03ITG VIP Rookie Debut-2
03O-Pee-Chee-336
03OPC Blue-336
03OPC Gold-336
03OPC Red-336
03Pacific-351
03Pacific Calder-162
Reflections-1
03Pacific Complete-518
Red-518
03Pacific Exhibit-226
03Pacific Heads-Up-101
Hobby LTD-101
Retail LTD-101
Jerseys-1
Prime Prospects-1
Prime Prospects LTD-1
03Pacific Invincible-101
Blue-101
Red-101
Retail-101
03Pacific Luxury Suite-81
Gold-81
03Pacific Prism-151
03Pacific Quest for the Cup-101
03Pacific Supreme-102
03Pacific Supreme-102A
Blue-102
Red-102
Retail-102
03Parkhurst Rookie-159
All-Rookie-ART-12
All-Rookie Autographs-ART-JLU
All-Rookie Gold-ART-12
Calder Candidates-CMC-6
Calder Candidate Autographs-CMC-JL
Calder Candidates Gold-CMC-6
Rookie Emblems-RE-3
Rookie Emblem Autographs-RE-JL
Rookie Emblems Gold-RE-3
Rookie Jerseys-RJ-3
Rookie Jersey Autographs-RJ-JL
Rookie Jerseys Gold-RJ-3
Rookie Numbers-RN-3
Rookie Number Autographs-RN-JL
Rookie Numbers Gold-RN-3
Teammates Gold-RT2
Teammates-RT2
03Private Stock Reserve-102
Blue-102
Red-102
Retail-102
Class Act-1
03SP Authentic-136
Limited-136
Signed Patches-JL
03SP Game Used-83
Gold-83
Rookie Exclusives-RE6
03SPx-224
Radiance-224
Spectrum-224
03Titanium-206
Patches-206
Right on Target-1
03Topps-336
Blue-336
Gold-336
Red-336
03Topps Pristine-185
03Topps Pristine-186
03Topps Pristine-187
Gold Refractor Die Cuts-185
Gold Refractor Die Cuts-186
Gold Refractor Die Cuts-187
Refractors-185
Refractors-186
Refractors-187
Mini-PM-JL
Press Plates Black-185
Press Plates Black-186
Press Plates Black-187
Press Plates Cyan-185
Press Plates Cyan-186
Press Plates Cyan-187
Press Plates Magenta-185
Press Plates Magenta-186
Press Plates Magenta-187
Press Plates Yellow-185
Press Plates Yellow-186
Press Plates Yellow-187
03Topps Traded Future Phenoms-FP-JOL
03UD Honor Roll-184
03UD Premier Collection-111

NHL Shields-SH-JL
Stars-ST-JL
Stars Patches-ST-JL
03Upper Deck-202
Canadian Exclusives-202
HG-202
Rookie Threads-RT-1
03Upper Deck Classic Portraits-170
03Upper Deck Ice-121
Glass Parallel-121
03Upper Deck MVP-445
03Upper Deck Rookie Update-156
YoungStars-YS13
03Upper Deck Trilogy-172
Limited-172
03Upper Deck Victory-201
04Pacific-5
Blue-5
Red-5
04Pacific NHL All-Star FANtasy-1
04Pacific NHL All-Star FANtasy Gold-1
04SP Authentic-2
Limited-2
Rookie Review-RR-JL
Sign of the Times-ST-JL
Sign of the Times-TS-LRZ
Sign of the Times-QS-BBLK
Sign of the Times-FS-PAC
04Upper Deck-5
Canadian Exclusives-5
HG Glossy Gold-5
HG Glossy Silver-5
YoungStars-YS-JL
04AHL Top Prospects-9
04Cincinnati Mighty Ducks-15
05Be A Player-2
First Period-2
Second Period-2
Third Period-2
Overtime-2
Signatures-JL
Signatures Gold-JL
05Beehive-2
Matte-2
Matted Materials-MMLU
05Black Diamond-1
Emerald-1
Gold-1
Onyx-1
Ruby-1
05Ducks Team Issue-9
05Hot Prospects-1
En Fuego-1
Red Hot-1
White Hot-1
05Panini Stickers-196
05Parkhurst-4
Facsimile Auto Parallel-4
True Colors-TCANA
True Colors-TCANA
05SP Authentic-2
Limited-2
Scripts to Success-SSLU
Sign of the Times-LU
Sign of the Times Duals-DLP
Sign of the Times Triples-TLPG
05SP Game Used Authentic Fabrics Quad-SGLC
05SP Game Used Authentic Patches Quad -SGLC
05SP Game Used Awesome Authentics-AA-LU
05SP Game Used Awesome Authentics Gold-DA-LU
05SP Game Used SIGnificance-JL
05SP Game Used SIGnificance Gold-S-JL
05SP Game Used Statscriptions-ST-LU
05The Cup Dual NHL Shields-DSJC
05The Cup Emblems of Endorsement-EELU
05The Cup Honorable Numbers-HNLU
05The Cup Scripted Swatches-SSLU
05The Cup Signature Patches-SPLU
05UD Artifacts-3
Blue-3
Gold-3
Green-3
Pewter-3
Red-3
Auto Facts-AF-JL
Auto Facts Blue-AF-JL
Auto Facts Copper-AF-JL
Auto Facts Pewter-AF-JL
Auto Facts Silver-AF-JL
Frozen Artifacts-FA-JL
Frozen Artifacts Autographed-FA-JL
Frozen Artifacts Copper-FA-JL
Frozen Artifacts Dual-FAD-JL
Frozen Artifacts Dual Autographed-FAD-JL
Frozen Artifacts Dual Copper-FAD-JL
Frozen Artifacts Dual Gold-FAD-JL
Frozen Artifacts Dual Maroon-FAD-JL
Frozen Artifacts Dual Pewter-FAD-JL
Frozen Artifacts Dual Silver-FAD-JL
Frozen Artifacts Gold-FA-JL
Frozen Artifacts Maroon-FA-JL
Frozen Artifacts Patches-FP-JL
Frozen Artifacts Patches Autographed-FP-JL
Frozen Artifacts Patches Dual-FPD-JL
Frozen Artifacts Patches Dual Autos-FPD-JL
Frozen Artifacts Patches Pewter-FP-JL
Frozen Artifacts Patches Silver-FP-JL
Frozen Artifacts Pewter-FA-JL
Frozen Artifacts Silver-FA-JL
Gold Autographed-3
Remarkable Artifacts-RA-JL
Remarkable Artifacts Dual-RA-JL
05UD PowerPlay-2
Rainbow-2
Specialists-TSJL
Specialists Patches-SPJL
05UD Toronto Fall Expo Priority Signings-PS-LU
05Ultimate Collection-3
Gold-3
Endorsed Emblems-EELU
Jerseys Dual-DJLS
Jerseys Triple-TJPGL
Ultimate Patches Dual-DPLS
Ultimate Patches Triple-TPPGL
05Ultra-7
Gold-7
Fresh Ink-FI-JL
Fresh Ink Blue-FI-JL
Ice-7
05Upper Deck-5
HG Glossy-5
Jerseys-J-JOL
Jerseys Series II-J2LU
Majestic Materials-MMJL
Notable Numbers-N-JL
Patches-P-JLU
05Upper Deck Ice-1
Rainbow-1
Fresh Ice-FILU
Fresh Ice Glass-FILU
Fresh Ice Glass Patches-FIPLU
05Upper Deck MVP-8
Gold-8
Platinum-8
05Upper Deck Rookie Update-3
05Upper Deck Trilogy-2
Honorary Patches-HP-LU
Honorary Patch Scripts-HSP-LU
Honorary Swatches-HS-LU
Honorary Swatch Scripts-HSS-LU
Scripts-SFS-JL
05Upper Deck Toronto Fall Expo-5
05Upper Deck Victory-2
Black-2
Gold-2
Silver-2
06Be A Player Portraits-45
06Beehive-63
Matte-63
Matted Materials-MMJL
06Black Diamond Jerseys-JJL
06Black Diamond Jerseys Black-JJL
06Black Diamond Jerseys Gold-JJL
06Black Diamond Jerseys Ruby-JJL
06Black Diamond Jerseys Black Autographs -JJL
06Flair Showcase-5
Parallel-5
Inks-IJL
Stitches-SSJL
Wave of the Future-WF1
06Fleer-77
Tiffany-77
06Gatorade-18
06Hot Prospects Hot Materials -HMLU
06Hot Prospects Hot Materials Red Hot-HMLU
06Hot Prospects Hot Materials White Hot-HMLU
06O-Pee-Chee-193
Rainbow-193
06Panini Stickers-271
06SP Authentic-63
Limited-63
06SP Game Used-41
Gold-41
Rainbow-41
Authentic Fabrics-AFLU
Authentic Fabrics Parallel-AFLU
Authentic Fabrics Patches-AFLU
Authentic Fabrics Dual-AF2HL
Authentic Fabrics Dual Patches-AF2HL
Inked Sweaters-ISJL
Inked Sweaters Patches-ISJL
Letter Marks-LMJL
06SPx-40
Spectrum-40
Winning Materials-WMJL
Winning Materials Spectrum-WMJL
06The Cup Autographed NHL Shields Duals-DASLS
06UD Artifacts-61
Blue-61
Gold-61
Platinum-61
Radiance-61
Autographed Radiance Parallel-61
Red-61
Auto-Facts-AFJL
Auto-Facts Gold-AFJL
Frozen Artifacts-FAJL
Frozen Artifacts Black-FAJL
Frozen Artifacts Blue-FAJL
Frozen Artifacts Gold-FAJL
Frozen Artifacts Platinum-FAJL
Frozen Artifacts Red-FAJL
Frozen Artifacts Autographed Black-FAJL
Frozen Artifacts Patches Black-FAJL
Frozen Artifacts Patches Blue-FAJL
Frozen Artifacts Patches Gold-FAJL
Frozen Artifacts Patches Platinum-FAJL
Frozen Artifacts Patches Red-FAJL
Frozen Artifacts Patches Autographed Black Tag Parallel-FAJL
Tundra Tandems-TTJJ
Tundra Tandems Black-TTJJ
Tundra Tandems Blue-TTJJ
Tundra Tandems Gold-TTJJ
Tundra Tandems Platinum-TTJJ
Tundra Tandems Red-TTJJ
Tundra Tandems Dual Patches Red-TTJJ
06UD Mini Jersey Collection-41
06UD Powerplay-40
Impact Rainbow-40
06Ultra-78
Gold Medallion-78
Ice Medallion-78
06Upper Deck Arena Giveaways-EDM5
06Upper Deck-328
Exclusives Parallel-328
High Gloss Parallel-328
Game Dated Moments-GD10
Game Jerseys-JJL
Game Patches-PJL
Generations Duals-G2IL
Generations Triples-G3IML
Generations Patches Dual-G2PIL
Generations Patches Triple-G3PIML
Masterpieces-328
06Upper Deck MVP-121
Gold Script-121
Super Script-121
Autographs-OALH
Jerseys-OJSV
06Upper Deck Ovation-52
06Upper Deck Sweet Shot Signature Sticks-STJL
06Upper Deck Sweet Shot Sweet Stitches-SSJL
06Upper Deck Sweet Shot Sweet Stitches Duals-SSJL
06Upper Deck Sweet Shot Sweet Stitches Triples-SSJL
06Upper Deck Trilogy-40
Combo Autographed Jerseys-CJHL
Combo Autographed Patches-CJHL
Honorary Scripted Patches-HSPJL
Honorary Scripted Swatches-HSSJL
Ice Scripts-ISJL
Scripts-TSLU
06Upper Deck Victory-2
06Upper Deck Victory-248
06Upper Deck Victory Black-2
06Upper Deck Victory Gold-2
06Upper Deck Victory Next In Line-NL2
07Upper Deck Ovation-84
07Upper Deck Victory-164
Black-164
Gold-164

Lupzig, Andreas
92Finnish Semic-189
94German DEL-210
95German DEL-210
95German DEL-429
95Swedish World Championships Stickers-64
96German DEL-355
98German DEL-104
98German DEL-320
99German DEL-113
00German DEL-133
01German Upper Deck-211

Lusignan, Hugo
93Quebec Pee-Wee Tournament-65

Lusnak, Patrik
06Sudbury Wolves-12

Lussier, Antoine
02Swiss HNL-215

Lussier, Jean
93Swiss HNL-412
95Swiss HNL-237

Lussier, Jonathan
01Swiss HNL-427

Lussier, Michael
01Swiss HNL-281
02Swiss HNL-123

Lussy, Silvan
00Swiss Panini Stickers-138
01Swiss HNL-136
02Swiss HNL-159

Lusth, Mats
83Swedish Semic Elitserien-106
84Swedish Semic Elitserien-106
85Swedish Panini Stickers-95
86Swedish Panini Stickers-87
87Swedish Panini Stickers-93
90Swedish Semic Elitserien Stickers-129
91Swedish Semic Elitserien Stickers-181
92Swedish Semic Elitserien Stickers-205
93Swiss HNL-469
94Swedish Leaf-236
95Swedish Leaf-300
95Swedish Upper Deck-192
97Swedish Collector's Choice-140
98Swedish UD Choice-155
99Swedish Upper Deck-153

Lustinec, Petr
99Czech Score Blue 2000-145
99Czech Score Red Ice 2000-145

Lutchenko, Vladimir
69Russian National Team Postcards-3
69Swedish Hockey-7
70Finnish Jaakiekko-6
70Russian National Team Postcards-3
70Swedish Hockey-316
70Swedish Masterserien-21
70Swedish Masterserien-69
70Swedish Masterserien-129
70Swedish Masterserien-132
71Finnish Suomi Stickers-7
71Swedish Hockey-31
72Finnish Jaakiekko-27
72Finnish Hellas-61
72Finnish Hellas-63
72Finnish Panda Toronto-54
72Finnish Semic World Championship-3
72Swedish Semic World Championship-3
73Finnish Jaakiekko-8
73Russian National Team-10
73Swedish Stickers-80
74Finnish Jenkki-48
74Russian National Team-11
74Swedish Semic World Champ Stickers-28
79Panini Stickers-142
79Russian National Team-6
81Swedish Semic Hockey VM Stickers-40
91Future Trends Canada '72-42
91Future Trends Canada '72 French-42

Lutes, Brett
04Bakersfield Condors-11
05Port Huron Flags-8
06Bakersfield Condors-4

Lutes, Craig
907th Inn. Sketch OHL-342
91Oshawa Generals Sheet-12
917th Inn. Sketch OHL-353
92Windsor Spitfires-6
93Windsor Spitfires-6
94Birmingham Bulls-17
95Birmingham Bulls-15

Luther, Gary
87Sault Ste. Marie Greyhounds-30

Luthi, Claude
93Swiss HNL-506
95Swiss HNL-455
00Swiss Panini Stickers-65
00Swiss Slapshot Mini-Cards-HCCF10

Luthi, Freddy
91Finnish Semic World Champ Stickers-189
91Swedish Semic World Champ Stickers-189
92Finnish Semic-210
93Swedish Semic World Champ Stickers-121
93Swiss HNL-201
95Swedish Globe World Championships-211
95Swiss HNL-76

Luthi, Peter
72Finnish Semic World Championship-144
72Swedish Semic World Championship-144

Luthi, Urs
93Swiss HNL-401

Lutkevich, Vitali
02Russian Transfert Promos-3

Lutter, Peter
94German DEL-362
95German DEL-317
96German DEL-98
98German DEL-15

Luttinen, Arttu
04Finnish Cardset-25
Parallel-18
05Finnish Cardset -21
06Finnish Cardset-22
06Binghamton Senators-13

Lutz, Jerod
93Quebec Pee-Wee Tournament-854

Lutz, Nathan
03Rockford Ice Hogs-9
05Milwaukee Admirals Pepsi-11
05Rockford Ice Hogs-8
06Rockford IceHogs -16

Lutz, Rainer
94German DEL-309
94German First League-309

Lutz, Stefan
95Swiss HNL-268

Luukkonen, Mattias
02Swedish SHL-277
Parallel-277
03Swedish Elite-27
Silver-27

Lux, Ralf
94German First League-77

Luza, Patrik
91Upper Deck Czech World Juniors-90
99Czech OFS-212
00Czech OFS-355
01Czech OFS Update-294
02Czech OFS Plus-71
03Czech OFS Plus-44
04Czech OFS Defence Points-12
05Czech HC Vsetin-15

Lyall, Matt
04Guelph Storm-18

Lyamin, Kirill
03Russian Hockey League-275
03Russian SL-33
03Russian Young Lions-7
04Russian Under-18 Team-4

Lyashenko, Roman
96Upper Deck Ice-144
99BAP Memorabilia-375
Gold-375
Silver-375
99Pacific Omega-78
Copper-78
Gold-78
Ice Blue-78
Premiere Date-78
99Pacific Prism-45
Holographic Blue-45
Holographic Gold-45
Holographic Mirror-45
Holographic Purple-45
Premiere Date-45
99Michigan K-Wings-21
00Paramount-78
Copper-78
Gold-78
Holo-Gold-78
Holo-Silver-78
Ice Blue-78
Premiere Date-78
00Stars Postcards-14
00Upper Deck-288
Exclusives Tier 1-288
Exclusives Tier 2-288
00Upper Deck Victory-80
01BAP Signature Series-36
Autographs-36
Autographs Gold-36
01Stars Postcards-14
01Utah Grizzlies-18
02BAP Sig Series Auto Buybacks 2001-36
02Russian World Championships-7
02AHL Top Prospects-27
02Hartford Wolf Pack-17

Lyck, Jan Erik
64Swedish Coralli ISHockey-80
65Swedish Coralli ISHockey-80
67Swedish Hockey-54
69Swedish Hockey-68
70Swedish Hockey-32
71Swedish Hockey-109
72Swedish Stickers-93
73Swedish Stickers-166

Lycka, Jaroslav
81Swedish Semic Hockey VM Stickers-62

Lydman, Toni
95Upper Deck-551
Electric Ice-551
Electric Ice Gold-551
98Finnish Kerailysarja-34
Leijonat-13
99Finnish Cardset-184
99Finnish Cardset-222
Par Avion-2
00BAP Memorabilia-488
Emerald-488
Ruby-488
Sapphire-488
00BAP Signature Series-255
Emerald-255
Ruby-255
Sapphire-255
Autographs-217
Autographs Gold-217
00Finnish Cardset-233
01BAP Memorabilia-146
Emerald-146
Ruby-146
Sapphire-146
01Upper Deck Victory-58
Gold-58
02BAP Sig Series Auto Buybacks 2000-217
02NHL Power Play Stickers-19
02O-Pee-Chee-80
02O-Pee-Chee Premier Blue Parallel-80
02O-Pee-Chee Premier Red Parallel-80
02O-Pee-Chee Factory Set-80
02Pacific-55
Blue-55
Red-55
02Pacific Complete-179
Red-179
02Topps-80
OPC Blue Parallel-80
OPC Red Parallel-80
Factory Set-80
02Topps Total-392
02Finnish Cardset-220
02Finnish Cardset Solid Gold Six-Pack-2
03ITG Action-96
03Pacific-53
Blue-53
Red-53
03Pacific Complete-132
Red-132
03Upper Deck-275
Canadian Exclusives-275
HG-275
UD Exclusives-275
05Finnish Cardset -13
Finnish Cardset Magicmakers-2

Lyerly, Ethan
04St. Cloud State Huskies-19

Lyke, R.C.
04Odessa Jackalopes-13

Lykke-Jorgensen, Soren
98Danish Hockey League-221
99Danish Hockey League-146

Lyle, George
80O-Pee-Chee-379
81O-Pee-Chee-100
82Post Cereal-7
82Whalers Junior Hartford Courant-11

Lyle, Justin
93Omaha Lancers-16

Lyle, Stevie
00UK Sekonda Superleague-51
01UK Cardiff Devils-16
01UK Manchester Storm-12
01UK Manchester Storm-21
02UK Cardiff Devils-16
02UK Manchester Storm-15
02UK Manchester Storm-20
03UK Guildford Flames-15

Lylyk, David
94Guelph Storm-21
99San Angelo Outlaws-9

Lymer, Mike
99Owen Sound Platers-11

Lynch, Brent
05Halifax Mooseheads-18

Lynch, Chad
98Kingston Frontenacs-9

Lynch, Chris
02Greenville Grrrowl-17
03ECHL All-Stars-250

Lynch, Darren
99Lethbridge Hurricanes-17
00Lethbridge Hurricanes-14
01Vancouver Giants-17
03Vancouver Giants-20
04Las Vegas Wranglers-15
05Las Vegas Wranglers-11

Lynch, Doug
00Red Deer Rebels-12
Signed-12
01Red Deer Rebels-11
01UD Prospects-24
Jerseys-J-DL
Jerseys Gold-J-DL
02Spokane Chiefs-16
03BAP Ultimate Memorabilia Autographs-118
Gold-118
03ITG VIP Rookie Debut-98
03Pacific Calder-118
Silver-118
03Pacific Complete-555
Red-555
03Parkhurst Rookie-170
03Upper Deck Rookie Update-129
03Pacific AHL Prospects-88
Gold-88
04AHL Top Prospects-13
05Peoria Rivermen-20
06Peoria Rivermen-9

Lynch, Jack
72O-Pee-Chee-160
73O-Pee-Chee-232
74NHL Action Stamps-107
74NHL Action Stamps Update-43
74O-Pee-Chee NHL-331
75O-Pee-Chee NHL-116
75Topps-116
76O-Pee-Chee NHL-288
77O-Pee-Chee NHL-369
78Capitals Team Issue-8
93Quebec Pee-Wee Tournament-692

Lynch, Jeff
01Spokane Chiefs-18
02Spokane Chiefs-17
04Spokane Chiefs Magnets-8

Lynch, John
93Quebec Pee-Wee Tournament-692

Lynch, P.J.
97Halifax Mooseheads I-8
97Halifax Mooseheads II-8
98Halifax Mooseheads-20
98Halifax Mooseheads Second Edition-7

Lynch, Scott
00Prince George Cougars-13
04Spokane Chiefs Magnets-3

Lynch, Steven
04UK Edinburgh Capitals-9

Lynes, Luke
04Brampton Battalion-15
05Brampton Battalion-13
06Brampton Battalion-14
06ITG Heroes and Prospects-107
Autographs-ALL

Lyness, Chris
99Quebec Remparts-8
Signed-8
99Bowman CHL-44
Gold-44
OPC International-44
00QMJHL All-Star Program Inserts-6
00Val d'Or Foreurs-3
Signed-3

Lynk, Mark
95Halifax Mooseheads-11
96Halifax Mooseheads I-12
96Halifax Mooseheads II-12
97Halifax Mooseheads I-9

Lynn, Matthew
03Erie Otters-15
04St. Francis Xavier X-Men-11

Lynn, Vic
44Beehive Group II Photos-421
45Quaker Oats Photos-29A
45Quaker Oats Photos-29B
45Quaker Oats Photos-29C
51Parkhurst-20
03BAP Ultimate Mem Linemates Autos-11

Lyons, Corey
88Lethbridge Hurricanes-15
89Lethbridge Hurricanes-13
90ProCards AHL/IHL-615
91ProCards-583
99Colorado Gold Kings Taco Bell-4
99Colorado Gold Kings Wendy's-2
01UK Hull Thunder-6
02UK Guildford Flames-13
02UK Guildford Flames-21

Lyons, Craig
907th Inn. Sketch WHL-301
917th Inn. Sketch WHL-85
98Colorado Gold Kings-11
98Colorado Gold Kings Postcards-10
99Colorado Gold Kings Taco Bell-14
99Colorado Gold Kings Wendy's-19
01Colorado Gold Kings-14
02UK Guildford Flames-5

Lyons, Derek
02Mississauga Ice Dogs-5
04Kingston Frontenacs-12

Lyons, Lynn
97Spokane Chiefs-20
99UD Prospects-49

Lyons, Marc
84Kingston Canadians-11
85Kingston Canadians-11
86Kingston Canadians-22
92Anaheim Bullfrogs RHI-4
92Thunder Bay Thunder Hawks-5
93Toledo Storm-21

Lyons, Mike
96Minnesota Golden Gophers-18
97Minnesota Golden Gophers-16
98Minnesota Golden Gophers-10
99Minnesota Golden Gophers-11

Lysak, Brett
96Regina Pats-20
97Regina Pats-4
99Black Diamond-114
Diamond Cut-114
Final Cut-114
99O-Pee-Chee-272
99O-Pee-Chee Chrome-272
99O-Pee-Chee Chrome Refractors-272
99SP Authentic-132
99Topps/OPC-272
99Topps/OPC Chrome-272
Refractors-272
99Upper Deck MVP SC Edition-204
Gold Script-204
Silver Script-204
Super Script-204
99Bowman CHL-16
99Bowman CHL-91
Gold-16
Gold-91
OPC International-16
OPC International-91
Autographs-BA36
Autographs Gold-BA36
Autographs Silver-BA36
02Lowell Lock Monsters-19
03UD Premier Collection-103
03Lowell Lock Monsters-6
03Lowell Lock Monsters Photo Album-15
04Pacific-273
Blue-273
Red-273
04German DEL-175

Lysen, Goran
57Swedish Alfabilder-93
64Swedish Coralli ISHockey-51
65Swedish Coralli ISHockey-51
67Swedish Hockey-106

Lysen, Ingemar
57Swedish Alfabilder-91

Lyseng, Cody
98Medicine Hat Tigers-15

Lysenko, Alexander
90O-Pee-Chee-500

Lysenko, Ilya
93Sudbury Wolves-18
93Sudbury Wolves Police-17

Lysiak, Tom
74NHL Action Stamps-18
74O-Pee-Chee NHL-14
74O-Pee-Chee NHL-68
74Topps-14
74Topps-68
75Nabisco Sugar Daddy-14
75O-Pee-Chee NHL-230
75O-Pee-Chee NHL-313
75Topps-230
75Topps-313
76O-Pee-Chee NHL-174
76O-Pee-Chee NHL-379
76Topps-174
77O-Pee-Chee NHL-127
77Topps-127
78Flames Majik Market-12
78O-Pee-Chee-97
78Topps-97
79Panini Stickers-59
79Blackhawks Postcards-10
79O-Pee-Chee-41
79Topps-41
80O-Pee-Chee-247
80Topps-247
81Blackhawks Borderless Postcards-13
81O-Pee-Chee-59
81O-Pee-Chee-73
81O-Pee-Chee Stickers-114
81Topps-49
81Topps-W71
82Blackhawks Postcards-12
82O-Pee-Chee-68
82O-Pee-Chee Stickers-14
82O-Pee-Chee Stickers-174
82Post Cereal-4
82Topps Stickers-14
82Topps Stickers-174
83Blackhawks Postcards-13
83NHL Key Tags-23
83O-Pee-Chee-107
83O-Pee-Chee Stickers-110
83Puffy Stickers-15
83Topps Stickers-110
84O-Pee-Chee-39
84O-Pee-Chee Stickers-31
84Topps-31
85Blackhawks Team Issue-22
85O-Pee-Chee-23
85Topps-23
04ITG Franchises Update-462
04ITG Franchises US East-301
Autographs-A-TLY

Lytwyn, Mark
03Guelph Storm-10

Lyubimov, Alexander
00Russian Hockey League-156
01Odessa Jackalopes-14
03Russian Hockey League-245

Lyubushin, Mikhail
02Russian Hockey League-202
02Russian SL-35
03Russian Hockey League-29

Lyulin, Andrei
95Swedish Upper Deck-189

Lyutkevich, Vitali
99Russian Hockey League-173
00Russian Hockey League-391
02Russian Transfert-7

Lyuzenkov, Yaroslav
98Russian Hockey League-32
01Russian Hockey League-148

Maag, Andy
93Swiss HNL-346
95Swiss HNL-401
96Swiss HNL-348

Maas, Joel
02Cape Breton Screaming Eagles-10

Maass, Michael
94German First League-39

Maatinen, Pasi
95Finnish SISU-240
03Swedish Elite Signatures II-12
05Swedish SHL Elitset-59

Maatta, Borje
67Swedish Hockey-242
69Swedish Hockey-285
70Swedish Hockey-183
71Swedish Hockey-269
72Swedish Stickers-245

Maatta, Eilert
64Swedish Coralli ISHockey-28
65Swedish Coralli ISHockey-28
65Swedish Coralli ISHockey-63
67Swedish Hockey-190
69Swedish Hockey-247
70Swedish Hockey-135
71Swedish Hockey-227
81Swedish Semic Hockey VM Stickers-119
97Swedish Alfabilder Autographs-3
98Swedish UD Choice-204
98Swedish UD Choice-209

Maatta, Soren
64Swedish Coralli ISHockey-71
65Swedish Coralli ISHockey-71
67Swedish Hockey-191
69Swedish Hockey-248
70Swedish Hockey-143
71Swedish Hockey-237

Maatta, Tero
00Finnish Cardset-125
01Finnish Cardset-3
02Finnish Cardset-228
03Finnish Cardset-4
04Finnish Cardset-203
05Finnish Cardset -178

Maattanen, Pasi
92Finnish Jyvas-Hyva Stickers-50
93Finnish Jyvas-Hyva Stickers-84
93Finnish SISU-129
94Finnish SISU-28
98Finnish Kerailysarja-194
99Finnish Cardset-114
00Finnish Cardset-270
01Finnish Cardset-34
02Swedish SHL-186
Parallel-186
03Swedish Elite-53
Silver-53
04Swedish Elitset-57
Gold-57
06Finnish Cardset-232
06Finnish Ilves Team Set-18

Maattanen, Raimo
65Finnish Hellas-75
70Finnish Jaakiekko-284

Mabey, Shane
98Guelph Storm-26
99Guelph Storm-28
01Guelph Storm-28
01Guelph Storm Memorial Cup-28
02Guelph Storm-29

MacAdam, Al
74NHL Action Stamps-65
74O-Pee-Chee NHL-301
75O-Pee-Chee NHL-253
75Topps-253
76O-Pee-Chee NHL-237
76O-Pee-Chee NHL-383
76Topps-237
77O-Pee-Chee NHL-149
77Topps-149A
77Topps-149B
78North Stars Cloverleaf Dairy-4
78O-Pee-Chee-381
79North Stars Postcards-6
79O-Pee-Chee-104
79Topps-104
80North Stars Postcards-10
80O-Pee-Chee-34
80O-Pee-Chee-139
80Topps-34
80Topps-139
81North Stars Postcards-12
81O-Pee-Chee-163
81O-Pee-Chee Stickers-90
81Topps-W107
82North Stars Postcards-13
82O-Pee-Chee-171
82Post Cereal-9
83North Stars Postcards-14
83O-Pee-Chee-173
84Canucks Team Issue-16
84O-Pee-Chee-324
84Topps-75
85O-Pee-Chee-209
85O-Pee-Chee Stickers-242
85Fredericton Express-27
97St. John's Maple Leafs-15
99St. John's Maple Leafs-12
02McDonald's Pacific Salt Lake Gold-3
03Blackhawks Postcards-12
04ITG Franchises US West-178
Autographs-A-AMA

MacAdam, Don
90ProCards AHL/IHL-240
94Milwaukee Admirals-14
99Charlotte Checkers-26
00Charlotte Checkers-16
02ECHL Update-U-14

MacAndrew, Larry
82Ottawa 67's-26

MacAngus, Michael
05Saskatoon Blades-13

MacArthur, Clarke
02Medicine Hat Tigers-16
03Medicine Hat Tigers-4
04Medicine Hat Tigers-12
04ITG Heroes and Prospects-217
04ITG Heroes/Prospects Toronto Expo '05-217
05ITG Heroes/Prosp Toronto Expo Parallel -209
05ITG Heroes and Prospects-209
Autographs Series II-CM
06Be A Player-236
06Beehive-108
Matte-108
06Flair Showcase-306
06Hot Prospects-198
06Rochester Americans-13
06SP Authentic-249
Limited-249
06The Cup-115
Autographed NHL Shields Duals-DASSM
Autographed Rookie Masterpiece Pressplates-115
Gold Rainbow Autographed Rookie Patches-115
Masterpiece Pressplates (Bee Hive)-108
Masterpiece Pressplates (SP Authentic)-249
Masterpiece Pressplates (Sweet Beginnings)-108
Masterpiece Pressplates (Ultimate Collection)-63
Rookies Black-115
Rookies Platinum-115
06UD Artifacts-272
06Ultimate Collection-63
06Upper Deck Sweet Shot-108
Rookie Jerseys Autographs-108
06AHL Top Prospects-38

MacArthur, Ken
90Alberta International Team Canada-6

MacArthur, Peter
03Waterloo Blackhawks-21

Macaskill, Ben
05Halifax Mooseheads-16
06Halifax Mooseheads-17

MacAulay, Anthony
94Hampton Roads Admirals-12

MacAulay, Blair
05Saskatoon Blades-14
06Saskatoon Blades-16

MacAulay, Jeff
01Quebec Remparts-17

Macauley, Jeff
03P.E.I. Rocket-14
04Halifax Mooseheads-12

MacAusland, Len
907th Inn. Sketch WHL-58
917th Inn. Sketch WHL-185

MacBride, Luke
93Quebec Pee-Wee Tournament-561

Maccarone, Matt
03Sudbury Wolves-15

Macchio, Ralph
91Pro Set Platinum-295

MacCormick, Roddy
98Fayetteville Force-9

MacDermid, Jeff
01Owen Sound Attack-11
03Owen Sound Attack-19

MacDermid, Ken
87Hull Olympiques-11

MacDermid, Lane
06Owen Sound Attack-11

MacDermid, Paul
85Whalers Junior Wendy's-11
86Whalers Junior Thomas'-15
87Whalers Jr. Burger King/Pepsi-14
88Panini Stickers-243
88Whalers Junior Ground Round-11
89O-Pee-Chee-183
89O-Pee-Chee Stickers-266
89Panini Stickers-227
89Topps-183
89Whalers Junior Milk-15
90Jets IGA-19
90O-Pee-Chee-338
90Pro Set-331
90Score-296
Canadian-296
90Topps-338
Tiffany-338
90Upper Deck-218
French-218
91Bowman-195
91Capitals Kodak-19
91Jets Panini Team Stickers-15
91Jets IGA-16
91O-Pee-Chee-463
91Panini Stickers-69
91Pinnacle-279
French-279
91Pro Set-269
French-269
91Score American-219
91Score Canadian Bilingual-219
91Score Canadian English-219
91Stadium Club-254
91Topps-463
92Bowman-282
92Capitals Kodak-19
92Score-59
Canadian-59
92Stadium Club-178
92Topps-391
Gold-391G
92Ultra-439
94Nordiques Burger King-18
00Owen Sound Attack-11

MacDermott, Matt
05Regina Pats-27

MacDonagh, Bill
51Laval Dairy QSHL-52

MacDonald, Aaron
95Swift Current Broncos-9
95Classic-32
95Classic Five-Sport *-142
Autographs-142

MacDonald, Andrew
05Moncton Wildcats-16
06Moncton Wildcats-2

MacDonald, Blair
76O-Pee-Chee WHA-93
77O-Pee-Chee WHA-16
79Oilers Postcards-15
80O-Pee-Chee-32
80Pepsi-Cola Caps-33
80Topps-32
81Canucks Team Issue-14
81O-Pee-Chee-340
81Fredericton Express-2
82O-Pee-Chee-350
82Fredericton Express-2
88Oilers Tenth Anniversary-99
89ProCards IHL-164
90ProCards AHL/IHL-390

MacDonald, Brendon

04Cape Breton Screaming Eagles-12
05Cape Breton Screaming Eagles-17
06Cape Breton Screaming Eagles-17

MacDonald, Brent
04Florida Everblades-7

MacDonald, Brett
83North Bay Centennials-17
85Kitchener Rangers-12
86Fredericton Express-17
87Flint Spirits-13
88Flint Spirits-13
91ProCards-430
95Flint Generals-20
96Flint Generals-13
97Flint Generals-13
97Flint Generals EBK-20
98Flint Generals-21

MacDonald, Brian
83Brantford Alexanders-12

MacDonald, Bruce
92Toledo Storm-18
92Toledo Storm Team Issue-15
93Toledo Storm-20
97Toledo Storm-21

MacDonald, C.J.
93Quebec Pee-Wee Tournament-620

MacDonald, Cameron
99Adirondack IceHawks-15
01Fort Worth Brahmas-14

MacDonald, Chris
92Quebec Pee-Wee Tournament-1341
95Slapshot-129

MacDonald, Clint
91British Columbia JHL-120
92British Columbia JHL-133

MacDonald, Connor
04P.E.I. Rocket-4

MacDonald, Craig
98New Haven Beast-4
99BAP Memorabilia-175
Gold-175
Silver-175
99Pacific-83
Copper-83
Emerald Green-83
Gold-83
Ice Blue-83
Premiere Date-83
Red-83
99Cincinnati Cyclones-13
00Cincinnati Cyclones-5
02Lowell Lock Monsters-7
04Lowell Lock Monsters-15
04Lowell Lock Monsters Photo Album-15
06New Mexico Scorpions-14
06Norfolk Admirals-7

MacDonald, Dave
94Sudbury Wolves-2
94Sudbury Wolves Police-25
95Slapshot-381
95Sudbury Wolves-20
95Sudbury Wolves Police-13
96Guelph Storm-3

MacDonald, David
04P.E.I. Rocket-6
05Moncton Wildcats-30
05PEI Rocket-26
06Saint Johns Sea Dogs-5

MacDonald, Doug
92Rochester Americans Dunkin' Donuts-10
92Rochester Americans Kodak-13
92Classic-92
Gold-92
93Upper Deck-97
93Rochester Americans Kodak-15
95Cincinnati Cyclones-15
96Cincinnati Cyclones-44
97Cincinnati Cyclones-11
98Cincinnati Cyclones-12
98Cincinnati Cyclones 2-5
01German Upper Deck-71

MacDonald, Franklin
03Halifax Mooseheads-20
04Halifax Mooseheads-6
05Halifax Mooseheads-22

MacDonald, Garett
92Northern Michigan Wildcats-17
93Northern Michigan Wildcats-20
94Richmond Renegades-10
95Richmond Renegades-16

MacDonald, Goalie
03London Knights-16
04London Knights-1

MacDonald, Jack
10Sweet Caporal Postcards-8
11C55-8
12C57-17

MacDonald, Jason
907th Inn. Sketch OHL-311
917th Inn. Sketch OHL-277
93Owen Sound Platers-6
93Owen Sound Platers-16
94Classic-118
Gold-118
95Adirondack Red Wings-12
98Manitoba Moose-D1
99Manitoba Moose-16
00Wilkes-Barre Scranton Penguins-13
01Wilkes-Barre Scranton Penguins-14
02Wilkes-Barre Scranton Penguins-17
03ITG VIP Rookie Debut-83
03Parkhurst Original Six New York-30
03Parkhurst Rookie-117
03Upper Deck Rookie Update-95
03Hartford Wolf Pack-15
05Providence Bruins-9
05Regina Pats-11
06Regina Pats-12

MacDonald, Jerry
71Johnstown Jets Acme-10
72Johnstown Jets-6

MacDonald, Joey
97Halifax Mooseheads I-10
97Halifax Mooseheads II-9
02Grand Rapids Griffins-18
03ITG Action-647
03ITG Used Signature Series-186
Gold-186
03ITG VIP Rookie Debut-80
03Parkhurst Rookie-75
03Upper Deck Rookie Update-101
03Grand Rapids Griffins-12
04AHL All-Stars-27
05ITG Heroes/Prosp Toronto Expo Parallel -51
05ITG Heroes and Prospects-51
Autographs-A-JM
06Between The Pipes The Mask-M11
06Between The Pipes The Mask Gold-M11
06Between The Pipes The Mask Silver-M11

MacDonald, Kevin
88ProCards IHL-54
89ProCards AHL-24
89Rayside-Balfour Jr. Canadians-15
90ProCards AHL/IHL-366
91ProCards-388
93Fort Wayne Komets-10
96Collector's Edge Ice-106
Prism-106
98Bakersfield Condors-23
99Bakersfield Condors-21
00Bakersfield Condors-22

MacDonald, Kilby
34Beehive Group I Photos-285
39O-Pee-Chee V301-1-87

MacDonald, Kris
04P.E.I. Rocket-12

MacDonald, Leonard
89Sudbury Wolves-14
907th Inn. Sketch OHL-184
917th Inn. Sketch OHL-185

MacDonald, Lowell
61Hamilton Red Wings-11
66Tulsa Oilers-6
68O-Pee-Chee-42
68Shirriff Coins-56
68Topps-42
70O-Pee-Chee-206
72O-Pee-Chee-214
73O-Pee-Chee-128
73Topps-128
74NHL Action Stamps-229
74O-Pee-Chee NHL-30
74O-Pee-Chee NHL-133
74O-Pee-Chee NHL-183
74Penguins Postcards-15
74Topps-30
74Topps-133
74Topps-183
75O-Pee-Chee NHL-204
75Topps-204
76O-Pee-Chee NHL-33
76O-Pee-Chee NHL-218
76Topps-33
76Topps-218
77O-Pee-Chee NHL-390
77Penguins Puck Bucks-18
94Parkhurst Tall Boys-60
04ITG Franchises US West-272
Autographs-A-LMD

MacDonald, Mickey
06Cape Breton Screaming Eagles-20

MacDonald, Parker
44Beehive Group II Photos-190
44Beehive Group II Photos-430
55Parkhurst-9
55Parkhurst-77
Quaker Oats-9
Quaker Oats-77
60Shirriff Coins-59
61Shirriff/Salada Coins-69
62York Iron-On Transfers-27
63Chex Photos-33
63Parkhurst-44
63Toronto Star-24
63York White Backs-40
64Beehive Group III Photos-17
64Beehive Group III Photos-83
64Coca-Cola Caps-53
64Topps-11
64Toronto Star-27
65Coca-Cola-14
65Topps-105
68O-Pee-Chee-55
68Shirriff Coins-70
68Topps-55
73North Stars Postcards-10
89New Haven Nighthawks-15
94Parkhurst Missing Link-104
94Parkhurst Tall Boys-44
95Parkhurst '66-67-55
Coins-55

MacDonald, Paul
917th Inn. Sketch QMJHL-200
05Kootenay Ice-14

MacDonald, Paul (WHL)
05Kootenay Ice-14

MacDonald, Ryan
94Detroit Jr. Red Wings-4
95Slapshot-212
95Slapshot Memorial Cup-78
05ITG Heroes/Prosp Toronto Expo Parallel -282
05Guelph Storm-A-05
05OHL Bell All-Star Classic-32
05ITG Heroes and Prospects-282
Autographs Series II-RMC

MacDonald, Shaun
04Penticton Vees-7

MacDonald, Steve
92Norwegian Elite Series-177

MacDonald, Todd
92Tacoma Rockets-12
93Tacoma Rockets-15
96Cincinnati Cyclones-1
96Collector's Edge Ice-24
Prism-24
97Cincinnati Cyclones-12
98New Haven Beast-8
00Amarillo Rattlers-11

MacDonald, Tom
907th Inn. Sketch OHL-166
917th Inn. Sketch OHL-322
917th Inn. Sketch Memorial Cup-14
93Sault Ste. Marie Greyhounds-15
93Sault Ste. Marie Greyhound Memorial Cup-17
96Louisville Riverfrogs-20

MacDonald, Wayne
90Fort Saskatchewan Traders-11

MacDonald, Willie
87Kamloops Blazers-11

MacDonell, Alex
00Brampton Battalion-23

MacDougald, Jeff
02Peterborough Petes-22
04Peterborough Petes Postcards-25

MacEachern, Ali
97Halifax Mooseheads I-11
97Halifax Mooseheads II-10
98Halifax Mooseheads-16
98Halifax Mooseheads Second Edition-16
99Halifax Mooseheads-15
00Halifax Mooseheads-15

MacEachern, Greg
907th Inn. Sketch QMJHL-77
907th Inn. Sketch Memorial Cup-57
92Tulsa Oilers-8

MacEachern, Liam
94Sudbury Wolves-18
94Sudbury Wolves Police-9
95Slapshot-397
95Sudbury Wolves-10
95Sudbury Wolves Police-14

MacEachern, Shane
88ProCards IHL-70
94Brantford Smoke-16

Macek, Petr
94Czech APS Extraliga-254
95Czech APS Extraliga-132
99Czech OFS-138

Macenauer, Maxime
05Rimouski Oceanic-16

Macera, Mark
98Wichita Thunder-14
99Wichita Thunder-13

MacFarland, Bill
69Seattle Totems-20

MacFarlane, Ben
05Shawinigan Cataractes-2

MacFarlane, Eon
92British Columbia JHL-200
98Pensacola Ice Pilots-17

MacGillivray, Bill
92Northern Michigan Wildcats-18
93Northern Michigan Wildcats-21

MacGillvray, John
52Juniors Blue Tint-165

MacGregor, Blair
83Medicine Hat Tigers-6

MacGregor, Brad
88ProCards AHL-96

MacGregor, Bruce
44Beehive Group II Photos-191
61Shirriff/Salada Coins-73
62Parkhurst-23
62York Iron-On Transfers-36
63Chex Photos-34
63Parkhurst-41
63York White Backs-51
64Beehive Group III Photos-84A
64Beehive Group III Photos-84B
64Coca-Cola Caps-49
64Topps-76
65Coca-Cola-48
65Topps-110
66Topps-104
66Topps USA Test-56
67Topps-102
68O-Pee-Chee-30
68Shirriff Coins-41
68Topps-30
69O-Pee-Chee-63
69Topps-63
70Dad's Cookies-72
70Esso Power Players-137
70O-Pee-Chee-27
70Red Wings Marathon-6
70Sargent Promotions Stamps-51
70Topps-27
71O-Pee-Chee-216
71Sargent Promotions Stamps-124
71Toronto Sun-176
72O-Pee-Chee-103
72Sargent Promotions Stamps-153
73O-Pee-Chee-201
74O-Pee-Chee WHA-2
75O-Pee-Chee WHA-22
88Oilers Tenth Anniversary-154
94Parkhurst Tall Boys-47
95Parkhurst '66-67-49
Coins-49
04ITG Franchises US West-218
Autographs-A-BMG

MacGuigan, Garth
81Indianapolis Checkers-14
82Indianapolis Checkers-15

Mach, Ales
96Czech APS Extraliga-49
00Czech OFS-211

Mach, Miroslav
94Czech APS Extraliga-63
95Czech APS Extraliga-91
96Czech APS Extraliga-300
97Czech DS Stickers-223

Machabee, Julien
05Kitchener Rangers-2

Machac, Oldrich
69Swedish Hockey-34
70Finnish Jaakiekko-53
70Swedish Hockey-349
70Swedish Masterserien-154
71Finnish Suomi Stickers-31
71Swedish Hockey-45
72Finnish Jaakiekko-14
72Finnish Hellas-83
72Finnish Panda Toronto-87
72Finnish Semic World Championship-24
72Swedish Semic World Championship-24
73Finnish Jaakiekko-55
73Swedish Stickers-29
74Finnish Jenkki-77
74Finnish Typotor-118
74Swedish Stickers-13
74Swedish Semic World Champ Stickers-55

Machacek, Martin
93Michigan Tech Huskies-24
98Fort Worth Brahmas-6

Machacek, Petr
06Czech OFS-11

Machacek, Spencer
05Vancouver Giants-15

Machalek, Robert
95Czech APS Extraliga-108

Machesney, Daren
04Brampton Battalion-2
04ITG Heroes and Prospects-227
04ITG Heroes/Prospects Toronto Expo '05-227
05ITG Heroes/Prosp Toronto Expo Parallel -128
05Brampton Battalion-5
05Extreme Top Prospects Signature Edition-S7
05ITG Heroes and Prospects-128
Autographs-A-DMA
06Hot Prospects-188
06SP Authentic-211
Limited-211
The Cup Masterpiece Pressplates (SP Authentic)-211
06The Cup Masterpiece Pressplates (Ultimate Collection)-102
06UD Artifacts-260
06Ultimate Collection-102

Macho, Michal
96Slovakian Quebec Pee-Wee Tournament-17

Machulda, Petr
01Czech OFS-188
02Czech OFS Plus-200
03Czech OFS Plus-137
04German DEL-202

Machulda, Vladimir
94Czech APS Extraliga-225
94German First League-147
95Czech APS Extraliga-172
96Czech APS Extraliga-69
97Czech APS Extraliga-325
97Czech DS Stickers-234
98Czech DS-73
98Czech OFS-220
99Czech DS-126
99Czech OFS-386
00Finnish Cardset-80
01Finnish Cardset-117
01Finnish Cardset Dueling Aces-1
02Finnish Cardset-66
03Finnish Cardset-136
05Swedish Lulea Hockey Postcards-17
05Swedish SHL Elitset-237
Gold-237
06Czech OFS-33
06Swedish SHL Elitset-92

Macias, Ray
03Kamloops Blazers-18
04Kamloops Blazers-5
05Kamloops Blazers-20
05ITG Heroes and Prospects-170
Autographs-A-RM
06Kamloops Blazers-14

Macijevskis, Alexanders
99Danish Hockey League-93

MacInnes, John
91Michigan Tech Huskies-10

MacInnis, Aaron
05Stockton Thunder-11
06New Mexico Scorpions-20

MacInnis, Al
82Kitchener Rangers-17
85Flames Red Rooster-16
85O-Pee-Chee-237
85O-Pee-Chee Stickers-211
86Flames Red Rooster-11
86O-Pee-Chee-173
86O-Pee-Chee Stickers-86
86Topps-173
87Flames Red Rooster-12
87O-Pee-Chee-72
87O-Pee-Chee Minis-26
87O-Pee-Chee Stickers-40
87O-Pee-Chee Stickers-123
87Panini Stickers-205
87Topps-72
87Topps Sticker Inserts-9
88Flames Postcards-25
88Frito-Lay Stickers-31
88O-Pee-Chee-231
88O-Pee-Chee Minis-22
88O-Pee-Chee Stickers-92
88Panini Stickers-5
89Kraft-3
89O-Pee-Chee-49
89O-Pee-Chee Stickers-5
89O-Pee-Chee Stickers-21
89O-Pee-Chee Stickers-95
89O-Pee-Chee Stickers-159
89O-Pee-Chee Stickers-161
89Panini Stickers-20
89Panini Stickers-32
89Sports Illustrated for Kids I-82
89Topps-49
89Topps Sticker Inserts-4
89Swedish Semic World Champ Stickers-56
90Bowman-93
Tiffany-93
90Flames IGA/McGavin's-9
90Flames IGA/McGavin's-13
90Kraft-33
90O-Pee-Chee-127
90O-Pee-Chee-197
90O-Pee-Chee Box Bottoms-H
90OPC Premier-65
90Panini Stickers-185
90Panini Stickers-328
90Pro Set-35
90Pro Set-337
90Score-5
90Score-314
90Score-335
Canadian-5
Canadian-314
Canadian-335
90Score Hottest/Rising Stars-36
90Topps-127
90Topps-197
Tiffany-127
Tiffany-197
90Topps Box Bottoms-H
90Upper Deck-143
90Upper Deck-319
90Upper Deck-497
French-143
French-319
French-497
91Pro Set Platinum-19
91Pro Set Platinum-276
91Bowman-262
91Flames Panini Team Stickers-7
91Flames IGA-7
91Gillette-7
91Kraft-32
91McDonald's Upper Deck-23
91O-Pee-Chee-262
91O-Pee-Chee-491
91OPC Premier-81
91Panini Stickers-50
91Panini Stickers-330
91Parkhurst-28
French-28
91Pinnacle-220
91Pinnacle-399
French-220
French-399
B-B8
B French-B8
91Pro Set-33
91Pro Set-275
French-33
French-275
Awards Special-AC8
Puck Candy-5
91Score National-4
91Score Ntnl Candy Wholesalers Convention-4
91Score Fanfest-4
91Score American-2
91Score American-409
91Score American-417
91Score Canadian Bilingual-2
91Score Canadian Bilingual-299
91Score Canadian Bilingual-333
91Score Canadian English-2
91Score Canadian English-299
91Score Canadian English-333
91Score Kellogg's-16
91Stadium Club-79
91Topps-262
91Topps-491
91Upper Deck-8
91Upper Deck-243
91Upper Deck-632
French-8
French-243
French-632
91Finnish Semic World Champ Stickers-57
91Swedish Semic World Champ Stickers-57
92Bowman-51
92Bowman-211
92Flames IGA-22
92Humpty Dumpty II-14
92McDonald's Upper Deck-10
92O-Pee-Chee-330
92Panini Stickers-49
92Panini Stickers-285
92Panini Stickers French-49
92Panini Stickers French-285
92Parkhurst-20
Emerald Ice-20
92Pinnacle-83
French-83
92Pro Set-22
92Score-302
92Score-421
92Score-496
Canadian-302
Canadian-421
Canadian-496
92Seasons Patches-60
92Stadium Club-128
92Topps-452
Gold-452G
92Ultra-23
All-Stars-8
92Upper Deck-257
92Finnish Semic-77
93Donruss-47
93Kraft Recipes-5
93Kraft Recipes French-5
93Leaf-180
93OPC Premier-276
Gold-276
93Panini Stickers-P
93Parkhurst-36
Emerald Ice-36
Cherry's Playoff Heroes-D3
93Pinnacle-155
Canadian-155
93PowerPlay-38
Slapshot Artists-7
93Score-121
Canadian-121
Dream Team-4
Franchise-3
93Stadium Club-105
Members Only Master Set-105
OPC-105
First Day Issue-105
First Day Issue OPC-105
93Topps/OPC Premier-276
Gold-276
93Ultra-113
93Upper Deck-412
NHLPA/Roots-19
SP-22
93Swedish Semic World Champ Stickers-193
94Be A Player 99 All-Stars-G14
94Canada Games NHL POGS-264
94Donruss Dominators-6
94EA Sports-20
94Finest Division's Finest Clear Cut-12
94Flair-157
94Fleer-190
Slapshot Artists-5
94Hockey Wit-90
94Leaf-461
94Leaf Limited-79
94McDonald's Upper Deck-McD15
94OPC Premier-110
94OPC Premier-127
94OPC Premier-347
94OPC Premier-488
Special Effects-110
Special Effects-127
Special Effects-347
Special Effects-488
94Parkhurst-35
Gold-35
94Parkhurst SE-SE152
Gold-SE152
94Pinnacle-387
Artist's Proofs-387
Rink Collection-387
Boomers-BR3
94Score-120
Gold-120
Platinum-120
Dream Team-DT7
94Select-28
Gold-28
94SP-104
Die Cuts-104
94Stadium Club Members Only-7
94Stadium Club-56
Members Only Master Set-56
First Day Issue-56
Super Team Winner Cards-56
94Topps/OPC Premier-110
94Topps/OPC Premier-127
94Topps/OPC Premier-347
94Topps/OPC Premier-488
Special Effects-110
Special Effects-127
Special Effects-347
Special Effects-488
94Ultra-185
94Upper Deck-150
94Upper Deck-232
Electric Ice-150
Electric Ice-232
Predictor Canadian-C33
94Upper Deck Predictor Canadian Exch Gold-C33
94Upper Deck Predictor Retail-R46
94Upper Deck Predictor Retail Exchange-R46
94Upper Deck SP Inserts-SP159
94Upper Deck SP Inserts Die Cuts-SP159
94Finnish Jaa Kiekko-84
94Finnish Jaa Kiekko-340
95Bashan Super Stickers-100
95Bashan Super Stickers-102
95Be A Player-134
Signatures-S134
Signatures Die Cuts-S134
95Bowman-16
All-Foil-16
95Canada Games NHL POGS-242
95Collector's Choice-313
Player's Club-313
Player's Club Platinum-313
95Donruss-205
Dominators-7
95Donruss Elite-15
Die Cut Stars-15
Die Cut Uncut-15
95Emotion-150
95Finest-48
Refractors-48
95Imperial Stickers-102
95Leaf-312
95Leaf Limited-95
95Metal-126
95NHL Aces Playing Cards-2D
95Panini Stickers-197
95Parkhurst International-178
Emerald Ice-178
95Pinnacle-79
Artist's Proofs-79
Rink Collection-79
95Playoff One on One-90
95Pro Magnets-13
95Score-46
Black Ice Artist's Proofs-46
Black Ice-46
95Select Certified-72
Mirror Gold-72
95SkyBox Impact-143
95SP-125
95Stadium Club Members Only-34
95Stadium Club-13
Members Only Master Set-13
95Summit-90
Artist's Proofs-90
Ice-90
GM's Choice-14
95Topps-145
OPC Inserts-145
Home Grown Canada-HGC22
95Topps SuperSkills-49
Platinum-49
95Ultra-300
95Upper Deck-290
Electric Ice-290
Electric Ice Gold-290
NHL All-Stars-AS9
NHL All-Stars Jumbo-AS9
Special Edition-SE71
Special Edition Gold-SE71
95Zenith-40
95Finnish Semic World Championships-85
95Swedish Globe World Championships-79
96SLU Hockey Canadian-9
96SLU Hockey American-13
96Blues Dispatch 30th Anniversary-3
96Collector's Choice-228
96Collector's Choice-329
96Donruss-12
Press Proofs-12
96Donruss Canadian Ice-15
Gold Press Proofs-15
Red Press Proofs-15
96Donruss Elite-67
Die Cut Stars-67
96Flair-82
Blue Ice-82
96Fleer-98
96Kenner Starting Lineup Cards-13
96Kraft Upper Deck-35
96Leaf-174
Press Proofs-174
96Maggers-59
96Metal Universe-133
96NHL Pro Stamps-13
96Pinnacle-153
Artist's Proofs-153
Foil-153
Premium Stock-153
Rink Collection-153
96Post Upper Deck-13
96Score-114
Artist's Proofs-114
Dealer's Choice Artist's Proofs-114
Special Artist's Proofs-114
Golden Blades-114
96SkyBox Impact-114
96Stadium Club Members Only-9
96Team Out-77
96Topps Picks-49
OPC Inserts-49
96Ultra-147
Gold Medallion-147
96Upper Deck-141
96Zenith-18
Artist's Proofs-18
96Swedish Semic Wien-81
97Be A Player-125
Autographs-125
Autographs Die-Cuts-125
Autographs Prismatic Die-Cuts-125
97Collector's Choice-234
97Donruss-122
Press Proofs Silver-122
Press Proofs Gold-122
97Donruss Canadian Ice-55
Dominion Series-55
Provincial Series-55
97Donruss Preferred-132
Cut to the Chase-132
97Donruss Priority-144
Stamp of Approval-144
97Katch-130
Gold-130
Silver-130
97Kraft Team Canada-5
97McDonald's Team Canada Coins-2
97Pacific-202
Copper-202
Emerald Green-202
Ice Blue-202
Red-202
Silver-202
97Pacific Omega-195
Copper-195
Dark Gray-195
Emerald Green-195
Gold-195
Ice Blue-195
97Pinnacle-116
Press Plates Back Black-116
Press Plates Back Cyan-116
Press Plates Back Magenta-116
Press Plates Back Yellow-116
Press Plates Front Black-116
Press Plates Front Cyan-116
Press Plates Front Magenta-116
Press Plates Front Yellow-116
97Pinnacle Certified-120
Red-120
Mirror Blue-120
Mirror Gold-120
Mirror Red-120
97Pinnacle Inside-161
97Pinnacle Tot Cert Platinum Blue-120
97Pinnacle Tot Certi Platinum Gold-120
97Pinnacle Totally Certified Platinum Red-120
97Pinnacle Tot Cert Mirror Platinum Gold-120
97Score-248
97Score Blues-6
Platinum-6
Premier-6
97SP Authentic-140
97Upper Deck-352
98Aurora-161
98Be A Player-274
Press Release-274
98BAP Gold-274
98BAP Autographs-274
98BAP Autographs Gold-274
98BAP AS Milestones-M22
98Black Diamond-77
Double Diamond-77
Triple Diamond-77
Quadruple Diamond-77
98Bowman's Best-57
Refractors-57
Atomic Refractors-57
98Crown Royale-115
Limited Series-115
98Finest-88
No Protectors-88
No Protectors Refractors-88
Refractors-88
98Kraft Peanut Butter-5
98OPC Chrome-100
Refractors-100
98Pacific-368
Ice Blue-368
Red-368
98Pacific Dynagon Ice-159
Blue-159
Red-159
98Pacific Omega-203
Red-203
Opening Day Issue-203
98Panini Photocards-50
98Paramount-204
Copper-204
Emerald Green-204
Holo-Electric-204
Ice Blue-204
Silver-204
98Revolution-123
Ice Shadow-123
Red-123
All-Star Die Cuts-19
98SP Authentic-72
Power Shift-72
98SPx Top Prospects-51
Radiance-51
Spectrum-51
98Topps-100
O-Pee-Chee-100
98Topps Gold Label Class 1-15
Black-15
Black One of One-15
One of One-15
Red-15
Red One of One-15
98Topps Gold Label Class 2-15
98Topps Gold Label Class 2 Black-15
98Topps Gold Label Class 2 Black 1 of 1-15
98Topps Gold Label Class 2 One of One-15
98Topps Gold Label Class 2 Red-15
98Topps Gold Label Class 2 Red One of One-15
98Topps Gold Label Class 3-15
98Topps Gold Label Class 3 Black-15
98Topps Gold Label Class 3 Black 1 of 1-15
98Topps Gold Label Class 3 One of One-15
98Topps Gold Label Class 3 Red-15
98Topps Gold Label Class 3 Red One of One-15
98UD Choice-188
Prime Choice Reserve-188
Reserve-188
98Upper Deck-176
Exclusives-176
Exclusives 1 of 1-176
Game Jerseys-GJ9
Gold Reserve-176
98Upper Deck MVP-179
Gold Script-179
Silver Script-179
Super Script-179
98Slovakian Eurotel-15
99Aurora-126
Striped-126
Premiere Date-126
Premiere Date Striped-126
99BAP Memorabilia-155
Gold-155
Silver-155
Jersey Cards-J13
Jersey Emblems-E13
Jersey Numbers-I13
Jersey and Stick Cards-S13
Selects Silver-SL11
Selects Gold-SL11
AS Heritage Ruby-H9
AS Heritage Sapphire-H9
AS Heritage Emerald-H9
99BAP Update Double AS Jersey Cards-D15
99BAP Update Teammates Jersey Cards-TM34
99BAP Millennium-203
Emerald-203
Ruby-203
Sapphire-203
Signatures-203
Signatures Gold-203
Jerseys-J6
Jersey Autographs-J6
Jersey and Stick Cards-JS6
Jersey Emblems-E6
Jersey Numbers-N6
99Blues Taco Bell-20
99Crown Royale-117
Limited Series-117
Premiere Date-117
99Jell-O Pudding Super Skills-4
99Kraft Peanut Butter-8
99O-Pee-Chee-13
99O-Pee-Chee All-Topps-AT4
99O-Pee-Chee Chrome-13
99O-Pee-Chee Chrome All Topps-AT4
99O-Pee-Chee Chrome All-Topps Refractors-AT4
99O-Pee-Chee Chrome Ice Masters-IM12
99O-Pee-Chee Chrome Ice Masters Refractor-IM12
99O-Pee-Chee Chrome Refractors-13
99O-Pee-Chee Chrome Positive Performers-PP5
99OPC Chrome Pos Performers Ref-PP5
99O-Pee-Chee Ice Masters-IM12
99O-Pee-Chee Positive Performers-PP5
99Oscar Mayer Lunchables-9
99Pacific-358
Copper-358
Emerald Green-358
Gold-358
Ice Blue-358
Premiere Date-358
Red-358
99Pacific Dynagon Ice-166
Blue-166
Copper-166
Gold-166
Premiere Date-166
99Pacific Omega-196
Copper-196
Gold-196
Ice Blue-196
Premiere Date-196
Cup Contenders-18
99Pacific Prism-119
Holographic Blue-119
Holographic Gold-119
Holographic Mirror-119
Holographic Purple-119
Premiere Date-119
99Panini Stickers-5
99Panini Stickers-287
99Panini Stickers-341
99Paramount-198
Copper-198
Emerald-198
Gold-198
Holographic Emerald-198
Holographic Gold-198
Holographic Silver-198
Ice Blue-198
Premiere Date-198
Red-198
Silver-198
99Revolution-123
Premiere Date-123
Red-123
Shadow Series-123
99SPx-133
Radiance-133
Spectrum-133
SPXtreme-XT1
99Stadium Club-14
First Day Issue-14
One of a Kind-14
Printing Plates Black-14
Printing Plates Cyan-14
Printing Plates Magenta-14
Printing Plates Yellow-14
Capture the Action-CA29
Capture the Action Game View-CAG29
Chrome-13
Chrome Refractors-13
Co-Signers-CS13
Co-Signers-CS14
Lone Star Signatures-LS5
Souvenirs-SAM
99Topps/OPC-13
All-Topps-AT4
Ice Masters-IM12
Positive Performers-PP5
99Topps/OPC Chrome-13
Refractors-13
All-Topps-AT4
All-Topps Refractors-AT4
Ice Masters-IM12
Ice Masters Refractors-IM12
Positive Performers-PP5
Positive Performers Refractors-PP5
99Topps Gold Label Class 1-2
Black-2
Black One of One-2
One of One-2
Red-2
Red One of One-2
99Topps Gold Label Class 2-2
99Topps Gold Label Class 2 Black-2
99Topps Gold Label Class 2 Black 1 of 1-2
99Topps Gold Label Class 2 One of One-2
99Topps Gold Label Class 2 Red-2
99Topps Gold Label Class 2 Red One of One-2
99Topps Gold Label Class 3-2
99Topps Gold Label Class 3 Black-2
99Topps Gold Label Class 3 Black 1 of 1-2
99Topps Gold Label Class 3 One of One-2
99Topps Gold Label Class 3 Red-2
99Topps Gold Label Class 3 Red One of One-2
99Topps Premier Plus-25
Parallel-25
99Upper Deck-114
Exclusives-114
Exclusives 1 of 1-114
All-Star Class-AS18
All-Star Class Quantum Gold-AS18
All-Star Class Quantum Silver-AS18

Crunch Time-CT15
Crunch Time Quantum Gold-CT15
Crunch Time Quantum Silver-CT15
Game Jerseys Series II-AM
99Upper Deck Gold Reserve-114
99Upper Deck HoloGrFx-52
Ausome-52
99Upper Deck MVP-183
Gold Script-183
Silver Script-183
Super Script-183
SC Edition ProSign-AM
99Upper Deck Ovation-49
Standing Ovation-49
99Upper Deck Retro-70
Gold-70
Platinum-70
99Upper Deck Victory-258
99Upper Deck Victory-260
99Upper Deck Victory-318
99Upper Deck Victory-341
99Wayne Gretzky Hockey-146
Changing The Game-CG8
99Slovakian Challengers-15
00Aurora-122
Premiere Date-122
00BAP Memorabilia-257
Emerald-257
Ruby-257
Sapphire-257
Promos-257
Jersey Cards-J8
Jersey Emblems-E8
Jersey Numbers-N8
Jersey and Stick Cards-JS8
00BAP Mem Chicago Sportsfest Copper-257
00BAP Memorabilia Chicago Sportsfest Blue-257
00BAP Memorabilia Chicago Sportsfest Gold-257
00BAP Memorabilia Chicago Sportsfest Ruby-257
00BAP Memorabilia Chicago Sun-Times Ruby-257
00BAP Memorabilia Chicago Sun-Times Gold-257
00BAP Mem Chicago Sun-Times Sapphire-257
00BAP Mem Toronto Fall Expo Copper-257
00BAP Memorabilia Toronto Fall Expo Gold-257
00BAP Memorabilia Toronto Fall Expo Ruby-257
00BAP Mem Update Heritage Jersey Cards-H13
00BAP Mem Update Heritage Jersey Gold-H13
00BAP Parkhurst 2000-P116
00BAP Signature Series-128
Emerald-128
Ruby-128
Sapphire-128
Autographs-28
Autographs Gold-28
Department of Defense-DD7
He Shoots-He Scores Prizes-17
Jersey Cards-J6
Jersey and Stick Cards-GSJ6
Jersey Cards Autographs-J6
Jersey Emblems-E6
Jersey Numbers-IN6
00BAP Ultimate Memorabilia Autographs-6
Gold-6
00BAP Ultimate Mem Game-Used Jerseys-GJ6
00BAP Ultimate Mem Game-Used Sticks-GS6
00BAP Ultimate Mem Journey Jerseys-JJ14
00BAP Ultimate Mem Journey Emblems-JE14
00BAP Ultimate Mem Journey Numbers-JI14
00BAP Ultimate Memorabilia Norris Trophy-N2
00BAP Ultimate Memorabilia Teammates-TM37
00O-Pee-Chee-62
00O-Pee-Chee Parallel-62
00Pacific-346
Copper-346
Gold-346
Ice Blue-346
Premiere Date-346
00Paramount-206
Copper-206
Gold-206
Holo-Gold-206
Holo-Silver-206
Ice Blue-206
Premiere Date-206
Game Used Sticks-16
00Private Stock-83
Gold-83
Premiere Date-83
Retail-83
Silver-83
00Revolution-123
Blue-123
Premiere Date-123
Red-123
00SP Game Used Tools of the Game-AM
00SP Game Used Tools of the Game Excl-AM
00SP Game Used Tools of the Game Combos-C-DM
00Stadium Club-172
00Topps/OPC-62
Parallel-62
1000 Point Club-PC13
00Topps Chrome-50
OPC Refractors-50
Refractors-50
1000 Point Club Refractors-13
00Topps Premier Plus-14
Blue Ice-14
00Topps Stars-45
Blue-45
00UD Heroes NHL Leaders-L10
00Upper Deck-380
Exclusives Tier 1-380
Exclusives Tier 2-380
Legends Legendary Game Jerseys-JAM
00Upper Deck MVP-153
First Stars-153
ProSign-AM
Second Stars-153
Third Stars-153
00Upper Deck Victory-201
00Upper Deck Victory-321
00Upper Deck Vintage-314
00Vanguard-82
Holographic Gold-82
Holographic Purple-82
Pacific Proofs-82
00Czech Stadion-149
01BAP Memorabilia-84
Emerald-84
Ruby-84
Sapphire-84
All-Star Jerseys-ASJ44
All-Star Emblems-ASE44
All-Star Numbers-ASN44
All-Star Jersey Doubles-DASJ23
All-Star Teammates-AST16
All-Star Teammates-AST30
Country of Origin-CO7
He Shoots-He Scores Prizes-20
Stanley Cup Playoffs-SC28
01BAP Signature Series Certified 100-C1
01BAP Signature Series Certified 50-C1
01BAP Signature Series Certified 1 of 1's-C1
01BAP Signature Series Autographs-LAM
01BAP Signature Series Autographs Gold-LAM
01BAP Sig Series Department of Defense-DD-6
01BAP Sig Series International Medals-IG-3
01BAP Signature Series Jerseys-GJ-58
01BAP Signature Series Jersey Autographs-GUAM
01BAP Sig Series Jersey and Stick Cards-GSJ-58
01BAP Signature Series Emblems-GUE-28
01BAP Signature Series Numbers-ITN-28
01BAP Ultimate Memorabilia Autographs-10
01BAP Ultimate Mem Autographs Gold-10
01BAP Ultimate Memorabilia Decades-22
01BAP Ultimate Memorabilia Gloves Are Off-14
01BAP Update Heritage-H15
01Bowman YoungStars-103
Gold-103
Ice Cubed-103
01McDonald's Pacific Hometown Pride-9
01O-Pee-Chee-96
01O-Pee-Chee Heritage Parallel-96
01O-Pee-Chee Heritage Parallel Limited-96
01O-Pee-Chee Premier Parallel-96
01Pacific-326
Extreme LTD-326
Hobby LTD-326
Premiere Date-326
Retail LTD-326
01Pacific Adrenaline-160
Blue-160
Premiere Date-160
Red-160
Retail-160
01Pacific Arena Exclusives-326
01Parkhurst-37
Gold-37
Silver-37
Jerseys-PJ20
Jersey and Stick-PSJ16
Milestones-M48
Sticks-PS20
01SP Authentic-108
Limited-108
Limited Gold-108
Sign of the Times-AM
Sign of the Times-WM
01SP Game Used Inked Sweaters-DSWM
01Sports Illustrated for Kids III-321
01Titanium-117
Hobby Parallel-117
Premiere Date-117
Retail-117
Retail Parallel-117
01Topps-96
Heritage Parallel-96
Heritage Parallel Limited-96
OPC Parallel-96
01Topps Chrome-96
Refractors-96
Black Border Refractors-96
01Topps Heritage-79
Refractors-79
01UD Challenge for the Cup Jerseys-TNAM
01UD Challenge for the Cup Jersey Autos-TNMA
01UD Honor Roll-22
01UD Honor Roll-52
Playoff Matchups-HS-TM
Playoff Matchups Gold-HS-TM
01UD Stanley Cup Champs-29
Sticks-S-AM
01Upper Deck-152
Exclusives-152
Game Jerseys-AAM
Game Jerseys Series II-SSAM
01Upper Deck MVP-167
Souvenirs-C-AM
Souvenirs Gold-C-AM
01Upper Deck Victory-308
Gold-308
01Upper Deck Vintage-223
01Upper Deck Vintage-226
02BAP All-Star Edition-57
He Shoots-He Score Prizes-17
Jerseys-57
Jerseys Gold-57
Jerseys Silver-57
02BAP First Edition-118
Jerseys-118
02BAP Memorabilia-12
Emerald-12
Ruby-12
Sapphire-12
All-Star Jerseys-ASJ-34
All-Star Triple Jerseys-ASTJ-13
NHL All-Star Game-12
NHL All-Star Game Blue-12
NHL All-Star Game Green-12
NHL All-Star Game Red-12
Teammates-TM-16
02BAP Memorabilia Toronto Fall Expo-12
02BAP Signature Series-159
Autographs-159
Autograph Buybacks 1998-274
Autograph Buybacks 1999-203
Autograph Buybacks 2000-28
Autograph Buybacks 2001-LAM
Autographs Gold-159
Defensive Wall-DW7
Jerseys-SGJ37
Jersey Autographs-SGJ37
Team Quads-TQ15
02BAP Ultimate Memorabilia Conn Smythe-17
02BAP Ultimate Mem Global Dominators-2
02BAP Ultimate Memorabilia Gloves Are Off-6
02BAP Ultimate Memorabilia Hat Tricks-16
02Blues Team Issue-14
02Bowman YoungStars-67
Gold-67
Silver-67
02ITG Used-66
02ITG Used-166
Jerseys-GUJ37
Jersey Autographs-GUJ37
Jerseys Gold-GUJ37
Emblems-E35
Jersey and Stick-SJ37
Jersey and Stick Gold-SJ37
Triple Memorabilia-TM10
Triple Memorabilia Gold-TM10
02O-Pee-Chee-199
02O-Pee-Chee Premier Blue Parallel-199
02O-Pee-Chee Premier Red Parallel-199
02O-Pee-Chee Factory Set-199
02Pacific-325
Blue-325
Red-325
02Pacific Complete-38
Red-38
02Pacific Exclusive-144
02Parkhurst-6
Bronze-6
Gold-6
Silver-6
Heroes-NH9
Jerseys-GJ11
Stick and Jerseys-SJ11
Teammates-TT16
02Parkhurst Retro-104
Minis-104
Hopefuls-NH4
02SPx-133
02Topps-199
OPC Blue Parallel-199
OPC Red Parallel-199
Topps/OPC Hometown Heroes-HHU14
Factory Set-199
Factory Set Hometown Heroes-HHU14
02Topps Chrome-112
Black Border Refractors-112
Refractors-112
02Topps Heritage Autographs-AM
02Topps Heritage Autographs Black-AM
02Topps Heritage Autographs Red-AM
02Topps Total-92
02UD Piece of History Awards Collection-AC26
02UD Top Shelf Clutch Performers-CPAM
02UD Top Shelf Hardware Heroes-HPMBL
02Upper Deck-152
Exclusives-152
Blow-Ups-C35
Good Old Days-GOAM
02Upper Deck MVP-161
Gold-161
Classics-161
Golden Classics-161
02Upper Deck Rookie Update-155A
02Upper Deck Victory-183
Bronze-183
Gold-183
Silver-183
02Upper Deck Vintage-225
Green Backs-225
03McFarlane Hockey-170
03McFarlane Hockey-172
03BAP Memorabilia-1
Emerald-1
Gold-1
Ruby-1
Sapphire-1
All-Star Emblems-ASE-19
All-Star Jerseys-ASJ-31
All-Star Numbers-ASN-19
Jersey and Stick-SJ-8
Jerseys-GJ-8
Practice Jerseys-PMP5
03BAP Ultimate Memorabilia Autographs-75
Gold-75
03BAP Ultimate Mem Auto Jerseys-75
03BAP Ultimate Mem Always An All-Star-5
03BAP Ultimate Mem Always An AS Gold-5
03BAP Ultimate Mem Blades of Steel-3
03BAP Ultimate Mem Complete Package-4
03BAP Ultimate Mem Complete Package Gold-4
03BAP Ultimate Memorabilia Hat Tricks-16
03BAP Ultimate Memorabilia Triple Threads-11
03BAP Ultimate Memorabilia Triple Threads-12
03Black Diamond-125
Black-125
Green-125
Red-125
03Blues Team Set-16
03eTopps-2
03ITG Action-501
Jerseys-M167
03ITG Used Signature Series-85
Gold-85
Autographs-AMA
Autographs Gold-AMA
Norris Trophy-3
Norris Trophy Gold-3
Oh Canada-5
Oh Canada Gold-5
Oh Canada Emblems-5
Oh Canada Emblems Gold-5
03ITG VIP Jerseys-27
03Kraft-6
03NHL Sticker Collection-277
03O-Pee-Chee-265
03O-Pee-Chee-298
03OPC Blue-265
03OPC Blue-298
03OPC Gold-265
03OPC Gold-298
03OPC Red-265
03OPC Red-298
03Pacific-284
Blue-284
Red-284
03Pacific Complete-128
Red-128
03Pacific Exhibit-122
Blue Backs-122
Yellow Backs-122
03Pacific Prism-84
Blue-84
Gold-84
Red-84
03Pacific Supreme Generations-9
03Parkhurst Rookie-27
Retro Rookies-RR-17
Retro Rookies Gold-RR-17
03Private Stock Reserve-85
Blue-85
Red-85
Retail-85
03SP Game Used-40
Gold-40
03SPx-84
Radiance-84
Spectrum-84
Fantasy Franchise-FF-TWM
Fantasy Franchise Limited-FF-TWM
03Topps-265
03Topps-298
Blue-265
Blue-298
Gold-265
Gold-298
Red-265
Red-298
03Topps C55-122
Minis-122
Minis American Back-122
Minis American Back Red-122
Minis Bazooka Back-122
Minis Brooklyn Back-122
Minis Hat Trick Back-122
Minis O Canada Back-122
Minis O Canada Back Red-122
Minis Stanley Cup Back-122
03Topps Pristine-63
Gold Refractor Die Cuts-63
Refractors-63
Press Plates Black-63
Press Plates Cyan-63
Press Plates Magenta-63
Press Plates Yellow-63
03Upper Deck-164
Canadian Exclusives-164
HG-164
Team Essentials-TP-AM
03Upper Deck Classic Portraits-83
Classic Colors-CC-AM
03Upper Deck Ice Icons-I-AM
03Upper Deck Ice Icons Jerseys-I-AM
03Upper Deck MVP-359
Gold Script-359
Silver Script-359
Canadian Exclusives-359
SportsNut-SN77
Threads-TC1
03Upper Deck Trilogy-83
Limited-83
03Upper Deck Victory-164
Bronze-164
Gold-164
Silver-164
Game Breakers-GB31
03Toronto Star-77
04Pacific-220
Blue-220
Red-220
04Ultimate Collection Dual Logos-UL2-MP
04Upper Deck-150
Canadian Exclusives-150
HG Glossy Gold-150
HG Glossy Silver-150
05Black Diamond-123
Emerald-123
Gold-123
Onyx-123
Ruby-123
Jerseys-J-AM
Jerseys Ruby-J-AM
Jersey Duals-DJ-AM
Jersey Triples-TJ-AM
Jersey Quads-QJ-AM
05SPx Winning Combos-WC-WM
05SPx Winning Combos Gold-WC-WM
05SPx Winning Combos Spectrum-WC-WM
05UD Artifacts Frozen Artifacts-FA-AM
05UD Artifacts Frozen Artifacts Autos-FA-AM
05UD Artifacts Frozen Artifacts Copper-FA-AM
05UD Artifacts Frozen Artifacts Dual-FAD-AM
05UD Artifacts Frozen Artifact Dual Auto-FAD-AM
05UD Artifact Frozen Artifact Dual Copper-FAD-AM
05UD Artifacts Frozen Artifacts Dual Gold-FAD-AM
05UD Artifact Frozen Artifact Dual Maroon-FAD-AM
05UD Artifact Frozen Artifact Dual Pewter-FAD-AM
05UD Artifact Frozen Artifact Dual Silver-FAD-AM
05UD Artifacts Frozen Artifacts Gold-FA-AM
05UD Artifacts Frozen Artifacts Maroon-FA-AM
05UD Artifacts Frozen Artifacts Patches-FP-AM
05UD Artifact Frozen Artifact Patch Autos-FP-AM
05UD Artifact Frozen Artifact Patch Dual-FPD-AM
05UD Artifacts Frozen Art Patch Dual Auto-FPD-AM
05UD Artifacts Frozen Art Patch Pewter-FP-AM
05UD Artifacts Frozen Art Patch Silver-FP-AM
05UD Artifacts Frozen Artifacts Pewter-FA-AM
05UD Artifacts Frozen Artifacts Silver-FA-AM
05Upper Deck Big Playmakers-B-AM
05Upper Deck Patches-P-AMA
05Upper Deck Trilogy Honorary Patches-HP-AM
05Upper Deck Tril Honorary Patch Script-HSP-AM
05Upper Deck Trilogy Honorary Swatches-HS-AM
05Upper Deck Tril Honorary Swatch Scripts-HSS-AM
05Upper Deck Victory-169
Black-169
Gold-169
Silver-169
06Parkhurst-68
06Parkhurst-226
Autographs-68
Autographs-226
06SP Game Used Inked Sweaters-ISMA
06SP Game Used Inked Sweaters Patches-ISMA
06SP Game Used Inked Sweaters Dual-IS2MM
06SP Game Used Inked Sweaters Dual Patches-IS2MM
06SPx-136
Spectrum-136
Winning Materials-WMAM
Winning Materials Spectrum-WMAM
Winning Materials Autographs-WMAM
06The Cup-16
Autographed Foundations-CQAM
Autographed Foundations Patches-CQAM
Autographed NHL Shields Duals-DASBM
Autographed Patches-16
Black Rainbow-16
Foundations-CQAM
Foundations Patches-CQAM
Gold-16
Gold Patches-16
Honorable Numbers-HNAM
Jerseys-16
Limited Logos-LLAM
Masterpiece Pressplates-16
Property of-POAM
Scripted Swatches Duals-DSMM
Signature Patches-SPAM
Stanley Cup Signatures-CSAM
Stanley Cup Titlists Patches-TAM
06UD Artifacts-145
Blue-145
Gold-145
Platinum-145
Radiance-145
Red-145
Treasured Patches Black-TSAM
Treasured Patches Blue-TSAM
Treasured Patches Gold-TSAM
Treasured Patches Platinum-TSAM
Treasured Patches Red-TSAM
Treasured Swatches-TSAM
Treasured Swatches Black-TSAM
Treasured Swatches Blue-TSAM
Treasured Swatches Gold-TSAM
Treasured Swatches Platinum-TSAM
Treasured Swatches Red-TSAM
Tundra Tandems-TTJA
Tundra Tandems-TTMM
Tundra Tandems Black-TTJA
Tundra Tandems Black-TTMM
Tundra Tandems Blue-TTJA
Tundra Tandems Blue-TTMM
Tundra Tandems Gold-TTJA
Tundra Tandems Gold-TTMM
Tundra Tandems Platinum-TTJA
Tundra Tandems Platinum-TTMM
Tundra Tandems Red-TTJA
Tundra Tandems Red-TTMM
Tundra Tandems Dual Patches Red-TTJA
Tundra Tandems Dual Patches Red-TTMM
06Ultimate Collection Jerseys Dual-UJ2-MM
06Ultimate Collection Patches Dual-UJ2-MM
06Ultimate Collection Premium Patches-PS-AM
06Ultimate Collection Premium Swatches-PS-AM
06Ultimate Collection Signatures-US-AM
06Upper Deck Sweet Shot Signature Sticks-STAM

MacInnis, Ian
81Kingston Canadians-7

MacInnis, Neill
01Belleville Bulls-14

MacInnis, Rob
83Kitchener Rangers-4
88ProCards AHL-73
90ProCards AHL/IHL-532
93Richmond Renegades-7

MacIntosh, Andy
92British Columbia JHL-153

MacIntyre, Andy
907th Inn. Sketch WHL-6
91Saskatoon Blades-18
917th Inn. Sketch WHL-98
93Saskatoon Blades-15
94Indianapolis Ice-14
95Indianapolis Ice-12
98Kentucky Thoroughblades-16
99Florida Everblades-21
00Florida Everblades-16

Macintyre, Cam
05Salmon Arm Silverbacks-12

MacIntyre, Colby
02Halifax Mooseheads-19
03Halifax Mooseheads-19

MacIntyre, Corey
98Oklahoma City Blazers-19

MacIntyre, Dave
91Johnstown Chiefs-8
95Peoria Rivermen-10
97Milwaukee Admirals-11
98German DEL-114
00Lubbock Cotton Kings-5
03Lubbock Cotton Kings-12

MacIntyre, Drew
00QMJHL All-Star Program Inserts-24
00Sherbrooke Castors-1
Signed-1
01Sherbrooke Castors-1
05ITG Heroes/Prosp Toronto Expo Parallel -244
05ITG Heroes and Prospects-244
Autographs Series II-DMI

MacIntyre, Dunc
83Belleville Bulls-12
84Belleville Bulls-4
85Fredericton Express-10
86Fredericton Express-18

MacIntyre, Jason
93Hampton Roads Admirals-8
94Hampton Roads Admirals-17
95Hampton Roads Admirals-8
98San Antonio Iguanas-6
99San Antonio Iguanas-3

MacIntyre, Rob
03Camrose Kodiaks-9

MacIntyre, Steve
00OCN Blizzard-23

MacIntyre, Steven
00OCN Blizzard-23
02Muskegon Fury-17
03Charlotte Checkers-72
04Hartford Wolf Pack-15

MacIsaac, Al
91Hampton Roads Admirals-9
93Hampton Roads Admirals-9
96Hampton Roads Admirals-HRA22
97Hampton Roads Admirals-23
98Hampton Roads Admirals-3
98Hampton Roads Admirals 10th Anniversary-20
99Hampton Roads Admirals-23
06Norfolk Admirals-26

MacIsaac, Bob
917th Inn. Sketch OHL-263
91Sudbury Wolves-7
92Sudbury Wolves-3
93Sudbury Wolves-23
93Sudbury Wolves Police-25
00Charlotte Checkers-22

MacIsaac, Dave
92Maine Black Bears-23
93Maine Black Bears-45
95Milwaukee Admirals-11
95Milwaukee Admirals Postcards-1
99Lowell Lock Monsters-2
00Kentucky Thoroughblades-17
01Hartford Wolf Pack-15
01Hershey Bears-15
02Russian Hockey League-65

MacIsaac, Todd
917th Inn. Sketch WHL-348
93Lethbridge Hurricanes-6
97Macon Whoopee-9
97Macon Whoopee Autographs-9
01Asheville Smoke-12
04Knoxville Ice Bears-4

Macissac, Kent
93Quebec Pee-Wee Tournament-1214

MacIver, Doug
99Kingston Frontenacs-12
00Kingston Frontenacs-10
01Kingston Frontenacs-11
03Peoria Rivermen-8
04Louisiana Ice Gators-11

Maciver, Norm
84Minnesota-Duluth Bulldogs-17
85Minnesota-Duluth Bulldogs-5
88Panini Stickers-302
89ProCards AHL-140
90ProCards AHL/IHL-224
91Bowman-99
91Oilers IGA-10
91Oilers Team Issue-12
91Parkhurst-282
French-282
91Score Canadian Bilingual-434
91Score Canadian English-434
92Bowman-425
92O-Pee-Chee-344
92OPC Premier-107
92Parkhurst-117
Emerald Ice-117
92Pinnacle-157
French-157
92Pro Set-50
92Score-349
Canadian-349
92Senators Team Issue-9
92Stadium Club-46
92Topps-96
Gold-96G
92Ultra-61
92Ultra-363
92Upper Deck-511
93Donruss-233
93Leaf-189
93OPC Premier-64
Gold-64
93Panini Stickers-112
93Parkhurst-137
Emerald Ice-137
93Pinnacle-120
Canadian-120
93PowerPlay-172
93Score-123
Canadian-123
93Senators Kraft Sheets-15
93Stadium Club-267
Members Only Master Set-267
First Day Issue-267
93Topps/OPC Premier-64
Gold-64
93Ultra-143
93Upper Deck-299
93Upper Deck-335
SP-111
94Be A Player Signature Cards-127
94Canada Games NHL POGS-175
94Donruss-273
94EA Sports-91
94Flair-122
94Leaf-68
94OPC Premier-49
Special Effects-49
94Parkhurst-154
Gold-154
94Pinnacle-80
Artist's Proofs-80
Rink Collection-80
94Score-24
Gold-24
Platinum-24
94Senators Team Issue-18
94Topps/OPC Premier-49
Special Effects-49
94Ultra-149
94Upper Deck-466
Electric Ice-466
95Collector's Choice-270
Player's Club-270
Player's Club Platinum-270
95Parkhurst International-171
95Parkhurst International-499
Emerald Ice-171
Emerald Ice-499
95Penguins Foodland-8
95Pinnacle-170
Artist's Proofs-170
Rink Collection-170
95Score-276
Black Ice Artist's Proofs-276
Black Ice-276
95Ultra-289
96Be A Player-133
Autographs-133
Autographs Silver-133
96Collector's Choice-208
96Coyotes Coca-Cola-18
96Donruss-69
Press Proofs-69
96Fleer Picks-112
96Leaf-35
Press Proofs-35
96Score-167
Artist's Proofs-167
Dealer's Choice Artist's Proofs-167
Special Artist's Proofs-167
Golden Blades-167
97Coyotes Face-Off Luncheon -13
97Pacific-60
Copper-60
Emerald Green-60
Ice Blue-60
Red-60
Silver-60
02Springfield Falcons-16

Mackay, Brian
52Juniors Blue Tint-133

Mackay, Calum
44Beehive Group II Photos-271
45Quaker Oats Photos-92
51Parkhurst-9
51Buffalo Bison-14
54Parkhurst-11
55Parkhurst-41
Quaker Oats-41

MacKay, Darrin
97Austin Ice Bats-10

Mackay, Dave
34Beehive Group I Photos-65

MacKay, Kevin
89Windsor Spitfires-9
907th Inn. Sketch OHL-186
917th Inn. Sketch OHL-190

MacKay, Mark
94German First League-574
94German First League-665
95German DEL-404
96German DEL-312
98German DEL-203
98German DEL-337
99German DEL-216
99German DEL-391
00German DEL-216
Game Jersey-MM
01German Upper Deck-233
Gate Attractions-GA4

MacKay, Mickey
83Hall of Fame Postcards-N8
85Hall of Fame-203

MacKay, Murdo
45Quaker Oats Photos-93

MacKay, Ryan
04St. Francis Xavier X-Men-12

Mackay, Tyler
97Saskatoon Blades-12
99Spokane Chiefs-16
00Spokane Chiefs-17
03ECHL Update RBI Sports-287
04Florida Everblades-1

Mackegard, Jens
87Swedish Panini Stickers-259

Mackeigan, Jack
82Victoria Cougars-14
83Victoria Cougars-15

Mackell, Fleming
44Beehive Group II Photos-45
44Beehive Group II Photos-422
45Quaker Oats Photos-30A
45Quaker Oats Photos-30B
48Exhibits Canadian-34
51Parkhurst-83
52Parkhurst-82
53Parkhurst-91A
53Parkhurst-91B
54Parkhurst-50
54Topps-36
55Bruins Photos-10
57Bruins Photos-12
57Topps-16
58Bruins Photos-8
58Topps-29
59Topps-19
59Topps-60
61Union Oil WHL-7
91Bruins Sports Action Legends-14
94Parkhurst Missing Link-3

MacKellar, Peter
93Sault Ste. Marie Greyhounds-9
93Sault Ste. Marie Greyhound Memorial Cup-5
94Owen Sound Platers-5
95Slapshot-289
95Owen Sound Platers-12
00Bakersfield Condors-13

MacKenzie, Aaron
03Worcester Ice Cats-19
04Worcester IceCats-14
05Peoria Rivermen-13
06Peoria Rivermen-10

MacKenzie, Bill
33V357 Ice Kings-61
34Beehive Group I Photos-199
36O-Pee-Chee V304D-111
37O-Pee-Chee V304E-151
37V356 Worldwide Gum-44
39O-Pee-Chee V301-1-81

MacKenzie, Brian
917th Inn. Sketch OHL-267

MacKenzie, Chris
97El Paso Buzzards-6
99Indianapolis Ice-12
00Finnish Cardset-169
00Indianapolis Ice-15
01Indianapolis Ice-14

MacKenzie, Derek
97Sudbury Wolves Police-12
98SP Authentic-127
Power Shift-127
Sign of the Times-DMA
Sign of the Times Gold-DMA
98Upper Deck-404
Exclusives-404
Exclusives 1 of 1-404
Gold Reserve-404
98Sudbury Wolves-6
99Sudbury Wolves-14
99Bowman CHL-10
Gold-10
OPC International-10
Autographs-BA30
Autographs Gold-BA30
Autographs Silver-BA30
00Sudbury Wolves-15
00UD CHL Prospects-39
01Chicago Wolves-10
02Chicago Wolves-15
03Chicago Wolves-13
04Chicago Wolves-23
05Chicago Wolves-10

MacKenzie, Jean-Marc
83Sault Ste. Marie Greyhounds-16
84Sault Ste. Marie Greyhounds-13
86London Knights-10

MacKenzie, Ken
907th Inn. Sketch OHL-399
917th Inn. Sketch OHL-265
98Sudbury Wolves-2

MacKenzie, Robert
917th Inn. Sketch OHL-285

MacKenzie, Roddie
95Slapshot Memorial Cup-66

MacKenzie, Shawn
95Halifax Mooseheads-23
96Halifax Mooseheads I-25
96Halifax Mooseheads II-25
97Halifax Mooseheads I-25
97Halifax Mooseheads II-24

Mackey, Dave
82Victoria Cougars-15
83Victoria Cougars-16
85Medicine Hat Tigers-22
88ProCards IHL-103
90ProCards AHL/IHL-328
91ProCards-31
92Peoria Rivermen-13
93Peoria Rivermen-17
94Leaf-280
94OPC Premier-48
Special Effects-48
94Parkhurst-202
Gold-202
94Topps/OPC Premier-48
Special Effects-48
94Milwaukee Admirals-15
95Milwaukee Admirals-13
95Milwaukee Admirals Postcards-9
96Milwaukee Admirals-16
98Orlando Solar Bears-12
98Orlando Solar Bears II-4
99Chicago Wolves-18

Mackey, Kevin
95North Iowa Huskies-18

MacKie, Brent
04Guelph Storm-8
05Ottawa 67's-11

Mackie, Dub
23V128-1 Paulin's Candy-14

Mackie, Kevin
96Swift Current Broncos-3
98Kamloops Blazers-17
99Kamloops Blazers-13
00San Diego Gulls-10

MacKinnon, Brett
01Minnesota Golden Gophers-26
02Minnesota Golden Gophers-13
03Minnesota Golden Gophers-20

Mackinnon, Donnie
93Quebec Pee-Wee Tournament-1222

MacKinnon, Paul
78Jets Postcards-14

MacKinnon, Steve
98Peoria Rivermen-19

MacKinnon, Zack
06Okotoks Oilers -10

MacLean, A.J.
00Halifax Mooseheads-16
01Halifax Mooseheads-7
02Halifax Mooseheads-7

MacLean, Adam
04Huntsville Havoc-3

MacLean, Anthony
93Quebec Pee-Wee Tournament-1698

MacLean, Brandon
04Sault Ste. Marie Greyhounds-10

MacLean, Brett
04Erie Otters-4
06Oshawa Generals-8

MacLean, Cail
93Kingston Frontenacs-12
95Slapshot-117
98ECHL All-Star Southern Conference-11
00Trenton Titans-5
01Trenton Titans-1-6
02Hershey Bears-13
03Bridgeport Sound Tigers-5B
04Hershey Bears Patriot News-20
04Reading Royals-9

MacLean, Dave
81Oshawa Generals-17
83Belleville Bulls-4
84Belleville Bulls-11

MacLean, Derek
97Portland Winter Hawks-11

Maclean, Donald
95Classic-30
95Signature Rookies Auto-Phonex-26
95Signature Rook Auto-Phonex Phone Cards-26
95Classic Five-Sport *-157
Autographs-157
97Be A Player-241
Autographs-241
Autographs Die-Cuts-241
Autographs Prismatic Die-Cuts-241
97Black Diamond-57
Double Diamond-57
Triple Diamond-57
Quadruple Diamond-57
97Crown Royale-63
Emerald Green-63
Ice Blue-63
Silver-63
97Katch-70
Gold-70
Silver-70
97Pinnacle-14
Artist's Proofs-14
Rink Collection-14
Press Plates Back Black-14
Press Plates Back Cyan-14
Press Plates Back Magenta-14
Press Plates Back Yellow-14
Press Plates Front Black-14
Press Plates Front Cyan-14
Press Plates Front Magenta-14
Press Plates Front Yellow-14
97SP Authentic-184
97Upper Deck-292
97Upper Deck Ice-53
Parallel-53
Power Shift-53
98Pacific-238
Ice Blue-238
Red-238
98UD Choice-102
Prime Choice Reserve-102
Reserve-102
98Upper Deck-106
Exclusives-106
Exclusives 1 of 1-106
Gold Reserve-106
99Lowell Lock Monsters-7
00Upper Deck NHLPA-PA82
00St. John's Maple Leafs-15
01Pacific-368
Extreme LTD-368
Hobby LTD-368
Premiere Date-368
Retail LTD-368
01Pacific Arena Exclusives-368
01St. John's Maple Leafs-13
03Syracuse Crunch-9
04Finnish Cardset-7
Parallel-7
05AHL All-Stars-19

MacLean, John
81Oshawa Generals-19
82Oshawa Generals-15
83Devils Postcards-18
84Devils Postcards-15
86Devils Police-14
86O-Pee-Chee-37
86Topps-37
87O-Pee-Chee-191
87Panini Stickers-80
87Topps-191
88Devils Caretta-18
88O-Pee-Chee-10
88O-Pee-Chee Stickers-78

88Panini Stickers-274
88Topps-10
89Devils Caretta-15
89O-Pee-Chee-102
89O-Pee-Chee Stickers-87
89Panini Stickers-249
89Topps-102
90Bowman-83
Tiffany-83
90Devils Team Issue-17
90O-Pee-Chee-224
90Panini Stickers-74
90Pro Set-170
90Score-190
Canadian-190
90Score Hottest/Rising Stars-83
90Topps-224
Tiffany-224
90Upper Deck-161
French-161
91Pro Set Platinum-70
91Bowman-272
91Bowman-289
91O-Pee-Chee-239
91OPC Premier-4
91Panini Stickers-213
91Pinnacle-115
French-115
91Pro Set-136
91Pro Set-307
French-136
French-307
91Score American-210
91Score Canadian Bilingual-210
91Score Canadian English-210
91Score Kellogg's-13
91Stadium Club-144
91Topps-239
Team Scoring Leaders-15
91Upper Deck-88
91Upper Deck-169
French-88
French-169
92Bowman-130
92Parkhurst-90
Emerald Ice-90
92Pinnacle-351
French-351
92Score-30
Canadian-30
92Stadium Club-28
92Topps-273
Gold-273G
92Ultra-115
92Upper Deck-521
93Donruss-184
93Leaf-264
93OPC Premier-193
Gold-193
93Panini Stickers-40
93Parkhurst-115
Emerald Ice-115
93Pinnacle-183
Canadian-183
93PowerPlay-138
93Score-81
Canadian-81
93Stadium Club-287
Members Only Master Set-287
First Day Issue-287
93Topps/OPC Premier-193
Gold-193
93Ultra-53
93Upper Deck-134
94Be A Player Signature Cards-134
94Canada Games NHL POGS-146
94Donruss-151
94Finest-90
Super Team Winners-90
Refractors-90
94Flair-95
94Fleer-114
94Leaf-204
94Leaf Limited-92
94OPC Premier-175
Special Effects-175
94Parkhurst-125
Gold-125
94Pinnacle-101
Artist's Proofs-101
Rink Collection-101
94Score-172
Gold-172
Platinum-172
94Select-136
Gold-136
94SP-65
Die Cuts-65
94Topps/OPC Premier-175
Special Effects-175
94Ultra-119
94Upper Deck-8
Electric Ice-8
SP Inserts-SP133
SP Inserts Die Cuts-SP133
95Bowman-27
All-Foil-27
95Canada Games NHL POGS-160
95Collector's Choice-34
Player's Club-34
Player's Club Platinum-34
95Donruss-88
95Donruss Elite-23
Die Cut Stars-23
Die Cut Uncut-23
95Emotion-98
95Finest-38
Refractors-38
95Leaf-176
95Metal-83
95Panini Stickers-83
95Parkhurst International-123
Emerald Ice-123
95Pinnacle-26
Artist's Proofs-26
Rink Collection-26
95Playoff One on One-278
95Pro Magnets-37
95Score-77
Black Ice Artist's Proofs-77
Black Ice-77
95Select Certified-92
Mirror Gold-92
95SkyBox Impact-93
95SP-78
95Stadium Club-26
Members Only Master Set-26
95Summit-106
Artist's Proofs-106
Ice-106
95Topps-140
OPC Inserts-140
95Topps SuperSkills-62
Platinum-62
95Ultra-89
95Ultra-193
Gold Medallion-89
Gold Medallion-193
95Upper Deck-74
Electric Ice-74
Electric Ice Gold-74
Special Edition-SE134
Special Edition Gold-SE134
95Zenith-69
96Devils Team Issue-15
96Donruss-146
Press Proofs-146
96Leaf-195
Press Proofs-195
96NHL Pro Stamps-37
96Pinnacle-149
Artist's Proofs-149
Foil-149
Premium Stock-149
Rink Collection-149
96Score-143
Artist's Proofs-143
Dealer's Choice Artist's Proofs-143
Special Artist's Proofs-143
Golden Blades-143
96Summit-143
Artist's Proofs-143
Ice-143
Metal-143
Premium Stock-143
96Upper Deck-95
97Black Diamond-68
Double Diamond-68
Triple Diamond-68
Quadruple Diamond-68
97Collector's Choice-146
97Devils Team Issue-10
97Donruss-155
Press Proofs Silver-155
Press Proofs Gold-155
97Donruss Limited-60
Exposure-60
97Pacific-169
Copper-169
Emerald Green-169
Ice Blue-169
Red-169
Silver-169
97Pacific Dynagon-71
Copper-71
Dark Grey-71
Emerald Green-71
Ice Blue-71
Red-71
Silver-71
Tandems-48
97Pacific Omega-202
Copper-202
Dark Gray-202
Emerald Green-202
Gold-202
Ice Blue-202
97Panini Stickers-70
97Paramount-104
Copper-104
Dark Grey-104
Emerald Green-104
Ice Blue-104
Red-104
Silver-104
97Pinnacle-184
Press Plates Back Black-184
Press Plates Back Cyan-184
Press Plates Back Magenta-184
Press Plates Back Yellow-184
Press Plates Front Black-184
Press Plates Front Cyan-184
Press Plates Front Magenta-184
Press Plates Front Yellow-184
97Pinnacle Certified-91
Red-91
Mirror Blue-91
Mirror Gold-91
Mirror Red-91
97Pinnacle Inside-145
97Pinnacle Tot Cert Platinum Blue-91
97Pinnacle Tot Certi Platinum Gold-91
97Pinnacle Totally Certified Platinum Red-91
97Pinnacle Tot Cert Mirror Platinum Gold-91
97Revolution-124
Copper-124
Emerald-124
Ice Blue-124
Silver-124
97Score-141
Artist's Proofs-141
Golden Blades-141
97Score Devils-4
Platinum-4
Premier-4
97Upper Deck-94
98Pacific-384
Ice Blue-384
Red-384
98Panini Stickers-212
98UD Choice-176
Prime Choice Reserve-176
Reserve-176
98Upper Deck-320
Exclusives-320
Exclusives 1 of 1-320
Gold Reserve-320
99Aurora-95
Premiere Date-95
99BAP Memorabilia-295
Gold-295
Silver-295
99BAP Millennium-162
Emerald-162
Ruby-162
Sapphire-162
Signatures-162
Signatures Gold-162
99O-Pee-Chee-81
99O-Pee-Chee Chrome-81
99O-Pee-Chee Chrome Refractors-81
99Pacific-273
Copper-273
Emerald Green-273
Gold-273
Ice Blue-273
Premiere Date-273
Red-273
99Panini Stickers-106
99Paramount-153
Copper-153
Emerald-153
Gold-153
Holographic Emerald-153
Holographic Gold-153
Holographic Silver-153
Ice Blue-153
Premiere Date-153
Red-153
Silver-153
99Revolution-98
Premiere Date-98
Red-98
Shadow Series-98
99Stadium Club-127
First Day Issue-127
One of a Kind-127
Printing Plates Black-127
Printing Plates Cyan-127
Printing Plates Magenta-127
Printing Plates Yellow-127
99Topps/OPC-81
99Topps/OPC Chrome-81
Refractors-81
99Upper Deck MVP-137
Gold Script-137
Silver Script-137
Super Script-137
00Pacific-266
Copper-266
Gold-266
Ice Blue-266
Premiere Date-266
00Manitoba Moose-16
02BAP Sig Series Auto Buybacks 1999-162
02Devils Team Issue-28
03Devils Team Issue-44
04ITG Franchises US East-362
Autographs-A-JMA
05Devils Team Issue-3
06Devils Team Set-31

MacLean, Paul
81Jets Postcards-12
81Swedish Semic Hockey VM Stickers-86
82Jets Postcards-15
82O-Pee-Chee-386
82O-Pee-Chee Stickers-208
82Post Cereal-21
82Topps Stickers-208
83Jets Postcards-14
83NHL Key Tags-137
83O-Pee-Chee-388
83O-Pee-Chee Stickers-283
83Puffy Stickers-6
83Topps Stickers-283
83Vachon-131
84Jets Police-13
84Kellogg's Accordion Discs-2
84O-Pee-Chee-342
84O-Pee-Chee-371
84O-Pee-Chee Stickers-289
847-Eleven Discs-59
85Jets Police-10
85Jets Silverwood Dairy-5
85O-Pee-Chee-145
85O-Pee-Chee Stickers-250
857-Eleven Credit Cards-21
85Topps-145
86Jets Postcards-12
86Kraft Drawings-38
86O-Pee-Chee-114
86O-Pee-Chee Stickers-108
86Topps-114
87Jets Postcards-12
87O-Pee-Chee-91
87O-Pee-Chee Stickers-252
87Panini Stickers-364
87Topps-91
88O-Pee-Chee-38
88O-Pee-Chee Minis-23
88O-Pee-Chee Stickers-144
88Panini Stickers-156
88Red Wings Little Caesars-14
88Topps-38
89Blues Kodak-15
89O-Pee-Chee-129
89O-Pee-Chee Stickers-18
89Topps-129
90Blues Kodak-13
90Bowman-18
Tiffany-18
90O-Pee-Chee-110
90Panini Stickers-271
90Pro Set-266
90Score-203
Canadian-203
90Topps-110
Tiffany-110
90Upper Deck-330
French-330
93Peoria Rivermen-18
96Coyotes Coca-Cola-34
98Kansas City Blades-25
99Kansas City Blades Supercuts-27
00Quad-City Mallards-25
01Quad-City Mallards-14
04ITG Franchises Canadian-150
Autographs-PML

MacLean, Paul (juniors)
87Brockville Braves-6
88Brockville Braves-9

Maclean, Ron
97Pinnacle Hockey Night in Canada-7
06Parkhurst-1

MacLean, Terry
88ProCards IHL-86
89ProCards IHL-10
92Tulsa Oilers-9

MacLeish, Dale
75Roanoke Valley Rebels-12

MacLeish, Rick
71O-Pee-Chee-207
71Toronto Sun-203
72O-Pee-Chee-105
72Sargent Promotions Stamps-167
73Flyers Linnett-11
73O-Pee-Chee-133
73O-Pee-Chee-138
73O-Pee-Chee-146
73Topps-1
73Topps-6
73Topps-135
74Lipton Soup-20
74NHL Action Stamps-210
74O-Pee-Chee NHL-6
74O-Pee-Chee NHL-163
74Topps-6
74Topps-163
75Flyers Canada Dry Cans-13
75Heroes Stand-Ups-23
75O-Pee-Chee NHL-20
75Topps-20
76O-Pee-Chee NHL-121
76Topps-121
77O-Pee-Chee NHL-7
77O-Pee-Chee NHL-15
77Topps-7
77Topps-15
77Topps/O-Pee-Chee Glossy-9
Square-9
78O-Pee-Chee-125
78Topps-125
79O-Pee-Chee-75
79Topps-75
80O-Pee-Chee-115
80Topps-115
81O-Pee-Chee-133
81Topps-E108
82O-Pee-Chee-273
82O-Pee-Chee Stickers-147
82Topps Stickers-147
92Parkhurst-472
Emerald Ice-472
01Greats of the Game-47
Autographs-47
01Topps Archives-36
02Topps Stanley Cup Heroes-RM
02Topps Stanley Cup Heroes Autographs-RM
04ITG Franchises Update-470
Memorabilia-USM6
Memorabilia Gold-USM6
04ITG Franchises US East-433
Autographs-A-RM
04ITG Ultimate Mem Broad St Bullie Jersey-5
04ITG Ult Mem Broad St Bullie Jersey Auto-5
04ITG Ultimate Mem Broad St Bullie Emblem-5
04ITG Ult Mem Broad St Bullie Emblem Auto-5
04ITG Ultimate Mem Broad St Bullie Number-5
04ITG Ult Mem Broad St Bullie Number Auto-5

Maclellan, Brent
99Rimouski Oceanic-6
Signed-6
00Rimouski Oceanic-8
Signed-8
00UD CHL Prospects-81
01Rimouski Oceanic-8
01UD Prospects-33
Jerseys-J-BM
Jerseys Gold-J-BM
03P.E.I. Rocket-16

MacLellan, Brian
84Kings Smokey-11
84O-Pee-Chee-87
85O-Pee-Chee-204
86North Stars 7-Eleven-2
86North Stars Postcards-18
86O-Pee-Chee-33
86Topps-33
87North Stars Postcards-19
87O-Pee-Chee-31
87Panini Stickers-294
87Topps-31
88North Stars ADA-16
88O-Pee-Chee-193
88O-Pee-Chee Stickers-197
88Panini Stickers-95
88Topps-193
89O-Pee-Chee-208
90Flames IGA/McGavin's-10
90O-Pee-Chee-286
90Pro Set-36
90Score Rookie/Traded-56T
90Topps-286
Tiffany-286
90Upper Deck-372
French-372
91Bowman-269
91Flames Panini Team Stickers-8
91O-Pee-Chee-50
91Score Canadian Bilingual-582
91Score Canadian English-582
91Score Rookie/Traded-32T
91Stadium Club-206
91Topps-50

Maclellan, Jevin
05Saint John's Sea Dogs-11

MacLellan, Scott
81Kingston Canadians-2
82Kingston Canadians-21
91Rayside-Balfour Jr. Canadians-10

MacLellan, Todd
86Saskatoon Blades Photos-17

MacLeod, Alex
04Penticton Vees-15
05Penticton Vees-10
06Penticton Vees-14

MacLeod, Carla
04Wisconsin Badgers Women-13
06ITG Going For Gold-5
06ITG Going For Gold Samples-5
06ITG Going For Gold Autographs-AM
06ITG Going For Gold Jerseys-GUJ5

MacLeod, Daniel
00QMJHL All-Star Program Inserts-28

MacLeod, Jeff
94Tampa Bay Tritons RHI-15
98German DEL-53
99German DEL-175
01German Upper Deck-130
03German DEL-159

MacLeod, Jeffrey John
02German DEL City Press-179

MacLeod, Pat
87Kamloops Blazers-12
88Kamloops Blazers-17
89ProCards IHL-90
90ProCards AHL/IHL-108
91OPC Premier-87
91Parkhurst-161
French-161
91Pro Set-559
French-559
91Score Canadian Bilingual-645
91Score Canadian English-645
91Score Rookie/Traded-95T
91Sharks Sports Action-14
91Upper Deck-578
French-578
91ProCards-525
92Bowman-433
92O-Pee-Chee-273
92Stadium Club-336
92Topps-317
Gold-317G
92Upper Deck-146
94Milwaukee Admirals-16
97Cincinnati Cyclones-13
98Cincinnati Cyclones-13
98Cincinnati Cyclones 2-16

MacIsaac, Dave
05Danbury Trashers-12

MacMillan, Bill
69Maple Leafs White Border Matte-3
70Esso Power Players-33
70Sargent Promotions Stamps-205
71Maple Leafs Postcards-10
71Sargent Promotions Stamps-198
71Toronto Sun-263
72Flames Postcards-7
72O-Pee-Chee-98
72Sargent Promotions Stamps-5
72Topps-77
74NHL Action Stamps-170
74O-Pee-Chee NHL-339
76O-Pee-Chee NHL-312
81Rockies Postcards-14

MacMillan, Bob
72Minnesota Fighting Saints Postcards WHA-13
76O-Pee-Chee NHL-38
76Topps-38
77O-Pee-Chee NHL-141
77Topps-141
78Flames Majik Market-11
78O-Pee-Chee-82
78Topps-82
79Panini Stickers-66
79Flames Postcards-8
79Flames Team Issue-9
79O-Pee-Chee-210
79Topps-210
80Flames Postcards-10
80O-Pee-Chee-267
80Pepsi-Cola Caps-8
81O-Pee-Chee-46
81Rockies Postcards-15
82O-Pee-Chee-143
82O-Pee-Chee Stickers-225
82Post Cereal-11
82Topps Stickers-225
83Devils Postcards-19
83NHL Key Tags-74
83O-Pee-Chee-234
83O-Pee-Chee Stickers-220
83Puffy Stickers-11
83Topps Stickers-220
84O-Pee-Chee-40
84O-Pee-Chee Stickers-72
85O-Pee-Chee-193
04ITG Franchises US East-302
Autographs-A-BMM
04ITG Franchises US West-191

MacMillan, Brad
04Missouri River Otters-27
05Missouri River Otters-19

MacMillan, Darren
91Air Canada SJHL-E38
03St. Francis Xavier X-Men-15

Macmillan, Garry
66Columbus Checkers-12

MacMillan, Jason
95Slapshot-315

MacMillan, Jeff
99Michigan K-Wings-7
00Utah Grizzlies-5
01Utah Grizzlies-22
02Utah Grizzlies-21
03ITG VIP Rookie Debut-77
03Pacific Complete-519
Red-519
03Parkhurst Rookie-69
03Stars Postcards-13
03Upper Deck Rookie Update-117
04Hartford Wolf Pack-16
05Syracuse Crunch-14

MacMillan, John
44Beehive Group II Photos-423
61Shirriff/Salada Coins-56
62Shirriff Coins-14
63Chex Photos-38
63Parkhurst-15

MacMillan, Logan
05Halifax Mooseheads-14
06Halifax Mooseheads-9

MacMillan, Malcolm
01Guelph Storm-8
01Guelph Storm Memorial Cup-8
02Guelph Storm-24
03Peoria Rivermen-16
05Reading Royals-9
06Reading Royals-6

MacMillan, Tavis
95Signature Rookies Auto-Phonex-27
95Signature Rook Auto-Phonex Phone Cards-27

MacMillan, Todd
91Air Canada SJHL-E15

MacMillan, Travis
95Alaska Gold Kings-13

MacMurchy, Ryan
03Wisconsin Badgers-21
04Wisconsin Badgers-18
05Wisconsin Badgers-19
06Peoria Rivermen-11

MacNab, Brent
56Quebec Aces-10

MacNair, Scott
94Raleigh Icecaps-11

MacNamara, Jerry
52Juniors Blue Tint-153

MacNeil, Al
44Beehive Group II Photos-118A
44Beehive Group II Photos-118B
44Beehive Group II Photos-263
44Beehive Group II Photos-424
57Parkhurst-T19
61Shirriff/Salada Coins-119
61York Yellow Backs-36
62Shirriff Coins-40
62Topps-32
63Topps-28
64Beehive Group III Photos-45
64Beehive Group III Photos-139
64Coca-Cola Caps-33
64Topps-26
64Toronto Star-28
65Coca-Cola-33
65Topps-57
66Topps-89
69Canadiens Postcards Color-16
76Nova Scotia Voyageurs-12
77Nova Scotia Voyageurs-14
79Flames Team Issue-10
94Parkhurst Missing Link-121
94Parkhurst Tall Boys-40
95Parkhurst '66-67-94
Coins-94

MacNeil, Bernie
75Stingers Kahn's-8

MacNeil, Ian
95Slapshot-247
98New Haven Beast-2
00Cincinnati Cyclones-10
02BAP Memorabilia-396
02BAP Ultimate Memorabilia-85
02SP Authentic-179
02UD Artistic Impressions-102
Gold-102
02UD Honor Roll-135
02UD Mask Collection-136
02Philadelphia Phantoms-15
03Philadelphia Phantoms-8

MacNeil, Nick
06Cape Breton Screaming Eagles-21

MacNevin, Josh
00Charlotte Checkers-14

MacNevin, Troy
84Kingston Canadians-29
85Kingston Canadians-29
86Kingston Canadians-15

Macoun, Jamie
83Vachon-12
84O-Pee-Chee-230
85Flames Red Rooster-17
85O-Pee-Chee-201
85O-Pee-Chee Stickers-212
86Flames Red Rooster-12
86O-Pee-Chee-203
86O-Pee-Chee Stickers-85
87O-Pee-Chee-214
87O-Pee-Chee Stickers-48
87Panini Stickers-208
88Flames Postcards-4
89O-Pee-Chee-207
89Panini Stickers-38
90Flames IGA/McGavin's-11
90O-Pee-Chee-265
90Panini Stickers-178
90Pro Set-37
90Score-216
Canadian-216
90Topps-265
Tiffany-265
90Upper Deck-101
French-101
91Pro Set Platinum-235
91Flames Panini Team Stickers-9
91Flames IGA-8
91O-Pee-Chee-168
91Panini Stickers-61
91Pinnacle-114
French-114
91Pro Set-38
French-38
91Score American-284
91Score Canadian Bilingual-504
91Score Canadian English-504
91Stadium Club-160
91Topps-168
91Upper Deck-412
French-412
92Bowman-9
92Maple Leafs Kodak-14
92O-Pee-Chee-371
92Pinnacle-294
French-294
92Pro Set-188
92Score-88
Canadian-88
92Stadium Club-309
92Topps-348
Gold-348G
92Ultra-212
93Maple Leafs Score Black's-11
93OPC Premier-517
Gold-517
93Panini Stickers-230
93Pinnacle-131
Canadian-131
93PowerPlay-451
93Score-224
Canadian-224
93Topps/OPC Premier-517
Gold-517
93Ultra-431
94Canada Games NHL POGS-240
94Leaf-418
94Maple Leafs Gangsters-11
94Maple Leafs Kodak-18
94Maple Leafs Pin-up Posters-10
94Maple Leafs Postcards-1
94OPC Premier-102
Special Effects-102
94Parkhurst SE-SE179
Gold-SE179
94Pinnacle-297
Artist's Proofs-297
Rink Collection-297
94Score-106
Gold-106
Platinum-106
94Topps/OPC Premier-102
Special Effects-102
94Ultra-217
95Be A Player-218
Signatures-S218
Signatures Die Cuts-S218
95Upper Deck-331
Electric Ice-331
Electric Ice Gold-331
96Upper Deck-166
97Pacific-231
Copper-231
Emerald Green-231
Ice Blue-231
Red-231
Silver-231
04ITG Franchises Canadian-5
Autographs-JMC

Macphee, Kris
93Quebec Pee-Wee Tournament-1225

Macphee, Wayne
83North Bay Centennials-18
94Brantford Smoke-13

MacPherson, Alex
93Quebec Pee-Wee Tournament-1216

MacPherson, B.J.
907th Inn. Sketch OHL-343
91Oshawa Generals-16
91Oshawa Generals Sheet-5
917th Inn. Sketch OHL-158
92Oshawa Generals Sheet-13
93North Bay Centennials-13
94Anaheim Bullfrogs RHI-11
94Toledo Storm-13
95Anaheim Bullfrogs RHI-11
95Toledo Storm-9
96Anaheim Bullfrogs RHI-9
99San Diego Gulls-8
00San Diego Gulls-9

MacPherson, Blair
85Kitchener Rangers-26

MacPherson, Bud
44Beehive Group II Photos-264
51Parkhurst-6
52Parkhurst-11
53Parkhurst-22
55Parkhurst-47
Quaker Oats-47
02Parkhurst Reprints-178

MacPherson, Donald
907th Inn. Sketch OHL-87

MacPherson, Duncan
83Saskatoon Blades-4
84Saskatoon Blades Stickers-12
88ProCards AHL-307

MacPherson, Forbes
97Mississippi Sea Wolves-22
01Bossier-Shreveport Mudbugs-12
02Bossier-Shreveport Mudbugs-12
03Bossier-Shreveport Mudbugs-11

MacPherson, James
45Quaker Oats Photos-94

Macpherson, Ryan
00Halifax Mooseheads-17

Macpherson, Scott
98Cincinnati Cyclones-26
98Cincinnati Cyclones 2-26

MacQueen, Dave
04Erie Otters-23

MacQuisten, Doug
37V356 Worldwide Gum-105

MacRae, Jim
81Fredericton Express-25
82Fredericton Express-25

MacRae, Myles
05Kelowna Rockets-18

MacRae, Stuart
01Cape Breton Screaming Eagles-5
03St. Francis Xavier X-Men-3
04St. Francis Xavier X-Men-13

Macri, Vincent
04Atlantic City Boardwalk Bullies-21

MacSwain, Steve
96Anchorage Aces-5
97Anchorage Aces-13
98Anchorage Aces-20
99Anchorage Aces-4

MacSween, Brent
04Chicoutimi Sagueneens-5
05Chicoutimi Sagueneens-19

MacSweyn, Kurt
99Brampton Battalion-19
00Brampton Battalion-17
05Idaho Steelheads-14

MacSweyn, Ralph
73Vancouver Blazers-14

MacTavish, Craig
85Oilers Red Rooster-14
86Oilers Red Rooster-14
86Oilers Team Issue-14
86O-Pee-Chee-178
86O-Pee-Chee Stickers-76
86Topps-178
87Oilers Team Issue-14
87O-Pee-Chee-203
87O-Pee-Chee Stickers-91
87Panini Stickers-267
88Oilers Tenth Anniversary-21
88Oilers Team Issue-19
88O-Pee-Chee-232
88O-Pee-Chee Stickers-217
88Panini Stickers-60
89Oilers Team Issue-16
89O-Pee-Chee-230
89O-Pee-Chee Stickers-226
89Panini Stickers-78
90Bowman-193
Tiffany-193
90Oilers IGA-15
90O-Pee-Chee-189
90Panini Stickers-220
90Pro Set-90
90Score-258
Canadian-258
90Topps-189
Tiffany-189
90Upper Deck-169
French-169
91Bowman-100
91Oilers Panini Team Stickers-13
91Oilers IGA-11
91Oilers Team Issue-13
91O-Pee-Chee-63
91Panini Stickers-132
91Parkhurst-276
French-276
91Pinnacle-215
French-215
91Pro Set-77
French-77
91Score American-202
91Score Canadian Bilingual-202
91Score Canadian English-202
91Stadium Club-133
91Topps-63
91Upper Deck-284
French-284
92Bowman-118
92Oilers IGA-12
92Oilers Team Issue-11
92O-Pee-Chee-118
92Panini Stickers-101
92Panini Stickers French-101
92Parkhurst-48
Emerald Ice-48
92Pinnacle-78
French-78
92Score-303
Canadian-303
92Stadium Club-125
92Topps-336
Gold-336G
92Ultra-294
92Upper Deck-425
93Donruss-462
93Kraft-48
93OPC Premier-23
Gold-23
93Panini Stickers-240
93Parkhurst-342
Emerald Ice-342
93Pinnacle-96
Canadian-96
Captains-8
Captains Canadian-8
93PowerPlay-82
93Score-8
Canadian-8
93Stadium Club-410
Members Only Master Set-410
First Day Issue-410
93Topps/OPC Premier-23
Gold-23
93Ultra-316
93Upper Deck-111
94Be A Player Signature Cards-72
94Finest Ring Leaders-8
94Leaf-514
94OPC Premier-103
Special Effects-103
94Parkhurst-145
Gold-145
94Parkhurst SE-SE132
Gold-SE132
94Pinnacle-392
Artist's Proofs-392
Rink Collection-392
94Score-85
Gold-85
Platinum-85
94Topps/OPC Premier-103
Special Effects-103
94Upper Deck-225
Electric Ice-225
95Pinnacle-148
Artist's Proofs-148
Rink Collection-148
95Score-249
Black Ice Artist's Proofs-249
Black Ice-249
96Collector's Choice-227
96Donruss-103
Press Proofs-103
96Leaf-192
Press Proofs-192
96Score-230
Artist's Proofs-230
Dealer's Choice Artist's Proofs-230
Special Artist's Proofs-230
Golden Blades-230
96Stadium Club Members Only-23
06Parkhurst-155
06Parkhurst-183
Autographs-155
Autographs-183
Autographs Dual-DAGC
06The Cup Stanley Cup Signatures-CSCM

MacVicar, Andy
89Sudbury Wolves-18

MacWilliams, Mike
88Flint Spirits-14
91ProCards-348

Macy, Erik
95North Iowa Huskies-19

Macy, Lindsay
04Wisconsin Badgers Women-14

Madach, Peter
92Norwegian Elite Series-23

Madden, Chris
93Quebec Pee-Wee Tournament-673
96Guelph Storm-21
97Guelph Storm-4
98Guelph Storm-3
99Guelph Storm-3
99Bowman CHL-162
Gold-162
OPC International-162
00Hamilton Bulldogs-1
01Macon Whoopee-12
02Milwaukee Admirals-2
02Milwaukee Admirals Postcards-11
05ITG Heroes/Prosp Toronto Expo Parallel -202
05ITG Heroes and Prospects-202
Autographs Series II-CMD

Madden, John
93Michigan Wolverines-15
97Albany River Rats-9
98Devils Team Issue-16
98Albany River Rats-11
99BAP Memorabilia-150
Gold-150
Silver-150
99Devils Team Issue-7
99O-Pee-Chee Chrome-294
99O-Pee-Chee Chrome Refractors-294
99Pacific-239
Copper-239
Emerald Green-239
Gold-239
Ice Blue-239
Premiere Date-239
Red-239
99Pacific Omega-139
Copper-139
Gold-139
Ice Blue-139
Premiere Date-139
99Paramount-134
Copper-134
Emerald-134
Gold-134

Holographic Emerald-134
Holographic Gold-134
Holographic Silver-134
Ice Blue-134
Premiere Date-134
Red-134
Silver-134
99SP Authentic-107
99Topps/OPC Chrome-294
Refractors-294
99Topps Premier Plus-104
Parallel-104
99Upper Deck-81
Exclusives-81
Exclusives 1 of 1-81
99Upper Deck Gold Reserve-81
99Upper Deck MVP-122
Gold Script-122
Silver Script-122
Super Script-122
99Upper Deck Retro-47
Gold-47
Platinum-47
99Upper Deck Victory-167
00Aurora-84
Premiere Date-84
00BAP Memorabilia-103
Emerald-103
Ruby-103
Sapphire-103
Promos-103
00BAP Mem Chicago Sportsfest Copper-103
00BAP Memorabilia Chicago Sportsfest Blue-103
00BAP Memorabilia Chicago Sportsfest Gold-103
00BAP Memorabilia Chicago Sportsfest Ruby-103
00BAP Memorabilia Chicago Sun-Times Ruby-103
00BAP Memorabilia Chicago Sun-Times Gold-103
00BAP Mem Chicago Sun-Times Sapphire-103
00BAP Mem Toronto Fall Expo Copper-103
00BAP Memorabilia Toronto Fall Expo Gold-103
00BAP Memorabilia Toronto Fall Expo Ruby-103
00BAP Parkhurst 2000-P4
00BAP Signature Series-243
Emerald-243
Ruby-243
Sapphire-243
Autographs-177
Autographs Gold-177
00Devils Team Issue-11
00O-Pee-Chee-215
00O-Pee-Chee Parallel-215
00Pacific-237
Copper-237
Gold-237
Ice Blue-237
Premiere Date-237
00Paramount-145
Copper-145
Gold-145
Holo-Gold-145
Holo-Silver-145
Ice Blue-145
Premiere Date-145
00Stadium Club-67
00Topps/OPC-215
Parallel-215
00Topps Chrome-138
OPC Refractors-138
Refractors-138
00Topps Heritage-234
00Upper Deck-105
Exclusives Tier 1-105
Exclusives Tier 2-105
00Upper Deck MVP-105
First Stars-105
Second Stars-105
Third Stars-105
00Upper Deck Victory-136
00Upper Deck Vintage-216
01BAP Memorabilia-143
Emerald-143
Ruby-143
Sapphire-143
01Devils Team Issue-12
01O-Pee-Chee-237
01O-Pee-Chee-321
01O-Pee-Chee Premier Parallel-237
01O-Pee-Chee Premier Parallel-321
01Pacific-232
Extreme LTD-232
Hobby LTD-232
Premiere Date-232
Retail LTD-232
01Pacific Adrenaline-115
Blue-115
Premiere Date-115
Red-115
Retail-115
01Pacific Arena Exclusives-232
01Parkhurst-23
Gold-23
Silver-23
01Topps-237
01Topps-321
OPC Parallel-237
OPC Parallel-321
01Topps Chrome-137
Refractors-137
Black Border Refractors-137
01Topps Heritage-136
01UD Honor Roll Defense First-DF5
01UD Stanley Cup Champs-79
01Upper Deck-107
Exclusives-107
01Upper Deck Victory-216
Gold-216
02BAP Sig Series Auto Buybacks 2000-177
02Bowman YoungStars-78
Gold-78
Silver-78
02Devils Team Issue-9
02Pacific-225
Blue-225
Red-225
02Pacific Complete-416
Red-416
02Titanium-64
Blue-64
Red-64
Retail-64
02Topps Total-339
02Upper Deck-351
Exclusives-351
02Upper Deck Beckett UD Promos-351
02Upper Deck MVP-107
Gold-107
Classics-107
Golden Classics-107
02Upper Deck Rookie Update-58
02Upper Deck Vintage-150
03BAP Memorabilia Stanley Cup Champions-SCC-5
03BAP Memorabilia Stanley Cup Playoffs-SCP-28
03Beehive-113
Gold-113
Silver-113
03Devils Team Issue-11
03ITG Action-323
Jerseys-M50
03O-Pee-Chee-86
03OPC Blue-86
03OPC Gold-86
03OPC Red-86
03Pacific-202
Blue-202
Red-202
03Pacific Complete-185
Red-185
03Pacific Exhibit-88
Blue Backs-88
Yellow Backs-88
03Pacific Prism-63
Blue-63
Gold-63
Red-63
03Pacific Supreme-59
Blue-59
Red-59
Retail-59
03Topps-86
Blue-86
Gold-86
Red-86
03Topps C55-12
Minis-12
Minis American Back-12
Minis American Back Red-12
Minis Bazooka Back-12
Minis Brooklyn Back-12
Minis Hat Trick Back-12
Minis O Canada Back-12
Minis O Canada Back Red-12
Minis Stanley Cup Back-12
03Upper Deck-357
Canadian Exclusives-357
HG-357
UD Exclusives-357
03Upper Deck MVP-252
Gold Script-252
Silver Script-252
Canadian Exclusives-252
03Upper Deck Victory-111
Bronze-111
Gold-111
Silver-111
03Bossier-Shreveport Mudbugs-20
04Pacific-160
Blue-160
Red-160
05Devils Team Issue-23
05Panini Stickers-89
05Parkhurst-292
Facsimile Auto Parallel-292
05Ultra-121
Gold-121
Ice-121
05Upper Deck-115
HG Glossy-115
05Upper Deck MVP-232
Gold-232
Platinum-232
05Upper Deck Toronto Fall Expo-115
06Devils Team Set-14
06O-Pee-Chee-294
Rainbow-294
06Panini Stickers-83
06Upper Deck-119
Exclusives Parallel-119
High Gloss Parallel-119
Masterpieces-119
06Upper Deck MVP-173
Gold Script-173
Super Script-173

Madder, Tucker
97OCN Blizzard-2

Madeley, Darrin
91Lake Superior State Lakers-15
92Lake Superior State Lakers-16
92Classic-65
Gold-65
92Classic Four-Sport *-193
Gold-193
93Donruss-229
93Leaf-299
93OPC Premier-283
Gold-283
93Parkhurst-142
Emerald Ice-142
93Pinnacle-211
Canadian-211
93PowerPlay-400
93Score-462
Canadian-462
93Senators Kraft Sheets-16
93Stadium Club-431
Members Only Master Set-431
First Day Issue-431
93Topps/OPC Premier-283
Gold-283
93Ultra-382
93Upper Deck-61
93Classic Pro Prospects-17
93Classic Pro Prospects-40
93Classic Four-Sport *-239
Gold-239
94Leaf-300
94OPC Premier-109
Special Effects-109
94Parkhurst SE-SE120
Gold-SE120
94Pinnacle-459
Artist's Proofs-459
Rink Collection-459
94Score-51
Gold-51
Platinum-51
94Senators Team Issue-19
94Topps/OPC Premier-109
Special Effects-109
94Ultra-340
95Upper Deck-158
Electric Ice-158
Electric Ice Gold-158
95PEI Senators-13

Mader, Bob
52Juniors Blue Tint-87

Mader, Mike
98Roanoke Express-18
00Rochester Americans-14

Mader, Patrick
01Swiss HNL-447
02Swiss HNL-429

Mader, Trevor
93Quebec Pee-Wee Tournament-1433

Madia, Rob
94Central Hockey League-14
94Dallas Freeze-14

Madill, Jeff
88ProCards AHL-335
89ProCards AHL-204
90ProCards AHL/IHL-571
91O-Pee-Chee Inserts-6S
91Kansas City Blades-8
91ProCards-521
92Cincinnati Cyclones-15
93Atlanta Knights-8
96Kansas City Blades-14
96Collector's Edge Ice-191
Prism-191

Madison, Steve
93Quebec Pee-Wee Tournament-85

Madl, Michal
98Czech OFS-166
99Czech DS-157
99Czech OFS-169
00Czech DS Extraliga-136
00Czech OFS-113
01Czech OFS-191
02Czech OFS Plus-286

Madore, Stephane
917th Inn. Sketch QMJHL-151
96Louisville Riverfrogs-16
97Louisville Riverfrogs-15
98Quad-City Mallards-16
99Colorado Gold Kings Taco Bell-7
99Colorado Gold Kings Wendy's-12

Madsen, Carter
06Okotoks Oilers -12

Madsen, Henrik B.
99Danish Hockey League-111

Madsen, Jesper
98Danish Hockey League-19
99Danish Hockey League-19

Madsen, Kenneth
98Danish Hockey League-129

Madsen, Michael
99Danish Hockey League-67
07Upper Deck Spectrum Spectrum of Stars Signatures-MM-1

Madsen, Morten
06Victoriaville Tigres-1

Madsen, Rene B.
98Danish Hockey League-94
99Danish Hockey League-127

Madsen, Tim
02Tri-City Stormfront-7

Madsen, Tom
83Pinebridge Bucks-8

Maenpaa, Mikko
06Finnish Cardset-212

Maetche, Scott
06Chilliwack Bruins-8

Magarrell, Adam
93Brandon Wheat Kings-8
94Brandon Wheat Kings-13
95Spokane Chiefs-22
95Signature Rookies-53
Signatures-53
96Spokane Chiefs-19

Magdosko, Jan
04UK Nottingham Panthers-11

Mageau, Fernand
43Parade Sportive *-76

Magers, Marty
02Owen Sound Attack-25

Maggs, Darryl
71Toronto Sun-71

Magill, Murray
04Lakehead University Thunderwolves-5

Magliarditi, Marc
95Donruss Elite World Juniors-24
96Spokane Chiefs-23
98Florida Everblades-13
99ECHL All-Star Southern Conference-15
99Florida Everblades-15
00Cincinnati Cyclones-22
00Florida Everblades-17
01Louisiana Ice Gators-13
03Las Vegas Wranglers-11
03Las Vegas Wranglers RBI-233
04Las Vegas Wranglers-12
05Las Vegas Wranglers-12
06Las Vegas Wranglers-11

Magnertoft, Marcus
93Swedish Semic Elitserien-181
94Swedish Leaf-237
95Swedish Leaf-89
95Swedish Upper Deck-143
98Swedish UD Choice-157
99Swedish Upper Deck-160
02Swedish Malmo Red Hawks-6
02Swedish SHL-75
Parallel-75
03Swedish Elite-243
Silver-243
04Swedish Elitset-88
Gold-88
04Swedish Malmo Red Hawks-5

Magneson, Brady
97Prince Albert Raiders-13

Magnowski, Mark
04Green Bay Gamblers-10
05Sioux Falls Stampede-2

Magnuson, Josh
00Lincoln Stars-12

Magnuson, Keith
70Blackhawks Postcards-7
70Dad's Cookies-73
70Esso Power Players-111
70O-Pee-Chee-151
70Sargent Promotions Stamps-35
71O-Pee-Chee-69
71Sargent Promotions Stamps-48
71Topps-69
71Toronto Sun-72
72O-Pee-Chee-71
72O-Pee-Chee-268
72Sargent Promotions Stamps-57
72Topps-65
72Topps-87
72Finnish Semic World Championship-230
72Swedish Semic World Championship-230
73O-Pee-Chee-151
73Topps-44
74NHL Action Stamps-88
74O-Pee-Chee NHL-75
74Topps-75
75O-Pee-Chee NHL-176
75Topps-176
76O-Pee-Chee NHL-125
76Topps-125
77O-Pee-Chee NHL-89
77Topps-89
78O-Pee-Chee-34
78Topps-34
79Blackhawks Postcards-11
80Blackhawks Postcards-5
81Blackhawks Borderless Postcards-14
81Blackhawks Brown Background-5
94Arizona Icecats-22
94Arizona Icecats-23
01Topps Archives-54
02Fleer Throwbacks-26
Gold-26
Platinum-26
02Topps Rookie Reprints-9
02Topps Rookie Reprint Autographs-9
03Parkhurst Original Six Chicago-55
Autographs-11

Magnussen, Trond
92Swedish Semic Elitserien Stickers-312
93Swedish Semic World Champ Stickers-244
94Finnish Jaa Kiekko-265
95Swedish Globe World Championships-196
95Swedish World Championships Stickers-246
96Swedish Semic Wien-207
97Swedish Collector's Choice-62
98Swedish UD Choice-92
99Norwegian National Team-15
99Swedish Upper Deck-61
00Swedish Upper Deck-87
01German Upper Deck-53
02German DEL City Press-54
Top Scorers-TS9
03German Deg Metro Stars-12
03German DEL-36
All-Stars-AS20
04German DEL-52
04German Dusseldorf Metro Stars Postcards-14
05German DEL-47

Magnusson, Ingemar
67Swedish Hockey-89

Magnusson, Mikael
92Swedish Semic Elitserien Stickers-85
93Swedish Semic Elitserien-58
94Swedish Leaf-3
95Swedish Leaf-29
95Swedish Upper Deck-43
98Swedish UD Choice-55
99Swedish Upper Deck-40
00Swedish Upper Deck-48
02Swedish SHL-15
Parallel-15
04German DEL-111

Magnusson, Rune
55Swedish Alfabilder-15

Magnusson, Steve
91Swedish Semic Elitserien Stickers-106
91Minnesota Golden Gophers-13
92Minnesota Golden Gophers-11
93Minnesota Golden Gophers-17
94Central Hockey League-51
95Central Hockey League-29

Magnusson, Torsten
55Swedish Alfabilder-8

Mago, Miroslav
94German First League-473

Magowan, Ken
03Boston University Terriers-22
06Toledo Storm-16

Maguire, Bill
82North Bay Centennials-14

Maguire, Derek
92Harvard Crimson-20
94Fredericton Canadiens-19
94Classic-56
Gold-56

Maguire, Kevin
87Sabres Blue Shield-17
87Sabres Wonder Bread/Hostess-18
88Sabres Blue Shield-15
88Sabres Wonder Bread/Hostess-16
89Sabres Blue Shield-11
89Sabres Campbell's-13
90Maple Leafs Postcards-12
90Pro Set-538
91Bowman-172
91Maple Leafs Panini Team Stickers-13
91ProCards-347

Magura, Tyler
02Lincoln Stars-9
03Lincoln Stars-8
03Lincoln Stars Update-39

Mah, Colin
93Quebec Pee-Wee Tournament-174

Mahaffy, Johnny
37V356 Worldwide Gum-133
51Laval Dairy QSHL-55

Mahalik, Pavol
04UK Coventry Blaze Champions-6

Maher, Jeff
98Calgary Hitmen-25
98Calgary Hitmen Autographs-25
99Calgary Hitmen-16
99Calgary Hitmen Autographs-16
00Calgary Hitmen-18
01Calgary Hitmen-14
01Calgary Hitmen Autographed-14

Maher, Jeremy
93Quebec Pee-Wee Tournament-22

Maher, Jim
92Phoenix Roadrunners-14
93Phoenix Roadrunners-17
94Toledo Storm-14

Maher, Ryan
93Quebec Pee-Wee Tournament-690

Maheux, Chantale
93Quebec Pee-Wee Tournament-1104

Maheux, Nicolas
95Halifax Mooseheads-21

Maheux, Vincent
93Quebec Pee-Wee Tournament-406

Mahon, Brent
02Plymouth Whalers-15
03Plymouth Whalers-5

Mahon, Craig
06Port Huron Flags-2

Mahon, Dan
82Kingston Canadians-14

Mahon, Mark
94German First League-465
96German DEL-219
99German Bundesliga 2-153

Mahoney, Bill
83North Stars Postcards-15

Mahoney, Darren
93Quebec Pee-Wee Tournament-551

Mahoney, Scott
89Sudbury Wolves-5

Mahood, Harry
81Billings Bighorns-NNO

Mahovlich, Frank
44Beehive Group II Photos-425
57Parkhurst-T17
58Parkhurst-33
59Parkhurst-24
60Parkhurst-2
60Shirriff Coins-12
60York Photos-22
61Parkhurst-2
61Shirriff/Salada Coins-43
61York Yellow Backs-3
62Wheaties Great Moments in Cdn Sport-7
62El Producto Discs-5
62Parkhurst-4
62Parkhurst-18
62Shirriff Coins-3
62Shirriff Coins-53
62York Iron-On Transfers-11
63Chex Photos-35
63Maple Leafs Team Issue-14
63Maple Leafs Team Issue-15
63Parkhurst-17
63Parkhurst-77
63Toronto Star-25
63York White Backs-5
64Beehive Group III Photos-174A
64Beehive Group III Photos-174B
64Coca-Cola Caps-108
64Topps-85
64Toronto Star-29
65Coca-Cola-107
65Topps-81
66Maple Leafs Hockey Talks-4
66Topps-77
66Topps-131
66Topps USA Test-51
67Post Flip Books-5
67Topps-79
67York Action Octagons-18
67York Action Octagons-20
67York Action Octagons-28
67York Action Octagons-35
68O-Pee-Chee-31
Puck Stickers-2
68Shirriff Coins-45
68Topps-31
69Canadiens Postcards Color-17
69Maple Leafs White Border Glossy-21
69O-Pee-Chee-62
69O-Pee-Chee-222
Four-in-One-4
Stamps-19
69Topps-62
70Canadiens Pins-10
70Dad's Cookies-74
70Esso Power Players-143
70O-Pee-Chee-22
70O-Pee-Chee-242
Deckle-17
70Post Shooters-10
70Red Wings Marathon-7
70Sargent Promotions Stamps-63
70Topps-22
Topps/OPC Sticker Stamps-21
71Bazooka-2
71Canadiens Postcards-14
71Colgate Heads-6
71Frito-Lay-3
71Letraset Action Replays-8
71Mattel Mini-Records-6
71O-Pee-Chee-105
71Sargent Promotions Stamps-104
71Topps-105
71Toronto Sun-157
72Canadiens Postcards-13
72Dimanche/Derniere Heure *-156
72Dimanche/Derniere Heure *-157
72Kellogg's Iron-On Transfers-5
72O-Pee-Chee-102
72O-Pee-Chee-128
Team Canada-17
72Sargent Promotions Stamps-120
72Topps-140
72Finnish Semic World Championship-195
72Swedish Stickers-119
72Swedish Semic World Championship-195
73Canadiens Postcards-15
73Mac's Milk-15
73O-Pee-Chee-145
73Topps-40
74O-Pee-Chee NHL-124
74O-Pee-Chee WHA-40
74Team Canada L'Equipe WHA-15
74Topps-124
75O-Pee-Chee WHA-110
76O-Pee-Chee WHA-111
77O-Pee-Chee WHA-61
81TCMA-10
83Hall of Fame-121
83Hall of Fame Postcards-I10
85Hall of Fame-121
88Esso All-Stars-28
91Future Trends Canada '72-26
91Future Trends Canada '72-30
91Future Trends Canada '72 French-26
91Future Trends Canada '72 French-30
91Kraft-87
91Ultimate Original Six-40
French-40
91Star Pics-27
92Parkhurst Parkie Reprints-PR29
92Zeller's Masters of Hockey-4
92Zeller's Masters of Hockey Signed-4
93O-Pee-Chee Canadiens Hockey Fest-24
93O-Pee-Chee Canadiens Hockey Fest-39
93Parkhurst Parkie Reprints-PR44
93Upper Deck Locker All-Stars-44
94Hockey Wit-56
94Parkhurst Missing Link Autographs-6
94Parkhurst Missing Link Future Stars-FS5
94Parkhurst Tall Boys-130
94Parkhurst Tall Boys-143
Mail-Ins-SL6
95Parkhurst '66-67-102
95Parkhurst '66-67-145
Coins-102
99BAP Memorabilia AS Canadian Hobby-CH4
99BAP Memorabilia AS Cdn Hobby Autos-CH4
99Topps Stanley Cup Heroes-SC6
99Topps Stanley Cup Heroes Refractors-SC6
99Topps Stanley Cup Heroes Autographs-SCA6
99Upper Deck Century Legends-27
Century Collection-27
Epic Signatures-FM
Epic Signatures 100-FM
00UD Heroes-138
Signs of Greatness-FM
00Upper Deck 500 Goal Club-500FM
00Upper Deck 500 Goal Club-500FM
00Upper Deck Legends-120
00Upper Deck Legends-126
Legendary Collection Bronze-120
Legendary Collection Bronze-126
Legendary Collection Gold-120
Legendary Collection Gold-126
Legendary Collection Silver-120
Legendary Collection Silver-126
Enshrined Stars-ES10
Epic Signatures-FM
01BAP Memorabilia 500 Goal Scorers-GS19
01BAP Signature Series 500 Goal Scorers-4
01BAP Sig Series 500 Goal Scorers Autos-4
01BAP Signature Series Vintage Autographs-VA-27
01BAP Ultimate Mem All-Star History-25
01BAP Ultimate Memorabilia Autographs-27
01BAP Ultimate Mem Autographs Gold-27
01BAP Ultimate Memorabilia Bloodlines-4
01BAP Ultimate Memorabilia Emblem Attic-11
01BAP Ultimate Mem 500 Goal Scorers-11
01BAP Ultimate Mem 500 Goal Scorers Autos-6
01BAP Ultimate Mem 500 Goal Jerseys/Stick-11
01BAP Ultimate Mem 500 Goal Emblems-11
01BAP Ultimate Memorabilia Les Canadiens-13
01BAP Ultimate Mem Retro Teammates-9
01BAP Ultimate Mem Stanley Cup Winners-14
01Fleer Legacy-21
Ultimate-21
01Greats of the Game-55
Autographs-55
01Parkhurst Autographs-PA1
01Parkhurst Autographs-PA4
01Parkhurst 500 Goal Scorers-PGS19
01Parkhurst Reprints-PR8
01Parkhurst Reprints-PR38
01Parkhurst Reprints-PR48
01Parkhurst Reprints-PR64
01Parkhurst Reprints-PR86
01Parkhurst Reprints-PR101
01Parkhurst Reprints-PR124
01Parkhurst Reprints-PR134
01Parkhurst Reprints-PR146
01UD Stanley Cup Champs-26
01Upper Deck Legends-58
Epic Signatures-FM
Sticks-PHFM
02BAP Memorabilia Mini Stanley Cups-9
02BAP NHL All-Star History-25
02BAP Ultimate Memorabilia All-Star MVP-7
02BAP Ultimate Memorabilia Emblem Attic-5
02BAP Ultimate Memorabilia Numerology-27
02BAP Ultimate Mem Storied Franchise-18
02BAP Ultimate Mem Vintage Jerseys-13
02BAP Ultimate Mem Vintage Jersey Autos-9
02Maple Leafs Platinum Collection-58
02Maple Leafs Platinum Collection-77
Autographs-77
02Parkhurst Vintage Memorabilia-VM10
02Parkhurst Vintage Teammates-VT7
02Parkhurst Retro Nicknames-RN12
02UD Foundations Signs of Greatness-SGFM
03BAP Ultimate Memorabilia Autographs-160
Gold-160
03BAP Ultimate Memorabilia Cornerstones-4
03BAP Ultimate Memorabilia Emblem Attic-19
03BAP Ultimate Mem Emblem Attic Gold-19
03BAP Ultimate Mem Hometown Heroes-9
03BAP Ultimate Mem Hometown Heroes Gold-9
03BAP Ultimate Memorabilia Triple Threads-26
03BAP Ultimate Mem Vintage Jerseys-18
03BAP Ultimate Mem Vintage Jerseys Gold-18
03Canada Post-19
03ITG Used Signature Series-112
Gold-112
Autographs-FM
Autographs Gold-FM
03ITG VIP Vintage Memorabilia-19
03Pacific Exhibit-224
03Parkhurst Original Six Montreal-58
Autographs-10
03Parkhurst Original Six Toronto-51
03Parkhurst Original Six Toronto-86
03Parkhurst Original Six Toronto-98
Autographs-7
Inserts-T6
Memorabilia-TM33
03Czech Stadion-550
04ITG NHL AS FANtasy AS History Jerseys-SB25
04ITG Franchises Canadian-57
04ITG Franchises Canadian-89
Autographs-FM2
Autographs-FM3
Double Memorabilia-DM15
Double Memorabilia Autographs-DM15
Double Memorabilia Gold-DM15
Memorabilia-SM19
Memorabilia Autographs-SM19
Memorabilia Gold-SM19
04ITG Franchises He Shoots/Scores Prizes-13
04ITG Franchises US West-201
Autographs-A-FM1
04ITG Ultimate Memorabilia-136
04ITG Ultimate Memorabilia-148
04ITG Ultimate Memorabilia-190
Gold-136
Gold-148
Gold-190
Day In History-4
Day In History-42
Day In History Gold-4
Day In History Gold-42
Jersey Autographs-32
Jersey Autographs Gold-32
Nicknames-19
Nickname Autographs-9
Original Six-16
Stick Autographs-26
Stick Autographs Gold-26
Triple Threads-13
04SP Authentic Sign of the Times-ST-FM
04SP Authentic Sign of the Times-SS-ORG
04UD Legendary Signatures-35
AKA Autographs-AKA-FM
Autographs-FM
Summit Stars-CDN10
Summit Stars Autographs-CDN-FM
04UD Legends Classics-21
04UD Legends Classics-94
Gold-21
Gold-94
Platinum-21
Platinum-94
Silver-21
Silver-94
Jersey Redemptions-JY8
Signature Moments-M36
Signatures-CS35
Signatures-TC2
Signatures-QC3
04ITG Heroes and Prospects-124
Aspiring-8
Autographs-FM
Hero Memorabilia-20
04ITG Heroes/Prospects Toronto Expo '05-124
04ITG Heroes/Prospects Expo Heroes/Pros-124
05ITG Heroes/Prosp Toronto Expo Parallel -35
05ITG Ultimate Memorabilia Level 1-36
05ITG Ultimate Memorabilia Level 2-36
05ITG Ultimate Memorabilia Level 3-36
05ITG Ultimate Memorabilia Level 4-36
05ITG Ultimate Memorabilia Level 5-36
05ITG Ultimate Mem Complete Jersey-7
05ITG Ultimate Mem Complete Jersey Gold-7
05ITG Ultimate Mem Double Mem Autos-15
05ITG Ultimate Mem Double Mem Autos Gold-15
05ITG Ultimate Memorabilia Emblem Attic-1
05ITG Ultimate Mem Emblem Attic Gold-1
05ITG Ultimate Memorabilia Emblems-9
05ITG Ultimate Memorabilia Emblems Gold-9
05ITG Ultimate Memorabilia In The Numbers-4
05ITG Ultimate Mem In The Numbers Gold-4
05ITG Ultimate Mem Jersey and Emblem-21
05ITG Ultimate Memorabilia Jersey Autos-19
05ITG Ultimate Mem Jersey Autos Gold-19
05ITG Ultimate Mem Jersey Emblems Gold-21
05ITG Ultimate Memorabilia Jerseys-14
05ITG Ultimate Memorabilia Jerseys Gold-14
05ITG Ultimate Mem Retro Teammate Jerseys-10
05ITG Ultimate Mem Retro Teammate Jerseys-12
05ITG Ult Mem Retro Teammates Jersey Gold-10
05ITG Ult Mem Retro Teammates Jersey Gold-12
05ITG Ultimate Mem Seams Unbelievable-17
05ITG Ultimate Mem Seam Unbelievable Gold-17
05ITG Ultimate Memorabilia Sextuple Autos-4
05ITG Ultimate Memorabilia Stick Autos-34
05ITG Ultimate Mem Stick Autos Gold-34
05ITG Ultimate Mem 3 Star of the Game Jsy-6
05ITG Ult Mem 3 Star of the Game Jsy Gold-6
05ITG Ultimate Mem Triple Threads Jerseys-6
05ITG Ultimate Mem Triple Thread Jsy Gold-6
05ITG Ultimate Memorabilia Ultimate Autos-17
05ITG Ultimate Mem Ultimate Autos Gold-17
05ITG Ultimate Memorabilia Vintage Lumber-24
05ITG Ultimate Mem Vintage Lumber Gold-24
05NHL Legends Medallions-12
05SP Authentic Immortal Inks-IIFM
05SP Authentic Sign of the Times Fives-LRMMG
05SP Authentic Sign of the Times Fives-SMSMK
05SP Authentic Six Star Signatures-SSMO
05SP Authentic Six Star Signatures-SSTO
05SPx Xcitement Legends-XL-FM
05SPx Xcitement Legends Gold-XL-FM
05SPx Xcitement Legends Spectrum-XL-FM
05The Cup Emblems of Endorsement-EEFM
05The Cup Hardware Heroes-HHFM
05The Cup Limited Logos-LLFM
05The Cup Noble Numbers-NNMS
05The Cup Property of-POFM
05The Cup Scripted Numbers-SNMS
05The Cup Scripted Numbers Dual-DSNSM
05The Cup Signature Patches-SPFM
05The Cup Stanley Cup Titlists-TFM1
05The Cup Stanley Cup Titlists-TFM2
05UD Artifacts-131
Blue-131
Gold-131
Green-131
Pewter-131
Red-131
Gold Autographed-131
05ITG Heroes and Prospects-35
Autographs-A-FM
Future Teammates-FT7
He Shoots-He Scores Prizes-46
Hero Memorabilia-HM-21
06ITG International Ice-118
Gold-118
Autographs-AFM
International Rivals-IR03
International Rivals Gold-IR03
Teammates-IT22
Teammates Gold-IT22
06ITG Ultimate Memorabilia-51
Artist Proof-51
Autos-48
Autos Gold-48
Bloodlines-4
Bloodlines Gold-4
Bowman Factor-2
Bowman Factor Gold-2
Bowman Factor Autos-2
Bowman Factor Autos Gold-2
Boys Will Be Boys-2
Boys Will Be Boys Gold-2
Emblem Attic-10
Emblem Attic Gold-10
Jerseys Autos-36
Jerseys Autos Gold-36
Ring Leaders-13
Ring Leaders Gold-13
Road to the Cup-3
Road to the Cup Gold-3
Stick Rack-3
Stick Rack Gold-3
06The Cup-83
Autographed Foundations-CQFM
Black Rainbow-83
Foundations-CQFM
Enshrinements-EFM
Gold-83
Masterpiece Pressplates-83
Stanley Cup Signatures-CSFM
Stanley Cup Signatures-CSFR
06Upper Deck Sweet Shot Signature Sticks-STFM
06Upper Deck Sweet Shot Sweet Stitches-SSFM
06Upper Deck Sweet Shot Sweet Stitches Duals-SSFM
06Upper Deck Sweet Shot Sweet Stitches Triples-SSFM
06ITG Heroes and Prospects Heroes Memorabilia-HM14
06ITG Heroes and Prospects Heroes Memorabilia Gold-HM14
07Maple Leafs 1967 Commemorative-15
07Maple Leafs 1967 Commemorative-16
Sticks-SFM

Mahovlich, Pete
64Beehive Group III Photos-85
66Topps-103
66Topps USA Test-21
68O-Pee-Chee-143
68Shirriff Coins-36
69Canadiens Postcards Color-18
70Canadiens Pins-11
70Esso Power Players-14
70O-Pee-Chee-58
70Post Shooters-11
70Sargent Promotions Stamps-102
70Topps-58
71Canadiens Postcards-15
71O-Pee-Chee-84
71Sargent Promotions Stamps-99
71Topps-84
71Toronto Sun-158
72Canadiens Postcards-14
72Canadiens Great West Life Prints-4
72Dimanche/Derniere Heure *-158
72Dimanche/Derniere Heure *-159
72O-Pee-Chee-124
Team Canada-18
72Sargent Promotions Stamps-114
72Topps-42
73Canadiens Postcards-16
73Mac's Milk-16
73O-Pee-Chee-164
73Topps-186
74Canadiens Postcards-16
74Lipton Soup-39
74NHL Action Stamps-146
74O-Pee-Chee NHL-97
74Topps-97
75Canadiens Postcards-13
75Heroes Stand-Ups-11
75O-Pee-Chee NHL-50
75O-Pee-Chee NHL-209
75O-Pee-Chee NHL-322
75Topps-50
75Topps-209
75Topps-322
76Canadiens Postcards-14
76O-Pee-Chee NHL-2
76O-Pee-Chee NHL-15
76O-Pee-Chee NHL-388
76Topps-2
76Topps-15
77O-Pee-Chee NHL-205
77Topps-205
78O-Pee-Chee-51
78Topps-51
79O-Pee-Chee-187
79Topps-187
80O-Pee-Chee-72
80O-Pee-Chee Super-6
80Topps-72
91Future Trends Canada '72-27
91Future Trends Canada '72-30
91Future Trends Canada '72 French-27
91Future Trends Canada '72 French-30
92Future Trends '76 Canada Cup-180
92Fort Worth Fire-12
95Parkhurst '66-67-46
Coins-46
99BAP Memorabilia AS Canadian Hobby-CH7
99BAP Memorabilia AS Cdn Hobby Autos-CH7
01BAP Ultimate Memorabilia Bloodlines-4
01BAP Ultimate Memorabilia Les Canadiens-14
01Parkhurst Autographs-PA47
01Topps Archives-80
Relics-JPM
02BAP Ultimate Memorabilia All-Star MVP-19
02BAP Ultimate Mem Vintage Jerseys-29
02Parkhurst Vintage Teammates-VT7
02Parkhurst Retro Nicknames-RN12
02Topps Rookie Reprints-3
02Topps Rookie Reprint Autographs-3
03BAP Ultimate Mem Hometown Heroes-9
03BAP Ultimate Mem Hometown Heroes Gold-9
03BAP Ultimate Memorabilia Linemates-8
03Parkhurst Orig Six Montreal Mem-MM62
04ITG Franchises Update-475
Linemates-ULI4
Linemates Gold-ULI4
04ITG Franchises US West-202
04UD Legendary Signatures-64
Autographs-PM
Linemates-SCPMGL
Summit Stars-CDN11
Summit Stars Autographs-CDN-PM
06ITG International Ice-91
06ITG International Ice-139
Gold-91
Gold-139
Autographs-APM
Autographs-APM2
Teammates-IT22
Teammates Gold-IT22
06ITG Ultimate Memorabilia Bloodlines-4
06ITG Ultimate Memorabilia Bloodlines Gold-4

Mahovsky, Dale
03Kootenay Ice-17
04Kootenay Ice-14
05Kootenay Ice-15

Mai, Michael
94German First League-577

Maia, Pierrick
94Finnish Jaa Kiekko-223
94French National Team-18
95Swedish Globe World Championships-202
95Swedish World Championships Stickers-111

Maiani, Domenic
04Ohio State Buckeyes-17
05Ohio State Buckeyes-11

06Ohio State Buckeyes-10
Maidl, Anton
94German DEL-138
95German DEL-131
Maier, Arno
93Swedish Semic World Champ Stickers-281
94Finnish Jaa Kiekko-245
Maier, Josef
94German First League-267
Maier, Kim
91Air Canada SJHL-A42
91Air Canada SJHL All-Stars-24
91Air Canada SJHL All-Stars-47
91Air Canada SJHL All-Stars-48
92Wheeling Thunderbirds-9
93Knoxville Cherokees-8
98Tacoma Sabercats-12
99Tacoma Sabercats-17
Mailhot, Jacques
88ProCards AHL-103
89ProCards IHL-119
91ProCards-431
97Central Texas Stampede-9
Mailhot, Kevin
02Drummondville Voltigeurs-16
03Drummondville Voltigeurs-12
04Drummondville Voltigeurs-26
05Drummondville Voltigeurs-6
Mailhot, Simon
93Quebec Pee-Wee Tournament-234
Maillat, Fabrice
00Swiss Panini Stickers-66
00Swiss Slapshot Mini-Cards-HCCF11
01Swiss HNL-297
02Swiss HNL-359
Maillet, Chris
93Red Deer Rebels-13
98Muskegon Fury-5
99Muskegon Fury-15
Maillet, Claude
92Greensboro Monarchs-14
Mailloux, Chris
93Detroit Jr. Red Wings-4
Mailloux, Guillaume
05Rimouski Oceanic-20
Mailloux, Robert
95Slapshot-114
98Bowman CHL-33
Golden Anniversary-33
OPC International-33
98Bowman Chrome CHL-33
Golden Anniversary-33
Golden Anniversary Refractors-33
OPC International-33
OPC International Refractors-33
Refractors-33
Main, Bryan
05Gatineau Olympiques-23
06Gatineau Olympiques-14
Main, Eric
06Stockton Thunder-17
Mainer, Petr
94Czech APS Extraliga-100
95Czech APS Extraliga-225
97Czech APS Extraliga-223
Mainguy, Francis
93Quebec Pee-Wee Tournament-1099
Mair, Adam
95Slapshot-298
95Owen Sound Platers-20
96Owen Sound Platers-19
97Owen Sound Platers-15
97Bowman CHL-144
OPC-144
Autographs-24
98Owen Sound Platers-16
98Owen Sound Platers-27
99BAP Memorabilia-199
Gold-199
Silver-199
99Black Diamond-80
Diamond Cut-80
Final Cut-80
99Pacific-412
Copper-412
Emerald Green-412
Gold-412
Ice Blue-412
Premiere Date-412
Red-412
99Pacific Omega-230
Copper-230
Gold-230
Ice Blue-230
Premiere Date-230
99SP Authentic-117
99St. John's Maple Leafs-15
99Bowman CHL-148
Gold-148
OPC International-148
00BAP Memorabilia-247
Emerald-247
Ruby-247
Sapphire-247
Promos-247
00BAP Mem Chicago Sportsfest Copper-247
00BAP Memorabilia Chicago Sportsfest Blue-247
00BAP Memorabilia Chicago Sportsfest Gold-247
00BAP Memorabilia Chicago Sportsfest Ruby-247
00BAP Memorabilia Chicago Sun-Times Ruby-247
00BAP Memorabilia Chicago Sun-Times Gold-247
00BAP Mem Chicago Sun-Times Sapphire-247
00BAP Mem Toronto Fall Expo Copper-247
00BAP Memorabilia Toronto Fall Expo Gold-247
00BAP Memorabilia Toronto Fall Expo Ruby-247
00O-Pee-Chee-296
00O-Pee-Chee Parallel-296
00Titanium-147
Retail-147
00Titanium Draft Day Edition-147
00Titanium Draft Day Promos-147
00Topps/OPC-296
Parallel-296
00Topps Chrome-191
OPC Refractors-191
Refractors-191
00St. John's Maple Leafs-16
01BAP Memorabilia-231
Emerald-231
Ruby-231
Sapphire-231
02Pacific Complete-454
Red-454
02Sabres Team Issue-8
03ITG Action-46
03Pacific Complete-19
Red-19
06O-Pee-Chee-57
Rainbow-57
Mair, James
72O-Pee-Chee-232
72Sargent Promotions Stamps-140
Mair, Michael
82Swedish Semic VM Stickers-135
83Swedish Semic VM Stickers-135
Maiser, Justin
04Peoria Rivermen-8
Maisonneuve, Roger
52Juniors Blue Tint-88
Maitland, Shane
907th Inn. Sketch WHL-194
917th Inn. Sketch WHL-15
917th Inn. Sketch Memorial Cup-93
Maj, Boguslaw
94German First League-582
Majaniemi, Tapio
65Finnish Hellas-97
66Finnish Jaakiekkosarja-114
Majapuro, Raimo
73Finnish Jaakiekko-224
Majaury, Craig
86London Knights-20
Majava, Kyosti
73Finnish Jaakiekko-207
78Finnish SM-Liiga-22
Majeske, Brian
94Anchorage Aces-16
Majesky, Boris
97Halifax Mooseheads II-11
Majesky, Igor
04Czech OFS Czech/Slovak-36
Majesky, Ivan
00Finnish Cardset-151
01Finnish Cardset-236
02BAP All-Star Edition-147
Gold-147
Silver-147
02BAP Memorabilia-277
Emerald-277
Ruby-277
Sapphire-277
NHL All-Star Game-277
NHL All-Star Game Blue-277
NHL All-Star Game Green-277
NHL All-Star Game Red-277
02BAP Memorabilia Toronto Fall Expo-277
02BAP Signature Series-182
Autographs-182
Autographs Gold-182
02BAP Ultimate Memorabilia-7
02Crown Royale-116
Blue-116
Purple-116
Red-116
Retail-116
02ITG Used-87
02Parkhurst-207
Bronze-207
Gold-207
Silver-207
02SP Authentic-146
02Topps Chrome-150
Black Border Refractors-150
Refractors-150
02Topps Total-424
02UD Mask Collection-132
02UD Top Shelf-92
02Upper Deck-438
Exclusives-438
02Upper Deck Classic Portraits-115
02Finnish Cardset-67
03Thrashers Postcards-12
04Czech OFS-320
Stars II-3
06Finnish Cardset-272
Majic, Ron
91Nashville Knights-6
93Huntington Blizzard-15
94Hampton Roads Admirals-20
97Hampton Roads Admirals-13
Majic, Xavier
93RPI Engineers-16
94Wheeling Thunderbirds-8
94Wheeling Thunderbirds-PC1
94Wheeling Thunderbirds Photo Album-18
94Classic-46
Gold-46
Previews-HK3
95Fredericton Canadiens-20
Majka, Bob
95Arizona Icecats-13
96Arizona Icecats-22
97Arizona Icecats-15
98Arizona Icecats-14
99Arizona Icecats-14
Major, Bruce
90ProCards AHL/IHL-545
Major, Mark
90ProCards AHL/IHL-380
91ProCards-294
92Cleveland Lumberjacks-24
95Adirondack Red Wings-13
95Buffalo Stampedes RHI-32
97Portland Pirates-15
98Portland Pirates-24
99Houston Aeros-14
Majorov, Boris
92Finnish Jyvas-Hyva Stickers-52
93Finnish Jyvas-Hyva Stickers-283
93Finnish SISU-57
94Finnish SISU-397
Makarov, Denis
01Russian Hockey League-22
Makarov, Evgeni
02Russian SL-30
Makarov, Konstantin
03Russian Under-18 Team-19
Makarov, Nikolai
82Swedish Semic VM Stickers-75
03Russian Hockey League-150
Makarov, Sergei
79Panini Stickers-157
79Russian National Team-22
81Swedish Semic Hockey VM Stickers-51
82Swedish Semic VM Stickers-60
83Swedish Semic VM Stickers-60
84Russian National Team-12
87Russian National Team-14
89Kraft-4
89Russian National Team-18
89Swedish Semic World Champ Stickers-96
90Bowman-92
Tiffany-92
90Flames IGA/McGavin's-12
90Flames IGA/McGavin's-13
90O-Pee-Chee-60
90O-Pee-Chee-503
90O-Pee-Chee Box Bottoms-P
90Panini Stickers-184
90Panini Stickers-334
90Pro Set-38
90Pro Set-379
90Pro Set-396
90Score-71
90Score-329
90Score-350
90Score-362
Canadian-71
Canadian-329
Canadian-350
Canadian-362
90Score Hottest/Rising Stars-99
90Topps-60
Tiffany-60
90Topps Box Bottoms-P
90Upper Deck-123
90Upper Deck-202
90Upper Deck-336
French-123
French-202
French-336
91Pro Set Platinum-15
91Bowman-250
91Bowman-264
91Flames Panini Team Stickers-10
91Flames IGA-9
91O-Pee-Chee-482
91OPC Premier-45
91Panini Stickers-57
91Parkhurst-247
French-247
91Pinnacle-271
French-271
91Pro Set-39
French-39
91Score American-51
91Score Canadian Bilingual-51
91Score Canadian English-51
91Stadium Club-31
91Topps-482
91Upper Deck-321
French-321
91Finnish Semic World Champ Stickers-216
91Russian Stars Red Ace-13
91Russian Sports Unite Hearts-7
91Russian Stars in NHL-7
91Swedish Semic World Champ Stickers-216
92Bowman-53
92Flames IGA-15
92O-Pee-Chee-90
92Panini Stickers-47
92Panini Stickers French-47
92Parkhurst-25
Emerald Ice-25
92Pinnacle-335
French-335
92Pro Set-24
92Score-382
Canadian-382
Sharpshooters-2
Sharpshooters Canadian-2
92Stadium Club-217
92Topps-467
Gold-467G
92Ultra-24
92Upper Deck-314
Euro-Stars-E16
93Donruss-304
93Leaf-384
93Panini Stickers-183
93Parkhurst-188
Emerald Ice-188
93Pinnacle-362
Canadian-362
93PowerPlay-222
93Score-33
93Score-531
Gold-531
Canadian-33
Canadian-531
Canadian Gold-531
Dynamic Duos U.S.-8
93Ultra-416
93Upper Deck-446
SP-145
94Action Packed Big Picture 24K Gold-1G
94Canada Games NHL POGS-217
94Donruss-103
94Flair-167
94Fleer-198
94Leaf-282
94OPC Premier-396
Special Effects-396
94Parkhurst-211
Gold-211
94Pinnacle-152
Artist's Proofs-152
Rink Collection-152
94Select-8
Gold-8
94SP-107
Die Cuts-107
94Stadium Club-123
Members Only Master Set-123
First Day Issue-123
Super Teams-21
Super Teams Members Only Master Set-21
Super Team Winner Cards-123
94Topps/OPC Premier-396
Special Effects-396
94Ultra-198
94Upper Deck-124
Electric Ice-124
SP Inserts-SP72
SP Inserts Die Cuts-SP72
94Finnish Jaa Kiekko-155
95Collector's Choice-207
Player's Club-207
Player's Club Platinum-207
95Emotion-158
95Leaf-293
95Panini Stickers-282
95Score-159
Black Ice Artist's Proofs-159
Black Ice-159
95Topps-171
OPC Inserts-171
95Ultra-148
Gold Medallion-148
95Upper Deck-24
Electric Ice-24
Electric Ice Gold-24
95Swedish Globe World Championships-238
95Swedish World Championships Stickers-284
99Russian Fetisov Tribute-5
03BAP Ultimate Memorabilia Linemates-12
06ITG International Ice Triple Memorabilia-TM07
06ITG International Ice Triple Memorabilia Gold-TM07
Makarov, Sergei B
90O-Pee-Chee-485
99Russian Hockey League-153
00Russian Hockey League-255
Makarov, Sergei C.
00Russian Hockey League-210
01Russian Hockey League-23
Makarov, Vladislav
98Russian Hockey League-83
99Russian Hockey League-59
01Russian Hockey League-66
Makatsch, Rainer
72Finnish Hellas-57
72Finnish Semic World Championship-116
72Swedish Semic World Championship-116
Makela, Erkki
91Finnish Jyvas-Hyva Stickers-52
92Finnish Jyvas-Hyva Stickers-148
93Finnish Jyvas-Hyva Stickers-259
98Danish Hockey League-171
Makela, Jaakko
99Finnish Cardset-344
Makela, Janne
00Finnish Cardset-108
Makela, Jarno
93Finnish SISU-228
94Finnish SISU-247
95Finnish SISU-158
Makela, Mikko
86Islanders Team Issue-22
87Panini Stickers-100
88O-Pee-Chee-44
88O-Pee-Chee Stickers-108
88Panini Stickers-291
88Topps-44
89Islanders Team Issue-12
89Kings Smokey-22
89O-Pee-Chee-247
89O-Pee-Chee Stickers-112
89Panini Stickers-270
89Swedish Semic World Champ Stickers-41
90O-Pee-Chee-229
90OPC Premier-66
90Panini Stickers-237
90Pro Set-418
90Sabres Blue Shield-13
90Sabres Campbell's-15
90Score Rookie/Traded-26T
90Topps-229
Tiffany-229
91Bowman-36
91O-Pee-Chee-503
91Panini Stickers-302
91Score Canadian Bilingual-549
91Score Canadian English-549
91Stadium Club-261
91Topps-503
92Finnish Jyvas-Hyva Stickers-181
92Finnish Semic-20
93Swedish Semic Elitserien-192
93Swedish Semic World Champ Stickers-68
94Leaf-515
94Ultra-258
94Finnish SISU-345
94Finnish SISU Guest Specials-5
94Finnish Jaa Kiekko-31
95Finnish SISU Limited-106
95Finnish Semic World Championships-42
95German DEL-98
95Swedish Globe World Championships-142
96German DEL-286
97Swedish Collector's Choice-180
Crash the Game Exchange-C28
Crash the Game Redemption-R28
98Finnish Kerailysarja-226
Makela, Pekka
78Finnish SM-Liiga-229
Makela, Pertti
66Finnish Jaakiekkosarja-34
70Finnish Jaakiekko-198
71Finnish Suomi Stickers-89
72Finnish Jaakiekko-253
73Finnish Jaakiekko-252
Makela, Seppo
93Finnish SISU-380
Makela, Tauno
78Finnish SM-Liiga-239
80Finnish Mallasjuoma-215
Makela, Timo
65Finnish Hellas-72
91Greensboro Monarchs-9
Makela, Tuukka
01Finnish Cardset-220
02Finnish Cardset-77
04Finnish Cardset-35
Parallel-25
05Finnish Cardset -282
06Finnish Cardset-108
Maki, Brent
83Oshawa Generals-23
Maki, Chico
44Beehive Group II Photos-119A
44Beehive Group II Photos-119B
57St. Catherine's Tee Pees-16
61Shirriff/Salada Coins-28
62Topps-37
63Chex Photos-36
63Topps-41
64Beehive Group III Photos-46A
64Beehive Group III Photos-46B
64Coca-Cola Caps-30
64Topps-73
64Toronto Star-30
65Coca-Cola-31
65Topps-117
66Topps-110
66Topps USA Test-53
67Topps-111
68Blackhawks Team Issue-3
68O-Pee-Chee-17
68Shirriff Coins-23
68Topps-17
69O-Pee-Chee-137
70Dad's Cookies-75
70Esso Power Players-122
70O-Pee-Chee-149
70Sargent Promotions Stamps-46
71Letraset Action Replays-2
71O-Pee-Chee-210
71Sargent Promotions Stamps-36
71Toronto Sun-73
72O-Pee-Chee-198
72Sargent Promotions Stamps-60
73O-Pee-Chee-227
74NHL Action Stamps-90
74O-Pee-Chee NHL-395
94Parkhurst Tall Boys-24
95Parkhurst '66-67-32
Coins-32
Maki, Timo
93Finnish Jyvas-Hyva Stickers-194
93Finnish SISU-257
94Finnish SISU-312
Maki, Tomi
04Finnish Cardset-243
05ITG Heroes/Prosp Toronto Expo Parallel -262
05Finnish Cardset -58
05ITG Heroes and Prospects-262
Autographs Series II-TMK
06ITG Heroes and Prospects Jerseys-GUJ11
06ITG Heroes and Prospects Jerseys Gold-GUJ11
06ITG Heroes and Prospects Emblems-GUE11
06ITG Heroes and Prospects Emblems Gold-GUE11
06ITG Heroes and Prospects Numbers-GUN11
06ITG Heroes and Prospects Numbers Gold-GUN11
07Upper Deck Victory-206
Black-206
Gold-206
Maki, Wayne
67Topps-55
68Shirriff Coins-19
70Canucks Royal Bank-10
70Esso Power Players-46
70O-Pee-Chee-116
70Sargent Promotions Stamps-210
70Topps-116
71Canucks Royal Bank-20
71O-Pee-Chee-56
71Sargent Promotions Stamps-217
71Topps-58
71Toronto Sun-284
72Canucks Nalley's-3
72Canucks Royal Bank-13
72O-Pee-Chee-84
72Sargent Promotions Stamps-216
72Topps-32
72Finnish Semic World Championship-221
72Swedish Semic World Championship-221
Maki-Kokkila, Kimmo
93Finnish Jyvas-Hyva Stickers-209
93Finnish SISU-270
94Finnish SISU-323
95Finnish SISU-207
Makia, Martti
66Finnish Jaakiekkosarja-93
72Finnish Jaakiekko-178
Makia, Veikko
66Finnish Jaakiekkosarja-96
Makiaho, Toni
94Finest-139
Super Team Winners-139
Refractors-139
94Finnish SISU-272
95Finnish SISU-27
96Finnish SISU Redline-23
98Finnish Kerailysarja-47
99Finnish Cardset-28
00Finnish Cardset-258
01Finnish Cardset-24
02Finnish Cardset-226
03Finnish Cardset-124
04Finnish Cardset-44
Parallel-32
06Finnish Cardset-222
Enforcers-7
Makila, Rainer
50Quebec Citadelles-15
51Laval Dairy Lac St. Jean-41
Makinen, Ari
78Finnish SM-Liiga-73
80Finnish Mallasjuoma-66
Makinen, Esko
70Finnish Jaakiekko-132
73Finnish Jaakiekko-185
Makinen, Juha
71Finnish Suomi Stickers-371
Makinen, Kari
65Finnish Hellas-154
66Finnish Jaakiekkosarja-153
70Finnish Jaakiekko-214
93Finnish Jyvas-Hyva Stickers-253
Makinen, Keijo
66Finnish Jaakiekkosarja-217
Makinen, Marko
95Finnish SISU-333
Drafted Dozen-4
97Louisville Riverfrogs-11
00Finnish Cardset-334
01Finnish Cardset-343
02Finnish Cardset-78
03Finnish Cardset-151
04Finnish Cardset-299
05Finnish Cardset -146
Makinen, Pekka
70Finnish Jaakiekko-215
71Finnish Suomi Stickers-137
72Finnish Jaakiekko-200
73Finnish Jaakiekko-161
78Finnish SM-Liiga-137
Makinen, Seppo I.
65Finnish Hellas-151
66Finnish Jaakiekkosarja-145
70Finnish Jaakiekko-216
71Finnish Suomi Stickers-138
72Finnish Jaakiekko-201
72Finnish Jaakiekko-271
73Finnish Jaakiekko-162
Makinen, Seppo S.
73Finnish Jaakiekko-163
Makinen, Tapio
66Finnish Jaakiekkosarja-218
Makinen, Timo
96Finnish SISU Redline-116
Makitalo, Jarmo
77Finnish Sportscasters-90-2152
78Finnish SM-Liiga-122
82Swedish Semic VM Stickers-41
83Swedish Semic Elitserien-217
84Swedish Semic Elitserien-230
85Swedish Panini Stickers-152
86Swedish Panini Stickers-152
87Swedish Panini Stickers-161
89Swedish Semic Elitserien Stickers-137
92Swedish Semic Elitserien Stickers-173
93Swedish Semic Elitserien-144
94Finnish SISU-368
94Swedish Leaf-77
98Danish Hockey League-179
Makitalo, Jouni
78Finnish SM-Liiga-237
Makitalo, Jukka
94Finnish SISU-340
Makitalo, Kari
78Finnish SM-Liiga-123
Makkonen, Jussi
05Finnish Cardset -333
06Finnish Cardset-161
Playmakers Rookies-3
Playmakers Rookies Gold-3
Playmakers Rookies Silver-3
Signature Sensations-30
Makkonen, Kari
78Finnish SM-Liiga-18
78Finnish SM-Liiga-240
79Oilers Postcards-16
80Finnish Mallasjuoma-216
83Swedish Semic VM Stickers-47
88Oilers Tenth Anniversary-144
Makkonen, Pasi
71Finnish Suomi Stickers-329
Maklaho, Toni
98Finnish Kerailysarja Leijonat-32
Makombo, Alexandre
99Rockford IceHogs-13
Makritzky, Alexander
99German DEL-311
Maksimov, Alexander
99Russian Hockey League-199
Maksimov, Dmitri
98Russian Hockey League-21
99Russian Hockey League-107
Maksym, Andrew
02Owen Sound Attack-13
03Owen Sound Attack-9
04Belleville Bulls-1
05Belleville Bulls-19
Makway, Steve
00Kootenay Ice-15
Malac, Pavel
94Czech APS Extraliga-182
95Czech APS Extraliga-30
99Czech Score Blue 2000-25
99Czech Score Blue 2000-73
99Czech Score Red Ice 2000-25
99Czech Score Red Ice 2000-73
01Czech OFS-237
Gold Inserts-G11
Malaison, Eric
93Quebec Pee-Wee Tournament-1361
Malakhov, Vladimir
90O-Pee-Chee Red Army-2R
91Upper Deck-1
French-1
91Finnish Semic World Champ Stickers-80
91Swedish Semic World Champ Stickers-80
92OPC Premier-89
92Parkhurst-339
Emerald Ice-339
92Pinnacle-409
French-409
92Ultra-346
Imports-14
92Upper Deck-554
92Upper Deck-577
Calder Candidates-CC12
Euro-Rookies-ER15
Gordie Howe Selects-G12
92Finnish Semic-104
92Russian Stars Red Ace-19
92Russian Stars Red Ace-28
92Russian Tri-Globe From Russia With Puck-19
92Russian Tri-Globe From Russia With Puck-20
93Donruss-207
93Leaf-32
Gold Rookies-9
93OPC Premier-129
93OPC Premier-445
93OPC Premier-515
Gold-129
Gold-445
Gold-515
93Parkhurst-125
93Parkhurst-239
Emerald Ice-125
Emerald Ice-239
93Pinnacle-104
Canadian-104
93PowerPlay-153
Second Year Stars-6
93Score-157
Canadian-157
93Stadium Club-248
Members Only Master Set-248
OPC-248
First Day Issue-248
First Day Issue OPC-248
93Topps/OPC Premier-129
93Topps/OPC Premier-445
93Topps/OPC Premier-515
Gold-129
Gold-445
Gold-515
93Ultra-235
93Upper Deck-29
93Upper Deck-283
SP-93
93Upper Deck Locker All-Stars-57
93Swedish Semic World Champ Stickers-142
93Classic Pro Prospects-55
BCs-BC4
94Be A Player-R125
Signature Cards-121
94Canada Games NHL POGS-162
94Donruss-307
94EA Sports-79
94Flair-105
94Fleer-126
94Leaf-194
94OPC Premier-546
Special Effects-546
94Parkhurst Vintage-V77
94Parkhurst SE-SE108
Gold-SE108
94Pinnacle-104
Artist's Proofs-104
Rink Collection-104
Boomers-BR2
94Score-62
Gold-62
Platinum-62
94SP-60
Die Cuts-60
94Stadium Club-144
Members Only Master Set-144
First Day Issue-144
Super Team Winner Cards-144
94Topps/OPC Premier-546
Special Effects-546
94Ultra-130
94Upper Deck-139
Electric Ice-139
SP Inserts-SP47
SP Inserts Die Cuts-SP47
94Finnish Jaa Kiekko-137
94Finnish Jaa Kiekko-341
95Canada Games NHL POGS-151
95Canadiens Postcards-9
95Canadiens Sheets-7
95Collector's Choice-143
Player's Club-143
Player's Club Platinum-143
95Donruss-4
95Emotion-88
95Leaf-149
95Panini Stickers-42
95Parkhurst International-115
Emerald Ice-115
95Playoff One on One-273
95Score-117
Black Ice Artist's Proofs-117
Black Ice-117
95SkyBox Impact-85
95Summit-157
Artist's Proofs-157
Ice-157
95Topps-113
OPC Inserts-113
95Ultra-81
Gold Medallion-81
95Upper Deck-466
Electric Ice-466
Electric Ice Gold-466
Special Edition-SE45
Special Edition Gold-SE45
95Swedish Globe World Championships-166
96Canadiens Postcards-16
96Canadiens Sheets-10
96Collector's Choice-139
96Fleer Picks-118
96Team Out-55
96Upper Deck-84
96Swedish Semic Wien-135
97Be A Player-133
Autographs-133
Autographs Die-Cuts-133
Autographs Prismatic Die-Cuts-133
97Canadiens Postcards-11
97Katch-76
Gold-76
Silver-76
97Pacific Invincible NHL Regime-103
97Pacific Omega-119
Copper-119
Dark Gray-119
Emerald Green-119
Gold-119
Ice Blue-119
97Panini Stickers-34
97Score-247
97Score Canadiens-11
Platinum-11
Premier-11
97SP Authentic-83
98Be A Player-222
Press Release-222
98BAP Gold-222
98BAP Autographs-222
98BAP Autographs Gold-222
98Canadiens Team Issue-10
98Finest-57
No Protectors-57
No Protectors Refractors-57
Refractors-57
98Katch-76
98Kraft Peanut Butter-4
98Pacific-253
Ice Blue-253
Red-253
98Panini Stickers-33
98Paramount-114
Copper-114
Emerald Green-114
Holo-Electric-114
Ice Blue-114
Silver-114
98UD Choice-104
Prime Choice Reserve-104
Reserve-104
98Upper Deck-112
Exclusives-112
Exclusives 1 of 1-112
Gold Reserve-112
99BAP Memorabilia-191
99BAP Memorabilia-395
Gold-191
Gold-395
Silver-191
Silver-395
99O-Pee-Chee-101
99O-Pee-Chee Chrome-101
99O-Pee-Chee Chrome Refractors-101
99Pacific-206
Copper-206
Emerald Green-206
Gold-206
Ice Blue-206
Premiere Date-206
Red-206
99Paramount-119
Copper-119
Emerald-119
Gold-119
Holographic Emerald-119
Holographic Gold-119
Holographic Silver-119
Ice Blue-119
Premiere Date-119
Red-119
Silver-119
99Revolution-76
Premiere Date-76
Red-76
Shadow Series-76
99Topps/OPC-101
99Topps/OPC Chrome-101
Refractors-101
99Upper Deck-242
Exclusives-242
Exclusives 1 of 1-242
99Upper Deck Gold Reserve-242
99Upper Deck MVP-102
Gold Script-102
Silver Script-102
Super Script-102
99Upper Deck Victory-148
99Russian Fetisov Tribute-10
00BAP Memorabilia-99
00BAP Memorabilia-433
Emerald-99
Emerald-433
Ruby-99
Ruby-433
Sapphire-99
Sapphire-433
Promos-99
00BAP Mem Chicago Sportsfest Copper-99
00BAP Memorabilia Chicago Sportsfest Blue-99
00BAP Memorabilia Chicago Sportsfest Gold-99
00BAP Memorabilia Chicago Sportsfest Ruby-99
00BAP Memorabilia Chicago Sun-Times Ruby-99
00BAP Memorabilia Chicago Sun-Times Gold-99
00BAP Mem Chicago Sun-Times Sapphire-99
00BAP Mem Toronto Fall Expo Copper-99
00BAP Memorabilia Toronto Fall Expo Gold-99
00BAP Memorabilia Toronto Fall Expo Ruby-99
00Pacific-238
Copper-238
Gold-238
Ice Blue-238
Premiere Date-238
00Stadium Club-218
00Upper Deck-346
Exclusives Tier 1-346
Exclusives Tier 2-346
00Upper Deck Vintage-240
02BAP First Edition-172
02BAP Sig Series Auto Buybacks 1998-222
02Pacific-254
Blue-254
Red-254
02Pacific Complete-370
Red-370
02Rangers Team Issue-9
02Upper Deck-362
Exclusives-362
02Upper Deck Beckett UD Promos-362
03ITG Action-360
03Pacific Complete-85
Red-85
03Parkhurst Original Six New York-23
Memorabilia-NM11
03Rangers Team Issue-14
03Upper Deck MVP-284
Gold Script-284
Silver Script-284
Canadian Exclusives-284
05Devils Team Issue-30
05Panini Stickers-82
Malandrino, Salvatore
02Mississauga Ice Dogs-17
Malarchuk, Clint
81Fredericton Express-6
82Nordiques Postcards-12
82Fredericton Express-6
83Nordiques Postcards-15
84Fredericton Express-10
85Nordiques General Foods-15
85Nordiques McDonald's-13
85Nordiques Placemats-6
85Nordiques Provigo-14
85Nordiques Team Issue-14
86Kraft Drawings-39
86Nordiques General Foods-15
86Nordiques McDonald's-15
86Nordiques Team Issue-13
86Nordiques Yum-Yum-6
86O-Pee-Chee-47
86O-Pee-Chee Stickers-33
86Topps-47
87Capitals Kodak-30
87Capitals Team Issue-15
87O-Pee-Chee-246
87Panini Stickers-158
88Capitals Borderless-13
88Capitals Smokey-13
88O-Pee-Chee-25
88O-Pee-Chee Stickers-72
88Panini Stickers-363
88Topps-25
89O-Pee-Chee-170
89Sabres Blue Shield-12
89Sabres Campbell's-14
89Topps-170
90O-Pee-Chee-371
90Panini Stickers-26
90Pro Set-25
90Sabres Blue Shield-14
90Sabres Campbell's-16
90Score-289
Canadian-289
90Topps-371
Tiffany-371
90Upper Deck-399
French-399
91Pro Set Platinum-159
91Bowman-23
91O-Pee-Chee-97
91Panini Stickers-301
91Parkhurst-244
French-244
91Pinnacle-103
91Pinnacle-397
French-103
French-397
91Sabres Blue Shield-11
91Sabres Pepsi/Campbell's-11
91Score American-438
91Score Canadian Bilingual-419

91Score Canadian English-419
91Stadium Club-251
91Topps-97
91Upper Deck-368
French-368
92Bowman-30
92Score-138
Canadian-138
92Stadium Club-186
92Topps-363
Gold-363G
92San Diego Gulls-16
93Las Vegas Thunder-19
94Las Vegas Thunder-14
94Classic Pro Prospects-85
95Las Vegas Thunder-24
96Las Vegas Thunder-14
97Las Vegas Thunder-25
98Idaho Steelheads-22
99Idaho Steelheads-13
06Parkhurst-69
Autographs-69

Malbasa, Matko
00OCN Blizzard-4

Malcolm, Bob
71Rochester Americans-12

Malcolm, Kevin
99Ottawa 67's-17

Malec, Tomas
00Rimouski Oceanic-7
Signed-7
01Rimouski Oceanic-7
02BAP Memorabilia-343
02BAP Ultimate Memorabilia-58
02Pacific Complete-535
Red-535
02Pacific Quest for the Cup-111
Gold-111
02Parkhurst Retro-213
Minis-213
02SP Authentic-168
02UD Artistic Impressions-127
Gold-127
02UD Honor Roll-144
02UD Premier Collection-64
Gold-64
02AHL Top Prospects-28
02Lowell Lock Monsters-23
03Lowell Lock Monsters-24
03Lowell Lock Monsters Photo Album-22
04Cincinnati Mighty Ducks-27
05Binghamton Senators-14
05Binghamton Senators Quickway-14
06Binghamton Senators-14

Malecek, Pavel
99Czech Score Blue 2000-9
99Czech Score Red Ice 2000-9
02Czech OFS Plus-159

Malecki, Stan
75HCA Steel City Vacuum-7

Malek, Roman
98Czech OFS-210
99Czech DS-114
99Czech OFS-538
99Czech Score Blue 2000-1
99Czech Score Red Ice 2000-1
00Czech DS Extraliga-110
Goalies-G10
00Czech OFS-84
00Czech OFS Star Emerald-36
00Czech OFS Star Pink-36
00Czech OFS Star Violet-36
01Czech DS-3
Goalies-G5
01Czech OFS-4
Gold Inserts-G1
02Czech DS-78
02Czech OFS Plus-244
02Czech OFS Plus Masks-M10
02Czech OFS Plus Trios-T12
02Czech OFS Plus Duos-D4
03Czech OFS Plus-179
03Czech OFS Plus-384
03Czech OFS Plus All-Star Game-H26
03Czech OFS Plus Checklists-9
03Czech OFS Plus Insert B-B1
03Czech OFS Plus Insert M-M7
03Czech OFS Plus Insert P-P1
03Czech OFS Plus Insert P-P15
03Czech OFS Plus MS Praha-SE23
04Czech OFS-381
Goals-Against Leaders-5
Save Percentage Leaders-5
Stars II-9
04Russian Legion-32
05Czech HC Plzen-7
06Czech CP Cup Postcards-12
06Czech HC Plzen Postcards-8
06Czech OFS-276
All Stars-2
Goalies I-7
Goalies II-10
Stars-9
Team Cards-7

Malena, Rostislav
99Czech OFS-459
99Czech Score Blue 2000-165
99Czech Score Red Ice 2000-165
00Czech OFS-356
01Czech OFS-81
03Czech OFS Plus-229
04Czech OFS-13

Malenfant, Dave
92Quebec Pee-Wee Tournament-108
96Rimouski Oceanic-18
96Rimouski Oceanic Quebec Police-17
97Rimouski Oceanic-14

Malenfant, Ken
91Air Canada SJHL-D27

Malenfant, Ray
37V356 Worldwide Gum-108

Malenfant, Sebastien
93Quebec Pee-Wee Tournament-271

Malenkikh, Vladimir
00Russian Hockey League-171
02Russian Hockey League-32
03Russian Hockey League-113
03Russian National Team-26

Malette, Maxime
05Gatineau Olympiques-17

Malette, Vince
01Ottawa 67's-22
02Ottawa 67's-26

Maley, Brennan
90ProCards AHL/IHL-562

Maley, David
85Canadiens Postcards-19
87Canadiens Postcards-16
88Devils Caretta-19
89Devils Caretta-16
90Devils Team Issue-16
90O-Pee-Chee-438
90Pro Set-171A
90Pro Set-171B
90Score-310A
Canadian-310A
91O-Pee-Chee-476
91Parkhurst-99
French-99
91Pinnacle-272
French-272
91Pro Set-421
French-421
91Score Canadian Bilingual-426
91Score Canadian English-426
91Topps-476
92Score-370
Canadian-370
93Stadium Club-259
Members Only Master Set-259
First Day Issue-259
99Albany River Rats-19
02Fleer Throwbacks-30
Gold-30
Platinum-30

Maleyko, Jason
99Brampton Battalion-6
99Brampton Battalion-31
00Brampton Battalion-6
03ECHL All-Stars-251
03Reading Royals-5
03Reading Royals RBI Sports-294
06Toledo Storm-3

Malgin, Albert
91O-Pee-Chee Inserts-54R
93Swiss HNL-308
95Swiss HNL-280
96Swiss HNL-463
98Swiss Power Play Stickers-346
99German DEL-302
01Swiss HNL-376
02Swiss HNL-423

Malgunas, Kevin
907th Inn. Sketch WHL-5
917th Inn. Sketch WHL-156
92Richmond Renegades-12
93Hampton Roads Admirals-10
95Houston Aeros-14

Malgunas, Stewart
90ProCards AHL/IHL-487
91ProCards-123
93Donruss-470
93Flyers J.C. Penney-14
93Flyers Lineup Sheets-24
93Flyers Lineup Sheets-40
93OPC Premier-516
Gold-516
93Parkhurst-420
Emerald Ice-420
93Score-612
Gold-612
Canadian-612
Canadian Gold-612
93Stadium Club-409
Members Only Master Set-409
First Day Issue-409
93Topps/OPC Premier-516
Gold-516
93Ultra-390
93Upper Deck-425
94Leaf-170
95Jets Team Issue-13
96Portland Pirates-4
97Portland Pirates-16
98Portland Pirates-21
99IHL All-Stars-10
99Utah Grizzlies-17
00Hershey Bears-9
01German Upper Deck-82
02German DEL City Press-78

Malhotra, Manny
96Guelph Storm-8
96Guelph Storm-32
96Guelph Storm Premier Collection-10
97Black Diamond-79
Double Diamond-79
Triple Diamond-79
Quadruple Diamond-79
97Upper Deck-413
97Zenith-96
Z-Gold-96
Z-Silver-96
97Zenith 5 x 7-76
Gold Impulse-76
Silver Impulse-76
97Guelph Storm-8
98Be A Player-241
Press Release-241
98BAP Gold-241
98BAP Autographs-241
98BAP Autographs Gold-241
98Black Diamond-57
Double Diamond-57
Triple Diamond-57
Quadruple Diamond-57
Myriad-M8
Myriad 2-M8
Winning Formula Gold-WF14
Winning Formula Platinum-WF14
98Bowman's Best-106
Refractors-106
Atomic Refractors-106
Autographs-A10A
Autographs-A10B
Autographs Refractors-A10A
Autographs Refractors-A10B
Autographs Atomic Refractors-A10A
Autographs Atomic Refractors-A10B
Performers-BP6
Performers Refractors-BP6
Performers Atomic Refractors-BP6
98Crown Royale-90
Limited Series-90
Rookie Class-6
98Finest Futures Finest-F2
98Finest Futures Finest Refractors-F2
98OPC Chrome-235
Refractors-235
98Pacific Dynagon Ice-124
Blue-124
Red-124
98Pacific Omega-159
Red-159
Opening Day Issue-159
98Revolution-95
Ice Shadow-95
Red-95
98SP Authentic-101
Power Shift-101
Sign of the Times-MM
Sign of the Times Gold-MM
98SPx Top Prospects-40
Radiance-40
Spectrum-40
98Topps-235
O-Pee-Chee-235
98Topps Gold Label Class 1-93
Black-93
Black One of One-93
One of One-93
Red-93
Red One of One-93
98Topps Gold Label Class 2-93
98Topps Gold Label Class 2 Black-93
98Topps Gold Label Class 2 Black 1 of 1-93
98Topps Gold Label Class 2 One of One-93
98Topps Gold Label Class 2 Red-93
98Topps Gold Label Class 2 Red One of One-93
98Topps Gold Label Class 3-93
98Topps Gold Label Class 3 Black-93
98Topps Gold Label Class 3 Black 1 of 1-93
98Topps Gold Label Class 3 One of One-93
98Topps Gold Label Class 3 Red-93
98Topps Gold Label Class 3 Red One of One-93
98UD Choice-255
Prime Choice Reserve-255
Reserve-255
98Upper Deck-420
Exclusives-420
Exclusives 1 of 1-420
Game Jerseys-GJ12
Generation Next-GN6
Generation Next Quantum 1-GN6
Generation Next Quantum 2-GN6
Generation Next Quantum 3-GN6
Profiles-P12
Profiles Quantum 1-P12
Profiles Quantum 2-P12
Profiles Quantum 3-P12
Gold Reserve-420
98Upper Deck MVP-134
Gold Script-134
Silver Script-134
Super Script-134
ProSign-MM
98Bowman CHL-10
98Bowman CHL-148
Golden Anniversary-10
Golden Anniversary-148
OPC International-10
OPC International-148
Autographs Blue-A5
Autographs Gold-A5
Autographs Silver-A5
Scout's Choice-SC2
98Bowman Chrome CHL-10
98Bowman Chrome CHL-148
Golden Anniversary-10
Golden Anniversary-148
Golden Anniversary Refractors-10
Golden Anniversary Refractors-148
OPC International-10
OPC International-148
OPC International Refractors-10
OPC International Refractors-148
Refractors-10
Refractors-148
99BAP Memorabilia-240
Gold-240
Silver-240
99BAP Millennium-163
Emerald-163
Ruby-163
Sapphire-163
Signatures-163
Signatures Gold-163
99O-Pee-Chee-51
99O-Pee-Chee Chrome-51
99O-Pee-Chee Chrome Refractors-51
99Pacific-274
Copper-274
Emerald Green-274
Gold-274
Ice Blue-274
Premiere Date-274
Red-274
99Paramount-154
Copper-154
Emerald-154
Gold-154
Holographic Emerald-154
Holographic Gold-154
Holographic Silver-154
Ice Blue-154
Premiere Date-154
Red-154
Silver-154
99SPx-101
Radiance-101
Spectrum-101
99Stadium Club-36
First Day Issue-36
One of a Kind-36
Printing Plates Black-36
Printing Plates Cyan-36
Printing Plates Magenta-36
Printing Plates Yellow-36
Capture the Action-CA6
Capture the Action Game View-CAG6
99Topps/OPC-51
99Topps/OPC Chrome-51
Refractors-51
99Upper Deck-89
Exclusives-89
Exclusives 1 of 1-89
99Upper Deck Arena Giveaways-NR2
99Upper Deck Gold Reserve-89
99Upper Deck MVP-136
Gold Script-136
Silver Script-136
Super Script-136
99Upper Deck Retro-50
Gold-50
Platinum-50
99Upper Deck Victory-188
99Wayne Gretzky Hockey-113
00BAP Memorabilia-160
Emerald-160
Ruby-160
Sapphire-160
Promos-160
00BAP Mem Chicago Sportsfest Copper-160
00BAP Memorabilia Chicago Sportsfest Blue-160
00BAP Memorabilia Chicago Sportsfest Gold-160
00BAP Memorabilia Chicago Sportsfest Ruby-160
00BAP Memorabilia Chicago Sun-Times Ruby-160
00BAP Memorabilia Chicago Sun-Times Gold-160
00BAP Mem Chicago Sun-Times Sapphire-160
00BAP Mem Toronto Fall Expo Copper-160
00BAP Memorabilia Toronto Fall Expo Gold-160
00BAP Memorabilia Toronto Fall Expo Ruby-160
00Titanium Game Gear-116
00Titanium Game Gear Patches-116
00Upper Deck MVP Excellence-ME9
00Upper Deck MVP Mark of Excellence-SGMY
00Upper Deck MVP ProSign-MM
00Hartford Wolf Pack-18
01BAP Memorabilia-473
Emerald-473
Ruby-473
Sapphire-473
01Crown Royale Triple Threads-13
01Pacific Heads-Up Quad Jerseys-25
01Upper Deck Game Jerseys-NGMM
01Upper Deck Game Jerseys Series II-GNMM
01Upper Deck Victory-238
Gold-238
02BAP Sig Series Auto Buybacks 1998-241
02BAP Sig Series Auto Buybacks 1999-163
02SP Game Used First Rounder Patches-MA
02SP Game Used Future Fabrics-FFMM
02SP Game Used Future Fabrics Gold-FFMM
02SP Game Used Future Fabrics Rainbow-FFMM
02Stars Postcards-11
02Topps Total-112
02Upper Deck Bright Futures-MM
03ITG Action-153
03Pacific Complete-498
Red-498
04Pacific-77
Blue-77
Red-77
04Swedish Pure Skills-37
Parallel-37
05Panini Stickers-240
05Parkhurst-141
Facsimile Auto Parallel-141
05Upper Deck-55
HG Glossy-55
05Upper Deck MVP-116
Gold-116
Platinum-116
05Upper Deck Toronto Fall Expo-55
06Be A Player-89
Autographs-89
Signatures-MA
Signatures Duals-DMS
06O-Pee-Chee-150
Rainbow-150
06Upper Deck-311
Exclusives Parallel-311
High Gloss Parallel-311
Masterpieces-311

Malia, Darren
93Quebec Pee-Wee Tournament-707

Malik, Jaroslav
93Quebec Pee-Wee Tournament-1549

Malik, Marek
94Parkhurst SE-SE212
Gold-SE212
94Upper Deck-482
94Upper Deck-506
94Upper Deck-558
Electric Ice-482
Electric Ice-506
Electric Ice-558
95Donruss-150
95Parkhurst International-99
Emerald Ice-99
95Score-298
Black Ice Artist's Proofs-298
Black Ice-298
95Topps-57
OPC Inserts-57
95Upper Deck-58
Electric Ice-58
Electric Ice Gold-58
95Whalers Bob's Stores-14
96Be A Player-110
Autographs-110
Autographs Silver-110
96Collector's Choice-118
96Leaf-227
Press Proofs-227
96Pinnacle-225
Artist's Proofs-225
Foil-225
Premium Stock-225
Rink Collection-225
96Whalers Kid's Club-7
97Pacific-322
Copper-322
Emerald Green-322
Ice Blue-322
Red-322
Silver-322
97Panini Stickers-22
97Swedish Collector's Choice-139
98Hurricanes Team Issue-5
98New Haven Beast-3
99Czech OFS-27
99Czech OFS Jagr Team Embossed-27
00BAP Memorabilia-23
Emerald-23
Ruby-23
Sapphire-23
Promos-23
00BAP Mem Chicago Sportsfest Copper-23
00BAP Memorabilia Chicago Sportsfest Blue-23
00BAP Memorabilia Chicago Sportsfest Gold-23
00BAP Memorabilia Chicago Sportsfest Ruby-23
00BAP Memorabilia Chicago Sun-Times Ruby-23
00BAP Memorabilia Chicago Sun-Times Gold-23
00BAP Mem Chicago Sun-Times Sapphire-23
00BAP Mem Toronto Fall Expo Copper-23
00BAP Memorabilia Toronto Fall Expo Gold-23
00BAP Memorabilia Toronto Fall Expo Ruby-23
00Panini Stickers-27
02Canucks Team Issue-9
02Upper Deck-278
Exclusives-278
02Upper Deck Beckett UD Promos-278
02Czech Stadion Cup Finals-489
03Canucks Postcards-16
03Canucks Sav-on-Foods-7
03ITG Action-539
03Upper Deck-191
Canadian Exclusives-191
HG-191
03Upper Deck MVP-419
Gold Script-419
Silver Script-419
Canadian Exclusives-419
04Czech OFS-233
Stars-31
04Czech Zuma-24
05Panini Stickers-114
05Parkhurst-327
Facsimile Auto Parallel-327
06O-Pee-Chee-335
Rainbow-335
06Panini Stickers-103
06Upper Deck MVP-194
Gold Script-194
Super Script-194

Malik, Milan
04Slovakian Skalica Team Set-14

Malin, Darren
93Quebec Pee-Wee Tournament-176

Malinoski, Gord
76Saginaw Gears-9

Malinowski, Merlin
81O-Pee-Chee-76
81O-Pee-Chee Stickers-228
81Rockies Postcards-16
81Topps-W81
82O-Pee-Chee-128
82O-Pee-Chee Stickers-229
82Post Cereal-11
82Topps Stickers-229
83O-Pee-Chee-142
01Swiss HNL-400
02Swiss HNL-165

Malinsky, Jiri
94Czech APS Extraliga-26
96Czech APS Extraliga-147
97Czech APS Extraliga-247
97Czech DS Stickers-249
98Czech DS Stickers-135
98Czech OFS-147
99Czech DS-75
99Czech OFS-321
99Czech OFS-354
00Czech DS Extraliga-88
00Czech OFS-35
01Czech OFS-224
02Czech OFS Plus-91
03Czech OFS Plus-293
04Czech OFS-213
Czech/Slovak-9
Defence Points-11
06Czech HC Plzen Postcards-4
06Czech OFS-277

Malinsky, Ondrej
04Czech OFS-323

Malkia, Heikki
80Finnish Mallasjuoma-148

Malkin, Evgeni
03Russian Hockey League-251
03Russian Under-18 Team-4
04Russian Hope-2
04Russian RHL-12
04Russian Under-18 Team-11
04Russian World Junior Team-9
05ITG Heroes/Prosp Toronto Expo Parallel -110
05ITG Heroes/Prosp Toronto Expo Parallel -278
05ITG Heroes/Prosp Toronto Expo Parallel -367
05ITG Sidney Crosby Series Memorabilia-SCM8
05ITG Sidney Crosby Series Memorabilia-SCM9
05ITG Sidney Crosby Series Memorabilia-SCM10
05ITG Ultimate Memorabilia Level 1-34
05ITG Ultimate Memorabilia Level 2-34
05ITG Ultimate Memorabilia Level 3-34
05ITG Ultimate Memorabilia Level 4-34
05ITG Ultimate Memorabilia Level 5-34
05ITG Ultimate Mem Complete Jersey-2
05ITG Ultimate Mem Complete Jersey Gold-2
05ITG Ultimate Memorabilia Double Autos-12
05ITG Ultimate Mem Double Autos Gold-12
05ITG Ultimate Mem Double Mem Autos-1
05ITG Ultimate Mem Double Mem Autos Gold-1
05ITG Ultimate Memorabilia Emblems-3
05ITG Ultimate Memorabilia Emblems Gold-3
05ITG Ultimate Mem First Rounders Jerseys-2
05ITG Ultimate Mem First Rounders Jerseys-6
05ITG Ultimate Mem 1st Round Jersey Gold-2
05ITG Ultimate Mem 1st Round Jersey Gold-6
05ITG Ultimate Mem Future Stars Autos-8
05ITG Ultimate Mem Future Star Autos Gold-8
05ITG Ultimate Mem Future Stars Jerseys-8
05ITG Ultimate Mem Fut Stars Jerseys Gold-8
05ITG Ultimate Mem Future Stars Mem Autos-8
05ITG Ultimate Mem Fut Star Mem Auto Gold-8
05ITG Ultimate Memorabilia In The Numbers-20
05ITG Ultimate Mem In The Numbers Gold-20
05ITG Ultimate Mem Jersey and Emblem-24
05ITG Ultimate Mem Jersey Emblems Gold-24
05ITG Ultimate Memorabilia Jerseys-13
05ITG Ultimate Memorabilia Jerseys Gold-13
05ITG Ultimate Memorabilia Triple Autos-18
05ITG Ultimate Mem Triple Autos Gold-18
05ITG Ultimate Mem Triple Threads Jerseys-1
05ITG Ultimate Mem Triple Thread Jsy Gold-1
05Russian Hockey League RHL-37
05ITG Heroes and Prospects-110
05ITG Heroes and Prospects-278
05ITG Heroes and Prospects-367
Aspiring-ASP2
Autograph Memorabilia-GA-08
Autograph Memorabilia Gold-GA-08
Autographs-A-EMA
Autographs-DA-ML
Autographs-DA-MO
Autographs Series II-EMA2
Autographs Series II-EMA3
Complete Jerseys-CJ-24
Complete Jerseys Gold-CJ-24
Future Teammates-FT13
He Shoots-He Scores Prizes-6
He Shoots-He Scores Prizes-11
He Shoots-He Scores Prizes-36
He Shoots-He Scores Prizes-42
Jerseys-GUJ-49
Jerseys-GUJ-89
Jerseys Gold-GUJ-49
Jerseys Gold-GUJ-89
Emblems-GUE-49
Emblems-GUE-89
Emblems Gold-GUE-49
Emblems Gold-GUE-89
Numbers-GUN-49
Numbers-GUN-89
Numbers Gold-GUN-49
Numbers Gold-GUN-89
Nameplates-N-30
Nameplates Gold-N-30
National Pride-NPR-10
National Pride-NPR-35
06Be A Player-201
06Be A Player Portraits-103
Signature Portraits-SPEM
06Beehive-144
Blue-144
Gold-144
Matte-144
Red Facsimile Signatures-144
Wood-144
5 X 7 Black and White-144
5 X 7 Dark Wood-144
06Black Diamond-210
Black-210
Gold-210
Ruby-210
06Flair Showcase-322
06Flair Showcase-FE-301
06Hot Prospects-142
Red Hot-142
White Hot-142
Hot Materials -HMEM
Hot Materials Red Hot-HMEM
Hot Materials White Hot-HMEM
Hotagraphs-HEM
06ITG International Ice-69
06ITG International Ice-160
Gold-69
Gold-160
Autographs-AEM
Autographs-AOM
Complete Jersey-CJ09
Complete Jersey Gold-CJ09
Cornerstones-IC02
Cornerstones Gold-IC02
International Rivals-IR19
International Rivals Gold-IR19
Passing The Torch-PTT13
Passing The Torch Gold-PTT13
Quad Patch-QP06
Quad Patch Gold-QP06
Teammates-IT21
Teammates Gold-IT21
06ITG Phenoms Teammates Gold-TMAO
06ITG Phenoms Teammates Silver-TMAO
06ITG Ultimate Memorabilia-48
Artist Proof-48
Complete Jersey-1
Complete Jersey Gold-1
Cornerstones-1
Cornerstones Gold-1
Decades-1
Decades Gold-1
Emblems-1
Emblems Gold-1
First Round Picks-1
First Round Picks Gold-1
Future Star-3
Future Star Gold-3
Going For Gold-8
Going For Gold Gold-8
In The Numbers-1
In The Numbers Gold-1
Jerseys-1
Jerseys Gold-1
Jerseys and Emblems-1
Jerseys and Emblems Gold-1
Passing The Torch-18
Passing The Torch Gold-18
R.O.Y. Autos-9
R.O.Y. Autos Gold-9
R.O.Y. Emblems-9
R.O.Y. Emblems Gold-9
R.O.Y. Jerseys-9
R.O.Y. Jerseys Gold-9
R.O.Y. Numbers-9
R.O.Y. Numbers Gold-9
Seams Unbelievable-1
Seams Unbelievable Gold-1
Triple Thread Jerseys-1
Triple Thread Jerseys Gold-1
06O-Pee-Chee-564
06O-Pee-Chee-621
06O-Pee-Chee-624
Rainbow-564
Rainbow-621
Rainbow-624
Autographs-A-EM
06SP Authentic-196
Chirography-EM
Limited-196
Sign of the Times-STEM
Sign of the Times Duals-STLM
Sign of the Times Triples-ST3LFM
Sign of the Times Quads-ST4MKSL
06SP Game Used-149
Gold-149
Rainbow-149
Autographs-149
Letter Marks-LMEM
Rookie Exclusives Autographs-REEM
SIGnificance-SEM
06SPx-193
Spectrum-193
06The Cup-171
Autographed Foundations-CQEM
Autographed Foundations Patches-CQEM
Autographed NHL Shields Duals-DASMK
Autographed NHL Shields Duals-DASMO
Autographed NHL Shields Duals-DASMR
Autographed NHL Shields Duals-DASMS
Autographed Rookie Masterpiece Pressplates-171
Foundations-CQEM
Foundations Patches-CQEM
Enshrinements-EEM
Gold Rainbow Autographed Rookie Patches-171
Honorable Numbers-HNEM
Limited Logos-LLEM
Masterpiece Pressplates (Be A Player Portraits)-103
Masterpiece Pressplates (Bee Hive)-144
Masterpiece Pressplates (Marquee Rookies)-564
Masterpiece Pressplates (MVP)-303
Masterpiece Pressplates (SP Authentic Autographs)-196
Masterpiece Pressplates (SP Game Used)-149
Masterpiece Pressplates (SPx Autographs)-193
Masterpiece Pressplates (Sweet Beginnings)-146
Masterpiece Pressplates (Trilogy)-149
Masterpiece Pressplates (Ultimate Collection Autographs)-125
Masterpiece Pressplates (Victory)-304
Property of-POEM
Rookies Black-171
Rookies Platinum-171
Scripted Swatches-SSEM
Scripted Swatches Duals-DSLM
Scripted Swatches Duals-DSOM
Signature Patches-SPEM
06UD Artifacts-254
06UD Biography of a Season-BOS4
06UD Biography of a Season-BOS5
06UD Mini Jersey Collection-126
Jerseys-EM
Jersey Variations-EM
06Ultimate Collection-125
Autographed Jerseys-AJ-EM
Autographed Patches-AJ-EM
Jerseys-UJ-EM
Jerseys Dual-UJ2-CM
Jerseys Triple-UJ3-CMS
Jerseys Triple-UJ3-OMK
Patches-UJ-EM
Patches Dual-UJ2-CM
Patches Triple-UJ3-CMS
Patches Triple-UJ3-OMK
Rookies Autographed NHL Shields-125
Rookies Autographed Patches-125
Signatures-US-EM
Ultimate Achievements-UA-EM
Ultimate Debut Threads Jerseys-DJ-EM
Ultimate Debut Threads Jerseys Autographs-DJ-EM
Ultimate Debut Threads Patches-DJ-EM
Ultimate Debut Threads Patches Autographs-DJ-EM
06Ultra-251
Gold Medallion-251
Ice Medallion-251
06Upper Deck-486
06Upper Deck-495
Exclusives Parallel-486
Exclusives Parallel-495
High Gloss Parallel-486
High Gloss Parallel-495
Diary of a Phenom-DP1
Diary of a Phenom-DP2
Diary of a Phenom-DP3
Diary of a Phenom-DP4
Diary of a Phenom-DP5
Diary of a Phenom-DP6
Diary of a Phenom-DP7
Diary of a Phenom-DP8
Diary of a Phenom-DP9
Diary of a Phenom-DP10
Diary of a Phenom-DP11
Diary of a Phenom-DP12
Diary of a Phenom-DP13
Diary of a Phenom-DP14
Diary of a Phenom-DP15
Diary of a Phenom-DP16
Diary of a Phenom-DP17
Diary of a Phenom-DP18
Diary of a Phenom-DP19
Diary of a Phenom-DP20
Diary of a Phenom-DP21
Diary of a Phenom-DP22
Diary of a Phenom-DP23
Diary of a Phenom-DP24
Diary of a Phenom-DP25
Masterpieces-486
Masterpieces-495
Rookie Game Dated Moments-RGD21
Rookie Headliners-RH21
Rookie Materials-RMEM
Rookie Materials Patches-RMEM
Signatures-SEM
06Upper Deck MVP-303
06Upper Deck MVP-303
Gold Script-303
Super Script-303
06Upper Deck Ovation-192
06Upper Deck Sweet Shot-146
Rookie Jerseys Autographs-146
Signature Shots/Saves-SSEM
Signature Shots/Saves Ice Signings-SSIEM
Signature Shots/Saves Sticks-SSSEM
Signature Sticks-STEM
06Upper Deck Trilogy-149
06Upper Deck Victory-304
06Russian Sport Collection Olympic Stars-9
06Russian Torino Olympic Team-2
06ITG Heroes and Prospects-135
Autographs-AEM
Quad Emblems-QE06
Quad Emblems Gold-QE06
Triple Memorabilia-TM03
Triple Memorabilia-TM04
Triple Memorabilia Gold-TM03
Triple Memorabilia Gold-TM04
07Sports Illustrated for Kids *-136
07Upper Deck National Convention *-NTL15
07Upper Deck National Convention VIP *-VIP15
07Upper Deck All-Star Game Redemptions-AS11
07Upper Deck Rookie Class -9
07Upper Deck Rookie Class C-Card Insert-CC1
07Upper Deck Victory-9
Black-9
Gold-9
GameBreakers-GB31
Oversize Cards-OS3
Stars on Ice-SI41

Malko, Don
00Fresno Falcons-9
01Indianapolis Ice-15

Malkoc, Dean
89Kamloops Blazers-13
907th Inn. Sketch WHL-69
907th Inn. Sketch Memorial Cup-16
91ProCards-409
94Indianapolis Ice-15
95Stadium Club-221
Members Only Master Set-221
95Upper Deck-330
Electric Ice-330
Electric Ice Gold-330
97Be A Player-23
Autographs-23
Autographs Die-Cuts-23
Autographs Prismatic Die-Cuts-23
99Chicago Wolves-17

Malkov, Andrei
00Russian Goalkeepers-6

Malkov, Petr
93Swiss HNL-153
95Swiss HNL-184

Mall, Station
82Sault Ste. Marie Greyhounds-24

Mallen, Ken
10Sweet Caporal Postcards-7
11C55-7

Mallett, Kurt
94Richmond Renegades-9
95Richmond Renegades-10
99Charlotte Checkers-10

Mallette, Carl
99UD Prospects-60
00QMJHL All-Star Program Inserts-13
00Victoriaville Tigres-2
Signed-2
00UD CHL Prospects-84
03Florida Everblades RBI Sports-167

Mallette, Jean
99Quebec Remparts-1
Signed-1
00Quebec Remparts-1
Signed-1

Mallette, Kris
01Asheville Smoke-2
03Elmira Jackals-11
04Colorado Eagles-10

Mallette, Maxim
05Drummondville Voltigeurs-7
06Gatineau Olympiques-3

Mallette, Troy
87Sault Ste. Marie Greyhounds-20
89Rangers Marine Midland Bank-26
90Bowman-219
Tiffany-219
90O-Pee-Chee-277
90Panini Stickers-100
90Pro Set-492
90Score-288
Canadian-288
90Topps-277
Tiffany-277
90Upper Deck-11
French-11
90Rayside-Balfour Jr. Canadians-13
91Bowman-65
91Oilers IGA-12
91Oilers Team Issue-14
91O-Pee-Chee-474
91OPC Premier-39
91Panini Stickers-295
91Pro Set-157
French-157
91Score American-178
91Score Canadian Bilingual-178
91Score Canadian Bilingual-601
91Score Canadian English-178
91Score Canadian English-601
91Stadium Club-134
91Topps-474
91Upper Deck-326
French-326
92Stadium Club-432
92Topps-335
Gold-335G
93Donruss-227
93Leaf-228
93Parkhurst-413
Emerald Ice-413
93PowerPlay-401
93Senators Kraft Sheets-17
93Stadium Club-444
Members Only Master Set-444
First Day Issue-444
93Upper Deck-418
94Canada Games NHL POGS-354
94Donruss-329
94Leaf-358
94OPC Premier-303
Special Effects-303
94Parkhurst-160
Gold-160
94Senators Team Issue-20
94Stadium Club-94
Members Only Master Set-94
First Day Issue-94
Super Team Winner Cards-94
94Topps/OPC Premier-303
Special Effects-303
94Ultra-150
94Upper Deck-196
Electric Ice-196
95Senators Team Issue-15
95Upper Deck-461
Electric Ice-461
Electric Ice Gold-461
96Be A Player-72
Autographs-72
Autographs Silver-72
97Pacific Invincible NHL Regime-14

Mallette, Vince
99Ottawa 67's-28
00Ottawa 67's-22

Mallgrave, Matt
92Harvard Crimson-21
93St. John's Maple Leafs-15
94Hampton Roads Admirals-19
94Classic Pro Prospects-109

Mallon, Jason
95Richmond Renegades-13

Malloy, Mike
88Brockville Braves-13

Malmberg, Ove
64Swedish Coralli ISHockey-2
64Swedish Coralli ISHockey-130
65Swedish Coralli ISHockey-2
65Swedish Coralli ISHockey-130

Malmio, Jyrki
65Finnish Hellas-54

Malmivaara, Olli
01Finnish Cardset-254
02Finnish Cardset-68
04Finnish Cardset-139
Parallel-103
05Finnish Cardset -126

Malmivuori, Olli
65Finnish Hellas-30

Malmstrom, Henrik
99Swedish Upper Deck-156
00Swedish Upper Deck-141
02Swedish Malmo Red Hawks-4
02Swedish SHL-71
Parallel-71
03Swedish Elite-149
Silver-149
04Swedish Elitset-5
Gold-5
05Swedish SHL Elitset-6
06Swedish SHL Elitset-6

Malmstrom, Par
71Swedish Hockey-99

Malo, Andre
95UK Sheffield Steelers-11
97UK Sheffield Steelers-15
97UK Sheffield Steelers-17

99UK Sheffield Steelers-10
00UK Sheffield Steelers Centurions-8

Malo, Gaeten
94German DEL-60
95German DEL-60
96German DEL-257

Malone, Brad
06Sioux Falls Stampede -1

Malone, Cliff
51Laval Dairy QSHL-91
52St. Lawrence Sales-15

Malone, Greg
77Penguins Puck Bucks-12
78O-Pee-Chee-233
78Topps-233
79O-Pee-Chee-9
79Topps-9
80O-Pee-Chee-186
80Topps-186
81O-Pee-Chee-264
82O-Pee-Chee-272
82Post Cereal-15
83NHL Key Tags-102
83O-Pee-Chee-284
83O-Pee-Chee Stickers-229
83Penguins Heinz Photos-17
83Puffy Stickers-7
83Topps Stickers-229
83Whalers Junior Hartford Courant-11
83Whalers Junior Hartford Courant-12
84O-Pee-Chee-74
84O-Pee-Chee Stickers-194
84Topps-57
84Whalers Junior Wendy's-11
85O-Pee-Chee-118
85O-Pee-Chee Stickers-166
85Topps-118
85Whalers Junior Wendy's-12
86Fredericton Express-19
04ITG Franchises US West-268
Autographs-A-GMA

Malone, Joe
10Sweet Caporal Postcards-4
11C55-4
12C57-48
23V145-1-13
60Topps-3
Stamps-34
83Hall of Fame Postcards-N9
85Hall of Fame-204
91Pro Set-332
French-332
93O-Pee-Chee Canadiens Hockey Fest-55
99Upper Deck Century Legends-41
Century Collection-41
04ITG Franchises Canadian-71
05ITG Ultimate Memorabilia Level 1-56
05ITG Ultimate Memorabilia Level 2-56
05ITG Ultimate Memorabilia Level 3-56
05ITG Ultimate Memorabilia Level 4-56
05ITG Ultimate Memorabilia Level 5-56
06ITG Ultimate Memorabilia-77
Artist Proof-77

Malone, Ryan
03BAP Memorabilia-204
03BAP Ultimate Memorabilia Autographs-115
Gold-115
03BAP Ultimate Mem Auto Jerseys-115
03BAP Ultimate Mem Auto Emblems-115
03BAP Ultimate Mem Auto Numbers-115
03BAP Ultimate Mem Calder Candidates-5
03BAP Ultimate Mem Calder Candidates Gold-5
03BAP Ultimate Mem Magnificent Prospects-5
03BAP Ultimate Mem Magnif Prospect Autos-5
03BAP Ultimate Mem Rookie Jersey Emblems-9
03BAP Ultimate Mem Rookie Jsy Emblem Gold-9
03BAP Ultimate Mem Rookie Jersey Numbers-9
03BAP Ultimate Mem Rookie Jsy Number Gold-9
03Bowman-123
Gold-123
03Bowman Chrome-123
Refractors-123
Gold Refractors-123
Xfractors-123
03ITG Action-615
03ITG Toronto Spring Expo Class of 2004-3
03ITG Used Signature Series-141
Autographs Gold-141
03ITG VIP Rookie Debut-34
03Pacific-367
03Pacific Calder-131
Silver-131
Reflections-8
03Pacific Complete-550
Red-550
03Pacific Exhibit-235
03Pacific Quest for the Cup-132
Calder Contenders-18
03Parkhurst Toronto Expo Rookie Preview-PRP-17
03Parkhurst Rookie-185
All-Rookie-ART-6
All-Rookie Gold-ART-6
Calder Candidates-CMC-5
Calder Candidates Gold-CMC-5
Rookie Emblems-RE-37
Rookie Emblem Autographs-RE-RM
Rookie Emblems Gold-RE-37
Rookie Jerseys-RJ-37
Rookie Jersey Autographs-RJ-RM
Rookie Jerseys Gold-RJ-37
Rookie Numbers-RN-37
Rookie Number Autographs-RN-RM
Rookie Numbers Gold-RN-37
03SP Authentic-113
Limited-113
03SPx-235
03Topps Traded-TT136
Blue-TT136
Gold-TT136
Red-TT136
03UD Honor Roll-160
03Upper Deck-236
Canadian Exclusives-236
HG-236
03Upper Deck Rookie Update-96
YoungStars-YS5
03Upper Deck Trilogy-164
Limited-164
04Pacific-214
Blue-214
Red-214
04UD All-World-23
Gold-23
04Upper Deck-140
Canadian Exclusives-140
HG Glossy Gold-140
HG Glossy Silver-140
05Black Diamond-70
Emerald-70
Gold-70
Onyx-70
Ruby-70
05Hot Prospects-81
En Fuego-81
Red Hot-81
White Hot-81
05Panini Stickers-149
05Parkhurst-388
Facsimile Auto Parallel-388
Signatures-RM
05SP Game Used Game Gear-GG-RM
05UD Toronto Fall Expo Priority Signings-PS-RM
05Ultimate Collection-72
Gold-72
05Ultra-158
Gold-158
Ice-158
05Upper Deck-152
HG Glossy-152
05Upper Deck MVP-308
Gold-308
Platinum-308
05Upper Deck Rookie Update-79
05Upper Deck Toronto Fall Expo-152
05Upper Deck Victory-159
Black-159
Gold-159
Silver-159
06Be A Player-88
Autographs-88
Signatures-RM
Signatures 10-95
Signatures Trios-TFSM
06Black Diamond-68
Black-68
Gold-68
Ruby-68
06Flair Showcase Inks-IRM
06Fleer-155
Tiffany-155
06Hot Prospects Hotagraphs-HRM
06ITG International Ice-126
Gold-126
Autographs-ARML
06O-Pee-Chee-400
Rainbow-400
Autographs-A-RM
06Panini Stickers-142
06SP Game Used Authentic Fabrics-AFRM
06SP Game Used Authentic Fabrics Parallel-AFRM
06SP Game Used Authentic Fabrics Patches-AFRM
06SP Game Used Authentic Fabrics Triple-AF3PIT
06SP Game Used Authentic Fabrics Triple Patches-AF3PIT
06SP Game Used SIGnificance-SMA
06UD Artifacts Auto-Facts-AFRM
06UD Artifacts Auto-Facts Gold-AFRM
06UD Artifacts Tundra Tandems-TTRM
06UD Artifacts Tundra Tandems Black-TTRM
06UD Artifacts Tundra Tandems Blue-TTRM
06UD Artifacts Tundra Tandems Gold-TTRM
06UD Artifacts Tundra Tandems Platinum-TTRM
06UD Artifacts Tundra Tandems Red-TTRM
06UD Artifacts Tundra Tandems Dual Patches Red-TTRM
06Ultra-156
Gold Medallion-156
Ice Medallion-156
Fresh Ink-IRM
06Upper Deck Arena Giveaways-PIT4
06Upper Deck-160
Exclusives Parallel-160
High Gloss Parallel-160
Masterpieces-160
06Upper Deck MVP-239
Gold Script-239
Super Script-239
Autographs-OAMC
Jerseys-OJHM
06Upper Deck Sweet Shot Signature Sticks-STRM
06Upper Deck Trilogy Ice Scripts-ISRM
06Upper Deck Trilogy Scripts-TSRM
06Upper Deck Victory-158
06Upper Deck Victory Black-158
06Upper Deck Victory Gold-158

Malone, Scott
94Binghamton Rangers-10
94Classic-66
Gold-66
Tri-Cards-T43
95Binghamton Rangers-15
97Pensacola Ice Pilots-13

Malone, Shane
06Prince Albert Raiders-23

Maloney, Brian
00Michigan State Spartans-14
03Chicago Wolves-14
04Chicago Wolves-11
05Chicago Wolves-11
06Binghamton Senators-15

Maloney, Dan
71Toronto Sun-74
72O-Pee-Chee-264
72Sargent Promotions Stamps-70
73O-Pee-Chee-32
73Topps-32
74NHL Action Stamps-121
74O-Pee-Chee NHL-172
74Topps-172
75O-Pee-Chee NHL-177
75Topps-177
76O-Pee-Chee NHL-101
76Topps-101
77O-Pee-Chee NHL-172
77Topps-172
78Maple Leafs Postcards-12
78O-Pee-Chee-21
78Topps-21
79Maple Leafs Postcards-17
79O-Pee-Chee-271
80O-Pee-Chee-118
80Pepsi-Cola Caps-90
80Topps-118
81Maple Leafs Postcards-10
81O-Pee-Chee-320
81O-Pee-Chee Stickers-102
82Maple Leafs Postcards-22
82O-Pee-Chee-326
82O-Pee-Chee Stickers-72
82Topps Stickers-72
83Maple Leafs Postcards-14
84Maple Leafs Postcards-16
86Jets Postcards-3
88Jets Police-13
88Jets Postcards-15
02Fleer Throwbacks-35
Gold-35
Platinum-35
05ITG Tough Customers-DM
Autographs-DM
Emblem and Numbers-DM
Jerseys-DM
Signed Memorabilia-DM

Maloney, Darren
91Air Canada SJHL-B22
91Air Canada SJHL All-Stars-43
92Saskatchewan JHL-71
93Western Michigan Broncos-20
96Peoria Rivermen-15
96Peoria Rivermen Photo Album-16
97Peoria Rivermen-5
98ECHL All-Star Northern Conference-4
98Peoria Rivermen-1
98Peoria Rivermen-27
99Peoria Rivermen-12
00Peoria Rivermen-6
01UK Nottingham Panthers-19

Maloney, Dave
76O-Pee-Chee NHL-181
76Topps-181
77Coca-Cola-14
77O-Pee-Chee NHL-41
77Topps-41
77Topps/O-Pee-Chee Glossy-10
Square-10
78O-Pee-Chee-221
78Topps-221
79O-Pee-Chee-159
79Topps-159
80O-Pee-Chee-7
80Topps-7
81O-Pee-Chee-227
81O-Pee-Chee Stickers-173
81Topps-E100
82O-Pee-Chee-228
82O-Pee-Chee Stickers-140
82Post Cereal-13
82Topps Stickers-140
83NHL Key Tags-89
83O-Pee-Chee-249
83O-Pee-Chee Stickers-211
83Topps Stickers-211
84O-Pee-Chee-146
85O-Pee-Chee-89
85O-Pee-Chee Stickers-177
85Topps-89

Maloney, Don
79O-Pee-Chee-42
79O-Pee-Chee-162
79Topps-42
79Topps-162
80O-Pee-Chee-231
80Topps-231
81O-Pee-Chee-228
81O-Pee-Chee Stickers-170
81Topps-E101
82O-Pee-Chee-229
82O-Pee-Chee Stickers-137
82Post Cereal-13
82Topps Stickers-137
83NHL Key Tags-87
83O-Pee-Chee-250
83O-Pee-Chee Stickers-212
83Puffy Stickers-21
83Topps Stickers-212
84O-Pee-Chee-147
84O-Pee-Chee Stickers-95
84O-Pee-Chee Stickers-96
84 7-Eleven Discs-36
84Topps-109
85O-Pee-Chee-94
85Topps-94
86O-Pee-Chee-81
86Topps-81
87O-Pee-Chee-49
87O-Pee-Chee Stickers-29
87Panini Stickers-117
87Topps-49
88Panini Stickers-308
89Islanders Team Issue-13
89Panini Stickers-231
90Bowman-117
Tiffany-117
90O-Pee-Chee-31
90Panini Stickers-84
90Pro Set-187
90Score-303A
Canadian-303A
90Topps-31
Tiffany-31
90Upper Deck-20
French-20

Maloney, Phil
44Beehive Group II Photos-46
44Beehive Group II Photos-426
45Quaker Oats Photos-31
74O-Pee-Chee NHL-104
74Topps-104

Malov, Roman
00Russian Hockey League-90
04Russian RHL-19

Maltais, Daniel
93Quebec Pee-Wee Tournament-379

Maltais, Dominic
90 7th Inn. Sketch QMJHL-85
91 7th Inn. Sketch QMJHL-108
93Fort Worth Fire-10
94Central Hockey League-25
95Hampton Roads Admirals-7
96Hampton Roads Admirals-HRA17
98Hampton Roads Admirals-22
99Hampton Roads Admirals-12
00Asheville Smoke-8
01Sorel Royaux-16
03St. Jean Mission-16

Maltais, Frederic
88Richelieu Riverains-17

Maltais, Steve
89Capitals Kodak-26
89ProCards AHL-85
90Score-417
Canadian-417
90ProCards AHL/IHL-205
91ProCards-156
92Lightning Sheraton-20
92Atlanta Knights-11
96Collector's Edge Ice-107
Prism-107
98Chicago Wolves-4
98Chicago Wolves Turner Cup-11
98IHL All-Star Western Conference-6
99Chicago Wolves-8
99IHL All-Stars-20
00Upper Deck NHLPA-PA27
00Chicago Wolves-16
01Chicago Wolves-11
02Chicago Wolves-16
03Chicago Wolves-15
04Chicago Wolves-22

Maltby, Kirk
90 7th Inn. Sketch OHL-287
91 7th Inn. Sketch OHL-278
92Classic-20
Gold-20
92Classic Four-Sport *-169
Gold-169
93Donruss-428
93OPC Premier-290
Gold-290
93Score-627
Gold-627
Canadian-627
Canadian Gold-627
93Stadium Club-299
Members Only Master Set-299
First Day Issue-299
93Topps/OPC Premier-290
Gold-290
93Upper Deck-520
93Owen Sound Platers-18
94Be A Player Signature Cards-38
94Donruss-53
94Leaf-230
94OPC Premier-72
Special Effects-72
94Pinnacle-441
Artist's Proofs-441
Rink Collection-441
94Topps/OPC Premier-72
Special Effects-72
94Upper Deck-472
Electric Ice-472
94Classic Pro Prospects-21
95Collector's Choice-191
Player's Club-191
Player's Club Platinum-191
95Pinnacle-126
Artist's Proofs-126
Rink Collection-126
95Playoff One on One-149
95Topps-133
OPC Inserts-133
95Upper Deck-41
Electric Ice-41
Electric Ice Gold-41
96Playoff One on One-373
96Red Wings Detroit News/Free Press-1
97Collector's Choice-84
97Pacific Dynagon Best Kept Secrets-33
97Pacific Invincible NHL Regime-71
97Score Red Wings-15
Platinum-15
Premier-15
97Upper Deck-61
97Owen Sound Platers-26
98Pacific-199
Ice Blue-199
Red-199
99BAP Millennium-93
Emerald-93
Ruby-93
Sapphire-93
Signatures-93
Signatures Gold-93
00Pacific-154
Copper-154
Gold-154
Ice Blue-154
Premiere Date-154
01UD Stanley Cup Champs-63
01Upper Deck Victory-129
Gold-129
02BAP Memorabilia-150
Emerald-150
Ruby-150
Sapphire-150
NHL All-Star Game-150
NHL All-Star Game Blue-150
NHL All-Star Game Green-150
NHL All-Star Game Red-150
02BAP Memorabilia Toronto Fall Expo-150
02BAP Sig Series Auto Buybacks 1999-93
02BAP Ultimate Mem Dynasty Jerseys-8
02BAP Ultimate Mem Dynasty Emblems-8
02BAP Ultimate Mem Dynasty Numbers-8
02Pacific Complete-277
Red-277
02Topps Total-382
02Upper Deck-312
Exclusives-312
02Upper Deck Beckett UD Promos-312
03ITG Action-205
03Pacific Complete-94
Red-94
03Parkhurst Original Six Detroit-20
04UD Toronto Fall Expo Pride of Canada-19
04Upper Deck-60
Canadian Exclusives-60
HG Glossy Gold-60
HG Glossy Silver-60
05Parkhurst-180
Facsimile Auto Parallel-180
06O-Pee-Chee-185
Rainbow-185

Maltby, Shawn
97Toledo Storm-24
02UK Manchester Storm-3
02Atlantic City Boardwalk Bullies-13
04UK EIHL All-Stars-16

Maltby, Stephen
98Abilene Aviators-15

Malts, Vince
02Augusta Lynx-71
02Charlotte Checkers-86
03Bakersfield Condors-13

Maltsev, Alexander
69Russian National Team Postcards-10
69Swedish Hockey-8
70Finnish Jaakiekko-7
70Russian National Team Postcards-10
70Swedish Hockey-325
70Swedish Masterserien-67
70Swedish Masterserien-100
70Swedish Masterserien-124
70Swedish Masterserien-131
70Swedish Masterserien-133
71Finnish Suomi Stickers-8
71Swedish Hockey-36
72Finnish Jaakiekko-28
72Finnish Hellas-70
72Finnish Panda Toronto-55
72Finnish Semic World Championship-10
72Swedish Stickers-31
72Swedish Stickers-49
72Swedish Semic World Championship-10
73Finnish Jaakiekko-9
73Russian National Team-20
73Swedish Stickers-89
74Finnish Jenkki-49
74Finnish Typotor-69
74Russian National Team-12
74Swedish Stickers-8
74Swedish Semic World Champ Stickers-36
79Panini Stickers-155
79Russian National Team-16
81Swedish Semic Hockey VM Stickers-46
82Swedish Semic VM Stickers-67
83Swedish Semic VM Stickers-67
84Russian National Team-13
91Future Trends Canada '72-20
91Future Trends Canada '72 French-20
91Finnish Semic World Champ Stickers-245
91Swedish Semic World Champ Stickers-245
92Future Trends '76 Canada Cup-161
92Future Trends '76 Canada Cup-190
92Future Trends '76 Canada Cup-200
92Future Trends Promo Sheet-1
96Swedish Semic Wien Hockey Legends-HL6
99Russian Stars of Hockey-42
03Czech Stadion-649
06ITG International Ice International Rivals-IR02
06ITG International Ice International Rivals Gold-IR02
06ITG International Ice Teammates-IT19
06ITG International Ice Teammates Gold-IT19
06ITG Phenoms Idols Gold-IDAO
06ITG Phenoms Idols Silver-IDAO

Maluta, Ray
77Rochester Americans-16

Maly, Miroslav
84Springfield Indians-20
94German DEL-331
95German DEL-293
96German DEL-321

Maly, Tomas
02Czech OFS Plus Trios-T9

Malykhin, Igor
90O-Pee-Chee Red Army-15R
91O-Pee-Chee Inserts-20R
93Fort Wayne Komets-11
93Classic Pro Prospects-86
00Fort Wayne Komets-11
00Fort Wayne Komets Shoe Carnival-5

Malysiak, Andrzej
79Panini Stickers-128

Mamane, Shawn
00Worcester Icecats-29

Manavian, Antonin
05Gatineau Olympiques-25

Manberg, Kenneth
69Swedish Hockey-177

Mancari, Mark
01Ottawa 67's-18
02Ottawa 67's-18
03Ottawa 67's-14
04Ottawa 67's-8
06Rochester Americans-14
07Upper Deck Victory-202
Black-202
Gold-202

Manchakowski, Chris
00Saskatoon Blades-18

Manchur, Trent
04Williams Lake Timberwolves-13

Mancini, Jeff
00Amarillo Rattlers-12

Mandel, Joshua
93Quebec Pee-Wee Tournament-728

Manderson, Denver
06Kitchener Rangers-14

Manderville, Kent
90Upper Deck-465
French-465
91Alberta International Team Canada-16
91Parkhurst-392
French-392
92Maple Leafs Kodak-15
92O-Pee-Chee-14
92OPC Premier-23
92Parkhurst-184
Emerald Ice-184
92Score-458
Canadian-458
Canadian Olympians-10
92Stadium Club-339
92Topps-148
Gold-148G
92Upper Deck-32
92St. John's Maple Leafs-11
93Maple Leafs Score Black's-10
93Parkhurst-204
Emerald Ice-204
93Stadium Club-417
Members Only Master Set-417
First Day Issue-417
93Upper Deck-420
94Be A Player Signature Cards-156
94Canada Games NHL POGS-235
94Leaf-526
94Maple Leafs Gangsters-12
94Maple Leafs Pin-up Posters-17
94OPC Premier-474
Special Effects-474
94Parkhurst-235
Gold-235
94Pinnacle-454
Artist's Proofs-454
Rink Collection-454
94Stadium Club-253
Members Only Master Set-253
First Day Issue-253
Super Team Winner Cards-253
94Topps/OPC Premier-474
Special Effects-474
94Upper Deck-131
Electric Ice-131
95St. John's Maple Leafs-15
96Whalers Kid's Club-28
96Springfield Falcons-10
96Collector's Edge Ice-83
Prism-83
97Be A Player-165
Autographs-165
Autographs Die-Cuts-165
Autographs Prismatic Die-Cuts-165
97Collector's Choice-118
97Hurricanes Team Issue-18
97Pacific-289
Copper-289
Emerald Green-289
Ice Blue-289
Red-289
Silver-289
98Hurricanes Team Issue-21
99BAP Millennium-52
Emerald-52
Ruby-52
Sapphire-52
Signatures-52
Signatures Gold-52
99Pacific-77
Copper-77
Emerald Green-77
Gold-77
Ice Blue-77
Premiere Date-77
Red-77
99Panini Stickers-49
99Upper Deck Retro-13
Gold-13
Platinum-13
00BAP Memorabilia-210
Emerald-210
Ruby-210
Sapphire-210
Promos-210
00BAP Mem Chicago Sportsfest Copper-210
00BAP Memorabilia Chicago Sportsfest Blue-210
00BAP Memorabilia Chicago Sportsfest Gold-210
00BAP Memorabilia Chicago Sportsfest Ruby-210
00BAP Memorabilia Chicago Sun-Times Ruby-210
00BAP Memorabilia Chicago Sun-Times Gold-210
00BAP Mem Chicago Sun-Times Sapphire-210
00BAP Mem Toronto Fall Expo Copper-210
00BAP Memorabilia Toronto Fall Expo Gold-210
00BAP Memorabilia Toronto Fall Expo Ruby-210
00Pacific-302
Copper-302
Gold-302
Ice Blue-302
Premiere Date-302
01Flyers Postcards-10
01Upper Deck Vintage-187
02BAP Sig Series Auto Buybacks 1999-52
04Swedish Pure Skills-95
Parallel-95

Mandeville, Louis
00Halifax Mooseheads-18
00Rouyn-Noranda Huskies-17
Signed-17
01Halifax Mooseheads-22

Mandeville, Martin
00Baie-Comeau Drakkar-21
Signed-21
01Baie-Comeau Drakkar-19
02Baie-Comeau Drakkar-21
03Baie Comeau Drakkar-20
04Baie-Comeau Drakkar-12

Mandich, Dan
82North Stars Postcards-14
83North Stars Postcards-16
84North Stars Postcards-13
85North Stars Postcards-18

Mando, Dean
95Slapshot-420
97Austin Ice Bats-11
99Charlotte Checkers-28
99Mississippi Sea Wolves Kelly Cup-14

Mandous, Vaclav
94German First League-342

Maneluk, George
88ProCards AHL-317
89ProCards AHL-241
90ProCards AHL/IHL-500
91ProCards-370
94Central Hockey League-117
95Louisiana Ice Gators-9
95Louisiana Ice Gators Playoffs-10

Maneluk, Mike
91 7th Inn. Sketch WHL-199
92Brandon Wheat Kings-15
93Brandon Wheat Kings-21
96Collector's Edge Ice-13
Prism-13
98Bowman's Best-112
Refractors-112
Atomic Refractors-112
98Pacific Dynagon Ice-139
Blue-139
Red-139
Rookies-5
98Pacific Omega-53
Red-53
Opening Day Issue-53
98SP Authentic-93
Power Shift-93
98Upper Deck-332
Exclusives-332
Exclusives 1 of 1-332
Gold Reserve-332
98Upper Deck MVP-49
Gold Script-49
Silver Script-49
Super Script-49
01Upper Deck Victory-107
Gold-107
01Swiss HNL-44
02Swiss HNL-91
02Swiss HNL-245
05Philadelphia Phantoms All-Decade Team-8

Manery, Kris
78North Stars Cloverleaf Dairy-8
78O-Pee-Chee-107
78Topps-107
79North Stars Postcards-7
79O-Pee-Chee-151
79Topps-151
80Jets Postcards-14
80Pepsi-Cola Caps-132
81O-Pee-Chee-371

Manery, Randy
72Flames Postcards-8
72O-Pee-Chee-260
72Sargent Promotions Stamps-10
73O-Pee-Chee-131
73Topps-131
74NHL Action Stamps-9
74O-Pee-Chee NHL-86
74Topps-86
75O-Pee-Chee NHL-44
75Topps-44
76O-Pee-Chee NHL-24
76Topps-24
77O-Pee-Chee NHL-389
78O-Pee-Chee-266
79O-Pee-Chee-317
80O-Pee-Chee-342

Mangan, Phil
03Ottawa 67's-15
04Kingston Frontenacs-13

Manganaro, Sal
96Dayton Bombers-21
99Greensboro Generals-3
01Greensboro Generals-3

Mangold, Pat
84Kamloops Blazers-14

Maniago, Cesare
44Beehive Group II Photos-265
44Beehive Group II Photos-427
60NHL Ceramic Tiles-29
61York Yellow Backs-41
63Parkhurst-40
63Parkhurst-99
64Beehive Group III Photos-140
68O-Pee-Chee-45
68Shirriff Coins-66
68Topps-45
69O-Pee-Chee-121
Four-in-One-11
69Topps-121
70Colgate Stamps-63
70Esso Power Players-180
70North Stars Postcards-5
70O-Pee-Chee-173
70Sargent Promotions Stamps-81
71Letraset Action Replays-24
71O-Pee-Chee-117
71Sargent Promotions Stamps-92
71Topps-5
71Topps-117
71Toronto Sun-136
72O-Pee-Chee-138
72Sargent Promotions Stamps-110
72Topps-104
73North Stars Action Posters-6
73North Stars Postcards-11
73O-Pee-Chee-127
73Topps-146
74Lipton Soup-27
74NHL Action Stamps-138
74O-Pee-Chee NHL-26
74Topps-26
75O-Pee-Chee NHL-261
75Topps-261
76Canucks Royal Bank-10
76O-Pee-Chee NHL-240
76Topps-240
77Canucks Canada Dry Cans-8
77Canucks Royal Bank-11
77O-Pee-Chee NHL-23
77Topps-23
95Parkhurst '66-67-97
Coins-97
04ITG Franchises US West-247
Autographs-A-CM
Original Sticks-WOS14
Original Sticks Gold-WOS14
06Parkhurst-70
Autographs-70

Maniago, Michael
05Kamloops Blazers-2

Manias, Matt
03Sarnia Sting-14

Maniatis, Chris
93Quebec Pee-Wee Tournament-828

Manitowich, Ryan
03Bossier-Shreveport Mudbugs-12
05Bossier-Shreveport Mudbugs-10

Manley, Billy
95Halifax Mooseheads-19
96Halifax Mooseheads I-13
96Halifax Mooseheads II-13
97Halifax Mooseheads I-12
97Halifax Mooseheads II-12
98Halifax Mooseheads-5
98Halifax Mooseheads Second Edition-19

Manley, Mike
04Kalamazoo Wings-24
05Kalamazoo Wings-20

Manley, Wayne
93Swiss HNL-309

Manlow, Eric
91 7th Inn. Sketch OHL-87
93Kitchener Rangers-1
93Kitchener Rangers-24
93Classic Four-Sport *-210
Gold-210
94Detroit Jr. Red Wings-11
94Kitchener Rangers-26
95Indianapolis Ice-13
95Slapshot Memorial Cup-85
96Collector's Edge Ice-137
Prism-137
97Indianapolis Ice-15
00Upper Deck Ice-110
00Providence Bruins-4
01Pacific-34
Extreme LTD-34
Hobby LTD-34
Premiere Date-34
Retail LTD-34
01Pacific Arena Exclusives-34
01Providence Bruins-6
03Bridgeport Sound Tigers-6A
06Hamilton Bulldogs-9

Mann, Cameron
93Peterborough Petes-16
95Slapshot-313
95Slapshot-NNO
95Signature Rookies Tetrad Autobilia *-47
96Upper Deck Ice-130
97Black Diamond-138
Double Diamond-138
Triple Diamond-138
Quadruple Diamond-138
97Collector's Choice-306
97Providence Bruins-9
97Bowman CHL-4
OPC-4
98Bowman's Best-127
Refractors-127
Atomic Refractors-127
98Katch-163
98McDonald's Upper Deck-26
98Pacific-85
Ice Blue-85
Red-85
98SPx Finite-126
Radiance-126
Spectrum-126
98UD Choice-17
98UD Choice Preview-17
98UD Choice Prime Choice Reserve-17
98UD Choice Reserve-17
98UD3-19
98UD3-79
98UD3-139
Die-Cuts-19
Die-Cuts-79
Die-Cuts-139
98Upper Deck-2
Exclusives-2
Exclusives 1 of 1-2
Gold Reserve-2
98Upper Deck MVP-11
Gold Script-11
Silver Script-11
Super Script-11
98Providence Bruins-13
99BAP Memorabilia-198
Gold-198
Silver-198
99BAP Millennium-26
Emerald-26
Ruby-26
Sapphire-26
Signatures-26
Signatures Gold-26
99Pacific-26
Copper-26
Emerald Green-26
Gold-26
Ice Blue-26
Premiere Date-26
Red-26
99Providence Bruins-16
00Upper Deck NHLPA-PA9
00Providence Bruins-6
01Utah Grizzlies-23
02BAP Sig Series Auto Buybacks 1999-26
02Milwaukee Admirals-11
02Milwaukee Admirals Postcards-12
03German DEL-82
04German DEL-91
All-Stars-AS9
04German Ingolstadt Panthers-15
05German DEL-151

Mann, Dallas
98BC Icemen-15
98BC Icemen II-22

Mann, Doug
97Columbus Cottonmouths-8
99Columbus Cottonmouths-12
00Columbus Cottonmouths-6
04Columbus Cottonmouths-20

Mann, Jimmy
79Jets Postcards-14
80Jets Postcards-15
80O-Pee-Chee-164
80O-Pee-Chee-353
80Pepsi-Cola Caps-133
80Topps-164
81Jets Postcards-13
81O-Pee-Chee-372
82Jets Postcards-16
83Jets Postcards-15
83Nordiques Postcards-16
84Nordiques Postcards-14
85Nordiques General Foods-16
85Nordiques Provigo-15
86Nordiques McDonald's-16
88ProCards IHL-21
02Fleer Throwbacks-36
Gold-36
Platinum-36
04ITG Franchises Canadian-138
Autographs-JMN
05ITG Tough Customers-JM
Autographs-JM

Mann, Norm
34Beehive Group I Photos-335A
34Beehive Group I Photos-335B

Mann, Pavel
94German DEL-344
95German DEL-318
95German DEL-430

Mann, Stephan
94German DEL-203
95German DEL-206
96German DEL-349
99German DEL-26

Mann, Stephen
00Spokane Chiefs-18
01Saskatoon Blades-20
02Saskatoon Blades-20
03Saskatoon Blades-28

Mann, Troy
96Mississippi Sea Wolves-12
97Mississippi Sea Wolves-15
99Mississippi Sea Wolves Kelly Cup-23
01Missouri River Otters-5
03Missouri River Otters-8

Mannberg, Niklas
83Swedish Semic Elitserien-187
84Swedish Semic Elitserien-210
86Swedish Panini Stickers-237
87Swedish Panini Stickers-228
89Swedish Semic Elitserien Stickers-209

Manness, Alan
96Kamloops Blazers-15
98Kamloops Blazers-18

Mannikko, Erkki
66Finnish Jaakiekkosarja-160

Mannikko, Miikka
99Finnish Cardset-322
05Finnish Cardset -248
06Finnish Cardset-76

Manninen, Kevin
00Michigan Tech Huskies-16

Manninen, Mika
93Finnish SISU-110
94Finnish SISU-108
94Finnish SISU Junior-7
94Finnish SISU NL Phenoms-1
95Finnish SISU-29

Manning, Blair
95Seattle Thunderbirds-14
96Louisiana Ice Gators-6
98Louisiana Ice Gators-7
99Topeka Scarecrows-7
03Oklahoma City Blazers-15
05Bossier-Shreveport Mudbugs-11

Manning, Josh
02Belleville Bulls-10
03Belleville Bulls-17

Manning, Paul
01Syracuse Crunch-4
02BAP Memorabilia-341
02BAP Ultimate Memorabilia-83
02Parkhurst Retro-243
Minis-243

02UD Artistic Impressions-135
Gold-135
02UD Honor Roll-129
02Syracuse Crunch-5
03German DEL-113
04German DEL-128
04German Hamburg Freezers Postcards-7
05German DEL-110
06German DEL-73

Manning, Tom
93Quebec Pee-Wee Tournament-627

Mannino, Tommy
03London Knights-19
05Saginaw Spirit-14
06Saginaw Spirit-6

Mannisto, Keijo
66Finnish Jaakiekkosarja-161
70Finnish Jaakiekko-217
71Finnish Suomi Stickers-139
73Finnish Jaakiekko-164
78Finnish SM-Liiga-191

Manno, Bob
77Canucks Royal Bank-12
78Canucks Royal Bank-15
78O-Pee-Chee-349
79Canucks Royal Bank-14
79O-Pee-Chee-270
80Canucks Silverwood Dairies-16
81Maple Leafs Postcards-11
81O-Pee-Chee-396
82O-Pee-Chee-325
82O-Pee-Chee Stickers-71
82Post Cereal-18
82Topps Stickers-71
83O-Pee-Chee-132
83Swedish Semic VM Stickers-129
84O-Pee-Chee-59
85O-Pee-Chee-134
85Topps-134
98German DEL-154
99German DEL-169

Manny, Ben
05Knoxville Ice Bears-8

Manny, Phil
03UK Cardiff Devils-6
05UK Cardiff Devils Challenge Cup-10

Manojlovic, Steven
06Mississauga Ice Dogs-15

Mansi, Moe
88Flint Spirits-15
93Swedish Semic World Champ Stickers-226
94Finnish Jaa Kiekko-304
95Swedish World Championships Stickers-95
96German DEL-121
96Swedish Semic Wien-179
01UK London Knights-10
02UK London Knights-6

Mansikka, Reijo
78Finnish SM-Liiga-91

Mansoff, Jason
92British Columbia JHL-78
93Maine Black Bears-40
97Hampton Roads Admirals-14
98Rochester Americans-14
99Indianapolis Ice-13
00UK Sekonda Superleague-35
01UK Sheffield Steelers-15

Manson, Dave
84Prince Albert Raiders Stickers-17
86Blackhawks Coke-8
87Blackhawks Coke-9
88Blackhawks Coke-9
89Blackhawks Coke-24
89O-Pee-Chee-150
89O-Pee-Chee Stickers-13
89Panini Stickers-47
89Topps-150
90Blackhawks Coke-24
90O-Pee-Chee-363
90O-Pee-Chee-397
90Panini Stickers-199
90Pro Set-54A
90Pro Set-54B
90Score-193
Canadian-193
90Topps-363
90Upper Deck-85
French-85
91Pro Set Platinum-172
91Bowman-389
91Oilers IGA-13
91Oilers Team Issue-15
91O-Pee-Chee-409
91OPC Premier-137
91Panini Stickers-15
91Parkhurst-49
French-49
91Pinnacle-62
French-62
91Pro Set-41
91Pro Set-389
French-41
French-389
91Score American-152
91Score Canadian Bilingual-152
91Score Canadian Bilingual-624
91Score Canadian English-152
91Score Canadian English-624
91Score Rookie/Traded-74T
91Stadium Club-308
91Topps-409
91Upper Deck-280
91Upper Deck-548
French-280
French-548
92Bowman-339
92Oilers IGA-14
92Oilers Team Issue-12
92O-Pee-Chee-56
92Panini Stickers-108
92Panini Stickers French-108
92Parkhurst-47
Emerald Ice-47
Cherry Picks-CP15
92Pinnacle-334
French-334
92Pro Set-55
92Score-214
Canadian-214
92Seasons Patches-56
92Stadium Club-436
92Topps-389
Gold-389G
92Ultra-62
92Upper Deck-84
93Donruss-109
93Donruss-509
93Leaf-159
93McDonald's Upper Deck-9
93OPC Premier-71
Gold-71
93Panini Stickers-242
93Parkhurst-335
Emerald Ice-335
93Pinnacle-363
Canadian-363
All-Stars-38
All-Stars Canadian-38
93PowerPlay-83
93Score-127
Canadian-127
93Stadium Club-183
Members Only Master Set-183
OPC-183
First Day Issue-183
First Day Issue OPC-183
All-Stars-14
All-Stars Members Only-14
All-Stars OPC-14
93Topps/OPC Premier-71
Gold-71
93Ultra-93
93Upper Deck-358
SP-50
93Upper Deck Locker All-Stars-30
94Be A Player-R41
Signature Cards-95
94Canada Games NHL POGS-257
94Donruss-242
94EA Sports-43
94Flair-207
94Fleer-243
94Leaf-239
94OPC Premier-121
Special Effects-121
94Parkhurst-262
Gold-262
Vintage-V9
94Pinnacle-51
Artist's Proofs-51
Rink Collection-51
94Select-13
Gold-13
94SP-134
Die Cuts-134
94Stadium Club-61
Members Only Master Set-61
First Day Issue-61
Super Team Winner Cards-61
94Topps/OPC Premier-121
Special Effects-121
94Ultra-243
94Upper Deck-63
Electric Ice-63
SP Inserts-SP180
SP Inserts Die Cuts-SP180
94Upper Deck NHLPA/Be A Player-30
95Canada Games NHL POGS-295
95Collector's Choice-230
Player's Club-230
Player's Club Platinum-230
95Donruss-317
95Emotion-194
95Jets Readers Club-7
95Jets Team Issue-14
95Leaf-158
95Panini Stickers-219
95Parkhurst International-233
Emerald Ice-233
95Pinnacle-103
Artist's Proofs-103
Rink Collection-103
95Playoff One on One-218
95Score-59
Black Ice Artist's Proofs-59
Black Ice-59
95SkyBox Impact-182
95Topps-120
OPC Inserts-120
95Ultra-181
Gold Medallion-181
95Upper Deck-51
Electric Ice-51
Electric Ice Gold-51
96Be A Player-57
Autographs-57
Autographs Silver-57
96Canadiens Postcards-17
96Canadiens Sheets-11
96Coyotes Coca-Cola-19
96Metal Universe-119
96Playoff One on One-401
96Ultra-133
Gold Medallion-133
96Upper Deck-317
97Canadiens Postcards-12
97Collector's Choice-136
97Pacific Dynagon Best Kept Secrets-49
97Score Canadiens-17
Platinum-17
Premier-17
98Be A Player-67
Press Release-67
98BAP Gold-67
98BAP Autographs-67
98BAP Autographs Gold-67
98BAP Tampa Bay All Star Game-67
98OPC Chrome-165
Refractors-165
98Pacific-254
Ice Blue-254
Red-254
98Paramount-115
Copper-115
Emerald Green-115
Holo-Electric-115
Ice Blue-115
Silver-115
98Topps-165
O-Pee-Chee-165
98UD Choice-108
Prime Choice Reserve-108
Reserve-108
98Upper Deck-113
Exclusives-113
Exclusives 1 of 1-113
Gold Reserve-113
99Blackhawks Chicago Sun-Times-5
99Pacific-91
Copper-91
Emerald Green-91
Gold-91
Ice Blue-91
Premiere Date-91
Red-91
00BAP Memorabilia-436
Emerald-436
Ruby-436
Sapphire-436
00Pacific-135
Copper-135
Gold-135
Ice Blue-135
Premiere Date-135
01Pacific-369
Extreme LTD-369
Hobby LTD-369
Premiere Date-369
Retail LTD-369
01Pacific Arena Exclusives-369
01Stars Postcards-15
02BAP Sig Series Auto Buybacks 1998-67
03Prince Albert Raiders-8
05Prince Albert Raiders-24
06Prince Albert Raiders-25

Manson, Grady
97Columbus Cottonmouths-9
98Columbus Cottonmouths-7

Manson, James
99UK Guildford Flames-21
03UK Cardiff Devils-16

Manson, Lane
01Moose Jaw Warriors-19
04Gwinnett Gladiators-17

Manson, Triston
05Shawinigan Cataractes-16

Mansson, Johan
91Swedish Semic Elitserien Stickers-178
92Swedish Semic Elitserien Stickers-201

Mansson, Mathias
05Swedish SHL Elitset-153
Series Two Signatures-1
06Swedish SHL Elitset-9

Mantere, Eero
78Finnish SM-Liiga-114
80Finnish Mallasjuoma-74

Mantha, Billy
24V145-2-50

Mantha, Carl
907th Inn. Sketch QMJHL-48
907th Inn. Sketch Memorial Cup-51

Mantha, Georges
28La Presse Photos-9
33O-Pee-Chee V304A-22
33V252 Canadian Gum-37
33V357 Ice Kings-26
34Beehive Group I Photos-166
34Diamond Matchbooks Silver-41
34Sweet Caporal-9
35Diamond Matchbooks Tan 1-41
35Diamond Matchbooks Tan 2-42
35Diamond Matchbooks Tan 3-38
37O-Pee-Chee V304E-153
37V356 Worldwide Gum-45
38Quaker Oats Photos-24
39O-Pee-Chee V301-1-26
43Parade Sportive *-78
43Parade Sportive *-81
06ITG Ultimate Memorabilia Bleu Blanc et Rouge Autos-2

Mantha, Maurice
52Juniors Blue Tint-169
60Cleveland Barons-11

Mantha, Moe
80Jets Postcards-16
80Pepsi-Cola Caps-134
81O-Pee-Chee-373
83Jets Postcards-16
83Vachon-132
85O-Pee-Chee-125
85O-Pee-Chee Stickers-98
85Topps-125
86O-Pee-Chee-45
86O-Pee-Chee Stickers-231
86Penguins Kodak-16
86Topps-45
87O-Pee-Chee-51
87O-Pee-Chee Stickers-171
87Panini Stickers-142
87Topps-51
88North Stars ADA-17
88Oilers Tenth Anniversary-34
88O-Pee-Chee-30
88O-Pee-Chee Stickers-200
88Topps-30
89Jets Safeway-19
90Jets IGA-20
90O-Pee-Chee-354
90Pro Set-332
90Score-310C
Canadian-310C
90Topps-354
Tiffany-354
91Bowman-205
91Jets Panini Team Stickers-16
91Jets IGA-17
91O-Pee-Chee-477
91Score Canadian Bilingual-506
91Score Canadian English-506
91Stadium Club-287
91Topps-477
98Cincinnati Mighty Ducks-6
99Cincinnati Mighty Ducks-2
03Saginaw Spirit-27

Mantha, Sylvio
23V145-1-12
24Anonymous NHL-3
24Anonymous NHL-4
24C144 Champ's Cigarettes-37
27La Patrie-1
27La Presse Photos-3
33V288 Hamilton Gum-18
33V357 Ice Kings-42
34Beehive Group I Photos-167
34Diamond Matchbooks Silver-42
34Sweet Caporal-10
35Diamond Matchbooks Tan 1-42
35Diamond Matchbooks Tan 2-43
35Diamond Matchbooks Tan 3-39
35O-Pee-Chee V304C-82
36Triumph Postcards-5
55Parkhurst-60
Quaker Oats-60
83Hall of Fame-84
83Hall of Fame Postcards-F9
85Hall of Fame-84
04ITG Ultimate Mem Bleu Blanc et Rouge-6
05ITG Ultimate Mem Bleu Blanc Rouge Autos-11

Mantione, Joe
83Kitchener Rangers-1

Mantua, Mike
99Des Moines Buccaneers-22

Mantyla, Tuukka
99Finnish Cardset-318
00Finnish Cardset-85
00Finnish Cardset Next Generation-2
01Finnish Cardset-337
02Finnish Cardset-227
02Finnish Cardset Dynamic Duos-6
03Swedish Elite-227
Silver-227
04Swedish Elitset-73
Gold-73
05Finnish Cardset-318
06Finnish Cardset-147

Mantymaa, Ville
05Finnish Cardset -139
06Finnish Cardset-146

Manzano, Ian
03Johnstown Chiefs-5
03Johnstown Chiefs RBI Sports-220
04Johnstown Chiefs-12
05Johnstown Chiefs-13

Manzato, Daniel
03Victoriaville Tigers-18

Mapes, Casey
02Tri-City Stormfront-22

Mapletoft, Justin
97Red Deer Rebels-10
98Red Deer Rebels-9
99O-Pee-Chee-265
99O-Pee-Chee Chrome-265
99O-Pee-Chee Chrome Refractors-265
99Topps/OPC-265
99Topps/OPC Chrome-265
Refractors-265
99Bowman CHL-33
Gold-33
OPC International-33
Autographs-BA8
Autographs Gold-BA8
Autographs Silver-BA8
00Red Deer Rebels-13
Signed-13
00UD CHL Prospects-60
Supremacy-CS6
02Crown Royale Rookie Royalty-15
02Pacific Calder-82
Silver-82
02Pacific Complete-589
Red-589
02Vanguard Prime Prospects-16
03ITG Action-349
03AHL Top Prospects-22
03Bridgeport Sound Tigers-6B
03Pacific AHL Prospects-11
Gold-11

Mara, Paul
93Quebec Pee-Wee Tournament-597
96Upper Deck Ice-149
96Sudbury Wolves-13
96Sudbury Wolves Police-16
97Sudbury Wolves Police-16
97Bowman CHL-16
97Bowman CHL-137
OPC-16
OPC-137
Bowman's Best-3
Bowman's Best Atomic Refractors-3
Bowman's Best Refractor-3
98UD Choice-297
Prime Choice Reserve-297
Reserve-297
99Aurora-132
Premiere Date-132
99BAP Memorabilia-22
Gold-22
Silver-22
99BAP Millennium-217
Emerald-217
Ruby-217
Sapphire-217
Signatures-217
Signatures Gold-217
99O-Pee-Chee-133
99O-Pee-Chee Chrome-133
99O-Pee-Chee Chrome Refractors-133
99Pacific-400
Copper-400
Emerald Green-400
Gold-400
Ice Blue-400
Premiere Date-400
Red-400
99Paramount-268
99SP Authentic Sign of the Times-PM
99SP Authentic Sign of the Times Gold-PM
99SPx-138
Radiance-138
Spectrum-138
99Topps Arena Giveaways-TB-PM
99Topps/OPC-133
99Topps/OPC Chrome-133
Refractors-133
99Upper Deck-118
99Upper Deck-150
Exclusives-118
Exclusives-150
Exclusives 1 of 1-118
Exclusives 1 of 1-150
Crunch Time-CT16
Crunch Time Quantum Gold-CT16
Crunch Time Quantum Silver-CT16
New Ice Age-N10
New Ice Age Quantum Gold-N10
New Ice Age Quantum Silver-N10
99Upper Deck Arena Giveaways-TL1
99Upper Deck Century Legends-76
Century Collection-76
99Upper Deck Gold Reserve-118
99Upper Deck Gold Reserve-150
99Upper Deck HoloGrFx-53
Ausome-53
99Upper Deck MVP-191
Gold Script-191
Silver Script-191
Super Script-191
21st Century NHL-7
99Upper Deck Ovation-54
Standing Ovation-54
99Upper Deck Retro-71
Gold-71
Platinum-71
99Upper Deck Victory-271
99Wayne Gretzky Hockey Signs of Greatness-PM
99Quebec PeeWee Tournament Coll Souv-17
99Bowman CHL-157
Gold-157
OPC International-157
00BAP Memorabilia-71
Emerald-71
Ruby-71
Sapphire-71
Promos-71
00BAP Mem Chicago Sportsfest Copper-71
00BAP Memorabilia Chicago Sportsfest Blue-71
00BAP Memorabilia Chicago Sportsfest Gold-71
00BAP Memorabilia Chicago Sportsfest Ruby-71
00BAP Memorabilia Chicago Sun-Times Ruby-71
00BAP Memorabilia Chicago Sun-Times Gold-71
00BAP Mem Chicago Sun-Times Sapphire-71
00BAP Mem Toronto Fall Expo Copper-71
00BAP Memorabilia Toronto Fall Expo Gold-71
00BAP Memorabilia Toronto Fall Expo Ruby-71
00O-Pee-Chee-187
00O-Pee-Chee Parallel-187
00Stadium Club-176
00Topps/OPC-187
Parallel-187
00UD Heroes-108
00Upper Deck-158
Exclusives Tier 1-158
Exclusives Tier 2-158
00Upper Deck Legends-119
Legendary Collection Bronze-119
Legendary Collection Gold-119
Legendary Collection Silver-119
00Upper Deck MVP-162
First Stars-162
Second Stars-162
Third Stars-162
00Upper Deck Victory-210
00Upper Deck Vintage-326
01Bowman YoungStars-158
Gold-158
Ice Cubed-158
Autographs-PM
Relics-JPM
Relics-SPM
Relics-DSPM
01Coyotes Team Issue-12
01Upper Deck-134
Exclusives-134
01Upper Deck MVP-144
02BAP Sig Series Auto Buybacks 1999-217
02Coyotes Team Issue-12
02Pacific Complete-251
Red-251
02Stadium Club YoungStars Relics-S19
02Upper Deck-134
Exclusives-134
03Coyotes Postcards-13
03ITG Action-474
03Pacific Complete-161
Red-161
03Upper Deck-395
Canadian Exclusives-395
HG-395
UD Exclusives-395
03Upper Deck MVP-328
Gold Script-328
Silver Script-328
Canadian Exclusives-328
04Pacific-203
Blue-203
Red-203
04German DEL Superstars-SU17
04German Hannover Scorpions Postcards-19
05Panini Stickers-324
05Parkhurst-372
Facsimile Auto Parallel-372
05Upper Deck-149
HG Glossy-149
05Upper Deck MVP-305
Gold-305
Platinum-305
05Upper Deck Toronto Fall Expo-149
06Hot Prospects Hotagraphs-HPM
06O-Pee-Chee-45
Rainbow-45
06Panini Stickers-24
06Upper Deck-270
Exclusives Parallel-270
High Gloss Parallel-270
Masterpieces-270
06Upper Deck MVP-29
Gold Script-29
Super Script-29

Marach, Nick
98Kootenay Ice-11
01Kelowna Rockets-11
01Vancouver Giants-18

Maracle, D.J.
98Kingston Frontenacs-10

Maracle, Ian
02Mississauga Ice Dogs-3
03St. Michael's Majors-14

Maracle, Norm
91Saskatoon Blades-3
917th Inn. Sketch WHL-117
93Saskatoon Blades-16
95Adirondack Red Wings-14
98Pacific-200
Ice Blue-200
Red-200
98Pacific Omega-89
Red-89
Opening Day Issue-89
98Revolution-49
Ice Shadow-49
Red-49
98SPx Finite-144
Radiance-144
Spectrum-144
98Upper Deck-3
Exclusives-3
Exclusives 1 of 1-3
Gold Reserve-3
98Upper Deck MVP-75
Gold Script-75
Silver Script-75
Super Script-75
99Pacific Dynagon Ice-17
Blue-17
Copper-17
Gold-17
Premiere Date-17
99Paramount-13
Copper-13
Emerald-13
Gold-13
Holographic Emerald-13
Holographic Gold-13
Holographic Silver-13
Ice Blue-13
Premiere Date-13
Red-13
Silver-13
99Upper Deck-180
Exclusives-180
Exclusives 1 of 1-180
99Upper Deck Gold Reserve-180
99Upper Deck MVP SC Edition-10
Gold Script-10
Silver Script-10
Super Script-10
99Upper Deck Victory-16
00BAP Memorabilia-164
Emerald-164
Ruby-164
Sapphire-164
Promos-164
00BAP Mem Chicago Sportsfest Copper-164
00BAP Memorabilia Chicago Sportsfest Blue-164
00BAP Memorabilia Chicago Sportsfest Gold-164
00BAP Memorabilia Chicago Sportsfest Ruby-164
00BAP Memorabilia Chicago Sun-Times Ruby-164
00BAP Memorabilia Chicago Sun-Times Gold-164
00BAP Mem Chicago Sun-Times Sapphire-164
00BAP Mem Toronto Fall Expo Copper-164
00BAP Memorabilia Toronto Fall Expo Gold-164
00BAP Memorabilia Toronto Fall Expo Ruby-164
01Between the Pipes-64
01Pacific-20
Extreme LTD-20
Hobby LTD-20
Premiere Date-20
Retail LTD-20
01Pacific Arena Exclusives-20
01Chicago Wolves-12
02Between the Pipes-44
Gold-44
Silver-44
02Chicago Wolves-17
03Russian Hockey League-221

Marak, Zbynek
94Czech APS Extraliga-238
95Czech APS Extraliga-19
95Czech APS Extraliga-382
96Czech APS Extraliga-40
97Czech APS Extraliga-112
97Czech DS Extraliga-24
97Czech DS Stickers-107
98Czech DS-84
98Czech DS Stickers-55
98Czech OFS-344
99Czech DS-138
99Czech OFS-440
00Czech DS Extraliga-105
00Czech OFS-201
01Czech OFS-102
All Stars-24

Marakhovski, Roman
00Louisiana Ice Gators-6
02Greensboro Generals RBI-13
06Augusta Lynx-11

Maranduik, Bill
93Kingston Frontenacs-13

Marble, Evan
907th Inn. Sketch WHL-59
917th Inn. Sketch WHL-321
98German DEL-79

Marc, Rob
96Kitchener Rangers-17

Marcaurelle, Brian
93Quebec Pee-Wee Tournament-838

Marcel, Paul
34Sweet Caporal-13

Marcellus, Todd
97New Mexico Scorpions-11
03Tulsa Oilers-11
04Tulsa Oilers-16

Marcetta, Milan
68Shirriff Coins-67
07Maple Leafs 1967 Commemorative-17

March, Harold
34Beehive Group I Photos-67
34Diamond Matchbooks Silver-43
34Sweet Caporal-34
35Diamond Matchbooks Tan 1-43
35Diamond Matchbooks Tan 2-44
35Diamond Matchbooks Tan 3-40
35Diamond Matchbooks Tan 4-11
35Diamond Matchbooks Tan 5-9
36Champion Postcards-2
37Diamond Matchbooks Tan 6-9
37V356 Worldwide Gum-13
39O-Pee-Chee V301-1-45
04ITG Ultimate Mem Chitown Immortals-3
05ITG Ultimate Mem Chi-Town Immortal Auto-6
06ITG Ultimate Memorabilia Chi-Town Immortals Autos-9

Marchand, Brad
04Moncton Wildcats-6
05ITG Heroes/Prosp Toronto Expo Parallel -136
05Moncton Wildcats-5
05ITG Heroes and Prospects-136
Autographs-A-BMA
07ITG Going For Gold World Juniors-15
Autographs-15
Emblems-GUE15
Jerseys-GUJ15
Numbers-GUN15

Marchand, Derek
97Columbus Cottonmouths-10
98Columbus Cottonmouths-8

Marchand, Hugo
99Louisiana Ice Gators-10
01South Carolina Stingrays-13

Marchand, Jonathan
93Quebec Pee-Wee Tournament-1593

Marchant, Eddy
91Air Canada SJHL-C47
93Red Deer Rebels-14

Marchant, Gordon
71Blues Postcards-12

Marchant, Terry
99Houston Aeros-9
00UK Sekonda Superleague-189
01Columbus Cottonmouths-12
02Arkansas Riverblades-9

Marchant, Todd
92Upper Deck-606
92Clarkson Knights-10
93PowerPlay-511
93Stadium Club Team USA-15
93Stadium Club Team USA Members Only-15
93Topps Premier Team USA-14
93Ultra-491
94Finest Bowman's Best-R19
94Finest Bowman's Best Refractors-R19
94Fleer-71
94Leaf-505
94Parkhurst SE-SE61
Gold-SE61
94Score-226
Gold-226
Platinum-226
94SP Premier-4
94SP Premier Die-Cuts-4
94Upper Deck-159
94Upper Deck-323
Electric Ice-159
Electric Ice-323
94Cape Breton Oilers-13
94Classic-88
Gold-88
Pro Prospects Ice Ambassadors-IA8
Pro Prospects International Heroes-LP8
94Classic Four-Sport *-140
Gold-140
Autographs-140A
Printers Proofs-140
94Images *-17
95Be A Player-190
Signatures-S190
Signatures Die Cuts-S190
95Canada Games NHL POGS-107
95Collector's Choice-210
Player's Club-210
Player's Club Platinum-210
95Donruss-200
Rookie Team-8
95Emotion-64
95Leaf-61
Studio Rookies-8
95Metal-54
95Panini Stickers-257
95Parkhurst International-347
Emerald Ice-347
95Pinnacle-76
Artist's Proofs-76
Rink Collection-76
95Pro Magnets-83
95Score-34
Black Ice Artist's Proofs-34
Black Ice-34
95SkyBox Impact-62
95SkyBox Impact-234
NHL On Fox-10
95Stadium Club Members Only-49
95Stadium Club-102
Members Only Master Set-102
95Topps-29
OPC Inserts-29
New To The Game-3NG
95Ultra-55
Gold Medallion-55
All-Rookies-8
All-Rookie Gold Medallion-8
95Upper Deck-71
Electric Ice-71
Electric Ice Gold-71
Special Edition-SE121
Special Edition Gold-SE121
95Images-8
Gold-8
Clear Excitement-CE8
95Images Four-Sport *-115
95Images Platinum Prospects-PR5
95Assets Gold *-5
95Assets Gold Phone Cards $2 *-5
96Collector's Choice-97
96Donruss-53
Press Proofs-53
96Leaf-153
Press Proofs-153
96NHL Pro Stamps-83
96Oilers Postcards-26
96Pinnacle-117
Artist's Proofs-117
Foil-117
Premium Stock-117
Rink Collection-117
96Score-217
Artist's Proofs-217
Dealer's Choice Artist's Proofs-217
Special Artist's Proofs-217
Golden Blades-217
96Upper Deck-59
96Collector's Edge Ice-34
Crucibles-C6
Prism-34
96Collector's Edge Ice Promos-PR1
97Be A Player-72
Autographs-72
Autographs Die-Cuts-72
Autographs Prismatic Die-Cuts-72
97Donruss-184
Press Proofs Silver-184
Press Proofs Gold-184
97Donruss Limited-144
Exposure-144
97Pacific-320
Copper-320
Emerald Green-320
Ice Blue-320
Red-320
Silver-320
97Pinnacle-127
Press Plates Back Black-127
Press Plates Back Cyan-127
Press Plates Back Magenta-127
Press Plates Back Yellow-127
Press Plates Front Black-127
Press Plates Front Cyan-127
Press Plates Front Magenta-127
Press Plates Front Yellow-127
97Score-243
97Upper Deck-64
Game Dated Moments-64
98Be A Player-55
Press Release-55
98BAP Gold-55
98BAP Autographs-55
98BAP Autographs Gold-55
98BAP Tampa Bay All Star Game-55
98OPC Chrome-64
Refractors-64
98Pacific-213
Ice Blue-213
Red-213
98Paramount-88
Copper-88
Emerald Green-88
Holo-Electric-88
Ice Blue-88
Silver-88
98Topps-64
O-Pee-Chee-64
98Upper Deck-275
Exclusives-275
Exclusives 1 of 1-275
Gold Reserve-275
99O-Pee-Chee-43
99O-Pee-Chee Chrome-43
99O-Pee-Chee Chrome Refractors-43
99Pacific-159
Copper-159
Emerald Green-159
Gold-159
Ice Blue-159
Premiere Date-159
Red-159
99Panini Stickers-248
99Topps/OPC-43
99Topps/OPC Chrome-43
Refractors-43
99Upper Deck Victory-117
00BAP Memorabilia-325
Emerald-325
Ruby-325
Sapphire-325
Promos-325
00BAP Mem Chicago Sportsfest Copper-325
00BAP Memorabilia Chicago Sportsfest Blue-325
00BAP Memorabilia Chicago Sportsfest Gold-325
00BAP Memorabilia Chicago Sportsfest Ruby-325
00BAP Memorabilia Chicago Sun-Times Ruby-325
00BAP Memorabilia Chicago Sun-Times Gold-325
00BAP Mem Chicago Sun-Times Sapphire-325
00BAP Mem Toronto Fall Expo Copper-325
00BAP Memorabilia Toronto Fall Expo Gold-325
00BAP Memorabilia Toronto Fall Expo Ruby-325
00BAP Parkhurst 2000-P173
00BAP Signature Series-208
Emerald-208
Ruby-208
Sapphire-208
Autographs-76
Autographs Gold-76
00O-Pee-Chee-73
00O-Pee-Chee Parallel-73
00Pacific-169
Copper-169
Gold-169
Ice Blue-169
Premiere Date-169
Autographs-169
00Paramount-96
Copper-96
Gold-96
Holo-Gold-96
Holo-Silver-96
Ice Blue-96
Premiere Date-96
00Revolution-57
Blue-57
Premiere Date-57
Red-57
00Stadium Club-93
00Topps/OPC-73
Parallel-73
00Topps Chrome-58
OPC Refractors-58
Refractors-58
00Upper Deck-298
Exclusives Tier 1-298
Exclusives Tier 2-298
00Upper Deck Vintage-139
01O-Pee-Chee-169
01O-Pee-Chee Premier Parallel-169
01Pacific-160
Extreme LTD-160
Hobby LTD-160
Premiere Date-160
Retail LTD-160
01Pacific Arena Exclusives-160
01Parkhurst-186
01Topps-169
OPC Parallel-169
01Upper Deck-69
Exclusives-69
01Upper Deck MVP-77
01Upper Deck Victory-136
Gold-136
02BAP Sig Series Auto Buybacks 1998-55
02BAP Sig Series Auto Buybacks 2000-76
02NHL Power Play Stickers-40
02Oilers Postcards-11
02Pacific-145
Blue-145
Red-145
02Pacific Complete-162
Red-162
02Topps Total-115
02Upper Deck-315
Exclusives-315
02Upper Deck Beckett UD Promos-315
02Upper Deck Specialists-STM
02Upper Deck Speed Demons-SDTM
02Upper Deck MVP-75
Gold-75
Classics-75
Golden Classics-75
03Beehive-60
Gold-60
Silver-60
03Black Diamond-114
Black-114
Green-114
Red-114
03Crown Royale-29
Blue-29
Retail-29
03O-Pee-Chee-29
03OPC Blue-29
03OPC Gold-29
03OPC Red-29
03Pacific-135
Blue-135
Red-135
03Pacific Complete-211
Red-211
03SP Authentic-25
Limited-25
03SP Game Used-99
Gold-99
Authentic Fabrics-DFNM
Authentic Fabrics Gold-DFNM
03SPx-28
Radiance-28
Spectrum-28
03Topps-29
Blue-29
Gold-29
Red-29
03Topps Traded-TT12
Blue-TT12
Gold-TT12
Red-TT12

03UD Honor Roll-23
03Upper Deck-297
Canadian Exclusives-297
HG-297
UD Exclusives-297
03Upper Deck Classic Portraits-27
03Upper Deck Ice-23
Gold-23
03Upper Deck MVP-122
Gold Script-122
Silver Script-122
Canadian Exclusives-122
03Upper Deck Rookie Update-23
03Upper Deck Trilogy-27
Limited-27
03Upper Deck Victory-72
Bronze-72
Gold-72
Silver-72
04Pacific-78
Blue-78
Red-78
05Be A Player-26
First Period-26
Second Period-26
Third Period-26
Overtime-26
Signatures-TM
Signatures Gold-TM
05Parkhurst-5
Facsimile Auto Parallel-5
05Upper Deck-56
HG Glossy-56
05Upper Deck MVP-114
Gold-114
Platinum-114
05Upper Deck Toronto Fall Expo-56
06O-Pee-Chee-14
Rainbow-14
06Upper Deck-256
Exclusives Parallel-256
High Gloss Parallel-256
Masterpieces-256

Marchessault, Alain
87Brockville Braves-8

Marchessault, Richard
87Brockville Braves-16

Marchetti, Giovanni
92Finnish Semic-250
94Finnish Jaa Kiekko-298
95Swedish World Championships Stickers-78

Marchi, De
79Panini Stickers-392

Marchinko, Brian
72O-Pee-Chee-179
72Sargent Promotions Stamps-136

Marchment, Bryan
89ProCards AHL-44
90Jets IGA-21
90Moncton Hawks-17
90ProCards AHL/IHL-250
91Blackhawks Coke-17
91Bowman-208
91O-Pee-Chee-116
91OPC Premier-99
91Score American-314
91Score Canadian Bilingual-344
91Score Canadian Bilingual-606
91Score Canadian English-344
91Score Canadian English-606
91Score Rookie/Traded-56T
91Stadium Club-384
91Topps-116
92Blackhawks Coke-10
92Bowman-418
92Parkhurst-267
Emerald Ice-267
92Score-288
Canadian-288
92Stadium Club-148
92Topps-501
Gold-501G
92Ultra-278
93Donruss-73
93Leaf-224
93Pinnacle-283
Canadian-283
93PowerPlay-352
93Score-386
93Score-577
Gold-577
Canadian-386
Canadian-577
Canadian Gold-577
93Stadium Club-161
Members Only Master Set-161
OPC-161
First Day Issue-161
First Day Issue OPC-161
93Ultra-335
93Whalers Coke-9
94Leaf-127
94Pinnacle-407
Artist's Proofs-407
Rink Collection-407
94Score-107
Gold-107
Platinum-107
94Stadium Club-84
Members Only Master Set-84
First Day Issue-84
Super Team Winner Cards-84
95Be A Player-39
Signatures-S39
Signatures Die Cuts-S39
95Collector's Choice-67
Player's Club-67
Player's Club Platinum-67
95Score-270
Black Ice Artist's Proofs-270
Black Ice-270
95Ultra-238
95Upper Deck-371
Electric Ice-371
Electric Ice Gold-371
96Collector's Choice-99
96Oilers Postcards-24
97Black Diamond-66
Double Diamond-66
Triple Diamond-66
Quadruple Diamond-66
97Pacific Invincible NHL Regime-79
97Upper Deck-69
97Upper Deck-392
98Pacific-385
Ice Blue-385
Red-385
98Pacific Omega-210
Red-210
Opening Day Issue-210
98Upper Deck-356
Exclusives-356
Exclusives 1 of 1-356
Gold Reserve-356
99O-Pee-Chee-54
99O-Pee-Chee Chrome-54
99O-Pee-Chee Chrome Refractors-54
99Pacific-374
Copper-374
Emerald Green-374
Gold-374
Ice Blue-374
Premiere Date-374
Red-374
99Topps/OPC-54
99Topps/OPC Chrome-54
Refractors-54
00BAP Memorabilia-378
Emerald-378
Ruby-378
Sapphire-378
Promos-378
00BAP Mem Chicago Sportsfest Copper-378
00BAP Memorabilia Chicago Sportsfest Blue-378
00BAP Memorabilia Chicago Sportsfest Gold-378
00BAP Memorabilia Chicago Sportsfest Ruby-378
00BAP Memorabilia Chicago Sun-Times Ruby-378
00BAP Memorabilia Chicago Sun-Times Gold-378
00BAP Mem Chicago Sun-Times Sapphire-378
00BAP Mem Toronto Fall Expo Copper-378
00BAP Memorabilia Toronto Fall Expo Gold-378
00BAP Memorabilia Toronto Fall Expo Ruby-378
01Pacific-338
01Pacific-421
Extreme LTD-338
Gold-421
Hobby LTD-338
Premiere Date-338
Retail LTD-338
01Pacific Arena Exclusives-338
01Pacific Arena Exclusives-421
01Sharks Postcards-15
02BAP Signature Series Golf-GS16
02Pacific-335
Blue-335
Red-335
02Pacific Complete-280
Red-280
02Upper Deck Rookie Update-24
03Black Diamond-10
Black-10
Green-10
Red-10
03Parkhurst Original Six Toronto-11
03Topps Traded-TT61
Blue-TT61
Gold-TT61
Red-TT61

Marcinczak, Marek
79Panini Stickers-125

Marcinko, Miroslav
94Finnish Jaa Kiekko-196
96Swedish Semic Wien-226

Marcinko, Thomas
06Barrie Colts-5

Marcinyshyn, Dave
85Kamloops Blazers-12
86Kamloops Blazers-10
88ProCards AHL-342
89ProCards AHL-215
90OPC Premier-67
90Pro Set-623
91ProCards-543
92Binghamton Rangers-16
94Milwaukee Admirals-17
95Cincinnati Cyclones-16
96Cincinnati Cyclones-27
98German DEL-213

Marcogliese, Jan
93Quebec Pee-Wee Tournament-35

Marcolini, Steve
84Kitchener Rangers-8
85Kitchener Rangers-7
86London Knights-19

Marcon, Lou
59Topps-49

Marcotte, Dan
97Tucson Gila Monsters-2
98Bakersfield Condors-12
99Idaho Steelheads-5
04UD Legendary Signatures Linemates-SJDMTO

Marcotte, Don
70Bruins Postcards-6
70Bruins Team Issue-6
70Esso Power Players-70
70O-Pee-Chee-138
71Bruins Postcards-16
71O-Pee-Chee-176
71Toronto Sun-13
72O-Pee-Chee-219
72Sargent Promotions Stamps-27
73Topps-89
74NHL Action Stamps-21
74O-Pee-Chee NHL-221
74Topps-221
75O-Pee-Chee NHL-269
75Topps-269
76O-Pee-Chee NHL-234
76Topps-234
77O-Pee-Chee NHL-165
77Topps-165
78O-Pee-Chee-236
78Topps-236
79O-Pee-Chee-99
79Topps-99
80O-Pee-Chee-36
81O-Pee-Chee-14
82O-Pee-Chee-14
82O-Pee-Chee Stickers-91
82Topps Stickers-91
91Bruins Sports Action Legends-15
98Bruins Alumni-21
Autographs-21
04ITG Franchises US East-325
Autographs-A-DMA
04UD Legendary Signatures-30
Autographs-DM

Marcotte, Frederick
92Quebec Pee-Wee Tournament-620
93Quebec Pee-Wee Tournament-291

Marcotte, Gaston
52Juniors Blue Tint-14

Marcotte, Jacques
52Juniors Blue Tint-82

Marcotte, Jerome
93Quebec Pee-Wee Tournament-446

Marcotte, Nicolas
01Chicoutimi Sagueneens-16
04Chicoutimi Sagueneens-20

Marcotte, Real
51Laval Dairy Lac St. Jean-13

Marcotte, Remy
93Quebec Pee-Wee Tournament-60

Marcou, James
05Waterloo Blackhawks-15

Marcoux, Andrew
05Mississauga Ice Dogs-12

Marcoux, Christian
93Drummondville Voltigeurs-16

Marcoux, Eric
907th Inn. Sketch QMJHL-201
917th Inn. Sketch QMJHL-289

Marcoux, Guillaume
93Quebec Pee-Wee Tournament-914

Marcoux, Henri
94German DEL-256
95German DEL-254
96German DEL-143
99German Bundesliga 2-175

Marcoux, Kevin
92Quebec Pee-Wee Tournament-51
93Quebec Pee-Wee Tournament-369

Marcoux, Pierre
98Thetford Mines Coyotes-21
01Thetford Mines Coyotes-19
02Thetford Mines Coyotes-13
03Thetford Mines Prolab-12

Marcus, Borje
69Swedish Hockey-157
70Swedish Hockey-125
71Swedish Hockey-215

Marcuzzi, Julian
03Salmon Arm Silverbacks-12
04Salmon Arm Silverbacks-19

Marczell, Arthur
95Austrian National Team-16

Marecek, Pavel
94Czech APS Extraliga-123
95Czech APS Extraliga-295
97Czech APS Extraliga-109
98Czech DS Stickers-54

Marek, Jan
99Czech OFS-408
00Czech OFS-233
01Czech OFS-65
02Czech OFS Plus-92
02Czech National Team Postcards-7
03Czech OFS Plus-157
03Czech OFS Plus All-Star Game-H36
03Czech OFS Plus Insert G-G5
03Czech OFS Plus Insert M-M12
03Czech OFS Plus Insert S-S2
03Czech OFS Plus MS Praha-SE4
04Czech HC Sparta Praha Postcards-11
04Czech OFS-190
Assist Leaders-5
Goals Leaders-8
Points Leaders-5
05Czech HC Sparta Praha-8
06Czech CP Cup Postcards-13
06Czech LG Hockey Games Postcards-11
06Czech OFS All Stars-15
06Czech OFS Goals Leaders-3
06Czech OFS Points Leaders-1

Marek, Ludwig
96Swiss HNL-354

Marek, Pavel
99Czech OFS-86

Marek, Petr
94Wheeling Thunderbirds-9
94Wheeling Thunderbirds Photo Album-1
99San Diego Gulls-9
00San Diego Gulls-11

Marengere, Steve
83Nova Scotia Voyageurs-6

Marentette, Mark
90Cincinnati Cyclones-34

Mares, Daniel
96Swiss HNL-488
01Swiss HNL-435

Mares, Jaroslav
99Czech Score Blue 2000-53
99Czech Score Red Ice 2000-53
03Czech OFS Plus-375
04Czech OFS-14

Marett, Geb
92Harvard Crimson-22

Margeson, Stephen
02New Mexico Scorpions-8
03Memphis RiverKings-10
04Memphis RiverKings-17

Margettie, Don
93London Knights-13
98Abilene Aviators-3
98Abilene Aviators-12
01Odessa Jackalopes-15
02Odessa Jackalopes-15
03Rockford Ice Hogs-10
04Odessa Jackalopes-14
05Odessa Jackalopes-16
06Odessa Jackalopes-14

Marha, Josef
93Parkhurst-516
Emerald Ice-516
94SP-157
Die Cuts-157
94Czech APS Extraliga-171
95Classic Autographs-13
97Score Avalanche-10
Platinum-10
Premier-10
97Upper Deck-256
98Pacific-59
Ice Blue-59
Red-59
98Panini Stickers-173
98Paramount-4
Copper-4
Emerald Green-4
Holo-Electric-4
Ice Blue-4
Silver-4
98SPx Finite-3
98SPx Finite-124
Radiance-3
Radiance-124
Spectrum-3
Spectrum-124
98UD Choice-3
98UD Choice Preview-3
98UD Choice Prime Choice Reserve-3
98UD Choice Reserve-3
98UD3-3
98UD3-63
98UD3-123
Die-Cuts-3
Die-Cuts-63
Die-Cuts-123
98Upper Deck-33
98Upper Deck-216
Exclusives-33
Exclusives-216
Exclusives 1 of 1-33
Exclusives 1 of 1-216
Gold Reserve-33
Gold Reserve-216
99Pacific-92
Copper-92
Emerald Green-92
Gold-92
Ice Blue-92
Premiere Date-92
Red-92
99Upper Deck-207
Exclusives-207
Exclusives 1 of 1-207
99Upper Deck Gold Reserve-207
00BAP Signature Series-69
Emerald-69
Ruby-69
Sapphire-69
Autographs-194
Autographs Gold-194
00Upper Deck Vintage-83
01Swiss HNL-117
02BAP Sig Series Auto Buybacks 2000-194
02Swiss HNL-8
04Swiss Davos Postcards-19
06Czech CP Cup Postcards-14

Maribo, Jens
98Danish Hockey League-86
99Danish Hockey League-33

Maric, Rob
94Kitchener Rangers-25
95Slapshot-136

Marier, Olivier
93Quebec Pee-Wee Tournament-1077

Marietti, Brett
917th Inn. Sketch OHL-371
95South Carolina Stingrays-17
96South Carolina Stingrays-24
01South Carolina Stingrays-14
02South Carolina Stingrays-14
02South Carolina Stingrays RBI-217

Marijarvi, Juha-Matti
93Finnish Jyvas-Hyva Stickers-81
93Finnish SISU-117

Marik, Michal
94Czech APS Extraliga-245
96Czech APS Extraliga-289
97Czech APS Extraliga-172
98Czech DS Stickers-148
98Czech OFS-194
98Czech DS-30
99Czech OFS-11
99Czech OFS Goalie Die-Cuts-11
00Czech DS Extraliga-73
00Czech OFS-6
00Czech OFS Star Emerald-15
00Czech OFS Star Pink-15
00Czech OFS Star Violet-15
01Czech OFS-125
Gold Inserts-G9
02Czech OFS Plus-138
02Czech OFS Plus-349
Trios-T2
Duos-D25
03Czech OFS Plus-335
03Czech OFS Plus MS Praha-SE47
04Czech OFS-100
Goals-Against Leaders-14
Save Percentage Leaders-15
Team Cards-5

Marin, Alexei
91Finnish Semic World Champ Stickers-78
91Swedish Semic World Champ Stickers-78

Marin, Jason
02OCN Blizzard-20

Marinari, Gregory
93Quebec Pee-Wee Tournament-1678

Marini, Hector
83Devils Postcards-20
83O-Pee-Chee-235
83O-Pee-Chee Stickers-221
83Puffy Stickers-8
83Topps Stickers-221

Marinier, Roch
84Chicoutimi Sagueneens-18

Marinucci, Chris
93Minnesota-Duluth Bulldogs-19
93Minnesota-Duluth Commemorative-1
94Classic-100
Gold-100
All-Americans-AA3
Autographs-NNO
Tri-Cards-T40
95Donruss-6
95Leaf-92
95Parkhurst International-401
Emerald Ice-401
95Pinnacle-206
Artist's Proofs-206
Rink Collection-206
95Score-309
Black Ice Artist's Proofs-309
Black Ice-309
95Topps-62
OPC Inserts-62
95Images-95
Gold-95
Autographs-95A
Clear Excitement-CE19
Platinum Prospects-PR7
96Collector's Edge Ice-193
Prism-193
98Chicago Wolves-12
98Chicago Wolves Turner Cup-14
99Chicago Wolves-9
01German Berlin Polar Bears Postcards-15
01German Upper Deck-38
04Minnesota-Duluth Bulldogs-30

Mario, Frank
51Laval Dairy Subset-14
52St. Lawrence Sales-51

Marion, Pierre-Alexandre
05Drummondville Voltigeurs-4
06Drummondville Voltigeurs-26

Maristuen, Mike
93St. Cloud State Huskies-16

Mariucci, John
34Beehive Group I Photos-68
85Hall of Fame-254
95AHCA-3

Marjamaki, Masi
02Red Deer Rebels-7
04Moose Jaw Warriors-15
06Flair Showcase-61
Parallel-61
06Hot Prospects Hotagraphs-HMM
06O-Pee-Chee-515
Rainbow-515
06SP Authentic-229
Limited-229
06SP Game Used-134
Gold-134
Rainbow-134
Rookie Exclusives Autographs-REMM
06SPx-148
Spectrum-148
06The Cup-142
Autographed Rookie Masterpiece Pressplates-142
Gold Rainbow Autographed Rookie Patches-142
Masterpiece Pressplates (Artifacts)-213
Masterpiece Pressplates (Marquee Rookies)-515
Masterpiece Pressplates (MVP)-345
Masterpiece Pressplates (Power Play)-114
Masterpiece Pressplates (SP Authentic)-229
Masterpiece Pressplates (SP Game Used)-134
Masterpiece Pressplates (SPx)-148
Masterpiece Pressplates (Sweet Beginnings)-110
Masterpiece Pressplates (Trilogy)-133
Masterpiece Pressplates (Victory)-228
Rookies Black-142
Rookies Platinum-142
06UD Artifacts-213
Blue-213
Gold-213
Platinum-213
Radiance-213
Red-213
06UD Powerplay-114
Impact Rainbow-114
06Ultimate Collection Ultimate Debut Threads Jerseys-DJ-MM
06Ultimate Collection Ultimate Debut Threads Jerseys Autographs-DJ-MM
06Ultimate Collection Ultimate Debut Threads Patches-DJ-MM
06Ultimate Collection Ultimate Debut Threads Patches Autographs-DJ-MM
06Ultra-216
Gold Medallion-216
Ice Medallion-216
06Upper Deck-228
Exclusives Parallel-228
High Gloss Parallel-228
Masterpieces-228
06Upper Deck MVP-345
Gold Script-345
Super Script-345
06Upper Deck Ovation-182
06Upper Deck Sweet Shot-110
Rookie Jerseys Autographs-110
06Upper Deck Trilogy-133
06Upper Deck Victory-228
06Upper Deck Victory Black-228
06Upper Deck Victory Gold-228

Marjamaki, Pekka
65Finnish Hellas-146
66Finnish Jaakiekkosarja-155
69Swedish Hockey-376
70Finnish Jaakiekko-68
70Finnish Jaakiekko-212
70Swedish Hockey-297
70Swedish Masterserien-163
71Finnish Suomi Stickers-135
71Swedish Hockey-64
72Finnish Jaakiekko-126
72Finnish Jaakiekko-198
72Finnish Hellas-5
72Finnish Panda Toronto-102
72Finnish Semic World Championship-75
72Swedish Stickers-34
72Swedish Semic World Championship-75
73Finnish Jaakiekko-159
74Finnish Jenkki-11
74Finnish Typotor-29
74Finnish Typotor-52
74Swedish Stickers-105
74Swedish Semic World Champ Stickers-78
77Finnish Sportscasters-19-436
78Finnish SM-Liiga-178
79Panini Stickers-167
96Finnish SISU Redline-195
05Finnish Tappara Legendat-22

Mark, Gordon
84Kamloops Blazers-15
94Parkhurst-80
Gold-80

Mark, Len
84Kamloops Blazers-16
85Kamloops Blazers-13
86Kamloops Blazers-11

Markarian, Ralph
52Juniors Blue Tint-178

Markell, John
00Ohio State Buckeyes-20
02Ohio State Buckeyes-18

Marker, Gus
34Beehive Group I Photos-280
34Beehive Group I Photos-336
34Sweet Caporal-22
35O-Pee-Chee V304C-78
37O-Pee-Chee V304E-173
39O-Pee-Chee V301-1-16
40O-Pee-Chee V301-2-113
05ITG Ultimate Mem Marvelous Maroons Auto-5

Market, Hasty
88Kamloops Blazers-25

Markgren, Lennart
56Swedish Alfabilder-64

Markham, Ryan
01Michigan Tech Huskies-18
05Port Huron Flags-15
06Port Huron Flags-14

Markhovski, Roman
98Columbus Cottonmouths-8

Marki, Michael
01Swiss HNL-448
02Swiss HNL-430

Markkanen, Jussi
94Finest-124
Super Team Winners-124
Refractors-124
94Parkhurst SE-SE215
Gold-SE215
95Finnish SISU-311
98Finnish Keraliysarja-184
Mad Masks-9
Off Duty-9
99Finnish Cardset-106
00Finnish Cardset-209
00Finnish Cardset Masquerade-7
01Between the Pipes-87
01Crown Royale-160
01Titanium-159
Retail-159
01Titanium Draft Day Edition-130
01Topps Chrome-144
Refractors-144
Black Border Refractors-144
01Vanguard-112
Blue-112
Red-112
One of Ones-112
Premiere Date-112
Proofs-112
01Finnish Cardset-121
01Finnish Cardset Haltmeisters-9
02BAP First Edition-296
02Between the Pipes-96
Gold-96
Silver-96
Jerseys-47
Tandems-18
02NHL Power Play Stickers-29
02Oilers Postcards-14
02Pacific-146
Blue-146
Red-146
02UD Mask Collection-34
02UD Mask Collection-35
02UD Mask Collection Beckett Promos-34
02UD Mask Collection Beckett Promos-35
02Finnish Cardset-69
02Finnish Cardset Solid Gold Six-Pack-1
03BAP Memorabilia-131
Emerald-131
Gold-131
Ruby-131
Sapphire-131
Deep in the Crease-D5
03Pacific-136
Blue-136
Red-136
03Pacific Complete-439
Red-439
03Parkhurst Original Six New York-6
03Rangers Team Issue-15
03Upper Deck-375
Canadian Exclusives-375
HG-375
UD Exclusives-375
04Russian Legion-12
05Parkhurst-193
Facsimile Auto Parallel-193
05Upper Deck-321
06Gatorade-30
06O-Pee-Chee-199
Rainbow-199
06Upper Deck-327
Exclusives Parallel-327
High Gloss Parallel-327
Masterpieces-327
06Upper Deck MVP-120
Gold Script-120
Super Script-120

Markkanen, Mikko
95Collector's Choice-326
Player's Club-326
Player's Club Platinum-326
95Finnish SISU-334
Drafted Dozen-12

Marklund, Johan
98Danish Hockey League-126
99Danish Hockey League-39

Marklund, Jorgen
83Swedish Semic Elitserien-193
84Swedish Semic Elitserien-216
86Swedish Panini Stickers-240
87Swedish Panini Stickers-227

Marklund, Lars
83Swedish Semic Elitserien-175
84Swedish Semic Elitserien-200
86Swedish Panini Stickers-222
87Swedish Panini Stickers-214
88Swedish Semic Elitserien Stickers-199

Markov, Andrei
96Upper Deck Ice-142
99Russian Dynamo Moscow-6
99Russian Stars of Hockey-5
00BAP Memorabilia-432
Emerald-432
Ruby-432
Sapphire-432
00BAP Parkhurst 2000-P205
00BAP Signature Series-294
Emerald-294
Ruby-294
Sapphire-294
Autographs-236
Autographs Gold-236
00Black Diamond-100
00Canadiens Postcards-18
00Crown Royale-129
21st Century Rookies-13
00Private Stock-128
Gold-128
Premiere Date-128
Retail-128
Silver-128
PS-2001 Rookies-12
00SP Authentic-47
00Titanium-130
Retail-130
00Titanium Draft Day Edition-130
00Titanium Draft Day Promos-130
00Topps Heritage-105
00Topps Premier Plus-103
Blue Ice-103
Rookies-PR9
Rookies Blue Ice-PR9
00Vanguard-130
Pacific Proofs-130
00Russian Champions-3
01BAP Memorabilia-52
Emerald-52
Ruby-52
Sapphire-52
01Parkhurst-109
01Upper Deck MVP-103
01Upper Deck Victory-192
Gold-192
01Upper Deck Vintage-136
01Quebec Citadelles-24
02BAP Sig Series Auto Buybacks 2000-236
02Canadiens Postcards-22
02NHL Power Play Stickers-65
02Pacific-199
Blue-199
Red-199
02Pacific Complete-249
Red-249
02Topps Total-266
02Upper Deck-91
Exclusives-91
02Upper Deck Vintage-137
03Beehive-101
Gold-101
Silver-101
03Canadiens Postcards-19
03ITG Action-307
03O-Pee-Chee-148
03OPC Blue-148
03OPC Gold-148
03OPC Red-148
03Pacific-179
Blue-179
Red-179
03Pacific Complete-293
Red-293
03Parkhurst Original Six Montreal-20
03Topps-148
Blue-148
Gold-148
Red-148
03Upper Deck-346
Canadian Exclusives-346
HG-346
UD Exclusives-346
03Upper Deck MVP-225
Gold Script-225
Silver Script-225
Canadian Exclusives-225
04Russian Back to Russia-4
04Russian Moscow Dynamo-19
05Canadiens Team Issue-14
05Parkhurst-254
Facsimile Auto Parallel-254
05Upper Deck-352
05Upper Deck MVP-213
Gold-213
Platinum-213
06Be A Player-87
Autographs-87
Signatures-AM
Signatures Duals-DSM
06Canadiens Postcards-13
06Gatorade-34
06ITG International Ice-159
Gold-159
Autographs-AAMK
06O-Pee-Chee-259
Rainbow-259
06Panini Stickers-70
06Upper Deck-104
Exclusives Parallel-104
High Gloss Parallel-104
Masterpieces-104
06Upper Deck MVP-154
Gold Script-154
Super Script-154
06Russian Sport Collection Olympic Stars-10
06Russian Torino Olympic Team-17

Markov, Daniil
97St. John's Maple Leafs-16
98Be A Player-283
Press Release-283
98BAP Gold-283
98BAP Autographs-283
98BAP Autographs Gold-283
98Bowman's Best-123
Refractors-123
Atomic Refractors-123
Mirror Image Fusion-F7
Mirror Image Fusion Refractors-F7
Mirror Image Fusion Atomic Refractors-F7
98Katch-166
98Pacific-417
Ice Blue-417
Red-417
98Pacific Omega-233
Red-233
Opening Day Issue-233
98Upper Deck-372
Exclusives-372
Exclusives 1 of 1-372
Gold Reserve-372
99Kraft Whiz Kid-6
99Maple Leafs Pizza Pizza-6
99O-Pee-Chee-63
99O-Pee-Chee Chrome-63
99O-Pee-Chee Chrome Refractors-63
99SPx-148
Radiance-148
Spectrum-148
99Topps/OPC-63
99Topps/OPC Chrome-63
Refractors-63
99Upper Deck-122
Exclusives-122
Exclusives 1 of 1-122
99Upper Deck Arena Giveaways-TM2
99Upper Deck Gold Reserve-122
99Upper Deck MVP-197
Gold Script-197
Silver Script-197
Super Script-197
99Upper Deck Victory-286
99Russian Fetisov Tribute-20
00BAP Memorabilia-396
Emerald-396
Ruby-396
Sapphire-396
Promos-396
00BAP Mem Chicago Sportsfest Copper-396
00BAP Memorabilia Chicago Sportsfest Blue-396
00BAP Memorabilia Chicago Sportsfest Gold-396
00BAP Memorabilia Chicago Sportsfest Ruby-396
00BAP Memorabilia Chicago Sun-Times Ruby-396
00BAP Memorabilia Chicago Sun-Times Gold-396
00BAP Mem Chicago Sun-Times Sapphire-396
00BAP Mem Toronto Fall Expo Copper-396
00BAP Memorabilia Toronto Fall Expo Gold-396
00BAP Memorabilia Toronto Fall Expo Ruby-396
01BAP Memorabilia-424
Emerald-424
Ruby-424
Sapphire-424
01Coyotes Team Issue-13
01Parkhurst-396
01Upper Deck Exclusives-364
02BAP Sig Series Auto Buybacks 1998-283
02Coyotes Team Issue-20
02O-Pee-Chee-93
02O-Pee-Chee Premier Blue Parallel-93
02O-Pee-Chee Premier Red Parallel-93
02O-Pee-Chee Factory Set-93
02Pacific-300
Blue-300
Red-300
02Pacific Complete-343
Red-343
02Parkhurst Retro-163
Minis-163
02Topps-93
OPC Red Parallel-93
Factory Set-93
02Topps Total-21
03Beehive-34
Gold-34
Silver-34
03Black Diamond-27
Black-27
Green-27
Red-27
03Flyers Program Inserts-5
03Flyers Postcards-14
03NHL Sticker Collection-269
03Pacific Complete-250
Red-250
03Topps Traded-TT54
Blue-TT54
Gold-TT54
Red-TT54
03Upper Deck-282
Canadian Exclusives-282
HG-282
UD Exclusives-282
04Upper Deck-130
Canadian Exclusives-130
HG Glossy Gold-130
HG Glossy Silver-130
05Parkhurst Facsimile Auto Parallel-284
05Upper Deck MVP-226
Gold-226
Platinum-226
06Russian Torino Olympic Team-25

Markov, Valentin
73Swedish Stickers-112

Markov, Vladimir
74Swedish Stickers-79

Markov, Zdenek
97St. John's Maple Leafs-17

Markovich, Mike
93Toledo Storm-11

Markovsky, Dmitri
93Portland Winter Hawks-15

Marks, Jack
12C57-38

Marks, John
74NHL Action Stamps-80
74O-Pee-Chee NHL-282
75O-Pee-Chee NHL-121
75Topps-121
76O-Pee-Chee NHL-114
76Topps-114
77O-Pee-Chee NHL-47
77Topps-47
78O-Pee-Chee-157
78Topps-157
79Blackhawks Postcards-12
79O-Pee-Chee-16
79Topps-16
80Blackhawks White Border-8
80O-Pee-Chee-194
80Topps-194
81Blackhawks Borderless Postcards-15
81O-Pee-Chee-70
81Indianapolis Checkers-15
90ProCards AHL/IHL-121
91ProCards-503
96Charlotte Checkers-19
97Charlotte Checkers-22
01Greenville Grrrowl-1
02ECHL Update-U-16
02Greenville Grrrowl-16
03Greenville Grrrowl-22
06Fayetteville FireAntz-8

Marks, Lloyd
02Fort Worth Brahmas-8

Markstrom, Chris
93St. Cloud State Huskies-17
96Madison Monsters-8

Markus, Todd
91Air Canada SJHL-B31

Markwart, Kelly
88Regina Pats-14
89Regina Pats-13
90Saskatoon Blades-17
907th Inn. Sketch WHL-175

Markwart, Nevin
82Regina Pats-15
83Regina Pats-15
84Bruins Postcards-11
84O-Pee-Chee-8
84Topps-7
89Bruins Sports Action-16
90Bruins Sports Action-15
90Pro Set-408
91O-Pee-Chee-238
91Topps-238

Marlan, Brandon
93Quebec Pee-Wee Tournament-769

Marleau, Patrick
95Seattle Thunderbirds-15
96Black Diamond-103
Gold-103
96Upper Deck-384
96Seattle Thunderbirds-12
97Be A Player-221
Autographs-221
Autographs Die-Cuts-221
Autographs Prismatic Die-Cuts-221
97Black Diamond-140
Double Diamond-140
Triple Diamond-140
Quadruple Diamond-140
97Collector's Choice-304
97Crown Royale-120
Emerald Green-120
Ice Blue-120
Silver-120
97Donruss Elite-99
97Donruss Elite-128
97Donruss Elite-145
Aspirations-99
Aspirations-128

Aspirations-145
Status-99
Status-128
Status-145
Back to the Future-3
Back to the Future Autographs-3
Craftsmen-11
Master Craftsmen-11
97Donruss Limited-200
Exposure-200
97Donruss Preferred-150
97Donruss Preferred-198
Cut to the Chase-150
Cut to the Chase-198
Line of the Times-5C
97Donruss Preferred Line of Times Promos-5C
97Donruss Priority-175
97Donruss Priority-195
97Donruss Priority-216
Stamp of Approval-175
Stamp of Approval-195
Stamp of Approval-216
Direct Deposit-18
Direct Deposit Promos-P18
Postcards-18
Postcards Opening Day Issues-29
Stamps-18
Stamps Bronze-18
Stamps Gold-18
Stamps Silver-18
97Katch-121
Gold-121
Silver-121
97Leaf-154
Fractal Matrix-154
Fractal Matrix Die Cuts-154
97McDonald's Upper Deck-34
97Pacific Dynagon-NNO
Copper-NNO
Dark Grey-NNO
Emerald Green-NNO
Ice Blue-NNO
Red-NNO
Silver-NNO
97Pacific Omega-203
Copper-203
Dark Gray-203
Emerald Green-203
Gold-203
Ice Blue-203
97Paramount-167
Copper-167
Dark Grey-167
Emerald Green-167
Ice Blue-167
Red-167
Silver-167
97Pinnacle-12
Artist's Proofs-12
Rink Collection-12
Press Plates Back Black-12
Press Plates Back Cyan-12
Press Plates Back Magenta-12
Press Plates Back Yellow-12
Press Plates Front Black-12
Press Plates Front Cyan-12
Press Plates Front Magenta-12
Press Plates Front Yellow-12
Certified Rookie Redemption-C
Certified Rookie Redemption Gold-C
Certified Rookie Redemption Mirror Gold-C
97Revolution-125
Copper-125
Emerald-125
Ice Blue-125
Silver-125
97SP Authentic-191
97Upper Deck-354
Game Dated Moments-354
Smooth Grooves-SG3
97Upper Deck Ice-41
Parallel-41
Power Shift-41
97Zenith-84
Z-Gold-84
Z-Silver-84
Rookie Reign-10
97Bowman CHL-88
97Bowman CHL-141
OPC-88
OPC-141
Bowman's Best-2
Bowman's Best Atomic Refractors-2
Bowman's Best Refractor-2
98Aurora-168
Championship Fever-43
Championship Fever Copper-43
Championship Fever Ice Blue-43
Championship Fever Red-43
Championship Fever Silver-43
98Be A Player-120
Press Release-120
98BAP Gold-120
98BAP Autographs-120
98BAP Autographs Gold-120
98BAP Tampa Bay All Star Game-120
98Black Diamond-72
Double Diamond-72
Triple Diamond-72
Quadruple Diamond-72
98Bowman's Best-60
Refractors-60
Atomic Refractors-60
Performers-BP4
Performers Refractors-BP4
Performers Atomic Refractors-BP4
98Crown Royale-119
Limited Series-119
98Finest-18
No Protectors-18
No Protectors Refractors-18
Refractors-18
Centurion-C12
Centurion Refractors-C12
98OPC Chrome-170
Refractors-170
Season's Best-SB10
Season's Best Refractors-SB10
98Pacific-386
Ice Blue-386
Red-386
Team Checklists-23
98Pacific Dynagon Ice-167
Blue-167
Red-167
98Pacific Omega-211
Red-211
Opening Day Issue-211
98Paramount-211
Copper-211
Emerald Green-211
Holo-Electric-211
Ice Blue-211
Silver-211
Team Checklists Die-Cuts-23
98Revolution-127
Ice Shadow-127
Red-127
98SP Authentic-75
Power Shift-75
98SPx Finite-73
98SPx Finite-130
Radiance-73
Radiance-130
Spectrum-73
Spectrum-130
98SPx Top Prospects-50
Radiance-50
Spectrum-50
98Topps-170
O-Pee-Chee-170
Season's Best-SB10
98Topps Gold Label Class 1-94
Black-94
Black One of One-94
One of One-94
Red-94
Red One of One-94
98Topps Gold Label Class 2-94
98Topps Gold Label Class 2 Black-94
98Topps Gold Label Class 2 Black 1 of 1-94
98Topps Gold Label Class 2 One of One-94
98Topps Gold Label Class 2 Red-94
98Topps Gold Label Class 2 Red One of One-94
98Topps Gold Label Class 3-94
98Topps Gold Label Class 3 Black-94
98Topps Gold Label Class 3 Black 1 of 1-94
98Topps Gold Label Class 3 One of One-94
98Topps Gold Label Class 3 Red-94
98Topps Gold Label Class 3 Red One of One-94
98UD Choice-173
98UD Choice Preview-173
98UD Choice Prime Choice Reserve-173
98UD Choice Reserve-173
98UD3-4
98UD3-64
98UD3-124
Die-Cuts-4
Die-Cuts-64
Die-Cuts-124
98Upper Deck-26
98Upper Deck-171
Exclusives-26
Exclusives-171
Exclusives 1 of 1-26
Exclusives 1 of 1-171
Generation Next-GN10
Generation Next Quantum 1-GN10
Generation Next Quantum 2-GN10
Generation Next Quantum 3-GN10
Gold Reserve-26
Gold Reserve-171
98Upper Deck MVP-170
Gold Script-170
Silver Script-170
Super Script-170
Power Game-PG13
99Aurora-121
Premiere Date-121
99BAP Memorabilia-133
Gold-133
Silver-133
99BAP Millennium-210
Emerald-210
Ruby-210
Sapphire-210
Signatures-210
Signatures Gold-210
99Black Diamond-74
Diamond Cut-74
Final Cut-74
99Crown Royale-124
Limited Series-124
Premiere Date-124
99O-Pee-Chee-134
99O-Pee-Chee Chrome-134
99O-Pee-Chee Chrome Refractors-134
99Pacific-375
Copper-375
Emerald Green-375
Gold-375
Ice Blue-375
Premiere Date-375
Red-375
99Pacific Dynagon Ice-173
Blue-173
Copper-173
Gold-173
Premiere Date-173
Checkmates American-14
Checkmates American-29
Checkmates Canadian-29
99Pacific Omega-208
Copper-208
Gold-208
Ice Blue-208
Premiere Date-208
99Pacific Prism-125
Holographic Blue-125
Holographic Gold-125
Holographic Mirror-125
Holographic Purple-125
Premiere Date-125
99Panini Stickers-301
99Paramount-206
Copper-206
Emerald-206
Gold-206
Holographic Emerald-206
Holographic Gold-206
Holographic Silver-206
Ice Blue-206
Premiere Date-206
Red-206
Silver-206
99Revolution-128
Premiere Date-128
Red-128
Shadow Series-128
Showstoppers-31
Copper-128
Gold-128
CSC Silver-128
99SPx-129
Radiance-129
Spectrum-129
99Stadium Club-72
First Day Issue-72
One of a Kind-72
Printing Plates Black-72
Printing Plates Cyan-72
Printing Plates Magenta-72
Printing Plates Yellow-72
99Topps/OPC-134
99Topps/OPC Chrome-134
Refractors-134
99Upper Deck-110
Exclusives-110
Exclusives 1 of 1-110
99Upper Deck Gold Reserve-110
99Upper Deck MVP-176
Gold Script-176
Silver Script-176
Super Script-176
99Upper Deck Victory-250
99Wayne Gretzky Hockey-151
00Aurora-128
Premiere Date-128
00BAP Memorabilia-229
Emerald-229
Ruby-229
Sapphire-229
Promos-229
00BAP Mem Chicago Sportsfest Copper-229
00BAP Memorabilia Chicago Sportsfest Blue-229
00BAP Memorabilia Chicago Sportsfest Gold-229
00BAP Memorabilia Chicago Sportsfest Ruby-229
00BAP Memorabilia Chicago Sun-Times Ruby-229
00BAP Memorabilia Chicago Sun-Times Gold-229
00BAP Mem Chicago Sun-Times Sapphire-229
00BAP Mem Toronto Fall Expo Copper-229
00BAP Memorabilia Toronto Fall Expo Gold-229
00BAP Memorabilia Toronto Fall Expo Ruby-229
00BAP Parkhurst 2000-P71
00BAP Signature Series-55
Emerald-55
Ruby-55
Sapphire-55
Autographs-51
Autographs Gold-51
00Crown Royale-93
Ice Blue-93
Limited Series-93
Premiere Date-93
Red-93
00O-Pee-Chee-223
00O-Pee-Chee Parallel-223
00Pacific-360
Copper-360
Gold-360
Ice Blue-360
Premiere Date-360
00Paramount-214
Copper-214
Gold-214
Holo-Gold-214
Holo-Silver-214
Ice Blue-214
Premiere Date-214
00Revolution-129
Blue-129
Premiere Date-129
Red-129
00SP Authentic-74
00SP Game Used Tools of the Game-PM
00SP Game Used Tools of the Game Excl-PM
00Titanium-85
Blue-85
Gold-85
Premiere Date-85
Red-85
Retail-85
00Topps/OPC-223
Parallel-223
00Topps Chrome-142
OPC Refractors-142
Refractors-142
00Topps Gold Label Class 1-12
Gold-12
00Topps Gold Label Class 2-12
00Topps Gold Label Class 2 Gold-12
00Topps Gold Label Class 3-12
00Topps Gold Label Class 3 Gold-12
00Topps Gold Label Bullion-B8
00Topps Gold Label Bullion One to One-B8
00Topps Gold Label Game-Worn Jerseys-GLJ-PM
00Topps Heritage-153
00UD Pros and Prospects-73
00Upper Deck-146
Exclusives Tier 1-146
Exclusives Tier 2-146
00Upper Deck Victory-195
00Upper Deck Vintage-305
01BAP Memorabilia-173
Emerald-173
Ruby-173
Sapphire-173
01BAP Signature Series-144
Autographs-144
Autographs Gold-144
01O-Pee-Chee-9
01O-Pee-Chee Heritage Parallel-9
01O-Pee-Chee Heritage Parallel Limited-9
01O-Pee-Chee Premier Parallel-9
01Pacific-339
Extreme LTD-339
Hobby LTD-339
Premiere Date-339
Retail LTD-339
01Pacific Adrenaline-166
Blue-166
Premiere Date-166
Red-166
Retail-166
01Pacific Arena Exclusives-339
01Pacific Heads-Up-83
Blue-83
Premiere Date-83
Red-83
Silver-83
01Parkhurst-80
Gold-80
Silver-80
01Private Stock-84
Gold-84
Premiere Date-84
Retail-84
Silver-84
01Private Stock Pacific Nights-84
01Sharks Postcards-6
01SP Game Used Authentic Fabric-AFPM
01SP Game Used Authentic Fabric Gold-AFPM
01Stadium Club-70
Award Winners-70
Master Photos-70
Souvenirs-PM
01Titanium Draft Day Edition-85
01Topps-9
Heritage Parallel-9
Heritage Parallel Limited-9
OPC Parallel-9
01Topps Chrome-9
Refractors-9
Black Border Refractors-9
01Topps Heritage-93
Refractors-93
Jerseys-JPM
01Topps Reserve Emblems-PM
01Topps Reserve Jerseys-PM
01Topps Reserve Name Plates-PM
01Topps Reserve Numbers-PM
01Topps Reserve Patches-PM
01Upper Deck-147
Exclusives-147
Game Jerseys Series II-GNPM
01Upper Deck Victory-291
Gold-291
01Vanguard-85
Blue-85
Red-85
One of Ones-85
Premiere Date-85
Proofs-85
02Atomic-85
Blue-85
Gold-85
Red-85
Hobby Parallel-85
02BAP First Edition-238
02BAP Memorabilia-105
Emerald-105
Ruby-105
Sapphire-105
NHL All-Star Game-105
NHL All-Star Game Blue-105
NHL All-Star Game Green-105
NHL All-Star Game Red-105
02BAP Memorabilia Toronto Fall Expo-105
02BAP Signature Series-69
Autographs-69
Autograph Buybacks 1998-120
Autograph Buybacks 1999-210
Autograph Buybacks 2000-51
Autograph Buybacks 2001-144
Autographs Gold-69
Golf-GS68
02Crown Royale Dual Patches-19
02O-Pee-Chee-63
02O-Pee-Chee Premier Blue Parallel-63
02O-Pee-Chee Premier Red Parallel-63
02O-Pee-Chee Factory Set-63
02Pacific-336
Blue-336
Red-336
02Pacific Complete-113
Red-113
02Pacific Exclusive-149
Jerseys-22
Jerseys Gold-22
02Pacific Heads-Up-107
Blue-107
Purple-107
Red-107
Quad Jerseys-24
Quad Jerseys Gold-24
02Parkhurst-147
Bronze-147
Gold-147
Silver-147
02Private Stock Reserve-87
Blue-87
Red-87
Retail-87
02Sharks Team Issue-3
02SP Game Used Authentic Fabrics-AFPM
02SP Game Used Authentic Fabrics Gold-AFPM
02SP Game Used Authentic Fabrics Rainbow-AFPM
02SP Game Used First Rounder Patches-PM
02SP Game Used Piece of History-PHPM
02SP Game Used Piece of History Gold-PHPM
02SP Game Used Piece of History Rainbow-PHPM
02Titanium-86
Blue-86
Red-86
Retail-86
Jerseys-62
Jerseys Retail-62
Patches-62
02Topps-63
OPC Blue Parallel-63
OPC Red Parallel-63
First Round Fabric-PM
Factory Set-63
02Topps Chrome-44
Black Border Refractors-44
Refractors-44
First Round Fabric Patches-PM
02Topps Total-328
02UD Piece of History-74
02Upper Deck-144
Exclusives-144
02Upper Deck Classic Portraits-81
02Upper Deck MVP-156
Gold-156
Classics-156
Golden Classics-156
02Upper Deck Victory-178
Bronze-178
Gold-178
Silver-178
02Upper Deck Vintage-210
02Upper Deck Vintage-285
Green Backs-210
02Vanguard Jerseys-40
02Vanguard Jerseys Gold-40
03BAP Memorabilia-65
Emerald-65
Gold-65
Ruby-65
Sapphire-65
03BAP Ultimate Memorabilia Heroes-17
03Beehive-164
Variations-164
Gold-164
Silver-164
03Black Diamond-62
Black-62
Green-62
Red-62
03Bowman-8
Gold-8
Future Rivals-MM
Future Rivals Patches-MM
03Bowman Chrome-8
Refractors-8
Gold Refractors-8
Xfractors-8
03eTopps-51
03ITG Action-415
Jerseys-M51
03NHL Sticker Collection-285
03O-Pee-Chee-188
03OPC Blue-188
03OPC Gold-188
03OPC Red-188
03Pacific-296
Blue-296
Red-296
03Pacific Calder-87
Silver-87
03Pacific Complete-101
Red-101
03Pacific Exhibit-129
Blue Backs-129
Yellow Backs-129
03Pacific Heads-Up-83
Hobby LTD-83
Retail LTD-83
03Pacific Invincible-83
Blue-83
Red-83
Retail-83
Featured Performers-26
03Pacific Prism-87
Blue-87
Gold-87
Red-87
03Pacific Quest for the Cup-89
Blue-89
03Pacific Supreme-84
Blue-84
Red-84
Retail-84
03Private Stock Reserve-90
Blue-90
Red-90
Retail-90
03Sharks Postcards-9
03SP Authentic-72
Limited-72
03Titanium-88
Hobby Jersey Number Parallels-88
Retail-88
Retail Jersey Number Parallels-88
03Topps-188
Blue-188
Gold-188
Red-188
03Topps C55-8
Minis-8
Minis American Back-8
Minis American Back Red-8
Minis Bazooka Back-8
Minis Brooklyn Back-8
Minis Hat Trick Back-8
Minis O Canada Back-8
Minis O Canada Back Red-8
Minis Stanley Cup Back-8
03Topps Pristine-61
Gold Refractor Die Cuts-61
Refractors-61
Jersey Portions-PPJ-PM
Jersey Portion Refractors-PPJ-PM
Press Plates Black-61
Press Plates Cyan-61
Press Plates Magenta-61
Press Plates Yellow-61
03Topps Traded Franchise Fabrics-FF-PM
03UD Honor Roll-71
03Upper Deck-404
All-Star Class-AS-24
Canadian Exclusives-404
HG-404
UD Exclusives-404
03Upper Deck Ice-72
Gold-72
03Upper Deck MVP-345
Gold Script-345
Silver Script-345
Canadian Exclusives-345
03Upper Deck Rookie Update-73
03Upper Deck Victory-157
Bronze-157
Gold-157
Silver-157
04Pacific-230
Blue-230
Red-230
All-Stars-11
04SP Authentic-75
04UD Toronto Fall Expo Pride of Canada-20
04Upper Deck-146
Canadian Exclusives-146
HG Glossy Gold-146
HG Glossy Silver-146
World Cup Tribute-DHPMSD
05Be A Player-73
First Period-73
Second Period-73
Third Period-73
Overtime-73
Dual Signatures-IM
Dual Signatures-MC
Outtakes-OT41
Quad Signatures-IMPL
Signatures-PM
Signatures Gold-PM
Triple Signatures-IBM
05Beehive-75
Matte-75
05Black Diamond-112
Emerald-112
Gold-112
Onyx-112
Ruby-112
05Hot Prospects-83
En Fuego-83
Red Hot-83
White Hot-83
05Panini Stickers-344
05Parkhurst-401
05Parkhurst-521
Facsimile Auto Parallel-401
Facsimile Auto Parallel-521
True Colors-TCSJS
True Colors-TCSJS
True Colors-TCSJLA
True Colors-TCSJLA
05SP Authentic-84
Limited-84
Sign of the Times Fives-TNCMC
05SP Game Used-84
Gold-84
Authentic Fabrics-AF-PM
Authentic Fabrics Dual-MC
Authentic Fabrics Gold-AF-PM
Authentic Patches-AP-PM
Authentic Patches Dual-MC
05SPx-76
Spectrum-76
Winning Materials-WM-PM
Winning Materials Gold-WM-PM
Winning Materials Spectrum-WM-PM
05The Cup-87
Gold-87
Black Rainbow-87
Emblems of Endorsement-EEPM
Honorable Numbers-HNPM
Limited Logos-LLPM
Masterpiece Pressplates-87
Noble Numbers-NNGM
Noble Numbers-NNSM
Patch Variation-P87
Patch Variation Autographs-AP87
Scripted Numbers-SNGM
Scripted Numbers-SNSM
Scripted Numbers Dual-DSNTM
Scripted Swatches-SSPM
05UD Artifacts-84
Blue-84
Gold-84
Green-84
Pewter-84
Red-84
Gold Autographed-84
05UD PowerPlay-75
05UD PowerPlay-116
Rainbow-75
05Ultimate Collection-77
Gold-77
Endorsed Emblems-EEPM
Jerseys-JPM
Premium Patches-PPPM
Premium Swatches-PSPM
Ultimate Patches-PPM
05Ultra-161
Gold-161
Ice-161
05Upper Deck-404
05Upper Deck All-Time Greatest-51
05Upper Deck Big Playmakers-B-PM
05Upper Deck Notable Numbers-N-PM
05Upper Deck Patches-P-PM
05Upper Deck Ice-83
Rainbow-83
Frozen Fabrics-FFPM
Frozen Fabrics Glass-FFPM
Frozen Fabrics Patches-FFPPM
05Upper Deck MVP-325
Gold-325
Platinum-325
05Upper Deck Rookie Update-82
05Upper Deck Trilogy-75
05Upper Deck Trilogy-151
Crystal-151
05Upper Deck Victory-160
Black-160
Gold-160
Silver-160
Blow-Ups-BU33
Game Breakers-GB37
06Be A Player-86
Autographs-86
Signatures-PM
Signatures 10-93
Signatures 25-93
Signatures Duals-DMG
Signatures Trios-TTCM
Signatures Foursomes-FMSRS
Up Close and Personal-UC43
Up Close and Personal Autographs-UC43
06Be A Player Portraits-85
Sensational Six-SSSJM
Signature Portraits-SPPM
06Beehive-16
Blue-16
Gold-16
Matte-16
Red Facsimile Signatures-16
Wood-16
Matted Materials-MMPM
Remarkable Matted Materials-MMPM
Signature Scrapbook-SSPM
06Black Diamond-122
Black-122
Gold-122
Ruby-122
Gemography-GPM
06Flair Showcase-85
06Flair Showcase-160
Parallel-85
Parallel-160
Inks-IPM
06Fleer-160
Tiffany-160
Fabricology-FPM
Speed Machines-SM21
06Hot Prospects-85
Red Hot-85
White Hot-85
Hot Materials -HMPM
Hot Materials Red Hot-HMPM
Hot Materials White Hot-HMPM
06McDonald's Upper Deck Autographs-APM
06NHL POG-57
06O-Pee-Chee-413
06O-Pee-Chee-695
Rainbow-413
Rainbow-695
Swatches-S-PM
06Panini Stickers-333
06SP Authentic-17
Chirography-PM
Limited-17
Sign of the Times-STPM
Sign of the Times Duals-STPJ
Sign of the Times Triples-ST3MTC
06SP Game Used-85
Gold-85
Rainbow-85
Authentic Fabrics-AFPM
Authentic Fabrics Parallel-AFPM
Authentic Fabrics Patches-AFPM
Authentic Fabrics Dual-AF2MT
Authentic Fabrics Dual Patches-AF2MT
Authentic Fabrics Triple-AF3SJS
Authentic Fabrics Triple Patches-AF3SJS
Authentic Fabrics Quads-AF4LMSB
Authentic Fabrics Quads Patches-AF4LMSB
Autographs-85
By The Letter-BLPM
Inked Sweaters-ISPM
Inked Sweaters Patches-ISPM
Inked Sweaters Dual-IS2MC
Inked Sweaters Dual Patches-IS2MC
Letter Marks-LMPM
06SPx-84
Spectrum-84
SPxcitement-X84
SPxcitement Spectrum-X84
Winning Materials-WMPM
Winning Materials Spectrum-WMPM
Winning Materials Autographs-WMPM
06The Cup-79
Autographed Foundations-CQPM
Autographed Foundations Patches-CQPM
Autographed NHL Shields Duals-DASMM
Autographed NHL Shields Duals-DASTM
Autographed Patches-79
Black Rainbow-79
Foundations-CQPM
Foundations Patches-CQPM
Gold-79
Gold Patches-79
Honorable Numbers-HNPM
Jerseys-79
Limited Logos-LLPM
Masterpiece Pressplates-79
Scripted Swatches-SSPM
Signature Patches-SPPM
06UD Artifacts-16
06UD Artifacts-194
Blue-16
Blue-194
Gold-16
Gold-194
Platinum-16
Platinum-194
Radiance-16
Radiance-194
Autographed Radiance Parallel-16
Autographed Radiance Parallel-194
Red-16
Red-194
Auto-Facts-AFPM
Auto-Facts Gold-AFPM
Frozen Artifacts-FAPM
Frozen Artifacts Black-FAPM
Frozen Artifacts Blue-FAPM
Frozen Artifacts Gold-FAPM
Frozen Artifacts Platinum-FAPM
Frozen Artifacts Red-FAPM
Frozen Artifacts Autographed Black-FAPM
Frozen Artifacts Patches Black-FAPM
Frozen Artifacts Patches Blue-FAPM
Frozen Artifacts Patches Gold-FAPM
Frozen Artifacts Patches Platinum-FAPM
Frozen Artifacts Patches Red-FAPM
Frozen Artifacts Patches Autographed Black Tag Parallel-FAPM
Tundra Tandems-TTPM
Tundra Tandems Black-TTPM
Tundra Tandems Blue-TTPM
Tundra Tandems Gold-TTPM
Tundra Tandems Platinum-TTPM
Tundra Tandems Red-TTPM
Tundra Tandems Dual Patches Red-TTPM
06UD Mini Jersey Collection-84
06UD Powerplay-84
Impact Rainbow-84
Power Marks-PMPM
Specialists-SPM
Specialists Patches-PPM
06Ultimate Collection-52
Autographed Jerseys-AJ-PM
Autographed Patches-AJ-PM
Premium Patches-PS-PM
Premium Swatches-PS-PM
Signatures-US-PM
Ultimate Signatures Logos-SL-PM
06Ultra-162
Gold Medallion-162
Ice Medallion-162
06Upper Deck Arena Giveaways-SJS4
06Upper Deck-410
Exclusives Parallel-410
High Gloss Parallel-410
Game Dated Moments-GD29
Game Jerseys-J2PM
Game Patches-P2PM
Hometown Heroes-HH44
Masterpieces-410
Oversized Wal-Mart Exclusives-410
Signature Sensations-SSPM
06Upper Deck MVP-246
Gold Script-246
Super Script-246
Autographs-OATM
06Upper Deck Ovation-193
06Upper Deck Sweet Shot-87
Signature Shots/Saves-SSPM
Signature Shots/Saves Sticks-SSSPM
Signature Sticks-STPM
Sweet Stitches-SSPM
Sweet Stitches Duals-SSPM
Sweet Stitches Triples-SSPM
06Upper Deck Trilogy-83
Combo Clearcut Autographs-C2PM
Combo Clearcut Autographs-C3MTC
Honorary Scripted Patches-HSPPM
Honorary Scripted Swatches-HSSPM
Scripts-S2PM
Scripts-TSPM
06Upper Deck Victory-165
06Upper Deck Victory Black-165
06Upper Deck Victory Gold-165
06Upper Deck Victory GameBreakers-GB43
07Upper Deck Victory-180
Black-180
Gold-180
GameBreakers-GB34
Stars on Ice-SI45

Marler, Jeff

03Minnesota State Mavericks-12

Marois, Daniel

88Maple Leafs PLAY-15
89Kraft-37
89O-Pee-Chee-273
89O-Pee-Chee Stickers-102
89O-Pee-Chee Stickers-176
89O-Pee-Chee Stickers-239
89Panini Stickers-137
90Bowman-160
Tiffany-160
90O-Pee-Chee-267
90Panini Stickers-284
90Pro Set-284
90Score-122
Canadian-122
90Score Young Superstars-3
90Topps-267
Tiffany-267
90Upper Deck-179
French-179
91Pro Set Platinum-118
91Bowman-165
91Maple Leafs Panini Team Stickers-14
91Maple Leafs PLAY-23
91O-Pee-Chee-212
91Panini Stickers-95
91Parkhurst-329
French-329
91Pinnacle-27
French-27
91Pro Set-223
French-223
91Score American-254
91Score Canadian Bilingual-474
91Score Canadian English-474
91Stadium Club-197
91Topps-212
91Upper Deck-331
French-331
92Bowman-245
92Durivage Panini-16
92O-Pee-Chee-58
92Pinnacle-139
French-139
92Score-63
Canadian-63
92Stadium Club-63
92Topps-49
Gold-49G
92Upper Deck-71
93Donruss-17
93Parkhurst-282
Emerald Ice-282
94Parkhurst-18
Gold-18
98Swiss Power Play Stickers-46
99Finnish Cardset-255
00Swiss Panini Stickers-23
00Swiss Slapshot Mini-Cards-HCAP16

Marois, Jean

43Parade Sportive *-82
51Laval Dairy QSHL-2
52St. Lawrence Sales-36

Marois, Jerome

98Quebec Remparts-13
Signed-13
00Rouyn-Noranda Huskies-13
Signed-13

Marois, Mario

80Pepsi-Cola Caps-113
81Nordiques Postcards-11
81O-Pee-Chee-279
82Nordiques Postcards-13
82O-Pee-Chee-287
82Post Cereal-16
83Nordiques Postcards-17
83O-Pee-Chee-295
83Vachon-67
84Nordiques Postcards-15
84O-Pee-Chee-282
84O-Pee-Chee Stickers-166
84O-Pee-Chee Stickers-167
85Jets Police-11
85Nordiques General Foods-17
85Nordiques Provigo-16
85O-Pee-Chee-194
85O-Pee-Chee Stickers-144
86Jets Postcards-13
86Kraft Drawings-40
87Jets Postcards-13
87O-Pee-Chee-220
87O-Pee-Chee Stickers-250
87Panini Stickers-359
88Jets Police-14
88Nordiques General Foods-26
88Nordiques Team Issue-40
88O-Pee-Chee-233
88O-Pee-Chee Stickers-142
88Panini Stickers-151
89Nordiques Team Issue-28
89Nordiques General Foods-22
89Nordiques Police-19
89O-Pee-Chee-260
89O-Pee-Chee Stickers-185
89Panini Stickers-336
90Blues Kodak-14
90Nordiques Team Issue-20
90O-Pee-Chee-158
90Pro Set-253
90Pro Set-524
90Score-229
Canadian-229
90Score Rookie/Traded-94T
90Topps-158
Tiffany-158
90Upper Deck-8
French-8
91Bowman-380
91O-Pee-Chee-82
91Pro Set-477
French-477
91Score Canadian Bilingual-546
91Score Canadian English-546
91Stadium Club-12
91Topps-82
92Hamilton Canucks-14
92Hamilton Canucks-29
04ITG Franchises Canadian-144
Autographs-MM

Maron, Oliver

01Belleville Bulls-15
02Belleville Bulls-11

Maroney, Katie

04Ohio State Buckeyes Women-11
05Ohio State Buckeyes Women-5
06Ohio State Buckeyes Women-2

Maroste, Mark

94German DEL-137
95German DEL-40

Marostega, Michael

01Anchorage Aces-8

Marotte, Gilles

66Topps-36
67Topps-59
68Bauer Ads-15
68Blackhawks Team Issue-4
68O-Pee-Chee-14
68Shirriff Coins-32
68Topps-14
69O-Pee-Chee-68

69Topps-68
70Colgate Stamps-65
70Dad's Cookies-76
70Esso Power Players-148
70O-Pee-Chee-34
70Sargent Promotions Stamps-78
70Topps-34
71Letraset Action Replays-1
71O-Pee-Chee-151
71Sargent Promotions Stamps-70
72O-Pee-Chee-27
72Sargent Promotions Stamps-89
72Topps-167
72Finnish Semic World Championship-202
72Swedish Semic World Championship-202
73O-Pee-Chee-5
73Topps-188
74NHL Action Stamps-197
74O-Pee-Chee NHL-373
75O-Pee-Chee NHL-164
75Topps-164
76O-Pee-Chee NHL-192
76Topps-192
91Ultimate Original Six-59
French-59
95Parkhurst '66-67-17
Coins-17

Marouelli, Dan
90Pro Set-692

Marple, Stan
97UK Guildford Flames-21
99UK Guildford Flames-22
99UK Guildford Flames-23
00UK Guildford Flames-14
00UK Guildford Flames-15
01UK Guildford Flames-4
01UK Guildford Flames-21
02UK Guildford Flames-2
02UK Guildford Flames-19
03UK Guildford Flames-3
03UK Guildford Flames-20
04UK Guildford Flames-21
05UK Guildford Flames-21
06UK Guildford Flames-23

Marquardt, Matt
05Moncton Wildcats-23
06Moncton Wildcats-9

Marquet, Sebastien
93Swedish Semic World Champ Stickers-256

Marquette, Dale
88ProCards IHL-104
89ProCards IHL-64

Marquis, Francois
93Swiss HNL-280
96Swiss HNL-353

Marquis, James
00Brandon Wheat Kings-11

Marquis, Philippe
95Swiss HNL-242
96Swiss HNL-212
98Swiss Power Play Stickers-87
99Swiss Panini Stickers-85
99Swiss Panini Stickers-257
00Swiss Panini Stickers-133
00Swiss Slapshot Mini-Cards-HCFG5
01Swiss HNL-128
02Swiss HNL-48

Marr, Steve
02Medicine Hat Tigers-13
04Medicine Hat Tigers-13

Marrietti, Brett
907th Inn. Sketch OHL-134

Marrin, Peter
76O-Pee-Chee WHA-96
77O-Pee-Chee WHA-51

Marriott, Jamie
91British Columbia JHL-38

Mars, Gunnar
69Swedish Hockey-121

Mars, Per
01Swedish Brynas Tigers-13
02Lincoln Stars-33
03Swedish Bjorkloven Umea-23

Marsch, Kenny
93Quebec Pee-Wee Tournament-1328

Marsh, Blair
92British Columbia JHL-235
93Maine Black Bears-56

Marsh, Brad
78Flames Majik Market-5
79Flames Postcards-9
79Flames Team Issue-8
80Flames Postcards-12
80O-Pee-Chee-338
80Pepsi-Cola Caps-9
81O-Pee-Chee-47
81O-Pee-Chee Stickers-225
82O-Pee-Chee-254
82Post Cereal-14
83Flyers J.C. Penney-15
83O-Pee-Chee-269
84O-Pee-Chee-163
85Flyers Postcards-18
85O-Pee-Chee-72
85Topps-72
86Flyers Postcards-15
86O-Pee-Chee-175
86O-Pee-Chee Stickers-235
86Topps-175
87Flyers Postcards-12
87O-Pee-Chee-128
87Panini Stickers-127
87Topps-128
88Maple Leafs PLAY-25
88O-Pee-Chee-64
88O-Pee-Chee Stickers-101
88Topps-64
89O-Pee-Chee-276
89O-Pee-Chee Stickers-175
89Panini Stickers-141
90Bowman-158
Tiffany-158
90Maple Leafs Postcards-13
90O-Pee-Chee-155
90Panini Stickers-277
90Pro Set-285
90Score-219
Canadian-219
90Topps-155
Tiffany-155
90Upper Deck-199
French-199
91Maple Leafs Panini Team Stickers-15
91O-Pee-Chee-19
91Pinnacle-361
91Pinnacle-401
French-361
French-401
91Pro Set-378
French-378
91Score Canadian Bilingual-416
91Score Canadian English-416
91Topps-19
92Parkhurst-123
Emerald Ice-123
92Pinnacle-378
French-378
92Pro Set-126
92Pro Set-264
92Score-293
Canadian-293
92Senators Team Issue-10
92Stadium Club-482
92Topps-215
Gold-215G
92Ultra-364
93Pinnacle All-Stars-10
93Pinnacle All-Stars Canadian-10
93Score-392
Canadian-392
93Senators Kraft Sheets-18
93Stadium Club All-Stars-15
93Stadium Club All-Stars Members Only-15
93Stadium Club All-Stars OPC-15
94Senators Team Issue-21
95Senators Team Issue-16
01Ottawa 67's-27
04ITG Franchises Update-486
04ITG Franchises US East-431
Autographs-A-BM
04UD Legendary Signatures-11
Autographs-BM
Rearguard Retrospectives-BMMH

Marsh, Kevin
98Red Deer Rebels-10
04Colorado Eagles-11

Marsh, Peter
79Jets Postcards-15
79O-Pee-Chee-147
79Topps-147
80Blackhawks Postcards-6
80O-Pee-Chee-314
81Blackhawks Borderless Postcards-16
81Blackhawks Brown Background-6
81O-Pee-Chee-71
82Blackhawks Postcards-13
83Blackhawks Postcards-14

Marsh, Ryan
94Tri-City Americans-7
01Louisiana Ice Gators-14

Marsh, Tyson
01Vancouver Giants-19
03Vancouver Giants-19

Marshall, Andrew
04Barrie Colts-21
05OHL Bell All-Star Classic-20
06Barrie Colts-20

Marshall, Anthony
00Brampton Battalion-24

Marshall, Bert
60NHL Ceramic Tiles-12
64Beehive Group III Photos-86
65Coca-Cola-39
66Topps-51
67Topps-46
68O-Pee-Chee-79
68Shirriff Coins-117
68Topps-79
69O-Pee-Chee-80
Four-in-One-17
69Topps-80
70Dad's Cookies-77
70O-Pee-Chee-188
70Sargent Promotions Stamps-131
71Bazooka-25
71O-Pee-Chee-73
71Sargent Promotions Stamps-134
71Topps-73
71Toronto Sun-52
72O-Pee-Chee-130
72Sargent Promotions Stamps-47
72Topps-162
73O-Pee-Chee-51
73Topps-51
74NHL Action Stamps-174
74O-Pee-Chee NHL-177
74Topps-177
75O-Pee-Chee NHL-72
75Topps-72
76O-Pee-Chee NHL-62
76Topps-62
77O-Pee-Chee NHL-206
77Topps-206
78O-Pee-Chee-49
78Topps-49
81Rockies Postcards-17

Marshall, Bobby
94Saint John Flames-12
97Columbus Cottonmouths-11
98German DEL-14
99German DEL-295
00Columbus Cottonmouths-7

Marshall, Bruce
00Connecticut Huskies-16

Marshall, Charles
52Juniors Blue Tint-20

Marshall, Chris
90Cincinnati Cyclones-29
91Cincinnati Cyclones-13
92Birmingham Bulls-12
92Raleigh Icecaps-25
93Birmingham Bulls-12

Marshall, David
03Chicago Steel-9

Marshall, Don
44Beehive Group II Photos-266
44Beehive Group II Photos-340
55Parkhurst-35
Quaker Oats-35
57Parkhurst-M8
58Parkhurst-44
59Parkhurst-37
60Parkhurst-42
60Parkhurst-57
60Parkhurst-59
60Shirriff Coins-23
60York Photos-23
61Parkhurst-40
61Shirriff/Salada Coins-103
61York Yellow Backs-6
62Parkhurst-43
62Shirriff Coins-33
62York Iron-On Transfers-28
63Topps-59
64Beehive Group III Photos-141
64Coca-Cola Caps-89
64Topps-97
65Coca-Cola-89
65Topps-29
66Topps-24
66Topps USA Test-24
67Topps-23
67Topps-130
68O-Pee-Chee-75
68Shirriff Coins-99
68Topps-75
69O-Pee-Chee-39
69Topps-39
70Colgate Stamps-27
70Dad's Cookies-78
70Esso Power Players-88
70O-Pee-Chee-129
70Topps-129
71Maple Leafs Postcards-11
71O-Pee-Chee-199
71Sargent Promotions Stamps-208
71Toronto Sun-264
72Finnish Semic World Championship-197
72Swedish Semic World Championship-197
91Ultimate Original Six-13
French-13
94Parkhurst Missing Link-76
94Parkhurst Tall Boys-88
95Parkhurst '66-67-82
Coins-82
04ITG Franchises US East-399
Autographs-A-DMR

Marshall, Grant
907th Inn. Sketch OHL-88
917th Inn. Sketch OHL-299
92Ottawa 67's-15
92Classic-13
Gold-13
92Classic Four-Sport *-162
Gold-162
93St. John's Maple Leafs-16
93Classic-140
93Classic Four-Sport *-240
Gold-240
94Classic Pro Prospects-188
95Bowman-162
All-Foil-162
95Leaf-327
95Parkhurst International-533
Emerald Ice-533
95Upper Deck-362
Electric Ice-362
Electric Ice Gold-362
96Be A Player-146
Autographs-146
Autographs Silver-146
96Collector's Choice-77
96Donruss-222
Press Proofs-222
96Leaf-169
Press Proofs-169
96Score-261
Artist's Proofs-261
Dealer's Choice Artist's Proofs-261
Special Artist's Proofs-261
Golden Blades-261
96Stars Postcards-19
96Upper Deck-47
98Upper Deck MVP-64
Gold Script-64
Silver Script-64
Super Script-64
99Pacific-125
Copper-125
Emerald Green-125
Gold-125
Ice Blue-125
Premiere Date-125
Red-125
99Stars Postcards-16
00Crown Royale Game-Worn Jerseys-10
00Crown Royale Game-Worn Jersey Patches-10
00Crown Royale Premium-Sized Jerseys-10
00Stars Postcards-15
00Titanium Game Gear-88
00Titanium Game Gear Patches-88
01Blue Jackets Donatos Pizza-2
01Pacific-130
01Pacific-409
Extreme LTD-130
Gold-409
Hobby LTD-130
Premiere Date-130
Retail LTD-130
01Pacific Arena Exclusives-130
01Pacific Arena Exclusives-409
01Private Stock Game Gear-32
01Private Stock Game Gear Patches-32
01UD Stanley Cup Champs-53
01Upper Deck Victory-117
Gold-117
02Pacific-102
Blue-102
Red-102
02Pacific Complete-448
Red-448
02Parkhurst-199
Bronze-199
Gold-199
Silver-199
02Topps Total-160
02Upper Deck-51
Exclusives-51
03Devils Team Issue-29
03ITG Action-337
03Pacific Complete-138
Red-138
03Upper Deck-115
Canadian Exclusives-115
HG-115
03Upper Deck MVP-255
Gold Script-255
Silver Script-255
Canadian Exclusives-255
03Czech Stadion-605
05Devils Team Issue-11
05Parkhurst-295
Facsimile Auto Parallel-295

Marshall, Jack
10C56-33
10C56-35
10Sweet Caporal Postcards-29
11C55-29
83Hall of Fame Postcards-C9
85Hall of Fame-39

Marshall, Jason
90Upper Deck-453
French-453
907th Inn. Sketch WHL-117
91Score American-388
91Score Canadian Bilingual-278
91Score Canadian English-278
91ProCards-25
92Upper Deck-68
92Peoria Rivermen-14
93Alberta International Team Canada-13
93PowerPlay-488
93Ultra-468
94Finnish Jaa Kiekko-105
95Leaf-190
96Ducks Team Issue-15
97Be A Player-54
Autographs-54
Autographs Die-Cuts-54
Autographs Prismatic Die-Cuts-54
97Pacific Invincible NHL Regime-5
98Be A Player-1
Press Release-1
98BAP Gold-1
98BAP Autographs-1
98BAP Autographs Gold-1
98BAP Tampa Bay All Star Game-1
98Pacific-60
Ice Blue-60
Red-60
99Ultimate Victory-3
1/1-3
Parallel-3
Parallel 100-3
00Upper Deck Vintage-8
02BAP Sig Series Auto Buybacks 1998-1
03Houston Aeros-13
05Ducks Team Issue-10
06Czech NHL ELH Postcards-6
06German DEL-127
New Arrivals-NA5

Marshall, Jeff
05Maine Black Bears-17

Marshall, Paul
81Maple Leafs Postcards-12
90ProCards AHL/IHL-297
92Birmingham Bulls-10
93Birmingham Bulls-10
93Birmingham Bulls Birmingham News-13

Marshall, Rick
907th Inn. Sketch OHL-10
917th Inn. Sketch OHL-105
92Windsor Spitfires-18

Marshall, Robert
00Asheville Smoke-21

Marshall, Scott
04Arizona Icecats-11

Marshall, Willie
55Parkhurst-17
Quaker Oats-17
58Parkhurst-19

Marson, Mike
74Capitals White Borders-19
74NHL Action Stamps-313
75O-Pee-Chee NHL-43
75Topps-43

Marsters, Nathan
04Louisiana Ice Gators-12
05ITG Heroes/Prosp Toronto Expo Parallel -252
05Portland Pirates-22
05ITG Heroes and Prospects-252
Autographs Series II-NM
06Augusta Lynx-12
06Portland Pirates-5
06ITG Heroes and Prospects-40
Autographs-ANM

Martak, Igor
95Slovakian-Quebec Pee-Wee Tournament-15

Martan, John
52Juniors Blue Tint-109

Martel, Jake
95Slapshot-215

Martel, Jocelyn
907th Inn. Sketch QMJHL-258

Martel, Richard
99Baie-Comeau Drakkar-26
00Baie-Comeau Drakkar-25
Signed-25
01Baie-Comeau Drakkar-NNO

Martell, Steve
897th Inn. Sketch OHL-34
907th Inn. Sketch OHL-135
91ProCards-559
92Hampton Roads Admirals-18

Martens, Darren
00Fort Wayne Komets-12

Martens, Henry
05German DEL-354

Martens, Mike
92Thunder Bay Thunder Hawks-11
95Roller Hockey Magazine RHI-4
98Columbus Cottonmouths-9
00Columbus Cottonmouths-8

Martens, Nick
02Michigan Wolverines-19
03Michigan Wolverines-14
04Michigan Wolverines-16

Martens, Norman
04German DEL Update-294
05German DEL-32

Martensson, Leif
71Swedish Hockey-297

Martensson, Tony
00Swedish Upper Deck-36
01Swedish Brynas Tigers-14
02Swedish SHL-6
Parallel-6
02Cincinnati Mighty Ducks-A-10
03Beehive-223
Gold-223
Silver-223
03ITG VIP Rookie Debut-71
03Pacific Complete-564
Red-564
03Pacific Luxury Suite-52
Gold-52
03Parkhurst Rookie-109
03SP Authentic-117
Limited-117
03Titanium-102
Hobby Jersey Number Parallels-102
Retail-102
Retail Jersey Number Parallels-102
03Topps Traded-TT116
Blue-TT116
Gold-TT116
Red-TT116
03Upper Deck Rookie Update-103
03Cincinnati Mighty Ducks-B9
03Pacific AHL Prospects-18
Gold-18
04Swedish Elitset-207
Gold-207
04Swedish Pure Skills-45
Parallel-45
05Swedish SHL Elitset-223
Series Two Signatures-18
Star Potential-9
06Swedish SHL Elitset-73
Performers-8
Playmakers-8

Martensson, Ulf
67Swedish Hockey-107
69Swedish Hockey-122
70Swedish Hockey-78
71Swedish Hockey-168
72Swedish Stickers-162
73Swedish Stickers-52
74Swedish Stickers-251

Marthinsen, Jim
92Finnish Semic-27
92Norwegian Elite Series-1
92Norwegian Elite Series-191
93Swedish Semic World Champ Stickers-229
94Finnish Jaa Kiekko-251
94Swedish Olympics Lillehammer*-311
95Finnish Semic World Championships-177
95Swedish Globe World Championships-190
95Swedish World Championships Stickers-236
96Swedish Semic Wien-202

Marthinsen, Pal
92Norwegian Elite Series-33

Marthinsen, Per
92Norwegian Elite Series-146

Martikainen, Kari
92Finnish Jyvas-Hyva Stickers-59
93Finnish Jyvas-Hyva Stickers-105
93Finnish SISU-11
94Finnish SISU-95
95Finnish SISU-48
96Swiss HNL-132
98Swiss Power Play Stickers-233
99Finnish Cardset-185
99Swiss Panini Stickers-232
00Swiss Panini Stickers-226
00Swiss Slapshot Mini-Cards-RJ3
01Swiss HNL-151
02Finnish Cardset-70
02Swiss HNL-96
04Finnish Cardset-65
Parallel-48
05Finnish Cardset -55
06Finnish Cardset-283

Martikainen, Pentti
71Finnish Suomi Stickers-266

Martikainen, Pertti
71Finnish Suomi Stickers-265

Martikainen, Roopertti
06Moncton Wildcats-3

Martin Jr., Pete
81Victoria Cougars-10

Martin, Andrew
06Toledo Storm-1

Martin, Benoit
99Rimouski Oceanic-9
Signed-9
00Rimouski Oceanic-11
Signed-11
01Rimouski Oceanic-10

Martin, Blake
907th Inn. Sketch OHL-64
04Sioux City Musketeers-15

Martin, Brian
83Belleville Bulls-7
89Hampton Roads Admirals-13A
89Hampton Roads Admirals-13H
90Hampton Roads Admirals-58
91Hampton Roads Admirals-10
92Hampton Roads Admirals-13
98Hampton Roads Admirals 10th Anniversary-4

Martin, Bruce
89Red Wings Little Caesars-23

Martin, Chris
82Kitchener Rangers-29

Martin, Christian
94German First League-364

Martin, Clare George
44Beehive Group II Photos-192
51Parkhurst-39

Martin, Craig
87Hull Olympiques-12
907th Inn. Sketch QMJHL-228
91ProCards-241
94Classic Enforcers-E6
94Classic Pro Prospects-78
95Leaf-189
95Parkhurst International-229
Emerald Ice-229
95Topps-94
OPC Inserts-94
95Buffalo Stampedes RHI-61
95Neepewa Natives-21
96Carolina Monarchs-17
98German DEL-118
00Bakersfield Condors-14

Martin, DEL
94German DEL-196
95German DEL-413

Martin, Derrick
99Hull Olympiques-6
Signed-6
00Hull Olympiques-7
Signed-7
01Hull Olympiques-7
04Wyoming-15

Martin, Don
86London Knights-16
88ProCards AHL-94
89ProCards IHL-102
01Memphis RiverKings-17
04Richmond Riverdogs-2

Martin, Eric
93Quebec Pee-Wee Tournament-1008

Martin, Frank
44Beehive Group II Photos-47
53Parkhurst-97
54Topps-30
62Quebec Aces-17
63Quebec Aces-16
92Quebec Pee-Wee Tournament-1687
94Parkhurst Missing Link-34

Martin, Gareth
03UK Belfast Giants-9

Martin, Grant
81Fredericton Express-15
82Fredericton Express-15
83Fredericton Express-18
84Fredericton Express-22
94German DEL-436
95German DEL-399
96German DEL-308

Martin, Hans
70Finnish Jaakiekko-301

Martin, Howie
03Brampton Batallion-12
04Brampton Battalion-14
05Brampton Battalion-12

Martin, Jacques
88Blackhawks Coke-10
89Blackhawks Coke-27
90Nordiques Petro-Canada-17
91Nordiques Petro-Canada-16
92Nordiques Petro-Canada-21
96Senators Pizza Hut-13
98Senators Team Issue-11
99Senators Team Issue-24
00Senators Team Issue-11
01Senators Team Issue-15
02Senators Team Issue-26
03Senators Postcards-25

Martin, James
02Tri City Stormfront-18

Martin, Jason
91Air Canada SJHL-D7

Martin, Jean-Michael
00Chicoutimi Sagueneens-22
Signed-22

Martin, Jeff
95Slapshot-423

Martin, Joel
00Lethbridge Hurricanes-15
03Columbus Cottonmouths-12
03Odessa Jackalopes-14
04Kalamazoo Wings-23
05Kalamazoo Wings-21

Martin, Joey
00Minnesota Golden Gophers-12
01Minnesota Golden Gophers-19
02Minnesota Golden Gophers-14
03Minnesota Golden Gophers-21

Martin, Justin
00Muskegon Fury-22

Martin, Louis-Philippe
01Baie-Comeau Drakkar-2
02Baie Comeau Drakkar-5
03Drummondville Voltigeurs-13
04Drummondville Voltigeurs-13

Martin, Matt
92Maine Black Bears-4
93Donruss-497
93Parkhurst-471
Emerald Ice-471
93Score-635
Gold-635
Canadian-635
Canadian Gold-635
93Stadium Club Team USA-16
93Stadium Club Team USA Members Only-16
93Topps Premier Team USA-23
93Ultra-432
93Upper Deck-447
93Classic-57
94Donruss-34
94Leaf-159
94Maple Leafs Pin-up Posters-23
94OPC Premier Special Effects-550
94Topps/OPC Premier Special Effects-550
94St. John's Maple Leafs-19
94Classic Pro Prospects-150
Ice Ambassadors-IA9
International Heroes-LP9
Jumbos-PP22
97Pacific Invincible NHL Regime-194
98Chicago Wolves Turner Cup-20
98Michigan K-Wings-16
99Michigan K-Wings-11
00Idaho Steelheads-13
06Sarnia Sting-10

Martin, Michael
03Russian Hockey League-258

Martin, Mike
92Windsor Spitfires-2
93Windsor Spitfires-4
94Windsor Spitfires-5
95Slapshot-408
95Slapshot-NNO
95Classic-9
95Classic-98
95Signature Rookies Auto-Phonex-28
95Signature Rook Auto-Phonex Phone Cards-28
96Binghamton Rangers-13
97Hartford Wolf Pack-12
98Fort Wayne Komets-14
98Hartford Wolf Pack-13
99Michigan K-Wings-5
04German DEL-176

Martin, Neal
93Sault Ste. Marie Greyhound Memorial Cup-10
94Sudbury Wolves-5
94Sudbury Wolves Police-21
95Slapshot-387
95Sudbury Wolves-14
95Sudbury Wolves Police-15
96Hampton Roads Admirals-HRA6
97Mississippi Sea Wolves-2
99UK London Knights-10
00UK Sekonda Superleague-73
01German Upper Deck-234
02German DEL City Press-291
04UK Coventry Blaze-9
04UK Coventry Blaze Champions-4
04UK EIHL All-Stars-3
05UK Coventry Blaze-3
06UK Coventry Blaze-1

Martin, P.J.
03Trenton Titans-362
06Toledo Storm-5

Martin, Paul
00Minnesota Golden Gophers-13
01Minnesota Golden Gophers-9
02SPx Rookie Redemption-R205
02Minnesota Golden Gophers-15
03BAP Memorabilia-189
Emerald-189
Gold-189
Ruby-189
Sapphire-189
03BAP Ultimate Memorabilia Autographs-103
Gold-103
03BAP Ultimate Mem Franch Present Future-18
03BAP Ultimate Mem Rookie Jersey Emblems-14
03BAP Ultimate Mem Rookie Jsy Emblem Gold-14
03BAP Ultimate Mem Rookie Jersey Numbers-14
03BAP Ultimate Mem Rookie Jsy Number Gold-14
03BAP Ultimate Memorabilia Triple Threads-31
03Bowman-143
Gold-143
03Bowman Chrome-143
Refractors-143
Gold Refractors-143
Xfractors-143
03Crown Royale-126
Red-126
Retail-126
03Devils Team Issue-7
03ITG Action-670
03ITG Used Signature Series-131
Autographs Gold-131
03ITG VIP Rookie Debut-5
03Pacific Complete-579
Red-579
03Pacific Heads-Up-125
Hobby LTD-125
Retail LTD-125
03Pacific Luxury Suite-71
Gold-71
03Pacific Quest for the Cup-126
03Pacific Supreme-128
Blue-128
Red-128
Retail-128
03Parkhurst Rookie-192
All-Rookie-ART-2
All-Rookie Autographs-ART-PM
All-Rookie Gold-ART-2
Rookie Emblems-RE-13
Rookie Emblem Autographs-RE-PM
Rookie Emblems Gold-RE-13
Rookie Jerseys-RJ-13
Rookie Jersey Autographs-RJ-PM
Rookie Jerseys Gold-RJ-13
Rookie Numbers-RN-13
Rookie Number Autographs-RN-PM
Rookie Numbers Gold-RN-13
03Private Stock Reserve-129
Blue-129
Red-129
Retail-129
03SP Authentic-112
Limited-112
03SP Game Used-71
Gold-71
03SPx-195
Radiance-195
Spectrum-195
03Titanium-127
Hobby Jersey Number Parallels-127
Retail-127
Retail Jersey Number Parallels-127
03Topps C55-144
Minis-144
Minis American Back-144
Minis American Back Red-144
Minis Bazooka Back-144
Minis Brooklyn Back-144
Minis Hat Trick Back-144
Minis O Canada Back-144
Minis O Canada Back Red-144
Minis Stanley Cup Back-144
03Topps Traded-TT122
Blue-TT122
Gold-TT122
Red-TT122
03UD Honor Roll-136
03Upper Deck-229
Canadian Exclusives-229
HG-229
Rookie Update YoungStars-YS9
03Upper Deck Trilogy-160
Limited-160
05Be A Player Signatures-PA
05Be A Player Signatures Gold-PA
05Devils Team Issue-27
05Parkhurst-300
Facsimile Auto Parallel-300
05SP Game Used Authentic Fabrics Quad-EMMR
05SP Game Used Authentic Patches Quad -EMMR
05SP Game Used Game Gear-GG-MA
05Upper Deck-117
HG Glossy-117
05Upper Deck MVP-234
Gold-234
Platinum-234
05Upper Deck Toronto Fall Expo-117
06Devils Team Set-15
06O-Pee-Chee-293
Rainbow-293
06Upper Deck-369
Exclusives Parallel-369
High Gloss Parallel-369
Masterpieces-369
06Upper Deck MVP-180
Gold Script-180
Super Script-180

Martin, Pete V.
37V356 Worldwide Gum-31

Martin, Peter
93Swiss HNL-289
96Swiss HNL-295

Martin, Pierre
79Montreal Juniors-17
06ITG Heroes and Prospects AHL All-Star Jerseys-AJ02

Martin, Pit
61Hamilton Red Wings-12
63Chex Photos-37
64Beehive Group III Photos-87
64Coca-Cola Caps-43
64Topps-1
65Topps-52
66Topps-41
67Topps-116
68O-Pee-Chee-18
68Shirriff Coins-22
68Topps-18
69O-Pee-Chee-75
69Topps-75
70Blackhawks Postcards-8
70Colgate Stamps-31
70Dad's Cookies-79
70Esso Power Players-114
70O-Pee-Chee-18
70O-Pee-Chee-253
70Sargent Promotions Stamps-39
70Topps-18
71O-Pee-Chee-39
71Sargent Promotions Stamps-42
71Topps-39
71Toronto Sun-75
72O-Pee-Chee-24
72Sargent Promotions Stamps-68
72Topps-99
72Finnish Semic World Championship-224
72Swedish Semic World Championship-224
73O-Pee-Chee-73
73Topps-164
74Lipton Soup-37
74NHL Action Stamps-87
74O-Pee-Chee NHL-58
74Topps-58
75O-Pee-Chee NHL-48
75Topps-48
76O-Pee-Chee NHL-76
76O-Pee-Chee NHL-382
76Topps-76
77Coca-Cola-15
77O-Pee-Chee NHL-135
77Topps-135
78Canucks Royal Bank-16
78O-Pee-Chee-286
90Upper Deck-513
French-513
94Parkhurst Tall Boys-51
95Parkhurst '66-67-1
Coins-1

Martin, Rick
71Colgate Heads-7
71O-Pee-Chee-161
Posters-6
71Sabres Postcards-76
71Toronto Sun-32
72O-Pee-Chee-157
72O-Pee-Chee-182
Player Crests-4
72Sabres Pepsi Pinback Buttons-3
72Sabres Pepsi Pinback Buttons-4
72Sabres Postcards-10
72Sargent Promotions Stamps-35
72Topps-145
73Mac's Milk-17
73O-Pee-Chee-173
73Sabres Bells-3
73Sabres Postcards-6
73Topps-155
74Lipton Soup-33
74NHL Action Stamps-53
74O-Pee-Chee NHL-42
74O-Pee-Chee NHL-127
74O-Pee-Chee NHL-190
74Sabres Postcards-14
74Topps-42
74Topps-127
74Topps-190
75O-Pee-Chee NHL-175
75O-Pee-Chee NHL-208
75O-Pee-Chee NHL-212
75O-Pee-Chee NHL-289
75O-Pee-Chee NHL-315
75Sabres Linnett-6
75Topps-175
75Topps-208
75Topps-212
75Topps-289
75Topps-315
76O-Pee-Chee NHL-5
76O-Pee-Chee NHL-210
76O-Pee-Chee NHL-214
76O-Pee-Chee NHL-380
76Sabres Glasses-2
76Topps-5
76Topps-210
76Topps-214
76Topps Glossy Inserts-19
77O-Pee-Chee NHL-180
77Topps-180
77Topps/O-Pee-Chee Glossy-11
Square-11
78O-Pee-Chee-80
78Topps-80
79O-Pee-Chee-149
79Sabres Bells-4
79Topps-149
80O-Pee-Chee-51
80Sabres Milk Panels-8
80Topps-51
91Future Trends Canada '72-49
92Future Trends '76 Canada Cup-125
93Sabres Noco-11
01Greats of the Game-49
Autographs-49
04ITG Franchises US East-338
Autographs-A-RMA
04ITG Ultimate Memorabilia-115
Gold-115
04UD Legendary Signatures-70
Autographs-RM
Linemates-RMGPRR
04UD Legends Classics-49
Gold-49
Platinum-49
Silver-49
Signature Moments-M14
Signatures-CS14
Signatures-TC10
05SPx Xcitement Legends-XL-RM
05SPx Xcitement Legends Gold-XL-RM
05SPx Xcitement Legends Spectrum-XL-RM
05UD Artifacts-132
Blue-132
Gold-132
Green-132
Pewter-132
Red-132
Gold Autographed-132
05Ultimate Coll Ultimate Sigs Trios-UTILN

Martin, Rob
93Quebec Pee-Wee Tournament-826

Martin, Ronnie
33V357 Ice Kings-7
34Diamond Matchbooks Silver-44

Martin, Ryan
01Calgary Hitmen-15
01Calgary Hitmen Autographed-15

Martin, Shawn
03Huntsville Channel Cats-11

Martin, Streit
98Czech OFS-93

Martin, Swiss
93Swiss HNL-289
95Swiss HNL-318
98Swiss Power Play Stickers-5
99Swiss Panini Stickers-5
00Swiss Panini Stickers-199

Martin, Terry
77O-Pee-Chee NHL-318
78O-Pee-Chee-118
78Topps-118

79Maple Leafs Postcards-18
80Maple Leafs Postcards-17
80Pepsi-Cola Caps-91
81Maple Leafs Postcards-13
81O-Pee-Chee-321
82Maple Leafs Postcards-23
82O-Pee-Chee-329
82O-Pee-Chee Stickers-66
82Post Cereal-18
82Topps Stickers-66
83Maple Leafs Postcards-15
83NHL Key Tags-118
83O-Pee-Chee-336
83Vachon-92
84O-Pee-Chee-306
84Nova Scotia Oilers-24
88Oilers Tenth Anniversary-146
89ProCards AHL-261
90ProCards AHL/IHL-292
91ProCards-22
91Rochester Americans Kodak-2
91Rochester Americans Postcards-14
92Rochester Americans Kodak-2
93Rochester Americans Kodak-2
94Maple Leafs Kodak-19

Martin, Tom
83Victoria Cougars-17
90ProCards AHL/IHL-419

Martin, Trevor
92Quebec Pee-Wee Tournament-1133
92Quebec Pee-Wee Tournament-1281
93Quebec Pee-Wee Tournament-1259

Martin, Tuomo
78Finnish SM-Liiga-90
80Finnish Mallasjuoma-134

Martine, Nathan
04Barrie Colts-2
05Mississauga Ice Dogs-20
06Mississauga Ice Dogs-18

Martineau, Andre
98Quebec Remparts-14
Signed-14
99Quebec Remparts-13
Signed-13
01Cape Breton Screaming Eagles-16
02Thetford Mines Coyotes-14
03Thetford Mines Prolab-13
04Thetford Mines Prolab-8

Martineau, Don
74NHL Action Stamps-144

Martineau, Eric
92Quebec Pee-Wee Tournament-443
93Quebec Pee-Wee Tournament-309

Martineau, Patrice
907th Inn. Sketch QMJHL-28
917th Inn. Sketch QMJHL-88
917th Inn. Sketch Memorial Cup-38

Martinec, Patrik
94Czech APS Extraliga-85
96Czech APS Extraliga-134
97Czech APS Extraliga-22
97Czech DS Extraliga-65
97Czech DS Stickers-69
98Czech DS-95
98Czech DS Stickers-216
98Czech OFS-138
99Czech DS-148
99Czech OFS-398
00Czech OFS-307
01Czech OFS All Stars-17
01Russian Hockey League-159
02Czech OFS Plus-10
03Czech OFS Plus-180
04Czech OFS-181

Martinec, Tomas
94Czech APS Extraliga-18
94German DEL-181
95Czech APS Extraliga-117
95German DEL-184
96Czech APS Extraliga-156
96Czech APS Extraliga-158
97Czech APS Extraliga-258
97Czech DS Extraliga-72
97Czech DS Stickers-260
98Czech DS-53
98Czech OFS-156
98Czech OFS-282
99Czech OFS-93
99Czech OFS-317
99German Bundesliga 2-214
00Czech OFS-153
00German DEL-104
01German Upper Deck-116
Skilled Stars-SS6
02Czech OFS Plus-201
02German DEL City Press-247
All-Stars-AS11
03Czech OFS Plus-99
03Czech OFS Plus Insert M-M11
03German DEL-8
03German Mannheim Eagles Postcards-16
04German DEL-252
04German Nuremburg Ice Tigers Postcards-11
05German DEL-272
05German DEL-295
06German DEL-150
German Forwards-GF1

Martinec, Vladimir
71Finnish Suomi Stickers-32
71Swedish Hockey-55
72Finnish Jaakiekko-15
72Finnish Hellas-89
72Finnish Panda Toronto-88
72Finnish Semic World Championship-30
72Swedish Semic World Championship-30
73Finnish Jaakiekko-56
73Swedish Stickers-30
74Finnish Jenkki-78
74Finnish Typotor-119
74Swedish Stickers-17
74Swedish Semic World Champ Stickers-56
79Panini Stickers-86
92Future Trends '76 Canada Cup-156
95Czech APS Extraliga-396
98Czech OFS Legends-6
99Czech OFS-253
01Czech DS Legends-L6

Martinec, Vladislav
70Finnish Jaakiekko-54
70Swedish Hockey-361
70Swedish Masterserien-151

Martinek, Petr
99Czech Score Blue 2000-27
99Czech Score Red Ice 2000-27
00Czech OFS-91
01Czech OFS-2
02Czech OFS Plus-354
Trios-T7
03Czech OFS Plus-100

Martinek, Radek
96Czech APS Extraliga-248
97Czech APS Extraliga-275
97Czech DS Extraliga-30
97Czech DS Stickers-79
98Czech DS-32
98Czech DS Stickers-71
98Czech OFS-199
99Czech DS-32
99Czech OFS-264
99Czech OFS-283
99Czech OFS-502
All-Star Game Blue-502
All-Star Game Gold-502
All-Star Game Red-502
All-Star Game Silver-502
00Czech DS Extraliga-75
Top Stars-TS2
World Champions-WCH3
00Czech OFS-8
01Atomic-115
Premiere Date-115
01Atomic Toronto Fall Expo-115
01BAP Memorabilia-384
Emerald-384
Ruby-384
Sapphire-384
01BAP Signature Series-240
Autographs-240
Autographs Gold-240
01Bowman YoungStars-118
Gold-118
Ice Cubed-118
01Crown Royale-169
01O-Pee-Chee-342
01Pacific Adrenaline-216
Blue-216
Premiere Date-216
Red-216
Retail-216
01Parkhurst-264
01Parkhurst Beckett Promos-264
01Private Stock-130
Gold-130
Premiere Date-130
Retail-130
Silver-130
01Private Stock Pacific Nights-130
01SP Authentic-163
Limited-163
Limited Gold-163
01SP Game Used-87
01SPx-116
01Titanium-169
Retail-169
01Titanium Draft Day Edition-150
01Topps-342
01Topps Chrome-160
Refractors-160
Black Border Refractors-160
01UD Challenge for the Cup-123
01UD Honor Roll-81
01UD Playmakers-129
01UD Premier Collection-72
01Upper Deck-435
Exclusives-435
01Upper Deck Ice-61
01Upper Deck Vintage-287
01Vanguard-120
Blue-120
Red-120
One of Ones-120
Premiere Date-120
Proofs-120
01Czech DS-53
02Pacific Complete-378
Red-378
02Topps Total-72
05Parkhurst-313
Facsimile Auto Parallel-313

Martinek, Vladimir
03Czech Stadion-653

Martinelle, Per
83Swedish Semic Elitserien-21
84Swedish Semic Elitserien-19
85Swedish Panini Stickers-18
87Swedish Panini Stickers-16

Martinelli, Mike
03Plymouth Whalers-6

Martinelli, Ryan
05London Knights-17
06London Knights-15

Martini, Darcy
90Michigan Tech Huskies-14
91Michigan Tech Huskies-11
91Michigan Tech Huskies-12
91Michigan Tech Huskies-34
94Cape Breton Oilers-14
98German DEL-187

Martini, Mario
83Belleville Bulls-15
84Sudbury Wolves-3

Martiniuk, Denis
99Russian Hockey League-40
00Russian Hockey League-27
02Columbia Inferno-104

Martino, Tony
92Tulsa Oilers-4
94Central Hockey League-101
95Central Hockey League-66
97New Mexico Scorpions-21
97New Mexico Scorpions II-5
97New Mexico Scorpions II-6
98Abilene Aviators-4
01New Mexico Scorpions-20

Martinov, Sergei
00Russian Hockey League-61

Martinovic, Sasha
04German DEL Update-307
04German Hamburg Freezers Postcards-8
05German DEL-111
05German DEL-348

Martinovich, Mihajlo
96Barrie Colts-14

Martins, Mark
99Columbus Cottonmouths-13

Martins, Steve
92Harvard Crimson-23
96Whalers Bob's Stores-15
96Springfield Falcons-12
98Senators Team Issue-12
98Chicago Wolves Turner Cup-19
99Pacific Omega-217
Copper-217
Gold-217
Ice Blue-217
Premiere Date-217
01BAP Signature Series-19
Autographs-19
Autographs Gold-19
01Grand Rapids Griffins-8
02BAP Sig Series Auto Buybacks 2001-19
03Blues Team Set-17
03ITG Action-585
03Upper Deck MVP-367
Gold Script-367
Silver Script-367
Canadian Exclusives-367
03Worcester Ice Cats-22
04Finnish Cardset-86
04Finnish Cardset Signatures-19
04Swedish Pure Skills-123
Parallel-123
05Binghamton Senators-7
05Binghamton Senators Quickway-7
06Binghamton Senators 5th Anniversary-17

Martinsen, Anders
92Norwegian Elite Series-166

Martinsen, Ketil
92Norwegian Elite Series-56

Martinsen, Remo
92Norwegian Elite Series-19

Martinson, Joel
91Air Canada SJHL-C29

Martinson, Steve
88Canadiens Postcards-19
88ProCards AHL-294
89Canadiens Postcards-23
90ProCards AHL/IHL-308
91ProCards-319
92San Diego Gulls-17
92San Diego Barracudas RHI-14
99San Diego Gulls-17
05Rockford Ice Hogs-24
06Rockford IceHogs -24

Martinsson, Per
85Swedish Panini Stickers-196
86Swedish Panini Stickers-128

Martinyuk, Alexander
71Finnish Suomi Stickers-9
72Finnish Panda Toronto-56
72Finnish Semic World Championship-15
72Swedish Semic World Championship-15
73Finnish Jaakiekko-10
73Russian National Team-17
73Swedish Stickers-92
74Finnish Jenkki-50
74Swedish Semic World Champ Stickers-39
91Future Trends Canada '72-50
91Future Trends Canada '72 French-50

Martone, Mike
95Slapshot-308
99Mississippi Sea Wolves-18
99Mississippi Sea Wolves Kelly Cup-18
03St. Francis Xavier X-Men-5

Martorelli, Marty
93Quebec Pee-Wee Tournament-764

Marts, Par
72Swedish Stickers-282
74Swedish Stickers-252

Marttila, Jukka
91Finnish Semic World Champ Stickers-8
91Finnish Jyvas-Hyva Stickers-59
91Swedish Semic World Champ Stickers-8
92Finnish Jyvas-Hyva Stickers-157

Marttila, Niko
91Finnish Jyvas-Hyva Stickers-53
92Finnish Jyvas-Hyva Stickers-30
93Finnish Jyvas-Hyva Stickers-50
93Finnish SISU-241
94Finnish SISU-12
95Finnish SISU-18

Marttinen, Jaakko
65Finnish Hellas-138
70Finnish Jaakiekko-163
71Finnish Suomi Stickers-119
72Finnish Jaakiekko-89
72Finnish Panda Toronto-7
73Finnish Jaakiekko-135
78Finnish SM-Liiga-30

Marttinen, Jyri
01Finnish Cardset-270
02Finnish Cardset-221
03Finnish Cardset-76
05Finnish Cardset -245
06Finnish Cardset-73

Martynek, Rostislav
02Czech OFS Plus-93
03Czech OFS Plus-294
03Czech OFS Plus Insert M-M15
04Czech OFS-214
06Czech OFS-162

Martynowski, Rafal
01Kitchener Rangers-14
03Kitchener Rangers-17
03Kitchener Rangers Memorial Cup-13
03Sudbury Wolves-16
04Sudbury Wolves-20
05Quad City Mallards-8

Martz, Nathan
05Stockton Thunder-12
06Stockton Thunder-14a

Maruca, David
96Regina Pats-5
97Regina Pats-13

Maruk, Dennis
76O-Pee-Chee NHL-86
76Topps-86
77O-Pee-Chee NHL-21
77Topps-21
78Capitals Team Issue-9
78O-Pee-Chee-141
78Topps-141
79Panini Stickers-60
79Capitals Team Issue-13
79O-Pee-Chee-223
79Topps-223
80O-Pee-Chee-284
81Capitals Team Issue-10
81O-Pee-Chee-350
81O-Pee-Chee-357
81O-Pee-Chee Stickers-191
81Topps-65
81Topps-E120
82Capitals Team Issue-15
82O-Pee-Chee-359
82O-Pee-Chee-369
82O-Pee-Chee-370
82O-Pee-Chee Stickers-151
82Topps Stickers-151
83NHL Key Tags-131
83North Stars Postcards-17
83O-Pee-Chee-174
83O-Pee-Chee Stickers-204
83O-Pee-Chee Stickers-205
83Puffy Stickers-18
83Topps Stickers-204
83Topps Stickers-205
84North Stars 7-Eleven-9
84North Stars Postcards-14
84O-Pee-Chee-101
84O-Pee-Chee Stickers-48
84Topps-76
85North Stars Postcards-19
85O-Pee-Chee-111
85Topps-111
86North Stars 7-Eleven-8
86North Stars Postcards-10
86O-Pee-Chee-60
86O-Pee-Chee Stickers-170
86Topps-60
87North Stars Postcards-20
87O-Pee-Chee-117
87O-Pee-Chee Stickers-50
87Panini Stickers-298
87Topps-117
01Greats of the Game-6
Autographs-6
01Upper Deck Legends-71
04ITG Franchises US East-444
Autographs-A-DMK1
04ITG Franchises US West-179
Autographs-A-DMK2

Maruk, Jon
01Notre Dame Fighting Irish-3

Marusak, Jiri
95Czech APS Extraliga-38
96Czech APS Extraliga-30
97Czech APS Extraliga-60
97Czech DS Stickers-100
98Czech DS Stickers-293
98Czech OFS-22
99Czech DS-5
99Czech OFS-213
99Czech OFS-520
All-Star Game Blue-520
All-Star Game Gold-520
All-Star Game Red-520
All-Star Game Silver-520
00Czech DS Extraliga-52
00Czech OFS-353
01Czech OFS-80
All Stars-26
02Czech DS-40
02Czech OFS Plus-33
02Czech OFS Plus All-Star Game-H14
02Czech OFS Plus Trios-T23
02Czech OFS Plus Duos-D16
03Russian Hockey League-190
04Russian Super League All-Stars-21
06Czech OFS-290

Maruschak, Duane
89Lethbridge Hurricanes-14
907th Inn. Sketch WHL-133

Marvel, Chris
93Omaha Lancers-17

Marvin, Lee
00Lincoln Stars-18
01Lincoln Stars-17
03North Dakota Fighting Sioux-14
04North Dakota Fighting Sioux-14

Marvin, Willy
96Minnesota Golden Gophers-19
97Minnesota Golden Gophers-13

Marx, Gord
95Las Vegas Thunder-7

Marziali, Morgan
06Ohio State Buckeyes Women-16

Marziani, Dan
03Chicago Steel-2

Masa, Martin
92British Columbia JHL-60
94Central Hockey League-26
96Johnstown Chiefs-11
97Johnstown Chiefs-8
98Johnstown Chiefs-15
01Greenville Grrrowl-17
02Greenville Grrrowl-15
03Louisiana Ice Gators-12
05UK Sheffield Steelers-10
Gold-10
Silver-10

Masak, Martin
95Czech APS Extraliga-63
96Czech APS Extraliga-247

Masalskis, Edgars
04Czech OFS-29

Mascioli, Mike
06Kitchener Rangers-8

Mascot, Mascot
88Nordiques General Foods-2
93Sherbrooke Faucons-24
95Kansas City Blades-25
96Rutgers-13
96Anaheim Bullfrogs RHI-2
96Carolina Monarchs-28
96Cleveland Lumberjacks Multi-Ad-28
96Fredericton Canadiens-29
96Mississippi Sea Wolves-22
96Richmond Renegades-5
96Rochester Americans-24
96Saint John Flames-24
96Spokane Chiefs-24
96Wheeling Nailers-23
96Wheeling Nailers Photo Pack-17
97Anchorage Aces-23
97Anchorage Aces-24
97Anchorage Aces-25
97Austin Ice Bats-23
97Cincinnati Cyclones-22
97Cleveland Lumberjacks-29
97Cleveland Lumberjacks Postcards-25
97El Paso Buzzards-21
97Grand Rapids Griffins-23
97Hartford Wolf Pack-29
97Kentucky Thoroughblades-23
97Long Beach Ice Dogs-20
97Louisville Riverfrogs-27
97Medicine Hat Tigers-25
97Mississippi Sea Wolves-13
97Wheeling Nailers Photo Pack-24
98Calgary Hitmen-26
98Calgary Hitmen Autographs-26
98Charlotte Checkers-20
98Dayton Bombers-21
98Dayton Bombers EBK-17
98Detroit Vipers-21
98Florida Everblades-26
98Grand Rapids Griffins-23
98Guelph Storm-28
98Huntington Blizzard-24
98Huntsville Channel Cats-15
98Idaho Steelheads-23
98Indianapolis Ice-17
98Kansas City Blades-29
98Kentucky Thoroughblades-24
98Las Vegas Thunder-29
98Long Beach Ice Dogs-20
98Medicine Hat Tigers-25
98Milwaukee Admirals-18
98Orlando Solar Bears-19
98Red Deer Rebels-23
98Roanoke Express-26
98Topeka Scarecrows-16
98Windsor Spitfires-3
99Senators Team Issue-25
99UK Guildford Flames-28
99Albany River Rats-24
99Calgary Hitmen-25
99Calgary Hitmen Autographs-25
99Cincinnati Mighty Ducks-23
99Cleveland Lumberjacks-2
99Fort Worth Brahmas-2
99Guelph Storm-30
99Halifax Mooseheads-23
99Kansas City Blades Supercuts-23
99Kitchener Rangers-9
99Long Beach Ice Dogs-9
99Mississippi Sea Wolves-3
99Peoria Rivermen-1
99San Angelo Outlaws-29
99Spokane Chiefs-4
00Panthers Team Issue-4
00Senators Team Issue-23
00Austin Ice Bats-28
00Baie-Comeau Drakkar-NNO
Signed-NNO
00Cincinnati Cyclones-26
00Indianapolis Ice-22
00Kelowna Rockets-21
00Lethbridge Hurricanes-23
00London Knights-U7
00Louisville Panthers-24
00Lowell Lock Monsters-26
00Ohio State Buckeyes-20
00Prince Albert Raiders-20
00Saskatoon Blades-31
00Sherbrooke Castors-22
Signed-22
00Sioux Falls Stampede-21
00Spokane Chiefs-30
00Sudbury Wolves-26
00Swift Current Broncos-24
00Syracuse Crunch-24
00Wilkes-Barre Scranton Penguins-27
00Worcester Icecats-15
01Devils Team Issue-17
01Flyers Postcards-30
01UK Guildford Flames-27
01UK Manchester Storm-22
01UK Nottingham Panthers-26
01Anchorage Aces-20
01Asheville Smoke-17
01Austin Ice Bats-22
01Barrie Colts-22
01BC Icemen-28
01BC Icemen-29
01Belleville Bulls-29
01Bossier-Shreveport Mudbugs-23
01Brandon Wheat Kings-23
01Calgary Hitmen-25
01Calgary Hitmen Autographed-25
01Chicago Wolves-25
01Cincinnati Mighty Ducks-28
01Colorado Gold Kings-22
01Fort Worth Brahmas-20
01Greensboro Generals-20
01Greenville Grrrowl-23
01Guelph Storm-27
01Guelph Storm Memorial Cup-27
01Hamilton Bulldogs-25
01Hartford Wolf Pack-26
01Hershey Bears-4
01Indianapolis Ice-22
01Johnstown Chiefs-29
01Louisiana Ice Gators-25
01Manchester Monarchs-15B
01Manitoba Moose-23
01Milwaukee Admirals Postcards-11
01Missouri River Otters-14
01New Mexico Scorpions-25
01Ohio State Buckeyes-20
01Quad-City Mallards-24
01Red Deer Rebels-21
01St. John's Maple Leafs-29
01Sudbury Wolves Police-26
01Syracuse Crunch-25
01Trenton Titans-2-12
01Utah Grizzlies-6
01Worcester Icecats-15
02Atlantic City Boardwalk Bullies-24
02Chicago Wolves-22
02Cincinnati Mighty Ducks-B-4
02Columbus Cottonmouths-23
02Florida Everblades-25
02Fort Worth Brahmas-20
02Grand Rapids Griffins-13
02Greenville Grrrowl-10
02Guelph Storm-31
02Hamilton Bulldogs-27
02Hartford Wolf Pack-30
02Hershey Bears-29
02Kalamazoo Wings-27
02Lincoln Stars-29
02Manchester Monarchs-24
02Philadelphia Phantoms-24
02Roanoke Express-4
02Spokane Chiefs-29
02Trenton Titans-A-12
02Trenton Titans-B-12
02Windsor Spitfires-14
02Windsor Spitfires-24
02Worcester IceCats-28
03Bruins Team Issue-13
03Canucks Postcards-28
03Senators Postcards-28
03UK London Racers-13
03UK Manchester Phoenix-21
03Huntsville Channel Cats-18
03Lewiston Maineiacs-27
03Owen Sound Attack-1
03St. Michael's Majors-26
04German Berlin Polar Bears Postcards-31
04German Dusseldorf Metro Stars Postcards-25
04German Ingolstadt Panthers-27
04UK Guildford Flames-26
04Atlantic City Boardwalk Bullies-30
04Austin Ice Bats-12
04Binghamton Senators-26
04Chicago Wolves-25
04Cleveland Barons-27
04Colorado Eagles-23
04Erie Otters-25
04Fort Worth Brahmas-20
04Guelph Storm-29
04Gwinnett Gladiators-28
04Hershey Bears Patriot News-31
04Huntsville Havoc-1
04Knoxville Ice Bears-7
04Lincoln Stars-28
04Manchester Monarchs-25
04Milwaukee Admirals-5
04Odessa Jackalopes-20
04Owen Sound Attack-24
04Peoria Rivermen-22
04Reading Royals-19
04Richmond Riverdogs-25
04Salmon Arm Silverbacks-21
04Syracuse Crunch-24
04Vernon Vipers-7
04Wilkes-Barre Scranton Penguins-27
05Chicoutimi Sagueneens-31
05Danbury Trashers-29
05Manchester Monarchs-24
06Saginaw Spirit-24
06Stockton Thunder-10

Maser, Josh
97Spokane Chiefs-23
98Spokane Chiefs-18
98Swift Current Broncos-21
99Medicine Hat Tigers-25
99Medicine Hat Tigers-32
00Austin Ice Bats-11
01Bakersfield Condors-14

Mashanov, Denis
04Russian RHL-7

Mashinter, Brandon
06Sarnia Sting-21

Masjin, Alexei
74Swedish Stickers-90

Maskarinec, Martin
91Finnish Semic World Champ Stickers-110
91Swedish Semic World Champ Stickers-110
94Czech APS Extraliga-183
95Czech APS Extraliga-128
96Czech APS Extraliga-10
97Czech APS Extraliga-104
97Czech DS Extraliga-23
97Czech DS Stickers-118
98Czech DS Stickers-49
98Czech OFS-96
99Czech DS-19
99Czech OFS-139
99Czech OFS-433

Maskarinec, Tomas
98Czech DS Stickers-139

Maslennikov, Igor
90O-Pee-Chee Red Army-14R
91O-Pee-Chee Inserts-21R
91Finnish Semic World Champ Stickers-91
91Swedish Semic World Champ Stickers-91
99German DEL-153
00German DEL-17
01German Upper Deck-10

Maslov, Nikolai
91O-Pee-Chee Inserts-55R

Maslyukov, Konstantin
98Russian Hockey League-39
99Russian Hockey League-150
00Russian Hockey League-373
02Russian Hockey League-17

Masnick, Paul
44Beehive Group II Photos-267
45Quaker Oats Photos-95
51Parkhurst-8
52St. Lawrence Sales-11
54Parkhurst-13

Masny, Radek
98Czech OFS-66
99Czech DS-86
99Czech OFS-537
99Czech OFS-549
00Czech DS Extraliga-146
00Czech OFS-265
02Czech OFS Plus-365
Trios-T21
03Czech OFS Plus-36
04Czech OFS-254

Mason, Bob
86Capitals Kodak-16
87Blackhawks Coke-10
87O-Pee-Chee Stickers-238
87Panini Stickers-175
88Nordiques General Foods-25
88Nordiques Team Issue-23
88Panini Stickers-20
89Capitals Team Issue-15
89O-Pee-Chee Stickers-188
89Panini Stickers-344
89ProCards AHL-88
91ProCards-617
92Hamilton Canucks-15
94Milwaukee Admirals-18
04ITG Franchises US East-442
Autographs-A-BMS

Mason, Brady
05Kamloops Blazers-14
06Kamloops Blazers-15

Mason, Charley
35Diamond Matchbooks Tan 1-44
35Diamond Matchbooks Tan 2-45
35Diamond Matchbooks Tan 3-41
35Diamond Matchbooks Tan 3-42

Mason, Chris
98Milwaukee Admirals-4
99Milwaukee Admirals Keebler-3
00Pacific-230
Copper-230
Gold-230
Ice Blue-230
Premiere Date-230
00SP Authentic-113
00UD Reserve-102
00Upper Deck Ice-93
00Milwaukee Admirals Keebler-9
00Milwaukee Admirals Postcards-9
01BAP Memorabilia-234
Emerald-234
Ruby-234
Sapphire-234
01Between the Pipes-47
01Parkhurst-269
01Parkhurst Beckett Promos-269
01Upper Deck Victory-378
Gold-378
01Milwaukee Admirals-12
02Between the Pipes-106
Gold-106
Silver-106
03BAP Memorabilia Deep in the Crease-D6
03Pacific Complete-469
Red-469
06O-Pee-Chee-284
Rainbow-284
06Upper Deck-363
Exclusives Parallel-363
High Gloss Parallel-363
Masterpieces-363
07Upper Deck Victory-107
Black-107
Gold-107

Mason, Dale
89Kamloops Blazers-14

Mason, Doug
917th Inn. Sketch OHL-256
98German DEL-41
99German DEL-147
01Swiss EV Zug Postcards-2
01Swiss HNL-167
02Swiss EV Zug Postcards-2
02Swiss HNL-64

Mason, Ron
92Michigan State Spartans-2
93Michigan State Spartans-12
95AHCA-6
00Michigan State Spartans-19

Mason, Steve
05London Knights-21
06Between The Pipes-48
Autographs-ASM
Prospect Trios-PT07
Prospect Trios Gold-PT07
06London Knights-3

Mason, Tyrell
03Salmon Arm Silverbacks-13
04Salmon Arm Silverbacks-8

Mason, Wes
94Sarnia Sting-19
95Bowman Draft Prospects-P24
95Slapshot-349
95Slapshot-435
95Sarnia Sting-19
96Sarnia Sting-15
99ECHL All-Star Southern Conference-19
03Pensacola Ice Pilots-349
04Louisiana Ice Gators-13

Mass, Louis
02Louisiana Ice Gators-11

Massa, Rob
94Sarnia Sting-15

Masse, Daniel
92Quebec Pee-Wee Tournament-800
93Quebec Pee-Wee Tournament-957

Masse, David
00Quebec Remparts-19
Signed-19
00Victoriaville Tigres-18
Signed-18
01Quebec Remparts-19
02Quebec Remparts-16
03ECHL All-Stars-252
03Quebec Remparts Memorial Cup-12
03Reading Royals-11
04Hershey Bears Patriot News-16
04Reading Royals-7
06Rio Grande Valley Killer Bees-16

Masse, Gerrard
92Windsor Spitfires-12

Masse, Mike
92Saskatchewan JHL-87
01Fort Wayne Komets Shoe Carnival-11

Masse, Patrice
80Quebec Remparts-16

Massen, James
00Sioux Falls Stampede-14
03North Dakota Fighting Sioux-3
04North Dakota Fighting Sioux-15

Massey, Jeff
93Oklahoma City Blazers-9
94Central Hockey League-27
95Central Hockey League-9
95Fort Worth Fire-11

Massicotte, Benoit
05Victoriaville Tigres-6

Massie, Michel
98Baton Rouge Kingfish-13
01Fort Wayne Komets-12
02Fort Wayne Komets-11
02Fort Wayne Komets Shoe Carnival-4
03Fort Wayne Komets-7
03Fort Wayne Komets 2003 Champions-14
03Fort Wayne Komets Shoe Carnival-11

Massinen, Vesa
71Finnish Suomi Stickers-330

Masson, Dale
907th Inn. Sketch WHL-294
907th Inn. Sketch Memorial Cup-24
917th Inn. Sketch WHL-86

Massy, Didier
91Finnish Semic World Champ Stickers-183
91Swedish Semic World Champ Stickers-183
92Finnish Semic-199
93Swiss HNL-220
01Swiss HNL-421

Mastad, Milt
91British Columbia JHL-111
93Seattle Thunderbirds-12
96Providence Bruins-28
97Charlotte Checkers-14
98Hampton Roads Admirals-21
00Jackson Bandits-5
01Macon Whoopee-13
03Louisiana Ice Gators-13

Masters, Casson
00UK Nottingham Panthers-23
00UK Sekonda Superleague-199

Masters, Chris
94Dubuque Fighting Saints-17

Masters, Kevin
907th Inn. Sketch WHL-147
917th Inn. Sketch WHL-267

Masters, Tyler
03ECHL Update RBI Sports-63
04Fort Wayne Komets-9
04Fort Wayne Komets Shoe Carnival-10

Masterson, Matt
95Slapshot-413

Masterton, Bill
04ITG Franchises US West-243
06Beehive 5 X 7 Cherry Wood-BMT

Mastic, Marek
04German DEL-272

Matalamaki, Kaj
65Finnish Hellas-46
66Finnish Jaakiekkosarja-46
70Finnish Jaakiekko-196
71Finnish Suomi Stickers-88
72Finnish Jaakiekko-252
72Finnish Panda Toronto-41
73Finnish Jaakiekko-251

Matalik, Radek
99Guelph Storm-8

Matatall, Bruce
91Air Canada SJHL-B47
92Saskatchewan JHL-64

Matatall, Craig
91Air Canada SJHL-C1
91Air Canada SJHL All-Stars-29
91Air Canada SJHL All-Stars-49

Matchefts, John
04Michigan Wolverines TK Legacy-1950A
04Michigan Wolverines TK Legacy-H2
04Michigan Wolverines TK Legacy-HL9
04Michigan Wolverines TK Legacy-VH1

Matczak, Wojciech
92Finnish Semic-285

Matechuk, Rod
84Saskatoon Blades Stickers-13

Matejny, Jan
97Czech APS Extraliga-138
99Czech OFS-426

Matejovsky, Radek
96Czech APS Extraliga-24
97Czech APS Extraliga-166
98Czech DS Stickers-203
98Czech OFS-301
99Czech DS-125
99Czech OFS-49
99Czech OFS-364
00Czech OFS-100
01Czech OFS-9
02Czech OFS Plus-264
03Czech OFS Plus-205
04Czech HC Plzen Postcards-10
04Czech OFS-148
05Czech HC Plzen-8
06Czech OFS-278

Mateka, Eddie
52Juniors Blue Tint-30

Materi, Lee
92Saskatchewan JHL-69

Materi, Lindsey
96Swift Current Broncos-2
97Swift Current Broncos-2
98Kelowna Rockets-16

Materna, Erwin
94German First League-460

Materukhin, Alex
03Louisiana Ice Gators-14
04Louisiana Ice Gators-14

Mather, Shawn
03Johnstown Chiefs-8
03Johnstown Chiefs RBI Sports-221
04Atlantic City Boardwalk Bullies-26
04Johnstown Chiefs-13
05Fresno Falcons-11

Mathers, Frank
44Beehive Group II Photos-428
45Quaker Oats Photos-32
88ProCards AHL-146
98Hershey Bears-36
04Hershey Bears Patriot News-17
04Hershey Bears Patriot News-18

Mathers, Mike
907th Inn. Sketch WHL-299
917th Inn. Sketch WHL-81
00Fresno Falcons-10
01Fresno Falcons-9
02Fresno Falcons-5
03Fresno Falcons-9

Matheson, Jeff
06Kotoks Oilers -13

Mathias, Matt
03New Mexico Scorpions-13
04Columbus Cottonmouths-13

Mathias, Trevor
91Air Canada SJHL-C42

Mathiasen, Dwight
87Penguins Kodak-18

Mathies, Jeremy
91Air Canada SJHL-D33

Mathieson, Jim
86Regina Pats-15
87Regina Pats-17
88Regina Pats-15
89Regina Pats-12
90ProCards AHL/IHL-197
91Baltimore Skipjacks-8
91ProCards-554
93Portland Pirates-9
94Portland Pirates-15
95Portland Pirates-14

Mathieson, T.J.
01Notre Dame Fighting Irish-10
02Notre Dame Fighting Irish-16
03Notre Dame Fighting Irish-6

Mathieu, Alexander
93Quebec Pee-Wee Tournament-1334
96Halifax Mooseheads I-14
96Halifax Mooseheads II-14
97Halifax Mooseheads I-13
97Halifax Mooseheads II-13
97Bowman CHL-123
OPC-123
Autographs-3
98Halifax Mooseheads-13
98Halifax Mooseheads Second Edition-24
98Bowman CHL-115
Golden Anniversary-115
OPC International-115
98Bowman Chrome CHL-115
Golden Anniversary-115
Golden Anniversary Refractors-115
OPC International-115
OPC International Refractors-115
Refractors-115
00Wilkes-Barre Scranton Penguins-14
01Wilkes-Barre Scranton Penguins-17
02Lexington Men O'War-12
03Memphis RiverKings-11

Mathieu, Gilbert
72Finnish Semic World Championship-160
72Swedish Semic World Championship-160

Mathieu, Marquis
907th Inn. Sketch QMJHL-114
917th Inn. Sketch QMJHL-162
93Wheeling Thunderbirds-13

94Toledo Storm-16
97Wheeling Nailers-16
97Wheeling Nailers Photo Pack-16
98Providence Bruins-14
99BAP Memorabilia-369
Gold-369
Silver-369
99Providence Bruins-17
00Providence Bruins-12
03Wilkes-Barre Scranton Penguins-16
04German DEL Update-325A
04Thetford Mines Prolab-10

Mathieu, Maxime
06Rio Grande Valley Killer Bees-8

Mathieu, Nando
72Finnish Semic World Championship-138
72Swedish Semic World Championship-138

Mathieu, Patrick
93Quebec Pee-Wee Tournament-467

Mathis, Scott
06Cedar Rapids RoughRiders-11

Mathisrud, Bjorn
92Norwegian Elite Series-54

Matic, Jovan
03Everett Silvertips-4

Matic, Steve
04Langley Hornets-12

Matier, Mark
90 7th Inn. Sketch OHL-167
91 7th Inn. Sketch OHL-326
91 7th Inn. Sketch Memorial Cup-18
93Sault Ste. Marie Greyhound Memorial Cup-3
99UK Sheffield Steelers-11
00UK Sekonda Superleague-36
03Laredo Bucks-12

Matijasic, Grega
93Quebec Pee-Wee Tournament-1802

Matikainen, Pentti
80Finnish Mallasjuoma-143
89Swedish Semic World Champ Stickers-27
92Finnish Semic-2
93Finnish Jyvas-Hyva Stickers-43
93Finnish SISU-233
93Swedish Semic World Champ Stickers-88
96German DEL-36

Matikainen, Petri
94Finnish SISU-233
95Finnish SISU-70
96German DEL-255

Matile, Sean
97New Hampshire Wildcats-17
98New Hampshire Wildcats-5
99ECHL All-Star Northern Conference-21
00Richmond Renegades-17
03Mississippi Sea Wolves-11

Matousek, Jiri
99Czech Score Blue 2000-82
99Czech Score Red Ice 2000-82

Matschke, Trevor
98San Antonio Iguanas-18
99San Antonio Iguanas-4

Matsijevski, Aleksander
98Finnish Keraileysarja-195

Matsos, David
89Sault Ste. Marie Greyhounds-23
90 7th Inn. Sketch OHL-168
91 7th Inn. Sketch OHL-329
91 7th Inn. Sketch Memorial Cup-10
93Sault Ste. Marie Greyhound Memorial Cup-12
99German Bundesliga 2-9
01UK Belfast Giants-11

Mattaa, Eilert
01Swedish Alfabilder-3

Matte, Christian
97Donruss-207
Press Proofs Silver-207
Press Proofs Gold-207
Rated Rookies-6
Medallist-6
97Donruss Canadian Ice-137
Dominion Series-137
Provincial Series-137
97Upper Deck-257
98Hershey Bears-21
99O-Pee-Chee-233
99O-Pee-Chee Chrome-233
99O-Pee-Chee Chrome Refractors-233
99Topps/OPC-233
99Topps/OPC Chrome-233
Refractors-233
99AHL All-Stars-6
00BAP Memorabilia-471
Emerald-471
Ruby-471
Sapphire-471
00Cleveland Lumberjacks-1
02Swiss HNL-271

Matte, David
93Quebec Pee-Wee Tournament-57

Matte, Joe
34Beehive Group I Photos-69

Matte, Sebastien
92Quebec Pee-Wee Tournament-795
93Quebec Pee-Wee Tournament-1052

Matteau, Philippe
93Quebec Pee-Wee Tournament-1126

Matteau, Stephane
87Hull Olympiques-14
89ProCards IHL-192
90Flames IGA/McGavin's-14
90OPC Premier-68
90Pro Set-593
90Score-381
Canadian-381
90Upper Deck-535
French-535
91Bowman-258
91Flames Panini Team Stickers-11
91Flames IGA-10
91O-Pee-Chee-383
91Panini Stickers-62
91Parkhurst-259
French-259
91Pro Set-27
French-27
91Score Canadian Bilingual-242
91Score Canadian English-242
91Stadium Club-391
91Topps-383
91Upper Deck-121
French-121
92Bowman-340
92O-Pee-Chee-69
92Parkhurst-268
Emerald Ice-268
92Pinnacle-180
French-180
92Score-543
Canadian-543
92Stadium Club-363
92Topps-463
Gold-463G
92Ultra-279
92Upper Deck-540
93Blackhawks Coke-13
93Donruss-463
93Durivage Score-44
93Leaf-114
93OPC Premier-415
Gold-415
93Panini Stickers-150
93Parkhurst-41
Emerald Ice-41
93Pinnacle-344
Canadian-344
93PowerPlay-313
93Score-398
Canadian-398
93Stadium Club-127
Members Only Master Set-127
OPC-127
First Day Issue-127
First Day Issue OPC-127
93Topps/OPC Premier-415
Gold-415
93Ultra-290
93Upper Deck-214
94Canada Games NHL POGS-165
94Donruss-15
94Leaf-32
94OPC Premier-317
Special Effects-317
94Parkhurst-150
Gold-150
94Pinnacle-329
Artist's Proofs-329
Rink Collection-329
94Stadium Club-216
Members Only Master Set-216
First Day Issue-216
Super Team Winner Cards-216
94Topps/OPC Premier-317
Special Effects-317
94Ultra-332
94Upper Deck-136
Electric Ice-136
95Be A Player-5
Signatures-S5
Signatures Die Cuts-S5
95Parkhurst International-446
Emerald Ice-446
95Score-227
Black Ice Artist's Proofs-227
Black Ice-227
95Upper Deck-60
Electric Ice-60
Electric Ice Gold-60
96Be A Player-169
Autographs-169
Autographs Silver-169
96Collector's Choice-230
96Upper Deck-326
97Pacific-280
Copper-280
Emerald Green-280
Ice Blue-280
Red-280
Silver-280
97Paramount-168
Copper-168
Dark Grey-168
Emerald Green-168
Ice Blue-168
Red-168
Silver-168
98Pacific-387
Ice Blue-387
Red-387
98Paramount-212
Copper-212
Emerald Green-212
Holo-Electric-212
Ice Blue-212
Silver-212
98Upper Deck-355
Exclusives-355
Exclusives 1 of 1-355
Gold Reserve-355
99Pacific-376
Copper-376
Emerald Green-376
Gold-376
Ice Blue-376
Premiere Date-376
Red-376
00Pacific-361
Copper-361
Gold-361
Ice Blue-361
Premiere Date-361
00Panini Stickers-202
01Upper Deck-379
Exclusives-379

Matter, Trevor
98Tacoma Sabercats-13

Mattersdorfer, Charlie
97Lethbridge Hurricanes-11

Mattersdorfer, Darcy
91 7th Inn. Sketch WHL-70

Matteucci, Mike
91Air Canada SJHL-D43
91Air Canada SJHL All-Stars-21
91Air Canada SJHL All-Stars-31
91Air Canada SJHL All-Stars-48
92Lake Superior State Lakers-17
97Long Beach Ice Dogs-11
98Long Beach Ice Dogs-12
99Long Beach Ice Dogs-6
00Cleveland Lumberjacks-3
01BAP Memorabilia-441
Emerald-441
Ruby-441
Sapphire-441
01SP Authentic-152
Limited-152
Limited Gold-152
01SPx-141
01SPx-141
Rookie Treasures-RTMM
01UD Challenge for the Cup-111
01Upper Deck-192
Exclusives-192
01Upper Deck MVP-203
01Upper Deck Victory-376
Gold-376
02Albany River Rats-17
02Albany River Rats AAP-18
03Albany River Rats-19
03Albany River Rats Kinko's-18

Matthews, Jamie
89Sudbury Wolves-8
90 7th Inn. Sketch OHL-387
90Sudbury Wolves-9
91Upper Deck-76
French-76
91 7th Inn. Sketch OHL-261
91 7th Inn. Sketch Memorial Cup-124
91Sudbury Wolves-19
91Classic-37
91Star Pics-6
91Ultimate Draft-32
91Ultimate Draft French-32
91Classic Four-Sport *-37
Autographs-37A
Autographs-40A
92Sudbury Wolves-10
93Sudbury Wolves-16
93Sudbury Wolves Police-9
97Sudbury Wolves Anniversary-12

Matthews, Jeff
93RPI Engineers-17

Matthews, Ronnie
51Laval Dairy Subset-40
52St. Lawrence Sales-86

Matthias, Shawn
04Belleville Bulls-22
05Belleville Bulls-21
06Belleville Bulls-9
06Belleville Bulls-LE2
06ITG Heroes and Prospects-124
Autographs-ASM

Matthiasson, Markus
97Swedish Collector's Choice-34
00Swedish Upper Deck-178
02Swedish SHL-105
Dynamic Duos-8
Parallel-105
Sharpshooters-SS7
03Swedish Elite-132
Hot Numbers-HN7
Signatures II-6
Silver-132
04Swedish Elitset-235
Gold-235
04Swedish Malmo Red Hawks-23
06Swedish SHL Elitset-101

Matthies, Jeremy
92Saskatchewan JHL-155

Mattie, James
00Sioux Falls Stampede-15

Mattila, Hannu
92Finnish Jyvas-Hyva Stickers-49
93Finnish Jyvas-Hyva Stickers-78
93Finnish SISU-127
94Finnish SISU-76
95Finnish SISU-38
96Finnish SISU Redline-35
98Finnish Keraileysarja-89

Mattila, Jukka
70Finnish Jaakiekko-131
71Finnish Suomi Stickers-181
72Finnish Jaakiekko-130
73Finnish Jaakiekko-184

Mattis, Mike
92Michigan State Spartans-15
93Michigan State Spartans-13

Mattiussi, Dick
69O-Pee-Chee-147
70Esso Power Players-96
70O-Pee-Chee-192
70Sargent Promotions Stamps-139

Mattsson, Andreas
98Danish Hockey League-77
99Danish Hockey League-222
05Swedish SHL Elitset-159

Mattsson, Ingvar
56Swedish Alfabilder-94

Mattsson, Jesper
91Swedish Semic Elitserien Stickers-198
91Swedish Semic Elitserien Stickers-332
92Swedish Semic Elitserien Stickers-217
93Swedish Semic Elitserien-188
93Classic-141
93Classic Four-Sport *-201
Gold-201
94Parkhurst SE-SE244
Gold-SE244
94SP-171
Die Cuts-171
94Upper Deck-519
Electric Ice-519
94Swedish Leaf-280
95Swedish Leaf-92
95Swedish Globe World Championships-61
95Saint John Flames-13
96Saint John Flames-12
96Collector's Edge Ice-76
Prism-76
97Saint John Flames-14
98Swedish UD Choice-163
99Swedish Upper Deck-165
00Swedish Upper Deck-145
02Swedish Malmo Red Hawks-11
02Swedish SHL-77
Parallel-77
Signatures-11
03Swedish Elite-96
Silver-96
04Swedish Elitset-185
Gold-185
05Swedish SHL Elitset-44
Gold-44
Series Two Signatures-9
06Swedish SHL Elitset-45

Mattsson, Markus
72Finnish Jaakiekko-311
77Finnish Sportscasters-51-1201
78Jets Postcards-15
80Jets Postcards-17
80O-Pee-Chee-394
80Pepsi-Cola Caps-135
81O-Pee-Chee-374
82Swedish Semic VM Stickers-159
82Birmingham South Stars-16
99Finnish Valio World Championships-4
05Finnish Tappara Legendat-23

Mattsson, Teppo
78Finnish SM-Liiga-155
80Finnish Mallasjuoma-111

Mattsson, Torbjorn
83Swedish Semic Elitserien-57
84Swedish Semic Elitserien-57
85Swedish Panini Stickers-54
86Swedish Panini Stickers-34
87Swedish Panini Stickers-256
90Swedish Semic Elitserien Stickers-83

Matulik, Ivan
89ProCards AHL-150
90ProCards AHL/IHL-527
91ProCards-537
93UK Sheffield Steelers-8
95Vancouver VooDoo RHI-12
00UK Sekonda Superleague-62
01UK Cardiff Devils-13
01UK Manchester Storm-8
02UK Cardiff Devils-13
02UK Ivan Matulik Testimonial-1
02UK Ivan Matulik Testimonial-2
02UK Ivan Matulik Testimonial-3
02UK Ivan Matulik Testimonial-4
02UK Ivan Matulik Testimonial-5
02UK Ivan Matulik Testimonial-6
02UK Ivan Matulik Testimonial-7
02UK Ivan Matulik Testimonial-8
02UK Ivan Matulik Testimonial-9
02UK Ivan Matulik Testimonial-10
02UK Ivan Matulik Testimonial-11
02UK Ivan Matulik Testimonial-12
02UK Manchester Storm-10
03UK Cardiff Devils-11

Maturo, Mike
93Quebec Pee-Wee Tournament-598

Matuschow, Dimitri
94German First League-592

Matushkin, Igor
98Swedish UD Choice-138

Matusovich, Scott
92Birmingham Bulls-6
92Nashville Knights-5
93Birmingham Bulls-6
94Wheeling Thunderbirds-18
94Wheeling Thunderbirds Photo Album-3

Matuszek, Mike
89 7th Inn. Sketch OHL-170

Matvichuk, Alexandre
93Seattle Thunderbirds-24
94North Bay Centennials-11
95Slapshot-216
96Toledo Storm-17
97Wheeling Nailers-18
97Wheeling Nailers Photo Pack-18
99Russian Hockey League-248

Matvichuk, Richard
89Saskatoon Blades-15
90Saskatoon Blades-14
90 7th Inn. Sketch WHL-83
91Upper Deck Czech World Juniors-48
91Saskatoon Blades-11
91 7th Inn. Sketch WHL-113
91 7th Inn. Sketch Memorial Cup-108
91Arena Draft Picks-6
91Arena Draft Picks French-6
91Arena Draft Picks Autographs-6
91Arena Draft Picks Autographs French-6
91Classic-7
91Star Pics-57
91Ultimate Draft-7
91Ultimate Draft-63
91Ultimate Draft French-7
91Classic Four-Sport *-7
92OPC Premier-83
92Parkhurst-74
Emerald Ice-74
92Pinnacle-391
French-391
92Ultra-321
92Upper Deck-505
93Donruss-418
93Pinnacle-182
Canadian-182
93Score-285
Canadian-285
93Ultra-180
93Upper Deck-55
94Donruss-303
94Leaf-269
94OPC Premier-187
Special Effects-187
94Parkhurst-57
Gold-57
94Stars Postcards-17
94Topps/OPC Premier-187
Special Effects-187
94Upper Deck-157
Electric Ice-157
94Classic Pro Prospects-151
95Parkhurst International-328
Emerald Ice-328
95Playoff One on One-249
95Upper Deck-37
Electric Ice-37
Electric Ice Gold-37
96Be A Player-195
Autographs-195
Autographs Silver-195
96Donruss-97
Press Proofs-97
96Score-229
Artist's Proofs-229
Dealer's Choice Artist's Proofs-229
Special Artist's Proofs-229
Golden Blades-229
96Stars Postcards-20
97Donruss-193
Press Proofs Silver-193
Press Proofs Gold-193
97Pacific Dynagon Best Kept Secrets-29
98OPC Chrome-210
Refractors-210
98Topps-210
O-Pee-Chee-210
98Upper Deck-255
Exclusives-255
Exclusives 1 of 1-255
Gold Reserve-255
99BAP Memorabilia-300
Gold-300
Silver-300
99Stars Postcards-17
00BAP Memorabilia-326
Emerald-326
Ruby-326
Sapphire-326
Promos-326
00BAP Mem Chicago Sportsfest Copper-326
00BAP Memorabilia Chicago Sportsfest Blue-326
00BAP Memorabilia Chicago Sportsfest Gold-326
00BAP Memorabilia Chicago Sportsfest Ruby-326
00BAP Memorabilia Chicago Sun-Times Ruby-326
00BAP Memorabilia Chicago Sun-Times Gold-326
00BAP Mem Chicago Sun-Times Sapphire-326
00BAP Mem Toronto Fall Expo Copper-326
00BAP Memorabilia Toronto Fall Expo Gold-326
00BAP Memorabilia Toronto Fall Expo Ruby-326
00O-Pee-Chee-219
00O-Pee-Chee Parallel-219
00Pacific-136
Copper-136
Gold-136
Ice Blue-136
Premiere Date-136
00Panini Stickers-147
00Stars Postcards-16
00Topps/OPC-219
Parallel-219
01Stars Postcards-16
02Pacific Complete-97
Red-97
02Stars Postcards-10
02Topps Total-324
02Upper Deck-304
Exclusives-304
02Upper Deck Beckett UD Promos-304
03ITG Action-122
03Pacific Complete-222
Red-222
03Stars Postcards-14
05Devils Team Issue-15
05Parkhurst-297
Facsimile Auto Parallel-297
06Devils Team Set-16

Matwijiw, Stan
91Prince Albert Raiders-12
91 7th Inn. Sketch WHL-261
93Lethbridge Hurricanes-7
94Flint Generals-16

Matzka, Scott
92Quebec Pee-Wee Tournament-1566
01Atlantic City Boardwalk Bullies-16
02Atlantic City Boardwalk Bullies-14

Mau'u, Manu
93Quebec Pee-Wee Tournament-1251

Mauch, Jill
04Ohio State Buckeyes Women-17
05Ohio State Buckeyes Women-13
06Ohio State Buckeyes Women-11

Maudie, Bob
93Kamloops Blazers-16
94Kamloops Blazers-8
95Kamloops Blazers-19
95Slapshot Memorial Cup-22
96Binghamton Rangers-14
00UK Sekonda Superleague-183
01UK Sheffield Steelers-16

Mauer, Nate
02New Mexico Scorpions-9

Mauldin, Greg
03BAP Memorabilia-240
03ITG VIP Rookie Debut-147
03Parkhurst Rookie-76
03Upper Deck Rookie Update-188
04Pacific-280
Blue-280
Red-280
04Syracuse Crunch-21
05Syracuse Crunch-23

Maund, Jeff
99ECHL All-Star Southern Conference-10
99Florida Everblades-1
01Providence Bruins-2
01Florida Everblades-15
03Florida Everblades RBI Sports-168

Maunu, Matt
04Northern Michigan Wildcats-12

Maunu, Mitchell
02Windsor Spitfires-6

Maurer, Andreas
94German First League-300
95German DEL-349

Maurer, Bruno
93Swiss HNL-50
95Swiss HNL-250
96Swiss HNL-264

Maurer, David
01Swiss HNL-137
02Swiss HNL-50

Maurer, Ulrich
04German DEL-253
04German Nuremburg Ice Tigers Postcards-12
05German DEL-366

Maurice, Mike
85Kingston Canadians-22
86Kingston Canadians-19
92Hamilton Canucks-16
94Classic Pro Prospects-64
95Houston Aeros-15
98Madison Monsters-8
99UHL All-Stars East-5T
03Cape Fear Fire Antz-7

Maurice, Paul
93Detroit Jr. Red Wings-23
94Detroit Jr. Red Wings-25
95Whalers Bob's Stores-16
95Slapshot Memorial Cup-99
97Hurricanes Team Issue-27

Mauron, Jaques
93Swiss HNL-320

Mavety, Larry
83Belleville Bulls-29
84Belleville Bulls-3
90 7th Inn. Sketch OHL-23
91 7th Inn. Sketch OHL-110
98Kingston Frontenacs-11

Maximenko, Andrei
00Russian Hockey League-66

Maxner, Wayne
85Sudbury Wolves-5
86London Knights-4
89 7th Inn. Sketch OHL-48
91 7th Inn. Sketch OHL-192

Maxwell, Ben
04Kootenay Ice-15
05ITG Heroes/Prosp Toronto Expo Parallel -173
05Kootenay Ice-16
05ITG Heroes and Prospects-173
Autographs-A-BMX
Team Cherry-TC8
06ITG Heroes and Prospects-101
Autographs-ABM
CHL Top Prospects-TP15
CHL Top Prospects Gold-TP15
Quad Emblems-QE01
Quad Emblems Gold-QE01

Maxwell, Brad
78North Stars Cloverleaf Dairy-6
78O-Pee-Chee-83
78Topps-83
79Panini Stickers-56
79North Stars Postcards-8
79O-Pee-Chee-231
79Topps-231
80North Stars Postcards-11
80O-Pee-Chee-152
80Topps-152
81North Stars Postcards-13
81O-Pee-Chee-102
82North Stars Postcards-15
82O-Pee-Chee-168
82Post Cereal-9
83NHL Key Tags-59
83North Stars Postcards-18
83O-Pee-Chee-175
84Nordiques Postcards-16
84North Stars Postcards-15
84O-Pee-Chee-102
84O-Pee-Chee Stickers-50
84Topps-77
85Maple Leafs Postcards-20
85Maple Leafs Postcards-21
85O-Pee-Chee-224
85O-Pee-Chee Stickers-154
86Canucks Team Issue-10
86O-Pee-Chee-242
86O-Pee-Chee Stickers-145

Maxwell, Bryan
76O-Pee-Chee WHA-54
78O-Pee-Chee-216
78Topps-216
81Jets Postcards-14
82Jets Postcards-17
82O-Pee-Chee-387
82Post Cereal-21
83NHL Key Tags-134
83Penguins Coke-15
84Penguins Heinz Photos-14
85Medicine Hat Tigers-16
88Kings Postcards-22
88Kings Smokey-16
90 7th Inn. Sketch WHL-209
91 7th Inn. Sketch WHL-3
91 7th Inn. Sketch Memorial Cup-95
93Spokane Chiefs-16
95Lethbridge Hurricanes-12
96Lethbridge Hurricanes-19

Maxwell, Dennis
91 7th Inn. Sketch OHL-205
92Sudbury Wolves-22
94Sarnia Sting-22
95Classic-96
99St. John's Maple Leafs-13
02UK London Knights-19
03UK Cardiff Devils-18
04UK London Racers-4
04UK London Racers Playoffs-10
05UK Sheffield Steelers Supplementary-1
Gold-1
Silver-1
06Rio Grande Valley Killer Bees-17

Maxwell, F.G.
83Hall of Fame-177
85Hall of Fame-177

Maxwell, Kevin
81North Stars Postcards-14
81Rockies Postcards-18
81Swedish Semic Hockey VM Stickers-83
82Post Cereal-11

Maxwell, Pete
74Sioux City Musketeers-9

Maxwell, Randy
98Danish Hockey League-30
99Danish Hockey League-208

Maxwell, Robert
52Juniors Blue Tint-29

Maxwell, Roger
96Louisiana Ice Gators-7
96Mississippi Sea Wolves-13
98Louisiana Ice Gators-8
00Louisiana Ice Gators-20
03Mississippi Sea Wolves-12

Maxwell, Steamer
83Hall of Fame Postcards-M13

Maxwell, Tim
04Maine Black Bears-16

Maxwell, Tommy
02Medicine Hat Tigers-14
04Medicine Hat Tigers-14
05Medicine Hat Tigers-14

Maxwell, Wayne
96UK Fife Flyers-10
97UK Fife Flyers-3

May, Alan
88Oilers Tenth Anniversary-159
88ProCards AHL-78
89Capitals Kodak-16
89Capitals Team Issue-16
90Bowman-78
Tiffany-78
90Capitals Kodak-16
90Capitals Postcards-16
90Capitals Smokey-15
90Panini Stickers-160
90Pro Set-317
90Upper Deck-240
French-240
91Bowman-295
91Capitals Junior 5x7-20
91Capitals Kodak-20
91O-Pee-Chee-57
91Parkhurst-417
French-417
91Pro Set-508
91Pro Set-614
French-508
French-614
91Score Canadian Bilingual-545
91Score Canadian English-545
91Stadium Club-288
91Topps-57
92Capitals Kodak-20
92Score-357
Canadian-357
93Donruss-419
93OPC Premier-518
Gold-518
93Score-430
Canadian-430
93Topps/OPC Premier-518
Gold-518
02Fleer Throwbacks-42
Gold-42
Platinum-42

May, Bob
93Huntington Blizzard-16

May, Brad
88Niagara Falls Thunder-2
89Niagara Falls Thunder-11
89 7th Inn. Sketch OHL-125
90Score-427
Canadian-427
90Upper Deck-455
French-455
90 7th Inn. Sketch OHL-264
91Parkhurst-10
French-10
91Pinnacle-302
French-302
91Pro Set-523
French-523
91Sabres Blue Shield-12
91Sabres Pepsi/Campbell's-12
91Score Canadian Bilingual-628
91Score Canadian English-628
91Score Rookie/Traded-78T
91Upper Deck-596
French-596
92Bowman-374
92O-Pee-Chee-256
92Panini Stickers-252
92Panini Stickers French-252
92Parkhurst-240
92Parkhurst-257
Emerald Ice-240
Emerald Ice-257
92Pinnacle-197
French-197
92Sabres Blue Shield-12
92Sabres Jubilee Foods-8
92Score-96
Canadian-96
92Stadium Club-51
92Topps-34
Gold-34G
92Ultra-17
92Upper Deck-74
93Donruss-38
93Leaf-47
93OPC Premier-192
Gold-192
93Parkhurst-27
Emerald Ice-27
93Pinnacle-141
Canadian-141
93PowerPlay-298
93Sabres Noco-12
93Score-269
Canadian-269
93Stadium Club-203
Members Only Master Set-203
OPC-203
First Day Issue-203
First Day Issue OPC-203
93Topps/OPC Premier-192
Gold-192
93Upper Deck-201
94Be A Player-R26
Signature Cards-22
94Canada Games NHL POGS-362
94Donruss-76
94Fleer-24
94Leaf-215
94OPC Premier-409
Special Effects-409
94Parkhurst-26
Gold-26
94Pinnacle-194
Artist's Proofs-194
Rink Collection-194
94Score-104
Gold-104
Platinum-104
94Stadium Club-2
Members Only Master Set-2
First Day Issue-2
Super Team Winner Cards-2
94Topps/OPC Premier-409
Special Effects-409
94Ultra-25
94Upper Deck-391
Electric Ice-391
95Canada Games NHL POGS-44
95Donruss-93
95Leaf-224
95Parkhurst International-289
Emerald Ice-289
95Score-288
Black Ice Artist's Proofs-288
Black Ice-288
95Stadium Club-79
Members Only Master Set-79
95Summit-70
Artist's Proofs-70
Ice-70
95Upper Deck-468
Electric Ice-468
Electric Ice Gold-468
96Be A Player-52
96Be A Player-P52
Autographs-52
Autographs Silver-52
96Collector's Choice-29
96Donruss-189
Press Proofs-189
96Leaf-4
Press Proofs-4
96Score-48
Artist's Proofs-48
Dealer's Choice Artist's Proofs-48
Special Artist's Proofs-48
Golden Blades-48
97Pacific Dynagon Best Kept Secrets-11
97Score Sabres-10
Platinum-10
Premier-10
98Be A Player-293
Press Release-293
98BAP Gold-293
98BAP Autographs-293
98BAP Autographs Gold-293
98Pacific-429
Ice Blue-429
Red-429
98Upper Deck-380
Exclusives-380
Exclusives 1 of 1-380
Gold Reserve-380
99BAP Millennium-237
Emerald-237
Ruby-237
Sapphire-237
Signatures-237
Signatures Gold-237
99Upper Deck MVP SC Edition-187
Gold Script-187
Silver Script-187
Super Script-187
00BAP Memorabilia-474
Emerald-474
Ruby-474
Sapphire-474
00Upper Deck Vintage-275
01Coyotes Team Issue-14
02BAP Sig Series Auto Buybacks 1998-293
02BAP Sig Series Auto Buybacks 1999-237
02Coyotes Team Issue-35
02Pacific Complete-274
Red-274
02Topps Total-200
02Upper Deck-132
Exclusives-132
03Canucks Postcards-17
03Canucks Sav-on-Foods-8
03ITG Action-559
03Pacific Complete-377
Red-377
05Be A Player Signatures-MA
05Be A Player Signatures Gold-MA
05Upper Deck MVP-104
Gold-104
Platinum-104

May, Danny
84Minnesota-Duluth Bulldogs-3

May, Darrell
88ProCards IHL-94
03Vancouver Giants-13

May, Jeff
03Prince Albert Raiders-11
04Prince Albert Raiders-6
05Prince Albert Raiders-15
06Prince Albert Raiders-4

May, Mike
91Ferris State Bulldogs-21
92Ferris State Bulldogs-21

May, Scott
00Ohio State Buckeyes-17
01Ohio State Buckeyes-10
02Ohio State Buckeyes-8
03Ohio State Buckeyes-10
05Milwaukee Admirals Pepsi-12

Mayasich, John
70Swedish Masterserien-177

Maye, Chris
93RPI Engineers-18

Mayer, Daniel
02OCN Blizzard-14
03OCN Blizzard-12

Mayer, Derek
89ProCards AHL-329
91ProCards-135
92Alberta International Team Canada-12
93Alberta International Team Canada-14
93Donruss-467
93OPC Premier Team Canada-6
93PowerPlay-489
93Ultra-469
94Parkhurst-156
Gold-156
Vintage-V60
94Score-23
Gold-223
Platinum-223
Team Canada-CT17
94Stadium Club-251
Members Only Master Set-251
First Day Issue-251
Super Team Winner Cards-251
94Upper Deck-107
Electric Ice-107
94Atlanta Knights-4
95Finnish SISU-315
95Finnish SISU-375
96Finnish SISU Redline Sledgehammers-5
96German DEL-30
98German DEL-160
99German DEL-66
00German Berlin Polar Bears Postcards-16
00German DEL-62
04German Berlin Eisbarens 50th Anniv-73

Mayer, Gil
60Cleveland Barons-12

Mayer, Hans-Jorg
91Upper Deck-682
French-682
91Upper Deck Czech World Juniors-45
94German DEL-184
95German DEL-185
96German DEL-123

Mayer, Markus
94German First League-263

Mayer, Oliver
94German First League-184

Mayer, Pat
88ProCards IHL-55

Mayer, Stefan
94German DEL-28
95German DEL-8
96German DEL-9
98German DEL-16
99German DEL-44

Mayer, Thierry
91 7th Inn. Sketch QMJHL-218
95German DEL-102

Mayers, J.R.
93Quebec Pee-Wee Tournament-1445

Mayers, Jamal
92Western Michigan Broncos-17
93Western Michigan Broncos-21
97Donruss-223
Press Proofs Silver-223
Press Proofs Gold-223
99BAP Millennium-206
Emerald-206
Ruby-206
Sapphire-206
Signatures-206
Signatures Gold-206
99Blues Taco Bell-21
99Pacific-359
Copper-359
Emerald Green-359
Gold-359
Ice Blue-359
Premiere Date-359
Red-359
99Stadium Club-74
First Day Issue-74
One of a Kind-74
Printing Plates Black-74

Printing Plates Cyan-74
Printing Plates Magenta-74
Printing Plates Yellow-74
00Paramount-207
Copper-207
Gold-207
Holo-Gold-207
Holo-Silver-207
Ice Blue-207
Premiere Date-207
00Upper Deck Vintage-317
01BAP Update Tough Customers-TC5
01BAP Update Tough Customers-TC35
01Upper Deck Victory-312
Gold-312
02BAP Sig Series Auto Buybacks 1999-206
02Blues Team Issue-15
02Pacific Complete-258
Red-258
02Topps Total-286
02Upper Deck-397
Exclusives-397
02Upper Deck Beckett UD Promos-397
03Blues Team Set-18
03ITG Action-537
05Blues Team Set-11
05Parkhurst-421
Facsimile Auto Parallel-421
05Upper Deck-413
05Upper Deck MVP-339
Gold-339
Platinum-339
06Be A Player-85
Autographs-85
Signatures-JM
06O-Pee-Chee-431
Rainbow-431

Mayes, David
96South Carolina Stingrays-12
98Thunder Bay Thunder Cats-3
99UHL All-Stars East-9T
00Knoxville Speed-6
01Fort Wayne Komets-13

Mayes, Jim
94Anchorage Aces-13

Mayes, Lance
03Alaska Aces-10

Mayhew, Mike
97Mobile Mysticks-2
97Mobile Mysticks Kellogg's-7
97Pensacola Ice Pilots-14
99Tupelo T-Rex-15
03Michigan Wolverines-2
04Michigan Wolverines-14

Mayko, Ryan
01Kelowna Rockets-12
02Kelowna Rockets-16
03Vancouver Giants-4
04Camrose Kodiaks-4

Maynard, Geordie
907th Inn. Sketch OHL-288
917th Inn. Sketch OHL-281

Maynard, Niall
95Slapshot-265

Maynort, Bruno
95Finnish Semic World Championships-196

Mayo, Kevin
85Brandon Wheat Kings-9

Mayo, Matthew
93Niagara Falls Thunder-18

Mayr, Jorg
92Finnish Semic-175
94German DEL-201
95German DEL-199
96German DEL-341
98German DEL-100
98German DEL-318
99German DEL-104
01German Upper Deck-141

Mayr, Roland
04German Augsburg Panthers Postcards-19
04German DEL-33
05German DEL-9
06German DEL-9

Mayrand, Dean
00Muskegon Fury-7

Mazanec, David
02Czech OFS Plus-346
06Czech OFS-279

Mazerolle, Bobby
03Moncton Wildcats-17

Mazhugin, Andrei
98Russian Hockey League-82

Maznick, Paul
48Exhibits Canadian-15

Mazur, Eddie
44Beehive Group II Photos-268
51Buffalo Bison-15
53Parkhurst-20
54Parkhurst-4
60Cleveland Barons-13
02Parkhurst Reprints-187

Mazur, Jay
89ProCards IHL-176
90Canucks Mohawk-17
91Bowman-322
91O-Pee-Chee-28
91Stadium Club-272
91Topps-28
91Upper Deck-378
French-378
91ProCards-612
92Hamilton Canucks-17
95Rochester Americans-10
99Alexandria Warthogs-9

Mazurak, Chad
02Roanoke Express-20
02Roanoke Express RBI Sports-199

Mazutinec, Shane
88Lethbridge Hurricanes-16

Mazzei, Tyler
04Williams Lake Timberwolves-14

Mazzoleni, Fausto
93Swiss HNL-15
95Swiss HNL-166
95Swiss HNL-519

Mazzoleni, Mark
04Green Bay Gamblers-11

Mazzoli, Pat
91Ferris State Bulldogs-22
92Ferris State Bulldogs-22
00UK Sekonda Superleague-194

Mazzuca, Mike
99Kitchener Rangers-22

Mazzuca, Rob
97Sudbury Wolves Anniversary-13

Mbaraga, Patrick
01Sherbrooke Castors-17

McAdam, Don
91ProCards-235

McAdam, Gary
77O-Pee-Chee NHL-253
77Topps-253
78O-Pee-Chee-42
78Topps-42
79O-Pee-Chee-72
79Topps-72
80O-Pee-Chee-288
81Flames Postcards-13
81O-Pee-Chee-93
81Topps-W93
82Post Cereal-3
84O-Pee-Chee-117

McAiney, Garrett
98Guelph Storm-13

McAleavy, Tony
97UK Kingston Hawks Stickers-16

McAlendin, Marlin
52Juniors Blue Tint-6

McAllister, Chris
95Classic-35
96Syracuse Crunch-28
99BAP Millennium-228
Emerald-228
Ruby-228
Sapphire-228
Signatures-228
Signatures Gold-228
99Stadium Club-114
First Day Issue-114
One of a Kind-114
Printing Plates Black-114
Printing Plates Cyan-114
Printing Plates Magenta-114
Printing Plates Yellow-114
99Upper Deck Gold Reserve-349
00Upper Deck NHLPA-PA64
01Flyers Postcards-12
01Topps Reserve-87
02BAP Sig Series Auto Buybacks 1999-228
02Flyers Postcards-9
03ITG Action-128

McAllister, Kyle
99Owen Sound Platers-21
01Owen Sound Attack-12

McAlpine, Chris
91Minnesota Golden Gophers-14
92Minnesota Golden Gophers-12
93Minnesota Golden Gophers-18
94Classic-54
Gold-54
All-Americans-AA4
95Donruss-113
95Leaf-14
95Pinnacle-210
Artist's Proofs-210
Rink Collection-210
95Score-293
Black Ice Artist's Proofs-293
Black Ice-293
95Topps-61
OPC Inserts-61
95Images-80
Gold-80
Autographs-80A
96Albany River Rats-9
96Collector's Edge Ice-7
Prism-7
97Be A Player-82
Autographs-82
Autographs Die-Cuts-82
Autographs Prismatic Die-Cuts-82
97Score Blues-14
Platinum-14
Premier-14
97Upper Deck-348
99BAP Millennium-207
Emerald-207
Ruby-207
Sapphire-207
Signatures-207
Signatures Gold-207
99Stadium Club-139
First Day Issue-139
One of a Kind-139
Printing Plates Black-139
Printing Plates Cyan-139
Printing Plates Magenta-139
Printing Plates Yellow-139
01O-Pee-Chee-263
01O-Pee-Chee Premier Parallel-263
01Topps-263
OPC Parallel-263
01Norfolk Admirals-5
02BAP Sig Series Auto Buybacks 1999-207

McAlpine, Mike
92Minnesota Golden Gophers-22
93Minnesota Golden Gophers-19

McAmmond, Dave
91Air Canada SJHL-B26

McAmmond, Dean
90Prince Albert Raiders-11
907th Inn. Sketch WHL-267
91Prince Albert Raiders-13
917th Inn. Sketch WHL-254
917th Inn. Sketch Memorial Cup-109
91Arena Draft Picks-17
91Arena Draft Picks French-17
91Arena Draft Picks Autographs-17
91Arena Draft Picks Autographs French-17
91Classic-19
91Star Pics-66
91Ultimate Draft-18
91Ultimate Draft-74
91Classic Four-Sport *-19
Autographs-19A
92Pro Set-224
92Score-469
Canadian-469
92Ultra-40
92Upper Deck-403
93Donruss-110
93Leaf-436
93OPC Premier-366
Gold-366
93Parkhurst-64
Emerald Ice-64
Calder Candidates-C9
Calder Candidates Gold-C9
93Topps/OPC Premier-366
Gold-366
93Ultra-317
93Upper Deck-480
SP-51
94Donruss-123
94Flair-59
94Leaf-298
94Parkhurst SE-SE62
Gold-SE62
94Pinnacle-358
Artist's Proofs-358
Rink Collection-358
94Stadium Club-147
Members Only Master Set-147
First Day Issue-147
Super Team Winner Cards-147
94Ultra-292
94Upper Deck-386
Electric Ice-386
95Playoff One on One-257
95Upper Deck-363
Electric Ice-363
Electric Ice Gold-363
96Be A Player-126
Autographs-126
Autographs Silver-126
96Oilers Postcards-37
96Playoff One on One-419
96Upper Deck-257
97Collector's Choice-97
97Pacific Invincible NHL Regime-80
97SP Authentic-62
97Upper Deck-275
98Bowman's Best-90
Refractors-90
Atomic Refractors-90
98Pacific-214
Ice Blue-214
Red-214
98Paramount-89
Copper-89
Emerald Green-89
Holo-Electric-89
Ice Blue-89
Silver-89
98UD Choice-79
98UD Choice Preview-79
98UD Choice Prime Choice Reserve-79
98UD Choice Reserve-79
98Upper Deck-271
Exclusives-271
Exclusives 1 of 1-271
Gold Reserve-271
99BAP Millennium-60
Emerald-60
Ruby-60
Sapphire-60
Signatures-60
Signatures Gold-60
99Blackhawks Lineup Cards-5
99Pacific-93
Copper-93
Emerald Green-93
Gold-93
Ice Blue-93
Premiere Date-93
Red-93
99Panini Stickers-202
99Paramount-56
Copper-56
Emerald-56
Gold-56
Holographic Emerald-56
Holographic Gold-56
Holographic Silver-56
Ice Blue-56
Premiere Date-56
Red-56
Silver-56
99Upper Deck MVP SC Edition-47
Gold Script-47
Silver Script-47
Super Script-47
00BAP Memorabilia-379
Emerald-379
Ruby-379
Sapphire-379
Promos-379
00BAP Mem Chicago Sportsfest Copper-379
00BAP Memorabilia Chicago Sportsfest Blue-379
00BAP Memorabilia Chicago Sportsfest Gold-379
00BAP Memorabilia Chicago Sportsfest Ruby-379
00BAP Memorabilia Chicago Sun-Times Ruby-379
00BAP Memorabilia Chicago Sun-Times Gold-379
00BAP Mem Chicago Sun-Times Sapphire-379
00BAP Mem Toronto Fall Expo Copper-379
00BAP Memorabilia Toronto Fall Expo Gold-379
00BAP Memorabilia Toronto Fall Expo Ruby-379
00Pacific-96
Copper-96
Gold-96
Ice Blue-96
Premiere Date-96
00Paramount-50
Copper-50
Gold-50
Holo-Gold-50
Holo-Silver-50
Ice Blue-50
Premiere Date-50
00Upper Deck-269
Exclusives Tier 1-269
Exclusives Tier 2-269
01BAP Memorabilia-461
Emerald-461
Ruby-461
Sapphire-461
01Crown Royale-21
Blue-21
Premiere Date-21
Red-21
Retail-21
01Parkhurst-371
01Titanium-19
Hobby Parallel-19
Premiere Date-19
Retail-19
Retail Parallel-19
01Upper Deck-261
Exclusives-261
02BAP Memorabilia-53
Emerald-53
Ruby-53
Sapphire-53
NHL All-Star Game-53
NHL All-Star Game Blue-53
NHL All-Star Game Green-53
NHL All-Star Game Red-53
02BAP Memorabilia Toronto Fall Expo-53
02BAP Sig Series Auto Buybacks 1999-60
02O-Pee-Chee-89
02O-Pee-Chee Premier Blue Parallel-89
02O-Pee-Chee Premier Red Parallel-89
02O-Pee-Chee Factory Set-89
02Pacific-56
Blue-56
Red-56
02Pacific Complete-420
Red-420
02Pacific Exclusive-42
02Pacific Heads-Up-17
Blue-17
Purple-17
Red-17
02Parkhurst Retro-74
Minis-74
02Private Stock Reserve-26
Blue-26
Red-26
Retail-26
02Topps-89
OPC Blue Parallel-89
OPC Red Parallel-89
Factory Set-89
02Upper Deck-25
Exclusives-25
02Upper Deck Victory-32
Bronze-32
Gold-32
Silver-32
03ITG Action-31
03Pacific-54
Blue-54
Red-54
03Pacific Complete-17
Red-17
03Upper Deck-28
Canadian Exclusives-28
HG-28
03Upper Deck MVP-71
Gold Script-71
Silver Script-71
Canadian Exclusives-71
04Albany River Rats-13
05Blues Team Set-12
05Parkhurst-417
Facsimile Auto Parallel-417
05Upper Deck MVP-342
Gold-342
Platinum-342
06Gatorade-54

McAndrew, Hazen
34Beehive Group I Photos-241

McAneeley, Ted
72O-Pee-Chee-242
73O-Pee-Chee-37
73Topps-37
74NHL Action Stamps-66
74O-Pee-Chee NHL-148
74Topps-148

McArdle, Kenndal
04Moose Jaw Warriors-9
05ITG Heroes/Prosp Toronto Expo Parallel -174
05Moose Jaw Warriors-14
05ITG Heroes and Prospects-174
Autographs-A-KMC
Complete Logos-CHL-5
Jerseys-GUJ-33
Jerseys Gold-GUJ-33
Emblems-GUE-33
Emblems Gold-GUE-33
Numbers-GUN-33
Numbers Gold-GUN-33
Nameplates-N-16
Nameplates Gold-N-16
06ITG Heroes and Prospects-181
Autographs-AKM
Update Autographs-AKM
07ITG Going For Gold World Juniors-13
Autographs-13
Emblems-GUE13
Jerseys-GUJ13
Numbers-GUN13

McArter, Joel
92Cornell Big Red-20
93Cornell Big Red-18

McArthur, Darryl
95Slapshot-84
95Guelph Storm-17
96Guelph Storm-16
97Guelph Storm-20
98Guelph Storm-18
01Austin Ice Bats-8
02Austin Ice Bats-9
03Austin Ice Bats-10

McArthur, Dean
82Medicine Hat Tigers-11

McArthur, Dustin
94Sarnia Sting-14
96Peoria Rivermen-16
96Peoria Rivermen Photo Album-17
99Corpus Christi IceRays-12

McArthur, Mark
93Guelph Storm-3
94Guelph Storm-2
95Signature Rookies-69A
95Signature Rookies-69B
Signatures-52
96Collector's Edge Future Legends-33
96Collector's Edge Ice-194
Prism-194
00UK Guildford Flames-16
01UK Guildford Flames-2
01UK Guildford Flames-30

McAslan, Sean
98Calgary Hitmen-8
98Calgary Hitmen Autographs-8
99Calgary Hitmen-17
99Calgary Hitmen Autographs-17
00Calgary Hitmen-19
01Columbus Cottonmouths-13
02Columbus Cottonmouths-12
06UK Nottingham Panthers-6

McAuley, Pat
06Lincoln Stars-19
06Lincoln Stars Upper DeckÂ Signature Series -21

McAusland, Darren
907th Inn. Sketch WHL-7
917th Inn. Sketch WHL-135
93Portland Pirates-16
94Portland Pirates-16
94Wheeling Thunderbirds-12
95Portland Pirates-15
96Portland Pirates-16
99Tallahassee Tiger Sharks-4
00UK Sekonda Superleague-115
01Columbus Cottonmouths-14
02Columbus Cottonmouths-13

McAvoy, Alexcei
03Lincoln Stars-13

McAvoy, Drew
05Mississauga Ice Dogs-21
06Mississauga Ice Dogs-19

McAvoy, Keegan
02Reading Royals-23

McAvoy, Spencer
05Swift Current Broncos-12
06Swift Current Broncos-15

McBain, Andrew
82North Bay Centennials-15
83Jets Postcards-17
83Vachon-133
84Jets Police-14
84O-Pee-Chee-343
85Jets Police-12
86Jets Postcards-14
87Jets Postcards-14
87Panini Stickers-370
88Frito-Lay Stickers-12
88Jets Police-15
88Jets Postcards-16
88O-Pee-Chee-105
88O-Pee-Chee Stickers-147
88Panini Stickers-157
88Topps-105
89O-Pee-Chee-38
89O-Pee-Chee-318
89O-Pee-Chee Stickers-135
89Penguins Foodland-13A
89Topps-38
90Canucks Mohawk-18
90O-Pee-Chee-248
90Panini Stickers-297
90Pro Set-301A
90Pro Set-301B
90Score-257
Canadian-257
90Topps-248
Tiffany-248
91Canucks Panini Team Stickers-15
91Pro Set-500
French-500
91ProCards-605
92Pro Set-120
92Senators Team Issue-11
92Ultra-147
93OPC Premier-238
Gold-238
93Topps/OPC Premier-238
Gold-238
94OPC Premier-77
Special Effects-77
94Topps/OPC Premier-77
Special Effects-77
94Las Vegas Thunder-15
95Fort Wayne Komets-10
96Collector's Edge Ice-127
Prism-127

McBain, Jason
907th Inn. Sketch WHL-132
917th Inn. Sketch WHL-48
92Classic-25
Gold-25
92Classic Four-Sport *-174
Gold-174
93Donruss Team USA-14
93Pinnacle-483
Canadian-483
93Upper Deck-552
93Portland Winter Hawks-16
96Upper Deck-189
96Springfield Falcons-25
96Collector's Edge Ice-72
Prism-72
97Cleveland Lumberjacks-19
97Cleveland Lumberjacks Postcards-18
98Las Vegas Thunder-12
00German DEL-157
01German Upper Deck-222
02Fresno Falcons-20
03Las Vegas Wranglers-12
03Las Vegas Wranglers RBI-234
04Las Vegas Wranglers-4

McBain, Mike
93Red Deer Rebels-15
94Parkhurst SE-SE252
Gold-SE252
94Select-167
Gold-167
94SP-176
Die Cuts-176
95Donruss Elite World Juniors-29
95Upper Deck-570
Electric Ice-570
Electric Ice Gold-570
95Red Deer Rebels-11
95Classic-27
96Red Deer Rebels-3
97Bowman CHL-103
OPC-103
98Pacific-401
Ice Blue-401
Red-401
99Quebec Citadelles-1
00Quebec Citadelles-8
Signed-8
03Las Vegas Wranglers-13
03Las Vegas Wranglers RBI-235
04Las Vegas Wranglers-1
05Las Vegas Wranglers-13
06Las Vegas Wranglers-12

McBean, Wayne
85Medicine Hat Tigers-18
88Kings Smokey-17
89ProCards AHL-237
90Pro Set-485
90ProCards AHL/IHL-502
91Bowman-217
91O-Pee-Chee-62
91Parkhurst-330
French-330
91Pro Set-144
French-144
91Score Canadian Bilingual-530
91Score Canadian English-530
91Stadium Club-353
91Topps-62
92O-Pee-Chee-50
92Stadium Club-397
92Topps-443
Gold-443G
93Leaf-413
93Stadium Club-493
Members Only Master Set-493
First Day Issue-493

McBride, Brandon
01Kingston Frontenacs-12
03Oshawa Generals-23
04Oshawa Generals-17
04Oshawa Generals Autographs-17

McBride, Daryn
90ProCards AHL/IHL-363
91Cincinnati Cyclones-14

McBrien, Paul
01Lethbridge Hurricanes-7

McBurney, Jim
52Juniors Blue Tint-182

McBurnie, Bob
91British Columbia JHL-107

McCabe, Bryan
917th Inn. Sketch WHL-331
93Donruss Team Canada-16
93Pinnacle-462
Canadian-462
93Upper Deck-549
93Spokane Chiefs-17
94Finest-150
Super Team Winners-150
Refractors-150
94Parkhurst SE-SE209
Gold-SE209
94Pinnacle-523
Artist's Proofs-523
Rink Collection-523
94SP-153
Die Cuts-153
94Upper Deck-502
Electric Ice-502
94Spokane Chiefs-22
95Bowman-96
All-Foil-96
95Canada Games NHL POGS-175
95Collector's Choice-404
95Donruss-333
Canadian World Junior Team-8
95Finest-54
Refractors-54
95Parkhurst International-256
Emerald Ice-256
95Select Certified-126
Mirror Gold-126
95SkyBox Impact-209
95SP-91
95Stadium Club-93
Members Only Master Set-93
95Summit-172
Artist's Proofs-172
Ice-172
95Topps-312
OPC Inserts-312
Canadian World Juniors-7CJ
95Ultra-348
95Upper Deck-496
Electric Ice-496
Electric Ice Gold-496
95Zenith-138
95Images-91
Gold-91
95Slapshot Memorial Cup-34
96Be A Player-162
Autographs-162
Autographs Silver-162
96Collector's Choice-161
96Donruss-217
Press Proofs-217
96Islander Postcards-13
96Leaf-161
Press Proofs-161
96Metal Universe-94
96Score-253
Artist's Proofs-253
Dealer's Choice Artist's Proofs-253
Special Artist's Proofs-253
Golden Blades-253
96Summit-157
Artist's Proofs-157
Ice-157
Metal-157
Premium Stock-157
96Topps Picks-175
OPC Inserts-175
96Upper Deck-99
97Collector's Choice-157
97Katch-89
Gold-89
Silver-89
97Pacific-118
Copper-118
Emerald Green-118
Ice Blue-118
Red-118
Silver-118
97Pacific Omega-138
Copper-138
Dark Gray-138
Emerald Green-138
Gold-138
Ice Blue-138
97Upper Deck-100
98Pacific-430
Ice Blue-430
Red-430
99BAP Memorabilia-43
Gold-43
Silver-43
99Blackhawks Chicago Sun-Times-6
99Blackhawks Lineup Cards-6
99Pacific-425
Copper-425
Emerald Green-425
Gold-425
Ice Blue-425
Premiere Date-425
Red-425
99Panini Stickers-197
99SPx-38
Radiance-38
Spectrum-38
99Stadium Club-160
First Day Issue-160
One of a Kind-160
Printing Plates Black-160
Printing Plates Cyan-160
Printing Plates Magenta-160
Printing Plates Yellow-160
99Upper Deck Arena Giveaways-CB2
99Upper Deck Victory-74
00BAP Memorabilia-14
00BAP Memorabilia-446
Emerald-14
Emerald-446
Ruby-14
Ruby-446
Sapphire-14
Sapphire-446
Promos-14
00BAP Mem Chicago Sportsfest Copper-14
00BAP Memorabilia Chicago Sportsfest Blue-14
00BAP Memorabilia Chicago Sportsfest Gold-14
00BAP Memorabilia Chicago Sportsfest Ruby-14
00BAP Memorabilia Chicago Sun-Times Ruby-14
00BAP Memorabilia Chicago Sun-Times Gold-14
00BAP Mem Chicago Sun-Times Sapphire-14
00BAP Mem Toronto Fall Expo Copper-14
00BAP Memorabilia Toronto Fall Expo Gold-14
00BAP Memorabilia Toronto Fall Expo Ruby-14
00O-Pee-Chee-68
00O-Pee-Chee Parallel-68
00Pacific-97
Copper-97
Gold-97
Ice Blue-97
Premiere Date-97
00Topps/OPC-68
Parallel-68
00UD Heroes-112
00Upper Deck-40
Exclusives Tier 1-40
Exclusives Tier 2-40
01BAP Signature Series-146
Autographs-146
Autographs Gold-146
01Upper Deck Victory-328
Gold-328
01Upper Deck Vintage-241
02BAP First Edition-126
Jerseys-126
02BAP Memorabilia-68
Emerald-68
Ruby-68
Sapphire-68
NHL All-Star Game-68
NHL All-Star Game Blue-68
NHL All-Star Game Green-68
NHL All-Star Game Red-68
02BAP Memorabilia Toronto Fall Expo-68
02BAP Signature Series-8
Autographs-8
Autograph Buybacks 2001-146
Autographs Gold-8
Defensive Wall-DW2
Golf-GS17
02Maple Leafs Platinum Collection-12
02NHL Power Play Stickers-143
02O-Pee-Chee-226
02O-Pee-Chee-322
02O-Pee-Chee Premier Blue Parallel-226
02O-Pee-Chee Premier Blue Parallel-322
02O-Pee-Chee Premier Red Parallel-226
02O-Pee-Chee Premier Red Parallel-322
02O-Pee-Chee Factory Set-226
02O-Pee-Chee Factory Set-322
02Pacific-363
Blue-363
Red-363
02Pacific Complete-338
Red-338
02Parkhurst-170
Bronze-170
Gold-170
Silver-170
Hardware-N6
02Parkhurst Retro-83
Minis-83
02Topps-226
02Topps-322
OPC Blue Parallel-226
OPC Blue Parallel-322
OPC Red Parallel-226
OPC Red Parallel-322
Factory Set-226
Factory Set-322
02Topps Chrome-124
Black Border Refractors-124
Refractors-124
02Topps Heritage Autographs-BM
02Topps Heritage Autographs Black-BM
02Topps Heritage Autographs Red-BM
02Topps Total-275
02Upper Deck-161
Exclusives-161
02Upper Deck Vintage-241
03ITG Action-523
03NHL Sticker Collection-139
03Pacific Complete-277
Red-277
03Parkhurst Orig Six He Shoots/Scores-5
03Parkhurst Orig Six He Shoots/Scores-5A
03Parkhurst Original Six Toronto-16
Memorabilia-TM3
Memorabilia-TM17
Memorabilia-TM57
03Upper Deck-427
Canadian Exclusives-427
HG-427
UD Exclusives-427
03Upper Deck MVP-401
Gold Script-401
Silver Script-401
Canadian Exclusives-401
04Pacific-246
Blue-246
Red-246
04Upper Deck-165
Canadian Exclusives-165
HG Glossy Gold-165
HG Glossy Silver-165
05Be A Player Quad Signatures-MAPL
05Be A Player Signatures-BY
05Be A Player Signatures Gold-BY
05Beehive Matted Materials-MMMC
05Beehive Matted Materials Remarkable-RMMC
05Hot Prospects-94
En Fuego-94
Red Hot-94
White Hot-94
05McDonalds Upper Deck-49
05Panini Stickers-168
05Parkhurst-449
05Parkhurst-583
Facsimile Auto Parallel-449
Facsimile Auto Parallel-583
True Colors-TCTOR
True Colors-TCTOR
True Colors-TCOTTO
True Colors-TCOTTO
05SP Game Used Authentic Fabrics Dual-BM
05SP Game Used Authentic Patches Dual-BM
05SP Game Used Awesome Authentics-AA-BM
05SP Game Used Statscriptions-ST-BM
05SPx Winning Materials-WM-MC
05SPx Winning Materials Autographs-AWM-MC
05SPx Winning Materials Gold-WM-MC
05SPx Winning Materials Spectrum-WM-MC
05The Cup Emblems of Endorsement-EEMC
05The Cup Honorable Numbers-HNBM
05The Cup Limited Logos-LLMC
05The Cup Master Pressplate Rookie Update-220
05UD Artifacts Auto Facts-AF-BM
05UD Artifacts Auto Facts Blue-AF-BM
05UD Artifacts Auto Facts Copper-AF-BM
05UD Artifacts Auto Facts Pewter-AF-BM
05UD Artifacts Auto Facts Silver-AF-BM
05Ultimate Collection-82
Gold-82
Endorsed Emblems-EEMC
National Heroes Jerseys-NHJMC
National Heroes Patches-NHPMC
05Ultra-183
Gold-183
Fresh Ink-FI-MC
Fresh Ink Blue-FI-MC
Ice-183
05Upper Deck-179
Big Playmakers-B-BMO
HG Glossy-179
Jerseys-J-BMC
Jerseys Series II-J2MC
Notable Numbers-N-BY
05Upper Deck MVP-356
Gold-356
Platinum-356
ProSign-P-BM
05Upper Deck Rookie Update-94
05Upper Deck Rookie Update-220
05Upper Deck Toronto Fall Expo-179
05Upper Deck Victory-182
Black-182
Gold-182
Silver-182
Blow-Ups-BU40
06Black Diamond Gemography-GBM
06Flair Showcase Stitches-SSMC
06Fleer-182
Tiffany-182
Fabricology-FMC
06Gatorade-66
06McDonald's Upper Deck Autographs-ABM
06NHL POG-10
06O-Pee-Chee-463
Rainbow-463
06Panini Stickers-166
06SP Game Used Authentic Fabrics Quads-AF4BPJM
06SP Game Used Authentic Fabrics Quads Patches-AF4BPJM
06SP Game Used Authentic Fabrics Fives-AF5DPT
06SP Game Used Authentic Fabrics Fives Patches-AF5DPT
06SP Game Used Inked Sweaters-ISBM
06SP Game Used Inked Sweaters Patches-ISBM
06SP Game Used SIGnificance-SBM
06SPx Winning Materials-WMBM
06SPx Winning Materials Spectrum-WMBM
06SPx Winning Materials Autographs-WMBM
06UD Artifacts Frozen Artifacts-FAMC
06UD Artifacts Frozen Artifacts Black-FAMC
06UD Artifacts Frozen Artifacts Blue-FAMC
06UD Artifacts Frozen Artifacts Gold-FAMC
06UD Artifacts Frozen Artifacts Platinum-FAMC
06UD Artifacts Frozen Artifacts Red-FAMC
06UD Artifacts Frozen Artifacts Patches Black-FAMC
06UD Artifacts Frozen Artifacts Patches Blue-FAMC
06UD Artifacts Frozen Artifacts Patches Gold-FAMC
06UD Artifacts Frozen Artifacts Patches Platinum-FAMC
06UD Artifacts Frozen Artifacts Patches Red-FAMC
06UD Artifacts Tundra Tandems-TTAB
06UD Artifacts Tundra Tandems-TTMT
06UD Artifacts Tundra Tandems Black-TTAB
06UD Artifacts Tundra Tandems Black-TTMT
06UD Artifacts Tundra Tandems Blue-TTAB
06UD Artifacts Tundra Tandems Blue-TTMT
06UD Artifacts Tundra Tandems Gold-TTAB
06UD Artifacts Tundra Tandems Gold-TTMT
06UD Artifacts Tundra Tandems Platinum-TTAB
06UD Artifacts Tundra Tandems Platinum-TTMT
06UD Artifacts Tundra Tandems Red-TTAB
06UD Artifacts Tundra Tandems Red-TTMT
06UD Artifacts Tundra Tandems Dual Patches Red-TTAB
06UD Artifacts Tundra Tandems Dual Patches Red-TTMT
06UD Mini Jersey Collection-92
06UD Powerplay-93
Impact Rainbow-93
Specialists-SBM
Specialists Patches-PBM
06Ultra-182
Gold Medallion-182
Ice Medallion-182
Uniformity-UMC
Uniformity Patches-UPMD
Uniformity Autographed Jerseys-UAMC
06Upper Deck Arena Giveaways-TOR6
06Upper Deck-187
Exclusives Parallel-187
High Gloss Parallel-187
Game Jerseys-J2BR
Game Patches-P2BR
Masterpieces-187
06Upper Deck MVP-271
Gold Script-271
Super Script-271
Jerseys-OJLM
06Upper Deck Ovation-46
06Upper Deck Victory-186
06Upper Deck Victory Black-186
06Upper Deck Victory Gold-186
07Upper Deck Ovation-5
07Upper Deck Victory-59
Black-59
Gold-59

McCabe, Jamie
03Drummondville Voltigeurs-14
03Quebec Remparts Memorial Cup-13

McCabe, John
98Mobile Mysticks-14
99Mobile Mysticks-6

McCabe, Scott
92Lake Superior State Lakers-18

McCabe, Tony
90Kitchener Rangers-11
907th Inn. Sketch OHL-236
917th Inn. Sketch OHL-77

McCaffrey, Albert
24C144 Champ's Cigarettes-38
24V145-2-57
25Dominion Chocolates-60

McCaffrey, Cam

04Portland Pirates-12
McCaffrey, Chad
01Kitchener Rangers-21
03Kitchener Rangers Memorial Cup-14
McCaffrey, Joe
96Arizona Icecats-12
97Arizona Icecats-13
98Arizona Icecats-15
99Arizona Icecats-15
McCaffrey, Kevin
92Western Michigan Broncos-18
McCaghey, Brad
92Anaheim Bullfrogs RHI-18
McCague, Mark
907th Inn. Sketch OHL-65
McCague, Peter
95Slapshot-224
McCaig, Doug
34Beehive Group I Photos-114
44Beehive Group II Photos-120
McCaig, Jamie
01Anchorage Aces-9
McCaig, Rob
94Central Hockey League-15
94Dallas Freeze-15
95Louisiana Ice Gators-10
95Louisiana Ice Gators Playoffs-11
96Louisiana Ice Gators II-8
98Colorado Gold Kings-12
99Colorado Gold Kings Taco Bell-23
99Colorado Gold Kings Wendy's-15
01UK Hull Thunder-19
McCain, John
03Arizona Icecats-30
04Arizona Icecats-32
McCallion, Paul
90Kitchener Rangers-21
907th Inn. Sketch OHL-237
917th Inn. Sketch OHL-86
96UK Guildford Flames-21
McCallum, Andy
52St. Lawrence Sales-93
McCallum, Dunc
61Sudbury Wolves-13
62Sudbury Wolves-15
68Shirriff Coins-143
70Esso Power Players-222
71Topps-132
McCallum, Scott
95Tri-City Americans-18
97Brandon Wheat Kings-17
98Brandon Wheat Kings-14
02Austin Ice Bats-10
03Austin Ice Bats-11
McCambridge, Keith
917th Inn. Sketch WHL-186
95Saint John Flames-14
95Slapshot Memorial Cup-5
96Saint John Flames-13
97Saint John Flames-15
99Providence Bruins-18
00Providence Bruins-2
01Providence Bruins-3
02Cleveland Barons-14
03Alaska Aces-11
McCammon, Bob
85Oilers Red Rooster-NNO
90Pro Set-678
McCamus, Brad
93Quebec Pee-Wee Tournament-556
McCann, Dave
92Quebec Pee-Wee Tournament-808
93Quebec Pee-Wee Tournament-958
97Las Vegas Thunder-27
McCann, Gordon
91Air Canada SJHL-C8
92Saskatchewan JHL-83
McCann, Joe
04Kitchener Rangers-13
05Plymouth Whalers-B-08
05Saginaw Spirit-15
06Plymouth Whalers-13
McCann, Sean
92Harvard Crimson-24
94Classic-55
Gold-55
All-Americans-AA5
96Grand Rapids Griffins-10
98Orlando Solar Bears-3
98Orlando Solar Bears II-5
McCartan, Jack
44Beehive Group II Photos-341
60Shirriff Coins-81
60Topps-39
72Minnesota Fighting Saints Postcards WHA-14
McCarthy, Brian
97Bakersfield Fog-8
98Bakersfield Condors-13
McCarthy, Doug
95Vancouver VooDoo RHI-5
96Anaheim Bullfrogs RHI-5
98Phoenix Mustangs-14
00UK Sekonda Superleague-49
McCarthy, Jeremiah
95Donruss Elite World Juniors-30
99Missouri River Otters-13
99Missouri River Otters Sheet-11
00Cincinnati Cyclones-2
03Springfield Falcons Postcards-23
McCarthy, Joe
93Raleigh Icecaps-11
06Topps Co-Signers Dual Cut Signatures-BHJM
McCarthy, Kevin
79Canucks Royal Bank-15
79O-Pee-Chee-287
80Canucks Silverwood Dairies-17
80Canucks Team Issue-16
80O-Pee-Chee-21
80Pepsi-Cola Caps-114
80Topps-21
81Canucks Team Issue-15
81O-Pee-Chee-341
81O-Pee-Chee Stickers-248
82Canucks Team Issue-14
82O-Pee-Chee-351
82O-Pee-Chee Stickers-246
82Post Cereal-19
82Topps Stickers-246
83Canucks Team Issue-13
83O-Pee-Chee-356
83O-Pee-Chee Stickers-279
83Puffy Stickers-6
83Topps Stickers-279
83Vachon-112
84O-Pee-Chee-178
84O-Pee-Chee Stickers-119
84Topps-126
88ProCards AHL-143
89ProCards AHL-360
03Hurricanes Postcards-12
06Hurricanes Postcards-19
McCarthy, Liam
04Knoxville Ice Bears-21
05Knoxville Ice Bears-9
McCarthy, Sandy
907th Inn. Sketch QMJHL-54
907th Inn. Sketch Memorial Cup-53
91Upper Deck-77
French-77
917th Inn. Sketch QMJHL-228
91Classic-42
91Classic Four-Sport *-42
Autographs-42A
92Salt Lake Golden Eagles-14
93Donruss-59
93Leaf-358
93Parkhurst-30
Emerald Ice-30
93PowerPlay-306
93Score-633
Gold-633
Canadian-633
Canadian Gold-633
93Upper Deck-493
93Classic-142
93Classic Four-Sport *-241
Gold-241
94Donruss-39
94Leaf-411
94Classic Pro Prospects-22
95Be A Player-217
Signatures-S217
Signatures Die Cuts-S217
95Upper Deck-361
Electric Ice-361
Electric Ice Gold-361
96Collector's Choice-43
96Donruss-42
Press Proofs-42
96Score-215
Artist's Proofs-215
Dealer's Choice Artist's Proofs-215
Special Artist's Proofs-215
Golden Blades-215
96Upper Deck-23
97Flames Collector's Photos-19
97Katch-22
Gold-22
Silver-22
97SP Authentic-21
97Upper Deck-25
98Be A Player-282
Press Release-282
98BAP Gold-282
98BAP Autographs-282
98BAP Autographs Gold-282
98Finest-124
No Protectors-124
No Protectors Refractors-124
Refractors-124
98Katch-134
98OPC Chrome-82
Refractors-82
98Pacific-402
Ice Blue-402
Red-402
98Pacific Omega-220
Red-220
Opening Day Issue-220
98Paramount-218
Copper-218
Emerald Green-218
Holo-Electric-218
Ice Blue-218
Silver-218
98Topps-82
O-Pee-Chee-82
98Upper Deck-184
Exclusives-184
Exclusives 1 of 1-184
Gold Reserve-184
99BAP Millennium-184
Emerald-184
Ruby-184
Sapphire-184
Signatures-184
Signatures Gold-184
99Pacific-308
Copper-308
Emerald Green-308
Gold-308
Ice Blue-308
Premiere Date-308
Red-308
00BAP Memorabilia-358
Emerald-358
Ruby-358
Sapphire-358
Promos-358
00BAP Mem Chicago Sportsfest Copper-358
00BAP Memorabilia Chicago Sportsfest Blue-358
00BAP Memorabilia Chicago Sportsfest Gold-358
00BAP Memorabilia Chicago Sportsfest Ruby-358
00BAP Memorabilia Chicago Sun-Times Ruby-358
00BAP Memorabilia Chicago Sun-Times Gold-358
00BAP Mem Chicago Sun-Times Sapphire-358
00BAP Mem Toronto Fall Expo Copper-358
00BAP Memorabilia Toronto Fall Expo Gold-358
00BAP Memorabilia Toronto Fall Expo Ruby-358
00BAP Memorabilia Update Tough Materials-T14
00BAP Mem Update Tough Materials Gold-T14
00Titanium Game Gear-37
00Topps Heritage-178
01BAP Update Tough Customers-TC15
01BAP Update Tough Customers-TC39
01Pacific-263
01Pacific-416
Extreme LTD-263
Gold-416
Hobby LTD-263
Premiere Date-263
Retail LTD-263
01Pacific Arena Exclusives-263
01Pacific Arena Exclusives-416
01SP Authentic Jerseys-NNMC
01Upper Deck Victory-240
Gold-240
02BAP Sig Series Auto Buybacks 1998-282
02BAP Sig Series Auto Buybacks 1999-184
02BAP Signature Series Famous Scraps-FS12
02O-Pee-Chee-79
02O-Pee-Chee Premier Blue Parallel-79
02O-Pee-Chee Premier Red Parallel-79
02O-Pee-Chee Factory Set-79
02Pacific-255
Blue-255
Red-255
02Pacific Complete-485
Red-485
02Rangers Team Issue-10
02Topps-79
OPC Blue Parallel-79
OPC Red Parallel-79
Factory Set-79
02Topps Total-235
02Upper Deck Vintage-165
03ITG Action-390
03Pacific Complete-354
Red-354
03Parkhurst Original Six Boston-22
03Topps Signs of Toughness-SM
03Topps Tough Materials-SM
03Topps Tough Materials Signed-SM
03Czech Stadion-532
McCarthy, Shaun
93Quebec Pee-Wee Tournament-146
McCarthy, Steve
98SP Authentic-119
Power Shift-119
Sign of the Times-SM
Sign of the Times Gold-SM
98Upper Deck-396
Exclusives-396
Exclusives 1 of 1-396
Gold Reserve-396
98Kootenay Ice-7
99BAP Memorabilia-319
Gold-319
Silver-319
99BAP Millennium Calder Candidates Ruby-C38
99BAP Millennium Calder Candidate Emerald-C38
99BAP Millennium Calder Cand Sapphire-C38
99Pacific Dynagon Ice-51
Blue-51
Copper-51
Gold-51
Premiere Date-51
99Pacific Omega-59
Copper-59
Gold-59
Ice Blue-59
Premiere Date-59
99Bowman CHL-20
99Bowman CHL-97
Gold-20
Gold-97
OPC International-20
OPC International-97
Autographs-BA40
Autographs Gold-BA40
Autographs Silver-BA40
00BAP Memorabilia-26
Emerald-26
Ruby-26
Sapphire-26
Promos-26
00BAP Mem Chicago Sportsfest Copper-26
00BAP Memorabilia Chicago Sportsfest Blue-26
00BAP Memorabilia Chicago Sportsfest Gold-26
00BAP Memorabilia Chicago Sportsfest Ruby-26
00BAP Memorabilia Chicago Sun-Times Ruby-26
00BAP Memorabilia Chicago Sun-Times Gold-26
00BAP Mem Chicago Sun-Times Sapphire-26
00BAP Mem Toronto Fall Expo Copper-26
00BAP Memorabilia Toronto Fall Expo Gold-26
00BAP Memorabilia Toronto Fall Expo Ruby-26
00BAP Signature Series-290
Emerald-290
Ruby-290
Sapphire-290
Autographs-220
Autographs Gold-220
00Crown Royale-117
21st Century Rookies-6
00O-Pee-Chee-293
00O-Pee-Chee Parallel-293
00Pacific-98
Copper-98
Gold-98
Ice Blue-98
Premiere Date-98
00Private Stock-110
Gold-110
Premiere Date-110
Retail-110
Silver-110
00Stadium Club-229
00Topps/OPC-293
Parallel-293
00Topps Chrome-188
OPC Refractors-188
Refractors-188
00Topps Premier Plus-86
Blue Ice-86
00Upper Deck MVP ProSign-SM
00Upper Deck Victory-275
00Vanguard-110
Pacific Proofs-110
01BAP Memorabilia-269
Emerald-269
Ruby-269
Sapphire-269
01Upper Deck Victory-75
Gold-75
01Norfolk Admirals-21
02BAP First Edition-108
Jerseys-108
02BAP Sig Series Auto Buybacks 2000-220
02Norfolk Admirals-15
03Blackhawks Postcards-13
03ITG Action-111
03Pacific Complete-284
Red-284
03Parkhurst Original Six Chicago-16
Memorabilia-CM6
03Topps Tough Materials-SMEC
06O-Pee-Chee-31
Rainbow-31
McCarthy, Tom
79North Stars Postcards-9
80North Stars Postcards-12
80O-Pee-Chee-93
80Topps-93
80Oshawa Generals-23
81North Stars Postcards-15
81O-Pee-Chee-164
81O-Pee-Chee Stickers-95
81Topps-W108
82North Stars Postcards-16
82O-Pee-Chee-169
82Post Cereal-9
83NHL Key Tags-59
83North Stars Postcards-19
83O-Pee-Chee-176
83O-Pee-Chee Stickers-115
83Topps Stickers-115
84North Stars 7-Eleven-10
84North Stars Postcards-16
84O-Pee-Chee-103
84O-Pee-Chee Stickers-52
84Topps-78
85North Stars Postcards-20
87O-Pee-Chee-38
87O-Pee-Chee Stickers-141
87Panini Stickers-13
87Topps-38
88Bruins Sports Action-12
McCarthy, Tom (50s)
57Topps-37
McCarthy, Tony
72Johnstown Jets-3
McCartin, Brendan
98Sioux City Musketeers-13
99Sioux City Musketeers-13
00Sioux City Musketeers-19
McCarty, Charles
97Arizona Icecats-14
McCarty, Darren
897th Inn. Sketch OHL-77
907th Inn. Sketch OHL-12
917th Inn. Sketch OHL-113
93Donruss-103
93Leaf-435
93OPC Premier-412
Gold-412
93Parkhurst-265
Emerald Ice-265
93PowerPlay-333
93Score-631
Gold-631
Canadian-631
Canadian Gold-631
93Stadium Club-441
Members Only Master Set-441
First Day Issue-441
93Topps/OPC Premier-412
Gold-412
93Ultra-307
93Upper Deck-508
93Classic Pro Prospects-147
94Canada Games NHL POGS-89
94Donruss-237
94Leaf-197
94OPC Premier-203
94O-Pee-Chee Finest Inserts-19
94OPC Premier Special Effects-203
94Pinnacle-180
Artist's Proofs-180
Rink Collection-180
94Score-258
Gold-258
Platinum-258
94Topps/OPC Premier-203
Special Effects-203
94Ultra-63
94Upper Deck-365
Electric Ice-365
94Classic Pro Prospects-23
95Canada Games NHL POGS-103
95Donruss-313
95Leaf-320
95Parkhurst International-341
Emerald Ice-341
95Pinnacle-176
Artist's Proofs-176
Rink Collection-176
95Topps-28
OPC Inserts-28
95Ultra-235
Crease Crashers-9
95Upper Deck-301
Electric Ice-301
Electric Ice Gold-301
96Be A Player-175
Autographs-175
Autographs Silver-175
96Collector's Choice-89
96Red Wings Detroit News/Free Press-1
96Upper Deck-55
96Collector's Edge Ice Crucibles-C19
97Collector's Choice-83
97Crown Royale-48
Emerald Green-48
Ice Blue-48
Silver-48
97Donruss-107
Press Proofs Silver-107
Press Proofs Gold-107
97Donruss Elite-84
Aspirations-84
Status-84
97Donruss Limited-72
Exposure-72
97Donruss Preferred-114
Cut to the Chase-114
97Donruss Priority-146
Stamp of Approval-146
97Katch-51
Gold-51
Silver-51
97Leaf-88
Fractal Matrix-88
Fractal Matrix Die Cuts-88
97Leaf International-88
Universal Ice-88
97Pacific-163
Copper-163
Emerald Green-163
Ice Blue-163
Red-163
Silver-163
97Pacific Omega-84
Copper-84
Dark Gray-84
Emerald Green-84
Gold-84
Ice Blue-84
97Paramount-68
Copper-68
Dark Grey-68
Emerald Green-68
Ice Blue-68
Red-68
Silver-68
97Pinnacle-176
Press Plates Back Black-176
Press Plates Back Cyan-176
Press Plates Back Magenta-176
Press Plates Back Yellow-176
Press Plates Front Black-176
Press Plates Front Cyan-176
Press Plates Front Magenta-176
Press Plates Front Yellow-176
97Revolution-48
Copper-48
Emerald-48
Ice Blue-48
Silver-48
97Score-190
97Score Red Wings-6
Platinum-6
Premier-6
97SP Authentic-57
Sign of the Times-DM
97Upper Deck-59
97Upper Deck-390
Game Dated Moments-59
98Aurora-66
98Be A Player-50
Press Release-50
98BAP Gold-50
98BAP Autographs-50
98BAP Autographs Gold-50
98BAP Tampa Bay All Star Game-50
98Bowman's Best-79
Refractors-79
Atomic Refractors-79
98Crown Royale-46
Limited Series-46
98Katch-50
98OPC Chrome-105
Refractors-105
98Pacific-201
Ice Blue-201
Red-201
Trophy Winners-7
98Pacific Dynagon Ice-66
Blue-66
Red-66
98Pacific Omega-84
Red-84
Opening Day Issue-84
98Paramount-79
Copper-79
Emerald Green-79
Holo-Electric-79
Ice Blue-79
Silver-79
98Revolution-50
Ice Shadow-50
Red-50
Three Pronged Attack-4
Three Pronged Attack Parallel-4
98Topps-105
O-Pee-Chee-105
98UD Choice-72
Prime Choice Reserve-72
Reserve-72
98Upper Deck-266
Exclusives-266
Exclusives 1 of 1-266
Gold Reserve-266
98Upper Deck MVP-73
Gold Script-73
Silver Script-73
Super Script-73
99Aurora-52
Premiere Date-52
99BAP Memorabilia-277
Gold-277
Silver-277
99O-Pee-Chee-188
99O-Pee-Chee Chrome-188
99O-Pee-Chee Chrome Refractors-188
99Pacific-144
Copper-144
Emerald Green-144
Gold-144
Ice Blue-144
Premiere Date-144
Red-144
99Pacific Dynagon Ice-76
Blue-76
Copper-76
Gold-76
Premiere Date-76
99Paramount-84
Copper-84
Emerald-84
Gold-84
Holographic Emerald-84
Holographic Gold-84
Holographic Silver-84
Ice Blue-84
Premiere Date-84
Red-84
Silver-84
99Topps/OPC-188
99Topps/OPC Chrome-188
Refractors-188
99Upper Deck Victory-107
00BAP Memorabilia-275
Emerald-275
Ruby-275
Sapphire-275
Promos-275
00BAP Mem Chicago Sportsfest Copper-275
00BAP Memorabilia Chicago Sportsfest Blue-275
00BAP Memorabilia Chicago Sportsfest Gold-275
00BAP Memorabilia Chicago Sportsfest Ruby-275
00BAP Memorabilia Chicago Sun-Times Ruby-275
00BAP Memorabilia Chicago Sun-Times Gold-275
00BAP Mem Chicago Sun-Times Sapphire-275
00BAP Mem Toronto Fall Expo Copper-275
00BAP Memorabilia Toronto Fall Expo Gold-275
00BAP Memorabilia Toronto Fall Expo Ruby-275
00BAP Memorabilia Update Teammates-TM13
00BAP Memorabilia Update Teammates Gold-TM13
00BAP Memorabilia Update Tough Materials-T11
00BAP Mem Update Tough Materials Gold-T11
00BAP Signature Series-59
Emerald-59
Ruby-59
Sapphire-59
Autographs-92
Autographs Gold-92
00BAP Ultimate Mem Dynasty Jerseys-D18
00BAP Ultimate Mem Dynasty Emblems-D18
00O-Pee-Chee-214
00O-Pee-Chee Parallel-214
00Pacific-155
Copper-155
Gold-155
Ice Blue-155
Premiere Date-155
00Stadium Club Souvenirs-SCS7
00Titanium Draft Day Edition-39
00Topps/OPC-214
Parallel-214
Game-Worn Sweaters-GWDM
00Topps Stars Game Gear-GGDM
00Upper Deck-64
Exclusives Tier 1-64
Exclusives Tier 2-64
00Upper Deck MVP-71
First Stars-71
Second Stars-71
Third Stars-71
00Upper Deck Vintage-131
00Vanguard Dual Game-Worn Jerseys-13
00Vanguard Dual Game-Worn Patches-13
01Atomic Jerseys-23
01Atomic Patches-23
01O-Pee-Chee-100
01O-Pee-Chee Heritage Parallel-100
01O-Pee-Chee Heritage Parallel Limited-100
01O-Pee-Chee Premier Parallel-100
01Pacific-147
01Pacific-410
Extreme LTD-147
Gold-410
Hobby LTD-147
Premiere Date-147
Retail LTD-147
01Pacific Arena Exclusives-147
01Pacific Arena Exclusives-410
01Parkhurst Jerseys-PJ36
01Parkhurst Sticks-PS43
01Stadium Club-53
Award Winners-53
Master Photos-53
Souvenirs-TDDM
01Topps-100
Heritage Parallel-100
Heritage Parallel Limited-100
OPC Parallel-100
01Topps Chrome-100
Refractors-100
Black Border Refractors-100
01Topps Reserve Emblems-DM
01Topps Reserve Jerseys-DM
01Topps Reserve Name Plates-DM
01Topps Reserve Numbers-DM
01Topps Reserve Patches-DM
01UD Stanley Cup Champs-62
01Upper Deck-64
Exclusives-64
01Upper Deck MVP-70
01Upper Deck Victory-128
Gold-128
01Upper Deck Vintage-94
02BAP First Edition-81
Jerseys-81
02BAP Memorabilia Stanley Cup Champions-SCC-11
02BAP Sig Series Auto Buybacks 1998-50
02BAP Sig Series Auto Buybacks 2000-92
02BAP Signature Series Gold-GS27
02BAP Ultimate Mem Dynasty Jerseys-5
02BAP Ultimate Mem Dynasty Emblems-5
02BAP Ultimate Mem Dynasty Numbers-5
02Pacific Complete-42
Red-42
02Topps Total-163
03ITG Action-221
03Parkhurst Original Six Detroit-21
Memorabilia-DM9
03Upper Deck-315
Canadian Exclusives-315
HG-315
Tough Customers-TC-6
UD Exclusives-315
03Upper Deck MVP-152
Gold Script-152
Silver Script-152
Canadian Exclusives-152
03Czech Stadion-543
05Beehive Signature Scrapbook-SSDM
05Black Diamond-13
Emerald-13
Gold-13
Onyx-13
Ruby-13
05Parkhurst-76
Facsimile Auto Parallel-76
True Colors-TCCGY
True Colors-TCCGY
05SP Game Used Auto Draft-AD-DM
05SP Game Used SIGnificance-DM
05SP Game Used SIGnificance Gold-S-DM
05UD Artifacts Auto Facts-AF-DM
05UD Artifacts Auto Facts Blue-AF-DM
05UD Artifacts Auto Facts Copper-AF-DM
05UD Artifacts Auto Facts Pewter-AF-DM
05UD Artifacts Auto Facts Silver-AF-DM
05Ultra-38
Gold-38
Ice-38
05Upper Deck Notable Numbers-N-DM
05Upper Deck Hockey Showcase-HS7
05Upper Deck Showcase Promos-HS7
05Upper Deck MVP-63
Gold-63
Platinum-63
ProSign-P-DM
06Flair Showcase Stitches-SSDM
06O-Pee-Chee-75
Rainbow-75
06Ultra Uniformity-UDM
06Ultra Uniformity Patches-UPDM
06Ultra Uniformity Autographed Jerseys-UADM
06Upper Deck-32
Exclusives Parallel-32
High Gloss Parallel-32
Masterpieces-32
McCaskill, Ted
72Los Angeles Sharks WHA-9
McCaughey, Brad
88ProCards IHL-80
92Phoenix Roadrunners-15
93Anaheim Bullfrogs RHI-12
94Anaheim Bullfrogs RHI-12
95Anaheim Bullfrogs RHI-3
96Alaska Gold Kings-9
96Anaheim Bullfrogs RHI-21
98Phoenix Mustangs-23
McCauley, Alex
98Sudbury Wolves-1
McCauley, Alyn
94Parkhurst SE-SE264
Gold-SE264
94Select-162
Gold-162
94SP-183
Die Cuts-183
94Classic Draft Prospects-DP5
95Donruss Elite World Juniors-18
95Slapshot-278
95SP-173
95Classic-53
95Classic-92
95Signature Rookies-47
Signatures-47
96Black Diamond-78
Gold-78
96Upper Deck Ice-129
97Be A Player-222
Autographs-222
Autographs Die-Cuts-222
Autographs Prismatic Die-Cuts-222
97Beehive-55
Authentic Autographs-55
Golden Portraits-55
97Black Diamond-128
Double Diamond-128
Triple Diamond-128
Quadruple Diamond-128
97Collector's Choice-299
97Crown Royale-130
Emerald Green-130
Ice Blue-130
Silver-130
97Donruss Elite-38
97Donruss Elite-117
Aspirations-38
Aspirations-117
Status-38
Status-117
97Donruss Preferred-153
Cut to the Chase-153
97Donruss Priority-181
97Donruss Priority-206
97Donruss Priority-220
Stamp of Approval-181
Stamp of Approval-206
Stamp of Approval-220
Direct Deposit-20
97Katch-141
Gold-141
Silver-141
97Leaf-152
Fractal Matrix-152
Fractal Matrix Die Cuts-152
97Pacific Dynagon-NNO
Copper-NNO
Dark Grey-NNO
Emerald Green-NNO
Ice Blue-NNO
Red-NNO
Silver-NNO
97Paramount-182
Copper-182
Dark Grey-182
Emerald Green-182
Ice Blue-182
Red-182
Silver-182
97Pinnacle-18
Artist's Proofs-18
Rink Collection-18
Press Plates Back Black-18
Press Plates Back Cyan-18
Press Plates Back Magenta-18
Press Plates Back Yellow-18
Press Plates Front Black-18
Press Plates Front Cyan-18
Press Plates Front Magenta-18
Press Plates Front Yellow-18
Certified Rookie Redemption-G
Certified Rookie Redemption Gold-G
Certified Rookie Redemption Mirror Gold-G
97Pinnacle Mint-28
Bronze-28
Gold Team-28
Silver Team-28
Coins Brass-28
Coins Brass Proofs-28
Coins Gold Plated-28
Coins Gold Plated Proofs-28
Coins Nickel Silver-28
Coins Nickel Silver Proofs-28
Coins Solid Gold-28
Coins Solid Silver-28
97Score-52
Artist's Proofs-52
Golden Blades-52
97Score Maple Leafs-17
Platinum-17
Premier-17
97SP Authentic-195
97Upper Deck-371
97Zenith-88
Z-Gold-88
Z-Silver-88
97Zenith 5 x 7-71
Silver Impulse-70
97Zenith Rookie Reign-11
97Bowman CHL-5
OPC-5
98Be A Player-138
Press Release-138
98BAP Gold-138
98BAP Autographs-138
98BAP Autographs Gold-138
98BAP Tampa Bay All Star Game-138
98OPC Chrome-79
Refractors-79
98Pacific-418
Ice Blue-418
Red-418
98Pacific Dynagon Ice-183
Blue-183
Red-183
98Pacific Omega-230
Red-230
Opening Day Issue-230
98SPx Finite-83
98SPx Finite-132
Radiance-83
Radiance-132
Spectrum-83
Spectrum-132
98Topps-79
O-Pee-Chee-79
98Topps Gold Label Class 1-79
Black-79
Black One of One-79
One of One-79
Red-79
Red One of One-79
98Topps Gold Label Class 2-79
98Topps Gold Label Class 2 Black-79
98Topps Gold Label Class 2 Black 1 of 1-79
98Topps Gold Label Class 2 One of One-79
98Topps Gold Label Class 2 Red-79
98Topps Gold Label Class 2 Red One of One-79
98Topps Gold Label Class 3-79
98Topps Gold Label Class 3 Black-79
98Topps Gold Label Class 3 Black 1 of 1-79
98Topps Gold Label Class 3 One of One-79
98Topps Gold Label Class 3 Red-79
98Topps Gold Label Class 3 Red One of One-79
98UD Choice-200
Prime Choice Reserve-200
Reserve-200
98UD3-8
98UD3-68
98UD3-128
Die-Cuts-8
Die-Cuts-68
Die-Cuts-128
98Upper Deck-185
Exclusives-185
Exclusives 1 of 1-185
Gold Reserve-185
98Upper Deck MVP-198
Gold Script-198
Silver Script-198
Super Script-198
ProSign-AM
99Maple Leafs Pizza Pizza-11
99Pacific-413
Copper-413
Emerald Green-413
Gold-413
Ice Blue-413
Premiere Date-413
Red-413
99Upper Deck MVP SC Edition-179
Gold Script-179
Silver Script-179
Super Script-179
00Upper Deck NHLPA-PA83
01BAP Signature Series-124
Autographs-124
Autographs Gold-124
02BAP First Edition-38
Jerseys-38
02BAP Memorabilia-38
Emerald-38
Ruby-38
Sapphire-38
NHL All-Star Game-38
NHL All-Star Game Blue-38
NHL All-Star Game Green-38
NHL All-Star Game Red-38
02BAP Memorabilia Toronto Fall Expo-38
02BAP Signature Series-36
Autographs-36
Autograph Buybacks 1998-138
Autograph Buybacks 2001-124
Autographs Gold-36
Golf-GS7
02Maple Leafs Platinum Collection-13
02NHL Power Play Stickers-129
02Pacific-364
Blue-364
Red-364
02Pacific Complete-31
Red-31
02Pacific Exclusive-160
02Pacific Heads-Up-115
Blue-115
Purple-115
Red-115
02Parkhurst-140
Bronze-140
Gold-140
Silver-140
02Topps Heritage-93
Chrome Parallel-93
02Topps Total-56
02Upper Deck-410
Exclusives-410
02Upper Deck Beckett UD Promos-410
02Upper Deck MVP-171
Gold-171
Classics-171
Golden Classics-171
02Upper Deck Vintage-242
03Bowman-65
Gold-65
03Bowman Chrome-65
Refractors-65
Gold Refractors-65
Xfractors-65
03Crown Royale-86
Blue-86
Retail-86
03ITG Action-492
03O-Pee-Chee-13
03OPC Blue-13
03OPC Gold-13
03OPC Red-13
03Pacific-297
Blue-297
Red-297
03Pacific Complete-3
Red-3
03Pacific Heads-Up-84
Hobby LTD-84
Retail LTD-84
03Sharks Postcards-10
03Topps-13
Blue-13
Gold-13
Red-13
03Topps C55-96
Minis-96
Minis American Back-96
Minis American Back Red-96
Minis Bazooka Back-96
Minis Brooklyn Back-96
Minis Hat Trick Back-96
Minis O Canada Back-96
Minis O Canada Back Red-96
Minis Stanley Cup Back-96
03Topps Pristine-27
Gold Refractor Die Cuts-27
Refractors-27
Press Plates Black-27
Press Plates Cyan-27
Press Plates Magenta-27
Press Plates Yellow-27
04Pacific-231
Blue-231
Red-231
04Upper Deck-144
Canadian Exclusives-144
HG Glossy Gold-144
HG Glossy Silver-144
05Be A Player Signatures-AM

05Be A Player Signatures Gold-AM
05Black Diamond-73
Emerald-73
Gold-73
Onyx-73
Ruby-73
05Panini Stickers-352
05Parkhurst-407
Facsimile Auto Parallel-407
05Upper Deck-159
HG Glossy-159
05Upper Deck MVP-321
Gold-321
Platinum-321
05Upper Deck Toronto Fall Expo-159
05Upper Deck Victory-165
Black-165
Gold-165
Silver-165

McCauley, Bill
92Quebec Pee-Wee Tournament-1879
93Detroit Jr. Red Wings-10
93Classic Four-Sport *-213
Gold-213
94Detroit Jr. Red Wings-12
95Slapshot Memorial Cup-86
96Providence Bruins-19
97Charlotte Checkers-20

McCauley, Dennis
04Sioux City Musketeers-16

McCauley, Wes
92Michigan State Spartans-16
93Knoxville Cherokees-9
94Muskegon Fury-15

McClanahan, Rob
80USA Olympic Team Mini Pics-5
80O-Pee-Chee-232
80Topps-232
81Swedish Semic Hockey VM Stickers-105
83NHL Key Tags-86
83O-Pee-Chee-251
83Puffy Stickers-20
84O-Pee-Chee-325
95Signature Rookies Miracle on Ice-19
95Signature Rookies Miracle on Ice-20
95Signature Rook Miracle on Ice Sigs-19
95Signature Rook Miracle on Ice Sigs-20
04UD Legendary Signatures-89
Miracle Men-USA3
Miracle Men Autographs-USA-RO

McCleary, Trent
907th Inn. Sketch WHL-50
917th Inn. Sketch WHL-190
93Thunder Bay Senators-5
95Bowman-135
All-Foil-135
95Parkhurst International-420
Emerald Ice-420
95Senators Team Issue-17
95Ultra-280
97Detroit Vipers-9
98Canadiens Team Issue-11
99O-Pee-Chee-212
99O-Pee-Chee Chrome-212
99O-Pee-Chee Chrome Refractors-212
99Topps/OPC-212
99Topps/OPC Chrome-212
Refractors-212

McClelland, Darwin
88Kamloops Blazers-18

McClelland, Kevin
83Oilers McDonald's-16
83Penguins Heinz Photos-18
84Oilers Red Rooster-24
84Oilers Team Issue-17
84O-Pee-Chee-253
85Oilers Red Rooster-24
85O-Pee-Chee Stickers-230
86Oilers Red Rooster-24
86Oilers Team Issue-24
86O-Pee-Chee Stickers-77
87Oilers Team Issue-24
87O-Pee-Chee-201
88Oilers Tenth Anniversary-109
88Oilers Team Issue-20
90O-Pee-Chee-389
90Score-287
Canadian-287
90Topps-389
Tiffany-389
91ProCards-344
92St. John's Maple Leafs-12
96Barrie Colts-15
97Barrie Colts-14
00St. John's Maple Leafs-17
01St. John's Maple Leafs-14
02Fleer Throwbacks-44
Gold-44
Platinum-44

McClement, Jay
99Brampton Battalion-17
00Brampton Battalion-16
00Brampton Battalion-31
00UD CHL Prospects-2
00UD CHL Prospects-96
01UD Prospects-8
Autographs-A-JM
Jersey Autographs-S-JM
Jerseys-J-JM
Jerseys-C-MS
Jerseys Gold-J-JM
Jerseys Gold-C-MS
03AHL Top Prospects-23
03Pacific AHL Prospects-98
Gold-98
03Worcester Ice Cats-17
04Worcester IceCats-12
04ITG Heroes and Prospects-33
Autographs-JM
04ITG Heroes/Prospects Toronto Expo '05-33
04ITG Heroes/Prospects Expo Heroes/Pros-33
05ITG Heroes/Prosp Toronto Expo Parallel -397
05Beehive-131
Beige -131
Blue -131
Gold-131
Red -131
Matte-131
Signature Scrapbook-SSJM
05Black Diamond-157
Emerald-157
Gold-157
Onyx-157
Ruby-157
05Blues Team Set-13
05Hot Prospects-213
Autographed Patch Variation-213
Autographed Patch Variation Gold-213
Red Hot-213
05Parkhurst-426
Facsimile Auto Parallel-426
True Colors-TCSTL
True Colors-TCSTL
05SP Authentic-185
Limited-185
Rarefied Rookies-RRJM
05SP Game Used-146
Autographs-146
Gold-146
Auto Draft-AD-MC
Rookie Exclusives-JM
Rookie Exclusives Silver-RE-JM
05SPx-135
Spectrum-135
Xcitement Rookies-XR-JM
Xcitement Rookies Gold-XR-JM
Xcitement Rookies Spectrum-XR-JM
05The Cup-182
Black Rainbow Rookies-182
Masterpiece Pressplates (Artifacts)-322
Masterpiece Pressplates (Bee Hive)-131
Masterpiece Pressplates (Black Diamond)-157
Masterpiece Pressplates (Ice)-166
Masterpiece Pressplates (Rookie Update)-248
Masterpiece Pressplates SPA Autos-185
Masterpiece Pressplates (SP Game Used)-146
Masterpiece Pressplates (SPx)-135
Masterpiece Pressplates (SPx)-135
Masterpiece Pressplates (Trilogy)-215
Masterpiece Pressplates Ult Coll-167
Masterpiece Pressplates (Victory)-256
Masterpiece Pressplates Autographs-182
Platinum Rookies-182
05UD Artifacts-322
05Ultimate Collection-167
Gold-167
Ultimate Debut Threads Jerseys-DTJJM
Ultimate Debut Threads Jerseys Autos-DAJJM
Ultimate Debut Threads Patches-DTPJM
Ultimate Debut Threads Patches Autos-DAPJM
05Ultra-243
Gold-243
Fresh Ink-FI-JM
Fresh Ink Blue-FI-JM
Ice-243
Rookie Uniformity Jerseys-RU-JM
Rookie Uniformity Jersey Autographs-ARU-JM
Rookie Uniformity Patches-RUP-JM
Rookie Uniformity Patch Autographs-ARP-JM
05Upper Deck-224
HG Glossy-224
Rookie Ink-RIJM
Rookie Threads-RTJM
Rookie Threads Autographs-ARTJM
05Upper Deck Ice-166
Fresh Ice-FIMC
Fresh Ice Glass-FIMC
Fresh Ice Glass Patches-FIPMC
Premieres Auto Patches-AIPJM
05Upper Deck Rookie Update-248
05Upper Deck Trilogy-215
05Upper Deck Toronto Fall Expo-224
05Upper Deck Victory-256
Black-256
Gold-256
Silver-256
05ITG Heroes and Prospects-397
06Flair Showcase Inks-IPA
06O-Pee-Chee-425
Rainbow-425
06Upper Deck-418
Exclusives Parallel-418
High Gloss Parallel-418
Masterpieces-418
07Upper Deck Victory-117
Black-117
Gold-117

McClennan, Don
90Knoxville Cherokees-111

McCloy, Aaron
03Lincoln Stars-24

McColgan, Gary
83Oshawa Generals-21
88ProCards IHL-37

McCollum, Thomas
06Between The Pipes Autographs-ATM
06Guelph Storm-1
06ITG Heroes and Prospects Net Prospects-NPR12

McComb, Dave
61Sudbury Wolves-14
62Sudbury Wolves-16

McConnell, Brian
03Boston University Terriers-8

McConnell, Don
87Sault Ste. Marie Greyhounds-10
89Niagara Falls Thunder-12
897th Inn. Sketch OHL-146
907th Inn. Sketch OHL-265

McConnell, Ryan
92Saskatchewan JHL-113

McConvey, D'Arcy
03Bowling Green Falcons-6
05ITG Heroes/Prosp Toronto Expo Parallel -356
05Idaho Steelheads-15
05ITG Heroes and Prospects-356
Autographs Series II-DMC
06Idaho Steelheads-8

McCooeye, Shane
93Quebec Pee-Wee Tournament-1148

McCool, Frank
45Quaker Oats Photos-33
03BAP Ultimate Mem Maple Leafs Forever-1
04ITG Franchises Canadian-99
06ITG Ultimate Memorabilia Paper Cuts Autos-10

McCord, Bob
52Juniors Blue Tint-130
63Topps-6
64Beehive Group III Photos-18
64Beehive Group III Photos-88
64Coca-Cola Caps-2
64Topps-10
65Topps-46
68O-Pee-Chee-146
68Shirriff Coins-73
69O-Pee-Chee-123
69Topps-123
70O-Pee-Chee-41
70Topps-41
72Blues White Border-10
94Parkhurst Tall Boys-10
95Parkhurst '66-67-43
Coins-43

McCormack, Brian
03SL Cloud State Huskies-19

McCormack, John
44Beehive Group II Photos-269
44Beehive Group II Photos-429
45Quaker Oats Photos-34
45Quaker Oats Photos-96A
45Quaker Oats Photos-96B
52Parkhurst-15
53Parkhurst-34
54Parkhurst-9

McCormick, Cam
02Florida Everblades-12
02Florida Everblades RBI-123

McCormick, Cody
00Belleville Bulls-7
01Belleville Bulls-16
01Belleville Bulls-28
02SPx Rookie Redemption-R197
02Belleville Bulls-12
03Black Diamond-163
Black-163
Green-163
Red-163
03Bowman-124
Gold-124
03Bowman Chrome-124
Refractors-124
Gold Refractors-124
Xfractors-124
03Crown Royale-111
Red-112
Retail-111
Retail-112
03ITG Action-612
03ITG Used Signature Series-198
Gold-198
03ITG VIP Rookie Debut-40
03Pacific Calder-110
Silver-110
03Pacific Complete-582
Red-582
03Pacific Heads-Up-109
Hobby LTD-109
Retail LTD-109
03Pacific Luxury Suite-59
Gold-59
03Pacific Supreme-113
Blue-113
Red-113
Retail-113
03Parkhurst Rookie-146
Rookie Emblems-RE-33
Rookie Emblems Gold-RE-33
Rookie Jerseys-RJ-33
Rookie Jerseys Gold-RJ-33
Rookie Numbers-RN-33
Rookie Numbers Gold-RN-33
03Private Stock Reserve-113
Blue-113
Red-113
Retail-113
03SP Authentic-95
Limited-95
03SP Game Used-59
Gold-59
03Titanium-111
Hobby Jersey Number Parallels-111
Retail-111
Retail Jersey Number Parallels-111
03Topps Traded-TT98
Blue-TT98
Gold-TT98
Red-TT98
03UD Honor Roll-150
03Upper Deck-211
Canadian Exclusives-211
HG-211
03Upper Deck Classic Portraits-188
03Upper Deck MVP-447
03Upper Deck Rookie Update-211
03Upper Deck Trilogy-148
Limited-148
04Hershey Bears Patriot News-19

McCormick, Eliott
03Brampton Batallion-13

McCormick, Joe
23V128-1 Paulin's Candy-43

McCormick, Mike
92Fort Worth Fire-13
93Fort Worth Fire-11
94Central Hockey League-28
97Fort Worth Brahmas-11

McCormick, Mike (OSU)
99Ohio State Buckeyes-11
00Ohio State Buckeyes-5
01Ohio State Buckeyes-11

McCormick, Morgan
98Kingston Frontenacs-12
99Guelph Storm-25
01Guelph Storm-20
01Guelph Storm Memorial Cup-21

McCosh, Shawn
88Niagara Falls Thunder-8
90ProCards AHL/IHL-436
91ProCards-390
92Phoenix Roadrunners-16
92Classic-111
Gold-111
92Classic Four-Sport *-217
Gold-217
94Binghamton Rangers-11
99German Adler Mannheim Eagles Postcards-5
99German DEL-6

McCosh, Shayne
90Kitchener Rangers-19
907th Inn. Sketch OHL-238
917th Inn. Sketch OHL-91
93Detroit Jr. Red Wings-20
93Windsor Spitfires-13
94Detroit Jr. Red Wings-22
95Slapshot Memorial Cup-96
99UK Sheffield Steelers-16
00UK Sekonda Superleague-145
00UK Sheffield Steelers-15
02German DEL City Press-15

McCourt, Dale
75Hamilton Fincups-12
78O-Pee-Chee-132
78Topps-132
79O-Pee-Chee-63
79Red Wings Postcards-12
79Topps-63
80O-Pee-Chee-245
80Topps-245
81O-Pee-Chee-86
81O-Pee-Chee-96
81O-Pee-Chee-105
81O-Pee-Chee Stickers-120
81Post Standups-4
81Sabres Milk Panels-17
81Topps-21
81Topps-51
81Topps-W129
82O-Pee-Chee-28
82O-Pee-Chee Stickers-119
82Post Cereal-2
82Sabres Milk Panels-14
82Topps Stickers-119
83NHL Key Tags-10
83O-Pee-Chee-66
83O-Pee-Chee Stickers-236
83Puffy Stickers-11
83Topps Stickers-236
83Vachon-93
84O-Pee-Chee Stickers-13
93Swiss HNL-135
98German DEL-131

McCourt, Danny
90Pro Set-693

McCourt, Mike
87Brockville Braves-5
88Brockville Braves-22
94Thunder Bay Senators-10
96Fort Worth Fire-16
99Muskegon Fury-17
99UHL All-Stars West-13T
00Fresno Falcons-11
01Fresno Falcons-10

McCoy, John
92North Dakota Fighting Sioux-19

McCoy, Mark
907th Inn. Sketch WHL-68
917th Inn. Sketch WHL-181
98UK Kingston Hawks-14

McCracken, Jake
96Sault Ste. Marie Greyhounds-11
96Sault Ste. Marie Greyhounds Autographed-11
97Upper Deck-400

McCrady, Scott
85Medicine Hat Tigers-10
88ProCards IHL-23
90ProCards AHL/IHL-614

McCrae, Justin
04Saskatoon Blades-3
05Saskatoon Blades-15
06Saskatoon Blades-17

McCready, Matt
05London Knights-12

McCreary, Bill
68O-Pee-Chee-182
69O-Pee-Chee-181
70Esso Power Players-247
71Blues Postcards-13
73Canucks Royal Bank-13

McCreary, Keith
68O-Pee-Chee-193A
68O-Pee-Chee-193B
68Shirriff Coins-144
69O-Pee-Chee-114
Four-in-One-12
Stamps-20
69Topps-114
70Colgate Stamps-34
70Dad's Cookies-80
70Esso Power Players-225
70O-Pee-Chee-93
70Sargent Promotions Stamps-168
70Topps-93
Topps/OPC Sticker Stamps-22
71O-Pee-Chee-188
71Penguins Postcards-12
71Sargent Promotions Stamps-174
71Toronto Sun-221
72Flames Postcards-9
72O-Pee-Chee-25
72Sargent Promotions Stamps-4
72Topps-27
73O-Pee-Chee-13
73Topps-13
74NHL Action Stamps-12
74O-Pee-Chee NHL-14
74O-Pee-Chee NHL-103
74Topps-14
74Topps-103
91Ultimate Original Six-98
French-98

McCreary, Mark
93Toledo Storm-15

McCreary, Ref
90Pro Set-694

McCreary, William
52Juniors Blue Tint-59

McCreedy, Johnny
34Beehive Group I Photos-337

McCrimmon, Brad
80O-Pee-Chee-354
81O-Pee-Chee-15
82O-Pee-Chee-255
82O-Pee-Chee Stickers-90
82Post Cereal-1
82Topps Stickers-90
83Flyers J.C. Penney-16
83NHL Key Tags-97
83O-Pee-Chee-270
83O-Pee-Chee Stickers-193
83Topps Stickers-193
84O-Pee-Chee-164
84Kelowna Wings-55
85Flyers Postcards-19
85O-Pee-Chee-158
85O-Pee-Chee Stickers-92
85Topps-158
86Flyers Postcards-16
86O-Pee-Chee-5
86O-Pee-Chee Stickers-247
86Topps-5
87Flames Red Rooster-13
87O-Pee-Chee-85
87O-Pee-Chee Minis-27
87O-Pee-Chee Stickers-99
87Panini Stickers-126
87Topps-85
88Flames Postcards-24
88O-Pee-Chee-178
88O-Pee-Chee Minis-24
88O-Pee-Chee Stickers-96
88O-Pee-Chee Stickers-120
88O-Pee-Chee Stickers-206
88Panini Stickers-6
88Panini Stickers-408
88Topps-178
88Topps Sticker Inserts-10
89O-Pee-Chee-203
89O-Pee-Chee Stickers-91
89Panini Stickers-33
89Swedish Semic World Champ Stickers-63
90O-Pee-Chee-320
90OPC Premier-69
90Panini Stickers-173
90Pro Set-39A
90Pro Set-39B
90Pro Set-438
90Score-184
Canadian-184
90Score Rookie/Traded-37T
90Topps-320
Tiffany-320
90Upper Deck-294
90Upper Deck-430
French-294
French-430
91Pro Set Platinum-170
91Bowman-48
91O-Pee-Chee-79
91Parkhurst-271
French-271
91Pinnacle-214
French-214
91Pro Set-377
91Pro Set-609
French-377
French-609
91Red Wings Little Caesars-12
91Score American-16
91Score Canadian Bilingual-16
91Score Canadian English-16
91Stadium Club-14
91Topps-79
92Bowman-67
92Pinnacle-124
French-124
92Score-141
Canadian-141
92Stadium Club-21
92Topps-301
Gold-301G
92Ultra-52
93Leaf-395
93OPC Premier-391
Gold-391
93Parkhurst-358
Emerald Ice-358
93Pinnacle-358
Canadian-358
93Score-54
93Score-527
Gold-527
Canadian-54
Canadian-527
Canadian Gold-527
93Topps/OPC Premier-391
Gold-391
93Whalers Coke-10
94Pinnacle-427
Artist's Proofs-427
Rink Collection-427
95Be A Player-51
Signatures-S51
Signatures Die Cuts-S51
95Whalers Bob's Stores-17
96Be A Player-168
Autographs-168
Autographs Silver-168
96Coyotes Coca-Cola-20
97Pacific Dynagon Best Kept Secrets-75
06Thrashers Postcards-4

McCrimmon, Kelly
88Brandon Wheat Kings-18
90Brandon Wheat Kings-7
907th Inn. Sketch WHL-214
917th Inn. Sketch WHL-216

McCrimmon, Mick
04Vernon Vipers-17

McCrimmon, Mickey
05Vernon Vipers-14

McCrone, Bernie
97UK Fife Flyers-2

McCrone, John
94Finnish Jaa Kiekko-313

McCrory, Scott
88ProCards AHL-46
89ProCards AHL-282
90ProCards AHL/IHL-275
95Houston Aeros-16
98German DEL-209
99German DEL-204

McCue, Matt
06Chilliwack Bruins-10

McCulloch, Dave
05Stockton Thunder-13

McCullough, Brian
00Richmond Renegades-19
01Quad-City Mallards-12
02ECHL All-Star Northern-28
02Reading Royals-24
02Reading Royals RBI Sports-177
03ECHL All-Stars-253
03Florida Everblades-16
03Florida Everblades RBI Sports-169
04Peoria Rivermen-5

McCullough, Dave
04Gwinnett Gladiators-18

McCullough, Scott
87Sudbury Wolves-18

McCullough, Zach
05Owen Sound Attack-14
06Owen Sound Attack-14
06Sudbury Wolves-19

McCune, Grant
97Prince Albert Raiders-14
98Prince Albert Raiders-16
99Kamloops Blazers-14
00Prince Albert Raiders-13
04Lakehead University Thunderwolves-18

McCusker, Don
91British Columbia JHL-123
92Northern Michigan Wildcats-19
93Northern Michigan Wildcats-22

McCusker, John
96OCN Blizzard-23
97OCN Blizzard-22
98OCN Blizzard-21

McCusker, Red
23V128-1 Paulin's Candy-24

McCutcheon, Darwin
86Moncton Golden Flames-8
88ProCards IHL-11
88Salt Lake Golden Eagles-13
98Rochester Americans-22

McCutcheon, David
98Halifax Mooseheads-11
98Halifax Mooseheads Second Edition-11

McCutcheon, Justin
00Kingston Frontenacs-12
01Kingston Frontenacs-13
03Saginaw Spirit-12

McCutcheon, Terry
90Richmond Renegades-11

McCutcheon, Warren
99Lethbridge Hurricanes-18
00Lethbridge Hurricanes-16

McCutheon, Jeff
92Saskatchewan JHL-60

McDade, Rory
98SP Authentic-128
Power Shift-128
Sign of the Times-RM
Sign of the Times Gold-RM
98Upper Deck-405
Exclusives-405
Exclusives 1 of 1-405
Gold Reserve-405
98Kelowna Rockets-17
99Kelowna Rockets-17
00Kelowna Rockets-2

McDermid, Jeff
02Owen Sound Attack-20

McDonagh, Bill
44Beehive Group II Photos-342

McDonald, Ab
44Beehive Group II Photos-121
58Parkhurst-30
59Parkhurst-20
60Parkhurst-56
60Parkhurst-60
60Shirriff Coins-72
60Topps-33
61Shirriff/Salada Coins-33
61Topps-27
62Topps-38
Hockey Bucks-15
63Topps-37
64Beehive Group III Photos-19
64Beehive Group III Photos-89
64Coca-Cola Caps-16
64Topps-16
65Coca-Cola-52
65Topps-50
68O-Pee-Chee-107
68O-Pee-Chee-180
68Shirriff Coins-158
68Topps-107
69O-Pee-Chee-18
69Topps-18
70Dad's Cookies-81
70Esso Power Players-250
70O-Pee-Chee-215
70Sargent Promotions Stamps-178
71Letraset Action Replays-6
71O-Pee-Chee-134
71Sargent Promotions Stamps-59
71Toronto Sun-99
72O-Pee-Chee-321
91Ultimate Original Six-60
French-60
92Blues UD Best of the Blues-8
94Parkhurst Tall Boys-14
95Parkhurst '66-67-50
Coins-50

McDonald, Alvin
44Beehive Group II Photos-270

McDonald, Andy
00SP Authentic-92
00SP Game Used-62
00UD Pros and Prospects-92
00Upper Deck Ice-103
01BAP Memorabilia-212
01BAP Memorabilia-397
Emerald-212
Emerald-397
Ruby-212
Ruby-397
Sapphire-212
Sapphire-397
01Parkhurst-352
01Titanium Draft Day Edition-102
01Upper Deck-4
Exclusives-4
01Cincinnati Mighty Ducks-14
02BAP First Edition-207
02BAP Signature Series-15
Autographs-15
Autographs Gold-15
Golf-GS8
02O-Pee-Chee-91
02O-Pee-Chee Premier Blue Parallel-91
02O-Pee-Chee Premier Red Parallel-91
02O-Pee-Chee Factory Set-91
02Pacific-6
Blue-6
Red-6
02Pacific Complete-272
Red-272
02SP Authentic-106
02Topps-91
OPC Blue Parallel-91
OPC Red Parallel-91
Factory Set-91
02Topps Total-48
02Upper Deck-5
Exclusives-5
02Upper Deck MVP-4
Gold-4
Classics-4
Golden Classics-4
02Upper Deck Vintage-8
03ITG Action-8
03Pacific Complete-174
Red-174
04Upper Deck-2
Canadian Exclusives-2
HG Glossy Gold-2
HG Glossy Silver-2
04German DEL-99
Superstars-SU10
04German Ingolstadt Panthers-16
05Ducks Team Issue-11
05Parkhurst-1
Facsimile Auto Parallel-1
05Upper Deck-4
HG Glossy-4
05Upper Deck MVP-9
Gold-9
Platinum-9
05Upper Deck Toronto Fall Expo-4
06Be A Player-84
Autographs-84
Signatures-MC
Signatures 25-91
Signatures Duals-DMK
Up Close and Personal-UC6
Up Close and Personal Autographs-UC6
06Flair Showcase Inks-IAM
06Fleer-2
Tiffany-2
06O-Pee-Chee-3
Rainbow-3
Autographs-A-AM
06Panini Stickers-188
06SP Game Used SIGnificance-SMD
06Ultra-3
Gold Medallion-3
Ice Medallion-3
06Upper Deck Arena Giveaways-ANA3
06Upper Deck-4
Exclusives Parallel-4
High Gloss Parallel-4
Masterpieces-4
06Upper Deck MVP-3
Gold Script-3
Super Script-3
Autographs-OAMK
06Upper Deck Victory-4
06Upper Deck Victory Black-4
06Upper Deck Victory Gold-4
07Upper Deck Ovation-49
07Upper Deck Victory-168
Black-168
Gold-168
Stars on Ice-SI20

McDonald, Bill
92Thunder Bay Thunder Hawks-2
95Central Hockey League-18
96Fort Worth Fire-18
97Fort Worth Brahmas-21
00Lubbock Cotton Kings-8
02New Mexico Scorpions-18
03New Mexico Scorpions-21

McDonald, Brad
93Quebec Pee-Wee Tournament-1191
04Huntsville Havoc-13

McDonald, Brent
95Red Deer Rebels-12
96Red Deer Rebels-9
97Red Deer Rebels-11
00Florida Everblades-18
01Florida Everblades-9
02Florida Everblades RBI-124
02Lowell Lock Monsters-11
03Florida Everblades-17

McDonald, Brett
98Red Deer Rebels-11

McDonald, Brian
91British Columbia JHL-131

McDonald, Bucko
34Beehive Group I Photos-115A
34Beehive Group I Photos-115B
34Beehive Group I Photos-334
37V356 Worldwide Gum-84
39O-Pee-Chee V301-1-13

McDonald, Dan
92Quebec Pee-Wee Tournament-1422
04Brampton Battalion-10

McDonald, Danny
93Quebec Pee-Wee Tournament-1585
01Plymouth Whalers-20
04Brampton Battalion-10

McDonald, David
01Regina Pats-14
02Regina Pats-18
03Regina Pats-9

McDonald, Dean
91Knoxville Cherokees-17

McDonald, Doug
94Classic Pro Prospects-211

McDonald, John
83Belleville Bulls-9

McDonald, Kevin
96Medicine Hat Tigers-11
97Medicine Hat Tigers-12
98Florida Everblades-14
04Colorado Eagles-12

McDonald, Lanny
73Maple Leafs Postcards-17
74Maple Leafs Postcards-12
74NHL Action Stamps-264
74O-Pee-Chee NHL-168
74Topps-168
75Heroes Stand-Ups-26
75Maple Leafs Postcards-12
75O-Pee-Chee NHL-23
75Topps-23
76Maple Leafs Postcards-9
76O-Pee-Chee NHL-348
77Maple Leafs Postcards-9
77O-Pee-Chee NHL-5
77O-Pee-Chee NHL-110
77Topps-5
77Topps-110
78Maple Leafs Postcards-13
78O-Pee-Chee-78
78Topps-78
79Maple Leafs Postcards-19
79O-Pee-Chee-153
79Rockies Team Issue-11
79Topps-153
80O-Pee-Chee-62
80O-Pee-Chee Super-5
80Topps-62
81Flames Postcards-12
81O-Pee-Chee-77
81O-Pee-Chee-85
81O-Pee-Chee Stickers-227
81Topps-50
81Topps-W82
82Flames Dollars-3
82O-Pee-Chee-38
82O-Pee-Chee-51
82O-Pee-Chee-52
82O-Pee-Chee Stickers-214
82Post Cereal-3
82Topps Stickers-214
83Esso-12
83NHL Key Tags-18
83O-Pee-Chee-74
83O-Pee-Chee-75
83O-Pee-Chee-87
83O-Pee-Chee-208
83O-Pee-Chee Stickers-8
83O-Pee-Chee Stickers-162
83O-Pee-Chee Stickers-263
83O-Pee-Chee Stickers-303
83Puffy Stickers-6
83Topps Stickers-8
83Topps Stickers-162
83Topps Stickers-263
83Topps Stickers-303
83Vachon-13
84Kellogg's Accordion Discs-4
84Kellogg's Accordion Discs Singles-25
84O-Pee-Chee-231
84O-Pee-Chee Stickers-237
84O-Pee-Chee Stickers-238
847-Eleven Discs-6
84Topps-26
85Flames Red Rooster-14
85Flames Red Rooster-15
85O-Pee-Chee-1
85O-Pee-Chee Stickers-215
857-Eleven Credit Cards-3
85Topps-1
86Flames Red Rooster-13
86Flames Red Rooster-14
86Kraft Drawings-41
86O-Pee-Chee-8
86O-Pee-Chee Box Bottoms-J
86O-Pee-Chee Stickers-80
86Topps-8
86Topps Box Bottoms-J
87Flames Red Rooster-14
87Flames Red Rooster-15
87O-Pee-Chee-20
87O-Pee-Chee Stickers-43
87Panini Stickers-215
87Topps-20
88Esso All-Stars-29
88Flames Postcards-20
88O-Pee-Chee-234
88O-Pee-Chee Stickers-85
88Panini Stickers-10
89O-Pee-Chee-7
89O-Pee-Chee Stickers-92
89Panini Stickers-39
89Topps-7
90Upper Deck-508
French-508
92Future Trends '76 Canada Cup-174
92Hall of Fame Legends-34
93Upper Deck Locker All-Stars-45
94Hockey Wit-85
94Zeller's Masters of Hockey-5
94Zeller's Masters of Hockey Signed-5
97Flames Collector's Photos-13
99BAP Memorabilia AS Canadian Hobby-CH6
99BAP Memorabilia AS Cdn Hobby Autos-CH6
99Topps Stanley Cup Heroes-SC5
99Topps Stanley Cup Heroes Refractors-SC5
99Topps Stanley Cup Heroes Autographs-SCA5
99Upper Deck Retro-95
Gold-95
Platinum-95
Distant Replay-DR13
Distant Replay Level 2-DR13
Inkredible-LM
Inkredible Level 2-LM
00Upper Deck 500 Goal Club-500LM
00Upper Deck 500 Goal Club-500LM
00Upper Deck Legends-19
Legendary Collection Bronze-19
Legendary Collection Gold-19
Legendary Collection Silver-19
Epic Signatures-LM
01BAP Memorabilia 500 Goal Scorers-GS27
01BAP Signature Series 500 Goal Scorers-23
01BAP Sig Series 500 Goal Scorers Autos-23
01BAP Signature Series Vintage Autographs-VA-39
01BAP Ultimate Mem All-Star History-30
01BAP Ultimate Memorabilia Cornerstones-1
01BAP Ultimate Mem 500 Goal Scorers-18
01BAP Ultimate Mem 500 Goal Scorers Autos-12
01BAP Ultimate Mem 500 Goal Jerseys/Stick-18
01BAP Ultimate Mem 500 Goal Emblems-18
01BAP Ultimate Memorabilia Retro Trophies-8
01Fleer Legacy-58
Ultimate-58
In the Corners-5
01Greats of the Game-53
Autographs-53
01Parkhurst Autographs-PA19
01Parkhurst 500 Goal Scorers-PGS27
01Parkhurst Sticks-PS65
01UD Stanley Cup Champs Pieces of Glory-G-LM
01Upper Deck Legends-9
Milestones-MLM
Milestones Platinum-MLM
02BAP NHL All-Star History-30
02BAP Ultimate Mem Retro Teammates-1
02BAP Ultimate Memorabilia Retro Trophies-17
02BAP Ultimate Mem Vintage Jerseys-24
02Fleer Throwbacks-20
Gold-20
Platinum-20
02Maple Leafs Platinum Collection-59
02Maple Leafs Platinum Collection-78
Autographs-78
02Parkhurst Vintage Teammates-VT20
02UD Foundations 1000 Point Club-MC
02UD Foundations Signs of Greatness-SGLM
03BAP Ultimate Mem Retro Teammates-9
03BAP Ultimate Memorabilia Triple Threads-28
03BAP Ultimate Mem Vintage Jerseys-32
03BAP Ultimate Mem Vintage Jerseys Gold-32
03ITG Toronto Fall Expo Forever Rivals-FR5
03Parkhurst Orig Six He Shoots/Scores-3
03Parkhurst Orig Six He Shoots/Scores-3A
03Parkhurst Original Six Toronto-64
Inserts-T17
Memorabilia-TM30
Memorabilia-TM53
03Parkhurst Rookie Jerseys-GJ-43
03Parkhurst Rookie Jerseys Gold-GJ-43
03SP Authentic Sign of the Times-LM
03SP Authentic Sign of the Times-IM
03SP Game Used Limited Threads-LTLM
03SPx-106
Radiance-106
Spectrum-106
03Upper Deck Trilogy-13
03Upper Deck Trilogy-133
Crest Variations-133
Limited-13
Limited-133
Scripts-S3LM
Scripts Limited-S3LM
Scripts Red-S3LM
04ITG NHL AS FANtasy AS History Jerseys-SB30
04ITG Franchises Canadian-13
04ITG Franchises Canadian-100
Autographs-LM2
Autographs-LM3
Barn Burners-BB1
Barn Burners Gold-BB1
Forever Rivals-FR10
Forever Rivals Gold-FR10
Memorabilia-SM9
Memorabilia Autographs-SM9

Memorabilia Gold-SM9
Original Sticks-OS4
Original Sticks Autographs-OS4
Original Sticks Gold-OS4
Teammates-TM5
Teammates Gold-TM5
04ITG Franchises He Shoots/Scores Prizes-15
04ITG Franchises US West-190
Autographs-A-LM1
04ITG Ultimate Memorabilia-117
04ITG Ultimate Memorabilia-193
Gold-117
Gold-193
Country of Origin-12
Country of Origin Gold-12
Jersey Autographs-37
Jersey Autographs Gold-37
Original Six-18
Original Six-19
Retro Teammates-4
04MasterCard Priceless Moments-5
04SP Authentic Buybacks-103
04SP Authentic Buybacks-104
04SP Authentic Sign of the Times-ST-LM
04UD Legendary Signatures-53
Autographs-LM
Linemates-ETDSLM
04UD Legends Classics-36
Gold-36
Platinum-36
Silver-36
Signature Moments-M19
Signatures-CS19
04ITG Heroes and Prospects-162
Autographs-LM
04ITG Heroes/Prospects Toronto Expo '05-162
04ITG Heroes/Prospects Expo Heroes/Pros-162
05Beehive-231
Signature Scrapbook-SSLM
05ITG Ultimate Memorabilia Level 1-61
05ITG Ultimate Memorabilia Level 2-61
05ITG Ultimate Memorabilia Level 3-61
05ITG Ultimate Memorabilia Level 4-61
05ITG Ultimate Memorabilia Level 5-61
05ITG Ultimate Mem Complete Jersey-25
05ITG Ultimate Mem Complete Jersey Gold-25
05ITG Ultimate Mem Double Mem Autos-14
05ITG Ultimate Mem Double Mem Autos Gold-14
05ITG Ultimate Memorabilia Emblems-29
05ITG Ultimate Memorabilia Emblems Gold-29
05ITG Ultimate Memorabilia In The Numbers-11
05ITG Ultimate Mem In The Numbers Gold-11
05ITG Ultimate Mem Jersey and Emblem-15
05ITG Ultimate Mem Jersey Autos-34
05ITG Ultimate Mem Jersey Autos Gold-34
05ITG Ultimate Mem Jersey Emblems Gold-15
05ITG Ultimate Memorabilia Jerseys-22
05ITG Ultimate Memorabilia Jerseys Gold-22
05ITG Ultimate Mem Raised to the Rafters-13
05ITG Ultimate Mem Raised Rafters Gold-13
05ITG Ultimate Mem Seams Unbelievable-14
05ITG Ultimate Mem Seam Unbelievable Gold-14
05ITG Ultimate Memorabilia Stick Autos-39
05ITG Ultimate Mem Stick Autos Gold-39
05ITG Ultimate Mem Sticks and Jerseys-15
05ITG Ultimate Mem Stick and Jerseys Gold-15
05ITG Ultimate Mem 3 Star of the Game Jsy-17
05ITG Ult Mem 3 Star of the Game Jsy Gold-17
05ITG Ultimate Memorabilia Triple Autos-6
05ITG Ultimate Mem Triple Autos Gold-6
05SP Authentic Sign of the Times Fives-SMSMK
05SP Authentic Six Star Signatures-SSTO
05SP Game Used Heritage Classic-HC-MC
05SP Game Used Heritage Classic Autos-HCA-MC
05SP Game Used Heritage Classic Patches-HCP-MC
05SP GameUsed Heritage Classic Patch Auto-HAP-MC
05SP Game Used Oldtimer's Challenge-OC-MC
05SP Game Used Oldtimer's Challenge Autos-OCA-MC
05SP Game Used Oldtimer's Challenge Patch-OCP-MC
05SP Game Used Oldtime Chall Patch Autoa-OAP-MC
05SPx-127
Spectrum-127
Xcitement Legends-XL-LM
Xcitement Legends Gold-XL-LM
Xcitement Legends Spectrum-XL-LM
05The Cup-18
Gold-18
Black Rainbow-18
Emblems of Endorsement-EEMU
Hardware Heroes-HHLM1
Hardware Heroes-HHLM2
Honorable Numbers-HNMC
Limited Logos-LLLM
Masterpiece Pressplates-18
Noble Numbers-NNHM
Noble Numbers-NNMM
Noble Numbers Dual-DNNMM
Noble Numbers Dual-DNNMS
Patch Variation-P18
Patch Variation Autographs-AP18
Scripted Numbers-SNHM
Scripted Numbers-SNMM
Scripted Numbers Dual-DSNCA
Scripted Swatches-SSMC
Signature Patches-SPLM
Stanley Cup Titlists-TMC
05UD Artifacts-133
Blue-133
Gold-133
Green-133
Pewter-133
Red-133
Gold Autographed-133
05Ultimate Collection Endorsed Emblems-EELM
05Ultimate Coll Ultimate Sigs Pairings-UPMM
05Upper Deck All-Time Greatest-10
05Upper Deck Patches-P-LM
05Upper Deck Trilogy Legendary Scripts-LEG-LM
05Upper Deck Trilogy Personal Scripts-PER-LM
05ITG Heroes and Prospects Hero Mem-HM-43
05ITG Heroes and Prospects National Pride-NPR-24
06ITG International Ice-144
Gold-144
Autographs-ALMC
Teammates-IT03
Teammates Gold-IT03
06ITG Ultimate Memorabilia-86
Artist Proof-86
Autos-23
Autos Gold-23
Captain-C-7
Captain-C Gold-7
Emblems-14
Emblems Gold-14
Jerseys Autos-37
Jerseys Autos Gold-37
Retro Teammates-14
Retro Teammates Gold-14
Stick Rack-22
Stick Rack Gold-22
06SPx-125
Spectrum-125
SPxcitement-X14
SPxcitement Spectrum-X14
Winning Materials-WMLM
Winning Materials Spectrum-WMLM
06The Cup Autographed Foundations-CQLM
06The Cup Autographed Foundations Patches-CQLM
06The Cup Foundations-CQLM
06The Cup Honorable Numbers-HNLM
06The Cup Limited Logos-LLLM
06The Cup Scripted Swatches Duals-DSMM
06The Cup Signature Patches-SPLM
06UD Artifacts-122
Blue-122
Gold-122
Platinum-122
Radiance-122
Red-122
Frozen Artifacts-FALM
Frozen Artifacts Black-FALM
Frozen Artifacts Blue-FALM
Frozen Artifacts Gold-FALM
Frozen Artifacts Platinum-FALM
Frozen Artifacts Red-FALM
Frozen Artifacts Patches Black-FALM
Frozen Artifacts Patches Blue-FALM
Frozen Artifacts Patches Gold-FALM
Frozen Artifacts Patches Platinum-FALM
Frozen Artifacts Patches Red-FALM
Tundra Tandems-TTME
Tundra Tandems-TTMM
Tundra Tandems Black-TTME
Tundra Tandems Black-TTMM
Tundra Tandems Blue-TTME
Tundra Tandems Blue-TTMM
Tundra Tandems Gold-TTME
Tundra Tandems Gold-TTMM
Tundra Tandems Platinum-TTME
Tundra Tandems Platinum-TTMM
Tundra Tandems Red-TTME
Tundra Tandems Red-TTMM
Tundra Tandems Dual Patches Red-TTME
Tundra Tandems Dual Patches Red-TTMM
06Ultimate Collection Autographed Jerseys-AJ-LM
06Ultimate Collection Autographed Patches-AJ-LM
06Ultimate Collection Jerseys-UJ-LM
06Ultimate Collection Jerseys Dual-UJ2-ME
06Ultimate Collection Patches-UJ-LM
06Ultimate Collection Patches Dual-UJ2-ME
06Ultimate Collection Premium Patches-PS-LM
06Ultimate Collection Premium Swatches-PS-LM
06Upper Deck Game Jerseys-J2LA
06Upper Deck Game Patches-P2LA
06Upper Deck Trilogy Combo Clearcut Autographs-C2MM
06Upper Deck Trilogy Combo Clearcut Autographs-C3MSS
06Upper Deck Trilogy Honorary Scripted Patches-HSPLM
06Upper Deck Trilogy Honorary Scripted Swatches-HSSLM
06Upper Deck Trilogy Honorary Swatches-HSLM

McDonald, Nolan
97Fort Worth Brahmas-12
99German Bundesliga 2-137
01Columbus Cottonmouths-15

McDonald, Randy
74Sioux City Musketeers-10

McDonald, Reid
90Michigan Tech Huskies-15
91Michigan Tech Huskies-13

McDonald, Ronald
83Oshawa Generals-24

McDonald, Ryan
04Regina Pats-12
05Regina Pats-26
06Regina Pats-13

McDonald, Walker
95Slapshot-46
96Barrie Colts-16
97Barrie Colts-15
98Kingston Frontenacs-13
98Wichita Thunder-15
99Wichita Thunder-14
00Lubbock Cotton Kings-17
02Charlotte Checkers-87
03New Mexico Scorpions-20

McDonell, Kacey
99Cornwall Colts-5

McDonell, Kent
96Guelph Storm-11
97Guelph Storm-14
98Guelph Storm-12
99Guelph Storm-12
99Bowman CHL-149
Gold-149
OPC International-149
01Syracuse Crunch-19
02Syracuse Crunch-16
02Syracuse Crunch Sheets-3
03ITG Action-149
03O-Pee-Chee-312
03OPC Blue-312
03OPC Gold-312
03OPC Red-312
03Pacific-95
Blue-95
Red-95
03Pacific Complete-526
Red-526
03Pacific Exhibit-43
Blue Backs-43
Yellow Backs-43
03Pacific Invincible-109
Blue-109
Red-109
Retail-109
03Pacific Luxury Suite-61
Gold-61
03Pacific Prism-30
Blue-30
Gold-30
Red-30
03Pacific Supreme-115
Blue-115
Red-115
Retail-115
03Parkhurst Rookie-62
03Private Stock Reserve-115
Blue-115
Red-115
Retail-115
03Titanium-113
Hobby Jersey Number Parallels-113
Retail-113
Retail Jersey Number Parallels-113
03Topps-312
Blue-312
Gold-312
Red-312
03Topps C55-137
Minis-137
Minis American Back-137
Minis American Back Red-137
Minis Bazooka Back-137
Minis Brooklyn Back-137
Minis Hat Trick Back-137
Minis O Canada Back-137
Minis O Canada Back Red-137
Minis Stanley Cup Back-137
03UD Honor Roll-155
03Upper Deck Classic Portraits-164
03Upper Deck MVP-126
Gold Script-126
Silver Script-126
Canadian Exclusives-126
03Upper Deck Victory-55
Bronze-55
Gold-55
Silver-55
03Syracuse Crunch-17

McDonnell, Joe
83Moncton Alpines-7
86Kitchener Rangers-30
87Kitchener Rangers-4
88Kitchener Rangers-4
89Kitchener Rangers-4
90Kitchener Rangers-3
907th Inn. Sketch OHL-248
907th Inn. Sketch Memorial Cup-26
917th Inn. Sketch OHL-97
93Kitchener Rangers-27

McDonough, Al
71O-Pee-Chee-150
71Toronto Sun-121
72O-Pee-Chee-235
73O-Pee-Chee-89
73Topps-176
75O-Pee-Chee WHA-33
76O-Pee-Chee WHA-77

McDonough, Brian
93Quebec Pee-Wee Tournament-1469

McDonough, Hubie
88ProCards AHL-195
89New Haven Nighthawks-8
90Bowman-120
Tiffany-120
90O-Pee-Chee-366
90Panini Stickers-92
90Pro Set-188
90Score-222
Canadian-222
90Topps-366
Tiffany-366
90Upper Deck-226
French-226
91Bowman-214
91O-Pee-Chee-389
91Score Canadian Bilingual-450
91Score Canadian English-450
91Stadium Club-260
91Topps-389
91Upper Deck-138
French-138
91ProCards-473
92Stadium Club-335
92San Diego Gulls-18
93San Diego Gulls-14
95Images-29
Gold-29
96Collector's Edge Ice QuantumMotion-5
98Orlando Solar Bears-5
98Orlando Solar Bears II-6

McDonough, Kyle
92Norwegian Elite Series-142

McDonough, Ryan
04Sudbury Wolves-16
05Saginaw Spirit-16
06Saginaw Spirit-22

McDougall, Bill
90ProCards AHL/IHL-481
91ProCards-133
93Donruss-323
93Leaf-379
93Parkhurst-463
Emerald Ice-463
93Ultra-426
93Upper Deck-324
93Atlanta Knights-10
93Classic Four-Sport *-242
Gold-242
96Swiss HNL-68
98Swiss Power Play Stickers-117
99German DEL-330

McDougall, Kevin
89Windsor Spitfires-10
907th Inn. Sketch OHL-289

McDougall, Terry
99Fort Wayne Komets Points Leaders-4

McDougall, Tom
51Bas Du Fleuve-20
51Laval Dairy QSHL-45
52St. Lawrence Sales-84

McDowell, Dave
90ProCards AHL/IHL-413

McDuffe, Peter
71O-Pee-Chee-225
71Toronto Sun-240
74NHL Action Stamps-292
74O-Pee-Chee NHL-173
74Topps-173
75O-Pee-Chee NHL-256
75Topps-256

McEachen, Tim
97Moose Jaw Warriors-9

McEachern, Shawn
91Parkhurst-355
French-355
92Bowman-415
92O-Pee-Chee-359
92OPC Premier-94
92Panini Stickers-222
92Panini Stickers French-222
92Parkhurst-142
Emerald Ice-142
92Penguins Coke/Clark-12
92Penguins Foodland-9
92Penguins Foodland Coupon Stickers-6
92Pinnacle-420
French-420
92Pro Set-237
92Score-459
Canadian-459
92Stadium Club-205
92Topps-481
Gold-481G
92Ultra-379
92Upper Deck-368
92Upper Deck-412
92Upper Deck-565
92Upper Deck-634
Calder Candidates-CC14
Gordie Howe Selects-G17
93Donruss-154
93Donruss-473
93Leaf-217
Gold Rookies-7
93OPC Premier-123
93OPC Premier-353
Gold-123
Gold-353
93Panini Stickers-84
93Parkhurst-242
93Parkhurst-364
Emerald Ice-242
Emerald Ice-364
93Pinnacle-105
Canadian-105
Team 2001-9
Team 2001 Canadian-9
93PowerPlay-119
Second Year Stars-7
93Score-67
93Score-497
Gold-497
Canadian-67
Canadian-497
Canadian Gold-497
93Seasons Patches-11
93Stadium Club-189
Members Only Master Set-189
OPC-189
First Day Issue-189
First Day Issue OPC-189
93Topps/OPC Premier-123
93Topps/OPC Premier-353
Gold-123
Gold-353
93Topps Premier Black Gold-4
93Ultra-133
93Ultra-345
93Upper Deck-454
SP-72
94Be A Player-R75
Signature Cards-101
94Canada Games NHL POGS-186
94Donruss-95
94Flair-136
94Fleer-164
94Leaf-232
94OPC Premier-354
Special Effects-354
94Parkhurst-173
Gold-173
94Penguins Foodland-3
94Pinnacle-127
Artist's Proofs-127
Rink Collection-127
94Score-108
Gold-108
Platinum-108
94Stadium Club-211
Members Only Master Set-211
First Day Issue-211
Super Team Winner Cards-211
94Topps/OPC Premier-354
Special Effects-354
94Ultra-166
94Upper Deck-163
Electric Ice-163
94Finnish SISU-348
94Finnish SISU Guest Specials-4
95Collector's Choice-145
Player's Club-145
Player's Club Platinum-145
95Donruss-373
95Finest-91
Refractors-91
95Metal-8
95Parkhurst International-280
Emerald Ice-280
95Score-81
Black Ice Artist's Proofs-81
Black Ice-81
95SP-10
95Stadium Club-83
Members Only Master Set-83
95Summit-155
Artist's Proofs-155
Ice-155
95Topps-321
OPC Inserts-321
95Ultra-205
95Upper Deck-360
Electric Ice-360
Electric Ice Gold-360
Special Edition-SE95
Special Edition Gold-SE95
96Be A Player-119
96Be A Player-P119
Autographs-119
Autographs Silver-119
96Collector's Choice-20
96Donruss-190
Press Proofs-190
96Leaf-9
Press Proofs-9
96Score-151
Artist's Proofs-151
Dealer's Choice Artist's Proofs-151
Special Artist's Proofs-151
Golden Blades-151
96Senators Pizza Hut-14
97Collector's Choice-180
97Crown Royale-91
Emerald Green-91
Ice Blue-91
Silver-91
97Pacific-224
Copper-224
Emerald Green-224
Ice Blue-224
Red-224
Silver-224
97Pacific Omega-156
Copper-156
Dark Gray-156
Emerald Green-156
Gold-156
Ice Blue-156
97Revolution-93
Copper-93
Emerald-93
Ice Blue-93
Silver-93
97SP Authentic-110
98Aurora-131
98Be A Player-248
Press Release-248
98BAP Gold-248
98BAP Autographs-248
98BAP Autographs Gold-248
98Crown Royale-94
Limited Series-94
98Pacific-313
Ice Blue-313
Red-313
98Pacific Dynagon Ice-128
Blue-128
Red-128
98Pacific Omega-166
Red-166
Opening Day Issue-166
98Paramount-164
Copper-164
Emerald Green-164
Holo-Electric-164
Ice Blue-164
Silver-164
98Revolution-100
Ice Shadow-100
Red-100
98Senators Team Issue-13
98UD Choice-138
Prime Choice Reserve-138
Reserve-138
98Upper Deck-142
Exclusives-142
Exclusives 1 of 1-142
Gold Reserve-142
98Upper Deck MVP-143
Gold Script-143
Silver Script-143
Super Script-143
99Aurora-100
Premiere Date-100
99BAP Memorabilia-108
Gold-108
Silver-108
99BAP Millennium-176
Emerald-176
Ruby-176
Sapphire-176
Signatures-176
Signatures Gold-176
99Pacific-291
Copper-291
Emerald Green-291
Gold-291
Ice Blue-291
Premiere Date-291
Red-291
99Pacific Omega-161
Copper-161
Gold-161
Ice Blue-161
Premiere Date-161
99Pacific Prism-97
Holographic Blue-97
Holographic Gold-97
Holographic Mirror-97
Holographic Purple-97
Premiere Date-97
99Panini Stickers-113
99Paramount-163
Copper-163
Emerald-163
Gold-163
Holographic Emerald-163
Holographic Gold-163
Holographic Silver-163
Ice Blue-163
Premiere Date-163
Red-163
Silver-163
99Revolution-103
Premiere Date-103
Red-103
Shadow Series-103
Copper-103
Gold-103
CSC Silver-103
99Senators Team Issue-13
99Upper Deck-93
Exclusives-93
Exclusives 1 of 1-93
99Upper Deck Gold Reserve-93
99Upper Deck MVP-145
Gold Script-145
Silver Script-145
Super Script-145
99Upper Deck Victory-202
00Aurora-102
Premiere Date-102
00BAP Memorabilia-148
Emerald-148
Ruby-148
Sapphire-148
Promos-148
00BAP Mem Chicago Sportsfest Copper-148
00BAP Memorabilia Chicago Sportsfest Blue-148
00BAP Memorabilia Chicago Sportsfest Gold-148
00BAP Memorabilia Chicago Sportsfest Ruby-148
00BAP Memorabilia Chicago Sun-Times Ruby-148
00BAP Memorabilia Chicago Sun-Times Gold-148
00BAP Mem Chicago Sun-Times Sapphire-148
00BAP Mem Toronto Fall Expo Copper-148
00BAP Memorabilia Toronto Fall Expo Gold-148
00BAP Memorabilia Toronto Fall Expo Ruby-148
00BAP Parkhurst 2000-P120
00BAP Signature Series-149
Emerald-149
Ruby-149
Sapphire-149
00O-Pee-Chee-160
00O-Pee-Chee Parallel-160
00Pacific-283
Copper-283
Gold-283
Ice Blue-283
Premiere Date-283
00Panini Stickers-71
00Paramount-175
Copper-175
Gold-175
Holo-Gold-175
Holo-Silver-175
Ice Blue-175
Premiere Date-175
00Revolution-105
Blue-105
Premiere Date-105
Red-105
00Senators Team Issue-12
00Stadium Club-80
00Topps/OPC-160
Parallel-160
00Upper Deck-125
Exclusives Tier 1-125
Exclusives Tier 2-125
00Upper Deck MVP-128
First Stars-128
Second Stars-128
Third Stars-128
00Upper Deck Victory-161
00Upper Deck Vintage-254
01BAP Memorabilia-81
Emerald-81
Ruby-81
Sapphire-81
01BAP Signature Series-45
Autographs-45
Autographs Gold-45
01O-Pee-Chee-206
01O-Pee-Chee Premier Parallel-206
01Pacific-276
Extreme LTD-276
Hobby LTD-276
Premiere Date-276
Retail LTD-276
01Pacific Adrenaline-136
Blue-136
Premiere Date-136
Red-136
Retail-136
01Pacific Arena Exclusives-276
01Parkhurst-120
01Senators Team Issue-16
01Topps-206
OPC Parallel-206
Reserve Emblems-SM
Reserve Jerseys-SM
Reserve Name Plates-SM
Reserve Numbers-SM
Reserve Patches-SM
01Upper Deck-350
Exclusives-350
01Upper Deck MVP-132
01Upper Deck Victory-243
Gold-243
01Upper Deck Vintage-180
02BAP First Edition-125
Jerseys-125
02BAP Signature Series-79
Autographs-79
Autograph Buybacks 1998-248
Autograph Buybacks 1999-176
Autograph Buybacks 2001-45
Autographs Gold-79
02Pacific-270
Blue-270
Red-270
02Pacific Complete-324
Red-324
02Topps Heritage-171
02Topps Total-71
02UD Honor Roll-72
02Upper Deck-256
Exclusives-256
02Upper Deck Beckett UD Promos-256
03ITG Action-86
03NHL Sticker Collection-9
03O-Pee-Chee-122
03OPC Blue-122
03OPC Gold-122
03OPC Red-122
03Pacific-18
Blue-18
Red-18
03Pacific Complete-198
Red-198
03Pacific Heads-Up-5
Hobby LTD-5
Retail LTD-5
03Thrashers Postcards-13
03Topps-122
Blue-122
Gold-122
Red-122
03Upper Deck-12
Canadian Exclusives-12
HG-12
03Upper Deck MVP-21
Gold Script-21
Silver Script-21
Canadian Exclusives-21
04Pacific-13
Blue-13
Red-13
05Be A Player Signatures-SH
05Be A Player Signatures Gold-SH
05Black Diamond-4
Emerald-4
Gold-4
Onyx-4
Ruby-4
05Panini Stickers-29
05Ultra-22
Gold-22
Ice-22
05Upper Deck MVP-33
Gold-33
Platinum-33
05Upper Deck Victory-10
Black-10
Gold-10
Silver-10

McEachran, Sean
98Thunder Bay Thunder Cats-21

McElhinney, Curtis
05ITG Heroes/Prosp Toronto Expo Parallel -249
05ITG Heroes and Prospects-249
Autographs Series II-CME
06Between The Pipes-11
Autographs-ACM
Emblems-GUE26
Emblems Gold-GUE26
Emblems Autographs-GUE26
Jerseys-GUJ26
Jerseys Gold-GUJ26
Jerseys Autographs-GUJ26
Numbers-GUN26
Numbers Gold-GUN26
Numbers Autographs-GUN26
Prospect Trios-PT05
Prospect Trios Gold-PT05
06AHL Top Prospects-31
06ITG Heroes and Prospects Jerseys-GUJ07
06ITG Heroes and Prospects Jerseys Gold-GUJ07
06ITG Heroes and Prospects Emblems-GUE07
06ITG Heroes and Prospects Emblems Gold-GUE07
06ITG Heroes and Prospects Numbers-GUN07
06ITG Heroes and Prospects Numbers Gold-GUN07

McElhinney, Spencer
06Okotoks Oilers-11

McElmury, Jim
72Finnish Semic World Championship-119
72Swedish Semic World Championship-119
75O-Pee-Chee NHL-14
75Topps-14
77O-Pee-Chee NHL-352

McElroy, Joey
03Wisconsin Badgers-22

McElroy, T.J.
01Lincoln Stars-18
03St. Cloud State Huskies-20
04St. Cloud State Huskies-20
05St. Cloud State Huskies-26
05St. Cloud State Huskies-19

McElwee, Matt
95Dayton Bombers-10

McEnaney, Pete
94Anchorage Aces-20

McEwan, Bill
72Johnstown Jets-17

McEwen, Bobby
97UK Kingston Hawks Stickers-2

McEwen, Brad
91Air Canada SJHL All-Stars-23
92Saskatchewan JHL-95

McEwen, Chris
04UK Milton Keynes Lightning-11

McEwen, Dennis
86London Knights-23
89Hampton Roads Admirals-14A
89Hampton Roads Admirals-14H
90Hampton Roads Admirals-50
91Hampton Roads Admirals-11
93Hampton Roads Admirals-11
94Hampton Roads Admirals-14
98Hampton Roads Admirals 10th Anniversary-5

McEwen, Doug
94Finnish Jaa Kiekko-326
02UK Peterborough Phantoms-16
03UK Cardiff Devils-19

McEwen, Hugh
90Michigan Tech Huskies-16
91Michigan Tech Huskies-14

McEwen, Mike
77O-Pee-Chee NHL-232
77Topps-232
78O-Pee-Chee-187
78Topps-187
79O-Pee-Chee-66
79Rockies Team Issue-12
79Topps-66
80O-Pee-Chee-185
80Topps-185
81O-Pee-Chee-215
82O-Pee-Chee-207
82Post Cereal-12
86Whalers Junior Thomas'-16
91ProCards-374
93Oklahoma City Blazers-18
94Central Hockey League-62

McFadden, Clay
03Oshawa Generals-7

McFadden, Jim
44Beehive Group II Photos-122
44Beehive Group II Photos-193
51Parkhurst-44
52Parkhurst-38
53Parkhurst-77

McFadyen, Don
35Diamond Matchbooks Tan 1-45
35Diamond Matchbooks Tan 2-46
35Diamond Matchbooks Tan 3-43

McFarland, Jeff
02Lincoln Stars-12
04Minnesota-Duluth Bulldogs-13

McFarland, Paul
03Kitchener Rangers-18
04Kitchener Rangers-24

McFarlane, Brian
06Parkhurst-72
Autographs-72
Autographs Dual-DAIM

McFarlane, Mark
907th Inn. Sketch WHL-51
96Quad-City Mallards-14
97Quad-City Mallards-9
98Quad-City Mallards-15
99Quad-City Mallards-16
00Quad-City Mallards-16
01Quad-City Mallards-13

McFatridge, Sean
91Saskatoon Blades-20
917th Inn. Sketch WHL-108
92Brandon Wheat Kings-16

McFee, Dale
84Prince Albert Raiders Stickers-18

McFeeters, Rob
05Fresno Falcons-12

McGarry, Pat
93Fort Worth Fire-12
94Central Hockey League-29

McGarvey, Willie
89Peterborough Petes-111
897th Inn. Sketch OHL-111

McGee, Frank
83Hall of Fame-56
83Hall of Fame Postcards-D10
85Hall of Fame-56
05ITG Ultimate Memorabilia Level 1-37
05ITG Ultimate Memorabilia Level 2-37
05ITG Ultimate Memorabilia Level 3-37
05ITG Ultimate Memorabilia Level 4-37
05ITG Ultimate Memorabilia Level 5-37

McGee, Grant
06Guelph Storm-6

McGee, Jay
03Fort Worth Brahmas-9

McGee, Jeff
99Kitchener Rangers-26

McGee, Oliver
93Quebec Pee-Wee Tournament-1146

McGeough, Jim
89ProCards IHL-116
90ProCards AHL/IHL-315
92Richmond Renegades-13
94Central Hockey League-16
94Dallas Freeze-16
99Wichita Thunder-15
00Wichita Thunder-15

McGeough, John
98Wichita Thunder-16

McGhan, Mike
93Prince Albert Raiders-15
94Prince Albert Raiders-14
95Prince Albert Raiders-14
03Colorado Eagles-11

McGibney, Kevin
94German First League-657

McGill, Bob
81Maple Leafs Postcards-14
82Maple Leafs Postcards-24
82O-Pee-Chee-327
82Post Cereal-18
84Maple Leafs Postcards-17
85Maple Leafs Postcards-22
85O-Pee-Chee Stickers-15
87Blackhawks Coke-11
88Blackhawks Coke-11
89Blackhawks Coke-10
90Blackhawks Coke-10
90Pro Set-55A
90Pro Set-55B
90Score Rookie/Traded-49T
91O-Pee-Chee-216
91OPC Premier-8
91Pinnacle-98
French-98
91Pro Set-47
91Pro Set-480
French-47
French-480
91Score American-368
91Score Canadian Bilingual-327
91Score Canadian Bilingual-560
91Score Canadian English-327
91Score Canadian English-560
91Score Rookie/Traded-10T
91Sharks Sports Action-15
91Topps-216
91Upper Deck-62
French-62
92Bowman-429
92Maple Leafs Kodak-28
92Score-386
Canadian-386
92Stadium Club-483
92Topps-209
Gold-209G
98Baton Rouge Kingfish-22

McGill, Jack
34Sweet Caporal-11
35Diamond Matchbooks Tan 1-46
35Diamond Matchbooks Tan 2-47
35Diamond Matchbooks Tan 3-44
35O-Pee-Chee V304C-74
37V356 Worldwide Gum-77

McGill, Ryan
89ProCards IHL-56
90ProCards AHL/IHL-394
91ProCards-498
92Flyers J.C. Penney-17
92Flyers Upper Deck Sheets-23
92Flyers Upper Deck Sheets-31
92Parkhurst-366
Emerald Ice-366
92Ultra-373
92Upper Deck-494
93Flyers J.C. Penney-15
93Flyers Lineup Sheets-25
93Parkhurst-415
Emerald Ice-415
93Score-649
Gold-649
Canadian-649
Canadian Gold-649
93Ultra-177
94Upper Deck-160
Electric Ice-160
02Hartford Wolf Pack-29

McGillis, Brock
03Kalamazoo Wings-22

McGillis, Cort
06Barrie Colts-21

McGillis, Dan
96Oilers Postcards-23
97Be A Player-131
Autographs-131
Autographs Die-Cuts-131
Autographs Prismatic Die-Cuts-131
97Pacific-294
Copper-294
Emerald Green-294
Ice Blue-294
Red-294
Silver-294
98Pacific-328
Ice Blue-328
Red-328
98Upper Deck MVP-153
Gold Script-153
Silver Script-153
Super Script-153
99BAP Memorabilia-99
Gold-99
Silver-99
99BAP Millennium-186
Emerald-186
Ruby-186
Sapphire-186
Signatures-186
Signatures Gold-186
99Pacific-309
Copper-309
Emerald Green-309
Gold-309
Ice Blue-309
Premiere Date-309
Red-309
99Upper Deck Victory-221
00BAP Memorabilia-383
Emerald-383
Ruby-383
Sapphire-383
Promos-383
00BAP Mem Chicago Sportsfest Copper-383
00BAP Memorabilia Chicago Sportsfest Blue-383
00BAP Memorabilia Chicago Sportsfest Gold-383

00BAP Memorabilia Chicago Sportsfest Ruby-383
00BAP Memorabilia Chicago Sun-Times Ruby-383
00BAP Memorabilia Chicago Sun-Times Gold-383
00BAP Mem Chicago Sun-Times Sapphire-383
00BAP Mem Toronto Fall Expo Copper-383
00BAP Memorabilia Toronto Fall Expo Gold-383
00BAP Memorabilia Toronto Fall Expo Ruby-383
00Pacific-303
Copper-303
Gold-303
Ice Blue-303
Premiere Date-303
00Upper Deck-357
Exclusives Tier 1-357
Exclusives Tier 2-357
01Flyers Postcards-13
01Pacific-291
Extreme LTD-291
Hobby LTD-291
Premiere Date-291
Retail LTD-291
01Pacific Arena Exclusives-291
01Upper Deck-360
Exclusives-360
01Upper Deck Victory-262
Gold-262
02BAP Sig Series Auto Buybacks 1999-186
02Topps Total-119
02Upper Deck Rookie Update-8
03Bruins Team Issue-5
03ITG Action-20
03Pacific Complete-124
Red-124
03Parkhurst Original Six Boston-21
03Upper Deck MVP-40
Gold Script-40
Silver Script-40
Canadian Exclusives-40
05Devils Team Issue-28
05Upper Deck MVP-233
Gold-233
Platinum-233

McGillivray, Jordan
02Regina Pats-19
03Regina Pats-19
04Regina Pats-18
05Regina Pats-12

McGillvary, Glen
92Saskatchewan JHL-85

McGimpsey, Chris
03UK Belfast Giants-10

McGimsie, Billy
83Hall of Fame Postcards-E11
85Hall of Fame-71

McGinn, Jamie
04Ottawa 67's-20
05ITG Heroes/Prosp Toronto Expo Parallel -406
05Ottawa 67's-20
05ITG Heroes and Prospects-406
Team Cherry-TC7
06Ottawa 67s-7
06ITG Heroes and Prospects-106
Autographs-AJM
Jerseys-GUJ31
Jerseys Gold-GUJ31
Emblems-GUE31
Emblems Gold-GUE31
Numbers-GUN31
Numbers Gold-GUN31

McGinn, Mark
92Oklahoma City Blazers-13
93Memphis RiverKings-8
94Central Hockey League-52
99Memphis RiverKings All-Time-4

Mcginnis, Brad
88Regina Pats-16

McGinnis, Ryan
03Plymouth Whalers-19
05Plymouth Whalers-A-11
06Plymouth Whalers-14

McGlynn, Dick
72Finnish Semic World Championship-133
72Swedish Semic World Championship-133

McGlynn, Pete
897th Inn. Sketch OHL-70
907th Inn. Sketch OHL-89
917th Inn. Sketch OHL-241

McGowan, Cal
88Kamloops Blazers-19
89Kamloops Blazers-15
907th Inn. Sketch WHL-293
907th Inn. Sketch Memorial Cup-9
91ProCards-152
95Binghamton Rangers-16
98Amarillo Rattlers-12

McGowan, Dwayne
93Quebec Pee-Wee Tournament-1309

McGowan, Everett
28V128-2 Paulin's Candy-81

McGrane, Ed
03ECHL Update RBI Sports-142
03Louisiana Ice Gators-15
04Wheeling Nailers Riesbeck's-9
05Colorado Eagles-12
06Colorado EaglesÂ -14

McGrath, Bobby
89Hampton Roads Admirals-15A
89Hampton Roads Admirals-15H

McGrath, Brett
00Ottawa 67's-11
01Ottawa 67's-13
02Owen Sound Attack-15

McGrath, Don
97Central Texas Stampede-10

McGrath, Evan
00Quebec Pee Wee Tournament-1276
02Kitchener Rangers Postcards-5
03Kitchener Rangers-19
03Kitchener Rangers Memorial Cup-15
04Kitchener Rangers-10
04ITG Heroes and Prospects-206
04ITG Heroes/Prospects Toronto Expo '05-206
05ITG Heroes/Prosp Toronto Expo Parallel -122
05Kitchener Rangers-7
05OHL Bell All-Star Classic-33
05ITG Heroes and Prospects-122
Autographs-A-EM

McGrath, J.J.
04UK London Racers-18
04UK London Racers Playoffs-11

McGrath, Peter
83North Bay Centennials-19

McGrattan, Brian
97Guelph Storm-19
98Sudbury Wolves-20
99Sudbury Wolves-18
00Mississauga Ice Dogs-16
03Binghamton Senators-14
03Binghamton Senators Postcards-8
04Binghamton Senators-11
04Binghamton Senators Hess-9
05Hot Prospects-154
En Fuego-154
Red Hot-154
White Hot-154
05Parkhurst Facsimile Auto Parallel-349
05SP Authentic-236
Limited-236
05SP Game Used-169
Gold-169
05SPx-201
Spectrum-201
05The Cup Masterpiece Pressplate Artifact-305
05The Cup Masterpiece Pressplates (Ice)-159
05The Cup Master Pressplate Rookie Update-161
05The Cup Masterpiece Pressplates SPA-236
05The Cup Masterpiece Pressplates SP GU-169
05The Cup Masterpiece Pressplates (SPx)-201
05The Cup Masterpiece Pressplates Trilogy-286
05The Cup Masterpiece Pressplate Ult Coll-159
05UD Artifacts-305
05Ultimate Collection-159
Gold-159
05Ultra-235
Gold-235
Ice-235
05Upper Deck Ice-159
05Upper Deck Rookie Update-161
05Upper Deck Trilogy-286
06Senators Postcards-8
06Binghamton Senators 5th Anniversary-18

McGregor, Brian
77Rochester Americans-17

McGregor, Bryan
04Minnesota-Duluth Bulldogs-14

McGregor, Mark
93Swiss HNL-338
95Swiss HNL-391
98Swiss Power Play Stickers-177

McGregor, Percy
23V128-1 Paulin's Candy-50

McGrinder, Steve
90Cincinnati Cyclones-19

McGuffin, Matt
907th Inn. Sketch OHL-39
917th Inn. Sketch OHL-6

McGuigan, Bill
94Slapshot Promos-3
94Kitchener Rangers-18
96Alaska Gold Kings-10
97Idaho Steelheads-4

McGuire, Conor
99Shawinigan Cataractes-19
Signed-19
00Halifax Mooseheads-19

McGuire, E.J.
85Flyers Postcards-20
86Flyers Postcards-17
88Blackhawks Coke-12
89Blackhawks Coke-26
90Blackhawks Coke-27
91ProCards-67
95Slapshot-105
96Guelph Storm-28

McGuire, John
93Quebec Pee-Wee Tournament-618

McGuire, Matthew
93Quebec Pee-Wee Tournament-190

McGuire, Mickey
91British Columbia JHL-54
92British Columbia JHL-136

McGuire, Pierre
93Whalers Coke-11

McHale, Gavin
05Lethbridge Hurricanes-16

McHugh, Justin
91Minnesota Golden Gophers-15
92Minnesota Golden Gophers-13
93Minnesota Golden Gophers-20
94Minnesota Golden Gophers-20
96Quad-City Mallards-7

McHugh, Mike
75HCA Steel City Vacuum-8
88ProCards IHL-35
89ProCards IHL-86
90ProCards AHL/IHL-113
910-Pee-Chee Inserts-7S
91Score Canadian Bilingual-651
91Score Canadian English-651

McHugh, Oriel
05Bakersfield Condors-10

McHugh, Tony
92Quebec Pee-Wee Tournament-623
93Quebec Pee-Wee Tournament-1374

Mclantyre, Ian
917th Inn. Sketch QMJHL-180

McIlhargey, Jack
75Flyers Canada Dry Cans-14
77Canucks Canada Dry Cans-9
77Canucks Royal Bank-13
78Canucks Royal Bank-17
780-Pee-Chee-294
79Canucks Royal Bank-16
790-Pee-Chee-367
91ProCards-618
92Hamilton Canucks-18
96Syracuse Crunch-NNO
03Canucks Postcards-18
04ITG Franchises Canadian-124
Autographs-JMI0

McIlvane, Matt
03Chicago Steel-1
04Ohio State Buckeyes-17
05Ohio State Buckeyes-22
06Ohio State Buckeyes-11

McIlveen, Paul
05Cape Breton Screaming Eagles-23
06Cape Breton Screaming Eagles-22

McInenly, Bert
330-Pee-Chee V304A-41
36Providence Reds-6
05The Cup Legendary Cuts-LCBM

McInerney, Eoin
95Slapshot-157
96Sarnia Sting-18
97Owen Sound Platers-24
00UK Nottingham Panthers-20
00UK Sekonda Superleague-125
02UK Hull Thunder-21

McInerney, Ryan
04Sault Ste. Marie Greyhounds-9

McInnes, Darin
86Regina Pats-16

McInness, Paul
94Sarnia Sting-12
95Slapshot-34

McInnis, Marty
91Parkhurst-327
French-327
92Bowman-352
920-Pee-Chee-135
92OPC Premier-12
92Parkhurst-106
Emerald Ice-106
92Pro Set-233
92Score-465
Canadian-465
92Stadium Club-213
92Topps-302
Gold-302G
92Ultra-347
92Upper Deck-394
92Upper Deck-410
93Donruss-457
93OPC Premier-57
Gold-57
93Panini Stickers-62
93Parkhurst-390
Emerald Ice-390
93PowerPlay-385
93Score-405
Canadian-405
93Stadium Club-257
Members Only Master Set-257
First Day Issue-257
93Topps/OPC Premier-57
Gold-57
93Ultra-370
93Upper Deck-392
SP-94
93Classic Pro Prospects-133
94Be A Player-R4
Signature Cards-14
94Canada Games NHL POGS-158
94Donruss-311
94Flair-106
94Leaf-157
94OPC Premier-244
Special Effects-244
94Parkhurst SE-SE104
Gold-SE104
94Pinnacle-153
Artist's Proofs-153
Rink Collection-153
94Score-88
Gold-88
Platinum-88
94Topps/OPC Premier-244
Special Effects-244
94Ultra-131
94Upper Deck-106
Electric Ice-106
95Collector's Choice-59
Player's Club-59
Player's Club Platinum-59
95Parkhurst International-134
Emerald Ice-134
95Score-217
Black Ice Artist's Proofs-217
Black Ice-217
95Topps-323
OPC Inserts-323
95Upper Deck-52
Electric Ice-52
Electric Ice Gold-52
96Collector's Choice-160
96Islander Postcards-14
96Pinnacle-62
Artist's Proofs-62
Foil-62
Premium Stock-62
Rink Collection-62
96Upper Deck-102
97Collector's Choice-42
97Flames Collector's Photos-14
97Panini Stickers-193
97Revolution-19
Copper-19
Emerald-19
Ice Blue-19
Silver-19
97Score-210
97Upper Deck-26
98Aurora-26
98Be A Player-19
Press Release-19
98BAP Gold-19
98BAP Autographs-19
98BAP Autographs Gold-19
98BAP Tampa Bay All Star Game-19
98OPC Chrome-103
Refractors-103
98Pacific-121
Ice Blue-121
Red-121
98Pacific Omega-5
Red-5
Opening Day Issue-5
98Paramount-29
Copper-29
Emerald Green-29
Holo-Electric-29
Ice Blue-29
Silver-29
98Revolution-3
Ice Shadow-3
Red-3
98Topps-103
O-Pee-Chee-103
98Upper Deck MVP-7
Gold Script-7
Silver Script-7
Super Script-7
99Aurora-3
Premiere Date-3
99BAP Memorabilia-144
Gold-144
Silver-144
990-Pee-Chee-48
990-Pee-Chee Chrome-48
990-Pee-Chee Chrome Refractors-48
99Pacific-9
Copper-9
Emerald Green-9
Gold-9
Ice Blue-9
Premiere Date-9
Red-9
99Pacific Omega-4
Copper-4
Gold-4
Ice Blue-4
Premiere Date-4
99Panini Stickers-180
99Paramount-4
Copper-4
Emerald-4
Gold-4
Holographic Emerald-4
Holographic Gold-4
Holographic Silver-4
Ice Blue-4
Premiere Date-4
Red-4
Silver-4
99Revolution-3
Premiere Date-3
Red-3
Shadow Series-3
99Stadium Club-147
First Day Issue-147
One of a Kind-147
Printing Plates Black-147
Printing Plates Cyan-147
Printing Plates Magenta-147
Printing Plates Yellow-147
99Topps/OPC-48
99Topps/OPC Chrome-48
Refractors-48
99Upper Deck Victory-10
00BAP Memorabilia-386
Promos-386
00BAP Mem Chicago Sportsfest Copper-386
00BAP Memorabilia Chicago Sportsfest Blue-386
00BAP Memorabilia Chicago Sportsfest Gold-386
00BAP Memorabilia Chicago Sportsfest Ruby-386
00BAP Memorabilia Chicago Sun-Times Ruby-386
00BAP Memorabilia Chicago Sun-Times Gold-386
00BAP Mem Chicago Sun-Times Sapphire-386
00BAP Mem Toronto Fall Expo Copper-386
00BAP Memorabilia Toronto Fall Expo Gold-386
00BAP Memorabilia Toronto Fall Expo Ruby-386
000-Pee-Chee-181
000-Pee-Chee Parallel-181
00Pacific-7
Copper-7
Gold-7
Ice Blue-7
Premiere Date-7
00Private Stock Game Gear-2
00Private Stock Game Gear Patches-2
00Revolution Game-Worn Jerseys-1
00Revolution Game-Worn Jersey Patches-1
00Topps/OPC-181
Parallel-181
00UD Heroes-2
00Upper Deck-236
Exclusives Tier 1-236
Exclusives Tier 2-236
00Vanguard Dual Game-Worn Jerseys-16
00Vanguard Dual Game-Worn Patches-16
01BAP Memorabilia-419
Emerald-419
Ruby-419
Sapphire-419
010-Pee-Chee-236
010-Pee-Chee Premier Parallel-236
01Pacific-8
Extreme LTD-8
Hobby LTD-8
Premiere Date-8
Retail LTD-8
01Pacific Adrenaline-4
Blue-4
Premiere Date-4
Red-4
Retail-4
01Pacific Arena Exclusives-8
01Parkhurst-364
01Topps-236
OPC Parallel-236
01Upper Deck-237
Exclusives-237
01Upper Deck Vintage-9
02BAP Sig Series Auto Buybacks 1998-19
02Pacific Complete-347
Red-347
02Upper Deck-262
Exclusives-262
02Upper Deck Beckett UD Promos-262

McInnis, Paul
99Bakersfield Condors-10

McIntosh, Bob
91Air Canada SJHL-D17
91Air Canada SJHL-D31

McIntosh, Don
52Juniors Blue Tint-90

McIntosh, Geoff
01Brandon Wheat Kings-13
02Brandon Wheat Kings-22
03Kamloops Blazers-1

McIntosh, Murray
94German DEL-162
95German DEL-154

McIntosh, Paul
78Saginaw Gears-15

McIntosh, Ryan
02Rockford Ice Hogs-22
03Elmira Jackals-12

McIntyre, Dan
99Asheville Smoke-9
01Austin Ice Bats-9
02Greenville Grrrowl-14
04UK Edinburgh Capitals-10
04Richmond Riverdogs-23

McIntyre, Drew
06Manitoba Moose-2

McIntyre, Eric
03St. Jean Mission-17

McIntyre, Ian
90Montreal-Bourassa AAA-15
96Syracuse Crunch-11
96Wheeling Nailers-13
96Wheeling Nailers Photo Pack-6
00UK Cardiff Devils-14
00UK Sekonda Superleague-63
01UK Cardiff Devils-12
01UK London Knights-17
02UK Cardiff Devils-12
02UK London Knights-11
04UK London Racers-9
04UK London Racers Playoffs-12

McIntyre, Jack
44Beehive Group II Photos-48
52Parkhurst-77
54Parkhurst-88
54Topps-43
57Topps-28
60Parkhurst-24
60Shirriff Coins-46
94Parkhurst Missing Link-27

McIntyre, John
89ProCards AHL-121
90Kings Smokey-22
900-Pee-Chee-382
90Pro Set-457
90Score Rookie/Traded-46T
90Topps-382
Tiffany-382
91Bowman-180
91Maple Leafs Panini Team Stickers-16
910-Pee-Chee-37
91Parkhurst-296
French-296
91Pro Set-401
French-401
91Score American-182
91Score Canadian Bilingual-182
91Score Canadian English-182
91Stadium Club-324
91Topps-37
91Upper Deck-218
French-218
92Bowman-336
92Pinnacle-214
French-214
92Score-347
Canadian-347
92Stadium Club-117
92Topps-369
Gold-369G
92Upper Deck-118
93Parkhurst-482
Emerald Ice-482
93Upper Deck-527
94Leaf-365
94Stadium Club-244
Members Only Master Set-244
First Day Issue-244
Super Team Winner Cards-244
94Upper Deck-478
Electric Ice-478
95Canucks Building the Dream Art-15

McIntyre, Larry
69Maple Leafs White Border Matte-4
72Maple Leafs Postcards-18

McIntyre, Lloyd
28V128-2 Paulin's Candy-48
37V356 Worldwide Gum-121

McIntyre, Many
51Bas Du Fleuve-54

McIntyre, Robb
91Ferris State Bulldogs-23
92Ferris State Bulldogs-23
94Knoxville Cherokees-21
94St. John's Maple Leafs-20

McIver, Chad
03Indianapolis Ice-14
06Austin Ice Bats-3

McIver, Nathan
02St. Michaels Majors-7
03St. Michael's Majors-5
04St. Michael's Majors-6
05Manitoba Moose-13
06Hot Prospects-180
Red Hot-180
White Hot-180
060-Pee-Chee-581
Rainbow-581
06SP Authentic-212
Limited-212
06SP Game Used Rookie Exclusives Autographs-RENM
06The Cup-108
Autographed Rookie Masterpiece Pressplates-108
Gold Rainbow Autographed Rookies-108
Masterpiece Pressplates (Marquee Rookies)-581
Masterpiece Pressplates (SP Authentic)-212
Masterpiece Pressplates (Victory)-330
Rookies Black-108
Rookies Platinum-108
06Upper Deck-493
Exclusives Parallel-493
High Gloss Parallel-493
Masterpieces-493
Victory-330
06Manitoba Moose-6
07Upper Deck Rookie Class -44

McIvor, Trevor
89Oshawa Generals-22
89Oshawa Generals 7th Inning Sketch-16
897th Inn. Sketch OHL-16
907th Inn. Sketch OHL-109
907th Inn. Sketch Memorial Cup-95

McKane, Chris
93Quebec Pee-Wee Tournament-1451

McKave, Todd
92British Columbia JHL-229

McKay, Bill
92Saskatchewan JHL-14
97New Orleans Brass-6

McKay, Bruce
81Milwaukee Admirals-7

McKay, Doug
88Devils Caretta-20
89ProCards AHL-287

McKay, Ken
95Red Deer Rebels-13
98Tri-City Americans-8
99Bowman CHL-111
Gold-111
OPC International-111

McKay, Kevin
97Saskatoon Blades-13

McKay, Konrad
96OCN Blizzard-21
97OCN Blizzard-20
98OCN Blizzard-19
02Charlotte Checkers-88
03Charlotte Checkers-73
04New Mexico Scorpions-14

McKay, Lyle
03OCN Blizzard-13

McKay, Martin
93UK Sheffield Steelers-15
94Finnish Jaa Kiekko-311
94UK Sheffield Steelers-24
95UK Sheffield Steelers-1
96UK Fife Flyers-15

McKay, Michael
95Slapshot Memorial Cup-75
00Fort Wayne Komets-13
00Fort Wayne Komets Shoe Carnival-8
01Fort Wayne Komets-14

McKay, Murdo
51Laval Dairy QSHL-5
52St. Lawrence Sales-45

McKay, Preston
98OCN Blizzard-23
99OCN Blizzard-24

McKay, Randy
88ProCards AHL-20
89ProCards AHL-318
90Bowman-227
Tiffany-227
91Pro Set-422
French-422
91Score Canadian Bilingual-604
91Score Canadian English-604
91Score Rookie/Traded-54T
91Upper Deck-313
French-313
92Bowman-296
92Parkhurst-331
Emerald Ice-331
92Score-339
Canadian-339
92Stadium Club-450
92Topps-106
Gold-106G
93Donruss-454
93Pinnacle-322
Canadian-322
93Score-319
Canadian-319
94Leaf-400
94OPC Premier-271
Special Effects-271
94Pinnacle-222
Artist's Proofs-222
Rink Collection-222
94Topps/OPC Premier-271
Special Effects-271
95Be A Player-52
Signatures-S52
Signatures Die Cuts-S52
95Canada Games NHL POGS-162
95Emotion-99
95Leaf-314
95Panini Stickers-84
95Pinnacle-92
Artist's Proofs-92
Rink Collection-92
95SkyBox Impact-94
95Stadium Club-153
Members Only Master Set-153
95Topps-201
OPC Inserts-201
Power Lines-10PL
95Upper Deck-444
Electric Ice-444
Electric Ice Gold-444
96Collector's Choice-154
96Devils Team Issue-21
97Be A Player-160
Autographs-160
Autographs Die-Cuts-160
Autographs Prismatic Die-Cuts-160
97Devils Team Issue-16
97Pacific Invincible NHL Regime-114
97Pacific Omega-131
Copper-131
Dark Gray-131
Emerald Green-131
Gold-131
Ice Blue-131
97Score Devils-12
Platinum-12
Premier-12
98Aurora-111
98Be A Player-80
Press Release-80
98BAP Gold-80
98BAP Autographs-80
98BAP Autographs Gold-80
98BAP Tampa Bay All Star Game-80
98Devils Team Issue-17
98OPC Chrome-90
Refractors-90
Season's Best-SB29
Season's Best Refractors-SB29
98Pacific-264
Ice Blue-264
Red-264
98Paramount-135
Copper-135
Emerald Green-135
Holo-Electric-135
Ice Blue-135
Silver-135
98Topps-90
O-Pee-Chee-90
Season's Best-SB29
98Topps Gold Label Class 1-28
Black-28
Black One of One-28
One of One-28
Red-28
Red One of One-28
98Topps Gold Label Class 2-28
98Topps Gold Label Class 2 Black-28
98Topps Gold Label Class 2 Black 1 of 1-28
98Topps Gold Label Class 2 One of One-28
98Topps Gold Label Class 2 Red-28
98Topps Gold Label Class 2 Red One of One-28
98Topps Gold Label Class 3-28
98Topps Gold Label Class 3 Black-28
98Topps Gold Label Class 3 Black 1 of 1-28
98Topps Gold Label Class 3 One of One-28
98Topps Gold Label Class 3 Red-28
98Topps Gold Label Class 3 Red One of One-28
99Devils Team Issue-14
99Pacific-240
Copper-240
Emerald Green-240
Gold-240
Ice Blue-240
Premiere Date-240
Red-240
99Paramount-135
Copper-135
Emerald-135
Gold-135
Holographic Emerald-135
Holographic Gold-135
Holographic Silver-135
Ice Blue-135
Premiere Date-135
Red-135
Silver-135
99Upper Deck MVP SC Edition-109
Gold Script-109
Silver Script-109
Super Script-109
99Russian Fetisov Tribute-35
00BAP Memorabilia-342
Emerald-342
Ruby-342
Sapphire-342
Promos-342
00BAP Mem Chicago Sportsfest Copper-342
00BAP Memorabilia Chicago Sportsfest Blue-342
00BAP Memorabilia Chicago Sportsfest Gold-342
00BAP Memorabilia Chicago Sportsfest Ruby-342
00BAP Memorabilia Chicago Sun-Times Ruby-342
00BAP Memorabilia Chicago Sun-Times Gold-342
00BAP Mem Chicago Sun-Times Sapphire-342
00BAP Mem Toronto Fall Expo Copper-342
00BAP Memorabilia Toronto Fall Expo Gold-342
00BAP Memorabilia Toronto Fall Expo Ruby-342
00BAP Signature Series-70
Emerald-70
Ruby-70
Sapphire-70
Autographs-205
Autographs Gold-205
00Devils Team Issue-12
00Pacific-239
Copper-239
Gold-239
Ice Blue-239
Premiere Date-239
00Topps Heritage-150
00Upper Deck-333
Exclusives Tier 1-333
Exclusives Tier 2-333
00Upper Deck Vintage-220
01BAP Memorabilia-482
Emerald-482
Ruby-482
Sapphire-482
01Devils Team Issue-13
010-Pee-Chee-192
010-Pee-Chee-321
010-Pee-Chee Premier Parallel-192
010-Pee-Chee Premier Parallel-321
01Pacific-233
Extreme LTD-233
Hobby LTD-233
Premiere Date-233
Retail LTD-233
01Pacific Adrenaline-116
Blue-116
Premiere Date-116
Red-116
Retail-116
01Pacific Arena Exclusives-233
01Topps-192
01Topps-321
OPC Parallel-192
OPC Parallel-321
01UD Stanley Cup Champs-71
01Upper Deck-337
Exclusives-337
01Upper Deck Victory-208
Gold-208
01Czech Stadion-245
02BAP Sig Series Auto Buybacks 1998-80
02BAP Sig Series Auto Buybacks 2000-205
02Canadiens Postcards-5
02NHL Power Play Stickers-56
02Pacific Complete-253
Red-253
02Topps Heritage-167
02Topps Total-66
03ITG Action-399
03NHL Sticker Collection-53

McKay, Ray
71Sabres Postcards-88
71Toronto Sun-33

McKay, Ross
90ProCards AHL/IHL-177

McKay, Ryan
02Sault Ste. Marie Greyhounds-23

McKay, Scott
897th Inn. Sketch OHL-35
907th Inn. Sketch OHL-136
917th Inn. Sketch OHL-376
93San Diego Gulls-15
94Greensboro Monarchs-12
94Classic Pro Prospects-216
97Louisiana Ice Gators-9

McKechney, Garnet
82Kitchener Rangers-13
83Kitchener Rangers-10
84Kitchener Rangers-3

McKechnie, Craig
91Air Canada SJHL-A8
92Saskatchewan JHL-149

McKechnie, Darrin
86Regina Pats-17
87Regina Pats-18

McKechnie, Walt
70Colgate Stamps-1
70Esso Power Players-177
700-Pee-Chee-172
70Sargent Promotions Stamps-89
71Bazooka-28
71Letraset Action Replays-5
710-Pee-Chee-124
Posters-17
71Sargent Promotions Stamps-129
71Toronto Sun-53
720-Pee-Chee-192
72Sargent Promotions Stamps-43
730-Pee-Chee-152
73Topps-127
74NHL Action Stamps-27
74NHL Action Stamps Update-11
740-Pee-Chee NHL-56
74Topps-56
750-Pee-Chee NHL-194
75Topps-194
760-Pee-Chee NHL-196
760-Pee-Chee NHL-385
76Topps-196
770-Pee-Chee NHL-32
77Topps-32
78Maple Leafs Postcards-14
780-Pee-Chee-344
79Maple Leafs Postcards-20
790-Pee-Chee-68
79Topps-68
800-Pee-Chee-378
820-Pee-Chee-91
820-Pee-Chee Stickers-186
82Post Cereal-5
82Topps Stickers-186
83NHL Key Tags-31
83Puffy Stickers-14

McKee, Brian
90ProCards AHL/IHL-552
91ProCards-40
92Peoria Rivermen-15
93Fort Wayne Komets-12

McKee, Corey
91Air Canada SJHL-A25

McKee, David
06Be A Player-242
06Beehive-101
Matte-101
06Flair Showcase-302
06Hot Prospects-143
Red Hot-143
White Hot-143
060-Pee-Chee-592
Rainbow-592
06SP Authentic-250
Limited-250
06The Cup-111
Autographed Rookie Masterpiece Pressplates-111
Gold Rainbow Autographed Rookie Patches-111
Masterpiece Pressplates (Bee Hive)-101
Masterpiece Pressplates (Marquee Rookies)-592
Masterpiece Pressplates (SP Authentic)-250
Masterpiece Pressplates (Sweet Beginnings)-103
Masterpiece Pressplates (Ultimate Collection)-61
Rookies Black-111
Rookies Platinum-111
06Ultimate Collection-61
06Upper Deck-451
Exclusives Parallel-451
High Gloss Parallel-451
Masterpieces-451
06Upper Deck Sweet Shot-103
Rookie Jerseys Autographs-103
06Augusta Lynx-13

McKee, Don
01Odessa Jackalopes-16
02Odessa Jackalopes-20
03Odessa Jackalopes-21
04Odessa Jackalopes-19
05Odessa Jackalopes-19
06Odessa Jackalopes-20

McKee, Jay
93Sudbury Wolves-3
93Sudbury Wolves Police-3
94Sudbury Wolves Police-22
95Slapshot-183
95Slapshot-NNO
95Classic Five-Sport *-135
Autographs-135
96Fleer-131
96Metal Universe-186
96Pinnacle-222
Artist's Proofs-222
Foil-222
Premium Stock-222
Rink Collection-222
96SkyBox Impact-154
96Ultra-18
Gold Medallion-18
Rookies-12
96Visions Signings *-72
Autographs-72A
Autographs Silver-72A
97Be A Player-122
Autographs-122
Autographs Die-Cuts-122
Autographs Prismatic Die-Cuts-122
97Upper Deck-231
97Rochester Americans-4-3
97Talk N' Sports *-48
Phone Cards $1-48
99Pacific-40
Copper-40
Emerald Green-40
Gold-40
Ice Blue-40
Premiere Date-40
Red-40
00Private Stock Game Gear-10
00Private Stock Game Gear Patches-10
00Upper Deck-252
Exclusives Tier 1-252
Exclusives Tier 2-252
00Upper Deck Victory-33
01Pacific Jerseys-3
01Pacific Adrenaline Jerseys-4
01Private Stock Game Gear-11
01Private Stock Game Gear Patches-11
01Upper Deck-253
Exclusives-253
02Pacific-45
Blue-45
Red-45
Heads-Up Quad Jerseys-4
Heads-Up Quad Jerseys Gold-4
02Sabres Team Issue-9
02Upper Deck-22
Exclusives-22
02Upper Deck Vintage-32
03ITG Action-40
03NHL Sticker Collection-28
03Pacific Complete-237
Red-237
05Parkhurst-64
Facsimile Auto Parallel-64
060-Pee-Chee-436
Rainbow-436
06Panini Stickers-343
06Upper Deck-421
Exclusives Parallel-421
High Gloss Parallel-421
Masterpieces-421
06Upper Deck MVP-257
Gold Script-257
Super Script-257

McKee, Mike
93Donruss-479
93PowerPlay-424
93Score-630
Gold-630
Canadian-630
Canadian Gold-630
94Classic Pro Prospects-91
97Rochester Americans-4-3

McKeever, Sean
93Quebec Pee-Wee Tournament-628

McKegney, Tony
79Sabres Bells-5
800-Pee-Chee-144
80Topps-144
810-Pee-Chee-22
810-Pee-Chee Stickers-57
81Sabres Milk Panels-11
81Topps-E76
820-Pee-Chee-29

82O-Pee-Chee Stickers-122
82Post Cereal-2
82Sabres Milk Panels-13
82Topps Stickers-122
83NHL Key Tags-11
83O-Pee-Chee-60
83O-Pee-Chee-296
83O-Pee-Chee Stickers-239
83Puffy Stickers-17
83Topps Stickers-239
83Vachon-68
84North Stars Postcards-17
84O-Pee-Chee-283
84O-Pee-Chee Stickers-171
85North Stars 7-Eleven-5
85North Stars Postcards-21
85O-Pee-Chee-156
85O-Pee-Chee Stickers-45
85Topps-156
87Blues Kodak-16
87Blues Team Issue-13
87O-Pee-Chee-172
87Panini Stickers-118
87Topps-172
88Blues Kodak-13
88Blues Team Issue-13
88O-Pee-Chee-4
88O-Pee-Chee Stickers-17
88Panini Stickers-109
88Topps-4
89Nordiques Team Issue-29
89O-Pee-Chee-4
89Topps-4
90Bowman-168
Tiffany-168
90Nordiques Petro-Canada-18
90Nordiques Team Issue-21
90O-Pee-Chee-333
90Panini Stickers-149
90Pro Set-254
90Score-311C
Canadian-311C
90Topps-333
Tiffany-333
90Upper Deck-340
French-340
91Bowman-387
91Nordiques Panini Team Stickers-15
91O-Pee-Chee-484
91Score American-104
91Score Canadian Bilingual-104
91Score Canadian English-104
91Stadium Club-281
91Topps-484

McKelvie, Ryan
03Minnesota State Mavericks-13

McKenna, Colin
93Quebec Pee-Wee Tournament-1468

McKenna, Mike
05Las Vegas Wranglers-14
06Las Vegas Wranglers-13

McKenna, Paul
92British Columbia JHL-7

McKenna, Sean
84Sabres Blue Shield-10
85Sabres Blue Shield-17
85Sabres Blue Shield Small-17
86Kings 20th Anniversary Team Issue-14
87Panini Stickers-284
88Maple Leafs PLAY-27
88ProCards AHL-226
89ProCards AHL-115
04ITG Franchises US East-340
Autographs-A-SMK

McKenna, Steve
92Saskatchewan JHL-108
97Be A Player-244
Autographs-244
Autographs Die-Cuts-244
Autographs Prismatic Die-Cuts-244
97Pacific Omega-109
Copper-109
Dark Gray-109
Emerald Green-109
Gold-109
Ice Blue-109
98Pacific-239
Ice Blue-239
Red-239
00BAP Signature Series-203
Emerald-203
Ruby-203
Sapphire-203
Autographs-25
Autographs Gold-25
01O-Pee-Chee-252
01O-Pee-Chee Premier Parallel-252
01Topps-252
OPC Parallel-252
02BAP Sig Series Auto Buybacks 2000-25
03ITG Action-401
03O-Pee-Chee-273
03OPC Blue-273
03OPC Gold-273
03OPC Red-273
03Pacific Complete-189
Red-189
03Topps-273
Blue-273
Gold-273
Red-273
03Upper Deck-400
Canadian Exclusives-400
HG-400
UD Exclusives-400
04UK Nottingham Panthers-12

McKenney, Don
44Beehive Group II Photos-49
44Beehive Group II Photos-343
44Beehive Group II Photos-431
52Juniors Blue Tint-111
54Topps-35
55Bruins Photos-11
57Bruins Photos-13
57Topps-13
58Bruins Photos-9
58Topps-62
59Topps-9
60Shirriff Coins-108
60Topps-40
Stamps-35
61Shirriff/Salada Coins-6
61Topps-12
62Topps-10
Hockey Bucks-16
63Maple Leafs Team Issue-16
63Topps-53
64Beehive Group III Photos-175A
64Beehive Group III Photos-175B
64Coca-Cola Caps-101
64Topps-83
64Toronto Star-31
65Topps-112
91Bruins Sports Action Legends-16
94Parkhurst Missing Link-6
94Parkhurst Tall Boys-112
98Bruins Alumni-31
Autographs-31

McKenney, Sam
90Dayton Bombers-14

McKenny, Jim
66Tulsa Oilers-7
68Shirriff Coins-174
69Maple Leafs White Border Glossy-22
70Dad's Cookies-82
70Esso Power Players-29
70Maple Leafs Postcards-8
70Sargent Promotions Stamps-201
71Maple Leafs Postcards-12
71O-Pee-Chee-43
71Sargent Promotions Stamps-194
71Topps-43
71Toronto Sun-265
72Maple Leafs Postcards-19
72Maple Leafs Postcards-20
72O-Pee-Chee-83
72Sargent Promotions Stamps-198
72Topps-54
72Finnish Semic World Championship-189
72Swedish Semic World Championship-189
73Mac's Milk-18
73Maple Leafs Postcards-18
73O-Pee-Chee-39
73Topps-39
74Lipton Soup-23
74Maple Leafs Postcards-13
74NHL Action Stamps-260
74O-Pee-Chee NHL-198
74Topps-198
75Maple Leafs Postcards-13
75O-Pee-Chee NHL-311
75Topps-311
76Maple Leafs Postcards-10
76O-Pee-Chee NHL-302
77Maple Leafs Postcards-10
77O-Pee-Chee NHL-374
02Maple Leafs Platinum Collection-79
02Maple Leafs Platinum Collection-86
Autographs-79
04ITG Franchises Canadian-97
Autographs-JMK
07Maple Leafs 1967 Commemorative-18

McKenzie, Aaron
04South Surrey Eagles-13
04Surrey Eagles-11
04Surrey Eagles-12

McKenzie, Bari
04UK Milton Keynes Lightning-5
04UK U-20 Team-13

McKenzie, Bill
76O-Pee-Chee NHL-267
78O-Pee-Chee-275
79Rockies Team Issue-13

McKenzie, Erica
04Minnesota Golden Gophers Women-4

McKenzie, Gordon
24Crescent Falcon-Tigers-12

McKenzie, Ian
04Moose Jaw Warriors-20
05Moose Jaw Warriors-15

McKenzie, Jim
89ProCards AHL-302
90Whalers Jr. 7-Eleven-19
90ProCards AHL/IHL-175
91Bowman-7
91O-Pee-Chee-24
91Pro Set-391
French-391
91Stadium Club-354
91Topps-24
91Upper Deck-494
French-494
91Whalers Jr. 7-Eleven-21
92Whalers Dairymart-15
93Parkhurst-357
Emerald Ice-357
93Upper Deck-23
94Parkhurst-178
Gold-178
94Penguins Foodland-20
95Jets Team Issue-15
96Be A Player-69
Autographs-69
Autographs Silver-69
96Coyotes Coca-Cola-21
97Coyotes Face-Off Luncheon -14
97Upper Deck-337
99Pacific-10
Copper-10
Emerald Green-10
Gold-10
Ice Blue-10
Premiere Date-10
Red-10
99Upper Deck Retro-3
Gold-3
Platinum-3
00Devils Team Issue-13
00Upper Deck NHLPA-PA53
01Devils Team Issue-14
01Pacific-234
Extreme LTD-234
Hobby LTD-234
Premiere Date-234
Retail LTD-234
01Pacific Arena Exclusives-234
02Devils Team Issue-15

McKenzie, John
57St. Catherine's Tee Pees-NNO
60Parkhurst-37
60Shirriff Coins-43
61Parkhurst-34
63Topps-42
64Beehive Group III Photos-47
64Coca-Cola Caps-32
64Topps-30
64Toronto Star-32
65Coca-Cola-84
65Topps-94
66Topps-97
66Topps USA Test-66
67Topps-39
68O-Pee-Chee-9
68Shirriff Coins-11
68Topps-9
69O-Pee-Chee-28
69Topps-28
70Bruins Postcards-12
70Bruins Team Issue-15
70Colgate Stamps-59
70Dad's Cookies-83
70Esso Power Players-68
70O-Pee-Chee-6
70O-Pee-Chee-241
70Sargent Promotions Stamps-9
70Topps-6
71Bruins Postcards-14
71O-Pee-Chee-82
71Sargent Promotions Stamps-3
71Topps-82
71Toronto Sun-14
72O-Pee-Chee-338
72 7-Eleven Slurpee Cups WHA-14
72Finnish Semic World Championship-185
72Swedish Semic World Championship-185
74Team Canada L'Equipe WHA-16
75O-Pee-Chee WHA-77
76O-Pee-Chee WHA-103
77O-Pee-Chee WHA-41
91Ultimate Original Six-52
French-52
94Parkhurst Tall Boys-36
95Parkhurst '66-67-10
Coins-10
98Bruins Alumni-19
Autographs-19

McKenzie, Mark
93Quebec Pee-Wee Tournament-1223

McKeown, Christopher
93Quebec Pee-Wee Tournament-1700

McKeown, Kevin
93Quebec Pee-Wee Tournament-1699

McKeown, Mike
02Peterborough Petes-21

McKeracher, Jamie
93Quebec Pee-Wee Tournament-1436

McKercher, Jeff
96Barrie Colts-17
97Barrie Colts-16
99Bowman CHL-139
Gold-139
OPC International-139

McKichan, Steve
90ProCards AHL/IHL-341

McKie, Rusty
97El Paso Buzzards-8
98Colorado Gold Kings-13
98Phoenix Mustangs-8
99Knoxville Speed-8

McKie, Ryan
95Slapshot-177
97Sudbury Wolves Police-18
98Sudbury Wolves-15

McKillop, Bob
907th Inn. Sketch OHL-66
91Michigan Falcons-19
92Anaheim Bullfrogs RHI-8
93Anaheim Bullfrogs RHI-13
98Port Huron Border Cats-6

McKillop, Larry
71Rochester Americans-11

McKim, Andrew
90ProCards AHL/IHL-626
91ProCards-343
93Classic Pro Prospects-14
94Parkhurst-16
Gold-16
95Swiss HNL-503
96German DEL-38
96Swedish Semic Wien All-Stars-AS6
96Swiss HNL-584
98German DEL-159
99Swiss Panini Stickers-118
00Swiss Panini Stickers-283
00Swiss Slapshot Mini-Cards-ZSCL12
04German Berlin Eisbarens 50th Anniv-56

McKinlay, Barry
92Thunder Bay Thunder Hawks-21
93Thunder Bay Senators-12
94Thunder Bay Senators-5
95Thunder Bay Senators-11
98Thunder Bay Thunder Cats-2
99Rockford IceHogs-14
03Port Huron Beacons-16

McKinlay, Derek
04Huntsville Havoc-19

McKinlay, Mike
91British Columbia JHL-125
92British Columbia JHL-164

McKinley, Lucas
06PEI Rocket-14

McKinley, Rob
84Kamloops Blazers-17
85Kamloops Blazers-14
86Kamloops Blazers-12
86Regina Pats-18
87Regina Pats-19

McKinley, Tyler
04Sault Ste. Marie Greyhounds-12
05Erie Otters-23

McKinney, Bryan
94Guelph Storm-4
95Slapshot-88
95Guelph Storm-18
99Johnstown Chiefs-22

McKinnon, Alex
24V145-2-16

McKinnon, Brian
82Ottawa 67's-13
83Ottawa 67's-18

McKinnon, Kenny
37V356 Worldwide Gum-118

McKinnon, Kevin
92North Dakota Fighting Sioux-20
94Erie Panthers-10
98Colorado Gold Kings-14
98Colorado Gold Kings Postcards-8
98San Angelo Outlaws-11
99Colorado Gold Kings Taco Bell-13
99Colorado Gold Kings Wendy's-10
99San Angelo Outlaws-10
01Colorado Gold Kings-21

McKinnon, Mike
02Fort Worth Brahmas-9
03UK London Racers-9

McKinnon, Paul
79Capitals Team Issue-12

McKinnon, Robert
24C144 Champ's Cigarettes-39

McKinnon, Tom
01Flint Generals-11

McKnight, Matt
03Camrose Kodiaks-6
04Minnesota-Duluth Bulldogs-15

McKnight, Wes
34Beehive Group I Photos-347

McLachlan, Darren
03Springfield Falcons Postcards-9
04Idaho Steelheads-10

McLaine, Mike
93Quebec Pee-Wee Tournament-1213

McLane, Mark
87Hull Olympiques-13

McLaren, Don
81Ottawa 67's-13
82Ottawa 67's-14
83Ottawa 67's-19
93Swiss HNL-402
95Swiss HNL-48
96Swiss HNL-309

McLaren, Frazer
03Portland Winter Hawks-19
04Portland Winter Hawks-7

McLaren, Kyle
93Tacoma Rockets-16
95Be A Player-173
Signatures-S173
Signatures Die Cuts-S173
95Bowman-151
All-Foil-151
95Canada Games NHL POGS-35
95Donruss-334
Elite Rookies-15
95Finest-111
Refractors-111
95Metal-184
95Parkhurst International-262
Emerald Ice-262
95Select Certified-139
Mirror Gold-139
95SkyBox Impact-189
95SP-8
95Stadium Club-63
Members Only Master Set-63
95Summit-194
Artist's Proofs-194
Ice-194
95Topps-309
OPC Inserts-309
SuperSkills Super Rookies-SR9
95Ultra-349
95Upper Deck-421
Electric Ice-421
Electric Ice Gold-421
95Zenith-127
Rookie Roll Call-17
96Collector's Choice-15
96Collector's Choice-341
96Donruss-219
Press Proofs-219
96Fleer-5
96Leaf-142
Press Proofs-142
96Metal Universe-8
96Score-258
Artist's Proofs-258
Dealer's Choice Artist's Proofs-258
Special Artist's Proofs-258
Golden Blades-258
96SkyBox Impact-6
96SP-8
96Summit-159
Artist's Proofs-159
Ice-159
Metal-159
Premium Stock-159
96Topps Picks Rookie Stars-RS13
96Topps Picks Rookie Stars OPC-RS13
96Ultra-9
Gold Medallion-9
96Upper Deck-9
Generation Next-X37
Superstar Showdown-SS25B
97Black Diamond-54
Double Diamond-54
Triple Diamond-54
Quadruple Diamond-54
97Collector's Choice-15
97Donruss Limited-106
Exposure-106
97Donruss Preferred-107
Cut to the Chase-107
97Pacific-42
Copper-42
Emerald Green-42
Ice Blue-42
Red-42
Silver-42
97Score Bruins-19
Platinum-19
Premier-19
97SP Authentic-11
97Upper Deck-13
98Pacific-86
Ice Blue-86
Red-86
98UD Choice-16
Prime Choice Reserve-16
Reserve-16
98Upper Deck-219
Exclusives-219
Exclusives 1 of 1-219
Gold Reserve-219
98Upper Deck MVP-15
Gold Script-15
Silver Script-15
Super Script-15
99BAP Memorabilia-47
Gold-47
Silver-47
Selects Silver-SL22
Selects Gold-SL22
99BAP Millennium-25
Emerald-25
Ruby-25
Sapphire-25
Signatures-25
Signatures Gold-25
99O-Pee-Chee-218
99O-Pee-Chee Chrome-218
99O-Pee-Chee Chrome Refractors-218
99Pacific-27
Copper-27
Emerald Green-27
Gold-27
Ice Blue-27
Premiere Date-27
Red-27
99Panini Stickers-29
99Topps/OPC-218
99Topps/OPC Chrome-218
Refractors-218
99Upper Deck-186
Exclusives-186
Exclusives 1 of 1-186
99Upper Deck Gold Reserve-186
99Upper Deck MVP-16
Gold Script-16
Silver Script-16
Super Script-16
99Upper Deck Victory-30
99Wayne Gretzky Hockey-18
00BAP Memorabilia-85
Emerald-85
Ruby-85
Sapphire-85
Promos-85
00BAP Mem Chicago Sportsfest Copper-85
00BAP Memorabilia Chicago Sportsfest Blue-85
00BAP Memorabilia Chicago Sportsfest Gold-85
00BAP Memorabilia Chicago Sportsfest Ruby-85
00BAP Memorabilia Chicago Sun-Times Ruby-85
00BAP Memorabilia Chicago Sun-Times Gold-85
00BAP Mem Chicago Sun-Times Sapphire-85
00BAP Mem Toronto Fall Expo Copper-85
00BAP Memorabilia Toronto Fall Expo Gold-85
00BAP Memorabilia Toronto Fall Expo Ruby-85
00BAP Memorabilia Update Teammates-TM11
00BAP Memorabilia Update Teammates Gold-TM11
00BAP Parkhurst 2000-P52
00BAP Signature Series-97
Emerald-97
Ruby-97
Sapphire-97
Department of Defense-DD8
Jersey Cards-J36
Jersey and Stick Cards-GSJ36
Jersey Cards Autographs-J36
Jersey Emblems-E36
Jersey Numbers-IN36
00BAP Ultimate Mem Game-Used Jerseys-GJ35
00BAP Ultimate Mem Game-Used Sticks-GS35
00O-Pee-Chee-126
00O-Pee-Chee Parallel-126
00Pacific-38
Copper-38
Gold-38
Ice Blue-38
Premiere Date-38
00Stadium Club-139
00Titanium Draft Day Edition-5
00Topps/OPC-126
Parallel-126
00Upper Deck-17
Exclusives Tier 1-17
Exclusives Tier 2-17
00Upper Deck MVP-18
First Stars-18
Second Stars-18
Third Stars-18
00Upper Deck Vintage-27
00Upper Deck Vintage-36
00Vanguard Dual Game-Worn Jerseys-14
00Vanguard Dual Game-Worn Patches-14
01BAP Memorabilia-203
Emerald-203
Ruby-203
Sapphire-203
01BAP Signature Series Certified 100-C22
01BAP Signature Series Certified 50-C22
01BAP Signature Series Certified 1 of 1's-C22
01BAP Signature Series Autographs-LKM
01BAP Signature Series Autographs Gold-LKM
01BAP Sig Series Department of Defense-DD-7
01Pacific Heads-Up Quad Jerseys-2
01Titanium Draft Day Edition-10
01Upper Deck-15
Exclusives-15
01Upper Deck MVP-15
01Upper Deck Victory-35
Gold-35
01Upper Deck Vintage-18
02BAP First Edition-25
Jerseys-25
02BAP Sig Series Auto Buybacks 1999-25
02BAP Sig Series Auto Buybacks 2001-LKM
02Pacific Heads-Up Quad Jerseys-3
02Pacific Heads-Up Quad Jerseys Gold-3
02Parkhurst Teammates-TT8
02Parkhurst Retro-157
Minis-157
02UD Premier Collection-46A
02Upper Deck Rookie Update-87
03Beehive-161
Gold-161
Silver-161
03ITG Action-457
03O-Pee-Chee-217
03OPC Blue-217
03OPC Gold-217
03OPC Red-217
03Pacific Complete-230
Red-230
03Sharks Postcards-11
03Topps-217
Blue-217
Gold-217
Red-217
03Topps C55-107
Minis-107
Minis American Back-107
Minis American Back Red-107
Minis Bazooka Back-107
Minis Brooklyn Back-107
Minis Hat Trick Back-107
Minis O Canada Back-107
Minis O Canada Back Red-107
Minis Stanley Cup Back-107
03Topps Pristine-28
Gold Refractor Die Cuts-28
Refractors-28
Press Plates Black-28
Press Plates Cyan-28
Press Plates Magenta-28
Press Plates Yellow-28
03Upper Deck-162
Canadian Exclusives-162
HG-162
03Upper Deck MVP-355
Gold Script-355
Silver Script-355
Canadian Exclusives-355
03Upper Deck Victory-160
Bronze-160
Gold-160
Silver-160
04Upper Deck-148
Canadian Exclusives-148
HG Glossy Gold-148
HG Glossy Silver-148
05Parkhurst-409
Facsimile Auto Parallel-409
05Upper Deck-160
HG Glossy-160
05Upper Deck MVP-329
Gold-329
Platinum-329
05Upper Deck Toronto Fall Expo-160
06O-Pee-Chee-418
Rainbow-418

McLaren, Steve
93North Bay Centennials-4
94North Bay Centennials-5
95Indianapolis Ice-14
97Indianapolis Ice-16
01Worcester Icecats-26
02Worcester IceCats-13
03ITG VIP Rookie Debut-88
03Parkhurst Rookie-101
03Upper Deck Rookie Update-109
03Worcester Ice Cats-18
04Springfield Falcons-25
05Springfield Falcons-20

McLarren, Rick
92British Columbia JHL-141

McLarty, Jim
91Air Canada SJHL-C20
91Air Canada SJHL All-Stars-9

McLaughlin, Blair
99Brampton Battalion-26

McLaughlin, Brian
03UK London Racers-10

McLaughlin, Cam
99Brampton Battalion-8

McLaughlin, Jordan
03Vancouver Giants-2

McLaughlin, Maj. F
83Hall of Fame Postcards-J9
85Hall of Fame-189

McLaughlin, Mike
92Rochester Americans Dunkin' Donuts-11
92Rochester Americans Kodak-14
94Binghamton Rangers-12

McLaughlin, Peter
92Harvard Crimson-25

McLay, Dave
86Portland Winter Hawks-12

McLean, Brett
95Upper Deck-506
Electric Ice-506
Electric Ice Gold-506
98UD Choice-270
Prime Choice Reserve-270
Reserve-270
98Kelowna Rockets-18
99Bowman CHL-112
Gold-112
OPC International-112
00Cleveland Lumberjacks-6
02Norfolk Admirals-16
03Blackhawks Postcards-14
03Crown Royale-20
Blue-20
Retail-20
03Parkhurst Original Six Chicago-26
03Topps Traded-TT34
Blue-TT34
Gold-TT34
Red-TT34
04Pacific-61
Blue-61
Red-61
04Swedish Malmo Red Hawks-19
05Parkhurst-131
Facsimile Auto Parallel-131
06Avalanche Team Postcards-10
06O-Pee-Chee-134
Rainbow-134

McLean, Cail
05South Carolina Stingrays-9

McLean, Carl
01Cape Breton Screaming Eagles-17
02Moncton Wildcats-23

McLean, Cory
01Notre Dame Fighting Irish-17
03Notre Dame Fighting Irish-3
04Notre Dame Fighting Irish-24

McLean, Darren
91Air Canada SJHL-C25
92Saskatchewan JHL-12
98Fayetteville Force-2
03Cape Fear Fire Antz-8

McLean, Greg
93Kitchener Rangers-4
94Kitchener Rangers-5
96Wheeling Nailers-14

McLean, Hugh
62Sudbury Wolves-17

McLean, Jack
34Beehive Group I Photos-338

McLean, Jason
97Lethbridge Hurricanes-12

McLean, Jeff
91UND Fighting Sioux Sports Collectors Card Set -15
92Kansas City Blades-6
92Classic-85
Gold-85
92Classic Autographs-NNO
92Classic Four-Sport *-205
Gold-205
93Kansas City Blades-4
94Classic Pro Prospects-139
95Kansas City Blades-13
96Kansas City Blades-15

McLean, Jim
91Air Canada SJHL-86
98Amarillo Rattlers-13

McLean, Keith
92Harvard Crimson-26

McLean, Kirk
83Oshawa Generals-2
87Canucks Shell Oil-12
88Canucks Mohawk-11
88O-Pee-Chee Stickers-11
88O-Pee-Chee Stickers-55
88O-Pee-Chee Stickers-136
88O-Pee-Chee Stickers-140
88Panini Stickers-132
89Canucks Mohawk-11
89Kraft-43
89O-Pee-Chee-61
89O-Pee-Chee Stickers-64
89Panini Stickers-155
89Topps-61
90Bowman-57
Tiffany-57
90Canucks Mohawk-19
90Canucks Molson-5
90Canucks Molson-6
90Kraft-70
90O-Pee-Chee-257
90OPC Premier-70
90Panini Stickers-296
90Pro Set-302
90Pro Set-355
90Score-93
Canadian-93
90Score Hottest/Rising Stars-46
90Topps-257
Tiffany-257
90Upper Deck-278
French-278
91Pro Set Platinum-239
91Bowman-310
91Canucks Panini Team Stickers-G
91Canucks Autograph Cards-14
91Canucks Molson-6
91Canucks Team Issue 8x10-14
91O-Pee-Chee-221
91OPC Premier-158
91Panini Stickers-45
91Parkhurst-181
91Parkhurst-440
French-181
French-440
91Pinnacle-158
French-158
91Pro Set-501
91Pro Set-603
91Pro Set-AU501
French-501
French-603
French-AU501
Player of the Month-P1
Puck Candy Promos-1
Puck Candy-28
91Score American-261
91Score Canadian Bilingual-481
91Score Canadian English-481
91Stadium Club-105
91Topps-221
91Upper Deck-191
French-191
92Bowman-212
92Bowman-285
92Canucks Road Trip Art-13
92Humpty Dumpty I-15
92Kraft-29
92O-Pee-Chee-342
92O-Pee-Chee-349
92Panini Stickers-27
92Panini Stickers French-27
92Parkhurst-192
Emerald Ice-192
92Pinnacle-246
92Pinnacle-330
French-246
French-330
92Pro Set-193
92Pro Set-250
92Pro Set-AU239
92Score-385
Canadian-385
92Seasons Patches-71
92Stadium Club-193
92Topps-130
92Topps-270
Gold-130G
Gold-270G
92Ultra-224
92Upper Deck-22
92Upper Deck-299
93Donruss-355
93Kraft-58
93Leaf-55
Painted Warriors-3
93OPC Premier-113
Gold-113
93Panini Stickers-177
93Parkhurst-213
Emerald Ice-213
93Pinnacle-158
Canadian-158
Team Pinnacle-7
Team Canadian-7
93PowerPlay-253
93Score-47
Canadian-47
93Stadium Club-163
Members Only Master Set-163
OPC-163
First Day Issue-163
First Day Issue OPC-163
93Topps/OPC Premier-113
Gold-113
93Ultra-29
93Upper Deck-156
NHLPA/Roots-7
SP-165
93Swedish Semic World Champ Stickers-190
94Action Packed Big Picture 24K Gold-2G
94Be A Player-R73
94Be A Player-R107
94Canada Games NHL POGS-270
94Canucks Program Inserts-15
94Donruss-22
Masked Marvels-6
94EA Sports-144
94Finest-61
Super Team Winners-61
Refractors-61
94Flair-193
94Fleer-227
Netminders-6
94Kraft-46
94Leaf-109
Crease Patrol-7
94Leaf Limited-23
94OPC Premier-85
94OPC Premier-397
Special Effects-85
Special Effects-397
94Parkhurst-238
Gold-238
SE Vintage-10
94Pinnacle-60
Artist's Proofs-60
Rink Collection-60
Goaltending Greats-GT11
94Score-60
Gold-60
Platinum-60
94Select-64
Gold-64
94SP-124
Die Cuts-124
94Stadium Club-188
94Stadium Club-223
Members Only Master Set-188
Members Only Master Set-223
First Day Issue-188
First Day Issue-223
Super Team Winner Cards-188
Super Team Winner Cards-223
94Topps/OPC Premier-85
94Topps/OPC Premier-397
Special Effects-85
Special Effects-397
94Ultra-228
94Upper Deck-133
Electric Ice-133
Predictor Hobby-H34
94Upper Deck Predictor Hobby Exch Gold-H34
94Upper Deck SP Inserts-SP84
94Upper Deck SP Inserts Die Cuts-SP84
95Bashan Super Stickers-127
95Be A Player-200
Signatures-S200
Signatures Die Cuts-S200
95Canada Games NHL POGS-278
95Canucks Building the Dream Art-1
95Collector's Choice-71
Player's Club-71
Player's Club Platinum-71
95Donruss-16
95Emotion-181
95Finest-161
Refractors-161
95Imperial Stickers-127
95Kraft-18
95Leaf-102
95Leaf Limited-67
95McDonald's Pinnacle-MCD-30
95Metal-152
95Panini Stickers-298
95Parkhurst International-213
Emerald Ice-213
Goal Patrol-11
95Pinnacle-132
Artist's Proofs-132
Rink Collection-132
95Playoff One on One-101
95Pro Magnets-28
95Score-49
Black Ice Artist's Proofs-49
Black Ice-49
95Select Certified-63
Mirror Gold-63
95SkyBox Impact-170
Deflectors-12
95SP-152
95Stadium Club-41
Members Only Master Set-41
95Stadium Club Master Photo Test-5
95Summit-69
Artist's Proofs-69
Ice-69
In The Crease-14
95Topps-277
OPC Inserts-277
Hidden Gems-13HG
95Topps SuperSkills-89
Platinum-89
95Ultra-170
95Ultra-373
Gold Medallion-170
95Upper Deck-136
Electric Ice-136
Electric Ice Gold-136
Special Edition-SE83
Special Edition Gold-SE83
95Zenith-57
96Canucks Postcards-1
96Collector's Choice-271
96Donruss-3
Press Proofs-3
96Donruss Canadian Ice-33
Gold Press Proofs-33
Red Press Proofs-33
96Donruss Elite-121
Die Cut Stars-121
96Fleer-113
96Leaf-43
Press Proofs-43
96Metal Universe-158
96NHL Pro Stamps-28
96Pinnacle-90
Artist's Proofs-90
Foil-90
Premium Stock-90
Rink Collection-90
96Score-155
Artist's Proofs-155
Dealer's Choice Artist's Proofs-155
Special Artist's Proofs-155
Golden Blades-155
96Select Certified-22
Artist's Proofs-22
Blue-22
Mirror Blue-22
Mirror Gold-22
Mirror Red-22
Red-22
96SkyBox Impact-134
96Summit-68
Artist's Proofs-68
Ice-68
Metal-68
Premium Stock-68
96Team Out-57
96Ultra-169
Gold Medallion-169
96Upper Deck-348
97Be A Player-118
Autographs-118
Autographs Die-Cuts-118
Autographs Prismatic Die-Cuts-118
97Black Diamond-31
Double Diamond-31
Triple Diamond-31
Quadruple Diamond-31
97Donruss-189
Press Proofs Silver-189
Press Proofs Gold-189
97Donruss Canadian Ice-79
Dominion Series-79
Provincial Series-79
97Donruss Limited-3

Exposure-3
97Donruss Priority-162
Stamp of Approval-162
97Katch-147
Gold-147
Silver-147
97Leaf-74
Fractal Matrix-74
Fractal Matrix Die Cuts-74
97Leaf International-74
Universal Ice-74
97Pacific-258
Copper-258
Emerald Green-258
Ice Blue-258
Red-258
Silver-258
97Pacific Dynagon-128
Copper-128
Dark Grey-128
Emerald Green-128
Ice Blue-128
Red-128
Silver-128
Tandems-56
97Pacific Invincible-143
Copper-143
Emerald Green-143
Ice Blue-143
Red-143
Silver-143
97Paramount-189
Copper-189
Dark Grey-189
Emerald Green-189
Ice Blue-189
Red-189
Silver-189
97Pinnacle-88
Artist's Proofs-88
Rink Collection-88
Press Plates Back Black-88
Press Plates Back Cyan-88
Press Plates Back Magenta-88
Press Plates Back Yellow-88
Press Plates Front Black-88
Press Plates Front Cyan-88
Press Plates Front Magenta-88
Press Plates Front Yellow-88
97Pinnacle Certified-27
Red-27
Mirror Blue-27
Mirror Gold-27
Mirror Red-27
97Pinnacle Inside-60
Coach's Collection-60
Executive Collection-60
97Pinnacle Tot Cert Platinum Blue-27
97Pinnacle Tot Certi Platinum Gold-27
97Pinnacle Totally Certified Platinum Red-27
97Pinnacle Tot Cert Mirror Platinum Gold-27
97Score-43
Artist's Proofs-43
Golden Blades-43
97Score Canucks-10
Platinum-10
Premier-10
97SP Authentic-159
97Studio-88
Press Proofs Silver-88
Press Proofs Gold-88
97Upper Deck-375
98SLU Hockey-130
98Kenner Starting Lineup Cards-21
98NHL Aces Playing Cards-29
98Pacific-225
Ice Blue-225
Red-225
99Pacific-177
Copper-177
Emerald Green-177
Gold-177
Ice Blue-177
Premiere Date-177
Red-177
99Upper Deck Victory-197
00Black Diamond Game Gear-CKM
00Pacific-267
Copper-267
Gold-267
Ice Blue-267
Premiere Date-267
00Titanium Game Gear-38
00Titanium Game Gear-39
01Between the Pipes-71
04ITG Franchises Canadian-128
Autographs-KML
04ITG Franchises US East Memorabilia-ESM26
04ITG Franchises US East Memorabilia Gold-ESM26
05ITG Ultimate Mem 3 Star of the Game Jsy-23
05ITG Ult Mem 3 Star of the Game Jsy Gold-23

McLean, Mike
03Oshawa Generals-16
04Guelph Storm-16
05Guelph Storm-D-04
06Guelph Storm-12

McLean, Sean
93Quebec Pee-Wee Tournament-47

McLeary, Mark
82Victoria Cougars-16

McLellan, Cam
89Regina Pats-13

McLellan, Dusty
91British Columbia JHL-25
91British Columbia JHL-155
92British Columbia JHL-130
93Johnstown Chiefs-11

Mclellan, Jim
61Hamilton Red Wings-13

McLellan, Todd
83Saskatoon Blades-14
84Saskatoon Blades Stickers-14
88ProCards AHL-303
00Cleveland Lumberjacks-20
06Houston Aeros RetroÂ -9

McLelland, Kevin
89Red Wings Little Caesars-12

McLemman, Jamal
99Pacific Copper-360
99Pacific Emerald Green-360
99Pacific Gold-360
99Pacific Red-360

McLennan, Jamie
89Lethbridge Hurricanes-15
907th Inn. Sketch WHL-129
91Richmond Renegades-20
91Richmond Renegades Set 2-8
917th Inn. Sketch CHL Award Winners-16
917th Inn. Sketch Memorial Cup-79
91Classic-40
91Star Pics-32
91Ultimate Draft-35
91Classic Four-Sport *-40
93Donruss-458
93PowerPlay-386
94Canada Games NHL POGS-286
94Donruss-88
94Flair-107
94Fleer-127
94Kraft-47
94Leaf-74
94OPC Premier-143
94O-Pee-Chee Finest Inserts-21
94OPC Premier Special Effects-143
94Pinnacle-250
Artist's Proofs-250
Rink Collection-250
94Score-224
Gold-224
Platinum-224
94Select-189
Gold-189
94Topps/OPC Premier-143
Special Effects-143
94Ultra-328
94Upper Deck-252
Electric Ice-252
SP Inserts-SP137
SP Inserts Die Cuts-SP137
94Classic Pro Prospects-112
95Parkhurst International-404
Emerald Ice-404
97Be A Player-107
Autographs-107
Autographs Die-Cuts-107
Autographs Prismatic Die-Cuts-107
97Score Blues-20
Platinum-20
Premier-20
98Aurora-162
98Be A Player-273
Press Release-273
98BAP Gold-273
98BAP Autographs-273
98BAP Autographs Gold-273
98NHL Aces Playing Cards-7
98Pacific-369
Ice Blue-369
Red-369
98Pacific Dynagon Ice-160
Blue-160
Red-160
98Pacific Omega-204
Red-204
Opening Day Issue-204
98Panini Stickers-228
98Paramount-205
Copper-205
Emerald Green-205
Holo-Electric-205
Ice Blue-205
Silver-205
98UD Choice-187
98UD Choice Preview-187
98UD Choice Prime Choice Reserve-187
98UD Choice Reserve-187
98Upper Deck-361
Exclusives-361
Exclusives 1 of 1-361
Gold Reserve-361
99Blues Taco Bell-3
99Pacific-360
Ice Blue-360
Premiere Date-360
99Pacific Omega-197
Copper-197
Gold-197
Ice Blue-197
Premiere Date-197
00Crown Royale-53
Ice Blue-53
Limited Series-53
Premiere Date-53
Red-53
00Pacific-347
Copper-347
Gold-347
Ice Blue-347
Premiere Date-347
00Paramount-120
Copper-120
Gold-120
Holo-Gold-120
Holo-Silver-120
Ice Blue-120
Premiere Date-120
00Revolution-72
Blue-72
Premiere Date-72
Red-72
00Stadium Club-206
00Topps Chrome-231
OPC Refractors-231
Refractors-231
00Topps Heritage-104
00UD Reserve-42
01Between the Pipes-49
01Crown Royale Triple Threads-18
01O-Pee-Chee-67
01O-Pee-Chee Heritage Parallel-67
01O-Pee-Chee Heritage Parallel Limited-67
01O-Pee-Chee Premier Parallel-67
01Pacific-199
Extreme LTD-199
Hobby LTD-199
Premiere Date-199
Retail LTD-199
Adrenaline Jerseys-21
01Pacific Arena Exclusives-199
01Private Stock Game Gear-53
01Private Stock Game Gear Patches-53
01Titanium Double-Sided Jerseys-15
01Titanium Double-Sided Jerseys-70
01Titanium Double-Sided Patches-70
01Titanium Draft Day Edition-47
01Topps-67
Heritage Parallel-67
Heritage Parallel Limited-67
OPC Parallel-67
01Upper Deck Victory-179
Gold-179
01Vanguard Memorabilia-29
02BAP Sig Series Auto Buybacks 1998-273
02Between the Pipes-67
Gold-67
Silver-67
02NHL Power Play Stickers-16
02Pacific Complete-392
Red-392
02Pacific Heads-Up Quad Jerseys-14
02Pacific Heads-Up Quad Jerseys Gold-14
02UD Mask Collection-13
02UD Mask Collection-14
02UD Mask Collection Beckett Promos-13
02UD Mask Collection Beckett Promos-14
02Vanguard Jerseys-8
02Vanguard Jerseys Gold-8
03Beehive-29
Gold-29
Silver-29
03ITG Action-61
03Pacific-55
Blue-55
Red-55
03Pacific Complete-479
Red-479
03Pacific Heads-Up-15
Hobby LTD-15
Retail LTD-15
03Pacific Invincible Jerseys-4
03Upper Deck-277
Canadian Exclusives-277
HG-277
UD Exclusives-277
03Upper Deck MVP-75
Gold Script-75
Silver Script-75
Canadian Exclusives-75
03Upper Deck Victory-31
Bronze-31
Gold-31
Silver-31
05Parkhurst-212
Facsimile Auto Parallel-212
05Upper Deck MVP-174
Gold-174
Platinum-174
06O-Pee-Chee-79
Rainbow-79

McLennen, Blondie
28V128-2 Paulin's Candy-45

McLeod, Al
75O-Pee-Chee WHA-88
75Phoenix Roadrunners WHA-15
76O-Pee-Chee WHA-47

McLeod, Cody
03Portland Winter Hawks-7
04Portland Winter Hawks-12
04Portland Winter Hawks-NNO
06Albany River Rats-16

McLeod, Don
74O-Pee-Chee WHA-48
74Team Canada L'Equipe WHA-17
75O-Pee-Chee WHA-32
76O-Pee-Chee WHA-129
77O-Pee-Chee WHA-14

McLeod, Gavin
98Kelowna Rockets-19
99Kelowna Rockets-16
00Kelowna Rockets-16

McLeod, Jack
44Beehive Group II Photos-344
51Parkhurst-98
52Parkhurst-102

McLeod, Jimmy
727-Eleven Slurpee Cups WHA-15
73Quaker Oats WHA-17

McLeod, Kiel
98Kelowna Rockets-20
99Kelowna Rockets-14
99UD Prospects-75
00Kelowna Rockets-1
00UD CHL Prospects-52
00UD CHL Prospects-95
01Kelowna Rockets-13
01UD Prospects-40
Autographs-A-KM
Jersey Autographs-S-KM
Jerseys-J-KM
Jerseys-C-HM
Jerseys Gold-J-KM
Jerseys Gold-C-HM
02Kelowna Rockets-3
03Kelowna Rockets Memorial Cup-12
03Springfield Falcons Postcards-3
04ITG Heroes and Prospects-28
Autographs-KM
Combos-6
Complete Emblems-24
Emblems-40
Emblems Gold-40
He Shoots-He Scores Prizes-26
Jersey Autographs-40
Jerseys-40
Jerseys Gold-40
Numbers-40
Numbers Gold-40
04ITG Heroes/Prospects Toronto Expo '05-28
04ITG Heroes/Prospects Expo Heroes/Pros-28

McLeod, Pat
91Kansas City Blades-1
99Cincinnati Cyclones-14

McLeod, Pete
85London Knights-15

McLeod, Ryan
03Salmon Arm Silverbacks-14
06New Mexico Scorpions-9

McLlwain, Dave
84Kitchener Rangers-21
87Penguins Kodak-19
88O-Pee-Chee-132
88Topps-132
88ProCards IHL-56
89Jets Safeway-20
90Bowman-136
Tiffany-136
90Jets IGA-22
90O-Pee-Chee-299
90Panini Stickers-319
90Pro Set-333
90Score-231A
90Score-231B
Canadian-231A
Canadian-231B
90Topps-299
Tiffany-299
90Upper Deck-216
French-216
91Bowman-196
91Jets Panini Team Stickers-17
91O-Pee-Chee-95
91Panini Stickers-73
91Pro Set-434
French-434
91Score Canadian Bilingual-233
91Score Canadian English-233
91Score Rookie/Traded-102T
91Stadium Club-202
91Topps-95
91Upper Deck-222
91Upper Deck-527
French-222
French-527
92Maple Leafs Kodak-16
92Maple Leafs Kodak-29
92Score-122
Canadian-122
92Stadium Club-491
92Topps-393
Gold-393G
92Upper Deck-93
93Maple Leafs Score Black's-9
93PowerPlay-402
93Score-418
93Score-583
Gold-583
Canadian-418
Canadian-583
Canadian Gold-583
93Senators Kraft Sheets-19
93Upper Deck-524
94Be A Player Signature Cards-9
94Canada Games NHL POGS-355
94Donruss-315
94Flair-123
94Leaf-260
94OPC Premier-446
Special Effects-446
94Parkhurst-157
Gold-157
94Pinnacle-54
Artist's Proofs-54
Rink Collection-54
94Senators Team Issue-22
94Stadium Club-31
Members Only Master Set-31
First Day Issue-31
Super Team Winner Cards-31
94Topps/OPC Premier-446
Special Effects-446
94Upper Deck-423
Electric Ice-423
95Cleveland Lumberjacks-18
95Cleveland Lumberjacks Postcards-17
96Cleveland Lumberjacks-16
96Cleveland Lumberjacks Multi-Ad-18
98Swiss Power Play Stickers-44
99Swiss Panini Stickers-45
00German DEL-140
01German Upper Deck-142
02German DEL City Press-199
03German DEL-174
All-Stars-AS19
03German Cologne Sharks Postcards-19
04German DEL-216
All-Stars-AS17
05German DEL-212
All-Star Jerseys-AS09
06German DEL-128
Team Leaders-TL7

McMahon, Mark
95Slapshot-137
96Kitchener Rangers-18
98Bowman CHL-3
Golden Anniversary-3
OPC International-3
98Bowman Chrome CHL-3
Golden Anniversary-3
Golden Anniversary Refractors-3
OPC International-3
OPC International Refractors-3
Refractors-3

McMahon, Mike
43Parade Sportive *-84
45Quaker Oats Photos-97
61Sudbury Wolves-15
62Sudbury Wolves-18
65Coca-Cola-78
65Topps-24
68O-Pee-Chee-46
68Shirriff Coins-72
68Topps-46
70Dad's Cookies-84
70O-Pee-Chee-143
70Sargent Promotions Stamps-28
72Minnesota Fighting Saints Postcards WHA-15
72O-Pee-Chee-305
74Minnesota Fighting Saints WHA-16

McMahon, Rory
03North Dakota Fighting Sioux-19
04North Dakota Fighting Sioux-16

McManus, Sammy
37V356 Worldwide Gum-79

McManus, Tyler
92Cornell Big Red-21
93Cornell Big Red-19

McMaster, Geoff
91Air Canada SJHL-D15

McMeekin, Ken
52Juniors Blue Tint-179

McMichel, Scott
83Belleville Bulls-18

McMillan, Carson
05Calgary Hitmen-11

McMillan, Casey
86Kamloops Blazers-13
88Lethbridge Hurricanes-17

McMillan, Darren
04St. Francis Xavier X-Men-14

McMillan, George
01Roanoke Express-24

McMillan, Paul
91British Columbia JHL-108

McMillan, Tyler
91Air Canada SJHL-A4
92Saskatchewan JHL-146
99Peoria Rivermen-26
01Asheville Smoke-3

McMillen, Dave
907th Inn. Sketch WHL-253
917th Inn. Sketch WHL-157
92Tacoma Rockets-13

McMonagle, Tom
93Quebec Pee-Wee Tournament-1576
04Columbus Cottonmouths-10

McMorran, Larry
93Lethbridge Hurricanes-8
93Seattle Thunderbirds-13

McMorris, Doyle
95Lethbridge Hurricanes-13

McMorrow, Sean
96Quebec Pee-Wee Tournament-975
99Kitchener Rangers-21
00Kingston Frontenacs-13
00Mississauga Ice Dogs-17
01London Knights-13
02BAP Memorabilia-344
02Upper Deck Rookie Update-146
02Rochester Americans-12
03Rochester Americans-13
04Rochester Americans-11

McMulkin, John
917th Inn. Sketch WHL-175

McMullen, Bryan
95Guelph Storm-23
97Flint Generals-14
97Flint Generals EBK-18
98Colorado Gold Kings-15
98Colorado Gold Kings Postcards-6
99Austin Ice Bats-9
00Austin Ice Bats-12
01Austin Ice Bats-10

McMullen, John
96Devils Team Issue-NNO
97Devils Team Issue-32
98Devils Team Issue-18

McMullen, Jordan
03Yarmouth Mariners-14

McMullin, Ben
99Medicine Hat Tigers-23
99Medicine Hat Tigers-30
00Medicine Hat Tigers-16
02Quebec Remparts-15

McMullin, Cody
05Vernon Vipers-15

McMunn, Harold
23Crescent Selkirks-13
24Holland Creameries-2
28V128-2 Paulin's Candy-70

McMurchy, Tom
82Brandon Wheat Kings-12
83Springfield Indians-10
85Nova Scotia Oilers-18
88Oilers Tenth Anniversary-31

McMurphy, Kyle
06Penticton Vees-15

McMurtry, Chris
917th Inn. Sketch OHL-340
93Sudbury Wolves-4
93Sudbury Wolves Police-4
94Central Hockey League-63
94Oklahoma City Blazers-9

McNab, Max
44Beehive Group II Photos-194

McNab, Peter
74Sabres Postcards-15
75O-Pee-Chee NHL-252
75Sabres Linnett-7
75Topps-252
76O-Pee-Chee NHL-118
76Topps-118
77O-Pee-Chee NHL-7
77O-Pee-Chee NHL-18
77Topps-7
77Topps-18
78O-Pee-Chee-212
78Topps-212
79O-Pee-Chee-39
79Topps-39
80O-Pee-Chee-94
80O-Pee-Chee-167
80O-Pee-Chee-220
80Topps-94
80Topps-167
80Topps-220
81O-Pee-Chee-5
81O-Pee-Chee Stickers-46
81Topps-E69
82O-Pee-Chee-16
82O-Pee-Chee Stickers-83
82O-Pee-Chee Stickers-84
82Post Cereal-1
82Topps Stickers-83
82Topps Stickers-84
83Bruins Team Issue-10
83O-Pee-Chee-53
83O-Pee-Chee Stickers-51
83Topps Stickers-51
84Canucks Team Issue-17
84O-Pee-Chee-326
85O-Pee-Chee Stickers-244
86Devils Police-15
01Topps Archives-73
Autographs-25
06Parkhurst-137
Autographs-137
Autographs Dual-DAOM

McNabb, Graham
04Brampton Battalion-16
05Brampton Battalion-14
06Brampton Battalion-15

McNabb, John
99ECHL All-Star Southern Conference-11
04Austin Ice Bats-8
06Austin Ice Bats-11

McNabney, Sid
51Buffalo Bison-16

McNamara, Chris
02ECHL All-Star Northern-29
02ECHL Update-U-15
04UK Coventry Blaze-10
04UK Coventry Blaze Champions-16

McNamara, George
83Hall of Fame-220
83Hall of Fame Postcards-O10
85Hall of Fame-220

McNamara, Gerry
80Maple Leafs Postcards-18

McNamara, Harold
10C56-32

McNamara, Len
907th Inn. Sketch OHL-299

McNamara, Michael
93Swiss HNL-262

McNaught, Todd
93Quebec Pee-Wee Tournament-1177

McNaughton, Declan
94UK Solihull Barons-9

McNeil, Al
76Nova Scotia Voyageurs-12
79Flames Team Issue-10

McNeil, Douglas
51Laval Dairy QSHL-99

McNeil, Gerry
43Parade Sportive *-89
44Beehive Group II Photos-272
45Quaker Oats Photos-60A
45Quaker Oats Photos-60D
45Quaker Oats Photos-98
48Exhibits Canadian-16
51Parkhurst-15
51Parkhurst-52
52Parkhurst-12
53Parkhurst-25
54Parkhurst-1
55Parkhurst-52
Quaker Oats-52
55Montreal Royals-5
93Parkhurst Parkie Reprints-PR35
02Parkhurst Reprints-157

McNeil, Ian
99Cincinnati Cyclones-15

McNeil, Kyle
06Victoriaville Tigres-21

McNeil, Shawn
94Kamloops Blazers-6
95Kamloops Blazers-7
95Slapshot Memorial Cup-24
96Kamloops Blazers-16
97Red Deer Rebels-12
97Bowman CHL-99
OPC-99
98Red Deer Rebels-12
98Bowman CHL-71
Golden Anniversary-71
OPC International-71
98Bowman Chrome CHL-71
Golden Anniversary-71
Golden Anniversary Refractors-71
OPC International-71
OPC International Refractors-71
Refractors-71
99Louisiana Ice Gators-7
00Louisiana Ice Gators-4
01Louisiana Ice Gators-15
02Louisiana Ice Gators-12
05German DEL-48

McNeil, Steve
94German DEL-264

McNeilance, Kyle
98Arizona Icecats-16
99Arizona Icecats-15
00Arizona Icecats-15

McNeill, Bill
57Topps-44
59Topps-41
63Parkhurst-56
94Parkhurst Missing Link-48

McNeill, Grant
00Prince Albert Raiders-14
01Prince Albert Raiders-14
02Prince Albert Raiders-15
03ITG VIP Rookie Debut-63
03Pacific Complete-529
Red-529
03Parkhurst Rookie-145
03SP Authentic-135
Limited-135
03UD Honor Roll-152
03Upper Deck-458
Canadian Exclusives-458
HG-458
UD Exclusives-458
03Upper Deck Rookie Update-99
03San Antonio Rampage-8
05Florida Everblades-18

McNeill, Jay
96Richmond Renegades-14

McNeill, Mike
89ProCards IHL-72
90Blackhawks Coke-15
90Pro Set-600
91Bowman-143
91Nordiques Petro-Canada-17
91O-Pee-Chee-408
91Pro Set-467
French-467
91Stadium Club-241
91Topps-408
91Upper Deck-524
French-524
92Bowman-424
92Stadium Club-294
92Topps-166
Gold-166G
94Milwaukee Admirals-19
95Milwaukee Admirals-12
95Milwaukee Admirals Postcards-7
96Milwaukee Admirals-17
97Milwaukee Admirals-12
98German DEL-4
99German DEL-299

McNeill, Patrick
03Saginaw Spirit-13
04Saginaw Spirit-1
05OHL Bell All-Star Classic-18
05Saginaw Spirit-17
06Saginaw Spirit-2
06Saginaw Spirit-LE1
06ITG Heroes and Prospects-195
Autographs-APMC
National Pride-NP15
National Pride Gold-NP15
Update Autographs-APMC

McNelis, Bill
93Waterloo Black Hawks-18

McNicoll, Dave
93Quebec Pee-Wee Tournament-381

McNicoll, Kaven
93Quebec Pee-Wee Tournament-13

McNicoll, Pascal
92Quebec Pee-Wee Tournament-874
93Quebec Pee-Wee Tournament-525

McNiven, Andrew
03UK Coventry Blaze History-11

McNutt, Steve
907th Inn. Sketch WHL-110

McParland, Mike
93Swiss HNL-337
95Swiss HNL-315
96Swiss HNL-294
98Swiss Power Play Stickers-311
99Swiss Panini Stickers-314
00Swiss Panini Stickers-77
01Swiss HNL-258
02Swiss HNL-284

McPhee, George
85O-Pee-Chee-252
02Fleer Throwbacks-24
Gold-24
Platinum-24
03Bowling Green Falcons-4

McPhee, Iain
02Windsor Spitfires-5

McPhee, Mike
83Nova Scotia Voyageurs-19
84Canadiens Postcards-16
85Canadiens Postcards-20
85Canadiens Provigo-10
85O-Pee-Chee-225
86Canadiens Postcards-13
86Kraft Drawings-42
86O-Pee-Chee-221
86O-Pee-Chee Stickers-15
87Canadiens Kodak-3
87Canadiens Postcards-12
87Canadiens Vachon Stickers-17
87Canadiens Vachon Stickers-29
87Canadiens Vachon Stickers-37
87Canadiens Vachon Stickers-38
87Panini Stickers-66
88Canadiens Postcards-20
88O-Pee-Chee-237
88O-Pee-Chee Stickers-47
88Panini Stickers-258
89Canadiens Kraft-16
89Canadiens Postcards-24
89Canadiens Provigo Figurines-35
89Kraft All-Stars Stickers-1
89O-Pee-Chee-84
89O-Pee-Chee Stickers-59
89Panini Stickers-243
89Topps-84
90Bowman-43
Tiffany-43
90Canadiens Postcards-21
90O-Pee-Chee-137
90Panini Stickers-63
90Pro Set-155
90Topps-137
Tiffany-137
90Upper Deck-384
French-384
91Bowman-339
91Canadiens Panini Team Stickers-16
91Canadiens Postcards-19
91O-Pee-Chee-252
91Panini Stickers-188
91Parkhurst-310
French-310
91Pinnacle-147
French-147
91Pro Set-129
French-129
91Score American-147
91Score Canadian Bilingual-147
91Score Canadian English-147
91Stadium Club-210
91Topps-252
91Upper Deck-487
French-487
92Bowman-89
92O-Pee-Chee-199
92Pinnacle-342
French-342
92Score-91
Canadian-91
92Stadium Club-452
92Topps-45
Gold-45G
92Ultra-322
92Upper Deck-538
93OPC Premier-214
Gold-214
93Parkhurst-51
Emerald Ice-51
93Pinnacle-163
Canadian-163
93PowerPlay-326
93Score-85
Canadian-85
93Stadium Club-6
Members Only Master Set-6
OPC-6
First Day Issue-6
First Day Issue OPC-6
93Topps/OPC Premier-214
Gold-214
93Ultra-300
93Upper Deck-43
94Canada Games NHL POGS-80
94Leaf-203
94OPC Premier-163
Special Effects-163
94Pinnacle-105
Artist's Proofs-105
Rink Collection-105
94Score-17
Gold-17
Platinum-17
94Stars HockeyKaps-20
94Stars Score Sheet-17
94Topps/OPC Premier-163
Special Effects-163
95Summit GM's Choice-21

McPhee, Scott
92Quebec Pee-Wee Tournament-1603
93Quebec Pee-Wee Tournament-514

McPherson, Andrew
03Roanoke Express-314

McPherson, Brock
03Brampton Battalion-14
04Brampton Battalion-12
05Brampton Battalion-25

McPherson, Bud
48Exhibits Canadian-14

McPherson, Darwin
84Brandon Wheat Kings-19
88Saskatoon Blades-25
89ProCards IHL-2
90ProCards AHL/IHL-94
92Dayton Bombers-18
93Dayton Bombers-16

McPolin, Justin
95Slapshot-172

McQuade, Sean
93Quebec Pee-Wee Tournament-1726

McQuaid, Adam
03Sudbury Wolves-17
04Sudbury Wolves-15
05ITG Heroes/Prosp Toronto Expo Parallel -114
05Sudbury Wolves-5
05ITG Heroes and Prospects-114
Autographs-A-AMQ
06Sudbury Wolves-20

McQuat, Jason
92Oshawa Generals Sheet-9
93Oshawa Generals-24
95Louisiana Ice Gators-11
95Louisiana Ice Gators Playoffs-12
96Louisiana Ice Gators-8
96Louisiana Ice Gators II-9
97Louisiana Ice Gators-2
98Louisiana Ice Gators-9
99Louisiana Ice Gators-13
00Louisiana Ice Gators-14

McQuat, Rob
92Oshawa Generals Sheet-6
93Oshawa Generals-18

McQueen, Dave
95Slapshot-330

McQueen, Scott
97Red Deer Rebels-13
98Red Deer Rebels-13
00Prince Albert Raiders-15

McRae, Basil
81Fredericton Express-10
82Fredericton Express-10
83Maple Leafs Postcards-16
86Nordiques Team Issue-14
87North Stars Postcards-21
87O-Pee-Chee Stickers-227
88North Stars ADA-18
89O-Pee-Chee-216
89Panini Stickers-109
90Bowman-187
Tiffany-187
90O-Pee-Chee-151
90Panini Stickers-249
90Pro Set-141
90Score-261
Canadian-261
90Topps-151
Tiffany-151
90Upper Deck-30
French-30
91Panini Stickers-119
91Pro Set-409
French-409
91Score Canadian Bilingual-391
91Score Canadian English-391
91Upper Deck-388
French-388
92Parkhurst-391
Emerald Ice-391
92Pro Set-176
92Score-356
92Score-509
Canadian-356
Canadian-509
93PowerPlay-430
93Score-436
Canadian-436
93Stadium Club-273
Members Only Master Set-273
First Day Issue-273
95Be A Player-6
Signatures-S6
Signatures Die Cuts-S6
01Fleer Legacy-27
Ultimate-27
02Fleer Throwbacks-46
Gold-46
Platinum-46
Autographs-14
Scraps-1
Tie Downs-1
04ITG Franchises US West-258
Autographs-A-BMC
05ITG Tough Customers-BM
Autographs-BM

McRae, Chris
89ProCards AHL-308
90ProCards AHL/IHL-472
91ProCards-240

McRae, Colin
99Brandon Wheat Kings-13
00Brandon Wheat Kings-12
01Brandon Wheat Kings-14
06Sports Illustrated for Kids *-117
07Sports Illustrated for Kids *-117

McRae, Gord
74Maple Leafs Postcards-14
75Maple Leafs Postcards-14
75O-Pee-Chee NHL-203
75Topps-203
76Maple Leafs Postcards-11
76O-Pee-Chee NHL-337
77Maple Leafs Postcards-11

McRae, Ken
85Sudbury Wolves-14
86Sudbury Wolves-12
88Nordiques General Foods-27
88Nordiques Team Issue-30
88ProCards AHL-99
89Nordiques Team Issue-30
89Nordiques General Foods-23
89Nordiques Police-20
90Nordiques Team Issue-22
90O-Pee-Chee-411
90Pro Set-255
91Nordiques Panini Team Stickers-16
91Nordiques Petro-Canada-18
91ProCards-542
92St. John's Maple Leafs-13
93St. John's Maple Leafs-17
95Phoenix Roadrunners-11
99Austin Ice Bats-27
00Austin Ice Bats-24
01Austin Ice Bats-21
02Indianapolis Ice-20
03Indianapolis Ice-21

McRae, Mark
03ECHL All-Stars-254
03Florence Pride-153

McRae, Philip
06London Knights-10

McRae, Stuart
02Cape Breton Screaming Eagles-23
02Halifax Mooseheads-5

McReavy, Pat
34Beehive Group I Photos-24
34Beehive Group I Photos-116

McReynolds, Brian
89Jets Safeway-21
89ProCards AHL-47
90ProCards AHL/IHL-24
91Upper Deck-434
French-434
91ProCards-209
92Binghamton Rangers-15
93Phoenix Roadrunners-18
95Swedish Leaf-260
95Swedish Upper Deck-147
98German DEL-103

McShan, Morgan

93Quebec Pee-Wee Tournament-616
McSheffrey, Bryan
72Canucks Royal Bank-14
73Canucks Royal Bank-14
73O-Pee-Chee-219
74NHL Action Stamps-285
74NHL Action Stamps Update-4
McSorley, Chris
87Flint Spirits-14
88ProCards IHL-8
90Richmond Renegades-18
92Anaheim Bullfrogs RHI-12
92Toledo Storm-2
92Toledo Storm Team Issue-2
93Toledo Storm-2
94Las Vegas Thunder-16
95Las Vegas Thunder-23
96Las Vegas Thunder-15
97Las Vegas Thunder-12
98Las Vegas Coyotes RHI-17
99UK London Knights-11
00UK Sekonda Superleague-69
01Swiss HNL-321
02Swiss HNL-336
McSorley, Marty
83Penguins Coke-16
84Penguins Heinz Photos-15
85Oilers Red Rooster-33
86Oilers Red Rooster-33
86Oilers Team Issue-33
87Oilers Team Issue-33
87O-Pee-Chee-205
88Kings Postcards-18
88Kings Smokey-18
88Oilers Tenth Anniversary-37
89Kings Smokey-17
89Panini Stickers-99
90Kings Smokey-18
90O-Pee-Chee-17
90O-Pee-Chee-392
90Panini Stickers-234
90Pro Set-124
90Score-271
Canadian-271
90Topps-17
90Topps-392
Tiffany-392
90Upper Deck-212
French-212
91Pro Set Platinum-184
91Bowman-184
91O-Pee-Chee-225
91O-Pee-Chee-322
91Panini Stickers-84
91Parkhurst-69
French-69
91Pinnacle-35
French-35
91Pro Set-100
French-100
NHL Sponsor Awards-AC21
91Score American-217
91Score American-407
91Score Canadian Bilingual-217
91Score Canadian Bilingual-297
91Score Canadian English-217
91Score Canadian English-297
91Stadium Club-267
91Topps-225
91Upper Deck-199
French-199
92Bowman-35
92O-Pee-Chee-261
92Panini Stickers-73
92Panini Stickers French-73
92Parkhurst-304
Emerald Ice-304
Cherry Picks-CP17
92Pinnacle-156
French-156
92Pro Set-69
92Score-26
Canadian-26
92Stadium Club-481
92Topps-171
Gold-171G
92Ultra-310
92Upper Deck-322
93Donruss-256
93Donruss-447
93Leaf-352
93OPC Premier-395
Gold-395
93Panini Stickers-208
93Parkhurst-161
Emerald Ice-161
93Penguins Foodland-5
93Pinnacle-374
Canadian-374
93PowerPlay-191
93Score-212
93Score-542
Gold-542
Canadian-212
Canadian-542
Canadian Gold-542
93Stadium Club-155
Members Only Master Set-155
OPC-155
First Day Issue-155
First Day Issue OPC-155
Finest-8
Finest Members Only-8
93Topps/OPC Premier-395
Gold-395
93Ultra-227
93Ultra-394
93Upper Deck-487
Gretzky's Great Ones-GG9
94Be A Player-R10
94Be A Player-R150
99 All-Stars-G15
94Canada Games NHL POGS-130
94Donruss-168
94EA Sports-62
94Finest Ring Leaders-11
94Flair-82
94Fleer-98
94Leaf-174
94OPC Premier-146
Special Effects-146
94Parkhurst-106
Gold-106
94Pinnacle-61
Artist's Proofs-61
Rink Collection-61
94Post Box Backs-16
94Score-20
Gold-20
Platinum-20
94Select-124
Gold-124
94Topps/OPC Premier-146
Special Effects-146
94Ultra-102
94Upper Deck-33
Electric Ice-33
SP Inserts-SP127
SP Inserts Die Cuts-SP127
95Be A Player-225
Signatures-S225
Signatures Die Cuts-S225
95Canada Games NHL POGS-140
95Collector's Choice-44
Player's Club-44
Player's Club Platinum-44
95Donruss-354
95Hoyle Western Playing Cards-45
95Leaf-309
95Panini Stickers-274
95Parkhurst International-105
Emerald Ice-105
95Pinnacle-36
Artist's Proofs-36
Rink Collection-36
95Playoff One on One-51
95Score-92
Black Ice Artist's Proofs-92
Black Ice-92
95Topps-162
OPC Inserts-162
95Ultra-76
Gold Medallion-76
95Upper Deck-193
Electric Ice-193
Electric Ice Gold-193
Special Edition-SE129
Special Edition Gold-SE129
96Collector's Choice-172
96Duracell All-Cherry Team-DC9
96Fleer Picks-166
96Kraft Upper Deck-62
96Pinnacle-67
Artist's Proofs-67
Foil-67
Premium Stock-67
Rink Collection-67
96Upper Deck-106
96Upper Deck Ice-60
Parallel-60
96Collector's Edge Ice Livin' Large-L2
97Collector's Choice-221
97Katch-122
Gold-122
Silver-122
97Pacific-333
Copper-333
Emerald Green-333
Ice Blue-333
Red-333
Silver-333
97Pacific Omega-204
Copper-204
Dark Gray-204
Emerald Green-204
Gold-204
Ice Blue-204
98Aurora-169
98Katch-121
98McDonalds Upper Deck Gretzkys Teammates-T3
98OPC Chrome-155
Refractors-155
98Pacific-388
Ice Blue-388
Red-388
98Paramount-213
Copper-213
Emerald Green-213
Holo-Electric-213
Ice Blue-213
Silver-213
98SP Authentic Sign of the Times-MMC
98SP Authentic Sign of the Times Gold-MMC
98Topps-155
O-Pee-Chee-155
98Upper Deck MVP SC Edition-21
Gold Script-21
Silver Script-21
Super Script-21
00Czech Stadion-64
00Grand Rapids Griffins-13
02Fleer Throwbacks-52
Gold-52
Platinum-52
Autographs-16
Drop the Gloves-4
Scraps-6
Tie Downs-6
Squaring Off-7
Squaring Off Memorabilia-7
Stickwork-9
02UD Foundations-33
02UD Foundations-43
Canadian Heroes-CMM
Canadian Heroes Gold-CMM
Canadian Heroes Silver-C-MM
Defense First-DMM
Defense First Gold-DMS
Defense First Silver-D-MM
Playoff Performers-PMM
Playoff Performers Gold-PMM
Playoff Performers Silver-P-MM
Power Stations-SMM
Power Stations Gold-SMM
Power Stations Silver-S-MM
02Springfield Falcons-17
03Springfield Falcons Postcards-26
04ITG Franchises Update-468
06Parkhurst-73
06Parkhurst-232
06Parkhurst-249
Autographs-73
Autographs-232
Autographs-249
Autographs Dual-DAMP
06Upper Deck Sweet Shot Signature Shots/Saves-SSMM
McSween, Don
88ProCards AHL-255
89ProCards AHL-280
90ProCards AHL/IHL-290
91ProCards-16
91Rochester Americans Dunkin' Donuts-11
91Rochester Americans Kodak-18
91Rochester Americans Postcards-15
92San Diego Gulls-19
93San Diego Gulls-16
94Canada Games NHL POGS-179
94Ducks Carl's Jr.-18
94Upper Deck-301
Electric Ice-301
95Swedish World Championships Stickers-215
96Grand Rapids Griffins-13
97Milwaukee Admirals-13
99Muskegon Fury-28
McSweeney, Shaun
93Quebec Pee-Wee Tournament-872
McSweyn, Ralph
69O-Pee-Chee-96
70Sargent Promotions Stamps-145
72Los Angeles Sharks WHA-8
McTamney, Joey
897th Inn. Sketch OHL-63
93Dallas Freeze-12
McTavish, Dale
89Peterborough Petes-110
897th Inn. Sketch OHL-110
907th Inn. Sketch OHL-365
91Peterborough Petes-16
917th Inn. Sketch OHL-127
96Saint John Flames-14
98Finnish Keraiilysarja-193
99Finnish Cardset-213
Aces High-D-9
00Finnish Cardset Master Blasters-5
00Swiss Panini Stickers-238
00Swiss Slapshot Mini-Cards-RJ13
01Swiss HNL-160
02Finnish Cardset-71
02Swiss HNL-316
McTavish, Gord
76Nova Scotia Voyageurs-13
77Nova Scotia Voyageurs-15
79Jets Postcards-16
McVeigh, Charley
23V128-1 Paulin's Candy-27
33O-Pee-Chee V304A-44
33V357 Ice Kings-38
34Diamond Matchbooks Silver-45
35Diamond Matchbooks Tan 1-47
37V356 Worldwide Gum-93
McVey, Ward
24Crescent Falcon-Tigers-7
McVicar, Rob
99Brandon Wheat Kings-14
00Brandon Wheat Kings-24
01Brandon Wheat Kings-15
02Brandon Wheat Kings-23
03Columbia Inferno-106
04SP Authentic Rookie Redemptions-RR29
05Beehive-100
Matte-100
05Black Diamond-290
05Hot Prospects-179
En Fuego-179
Red Hot-179
White Hot-179
05SP Authentic-249
Limited-249
05SP Game Used-189
Gold-189
05SPx-220
Spectrum-220
05The Cup Masterpiece Pressplate Artifact-229
05The Cup Masterpiece Pressplate Artifact-338
05The Cup Masterpiece Pressplate Bee Hive-100
05The Cup Master Pressplate Black Diamond-290
05The Cup Masterpiece Pressplates (Ice)-182
05The Cup Master Pressplate Rookie Update-188
05The Cup Masterpiece Pressplates SPA-249
05The Cup Masterpiece Pressplates SP GU-189
05The Cup Masterpiece Pressplates (SPx)-220
05The Cup Masterpiece Pressplates Trilogy-314
05The Cup Masterpiece Pressplate Ult Coll-181
05UD Artifacts-229
05UD Artifacts-338
05Ultimate Collection-181
Gold-181
05Upper Deck Rookie Showcase-RS29
05Upper Deck Rookie Showcase Promos-RS29
05Upper Deck Ice-182
05Upper Deck Rookie Update-188
05Upper Deck Trilogy-314
McVie, Tom
68Seattle Totems-14
72Johnstown Jets-15
79Jets Postcards-17
88ProCards AHL-341
89ProCards AHL-214
90ProCards AHL/IHL-564
96Wheeling Nailers-22
96Wheeling Nailers Photo Pack-18
97Providence Bruins-23
McWhinney, Dan
06Fort Wayne Komets-13
Mead, Scott
92Saskatchewan JHL-123
Meadmore, Neil
88ProCards AHL-173
89ProCards AHL-39
Meadows, Brock
04South Surrey Eagles-14
04Surrey Eagles-12
04Surrey Eagles-12
06Westside Warriors-5
Meagher, Bryan
03Arizona Icecats-14
Meagher, Maurice
917th Inn. Sketch WHL-345
Meagher, Rick
77Nova Scotia Voyageurs-16
82O-Pee-Chee-144
83Devils Postcards-21
83NHL Key Tags-76
84Devils Postcards-16
87Blues Kodak-17
87Blues Team Issue-14
87Panini Stickers-316
88Blues Kodak-14
88Blues Team Issue-14
88O-Pee-Chee-235
88Panini Stickers-110
89Blues Kodak-22
89O-Pee-Chee-116
89Panini Stickers-125
89Topps-116
90Blues Kodak-15
90O-Pee-Chee-125
90O-Pee-Chee-198
90Panini Stickers-273
90Pro Set-267
90Pro Set-389
90Score-267
90Score-359
Canadian-267
Canadian-359
90Topps-125
Tiffany-125
90Upper Deck-208
90Upper Deck-285
French-285
91O-Pee-Chee-58
91Pro Set St. Louis Midwest-3
91Stadium Club-85
91Topps-58
92Blues UD Best of the Blues-23
92Peoria Rivermen-16
Mealey, Travis
03Lewiston Maineiacs-13
Mealy, Travis
05PEI Rocket-4
Meanchoff, Robert
93Quebec Pee-Wee Tournament-495
03Tulsa Oilers-12
Means, Eric
91Minnesota Golden Gophers-16
92Minnesota Golden Gophers-14
93Minnesota Golden Gophers-21
Mearns, Rick
917th Inn. Sketch WHL-33
Mears, Glen
94Flint Generals-17
95Toledo Storm-5
97Bakersfield Fog-9
98Bakersfield Condors-14
99Bakersfield Condors-11
00Bakersfield Condors-15
01Bakersfield Condors-15
03Bakersfield Condors-15
Measures, Allan
92Finnish Jyvas-Hyva Stickers-123
93Finnish Jyvas-Hyva Stickers-86
93Finnish SISU-119
94Finnish SISU-31
95Finnish SISU-33
95Finnish SISU-376
95Finnish SISU Limited-103
98Finnish Keraiilysarja-80
99Finnish Cardset-283
00Finnish Cardset-62
Meciar, Stanislav
93Finnish Jyvas-Hyva Stickers-350
93Finnish SISU-216
93Finnish SISU-193
94Swedish Leaf-174
95Czech APS Extraliga-224
Meckler, David
03Waterloo Blackhawks-20
06London Knights-20
Meckling, Brent
82Medicine Hat Tigers-12
83Medicine Hat Tigers-16
Mecteau, Francois
92Quebec Pee-Wee Tournament-144
93Quebec Pee-Wee Tournament-1100
Medak, Judd
93Quebec Pee-Wee Tournament-1450
02ECHL All-Star Southern-48
02Greenville Grrrowl-13
03Reading Royals-10
03Reading Royals RBI Sports-295
Mede, Roger
94German DEL-146
Medeiros, Brian
93Owen Sound Platers-19
94Owen Sound Platers-8
Medicus, Dieter
94German DEL-8
95German DEL-169
Medina, Damien
93Quebec Pee-Wee Tournament-568
Medley, Matt
06Rio Grande Valley Killer Bees-12
Medley, Mike
06Rio Grande Valley Killer Bees-13
Medrik, Stanislav
91Finnish Semic World Champ Stickers-112
91Swedish Semic World Champ Stickers-112
94Finnish Jaa Kiekko-197
95Czech APS Extraliga-33
95Slovakian APS National Team-10
96Czech APS Extraliga-33
96Swedish Semic Wien-225
97Czech DS Stickers-97
Medvedev, Alexei
02Russian Hockey League-3
03Russian Hockey League-193
Medvedev, Andrei
00Russian Hockey League-266
00Russian Hockey League-301
02Russian Future Stars-15
02Russian Hockey League-196
02Russian Ultimate Line-12
Medzihorsky, Branislav
95Slovakian-Quebec Pee-Wee Tournament-16
Meech, Derek
00Red Deer Rebels-14
Signed-14
01Red Deer Rebels-12
02Red Deer Rebels-2
03Red Deer Rebels-1
06Hot Prospects-196
06UD Artifacts-241
Meehan, Brian
95Arizona Icecats-12
96Arizona Icecats-13
97Arizona Icecats-16
98Arizona Icecats-17
99Arizona Icecats-17
00Arizona Icecats-26
01Arizona Icecats-12
02Arizona Icecats-28
03Arizona Icecats-16
04Arizona Icecats-12
Meehan, Gerry
69Seattle Totems-15
70Colgate Stamps-20
70Esso Power Players-83
70O-Pee-Chee-125
70Sargent Promotions Stamps-20
70Topps-125
71O-Pee-Chee-160
71Sabres Postcards-82
71Sargent Promotions Stamps-17
71Topps-74
71Toronto Sun-34
72O-Pee-Chee-22
72Sabres Postcards-11
72Sargent Promotions Stamps-29
72Topps-16
73O-Pee-Chee-22
73Sabres Postcards-7
73Topps-22
74Canucks Royal Bank-12
74NHL Action Stamps-54
74NHL Action Stamps Update-39
74O-Pee-Chee NHL-99
74Topps-99
75Sabres Linnett-8
76O-Pee-Chee NHL-35
76O-Pee-Chee NHL-396
76Topps-35
77O-Pee-Chee NHL-53
77Topps-53
78O-Pee-Chee-128
78Topps-128
Meehan, Jeremy
93Detroit Jr. Red Wings-11
Meehan, Kevin
92Quebec Pee-Wee Tournament-1425
93Quebec Pee-Wee Tournament-1571
98Arizona Icecats-18
99Arizona Icecats-18
00Arizona Icecats-16
01Arizona Icecats-13
Meehan, Mickey
01Arizona Icecats-15
02Arizona Icecats-14
03Arizona Icecats-15
04Arizona Icecats-13
Meehan, Pat
91British Columbia JHL-68
92British Columbia JHL-84
Meek, Darren
98Las Vegas Coyotes RHI-6
Meeker, Howie
44Beehive Group II Photos-432
45Quaker Oats Photos-35A
45Quaker Oats Photos-35B
45Quaker Oats Photos-35C
45Quaker Oats Photos-60A
48Exhibits Canadian-35
51Parkhurst-72
52Parkhurst-42
94Parkhurst Missing Link-133
03BAP Ultimate Mem Linemates Autos-11
04ITG Franchises Canadian-108
Autographs-HM
04ITG Ultimate Memorabilia Autographs-61
04ITG Ultimate Mem Autographs Gold-61
05ITG Ultimate Memorabilia Level 1-49
05ITG Ultimate Memorabilia Level 2-49
05ITG Ultimate Memorabilia Level 3-49
05ITG Ultimate Memorabilia Level 4-49
05ITG Ultimate Memorabilia Level 5-49
06Parkhurst-74
Autographs-74
Meger, Paul
44Beehive Group II Photos-273
45Quaker Oats Photos-99
48Exhibits Canadian-17
51Parkhurst-2
52Parkhurst-4
53Parkhurst-21
54Parkhurst-94
55Parkhurst-51
Quaker Oats-51
Mehalko, Brad
93Lethbridge Hurricanes-9
94Parkhurst SE-SE265
Gold-SE265
94SP-184
Die Cuts-184
95Lethbridge Hurricanes-14
98Tacoma Sabercats-14
00Charlotte Checkers-8
00Hartford Wolf Pack-19
01Hartford Wolf Pack-16
03Wheeling Nailers-90
04Bakersfield Condors-12
Meichtry, Patrick
02Swiss HNL-379
Meidl, Vaclav
03Plymouth Whalers-7
04ITG Top Prospects Spring Expo-9
04ITG Heroes and Prospects-109
Autographs-VM
Top Prospects-9
04ITG Heroes/Prospects Toronto Expo '05-109
04ITG Heroes/Prospects Expo Heroes/Pros-109
05Plymouth Whalers-A-10
Meier, Beat
98Swiss Power Play Stickers-109
Meier, Daniel
93Swiss HNL-126
95Swiss HNL-77
96Swiss HNL-219
98Swiss Power Play Stickers-216
99Swiss Panini Stickers-216
00Swiss Panini Stickers-260
00Swiss Slapshot Mini-Cards-EVZ12
02Swiss HNL-120
Meier, Dominic
95Swiss HNL-422
96Swiss HNL-133
98Swiss Power Play Stickers-182
99Swiss Panini Stickers-181
00Swiss Panini Stickers-34
00Swiss Slapshot Mini-Cards-SCB4
01Swiss HNL-82
02Swiss HNL-259
Meier, Michael
93Swiss HNL-75
95Swiss HNL-227
96Swiss HNL-141
99Swiss Panini Stickers-316
00Swiss Panini Stickers-88
00Swiss Slapshot Mini-Cards-EHCC9
01Swiss HNL-248
Meier, Patrick
99Swiss Panini Stickers-353
Meier, Roger
93Swiss HNL-26
95Swiss HNL-24
Meier, Stefan
93Swiss HNL-395
94German First League-351
Meier, Trevor
93Swiss HNL-157
95Swiss HNL-102
96Swiss HNL-43
98Swiss Power Play Stickers-171
99Swiss Panini Stickers-172
00Swiss Panini Stickers-215
01Swiss HNL-275
02Swiss HNL-302
Meighan, Ron
82North Bay Centennials-16
83Penguins Heinz Photos-19
Meijer, Sebastien
02Swedish SHL-183
Parallel-183
03Swedish Elite Rookies-5
05Swedish SHL Elitset-211
Meikle, Derek
91Air Canada SJHL-D48
Meiler, Christian
04German Weiden Blue Devils-17
Meins, Jerry
99Houston Aeros-NNO
Meisenheimer, Harvey
61Hamilton Red Wings-14
Meisner, Kevin
88Sudbury Wolves-8
Meissner, Dick
44Beehive Group II Photos-50
60Shirriff Coins-111
61Shirriff/Salada Coins-15
61Topps-6
61Topps-64
63Topps-60
Meister, Mark
98Arizona Icecats-19
99Arizona Icecats-19
Meister, Rupert
94German DEL-51
95German DEL-2
96German DEL-48
99German EV Landshut-2
04German Cologne Sharks Postcards-20
Meitinger, Holger
82Swedish Semic VM Stickers-113
83Swedish Semic VM Stickers-113
Meixner, Michael
94German First League-462
Mejzlik, Roman
94Czech APS Extraliga-196
95Czech APS Extraliga-212
97Czech APS Extraliga-302
97Czech DS Extraliga-37
98Czech DS-41
98Czech DS Stickers-116
98Czech OFS-300
Melametsa, Anssi
80Finnish Mallasjuoma-51
83Swedish Semic VM Stickers-44
85Jets Police-13
Melancon, Sebastian
93Quebec Pee-Wee Tournament-1124
Melancon, Tyler
06Guelph Storm-10
Melanson, A.J.
94Dubuque Fighting Saints-18
Melanson, Bruce
83Oshawa Generals-19
Melanson, Dean
907th Inn. Sketch QMJHL-209
917th Inn. Sketch QMJHL-19
93Rochester Americans Kodak-16
93Classic-143
93Classic Four-Sport *-243
Gold-243
94Classic Pro Prospects-102
95Rochester Americans-11
97Rochester Americans-4-4
98Rochester Americans-13
00Chicago Wolves-17
01BAP Memorabilia-416
Emerald-416
Ruby-416
Sapphire-416
01Upper Deck Ice-150
04German DEL-195
Melanson, Jules
02Drummondville Voltigeurs-15
03Drummondville Voltigeurs-15
04Drummondville Voltigeurs-5
05Drummondville Voltigeurs-5
Melanson, Luc
05Saint John's Sea Dogs-24
Melanson, Mathieu
03Quebec Remparts-19
04Quebec Remparts-15
05Quebec Remparts-15
05Quebec Remparts Signature Series-25
06ITG Heroes and Prospects Memorial Cup Champions-MC07
Melanson, Robert
907th Inn. Sketch QMJHL-153
91Knoxville Cherokees-20
92Cleveland Lumberjacks-23
93Muskegon Fury-9
95Muskegon Fury-14
98Muskegon Fury-15
99Muskegon Fury-6
00Muskegon Fury-15
Melanson, Rollie
83Islanders Team Issue-9
83O-Pee-Chee-12
83O-Pee-Chee Stickers-88
83O-Pee-Chee Stickers-317
83Topps Stickers-88
83Topps Stickers-317
84Islanders News-22
84North Stars Postcards-18
84O-Pee-Chee-130
84O-Pee-Chee-387
84O-Pee-Chee Stickers-92
85North Stars Postcards-22
85O-Pee-Chee-230
86Kings 20th Anniversary Team Issue-15
87O-Pee-Chee-19
87O-Pee-Chee Stickers-213
87Panini Stickers-271
87Topps-19
88O-Pee-Chee-160
88O-Pee-Chee Stickers-151
88Panini Stickers-69
88Topps-160
89ProCards AHL-213
90ProCards AHL/IHL-579
91Canadiens Postcards-32
91OPC Premier-97
91Upper Deck-575
French-575
92Bowman-187
92Stadium Club-184
92Topps-298
Gold-298G
02Canadiens Postcards-31
Melanson, Stan
907th Inn. Sketch QMJHL-231
917th Inn. Sketch QMJHL-28
96Louisiana Ice Gators-9
96Louisiana Ice Gators II-10
97Louisiana Ice Gators-11
98Louisiana Ice Gators-10
99Louisiana Ice Gators-6
00Louisiana Ice Gators-1
Melas, Mike
98Quad-City Mallards-17
98UHL All-Stars-21
99Quad-City Mallards-5
Melenovsky, Marek
95Upper Deck-543
Electric Ice-543
Electric Ice Gold-543
95Czech APS Extraliga-195
96Czech APS Extraliga-329
97Czech APS Extraliga-307
97Czech DS Extraliga-40
98Czech DS-39
98Czech DS Stickers-121
98Czech OFS-59
99Czech DS-52
99Czech OFS-240
00Czech OFS-279
01Czech OFS-32
02Czech OFS Plus-57
02Czech OFS Plus All-Star Game-H15
03Czech OFS Plus-292
04Czech OFS-215
Goals Leaders-7
Points Leaders-13
05Czech HC Hame Zlin-9
06Czech HC Zlin Hame Postcards-8
06Czech OFS-233
Melfi, Patrick
917th Inn. Sketch QMJHL-72
Melichar, Josef
98Tri-City Americans-2
00BAP Memorabilia-494
Emerald-494
Ruby-494
Sapphire-494
00Wilkes-Barre Scranton Penguins-15
01Titanium-177
Retail-177
01Titanium Draft Day Edition-161
01Czech DS-28
02Czech DS-54
02Czech DS-68
03Pacific Complete-361
Red-361
05Parkhurst-394
Facsimile Auto Parallel-394
06O-Pee-Chee-404
Rainbow-404
06Czech OFS Jagr Team-10
Melichercik, Jan
95Halifax Mooseheads-20
00Lubbock Cotton Kings-3
03Lubbock Cotton Kings-13
Melicherik, Milos
00Czech OFS-285
03UK Guildford Flames-10
03UK Guildford Flames-28
04UK Guildford Flames-9
05UK Guildford Flames-11
06UK Guildford Flames-11
Melin, Bjorn
02Swedish SHL-43
Next Generation-NG8
Parallel-43
03Swedish Elite-198
Silver-198
04Swedish Elitset-228
Gold-228
High Expectations-5
04Swedish Malmo Red Hawks-3
04Swedish Pure Skills-59
Parallel-59
05Swedish SHL Elitset-199
06Swedish SHL Elitset-63
06Portland Pirates-19
Melin, Brad
84Victoria Cougars-13
Melin, Roger
84Swedish Semic Elitserien-139
01Swedish Brynas Tigers-15
Melinko, Mike
03Erie Otters-16
Melischko, Christoph
02German DEL City Press-141
04German DEL-101
04German Ingolstadt Panthers-17
05German DEL-152
Melkersson, Tommy
88Swedish Semic Elitserien Stickers-35
90Swedish Semic Elitserien Stickers-184
91Swedish Semic Elitserien Stickers-35
92Swedish Semic Elitserien Stickers-55
93Swedish Semic Elitserien-31
94Swedish Leaf-119
95Swedish Leaf-180
95Swedish Upper Deck-23
96Swedish Brynas Tigers-7
97Swedish Collector's Choice-19
98Swedish UD Choice-34
Mellanby, Scott
86Flyers Postcards-18
87Flyers Postcards-19
88Flyers Postcards-14
88O-Pee-Chee-21
88Panini Stickers-322
88Topps-21
89Flyers Postcards-15
89O-Pee-Chee-253
90Flyers Postcards-17
90O-Pee-Chee-173
90Pro Set-220
90Score-242
Canadian-242
90Topps-173
Tiffany-173
91Pro Set Platinum-173
91Bowman-236
91Oilers IGA-14
91Oilers Team Issue-16
91O-Pee-Chee-200
91OPC Premier-191
91Panini Stickers-238
91Parkhurst-50
French-50
91Pinnacle-45
French-45
91Pro Set-172
91Pro Set-383
French-172
French-383
91Score American-279
91Score Canadian Bilingual-575
91Score Canadian English-575
91Score Rookie/Traded-25T
91Stadium Club-110
91Topps-200
91Upper Deck-542
French-542
92Bowman-163
92Durivage Panini-17
92Oilers IGA-15
92O-Pee-Chee-140
92Parkhurst-52
Emerald Ice-52
92Pinnacle-346
French-346
92Pro Set-54
92Score-148
Canadian-148
92Stadium Club-462
92Topps-444
Gold-444G
92Ultra-295
92Upper Deck-119
93Donruss-126
93Durivage Score-46
93Leaf-262
93OPC Premier-249
Gold-249
93Panini Stickers-243
93Panthers Team Issue-7
93Parkhurst-81
Emerald Ice-81
93Pinnacle-168
Canadian-168
Expansion-6
93PowerPlay-98
93Score-63
93Score-503
Gold-503
Canadian-63
Canadian-503
Canadian Gold-503
93Stadium Club-31
93Stadium Club-369
Members Only Master Set-31
Members Only Master Set-369
OPC-31
First Day Issue-31
First Day Issue-369
First Day Issue OPC-31
93Topps/OPC Premier-249
Gold-249
93Ultra-328
93Upper Deck-107
SP-57
94Be A Player Signature Cards-170
94Canada Games NHL POGS-108
94Donruss-42
94EA Sports-53
94Flair-65
94Fleer-80
94Leaf-182
94Leaf Limited-103
94OPC Premier-144
Special Effects-144
94Panthers Pop-ups-3
94Parkhurst-85
Gold-85
94Pinnacle-73
Artist's Proofs-73
Rink Collection-73
94Score-102
Gold-102
Platinum-102
94Select-85
Gold-85
94SP-47
Die Cuts-47
94Topps/OPC Premier-144
Special Effects-144
94Ultra-298
94Upper Deck-92
Electric Ice-92
SP Inserts-SP121
SP Inserts Die Cuts-SP121
95Bashan Super Stickers-49
95Bowman-37
All-Foil-37
95Canada Games NHL POGS-116
95Collector's Choice-171
Player's Club-171
Player's Club Platinum-171
95Donruss-37
95Donruss Elite-86
Die Cut Stars-86
Die Cut Uncut-86
95Finest-136
Refractors-136
95Imperial Stickers-49
95Leaf-87
95Leaf Limited-114
95Metal-60
95Panini Stickers-75
95Parkhurst International-355
Emerald Ice-355
95Pinnacle-78
Artist's Proofs-78
Rink Collection-78
95Playoff One on One-154
95Pro Magnets-88
95Score-134
Black Ice Artist's Proofs-134
Black Ice-134
95Select Certified-3
Mirror Gold-3
95SP-55
95Stadium Club-170
Members Only Master Set-170
95Summit-57
Artist's Proofs-57
Ice-57
95Topps-260
OPC Inserts-260
95Ultra-242
Crease Crashers-10
95Upper Deck-399
Electric Ice-399
Electric Ice Gold-399
Special Edition-SE34
Special Edition Gold-SE34
95Zenith-25
96SLU Hockey Canadian-10
96SLU Hockey American-14
96Be A Player-171
Autographs-171
Autographs Silver-171
96Black Diamond-127

Gold-127
96Collector's Choice-102
96Donruss-49
Press Proofs-49
96Donruss Canadian Ice-107
Gold Press Proofs-107
Red Press Proofs-107
96Donruss Elite-32
Die Cut Stars-32
96Fleer-40
96Kenner Starting Lineup Cards-14
96Leaf-132
Press Proofs-132
96Leaf Limited-50
Gold-50
Stubble-17
96Leaf Preferred-111
Press Proofs-111
Steel-8
Steel Gold-8
96Metal Universe-60
96NHL Pro Stamps-88
96Pinnacle-126
Artist's Proofs-126
Foil-126
Premium Stock-126
Rink Collection-126
96Playoff One on One-387
96Score-31
Artist's Proofs-31
Dealer's Choice Artist's Proofs-31
Special Artist's Proofs-31
Golden Blades-31
Superstitions-13
96Select Certified-84
Artist's Proofs-84
Blue-84
Mirror Blue-84
Mirror Gold-84
Mirror Red-84
Red-84
96SkyBox Impact-46
96SP-65
96Stadium Club Members Only-32
96Summit-8
Artist's Proofs-8
Ice-8
Metal-8
Premium Stock-8
96Team Out-5
96Topps Picks-101
OPC Inserts-101
96Ultra-66
Gold Medallion-66
96Upper Deck-200
96Upper Deck-265
Generation Next-X25
96Zenith-16
Artist's Proofs-16
97Black Diamond-92
Double Diamond-92
Triple Diamond-92
Quadruple Diamond-92
97Collector's Choice-100
Star Quest-SQ37
97Crown Royale-59
Emerald Green-59
Ice Blue-59
Silver-59
97Donruss-171
Press Proofs Silver-171
Press Proofs Gold-171
97Donruss Elite-76
Aspirations-76
Status-76
97Donruss Limited-110
Exposure-110
97Donruss Preferred-135
Cut to the Chase-135
97Donruss Priority-129
Stamp of Approval-129
97Katch-62
Gold-62
Silver-62
97Leaf-110
Fractal Matrix-110
Fractal Matrix Die Cuts-110
97Leaf International-110
Universal Ice-110
97Pacific-321
Copper-321
Emerald Green-321
Ice Blue-321
Red-321
Silver-321
97Pacific Dynagon-54
Copper-54
Dark Grey-54
Emerald Green-54
Ice Blue-54
Red-54
Silver-54
Tandems-53
97Pacific Invincible-61
Copper-61
Emerald Green-61
Ice Blue-61
Red-61
Silver-61
97Pacific Omega-100
Copper-100
Dark Gray-100
Emerald Green-100
Gold-100
Ice Blue-100
97Panini Stickers-63
97Paramount-81
Copper-81
Dark Grey-81
Emerald Green-81
Ice Blue-81
Red-81
Silver-81
97Pinnacle Certified-107
Red-107
Mirror Blue-107
Mirror Gold-107
Mirror Red-107
97Pinnacle Inside-165
97Pinnacle Tot Cert Platinum Blue-107
97Pinnacle Tot Cert Platinum Gold-107
97Pinnacle Totally Certified Platinum Red-107
97Pinnacle Tot Cert Mirror Platinum Gold-107
97Score-177
97SP Authentic-68
97Studio-41
Press Proofs Silver-41
Press Proofs Gold-41
97Upper Deck-282
Game Dated Moments-282
98Aurora-83
98Be A Player-58
Press Release-58
98BAP Gold-58
98BAP Autographs-58
98BAP Autographs Gold-58
98BAP Tampa Bay All Star Game-58
98Katch-62
98OPC Chrome-13
Refractors-13
98Pacific-226
Ice Blue-226
Red-226
98Paramount-99
Copper-99
Emerald Green-99
Holo-Electric-99
Ice Blue-99
Silver-99
98Topps-13
O-Pee-Chee-13
98UD Choice-90
98UD Choice Preview-90
98UD Choice Prime Choice Reserve-90
98UD Choice Reserve-90
98Upper Deck-279
Exclusives-279
Exclusives 1 of 1-279
Gold Reserve-279
99BAP Memorabilia-14
Gold-14
Silver-14
99O-Pee-Chee-75
99O-Pee-Chee Chrome-75
99O-Pee-Chee Chrome Refractors-75
99Pacific-178
Copper-178
Emerald Green-178
Gold-178
Ice Blue-178
Premiere Date-178
Red-178
99Panini Stickers-62
99Paramount-102
Copper-102
Emerald-102
Gold-102
Holographic Emerald-102
Holographic Gold-102
Holographic Silver-102
Ice Blue-102
Premiere Date-102
Red-102
Silver-102
99Topps/OPC-75
99Topps/OPC Chrome-75
Refractors-75
99Upper Deck-60
Exclusives-60
Exclusives 1 of 1-60
99Upper Deck Gold Reserve-60
99Upper Deck MVP-90
Gold Script-90
Silver Script-90
Super Script-90
99Upper Deck Victory-122
99Wayne Gretzky Hockey-77
00BAP Memorabilia-2
Emerald-2
Ruby-2
Sapphire-2
Promos-2
00BAP Mem Chicago Sportsfest Copper-2
00BAP Memorabilia Chicago Sportsfest Blue-2
00BAP Memorabilia Chicago Sportsfest Gold-2
00BAP Memorabilia Chicago Sportsfest Ruby-2
00BAP Memorabilia Chicago Sun-Times Ruby-2
00BAP Memorabilia Chicago Sun-Times Gold-2
00BAP Mem Chicago Sun-Times Sapphire-2
00BAP Mem Toronto Fall Expo Copper-2
00BAP Memorabilia Toronto Fall Expo Gold-2
00BAP Memorabilia Toronto Fall Expo Ruby-2
00BAP Parkhurst 2000-P193
00BAP Signature Series-202
Emerald-202
Ruby-202
Sapphire-202
Autographs-14
Autographs Gold-14
00O-Pee-Chee-216
00O-Pee-Chee Parallel-216
00Pacific-182
Copper-182
Gold-182
Ice Blue-182
Premiere Date-182
00Panini Stickers-32
00Panthers Team Issue-27
00Paramount-106
Copper-106
Gold-106
Holo-Gold-106
Holo-Silver-106
Ice Blue-106
Premiere Date-106
00Private Stock Game Gear-53
00Revolution-64
Blue-64
Premiere Date-64
Red-64
00Topps/OPC-216
Parallel-216
00Upper Deck MVP-81
First Stars-81
Second Stars-81
Third Stars-81
00Upper Deck Victory-103
00Upper Deck Vintage-154
01Pacific-327
Extreme LTD-327
Hobby LTD-327
Premiere Date-327
Retail LTD-327
01Pacific Arena Exclusives-327
02BAP Memorabilia-197
Emerald-197
Ruby-197
Sapphire-197
NHL All-Star Game-197
NHL All-Star Game Blue-197
NHL All-Star Game Green-197
NHL All-Star Game Red-197
02BAP Memorabilia Toronto Fall Expo-197
02BAP Sig Series Auto Buybacks 1998-58
02BAP Sig Series Auto Buybacks 2000-14
02Blues Team Issue-16
02Pacific-326
Blue-326
Red-326
02Pacific Complete-134
Red-134
02Topps Total-27
02Upper Deck-400
Exclusives-400
02Upper Deck Beckett UD Promos-400
03Blues Team Set-19
03ITG Action-502
03Pacific-285
Blue-285
Red-285
03Pacific Complete-39
Red-39
03Upper Deck-165
Canadian Exclusives-165
HG-165
03Upper Deck MVP-362
Gold Script-362
Silver Script-362
Canadian Exclusives-362
05Be A Player Signatures-SM
05Be A Player Signatures Gold-SM
05Parkhurst-33
05Parkhurst-502
Facsimile Auto Parallel-33
Facsimile Auto Parallel-502
True Colors-TCATL
True Colors-TCATL
05Upper Deck Jerseys-J-SM
05Upper Deck MVP-25
Gold-25
Platinum-25
06O-Pee-Chee-23
Rainbow-23
06Panini Stickers-8
06Upper Deck-264
Exclusives Parallel-264
High Gloss Parallel-264
Masterpieces-264
07Upper Deck Victory-78
Black-78
Gold-78

Mellbin, Bo
71Swedish Hockey-356

Mellinger, Hasse
65Swedish Coralli ISHockey-210
67Swedish Hockey-272
69Swedish Hockey-325

Mellios, Loui
91British Columbia JHL-117
92British Columbia JHL-180
92British Columbia JHL-184

Mello, Mike
93Quebec Pee-Wee Tournament-824

Mellor, Tom
72Finnish Semic World Championship-121
72Swedish Semic World Championship-121
73Red Wings McCarthy Postcards-13

Mellstrom, Johan
83Swedish Semic Elitserien-210
84Swedish Semic Elitserien-235

Melly, Cedric
01Swiss HNL-436

Melnechuk, Jeff
93Sudbury Wolves-2
93Sudbury Wolves Police-23
95Waterloo Blackhawks-11

Melnechuk, Ryan
93Quebec Pee-Wee Tournament-853

Melnyk, Chop
02OCN Blizzard-22

Melnyk, Don
03OCN Blizzard-14
06Richmond Renegades-9

Melnyk, Doug
90Cincinnati Cyclones-30
91Cincinnati Cyclones-15

Melnyk, Gerry
44Beehive Group II Photos-124
44Beehive Group II Photos-195
60Parkhurst-28
60Shirriff Coins-51
61Shirriff/Salada Coins-38
64Beehive Group III Photos-48
68O-Pee-Chee-120
68Topps-120

Melnyk, Larry
82Post Cereal-1
84Oilers Red Rooster-28
84Oilers Team Issue-18
84Nova Scotia Oilers-15
86O-Pee-Chee-95
86O-Pee-Chee Stickers-224
86Topps-95
87Canucks Shell Oil-13
87Panini Stickers-111
88Canucks Mohawk-13
88Oilers Tenth Anniversary-14
88O-Pee-Chee Stickers-53
89Canucks Mohawk-12
89O-Pee-Chee-288
89O-Pee-Chee Stickers-73
90O-Pee-Chee-419

Melnyk, Scott
86Portland Winter Hawks-13

Meloche, Denis
73Vancouver Blazers-15

Meloche, Eric
90 7th Inn. Sketch QMJHL-18
91 7th Inn. Sketch QMJHL-280
91 7th Inn. Sketch Memorial Cup-69
99Ohio State Buckeyes-12
00Wilkes-Barre Scranton Penguins-16
01BAP Memorabilia-396
Emerald-396
Ruby-396
Sapphire-396
01UD Playmakers-137
01UD Premier Collection-78
01Upper Deck Ice-147
01Wilkes-Barre Scranton Penguins-22
02Wilkes-Barre Scranton Penguins-24
03ITG Action-428
03Wilkes-Barre Scranton Penguins-17
04Philadelphia Phantoms-9
05Norfolk Admirals-18
05Philadelphia Phantoms-14
06Philadelphia Phantoms-7

Meloche, Gilles
71Letraset Action Replays-18
72O-Pee-Chee-112
72Sargent Promotions Stamps-50
72Topps-69
73O-Pee-Chee-2
73Topps-175
74NHL Action Stamps-70
74O-Pee-Chee NHL-205
74Topps-205
75O-Pee-Chee NHL-190
75Topps-190
76O-Pee-Chee NHL-36
76Topps-36
77O-Pee-Chee NHL-109
77Topps-109
78North Stars Cloverleaf Dairy-1
78O-Pee-Chee-28
78Topps-28
79North Stars Postcards-10
79O-Pee-Chee-136
79Topps-136
80North Stars Postcards-13
80O-Pee-Chee-47
80Topps-47
81North Stars Postcards-16
81O-Pee-Chee-165
81O-Pee-Chee Stickers-93
81Topps-W109
82McDonald's Stickers-3
82North Stars Postcards-17
82O-Pee-Chee-170
82O-Pee-Chee Stickers-195
82Post Cereal-9
82Topps Stickers-195
83North Stars Postcards-20
83O-Pee-Chee-177
84North Stars 7-Eleven-8
84North Stars Postcards-19
84O-Pee-Chee-104
84O-Pee-Chee Stickers-51
84Topps-79
86Penguins Kodak-17
87O-Pee-Chee-107
87O-Pee-Chee Stickers-168
87Panini Stickers-140
87Penguins Masks-7
87Penguins Kodak-20
87Topps-107
88O-Pee-Chee-8
88O-Pee-Chee Stickers-238
88Topps-8
04ITG Franchises US West-154
04ITG Franchises US West-182
Autographs-A-GME1
Autographs-A-GME2
06Parkhurst-75
Autographs-75
Autographs Dual-DAMB

Meloche, Jason
91Cornwall Royals-1
91 7th Inn. Sketch OHL-2

Melrose, Barry
79Jets Postcards-18
79O-Pee-Chee-386
80Pepsi-Cola Caps-92
81Maple Leafs Postcards-15
82O-Pee-Chee-328
82Post Cereal-18
89ProCards AHL-321
90ProCards AHL/IHL-476
91ProCards-140
93Kraft-42
01Topps Archives-45
01Topps Chrome Reprints-3
01Topps Chrome Reprint Refractors-3
01Topps Chrome Reprint Autographs-3
06Parkhurst-76
Autographs-76
06Upper Deck Sweet Shot Signature Shots/Saves-SSME

Melrose, Kevan
90ProCards AHL/IHL-613
91ProCards-574

Melson, Taj
93St. Cloud State Huskies-18
98Las Vegas Thunder-13
99San Diego Gulls-10
00San Diego Gulls-12

Melton, Kelly
96Dayton Ice Bandits-12

Meluzin, Roman
91Upper Deck Czech World Juniors-94
94Czech APS Extraliga-198
95Czech APS Extraliga-41
95Czech APS Extraliga-379
96Czech APS Extraliga-42
96Czech APS Extraliga-350
96Swedish Semic Wien-119
97Czech APS Extraliga-62
97Czech DS Extraliga-9
97Czech DS Stickers-15
97Czech DS Stickers-109
98Czech DS-110
98Czech DS Stickers-294
98Czech OFS-25
99Czech OFS-429
99Czech OFS-483
99Finnish Cardset-321
00German DEL-161
01Czech OFS-64
02Czech OFS Plus-94
03Czech OFS Plus-295

Melyakov, Igor
94Classic Draft Prospects-DP6
00Russian Hockey League-110

Menard, Carl
90 7th Inn. Sketch QMJHL-80
91 7th Inn. Sketch QMJHL-19
92Quebec Pee-Wee Tournament-1064
93Quebec Pee-Wee Tournament-346
95Central Hockey League-30
97Idaho Steelheads-20

Menard, Daniel
77Granby Vics-15

Menard, Derry
93Oklahoma City Blazers-10
94Central Hockey League-64
94Oklahoma City Blazers-10
98Finnish Keraílysarja-144

Menard, Howie
61Hamilton Red Wings-15
69O-Pee-Chee-73
70O-Pee-Chee-124
70Topps-124

Menard, Martin
95Slapshot Memorial Cup-68
97Rochester Americans-2-3
97Bowman CHL-54
OPC-54
00Columbus Cottonmouths-9

Menard, Stephane
90 7th Inn. Sketch QMJHL-235
91 7th Inn. Sketch QMJHL-5
94Knoxville Cherokees-5

Menard, Terry
92Thunder Bay Thunder Hawks-28
93Thunder Bay Senators-19
94Thunder Bay Senators-9
95Thunder Bay Senators-12
96Fort Worth Fire-12
97Fort Worth Brahmas-13
98Fort Worth Brahmas-1
99Fort Worth Brahmas-12

Menauer, Josef
03German Nuremberg Ice Tigers Postcards-18
04German DEL-254
05German DEL-10
06German DEL-10

Mencicky, Tomas
03Czech OFS Plus-75

Mende, Karsten
94Finnish Jaa Kiekko-278
94German DEL-211
95German DEL-203
96German DEL-344
99German Bundesliga 2-155

Mendel, Bob
90ProCards AHL/IHL-198
91ProCards-335
95German DEL-6
96German DEL-5

Menei, Ryan
04Saskatoon Blades-21
05Saskatoon Blades-16
06Saskatoon Blades-18

Menges, Greg
91Greensboro Monarchs-10
92Greensboro Monarchs-19

Menhart, Marian
95Prince Albert Raiders-15
96Prince Albert Raiders-14
98Czech OFS-8
99Czech OFS-152

Menicci, Tom
94Hampton Roads Admirals-11
95Anaheim Bullfrogs RHI-19
96Anaheim Bullfrogs RHI-12
98Phoenix Mustangs-15
99Idaho Steelheads-7
00Lubbock Cotton Kings-15

Mensator, Lukas
02Ottawa 67's-20
03Ottawa 67's-16
03Ottawa 67's-NNO
04Czech OFS-46
05Czech HC Karlovy Vary-9
06Czech OFS-34
Goalies I-2
Goalies II-6
Stars-4
Team Cards-2

Menschig, Markus
94German First League-524

Mensonen, Jarno
98BC Icemen-10
98BC Icemen II-11

Mentis, Jim
84Victoria Cougars-14

Menzul, Curtis
00Tacoma Sabercats-18
01Asheville Smoke-18
04Knoxville Ice Bears-13
05Knoxville Ice Bears-10

Mercer, Dan
03Red Deer Rebels-4

Mercer, Jeff
99Tupelo T-Rex-9

Mercer, Lee
96UK Fife Flyers-20
97UK Fife Flyers-16

Mercer, Randy
96St. John's Maple Leafs-20

Merchese, Paul
04Mississauga Ice Dogs-16

Mercier, Chad
96Regina Pats-7
01Regina Pats-15

Mercier, Don
88Moncton Golden Flames-15

Mercier, Martin
92Maine Black Bears-32

Mercier, Pascal
92Quebec Pee-Wee Tournament-1263
93Quebec Pee-Wee Tournament-1375

Mercure, Andre
99Baie-Comeau Drakkar-17

Meredith, Greg
83O-Pee-Chee-88

Meredith, Mark
93Quebec Pee-Wee Tournament-1432

Merinov, Vladimir
74Swedish Stickers-39

Merk, Klaus
92Finnish Semic-171
93Swedish Semic World Champ Stickers-150
94Finnish Jaa Kiekko-271
94German DEL-70
95German DEL-50
96German DEL-440
95Swedish Globe World Championships-217
95Swedish World Championships Stickers-52
96German DEL-247
96Swedish Semic Wien-192
98German DEL-273
98German DEL-327
99German DEL-168
00German Berlin Polar Bears Postcards-17
00German DEL-69
01German Berlin Polar Bears Postcards-16
01German Upper Deck-39
Goalies in Action-G2
02German Berlin Polar Bears Postcards-18
04German Berlin Eisbarens 50th Anniv-10

Merkley, Riley
03Calgary Hitmen-13
04Calgary Hitmen-12
05Calgary Hitmen-12

Merkosky, Glenn
88ProCards AHL-4
89ProCards AHL-323
90ProCards AHL/IHL-470
91ProCards-141
94Sudbury Wolves-24

Merli, Brandon
99Kitchener Rangers-18

Merlini, Derek
03Erie Otters-17
04Erie Otters-3
05Plymouth Whalers-B-06

Meropoulis, Matt
06Chilliwack Bruins-17

Merra, Martti
92Finnish Jyvas-Hyva Stickers-103
93Finnish Jyvas-Hyva Stickers-193
93Finnish SISU-255

Merrell, Barry
71Rochester Americans-13

Merrett, Andrew
05Mississauga Ice Dogs-13
06Mississauga Ice Dogs-8

Merrick, Andrew
92Quebec Pee-Wee Tournament-1832
00Muskegon Fury-13

Merrick, Wayne
72Blues White Border-11
73Blues White Border-12
74NHL Action Stamps-248
74O-Pee-Chee NHL-66
74Topps-66
75O-Pee-Chee NHL-228
75Topps-228
76O-Pee-Chee NHL-18
76O-Pee-Chee NHL-383
76Topps-18
77O-Pee-Chee NHL-176
77Topps-176
78O-Pee-Chee-258
78Topps-258
79Islanders Transparencies-11
79O-Pee-Chee-169
79Topps-169
80O-Pee-Chee-345
81O-Pee-Chee-216
82O-Pee-Chee-205
82Post Cereal-12
83Islanders Team Issue-10
84Islanders News-10
92Quebec Pee-Wee Tournament-1846
93Islanders Chemical Bank Alumni-5

Merrill, Doug
04Huntsville Havoc-16

Merritt, Brett
93Quebec Pee-Wee Tournament-672

Merritt, Jeff
03Arizona Icecats-16

Merritt, Ryan
89Windsor Spitfires-11
90 7th Inn. Sketch OHL-187
91 7th Inn. Sketch OHL-61

Mersch, Mike
87Flint Spirits-15
88Flint Spirits-16
88Flint Spirits-19
89ProCards IHL-161
90ProCards AHL/IHL-386

Merta, Jerry
93Quebec Pee-Wee Tournament-1605

Mertzig, Jan
95Swedish Leaf-253
Rookies-6
95Swedish Upper Deck-117
97Swedish Collector's Choice-120
Crash the Game Exchange-C8
Crash the Game Redemption-R8
02Swedish SHL-208
Parallel-208
03Swedish Elite-68
Silver-68

Merz, Loic
04Swiss Lausanne HC Postcards-12

Merz, Suzanne
94Classic Women of Hockey-W28

Mesh, Eugene
98Arizona Icecats-20

Mesicek, Radek
94Czech APS Extraliga-234
95Czech APS Extraliga-321
96Czech APS Extraliga-103
97Czech DS Stickers-270

Mesikammen, Ilkka
65Finnish Hellas-2
66Finnish Jaakiekkosarja-75
70Finnish Jaakiekko-197
71Finnish Suomi Stickers-232
72Finnish Jaakiekko-216
73Finnish Jaakiekko-291
78Finnish SM-Liiga-203

Messa, Peter
03Swedish Elite-260
Silver-260

Messer, Kevin
91Air Canada SJHL-D6
92Saskatchewan JHL-120

Messier, Charles-Antoine
05Baie-Comeau Drakkar-2

Messier, Doug
83Moncton Alpines-1
94Tampa Bay Tritons RHI-20

Messier, Eric
91 7th Inn. Sketch QMJHL-111
93Sherbrooke Faucons-14
97Be A Player-204
Autographs-204
Autographs Die-Cuts-204
Autographs Prismatic Die-Cuts-204
97Black Diamond-13
Double Diamond-13
Triple Diamond-13
Quadruple Diamond-13
97Donruss Limited-125
Exposure-125
97Katch-167
Gold-167
Silver-167
97Pacific Invincible NHL Regime-55
97Pacific Omega-61
Copper-61
Dark Gray-61
Emerald Green-61
Gold-61
Ice Blue-61
97Revolution-36
Copper-36
Emerald-36
Ice Blue-36
Silver-36
97SP Authentic-178
97Upper Deck-45
97Zenith 5 x 7-70
Gold Impulse-70
98Aurora-49
98Pacific-165
Ice Blue-165
Red-165
98Paramount-58
Copper-58
Emerald Green-58
Holo-Electric-58
Ice Blue-58
Silver-58
98UD Choice-53
98UD Choice Preview-53
98UD Choice Prime Choice Reserve-53
98UD Choice Reserve-53
98Upper Deck-70
Exclusives-70
Exclusives 1 of 1-70
Gold Reserve-70
99Avalanche Team Issue-13
00Pacific-116
Copper-116
Gold-116
Ice Blue-116
Premiere Date-116
Jerseys-2
Jersey Patches-2
00Private Stock Game Gear-26
00Private Stock Game Gear Patches-26
00Stadium Club-122
01Avalanche Team Issue-14
01BAP Memorabilia Stanley Cup Champions-CA11
01Vanguard Memorabilia-37
01Vanguard Patches-37
02Avalanche Postcards-7
02Pacific Complete-329
Red-329
02Topps Total-213
03Panthers Team Issue-12
03Upper Deck-327
Canadian Exclusives-327
HG-327
UD Exclusives-327
03Upper Deck MVP-109
Gold Script-109
Silver Script-109
Canadian Exclusives-109

Messier, Joby
92Binghamton Rangers-12
92Classic-72
Gold-72
LPs-LP10
92Classic Four-Sport *-196
Gold-196
Autographs-196A
93Leaf-298
93OPC Premier-522
Gold-522
93Parkhurst-399
Emerald Ice-399
93PowerPlay-161
93Stadium Club-339
Members Only Master Set-339
First Day Issue-339
93Topps/OPC Premier-522
Gold-522
93Ultra-170
All-Rookies-6
93Upper Deck-73
93Classic Pro Prospects-76
93Classic Pro Prospects-127
BCs-BC13
94Leaf-375
94OPC Premier-476
Special Effects-476
94Pinnacle-497
Artist's Proofs-497
Rink Collection-497
94Topps/OPC Premier-476
Special Effects-476
94Binghamton Rangers-13
97Long Beach Ice Dogs-12

Messier, Lyon
06Texas Tornados-2

Messier, Mark
79Oilers Postcards-17
80O-Pee-Chee-289
80Pepsi-Cola Caps-34
81Oilers Red Rooster-11
81O-Pee-Chee-118
81O-Pee-Chee Stickers-210
81Post Standups-15
82McDonald's Stickers-15
82Neilson's Gretzky-45
82Oilers Red Rooster-11
82O-Pee-Chee-117
82O-Pee-Chee Stickers-94
82O-Pee-Chee Stickers-159
82Post Cereal-6
82Topps Stickers-94
82Topps Stickers-159
83Esso-13
83NHL Key Tags-37
83Oilers Dollars-H20
83Oilers McDonald's-18
83O-Pee-Chee-23
83O-Pee-Chee-39
83O-Pee-Chee Stickers-97
83O-Pee-Chee Stickers-98
83O-Pee-Chee Stickers-157
83Puffy Stickers-4
83Topps Stickers-97
83Topps Stickers-98
83Topps Stickers-157
83Vachon-36
84Oilers Red Rooster-11
84Oilers Team Issue-19
84O-Pee-Chee-213
84O-Pee-Chee-254
84O-Pee-Chee Stickers-5
84O-Pee-Chee Stickers-261
84 7-Eleven Discs-21
84Topps-159
85Oilers Red Rooster-11
85O-Pee-Chee-177
85O-Pee-Chee Stickers-228
86Kraft Drawings-43
86Oilers Red Rooster-11
86Oilers Team Issue-11
86O-Pee-Chee-186
86O-Pee-Chee Stickers-79
86Topps-186
87Oilers Team Issue-11
87O-Pee-Chee-112
87O-Pee-Chee Minis-28
87O-Pee-Chee Stickers-92
87Panini Stickers-194
87Panini Stickers-263
87Pro-Sport All-Stars-13
87Topps-112
88Esso All-Stars-30
88Frito-Lay Stickers-35
88Oilers Tenth Anniversary-89
88Oilers Team Issue-21
88O-Pee-Chee-93
88O-Pee-Chee Minis-25
88O-Pee-Chee Stickers-230
88Panini Stickers-61
88Topps-93
89Kraft-15
89Oilers Team Issue-17
89O-Pee-Chee-65
89O-Pee-Chee Stickers-227
89Panini Stickers-74
89Sports Illustrated for Kids I-100
89Topps-65
89Swedish Semic World Champ Stickers-69
90Bowman-199
Tiffany-199
90Bowman Hat Tricks-4
Tiffany-4
90Kraft-32
90Kraft-71
90Oilers IGA-16
90O-Pee-Chee-130
90O-Pee-Chee-193
90O-Pee-Chee-519
90OPC Premier-71
90Panini Stickers-219
90Pro Set-91
90Pro Set-349
90Pro Set-381
90Pro Set-386
90Pro Set-397
90Score Promos-100A
90Score Promos-100B
90Score-100
90Score-315
90Score-331
90Score-360
Canadian-100
Canadian-315
Canadian-360
90Score Hottest/Rising Stars-33
90Topps-130
90Topps-193
Tiffany-130
Tiffany-193
Team Scoring Leaders-16
Team Scoring Leaders Tiffany-16
90Upper Deck-44
90Upper Deck-206
90Upper Deck-321
90Upper Deck-494
French-44
French-206
French-321
French-494
90Upper Deck Holograms-5
90Upper Deck Holograms-6
90Upper Deck Holograms-7
91Pro Set Platinum-81
91Bowman-114
91Gillette-31
91Kraft-16
91Oilers Panini Team Stickers-14
91Oilers Panini Team Stickers-G
91O-Pee-Chee-346
91OPC Premier-51
91Panini Stickers-124
91Parkhurst-121
91Parkhurst-213
91Parkhurst-468
91Parkhurst-475
French-121
French-213
French-468
French-475
PHC-PHC8
PHC French-PHC8
91Pinnacle-285
91Pinnacle-390
French-50
French-390
91Pro Set-74
91Pro Set-282
91Pro Set-439
91Pro Set-579
French-74
French-282
French-439
French-579
Platinum PC-PC20
Puck Candy-19
91Score American-285
91Score American-373
91Score American-420
91Score Canadian Bilingual-263
91Score Canadian Bilingual-310
91Score Canadian Bilingual-505
91Score Canadian Bilingual-635
91Score Canadian English-263
91Score Canadian English-310
91Score Canadian English-505
91Score Canadian English-635
91Score Rookie/Traded-85T
91Stadium Club Members Only-49
91Stadium Club-111
91Topps-346
Topps/Bowman Preview Sheet-6
91Upper Deck-14
91Upper Deck-246
91Upper Deck-545
91Upper Deck-610
91Upper Deck-620
French-14
French-246
French-545
French-610
French-620
Box Bottoms-3
Box Bottoms-4

91Finnish Semic World Champ Stickers-63
91Swedish Semic World Champ Stickers-63
92Bowman-113
92Bowman-234
92Enor Mark Messier-1
92Enor Mark Messier-2
92Enor Mark Messier-3
92Enor Mark Messier-4
92Enor Mark Messier-5
92Enor Mark Messier-6
92Enor Mark Messier-7
92Enor Mark Messier-8
92Enor Mark Messier-9
92Enor Mark Messier-10
92High-5 Previews-P4
92Humpty Dumpty II-15
92Kellogg's Posters-2
92Kraft-45
92McDonald's Upper Deck-H1
92O-Pee-Chee-208
92O-Pee-Chee-258
25th Anniv. Inserts-13
Trophy Winners-3
92OPC Premier Star Performers-15
92Panini Stickers-233
92Panini Stickers French-233
92Parkhurst-111
Emerald Ice-111
Cherry Picks-CP4
92Pinnacle-1
French-1
92Pro Set-111
Award Winners-CC1
92Score-300
92Score-431
92Score-493
92Score-521
Canadian-300
Canadian-431
Canadian-493
Canadian-521
92Seasons Patches-26
92Sports Illustrated for Kids II-42
92Sports Illustrated for Kids II-347
92Stadium Club-241
92Stadium Club-443
92Topps-258
92Topps-274
Gold-258G
Gold-274G
92Ultra-139
Award Winners-1
Award Winners-10
92Upper Deck-34
92Upper Deck-242
92Upper Deck-432
92Upper Deck-437
92Upper Deck-453
92Finnish Semic-85
93SLU Hockey Canadian-8
93SLU Hockey American-9
93Donruss-222
Special Print-O
93Kenner Starting Lineup Cards-9
93Kraft-43
93Leaf-158
93OPC Premier-430
Gold-430
93Panini Stickers-I
93Parkhurst-127
Emerald Ice-127
Cherry's Playoff Heroes-D4
93Pinnacle-125
93Pinnacle-238
Canadian-125
Canadian-238
Captains-15
Captains Canadian-15
93PowerPlay-162
Point Leaders-9
93Score-200
Canadian-200
Dynamic Duos U.S.-5
93Stadium Club-35
Members Only Master Set-35
OPC-35
First Day Issue-35
First Day Issue OPC-35
93Topps Premier Promo Sheet-601
93Topps/OPC Premier-430
Gold-430
93Ultra-183
Premier Pivots-6
93Upper Deck-51
93Upper Deck-298
Gretzky's Great Ones-GG5
SP-103
93Upper Deck Locker All-Stars-7
93Swedish Semic World Champ Stickers-202
94SLU Hockey American-13
94Action Packed Big Picture 24K Gold-3G
94Canada Games NHL POGS-166
94Donruss-9
Dominators-1
Ice Masters-7
94EA Sports-87
94Finest-16
Super Team Winners-16
Refractors-16
Bowman's Best-B2
Bowman's Best Refractors-B2
Ring Leaders-1
94Flair-115
Center Spotlight-8
94Fleer-136
Headliners-7
94Hockey Wit-102
94Kenner Starting Lineup Cards-14
94Kraft-22
94Leaf-11
Gold Stars-5
Limited Inserts-15
94Leaf Limited-89
94OPC Premier-1
94OPC Premier-278
Special Effects-1
Special Effects-278
94Parkhurst Crash the Game Green-27
94Parkhurst Crash the Game Blue-27
94Parkhurst Crash the Game Gold-27
94Parkhurst Crash the Game Red-27
94Parkhurst Vintage-V33
94Parkhurst SE-SE113
Gold-SE113
94Pinnacle-300
Artist's Proofs-300
Rink Collection-300
Gamers-GR9
Team Pinnacle-TP9
Team Dufex Parallel-TP9
94Score Dream Team-DT16
94Score Franchise-TF15
94Select-1
Gold-1
94SP-73
Die Cuts-73
Premier-28
Premier Die-Cuts-28
94Stadium Club Members Only-27
94Stadium Club-1
Members Only Master Set-1
First Day Issue-1
Dynasty and Destiny-2
Dynasty and Destiny Members Only-2
Finest Inserts-3
Finest Inserts Members Only-3
Super Teams-15
Super Teams Members Only Master Set-15
Super Team Winner Cards-1
94Topps/OPC Premier-1
94Topps/OPC Premier-120
94Topps/OPC Premier-278
Special Effects-1
Special Effects-278
The Go To Guy-15
94Topps Finest Bronze-15
94Ultra-140
All-Stars-4
Premier Pivots-7
94Upper Deck-62
94Upper Deck-234
94Upper Deck-563
Electric Ice-62
Electric Ice-234
Electric Ice-563
Predictor Canadian-C22
94Upper Deck Predictor Canadian Exch Gold-C22
94Upper Deck Predictor Hobby-H4
94Upper Deck Predictor Hobby Exch Gold-H4
94Upper Deck Predictor Hobby Exch Silver-H4
94Upper Deck Predictor Retail-R34
94Upper Deck Predictor Retail-R54
94Upper Deck Predictor Retail Exchange-R34
94Upper Deck Predictor Retail Exchange-R54
94Upper Deck SP Inserts-SP51
94Upper Deck SP Inserts Die Cuts-SP51
94Finnish Jaa Kiekko-94
94Finnish Jaa Kiekko-350
94Tampa Bay Tritons RHI-2
95Bashan Super Stickers-78
95Bashan Super Stickers-80
95Bowman-8
All-Foil-8
Bowman's Best-BB6
Bowman's Best Refractors-BB6
95Canada Games NHL POGS-6
95Canada Games NHL POGS-24
95Canada Games NHL POGS-180
95Collector's Choice-220
Player's Club-220
Player's Club Platinum-220
Crash The Game-C6A
Crash The Game-C6B
Crash The Game-C6C
Crash The Game Gold-C6A
Crash The Game Gold-C6B
Crash The Game Gold-C6C
Crash the Game Silver Redeemed-C6
Crash the Game Silver Bonus-C6
Crash the Game Gold Redeemed-C6
Crash the Game Gold Bonus-C6
95Donruss-271
Igniters-5
95Donruss Elite-46
Die Cut Stars-46
Die Cut Uncut-46
Cutting Edge-8
95Emotion-116
Ntense Power-3
95Finest-50
95Finest-99
Refractors-50
Refractors-99
95Hoyle Eastern Playing Cards-40
95Imperial Stickers-80
95Kraft-70
95Leaf-68
95Leaf Limited-75
95McDonald's Pinnacle-MCD-5
95Metal-97
Iron Warriors-8
95NHL Aces Playing Cards-11C
95NHL Cool Trade-5
95NHL Cool Trade-RP5
95Panini Stickers-102
95Parkhurst International-136
Emerald Ice-136
Crown Collection Silver Series 2-7
Crown Collection Gold Series 2-7
Parkie's Trophy Picks-PP6
Parkie's Trophy Picks-PP12
95Pinnacle-5
Artist's Proofs-5
Rink Collection-5
First Strike-1
Full Contact-12
95Pinnacle FANtasy-18
95Playoff One on One-175
95Playoff One on One-284
95Pro Magnets-98
95Score-50
Black Ice Artist's Proofs-50
Black Ice-50
Dream Team-4
Golden Blades-15
95Select Certified-14
Mirror Gold-14
Double Strike-15
Double Strike Gold-15
95SkyBox Impact-111
Countdown to Impact-5
Ice Quake-5
95SP-92
Holoviews-FX14
Holoviews Special FX-FX14
Stars/Etoiles-E19
Stars/Etoiles Gold-E19
95Stadium Club Members Only-19
95Stadium Club-178
Members Only Master Set-178
Metalists-M9
Metalists Members Only Master Set-M9
Nemeses-N8
Nemeses Members Only Master Set-N8
95Summit-1
Artist's Proofs-1
Ice-1
GM's Choice-16
95Topps-5
95Topps-240
OPC Inserts-5
OPC Inserts-240
Home Grown Canada-HGC29
Marquee Men Power Boosters-5
Mystery Finest-M3
Mystery Finest Refractors-M3
Power Lines-3PL
Rink Leaders-1RL
95Topps SuperSkills-60
Platinum-60
95Ultra-105
95Ultra-393
Gold Medallion-105
Crease Crashers-11
Premier Pivots-5
Premier Pivots Gold Medallion-5
95Upper Deck-169
95Upper Deck-217
Electric Ice-169
Electric Ice-217
Electric Ice Gold-169
Electric Ice Gold-217
95Upper Deck All-Star Game Predictors-19
Redemption Winners-19
95Upper Deck Freeze Frame-F7
95Upper Deck Freeze Frame Jumbo-F7
95Upper Deck NHL All-Stars-AS16
95Upper Deck NHL All-Stars Jumbo-AS16
95Upper Deck Predictor Hobby-H9
95Upper Deck Predictor Hobby Exchange-H9
95Upper Deck Predictor Retail-R39
95Upper Deck Predictor Retail-R56
95Upper Deck Predictor Retail Exchange-R39
95Upper Deck Predictor Retail Exchange-R56
95Upper Deck Special Edition-SE141
95Upper Deck Special Edition Gold-SE141
95Zenith-18
Z-Team-5
95Finnish Semic World Championships-97
95Swedish Globe World Championships-84
95Swedish World Championships Stickers-279
96SLU Hockey Canadian-11
96Headliners Hockey-13
96SLU Hockey American-15
96Be A Player-111
Autographs-111
Autographs Silver-111
Biscuit In The Basket-19
Messier Die Cut-1
Messier Die Cut-2
96Black Diamond-100
Gold-100
Run for the Cup-RC11
96Collector's Choice-166
96Collector's Choice-296
96Collector's Choice-335
Slick'Ums-S10
Crash the Game-C30A
Crash the Game-C30B
Crash the Game-C30C
Crash the Game Gold-C30A
Crash the Game Gold-C30B
Crash the Game Gold-C30C
Crash the Game Exchange-CR30
Crash the Game Exchange Gold-CR30
96Donruss-16
Press Proofs-16
Elite Inserts-5
Elite Inserts Gold-5
Hit List-8
96Donruss Canadian Ice-87
Gold Press Proofs-87
Red Press Proofs-87
O Canada-3
96Donruss Elite-22
Die Cut Stars-22
Perspective-2
96Flair-61
Blue Ice-61
Hot Numbers-9
Now And Then-1
96Fleer-71
Art Ross-15
Picks Captain's Choice-5
Picks Fabulous 50-29
96Hockey Greats Coins-15
Gold-15
96Kenner Starting Lineup Cards-15
96Leaf-180
Press Proofs-180
Fire On Ice-15
Sweaters Away-8
Sweaters Home-8
96Leaf Limited-65
Gold-65
96Leaf Limited Bash the Boards Promos-P2
96Leaf Limited Bash The Boards-2
96Leaf Limited Bash The Boards Ltd Ed-2
96Leaf Preferred-66
Press Proofs-66
Steel-42
Steel Gold-42
Steel Power-4
96Maggers-60
96McDonald's Pinnacle-22
96Metal Universe-99
Cool Steel-8
Cool Steel Super Power-8
Lethal Weapons-13
Lethal Weapons Super Power-13
96NHL Aces Playing Cards-32
96NHL Pro Stamps-98
96Pinnacle-2
Artist's Proofs-2
Foil-2
Premium Stock-2
Rink Collection-2
By The Numbers-12
By The Numbers Premium-12
Team Pinnacle-4
96Pinnacle Fantasy-FC6
96Pinnacle Mint-16
Bronze-16
Gold-16
Silver-16
Coins Brass-16
Coins Solid Gold-16
Coins Gold Plated-16
Coins Nickel-16
Coins Silver-16
96Playoff One on One-424
96Score-24
Artist's Proofs-24
Dealer's Choice Artist's Proofs-24
Special Artist's Proofs-24
Golden Blades-24
Dream Team-5
Sudden Death-10
96Select Certified-36
Artist's Proofs-36
Blue-36
Mirror Blue-36
Mirror Gold-36
Mirror Red-36
Red-36
Cornerstones-5
96SkyBox Impact-82
BladeRunners-14
96SP-98
Clearcut Winner-CW11
Game Film-GF10
96SPx-27
Gold-27
Holoview Heroes-HH5
96Stadium Club Members Only-40
96Summit-111
Artist's Proofs-111
Ice-111
Metal-111
Premium Stock-111
High Voltage-1
High Voltage Mirage-1
96Team Out-20
96Topps Picks-25
500 Club-FC6
OPC Inserts-25
Top Shelf-TS5
96Ultra-109
Gold Medallion-109
Clear the Ice-7
Mr. Momentum-8
96Upper Deck-299
Game Jerseys-GJ11
Hart Hopefuls Bronze-HH2
Hart Hopefuls Gold-HH2
Hart Hopefuls Silver-HH2
Lord Stanley's Heroes Finals-LS2
Lord Stanley's Heroes Quarterfinals-LS2
Lord Stanley's Heroes Semifinals-LS2
Superstar Showdown-SS9A
96Upper Deck Ice-111
Parallel-111
Stanley Cup Foundation-S1
Stanley Cup Foundation Dynasty-S1
96Zenith-94
Artist's Proofs-94
Champion Salute-1
Champion Salute Diamond-1
96Swedish Semic Wien-86
97SLU Hockey Canadian-11
97SLU Hockey American-13
97Headliners Hockey-18
97Be A Player Take A Number-17
97Beehive-30
Golden Portraits-30
Team-2
Team Gold-2
97Black Diamond-7
Double Diamond-7
Triple Diamond-7
Quadruple Diamond-7
Premium Cut-PC23
Premium Cut Double Diamond-PC23
Premium Cut Quadruple Diamond Horiz-PC23
Premium Cut Triple Diamond-PC23
Premium Cut Quadruple Diamond Verticals-PC23
97Collector's Choice-168
Star Quest-SQ49
World Domination-W2
97Crown Royale-136
Emerald Green-136
Ice Blue-136
Silver-136
Blades of Steel Die-Cuts-20
Hat Tricks Die-Cuts-19
Lamplighters Cel-Fusion Die-Cuts-20
97Donruss-4
Press Proofs Silver-4
Press Proofs Gold-4
Line 2 Line-23
Line 2 Line Die Cut-23
97Donruss Canadian Ice-50
Dominion Series-50
Provincial Series-50
National Pride-2
Stanley Cup Scrapbook-23
97Donruss Elite-5
97Donruss Elite-127
97Donruss Elite-150
Aspirations-5
Aspirations-127
Aspirations-150
Status-5
Status-127
Status-150
Craftsmen-4
Master Craftsmen-4
Prime Numbers-3A
Prime Numbers-3B
Prime Numbers-3C
Prime Numbers Die-Cuts-3A
Prime Numbers Die-Cuts-3B
Prime Numbers Die-Cuts-3C
97Donruss Limited-25
97Donruss Limited-84
97Donruss Limited-187
Exposure-25
Exposure-84
Exposure-187
Fabric of the Game-44
Fabric of the Game-59
97Donruss Preferred-7
97Donruss Preferred-177
Cut to the Chase-7
Cut to the Chase-177
Line of the Times-7C
97Donruss Preferred Line of Times Promos-7C
97Donruss Preferred Precious Metals-4
97Donruss Priority-16
97Donruss Priority-189
Stamp of Approval-16
Stamp of Approval-189
Direct Deposit-7
Direct Deposit Promos-P7
Postcards-6
Postcards Opening Day Issues-14
Stamps-6
Stamps Bronze-6
Stamps Gold-6
Stamps Silver-6
97Esso Olympic Hockey Heroes-20
97Esso Olympic Hockey Heroes French-20
97Gatorade Stickers-2
97Highland Mint Mint-Cards Topps-19
97Highland Mint Mint-Cards Topps-20
97Jell-O Juniors To Pros-4
97Katch-148
Gold-148
Silver-148
97Kenner Starting Lineup Cards-13
97Kraft-7
97Kraft 3-D World's Best-6
97Leaf-9
97Leaf-176
Fractal Matrix-9
Fractal Matrix-176
Fractal Matrix Die Cuts-9
Fractal Matrix Die Cuts-176
Fire On Ice-11
97Leaf International-9
Universal Ice-9
97NHL Aces Playing Cards-12
97Pacific-11
97Pacific-CM1
Copper-11
Emerald Green-11
Ice Blue-11
Red-11
Silver-11
Card-Supials-13
Card-Supials Minis-13
Cramer's Choice-8
Gold Crown Die-Cuts-16
Slap Shots Die-Cuts-5B
97Pacific Dynagon-81
97Pacific Dynagon-140
Copper-81
Copper-140
Dark Grey-81
Dark Grey-140
Emerald Green-81
Emerald Green-140
Ice Blue-81
Ice Blue-140
Red-81
Red-140
Silver-81
Silver-140
Best Kept Secrets-63
Dynamic Duos-10B
Kings of the NHL-7
Tandems-3
Tandems-19
97Pacific Invincible-89
Copper-89
Emerald Green-89
Ice Blue-89
Red-89
Silver-89
Attack Zone-16
Feature Performers-22
NHL Regime-131
Off The Glass-13
97Pacific Omega-231
Copper-231
Dark Gray-231
Emerald Green-231
Gold-231
Gold-250
Ice Blue-231
Game Face-19
Silks-12
Stick Handle Laser Cuts-20
Team Leaders-20
97Panini Stickers-83
97Paramount-190
Copper-190
Dark Grey-190
Emerald Green-190
Ice Blue-190
Red-190
Silver-190
Big Numbers Die-Cuts-20
Canadian Greats-12
Photoengravings-20
97Pinnacle-27
97Pinnacle-194
Artist's Proofs-27
Rink Collection-27
Epix Game Emerald-12
Epix Game Orange-12
Epix Game Purple-12
Epix Moment Emerald-12
Epix Moment Orange-12
Epix Moment Purple-12
Epix Play Emerald-12
Epix Play Orange-12
Epix Play Purple-12
Epix Season Emerald-12
Epix Season Orange-12
Epix Season Purple-12
Press Plates Back Black-27
Press Plates Back Black-194
Press Plates Back Cyan-27
Press Plates Back Cyan-194
Press Plates Back Magenta-27
Press Plates Back Magenta-194
Press Plates Back Yellow-27
Press Plates Back Yellow-194
Press Plates Front Black-27
Press Plates Front Black-194
Press Plates Front Cyan-27
Press Plates Front Cyan-194
Press Plates Front Magenta-27
Press Plates Front Magenta-194
Press Plates Front Yellow-27
Press Plates Front Yellow-194
Team Pinnacle-5
Team Mirror-5
Team Parallel-5
Team Parallel Mirror-5
97Pinnacle Certified-43
Red-43
Mirror Blue-43
Mirror Gold-43
Mirror Red-43
Team-12
Gold Team Promo-12
Gold Team-12
97Pinnacle Inside-50
Coach's Collection-50
Executive Collection-50
Track-18
Cans-21
Cans Gold-21
97Pinnacle Mint-13
Bronze-13
Gold Team-13
Silver Team-13
Coins Brass-13
Coins Brass Proofs-13
Coins Gold Plated-13
Coins Gold Plated Proofs-13
Coins Nickel Silver-13
Coins Nickel Silver Proofs-13
Coins Solid Gold-13
Coins Solid Silver-13
97Pinnacle Power Pack Blow-Ups-9
97Pinnacle Tot Cert Platinum Blue-43
97Pinnacle Tot Certi Platinum Gold-43
97Pinnacle Totally Certified Platinum Red-43
97Pinnacle Tot Cert Mirror Platinum Gold-43
97Post Pinnacle-5
97Revolution-142
Copper-142
Emerald-142
Ice Blue-142
Silver-142
1998 All-Star Game Die-Cuts-19
97Score-85
Artist's Proofs-85
Golden Blades-85
97Score Canucks-3
Platinum-3
Premier-3
97SP Authentic-157
Icons-I16
Icons Die-Cuts-I16
Icons Embossed-I16
97SPx-32
Bronze-32
Gold-32
Silver-32
Steel-32
Dimension-SPX3
Grand Finale-32
97Studio-9
Press Proofs Silver-9
Press Proofs Gold-9
Portraits-9
Silhouettes-6
Silhouettes 8x10-6
97Upper Deck-374
Blow-Ups 3 x 5-2-6
Blow-Ups 5 x 7-1A
Game Dated Moments-374
Sixth Sense Masters-SS11
Sixth Sense Wizards-SS11
Smooth Grooves-SG11
The Specialists-5
The Specialists Level 2 Die Cuts-5
Three Star Selects-11B
97Upper Deck Crash the All-Star Game-14
97Upper Deck Crash the All-Star Game-AR14
97Upper Deck Ice-71
Parallel-71
Champions-IC11
Champions 2 Die Cuts-IC11
Lethal Lines-L3B
Lethal Lines 2-L3B
Power Shift-71
97Zenith-16
Z-Gold-16
Z-Silver-16
97Zenith 5 x 7-64
Gold Impulse-64
Silver Impulse-64
97Pinnacle Collector's Club Team Pinnacle-H10
98SLU Hockey Classic Doubles-3
98SLU Hockey One on One-3
98SLU Hockey-140
98Aurora-189
Atomic Laser Cuts-19
Championship Fever-48
Championship Fever Copper-48
Championship Fever Ice Blue-48
Championship Fever Red-48
Championship Fever Silver-48
Cubes-18
Man Advantage-19
98Be A Player-290
Press Release-290
98BAP Gold-290
98BAP Autographs-290
98BAP Autographs Gold-290
98BAP AS Game Used Stick Cards-S10
98BAP AS Game Used Jersey Cards-AS10
98BAP AS Milestones-M2
98BAP AS Milestones-M8
98BAP Playoff Game Used Jerseys-G20
98BAP Playoff Highlights-H1
98BAP Playoff Practice Used Jerseys-P17
98Black Diamond-85
Double Diamond-85
Triple Diamond-85
Quadruple Diamond-85
Winning Formula Gold-WF24
Winning Formula Platinum-WF24
98Bowman's Best-5
Refractors-5
Atomic Refractors-5
98Crown Royale-135
Limited Series-135
Master Performers-19
Pillars of the Game-24
Pivotal Players-23
98Donruss Elite Promos-4
98Finest-68
No Protectors-68
No Protectors Refractors-68
Refractors-68
Double Sided Mystery Finest-M41
Double Sided Mystery Finest-M42
Double Sided Mystery Finest-M43
Double Sided Mystery Finest-M44
Double Sided Mystery Refractors-M41
Double Sided Mystery Refractors-M42
Double Sided Mystery Refractors-M43
Double Sided Mystery Refractors-M44
Red Lighters-R18
Red Lighters Refractors-R18
98Katch-146
98Kenner Starting Lineup Cards-22
98OPC Chrome-138
Refractors-138
Blast From the Past-2
Blast From the Past Refractors-2
98Pacific-11
Ice Blue-11
Red-11
Dynagon Ice Inserts-18
Titanium Ice-18
Gold Crown Die-Cuts-34
Timelines-20
98Pacific Dynagon Ice-189
Blue-189
Red-189
Forward Thinking-19
Team Checklists-26
98Pacific Omega-236
Red-236
Opening Day Issue-236
EO Portraits-20
EO Portraits 1 of 1-20
Face to Face-10
Online-34
Planet Ice-10
Planet Ice Parallel-10
Prism-20
98Panini Photocards-51
98Panini Photocards-105
98Panini Stickers-219
98Paramount-236
Copper-236
Emerald Green-236
Holo-Electric-236
Ice Blue-236
Silver-236
Hall of Fame Bound-10
Hall of Fame Bound Proofs-10
Special Delivery Die-Cuts-19
Team Checklists Die-Cuts-26
98Post-15
98Revolution-141
Ice Shadow-141
Red-141
Chalk Talk Laser-Cuts-19
Showstoppers-35
98SP Authentic-85
Power Shift-85
Stat Masters-S12
98SPx Finite-160
Radiance-160
Spectrum-160
98SPx Top Prospects-57
Radiance-57
Spectrum-57
Premier Stars-PS30
98Topps-138
O-Pee-Chee-138
Blast From The Past-2
Local Legends-L11
Mystery Finest Bronze-M19
Mystery Finest Bronze Refractors-M19
Mystery Finest Gold-M19
Mystery Finest Gold Refractors-M19
Mystery Finest Silver-M19
Mystery Finest Silver Refractors-M19
98Topps Gold Label Class 1-6
Black-6
Black One of One-6
One of One-6
Red-6
Red One of One-6
98Topps Gold Label Class 2-6
98Topps Gold Label Class 2 Black-6
98Topps Gold Label Class 2 Black 1 of 1-6
98Topps Gold Label Class 2 One of One-6
98Topps Gold Label Class 2 Red-6
98Topps Gold Label Class 2 Red One of One-6
98Topps Gold Label Class 3-6
98Topps Gold Label Class 3 Black-6
98Topps Gold Label Class 3 Black 1 of 1-6
98Topps Gold Label Class 3 One of One-6
98Topps Gold Label Class 3 Red-6
98Topps Gold Label Class 3 Red One of One-6
98UD Choice-211
Mini Bobbing Head-BH9
98UD Choice Preview-211
98UD Choice Prime Choice Reserve-211
98UD Choice Reserve-211
98UD Choice StarQuest Blue-SQ29
98UD Choice StarQuest Gold-SQ29
98UD Choice StarQuest Green-SQ29
98UD Choice StarQuest Red-SQ29
98UD3-53
98UD3-113
98UD3-173
Die-Cuts-53
Die-Cuts-113
Die-Cuts-173
98Upper Deck-195
Exclusives-195
Exclusives 1 of 1-195
Lord Stanley's Heroes-LS11
Lord Stanley's Heroes Quantum 1-LS11
Lord Stanley's Heroes Quantum 2-LS11
Lord Stanley's Heroes Quantum 3-LS11
Gold Reserve-195
98Upper Deck MVP-201
Gold Script-201
Silver Script-201
Super Script-201
Power Game-PG7
99SLU Hockey Classic Doubles-2
99SLU Hockey 12" Figures-5
99SLU Hockey Pro Action-50
99Aurora-140
Striped-140
Premiere Date-140
Premiere Date Striped-140
Styrotechs-20
99BAP Memorabilia-265
Gold-265
Silver-265
Jersey Cards-J10
Jersey Emblems-E10
Jersey Numbers-I10
Jersey and Stick Cards-S10
AS Heritage Ruby-H14
AS Heritage Sapphire-H14
AS Heritage Emerald-H14
99BAP Update Double AS Jersey Cards-D18
99BAP Update Teammates Jersey Cards-TM3
99BAP Update Teammates Jersey Cards-TM8
99BAP Update Teammates Jersey Cards-TM36
99BAP Millennium-235
Emerald-235
Ruby-235
Sapphire-235
Signatures-235
Signatures Gold-235
Jerseys-J11
Jersey and Stick Cards-JS11
Jersey Emblems-E11
Jersey Numbers-N11
Pearson-P6
Pearson Autographs-P6
Players of the Decade-D2
Players of the Decade Autographs-D2
99Black Diamond-86
Diamond Cut-86
Final Cut-86
Diamond Might-DM9
99Crown Royale-137
Limited Series-137
Premiere Date-137
Team Captain Die-Cuts-10
99Kraft Stanley Cup Moments-1
99O-Pee-Chee-92
99O-Pee-Chee-283A
99O-Pee-Chee-283B
99O-Pee-Chee-283C
99O-Pee-Chee-283D
99O-Pee-Chee-283E
99O-Pee-Chee Chrome-92
99O-Pee-Chee Chrome-283A
99O-Pee-Chee Chrome-283B
99O-Pee-Chee Chrome-283C
99O-Pee-Chee Chrome-283D
99O-Pee-Chee Chrome-283E
99O-Pee-Chee Chrome Refractors-92
99O-Pee-Chee Chrome Refractors-283A
99O-Pee-Chee Chrome Refractors-283B
99O-Pee-Chee Chrome Refractors-283C
99O-Pee-Chee Chrome Refractors-283D
99O-Pee-Chee Chrome Refractors-283E
99Oscar Mayer Lunchables-10
99Pacific-426
Copper-426
Emerald Green-426
Gold-426
Ice Blue-426
Premiere Date-426
Red-426
Center Ice-20
Center Ice Proofs-20
Gold Crown Die-Cuts-36
Team Leaders-27
99Pacific Dynagon Ice-194
Blue-194
Copper-194
Gold-194
Premiere Date-194
99Pacific Omega-234
Copper-234
Gold-234
Ice Blue-234
Premiere Date-234
Cup Contenders-20
EO Portraits-20
EO Portraits 1/1-20
North American All-Stars-10
5 Star Talents-12
5 Star Talents Parallel-12
99Pacific Prism-141
Holographic Blue-141
Holographic Gold-141
Holographic Mirror-141
Holographic Purple-141
Premiere Date-141
Dial-a-Stats-10
99Panini Stickers-307
99Panini Stickers-331
99Paramount-235
Copper-235
Emerald-235
Gold-235
Holographic Emerald-235
Holographic Gold-235
Holographic Silver-235
Ice Blue-235
Premiere Date-235
Red-235
Silver-235
Hall of Fame Bound-10
Hall of Fame Bound Proofs-10
Ice Advantage-20
Ice Advantage Proofs-20
Ice Alliance-27
Personal Best-36
99Revolution-142
Premiere Date-142
Red-142
Shadow Series-142
NHL Icons-20
Ornaments-20
Showstoppers-35
Top of the Line-20
Copper-142
Gold-142
CSC Silver-142
99SP Authentic-85
99SPx-149
Radiance-149
Spectrum-149
99Stadium Club-3
First Day Issue-3
One of a Kind-3
Printing Plates Black-3
Printing Plates Cyan-3
Printing Plates Magenta-3
Printing Plates Yellow-3
Capture the Action-CA24
Capture the Action Game View-CAG24
Chrome-3
Chrome Refractors-3
99Topps/OPC-92
99Topps/OPC-283A
99Topps/OPC-283B
99Topps/OPC-283C
99Topps/OPC-283D
99Topps/OPC-283E
99Topps Stanley Cup Heroes-SC8
99Topps Stanley Cup Heroes Refractors-SC8
99Topps/OPC Chrome-92
99Topps/OPC Chrome-283A
99Topps/OPC Chrome-283B
99Topps/OPC Chrome-283C
99Topps/OPC Chrome-283D
99Topps/OPC Chrome-283E
Refractors-92
Refractors-283A
Refractors-283B
Refractors-283C
Refractors-283D
Refractors-283E
99Topps Gold Label Class 1-36

Black-36
Black One of One-36
One of One-36
Red-36
Red One of One-36
99Topps Gold Label Class 2-36
99Topps Gold Label Class 2 Black-36
99Topps Gold Label Class 2 Black 1 of 1-36
99Topps Gold Label Class 2 One of One-36
99Topps Gold Label Class 2 Red-36
99Topps Gold Label Class 2 Red One of One-36
99Topps Gold Label Class 3-36
99Topps Gold Label Class 3 Black-36
99Topps Gold Label Class 3 Black 1 of 1-36
99Topps Gold Label Class 3 One of One-36
99Topps Gold Label Class 3 Red-36
99Topps Gold Label Class 3 Red One of One-36
99Topps Premier Plus-24
Parallel-24
Feature Presentations-FP2
99Ultimate Victory-85
1/1-85
Parallel-85
Parallel 100-85
The Victors-V1
99Upper Deck-126
Exclusives-126
Exclusives 1 of 1-126
Headed for the Hall-HOF11
Headed for the Hall Quantum Gold-HOF11
Headed for the Hall Quantum Silver-HOF11
99Upper Deck Century Legends-12
Century Collection-12
99Upper Deck Gold Reserve-126
99Upper Deck MVP-204
Gold Script-204
Silver Script-204
Super Script-204
99Upper Deck MVP SC Edition-182
Gold Script-182
Silver Script-182
Super Script-182
Playoff Heroes-PH10
Second Season Snipers-SS12
Stanley Cup Talent-SC19
99Upper Deck Ovation-58
Standing Ovation-58
99Upper Deck Retro-77
Gold-77
Platinum-77
Distant Replay-DR6
Distant Replay Level 2-DR6
99Upper Deck Victory-292
99Upper Deck Victory-293
99Wayne Gretzky Hockey-167
Will to Win-W10
00McFarlane Hockey-120
00Aurora-96
Pinstripes-96
Pinstripes Premiere Date-96
Premiere Date-96
Championship Fever-16
Championship Fever Copper-16
Championship Fever Platinum Blue-16
Championship Fever Silver-16
Game-Worn Jerseys-7
Game-Worn Jersey Patches-7
00BAP Memorabilia-133
00BAP Memorabilia-443
Emerald-133
Emerald-443
Ruby-133
Ruby-443
Sapphire-133
Sapphire-443
Promos-133
Jersey Cards-J23
Jersey Emblems-E23
Jersey Numbers-N23
Jersey and Stick Cards-JS23
00BAP Mem Chicago Sportsfest Copper-133
00BAP Memorabilia Chicago Sportsfest Blue-133
00BAP Memorabilia Chicago Sportsfest Gold-133
00BAP Memorabilia Chicago Sportsfest Ruby-133
00BAP Memorabilia Chicago Sun-Times Ruby-133
00BAP Memorabilia Chicago Sun-Times Gold-133
00BAP Mem Chicago Sun-Times Sapphire-133
00BAP Mem Toronto Fall Expo Copper-133
00BAP Memorabilia Toronto Fall Expo Gold-133
00BAP Memorabilia Toronto Fall Expo Ruby-133
00BAP Mem Update Heritage Jersey Cards-H1
00BAP Mem Update Heritage Jersey Gold-H1
00BAP Memorabilia Update Teammates-TM7
00BAP Memorabilia Update Teammates-TM32
00BAP Memorabilia Update Teammates Gold-TM7
00BAP Memorabilia Update Teammates Gold-TM32
00BAP Parkhurst 2000-P234
00BAP Signature Series-98
Emerald-98
Ruby-98
Sapphire-98
He Shoots-He Scores Points-12
He Shoots-He Scores Prizes-31
Jersey Cards-J11
Jersey and Stick Cards-GSJ11
Jersey Cards Autographs-J11
Jersey Emblems-E11
Jersey Numbers-IN11
00BAP Ultimate Memorabilia Active Eight-AE1
00BAP Ultimate Memorabilia Active Eight-AE2
00BAP Ultimate Memorabilia Captain's C-C7
00BAP Ultimate Mem Dynasty Jerseys-D2
00BAP Ultimate Mem Dynasty Emblems-D2
00BAP Ultimate Mem Game-Used Jerseys-GJ11
00BAP Ultimate Mem Game-Used Emblems-E9
00BAP Ultimate Mem Game-Used Numbers-N9
00BAP Ultimate Mem Game-Used Sticks-GS11
00BAP Ultimate Memorabilia Hart Trophy-H9
00BAP Ultimate Memorabilia Hart Trophy-H11
00BAP Ultimate Mem Journey Jerseys-JJ2
00BAP Ultimate Mem Journey Emblems-JE2
00BAP Ultimate Mem Journey Numbers-JI2
00BAP Ultimate Mem Magnificent Ones-ML4
00BAP Ultimate Mem Magnificent Ones Autos-ML4
00BAP Ultimate Memorabilia Retro-Active-RA10
00BAP Ultimate Memorabilia Teammates-TM36
00Black Diamond-38
Gold-38
Game Gear-SMM
00Crown Royale-71
Ice Blue-71
Limited Series-71
Premiere Date-71
Red-71
Jewels of the Crown-18
00Kraft-28
00O-Pee-Chee-20
00O-Pee-Chee Parallel-20
00Pacific-411
Copper-411
Gold-411
Ice Blue-411
Premiere Date-411
Jerseys-14
Jersey Patches-14
Gold Crown Die Cuts-35
Reflections-20
00Panini Stickers-208
00Paramount-165
Copper-165
Gold-165
Holo-Gold-165
Holo-Silver-165
Ice Blue-165
Premiere Date-165
00Private Stock-66
Gold-66
Premiere Date-66
Retail-66
Silver-66
Artist's Canvas-15
Artist's Canvas Proofs-15
Game Gear-77
Game Gear Patches-77
PS-2001 Action-38
PS-2001 Stars-18
Reserve-15
00Revolution-97
Blue-97
Premiere Date-97
Red-97
NHL Game Gear-7
00SP Authentic-55
BuyBacks-69
BuyBacks-70
BuyBacks-71
BuyBacks-72
BuyBacks-73
BuyBacks-74
Honor-SP5
Sign of the Times-MM
Sign of the Times-M/G
Sign of the Times-GMF
Significant Stars-ST5
00SP Game Used-41
Patch Cards-D-MG
Patch Cards-P-MM
Tools of the Game-MM
Tools of the Game Exclusives-MM
Tools of the Game Combos-C-MG
00SPx-43
00SPx-74
Spectrum-43
Spectrum-74
Prolifics-P5
SPXtreme-S5
00Stadium Club-213
Beam Team-BT19
00Titanium-62
Blue-62
Gold-62
Premiere Date-62
Red-62
Retail-62
00Topps/OPC-20
Parallel-20
1000 Point Club-PC1
00Topps Chrome-19
OPC Refractors-19
Refractors-19
1000 Point Club Refractors-1
00Topps Gold Label Class 1-47
Gold-47
00Topps Gold Label Class 2-47
00Topps Gold Label Class 2 Gold-47
00Topps Gold Label Class 3-47
00Topps Gold Label Class 3 Gold-47
00Topps Gold Label Bullion-B9
00Topps Gold Label Bullion One to One-B9
00Topps Heritage-7
Chrome Parallel-7
Arena Relics-OSA-MM
Heroes-HH7
Original Six Relics-OSS-MM
00Topps Premier Plus-11
Blue Ice-11
Trophy Tribute-TT7
00Topps Stars-92
Blue-92
All-Star Authority-ASA3
00UD Heroes-151
00UD Heroes-179
Game-Used Twigs-T-MM
Game-Used Twigs Gold-C-GM
NHL Leaders-L5
Player Idols-PI1
Second Season Heroes-SS8
Signs of Greatness-MM
00UD Pros and Prospects-58
00UD Pros and Prospects-89
Championship Rings-CR7
Game Jersey Autograph Exclusives-S-MM
Game Jersey Autographs-S-MM
NHL Passion-NP4
00UD Reserve-57
00UD Reserve-119
Buyback Autographs-72
Buyback Autographs-73
Buyback Autographs-74
Buyback Autographs-75
Buyback Autographs-76
Buyback Autographs-77
Buyback Autographs-78
On-Ice Success-OS6
Power Portfolios-PP5
Practice Session Jerseys-MA
Practice Session Jerseys Autographs-MA
00Upper Deck-119
00Upper Deck-410
Exclusives Tier 1-119
Exclusives Tier 1-410
Exclusives Tier 2-119
Exclusives Tier 2-410
500 Goal Club-500MM
500 Goal Club-500MM
500 Goal Club-500MM
500 Goal Club-500MM
Dignitaries-D10
e-Cards-EC8
e-Card Prizes-AMM
e-Card Prizes-SEMM
Frozen in Time-FT5
Game Jersey Autographs Canadian-CMM
Game Jersey Combos-DGM
Game Jersey Patches-MMP
Game Jersey Patch Autographs Exclusives-MMP
Lord Stanley's Heroes-L8
Number Crunchers-NC10
Triple Threat-TT6
00Upper Deck Ice-39
00Upper Deck Ice-73
Immortals-39
Legends-39
Stars-39
00Upper Deck Legends-51
00Upper Deck Legends-92
Legendary Collection Bronze-51
Legendary Collection Bronze-92
Legendary Collection Gold-51
Legendary Collection Gold-92
Legendary Collection Silver-51
Legendary Collection Silver-92
Epic Signatures-MM
Playoff Heroes-PH6
Supreme Milestones-SM8
00Upper Deck MVP Game-Used Souvenirs-GSMM
00Upper Deck MVP Super Game-Used Souvenir-GSMM
00Upper Deck Victory-225
00Upper Deck Victory-226
00Upper Deck Victory-328
00Upper Deck Vintage-237
00Upper Deck Vintage-246
00Upper Deck Vintage-247
Dynasty: A Piece of History-GK
Dynasty: A Piece of History Gold-GK
Messier Heroes of Hockey-HH37
Messier Heroes of Hockey-HH38
Messier Heroes of Hockey-HH39
Messier Heroes of Hockey-HH40
Messier Heroes of Hockey-HH41
Messier Heroes of Hockey-HH42
Messier Heroes of Hockey-HH43
Messier Heroes of Hockey-HH44
Messier Heroes of Hockey-HH45
Messier Heroes of Hockey-HH46
National Heroes-NH16
00Vanguard-66
High Voltage-23
High Voltage Gold-23
High Voltage Green-23
High Voltage Red-23
High Voltage Silver-23
Holographic Gold-66
Holographic Purple-66
Pacific Proofs-66
Press East/West-15
00Czech Stadion-67
00Czech Stadion-150
01Atomic-66
Blue-66
Gold-66
Premiere Date-66
Red-66
Core Players-12
Power Play-24
Team Nucleus-10
01BAP Memorabilia-97
Emerald-97
Ruby-97
Sapphire-97
All-Star Jerseys-ASJ31
All-Star Emblems-ASE31
All-Star Numbers-ASN31
All-Star Jersey Doubles-DASJ17
All-Star Teammates-AST24
All-Star Teammates-AST39
500 Goal Scorers-GS6
He Shoots-He Scores Points-6
01BAP Signature Series Certified 100-C55
01BAP Signature Series Certified 50-C55
01BAP Signature Series Certified 1 of 1's-C55
01BAP Signature Series Autographs-XLMM
01BAP Signature Series Autographs Gold-LMM
01BAP Signature Series 500 Goal Scorers-25
01BAP Signature Series 500 Goal Scorers-MM
01BAP Sig Series He Shoots/Scores Points-6
01BAP Sig Series He Shoots/Scores Prizes-20
01BAP Signature Series Jerseys-GJ-40
01BAP Signature Series Jersey Autographs-GUMME
01BAP Sig Series Jersey and Stick Cards-GSJ-40
01BAP Signature Series Emblems-GUE-38
01BAP Signature Series Numbers-ITN-38
01BAP Signature Series Teammates-TM-19
01BAP Ultimate Memorabilia Active Eight-3
01BAP Ultimate Memorabilia Active Eight-5
01BAP Ultimate Memorabilia Active Eight-7
01BAP Ultimate Mem All-Star History-34
01BAP Ultimate Memorabilia Autographs-32
01BAP Ultimate Mem Autographs Gold-32
01BAP Ultimate Memorabilia Dynamic Duos-9
01BAP Ultimate Memorabilia Emblems-13
01BAP Ultimate Memorabilia Emblem Attic-12
01BAP Ultimate Mem 500 Goal Scorers-12
01BAP Ultimate Mem 500 Goal Jerseys/Stick-12
01BAP Ultimate Mem 500 Goal Emblems-12
01BAP Ultimate Memorabilia Jerseys-13
01BAP Ultimate Mem Jerseys and Sticks-13
01BAP Ultimate Mem Journey Jerseys-1
01BAP Ultimate Mem Journey Emblems-1
01BAP Ultimate Memorabilia Numbers-11
01BAP Ultimate Memorabilia Name Plates-14
01BAP Ultimate Mem Playoff Records-4
01BAP Ultimate Mem Playoff Records-17
01BAP Ultimate Mem Retro Teammates-4
01BAP Ultimate Mem Retro Teammates-12
01BAP Ultimate Mem Stanley Cup Winners-11
01BAP Update Heritage-H4
01Bowman YoungStars-82
Gold-82
Ice Cubed-82
01Crown Royale-97
Blue-97
Premiere Date-97
Red-97
Retail-97
All-Star Honors-16
Jewels of the Crown-22
Legendary Heroes-7
01eTopps-18
01McDonald's Pacific Hockey Greats-6
01O-Pee-Chee-55
01O-Pee-Chee Heritage Parallel-55
01O-Pee-Chee Heritage Parallel Limited-55
01O-Pee-Chee Premier Parallel-55
01Pacific-264
Extreme LTD-264
Hobby LTD-264
Premiere Date-264
Retail LTD-264
Gold Crown Die-Cuts-14
01Pacific Adrenaline-128
Blue-128
Premiere Date-128
Red-128
Retail-128
01Pacific Arena Exclusives-264
01Pacific Heads-Up-65
Blue-65
Premiere Date-65
Red-65
Silver-65
01Parkhurst-50
Gold-50
Silver-50
500 Goal Scorers-PGS6
He Shoots-He Scores Prizes-20
Jerseys-PJ6
Milestones-M12
Milestones-M35
Sticks-PS6
Teammates-T3
Teammates-T24
01Private Stock-64
Gold-64
Premiere Date-64
Retail-64
Silver-64
01Private Stock Pacific Nights-64
01Private Stock PS-2002-49
01SP Authentic-54
01SP Authentic-103
Limited-54
Limited-103
Limited Gold-54
Limited Gold-103
Jerseys-NNMM
01SP Game Used-35
Tools of the Game-TMM
01SPx-42
Signs of Xcellence-MM
01Sports Illustrated for Kids III-11
01Stadium Club-10
Award Winners-10
Master Photos-10
Gallery-G40
Gallery Gold-G40
Heart and Soul-HS1
01Titanium-95
Hobby Parallel-95
Premiere Date-95
Retail-95
Retail Parallel-95
Double-Sided Jerseys-27
Double-Sided Patches-27
01Titanium Draft Day Edition-62
01Topps-55
Heritage Parallel-55
Heritage Parallel Limited-55
OPC Parallel-55
01Topps Chrome-55
Refractors-55
Black Border Refractors-55
01Topps Heritage-14
Refractors-14
01Topps Reserve-9
01UD Challenge for the Cup-57
Century Men-CM6
Future Famers-FF6
01UD Honor Roll Pucks-P-MM
01UD Honor Roll Pucks Gold-P-MM
01UD Mask Collection Gloves-GGMM
01UD Playmakers-66
01UD Premier Collection Dual Jerseys-DGM
01UD Premier Collection Dual Jersey Black-DGM
01UD Stanley Cup Champs-84
Jerseys-T-ME
Pieces of Glory-G-MA
01UD Top Shelf Sticks-SMM
01UD Top Shelf Sticks Gold-SMM
01Upper Deck-114
01Upper Deck-217
Exclusives-114
Exclusives-217
Gate Attractions-GA1
Leaders of the Pack-LP8
Skilled Stars-SS17
01Upper Deck Ice-30
01Upper Deck MVP-123
Souvenirs-S-MM
Souvenirs Gold-S-MM
Watch-MW6
01Upper Deck Victory-230
Gold-230
01Upper Deck Vintage-166
01Upper Deck Vintage-173
01Vanguard-65
Blue-65
Red-65
One of Ones-65
Premiere Date-65
Proofs-65
02McFarlane Hockey-30
02McFarlane Hockey-32
02McFarlane Hockey-230
02McFarlane Hockey-232
02Atomic Jerseys-16
02Atomic Jerseys Gold-16
02Atomic Patches-16
02BAP All-Star Edition-58
02BAP All-Star Edition-59
He Shoots-He Scores Points-3
He Shoots-He Score Prizes-18
Jerseys-58
Jerseys-59
Jerseys Gold-58
Jerseys Gold-59
Jerseys Silver-58
Jerseys Silver-59
02BAP First Edition-133
Debut Jerseys-18
He Shoots-He Score Points-9
He Shoots-He Scores Prizes-10
Jerseys-133
02BAP Memorabilia-118
Emerald-118
Ruby-118
Sapphire-118
All-Star Jerseys-ASJ-35
All-Star Emblems-ASE-15
All-Star Numbers-ASN-15
All-Star Teammates-AST-3
All-Star Teammates-AST-4
All-Star Teammates-AST-20
All-Star Triple Jerseys-ASTJ-14
He Shoots-He Scores Prizes-27
Mini Stanley Cups-22
NHL All-Star Game-118
NHL All-Star Game Blue-118
NHL All-Star Game Green-118
NHL All-Star Game Red-118
Teammates-TM-7
02BAP Memorabilia Toronto Fall Expo-118
02BAP NHL All-Star History-34
02BAP Sig Series Auto Buybacks 1998-290
02BAP Sig Series Auto Buybacks 1999-235
02BAP Signature Series Jerseys-SGJ17
02BAP Signature Series Jersey Autographs-SGJ17
02BAP Ultimate Memorabilia Active Eight-1
02BAP Ultimate Memorabilia Active Eight-4
02BAP Ultimate Memorabilia Active Eight-5
02BAP Ultimate Memorabilia Emblems-26
02BAP Ultimate Memorabilia Great Moments-9
02BAP Ultimate Memorabilia Jerseys-21
02BAP Ultimate Mem Jersey and Stick-4
02BAP Ultimate Mem Lifetime Achievers-17
02BAP Ultimate Memorabilia Numbers-17
02BAP Ultimate Memorabilia Numerology-16
02BAP Ultimate Mem Playoff Scorers-11
02BAP Ultimate Memorabilia Retro Trophies-14
02Bowman YoungStars-69
Gold-69
Silver-69
02ITG Used-49
02ITG Used-149
Jerseys-GUJ17
Jersey Autographs-GUJ17
Jerseys Gold-GUJ17
Emblems-E17
Jersey and Stick-SJ17
Jersey and Stick Gold-SJ17
Teammates-T11
Teammates Gold-T11
02O-Pee-Chee-242
02O-Pee-Chee Premier Blue Parallel-242
02O-Pee-Chee Premier Red Parallel-242
02O-Pee-Chee Factory Set-242
02Pacific-256
Blue-256
Red-256
Jerseys-36
Jerseys Holo-Silver-36
02Pacific Calder-47
Silver-47
Hardware Heroes-9
02Pacific Complete-24
Red-24
02Pacific Exclusive-117
02Pacific Quest for the Cup-67
Gold-67
Jerseys-11
Raising the Cup-10
02Parkhurst-23
Bronze-23
Gold-23
Silver-23
Heroes-NH3
Heroes-NH6
He Shoots-He Scores Points-3
He Shoots-He Scores Prizes-13
Jerseys-GJ21
Patented Power-PP9
Stick and Jerseys-SJ21
02Parkhurst Retro-145
Minis-145
Jerseys-RJ4
Jersey and Sticks-RSJ4
02Rangers Team Issue-11
02SPx-126
02Titanium Jerseys-45
02Titanium Jerseys Retail-45
02Titanium Patches-44
02Topps-242
OPC Blue Parallel-242
OPC Red Parallel-242
Factory Set-242
02Topps Chrome-133
Black Border Refractors-133
Refractors-133
02Topps Total-314
02UD Artistic Impressions Performers-SSMM
02UD Artistic Impressions Performers Gold-SSMM
02UD Foundations-32
02UD Foundations-65
02UD Foundations-80
02UD Piece of History-108
Exquisite Combos-ECBM
Exquisite Combos-ECLM
02UD Top Shelf Dual Player Jerseys-STGM
02UD Top Shelf Milestones Jerseys-MGBYM
02UD Top Shelf Milestones Jerseys-MMHYR
02UD Top Shelf Milestones Jerseys-MSFRM
02Upper Deck-364
Exclusives-364
02Upper Deck Beckett UD Promos-364
02Upper Deck MVP Skate Around Jerseys-SDJM
02Upper Deck MVP Skate Around Jerseys-STMMT
02Upper Deck MVP Souvenirs-S-MM
02Upper Deck Rookie Update-67
02Upper Deck Victory-139
Bronze-139
Gold-139
Silver-139
02Upper Deck Vintage-170
02Upper Deck Vintage-280
Green Backs-170
02Vanguard Jerseys-30
02Vanguard Jerseys Gold-30
02UD SuperStars Leg Leaders Triple Jersey-JDM
02UD SuperStars Rookie Review *-R1
03McFarlane Hockey NHL 2-Pack-10
03BAP Memorabilia-49
Emerald-49
Gold-49
Ruby-49
Sapphire-49
Jerseys-GJ-44
03BAP Ultimate Memorabilia Active Eight-5
03BAP Ultimate Mem Always An All-Star-13
03BAP Ultimate Mem Always An AS Gold-13
03BAP Ultimate Memorabilia Dynamic Duos-10
03BAP Ultimate Mem French Present Future-20
03BAP Ultimate Memorabilia Great Moments-10
03BAP Ultimate Memorabilia Great Moments-11
03BAP Ultimate Memorabilia Heroes-3
03BAP Ultimate Mem Hometown Heroes-14
03BAP Ultimate Mem Hometown Heroes Gold-14
03BAP Ultimate Mem Journey Jerseys-8
03BAP Ultimate Mem Journey Jerseys Gold-8
03BAP Ultimate Mem Journey Emblems-8
03BAP Ultimate Mem Journey Emblems Gold-8
03BAP Ultimate Mem Lifetime Achievers-5
03BAP Ultimate Memorabilia Nameplates-8
03BAP Ultimate Mem Nameplates Gold-8
03BAP Ultimate Mem Retro Teammates-4
03BAP Ultimate Mem Retro-Active Trophies-8
03Beehive-132
Variations-132
Gold-132
Silver-132
Sticks Blue Border-BL11
Sticks Red Border-RE7
03Black Diamond Threads-DT-MM
03Black Diamond Threads Green-DT-MM
03Black Diamond Threads Red-DT-MM
03Black Diamond Threads Black-DT-MM
03Crown Royale-68
Blue-68
Retail-68
03ITG Action-310
Homeboys-HB5
Jerseys-M168
Oh Canada-OC7
03ITG Used Sig Series Jersey and Stick-21
03ITG Used Sig Ser Jersey and Stick Gold-21
03ITG Used Sig Series Retrospectives-10A
03ITG Used Sig Series Retrospectives-10B
03ITG Used Sig Series Retrospectives-10C
03ITG Used Sig Series Retrospectives-10D
03ITG Used Sig Series Retrospectives-10E
03ITG Used Sig Series Retrospectives-10F
03ITG Used Sig Series Retrospectives Gold-10A
03ITG Used Sig Series Retrospectives Gold-10B
03ITG Used Sig Series Retrospectives Gold-10C
03ITG Used Sig Series Retrospectives Gold-10D
03ITG Used Sig Series Retrospectives Gold-10E
03ITG Used Sig Series Retrospectives Gold-10F
03ITG Used Signature Series Teammates-12
03ITG Used Sig Series Teammates Gold-12
03ITG VIP Collages-9
03ITG VIP MVP-24
03McDonald's Pacific-34
Etched in Time-1
03NHL Sticker Collection-86
03O-Pee-Chee-101
03OPC Blue-101
03OPC Gold-101
03OPC Red-101
03Pacific-228
Blue-228
Red-228
Maximum Impact-7
03Pacific Calder-69
Silver-69
03Pacific Complete-221
Red-221
03Pacific Exhibit-182
Blue Backs-182
03Pacific Heads-Up-67
Hobby LTD-67
Retail LTD-67
Rink Immortals-8
Rink Immortals LTD-8
03Pacific Invincible-67
Blue-67
Red-67
Retail-67
03Pacific Prism-72
Blue-72
Gold-72
Red-72
03Pacific Quest 4 the Cup Raising the Cup-14
03Parkhurst Orig Six He Shoots/Scores-22
03Parkhurst Orig Six He Shoots/Scores-22A
03Parkhurst Original Six New York-25
03Parkhurst Original Six New York-61
03Parkhurst Original Six New York-71
03Parkhurst Original Six New York-98
Inserts-N9
Memorabilia-NM4
Memorabilia-NM15
03Parkhurst Rookie Jerseys-GJ-31
03Parkhurst Rookie Jerseys Gold-GJ-31
03Parkhurst Rookie Jersey and Sticks-SJ-3
03Parkhurst Rookie Jersey and Sticks Gold-SJ-3
03Parkhurst Rookie Retro Rookies-RR-16
03Parkhurst Rookie Retro Rookies Gold-RR-16
03Parkhurst Rookie Teammates-RT21
03Parkhurst Rookie Teammates Gold-RT21
03Private Stock Reserve-71
Blue-71
Red-71
Retail-71
03Rangers Team Issue-16
03Serious NHL Starz-2
03SP Authentic-59
Limited-59
03SPx-115
Radiance-115
Spectrum-115
Hall Pass-HP-MM
Hall Pass Limited-HP-MM
Winning Materials-WM-MM
Winning Materials Limited-WM-MM
03Titanium-69
Hobby Jersey Number Parallels-69
Retail-69
Retail Jersey Number Parallels-69
03Topps-101
Blue-101
Gold-101
Red-101
Topps/OPC Idols-CI16
Pristine Stick Portions-PPS-MM
Pristine Stick Portion Refractors-PPS-MM
03UD Honor Roll-56
Grade A Jerseys-GAMM
03UD Premier Collection-36
Teammates-PT-EO1
Teammates-PT-NR
Teammates Patches-PT-EO1
Teammates Patches-PT-NR
03Upper Deck-126
03Upper Deck-472
Canadian Exclusives-126
Canadian Exclusives-472
HG-126
HG-472
UD Exclusives-472
03Upper Deck Ice-58
Gold-58
Breakers-IB-MR
Breaker Patches-IB-MR
Clear Cut Winners-CC-MR
03Upper Deck Rookie Update-59
Skills-SKMK
Super Stars-SSMK
03Upper Deck Victory-125
Bronze-125
Gold-125
Silver-125
03Toronto Star-61
04ITG NHL AS FANtasy AS History Jerseys-SB34
04MasterCard Priceless Moments-7
04Pacific-177
Blue-177
Red-177
Milestones-4
Philadelphia-10
04SP Authentic-56
04Ultimate Collection-27
Dual Logos-UL2-GM
Jerseys-UGJ-MM
Jerseys Gold-UGJ-MM
Patches-UP-MM
04Upper Deck-116
04Upper Deck-184
Canadian Exclusives-116
Canadian Exclusives-184
Heritage Classic-CC-MM
HG Glossy Gold-116
HG Glossy Gold-184
HG Glossy Silver-116
HG Glossy Silver-184
Patches-GJPA-MM
Patches-GJPL-MM
Patches-GJPN-MM
Swatch of Six-SS-MM
05Be A Player Class Action-CA16
05Be A Player Outtakes-OT33
05Black Diamond-179
Emerald-179
Gold-179
Onyx-179
Ruby-179
Jerseys-J-MS
Jerseys Ruby-J-MS
Jersey Duals-DJ-MS
Jersey Triples-TJ-MS
Jersey Quads-QJ-MS
05SP Game Used Authentic Fabrics Quad-GMCF
05SP Game Used Authentic Fabrics Quad-MLYS
05SP Game Used Authentic Patches Quad -MLYS
05SP Game Used Authentic Patches Triple-KGM
05SPx Winning Combos-WC-GM
05SPx Winning Combos-WC-JM
05SPx Winning Combos-WC-MT
05SPx Winning Combos Gold-WC-GM
05SPx Winning Combos Gold-WC-JM
05SPx Winning Combos Gold-WC-MT
05SPx Winning Combos Spectrum-WC-GM
05SPx Winning Combos Spectrum-WC-JM
05SPx Winning Combos Spectrum-WC-MT
05SPx Winning Materials-WM-MS
05SPx Winning Materials Gold-WM-MS
05SPx Winning Materials Spectrum-WM-MS
05SPx Xcitement Superstars-XS-MM
05SPx Xcitement Superstars Gold-XS-MM
05SPx Xcitement Superstars Spectrum-XS-MM
05UD Artifacts-63
05UD Artifacts-178
Blue-63
Blue-178
Gold-63
Gold-178
Green-63
Green-178
Pewter-63
Pewter-178
Red-63
Red-178
Gold Autographed-63
Gold Autographed-178
Treasured Patches-TP-MS
Treasured Patches Autographed-TP-MS
Treasured Patches Dual-TPD-MS
Treasured Patches Dual Autographed-TPD-MS
Treasured Patches Pewter-TP-MS
Treasured Patches Silver-TP-MS
Treasured Swatches-TS-MS
Treasured Swatches Autographed-TS-MS
Treasured Swatches Blue-TS-MS
Treasured Swatches Copper-TS-MS
Treasured Swatches Dual-TSD-MS
Treasured Swatches Dual Autographed-TSD-MS
Treasured Swatches Dual Blue-TSD-MS
Treasured Swatches Dual Copper-TSD-MS
Treasured Swatches Dual Maroon-TSD-MS
Treasured Swatches Dual Pewter-TSD-MS
Treasured Swatches Dual Silver-TSD-MS
Treasured Swatches Maroon-TS-MS
Treasured Swatches Pewter-TS-MS
Treasured Swatches Silver-TS-MS
05UD PowerPlay-56
05UD PowerPlay-112
05UD PowerPlay-124
Rainbow-56
05Upper Deck Big Playmakers-B-MME
05Upper Deck Hometown Heroes-HH12
05Upper Deck NHL Generations-DML
05Upper Deck NHL Generations-TMST
05Upper Deck Patches-P-MME
05Upper Deck Scrapbooks-HS11
05Upper Deck Shooting Stars-S-MME
05Upper Deck Trilogy-119
Crystal-119
Honorary Patches-HP-MM
Honorary Swatches-HS-MM
05Upper Deck Victory-128
Black-128
Gold-128
Silver-128
Blow-Ups-BU23
05ITG Heroes and Prospects He Shoots-He Scores Prizes-45
05ITG Heroes and Prospects He Shoots-He Scores Prizes-55
06ITG International Ice-85
06ITG International Ice-94
06ITG International Ice-102
06ITG International Ice-158
Gold-85
Gold-94
Gold-102
Gold-158
Autographs-AMM
Autographs-AMM2
Autographs-AMM3
Autographs-AMM4
Best of the Best-BB04
Best of the Best Gold-BB04
Canadian Dream Team-DT02
Canadian Dream Team Gold-DT02
Complete Jersey-CJ19
Complete Jersey Gold-CJ19
Greatest Moments-GM07
Greatest Moments Gold-GM07
Hockey Passport-HP08
Hockey Passport Gold-HP08
International Rivals-IR16
International Rivals Gold-IR16
Passing The Torch-PTT9
Passing The Torch Gold-PTT9
Quad Patch-QP05
Quad Patch Gold-QP05
Stick and Jersey-SJ02
Stick and Jersey Gold-SJ02
Teammates-IT02
Teammates-IT08
Teammates Gold-IT02
Teammates Gold-IT08
Triple Memorabilia-TM05
Triple Memorabilia Gold-TM05
06ITG Ultimate Memorabilia-97
Artist Proof-97
Autos-25
Autos Gold-25
Autos Dual-8
Autos Dual Gold-8
Complete Jersey-7
Complete Jersey Gold-7
Cornerstones-6
Cornerstones-8
Cornerstones Gold-6
Cornerstones Gold-8
Decades-1
Decades-4
Decades Gold-1
Decades Gold-4
Double Memorabilia-1
Double Memorabilia Gold-1
Double Memorabilia Autos-9
Double Memorabilia Autos Gold-9
Emblems-3
Emblems Gold-3
Going For Gold-18
Going For Gold Gold-18
In The Numbers-7
In The Numbers Gold-7
Jerseys-9
Jerseys Gold-9
Jerseys and Emblems-7
Jerseys and Emblems Gold-7
Jerseys Autos-38
Jerseys Autos Gold-38
Journey Emblem-13
Journey Emblem Gold-13
Journey Jersey-13
Journey Jersey Gold-13
Legendary Captains-6
Legendary Captains Gold-6
Passing The Torch-9
Passing The Torch Gold-9
Raised to the Rafters-2
Raised to the Rafters Gold-2
Retro Teammates-16
Retro Teammates-20
Retro Teammates-23
Retro Teammates Gold-16
Retro Teammates Gold-20
Retro Teammates Gold-23
Retrospective-8
Retrospective Gold-8
Ring Leaders-6
Ring Leaders Gold-6
Road to the Cup-7
Road to the Cup Gold-7
Seams Unbelievable-7
Seams Unbelievable Gold-7
Sticks Autos-8
Sticks Autos Gold-8
Triple Thread Jerseys-3
Triple Thread Jerseys Gold-3
Ultimate Hero Single Jerseys-5
Ultimate Hero Single Jerseys Gold-5
Ultimate Hero Double Jerseys-5
Ultimate Hero Double Jerseys Gold-5
Ultimate Hero Triple Jerseys-5
Ultimate Hero Triple Jerseys Gold-5
06ITG Heroes and Prospects-5
Autographs-AMM
Double Memorabilia-DM06
Double Memorabilia Gold-DM06
Heroes Memorabilia-HM08
Heroes Memorabilia Gold-HM08
Triple Memorabilia-TM01
Triple Memorabilia Gold-TM01

Messier, Mitch
88ProCards IHL-66
89ProCards IHL-98
90ProCards AHL/IHL-102
91ProCards-154
93Fort Wayne Komets-13
93Classic Pro Prospects-76
95Fort Wayne Komets-11

Messier, Paul
94Tampa Bay Tritons RHI-1

Messthaler, Ernst
94German First League-99

Messuri, John
88Johnstown Chiefs-21
91ProCards-439

Meszaros, Andrej
04SP Authentic Rookie Redemptions-RR21
04Vancouver Giants-12
04ITG Heroes and Prospects-208
04ITG Heroes/Prospects Toronto Expo '05-208
05Beehive-128
Beige -128
Blue -128
Gold-128
Red -128
Matte-128
Signature Scrapbook-SSAM
05Black Diamond-208
Emerald-208
Gold-208
Onyx-208
Ruby-208
05Hot Prospects-255
En Fuego-255
Hot Materials-HMAM
Red Hot-255
White Hot-255
05Parkhurst-650
Facsimile Auto Parallel-650

Signatures-AM
True Colors-TCOTT
True Colors-TCOTT
05SP Authentic-176
Limited-176
Rarefied Rookies-RRAM
Rookie Authentics-RAAM
05SP Game Used-140
Autographs-140
Gold-140
Rookie Exclusives-AM
Rookie Exclusives Silver-RE-AM
05SPx-178
Spectrum-178
Xcitement Rookies-XR-AM
Xcitement Rookies Gold-XR-AM
Xcitement Rookies Spectrum-XR-AM
05The Cup-115
Autographed Rookie Patches Gold Rainbow-115
Black Rainbow Rookies-115
Masterpiece Pressplates (Artifacts)-221
Masterpiece Pressplates (Bee Hive)-128
Masterpiece Pressplates (Black Diamond)-208
Masterpiece Pressplates (Ice)-139
Masterpiece Pressplates (MVP)-424
Masterpiece Pressplates (Power Play)-170
Masterpiece Pressplates Rookie Upd Auto-271
Masterpiece Pressplates SPA Autos-176
Masterpiece Pressplates (SP Game Used)-140
Masterpiece Pressplates SPx Autos-178
Masterpiece Pressplates (Trilogy)-205
Masterpiece Pressplates Ult Coll Autos-127
Masterpiece Pressplates (Victory)-293
Masterpiece Pressplates Autographs-115
Platinum Rookies-115
05UD Artifacts-221
Gold-RED21
05UD PowerPlay-170
05UD Rookie Class-15
05Ultimate Collection-127
Autographed Patches-127
Autographed Shields-127
Ultimate Debut Threads Jerseys-DTJAM
Ultimate Debut Threads Jerseys Autos-DAJAM
Ultimate Debut Threads Patches Autos-DAPAM
05Ultra-234
Gold-234
Ice-234
Rookie Uniformity Jerseys-RU-AM
Rookie Uniformity Jersey Autographs-ARU-AM
Rookie Uniformity Patches-RUP-AM
Rookie Uniformity Patch Autographs-ARP-AM
05Upper Deck-228
HG Glossy-228
Rookie Ink-RIAM
05Upper Deck Rookie Showcase-RS21
05Upper Deck Rookie Showcase Promos-RS21
05Upper Deck Rookie Threads-RTAM
05Upper Deck Rookie Threads Autographs-ARTAM
05Upper Deck Ice-139
Premieres Auto Patches-AIPAM
05Upper Deck MVP-424
Gold-424
Platinum-424
05Upper Deck Rookie Update-271
05Upper Deck Trilogy-205
05Upper Deck Toronto Fall Expo-228
05Upper Deck Victory-293
Black-293
Gold-293
Silver-293
06Be A Player-83
Autographs-83
Signatures-MZ
Signatures Duals-DRM
Portraits First Exposures-FEAM
06Black Diamond Jerseys-JAM
06Black Diamond Jerseys Black-JAM
06Black Diamond Jerseys Gold-JAM
06Black Diamond Jerseys Ruby-JAM
06Fleer Fabricology-FAM
06Gatorade-59
06McDonald's Upper Deck Rookie Review-RR8
06O-Pee-Chee-348
06O-Pee-Chee-626
Rainbow-348
Rainbow-626
Swatches-S-AM
06Senators Postcards-9
06UD Artifacts Tundra Tandems-TTWA
06UD Artifacts Tundra Tandems Black-TTWA
06UD Artifacts Tundra Tandems Blue-TTWA
06UD Artifacts Tundra Tandems Gold-TTWA
06UD Artifacts Tundra Tandems Platinum-TTWA
06UD Artifacts Tundra Tandems Red-TTWA
06UD Artifacts Tundra Tandems Dual Patches Red-TTWA
06UD Powerplay Power Marks-PMAM
06Upper Deck-137
Exclusives Parallel-137
High Gloss Parallel-137
Game Jerseys-JAM
Game Patches-PAM
Generations Duals-G2RM
Generations Patches Dual-G2PRM
Masterpieces-137
06Upper Deck MVP-208
Gold Script-208
Super Script-208
Jerseys-OJMJ
Meszaros, Dave
84Moncton Golden Flames-21
85Moncton Golden Flames-5
Metcalf, Nate
03Minnesota State Mavericks-14
Metcalf, Peter
93Quebec Pee-Wee Tournament-839
02Providence Bruins-15
03Providence Bruins-13
04Idaho Steelheads-17
Metcalfe, Charles
93Quebec Pee-Wee Tournament-1147
Metcalfe, Jason
95Slapshot-244
00Florida Everblades-19
01Greensboro Generals-12
02Pee Dee Pride RBI-143
03Greenville Grrrowl-16
05Stockton Thunder-14
Metcalfe, Scott
83Kingston Canadians-10
84Kingston Canadians-6
85Kingston Canadians-6
86Kingston Canadians-10
88Oilers Tenth Anniversary-127
88ProCards AHL-258
89ProCards AHL-262
90ProCards AHL/IHL-267
93Knoxville Cherokees-10
95Rochester Americans-12
96Rochester Americans-5
97Rochester Americans-1-2
98German DEL-190
99German DEL-231
00UK Sekonda Superleague-155
00UK Sheffield Steelers-16
Methot, Francois
92Quebec Pee-Wee Tournament-562
95Bowman Draft Prospects-P25
95Upper Deck-521
Electric Ice-521
Electric Ice Gold-521
97Bowman CHL-57
OPC-57
98Rochester Americans-12
98Bowman CHL-95
Golden Anniversary-95
OPC International-95
98Bowman Chrome CHL-95
Golden Anniversary-95
Golden Anniversary Refractors-95
OPC International-95
OPC International Refractors-95
Refractors-95
00Rochester Americans-15
02Rochester Americans-13
04German Augsburg Panthers Postcards-20
04German DEL-34
05German DEL-273
All-Star Jerseys-AS10
06German DEL-151
Methot, Marc
02London Knights-20
03London Knights-10
04London Knights-21
05Syracuse Crunch-2
05ITG Heroes and Prospects Memorial Cup-MC-13
06Syracuse Crunch-2
07Upper Deck Victory-209
Black-209
Gold-209
Methot, Matthieu
06Ottawa 67s-8
Metlicka, Pavel
95Czech APS Extraliga-259
97Czech APS Extraliga-232
98Czech OFS-92
99Czech OFS-315
Metliuk, Philip
02Russian Hockey League-52
03Russian Hockey League-244
Metlyuk, Denis
91Upper Deck-653
French-653
91Upper Deck Czech World Juniors-14
92Classic-45
Gold-45
92Classic Four-Sport *-186
Gold-186
94Classic-91
Gold-91
Tri-Cards-T49
94Classic Pro Prospects-215
94Classic Four-Sport *-157
Gold-157
Autographs-157A
Printers Proofs-157
99Russian Hockey League-44
00Russian Hockey League-154
01Russian Lightnings-7
02Russian Hockey League-19
Metrailler, Cedric
01Swiss HNL-357
02Swiss HNL-161
Metrailler, Thierry
01Swiss HNL-437
02Swiss HNL-461
Metro, Rich
93Waterloo Black Hawks-19
Metro, Terry
91Air Canada SJHL-C22
Metropolit, Glen
96Pensacola Ice Pilots-7
97Grand Rapids Griffins-9
98Grand Rapids Griffins-12
99BAP Memorabilia-303
Gold-303
Silver-303
99BAP Millennium Calder Candidates Ruby-C42
99BAP Millennium Calder Candidate Emerald-C42
99BAP Millennium Calder Cand Sapphire-C42
99Pacific Omega-246
Copper-246
Gold-246
Ice Blue-246
Premiere Date-246
99Pacific Prism-149
Holographic Blue-149
Holographic Gold-149
Holographic Mirror-149
Holographic Purple-149
Premiere Date-149
99Topps Premier Plus-88
Parallel-88
99Ultimate Victory-105
1/1-105
Parallel-105
Parallel 100-105
99Portland Pirates-14
00BAP Signature Series-85
Emerald-85
Ruby-85
Sapphire-85
Autographs-101
Autographs Gold-101
00O-Pee-Chee-275
00O-Pee-Chee Parallel-275
00Pacific-427
Copper-427
Gold-427
Ice Blue-427
Premiere Date-427
00Topps/OPC-275
Parallel-275
00Topps Chrome-170
OPC Refractors-170
Refractors-170
00Portland Pirates-9
02BAP Sig Series Auto Buybacks 2000-101
02Pacific Complete-196
Red-196
03Finnish Cardset-68
04Finnish Cardset-77
Parallel-59
04Swedish Pure Skills-121
Parallel-121
Metsaranta, Matias
04Finnish Cardset-307
Metsch, Rudiger
94German First League-346
Mettavainio, Jan Ove
85Swedish Panini Stickers-52
86Swedish Panini Stickers-39
87Swedish Panini Stickers-51
89Swedish Semic Elitserien Stickers-149
90Swedish Semic Elitserien Stickers-232
Mettler, Peter
01Swiss HNL-463
02Swiss EV Zug Postcards-7
02Swiss HNL-212
Mettovaara, Sami
93Finnish Jyvas-Hyva Stickers-177
93Finnish SISU-176
94Finnish SISU-44
95Finnish SISU-337
98Finnish Kerailysarja-107
00Swedish Upper Deck-134
02Finnish Cardset-72
Metz, Don
34Beehive Group I Photos-339
39O-Pee-Chee V301-1-8
40O-Pee-Chee V301-2-111
44Beehive Group II Photos-433
45Quaker Oats Photos-36A
45Quaker Oats Photos-36B
45Quaker Oats Photos-36C
06Parkhurst-142
Metz, Nick
34Beehive Group I Photos-340
35O-Pee-Chee V304C-84
36Triumph Postcards-6
37O-Pee-Chee V304E-144
37V356 Worldwide Gum-28
38Quaker Oats Photos-25
39O-Pee-Chee V301-1-51
40O-Pee-Chee V301-2-133
40O-Pee-Chee V301-2-141
44Beehive Group II Photos-434
45Quaker Oats Photos-37A
45Quaker Oats Photos-37B
45Quaker Oats Photos-37C
Metzger, Ben
99Adirondack IceHawks-23
Metzger, Steve
93Swiss HNL-254
Meulenbroeks, John
83Brantford Alexanders-28
85Moncton Golden Flames-21
Meunier, Laurent
92Quebec Pee-Wee Tournament-1196
93Quebec Pee-Wee Tournament-1486
02ECHL All-Star Southern-49
02Florida Everblades-13
02Florida Everblades RBI-125
Meunier, Yves
907th Inn. Sketch QMJHL-204
917th Inn. Sketch QMJHL-22
917th Inn. Sketch QMJHL-59
Meurer, Peter
24Crescent Selkirks-13
Meuwly, Steve
95Swiss HNL-60
96Swiss HNL-204
98Swiss Power Play Stickers-321
Mews, Harry
90Hampton Roads Admirals-56
91ProCards-565
92Hampton Roads Admirals-15
98Hampton Roads Admirals 10th Anniversary-19
Meyer, Adam
06Fayetteville FireAntz-10
Meyer, Alexander
94German First League-221
Meyer, Andrew
04Green Bay Gamblers-12
Meyer, Dennis
95German DEL-72
99German DEL-274
Meyer, Doug
98Minnesota Golden Gophers-15
99Minnesota Golden Gophers-12
Meyer, Freddy
99Quebec Pee-Wee Tournament-1202
03ITG VIP Rookie Debut-131
03Parkhurst Rookie-92
03Upper Deck Rookie Update-168
03Philadelphia Phantoms-7
04Philadelphia Phantoms-10
05Philadelphia Phantoms-15
05Philadelphia Phantoms All-Decade Team-10
06O-Pee-Chee-365
Rainbow-365
06Upper Deck-395
Exclusives Parallel-395
High Gloss Parallel-395
Masterpieces-395
Meyer, Fritz
94German DEL-14
95German DEL-5
Meyer, Herve
96Swiss HNL-511
Meyer, Jayson
81Regina Pats-11
82Regina Pats-21
83Regina Pats-21
94Finnish Jaa Kiekko-276
95Finnish Semic World Championships-167
95German DEL-322
95Swedish World Championships Stickers-56
96German DEL-343
96Swedish Semic Wien-195
98German DEL-30
99German Bundesliga 2-160
Meyer, Jonathon
02OCN Blizzard-25
03OCN Blizzard-15
Meyer, Jorg
94German First League-607
Meyer, Martin
02Swiss HNL-472
Meyer, Roland
93Swiss HNL-61
95Swiss HNL-368
96Swiss HNL-228
01Swiss HNL-423
02Swiss HNL-208
Meyer, Scott
01Hartford Wolf Pack-17
02Charlotte Checkers-89
03Parkhurst Rookie-66
03Charlotte Checkers-74
Meyer, Serge
96Swiss HNL-400
01Swiss HNL-305
02Swiss HNL-367
Meyer, Stefan
02Medicine Hat Tigers-15
03Medicine Hat Tigers-5
04Medicine Hat Tigers-15
06Rochester Americans-15
Meyers, Bret
98ECHL All-Star Northern Conference-5
99Peoria Rivermen-21
00Peoria Rivermen-9
01Peoria Rivermen-12
Meyers, Dan
91Air Canada SJHL-A2
95German DEL-432
99UK Basingstoke Bison-3
Meyers, Danny
06UK Nottingham Panthers-7
Meyers, Josh
04Sioux City Musketeers-17
Meyers, Scott
99Prince George Cougars-1
Meyhoff, Chad
94Anchorage Aces-17
Meylan, Camille
95Swiss HNL-493
Mezei, Branislav
99Black Diamond-95
Diamond Cut-95
Final Cut-95
99O-Pee-Chee-269
99O-Pee-Chee Chrome-269
99O-Pee-Chee Chrome Refractors-269
99SP Authentic-124
99Topps/OPC-269
99Topps/OPC Chrome-269
Refractors-269
99Ultimate Victory-108
1/1-108
Parallel-108
Parallel 100-108
99Upper Deck-314
Exclusives-314
Exclusives 1 of 1-314
99Upper Deck Gold Reserve-314
99Upper Deck MVP SC Edition-196
Gold Script-196
Silver Script-196
Super Script-196
99Upper Deck Ovation-67
Standing Ovation-67
99Upper Deck Victory-366
99Bowman CHL-15
99Bowman CHL-136
Gold-15
Gold-136
OPC International-15
OPC International-136
Autographs-BA35
Autographs Gold-BA35
Autographs Silver-BA35
99UD Prospects Signatures of Tradition-BM
00BAP Memorabilia-504
00Lowell Lock Monsters-22
01BAP Memorabilia-199
Emerald-199
Ruby-199
Sapphire-199
01BAP Signature Series-94
Autographs-94
Autographs Gold-94
01O-Pee-Chee-282
01O-Pee-Chee Premier Parallel-282
01Topps-282
OPC Parallel-282
02BAP Sig Series Auto Buybacks 2001-94
03Panthers Team Issue-13
03Upper Deck-328
Canadian Exclusives-328
HG-328
UD Exclusives-328
04Czech OFS-318
Stars-29
Mezei, Shawn
04Lethbridge Hurricanes-2
Mezin, Andrei
95Flint Generals-13
96Flint Generals-14
97Flint Generals-15
98German DEL-249
99German DEL-267
00German DEL-30
Profiles-P2
01German Upper Deck-21
Goalies in Action-G1
Jersey Cards-AM-J
03Czech OFS Plus-328
Miaskowski, Phil
98Fort Worth Brahmas-15
Micalef, Corrado
83NHL Key Tags-35
83O-Pee-Chee-116
83O-Pee-Chee-126
83O-Pee-Chee Stickers-147
83Topps Stickers-147
85O-Pee-Chee-200
05German SC Bietigheim-Bissingen Steelers-10
Micflikier, Jacob
01Sioux Falls Stampede-7
Michaels, J.J.
96Anchorage Aces-7
Michalchuk, Chad
91Saskatoon Blades-15
917th Inn. Sketch WHL-114
Michalek, Milan
01Czech OFS-140
02SPx Rookie Redemption-R223
02Czech DS-12
02Czech OFS Plus-178
03BAP Memorabilia-181
03BAP Memorabilia-213
Emerald-181
Gold-181
Ruby-181
Sapphire-181
Draft Redemptions-6
03BAP Ultimate Memorabilia Autographs-125
Gold-125
03Beehive-232
Gold-232
Silver-232
03Black Diamond-186
Black-186
Green-186
Red-186
03Bowman-116
Gold-116
03Bowman Chrome-116
Refractors-116
Gold Refractors-116
Xfractors-116
03Crown Royale-133
Red-133
Retail-133
Royal Portraits-9
03ITG Used Signature Series-148
Autographs Gold-148
03ITG VIP Rookie Debut-28
03Pacific-359
03Pacific Calder-134
Silver-134
03Pacific Complete-551
Red-551
03Pacific Heads-Up-133
Hobby LTD-133
Retail LTD-133
Prime Prospects-18
Prime Prospects LTD-18
03Pacific Invincible-123
Blue-123
Red-123
Retail-123
03Pacific Luxury Suite-98
Gold-98
03Pacific Quest for the Cup-135
03Pacific Supreme-136
03Pacific Supreme-136A
Blue-136
Red-136
Retail-136
03Parkhurst Rookie-71
03Parkhurst Rookie-169
03Private Stock Reserve-137
Blue-137
Red-137
Retail-137
Class Act-11
03SP Authentic-155
Limited-155
03SP Game Used-92
Gold-92
03SPx-210
Radiance-210
Spectrum-210
03Titanium-136
Hobby Jersey Number Parallels-136
Retail-136
Retail Jersey Number Parallels-136
03Topps C55-154
Minis-154
Minis American Back-154
Minis American Back Red-154
Minis Bazooka Back-154
Minis Brooklyn Back-154
Minis Hat Trick Back-154
Minis O Canada Back-154
Minis O Canada Back Red-154
Minis Stanley Cup Back-154
03Topps Pristine-110
03Topps Pristine-111
03Topps Pristine-112
Gold Refractor Die Cuts-110
Gold Refractor Die Cuts-111
Gold Refractor Die Cuts-112
Refractors-110
Refractors-111
Refractors-112
Press Plates Black-110
Press Plates Black-111
Press Plates Black-112
Press Plates Cyan-110
Press Plates Cyan-111
Press Plates Cyan-112
Press Plates Magenta-110
Press Plates Magenta-111
Press Plates Magenta-112
Press Plates Yellow-110
Press Plates Yellow-111
Press Plates Yellow-112
03Topps Traded-TT150
Blue-TT150
Gold-TT150
Red-TT150
03UD Honor Roll-170
03UD Premier Collection-78
03Upper Deck-238
Canadian Exclusives-238
HG-238
03Upper Deck Classic Portraits-174
03Upper Deck Ice-99
Glass Parallel-99
03Upper Deck MVP-464
03Upper Deck Rookie Update-115
03Upper Deck Trilogy-181
Limited-181
03Upper Deck Victory-208
05Beehive Matted Materials-MMMI
05Parkhurst-406
Facsimile Auto Parallel-406
Signatures-MM
True Colors-TCSJS
True Colors-TCSJS
05UD Rookie Class-18
05Upper Deck-408
Ice Fresh Ice-FIMM
Ice Fresh Ice Glass-FIMM
Ice Fresh Ice Glass Patches-FIPMM
Ice Frozen Fabrics-FFMM
Ice Frozen Fabrics Autographs-AFFMM
Ice Frozen Fabrics Glass-FFMM
Ice Frozen Fabrics Patch-FFPMM
Ice Frozen Fabrics Patch Autographs-FAPMM
05Upper Deck MVP-322
Gold-322
Platinum-322
05Upper Deck Victory-242
Black-242
Gold-242
Silver-242
06Be A Player-82
Autographs-82
Signatures-MI
Signatures 10-89
Signatures Trios-TTBM
06Flair Showcase Inks-IMM
06O-Pee-Chee-416
Rainbow-416
06Panini Stickers-336
06SP Game Used Inked Sweaters-ISMM
06SP Game Used Inked Sweaters Patches-ISMM
06SP Game Used SIGnificance-SMM
06The Cup Autographed NHL Shields Duals-DASMM
06Upper Deck-163
Exclusives Parallel-163
High Gloss Parallel-163
Masterpieces-163
06Upper Deck MVP-248
Gold Script-248
Super Script-248
Autographs-OABM
06Upper Deck Trilogy Combo Clearcut Autographs-C2PM
06Upper Deck Trilogy Ice Scripts-ISMM
06Upper Deck Trilogy Scripts-TSMM
07Upper Deck Victory-179
Black-179
Gold-179
Michalek, Vladimir
95Czech APS Extraliga-238
Michalek, Zbynek
00Shawinigan Cataractes-2
01Shawinigan Cataractes-2
02Czech National Team Postcards-8
03Beehive-237
Gold-237
Silver-237
03ITG VIP Rookie Debut-107
03Pacific Complete-511
Red-511
03Parkhurst Rookie-71
03UD Premier Collection-90
03Upper Deck Rookie Update-166
03Houston Aeros-14
04Houston Aeros-13
05Parkhurst-377
Facsimile Auto Parallel-377
Signatures-ZM
06O-Pee-Chee-385
Rainbow-385
06Czech IIHF World Championship Postcards-14
06Czech LG Hockey Games Postcards-12
07Upper Deck Ovation-64
07Upper Deck Victory-200
Black-200
Gold-200
Michalenko, Wade
84Nanaimo Clippers-14
Michalski, Troy
00Missouri River Otters-12
Michaud, Alfie
99BAP Memorabilia-366
Gold-366
Silver-366
99Pacific Omega-240
Copper-240
Gold-240
Ice Blue-240
Premiere Date-240
99Pacific Prism-142
Holographic Blue-142
Holographic Gold-142
Holographic Mirror-142
Holographic Purple-142
Premiere Date-142
99Syracuse Crunch-18
00Pacific-417
Copper-417
Gold-417
Ice Blue-417
Premiere Date-417
00Upper Deck-230
Exclusives Tier 1-230
Exclusives Tier 2-230
00Upper Deck MVP-207
First Stars-207
Second Stars-207
Third Stars-207
00Upper Deck Victory-271
00Kansas City Blades-22
01Manitoba Moose-17
02Peoria Rivermen-24
02Peoria Rivermen Photo Pack-7
02Peoria Rivermen RBI Sports-163
03German DEL-208
03German Nuremberg Ice Tigers Postcards-19
04Peoria Rivermen-11
Michaud, Dany
917th Inn. Sketch QMJHL-229
Michaud, Francois
93Lakeland Ice Warriors-19
Michaud, Frederic
92Quebec Pee-Wee Tournament-755
93Quebec Pee-Wee Tournament-334
Michaud, Hughes
93Quebec Pee-Wee Tournament-1209
Michaud, Mark
87Brockville Braves-7
92Thunder Bay Thunder Hawks-4
93Hampton Roads Admirals-12
94Birmingham Bulls-18
98Hampton Roads Admirals 10th Anniversary-27
Michaud, Olivier
00Shawinigan Cataractes-16
Signed-16
01BAP Memorabilia-389
Emerald-389
Ruby-389
Sapphire-389
01Between the Pipes-85
01Bowman YoungStars-115
Gold-115
Ice Cubed-115
01Parkhurst-321
01SPx-207
01UD Honor Roll-77
01UD Mask Collection-150
Gold-150
01UD Playmakers-124
01UD Premier Collection-98
01UD Top Shelf-129
01Upper Deck Ice-141
01Upper Deck MVP-233
01Upper Deck Victory-453
01Shawinigan Cataractes-15
02BAP First Edition-271
02Between the Pipes-101
Gold-101
Silver-101
03BAP Memorabilia Deep in the Crease-D3
03Parkhurst Original Six Montreal-21
03Columbus Cottonmouths-13
03ECHL Update RBI Sports-116
05Hamilton Bulldogs-17
Michaud, Sylvain
01Drummondville Voltigeurs-21
02Drummondville Voltigeurs-22
03Drummondville Voltigeurs-16
04Drummondville Voltigeurs-29
05Chicoutimi Sagueneens-8
Michayluk, Dave
81Regina Pats-20
83Springfield Indians-11
88ProCards IHL-57
89ProCards IHL-153
90ProCards AHL/IHL-389
91ProCards-288
92Cleveland Lumberjacks-13
93Cleveland Lumberjacks-18
93Cleveland Lumberjacks Postcards-15
93Classic Pro Prospects-123
94Cleveland Lumberjacks-21
94Cleveland Lumberjacks Postcards-21
95Cleveland Lumberjacks-19
95Cleveland Lumberjacks Postcards-18
96Cleveland Lumberjacks-17
96Cleveland Lumberjacks Multi-Ad-19
Michel, Steffen
94German DEL-278
95German DEL-269
99German Bundesliga 2-5
Micheletti, Joe
81Rockies Postcards-19
82Post Cereal-11
Micheli, Claudio
93Swiss HNL-176
95Swiss HNL-49
96Swiss HNL-195
98Swiss Power Play Stickers-241
98Swiss Power Play Stickers-260
99Swiss Panini Stickers-243
00Swiss Panini Stickers-284
00Swiss Panini Stickers National Team-P19
00Swiss Slapshot Mini-Cards-ZSCL13
01Swiss HNL-18
02Swiss HNL-59
Micheli, Damien
02Swiss HNL-360
Michelin, Leon
52Juniors Blue Tint-36
Micheller, Holger
94German First League-198
Micheller, Klaus
94German DEL-239
95German DEL-223
96German DEL-74
99German Bundesliga 2-237
Michie, Geordie
03Brampton Batallion-15
Michie, Jack
69Seattle Totems-9
Michnac, Peter
03UK Guildford Flames-2
04UK Guildford Flames-2
Michon, Michel
907th Inn. Sketch WHL-332
Miciak, Darren
89Hampton Roads Admirals-16A
89Hampton Roads Admirals-16H
91ProCards-435
94Central Hockey League-53
Mick, Troy
86Portland Winter Hawks-14
87Portland Winter Hawks-15
88Portland Winter Hawks-15
89Regina Pats-14
90Knoxville Cherokees-113
91Knoxville Cherokees-16
92Nashville Knights-21
Micka, Tomas
02Czech OFS Plus-306
03Columbus Cottonmouths-14
03ECHL Update RBI Sports-117
Mickey, Larry
68O-Pee-Chee-195
69Maple Leafs White Border Glossy-23
70Dad's Cookies-85
70Esso Power Players-154
70O-Pee-Chee-162
70Sargent Promotions Stamps-74
71O-Pee-Chee-167
71Sargent Promotions Stamps-149
71Toronto Sun-204
72Sabres Postcards-12
73Sabres Postcards-8
74NHL Action Stamps-44
74Sabres Postcards-16
Mickolajak, Todd
93Minnesota-Duluth Bulldogs-20
Mickoski, Nick
44Beehive Group II Photos-345
51Parkhurst-97
52Parkhurst-101
53Parkhurst-62
54Parkhurst-75
54Topps-29
57Topps-32
58Topps-27
59Topps-37
59Topps-53
94Parkhurst Missing Link-25
Micks, Mackenzie
06Drummondville Voltigeurs-3
Micuda, Miroslav
95Slovakian-Quebec Pee-Wee Tournament-17
Miculinic, Jeremy
94Sarnia Sting-7
95Slapshot-28
95Barrie Colts-17
95Classic-82
Middendorf, Max
84Sudbury Wolves-12
85Sudbury Wolves-22
86Sudbury Wolves-22
87Nordiques General Foods-21
87Nordiques Team Issue-8
88ProCards AHL-113
89Halifax Citadels-15
89ProCards AHL-172
91ProCards-217
93Fort Wayne Komets-14
95San Diego Barracudas RHI-12
97Fort Worth Brahmas-14
Middlebrook, Lindsay
88Oilers Tenth Anniversary-102
Middleton, Marcus
89Sudbury Wolves-12
907th Inn. Sketch OHL-40
Middleton, Rick
74NHL Action Stamps Update-26
74O-Pee-Chee NHL-304
75O-Pee-Chee NHL-37
75Topps-37
76O-Pee-Chee NHL-127
76Topps-127
77O-Pee-Chee NHL-246
77Topps-246
78O-Pee-Chee-113
78Topps-113
79O-Pee-Chee-10
79Topps-10
80O-Pee-Chee-94
80O-Pee-Chee-251
80Topps-94
80Topps-251
81O-Pee-Chee-2
81O-Pee-Chee-18
81O-Pee-Chee-19
81O-Pee-Chee Stickers-45
81Topps-22
81Topps-46
81Topps-E129
82McDonald's Stickers-9
82O-Pee-Chee-6
82O-Pee-Chee-15
82O-Pee-Chee Stickers-78
82O-Pee-Chee Stickers-79
82O-Pee-Chee Stickers-262
82Post Cereal-1
82Topps Stickers-78
82Topps Stickers-79
82Topps Stickers-262
83Bruins Team Issue-11
83NHL Key Tags-3
83O-Pee-Chee-43
83O-Pee-Chee-54
83O-Pee-Chee-214
83O-Pee-Chee Stickers-14
83O-Pee-Chee Stickers-44
83O-Pee-Chee Stickers-45
83O-Pee-Chee Stickers-329
83O-Pee-Chee Stickers-330
83Puffy Stickers-10
83Topps Stickers-14
83Topps Stickers-44
83Topps Stickers-45
83Topps Stickers-329
83Topps Stickers-330
84Bruins Postcards-12
84Kellogg's Accordion Discs-3A
84Kellogg's Accordion Discs-38
84Kellogg's Accordion Discs Singles-26
84O-Pee-Chee-9
84O-Pee-Chee-352
84O-Pee-Chee Stickers-142
84O-Pee-Chee Stickers-181
84O-Pee-Chee Stickers-182
847-Eleven Discs-2
84Topps-8
85O-Pee-Chee-64
85O-Pee-Chee Stickers-159
857-Eleven Credit Cards-1
85Topps-64
86O-Pee-Chee-157
86O-Pee-Chee Stickers-35
86Topps-157
87O-Pee-Chee-115
87O-Pee-Chee Stickers-138
87Panini Stickers-12
87Topps-115
88Bruins Sports Action-13
88Bruins Postcards-12
88O-Pee-Chee-87
88O-Pee-Chee Stickers-26
88Topps-87
91Bruins Sports Action Legends-17
01Greats of the Game-70
Autographs-70
01Topps Archives-18
Autographs-24
03Parkhurst Original Six Boston-53
03Parkhurst Original Six Boston-77
Autographs-9
04ITG Franchises US East-335
Autographs-A-RMI
Double Memorabilia-EDM21
Double Memorabilia Autographs-EDM-RM
Double Memorabilia Gold-EDM21
Forever Rivals-EFR2
Forever Rivals Gold-EFR2
Memorabilia-ESM23
Memorabilia Autographs-ESM-RM
Memorabilia Gold-ESM23
Original Sticks-EOS19
Original Sticks Autographs-EOS-RM
Original Sticks Gold-EOS19
Teammates-ETM5
Teammates Gold-ETM5
04ITG Ultimate Memorabilia Original Six-11
04ITG Ultimate Mem Retro Teammates-1
05ITG Ultimate Mem 3 Star of the Game Jsy-18
05ITG Ult Mem 3 Star of the Game Jsy Gold-18
06ITG International Ice-122
Gold-122
Autographs-ARM
Teammates-IT06
Teammates Gold-IT06
06Parkhurst-138
Autographs-138
Autographs Dual-DAPM
Midgley, Jim
95Slapshot-213
02Fort Worth Brahmas-10
Miehm, Kevin
89ProCards IHL-11
90ProCards AHL/IHL-93
91ProCards-28
92Upper Deck-543
92Peoria Rivermen-17
93OPC Premier Gold-264
93Parkhurst-447
Emerald Ice-447
93Topps/OPC Premier Gold-264G
93Ultra-205

Prospects-6
93Classic Pro Prospects-63
96Collector's Edge Ice-128
Prism-128
98Swiss Power Play Stickers-360
00German DEL-194
01UK Sheffield Steelers-17

Mielczarek, Ted
86Sudbury Wolves-1
87Sudbury Wolves-2
88Sudbury Wolves-3

Mielko, Brian
917th Inn. Sketch OHL-118

Mielonen, Juho
06Finnish Cardset-44
06Finnish Ilves Team Set-17

Miettinen, Antti
99Finnish Cardset-240
00Finnish Cardset-27
00Finnish Cardset Next Generation-7
01Finnish Cardset-31
02SPx Rookie Redemption-R199
02Finnish Cardset-73
02Finnish Cardset Dynamic Duos-9
03BAP Memorabilia-199
Emerald-199
Gold-199
Ruby-199
Sapphire-199
03BAP Ultimate Memorabilia Autographs-117
Gold-117
03BAP Ultimate Mem Rookie Jersey Emblems-7
03BAP Ultimate Mem Rookie Jsy Emblem Gold-7
03BAP Ultimate Mem Rookie Jersey Numbers-7
03BAP Ultimate Mem Rookie Jsy Number Gold-7
03Beehive-211
Gold-211
Silver-211
03Black Diamond-152
Black-152
Green-152
Red-152
03Bowman-150
Gold-150
Premier Performance-PP-AM
Premier Performance Patches-PP-AM
Signs of the Future-SOF-AM
03Bowman Chrome-150
Refractors-150
Gold Refractors-150
Xfractors-150
03Crown Royale-115
Red-115
Retail-115
03ITG Used Signature Series-126
Autographs Gold-126
03ITG VIP Rookie Debut-11
03O-Pee-Chee-333
03OPC Blue-333
03OPC Gold-333
03OPC Red-333
03Pacific Calder-165
03Pacific Complete-565
Red-565
03Pacific Heads-Up-112
Hobby LTD-112
Retail LTD-112
Jerseys-9
03Pacific Invincible-110
Blue-110
Red-110
Retail-110
03Pacific Luxury Suite-86
Gold-86
03Pacific Quest for the Cup-113
03Pacific Supreme-116
Blue-116
Red-116
Retail-116
03Parkhurst Rookie-183
Rookie Emblems-RE-4
Rookie Emblem Autographs-RE-AM
Rookie Emblems Gold-RE-4
Rookie Jerseys-RJ-4
Rookie Jerseys Gold-RJ-4
Rookie Numbers-RN-4
Rookie Numbers Gold-RN-4
03Private Stock Reserve-117
Blue-117
Red-117
Retail-117
03SP Authentic-141
Limited-141
Signed Patches-AM
03SP Game Used-61
Gold-61
03SPx-214
Radiance-214
Spectrum-214
03Stars Postcards-15
03Titanium-116
Hobby Jersey Number Parallels-116
Retail-116
Retail Jersey Number Parallels-116
03Topps-333
Blue-333
Gold-333
Red-333
03Topps C55-138
Minis-138
Minis American Back-138
Minis American Back Red-138
Minis Bazooka Back-138
Minis Brooklyn Back-138
Minis Hat Trick Back-138
Minis O Canada Back-138
Minis O Canada Back Red-138
Minis Stanley Cup Back-138
03Topps Pristine-125
03Topps Pristine-126
03Topps Pristine-127
Gold Refractor Die Cuts-125
Gold Refractor Die Cuts-126
Gold Refractor Die Cuts-127
Refractors-125
Refractors-126
Refractors-127
Mini-PM-AM
Press Plates Black-125
Press Plates Black-126
Press Plates Black-127
Press Plates Cyan-125
Press Plates Cyan-126
Press Plates Cyan-127
Press Plates Magenta-125
Press Plates Magenta-126
Press Plates Magenta-127
Press Plates Yellow-125
Press Plates Yellow-126
Press Plates Yellow-127
03Topps Traded Future Phenoms-FP-AM
03UD Honor Roll-174
03Upper Deck-215
Canadian Exclusives-215
HG-215
03Upper Deck Classic Portraits-179
03Upper Deck Ice-92
Glass Parallel-92
03Upper Deck MVP-457
03Upper Deck Rookie Update-104
03Upper Deck Trilogy-150
Limited-150
03Finnish Cardset D-Day-DD6
04Finnish Cardset-232
04Hamilton Bulldogs-19
05Panini Stickers-257
05Parkhurst-156
Facsimile Auto Parallel-156
05UD Artifacts Auto Facts-AF-AM
05UD Artifacts Auto Facts Blue-AF-AM
05UD Artifacts Auto Facts Copper-AF-AM
05UD Artifacts Auto Facts Pewter-AF-AM
05UD Artifacts Auto Facts Silver-AF-AM
05UD Rookie Class-19
05Upper Deck-310
Trilogy Scripts-SFS-AM
05Upper Deck Victory-214
Black-214
Gold-214
Silver-214
06O-Pee-Chee-167
Rainbow-167
06Stars Team Postcards-14
06Upper Deck-314
Exclusives Parallel-314
High Gloss Parallel-314
Masterpieces-314

Miettinen, Tommi
93Parkhurst-522
Emerald Ice-522
93Finnish Jyvas-Hyva Stickers-173
94Finest-133
Super Team Winners-133
Refractors-133
94Parkhurst SE-SE221
Gold-SE221
94Finnish SISU-86
94Finnish SISU Junior-3
94Finnish SISU NHL Draft-7
95Finnish SISU-330
95Finnish Semic World Championships-236
96Finnish SISU Redline-144
98Finnish Kerailysarja-245
99Finnish Cardset-253
00Finnish Cardset-273
01Finnish Cardset-238
02Swedish SHL-152
Parallel-152
03Swedish Elite-11
Signatures-8
Silver-11
04Swedish Elitset-11
Gold-11
Signatures Series A-11
04Swedish Pure Skills-5
Parallel-5
05Swedish SHL Elitset-10
Gold-10

Mifek, Jiri
99Czech Score Blue 2000-135
99Czech Score Red Ice 2000-135

Mifflen, Chris
06Sarnia Sting-20

Migay, Rudy
44Beehive Group II Photos-435
45Quaker Oats Photos-38
52Parkhurst-96
53Parkhurst-17
54Parkhurst-21
55Parkhurst-12
Quaker Oats-12
57Parkhurst-T6
60Shirriff Coins-18
94Parkhurst Missing Link-111

Migdal, Thomas
98Wichita Thunder-17
99Wichita Thunder-16

Migliore, Chris
93Quebec Pee-Wee Tournament-1288
03Cape Fear Fire Antz-9

Mignacca, Sonny
907th Inn. Sketch WHL-23
917th Inn. Sketch WHL-314

Mignardi, Bobby
06Kingston Frontenacs-3

Migneault, John
73Vancouver Blazers-16
75Phoenix Roadrunners WHA-17

Mihalech, Peter
93Quebec Pee-Wee Tournament-1241

Mihalik, Jason
93Quebec Pee-Wee Tournament-418

Mihalik, Pavol
04UK Coventry Blaze-11
05UK Coventry Blaze-4

Mihalik, Tomas
95Slovakian-Quebec Pee-Wee Tournament-18

Mihalik, Vladimir
05Red Deer Rebels-12

Mihaly, Arpad
04Binghamton Senators-12
05WBS Penguins-19
06Las Vegas Wranglers-14

Miikkulainen, Jarno
92Finnish Jyvas-Hyva Stickers-201
93Finnish Jyvas-Hyva Stickers-351
93Finnish SISU-213
94Finnish SISU-80
95Finnish SISU-152
95Finnish SISU-300
99German Bundesliga 2-64

Mika, David
99Czech Score Blue 2000-113
99Czech Score Red Ice 2000-113

Mika, Petr
98Czech OFS-221
99Lowell Lock Monsters-6
00BAP Memorabilia-193
Emerald-193
Ruby-193
Sapphire-193
Promos-193
00BAP Mem Chicago Sportsfest Copper-193
00BAP Memorabilia Chicago Sportsfest Blue-193
00BAP Memorabilia Chicago Sportsfest Gold-193
00BAP Memorabilia Chicago Sportsfest Ruby-193
00BAP Memorabilia Chicago Sun-Times Ruby-193
00BAP Memorabilia Chicago Sun-Times Gold-193
00BAP Mem Chicago Sun-Times Sapphire-193
00BAP Mem Toronto Fall Expo Copper-193
00BAP Memorabilia Toronto Fall Expo Gold-193
00BAP Memorabilia Toronto Fall Expo Ruby-193
00Pacific-254
Copper-254
Gold-254
Ice Blue-254
Premiere Date-254
00SPx-103
Spectrum-103
00UD Pros and Prospects-113
00Upper Deck-190
Exclusives Tier 1-190
Exclusives Tier 2-190
00Upper Deck Victory-265
00Lowell Lock Monsters-5
01Czech DS-34
02Czech OFS Plus-245
02Czech OFS Plus-307
03Czech OFS Plus-20
04Czech OFS-30

Mika, Radek
03Czech OFS Plus-170

Mikaelsson, Par
89Swedish Semic Elitserien Stickers-214

Mikan, Erik
93Quebec Pee-Wee Tournament-1294

Mikel, Jan
00UK Sekonda Superleague-9
01UK Dundee Stars-10
02UK Dundee Stars-10

Mikes, Josef
99Czech OFS-442

Mikesch, Jeff
93Michigan Tech Huskies-16

Mikesch, Pat
93Michigan Tech Huskies-1
96Kentucky Thoroughblades-13
98Florida Everblades-15
99German Bundesliga 2-213
00German DEL-117
01German Upper Deck-131
Skilled Stars-SS7
02German DEL City Press-180
03German Deg Metro Stars-13
03German DEL-37

Mikesch, Scott
95Waterloo Blackhawks -23

Mikeska, Michal
98Czech OFS-160
99Czech OFS-298
99Czech OFS-365
00Czech DS Extraliga-94
00Czech OFS-46
01Czech OFS-254
02Czech OFS Plus-220
03Czech OFS Plus-319
03Czech OFS Plus Insert H-H16
03Czech OFS Plus MS Praha-SE11
03Czech Pardubice Postcards-9
04Czech OFS-124
05Czech HC Pardubice-10
06Czech OFS All Stars-14
06Czech Super Six Postcards-8

Mikesz, Lubomir
94German First League-660

Mikhailev, Sergei
02Russian Hockey League-91
03Russian Hockey League-200

Mikhailov, Boris
69Russian National Team Postcards-7
69Swedish Hockey-9
70Finnish Jaakiekko-8
70Russian National Team Postcards-13
70Swedish Hockey-119
70Swedish Hockey-326
70Swedish Masterserien-128
70Swedish Masterserien-131
71Finnish Suomi Stickers-10
71Swedish Hockey-37
72Finnish Jaakiekko-29
72Finnish Hellas-72
72Finnish Panda Toronto-57
72Finnish Semic World Championship-13
72Swedish Semic World Championship-13
73Finnish Jaakiekko-11
73Russian National Team-6
73Russian National Team-9
73Russian National Team-24
73Swedish Stickers-86
74Finnish Jenkki-51
74Finnish Typotor-70
74Russian National Team-13
74Russian National Team-14
74Swedish Stickers-7
74Swedish Semic World Champ Stickers-33
77Finnish Sportscasters-26-673
79Panini Stickers-150
79Russian National Team-13
80USSR Olympic Team Mini Pics-6
91Future Trends Canada '72-43
91Future Trends Canada '72 French-43
95Swedish Globe World Championships-243
99Russian Stars of Hockey-39
03Czech Stadion-553
03Russian Hockey League-85
06ITG International Ice Cornerstones-IC07
06ITG International Ice Cornerstones Gold-IC07
06ITG International Ice Emblems-GUE37
06ITG International Ice Emblems Gold-GUE37
06ITG International Ice Jerseys-GUJ37
06ITG International Ice Jerseys Gold-GUJ37
06ITG International Ice Numbers-GUN37
06ITG International Ice Numbers Gold-GUN37
06ITG International Ice Triple Memorabilia-TM03
06ITG International Ice Triple Memorabilia Gold-TM03
06ITG Ultimate Memorabilia Autos-65
06ITG Ultimate Memorabilia Autos Gold-65

Mikhailov, Dmitri
99Russian Hockey League-253

Mikhailov, Igor
96Spokane Chiefs-5
98Russian Hockey League-65
99Russian Hockey League-66
99Russian Stars Postcards-15
00Russian Hockey League-259
01Russian Hockey League-76
03Russian Hockey League-75
03Russian Hockey League-182
04Russian Super League All-Stars-12

Mikhailov, Konstantin
01Russian Hockey League-74
02Russian Young Lions-11
03Russian Hockey League-169

Mikhailovski, Mikhail
00Russian Hockey League-329

Mikhailovsky, Maxim
90O-Pee-Chee Red Army-9R
91O-Pee-Chee Inserts-22R
92Russian Stars Red Ace-20
99Russian Hockey League-155
99Russian Stars of Hockey-15
00Russian Goalkeepers-9
02Russian Hockey League-37
03Russian Hockey League-164

Mikhnov, Alexei
02Russian Future Stars-19
02Russian Hockey League-73
02Russian Young Lions-14
03Russian Hockey League-171
06Beehive-120
Matte-120
06Hot Prospects-156
06O-Pee-Chee-568
Rainbow-568
06SP Authentic-214
Limited-214
06SP Game Used-115
Gold-115
Rainbow-115
06SPx-207
Spectrum-207
06The Cup Masterpiece Pressplates (Bee Hive)-120
06The Cup Masterpiece Pressplates (Marquee Rookies)-568
06The Cup Masterpiece Pressplates (SP Game Used)-115
06The Cup Masterpiece Pressplates (Victory)-321
06Ultra-239
06Ultra-240
Gold Medallion-239
Ice Medallion-239
06Upper Deck-467
Exclusives Parallel-467
High Gloss Parallel-467
Masterpieces-467
Rookie Headliners-RH16
Victory-321
06Wilkes-Barre Scranton Penguins-2
07Upper Deck Rookie Class -31

Mikhnov, Andrei
01Sudbury Wolves-11
01Sudbury Wolves Police-9

Mikita, Stan
44Beehive Group II Photos-125
57St. Catherine's Tee Pees-NNO
60Shirriff Coins-71
60Topps-14
Stamps-36
61Shirriff/Salada Coins-22
61Topps-36
62Shirriff Coins-46
62Topps-34
Hockey Bucks-17
63Chex Photos-39
63Topps-36
63Toronto Star-26
64Beehive Group III Photos-49
64Coca-Cola Caps-35
64Topps-31
64Topps-106
64Toronto Star-33
65Coca-Cola-35
65Topps-60
66Topps-62
66Topps-124
66Topps USA Test-62
67General Mills-4
67Post Cereal Box Backs-7
67Post Cereal Box Backs-8
67Topps-64
67Topps-114
67Topps-126
68Blackhawks Team Issue-5
68O-Pee-Chee-155
68O-Pee-Chee-202
68O-Pee-Chee-211
Puck Stickers-1
68Shirriff Coins-25
68Topps-20
69Equitable Sports Hall of Fame-5
69O-Pee-Chee-76
Four-in-One-13
Stamps-21
69Topps-76
70Blackhawks Postcards-3
70Blackhawks Postcards-9
70Dad's Cookies-86
70Esso Power Players-125
70O-Pee-Chee-20
70O-Pee-Chee-240
70Sargent Promotions Stamps-48
70Topps-20
Topps/OPC Sticker Stamps-23
71Bazooka-35
71Colgate Heads-2
71Letraset Action Replays-10
71O-Pee-Chee-125
71Sargent Promotions Stamps-33
71Topps-125
71Toronto Sun-76
72Kellogg's Iron-On Transfers-6
72O-Pee-Chee-156
72O-Pee-Chee-177
Player Crests-5
Team Canada-19
72Sargent Promotions Stamps-63
72Topps-56
72Finnish Semic World Championship-227
72Swedish Semic World Championship-227
73O-Pee-Chee-6
73Topps-145
74NHL Action Stamps-81
74O-Pee-Chee NHL-20
74O-Pee-Chee NHL-69
74Topps-20
74Topps-69
75O-Pee-Chee NHL-30
75O-Pee-Chee NHL-317
75Topps-30
75Topps-317
76O-Pee-Chee NHL-225
76Topps-225
77O-Pee-Chee NHL-195
77Sportscasters-1222
77Topps-195
77Finnish Sportscasters-51-1224
78O-Pee-Chee-75
78Topps-75
79Blackhawks Postcards-13
79O-Pee-Chee-155
79Topps-155
81TCMA-13
83Hall of Fame-226
83Hall of Fame Postcards-O11
85Hall of Fame-226
88Esso All-Stars-31
90Pro Set-405
90Pro Set-655
91Future Trends Canada '72-61
91Future Trends Canada '72 French-61
92Hall of Fame Legends-15
92Zeller's Masters of Hockey-5
92Zeller's Masters of Hockey Signed-5
93American Licorice Sour Punch Caps-4
93Upper Deck Locker All-Stars-46
94Hockey Wit-39
94Parkhurst Missing Link Future Stars-FS3
94Parkhurst Tall Boys-26
94Parkhurst Tall Boys-138
94Parkhurst Tall Boys-147
94Parkhurst Tall Boys-170
Mail-Ins-SL2
Mail-Ins-TW3
94Arizona Icecats-23
95Parkhurst '66-67 Promos-4
95Parkhurst '66-67-24
95Parkhurst '66-67-125
95Parkhurst '66-67-PR125
Coins-24
96Arizona Icecats-25
97Beehive-59
Golden Portraits-59
Golden Originals Autographs-59
98OPC Chrome Blast From the Past-8
98OPC Chrome Blast From Past Refractors-8
98Topps Blast From The Past-8
98Topps Blast From The Past Autographs-8
99BAP Memorabilia AS Retail-R5
99BAP Memorabilia AS Retail Autographs-R5
99Upper Deck 500 Goal Club-500SM
99Upper Deck 500 Goal Club-500SM
99Upper Deck Century Legends-18
Century Collection-18
Epic Signatures-SM
Epic Signatures 100-SM
99Upper Deck Retro-91
Gold-91
Platinum-91
Generation-G7A
Generation Level 2-G7A
Inkredible-SM
Inkredible Level 2-SM
00UD Heroes-123
Signs of Greatness-SM
00Upper Deck Legends-26
Legendary Collection Bronze-26
Legendary Collection Gold-26
Legendary Collection Silver-26
Enshrined Stars-ES14
Epic Signatures-SM
01BAP Memorabilia 500 Goal Scorers-GS18
01BAP Signature Series 500 Goal Scorers-5
01BAP Sig Series 500 Goal Scorers Autos-5
01BAP Signature Series Vintage Autographs-VA-33
01BAP Ultimate Mem All-Star History-18
01BAP Ultimate Memorabilia Autographs-25
01BAP Ultimate Mem Autographs Gold-25
01BAP Ultimate Memorabilia Cornerstones-3
01BAP Ultimate Memorabilia Decades-12
01BAP Ultimate Memorabilia Emblem Attic-13
01BAP Ultimate Mem 500 Goal Scorers-8
01BAP Ultimate Mem 500 Goal Scorers Autos-23
01BAP Ultimate Mem 500 Goal Jerseys/Stick-8
01BAP Ultimate Mem 500 Goal Emblems-8
01BAP Ultimate Mem Retired Numbers-16
01BAP Ultimate Mem Retro Teammates-7
01BAP Update Tough Customers-TC32
01Fleer Legacy-34
Ultimate-34
Memorabilia-17
Memorabilia Autographs-6
01Greats of the Game-31
Autographs-31
01Parkhurst Autographs-PA35
01Parkhurst 500 Goal Scorers-PGS18
01Parkhurst He Shoots-He Scores Points-6
01Parkhurst Heroes-H8
01Parkhurst Sticks-PS63
01Topps Archives-14
Arena Seats-ASSM
Autographs-10
Relics-JSM
01Upper Deck Legends-13
Epic Signatures-SM
Fiorentino Collection-FCSM
Jerseys-TTSM
Jerseys-TTHM
Jerseys Platinum-TTSM
Jerseys Platinum-TTHM
Sticks-PHSM
02BAP NHL All-Star History-18
02BAP Signature Series Golf-GS86
02BAP Ultimate Memorabilia Emblem Attic-18
02BAP Ultimate Memorabilia Great Moments-20
02BAP Ultimate Memorabilia Numerology-24
02BAP Ultimate Mem Retro Teammates-3
02BAP Ultimate Memorabilia Retro Trophies-6
02BAP Ultimate Mem Scoring Leaders-24
02BAP Ultimate Mem Scoring Leaders-25
02BAP Ultimate Mem Scoring Leaders-27
02BAP Ultimate Mem Scoring Leaders-28
02BAP Ultimate Mem Vintage Jerseys-1
02BAP Ultimate Mem Vintage Jersey Autos-10
02Parkhurst Vintage Memorabilia-VM4
02Parkhurst Vintage Teammates-VT5
02Parkhurst Retro Nicknames-RN16
02UD Foundations 1000 Point Club-MI
02UD Foundations Signs of Greatness-SGSM
03BAP Ultimate Memorabilia Gloves Are Off-11
03BAP Ultimate Memorabilia Great Moments-2
03BAP Ultimate Memorabilia Linemates-1
03BAP Ultimate Memorabilia Linemates-5
03BAP Ultimate Mem Raised to the Rafters-13
03BAP Ultimate Mem Vint Complete Package-5
03BAP Ultimate Mem Vint Comp Package Gold-5
03BAP Ultimate Mem Vintage Hat Tricks-5
03BAP Ultimate Mem Vintage Jerseys-36
03BAP Ultimate Mem Vintage Jerseys Gold-36
03Canada Post-22
03ITG Used Sig Series Triple Mem-6
03ITG Used Sig Series Triple Mem Gold-6
03ITG Used Sig Series Vintage Mem -18
03ITG Used Sig Series Vintage Mem Gold-18
03ITG VIP MVP-9
03ITG VIP Vintage Memorabilia-22
03Parkhurst Original Six Chicago-45
03Parkhurst Original Six Chicago-65
03Parkhurst Original Six Chicago-78
03Parkhurst Original Six Chicago-83
03Parkhurst Original Six Chicago-92
03Parkhurst Original Six Chicago-93
Autographs-12
Inserts-C1
Inserts-C11
Memorabilia-CM30
Memorabilia-CM37
Memorabilia-CM53
03Parkhurst Orig Six He Shoots/Scores-20
03Parkhurst Orig Six He Shoots/Scores-20A
03SP Authentic Sign of the Times-SM
03SPx-107
Radiance-107
Spectrum-107
03Upper Deck Trilogy-134
Crest Variations-134
Limited-134
Scripts-S3SM
Scripts Limited-S3SM
Scripts Red-S3SM
03Czech Stadion-554
04ITG NHL AS FANtasy AS History Jerseys-SB18
04ITG Franchises He Shoots/Scores Prizes-19
04ITG Franchises US West-161
Autographs-A-SM
Complete Jerseys-WCJ4
Complete Jerseys Gold-WCJ4
Double Memorabilia-WDM11
Double Memorabilia Autographs-WDMSM
Double Memorabilia Gold-WDM11
Forever Rivals-WFR4
Forever Rivals Gold-WFR4
Memorabilia-WSM15
Memorabilia Autographs-WSMSM
Memorabilia Gold-WSM15
Original Sticks-WOS7
Original Sticks Autographs-WOSSM
Original Sticks Gold-WOS7
Teammates-WTM2
Teammates Gold-WTM2
Triple Memorabilia Autographs-WTMSM
Triple Memorabilia Gold-WTM9
Trophy Winners-WTW1
Trophy Winners Gold-WTW1
04ITG Ultimate Memorabilia-30
Gold-30
Art Ross Trophy-4
Auto Threads-14
Autographs-11
Autographs Gold-11
Complete Package-11
Cornerstones-2
Cornerstones Gold-2
Day In History-16
Day In History-40
Day In History Gold-16
Day In History Gold-40
Hart Trophy-4
Jersey Autographs-34
Jersey Autographs Gold-34
Nicknames-1
Nickname Autographs-10
Original Six-1
Original Six-20
Raised to the Rafters-6
Retro Teammates-3
Stick Autographs-30
Stick Autographs Gold-30
Vintage Lumber-5
04SP Authentic Buybacks-185
04SP Authentic Buybacks-186
04SP Authentic Buybacks-187
04SP Authentic Octographs-OS-ART
04SP Authentic Sign of the Times-QS-MHCL
04UD Legendary Signatures-78
Autographs-SM
Summit Stars-CDN14
Summit Stars Autographs-CDN-SM
04UD Legends Classics-50
04UD Legends Classics-72
04UD Legends Classics-99
Gold-50
Gold-72
Gold-99
Platinum-50
Platinum-72
Platinum-99
Silver-50
Silver-72
Silver-99
Jersey Redemptions-JY17
Signature Moments-M11
Signatures-CS11
Signatures-DC3
Signatures-DC22
04ITG Heroes and Prospects-133
Aspiring-14
Autographs-SM
Hero Memorabilia-2
04ITG Heroes/Prospects Toronto Expo '05-133
04ITG Heroes/Prospects Expo Heroes/Pros-133
05ITG Heroes/Prosp Toronto Expo Parallel -36
05Beehive-239
05ITG Ultimate Memorabilia Level 1-88
05ITG Ultimate Memorabilia Level 2-88
05ITG Ultimate Memorabilia Level 3-88
05ITG Ultimate Memorabilia Level 4-88
05ITG Ultimate Memorabilia Level 5-88
05ITG Ultimate Mem Complete Package-2
05ITG Ultimate Mem Complete Package Gold-2
05ITG Ultimate Mem Cornerstones Jerseys-1
05ITG Ultimate Mem Cornerst Jerseys Gold-1
05ITG Ultimate Mem Double Mem-6
05ITG Ultimate Mem Double Mem Autos-17
05ITG Ultimate Mem Double Mem Autos Gold-17
05ITG Ultimate Mem Double Mem Gold-6
05ITG Ultimate Memorabilia Emblem Attic-11
05ITG Ultimate Mem Emblem Attic Gold-11
05ITG Ultimate Memorabilia Emblems-18
05ITG Ultimate Memorabilia Emblems Gold-18
05ITG Ultimate Memorabilia Gloves Are Off-17
05ITG Ultimate Mem Gloves Are Off Gold-17
05ITG Ultimate Memorabilia Jersey Autos-20
05ITG Ultimate Mem Jersey Autos Gold-20
05ITG Ultimate Memorabilia Jerseys-35
05ITG Ultimate Memorabilia Jerseys Gold-35
05ITG Ultimate Mem Pass the Torch Jerseys-11
05ITG Ultimate Mem Passing Torch Jsy Gold-11
05ITG Ultimate Mem Raised to the Rafters-18
05ITG Ultimate Mem Raised Rafters Gold-18
05ITG Ultimate Mem Record Breaker Jerseys-4
05ITG Ultimate Mem Record Breaker Jerseys-16
05ITG Ultimate Mem RecBreak Jerseys Gold-4
05ITG Ultimate Mem RecBreak Jerseys Gold-16
05ITG Ultimate Mem Retro Teammate Jerseys-27
05ITG Ult Mem Retro Teammates Jersey Gold-27
05ITG Ultimate Memorabilia Sextuple Autos-4
05ITG Ultimate Memorabilia Stick Autos-40
05ITG Ultimate Mem Stick Autos Gold-40
05ITG Ultimate Mem 3 Star of the Game Jsy-9
05ITG Ult Mem 3 Star of the Game Jsy Gold-9
05ITG Ultimate Memorabilia Triple Autos-1
05ITG Ultimate Mem Triple Autos Gold-1
05ITG Ultimate Mem Triple Threads Jerseys-7
05ITG Ultimate Mem Triple Thread Jsy Gold-7
05ITG Ultimate Memorabilia Ultimate Autos-16
05ITG Ultimate Mem Ultimate Autos Gold-16
05ITG Ultimate Memorabilia Vintage Lumber-11
05ITG Ultimate Mem Vintage Lumber Gold-11
05SPx Xcitement Legends-XL-SM
05SPx Xcitement Legends Gold-XL-SM
05SPx Xcitement Legends Spectrum-XL-SM
05UD Artifacts-134
Blue-134
Gold-134
Green-134
Pewter-134
Red-134
Gold Autographed-134
05UD Toronto Fall Expo Priority Signings-PS-SM
05Upper Deck All-Time Greatest-14
05Upper Deck Trilogy Legendary Scripts-LEG-SM
05Upper Deck Trilogy Personal Scripts-PER-SM
05ITG Heroes and Prospects-36
Autographs-A-SM
Hero Memorabilia-HM-6
Hero Memorabilia Dual-HDM-16
06ITG International Ice-23
Gold-23
Autographs-ASM
06ITG Ultimate Memorabilia-130
Artist Proof-130
Autos-26
Autos Gold-26
Blades of Steel-29
Blades of Steel Gold-29
Captain-C-8
Captain-C Gold-8
Complete Package-4
Complete Package Gold-4
Cornerstones-4
Cornerstones Gold-4
Double Memorabilia-30
Double Memorabilia Gold-30
Emblems-22
Emblems Gold-22
Gloves Are Off-19
Gloves Are Off Gold-19
Jerseys Autos-39
Jerseys Autos Gold-39
Retro Teammates-7
Retro Teammates Gold-7
Sensational Season-3
Sensational Season Gold-3
Stick Rack-12
Stick Rack Gold-12
06The Cup-21
Autographed Foundations-CQMA
Autographed Foundations Patches-CQMA
Autographed Patches-21
Black Rainbow-21
Foundations-CQMA
Foundations Patches-CQMA
Gold-21
Gold Patches-21
Hardware Heroes Patches-HHSM
Honorable Numbers-HNMA
Jerseys-21
Masterpiece Pressplates-21
Signature Patches-SPSM
Stanley Cup Signatures-CSSM
06Ultimate Collection Jerseys-UJ-SM
06Ultimate Collection Patches-UJ-SM
06ITG Heroes and Prospects Heroes Memorabilia-HM17
06ITG Heroes and Prospects Heroes Memorabilia Gold-HM17

Mikkelson, Bill
72O-Pee-Chee-79
72Topps-118
74Capitals White Borders-20
74NHL Action Stamps-307
74O-Pee-Chee NHL-23
74Topps-23
75O-Pee-Chee NHL-207
75Topps-207

Mikkelson, Brendan
03Portland Winter Hawks-6
05ITG Heroes/Prosp Toronto Expo Parallel -165
05Vancouver Giants-16
05ITG Heroes and Prospects-165
Autographs-A-BMI

Mikkelson, Meaghan
04Wisconsin Badgers Women-15

Mikko, Ingemar
84Swedish Semic Elitserien-187

Mikko, Roger
84Swedish Semic Elitserien-188
85Swedish Panini Stickers-163
86Swedish Panini Stickers-182

Mikkola, Ari
72Finnish Jaakiekko-177
78Finnish SM-Liiga-81

Mikkola, Heikki
66Finnish Jaakiekkosarja-104

Mikkola, Ilkka
98Black Diamond-98
Double Diamond-98
Triple Diamond-98
Quadruple Diamond-98
98SPx Top Prospects-71
Radiance-71
Spectrum-71
98Finnish Kerailysarja-232
99Finnish Cardset-135
00Finnish Cardset-338
01Finnish Cardset-252
02Finnish Cardset-222
03Finnish Cardset-87
04Finnish Cardset-258
05Finnish Cardset -90
06Finnish Cardset-95

Mikkola, Niko
93Finnish SISU-50
94Finnish SISU-88
95Finnish Semic World Championships-240
98Finnish Kerailysarja-264
99Finnish Cardset-153
00Finnish Cardset-166
01Finnish Cardset-59
02Finnish Cardset-74
03Finnish Cardset-168

Mikkolainen, Reijo
89Swedish Semic World Champ Stickers-38
92Finnish Jyvas-Hyva Stickers-180
93Finnish SISU-53
94Finnish SISU-206
95Finnish SISU-37
95Finnish SISU-187

Mikkonen, Tuomas
04Finnish Cardset-254
05Finnish Cardset -72
06Idaho Steelheads-9

Mikkonen, Ville
98Finnish Kerailysarja-175
99Finnish Cardset-87

Miklenda, Jaroslav
93Parkhurst-519
Emerald Ice-519
93Upper Deck-573

Miklik, Martin
99Czech OFS-241

Miklulik, Milan
04Czech OFS-405
06Czech OFS-59

Mikol, Jim
44Beehive Group II Photos-436
60Cleveland Barons-14
64Beehive Group III Photos-142
64Coca-Cola Caps-82
64Topps-36
94Parkhurst Tall Boys-99

Mikola, Julian
06Texas Tornados-8

Mikolas, Josef
97Czech APS Extraliga-379

Mikolasek, Tomas
94Czech APS Extraliga-66
95Czech APS Extraliga-92
96Czech APS Extraliga-88
97Czech APS Extraliga-217
97Czech DS Stickers-144
98Czech DS Stickers-239
98Czech OFS-168
99Czech Score Blue 2000-24
99Czech Score Red Ice 2000-24

Mikulchik, Oleg
95Upper Deck-471
98Russian Hockey League-3
98Russian Hockey League-130
99Russian Hockey League-16
99Russian Metallurg Magnetogorsk-35
00Russian Hockey League-52
01Russian Hockey League-24

Mikulchik, Pavel
99Tacoma Sabercats-3
00Bakersfield Condors-16

Mikulik, Jan
02Czech OFS Plus-113

Mikus, Juraj
04Slovakian Skalica Team Set-22
06Chicoutimi Sagueneens-15

Mikus, Tomas
96Slovakian Quebec Pee-Wee Tournament-18

Milam, Jamie
04Northern Michigan Wildcats-13

Milam, Troy
03ECHL All-Stars-275
03Gwinnett Gladiators-18
03Gwinnett Gladiators RBI Sports-204
04Manchester Monarchs-23
04Manchester Monarchs Tobacco-23

Milan, Corey
04Penticton Vees-22
05Penticton Vees-11
06Penticton Vees-16

Milani, Tom
77Kalamazoo Wings-9
82Swedish Semic VM Stickers-138
83Swedish Semic VM Stickers-138

Milanovic, Ryan
96Kitchener Rangers-19

Milbert, Megan
98Minnesota Golden Gophers Women-14

Milburn, Marc
03Cape Fear Fire Antz-10

Milbury, Mike
77O-Pee-Chee NHL-134
77Topps-134
78O-Pee-Chee-59
78Topps-59
79O-Pee-Chee-114
79Topps-114
80O-Pee-Chee-191
80Topps-191
81O-Pee-Chee-16
82Post Cereal-1
83Bruins Team Issue-12
83NHL Key Tags-5
83O-Pee-Chee-55
84Bruins Postcards-13
84O-Pee-Chee-10
87Panini Stickers-8
90Pro Set-661
92Future Trends Promo Sheet-1
96Islander Postcards-15
01Topps Archives-70

Mild, Hans
64Swedish Coralli ISHockey-127
65Swedish Coralli ISHockey-127
98Swedish UD Choice-202

Milek, David
01Bakersfield Condors-16

Miles, Jeff
04Reading Royals-21

Milette, Charles
05Shawinigan Cataractes-20

Milford, John C
85Hall of Fame-253

Milhench, Keith
97UK Kingston Hawks Stickers-1
98UK Kingston Hawks-24
Milhouse, Jonathan
05Everett Silvertips-17
Milks, Hib
24Anonymous NHL-48
24Anonymous NHL-52
Mill, Jim
92Raleigh Icecaps-8
92Raleigh Icecaps-29
93Birmingham Bulls Birmingham News-14
93Huntington Blizzard-17
93Roanoke Express-13
Millar, Aaron
95Medicine Hat Tigers-10
96Medicine Hat Tigers-12
97Medicine Hat Tigers-13
98Medicine Hat Tigers-16
03Tulsa Oilers-13
Millar, Al
56Quebec Aces-11
66Tulsa Oilers-8
Millar, Craig
95Swift Current Broncos-10
96Rochester Americans-4
97Be A Player-239
Autographs-239
Autographs Die-Cuts-239
Autographs Prismatic Die-Cuts-239
97SP Authentic-182
98Pacific-215
Ice Blue-215
Red-215
98Pacific Omega-98
Red-98
Opening Day Issue-98
98Upper Deck-95
Exclusives-95
Exclusives 1 of 1-95
Gold Reserve-95
00Pacific-224
Copper-224
Gold-224
Ice Blue-224
Premiere Date-224
Millar, Mike
83Brantford Alexanders-20
88ProCards AHL-47
89Bruins Sports Action Update-6
89ProCards AHL-67
90Newmarket Saints-15
90ProCards AHL/IHL-168
94German DEL-159
95German DEL-159
96German DEL-235
99German Bundesliga 2-150
Millen, Corey
89Rangers Marine Midland Bank-23
89ProCards IHL-44
91Pro Set Platinum-185
91Bowman-60
91O-Pee-Chee-461
91Parkhurst-292
French-292
91Score American-318
91Score Canadian Bilingual-348
91Score Canadian English-348
91Stadium Club-71
91Topps-461
91Upper Deck-110
91Upper Deck-604
French-110
French-604
92Bowman-57
92O-Pee-Chee-334
92Panini Stickers-70
92Panini Stickers French-70
92Parkhurst-306
Emerald Ice-306
92Pinnacle-138
French-138
92Score-111
Canadian-111
Sharpshooters-26
Sharpshooters Canadian-26
92Stadium Club-296
92Topps-326
Gold-326G
92Ultra-86
92Upper Deck-48
93Donruss-181
93Leaf-361
93OPC Premier-493
Gold-493
93Panini Stickers-207
93Parkhurst-381
Emerald Ice-381
93Pinnacle-350
Canadian-350
93PowerPlay-379
93Score-62
93Score-519
Gold-519
Canadian-62
Canadian-519
Canadian Gold-519
93Stadium Club-437
Members Only Master Set-437
First Day Issue-437
93Topps/OPC Premier-493
Gold-493
93Ultra-361
93Upper Deck-483
SP-84
94Canada Games NHL POGS-147
94Donruss-148
94Leaf-187
94Parkhurst-122
Gold-122
94Pinnacle-425
Artist's Proofs-425
Rink Collection-425
94Score-99
Gold-99
Platinum-99
94Stars Postcards-18
94Ultra-120
94Upper Deck-25
Electric Ice-25
95Canada Games NHL POGS-84
95Collector's Choice-274
Player's Club-274
Player's Club Platinum-274
95Parkhurst International-304
Emerald Ice-304
95Score-172
Black Ice Artist's Proofs-172
Black Ice-172
95Upper Deck-105
Electric Ice-105
Electric Ice Gold-105
96Upper Deck-231
97Pacific-107
Copper-107
Emerald Green-107
Ice Blue-107
Red-107
Silver-107
98German DEL-87
99German DEL-119
00German DEL-142
All-Star Class-A8
01German Upper Deck-143
02Swiss HNL-30
Millen, Greg
79O-Pee-Chee-281
80O-Pee-Chee-158
80Topps-158
81O-Pee-Chee-134
81Topps-E115
82O-Pee-Chee-126
82O-Pee-Chee Stickers-130
82Post Cereal-7
82Topps Stickers-130
82Whalers Junior Hartford Courant-12
83NHL Key Tags-49
83O-Pee-Chee-143
83O-Pee-Chee Stickers-262
83Puffy Stickers-16
83Topps Stickers-262
84O-Pee-Chee-75
84O-Pee-Chee Stickers-198
84Topps-58
84Whalers Junior Wendy's-12
85O-Pee-Chee-221
85O-Pee-Chee Stickers-51
87Blues Kodak-18
87Blues Team Issue-15
88Blues Kodak-15
88Blues Team Issue-15
88O-Pee-Chee-117
88Panini Stickers-100
88Topps-117
89Nordiques Team Issue-31
89O-Pee-Chee-137
89O-Pee-Chee-314
89Panini Stickers-129
89Topps-137
90Blackhawks Coke-18
90Bowman-3
Tiffany-3
90O-Pee-Chee-335
90Panini Stickers-188
90Pro Set-56
90Score-42
Canadian-42
90Topps-335
Tiffany-335
90Upper Deck-213
French-213
97Pinnacle Hockey Night in Canada-8
06Parkhurst-90
Autographs-90
Miller, Aaron
94Classic Pro Prospects-105
96Collector's Edge Ice-29
Prism-29
97Be A Player-75
Autographs-75
Autographs Die-Cuts-75
Autographs Prismatic Die-Cuts-75
97Pacific-317
Copper-317
Emerald Green-317
Ice Blue-317
Red-317
Silver-317
97Upper Deck-258
99Avalanche Team Issue-14
99Pacific-111
Copper-111
Emerald Green-111
Gold-111
Ice Blue-111
Premiere Date-111
Red-111
99Upper Deck MVP SC Edition-49
Gold Script-49
Silver Script-49
Super Script-49
00Private Stock Game Gear-27
00Private Stock Game Gear Patches-27
00Titanium Game Gear-76
00Titanium Game Gear Patches-76
00Upper Deck-49
Exclusives Tier 1-49
Exclusives Tier 2-49
01BAP Memorabilia-39
Emerald-39
Ruby-39
Sapphire-39
01BAP Signature Series-13
Autographs-13
Autographs Gold-13
01Pacific Jerseys-16
01Pacific Heads-Up Quad Jerseys-8
01Parkhurst-141
01Private Stock Game Gear-51
01Private Stock Game Gear Patches-51
01Titanium Double-Sided Jerseys-19
01Upper Deck Avalanche NHL All-Star Game-CA5
01Upper Deck Victory-164
Gold-164
02Kings Team Issue-7
02BAP Sig Series Auto Buybacks 2001-13
02Kings Game Sheets-31
02Kings Game Sheets-32
02Pacific-169
Blue-169
Red-169
Jerseys-22
Jerseys Holo-Silver-22
02Pacific Complete-48
Red-48
02Upper Deck-325
Exclusives-325
02Upper Deck Beckett UD Promos-325
02Upper Deck Vintage-122
03ITG Action-295
03Pacific Complete-389
Red-389
03Upper Deck MVP-201
Gold Script-201
Silver Script-201
Canadian Exclusives-201
04Upper Deck-80
Canadian Exclusives-80
HG Glossy Gold-80
HG Glossy Silver-80
05Kings Team Issue-10
05Upper Deck MVP-188
Gold-188
Platinum-188
06O-Pee-Chee-231
Rainbow-231
Miller, Al
51Laval Dairy QSHL-57
51Laval Dairy Subset-7
Miller, Andrew
99Memphis RiverKings All-Time-6
06ITG Heroes and Prospects-164
Miller, Anya
04Minnesota Golden Gophers Women-3
Miller, Aren
95Spokane Chiefs-30
96Spokane Chiefs-1
97Beehive-70
Authentic Autographs-70
Golden Portraits-70
97Spokane Chiefs-1
99Cincinnati Mighty Ducks-8
Miller, Austin
01Western Michigan Broncos-6
03Mississippi Sea Wolves-7
Miller, Ben
06Texas Tornados-16
Miller, Bob
79O-Pee-Chee-196
79Topps-196
80O-Pee-Chee-236
80Topps-236
81Rockies Postcards-20
82Post Cereal-11
84Kings Smokey-20
98Bruins Alumni-11
Autographs-11
Miller, Brad
86Regina Pats-19
87Regina Pats-20
88Sabres Wonder Bread/Hostess-17
88Regina Pats-17
89ProCards AHL-264
90Pro Set-591
90Sabres Campbell's-17
90ProCards AHL/IHL-272
91Parkhurst-243
French-243
91Pro Set-354
French-354
91Sabres Blue Shield-13
91Sabres Pepsi/Campbell's-13
91Rochester Americans Kodak-19
92Stadium Club-475
92St. John's Maple Leafs-14
93Parkhurst-306
Emerald Ice-306
94Minnesota Moose-11
95Minnesota Moose-13
98Las Vegas Thunder-14
99Utah Grizzlies-30
Miller, Brad USHL
04Green Bay Gamblers-13
Miller, Brant
04Victoriaville Tigres-26
05Victoriaville Tigres-14
Miller, Bryan
03Boston University Terriers-11
05Albany River Rats-14
Miller, Clint
96OCN Blizzard-4
Miller, Colin
88Niagara Falls Thunder-13
89Sault Ste. Marie Greyhounds-11
907th Inn. Sketch OHL-169
917th Inn. Sketch OHL-321
917th Inn. Sketch Memorial Cup-23
92Atlanta Knights-6
93Atlanta Knights-4
94Atlanta Knights-7
95Dayton Bombers-13
96Dayton Bombers-24
97Dayton Bombers-20
98Dayton Bombers-12
98Dayton Bombers EBK-4
98Dayton Bombers EBK-16
Miller, Cory
96Minnesota Golden Gophers-20
97Minnesota Golden Gophers-10
98Minnesota Golden Gophers-11
Miller, Craig
00Upper Deck NHLPA-PA81
05Florida Seals Team Issue-10
Miller, Dan
03Plymouth Whalers-23
Miller, Dennis
91ProCards-434
95Central Hockey League-10
95Fort Worth Fire-17
Miller, Drew
06Portland Pirates-15
06ITG Heroes and Prospects-164
Autographs-ADM
Miller, Gary
897th Inn. Sketch OHL-160
907th Inn. Sketch OHL-312
917th Inn. Sketch OHL-89
Miller, Gus
92British Columbia JHL-228
Miller, Jason
90Upper Deck-335
French-335
907th Inn. Sketch WHL-28
91O-Pee-Chee-163
91Score American-312
91Score Canadian Bilingual-342
91Score Canadian English-342
91Topps-163
91ProCards-420
92Quebec Pee-Wee Tournament-279
93Classic Pro Prospects-13
95Finnish SISU-222
95Finnish SISU-377
95Peoria Rivermen-11
98German DEL-254
99German DEL-37
00German DEL-192
01German Upper Deck Gate Attractions-GA10
02German DEL City Press-97
03Salmon Arm Silverbacks-15
Miller, Jason (BCHL)
03Salmon Arm Silverbacks-15
Miller, Jay
85Moncton Golden Flames-23
87Panini Stickers-18
88Bruins Sports Action-14
88Panini Stickers-212
89Kings Smokey-15
90Kings Smokey-16
90Upper Deck-414
French-414
91Bowman-178
91O-Pee-Chee-467
91Pro Set-402
French-402
91Score Canadian Bilingual-543
91Score Canadian English-543
91Stadium Club-63
91Topps-467
02Fleer Throwbacks-70
Gold-70
Platinum-70
Miller, Joey
06Lincoln Stars Traded-3T
06Lincoln Stars Upper DeckÂ Signature Series -22
06Sioux Falls Stampede -7
Miller, John
99Sioux City Musketeers-14
04Northern Michigan Wildcats-14
Miller, Keith
88ProCards AHL-137
89ProCards IHL-137
92Quebec Pee-Wee Tournament-1538
Miller, Kelly
86Capitals Kodak-17
87Capitals Kodak-10
87Capitals Team Issue-16
87O-Pee-Chee-189
87Panini Stickers-186
87Topps-189
88Capitals Borderless-14
88Capitals Smokey-14
88O-Pee-Chee-130
88Panini Stickers-373
88Topps-130
89Capitals Kodak-10
89Capitals Team Issue-17
89O-Pee-Chee-131
89O-Pee-Chee Stickers-74
89Panini Stickers-348
89Topps-131
90Bowman-76
Tiffany-76
90Capitals Kodak-17
90Capitals Postcards-17
90Capitals Smokey-16
90O-Pee-Chee-81
90OPC Premier-72
90Panini Stickers-156
90Pro Set-318
90Score-168
Canadian-168
90Topps-81
Tiffany-81
90Upper Deck-130
French-130
91Bowman-292
91Capitals Junior 5x7-21
91Capitals Kodak-21
91O-Pee-Chee-342
91Panini Stickers-202
91Parkhurst-414
French-414
91Pinnacle-23
91Pinnacle-372
French-23
French-372
91Pro Set-256
91Pro Set-611
91Pro Set-615
French-256
French-611
French-615
91Score American-81
91Score American-309
91Score Canadian Bilingual-81
91Score Canadian Bilingual-339
91Score Canadian English-81
91Score Canadian English-339
91Stadium Club-106
91Topps-342
91Upper Deck-133
French-133
92Bowman-338
92Capitals Kodak-21
92O-Pee-Chee-142
92Panini Stickers-166
92Panini Stickers French-166
92Pinnacle-160
French-160
92Score-55
Canadian-55
USA Greats-14
92Stadium Club-361
92Topps-479
Gold-479G
92Ultra-236
92Upper Deck-179
93Donruss-365
93Leaf-254
93OPC Premier-474
Gold-474
93Panini Stickers-30
93Parkhurst-491
Emerald Ice-491
93Pinnacle-284
Canadian-284
93PowerPlay-468
93Score-30
Canadian-30
93Stadium Club-17
Members Only Master Set-17
OPC-17
First Day Issue-17
First Day Issue OPC-17
93Topps/OPC Premier-474
Gold-474
93Ultra-88
93Upper Deck-384
94Canada Games NHL POGS-247
94Donruss-52
94Leaf-519
94OPC Premier-222
Special Effects-222
94Parkhurst-256
Gold-256
Vintage-V72
94Pinnacle-158
Artist's Proofs-158
Rink Collection-158
94Score-63
Gold-63
Platinum-63
94Topps/OPC Premier-222
Special Effects-222
94Ultra-390
94Upper Deck-151
Electric Ice-151
95Canada Games NHL POGS-280
95Capitals Team Issue-18
95Collector's Choice-82
Player's Club-82
Player's Club Platinum-82
95Donruss-159
95Parkhurst International-219
Emerald Ice-219
95Playoff One on One-324
95Score-271
Black Ice Artist's Proofs-271
Black Ice-271
95Topps-126
OPC Inserts-126
95Upper Deck-346
Electric Ice-346
Electric Ice Gold-346
96Be A Player-46
Autographs-46
Autographs Silver-46
97Pacific Invincible NHL Regime-211
98Pacific-444
Ice Blue-444
Red-444
01Fort Wayne Komets-15
03Rockford Ice Hogs-11
05Fort Wayne Komets Choice-10
Miller, Kevin
89ProCards IHL-29
90OPC Premier-73
90Pro Set-493
90Score Rookie/Traded-18T
90Upper Deck-444
French-444
91Pro Set Platinum-168
91Bowman-57
91O-Pee-Chee-125
91Parkhurst-40
French-40
91Pinnacle-133
French-133
91Pro Set-60
French-60
91Score American-126
91Score American-309
91Score Canadian Bilingual-126
91Score Canadian Bilingual-339
91Score Canadian English-126
91Score Canadian English-339
91Score Young Superstars-40
91Stadium Club-286
91Topps-125
91Upper Deck-142
French-142
92Bowman-391
92O-Pee-Chee-291
92Panini Stickers-115
92Panini Stickers French-115
92Pinnacle-313
French-313
92Score-229
Canadian-229
92Stadium Club-229
92Topps-129
Gold-129G
92Ultra-396
92Upper Deck-482
92Finnish Semic-166
93Donruss-298
93Leaf-192
93OPC Premier-8
Gold-8
93Parkhurst-178
Emerald Ice-178
93Pinnacle-126
Canadian-126
93PowerPlay-215
93Score-89
Canadian-89
93Stadium Club-193
Members Only Master Set-193
OPC-193
First Day Issue-193
First Day Issue OPC-193
93Topps/OPC Premier-8
Gold-8
93Ultra-218
93Upper Deck-408
94Canada Games NHL POGS-205
94Donruss-11
94Leaf-129
94OPC Premier-21
Special Effects-21
94Parkhurst SE-SE150
Gold-SE150
94Pinnacle-289
Artist's Proofs-289
Rink Collection-289
94Score-25
Gold-25
Platinum-25
94Topps/OPC Premier-21
Special Effects-21
94Ultra-186
94Upper Deck-451
Electric Ice-451
94Finnish Jaa Kiekko-116
95Canada Games NHL POGS-224
95Collector's Choice-275
Player's Club-275
Player's Club Platinum-275
95Pinnacle-146
Artist's Proofs-146
Rink Collection-146
95Swedish Globe World Championships-119
96Be A Player-165
Autographs-165
Autographs Silver-165
96Pinnacle-15
Artist's Proofs-15
Foil-15
Premium Stock-15
Rink Collection-15
96Upper Deck-236
97Collector's Choice-50
97Pacific-46
Copper-46
Emerald Green-46
Ice Blue-46
Red-46
Silver-46
97Indianapolis Ice-17
98Chicago Wolves-24
99Grand Rapids Griffins-13
99IHL All-Stars-6
00Swiss Panini Stickers-108
00Swiss Slapshot Mini-Cards-HCD10
01Swiss HNL-118
02Swiss HNL-258
03Grand Rapids Griffins-13
Miller, Kip
90Score-330A
90Score-330B
Canadian-330A
Canadian-330B
90Upper Deck-522
French-522
90Halifax Citadels-17
90ProCards AHL/IHL-452
91Bowman-139
91Nordiques Petro-Canada-19
91O-Pee-Chee-387
91OPC Premier-42
91Parkhurst-142
French-142
91Pinnacle-306
French-306
91Pro Set-555
French-555
91Score American-384
91Score Canadian Bilingual-274
91Score Canadian English-274
91Topps-387
91Upper Deck-431
French-431
92Upper Deck-35
92Upper Deck-247
92Upper Deck-421
93Kansas City Blades-5
95Indianapolis Ice-15
96Collector's Edge Ice-138
Prism-138
99BAP Millennium-199
Emerald-199
Ruby-199
Sapphire-199
Signatures-199
Signatures Gold-199
99O-Pee-Chee-40
99O-Pee-Chee Chrome-40
99O-Pee-Chee Chrome Refractors-40
99Pacific-343
Copper-343
Emerald Green-343
Gold-343
Ice Blue-343
Premiere Date-343
Red-343
99Topps/OPC-40
99Topps/OPC Chrome-40
Refractors-40
99Upper Deck Victory-244
00BAP Memorabilia-303
Emerald-303
Ruby-303
Sapphire-303
Promos-303
00BAP Mem Chicago Sportsfest Copper-303
00BAP Memorabilia Chicago Sportsfest Blue-303
00BAP Memorabilia Chicago Sportsfest Gold-303
00BAP Memorabilia Chicago Sportsfest Ruby-303
00BAP Memorabilia Chicago Sun-Times Ruby-303
00BAP Memorabilia Chicago Sun-Times Gold-303
00BAP Mem Chicago Sun-Times Sapphire-303
00BAP Mem Toronto Fall Expo Copper-303
00BAP Memorabilia Toronto Fall Expo Gold-303
00BAP Memorabilia Toronto Fall Expo Ruby-303
00Pacific-8
Copper-8
Gold-8
Ice Blue-8
Premiere Date-8
00Grand Rapids Griffins-14
01Pacific Jerseys-29
01Pacific Heads-Up Quad Jerseys-15
01Titanium Draft Day Edition-57
01Vanguard Memorabilia-39
01Vanguard Patches-39
01Grand Rapids Griffins-4
02BAP Sig Series Auto Buybacks 1999-199
02Pacific-239
Blue-239
Red-239
02Pacific Complete-232
Red-232
03ITG Action-551
03Pacific-348
Blue-348
Red-348
03Pacific Complete-133
Red-133
04Pacific-265
Blue-265
Red-265
05Chicago Wolves-12
Miller, Kris
91ProCards-394
92Raleigh Icecaps-9
92Raleigh Icecaps-26
92Salt Lake Golden Eagles-15
94Minnesota Moose-2
95Minnesota Moose-14
01UK Manchester Storm-17
01UK Manchester Storm Retro-20
Miller, Kurt
91Lake Superior State Lakers-16
92Lake Superior State Lakers-19
95Adirondack Red Wings-15
99German DEL-155
02Kalamazoo Wings-14
03Kalamazoo Wings-12
Miller, Lucas
94Kitchener Rangers-23
98UK Kingston Hawks-22
Miller, Mark
97Louisville Riverfrogs-25
Miller, Matt
97Saskatoon Blades-14
05Roanoke Valley Vipers-6
Miller, Nate
96Minnesota Golden Gophers-21
97Minnesota Golden Gophers-6
98Minnesota Golden Gophers-6
99Minnesota Golden Gophers-13
00Lowell Lock Monsters-21
01Manchester Monarchs-4A
Miller, Nick
02Topeka Scarecrows-18
Miller, Pat
93Quebec Pee-Wee Tournament-515
Miller, Paul
83Moncton Alpines-15
Miller, Perry
75O-Pee-Chee WHA-6
78O-Pee-Chee-16
78Topps-16
79O-Pee-Chee-157
79Topps-157
81O-Pee-Chee-101
Miller, Rob
04Knoxville Ice Bears-23
05Knoxville Ice Bears-11
Miller, Rod
93Minnesota-Duluth Bulldogs-21
Miller, Ryan
00Michigan State Spartans-15
02BAP All-Star Edition-113
Gold-113
Silver-113
02BAP Memorabilia-320
02BAP Signature Series All-Rookie-AR1
02BAP Ultimate Memorabilia-50
Calder Candidates-16
02Between the Pipes-105
Gold-105
Silver-105
02Bowman YoungStars-118
Gold-118
Silver-118
Autographs-RM
Jerseys-RM
Patches-RM
Double Stuff-RM
Triple Stuff-RM
Rivals-DARM
Rivals Patches-2
Sticks-RM
02Crown Royale-105
Blue-105
Purple-105
Red-105
Retail-105
02eTopps-54
02ITG Used-92
Calder Jerseys-C12
Calder Jerseys Gold-C12
02Pacific Calder-106
Silver-106
Reflections-4
02Pacific Complete-547
Red-547
02Pacific Quest for the Cup-107
Gold-107
Calder Contenders-3
02Parkhurst-210
Bronze-210
Gold-210
Silver-210
02Parkhurst Retro-249
Minis-249
Hopefuls-CH3
02SP Authentic-166
02SP Game Used-97
02SPx-187
02Titanium-107
Blue-107
Red-107
Retail-107
02UD Artistic Impressions-126
Gold-126
02UD Honor Roll-131
02UD Mask Collection-165
Masked Marvels-MMRM
Nation's Best-NRDM
02UD Premier Collection-46B
Gold-46
02Upper Deck-436
Exclusives-436
02Upper Deck Classic Portraits-137
02Upper Deck Rookie Update-139
02Vanguard-105
LTD-105
Prime Prospects-4
02AHL Top Prospects-29
02Rochester Americans-14
02Rochester Americans-22
03BAP Memorabilia-161
Emerald-161
Gold-161
Ruby-161
Sapphire-161
Deep in the Crease-D13
Future of the Game-FG-5
Future Wave-FW-7
Masks III-5
Masks III Gold-5
Masks III Silver-5
Masks III Autographs-M-RM
Masks III Memorabilia-5
Tandems-T-4
03BAP Ultimate Memorabilia Autographs-57
Gold-57
03BAP Ultimate Mem Auto Jerseys-57
03Bowman Future Fabrics-FF-RM
03Bowman Future Fabric Patches-RM
03Bowman Future Rivals-NML
03Bowman Future Rivals Patches-ML
03Crown Royale Jerseys-4
03Crown Royale Patches-4
03ITG Action-81
Jerseys-M137
Jerseys-M232
03ITG Used Signature Series-80
Gold-80
Autographs-RM
Autographs Gold-RM
03ITG VIP Netminders-11
03ITG VIP Sophomores-5
03O-Pee-Chee-57
03OPC Blue-57
03OPC Gold-57
03OPC Red-57
03Pacific-42
Blue-42
Red-42
03Pacific Atlantic City National-3
03Pacific Calder Contenders Entry Draft-3
03Pacific Complete-481
Red-481
03Pacific Exhibit-21
Blue Backs-21
Yellow Backs-21
03Pacific Heads-Up Jerseys-5
03Pacific Heads-Up Prime Prospects-3
03Pacific Heads-Up Prime Prospects LTD-3
03Pacific Invincible-10
Blue-10
Red-10
Retail-10
Freeze Frame-2
New Sensations-5
03Pacific Luxury Suite-27A
03Pacific Luxury Suite-27B
03Pacific Prism-16
Blue-16
Gold-16
Red-16
Rookie Revolution-3
03Pacific Supreme-12
Blue-12
Red-12
Retail-12
03Pacific Toronto Spring Expo-2
Gold-2
03Private Stock Reserve-14
Blue-14
Red-14
Retail-14
Increase Security-3
Rising Stock-3
03SPx-172
Radiance-172
Spectrum-172
03Titanium-145
Hobby Jersey Number Parallels-145
Patches-145
Retail-145
03Topps-57
Blue-57
Gold-57
Red-57
C55 Relics-TRRM
Traded Future Phenoms-FP-RM
03Upper Deck-270
All-Star Lineup-AS10
Canadian Exclusives-270
HG-270
Shooting Stars-ST-RM
UD Exclusives-270
03Upper Deck MVP-63
Gold Script-63
Silver Script-63
Canadian Exclusives-63
03Upper Deck Victory-25
Bronze-25
Gold-25
Silver-25
Freshman Flashback-FF7
03AHL Top Prospects-24
03Pacific AHL Prospects-70
Gold-70
Autographs-2
Crease Lightning-7
03Rochester Americans-14
03Toronto Star-11
04AHL All-Stars-28
04Rochester Americans-12
04Rochester Americans-27
04ITG Heroes and Prospects-38
Autographs-RM
Combos-3
Emblems-9
Emblems Gold-9
He Shoots-He Scores Prizes-32
Jersey Autographs-9
Jerseys-9
Jerseys Gold-9
Net Prospects-7
Net Prospects Gold-7
Numbers-9
Numbers Gold-9
04ITG Heroes/Prospects Toronto Expo '05-38
05Beehive Matted Materials-MMRM
05Beehive Signature Scrapbook-SSRM
05Hot Prospects-11
En Fuego-11
Red Hot-11
White Hot-11
05Panini Stickers-35
05Parkhurst-54
05Parkhurst-674
Facsimile Auto Parallel-54
Facsimile Auto Parallel-674
True Colors-TCBUF
True Colors-TCBUF
05SP Authentic Prestigious Pairings-PPMB
05SP Authentic Scripts to Success-SSRM
05SP Authentic Sign of the Times-RM
05SP Game Used Authentic Fabrics Quad-MNDB
05SP Game Used Authentic Patches Quad -MNDB
05SP Game Used SIGnificance-RM
05SP Game Used SIGnificance Gold-S-RM
05SP Game Used SIGnificance Extra-MS
05SP Game Used SIGnificance Extra Gold-MS
05SP Game Used Statscriptions-ST-RM
05The Cup-16
Gold-16
Black Rainbow-16
Emblems of Endorsement-EERM
Limited Logos-LLRM
Masterpiece Pressplates-16
Noble Numbers-NNLM
Patch Variation-P16
Patch Variation Autographs-AP16
Scripted Numbers-SNLM
Scripted Numbers Dual-DSNDM
Scripted Swatches-SSRM
Signature Patches-SPRM
05UD Artifacts Auto Facts-AF-RM
05UD Artifacts Auto Facts Blue-AF-RM
05UD Artifacts Auto Facts Copper-AF-RM
05UD Artifacts Auto Facts Pewter-AF-RM
05UD Artifacts Auto Facts Silver-AF-RM
05UD PowerPlay-11
Rainbow-11

05UD Rookie Class-26
05Ultimate Collection Endorsed Emblems-EERM
05Upper Deck-264
Jerseys-J-RM
Jerseys Series II-J2RY
Majestic Materials-MMRM
Notable Numbers-N-RM
05Upper Deck Ice-12
Rainbow-12
Fresh Ice-FIRM
Fresh Ice Glass-FIRM
Fresh Ice Glass Patches-FIPRM
Glacial Graphs-GGRM
05Upper Deck MVP-54
Gold-54
Platinum-54
05Upper Deck Rookie Update-12
05Upper Deck Trilogy Scripts-SFS-RM
05Upper Deck Victory-207
Black-207
Gold-207
05ITG Heroes and Prospects-92
Autographs-A-RMI
He Shoots-He Scores Prizes-21
Measuring Up-MU10
Measuring Up Gold-MU10
Nameplates-N-60
Nameplates Gold-N-60
Net Prospects-NP-11
Net Prospects Gold-NP-11
06Be A Player-81
Autographs-81
Signatures-RY
Signatures 10-88
Signatures 25-88
Signatures Duals-DMC
Signatures Trios-TMAR
Unmasked Warriors-UM1
Unmasked Warriors Autographs-UM1
Up Close and Personal-UC14
Up Close and Personal Autographs-UC14
06Be A Player Portraits-15
Signature Portraits-SPRM
Triple Signature Portraits-TBUF
06Beehive-90
06Beehive-227
Blue-90
Gold-90
Matte-90
Red Facsimile Signatures-90
Wood-90
5 X 7 Black and White-90
5 X 7 Dark Wood-90
Matted Materials-MMRM
Remarkable Matted Materials-MMRM
Signature Scrapbook-SSRM
06Between The Pipes-76
Aspiring-AS03
Aspiring Gold-AS03
Autographs-ARM
Complete Jersey-CJ15
Complete Jersey Gold-CJ15
Double Jerseys-DJ06
Double Jerseys Gold-DJ06
Emblems-GUE47
Emblems Gold-GUE47
Emblems Autographs-GUE47
Jerseys-GUJ47
Jerseys Gold-GUJ47
Jerseys Autographs-GUJ47
Numbers-GUN47
Numbers Gold-GUN47
Numbers Autographs-GUN47
Stick and Jersey-SJ20
Stick and Jersey Gold-SJ20
Stick and Jersey Autographs-SJ20
Stick Work-SW02
Stick Work Gold-SW02
The Mask-M07
The Mask Gold-M07
The Mask Silver-M07
The Mask Game-Used-MGU12
The Mask Game-Used Gold-MGU12
06Black Diamond-91
Black-91
Gold-91
Ruby-91
Gemography-GRM
Jerseys-JRM
Jerseys Black-JRM
Jerseys Gold-JRM
Jerseys Ruby-JRM
Jerseys Black Autographs -JRM
06Flair Showcase-14
06Flair Showcase-111
06Flair Showcase-210
Parallel-14
Parallel-111
Parallel-210
Hot Gloves-HG4
Inks-IMI
Stitches-SSRM
Wave of the Future-WF6
06Fleer-24
Tiffany-24
Fabricology-FRM
Netminders-N3
06Hot Prospects-11
Red Hot-11
White Hot-11
06ITG International Ice-147
Gold-147
Autographs-ARMI
06ITG Ultimate Memorabilia-126
Artist Proof-126
Autos-64
Autos Gold-64
Passing The Torch-15
Passing The Torch Gold-15
06McDonald's Upper Deck-4
Autographs-ARM
06O-Pee-Chee-60
06O-Pee-Chee-674
Rainbow-60
Rainbow-674
Swatches-S-RM
06Panini Stickers-28
06SP Authentic-89
06SP Authentic-152
Chirography-RM
Limited-89
Limited-152
Sign of the Times-STMI
Sign of the Times Duals-STGR
Sign of the Times Triples-ST3DBM
06SP Game Used-11
Gold-11
Rainbow-11
Authentic Fabrics Dual-AF2DM
Authentic Fabrics Dual Patches-AF2DM
Authentic Fabrics Triple-AF3BUF
Authentic Fabrics Triple Patches-AF3BUF
Autographs-11
By The Letter-BLRM
Inked Sweaters-ISMI
Inked Sweaters Patches-ISMI
Inked Sweaters Dual-IS2DM
Inked Sweaters Dual Patches-IS2DM
Letter Marks-LMRY
SIGnificance-SRM
06SPx-10
Spectrum-10
SPxcitement-X12
SPxcitement Spectrum-X12
06The Cup-12
Autographed Foundations-CQRM
Autographed Foundations Patches-CQRM
Autographed NHL Shields Duals-DASMB
Autographed NHL Shields Duals-DASMD
Autographed Patches-12
Black Rainbow-12
Foundations-CQRM
Foundations Patches-CQRM
Enshrinements-ERM
Gold-12
Gold Patches-12
Honorable Numbers-HNRM
Jerseys-12
Limited Logos-LLRM
Masterpiece Pressplates-12
Scripted Swatches-SSRM
Signature Patches-SPRM
06UD Artifacts-88
06UD Artifacts-156
Blue-88
Blue-156
Gold-88
Gold-156
Radiance-88
Radiance-156
Autographed Radiance Parallel-88
Autographed Radiance Parallel-156
Red-88
Red-156
Auto-Facts-AFRY
Auto-Facts Gold-AFRY
Frozen Artifacts-FARM
Frozen Artifacts Black-FARM
Frozen Artifacts Blue-FARM
Frozen Artifacts Platinum-FARM
Frozen Artifacts Red-FARM
Frozen Artifacts Autographed Black-FARM
Frozen Artifacts Patches Blue-FARM
Frozen Artifacts Patches Gold-FARM
Frozen Artifacts Patches Red-FARM
Tundra Tandems-TTMB
Tundra Tandems Black-TTMB
Tundra Tandems Blue-TTMB
Tundra Tandems Gold-TTMB
Tundra Tandems Red-TTMB
Tundra Tandems Dual Patches Red-TTMB
06UD Biography of a Season-BOS6
06UD Mini Jersey Collection-11
06UD Powerplay-12
Impact Rainbow-12
Goal Robbers-GR3
Specialists-SRM
Specialists Patches-PRM
06Ultimate Collection-8
Autographed Jerseys-AJ-RM
Autographed Patches-AJ-RM
Premium Patches-PS-RM
Premium Swatches-PS-RM
Signatures-US-RM
06Ultra-22
Gold Medallion-22
Ice Medallion-22
Difference Makers-DM4
06Upper Deck Arena Giveaways-BUF1
06Upper Deck-21
Exclusives Parallel-21
High Gloss Parallel-21
Game Dated Moments-GD11
Game Jerseys-JRM
Game Patches-PRM
Hometown Heroes-HH31
Masterpieces-21
06Upper Deck MVP-32
Gold Script-32
Super Script-32
Clutch Performers-CP9
Last Line of Defense-LL9
06Upper Deck Ovation-107
06Upper Deck Sweet Shot-13
Signature Shots/Saves-SSRM
Signature Shots/Saves Ice Signings-SSIRM
Signature Shots/Saves Sticks-SSSRM
Signature Sticks-STRY
Sweet Stitches-SSRM
Sweet Stitches Duals-SSRM
Sweet Stitches Triples-SSRM
06Upper Deck Trilogy-11
Combo Clearcut Autographs-C2MV
Honorary Scripted Patches-HSPRM
Honorary Scripted Swatches-HSSRM
Honorary Swatches-HSRM
Ice Scripts-ISRY
Scripts-TSMI
06Upper Deck Victory-21
06Upper Deck Victory Black-21
06Upper Deck Victory Gold-21
06Upper Deck Victory Next In Line-NL10
06Upper Deck Victory Oversize Cards-RM
06ITG Heroes and Prospects Complete AHL Logos-AHL07
06ITG Heroes and Prospects Complete Jerseys-CJ10
06ITG Heroes and Prospects Complete Jerseys Gold-CJ10
06ITG Heroes and Prospects Making The Bigs-MTB04
06ITG Heroes and Prospects Making The Bigs Gold-MTB04
06ITG Heroes and Prospects Net Prospects-NPR06
06ITG Heroes and Prospects Net Prospects Gold-NPR06
06ITG Heroes and Prospects Quad Emblems-QE04
06ITG Heroes and Prospects Quad Emblems Gold-QE04
06ITG Heroes and Prospects Sticks and Jerseys-SJ09
06ITG Heroes and Prospects Sticks and Jerseys Gold-SJ09
07Upper Deck Ovation-95
07Upper Deck Victory-33
Black-33
Gold-33
GameBreakers-GB24
Oversize Cards-OS10
Stars on Ice-SI4

Miller, Ryan FWD
02Topeka Scarecrows-14

Miller, Sam
03Port Huron Beacons-17

Miller, Scott
92Windsor Spitfires-23

Miller, Stephen
04Sudbury Wolves-13
06Sudbury Wolves-18

Miller, T.J.
04South Surrey Eagles-15
04Surrey Eagles-13
04Surrey Eagles-13
05Penticton Vees-12

Miller, Todd
95Slapshot-343
95Sarnia Sting-13
96Owen Sound Platers-23

Miller, Tom
72O-Pee-Chee-32
72Sargent Promotions Stamps-137
72Topps-76
73O-Pee-Chee-249

Miller, Tyrone
00UK Guildford Flames-17

Miller, Warren
81O-Pee-Chee-130
81Topps-E84
82O-Pee-Chee-127
82Post Cereal-7
82Whalers Junior Hartford Courant-13

Millette, Andre
88Richelieu Riverains-18

Milley, Norm
94Quebec Pee-Wee Tournament-1025
96Sudbury Wolves-14
96Sudbury Wolves Police-17
97Upper Deck-414
97Sudbury Wolves Police-7
98Sudbury Wolves-5
98Bowman CHL-38
98Bowman CHL-129
Golden Anniversary-38
Golden Anniversary-129
OPC International-38
OPC International-129
Autographs Blue-A16
Autographs Gold-A16
Autographs Silver-A16
98Bowman Chrome CHL-38
98Bowman Chrome CHL-129
Golden Anniversary-38
Golden Anniversary-129
Golden Anniversary Refractors-38
Golden Anniversary Refractors-129
OPC International-38
OPC International-129
OPC International Refractors-38
OPC International Refractors-129
Refractors-38
Refractors-129
99Black Diamond-109
Diamond Cut-109
Final Cut-109
99Upper Deck-320
Exclusives-320
Exclusives 1 of 1-320
99Upper Deck Gold Reserve-320
99Upper Deck Ovation-66
Standing Ovation-66
99Sudbury Wolves-9
99Bowman CHL-126
Gold-126
OPC International-126
00Rochester Americans-16
02O-Pee-Chee-295
02O-Pee-Chee Premier Blue Parallel-295
02O-Pee-Chee Premier Red Parallel-295
02O-Pee-Chee Factory Set-295
02Topps-295
OPC Blue Parallel-295
OPC Red Parallel-295
Factory Set-295
02Rochester Americans-15
03Rochester Americans-16
04Rochester Americans-13
05Springfield Falcons-18
06Springfield Falcons-17

Millham, Mike
92Wheeling Thunderbirds-10

Millie, Les
93UK Sheffield Steelers-12
94UK Sheffield Steelers-12
95UK Sheffield Steelers-12

Millier, Pierre
84Chicoutimi Sagueneens-19

Milliken, Rob
92British Columbia JHL-232
97Bakersfield Fog-10
99Asheville Smoke-10

Mills, Craig
95Bowman-99
All-Foil-99
95Donruss-292
Elite World Juniors-19
95Parkhurst International-497
Emerald Ice-497
95Slapshot-52
95Upper Deck-527
Electric Ice-527
Electric Ice Gold-527
97SP Authentic-176
97Upper Deck-251
97Indianapolis Ice-18
98Portland Pirates-20
01St. John's Maple Leafs-15
02St. John's Maple Leafs Aliant-6

Mills, David
01Bossier-Shreveport Mudbugs-13

Mills, Dylan
97Minnesota Golden Gophers-18
98Minnesota Golden Gophers-5
99Minnesota Golden Gophers-14
00Minnesota Golden Gophers-14
01Quad-City Mallards-15
04Bakersfield Condors-13

Mills, Kelly
90Richmond Renegades-6

Mills, Mark
95Cincinnati Cyclones-22
97Cincinnati Cyclones-24
98Cincinnati Cyclones-25
98Cincinnati Cyclones 2-27
99Cincinnati Cyclones-24
00Cincinnati Cyclones-24

Mills, Mike
03Sudbury Wolves-18
04Sudbury Wolves-18
05Sudbury Wolves-15

Milne, Andrew
96Swift Current Broncos-22
97Swift Current Broncos-25

Milo, Dusan
02Slovakian Kvarteto-8
02Swedish SHL-241
Parallel-241
03Swedish Elite-101
Silver-101
06German DEL-136
New Arrivals-NA6

Milo, Justin
04Sioux Falls Stampede-4-1
05Lincoln Stars Update Traded-3T

Milot, Jean-Claude
05Chicoutimi Sagueneens-18
05PEI Rocket-18

Milroy, Duncan
99Swift Current Broncos-10
00Swift Current Broncos-12
00UD CHL Prospects-67
00UD CHL Prospects-94
01Swift Current Broncos-20
01UD Prospects-37
Autographs-A-DM
Jersey Autographs-S-DM
Jerseys-J-DM
Jerseys-C-BD
Jerseys-C-PM
Jerseys-C-SM
Jerseys-C-WM
Jerseys Gold-J-DM
Jerseys Gold-C-BD
Jerseys Gold-C-PM
Jerseys Gold-C-SM
Jerseys Gold-C-WM
02Kootenay Ice-2
04Hamilton Bulldogs-20
04ITG Heroes and Prospects-9
Autographs-DM
04ITG Heroes/Prospects Toronto Expo '05-9
04ITG Heroes/Prospects Expo Heroes/Pros-9
05Hamilton Bulldogs-18
06Hamilton Bulldogs-21
07Upper Deck Victory-238
Black-238
Gold-238

Milton, Andrew
93Quebec Pee-Wee Tournament-1199

Milton, Kjell-Rune
67Swedish Hockey-208
69Swedish Hockey-192
70Finnish Jaakiekko-32
70Swedish Hockey-86
70Swedish Hockey-279
70Swedish Masterserien-43
70Swedish Masterserien-109
71Finnish Suomi Stickers-52
71Swedish Hockey-8
71Swedish Hockey-179
72Finnish Semic World Championship-62
72Swedish Stickers-6
72Swedish Stickers-169
72Swedish Semic World Championship-62
73Swedish Stickers-21
73Swedish Stickers-143
74Finnish Typotor-98
74Swedish Stickers-22
74Swedish Stickers-176
74Swedish Semic World Champ Stickers-16

Minakov, Oleg
02Russian Hockey League-33
03Russian Hockey League-19

Minard, Chris
98Owen Sound Platers-9
99Owen Sound Platers-30

Minard, Craig
02Bossier-Shreveport Mudbugs-13
03Bossier-Shreveport Mudbugs-14
05Bossier-Shreveport Mudbugs-12

Minard, Mike
95Slapshot-56
96Wheeling Nailers-15
96Wheeling Nailers Photo Pack-20
97New Orleans Brass-14
99Hamilton Bulldogs-1
00BAP Memorabilia-21
Emerald-21
Ruby-21
Sapphire-21
Promos-21
00BAP Mem Chicago Sportsfest Copper-21
00BAP Memorabilia Chicago Sportsfest Blue-21
00BAP Memorabilia Chicago Sportsfest Gold-21
00BAP Memorabilia Chicago Sportsfest Ruby-21
00BAP Memorabilia Chicago Sun-Times Ruby-21
00BAP Memorabilia Chicago Sun-Times Gold-21
00BAP Mem Chicago Sun-Times Sapphire-21
00BAP Mem Toronto Fall Expo Copper-21
00BAP Memorabilia Toronto Fall Expo Gold-21
00BAP Memorabilia Toronto Fall Expo Ruby-21
00SPx-96
Spectrum-96
00Upper Deck-184
Exclusives Tier 1-184
Exclusives Tier 2-184
00St. John's Maple Leafs-18
01St. John's Maple Leafs-16
03Memphis RiverKings-13

Minchella, Jamie
00Kitchener Rangers-18

Mindel, Chuck
99Johnstown Chiefs-16

Mindjimba, Antoine
03Memphis RiverKings-9
93San Diego Gulls-17
94French National Team-19
99Memphis RiverKings All-Time-5

Mineault, Alexandre
04Quebec Remparts-22
05Quebec Remparts-10
05Quebec Remparts Signature Series-10
06Quebec Remparts-12

Minella, Christian
04Sioux City Musketeers-18

Miner, John
82Regina Pats-5
83Regina Pats-5
85Nova Scotia Oilers-14
88Oilers Tenth Anniversary-30
93Swiss HNL-270
95Swiss HNL-167
96Swiss HNL-61
98German DEL-97
99German DEL-121
00German DEL-139
01German Upper Deck-144
02Swiss HNL-403
02Swiss HNL-404
03German DEL-25
04German Augsburg Panthers Postcards-21
04German DEL-35
All-Stars-AS8

Minetti, Tino
71Finnish Suomi Stickers-349

Minge, Leszek
89Swedish Semic World Champ Stickers-147

Minichiello, Mike
94Dubuque Fighting Saints-19

Ministr, Milan
97Czech APS Extraliga-121
99Czech Score Blue 2000-125
99Czech Score Red Ice 2000-125
01Czech OFS-90
02Czech OFS Plus-34
05Czech HC Znojmo-8

Mink, Graham
03ITG VIP Rookie Debut-115
03Parkhurst Rookie-74
03Upper Deck Rookie Update-106
03Pacific AHL Prospects-65
Gold-65
04Portland Pirates-10
05Hershey Bears-13
06ITG Heroes and Prospects Calder Cup Champions-CC06

Mink, Mark
02Michigan Wolverines-18

Minkhorst, Bill
95Slapshot-126

Minkkila, Timo
71Finnish Suomi Stickers-331

Minnis, Mike
92British Columbia JHL-83

Minor, Doug
89Sault Ste. Marie Greyhounds-9
907th Inn. Sketch OHL-188

Minor, Gerald
80Canucks Silverwood Dairies-18
80Canucks Team Issue-17
80Pepsi-Cola Caps-115
81Canucks Team Issue-16
81O-Pee-Chee-342
82Canucks Team Issue-15
82O-Pee-Chee-352

Mintenko, Kurtis
94Thunder Bay Flyers-15

Mio, Ed
79Oilers Postcards-18A
79Oilers Postcards-18B
80O-Pee-Chee-341
80Pepsi-Cola Caps-35
81O-Pee-Chee-119
81O-Pee-Chee Stickers-216
82O-Pee-Chee-230
82O-Pee-Chee Stickers-142
82Topps Stickers-142
83O-Pee-Chee-127
83O-Pee-Chee Stickers-209
83Topps Stickers-209
84O-Pee-Chee-61
84Topps-45
88Oilers Tenth Anniversary-51
91Upper Deck-639
French-639
04ITG Franchises Canadian-32
Autographs-EM

Mior, Ryan
03P.E.I. Rocket-17
04P.E.I. Rocket-19
05PEI Rocket-1
06Gatineau Olympiques-27
06PEI Rocket-3

Mirabile, Steve
92Hampton Roads Admirals-7

Miracolo, Matt
93Quebec Pee-Wee Tournament-1739

Mirao, Silverio
91British Columbia JHL-39
92British Columbia JHL-46

Mirasty, Jon
00Prince Albert Raiders-16
03Bakersfield Condors-17
03ECHL Update RBI Sports-58

Mireau, Brent
84Brandon Wheat Kings-2
85Brandon Wheat Kings-2

Mirnov, Igor
98Quebec Pee Wee Tournament-1032
01Russian Dynamo Moscow-19
02Russian Future Stars-11
02Russian SL-10
02Russian Young Lions-3
03Russian Hockey League-32
04Russian Moscow Dynamo-20

Mironov, Boris
91Upper Deck-662
French-662
91Upper Deck Czech World Juniors-23
92Russian Stars Red Ace-21
92Russian Stars Red Ace-15
92Russian Tri-Globe From Russia With Puck-21
92Russian Tri-Globe From Russia With Puck-22
92Classic-44
Gold-44
92Classic Four-Sport *-185
Gold-185
Autographs-185A
93Donruss-384
93Donruss-429
Rated Rookies-9
93Jets Readers Club-13
93Jets Ruffles-16
93Leaf-364
93OPC Premier-394
Gold-394
93Parkhurst-264
Emerald Ice-264
93PowerPlay-474
Rookie Standouts-6
93Score-607
Gold-607
Canadian-607
Canadian Gold-607
93Stadium Club-338
Members Only Master Set-338
First Day Issue-338
93Topps/OPC Premier-394
Gold-394
93Ultra-454
Wave of the Future-8
93Upper Deck-492
SP-176
94Canada Games NHL POGS-102
94Donruss-218
94Leaf-179
Gold Rookies-8
94OPC Premier-288
94O-Pee-Chee Finest Inserts-17
94OPC Premier Special Effects-288
94Parkhurst SE-SE57
Gold-SE57
94Pinnacle-188
Artist's Proofs-188
Rink Collection-188
94Score-255
Gold-255
Platinum-255
94Stadium Club-85
Members Only Master Set-85
First Day Issue-85
Super Team Winner Cards-85
94Topps/OPC Premier-288
Special Effects-288
94Ultra-73
All-Rookies-5
All-Rookies Parallel-5
94Upper Deck-172
Electric Ice-172
95Parkhurst International-75
Emerald Ice-75
95Playoff One on One-150
95Ultra-239
96Be A Player-88
Autographs-88
Autographs Silver-88
96Flair-34
Blue Ice-34
96Oilers Postcards-2
97Pacific Invincible NHL Regime-81
97Pacific Omega-94
Copper-94
Dark Gray-94
Emerald Green-94
Gold-94
Ice Blue-94
97Panini Stickers-216
97Upper Deck-276
98Aurora-74
98Be A Player-51
Press Release-51
98BAP Gold-51
98BAP Autographs-51
98BAP Autographs Gold-51
98BAP Tampa Bay All Star Game-51
98Finest-60
No Protectors-60
No Protectors Refractors-60
Refractors-60
98Kraft Peanut Butter-6
98Pacific-216
Ice Blue-216
Red-216
98Panini Stickers-192
98Paramount-90
Copper-90
Emerald Green-90
Holo-Electric-90
Ice Blue-90
Silver-90
98UD Choice-83
98UD Choice Preview-83
98UD Choice Prime Choice Reserve-83
98UD Choice Reserve-83
98Upper Deck-273
Exclusives-273
Exclusives 1 of 1-273
Gold Reserve-273
99BAP Memorabilia-16
Gold-16
Silver-16
99Blackhawks Chicago Sun-Times-7
99Blackhawks Lineup Cards-7
99Pacific-94
Copper-94
Emerald Green-94
Gold-94
Ice Blue-94
Premiere Date-94
Red-94
99Paramount-57
Copper-57
Emerald-57
Gold-57
Holographic Emerald-57
Holographic Gold-57
Holographic Silver-57
Ice Blue-57
Premiere Date-57
Red-57
Silver-57
00BAP Memorabilia-84
Emerald-84
Ruby-84
Sapphire-84
Promos-84
00BAP Mem Chicago Sportsfest Copper-84
00BAP Memorabilia Chicago Sportsfest Blue-84
00BAP Memorabilia Chicago Sportsfest Gold-84
00BAP Memorabilia Chicago Sportsfest Ruby-84
00BAP Memorabilia Chicago Sun-Times Ruby-84
00BAP Memorabilia Chicago Sun-Times Gold-84
00BAP Mem Chicago Sun-Times Sapphire-84
00BAP Mem Toronto Fall Expo Copper-84
00BAP Memorabilia Toronto Fall Expo Gold-84
00BAP Memorabilia Toronto Fall Expo Ruby-84
00BAP Parkhurst 2000-P35
00BAP Signature Series-187
Emerald-187
Ruby-187
Sapphire-187
Autographs-118
Autographs Gold-118
00BAP Ultimate Memorabilia Teammates-TM18
00Pacific-99
Copper-99
Gold-99
Ice Blue-99
Premiere Date-99
00Panini Stickers-124
00Paramount-51
Copper-51
Gold-51
Holo-Gold-51
Holo-Silver-51
Ice Blue-51
Premiere Date-51
00Titanium Game Gear-72
00Titanium Game Gear Patches-72
00Titanium Draft Day Edition-18
Patches-18
00Upper Deck-268
Exclusives Tier 1-268
Exclusives Tier 2-268
00Upper Deck Victory-54
00Upper Deck Vintage-78
01BAP Memorabilia-148
Emerald-148
Ruby-148
Sapphire-148
01BAP Signature Series-179
Autographs-179
Autographs Gold-179
01Pacific Heads-Up Quad Jerseys-7
01Private Stock Game Gear-23
01Private Stock Game Gear Patches-23
01Titanium Double-Sided Jerseys-8
01Upper Deck-42
Exclusives-42
01Vanguard Memorabilia-7
02BAP Sig Series Auto Buybacks 1998-51
02BAP Sig Series Auto Buybacks 2000-118
02BAP Sig Series Auto Buybacks 2001-179
02Pacific-79
Blue-79
Red-79
02Pacific Complete-262
Red-262
02Parkhurst Retro-190
Minis-190
03ITG Action-316
03Parkhurst Original Six New York-8
03Rangers Team Issue-17
04Pacific-178
Blue-178
Red-178

Mironov, Dmitri
90O-Pee-Chee-514
91O-Pee-Chee-515
91O-Pee-Chee Inserts-23R
91Parkhurst-391
French-391
91Topps-515
91Finnish Semic World Champ Stickers-84
91Swedish Semic World Champ Stickers-84
91Star Pics-58
92Maple Leafs Kodak-17
92O-Pee-Chee-71
92Parkhurst-417
Emerald Ice-417
92Pinnacle-247
92Pinnacle-419
French-247
French-419
92Score-468
Canadian-468
92Stadium Club-5
92Topps-144
Gold-144G
92Ultra-422
Imports-15
92Upper Deck-83
92Finnish Semic-107
92Russian Stars Red Ace-22
92Russian Stars Red Ace-22
93Maple Leafs Score Black's-8
93OPC Premier-419
Gold-419
93Parkhurst-477
Emerald Ice-477
93PowerPlay-245
93Score-209
Canadian-209
93Topps/OPC Premier-419
Gold-419
93Ultra-127
93Upper Deck-513
94Be A Player Signature Cards-19
94Canada Games NHL POGS-241
94Donruss-58
94Flair-183
94Fleer-217
94Leaf-254
94Maple Leafs Gangsters-13
94Maple Leafs Kodak-20
94Maple Leafs Pin-up Posters-20
94Maple Leafs Postcards-3
94OPC Premier-165
Special Effects-165
94Parkhurst-232
Gold-232
94Pinnacle-229
Artist's Proofs-229
Rink Collection-229
94SP-120
Die Cuts-120
94Topps/OPC Premier-165
Special Effects-165
94Ultra-218
94Upper Deck-222
Electric Ice-222
SP Inserts-SP79
SP Inserts Die Cuts-SP79
95Canada Games NHL POGS-219
95Collector's Choice-125
Player's Club-125
Player's Club Platinum-125
95Emotion-139
95Leaf-96
95Panini Stickers-67
95Parkhurst International-437
Emerald Ice-437
95Penguins Foodland-25
95Playoff One on One-189
95Score-180
Black Ice Artist's Proofs-180
Black Ice-180
95Ultra-290
95Upper Deck-322
Electric Ice-322
Electric Ice Gold-322
96Collector's Choice-221
96Ducks Team Issue-7
96Topps Picks-167
OPC Inserts-167
96Upper Deck-138
96Swedish Semic Wien-133
97Be A Player-170
Autographs-170
Autographs Die-Cuts-170
Autographs Prismatic Die-Cuts-170
97Collector's Choice-3
97Donruss-130
Press Proofs Silver-130
Press Proofs Gold-130
97Pacific-234
Copper-234
Emerald Green-234
Ice Blue-234
Red-234
Silver-234
97Pacific Omega-4
Copper-4
Dark Gray-4
Emerald Green-4
Gold-4
Ice Blue-4
97Panini Stickers-182
97Paramount-4
Copper-4
Dark Grey-4
Emerald Green-4
Ice Blue-4
Red-4
Silver-4
97Pinnacle-125
Press Plates Back Black-125
Press Plates Back Cyan-125
Press Plates Back Magenta-125
Press Plates Back Yellow-125
Press Plates Front Black-125
Press Plates Front Cyan-125
Press Plates Front Magenta-125
Press Plates Front Yellow-125
97Revolution-3
Copper-3
Emerald-3
Ice Blue-3
Silver-3
97Score-240
97Score Mighty Ducks-4
Platinum-4
Premier-4
97Upper Deck-213
98Be A Player-295
Press Release-295
98BAP Gold-295
98BAP Autographs-295
98BAP Autographs Gold-295
98Pacific-202
Ice Blue-202
Red-202
98SPx Finite-31
Radiance-31
Spectrum-31
98Upper Deck-385
Exclusives-385
Exclusives 1 of 1-385
Gold Reserve-385
99BAP Memorabilia-27
Gold-27
Silver-27
99O-Pee-Chee-228
99O-Pee-Chee Chrome-228
99O-Pee-Chee Chrome Refractors-228
99Panini Stickers-165
99Topps/OPC-228
99Topps/OPC Chrome-228
Refractors-228
99Upper Deck MVP SC Edition-190
Gold Script-190
Silver Script-190
Super Script-190
00Upper Deck NHLPA-PA89
02BAP Sig Series Auto Buybacks 1998-295

Mironovics, Aigars
97Tucson Gila Monsters-10
98San Angelo Outlaws-12
00Indianapolis Ice-16

Miroshnikov, Alexei
99Russian Hockey League-159

Misal, Peter
04Slovakian Poprad Team Set-22

Mischer, Bodo
94German First League-449

Mischler, Graig
92Quebec Pee-Wee Tournament-1837
01Cleveland Barons-15
02Cleveland Barons-15
03Reading Royals-15
03Reading Royals RBI Sports-296
04Reading Royals-11

Misek, Petr
82Swedish Semic VM Stickers-85

Mishakov, Yevgeny
69Russian National Team Postcards-16
69Swedish Hockey-10
70Finnish Jaakiekko-9
70Russian National Team Postcards-12
70Swedish Hockey-327
70Swedish Masterserien-21
70Swedish Masterserien-64
71Finnish Suomi Stickers-11
71Swedish Hockey-38
72Finnish Jaakiekko-30
72Finnish Hellas-71
72Finnish Semic World Championship-12
72Swedish Semic World Championship-12
73Swedish Stickers-104
74Swedish Semic World Champ Stickers-48
91Future Trends Canada '72-75

Misharin, Georgi
03Russian Under-18 Team-14
03Saginaw Spirit-14

Mishukov, Igor
92Norwegian Elite Series-81

Misita, Lorne
04Columbus Cottonmouths-12

Miskolczi, Ted
897th Inn. Sketch OHL-78
907th Inn. Sketch OHL-290
91Johnstown Chiefs-14

94Brantford Smoke-18
Miskovich, Aaron
97Minnesota Golden Gophers-22
98Minnesota Golden Gophers-26
99Minnesota Golden Gophers-15
00Minnesota Golden Gophers-15
01Quad-City Mallards-16
02Lexington Men O'War-20
Miskovich, Josh
04Minnesota-Duluth Bulldogs-16
Mistrik, Stanislav
95Slovakian-Quebec Pee-Wee Tournament-19
Miszuk, John
680-Pee-Chee-93
68Shirriff Coins-123
68Topps-93
690-Pee-Chee-124
Four-in-One-3
69Topps-124
760-Pee-Chee WHA-57
Mitani, Darcy
92North Dakota Fighting Sioux-21
96Charlotte Checkers-11
Mitchell, Bobby-Chad
01Moose Jaw Warriors-5
03Laredo Bucks-13
Mitchell, Dale
06Oshawa Generals-2
Mitchell, Dan
95Spokane Chiefs-29
96Spokane Chiefs-29
97Spokane Chiefs-30
99Spokane Chiefs-17
00Spokane Chiefs-19
01Spokane Chiefs-25
02Spokane Chiefs-28
Mitchell, Daryll
91Nashville Knights-5
Mitchell, Dave
92Western Michigan Broncos-19
92Windsor Spitfires-30
93Western Michigan Broncos-22
00Fresno Falcons-12
01Fresno Falcons-11
Mitchell, David
06Richmond Renegades-10
Mitchell, Greg
91Arizona Icecats-14
92Arizona Icecats-11
93Arizona Icecats-3
93Quebec Pee-Wee Tournament-691
94Arizona Icecats-7
Mitchell, Herbie
24Anonymous NHL-38
24Anonymous NHL-39
24C144 Champ's Cigarettes-40
24V145-2-29
Mitchell, Jeff
93Detroit Jr. Red Wings-14
94Finest-121
Super Team Winners-121
Refractors-121
94Leaf Limited World Juniors USA-8
94SP-195
Die Cuts-195
94Detroit Jr. Red Wings-15
95Classic-84
95Slapshot Memorial Cup-89
96Michigan K-Wings-13
98Michigan K-Wings-9
99ECHL All-Star Northern Conference-14
Mitchell, John
01Plymouth Whalers-14
02Plymouth Whalers-4
03Plymouth Whalers-8
06Toronto Marlies-17
Mitchell, Keith
02Arizona Icecats-15
03Arizona Icecats-17
04Arizona Icecats-14
Mitchell, Kevin
97Guelph Storm-5
98Guelph Storm-4
99Guelph Storm-4
99Bowman CHL-158
Gold-158
OPC International-158
01Louisiana Ice Gators-16
02Louisiana Ice Gators-13
03Houston Aeros-15
03Louisiana Ice Gators-16
04German DEL-177
Mitchell, Lee
04UK U-20 Team-14
05UK Hull Stingrays-12
Mitchell, Red
34Beehive Group I Photos-70
Mitchell, Roy
86Portland Winter Hawks-15
87Portland Winter Hawks-16
88Portland Winter Hawks-16
89ProCards AHL-192
90ProCards AHL/IHL-65
91ProCards-144
99Idaho Steelheads-8
00Idaho Steelheads-14
Mitchell, Tote
24Crescent Falcon-Tigers-8
Mitchell, Willie
99Albany River Rats-20
00BAP Memorabilia-174
Emerald-174
Ruby-174
Sapphire-174
Promos-174
00BAP Mem Chicago Sportsfest Copper-174
00BAP Memorabilia Chicago Sportsfest Blue-174
00BAP Memorabilia Chicago Sportsfest Gold-174
00BAP Memorabilia Chicago Sportsfest Ruby-174
00BAP Memorabilia Chicago Sun-Times Ruby-174
00BAP Memorabilia Chicago Sun-Times Gold-174
00BAP Mem Chicago Sun-Times Sapphire-174
00BAP Mem Toronto Fall Expo Copper-174
00BAP Memorabilia Toronto Fall Expo Gold-174
00BAP Memorabilia Toronto Fall Expo Ruby-174
000-Pee-Chee-320
000-Pee-Chee Parallel-320
00Pacific-246
Copper-246
Gold-246
Ice Blue-246
Premiere Date-246
00SPx-100
Spectrum-100
00Topps/OPC-320
Parallel-320
00Topps Chrome-215
OPC Refractors-215
Refractors-215
00UD Pros and Prospects-111
00UD Reserve-103
00Upper Deck-188
Exclusives Tier 1-188
Exclusives Tier 2-188
00Upper Deck MVP-197
First Stars-197
Second Stars-197
Third Stars-197
00Upper Deck Vintage-384
00Albany River Rats-15
01BAP Memorabilia-207
Emerald-207
Ruby-207
Sapphire-207
01BAP Signature Series-62
Autographs-62
Autographs Gold-62
01Parkhurst-125
01Wild Crime Prevention-17
01Wild Team Issue-3
02BAP Sig Series Auto Buybacks 2001-62
03Black Diamond-131
Black-131
Green-131
Red-131
03ITG Action-241
03NHL Sticker Collection-249
03Pacific Complete-86
Red-86
03Upper Deck-97
Canadian Exclusives-97
HG-97
03Upper Deck MVP-215
Gold Script-215
Silver Script-215
Canadian Exclusives-215
03Wild Law Enforcement Cards-5
05Panini Stickers-300
05Parkhurst-154
Facsimile Auto Parallel-245
Facsimile Auto Parallel-529
06Canucks Postcards-13
06Fleer-193
Tiffany-193
06Gatorade-89
060-Pee-Chee-480
Rainbow-480
06Upper Deck-437
Exclusives Parallel-437
High Gloss Parallel-437
Masterpieces-437
Mitew, Thomas
95German DEL-47
04German Berlin Eisbarens 50th Anniv-33
Mitroshkin, Konstantin
99Russian Hockey League-122
00Russian Hockey League-20
Mitrovic, Savo
92Anaheim Bullfrogs RHI-11
93Anaheim Bullfrogs RHI-14
93Greensboro Monarchs-8
94Anaheim Bullfrogs RHI-13
95Anaheim Bullfrogs RHI-6
98Phoenix Mustangs-16
99Odessa Jackalopes-17
Mitsou, Pierre
00Ottawa 67's-6
01Ottawa 67's-7
02Ottawa 67's-6
03Ottawa 67's-17
Mittelsteadt, Joey
87Portland Winter Hawks-17
88Portland Winter Hawks-17
89Kamloops Blazers-16
907th Inn. Sketch WHL-295
907th Inn. Sketch Memorial Cup-17
92Dallas Freeze-13
93Dallas Freeze-13
96Louisiana Ice Gators II-11
Mitterfellner, Vitus
95German DEL-370
Mittleholt, Craig
96Anchorage Aces-9
Mitton, Paul
89Peterborough Petes-107
897th Inn. Sketch OHL-107
907th Inn. Sketch OHL-110
94Brantford Smoke-12
Mix, Holger
94German DEL-42
95German DEL-39
04German Berlin Eisbarens 50th Anniv-30
Mix, Tom
92British Columbia JHL-74
Miyazoe, Takeshi
93Quebec Pee-Wee Tournament-157
Mizera, Vladimir
99Czech Score Blue 2000-119
99Czech Score Red Ice 2000-119
Mizerek, Josh
95North Iowa Huskies-20
02Lexington Men O'War-24
03Louisiana Ice Gators-17
05Rockford Ice Hogs-21
Mizzi, Gregg
00Barrie Colts-17
Mizzi, Preston
00Sarnia Sting-18
03Atlantic City Boardwalk Bullies-14
04Atlantic City Boardwalk Bullies Kinko's-21
04Reading Royals-16
05Rockford Ice Hogs-9
06Rockford IceHogs -17
Mjelleli, Marty
04St. Cloud State Huskies-21
05St. Cloud State Huskies-15
06St. Cloud State Huskies-20
Mjoberg, Lars
69Swedish Hockey-158
70Swedish Hockey-116
71Swedish Hockey-206
72Swedish Stickers-192
Mlinchenko, Evgeni
98Russian Hockey League-80
Moberg, Dan
82Victoria Cougars-17
Moberg, Larry
96Roanoke Express-35
Mobile, R.A.
99Sudbury Wolves-23
Moborg, Andreas
01Trenton Titans-2-6
02UK Coventry Blaze-6
05UK Coventry Blaze-5
Mocek, David
03Czech OFS Plus-349
Mocek, Petr
02Czech OFS Plus-221
Mocgut, Russell
93Quebec Pee-Wee Tournament-1579
Mock, Trevor
04Victoriaville Tigres-22
05Victoriaville Tigres-19
Mockl, Andreas
94German First League-91
Modano, Mike
90Bowman-188
Tiffany-188
90Kraft-34
900-Pee-Chee-348
900-Pee-Chee Box Bottoms-F
90OPC Premier-74
90Panini Stickers-253
90Panini Stickers-340
90Pro Set-142
90Score-120
90Score-327
Canadian-120
Canadian-327
90Score Hottest/Rising Stars-97
90Score Young Superstars-20
90Topps-348
Tiffany-348
90Topps Box Bottoms-F
90Upper Deck-46
90Upper Deck-346
French-46
French-346
91Pro Set Platinum-55
91Pro Set Platinum-143
91Bowman-125
91Bowman-415
91Gillette-15
91Kraft-48
910-Pee-Chee-367
91Panini Stickers-116
91Parkhurst-81
French-81
91Pinnacle-5
French-5
91Pro Set-105
French-105
91Score American-247
91Score American-423
91Score Canadian Bilingual-313
91Score Canadian Bilingual-467
91Score Canadian English-313
91Score Canadian English-467
91Score Kellogg's-4
91Score Young Superstars-35
91Stadium Club-187
91Topps-367
91Upper Deck-32
91Upper Deck-160
French-32
French-160
91Finnish Semic World Champ Stickers-141
91Swedish Semic World Champ Stickers-141
92Bowman-151
920-Pee-Chee-313
92Panini Stickers-91
92Panini Stickers French-91
92Parkhurst-75
Emerald Ice-75
92Pinnacle-155
92Pinnacle-260
French-155
French 260
Team 2000-2
Team 2000 French-2
92Pro Set-76
Gold Team Leaders-7
92Score-139
92Score-427
Canadian-139
Canadian-427
USA Greats-5
Young Superstars-40
92Seasons Patches-65
92Stadium Club-4
92Topps-441
Gold-441G
92Ultra-96
92Upper Deck-9
92Upper Deck-305
92Finnish Semic-157
93Donruss-76
Special Print-F
93Leaf-202
93McDonald's Upper Deck-10
93OPC Premier-46
Gold-46
93Panini Stickers-X
93Parkhurst-49
Emerald Ice-49
First Overall-F6
93Pinnacle-40
Canadian-40
All-Stars-28
All-Stars Canadian-28
Team 2001-17
Team 2001 Canadian-17
93PowerPlay-63
Slapshot Artists-8
93Score-142
Canadian-142
Franchise-5
93Stadium Club-130
Members Only Master Set-130
OPC-130
First Day Issue-130
First Day Issue OPC-130
All-Stars-21
All-Stars Members Only-21
All-Stars OPC-21
93Topps/OPC Premier-46
Gold-46
93Topps Premier Finest-6
93Ultra-194
93Upper Deck-294
93Upper Deck-397
NHLPA/Roots-24
SP-38
93Upper Deck Locker All-Stars-31
93Swedish Semic World Champ Stickers-182
94Action Packed Badge of Honor Promos-3
94Action Packed Big Picture 24K Gold-4G
94Be A Player-R8
94Be A Player-R114
94Canada Games NHL POGS-81
94Donruss-193
Ice Masters-8
94EA Sports-33
94Finest-106
Super Team Winners-106
Refractors-106
Bowman's Best-B6
Bowman's Best Refractors-B6
94Flair-43
Center Spotlight-9
Scoring Power-7
94Fleer-55
Slapshot Artists-6
94Hockey Wit-60
94Kraft-23
94Leaf-9
Gold Stars-10
Limited Inserts-6
94Leaf Limited-60
94OPC Premier-230
Special Effects-230
94Parkhurst-308
Gold-308
Crash the Game Green-6
Crash the Game Blue-6
Crash the Game Gold-6
Crash the Game Red-6
Vintage-V2
94Parkhurst SE-SE47
Gold-SE47
94Pinnacle I Hobby Samples-3
94Pinnacle-3
Artist's Proofs-3
Rink Collection-3
Boomers-BR5
Gamers-GR8
World Edition-WE9
94Score-188
Gold-188
Platinum-188
Dream Team-DT17
Franchise-TF6
90 Plus Club-16
94Select-38
94Select-NNO
Gold-38
94SP-28
Die Cuts-28
94Stadium Club Super Teams-6
94Stadium Club Super Team MemberOnly Set-6
94Stars HockeyKaps-21
94Stars Pinnacle Sheet-3
94Stars Pinnacle Sheet-NNO
94Stars Postcards-19
94Stars Score Sheet-188
94Topps/OPC Premier-230
Special Effects-230
94Topps Finest Inserts-9
94Topps/OPC Premier The Go To Guy-4
94Ultra-55
Premier Pivots-8
Speed Merchants-7
94Upper Deck-58
Electric Ice-58
Ice Gallery-IG8
Predictor Retail-R37
94Upper Deck Predictor Retail Exchange-R37
94Upper Deck SP Inserts-SP21
94Upper Deck SP Inserts Die Cuts-SP21
94Upper Deck NHLPA/Be A Player-31
94Finnish Jaa Kiekko-125
95SLU Hockey Canadian-9
95SLU Hockey American-11
95Bashan Super Stickers-32
95Bashan Super Stickers-33
95Be A Player-153
Signatures-S153
Signatures Die Cuts-S153
95Bowman-35
All-Foil-35
95Canada Games NHL POGS-85
95Collector's Choice-238
Player's Club-238
Player's Club Platinum-238
Crash The Game-C16A
Crash The Game-C16B
Crash The Game-C16C
Crash The Game Gold-C16A
Crash The Game Gold-C16B
Crash The Game Gold-C16C
Crash the Game Silver Redeemed-C16
Crash the Game Silver Bonus-C16
Crash the Game Gold Redeemed-C16
Crash the Game Gold Bonus-C16
95Donruss-62
Pro Pointers-8
95Donruss Elite-32
Die Cut Stars-32
Die Cut Uncut-32
95Emotion-49
Xcited-3
95Finest-128
Refractors-128
95Hoyle Western Playing Cards-46
95Imperial Stickers-33
95Kenner Starting Lineup Cards-13
95Leaf-227
95Leaf Limited-51
95Metal-42
Heavy Metal-10
95NHL Aces Playing Cards-3D
95Panini Stickers-168
95Parkhurst International-55
Emerald Ice-55
95Pinnacle-108
Artist's Proofs-108
Rink Collection-108
Roaring 20s-5
95Pinnacle FANtasy-14
95Playoff One on One-31
95Playoff One on One-142
95Playoff One on One-250
95Pro Magnets-124
95Score-120
Black Ice Artist's Proofs-120
Black Ice-120
Border Battle-9
Golden Blades-6
95Select Certified Promos-17
95Select Certified-17
Mirror Gold-17
95SkyBox Impact-48
95SP-36
Stars/Etoiles-E11
Stars/Etoiles Gold-E11
95Stadium Club Members Only-25
95Stadium Club-168
Members Only Master Set-168
95Stars Score Sheet-120
95Summit-14
Artist's Proofs-14
Ice-14
95Topps-80
OPC Inserts-80
Home Grown USA-HGA3
95Topps SuperSkills-46
Platinum-46
95Ultra-41
95Ultra-394
Gold Medallion-41
Extra Attackers-14
95Upper Deck-220
95Upper Deck-420
Electric Ice-220
Electric Ice-420
Electric Ice Gold-220
Electric Ice Gold-420
95Upper Deck All-Star Game Predictors-14
Redemption Winners-14
95Upper Deck Predictor Retail-R59
95Upper Deck Predictor Retail Exchange-R59
95Upper Deck Special Edition-SE26
95Upper Deck Special Edition Gold-SE26
95Zenith-24
Z-Team-10
95Finnish Semic World Championships-116
95Swedish Globe World Championships-111
96SLU Hockey American-16
96Be A Player Biscuit In The Basket-8
96Black Diamond-99
Gold-99
Run for the Cup-RC16
96Collector's Choice-69
96Collector's Choice-315
MVP-UD17
MVP Gold-UD17
Stick'Ums-S15
96Collector's Choice Blow-Ups-69
96Donruss-22
Press Proofs-22
Dominators-9
Go Top Shelf-7
96Donruss Canadian Ice-25
Gold Press Proofs-25
Red Press Proofs-25
96Donruss Elite-116
Die Cut Stars-116
96Flair-23
Blue Ice-23
96Fleer-27
Picks Dream Lines-7
Picks Fabulous 50-30
Picks Jagged Edge-11
96Kenner Starting Lineup Cards-16
96Kraft Upper Deck-35
96Leaf-12
Press Proofs-12
Fire On Ice-14
96Leaf Leather And Laces Promos-P15
96Leaf Leather And Laces-15
96Leaf Limited-13
Gold-13
Stubble-8
96Leaf Preferred-44
96Leaf Preferred-150
Press Proofs-44
Press Proofs-150
Steel-28
Steel Gold-28
96Maggers-61
96Metal Universe-40
96NHL Aces Playing Cards-33
96NHL Pro Stamps-124
96Pinnacle-154
Artist's Proofs-154
Foil-154
Premium Stock-154
Rink Collection-154
96Playoff One on One-352
96Score-72
Artist's Proofs-72
Dealer's Choice Artist's Proofs-72
Special Artist's Proofs-72
Golden Blades-72
Superstitions-4
96Select Certified-2
Artist's Proofs-2
Blue-2
Mirror Blue-2
Mirror Gold-2
Mirror Red-2
Red-2
96SkyBox Impact-30
96SP-40
Holoview Collection-HC25
96SPx-11
Gold-11
96Stars Postcards-21
96Stars Score Sheet-72
96Summit-23
Artist's Proofs-23
Ice-23
Metal-23
Premium Stock-23
96Team Out-25
96Topps Picks-51
OPC Inserts-51
96Ultra-44
Gold Medallion-44
96Upper Deck-43
96Upper Deck-363
Game Jerseys-GJ9
Generation Next-X21
Superstar Showdown-SS19A
96Upper Deck Ice-82
Parallel-82
96Zenith-1
Artist's Proofs-1
Assailants-2
96Swedish Semic Wien-166
97Be A Player One Timers-10
97Beehive-26
Golden Portraits-26
Team-3
Team Gold-3
97Black Diamond-80
Double Diamond-80
Triple Diamond-80
Quadruple Diamond-80
Premium Cut-PC25
Premium Cut Double Diamond-PC25
Premium Cut Quadruple Diamond Horiz-PC25
Premium Cut Triple Diamond-PC25
Premium Cut Quadruple Diamond Verticals-PC25
97Collector's Choice-65
Crash the Game-C2A
Crash the Game-C2B
Crash the Game-C2C
Crash the Game Exchange-CR2
Star Quest-SQ82
Stick'Ums-S8
97Crown Royale-41
Emerald Green-41
Ice Blue-41
Silver-41
Blades of Steel Die-Cuts-7
Hat Tricks Die-Cuts-6
Lamplighters Cel-Fusion Die-Cuts-7
97Donruss-104
Press Proofs Silver-104
Press Proofs Gold-104
Line 2 Line-14
Line 2 Line Die Cut-14
97Donruss Canadian Ice-13
Dominion Series-13
Provincial Series-13
Stanley Cup Scrapbook-1
97Donruss Elite-2
97Donruss Elite-129
Aspirations-2
Aspirations-129
Status-2
Status-129
Craftsmen-18
Master Craftsmen-18
97Donruss Limited-19
97Donruss Limited-42
97Donruss Limited-193
Exposure-19
Exposure-42
Exposure-193
Fabric of the Game-67
97Donruss Preferred-8
97Donruss Preferred-176
Cut to the Chase-8
Cut to the Chase-176
Line of the Times-5A
97Donruss Preferred Line of Times Promos-5A
97Donruss Priority-11
97Donruss Priority-192
Stamp of Approval-11
Stamp of Approval-192
Direct Deposit-13
Postcards-12
Postcards Opening Day Issues-11
Stamps-12
Stamps Bronze-12
Stamps Gold-12
Stamps Silver-12
97Esso Olympic Hockey Heroes-24
97Esso Olympic Hockey Heroes French-24
97Katch-46
Gold-46
Silver-46
97Kraft-24
97Leaf-15
97Leaf-181
Fractal Matrix-15
Fractal Matrix-181
Fractal Matrix Die Cuts-15
Fractal Matrix Die Cuts-181
Banner Season-9
Fire On Ice-6
97Leaf International-15
Universal Ice-15
97NHL Aces Playing Cards-20
97Pacific-4
Copper-4
Emerald Green-4
Ice Blue-4
Red-4
Silver-4
Card-Supials-5
Card-Supials Minis-5
Team Checklists-8
97Pacific Dynagon-37
Copper-37
Dark Grey-37
Emerald Green-37
Ice Blue-37
Red-37
Silver-37
Best Kept Secrets-30
Tandems-42
97Pacific Invincible-41
Copper-41
Emerald Green-41
Ice Blue-41
Red-41
Silver-41
Attack Zone-8
Feature Performers-11
NHL Regime-63
97Pacific Omega-73
97Pacific Omega-246
97Pacific Omega-S73
Copper-73
Copper-246
Dark Gray-73
Dark Gray-246
Emerald Green-73
Emerald Green-246
Gold-73
Gold-246
Ice Blue-73
Ice Blue-246
Game Face-5
Stick Handle Laser Cuts-7
97Panini Stickers-139
97Paramount-60
97Paramount-P60
Copper-60
Dark Grey-60
Emerald Green-60
Ice Blue-60
Red-60
Silver-60
Photoengravings-8
97Pinnacle-91
Artist's Proofs-91
Rink Collection-91
Press Plates Back Black-91
Press Plates Back Cyan-91
Press Plates Back Magenta-91
Press Plates Back Yellow-91
Press Plates Front Black-91
Press Plates Front Cyan-91
Press Plates Front Magenta-91
Press Plates Front Yellow-91
97Pinnacle Certified-33
Red-33
Mirror Blue-33
Mirror Gold-33
Mirror Red-33
97Pinnacle Inside-15
Coach's Collection-15
Executive Collection-15
97Pinnacle Tot Cert Platinum Blue-33
97Pinnacle Tot Certi Platinum Gold-33
97Pinnacle Totally Certified Platinum Red-33
97Pinnacle Tot Cert Mirror Platinum Gold-33
97Revolution-43
Copper-43
Emerald-43
Ice Blue-43
Silver-43
1998 All-Star Game Die-Cuts-10
Team Checklist Laser Cuts-8
97Score-92
97Score-262
Artist's Proofs-92
Golden Blades-92
97SP Authentic-43
Icons-I37
Icons Die-Cuts-I37
Icons Embossed-I37
97SPx-13
Bronze-13
Gold-13
Silver-13
Steel-13
Grand Finale-13
97Studio-13
Press Proofs Silver-13
Press Proofs Gold-13
Portraits-13
Silhouettes-19
Silhouettes 8x10-19
97Upper Deck-56
Sixth Sense Masters-SS29
Sixth Sense Wizards-SS29
Smooth Grooves-SG29
The Specialists-26
The Specialists Level 2 Die Cuts-26
Three Star Selects-16B
97Upper Deck Ice-62
Parallel-62
Lethal Lines-L8B
Lethal Lines 2-L8B
Power Shift-62
97Zenith-37
Z-Gold-37
Z-Silver-37
97Zenith 5 x 7-58
Gold Impulse-58
Silver Impulse-58
97Zenith Chasing The Cup-5
98SLU Hockey One on One-4
98NHL Pro Zone-40
98Aurora-58
Atomic Laser Cuts-8
Championship Fever-15
Championship Fever Copper-15
Championship Fever Ice Blue-15
Championship Fever Red-15
Championship Fever Silver-15
Cubes-7
Man Advantage-7
NHL Command-5
98Be A Player-40
Press Release-40
98BAP Gold-40
98BAP Autographs-40
98BAP Autographs Gold-40
98BAP AS Game Used Stick Cards-S4
98BAP AS Game Used Jersey Cards-AS4
98BAP Playoff Game Used Jerseys-G17
98BAP Playoff Practice Used Jerseys-P14
98BAP Tampa Bay All Star Game-40
98Black Diamond-27
Double Diamond-27
Triple Diamond-27
Quadruple Diamond-27
Myriad-M5
Myriad 2-M5
Winning Formula Gold-WF30
Winning Formula Platinum-WF30
98Bowman's Best-48
Refractors-48
Atomic Refractors-48
98Crown Royale-41
Limited Series-41
Master Performers-8
Pillars of the Game-11
Pivotal Players-7
98Finest-75
No Protectors-75
No Protectors Refractors-75
Refractors-75
Double Sided Mystery Finest-M31
Double Sided Mystery Finest-M32
Double Sided Mystery Finest-M33
Double Sided Mystery Finest-M34
Double Sided Mystery Refractors-M31
Double Sided Mystery Refractors-M32
Double Sided Mystery Refractors-M33
Double Sided Mystery Refractors-M34
Red Lighters-R2
Red Lighters Refractors-R2
98Katch-46
98Kraft Fearless Forwards-8
98OPC Chrome-50
Refractors-50
98Pacific-181
98Pacific-S181
Ice Blue-181
Red-181
Cramer's Choice-5
Dynagon Ice Inserts-8
Titanium Ice-8
Gold Crown Die-Cuts-12
Team Checklists-8
Timelines-9
98Pacific Dynagon Ice-59
Blue-59
Red-59
Forward Thinking-8
Preeminent Players-5
Team Checklists-8
98Pacific Omega-73
Red-73
Opening Day Issue-73
EO Portraits-8
EO Portraits 1 of 1-8
Face to Face-9
Online-13
Planet Ice-16
Planet Ice Parallel-16
Prism-7
98Panini Photocards-52
98Panini Stickers-123
98Paramount-68
Copper-68
Emerald Green-68
Holo-Electric-68
Ice Blue-68
Silver-68
Special Delivery Die-Cuts-6
Team Checklists Die-Cuts-8
98Revolution-44
Ice Shadow-44
Red-44
All-Star Die Cuts-20
Chalk Talk Laser-Cuts-7
NHL Icons-5
Showstoppers-15
Three Pronged Attack-25
Three Pronged Attack Parallel-25
98SP Authentic-25
Power Shift-25
Snapshots-SS12
Stat Masters-S14
98SPx Finite-109
98SPx Finite-169
Radiance-109
Radiance-169
Spectrum-109
Spectrum-169
98SPx Top Prospects-18
Radiance-18
Spectrum-18
Highlight Heroes-H11
Lasting Impressions-L5
Premier Stars-PS24
98Topps-50
O-Pee-Chee-50
Local Legends-L12
Mystery Finest Bronze-M5
Mystery Finest Bronze Refractors-M5
Mystery Finest Gold-M5
Mystery Finest Gold Refractors-M5
Mystery Finest Silver-M5
Mystery Finest Silver Refractors-M5
98Topps Gold Label Class 1-2
Black-2
Black One of One-2
One of One-2
Red-2
Red One of One-2
98Topps Gold Label Class 2-2
98Topps Gold Label Class 2 Black-2
98Topps Gold Label Class 2 Black 1 of 1-2
98Topps Gold Label Class 2 One of One-2
98Topps Gold Label Class 2 Red-2
98Topps Gold Label Class 2 Red One of One-2
98Topps Gold Label Class 3-2
98Topps Gold Label Class 3 Black-2
98Topps Gold Label Class 3 Black 1 of 1-2
98Topps Gold Label Class 3 One of One-2
98Topps Gold Label Class 3 Red-2
98Topps Gold Label Class 3 Red One of One-2
98UD Choice-69
Mini Bobbing Head-BH16
98UD Choice Preview-69
98UD Choice Prime Choice Reserve-69
98UD Choice Reserve-69
98UD Choice StarQuest Blue-SQ24
98UD Choice StarQuest Gold-SQ24
98UD Choice StarQuest Green-SQ24
98UD Choice StarQuest Red-SQ24
98UD3-39
98UD3-99
98UD3-159
Die-Cuts-39
Die-Cuts-99
Die-Cuts-159
98Upper Deck-30
98Upper Deck-256
Exclusives-30
Exclusives-256
Exclusives 1 of 1-30
Exclusives 1 of 1-256
Fantastic Finishers-FF12
Fantastic Finishers Quantum 1-FF12
Fantastic Finishers Quantum 2-FF12
Fantastic Finishers Quantum 3-FF12
Frozen In Time-FT13
Frozen In Time Quantum 1-FT13
Frozen In Time Quantum 2-FT13
Frozen In Time Quantum 3-FT13
Lord Stanley's Heroes-LS28
Lord Stanley's Heroes Quantum 1-LS28
Lord Stanley's Heroes Quantum 2-LS28
Lord Stanley's Heroes Quantum 3-LS28
Profiles-P18
Profiles Quantum 1-P18
Profiles Quantum 2-P18
Profiles Quantum 3-P18
Gold Reserve-30
Gold Reserve-256
98Upper Deck MVP-61
Gold Script-61
Silver Script-61
Super Script-61
Game Souvenirs-MM
Power Game-PG4
99SLU Hockey-13
99Aurora-47
Striped-47
Premiere Date-47
Premiere Date Striped-47
Championship Fever-11
Championship Fever Copper-11
Championship Fever Ice Blue-11
Championship Fever Silver-11
Complete Players-6
Complete Players Parallel-6
Complete Players Retail-6
Complete Players Retail Parallel-6
Styrotechs-8
99BAP Memorabilia-217
Gold-217
Silver-217

Jersey Cards-J4
Jersey Emblems-E4
Jersey Numbers-I4
Jersey and Stick Cards-S4
99BAP Update Teammates Jersey Cards-TM22
99BAP Update Teammates Jersey Cards-TM26
99BAP Update Teammates Jersey Cards-TM46
99BAP Update Teammates Jersey Cards-TM48
99BAP Millennium Prototypes-3
99BAP Millennium-76
Emerald-76
Ruby-76
Sapphire-76
Signatures-76
Signatures Gold-76
Jerseys-J27
Jersey Autographs-J27
Jersey and Stick Cards-JS27
Jersey Emblems-E27
Jersey Numbers-N27
99Black Diamond-29
Diamond Cut-29
Final Cut-29
A Piece of History-MM
A Piece of History Double-MM
A Piece of History Triple-MM
Diamonation-D6
99Crown Royale-46
Limited Series-46
Premiere Date-46
Card-Supials-9
Card-Supials Minis-9
Cramer's Choice Jumbos-5
Cramer's Choice Jumbos Dark Blue-5
Cramer's Choice Jumbos Gold-5
Cramer's Choice Jumbos Green-5
Cramer's Choice Jumbos Light Blue-5
Cramer's Choice Jumbos Purple-5
Cramer's Choice Jumbos Red-5
International Glory-8
International Glory Parallel-8
99Hasbro Starting Lineup Cards-13
99Jell-O Pudding Super Skills-5
99Kraft Dinner-6
99Kraft Face Off Rivals-6
99Kraft Overtime Winners-3
99McDonald's Upper Deck Game Jerseys-GJMM
99O-Pee-Chee-6
99O-Pee-Chee Chrome-6
99O-Pee-Chee Chrome Ice Masters-IM8
99O-Pee-Chee Chrome Ice Masters Refractor-IM8
99O-Pee-Chee Chrome Refractors-6
99O-Pee-Chee Ice Masters-IM8
99O-Pee-Chee Top of the World-TW12
99Pacific-126
Copper-126
Emerald Green-126
Gold-126
Ice Blue-126
Premiere Date-126
Red-126
Center Ice-9
Center Ice Proofs-9
Cramer's Choice-6
Gold Crown Die-Cuts-15
Home and Away-6
Home and Away-16
Past and Present-11
Team Leaders-9
99Pacific Dynagon Ice-68
Blue-68
Copper-68
Gold-68
Premiere Date-68
2000 All-Star Preview-11
Checkmates American-9
Checkmates American-24
Checkmates Canadian-24
99Pacific Omega-74
Copper-74
Gold-74
Ice Blue-74
Premiere Date-74
Cup Contenders-7
EO Portraits-7
EO Portraits 1/1-7
Game-Used Jerseys-2
NHL Generations-5
North American All-Stars-4
5 Star Talents-20
5 Star Talents Parallel-20
99Pacific Prism-46
Holographic Blue-46
Holographic Gold-46
Holographic Mirror-46
Holographic Purple-46
Premiere Date-46
Dial-a-Stats-6
Sno-Globe Die-Cuts-9
99Panini Stickers-226
99Paramount-75
Copper-75
Emerald-75
Gold-75
Holographic Emerald-75
Holographic Gold-75
Holographic Silver-75
Ice Blue-75
Premiere Date-75
Red-75
Silver-75
Ice Alliance-9
Personal Best-14
Toronto Fall Expo '99-75
99Revolution-48
Premiere Date-48
Red-48
Shadow Series-48
NHL Icons-9
Ornaments-9
Showstoppers-14
Top of the Line-15
Copper-48
Gold-48
CSC Silver-48
99SP Authentic-27
Special Forces-SF5
99SPx-47
Radiance-47
Spectrum-47
Prolifics-P11
SPXcitement-X18
SPXtreme-XT8
Winning Materials-WM1
99Stadium Club-20
First Day Issue-20
One of a Kind-20
Printing Plates Black-20
Printing Plates Cyan-20
Printing Plates Magenta-20
Printing Plates Yellow-20
Capture the Action-CA19
Capture the Action Game View-CAG19
Chrome-18
Chrome Refractors-18
Chrome Oversized-10
Chrome Oversized Refractors-10
99Stars Postcards-18
99Topps/OPC-6
Ice Masters-IM8
Top of the World-TW12
99Topps/OPC Chrome-6
Refractors-6
Ice Masters-IM8
Ice Masters Refractors-IM8
99Topps Gold Label Class 1-85
Black-85
Black One of One-85
One of One-85
Red-85
Red One of One-85
99Topps Gold Label Class 2-85
99Topps Gold Label Class 2 Black-85
99Topps Gold Label Class 2 Black 1 of 1-85
99Topps Gold Label Class 2 One of One-85
99Topps Gold Label Class 2 Red-85
99Topps Gold Label Class 2 Red One of One-85
99Topps Gold Label Class 3-85
99Topps Gold Label Class 3 Black-85
99Topps Gold Label Class 3 Black 1 of 1-85
99Topps Gold Label Class 3 One of One-85
99Topps Gold Label Class 3 Red-85
99Topps Gold Label Class 3 Red One of One-85
99Topps Gold Label Prime Gold-PG13
99Topps Gold Label Prime Gold One of One -PG13
99Topps Gold Label Prime Gold Black-PG13
99Topps Gold Label Prime Gold Black One of One -PG13
99Topps Gold Label Prime Gold Red-PG13
99Topps Gold Label Prime Gold Red One of One -PG13
99Topps Premier Plus-57
Parallel-57
Feature Presentations-FP4
Premier Team-PT4
Premier Team Parallel-PT4
99Ultimate Victory-27
1/1-27
Parallel-27
Parallel 100-27
Frozen Fury-FF5
Stature-S4
99Upper Deck-152
99Upper Deck-216
Exclusives-152
Exclusives-216
Exclusives 1 of 1-152
Exclusives 1 of 1-216
Crunch Time-CT14
Crunch Time Quantum Gold-CT14
Crunch Time Quantum Silver-CT14
Game Jerseys-MM
Game Jersey Patch-MMP
Game Jersey Patch 1 of 1-MMSP
Marquee Attractions-MA13
Marquee Attractions Quantum Gold-MA13
Marquee Attractions Quantum Silver-MA13
Sixth Sense-SS20
Sixth Sense Quantum Gold-SS20
Sixth Sense Quantum Silver-SS20
99Upper Deck Century Legends-60
Century Collection-60
99Upper Deck Gold Reserve-152
99Upper Deck Gold Reserve-216
99Upper Deck HoloGrFx-19
Ausome-19
99Upper Deck MVP-59
Gold Script-59
Silver Script-59
Super Script-59
Hands of Gold-H11
Talent-MVP10
99Upper Deck MVP SC Edition-58
Gold Script-58
Silver Script-58
Super Script-58
Golden Memories-GM4
Great Combinations-GCHM
Great Combinations Parallel-GCHM
Playoff Heroes-PH4
99Upper Deck Ovation-19
Standing Ovation-19
Lead Performers-LP1
99Upper Deck PowerDeck-10
Auxiliary-10
Auxiliary 1 of 1-10
99Upper Deck Retro-24
Gold-24
Platinum-24
99Upper Deck Victory-88
99Wayne Gretzky Hockey-53
00SP Authentic Autographed Replica Jersey-4
00Aurora-45
Pinstripes-45
Pinstripes Premiere Date-45
Premiere Date-45
Canvas Creations-4
Championship Fever-9
Championship Fever Copper-9
Championship Fever Platinum Blue-9
Championship Fever Silver-9
Styrotechs-5B
00BAP Memorabilia-67
Emerald-67
Ruby-67
Sapphire-67
Promos-67
Jersey Cards-J20
Jersey Emblems-E20
Jersey Numbers-N20
Jersey and Stick Cards-JS20
00BAP Mem Chicago Sportsfest Copper-67
00BAP Memorabilia Chicago Sportsfest Blue-67
00BAP Memorabilia Chicago Sportsfest Gold-67
00BAP Memorabilia Chicago Sportsfest Ruby-67
00BAP Memorabilia Chicago Sun-Times Ruby-67
00BAP Memorabilia Chicago Sun-Times Gold-67
00BAP Mem Chicago Sun-Times Sapphire-67
00BAP Mem Toronto Fall Expo Copper-67
00BAP Memorabilia Toronto Fall Expo Gold-67
00BAP Memorabilia Toronto Fall Expo Ruby-67
00BAP Mem Update Heritage Jersey Cards-H7
00BAP Mem Update Heritage Jersey Gold-H7
00BAP Memorabilia Update Teammates-TM15
00BAP Memorabilia Update Teammates-TM36
00BAP Memorabilia Update Teammates Gold-TM15
00BAP Memorabilia Update Teammates Gold-TM36
00BAP Parkhurst 2000-P232
00BAP Signature Series-89
Emerald-89
Ruby-89
Sapphire-89
Autographs-142
Autographs Gold-142
Franchise Players-F10
He Shoots-He Scores Points-13
He Shoots-He Scores Prizes-10
Jersey Cards-J27
Jersey and Stick Cards-GSJ27
Jersey Cards Autographs-J27
Jersey Emblems-E27
Jersey Numbers-IN27
00BAP Ultimate Memorabilia Autographs-27
Gold-27
00BAP Ultimate Mem Game-Used Jerseys-GJ27
00BAP Ultimate Mem Game-Used Emblems-E24
00BAP Ultimate Mem Game-Used Numbers-N24
00BAP Ultimate Mem Game-Used Sticks-GS27
00BAP Ultimate Mem Journey Jerseys-JJ8
00BAP Ultimate Mem Journey Emblems-JE8
00BAP Ultimate Mem Journey Numbers-JI8
00BAP Ultimate Memorabilia Teammates-TM24
00BAP Ultimate Memorabilia Teammates-TM26
00Black Diamond-20
Gold-20
Diamond Might-FP4
Diamond Skills-IC2
00Crown Royale-36
Ice Blue-36
Limited Series-36
Premiere Date-36
Red-36
Game-Worn Jerseys-11
Game-Worn Jersey Patches-11
Premium-Sized Game-Worn Jerseys-11
Jewels of the Crown-12
00Kraft-5
00McDonald's Pacific-12
Blue-12
Game Jerseys-4
00O-Pee-Chee-18
00O-Pee-Chee Parallel-18
00Pacific-137
Copper-137
Gold-137
Ice Blue-137
Premiere Date-137
Autographs-137
Jerseys-5
Jersey Patches-5
Gold Crown Die Cuts-13
North American Stars-4
Reflections-8
00Panini Stickers-144
00Paramount-79
Copper-79
Gold-79
Holo-Gold-79
Holo-Silver-79
Ice Blue-79
Premiere Date-79
Epic Scope-9
Freeze Frame-13
00Private Stock-32
Gold-32
Premiere Date-32
Retail-32
Silver-32
Artist's Canvas-10
Artist's Canvas Proofs-10
Extreme Action-8
Game Gear-39
Game Gear Patches-39
PS-2001 Action-18
PS-2001 Stars-10
Reserve-8
00Revolution-47
Blue-47
Premiere Date-47
Red-47
Ice Immortals-9
NHL Game Gear-3
NHL Icons-10
Stat Masters-25
00SP Authentic-29
BuyBacks-18
BuyBacks-19
BuyBacks-20
BuyBacks-21
BuyBacks-22
BuyBacks-23
BuyBacks-24
BuyBacks-25
BuyBacks-B-MM
Parents' Scrapbook-PS3
Sign of the Times-MO
Sign of the Times-LMB
Special Forces-SF2
00SP Game Used-18
Patch Cards-P-MO
Tools of the Game-MO
Tools of the Game Exclusives-MO
Tools of the Game Combos-C-MN
00SPx-21
00SPx-85
Spectrum-21
Spectrum-85
SPXcitement-X5
SPXtreme-SPX8
Winning Materials-MM
00Stadium Club-86
Beam Team-BT3
Special Forces-SF5
00Stars Postcards-17
00Titanium-29
Blue-29
Gold-29
Premiere Date-29
Red-29
Retail-29
Game Gear-89
Game Gear-154
Game Gear Patches-89
Three-Star Selections-13
00Titanium Draft Day Edition-33
Patches-33
00Topps/OPC-18
Parallel-18
Autographs-AMM
Combos-TC5
Combos Jumbos-TC5
Hobby Masters-HM8
NHL Draft-D3
Own the Game-OTG8
00Topps Chrome-18
00Topps Chrome-164
OPC Refractors-18
OPC Refractors-164
Refractors-18
Refractors-164
Combos-TC5
Combos Refractors-TC5
Hobby Masters Refractors-HM8
00Topps Gold Label Class 1-64
Gold-64
00Topps Gold Label Class 2-64
00Topps Gold Label Class 2 Gold-64
00Topps Gold Label Class 3-64
00Topps Gold Label Class 3 Gold-64
00Topps Gold Label Bullion-B2
00Topps Gold Label Bullion One to One-B2
00Topps Gold Label Golden Greats-GG13
00Topps Gold Label Golden Greats 1 to 1-GG13
00Topps Heritage-45
00Topps Heritage-217
Chrome Parallel-45
Heroes-HH4
00Topps Premier Plus-69
Blue Ice-69
Masters of the Break-MB10
Team-PT4
Team Blue Ice-PR4
World Premier-WP15
00Topps Stars-7
Blue-7
Autographs-AMM
Game Gear-GGMM
Game Gear-GGMM
Progression-P1
Walk of Fame-WF5
00UD Heroes-145
Second Season Heroes-SS3
00UD Pros and Prospects-27
Game Jerseys-MM
Game Jersey Exclusives-MM
ProMotion-PM5
00UD Reserve-27
Buyback Autographs-52
Buyback Autographs-53
Buyback Autographs-54
Buyback Autographs-55
Buyback Autographs-56
Buyback Autographs-57
Buyback Autographs-58
Buyback Autographs-59
Buyback Autographs-60
Buyback Autographs-61
Buyback Autographs-62
Buyback Autographs-63
Buyback Autographs-64
Buyback Autographs-65
Buyback Autographs-66
Gold Strike-GS3
Practice Session Jerseys-MM
Practice Session Jerseys Autographs-MM
00Upper Deck-55
Exclusives Tier 1-55
Exclusives Tier 2-55
All-Star Class-A4
Fun-Damentals-F4
Gate Attractions-GA5
Profiles-P3
Skilled Stars-SS8
Triple Threat-TT5
00Upper Deck Ice-15
Immortals-15
Legends-15
Stars-15
Champions-IC2
Game Jerseys-JCMM
Rink Favorites-FP4
00Upper Deck Legends-39
00Upper Deck Legends-40
Legendary Collection Bronze-39
Legendary Collection Bronze-40
Legendary Collection Gold-39
Legendary Collection Gold-40
Legendary Collection Silver-39
Legendary Collection Silver-40
Legendary Game Jerseys-JMM
Playoff Heroes-PH4
00Upper Deck MVP-61
First Stars-61
Second Stars-61
Third Stars-61
Top Playmakers-TP4
Valuable Commodities-VC4
00Upper Deck Victory-70
00Upper Deck Victory-77
00Upper Deck Victory-298
00Upper Deck Vintage-112
00Upper Deck Vintage-123
00Upper Deck Vintage-124
National Heroes-NH10
00Vanguard-35
Dual Game-Worn Jerseys-4
Dual Game-Worn Patches-4
High Voltage-12
High Voltage Gold-12
High Voltage Green-12
High Voltage Red-12
High Voltage Silver-12
Holographic Gold-35
Holographic Purple-35
Pacific Proofs-35
00Czech Stadion-87
01Atomic-32
Blue-32
Gold-32
Premiere Date-32
Red-32
Core Players-4
Jerseys-19
Patches-19
Power Play-11
Team Nucleus-5
01BAP Memorabilia-147
Emerald-147
Ruby-147
Sapphire-147
All-Star Jerseys-ASJ32
All-Star Emblems-ASE32
All-Star Numbers-ASN32
All-Star Jersey Doubles-DASJ16
All-Star Teammates-AST17
All-Star Teammates-AST22
All-Star Teammates-AST25
All-Star Teammates-AST33
All-Star Teammates-AST34
All-Star Teammates-AST41
Country of Origin-CO15
He Shoots-He Scores Points-7
He Shoots-He Scores Prizes-27
Patented Power-PP4
Stanley Cup Playoffs-SC20
01BAP Signature Series Certified 100-C27
01BAP Signature Series Certified 50-C27
01BAP Signature Series Certified 1 of 1's-C27
01BAP Signature Series Franchise Jerseys-FP-10
01BAP Sig Series He Shoots/Scores Points-7
01BAP Sig Series He Shoots/Scores Prizes-13
01BAP Sig Series International Medals-IS-6
01BAP Signature Series Jerseys-GJ-20
01BAP Sig Series Jersey and Stick Cards-GSJ-20
01BAP Signature Series Emblems-GUE-19
01BAP Signature Series Numbers-ITN-19
01BAP Signature Series Teammates-TM-10
01BAP Ultimate Mem All-Star History-48
01BAP Ultimate Memorabilia Dynamic Duos-1
01BAP Ultimate Memorabilia Emblems-19
01BAP Ultimate Memorabilia Jerseys-19
01BAP Ultimate Mem Jerseys and Sticks-19
01BAP Ultimate Mem Journey Jerseys-10
01BAP Ultimate Mem Journey Emblems-10
01BAP Ultimate Memorabilia Numbers-14
01BAP Ultimate Memorabilia Name Plates-29
01BAP Update Heritage-H12
01Bowman YoungStars-6
Gold-6
Ice Cubed-6
01Crown Royale-48
Blue-48
Premiere Date-48
Red-48
Retail-48
All-Star Honors-6
Jewels of the Crown-9
Triple Threads-8
01eTopps-12
01McDonald's Pacific-10
Jersey Patches Silver-7
Jersey Patches Gold-7
01O-Pee-Chee-52
01O-Pee-Chee Heritage Parallel-52
01O-Pee-Chee Heritage Parallel Limited-52
01O-Pee-Chee Premier Parallel-52
01Pacific-131
01Pacific-409
01Pacific-428
Extreme LTD-131
Gold-409
Gold-428
Hobby LTD-131
Premiere Date-131
Retail LTD-131
Gold Crown Die-Cuts-8
Impact Zone-10
Top Draft Picks-8
01Pacific Top Draft Picks Draft Day Promo-8
01Pacific Adrenaline-59
Blue-59
Premiere Date-59
Red-59
Retail-59
Playmakers-3
World Beaters-4
01Pacific Arena Exclusives-131
01Pacific Arena Exclusives-409
01Pacific Arena Exclusives-428
01Pacific Heads-Up-31
Blue-31
Premiere Date-31
Red-31
Silver-31
HD NHL-4
Quad Jerseys-10
Quad Jerseys-21
Stat Masters-6
01Parkhurst-10
Gold-10
Silver-10
He Shoots-He Scores Prizes-4
Jerseys-PJ16
Milestones-M31
Sticks-PS16
Teammates-T12
Teammates-T21
World Class Jerseys-WCJ6
World Class Emblems-WCE6
World Class Numbers-WCN6
Waving the Flag-25
01Private Stock-29
Gold-29
Premiere Date-29
Retail-29
Silver-29
Game Gear-37
Game Gear Patches-37
01Private Stock Pacific Nights-29
01Private Stock PS-2002-24
01SP Authentic-23
01SP Authentic-95
Limited-23
Limited-95
Limited Gold-23
Limited Gold-95
Buybacks-19
Buybacks-20
Jerseys-NNMO
Sign of the Times-MM
01SP Game Used-14
Authentic Fabric-AFMM
Authentic Fabric-AFMO
Authentic Fabric-DFMB
Authentic Fabric-TFMNB
Authentic Fabric Gold-AFMM
Authentic Fabric Gold-AFMO
Inked Sweaters-ISMM
Inked Sweaters-DSMA
Patches-PMM
01SPx-19
01SPx-73
01SPx-84
Hockey Treasures-HTMM
Hockey Treasures-HTMO
01Stadium Club-5
Award Winners-5
Master Photos-5
Gallery-G7
Gallery Gold-G7
Heart and Soul-HS9
NHL Passport-NHLP16
01Stars Postcards-17
01Titanium-45
Hobby Parallel-45
Premiere Date-45
Retail-45
Retail Parallel-45
Double-Sided Jerseys-16
Double-Sided Jerseys-52
Double-Sided Patches-16
Double-Sided Patches-52
01Titanium Draft Day Edition-34
01Topps-52
Heritage Parallel-52
Heritage Parallel Limited-52
OPC Parallel-52
Stars of the Game-SG6
01Topps Chrome-52
Refractors-52
Black Border Refractors-52
01Topps Heritage-8
Refractors-8
01Topps Reserve-47
01UD Challenge for the Cup-25
Cornerstones-CR4
Jerseys-UCMB
01UD Honor Roll-99
Defense First-DF1
Jerseys-J-MM
Jerseys Gold-J-MM
Sharp Skaters-SS2
Student of the Game-SG3
01UD Mask Collection-30
Gold-30
Double Patches-DPMM
Dual Jerseys-PMMJ
Jerseys-J-MM
Jersey and Patch-JPMM
01UD Playmakers-33
01UD Premier Collection-17
Dual Jerseys-DDM
Dual Jerseys-DMB
Dual Jerseys Black-DDM
Dual Jerseys Black-DMB
Jerseys-SMM
Jerseys Black-S-MM
01UD Stanley Cup Champs-46
Jerseys-T-MM
Pieces of Glory-G-MM
Sticks-S-MM
01UD Top Shelf-14
Jerseys-MM
Jersey Autographs-MM
Patches-PMM
01Upper Deck-55
01Upper Deck-218
Exclusives-55
Exclusives-218
Crunch Timers-CT4
Franchise Cornerstones-FC11
Game Jerseys-AMM
Game Jerseys-CMN
Game Jerseys-MNB
Game Jerseys Series II-FJMM
Game Jerseys Series II-SSMM
Game Jerseys Series II-DJMN
Game Jerseys Series II-TJNMB
Game Jersey Autographs-SMM
Gate Attractions-GA14
Leaders of the Pack-LP4
Patches-PMM
Patches-PMO
Patches Series II-PNMM
Patches Series II-PLMM
Pride of a Nation-DPLM
Skilled Stars-SS8
01Upper Deck Ice-12
Autographs-MM
Combos-C-MM
Combos Gold-G-MM
First Rounders-F-MM
01Upper Deck MVP-57
Morning Skate Jerseys-J-MM
Morning Skate Jersey Autographs-SJ-MM
Souvenirs-C-MM
Souvenirs Gold-C-MM
Talent-MT3
Valuable Commodities-VC7
01Upper Deck Victory-109
01Upper Deck Victory-414
Gold-109
Gold-414
01Upper Deck Vintage-79
01Upper Deck Vintage-86
01Upper Deck Vintage-87
01Vanguard-32
Blue-32
Red-32
Memorabilia-11
One of Ones-32
Premiere Date-32
Proofs-32
Quebec Tournament Heroes-5
02McFarlane Hockey-40
02McFarlane Hockey-42
02Atomic-33
Blue-33
Gold-33
Red-33
Hobby Parallel-33
National Pride-U2
02BAP All-Star Edition-60
02BAP All-Star Edition-61
He Shoots-He Scores Points-15
He Shoots-He Score Prizes-19
Jerseys-60
Jerseys-61
Jerseys Gold-60
Jerseys Gold-61
Jerseys Silver-60
Jerseys Silver-61
02BAP First Edition-153
02BAP First Edition-326
02BAP First Edition-350
02BAP First Edition-401H
He Shoots-He Score Points-17
He Shoots-He Scores Prizes-9
Jerseys-153
Scoring Leaders-8
02BAP Memorabilia-180
02BAP Memorabilia-210
Emerald-180
Emerald-210
Ruby-180
Ruby-210
Sapphire-180
Sapphire-210
All-Star Jerseys-ASJ-36
All-Star Emblems-ASE-16
All-Star Numbers-ASN-16
All-Star Teammmates-AST-12
All-Star Triple Jerseys-ASTJ-15
Franchise Players-FP-10
He Shoots-He Scores Points-1
He Shoots-He Scores Prizes-20
Mini Stanley Cups-37
NHL All-Star Game-180
NHL All-Star Game-210
NHL All-Star Game Blue-180
NHL All-Star Game Blue-210
NHL All-Star Game Green-180
NHL All-Star Game Green-210
NHL All-Star Game Red-180
NHL All-Star Game Red-210
02BAP Memorabilia Toronto Fall Expo-180
02BAP Memorabilia Toronto Fall Expo-210
02BAP NHL All-Star History-48
02BAP Sig Series Auto Buybacks 1998-40
02BAP Sig Series Auto Buybacks 1999-76
02BAP Sig Series Auto Buybacks 2000-142
02BAP Signature Series Franchise Players-FJ10
02BAP Signature Series Jerseys-SGJ11
02BAP Signature Series Jersey Autographs-SGJ11
02BAP Signature Series Team Quads-TQ16
02BAP Ultimate Memorabilia Dynamic Duos-5
02BAP Ultimate Memorabilia Emblems-20
02BAP Ultimate Memorabilia First Overall-9
02BAP Ultimate Memorabilia Jerseys-25
02BAP Ultimate Mem Jersey and Stick-2
02BAP Ultimate Mem Magnificent Ones-4
02BAP Ultimate Mem Magnificent Ones Autos-4
02BAP Ultimate Memorabilia Nameplates-2
02BAP Ultimate Memorabilia Numbers-1
02BAP Ultimate Memorabilia Numerology-12
02Bowman YoungStars-16
Gold-16
Silver-16
02Crown Royale-30
Blue-30
Red-30
Retail-30
Dual Patches-8
Lords of the Rink-8
02eTopps-11
02ITG Used-21
02ITG Used-121
Franchise Players-F10
Franchise Players Autographs-F10
Franchise Players Gold-F10
International Experience-IE6
International Experience Gold-IE6
Jerseys-GUJ11
Jersey Autographs-GUJ11
Jerseys Gold-GUJ11
Emblems-E11
Jersey and Stick-SJ11
Jersey and Stick Gold-SJ11
Teammates-T13
Teammates Gold-T13
02O-Pee-Chee-13
02O-Pee-Chee Premier Blue Parallel-13
02O-Pee-Chee Premier Red Parallel-13
02O-Pee-Chee Factory Set-13
02Pacific-114
Blue-114
Red-114
Jerseys-15
Jerseys Holo-Silver-15
Main Attractions-6
02Pacific Calder-23
Silver-23
Chasing Glory-4
Hart Stoppers-4
02Pacific Chicago National *-5
02Pacific Complete-103
Red-103
02Pacific Exclusive-57
Maximum Overdrive-8
02Pacific Heads-Up-39
Blue-39
Purple-39
Red-39
Inside the Numbers-9
Quad Jerseys-11
Quad Jerseys-29
Quad Jerseys Gold-11
Quad Jerseys Gold-29
02Pacific Quest for the Cup-29
Gold-29
Jerseys-7
Raising the Cup-4
02Parkhurst-22
Bronze-22
Gold-22
Silver-22
Franchise Players-FP10
He Shoots-He Scores Points-16
He Shoots-He Scores Prizes-7
Jerseys-GJ33
Patented Power-PP5
Stick and Jerseys-SJ33
02Parkhurst Retro-12
Minis-12
Franchise Players-RF10
He Shoots-He Scores Points-4
He Shoots-He Scores Prizes-20
Jerseys-RJ2
Jersey and Sticks-RSJ2
Memorabilia-RM20
02Private Stock Reserve-115
Red-115
Retail-115
Patches-115
02SP Authentic-30
Beckett Promos-30
Super Premiums-SPMM
Super Premiums-DPMG
02SP Game Used-16
Authentic Fabrics-AFMM
Authentic Fabrics-AFMO
Authentic Fabrics-CFMO
Authentic Fabrics Gold-AFMM
Authentic Fabrics Gold-AFMO
Authentic Fabrics Gold-CFMO
Authentic Fabrics Rainbow-AFMM
Authentic Fabrics Rainbow-AFMO
Authentic Fabrics Rainbow-CFMO
First Rounder Patches-MM
Piece of History-PHMM
Piece of History-PHMO
Piece of History Gold-PHMM
Piece of History Gold-PHMO
Piece of History Rainbow-PHMM
Piece of History Rainbow-PHMO
02SPx-23
02SPx-87
02SPx-139
Spectrum Gold-23
Spectrum Gold-87
Spectrum Silver-23
Spectrum Silver-87
Milestones-MMM
Milestones Gold-MM
Milestones Silver-MM
Smooth Skaters-MM
Smooth Skaters Gold-MM
Smooth Skaters Silver-MM
Winning Materials-WMMM
Winning Materials Gold-MM
Winning Materials Silver-MM
Xtreme Talents-MM
Xtreme Talents Gold-MM
Xtreme Talents Silver-MM
02Stadium Club-11
Silver Decoy Cards-11
Proofs-11
Champions Fabric-FC6
Champions Patches-PC-6
World Stage-WS5
02Stars Postcards-9
02Titanium-32
Blue-32
Red-32
Retail-32
02Topps-13
OPC Blue Parallel-13
OPC Red Parallel-13
Captain's Cloth-CC3
First Round Fabric-MM
First Round Fabric Autographs-MM
Topps/OPC Hometown Heroes-HHU6
Factory Set-13
Factory Set Hometown Heroes-HHU6
02Topps Chrome-13
Black Border Refractors-13
Refractors-13
First Round Fabric Patches-MM
02Topps Heritage-33
Chrome Parallel-33
02Topps Total-39
Team Checklists-TTC9
Topps-TT9
02UD Artistic Impressions-30
Gold-30
Artist's Touch-ATMM
Artist's Touch Gold-ATMM
02UD Artistic Impressions Beckett Promos-30
02UD Artistic Impress Common Ground-CG20
02UD Artistic Impress Common Ground Gold-CG20
02UD Artistic Impressions Flashbacks-UD2
02UD Artistic Impressions Flashbacks Gold-UD2
02UD Artistic Impressions Retrospectives-R30
02UD Artistic Impress Retrospect Gold-R30
02UD Artistic Impress Retrospect Silver-R30
02UD Foundations-48
02UD Foundations-148
02UD Honor Roll-21
Grade A Jerseys-GAMM
Students of the Game-SG10
Team Warriors-TW5
02UD Mask Collection-28
02UD Mask Collection Beckett Promos-28
02UD Mask Collection Instant Offense-IOMM
02UD Mask Collection Patches-PGMM
02UD Piece of History-29
Patches-PHMM
Stellar Stitches-SSMM
02UD Premier Collection-18
Jerseys Bronze-MM
Jerseys Bronze-MO
Jerseys Gold-MM
Jerseys Gold-MO
Jerseys Silver-MM
Jerseys Silver-MO
NHL Patches-MM1
Patches-PMM
02UD Top Shelf-26
Clutch Performers-CPMM
Dual Player Jerseys-RMC
Goal Oriented-GOMM
Milestones Jerseys-MBMBS
Shooting Stars-SHMM
Sweet Sweaters-SWMM
Triple Jerseys-TSMMB
02Upper Deck-56
Exclusives-56
All-Star Performers-ASMM
Blow-Ups-C11
CHL Graduates-CGMM
CHL Graduates Gold-CGMM
Difference Makers-MM
Fan Favorites-MM
Gifted Greats-GG6
Letters of Note-LNMM
Letters of Note Gold-LNMM
Patch Card Numbers-MM
Patchwork-PWMM
Pinpoint Accuracy-PAMM
Playbooks Series II-MT
Reaching Fifty-50MM
Reaching Fifty Gold-50MM
Shooting Stars-SS5
Sizzling Scorers-SS6
Specialists-SMM
02Upper Deck Classic Portraits-33
Etched in Time-ET4
Hockey Royalty-MML
Hockey Royalty Limited-MML
Pillars of Strength-PS4
Starring Cast-CMM
Starring Cast Limited-CMM
02Upper Deck MVP-59
Gold-59
Classics-59
Golden Classics-59
Overdrive-SO7
Skate Around Jerseys-SAMM
Skate Around Jerseys-SDMS
Skate Around Jerseys-SDMT
Skate Around Jerseys-STMMT
Skate Around Jerseys-STSMJ
Souvenirs-S-MO
Vital Forces-VF7
02Upper Deck Rookie Update-31
02Upper Deck Rookie Update-116
Jerseys-DMM
Jerseys Gold-DMM

02Upper Deck Victory-69
Bronze-69
Gold-69
Silver-69
National Pride-NP54
02Upper Deck Vintage-81
02Upper Deck Vintage-270
02Upper Deck Vintage-293
Tall Boys-T22
Tall Boys Gold-T22
02Vanguard-33
LTD-33
East Meets West-5
Jerseys-15
Jerseys Gold-15
02UD SuperStars *-75
Gold-75
City All-Stars Dual Jersey-MMAR
City All-Stars Triple Jersey-IMD
Legendary Leaders Triple Jersey-AEM
03McFarlane Hockey 3-Inch Duals-20
03BAP Memorabilia-58
Emerald-58
Gold-58
Ruby-58
Sapphire-58
All-Star Complete Jerseys-ASCJ5
All-Star Emblems-ASE-1
All-Star Jerseys-ASJ-3
All-Star Jerseys-ASJ-35
All-Star Numbers-ASN-1
All-Star Staring Lineup-10
All-Star Teammates-AST3
He Shoots-He Scores Points-15
He Shoots-He Scores Prizes-2
Jersey and Stick-SJ-28
Jerseys-GJ-37
Jersey Autographs-GJ-37
Stanley Cup Playoffs-SCP-7
03BAP Ultimate Memorabilia Autographs-138
Gold-138
03BAP Ultimate Mem Auto Jerseys-138
03BAP Ultimate Mem Auto Emblems-138
03BAP Ultimate Mem Auto Sticks-138
03BAP Ultimate Memorabilia Active Eight-7
03BAP Ultimate Mem Always An All-Star-2
03BAP Ultimate Mem Always An AS Gold-2
03BAP Ultimate Mem Complete Jersey-17
03BAP Ultimate Mem Complete Jersey Gold-17
03BAP Ultimate Memorabilia Dynamic Duos-9
03BAP Ultimate Memorabilia Emblems-18
03BAP Ultimate Memorabilia Emblems Gold-18
03BAP Ultimate Mem Franch Present Future-10
03BAP Ultimate Memorabilia Jerseys-14
03BAP Ultimate Memorabilia Jerseys Gold-14
03BAP Ultimate Mem Jersey and Emblems-28
03BAP Ultimate Mem Jersey and Emblem Gold-28
03BAP Ultimate Mem Jersey and Numbers-28
03BAP Ultimate Mem Jersey and Number Gold-28
03BAP Ultimate Mem Jersey and Stick-7
03BAP Ultimate Mem Jersey and Stick Gold-7
03BAP Ultimate Memorabilia Nameplates-6
03BAP Ultimate Mem Nameplates Gold-6
03BAP Ultimate Memorabilia Numbers-11
03BAP Ultimate Memorabilia Numbers Gold-11
03BAP Ultimate Memorabilia Triple Threads-15
03Beehive-68
Variations-68
Gold-68
Silver-68
Jumbo Jerseys-BH10
Jerseys-JT1
Sticks Beige Border-BE7
Sticks Red Border-RE6
03Black Diamond-52
Black-52
Green-52
Red-52
Threads-DT-MO
Threads Green-DT-MO
Threads Red-DT-MO
Threads Black-DT-MO
03Bowman-99
Gold-99
Goal to Goal-MN
03Bowman Chrome-99
Refractors-99
Gold Refractors-99
Xfractors-99
03Crown Royale-33
Blue-33
Retail-33
Global Conquest-10
Jerseys-8
Patches-8
Lords of the Rink-10
03ITG Action-163
Center of Attention-CA8
Jerseys-M194
Jerseys-M214
Jerseys-M250
03ITG Toronto Fall Expo Jerseys-FE19
03ITG Used Signature Series-104
Gold-104
Autographs-MM
Autographs Gold-MM
Franchise-10
Franchise Autographs-10
Franchise Gold-10
Game-Day Jerseys-2
Game-Day Jerseys Gold-2
International Experience-26
International Experience Autographs-26
International Experience Emblems Gold-26
International Experience Emblems-26
International Experience Gold-26
Jerseys-28
Jerseys Gold-28
Jersey Autos-28
Emblems-20
Emblems Gold-20
Jersey and Stick-28
Jersey and Stick Gold-28
Teammates-19
Teammates Gold-19
03ITG VIP Collages-11
03ITG VIP International Experience-4
03ITG VIP Jerseys-14
03ITG VIP Jersey and Emblems-10
03ITG VIP Jersey and Numbers-10
03McDonald's Pacific-15
Patches Silver-8
Patches Gold-8
Patches and Sticks-8
03NHL Sticker Collection-205
03O-Pee-Chee-9
03OPC Blue-9
03OPC Gold-9
03OPC Red-9
03Pacific-107
Blue-107
Red-107
Cramer's Choice-4
Jerseys-13
Jerseys Gold-13
Main Attractions-5
Milestones-3
View from the Crease-4
03Pacific Calder-32
Silver-32
03Pacific Complete-135
Red-135
03Pacific Exhibit-165
Blue Backs-165
03Pacific Heads-Up-32
Hobby LTD-32
Retail LTD-32
Fast Forwards-4
Fast Forwards LTD-4
03Pacific Invincible-30
Blue-30
Red-30
Retail-30
Afterburners-4
Featured Performers-10
03Pacific Luxury Suite-8A
03Pacific Luxury Suite-8B
03Pacific Luxury Suite-8C
03Pacific Luxury Suite-8D
03Pacific Luxury Suite-32A
03Pacific Luxury Suite-32B
03Pacific Luxury Suite-32C
03Pacific Prism-114
Blue-114
Patches-114
Red-114
Retail-114
Stat Masters-5
03Pacific Quest for the Cup-32
Blue-32
Raising the Cup-6
03Pacific Supreme-30
Blue-30
Red-30
Retail-30
03Parkhurst Orig Six Boston Mem -BM46
03Parkhurst Orig Six Chicago Mem -CM46
03Parkhurst Orig Six Detroit Mem-DM46
03Parkhurst Orig Six Montreal Mem-MM46
03Parkhurst Orig Six New York Mem-NM46
03Parkhurst Original Six Shooters-OSM6
03Parkhurst Orig Six Toronto Mem-TM46
03Parkhurst Rookie-42
High Expectations-HE-8
High Expectations Gold-HE-8
Jerseys-GJ-20
Jerseys Gold-GJ-20
Jersey and Sticks-SJ-18
Jersey and Sticks Gold-SJ-18
Retro Rookies-RR-1
Retro Rookie Autographs-RR-MM
Retro Rookies Gold-RR-1
Teammates Gold-RT5
Teammates-RT5
03Private Stock Reserve-163
Blue-163
Patches-163
Red-163
Retail-163
Moments in Time-6
03SP Authentic-28
Limited-28
10th Anniversary-SP9
10th Anniversary Limited-SP9
Breakout Seasons-B13
Breakout Seasons Limited-B13
Foundations-F7
Foundations Limited-F7
Honors-H20
Honors Limited-H20
03SP Game Used-16
03SP Game Used-116
Gold-16
Gold-116
Authentic Fabrics-DFMT
Authentic Fabrics-QMGTM
Authentic Fabrics Gold-DFMT
Authentic Fabrics Gold-QMGTM
Authentic Patches-APMM
Double Threads-DTMG
Double Threads-DTMT
Limited Threads-LTMM
Limited Threads Gold-LTMM
Team Threads-TTMGT
03SPx-31
03SPx-119
03SPx-147
03SPx-186
Radiance-31
Radiance-119
Radiance-147
Radiance-186
Spectrum-31
Spectrum-119
Spectrum-147
Spectrum-186
Fantasy Franchise-FF-MGT
Fantasy Franchise Limited-FF-MGT
VIP-VIP-MG
VIP Limited-VIP-MG
Winning Materials-WM-MO
Winning Materials Limited-WM-MO
03Stars Postcards-16
03Titanium-151
Hobby Jersey Number Parallels-151
Patches-151
Retail-151
03Topps-9
03Topps-PP4
Blue-9
Gold-9
Red-9
Box Toppers-19
First Overall Fabrics-MM
First Overall Fabrics-MLMM
First Overall Fabrics-MMMS
Topps/OPC Idols-UI5
Lost Rookies-MM
03Topps C55-9
Minis-9
Minis American Back-9
Minis American Back Red-9
Minis Bazooka Back-9
Minis Brooklyn Back-9
Minis Hat Trick Back-9
Minis O Canada Back-9
Minis O Canada Back Red-9
Minis Stanley Cup Back-9
Relics-TRMM
03Topps Pristine-44
Gold Refractor Die Cuts-44
Refractors-44
Patches-PP-MM
Patch Refractors-PP-MM
Popular Demand Relics-PD-MM
Popular Demand Relic Refractors-PD-MM
Press Plates Black-44
Press Plates Cyan-44
Press Plates Magenta-44
Press Plates Yellow-44
03UD Honor Roll-26
03UD Honor Roll-113
03UD Honor Roll-132
03UD Premier Collection-19
Teammates-PT-DS1
Teammates-PT-DS2
Teammates Patches-PT-DS1
Teammates Patches-PT-DS2
03Upper Deck-59
All-Star Class-AS-8
Big Playmakers-BP-MM
Canadian Exclusives-59
Fan Favorites-FF7
HG-59
NHL Best-NB-MM
Patches-LD2
Performers-PS10
Superstar Spotlight-SS8
Team Essentials-TP-MM
03Upper Deck Classic Portraits-28
03Upper Deck Classic Portraits-155
Starring Cast-SC-MM
03Upper Deck Ice-26
Gold-26
Breakers-IB-MM
Breaker Patches-IB-MM
Clear Cut Winners-CC-MM
Icons-I-MM
Icons Jerseys-I-MM
03Upper Deck MVP-127
Gold Script-127
Silver Script-127
Canadian Exclusives-127
SportsNut-SN28
Talent-MT15
Winning Formula-WF8
03Upper Deck Rookie Update-28
Skills-SKMM
Super Stars-SSMM
03Upper Deck Trilogy-28
03Upper Deck Trilogy-120
Authentic Patches-AP3
Crest Variations-120
Limited-28
Limited-120
Limited Threads-LT9
03Upper Deck Victory-56
Bronze-56
Gold-56
Silver-56
Freshman Flashback-FF16
Game Breakers-GB22
03Toronto Star-28
Foil-8
04ITG NHL AS FANtasy AS History Jerseys-SB48
04ITG All-Star FANtasy Hall Minnesota-3
04Pacific-86
Blue-86
Red-86
All-Stars-5
04Pacific NHL All-Star Nets-2
Gold-2
04SP Authentic-28
04SP Authentic-110
04SP Game Used Hawaii Conference Patch-PP22
04Ultimate Collection-13
04Ultimate Collection-81
Dual Logos-UL2-MT
Jerseys-UGJ-MO
Jerseys Gold-UGJ-MO
Patches-UP-MO
04Upper Deck-54
04Upper Deck-195
1997 Game Jerseys-MM
Big Playmakers-BP-MM
Canadian Exclusives-54
Canadian Exclusives-195
HG Glossy Gold-54
HG Glossy Gold-195
HG Glossy Silver-54
HG Glossy Silver-195
Patches-GJPA-MO
Patches-GJPL-MO
Patches-GJPN-MO
Three Stars-AS4
World's Best-WB29
World Cup Tribute-MM
World Cup Tribute-DWMOCD
05Be A Player-29
First Period-29
Second Period-29
Third Period-29
Overtime-29
Class Action-CA9
Outtakes-OT18
World Cup Salute-WCS8
05Beehive-28
05Beehive-185
Beige -28
Blue -28
Gold-28
Red -28
Matte-28
Matted Materials-MMMM
PhotoGraphs-PGMM
Signature Scrapbook-SSMM
05Black Diamond-132
Emerald-132
Gold-132
Onyx-132
Ruby-132
Jerseys-J-MM
Jerseys Ruby-J-MM
Jersey Duals-DJ-MM
Jersey Triples-TJ-MM
Jersey Quads-QJ-MM
05Hot Prospects-30
En Fuego-30
Red Hot-30
White Hot-30
05McDonalds Upper Deck-40
Top Scorers-TS7
05Panini Stickers-247
05Parkhurst-162
05Parkhurst-510
05Parkhurst-680
Facsimile Auto Parallel-162
Facsimile Auto Parallel-510
Facsimile Auto Parallel-680
True Colors-TCDAL
True Colors-TCDAL
True Colors-TCMIDA
True Colors-TCMIDA
05SP Authentic-31
05SP Authentic-104
Limited-31
Limited-104
Chirography-SPMM
Exquisite Endorsements-EEMM
Marks of Distinction-MDMM
Sign of the Times Duals-DMA
Sign of the Times Fives-MMZTJ
05SP Game Used-31
Autographs-31
Gold-31
Authentic Fabrics-AF-MM
Authentic Fabrics Dual-TM
Authentic Fabrics Dual Autographs-TM
Authentic Fabrics Gold-AF-MM
Authentic Fabrics Quad-MTGA
Authentic Patches Quad -MTGA
Authentic Fabrics Triple-MLR
Authentic Patches-AP-MM
Authentic Patches Dual-TM
Authentic Patches Dual Autographs-TM
Authentic Patches Triple-MLR
Auto Draft-AD-MM
Awesome Authentics-AA-MM
Awesome Authentics Gold-DA-MM
Game Gear-GG-MM
Game Gear Autographs-AG-MM
Significant Numbers-SN-MM
05SPx-25
05SPx-114
Spectrum-25
Spectrum-114
Winning Combos-WC-DA
Winning Combos-WC-MM
Winning Combos-WC-TM
Winning Combos Autographs-AWC-MM
Winning Combos Gold-WC-DA
Winning Combos Gold-WC-MM
Winning Combos Gold-WC-TM
Winning Combos Spectrum-WC-DA
Winning Combos Spectrum-WC-MM
Winning Combos Spectrum-WC-TM
Winning Materials-WM-MM
Winning Materials Autographs-AWM-MO
Winning Materials Gold-WM-MM
Winning Materials Spectrum-WM-MM
Xcitement Superstars-XS-MO
Xcitement Superstars Gold-XS-MO
Xcitement Superstars Spectrum-XS-MO
05The Cup-35
Gold-35
Black Rainbow-35
Dual NHL Shields-DSMG
Dual NHL Shields-DSMT
Dual NHL Shields Autographs-ADSMT
Emblems of Endorsement-EEMM
Limited Logos-LLMM
Masterpiece Pressplates-35
Masterpiece Pressplates Rookie Upd Auto-273
Noble Numbers-NNMK
Noble Numbers Dual-DNNMG
Noble Numbers Dual-DNNMR
Patch Variation-P35
Patch Variation Autographs-AP35
Scripted Numbers-SNMH
Scripted Numbers Dual-DSNDA
Scripted Numbers Dual-DSNMM
Scripted Swatches-SSMM
Signature Patches-SPMM
05UD Artifacts-32
05UD Artifacts-163
Blue-32
Blue-163
Gold-32
Gold-163
Green-32
Green-163
Pewter-32
Pewter-163
Red-32
Red-163
Auto Facts-AF-MM
Auto Facts Blue-AF-MM
Auto Facts Copper-AF-MM
Auto Facts Pewter-AF-MM
Auto Facts Silver-AF-MM
Gold Autographed-32
Gold Autographed-163
Remarkable Artifacts-RA-MM
Remarkable Artifacts Dual-RA-MM
Treasured Patches-TP-MM
Treasured Patches Autographed-TP-MM
Treasured Patches Dual-TPD-MM
Treasured Patches Dual Autographed-TPD-MM
Treasured Patches Pewter-TP-MM
Treasured Patches Silver-TP-MM
Treasured Swatches-TS-MM
Treasured Swatches Autographed-TS-MM
Treasured Swatches Blue-TS-MM
Treasured Swatches Copper-TS-MM
Treasured Swatches Dual-TSD-MM
Treasured Swatches Dual Autographed-TSD-MM
Treasured Swatches Dual Blue-TSD-MM
Treasured Swatches Dual Copper-TSD-MM
Treasured Swatches Dual Maroon-TSD-MM
Treasured Swatches Dual Pewter-TSD-MM
Treasured Swatches Dual Silver-TSD-MM
Treasured Swatches Maroon-TS-MM
Treasured Swatches Pewter-TS-MM
Treasured Swatches Silver-TS-MM
05UD PowerPlay-29
Rainbow-29
Specialists-TSMM
Specialists Patches-SPMM
05UD Toronto Fall Expo Priority Signings-PS-MM
05Ultimate Collection-29
Gold-29
Endorsed Emblems-EEMM
Jerseys-JMM
Marquee Attractions-MA17
Marquee Attractions Signatures-SMA17
National Heroes Jerseys-NHJMM
National Heroes Patches-NHPMM
Premium Patches-PPMM
Premium Swatches-PSMM
Ultimate Achievements-UAMM
Ultimate Patches-PMM
Ultimate Signatures-USMM
Ultimate Signatures Logos-SLMM
Ultimate Signatures Pairings-UPMT
05Ultra-68
Gold-68
Ice-68
Scoring Kings-SK6
Scoring Kings Jerseys-SKJ-MM
Scoring Kings Jersey Autographs-KAJ-MM
Scoring Kings Patches-SKP-MM
Scoring Kings Patch Autographs-KAP-MM
05Upper Deck-305
05Upper Deck All-Time Greatest-19
05Upper Deck All-Time Greatest-75
05Upper Deck Big Playmakers-B-MM
05Upper Deck Goal Rush-GR12
05Upper Deck Hometown Heroes-HH10
05Upper Deck Jerseys-J-MM
05Upper Deck Jerseys Series II-J2MM
05Upper Deck Majestic Materials-MMMM
05Upper Deck Notable Numbers-N-MM
05Upper Deck Patches-P-MMO
05Upper Deck Scrapbooks-HS9
05Upper Deck Shooting Stars-S-MMO
05Upper Deck Ice-28
Rainbow-28
Cool Threads-CTMM
Cool Threads Autographs-ACTMM
Cool Threads Glass-CTMM
Cool Threads Patches-CTPMM
Cool Threads Patch Autographs-CAPMM
Glacial Graphs-GGMM
Signature Swatches-SSMM
05Upper Deck MVP-125
Gold-125
Platinum-125
Rising to the Occasion-RO9
05Upper Deck Rookie Update-30
05Upper Deck Rookie Update-273
05Upper Deck Trilogy-29
05Upper Deck Trilogy-108
Crystal-108
Honorary Patches-HP-MO
Honorary Patch Scripts-HSP-MO
Honorary Swatches-HS-MO
Honorary Swatch Scripts-HSS-MO
Ice Scripts-IS-MM
05Upper Deck Victory-60
Black-60
Gold-60
Silver-60
Blow-Ups-BU12
Game Breakers-GB14
Stars on Ice-SI19
06Be A Player Portraits-35
Dual Signature Portraits-DSMT
Dual Signature Portraits-DSSM
Sensational Six-SS1ST
Sensational Six-SSSTR
Signature Portraits-SPMM
Triple Signature Portraits-TSSM
06Beehive-68
06Beehive-208
Blue-68
Gold-68
Matte-68
Red Facsimile Signatures-68
Wood-68
5 X 7 Black and White-68
5 X 7 Dark Wood-68
Matted Materials-MMMM
PhotoGraphs-PGMM
Remarkable Matted Materials-MMMM
06Black Diamond-134
Black-134
Black-154B
Gold-134
Ruby-134
Jerseys-JMM
Jerseys Black-JMM
Jerseys Gold-JMM
Jerseys Ruby-JMM
06Flair Showcase-34
06Flair Showcase-181
06Flair Showcase-225
06Flair Showcase-279
Parallel-34
Parallel-181
Parallel-225
Parallel-279
Hot Numbers-HN15
Hot Numbers Parallel-HN15
Stitches-SSMM
06Fleer-62
Tiffany-62
Fabricology-FMM
Speed Machines-SM11
Total O-O7
06Hot Prospects-33
Red Hot-33
White Hot-33
Hot Materials -HMMM
Hot Materials Red Hot-HMMM
Hot Materials White Hot-HMMM
06ITG Ultimate Memorabilia-105
Artist Proof-105
Autos-49
Autos Gold-49
Autos Dual-10
Autos Dual Gold-10
Autos Triple-8
Autos Triple Gold-8
Captain-C-11
Captain-C Gold-11
Complete Jersey-20
Complete Jersey Gold-20
Double Memorabilia-4
Double Memorabilia Gold-4
Double Memorabilia Autos-11
Double Memorabilia Autos Gold-11
Emblems-10
Emblems Gold-10
First Round Picks-21
First Round Picks Gold-21
Going For Gold-2
Going For Gold Gold-2
In The Numbers-14
In The Numbers Gold-14
Jerseys Autos-40
Jerseys Autos Gold-40
Legendary Captains-14
Legendary Captains Gold-14
Retrospective-9
Retrospective Gold-9
Sticks Autos-21
Sticks Autos Gold-21
06McDonald's Upper Deck-13
06NHL POG-56
06O-Pee-Chee-172
06O-Pee-Chee-648
06O-Pee-Chee-680
Rainbow-172
Rainbow-648
Rainbow-680
Swatches-S-MM
06Panini Stickers-245
06SP Authentic-70
06SP Authentic-140
Chirography-MM
Limited-70
Limited-140
Sign of the Times-STMM
Sign of the Times Duals-STMM
Sign of the Times Duals-STMR
Sign of the Times Triples-ST3MTM
06SP Game Used-31
Gold-31
Rainbow-31
Authentic Fabrics-AFMM
Authentic Fabrics Parallel-AFMM
Authentic Fabrics Patches-AFMM
Authentic Fabrics Dual-AF2ML
Authentic Fabrics Dual Patches-AF2ML
Authentic Fabrics Triple-AF3DAL
Authentic Fabrics Triple Patches-AF3DAL
Authentic Fabrics Quads-AF4MWGD
Authentic Fabrics Quads Patches-AF4MWGD
Autographs-31
By The Letter-BLMM
Inked Sweaters-ISMO
Inked Sweaters Patches-ISMO
Inked Sweaters Dual-IS2MT
Inked Sweaters Dual Patches-IS2MT
Letter Marks-LMMM
06SPx-30
06SPx-108
Spectrum-30
Spectrum-108
SPxcitement-X29
SPxcitement Spectrum-X29
Winning Materials-WMMM
Winning Materials Spectrum-WMMM
06Stars Team Postcards-15
06The Cup-26
Autographed Foundations-CQMM
Autographed Foundations Patches-CQMM
Autographed NHL Shields Duals-DASBR
Autographed NHL Shields Duals-DASMI
Autographed NHL Shields Duals-DASMT
Autographed Patches-26
Black Rainbow-26
Foundations-CQMM
Foundations Patches-CQMM
Gold-26
Gold Patches-26
Honorable Numbers-HNMM
Jerseys-26
Limited Logos-LLMM
Masterpiece Pressplates-26
NHL Shields Duals-DSHML
Property of-POMM
Scripted Swatches-SSMM
Signature Patches-SPMM
Stanley Cup Signatures-CSMM
06UD Artifacts-67
06UD Artifacts-164
Blue-67
Blue-164
Gold-67
Gold-164
Platinum-67
Platinum-164
Radiance-67
Radiance-164
Red-67
Red-164
Frozen Artifacts-FAMM
Frozen Artifacts Black-FAMM
Frozen Artifacts Blue-FAMM
Frozen Artifacts Gold-FAMM
Frozen Artifacts Platinum-FAMM
Frozen Artifacts Red-FAMM
Frozen Artifacts Patches Black-FAMM
Frozen Artifacts Patches Blue-FAMM
Frozen Artifacts Patches Gold-FAMM
Frozen Artifacts Patches Platinum-FAMM
Frozen Artifacts Patches Red-FAMM
Treasured Patches Black-TSMM
Treasured Patches Blue-TSMM
Treasured Patches Gold-TSMM
Treasured Patches Platinum-TSMM
Treasured Patches Red-TSMM
Treasured Swatches-TSMM
Treasured Swatches Black-TSMM
Treasured Swatches Blue-TSMM
Treasured Swatches Gold-TSMM
Treasured Swatches Platinum-TSMM
Treasured Swatches Red-TSMM
Tundra Tandems-TTML
Tundra Tandems Black-TTML
Tundra Tandems Blue-TTML
Tundra Tandems Gold-TTML
Tundra Tandems Platinum-TTML
Tundra Tandems Red-TTML
Tundra Tandems Dual Patches Red-TTML
06UD Mini Jersey Collection-33
06UD Powerplay-32
Impact Rainbow-32
Cup Celebrations-CC4
Specialists-SMM
Specialists Patches-PMM
06Ultimate Collection-20
Autographed Jerseys-AJ-MM
Autographed Patches-AJ-MM
Jerseys-UJ-MM
Jerseys Dual-UJ2-ML
Patches-UJ-MM
Patches Dual-UJ2-ML
Premium Patches-PS-MM
Premium Swatches-PS-MM
Signatures-US-MM
Ultimate Achievements-UA-MM
Ultimate Signatures Logos-SL-MM
06Ultra-63
Gold Medallion-63
Ice Medallion-63
Action-UA8
Scoring Kings-SK21
Uniformity-UMM
Uniformity Patches-UPMN
06Upper Deck Arena Giveaways-DAL4
06Upper Deck Arena Giveaways-DAL4
06Upper Deck-313
Exclusives Parallel-313
High Gloss Parallel-313
All-Time Greatest-ATG7
All World-AW1
Game Jerseys-JMM
Game Patches-PMM
Masterpieces-313
Oversized Wal-Mart Exclusives-313
Signatures-SMM
06Upper Deck MVP-97
Gold Script-97
Super Script-97
Clutch Performers-CP12
International Icons-II7
Jerseys-OJMT
Jerseys-OJSM
06Upper Deck Ovation-116
06Upper Deck Sweet Shot-34
Signature Shots/Saves-SSMO
Signature Shots/Saves Ice Signings-SSIMM
Signature Shots/Saves Sticks-SSSMM
Signature Sticks-STMM
Sweet Stitches-SSMM
Sweet Stitches Duals-SSMM
Sweet Stitches Triples-SSMM
06Upper Deck Trilogy-32
Combo Clearcut Autographs-C3MTM
Frozen In Time-FT14
06Upper Deck Victory-60
06Upper Deck Victory Black-60
06Upper Deck Victory Gold-60
06Upper Deck Victory GameBreakers-GB14
06Upper Deck Victory Oversize Cards-MM
06Russian Sport Collection Olympic Stars-51
07Upper Deck All-Star Game Redemptions-AS12
07Upper Deck Ovation-87
07Upper Deck Victory-188
Black-188
Gold-188
GameBreakers-GB11
Oversize Cards-OS41

Modes, Werner

72Finnish Semic World Championship-99
72Swedish Semic World Championship-99

Modig, Lars

84Swedish Semic Elitserien-177
85Swedish Panini Stickers-157
86Swedish Panini Stickers-169
87Swedish Panini Stickers-176
89Swedish Semic Elitserien Stickers-148
90Swedish Semic Elitserien Stickers-228
91Swedish Semic Elitserien Stickers-155
92Swedish Semic Elitserien Stickers-177
93Swedish Semic Elitserien-148
94Swedish Leaf-101
95Swedish Leaf-76
95Swedish Upper Deck-114

Modig, Mattias

05Swedish SHL Elitset-229
Gold-229
06Swedish SHL Elitset Goal Patrol-12
06Swedish SHL Elitset In The Crease-7

Modin, Fredrik

94Swedish Leaf-273
NHL Draft-3
Rookie Rockets-1
95Swedish Leaf-19
95Swedish Upper Deck-35
95Swedish Upper Deck-220
Ticket to North America-NA4
95Swedish Globe World Championships-59
95Signature Rookies-7
Signatures-7
96Be A Player-216
Autographs-216
Autographs Silver-216
96Donruss Canadian Ice-130
Gold Press Proofs-130
Red Press Proofs-130
96Select Certified-112
Artist's Proofs-112
Blue-112
Mirror Blue-112
Mirror Gold-112
Mirror Red-112
Red-112
96Upper Deck-345
96Swedish Semic Wien-73
97Collector's Choice-249
97Pacific-127
Copper-127
Emerald Green-127
Ice Blue-127
Red-127
Silver-127
97Panini Stickers-181
97Score Maple Leafs-13
Platinum-13
Premier-13
97Upper Deck-162
98Be A Player-134
Press Release-134
98BAP Gold-134
98BAP Autographs-134
98BAP Autographs Gold-134
98BAP Tampa Bay All Star Game-134
98Katch-143
98Pacific-419
Ice Blue-419
Red-419
98Panini Stickers-160
98Upper Deck-192
Exclusives-192
Exclusives 1 of 1-192
Gold Reserve-192
98Upper Deck MVP-193
Gold Script-193
Silver Script-193
Super Script-193
99BAP Millennium-218
Emerald-218
Ruby-218
Sapphire-218
Signatures-218
Signatures Gold-218
99Pacific Dynagon Ice-182
Blue-182
Copper-182
Gold-182
Premiere Date-182
99Pacific Omega-218
Copper-218
Gold-218
Ice Blue-218
Premiere Date-218
99Panini Stickers-147
99Wayne Gretzky Hockey-159
00BAP Memorabilia-191
Emerald-191
Ruby-191
Sapphire-191
Promos-191
00BAP Mem Chicago Sportsfest Copper-191
00BAP Memorabilia Chicago Sportsfest Blue-191
00BAP Memorabilia Chicago Sportsfest Gold-191
00BAP Memorabilia Chicago Sportsfest Ruby-191
00BAP Memorabilia Chicago Sun-Times Ruby-191
00BAP Memorabilia Chicago Sun-Times Gold-191
00BAP Mem Chicago Sun-Times Sapphire-191
00BAP Mem Toronto Fall Expo Copper-191
00BAP Memorabilia Toronto Fall Expo Gold-191
00BAP Memorabilia Toronto Fall Expo Ruby-191
00BAP Parkhurst 2000-P176
00Crown Royale-97
Ice Blue-97
Limited Series-97
Premiere Date-97
Red-97
00O-Pee-Chee-92
00O-Pee-Chee Parallel-92
00Pacific-378
Copper-378
Gold-378
Ice Blue-378
Premiere Date-378
00Panini Stickers-89
00Paramount-223
Copper-223
Gold-223
Holo-Gold-223
Holo-Silver-223
Ice Blue-223
Premiere Date-223
00SP Authentic-81
00Stadium Club-138
00Topps/OPC-92
Parallel-92
00UD Pros and Prospects-78
00Upper Deck-160
Exclusives Tier 1-160
Exclusives Tier 2-160
00Upper Deck MVP-160
First Stars-160
Second Stars-160
Third Stars-160
00Upper Deck Victory-215
00Upper Deck Vintage-327
01BAP Memorabilia-65
Emerald-65
Ruby-65
Sapphire-65
01BAP Signature Series-70
Autographs-70
Autographs Gold-70
01O-Pee-Chee-246
01O-Pee-Chee Premier Parallel-246
01Pacific-356
Extreme LTD-356
Hobby LTD-356
Premiere Date-356
Retail LTD-356
01Pacific Adrenaline-175
Blue-175
Premiere Date-175
Red-175
Retail-175
01Pacific Arena Exclusives-356
01Parkhurst-167
Jerseys-PJ31
01Topps-246
OPC Parallel-246
01Topps Heritage-109
Refractors-109
01UD Mask Collection-87
Gold-87
01Upper Deck-159
Exclusives-159
01Upper Deck MVP-172
01Upper Deck Victory-318
Gold-318
01Upper Deck Vintage-230
01Upper Deck Vintage-234
02BAP First Edition-164
02BAP Sig Series Auto Buybacks 1998-134
02BAP Sig Series Auto Buybacks 1999-218
02BAP Sig Series Auto Buybacks 2001-70
02Crown Royale Jerseys-21
02Crown Royale Jerseys Gold-21
02Lightning Team Issue-9
02O-Pee-Chee-189
02O-Pee-Chee Premier Blue Parallel-189
02O-Pee-Chee Premier Red Parallel-189
02O-Pee-Chee Factory Set-189
02Pacific-352
Blue-352
Red-352
Jerseys-46
Jerseys Holo-Silver-46
02Pacific Complete-71
Red-71
02Parkhurst-127
Bronze-127
Gold-127
Silver-127
02Parkhurst Retro-114
Minis-114
02Titanium Jerseys-65
02Titanium Jerseys Retail-65
02Titanium Patches-65
02Topps-189
OPC Blue Parallel-189
OPC Red Parallel-189
Factory Set-189
02Topps Total-256
02Upper Deck-403
Exclusives-403
02Upper Deck Beckett UD Promos-403
02Upper Deck MVP-168
Gold-168
Classics-168
Golden Classics-168
02Upper Deck Victory-196
Bronze-196

Gold-196
Silver-196
02Upper Deck Vintage-232
03Beehive-177
Gold-177
Silver-177
03ITG Action-541
03Lightning Team Issue-30
03Pacific-309
Blue-309
Red-309
Jerseys-36
Jerseys Gold-36
03Pacific Complete-352
Red-352
03Private Stock Reserve-201
Blue-201
Patches-201
Red-201
Retail-201
03Upper Deck-418
Canadian Exclusives-418
HG-418
UD Exclusives-418
03Upper Deck MVP-381
Gold Script-381
Silver Script-381
Canadian Exclusives-381
04Pacific-240
Blue-240
Red-240
04UD All-World-75
Gold-75
04Swedish Alfabilder Alfa Stars-33
04Swedish Alfabilder Alfa Star Golden Ice-12
04Swedish Alfabilder Autographs-115
04Swedish Alfabilder Limited Autographs-115
04Swedish Alfabilder Proof Parallels-33
05Be A Player World Cup Salute-WCS1
05Black Diamond-76
Emerald-76
Gold-76
Onyx-76
Ruby-76
05Panini Stickers-157
05Parkhurst-436
Facsimile Auto Parallel-436
05UD Artifacts-90
Blue-90
Gold-90
Green-90
Pewter-90
Red-90
Gold Autographed-90
05Ultra-176
Gold-176
Ice-176
05Upper Deck-171
HG Glossy-171
05Upper Deck MVP-344
Gold-344
Platinum-344
05Upper Deck Toronto Fall Expo-171
05Upper Deck Victory-175
Black-175
Gold-175
Silver-175
06Black Diamond-23
Black-23
Gold-23
Ruby-23
06Fleer-57
Tiffany-57
06O-Pee-Chee-153
Rainbow-153
06Panini Stickers-234
06SPx-28
Spectrum-28
06UD Artifacts-71
Blue-71
Gold-71
Platinum-71
Radiance-71
Red-71
06UD Mini Jersey Collection-28
06Ultra-55
Gold Medallion-55
Ice Medallion-55
06Upper Deck Arena Giveaways-CLB4
06Upper Deck-306
Exclusives Parallel-306
High Gloss Parallel-306
Masterpieces-306
06Upper Deck MVP-86
Gold Script-86
Super Script-86
06Upper Deck Ovation-144
06Upper Deck Trilogy-30
06Upper Deck Victory-181
06Upper Deck Victory-240
06Upper Deck Victory Black-181
06Upper Deck Victory Gold-181
07Upper Deck Victory-127
Black-127
Gold-127

Modry, Jaroslav

93Donruss-455
93OPC Premier-307
Gold-307
93Parkhurst-386
Emerald Ice-386
93PowerPlay-380
Rookie Standouts-7
93Score-616
Gold-616
Canadian-616
Canadian Gold-616
93Stadium Club-411
Members Only Master Set-411
First Day Issue-411
93Topps/OPC Premier-307
Gold-307
93Ultra-362
Wave of the Future-9
93Upper Deck-319
93Classic Pro Prospects-146
94Donruss-197
94Leaf-496
94OPC Premier-512
Special Effects-512
94Parkhurst-123
94Parkhurst-290
Gold-123
Gold-290
94Topps/OPC Premier-512
Special Effects-512
94Upper Deck-473
Electric Ice-473
94Czech APS Extraliga-97
94Classic Pro Prospects-24
95Parkhurst International-418
Emerald Ice-418
95Senators Team Issue-18
99Pacific Omega-108
Copper-108
Gold-108
Ice Blue-108
Premiere Date-108
00BAP Signature Series-144
Emerald-144
Ruby-144
Sapphire-144
Autographs-191
Autographs Gold-191
00Czech Stadion-126
01Upper Deck Victory-166
Gold-166
02BAP Memorabilia-90
Emerald-90
Ruby-90
Sapphire-90
NHL All-Star Game-90
NHL All-Star Game Blue-90
NHL All-Star Game Green-90
NHL All-Star Game Red-90
02BAP Memorabilia Toronto Fall Expo-90
02BAP Sig Series Auto Buybacks 2000-191
02Kings Game Sheets-7
02Kings Game Sheets-8
02O-Pee-Chee-101
02O-Pee-Chee Premier Blue Parallel-101
02O-Pee-Chee Premier Red Parallel-101
02O-Pee-Chee Factory Set-101
02Pacific-170
Blue-170
Red-170
02Pacific Complete-265
Red-265
02Parkhurst Retro-151
Minis-151
02Topps-101
OPC Blue Parallel-101
OPC Red Parallel-101
Factory Set-101
02Topps Total-170
02Czech National Team Postcards-9
03ITG Action-243
03NHL Sticker Collection-237
03O-Pee-Chee-26
03OPC Blue-26
03OPC Gold-26
03OPC Red-26
03Pacific-157
Blue-157
Red-157
03Pacific Complete-6
Red-6
03Topps-26
Blue-26
Gold-26
Red-26
03Upper Deck MVP-191
Gold Script-191
Silver Script-191
Canadian Exclusives-191
03Czech National Team Postcards-9
04Upper Deck-10
Canadian Exclusives-10
HG Glossy Gold-10
HG Glossy Silver-10
04Czech OFS-342
Stars II-12
05Panini Stickers-12
05Parkhurst-23
Facsimile Auto Parallel-23
05Upper Deck MVP-21
Gold-21
Platinum-21
05Czech Kvarteto Bonaparte-3d
06O-Pee-Chee-159
Rainbow-159
06Panini Stickers-250

Modzelewski, Jan

70Swedish Masterserien-195
70Swedish Masterserien-199

Moe, Asgaut

92Norwegian Elite Series-8

Moe, Billy

44Beehive Group II Photos-346

Moen, Jeff

92Minnesota Golden Gophers-15
93Minnesota Golden Gophers-22
94Minnesota Golden Gophers-21
95Minnesota Golden Gophers-21

Moen, Travis

00Kelowna Rockets-26
01Kelowna Rockets-14
02Norfolk Admirals-17
03Blackhawks Postcards-15
03Bowman-141
Gold-141
03Bowman Chrome-141
Refractors-141
Gold Refractors-141
Xfractors-141
03ITG VIP Rookie Debut-7
03Pacific Complete-596
Red-596
03Pacific Luxury Suite-56
Gold-56
03Pacific Supreme-110
Blue-110
Red-110
Retail-110
03Parkhurst Original Six Chicago-29
03Parkhurst Rookie-91
03Private Stock Reserve-110
Blue-110
Red-110
Retail-110
03SP Game Used-56
Gold-56
03SPx-218
Radiance-218
Spectrum-218
03Titanium-107
Hobby Jersey Number Parallels-107
Retail-107
Retail Jersey Number Parallels-107
03Topps Traded-TT95
Blue-TT95
Gold-TT95
Red-TT95
03UD Honor Roll-178
03Upper Deck-209
Canadian Exclusives-209
HG-209
04Norfolk Admirals-14
05Black Diamond Gemography-G-TM
05Black Diamond Gemography Emerald-G-TM
05Black Diamond Gemography Gold-G-TM
05Black Diamond Gemography Onyx-G-TM
05Black Diamond Gemography Ruby-G-TM
05Ducks Team Issue-12
05Upper Deck Trilogy Scripts-SFS-TM

Moes, Mike

90Newmarket Saints-16
90ProCards AHL/IHL-148

Moeser, Duanne

94German DEL-9
95German DEL-12
96German DEL-12
98German DEL-287
99German DEL-151
00German DEL-24
Game Jersey-DM
01German Upper Deck-11
02German DEL City Press-16
03German DEL-26
04German Augsburg Panthers Postcards-22
04German DEL-36
05German DEL All-Star Jerseys-AS11

Moffat, Andy

01UK Hull Thunder-4

Moffat, Caleb

01Baie-Comeau Drakkar-17
02Baie Comeau Drakkar-18

Moffat, Corri

91Air Canada SJHL-A10
91Air Canada SJHL All-Stars-18
92Saskatchewan JHL-77
97El Paso Buzzards-5
98El Paso Buzzards-19

Moffat, Lyle

74Maple Leafs Postcards-15
74O-Pee-Chee NHL-379
77O-Pee-Chee WHA-64
78Jets Postcards-16
79Jets Postcards-19
79O-Pee-Chee-277

Moffat, Mike

81Kingston Canadians-23

Moffatt, Rob

83Brantford Alexanders-7

Moffatt, Steve

99Florida Everblades-9

Moffett, Greg

83Nova Scotia Voyageurs-24

Moger, Sandy

91Lake Superior State Lakers-17
92Hamilton Canucks-19
92Classic-67
Gold-67
92Classic Four-Sport *-192
Gold-192
Autographs-192A
94Classic Pro Prospects-187
95Donruss-245
95Leaf-272
95Panini Stickers-6
95Select Certified-140
Mirror Gold-140
95Summit-185
Artist's Proofs-185
Ice-185
95Ultra-11
Gold Medallion-11
95Upper Deck-332
Electric Ice-332
Electric Ice Gold-332
96Be A Player-172
Autographs-172
Autographs Silver-172
96Summit-53
Artist's Proofs-53
Ice-53
Metal-53
Premium Stock-53
97Pacific Invincible NHL Regime-15
98Be A Player-64
Press Release-64
98BAP Gold-64
98BAP Autographs-64
98BAP Autographs Gold-64
98BAP Tampa Bay All Star Game-64
98OPC Chrome-59
Refractors-59
98Pacific-240
Ice Blue-240
Red-240
98Topps-59
O-Pee-Chee-59
99Houston Aeros-19
01Finnish Cardset-377
02BAP Sig Series Auto Buybacks 1998-64
02German DEL City Press-224

Moggi, Claudio

01Swiss HNL-161
02Swiss HNL-382

Moggi, Sandro

01Swiss HNL-162
02Swiss HNL-150

Mogilny, Alexander

89Sabres Blue Shield-13
89Sabres Campbell's-15
90Bowman-240
Tiffany-240
90O-Pee-Chee-42
90O-Pee-Chee Box Bottoms-A
90OPC Premier-75
90Panini Stickers-338
90Pro Set-26
90Sabres Blue Shield-15
90Sabres Campbell's-18
90Score-43
Canadian-43
90Score Young Superstars-26
90Topps-42
Tiffany-42
90Topps Box Bottoms-A
90Upper Deck-24
French-24
91Pro Set Platinum-14
91Pro Set Platinum-283
91Bowman-30
91Kraft-60
91O-Pee-Chee-32
91O-Pee-Chee-171
91Panini Stickers-304
91Parkhurst-12
French-12
91Pinnacle-163
French-163
91Pro Set-16
French-16
91Sabres Blue Shield-14
91Sabres Pepsi/Campbell's-14
91Score American-236
91Score Canadian Bilingual-456
91Score Canadian English-456
91Score Young Superstars-13
91Stadium Club-195
91Topps-171
91Upper Deck-267
91Upper Deck-618
French-267
French-618
Euro-Stars-2
Euro-Stars French-2
91Finnish Semic World Champ Stickers-218
91Russian Stars Red Ace-14
91Russian Sports Unite Hearts-8
91Russian Stars in NHL-8
91Swedish Semic World Champ Stickers-218
92Bowman-34
92Bowman-235
92Humpty Dumpty I-16
92McDonald's Upper Deck-22
92O-Pee-Chee-279
92Panini Stickers-248
92Panini Stickers-299
92Panini Stickers French-248
92Panini Stickers French-299
92Parkhurst-13
92Parkhurst-218
Emerald Ice-13
Emerald Ice-218
92Pinnacle Canadian Promo Panels-3
92Pinnacle-77
French-77
Team 2000-28
Team 2000 French-28
92Pro Set-19
92Sabres Blue Shield-13
92Sabres Jubilee Foods-9
92Score-248
Canadian-248
Young Superstars-8
92Sports Illustrated for Kids II-154
92Stadium Club-320
92Topps-382
Gold-382G
92Ultra-18
Imports-16
92Upper Deck-167
92Upper Deck-456
World Junior Grads-WG18
93Donruss-39
Elite Inserts-8
Special Print-C
93Kraft-16
93Leaf-91
Gold All-Stars-8
Hat Trick Artists-2
93McDonald's Upper Deck-19
93OPC Premier-148
93OPC Premier-172
93OPC Premier-245
Gold-148
Gold-172
Gold-245
Black Gold-10
93Panini Stickers-J
93Parkhurst-21
Emerald Ice-21
93Pinnacle II Samples-NF9
93Pinnacle-10
Canadian-10
All-Stars-22
All-Stars Canadian-22
Nifty Fifty-2
Team Pinnacle-12
Team Canadian-12
Team 2001-2
Team 2001 Canadian-2
93PowerPlay-32
Global Greats-5
Point Leaders-10
93Sabres Limited Edition Team Issue-4
93Sabres Noco-13
93Score-222
93Score-477
Canadian-222
Canadian-477
Dream Team-20
Dynamic Duos U.S.-2
International Stars-8
International Stars Canadian-8
93Seasons Patches-12
93Stadium Club-91
Members Only Master Set-91
OPC-91
First Day Issue-91
First Day Issue OPC-91
All-Stars-12
All-Stars Members Only-12
All-Stars OPC-12
93Topps/OPC Premier-148
93Topps/OPC Premier-172
93Topps/OPC Premier-245
Gold-148
Gold-172
Gold-245
93Ultra-238
All-Stars-5
Red Light Specials-7
Speed Merchants-7
93Upper Deck-234
93Upper Deck-488
Future Heroes-34
Hat Tricks-HT15
NHL's Best-HB1
Silver Skates-H10
Silver Skates Gold-H10
SP-18
93Upper Deck Locker All-Stars-8
93Classic-122
Autographs-AU5
Crash Numbered-N7
94Hockey Canadian-8
94SLU Hockey Canadian-8
94SLU Hockey American-14
94Action Packed Big Picture 24K Gold-5G
94Be A Player-R68
94Canada Games NHL POGS-44
94Donruss-92
94EA Sports-17
94EA Sports-191
94Finest-68
94Finest-99
Super Team Winners-68
Super Team Winners-99
Refractors-68
Refractors-99
94Flair-20
Scoring Power-8
94Fleer-25
94Hockey Wit-75
94Kenner Starting Lineup Cards-15
94Kraft-24
94Leaf-256
Fire on Ice-10
94Leaf Limited-36
94McDonald's Upper Deck-McD8
94OPC Premier-50
Special Effects-50
94Parkhurst-21
Gold-21
SE Euro-Stars-ES14
SE Vintage-34
94Pinnacle-125
Artist's Proofs-125
Rink Collection-125
Boomers-BR17
94Post Box Backs-17
94Score-200
Gold-200
Platinum-200
94Select-22
Gold-22
94SP-13
Die Cuts-13
94Stadium Club Members Only-26
94Topps/OPC Premier-50
Special Effects-50
The Go To Guy-13
94Topps Finest Bronze-19
94Ultra-26
All-Stars-5
Global Greats-6
Speed Merchants-8
94Upper Deck-334
94Upper Deck-552
Electric Ice-334
Electric Ice-552
Predictor Hobby-H9
94Upper Deck Predictor Hobby Exch Gold-H9
94Upper Deck Predictor Hobby Exch Silver-H9
94Upper Deck SP Inserts-SP10
94Upper Deck SP Inserts Die Cuts-SP10
94Classic Pro Prospects Jumbos-PP8
95Bashan Super Stickers-122
95Bashan Super Stickers-124
95Be A Player-204
Signatures-S204
Signatures Die Cuts-S204
Lethal Lines-LL9
95Bowman-5
All-Foil-5
Bowman's Best-BB9
Bowman's Best Refractors-BB9
95Canada Games NHL POGS-272
95Collector's Choice-163
Player's Club-163
Player's Club Platinum-163
95Donruss-275
95Donruss Elite-18
Die Cut Stars-18
Die Cut Uncut-18
Cutting Edge-7
95Emotion-182
95Finest-140
95Finest-160
Refractors-140
Refractors-160
95Hoyle Eastern Playing Cards-42
95Imperial Stickers-124
95Kraft-56
95Leaf-187
Freeze Frame-8
95Leaf Limited-83
Stars of the Game-6
95McDonald's Pinnacle-MCD-21
95Metal-153
International Steel-15
Winners-5
95NHL Cool Trade-19
95NHL Cool Trade-RP19
95Panini Stickers-294
95Parkhurst International-212
95Parkhurst International-246
Emerald Ice-212
Emerald Ice-246
Crown Collection Silver Series 2-3
Crown Collection Gold Series 2-3
Parkie's Trophy Picks-PP18
Parkie's Trophy Picks-PP48
95Playoff One on One-102
95Playoff One on One-209
95Playoff One on One-318
95Pro Magnets-29
95Score-21
Black Ice Artist's Proofs-21
Black Ice-21
Golden Blades-3
95Select Certified Promos-43
95Select Certified-43
Mirror Gold-43
95SkyBox Impact-171
95SP-148
Stars/Etoiles-E28
Stars/Etoiles Gold-E28
95Stadium Club Members Only-6
95Stadium Club-1
Members Only Master Set-1
Extreme North-EN9
Extreme North Members Only Master Set-EN9
95Stadium Club Master Photo Test-6
95Summit-48
Artist's Proofs-48
Ice-48
95Topps-225
95Topps-376
OPC Inserts-225
OPC Inserts-376
Marquee Men Power Boosters-376
Power Lines-6PL
95Topps SuperSkills-36
Platinum-36
95Ultra-21
95Ultra-317
Gold Medallion-21
Extra Attackers-15
95Upper Deck-188
95Upper Deck-221
Electric Ice-188
Electric Ice-221
Electric Ice Gold-188
Electric Ice Gold-221
95Upper Deck All-Star Game Predictors-4
Redemption Winners-4
95Upper Deck NHL All-Stars-AS10
95Upper Deck NHL All-Stars Jumbo-AS10
95Upper Deck Predictor Retail-R6
95Upper Deck Predictor Retail-R35
95Upper Deck Predictor Retail Exchange-R6
95Upper Deck Predictor Retail Exchange-R35
95Upper Deck Special Edition-SE173
95Upper Deck Special Edition Gold-SE173
95Zenith-31
95Swedish World Championships Stickers-285
96Be A Player Biscuit In The Basket-24
96Black Diamond-89
Gold-89
96Canucks Postcards-89
96Collector's Choice-267
96Collector's Choice-333
MVP-UD4
MVP Gold-UD4
Crash the Game-C3A
Crash the Game-C3B
Crash the Game-C3C
Crash the Game Gold-C3A
Crash the Game Gold-C3B
Crash the Game Gold-C3C
Crash the Game Exchange-CR3
Crash the Game Exchange Gold-CR3
96Collector's Choice Blow-Ups Bi-Way-8
96Donruss-181
Press Proofs-181
Dominators-7
Go Top Shelf-4
96Donruss Canadian Ice-91
Gold Press Proofs-91
Red Press Proofs-91
96Donruss Elite-56
Die Cut Stars-56
Status-9
96Flair-96
Blue Ice-96
96Fleer-114
96Fleer-138
Art Ross-16
Picks Dream Lines-4
Picks Fabulous 50-31
Picks Jagged Edge-3
96Hockey Greats Coins-16
Gold-16
96Kraft Upper Deck-24
96Kraft Upper Deck-69
96Leaf-162
Press Proofs-162
Fire On Ice-2
96Leaf Leather And Laces Promos-P11
96Leaf Leather And Laces-11
96Leaf Limited-8
Gold-8
Stubble-13
96Leaf Preferred-2
Press Proofs-2
Steel-51
Steel Gold-51
96Maggers-62
96McDonald's Pinnacle-11
96Metal Universe-159
Ice Carvings-11
Ice Carvings Super Power-11
Lethal Weapons-14
Lethal Weapons Super Power-14
96NHL Aces Playing Cards-34
96NHL Pro Stamps-29
96Pinnacle-87
Artist's Proofs-87
Foil-87
Premium Stock-87
Rink Collection-87
96Playoff One on One-422
96Score Samples-16
96Score-16
Artist's Proofs-16
Dealer's Choice Artist's Proofs-16
Special Artist's Proofs-16
Golden Blades-16
Dream Team-9
Sudden Death-8
96Select Certified-70
Artist's Proofs-70
Blue-70
Mirror Blue-70
Mirror Gold-70
Mirror Red-70
Red-70
96SkyBox Impact-135
BladeRunners-15
96SP-158
Game Film-GF12
96SPx-47
Gold-47
96Stadium Club Members Only-10
96Summit-107
Artist's Proofs-107
Ice-107
Metal-107
Premium Stock-107
High Voltage-11
High Voltage Mirage-11
Untouchables-9
96Team Out-39
96Topps Picks-9
Fantasy Team-FT19
OPC Inserts-9
Top Shelf-TS9
96Ultra-170
Gold Medallion-170
Power-13
Power Red Line-5
96Upper Deck-167
Generation Next-X29
Hart Hopefuls Bronze-HH12
Hart Hopefuls Gold-HH12
Hart Hopefuls Silver-HH12
Superstar Showdown-SS10B
96Upper Deck Ice-104
Parallel-104
96Zenith-34
Artist's Proofs-34
Z-Team-9
97Be A Player-247
Autographs-247
Autographs Die-Cuts-247
Autographs Prismatic Die-Cuts-247
Take A Number-18
97Black Diamond-97
Double Diamond-97
Triple Diamond-97
Quadruple Diamond-97
97Collector's Choice-256
Star Quest-SQ69
97Crown Royale-137
Emerald Green-137
Ice Blue-137
Silver-137
97Donruss-106
Press Proofs Silver-106
Press Proofs Gold-106
97Donruss Canadian Ice-45
Dominion Series-45
Provincial Series-45
97Donruss Elite-69
Aspirations-69
Status-69
97Donruss Limited-68
97Donruss Limited-104
97Donruss Limited-122
Exposure-68
Exposure-104
Exposure-122
Fabric of the Game-51
97Donruss Preferred-39
97Donruss Preferred-170
Cut to the Chase-39
Cut to the Chase-170
97Donruss Priority-119
Stamp of Approval-119
97Esso Olympic Hockey Heroes-39
97Esso Olympic Hockey Heroes French-39
97Gatorade Stickers-3
97Katch-149
Gold-149
Silver-149
97Leaf-25
Fractal Matrix-25
Fractal Matrix Die Cuts-25
97Leaf International-25
Universal Ice-25
97McDonald's Upper Deck Game Film-2
97Pacific-89
Copper-89
Emerald Green-89
Ice Blue-89
Red-89
Silver-89
Slap Shots Die-Cuts-11C
97Pacific Dynagon-129
Copper-129
Dark Grey-129
Emerald Green-129
Ice Blue-129
Red-129
Silver-129
Dynamic Duos-15B
Tandems-55
97Pacific Invincible-144
Copper-144
Emerald Green-144
Ice Blue-144
Red-144
Silver-144
Attack Zone-24
Feature Performers-35
NHL Regime-203
97Pacific Omega-232
Copper-232
Dark Gray-232
Emerald Green-232
Gold-232
Ice Blue-232
97Panini Stickers-237
97Pinnacle-58
Artist's Proofs-58
Rink Collection-58
Press Plates Back Black-58
Press Plates Back Cyan-58
Press Plates Back Magenta-58
Press Plates Back Yellow-58
Press Plates Front Black-58
Press Plates Front Cyan-58
Press Plates Front Magenta-58
Press Plates Front Yellow-58
97Pinnacle Certified-60
Red-60
Mirror Blue-60
Mirror Gold-60
Mirror Red-60
97Pinnacle Inside-34
Coach's Collection-34
Executive Collection-34
Track-27
97Pinnacle Tot Cert Platinum Blue-60
97Pinnacle Tot Certi Platinum Gold-60
97Pinnacle Totally Certified Platinum Red-60
97Pinnacle Tot Cert Mirror Platinum Gold-60
97Revolution-143
Copper-143
Emerald-143
Ice Blue-143
Silver-143
97Score-129
Artist's Proofs-129
Golden Blades-129
97Score Canucks-2
Platinum-2
Premier-2
97SP Authentic-155
97Upper Deck Three Star Selects-19B
97Zenith-79
Z-Gold-79
Z-Silver-79
98Aurora-190
98Be A Player-141
Press Release-141
98BAP Gold-141
98BAP Autographs-141
98BAP Autographs Gold-141
98BAP AS Game Used Stick Cards-S13
98BAP AS Game Used Jersey Cards-AS14
98BAP Playoff Game Used Jerseys-G21
98BAP Playoff Highlights-P2
98BAP Tampa Bay All Star Game-141
98Bowman's Best-40
Refractors-40
Atomic Refractors-40
98Crown Royale-136
Limited Series-136
98Finest-129
No Protectors-129
No Protectors Refractors-129
Refractors-129
98OPC Chrome-207
Refractors-207
98Pacific-89
Ice Blue-89
Red-89
98Pacific Dynagon Ice-190
Blue-190
Red-190
98Pacific Omega-237
Red-237
Opening Day Issue-237
98Panini Photocards-53
98Panini Stickers-217
98Paramount-237
Copper-237
Emerald Green-237
Holo-Electric-237
Ice Blue-237
Silver-237
98Revolution-142
Ice Shadow-142
Red-142
98SP Authentic Sign of the Times-AM
98SP Authentic Sign of the Times Gold-AM
98Topps-207
O-Pee-Chee-207
98Topps Gold Label Class 1-62
Black-62
Black One of One-62
One of One-62
Red-62
Red One of One-62
98Topps Gold Label Class 2-62
98Topps Gold Label Class 2 Black-62
98Topps Gold Label Class 2 Black 1 of 1-62
98Topps Gold Label Class 2 One of One-62
98Topps Gold Label Class 2 Red-62
98Topps Gold Label Class 2 Red One of One-62
98Topps Gold Label Class 3-62
98Topps Gold Label Class 3 Black-62
98Topps Gold Label Class 3 Black 1 of 1-62
98Topps Gold Label Class 3 One of One-62
98Topps Gold Label Class 3 Red-62
98Topps Gold Label Class 3 Red One of One-62
98UD Choice-210
Prime Choice Reserve-210
Reserve-210
98Upper Deck-376
Exclusives-376
Exclusives 1 of 1-376
Gold Reserve-376
98Upper Deck MVP-204
Gold Script-204
Silver Script-204
Super Script-204
99Aurora-142
Premiere Date-142
99BAP Memorabilia-286
99BAP Memorabilia-349
Gold-286
Gold-349
Silver-286
Silver-349
99BAP Update Teammates Jersey Cards-TM36
99BAP Millennium-243
Emerald-243
Ruby-243
Sapphire-243
Signatures-243
Signatures Gold-243
Jerseys-J31
Jersey and Stick Cards-JS31
Jersey Emblems-E31
Jersey Numbers-N31
99Black Diamond-87
Diamond Cut-87
Final Cut-87
99Pacific-427
Copper-427
Emerald Green-427
Gold-427
Ice Blue-427
Premiere Date-427
Red-427
99Pacific Dynagon Ice-195
Blue-195
Copper-195
Gold-195
Premiere Date-195
99Pacific Omega-235
Copper-235
Gold-235
Ice Blue-235
Premiere Date-235
99Pacific Prism-143
Holographic Blue-143
Holographic Gold-143
Holographic Mirror-143
Holographic Purple-143
Premiere Date-143
99Panini Stickers-309
99Paramount-236
Copper-236
Emerald-236
Gold-236
Holographic Emerald-236
Holographic Gold-236
Holographic Silver-236
Ice Blue-236
Premiere Date-236
Red-236
Silver-236
99SP Authentic-87
99Topps Gold Label Class 1-77
Black-77
Black One of One-77
One of One-77
Red-77
Red One of One-77
99Topps Gold Label Class 2-77
99Topps Gold Label Class 2 Black-77
99Topps Gold Label Class 2 Black 1 of 1-77
99Topps Gold Label Class 2 One of One-77
99Topps Gold Label Class 2 Red-77
99Topps Gold Label Class 2 Red One of One-77
99Topps Gold Label Class 3-77
99Topps Gold Label Class 3 Black-77
99Topps Gold Label Class 3 Black 1 of 1-77

99Topps Gold Label Class 3 One of One-77
99Topps Gold Label Class 3 Red-77
99Topps Gold Label Class 3 Red One of One-77
99Upper Deck-300
Exclusives-300
Exclusives 1 of 1-300
99Upper Deck Gold Reserve-300
99Upper Deck MVP-210
Gold Script-210
Silver Script-210
Super Script-210
99Upper Deck Victory-299
99Wayne Gretzky Hockey-168
99Russian Stars of Hockey-29
99Slovakian Challengers-6
00BAP Memorabilia-219
Emerald-219
Ruby-219
Sapphire-219
Promos-219
00BAP Mem Chicago Sportsfest Copper-219
00BAP Memorabilia Chicago Sportsfest Blue-219
00BAP Memorabilia Chicago Sportsfest Gold-219
00BAP Memorabilia Chicago Sportsfest Ruby-219
00BAP Memorabilia Chicago Sun-Times Ruby-219
00BAP Memorabilia Chicago Sun-Times Gold-219
00BAP Mem Chicago Sun-Times Sapphire-219
00BAP Mem Toronto Fall Expo Copper-219
00BAP Memorabilia Toronto Fall Expo Gold-219
00BAP Memorabilia Toronto Fall Expo Ruby-219
00BAP Parkhurst 2000-P114
00BAP Signature Series-46
Emerald-46
Ruby-46
Sapphire-46
00Crown Royale-65
Ice Blue-65
Limited Series-65
Premiere Date-65
Red-65
00Devils Team Issue-14
00O-Pee-Chee-19
00O-Pee-Chee Parallel-19
00Pacific-240
Copper-240
Gold-240
Ice Blue-240
Premiere Date-240
00Panini Stickers-46
00Paramount-146
Copper-146
Gold-146
Holo-Gold-146
Holo-Silver-146
Ice Blue-146
Premiere Date-146
Game Used Sticks-13
00Stadium Club-157
00Titanium-56
Blue-56
Gold-56
Premiere Date-56
Red-56
Retail-56
Game Gear-30
00Topps/OPC-19
Parallel-19
00Topps Gold Label Class 1-55
Gold-55
00Topps Gold Label Class 2-55
00Topps Gold Label Class 2 Gold-55
00Topps Gold Label Class 3-55
00Topps Gold Label Class 3 Gold-55
00Topps Gold Label Golden Greats-GG7
00Topps Gold Label Golden Greats 1 to 1-GG7
00Topps Heritage-71
Chrome Parallel-71
00UD Heroes-70
00Upper Deck-104
Exclusives Tier 1-104
Exclusives Tier 2-104
00Upper Deck MVP-103
First Stars-103
Second Stars-103
Third Stars-103
00Upper Deck Victory-141
00Upper Deck Vintage-214
00Vanguard-60
Holographic Gold-60
Holographic Purple-60
Pacific Proofs-60
00Czech Stadion-114
01Atomic-92
Blue-92
Gold-92
Premiere Date-92
Red-92
Team Nucleus-13
01BAP Memorabilia-96
01BAP Memorabilia-395
Emerald-96
Emerald-395
Ruby-96
Ruby-395
Sapphire-96
Sapphire-395
01BAP Sig Series He Shoots/Scores Prizes-23
01BAP Signature Series Jerseys-GJ-71
01BAP Ultimate Memorabilia Dynamic Duos-10
01BAP Ultimate Mem Journey Jerseys-18
01BAP Ultimate Mem Journey Emblems-18
01BAP Ultimate Mem Scoring Leaders-12
01BAP Update He Shoots-He Scores Prizes-13
01BAP Update Heritage-H25
01BAP Update Travel Plans-TP7
01Bowman YoungStars-78
Gold-78
Ice Cubed-78
01Crown Royale-132
Blue-132
Premiere Date-132
Red-132
Retail-132
01O-Pee-Chee-58
01O-Pee-Chee-58U
01O-Pee-Chee Heritage Parallel-58
01O-Pee-Chee Heritage Parallel Limited-58
01O-Pee-Chee Premier Parallel-58
01Pacific-235
01Pacific-433
Extreme LTD-235
Gold-433
Hobby LTD-235
Premiere Date-235
Retail LTD-235
01Pacific Adrenaline-183
Blue-183
Premiere Date-183
Red-183
Retail-183
01Pacific Arena Exclusives-235
01Pacific Arena Exclusives-433
01Pacific Heads-Up-90
Blue-90
Premiere Date-90
Red-90
Silver-90
01Parkhurst-56
Gold-56
Silver-56
He Shoots-He Scores Prizes-29
Milestones-M27
Sticks-PS70
01Private Stock-91
Gold-91
Premiere Date-91
Retail-91
Silver-91
01Private Stock Pacific Nights-91
01SP Authentic-84
Limited-84
Limited Gold-84
01SP Game Used-54
01SPx-194
01Stadium Club-108
Award Winners-108
Master Photos-108
01Titanium-130
Hobby Parallel-130
Premiere Date-130
Retail-130
Retail Parallel-130
01Topps-58
01Topps-58U
Heritage Parallel-58
Heritage Parallel Limited-58
OPC Parallel-58
Shot Masters-SM18
01Topps Chrome-58
Refractors-58
Black Border Refractors-58
01Topps Heritage-165
01Topps Reserve-78
01UD Challenge for the Cup-83
01UD Mask Collection-91
Gold-91
Gloves-GGAM
01UD Playmakers-92
01UD Stanley Cup Champs-73
Sticks-S-MO
01Upper Deck-392
Exclusives-392
Shooting Stars-SS17
MVP Souvenirs-S-AM
MVP Souvenirs Gold-S-AM
01Upper Deck Victory-210
01Upper Deck Victory-427
Gold-210
Gold-427
01Vanguard-93
Blue-93
Red-93
One of Ones-93
Premiere Date-93
Proofs-93
02McFarlane Hockey Maple Leafs-10
02McFarlane Hockey-50
02McFarlane Hockey-52
02Atomic-92
Blue-92
Gold-92
Red-92
Hobby Parallel-92
02BAP All-Star Edition-62
Jerseys-62
Jerseys Gold-62
Jerseys Silver-62
02BAP First Edition-102
Jerseys-102
02BAP Memorabilia-8
02BAP Memorabilia-248
Emerald-8
Emerald-248
Ruby-8
Ruby-248
Sapphire-8
Sapphire-248
All-Star Jerseys-ASJ-37
All-Star Teammmates-AST-6
NHL All-Star Game-8
NHL All-Star Game-248
NHL All-Star Game Blue-8
NHL All-Star Game Blue-248
NHL All-Star Game Green-8
NHL All-Star Game Green-248
NHL All-Star Game Red-8
NHL All-Star Game Red-248
Stanley Cup Playoffs-SC-19
02BAP Memorabilia Toronto Fall Expo-8
02BAP Memorabilia Toronto Fall Expo-248
02BAP Sig Series Auto Buybacks 1998-141
02BAP Sig Series Auto Buybacks 1999-243
02BAP Signature Series Golf-GS5
02BAP Signature Series Jerseys-SGJ41
02BAP Signature Series Jersey Autographs-SGJ41
02BAP Signature Series Team Quads-TQ2
02BAP Ultimate Mem Global Dominators-8
02BAP Ultimate Mem Journey Jerseys-10
02BAP Ultimate Mem Journey Emblems-10
02Bowman YoungStars-35
Gold-35
Silver-35
02Crown Royale-92
Blue-92
Red-92
Retail-92
Jerseys-22
Jerseys Gold-22
Dual Patches-21
02ITG Used International Experience-IE12
02ITG Used International Experience Gold-IE12
02ITG Used Jerseys-GUJ41
02ITG Used Jersey Autographs-GUJ41
02ITG Used Jerseys Gold-GUJ41
02ITG Used Emblems-E33
02ITG Used Jersey and Stick-SJ41
02ITG Used Jersey and Stick Gold-SJ41
02ITG Used Teammates-T12
02ITG Used Teammates Gold-T12
02Maple Leafs Platinum Collection-14
02Maple Leafs Team Issue-8
02McDonald's Pacific Jersey Patch Silver-17
02McDonald's Pacific Jersey Patches Gold-17
02NHL Power Play Stickers-138
02O-Pee-Chee-187
02O-Pee-Chee Premier Blue Parallel-187
02O-Pee-Chee Premier Red Parallel-187
02O-Pee-Chee Factory Set-187
02Pacific-365
Blue-365
Red-365
Jerseys-47
Jerseys Holo-Silver-47
02Pacific Complete-28
Red-28
02Pacific Exclusive-161
02Pacific Heads-Up-116
Blue-116
Purple-116
Red-116
Quad Jerseys-26
Quad Jerseys Gold-26
02Pacific Quest for the Cup-92
Gold-92
02Parkhurst-71
Bronze-71
Gold-71
Silver-71
Jerseys-GJ14
Stick and Jerseys-SJ14
Teammates-TT3
02Parkhurst Retro-35
Minis-35
02Private Stock Reserve-92
Blue-92
Red-92
Retail-92
02SP Authentic-82
Beckett Promos-82
02SP Game Used Tools of the Game-AM
02SPx-69
Spectrum Gold-69
Spectrum Silver-69
02Stadium Club-44
Silver Decoy Cards-44
Proofs-44
02Titanium-93
Blue-93
Red-93
Retail-93
Jerseys-66
Jerseys Retail-66
Patches-66
02Topps-187
OPC Blue Parallel-187
OPC Red Parallel-187
Factory Set-187
02Topps Chrome-108
Black Border Refractors-108
Refractors-108
02Topps Heritage-82
Chrome Parallel-82
02Topps Total-127
Production-TP12
02UD Artistic Impressions-84
Gold-84
02UD Artistic Impressions Beckett Promos-84
02UD Artistic Impressions Retrospectives-R84
02UD Artistic Impressions Retrospect Gold-R84
02UD Artistic Impress Retrospect Silver-R84
02UD Piece of History-82
02UD Top Shelf-82
02Upper Deck-166
Exclusives-166
02Upper Deck Classic Portraits-94
02Upper Deck MVP-176
Gold-176
Classics-176
Golden Classics-176
02Upper Deck Victory-198
Bronze-198
Gold-198
Silver-198
02Upper Deck Vintage-243
02Upper Deck Vintage-288
Green Backs-243
Tall Boys-T61
Tall Boys Gold-T61
02Vanguard-92
LTD-92
Jerseys-43
Jerseys Gold-43
03BAP Memorabilia-7
Emerald-7
Gold-7
Ruby-7
Sapphire-7
Jerseys-GJ-15
Stanley Cup Playoffs-SCP-16
03BAP Ultimate Memorabilia Active Eight-3
03BAP Ultimate Mem Jersey and Emblems-1
03BAP Ultimate Mem Jersey and Emblem Gold-1
03BAP Ultimate Mem Jersey and Numbers-1
03BAP Ultimate Mem Jersey and Number Gold-1
03BAP Ultimate Memorabilia Triple Threads-17
03Beehive-181
Gold-181
Silver-181
03Black Diamond-26
Black-26
Green-26
Red-26
03Bowman-82
Gold-82
03Bowman Chrome-82
Refractors-82
Gold Refractors-82
Xfractors-82
03Crown Royale-93
Blue-93
Retail-93
03ITG Action-505
Jerseys-M169
03ITG Used Sig Series Intl Experience-19
03ITG Used Sig Ser Intl Exper Emblem Gold-19
03ITG Used Sig Ser Intl Experience Emblem-19
03ITG Used Sig Ser Intl Experience Gold-19
03NHL Sticker Collection-136
03O-Pee-Chee-169
03OPC Blue-169
03OPC Gold-169
03OPC Red-169
03Pacific-320
Blue-320
Red-320
03Pacific Complete-235
Red-235
03Pacific Exhibit-137
Blue Backs-137
Yellow Backs-137
03Pacific Heads-Up-91
Hobby LTD-91
Retail LTD-91
Fast Forwards-8
Fast Forwards LTD-8
03Pacific Invincible-90
Blue-90
Red-90
Retail-90
03Pacific Luxury Suite-48A
03Pacific Luxury Suite-48B
03Pacific Luxury Suite-48C
03Pacific Prism-92
Blue-92
Gold-92
Red-92
03Pacific Supreme-91
Blue-91
Red-91
Retail-91
03Parkhurst Orig Six He Shoots/Scores-3
03Parkhurst Orig Six He Shoots/Scores-3A
03Parkhurst Original Six Toronto-18
Memorabilia-TM7
Memorabilia-TM15
Memorabilia-TM53
03Private Stock Reserve-94
Blue-94
Red-94
Retail-94
03SP Authentic-80
Limited-80
03SP Game Used Authentic Fabrics-QSNBM
03SP Game Used Authentic Fabrics Gold-QSNBM
03SPx-91
Radiance-91
Spectrum-91
Fantasy Franchise-FF-NSM
Fantasy Franchise Limited-FF-NSM
03Topps-169
Blue-169
Gold-169
Red-169
Topps/OPC Idols-II9
03Topps C55-89
Minis-89
Minis American Back-89
Minis American Back Red-89
Minis Bazooka Back-89
Minis Brooklyn Back-89
Minis Hat Trick Back-89
Minis O Canada Back-89
Minis O Canada Back Red-89
Minis Stanley Cup Back-89
Award Winners-8
03Topps Pristine-97
Gold Refractor Die Cuts-97
Refractors-97
Press Plates Black-97
Press Plates Cyan-97
Press Plates Magenta-97
Press Plates Yellow-97
03UD Honor Roll-80
03UD Premier Collection Stars-ST-AM
03UD Premier Collection Stars Patches-ST-AM
03Upper Deck-177
Canadian Exclusives-177
HG-177
Highlight Heroes-HH-AM
Highlight Heroes Jerseys-HH-AM
03Upper Deck Classic Portraits-90
Hockey Royalty-BSM
03Upper Deck Ice-82
Gold-82
03Upper Deck MVP-390
Gold Script-390
Silver Script-390
Canadian Exclusives-390
SportsNut-SN84
03Upper Deck Rookie Update-81
Super Stars-SSAM
03Upper Deck Trilogy-90
Limited-90
03Upper Deck Victory-176
Bronze-176
Gold-176
Silver-176
Freshman Flashback-FF45
Game Breakers-GB35
03Toronto Star-87
04Pacific-247
Blue-247
Red-247
Global Connection-8
04Upper Deck-162
Canadian Exclusives-162
HG Glossy Gold-162
HG Glossy Silver-162
05Beehive-55
Matte-55
05Black Diamond-54
Emerald-54
Gold-54
Onyx-54
Ruby-54
05Devils Team Issue-7
05Panini Stickers-81
05SP Game Used-61
Gold-61
Authentic Fabrics Quad-EMMR
Authentic Patches Quad -EMMR
Game Gear-GG-AM
05SPx-52
Spectrum-52
05UD Artifacts Frozen Artifacts-FA-MO
05UD Artifacts Frozen Artifacts Autos-FA-MO
05UD Artifacts Frozen Artifacts Copper-FA-MO
05UD Artifacts Frozen Artifacts Dual-FAD-MO
05UD Artifact Frozen Artifact Dual Auto-FAD-MO
05UD Artifact Frozen Artifact Dual Copper-FAD-MO
05UD Artifact Frozen Artifact Dual Gold-FAD-MO
05UD Artifact Frozen Artifact Dual Maroon-FAD-MO
05UD Artifact Frozen Artifact Dual Pewter-FAD-MO
05UD Artifact Frozen Artifact Dual Silver-FAD-MO
05UD Artifacts Frozen Artifacts Gold-FA-MO
05UD Artifacts Frozen Artifacts Maroon-FA-MO
05UD Artifacts Frozen Artifacts Patches-FP-MO
05UD Artifact Frozen Artifact Patch Autos-FP-MO
05UD Artifact Frozen Artifact Patch Dual-FPD-MO
05UD Artifacts Frozen Art Patch Dual Auto-FPD-MO
05UD Artifacts Frozen Art Patch Pewter-FP-MO
05UD Artifacts Frozen Art Patch Silver-FP-MO
05UD Artifacts Frozen Artifacts Pewter-FA-MO
05UD Artifacts Frozen Artifacts Silver-FA-MO
05Ultra-119
Gold-119
Ice-119
05Upper Deck Big Playmakers-B-AT
05Upper Deck Jerseys-J-AM
05Upper Deck Notable Numbers-N-AM
05Upper Deck Patches-P-AMO
05Upper Deck Shooting Stars-S-AM
05Upper Deck Hockey Showcase-HS18
05Upper Deck Showcase Promos-HS18
05Upper Deck MVP-235
Gold-235
Platinum-235
05Upper Deck Victory Game Breakers-GB43
05ITG Heroes and Prospects Jerseys-GUJ-112
05ITG Heroes and Prospects Jerseys Gold-GUJ-112
05ITG Heroes and Prospects Emblems-GUE-95
05ITG Heroes and Prospects Emblems Gold-GUE-95
05ITG Heroes and Prospects Numbers-GUN-95
05ITG Heroes and Prospects Numbers Gold-GUN-95
06Devils Team Set-17

Mohagen, Tony

95Seattle Thunderbirds-17
96Seattle Thunderbirds-17
97Swift Current Broncos-14
98Cincinnati Mighty Ducks-23

Moher, Chris

00Hull Olympiques-1
Signed-1
01Hull Olympiques-1

Moher, Mike

02Sault Ste. Marie Greyhounds-8

Moher, Riley

02Barrie Colts-10

Mohlander, Borje

64Swedish Coralli ISHockey-111

Mohlin, Dan

83Swedish Semic Elitserien-122
84Swedish Semic Elitserien-114

Mohlin, Ove

91Swedish Semic Elitserien Stickers-48

Mohninger, Bret

91Air Canada SJHL-C26

Mohns, Doug

44Beehive Group II Photos-51
52Juniors Blue Tint-107
54Parkhurst-57
54Topps-18
55Bruins Photos-12
57Bruins Photos-14
57Topps-12
58Topps-50
59Topps-58
60Shirriff Coins-106
60Topps-52
Stamps-37
61Shirriff/Salada Coins-10
61Topps-10
62Topps-6
Hockey Bucks-18
63Topps-3
64Beehive Group III Photos-50
64Coca-Cola Caps-20
64Topps-25
65Coca-Cola-20
65Topps-118
66Topps-61
66Topps USA Test-61
67Topps-63
68Bauer Ads-16
68O-Pee-Chee-19
68Shirriff Coins-24
68Topps-19
69O-Pee-Chee-72
Four-in-One-14
69Topps-72
70Dad's Cookies-87
70Esso Power Players-118
70O-Pee-Chee-16
Deckle-29
70Sargent Promotions Stamps-47
70Topps-16
71O-Pee-Chee-242
71Sargent Promotions Stamps-84
71Toronto Sun-137
72O-Pee-Chee-75
72Sargent Promotions Stamps-102
72Topps-78
73O-Pee-Chee-241
74Capitals White Borders-21
74NHL Action Stamps-309
74O-Pee-Chee NHL-181
74Topps-181
91Bruins Sports Action Legends-18
91Ultimate Original Six-53
French-53
94Parkhurst Missing Link-18
94Parkhurst Tall Boys-27
95Parkhurst '66-67-35
Coins-35
98Bruins Alumni-34
Autographs-34
03BAP Ultimate Memorabilia Linemates-1

Mohoric, Klemen

96Johnstown Chiefs-12

Mohr, Mike

04Austin Ice Bats-18

Moir, Kyle

03Swift Current Broncos-9
04Swift Current Broncos-14
05Swift Current Broncos-10
05ITG Heroes and Prospects Net Prospects-NP-16
05ITG Heroes and Prosp Net Prospects Gold-NP-16
06Between The Pipes-34
Autographs-AKM
Prospect Trios-PT10
Prospect Trios Gold-PT10
06Swift Current Broncos-2

Moir, Sean

01Saskatoon Blades-21
02Saskatoon Blades-2
03Saskatoon Blades-25

Moira, Steve

01UK Nottingham Panthers-10

Moise, Martin

97Bowman CHL-72
OPC-72
98Quebec Remparts-15
Signed-15
98Bowman CHL-113
Golden Anniversary-113
OPC International-113
98Bowman Chrome CHL-113
Golden Anniversary-113
Golden Anniversary Refractors-113
OPC International-113
OPC International Refractors-113
Refractors-113
99Quebec Remparts-15
Signed-15
99Bowman CHL-56
Gold-56
OPC International-56

Moiseev, Yuri

02Russian SL-17

Moisio, Markku

71Finnish Suomi Stickers-213
72Finnish Jaakiekko-159
73Finnish Jaakiekko-225

Moisio, Pekka

66Finnish Jaakiekkosarja-92

Mojzis, Pavel

98Czech OFS-23
99Czech OFS-214
00Czech OFS-11
00Czech OFS-373
01Czech OFS-79
03Czech OFS Plus-251
04Czech OFS-310
04Czech OFS-410
05Czech HC Znojmo-9
06Czech OFS-208
Stars-23

Mojzis, Tomas

02Czech DS-52
02Czech DS-73
03Manitoba Moose-4
04Manitoba Moose-2
05Black Diamond-291
05Hot Prospects-178
En Fuego-178
Red Hot-178
White Hot-178
05SP Game Used-238
05SPx-290
05The Cup Masterpiece Pressplate Artifact-339
05The Cup Master Pressplate Black Diamond-291
05The Cup Master Pressplate Rookie Update-190
05The Cup Masterpiece Pressplates SP GU-238
05The Cup Masterpiece Pressplates (SPx)-290
05The Cup Masterpiece Pressplates Trilogy-315
05The Cup Masterpiece Pressplate Ult Coll-232
05UD Artifacts-339
05Ultimate Collection-232
Gold-232
05Upper Deck Rookie Update-190
05Upper Deck Trilogy-315
05Manitoba Moose-14
06Peoria Rivermen-12

Mokhov, Stepan

99Russian Hockey League-236

Mokosak, Carl

88ProCards AHL-156
89ProCards IHL-132
90ProCards AHL/IHL-304
90ProCards AHL/IHL-412

Mokosak, John

81Victoria Cougars-11
82Victoria Cougars-18
88ProCards AHL-11
90ProCards AHL/IHL-127
91ProCards-192
92Phoenix Roadrunners-17

Mokrejs, Pavel

06Czech OFS-234

Mokrejs, Petr

98Czech OFS-61
99Czech Score Blue 2000-41
99Czech Score Red Ice 2000-41
02Czech OFS Plus-35
03Czech OFS Plus-138
04Czech OFS-284
05Czech HC Hame Zlin-10

Mokros, Milan

94German DEL-153
95German DEL-149
96German DEL-245

Molander, Borje

65Swedish Coralli ISHockey-111
67Swedish Hockey-37
69Swedish Hockey-48

Molander, Lars

64Swedish Coralli ISHockey-114
65Swedish Coralli ISHockey-114
67Swedish Hockey-177
69Swedish Hockey-178

Molander, Pontus

84Swedish Semic Elitserien-85
86Swedish Panini Stickers-75
87Swedish Panini Stickers-77

Molander, Urban

90Swedish Semic Elitserien Stickers-181
91Swedish Semic Elitserien Stickers-37

Molby, Jesper

98Danish Hockey League-164
99Danish Hockey League-61

Mole, Kevin

06Kingston Frontenacs-17

Mole, Michael

00Mississauga Ice Dogs-18
01Belleville Bulls Update-3
02Belleville Bulls-13
02Belleville Bulls-25
03St. Francis Xavier X-Men-22
04St. Francis Xavier X-Men-15

Molenda, Jaroslaw

93Quebec Pee-Wee Tournament-1507

Molgaard, Lars

98Danish Hockey League-165
99Danish Hockey League-157

Molin, Johan

97Swedish Collector's Choice-190
98Swedish UD Choice-192
99Swedish Upper Deck-196
00Swedish Upper Deck-35
03German Deg Metro Stars-14

Molin, Lars

81Canucks Team Issue-17
81Swedish Semic Hockey VM Stickers-17
82Canucks Team Issue-16
82O-Pee-Chee-353
82O-Pee-Chee Stickers-245
82Post Cereal-19
82Topps Stickers-245
82Swedish Semic VM Stickers-149
83Canucks Team Issue-14
83NHL Key Tags-124
83Vachon-113
85Swedish Panini Stickers-216
86Swedish Panini Stickers-204
87Swedish Panini Stickers-203

Molin, Ove

92Swedish Semic Elitserien Stickers-68
93Swedish Semic Elitserien-44
94Swedish Leaf-85
95Swedish Leaf-20
Goldies-2
95Swedish Upper Deck-33
97Swedish Collector's Choice-27
98Swedish UD Choice-41
99Swedish Upper Deck-25
Snapshots-3
00Swedish Upper Deck-39
00Swedish Upper Deck-185
SHL Signatures-OM
Top Draws-T2
01Swedish Brynas Tigers-16
02Swedish SHL-8
Parallel-8
Signatures-2
03Swedish Elite-9
Silver-9
04Swedish Elitset-9
04Swedish Elitset-134
Gold-9
Gold-134
05Swedish SHL Elitset-8
Gold-8
Icons-7
06Swedish SHL Elitset-10

Molin, Sacha

94Swedish Leaf-166
98Long Beach Ice Dogs-13

Molina, Alfio

72Finnish Semic World Championship-157
72Swedish Semic World Championship-157
74Finnish Typotor-109

Molina, Sean

00Trenton Titans-18

Mollard, Larry

83Pinebridge Bucks-9

Molle, Bryant

06Penticton Vees-17

Molle, Dustin

03Waterloo Blackhawks-19
04Waterloo Blackhawks-7

Molle, Ryan

06Swift Current Broncos-6

Molle, Tim

94Anchorage Aces-23

Molleken, Lorne

84Springfield Indians-2
91Saskatoon Blades-1
917th Inn. Sketch WHL-100
99Blackhawks Chicago Sun-Times-10

Moller, Fredrik

93Swedish Semic Elitserien-238

Moller, Mads

98Danish Hockey League-69
99Danish Hockey League-95

Moller, Mike

84Sabres Blue Shield-11
85Nova Scotia Oilers-3
88Oilers Tenth Anniversary-136
89ProCards AHL-305
93Red Deer Rebels-16

Moller, Oscar

06Chilliwack Bruins-19
06Chilliwack Bruins-20

Moller, Randy

82Nordiques Postcards-14
83NHL Key Tags-109
83Nordiques Postcards-18
83O-Pee-Chee-297
83O-Pee-Chee Stickers-248
83Topps Stickers-248
83Vachon-69
84Nordiques Postcards-17
84O-Pee-Chee-284
84O-Pee-Chee Stickers-174
85Nordiques General Foods-18
85Nordiques McDonald's-14
85Nordiques Placemats-6
85Nordiques Provigo-17
85Nordiques Team Issue-15
85O-Pee-Chee-240
85O-Pee-Chee Stickers-145
86Kraft Drawings-44
86Nordiques General Foods-16
86Nordiques McDonald's-17
86Nordiques Team Issue-15
87Nordiques General Foods-22
87Nordiques Team Issue-16
87O-Pee-Chee-251
87O-Pee-Chee Stickers-229
87Panini Stickers-162
88Nordiques General Foods-28
88Nordiques Team Issue-24
88Panini Stickers-351
89Nordiques Team Issue-32
89O-Pee-Chee-259
89O-Pee-Chee Stickers-195
89Panini Stickers-331
89Rangers Marine Midland Bank-24
90O-Pee-Chee-515
90Pro Set-202
90Score-45
Canadian-45
90Upper Deck-418
French-418
91Bowman-58
91O-Pee-Chee-371
91Pinnacle-256
French-256
91Pro Set-163
French-163
91Score American-79
91Score Canadian Bilingual-79
91Score Canadian English-79
91Stadium Club-2
91Topps-371
92Pinnacle-176
French-176
92Sabres Blue Shield-14
92Sabres Jubilee Foods-10
92Score-289
Canadian-289
92Stadium Club-484
92Topps-407
Gold-407G
93Score-422
Canadian-422
93Stadium Club-435
Members Only Master Set-435
First Day Issue-435
94Leaf-344
94Pinnacle-401
Artist's Proofs-401
Rink Collection-401

Moller, Tommy

83Swedish Semic Elitserien-107
84Swedish Semic Elitserien-107

Mollerstedt, Ola

02Swedish SHL-90
Parallel-90

Molling, Jochen

94German DEL-55
95German DEL-409
96German DEL-251
98German DEL-55
99German DEL-171
99German DEL-373
01German Upper Deck-132
02German DEL City Press-292
03German DEL-9
03German Mannheim Eagles Postcards-15
04German DEL-129
04German Hamburg Freezers Postcards-9

Molloy, Mitch

88ProCards AHL-151
89Johnstown Chiefs-29
90ProCards AHL/IHL-283
92San Diego Gulls-20

Molnar, Aaron

00London Knights-14

Molnar, Petr

94Czech APS Extraliga-207
95Czech APS Extraliga-159
97Czech APS Extraliga-83

Molodstov, Konstantin

00Russian Hockey League-280

Molotilov, Vadim

98Russian Hockey League-149

Molson, Sen.H.de M

83Hall of Fame Postcards-012
85Hall of Fame-221

Molyneaux, Larry

34Beehive Group I Photos-286

Momesso, Sergio

85Canadiens Postcards-21
85Canadiens Provigo-11
86Canadiens Postcards-14
86Kraft Drawings-45
87Blues Team Issue-16
87Canadiens Postcards-18
87Canadiens Vachon Stickers-55
87Canadiens Vachon Stickers-56
88Blues Kodak-16
88Blues Team Issue-16
89Blues Kodak-27
90Blues Kodak-16
90Bowman-17
Tiffany-17
90O-Pee-Chee-244
90Panini Stickers-263
90Pro Set-268
90Score-224
Canadian-224
90Topps-244
Tiffany-244
90Upper Deck-19
French-19
91Pro Set Platinum-240
91Bowman-309
91Canucks Autograph Cards-15
91Canucks Team Issue 8x10-15
91O-Pee-Chee-462
91OPC Premier-55
91Panini Stickers-44
91Parkhurst-185
French-185
91Pinnacle-34
French-34
91Pro Set-242
French-242
91Score American-121
91Score Canadian Bilingual-121
91Score Canadian English-121
91Stadium Club-17
91Topps-462
91Upper Deck-571
French-571
92Bowman-316
92Canucks Road Trip Art-14
92Durivage Panini-26
92O-Pee-Chee-377
92Parkhurst-421
Emerald Ice-421
92Pinnacle-163
French-163
92Pro Set-194
92Score-79
Canadian-79
92Stadium Club-42
92Topps-214
Gold-214G
92Ultra-225
92Upper Deck-85
93Donruss-349
93Durivage Score-33
93Leaf-250
93Parkhurst-212
Emerald Ice-212
93Pinnacle-393
Canadian-393
93Score-255
Canadian-255
93Stadium Club-323
Members Only Master Set-323
First Day Issue-323
93Ultra-47
93Upper Deck-104
94Be A Player Signature Cards-178
94Canada Games NHL POGS-342
94Leaf-499
94OPC Premier-356
Special Effects-356
94Parkhurst-249
Gold-249
94Pinnacle-307
Artist's Proofs-307
Rink Collection-307
94Stadium Club-65
Members Only Master Set-65
First Day Issue-65
Super Team Winner Cards-65
94Topps/OPC Premier-356

Special Effects-356
94Ultra-384
94Upper Deck-85
Electric Ice-85
95Canucks Building the Dream Art-12
95Collector's Choice-99
Player's Club-99
Player's Club Platinum-99
95Donruss-380
95Leaf-58
95Parkhurst International-473
Emerald Ice-473
95Score-161
Black Ice Artist's Proofs-161
Black Ice-161
95Stadium Club-123
Members Only Master Set-123
95Summit-163
Artist's Proofs-163
Ice-163
95Ultra-313
95Upper Deck-125
Electric Ice-125
Electric Ice Gold-125
97Pacific Invincible-121
Copper-121
Emerald Green-121
Ice Blue-121
Red-121
Silver-121
98German DEL-248
99German DEL-122

Mona, Gianluca
00Swiss Panini Stickers-7
01Swiss HNL-123
02Swiss HNL-45

Monahan, Alexandre
05Saint John's Sea Dogs-3

Monahan, Garry
64Canadiens Postcards-13
67Canadiens IGA-20
67Topps-8
68Canadiens IGA-20
68Canadiens Postcards BW-10
69O-Pee-Chee-160
70Colgate Stamps-13
70Esso Power Players-31
70Maple Leafs Postcards-9
70O-Pee-Chee-112
70Sargent Promotions Stamps-207
70Topps-112
71Maple Leafs Postcards-13
71Sargent Promotions Stamps-199
71Toronto Sun-266
72Maple Leafs Postcards-21
72O-Pee-Chee-207
72Sargent Promotions Stamps-202
73Maple Leafs Postcards-19
73O-Pee-Chee-226
74Canucks Royal Bank-13
75Canucks Royal Bank-13
75O-Pee-Chee NHL-357
76Canucks Royal Bank-11
76O-Pee-Chee NHL-295
77Canucks Canada Dry Cans-10
77Canucks Royal Bank-14
77O-Pee-Chee NHL-341
78Maple Leafs Postcards-15
78O-Pee-Chee-268

Monahan, Hartland
76O-Pee-Chee NHL-203
76Topps-203
77O-Pee-Chee NHL-96
77Topps-96
78O-Pee-Chee-393

Monberg, Nicklas
98Danish Hockey League-40
99Danish Hockey League-225

Moncour, David
04Surrey Eagles-14

Moncur, David
04South Surrey Eagles-16
04Surrey Eagles-14

Mondou, Armand
28La Presse Photos-10
33O-Pee-Chee V304A-48
33V129-44
33V357 Ice Kings-17
34Beehive Group I Photos-169
34Sweet Caporal-12
35Diamond Matchbooks Tan 1-48
35Diamond Matchbooks Tan 2-48
35Diamond Matchbooks Tan 3-45
37O-Pee-Chee V304E-177
39O-Pee-Chee V301-1-27
05ITG Ultimate Mem Bleu Blanc Rouge Autos-12
06ITG Ultimate Memorabilia Bleu Blanc et Rouge Autos-6

Mondou, Benoit
01Baie-Comeau Drakkar-23
02Baie Comeau Drakkar-23
02Shawinigan Cataractes-22
03Shawinigan Cataractes-18
05Shawinigan Cataractes-4

Mondou, Pierre
76Nova Scotia Voyageurs-14
77Canadiens Postcards-17
78Canadiens Postcards-19
78O-Pee-Chee-102
78Topps-102
79Canadiens Postcards-17
79O-Pee-Chee-211
79Topps-211
80Canadiens Postcards-16
80O-Pee-Chee-42
80Pepsi-Cola Caps-52
80Topps-42
81Canadiens Postcards-18
81O-Pee-Chee-188
82Canadiens Postcards-14
82Canadiens Steinberg-10
82O-Pee-Chee-188
82O-Pee-Chee Stickers-35
82Post Cereal-10
82Topps Stickers-35
83Canadiens Postcards-17
83O-Pee-Chee-191
83O-Pee-Chee Stickers-68
83Topps Stickers-68
83Vachon-49
84Canadiens Postcards-17
84O-Pee-Chee-266
84O-Pee-Chee Stickers-162
85O-Pee-Chee-211
85O-Pee-Chee Stickers-133
92Sport-Flash-11
92Sport-Flash Autographs-11

Mondt, Niki
95German DEL-99
01German Upper Deck-246

Mondt, Nikolaus
95German DEL-99
96German DEL-287
98German DEL-58
99German DEL-178
99German DEL-375
00German DEL-46
01German Upper Deck-246
02German DEL City Press-55
03German DEL-83
04German DEL-92
04German Ingolstadt Panthers-18
05German DEL-213

Monette, Jacques
51Bas Du Fleuve-45
52Bas Du Fleuve-35

Monette, Russell
04Saskatoon Blades-4

Mongeau, Michel
88Flint Spirits-17
89ProCards IHL-17
90Score-395
Canadian-395
90Upper Deck-345
French-345
90ProCards AHL/IHL-91
91Blues Postcards-15
91Upper Deck-213
French-213
91ProCards-26
92Pinnacle-388
French-388
92Stadium Club-415
92Ultra-203
93Peoria Rivermen-19
95Peoria Rivermen-12
96Milwaukee Admirals-18
96Collector's Edge Ice-178
Prism-178
99Swiss Panini Stickers-304

Mongeon, Hughes
907th Inn. Sketch QMJHL-189
917th Inn. Sketch QMJHL-32

Mongrain, Bob
79Rochester Americans-11
93Swiss HNL-313

Mongrain, Francis
93Quebec Pee-Wee Tournament-208

Mongrain, Steve
93Quebec Pee-Wee Tournament-206
95Halifax Mooseheads-13
97Halifax Mooseheads I-14

Monias, Reynold
96OCN Blizzard-2

Monier, Francois
93Quebec Pee-Wee Tournament-1012

Monkman, Bill
99Topeka Scarecrows-4

Monnet, Thibaut
00Swiss Panini Stickers-67
00Swiss Slapshot Mini-Cards-HCCF16
01Swiss HNL-138
02Swiss HNL-162

Monnier, Frank
93Swiss HNL-51
95Swiss HNL-251
96Swiss HNL-266
96Swiss HNL-576
98Swiss Power Play Stickers-193
99Swiss Panini Stickers-194

Monohan, Alexandre
06Saint Johns Sea Dogs-18

Mononen, Erkki
66Finnish Jaakiekkosarja-107
70Finnish Jaakiekko-181
71Finnish Suomi Stickers-69
71Finnish Suomi Stickers-105
71Swedish Hockey-68
72Finnish Jaakiekko-149
72Finnish Panda Toronto-103
72Finnish Semic World Championship-81
72Swedish Semic World Championship-81

Mononen, Lauri
69Swedish Hockey-377
70Finnish Jaakiekko-69
70Finnish Jaakiekko-182
70Swedish Hockey-306
71Finnish Suomi Stickers-70
71Finnish Suomi Stickers-288
71Swedish Hockey-69
72Finnish Jaakiekko-66
72Finnish Hellas-6
72Finnish Panda Toronto-104
72Finnish Semic World Championship-82
72Swedish Stickers-37
72Swedish Semic World Championship-82
73Finnish Jaakiekko-72
73Finnish Jaakiekko-115
73Swedish Stickers-35
74Swedish Semic World Champ Stickers-99
75Phoenix Roadrunners WHA-18
76Phoenix Roadrunners WHA-13
78Finnish SM-Liiga-32

Mononen, Pekka
71Finnish Suomi Stickers-68

Monrisson, Sandy
52Juniors Blue Tint-164

Montador, Steve
93Quebec Pee-Wee Tournament-563
01BAP Memorabilia-340
Emerald-340
Ruby-340
Sapphire-340
01Upper Deck Ice-130
02O-Pee-Chee-303
02O-Pee-Chee Premier Blue Parallel-303
02O-Pee-Chee Premier Red Parallel-303
02O-Pee-Chee Factory Set-303
02Topps-303
OPC Blue Parallel-303
OPC Red Parallel-303
Factory Set-303
03ITG Action-4
06Be A Player-80
Autographs-80
Signatures-SM
Signatures Trios-TJBM

Montan, Carl-Fredrik
67Swedish Hockey-294
69Swedish Hockey-340
70Swedish Hockey-256

Montanari, Mark
86Kitchener Rangers-18
87Kitchener Rangers-19
88Kitchener Rangers-19
89ProCards AHL-57
90ProCards AHL/IHL-142
907th Inn. Sketch Memorial Cup-30
95Swedish World Championships Stickers-91
96German DEL-102
00UK Sekonda Superleague-19

Montandon, Gil
91Finnish Semic World Champ Stickers-198
91Swedish Semic World Champ Stickers-198
92Finnish Semic-214
93Swedish Semic World Champ Stickers-128
93Swiss HNL-76
95Finnish Semic World Championships-193
95Swedish Globe World Championships-215
95Swedish World Championships Stickers-131
95Swiss HNL-103
96Swiss HNL-44
96Swiss HNL-520
98Swiss Power Play Stickers-45
99Swiss Panini Stickers-93
00Swiss Panini Stickers-139
00Swiss Slapshot Mini-Cards-HCFG10
01Swiss HNL-139
02Swiss HNL-164

Monteith, Russell
97Mobile Mysticks-7
97Mobile Mysticks Kellogg's-21
98Mobile Mysticks-1
01UK Fife Flyers-11

Monteleone, Phoebe
04Wisconsin Badgers Women-16

Montemurro, Carlo
52Juniors Blue Tint-92

Montgomery, Chris
00UD CHL Prospects-80
02Quebec Remparts-22
03Quebec Remparts Memorial Cup-14

Montgomery, Jason
99Quesnel Millionaires-1
03St. Cloud State Huskies-21
04St. Cloud State Huskies-22
05St. Cloud State Huskies-2
05St. Cloud State Huskies-21

Montgomery, Jim
92Maine Black Bears-12
92Maine Black Bears-27
93Donruss-300
Rated Rookies-13
93OPC Premier-488
Gold-488
93Parkhurst-176
Emerald Ice-176
93Pinnacle-438
Canadian-438
93PowerPlay-431
93Score-621
Gold-621
Canadian-621
Canadian Gold-621
93Topps/OPC Premier-488
Gold-488
93Ultra-413
93Upper Deck-472
93Maine Black Bears-61
93Classic-55
Autographs-AU6
94Canadiens Postcards-15
94Leaf-258
94Leaf-348
94OPC Premier-91
Special Effects-91
94Parkhurst-198
Gold-198
94Parkhurst SE-SE93
Gold-SE93
94Pinnacle-159
Artist's Proofs-159
Rink Collection-159
94Topps/OPC Premier-91
Special Effects-91
94Ultra-187
94Ultra-312
94Upper Deck-132
Electric Ice-132
94Classic Pro Prospects-25
94Images *-16
96German DEL-348
96Collector's Edge Future Legends-11
96Collector's Edge Ice-46
Prism-46
99Manitoba Moose-20
00Upper Deck NHLPA-PA75
00Kentucky Thoroughblades-18
01Utah Grizzlies-25
02Utah Grizzlies-11
04Missouri River Otters-12

Montgomery, Mike
04Peterborough Petes Postcards-12

Montgomery, Scott
86Kitchener Rangers-26
87Kitchener Rangers-29

Montoya, Al
02Michigan Wolverines-28
03Michigan Wolverines-18
04Michigan Wolverines-4
05ITG Heroes/Prosp Toronto Expo Parallel -107
05ITG Heroes/Prosp Toronto Expo Parallel -374
05Beehive-179
Matte-179
05Black Diamond-264
05Hot Prospects-253
En Fuego-253
Hot Materials-HMMO
Red Hot-253
White Hot-253
05ITG Ultimate Memorabilia Emblems-4
05ITG Ultimate Memorabilia Emblems Gold-4
05ITG Ultimate Mem First Rounders Jerseys-5
05ITG Ultimate Mem 1st Round Jersey Gold-5
05ITG Ultimate Mem Future Stars Autos-11
05ITG Ultimate Mem Future Star Autos Gold-11
05ITG Ultimate Mem Fut Stars Jerseys Gold-11
05ITG Ultimate Mem Future Stars Jerseys-11
05ITG Ultimate Mem Future Stars Mem Autos-11
05ITG Ultimate Mem Fut Star Mem Auto Gold-11
05ITG Ultimate Mem Jersey and Emblem-25
05ITG Ultimate Mem Jersey Emblems Gold-25
05Parkhurst-648
Facsimile Auto Parallel-648
Signatures-AM
05SP Authentic-170
Limited-170
Prestigious Pairings-PPLM
Rarefied Rookies-RRMO
05SP Game Used-162
Autographs-162
Gold-162
Auto Draft-AD-AM
Rookie Exclusives-AL
Rookie Exclusives Silver-RE-AL
Significant Numbers-SN-AM
05SPx-159
Spectrum-159
Xcitement Rookies-XR-MO
Xcitement Rookies Gold-XR-MO
Xcitement Rookies Spectrum-XR-MO
05The Cup-147
Autographed Rookie Patches Gold Rainbow-147
Black Rainbow Rookies-147
Masterpiece Pressplates (Artifacts)-304
Masterpiece Pressplates (Bee Hive)-179
Masterpiece Pressplates (Black Diamond)-264
Masterpiece Pressplates (Ice)-136
Masterpiece Pressplates (Rookie Update)-221
Masterpiece Pressplates SPA Autos-170
Masterpiece Pressplates (SP Game Used)-162
Masterpiece Pressplates SPx Autos-159
Masterpiece Pressplates (Trilogy)-204
Masterpiece Pressplates Ult Coll Autos-124
Masterpiece Pressplates (Victory)-289
Masterpiece Pressplates Autographs-147
Platinum Rookies-147
05UD Artifacts-304
05UD Rookie Class-11
05Ultimate Collection-124
Autographed Patches-124
Autographed Shields-124
Jerseys Dual-DJML
Ultimate Debut Threads Jerseys-DTJMO
Ultimate Debut Threads Jerseys Autos-DAJMO
Ultimate Debut Threads Patches-DTPMO
Ultimate Debut Threads Patches Autos-DAPMO
Ultimate Patches Dual-DPML
Ultimate Signatures Pairings-UPLM
05Ultra-231
Gold-231
Fresh Ink-FI-AM
Fresh Ink Blue-FI-AM
Ice-231
Rookie Uniformity Jerseys-RU-MO
Rookie Uniformity Jersey Autographs-ARU-AM
Rookie Uniformity Patches-RUP-AM
Rookie Uniformity Patch Autographs-ARP-AM
05Upper Deck-455
Rookie Ink-RIMO
Rookie Threads-RTMO
Rookie Threads Autographs-ARTMO
05Upper Deck Ice-136
Premieres Auto Patches-AIPMO
05Upper Deck Rookie Update-221
Inspirations Patch Rookies-221
05Upper Deck Trilogy-204
05Upper Deck Victory-289
Black-289
Gold-289
Silver-289
05AHL All-Stars-20
05AHL Top Prospects-25
05Hartford Wolf Pack-16
05ITG Heroes and Prospects-107
05ITG Heroes and Prospects-374
Autographs-A-AM
Autographs Series II-AM2
Autographs Series II-CM2
Complete Jerseys-CJ-1
Complete Jerseys Gold-CJ-1
Complete Logos-AHL-16
Jerseys-GUJ-55
Jerseys Gold-GUJ-55
Emblems-GUE-55
Emblems Gold-GUE-55
Numbers-GUN-55
Numbers Gold-GUN-55
Measuring Up-MU18
Measuring Up Gold-MU18
Nameplates-N-33
Nameplates Gold-N-33
National Pride-NPR-40
Net Prospects Dual-NPD5
Net Prospects Dual Gold-NPD5
06Between The Pipes-1
06Between The Pipes-105
Autographs-AAM2
Autographs-AAM
Double Jerseys-DJ01
Double Jerseys Gold-DJ01
Double Memorabilia-DM11
Double Memorabilia Gold-DM11
Gloves-GG14
Gloves Gold-GG14
Playing For Your Country-PC15
Playing For Your Country Gold-PC15
Prospect Trios-PT18
Prospect Trios Gold-PT18
Shooting Gallery-SG05
Shooting Gallery Gold-SG05
Stick and Jersey-SJ21
Stick and Jersey Gold-SJ21
Stick and Jersey Autographs-SJ21
The Mask-M01
The Mask Gold-M01
The Mask Silver-M01
The Mask Game-Used-MGU13
The Mask Game-Used Gold-MGU13
06ITG International Ice-84
Gold-84
Autographs-AAM
Cornerstones-IC08
Cornerstones Gold-IC08
Goaltending Glory-GG18
Goaltending Glory Gold-GG18
International Rivals-IR18
International Rivals Gold-IR18
Passing The Torch-PTT4
Passing The Torch Gold-PTT4
06ITG Ultimate Memorabilia-2
Artist Proof-2
Future Star-20
Future Star Gold-20
Future Star Patches Autos-11
Future Star Patches Autos Gold-11
06SP Game Used SIGnificance-SAM
06Ultra Fresh Ink-IAM
06Hartford Wolf Pack-26
06ITG Heroes and Prospects-76
Autographs-AAMO
Sticks and Jerseys-SJ15
Sticks and Jerseys Gold-SJ15

Montreuil, Eric
96Carolina Monarchs-18
97New Orleans Brass-3
98Baton Rouge Kingfish-14
99Knoxville Speed-9

Monych, Lance
00Brandon Wheat Kings-16
01Brandon Wheat Kings-16
02Brandon Wheat Kings-14
03Brandon Wheat Kings-5
04Brandon Wheat Kings-14

Moodie, Lane
01Ottawa 67's-11

Moody, Bill
92British Columbia JHL-140
97UK Fife Flyers-6

Moog, Andy
81Oilers Red Rooster-35
81O-Pee-Chee-120
82Oilers Red Rooster-35
83NHL Key Tags-41
83Oilers Dollars-H15
83Oilers McDonald's-3
83O-Pee-Chee-40
83O-Pee-Chee Stickers-99
83O-Pee-Chee Stickers-155
83Topps Stickers-99
83Topps Stickers-155
83Vachon-37
84Oilers Red Rooster-35
84Oilers Team Issue-20
84O-Pee-Chee-255
84O-Pee-Chee Stickers-262
85Oilers Red Rooster-35
85O-Pee-Chee-12
85O-Pee-Chee Stickers-123
85O-Pee-Chee Stickers-220
85Topps-12
86Kraft Drawings-46
86Oilers Red Rooster-35A
86Oilers Red Rooster-35B
86Oilers Team Issue-35
86O-Pee-Chee-212
86O-Pee-Chee Stickers-66
87O-Pee-Chee-204
87O-Pee-Chee Stickers-93
87Panini Stickers-255
88Bruins Sports Action-15
88Bruins Postcards-13
88Oilers Tenth Anniversary-91
89Bruins Sports Action-15
89O-Pee-Chee-160
89O-Pee-Chee Stickers-30
89Panini Stickers-191
89Topps-160
90Bowman-35
Tiffany-35
90Bruins Sports Action-16
90Bruins Sports Action-26
90Kraft-35
90O-Pee-Chee-294
90O-Pee-Chee-486
90OPC Premier-76
90Panini Stickers-11
90Pro Set-10
90Pro Set-382
90Score-140
90Score-365
Canadian-140
Canadian-365
90Score Hottest/Rising Stars-62
90Topps-294
Tiffany-294
90Upper Deck-209
90Upper Deck-232
French-209
French-232
91Pro Set Platinum-4
91Bowman-361
91Bowman-418
91Bruins Sports Action-11
91Bruins Sports Action-24
91Gillette-29
91Kraft-59
91McDonald's Upper Deck-9
91O-Pee-Chee-338
91OPC Premier-133
91Panini Stickers-179
91Parkhurst-8
91Parkhurst-459
French-8
91Pinnacle-126
91Pinnacle-379
French-126
French-379
91Pro Set-10
91Pro Set-299
French-10
French-299
Player of the Month-P4
Puck Candy Promos-2
Puck Candy-2
91Score American-90
91Score Canadian Bilingual-90
91Score Canadian English-90
91Score Kellogg's-10
91Stadium Club-211
91Topps-338
91Upper Deck-147
French-147
92Bowman-79
92Bruins Postcards-6
92Kraft-32
92O-Pee-Chee-184
92Panini Stickers-135
92Panini Stickers French-135
92Parkhurst-3
Emerald Ice-3
92Pinnacle American Promo Panel-1
92Pinnacle-91
92Pinnacle-263
French-91
French-263
92Pro Set-7
92Score-120
Canadian-120
92Seasons Patches-19
92Stadium Club-430
92Topps-394
Gold-394G
92Ultra-6
92Upper Deck-1
92Upper Deck-329
93Anti-Gambling Postcards-NNO
93Donruss-87
93Leaf-369
93OPC Premier-476
Gold-476
93Panini Stickers-9
93Parkhurst-47
Emerald Ice-47
93Pinnacle-347
Canadian-347
93PowerPlay-64
93Score-11
93Score-516
Gold-516
Canadian-11
Canadian-516
Canadian Gold-516
93Stadium Club-470
Members Only Master Set-470
First Day Issue-470
93Topps/OPC Premier-476
Gold-476
93Ultra-2
93Ultra-301
93Upper Deck-478
SP-39
94Be A Player Signature Cards-30
94Canada Games NHL POGS-277
94Donruss-108
94EA Sports-12
94Flair-44
94Fleer-56
94Kraft-48
94Kraft Goalie Masks-4
94Leaf-47
94OPC Premier-81
94OPC Premier-511
Special Effects-81
Special Effects-511
94Parkhurst-51
Gold-51
94Pinnacle-315
Artist's Proofs-315
Rink Collection-315
Goaltending Greats-GT14
Masks-MA8
94Score-173
Gold-173
Platinum-173
94Select-94
Gold-94
94SP-32
Die Cuts-32
94Stadium Club-231
Members Only Master Set-231
First Day Issue-231
Super Team Winner Cards-231
94Stars HockeyKaps-22
94Stars Pinnacle Sheet-315
94Stars Pinnacle Sheet-NNO
94Stars Postcards-20
94Stars Score Sheet-173
94Topps/OPC Premier-81
94Topps/OPC Premier-511
Special Effects-81
Special Effects-511
94Ultra-56
94Upper Deck-81
Electric Ice-81
SP Inserts-SP111
SP Inserts Die Cuts-SP111
95Bashan Super Stickers-35
95Canada Games NHL POGS-92
95Collector's Choice-62
Player's Club-62
Player's Club Platinum-62
95Donruss-290
95Emotion-50
95Imperial Stickers-35
95Kraft-30
95Metal-43
95Panini Stickers-177
95Parkhurst International-59
Emerald Ice-59
95Pinnacle-114
Artist's Proofs-114
Rink Collection-114
Masks-5
95Playoff One on One-32
95Pro Magnets-125
95Score-64
Black Ice Artist's Proofs-64
Black Ice-64
95Select Certified-77
Mirror Gold-77
95SkyBox Impact-49
95Stars Score Sheet-64
95Summit-96
Artist's Proofs-96
Ice-96
In The Crease-12
95Topps-53
OPC Inserts-53
Hidden Gems-14HG
95Topps SuperSkills-83
Platinum-83
95Ultra-42
Gold Medallion-42
Premier Pad Men-8
Premier Pad Men Gold Medallion-8
95Upper Deck-191
Electric Ice-191
Electric Ice Gold-191
95Zenith-105
96Be A Player-7
Autographs-7
Autographs Silver-7
Stacking the Pads-12
96Donruss-166
Press Proofs-166
96Donruss Canadian Ice-90
Gold Press Proofs-90
Red Press Proofs-90
96Donruss Elite-3
Die Cut Stars-3
96Flair-24
Blue Ice-24
96Leaf-99
Press Proofs-99
96Maggers-63
96Metal Universe-41
96NHL Pro Stamps-125
96Pinnacle-166
Artist's Proofs-166
Foil-166
Premium Stock-166
Rink Collection-166
96Playoff One on One-382
96Score-104
Artist's Proofs-104
Dealer's Choice Artist's Proofs-104
Special Artist's Proofs-104
Golden Blades-104
96Select Certified-25
Artist's Proofs-25
Blue-25
Mirror Blue-25
Mirror Gold-25
Mirror Red-25
Red-25
96SP-44
96Stars Postcards-23
96Stars Score Sheet-104
96Summit-130
Artist's Proofs-130
Ice-130
Metal-130
Premium Stock-130
96Ultra-45
Gold Medallion-45
96Zenith-110
Artist's Proofs-110
97Black Diamond-113
Double Diamond-113
Triple Diamond-113
Quadruple Diamond-113
97Canadiens Postcards-13
97Collector's Choice-67
Star Quest-SQ34
97Crown Royale-70
Emerald Green-70
Ice Blue-70
Silver-70
Freeze Out Die-Cuts-10
97Donruss-40
Press Proofs Silver-40
Press Proofs Gold-40
97Donruss Canadian Ice-85
Dominion Series-85
Provincial Series-85
97Donruss Elite-66
Aspirations-66
Status-66
97Donruss Limited-28
Exposure-28
Fabric of the Game-36
97Donruss Preferred-113
Cut to the Chase-113
97Donruss Priority-108
Stamp of Approval-108
97McDonald's Upper Deck-28
97Pacific-35
Copper-35
Emerald Green-35
Ice Blue-35
Red-35
Silver-35
In The Cage Laser Cuts-6
Dynagon Best Kept Secrets-31
97Pacific Invincible-42
Copper-42
Emerald Green-42
Ice Blue-42
Red-42
Silver-42
NHL Regime-64
97Pacific Omega-120
Copper-120
Dark Gray-120
Emerald Green-120
Gold-120
Ice Blue-120
No Scoring Zone-6
97Paramount-96
Copper-96
Dark Grey-96
Emerald Green-96
Ice Blue-96
Red-96
Silver-96
Glove Side Laser Cuts-10
97Pinnacle-70
Artist's Proofs-70
Rink Collection-70
Press Plates Back Black-70
Press Plates Back Cyan-70
Press Plates Back Magenta-70
Press Plates Back Yellow-70
Press Plates Front Black-70
Press Plates Front Cyan-70
Press Plates Front Magenta-70
Press Plates Front Yellow-70
97Pinnacle Certified-5
Red-5
Mirror Blue-5
Mirror Gold-5
Mirror Red-5
97Pinnacle Inside-47
Coach's Collection-47
Executive Collection-47
97Pinnacle Tot Cert Platinum Blue-5
97Pinnacle Tot Cert Platinum Gold-5
97Pinnacle Totally Certified Platinum Red-5
97Pinnacle Tot Cert Mirror Platinum Gold-5
97Revolution-72
Copper-72
Emerald-72
Ice Blue-72
Silver-72
Return to Sender Die-Cuts-10
97Score-8
Artist's Proofs-8
Golden Blades-8
97Score Canadiens-1
Platinum-1
Premier-1
97SP Authentic-81
97Upper Deck-294
98SLU Hockey One on One-2
98Pacific-255
Ice Blue-255
Red-255
98SPx Finite-44
Radiance-44
Spectrum-44
98UD Choice-106
Prime Choice Reserve-106
Reserve-106
01Topps Archives-24
Relics-JAM
01Upper Deck Vintage Jerseys-GGAM
02BAP Memorabilia Mini Stanley Cups-23
02BAP Ultimate Memorabilia Cup Duels-12
02BAP Ultimate Memorabilia Cup Duels-14
02Topps Rookie Reprints-8
02Topps Rookie Reprint Autographs-8
02UD Foundations-1
02UD Foundations-19
02UD Foundations-29
02UD Mask Collection Career Wins-CWAM
02UD Mask Collection Mini Masks-AM
03Parkhurst Original Six Boston-57
Autographs-10
Memorabilia-BM29
04ITG Franchises Canadian-19
Autographs-AM2
04ITG Franchises Update-463
04ITG Franchises US East-328
Autographs-A-AM1
Goalie Gear-EGG7
Goalie Gear Gold-EGG7
Memorabilia-ESM27
Memorabilia Gold-ESM27
04ITG Ultimate Memorabilia Complete Logo-18
04ITG Ultimate Memorabilia Original Six-7
04ITG Ultimate Mem Retro Teammates-1
06Between The Pipes-78
Autographs-AAMO
Emblems-GUE35
Emblems Gold-GUE35
Emblems Autographs-GUE35
Jerseys-GUJ35
Jerseys Gold-GUJ35
Jerseys Autographs-GUJ35
Numbers-GUN35
Numbers Gold-GUN35
Numbers Autographs-GUN35
Shooting Gallery-SG03
Shooting Gallery Gold-SG03
06ITG Ultimate Memorabilia Retro Teammates-19
06ITG Ultimate Memorabilia Retro Teammates Gold-19

Moon, Cam
89Saskatoon Blades-2
90Saskatoon Blades-3
907th Inn. Sketch WHL-87

Moon, Nathan
06Kingston Frontenacs-4

Mooney, Francis
93Quebec Pee-Wee Tournament-186

Mooney, Matt
90Rayside-Balfour Jr. Canadians-14
91Rayside-Balfour Jr. Canadians-11

Mooney, Mike
89Rayside-Balfour Jr. Canadians-16

Mooney, Shane
93Quebec Pee-Wee Tournament-158

Moor, Daryl
02Lexington Men O'War-11
04Columbus Cottonmouths-19
04New Mexico Scorpions-17

Moor, Jeff
05Owen Sound Attack-6

Moore, Barrie
917th Inn. Sketch OHL-259
91Sudbury Wolves-20
92Sudbury Wolves-17
93Sudbury Wolves-15
93Sudbury Wolves Police-15
94Sudbury Wolves-14
94Sudbury Wolves Police-10
95Rochester Americans-13
96Rochester Americans-9
96Collector's Edge Ice-65
Prism-65
98Indianapolis Ice-20
99Portland Pirates-15
00UK Sekonda Superleague-195
02Columbia Inferno-105
03Columbia Inferno-107
04Missouri River Otters-5
05UK Coventry Blaze-13
06UK Coventry Blaze-6

Moore, Blaine
92British Columbia JHL-238
94Richmond Renegades-7
95Las Vegas Thunder-8
96Las Vegas Thunder-16
00Fresno Falcons-22
01Fresno Falcons-22
02Fresno Falcons-22
03Fresno Falcons-10

Moore, Chad
03Missouri River Otters-11

Moore, Charlie
83Belleville Bulls-13
84Belleville Bulls-8

Moore, David
91Cincinnati Cyclones-16
93Memphis RiverKings-10
94Central Hockey League-102
98Danish Hockey League-93
98Danish Hockey League-109
99Austin Ice Bats-5
99Austin Ice Bats-33

Moore, Dean
91Air Canada SJHL-A15
92Saskatchewan JHL-106
96Knoxville Cherokees-17
97Charlotte Checkers-15

Moore, Dickie
44Beehive Group II Photos-274
45Quaker Oats Photos-100
48Exhibits Canadian-18
52Parkhurst-10
53Parkhurst-28
54Parkhurst-2
55Parkhurst-38
Quaker Oats-38
57Parkhurst-M14
58Parkhurst-8
59Parkhurst-14
60NHL Ceramic Tiles-24
60Parkhurst-38
60Parkhurst-57
60Shirriff Coins-22
60York Photos-24
61Parkhurst-36
61Shirriff/Salada Coins-107
61York Yellow Backs-5
62Parkhurst-42
62Shirriff Coins-37
62York Iron-On Transfers-22
63Maple Leafs Team Issue-17
63Toronto Star-27

64Beehive Group III Photos-176
64Coca-Cola Caps-100
83Hall of Fame-190
83Hall of Fame Postcards-J10
85Hall of Fame-190
92Parkhurst Parkie Reprints-PR26
93O-Pee-Chee Canadiens Hockey Fest-59
93O-Pee-Chee Canadiens Hockey Fest-63
93Parkhurst Parkie Reprints Case Inserts-12
94Parkhurst Missing Link-70
94Parkhurst Tall Boys-116
99BAP Memorabilia AS Canadian Hobby-CH8
99BAP Memorabilia AS Cdn Hobby Autos-CH8
99Upper Deck Century Legends-31
Century Collection-31
01BAP Memorabilia Rocket's Mates-RM8
01BAP Signature Series Vintage Autographs-VA-24
01BAP Ultimate Memorabilia Gloves Are Off-25
01Parkhurst Autographs-PA16
01Parkhurst Reprints-PR19
01Parkhurst Reprints-PR29
01Parkhurst Reprints-PR61
01Parkhurst Reprints-PR77
01Parkhurst Reprints-PR94
01Parkhurst Reprints-PR102
01Parkhurst Reprints-PR120
01Parkhurst Reprints-PR145
02BAP Ultimate Memorabilia Gloves Are Off-7
02BAP Ultimate Mem Scoring Leaders-32
02BAP Ultimate Mem Scoring Leaders-33
03BAP Memorabilia Gloves-GUG17
03BAP Ultimate Memorabilia Gloves Are Off-15
03BAP Ultimate Memorabilia Linemates-4
03Parkhurst Original Six Montreal-60
Autographs-11
Memorabilia-MM16
04ITG Franchises Canadian-49
Autographs-DM2
04ITG Franchises Update Linemates-ULI5
04ITG Franchises Update Linemates Gold-ULI5
04ITG Franchises US West-286
Autographs-A-DM1
04ITG Ultimate Memorabilia-75
Gold-75
Day In History-39
Day In History Gold-39
Original Six-10
04UD Legends Classics-18
04UD Legends Classics-98
Gold-18
Gold-98
Platinum-18
Platinum-98
Silver-18
Silver-98
Jersey Redemptions-JY4
Signature Moments-M5
Signatures-CS5
Signatures-DC9
Signatures-TC12
05Beehive Signature Scrapbook-SSDI
05ITG Ultimate Mem 3 Star of the Game Jsy-5
05ITG Ult Mem 3 Star of the Game Jsy Gold-5
05SP Authentic Sign of the Times Fives-LRMMG
05SPx Xcitement Legends-XL-DM
05SPx Xcitement Legends Gold-XL-DM
05SPx Xcitement Legends Spectrum-XL-DM
05UD Artifacts-135
Blue-135
Gold-135
Green-135
Pewter-135
Red-135
Gold Autographed-135
06Parkhurst-117
Autographs Dual-DABM

Moore, Dominic
94Quebec Pee-Wee Tournament-1607
03Bowman-126
Gold-126
03Bowman Chrome-126
Refractors-126
Gold Refractors-126
Xtractors-126
03ITG Action-636
03ITG Used Signature Series-194
Gold-194
03ITG VIP Rookie Debut-55
03Pacific Calder-127
Silver-127
03Pacific Complete-547
Red-547
03Pacific Heads-Up-126
Hobby LTD-126
Retail LTD-126
03Pacific Luxury Suite-72
Gold-72
03Pacific Quest for the Cup-127
03Parkhurst Original Six New York-16
03Parkhurst Rookie-155
Rookie Emblems-RE-24
Rookie Emblems Gold-RE-24
Rookie Jerseys-RJ-24
Rookie Jerseys Gold-RJ-24
Rookie Numbers-RN-24
Rookie Numbers Gold-RN-24
Teammates Gold-RT21
Teammates-RT21
03SP Authentic-127
Limited-127
03SPx-233
03Titanium-129
Hobby Jersey Number Parallels-129
Retail-129
Retail Jersey Number Parallels-129
03Topps Pristine-113
03Topps Pristine-114
03Topps Pristine-115
Gold Refractor Die Cuts-113
Gold Refractor Die Cuts-114
Gold Refractor Die Cuts-115
Refractors-113
Refractors-114
Refractors-115
Press Plates Black-113
Press Plates Black-114
Press Plates Black-115
Press Plates Cyan-113
Press Plates Cyan-114
Press Plates Cyan-115
Press Plates Magenta-113
Press Plates Magenta-114
Press Plates Magenta-115
Press Plates Yellow-113
Press Plates Yellow-114
Press Plates Yellow-115
03Topps Traded-TT128
Blue-TT128
Gold-TT128
Red-TT128
03UD Honor Roll-167
03Upper Deck-462
03Upper Deck-475
Canadian Exclusives-462
Canadian Exclusives-475
HG-462
HG-475
UD Exclusives-462
UD Exclusives-475
03Upper Deck Ice-106
Glass Parallel-106
03Upper Deck Rookie Update-196
03Hartford Wolf Pack-16
03Pacific AHL Prospects-34
Gold-34
04Hartford Wolf Pack-17
05Parkhurst-329
Facsimile Auto Parallel-329
True Colors-TCNYR
True Colors-TCNYR
True Colors-TCNJNY
True Colors-TCNJNY
05Upper Deck-379
Jerseys Series II-J2DM
06Fleer Fabricology-FDM
06O-Pee-Chee-392
Rainbow-392
06Upper Deck-408
Exclusives Parallel-408
High Gloss Parallel-408
Masterpieces-408

Moore, Greg
92Saskatchewan JHL-98
06Hartford Wolf Pack-21

Moore, Greg NCAA
04Maine Black Bears-12
05Maine Black Bears-18
06Hartford Wolf Pack-21

Moore, James
02UK Peterborough Phantoms-2

Moore, Jimmy
51Laval Dairy QSHL-36
52St. Lawrence Sales-3

Moore, Kevin
91Ferris State Bulldogs-24
92Ferris State Bulldogs-24

Moore, Mark
00Charlotte Checkers-34

Moore, Matt
04Knoxville Ice Bears-17
05Knoxville Ice Bears-12

Moore, Mike
97Portland Winter Hawks-18
88Portland Winter Hawks-18

Moore, Ryan
03Halifax Mooseheads-14
04Halifax Mooseheads-14
05Saint John's Sea Dogs-19

Moore, Scott
90Swedish Semic Elitserien Stickers-71
91Swedish Semic Elitserien Stickers-241

Moore, Shaden
05Calgary Hitmen-13

Moore, Shane
04UK U-20 Team-6

Moore, Skeeter
84Minnesota-Duluth Bulldogs-27
85Minnesota-Duluth Bulldogs-1
98San Angelo Outlaws-13
99San Angelo Outlaws-11

Moore, Steve
95Central Hockey League-48
98Oklahoma City Blazers-9
99Topeka Scarecrows-8
01BAP Memorabilia-342
Emerald-342
Ruby-342
Sapphire-342
01UD Premier Collection-56
01Hershey Bears-16
01Kalamazoo K-Wings-16
02Hershey Bears-14
03Hershey Bears Patriot News-15

Moore, Taylor
04Langley Hornets-13

Moore, Teegan
02Brandon Wheat Kings-11
03Brandon Wheat Kings-11
04Brandon Wheat Kings-12
05Brandon Wheat Kings-17

Moores, Tom
917th Inn. Sketch OHL-214
93Niagara Falls Thunder-17

Moorhead, Jaime
93Quebec Pee-Wee Tournament-750

Moraal, Arie
83Kingston Canadians-4
84Kingston Canadians-3
85Kingston Canadians-3
86Kingston Canadians-3
87Kingston Canadians-1

Morabito, John
91British Columbia JHL-12
92British Columbia JHL-190
95Birmingham Bulls-11

Moran, Amby
23V128-1 Paulin's Candy-29
24Anonymous NHL-11

Moran, Brad
98Calgary Hitmen-14
98Calgary Hitmen Autographs-14
98Bowman CHL-72
Golden Anniversary-72
OPC International-72
98Bowman Chrome CHL-72
Golden Anniversary-72
Golden Anniversary Refractors-72
OPC International-72
OPC International Refractors-72
Refractors-72
99SP Authentic-130
99Upper Deck MVP SC Edition-203
Gold Script-203
Silver Script-203
Super Script-203
99Upper Deck Ovation-77
Standing Ovation-77
99Calgary Hitmen-18
99Calgary Hitmen Autographs-18
99Bowman CHL-92
Gold-92
OPC International-92
00Syracuse Crunch-15
01Syracuse Crunch-14
02Upper Deck MVP-51
Gold-51
Classics-51
Golden Classics-51
02Syracuse Crunch-13
02Syracuse Crunch Sheets-8
03Pacific AHL Prospects-87
Gold-87
03Syracuse Crunch-13
04Syracuse Crunch-14
06Manitoba Moose-14

Moran, Ian
93PowerPlay-512
93Stadium Club Team USA-17
93Stadium Club Team USA Members Only-17
93Topps Premier Team USA-2
93Ultra-492
94Cleveland Lumberjacks-10
94Cleveland Lumberjacks Postcards-10
94Classic-101
Gold-101
95Penguins Foodland-20
95SkyBox Impact-216
95Stadium Club-219
Members Only Master Set-219
96Cleveland Lumberjacks-18
96Cleveland Lumberjacks Multi-Ad-20
97Be A Player-93
Autographs-93
Autographs Die-Cuts-93
Autographs Prismatic Die-Cuts-93
97Pacific Dynagon Best Kept Secrets-79
99Paramount-191
Copper-191
Emerald-191
Gold-191
Holographic Emerald-191
Holographic Gold-191
Holographic Silver-191
Ice Blue-191
Premiere Date-191
Red-191
Silver-191
01Pacific Jerseys-30
01Private Stock Game Gear-80
01Private Stock Game Gear Patches-80
01Titanium Double-Sided Jerseys-35
01Titanium Double-Sided Patches-35
02Topps Total-222
03Parkhurst Original Six Boston-29

Moran, Keith
97Austin Ice Bats-12

Moran, Paddy
10C56-28
10Sweet Caporal Postcards-1
11C55-1
12C57-18
60Topps-2
Stamps-38
83Hall of Fame-144
83Hall of Fame Postcards-K10
85Hall of Fame-144
03BAP Ultimate Mem Vintage Blade of Steel-19
04ITG Ultimate Mem Blades of Steel-16
06Between The Pipes Forgotten Franchises-FF10
06ITG Ultimate Memorabilia Blades of Steel-26
06ITG Ultimate Memorabilia Blades of Steel Gold-26

Moran, Patrick
06Guelph Storm-13

Moran, Paul
00UK Nottingham Panthers-3
01UK Nottingham Panthers-17
02UK Nottingham Panthers-14
03UK Nottingham Panthers-14
04UK Nottingham Panthers-14
05UK Nottingham Panthers-14
06UK Nottingham Panthers-8

Moran, Tim
93Quebec Pee-Wee Tournament-516

Moran, Travis
02Chicago Steel-15

Morava, Marian
96Czech APS Extraliga-318
97Czech APS Extraliga-296
97Czech DS Stickers-152
98Czech DS Stickers-112
98Czech OFS-52
99Czech Score Blue 2000-39
99Czech Score Red Ice 2000-39
02Czech OFS Plus-95
06Czech OFS-141

Moravec, David
95Czech APS Extraliga-309
96Czech APS Extraliga-206
97Czech APS Extraliga-134
97Czech DS Extraliga-100
97Czech DS Stickers-202
98Czech DS-6
98Czech DS Stickers-257
98Czech OFS-243
99Czech OFS-355
99Czech OFS-482
Olympic Winners-11
98Czech Bonaparte-7D
98Czech Pexeso-25
98Czech Pexeso Series Two-7
99Pacific Omega-33
Copper-33
Gold-33
Ice Blue-33
Premiere Date-33
99Upper Deck-192
Exclusives-192
Exclusives 1 of 1-192
99Upper Deck Gold Reserve-192
99Czech DS National Stars-NS19
99Czech OFS-434
99Czech OFS-479
99Czech OFS-521
All-Star Game Blue-521
All-Star Game Gold-521
All-Star Game Red-521
All-Star Game Silver-521
00Czech DS Extraliga-162
00Czech OFS-250
01Czech DS-18
01Czech DS-61
Best of the Best-BB5
01Czech National Team Postcards-9
01Czech OFS-30
All Stars-23
01Czech OFS Red Inserts-RE7D
02Czech DS-26
02Czech OFS Plus-58
02Czech OFS Plus All-Star Game-H16
02Czech OFS Plus Trios-T18
02Czech OFS Plus Duos-D6
02Czech IQ Sports Blue-17
02Czech IQ Sports Yellow-18
03Czech OFS Plus-68
03Czech OFS Plus All-Star Game-H40
03Czech OFS Plus Insert S-S4
03Czech OFS Plus MS Praha-SE31
03Russian Hockey League-259
03Russian SL-29
04Czech OFS-234
04Czech OFS-349
Checklist Cards-11
Stars-46
05Czech HC Plzen-9
06Czech OFS All Stars-20
06Swedish SHL Elitset-236

Moravec, Jiri
02Czech OFS Plus-160
03Czech OFS Plus-119
04Czech OFS-72
06Czech OFS-95

Morczinietz, Andreas
99German Bundesliga 2-262
01German Upper Deck-241
02German DEL City Press-200
Top Scorers-TS4
03German DEL-175
04German DEL-155
04German Hannover Scorpions Postcards-20
05German DEL-134
05German DEL-299
06German DEL-84
German Forwards-GF3

Morden, Steve
99UK Hull Thunder-16

More, Jayson
90ProCards AHL/IHL-998
91Parkhurst-387
French-387
91Pinnacle-342
French-342
92Bowman-388
92O-Pee-Chee-312
92Parkhurst-394
Emerald Ice-394
92Pro Set-169
92Score-147
Canadian-147
92Stadium Club-60
92Topps-245
Gold-245G
92Upper Deck-488
93OPC Premier-227
Gold-227
93Parkhurst-452
Emerald Ice-452
93Stadium Club-208
Members Only Master Set-208
OPC-208
First Day Issue-208
First Day Issue OPC-208
93Topps/OPC Premier-227
Gold-227
94Leaf-509
94Stadium Club-165
Members Only Master Set-165
First Day Issue-165
Super Team Winner Cards-165
95Playoff One on One-303
96Playoff One on One-417
97Be A Player-70
Autographs-70
Autographs Die-Cuts-70
Autographs Prismatic Die-Cuts-70
97Coyotes Face-Off Luncheon -15
98Pacific-98
Ice Blue-98
Red-98
98Paramount-126
Copper-126
Emerald Green-126
Holo-Electric-126
Ice Blue-126
Silver-126
98Predators Team Issue-16

More, Paul
83Brandon Wheat Kings-15
84Brandon Wheat Kings-23

Moreau, Eric
917th Inn. Sketch QMJHL-191
92Quebec Pee-Wee Tournament-1262
93Niagara Falls Thunder-28
93Quebec Pee-Wee Tournament-1373

Moreau, Ethan
917th Inn. Sketch OHL-212
93Niagara Falls Thunder-13
94Sudbury Wolves-20
94Classic-12
Gold-12
Tri-Cards-T13
94Classic Four-Sport *-128
Gold-128
BCs-BC20
Classic Picks-25
Printers Proofs-128
95Parkhurst International-540
Emerald Ice-540
95Indianapolis Ice-16
95Classic-97
CHL All-Stars-AS12
95Images-50
Gold-50
95Images Four-Sport *-105
96Be A Player Link to History-4A
96Be A Player Link to History Autographs-4A
96Be A Player Link to History Auto Silver-4A
96Black Diamond-69
Gold-69
96Collector's Choice-354
96Donruss-228
Press Proofs-228
96Donruss Canadian Ice-127
Gold Press Proofs-127
Red Press Proofs-127
96Donruss Elite-136
Die Cut Stars-136
Aspirations-20
96Flair-104
Blue Ice-104
96Leaf Gold Rookies-1
96Leaf Limited Rookies-1
96Leaf Limited Rookies Gold-1
96Leaf Preferred-139
Press Proofs-139
96Metal Universe-187
96Pinnacle-239
Artist's Proofs-239
Foil-239
Premium Stock-239
Rink Collection-239
96Score-268
Artist's Proofs-268
Dealer's Choice Artist's Proofs-268
Special Artist's Proofs-268
Golden Blades-268
96Select Certified-116
Artist's Proofs-116
Blue-116
Mirror Blue-116
Mirror Gold-116
Mirror Red-116
Red-116
96SP-31
96Summit-184
Artist's Proofs-184
Ice-184
Metal-184
Premium Stock-184
96Ultra-32
Gold Medallion-32
Rookies-13
96Upper Deck-187
96Zenith-133
Artist's Proofs-133
96Collector's Edge Future Legends-34
96Collector's Edge Ice-134
Platinum Club-7
Prism-134
96Visions *-88
97Collector's Choice-51
97Donruss-50
Press Proofs Silver-50
Press Proofs Gold-50
97Donruss Canadian Ice-83
Dominion Series-83
Provincial Series-83
97Donruss Elite-52
Aspirations-52
Status-52
97Donruss Limited-60
97Donruss Limited-87
97Donruss Limited-94
Exposure-60
Exposure-87
Exposure-94
97Donruss Preferred-35
Cut to the Chase-35
97Donruss Priority-116
Stamp of Approval-116
97Katch-35
Gold-35
Silver-35
97Leaf-143
Fractal Matrix-143
Fractal Matrix Die Cuts-143
97Leaf International-143
Universal Ice-143
97Pacific Dynagon-28
Copper-28
Dark Grey-28
Emerald Green-28
Ice Blue-28
Red-28
Silver-28
Tandems-40
97Pacific Invincible-31
Copper-31
Emerald Green-31
Ice Blue-31
Red-31
Silver-31
97Paramount-46
Copper-46
Dark Grey-46
Emerald Green-46
Ice Blue-46
Red-46
Silver-46
97Pinnacle-189
Press Plates Back Black-189
Press Plates Back Cyan-189
Press Plates Back Magenta-189
Press Plates Back Yellow-189
Press Plates Front Black-189
Press Plates Front Cyan-189
Press Plates Front Magenta-189
Press Plates Front Yellow-189
97Pinnacle Inside-184
97Score-151
Artist's Proofs-151
Golden Blades-151
97Studio-83
Press Proofs Silver-83
Press Proofs Gold-83
Hard Hats-23
97Upper Deck-250
98Finest-71
No Protectors-71
No Protectors Refractors-71
Refractors-71
99Pacific-160
Copper-160
Emerald Green-160
Gold-160
Ice Blue-160
Premiere Date-160
Red-160
99Upper Deck MVP SC Edition-76
Gold Script-76
Silver Script-76
Super Script-76
00O-Pee-Chee-257B
00O-Pee-Chee Parallel-257B
00Pacific-170
Copper-170
Gold-170
Ice Blue-170
Premiere Date-170
00Stadium Club-173
00Topps/OPC-257B
Parallel-257B
00Upper Deck-71
Exclusives Tier 1-71
Exclusives Tier 2-71
02NHL Power Play Stickers-36
02Oilers Postcards-6
02Pacific Complete-44
Red-44
02Upper Deck Vintage-104
03ITG Action-228
03Oilers Postcards-12
03Pacific Complete-317
Red-317
03Upper Deck-317
Canadian Exclusives-317
HG-317
UD Exclusives-317
04Pacific-104
Blue-104
Red-104
06O-Pee-Chee-197
Rainbow-197
06Upper Deck-80
Exclusives Parallel-80
High Gloss Parallel-80
Masterpieces-80

Moreau, Marguerite
92Disney Mighty Ducks Movie-4

Moreau, Olivier
93Quebec Pee-Wee Tournament-1059

Moreau, Patrick
97Idaho Steelheads-3

Moreau, Sebastien
917th Inn. Sketch QMJHL-106
92Saskatchewan JHL-165

Morehouse, Chris
05Moncton Wildcats-24
06Moncton Wildcats-18

Morel, Alexandre
98Quebec Remparts-16
Signed-16
00Rouyn-Noranda Huskies-9
Signed-9

Morel, Denis
90Pro Set-695

Morel, Kelly
97New Mexico Scorpions-19

Moreland, Jake
98Sioux City Musketeers-14
03Atlantic City Boardwalk Bullies-15
03Atlantic City Boardwalk Bullies RBI-23
04Atlantic City Boardwalk Bullies-22
04Atlantic City Boardwalk Bullies Kinko's-2
05Stockton Thunder-15
06Rockford IceHogs-18

Moren, Darren
83Victoria Cougars-18
84Saskatoon Blades Stickers-15

Moren, Ryan
03Alaska Aces-12

Morency, Pascal
01Cape Breton Screaming Eagles-18
04Wheeling Nailers Riesbeck's-15
04Wheeling Nailers SGA-9
06Fort Wayne Komets-14

Morency, Steve
98Val d'Or Foreurs-18
00Sherbrooke Castors-6
Signed-6

Morenz , Howie, Jr.
37V356 Worldwide Gum-100

Morenz, Brian
74San Diego Mariners WHA-3

Morenz, Howie
23V145-1-15
24Anonymous NHL-9
24C144 Champ's Cigarettes-41
24V130 Maple Crispette-12
24V145-2-47
27La Patrie-14
27La Presse Photos-1
33Sport Kings R338 *-24
33O-Pee-Chee V304A-23
33Sport Kings R338 *-24
33V129-41
33V252 Canadian Gum-38
33V288 Hamilton Gum-8
33V357 Ice Kings-36
33V357-2 Ice Kings Premiums-4
34Beehive Group I Photos-170
34Diamond Matchbooks Silver-46
34Sweet Caporal-35
35Diamond Matchbooks Tan 1-49
35Diamond Matchbooks Tan 2-49
35Diamond Matchbooks Tan 3-46
36O-Pee-Chee V304D-121
37V356 Worldwide Gum-18
43Parade Sportive *-40
55Parkhurst-57
Quaker Oats-57
60Topps-59
Stamps-39
83Hall of Fame Postcards-H12
85Hall of Fame-106
91Pro Set-336
French-336
93O-Pee-Chee Canadiens Hockey Fest-13
94Hall of Fame Tickets-7
94Parkhurst Missing Link Pop-Ups-P1
99Upper Deck Century Legends-14
Century Collection-14
02BAP Ultimate Memorabilia Retro Trophies-9
02BAP Ultimate Mem Storied Franchise-3
03BAP Ultimate Memorabilia Gloves Are Off-16
03BAP Ultimate Memorabilia Paper Cuts-43
03BAP Ultimate Memorabilia Vintage Lumber-12
03Canada Post-15
03ITG Toronto Fall Expo Forever Rivals-FR10
03Parkhurst Original Six Chicago-37
04ITG Franchises Canadian-42
04ITG Franchises Update Exceptions-1
04ITG Franchises Update Exceptions Gold-1
04ITG Franchises Update Original Sticks-UOS9
04ITG Franchises Upd Original Sticks Gold-UOS9
04ITG Ultimate Memorabilia-36
04ITG Ultimate Memorabilia-123
Gold-36
Gold-123
Changing the Game-10
Cornerstones-4
Cornerstones Gold-4
Hart Trophy-8
Nicknames-27
Paper Cuts Memorabilia-13
Vintage Lumber-7
04ITG Heroes and Prospects-168
04ITG Heroes/Prospects Toronto Expo '05-168
05ITG Ultimate Memorabilia Level 1-50
05ITG Ultimate Memorabilia Level 3-50
05ITG Ultimate Memorabilia Level 4-50
05ITG Ultimate Mem Bleu Blanc Rouge Autos-4
05ITG Ultimate Mem Cornerstones Jerseys-9
05ITG Ult Mem Cornerst Jerseys Gold-9
05ITG Ultimate Memorabilia Gloves Are Off-19
05ITG Ultimate Mem Gloves Are Off Gold-19
05ITG Ultimate Mem Paper Cut Autos-1
05ITG Ultimate Memorabilia Vintage Lumber-1
05ITG Ultimate Mem Vintage Lumber Gold-1
06ITG Ultimate Memorabilia-68
Artist Proof-68
Boys Will Be Boys-4
Boys Will Be Boys Gold-4
Decades-4
Decades Gold-1
Decades Gold-4
Lumbergraphs-5
Paper Cuts Autos-1
Retro Teammates-1
Retro Teammates Gold-1
Stick Rack-21
Stick Rack Gold-21
Vintage Lumber-1
Vintage Lumber Gold-1

Moret, Leo
28V128-2 Paulin's Candy-44

Moret, Thierry
93Swiss HNL-331
95Swiss HNL-477
96Swiss HNL-375
98Swiss Power Play Stickers-342

Morf, Markus
93Swiss HNL-227

Morf, Stephan
93Swiss HNL-339
95Swiss HNL-290

Morgan, Brad
97Barrie Colts-17
97Sudbury Wolves Police-20
98Sudbury Wolves-19
99Sudbury Wolves-21

Morgan, Chris
91Air Canada SJHL-A18

Morgan, Cory
96Prince Albert Raiders-15
97Prince Albert Raiders-15
98Prince Albert Raiders-17
99Tacoma Sabercats-6
00Tacoma Sabercats-1

Morgan, Gavin
99Idaho Steelheads-11
00Utah Grizzlies-26
01Utah Grizzlies-32
02Utah Grizzlies-25
03Beehive-231
Gold-231
Silver-231
03ITG VIP Rookie Debut-75
03Parkhurst Rookie-81
03SP Authentic-129
Limited-129
03Stars Postcards-17
03Upper Deck Rookie Update-147
03Hershey Bears-8
03Hershey Bears Patriot News-16
04Hamilton Bulldogs-21
05Peoria Rivermen-6
06Peoria Rivermen-13

Morgan, James
03UK Nottingham Panthers-4

Morgan, Jason
93Kitchener Rangers-13
94Kitchener Rangers-14
95Slapshot-121
97Springfield Falcons-17
98Upper Deck-109
Exclusives-109
Exclusives 1 of 1-109
Gold Reserve-109
98Arizona Icecats-21
99Arizona Icecats-20
99Florida Everblades-22
00Arizona Icecats-17
00Florida Everblades-20
03Lowell Lock Monsters-10
03Lowell Lock Monsters Photo Album-5
04Norfolk Admirals-15
05Norfolk Admirals-12

Morgan, Jordan
03Prince Albert Raiders-13

Morger, Patrizio
93Swiss HNL-177
95Swiss HNL-50
96Swiss HNL-196
98Swiss Power Play Stickers-242
99Swiss Panini Stickers-244
00Swiss Panini Stickers-239
00Swiss Slapshot Mini-Cards-RJ14
01Swiss HNL-163
02Swiss HNL-100

Mori, Aaron
96Regina Pats-10
97Regina Pats-23

Moria, Steve
00UK Cardiff Devils-11
00UK Sekonda Superleague-64
01UK Cardiff Devils-10
02UK Cardiff Devils-10
03UK Basingstoke Bison-13
04UK London Racers-11
04UK London Racers Playoffs-13

Moriarty, Gerald
95Slapshot-333
95Sarnia Sting-3
96Sudbury Wolves-15

Morin, Benoit
00Trenton Titans-19

Morin, Claude
03St. Georges de Beauce Garaga-14
04St. Georges de Beauce Garaga-5

Morin, Derek
897th Inn. Sketch OHL-89
907th Inn. Sketch OHL-13

Morin, Etienne
92Quebec Pee-Wee Tournament-677
02Indianapolis Ice-11

Morin, Francis
92Quebec Pee-Wee Tournament-1032
93Quebec Pee-Wee Tournament-1336

Morin, Guillaume
917th Inn. Sketch QMJHL-173

Morin, J.P.
93Quebec Pee-Wee Tournament-1027
02Louisiana Ice Gators-14

Morin, Jean Junior
01Baie-Comeau Drakkar-14
01Hull Olympiques-23

Morin, Jean-Martin
917th Inn. Sketch QMJHL-138

Morin, Jerome
92Quebec Pee-Wee Tournament-759
93Quebec Pee-Wee Tournament-237
93Quebec Pee-Wee Tournament-328

Morin, Jesper
98German DEL-9

Morin, Joel
87Kingston Canadians-10
897th Inn. Sketch OHL-165

Morin, Karl
99Quebec Remparts-12
Signed-12
02Shawinigan Cataractes-6

Morin, Marc
84Chicoutimi Sagueneens-20

Morin, Mike
84Saskatoon Blades Stickers-16
85Brandon Wheat Kings-19
91Lake Superior State Lakers-18
92Lake Superior State Lakers-20
93Quebec Pee-Wee Tournament-1614
95Richmond Renegades-20
00UK Sekonda Superleague-104
01UK Manchester Storm-4
01UK Manchester Storm Retro-7
02UK Hull Thunder-12
02UK Sheffield Steelers-13
03UK Manchester Phoenix-10

Morin, Nathan
90Montreal-Bourassa AAA-16
917th Inn. Sketch QMJHL-158
98Thetford Mines Coyotes-22

Morin, Olivier
93Quebec Pee-Wee Tournament-462
97Bowman CHL-74
OPC-74
99ECHL All-Star Southern Conference-21

Morin, Patrice
93Quebec Pee-Wee Tournament-375

Morin, Pete
34Beehive Group I Photos-171
37V356 Worldwide Gum-129
43Parade Sportive *-53
43Parade Sportive *-90
52St. Lawrence Sales-16

Morin, Philippe
98Thetford Mines Coyotes-11

Morin, Stephane
89Halifax Citadels-16
89ProCards AHL-167
90Nordiques Petro-Canada-34
90Upper Deck-524
French-524
90Halifax Citadels-18
90ProCards AHL/IHL-455
91Pro Set Platinum-100
91Bowman-148
91Nordiques Petro-Canada-20
91O-Pee-Chee-159
91Panini Stickers-263
91Parkhurst-147
French-147
91Pinnacle-245
French-245
91Pro Set-201
French-201
91Score American-361
91Score Canadian Bilingual-254
91Score Canadian English-254
91Score Young Superstars-39
91Stadium Club-216
91Topps-159
91Upper Deck-433
French-433
92Durivage Panini-9
92Panini Stickers-214
92Panini Stickers French-214
92Stadium Club-469
92Topps-316
Gold-316G
92Hamilton Canucks-20
92Quebec Pee-Wee Tournament-746
94Minnesota Moose-13
95Minnesota Moose-4
96Collector's Edge Ice-169
Prism-169
97Long Beach Ice Dogs-13
98German DEL-109

Morin, Vic
80Sault Ste. Marie Greyhounds-12

Morin, Vincent
92Quebec Pee-Wee Tournament-744
93Quebec Pee-Wee Tournament-329

Morisset, David
97Seattle Thunderbirds-9

Morissette, Alain
91ProCards-303
95Roller Hockey Magazine RHI-5

Morissette, Dave
907th Inn. Sketch QMJHL-199
91Hampton Roads Admirals-12
92Hampton Roads Admirals-14
93Roanoke Express-14
93Roanoke Express-23
95Minnesota Moose-12
98Canadiens Team Issue-12
98SP Authentic-129
Power Shift-129
Sign of the Times-DM
Sign of the Times Gold-DM
98Upper Deck-406
Exclusives-406
Exclusives 1 of 1-406
Gold Reserve-406
98Upper Deck MVP-106
Gold Script-106
Silver Script-106
Super Script-106
99Quebec Citadelles-18

Morissette, Sebastian
00Quebec Remparts-7
Signed-7
00Victoriaville Tigres-21
Signed-21

Mork, Gary
66Columbus Checkers-13

Morlang, John
02Columbus Cottonmouths-14
03Columbus Cottonmouths-22
05Reading Royals-10

Morley, Peter

94UK Guildford Flames-11
97UK Guildford Flames-1
02UK Peterborough Phantoms-6

Mormina, Bob
83Springfield Indians-12

Mormina, Joey
05Manchester Monarchs-10
06Manchester Monarchs-9

Morneau, Adam
01Val d'Or Foreurs-23

Moro, Marc
93Kingston Frontenacs-4
95Slapshot-116
95Classic-24
95Classic Five-Sport *-140
Autographs-140
96Sault Ste. Marie Greyhounds-12
96Sault Ste. Marie Greyhounds Autographed-12
97Bowman CHL-17
OPC-17
98Milwaukee Admirals-21
99Milwaukee Admirals Keebler-14
00BAP Memorabilia-50
Emerald-50
Ruby-50
Sapphire-50
Promos-50
00BAP Mem Chicago Sportsfest Copper-50
00BAP Memorabilia Chicago Sportsfest Blue-50
00BAP Memorabilia Chicago Sportsfest Gold-50
00BAP Memorabilia Chicago Sportsfest Ruby-50
00BAP Memorabilia Chicago Sun-Times Ruby-50
00BAP Memorabilia Chicago Sun-Times Gold-50
00BAP Mem Chicago Sun-Times Sapphire-50
00BAP Mem Toronto Fall Expo Copper-50
00BAP Memorabilia Toronto Fall Expo Gold-50
00BAP Memorabilia Toronto Fall Expo Ruby-50
00Pacific-229
Copper-229
Gold-229
Ice Blue-229
Premiere Date-229
00Upper Deck-418
Exclusives Tier 1-418
Exclusives Tier 2-418
00Milwaukee Admirals Keebler-10
01BAP Signature Series-215
Autographs-215
Autographs Gold-215
01Milwaukee Admirals-18
01Milwaukee Admirals Postcards-8
02BAP Sig Series Auto Buybacks 2001-215
06Toronto Marlies-18

Morocco, Rick
80Sault Ste. Marie Greyhounds-20
82North Bay Centennials-17
92Finnish Semic-259

Moroder, Mirko
95Swedish World Championships Stickers-93

Moroney, Des
64Swedish Coralli ISHockey-57
67Swedish Hockey-273
69Swedish Hockey-284
70Swedish Hockey-182
71Swedish Hockey-268

Morozhov, Valentin
95Signature Rookies-68
Signatures-68
00Russian Hockey League-153

Morozov, Alexei
94Select-158
Gold-158
95Upper Deck-553
Electric Ice-553
Electric Ice Gold-553
95Signature Rookies Future Flash-FF10
95Signature Rook Future Flash Sigs-FF10
95Signature Rookies Tetrad *-61
95Signature Rookies Tetrad Autobilia *-48
95Signature Rookies Tetrad Signatures *-61
96Upper Deck Ice-139
97Be A Player-212
Autographs-212
Autographs Die-Cuts-212
Autographs Prismatic Die-Cuts-212
97Beehive Team-24
97Beehive Team Gold-24
97Black Diamond-130
Double Diamond-130
Triple Diamond-130
Quadruple Diamond-130
Premium Cut-PC5
Premium Cut Double Diamond-PC5
Premium Cut Quadruple Diamond Horiz-PC5
Premium Cut Triple Diamond-PC5
Premium Cut Quadruple Diamond Verticals-PC5
97Crown Royale-111
Emerald Green-111
Ice Blue-111
Silver-111
97Donruss Elite-108
Aspirations-108
Status-108
97Donruss Preferred-155
Cut to the Chase-155
97Donruss Priority-183
Stamp of Approval-183
97Katch-119
Gold-119
Silver-119
97Leaf-164
Fractal Matrix-164
Fractal Matrix Die Cuts-164
97McDonald's Upper Deck-38
97Pacific Omega-187
Copper-187
Dark Gray-187
Emerald Green-187
Gold-187
Ice Blue-187
97Paramount-152
Copper-152
Dark Grey-152
Emerald Green-152
Ice Blue-152
Red-152
Silver-152
97Pinnacle-6
Artist's Proofs-6
Rink Collection-6
Press Plates Back Black-6
Press Plates Back Cyan-6
Press Plates Back Magenta-6
Press Plates Back Yellow-6
Press Plates Front Black-6
Press Plates Front Cyan-6
Press Plates Front Magenta-6
Press Plates Front Yellow-6
Certified Rookie Redemption-H
Certified Rookie Redemption Gold-H
Certified Rookie Redemption Mirror Gold-H
97Pinnacle Mint-27
Bronze-27
Gold Team-27
Silver Team-27
Coins Brass-27
Coins Brass Proofs-27
Coins Gold Plated-27
Coins Gold Plated Proofs-27
Coins Nickel Silver-27
Coins Nickel Silver Proofs-27
Coins Solid Gold-27
Coins Solid Silver-27
97Score-74
Artist's Proofs-74
Golden Blades-74
97Score Penguins-18
Platinum-18
Premier-18
97SP Authentic-190
Icons-I15
Icons Die-Cuts-I15
Icons Embossed-I15
97Upper Deck-341
97Upper Deck Ice-56
Parallel-56
Lethal Lines-L7B
Lethal Lines 2-L7B
Power Shift-56
97Zenith-94
Z-Gold-94
Z-Silver-94
97Zenith 5 x 7-67
Gold Impulse-67
Silver Impulse-67
97Zenith Rookie Reign-8
97Zenith Z-Team-18
97Zenith Z-Team Gold-18
98Aurora-156
98Be A Player-111
Press Release-111
98BAP Gold-111
98BAP Autographs-111
98BAP Autographs Gold-111
98BAP Tampa Bay All Star Game-111
98Black Diamond-71
Double Diamond-71
Triple Diamond-71
Quadruple Diamond-71
98Crown Royale-111
Limited Series-111
98Katch-118
98OPC Chrome-70
Refractors-70
98Pacific-95
Ice Blue-95
Red-95
98Pacific Dynagon Ice-152
Blue-152
Red-152
98Pacific Omega-198
Red-198
Opening Day Issue-198
98Panini Stickers-53
98Paramount-194
Copper-194
Emerald Green-194
Holo-Electric-194
Ice Blue-194
Silver-194
98SPx Finite-68
98SPx Finite-149
Radiance-68
Radiance-149
Spectrum-68
Spectrum-149
98Topps-70
O-Pee-Chee-70
98UD Choice-166
Prime Choice Reserve-166
Reserve-166
98UD3-22
98UD3-82
98UD3-142
Die-Cuts-22
Die-Cuts-82
Die-Cuts-142
98Upper Deck-158
Exclusives-158
Exclusives 1 of 1-158
Frozen In Time-FT14
Frozen In Time Quantum 1-FT14
Frozen In Time Quantum 2-FT14
Frozen In Time Quantum 3-FT14
Gold Reserve-158
98Upper Deck MVP-165
Gold Script-165
Silver Script-165
Super Script-165
99BAP Memorabilia-187
Gold-187
Silver-187
99BAP Millennium-201
Emerald-201
Ruby-201
Sapphire-201
Signatures-201
Signatures Gold-201
99Pacific-344
Copper-344
Emerald Green-344
Gold-344
Ice Blue-344
Premiere Date-344
Red-344
99Pacific Dynagon Ice-161
Blue-161
Copper-161
Gold-161
Premiere Date-161
99Panini Stickers-136
99Upper Deck-277
Exclusives-277
Exclusives 1 of 1-277
99Upper Deck Gold Reserve-277
99Upper Deck Victory-245
99Wayne Gretzky Hockey-138
99Russian Fetisov Tribute-3
00BAP Memorabilia-7
Emerald-7
Ruby-7
Sapphire-7
Promos-7
00BAP Mem Chicago Sportsfest Copper-7
00BAP Memorabilia Chicago Sportsfest Blue-7
00BAP Memorabilia Chicago Sportsfest Gold-7
00BAP Memorabilia Chicago Sportsfest Ruby-7
00BAP Memorabilia Chicago Sun-Times Ruby-7
00BAP Memorabilia Chicago Sun-Times Gold-7
00BAP Mem Chicago Sun-Times Sapphire-7
00BAP Mem Toronto Fall Expo Copper-7
00BAP Memorabilia Toronto Fall Expo Gold-7
00BAP Memorabilia Toronto Fall Expo Ruby-7
00Pacific-334
Copper-334
Gold-334
Ice Blue-334
Premiere Date-334
00Panini Stickers-83
00Titanium Game Gear-137
00Titanium Game Gear Patches-137
00Upper Deck-369
Exclusives Tier 1-369
Exclusives Tier 2-369
00Upper Deck Vintage-287
01Pacific Heads-Up Quad Jerseys-28
01Private Stock Game Gear-81
01Private Stock Game Gear Patches-81
01Titanium Double-Sided Jerseys-32
01Upper Deck-370
Exclusives-370
01Upper Deck Victory-284
Gold-284
02Atomic-81
Blue-81
Gold-81
Red-81
Hobby Parallel-81
02BAP First Edition-56
Jerseys-56
02BAP Signature Series-95
Autographs-95
Autograph Buybacks 1998-111
Autograph Buybacks 1999-201
Autographs Gold-95
02Crown Royale-79
Blue-79
Red-79
Retail-79
Jerseys-17
Jerseys Gold-17
Dual Patches-17
02O-Pee-Chee-172
02O-Pee-Chee Premier Blue Parallel-172
02O-Pee-Chee Premier Red Parallel-172
02O-Pee-Chee Factory Set-172
02Pacific-313
Blue-313
Red-313
02Pacific Complete-452
Red-452
02Pacific Exclusive-139
02Pacific Heads-Up-101
Blue-101
Purple-101
Red-101
02Parkhurst-188
Bronze-188
Gold-188
Silver-188
02Private Stock Reserve-81
Blue-81
Red-81
Retail-81
02SP Authentic Super Premiums-SPAM
02Topps-172
OPC Blue Parallel-172
OPC Red Parallel-172
Factory Set-172
02Topps Total-123
02Upper Deck-386
Exclusives-386
02Upper Deck Beckett UD Promos-386
02Upper Deck Bright Futures-AM
02Upper Deck Classic Portraits Headliners-LM
02Upper Deck Classic Portraits Headliners Limited-LM
02Upper Deck Rookie Update-82
02Upper Deck Victory-175
Bronze-175
Gold-175
Silver-175
02Upper Deck Vintage-207
02Upper Deck Vintage-284
03BAP Memorabilia-2
Emerald-2
Gold-2
Ruby-2
Sapphire-2
03Bowman-45
Gold-45
03Bowman Chrome-45
Refractors-45
Gold Refractors-45
Xfractors-45
03ITG Action-412
Jerseys-M52
03ITG Used Signature Series-92
Gold-92
Autographs-AM
Autographs Gold-AM
03NHL Sticker Collection-116
03O-Pee-Chee-74
03OPC Blue-74
03OPC Gold-74
03OPC Red-74
03Pacific-275
Blue-275
Red-275
03Pacific Complete-98
Red-98
03Pacific Exhibit-118
Blue Backs-118
Yellow Backs-118
03Private Stock Reserve-83
Blue-83
Red-83
Retail-83
03Topps-74
Blue-74
Gold-74
Red-74
03Topps C55-88
Minis-88
Minis American Back-88
Minis American Back Red-88
Minis Bazooka Back-88
Minis Brooklyn Back-88
Minis Hat Trick Back-88
Minis O Canada Back-88
Minis O Canada Back Red-88
Minis Stanley Cup Back-88
03Upper Deck-152
Canadian Exclusives-152
HG-152
03Upper Deck MVP-336
Gold Script-336
Silver Script-336
Canadian Exclusives-336
04Pacific-215
Blue-215
Red-215
04Russian Back to Russia-21
04Russian World Championship Team-7

Morozov, Vladislav
98Russian Hockey League-104
99Russian Hockey League-212

Morque, Chris
94Huntington Blizzard-17
95Central Hockey League-31
98Odessa Jackalopes-16
99Odessa Jackalopes-3

Morrell, Tony
93Quebec Pee-Wee Tournament-782

Morris, Allen
93Quebec Pee-Wee Tournament-134

Morris, Bernie
23V128-1 Paulin's Candy-64
28V128-2 Paulin's Candy-73

Morris, Derek
96Regina Pats-16
97Be A Player-245
Autographs-245
Autographs Die-Cuts-245
Autographs Prismatic Die-Cuts-245
97Black Diamond-104
Double Diamond-104
Triple Diamond-104
Quadruple Diamond-104
97Donruss Elite-114
97Donruss Elite-132
Aspirations-114
Aspirations-132
Status-114
Status-132
97Donruss Priority-182
Stamp of Approval-182
97Flames Collector's Photos-6
97Pacific Omega-31
Copper-31
Dark Gray-31
Emerald Green-31
Gold-31
Ice Blue-31
97SP Authentic-175
97Upper Deck-233
97Upper Deck Ice-51
Parallel-51
Power Shift-51
97Regina Pats-22
97Bowman CHL-109
OPC-109
98Aurora-27
98Bowman's Best-78
Refractors-78
Atomic Refractors-78
98Finest-136
No Protectors-136
No Protectors Refractors-136
Refractors-136
98OPC Chrome-69
Refractors-69
98Pacific-53
Ice Blue-53
Red-53
98Paramount-30
Copper-30
Emerald Green-30
Holo-Electric-30
Ice Blue-30
Silver-30
98SP Authentic-11
Power Shift-11
98SPx Finite-13
98SPx Finite-136
Radiance-13
Radiance-136
Spectrum-13
Spectrum-136
98Topps-69
O-Pee-Chee-69
98UD Choice-29
98UD Choice Preview-29
98UD Choice Prime Choice Reserve-29
98UD Choice Reserve-29
98UD3-5
98UD3-65
98UD3-125
Die-Cuts-5
Die-Cuts-65
Die-Cuts-125
98Upper Deck-51
Exclusives-51
Exclusives 1 of 1-51
Gold Reserve-51
98Upper Deck MVP-28
Gold Script-28
Silver Script-28
Super Script-28
99O-Pee-Chee-197
99O-Pee-Chee Chrome-197
99O-Pee-Chee Chrome Refractors-197
99Pacific-58
Copper-58
Emerald Green-58
Gold-58
Ice Blue-58
Premiere Date-58
Red-58
99Pacific Dynagon Ice-37
Blue-37
Copper-37
Gold-37
Premiere Date-37
99Panini Stickers-192
99Paramount-41
Copper-41
Emerald-41
Gold-41
Holographic Emerald-41
Holographic Gold-41
Holographic Silver-41
Ice Blue-41
Premiere Date-41
Red-41
Silver-41
99SPx-22
Radiance-22
Spectrum-22
99Stadium Club-84
First Day Issue-84
One of a Kind-84
Printing Plates Black-84
Printing Plates Cyan-84
Printing Plates Magenta-84
Printing Plates Yellow-84
99Topps/OPC-197
99Topps/OPC Chrome-197
Refractors-197
99Upper Deck-27
Exclusives-27
Exclusives 1 of 1-27
99Upper Deck Arena Giveaways-CF2
99Upper Deck Gold Reserve-27
99Upper Deck MVP-31
Gold Script-31
Silver Script-31
Super Script-31
ProSign-DM
99Upper Deck MVP SC Edition-30
Gold Script-30
Silver Script-30
Super Script-30
99Upper Deck Victory-48
00Aurora-25
Pinstripes-25
Pinstripes Premiere Date-25
Premiere Date-25
00BAP Memorabilia-300
Emerald-300
Ruby-300
Sapphire-300
Promos-300
00BAP Mem Chicago Sportsfest Copper-300
00BAP Memorabilia Chicago Sportsfest Blue-300
00BAP Memorabilia Chicago Sportsfest Gold-300
00BAP Memorabilia Chicago Sportsfest Ruby-300
00BAP Memorabilia Chicago Sun-Times Ruby-300
00BAP Memorabilia Chicago Sun-Times Gold-300
00BAP Mem Chicago Sun-Times Sapphire-300
00BAP Mem Toronto Fall Expo Copper-300
00BAP Memorabilia Toronto Fall Expo Gold-300
00BAP Memorabilia Toronto Fall Expo Ruby-300
00O-Pee-Chee-74
00O-Pee-Chee Parallel-74
00Pacific-70
Copper-70
Gold-70
Ice Blue-70
Premiere Date-70
00Panini Stickers-121
00Topps/OPC-74
Parallel-74
00Upper Deck-27
Exclusives Tier 1-27
Exclusives Tier 2-27
00Upper Deck MVP-29
First Stars-29
Second Stars-29
Third Stars-29
00Upper Deck Victory-39
00Upper Deck Vintage-58
01BAP Memorabilia-127
Emerald-127
Ruby-127
Sapphire-127
01BAP Signature Series-177
Autographs-177
Autographs Gold-177
01Bowman YoungStars-72
Gold-72
Ice Cubed-72
01Crown Royale-22
Blue-22
Premiere Date-22
Red-22
Retail-22
01O-Pee-Chee-171
01O-Pee-Chee Premier Parallel-171
01Pacific-63
Extreme LTD-63
Hobby LTD-63
Premiere Date-63
Retail LTD-63
01Pacific Adrenaline-26
Blue-26
Premiere Date-26
Red-26
Retail-26
01Pacific Arena Exclusives-63
01Private Stock PS-2002-11
01Titanium-20
Hobby Parallel-20
Premiere Date-20
Retail-20
Retail Parallel-20
01Topps-171
OPC Parallel-171
01Topps Chrome-118
Refractors-118
Black Border Refractors-118
01Upper Deck-27
Exclusives-27
01Upper Deck MVP-27
01Upper Deck Victory-52
Gold-52
01Upper Deck Vintage-38
01Upper Deck Vintage-43
02Avalanche Postcards-12
02BAP Memorabilia-71
Emerald-71
Ruby-71
Sapphire-71
NHL All-Star Game-71
NHL All-Star Game Blue-71
NHL All-Star Game Green-71
NHL All-Star Game Red-71
02BAP Memorabilia Toronto Fall Expo-71
02BAP Signature Series-124
Autographs-124
Autograph Buybacks 2001-177
Autographs Gold-124
Golf-GS32
02McDonald's Pacific-6
02O-Pee-Chee-238
02O-Pee-Chee Premier Blue Parallel-238
02O-Pee-Chee Premier Red Parallel-238
02O-Pee-Chee Factory Set-238
02Pacific-57
Blue-57
Red-57
02Pacific Complete-226
Red-226
02Pacific Exclusive-43
02Parkhurst Retro-139
Minis-139
02Topps-238
OPC Blue Parallel-238
OPC Red Parallel-238
Factory Set-238
02Topps Chrome-131
Black Border Refractors-131
Refractors-131
02Topps Total-290
02Upper Deck-27
02Upper Deck-292
Exclusives-27
Exclusives-292
02Upper Deck Beckett UD Promos-292
02Upper Deck MVP-27
Gold-27
Classics-27
Golden Classics-27
02Upper Deck Victory-34
Bronze-34
Gold-34
Silver-34
02Upper Deck Vintage-40
02Upper Deck Vintage-265
03Beehive-49
Gold-49
Silver-49
03ITG Action-180
Jerseys-M53
03NHL Sticker Collection-189
03O-Pee-Chee-162
03OPC Blue-162
03OPC Gold-162
03OPC Red-162
03Pacific-85
Blue-85
Red-85
03Pacific Complete-11
Red-11
03Pacific Exhibit-38
Blue Backs-38
Yellow Backs-38
03Topps-162
Blue-162
Gold-162
Red-162
03Topps Traded-TT78
Blue-TT78
Gold-TT78
Red-TT78
03Upper Deck-47
Canadian Exclusives-47
HG-47
03Upper Deck MVP-106
Gold Script-106
Silver Script-106
Canadian Exclusives-106
04Pacific-204
Blue-204
Red-204
04Upper Deck-136
Canadian Exclusives-136
HG Glossy Gold-136
HG Glossy Silver-136
05Panini Stickers-330
05Parkhurst-382
Facsimile Auto Parallel-382
05Upper Deck-147
HG Glossy-147
05Upper Deck MVP-296
Gold-296
Platinum-296
05Upper Deck Toronto Fall Expo-147
06O-Pee-Chee-377
Rainbow-377
06Panini Stickers-323

Morris, Elwyn
45Quaker Oats Photos-39

Morris, Emily
04Wisconsin Badgers Women-17

Morris, Frank
96UK Fife Flyers-18
97UK Fife Flyers-19
01UK Fife Flyers-12

Morris, Jamie
99Indianapolis Ice-14
00Indianapolis Ice-17
01Indianapolis Ice-16
02Indianapolis Ice-13

Morris, Jon
89ProCards AHL-207
90Bowman-84
Tiffany-84
90Devils Team Issue-18
90O-Pee-Chee-457
90Pro Set-621
90Score-401
Canadian-401
90Upper Deck-65
French-65
91Bowman-286
91O-Pee-Chee-332
91Pro Set-424
French-424
91Score Canadian Bilingual-548
91Score Canadian English-548
91Stadium Club-360
91Topps-332
91Upper Deck-216
French-216
91ProCards-426
92Cincinnati Cyclones-16

Morris, Keith
92Alberta International Team Canada-13

Morris, Rick
75O-Pee-Chee WHA-91

Morris, Stephen
00Barrie Colts-18

Morris, Steven
01Barrie Colts-6

Morris, Ty
03Swift Current Broncos-10
03Vancouver Giants-22

Morrisett, David
04Idaho Steelheads-13

Morrison, Aaron
907th Inn. Sketch OHL-267
917th Inn. Sketch OHL-106

Morrison, Adam
83Victoria Cougars-19
84Victoria Cougars-15
06Press Pass-35
06Press Pass-45

Morrison, Andrew
95Slapshot-29
95Barrie Colts-18

Morrison, Bill
98Danish Hockey League-205
99Danish Hockey League-129

Morrison, Brady
04Kingston Frontenacs-24
05Ottawa 67's-17
06Ottawa 67s-22

Morrison, Brendan
92British Columbia JHL-117
93Michigan Wolverines-16
97Beehive-56
Authentic Autographs-56
Golden Portraits-56
97SP Authentic-193
97Zenith-90
Z-Gold-90
Z-Silver-90
Rookie Reign-4
97Albany River Rats-10
98Black Diamond-51
Double Diamond-51
Triple Diamond-51
Quadruple Diamond-51
98Bowman's Best-105
Refractors-105
Atomic Refractors-105
Autographs-A7A
Autographs-A7B
Autographs Refractors-A7A
Autographs Refractors-A7B
Autographs Atomic Refractors-A7A
Autographs Atomic Refractors-A7B
Mirror Image Fusion-F15
Mirror Image Fusion Refractors-F15
Mirror Image Fusion Atomic Refractors-F15
Performers-BP9
Performers Refractors-BP9
Performers Atomic Refractors-BP9
98Crown Royale-81
Limited Series-81
Rookie Class-5
98Devils Team Issue-19
98Finest Futures Finest-F19
98Finest Futures Finest Refractors-F19
98Katch-165
98McDonald's Upper Deck-24
98Pacific-265
Ice Blue-265
Red-265
98Pacific Dynagon Ice-111
Blue-111
Red-111
Rookies-4
98Pacific Omega-139
Red-139
Opening Day Issue-139
Online-20
98Panini Photocards-54
98Revolution-86
Ice Shadow-86
Red-86
98SP Authentic-47
Power Shift-47
98SPx Finite-48
98SPx Finite-145
Radiance-48
Radiance-145
Spectrum-48
Spectrum-145
98Topps Gold Label Class 1-82
Black-82
Black One of One-82
One of One-82
Red-82
Red One of One-82
98Topps Gold Label Class 2-82
98Topps Gold Label Class 2 Black-82
98Topps Gold Label Class 2 Black 1 of 1-82
98Topps Gold Label Class 2 One of One-82
98Topps Gold Label Class 2 Red-82
98Topps Gold Label Class 2 Red One of One-82
98Topps Gold Label Class 3-82
98Topps Gold Label Class 3 Black-82
98Topps Gold Label Class 3 Black 1 of 1-82
98Topps Gold Label Class 3 One of One-82
98Topps Gold Label Class 3 Red-82
98Topps Gold Label Class 3 Red One of One-82
98UD Choice-120
Prime Choice Reserve-120
Reserve-120
98UD3-30
98UD3-90
98UD3-150
Die-Cuts-30
Die-Cuts-90
Die-Cuts-150
98Upper Deck-5
Exclusives-5
Exclusives 1 of 1-5
Generation Next-GN4
Generation Next-GN27
Generation Next Quantum 1-GN4
Generation Next Quantum 1-GN27
Generation Next Quantum 2-GN4
Generation Next Quantum 2-GN27
Generation Next Quantum 3-GN4
Generation Next Quantum 3-GN27
Gold Reserve-5
98Upper Deck MVP-118
Gold Script-118
Silver Script-118
Super Script-118
ProSign-BM
99Aurora-87
Premiere Date-87
99BAP Memorabilia-146
Gold-146
Silver-146
99BAP Millennium-149
Emerald-149
Ruby-149
Sapphire-149
Signatures-149
Signatures Gold-149
99Devils Team Issue-6
99Kraft Whiz Kid-8
99O-Pee-Chee-156
99O-Pee-Chee Chrome-156
99O-Pee-Chee Chrome Refractors-156
99O-Pee-Chee Chrome Ice Futures-IF6
99O-Pee-Chee Chrome Ice Futures Refractor-IF6
99O-Pee-Chee Ice Futures-IF6
99Pacific-241
Copper-241
Emerald Green-241
Gold-241
Ice Blue-241
Premiere Date-241
Red-241
99Paramount-136
Copper-136
Emerald-136
Gold-136
Holographic Emerald-136
Holographic Gold-136
Holographic Silver-136
Ice Blue-136
Premiere Date-136
Red-136
Silver-136
99Revolution-87
Premiere Date-87
Red-87
Shadow Series-87
99SPx-87
Radiance-87
Spectrum-87
99Stadium Club Co-Signers-CS1
99Stadium Club Co-Signers-CS2
99Stadium Club Lone Star Signatures-LS12
99Topps/OPC-156
Ice Futures-IF6
99Topps/OPC Chrome-156
Refractors-156
Ice Futures-IF6
Ice Futures Refractors-IF6
99Topps Gold Label Fresh Gold-FG13
99Topps Gold Label Fresh Gold Black-FG13
99Topps Gold Label Fresh Gold Black 1of1-FG13
99Topps Gold Label Fresh Gold One of One-FG13
99Topps Gold Label Fresh Gold Red-FG13
99Topps Gold Label Fresh Gold Red 1 of 1-FG13
99Upper Deck-248
Exclusives-248
Exclusives 1 of 1-248
99Upper Deck Gold Reserve-248
99Upper Deck MVP-117
Gold Script-117
Silver Script-117
Super Script-117
99Upper Deck Victory-173
99Upper Deck Victory-352
99Wayne Gretzky Hockey-95
99Czech DS-78
99Czech OFS-94
99Czech Score Blue 2000-157
99Czech Score Red Ice 2000-157
00BAP Memorabilia-91
Emerald-91
Ruby-91
Sapphire-91
Promos-91
00BAP Mem Chicago Sportsfest Copper-91
00BAP Memorabilia Chicago Sportsfest Blue-91
00BAP Memorabilia Chicago Sportsfest Gold-91
00BAP Memorabilia Chicago Sportsfest Ruby-91
00BAP Memorabilia Chicago Sun-Times Ruby-91
00BAP Memorabilia Chicago Sun-Times Gold-91
00BAP Mem Chicago Sun-Times Sapphire-91
00BAP Mem Toronto Fall Expo Copper-91
00BAP Memorabilia Toronto Fall Expo Gold-91
00BAP Memorabilia Toronto Fall Expo Ruby-91
00BAP Parkhurst 2000-P23
00BAP Signature Series-126
Emerald-126
Ruby-126
Sapphire-126
Autographs-5
Autographs Gold-5
00O-Pee-Chee-145
00O-Pee-Chee Parallel-145
00Titanium-95
Blue-95
Gold-95
Premiere Date-95
Red-95
Retail-95
00Topps/OPC-145
Parallel-145
00Topps Chrome-105
OPC Refractors-105
Refractors-105
00Topps Heritage-146
00Upper Deck-399
Exclusives Tier 1-399
Exclusives Tier 2-399
00Upper Deck MVP-172
First Stars-172
Second Stars-172
Third Stars-172
00Upper Deck Victory-228
00Upper Deck Vintage-348
01BAP Memorabilia-58
Emerald-58
Ruby-58
Sapphire-58
01Bowman YoungStars-90
Gold-90
Ice Cubed-90
01Canucks Postcards-9
01Crown Royale-137
Blue-137
Premiere Date-137
Red-137
Retail-137
01McDonald's Pacific Hometown Pride-2
01O-Pee-Chee-144
01O-Pee-Chee Premier Parallel-144
01Pacific-383
Extreme LTD-383
Hobby LTD-383
Premiere Date-383
Retail LTD-383
01Pacific Adrenaline-190
Blue-190
Premiere Date-190
Red-190
Retail-190
01Pacific Arena Exclusives-383
01Parkhurst-133
01Private Stock PS-2002-73
01SPx-195
01Titanium-136

Hobby Parallel-136
Premiere Date-136
Retail-136
Retail Parallel-136
Double-Sided Jerseys-55
Double-Sided Jerseys-57
Double-Sided Patches-55
Double-Sided Patches-57
01Titanium Draft Day Edition-95
01Topps-144
OPC Parallel-144
01UD Challenge for the Cup-87
01UD Mask Collection-93
Gold-93
01UD Playmakers-95
01Upper Deck-170
Exclusives-170
01Upper Deck MVP-180
01Upper Deck Victory-343
Gold-343
01Upper Deck Vintage-248
01Vanguard-96
Blue-96
Red-96
One of Ones-96
Premiere Date-96
Proofs-96
02BAP First Edition-214
02BAP Memorabilia-6
Emerald-6
Ruby-6
Sapphire-6
NHL All-Star Game-6
NHL All-Star Game Blue-6
NHL All-Star Game Green-6
NHL All-Star Game Red-6
02BAP Memorabilia Toronto Fall Expo-6
02BAP Signature Series-56
Autographs-56
Autograph Buybacks 1999-149
Autograph Buybacks 2000-5
Autographs Gold-56
Golf-GS13
02Bowman YoungStars-86
Gold-86
Silver-86
02Canucks Team Issue-10
02Crown Royale-96
Blue-96
Red-96
Retail-96
02McDonald's Pacific-40
02NHL Power Play Stickers-165
02O-Pee-Chee-149
02O-Pee-Chee Premier Blue Parallel-149
02O-Pee-Chee Premier Red Parallel-149
02O-Pee-Chee Factory Set-149
02Pacific-380
Blue-380
Red-380
02Pacific Complete-227
Red-227
02Pacific Exclusive-168
02Pacific Heads-Up-121
Blue-121
Purple-121
Red-121
02Pacific Quest for the Cup-96
Gold-96
Chasing the Cup-19
02Parkhurst-186
Bronze-186
Gold-186
Silver-186
02Parkhurst Retro-58
Minis-58
02Private Stock Reserve-96
Blue-96
Red-96
Retail-96
02Stadium Club-89
Silver Decoy Cards-89
Proofs-89
02Titanium-97
Blue-97
Red-97
Retail-97
Jerseys-70
Jerseys Retail-70
Patches-70
02Topps-149
OPC Blue Parallel-149
OPC Red Parallel-149
Factory Set-149
02Topps Chrome-91
Black Border Refractors-91
Refractors-91
02Topps Heritage-57
Chrome Parallel-57
Great Skates-BM
Great Skates Patches-BM
02Topps Total-283
02UD Top Shelf-86
02Upper Deck-414
Exclusives-414
02Upper Deck Beckett UD Promos-414
02Upper Deck Classic Portraits-96
02Upper Deck MVP-178
Gold-178
Classics-178
Golden Classics-178
02Upper Deck Victory-205
Bronze-205
Gold-205
Silver-205
02Upper Deck Vintage-251
02Vanguard-96
LTD-96
Jerseys-47
Jerseys Gold-47
03Beehive-189
Gold-189
Silver-189
03Black Diamond-30
Black-30
Green-30
Red-30
03Bowman Future Rivals-MM
03Bowman Future Rivals Patches-MM
03Canucks Postcards-19
03Canucks Sav-on-Foods-4
03Canucks Sav-on-Foods-9
03Canucks Sav-on-Foods-NNO
03eTopps-18
03ITG Action-519
Jerseys-M54

03McDonald's Pacific-53
Saturday Night Rivals-3
03NHL Sticker Collection-295
03O-Pee-Chee-104
03OPC Blue-104
03OPC Gold-104
03OPC Red-104
03Pacific-333
Blue-333
Red-333
03Pacific Calder-99
03Pacific Calder-160
Silver-99
03Pacific Complete-146
Red-146
03Pacific Exhibit-143
Blue Backs-143
Yellow Backs-143
03Pacific Heads-Up-97
Hobby LTD-97
Retail LTD-97
03Pacific Invincible-96
Blue-96
Red-96
Retail-96
03Pacific Luxury Suite-49A
03Pacific Luxury Suite-49B
03Pacific Prism-148
Blue-148
Patches-148
Red-148
Retail-148
03Pacific Quest for the Cup-99
Blue-99
03Pacific Supreme-96
Blue-96
Red-96
Retail-96
03Private Stock Reserve-209
Blue-209
Patches-209
Red-209
Retail-209
03SP Game Used Authentic Fabrics-QNBJM
03SP Game Used Authentic Fabrics Gold-QNBJM
03SP Game Used Top Threads-NBJM
03SPx Fantasy Franchise-FF-NBM
03SPx Fantasy Franchise Limited-FF-NBM
03Titanium-188
Hobby Jersey Number Parallels-188
Patches-188
Retail-188
03Topps-104
Blue-104
Gold-104
Red-104
03Topps C55-97
Minis-97
Minis American Back-97
Minis American Back Red-97
Minis Bazooka Back-97
Minis Brooklyn Back-97
Minis Hat Trick Back-97
Minis O Canada Back-97
Minis O Canada Back Red-97
Minis Stanley Cup Back-97
Relics-TRBM
03Topps Pristine-33
Gold Refractor Die Cuts-33
Refractors-33
Jersey Portions-PPJ-BMN
Jersey Portion Refractors-PPJ-BMN
Patches-PP-BM
Patch Refractors-PP-BM
Press Plates Black-33
Press Plates Cyan-33
Press Plates Magenta-33
Press Plates Yellow-33
03UD Premier Collection-58
03Upper Deck-186
Canadian Exclusives-186
HG-186
Classic Portraits Hockey Royalty-BNM
03Upper Deck MVP-410
Gold Script-410
Silver Script-410
Canadian Exclusives-410
03Upper Deck Rookie Update Super Stars-SSBM
03Upper Deck Victory-188
Bronze-188
Gold-188
Silver-188
04Pacific-257
Blue-257
Red-257
04SP Authentic Sign of the Times-ST-MO
04SP Authentic Sign of the Times-QS-VANC
04SP Authentic Sign of the Times-FS-VAN
04UD All-World-60
Gold-60
Autographs-60
Triple Autographs-AT-RCM
04Ultimate Collection Dual Logos-UL2-NM
04Upper Deck-169
Canadian Exclusives-169
HG Glossy Gold-169
HG Glossy Silver-169
04Swedish Elitset-209
Dominators-5
Gold-209
04Swedish Pure Skills-46
Parallel-46
Signatures-4
04Michigan Wolverines TK Legacy-1996B
04Michigan Wolverines TK Legacy-H4
04Michigan Wolverines TK Legacy-VH5
05Be A Player-88
First Period-88
Second Period-88
Third Period-88
Overtime-88
Signatures-BM
Signatures Gold-BM
Triple Signatures-NMS
05Beehive-88
Matte-88
Matted Materials-MMBM
Matted Materials Remarkable-RMBM
05Black Diamond-81
Emerald-81
Gold-81
Onyx-81
Ruby-81
05Hot Prospects-99
En Fuego-99
Red Hot-99

White Hot-99
05McDonalds Upper Deck-29
05Panini Stickers-356
05Parkhurst-470
Facsimile Auto Parallel-470
True Colors-TCVAN
True Colors-TCVAN
05SP Authentic-99
Limited-99
Sign of the Times Duals-DMC
Sign of the Times Triples-TNMB
05SP Game Used-97
Autographs-97
Gold-97
Authentic Fabrics-AF-BM
Authentic Fabrics Autographs-AAF-BM
Authentic Fabrics Gold-AF-BM
Authentic Patches-AP-BM
Authentic Patches Autographs-AAP-BM
Awesome Authentics-AA-MO
SIGnificance-BM
SIGnificance Gold-S-BM
SIGnificance Extra-NM
SIGnificance Extra Gold-NM
Significant Numbers-SN-BM
Statscriptions-ST-BR
05SPx-89
Spectrum-89
Winning Combos-WC-BM
Winning Combos-WC-MN
Winning Combos-WC-VA
Winning Combos Autographs-AWC-JM
Winning Combos Autographs-AWC-MN
Winning Combos Gold-WC-BM
Winning Combos Gold-WC-MN
Winning Combos Gold-WC-VA
Winning Combos Spectrum-WC-BM
Winning Combos Spectrum-WC-MN
Winning Combos Spectrum-WC-VA
Winning Materials-WM-BM
Winning Materials Gold-WM-BM
Winning Materials Spectrum-WM-BM
05The Cup Dual NHL Shields-DSMN
05The Cup Honorable Numbers-HNMO
05The Cup Limited Logos-LLMO
05The Cup Master Pressplate Rookie Update-228
05The Cup Scripted Swatches-SSMO
05UD Artifacts Auto Facts-AF-MO
05UD Artifacts Auto Facts Blue-AF-MO
05UD Artifacts Auto Facts Copper-AF-MO
05UD Artifacts Auto Facts Pewter-AF-MO
05UD Artifacts Auto Facts Silver-AF-MO
05UD Artifacts Frozen Artifacts-FA-BM
05UD Artifacts Frozen Artifacts Autos-FA-BM
05UD Artifacts Frozen Artifacts Copper-FA-BM
05UD Artifacts Frozen Artifacts Dual-FAD-BM
05UD Artifacts Frozen Artifact Dual Auto-FAD-BM
05UD Artifact Frozen Artifact Dual Copper-FAD-BM
05UD Artifact Frozen Artifact Dual Gold-FAD-BM
05UD Artifact Frozen Artifact Dual Maroon-FAD-BM
05UD Artifact Frozen Artifact Dual Pewter-FAD-BM
05UD Artifact Frozen Artifact Dual Silver-FAD-BM
05UD Artifacts Frozen Artifacts Gold-FA-BM
05UD Artifacts Frozen Artifacts Maroon-FA-BM
05UD Artifacts Frozen Artifacts Patches-FP-BM
05UD Artifacts Frozen Artifact Patch Autos-FP-BM
05UD Artifact Frozen Artifact Patch Dual-FPD-BM
05UD Artifact Frozen Art Patch Dual Auto-FPD-BM
05UD Artifacts Frozen Art Patch Pewter-FP-BM
05UD Artifacts Frozen Art Patch Silver-FP-BM
05UD Artifacts Frozen Artifacts Pewter-FA-BM
05UD Artifacts Frozen Artifacts Silver-FA-BM
05UD Artifacts Remarkable Artifacts-RA-MO
05UD Artifacts Remarkable Artifacts Dual-RA-MO
05UD PowerPlay-87
Rainbow-87
05Ultimate Collection-87
Gold-87
Endorsed Emblems-EEBM
05Ultra-190
Gold-190
Fresh Ink-FI-MO
Fresh Ink Blue-FI-MO
Ice-190
05Upper Deck-433
Big Playmakers-B-BMC
Jerseys-J-BM
Jerseys Series II-J2BM
Notable Numbers-N-MB
Patches-P-BMO
05Upper Deck Ice-97
Rainbow-97
05Upper Deck MVP-379
Gold-379
Platinum-379
ProSign-P-MO
05Upper Deck Rookie Update-99
05Upper Deck Rookie Update-228
Inspirations Patch Rookies-228
05Upper Deck Victory-190
Black-190
Gold-190
Silver-190
05Swedish SHL Elitset Playmakers-7
06Be A Player-79
Autographs-79
Signatures-MO
Signatures 10-86
Signatures Duals-DMB
Signatures Trios-TLNM
06Be A Player Portraits-97
Signature Portraits-SPMO
06Black Diamond-82
Black-82
Gold-82
Ruby-82
Jerseys-JBM
Jerseys Black-JBM
Jerseys Gold-JBM
Jerseys Ruby-JBM
06Canucks Postcards-14
06Flair Showcase Inks-IMO
06Flair Showcase Stitches-SSMO
06Fleer-192
Tiffany-192
Fabricology-FBM
06Gatorade-80
06McDonald's Upper Deck-49
06O-Pee-Chee-476
Rainbow-476
Autographs-A-BM
Swatches-S-BM
06Panini Stickers-355
06SP Authentic-5
Limited-5
Sign of the Times Triples-ST3NLM

06SP Game Used-98
Gold-98
Rainbow-98
Authentic Fabrics-AFMO
Authentic Fabrics Parallel-AFMO
Authentic Fabrics Patches-AFMO
Inked Sweaters Dual-IS2NM
Inked Sweaters Dual Patches-IS2NM
06SPx-98
Spectrum-98
Winning Materials-WMMO
Winning Materials Spectrum-WMMO
06The Cup Autographed NHL Shields Duals-DASNM
06UD Artifacts-5
Blue-5
Gold-5
Platinum-5
Radiance-5
Red-5
Frozen Artifacts-FAMO
Frozen Artifacts Black-FAMO
Frozen Artifacts Blue-FAMO
Frozen Artifacts Gold-FAMO
Frozen Artifacts Platinum-FAMO
Frozen Artifacts Red-FAMO
Frozen Artifacts Patches Black-FAMO
Frozen Artifacts Patches Blue-FAMO
Frozen Artifacts Patches Gold-FAMO
Frozen Artifacts Patches Platinum-FAMO
Frozen Artifacts Patches Red-FAMO
06UD Mini Jersey Collection-98
06UD Powerplay-97
Impact Rainbow-97
Specialists-SMO
Specialists Patches-PMO
06Ultra-192
Gold Medallion-192
Ice Medallion-192
Uniformity-UBM
Uniformity Patches-UPBO
Uniformity Autographed Jerseys-UABM
06Upper Deck Arena Giveaways-VAN4
06Upper Deck-439
Exclusives Parallel-439
High Gloss Parallel-439
Game Jerseys-JMO
Game Patches-PMO
Masterpieces-439
06Upper Deck MVP-288
Gold Script-288
Super Script-288
Autographs-OANM
06Upper Deck Ovation-98
06Upper Deck Trilogy Combo Clearcut Autographs-C2NM
06Upper Deck Victory-193
06Upper Deck Victory Black-193
06Upper Deck Victory Gold-193
07Upper Deck Ovation-52
07Upper Deck Victory-133
Black-133
Gold-133

Morrison, Brett
04Gatineau Olympiques-14
05Gatineau Olympiques-20
06Gatineau Olympiques-10

Morrison, Brian
00San Diego Gulls-13

Morrison, Chris
95Vancouver VooDoo RHI-15
03Barrie Colts-7
04Barrie Colts-9

Morrison, Craig
83Oshawa Generals-17

Morrison, Crutchy
23V128-1 Paulin's Candy-48

Morrison, Dave
84Fredericton Express-1
94German DEL-157
95German DEL-158
96German DEL-23
04German Berlin Eisbarens 50th Anniv-3

Morrison, Don
44Beehive Group II Photos-196
06Philadelphia Phantoms-25

Morrison, Don (NHL)
44Beehive Group II Photos-196

Morrison, George
70Esso Power Players-243
71O-Pee-Chee-223
71Sargent Promotions Stamps-191
71Toronto Sun-241
72Minnesota Fighting Saints Postcards WHA-16
72O-Pee-Chee-314

Morrison, Goalie
02Columbus Cottonmouths-15
03ITG VIP Rookie Debut-121
03Parkhurst Rookie-75
03Upper Deck Rookie Update-121
03Pacific AHL Prospects-89
Gold-89

Morrison, Ikey
28V128-2 Paulin's Candy-50

Morrison, Jeffrey
93Quebec Pee-Wee Tournament-1165

Morrison, Jim
44Beehive Group II Photos-437
45Quaker Oats Photos-40
52Parkhurst-28
53Parkhurst-15
54Parkhurst-18
54Parkhurst-94
55Parkhurst-8
55Parkhurst-76
Quaker Oats-8
Quaker Oats-76
57Bruins Photos-15
57Parkhurst-T11
58Bruins Photos-10
59Topps-36
60Parkhurst-61
60Shirriff Coins-95
60Topps-9
62Quebec Aces-18
64Quebec Aces-13
65Quebec Aces-13
69O-Pee-Chee-156
70Esso Power Players-233
70O-Pee-Chee-90
70Sargent Promotions Stamps-169
70Topps-90
81Kingston Canadians-24
82Kingston Canadians-1
94Parkhurst Missing Link-115

Morrison, Jordan
02Peterborough Petes-7
04Peterborough Petes Postcards-7

Morrison, Justin
907th Inn. Sketch OHL-67
917th Inn. Sketch OHL-229
91Star Pics-45
91Ultimate Draft-52
91Ultimate Draft French-52
92Quebec Pee-Wee Tournament-1220
93Muskegon Fury-15
93Quebec Pee-Wee Tournament-1252
94Muskegon Fury-4
95Madison Monsters-22
96Madison Monsters-13
01Manitoba Moose-18
02Columbia Inferno-106
02ECHL All-Star Southern-50
03Manitoba Moose-16
04Manitoba Moose-6
05Chicago Wolves-13

Morrison, Ken
84Prince Albert Raiders Stickers-19
85Kamloops Blazers-15

Morrison, Kevin
74San Diego Mariners WHA-4
75O-Pee-Chee WHA-63
75O-Pee-Chee WHA-80
76O-Pee-Chee WHA-10
76O-Pee-Chee WHA-68
76San Diego Mariners WHA-7
79Rockies Team Issue-14

Morrison, Lance
00Kootenay Ice-16
01Calgary Hitmen-16
01Calgary Hitmen Autographed-16
02Calgary Hitmen-1
03Regina Pats-7

Morrison, Lew
70Esso Power Players-205
70Flyers Postcards-8
70O-Pee-Chee-197
71O-Pee-Chee-89
72Flames Postcards-10
72O-Pee-Chee-143
72Sargent Promotions Stamps-13
72Topps-58
74NHL Action Stamps-314
74NHL Action Stamps Update-27
74O-Pee-Chee NHL-125
74Topps-125
76O-Pee-Chee NHL-307
77O-Pee-Chee NHL-300

Morrison, Mark
81Victoria Cougars-12
82Victoria Cougars-19
83Canadian National Juniors-10
83Victoria Cougars-16
96UK Fife Flyers-17
97UK Fife Flyers-14
01UK Fife Flyers-6
03UK Belfast Giants-11

Morrison, Mike
05ITG Heroes/Prosp Toronto Expo Parallel -360
05Parkhurst Facsimile Auto Parallel-200
05ITG Heroes and Prospects-360
Autographs Series II-MM

Morrison, Mike (80's)
85Kitchener Rangers-15
93Quebec Pee-Wee Tournament-595

Morrison, Mike (PW)
93Quebec Pee-Wee Tournament-595

Morrison, Rod
44Beehive Group II Photos-197

Morrison, Scott
94Finnish Jaa Kiekko-321
94UK Humberside Hawks-19

Morrison, Tavis
96Dayton Bombers-11

Morrison, Taylor
93Quebec Pee-Wee Tournament-630

Morrisonn, Shaone
99Kamloops Blazers-15
00Kamloops Blazers-15
01BAP Memorabilia Draft Redemptions-19
01UD Prospects-25
Jerseys-J-SM
Jerseys Gold-J-SM
02BAP All-Star Edition-112
Gold-112
Silver-112
02BAP First Edition-432R
02BAP Memorabilia-347
02BAP Ultimate Memorabilia-61
02ITG Used-181
02Pacific Calder-104
Silver-104
02Pacific Complete-580
Red-580
02Pacific Quest for the Cup-105
Gold-105
02Parkhurst-221
Bronze-221
Gold-221
Silver-221
02Parkhurst Retro-235
Minis-235
02SP Authentic-161
02SP Game Used-96
02Titanium-105
Blue-105
Red-105
Retail-105
02UD Artistic Impressions-106
Gold-106
02UD Honor Roll-130
02UD Mask Collection-170
02UD Premier Collection-48B
Gold-48
02Upper Deck-441
Exclusives-441
02AHL Top Prospects-30
02Providence Bruins-13
03ITG Action-85
03O-Pee-Chee-319
03OPC Blue-319
03OPC Gold-319
03OPC Red-319
03Parkhurst Original Six Boston-12
Memorabilia-BM11
03Topps-319
Blue-319
Gold-319
Red-319
03Topps Traded-TT81

Blue-TT81
Gold-TT81
Red-TT81
03AHL Top Prospects-25
04Portland Pirates-16
05Parkhurst-496
Facsimile Auto Parallel-496
True Colors-TCWAS
True Colors-TCWAS
05Upper Deck-440
06Black Diamond Jerseys-JMO
06Black Diamond Jerseys Black-JMO
06Black Diamond Jerseys Gold-JMO
06Black Diamond Jerseys Ruby-JMO
06Upper Deck Arena Giveaways-WSH1
06Upper Deck-196
Exclusives Parallel-196
High Gloss Parallel-196
Masterpieces-196

Morrissey, Dan
91British Columbia JHL-78
92British Columbia JHL-88

Morrissey, Paul
99Des Moines Buccaneers-23

Morrone, Mike
93Owen Sound Platers-20
94Detroit Jr. Red Wings-9
95Slapshot-65
95Slapshot Memorial Cup-83
96Detroit Whalers-12

Morrow, Brenden
97Portland Winter Hawks-10
97Bowman CHL-98
97Bowman CHL-147
OPC-98
OPC-147
Autographs-147
Bowman's Best-16
Bowman's Best Atomic Refractors-16
Bowman's Best Refractor-16
98Black Diamond-94
Double Diamond-94
Triple Diamond-94
Quadruple Diamond-94
98SPx Top Prospects-66
Radiance-66
Spectrum-66
98Bowman CHL-60
Golden Anniversary-60
OPC International-60
98Bowman Chrome CHL-60
Golden Anniversary-60
Golden Anniversary Refractors-60
OPC International-60
OPC International Refractors-60
Refractors-60
99BAP Memorabilia-322
Gold-322
Silver-322
99Pacific Omega-75
Copper-75
Gold-75
Ice Blue-75
Premiere Date-75
99Paramount-256
99Topps Arena Giveaways-DAL-BM
99Upper Deck Arena Giveaways-DS1
99Upper Deck MVP SC Edition-61
Gold Script-61
Silver Script-61
Super Script-61
99Michigan K-Wings-17
99Bowman CHL-113
Gold-113
OPC International-113
00Aurora-46
Pinstripes-46
Pinstripes Premiere Date-46
Premiere Date-46
Autographs-46
00BAP Memorabilia-196
Emerald-196
Ruby-196
Sapphire-196
Promos-196
00BAP Mem Chicago Sportsfest Copper-196
00BAP Memorabilia Chicago Sportsfest Blue-196
00BAP Memorabilia Chicago Sportsfest Gold-196
00BAP Memorabilia Chicago Sportsfest Ruby-196
00BAP Memorabilia Chicago Sun-Times Ruby-196
00BAP Memorabilia Chicago Sun-Times Gold-196
00BAP Mem Chicago Sun-Times Sapphire-196
00BAP Mem Toronto Fall Expo Copper-196
00BAP Memorabilia Toronto Fall Expo Gold-196
00BAP Memorabilia Toronto Fall Expo Ruby-196
00BAP Parkhurst 2000-P19
00BAP Signature Series-58
Emerald-58
Ruby-58
Sapphire-58
Autographs-82
Autographs Gold-82
00O-Pee-Chee-246
00O-Pee-Chee Parallel-246
00Pacific-138
Copper-138
Gold-138
Ice Blue-138
Premiere Date-138
Autographs-138
00Paramount-80
Copper-80
Gold-80
Holo-Gold-80
Holo-Silver-80
Ice Blue-80
Premiere Date-80
00Private Stock-33
Gold-33
Premiere Date-33
Retail-33
Silver-33
PS-2001 New Wave-10
00Revolution-48
Blue-48
Premiere Date-48
Red-48
00Stadium Club-171
00Stars Postcards-18
00Topps/OPC-246
Parallel-246
00Topps Chrome-154
OPC Refractors-154
Refractors-154
00Topps Heritage-116

00Upper Deck-59
Exclusives Tier 1-59
Exclusives Tier 2-59
Prospects In Depth-P4
00Upper Deck MVP-56
First Stars-56
ProSign-BM
Second Stars-56
Third Stars-56
00Upper Deck Victory-74
00Upper Deck Vintage-119
01BAP Memorabilia-14
Emerald-14
Ruby-14
Sapphire-14
01BAP Signature Series-9
Autographs-9
Autographs Gold-9
01Bowman YoungStars-144
Gold-144
Ice Cubed-144
Autographs-BM
Relics-JBM
Relics-SBM
Relics-DSBM
Rivals-R10
01O-Pee-Chee-154
01O-Pee-Chee Premier Parallel-154
01Pacific-132
Extreme LTD-132
Hobby LTD-132
Premiere Date-132
Retail LTD-132
01Pacific Arena Exclusives-132
01Parkhurst-138
01Stars Postcards-18
01Stars Team Issue-1
01Topps-154
OPC Parallel-154
01Topps Heritage-110
Refractors-110
01Upper Deck-59
Exclusives-59
01Upper Deck Ice-93
01Upper Deck MVP-60
01Upper Deck Victory-111
Gold-111
02BAP First Edition-234
02BAP Memorabilia-43
Emerald-43
Ruby-43
Sapphire-43
NHL All-Star Game-43
NHL All-Star Game Blue-43
NHL All-Star Game Green-43
NHL All-Star Game Red-43
02BAP Memorabilia Toronto Fall Expo-43
02BAP Signature Series-142
Autographs-142
Autograph Buybacks 2000-82
Autograph Buybacks 2001-9
Autographs Gold-142
02Bowman YoungStars-53
Gold-53
Silver-53
02O-Pee-Chee-152
02O-Pee-Chee Premier Blue Parallel-152
02O-Pee-Chee Premier Red Parallel-152
02O-Pee-Chee Factory Set-152
02Pacific-115
Blue-115
Red-115
02Pacific Complete-421
Red-421
02Parkhurst Retro-167
Minis-167
02SP Game Used Future Fabrics-FFBM
02SP Game Used Future Fabrics Gold-FFBM
02SP Game Used Future Fabrics Rainbow-FFBM
02Stadium Club YoungStars Relics-S14
02Stars Postcards-8
02Topps-152
OPC Blue Parallel-152
OPC Red Parallel-152
Factory Set-152
02Topps Chrome-93
Black Border Refractors-93
Refractors-93
02Topps Total-99
02UD Top Shelf Dual Player Jerseys-STMM
02UD Top Shelf Shooting Stars-SHBM
02UD Top Shelf Triple Jerseys-TSMMB
02Upper Deck Number Crunchers-NC3
02Upper Deck On the Rise-ORBM
02Upper Deck Classic Portraits-32
Hockey Royalty-MML
Hockey Royalty Limited-MML
02Upper Deck MVP-61
Gold-61
Classics-61
Golden Classics-61
02Upper Deck Victory-70
Bronze-70
Gold-70
Silver-70
02Upper Deck Vintage-87
Jerseys-FSBM
Jerseys Gold-FS-BM
03Beehive-61
Gold-61
Silver-61
03Black Diamond-179
Black-179
Green-179
Red-179
Threads-DT-BM
Threads Green-DT-BM
Threads Red-DT-BM
Threads Black-DT-BM
03ITG Action-190
Jerseys-M55
03Pacific-108
Blue-108
Red-108
03Pacific Complete-5
Red-5
03Pacific Exhibit-49
Blue Backs-49
Yellow Backs-49
03SP Game Used Authentic Fabrics-QMGTM
03SP Game Used Authentic Fabrics Gold-QMGTM
03Stars Postcards-18
03Topps Pristine Jersey Portions-PPJ-BMW
03Topps Pristine Jersey Portion Refractor-PPJ-BMW
03Upper Deck-302

Canadian Exclusives-302
HG-302
UD Exclusives-302
03Upper Deck MVP-132
Gold Script-132
Silver Script-132
Canadian Exclusives-132
04Pacific-87
Blue-87
Red-87
04SP Authentic Sign of the Times-ST-BM
04SP Authentic Sign of the Times-DS-MT
04SP Authentic Sign of the Times-FS-PAC
04UD Toronto Fall Expo Pride of Canada-21
04Oklahoma City Blazers-4
05Be A Player-28
First Period-28
Second Period-28
Third Period-28
Overtime-28
Dual Signatures-GB
Signatures-BE
Signatures Gold-BE
Triple Signatures-DAL
05Beehive Matted Materials-MMMW
05Beehive Signature Scrapbook-SSBM
05Black Diamond-27
Emerald-27
Gold-27
Onyx-27
Ruby-27
05Hot Prospects-32
En Fuego-32
Red Hot-32
White Hot-32
05Panini Stickers-253
05Parkhurst-164
Facsimile Auto Parallel-164
True Colors-TCDAL
True Colors-TCDAL
True Colors-TCMIDA
True Colors-TCMIDA
05SP Authentic Sign of the Times-MW
05SP Authentic Sign of the Times Fives-MMZTJ
05SP Game Used Authentic Fabrics-AF-MW
05SP Game Used Authentic Fabrics Autos-AAF-MW
05SP Game Used Authentic Fabrics Gold-AF-MW
05SP Game Used Authentic Patches-AP-MW
05SP Game Used Authentic Patch Autos-AAP-MW
05SP Game Used Auto Draft-AD-MW
05SP Game Used Awesome Authentics-AA-MW
05SP Game Used SIGnificance-MW
05SP Game Used SIGnificance Gold-S-MW
05SP Game Used SIGnificance Extra-MT
05SP Game Used SIGnificance Extra Gold-MT
05SP Game Used Significant Numbers-SN-MW
05SP Game Used Statscriptions-ST-MW
05SPx Winning Combos-WC-MM
05SPx Winning Combos-WC-ST
05SPx Winning Combos Autographs-AWC-MM
05SPx Winning Combos Autographs-AWC-TM
05SPx Winning Combos Gold-WC-MM
05SPx Winning Combos Gold-WC-ST
05SPx Winning Combos Spectrum-WC-MM
05SPx Winning Combos Spectrum-WC-ST
05SPx Winning Materials-WM-MW
05SPx Winning Materials Autographs-AWM-BM
05SPx Winning Materials Gold-WM-MW
05SPx Winning Materials Spectrum-WM-MW
05The Cup-37
Gold-37
Black Rainbow-37
Emblems of Endorsement-EEMW
Honorable Numbers-HNMW
Limited Logos-LLMW
Masterpiece Pressplates-37
Patch Variation-P37
Patch Variation Autographs-AP37
Scripted Numbers Dual-DSNDA
Scripted Swatches-SSMW
05UD Artifacts-34
Blue-34
Gold-34
Green-34
Pewter-34
Red-34
Gold Autographed-34
Remarkable Artifacts-RA-BM
Remarkable Artifacts Dual-RA-BM
05Ultimate Collection Endorsed Emblems-EEMW
05Ultimate Collection Marquee Attractions-MA18
05Ultimate Coll Marquee Attractions Sigs-SMA18
05Ultimate Collection Ultimate Signatures-USBM
05Ultra-69
Gold-69
Fresh Ink-FI-BM
Fresh Ink Blue-FI-BM
Ice-69
05Upper Deck-59
HG Glossy-59
Jerseys Series II-J2MW
Majestic Materials-MMMW
Patches-P-BMW
05Upper Deck MVP-126
Gold-126
Platinum-126
ProSign-P-MW
05Upper Deck Rookie Update-31
05Upper Deck Trilogy Scripts-SFS-BM
05Upper Deck Toronto Fall Expo-59
05Upper Deck Victory-63
Black-63
Gold-63
Silver-63
06Be A Player Portraits-37
Signature Portraits-SPBM
06Black Diamond-26
Black-26
Gold-26
Ruby-26
06Flair Showcase-36
06Flair Showcase-123
06Flair Showcase-227
Parallel-36
Parallel-123
Parallel-227
Inks-IBR
Stitches-SSBM
06Fleer-64
Tiffany-64
06Hot Prospects Hot Materials -HMBM
06Hot Prospects Hot Materials Red Hot-HMBM
06Hot Prospects Hot Materials White Hot-HMBM
06Hot Prospects Hotographs-HBM
06O-Pee-Chee-166
Rainbow-166

06Panini Stickers-249
06SP Authentic Sign of the Times-STMO
06SP Authentic Sign of the Times Duals-STMM
06SP Authentic Sign of the Times Triples-ST3MTM
06SP Game Used Authentic Fabrics-AFBM
06SP Game Used Authentic Fabrics Parallel-AFBM
06SP Game Used Authentic Fabrics Patches-AFBM
06SP Game Used Authentic Fabrics Dual-AF2TM
06SP Game Used Authentic Fabrics Dual Patches-AF2TM
06SP Game Used Letter Marks-LMBM
06SPx-31
Spectrum-31
SPxcitement-X32
SPxcitement Spectrum-X32
Winning Materials-WMMW
Winning Materials Spectrum-WMMW
06Stars Team Postcards-16
06The Cup Autographed NHL Shields Duals-DASBR
06UD Artifacts-69
Blue-69
Gold-69
Platinum-69
Radiance-69
Red-69
Frozen Artifacts-FABM
Frozen Artifacts Black-FABM
Frozen Artifacts Blue-FABM
Frozen Artifacts Gold-FABM
Frozen Artifacts Platinum-FABM
Frozen Artifacts Red-FABM
Frozen Artifacts Patches Black-FABM
Frozen Artifacts Patches Blue-FABM
Frozen Artifacts Patches Gold-FABM
Frozen Artifacts Patches Platinum-FABM
Frozen Artifacts Patches Red-FABM
Tundra Tandems-TTTM
Tundra Tandems Black-TTTM
Tundra Tandems Blue-TTTM
Tundra Tandems Gold-TTTM
Tundra Tandems Platinum-TTTM
Tundra Tandems Red-TTTM
Tundra Tandems Dual Patches Red-TTTM
06UD Mini Jersey Collection-35
06UD Powerplay-33
Impact Rainbow-33
06Ultimate Collection Autographed Jerseys-AJ-BM
06Ultimate Collection Autographed Patches-AJ-BM
06Ultra-65
Gold Medallion-65
Ice Medallion-65
Fresh Ink-IBM
06Upper Deck Arena Giveaways-DAL1
06Upper Deck Arena Giveaways-DAL1
06Upper Deck-62
Exclusives Parallel-62
High Gloss Parallel-62
Game Jerseys-J2BM
Game Patches-P2BM
Generations Triples-G3IML
Generations Patches Triple-G3PIML
Masterpieces-62
Walmart Tins Oversize-62
06Upper Deck MVP-93
Gold Script-93
Super Script-93
Jerseys-OJDM
06Upper Deck Ovation-117
06Upper Deck Sweet Shot Signature Shots/Saves-SSBM
06Upper Deck Sweet Shot Signature Shots/Saves Sticks-SSSBM
06Upper Deck Trilogy Combo Autographed Jerseys-CJTM
06Upper Deck Trilogy Combo Autographed Patches-CJTM
06Upper Deck Trilogy Combo Clearcut Autographs-C3MTM
06Upper Deck Trilogy Honorary Scripted Patches-HSPBM
06Upper Deck Trilogy Honorary Scripted Swatches-HSSBM
06Upper Deck Trilogy Honorary Swatches-HSBM
06Upper Deck Victory-63
06Upper Deck Victory Black-63
06Upper Deck Victory Gold-63
07Upper Deck All-Star Game Redemptions-AS9
07Upper Deck Ovation-33
07Upper Deck Victory-186
Black-186
Gold-186

Morrow, Charles B.
97Columbus Cottonmouths-23

Morrow, Dave
84Minnesota-Duluth Bulldogs-4

Morrow, Jon
06Lincoln Stars-20

Morrow, Josh
99Medicine Hat Tigers-4
00Medicine Hat Tigers-17
02Kamloops Blazers-11
03Kootenay Ice-12

Morrow, Ken
80O-Pee-Chee-9
80Topps-9
81O-Pee-Chee-205
81O-Pee-Chee Stickers-165
81Topps-E91
81Swedish Semic Hockey VM Stickers-93
82O-Pee-Chee-206
82O-Pee-Chee Stickers-58
82Post Cereal-12
82Topps Stickers-58
83Islanders Team Issue-11
83O-Pee-Chee-13
83O-Pee-Chee Stickers-73
83Topps Stickers-73
84Islanders News-19
84O-Pee-Chee-131
84O-Pee-Chee Stickers-93
84Topps-97
85Islanders News-23
85O-Pee-Chee-93
85Topps-93
86Islanders Team Issue-20
86O-Pee-Chee-65
86O-Pee-Chee Stickers-215
86Topps-65
87O-Pee-Chee-66
87O-Pee-Chee Stickers-246
87Panini Stickers-94
87Topps-66
88O-Pee-Chee-53
88Panini Stickers-285
88Topps-53
91Upper Deck-637
French-637
95Signature Rookies Miracle on Ice-21
95Signature Rookies Miracle on Ice-22
95Signature Rook Miracle on Ice Sigs-21
95Signature Rook Miracle on Ice Sigs-22
01UD Stanley Cup Champs-21
Jerseys-T-KM
04UD Legendary Signatures-52
Autographs-KM
Miracle Men-USA10
Miracle Men Autographs-USA-KM
Rearguard Retrospectives-DPKM
04UD Legends Classics-35
04UD Legends Classics-76
Gold-35
Gold-76
Platinum-35
Platinum-76
Silver-35
Silver-76
Signature Moments-M22
Signature Moments-M62
Signatures-CS22
05Beehive Signature Scrapbook-SSKM
05SPx Xcitement Legends-XL-KM
05SPx Xcitement Legends Gold-XL-KM
05SPx Xcitement Legends Spectrum-XL-KM
05UD Artifacts-136
Blue-136
Gold-136
Green-136
Pewter-136
Red-136
Gold Autographed-136

Morrow, Scott
94Saint John Flames-13
96Cincinnati Cyclones-28
97Cincinnati Cyclones-14
98Cincinnati Cyclones-14
98Cincinnati Cyclones 2-9
01Augusta Lynx-2

Morrow, Steve
91ProCards-284

Morrow, Thomas
03Boston University Terriers-5

Morsch, Boris
94German First League-508

Morschauser, Gus
87Kitchener Rangers-6
88Kitchener Rangers-10

Morse, Jonathan
93Quebec Pee-Wee Tournament-697

Mortensen, Claus
98Danish Hockey League-162
99Danish Hockey League-48

Mortensen, Thomas
99Danish Hockey League-102

Morth, Tommy
82Swedish Semic VM Stickers-19
83Swedish Semic Elitserien-90
83Swedish Semic VM Stickers-19
84Swedish Semic Elitserien-90
85Swedish Panini Stickers-82
86Swedish Panini Stickers-72
87Swedish Panini Stickers-78

Mortier, Darren
94Sarnia Sting-8
95Slapshot-337
95Sarnia Sting-7
96Sarnia Sting-16

Morton, Dean
88ProCards AHL-17
89ProCards AHL-328
90ProCards AHL/IHL-314
91Michigan Falcons-9
92Cincinnati Cyclones-17

Morton, Douglas
94German First League-656

Morton, Rick
907th Inn. Sketch OHL-189
917th Inn. Sketch OHL-272

Mortson, Cleland
63Quebec Aces-18
64Quebec Aces-14
65Quebec Aces-14

Mortson, Gus
44Beehive Group II Photos-127
44Beehive Group II Photos-438
45Quaker Oats Photos-41A
45Quaker Oats Photos-41B
48Exhibits Canadian-36
51Parkhurst-73
52Parkhurst-39
53Parkhurst-81
54Parkhurst-81
54Topps-17
57Topps-25
58Topps-38
94Parkhurst Missing Link-30

Morusyk, Wayne
71Rochester Americans-14

Morvan, Pierre
00Val d'Or Foreurs-16
Signed-16
01Val d'Or Foreurs-14
03Drummondville Voltigeurs-17
03Quebec Remparts Memorial Cup-15

Morz, Johann
82Swedish Semic VM Stickers-117
83Swedish Semic VM Stickers-117

Mosca, Nick
93Quebec Pee-Wee Tournament-596

Moscaluk, Darryl
02Swift Current Broncos-11
03Swift Current Broncos-11
04Calgary Hitmen-13

Moscaluk, Gary
88ProCards IHL-105
89ProCards IHL-65

Moscevsky, Yuri
02Cleveland Barons-16
03Cleveland Barons-14
05Manitoba Moose-15

Mosdell, Ken
34Beehive Group I Photos-243
43Parade Sportive *-91
44Beehive Group II Photos-275
45Quaker Oats Photos-101A
45Quaker Oats Photos-101B
45Quaker Oats Photos-101C
45Quaker Oats Photos-101D
48Exhibits Canadian-19
51Parkhurst-11
52Parkhurst-8
53Parkhurst-33
54Parkhurst-12
55Parkhurst-39
Quaker Oats-39
94Parkhurst Missing Link-41

Mosdell, Wayne
75Roanoke Valley Rebels-8

Mosele, Andrea
94Italian Milano-4

Moser, Jay
94Minnesota Golden Gophers-22
95Minnesota Golden Gophers-22
96Providence Bruins-18
96South Carolina Stingrays-29

Moser, Marcel
02Swiss HNL-397

Moser, Stefan
96Swiss HNL-42
01Swiss HNL-313
02Swiss HNL-141

Moses, Jason
00UK Guildford Flames-18

Mosewich, Preston
04Regina Pats-24

Mosey, Scott
84Sault Ste. Marie Greyhounds-14

Mosher, Jody
03Yarmouth Mariners-15

Mosienko, Bill
43Parade Sportive *-92
44Beehive Group II Photos-128
51Parkhurst-49
52Parkhurst-27
53Parkhurst-80
54Topps-54
83Hall of Fame-11
83Hall of Fame Postcards-A11
85Hall of Fame-11
91Ultimate Original Six-61
French-61
92Hall of Fame Legends-22
92Parkhurst Parkie Reprints-PR20
00BAP Ultimate Memorabilia NHL Records-R5
00BAP Ultimate Memorabilia Retro-Active-RA7
01BAP Ultimate Mem All-Star History-6
01BAP Update Rocket's Rivals-RR-10
01Parkhurst Reprints-PR4
01Parkhurst Reprints-PR135
01Parkhurst Vintage Memorabilia-PV16
02BAP NHL All-Star History-6
02BAP Ultimate Memorabilia Great Moments-17
02BAP Ultimate Mem Paper Cuts Autos-15
02BAP Ultimate Mem Seams Unbelievable-8
02ITG Used Vintage Memorabilia-VM12
02ITG Used Vintage Memorabilia Gold-VM12
02Parkhurst Vintage Teammates-VT16
03BAP Memorabilia Vintage Memorabilia-VM-12
03BAP Ultimate Mem Hometown Heroes-18
03BAP Ultimate Mem Hometown Heroes Gold-18
03BAP Ultimate Mem Linemates Autos-6
03BAP Ultimate Memorabilia Paper Cuts-5
03BAP Ultimate Mem Retro-Active Trophies-13
03BAP Ultimate Mem Vint Complete Jersey-8
03BAP Ultimate Mem Vint Comp Jersey Gold-8
03BAP Ultimate Mem Vintage Jerseys-13
03BAP Ultimate Mem Vintage Jerseys Gold-13
03ITG Used Sig Series Vintage Mem -26
03ITG Used Sig Series Vintage Mem Gold-26
03Parkhurst Original Six Chicago-52
03Parkhurst Original Six Chicago-84
Memorabilia-CM16
Memorabilia-CM23
Memorabilia-CM56
04ITG NHL AS FANtasy AS History Jerseys-SB6
04ITG Franchises US West-166
Barn Burners-WBB2
Barn Burners Gold-WBB2
Double Memorabilia-WDM1
Double Memorabilia Gold-WDM1
Forever Rivals-WFR2
Forever Rivals Gold-WFR2
Memorabilia-WSM1
Memorabilia Gold-WSM1
04ITG Ultimate Memorabilia-95
Gold-95
Chitown Immortals-1
Day In History-14
Day In History Gold-14
Original Six-3
Original Six-13
Paper Cuts Memorabilia-15
04Ultimate Collection Ultimate Cuts-UC-BM
05ITG Ultimate Mem Chi-Town Immortal Auto-1
05ITG Ultimate Mem Cornerstones Jerseys-1
05ITG Ultimate Mem Cornerst Jerseys Gold-1
05ITG Ultimate Mem Pass the Torch Jerseys-11
05ITG Ultimate Mem Passing Torch Jsy Gold-11
05ITG Ultimate Mem Record Breaker Jerseys-5
05ITG Ultimate Mem RecBreak Jerseys Gold-5
05ITG Ultimate Mem Retro Teammate Jerseys-28
05ITG Ult Mem Retro Teammates Jersey Gold-28
05ITG Ultimate Mem 3 Star of the Game Jsy-3
05ITG Ult Mem 3 Star of the Game Jsy Gold-3
05The Cup Legendary Cuts-LCMO
05ITG Heroes and Prospects Aspiring-ASP4
05ITG Heroes/Prospects He Shoots/Scores-12
05ITG Heroes and Prospects Hero Mem Dual-HDM-1
06ITG Ultimate Memorabilia Chi-Town Immortals Autos-2
06ITG Ultimate Memorabilia Cornerstones-4
06ITG Ultimate Memorabilia Cornerstones Gold-4

Mosienko, Tyler
00Kelowna Rockets-11
01Kelowna Rockets-15
02Kelowna Rockets-23
03Kelowna Rockets Memorial Cup-13
03Kelowna Rockets-14
04Kelowna Rockets-14
05ITG Heroes/Prosp Toronto Expo Parallel -179
05ITG Heroes and Prospects-179
Aspiring-ASP4
Aspiring-ASP5
Autographs-A-TM
Complete Logos-CHL-21
He Shoots-He Scores Prizes-12
Jerseys-GUJ-40
Jerseys Gold-GUJ-40
Emblems-GUE-40
Emblems Gold-GUE-40
Numbers-GUN-40
Numbers Gold-GUN-40
Nameplates-N-21
Nameplates Gold-N-21
06Las Vegas Wranglers-15

Mosjkarov, Sergei
74Swedish Stickers-85

Moskal, Patrik
98Czech OFS-191
00Czech OFS-231
01Czech OFS-219
02Czech OFS Plus-331

Moskaleev, Sergei
98Russian Hockey League-98
99Russian Hockey League-214
00Russian Hockey League-179
03Russian Hockey League-192
04Russian Super League All-Stars-29

Mosnar, Miroslav
99Czech OFS-355
00UK Sekonda Superleague-114

Mosovsky, Karel
02Rochester Americans-16
03Rochester Americans-17

Moss, David
02Michigan Wolverines-8
03Michigan Wolverines-3
04Michigan Wolverines-17
07Upper Deck Victory-217
Black-217
Gold-217

Moss, Jim
99Huntington Blizzard-9

Moss, Joey
90Oilers IGA-17

Moss, Tyler
93Kingston Frontenacs-3
95Atlanta Knights-14
95Classic-86
CHL All-Stars-AS7
95Classic Five-Sport *-144
Autographs-144
96Grand Rapids Griffins-14
97Be A Player-230
Autographs-230
Autographs Die-Cuts-230
Autographs Prismatic Die-Cuts-230
97Black Diamond-108
Double Diamond-108
Triple Diamond-108
Quadruple Diamond-108
97Crown Royale-20
Emerald Green-20
Ice Blue-20
Silver-20
Freeze Out Die-Cuts-4
97Donruss Priority-179
Stamp of Approval-179
97Katch-23
Gold-23
Silver-23
97Pacific Omega-32
Copper-32
Dark Gray-32
Emerald Green-32
Gold-32
Ice Blue-32
97SP Authentic-174
97Upper Deck Ice-32
Parallel-32
Power Shift-32
97Saint John Flames-16
98Be A Player-17
Press Release-17
98BAP Gold-17
98BAP Autographs-17
98BAP Autographs Gold-17
98BAP Tampa Bay All Star Game-17
98Bowman's Best Mirror Image Fusion-F10
98Bowmans Best Mirror Im Fusion Ref-F10
98Bowmans Best Mirror Im Fusion Atom Ref-F10
98Katch-23
98Pacific-122
Ice Blue-122
Red-122
98Pacific Omega-34
Red-34
Opening Day Issue-34
98Revolution-21
Ice Shadow-21
Red-21
98Upper Deck-56
Exclusives-56
Exclusives 1 of 1-56
Gold Reserve-56
99Kansas City Blades Supercuts-11
00Upper Deck NHLPA-PA18
01Between the Pipes-66
01O-Pee-Chee-295
01O-Pee-Chee Premier Parallel-295
01Pacific-77
Extreme LTD-77
Hobby LTD-77
Premiere Date-77
Retail LTD-77
01Pacific Arena Exclusives-77
01Topps-295
OPC Parallel-295
02BAP Sig Series Auto Buybacks 1998-17
02Between the Pipes-68
Gold-68
Silver-68
02Manitoba Moose-14
03BAP Memorabilia Deep in the Crease-D10
03Manitoba Moose-18
05Russian Hockey League RHL-50

Mota, Kevin
96Sarnia Sting-17
98Sudbury Wolves-23
99Sudbury Wolves-8

Motkov, Dmitri
90O-Pee-Chee Red Army-5R
93Classic Pro Prospects-57

Motovilov, Anatoli
73Swedish Stickers-131

Mott, Morris
69Swedish Hockey-359
70Swedish Masterserien-33
70Swedish Masterserien-94
70Swedish Masterserien-189
74NHL Action Stamps Update-7
74O-Pee-Chee NHL-48
74Topps-48

Mottau, Mike
98UD Choice-300
Prime Choice Reserve-300
Reserve-300
00BAP Memorabilia-483
Emerald-483
Ruby-483
Sapphire-483
00Black Diamond-102
00Topps Heritage-117
00Topps Premier Plus-102
Blue Ice-102
00Hartford Wolf Pack-20
01BAP Memorabilia-57
Emerald-57
Ruby-57
Sapphire-57
01BAP Signature Series-44
Autographs-44
Autographs Gold-44
01O-Pee-Chee-266
01O-Pee-Chee Premier Parallel-266
01Stadium Club Souvenirs-TKMM
01Topps-266
OPC Parallel-266
Reserve Emblems-MM
Reserve Jerseys-MM
Reserve Name Plates-MM
Reserve Numbers-MM
Reserve Patches-MM
01Upper Deck-119
Exclusives-119
01Hartford Wolf Pack-18
02BAP Sig Series Auto Buybacks 2001-44
02O-Pee-Chee-276
02O-Pee-Chee Premier Blue Parallel-276
02O-Pee-Chee Premier Red Parallel-276
02O-Pee-Chee Factory Set-276
02Topps-276
OPC Blue Parallel-276
OPC Red Parallel-276
Factory Set-276
03Cincinnati Mighty Ducks-A3
04Worcester IceCats-2
05AHL All-Stars-21
05Peoria Rivermen-2

Motter, Alex
34Beehive Group I Photos-25
40O-Pee-Chee V301-2-115

Motz, Tyson
97Swift Current Broncos-3
98Swift Current Broncos-15
99Swift Current Broncos-11
00Swift Current Broncos-13

Motzko, Bob
05St. Cloud State Huskies-28
06St. Cloud State Huskies-28

Motzko, Joe
03ITG VIP Rookie Debut-114
03Parkhurst Rookie-93
03Upper Deck Rookie Update-172
03Syracuse Crunch-12
04Syracuse Crunch-13
05Syracuse Crunch-11
06Syracuse Crunch-13

Mougenel, Ryan
93Owen Sound Platers-21
94Owen Sound Platers-18
95Slapshot-133
96Kitchener Rangers-20
97Cleveland Lumberjacks-20
97Bowman CHL-27
OPC-27
00Jackson Bandits-12
02Atlantic City Boardwalk Bullies-16
05Fresno Falcons-21

Moul, Jason
01Sioux Falls Stampede-8

Moulson, Matt
06AHL Top Prospects-21
06Manchester Monarchs-13

Moulton, Tyrell
01Lethbridge Hurricanes-23
03Prince George Cougars-22
04South Surrey Eagles-17
05Idaho Steelheads-16

Moulton, Tyson
01Regina Pats-16
02Regina Pats-21
04Surrey Eagles-15
04Surrey Eagles-15

Mourier, Christian
98Danish Hockey League-44
99Danish Hockey League-219

Mouser, Tim
92Toledo Storm-5
92Toledo Storm Team Issue-5

Mouther, Michel
96Swiss HNL-45
98Swiss Power Play Stickers-47
98Swiss Power Play Stickers-281
99Swiss Panini Stickers-335
00Swiss Panini Stickers-140
00Swiss Slapshot Mini-Cards-HCFG16
01Swiss HNL-140
02Swiss HNL-52

Mouton, Claude
87Canadiens Postcards-19

Movsessian, Vicki
94Classic Women of Hockey-W23

Mowbray, Mike
96UK Guildford Flames-13

Mowers, Johnny
34Beehive Group I Photos-118
40O-Pee-Chee V301-2-105
04ITG Ultimate Memorabilia Motown Heroes-1

Mowers, Mark
96New Hampshire Wildcats-26
98IHL All-Star Western Conference-14
98Milwaukee Admirals-16
99Pacific-230
Copper-230
Emerald Green-230
Gold-230
Ice Blue-230
Premiere Date-230
Red-230
99Upper Deck MVP-112
Gold Script-112
Silver Script-112
Super Script-112
99Upper Deck Victory-161
99Milwaukee Admirals Keebler-6
00Milwaukee Admirals Keebler-11
00Milwaukee Admirals Postcards-10
01Milwaukee Admirals-19
02Grand Rapids Griffins-19
03Parkhurst Original Six Detroit-8
03Grand Rapids Griffins-14
06O-Pee-Chee-44
Rainbow-44

Moxam, Darren
84Belleville Bulls-12
86Kitchener Rangers-13

Moxam, Darryl
93Oshawa Generals-15
93Peterborough Petes-7
95Slapshot-390
95Sudbury Wolves-17
95Sudbury Wolves Police-16
00UK Nottingham Panthers-12
00UK Sekonda Superleague-137

Moxey, Jim
76O-Pee-Chee NHL-349

Moxness, Rob
91Rayside-Balfour Jr. Canadians-12

Moyer, Russ
99Ottawa 67's-19
00Ottawa 67's-5
01Ottawa 67's-6
02Ottawa 67's-5

Moylan, Corey
93Sault Ste. Marie Greyhounds-26

Moylan, Dave
84Sudbury Wolves-13
85Sudbury Wolves-10
86Sudbury Wolves-5
90ProCards AHL/IHL-439
91ProCards-159

Moyon, Christophe
94Finnish Jaa Kiekko-214
94French National Team-20
95Swedish World Championships Stickers-99

Mozak, Trent
98Sioux City Musketeers-15
99Sioux City Musketeers-15
00Sioux City Musketeers-20

Mozyakin, Sergei
99Russian Hockey League-86
00Russian Hockey League-352
02Russian Hockey League-97
03Russian Hockey League-9
03Russian National Team-3
03Russian Postcards-4
03Russian SL-40

Mozzini, Marco
93Swiss HNL-281
96Swiss HNL-490

Mracka, Daniel
03Czech OFS Plus-354

Mraz, Zdenek
98Czech OFS-176

Mrazek, Frantisek
97Red Deer Rebels-14
98Red Deer Rebels-14
99Bowman CHL-93
Gold-93
OPC International-93
00St. John's Maple Leafs-19
01St. John's Maple Leafs-17
02Czech OFS Plus-179
03Czech OFS Plus-53
03Czech Pardubice Postcards-10
04Czech HC Plzen Postcards-11
04Czech OFS-347
04Czech OFS-384
05Czech HC Pardubice-11
06Czech HC Pardubice Postcards-13
06Czech OFS-325
06Czech OFS-327

Mrazek, Jaroslav
03Czech OFS Plus-154
04St. Michael's Majors-22
06Czech OFS-78

Mrazek, Radek
94Czech APS Extraliga-210
95Czech APS Extraliga-160
96Czech APS Extraliga-170
97Czech APS Extraliga-82
97Czech DS Stickers-42
98Czech DS Stickers-93
98Czech OFS-4
99Czech DS-62
99Czech OFS-153
00Czech DS Extraliga-41
00Czech OFS-139
02Czech OFS Plus-342

Mrena, Andrej
95Slovakian-Quebec Pee-Wee Tournament-20

Mrena, Jozef
98Prince George Cougars-14
99Prince George Cougars-9
04Slovakian Skalica Team Set-4

Mrhalek, Roman
91Air Canada SJHL-C28

Mroz, Jim
95Waterloo Blackhawks -12
99Alexandria Warthogs-10

Mrozik, Rick
93Minnesota-Duluth Bulldogs-22
97Portland Pirates-17
98Portland Pirates-22
03Bowman-155
Gold-155
03Bowman Chrome-155
Refractors-155
Gold Refractors-155
Xfractors-155
03ITG Action-76
03O-Pee-Chee-311
03OPC Blue-311
03OPC Gold-311
03OPC Red-311
03Parkhurst Rookie-65
03Topps-311
Blue-311
Gold-311
Red-311
03Topps C55-136
Minis-136
Minis American Back-136
Minis American Back Red-136
Minis Bazooka Back-136
Minis Brooklyn Back-136
Minis Hat Trick Back-136
Minis O Canada Back-136
Minis O Canada Back Red-136
Minis Stanley Cup Back-136
03Upper Deck Classic Portraits-163
03Upper Deck MVP-76
Gold Script-76
Silver Script-76
Canadian Exclusives-76
03Upper Deck Victory-26
Bronze-26
Gold-26
Silver-26
03Rochester Americans-18

Mruk, Jerzy
89Swedish Semic World Champ Stickers-128

Mrukvia, Milan
95Swiss HNL-438

Mucha, Jan
02Czech OFS Plus-180
03Czech OFS Plus-266
05Czech HC Ceski Budejovice-11
06Czech HC Ceske Budejovice Postcards-5
06Czech OFS-12

Mucha, Jaro
94German DEL-158
95German DEL-153

Mucha, Kurt
06Between The Pipes-33
Autographs-AKMU

Muckalt, Bill
91British Columbia JHL-82
92British Columbia JHL-77
98Be A Player-291
Press Release-291
98BAP Gold-291
98BAP Autographs-291
98BAP Autographs Gold-291
98Black Diamond-86
Double Diamond-86
Triple Diamond-86
Quadruple Diamond-86
98Bowman's Best-124
Refractors-124
Atomic Refractors-124
Autographs-A6A
Autographs-A6B
Autographs Refractors-A6A
Autographs Refractors-A6B
Autographs Atomic Refractors-A6A
Autographs Atomic Refractors-A6B
Mirror Image Fusion-F14
Mirror Image Fusion Refractors-F14
Mirror Image Fusion Atomic Refractors-F14
98Crown Royale-137
Limited Series-137
Rookie Class-10
98Pacific Dynagon Ice Rookies-10
98Pacific Omega-238
Red-238
Opening Day Issue-238
Online-35
98Revolution-143
Ice Shadow-143
Red-143
98SP Authentic-111
Power Shift-111
98SPx Top Prospects-59
Radiance-59
Spectrum-59
98Topps Gold Label Class 1-73
Black-73
Black One of One-73
One of One-73
Red-73
Red One of One-73
98Topps Gold Label Class 2-73
98Topps Gold Label Class 2 Black-73
98Topps Gold Label Class 2 Black 1 of 1-73
98Topps Gold Label Class 2 One of One-73
98Topps Gold Label Class 2 Red-73
98Topps Gold Label Class 2 Red One of One-73
98Topps Gold Label Class 3-73
98Topps Gold Label Class 3 Black-73
98Topps Gold Label Class 3 Black 1 of 1-73
98Topps Gold Label Class 3 One of One-73
98Topps Gold Label Class 3 Red-73
98Topps Gold Label Class 3 Red One of One-73
98Upper Deck-377
Exclusives-377
Exclusives 1 of 1-377
Gold Reserve-377
98Upper Deck MVP-205
Gold Script-205
Silver Script-205
Super Script-205
99Aurora-141
Premiere Date-141
99BAP Memorabilia-238
Gold-238
Silver-238
99BAP Millennium-236
Emerald-236
Ruby-236
Sapphire-236
Signatures-236
Signatures Gold-236
99O-Pee-Chee-224
99O-Pee-Chee Chrome-224
99O-Pee-Chee Chrome Refractors-224
99O-Pee-Chee Chrome Ice Futures-IF3
99O-Pee-Chee Chrome Ice Futures Refractor-IF3
99O-Pee-Chee Ice Futures-IF3
99Pacific-428
Copper-428
Emerald Green-428
Gold-428
Ice Blue-428
Premiere Date-428
Red-428
99Pacific Dynagon Ice-196
Blue-196
Copper-196
Gold-196
Premiere Date-196
99Pacific Omega-144
Copper-144
Gold-144
Ice Blue-144
Premiere Date-144
99Paramount-237
Copper-237
Emerald-237
Gold-237
Holographic Emerald-237
Holographic Gold-237
Holographic Silver-237
Ice Blue-237
Premiere Date-237
Red-237
Silver-237
99Revolution-143
Premiere Date-143
Red-143
Shadow Series-143
99SP Authentic Sign of the Times-BM
99SP Authentic Sign of the Times Gold-BM
99SPx-150
Radiance-150
Spectrum-150
99Stadium Club-34
First Day Issue-34
One of a Kind-34
Printing Plates Black-34
Printing Plates Cyan-34
Printing Plates Magenta-34
Printing Plates Yellow-34
Capture the Action-CA1
Capture the Action Game View-CAG1
99Topps/OPC-224
Ice Futures-IF3
99Topps/OPC Chrome-224
Refractors-224
Ice Futures-IF3
Ice Futures Refractors-IF3
99Upper Deck-127
Exclusives-127
Exclusives 1 of 1-127
99Upper Deck Gold Reserve-127
UD Authentics-BM
99Upper Deck HoloGrFx UD Authentics-BM
99Upper Deck MVP-205
Gold Script-205
Silver Script-205
Super Script-205
Draft Report-DR2
ProSign-BM
99Upper Deck Retro-78
Gold-78
Platinum-78
99Upper Deck Victory-294
00BAP Memorabilia-341
Emerald-341
Ruby-341
Sapphire-341
Promos-341
00BAP Mem Chicago Sportsfest Copper-341
00BAP Memorabilia Chicago Sportsfest Blue-341
00BAP Memorabilia Chicago Sportsfest Gold-341
00BAP Memorabilia Chicago Sportsfest Ruby-341
00BAP Memorabilia Chicago Sun-Times Ruby-341
00BAP Memorabilia Chicago Sun-Times Gold-341
00BAP Mem Chicago Sun-Times Sapphire-341
00BAP Mem Toronto Fall Expo Copper-341
00BAP Memorabilia Toronto Fall Expo Gold-341
00BAP Memorabilia Toronto Fall Expo Ruby-341
00Paramount-157
Copper-157
Gold-157
Holo-Gold-157
Holo-Silver-157
Ice Blue-157
Premiere Date-157
00Upper Deck Vintage-229
01Parkhurst-214
01Senators Team Issue-17
01Topps Heritage-180
01Upper Deck-352
Exclusives-352
02BAP Sig Series Auto Buybacks 1998-291
02BAP Sig Series Auto Buybacks 1999-236
02Crown Royale-49
Blue-49
Red-49
Retail-49
02Pacific Complete-351
Red-351
03ITG Action-272
03Houston Aeros-16

Muckler, John
52Juniors Blue Tint-175
82Oilers Red Rooster-NNO
83Oilers McDonald's-20
84Oilers Red Rooster-NNO
85Oilers Red Rooster-NNO
86Oilers Red Rooster-NNO
88Oilers Tenth Anniversary-68
90Oilers IGA-18
90Pro Set-665
92Sabres Blue Shield-15
93Kraft-44

Mudra, Rudolf
99Czech Score Blue 2000-64
99Czech Score Red Ice 2000-64

Mudroch, Petr
96Czech APS Extraliga-152
97Czech APS Extraliga-252
98Czech DS Stickers-133
98Czech OFS-152
99Czech OFS-366
99Czech Score Blue 2000-6
99Czech Score Red Ice 2000-6
00Czech OFS-41
01Czech OFS-218
01Czech OFS-223
02Czech DS-11
02Czech OFS Plus-222
03Czech OFS Plus-54
04Czech OFS-125
05Czech HC Pardubice-12
06Czech OFS-35

Mueggler, Brian
89Niagara Falls Thunder-13
897th Inn. Sketch OHL-127

Mueller, Brad
84Brandon Wheat Kings-6
01Memphis RiverKings-3
03Memphis RiverKings-13
04Memphis RiverKings-4

Mueller, Brian
91Upper Deck Czech World Juniors-66
92Clarkson Knights-11
95Classic-77
Autographs-14
95Classic Five-Sport *-146
Autographs-146
98UHL All-Stars-11
99Saginaw Gears-1

Mueller, Peter
05ITG Heroes/Prosp Toronto Expo Parallel -323
05Everett Silvertips-18
05ITG Heroes and Prospects-323
Autographs Series II-PM
He Shoots-He Scores Prizes-55
Team Cherry-TC6
06ITG International Ice-149
Gold-149
Autographs-APMU
06ITG Ultimate Memorabilia Future Star-11
06ITG Ultimate Memorabilia Future Star Gold-11

06ITG Ultimate Memorabilia Future Star Autos-2
06ITG Ultimate Memorabilia Future Star Autos Gold-2
06ITG Ultimate Memorabilia Future Star Patches Autos-2
06ITG Ultimate Memorabilia Future Star Patches Autos Gold-2
06ITG Ultimate Memorabilia Triple Thread Jerseys-12
06ITG Ultimate Memorabilia Triple Thread Jerseys Gold-12
06ITG Heroes and Prospects-85
Autographs-APM
Class of 2006-CL04
Complete CHL Logos-CHL06
Complete Jerseys-CJ13
Jerseys-GUJ39
Jerseys Gold-GUJ39
Emblems-GUE39
Emblems Gold-GUE39
Numbers-GUN39
Numbers Gold-GUN39
Sticks and Jerseys-SJ05
Sticks and Jerseys Gold-SJ05

Mueller, Regan
93Seattle Thunderbirds-15

Mueller, Richard
98Brandon Wheat Kings-15
99Brandon Wheat Kings-15
00Brandon Wheat Kings-8
01Saskatoon Blades-11
04German DEL Update-297
05German DEL-33

Mueller-Boenigk, Bodo
99German DEL-342

Muench, Kelsey
04Atlantic City Boardwalk Bullies-7
05Fresno Falcons-13

Muffler, Oliver
93Swiss HNL-482

Muftiev, Rail
95Swedish World Championships Stickers-39
97Czech APS Extraliga-98
98Czech DS Stickers-101
99Russian Hockey League-187
01Russian Hockey League-52
02Russian Hockey League-104

Muhlbauer, Thomas
94German DEL-115
95German DEL-327

Muhlegger, Manfred
94German First League-272

Muhr, Manfred
95Austrian National Team-17
95Finnish Semic World Championships-187
95Swedish World Championships Stickers-272

Muikku, Jorma
70Finnish Jaakiekko-260

Muir, Bryan
98Upper Deck-314
Exclusives-314
Exclusives 1 of 1-314
Gold Reserve-314
99BAP Millennium-59
Emerald-59
Ruby-59
Sapphire-59
Signatures-59
Signatures Gold-59
99Panini Stickers-206
00Upper Deck Vintage-328
01O-Pee-Chee-248
01O-Pee-Chee Premier Parallel-248
01Topps-248
OPC Parallel-248
01Hershey Bears-17
02Avalanche Postcards-18
02BAP Sig Series Auto Buybacks 1999-59
02Hershey Bears-15
03Manchester Monarchs-10
03Manchester Monarchs Team Issue-10
05Be A Player Signatures-MU
05Be A Player Signatures Gold-MU
05Parkhurst-494
Facsimile Auto Parallel-494
06Be A Player-78
Autographs-78
Signatures-BM
06O-Pee-Chee-493
Rainbow-493

Muir, Jimmy
37V356 Worldwide Gum-128

Muir, Wayne
87Sault Ste. Marie Greyhounds-28
89Sault Ste. Marie Greyhounds-21
92Greensboro Monarchs-8
94Brantford Smoke-17
97Quad-City Mallards-7
98Port Huron Border Cats-1
98UHL All-Stars-10

Muise, Randy
91Air Canada SJHL-B33

Mujcin, Mirsad
917th Inn. Sketch WHL-296

Mukhachev, Andrei
99Russian Hockey League-84
01Russian Hockey League-4
02Russian Hockey League-93
03Russian National Team-4
05Russian Hockey League RHL-22

Mukhanov, Alex
98Tacoma Sabercats-15

Mukhometov, Ildar
91Upper Deck Czech World Juniors-10
98Russian Hockey League-143
99German DEL-233
99Russian Stars Postcards-16
00Russian Hockey League-388
02Russian Hockey League-80
03Russian Hockey League-277

Mulcahey, Bill
79Montreal Juniors-18

Muldoon, Colin
98Fayetteville Force-16

Muldoon, Michael
93Quebec Pee-Wee Tournament-1188

Mulhern, Richard
76O-Pee-Chee NHL-265
77O-Pee-Chee NHL-373
78O-Pee-Chee-256
78Topps-256
79O-Pee-Chee-133
79Topps-133
80Jets Postcards-18
80O-Pee-Chee-350

Mulhern, Ryan
96Hampton Roads Admirals-HRA7
97Portland Pirates-18
98Kansas City Blades-17
99Portland Pirates-16

Mulick, Robert
93Quebec Pee-Wee Tournament-1414
95Slapshot-378
95Sault Ste. Marie Greyhounds-12
96Sault Ste. Marie Greyhounds-13
96Sault Ste. Marie Greyhounds Autographed-13
99Kentucky Thoroughblades-21
00Kentucky Thoroughblades-19
01Cleveland Barons-16
02Cleveland Barons-17
03Cleveland Barons-15

Mull, Gerald
94German First League-399

Mullahy, Brad
93Birmingham Bulls Birmingham News-15
94Raleigh Icecaps-13

Mullen, Brian
82Jets Postcards-18
83Jets Postcards-18
83O-Pee-Chee-389
83O-Pee-Chee Stickers-148
83Puffy Stickers-4
83Topps Stickers-148
83Vachon-134
84Jets Police-15
84O-Pee-Chee-344
847-Eleven Discs-60
85Jets Police-14
85Jets Silverwood Dairy-6
85O-Pee-Chee-195
86Jets Postcards-15
86Kraft Drawings-47
86O-Pee-Chee-38
86O-Pee-Chee Stickers-109
86Topps-38
88O-Pee-Chee-91
88Topps-91
89O-Pee-Chee-24
89O-Pee-Chee Stickers-243
89Panini Stickers-286
89Rangers Marine Midland Bank-19
89Topps-24
90Bowman-217
Tiffany-217
90O-Pee-Chee-292
90Panini Stickers-96
90Pro Set-203
90Score-84
Canadian-84
90Topps-292
Tiffany-292
90Upper Deck-182
French-182
91Pro Set Platinum-106
91Bowman-61
91O-Pee-Chee-129
91OPC Premier-166
91Panini Stickers-289
91Parkhurst-166
French-166
91Pinnacle-135
French-135
91Pro Set-165
French-165
91Score American-59
91Score American-379
91Score Canadian Bilingual-59
91Score Canadian Bilingual-269
91Score Canadian Bilingual-552
91Score Canadian English-59
91Score Canadian English-269
91Score Canadian English-552
91Score Rookie/Traded-2T
91Sharks Sports Action-16
91Stadium Club-222
91Topps-129
91Upper Deck-57
French-57
92Bowman-139
92O-Pee-Chee-260
92OPC Premier-111
92Panini Stickers-125
92Panini Stickers French-125
92Pinnacle-333
French-333
92Score-278
Canadian-278
USA Greats-12
92Stadium Club-420
92Topps-104
Gold-104G
92Ultra-348
92Upper Deck-317
92Upper Deck-468
93OPC Premier-154
Gold-154
93Panini Stickers-61
93Pinnacle-122
93Pinnacle-324
Canadian-122
Canadian-324
93Score-347
Canadian-347
93Stadium Club-227
Members Only Master Set-227
OPC-227
First Day Issue-227
First Day Issue OPC-227
93Topps/OPC Premier-154
Gold-154
94Leaf-419
94Stadium Club-213
Members Only Master Set-213
First Day Issue-213
Super Team Winner Cards-213
94Finnish Jaa Kiekko-128
95Finnish Semic World Championships-120
01Topps Archives-30
Relics-JBM
06Parkhurst-78
Autographs-78
Autographs Dual-DAMM

Mullen, Dennis
95Lethbridge Hurricanes-15
97Saskatoon Blades-15

Mullen, Joe
82O-Pee-Chee-307
82O-Pee-Chee Stickers-200
82Topps Stickers-200
83O-Pee-Chee-317
84O-Pee-Chee-188
84O-Pee-Chee-367
84O-Pee-Chee Stickers-61
84Topps-133
85O-Pee-Chee-7
85O-Pee-Chee Stickers-47
85Topps-7
86Flames Red Rooster-15
86Flames Red Rooster-16
86Kraft Drawings-48
86O-Pee-Chee-44
86O-Pee-Chee Stickers-82
86Topps-44
87Flames Red Rooster-16
87O-Pee-Chee-126
87O-Pee-Chee Box Bottoms-G
87O-Pee-Chee Minis-29
87O-Pee-Chee Stickers-36
87O-Pee-Chee Stickers-186
87Panini Stickers-210
87Panini Stickers-384
87Pro-Sport All-Stars-8
87Topps-126
87Topps Box Bottoms-G
88Flames Postcards-21
88O-Pee-Chee-76
88O-Pee-Chee Stickers-95
88Panini Stickers-11
88Topps-76
89Kraft-60
89O-Pee-Chee-196
89O-Pee-Chee-324
89O-Pee-Chee Box Bottoms-O
89O-Pee-Chee Stickers-61
89O-Pee-Chee Stickers-90
89O-Pee-Chee Stickers-160
89O-Pee-Chee Stickers-214
89Panini Stickers-27
89Panini Stickers-380
89Panini Stickers-384
89Sports Illustrated for Kids I-252
89Topps-196
89Topps Box Bottoms-O
89Topps Sticker Inserts-5
89Swedish Semic World Champ Stickers-170
90Bowman-97
Tiffany-97
90Kraft-36
90Kraft-72
90O-Pee-Chee-218
90OPC Premier-77
90Panini Stickers-183
90Penguins Foodland-8
90Pro Set-40A
90Pro Set-40B
90Pro Set-343
90Pro Set-508
90Score-208
Canadian-208
90Score Hottest/Rising Stars-88
90Score Rookie/Traded-7T
90Topps-218
Tiffany-218
90Upper Deck-252
90Upper Deck-423
French-252
French-423
91Bowman-79
91O-Pee-Chee-69
91OPC Premier-153
91Panini Stickers-278
91Parkhurst-141
French-141
91Penguins Coke/Elby's-7
91Penguins Foodland-6
91Penguins Foodland Coupon Stickers-2
91Pinnacle-176
French-176
91Pro Set-191
French-191
91Score American-268
91Score American-379
91Score Canadian Bilingual-269
91Score Canadian Bilingual-488
91Score Canadian English-269
91Score Canadian English-488
91Stadium Club-7
91Topps-69
91Upper Deck-201
French-201
91Finnish Semic World Champ Stickers-146
91Swedish Semic World Champ Stickers-146
92Blues UD Best of the Blues-16
92Bowman-58
92O-Pee-Chee-23
92Panini Stickers-223
92Panini Stickers French-223
92Parkhurst-368
Emerald Ice-368
92Penguins Coke/Clark-13
92Penguins Foodland-6
92Penguins Foodland Coupon Stickers-7
92Pinnacle-360
French-360
92Pro Set-142
92Pro Set-262
92Score-3
Canadian-3
USA Greats-9
92Stadium Club-20
92Topps-113
Gold-113G
92Ultra-166
92Upper Deck-144
92Finnish Semic-163
93Donruss-257
93Leaf-300
93OPC Premier-498
Gold-498
93Panini Stickers-83
93Parkhurst-159
Emerald Ice-159
93Penguins Foodland-25
93Pinnacle-240
Canadian-240
93PowerPlay-192
93Score-7
Canadian-7
93Stadium Club-19
Members Only Master Set-19
OPC-19
First Day Issue-19
First Day Issue OPC-19
93Topps/OPC Premier-498
Gold-498
93Ultra-171
93Upper Deck-186
93Swedish Semic World Champ Stickers-178
94Canada Games NHL POGS-187
94Finest Ring Leaders-10
94Fleer-165
94Hockey Wit-78
94Leaf-385
94OPC Premier-517
Special Effects-517
94Parkhurst-180
Gold-180
94Penguins Foodland-6
94Pinnacle-149
Artist's Proofs-149
Rink Collection-149
94Score-57
Gold-57
Platinum-57
94Select-16
Gold-16
94Stadium Club Members Only-33
94Stadium Club-50
Members Only Master Set-50
First Day Issue-50
Super Teams-18
Super Teams Members Only Master Set-18
Super Team Winner Cards-50
94Topps/OPC Premier-517
Special Effects-517
94Ultra-167
94Upper Deck-346
Electric Ice-346
94Finnish Jaa Kiekko-118
95Be A Player-154
Signatures-S154
Signatures Die Cuts-S154
95Collector's Choice-25
Player's Club-25
Player's Club Platinum-25
95Donruss-38
95Donruss-251
95Emotion-9
95Leaf-155
95Panini Stickers-64
95Score-252
Black Ice Artist's Proofs-252
Black Ice-252
Border Battle-8
95SkyBox Impact-10
95Stadium Club Metalists-M7
95Stadium Club Metalists MembersOnly Set-M7
95Summit-92
Artist's Proofs-92
Ice-92
95Ultra-124
95Ultra-206
Gold Medallion-124
95Upper Deck-16
Electric Ice-16
Electric Ice Gold-16
95Swedish Globe World Championships-112
96Collector's Choice-22
96Donruss-191
Press Proofs-191
96Leaf-14
Press Proofs-14
96Penguins Tribune-Review-2
96Pinnacle-61
Artist's Proofs-61
Foil-61
Premium Stock-61
Rink Collection-61
96Score-201
Artist's Proofs-201
Dealer's Choice Artist's Proofs-201
Special Artist's Proofs-201
Golden Blades-201
96SP-131
96Swedish Semic Wien-169
00Upper Deck 500 Goal Club-500JM
00Upper Deck 500 Goal Club-500JM
00Upper Deck Legends-106
Legendary Collection Bronze-106
Legendary Collection Gold-106
Legendary Collection Silver-106
Epic Signatures-JM
01BAP Memorabilia 500 Goal Scorers-GS26
01BAP Signature Series 500 Goal Scorers-22
01BAP Ultimate Mem 500 Goal Scorers-25
01BAP Ultimate Mem 500 Goal Scorers Autos-25
01BAP Ultimate Mem 500 Goal Jerseys/Stick-25
01BAP Ultimate Mem 500 Goal Emblems-25
01Greats of the Game-79
Autographs-79
01Parkhurst 500 Goal Scorers-PGS26
04ITG Franchises Canadian-12
Double Memorabilia-DM16
Double Memorabilia Gold-DM16
Forever Rivals-FR5
Forever Rivals Gold-FR5
Memorabilia-SM15
Memorabilia Gold-SM15
04ITG Franchises He Shoots/Scores Prizes-1
04ITG Franchises US West-294
Autographs-A-JM2
04ITG Ultimate Memorabilia-92
Gold-92
Autographs-19
Autographs Gold-19
Country of Origin-11
Country of Origin Gold-11
Day In History-47
Day In History Gold-47
Jersey Autographs-18
Jersey Autographs Gold-18
Stick Autographs-36
Stick Autographs Gold-36
05The Cup-20
Gold-20
Black Rainbow-20
Emblems of Endorsement-EEJM
Hardware Heroes-HHJM
Masterpiece Pressplates-20
Noble Numbers-NNMM
Noble Numbers-NNMT
Noble Numbers Dual-DNNMM
Patch Variation-P20
Patch Variation Autographs-AP20
Scripted Numbers-SNMM
Scripted Numbers Dual-DSNCA
Scripted Numbers Dual-DSNMM
Signature Patches-SPJM
Stanley Cup Titlists-TJM1
Stanley Cup Titlists-TJM2
05Ultimate Coll Ultimate Sigs Pairings-UPMM
05WBS Penguins-28
06Parkhurst-79
Autographs-79
Autographs Dual-DAFM
Autographs Dual-DAMM
06SP Authentic Sign of the Times-STJM
06SP Authentic Sign of the Times Duals-STFM
06SP Game Used Inked Sweaters Dual-IS2MM
06SP Game Used Inked Sweaters Dual Patches-IS2MM
06SPx SPxcitement-X87
06SPx SPxcitement Spectrum-X87
06The Cup Enshrinements-EJM
06The Cup Honorable Numbers-HNJM
06The Cup Limited Logos-LLJM
06The Cup Scripted Swatches-SSJM
06The Cup Stanley Cup Signatures-CSJM
06The Cup Stanley Cup Signatures-CSMU
06UD Artifacts-123
Blue-123
Gold-123
Platinum-123
Radiance-123
Autographed Radiance Parallel-123
Red-123
Auto-Facts-AFJM
Auto-Facts Gold-AFJM
Tundra Tandems-TTJA
Tundra Tandems Black-TTJA
Tundra Tandems Blue-TTJA
Tundra Tandems Gold-TTJA
Tundra Tandems Platinum-TTJA
Tundra Tandems Red-TTJA
Tundra Tandems Dual Patches Red-TTJA
06Ultimate Collection Jerseys Dual-UJ2-MM
06Ultimate Collection Patches Dual-UJ2-MM
06Ultimate Collection Premium Patches-PS-JM
06Ultimate Collection Premium Swatches-PS-JM
06Ultimate Collection Signatures-US-JM
06Upper Deck Sweet Shot Signature Sticks-STJM
06Upper Deck Sweet Shot Sweet Stitches-SSJM
06Upper Deck Sweet Shot Sweet Stitches Duals-SSJM
06Upper Deck Sweet Shot Sweet Stitches Triples-SSJM
06Upper Deck Trilogy Combo Clearcut Autographs-C2MM
06Upper Deck Trilogy Legendary Scripts-LSJM
06Upper Deck Trilogy Scripts-TSJM
06Philadelphia Phantoms-1

Mullen, Mark
99Des Moines Buccaneers-19
03Boston University Terriers-1

Mullen, Patrick
04Sioux Falls Stampede-4-4

Muller, Benjamin
93Swiss HNL-454
95Swiss HNL-504

Muller, Blair
93Swiss HNL-143
95Swiss HNL-220
96Swiss HNL-134

Muller, Colin
93Swiss HNL-127
95Swiss HNL-175
96Swiss HNL-69
98Swiss Power Play Stickers-217
99Swiss Panini Stickers-94
01Swiss HNL-144
02Swiss HNL-137
03Swiss EV Zug Postcards-15
04Swiss EV Zug Postcards-27

Muller, Gerhard
83Swedish Semic VM Stickers-160
99German DEL-409
04German Berlin Eisbarens 50th Anniv-41

Muller, Greg
94German DEL-298
95German DEL-319

Muller, Jaroslav
99Czech Score Blue 2000-65
99Czech Score Red Ice 2000-65

Muller, Josef
96German DEL-193

Muller, Kirk
81Kingston Canadians-15
84Devils Postcards-27
85Devils Postcards-7
85O-Pee-Chee-84
85O-Pee-Chee Stickers-64
85Topps-84
86Devils Police-16
86O-Pee-Chee-94
86O-Pee-Chee Stickers-201
86Topps-94
87O-Pee-Chee-157
87O-Pee-Chee Stickers-65
87Panini Stickers-79
87Topps-157
88Devils Caretta-21
88Frito-Lay Stickers-33
88O-Pee-Chee-84
88O-Pee-Chee Box Bottoms-F
88O-Pee-Chee Stickers-75
88Panini Stickers-275
88Topps-84
88Topps Box Bottoms-F
89Devils Caretta-17
89O-Pee-Chee-117
89O-Pee-Chee Stickers-83
89Panini Stickers-251
89Topps-117
90Bowman-82
Tiffany-82
90Devils Team Issue-19
90Kraft-37
90Kraft-88
90O-Pee-Chee-245
90O-Pee-Chee-394
90OPC Premier-78
90Panini Stickers-73
90Pro Set-172
90Pro Set-371
90Score-160
Canadian-160
90Score Hottest/Rising Stars-71
90Topps-245
90Topps-394
Tiffany-245
Team Scoring Leaders-7
Team Scoring Leaders Tiffany-7
90Upper Deck-267
90Upper Deck-311
French-267
French-311
91Pro Set Platinum-66
91Pro Set Platinum-281
91Bowman-274
91Canadiens Postcards-20
91Gillette-21
91Kraft-12
91O-Pee-Chee-22
91O-Pee-Chee-191
91OPC Premier-86
91OPC Premier-145
91Panini Stickers-219
91Parkhurst-89
French-89
91Pinnacle-3
French-3
91Pro Set-134
91Pro Set-412
French-134
French-412
91Score American-110
91Score American-331
91Score Canadian Bilingual-110
91Score Canadian Bilingual-361
91Score Canadian Bilingual-614
91Score Canadian English-110
91Score Canadian English-361
91Score Canadian English-614
91Score Rookie/Traded-64T
91Stadium Club-193
91Topps-22
91Upper Deck-149
91Upper Deck-519
French-149
French-519
92Bowman-138
92Bowman-236
92Canadiens Postcards-18
92McDonald's Upper Deck-23
92O-Pee-Chee-327
92Panini Stickers-148
92Panini Stickers French-148
92Parkhurst-83
92Parkhurst-504
Emerald Ice-83
Emerald Ice-504
Cherry Picks-CP5
92Pinnacle Canadian Promo Panels-2
92Pinnacle-111
French-111
92Pro Set-87
92Score-225
Canadian-225
Sharpshooters-29
Sharpshooters Canadian-29
92Seasons Patches-25
92Stadium Club-387
92Topps-490
Gold-490G
92Ultra-107
92Upper Deck-180
93Canadiens Molson-8
93Canadiens Postcards-16
93Donruss-177
93Kraft-17
93Kraft-59
93Leaf-182
93McDonald's Upper Deck-20A
93McDonald's Upper Deck-20B
93O-Pee-Chee Canadiens Hockey Fest-26
93OPC Premier-509
Gold-509
Black Gold-24
93Panini Stickers-14
93Parkhurst-378
Emerald Ice-378
93Pinnacle-180
Canadian-180
All-Stars-7
All-Stars Canadian-7
93PowerPlay-131
93Score-234
Canadian-234
Dynamic Duos Canadian-6
93Stadium Club-67
Members Only Master Set-67
OPC-67
First Day Issue-67
First Day Issue OPC-67
All-Stars-16
All-Stars Members Only-16
All-Stars OPC-16
93Topps/OPC Premier-509
Gold-509
93Ultra-21
All-Stars-9
93Upper Deck-148
SP-80
93Upper Deck Locker All-Stars-9
94Be A Player-R3
99 All-Stars-G17
Signature Cards-40
94Canada Games NHL POGS-137
94Canadiens Postcards-16
94Donruss-255
94EA Sports-69
94Finest-44
Super Team Winners-44
Refractors-44
Bowman's Best-B10
Bowman's Best Refractors-B10
94Flair-89
94Fleer-104
94Hockey Wit-19
94Kraft-9
94Leaf-163
94Leaf Limited-37
94OPC Premier-305
Special Effects-305
94Parkhurst Vintage-V4
94Parkhurst SE-SE88
Gold-SE88
94Pinnacle-82
Artist's Proofs-82
Rink Collection-82
Gamers-GR7
Northern Lights-NL2
94Post Box Backs-18
94Score-146
Gold-146
Platinum-146
Check It-CI10
94Select-107
Gold-107
94SP-68
Die Cuts-68
94Stadium Club-130
Members Only Master Set-130
First Day Issue-130
Super Team Winner Cards-130
94Topps/OPC Premier-305
Special Effects-305
The Go To Guy-11
94Ultra-313
94Upper Deck-66
Electric Ice-66
Ice Gallery-IG9
SP Inserts-SP40
SP Inserts Die Cuts-SP40
95SLU Hockey American-12
95Bashan Super Stickers-74
95Canada Games NHL POGS-168
95Collector's Choice-142
Player's Club-142
Player's Club Platinum-142
95Donruss-129
95Donruss Elite-54
Die Cut Stars-54
Die Cut Uncut-54
95Emotion-106
95Hoyle Eastern Playing Cards-43
95Imperial Stickers-74
95Kenner Starting Lineup Cards-14
95Leaf-41
95Metal-91
95NHL Aces Playing Cards-2S
95Panini Stickers-91
95Parkhurst International-129
95Parkhurst International-474
Emerald Ice-129
Emerald Ice-474
95Playoff One on One-65
95Pro Magnets-59
95Score-96
Black Ice Artist's Proofs-96
Black Ice-96
95Select Certified-103
Mirror Gold-103
95SkyBox Impact-103
95SP-142
95Stadium Club-177
Members Only Master Set-177
95Summit-121
Artist's Proofs-121
Ice-121
95Topps-115
OPC Inserts-115
95Ultra-96
95Ultra-268
Gold Medallion-96
95Upper Deck Special Edition-SE52
95Upper Deck Special Edition Gold-SE52
95Zenith-45
Gifted Grinders-13
96Collector's Choice-259
96Donruss-161
Press Proofs-161
96Donruss Canadian Ice-47
Gold Press Proofs-47
Red Press Proofs-47
O Canada-10
96Duracell All-Cherry Team-DC10
96Flair Now And Then-2
96Fleer Picks-138
96Leaf-72
Press Proofs-72
96Metal Universe-150
96NHL Pro Stamps-59
96Pinnacle-147
Artist's Proofs-147
Foil-147
Premium Stock-147
Rink Collection-147
96Playoff One on One-344
96Score-103
Artist's Proofs-103
Dealer's Choice Artist's Proofs-103
Special Artist's Proofs-103
Golden Blades-103
96SkyBox Impact-127
96SP-156
96Upper Deck-165
97Be A Player-121
Autographs-121
Autographs Die-Cuts-121
Autographs Prismatic Die-Cuts-121
97Collector's Choice-98
97Donruss-38
Press Proofs Silver-38
Press Proofs Gold-38
97Donruss Canadian Ice-47
Dominion Series-47
Provincial Series-47
97Donruss Limited-156
Exposure-156
97Donruss Preferred-120
Cut to the Chase-120
97Pacific-217
Copper-217
Emerald Green-217
Ice Blue-217
Red-217
Silver-217
97Pacific Invincible-62
Copper-62
Emerald Green-62
Ice Blue-62
Red-62
Silver-62
97Panini Stickers-58
97Paramount-82
Copper-82
Dark Grey-82
Emerald Green-82
Ice Blue-82
Red-82
Silver-82
97Pinnacle-190
Press Plates Back Black-190
Press Plates Back Cyan-190
Press Plates Back Magenta-190
Press Plates Back Yellow-190
Press Plates Front Black-190
Press Plates Front Cyan-190
Press Plates Front Magenta-190
Press Plates Front Yellow-190
97Pinnacle Certified-117
Red-117
Mirror Blue-117
Mirror Gold-117
Mirror Red-117
97Pinnacle Inside-108
97Pinnacle Tot Cert Platinum Blue-117
97Pinnacle Tot Certi Platinum Gold-117
97Pinnacle Totally Certified Platinum Red-117
97Pinnacle Tot Cert Mirror Platinum Gold-117
97Score-105
Artist's Proofs-105
Golden Blades-105
97Upper Deck-76
98OPC Chrome-145
Refractors-145
98Pacific-227
Ice Blue-227
Red-227
98Topps-145
O-Pee-Chee-145
99Upper Deck MVP Draw Your Own-W23
99Upper Deck MVP SC Edition-60
Gold Script-60
Silver Script-60
Super Script-60
00Stars Postcards-19
00Upper Deck NHLPA-PA30
01Pacific-133
Extreme LTD-133
Hobby LTD-133
Premiere Date-133
Retail LTD-133
01Pacific Arena Exclusives-133
01Stars Postcards-19
02Pacific-116
Blue-116
Red-116
02Pacific Complete-278
Red-278
02Stars Postcards-7
02Upper Deck-305
Exclusives-305
02Upper Deck Beckett UD Promos-305
03ITG Action Homeboys-HB6
04ITG Franchises US East-361
Autographs-A-KM2
04ITG Franchises US West-194
Autographs-A-KM1
05SP Game Used Heritage Classic-HC-KM
05SP Game Used Heritage Classic Autos-HCA-KM
05SP Game Used Heritage Classic Patches-HCP-KM
05SP GameUsed Heritage Classic Patch Auto-HAP-KM
05SP Game Used Oldtimer's Challenge-OC-KM
05SP Game Used Oldtimer's Challenge Autos-OCA-KM
05SP Game Used Oldtimer's Challenge Patch-OCP-KM
05SP Game Used Oldtime Chall Patch Autoa-OAP-KM
05The Cup Stanley Cup Titlists-TKM
06Devils Team Set-37
06UD Artifacts-124
Blue-124
Gold-124
Platinum-124
Radiance-124
Autographed Radiance Parallel-124
Red-124
Auto-Facts-AFKM
Auto-Facts Gold-AFKM
Tundra Tandems-TTPK
Tundra Tandems Black-TTPK
Tundra Tandems Blue-TTPK
Tundra Tandems Gold-TTPK
Tundra Tandems Platinum-TTPK
Tundra Tandems Red-TTPK
Tundra Tandems Dual Patches Red-TTPK
06Upper Deck Game Jerseys-J2KM
06Upper Deck Game Patches-P2KM
06Upper Deck Trilogy Scripts-TSKM

Muller, Klaus
94German First League-76
99German DEL-397

Muller, Laurent
96Swiss HNL-46
98Swiss Power Play Stickers-243
98Swiss Power Play Stickers-282
99Swiss Panini Stickers-245
99Swiss Panini Stickers-270
00Swiss Panini Stickers-285
00Swiss Slapshot Mini-Cards-ZSCL14
01Swiss HNL-90
02Swiss HNL-81
04Swiss Davos Postcards-20

Muller, Marc
94German First League-411

Muller, Matt
02Arizona Icecats-16

Muller, Matthias
95Swiss HNL-5
01Swiss HNL-442
02Swiss HNL-186

Muller, Mike
91Minnesota Golden Gophers-17
94Classic Pro Prospects-71
96Mississippi Sea Wolves-14
99German Bundesliga 2-217

Muller, Moritz
04German Cologne Sharks Postcards-21
05German DEL-220

Muller, Oliver
95Swiss HNL-281
01Swiss HNL-377
02Swiss HNL-424

Muller, Pascal
98Swiss Power Play Stickers-133
99Swiss Panini Stickers-136
99Swiss Panini Stickers-283
00Swiss Panini Stickers-180
00Swiss Slapshot Mini-Cards-LT7
01Swiss EV Zug Postcards-10
01Swiss HNL-174
02Swiss EV Zug Postcards-13
02Swiss HNL-219
03Swiss EV Zug Postcards-16
04Swiss EV Zug Postcards-10

Muller, Philippe
95Swiss HNL-104
96Swiss HNL-47
01Swiss HNL-91
02Swiss HNL-277

Muller, Rene
93Swiss HNL-228
95Swiss HNL-125
96Swiss HNL-115
98Swiss Power Play Stickers-65
99Swiss Panini Stickers-69
00Swiss Panini Stickers-116
00Swiss Slapshot Mini-Cards-HCD11
01Swiss HNL-119

Muller, Reto
93Swiss HNL-442
Muller, Robert
98German DEL-297
98German DEL-NNO
99German DEL-264
99German DEL-367
00German DEL-226
01German Adler Mannheim Eagles Postcards-1
01German Upper Deck-260
02German DEL City Press-225
All-Stars-AS5
03German DEL-190
04German DEL-237
04German Krefeld Penguins Postcards-17
05German DEL-236
05German DEL-375
Goalies-G10
06German DEL-152
06German DEL-190
Muller, Viktor
93Swiss HNL-255
Muller, Zdenek
94Czech APS Extraliga-282
95Czech APS Extraliga-76
06Czech OFS Coaches-6
Mullin, Jim
96Denver University Pioneers-2
Mullin, Kory
917th Inn. Sketch WHL-301
93Tacoma Rockets-17
95St. John's Maple Leafs-16
00Fresno Falcons-13
01Fresno Falcons-12
03Fresno Falcons-11
Mullin, Matt
917th Inn. Sketch OHL-181
92Windsor Spitfires-29
94Sudbury Wolves-21
94Sudbury Wolves Police-26
97Flint Generals-16
97Quad-City Mallards-17
97Sudbury Wolves Anniversary-14
98ECHL All-Star Northern Conference-18
00Bakersfield Condors-17
Mullin, Steve
04Maine Black Bears-3
05Maine Black Bears-19
Mullins, Dwight
94Central Hockey League-30
95Central Hockey League-11
95Fort Worth Fire-12
96Fort Worth Fire-11
97Fort Worth Brahmas-20
Mulock, T.J.
04South Surrey Eagles-18
04South Surrey Eagles-19
04Surrey Eagles-16a
04Surrey Eagles-16b
04Surrey Eagles-16
05Kamloops Blazers-13
Mulock, Tyson
99Medicine Hat Tigers-6
00Medicine Hat Tigers-18
01Vancouver Giants-20
02Regina Pats-16
Muloin, Wayne
70Dad's Cookies-88
70Esso Power Players-94
70Sargent Promotions Stamps-135
72Cleveland Crusaders WHA-10
75O-Pee-Chee WHA-102
Mulroy, Terry
74Sioux City Musketeers-11
Multanen, Jari
93Finnish Jyvas-Hyva Stickers-258
93Finnish SISU-299
Mulvaney, Meaghan
04Ohio State Buckeyes Women-5
Mulvenna, Glenn
87Kamloops Blazers-13
88ProCards IHL-58
89ProCards IHL-162
90ProCards AHL/IHL-387
91ProCards-289
92OPC Premier-97
92Upper Deck-490
95Peoria Rivermen-13
Mulvey, Grant
75O-Pee-Chee NHL-272
75Topps-272
76O-Pee-Chee NHL-167
76Topps-167
77O-Pee-Chee NHL-101
77Topps-101
78O-Pee-Chee-261
78Topps-261
79Blackhawks Postcards-14
79O-Pee-Chee-88
79Topps-88
80Blackhawks Postcards-7
80Blackhawks White Border-9
80O-Pee-Chee-27
80O-Pee-Chee-212
80Topps-27
80Topps-212
81Blackhawks Borderless Postcards-17
81Blackhawks Brown Background-7
81O-Pee-Chee-60
81Topps-W72
82Blackhawks Postcards-14
82O-Pee-Chee-69
82O-Pee-Chee Stickers-173
82Post Cereal-4
82Topps Stickers-173
83Devils Postcards-22
92Seasons Patches-22
Mulvey, Paul
78Capitals Team Issue-10
79Capitals Team Issue-14
Mulvihill, Dana
98ECHL All-Star Southern Conference-4
Mumby, Craig
93Quebec Pee-Wee Tournament-484
Mummery, Harry
04ITG Franchises Canadian-72
Munce, Ryan
03Sarnia Sting-15
05Bakersfield Condors-13
Munck, Jari
85Swedish Panini Stickers-5
92Finnish Jyvas-Hyva Stickers-76
93Finnish Jyvas-Hyva Stickers-20
93Finnish SISU-92
94Finnish SISU-256
Munday, Travis
917th Inn. Sketch WHL-355
Munden, Justin
03Halifax Mooseheads-4
Mundt, Ryan
01Notre Dame Fighting Irish-12
Mundy, Buster
37V356 Worldwide Gum-101
Muni, Craig
86Oilers Red Rooster-28
86Oilers Team Issue-28
87Oilers Team Issue-28
87O-Pee-Chee-206
87O-Pee-Chee Minis-30
87Panini Stickers-258
88Oilers Tenth Anniversary-33
88Oilers Team Issue-22
88O-Pee-Chee-236
89Oilers Team Issue-18
89O-Pee-Chee-231
89O-Pee-Chee Stickers-229
89Panini Stickers-80
90Oilers IGA-19
90O-Pee-Chee-423
90Panini Stickers-217
90Pro Set-92
90Score-38A
90Score-38B
Canadian-38A
Canadian-38B
90Upper Deck-21
French-21
91Oilers Panini Team Stickers-15
91Oilers IGA-15
91Oilers Team Issue-17
91O-Pee-Chee-479
91Panini Stickers-133
91Parkhurst-460
91Pinnacle-262
French-262
91Pro Set-382
French-382
91Score American-67
91Score Canadian Bilingual-67
91Score Canadian English-67
91Topps-479
91Upper Deck-372
French-372
92Oilers IGA-16
92Score-81
Canadian-81
92Ultra-296
93Donruss-405
93Parkhurst-291
Emerald Ice-291
93Pinnacle-298
Canadian-298
93PowerPlay-299
93Score-266
93Score-579
Gold-579
Canadian-266
Canadian-579
Canadian Gold-579
94Flair-21
94Leaf-373
94OPC Premier-216
Special Effects-216
94Pinnacle-143
Artist's Proofs-143
Rink Collection-143
94Score-29
Gold-29
Platinum-29
94Topps/OPC Premier-216
Special Effects-216
94Ultra-265
95Be A Player-14
Signatures-S14
Signatures Die Cuts-S14
97Be A Player-19
Autographs-19
Autographs Die-Cuts-19
Autographs Prismatic Die-Cuts-19
Munn, Steve
02Atlantic City Boardwalk Bullies-17
03Atlantic City Boardwalk Bullies-16
03Atlantic City Boardwalk Bullies RBI-24
04Atlantic City Boardwalk Bullies Kinko's-4
04Providence Bruins-14
05Norfolk Admirals-2
06Norfolk Admirals-19
Munro, Adam
01BAP Memorabilia Draft Redemptions-29
01UD Prospects-22
Autographs-A-AM
Jersey Autographs-S-AM
Jerseys-J-AM
Jerseys-C-BM
Jerseys Gold-J-AM
Jerseys Gold-C-BM
02Sault Ste. Marie Greyhounds-1
03ITG Action-666
03ITG Toronto Spring Expo Class of 2004-10
03ITG Used Signature Series-165
Gold-165
03ITG VIP Rookie Debut-124
03Pacific Calder-107
Silver-107
03Pacific Complete-580
Red-580
03Parkhurst Rookie-98
03Upper Deck Rookie Update-199
03Gwinnett Gladiators-19
03Gwinnett Gladiators RBI Sports-205
03Norfolk Admirals-15
04Pacific-275
Blue-275
Red-275
05Norfolk Admirals-22
05ITG Heroes and Prospects Complete Logos-AHL-15
05ITG Heroes and Prospects Jerseys-GUJ-47
05ITG Heroes and Prospects Jerseys Gold-GUJ-47
05ITG Heroes and Prospects Emblems-GUE-47
05ITG Heroes and Prospects Emblems Gold-GUE-47
05ITG Heroes and Prospects Numbers-GUN-47
05ITG Heroes and Prospects Numbers Gold-GUN-47
05ITG Heroes and Prospects Nameplates-N-71
05ITG Heroes and Prospects Nameplate Gold-N-71
05ITG Heroes and Prospects Net Prospects-NP-8
05ITG Heroes and Prosp Net Prospects Gold-NP-08
06Between The Pipes Prospect Trios-PT19
06Between The Pipes Prospect Trios Gold-PT19
Munro, Bryce
92British Columbia JHL-30
Munro, Dunc
24Anonymous NHL-91
24Anonymous NHL-92
24C144 Champ's Cigarettes-42
24V-122-52
24V130 Maple Crispette-1
24V145-2-34
25Dominion Chocolates-57
Munro, Gerald
24C144 Champ's Cigarettes-43
24V145-2-33
Munro, Mike
99Kamloops Blazers-16
Munroe, Andy
01UK Hull Thunder-7
02UK Hull Thunder-9
Munroe, Scott
06Philadelphia Phantoms-11
Munster, Jan
99German DEL-236
00German DEL-99
01German Upper Deck-22
04German DEL-194
Munther, Lars
71Swedish Hockey-216
72Swedish Stickers-193
Muntz, John
94Arizona Icecats-10
95Arizona Icecats-4
Murakami, Hiroyuki
99Czech Score Blue 2000-86
99Czech Score Red Ice 2000-86
Murano, Eric
90ProCards AHL/IHL-338
91Upper Deck-50
French-50
91ProCards-606
92Hamilton Canucks-21
94Cleveland Lumberjacks-8
94Cleveland Lumberjacks Postcards-8
95Peoria Rivermen-14
98German DEL-296
00Missouri River Otters-14
01Missouri River Otters-19
Muratov, Evgeni
99Russian Hockey League-135
00Russian Hockey League-286
01Russian Hockey League-70
02Russian Hockey League-139
Murcheson, Brent
92British Columbia JHL-97
Murchison, Ken
92Anaheim Bullfrogs RHI-17
93Anaheim Bullfrogs RHI-15
Murdoch, Don
77O-Pee-Chee NHL-244
77Topps-244
77Topps/O-Pee-Chee Glossy-12
Square-12
78O-Pee-Chee-11
78Topps-11
79O-Pee-Chee-168
79Topps-168
80O-Pee-Chee-203
80Pepsi-Cola Caps-36
80Topps-203
88Oilers Tenth Anniversary-120
99Louisiana Ice Gators-25
04ITG Franchises US East-403
Autographs-A-DMU
Murdoch, Murray
24Crescent Falcon-Tigers-4
33O-Pee-Chee V304A-37
33V129-29
33V252 Canadian Gum-39
33V357 Ice Kings-68
34Beehive Group I Photos-287
34Diamond Matchbooks Silver-47
35Diamond Matchbooks Tan 1-50
35Diamond Matchbooks Tan 2-50
35Diamond Matchbooks Tan 3-47
37V356 Worldwide Gum-88
Murdoch, Robert John
72Canadiens Postcards-15
72Dimanche/Derniere Heure *-160
74NHL Action Stamps-115
74O-Pee-Chee NHL-194
74Topps-194
75O-Pee-Chee NHL-33
75Topps-33
76O-Pee-Chee NHL-74
76O-Pee-Chee NHL-383
76Topps-74
77O-Pee-Chee NHL-39
77O-Pee-Chee NHL-371
77Topps-39
78Blues Postcards-15
78Flames Majik Market-20
78O-Pee-Chee-91
78Topps-91
79Flames Postcards-10
79Flames Team Issue-11
79O-Pee-Chee-276
80Flames Postcards-11
80Pepsi-Cola Caps-10
81Flames Postcards-14
81O-Pee-Chee-48
82O-Pee-Chee-53
82Post Cereal-3
85Flames Red Rooster-18
86Flames Red Rooster-17
87Blackhawks Coke-12
90Pro Set-377
90Pro Set-680
94German DEL-296
95German DEL-193
96German DEL-336
Murdoch, Robert Lowell
76O-Pee-Chee NHL-54
76Topps-54
79O-Pee-Chee-351
89Jets Safeway-29
90Jets IGA-23
Murdoch, Sean
03UK London Racers-11
Murdock, Lorin
92British Columbia JHL-181
Murdock, Murdock
06Moncton Wildcats-12
Murer, Michael
01Swiss HNL-474
Murin, Igor
01Slovakian Kvarteto-5A
03Czech OFS Plus-316
03Czech OFS Plus Insert H-H6
04Czech OFS-285
Goals-Against Leaders-1
Goals-Against Leaders-NNO
Save Percentage Leaders-1
05Czech HC Hame Zlin-11
06Czech HC Zlin Hame Postcards-9
06Czech OFS-235
Goalies I-1
Goalies II-2
Stars-6
Team Cards-13
Murisier, Thierry
93Swiss HNL-493
95Swiss HNL-374
96Swiss HNL-233
Murley, Matt
93Quebec Pee-Wee Tournament-675
02Wilkes-Barre Scranton Penguins-15
03BAP Memorabilia-244
03Bowman-132
Gold-132
03Bowman Chrome-132
Refractors-132
Gold Refractors-132
Xfractors-132
03ITG Used Signature Series-156
Gold-156
03ITG VIP Rookie Debut-35
03Pacific Calder-132
Silver-132
03Pacific Complete-544
Red-544
03Pacific Luxury Suite-74
Gold-74
03Pacific Supreme-134
Blue-134
Red-134
Retail-134
03Parkhurst Rookie-128
03Private Stock Reserve-135
Blue-135
Red-135
Retail-135
03SP Authentic-109
Limited-109
03SP Game Used-75
Gold-75
03Titanium-133
Hobby Jersey Number Parallels-133
Retail-133
Retail Jersey Number Parallels-133
03Topps Traded-TT137
Blue-TT137
Gold-TT137
Red-TT137
03UD Honor Roll-157
03Upper Deck-235
Canadian Exclusives-235
HG-235
03Upper Deck Rookie Update-213
03Pacific AHL Prospects Jerseys-6
03Wilkes-Barre Scranton Penguins-18
04Wilkes-Barre Scranton Penguins-19
06Albany River Rats-17
Murman, Barry
67Swedish Hockey-161
Murnaghan, Kevin
95Slapshot-359
95Sault Ste. Marie Greyhounds-13
Murnaghan, Kyle
01Moncton Wildcats-4
02Moncton Wildcats-18
Murovic, Mirko
98SP Authentic-130
Power Shift-130
Sign of the Times-MIM
Sign of the Times Gold-MIM
98Upper Deck-407
Exclusives-407
Exclusives 1 of 1-407
Gold Reserve-407
99Bowman CHL-19
Gold-19
OPC International-19
Autographs-BA39
Autographs Gold-BA39
Autographs Silver-BA39
02Swiss HNL-286
Murphy, Al
89Hampton Roads Admirals-17A
89Hampton Roads Admirals-17H
90Hampton Roads Admirals-55
91Michigan Falcons-3
92Tulsa Oilers-10
98Bakersfield Condors-15
Murphy, Ben
04Maine Black Bears-14
Murphy, Billy
93Quebec Pee-Wee Tournament-1218
Murphy, Blake
98German DEL-1
Murphy, Burke
96Saint John Flames-15
97Saint John Flames-17
99German DEL-304
Murphy, Chris
04Lincoln Stars Update-36
06Austin Ice Bats-4
Murphy, Colin
01Michigan Tech Huskies-20
05ITG Heroes/Prosp Toronto Expo Parallel -248
05ITG Heroes and Prospects-248
Autographs Series II-CMU
06AHL Top Prospects-44
06Toronto Marlies-19
Murphy, Cory
92Ottawa 67's-16
95Slapshot-358
95Sault Ste. Marie Greyhounds-14
00Fresno Falcons-14
01Fresno Falcons-13
02Finnish Cardset-75
02Fresno Falcons-4
03Finnish Cardset-45
04Finnish Cardset-49
Parallel-36
05Fresno Falcons-14
06Finnish Cardset-197
Murphy, Curtis
98IHL All-Star Eastern Conference-17
98Orlando Solar Bears II-17
99IHL All-Stars-11
02BAP Memorabilia-325
02BAP Ultimate Memorabilia-89
02SP Authentic-177
02UD Artistic Impressions-128
Gold-128
02UD Honor Roll-137
03Milwaukee Admirals-7
03Milwaukee Admirals Postcards-15
04Russian Legion-14
05AHL All-Stars-22
06Houston Aeros RetroÂ -8
Murphy, Dan
91British Columbia JHL-48
92British Columbia JHL-110
92Maine Black Bears-8
92Maine Black Bears-22
98Peoria Rivermen-12
01Trenton Titans-2-7
02Lexington Men O'War-10
03Alaska Aces-13
04Fort Worth Brahmas-11
Murphy, Gord
88Flyers Postcards-4
89Flyers Postcards-16
89O-Pee-Chee Stickers-88
89O-Pee-Chee Stickers-229
89Panini Stickers-303
90Bowman-106
Tiffany-106
90Flyers Postcards-18
90O-Pee-Chee-302
90Panini Stickers-115
90Pro Set-221
90Score-117
Canadian-117
90Score Hottest/Rising Stars-56
90Score Young Superstars-13
90Topps-302
Tiffany-302
90Upper Deck-86
French-86
91Pro Set Platinum-156
91Bowman-235
91Bruins Sports Action-12
91Flyers J.C. Penney-19
91O-Pee-Chee-89
91Panini Stickers-230
91Parkhurst-227
French-227
91Pinnacle-140
French-140
91Pro Set Preview-171
91Pro Set-171
French-171
91Score American-43
91Score Canadian Bilingual-43
91Score Canadian English-43
91Stadium Club-248
91Topps-89
91Upper Deck-392
French-392
92Bowman-315
92O-Pee-Chee-101
92Pinnacle-132
French-132
92Pro Set-11
92Score-29
Canadian-29
92Stadium Club-445
92Topps-114
Gold-114G
92Ultra-253
93Donruss-131
93Leaf-284
93OPC Premier-465
Gold-465
93Parkhurst-345
Emerald Ice-345
93Pinnacle-380
Canadian-380
Expansion-2
93PowerPlay-99
93Score-95
93Score-548
Gold-548
Canadian-95
Canadian-548
Canadian Gold-548
93Stadium Club-439
Members Only Master Set-439
First Day Issue-439
93Topps/OPC Premier-465
Gold-465
93Ultra-329
93Upper Deck-521
94Canada Games NHL POGS-112
94Donruss-55
94EA Sports-50
94EA Sports-197
94EA Sports-207
94EA Sports-210
94Flair-66
94Fleer-81
94Leaf-250
94OPC Premier-19
Special Effects-19
94Pinnacle-141
Artist's Proofs-141
Rink Collection-141
94Score-117
Gold-117
Platinum-117
94Stadium Club-128
Members Only Master Set-128
First Day Issue-128
Super Team Winner Cards-128
94Topps/OPC Premier-19
Special Effects-19
94Ultra-83
94Upper Deck-438
Electric Ice-438
95Canada Games NHL POGS-122
95Collector's Choice-190
Player's Club-190
Player's Club Platinum-190
95Donruss-161
95Emotion-70
95Leaf-146
95Panini Stickers-77
95Parkhurst International-357
Emerald Ice-357
95Pinnacle-181
Artist's Proofs-181
Rink Collection-181
95Playoff One on One-262
95Score-104
Black Ice Artist's Proofs-104
Black Ice-104
95SkyBox Impact-68
95Ultra-61
95Ultra-243
Gold Medallion-61
95Upper Deck-21
Electric Ice-21
Electric Ice Gold-21
96Be A Player-44
96Be A Player-P44
Autographs-44
Autographs Silver-44
96Fleer Picks-162
96Upper Deck-68
97Pacific Invincible NHL Regime-88
97Upper Deck-285
99Stadium Club-165
First Day Issue-165
One of a Kind-165
Printing Plates Black-165
Printing Plates Cyan-165
Printing Plates Magenta-165
Printing Plates Yellow-165
99Upper Deck Retro-34
Gold-34
Platinum-34
01O-Pee-Chee-257
01O-Pee-Chee Premier Parallel-257
01Topps-257
OPC Parallel-257
Murphy, Jay
94Richmond Renegades-11
95Richmond Renegades-3
96Alaska Gold Kings-11
96Louisiana Ice Gators-10
97Louisiana Ice Gators-7
98Louisiana Ice Gators-11
99Louisiana Ice Gators-19
00Louisiana Ice Gators-2
01Louisiana Ice Gators-17
02Greensboro Generals RBI-14
Murphy, Jim
05Missouri River Otters-6
05Port Huron Flags-11
Murphy, Jodie
917th Inn. Sketch WHL-291
93Muskegon Fury-7
93Sault Ste. Marie Greyhound Memorial Cup-18
97Bakersfield Fog-11
00Amarillo Rattlers-13
Murphy, Joe
87Red Wings Little Caesars-19
89Oilers Team Issue-19
90Bowman-196
Tiffany-196
90Oilers IGA-20
90O-Pee-Chee-429
90Pro Set-93
90Score-293
Canadian-293
90Upper Deck-190
French-190
91Pro Set Platinum-171
91Bowman-109
91Oilers Panini Team Stickers-16
91Oilers IGA-16
91Oilers Team Issue-18
91O-Pee-Chee-48
91Parkhurst-52
91Parkhurst-458
French-52
91Pinnacle-206
French-206
91Pro Set-68
French-68
91Score American-299
91Score Canadian Bilingual-519
91Score Canadian English-519
91Stadium Club-313
91Topps-48
91Upper Deck-474
French-474
92Bowman-174
92O-Pee-Chee-100
92Panini Stickers-100
92Panini Stickers French-100
92Parkhurst-273
Emerald Ice-273
92Pinnacle-23
French-23
92Pro Set-49
92Score-321
Canadian-321
92Stadium Club-34
92Topps-38
Gold-38G
92Ultra-63
92Upper Deck-152
93Blackhawks Coke-1
93Donruss-66
93Leaf-179
93OPC Premier-273
Gold-273
93Parkhurst-38
Emerald Ice-38
First Overall-F8
93Pinnacle-45
Canadian-45
93PowerPlay-53
93Score-348
Canadian-348
Dynamic Duos U.S.-6
93Topps/OPC Premier-273
Gold-273
93Topps Premier Finest-8
93Ultra-163
93Upper Deck-47
SP-29
94Be A Player Signature Cards-87
94Blackhawks Coke-11
94Canada Games NHL POGS-67
94Donruss-38
94Flair-34
94Fleer-42
94Leaf-284
94OPC Premier-34
Special Effects-34
94Parkhurst-44
Gold-44
94Pinnacle-68
Artist's Proofs-68
Rink Collection-68
94Score-170
Gold-170
Platinum-170
94Select-44
Gold-44
94SP-27
Die Cuts-27
94Topps/OPC Premier-34
Special Effects-34
94Upper Deck-416
Electric Ice-416
95Bashan Super Stickers-24
95Blackhawks Coke-10
95Canada Games NHL POGS-66
95Collector's Choice-156
Player's Club-156
Player's Club Platinum-156
95Donruss-146
95Emotion-30
95Finest-58
Refractors-58
95Imperial Stickers-24
95Leaf-109
95Metal-25
95Panini Stickers-162
95Parkhurst International-309
Emerald Ice-309
95Pinnacle-8
Artist's Proofs-8
Rink Collection-8
95Pro Magnets-8
95Score-110
Black Ice Artist's Proofs-110
Black Ice-110
95Select Certified-50
Mirror Gold-50
95SkyBox Impact-30
95Stadium Club-52
Members Only Master Set-52
95Summit-10
Artist's Proofs-10
Ice-10
95Topps-280
OPC Inserts-280
95Ultra-217
95Upper Deck-278
Electric Ice-278
Electric Ice Gold-278
95Zenith-4
96Be A Player-28
Autographs-28
Autographs Silver-28
96Collector's Choice-48
96Donruss-144
Press Proofs-144
96Donruss Elite-102
Die Cut Stars-102
96Leaf-185
Press Proofs-185
96Maggers-64
96Metal Universe-134
96NHL Pro Stamps-8
96Pinnacle-200
Artist's Proofs-200
Foil-200
Premium Stock-200
Rink Collection-200
96Score-100
Artist's Proofs-100
Dealer's Choice Artist's Proofs-100
Special Artist's Proofs-100
Golden Blades-100
96SP-132
96Summit-86
Artist's Proofs-86
Ice-86
Metal-86
Premium Stock-86
96Topps Picks-143
OPC Inserts-143
96Upper Deck-325
97Collector's Choice-231
97Pacific-150
Copper-150
Emerald Green-150
Ice Blue-150
Red-150
Silver-150
97Panini Stickers-171
97Paramount-160
Copper-160
Dark Grey-160
Emerald Green-160
Ice Blue-160
Red-160
Silver-160
97Score-163
97Score Blues-3
Platinum-3
Premier-3
97Upper Deck-349
98Be A Player-271
Press Release-271
98BAP Gold-271
98BAP Autographs-271
98BAP Autographs Gold-271
99Pacific-377
Copper-377
Emerald Green-377
Gold-377
Ice Blue-377
Premiere Date-377
Red-377
00Upper Deck-403
Exclusives Tier 1-403
Exclusives Tier 2-403
01Grand Rapids Griffins-15
02BAP Sig Series Auto Buybacks 1998-271
03Finnish Cardset-109
06Binghamton Senators 5th Anniversary-19
Murphy, Joe A.
19W519 No Numbers-9
00Rochester Americans-17
Murphy, John
02Fort Worth Brahmas-11
04St Georges de Beauce Garaga-18
Murphy, Jonathan
93Peterborough Petes-2
95Slapshot-309
Murphy, Keith
91Air Canada SJHL-B40
91Air Canada SJHL All-Stars-30
92North Dakota Fighting Sioux-22
Murphy, Ken
73Red Wings Team Issue-16
Murphy, Kevin
92Clarkson Knights-12
Murphy, Larry
81O-Pee-Chee-148
81O-Pee-Chee-393
81O-Pee-Chee Stickers-239
81Topps-W100
82O-Pee-Chee-158
82O-Pee-Chee Stickers-232
82Post Cereal-8
82Topps Stickers-232
83NHL Key Tags-51
83O-Pee-Chee-159
83O-Pee-Chee Stickers-298
83Puffy Stickers-9
83Topps Stickers-298
84Capitals Pizza Hut-13
84O-Pee-Chee-204
84O-Pee-Chee Stickers-127
85Capitals Pizza Hut-12
85O-Pee-Chee-236
86Capitals Kodak-18
86Capitals Police-17
86O-Pee-Chee-185
86Topps-185
87Capitals Kodak-8
87Capitals Team Issue-17
87O-Pee-Chee-133
87O-Pee-Chee Box Bottoms-H
87O-Pee-Chee Minis-31
87O-Pee-Chee Stickers-119
87O-Pee-Chee Stickers-232
87Panini Stickers-176
87Topps-133
87Topps Box Bottoms-H
87Topps Sticker Inserts-7
88Capitals Borderless-15
88Capitals Smokey-15
88O-Pee-Chee-141
88O-Pee-Chee Stickers-71
88Panini Stickers-367
88Topps-141
89O-Pee-Chee-128
89O-Pee-Chee Stickers-199
89Panini Stickers-108
89Topps-128
90Bowman-177
Tiffany-177
90O-Pee-Chee-47
90Panini Stickers-251
90Pro Set-143
90Score-206
Canadian-206
90Topps-47
Tiffany-47
90Upper Deck-229
French-229
91Pro Set Platinum-213
91Bowman-78
91Kraft-71
91O-Pee-Chee-277
91Panini Stickers-270
91Parkhurst-358
91Parkhurst-456
French-358
91Penguins Coke/Elby's-55
91Penguins Foodland-10
91Penguins Foodland Coupon Stickers-3
91Pinnacle-143
French-143
91Pro Set-193
French-193
91Score American-31
91Score Canadian Bilingual-31
91Score Canadian English-31
91Stadium Club-112
91Topps-277
91Upper Deck-302
French-302
92Bowman-153
92O-Pee-Chee-209
92Panini Stickers-228
92Panini Stickers French-228
92Parkhurst-137
Emerald Ice-137
92Penguins Coke/Clark-14
92Penguins Foodland-10
92Penguins Foodland Coupon Stickers-8
92Pinnacle-292
French-292
92Pro Set-146
92Score-45
Canadian-45
92Stadium Club-375
92Topps-447
Gold-447G
92Ultra-167
92Upper Deck-241
92Finnish Semic-82
93Donruss-263
93Leaf-16
Gold All-Stars-2
93OPC Premier-173
93OPC Premier-189
Gold-173
Gold-189
93Panini Stickers-86
93Panini Stickers-135
93Parkhurst-162
Emerald Ice-162
93Penguins Foodland-13
93Pinnacle-52
Canadian-52
93PowerPlay-193
93Score-23
Canadian-23
93Stadium Club-283
Members Only Master Set-283
First Day Issue-283
93Topps/OPC Premier-173
93Topps/OPC Premier-189
Gold-173
Gold-189
93Topps Premier Black Gold-23
93Ultra-184
93Upper Deck-374
NHLPA/Roots-8
93Swedish Semic World Champ Stickers-191
94Be A Player-R170
Signature Cards-148
94Canada Games NHL POGS-191
94Donruss-27
94EA Sports-103
94Finest Ring Leaders-18
94Flair-137
94Fleer-166
94Hockey Wit-48
94Leaf-249
94Leaf Limited-12
94OPC Premier-10
94OPC Premier-492
Special Effects-10
Special Effects-492
94Parkhurst-179
Gold-179
94Penguins Foodland-24
94Pinnacle-215
Artist's Proofs-215
Rink Collection-215
94Score Samples-5
94Score-5
Gold-5

Platinum-5
94Select-143
Gold-143
94Stadium Club Members Only-32
94Topps/OPC Premier-10
94Topps/OPC Premier-492
Special Effects-10
Special Effects-492
94Ultra-168
94Upper Deck-99
Electric Ice-99
94Finnish Jaa Kiekko-81
95Bashan Super Stickers-121
95Bowman-34
All-Foil-34
95Canada Games NHL POGS-19
95Canada Games NHL POGS-266
95Collector's Choice-151
95Collector's Choice-386
Player's Club-151
Player's Club-386
Player's Club Platinum-151
Player's Club Platinum-386
95Donruss-366
95Donruss Elite-8
Die Cut Stars-8
Die Cut Uncut-8
95Emotion-173
95Finest-42
Refractors-42
95Imperial Stickers-121
95Kraft-50
95Leaf-186
95Leaf Limited-97
95Metal-145
95Panini Stickers-209
95Parkhurst International-207
Emerald Ice-207
Parkie's Trophy Picks-PP23
95Playoff One on One-97
95Post Upper Deck-21
95Score-260
Black Ice Artist's Proofs-260
Black Ice-260
95Select Certified-90
Mirror Gold-90
95SkyBox Impact-163
95SP-143
95Stadium Club-144
Members Only Master Set-144
95Summit-126
Artist's Proofs-126
Ice-126
95Topps-255
OPC Inserts-255
95Ultra-125
95Ultra-314
Gold Medallion-125
95Upper Deck-86
Electric Ice-86
Electric Ice Gold-86
Predictor Hobby-H38
Predictor Hobby Exchange-H38
Special Edition-SE170
Special Edition Gold-SE170
95Zenith-106
95Finnish Semic World Championships-83
96Collector's Choice-265
MVP-UD32
96Donruss-39
Press Proofs-39
96Donruss Canadian Ice-86
Gold Press Proofs-86
Red Press Proofs-86
96Fleer-108
Norris-9
96Fleer Picks-52
96Leaf-100
Press Proofs-100
96Metal Universe-151
96Pinnacle-189
Artist's Proofs-189
Foil-189
Premium Stock-189
Rink Collection-189
96Score-75
Artist's Proofs-75
Dealer's Choice Artist's Proofs-75
Special Artist's Proofs-75
Golden Blades-75
96SkyBox Impact-128
NHL on Fox-15
96SP-154
96Stadium Club Members Only-16
96Summit-11
Artist's Proofs-11
Ice-11
Metal-11
Premium Stock-11
96Team Out-53
96Ultra-164
Gold Medallion-164
96Upper Deck-161
Generation Next-X39
96Zenith-111
Artist's Proofs-111
96Swedish Semic Wien-82
97Be A Player-141
Autographs-141
Autographs Die-Cuts-141
Autographs Prismatic Die-Cuts-141
97Pacific Omega-85
Copper-85
Dark Gray-85
Emerald Green-85
Gold-85
Ice Blue-85
97Revolution-49
Copper-49
Emerald-49
Ice Blue-49
Silver-49
97Score Red Wings-8
Platinum-8
Premier-8
98Be A Player-48
Press Release-48
98BAP Gold-48
98BAP Autographs-48
98BAP Autographs Gold-48
98BAP AS Milestones-M20
98BAP Tampa Bay All Star Game-48
98Kraft Peanut Butter-1
98OPC Chrome-33
Refractors-33
Board Members-B9
Board Members Refractors-B9
Season's Best-SB26
Season's Best Refractors-SB26
98Pacific-203
Ice Blue-203
Red-203
98Pacific Omega-85
Red-85
Opening Day Issue-85
98Paramount-80
Copper-80
Emerald Green-80
Holo-Electric-80
Ice Blue-80
Silver-80
98Topps-33
O-Pee-Chee-33
Board Members-B9
Season's Best-SB26
98UD Choice-70
Prime Choice Reserve-70
Reserve-70
98Upper Deck-265
Exclusives-265
Exclusives 1 of 1-265
Gold Reserve-265
99BAP Memorabilia-42
Gold-42
Silver-42
99Pacific-145
Copper-145
Emerald Green-145
Gold-145
Ice Blue-145
Premiere Date-145
Red-145
99Panini Stickers-235
99Paramount-85
Copper-85
Emerald-85
Gold-85
Holographic Emerald-85
Holographic Gold-85
Holographic Silver-85
Ice Blue-85
Premiere Date-85
Red-85
Silver-85
99Stadium Club Capture the Action-CA30
99Stadium Club Capture Action Game View-CAG30
99Ultimate Victory-34
1/1-34
Parallel-34
Parallel 100-34
00BAP Memorabilia-194
Emerald-194
Ruby-194
Sapphire-194
Promos-194
00BAP Mem Chicago Sportsfest Copper-194
00BAP Memorabilia Chicago Sportsfest Blue-194
00BAP Memorabilia Chicago Sportsfest Gold-194
00BAP Memorabilia Chicago Sportsfest Ruby-194
00BAP Memorabilia Chicago Sun-Times Ruby-194
00BAP Memorabilia Chicago Sun-Times Gold-194
00BAP Mem Chicago Sun-Times Sapphire-194
00BAP Mem Toronto Fall Expo Copper-194
00BAP Memorabilia Toronto Fall Expo Gold-194
00BAP Memorabilia Toronto Fall Expo Ruby-194
00BAP Ultimate Mem Dynasty Jerseys-D11
00BAP Ultimate Mem Dynasty Emblems-D11
00Pacific-156
Copper-156
Gold-156
Ice Blue-156
Premiere Date-156
00Topps/OPC 1000 Point Club-PC8
00Topps Chrome 1000 Point Club Refractors-8
00Upper Deck-294
Exclusives Tier 1-294
Exclusives Tier 2-294
00Upper Deck Vintage-130
02BAP Sig Series Auto Buybacks 1998-48
04ITG Franchises US East-441
Autographs-A-LMU2
Original Sticks-EOS2
Original Sticks Gold-EOS2
04ITG Franchises US West-242
Autographs-A-LMU1
Memorabilia-WSM32
Memorabilia Autographs-WSMLM
Memorabilia Gold-WSM32
04ITG Ultimate Memorabilia-179
Gold-179
Complete Logo-17
Heroes Mario Lemieux-5
04UD Legends Classics-37
Gold-37
Platinum-37
Silver-37
Signature Moments-M68
Signatures-CS55
Signatures-DC16
Signatures-TC9
05Beehive Signature Scrapbook-SSMU
05SP Game Used Heritage Classic-HC-LM
05SP Game Used Heritage Classic Autos-HCA-LM
05SP Game Used Heritage Classic Patches-HCP-LM
05SP GameUsed Heritage Classic Patch Auto-HAP-LM
05SP Game Used Statscriptions-ST-LM
05The Cup Emblems of Endorsement-EELM
05The Cup Noble Numbers-NNMJ
05The Cup Noble Numbers-NNPM
05The Cup Stanley Cup Titlists-TLM1
05The Cup Stanley Cup Titlists-TLM2
05UD Artifacts-137
Blue-137
Gold-137
Green-137
Pewter-137
Red-137
Gold Autographed-137
05Ultimate Collection Endorsed Emblems-EEMU
05Upper Deck Notable Numbers-N-LM
06ITG International Ice-57
06ITG International Ice-123
Gold-57
Gold-123
Autographs-ALM
Autographs-ALM2
06Parkhurst-147
06SP Authentic Sign of the Times Duals-STBM
06The Cup Honorable Numbers-HNMU
06The Cup Limited Logos-LLMU
06The Cup Stanley Cup Signatures-CSLA
06UD Artifacts Tundra Tandems-TTMC
06UD Artifacts Tundra Tandems Black-TTMC
06UD Artifacts Tundra Tandems Blue-TTMC
06UD Artifacts Tundra Tandems Gold-TTMC
06UD Artifacts Tundra Tandems Platinum-TTMC
06UD Artifacts Tundra Tandems Red-TTMC
06UD Artifacts Tundra Tandems Dual Patches Red-TTMC
06Ultimate Collection Premium Swatches-PS-MU
06Upper Deck Game Jerseys-J2LM
06Upper Deck Game Patches-P2LM
06Upper Deck Sweet Shot Signature Sticks-STLM

Murphy, Luke
01Macon Whoopee-14
02Macon Trax-13

Murphy, Mark
99Des Moines Buccaneers-12
99ECHL All-Star Northern Conference-17
00Portland Pirates-4
03Philadelphia Phantoms-13
04Philadelphia Phantoms-11

Murphy, Mike
71Blues Postcards-11
72Blues White Border-12
72O-Pee-Chee-215
72Sargent Promotions Stamps-195
74NHL Action Stamps-122
74O-Pee-Chee NHL-224
74Topps-224
75O-Pee-Chee NHL-52
75Topps-52
76O-Pee-Chee NHL-21
76Topps-21
77O-Pee-Chee NHL-22
77Topps-22
78O-Pee-Chee-229
78Topps-229
79Panini Stickers-69
79O-Pee-Chee-31
79Topps-31
80Kings Card Night-9
80O-Pee-Chee-286
81O-Pee-Chee-149
81O-Pee-Chee Stickers-241
81Topps-W101
83NHL Key Tags-52
90ProCards AHL/IHL-335
04ITG Franchises US West-236
Autographs-A-MIM
06Belleville Bulls-22

Murphy, Mike (Goalie)
06Belleville Bulls-22

Murphy, Patrick
04Northern Michigan Wildcats-15

Murphy, Randy
97Columbus Cottonmouths-12
98Danish Hockey League-98
03Elmira Jackals-13
04New Mexico Scorpions-18
06New Mexico Scorpions-2

Murphy, Rob
89ProCards IHL-172
90Canucks Mohawk-20
90O-Pee-Chee-37
90Pro Set-546
90Topps-37
Tiffany-37
91Canucks Panini Team Stickers-16
91Canucks Autograph Cards-16
91Canucks Team Issue 8x10-16
91Score Canadian Bilingual-397
91Score Canadian English-397
91ProCards-607
92Pro Set-121
92Upper Deck-108
93Phoenix Roadrunners-19
95Fort Wayne Komets-12
98German DEL-73
99German DEL-62
00German DEL-95
01German Upper Deck-99
02German DEL City Press-119
03St. Jean Mission-18

Murphy, Ron
44Beehive Group II Photos-129
44Beehive Group II Photos-348
52Juniors Blue Tint-61
54Parkhurst-76
54Parkhurst-93
57Topps-29
58Topps-59
59Topps-66
60Shirriff Coins-75
60Topps-41
Stamps-40
61Shirriff/Salada Coins-36
61Topps-34
62Topps-40
63Topps-40
64Beehive Group III Photos-90
64Coca-Cola Caps-46
64Topps-56
65Coca-Cola-46
65Topps-111
66Topps-96
66Topps USA Test-33
67Topps-100
68O-Pee-Chee-139
69O-Pee-Chee-204
94Parkhurst Missing Link-102
94Parkhurst Tall Boys-48
95Parkhurst '66-67-15
Coins-15

Murphy, Ryan
01Florida Everblades-20
02Florida Everblades-14
02Florida Everblades RBI-126
03Albany River Rats-20
03Albany River Rats Kinko's-19
03Lewiston Maineiacs-14
04Albany River Rats-14
05Albany River Rats-15
05Manchester Monarchs-11
06Manchester Monarchs-19

Murphy, Sean
93Quebec Pee-Wee Tournament-761

Murphy, Stephen
93Quebec Pee-Wee Tournament-183
01UK Dundee Stars-15
02UK Dundee Stars-15

Murphy, Thomas
06Texas Tornados-1

Murphy, Todd
91Air Canada SJHL-D22
92Saskatchewan JHL-116

Murray, Adam
917th Inn. Sketch WHL-29
93Quebec Pee-Wee Tournament-1425

Murray, Adrian
93Peterborough Petes-26
95Slapshot-310

Murray, Al
34Beehive Group I Photos-244
35Diamond Matchbooks Tan 1-51
35Diamond Matchbooks Tan 2-51
35Diamond Matchbooks Tan 3-48
36O-Pee-Chee V304D-104
37V356 Worldwide Gum-54

Murray, Andrew
06Syracuse Crunch-8

Murray, Andy
89Flyers Postcards-17
93Jets Ruffles-17

Murray, Brady
03North Dakota Fighting Sioux-17
04North Dakota Fighting Sioux-17

Murray, Bryan
82Capitals Team Issue-16
83NHL Key Tags-23
86Capitals Kodak-19
86Capitals Police-18
87Capitals Kodak-xx
88Capitals Smokey-16
90Pro Set-664
91Red Wings Little Caesars-13

Murray, Chris
93Kamloops Blazers-17
94Fredericton Canadiens-20
95Fredericton Canadiens-21
96Canadiens Postcards-18
96Canadiens Sheets-12
96Collector's Edge Future Legends-12
97Pacific Invincible NHL Regime-39
98Senators Team Issue-14
99Stars Postcards-19
00Stadium Club-216
00Worcester Icecats-20

Murray, Darwin
01Rockford IceHogs-4
02Rockford Ice Hogs-2

Murray, Doug
94German First League-469
94German First League-479
94German First League-610
99German Bundesliga 2-67
03Cleveland Barons-16
04Cleveland Barons-15
05Hot Prospects-162
En Fuego-162
Red Hot-162
White Hot-162
05SP Authentic-277
Limited-277
05SP Game Used-231
05SPx-280
05The Cup Masterpiece Pressplate Artifact-321
05The Cup Masterpiece Pressplates (Ice)-223
05The Cup Master Pressplate Rookie Update-169
05The Cup Masterpiece Pressplates SPA-277
05The Cup Masterpiece Pressplates SP GU-231
05The Cup Masterpiece Pressplates (SPx)-280
05The Cup Masterpiece Pressplates Trilogy-298
05The Cup Masterpiece Pressplate Ult Coll-221
05UD Artifacts-321
05Ultimate Collection-221
Gold-221
05Upper Deck Ice-223
05Upper Deck Rookie Update-169
05Upper Deck Trilogy-298
05Cleveland Barons-14

Murray, Douglas
94German First League-469
94German First League-479
94German First League-610
99German Bundesliga 2-67

Murray, Garth
00UD CHL Prospects-62
01Regina Pats-17
01UD Prospects-9
Jerseys-J-GM
Jerseys-C-MT
Jerseys Gold-J-GM
Jerseys Gold-C-MT
02Hartford Wolf Pack-18
03BAP Memorabilia-224
03ITG Used Signature Series-180
Gold-180
03ITG VIP Rookie Debut-112
03Parkhurst Rookie-148
Rookie Emblems-RE-12
Rookie Emblems Gold-RE-12
Rookie Jerseys-RJ-12
Rookie Jerseys Gold-RJ-12
Rookie Numbers-RN-12
Rookie Numbers Gold-RN-12
03Topps Traded-TT130
Blue-TT130
Gold-TT130
Red-TT130
03Upper Deck Rookie Update-136
03Hartford Wolf Pack-17
04Hartford Wolf Pack-18
04ITG Heroes/Prospects Complete Emblems-28
04ITG Heroes and Prospects Emblems-27
04ITG Heroes and Prospects Emblems Gold-27
04ITG Heroes/Prospects He Shoots/Scores-23
04ITG Heroes and Prospects Jerseys-27
04ITG Heroes and Prospects Jerseys Gold-27
04ITG Heroes and Prospects Numbers-27
04ITG Heroes and Prospects Numbers Gold-27
05Hamilton Bulldogs-19
06Canadiens Postcards-14

Murray, Glen
89Sudbury Wolves-6
907th Inn. Sketch OHL-388
90Sudbury Wolves-13
91Parkhurst-229
French-229
91Upper Deck-69
French-69
917th Inn. Sketch OHL-245
917th Inn. Sketch Memorial Cup-111
91Sudbury Wolves-21
91Arena Draft Picks-14
91Arena Draft Picks French-14
91Arena Draft Picks Autographs-14
91Arena Draft Picks Autographs French-14
91Classic-15
91Star Pics-64
91Ultimate Draft-15
91Ultimate Draft-71
91Ultimate Draft-84
91Ultimate Draft French-15
91Classic Four-Sport *-15
Autographs-15A
92O-Pee-Chee-74
92OPC Premier-52
92Panini Stickers-142
92Panini Stickers French-142
92Parkhurst-9
Emerald Ice-9
92Pinnacle-224
French-224
92Pro Set-222
92Score-484
Canadian-484
92Stadium Club-393
92Topps-370
Gold-370G
92Upper Deck-401
93Donruss-22
93Leaf-317
93OPC Premier-477
Gold-477
93Parkhurst-16
Emerald Ice-16
93Stadium Club-59
Members Only Master Set-59
OPC-59
First Day Issue-59
First Day Issue OPC-59
93Topps/OPC Premier-477
Gold-477
93Upper Deck-189
93Classic Pro Prospects-89
94Canada Games NHL POGS-41
94Donruss-246
94Leaf-4
94OPC Premier-173
Special Effects-173
94Parkhurst SE-SE11
Gold-SE11
94Pinnacle-169
Artist's Proofs-169
Rink Collection-169
94Topps/OPC Premier-173
Special Effects-173
94Upper Deck-23
Electric Ice-23
95Be A Player-144
Signatures-S144
Signatures Die Cuts-S144
95Parkhurst International-440
Emerald Ice-440
95Penguins Foodland-2
95Playoff One on One-299
95Upper Deck-394
Electric Ice-394
Electric Ice Gold-394
97Pacific Omega-110
Copper-110
Dark Gray-110
Emerald Green-110
Gold-110
Ice Blue-110
97Upper Deck-81
97Sudbury Wolves Anniversary-15
98Finest-103
No Protectors-103
No Protectors Refractors-103
Refractors-103
98Pacific-241
Ice Blue-241
Red-241
98Pacific Omega-111
Red-111
Opening Day Issue-111
98Panini Stickers-203
98Paramount-105
Copper-105
Emerald Green-105
Holo-Electric-105
Ice Blue-105
Silver-105
98Post-11
98SP Authentic-40
Power Shift-40
98UD Choice-99
98UD Choice Preview-99
98UD Choice Prime Choice Reserve-99
98UD Choice Reserve-99
98Upper Deck-284
Exclusives-284
Exclusives 1 of 1-284
Gold Reserve-284
99BAP Memorabilia-2
Gold-2
Silver-2
99O-Pee-Chee-65
99O-Pee-Chee Chrome-65
99O-Pee-Chee Chrome Refractors-65
99Pacific-193
Copper-193
Emerald Green-193
Gold-193
Ice Blue-193
Premiere Date-193
Red-193
99Pacific Omega-109
Copper-109
Gold-109
Ice Blue-109
Premiere Date-109
99Panini Stickers-261
99Paramount-110
Copper-110
Emerald-110
Gold-110
Holographic Emerald-110
Holographic Gold-110
Holographic Silver-110
Ice Blue-110
Premiere Date-110
Red-110
Silver-110
99Topps/OPC-65
99Topps/OPC Chrome-65
Refractors-65
99Upper Deck MVP ProSign-GM
99Upper Deck Victory-138
00BAP Memorabilia-122
Emerald-122
Ruby-122
Sapphire-122
Promos-122
00BAP Mem Chicago Sportsfest Copper-122
00BAP Memorabilia Chicago Sportsfest Blue-122
00BAP Memorabilia Chicago Sportsfest Gold-122
00BAP Memorabilia Chicago Sportsfest Ruby-122
00BAP Memorabilia Chicago Sun-Times Ruby-122
00BAP Memorabilia Chicago Sun-Times Gold-122
00BAP Mem Chicago Sun-Times Sapphire-122
00BAP Mem Toronto Fall Expo Copper-122
00BAP Memorabilia Toronto Fall Expo Gold-122
00BAP Memorabilia Toronto Fall Expo Ruby-122
00BAP Parkhurst 2000-P104
00BAP Signature Series-79
Emerald-79
Ruby-79
Sapphire-79
Autographs-40
Autographs Gold-40
00O-Pee-Chee-123
00O-Pee-Chee Parallel-123
00Pacific-198
Copper-198
Gold-198
Ice Blue-198
Premiere Date-198
00Panini Stickers-169
00Paramount-112
Copper-112
Gold-112
Holo-Gold-112
Holo-Silver-112
Ice Blue-112
Premiere Date-112
00Stadium Club-195
00Topps/OPC-123
Parallel-123
00Topps Chrome-94
OPC Refractors-94
Refractors-94
00UD Heroes-58
00Upper Deck-85
Exclusives Tier 1-85
Exclusives Tier 2-85
00Upper Deck Victory-113
00Upper Deck Vintage-167
01BAP Memorabilia-134
01BAP Memorabilia-463
Emerald-134
Emerald-463
Ruby-134
Ruby-463
Sapphire-134
Sapphire-463
01Crown Royale-10
Blue-10
Premiere Date-10
Red-10
Retail-10
01Pacific-183
Extreme LTD-183
Hobby LTD-183
Premiere Date-183
Retail LTD-183
01Pacific Arena Exclusives-183
01Parkhurst-126
01SPx-158
01Upper Deck-249
Exclusives-249
01Upper Deck Ice-86
01Upper Deck Victory-163
Gold-163
01Upper Deck Vintage-117
01Vanguard-6
Blue-6
Red-6
One of Ones-6
Premiere Date-6
Proofs-6
02Atomic-6
Blue-6
Gold-6
Red-6
Hobby Parallel-6
02BAP First Edition-208
02BAP First Edition-372
02BAP First Edition-374
02BAP First Edition-378
02BAP Memorabilia-67
Emerald-67
Ruby-67
Sapphire-67
NHL All-Star Game-67
NHL All-Star Game Blue-67
NHL All-Star Game Green-67
NHL All-Star Game Red-67
02BAP Memorabilia Toronto Fall Expo-67
02BAP Signature Series-53
Autographs-53
Autograph Buybacks 2000-40
Autographs Gold-53
Team Quads-TQ11
02Bruins Team Issue-4
02Crown Royale-6
Blue-6
Red-6
Retail-6
02O-Pee-Chee-142
02O-Pee-Chee Premier Blue Parallel-142
02O-Pee-Chee Premier Red Parallel-142
02O-Pee-Chee Factory Set-142
02Pacific-30
Blue-30
Red-30
02Pacific Complete-299
Red-299
02Pacific Exclusive-11
02Pacific Heads-Up-8
Blue-8
Purple-8
Red-8
02Pacific Quest for the Cup-7
Gold-7
Jerseys-2
02Parkhurst-12
Bronze-12
Gold-12
Silver-12
02Parkhurst Retro-36
Minis-36
02Private Stock Reserve-6
Blue-6
Red-6
Retail-6
02SP Game Used Authentic Fabrics-AFGM
02SP Game Used Authentic Fabrics Gold-AFGM
02SP Game Used Authentic Fabrics Rainbow-AFGM
02Titanium-7
Blue-7
Red-7
Retail-7
02Topps-142
OPC Blue Parallel-142
OPC Red Parallel-142
Own The Game-OTG9
Factory Set-142
02Topps Chrome-87
Black Border Refractors-87
Refractors-87
02Topps Heritage-85
Chrome Parallel-85
02Topps Total-259
02UD Honor Roll Grade A Jerseys-TSTM
02UD Mask Collection Patches-PGGM
02UD Piece of History-7
02UD Premier Collection Jerseys Bronze-GM
02UD Premier Collection Jerseys Gold-GM
02UD Premier Collection Jerseys Silver-GM
02UD Top Shelf Goal Oriented-GOGM
02UD Top Shelf Shooting Stars-SHGM
02Upper Deck-16
Exclusives-16
CHL Graduates-CGGM
CHL Graduates Gold-CGGM
Classic Portraits Hockey Royalty-GTM
Classic Portraits Hockey Royalty Limited-GTM
02Upper Deck Rookie Update-12
02Upper Deck Vintage-24
02Upper Deck Vintage-263
02Upper Deck Vintage-306
Green Backs-24
Jerseys-OSGM
02Vanguard-7
LTD-7
03BAP Memorabilia-29
Emerald-29
Gold-29
Ruby-29
Sapphire-29
03BAP Ultimate Memorabilia Autographs-34
Gold-34
03Beehive-14
Gold-14
Silver-14
03Black Diamond-79
Black-79
Green-79
Red-79
03Bowman-85
Gold-85
03Bowman Chrome-85
Refractors-85
Gold Refractors-85
Xfractors-85
03Bruins Team Issue-6
03Crown Royale-7
Blue-7
Retail-7
03ITG Action-14
First Time All-Star-FT8
Jerseys-M138
03ITG Used Signature Series-10
Gold-10
Autographs-GM
Autographs Gold-GM
Teammates-17
Teammates Gold-17
03NHL Sticker Collection-14
03O-Pee-Chee-276
03OPC Blue-276
03OPC Gold-276
03OPC Red-276
03Pacific-28
Blue-28
Red-28
03Pacific Calder-7
Silver-7
03Pacific Complete-18
Red-18
03Pacific Exhibit-14
Blue Backs-14
Yellow Backs-14
03Pacific Invincible-6
Blue-6
Red-6
Retail-6
03Pacific Prism-104
Blue-104
Patches-104
Red-104
Retail-104
03Pacific Quest for the Cup-8
Blue-8
03Pacific Supreme-6
Blue-6
Red-6
Retail-6
03Parkhurst Original Six Boston-23
Memorabilia-BM10
Memorabilia-BM54
03Private Stock Reserve-144
Blue-144
Patches-144
Red-144
Retail-144
03SP Game Used Authentic Fabrics-DFTM
03SP Game Used Authentic Fabrics Gold-DFTM
03SP Game Used Double Threads-DTTM
03SPx-8
Radiance-8
Spectrum-8
Fantasy Franchise-FF-TMS
Fantasy Franchise Limited-FF-TMS
VIP-VIP-TM
VIP Limited-VIP-TM
03Titanium-9
Hobby Jersey Number Parallels-9
Retail-9
Retail Jersey Number Parallels-9
03Topps-276
Blue-276
Gold-276
Red-276
03Topps C55-47
Minis-47
Minis American Back-47
Minis American Back Red-47
Minis Bazooka Back-47
Minis Brooklyn Back-47
Minis Hat Trick Back-47
Minis O Canada Back-47
Minis O Canada Back Red-47
Minis Stanley Cup Back-47
03Topps Pristine-69
Gold Refractor Die Cuts-69
Refractors-69
Press Plates Black-69
Press Plates Cyan-69
Press Plates Magenta-69
Press Plates Yellow-69
03UD Honor Roll Grade A Jerseys-TBOS
03UD Premier Collection Stars-ST-GM
03UD Premier Collection Stars Patches-ST-GM
03Upper Deck-261
Canadian Exclusives-261
HG-261
NHL Best-NB-GM
Patches-SP10
UD Exclusives-261
03Upper Deck Classic Portraits-7
Classic Stitches-CS-GM
03Upper Deck MVP-32
Gold Script-32
Silver Script-32
Canadian Exclusives-32
Lethal Lineups-LL3
SportsNut-SN9
03Upper Deck Rookie Update Skills-SKGM
03Upper Deck Rookie Update Super Stars-SSGM
03Upper Deck Trilogy-7
Limited-7
03Upper Deck Victory-13
Bronze-13
Gold-13
Silver-13
03Toronto Star-6
04Pacific-22
Blue-22
Red-22
04SP Authentic-10
04SP Authentic-100
05Be A Player-6
First Period-6
Second Period-6
Third Period-6
Overtime-6
Dual Signatures-TM
Quad Signatures-BOST
Signatures-GM
Signatures Gold-GM
05Beehive-11
Matte-11
Matted Materials-MMGM
05Black Diamond-117
Emerald-117
Gold-117
Onyx-117
Ruby-117
05Bruins Boston Globe-1
05Hot Prospects-10
En Fuego-10
Red Hot-10
White Hot-10
05Panini Stickers-23
05Parkhurst-37
Facsimile Auto Parallel-37
True Colors-TCBOS
True Colors-TCBOS
True Colors-TCMOBO
True Colors-TCMOBO
05SP Authentic-12
Limited-12
Sign of the Times-GM
Sign of the Times Duals-DBM
05SP Game Used-8
Gold-8
Authentic Fabrics-AF-GM
Authentic Fabrics Autographs-AAF-GM
Authentic Fabrics Gold-AF-GM
Authentic Fabrics Triple-TBM
Authentic Patches-AP-GM
Authentic Patches Autographs-AAP-GM
Authentic Patches Triple-TBM
Awesome Authentics-AA-GM
Awesome Authentics Gold-DA-GM
SIGnificance-GM
SIGnificance Gold-S-GM
Significant Numbers-SN-GM
Statscriptions-ST-GM
05SPx-9
Spectrum-9
Winning Combos-WC-BO
05The Cup Dual NHL Shields-DSMB
05The Cup Dual NHL Shields Autographs-ADSMB
05The Cup Emblems of Endorsement-EEGM
05The Cup Honorable Numbers-HNGM
05The Cup Limited Logos-LLGM
05The Cup Scripted Numbers-SNMN
05The Cup Scripted Swatches-SSGM
05The Cup Signature Patches-SPGM
05UD Artifacts-9
05UD Artifacts-155
Blue-9
Blue-155
Gold-9
Gold-155
Green-9
Green-155
Pewter-9
Pewter-155
Red-9
Red-155
Gold Autographed-9
Gold Autographed-155
05UD PowerPlay-10
Rainbow-10
Specialists-TSGM
Specialists Patches-SPGM
05Ultimate Collection-11
Gold-11
Endorsed Emblems-EEGM
05Ultra-18
Gold-18
Fresh Ink-FI-GM
Fresh Ink Blue-FI-GM
Ice-18
Scoring Kings-SK33
Scoring Kings Jerseys-SKJ-GM
Scoring Kings Jersey Autographs-KAJ-GM
Scoring Kings Patches-SKP-GM
Scoring Kings Patch Autographs-KAP-GM
05Upper Deck-256
Big Playmakers-B-GM
Jerseys-J-GM
Jerseys Series II-J2GM
Notable Numbers-N-GM
Patches-P-GM
Shooting Stars-S-GM
05Upper Deck Ice-11
Rainbow-11
Frozen Fabrics-FFGM
Frozen Fabrics Autographs-AFFGM
Frozen Fabrics Glass-FFGM
Frozen Fabrics Patches-FFPGM
Frozen Fabrics Patch Autographs-FAPGM
05Upper Deck MVP-27
Gold-27
Platinum-27
Materials-M-GM
05Upper Deck Rookie Update-10
05Upper Deck Trilogy-10
Honorary Patches-HP-GM
Honorary Patch Scripts-HSP-GM
Honorary Swatches-HS-GM
Honorary Swatch Scripts-HSS-GM
05Upper Deck Victory-13
Black-13

Gold-13
Silver-13
Game Breakers-GB4
06Be A Player-77
Autographs-77
Signatures-GM
Signatures 10-83
Signatures 25-83
Signatures Duals-DBO
Portraits Signature Portraits-SPGM
Portraits Triple Signature Portraits-TBOS
06Black Diamond-9
Black-9
Gold-9
Ruby-9
Gemography-GGM
06Flair Showcase-107
Parallel-107
Stitches-SSGM
06Fleer-20
Tiffany-20
06Hot Prospects Hot Materials -HMGM
06Hot Prospects Hot Materials Red Hot-HMGM
06Hot Prospects Hot Materials White Hot-HMGM
06NHL POG-36
06O-Pee-Chee-40
Rainbow-40
Swatches-S-GM
06Panini Stickers-19
06SP Game Used Inked Sweaters Dual-IS2MS
06SP Game Used Inked Sweaters Dual Patches-IS2MS
06The Cup Autographed NHL Shields Duals-DASBO
06The Cup Autographed NHL Shields Duals-DASPG
06UD Artifacts Tundra Tandems-TTMS
06UD Artifacts Tundra Tandems Black-TTMS
06UD Artifacts Tundra Tandems Blue-TTMS
06UD Artifacts Tundra Tandems Gold-TTMS
06UD Artifacts Tundra Tandems Red-TTMS
06UD Artifacts Tundra Tandems Dual Patches Red-TTMS
06UD Powerplay Specialists-SGM
06UD Powerplay Specialists Patches-PGM
06Ultra-19
Gold Medallion-19
Ice Medallion-19
Fresh Ink-IGM
06Upper Deck Arena Giveaways-BOS6
06Upper Deck-20
Exclusives Parallel-20
High Gloss Parallel-20
Game Jerseys-J2GM
Game Patches-P2GM
Masterpieces-20
Signatures-SGM
Signature Sensations-SSGM
06Upper Deck MVP-28
Gold Script-28
Super Script-28
06Upper Deck Ovation-153
06Upper Deck Victory-15
06Upper Deck Victory Black-15
06Upper Deck Victory Gold-15
07Upper Deck Victory-65
Black-65
Gold-65

Murray, Herman
37V356 Worldwide Gum-113

Murray, John
91ProCards-361
04Sioux Falls Stampede-3-4
05Sioux Falls Stampede-8
06Between The Pipes-23
Autographs-AJM
06Kitchener Rangers-16

Murray, Josh
04Williams Lake Timberwolves-15
04Williams Lake Timberwolves-22

Murray, Ken
37V356 Worldwide Gum-109

Murray, Marty
917th Inn. Sketch WHL-206
92Brandon Wheat Kings-17
93Donruss Team Canada-17
93Pinnacle-477
Canadian-477
93Upper Deck-550
93Brandon Wheat Kings-24
94Finest-161
Super Team Winners-161
Refractors-161
94Pinnacle-536
Artist's Proofs-536
Rink Collection-536
94SP-148
Die Cuts-148
94Brandon Wheat Kings-14
95Bowman-152
All-Foil-152
95Collector's Choice-405
95Donruss-284
Canadian World Junior Team-10
Rated Rookies-11
95Metal-185
95Parkhurst International-530
Emerald Ice-530
95Select Certified-141
Mirror Gold-141
95SkyBox Impact-192
95Stadium Club-198
Members Only Master Set-198
95Summit-191
Artist's Proofs-191
Ice-191
95Topps-338
OPC Inserts-338
Canadian World Juniors-6CJ
95Ultra-350
95Upper Deck-500
Electric Ice-500
Electric Ice Gold-500
95Zenith-142
95Saint John Flames-15
95Slapshot Memorial Cup-48
96Fleer Picks-178
96SkyBox Impact-155
96Saint John Flames-16
96Collector's Edge Future Legends-35
97Be A Player-199
Autographs-199
Autographs Die-Cuts-199
Autographs Prismatic Die-Cuts-199
97Donruss-221
Press Proofs Silver-221
Press Proofs Gold-221
97Donruss Limited-39
Exposure-39
97Saint John Flames-18
99German DEL-105
00BAP Memorabilia-468
Emerald-468
Ruby-468
Sapphire-468
00Topps Heritage-198
01Flyers Postcards-14
01Parkhurst-394
01Upper Deck Victory-365
Gold-365
02Flyers Postcards-17
02Pacific Complete-267
Red-267
03Hurricanes Postcards-13
03Pacific Complete-340
Red-340
05German DEL-335

Murray, Mike (Center)
90Knoxville Cherokees-108
93Knoxville Cherokees-11
93Quebec Pee-Wee Tournament-594
94Knoxville Cherokees-9
94Classic-114
Gold-114
95Dayton Bombers-16
99Knoxville Speed-10
00Knoxville Speed-24

Murray, Pat
90OPC Premier-79
90Pro Set-630
91Score American-321
91Score Canadian Bilingual-351
91Score Canadian English-351
91Upper Deck-451
French-451
91ProCards-276
94Knoxville Cherokees-20

Murray, Rem
92Michigan State Spartans-17
93Michigan State Spartans-14
96Be A Player Link to History-5A
96Be A Player Link to History Autographs-5A
96Be A Player Link to History Auto Silver-5A
96Black Diamond-17
Gold-17
96Collector's Choice-352
96Donruss Canadian Ice-123
Gold Press Proofs-123
Red Press Proofs-123
96Donruss Elite-145
Die Cut Stars-145
Aspirations-22
96Flair-111
Blue Ice-111
96Hockey Greats Coins-24
Gold-24
96Leaf Preferred-136
Press Proofs-136
96Metal Universe-188
96Oilers Postcards-17
96Select Certified-119
Artist's Proofs-119
Blue-119
Mirror Blue-119
Mirror Gold-119
Mirror Red-119
Red-119
96SP-178
96Ultra-60
Gold Medallion-60
Rookies-14
96Upper Deck-261
96Upper Deck Ice-19
Parallel-19
96Zenith-146
Artist's Proofs-146
96Collector's Edge Future Legends-14
97Collector's Choice-91
97Donruss-127
Press Proofs Silver-127
Press Proofs Gold-127
97Donruss Limited-141
97Donruss Limited-173
Exposure-141
Exposure-173
97Donruss Preferred-56
Cut to the Chase-56
97Leaf-140
Fractal Matrix-140
Fractal Matrix Die Cuts-140
97Leaf International-140
Universal Ice-140
97Pacific-112
Copper-112
Emerald Green-112
Ice Blue-112
Red-112
Silver-112
97Pacific Dynagon-50
Copper-50
Dark Grey-50
Emerald Green-50
Ice Blue-50
Red-50
Silver-50
Tandems-50
97Pacific Invincible-57
Copper-57
Emerald Green-57
Ice Blue-57
Red-57
Silver-57
97Pinnacle-133
Press Plates Back Black-133
Press Plates Back Cyan-133
Press Plates Back Magenta-133
Press Plates Back Yellow-133
Press Plates Front Black-133
Press Plates Front Cyan-133
Press Plates Front Magenta-133
Press Plates Front Yellow-133
97Pinnacle Inside-94
97Score-227
97Upper Deck-70
98Finest-84
No Protectors-84
No Protectors Refractors-84
Refractors-84
99BAP Memorabilia-63
Gold-63
Silver-63
99BAP Millennium-104
Emerald-104
Ruby-104
Sapphire-104
Signatures-104
Signatures Gold-104
99O-Pee-Chee-183
99O-Pee-Chee Chrome-183
99O-Pee-Chee Chrome Refractors-183
99Pacific-161
Copper-161
Emerald Green-161
Gold-161
Ice Blue-161
Premiere Date-161
Red-161
99Paramount-93
Copper-93
Emerald-93
Gold-93
Holographic Emerald-93
Holographic Gold-93
Holographic Silver-93
Ice Blue-93
Premiere Date-93
Red-93
Silver-93
99Topps/OPC-183
99Topps/OPC Chrome-183
Refractors-183
00Upper Deck NHLPA-PA34
01BAP Memorabilia-484
Emerald-484
Ruby-484
Sapphire-484
01Pacific-161
Extreme LTD-161
Hobby LTD-161
Premiere Date-161
Retail LTD-161
01Pacific Arena Exclusives-161
01Upper Deck-300
Exclusives-300
01Upper Deck Victory-141
Gold-141
02BAP Sig Series Auto Buybacks 1999-104
02Pacific Complete-100
Red-100
02Topps Total-33
03ITG Action-397
03Pacific Complete-320
Red-320
03Upper Deck-351
Canadian Exclusives-351
HG-351
UD Exclusives-351
06Finnish Cardset-202

Murray, Rob
88ProCards AHL-40
90Bowman-74
Tiffany-74
90Capitals Postcards-18
90Capitals Smokey-17
90O-Pee-Chee-460
90Pro Set-553
91Jets IGA-18
91Moncton Hawks-20
91ProCards-164
96Springfield Falcons-23
96Collector's Edge Future Legends-15
97Springfield Falcons-18
02Springfield Falcons-18
04Providence Bruins-24
05Providence Bruins-24

Murray, Robert
79Panini Stickers-99
82Swedish Semic VM Stickers-103

Murray, Robert Frederick
74NHL Action Stamps-5
75Canucks Royal Bank-14
76Canucks Royal Bank-12
76O-Pee-Chee NHL-309
77O-Pee-Chee NHL-12
77Topps-12
78O-Pee-Chee-89
78Topps-89
79Blackhawks Postcards-15
79O-Pee-Chee-55
79Topps-55
80O-Pee-Chee-181
80Topps-181
81Blackhawks Borderless Postcards-18
81O-Pee-Chee-61
81O-Pee-Chee Stickers-119
81Topps-W73
82Blackhawks Postcards-15
82O-Pee-Chee-70
83Blackhawks Postcards-15
83O-Pee-Chee-108
83O-Pee-Chee Stickers-109
83Topps Stickers-109
84O-Pee-Chee-41
84O-Pee-Chee Stickers-26
84Topps-32
85O-Pee-Chee-114
85Topps-114
86Blackhawks Coke-9
86O-Pee-Chee-64
86Topps-64
87Blackhawks Coke-13
87O-Pee-Chee-156
87Panini Stickers-223
87Topps-156
88Panini Stickers-22
89Blackhawks Coke-5
90O-Pee-Chee-138
90Score-376
Canadian-376
90Topps-138
Tiffany-138

Murray, Robert John
74O-Pee-Chee NHL-336
75O-Pee-Chee NHL-385
76O-Pee-Chee NHL-363

Murray, RW
94Saint John Flames-14
95Saint John Flames-16
96Louisiana Ice Gators-11
98Louisiana Ice Gators-2
99Louisiana Ice Gators-2
00Louisiana Ice Gators-13

Murray, Ryan
93Quebec Pee-Wee Tournament-593

Murray, Scott
91Air Canada SJHL-B38

Murray, Terry
73O-Pee-Chee-259
74O-Pee-Chee NHL-126
74Topps-126
81Capitals Team Issue-11
82Capitals Team Issue-17
82Post Cereal-20
88ProCards AHL-41
89Capitals Kodak-xx
89ProCards AHL-92
90Capitals Kodak-18
90Pro Set-679

Murray, Tim
92Saskatchewan JHL-110
96New Hampshire Wildcats-28
97Detroit Vipers-14
98Detroit Vipers-3
98Detroit Vipers Freschetta-10
99UK London Knights-12

Murray, Troy
82Blackhawks Postcards-16
83Blackhawks Postcards-16
83Canadian National Juniors-NNO
84O-Pee-Chee-42
85Blackhawks Team Issue-17
85O-Pee-Chee-146
85O-Pee-Chee Stickers-29
85Topps-146
86Blackhawks Coke-10
86O-Pee-Chee-25
86O-Pee-Chee Stickers-154
86O-Pee-Chee Stickers-189
86Topps-25
87Blackhawks Coke-14
87O-Pee-Chee-74
87O-Pee-Chee Stickers-79
87Panini Stickers-227
87Topps-74
88Blackhawks Coke-13
88Frito-Lay Stickers-32
88O-Pee-Chee-106
88O-Pee-Chee Stickers-10
88Panini Stickers-27
88Topps-106
89Blackhawks Coke-2
89O-Pee-Chee-219
89O-Pee-Chee Stickers-11
89Panini Stickers-48
90Blackhawks Coke-2
90Bowman-13
Tiffany-13
90O-Pee-Chee-160
90Panini Stickers-200
90Pro Set-57A
90Pro Set-57B
90Score-243
Canadian-243
90Topps-160
Tiffany-160
90Upper Deck-112
French-112
91Pro Set Platinum-247
91Bowman-388
91Jets IGA-19
91O-Pee-Chee-87
91OPC Premier-75
91Panini Stickers-17
91Parkhurst-206
French-206
91Pinnacle-33
French-33
91Pro Set-46
91Pro Set-514
91Pro Set-588
French-46
French-514
French-588
91Score American-53
91Score Canadian Bilingual-53
91Score Canadian Bilingual-585
91Score Canadian English-53
91Score Canadian English-585
91Score Rookie/Traded-35T
91Stadium Club-167
91Topps-87
91Upper Deck-565
French-565
92Bowman-93
92Humpty Dumpty I-17
92O-Pee-Chee-54
92Panini Stickers-57
92Panini Stickers French-57
92Pinnacle-49
French-49
92Pro Set-215
92Score-189
Canadian-189
92Seasons Patches-58
92Stadium Club-31
92Topps-284
Gold-284G
92Ultra-242
92Ultra-443
92Upper Deck-129
92North Dakota Fighting Sioux-36
93Blackhawks Coke-23
93OPC Premier-182
Gold-182
93Pinnacle-318
Canadian-318
93Score-272
Canadian-272
93Stadium Club-230
Members Only Master Set-230
OPC-230
First Day Issue-230
First Day Issue OPC-230
93Topps/OPC Premier-182
Gold-182
94Be A Player Signature Cards-176
94OPC Premier-188
Special Effects-188
94Pinnacle-139
Artist's Proofs-139
Rink Collection-139
94Senators Team Issue-23
94Topps/OPC Premier-188
Special Effects-188
04Sudbury Wolves-21
05Sudbury Wolves-6

Murray, Tyler
97Swift Current Broncos-13
98Swift Current Broncos-8

Mursak, Jan
06Saginaw Spirit-9

Murto, Matti
70Finnish Jaakiekko-70
70Finnish Jaakiekko-111
70Swedish Hockey-307
70Swedish Masterserien-159
70Swedish Masterserien-168
71Finnish Suomi Stickers-71
71Finnish Suomi Stickers-120
71Swedish Hockey-70
72Finnish Jaakiekko-67
72Finnish Jaakiekko-90
72Finnish Hellas-7
72Finnish Panda Toronto-8
72Finnish Panda Toronto-105
72Finnish Semic World Championship-83
72Swedish Semic World Championship-83
73Finnish Jaakiekko-136
74Finnish Jenkki-12
74Finnish Typotor-1
74Finnish Typotor-53
74Swedish Stickers-35
74Swedish Semic World Champ Stickers-86
77Finnish Sportscasters-41-961
78Finnish SM-Liiga-37
80Finnish Mallasjuoma-13
96Finnish SISU Redline-197

Murtovaara, Petri
95Finnish SISU-241

Murzin, Alexei
98Russian Hockey League-113
99Russian Hockey League-203
01Russian Hockey League-162

Murzyn, Dana
85Whalers Junior Wendy's-13
86O-Pee-Chee-58
86Topps-58
86Whalers Junior Thomas'-17
87Flames Red Rooster-17
87O-Pee-Chee-138
87Panini Stickers-42
87Topps-138
87Whalers Jr. Burger King/Pepsi-15
88Flames Postcards-23
90Flames IGA/McGavin's-15
90O-Pee-Chee-304
90Pro Set-41
90Score-274
Canadian-274
90Topps-304
Tiffany-304
90Upper Deck-348
French-348
91Canucks Autograph Cards-17
91Canucks Team Issue 8x10-17
91Flames Panini Team Stickers-12
91Pinnacle-260
French-260
91Pro Set-498
French-498
91Score American-357
91Score Canadian Bilingual-231
91Score Canadian English-231
92Bowman-71
92Canucks Road Trip Art-15
92O-Pee-Chee-241
92Pinnacle-172
French-172
92Score-168
Canadian-168
92Stadium Club-353
92Topps-194
Gold-194G
93Donruss-348
93Leaf-292
93OPC Premier-311
Gold-311
93Parkhurst-486
Emerald Ice-486
93Pinnacle-273
Canadian-273
93Score-298
Canadian-298
93Topps/OPC Premier-311
Gold-311
93Ultra-441
94Canucks Program Inserts-16
94Pinnacle-198
Artist's Proofs-198
Rink Collection-198
94Score-134
Gold-134
Platinum-134
95Canucks Building the Dream Art-5
96Be A Player-160
Autographs-160
Autographs Silver-160
96Canucks Postcards-5
97Pacific Dynagon Best Kept Secrets-97

Musa, Ivo
05Penticton Vees-13

Musakka, Joakim
93Swedish Semic Elitserien-54
94Swedish Leaf-282
95Swedish Leaf-33

Musatov, Vadim
99Russian Hockey League-244

Muscutt, Scott
01Bossier-Shreveport Mudbugs-14
02Bossier-Shreveport Mudbugs-20
03Bossier-Shreveport Mudbugs-19
05Bossier-Shreveport Mudbugs-21

Mushaluk, Jeff
04Maine Black Bears-28

Musial, David
94German DEL-292
95German DEL-282
99German Bundesliga 2-300
01German Upper Deck-118
02German DEL City Press-226
04German DEL-273

Musil, Frank
87North Stars Postcards-22
87Panini Stickers-292
88North Stars ADA-19
88Panini Stickers-87
89O-Pee-Chee-217
90Flames IGA/McGavin's-16
90Panini Stickers-258
90Pro Set-425
90Score-223
Canadian-223
90Score Rookie/Traded-19T
90Upper Deck-383
French-383
91Bowman-259
91Flames IGA-11
91O-Pee-Chee-68
91Pinnacle-282
French-282
91Pro Set-368
French-368
91Score American-142
91Score Canadian Bilingual-142
91Score Canadian English-142
91Stadium Club-235
91Topps-68
92Bowman-157
92Flames IGA-16
92O-Pee-Chee-66
92Pinnacle-51
French-51
92Score-83
Canadian-83
92Stadium Club-67
92Topps-142
Gold-142G
92Ultra-270
92Finnish Semic-126
93Leaf-236
93OPC Premier-229
Gold-229
93Pinnacle-101
Canadian-101
93PowerPlay-307
93Score-303
Canadian-303
93Stadium Club-169
Members Only Master Set-169
OPC-169
First Day Issue-169
First Day Issue OPC-169
93Topps/OPC Premier-229
Gold-229
93Ultra-283
94Leaf-545
94OPC Premier-258
Special Effects-258
94Pinnacle-64
Artist's Proofs-64
Rink Collection-64
94Score-139
Gold-139
Platinum-139
94Topps/OPC Premier-258
Special Effects-258
94Ultra-31
94Czech APS Extraliga-75
95Senators Team Issue-19
95Finnish Semic World Championships-162
95Swedish World Championships Stickers-197
96Senators Pizza Hut-15
96Swedish Semic Wien-111
97Pacific Invincible NHL Regime-136
97Panini Stickers-44
97Indianapolis Ice-19
99Upper Deck-227
Exclusives-227
Exclusives 1 of 1-227
99Upper Deck Gold Reserve-227
00Topps Heritage-210
00Upper Deck NHLPA-PA35
01BAP Signature Series-99
Autographs-99
Autographs Gold-99
02BAP Sig Series Auto Buybacks 2001-99

Musil, Lukas
04Czech OFS-170

Musil, Mojmir
97Czech APS Extraliga-189
98Czech DS Stickers-162
99Czech OFS-370
02Czech OFS Plus-161
03Czech OFS Plus-121
03UK London Racers-12
04Czech OFS-395

Muspratt, Ryan
03Camrose Kodiaks-12

Muss, Benedikt
94German First League-369

Musselman, Kody
06Oshawa Generals-11

Musselman, Kyle
04Sudbury Wolves-10

Mustaniemi, Ari
70Finnish Jaakiekko-374

Mustonen, Jouni
91Finnish Jyvas-Hyva Stickers-39

Mustonen, Pasi
80Finnish Mallasjuoma-59

Mustonen, Tomi
05Finnish Cardset -278
06Finnish Cardset-105

Mustukovs, Ervins
03Drummondville Voltigeurs-18

Muswagon, Jamie
99OCN Blizzard-10
00OCN Blizzard-9
01OCN Blizzard-12

Mutch, Tom
91ProCards-441
99Memphis RiverKings All-Time-1

Muth, Ryan
03Camrose Kodiaks-24

Muukkonen, Jarmo
92Finnish Jyvas-Hyva Stickers-118
93Finnish SISU-267
94Finnish SISU-81
95Finnish SISU-90
96Finnish SISU Redline-85

Muzechka, Mike
97Portland Winter Hawks-3
98Tri-City Americans-18

Muzerall, Nadine
98Minnesota Golden Gophers Women-15
01Sports Illustrated for Kids III-31

Muzzatti, Jason
91ProCards-592
92Salt Lake Golden Eagles-16
92Classic-114
Gold-114
92Classic Four-Sport *-221
Gold-221
93Ultra-284
93Upper Deck-482
94Leaf-470
94OPC Premier-373
Special Effects-373
94Topps/OPC Premier-373
Special Effects-373
94Saint John Flames-15
95Parkhurst International-362
Emerald Ice-362
95Upper Deck-491
Electric Ice-491
Electric Ice Gold-491
95Whalers Bob's Stores-18
95Images-52
Gold-52
96Be A Player-131
Autographs-131
Autographs Silver-131
96Collector's Choice-117
96Flair-42
Blue Ice-42
96Upper Deck-71
96Whalers Kid's Club-2
97Pacific Invincible NHL Regime-40
97Score Rangers-17
Platinum-17
Premier-17
97Hartford Wolf Pack-13
99Finnish Cardset-314
Puck Stoppers-5
00German DEL-25
02Finnish Cardset-76

Myagkikh, Alexei
99Russian Hockey League-263

Mydan, Scott
87Portland Winter Hawks-19
88Portland Winter Hawks-19
89Portland Winter Hawks-17
907th Inn. Sketch WHL-333

Myers, Aran
99Guelph Storm-21

Myers, Josh
07Dubuque Fighting Saints-19

Myers, Matt
03UK Cardiff Devils-3
04UK Nottingham Panthers-15
06UK Nottingham Panthers-9

Myers, Mike
92Alberta International Team Canada-14

Myers, Murray
73Vancouver Blazers-17

Myers, Scott
98Prince George Cougars-15
00Muskegon Fury-29
00Quad-City Mallards-21
01New Mexico Scorpions-13
02New Mexico Scorpions-10

Myhre, Geir
92Norwegian Elite Series-18

Myhres, Brantt
907th Inn. Sketch WHL-317
917th Inn. Sketch WHL-360
94Lightning Photo Album-19
94Lightning Postcards-13
94Atlanta Knights-24
95Donruss-45
95Leaf-75
95Ultra-154
Gold Medallion-154
95Upper Deck-23
Electric Ice-23
Electric Ice Gold-23
95Atlanta Knights-9
97Be A Player-203
Autographs-203
Autographs Die-Cuts-203
Autographs Prismatic Die-Cuts-203
97Pacific-334
Copper-334
Emerald Green-334
Ice Blue-334
Red-334
Silver-334
00Topps Heritage-208
02Providence Bruins-17
04Lowell Lock Monsters-16
04Lowell Lock Monsters Photo Album-16

Mylander, Kevin
93Seattle Thunderbirds-16

Mylek, Larry
93Quebec Pee-Wee Tournament-852

Myles, David
89Windsor Spitfires-12
907th Inn. Sketch OHL-111
917th Inn. Sketch OHL-191

Myles, Mark
89Peterborough Petes-113
897th Inn. Sketch OHL-113
907th Inn. Sketch OHL-366

Myles, Vic
34Beehive Group I Photos-288

Myllari, Roy
83Ottawa 67's-20

Myllykoski, Mikko
93Finnish Jyvas-Hyva Stickers-45
93Finnish SISU-237
94Finnish SISU-317
95Finnish SISU-22
96Finnish SISU Redline-110
98Finnish Kerailysarja-190
99Finnish Cardset-110
00Swiss Panini Stickers-301
01Finnish Cardset-281
02Finnish Cardset-223
03Finnish Cardset-91
04Finnish Cardset-156
04Finnish Cardset Signatures-31

Myllymaki, Ari
66Finnish Jaakiekkosarja-117

Myllyniemi, Jere
02Finnish Cardset-224
03Finnish Cardset-1
04Finnish Cardset-1
Parallel-1

Myllyniemi, Mikko
65Finnish Hellas-40
66Finnish Jaakiekkosarja-50

Myllys, Jarmo
88ProCards IHL-26
89ProCards IHL-95
90OPC Premier-80
91O-Pee-Chee Inserts-8S
91OPC Premier-15
91Parkhurst-162
French-162
91Sharks Sports Action-17
91Upper Deck-537
French-537
91ProCards-509
92Bowman-125
92Stadium Club-113
92Topps-251
Gold-251G
92Upper Deck Euro-Stars-E19
93Finnish Jyvas-Hyva Stickers-224
93Finnish SISU-183
93Swedish Semic World Champ Stickers-47
94Finnish SISU-160
94Finnish SISU Specials-9
94Finnish Jaa Kiekko-1
94Finnish Jaa Kiekko-332
94Swedish Leaf-260
Foreign Affairs-4
95Finnish Jaa Kiekko Lehti Ad Cards-1
95Finnish SISU Gold Cards-2
95Finnish SISU Limited-28
95Finnish Karjala World Champ Labels-11
95Finnish Kellogg's-1
95Finnish Semic World Championships-35
95Finnish Semic World Championships-207
95Swedish Leaf-74
95Swedish Leaf-302
Mega-12
Spidermen-8
95Swedish Upper Deck-113
95Swedish Upper Deck-230
95Swedish Globe World Championships-128
95Swedish World Championships Stickers-161
96Swedish Semic Wien-1
All-Stars-AS1
Super Goalies-SG3
97Swedish Collector's Choice-117
Stick'Ums-S7
98Finnish Kerailysarja Leijonat-2
98Swedish UD Choice-133
Day in the Life-7
99Finnish Cardset Aces High-D-A
99Swedish Upper Deck-135
SHL Signatures-13
Snapshots-10
00Swedish Upper Deck-120
00Swedish Upper Deck-202
Masked Men-M5
SHL Excellence-S4
01Finnish Cardset-159
01Finnish Cardset-182
01Finnish Cardset Haltmeisters-6
02Finnish Cardset-225
03Finnish Cardset-128
04Finnish Cardset-136
04Finnish Cardset Signatures-26
04Swedish Pure Skills-135
Parallel-135
05Finnish Cardset Super Snatchers-13

Mylnikov Jr., Sergei
99Russian Hockey League-47
99Russian Hockey League-60
00Russian Hockey League-44
06ITG International Ice Cornerstones-IC10
06ITG International Ice Passing The Torch-PTT5
06ITG International Ice Passing The Torch Gold-PTT5

Mylnikov, Dmitri
98Russian Hockey League-22
99Russian Hockey League-51
99Russian Hockey League-60

Mylnikov, Sergei
87Russian National Team-15
89Nordiques Team Issue-33
89Nordiques General Foods-24
89Nordiques Police-21
89Russian National Team-20
89Swedish Semic World Champ Stickers-79
90O-Pee-Chee-445
06ITG International Ice Cornerstones-IC10
06ITG International Ice Cornerstones Gold-IC10
06ITG International Ice Emblems-GUE18
06ITG International Ice Emblems Gold-GUE18
06ITG International Ice Goaltending Glory-GG20
06ITG International Ice Goaltending Glory Gold-GG20
06ITG International Ice International Rivals-IR07
06ITG International Ice Jerseys-GUJ18
06ITG International Ice Jerseys Gold-GUJ18
06ITG International Ice Numbers-GUN18
06ITG International Ice Numbers Gold-GUN18
06ITG International Ice Passing The Torch-PTT5
06ITG International Ice Passing The Torch Gold-PTT5
06ITG International Ice Quad Patch-QP04
06ITG International Ice Quad Patch Gold-QP04

Mylymok, Jeremy
91Air Canada SJHL-C5
96Pensacola Ice Pilots-4
96Toledo Storm-29
98Chicago Wolves-20
98Chicago Wolves Turner Cup-6
00Idaho Steelheads-15
01Idaho Steelheads-23
01Idaho Steelheads-4
04Idaho Steelheads-5
05Idaho Steelheads-17

Myntinen, Mikko
70Finnish Jaakiekko-213
71Finnish Suomi Stickers-136
72Finnish Jaakiekko-199
73Finnish Jaakiekko-160

Myre, Dan
98Thunder Bay Thunder Cats-13
99Knoxville Speed-11
00Knoxville Speed-23

Myre, Marc
05Chicoutimi Sagueneens-13

Myre, Phil
69Canadiens Postcards Color-19
70Esso Power Players-18
70Sargent Promotions Stamps-112
71Canadiens Postcards-16
71Sargent Promotions Stamps-101
71Toronto Sun-159
72Flames Postcards-11
72O-Pee-Chee-43
72Sargent Promotions Stamps-2
72Topps-109
73O-Pee-Chee-77
73Topps-77
74NHL Action Stamps-10
74O-Pee-Chee NHL-270
75O-Pee-Chee NHL-308
75Topps-308
76O-Pee-Chee NHL-17
76Topps-17
77O-Pee-Chee NHL-193
77Topps-193
78Blues Postcards-16
78O-Pee-Chee-87
78Topps-87
79O-Pee-Chee-189
79Topps-189
80O-Pee-Chee-8
80Topps-8
81Rockies Postcards-21
89Red Wings Little Caesars-22
93Blackhawks Coke-30
96Senators Pizza Hut-16
02Senators Team Issue-30
04ITG Franchises US East-308
Autographs-A-PMY

Myre, Sam
99UHL All-Stars East-4T

Myreng, Kjell Erik
92Norwegian Elite Series-78

Myres, Johnny
24Crescent Falcon-Tigers-11

Myrra, Jouko
94Finnish SISU-344
95Finnish SISU-147

00Finnish Cardset-317

Myrvold, Anders
94Finnish Jaa Kiekko-254
95Donruss-228
95Parkhurst International-517
Emerald Ice-517
96Leaf-220
Press Proofs-220
96Summit-197
Artist's Proofs-197
Ice-197
Metal-197
Premium Stock-197
97Providence Bruins-10
98Swedish UD Choice-54
99Norwegian National Team-19
99Swedish Upper Deck-6
Snapshots-1
00Upper Deck NHLPA-PA56
02German DEL City Press-248
03Grand Rapids Griffins-15

Myshkin, Vladimir
80USSR Olympic Team Mini Pics-7
81Swedish Semic Hockey VM Stickers-38
82Swedish Semic VM Stickers-52
83Swedish Semic VM Stickers-52
84Russian National Team-14
89Russian National Team-19
06Between The Pipes Double Jerseys-DJ09
06Between The Pipes Double Jerseys Gold-DJ09
06Between The Pipes Playing For Your Country-PC16
06Between The Pipes Playing For Your Country Gold-PC16
06ITG International Ice-136
Gold-136
Autographs-AVM
Cornerstones-IC10
Cornerstones Gold-IC10
Emblems-GUE07
Emblems Gold-GUE07
Goaltending Glory-GG16
Goaltending Glory Gold-GG16
International Rivals-IR13
International Rivals Gold-IR13
Jerseys-GUJ07
Jerseys Gold-GUJ07
Numbers-GUN07
Numbers Gold-GUN07
Passing The Torch-PTT8
Passing The Torch Gold-PTT8
Quad Patch-QP04
Quad Patch Gold-QP04

Myson, Bobby
93Quebec Pee-Wee Tournament-155

Mytta, Jouko
99Finnish Cardset-105

Myyrylainen, Reijo
70Finnish Jaakiekko-283

N'Goy, Michel
01Swiss HNL-264
02Swiss HNL-294

Naatanen, Matti
02Finnish Cardset-238
04Finnish Cardset-208

Nabokov, Dmitri
94Select-159
Gold-159
95SP-177
95Upper Deck-552
Electric Ice-552
Electric Ice Gold-552
95Signature Rookies Auto-Phonex-30
95Signature Rook Auto-Phonex Phone Cards-30
95Signature Rookies Tetrad *-70
Signatures-69
96Regina Pats-25
97Black Diamond-85
Double Diamond-85
Triple Diamond-85
Quadruple Diamond-85
97Revolution-31
Copper-31
Emerald-31
Ice Blue-31
Silver-31
97Indianapolis Ice-20
97Bowman CHL-119
OPC-119
98Pacific-150
Ice Blue-150
Red-150
98SPx Finite-19
Radiance-19
Spectrum-19
98UD Choice-50
Prime Choice Reserve-50
Reserve-50
98Upper Deck-319
Exclusives-319
Exclusives 1 of 1-319
Generation Next-GN29
Generation Next Quantum 1-GN29
Generation Next Quantum 2-GN29
Generation Next Quantum 3-GN29
Gold Reserve-319
MVP ProSign-DN
99BAP Memorabilia-263
Gold-263
Silver-263
99Upper Deck-83
Exclusives-83
Exclusives 1 of 1-83
99Upper Deck Gold Reserve-83
99Upper Deck MVP-127
Gold Script-127
Silver Script-127
Super Script-127
99Upper Deck Victory-180
99Lowell Lock Monsters-13
00BAP Memorabilia-363
Emerald-363
Ruby-363
Sapphire-363
Promos-363
00BAP Mem Chicago Sportsfest Copper-363
00BAP Memorabilia Chicago Sportsfest Blue-363
00BAP Memorabilia Chicago Sportsfest Gold-363
00BAP Memorabilia Chicago Sportsfest Ruby-363
00BAP Memorabilia Chicago Sun-Times Ruby-363
00BAP Memorabilia Chicago Sun-Times Gold-363
00BAP Mem Chicago Sun-Times Sapphire-363
00BAP Mem Toronto Fall Expo Copper-363
00BAP Memorabilia Toronto Fall Expo Gold-363
00BAP Memorabilia Toronto Fall Expo Ruby-363
00O-Pee-Chee-281
00O-Pee-Chee Parallel-281
00Topps/OPC-281
Parallel-281
00Topps Chrome-176
OPC Refractors-176
Refractors-176
00Russian Hockey League-152

Nabokov, Evgeni
97Kentucky Thoroughblades-10
98Kentucky Thoroughblades-17
99BAP Memorabilia-328
Gold-328
Silver-328
99Pacific Omega-212
Copper-212
Gold-212
Ice Blue-212
Premiere Date-212
99Cleveland Lumberjacks-14
00BAP Memorabilia-140
Emerald-140
Ruby-140
Sapphire-140
Promos-140
00BAP Mem Chicago Sportsfest Copper-140
00BAP Memorabilia Chicago Sportsfest Blue-140
00BAP Memorabilia Chicago Sportsfest Gold-140
00BAP Memorabilia Chicago Sportsfest Ruby-140
00BAP Memorabilia Chicago Sun-Times Ruby-140
00BAP Memorabilia Chicago Sun-Times Gold-140
00BAP Mem Chicago Sun-Times Sapphire-140
00BAP Mem Toronto Fall Expo Copper-140
00BAP Memorabilia Toronto Fall Expo Gold-140
00BAP Memorabilia Toronto Fall Expo Ruby-140
00BAP Parkhurst 2000-P241
00BAP Signature Series-292
Emerald-292
Ruby-292
Sapphire-292
00Black Diamond-108
00Crown Royale-140
21st Century Rookies-22
00O-Pee-Chee-303
00O-Pee-Chee Parallel-303
00Pacific-362
Copper-362
Gold-362
Ice Blue-362
Premiere Date-362
00Private Stock-144
Gold-144
Premiere Date-144
Retail-144
Silver-144
00SP Authentic-75
00SPx-146
00Titanium-143
Retail-143
All-Stars-8W
Three-Star Selections-27
00Titanium Draft Day Edition-143
00Titanium Draft Day Promos-143
00Topps/OPC-303
Parallel-303
00Topps Chrome-198
OPC Refractors-198
Refractors-198
00Topps Gold Label Class 1-92
Gold-92
00Topps Gold Label Class 2-92
00Topps Gold Label Class 2 Gold-92
00Topps Gold Label Class 3-92
00Topps Gold Label Class 3 Gold-92
00Topps Heritage-145
00Topps Premier Plus Private Signings-PSEN
00UD Reserve-73
00Upper Deck Ice-76
00Upper Deck MVP-203
First Stars-203
Second Stars-203
Third Stars-203
00Upper Deck Victory-278
00Vanguard-145
Pacific Proofs-145
00Czech Stadion-125
00Kentucky Thoroughblades-SP2
01McFarlane Hockey-90
01McFarlane Hockey-91
01Atomic-85
Blue-85
Gold-85
Premiere Date-85
Red-85
Statosphere-9
Team Nucleus-12
01BAP Memorabilia-4
Emerald-4
Ruby-4
Sapphire-4
All-Star Jerseys-ASJ1
All-Star Emblems-ASE1
All-Star Numbers-ASN1
All-Star Teammates-AST1
All-Star Teammates-AST9
He Shoots-He Scores Points-8
01BAP Signature Series-24
Autographs-24
Autographs Gold-24
Jerseys-GJ-98
01BAP Ultimate Memorabilia Calder Trophy-1
01BAP Ultimate Mem Legend Terry Sawchuk-15
01BAP Ultimate Memorabilia Retro Trophies-11
01BAP Update He Shoots-He Scores Prizes-10
01Between the Pipes-27
All-Star Jerseys-ASJ10
Double Memorabilia-DM13
Future Wave-FW7
Goalie Gear-GG18
He Shoots-He Saves Points-7
He Shoots-He Saves Prizes-12
Jerseys-GJ31
Emblems-GUE10
Jersey and Stick Cards-GSJ29
Masks-27
Masks Silver-27
Masks Gold-27
Tandems-GT1
Trophy Winners-TW3
01Bowman YoungStars-163
Gold-163
Ice Cubed-163
01Crown Royale Calder Collection Gold Ed-1
01Crown Royale Calder Collection AS Ed-C5
01Crown Royale-124
Blue-124
Premiere Date-124
Red-124
Retail-124
01Crown Royale Toronto Expo Rookie Coll-G7
01eTopps-6
01McDonald's Pacific-35
Future Legends-4
01O-Pee-Chee-82
01O-Pee-Chee Heritage Parallel-82
01O-Pee-Chee Heritage Parallel Limited-82
01O-Pee-Chee Premier Parallel-82
01Pacific-340
01Pacific-441
01Pacific-450
Extreme LTD-340
Gold-441
Hobby LTD-340
Premiere Date-340
Retail LTD-340
All-Stars-W9
Gold Crown Die-Cuts-19
Steel Curtain-18
01Pacific Adrenaline-167
Blue-167
Premiere Date-167
Red-167
Retail-167
Creased Lightning-19
Power Play-32
01Pacific Arena Exclusives-340
01Pacific Arena Exclusives-441
01Pacific Heads-Up-84
Blue-84
Premiere Date-84
Red-84
Silver-84
All-Star Net-1
Breaking the Glass-17
Prime Picks-7
Showstoppers-18
01Parkhurst-93
Gold-93
Silver-93
01Private Stock-85
Gold-85
Premiere Date-85
Retail-85
Silver-85
01Private Stock Pacific Nights-85
01Private Stock PS-2002-64
01Private Stock Reserve-G9
01SP Authentic-73
Limited-73
Limited Gold-73
01SP Game Used-47
01SPx-55
01Sports Illustrated for Kids III-225
01Sports Illustrated for Kids III-413
01Stadium Club-48
Award Winners-48
Master Photos-48
Gallery-G31
Gallery Gold-G31
New Regime-NR4
New Regime-NRAEN
01Titanium-122
Hobby Parallel-122
Premiere Date-122
Retail-122
Retail Parallel-122
Three-Star Selections-8
01Titanium Draft Day Edition-86
01Topps-82
Heritage Parallel-82
Heritage Parallel Limited-82
OPC Parallel-82
Autographs-AEN
01Topps Chrome-82
Refractors-82
Black Border Refractors-82
01Topps Heritage-2
01Topps Heritage-133
Refractors-2
01Topps Reserve-10
01UD Challenge for the Cup-72
Backstops-BB8
01UD Mask Collection-125
01UD Mask Collection-187
Gold-125
Gold-187
01UD Playmakers-83
01UD Premier Collection-42
01UD Top Shelf-36
All-Star Nets-NEN
01Upper Deck-374
Exclusives-374
Goalies in Action-GL4
Last Line of Defense-LL8
01Upper Deck Ice-37
01Upper Deck MVP-160
Masked Men-MM8
01Upper Deck Victory-289
01Upper Deck Victory-300
01Upper Deck Victory-437
Gold-289
Gold-300
Gold-437
01Upper Deck Vintage-209
01Upper Deck Vintage-216
01Vanguard-86
Blue-86
Red-86
One of Ones-86
Premiere Date-86
Proofs-86
Stonewallers-17
V-Team-9
02Atomic-86
Blue-86
Gold-86
Red-86
Denied-18
Hobby Parallel-86
02BAP All-Star Edition-63
Jerseys-63
Jerseys Gold-63
Jerseys Silver-63
02BAP First Edition-72
02BAP First Edition-380
Jerseys-72
02BAP Memorabilia-14
Emerald-14
Ruby-14
Sapphire-14
All-Star Jerseys-ASJ-38
All-Star Teammates-AST-23
NHL All-Star Game-14
NHL All-Star Game Blue-14
NHL All-Star Game Green-14
NHL All-Star Game Red-14
02BAP Memorabilia Toronto Fall Expo-14
02BAP Signature Series-7
Autographs-7
Autograph Buybacks 2001-24
Autographs Gold-7
Phenoms-YP10
Team Quads-TQ18
02Between the Pipes-9
02Between the Pipes-146
Gold-9
Silver-9
All-Star Stick and Jersey-6
Blockers-3
Emblems-7
Goalie Autographs-16
He Shoots-He Saves Points-7
He Shoots-He Saves Prizes-12
Jerseys-7
Masks II-24
Masks II Gold-24
Masks II Silver-24
Numbers-7
Stick and Jerseys-7
Tandems-4
02Bowman YoungStars-84
Gold-84
Silver-84
02Crown Royale-85
Blue-85
Red-85
Retail-85
Dual Patches-19
02eTopps-24
02ITG Used-63
02ITG Used-163
02McDonald's Pacific-34
Glove Side Net-Fusions-6
02O-Pee-Chee-234
02O-Pee-Chee Premier Blue Parallel-234
02O-Pee-Chee Premier Red Parallel-234
02O-Pee-Chee Factory Set-234
02Pacific-337
Blue-337
Red-337
Jerseys-45
Jerseys Holo-Silver-45
Maximum Impact-7
02Pacific Calder-3
Silver-3
02Pacific Complete-431
Red-431
02Pacific Exclusive-150
Advantage-14
02Pacific Heads-Up-108
Blue-108
Purple-108
Red-108
Bobble Heads-9
Inside the Numbers-19
Quad Jerseys-24
Quad Jerseys Gold-24
Showstoppers-18
02Pacific Quest for the Cup-86
Gold-86
02Pacific Toronto Fall Expo-10
Gold-10
02Parkhurst-11
Bronze-11
Gold-11
Silver-11
Hardware-V2
Teammates-TT15
02Parkhurst Retro-107
Minis-107
02Private Stock Reserve-141
Red-141
Retail-141
InCrease Security-19
Patches-141
02Sharks Team Issue-4
02SP Authentic-74
Beckett Promos-74
Sign of the Times-EN
Sign of the Times-KN
02SP Game Used-42
02SPx-63
02SPx-98
Spectrum Gold-63
Spectrum Gold-98
Spectrum Silver-63
Spectrum Silver-98
02Stadium Club-51
Silver Decoy Cards-51
Proofs-51
Puck Stops Here-PSH3
02Titanium-87
Blue-87
Red-87
Retail-87
02Topps-234
OPC Blue Parallel-234
OPC Red Parallel-234
Own The Game-OTG18
Factory Set-234
02Topps Chrome-128
Black Border Refractors-128
Refractors-128
02Topps Heritage-98
Chrome Parallel-98
02Topps Total-19
02UD Artistic Impressions-74
Gold-74
02UD Artistic Impressions Beckett Promos-74
02UD Artistic Impressions Retrospectives-R74
02UD Artistic Impressions Retrospect Gold-R74
02UD Artistic Impressions Retrospect Silver-R74
02UD Honor Roll-60
02UD Mask Collection-72
02UD Mask Collection-73
02UD Mask Collection-74
02UD Mask Collection-104
02UD Mask Collection Beckett Promos-72
02UD Mask Collection Beckett Promos-73
02UD Mask Collection Beckett Promos-74
02UD Mask Collection Mini Masks-EN
02UD Mask Collection Mini Masks Autos-EN
02UD Piece of History-76
Awards Collection-AC23
02UD Premier Collection-45A
02UD Top Shelf-73
02Upper Deck-147
Exclusives-147
Last Line of Defense-LL11
Super Saviors-SA12
02Upper Deck Classic Portraits-83
02Upper Deck MVP-154
Gold-154
Classics-154
Golden Classics-154
02Upper Deck Rookie Update-88
02Upper Deck Victory-179
Bronze-179
Gold-179
Silver-179
02Upper Deck Vintage-215
02Upper Deck Vintage-285
02Upper Deck Vintage-316
Tall Boys-T55
Tall Boys Gold-T55
02Vanguard-85
LTD-85
Jerseys-41
Jerseys Gold-41
03BAP Memorabilia-118
Emerald-118
Gold-118
Ruby-118
Sapphire-118
03BAP Ultimate Memorabilia Autographs-73
Gold-73
03BAP Ultimate Mem Franch Present Future-26
03BAP Ultimate Memorabilia Triple Threads-6
03Beehive-163
Gold-163
Silver-163
03Black Diamond-78
Black-78
Green-78
Red-78
03Bowman-51
Gold-51
03Bowman Chrome-51
Refractors-51
Gold Refractors-51
Xfractors-51
03Crown Royale-87
Blue-87
Retail-87
Gauntlet of Glory-17
Global Conquest-5
03ITG Action-464
Jerseys-M139
Jerseys-M266
03ITG Used Signature Series-88
Gold-88
Autographs-EN
Autographs Gold-EN
Franchise-25
Franchise Autographs-25
Franchise Gold-25
Goalie Gear-15
Goalie Gear Autographs-15
Goalie Gear Gold-15
Triple Memorabilia-19
Triple Memorabilia Gold-19
03NHL Sticker Collection-290
03O-Pee-Chee-168
03OPC Blue-168
03OPC Gold-168
03OPC Red-168
03Pacific-298
Blue-298
Red-298
03Pacific Calder-88
Silver-88
03Pacific Complete-446
Red-446
03Pacific Exhibit-191
Blue Backs-191
03Pacific Invincible-84
Blue-84
Red-84
Retail-84
Freeze Frame-19
Jerseys-28
03Pacific Prism-88
Blue-88
Gold-88
Red-88
03Pacific Quest for the Cup-90
Blue-90
03Pacific Supreme-85
Blue-85
Red-85
Retail-85
03Parkhurst Rookie Jerseys-GJ-9
03Parkhurst Rookie Jersey Autographs-GUJ-EN
03Parkhurst Rookie Jerseys Gold-GJ-9
03Parkhurst Rookie ROYalty-VR-20
03Parkhurst Rookie ROYalty Gold-VR-20
03Private Stock Reserve-91
Blue-91
Red-91
Retail-91
Increase Security-14
03Sharks Postcards-12
03SP Authentic-71
Limited-71
03SP Game Used-39
Gold-39
03SPx-81
Radiance-81
Spectrum-81
03Titanium-89
Hobby Jersey Number Parallels-89
Retail-89
Retail Jersey Number Parallels-89
03Topps-168
Blue-168
Gold-168
Red-168
03Topps Pristine-94
Gold Refractor Die Cuts-94
Refractors-94
Mini-PM-EN
Press Plates Black-94
Press Plates Cyan-94
Press Plates Magenta-94
Press Plates Yellow-94
03UD Honor Roll-70
03UD Premier Collection-46
03Upper Deck-163
Canadian Exclusives-163
HG-163
03Upper Deck Classic Portraits-82
03Upper Deck Ice-73
Gold-73
03Upper Deck MVP-357
Gold Script-357
Silver Script-357
Canadian Exclusives-357
SportsNut-SN73
03Upper Deck Rookie Update-72
Top Draws-TD1
03Upper Deck Trilogy-82
Limited-82
03Upper Deck Victory-161
Bronze-161
Gold-161
Silver-161
03Toronto Star-75
04Pacific-232
Blue-232
Red-232
04SP Authentic-74
Limited-74
Buybacks-56
Buybacks-57
Sign of the Times-DS-NK
04UD All-World-35
Gold-35
Quad Autographs-AQ-GOL
Five Autographs-AF-GOL
04Ultimate Collection-35
04Upper Deck-149
Canadian Exclusives-149
HG Glossy Gold-149
HG Glossy Silver-149
04Russian Back to Russia-33
05Be A Player-75
First Period-75
Second Period-75
Third Period-75
Overtime-75
05Beehive-77
05Beehive-210
Beige -77
Blue -77
Gold-77
Red -77
Matte-77
05Black Diamond-141
Emerald-141
Gold-141
Onyx-141
Ruby-141
05Hot Prospects-84
En Fuego-84
Red Hot-84
White Hot-84
05Panini Stickers-343
05Parkhurst-403
Facsimile Auto Parallel-403
True Colors-TCSJS
True Colors-TCSJS
True Colors-TCSJLA
True Colors-TCSJLA
05SP Authentic-83
05SP Authentic-126
Limited-83
Limited-126
Chirography-SPEN
Octographs-OG
Prestigious Pairings-PPKN
Sign of the Times Duals-DNC
Sign of the Times Fives-TNCMC
05SP Game Used-83
Autographs-83
Gold-83
SIGnificance-EN
SIGnificance Gold-S-EN
05SPx-75
Spectrum-75
Winning Combos-WC-KN
Xcitement Superstars-XS-EN
Xcitement Superstars Gold-XS-EN
Xcitement Superstars Spectrum-XS-EN
05The Cup-85
Gold-85
Black Rainbow-85
Emblems of Endorsement-EEEN
Hardware Heroes-HHEN
Limited Logos-LLEN
Masterpiece Pressplates-85
Masterpiece Pressplates (Rookie Update)-244
Noble Numbers Dual-DNNNK
Patch Variation-P85
Patch Variation Autographs-AP85
Scripted Numbers-SNBN
Scripted Swatches-SSEN
05UD Artifacts-83
05UD Artifacts-191
Blue-83
Blue-191
Gold-83
Gold-191
Green-83
Green-191
Pewter-83
Pewter-191
Red-83
Red-191
Gold Autographed-83
Gold Autographed-191
05UD PowerPlay-74
Rainbow-74
Power Marks-PMEN
05Ultimate Collection-75
Gold-75
Ultimate Achievements-UAEN
Ultimate Signatures-USNA
Ultimate Signatures Pairings-UPKN
Ultimate Signatures Pairings-UPNC
Ultimate Signatures Trios-UTTNC
05Ultra-160
Gold-160
Ice-160
05Upper Deck-158
05Upper Deck All-Time Greatest-52
05Upper Deck All-Time Greatest-89
05Upper Deck HG Glossy-158
05Upper Deck Hometown Heroes-HH16
05Upper Deck Notable Numbers-N-EN
05Upper Deck Ice-82
Rainbow-82
05Upper Deck MVP-320
Gold-320
Platinum-320
05Upper Deck Rookie Update-83
05Upper Deck Rookie Update-244
Inspirations Patch Rookies-244
05Upper Deck Trilogy-74
05Upper Deck Trilogy-150
Crystal-150
05Upper Deck Toronto Fall Expo-158
05Upper Deck Victory-163
Black-163
Gold-163
Silver-163
Blow-Ups-BU32
Stars on Ice-SI36
06Be A Player Portraits Signature Portraits-SPEN
06Be A Player Portraits Timeless Tens-TTNET
06Black Diamond-70
Black-70
Gold-70
Ruby-70
06Flair Showcase-83
06Flair Showcase-158
06Flair Showcase-259
Parallel-83
Parallel-158
Parallel-259
Hot Gloves-HG25
Inks-IEN
Stitches-SSEN
06Fleer-164
Tiffany-164
06Hot Prospects Red Hot-86
06Hot Prospects White Hot-86
06O-Pee-Chee-408
Rainbow-408
Swatches-S-EN
06Panini Stickers-329
06SP Game Used Authentic Fabrics Sevens-AF7CAL
06SP Game Used Authentic Fabrics Sevens Patches-AF7CAL
06SP Game Used Authentic Fabrics Eights-AF8RUS
06SP Game Used Authentic Fabrics Eights Patches-AF8RUS
06The Cup Autographed Foundations-CQEN
06The Cup Autographed Foundations Patches-CQEN
06The Cup Foundations-CQEN
06The Cup Foundations Patches-CQEN
06The Cup Honorable Numbers-HNEN
06Ultra-160
Gold Medallion-160
Ice Medallion-160
Action-UA25
Fresh Ink-IEN
Uniformity-UEN
Uniformity Patches-UPEN
06Upper Deck Arena Giveaways-SJS5
06Upper Deck-415
Exclusives Parallel-415
High Gloss Parallel-415
All-Time Greatest-ATG19
Masterpieces-415
Oversized Wal-Mart Exclusives-415
Signature Sensations-SSEN
06Upper Deck MVP-249
Gold Script-249
Super Script-249
06Upper Deck Ovation-42
06Upper Deck Victory-164
06Upper Deck Victory Black-164
06Upper Deck Victory Gold-164
06Russian Sport Collection Olympic Stars-11
06Russian Torino Olympic Team-20
07Upper Deck Victory-178
Black-178
Gold-178

Nachbaur, Don
81O-Pee-Chee-138
82Post Cereal-7
88Oilers Tenth Anniversary-113
88ProCards AHL-345
89ProCards AHL-345
95Seattle Thunderbirds-18
96Seattle Thunderbirds-NNO
97Seattle Thunderbirds-25

Nachtmann, Markus
96German DEL-136

Nadazdi, Tomas
03Czech OFS Plus All-Star Game-H19

Nade, Ryan
93Quebec Pee-Wee Tournament-775

Nadeau, Bobby
06Chicoutimi Sagueneens-16

Nadeau, Frederic
92Quebec Pee-Wee Tournament-158
93Quebec Pee-Wee Tournament-1022

Nadeau, Jerome
93Quebec Pee-Wee Tournament-366

Nadeau, Patrick
90 7th Inn. Sketch QMJHL-91
91 7th Inn. Sketch QMJHL-120
99Quad-City Mallards-8
00Quad-City Mallards-8
01Quad-City Mallards-17
05Quad City Mallards-9
06Quad City Mallards-8

Nadjiwan, Jamie
84Sudbury Wolves-14

Nadrchal, Vladimir
72Finnish Panda Toronto-89

Naef, Markus
93Swiss HNL-373

Nagel, Lars Peder
04Bakersfield Condors-14

Nagle, Jim
01BC Icemen-15

Nagler, Martin
95German DEL-13

Nagurny, Shawn
82Medicine Hat Tigers-13

Nagy, Aaron
89 7th Inn. Sketch OHL-32
90 7th Inn. Sketch OHL-137
91 7th Inn. Sketch OHL-365

Nagy, Kory
06Oshawa Generals-7

Nagy, Ladislav
93Quebec Pee-Wee Tournament-1704
98Halifax Mooseheads-6
98Halifax Mooseheads Second Edition-23
99BAP Memorabilia-385
Gold-385
Silver-385
99Crown Royale-118
Limited Series-118
Premiere Date-118
Prospects Parallel-118
99Pacific Omega-203
Copper-203
Gold-203
Ice Blue-203
Premiere Date-203
99SP Authentic-115
99Topps Premier Plus-82
Parallel-82
99Quebec PeeWee Tournament Coll Souv-21
99Bowman CHL-54
Gold-54
OPC International-54
Scout's Choice-SC20
00BAP Memorabilia-286
Emerald-286
Ruby-286
Sapphire-286
Promos-286
00BAP Mem Chicago Sportsfest Copper-286
00BAP Memorabilia Chicago Sportsfest Blue-286
00BAP Memorabilia Chicago Sportsfest Gold-286
00BAP Memorabilia Chicago Sportsfest Ruby-286
00BAP Memorabilia Chicago Sun-Times Ruby-286
00BAP Memorabilia Chicago Sun-Times Gold-286
00BAP Mem Chicago Sun-Times Sapphire-286
00BAP Mem Toronto Fall Expo Copper-286
00BAP Memorabilia Toronto Fall Expo Gold-286
00BAP Memorabilia Toronto Fall Expo Ruby-286
00O-Pee-Chee-297
00O-Pee-Chee Parallel-297
00Pacific-355
Copper-355
Gold-355
Ice Blue-355
Premiere Date-355
00Private Stock-141
Gold-141
Premiere Date-141
Retail-141
Silver-141
PS-2001 Rookies-20
00Topps/OPC-297
Parallel-297
00Topps Chrome-192
OPC Refractors-192
Refractors-192
00Upper Deck MVP-204
Excellence-ME8
First Stars-204
Mark of Excellence-SGSL
ProSign-LN
Second Stars-204
Third Stars-204
00Vanguard-144
Pacific Proofs-144
00Worcester Icecats-5
01Coyotes Team Issue-15
01SP Authentic-129
Limited-128
Limited Gold-128
01Upper Deck-136
Exclusives-136
01Upper Deck MVP-149
01Upper Deck Victory-276
Gold-276
01Upper Deck Vintage-196
02BAP First Edition-256
02BAP Signature Series-92
Autographs-92
Autographs Gold-92
02Coyotes Team Issue-10
02Pacific-301
Blue-301
Red-301
02Pacific Complete-138
Red-138
02Parkhurst Retro-142
Minis-142
02Topps Total-390
02UD Top Shelf-67
02Upper Deck-382
Exclusives-382
02Upper Deck Beckett UD Promos-382
02Upper Deck MVP-142
Gold-142
Classics-142
Golden Classics-142
02Upper Deck Victory-166
Bronze-166
Gold-166
Silver-166
02Upper Deck Vintage-195
02Slovakian Kvarteto-21
03Coyotes Postcards-14
03Crown Royale-78
Blue-78
Retail-78
03ITG Action-458
03NHL Sticker Collection-267
03O-Pee-Chee-7
03OPC Blue-7
03OPC Gold-7
03OPC Red-7
03Pacific-266
Blue-266
Red-266
03Pacific Calder-79
Silver-79
03Pacific Complete-239
Red-239
03Pacific Heads-Up-77
Hobby LTD-77
Retail LTD-77
03Pacific Quest for the Cup-82
Blue-82
03Private Stock Reserve-81
Blue-81
Red-81
Retail-81
03Titanium-79
Hobby Jersey Number Parallels-79
Retail-79
Retail Jersey Number Parallels-79
03Topps-7
Blue-7
Gold-7
Red-7
03Topps C55-42
Minis-42
Minis American Back-42
Minis American Back Red-42
Minis Bazooka Back-42
Minis Brooklyn Back-42
Minis Hat Trick Back-42
Minis O Canada Back-42
Minis O Canada Back Red-42
Minis Stanley Cup Back-42
03Upper Deck-391
Canadian Exclusives-391
HG-391
UD Exclusives-391
03Upper Deck Ice-67
Gold-67
03Upper Deck MVP-322
Gold Script-322
Silver Script-322
Canadian Exclusives-322
03Upper Deck Victory-146
Bronze-146
Gold-146
Silver-146
03Worcester Ice Cats 10th Anniversary-14
04Pacific-205
Blue-205
Red-205
04SP Authentic Buybacks-102
04SP Authentic Sign of the Times-ST-LN
04UD All-World-69
Gold-69

Autographs-69
04Upper Deck-134
Canadian Exclusives-134
HG Glossy Gold-134
HG Glossy Silver-134
04Swedish Pure Skills-79
Parallel-79
05Beehive Matted Materials-MMLN
05Black Diamond-68
Emerald-68
Gold-68
Onyx-68
Ruby-68
05Hot Prospects-77
En Fuego-77
Red Hot-77
White Hot-77
05Parkhurst-368
Facsimile Auto Parallel-368
True Colors-TCPHX
True Colors-TCPHX
05SP Game Used Authentic Fabrics Triple-HND
05SP Game Used Authentic Patches Triple-HND
05SP Game Used Awesome Authentics-AA-LN
05SP Game Used Awesome Authentics Gold-DA-LN
05SPx Winning Combos-WC-ND
05SPx Winning Combos Autographs-AWC-ND
05SPx Winning Combos Gold-WC-ND
05SPx Winning Combos Spectrum-WC-ND
05SPx Winning Materials-WM-LN
05SPx Winning Materials Gold-WM-LN
05SPx Winning Materials Spectrum-WM-LN
05UD Artifacts Auto Facts-AF-LN
05UD Artifacts Auto Facts Blue-AF-LN
05UD Artifacts Auto Facts Copper-AF-LN
05UD Artifacts Auto Facts Pewter-AF-LN
05UD Artifacts Auto Facts Silver-AF-LN
05UD PowerPlay-68
Rainbow-68
05Ultra-150
Gold-150
Fresh Ink-FI-LN
Fresh Ink Blue-FI-LN
Ice-150
05Upper Deck-393
Notable Numbers-N-LN
05Upper Deck MVP-301
Gold-301
Platinum-301
05Upper Deck Rookie Update-77
05Upper Deck Trilogy-68
Scripts-SFS-LN
05Upper Deck Victory-150
Black-150
Gold-150
Silver-150
06Beehive Matted Materials-MMLN
06Beehive Remarkable Matted Materials-MMLN
06Beehive Signature Scrapbook-SSLN
06Black Diamond-64
Black-64
Gold-64
Ruby-64
06Flair Showcase-78
06Flair Showcase-154
Parallel-78
Parallel-154
Stitches-SSLN
06Fleer-150
Tiffany-150
06Hot Prospects Hotagraphs-HLN
06O-Pee-Chee-374
Rainbow-374
06Panini Stickers-321
06SP Game Used Inked Sweaters-ISLN
06SP Game Used Inked Sweaters Patches-ISLN
06SP Game Used SIGnificance-SLN
06The Cup NHL Shields Duals-DSHJN
06UD Artifacts Auto-Facts-AFLN
06UD Artifacts Auto-Facts Gold-AFLN
06UD Artifacts Tundra Tandems-TTCN
06UD Artifacts Tundra Tandems Black-TTCN
06UD Artifacts Tundra Tandems Blue-TTCN
06UD Artifacts Tundra Tandems Gold-TTCN
06UD Artifacts Tundra Tandems Platinum-TTCN
06UD Artifacts Tundra Tandems Red-TTCN
06UD Artifacts Tundra Tandems Dual Patches Red-TTCN
06Ultra-148
Gold Medallion-148
Ice Medallion-148
Uniformity-ULN
Uniformity Patches-UPLN
06Upper Deck Arena Giveaways-PHX2
06Upper Deck-151
Exclusives Parallel-151
High Gloss Parallel-151
Masterpieces-151
06Upper Deck MVP-224
Gold Script-224
Super Script-224
Jerseys-OJFN
06Upper Deck Ovation-139
06Upper Deck Trilogy Scripts-TSLN
06Upper Deck Victory-153
06Upper Deck Victory Black-153
06Upper Deck Victory Gold-153
07Upper Deck Victory-187
Black-187
Gold-187

Nagy, Richard
91Air Canada SJHL-A38
91Air Canada SJHL All-Stars-36
91Air Canada SJHL All-Stars-47

Nahigian, Paul
93Quebec Pee-Wee Tournament-592

Nail, John
00Michigan State Spartans-16
01Trenton Titans-1-7
02Greenville Grrrowl-22
02Trenton Titans-A-6
03Greenville Grrrowl-24

Najda, Anatoli
91O-Pee-Chee Inserts-56R
94Czech APS Extraliga-271
95Czech APS Extraliga-263

Najdek, Robert
04Czech OFS-396

Nakaoka, Daniel
98Swiss Power Play Stickers-336
00Swiss Panini Stickers-68
00Swiss Slapshot Mini-Cards-HCCF12
01Swiss HNL-298
02Swiss HNL-131

Namd, Harry
71Swedish Hockey-346

Namestnikov, Oleg
00Russian Hockey League-86

Namestnikov, Yevgeny
93Donruss-502
94Parkhurst-246
Gold-246
94Score-218
Gold-218
Platinum-218
94Classic Pro Prospects-153
95Topps-46
OPC Inserts-46
96Syracuse Crunch-26
00Milwaukee Admirals Keebler-12
02Russian Hockey League-253

Nanne, Lou
69O-Pee-Chee-198
70Esso Power Players-178
71O-Pee-Chee-240
71Sargent Promotions Stamps-93
71Toronto Sun-138
72O-Pee-Chee-10
72Sargent Promotions Stamps-111
72Topps-93
73North Stars Action Posters-7
73North Stars Postcards-12
73O-Pee-Chee-246
74NHL Action Stamps-131
74O-Pee-Chee NHL-325
75O-Pee-Chee NHL-143
75Topps-143
76O-Pee-Chee NHL-173
76Topps-173
77Coca-Cola-16
77O-Pee-Chee NHL-36
77Topps-36
86North Stars Postcards-19
94Minnesota Golden Gophers-23
04ITG Franchises US West-253
Autographs-A-LN

Nanne, Marty
88ProCards IHL-106
89ProCards IHL-54
90ProCards AHL/IHL-397

Nansen, Tomas
95Swedish Leaf-276
95Swedish Upper Deck-157

Nansen, Tord
72Swedish Stickers-230
83Swedish Semic Elitserien-78
84Swedish Semic Elitserien-78

Nantais, Richard
76O-Pee-Chee NHL-357

Nanzen, Tomas
90Swedish Semic Elitserien Stickers-12
91Swedish Semic Elitserien Stickers-209
92Swedish Semic Elitserien Stickers-232
93Swedish Semic Elitserien-202
94Swedish Leaf-56

Napier, Mark
75O-Pee-Chee WHA-78
76O-Pee-Chee WHA-108
77O-Pee-Chee WHA-12
78Canadiens Postcards-20
79Canadiens Postcards-18
79O-Pee-Chee-222
79Topps-222
80Canadiens Postcards-17
80O-Pee-Chee-111
80Pepsi-Cola Caps-53
80Topps-111
81Canadiens Postcards-19
81O-Pee-Chee-178
81O-Pee-Chee Stickers-36
81Topps-23
82Canadiens Postcards-15
82Canadiens Steinberg-11
82O-Pee-Chee-178
82O-Pee-Chee-189
82O-Pee-Chee Stickers-38
82O-Pee-Chee Stickers-39
82Post Cereal-10
82Topps Stickers-38
82Topps Stickers-39
83NHL Key Tags-69
83North Stars Postcards-21
83O-Pee-Chee-182
83O-Pee-Chee-192
83O-Pee-Chee Stickers-64
83O-Pee-Chee Stickers-65
83Topps Stickers-64
83Topps Stickers-65
84North Stars Postcards-20
84Oilers Red Rooster-18
84Oilers Team Issue-21
84O-Pee-Chee-105
85Oilers Red Rooster-18
85O-Pee-Chee-253
86Kraft Drawings-49
86Oilers Red Rooster-65
86Oilers Team Issue-65
86O-Pee-Chee-183
86O-Pee-Chee Stickers-75
86Topps-183
87Sabres Blue Shield-18
87Sabres Wonder Bread/Hostess-19
88Oilers Tenth Anniversary-28
88Sabres Blue Shield-16
88Sabres Wonder Bread/Hostess-18
89Sabres Campbell's-16
04ITG Franchises Canadian-22
Autographs-MN

Napolitano, Joseph
88Richelieu Riverains-19
907th Inn. Sketch QMJHL-249
917th Inn. Sketch QMJHL-268

Nardella, Robert
96German DEL-163
96Swedish Semic Wien-177
98Chicago Wolves-16
98Chicago Wolves Turner Cup-7
99Chicago Wolves-5
00Chicago Wolves-18
01Chicago Wolves-13
03Rockford Ice Hogs-12
05Rockford Ice Hogs-10

Narhi, Markku
71Finnish Suomi Stickers-307

Narinen, Martti
72Finnish Jaakiekko-179

Naroska, Rene
94German First League-523

Narvanen, Reijo
72Finnish Jaakiekko-273

Narvanmaa, Jouko
86Swedish Panini Stickers-195
87Swedish Panini Stickers-195
89Swedish Semic World Champ Stickers-35
91Finnish Jyvas-Hyva Stickers-65
92Finnish Jyvas-Hyva Stickers-178
93Finnish Jyvas-Hyva Stickers-320
93Finnish SISU-31

Nasato, Lucio
94Kitchener Rangers-15
95Slapshot-13
95Barrie Colts-19
96Barrie Colts-18
97Barrie Colts-18
98Flint Generals-13
01Memphis RiverKings-14
04Barrie Colts 10th Anniversary-9
04Richmond Riverdogs-14

Nasby, Bret
03Oshawa Generals-6
04Oshawa Generals-5
04Oshawa Generals Autographs-5
05Erie Otters-21

Naser, Andy
93Swiss HNL-229
95Swiss HNL-126
96Swiss HNL-116
98Swiss Power Play Stickers-172
99Swiss Panini Stickers-173
00Swiss Panini Stickers-216
01Swiss HNL-45
02Swiss HNL-95

Nash, Brendon
04Salmon Arm Silverbacks-2
05Salmon Arm Silverbacks-13

Nash, Colin
93Quebec Pee-Wee Tournament-502

Nash, Don
52Juniors Blue Tint-28

Nash, Rick
00London Knights-9
00London Knights-U8
00UD CHL Prospects-42
01SPx Rookie Redemption-R9
01UD Top Shelf Rookie Redemption-TS2
01London Knights-18
02Atomic-105
Blue-105
Gold-105
Red-105
Hobby Parallel-105
02BAP All-Star Edition-134
Gold-134
Silver-134
02BAP First Edition-439H
02BAP Memorabilia-272
Emerald-272
Ruby-272
Sapphire-272
Draft Redemptions-1
NHL All-Star Game-272
NHL All-Star Game Blue-272
NHL All-Star Game Green-272
NHL All-Star Game Red-272
02BAP Memorabilia Toronto Fall Expo-272
02BAP Signature Series-183
All-Rookie-AR12
Autographs-183
Autographs Gold-183
Franchise Players-FJ8
Jerseys-SGJ66
Jersey Autographs-SGJ66
02BAP Ultimate Memorabilia-2
Autographs-10
Autographs Gold-10
Calder Candidates-13
First Overall-13
Jerseys-32
Jersey and Stick-10
02Bowman YoungStars-155
Gold-155
Silver-155
Autographs-RN
Jerseys-RN
Patches-RN
Double Stuff-RN
Triple Stuff-RN
Rivals-RNJB
Rivals Patches-3
Sticks-RN
02Crown Royale-109
Blue-109
Purple-109
Red-109
Retail-109
Rookie Royalty-7
Royal Portraits-5
02eTopps-39
02ITG Used-82
Calder Jerseys-C2
Calder Jerseys Gold-C2
Emblems-E38
02O-Pee-Chee-338
02O-Pee-Chee Premier Blue Parallel-338
02O-Pee-Chee Premier Red Parallel-338
02O-Pee-Chee Factory Set-338
02Pacific-404
02Pacific Calder-112
02Pacific Calder-112A
Silver-112
Reflections-8
02Pacific Complete-557
Red-557
02Pacific Exclusive-196
Blue-196
Gold-196
Destined-5
02Pacific Heads-Up-130
02Pacific Quest for the Cup-113
Gold-113
Calder Contenders-6
02Parkhurst-202
Bronze-202
Gold-202
Silver-202
Hardware-C7
Heroes-NH8
Jerseys-GJ57
02Parkhurst Retro-202
Minis-202
Franchise Players-RF8
He Shoots-He Scores Points-5
He Shoots-He Scores Prizes-17
Hopefuls-CH2
Jerseys-RJ10
Memorabilia-RM28
02Private Stock Reserve-157
Blue-157
Red-157
Retail-157
Class Act-6
Moments in Time-2
02SP Authentic-184
Sign of the Times-RN
Signed Patches-PRN
02SP Game Used-73
02SPx-149
02Stadium Club-126
Silver Decoy Cards-126
Proofs-126
02Titanium-111
Blue-111
Red-111
Retail-111
Right on Target-6
02Topps-338
OPC Blue Parallel-338
OPC Red Parallel-338
Factory Set-338
02Topps Chrome-175
Black Border Refractors-175
Refractors-175
02Topps Heritage-140
02Topps Total-414
Team Checklists-TTC8
02UD Artistic Impressions-95
Gold-95
Common Ground-CG6
Common Ground-CG9
Common Ground Gold-CG6
Common Ground Gold-CG9
Retrospectives-R92
Retrospectives Gold-R92
Retrospectives Signed-R92
Retrospectives Silver-R92
02UD Foundations-149
02UD Honor Roll-150
Students of the Game-SG9
02UD Mask Collection-178
02UD Piece of History-127
02UD Premier Collection-80
Gold-80
Jerseys Bronze-JR
Jerseys Gold-JR
Jerseys Silver-JR
Signatures Bronze-SNA
Signatures Bronze-SRN
Signatures Gold-SNA
Signatures Gold-SRN
Signatures Silver-SNA
Signatures Silver-SRN
02UD Top Shelf-126
02Upper Deck-232
Exclusives-232
02Upper Deck Classic Portraits-109
02Upper Deck Rookie Update-172
02Vanguard-109
LTD-109
In Focus-5
Prime Prospects-8
02UD SuperStars *-261
Gold-261
03BAP Memorabilia-76
Emerald-76
Gold-76
Ruby-76
Sapphire-76
Brush with Greatness-12
Brush with Greatness Contest Cards-12
Future of the Game-FG-3
Jersey and Stick-SJ-9
Jerseys-GJ-10
Jersey Autographs-GJ-10
03BAP Ultimate Memorabilia Autographs-132
Gold-132
03BAP Ultimate Mem Auto Jerseys-132
03BAP Ultimate Mem Auto Emblems-132
03BAP Ultimate Mem Auto Sticks-132
03BAP Ultimate Memorabilia Career Year-5
03BAP Ultimate Mem Complete Jersey-9
03BAP Ultimate Mem Complete Jersey Gold-9
03BAP Ultimate Memorabilia Dynamic Duos-8
03BAP Ultimate Memorabilia Emblems-23
03BAP Ultimate Memorabilia Emblems Gold-23
03BAP Ultimate Mem Franch Present Future-9
03BAP Ultimate Memorabilia Heroes-6
03BAP Ultimate Mem Heroes Autos-3
03BAP Ultimate Memorabilia Jerseys-13
03BAP Ultimate Memorabilia Jerseys Gold-13
03BAP Ultimate Mem Jersey and Emblems-35
03BAP Ultimate Mem Jersey and Emblem Gold-35
03BAP Ultimate Mem Jersey and Numbers-35
03BAP Ultimate Mem Jersey and Number Gold-35
03BAP Ultimate Mem Jersey and Stick-8
03BAP Ultimate Mem Jersey and Stick Gold-8
03BAP Ultimate Memorabilia Numbers-10
03BAP Ultimate Memorabilia Numbers Gold-10
03BAP Ultimate Mem Redemption Cards-4
03BAP Ultimate Mem Seams Unbelievable-8
03BAP Ultimate Memorabilia Triple Threads-24
03Beehive-59
Variations-59
Gold-59
Silver-59
Jumbos-9
Jumbo Variations-9
Jumbo Jerseys-BH22
Jerseys-JT19
Signatures-RF21
03Black Diamond-132
Black-132
Green-132
Red-132
Signature Gems-SG-8
Threads-DT-RN
Threads Green-DT-RN
Threads Red-DT-RN
Threads Black-DT-RN
03Bowman-1
Gold-1
Future Rivals-NC
Future Rivals-NG
Future Rivals Patches-NC
Future Rivals Patches-NG
Goal to Goal-KN
Signs of the Future-SOF-RN
03Bowman Chrome-1
Refractors-1
Gold Refractors-1
Xfractors-1
03Crown Royale-30
Blue-30
Retail-30
Lords of the Rink-9
03eTopps-39
03ITG Action-123
Highlight Reel-HR10
Jerseys-M170
Jerseys-M249
03ITG Toronto Fall Expo Jerseys-FE6
03ITG Used Signature Series-1
Gold-1
Autographs-RN
Autographs Gold-RN
Franchise-9
Franchise Autographs-9
Franchise Gold-9
Jerseys-38
Jerseys Gold-38
Jersey Autos-38
Emblems-2
Emblems Gold-2
Jersey and Stick-38
Jersey and Stick Gold-38
03ITG VIP Collages-17
03ITG VIP Collage Autographs-17
03ITG VIP Jerseys-7
03ITG VIP Jersey Autographs-7
03ITG VIP Jersey and Emblems-5
03ITG VIP Jersey and Numbers-5
03ITG VIP Making the Bigs-2
03ITG VIP Sophomores-1
03McDonald's Pacific-14
Canadian Pride-3
Hockey Roots Checklists-3
03NHL Sticker Collection-193
03O-Pee-Chee-31
03OPC Blue-31
03OPC Gold-31
03OPC Red-31
03Pacific-96
Blue-96
Red-96
Cramer's Choice-3
Maximum Impact-3
03Pacific Atlantic City National-1
03Pacific Calder Contenders Entry Draft-6
03Pacific Calder-29
03Pacific Calder-147
Silver-29
03Pacific Calder Collection NHL All-Star Block Party Gold-4
03Pacific Complete-107
Red-107
03Pacific Exhibit-164
Blue Backs-164
Pursuing Prominence-4
03Pacific Heads-Up-29
Hobby LTD-29
Retail LTD-29
Fast Forwards-3
Fast Forwards LTD-3
In Focus-6
In Focus LTD-6
03Pacific Invincible-28
Blue-28
Red-28
Retail-28
Featured Performers-9
New Sensations-9
03Pacific Montreal Olympic Stadium Show-3
Gold-3
03Pacific Prism-31
Blue-31
Gold-31
Red-31
Paramount Prodigies-6
Rookie Revolution-5
03Pacific Quest for the Cup-30
Blue-30
Chasing the Cup-5
Jerseys-7
03Pacific Supreme-27
Blue-27
Red-27
Retail-27
Generations-3
03Pacific Toronto Spring Expo-3
Gold-3
03Parkhurst Rookie-46
Emblems-GUE-3
Emblem Autographs-GUE-RN
Emblems Gold-GUE-3
High Expectations-HE-2
High Expectations Gold-HE-2
Jerseys-GJ-11
Jersey Autographs-GUJ-RN
Jerseys Gold-GJ-11
Jersey and Sticks-SJ-17
Jersey and Sticks Gold-SJ-17
Road to the NHL-RNJ-3
Road to the NHL Gold-RTN-3
Road to the NHL Emblems-RTNE-3
Road to the NHL Emblems Gold-RTNE-3
Teammates Gold-RT4
Teammates-RT4
03Private Stock Reserve-27
Blue-27
Red-27
Retail-27
Rising Stock-5
03SP Authentic-24
Limited-24
10th Anniversary-SP13
10th Anniversary Limited-SP13
Honors-H21
Honors Limited-H21
Sign of the Times-RN
Sign of the Times-NL
Sign of the Times-NSZ
03SP Game Used-14
Gold-14
Authentic Fabrics-AFRN
Authentic Fabrics-DFND
Authentic Fabrics-DFNM
Authentic Fabrics-QSNZH
Authentic Fabrics Gold-AFRN
Authentic Fabrics Gold-DFND
Authentic Fabrics Gold-DFNM
Authentic Fabrics Gold-QSNZH
Authentic Patches-APRN
Double Threads-DTND
Limited Threads-LTRN
Limited Threads Gold-LTRN
Premium Patches-PPRN
Signers-SPSRN
03SPx-27
03SPx-161
Radiance-27
Radiance-161
Spectrum-27
Spectrum-161
Big Futures-BF-RN
Big Futures Limited-BF-RN
Fantasy Franchise-FF-NSZ
Fantasy Franchise Limited-FF-NSZ
Signature Threads-ST-RN
Style-SPX-HN
Style Limited-SPX-HN
Winning Materials-WM-RN
Winning Materials Limited-WM-RN
03Titanium-31
Hobby Jersey Number Parallels-31
Retail-31
Retail Jersey Number Parallels-31
Right on Target-4
Stat Masters-4
03Topps-31
Blue-31
Gold-31
Red-31
Box Toppers-5
First Overall Fabrics-RN
First Overall Fabrics-MLRN
First Overall Fabrics-RNIK
Topps/OPC Idols-CI13
Own the Game-OTG8
Signs of Youth-RN
03Topps All-Star Block Party-5
03Topps C55-21
03Topps C55-21B
Minis-21
Minis American Back-21
Minis American Back Red-21
Minis Bazooka Back-21
Minis Brooklyn Back-21
Minis Hat Trick Back-21
Minis O Canada Back-21
Minis O Canada Back Red-21
Minis Stanley Cup Back-21
Autographs-TA-RN
Relics-TRRN
03Topps Pristine Autographs-PE-RN
03Topps Pristine Autographs Gold-PE-RN
03Topps Traded Franchise Fabrics-FF-RN
03UD Honor Roll-22
03UD Honor Roll-97
03UD Premier Collection-17
NHL Shields-SH-RN
Signatures-PS-RN
Signatures Gold-PS-RN
Teammates-PT-CB1
Teammates-PT-CB2
Teammates Patches-PT-CB1
Teammates Patches-PT-CB2
03Upper Deck-55
All-Star Lineup-AS7
Big Playmakers-BP-RN
BuyBacks-50
BuyBacks-51
Canadian Exclusives-55
HG-55
Highlight Heroes-HH-RN
Highlight Heroes Jerseys-HH-RN
Jersey Autographs-SJ-RN
Patches-PLG-RN
Patches-PNM-RN
Patches-PNR-RN
Power Zone-PZ-6
Shooting Stars-ST-RN
Superstar Spotlight-SS4
03Upper Deck All-Star Promos-S1
03Upper Deck All-Star Promos-AS2
03Upper Deck Classic Portraits-25
03Upper Deck Classic Portraits-153
Classic Colors-CC-RN
Genuine Greatness-GG-RN
Starring Cast-SC-RN
03Upper Deck Ice-24
Gold-24
Authentics-IA-RN
Breakers-IB-RN
Breaker Patches-IB-RN
Frozen Fabrics-FF-RN
Frozen Fabric Patches-FF-RN
Under Glass Autographs-UG-RN
03Upper Deck MVP-120
Gold Script-120
Silver Script-120
Canadian Exclusives-120
SportsNut-SN26
Winning Formula-WF1
03Upper Deck Rookie Update-24
03Upper Deck Rookie Update-163
03Upper Deck Rookie Update-174
Skills-SKRN
Top Draws-TD13
03Upper Deck Trilogy-25
03Upper Deck Trilogy-122
Crest Variations-122
Limited-25
Limited-122
Scripts-CSRN
03Upper Deck Victory-53
Bronze-53
Gold-53
Silver-53
Freshman Flashback-FF15
Game Breakers-GB17
03Toronto Star-15
Foil-23
04Pacific-79
Blue-79
Red-79
All-Stars-4
Cramer's Choice-5
04Pacific NHL Draft All-Star Nets-1
04Pacific National Convention-3
04SP Authentic-26
Limited-26
Buybacks-166
Buybacks-167
Buybacks-168
Buybacks-169
Buybacks-170
Octographs-OS-ROK
Rookie Review-RR-RN
Sign of the Times-ST-RN
Sign of the Times-DS-NZ
Sign of the Times-TS-IKN
Sign of the Times-TS-ILN
Sign of the Times-TS-NSS
Sign of the Times-QS-HINS
Sign of the Times-QS-NHKS
04UD All-World-79
04UD All-World-95
Gold-79
Autographs-79
Autographs-95
Dual Autographs-AD-NT
Quad Autographs-AQ-GSC
Six Autographs-AS-SWT
04UD Toronto Fall Expo Priority Signings-RN
04Ultimate Collection-12
Buybacks-77
Dual Logos-UL2-NZ
Jerseys-UGJ-RN
Jerseys Gold-UGJ-RN
Jersey Autographs-UGJA-RN
Patches-UP-RN
Patch Autographs-UPA-RN
Patch Autographs-UPA-IKRN
Signatures-US-RN
Signature Logos-ULA-RN
Signature Patches-SP-RN
04Upper Deck-50
Canadian Exclusives-50
Hardware Heroes-AW6
HG Glossy Gold-50
HG Glossy Silver-50
Jersey Autographs-GJA-RN
NHL's Best-NB-RN
04Swiss Davos Postcards-21
04National Trading Card Day *-T7
05Be A Player-24
First Period-24
Second Period-24
Third Period-24
Overtime-24
Class Action-CA8
Dual Signatures-ND
Dual Signatures-NT
Outtakes-OT17
Quad Signatures-HSNT
Signatures-RN
Signatures Gold-RN
05Beehive-26
05Beehive-184
Beige -26
Blue -26
Gold-26
Red -26
Matte-26
Matted Materials-MMRN
Matted Materials Remarkable-RMRN
PhotoGraphs-PGRN
Signature Scrapbook-SSRN
05Black Diamond-174
Emerald-174
Gold-174
Onyx-174
Ruby-174
Jerseys-J-RN
Jerseys Ruby-J-RN
Jersey Duals-DJ-RN
Jersey Triples-TJ-RN
Jersey Quads-QJ-RN
05Hot Prospects-29
En Fuego-29
Red Hot-29
White Hot-29
05McDonalds Upper Deck-9
Autographs-MA7
CHL Graduates-CG6
Top Scorers-TS14
05Panini Stickers-235
05Parkhurst-137
05Parkhurst-576
05Parkhurst-679
Facsimile Auto Parallel-137
Facsimile Auto Parallel-576
Facsimile Auto Parallel-679
True Colors-TCCLB
True Colors-TCCLB
05SP Authentic-29
05SP Authentic-119
Limited-29
Limited-119
Chirography-SPRN
Marks of Distinction-MDRN
Octographs-OF
Prestigious Pairings-PPNZ
Sign of the Times Duals-DNB
Sign of the Times Fives-ISNKN
05SP Game Used-28
Autographs-28
Gold-28
Authentic Fabrics-AF-RN
Authentic Fabrics Autographs-AAF-RN
Authentic Fabrics Dual-NT
Authentic Fabrics Dual Autographs-NT
Authentic Fabrics Gold-AF-RN
Authentic Fabrics Quad-NSZB
Authentic Fabrics Quad-NZDF
Authentic Patches Quad -NSZB
Authentic Patches Quad -NZDL
Authentic Fabrics Triple-INK
Authentic Patches-AP-RN
Authentic Patches Autographs-AAP-RN
Authentic Patches Dual-NT
Authentic Patches Dual Autographs-NT
Authentic Patches Triple-INK
Auto Draft-AD-RN
Awesome Authentics-AA-RN
Game Gear-GG-RN
Game Gear Autographs-AG-RN
SIGnificance-RN
SIGnificance Gold-S-RN
SIGnificance Extra-ZN
SIGnificance Extra Gold-ZN
Significant Numbers-SN-RN
05SPx-23
Spectrum-23
Winning Combos-WC-DN
Winning Combos-WC-NZ
Winning Combos Autographs-AWC-NZ
Winning Combos Gold-WC-DN
Winning Combos Gold-WC-NZ
Winning Combos Spectrum-WC-DN
Winning Combos Spectrum-WC-NZ
Winning Materials-WM-RN
Winning Materials Autographs-AWM-RN
Winning Materials Gold-WM-RN
Winning Materials Spectrum-WM-RN
Xcitement Superstars-XS-RN
Xcitement Superstars Gold-XS-RN
Xcitement Superstars Spectrum-XS-RN
05The Cup-33
Gold-33
Black Rainbow-33
Dual NHL Shields-DSIN
Dual NHL Shields Autographs-ADSRG
Emblems of Endorsement-EERN
Hardware Heroes-HHRN
Honorable Numbers-HNRN
Limited Logos-LLRN
Masterpiece Pressplates-33
Noble Numbers-NNNP
Noble Numbers Dual-DNNFN
Patch Variation Autographs-AP33
Property of-PORN
Scripted Numbers-SNNP
Scripted Numbers Dual-DSNIN
Scripted Numbers Dual-DSNNS
Signature Patches-SPRN
05UD Artifacts-30
05UD Artifacts-162
Blue-30
Blue-162
Gold-30
Gold-162
Green-30
Green-162
Pewter-30
Pewter-162
Red-30
Red-162
Auto Facts-AF-RN
Auto Facts Blue-AF-RN
Auto Facts Copper-AF-RN
Auto Facts Pewter-AF-RN
Auto Facts Silver-AF-RN
Gold Autographed-30
Gold Autographed-162
Remarkable Artifacts-RA-RN
Remarkable Artifacts Dual-RA-RN
Treasured Patches-TP-RN
Treasured Patches Autographed-TP-RN
Treasured Patches Dual-TPD-RN
Treasured Patches Dual Autographed-TPD-RN
Treasured Patches Pewter-TP-RN
Treasured Patches Silver-TP-RN
Treasured Swatches-TS-RN
Treasured Swatches Autographed-TS-RN
Treasured Swatches Blue-TS-RN
Treasured Swatches Copper-TS-RN
Treasured Swatches Dual-TSD-RN
Treasured Swatches Dual Autographed-TSD-RN
Treasured Swatches Dual Blue-TSD-RN
Treasured Swatches Dual Copper-TSD-RN
Treasured Swatches Dual Maroon-TSD-RN
Treasured Swatches Dual Pewter-TSD-RN
Treasured Swatches Dual Silver-TSD-RN
Treasured Swatches Maroon-TS-RN
Treasured Swatches Pewter-TS-RN
Treasured Swatches Silver-TS-RN
05UD PowerPlay-26
05UD PowerPlay-108
Rainbow-26
Power Marks-PMRN
05UD Toronto Fall Expo Priority Signings-PS-RN
05Ultimate Collection-27
Gold-27
Endorsed Emblems-EERN
Jerseys Dual-DJNB
Jerseys Triple-TJNOC
Marquee Attractions-MA16
Marquee Attractions Signatures-SMA16
National Heroes Patches-NHPRN
Premium Patches-PPRN
Ultimate Achievements-UARN
Ultimate Patches Dual-DPNB
Ultimate Patches Triple-TPNOC
Ultimate Signatures-USRN
Ultimate Signatures Foursomes-UFINNL
Ultimate Signatures Logos-SLRN
Ultimate Signatures Pairings-UPRG
Ultimate Signatures Trios-UTNBZ
05Ultra-62
Gold-62
Difference Makers-DM1
Difference Makers Jerseys-DMJ-RN
Difference Makers Jersey Autographs-DAJ-RN
Difference Makers Patches-DMP-RN
Difference Makers Patch Autographs-DAP-RN
Fresh Ink-FI-RN
Fresh Ink Blue-FI-RN
Ice-62
05Upper Deck-51
05Upper Deck All-Time Greatest-17
05Upper Deck All-Time Greatest-68
05Upper Deck Big Playmakers-B-RN
05Upper Deck Goal Celebrations-GC6
05Upper Deck Goal Rush-GR1
05Upper Deck HG Glossy-51
05Upper Deck Hometown Heroes-HH18
05Upper Deck Jerseys Series II-J2RN
05Upper Deck Majestic Materials-MMRN
05Upper Deck NHL Generations-DIN
05Upper Deck NHL Generations-TBTN
05Upper Deck NHL Generations-TNSN
05Upper Deck Notable Numbers-N-RN
05Upper Deck Patches-P-RN
05Upper Deck Scrapbooks-HS10
05Upper Deck Shooting Stars-S-RN
05Upper Deck Ice-26
Rainbow-26
Cool Threads-CTRN
Cool Threads Autographs-ACTRN
Cool Threads Glass-CTRN
Cool Threads Patches-CTPRN
Cool Threads Patch Autographs-CAPRN
Glacial Graphs-GGNA
Signature Swatches-SSRN
05Upper Deck MVP-112
Gold-112
Platinum-112
ProSign-P-RN
05Upper Deck Rookie Update-28
05Upper Deck Trilogy-27
05Upper Deck Trilogy-107
Crystal-107
Honorary Patches-HP-RN
Honorary Patch Scripts-HSP-RN
Honorary Swatches-HS-RN
Honorary Swatch Scripts-HSS-RN
Ice Scripts-IS-RN
Personal Scripts-PER-RN
Scripts-SCS-RN
05Upper Deck Toronto Fall Expo-51
05Upper Deck Victory-54
Black-54
Gold-54
Silver-54
Blow-Ups-BU11
Game Breakers-GB13
Stars on Ice-SI16
06Be A Player Portraits-31
Dual Signature Portraits-DSFN
Quadruple Signature Portraits-QKIHN
Sensational Six-SS1ST
Sensational Six-SSCDN
Signature Portraits-SPRN
Timeless Tens-TTCAN
Triple Signature Portraits-TCLB
Triple Signature Portraits-TNSS
06Beehive-71
06Beehive-211
Blue-71
Gold-71
Matte-71
Red Facsimile Signatures-71
Wood-71

5 X 7 Black and White-71
5 X 7 Dark Wood-71
Matted Materials-MMRN
PhotoGraphs-PGRN
Remarkable Matted Materials-MMRN
06Black Diamond-154B
Black-153B
Gold-154B
Ruby-154B
Gemography-GRN
06Flair Showcase-32
06Flair Showcase-180
06Flair Showcase-223
06Flair Showcase-278
Parallel-32
Parallel-180
Parallel-223
Parallel-278
Hot Numbers-HN13
Hot Numbers Parallel-HN13
Wave of the Future-WF11
06Fleer-58
Tiffany-58
Total O-O6
06Hot Prospects-29
Red Hot-29
White Hot-29
Hot Materials -HMRN
Hot Materials Red Hot-HMRN
Hot Materials White Hot-HMRN
06McDonald's Upper Deck-12
Autographs-ARN
Clear Cut Winners-CC3
Jerseys-JRN
Patches-PRN
06O-Pee-Chee-139
06O-Pee-Chee-678
Rainbow-139
Rainbow-678
Autographs-A-NA
Swatches-S-RN
06Panini Stickers-232
06SP Authentic-72
06SP Authentic-149
Chirography-RN
Limited-72
Limited-149
Sign of the Times-STRN
Sign of the Times Duals-STNB
Sign of the Times Triples-ST3HNS
06SP Game Used-28
Gold-28
Rainbow-28
Authentic Fabrics-AFRN
Authentic Fabrics Parallel-AFRN
Authentic Fabrics Patches-AFRN
Authentic Fabrics Dual-AF2NF
Authentic Fabrics Dual Patches-AF2NF
Authentic Fabrics Triple-AF3CLB
Authentic Fabrics Triple Patches-AF3CLB
Authentic Fabrics Quads-AF4SKGN
Authentic Fabrics Quads Patches-AF4SKGN
Authentic Fabrics Fives-AF51ST
Authentic Fabrics Fives Patches-AF51ST
Authentic Fabrics Sixes-AF6MRT
Authentic Fabrics Sixes Patches-AF6MRT
Autographs-28
By The Letter-BLRN
Inked Sweaters-ISRN
Inked Sweaters Patches-ISRN
Inked Sweaters Dual-IS2NH
Inked Sweaters Dual Patches-IS2NH
SIGnificance-SRN
06SPx-26
Spectrum-26
SPxcitement-X26
SPxcitement Spectrum-X26
SPxcitement Autographs-X26
Winning Materials-WMRN
Winning Materials Spectrum-WMRN
Winning Materials Autographs-WMRN
06The Cup-24
Autographed Foundations-CQRN
Autographed Foundations Patches-CQRN
Autographed NHL Shields Duals-DASHN
Autographed NHL Shields Duals-DASNZ
Autographed Patches-24
Black Rainbow-24
Foundations-CQRN
Foundations Patches-CQRN
Enshrinements-ERN
Gold-24
Gold Patches-24
Honorable Numbers-HNRN
Jerseys-24
Limited Logos-LLRN
Masterpiece Pressplates-24
NHL Shields Duals-DSHNL
Scripted Swatches-SSRN
Signature Patches-SPRN
06UD Artifacts-72
06UD Artifacts-163
Blue-72
Blue-163
Gold-72
Gold-163
Platinum-72
Platinum-163
Radiance-72
Radiance-163
Autographed Radiance Parallel-72
Autographed Radiance Parallel-163
Red-72
Red-163
Treasured Patches Black-TSRN
Treasured Patches Blue-TSRN
Treasured Patches Gold-TSRN
Treasured Patches Platinum-TSRN
Treasured Patches Red-TSRN
Treasured Patches Autographed Black Tag
Parallel-TSRN
Treasured Swatches-TSRN
Treasured Swatches Black-TSRN
Treasured Swatches Blue-TSRN
Treasured Swatches Gold-TSRN
Treasured Swatches Platinum-TSRN
Treasured Swatches Red-TSRN
Treasured Swatches Autographed Black-TSRN
Tundra Tandems-TTNF
Tundra Tandems Black-TTNF
Tundra Tandems Blue-TTNF
Tundra Tandems Gold-TTNF
Tundra Tandems Platinum-TTNF
Tundra Tandems Red-TTNF
Tundra Tandems Dual Patches Red-TTNF
06UD Mini Jersey Collection-29
Jerseys-RN
Jersey Variations-RN
06UD Powerplay-29
Impact Rainbow-29
In Action-IA3
Power Marks-PMRN
06Ultimate Collection-19
Autographed Jerseys-AJ-RN
Autographed Patches-AJ-RN
Jerseys-UJ-RN
Jerseys Dual-UJ2-NL
Patches-UJ-RN
Patches Dual-UJ2-NL
Signatures-US-RN
Ultimate Achievements-UA-RN
Ultimate Signatures Logos-SL-RN
06Ultra-57
Gold Medallion-57
Ice Medallion-57
Action-UA7
Difference Makers-DM11
Scoring Kings-SK26
06Upper Deck Arena Giveaways-CLB1
06Upper Deck-55
Exclusives Parallel-55
High Gloss Parallel-55
All-Time Greatest-ATG6
All World-AW12
Game Jerseys-J2RN
Game Patches-P2RN
Generations Duals-G2SN
Generations Patches Dual-G2PSN
Goal Rush-GR5
Masterpieces-55
Signature Sensations-SSRN
Walmart Tins Oversize-55
06Upper Deck Entry Draft-DR4
06Upper Deck MVP-81
Gold Script-81
Super Script-81
Autographs-OANI
Clutch Performers-CP21
Gotta Have Hart-HH18
Jerseys-OJNT
Jerseys-OJZN
06Upper Deck Ovation-63
06Upper Deck Sweet Shot-31
Signature Shots/Saves-SSRN
Signature Shots/Saves Ice Signings-SSIRN
Signature Shots/Saves Sticks-SSSRN
Signature Sticks-STRN
Sweet Stitches-SSRN
Sweet Stitches Duals-SSRN
Sweet Stitches Triples-SSRN
06Upper Deck Trilogy-29
Combo Autographed Jerseys-CJHN
Combo Autographed Patches-CJHN
Combo Clearcut Autographs-C3NZB
Honorary Scripted Patches-HSPRN
Honorary Scripted Swatches-HSSRN
Honorary Swatches-HSRN
Scripts-S1RN
Scripts-S3RN
06Upper Deck Victory-54
06Upper Deck Victory Black-54
06Upper Deck Victory Gold-54
06Upper Deck Victory GameBreakers-GB13
06Upper Deck Victory Next In Line-NL16
06Upper Deck Victory Oversize Cards-RN
06Russian Sport Collection Olympic Stars-37
07Upper Deck National Convention *-NTL13
07Upper Deck National Convention VIP *-VIP13
07Upper Deck Ovation-88
3x5s-XL18
Autographed 3x5s-XLARN
07Upper Deck Victory-130
Black-130
Gold-130
Oversize Cards-OS30
Stars on Ice-SI33

Nash, Shane

93Quebec Pee-Wee Tournament-1407
95Slapshot-194

Nash, Tom

89ProCards IHL-18

Nash, Tyson

93Kamloops Blazers-18
94Kamloops Blazers-19
95Slapshot Memorial Cup-14
96Syracuse Crunch-18
99BAP Memorabilia-344
Gold-344
Silver-344
99Blues Taco Bell-23
99Pacific-368
Copper-368
Emerald Green-368
Gold-368
Ice Blue-368
Premiere Date-368
Red-368
99Pacific Omega-198
Copper-198
Gold-198
Ice Blue-198
Premiere Date-198
99SP Authentic-114
99Topps Arena Giveaways-STL-TN
99Topps Premier Plus-98
Parallel-98
00BAP Memorabilia-344
Emerald-344
Ruby-344
Sapphire-344
Promos-344
00BAP Mem Chicago Sportsfest Copper-344
00BAP Memorabilia Chicago Sportsfest Blue-344
00BAP Memorabilia Chicago Sportsfest Gold-344
00BAP Memorabilia Chicago Sportsfest Ruby-344
00BAP Memorabilia Chicago Sun-Times Ruby-344
00BAP Memorabilia Chicago Sun-Times Gold-344
00BAP Mem Chicago Sun-Times Sapphire-344
00BAP Mem Toronto Fall Expo Copper-344
00BAP Memorabilia Toronto Fall Expo Gold-344
00BAP Memorabilia Toronto Fall Expo Ruby-344
00BAP Signature Series-54
Emerald-54
Ruby-54
Sapphire-54
Autographs-41
Autographs Gold-41
00Pacific-348
Copper-348
Gold-348
Ice Blue-348
Premiere Date-348
00Topps Heritage-175
01O-Pee-Chee-213
01O-Pee-Chee Premier Parallel-213
01Topps-213
OPC Parallel-213
01Upper Deck Victory-311
Gold-311
01Worcester Icecats-14
02BAP Sig Series Auto Buybacks 2000-41
02Blues Team Issue-17
02Upper Deck MVP-164
Gold-164
Classics-164
Golden Classics-164
02Upper Deck Vintage-217
02Upper Deck Vintage-286
03Coyotes Postcards-15
03Upper Deck-149
Canadian Exclusives-149
HG-149
03Upper Deck MVP-329
Gold Script-329
Silver Script-329
Canadian Exclusives-329
05Be A Player Signatures-TN
05Be A Player Signatures Gold-TN
05Parkhurst-381
05Upper Deck-145
HG Glossy-145
Notable Numbers-N-TN
05Upper Deck MVP-302
Gold-302
Platinum-302
05Upper Deck Toronto Fall Expo-145

Nasheim, Richard

93Swedish Semic World Champ Stickers-282
94Finnish Jaa Kiekko-244
95Austrian National Team-18
96Swedish Semic Wien-216

Nasib, Erkan

65Finnish Hellas-122
66Finnish Jaakiekkosarja-68

Naslund, Bert-Roland

85Swedish Panini Stickers-180
86Swedish Panini Stickers-117
87Swedish Panini Stickers-116

Naslund, Ingvar

57Swedish Alfabilder-80

Naslund, Markus

90Swedish Semic Elitserien Stickers-23
91Swedish Semic Elitserien Stickers-214
91Arena Draft Picks-12
91Arena Draft Picks French-12
91Arena Draft Picks Autographs-12
91Arena Draft Picks Autographs French-12
91Classic-13
91Star Pics-41
91Ultimate Draft-13
91Ultimate Draft-69
91Ultimate Draft-76
91Ultimate Draft-83
91Ultimate Draft French-13
91Classic Four-Sport *-13
92Upper Deck-234
92Finnish Semic-67
92Swedish Semic Elitserien Stickers-240
93Donruss-269
Rated Rookies-8
93Leaf-289
Freshman Phenoms-4
93Parkhurst-245
Emerald Ice-245
Calder Candidates-C5
Calder Candidates Gold-C5
93Penguins Foodland-20
93Pinnacle-449
Canadian-449
Super Rookies-8
Super Rookies Canadian-8
93PowerPlay-412
93Score-597
Gold-597
Canadian-597
Canadian Gold-597
93Stadium Club-393
Members Only Master Set-393
First Day Issue-393
93Ultra-395
Wave of the Future-10
93Upper Deck-500
SP-123
93Swedish Semic World Champ Stickers-14
94Be A Player Signature Cards-68
94Donruss-51
94Leaf-211
94OPC Premier-44
Special Effects-44
94Parkhurst-287
Gold-287
94Parkhurst SE-SE136
Gold-SE136
Vintage-4
94Penguins Foodland-15
94Pinnacle-370
Artist's Proofs-370
Rink Collection-370
94Topps/OPC Premier-44
Special Effects-44
94Ultra-349
94Upper Deck-190
Electric Ice-190
SP Inserts-SP151
SP Inserts Die Cuts-SP151
94Swedish Olympics Lillehammer*-290
94Classic Pro Prospects-26
95Finest-154
Refractors-154
95Parkhurst International-163
Emerald Ice-163
95Penguins Foodland-4
95Select Certified-106
Mirror Gold-106
95SP-116
95Ultra-291
95Upper Deck-73
Electric Ice-73
Electric Ice Gold-73
Special Edition-SE67
Special Edition Gold-SE67
95Swedish Upper Deck-245
95Swedish Globe World Championships-43
96Be A Player-123
Autographs-123
Autographs Silver-123
96Canucks Postcards-19
96Collector's Choice-275
96Upper Deck-170
97Collector's Choice-261
97Pacific-128
Copper-128
Emerald Green-128
Ice Blue-128
Red-128
Silver-128
97Pacific Omega-233
Copper-233
Dark Gray-233
Emerald Green-233
Gold-233
Ice Blue-233
97Panini Stickers-239
97Score-150
Artist's Proofs-150
Golden Blades-150
97Score Canucks-7
Platinum-7
Premier-7
97Upper Deck-173
98Be A Player-140
Press Release-140
98BAP Gold-140
98BAP Autographs-140
98BAP Autographs Gold-140
98BAP Tampa Bay All Star Game-140
98Finest-90
No Protectors-90
No Protectors Refractors-90
Refractors-90
98Pacific-431
Ice Blue-431
Red-431
98Pacific Omega-239
Red-239
Opening Day Issue-239
98Panini Stickers-220
98Upper Deck-379
Exclusives-379
Exclusives 1 of 1-379
Gold Reserve-379
99Aurora-143
Premiere Date-143
99BAP Memorabilia-289
Gold-289
Silver-289
99BAP Millennium-242
Emerald-242
Ruby-242
Sapphire-242
Signatures-242
Signatures Gold-242
99Crown Royale-138
Limited Series-138
Premiere Date-138
99O-Pee-Chee-171
99O-Pee-Chee Chrome-171
99O-Pee-Chee Chrome Refractors-171
99Pacific-429
Copper-429
Emerald Green-429
Gold-429
Ice Blue-429
Premiere Date-429
Red-429
99Pacific Dynagon Ice-197
Blue-197
Copper-197
Gold-197
Premiere Date-197
99Pacific Omega-236
Copper-236
Gold-236
Ice Blue-236
Premiere Date-236
99Panini Stickers-310
99Paramount-238
Copper-238
Emerald-238
Gold-238
Holographic Emerald-238
Holographic Gold-238
Holographic Silver-238
Ice Blue-238
Premiere Date-238
Red-238
Silver-238
99Revolution-144
Premiere Date-144
Red-144
Shadow Series-144
99SPx-151
Radiance-151
Spectrum-151
99Stadium Club-83
First Day Issue-83
One of a Kind-83
Printing Plates Black-83
Printing Plates Cyan-83
Printing Plates Magenta-83
Printing Plates Yellow-83
99Topps/OPC-171
99Topps/OPC Chrome-171
Refractors-171
99Topps Gold Label Class 1-58
Black-58
Black One of One-58
One of One-58
Red-58
Red One of One-58
99Topps Gold Label Class 2-58
99Topps Gold Label Class 2 Black-58
99Topps Gold Label Class 2 Black 1 of 1-58
99Topps Gold Label Class 2 One of One-58
99Topps Gold Label Class 2 Red-58
99Topps Gold Label Class 2 Red One of One-58
99Topps Gold Label Class 3-58
99Topps Gold Label Class 3 Black-58
99Topps Gold Label Class 3 Black 1 of 1-58
99Topps Gold Label Class 3 One of One-58
99Topps Gold Label Class 3 Red-58
99Topps Gold Label Class 3 Red One of One-58
99Topps Premier Plus-42
Parallel-42
99Upper Deck-298
Exclusives-298
Exclusives 1 of 1-298
99Upper Deck Gold Reserve-298
99Upper Deck MVP-206
Gold Script-206
Silver Script-206
Super Script-206
99Upper Deck MVP SC Edition-183
Gold Script-183
Silver Script-183
Super Script-183
99Upper Deck Retro-76
Gold-76
Platinum-76
99Upper Deck Victory-296
99Wayne Gretzky Hockey-170
00Aurora-144
Premiere Date-144
00BAP Memorabilia-41
Emerald-41
Ruby-41
Sapphire-41
Promos-41
00BAP Mem Chicago Sportsfest Copper-41
00BAP Memorabilia Chicago Sportsfest Blue-41
00BAP Memorabilia Chicago Sportsfest Gold-41
00BAP Memorabilia Chicago Sportsfest Ruby-41
00BAP Memorabilia Chicago Sun-Times Ruby-41
00BAP Memorabilia Chicago Sun-Times Gold-41
00BAP Mem Chicago Sun-Times Sapphire-41
00BAP Mem Toronto Fall Expo Copper-41
00BAP Memorabilia Toronto Fall Expo Gold-41
00BAP Memorabilia Toronto Fall Expo Ruby-41
00BAP Parkhurst 2000-P216
00BAP Signature Series-247
Emerald-247
Ruby-247
Sapphire-247
00Black Diamond-57
Gold-57
00Crown Royale-104
Ice Blue-104
Limited Series-104
Premiere Date-104
Red-104
00Kraft-2
00O-Pee-Chee-188
00O-Pee-Chee Parallel-188
00Pacific-412
00Pacific-449
Copper-412
Copper-449
Gold-412
Gold-449
Ice Blue-412
Ice Blue-449
Premiere Date-412
Premiere Date-449
00Panini Stickers-212
00Paramount-240
Copper-240
Gold-240
Holo-Gold-240
Holo-Silver-240
Ice Blue-240
Premiere Date-240
00Private Stock-96
Gold-96
Premiere Date-96
Retail-96
Silver-96
PS-2001 Action-58
00Revolution-144
Blue-144
Premiere Date-144
Red-144
00SP Authentic-87
00SPx-68
Spectrum-68
00Stadium Club-153
00Titanium-96
Blue-96
Gold-96
Premiere Date-96
Red-96
Retail-96
00Topps/OPC-188
Parallel-188
00Topps Chrome-125
OPC Refractors-125
Refractors-125
00Topps Gold Label Class 1-13
Gold-13
00Topps Gold Label Class 2-13
00Topps Gold Label Class 2 Gold-13
00Topps Gold Label Class 3-13
00Topps Gold Label Class 3 Gold-13
00Topps Gold Label Bullion-B10
00Topps Gold Label Bullion One to One-B10
00Topps Heritage-136
00Topps Premier Plus-68
Blue Ice-68
00Topps Stars-79
Blue-79
00UD Pros and Prospects-83
00UD Reserve-83
00Upper Deck-167
Exclusives Tier 1-167
Exclusives Tier 2-167
00Upper Deck Legends-128
Legendary Collection Bronze-128
Legendary Collection Gold-128
Legendary Collection Silver-128
00Upper Deck MVP-177
First Stars-177
Second Stars-177
Third Stars-177
00Upper Deck Victory-229
00Upper Deck Vintage-347
00Upper Deck Vintage-357
00Upper Deck Vintage-358
00Vanguard-96
Holographic Gold-96
Holographic Purple-96
Pacific Proofs-96
01Atomic-94
Blue-94
Gold-94
Premiere Date-94
Red-94
Team Nucleus-14
01BAP Memorabilia-193
Emerald-193
Ruby-193
Sapphire-193
All-Star Jerseys-ASJ40
All-Star Emblems-ASE40
All-Star Numbers-ASN40
All-Star Teammates-AST27
All-Star Teammates-AST29
Country of Origin-CO32
01BAP Signature Series-80
Autographs-80
Autographs Gold-80
Franchise Jerseys-FP-29
He Shoots-He Scores Prizes-35
Jerseys-GJ-70
Jersey Autographs-GUMN
Jersey and Stick Cards-GSJ-70
Teammates-TM-29
01BAP Update He Shoots-He Scores Prizes-9
01Bowman YoungStars-18
Gold-18
Ice Cubed-18
01Canucks Postcards-10
01Crown Royale-138
Blue-138
Premiere Date-138
Red-138
Retail-138
01EA Sports-7
01McDonald's Pacific-41
01O-Pee-Chee-15
01O-Pee-Chee Heritage Parallel-15
01O-Pee-Chee Heritage Parallel Limited-15
01O-Pee-Chee Premier Parallel-15
01Pacific-384
01Pacific-424
Extreme LTD-384
Gold-424
Hobby LTD-384
Premiere Date-384
Retail LTD-384
01Pacific Adrenaline-191
Blue-191
Premiere Date-191
Red-191
Retail-191
01Pacific Arena Exclusives-384
01Pacific Arena Exclusives-424
01Pacific Heads-Up-94
Blue-94
Premiere Date-94
Red-94
Silver-94
01Parkhurst-29
Gold-29
Silver-29
He Shoots-He Scores Prizes-12
Sticks-PS36
Teammates-T17
Teammates-T26
01Private Stock-94
Gold-94
Premiere Date-94
Retail-94
Silver-94
01Private Stock Pacific Nights-94
01SP Authentic-85
Limited-85
Limited Gold-85
Sign of the Times-MN
Sign of the Times-SSN
01SP Game Used-56
Authentic Fabric-AFMN
Authentic Fabric-DFNB
Authentic Fabric Gold-AFMN
01SPx-66
01SPx-80
01Sports Illustrated for Kids III-251
01Stadium Club-49
Award Winners-49
Master Photos-49
01Titanium-137
Hobby Parallel-137
Premiere Date-137
Retail-137
Retail Parallel-137
Double-Sided Jerseys-56
Double-Sided Jerseys-58
Double-Sided Patches-56
Double-Sided Patches-58
01Titanium Draft Day Edition-96
01Topps-15
Heritage Parallel-15
Heritage Parallel Limited-15
OPC Parallel-15
01Topps Chrome-15
Refractors-15
Black Border Refractors-15
01Topps Heritage-16
Refractors-16
01Topps Reserve-65
01UD Challenge for the Cup-86
01UD Honor Roll Jerseys-J-MN
01UD Honor Roll Jerseys Gold-J-MN
01UD Mask Collection-95
Gold-95
01UD Playmakers-97
01UD Premier Collection-49
Signatures-MN
Signatures Black-MN
01UD Top Shelf-43
01Upper Deck-167
Exclusives-167
Crunch Timers-CT13
Fantastic Finishers-FF3
Game Jerseys Series II-PFMN
Shooting Stars-SS18
EA Sports Gold-7
01Upper Deck Ice-41
01Upper Deck MVP-179
01Upper Deck Victory-338
01Upper Deck Victory-419
Gold-338
Gold-419
01Upper Deck Vintage-244
01Upper Deck Vintage-250
01Upper Deck Vintage-251
01Vanguard-97
Blue-97
Red-97
One of Ones-97
Premiere Date-97
Proofs-97
01Czech Stadion-246
02Atomic-97
Blue-97
Gold-97
Red-97
Cold Fusion-23
Hobby Parallel-97
Power Converters-19
02BAP All-Star Edition-64
He Shoots-He Score Prizes-20
Jerseys-64
Jerseys Gold-64
Jerseys Silver-64
02BAP First Edition-148
02BAP First Edition-301
02BAP First Edition-369
02BAP First Edition-371
02BAP First Edition-407H
He Shoots-He Scores Prizes-30
Jerseys-148
Scoring Leaders-19
02BAP Memorabilia-189
02BAP Memorabilia-229
Emerald-189
Emerald-229
Ruby-189
Ruby-229
Sapphire-189
Sapphire-229
All-Star Jerseys-ASJ-39
Franchise Players-FP-29
NHL All-Star Game-189
NHL All-Star Game-229
NHL All-Star Game Blue-189
NHL All-Star Game Blue-229
NHL All-Star Game Green-189
NHL All-Star Game Green-229
NHL All-Star Game Red-189
NHL All-Star Game Red-229
Teammates-TM-19
02BAP Memorabilia Toronto Fall Expo-189
02BAP Memorabilia Toronto Fall Expo-229
02BAP Signature Series-31
Autographs-31
Autograph Buybacks 1998-140
Autograph Buybacks 1999-242
Autograph Buybacks 2001-80
Autographs Gold-31
Franchise Players-FJ29
Jerseys-SGJ33
Jersey Autographs-SGJ33
Team Quads-TQ14
02BAP Ultimate Memorabilia Captains-5
02BAP Ultimate Memorabilia Emblems-7
02BAP Ultimate Memorabilia Jerseys-22
02BAP Ultimate Mem Jersey and Stick-16
02BAP Ultimate Memorabilia Nameplates-18
02BAP Ultimate Memorabilia Numbers-11
02Bowman YoungStars-68
Gold-68
Silver-68
02Canucks Team Issue-11
02Crown Royale-97
Blue-97
Red-97
Retail-97
Jerseys-23
Jerseys Gold-23
02eTopps-53
02ITG Used-75
02ITG Used-175
Franchise Players-F29
Franchise Players Autographs-F29
Franchise Players Gold-F29
Jerseys-GUJ33
Jersey Autographs-GUJ33
Jerseys Gold-GUJ33
Emblems-E31
Jersey and Stick-SJ33
Jersey and Stick Gold-SJ33
Teammates-T19
Teammates Gold-T19
02McDonald's Pacific-41
Jersey Patches Silver-19
Jersey Patches Gold-19
02NHL Power Play Stickers-153
02O-Pee-Chee-32
02O-Pee-Chee Jumbos-24
02O-Pee-Chee Premier Blue Parallel-32
02O-Pee-Chee Premier Red Parallel-32
02O-Pee-Chee Factory Set-32
02O-Pee-Chee Factory Set Hometown Heroes-HHC7
02Pacific-381
Blue-381
Red-381
Main Attractions-19
02Pacific Calder-51
Silver-51
Chasing Glory-10
Hart Stoppers-8
02Pacific Complete-202
Red-202
02Pacific Exclusive-169
Maximum Overdrive-19
02Pacific Heads-Up-122
Blue-122
Purple-122
Red-122
Inside the Numbers-23
02Pacific Quest for the Cup-97
Gold-97
Chasing the Cup-20
Jerseys-23
02Parkhurst-103
Bronze-103
Gold-103
Silver-103
Franchise Players-FP29
Hardware-A5
Hardware-H6
Hardware-P5
Jerseys-GJ50
Stick and Jerseys-SJ50
Teammates-TT18
02Parkhurst Retro-8
Minis-8
Franchise Players-RF29
He Shoots-He Scores Prizes-27
Hopefuls-HH3
Hopefuls-RR5
Jerseys-RJ16
02Private Stock Reserve-97
Blue-97
Red-97
Retail-97
02SP Authentic-85
Beckett Promos-85
Sign of the Times-MN
Super Premiums-SPMN
02SP Game Used-48
Authentic Fabrics-AFMN
Authentic Fabrics-AFNA
Authentic Fabrics Gold-AFMN
Authentic Fabrics Gold-AFNA
Authentic Fabrics Rainbow-AFMN
Authentic Fabrics Rainbow-AFNA
First Rounder Patches-MN
Piece of History-PHMN
Piece of History-PHNA
Piece of History Gold-PHMN
Piece of History Gold-PHNA
Piece of History Rainbow-PHMN
Piece of History Rainbow-PHNA
02SPx-73
Spectrum Gold-73
Spectrum Silver-73
Smooth Skaters-MN
Smooth Skaters Gold-MN
Smooth Skaters Silver-MN
Winning Materials-WMMN
Winning Materials Gold-MN
Winning Materials Silver-MN
Xtreme Talents-MN
Xtreme Talents Gold-MN
Xtreme Talents Silver-MN
02Stadium Club-15
Silver Decoy Cards-15
Proofs-15
Passport-11
02Titanium-98
Blue-98
Red-98
Retail-98
02Topps-32
OPC Blue Parallel-32
OPC Red Parallel-32
Captain's Cloth-CC5
Captain's Cloth-CC10
First Round Fabric-MN
Topps/OPC Hometown Heroes-HHC7
Own The Game-OTG2
Own The Game-OTG10
Factory Set-32
02Topps Chrome-32
Black Border Refractors-32
Refractors-32
First Round Fabric Patches-MN
02Topps Heritage-45
02Topps Heritage-120
Chrome Parallel-45
02Topps Total-102
Production-TP13
02UD Artistic Impressions-87
Gold-87
02UD Artistic Impressions Beckett Promos-87
02UD Artistic Impressions Retrospectives-R87
02UD Artistic Impressions Retrospect Gold-R87
02UD Artistic Impress Retrospect Auto-R87
02UD Artistic Impress Retrospect Silver-R87
02UD Honor Roll-68
02UD Honor Roll-99
02UD Mask Collection Instant Offense-IOMN
02UD Mask Collection Patches-PGMN
02UD Piece of History-87
Marks of Distinction-MN
Patches-PHMN
02UD Premier Collection-53
Signatures Bronze-SMN
Signatures Gold-SMN
Signatures Silver-SMN
02UD Top Shelf-87
Dual Player Jerseys-STNL
Signatures-MN
Triple Jerseys-HTNTH
02Upper Deck-171
Exclusives-171
All-Star Jerseys-ASMN
All-Star Performers-ASMN
Blow-Ups-C41
Fan Favorites-MN
Letters of Note-LNMN
Letters of Note Gold-LNMN
Patch Card Logo-MN
Patchwork-PWMN
Playbooks-PL15
02Upper Deck Classic Portraits-97
Hockey Royalty-SNL
Hockey Royalty Limited-SNL
Starring Cast-CMN
Starring Cast Limited-CMN
02Upper Deck MVP-179
Gold-179
Classics-179
Golden Classics-179
Highlight Nights-HN7
Overdrive-SO13
02Upper Deck Rookie Update-96
Autographs-MN
02Upper Deck Victory-211
Bronze-211
Gold-211
Silver-211
National Pride-NP50
02Upper Deck Vintage-246
02Upper Deck Vintage-289
02Upper Deck Vintage-308
Green Backs-246
Tall Boys-T62
Tall Boys Gold-T62
02Vanguard-97
LTD-97
East Meets West-1
Jerseys-48
Jerseys Gold-48
03McFarlane Hockey-60
03McFarlane Hockey-62
03BAP Memorabilia-50
Emerald-50
Gold-50
Ruby-50
Sapphire-50
All-Star Emblems-ASE-17
All-Star Jerseys-ASJ-27
All-Star Numbers-ASN-17
He Shoots-He Scores Points-4
He Shoots-He Scores Prizes-16
Jersey and Stick-SJ-15
Jerseys-GJ-17
Stanley Cup Playoffs-SCP-20
03BAP Ultimate Memorabilia Autographs-22
Gold-22
03BAP Ultimate Mem Auto Jerseys-22
03BAP Ultimate Mem Auto Emblems-22
03BAP Ultimate Memorabilia Emblems-15
03BAP Ultimate Memorabilia Emblems Gold-15
03BAP Ultimate Mem French Present Future-29
03BAP Ultimate Mem Hometown Heroes-4
03BAP Ultimate Mem Hometown Heroes Gold-4
03BAP Ultimate Memorabilia Jerseys-33
03BAP Ultimate Memorabilia Jerseys Gold-33
03BAP Ultimate Mem Jersey and Emblems-23
03BAP Ultimate Mem Jersey and Emblem Gold-23
03BAP Ultimate Mem Jersey and Numbers-23
03BAP Ultimate Mem Jersey and Number Gold-23
03BAP Ultimate Memorabilia Nameplates-4
03BAP Ultimate Mem Nameplates Gold-4
03BAP Ultimate Memorabilia Numbers-26
03BAP Ultimate Memorabilia Numbers Gold-26
03BAP Ultimate Memorabilia Triple Threads-22
03Beehive-194
Gold-194
Silver-194
Jumbos-24
Jumbo Variations-24
Jerseys-JT11
Signatures-RF17
03Black Diamond-100
Black-100
Green-100
Red-100
Threads-DT-MN
Threads Green-DT-MN
Threads Red-DT-MN
Threads Black-DT-MN

03Bowman-38
Gold-38
Goal to Goal-MN
03Bowman Chrome-38
Refractors-38
Gold Refractors-38
Xfractors-38
03Canucks Postcards-20
03Canucks Sav-on-Foods-4
03Canucks Sav-on-Foods-5
03Canucks Sav-on-Foods-NNO
03Crown Royale-98
Blue-98
Retail-98
Jerseys-25
Patches-25
Lords of the Rink-23
03ITG Action-536
Homeboys-HB1
Jerseys-M171
Jerseys-M269
League Leaders-L9
Trophy Winners-TW5
03ITG Used Signature Series-63
Gold-63
Autographs-MN
Autographs Gold-MN
Franchise-29
Franchise Autographs-29
Franchise Gold-29
Jerseys-47
Jerseys Gold-47
Jersey Autos-47
Emblems-34
Emblems Gold-34
Jersey and Stick-47
Jersey and Stick Gold-47
Teammates-5
Teammates Gold-5
03ITG VIP Jerseys-9
03McDonald's Pacific-54
Patches Silver-25
Patches Gold-25
Patches and Sticks-25
03NHL Sticker Collection-296
03O-Pee-Chee-40
03OPC Blue-40
03OPC Gold-40
03OPC Red-40
03Pacific-334
Blue-334
Red-334
Cramer's Choice-9
Main Attractions-15
03Pacific Calder-100
Silver-100
03Pacific Complete-45
Red-45
03Pacific Exhibit-198
Blue Backs-198
History Makers-8
03Pacific Heads-Up-98
Hobby LTD-98
Retail LTD-98
Fast Forwards-9
Fast Forwards LTD-9
03Pacific Invincible-97
Blue-97
Red-97
Retail-97
Afterburners-10
Top Line-9
03Pacific Luxury Suite-22A
03Pacific Luxury Suite-22B
03Pacific Luxury Suite-22C
03Pacific Luxury Suite-22D
03Pacific Prism-149
Blue-149
Patches-149
Red-149
Retail-149
Stat Masters-9
03Pacific Quest for the Cup-100
Blue-100
03Pacific Supreme-97
Blue-97
Red-97
Retail-97
Generations-12
Jerseys-24
Team-9
03Parkhurst Rookie-50
Jerseys-GJ-23
Jersey Autographs-GUJ-MN
Jerseys Gold-GJ-23
03Private Stock Reserve-210
Blue-210
Patches-210
Red-210
Retail-210
03SP Authentic-86
Limited-86
10th Anniversary-SP20
10th Anniversary Limited-SP20
Breakout Seasons-B7
Breakout Seasons Limited-B7
Foundations-F6
Foundations Limited-F6
Honors-H29
Honors Limited-H29
Sign of the Times-NB
03SP Game Used-48
Gold-48
Authentic Fabrics-DFNB
Authentic Fabrics-QNBJM
Authentic Fabrics Gold-DFNB
Authentic Fabrics Gold-QNBJM
Authentic Patches-APMN
Double Threads-DTNB
Limited Threads-LTMN
Limited Threads Gold-LTMN
Team Threads-TTNBJ
Top Threads-NBJM
03SPx-94
03SPx-152
03SPx-190
Radiance-94
Radiance-152
Radiance-190
Spectrum-94
Spectrum-152
Spectrum-190
Fantasy Franchise-FF-NBM
Fantasy Franchise Limited-FF-NBM
Origins-O-MN
Signature Threads-ST-MN
Style-SPX-NZ
Style Limited-SPX-NZ

VIP-VIP-NB
VIP Limited-VIP-NB
Winning Materials-WM-MN
Winning Materials Limited-WM-MN
03Titanium-189
Hobby Jersey Number Parallels-189
Patches-189
Retail-189
Stat Masters-10
03Topps-40
03Topps-PP5
Blue-40
Gold-40
Red-40
Box Toppers-6
Topps/OPC Idols-II17
Own the Game-OTG2
03Topps C55-58
Minis-58
Minis American Back-58
Minis American Back Red-58
Minis Bazooka Back-58
Minis Brooklyn Back-58
Minis Hat Trick Back-58
Minis O Canada Back-58
Minis O Canada Back Red-58
Minis Stanley Cup Back-58
Award Winners-11
Relics-TRMN
03Topps Pristine-80
Gold Refractor Die Cuts-80
Refractors-80
Autographs-PE-MN
Autographs Gold-BE-MN
Patches-PP-MN
Patch Refractors-PP-MN
Popular Demand Relics-PD-MN
Popular Demand Relic Refractors-PD-MN
Press Plates Black-80
Press Plates Cyan-80
Press Plates Magenta-80
Press Plates Yellow-80
03UD Honor Roll-86
03UD Honor Roll-121
Grade A Jerseys-TVAN
03UD Premier Collection-56
NHL Shields-SH-MN
Signatures-PS-MNH
Stars-ST-MN
Stars Patches-ST-MN
Teammates-PT-VC
Teammates Patches-PT-VC
03Upper Deck-185
Big Playmakers-BP-MN
BuyBacks-8
BuyBacks-9
BuyBacks-10
BuyBacks-11
BuyBacks-12
BuyBacks-13
BuyBacks-14
BuyBacks-15
BuyBacks-16
BuyBacks-17
BuyBacks-18
Canadian Exclusives-185
Franchise Fabrics-FF-MN
HG-185
Patches-LD7
Patches-PLG-MN
Patches-PNM-MN
Patches-PNR-MN
Team Essentials-TL-MN
Three Stars-TS14
03Upper Deck Classic Portraits-95
Headliners-HH-MN
Hockey Royalty-BNM
03Upper Deck Ice-87
Gold-87
Authentics-IA-MN
Breakers-IB-MN
Breaker Patches-IB-MN
Frozen Fabrics-FF-MN
Frozen Fabric Patches-FF-MN
03Upper Deck MVP-408
Gold Script-408
Silver Script-408
Canadian Exclusives-408
Clutch Performers-CP2
Lethal Lineups-LL4
ProSign-PS-MN
SportsNut-SN87
Talent-MT3
03Upper Deck Rookie Update-86
03Upper Deck Rookie Update-164
All-Star Lineup-AS8
Skills-SKMN
03Upper Deck Trilogy-95
03Upper Deck Trilogy-110
Authentic Patches-AP16
Crest Variations-110
Limited-95
Limited-110
Limited Threads-LT22
Scripts-S2MN
Scripts Limited-S2MN
Scripts Red-S2MN
03Upper Deck Victory-186
Bronze-186
Gold-186
Silver-186
Game Breakers-GB44
03Toronto Star-96
Foil-20
04Pacific-258
Blue-258
Red-258
04SP Authentic-88
04SP Authentic-149
Limited-88
Limited-149
Buybacks-115
Buybacks-116
Buybacks-117
Buybacks-118
Buybacks-119
Buybacks-120
Buybacks-121
Buybacks-122
Buybacks-123
Buybacks-124
Buybacks-125
Buybacks-126
Octographs-OS-CAP
Rookie Review-RR-MN
Sign of the Times-ST-MN
Sign of the Times-DS-MZ
Sign of the Times-DS-NJ

Sign of the Times-QS-LKSN
Sign of the Times-QS-VANC
Sign of the Times-FS-RGT
Sign of the Times-FS-VAN
04UD All-World-66
04UD All-World-102
Gold-66
Autographs-66
Autographs-102
Dual Autographs-AD-NN
Quad Autographs-AQ-NAM
Six Autographs-AS-SWD
04UD Toronto Fall Expo Priority Signings-MN
04Ultimate Collection-41
Buybacks-51
Buybacks-52
Buybacks-53
Buybacks-54
Buybacks-55
Buybacks-56
Buybacks-57
Dual Logos-UL2-NM
Jerseys-UGJ-MN
Jerseys Gold-UGJ-MN
Jersey Autographs-UGJA-MN
Patches-UP-MNA
Patches-UP-MNB
Patch Autographs-UPA-MN
Signatures-US-MN
Signature Logos-ULA-MN
Signature Patches-SP-MN
04Upper Deck-168
Big Playmakers-BP-MN
Canadian Exclusives-168
HG Glossy Gold-168
HG Glossy Silver-168
Jersey Autographs-GJA-MK
Jersey Autographs-GJA-MN
Three Stars-AS9
04Swedish Alfabilder Alfa Stars-19
04Swedish Alfabilder Autographs-101
04Swedish Alfabilder Limited Autographs-101
04Swedish Alfabilder Next In Line-5
04Swedish Alfabilder Proof Parallels-19
04Swedish MoDo Postcards-10
04Swedish Pure Skills-67
Parallel-67
Professional Power-MN
05Be A Player-87
First Period-87
Second Period-87
Third Period-87
Overtime-87
Class Action-CA17
Dual Signatures-NL
Outtakes-OT48
Signatures-NA
Signatures Gold-NA
Triple Signatures-HSN
Triple Signatures-NKI
Triple Signatures-NMS
Triple Signatures-SNL
05Beehive-87
05Beehive-219
Beige -87
Blue -87
Gold-87
Red -87
Matte-87
Matted Materials-MMMN
Matted Materials Remarkable-RMMN
PhotoGraphs-PGMN
Signature Scrapbook-SSMN
05Black Diamond-145
Emerald-145
Gold-145
Onyx-145
Ruby-145
Gemography-G-MN
Gemography Emerald-G-MN
Gemography Gold-G-MN
Gemography Onyx-G-MN
Gemography Ruby-G-MN
05Hot Prospects-96
En Fuego-96
Red Hot-96
White Hot-96
05McDonalds Upper Deck-50
Autographs-MA2
Chasing the Cup-CC4
Jerseys-MJ4
Patches-MP4
Top Scorers-TS10
05Panini Stickers-355
05Parkhurst-465
05Parkhurst-524
05Parkhurst-699
Facsimile Auto Parallel-465
Facsimile Auto Parallel-524
Facsimile Auto Parallel-699
True Colors-TCVAN
True Colors-TCVAN
05SP Authentic-98
05SP Authentic-128
Limited-98
Limited-128
Chirography-SPMN
Marks of Distinction-MDMN
Octographs-OF
Prestigious Pairings-PPNL
Sign of the Times Triples-TNMB
Sign of the Times Fives-ISNKN
05SP Game Used-96
Autographs-96
Gold-96
Authentic Fabrics-AF-MN
Authentic Fabrics Autographs-AAF-MN
Authentic Fabrics Dual-MT
Authentic Fabrics Dual Autographs-MT
Authentic Fabrics Gold-AF-MN
Authentic Fabrics Triple-KNS
Authentic Fabrics Triple-SFN
Authentic Fabrics Triple-SNI
Authentic Patches-AP-MN
Authentic Patches Autographs-AAP-MN
Authentic Patches Dual-MT
Authentic Patches Dual Autographs-MT
Authentic Patches Triple-KNS
Authentic Patches Triple-SFN
Authentic Patches Triple-SNI
Auto Draft-AD-MN
Awesome Authentics-AA-MN
Awesome Authentics Gold-DA-MN
SIGnificance-MN
SIGnificance Gold-S-MN
SIGnificance Extra-NM
SIGnificance Extra Gold-NM
Significant Numbers-SN-MN

05SPx-88
Spectrum-88
Winning Combos-WC-CN
Winning Combos-WC-MN
Winning Combos Autographs-AWC-MN
Winning Combos Gold-WC-CN
Winning Combos Gold-WC-MN
Winning Combos Spectrum-WC-CN
Winning Combos Spectrum-WC-MN
Winning Materials-WM-MN
Winning Materials Autographs-AWM-MN
Winning Materials Gold-WM-MN
Winning Materials Spectrum-WM-MN
Xcitement Superstars-XS-MN
Xcitement Superstars Gold-XS-MN
Xcitement Superstars Spectrum-XS-MN
05The Cup-97
Gold-97
Black Rainbow-97
Dual NHL Shields-DSMN
Dual NHL Shields-DSNB
Dual NHL Shields-DSNZ
Dual NHL Shields Autographs-ADSNB
Dual NHL Shields Autographs-ADSNZ
Emblems of Endorsement-EEMN
Hardware Heroes-HHMN
Honorable Numbers-HNMN
Limited Logos-LLMN
Masterpiece Pressplates-97
Masterpiece Pressplates (Rookie Update)-219
Noble Numbers-NNTN
Patch Variation-P97
Patch Variation Autographs-AP97
Property of-POMN
Scripted Numbers-SNND
Scripted Numbers-SNTN
Scripted Numbers Dual-DSNBN
Scripted Numbers Dual-DSNZN
Scripted Swatches-SSMN
Signature Patches-SPMN
05UD Artifacts-98
05UD Artifacts-198
Blue-98
Blue-198
Gold-98
Gold-198
Green-98
Green-198
Pewter-98
Pewter-198
Red-98
Red-198
Auto Facts-AF-MN
Auto Facts Blue-AF-MN
Auto Facts Copper-AF-MN
Auto Facts Pewter-AF-MN
Auto Facts Silver-AF-MN
Gold Autographed-98
Gold Autographed-198
Remarkable Artifacts-RA-NA
Remarkable Artifacts Dual-RA-NA
Treasured Patches-TP-MN
Treasured Patches Autographed-TP-MN
Treasured Patches Dual-TPD-MN
Treasured Patches Dual Autographed-TPD-MN
Treasured Patches Pewter-TP-MN
Treasured Patches Silver-TP-MN
Treasured Swatches-TS-MN
Treasured Swatches Autographed-TS-MN
Treasured Swatches Blue-TS-MN
Treasured Swatches Copper-TS-MN
Treasured Swatches Dual-TSD-MN
Treasured Swatches Dual Autographed-TSD-MN
Treasured Swatches Dual Blue-TSD-MN
Treasured Swatches Dual Copper-TSD-MN
Treasured Swatches Dual Maroon-TSD-MN
Treasured Swatches Dual Pewter-TSD-MN
Treasured Swatches Dual Silver-TSD-MN
Treasured Swatches Maroon-TS-MN
Treasured Swatches Pewter-TS-MN
Treasured Swatches Silver-TS-MN
05UD PowerPlay-88
05UD PowerPlay-118
Rainbow-88
Power Marks-PMMN
05UD Toronto Fall Expo Priority Signings-PS-MN
05Ultimate Collection-86
Gold-86
Endorsed Emblems-EEMN
Jerseys-JMN
Marquee Attractions-MA47
Marquee Attractions Signatures-SMA47
Premium Patches-PPMN
Premium Swatches-PSMN
Ultimate Achievements-UAMN
Ultimate Patches-PMN
Ultimate Signatures-USMN
Ultimate Signatures Foursomes-UFINNL
Ultimate Signatures Pairings-UPNB
05Ultra-189
Gold-189
Ice-189
Scoring Kings-SK17
Scoring Kings Jerseys-SKJ-MN
Scoring Kings Jersey Autographs-KAJ-MN
Scoring Kings Patches-SKP-MN
Scoring Kings Patch Autographs-KAP-MN
05Upper Deck-429
05Upper Deck All-Time Greatest-57
05Upper Deck Big Playmakers-B-MN
05Upper Deck Goal Rush-GR10
05Upper Deck Hometown Heroes-HH25
05Upper Deck Jerseys Series II-J2MN
05Upper Deck Majestic Materials-MMMN
05Upper Deck NHL Generations-DNZ
05Upper Deck Notable Numbers-N-MN
05Upper Deck Patches-P-MN
05Upper Deck Scrapbooks-HS22
05Upper Deck Shooting Stars-S-MN
05Upper Deck Ice-95
Rainbow-95
Cool Threads-CTMN
Cool Threads Autographs-ACTMN
Cool Threads Glass-CTMN
Cool Threads Patches-CTPMN
Cool Threads Patch Autographs-CAPMN
Signature Swatches-SSMN
05Upper Deck MVP-369
Gold-369
Platinum-369
Materials Triples-T-VAN
05Upper Deck Rookie Update-96
05Upper Deck Rookie Update-219
Inspirations Patch Rookies-219
05Upper Deck Trilogy-88
05Upper Deck Trilogy-130
Crystal-130
Crystal Autographs-130

Honorary Patches-HP-MN
Honorary Patch Scripts-HSP-MN
Honorary Swatches-HS-MN
Honorary Swatch Scripts-HSS-MN
Ice Scripts-IS-MN
Scripts-SCS-MN
05Upper Deck Victory-189
Black-189
Gold-189
Silver-189
Blow-Ups-BU41
Game Breakers-GB45
Stars on Ice-SI44
05Swedish SHL Elitset-100
06Be A Player-76
Autographs-76
Profiles-PP15
Profiles Autographs-PP15
Signatures-NA
Signatures 10-82
Signatures 25-82
Signatures Duals-DLN
Signatures Trios-TLNM
Signatures Foursomes-FFLNA
Up Close and Personal-UC32
Up Close and Personal Autographs-UC32
06Be A Player Portraits-96
Dual Signature Portraits-DSLN
Sensational Six-SSSJM
Signature Portraits-SPMN
06Beehive-3
06Beehive-163
Blue-3
Gold-3
Matte-3
Red Facsimile Signatures-3
Wood-3
5 X 7 Black and White-3
5 X 7 Dark Wood-3
06Black Diamond-146
Black-146
Black-167B
Gold-146
Ruby-146
Jerseys-JMN
Jerseys Black-JMN
Jerseys Gold-JMN
Jerseys Ruby-JMN
Jerseys Black Autographs -JMN
06Canucks Postcards-15
06Flair Showcase-96
06Flair Showcase-199
06Flair Showcase-267
06Flair Showcase-299
Parallel-96
Parallel-199
Parallel-267
Parallel-299
Hot Numbers-HN41
Hot Numbers Parallel-HN41
Inks-IMN
Stitches-SSMN
06Fleer-188
Tiffany-188
Fabricology-FMN
Speed Machines-SM24
Total O-024
06Gatorade-76
06Hot Prospects-95
Red Hot-95
White Hot-95
Hot Materials -HMMN
Hot Materials Red Hot-HMMN
Hot Materials White Hot-HMMN
06McDonald's Upper Deck-47
06McDonald's Upper Deck-54
Autographs-AMN
Jerseys-JMN
Patches-PMN
06NHL POG-46
06O-Pee-Chee-486
06O-Pee-Chee-670
06O-Pee-Chee-699
Rainbow-486
Rainbow-670
Rainbow-699
Swatches-S-MN
06Panini Stickers-354
06SP Authentic-3
06SP Authentic-132
Limited-3
Limited-132
Sign of the Times Triples-ST3NLM
06SP Game Used-96
Gold-96
Rainbow-96
Authentic Fabrics-AFMN
Authentic Fabrics Parallel-AFMN
Authentic Fabrics Patches-AFMN
Authentic Fabrics Dual-AF2NL
Authentic Fabrics Dual Patches-AF2NL
Authentic Fabrics Triple-AF3VAN
Authentic Fabrics Triple Patches-AF3VAN
Authentic Fabrics Sevens-AF7LBP
Authentic Fabrics Sevens Patches-AF7LBP
Authentic Fabrics Eights-AF8SWE
Authentic Fabrics Eights Patches-AF8SWE
By The Letter-BLMN
Inked Sweaters Dual-IS2NM
Inked Sweaters Dual Patches-IS2NM
Letter Marks-LMMN
06SPx-97
Spectrum-97
SPxcitement-X96
SPxcitement Spectrum-X96
SPxcitement Autographs-X96
Winning Materials-WMMN
Winning Materials Spectrum-WMMN
Winning Materials Autographs-WMMN
06Sunkist-6
06The Cup-88
Autographed Foundations-CQMN
Autographed Foundations Patches-CQMN
Autographed NHL Shields Duals-DASLN
Autographed NHL Shields Duals-DASNM
Autographed NHL Shields Duals-DASZN
Autographed Patches-88
Black Rainbow-88
Foundations-CQMN
Foundations Patches-CQMN
Gold-88
Gold Patches-88
Honorable Numbers-HNMN
Jerseys-88
Masterpiece Pressplates-88
Scripted Swatches-SSMN
Scripted Swatches Duals-DSLN
06UD Artifacts-4

06UD Artifacts-200
Blue-4
Blue-200
Gold-4
Gold-200
Platinum-4
Platinum-200
Radiance-4
Radiance-200
Autographed Radiance Parallel-4
Autographed Radiance Parallel-200
Red-4
Red-200
Treasured Patches Black-TSMN
Treasured Patches Blue-TSMN
Treasured Patches Gold-TSMN
Treasured Patches Platinum-TSMN
Treasured Patches Red-TSMN
Treasured Patches Autographed Black Tag Parallel-TSMN
Treasured Swatches-TSMN
Treasured Swatches Black-TSMN
Treasured Swatches Blue-TSMN
Treasured Swatches Gold-TSMN
Treasured Swatches Platinum-TSMN
Treasured Swatches Red-TSMN
Treasured Swatches Autographed Black-TSMN
Tundra Tandems-TTLN
Tundra Tandems-TTNO
Tundra Tandems Black-TTLN
Tundra Tandems Black-TTNO
Tundra Tandems Blue-TTLN
Tundra Tandems Blue-TTNO
Tundra Tandems Gold-TTLN
Tundra Tandems Gold-TTNO
Tundra Tandems Platinum-TTLN
Tundra Tandems Platinum-TTNO
Tundra Tandems Red-TTLN
Tundra Tandems Red-TTNO
Tundra Tandems Dual Patches Red-TTLN
Tundra Tandems Dual Patches Red-TTNO
06UD Mini Jersey Collection-95
Jerseys-MN
Jersey Variations-MN
Jersey Autographs-MN
06UD Powerplay-95
Impact Rainbow-95
In Action-IA13
Specialists-SMN
Specialists Patches-PMN
06Ultimate Collection-58
Jerseys-UJ-MN
Jerseys Dual-UJ2-LN
Patches-UJ-MN
Patches Dual-UJ2-LN
Premium Patches-PS-MN
Premium Swatches-PS-MN
Ultimate Signatures Logos-SL-MN
06Ultra-188
Gold Medallion-188
Ice Medallion-188
Action-UA30
Difference Makers-DM8
Scoring Kings-SK18
Uniformity-UMN
Uniformity Patches-UPMO
Uniformity Autographed Jerseys-UAMN
06Upper Deck Arena Giveaways-VAN1
06Upper Deck-188
Exclusives Parallel-188
High Gloss Parallel-188
All World-AW20
Game Jerseys-JMN
Game Patches-PMN
Generations Duals-G2NZ
Generations Triples-G3NZS
Generations Patches Dual-G2PNZ
Generations Patches Triple-G3PNZS
Goal Rush-GR7
Masterpieces-188
Signatures-SMN
Walmart Tins Oversize-188
06Upper Deck MVP-283
Gold Script-283
Super Script-283
Autographs-OANM
Clutch Performers-CP23
Gotta Have Hart-HH24
Jerseys-OJTN
06Upper Deck Ovation-48
06Upper Deck Sweet Shot-99
Signature Sticks-STMN
Sweet Stitches-SSMN
Sweet Stitches Duals-SSMN
Sweet Stitches Triples-SSMN
06Upper Deck Trilogy-96
Combo Autographed Jerseys-CJNL
Combo Autographed Patches-CJNL
Combo Clearcut Autographs-C2NM
Honorary Scripted Patches-HSPMN
Honorary Scripted Swatches-HSSMN
Honorary Swatches-HSMN
Ice Scripts-ISMN
Scripts-S3MN
Scripts-TSMN
06Upper Deck Victory-192
06Upper Deck Victory Black-192
06Upper Deck Victory Gold-192
06Upper Deck Victory GameBreakers-GB49
06Upper Deck Victory Oversize Cards-MN
07Upper Deck Victory-137
Black-137
Gold-137
GameBreakers-GB45
Oversize Cards-OS32
Stars on Ice-SI38

Naslund, Mats

81Swedish Semic Hockey VM Stickers-11
82Canadiens Postcards-16
82Canadiens Steinberg-12
82Swedish Semic VM Stickers-13
83Canadiens Postcards-18
83NHL Key Tags-68
83O-Pee-Chee-193
83O-Pee-Chee Stickers-71
83Puffy Stickers-1
83Topps Stickers-71
83Vachon-50
84Canadiens Postcards-18
84O-Pee-Chee-267
84O-Pee-Chee Stickers-155
84O-Pee-Chee Stickers-156
85Canadiens Placemats-2
85Canadiens Placemats-7
85Canadiens Postcards-22
85Canadiens Provigo-12
85O-Pee-Chee-102
85O-Pee-Chee Stickers-131
85Topps-102
86Canadiens Postcards-15
86Kraft Drawings-50
86O-Pee-Chee-161
86O-Pee-Chee Stickers-11
86O-Pee-Chee Stickers-122
86Topps-161
86Topps Sticker Inserts-8
87Canadiens Kodak-4
87Canadiens Postcards-20
87Canadiens Vachon Stickers-27
87Canadiens Vachon Stickers-45
87Canadiens Vachon Stickers-46
87Canadiens Vachon Stickers-47
87Canadiens Vachon Stickers-48
87Canadiens Vachon Stickers-87
87O-Pee-Chee-16
87O-Pee-Chee Box Bottoms-L
87O-Pee-Chee Stickers-6
87Panini Stickers-61
87Pro-Sport All-Stars-18
87Topps-16
87Topps Box Bottoms-L
88Canadiens Postcards-21
88Esso All-Stars-32
88Frito-Lay Stickers-25
88O-Pee-Chee-156
88O-Pee-Chee Minis-26
88O-Pee-Chee Stickers-50
88O-Pee-Chee Stickers-215
88Panini Stickers-259
88Panini Stickers-406
88Topps-156
89Canadiens Kraft-17
89Canadiens Postcards-25
89Canadiens Provigo Figurines-26
89Kraft-23
89O-Pee-Chee-118
89O-Pee-Chee Box Bottoms-H
89O-Pee-Chee Stickers-46
89Panini Stickers-234
89Topps-118
89Topps Box Bottoms-H
90Panini Stickers-62
91Pinnacle-389
French-389
91Finnish Semic World Champ Stickers-49
91Swedish Semic Elitserien Stickers-188
91Swedish Semic Elitserien Stickers-349
91Swedish Semic World Champ Stickers-49
92Finnish Semic-63
92Swedish Semic Elitserien Stickers-220
93Swedish Semic Elitserien-191
94Fleer-14
94Swedish Leaf Gold Cards-14
95Collector's Choice-321
Player's Club-321
Player's Club Platinum-321
95Donruss-53
95Swedish Globe World Championships-72
95Swedish Globe World Championships-245
97Swedish Alfabilder Autographs-15
01Swedish Alfabilder-15
02UD Foundations-52
Lasting Impressions Sticks-L-MN
Signs of Greatness-SGMN
03Crown Royale Global Conquest-8
03UD All-World-47
04UD All-World-113
Gold-47
Autographs-47
Autographs-113
Dual Autographs-AD-NN
Triple Autographs-AT-KSN
Triple Autographs-AT-NLN
Quad Autographs-AQ-NAM
Quad Autographs-AQ-OAS
04Swedish Alfabilder Alfa Stars-51
04Swedish Alfabilder Proof Parallels-51
05SPx Xcitement Legends-XL-MN
05SPx Xcitement Legends Gold-XL-MN
05SPx Xcitement Legends Spectrum-XL-MN
05UD Artifacts-139
Blue-139
Gold-139
Green-139
Pewter-139
Red-139
Gold Autographed-139
06ITG International Ice-49
06ITG International Ice-96
06ITG International Ice-113
Gold-49
Gold-96
Gold-113
Autographs-AMN
Autographs-AMN2
Autographs-AMN3
Cornerstones-IC03
Cornerstones Gold-IC03
Emblem Autographs-GUE26
Emblem Autographs Gold-GUE26
Emblems-GUE26
Emblems Gold-GUE26
International Rivals-IR08
Jersey Autographs-GUJ26
Jersey Autographs Gold-GUJ26
Jerseys-GUJ26
Jerseys Gold-GUJ26
My Country My Team-MC16
My Country My Team Gold-MC16
Numbers-GUN26
Numbers Autographs-GUN26
Numbers Autographs Gold-GUN26
Numbers Gold-GUN26
Teammates-IT15
Teammates Gold-IT15
06ITG Ultimate Memorabilia-100
Artist Proof-100
06Parkhurst-140
Autographs-140

Nason, Kyle

03Regina Pats-14
04South Surrey Eagles-20
04Surrey Eagles-17
04Regina Pats-14
04Surrey Eagles-17

Nasreddine, Alain

917th Inn. Sketch QMJHL-277
93Classic Four-Sport *-225
Gold-225
97Indianapolis Ice-21
98Bowman's Best-130
Refractors-130
Atomic Refractors-130
98Canadiens Team Issue-13
00Hamilton Bulldogs-22
01Hamilton Bulldogs-17
03Bridgeport Sound Tigers-7B
04Wilkes-Barre Scranton Penguins-24
05WBS Penguins-20
06Wilkes-Barre Scranton Penguins-1
06Wilkes-Barre Scranton Penguins Jerseys-21

Nasreddine, Samy

97Peoria Rivermen-3
97Bowman CHL-45
OPC-45
00San Diego Gulls-14
05Quad City Mallards-10
06UK Coventry Blaze-4

Nasstrom, Anders

92Swedish Semic Elitserien Stickers-224

Nastasi, Tommy

93Quebec Pee-Wee Tournament-727

Naster, Mario

94German DEL-167
99German Bundesliga 2-239

Nastiuk, Kevin

02Medicine Hat Tigers-17
03Medicine Hat Tigers-6
04SP Authentic Rookie Redemptions-PP41
04Medicine Hat Tigers-16
04ITG Heroes and Prospects-205
04ITG Heroes/Prospects Toronto Expo '05-205
05Beehive Signature Scrapbook-SSKN
05Black Diamond-222
05Hot Prospects-228
En Fuego-228
Hot Materials-HMKN
Red Hot-228
White Hot-228
05Parkhurst Signatures-KN
05SP Authentic-143
Limited-143
05SP Game Used-120
Autographs-120
Gold-120
Rookie Exclusives-KN
Rookie Exclusives Silver-RE-KN
05SPx-142
Spectrum-142
Xcitement Rookies-XR-KN
Xcitement Rookies Gold-XR-KN
Xcitement Rookies Spectrum-XR-KN
05The Cup-155
Autographed Rookie Patches Gold Rainbow-155
Black Rainbow Rookies-155
Masterpiece Pressplates (Artifacts)-236
Masterpiece Pressplates (Black Diamond)-222
Masterpiece Pressplates (Ice)-122
Masterpiece Pressplates (MVP)-409
Masterpiece Pressplates (Power Play)-139
Masterpiece Pressplates (Rookie Update)-201
Masterpiece Pressplates SPA Autos-143
Masterpiece Pressplates (SP Game Used)-120
Masterpiece Pressplates (SPx)-142
Masterpiece Pressplates (SPx)-142
Masterpiece Pressplates Ult Coll-140
Masterpiece Pressplates Autographs-155
Platinum Rookies-155
05UD Artifacts-236
Gold-RED36
05UD PowerPlay-139
05Ultimate Collection-140
Gold-140
Jerseys Dual-DJWN
Ultimate Patches Dual-DPWN
05Ultra-208
Gold-208
Ice-208
Rookie Uniformity Jerseys-RU-KN
Rookie Uniformity Jersey Autographs-ARU-KN
Rookie Uniformity Patches-RUP-KN
Rookie Uniformity Patch Autographs-ARP-KN
05Upper Deck Rookie Ink-RIKN
05Upper Deck Rookie Threads-RTKN
05Upper Deck Rookie Threads Autographs-ARTKN
05Upper Deck Ice-122
Premieres Auto Patches-AIPKN
05Upper Deck MVP-409
Gold-409
Platinum-409
05Upper Deck Rookie Update-201
Inspirations Patch Rookies-201
05ITG Heroes and Prospects Net Prospects-NP-18
05ITG Heroes and Prospects Net Prospects Gold-NP-18
06Las Vegas Wranglers-16

Nasvall, Fredrick

96Quad-City Mallards-8
97Mobile Mysticks-15
97Mobile Mysticks Kellogg's-15
00Swedish Upper Deck-28

Natale, Cerrone P

93Quebec Pee-Wee Tournament-1421

Nater, Roger

93Swiss HNL-358
95Swiss HNL-410

Nathe, Bryan

02Brandon Wheat Kings-4
03Everett Silvertips-2

Nathe, Chris

02Tri-City Stormfront-9

Nattrass, Ralph

44Beehive Group II Photos-130

Nattress, Ric

82Canadiens Postcards-17
82Canadiens Steinberg-13
83Canadiens Postcards-19
84Canadiens Postcards-19
87Flames Red Rooster-18
87Panini Stickers-307
88Flames Postcards-22
88O-Pee-Chee-238
88O-Pee-Chee Stickers-91
90Flames IGA/McGavin's-17
90O-Pee-Chee-459
90Pro Set-426
90Score-302C
Canadian-302C
91Bowman-266
91Flames Panini Team Stickers-13
91Flames IGA-12
91Pro Set-363
French-363
91Score Canadian Bilingual-249
91Score Canadian English-249
91Stadium Club-217
92Bowman-63
92Flyers J.C. Penney-18
92Flyers Upper Deck Sheets-26
92O-Pee-Chee-98
92Score-344
Canadian-344
92Stadium Club-328
92Topps-219

Gold-219G
92Ultra-374
93Score-381
Canadian-381
Natyshak, Mike
88ProCards AHL-116
Natywary, Steve
05PEI Rocket-22
Naud, Daniel
94German DEL-10
Naud, Eric
93Amos Les Forestiers-15
97Providence Bruins-11
98Abilene Aviators-11
99ECHL All-Star Southern Conference-7
99Jacksonville Lizard Kings-10
02Pee Dee Pride RBI-142
03Columbus Stars-2
Naud, Jasmin
93Quebec Pee-Wee Tournament-61
Naud, Martin
93Quebec Pee-Wee Tournament-54
Naud, Sylvain
907th Inn. Sketch QMJHL-52
907th Inn. Sketch Memorial Cup-63
92Tulsa Oilers-11
94Central Hockey League-103
95Central Hockey League-67
97New Mexico Scorpions-6
97New Mexico Scorpions II-3
97New Mexico Scorpions II-4
Naughton, Stephen
98Pensacola Ice Pilots-6
Naukkarinen, Seppo
65Finnish Hellas-132
Nault, Francis
98Muskegon Fury-8
99Muskegon Fury-10
00Muskegon Fury-18
01Flint Generals-12
03Reading Royals-14
03Reading Royals RBI Sports-297
Naumann, Andreas
91Upper Deck-678
French-678
91Upper Deck Czech World Juniors-41
94German First League-589
95German DEL-44
99German Bundesliga 2-57
Naumenko, Gregg
95North Iowa Huskies-22
99Cincinnati Mighty Ducks-32
00BAP Memorabilia-516
01BAP Memorabilia-205
Emerald-205
Ruby-205
Sapphire-205
01Between the Pipes-37
Jerseys-GJ34
01O-Pee-Chee-306
01O-Pee-Chee Premier Parallel-308
01Topps-308
OPC Parallel-308
01Upper Deck MVP-189
01Upper Deck Victory-361
Gold-361
03BAP Memorabilia Deep in the Crease-D7
03Augusta Lynx-46
Naumenko, Nick
92North Dakota Fighting Sioux-23
98Las Vegas Thunder-15
99Kansas City Blades Supercuts-12
00Cleveland Lumberjacks-5
02German Adler Mannheim Eagles Postcards-14
02German DEL City Press-249
05Chicago Wolves-14
Naumenko, Oleg
00Russian Hockey League-14
Naumov, Sergei
94Central Hockey League-65
94Oklahoma City Blazers-11
99San Diego Gulls-11
02Russian SL-31
02Swedish SHL-12
Netminders-NM2
Parallel-12
03Russian Hockey League-60
03Russian Hockey League-201
03Russian SL-18
03Russian World Championship Stars-5
Naurov, Alexander
03Russian Under-18 Team-10
06Finnish Cardset-353
06Finnish Porin Assat Pelaajakortit-24
Nauser, Andreas
99Swiss Panini Stickers-119
00Swiss Panini Stickers-162
01Swiss HNL-314
02Swiss HNL-383
Nauss, Ryan
93Peterborough Petes-19
Navratil, Milan
94Czech APS Extraliga-12
95Czech APS Extraliga-115
96Czech APS Extraliga-257
97Czech APS Extraliga-188
97Czech DS Stickers-88
98Czech DS-64
98Czech DS Stickers-161
98Czech OFS-47
99Czech OFS-215
00Czech OFS-374
Navrotskin, Vadim
00Russian Hockey League-350
Naylor, Bobby
99Kitchener Rangers-16
Naylor, Matt
01Arizona Icecats-16
02Arizona Icecats-17
Naylor, Mike
95Dayton Bombers-11
Nazarov, Andrei
92Russian Stars Red Ace-23
92Russian Stars Red Ace-26
92Classic-7
Gold-7
92Classic Four-Sport *-157
Gold-157
93Donruss-490
93Kansas City Blades-14
94Fleer-199
94Leaf-328
94OPC Premier-461
Special Effects-461
94Parkhurst-216
Gold-216
94Score-239
Gold-239
Platinum-239
94Topps/OPC Premier-461
Special Effects-461
94Ultra-367
94Upper Deck-270
Electric Ice-270
94Kansas City Blades-17
94Classic-87
Gold-87
94Classic Pro Prospects-180
95Donruss-187
95Leaf-131
95Metal-132
95Parkhurst International-186
Emerald Ice-186
95Pinnacle-190
Artist's Proofs-190
Rink Collection-190
95Topps-121
OPC Inserts-121
95Ultra-303
95Upper Deck Special Edition-SE164
95Upper Deck Special Edition Gold-SE164
95Images-93
Gold-93
96Collector's Choice-242
96Collector's Edge Ice-146
Prism-146
97Pacific-307
Copper-307
Emerald Green-307
Ice Blue-307
Red-307
Silver-307
97Panini Stickers-235
99Pacific-59
Copper-59
Emerald Green-59
Gold-59
Ice Blue-59
Premiere Date-59
Red-59
99Panini Stickers-195
99Upper Deck MVP SC Edition-34
Gold Script-34
Silver Script-34
Super Script-34
00BAP Memorabilia-417
Emerald-417
Ruby-417
Sapphire-417
00O-Pee-Chee-249
00O-Pee-Chee Parallel-249
00Pacific-71
Copper-71
Gold-71
Ice Blue-71
Premiere Date-71
00Panini Stickers-119
00Topps/OPC-249
Parallel-249
01BAP Update Tough Customers-TC9
01BAP Update Tough Customers-TC28
01Pacific-35
Extreme LTD-35
Hobby LTD-35
Premiere Date-35
Retail LTD-35
01Pacific Arena Exclusives-35
01Parkhurst-363
02Coyotes Team Issue-18
02Pacific-302
Blue-302
Red-302
03Coyotes Postcards-16
03ITG Action-493
03Upper Deck Tough Customers-TC-2
04Russian Back to Russia-18
Nazarov, Dmitri
98Russian Hockey League-150
99Russian Hockey League-158
Nazarov, Slava
74Swedish Stickers-71
Nazarov, Valeri
73Swedish Stickers-125
NcNamee, Peter
75Phoenix Roadrunners WHA-16
NcWana, Llew
92Thunder Bay Thunder Hawks-7
93Thunder Bay Senators-3
94Thunder Bay Senators-13
95Thunder Bay Senators-14
Ndunigidi, Netema
93Quebec Pee-Wee Tournament-1393
Ndur, Rumun
93Guelph Storm-25
94Guelph Storm-24
95Rochester Americans-15
95Signature Rookies-37
Signatures-37
96Rochester Americans-20
97Upper Deck-184
97Rochester Americans-5-4
98SP Authentic Sign of the Times-RN
98SP Authentic Sign of the Times Gold-RN
98Upper Deck-229
Exclusives-229
Exclusives 1 of 1-229
Gold Reserve-229
99Pacific-275
Copper-275
Emerald Green-275
Gold-275
Ice Blue-275
Premiere Date-275
Red-275
01Pacific-21
Extreme LTD-21
Hobby LTD-21
Premiere Date-21
Retail LTD-21
01Pacific Arena Exclusives-21
01Norfolk Admirals-19
03Columbus Cottonmouths-7
06UK Coventry Blaze-18
Neal, Frank
78Finnish SM-Liiga-113
80Finnish Mallasjuoma-3
Neal, Harry
24Crescent Falcon-Tigers-13
24Holland Creameries-7
97Pinnacle Hockey Night in Canada-9
Neal, James
05ITG Heroes/Prosp Toronto Expo Parallel -119
05Plymouth Whalers-A-09
05ITG Heroes and Prospects-119
Autographs-A-JN
06Plymouth Whalers-15
06Plymouth Whalers-27
06ITG Heroes and Prospects-183
Autographs-AJN
Update Autographs-AJN
07ITG Going For Gold World Juniors-16
Autographs-16
Emblems-GUE16
Jerseys-GUJ16
Numbers-GUN16
Neal, Jay
94Toledo Storm-15
95Buffalo Stampedes RHI-44
97Bakersfield Fog-12
98Bakersfield Condors-16
98Las Vegas Coyotes RHI-2
99UHL All-Stars East-13T
00UK Sekonda Superleague-81
01Memphis RiverKings-8
03Memphis RiverKings-14
Neal, John
03Oshawa Generals-3
04Oshawa Generals-3
04Oshawa Generals Autographs-3
Neal, Michael
05Belleville Bulls-7
06Belleville Bulls-10
Neale, Joey
00Sherbrooke Castors-14
Signed-14
Neary, Kyle
93Quebec Pee-Wee Tournament-1669
98Arizona Icecats-22
99Arizona Icecats-21
00Arizona Icecats-18
01Arizona Icecats-17
Neary, Tim
93Quebec Pee-Wee Tournament-749
Neaton, Pat
91Michigan Wolverines-10
93PowerPlay-413
93Score-632
Gold-632
Canadian-632
Canadian Gold-632
93Cleveland Lumberjacks-21
93Cleveland Lumberjacks Postcards-16
94Leaf-469
94OPC Premier-483
Special Effects-483
94Topps/OPC Premier-483
Special Effects-483
94Classic-107
Gold-107
Tri-Cards-T52
94Classic Pro Prospects-10
95Swedish World Championships Stickers-216
96Collector's Edge Ice-174
Prism-174
98IHL All-Star Eastern Conference-9
98Orlando Solar Bears-2
98Orlando Solar Bears II-7
99Utah Grizzlies-19
00Utah Grizzlies-9
Neave, Adam
93Quebec Pee-Wee Tournament-1420
Necas, Antonin
94Czech APS Extraliga-164
95Central Hockey League-79
Neckar, Stanislav
93Classic-106
94Senators Team Issue-24
94Upper Deck-377
Electric Ice-377
94Classic Autographs-NNO
95Canada Games NHL POGS-199
95Collector's Choice-170
Player's Club-170
Player's Club Platinum-170
95Donruss-131
95Leaf-43
95Parkhurst International-148
Emerald Ice-148
95Pinnacle-49
Artist's Proofs-49
Rink Collection-49
95Senators Team Issue-20
95Stadium Club-112
Members Only Master Set-112
95Topps-91
OPC Inserts-91
95Ultra-113
Gold Medallion-113
95Upper Deck-68
Electric Ice-68
Electric Ice Gold-68
96Be A Player-184
Autographs-184
Autographs Silver-184
96Collector's Choice-185
96Senators Pizza Hut-17
96Czech APS Extraliga-348
99Panini Stickers-278
99Paramount-266
99Upper Deck Victory-232
00Paramount-191
Copper-191
Gold-191
Holo-Gold-191
Holo-Silver-191
Ice Blue-191
Premiere Date-191
01Topps Reserve-73
02Pacific Complete-149
Red-149
05Swedish SHL Elitset-268
Gold-268
Neckar, Zbynek
98Bakersfield Condors-17
99Bakersfield Condors-12
03Czech OFS Plus-267
Nedbalek, Michal
04Czech OFS-397
Nedielski, Sheldon
96Saskatoon Blades-16
04Fort Worth Brahmas-12
Nedoma, Milan
91Upper Deck Czech World Juniors-89
94Czech APS Extraliga-102
95Czech APS Extraliga-56
96Czech APS Extraliga-243
97Czech APS Extraliga-270
97Czech DS Extraliga-4
97Czech DS Stickers-78
98Czech DS-31
98Czech DS Stickers-11
98Czech DS Stickers-70
98Czech OFS-196
99Czech DS-31
99Czech OFS-184
00Czech DS Extraliga-16
00Czech OFS-324
01Czech OFS-131
02Czech OFS Plus-181
Duos-D19
03Czech OFS Plus-308
04Czech HC Plzen Postcards-12
04Czech OFS-150
06Czech HC Plzen Postcards-11
06Czech OFS-280
Nedomansky Jr., Vaclav
94Knoxville Cherokees-22
94Los Angeles Blades RHI-5
95Las Vegas Thunder-9
96Knoxville Cherokees-10
98Grand Rapids Griffins-13
99Louisiana Ice Gators-1
99Mississippi Sea Wolves Kelly Cup-9
Nedomansky, Vaclav
69Swedish Hockey-35
70Finnish Jaakiekko-55
70Swedish Hockey-362
70Swedish Masterserien-4
70Swedish Masterserien-6
70Swedish Masterserien-8
70Swedish Masterserien-148
70Swedish Masterserien-152
71Finnish Suomi Stickers-33
71Swedish Hockey-56
72Finnish Jaakiekko-16
72Finnish Hellas-92
72Finnish Panda Toronto-90
72Finnish Semic World Championship-33
72Swedish Stickers-26
72Swedish Semic World Championship-33
73Finnish Jaakiekko-57
73Swedish Stickers-31
74O-Pee-Chee WHA-49
74Finnish Jenkki-79
74Swedish Stickers-15
74Swedish Semic World Champ Stickers-57
75O-Pee-Chee WHA-27
76O-Pee-Chee WHA-1
76O-Pee-Chee WHA-64
76O-Pee-Chee WHA-120
77Sportscasters-7424
77Finnish Sportscasters-20-469
79O-Pee-Chee-132
79Red Wings Postcards-13
79Topps-132
80O-Pee-Chee-202
80Topps-202
81O-Pee-Chee-94
81O-Pee-Chee Stickers-125
81Topps-W94
82Post Cereal-5
91Finnish Semic World Champ Stickers-249
91Swedish Semic World Champ Stickers-249
96Swedish Semic Wien Hockey Legends-HL18
98Czech OFS Legends-1
03Czech Stadion-650
Nedorost, Andrej
99German DEL-362
00Czech OFS-74
01BAP Memorabilia-403
Emerald-403
Ruby-403
Sapphire-403
01Parkhurst-313
01UD Mask Collection-142
Gold-142
01Syracuse Crunch-21
02Pacific Complete-511
Red-511
02SPx-108
02UD Foundations-127
02UD Piece of History-126
02Upper Deck-203
Exclusives-203
02Upper Deck MVP-200
Gold-200
Classics-200
Golden Classics-200
02Upper Deck Vintage-329
02Syracuse Crunch-18
02Syracuse Crunch Sheets-19
04Czech OFS-382
05Czech HC Karlovy Vary-10
Nedorost, David
99Czech OFS-185
Nedorost, Vaclav
98Czech OFS-417
99Czech OFS-284
00SPx Rookie Redemption-RR8
01Atomic-107
Premiere Date-107
Rookie Reaction-3
01Atomic Toronto Fall Expo-107
01BAP Memorabilia-308
Emerald-308
Ruby-308
Sapphire-308
01BAP Signature Series-204
Autographs-204
Autographs Gold-204
01Bowman YoungStars-147
Gold-147
Ice Cubed-147
01Crown Royale-151
Rookie Royalty-5
01O-Pee-Chee-333
01Pacific-455
01Pacific Adrenaline-206
Blue-206
Premiere Date-206
Red-206
Retail-206
Rookie Report-6
01Pacific Heads-Up-109
01Pacific High Voltage-4
01Parkhurst-284
01Parkhurst Beckett Promos-284
01Private Stock-118
Gold-118
Premiere Date-118
Retail-118
Silver-118
Moments in Time-3
01Private Stock Pacific Nights-118
01Private Stock PS-2002-95
01Private Stock Reserve-R3
01SP Authentic-176
Limited-176
Limited Gold-176
01SP Game Used-71
01SPx-101
01Stadium Club-126
Award Winners-126
Master Photos-126
01Titanium-153
Retail-153
Double-Sided Jerseys-14
Double-Sided Patches-14
01Titanium Draft Day Edition-27
01Titanium Draft Day Edition-116
01Topps-333
01Topps Chrome-151
Refractors-151
Black Border Refractors-151
01Topps Heritage-145
01Topps Reserve-105
01UD Challenge for the Cup-102
01UD Honor Roll-69
01UD Mask Collection-140
Gold-140
01UD Playmakers-112
01UD Premier Collection-110
01UD Top Shelf-69
01Upper Deck-215
01Upper Deck Ice-50
01Upper Deck Vintage-278
01Vanguard-107
Blue-107
Red-107
One of Ones-107
Premiere Date-107
Prime Prospects-3
Proofs-107
01Czech DS-56
01Hershey Bears-18
02BAP First Edition-255
02BAP Sig Series Auto Buybacks 2001-204
02O-Pee-Chee-307
02O-Pee-Chee Premier Blue Parallel-307
02O-Pee-Chee Premier Red Parallel-307
02O-Pee-Chee Factory Set-307
02Pacific Calder Collection AS Fantasy-4
02Pacific Calder Collection All-Star Fantasy Gold-4
02Pacific Calder-65
Silver-65
02Pacific Complete-534
Red-534
02Pacific Heads-Up Quad Jerseys-8
02Pacific Heads-Up Quad Jerseys Gold-8
02Topps-307
OPC Blue Parallel-307
OPC Red Parallel-307
Factory Set-307
02Topps Total-151
02UD Piece of History Mark of Distinction-VN
03Pacific-86
Blue-86
Red-86
03San Antonio Rampage-9
04Czech OFS-73
Stars-4
04Czech Zuma-31
05Upper Deck Notable Numbers-N-VN
06Czech HC Ceske Budejovice Postcards-6
06Czech OFS-13
Stars-14
Team Cards-1
06Czech NHL ELH Postcards-7
Nedved, Jaroslav
93Cincinnati Cyclones-18
94Czech APS Extraliga-76
94Classic Pro Prospects-6
95Czech APS Extraliga-278
96Czech APS Extraliga-125
97Czech APS Extraliga-7
97Czech DS Extraliga-82
97Czech DS Stickers-58
98Czech DS Stickers-218
98Finnish Kerailysarja-58
99Czech DS-146
99Czech OFS-109
99Czech OFS-503
All-Star Game Blue-503
All-Star Game Gold-503
All-Star Game Red-503
All-Star Game Silver-503
00Czech OFS-298
01Czech OFS-35
01Czech OFS Plus-11
02Czech OFS Plus All-Star Game-H31
02Czech OFS Plus Trios-T14
03Czech OFS Plus-312
03Czech OFS Plus Insert H-H5
Nedved, Petr
90Canucks Mohawk-21
90Kraft-38
90OPC Premier-81
90Pro Set-402
90Pro Set-643
90Score Rookie/Traded-50T
90Score Young Superstars-37
90Upper Deck-351
90Upper Deck-353
French-351
French-353
91Bowman-324
91Canucks Panini Team Stickers-17
91Canucks Autograph Cards-18
91Canucks Team Issue 8x10-18
91Kraft-11
91O-Pee-Chee-141
91Panini Stickers-49
91Parkhurst-178
French-178
91Pinnacle-192
French-192
91Pro Set-235
French-235
91Score American-124
91Score Canadian Bilingual-124
91Score Canadian English-124
91Stadium Club-280
91Topps-141
91Upper Deck-227
French-227
Euro-Stars-5
Euro-Stars French-5
92Bowman-396
92Canucks Road Trip Art-16
92O-Pee-Chee-89
92Panini Stickers-31
92Panini Stickers-300
92Panini Stickers French-31
92Panini Stickers French-300
92Parkhurst-418
92Parkhurst-449
Emerald Ice-418
Emerald Ice-449
92Pinnacle-127
92Pinnacle-249
French-127
French-249
92Score-101
Canadian-101
92Stadium Club-457
92Topps-422
Gold-422G
92Ultra-226
Imports-17
92Upper Deck-263
93Donruss-356
93Donruss-486
93Leaf-78
93OPC Premier-6
Gold-6
Team Canada-15
93Panini Stickers-171
93Pinnacle-106
Canadian-106
93PowerPlay-254
93PowerPlay-490
93Score-231
Canadian-231
International Stars-22
International Stars Canadian-22
93Stadium Club-18
Members Only Master Set-18
OPC-18
First Day Issue-18
First Day Issue OPC-18
93Topps/OPC Premier-6
Gold-6
93Ultra-68
94Canada Games NHL POGS-169
94Finest-101
Super Team Winners-101
Refractors-101
94Fleer-137
94Leaf-360
94Leaf Limited-67
94OPC Premier-286
Special Effects-286
94Parkhurst Vintage-V44
94Parkhurst SE-SE116
Gold-SE116
94Pinnacle-58
Artist's Proofs-58
Rink Collection-58
World Edition-WE18
94Score Team Canada-CT2
94Select-120
Gold-120
94Stadium Club-205
Members Only Master Set-205
First Day Issue-205
Super Team Winner Cards-205
94Topps/OPC Premier-286
Special Effects-286
94Ultra-141
94Ultra-333
Global Greats-7
94Upper Deck-164
Electric Ice-164
SP Inserts-SP141
SP Inserts Die Cuts-SP141
95Be A Player-156
Signatures-S156
Signatures Die Cuts-S156
95Canada Games NHL POGS-212
95Collector's Choice-323
Player's Club-323
Player's Club Platinum-323
95Donruss-252
95Emotion-140
95Leaf-301
95Panini Stickers-104
95Parkhurst International-438
Emerald Ice-438
95Penguins Foodland-17
95Playoff One on One-300
95Score-220
Black Ice Artist's Proofs-220
Black Ice-220
95SkyBox Impact-133
95Stadium Club-64
Members Only Master Set-64
95Summit-91
Artist's Proofs-91
Ice-91
95Topps-304
OPC Inserts-304
95Ultra-292
95Upper Deck-462
Electric Ice-462
Electric Ice Gold-462
Special Edition-SE154
Special Edition Gold-SE154
95Zenith-103
95Swedish Globe World Championships-97
96Black Diamond-95
Gold-95
96Collector's Choice-219
96Collector's Choice-328
96Donruss-76
Press Proofs-76
96Flair-79
Blue Ice-79
96Fleer-88
96Fleer-143
Art Ross-17
Picks Fabulous 50-32
Picks Fantasy Force-10
Picks Jagged Edge-9
96Leaf-71
Press Proofs-71
96Leaf Limited-39
Gold-39
Stubble-12
96Leaf Preferred-82
Press Proofs-82
Steel-56
Steel Gold-56
96Maggers-65
96Metal Universe-129
96Pinnacle-108
Artist's Proofs-108
Foil-108
Premium Stock-108
Rink Collection-108
96Score-38
Artist's Proofs-38
Dealer's Choice Artist's Proofs-38
Special Artist's Proofs-38
Golden Blades-38
96SkyBox Impact-103
BladeRunners-16
96SP-128
96Summit-148
Artist's Proofs-148
Ice-148
Metal-148
Premium Stock-148
96Topps Picks-37
OPC Inserts-37
96Upper Deck-134
Superstar Showdown-SS26B
96Upper Deck Ice-56
Parallel-56
96Zenith-54
Artist's Proofs-54
Assailants-13
97Collector's Choice-209
Star Quest-SQ3
97Donruss-152
Press Proofs Silver-152
Press Proofs Gold-152
97Donruss Canadian Ice-71
Dominion Series-71
Provincial Series-71
97Donruss Limited-156
Exposure-156
97Donruss Preferred-33
Cut to the Chase-33
97Katch-120
Gold-120
Silver-120
97Leaf-51
Fractal Matrix-51
Fractal Matrix Die Cuts-51
97Leaf International-51
Universal Ice-51
97Pacific-13
Copper-13
Emerald Green-13
Ice Blue-13
Red-13
Silver-13
Slap Shots Die-Cuts-8A
97Pacific Dynagon-104
Copper-104
Dark Grey-104
Emerald Green-104
Ice Blue-104
Red-104
Silver-104
Best Kept Secrets-80
Tandems-22
97Pacific Invincible-115
Copper-115
Emerald Green-115
Ice Blue-115
Red-115
Silver-115
NHL Regime-163
97Panini Stickers-52
97Paramount-153
Copper-153
Dark Grey-153
Emerald Green-153
Ice Blue-153
Red-153
Silver-153
97Pinnacle-124
Press Plates Back Black-124
Press Plates Back Cyan-124
Press Plates Back Magenta-124
Press Plates Back Yellow-124
Press Plates Front Black-124
Press Plates Front Cyan-124
Press Plates Front Magenta-124
Press Plates Front Yellow-124
97Pinnacle Certified-95
Red-95
Mirror Blue-95
Mirror Gold-95
Mirror Red-95
97Pinnacle Inside-133
97Pinnacle Tot Cert Platinum Blue-95
97Pinnacle Tot Cert Platinum Gold-95
97Pinnacle Totally Certified Platinum Red-95
97Pinnacle Tot Cert Mirror Platinum Gold-95
97Score-143
Artist's Proofs-143
Golden Blades-143
97Score Penguins-6
Platinum-6
Premier-6
97Upper Deck-137
97Czech APS Extraliga-25
98Be A Player-243
Press Release-243
98BAP Gold-243
98BAP Autographs-243
98BAP Autographs Gold-243
98Pacific Omega-160
Red-160
Opening Day Issue-160
98Revolution-96
Ice Shadow-96
Red-96
98SPx Top Prospects-41
Radiance-41
Spectrum-41
98Czech DS Stickers-223
98Las Vegas Thunder-16
99Aurora-96
Premiere Date-96
99BAP Memorabilia-49
Gold-49
Silver-49
99BAP Millennium-161
Emerald-161
Ruby-161
Sapphire-161
Signatures-161
Signatures Gold-161
99O-Pee-Chee-182
99O-Pee-Chee Chrome-182
99O-Pee-Chee Chrome Refractors-182
99Pacific-276
Copper-276
Emerald Green-276
Gold-276
Ice Blue-276
Premiere Date-276
Red-276
99Pacific Dynagon Ice-133
Blue-133
Copper-133
Gold-133
Premiere Date-133
99Pacific Omega-152
Copper-152
Gold-152
Ice Blue-152
Premiere Date-152
99Paramount-155
Copper-155
Emerald-155
Gold-155
Holographic Emerald-155
Holographic Gold-155
Holographic Silver-155
Ice Blue-155
Premiere Date-155
Red-155
Silver-155
99Revolution-99
Premiere Date-99
Red-99
Shadow Series-99
99SPx-99
Radiance-99
Spectrum-99
99Stadium Club-58
First Day Issue-58
One of a Kind-58
Printing Plates Black-58
Printing Plates Cyan-58
Printing Plates Magenta-58
Printing Plates Yellow-58
99Topps/OPC-182
99Topps/OPC Chrome-182
Refractors-182
99Topps Gold Label Class 1-61
Black-61
Black One of One-61
One of One-61
Red-61
Red One of One-61
99Topps Gold Label Class 2-61
99Topps Gold Label Class 2 Black-61
99Topps Gold Label Class 2 Black 1 of 1-61
99Topps Gold Label Class 2 One of One-61
99Topps Gold Label Class 2 Red-61
99Topps Gold Label Class 2 Red One of One-61
99Topps Gold Label Class 3-61
99Topps Gold Label Class 3 Black-61
99Topps Gold Label Class 3 Black 1 of 1-61
99Topps Gold Label Class 3 One of One-61
99Topps Gold Label Class 3 Red-61
99Topps Gold Label Class 3 Red One of One-61
99Topps Premier Plus-51
Parallel-51
99Upper Deck-259
Exclusives-259
Exclusives 1 of 1-259
99Upper Deck Gold Reserve-259
99Upper Deck MVP-134
Gold Script-134
Silver Script-134
Super Script-134
99Upper Deck MVP SC Edition-121
Gold Script-121
Silver Script-121
Super Script-121
99Upper Deck Victory-193
99Wayne Gretzky Hockey-110
00Aurora-97
Premiere Date-97
00BAP Memorabilia-136
Emerald-136
Ruby-136
Sapphire-136
Promos-136
00BAP Mem Chicago Sportsfest Copper-136
00BAP Memorabilia Chicago Sportsfest Blue-136
00BAP Memorabilia Chicago Sportsfest Gold-136
00BAP Memorabilia Chicago Sportsfest Ruby-136
00BAP Memorabilia Chicago Sun-Times Ruby-136
00BAP Memorabilia Chicago Sun-Times Gold-136
00BAP Mem Chicago Sun-Times Sapphire-136
00BAP Mem Toronto Fall Expo Copper-136
00BAP Memorabilia Toronto Fall Expo Gold-136
00BAP Memorabilia Toronto Fall Expo Ruby-136
00BAP Parkhurst 2000-P220
00BAP Signature Series-154
Emerald-154
Ruby-154
Sapphire-154
Autographs-37
Autographs Gold-37
00O-Pee-Chee-80
00O-Pee-Chee Parallel-80
00Pacific-268
Copper-268
Gold-268
Ice Blue-268
Premiere Date-268
00Panini Stickers-61
00Paramount-166
Copper-166
Gold-166
Holo-Gold-166
Holo-Silver-166
Ice Blue-166
Premiere Date-166
00Revolution-98
Blue-98
Premiere Date-98
Red-98
00Stadium Club-159
00Titanium Game Gear-40
00Titanium Game Gear-117
00Titanium Game Gear Patches-117
00Titanium Draft Day Edition-67
Patches-67
00Topps/OPC-80
Parallel-80
00Topps Chrome-63
OPC Refractors-63
Refractors-63
00Upper Deck-343
Exclusives Tier 1-343
Exclusives Tier 2-343
00Upper Deck MVP-120
First Stars-120
Second Stars-120
Third Stars-120
00Upper Deck Victory-155
00Upper Deck Vintage-243
00Czech DS Extraliga Team Jagr-JT7
00Czech DS Extraliga Team Jagr Parallel-JT6
00Czech OFS-388
00Czech Stadion-80
01BAP Memorabilia-80
Emerald-80
Ruby-80
Sapphire-80
01Crown Royale Triple Threads-15

01O-Pee-Chee-83
01O-Pee-Chee Heritage Parallel-83
01O-Pee-Chee Heritage Parallel Limited-83
01O-Pee-Chee Premier Parallel-83
01Pacific-265
Extreme LTD-265
Hobby LTD-265
Premiere Date-265
Retail LTD-265
01Pacific Adrenaline-129
Blue-129
Premiere Date-129
Red-129
Retail-129
Jerseys-29
01Pacific Arena Exclusives-265
01Pacific Heads-Up Quad Jerseys-14
01Parkhurst-101
01Private Stock Game Gear-68
01Private Stock Game Gear Patches-68
01Private Stock PS-2002-50
01SP Authentic-56
Limited-56
Limited Gold-56
01Stadium Club-88
Award Winners-88
Master Photos-88
01Topps-83
Heritage Parallel-83
Heritage Parallel Limited-83
OPC Parallel-83
01Topps Chrome-83
Refractors-83
Black Border Refractors-83
01Topps Heritage-94
Refractors-94
01UD Mask Collection-62
Gold-62
01Upper Deck-347
Exclusives-347
01Upper Deck MVP-128
01Upper Deck Victory-234
Gold-234
01Czech DS-40
Ice Heroes-IH6
02BAP Sig Series Auto Buybacks 1998-243
02BAP Sig Series Auto Buybacks 1999-161
02BAP Sig Series Auto Buybacks 2000-37
02O-Pee-Chee-96
02O-Pee-Chee Premier Blue Parallel-96
02O-Pee-Chee Premier Red Parallel-96
02O-Pee-Chee Factory Set-96
02Pacific-257
Blue-257
Red-257
02Pacific Complete-90
Red-90
02Parkhurst Retro-129
Minis-129
02Topps-96
OPC Blue Parallel-96
OPC Red Parallel-96
Factory Set-96
02Topps Total-205
02Upper Deck-114
Exclusives-114
02Upper Deck MVP-123
Gold-123
Classics-123
Golden Classics-123
02Upper Deck Victory-142
Bronze-142
Gold-142
Silver-142
02Upper Deck Vintage-167
Green Backs-167
03Beehive-130
Gold-130
Silver-130
03ITG Action-356
03NHL Sticker Collection-87
03O-Pee-Chee-191
03OPC Blue-191
03OPC Gold-191
03OPC Red-191
03Pacific-229
Blue-229
Red-229
03Pacific Complete-315
Red-315
03Pacific Supreme-68
Blue-68
Red-68
Retail-68
03Parkhurst Original Six New York-28
03Rangers Team Issue-18
03Topps-191
Blue-191
Gold-191
Red-191
03Topps C55-39
Minis-39
Minis American Back-39
Minis American Back Red-39
Minis Bazooka Back-39
Minis Brooklyn Back-39
Minis Hat Trick Back-39
Minis O Canada Back-39
Minis O Canada Back Red-39
Minis Stanley Cup Back-39
03Topps Traded-TT67
Blue-TT67
Gold-TT67
Red-TT67
03Upper Deck-127
Canadian Exclusives-127
HG-127
03Upper Deck MVP-278
Gold Script-278
Silver Script-278
Canadian Exclusives-278
04Pacific-105
Blue-105
Red-105
04UD All-World-8
Gold-8
04Czech HC Sparta Praha Postcards-12
04Czech NHL ELH Postcards-9
04Czech OFS-191
Checklist Cards-9
Stars-26
04Czech Zuma-39
05Panini Stickers-329
05Parkhurst-365
Facsimile Auto Parallel-365
05Ultra-152
Gold-152
Ice-152
05Upper Deck-397
05Upper Deck MVP-298
Gold-298
Platinum-298
06Panini Stickers-127

Nedved, Zdenek

92Sudbury Wolves-11
93Parkhurst-518
Emerald Ice-518
93Sudbury Wolves-9
93Sudbury Wolves Police-10
94Slapshot Promos-7
94Sudbury Wolves-8
94Sudbury Wolves Police-11
95Bowman-91
All-Foil-91
95Donruss-157
Rated Rookies-5
95Parkhurst International-254
Emerald Ice-254
95Stadium Club-139
Members Only Master Set-139
95Upper Deck-441
Electric Ice-441
Electric Ice Gold-441
95Classic-97
96Leaf-230
Press Proofs-230
96Pinnacle-243
Artist's Proofs-243
Foil-243
Premium Stock-243
Rink Collection-243
96Summit-193
Artist's Proofs-193
Ice-193
Premium Stock-193
97Sudbury Wolves Anniversary-16
99Finnish Cardset-84
00Finnish Cardset-306
00Finnish Cardset Master Blasters-7
01Finnish Cardset-227
02German DEL City Press-181
03German DEL-131

Nedvidek, Michal

06Czech HC Liberec Postcards-5
06Czech OFS-96

Needham, Bill

60Cleveland Barons-15
72Cleveland Crusaders WHA-11

Needham, Bob

92British Columbia JHL-54

Needham, Brett

03OCN Blizzard-16

Needham, Mike

87Kamloops Blazers-14
88Kamloops Blazers-20
89Kamloops Blazers-17
90ProCards AHL/IHL-375
907th Inn. Sketch Memorial Cup-10
91ProCards-297
92OPC Premier-106
92Parkhurst-370
Emerald Ice-370
92Penguins Coke/Clark-15
92Ultra-380
92Upper Deck-489
92Classic-108
Gold-108
93Leaf-214
93OPC Premier-472
Gold-472
93Penguins Foodland-15
93Stadium Club-452
Members Only Master Set-452
First Day Issue-452
93Topps/OPC Premier-472
Gold-472
95Adirondack Red Wings-16

Neeld, John

94German First League-446

Neely, Bob

73Maple Leafs Postcards-20
74Maple Leafs Postcards-16
74NHL Action Stamps-263
74O-Pee-Chee NHL-272
75Maple Leafs Postcards-15
75O-Pee-Chee NHL-245
75Topps-245
76Maple Leafs Postcards-12
76O-Pee-Chee NHL-194
76Topps-194
77O-Pee-Chee NHL-347

Neely, Cam

84Canucks Team Issue-18
84O-Pee-Chee-327
84Kelowna Wings-43
85Canucks Team Issue-17
85O-Pee-Chee-228
86O-Pee-Chee-250
87O-Pee-Chee-69
87O-Pee-Chee Stickers-143
87Panini Stickers-10
87Topps-69
88Bruins Sports Action-16
88Bruins Sports Action-24
88Bruins Postcards-14
88Frito-Lay Stickers-17
88O-Pee-Chee-58
88O-Pee-Chee Minis-27
88O-Pee-Chee Stickers-22
88Panini Stickers-191
88Topps-58
88Topps Sticker Inserts-9
89Bruins Sports Action-17
89Bruins Sports Action Update-12
89Kraft-56
89O-Pee-Chee-15
89O-Pee-Chee Box Bottoms-K
89O-Pee-Chee Stickers-33
89Panini Stickers-182
89Panini Stickers-192
89Topps-15
89Topps Box Bottoms-K
89Swedish Semic World Champ Stickers-71
90Bowman-29
Tiffany-29
90Bruins Sports Action-17
90Kraft-39
90Kraft-84
90O-Pee-Chee-69
90O-Pee-Chee-201
90OPC Premier-82
90Panini Stickers-9
90Panini Stickers-327
90Pro Set-11
90Pro Set-358
90Score-4
90Score-323
90Score-340
Canadian-4
Canadian-323
Canadian-340
90Score Hottest/Rising Stars-67
90Topps-69
90Topps-201
Tiffany-69
Tiffany-201
Team Scoring Leaders-3
Team Scoring Leaders Tiffany-3
90Upper Deck-156
90Upper Deck-493
French-156
French-493
91Pro Set Platinum-1
91Bowman-348
91Bowman-366
91Bruins Sports Action-13
91Bruins Sports Action-24
91McDonald's Upper Deck-1
91McDonald's Upper Deck-H5
91O-Pee-Chee-170
91O-Pee-Chee-192
91O-Pee-Chee-266
91OPC Premier-107
91Panini Stickers-176
91Panini Stickers-332
91Parkhurst French-248
91Pinnacle-78
French-78
B-B6
B French-B6
91Pro Set-5
91Pro Set-300
French-5
French-300
91Score National-8
91Score Ntnl Candy Wholesalers Convention-8
91Score Fanfest-8
91Score American-6
91Score American-301
91Score Canadian Bilingual-6
91Score Canadian Bilingual-305
91Score Canadian English-6
91Score Canadian English-305
91Stadium Club-64
91Topps-192
91Topps-266
91Upper Deck-78
91Upper Deck-234
French-78
French-234
91Finnish Semic World Champ Stickers-68
91Swedish Semic World Champ Stickers-68
92Bowman-62
92Humpty Dumpty II-16
92O-Pee-Chee-174
92Panini Stickers-143
92Panini Stickers French-143
92Parkhurst-248
Emerald Ice-248
Cherry Picks-CP14
92Pinnacle-25
92Pinnacle-232
French-25
French-232
92Pro Set-8
92Score-10
Canadian-10
92Sports Illustrated for Kids II-265
92Stadium Club-316
92Topps-32
Gold-32G
92Ultra-7
92Upper Deck-86
93Donruss-29
Elite Inserts-U4
93Leaf-99
93OPC Premier-254
Gold-254
93Panini Stickers-3
93Parkhurst-10
Emerald Ice-10
93Pinnacle-30
Canadian-30
93PowerPlay-22
93Score-342
Canadian-342
Dynamic Duos U.S.-3
93Stadium Club-216
Members Only Master Set-216
OPC-216
First Day Issue-216
First Day Issue OPC-216
93Topps/OPC Premier-254
Gold-254
93Ultra-138
93Upper Deck-356
SP-10
94Action Packed Big Picture 24K Gold-6G
94Be A Player-R143
94Canada Games NHL POGS-39
94Canada Games NHL POGS-328
94Canada Games NHL POGS-336
94Donruss-269
Dominators-4
94EA Sports-11
94EA Sports-212
94Finest-22
Super Team Winners-22
Refractors-22
Bowman's Best-B3
Bowman's Best-X25
Bowman's Best Refractors-B3
Bowman's Best Refractors-X25
94Flair-11
94Fleer-15
Headliners-8
94Hockey Wit-36
94Kraft-65
94Leaf-267
Gold Stars-9
94Leaf Limited-49
94McDonald's Upper Deck-McD22
94OPC Premier-129
94OPC Premier-419
94OPC Premier-505
Special Effects-129
Special Effects-419
Special Effects-505
94Parkhurst-11
Gold-11
Vintage-V64
94Pinnacle-65
Artist's Proofs-65
Rink Collection-65
Boomers-BR12
Gamers-GR17
Team Pinnacle-TP12
Team Dufex Parallel-TP12
94Score Samples-4
94Score-4
Gold-4
Platinum-4
Check It-CI8
Dream Team-DT23
Franchise-TF2
94Select-39
Gold-39
94SP-9
Die Cuts-9
Premier-23
Premier Die-Cuts-23
94Stadium Club-8
94Stadium Club-266
Members Only Master Set-8
Members Only Master Set-266
First Day Issue-8
First Day Issue-266
Super Teams-2
Super Teams Members Only Master Set-2
Super Team Winner Cards-8
Super Team Winner Cards-266
94Topps/OPC Premier-129
94Topps/OPC Premier-419
94Topps/OPC Premier-505
Special Effects-129
Special Effects-419
Special Effects-505
94Topps Finest Inserts-8
94Topps Finest Bronze-10
94Ultra-13
Award Winners-8
Power-6
Red Light Specials-6
94Upper Deck-364
Electric Ice-364
Predictor Retail-R33
94Upper Deck Predictor Retail Exchange-R33
94Upper Deck SP Inserts-SP6
94Upper Deck SP Inserts Die Cuts-SP6
94Classic-AU2
95SLU Hockey Canadian-10
95SLU Hockey American-13
95Bashan Super Stickers-7
95Bowman-17
All-Foil-17
95Canada Games NHL POGS-3
95Canada Games NHL POGS-25
95Collector's Choice-102
95Collector's Choice-355
Player's Club-102
Player's Club-355
Player's Club Platinum-102
Player's Club Platinum-355
Crash The Game-C14A
Crash The Game-C14B
Crash The Game-C14C
Crash The Game Gold-C14A
Crash The Game Gold-C14B
Crash The Game Gold-C14C
Crash the Game Silver Redeemed-C14
Crash the Game Silver Bonus-C14
Crash the Game Gold Redeemed-C14
Crash the Game Gold Bonus-C14
95Donruss-165
95Donruss Elite-14
Die Cut Stars-14
Die Cut Uncut-14
95Emotion-10
Ntense Power-1
95Finest-9
95Finest-110
Refractors-9
Refractors-110
95Hoyle Eastern Playing Cards-44
95Imperial Stickers-7
95Kenner Starting Lineup Cards-15
95Kraft-7
95Leaf-113
95Leaf Limited-81
95Metal-9
Iron Warriors-9
95NHL Aces Playing Cards-10S
95NHL Cool Trade-1
95NHL Cool Trade-RP1
95Panini Stickers-8
95Panini Stickers-153
95Parkhurst International-12
Emerald Ice-12
95Pinnacle Clear Shots-5
95Pinnacle First Strike-5
95Pinnacle Full Contact-1
95Pinnacle FANtasy-1
95Playoff One on One-8
95Playoff One on One-120
95Playoff One on One-228
95Pro Magnets-18
95Score Promos-3
95Score-209
Black Ice Artist's Proofs-209
Black Ice-209
Border Battle-3
Lamplighters-3
95Select Certified-57
Mirror Gold-57
Gold Team-7
95SkyBox Impact-11
95SkyBox Impact-238
Ice Quake-10
95SP-6
Stars/Etoiles-E4
Stars/Etoiles Gold-E4
95Stadium Club Members Only-4
95Stadium Club-163
Members Only Master Set-163
Nemeses-N3
Nemeses Members Only Master Set-N3
95Summit-81
Artist's Proofs-81
Ice-81
GM's Choice-12
Mad Hatters-4
95Topps-15
95Topps-221
OPC Inserts-15
OPC Inserts-221
Home Grown Canada-HGC23
Marquee Men Power Boosters-15
Mystery Finest-M11
Mystery Finest Refractors-M11
Power Lines-7PL
Profiles-PF10
95Topps SuperSkills-63
Platinum-63
95Ultra-12
Gold Medallion-12
Crease Crashers-12
Red Light Specials-7
Red Light Specials Gold Medallion-7
95Upper Deck-1
95Upper Deck-237
Electric Ice-1
Electric Ice-237
Electric Ice Gold-1
Electric Ice Gold-237
95Upper Deck All-Star Game Predictors-22
Redemption Winners-22
95Upper Deck Freeze Frame-F5
95Upper Deck Freeze Frame Jumbo-F5
95Upper Deck NHL All-Stars-AS10
95Upper Deck NHL All-Stars Jumbo-AS10
95Upper Deck Predictor Retail-R1
95Upper Deck Predictor Retail Exchange-R1
95Upper Deck Special Edition-SE94
95Upper Deck Special Edition Gold-SE94
95Zenith-61
96Collector's Choice-16
96Collector's Choice-310
MVP-UD41
MVP Gold-UD41
Stick'Ums-S5
96Donruss-205
Press Proofs-205
96Leaf-86
Press Proofs-86
96Maggers-66
96NHL Pro Stamps-18
96Pinnacle-136
Artist's Proofs-136
Foil-136
Premium Stock-136
Rink Collection-136
96Score-111
Artist's Proofs-111
Dealer's Choice Artist's Proofs-111
Special Artist's Proofs-111
Check It-4
Golden Blades-111
96SPx-4
Gold-4
96Stadium Club Members Only-36
96Summit-29
Artist's Proofs-29
Ice-29
Premium Stock-29
96Topps Picks-137
OPC Inserts-137
96Upper Deck-13
97Highland Mint Mint-Cards Pinnacle/Score-11
97Highland Mint Mint-Cards Pinnacle/Score-12
97SP Authentic Mark of a Legend-M3
97SP Authentic Tradition-T3
97SP Authentic Tradition-T6
98Bruins Alumni-8
Autographs-8
99BAP Memorabilia AS American Hobby-AH2
99BAP Memorabilia AS American Hobby Autos-AH2
99Topps Premier Plus Club Signings-CS2
99Topps Premier Plus Club Signings-CSC1
00UD Heroes-120
Signs of Greatness-CN
00Upper Deck Legends-9
00Upper Deck Legends-13
Legendary Collection Bronze-9
Legendary Collection Bronze-13
Legendary Collection Gold-9
Legendary Collection Gold-13
Legendary Collection Silver-9
Legendary Collection Silver-13
Epic Signatures-CN
Essence of the Game-EG6
01BAP Ultimate Memorabilia Cornerstones-6
01BAP Ultimate Memorabilia Decades-23
01BAP Update Passing the Torch-PTT1
01Fleer Legacy-5
01Fleer Legacy-53
Ultimate-5
Ultimate-53
In the Corners-6
Memorabilia-18
01Greats of the Game-56
Autographs-56
Board Certified-4
Sticks-6
01Parkhurst Autographs-PA49
01UD Premier Collection Signatures-CN
01UD Premier Collection Signatures Black-CN
01Upper Deck Legends-5
Epic Signatures-CN
Jerseys-TTCN
Jerseys Platinum-TTCN
Milestones-MCN
Milestones Platinum-MCN
02Fleer Throwbacks-81
Gold-81
Platinum-81
Squaring Off-3
Squaring Off Memorabilia-3
Stickwork-11
02SP Authentic Super Premiums-TPTBN
02UD Foundations-3
02UD Foundations-107
Canadian Heroes-CCN
Canadian Heroes Gold-CCN
Canadian Heroes Silver-C-CN
Classic Greats-GCN
Classic Greats Gold-GCN
Classic Greats Silver-G-CN
Lasting Impressions Sticks-L-CN
Milestones-NCN
Milestones Gold-NCN
Milestones Silver-N-CN
Playoff Performers-PCN
Playoff Performers Gold-PCN
Playoff Performers Silver-P-CN
Power Stations-SCN
Power Stations Gold-SCN
Power Stations Silver-S-CN
Signs of Greatness-SGCN
02UD Piece of History Exquisite Combos-ECNB
02UD Piece of History Historical Swatches-HSCN
02UD Piece of History Mark of Distinction-CN
03BAP Ultimate Memorabilia Career Year-2
03BAP Ultimate Memorabilia Great Moments-12
03BAP Ultimate Memorabilia Nameplates-29
03BAP Ultimate Mem Nameplates Gold-29
03BAP Ultimate Mem Raised to the Rafters-1
03BAP Ultimate Mem Retro Teammates-1
03BAP Ultimate Memorabilia Triple Threads-28
03BAP Ultimate Mem Vintage Hat Tricks-2
03BAP Ultimate Mem Vintage Jerseys-40
03BAP Ultimate Mem Vintage Jerseys Gold-40
03ITG Used Signature Series Teammates-18
03ITG Used Sig Series Teammates Gold-18
03ITG Used Sig Series Triple Mem-21
03ITG Used Sig Series Triple Mem Gold-21
03Parkhurst Original Six Boston-32
03Parkhurst Original Six Boston-65
03Parkhurst Original Six Boston-95
03Parkhurst Original Six Boston-98
Autographs-11
Memorabilia-BM32
Memorabilia-BM40
Memorabilia-BM55
03Parkhurst Orig Six He Shoots/Scores-15
03Parkhurst Orig Six He Shoots/Scores-15A
03Parkhurst Orig Six He Shoots/Scores-18
03Parkhurst Orig Six He Shoots/Scores-18A
03Parkhurst Rookie Jerseys-GJ-50
03Parkhurst Rookie Jerseys Gold-GJ-50
03Parkhurst Rookie Jersey and Sticks-SJ-26
03Parkhurst Rookie Jersey and Sticks Gold-SJ-26
04ITG Franchises Canadian-121
Autographs-CN2
04ITG Franchises He Shoots/Scores Prizes-48
04ITG Franchises US East-326
Autographs-A-CN1
Barn Burners-EBB8
Barn Burners Gold-EBB8
Complete Jerseys-ECJ5
Complete Jerseys Gold-ECJ5
Double Memorabilia-EDM4
Double Memorabilia Autographs-EDM-CN
Double Memorabilia Gold-EDM4
Forever Rivals-EFR4
Forever Rivals Gold-EFR4
Memorabilia-ESM8
Memorabilia Autographs-ESM-CN
Memorabilia Gold-ESM8
Original Sticks-EOS1
Original Sticks Autographs-EOS-CN
Original Sticks Gold-EOS1
Teammates-ETM4
Teammates Gold-ETM4
Triple Memorabilia-ETM5
Triple Memorabilia Autographs-ETM-CN
Triple Memorabilia Gold-ETM5
04ITG Ultimate Memorabilia-102
04ITG Ultimate Memorabilia-199
Gold-102
Gold-199
Auto Threads-19
Autographs-6
Autographs-17
Autographs Gold-6
Autographs Gold-17
Complete Jerseys-5
Complete Logo-30
Complete Package-10
Gloves are Off-2
Jersey Autographs-20
Jersey Autographs Gold-20
Jersey and Sticks-15
Jersey and Sticks Gold-15
Original Six-5
Original Six-14
Retro Teammates-1
Stick Autographs-3
Stick Autographs Gold-3
Triple Threads-9
04SP Authentic Sign of the Times-DS-NH
04SP Authentic Sign of the Times-DS-RP
04SP Authentic Sign of the Times-DS-TN
04SP Authentic Sign of the Times-TS-BNT
04SP Authentic Sign of the Times-FS-BOS
04UD Legendary Signatures-16
Autographs-CA
04UD Legends Classics-12
Gold-12
Platinum-12
Silver-12
Signature Moments-M27
Signature Moments-M66
Signatures-CS27
Signatures-DC4
Signatures-DC8
Signatures-QC5
Signatures-QC6
04Ultimate Collection Dual Logos-UL2-NT
04Ultimate Collection Patch Autographs-UPA-CNRB
04Ultimate Collection Patch Autographs-UPA-GHCN
04ITG Heroes and Prospects-151
Aspiring-6
Autographs-CN
Hero Memorabilia-19
04ITG Heroes/Prospects Toronto Expo '05-151
04ITG Heroes/Prospects Expo Heroes/Pros-151
05ITG Heroes/Prosp Toronto Expo Parallel -8
05Black Diamond-189
Emerald-189
Gold-189
Onyx-189
Ruby-189
05ITG Tough Customers-CN
Double Memorabilia-CN
Signed Memorabilia-CN
Stickwork-CN
05ITG Ultimate Memorabilia Level 1-16
05ITG Ultimate Memorabilia Level 2-16
05ITG Ultimate Memorabilia Level 3-16
05ITG Ultimate Memorabilia Level 4-16
05ITG Ultimate Memorabilia Level 5-16
05ITG Ultimate Mem Complete Jersey-18
05ITG Ultimate Mem Complete Jersey Gold-18
05ITG Ultimate Mem Complete Package-13
05ITG Ultimate Mem Complete Package Gold-13
05ITG Ultimate Mem Double Mem-8
05ITG Ultimate Mem Double Mem Gold-8
05ITG Ultimate Memorabilia Emblems-16
05ITG Ultimate Memorabilia Emblems Gold-16
05ITG Ultimate Mem First Rounders Jerseys-7
05ITG Ultimate Mem 1st Round Jersey Gold-7
05ITG Ultimate Memorabilia Gloves Are Off-9
05ITG Ultimate Mem Gloves Are Off Gold-9
05ITG Ultimate Mem Jersey and Emblem-11
05ITG Ultimate Mem Jersey Emblems Gold-11
05ITG Ultimate Memorabilia Jerseys-8
05ITG Ultimate Memorabilia Jerseys Gold-8
05ITG Ultimate Mem Raised to the Rafters-17
05ITG Ultimate Mem Raised Rafters Gold-17
05ITG Ultimate Mem Retro Teammate Jerseys-19
05ITG Ult Mem Retro Teammates Jersey Gold-19
05ITG Ultimate Memorabilia Stick Autos-20
05ITG Ultimate Mem Stick Autos Gold-20
05ITG Ultimate Mem Sticks and Jerseys-16
05ITG Ultimate Mem Stick and Jerseys Gold-16
05ITG Ultimate Memorabilia Triple Autos-11
05ITG Ultimate Mem Triple Autos Gold-11
05ITG Ultimate Mem Triple Threads Jerseys-3
05ITG Ultimate Mem Triple Thread Jsy Gold-3
05ITG Ultimate Memorabilia Ultimate Autos-15
05ITG Ultimate Mem Ultimate Autos Gold-15
05SP Authentic Exquisite Endorsements-EECN
05SP Authentic Immortal Inks-IICN
05SP Authentic Prestigious Pairings-PPBN
05SP Authentic Sign of the Times Quads-QTNBB
05SP Authentic Six Star Signatures-SSBO
05SP Game Used Authentic Fabrics-AF-CN
05SP Game Used Authentic Fabrics Autos-AAF-CN
05SP Game Used Authentic Fabrics Dual-NB
05SP Game Used Authentic Fabric Dual Auto-NB
05SP Game Used Authentic Fabrics Gold-AF-CN
05SP Game Used Authentic Patches-AP-CN
05SP Game Used Authentic Patch Autos-AAP-CN
05SP Game Used Authentic Patches Dual-NB
05SP Game Used Authentic Patch Dual Autos-NB
05SP Game Used Auto Draft-AD-CN
05SP Game Used Game Gear-GG-CN
05SP Game Used Game Gear Autographs-AG-CN
05SPx-97
Spectrum-97
Xcitement Legends-XL-CN
Xcitement Legends Gold-XL-CN
Xcitement Legends Spectrum-XL-CN
05The Cup-6
Gold-6
Black Rainbow-6
Emblems of Endorsement-EECN
Hardware Heroes-HHCN
Honorable Numbers-HNCN
Limited Logos-LLCN
Masterpiece Pressplates-6
Patch Variation-P6
Patch Variation Autographs-AP6
Scripted Numbers-SNNO
Scripted Numbers Dual-DSNNB
Scripted Swatches-SSCN
Signature Patches-SPCN
05UD Artifacts-138
Blue-138
Gold-138
Green-138
Pewter-138
Red-138
Auto Facts-AF-CN
Auto Facts Blue-AF-CN
Auto Facts Copper-AF-CN
Auto Facts Pewter-AF-CN
Auto Facts Silver-AF-CN
Gold Autographed-138
Remarkable Artifacts-RA-CN
Remarkable Artifacts Dual-RA-CN
05Ultimate Collection Endorsed Emblems-EECN
05Ultimate Coll Ultimate Achievements-UACN
05Ultimate Collection Ultimate Signatures-USCN
05Ultimate Coll Ultimate Sigs Pairings-UPBO
05Ultimate Coll Ultimate Sigs Trios-UTBNE
05Upper Deck All-Time Greatest-6
05Upper Deck Big Playmakers-B-CN
05Upper Deck NHL Generations-TNSN
05Upper Deck Patches-P-CN
05Upper Deck Trilogy-156
Crystal-156
Ice Scripts-IS-CN
Legendary Scripts-LEG-CN
Personal Scripts-PER-CN
05ITG Heroes and Prospects-8
Aspiring-ASP6
Autographs-A-CN
Future Teammates-FT11
Hero Memorabilia-HM-3
Hero Memorabilia Dual-HDM-6
Spectrum-STM-07
Spectrum Gold-STM-07
06Beehive-229
5 X 7 Black and White-229
Matted Materials-MMCN
06Black Diamond-150B
Gold-150B
Ruby-150B
06ITG Ultimate Memorabilia-25
Artist Proof-25
Autos-27
Autos Gold-27
Complete Package-10
Complete Package Gold-10
Decades-7
Decades Gold-7
Double Memorabilia-18
Double Memorabilia Gold-18
Emblems-15
Emblems Gold-15
Gloves Are Off-5
Gloves Are Off Gold-5
Jerseys Autos-41
Jerseys Autos Gold-41
Retro Teammates-19
Retro Teammates Gold-19
Sticks Autos-7
Sticks Autos Gold-7
Triple Thread Jerseys-9
Triple Thread Jerseys Gold-9
06Parkhurst-80
Autographs-80
Autographs Dual-DANO
06SP Authentic Sign of the Times Duals-STNK
06SP Game Used Authentic Fabrics Quads-AF4NMBT
06SP Game Used Authentic Fabrics Quads Patches-AF4NMBT
06SP Game Used Authentic Fabrics Sixes-AF6MAS
06SP Game Used Authentic Fabrics Sixes Patches-AF6MAS
06SP Game Used Inked Sweaters-ISCN
06SP Game Used Inked Sweaters Patches-ISCN
06SP Game Used Letter Marks-LMCN
06SP Game Used SIGnificance-SCN
06SPx-122
Spectrum-122
SPxcitement-X7
SPxcitement Spectrum-X7
SPxcitement Autographs-X7
Winning Materials-WMCN
Winning Materials Spectrum-WMCN
Winning Materials Autographs-WMCN
06The Cup-9
Autographed Foundations-CQCN
Autographed Foundations Patches-CQCN
Autographed NHL Shields Duals-DASNB
Autographed Patches-9
Black Rainbow-9
Foundations-CQCN
Foundations Patches-CQCN
Enshrinements-ECN
Gold-9
Gold Patches-9
Honorable Numbers-HNCN
Jerseys-9
Limited Logos-LLCN
Masterpiece Pressplates-9
Scripted Swatches-SSCN
Scripted Swatches Duals-DSNB
Signature Patches-SPCN
06UD Artifacts-125
Blue-125
Gold-125
Platinum-125
Radiance-125
Autographed Radiance Parallel-125
Red-125
Auto-Facts-AFCN
Auto-Facts Gold-AFCN
Treasured Patches Black-TSCN
Treasured Patches Blue-TSCN
Treasured Patches Gold-TSCN
Treasured Patches Platinum-TSCN
Treasured Patches Red-TSCN
Treasured Patches Autographed Black Tag Parallel-TSCN
Treasured Swatches-TSCN
Treasured Swatches Black-TSCN
Treasured Swatches Blue-TSCN
Treasured Swatches Gold-TSCN
Treasured Swatches Platinum-TSCN
Treasured Swatches Red-TSCN
Treasured Swatches Autographed Black-TSCN
Tundra Tandems-TTCA
Tundra Tandems-TTCR
Tundra Tandems Black-TTCA
Tundra Tandems Black-TTCR
Tundra Tandems Blue-TTCA
Tundra Tandems Blue-TTCR
Tundra Tandems Gold-TTCA
Tundra Tandems Gold-TTCR
Tundra Tandems Platinum-TTCA
Tundra Tandems Platinum-TTCR
Tundra Tandems Red-TTCA
Tundra Tandems Red-TTCR
Tundra Tandems Dual Patches Red-TTCA
Tundra Tandems Dual Patches Red-TTCR
06Ultimate Collection Autographed Jerseys-AJ-CN
06Ultimate Collection Autographed Patches-AJ-CN
06Ultimate Collection Jerseys-UJ-CN
06Ultimate Collection Jerseys Dual-UJ2-NB
06Ultimate Collection Jerseys Triple-UJ3-ENK
06Ultimate Collection Patches-UJ-CN
06Ultimate Collection Patches Dual-UJ2-NB
06Ultimate Collection Patches Triple-UJ3-ENK
06Ultimate Collection Premium Patches-PS-CN
06Ultimate Collection Premium Swatches-PS-CN
06Ultimate Collection Signatures-US-CN
06Ultimate Collection Ultimate Achievements-UA-CN
06Upper Deck Game Jerseys-J2CN
06Upper Deck Game Patches-P2CN
06Upper Deck Sweet Shot-9
Signature Shots/Saves-SSCN
Signature Shots/Saves Sticks-SSSCN
Sweet Stitches-SSCN
Sweet Stitches Duals-SSCN
Sweet Stitches Triples-SSCN
06Upper Deck Trilogy Combo Autographed Jerseys-CJNB
06Upper Deck Trilogy Combo Autographed Patches-CJNB
06Upper Deck Trilogy Combo Clearcut Autographs-C3NOB
06Upper Deck Trilogy Frozen In Time-FT4
06Upper Deck Trilogy Honorary Scripted Patches-HSPCN
06Upper Deck Trilogy Honorary Scripted Swatches-HSSCN
06Upper Deck Trilogy Honorary Swatches-HSCN
06Upper Deck Trilogy Legendary Scripts-LSCN
06Upper Deck Trilogy Scripts-S2CN
06Upper Deck Trilogy Scripts-TSCN

Neff, Claudio

99Swiss Panini Stickers-70
00Swiss Panini Stickers-117
04Swiss Davos Postcards-22

Negrin, John

05Kootenay Ice-17

Nehrling, Lucas

96Sarnia Sting-19
98Guelph Storm-23
99Muskegon Fury-30
00Albany River Rats-16

Neidermayer, Scott

03BAP Memorabilia Practice Jerseys-PMP4

Neighbour, Rob

91Air Canada SJHL-E39

Neil, Chris

99Grand Rapids Griffins-14
00Grand Rapids Griffins-15
01Atomic-118
Premiere Date-118
01Atomic Toronto Fall Expo-118
01BAP Memorabilia-325
Emerald-325
Ruby-325
Sapphire-325
01BAP Signature Series-219
Autographs-219
Autographs Gold-219
01BAP Update Tough Customers-TC8
01BAP Update Tough Customers-TC38
01Crown Royale-172
01O-Pee-Chee-351
01Pacific Adrenaline-218
Blue-218
Premiere Date-218
Red-218
Retail-218
01Pacific Heads-Up-113
01Parkhurst-259
01Parkhurst Beckett Promos-259
01Private Stock-133
Gold-133
Premiere Date-133
Retail-133
Silver-133
01Private Stock Pacific Nights-133
01Senators Team Issue-18
01SP Authentic-166
Limited-166
Limited Gold-166
01SP Game Used-91
01SPx-118
01Titanium-173
Retail-173
01Titanium Draft Day Edition-154
01Topps-351
01Topps Chrome-169
Refractors-169
Black Border Refractors-169

01Topps Heritage-153
01Upper Deck Ice-80
01Upper Deck Vintage-291
01Vanguard-123
Blue-123
Red-123
One of Ones-123
Premiere Date-123
Proofs-123
02BAP First Edition-375
02BAP Sig Series Auto Buybacks 2001-219
02BAP Signature Series Golf-GS21
02NHL Power Play Stickers-115
02Pacific Complete-259
Red-259
02Senators Team Issue-11
02Senators Team Issue-17
02Topps Total-107
02Upper Deck-370
Exclusives-370
02Upper Deck Beckett UD Promos-370
02Upper Deck Vintage-313
03Pacific Complete-413
Red-413
03Senators Postcards-18
03Upper Deck Tough Customers-TC-10
05Parkhurst-342
Facsimile Auto Parallel-342
06Gatorade-56
06O-Pee-Chee-352
Rainbow-352
06Upper Deck-387
Exclusives Parallel-387
High Gloss Parallel-387
Masterpieces-387
Neil, Connie
23Crescent Selkirks-14
24Holland Creameries-9
Neil, James
06UK Nottingham Panthers-10
Neil, Mike
05Saint John's Sea Dogs-16
Neil, Scott
93UK Sheffield Steelers-5
94Finnish Jaa Kiekko-327
94UK Sheffield Steelers-4
95UK Sheffield Steelers-18
00UK Sheffield Steelers Centurions-10
Neill, Mike
82Sault Ste. Marie Greyhounds-17
88ProCards AHL-157
Neilson, Chris
02Syracuse Crunch Sheets-11
Neilson, Corey
93North Bay Centennials-6
94North Bay Centennials-7
95Slapshot-59
97Barrie Colts-19
97Quad-City Mallards-22
99Louisiana Ice Gators-11
00Louisiana Ice Gators-10
01Louisiana Ice Gators-18
03ECHL All-Stars-276
03Pensacola Ice Pilots-350
05Florida Everblades-17
06UK Nottingham Panthers-11
Neilson, David
90Prince Albert Raiders-12
907th Inn. Sketch WHL-265
91Prince Albert Raiders-14
917th Inn. Sketch WHL-250
94Knoxville Cherokees-13
94Las Vegas Thunder-17
95Saint John Flames-17
96Knoxville Cherokees-18
98Columbus Cottonmouths-10
Neilson, Eric
01Rimouski Oceanic-18
02Rimouski Oceanic-10
03Rimouski Oceanic-15
04Rimouski Oceanic-16
05Bakersfield Condors-18
Neilson, Jeff
94Classic-89
Gold-89
Neilson, Jim
62Topps-49
63Topps-50
64Beehive Group III Photos-143
64Coca-Cola Caps-84
64Topps-103
64Toronto Star-34
65Coca-Cola-85
65Topps-89
66Topps-88
66Topps USA Test-55
67Topps-91
68O-Pee-Chee-172
68O-Pee-Chee-207
68Shirriff Coins-104
68Topps-70
69O-Pee-Chee-35
Four-in-One-3
69Topps-35
70Dad's Cookies-89
70Esso Power Players-190
70O-Pee-Chee-185
70Sargent Promotions Stamps-121
71O-Pee-Chee-112
71Sargent Promotions Stamps-122
71Topps-112
71Toronto Sun-177
72O-Pee-Chee-60
72Sargent Promotions Stamps-154
72Topps-66
72Finnish Semic World Championship-211
72Swedish Semic World Championship-211
73O-Pee-Chee-123
73Topps-123
74NHL Action Stamps-67
74O-Pee-Chee NHL-109
74Topps-109
75O-Pee-Chee NHL-270
75Topps-270
76O-Pee-Chee NHL-344
77O-Pee-Chee NHL-317
91Ultimate Original Six-25
French-25
94Parkhurst Tall Boys-102
95Parkhurst '66-67-81
Coins-81
04ITG Franchises US East-409
Autographs-A-JN
06Parkhurst-141
Autographs-141
Neilson, Roger
78Maple Leafs Postcards-16
85Blackhawks Team Issue-4
89Rangers Marine Midland Bank-NNO
90Pro Set-672
00Senators Team Issue-13
01Senators Team Issue-19
02Senators Team Issue-27
04ITG Ultimate Memorabilia-200
Gold-200
Neininger, Michael
99Swiss Panini Stickers-95
00Swiss Panini Stickers-189
01Swiss HNL-299
02Swiss HNL-347
Neininger, Tony
72Finnish Semic World Championship-147
72Swedish Semic World Championship-147
74Finnish Typotor-110
Neish, Greg
93Wichita Thunder-12
94Central Hockey League-118
Neiszner, Chris
01Red Deer Rebels-13
02Red Deer Rebels-24
03Red Deer Rebels-19
05Las Vegas Wranglers-15
06Las Vegas Wranglers-17
Nejdsater, Anders
83Swedish Semic Elitserien-15
Neliba, Jan
81Swedish Semic Hockey VM Stickers-60
82Swedish Semic VM Stickers-84
94Czech APS Extraliga-281
95Czech APS Extraliga-75
96Czech APS Extraliga-212
97Czech APS Extraliga-26
Nelli, Toni
92Quebec Pee-Wee Tournament-1393
95Swiss HNL-494
Nelligan, Sam
74Sioux City Musketeers-12
Nellis, Jim
91Air Canada SJHL-D39
92Saskatchewan JHL-89
Nelson, A.J.
04Camrose Kodiaks-14
Nelson, Berk
94Dubuque Fighting Saints-20
Nelson, Brad
93St. Cloud State Huskies-19
Nelson, Brian
84Minnesota-Duluth Bulldogs-6
84Minnesota-Duluth Bulldogs-8
85Minnesota-Duluth Bulldogs-27
Nelson, Chad
95Louisiana Ice Gators Playoffs-13
95Louisiana Ice Gators Glossy-3
96Louisiana Ice Gators II-12
97Louisiana Ice Gators-20
01Greenville Grrrowl-22
Nelson, Chris
92Cincinnati Cyclones-18
93Raleigh Icecaps-12
94Atlanta Knights-3
94Los Angeles Blades RHI-2
98Tacoma Sabercats-16
Nelson, Craig
95Slapshot-152
97Louisville Riverfrogs-2
01UK Dundee Stars-11
02UK Dundee Stars-11
Nelson, Eric
03Rimouski Oceanic Sheets-1
04Atlantic City Boardwalk Bullies-14
Nelson, Francis
83Hall of Fame-160
83Hall of Fame Postcards-L11
85Hall of Fame-160
Nelson, Jeff
90Prince Albert Raiders-13
907th Inn. Sketch WHL-281
91Upper Deck-689
French-689
91Upper Deck Czech World Juniors-63
91Prince Albert Raiders-15
917th Inn. Sketch WHL-265
917th Inn. Sketch Memorial Cup-104
91Arena Draft Picks-27
91Arena Draft Picks French-27
91Arena Draft Picks Autographs-27
91Arena Draft Picks Autographs French-27
91Classic-32
91Star Pics-43
91Ultimate Draft-28
91Ultimate Draft-75
91Ultimate Draft French-28
91Classic Four-Sport *-32
Autographs-32A
92Iowa-55
93Portland Pirates-11
94Parkhurst SE-SE199
Gold-SE199
94Upper Deck-250
Electric Ice-250
94Portland Pirates-17
94Classic-48
Gold-48
94Classic Pro Prospects-155
94Classic Four-Sport *-146
Gold-146
Printers Proofs-146
95Upper Deck World Junior Alumni-3
95Capitals Team Issue-19
95Donruss-128
95Leaf-246
95Portland Pirates-16
95Images-66
Gold-66
Clear Excitement-CE15
Platinum Prospects-PR1
96Grand Rapids Griffins-15
96Collector's Edge Ice-54
Prism-54
97Milwaukee Admirals-14
98Milwaukee Admirals-12
99Portland Pirates-17
00Portland Pirates-2
01German Upper Deck-235
02Cleveland Barons-18
03Grand Rapids Griffins-27
03Muskegon Fury-13
05Muskegon Fury-13
Nelson, Kodie
82Medicine Hat Tigers-14
84Victoria Cougars-17
Nelson, Levi
05Swift Current Broncos-15
06Swift Current Broncos-7
06Swift Current Broncos-23
Nelson, Mark
03Vernon Vipers-11
04Vernon Vipers-2
Nelson, Mike
02Plymouth Whalers-22
03Greenville Grrrowl-17
03Toledo Storm-3
Nelson, Riley
00Columbus Cottonmouths-10
03Colorado Eagles-12
04Colorado Eagles-13
05Colorado Eagles-13
06Colorado EaglesÂ -15
Nelson, Scott
93Quebec Pee-Wee Tournament-1179
Nelson, Todd
90ProCards AHL/IHL-383
91ProCards-307
92Topps-50
Gold-50G
92Cleveland Lumberjacks-12
93Portland Pirates-24
93Classic Pro Prospects-42
94Donruss-238
94Flair-202
94Leaf-273
94Portland Pirates-18
96Grand Rapids Griffins-16
97Grand Rapids Griffins-10
98German DEL-116
99Grand Rapids Griffins-15
00Rochester Americans-18
02Grand Rapids Griffins-20
03Muskegon Fury-21
05Muskegon Fury-22
Nelson, Tom
02Florida Everblades-15
02Florida Everblades RBI-127
03Las Vegas Wranglers-14
03Las Vegas Wranglers RBI-236
04Fort Wayne Komets-10
Nelson, Willie
04Arizona Icecats-33
Nemcak, Juraj
96Slovakian Quebec Pee-Wee Tournament-19
Nemchinov, Sergei
89Russian National Team-21
89Swedish Semic World Champ Stickers-95
90O-Pee-Chee-493
91Pro Set Platinum-205
91O-Pee-Chee-514
91O-Pee-Chee Inserts-24R
91OPC Premier-25
91Parkhurst-334
French-334
91Pinnacle-317
French-317
91Pro Set-441
French-441
91Score Canadian Bilingual-617
91Score Canadian English-617
91Score Rookie/Traded-67T
91Topps-514
91Upper Deck-355
French-355
91Finnish Semic World Champ Stickers-96
91Russian Stars Red Ace-15
91Swedish Semic World Champ Stickers-96
92Bowman-426
92O-Pee-Chee-316
92Panini Stickers-234
92Panini Stickers French-234
92Parkhurst-114
92Parkhurst-236
92Parkhurst-447
Emerald Ice-114
Emerald Ice-236
Emerald Ice-447
92Pinnacle-158
French-158
92Pro Set-117
92Score-115
Canadian-115
Sharpshooters-5
Sharpshooters Canadian-5
92Stadium Club-340
92Topps-287
Gold-287G
92Ultra-140
92Upper Deck-298
Euro-Stars-E13
93Donruss-214
93Leaf-252
93OPC Premier-42
Gold-42
93Panini Stickers-93
93Parkhurst-128
Emerald Ice-128
93Pinnacle-51
Canadian-51
93PowerPlay-163
93Score-218
Canadian-218
International Stars-16
International Stars Canadian-16
93Stadium Club-245
Members Only Master Set-245
OPC-245
First Day Issue-245
First Day Issue OPC-245
93Topps/OPC Premier-42
Gold-42
93Ultra-203
93Upper Deck-371
94Canada Games NHL POGS-167
94Donruss-125
94Flair-116
94Fleer-138
94Leaf-153
94OPC Premier-443
Special Effects-443
94Parkhurst SE-SE115
Gold-SE115
94Pinnacle-220
Artist's Proofs-220
Rink Collection-220
94Score-14
Gold-14
Platinum-14
94Stadium Club-41
Members Only Master Set-41
First Day Issue-41
Super Team Winner Cards-41
94Topps/OPC Premier-443
Special Effects-443
94Ultra-142
94Upper Deck-156
Electric Ice-156
95Be A Player-209
Signatures-S209
Signatures Die Cuts-S209
95Canada Games NHL POGS-181
95Collector's Choice-283
Player's Club-283
Player's Club Platinum-283
95Donruss-378
95Leaf-236
95Parkhurst International-141
Emerald Ice-141
95Pinnacle-152
Artist's Proofs-152
Rink Collection-152
Global Gold-20
95Playoff One on One-285
95Score-41
Black Ice Artist's Proofs-41
Black Ice-41
95Topps-141
OPC Inserts-141
95Upper Deck-166
Electric Ice-166
Electric Ice Gold-166
96Collector's Choice-175
96Pinnacle-11
Artist's Proofs-11
Foil-11
Premium Stock-11
Rink Collection-11
96Upper Deck-298
97Pacific-102
Copper-102
Emerald Green-102
Ice Blue-102
Red-102
Silver-102
97Pacific Omega-139
Copper-139
Dark Gray-139
Emerald Green-139
Gold-139
Ice Blue-139
98Be A Player-237
Press Release-237
98BAP Gold-237
98BAP Autographs-237
98BAP Autographs Gold-237
98Finest-16
No Protectors-16
No Protectors Refractors-16
Refractors-16
98Pacific-283
Ice Blue-283
Red-283
98Panini Stickers-76
99Devils Team Issue-8
99Panini Stickers-77
99Upper Deck-247
Exclusives-247
Exclusives 1 of 1-247
99Upper Deck Gold Reserve-247
99Russian Fetisov Tribute-19
00Devils Team Issue-15
01Devils Team Issue-15
01Pacific-236
Extreme LTD-236
Hobby LTD-236
Premiere Date-236
Retail LTD-236
01Pacific Arena Exclusives-236
02BAP Sig Series Auto Buybacks 1998-237
02Russian Hockey League-230
Nemcicky, Tomas
93Upper Deck-264
95Czech APS Extraliga-47
96Czech APS Extraliga-37
97Czech APS Extraliga-25
97Czech DS Extraliga-107
97Czech DS Stickers-112
98Czech DS-112
98Czech DS Stickers-299
98Czech OFS-28
99German DEL-361
00Czech OFS-230
01Czech OFS-217
02Czech OFS Plus-287
02Czech OFS Plus All-Star Game-H32
02Czech OFS Plus Trios-T4
Nemec, Ondrej
01Czech OFS-58
02Czech OFS Plus-72
03Czech OFS Plus-32
04Czech OFS-255
05Czech HC Karlovy Vary-11
06Czech OFS-36
Nemec, Vladimir
00Idaho Steelheads-16
01Johnstown Chiefs-26
02Johnstown Chiefs-10
Nemecek, Jan
94Czech APS Extraliga-275
95Slapshot Memorial Cup-52
98Long Beach Ice Dogs-14
99BAP Memorabilia-326
Gold-326
Silver-326
00Pacific-199
Copper-199
Gold-199
Ice Blue-199
Premiere Date-199
01German Upper Deck-209
02Czech OFS Plus-339
03Swedish Elite-269
Global Impact-GI12
Silver-269
Nemecek, Roman
03Czech OFS Plus-245
04Czech OFS-406
06Czech OFS-209
Nemeth, Adam
02London Knights-15
03London Knights-3
04Kingston Frontenacs-14
05Kingston Frontenacs-5
06Kingston Frontenacs-18
Nemeth, Marian
95Slovakian-Quebec Pee-Wee Tournament-21
Nemeth, Steve
93UK Sheffield Steelers-6
94UK Sheffield Steelers-25
95UK Sheffield Steelers-4
98UK Kingston Hawks-8
00UK Sheffield Steelers Centurions-16
Nemeth, Tom
907th Inn. Sketch OHL-41
91Cornwall Royals-21
917th Inn. Sketch OHL-17
92Dayton Bombers-19
93Dayton Bombers-11
95Buffalo Stampedes RHI-16
96Dayton Bombers-22
97Fort Wayne Komets-7
98Cincinnati Cyclones-15
98Cincinnati Cyclones 2-21
98Dayton Bombers-13
98Dayton Bombers EBK-7
98Dayton Bombers EBK-16
03Columbus Stars-1
03Toledo Storm-7
04Fort Wayne Komets-11
Nemirovsky, David
95Bowman-119
All-Foil-119
95Parkhurst International-359
Emerald Ice-359
95Slapshot-272
95Slapshot-346
95Stadium Club-223
Members Only Master Set-223
95Sarnia Sting-16
96Leaf-219
Press Proofs-219
96Pinnacle-236
Artist's Proofs-236
Foil-236
Premium Stock-236
Rink Collection-236
96Summit-191
Artist's Proofs-191
Ice-191
Metal-191
Premium Stock-191
96Carolina Monarchs-19
97Be A Player-167
Autographs-167
Autographs Die-Cuts-167
Autographs Prismatic Die-Cuts-167
97Collector's Choice-106
97Katch-63
Gold-63
Silver-63
97Pacific-191
Copper-191
Emerald Green-191
Ice Blue-191
Red-191
Silver-191
97Upper Deck-77
98Katch-63
98Fort Wayne Komets-13
99St. John's Maple Leafs-14
02Finnish Cardset-79
03Russian Hockey League-238
05Russian Hockey League RHL-31
Nemirovsky, Mikhail
95Flint Generals-10
97New Orleans Brass-16
98Flint Generals-14
99Muskegon Fury-27
04German DEL-160
Nenonen, Esko
65Finnish Hellas-82
Nenonen, Martti
78Finnish SM-Liiga-236
80Finnish Mallasjuoma-219
Nenovich, Mark
98Minnesota Golden Gophers-3
99Minnesota Golden Gophers-16
00Minnesota Golden Gophers-16
01Minnesota Golden Gophers-14
Nepryaev, Ivan
00Russian Hockey League-306
06Russian Torino Olympic Team-16
Nepveu, Stephane
98Thetford Mines Coyotes-3
ner Mitterfell, Vitus
94German First League-151
Nerell, Erik
92Norwegian Elite Series-39
Neron, Alexandre
06Rimouski Oceanic-15
Neruda, Stanislav
99Czech Score Blue 2000-155
99Czech Score Red Ice 2000-155
Nesbitt, Derek
06Idaho Steelheads-10
Nesbitt, Thomas
06Ottawa 67s-9
Nesdill, Mike
02Lincoln Stars-14
03Lincoln Stars-11
03Lincoln Stars Update-41
Nesich, Jim
88ProCards AHL-269
89ProCards AHL-182
90ProCards AHL/IHL-61
91ProCards-148
Ness, Jay
91Lake Superior State Lakers-19
92Lake Superior State Lakers-21
Nessman, Ryan
91British Columbia JHL-22
Nestak, Pavel
95Czech APS Extraliga-201
97Czech APS Extraliga-103
98Czech DS Stickers-48
98Johnstown Chiefs-19
Nester, Kelly
87Hull Olympiques-15
Nesterenko, Eric
44Beehive Group II Photos-131
44Beehive Group II Photos-439
45Quaker Oats Photos-42
53Parkhurst-10
54Parkhurst-19
54Parkhurst-95
55Parkhurst-15
55Parkhurst-75
Quaker Oats-15
Quaker Oats-75
57Topps-24
58Topps-53
59Topps-1
60Shirriff Coins-69
61Shirriff/Salada Coins-23
61Topps-28
62Topps-41
63Topps-39
63Toronto Star-28
64Beehive Group III Photos-51A
64Beehive Group III Photos-51B
64Coca-Cola Caps-29
64Topps-91
65Coca-Cola-30
65Topps-119
66Topps-60
66Topps USA Test-60
67Topps-60
68O-Pee-Chee-154
68Shirriff Coins-31
69O-Pee-Chee-136
70Blackhawks Postcards-10
70Esso Power Players-121
70O-Pee-Chee-19
70Sargent Promotions Stamps-38
70Topps-19
71O-Pee-Chee-213
71Toronto Sun-77
90Upper Deck-503
French-503
94Parkhurst Missing Link-39
94Parkhurst Tall Boys-33
95Parkhurst '66-67-26
Coins-26
02Parkhurst Reprints-189
06Parkhurst-81
Autographs-81
Nesterov, Alexander
00Russian Hockey League-168
02Russian Hockey League-57
Nethery, Lance
88Oilers Tenth Anniversary-70
94German DEL-271
95German DEL-262
96German DEL-156
98German DEL-247
99German DEL-123
Netik, Tomas
01Czech OFS-117
03Czech OFS Plus-84
04Czech HC Sparta Praha Postcards-13
04Czech OFS-192
06Czech HC Sparta Praha Postcards-14
06Czech OFS-77
Netsch, Peter
94German First League-318
Neubauer, R.
95German DEL-288
Neuenschwander, Philipp
93Swiss HNL-128
95Swiss HNL-176
96Swiss HNL-70
Neufeld, Blaine
05Medicine Hat Tigers-15
Neufeld, Jeff
04Austin Ice Bats-16
Neufeld, Kyle
00London Knights-7
01Kingston Frontenacs-14
01Plymouth Whalers-8
Neufeld, Perry
95Oklahoma Coyotes RHI-12
Neufeld, Ray
82Whalers Junior Hartford Courant-14
83NHL Key Tags-45
83O-Pee-Chee-144
83O-Pee-Chee Stickers-260
83Topps Stickers-260
83Whalers Junior Hartford Courant-13
84O-Pee-Chee-76
84O-Pee-Chee Stickers-199
84Topps-59
84Whalers Junior Wendy's-13
84Kelowna Wings-33
85Jets Police-15
85O-Pee-Chee-58
85O-Pee-Chee Stickers-171
85Topps-58
85Whalers Junior Wendy's-14
86Jets Postcards-16
86O-Pee-Chee-177
86O-Pee-Chee Stickers-106
86Topps-177
87Jets Postcards-15
87Panini Stickers-369
88Jets Police-16
88O-Pee-Chee-239
88O-Pee-Chee Stickers-141
89ProCards AHL-69
Neukom, Patrik
93Swiss HNL-321
95Swiss HNL-469
96Swiss HNL-368
99Swiss Panini Stickers-346
Neumann, Karsten
94German First League-157
Neumann, Steve
94German First League-321
Neumeier, Troy
90Prince Albert Raiders-14
907th Inn. Sketch WHL-269
91ProCards-602
92Hamilton Canucks-22
95Adirondack Red Wings-17
00UK Sekonda Superleague-94
02Fort Wayne Komets-12
03Fort Wayne Komets-19
03Fort Wayne Komets Shoe Carnival-5
04Fort Wayne Komets Shoe Carnival-11
05Fort Wayne Komets Choice-23
05Fort Wayne Komets Sprint-14
Neumuller, Markus
94German First League-60
Neuvirth, Michal
06Plymouth Whalers-16
Neuvonen, Jari
93Finnish SISU-128
Nevalainen, Matti
96Finnish SISU Redline-118
Nevalainen, Seppo
71Finnish Suomi Stickers-257
Nevers, Tom
95Minnesota Golden Gophers-23
Nevesely, Stanislav
98Czech OFS-65
Neveu, Christian
93Amos Les Forestiers-16
Nevill, Rhett
98Red Deer Rebels-15
Neville, Dave
37V356 Worldwide Gum-111
Nevin, Bob
44Beehive Group II Photos-440
58Parkhurst-13
60York Photos-25
61Parkhurst-10
61Shirriff/Salada Coins-47
61York Yellow Backs-26
62Parkhurst-10
62Shirriff Coins-7
63Chex Photos-40
63Maple Leafs Team Issue-18
63Parkhurst-10
63Parkhurst-70
63York White Backs-8
64Beehive Group III Photos-144
64Coca-Cola Caps-78
64Topps-77
65Coca-Cola-80
65Topps-93
66Topps-27
66Topps USA Test-27
67Topps-28
68O-Pee-Chee-76
68Shirriff Coins-101
68Topps-76
69O-Pee-Chee-40
Four-in-One-15
69Topps-40
70Colgate Stamps-38
70Dad's Cookies-90
70Esso Power Players-186
70O-Pee-Chee-60
70Sargent Promotions Stamps-127
70Topps-60
71Bazooka-14
71O-Pee-Chee-44
71Sargent Promotions Stamps-90
71Topps-44
71Toronto Sun-139
72O-Pee-Chee-267
72Sargent Promotions Stamps-112
74NHL Action Stamps-125
74O-Pee-Chee NHL-378
75O-Pee-Chee NHL-123
75O-Pee-Chee NHL-320
75Topps-123
75Topps-320
76O-Pee-Chee WHA-73
91Ultimate Original Six-26
French-26
94Parkhurst Tall Boys-103
95Parkhurst '66-67 Promos-2
95Parkhurst '66-67-143
95Parkhurst '66-67-144
95Parkhurst '66-67-PR144
Coins-85
02Maple Leafs Platinum Collection-33
02Parkhurst Reprints-226
02Parkhurst Reprints-259
02Parkhurst Reprints-275
02Parkhurst Reprints-286
04ITG Franchises Canadian-95
Autographs-BN2
04ITG Franchises US East-394
Autographs-A-BN1
Newans, Chris
96Anaheim Bullfrogs RHI-19
96Anchorage Aces-10
97Anchorage Aces-14
01Anchorage Aces-10
Newberry, John
83Nova Scotia Voyageurs-8
Newberry, Scot
92Saskatchewan JHL-125
Newbury, Kris
99UD Prospects-17
99UD Prospects-76
00Sarnia Sting-19
06Beehive-156
Matte-156
06Hot Prospects-194
06SP Authentic-215
Limited-215
06The Cup Masterpiece Pressplates (Bee Hive)-156
06The Cup Masterpiece Pressplates (SP Authentic)-215
06The Cup Masterpiece Pressplates (Ultimate Collection)-98
06UD Artifacts-258
06Ultimate Collection-98
06Toronto Marlies-20
Newhook, Ron
94Sudbury Wolves-23
94Sudbury Wolves Police-12
95Slapshot-403
95Sudbury Wolves-12
95Sudbury Wolves Police-17
97Toledo Storm-12
Newman, Dan
77O-Pee-Chee NHL-362
78O-Pee-Chee-270
88Oilers Tenth Anniversary-129
Newman, Darrel
93Muskegon Fury-4
Newman, Dwayne
88Brandon Wheat Kings-3
89Brandon Wheat Kings-12
907th Inn. Sketch WHL-237
917th Inn. Sketch WHL-321
99UK Basingstoke Bison-14
04UK Milton Keynes Lightning-12
Newman, Jared
99Upper Deck Sobey's Memorial Cup-14
99UD Prospects-18
01Plymouth Whalers-2
02Florida Everblades RBI-128
03Florida Everblades-18
03Florida Everblades RBI Sports-170
04Florida Everblades-2
Newman, Mike
91British Columbia JHL-89
92British Columbia JHL-124
Newman, Tom
91Minnesota Golden Gophers-18
92Minnesota Golden Gophers-16
93Greensboro Monarchs-9
Newsom, Billy
00Amarillo Rattlers-14
Newsom, Matt
92Hamilton Canucks-23
Newton, Cam
75O-Pee-Chee WHA-119
Newton, Craig
94Brantford Smoke-24
Newton, Jake
06Texas Tornados-4
Newton, Todd
96Quad-City Mallards-1
Neziol, Tom
90Cincinnati Cyclones-36
91Cincinnati Cyclones-17
93Birmingham Bulls Birmingham News-16
97Mobile Mysticks Kellogg's-12
98Mobile Mysticks-3
99Mobile Mysticks-22
Ngoy, Michael
04Swiss Lausanne HC Postcards-15
Ngui, Ben
93Quebec Pee-Wee Tournament-1449
Nice, Derry
98Prince Albert Raiders-18
Nichol, Mike
03Brandon Wheat Kings-24
04Brandon Wheat Kings-1
05Vernon Vipers-16
Nichol, Scott
93Portland Winter Hawks-17
95Rochester Americans-14
96Rochester Americans-10
97Rochester Americans-2-2
98Rochester Americans-11
00SPx Rookie Redemption-RR5
01BAP Memorabilia-446
Emerald-446
Ruby-446
Sapphire-446
01BAP Signature Series-209
Autographs-209
Autographs Gold-209
01O-Pee-Chee-338
01SP Authentic-137
Limited-137
Limited Gold-137
01SP Game Used-68
01SPx-98
01Stadium Club-130
Award Winners-130
Master Photos-130
01Topps-338
01Topps Chrome-156
Refractors-156
Black Border Refractors-156
01Topps Reserve-121
01UD Challenge for the Cup-99
01UD Honor Roll-67
01UD Playmakers-108
01Upper Deck-417
Exclusives-417
01Upper Deck Ice-47
02BAP Sig Series Auto Buybacks 2001-209
02NHL Power Play Stickers-8
02Pacific Complete-388
Red-388
03Blackhawks Postcards-16
03Pacific Complete-345
Red-345
03Parkhurst Original Six Chicago-12
04UK EIHL All-Stars-18
04UK London Racers-1
04UK London Racers Playoffs-14
05Upper Deck MVP-223
Gold-223
Platinum-223
Nicholas, Crystal
98Minnesota Golden Gophers Women-16
Nicholishen, Mike
98Orlando Solar Bears II-18
01Colorado Gold Kings-15
02Atlantic City Boardwalk Bullies-18
Nicholls, Bernie
83NHL Key Tags-52
83O-Pee-Chee-160
83O-Pee-Chee Stickers-292
83Puffy Stickers-10
83Topps Stickers-292
84Kings Smokey-12
84O-Pee-Chee-88
84O-Pee-Chee Stickers-269
84Topps-67
85O-Pee-Chee-148
85O-Pee-Chee Stickers-232
85Topps-148
86Kings 20th Anniversary Team Issue-16
86O-Pee-Chee-159
86O-Pee-Chee Box Bottoms-K
86O-Pee-Chee Stickers-95
86Topps-159
86Topps Box Bottoms-K
87O-Pee-Chee-183
87O-Pee-Chee Stickers-214
87Panini Stickers-278
87Topps-183
88Frito-Lay Stickers-23
88Kings Postcards-10
88Kings Smokey-19
88O-Pee-Chee-169
88O-Pee-Chee Minis-28
88O-Pee-Chee Stickers-156
88Panini Stickers-77
88Topps-169
89O-Pee-Chee-47
89O-Pee-Chee Stickers-155
89Panini Stickers-88
89Rangers Marine Midland Bank-9
89Sports Illustrated for Kids I-228
89Topps-47
89Swedish Semic World Champ Stickers-73
90Bowman-221
Tiffany-221
90Bowman Hat Tricks-20
Tiffany-20
90Kraft-40
90Kraft-73
90O-Pee-Chee-13
90OPC Premier-83
90Panini Stickers-106
90Pro Set-204
90Pro Set-352
90Score-9
Canadian-9
90Score Hottest/Rising Stars-5
90Topps-13
Tiffany-13
90Upper Deck-34
French-34
91Pro Set Platinum-174
91Bowman-76
91O-Pee-Chee-174
91Panini Stickers-288
91Parkhurst-278
91Parkhurst-458
French-278
91Pinnacle-300
French-300
91Pro Set-166
91Pro Set-386
French-166
French-386
91Score American-240
91Score Canadian Bilingual-460
91Score Canadian English-460

91Stadium Club-245
91Topps-174
91Upper Deck-356
91Upper Deck-566
French-356
French-566
91Finnish Semic World Champ Stickers-67
91Swedish Semic World Champ Stickers-67
92Bowman-161
92Oilers IGA-17
92O-Pee-Chee-52
92Panini Stickers-109
92Panini Stickers French-109
92Parkhurst-49
92Parkhurst-328
Emerald Ice-49
Emerald Ice-328
92Pinnacle-120
French-120
92Pro Set-52
92Score-340
Canadian-340
92Stadium Club-448
92Topps-438
Gold-438G
92Ultra-64
92Upper Deck-290
92Upper Deck-624
93Donruss-188
93Leaf-169
93OPC Premier-274
Gold-274
93Panini Stickers-39
93Parkhurst-117
Emerald Ice-117
93Pinnacle-165
Canadian-165
93PowerPlay-139
93Score-19
Canadian-19
93Stadium Club-111
Members Only Master Set-111
OPC-111
First Day Issue-111
First Day Issue OPC-111
93Topps/OPC Premier-274
Gold-274
93Ultra-86
93Upper Deck-58
SP-85
94Blackhawks Coke-12
94Canada Games NHL POGS-68
94Finest-87
Super Team Winners-87
Refractors-87
94Flair-35
94Fleer-43
94Hockey Wit-64
94Leaf-362
94OPC Premier-403
Special Effects-403
94Parkhurst SE-SE38
Gold-SE38
94Pinnacle-499
Artist's Proofs-499
Rink Collection-499
94Score-74
94Score-245
Gold-74
Gold-245
Platinum-74
Platinum-245
94Select-17
Gold-17
94SP-25
Die Cuts-25
Premier-25
Premier Die-Cuts-25
94Topps/OPC Premier-403
Special Effects-403
94Ultra-42
94Ultra-275
94Upper Deck-83
Electric Ice-83
SP Inserts-SP106
SP Inserts Die Cuts-SP106
95Blackhawks Coke-11
95Canada Games NHL POGS-64
95Collector's Choice-169
Player's Club-169
Player's Club Platinum-169
Crash The Game-C17A
Crash The Game-C17B
Crash The Game-C17C
Crash The Game Gold-C17A
Crash The Game Gold-C17B
Crash The Game Gold-C17C
Crash the Game Silver Redeemed-C17
Crash the Game Silver Bonus-C17
Crash the Game Gold Redeemed-C17
Crash the Game Gold Bonus-C17
95Donruss-24
95Emotion-31
95Hoyle Western Playing Cards-47
95Kraft-67
95Leaf-84
95Metal-26
95Panini Stickers-156
95Parkhurst International-37
Emerald Ice-37
95Playoff One on One-23
95Pro Magnets-9
95Score-29
Black Ice Artist's Proofs-29
Black Ice-29
95SkyBox Impact-31
95SP-26
95Stadium Club-28
Members Only Master Set-28
95Summit-135
Artist's Proofs-135
Ice-135
Mad Hatters-1
95Topps-122
OPC Inserts-122
95Topps SuperSkills-72
Platinum-72
95Ultra-34
Gold Medallion-34
95Upper Deck-97
Electric Ice-97
Electric Ice Gold-97
Special Edition-SE16
Special Edition Gold-SE16
95Zenith-46
96Black Diamond-59
Gold-59
96Collector's Choice-50
96Donruss-198
Press Proofs-198
96Donruss Canadian Ice-106
Gold Press Proofs-106
Red Press Proofs-106
96Donruss Elite-75
Die Cut Stars-75
96Leaf-50
Press Proofs-50
96Leaf Preferred-60
Press Proofs-60
96Maggers-67
96Metal Universe-138
96NHL Pro Stamps-9
96Pinnacle-41
Artist's Proofs-41
Foil-41
Premium Stock-41
Rink Collection-41
96Playoff One on One-355
96Score-65
Artist's Proofs-65
Dealer's Choice Artist's Proofs-65
Special Artist's Proofs-65
Golden Blades-65
96SP-139
96Summit-115
Artist's Proofs-115
Ice-115
Metal-115
Premium Stock-115
96Topps Picks-131
OPC Inserts-131
96Ultra-152
Gold Medallion-152
96Upper Deck-334
Generation Next-X31
96Upper Deck Ice-57
Parallel-57
96Zenith-32
Artist's Proofs-32
97Donruss-34
Press Proofs Silver-34
Press Proofs Gold-34
97Donruss Limited-36
Exposure-36
97Katch-123
Gold-123
Silver-123
97Pacific-255
Copper-255
Emerald Green-255
Ice Blue-255
Red-255
Silver-255
97Pacific Invincible-127
Copper-127
Emerald Green-127
Ice Blue-127
Red-127
Silver-127
97Panini Stickers-228
97Pinnacle-165
Press Plates Back Black-165
Press Plates Back Cyan-165
Press Plates Back Magenta-165
Press Plates Back Yellow-165
Press Plates Front Black-165
Press Plates Front Cyan-165
Press Plates Front Magenta-165
Press Plates Front Yellow-165
97Pinnacle Certified-109
Red-109
Mirror Blue-109
Mirror Gold-109
Mirror Red-109
97Pinnacle Inside-185
97Pinnacle Tot Cert Platinum Blue-109
97Pinnacle Tot Certi Platinum Gold-109
97Pinnacle Totally Certified Platinum Red-109
97Pinnacle Tot Cert Mirror Platinum Gold-109
97Score-180
97Sharks Fleer All-Star Sheet-4
97SP Authentic-132
97Upper Deck-150
98BAP AS Milestones-M11
98OPC Chrome-78
Refractors-78
98Pacific-389
Ice Blue-389
Red-389
98Topps-78
O-Pee-Chee-78
04ITG Franchises Canadian-18
04ITG Franchises US West-241
Autographs-A-BNI
06Parkhurst-82
Autographs-82
Autographs Dual-DADN

Nicholls, Bob

93Lakeland Ice Warriors-20

Nicholls, Dave

82Kitchener Rangers-18

Nichols, Don

05Dutch Vadeko Flyers -12

Nichols, Rob

83North Bay Centennials-20
88ProCards AHL-1
89ProCards IHL-111
90ProCards AHL/IHL-299
91ProCards-329
92San Diego Gulls-21
95Flint Generals-9
96Flint Generals-23
97Flint Generals-24
97Flint Generals EBK-23
98Flint Generals-7
99Adirondack IceHawks-24

Nicholson, Al

61Union Oil WHL-10

Nicholson, Dan

81Oshawa Generals-9
82Oshawa Generals-18

Nickel, Hartmut

70Finnish Jaakiekko-89
70Swedish Hockey-378
70Swedish Masterserien-175
74Finnish Jenkki-108
74Finnish Typotor-61
94German DEL-127
01German Berlin Polar Bears Postcards-17
02German Berlin Polar Bears Postcards-19
03German Berlin Polar Bears Postcards-21
04German Berlin Eisbarens 50th Anniv-55
04German Berlin Polar Bears Postcards-21

Nickel, Stacey

84Kelowna Wings-3
86Regina Pats-20

Nickerson, Matt

04Victoriaville Tigres-15
05Finnish Cardset -343
06Finnish Cardset-173
06Iowa Stars-16

Nicklin, Brant

01Quad-City Mallards-18
02Rockford Ice Hogs-21

Nickulas, Eric

96New Hampshire Wildcats-27
98Providence Bruins-15
99Providence Bruins-19
00BAP Memorabilia-348
Emerald-348
Ruby-348
Sapphire-348
Promos-348
00BAP Mem Chicago Sportsfest Copper-348
00BAP Memorabilia Chicago Sportsfest Blue-348
00BAP Memorabilia Chicago Sportsfest Gold-348
00BAP Memorabilia Chicago Sportsfest Ruby-348
00BAP Memorabilia Chicago Sun-Times Ruby-348
00BAP Memorabilia Chicago Sun-Times Gold-348
00BAP Mem Chicago Sun-Times Sapphire-348
00BAP Mem Toronto Fall Expo Copper-348
00BAP Memorabilia Toronto Fall Expo Gold-348
00BAP Memorabilia Toronto Fall Expo Ruby-348
00Black Diamond-76
Gold-76
00O-Pee-Chee-292
00O-Pee-Chee Parallel-292
00Pacific-39
Copper-39
Gold-39
Ice Blue-39
Premiere Date-39
00Panini Stickers-14
00SPx-92
Spectrum-92
00Topps/OPC-292
Parallel-292
00Topps Chrome-187
OPC Refractors-187
Refractors-187
00UD Pros and Prospects-93
00Upper Deck-181
Exclusives Tier 1-181
Exclusives Tier 2-181
00Upper Deck Ice-55
Immortals-55
Legends-55
Stars-55
00Upper Deck MVP-186
First Stars-186
Second Stars-186
Third Stars-186
00Upper Deck Victory-268
00Upper Deck Vintage-373
00Providence Bruins-7
01Worcester Icecats-27
02Worcester IceCats-7
03Blues Team Set-20
03Pacific Complete-321
Red-321
04Norfolk Admirals-16
05Providence Bruins-10
06German DEL-85
New Arrivals-NA7

Nicol, Brett

907th Inn. Sketch OHL-138

Nicol, Cregg

86Regina Pats-21
87Regina Pats-21

Nicoletti, Danny

93Quebec Pee-Wee Tournament-573

Nicoletti, Martin

88ProCards AHL-279

Nicolls, Jamie

86Portland Winter Hawks-16
88ProCards AHL-77
92Greensboro Monarchs-11
93Greensboro Monarchs-10

Nicolls, Paul

92British Columbia JHL-33

Nicolson, Derek

95Thunder Bay Senators-13
97Central Texas Stampede-11
99Austin Ice Bats-23
00Austin Ice Bats-13

Nicolson, Graeme

81Rockies Postcards-22

Niderost, Ruedi

93Swiss HNL-93
95Swiss HNL-140
96Swiss HNL-157
99Swiss Panini Stickers-309
00Swiss Panini Stickers-59
00Swiss Slapshot Mini-Cards-HCCF5
01Swiss EV Zug Postcards-6
01Swiss HNL-175
02Swiss EV Zug Postcards-8
02Swiss HNL-66

Nie, Ryan

03Plymouth Whalers-24
05Plymouth Whalers-A-08

Niec, Andre

06Bloomington PrairieThunder-13

Nieckar, Barry

93Raleigh Icecaps-13
94Saint John Flames-16
00UK Nottingham Panthers-24
00UK Sekonda Superleague-138
01UK Nottingham Panthers-18
02UK Nottingham Panthers-15

Niederberger, Andreas

89Swedish Semic World Champ Stickers-106
93Swedish Semic World Champ Stickers-154
94Finnish Jaa Kiekko-279
94German DEL-88
95German DEL-82
95German DEL-438
95Swedish Globe World Championships-222
95Swedish World Championships Stickers-60
96German DEL-273

Niedermayer, Rob

907th Inn. Sketch WHL-29
917th Inn. Sketch WHL-327
92Upper Deck-593
93Donruss-134
Rated Rookies-4
Special Print-I
93Kraft-68
93Leaf-293
Freshman Phenoms-6
93OPC Premier-270
Gold-270
93Parkhurst-246
Emerald Ice-246
Calder Candidates-C4
Calder Candidates Gold-C4
East/West Stars-E5
USA/Canada Gold-G5
93Pinnacle-439
Canadian-439
Super Rookies-4
Super Rookies Canadian-4
93PowerPlay-349
Rookie Standouts-8
93Score-592
Gold-592
Canadian-592
Canadian Gold-592
93Stadium Club-449
Members Only Master Set-449
First Day Issue-449
93Topps/OPC Premier-270
Gold-270
93Ultra-330
Speed Merchants-8
Wave of the Future-11
93Upper Deck-98
Program of Excellence-E11
Silver Skates-H4
Silver Skates Gold-H4
SP-58
93Classic-5
Autographs-AU7
Top Ten-DP5
93Classic Four-Sport *-189
Gold-189
94Be A Player-R55
94Be A Player-R119
94Canada Games NHL POGS-109
94Donruss-113
94Flair-67
94Fleer-82
94Leaf-225
Gold Rookies-7
94Leaf Limited-11
94OPC Premier-306
94O-Pee-Chee Finest Inserts-9
94OPC Premier Special Effects-306
94Parkhurst-294
Gold-294
Vintage-V22
94Parkhurst SE-SE68
Gold-SE68
94Pinnacle-168
94Pinnacle-469
Artist's Proofs-168
Artist's Proofs-469
Rink Collection-168
Rink Collection-469
94Post Box Backs-19
94Select-25
Gold-25
94Stadium Club-22
94Stadium Club-117
Members Only Master Set-22
Members Only Master Set-117
First Day Issue-22
First Day Issue-117
Super Teams-9
Super Teams Members Only Master Set-9
Super Team Winner Cards-22
Super Team Winner Cards-117
94Topps/OPC Premier-306
Special Effects-306
94Ultra-84
94Upper Deck-287
Electric Ice-287
SP Inserts-SP30
SP Inserts Die Cuts-SP30
94Upper Deck NHLPA/Be A Player-10
94Classic Autographs-NNO
94Classic Pro Prospects-27
94Images *-30
Sudden Impact-SI6
95Bashan Super Stickers-50
95Be A Player-184
Signatures-S184
Signatures Die Cuts-S184
95Bowman-76
All-Foil-76
95Collector's Choice-40
Player's Club-40
Player's Club Platinum-40
95Donruss-51
95Donruss Elite-65
Die Cut Stars-65
Die Cut Uncut-65
95Finest-98
Refractors-98
95Hoyle Eastern Playing Cards-45
95Imperial Stickers-50
95Leaf-197
95Leaf Limited-35
95Metal-61
95Panini Stickers-71
95Parkhurst International-82
Emerald Ice-82
95Pinnacle-100
Artist's Proofs-100
Rink Collection-100
95Playoff One on One-42
95Playoff One on One-263
95Pro Magnets-89
95Score-48
Black Ice Artist's Proofs-48
Black Ice-48
95Select Certified-96
Mirror Gold-96
95SP-60
95Stadium Club-94
Members Only Master Set-94
95Summit-105
Artist's Proofs-105
Ice-105
95Topps-31
OPC Inserts-31
95Topps SuperSkills-22
Platinum-22
95Ultra-62
Gold Medallion-62
95Upper Deck-310
Electric Ice-310
Electric Ice Gold-310
Special Edition-SE35
Special Edition Gold-SE35
95Zenith-110
96Black Diamond-140
Gold-140
96Collector's Choice-103
96Collector's Choice-318
96Donruss-24
Press Proofs-24
96Donruss Canadian Ice-13
Gold Press Proofs-13
Red Press Proofs-13
96Donruss Elite-15
Die Cut Stars-15
96Fleer-41
96Kraft Upper Deck-63
96Leaf-22
Press Proofs-22
96Leaf Limited-78
Gold-78
Stubble-19
96Leaf Preferred-12
Press Proofs-12
Steel-61
Steel Gold-61
96Metal Universe-61
96NHL Pro Stamps-89
96Pinnacle-32
Artist's Proofs-32
Foil-32
Premium Stock-32
Rink Collection-32
96Playoff One on One-435
96Score-3
Artist's Proofs-3
Dealer's Choice Artist's Proofs-3
Special Artist's Proofs-3
Golden Blades-3
96Select Certified-7
Artist's Proofs-7
Blue-7
Mirror Blue-7
Mirror Gold-7
Mirror Red-7
Red-7
96SkyBox Impact-47
96SP-62
96Summit-147
Artist's Proofs-147
Ice-147
Metal-147
Premium Stock-147
96Topps Picks-99
OPC Inserts-99
96Ultra-67
Gold Medallion-67
96Upper Deck-262
Generation Next-X3
Superstar Showdown-SS28A
96Zenith-84
Artist's Proofs-84
97Black Diamond-22
Double Diamond-22
Triple Diamond-22
Quadruple Diamond-22
97Collector's Choice-105
Star Quest-SQ18
97Donruss-191
Press Proofs Silver-191
Press Proofs Gold-191
97Donruss Limited-79
Exposure-79
97Donruss Preferred-61
Cut to the Chase-61
97Katch-64
Gold-64
Silver-64
97Leaf-58
Fractal Matrix-58
Fractal Matrix Die Cuts-58
97Leaf International-58
Universal Ice-58
97Pacific-269
Copper-269
Emerald Green-269
Ice Blue-269
Red-269
Silver-269
97Paramount-83
Copper-83
Dark Grey-83
Emerald Green-83
Ice Blue-83
Red-83
Silver-83
97Pinnacle-157
Press Plates Back Black-157
Press Plates Back Cyan-157
Press Plates Back Magenta-157
Press Plates Back Yellow-157
Press Plates Front Black-157
Press Plates Front Cyan-157
Press Plates Front Magenta-157
Press Plates Front Yellow-157
97Pinnacle Inside-182
97Score-253
97SP Authentic-67
Sign of the Times-RN
97Upper Deck-281
Smooth Grooves-SG44
97Upper Deck Ice-14
Parallel-14
Power Shift-14
98SLU Hockey-150
98Be A Player-208
Press Release-208
98BAP Gold-208
98BAP Autographs-208
98BAP Autographs Gold-208
98Black Diamond-39
Double Diamond-39
Triple Diamond-39
Quadruple Diamond-39
98Finest-41
No Protectors-41
No Protectors Refractors-41
Refractors-41
98Kenner Starting Lineup Cards-23
98OPC Chrome-37
Refractors-37
98Pacific Omega-105
Red-105
Opening Day Issue-105
98Revolution-63
Ice Shadow-63
Red-63
98SP Authentic-36
Power Shift-36
98Topps-37
O-Pee-Chee-37
98UD Choice-94
Prime Choice Reserve-94
Reserve-94
98Upper Deck-277
Exclusives-277
Exclusives 1 of 1-277
Gold Reserve-277
98Upper Deck MVP-87
Gold Script-87
Silver Script-87
Super Script-87
ProSign-RN
99Aurora-64
Premiere Date-64
99BAP Memorabilia-237
Gold-237
Silver-237
99BAP Millennium-107
Emerald-107
Ruby-107
Sapphire-107
Signatures-107
Signatures Gold-107
99O-Pee-Chee-45
99O-Pee-Chee Chrome-45
99O-Pee-Chee Chrome Refractors-45
99Pacific-179
Copper-179
Emerald Green-179
Gold-179
Ice Blue-179
Premiere Date-179
Red-179
99Panini Stickers-59
99Paramount-103
Copper-103
Emerald-103
Gold-103
Holographic Emerald-103
Holographic Gold-103
Holographic Silver-103
Ice Blue-103
Premiere Date-103
Red-103
Silver-103
99Stadium Club-140
First Day Issue-140
One of a Kind-140
Printing Plates Black-140
Printing Plates Cyan-140
Printing Plates Magenta-140
Printing Plates Yellow-140
99Topps/OPC-45
99Topps/OPC Chrome-45
Refractors-45
99Upper Deck-233
Exclusives-233
Exclusives 1 of 1-233
99Upper Deck Gold Reserve-233
99Upper Deck MVP-88
Gold Script-88
Silver Script-88
Super Script-88
99Upper Deck Victory-125
99Slovakian Challengers-1
00BAP Memorabilia-259
Emerald-259
Ruby-259
Sapphire-259
Promos-259
00BAP Mem Chicago Sportsfest Copper-259
00BAP Memorabilia Chicago Sportsfest Blue-259
00BAP Memorabilia Chicago Sportsfest Gold-259
00BAP Memorabilia Chicago Sportsfest Ruby-259
00BAP Memorabilia Chicago Sun-Times Ruby-259
00BAP Memorabilia Chicago Sun-Times Gold-259
00BAP Mem Chicago Sun-Times Sapphire-259
00BAP Mem Toronto Fall Expo Copper-259
00BAP Memorabilia Toronto Fall Expo Gold-259
00BAP Memorabilia Toronto Fall Expo Ruby-259
00Crown Royale-46
Ice Blue-46
Limited Series-46
Premiere Date-46
Red-46
00O-Pee-Chee-198
00O-Pee-Chee Parallel-198
00Pacific-183
Copper-183
Gold-183
Ice Blue-183
Premiere Date-183
00Panthers Team Issue-31
00Topps/OPC-198
Parallel-198
00Topps Chrome-132
OPC Refractors-132
Refractors-132
00Topps Heritage-190
00Upper Deck Vintage-156
01BAP Signature Series-151
Autographs-151
Autographs Gold-151
01BAP Ultimate Memorabilia Bloodlines-2
01O-Pee-Chee-184
01O-Pee-Chee Premier Parallel-184
01Pacific-174
Extreme LTD-174
Hobby LTD-174
Premiere Date-174
Retail LTD-174
01Pacific Adrenaline-27
Blue-27
Premiere Date-27
Red-27
Retail-27
01Pacific Arena Exclusives-174
01Topps-184
OPC Parallel-184
01Topps Heritage-178
01Upper Deck-260
Exclusives-260
02BAP First Edition-116
Jerseys-116
02BAP Memorabilia-260
Emerald-260
Ruby-260
Sapphire-260
NHL All-Star Game-260
NHL All-Star Game Blue-260
NHL All-Star Game Green-260
NHL All-Star Game Red-260
02BAP Memorabilia Toronto Fall Expo-260
02BAP Sig Series Auto Buybacks 1998-208
02BAP Sig Series Auto Buybacks 1999-107
02BAP Sig Series Auto Buybacks 2001-151
02NHL Power Play Stickers-17
02Pacific-58
Blue-58
Red-58
02Pacific Complete-88
Red-88
02Topps Total-271
02Upper Deck Vintage-37
03ITG Action-77
Jerseys-M56
03Pacific Complete-109
Red-109
03SP Game Used Double Threads-DTNN
03Upper Deck-6
Canadian Exclusives-6
HG-6
Memorable Matchups-MM-NN
03Upper Deck MVP-9
Gold Script-9
Silver Script-9
Canadian Exclusives-9
03Czech Stadion-618
05Be A Player Signatures-NI
05Be A Player Signatures Gold-NI
05Ducks Team Issue-13
05Panini Stickers-190
05Parkhurst-12
Facsimile Auto Parallel-12
True Colors-TCANA
True Colors-TCANA
05SP Authentic Sign of the Times-RN
05SP Authentic Sign of the Times Duals-DNN
05SP Game Used SIGnificance-RO
05SP Game Used SIGnificance Gold-S-RO
05SP Game Used Statscriptions-ST-RN
05Ultra-4
Gold-4
Fresh Ink-FI-NI
Fresh Ink Blue-FI-NI
Ice-4
05Upper Deck-3
Big Playmakers-B-RNI
HG Glossy-3
Jerseys-J-RN
Jerseys Series II-J2NI
Notable Numbers-N-RON
Patches-P-RON
05Upper Deck MVP-4
Gold-4
Platinum-4
05Upper Deck Toronto Fall Expo-3
06Fleer Fabricology-FRN
06O-Pee-Chee-13
Rainbow-13
06Panini Stickers-189
06Upper Deck-255
Exclusives Parallel-255
High Gloss Parallel-255
Masterpieces-255

Niedermayer, Scott

89Kamloops Blazers-18
90Upper Deck-461
French-461
907th Inn. Sketch WHL-289
907th Inn. Sketch Memorial Cup-18
91OPC Premier-35
91Parkhurst-94
French-94
91Pinnacle-349
French-349
91Pro Set-547
French-547
CC-CC4
CC French-CC4
91Score Canadian Bilingual-577
91Score Canadian English-577
91Score Rookie/Traded-27T
91Upper Deck Czech World Juniors-53
917th Inn. Sketch CHL Award Winners-11
917th Inn. Sketch CHL Award Winners-13
917th Inn. Sketch Memorial Cup-97
91Arena Draft Picks-2
91Arena Draft Picks French-2
91Arena Draft Picks Autographs-2
91Arena Draft Picks Autographs French-2
91Classic-3
91Star Pics-13
91Ultimate Draft-3
91Ultimate Draft-56
91Ultimate Draft-59
91Ultimate Draft-75
91Ultimate Draft-79
91Ultimate Draft-80
91Ultimate Draft French-3
91Classic Four-Sport *-3
Autographs-3A
92Bowman-313
92OPC Premier-113
92Panini Stickers-179
92Panini Stickers French-179
92Parkhurst-95
Emerald Ice-95
92Pinnacle-241
92Pinnacle-304
French-304
Team 2000-12
Team 2000 French-12
92Pro Set-232
92Score-401
Canadian-401
Young Superstars-33
92Stadium Club-209
92Topps-223
Gold-223G
92Ultra-116
92Upper Deck-406
92Upper Deck-562
Ameri/Can Holograms-5
Calder Candidates-CC5
World Junior Grads-WG1
93Donruss-189
Special Print-M
93Leaf-80
Gold Rookies-14
93OPC Premier-470
Gold-470
93Panini Stickers-42
93Parkhurst-111
93Parkhurst-240
Emerald Ice-111
Emerald Ice-240
93Pinnacle-111
Canadian-111
Team 2001-14
Team 2001 Canadian-14
93PowerPlay-140
93Score-217
Canadian-217
93Stadium Club-403
Members Only Master Set-403
First Day Issue-403
93Topps/OPC Premier-470
Gold-470
93Ultra-95
93Upper Deck-25
93Upper Deck-284
SP-86
94Action Packed Big Picture 24K Gold-7G
94Be A Player-R37
94Be A Player-R128
Signature Cards-88
94Canada Games NHL POGS-351
94Donruss-161
94Flair-96
94Fleer-115
94Hockey Wit-54
94Leaf-237
94Leaf Limited-40
94OPC Premier-240
94OPC Premier-539
Special Effects-240
Special Effects-539
94Parkhurst SE-SE95
Gold-SE95
Vintage-12
94Pinnacle-75
Artist's Proofs-75
Rink Collection-75
94Score-22
Gold-22
Platinum-22
94Select-101
Gold-101
94SP-67
Die Cuts-67
94Stadium Club-93
Members Only Master Set-93
First Day Issue-93
Super Team Winner Cards-93
94Topps/OPC Premier-240
94Topps/OPC Premier-539
Special Effects-240
Special Effects-539
94Ultra-121
94Upper Deck-324
Electric Ice-324
Ice Gallery-IG6
Predictor Canadian-C34
94Upper Deck Predictor Canadian Exch Gold-C34
94Upper Deck SP Inserts-SP134
94Upper Deck SP Inserts Die Cuts-SP134
94Upper Deck NHLPA/Be A Player-32
94Classic Pro Prospects Jumbos-PP6
95Upper Deck World Junior Alumni-12
95Bashan Super Stickers-71
95Bowman-64
All-Foil-64
95Canada Games NHL POGS-164
95Collector's Choice-3
Player's Club-3
Player's Club Platinum-3
95Donruss-105
95Emotion-100
95Finest-103
Refractors-103
95Hoyle Eastern Playing Cards-46
95Imperial Stickers-71
95Leaf-150
Road To The Cup-9
95Leaf Limited-43
95Metal-84
95Panini Stickers-88
95Parkhurst International-388
Emerald Ice-388
95Playoff One on One-59
95Pro Magnets-38
95Score-52
Black Ice Artist's Proofs-52
Black Ice-52
95Select Certified-70
Mirror Gold-70
95SkyBox Impact-95
95SP-84
95Stadium Club-76
Members Only Master Set-76
Generation TSC-GT8
Generation TSC Members Only Master Set-GT8
95Summit-50
Artist's Proofs-50
Ice-50
95Topps-164
OPC Inserts-164
Young Stars-YS14
95Topps SuperSkills-27
Platinum-27
95Ultra-90
95Ultra-194
Gold Medallion-90
Gold Medallion-194
Rising Stars-5
Rising Stars Gold Medallion-5
95Upper Deck-383
Electric Ice-383
Electric Ice Gold-383
Special Edition-SE137
Special Edition Gold-SE137
95Zenith-27
96Be A Player-59
Autographs-59
Autographs Silver-59
96Black Diamond-137
Gold-137
96Collector's Choice-149
96Devils Team Issue-27
96Donruss-188
Press Proofs-188
96Flair Now And Then-3
96Fleer-60
96Fleer Picks-116
96Leaf-198
Press Proofs-198
96Metal Universe-87
96NHL Pro Stamps-38
96Score-108
Artist's Proofs-108
Dealer's Choice Artist's Proofs-108
Special Artist's Proofs-108
Golden Blades-108
96SkyBox Impact-70
96SP-90
96Summit-57
Artist's Proofs-57
Ice-57
Metal-57
Premium Stock-57
96Team Out-52
96Ultra-94
Gold Medallion-94
96Upper Deck-92
Superstar Showdown-SS28B
96Upper Deck Ice-36
Parallel-36
97Collector's Choice-148
World Domination-W12

97Donruss-72
Press Proofs Silver-72
Press Proofs Gold-72
97Donruss Priority-37
Stamp of Approval-37
97Esso Olympic Hockey Heroes-14
97Esso Olympic Hockey Heroes French-14
97Katch-83
Gold-83
Silver-83
97Pacific-247
Copper-247
Emerald Green-247
Ice Blue-247
Red-247
Silver-247
97Pacific Omega-132
Copper-132
Dark Gray-132
Emerald Green-132
Gold-132
Ice Blue-132
97Panini Stickers-72
97Pinnacle-115
Press Plates Back Black-115
Press Plates Back Cyan-115
Press Plates Back Magenta-115
Press Plates Back Yellow-115
Press Plates Front Black-115
Press Plates Front Cyan-115
Press Plates Front Magenta-115
Press Plates Front Yellow-115
97Pinnacle Inside-95
97Revolution-79
Copper-79
Emerald-79
Ice Blue-79
Silver-79
97Score-229
97Score Devils-7
Platinum-7
Premier-7
97Upper Deck-301
98Aurora-112
98Be A Player-232
Press Release-232
98BAP Gold-232
98BAP Autographs-232
98BAP Autographs Gold-232
98Bowman's Best-99
Refractors-99
Atomic Refractors-99
98Devils Power Play-NJD1
98Devils Team Issue-20
98Finest-120
No Protectors-120
No Protectors Refractors-120
Refractors-120
98Katch-80
98Kraft Peanut Butter-3
98OPC Chrome-143
Refractors-143
Board Members-B8
Board Members Refractors-B8
98Pacific-266
Ice Blue-266
Red-266
98Panini Photocards-55
98Panini Stickers-65
98Paramount-136
Copper-136
Emerald Green-136
Holo-Electric-136
Ice Blue-136
Silver-136
98Topps-143
O-Pee-Chee-143
Board Members-B8
98UD Choice-119
98UD Choice Preview-119
98UD Choice Prime Choice Reserve-119
98UD Choice Reserve-119
98Upper Deck-308
Exclusives-308
Exclusives 1 of 1-308
Gold Reserve-308
98Upper Deck MVP-120
Gold Script-120
Silver Script-120
Super Script-120
99BAP Memorabilia-113
Gold-113
Silver-113
99BAP Millennium-144
Emerald-144
Ruby-144
Sapphire-144
Signatures-144
Signatures Gold-144
99Devils Team Issue-20
99O-Pee-Chee-229
99O-Pee-Chee Chrome-229
99O-Pee-Chee Chrome Refractors-229
99Pacific-242
Copper-242
Emerald Green-242
Gold-242
Ice Blue-242
Premiere Date-242
Red-242
99Pacific Dynagon Ice-118
Blue-118
Copper-118
Gold-118
Premiere Date-118
99Paramount-137
Copper-137
Emerald-137
Gold-137
Holographic Emerald-137
Holographic Gold-137
Holographic Silver-137
Ice Blue-137
Premiere Date-137
Red-137
Silver-137
99Revolution-88
Premiere Date-88
Red-88
Shadow Series-88
99SPx-88
Radiance-88
Spectrum-88
99Stadium Club-45
First Day Issue-45
One of a Kind-45
Printing Plates Black-45
Printing Plates Cyan-45
Printing Plates Magenta-45
Printing Plates Yellow-45
99Topps/OPC-229
99Topps/OPC Chrome-229
Refractors-229
99Topps Gold Label Class 1-33
Black-33
Black One of One-33
One of One-33
Red-33
Red One of One-33
99Topps Gold Label Class 2-33
99Topps Gold Label Class 2 Black-33
99Topps Gold Label Class 2 Black 1 of 1-33
99Topps Gold Label Class 2 One of One-33
99Topps Gold Label Class 2 Red-33
99Topps Gold Label Class 2 Red One of One-33
99Topps Gold Label Class 3-33
99Topps Gold Label Class 3 Black-33
99Topps Gold Label Class 3 Black 1 of 1-33
99Topps Gold Label Class 3 One of One-33
99Topps Gold Label Class 3 Red-33
99Topps Gold Label Class 3 Red One of One-33
99Topps Premier Plus-32
Parallel-32
99Upper Deck-249
Exclusives-249
Exclusives 1 of 1-249
99Upper Deck Gold Reserve-249
99Upper Deck MVP-118
Gold Script-118
Silver Script-118
Super Script-118
99Upper Deck Victory-174
99Wayne Gretzky Hockey-101
00BAP Memorabilia-82
Emerald-82
Ruby-82
Sapphire-82
Promos-82
00BAP Mem Chicago Sportsfest Copper-82
00BAP Memorabilia Chicago Sportsfest Blue-82
00BAP Memorabilia Chicago Sportsfest Gold-82
00BAP Memorabilia Chicago Sportsfest Ruby-82
00BAP Memorabilia Chicago Sun-Times Ruby-82
00BAP Memorabilia Chicago Sun-Times Gold-82
00BAP Mem Chicago Sun-Times Sapphire-82
00BAP Mem Toronto Fall Expo Copper-82
00BAP Memorabilia Toronto Fall Expo Gold-82
00BAP Memorabilia Toronto Fall Expo Ruby-82
00BAP Memorabilia Update Teammates-TM10
00BAP Memorabilia Update Teammates-TM31
00BAP Memorabilia Update Teammates Gold-TM10
00BAP Memorabilia Update Teammates Gold-TM31
00BAP Parkhurst 2000-P169
00BAP Signature Series-148
Emerald-148
Ruby-148
Sapphire-148
Department of Defense-DD12
Jersey Cards-J9
Jersey and Stick Cards-GSJ9
Jersey Cards Autographs-J9
Jersey Emblems-E9
Jersey Numbers-IN9
00Crown Royale Jersey Redemptions-5
00Devils Team Issue-16
00O-Pee-Chee-170
00O-Pee-Chee Parallel-170
00Pacific-241
Copper-241
Gold-241
Ice Blue-241
Premiere Date-241
00Paramount-147
Copper-147
Gold-147
Holo-Gold-147
Holo-Silver-147
Ice Blue-147
Premiere Date-147
00Private Stock Game Gear-64
00Private Stock Game Gear Patches-64
00SPx-141
00Stadium Club-131
00Titanium Game Gear-106
00Titanium Game Gear Patches-106
00Titanium Draft Day Edition-60
Patches-60
00Topps/OPC-170
Parallel-170
00Vanguard Dual Game-Worn Jerseys-20
00Vanguard Dual Game-Worn Patches-20
01Atomic Jerseys-37
01Atomic Patches-37
01BAP Memorabilia-119
Emerald-119
Ruby-119
Sapphire-119
Country of Origin-CO13
01BAP Signature Series-162
Autographs-162
Autographs Gold-162
Jerseys-GJ-37
Jersey Autographs-GUSN
Jersey and Stick Cards-GSJ-37
Teammates-TM-18
01BAP Ultimate Memorabilia Bloodlines-2
01BAP Ultimate Memorabilia Gloves Are Off-17
01Crown Royale Triple Threads-13
01Devils Team Issue-16
01O-Pee-Chee-197
01O-Pee-Chee Premier Parallel-197
01Pacific-237
Extreme LTD-237
Hobby LTD-237
Premiere Date-237
Retail LTD-237
01Pacific Arena Exclusives-237
01Pacific Heads-Up Quad Jerseys-3
01Parkhurst-46
Gold-46
Silver-46
01Topps-197
OPC Parallel-197
01UD Challenge for the Cup-51
01UD Stanley Cup Champs-80
01Upper Deck-104
Exclusives-104
01Upper Deck MVP-113
01Upper Deck Victory-217
Gold-217
01Upper Deck Vintage-152
01Vanguard Memorabilia-17
01Czech Stadion-238
02BAP All-Star Edition-65
Jerseys-65
Jerseys Gold-65
Jerseys Silver-65
02BAP First Edition-99
02BAP First Edition-406H
Jerseys-99
02BAP Memorabilia-136
Emerald-136
Ruby-136
Sapphire-136
All-Star Jerseys-ASJ-40
NHL All-Star Game-136
NHL All-Star Game Blue-136
NHL All-Star Game Green-136
NHL All-Star Game Red-136
02BAP Memorabilia Toronto Fall Expo-136
02BAP Sig Series Auto Buybacks 1998-232
02BAP Sig Series Auto Buybacks 1999-144
02BAP Sig Series Auto Buybacks 2001-162
02BAP Signature Series Defensive Wall-DW6
02BAP Signature Series Team Quads-TQ7
02Devils Team Issue-21
02ITG Used Teammates-T14
02ITG Used Teammates Gold-T14
02ITG Used Triple Memorabilia-TM16
02ITG Used Triple Memorabilia Gold-TM16
02McDonald's Pacific Salt Lake Gold-2
02O-Pee-Chee-167
02O-Pee-Chee Premier Blue Parallel-167
02O-Pee-Chee Premier Red Parallel-167
02O-Pee-Chee Factory Set-167
02Pacific-226
Blue-226
Red-226
02Pacific Complete-152
Red-152
02Parkhurst-60
Bronze-60
Gold-60
Silver-60
02Parkhurst Retro-162
Minis-162
02Stadium Club Champions Fabric-FC7
02Stadium Club Champions Patches-PC-7
02Topps-167
OPC Blue Parallel-167
OPC Red Parallel-167
First Round Fabric-SN
First Round Fabric Autographs-SN
Factory Set-167
Chrome First Round Fabric Patches-SN
02Topps Total-367
02UD Top Shelf-53
02Upper Deck Classic Portraits-60
02Upper Deck MVP-111
Gold-111
Classics-111
Golden Classics-111
02Upper Deck Rookie Update-155C
02Upper Deck Victory-126
Bronze-126
Gold-126
Silver-126
02Upper Deck Vintage-149
Green Backs-149
03BAP Memorabilia-83
Emerald-83
Gold-83
Ruby-83
Sapphire-83
Stanley Cup Champions-SCC-6
Stanley Cup Playoffs-SCP-11
03BAP Ultimate Memorabilia Hat Tricks-20
03BAP Ultimate Mem Redemption Cards-2
03Beehive-114
Gold-114
Silver-114
03Black Diamond Threads-DT-SN
03Black Diamond Threads Green-DT-SN
03Black Diamond Threads Red-DT-SN
03Black Diamond Threads Black-DT-SN
03Devils Team Issue-27
03ITG Action-355
Homeboys-HB4
Jerseys-M57
03ITG Used Signature Series Oh Canada-4
03ITG Used Sig Series Oh Canada Gold-4
03ITG Used Sig Series Oh Canada Emblems-4
03ITG Used Sig Ser Oh Canada Emblems Gold-4
03NHL Sticker Collection-69
03O-Pee-Chee-231
03OPC Blue-231
03OPC Gold-231
03OPC Red-231
03Pacific-203
Blue-203
Red-203
03Pacific Complete-12
Red-12
03SP Game Used Double Threads-DTNN
03Titanium-62
Hobby Jersey Number Parallels-62
Retail-62
Retail Jersey Number Parallels-62
03Topps-231
Blue-231
Gold-231
Red-231
C55 Relics-TRSN
Pristine Popular Demand Relics-PD-SN
Pristine Popular Demand Relic Refractor-PD-SN
03Upper Deck-114
Canadian Exclusives-114
HG-114
Memorable Matchups-MM-NN
03Upper Deck MVP-254
Gold Script-254
Silver Script-254
Canadian Exclusives-254
03Upper Deck Rookie Update AS Lineup-AS5
03Czech Stadion-608
03Toronto Star-53
04Pacific-161
Blue-161
Red-161
04SP Authentic-123
04UD Toronto Fall Expo Pride of Canada-9
04Upper Deck-105
Canadian Exclusives-105
Hardware Heroes-AW1
HG Glossy Gold-105
HG Glossy Silver-105
NHL's Best-NB-SN
World Cup Tribute-SNEJ
05Be A Player Dual Signatures-BS
05Be A Player Signatures-SC
05Be A Player Signatures Gold-SC
05Be A Player Triple Signatures-DEV
05Black Diamond-52
Emerald-52
Gold-52
Onyx-52
Ruby-52
05Ducks Team Issue-14
05McDonalds Upper Deck-6
05Panini Stickers-189
05Parkhurst-3
05Parkhurst-501
05Parkhurst-585
Facsimile Auto Parallel-3
Facsimile Auto Parallel-501
Facsimile Auto Parallel-585
True Colors-TCANA
True Colors-TCANA
05SP Authentic-4
Limited-4
Marks of Distinction-MDSN
Sign of the Times-SN
Sign of the Times Duals-DNN
05SP Game Used-3
Gold-3
Authentic Fabrics Triple-CNP
Authentic Fabrics Triple-GNP
Auto Draft-AD-SN
SIGnificance-SN
SIGnificance Gold-S-SN
Significant Numbers-SN-SN
Statscriptions-ST-SN
05The Cup Emblems of Endorsement-EESN
05The Cup Hardware Heroes-HHSN
05The Cup Limited Logos-LLSN
05The Cup Master Pressplate Rookie Update-226
05The Cup Scripted Numbers-SNMN
05The Cup Scripted Numbers Dual-DSNGN
05The Cup Scripted Swatches-SSSN
05The Cup Signature Patches-SPSN
05The Cup Stanley Cup Titlists-TSN
05UD PowerPlay-54
Rainbow-54
05Ultimate Coll Ultimate Achievements-UASN
05Ultimate Collection Ultimate Signatures-USSN
05Ultimate Coll Ultimate Sigs Pairings-UPGN
05Ultra-5
Gold-5
Fresh Ink-FI-SN
Fresh Ink Blue-FI-SN
Ice-5
05Upper Deck-244
Jerseys Series II-J2SN
Majestic Materials-MMSN
Notable Numbers-N-SN
05Upper Deck Hockey Showcase-HS28
05Upper Deck Showcase Promos-HS28
05Upper Deck Ice-2
Rainbow-2
05Upper Deck MVP-3
Gold-3
Platinum-3
Materials-M-SN
Materials Duals-D-RN
05Upper Deck Rookie Update-226
Inspirations Patch Rookies-226
05Upper Deck Victory-119
05Upper Deck Victory-202
Black-119
Black-202
Gold-119
Gold-202
Silver-119
Silver-202
06Be A Player-75
Autographs-75
Profiles-PP6
Profiles Autographs-PP6
Signatures-SN
Signatures 10-81
Signatures 25-81
Signatures Duals-DSN
Signatures Foursomes-FNBRB
Up Close and Personal-UC52
Up Close and Personal Autographs-UC52
06Be A Player Portraits-4
Dual Signature Portraits-DSGN
Signature Portraits-SPSN
06Black Diamond-3
Black-3
Gold-3
Ruby-3
06Devils Team Set-38
06Flair Showcase-4
06Flair Showcase-102
Parallel-4
Parallel-102
Stitches-SSSN
06Fleer-4
Tiffany-4
Fabricology-FSN
Speed Machines-SM1
06NHL POG-7
06O-Pee-Chee-7
Rainbow-7
06Panini Stickers-185
06SP Game Used Authentic Fabrics-AFSN
06SP Game Used Authentic Fabrics Parallel-AFSN
06SP Game Used Authentic Fabrics Patches-AFSN
06SP Game Used Authentic Fabrics Triple-AF3ANA
06SP Game Used Authentic Fabrics Triple Patches-AF3ANA
06SP Game Used Authentic Fabrics Fives-AF5DPT
06SP Game Used Authentic Fabrics Fives Patches-AF5DPT
06SP Game Used Authentic Fabrics Sixes-AF6NOR
06SP Game Used Authentic Fabrics Sixes Patches-AF6NOR
06The Cup NHL Shields Duals-DSHPN
06UD Artifacts Treasured Patches Black-TSSN
06UD Artifacts Treasured Patches Blue-TSSN
06UD Artifacts Treasured Patches Gold-TSSN
06UD Artifacts Treasured Patches Platinum-TSSN
06UD Artifacts Treasured Patches Red-TSSN
06UD Artifacts Treasured Swatches-TSSN
06UD Artifacts Treasured Swatches Black-TSSN
06UD Artifacts Treasured Swatches Blue-TSSN
06UD Artifacts Treasured Swatches Gold-TSSN
06UD Artifacts Treasured Swatches Platinum-TSSN
06UD Artifacts Treasured Swatches Red-TSSN
06UD Artifacts Tundra Tandems-TTNG
06UD Artifacts Tundra Tandems-TTNP
06UD Artifacts Tundra Tandems Black-TTNG
06UD Artifacts Tundra Tandems Black-TTNP
06UD Artifacts Tundra Tandems Blue-TTNG
06UD Artifacts Tundra Tandems Blue-TTNP
06UD Artifacts Tundra Tandems Gold-TTNG
06UD Artifacts Tundra Tandems Gold-TTNP
06UD Artifacts Tundra Tandems Platinum-TTNP
06UD Artifacts Tundra Tandems Red-TTNG
06UD Artifacts Tundra Tandems Red-TTNP
06UD Artifacts Tundra Tandems Dual Patches Red-TTNG
06UD Artifacts Tundra Tandems Dual Patches Red-TTNP
06UD Powerplay Specialists-SSN
06UD Powerplay Specialists Patches-PSN
06Ultra-7
Gold Medallion-7
Ice Medallion-7
06Upper Deck Arena Giveaways-ANA4
06Upper Deck-7
Exclusives Parallel-7
High Gloss Parallel-7
Game Jerseys-JSN
Game Patches-PSN
Generations Duals-G2NB
Generations Patches Dual-G2PNB
Masterpieces-7
06Upper Deck MVP-8
Gold Script-8
Super Script-8
Jerseys-OJNJ
Jerseys-OJPN
06Upper Deck Ovation-51
06Upper Deck Trilogy Honorary Scripted Patches-HSPSN
06Upper Deck Trilogy Honorary Scripted Swatches-HSSSN
06Upper Deck Trilogy Honorary Swatches-HSSN
06Upper Deck Victory-5
06Upper Deck Victory Black-5
06Upper Deck Victory Gold-5
07Upper Deck Ovation-99
07Upper Deck Victory-169
Black-169
Gold-169
Stars on Ice-SI24

Niedermeier, Bastian
99German DEL-92
99German Bundesliga 2-81

Niedomyst, Tadeusz
72Swedish Stickers-252
74Swedish Stickers-253

Niekamp, James
71Toronto Sun-100
72Los Angeles Sharks WHA-10
75Phoenix Roadrunners WHA-19
76Phoenix Roadrunners WHA-14

Nieleck, Dirk
94German First League-475

Nielikainen, Pasi
99Finnish Cardset-231
00Finnish Cardset-18
01Finnish Cardset-22
02UK Manchester Storm-6
03Finnish Cardset-137
04Finnish Cardset-197
Parallel-145
05Finnish Cardset -171
06Finnish Cardset-208
Enforcers-11

Nielsen, Benny
99Danish Hockey League-197

Nielsen, Chris
98Calgary Hitmen-7
98Calgary Hitmen Autographs-7
98Bowman CHL-130
Golden Anniversary-130
OPC International-130
Autographs Blue-A28
Autographs Gold-A28
Autographs Silver-A28
98Bowman Chrome CHL-130
Golden Anniversary-130
Golden Anniversary Refractors-130
OPC International-130
OPC International Refractors-130
Refractors-130
99Calgary Hitmen-19
99Calgary Hitmen Autographs-19
00Black Diamond-62
Gold-62
00SP Authentic-141
00SPx-135
00Titanium-114
Retail-114
00Titanium Draft Day Edition-114
00Titanium Draft Day Promos-114
00Upper Deck-197
Exclusives Tier 1-197
Exclusives Tier 2-197
00Upper Deck Ice-42
Immortals-42
Legends-42
Stars-42
00Upper Deck MVP-210
First Stars-210
Second Stars-210
Third Stars-210
00Upper Deck Victory-280
00Syracuse Crunch-8
01BAP Memorabilia-150
Emerald-150
Ruby-150
Sapphire-150
01Blue Jackets Donatos Pizza-22
01O-Pee-Chee-279
01O-Pee-Chee Premier Parallel-279
01Pacific-115
Extreme LTD-115
Hobby LTD-115
Premiere Date-115
Retail LTD-115
01Pacific Arena Exclusives-115
01Topps-279
OPC Parallel-279
01Upper Deck MVP-195
02Upper Deck Victory-64
Bronze-64
Gold-64
Silver-64
03Manitoba Moose-7
04San Antonio Rampage-9
05German DEL-349

Nielsen, Daniel
98Danish Hockey League-170
99Danish Hockey League-49

Nielsen, Devon
92Cornell Big Red-22

Nielsen, Evan
01Notre Dame Fighting Irish-9
02Notre Dame Fighting Irish-7
03Gwinnett Gladiators-16
03Gwinnett Gladiators RBI Sports-206

Nielsen, Frans
02Swedish Malmo Red Hawks-8
02Swedish SHL-234
Parallel-234
03Swedish Elite-93
Rookies-7
Silver-93
04Swedish Elitset-89
Gold-89
Signatures Series A-1
04Swedish Malmo Red Hawks-6
05Swedish SHL Elitset-284
Gold-284
06Swedish SHL Elitset-138
Playmakers-12
07Upper Deck Victory-212
Black-212
Gold-212

Nielsen, Jeff
91Minnesota Golden Gophers-19
92Minnesota Golden Gophers-17
93Minnesota Golden Gophers-23
94Binghamton Rangers-14
95Binghamton Rangers-17
96Binghamton Rangers-15
98Pacific-61
Ice Blue-61
Red-61
99Wayne Gretzky Hockey-7
99Cincinnati Mighty Ducks-4
00BAP Memorabilia-61
Emerald-61
Ruby-61
Sapphire-61
Promos-61
00BAP Mem Chicago Sportsfest Copper-61
00BAP Memorabilia Chicago Sportsfest Blue-61
00BAP Memorabilia Chicago Sportsfest Gold-61
00BAP Memorabilia Chicago Sportsfest Ruby-61
00BAP Memorabilia Chicago Sun-Times Ruby-61
00BAP Memorabilia Chicago Sun-Times Gold-61
00BAP Mem Chicago Sun-Times Sapphire-61
00BAP Mem Toronto Fall Expo Copper-61
00BAP Memorabilia Toronto Fall Expo Gold-61
00BAP Memorabilia Toronto Fall Expo Ruby-61
00Paramount-121
Copper-121
Gold-121
Holo-Gold-121
Holo-Silver-121
Ice Blue-121
Premiere Date-121
00Topps Chrome-232
OPC Refractors-232
Refractors-232
00Upper Deck Vintage-178
01BAP Signature Series-91
Autographs-91
Autographs Gold-91
02BAP Sig Series Auto Buybacks 2001-91

Nielsen, Jens
89Swedish Semic Elitserien Stickers-141
90Swedish Semic Elitserien Stickers-214
91Swedish Semic Elitserien Stickers-142
92Swedish Semic Elitserien Stickers-163
93Swedish Semic Elitserien-258
94Swedish Leaf-287
95Swedish Leaf-286
95Swedish Upper Deck-184
97Swedish Collector's Choice-111
98Swedish UD Choice-129
99Swedish Upper Deck-115
00Swedish Upper Deck-112
SHL Signatures-JN
Top Draws-T7
02Swedish SHL-195
Parallel-195
Signatures Series II-18
03Swedish Elite-60
Signatures II-21
Silver-60

Nielsen, Kirk
92Harvard Crimson-27
96Providence Bruins-14
97Providence Bruins-12
98Cincinnati Cyclones-16
98Cincinnati Cyclones 2-2

Nielsen, Klaus
98Danish Hockey League-141
99Danish Hockey League-170

Nielsen, Rasmus
99Danish Hockey League-150

Nielsen, Robert
92Norwegian Elite Series-115

Nielsen, Soren
98Danish Hockey League-197
99Danish Hockey League-79

Nielsen, Tye
93Quebec Pee-Wee Tournament-615

Nielsen, Ulrick
98Danish Hockey League-184

Nielson, Corey
95Signature Rookies-48
Signatures-48

Nielson, Len
86Regina Pats-22
87Moncton Hawks-17
88ProCards AHL-172

Nielsson, Jimmy
98Danish Hockey League-156
99Danish Hockey League-200

Niemegeers, Kyle
91Air Canada SJHL-C10
92Saskatchewan JHL-11

Niemela, Jouni
70Finnish Jaakiekko-352

Niemela, Riku
99Finnish Cardset-49

Niemenranta, Olavi
78Finnish SM-Liiga-124
80Finnish Mallasjuoma-78

Niemi, Antti
05Finnish Cardset -291
06Finnish Cardset-119
Between the Pipes-17
Signature Sensations-23
Superior Snatchers-6
Superior Snatchers Gold-6
Superior Snatchers Silver-6

Niemi, Antti-Jussi
95Upper Deck-549
Electric Ice-549
Electric Ice Gold-549
95Finnish SISU-250
98Finnish Kerailysarja-100
Leijonat-14
99Finnish Cardset-58
99Finnish Cardset-186
00Finnish Cardset-113
01BAP Memorabilia-251
Emerald-251
Ruby-251
Sapphire-251
01O-Pee-Chee-301
01O-Pee-Chee Premier Parallel-301
01Topps-301
OPC Parallel-301
01Finnish Cardset-166
01Cincinnati Mighty Ducks-15
02Finnish Cardset-229
03Swedish Elite-172
Silver-172
04Swedish Elitset-25
Gold-25
Signatures Series A-17
05Swedish SHL Elitset-24
Gold-24
06Swedish SHL Elitset-28

Niemi, Esko
96Finnish SISU Redline-188
05Finnish Tappara Legendat-9

Niemi, Heikki
72Finnish Jaakiekko-272

Niemi, Jaakko
73Finnish Jaakiekko-253
78Finnish SM-Liiga-224

Niemi, Kari
72Finnish Jaakiekko-289

Niemi, Lars-Goran
84Swedish Semic Elitserien-185
86Swedish Panini Stickers-179
87Swedish Panini Stickers-180

Niemi, Marko
70Finnish Jaakiekko-317

Niemi, Mika
04Finnish Cardset-191
04Finnish Cardset Signatures-38
05Finnish Cardset -168

Niemi, Mikko
93Finnish SISU-116
99Danish Hockey League-30

Niemi, Tauno
65Finnish Hellas-121

Niemi, Toni
05Finnish Cardset -213
06Finnish Cardset-40
06Finnish Ilves Team Set-19

Nieminen, Jani
04Finnish Cardset-209

Nieminen, Lasse
92Finnish Jyvas-Hyva Stickers-78
93Finnish Jyvas-Hyva Stickers-138
93Finnish SISU-147
94Finnish SISU-57
95Finnish SISU-65
96Swiss HNL-288

Nieminen, Mika
89Swedish Semic World Champ Stickers-50
91Finnish Semic World Champ Stickers-17
91Finnish Jyvas-Hyva Stickers-44
91Swedish Semic World Champ Stickers-17
92Finnish Semic-19
92Swedish Semic Elitserien Stickers-197
93Swedish Semic Elitserien-168
93Swedish Semic World Champ Stickers-69
94Finnish SISU-369
94Finnish SISU-385
94Finnish Jaa Kiekko-36
94Swedish Leaf-22
Playmakers-3
95Finnish Jaa Kiekko Lehti Ad Cards-7
95Finnish SISU Gold Cards-18
95Finnish Karjala World Champ Labels-12
95Finnish Semic World Championships-40
95Swedish Globe World Championships-135
95Swedish World Championships Stickers-185
95Swiss HNL-305
96Swedish Semic Wien-22
98Finnish Kerailysarja-48
Leijonat-33
99Finnish Cardset-29
99Finnish Cardset-166
00Finnish Cardset-20
01Finnish Cardset-23
01Finnish Cardset-243
02Finnish Cardset-230

Nieminen, Niko
05Finnish Cardset -9
06Finnish Cardset-325

Nieminen, Pekka
72Finnish Jaakiekko-180

Nieminen, Pertti
65Finnish Hellas-6

Nieminen, Ville
95Finnish SISU-113
98Hershey Bears-25
00O-Pee-Chee-287
00O-Pee-Chee Parallel-287
00Pacific-125
Copper-125
Gold-125
Ice Blue-125
Premiere Date-125
00SP Authentic-99
00Topps/OPC-287
Parallel-287
00Topps Chrome-182
OPC Refractors-182
Refractors-182
00Hershey Bears-10
01BAP Memorabilia-56
01BAP Memorabilia-497
Emerald-56
Emerald-497
Ruby-56
Ruby-497
Sapphire-56
Sapphire-497
01BAP Signature Series-130
Autographs-130
Autographs Gold-130
01Pacific-103
Extreme LTD-103
Hobby LTD-103
Premiere Date-103
Retail LTD-103
01Pacific Arena Exclusives-103
01Parkhurst-248
01SPx Hidden Treasures-DTBN
01SPx Hidden Treasures-TTTHN
01UD Mask Collection Double Patches-DPVN
01UD Mask Collection Jerseys-J-VN
01UD Mask Collection Jersey and Patch-JPVN
01UD Premier Collection Dual Jerseys-DSN
01UD Premier Collection Dual Jerseys Black-DSN
01UD Stanley Cup Champs-39
01Upper Deck-43
Exclusives-43
01Upper Deck Victory-93
Gold-93
01Finnish Cardset-NNO
02BAP Sig Series Auto Buybacks 2001-130
02Pacific Complete-352
Red-352
02SP Authentic-129
02SP Game Used Future Fabrics-FFVN
02SP Game Used Future Fabrics Gold-FFVN
02SP Game Used Future Fabrics Rainbow-FFVN
02Topps Total-263
02UD Top Shelf Sweet Sweaters-SWVN
02Upper Deck-384
Exclusives-384
02Upper Deck Beckett UD Promos-384
02Upper Deck Bright Futures-VN
02Upper Deck Classic Portraits Hockey Royalty-LLN
02Upper Deck Classic Portraits Hockey Royalty-SLN
02Upper Deck Classic Portraits Hockey Royalty Limited-LLN
02Upper Deck Classic Portraits Hockey Royalty Limited-SLN
02Upper Deck MVP Souvenirs-S-VN
02Upper Deck Victory National Pride-NP23
02Upper Deck Vintage-200
Jerseys-HSVN
Jerseys Gold-HS-VN
02Finnish Cardset-80
02Finnish Cardset Dynamic Duos-6
03BAP Memorabilia-226
03Blackhawks Postcards-17
03ITG Action-418
03O-Pee-Chee-38
03OPC Blue-38
03OPC Gold-38
03OPC Red-38
03Pacific Complete-279
Red-279
03Parkhurst Original Six Chicago-15
03Topps-38
Blue-38
Gold-38
Red-38
03Topps Traded-TT69
Blue-TT69
Gold-TT69
Red-TT69
03Upper Deck MVP-338
Gold Script-338
Silver Script-338
Canadian Exclusives-338
Souvenirs-S24
04Finnish Cardset-162
04Finnish Cardset Signatures-33
04Finnish Cardset Stars of the Game-6
04Swedish Pure Skills-137
Jerseys-VN
Parallel-137
Professional Power-VN
05Parkhurst True Colors-TCNYR
05Parkhurst True Colors-TCNYR
05UD Powerplay Specialists-TSVN
05UD Powerplay Specialists Patches-SPVN
05Upper Deck Big Playmakers-B-VN
05Upper Deck Jerseys-J-VN
05Upper Deck MVP-263
Gold-263
Platinum-263
05Upper Deck Victory-32
Black-32
Gold-32
Silver-32
05Finnish Tappara Legendat-8
05Finnish Cardset -147
Finnish Cardset Magicmakers-15
06Black Diamond Jerseys-JVN
06Black Diamond Jerseys Black-JVN
06Black Diamond Jerseys Gold-JVN
06Black Diamond Jerseys Ruby-JVN
06O-Pee-Chee-417
Rainbow-417

Nienhuis, Kraig
86Moncton Golden Flames-11
94Los Angeles Blades RHI-7
95Austrian National Team-19
96German DEL-42
98Port Huron Border Cats-19

Nieuwendyk, Joe
87Flames Red Rooster-19
87Flames Red Rooster-20
88Flames Postcards-9
88Frito-Lay Stickers-36
88O-Pee-Chee-16
88O-Pee-Chee Minis-29
88O-Pee-Chee Stickers-90
88O-Pee-Chee Stickers-125
88O-Pee-Chee Stickers-134
88O-Pee-Chee Stickers-205
88O-Pee-Chee Stickers-216
88O-Pee-Chee Stickers-270
88Panini Stickers-12
88Panini Stickers-404
88Topps-16
89Kraft-5
89O-Pee-Chee-138
89O-Pee-Chee Stickers-101
89Panini Stickers-29
89Sports Illustrated for Kids I-15
89Topps-138
89Swedish Semic World Champ Stickers-74
90Bowman-91
Tiffany-91
90Flames IGA/McGavin's-18
90Kraft-41
90Kraft-74
90O-Pee-Chee-87
90OPC Premier-84
90Panini Stickers-174
90Pro Set-42A
90Pro Set-42B
90Pro Set-344
90Score-30A
90Score-30B
Canadian-30A
Canadian-30B
90Score Hottest/Rising Stars-45
90Topps-87
Tiffany-87
Team Scoring Leaders-8
Team Scoring Leaders Tiffany-8
90Upper Deck-26
French-26
91Pro Set Platinum-18
91Bowman-252
91Flames Panini Team Stickers-14
91Flames IGA-13
91O-Pee-Chee-223
91OPC Premier-48

91Panini Stickers-53
91Parkhurst-23
French-23
91Pinnacle-54
French-54
91Pro Set-29
91Pro Set-569
French-29
French-569
91Score American-170
91Score Canadian Bilingual-170
91Score Canadian English-170
91Stadium Club-60
91Topps-223
91Upper Deck-263
French-263
91Finnish Semic World Champ Stickers-69
91Swedish Semic World Champ Stickers-69
92Bowman-59
92Flames IGA-17
92O-Pee-Chee-354
92Panini Stickers-40
92Panini Stickers French-40
92Parkhurst-21
Emerald Ice-21
92Pinnacle-31
French-31
92Pro Set-26
92Score-193
Canadian-193
92Stadium Club-37
92Topps-105
Gold-105G
92Ultra-25
92Upper Deck-128
93Donruss-48
93Kraft-45
93Kraft-60
93Leaf-126
93OPC Premier-205
Gold-205
93Panini Stickers-182
93Parkhurst-31
Emerald Ice-31
93Pinnacle-198
Canadian-198
Captains-4
Captains Canadian-4
93PowerPlay-39
93Score-199
Canadian-199
Dynamic Duos Canadian-4
93Stadium Club-96
Members Only Master Set-96
OPC-96
First Day Issue-96
First Day Issue OPC-96
93Topps/OPC Premier-205
Gold-205
93Ultra-130
93Upper Deck-396
SP-23
94Action Packed Big Picture 24K Gold-8G
94Be A Player Signature Cards-56
94Canada Games NHL POGS-56
94Donruss-56
94EA Sports-21
94Fleer-32
94Hockey Wit-82
94Leaf-228
94Leaf Limited-82
94McDonald's Upper Deck-McD21
94OPC Premier-537
Special Effects-537
94Parkhurst-33
Gold-33
Crash the Game Green-4
Crash the Game Blue-4
Crash the Game Gold-4
Crash the Game Red-4
94Pinnacle-90
Artist's Proofs-90
Rink Collection-90
94Score-159
Gold-159
Platinum-159
94Select-131
Gold-131
94SP-20
Die Cuts-20
94Stadium Club Members Only-18
94Stadium Club-166
Members Only Master Set-166
First Day Issue-166
Super Team Winner Cards-166
94Topps/OPC Premier-537
Special Effects-537
94Upper Deck-276
Electric Ice-276
SP Inserts-SP13
SP Inserts Die Cuts-SP13
95Bashan Super Stickers-18
95Canada Games NHL POGS-49
95Collector's Choice-133
Player's Club-133
Player's Club Platinum-133
95Donruss-40
Igniters-9
95Donruss Elite-50
Die Cut Stars-50
Die Cut Uncut-50
95Emotion-24
95Finest-168
Refractors-168
95Hoyle Western Playing Cards-48
95Imperial Stickers-18
95Leaf-305
95Leaf Limited-56
95McDonald's Pinnacle-MCD-12
95Metal-21
95NHL Aces Playing Cards-10C
95Panini Stickers-233
95Parkhurst International-33
95Parkhurst International-329
Emerald Ice-33
Emerald Ice-329
95Playoff One on One-18
95Pro Magnets-48
95Score-229
Black Ice Artist's Proofs-229
Black Ice-229
95Select Certified-32
Mirror Gold-32
Double Strike-10
Double Strike Gold-10
95SkyBox Impact-24
95SP-38
95Stadium Club-18
Members Only Master Set-18
95Stars Score Sheet-229
95Summit-162
Artist's Proofs-162
Ice-162
Mad Hatters-13
95Topps-233
OPC Inserts-233
95Upper Deck-285
Electric Ice-285
Electric Ice Gold-285
Special Edition-SE12
Special Edition Gold-SE12
95Zenith-112
Gifted Grinders-14
96Be A Player-53
Autographs-53
Autographs Silver-53
96Collector's Choice-68
96Collector's Choice-315
96Donruss-195
Press Proofs-195
96Donruss Canadian Ice-63
Gold Press Proofs-63
Red Press Proofs-63
96Donruss Elite-62
Die Cut Stars-62
96Fleer Picks Fabulous 50-33
96Kraft Upper Deck-13
96Leaf-34
Press Proofs-34
96Leaf Limited-75
Gold-75
96Leaf Preferred-27
Press Proofs-27
Steel-45
Steel Gold-45
96Maggers-68
96Metal Universe-42
96NHL Pro Stamps-48
96Pinnacle-183
Artist's Proofs-183
Foil-183
Premium Stock-183
Rink Collection-183
96Playoff One on One-334
96Score-152
Artist's Proofs-152
Dealer's Choice Artist's Proofs-152
Special Artist's Proofs-152
Golden Blades-152
96Select Certified-88
Artist's Proofs-88
Blue-88
Mirror Blue-88
Mirror Gold-88
Mirror Red-88
Red-88
96SkyBox Impact-31
96SPx-12
Gold-12
96Stars Postcards-22
96Stars Score Sheet-152
96Summit-65
Artist's Proofs-65
Ice-65
Metal-65
Premium Stock-65
96Topps Picks-61
OPC Inserts-61
96Ultra-46
Gold Medallion-46
96Upper Deck-245
Power Performers-P20
96Zenith-63
Artist's Proofs-63
97Beehive-20
Golden Portraits-20
97Black Diamond-16
Double Diamond-16
Triple Diamond-16
Quadruple Diamond-16
97Collector's Choice-68
97Crown Royale-42
Emerald Green-42
Ice Blue-42
Silver-42
97Donruss-186
Press Proofs Silver-186
Press Proofs Gold-186
97Donruss Canadian Ice-51
Dominion Series-51
Provincial Series-51
97Donruss Elite-61
Aspirations-61
Status-61
97Donruss Limited-43
Exposure-43
97Donruss Preferred-115
Cut to the Chase-115
97Donruss Priority-140
Stamp of Approval-140
97Flames Collector's Photos-9
97Gatorade Stickers-4
97Katch-47
Gold-47
Silver-47
97Kraft Team Canada-9
97Leaf-108
Fractal Matrix-108
Fractal Matrix Die Cuts-108
97Leaf International-108
Universal Ice-108
97McDonald's Team Canada Coins-9
97Pacific-266
Copper-266
Emerald Green-266
Ice Blue-266
Red-266
Silver-266
97Pacific Dynagon-38
Copper-38
Dark Grey-38
Emerald Green-38
Ice Blue-38
Red-38
Silver-38
Tandems-43
97Pacific Invincible-43
Copper-43
Emerald Green-43
Ice Blue-43
Red-43
Silver-43
97Pacific Omega-74
Copper-74
Dark Gray-74
Emerald Green-74
Gold-74
Ice Blue-74
Team Leaders-7
97Panini Stickers-144
97Paramount-61
Copper-61
Dark Grey-61
Emerald Green-61
Ice Blue-61
Red-61
Silver-61
97Pinnacle-110
Press Plates Back Black-110
Press Plates Back Cyan-110
Press Plates Back Magenta-110
Press Plates Back Yellow-110
Press Plates Front Black-110
Press Plates Front Cyan-110
Press Plates Front Magenta-110
Press Plates Front Yellow-110
97Pinnacle Certified-76
Red-76
Mirror Blue-76
Mirror Gold-76
Mirror Red-76
97Pinnacle Inside-115
97Pinnacle Tot Cert Platinum Blue-76
97Pinnacle Tot Certi Platinum Gold-76
97Pinnacle Totally Certified Platinum Red-76
97Pinnacle Tot Cert Mirror Platinum Gold-76
97Revolution-44
Copper-44
Emerald-44
Ice Blue-44
Silver-44
97Score-135
Artist's Proofs-135
Golden Blades-135
97SP Authentic-49
97Studio-55
Press Proofs Silver-55
Press Proofs Gold-55
97Upper Deck-50
97Zenith-63
Z-Gold-63
Z-Silver-63
97Zenith 5 x 7-15
Gold Impulse-15
Silver Impulse-15
98Aurora-59
Man Advantage-8
98Be A Player-193
Press Release-193
98BAP Gold-193
98BAP Autographs-193
98BAP Autographs Gold-193
98Bowman's Best-62
Refractors-62
Atomic Refractors-62
98Crown Royale-42
Limited Series-42
98Finest-112
No Protectors-112
No Protectors Refractors-112
Refractors-112
Red Lighters-R14
Red Lighters Refractors-R14
98Katch-47
98OPC Chrome-161
Refractors-161
98Pacific-25
Ice Blue-25
Red-25
98Pacific Dynagon Ice-60
Blue-60
Red-60
98Pacific Omega-74
Red-74
Opening Day Issue-74
98Panini Photocards-56
98Panini Stickers-121
98Paramount-69
Copper-69
Emerald Green-69
Holo-Electric-69
Ice Blue-69
Silver-69
98Post-3
98Revolution-45
Ice Shadow-45
Red-45
98SPx Finite-26
Radiance-26
Spectrum-26
98Topps-161
O-Pee-Chee-161
98Topps Gold Label Class 1-44
Black-44
Black One of One-44
One of One-44
Red-44
Red One of One-44
98Topps Gold Label Class 2-44
98Topps Gold Label Class 2 Black-44
98Topps Gold Label Class 2 Black 1 of 1-44
98Topps Gold Label Class 2 One of One-44
98Topps Gold Label Class 2 Red-44
98Topps Gold Label Class 2 Red One of One-44
98Topps Gold Label Class 3-44
98Topps Gold Label Class 3 Black-44
98Topps Gold Label Class 3 Black 1 of 1-44
98Topps Gold Label Class 3 One of One-44
98Topps Gold Label Class 3 Red-44
98Topps Gold Label Class 3 Red One of One-44
98UD Choice-62
Prime Choice Reserve-62
Reserve-62
98Upper Deck-78
Exclusives-78
Exclusives 1 of 1-78
Fantastic Finishers-FF30
Fantastic Finishers Quantum 1-FF30
Fantastic Finishers Quantum 2-FF30
Fantastic Finishers Quantum 3-FF30
Game Jerseys-GJ24
Gold Reserve-78
98Upper Deck MVP-63
Gold Script-63
Silver Script-63
Super Script-63
98Slovakian Eurotel-16
99Aurora-48
Premiere Date-48
99BAP Memorabilia-197
Gold-197
Silver-197
AS Heritage Ruby-H22
AS Heritage Sapphire-H22
AS Heritage Emerald-H22
99BAP Millennium-78
Emerald-78
Ruby-78
Sapphire-78
Signatures-78
Signatures Gold-78
99Crown Royale-47
Limited Series-47
Premiere Date-47
99Kraft Face Off Rivals-2
99O-Pee-Chee-215
99O-Pee-Chee-278A
99O-Pee-Chee-278B
99O-Pee-Chee-278C
99O-Pee-Chee-278D
99O-Pee-Chee-278E
99O-Pee-Chee Chrome-215
99O-Pee-Chee Chrome-278A
99O-Pee-Chee Chrome-278B
99O-Pee-Chee Chrome-278C
99O-Pee-Chee Chrome-278D
99O-Pee-Chee Chrome-278E
99O-Pee-Chee Chrome Refractors-215
99O-Pee-Chee Chrome Refractors-278A
99O-Pee-Chee Chrome Refractors-278B
99O-Pee-Chee Chrome Refractors-278C
99O-Pee-Chee Chrome Refractors-278D
99O-Pee-Chee Chrome Refractors-278E
99Pacific-127
Copper-127
Emerald Green-127
Gold-127
Ice Blue-127
Premiere Date-127
Red-127
99Pacific Dynagon Ice-69
Blue-69
Copper-69
Gold-69
Premiere Date-69
99Pacific Omega-76
Copper-76
Gold-76
Ice Blue-76
Premiere Date-76
99Pacific Prism-47
Holographic Blue-47
Holographic Gold-47
Holographic Mirror-47
Holographic Purple-47
Premiere Date-47
99Panini Stickers-8
99Panini Stickers-222
99Paramount-76
Copper-76
Emerald-76
Gold-76
Holographic Emerald-76
Holographic Gold-76
Holographic Silver-76
Ice Blue-76
Premiere Date-76
Red-76
Silver-76
Ice Advantage-8
Ice Advantage Proofs-8
Personal Best-15
99Revolution-49
Premiere Date-49
Red-49
Shadow Series-49
Showstoppers-15
Top of the Line-16
Copper-49
Gold-49
CSC Silver-49
99SPx-53
Radiance-53
Spectrum-53
99Stadium Club-143
First Day Issue-143
One of a Kind-143
Printing Plates Black-143
Printing Plates Cyan-143
Printing Plates Magenta-143
Printing Plates Yellow-143
Chrome-39
Chrome Refractors-39
99Stars Postcards-20
99Topps/OPC-215
99Topps/OPC-278A
99Topps/OPC-278B
99Topps/OPC-278C
99Topps/OPC-278D
99Topps/OPC-278E
99Topps Stanley Cup Heroes-SC20
99Topps Stanley Cup Heroes Refractors-SC20
99Topps/OPC Chrome-215
99Topps/OPC Chrome-278A
99Topps/OPC Chrome-278B
99Topps/OPC Chrome-278C
99Topps/OPC Chrome-278D
99Topps/OPC Chrome-278E
Refractors-215
Refractors-278A
Refractors-278B
Refractors-278C
Refractors-278D
Refractors-278E
99Topps Gold Label Class 1-60
Black-60
Black One of One-60
One of One-60
Red-60
Red One of One-60
99Topps Gold Label Class 2-60
99Topps Gold Label Class 2 Black-60
99Topps Gold Label Class 2 Black 1 of 1-60
99Topps Gold Label Class 2 One of One-60
99Topps Gold Label Class 2 Red-60
99Topps Gold Label Class 2 Red One of One-60
99Topps Gold Label Class 3-60
99Topps Gold Label Class 3 Black-60
99Topps Gold Label Class 3 Black 1 of 1-60
99Topps Gold Label Class 3 One of One-60
99Topps Gold Label Class 3 Red-60
99Topps Gold Label Class 3 Red One of One-60
99Topps Premier Plus-28
Parallel-28
Calling All Calders-CAC9
99Upper Deck-48
Exclusives-48
Exclusives 1 of 1-48
99Upper Deck Gold Reserve-48
99Upper Deck MVP-67
Gold Script-67
Silver Script-67
Super Script-67
99Upper Deck Victory-91
99Wayne Gretzky Hockey-58
00Aurora-47
Premiere Date-47
00BAP Memorabilia-149
Emerald-149
Ruby-149
Sapphire-149
Promos-149
00BAP Mem Chicago Sportsfest Copper-149
00BAP Memorabilia Chicago Sportsfest Blue-149
00BAP Memorabilia Chicago Sportsfest Gold-149
00BAP Memorabilia Chicago Sportsfest Ruby-149
00BAP Memorabilia Chicago Sun-Times Ruby-149
00BAP Memorabilia Chicago Sun-Times Gold-149
00BAP Mem Chicago Sun-Times Sapphire-149
00BAP Mem Toronto Fall Expo Copper-149
00BAP Memorabilia Toronto Fall Expo Gold-149
00BAP Memorabilia Toronto Fall Expo Ruby-149
00BAP Parkhurst 2000-P218
00BAP Signature Series-205
Emerald-205
Ruby-205
Sapphire-205
Autographs-45
Autographs Gold-45
00Crown Royale-37
Ice Blue-37
Limited Series-37
Premiere Date-37
Red-37
Game-Worn Jerseys-12
Game-Worn Jersey Patches-12
Premium-Sized Game-Worn Jerseys-12
00O-Pee-Chee-183
00O-Pee-Chee Parallel-183
00Pacific-139
Copper-139
Gold-139
Ice Blue-139
Premiere Date-139
00Panini Stickers-145
00Paramount-81
Copper-81
Gold-81
Holo-Gold-81
Holo-Silver-81
Ice Blue-81
Premiere Date-81
00Private Stock-34
Gold-34
Premiere Date-34
Retail-34
Silver-34
00Revolution-49
Blue-49
Premiere Date-49
Red-49
00SP Game Used Tools of the Game-JN
00SP Game Used Tools of the Game Excl-JN
00SP Game Used Tools of the Game Combos-C-MN
00Stadium Club-145
00Stars Postcards-20
00Titanium-30
Blue-30
Gold-30
Premiere Date-30
Red-30
Retail-30
Game Gear-90
Game Gear Patches-90
00Titanium Draft Day Edition-34
Patches-34
00Topps/OPC-183
Parallel-183
00Topps Chrome-122
OPC Refractors-122
Refractors-122
00Topps Gold Label Class 1-32
Gold-32
00Topps Gold Label Class 2-32
00Topps Gold Label Class 2 Gold-32
00Topps Gold Label Class 3-32
00Topps Gold Label Class 3 Gold-32
00Topps Heritage-147
00Topps Stars-67
Blue-67
00UD Heroes-39
00Upper Deck-56
Exclusives Tier 1-56
Exclusives Tier 2-56
Game Jerseys-JN
Game Jersey Autographs Exclusives-EJN
Game Jersey Autographs Exclusives-ESJN
Game Jersey Doubles-DJN
Ice Game Jerseys-JCJN
Legends Epic Signatures-JN
00Upper Deck MVP-63
First Stars-63
Second Stars-63
Third Stars-63
00Upper Deck Victory-76
00Upper Deck Vintage-121
00Vanguard-36
Holographic Gold-36
Holographic Purple-36
Pacific Proofs-36
01Atomic-33
Blue-33
Gold-33
Premiere Date-33
Red-33
Team Nucleus-5
01BAP Memorabilia-287
01BAP Memorabilia-468
Emerald-287
Emerald-468
Ruby-287
Ruby-468
Sapphire-287
Sapphire-468
01BAP Ultimate Memorabilia Active Eight-6
01BAP Ultimate Memorabilia Calder Trophy-14
01Bowman YoungStars-102
Gold-102
Ice Cubed-102
01Crown Royale-49
Blue-49
Premiere Date-49
Red-49
Retail-49
01McDonald's Pacific Jersey Patch Silver-8
01McDonald's Pacific Jersey Patches Gold-8
01O-Pee-Chee-99
01O-Pee-Chee Heritage Parallel-99
01O-Pee-Chee Heritage Parallel Limited-99
01O-Pee-Chee Premier Parallel-99
01Pacific-134
Extreme LTD-134
Hobby LTD-134
Premiere Date-134
Retail LTD-134
01Pacific Adrenaline-60
Blue-60
Premiere Date-60
Red-60
Retail-60
Jerseys-13
01Pacific Arena Exclusives-134
01Pacific Heads-Up-32
Blue-32
Premiere Date-32
Red-32
Silver-32
Quad Jerseys-10
01Parkhurst-122
01Parkhurst-386
Jerseys-PJ58
Milestones-M23
Sticks-PS69
01Private Stock-30
Gold-30
Premiere Date-30
Retail-30
Silver-30
Game Gear-38
Game Gear Patches-38
01Private Stock Pacific Nights-30
01SP Game Used Authentic Fabric-AFJN
01SP Game Used Authentic Fabric-TFMNB
01SP Game Used Authentic Fabric Gold-AFJN
01SPx Hockey Treasures-HTJN
01Stadium Club-96
Award Winners-96
Master Photos-96
01Stars Postcards-20
01Titanium-46
Hobby Parallel-46
Premiere Date-46
Retail-46
Retail Parallel-46
01Topps-99
Heritage Parallel-99
Heritage Parallel Limited-99
OPC Parallel-99
01Topps Chrome-99
Refractors-99
Black Border Refractors-99
01Topps Heritage-100
Refractors-100
01UD Honor Roll Jerseys-J-JN
01UD Honor Roll Jerseys Gold-J-JN
01UD Mask Collection-56
Gold-56
Double Patches-DPJN
Jerseys-J-JN
Jersey and Patch-JPJN
01UD Premier Collection Dual Jerseys-DTN
01UD Premier Collection Dual Jersey Black-DTN
01UD Stanley Cup Champs-48
Pieces of Glory-G-JN
Sticks-S-JN
01UD Top Shelf-99
01Upper Deck-286
Exclusives-286
Game Jerseys-CMN
Game Jerseys-MNB
Game Jerseys Series II-FJJN
Game Jerseys Series II-DJMN
Game Jerseys Series II-TJNMB
01Upper Deck MVP-62
01Upper Deck Victory-112
Gold-112
01Upper Deck Vintage-82
01Upper Deck Vintage-87
02Atomic-62
Blue-62
Gold-62
Red-62
Hobby Parallel-62
02BAP First Edition-243
02BAP Memorabilia-58
02BAP Memorabilia-239
02BAP Memorabilia-257
Emerald-58
Emerald-239
Emerald-257
Ruby-58
Ruby-239
Ruby-257
Sapphire-58
Sapphire-239
Sapphire-257
NHL All-Star Game-58
NHL All-Star Game-239
NHL All-Star Game-257
NHL All-Star Game Blue-58
NHL All-Star Game Blue-239
NHL All-Star Game Blue-257
NHL All-Star Game Green-58
NHL All-Star Game Green-239
NHL All-Star Game Green-257
NHL All-Star Game Red-58
NHL All-Star Game Red-239
NHL All-Star Game Red-257
02BAP Memorabilia Toronto Fall Expo-58
02BAP Memorabilia Toronto Fall Expo-239
02BAP Memorabilia Toronto Fall Expo-257
02BAP Signature Series-131
Autographs-131
Autograph Buybacks 1998-193
Autograph Buybacks 1999-78
Autograph Buybacks 2000-45
Autographs Gold-131
02BAP Ultimate Memorabilia Conn Smythe-27
02BAP Ultimate Mem 500 Goal Scorers-1
02BAP Ultimate Mem 500 Goal Jersey/Stick-1
02BAP Ultimate Mem 500 Goal Emblems-1
02Crown Royale-59
Blue-59
Red-59
Retail-59
02Devils Team Issue-19
02McDonald's Pacific Salt Lake Gold-7
02O-Pee-Chee-255
02O-Pee-Chee Premier Blue Parallel-255
02O-Pee-Chee Premier Red Parallel-255
02O-Pee-Chee Factory Set-255
02Pacific-227
Blue-227
Red-227
Jerseys-31
Jerseys Holo-Silver-31
02Pacific Calder-25
Silver-25
02Pacific Complete-118
Red-118
02Pacific Exclusive-105
02Pacific Heads-Up-72
Blue-72
Purple-72
Red-72
02Parkhurst-89
Bronze-89
Gold-89
Silver-89
02Parkhurst Retro-73
Minis-73
02Private Stock Reserve-62
Blue-62
Red-62
Retail-62
02SP Game Used Authentic Fabrics-CFNB
02SP Game Used Authentic Fabrics Gold-CFNB
02SP Game Used Authentic Fabrics Rainbow-CFNB
02SP Game Used Piece of History-PHJN
02SP Game Used Piece of History Gold-PHJN
02SP Game Used Piece of History Rainbow-PHJN
02Topps-255
OPC Blue Parallel-255
OPC Red Parallel-255
Factory Set-255
02Topps Chrome-138
Black Border Refractors-138
Refractors-138
02Topps Total-357
02UD Artistic Impressions-54
Gold-54
02UD Artistic Impressions Beckett Promos-54
02UD Artistic Impressions Retrospectives-R54
02UD Artistic Impress Retrospect Gold-R54
02UD Artistic Impress Retrospect Silver-R54
02UD Piece of History-52
Awards Collection-AC17
02UD Top Shelf-51
Clutch Performers-CPJN
Dual Player Jerseys-RNL
Hardware Heroes-HYNLR
Shooting Stars-SHJN
02Upper Deck-106
Exclusives-106
Good Old Days-GOJN
02Upper Deck Classic Portraits-59
02Upper Deck MVP-112
Gold-112
Classics-112
Golden Classics-112
Skate Around Jerseys-SDBN
Skate Around Jerseys-SDNL
Skate Around Jerseys-STLNT
Souvenirs-S-JN
02Upper Deck Victory-129
Bronze-129
Gold-129
Silver-129
02Upper Deck Vintage-153
02Upper Deck Vintage-297
Green Backs-153
03BAP Memorabilia-250
Practice Jerseys-PMP15
Stanley Cup Champions-SCC-4
03BAP Ultimate Memorabilia Autographs-25
Gold-25
03Beehive-179
Gold-179
Silver-179
03ITG Action-386
Highlight Reel-HR7
Jerseys-M58
03ITG Used Sig Series Intl Experience-9
03ITG Used Sig Ser Intl Experience Autos-9
03ITG Used Sig Ser Intl Exper Emblem Gold-9
03ITG Used Sig Ser Intl Experience Emblem-9
03ITG Used Sig Ser Intl Experience Gold-9
03ITG Used Signature Series Oh Canada-15
03ITG Used Sig Series Oh Canada Gold-15
03ITG Used Sig Ser Oh Canada Emblems-15
03ITG Used Sig Ser Oh Canada Emblems Gold-15
03NHL Sticker Collection-65
03O-Pee-Chee-49
03OPC Blue-49
03OPC Gold-49
03OPC Red-49
03Pacific-204
Blue-204
Red-204
Milestones-6
03Pacific Complete-152
Red-152
03Pacific Exhibit-89
Blue Backs-89
Yellow Backs-89
03Pacific Prism-64
Blue-64
Gold-64
Red-64
03Parkhurst Original Six Toronto-15
03Parkhurst Rookie Records-RRE-4
03Parkhurst Rookie Records Gold-RRE-4
03Parkhurst Rookie ROYalty-VR-27
03Parkhurst Rookie ROYalty Gold-VR-27
03SP Authentic Sign of the Times-JN
03Titanium-93
Hobby Jersey Number Parallels-93
Retail-93
Retail Jersey Number Parallels-93
03Topps-49
Blue-49
Gold-49
Red-49
03Topps C55-74
Minis-74
Minis American Back-74
Minis American Back Red-74
Minis Bazooka Back-74
Minis Brooklyn Back-74
Minis Hat Trick Back-74
Minis O Canada Back-74
Minis O Canada Back Red-74
Minis Stanley Cup Back-74
03Topps Traded-TT29
Blue-TT29
Gold-TT29
Red-TT29
03UD Honor Roll Signature Class-SC19
03Upper Deck-113
03Upper Deck-424
500 Goal Club-500-JN
500 Goal Club-500-JNA
BuyBacks-126
BuyBacks-127
BuyBacks-128
BuyBacks-129
BuyBacks-130
BuyBacks-131
BuyBacks-132
BuyBacks-133
BuyBacks-134
BuyBacks-135
BuyBacks-136
BuyBacks-137
BuyBacks-138
Canadian Exclusives-113
Canadian Exclusives-424
HG-113
HG-424
UD Exclusives-424
03Upper Deck MVP-251
Gold Script-251
Silver Script-251
Canadian Exclusives-251
03Upper Deck Victory-110
Bronze-110
Gold-110
Silver-110
04Pacific-248
Blue-248
Red-248
04SP Authentic-147
04Upper Deck-167
Canadian Exclusives-167
HG Glossy Gold-167
HG Glossy Silver-167
05Be A Player-86
First Period-86
Second Period-86
Third Period-86
Overtime-86
05Black Diamond-124
Emerald-124
Gold-124
Onyx-124
Ruby-124
Jerseys-J-JN
Jerseys Ruby-J-JN
Jersey Triples-TJ-JN
Jersey Quads-QJ-JN
05Panini Stickers-58
05Parkhurst-204
Facsimile Auto Parallel-204
True Colors-TCFLA
True Colors-TCFLA
05SP Game Used-43
Gold-43
05SPx-37
Spectrum-37
05UD PowerPlay-83
Rainbow-83
Specialists-TSJN
Specialists Patches-SPJN
05Ultra-87
Gold-87
Ice-87
05Upper Deck-328
Big Playmakers-B-JN
Patches-P-JN
05Upper Deck Hockey Showcase-HS30
05Upper Deck Showcase Promos-HS30
05Upper Deck Ice-41
Rainbow-41
05Upper Deck MVP-172
Gold-172
Platinum-172
05Upper Deck Victory-183
05Upper Deck Victory-220
Black-183
Black-220
Gold-183
Gold-220
Silver-183
Silver-220
06Black Diamond Jerseys-JJN
06Black Diamond Jerseys Black-JJN
06Black Diamond Jerseys Gold-JJN
06Black Diamond Jerseys Ruby-JJN
06Fleer-87
Tiffany-87
06O-Pee-Chee-218
06O-Pee-Chee-653
Rainbow-218
Rainbow-653
06Panini Stickers-55
06SP Game Used Authentic Fabrics-AFJN
06SP Game Used Authentic Fabrics Parallel-AFJN
06SP Game Used Authentic Fabrics Patches-AFJN
06SP Game Used Authentic Fabrics Sixes-AF6500
06SP Game Used Authentic Fabrics Sixes Patches-AF6500
06The Cup NHL Shields Duals-DSHBN
06The Cup NHL Shields Duals-DSHNR
06UD Artifacts Treasured Patches Black-TSJN
06UD Artifacts Treasured Patches Blue-TSJN
06UD Artifacts Treasured Patches Gold-TSJN
06UD Artifacts Treasured Patches Platinum-TSJN
06UD Artifacts Treasured Patches Red-TSJN
06UD Artifacts Treasured Swatches-TSJN
06UD Artifacts Treasured Swatches Black-TSJN
06UD Artifacts Treasured Swatches Blue-TSJN
06UD Artifacts Treasured Swatches Gold-TSJN
06UD Artifacts Treasured Swatches Platinum-TSJN
06UD Artifacts Treasured Swatches Red-TSJN
06UD Artifacts Tundra Tandems-TTNR
06UD Artifacts Tundra Tandems Black-TTNR
06UD Artifacts Tundra Tandems Blue-TTNR
06UD Artifacts Tundra Tandems Gold-TTNR
06UD Artifacts Tundra Tandems Platinum-TTNR
06UD Artifacts Tundra Tandems Red-TTNR
06UD Artifacts Tundra Tandems Dual Patches Red-TTNR
06Ultra-89
Gold Medallion-89
Ice Medallion-89
06Upper Deck-82
Exclusives Parallel-82
High Gloss Parallel-82
Game Jerseys-JJN
Game Patches-PJN
Masterpieces-82
06Upper Deck MVP-128
Gold Script-128
Super Script-128
06Upper Deck Ovation-22
06Upper Deck Victory-88
06Upper Deck Victory Black-88
06Upper Deck Victory Gold-88

Niggli, Stefan

99Swiss Panini Stickers-217
00Swiss Panini Stickers-261
01Swiss EV Zug Postcards-17
01Swiss HNL-184
02Swiss EV Zug Postcards-17

02Swiss HNL-234
Nighbor, Frank
23V145-1-2
24Anonymous NHL-16
24C144 Champ's Cigarettes-44
24V145-2-6
60Topps-35
Stamps-41
83Hall of Fame-72
83Hall of Fame Postcards-E12
85Hall of Fame-72
03BAP Ultimate Mem Vintage Blade of Steel-6
04ITG Ultimate Mem Blades of Steel-20
05ITG Ultimate Memorabilia Level 1-38
05ITG Ultimate Memorabilia Level 2-38
05ITG Ultimate Memorabilia Level 3-38
05ITG Ultimate Memorabilia Level 4-38
05ITG Ultimate Memorabilia Level 5-38
05ITG Ultimate Mem Blades of Steel-10
05ITG Ultimate Mem Blades of Steel Gold-10
06ITG Ultimate Memorabilia Blades of Steel-11
06ITG Ultimate Memorabilia Blades of Steel Gold-11
06ITG Ultimate Memorabilia Paper Cuts Autos-7
Nighingale, Jared
06Idaho Steelheads-18
Nigmatullin, Khalim
01Russian Hockey League-164
Nigro, Anthony
06Guelph Storm-8
Nigro, Frank
82Maple Leafs Postcards-25
83Maple Leafs Postcards-17
83O-Pee-Chee-337
83O-Pee-Chee Stickers-149
83Topps Stickers-149
92Finnish Semic-256
Niinikoski, Mikko
04Finnish Cardset-278
Niinimaa, Janne
93Parkhurst-520
Emerald Ice-520
93Finnish SISU-390
93Classic-44
93Classic Four-Sport *-207
Gold-207
94Finest-128
Super Team Winners-128
Refractors-128
94Parkhurst SE-SE217
Gold-SE217
94SP-162
Die Cuts-162
94Finnish SISU-58
94Classic-105
Gold-105
Tri-Cards-T49
95Finnish SISU-251
95Finnish SISU-NNO
Gold Cards-8
95Finnish SISU Limited-13
95Finnish Karjala World Champ Labels-13
95Finnish Semic World Championships-227
96Black Diamond-154
Gold-154
96Collector's Choice-361
96Donruss Canadian Ice-128
Gold Press Proofs-128
Red Press Proofs-128
96Donruss Elite Aspirations-16
96Flair-120
Blue Ice-120
96Flyers Postcards-16
96Leaf Preferred-127
Press Proofs-127
96Metal Universe-189
96Select Certified-104
Artist's Proofs-104
Blue-104
Mirror Blue-104
Mirror Gold-104
Mirror Red-104
Red-104
96SP-186
96Ultra-127
Gold Medallion-127
Rookies-15
96Upper Deck-310
96Upper Deck Ice-49
Parallel-49
96Zenith-124
Artist's Proofs-124
96Swedish Semic Wien-6
97Be A Player-144
Autographs-144
Autographs Die-Cuts-144
Autographs Prismatic Die-Cuts-144
97Collector's Choice-183
Star Quest-SQ26
97Donruss-99
Press Proofs Silver-99
Press Proofs Gold-99
Canadian Ice Stanley Cup Scrapbook-21
97Donruss Elite-92
Aspirations-92
Status-92
97Donruss Limited-16
97Donruss Limited-136
97Donruss Limited-168
Exposure-16
Exposure-136
Exposure-168
Fabric of the Game-69
97Donruss Preferred-26
Cut to the Chase-26
97Donruss Priority-84
Stamp of Approval-84
97Leaf-75
Fractal Matrix-75
Fractal Matrix Die Cuts-75
97Leaf International-75
Universal Ice-75
97Pacific-173
Copper-173
Emerald Green-173
Ice Blue-173
Red-173
Silver-173
97Pacific Dynagon-92
Copper-92
Dark Grey-92
Emerald Green-92
Ice Blue-92
Red-92
Silver-92
Tandems-16
97Pacific Invincible-103
Copper-103
Emerald Green-103
Ice Blue-103
Red-103
Silver-103
Feature Performers-26
97Panini Stickers-94
97Panini Stickers-245
97Paramount-135
Copper-135
Dark Grey-135
Emerald Green-135
Ice Blue-135
Red-135
Silver-135
97Pinnacle Inside-179
97Score-165
97Score Flyers-9
Platinum-9
Premier-9
97SPx-37
Bronze-37
Gold-37
Silver-37
Steel-37
Grand Finale-37
97Studio-100
Press Proofs Silver-100
Press Proofs Gold-100
97Upper Deck-124
Game Dated Moments-124
Smooth Grooves-SG41
Three Star Selects-8A
97Upper Deck Ice-21
Parallel-21
Power Shift-21
98Aurora-75
98Crown Royale-52
Limited Series-52
98Finest-108
No Protectors-108
No Protectors Refractors-108
Refractors-108
98Pacific-24
Ice Blue-24
Red-24
98Pacific Dynagon Ice-74
Blue-74
Red-74
98Pacific Omega-94
Red-94
Opening Day Issue-94
98Panini Stickers-198
98Paramount-91
Copper-91
Emerald Green-91
Holo-Electric-91
Ice Blue-91
Silver-91
98SPx Finite-35
Radiance-35
Spectrum-35
98UD Choice-86
Prime Choice Reserve-86
Reserve-86
98Upper Deck-91
Exclusives-91
Exclusives 1 of 1-91
Gold Reserve-91
98Upper Deck MVP-78
Gold Script-78
Silver Script-78
Super Script-78
98Finnish Kerailysarja Dream Team-4
99BAP Memorabilia-76
Gold-76
Silver-76
99O-Pee-Chee-112
99O-Pee-Chee Chrome-112
99O-Pee-Chee Chrome Refractors-112
99Pacific-162
Copper-162
Emerald Green-162
Gold-162
Ice Blue-162
Premiere Date-162
Red-162
99Panini Stickers-245
99Topps/OPC-112
99Topps/OPC Chrome-112
Refractors-112
99Upper Deck-228
Exclusives-228
Exclusives 1 of 1-228
99Upper Deck Gold Reserve-228
99Upper Deck Victory-118
99Finnish Cardset Aces High-S-3
00BAP Memorabilia-282
Emerald-282
Ruby-282
Sapphire-282
Promos-282
00BAP Mem Chicago Sportsfest Copper-282
00BAP Memorabilia Chicago Sportsfest Blue-282
00BAP Memorabilia Chicago Sportsfest Gold-282
00BAP Memorabilia Chicago Sportsfest Ruby-282
00BAP Memorabilia Chicago Sun-Times Ruby-282
00BAP Memorabilia Chicago Sun-Times Gold-282
00BAP Mem Chicago Sun-Times Sapphire-282
00BAP Mem Toronto Fall Expo Copper-282
00BAP Memorabilia Toronto Fall Expo Gold-282
00BAP Memorabilia Toronto Fall Expo Ruby-282
00BAP Parkhurst 2000-P31
00BAP Signature Series-28
Emerald-28
Ruby-28
Sapphire-28
Autographs-32
Autographs Gold-32
00O-Pee-Chee-245
00O-Pee-Chee Parallel-245
00Pacific-437
Copper-437
Gold-437
Ice Blue-437
Premiere Date-437
00Panini Stickers-160
00Topps/OPC-245
Parallel-245
00Upper Deck Vintage-145
00Finnish Cardset-114
01BAP Memorabilia-76
Emerald-76
Ruby-76
Sapphire-76
01BAP Signature Series-132
Autographs-132
Autographs Gold-132
01O-Pee-Chee-139
01O-Pee-Chee Premier Parallel-139
01Pacific-162
Extreme LTD-162
Hobby LTD-162
Premiere Date-162
Retail LTD-162
01Pacific Arena Exclusives-162
01Parkhurst-123
01Topps-139
OPC Parallel-139
01Upper Deck-299
Exclusives-299
01Upper Deck Victory-140
Gold-140
01Upper Deck Vintage-101
01Finnish Cardset Salt Lake City-5
02BAP Sig Series Auto Buybacks 2000-32
02BAP Sig Series Auto Buybacks 2001-132
02NHL Power Play Stickers-33
02Oilers Postcards-19
02O-Pee-Chee-125
02O-Pee-Chee Premier Blue Parallel-125
02O-Pee-Chee Premier Red Parallel-125
02O-Pee-Chee Factory Set-125
02Pacific-147
Blue-147
Red-147
02Pacific Complete-94
Red-94
02Parkhurst Retro-154
Minis-154
02Topps-125
OPC Blue Parallel-125
OPC Red Parallel-125
Factory Set-125
02Topps Total-142
02Upper Deck-74
Exclusives-74
02Upper Deck Rookie Update-63
02Finnish Cardset-231
02Finnish Cardset Dynamic Duos-4
02Finnish Cardset Solid Gold-2
03ITG Action-353
03NHL Sticker Collection-229
03O-Pee-Chee-94
03OPC Blue-94
03OPC Gold-94
03OPC Red-94
03Pacific Complete-357
Red-357
03Topps-94
Blue-94
Gold-94
Red-94
03Upper Deck-368
Canadian Exclusives-368
HG-368
UD Exclusives-368
03Upper Deck MVP-271
Gold Script-271
Silver Script-271
Canadian Exclusives-271
03Upper Deck Victory-118
Bronze-118
Gold-118
Silver-118
04Finnish Cardset-96
Stars of the Game-7
04Swedish Malmo Red Hawks-15
04Swedish Pure Skills-127
Parallel-127
Professional Power-JN
05Upper Deck-123
HG Glossy-123
05Upper Deck MVP-247
Gold-247
Platinum-247
05Upper Deck Toronto Fall Expo-123
05Finnish Cardset -92
06Canadiens Postcards-15
06O-Pee-Chee-266
Rainbow-266
Niinimaki, Jari
72Finnish Jaakiekko-312
Niinimaki, Jesse
02Finnish Cardset-232
Bound for Glory-5
Signatures-5
03Finnish Cardset-49
04Finnish Cardset-52
05Finnish Cardset -235
06Swedish SHL Elitset-219
Niiniviita, Timo
72Finnish Jaakiekko-290
Niinivirta, Timo
78Finnish SM-Liiga-104
Niitoaho, Hannu
70Finnish Jaakiekko-145
74Finnish Typotor-40
78Finnish SM-Liiga-205
80Finnish Mallasjuoma-195
Niittoaho, Hannu
66Finnish Jaakiekkosarja-58
71Finnish Suomi Stickers-195
72Finnish Jaakiekko-233
73Finnish Jaakiekko-267
Niittymaki, Antero
99Finnish Cardset-326
Puck Stoppers-1
00Finnish Cardset-336
00Finnish Cardset Masquerade-5
00Finnish Cardset Next Generation-9
01Finnish Cardset-134
01Finnish Cardset-NNO
02Finnish Cardset-81
02Philadelphia Phantoms-1
03BAP Ultimate Mem Rookie Jersey Emblems-37
03BAP Ultimate Mem Rookie Jsy Emblem Gold-37
03BAP Ultimate Mem Rookie Jersey Numbers-37
03BAP Ultimate Mem Rookie Jsy Number Gold-37
03ITG Action-648
03ITG Used Signature Series-178
Gold-178
03ITG VIP Rookie Debut-78
03Parkhurst Rookie-142
Rookie Emblems-RE-21
Rookie Emblems Gold-RE-21
Rookie Jerseys-RJ-21
Rookie Jerseys Gold-RJ-21
Rookie Numbers-RN-21
Rookie Numbers Gold-RN-21
03Topps Traded-TT133
Blue-TT133
Gold-TT133
Red-TT133
03Upper Deck Rookie Update-139
03Pacific AHL Prospects-64
Gold-64
03Philadelphia Phantoms-2
04Pacific-294
Blue-294
Red-294
04AHL All-Stars-29
04AHL All-Stars-47
04AHL Top Prospects-40
04Philadelphia Phantoms-12
04ITG Heroes and Prospects-48
Autographs-U-AN
Net Prospects-6
Net Prospects Gold-6
04ITG Heroes/Prospects Toronto Expo '05-48
04ITG Heroes/Prospects Expo Heroes/Pros-48
05ITG Heroes/Prosp Toronto Expo Parallel -57
05Flyers Team Issue-13
05Hot Prospects-74
En Fuego-74
Red Hot-74
White Hot-74
05ITG Ultimate Memorabilia Level 1-4
05ITG Ultimate Memorabilia Level 2-4
05ITG Ultimate Memorabilia Level 3-4
05ITG Ultimate Memorabilia Level 4-4
05ITG Ultimate Memorabilia Level 5-4
05ITG Ultimate Memorabilia Double Autos-5
05ITG Ultimate Mem Double Autos Gold-5
05ITG Ultimate Mem Double Mem Autos-9
05ITG Ultimate Mem Double Mem Autos Gold-9
05ITG Ultimate Mem Future Star Autos-22
05ITG Ultimate Mem Future Star Autos Gold-22
05ITG Ultimate Mem Future Stars Jerseys-9
05ITG Ultimate Mem Fut Stars Jerseys Gold-9
05ITG Ultimate Mem Fut Stars Mem Autos-9
05ITG Ultimate Mem Fut Star Mem Auto Gold-9
05ITG Ultimate Memorabilia Jersey Autos-40
05ITG Ultimate Mem Jersey Autos Gold-40
05ITG Ultimate Memorabilia R.O.Y. Autos-19
05ITG Ultimate Mem R.O.Y. Autos Gold-19
05ITG Ultimate Memorabilia Stick Autos-33
05ITG Ultimate Mem Stick Autos Gold-33
05Parkhurst-350
Facsimile Auto Parallel-350
Signatures-AN
05UD Rookie Class-46
05Upper Deck Rookie Update-72
05Philadelphia Phantoms All-Decade Team-12
05ITG Heroes and Prospects-57
Aspiring-ASP10
Autographs-A-AN
Autographs Series II-LN
Complete Jerseys-CJ-16
Complete Jerseys Gold-CJ-16
Future Teammates-FT2
He Shoots-He Scores Prizes-34
Jerseys-GUJ-22
Jerseys Gold-GUJ-22
Emblems-GUE-22
Emblems Gold-GUE-22
Numbers-GUN-22
Numbers Gold-GUN-22
Measuring Up-MU11
Measuring Up Gold-MU11
Nameplates-N-9
Nameplates Gold-N-09
Net Prospects-NP-3
Net Prospects Dual-NPD3
Net Prospects Dual Gold-NPD3
Net Prospects Gold-NP-03
06Be A Player-74
Autographs-74
Signatures-AN
Signatures Duals-DNE
06Be A Player Portraits-76
06Between The Pipes-57
Autographs-AAN
Double Jerseys-DJ16
Double Jerseys Gold-DJ16
Emblems-GUE11
Emblems Gold-GUE11
Emblems Autographs-GUE11
Jerseys-GUJ11
Jerseys Gold-GUJ11
Jerseys Autographs-GUJ11
Numbers-GUN11
Numbers Gold-GUN11
Numbers Autographs-GUN11
Playing For Your Country-PC17
Playing For Your Country Gold-PC17
Prospect Trios-PT04
Prospect Trios Gold-PT04
Shooting Gallery-SG07
Shooting Gallery Gold-SG07
Stick and Jersey-SJ22
Stick and Jersey Gold-SJ22
Stick and Jersey Autographs-SJ22
The Mask-M04
The Mask Gold-M04
The Mask Silver-M04
The Mask Game-Used-MGU14
The Mask Game-Used Gold-MGU14
06Black Diamond-62
Black-62
Gold-62
Ruby-62
06Flair Showcase Hot Gloves-HG22
06Flair Showcase Inks-IAN
06Fleer-142
Tiffany-142
Netminders-N19
06Flyers Postcards-16
06Hot Prospects-73
Red Hot-73
White Hot-73
06ITG International Ice-16
Gold-16
Autographs-AAN
Cornerstones-IC04
Cornerstones Gold-IC04
Goaltending Glory-GG12
Goaltending Glory Gold-GG12
Passing The Torch-PTT6
Passing The Torch Gold-PTT6
Triple Memorabilia-TM08
Triple Memorabilia Gold-TM08
06ITG Ultimate Memorabilia-8
Artist Proof-8
Stick Rack-23
Stick Rack Gold-23
06O-Pee-Chee-357
Rainbow-357
Autographs-A-AN
06SP Game Used Inked Sweaters-ISAN
06SP Game Used Inked Sweaters Patches-ISAN
06SP Game Used Letter Marks-LMAN
06SP Game Used SIGnificance-SAN
06UD Mini Jersey Collection-75
06Ultra-141
Gold Medallion-141
Ice Medallion-141
06Upper Deck Arena Giveaways-PHI5
06Upper Deck-393
Exclusives Parallel-393
High Gloss Parallel-393
Masterpieces-393
06Upper Deck MVP-216
Gold Script-216
Super Script-216
Jerseys-OJBN
06Upper Deck Ovation-187
06Upper Deck Sweet Shot Sweet Stitches-SSAN
06Upper Deck Sweet Shot Sweet Stitches Duals-SSAN
06Upper Deck Sweet Shot Sweet Stitches Triples-SSAN
06Upper Deck Trilogy Combo Clearcut Autographs-C2KN
06Upper Deck Trilogy Ice Scripts-ISAN
06Upper Deck Trilogy Scripts-TSAN
06Upper Deck Victory-144
06Upper Deck Victory Black-144
06Upper Deck Victory Gold-144
06Russian Sport Collection Olympic Stars-25
06ITG Heroes and Prospects-22
Autographs-AAN
Quad Emblems-QE09
Quad Emblems Gold-QE09
Sticks and Jerseys-SJ11
Sticks and Jerseys Gold-SJ11
Niittymaki, Mika
94Finnish SISU-307
96Finnish SISU Redline-133
Nijland, Marcel
05Dutch Vadeko Flyers -13
Nikander, Harry
78Finnish SM-Liiga-227
80Finnish Mallasjuoma-217
91Finnish Jyvas-Hyva Stickers-72
92Finnish Jyvas-Hyva Stickers-200
Nikander, Jarkko
92Finnish Jyvas-Hyva Stickers-27
93Finnish Jyvas-Hyva Stickers-47
93Finnish SISU-247
94Finnish SISU-52
95Finnish SISU-317
96Finnish SISU Redline-129
98Finnish Kerailysarja-182
99Finnish Cardset-254
00Finnish Cardset-34
01Finnish Cardset-45
Nikitenko, Andrei
02Russian Hockey League-173
03Russian Hockey League-208
Nikitin, Igor
98Russian Hockey League-44
00Russian Hockey League-232
03Russian Avangard Omsk-12
Nikitin, Valerij
70Finnish Jaakiekko-10
70Russian National Team Postcards-4
70Swedish Hockey-321
70Swedish Masterserien-132
70Swedish Masterserien-134
74Swedish Stickers-42
Nikkila, Seppo
65Finnish Hellas-112
66Finnish Jaakiekkosarja-183
Nikkila, Tommi
03Finnish Cardset-72
04Finnish Cardset-79
Parallel-60
05Finnish Cardset -63
06Finnish Cardset-318
Between the Pipes-21
Nikko, Jani
92Finnish Jyvas-Hyva Stickers-37
93Parkhurst-524
Emerald Ice-524
93Finnish Jyvas-Hyva Stickers-75
93Finnish SISU-111
94Finnish SISU-203
95Finnish SISU-220
95Finnish SISU Limited-84
95Finnish Semic World Championships-226
96Finnish SISU Redline-18
98Finnish Kerailysarja-35
99Swedish Upper Deck-90
00Finnish Cardset-272
01Finnish Cardset-37
Nikolaev, Andrei
98Russian Hockey League-114
Nikolaev, Igor
98Russian Hockey League-62
99Russian Hockey League-89
00Russian Hockey League-15
03Russian Hockey League-100
Nikolayev, Sergei
00Russian Goalkeepers-7
00Russian Hockey League-114
02Russian Ultimate Line-4
Nikolic, Alex
92Salt Lake Golden Eagles-17
95Fort Wayne Komets-13
Nikolishin, Andrei
91Upper Deck Czech World Juniors-7
92Upper Deck-340
92Classic-48
Gold-48
92Classic Four-Sport *-189
Gold-189
94Finest-10
Super Team Winners-10
Refractors-10
94Fleer-87
94OPC Premier-421
Special Effects-421
94Parkhurst SE-SE72
Gold-SE72
94Pinnacle-487
Artist's Proofs-487
Rink Collection-487
94Select-184
Gold-184
94Topps/OPC Premier-421
Special Effects-421
94Ultra-301
94Upper Deck-241
Electric Ice-241
Predictor Canadian-C9
94Upper Deck Predictor Canadian Exch Gold-C9
94Upper Deck Predictor Cdn Exch Silver-C9
94Upper Deck SP Inserts-SP122
94Upper Deck SP Inserts Die Cuts-SP122
94Classic-70
Gold-70
ROY Sweepstakes-R14
Tri-Cards-T28
Pro Prospects Ice Ambassadors-IA18
95Collector's Choice-21
Player's Club-21
Player's Club Platinum-21
95Donruss-124
95Emotion-76
95Leaf-11
95Panini Stickers-29
95Parkhurst International-94
Emerald Ice-94
95Pinnacle-98
Artist's Proofs-98
Rink Collection-98
95Score-169
Black Ice Artist's Proofs-169
Black Ice-169
95SkyBox Impact-74
95Stadium Club-149
Members Only Master Set-149
95Topps-361
OPC Inserts-361
New To The Game-22NG
95Ultra-68
Gold Medallion-68
95Upper Deck-55
Electric Ice-55
Electric Ice Gold-55
Special Edition-SE38
Special Edition Gold-SE38
95Whalers Bob's Stores-19
95Finnish Semic World Championships-123
96Be A Player-137
Autographs-137
Autographs Silver-137
96Collector's Choice-114
96Fleer Picks-172
96Pinnacle-179
Artist's Proofs-179
Foil-179
Premium Stock-179
Rink Collection-179
97Pacific Dynagon Best Kept Secrets-102
97Panini Stickers-117
98Be A Player-300
Press Release-300
98BAP Gold-300
98BAP Autographs-300
98BAP Autographs Gold-300
98Panini Stickers-110
99BAP Memorabilia-106
Gold-106
Silver-106
99Pacific-445
Copper-445
Emerald Green-445
Gold-445
Ice Blue-445
Premiere Date-445
Red-445
99Panini Stickers-173
99Paramount-247
Copper-247
Emerald-247
Gold-247
Holographic Emerald-247
Holographic Gold-247
Holographic Silver-247
Ice Blue-247
Premiere Date-247
Red-247
Silver-247
99Upper Deck MVP SC Edition-192
Gold Script-192
Silver Script-192
Super Script-192
00BAP Memorabilia-391
Emerald-391
Ruby-391
Sapphire-391
Promos-391
00BAP Mem Chicago Sportsfest Copper-391
00BAP Memorabilia Chicago Sportsfest Blue-391
00BAP Memorabilia Chicago Sportsfest Gold-391
00BAP Memorabilia Chicago Sportsfest Ruby-391
00BAP Memorabilia Chicago Sun-Times Ruby-391
00BAP Memorabilia Chicago Sun-Times Gold-391
00BAP Mem Chicago Sun-Times Sapphire-391
00BAP Mem Toronto Fall Expo Copper-391
00BAP Memorabilia Toronto Fall Expo Gold-391
00BAP Memorabilia Toronto Fall Expo Ruby-391
00Upper Deck-177
Exclusives Tier 1-177
Exclusives Tier 2-177
00Upper Deck Vintage-362
01Upper Deck-177
Exclusives-177
01Upper Deck Victory-360
Gold-360
01Upper Deck Vintage-258
02BAP Sig Series Auto Buybacks 1998-300
02Pacific-397
Blue-397
Red-397
02Topps Total-363
02Upper Deck Vintage-259
03Avalanche Team Issue-13
03Pacific Complete-414
Red-414
04Russian Back to Russia-13
05Russian Hockey League RHL-52
Nikolov, Angel
94Czech APS Extraliga-206
95Czech APS Extraliga-153
95Classic Autographs-15
96Czech APS Extraliga-172
97Czech APS Extraliga-79
97Czech DS Extraliga-42
97Czech DS Stickers-43
98Czech DS-43
98Czech DS Stickers-90
98Czech OFS-3
99Czech DS-60
99Czech OFS-154
99Czech OFS-480
00Czech DS Extraliga-39
00Czech OFS-137
01Czech DS-7
01Finnish Cardset-272
02Finnish Cardset-82
03Russian Hockey League-187
06Czech OFS-142
Nikulin, Igor
95Swedish World Championships Stickers-35
98Cincinnati Mighty Ducks-21
00Russian Hockey League-236
Nikulin, Ilya
00Russian Dynamo Moscow-9
00Russian Hockey League-312
01Russian Dynamo Moscow-9
01Russian Dynamo Moscow Mentos-14
01Russian Young Lions-10
02Russian Future Stars-20
02Russian Young Lions-12
03Russian Hockey League-30
04Russian Moscow Dynamo-21
05Russian Hockey League RHL-46
Nikulin, Valeri
98Russian Hockey League-19
99Russian Hockey League-11
99Russian Metallurg Magnetogorsk-31
Nilan, Chris
80Canadiens Postcards-18
80Pepsi-Cola Caps-54
81Canadiens Postcards-20
82Canadiens Postcards-18
82Canadiens Steinberg-14
83Canadiens Postcards-20
83O-Pee-Chee-194
83Vachon-51
84Canadiens Postcards-20
84O-Pee-Chee-268
85Canadiens Placemats-3
85Canadiens Placemats-7
85Canadiens Postcards-23
85Canadiens Postcards-24
85Canadiens Provigo-13
85O-Pee-Chee Stickers-127
86Canadiens Postcards-16
86Kraft Drawings-51
86O-Pee-Chee-199
87Canadiens Kodak-5
87Canadiens Postcards-21
87Canadiens Vachon Stickers-19
87Canadiens Vachon Stickers-20
87O-Pee-Chee Stickers-15
87Panini Stickers-68
87Pro-Sport All-Stars-17
88O-Pee-Chee-31
88O-Pee-Chee Stickers-245
88Topps-31
89Rangers Marine Midland Bank-30
89Swedish Semic World Champ Stickers-175
90Bruins Sports Action-18
90O-Pee-Chee-454
90OPC Premier-85
90Pro Set-205A
90Pro Set-205B
90Pro Set-409
90Score-311A
Canadian-311A
90Score Rookie/Traded-22T
90Upper Deck-368
90Upper Deck-442
French-368
French-442
91Bowman-351
91O-Pee-Chee-311
91Panini Stickers-183
91Pinnacle-289
French-289
91Score American-197
91Score Canadian Bilingual-197
91Score Canadian English-197
91Stadium Club-244
91Topps-311
91Upper Deck-237
French-237
92Score-76
Canadian-76
02Fleer Throwbacks-66
Gold-66
Platinum-66
04UD Legendary Signatures-91
AKA Autographs-AKA-CN
Autographs-CN
05ITG Tough Customers-CNI
Autographs-CN
Famous Battles Autographs-HN
Stickwork-CNI
Nilimaa, Mattias
98Swedish UD Choice-73
99Swedish Upper Deck-132
Nill, Jim
81Swedish Semic Hockey VM Stickers-84
82Canucks Team Issue-17
83Canucks Team Issue-15
83NHL Key Tags-121
83O-Pee-Chee-357
83Vachon-114
84O-Pee-Chee-11
85Jets Police-16
86Jets Postcards-17
88Red Wings Little Caesars-15
89O-Pee-Chee-224
90ProCards AHL/IHL-475
Nilsater, Olle
67Swedish Hockey-209
Nilsen, Erik Skoglund
92Norwegian Elite Series-172
Nilsen, Johnny
92Norwegian Elite Series-147
92Norwegian Elite Series-209
Nilsen, N.
74Finnish Typotor-79
Nilsen, Odd
92Norwegian Elite Series-145
Nilsen, Sjur Robert
92Norwegian Elite Series-99
95Swedish World Championships Stickers-251
99Norwegian National Team-18
Nilsen, Tor
92Norwegian Elite Series-96
Nilson, Marcus
95Collector's Choice-345
Player's Club-345
Player's Club Platinum-345
95SP-185
95Upper Deck-560
Electric Ice-560
Electric Ice Gold-560
96Coll Edge Future Legends Auto Hot Pick-4
97Black Diamond-137
Double Diamond-137
Triple Diamond-137
Quadruple Diamond-137
97Swedish Collector's Choice-43
Stick'Ums-S2
97Talk N' Sports *-49
Phone Cards $1-49
98UD Choice-296
Prime Choice Reserve-296
Reserve-296
98Swedish UD Choice-221
98New Haven Beast-20
99BAP Memorabilia-163
Gold-163
Silver-163
99BAP Millennium-115
Emerald-115
Ruby-115
Sapphire-115
Signatures-115
Signatures Gold-115
99O-Pee-Chee-125
99O-Pee-Chee Chrome-125
99O-Pee-Chee Chrome Refractors-125
99Pacific-185
Copper-185
Emerald Green-185
Gold-185
Ice Blue-185
Premiere Date-185
Red-185
99Paramount-104
Copper-104
Emerald-104
Gold-104
Holographic Emerald-104
Holographic Gold-104
Holographic Silver-104
Ice Blue-104
Premiere Date-104
Red-104
Silver-104
99Topps/OPC-125
99Topps/OPC Chrome-125
Refractors-125
99Louisville Panthers-12
00Panthers Team Issue-21
01Pacific-175
Extreme LTD-175
Hobby LTD-175
Premiere Date-175
Retail LTD-175
01Pacific Adrenaline-84
Blue-84
Premiere Date-84
Red-84
Retail-84
01Pacific Arena Exclusives-175
01Titanium-62
Hobby Parallel-62
Premiere Date-62
Retail-62
Retail Parallel-62
01UD Mask Collection-40
Gold-40
01Upper Deck-74
Exclusives-74
01Upper Deck MVP-80
01Upper Deck Victory-149
Gold-149
01Upper Deck Vintage-108
01Upper Deck Vintage-113
02BAP Sig Series Auto Buybacks 1999-115
02O-Pee-Chee-224
02O-Pee-Chee Premier Blue Parallel-224
02O-Pee-Chee Premier Red Parallel-224
02O-Pee-Chee Factory Set-224
02Pacific-157
Blue-157
Red-157
02Pacific Complete-141
Red-141
02SP Authentic-117
02Topps-224
OPC Blue Parallel-224
OPC Red Parallel-224
Factory Set-224
02Topps Total-180
02Upper Deck-323
Exclusives-323
02Upper Deck Beckett UD Promos-323
02Upper Deck MVP-78
Gold-78
Classics-78
Golden Classics-78
02Upper Deck Victory-93
Bronze-93
Gold-93
Silver-93
03BAP Memorabilia-212
03ITG Action-248
03NHL Sticker Collection-45
03Pacific-148
Blue-148
Red-148
03Pacific Complete-203
Red-203
03Upper Deck-324
Canadian Exclusives-324
HG-324
UD Exclusives-324
03Upper Deck MVP-180
Gold Script-180
Silver Script-180
Canadian Exclusives-180
04Swedish Alfabilder Alfa Stars-18
04Swedish Alfabilder Autographs-124
04Swedish Alfabilder Limited Autographs-124
04Swedish Alfabilder Proof Parallels-18
04Swedish Elitset-165
Gold-165
04Swedish Pure Skills-12
Parallel-12
Professional Power-MN
05Parkhurst-82
Facsimile Auto Parallel-82
05Upper Deck-28
HG Glossy-28
Jerseys-J-MNI
05Upper Deck MVP-69
Gold-69
Platinum-69
05Upper Deck Toronto Fall Expo-28
05Swedish SHL Elitset-20
Gold-20
Playmakers-2
06Gatorade-14
06O-Pee-Chee-77
Rainbow-77
Nilson, Patrik
03Laredo Bucks-14
Nilsson, Ake
56Swedish Alfabilder-74
Nilsson, Anders
04Swedish Elitset-261
Gold-261
05Swedish SHL Elitset-116
Gold-116
Teammates-10
Nilsson, Andreas

06Swedish SHL Elitset-123
Nilsson, Axel
38Swedish Liv's Magazine-57
Nilsson, Bengt
57Swedish Alfabilder-125
Nilsson, Billy
92Swedish Semic Elitserien Stickers-250
Nilsson, Birger
55Swedish Alfabilder-14
Nilsson, Casper
98Danish Hockey League-91
99Danish Hockey League-109
Nilsson, Christer
67Swedish Hockey-123
69Swedish Hockey-136
70Swedish Hockey-93
71Swedish Hockey-187
72Swedish Stickers-174
Nilsson, Fredrik
89Swedish Semic Elitserien Stickers-252
90Swedish Semic Elitserien Stickers-170
91Swedish Semic Elitserien Stickers-272
92Swedish Semic Elitserien Stickers-290
93Swedish Semic World Champ Stickers-17
94Finnish Jaa Kiekko-59
95Kansas City Blades-14
97Swedish Collector's Choice-132
98Finnish Keraillysarja-108
99Finnish Cardset-62
00Swiss Panini Stickers-163
00Swiss Slapshot Mini-Cards-EHCK7
01Swiss HNL-69
02German DEL City Press-201
Nilsson, Goran
81Swedish Semic Hockey VM Stickers-4
83Swedish Semic Elitserien-220
83Swedish Semic Elitserien-223
Nilsson, Hans-Ake
67Swedish Hockey-90
84Swedish Semic Elitserien-206
Nilsson, Hardy
72Swedish Stickers-209
74Swedish Stickers-254
83Swedish Semic Elitserien-171
96German DEL-268
Nilsson, Henrik
90Swedish Semic Elitserien Stickers-172
91Swedish Semic Elitserien Stickers-267
92Swedish Semic Elitserien Stickers-288
93Swedish Semic Elitserien-255
94Swedish Leaf-59
95German DEL-74
95Swedish Leaf-205
95Swedish Upper Deck-218
97Swedish Collector's Choice-71
98Swedish UD Choice-81
99Swedish Upper Deck-84
00Swedish Upper Deck-73
Nilsson, Jan Erik
64Swedish Coralli ISHockey-27
65Swedish Coralli ISHockey-27
67Swedish Hockey-225
69Swedish Hockey-265
70Swedish Hockey-151
71Swedish Hockey-244
72Swedish Stickers-228
73Swedish Stickers-229
74Swedish Stickers-177
84Swedish Semic Elitserien-193
Nilsson, Johan
06Swedish SHL Elitset-246
Nilsson, Kent
78Jets Postcards-17
79Flames Postcards-11
79Flames Team Issue-12
80Flames Postcards-13
80O-Pee-Chee-106
80O-Pee-Chee-197
80O-Pee-Chee Super-3
80Pepsi-Cola Caps-11
80Topps-106
80Topps-197
81O-Pee-Chee-34
81O-Pee-Chee-52
81O-Pee-Chee-53
81O-Pee-Chee Stickers-218
81Post Standups-28
81Topps-24
81Topps-48
82Flames Dollars-4
82O-Pee-Chee-54
82O-Pee-Chee Stickers-217
82Post Cereal-3
82Topps Stickers-217
82Swedish Semic VM Stickers-147
83NHL Key Tags-18
83O-Pee-Chee-89
83O-Pee-Chee Stickers-267
83O-Pee-Chee Stickers-268
83Puffy Stickers-3
83Topps Stickers-267
83Topps Stickers-268
83Vachon-14
84O-Pee-Chee-232
84O-Pee-Chee Stickers-245
85O-Pee-Chee Stickers-208
86North Stars Postcards-11
87O-Pee-Chee Stickers-88
88Oilers Tenth Anniversary-27
89Swedish Semic World Champ Stickers-24
91Finnish Semic World Champ Stickers-50
91Swedish Semic World Champ Stickers-50
92Swedish Semic Elitserien Stickers-93
95Swedish Globe World Championships-71
97Swedish Alfabilder Autographs-16
01Greats of the Game-89
Autographs-89
01Upper Deck Legends-69
01Swedish Alfabilder-16
02UD Foundations-11
04ITG Franchises Canadian-6
04ITG Franchises Canadian-26
Autographs-KN
04UD All-World-50
04UD All-World-117
Gold-50
Autographs-50
Autographs-117
Dual Autographs-AD-SN
Triple Autographs-AT-NLN
Quad Autographs-AQ-ALS
Quad Autographs-AQ-SWE
04Swedish Alfabilder Alfa Stars-53
04Swedish Alfabilder Next In Line-6
04Swedish Alfabilder Proof Parallels-53
06ITG International Ice-65
Gold-65
Autographs-AKN
06Parkhurst-83
Nilsson, Kjell
67Swedish Hockey-38
73Swedish Stickers-218
Nilsson, Klas Goran
67Swedish Hockey-162
Nilsson, Lars-Goran
67Swedish Hockey-16
67Swedish Hockey-55
69Swedish Hockey-70
69Swedish Hockey-193
70Finnish Jaakiekko-33
70Swedish Hockey-17
70Swedish Hockey-33
70Swedish Hockey-287
70Swedish Masterserien-36
70Swedish Masterserien-61
70Swedish Masterserien-117
71Finnish Suomi Stickers-53
71Swedish Hockey-20
71Swedish Hockey-110
71Swedish Hockey-140
72Finnish Hellas-33
72Finnish Panda Toronto-73
72Finnish Semic World Championship-54
72Swedish Stickers-18
72Swedish Stickers-90
72Swedish Stickers-124
72Swedish Semic World Championship-54
74Swedish Semic World Champ Stickers-9
81Swedish Semic Hockey VM Stickers-120
83Swedish Semic Elitserien-104
Nilsson, Leif
69Swedish Hockey-341
70Swedish Hockey-257
71Swedish Hockey-317
Nilsson, Magnus
97Swedish Collector's Choice-137
98UD Choice-288
Prime Choice Reserve-288
Reserve-288
98Swedish UD Choice-159
98Swedish UD Choice-213
99Swedish Upper Deck-162
00Louisiana Ice Gators-17
02Swedish SHL-227
Parallel-227
02Swiss SCL Tigers-4
03Swedish Elite-234
Silver-234
04Swedish Elitset-287
Gold-287
05Swedish SHL Elitset-143
Gold-143
06Swedish SHL Elitset-141
Nilsson, Mats
89Swedish Semic Elitserien Stickers-106
90Swedish Semic Elitserien Stickers-109
Nilsson, Mikael
95Swedish Leaf-153
Nilsson, Nils
64Swedish Coralli ISHockey-19
65Swedish Coralli ISHockey-19
81Swedish Semic Hockey VM Stickers-121
Nilsson, Nisse
55Swedish Alfabilder-23
64Swedish Coralli ISHockey-55
65Swedish Coralli ISHockey-55
67Swedish Hockey-108
69Swedish Hockey-123
97Swedish Alfabilder Autographs-5
01Swedish Alfabilder-5
Nilsson, Odd
84Swedish Semic Elitserien-22
85Swedish Panini Stickers-22
87Swedish Panini Stickers-20
89Swedish Semic Elitserien Stickers-22
Nilsson, Olle
69Swedish Hockey-88
72Swedish Stickers-79
Nilsson, Orjan
91Swedish Semic Elitserien Stickers-137
92Swedish Semic Elitserien Stickers-157
Nilsson, Peder
73Swedish Stickers-221
74Swedish Stickers-148
Nilsson, Per
83Swedish Semic Elitserien-163
84Swedish Semic Elitserien-61
85Swedish Panini Stickers-59
86Swedish Panini Stickers-207
87Swedish Panini Stickers-201
89Swedish Semic Elitserien Stickers-186
Nilsson, Peter
71Swedish Hockey-116
83Swedish Semic Elitserien-87
84Swedish Semic Elitserien-87
85Swedish Panini Stickers-78
86Swedish Panini Stickers-71
87Swedish Panini Stickers-84
89Swedish Semic Elitserien Stickers-64
90Swedish Semic Elitserien Stickers-288
91Swedish Semic Elitserien Stickers-71
92Swedish Semic Elitserien Stickers-91
93Swedish Semic Elitserien-64
94Swedish Leaf-50
95Swedish Upper Deck 1st Division Stars-DS8
Nilsson, Petr
02Swedish SHL Dynamic Duos-5
Nilsson, Petter
91Swedish Semic Elitserien Stickers-161
92Swedish Semic Elitserien Stickers-182
93Swedish Semic Elitserien-153
94Swedish Leaf-7
95Swedish Leaf-254
95Swedish Upper Deck-118
96German DEL-347
98Swedish UD Choice-68
99Swedish Upper Deck-70
00Swedish Upper Deck-122
00Swedish Upper Deck-201
SHL Signatures-PN
02Swedish SHL-59
Parallel-59
03Swedish Elite-80
Silver-80
Nilsson, Robert
02Swedish SHL-198
03BAP Memorabilia Draft Redemptions-15
03Swedish Elite-204
Hot Numbers-HN2
Rookies-6
Signatures-16
Silver-204
04SP Authentic Rookie Redemptions-RR19
04Swedish Alfabilder Alfa Stars-38
04Swedish Alfabilder Next In Line-6
04Swedish Alfabilder Proof Parallels-38
04Swedish Djurgardens Postcards-6
04Swedish Elitset-163
Future Stars-5
Gold-163
05ITG Heroes/Prosp Toronto Expo Parallel -392
05Beehive-118
Beige -118
Blue -118
Gold-118
Red -118
Matte-118
05Black Diamond-200
Emerald-200
Gold-200
Onyx-200
Ruby-200
05Hot Prospects-252
En Fuego-252
Hot Materials-HMRN
Red Hot-252
White Hot-252
05Parkhurst-305
Facsimile Auto Parallel-642
Signatures-RN
05SP Authentic-168
Limited-168
Rarefied Rookies-RRRN
Rookie Authentics-RARN
Sign of the Times Triples-TYPN
05SP Game Used-119
Autographs-119
Gold-119
Rookie Exclusives-RN
Rookie Exclusives Silver-RE-RN
Significant Numbers-SN-NI
05SPx-167
Spectrum-167
Xcitement Rookies-XR-RN
Xcitement Rookies Gold-XR-RN
Xcitement Rookies Spectrum-XR-RN
05The Cup-109
Autographed Rookie Patches Gold Rainbow-109
Black Rainbow Rookies-109
Masterpiece Pressplates (Artifacts)-220
Masterpiece Pressplates (Bee Hive)-118
Masterpiece Pressplates (Black Diamond)-200
Masterpiece Pressplates (Ice)-173
Masterpiece Pressplates (MVP)-411
Masterpiece Pressplates (Power Play)-168
Masterpiece Pressplates (Rookie Update)-219
Masterpiece Pressplates SPA Autos-168
Masterpiece Pressplates (SP Game Used)-119
Masterpiece Pressplates SPx Autos-167
Masterpiece Pressplates (Trilogy)-199
Masterpiece Pressplates Ult Coll Autos-123
Masterpiece Pressplates (Victory)-275
Masterpiece Pressplates Autographs-109
Platinum Rookies-109
05UD Artifacts-220
Gold-RED20
05UD PowerPlay-168
05Ultimate Collection-123
Autographed Patches-123
Autographed Shields-123
Ultimate Debut Threads Jerseys-DTJRN
Ultimate Debut Threads Jerseys Autos-DAJRN
Ultimate Debut Threads Patches-DTPRN
Ultimate Debut Threads Patches Autos-DAPRN
05Ultra-264
Gold-264
Fresh Ink-FI-NS
Fresh Ink Blue-FI-NS
Ice-264
Rookie Uniformity Jerseys-RU-RN
Rookie Uniformity Jersey Autographs-ARU-RN
Rookie Uniformity Patches-RUP-RN
Rookie Uniformity Patch Autographs-ARP-RN
05Upper Deck-451
Rookie Ink-RIRN
05Upper Deck Rookie Showcase-RS19
05Upper Deck Rookie Showcase Promos-RS19
05Upper Deck Rookie Threads-RTRN
05Upper Deck Rookie Threads Autographs-ARTRN
05Upper Deck Ice-173
Cool Threads-CTNI
Cool Threads Autographs-ACTNI
Cool Threads Glass-CTNI
Cool Threads Patches-CTPNI
Cool Threads Patch Autographs-CAPNI
Glacial Graphs-GGRN
Glacial Graphs Labels-GGRN
Premieres Auto Patches-AIPRN
05Upper Deck MVP-411
Gold-411
Platinum-411
Rookie Breakthrough-RB14
05Upper Deck Rookie Update-219
Inspirations Patch Rookies-219
05Upper Deck Trilogy-199
05Upper Deck Victory-275
Black-275
Gold-275
Silver-275
05Swedish SHL Elitset-17
Gold-17
Star Potential-3
05ITG Heroes and Prospects-392
Autographs Update-A-RN
06Black Diamond-53
Black-53
Gold-53
Ruby-53
06O-Pee-Chee Autographs-A-RN
06UD Toronto Fall Expo Priority Signings -PSRN
06AHL Top Prospects-6
Nilsson, Roger
67Swedish Hockey-259
69Swedish Hockey-305
72Swedish Stickers-80
Nilsson, Rolf
98Danish Hockey League-25
Nilsson, Ronny
91Swedish Semic Elitserien Stickers-127
Nilsson, Rune
67Swedish Hockey-91
Nilsson, S.A.
56Swedish Alfabilder-80
Nilsson, Stefan
83Swedish Semic Elitserien-38
84Swedish Semic Elitserien-38
84Swedish Semic Elitserien-155
85Swedish Panini Stickers-138
86Swedish Panini Stickers-18
86Swedish Panini Stickers-130
86Swedish Panini Stickers-142
86Swedish Panini Stickers-187
87Swedish Panini Stickers-124
87Swedish Panini Stickers-152
89Swedish Semic Elitserien Stickers-114
89Swedish Semic Elitserien Stickers-160
90Swedish Semic Elitserien Stickers-240
91Swedish Semic Elitserien Stickers-167
92Swedish Semic Elitserien Stickers-186
92Swedish Semic Elitserien Stickers-258
93Swedish Semic Elitserien-156
94Finnish Jaa Kiekko-63
94Swedish Leaf-18
94Swedish Leaf-258
Playmakers-2
Rookie Rockets-10
95Swedish Leaf-42
95Swedish Leaf-252
95Swedish Upper Deck-65
95Swedish Upper Deck-122
97Swedish Collector's Choice-58
97Swedish Collector's Choice-124
97Swedish Collector's Choice-200
97Swedish Collector's Choice-212
Crash the Game Exchange-C7
Crash the Game Redemption-R7
Select-UD12
00Swiss Panini Stickers-69
00Swiss Slapshot Mini-Cards-HCCF13
02Swedish SHL-61
Dynamic Duos-5
Parallel-61
Signatures-9
03Swedish Elite-83
Silver-83
04Swedish Elitset-74
Gold-74
Nilsson, Tommy
84Swedish Semic Elitserien-146
91Swedish Semic Elitserien Stickers-10
Nilsson, Tyler
03Fort Worth Brahmas-10
Nilsson, Ulf
69Swedish Hockey-49
70Swedish Hockey-11
71Swedish Hockey-88
72Swedish Stickers-63
73Finnish Jaakiekko-33
73Swedish Stickers-10
73Swedish Stickers-202
74O-Pee-Chee WHA-4
74Finnish Jenkki-31
74Finnish Typotor-99
74Swedish Stickers-26
74Swedish Stickers-256
74Swedish Semic World Champ Stickers-8
75O-Pee-Chee WHA-83
76O-Pee-Chee WHA-2
76O-Pee-Chee WHA-3
76O-Pee-Chee WHA-5
76O-Pee-Chee WHA-9
77O-Pee-Chee WHA-15
77Sportscasters-7112
77Finnish Sportscasters-80-1911
78O-Pee-Chee-255
78Topps-255
79O-Pee-Chee-30
79Topps-30
79Topps-103
80O-Pee-Chee-116
80Topps-116
81O-Pee-Chee-229
81O-Pee-Chee Stickers-172
81Topps-E102
82Swedish Semic VM Stickers-145
83Swedish Semic Elitserien-32
84Swedish Semic Elitserien-35
85Swedish Panini Stickers-31
91Upper Deck-643
French-643
92Future Trends '76 Canada Cup-143
96Swedish Semic Wien Hockey Legends-HL11
01Greats of the Game-26
Autographs-26
04UD All-World-45
04UD All-World-110A
Gold-45
Autographs-45
Autographs-110
Triple Autographs-AT-SLN
Quad Autographs-AQ-OAS
06ITG International Ice-89
Gold-89
Autographs-AUN
06ITG Ultimate Memorabilia-145
Artist Proof-145
06Parkhurst-84
Autographs-84
Nilsson, Ulf (goalie)
83Swedish Semic Elitserien-173
84Swedish Semic Elitserien-196
86Swedish Panini Stickers-220
87Swedish Panini Stickers-212
Nilstorp, Christopher
03Swedish Elite-237
Silver-237
04Swedish Elitset-226
Gold-226
04Swedish Malmo Red Hawks-14
Nimigon, Steve
93Niagara Falls Thunder-9
95Slapshot-188
96Visions Signings *-71
Autographs-71A
Autographs Silver-71A
Ninham, Jeff
75HCA Steel City Vacuum-9
Niro, Dominic
93Flint Generals-8
Nises, Ulf
67Swedish Hockey-145
69Swedish Hockey-159
70Swedish Hockey-126
71Swedish Hockey-217
72Swedish Stickers-194
Niskala, Janne
01Finnish Cardset-296
02Finnish Cardset-83
03Finnish Cardset-103
04Finnish Cardset-112
Parallel-83
06Swedish SHL Elitset-185
Niskanen, Mika
99Finnish Cardset-96
00Finnish Cardset-72
01Finnish Cardset-98
02Swedish SHL-179
Parallel-179
03Swedish Elite-192
Silver-192
05Swedish SHL Elitset-195
Gold-195
Niskanen, Petri
70Finnish Jaakiekko-334
Niskavaara, Jakko
95Collector's Choice-332
Player's Club-332
Player's Club Platinum-332
00Finnish Cardset-56
05Finnish Cardset -242
06Finnish Cardset-69
Nissinen, Pekka
78Finnish SM-Liiga-127
Nissinen, Tero
96Finnish SISU Redline-86
Nissinen, Tuomas
02Finnish Cardset-233
03Finnish Cardset-44
04Finnish Cardset-184
Parallel-137
05Finnish Cardset -164
Finnish Cardset Super Snatchers-18
06Finnish Cardset-258
Between the Pipes-13
Nistas, George
01Plymouth Whalers-16
Nistico, Lou
75O-Pee-Chee WHA-13
Nitel, Adam
95Slapshot-203
Nittel, Adam
99Kentucky Thoroughblades-22
00Kentucky Thoroughblades-20
00Kentucky Thoroughblades-P1
01Cleveland Barons-17
Nittel, Ahren
02Windsor Spitfires-15
03Albany River Rats-21
03Albany River Rats Kinko's-20
04Albany River Rats-15
05Albany River Rats-16
Niukkanen, Petri
80Finnish Mallasjuoma-174
Nixon, Brock
03Kamloops Blazers-12
05Kamloops Blazers-15
06Kamloops Blazers-16
Nixon, Danny
51Laval Dairy Subset-15
52St. Lawrence Sales-38
Nixon, Jaret
95Slapshot-324
Nixon, Julian
74Sioux City Musketeers-13
Nixon, Kyle
03Minnesota State Mavericks-15
Nizivij, Alexander
01Russian Dynamo Moscow-13
Noack, Erik
98Abilene Aviators-1
99San Angelo Outlaws-12
00Austin Ice Bats-14
Noack, Rudiger
70Finnish Jaakiekko-90
70Swedish Hockey-379
74Finnish Typotor-62
Noak, Ron
94German First League-427
Nobili, Jason
00Owen Sound Attack-12
04Florida Everblades-24
Nobili, Mario
907th Inn. Sketch QMJHL-233
917th Inn. Sketch QMJHL-146
91Star Pics-34
91Ultimate Draft-51
91Ultimate Draft French-51
92Tulsa Oilers-12
Noble, Jeff
85Kitchener Rangers-18
86Kitchener Rangers-17
87Kitchener Rangers-18
Noble, Kip
91Michigan Falcons-7
99UK Sheffield Steelers-14
00UK Cardiff Devils-7
00UK Sekonda Superleague-54
01UK Cardiff Devils-18
02UK Cardiff Devils-18
Noble, Reg
23V145-1-26
24Anonymous NHL-96
24C144 Champ's Cigarettes-45
24V145-2-51
83Hall of Fame-22
83Hall of Fame Postcards-B8
85Hall of Fame-22
04ITG Franchises Canadian-85
Noble, Tom
93Classic Four-Sport *-229
Gold-229
98Pensacola Ice Pilots-16
Noctor, John
94UK Guildford Flames-9
Nodl, Andreas
04Sioux Falls Stampede-2-6
05Sioux Falls Stampede-7
Noel, Cedrick
93Quebec Pee-Wee Tournament-92
Noel, Claude
897th Inn. Sketch OHL-176
92Dayton Bombers-20
96Michigan K-Wings-23
98Milwaukee Admirals-14
99Milwaukee Admirals Keebler-20
03Milwaukee Admirals-15
04Milwaukee Admirals-30
05Milwaukee Admirals Choice-19
05Milwaukee Admirals Pepsi-24
06Milwaukee Admirals -22
Noel, Dominic
01Cape Breton Screaming Eagles-6
Noel, Mike
74Sioux City Musketeers-14
Noel, Thierry
01Swiss HNL-283
Noel-Bernier, Dave
03Muskegon Fury-14
Noga, Chris
92Arizona Icecats-17
93Arizona Icecats-16
94Arizona Icecats-5
95Arizona Icecats-3
Noga, Matt
95North Iowa Huskies-23
00Richmond Renegades-15
04Kalamazoo Wings-14
Nogier, Pat
85Kamloops Blazers-16
Nogues, Jean-Francois
00Victoriaville Tigres-16
Signed-16
Nohejl, Michal
99Czech Score Blue 2000-151
99Czech Score Red Ice 2000-151
Nohel, Pavel
94Czech APS Extraliga-16
95Czech APS Extraliga-112
96Czech APS Extraliga-275
97Czech DS Extraliga-17
97Czech DS Stickers-183
98Czech DS Stickers-35
98Czech OFS-71
99Czech DS-50
99Czech OFS-242
Noiseux, Yannick
99Shawinigan Cataractes-17
Signed-17
00Shawinigan Cataractes-11
Signed-11
Noivo, Bruce
04Victoriaville Tigres-12
Nokelainen, Esko
92Finnish Jyvas-Hyva Stickers-137
Nokelainen, Petteri
04SP Authentic Rookie Redemptions-PP42
04Finnish Cardset-146
04Finnish Cardset Signatures-27
05Beehive-135
Beige -135
Blue -135
Gold-135
Red -135
Matte-135
Signature Scrapbook-SSPN
05Black Diamond-165
Emerald-165
Gold-165
Onyx-165
Ruby-165
05Hot Prospects-251
En Fuego-251
Hot Materials-HMPN
Red Hot-251
White Hot-251
05Parkhurst Signatures-PN
05SP Authentic-169
Limited-169
05SP Game Used-153
Autographs-153
Gold-153
Rookie Exclusives-PN
Rookie Exclusives Silver-RE-PN
05SPx-168
Spectrum-168
Xcitement Rookies-XR-PN
Xcitement Rookies Gold-XR-PN
Xcitement Rookies Spectrum-XR-PN
05The Cup-184
Black Rainbow Rookies-184
Masterpiece Pressplates (Artifacts)-237
Masterpiece Pressplates (Bee Hive)-135
Masterpiece Pressplates (Black Diamond)-165
Masterpiece Pressplates (Ice)-134
Masterpiece Pressplates (MVP)-410
Masterpiece Pressplates (Power Play)-161
Masterpiece Pressplates (Power Play)-161
Masterpiece Pressplates (Rookie Update)-218
Masterpiece Pressplates SPA Autos-169
Masterpiece Pressplates (SP Game Used)-153
Masterpiece Pressplates SPx Autos-168
Masterpiece Pressplates (Trilogy)-200
Masterpiece Pressplates Ult Coll-155
Masterpiece Pressplates Autographs-184
Platinum Rookies-184
05UD Artifacts-237
Gold-RED37
05UD PowerPlay-161
05Ultimate Collection-155
Gold-155
05Ultra-227
Gold-227
Ice-227
Rookie Uniformity Jerseys-RU-PN
Rookie Uniformity Jersey Autographs-ARU-PN
Rookie Uniformity Patches-RUP-PN
Rookie Uniformity Patch Autographs-ARP-PN
05Upper Deck-211
HG Glossy-211
Rookie Ink-RIPN
Rookie Threads-RTPN
Rookie Threads Autographs-ARTPN
05Upper Deck Ice-134
Fresh Ice-FIPN
Fresh Ice Glass-FIPN
Fresh Ice Glass Patches-FIPPN
Premieres Auto Patches-AIPPN
05Upper Deck MVP-410
Gold-410
Platinum-410
05Upper Deck Rookie Update-218
Inspirations Patch Rookies-218
05Upper Deck Trilogy-200
05Upper Deck Toronto Fall Expo-211
06Be A Player Portraits First Exposures-FEPN
06Fleer Signing Day-SDPN
Nokikuru, Kimmo
66Finnish Jaakiekkosarja-39
Nokkosmaki, Nemo
93Finnish SISU-217
94Finnish SISU-232
Nolan, Adam
93Quebec Pee-Wee Tournament-188
Nolan, Alan
02St. Michaels Majors-19
Nolan, Billy
90Hampton Roads Admirals-51
91Hampton Roads Admirals-13
98Hampton Roads Admirals 10th Anniversary-24
Nolan, Brandon
03Columbia Inferno-108
04Manitoba Moose-13
04ITG Heroes and Prospects-13
Autographs-BN
04ITG Heroes/Prospects Toronto Expo '05-13
04ITG Heroes/Prospects Expo Heroes/Pros-13
Nolan, Doug
03Manchester Monarchs-11
03Manchester Monarchs Team Issue-11
03Reading Royals-30
03Reading Royals RBI Sports-298
04Manchester Monarchs-7
04Manchester Monarchs Tobacco-8
05Manchester Monarchs-12
06Manchester Monarchs-5
Nolan, Jeffery
907th Inn. Sketch OHL-112
Nolan, Jordan
05Erie Otters-7
Nolan, Owen
897th Inn. Sketch OHL-180
90Nordiques Petro-Canada-19
90OPC Premier-86
90Pro Set-401
90Pro Set-635
90Score-435
Canadian-435
90Score Rookie/Traded-80T
90Score Young Superstars-36
90Upper Deck-351
90Upper Deck-352
French-351
French-352
91Pro Set Platinum-101
91Bowman-134
91Gillette-25
91Kraft-55
91Nordiques Panini Team Stickers-17
91Nordiques Petro-Canada-21
91O-Pee-Chee-64
91OPC Premier-193
91Panini Stickers-266
91Parkhurst-143
French-143
91Pinnacle-156
French-156
91Pro Set-196
French-196
91Score American-143
91Score Canadian Bilingual-143
91Score Canadian English-143
91Stadium Club-259
91Topps-64
91Upper Deck-367
91Upper Deck-619
French-367
French-619
92Bowman-237
92Bowman-328
92Humpty Dumpty II-17
92McDonald's Upper Deck-24
92Nordiques Petro-Canada-22
92O-Pee-Chee-382
92Panini Stickers-210
92Panini Stickers French-210
92Parkhurst-145
92Parkhurst-455
Emerald Ice-145
Emerald Ice-455
Cherry Picks-CP13
92Pinnacle American Promo Panel-1
92Pinnacle-6
French-6
Team 2000-10
Team 2000 French-10
92Pro Set-153
92Score-286
Canadian-286
Sharpshooters-12
Sharpshooters Canadian-12
Young Superstars-37
92Seasons Patches-46
92Stadium Club-78
92Topps-349
Gold-349G
92Ultra-177
92Upper Deck-17
92Upper Deck-321
93Donruss-279
93Leaf-42
93OPC Premier-267
Gold-267
93Panini Stickers-70
93Parkhurst-163
Emerald Ice-163
First Overall-F4
93Pinnacle-151
Canadian-151
Team 2001-28
Team 2001 Canadian-28
93PowerPlay-201
93Score-32
Canadian-32
93Stadium Club-397
Members Only Master Set-397
First Day Issue-397
93Topps/OPC Premier-267
Gold-267
93Topps Premier Finest-4
93Ultra-154
93Upper Deck-175
Hat Tricks-HT16
SP-128
93Swedish Semic World Champ Stickers-207
94Be A Player-R51
Signature Cards-59
94Canada Games NHL POGS-197
94Donruss-45
94EA Sports-113
94Fleer-181
94Hockey Wit-57
94Leaf-144
94Leaf Limited-41
94Nordiques Burger King-19
94OPC Premier-457
Special Effects-457
94Parkhurst Vintage-V43
94Parkhurst SE-SE143
Gold-SE143
94Pinnacle-76
Artist's Proofs-76
Rink Collection-76
94Select-4
Gold-4
94SP-95
Die Cuts-95
94Stadium Club-102
Members Only Master Set-102
First Day Issue-102
Super Team Winner Cards-102
94Topps/OPC Premier-457
Special Effects-457
94Ultra-177
94Upper Deck-103
Electric Ice-103
SP Inserts-SP63
SP Inserts Die Cuts-SP63
94Upper Deck NHLPA/Be A Player-33
95Bashan Super Stickers-110
95Bowman-58
All-Foil-58
95Canada Games NHL POGS-76
95Collector's Choice-259
Player's Club-259
Player's Club Platinum-259
Crash The Game-C12A
Crash The Game-C12B
Crash The Game-C12C
Crash The Game Gold-C12A
Crash The Game Gold-C12B
Crash The Game Gold-C12C
Crash the Game Silver Redeemed-C12
Crash the Game Silver Bonus-C12
Crash the Game Gold Redeemed-C12
Crash the Game Gold Bonus-C12
95Donruss-153
95Donruss-268
Marksmen-2
95Donruss Elite-26
Die Cut Stars-26
Die Cut Uncut-26
95Emotion-40
Ntense Power-6
95Finest-142
Refractors-142
95Hoyle Eastern Playing Cards-47
95Imperial Stickers-110
95Leaf-240
95Leaf Limited-93
95McDonald's Pinnacle-MCD-10
95Metal-133
95Panini Stickers-249
95Parkhurst International-49
95Parkhurst International-453
Emerald Ice-49
Emerald Ice-453
95Pinnacle-12
Artist's Proofs-12
Rink Collection-12
Full Contact-3
95Playoff One on One-27
95Playoff One on One-241
95Score-83
Black Ice Artist's Proofs-83
Black Ice-83
Check It-2
Lamplighters-4
95Select Certified Promos-19
95Select Certified-19
Mirror Gold-19
95SkyBox Impact-150
95SkyBox Impact-240
Ice Quake-11
95SP-129
95Stadium Club-65
Members Only Master Set-65
95Summit-12
Artist's Proofs-12
Ice-12
Mad Hatters-1
95Topps-305
OPC Inserts-305
95Ultra-134
95Ultra-304
Gold Medallion-134
Crease Crashers-13
Red Light Specials-8
Red Light Specials Gold Medallion-8
95Upper Deck-176
95Upper Deck-225
95Upper Deck-246
95Upper Deck-495
Electric Ice-176
Electric Ice-225
Electric Ice-246
Electric Ice-495
Electric Ice Gold-176
Electric Ice Gold-225
Electric Ice Gold-246
Electric Ice Gold-495
NHL All-Stars-AS13
NHL All-Stars Jumbo-AS13
Predictor Retail-R7
Predictor Retail Exchange-R7
Special Edition-SE163
Special Edition Gold-SE163
95Zenith-16
Gifted Grinders-9
96Be A Player Biscuit In The Basket-25
96Black Diamond-111
Gold-111
96Collector's Choice-233
96Collector's Choice-330
MVP-UD42
MVP Gold-UD42
Stick'Ums-S25
96Donruss-6
Press Proofs-6
Hit List-17
96Donruss Canadian Ice-54
Gold Press Proofs-54
Red Press Proofs-54
96Donruss Elite-14
Die Cut Stars-14
Status-6
96Duracell All-Cherry Team-DC19
96Flair-85
Blue Ice-85
Hot Numbers-10
96Fleer-100
Picks Fabulous 50-34
96Kraft Upper Deck-4
96Kraft Upper Deck-36
96Leaf-128
Press Proofs-128
96Leaf Limited-20
Gold-20
96Leaf Limited Bash the Boards Promos-P3
96Leaf Limited Bash The Boards-14
96Leaf Limited Bash The Boards Ltd Ed-3
96Leaf Preferred-6
Press Proofs-6
Steel-62
Steel Gold-62
96Maggers-69
96Metal Universe-139
96NHL Aces Playing Cards-35
96Pinnacle-186
Artist's Proofs-186
Foil-186
Premium Stock-186
Rink Collection-186
96Pinnacle Fantasy-FC18
96Playoff One on One-335
96Score-69
Artist's Proofs-69
Dealer's Choice Artist's Proofs-69

Special Artist's Proofs-69
Check It-8
Golden Blades-69
96Select Certified-56
Artist's Proofs-56
Blue-56
Mirror Blue-56
Mirror Gold-56
Mirror Red-56
Red-56
96SkyBox Impact-117
96SP-138
96SPx-41
Gold-41
96Stadium Club Members Only-8
96Summit-45
Artist's Proofs-45
Ice-45
Metal-45
Premium Stock-45
96Team Out-43
96Topps Picks-57
OPC Inserts-57
96Ultra-153
Gold Medallion-153
96Upper Deck-146
Generation Next-X19
Power Performers-P18
96Upper Deck Ice-59
Parallel-59
96Zenith-37
Artist's Proofs-37
Assailants-14
97SLU Hockey One on One-4
97Beehive-22
Golden Portraits-22
97Black Diamond-9
Double Diamond-9
Triple Diamond-9
Quadruple Diamond-9
97Collector's Choice-214
Crash the Game-C30A
Crash the Game-C30B
Crash the Game-C30C
Crash the Game Exchange-CR30
Star Quest-SQ78
97Crown Royale-121
Emerald Green-121
Ice Blue-121
Silver-121
97Donruss-84
Press Proofs Silver-84
Press Proofs Gold-84
97Donruss Canadian Ice-108
Dominion Series-108
Provincial Series-108
National Pride-30
97Donruss Limited-117
97Donruss Limited-196
Exposure-117
Exposure-196
97Donruss Preferred-108
Cut to the Chase-108
97Donruss Priority-46
Stamp of Approval-46
97Katch-124
Gold-124
Silver-124
97Leaf-23
Fractal Matrix-23
Fractal Matrix Die Cuts-23
97Leaf International-23
Universal Ice-23
97NHL Aces Playing Cards-31
97Pacific-151
Copper-151
Emerald Green-151
Ice Blue-151
Red-151
Silver-151
Team Checklists-22
97Pacific Dynagon-114
Copper-114
Dark Grey-114
Emerald Green-114
Ice Blue-114
Red-114
Silver-114
Tandems-50
97Pacific Invincible-128
Copper-128
Emerald Green-128
Ice Blue-128
Red-128
Silver-128
97Pacific Omega-205
Copper-205
Dark Gray-205
Emerald Green-205
Gold-205
Ice Blue-205
97Panini Stickers-230
97Paramount-169
Copper-169
Dark Grey-169
Emerald Green-169
Ice Blue-169
Red-169
Silver-169
97Pinnacle-49
Artist's Proofs-49
Rink Collection-49
Press Plates Back Black-49
Press Plates Back Cyan-49
Press Plates Back Magenta-49
Press Plates Back Yellow-49
Press Plates Front Black-49
Press Plates Front Cyan-49
Press Plates Front Magenta-49
Press Plates Front Yellow-49
97Pinnacle Certified-59
Red-59
Mirror Blue-59
Mirror Gold-59
Mirror Red-59
97Pinnacle Inside-27
Coach's Collection-27
Executive Collection-27
97Pinnacle Tot Cert Platinum Blue-59
97Pinnacle Tot Cert Platinum Gold-59
97Pinnacle Totally Certified Platinum Red-59
97Pinnacle Tot Cert Mirror Platinum Gold-59
97Revolution-126
Copper-126
Emerald-126
Ice Blue-126
Silver-126
97Score-102
Artist's Proofs-102
Golden Blades-102
Check It-17
97Sharks Fleer All-Star Sheet-5
97SP Authentic-131
97SPx-44
Bronze-44
Gold-44
Silver-44
Steel-44
Grand Finale-44
97Upper Deck-147
Blow-Ups 3 x 5-1-4
Game Dated Moments-147
Smooth Grooves-SG24
Three Star Selects-6A
97Upper Deck Crash the All-Star Game-6
97Upper Deck Crash the All-Star Game-AR6
97Upper Deck Diamond Vision-13
Signature Moves-13
97Upper Deck Ice-10
Parallel-10
Lethal Lines-L3C
Lethal Lines 2-L3C
Power Shift-10
97Zenith-27
Z-Gold-27
Z-Silver-27
97Zenith 5 x 7-60
Gold Impulse-60
Silver Impulse-60
98Aurora-170
98Black Diamond-75
Double Diamond-75
Triple Diamond-75
Quadruple Diamond-75
98Bowman's Best-70
Refractors-70
Atomic Refractors-70
98Crown Royale-120
Limited Series-120
98Finest-23
No Protectors-23
No Protectors Refractors-23
Refractors-23
98OPC Chrome-156
Refractors-156
98Pacific-390
Ice Blue-390
Red-390
98Pacific Dynagon Ice-168
Blue-168
Red-168
98Pacific Omega-212
Red-212
Opening Day Issue-212
98Panini Stickers-210
98Paramount-214
Copper-214
Emerald Green-214
Holo-Electric-214
Ice Blue-214
Silver-214
98Revolution-128
Ice Shadow-128
Red-128
98SP Authentic-77
Power Shift-77
Sign of the Times-ON
Sign of the Times Gold-ON
98SPx Finite-71
Radiance-71
Spectrum-71
98Topps-156
O-Pee-Chee-156
98Topps Gold Label Class 1-14
Black-14
Black One of One-14
One of One-14
Red-14
Red One of One-14
98Topps Gold Label Class 2-14
98Topps Gold Label Class 2 Black-14
98Topps Gold Label Class 2 Black 1 of 1-14
98Topps Gold Label Class 2 One of One-14
98Topps Gold Label Class 2 Red-14
98Topps Gold Label Class 2 Red One of One-14
98Topps Gold Label Class 3-14
98Topps Gold Label Class 3 Black-14
98Topps Gold Label Class 3 Black 1 of 1-14
98Topps Gold Label Class 3 One of One-14
98Topps Gold Label Class 3 Red-14
98Topps Gold Label Class 3 Red One of One-14
98UD Choice-175
98UD Choice Preview-175
98UD Choice Prime Choice Reserve-175
98UD Choice Reserve-175
98Upper Deck-354
Exclusives-354
Exclusives 1 of 1-354
Fantastic Finishers-FF24
Fantastic Finishers Quantum 1-FF24
Fantastic Finishers Quantum 2-FF24
Fantastic Finishers Quantum 3-FF24
Frozen In Time-FT17
Frozen In Time Quantum 1-FT17
Frozen In Time Quantum 2-FT17
Frozen In Time Quantum 3-FT17
Gold Reserve-354
98Upper Deck MVP-173
Gold Script-173
Silver Script-173
Super Script-173
99BAP Memorabilia-245
Gold-245
Silver-245
99BAP Update Teammates Jersey Cards-TM16
99Black Diamond-75
Diamond Cut-75
Final Cut-75
99Crown Royale-125
Limited Series-125
Premiere Date-125
Ice Elite-22
Ice Elite Parallel-22
Team Captain Die-Cuts-8
99Jell-O Partners of Power-12
99O-Pee-Chee-206
99O-Pee-Chee Chrome-206
99O-Pee-Chee Chrome Refractors-206
99Pacific-378
Copper-378
Emerald Green-378
Gold-378
Ice Blue-378
Premiere Date-378
Red-378
99Pacific Dynagon Ice-174
Blue-174
Copper-174
Gold-174
Premiere Date-174
Checkmates American-14
Checkmates American-29
Checkmates Canadian-14
99Pacific Omega-209
Copper-209
Gold-209
Ice Blue-209
Premiere Date-209
5 Star Talents-11
5 Star Talents Parallel-11
99Pacific Prism-126
Holographic Blue-126
Holographic Gold-126
Holographic Mirror-126
Holographic Purple-126
Premiere Date-126
99Panini Stickers-300
99Paramount-207
Copper-207
Emerald-207
Gold-207
Holographic Emerald-207
Holographic Gold-207
Holographic Silver-207
Ice Blue-207
Premiere Date-207
Red-207
Silver-207
99SP Authentic-73
99SPx-127
Radiance-127
Spectrum-127
99Stadium Club-44
First Day Issue-44
One of a Kind-44
Printing Plates Black-44
Printing Plates Cyan-44
Printing Plates Magenta-44
Printing Plates Yellow-44
99Topps/OPC-206
99Topps/OPC Chrome-206
Refractors-206
99Topps Gold Label Class 1-49
Black-49
Black One of One-49
One of One-49
Red-49
Red One of One-49
99Topps Gold Label Class 2-49
99Topps Gold Label Class 2 Black-49
99Topps Gold Label Class 2 Black 1 of 1-49
99Topps Gold Label Class 2 One of One-49
99Topps Gold Label Class 2 Red-49
99Topps Gold Label Class 2 Red One of One-49
99Topps Gold Label Class 3-49
99Topps Gold Label Class 3 Black-49
99Topps Gold Label Class 3 Black 1 of 1-49
99Topps Gold Label Class 3 One of One-49
99Topps Gold Label Class 3 Red-49
99Topps Gold Label Class 3 Red One of One-49
99Topps Gold Label Quest for the Cup-QC8
99Topps Gold Label Quest for the Cup One of One -QC8
99Topps Gold Label Quest 4 the Cup Black-QC8
99Topps Gold Label Quest for the Cup Black One of One -QC8
99Topps Gold Label Quest for the Cup Red-QC8
99Topps Gold Label Quest for the Cup Red One of One -QC8
99Topps Premier Plus-15
Parallel-15
99Ultimate Victory-74
1/1-74
Parallel-74
Parallel 100-74
99Upper Deck-282
Exclusives-282
Exclusives 1 of 1-282
99Upper Deck Gold Reserve-282
99Upper Deck MVP-174
Gold Script-174
Silver Script-174
Super Script-174
99Upper Deck MVP SC Edition-153
Gold Script-153
Silver Script-153
Super Script-153
99Upper Deck Ovation-50
Standing Ovation-50
99Upper Deck Victory-252
00Aurora-129
Pinstripes-129
Pinstripes Premiere Date-129
Premiere Date-129
00BAP Memorabilia-227
Emerald-227
Ruby-227
Sapphire-227
Promos-227
Jersey Cards-J26
Jersey Emblems-E26
Jersey Numbers-N26
Jersey and Stick Cards-JS26
00BAP Mem Chicago Sportsfest Copper-227
00BAP Memorabilia Chicago Sportsfest Blue-227
00BAP Memorabilia Chicago Sportsfest Gold-227
00BAP Memorabilia Chicago Sportsfest Ruby-227
00BAP Memorabilia Chicago Sun-Times Ruby-227
00BAP Memorabilia Chicago Sun-Times Gold-227
00BAP Mem Chicago Sun-Times Sapphire-227
00BAP Mem Toronto Fall Expo Copper-227
00BAP Memorabilia Toronto Fall Expo Gold-227
00BAP Memorabilia Toronto Fall Expo Ruby-227
00BAP Mem Update Heritage Jersey Cards-H18
00BAP Mem Update Heritage Jersey Gold-H18
00BAP Parkhurst 2000-P17
00BAP Signature Series-73
Emerald-73
Ruby-73
Sapphire-73
Franchise Players-F26
00BAP Ultimate Mem Game-Used Jerseys-GJ18
00BAP Ultimate Mem Game-Used Emblems-E16
00BAP Ultimate Mem Game-Used Numbers-N16
00BAP Ultimate Mem Game-Used Sticks-GS18
00BAP Ultimate Mem Journey Jerseys-JJ19
00BAP Ultimate Mem Journey Emblems-JE19
00BAP Ultimate Mem Journey Numbers-JI19
00BAP Ultimate Memorabilia Teammates-TM34
00Crown Royale-94
Ice Blue-94
Limited Series-94
Premiere Date-94
Red-94
00Kraft-21
00O-Pee-Chee-11
00O-Pee-Chee Parallel-11
00Pacific-363
Copper-363
Gold-363
Ice Blue-363
Premiere Date-363
Gold Crown Die Cuts-31
00Panini Stickers-204
00Paramount-215
Copper-215
Gold-215
Holo-Gold-215
Holo-Silver-215
Ice Blue-215
Premiere Date-215
Freeze Frame-32
00Private Stock-89
Gold-89
Premiere Date-89
Retail-89
Silver-89
PS-2001 Action-50
00Revolution-130
Blue-130
Premiere Date-130
Red-130
HD NHL-31
Stat Masters-10
00SP Authentic-73
00SP Game Used-51
00SPx-79
Spectrum-79
00Stadium Club-43
Special Forces-SF11
00Titanium-86
Blue-86
Gold-86
Premiere Date-86
Red-86
Retail-86
00Topps/OPC-11
Parallel-11
NHL Draft-D4
Own the Game-OTG6
00Topps Chrome-11
OPC Refractors-11
Refractors-11
00Topps Gold Label Class 1-26
Gold-26
00Topps Gold Label Class 2-26
00Topps Gold Label Class 2 Gold-26
00Topps Gold Label Class 3-26
00Topps Gold Label Class 3 Gold-26
00Topps Gold Label Bullion-B8
00Topps Gold Label Bullion One to One-B8
00Topps Heritage-17
00Topps Heritage-230
00Topps Heritage-232
Chrome Parallel-17
00Topps Premier Plus-7
Blue Ice-7
00Topps Stars-11
Blue-11
00UD Heroes-101
00UD Pros and Prospects-71
00UD Reserve-71
00Upper Deck-144
Exclusives Tier 1-144
Exclusives Tier 2-144
Fantastic Finishers-FF10
Number Crunchers-NC8
00Upper Deck Legends-113
Legendary Collection Bronze-113
Legendary Collection Gold-113
Legendary Collection Silver-113
00Upper Deck MVP-150
First Stars-150
Second Stars-150
Third Stars-150
00Upper Deck Victory-197
00Upper Deck Victory-320
00Upper Deck Vintage-298
00Upper Deck Vintage-307
00Vanguard-88
Holographic Gold-88
Holographic Purple-88
Pacific Proofs-88
00Czech Stadion-74
01Atomic-86
Blue-86
Gold-86
Premiere Date-86
Red-86
Team Nucleus-12
01BAP Memorabilia-63
Emerald-63
Ruby-63
Sapphire-63
All-Star Jerseys-ASJ33
All-Star Emblems-ASE33
All-Star Numbers-ASN33
All-Star Jersey Doubles-DASJ28
Country of Origin-CO49
He Shoots-He Scores Prizes-12
Stanley Cup Playoffs-SC16
01BAP Signature Series Certified 100-C57
01BAP Signature Series Certified 50-C57
01BAP Signature Series Certified 1 of 1's-C57
01BAP Signature Series Autographs-XLON
01BAP Signature Series Autographs Gold-XLON
01BAP Signature Series Franchise Jerseys-FP-25
01BAP Sig Series He Shoots/Scores Prizes-33
01BAP Signature Series Jerseys-GJ-55
01BAP Signature Series Jersey Autographs-GUON
01BAP Sig Series Jersey and Stick Cards-GSJ-55
01BAP Signature Series Emblems-GUE-41
01BAP Signature Series Numbers-ITN-41
01BAP Signature Series Teammates-TM-25
01BAP Ultimate Memorabilia Autographs-31
01BAP Ultimate Mem Autographs Gold-31
01BAP Ultimate Memorabilia Emblems-12
01BAP Ultimate Memorabilia Jerseys-12
01BAP Ultimate Mem Jerseys and Sticks-12
01BAP Ultimate Memorabilia Numbers-19
01BAP Ultimate Memorabilia Name Plates-17
01BAP Update Heritage-H21
01Bowman YoungStars-46
Gold-46
Ice Cubed-46
01Crown Royale-125
Blue-125
Premiere Date-125
Red-125
Retail-125
01EA Sports-3
01eTopps-21
01O-Pee-Chee-30
01O-Pee-Chee Heritage Parallel-30
01O-Pee-Chee Heritage Parallel Limited-30
01O-Pee-Chee Premier Parallel-30
01Pacific-341
Extreme LTD-341
Hobby LTD-341
Premiere Date-341
Retail LTD-341
Top Draft Picks-6
01Pacific Top Draft Picks Draft Day Promo-6
01Pacific Adrenaline-168
Blue-168
Premiere Date-168
Red-168
Retail-168
01Pacific Arena Exclusives-341
01Parkhurst-55
Gold-55
Silver-55
Heroes-H10
Jerseys-PJ23
Sticks-PS23
01Private Stock-86
Gold-86
Premiere Date-86
Retail-86
Silver-86
01Private Stock Pacific Nights-86
01Private Stock PS-2002-65
01Sharks Postcards-5
01SP Authentic-72
Limited-72
Limited Gold-72
01SP Game Used Authentic Fabric-AFON
01SP Game Used Authentic Fabric Gold-AFON
01SPx-57
01Sports Illustrated for Kids III-238
01Stadium Club-11
Award Winners-11
Master Photos-11
01Titanium-123
Hobby Parallel-123
Premiere Date-123
Retail-123
Retail Parallel-123
All-Stars-16
01Titanium Draft Day Edition-87
01Topps-30
Heritage Parallel-30
Heritage Parallel Limited-30
OPC Parallel-30
01Topps Chrome-30
Refractors-30
Black Border Refractors-30
01Topps Heritage-47
Refractors-47
01Topps Reserve-45
01UD Challenge for the Cup-71
01UD Honor Roll Tough Customers-TC5
01UD Mask Collection-81
Gold-81
01UD Playmakers-81
01UD Top Shelf-114
01Upper Deck-144
Exclusives-144
Leaders of the Pack-LP12
Shooting Stars-SS15
Skilled Stars-SS5
Tandems-T8
EA Sports Gold-3
01Upper Deck Ice-116
01Upper Deck MVP-156
01Upper Deck Victory-292
01Upper Deck Victory-405
Gold-292
Gold-405
01Upper Deck Vintage-211
01Upper Deck Vintage-217
01Vanguard-87
Blue-87
Red-87
One of Ones-87
Premiere Date-87
Proofs-87
02Atomic-87
Blue-87
Gold-87
Red-87
Hobby Parallel-87
Super Colliders-14
02BAP All-Star Edition-66
He Shoots-He Scores Points-4
He Shoots-He Score Prizes-21
Jerseys-66
Jerseys Gold-66
Jerseys Silver-66
02BAP First Edition-156
02BAP First Edition-340
02BAP First Edition-366
02BAP First Edition-393
02BAP First Edition-404H
Debut Jerseys-8
He Shoots-He Score Points-10
He Shoots-He Scores Prizes-14
Jerseys-156
Scoring Leaders-16
02BAP Memorabilia-74
02BAP Memorabilia-226
02BAP Memorabilia-254
02BAP Memorabilia-364
Emerald-74
Emerald-226
Emerald-254
Ruby-74
Ruby-226
Ruby-254
Sapphire-74
Sapphire-226
Sapphire-254
All-Star Jerseys-ASJ-41
All-Star Emblems-ASE-17
All-Star Numbers-ASN-17
All-Star Starting Lineup-AS-5
All-Star Teammates-AST-7
All-Star Teammates-AST-27
All-Star Triple Jerseys-ASTJ-16
Franchise Players-FP-26
He Shoots-He Scores Points-3
He Shoots-He Scores Prizes-18
NHL All-Star Game-74
NHL All-Star Game-226
NHL All-Star Game-254
NHL All-Star Game Blue-74
NHL All-Star Game Blue-226
NHL All-Star Game Blue-254
NHL All-Star Game Green-74
NHL All-Star Game Green-226
NHL All-Star Game Green-254
NHL All-Star Game Red-74
NHL All-Star Game Red-226
NHL All-Star Game Red-254
Stanley Cup Playoffs-SC-9
Teammates-TM-18
02BAP Memorabilia Toronto Fall Expo-74
02BAP Memorabilia Toronto Fall Expo-226
02BAP Memorabilia Toronto Fall Expo-254
02BAP Sig Series Auto Buybacks 2001-XLON
02BAP Signature Series Famous Scraps-FS9
02BAP Signature Series Golf-GS66
02BAP Signature Series Jerseys-SGJ21
02BAP Signature Series Jersey Autographs-SGJ21
02BAP Signature Series Team Quads-TQ18
02BAP Ultimate Memorabilia First Overall-10
02Bowman YoungStars-21
Gold-21
Silver-21
02Crown Royale Jerseys-20
02Crown Royale Jerseys Gold-20
02ITG Used-64
02ITG Used-164
Franchise Players-F26
Franchise Players Autographs-F26
Franchise Players Gold-F26
Jerseys-GUJ21
Jersey Autographs-GUJ21
Jerseys Gold-GUJ21
Emblems-E21
Jersey and Stick-SJ21
Jersey and Stick Gold-SJ21
Teammates-T16
Teammates Gold-T16
02McDonald's Pacific Salt Lake Gold-8
02Nextel NHL All-Star Game-2
02O-Pee-Chee-30
02O-Pee-Chee Jumbos-20
02O-Pee-Chee Premier Blue Parallel-28
02O-Pee-Chee Premier Red Parallel-28
02O-Pee-Chee Factory Set-28
02Pacific-338
Blue-338
Red-338
02Pacific Complete-112
Red-112
02Pacific Exclusive-151
02Pacific Heads-Up-109
Blue-109
Purple-109
Red-109
Quad Jerseys-24
Quad Jerseys Gold-24
02Pacific Quest 4 the Cup Chasing the Cup-16
02Parkhurst-111
Bronze-111
Gold-111
Silver-111
Franchise Players-FP26
He Shoots-He Scores Points-4
He Shoots-He Scores Prizes-19
Jerseys-GJ37
Stick and Jerseys-SJ37
Teammates-TT15
02Parkhurst Retro-45
Minis-45
02Private Stock Reserve-142
Red-142
Retail-142
Patches-142
02SP Authentic-75
Beckett Promos-75
02SP Game Used-41
First Rounder Patches-ON
02SPx-62
Spectrum Gold-62
Spectrum Silver-62
02Stadium Club-7
Silver Decoy Cards-7
Proofs-7
Beam Team-BT12
02Titanium Jerseys-63
02Titanium Jerseys Retail-63
02Titanium Patches-63
02Topps-28
OPC Blue Parallel-28
OPC Red Parallel-28
Topps/OPC Hometown Heroes-HHU13
Factory Set-28
Factory Set Hometown Heroes-HHU13
02Topps Chrome-28
Black Border Refractors-28
Refractors-28
02Topps Heritage-44
Chrome Parallel-44
02Topps Total-261
Team Checklists-TTC25
Topps-TT19
02UD Artistic Impressions-75
Gold-75
02UD Artistic Impressions Beckett Promos-75
02UD Artistic Impressions Retrospectives-R75
02UD Artistic Impress Retrospect Gold-R75
02UD Artistic Impress Retrospect Silver-R75
02UD Honor Roll-59
02UD Honor Roll-95
Team Warriors-TW13
02UD Piece of History-75
02UD Top Shelf-74
Dual Player Jerseys-STSN
Milestones Jerseys-MLNLA
02Upper Deck-145
02Upper Deck-242
Exclusives-145
Exclusives-242
Blow-Ups-C34
Letters of Note-LNON
Letters of Note Gold-LNON
02Upper Deck Classic Portraits-84
02Upper Deck MVP-152
Gold-152
Classics-152
Golden Classics-152
02Upper Deck Rookie Update-93
02Upper Deck Victory-177
Bronze-177
Gold-177
Silver-177
02Upper Deck Vintage-211
02Upper Deck Vintage-285
Green Backs-211
Tall Boys-T54
Tall Boys Gold-T54
02Vanguard-86
LTD-86
03McFarlane Hockey-180
03McFarlane Hockey-182
03BAP Memorabilia-63
Emerald-63
Gold-63
Ruby-63
Sapphire-63
Jerseys-GJ-29
Jersey Autographs-GJ-29
Practice Jerseys-PMP8
03BAP Ultimate Memorabilia Autographs-141
Gold-141
03BAP Ultimate Mem Auto Jerseys-141
03BAP Ultimate Mem Auto Emblems-141
03BAP Ultimate Mem Jersey and Emblems-30
03BAP Ultimate Mem Jersey and Emblem Gold-30
03BAP Ultimate Mem Jersey and Numbers-30
03BAP Ultimate Mem Jersey and Number Gold-30
03BAP Ultimate Memorabilia Triple Threads-23
03Beehive-184
Gold-184
Silver-184
Signatures-RF22
Sticks Beige Border-BE11
Sticks Blue Border-BL15
Sticks Red Border-RE19
03Black Diamond-83
Black-83
Green-83
Red-83
03Crown Royale-94
Blue-94
Retail-94
Jerseys-24
Patches-24
03eTopps-15
03ITG Action-557
Jerseys-M172
03ITG Toronto Fall Expo Jerseys-FE7
03ITG Used Signature Series-103
Gold-103
Autographs-ON
Autographs Gold-ON
Oh Canada-8
Oh Canada Gold-8
Oh Canada Emblems-8
Oh Canada Emblems Gold-8
03Maple Leafs Team Issue-1
03McDonald's Pacific-48
03NHL Sticker Collection-286
03O-Pee-Chee-75
03OPC Blue-75
03OPC Gold-75
03OPC Red-75
03Pacific-321
Blue-321
Red-321
Maximum Impact-9
03Pacific Calder-93
Silver-93
03Pacific Complete-206
Red-206
03Pacific Exhibit-195
Blue Backs-195
03Pacific Heads-Up-92
Hobby LTD-92
Retail LTD-92
Jerseys-24
03Pacific Invincible-91
Blue-91
Red-91
Retail-91
03Pacific Prism-93
Blue-93
Gold-93
Red-93
03Pacific Quest for the Cup-95
Blue-95
03Pacific Supreme-92
Blue-92
Red-92
Retail-92
03Parkhurst Orig Six He Shoots/Scores-4
03Parkhurst Orig Six He Shoots/Scores-4A
03Parkhurst Original Six Toronto-6
Memorabilia-TM10
Memorabilia-TM52
03Parkhurst Rookie-8
High Expectations-HE-14
High Expectations Gold-HE-14
03Private Stock Reserve-95
Blue-95
Red-95
Retail-95
03SP Authentic-83
Limited-83
03SP Game Used-45
Gold-45
Authentic Fabrics-AFON
Authentic Fabrics-QSNBM
Authentic Fabrics Gold-AFON
Authentic Fabrics Gold-QSNBM
Authentic Patches-APON
Double Threads-DTSN
Team Threads-TTSNB
03SPx-90
03SPx-150
Radiance-90
Radiance-150
Spectrum-90
Spectrum-150
Fantasy Franchise-FF-NSM
Fantasy Franchise Limited-FF-NSM
Origins-O-ON
03Titanium-184
Hobby Jersey Number Parallels-184
Patches-184
Retail-184
03Topps-75
Blue-75
Gold-75
Red-75
03Topps C55-11
Minis-11
Minis American Back-11
Minis American Back Red-11
Minis Bazooka Back-11
Minis Brooklyn Back-11
Minis Hat Trick Back-11
Minis O Canada Back-11
Minis O Canada Back Red-11
Minis Stanley Cup Back-11
03Topps Pristine-98
Gold Refractor Die Cuts-98
Refractors-98
Press Plates Black-98
Press Plates Cyan-98
Press Plates Magenta-98
Press Plates Yellow-98
03UD Honor Roll-83
03UD Honor Roll-118
Grade A Jerseys-TTOR
03UD Premier Collection-52
NHL Shields-SH-ON
Signatures-PS-ON
Signatures Gold-PS-ON
Teammates-PT-TM1
Teammates Patches-PT-TM1
03Upper Deck-178
Big Playmakers-BP-ON
Canadian Exclusives-178
HG-178
Jerseys-GJ-JB
Jerseys-UD-ON
Power Zone-PZ-8
03Upper Deck Classic Portraits-92
03Upper Deck Classic Portraits-144
03Upper Deck Ice-83
Gold-83
Authentics-IA-ON
Under Glass Autographs-UG-ON
03Upper Deck MVP-392
Gold Script-392
Silver Script-392
Canadian Exclusives-392
Lethal Lineups-LL5
SportsNut-SN83
03Upper Deck Rookie Update-82
03Upper Deck Rookie Update-165
03Upper Deck Rookie Update-175
Skills-SKON
Super Stars-SSON
03Upper Deck Trilogy-92
Limited-92
03Upper Deck Victory-178
Bronze-178
Gold-178
Silver-178
Freshman Flashback-FF43
Game Breakers-GB7
03Toronto Star-86
Foil-11
04Pacific-249
Blue-249
Red-249
04SP Authentic-83
04Upper Deck-163
Canadian Exclusives-163
HG Glossy Gold-163
HG Glossy Silver-163
05Beehive Signature Scrapbook-SSON
05Black Diamond Jerseys-J-ON
05Black Diamond Jerseys Ruby-J-ON
05Black Diamond Jersey Duals-DJ-ON
05Black Diamond Jersey Triples-TJ-ON
05Black Diamond Jersey Quads-QJ-ON
05SP Game Used Authentic Fabrics Dual-MO
05SP Game Used Authentic Fabric Dual Auto-MO
05SP Game Used Authentic Fabrics Quad-DLBN
05SP Game Used Authentic Fabrics Quad-SNSA
05SP Game Used Authentic Patches Quad -DLBN
05SP Game Used Authentic Patches Quad -SNSA
05SP Game Used Authentic Fabrics Triple-NPJ
05SP Game Used Authentic Fabrics Triple-NSL
05SP Game Used Authentic Patches Dual-MO
05SP Game Used Authentic Patch Dual Autos-MO
05SP Game Used Authentic Patches Triple-NPJ
05SP Game Used Authentic Patches Triple-NSL
05SPx-117
Spectrum-117
Winning Combos-WC-NA
Winning Combos-WC-SN
Winning Combos Autographs-AWC-NA
Winning Combos Gold-WC-NA
Winning Combos Gold-WC-SN
Winning Combos Spectrum-WC-NA
Winning Combos Spectrum-WC-SN
Winning Materials-WM-ON
Winning Materials Gold-WM-ON
Winning Materials Spectrum-WM-ON
Xcitement Superstars-XS-ON
Xcitement Superstars Gold-XS-ON
Xcitement Superstars Spectrum-XS-ON
05UD Artifacts-94
05UD Artifacts-197
Blue-94
Blue-197
Gold-94
Gold-197
Green-94
Green-197
Pewter-94
Pewter-197
Red-94
Red-197
Frozen Artifacts-FA-ON
Frozen Artifacts Autographed-FA-ON
Frozen Artifacts Copper-FA-ON
Frozen Artifacts Dual-FAD-ON
Frozen Artifacts Dual Autographed-FAD-ON
Frozen Artifacts Dual Copper-FAD-ON
Frozen Artifacts Dual Gold-FAD-ON
Frozen Artifacts Dual Maroon-FAD-ON
Frozen Artifacts Dual Pewter-FAD-ON
Frozen Artifacts Dual Silver-FAD-ON
Frozen Artifacts Gold-FA-ON
Frozen Artifacts Maroon-FA-ON
Frozen Artifacts Patches-FP-ON
Frozen Artifacts Patches Autographed-FP-ON
Frozen Artifacts Patches Dual-FPD-ON
Frozen Artifacts Patches Dual Autos-FPD-ON
Frozen Artifacts Patches Pewter-FP-ON
Frozen Artifacts Patches Silver-FP-ON
Frozen Artifacts Pewter-FA-ON
Frozen Artifacts Silver-FA-ON
Gold Autographed-94
Gold Autographed-197
05Ultra Fresh Ink-FI-ON
05Ultra Fresh Ink Blue-FI-ON
05Upper Deck-182
Big Playmakers-B-ON
HG Glossy-182
Jerseys-J-ON
Notable Numbers-N-NA
Patches-P-ON
MVP ProSign-P-ON
05Upper Deck Toronto Fall Expo-182
06Beehive-26
Blue-26
Matte-26
Red Facsimile Signatures-26
Wood-26
06O-Pee-Chee-386
Rainbow-386
06SP Authentic-26
Limited-26
06SP Game Used-78
Gold-78
Rainbow-78

Authentic Fabrics Dual-AF2ND
Authentic Fabrics Dual Patches-AF2ND
06SPx SPxcitement-X78
06SPx SPxcitement Spectrum-X78
06Upper Deck Arena Giveaways-PHX5
06Upper Deck-403
Exclusives Parallel-403
High Gloss Parallel-403
Masterpieces-403
Oversized Wal-Mart Exclusives-403
06Upper Deck MVP-230
Gold Script-230
Super Script-230
06Upper Deck Trilogy Honorary Scripted Patches-HSPON
06Upper Deck Trilogy Honorary Scripted Swatches-HSSON
06Upper Deck Victory-265
07Upper Deck Ovation-54
07Upper Deck Victory-196
Black-196
Gold-196

Nolan, Ted
87Sault Ste. Marie Greyhounds-33
89Sault Ste. Marie Greyhounds-3
907th Inn. Sketch OHL-176
917th Inn. Sketch OHL-318
917th Inn. Sketch Memorial Cup-24
93Sault Ste. Marie Greyhounds-29
93Sault Ste. Marie Greyhound Memorial Cup-30

Nolan, Tom
96New Hampshire Wildcats-29
97New Hampshire Wildcats-20
99Mobile Mysticks-8

Nolander, Peter
04Swedish Elitset-256
Gold-256
05Swedish SHL Elitset-107
Gold-107
06Swedish SHL Elitset-149

Nolet, Danny
907th Inn. Sketch QMJHL-266

Nolet, Sebastien
02Rimouski Oceanic-11
03Halifax Mooseheads-16
03P.E.I. Rocket-18

Nolet, Simon
65Quebec Aces-15
68O-Pee-Chee-187
70Colgate Stamps-51
70Flyers Postcards-9
70O-Pee-Chee-194
70Sargent Promotions Stamps-150
71O-Pee-Chee-206
71Sargent Promotions Stamps-145
71Toronto Sun-205
72O-Pee-Chee-125
72Sargent Promotions Stamps-158
72Topps-26
72Finnish Semic World Championship-174
72Swedish Semic World Championship-174
73Flyers Linnett-12
73O-Pee-Chee-222
74NHL Action Stamps-293
74O-Pee-Chee NHL-187
74Topps-187
75O-Pee-Chee NHL-220
75O-Pee-Chee NHL-319
75Topps-220
75Topps-319
76O-Pee-Chee NHL-64
76Rockies Coke Cans-14
76Rockies Puck Bucks-13
76Topps-64
84Nordiques Postcards-18
85Nordiques General Foods-19
85Nordiques Team Issue-16
86Nordiques General Foods-17
01Upper Deck Legends-74

Nolin, Dave
06Victoriaville Tigres-10

Noonan, Brian
87Blackhawks Coke-15
88Blackhawks Coke-14
88O-Pee-Chee-165
88O-Pee-Chee Stickers-11
88O-Pee-Chee Stickers-147
88Panini Stickers-28
88Topps-165
88ProCards IHL-107
90OPC Premier-87
90Pro Set-433
91Pro Set Platinum-165
91Blackhawks Coke-19
91Parkhurst-264
French-264
91Upper Deck-380
French-380
92Bowman-98
92O-Pee-Chee-234
92Panini Stickers-9
92Panini Stickers French-9
92Pinnacle-194
French-194
92Score-89
Canadian-89
92Stadium Club-400
92Topps-159
Gold-159G
92Ultra-280
92Upper Deck-117
93Blackhawks Coke-6
93Donruss-464
93Leaf-398
93OPC Premier-13
Gold-13
93Panini Stickers-149
93Pinnacle-162
Canadian-162
93PowerPlay-314
93Score-411
Canadian-411
93Topps/OPC Premier-13
Gold-13
93Ultra-291
94Canada Games NHL POGS-168
94Donruss-140
94Leaf-217
94OPC Premier-28
Special Effects-28
94Parkhurst-143
Gold-143
94Pinnacle-131
Artist's Proofs-131
Rink Collection-131
94Topps/OPC Premier-28
Special Effects-28
94Upper Deck-302
Electric Ice-302
95Canada Games NHL POGS-237
95Collector's Choice-116
Player's Club-116
Player's Club Platinum-116
95Donruss-242
95Parkhurst International-445
Emerald Ice-445
95Score-156
Black Ice Artist's Proofs-156
Black Ice-156
95Stadium Club-121
Members Only Master Set-121
95Ultra-301
95Upper Deck-272
Electric Ice-272
Electric Ice Gold-272
96Be A Player-201
Autographs-201
Autographs Silver-201
96Collector's Choice-232
96Pinnacle-30
Artist's Proofs-30
Foil-30
Premium Stock-30
Rink Collection-30
97Pacific-339
Copper-339
Emerald Green-339
Ice Blue-339
Red-339
Silver-339
97Score Canucks-18
Platinum-18
Premier-18
98Pacific-432
Ice Blue-432
Red-432
98Upper Deck-378
Exclusives-378
Exclusives 1 of 1-378
Gold Reserve-378
98IHL All-Star Eastern Conference-4
98Indianapolis Ice-1
99Chicago Wolves-10
00Chicago Wolves-19

Noonan, Rick
74Team Canada L'Equipe WHA-18

Norback, Erik
98Swedish UD Choice-14
99Swedish Upper Deck-14
02Swedish SHL-96
Parallel-96
04Swedish Elitset-113
Gold-113
05Swedish SHL Elitset-128

Norberg, Agne
71Swedish Hockey-399

Norberg, Anders
69Swedish Hockey-210

Norberg, Hans
83Swedish Semic Elitserien-23
84Swedish Semic Elitserien-21
85Swedish Panini Stickers-174
86Swedish Panini Stickers-180
87Swedish Panini Stickers-183

Norberg, Kent
89Swedish Semic Elitserien Stickers-189

Norberg, Lennart
69Swedish Hockey-137
69Swedish Hockey-266
70Swedish Hockey-94
70Swedish Hockey-162
71Swedish Hockey-257
72Swedish Stickers-236
73Swedish Stickers-232
81Swedish Semic Hockey VM Stickers-12

Norberg, Niklas
93Swedish Semic Elitserien-13

Norberg, Ulf
83Swedish Semic Elitserien-161
85Swedish Panini Stickers-208

Nord, Bjorn
92Upper Deck-231
92Swedish Semic Elitserien Stickers-84
93Swedish Semic Elitserien-57
94Swedish Leaf-133
95Swedish Leaf-192
95Swedish Upper Deck-42
95Swedish Globe World Championships-24
97Swedish Collector's Choice-38
98Swedish UD Choice-50
99Swedish Upper Deck-36
00German DEL-193
02Swedish SHL-14
Parallel-14
Signatures Series II-4
03Swedish Elite-15
Enforcers-EF8
Signatures II-9
Silver-15

Nord, Nils
56Swedish Alfabilder-106

Nord, Tomas
83Swedish Semic Elitserien-8
84Swedish Semic Elitserien-4
85Swedish Panini Stickers-140
86Swedish Panini Stickers-148
87Swedish Panini Stickers-154
89Swedish Semic Elitserien Stickers-128
90Swedish Semic Elitserien Stickers-205

Nordback, Erik
02Swedish SHL Signatures Series II-3

Nordberg, Robert
90Swedish Semic Elitserien Stickers-245
91Swedish Semic Elitserien Stickers-170
92Swedish Semic Elitserien Stickers-188
93Swedish Semic Elitserien-160
94Swedish Leaf-42
95Swedish Leaf-82
95Swedish Upper Deck-128
97Swedish Collector's Choice-127
98Finnish Keräilysarja-129
99Danish Hockey League-24

Nordblad, Christer
71Finnish Suomi Stickers-289

Nordby, Mikka
04Wisconsin Badgers Women-18

Nordenberg, Kenneth
71Swedish Hockey-188

Nordfeldt, Henrik
93Swedish Semic Elitserien-264
94Swedish Leaf-281
95Swedish Leaf-132
97Swedish Collector's Choice-192
98Swedish UD Choice-194
99Swedish Upper Deck-126
00Swedish Upper Deck-116
02Swedish SHL-203
Parallel-203
03Swedish Elite-66
Enforcers-EF9
Silver-66
05Swedish SHL Elitset-164
Gold-164
06Swedish SHL Elitset-18

Nordgren, Niklas
02Swedish SHL-104
Parallel-104
03Swedish Elite-128
Silver-128
Stars of the Game-9
04Swedish Elitset-128
Gold-128
04Swedish Pure Skills-92
Parallel-92
05Black Diamond-163
Emerald-163
Gold-163
Onyx-163
Ruby-163
05Hot Prospects-192
Autographed Patch Variation-192
Autographed Patch Variation Gold-192
Hot Materials-HMNN
Red Hot-192
05Parkhurst-383
Facsimile Auto Parallel-98
Signatures-NN
05SP Authentic-144
Limited-144
Sign of the Times-NN
05SP Game Used-124
Autographs-124
Gold-124
Rookie Exclusives-NN
Rookie Exclusives Silver-RE-NN
05SPx-141
Spectrum-141
05The Cup-154
Autographed Rookie Patches Gold Rainbow-154
Black Rainbow Rookies-154
Masterpiece Pressplates (Artifacts)-255
Masterpiece Pressplates (Black Diamond)-163
Masterpiece Pressplates (Ice)-147
Masterpiece Pressplates (Rookie Update)-252
Masterpiece Pressplates SPA Autos-144
Masterpiece Pressplates (SP Game Used)-124
Masterpiece Pressplates (SPx)-141
Masterpiece Pressplates (SPx)-141
Masterpiece Pressplates (Trilogy)-235
Masterpiece Pressplates Ult Coll-139
Masterpiece Pressplates Autographs-154
Platinum Rookies-154
05UD Artifacts-255
05Ultimate Collection-139
Gold-139
05Ultra-207
Gold-207
Fresh Ink-FI-NN
Fresh Ink Blue-FI-NN
Ice-207
Rookie Uniformity Jerseys-RU-NN
Rookie Uniformity Jersey Autographs-ARU-NN
Rookie Uniformity Patches-RUP-NN
Rookie Uniformity Patch Autographs-ARP-NN
05Upper Deck-223
HG Glossy-223
Rookie Threads-RTNN
Rookie Threads Autographs-ARTNN
05Upper Deck Ice-147
Premieres Auto Patches-AIPNN
05Upper Deck Rookie Update-252
Inspirations Patch Rookies-252
05Upper Deck Trilogy-235
05Upper Deck Toronto Fall Expo-223
05Swedish SHL Elitset-139
Gold-139

Nordhagen, Chad
98Sioux City Musketeers-16
99Sioux City Musketeers-16

Nordhus, Morten
92Norwegian Elite Series-132

Nordin, Anders
65Swedish Coralli ISHockey-177
67Swedish Hockey-17
67Swedish Hockey-124
69Swedish Hockey-138
70Finnish Jaakiekko-34
70Swedish Hockey-95
70Swedish Hockey-288
70Swedish Masterserien-119
71Swedish Hockey-189
72Swedish Stickers-175
74Swedish Stickers-257
87Swedish Panini Stickers-190

Nordin, Hakan
83Swedish Semic Elitserien-110
84Swedish Semic Elitserien-101
85Swedish Panini Stickers-98
86Swedish Panini Stickers-89
87Swedish Panini Stickers-96
89Swedish Semic Elitserien Stickers-272
90Swedish Semic Elitserien Stickers-31
91Swedish Semic Elitserien Stickers-279

Nordin, Jan-Olof
69Swedish Hockey-89

Nordin, Lars-Ake
69Swedish Hockey-286
70Swedish Hockey-202
71Swedish Hockey-298

Nordin, Stig
71Swedish Hockey-169
73Swedish Stickers-57

Nordin, Urban
89Swedish Semic Elitserien Stickers-181
90Swedish Semic Elitserien Stickers-15

Nordlander, Bert-Ola
57Swedish Alfabilder-84
57Swedish Alfabilder-133
64Swedish Coralli ISHockey-26
64Swedish Coralli ISHockey-34
65Swedish Coralli ISHockey-26
65Swedish Coralli ISHockey-34
67Swedish Hockey-18
67Swedish Hockey-39
69Swedish Hockey-50
69Swedish Hockey-194
70Swedish Hockey-7
70Swedish Masterserien-52
71Finnish Suomi Stickers-54
71Swedish Hockey-9
71Swedish Hockey-81
72Finnish Panda Toronto-74
72Finnish Semic World Championship-48
72Swedish Stickers-56
72Swedish Semic World Championship-48
73Swedish Stickers-195
81Swedish Semic Hockey VM Stickers-112
98Swedish UD Choice-203

Nordlinder, Per
83Swedish Semic Elitserien-137

Nordlund, Birger
67Swedish Hockey-210

Nordlund, Markus
06Finnish Cardset-106

Nordmark, Robert
83Swedish Semic Elitserien-60
84Swedish Semic Elitserien-173
85Swedish Panini Stickers-160
86Swedish Panini Stickers-167
87Blues Kodak-19
88Canucks Mohawk-14
89Canucks Mohawk-13
89O-Pee-Chee Stickers-66
90Canucks Mohawk-22
90O-Pee-Chee-433
90Pro Set-547
91Canucks Panini Team Stickers-18
91Swedish Semic Elitserien Stickers-256
92Swedish Semic Elitserien Stickers-285
93Swedish Semic Elitserien-59
94Swedish Leaf-131
95Finnish SISU-302
95Finnish SISU-378
Double Trouble-4
95Finnish SISU Limited-32
96Finnish SISU Redline Sledgehammers-2
96Swiss HNL-182
00UK Nottingham Panthers-21
00UK Nottingham Panthers-NA
00UK Sekonda Superleague-200

Nordnes, Kare
92Norwegian Elite Series-117

Nordnes, Magne
92Norwegian Elite Series-118

Nordquist, Jonas
03Swedish Elite-232
Silver-232
04Swedish Elitset-221
Gold-221
05Swedish Lulea Hockey Postcards-12
05Swedish SHL Elitset-89
Gold-89
06Norfolk Admirals-12

Nordqvist, Nicklas
94Swedish Leaf-277
95Swedish Leaf-244
98Swedish UD Choice-121
99Swedish Upper Deck-123

Nordstrom, Carlin
91Air Canada SJHL-A46
97Fort Wayne Komets-17

Nordstrom, Jan Hroar
92Norwegian Elite Series-21

Nordstrom, Peter
94Swedish Leaf-180
95Swedish Leaf-214
95Swedish Upper Deck-73
97Swedish Collector's Choice-52
98Pacific Dynagon Ice-13
Blue-13
Red-13
98Upper Deck-220
Exclusives-220
Exclusives 1 of 1-220
Gold Reserve-220
98Providence Bruins-16
99Danish Hockey League-25
99Swedish Upper Deck-59
SHL Signatures-5
Snapshots-6
00Swedish Upper Deck-88
02Swedish SHL-173
Parallel-173
03Swedish Elite-39
Silver-39
04Swedish Elitset-42
Gold-42
04Swedish Pure Skills-31
Parallel-31
05Swedish SHL Elitset-47
06Swedish SHL Elitset-49

Nordstrom, Roger
90Swedish Semic Elitserien Stickers-126
91Swedish Semic Elitserien Stickers-177
92Swedish Semic Elitserien Stickers-200
93Swedish Semic Elitserien-171
94Swedish Leaf-188
Studio Signatures-8
95Finnish Semic World Championships-52
95Finnish Semic World Championships-209
95Swedish Leaf-258
Mega-7
Spidermen-14
95Swedish Upper Deck-133
95Swedish Globe World Championships-2
95Swedish World Championships Stickers-136
97Swedish Collector's Choice-133
98German DEL-39
99German DEL-145
00German DEL-152
01German Upper Deck-161
Goalies in Action-G6
Jersey Cards-RN-J
02German DEL City Press-227

Nordstrom, Ronny
64Swedish Coralli ISHockey-163
65Swedish Coralli ISHockey-163

Noreau, Maxim
04Victoriaville Tigres-1
05Victoriaville Tigres-13
06Victoriaville Tigres-5

Norell, Rolf
67Swedish Hockey-163

Noren, Darryl
90ProCards AHL/IHL-525
91Greensboro Monarchs-11
92Greensboro Monarchs-12
97Charlotte Checkers-16
97Charlotte Checkers-25
98Charlotte Checkers-11
99Charlotte Checkers-17
99Charlotte Checkers-35

Norgaard, Rasmus
98Danish Hockey League-137

Norgren, Christoffer
02Swedish SHL-48
Parallel-48
02Bakersfield Condors-12
03Swedish Elite-213
Silver-213
04Swedish Elitset-204
Gold-204
05Swedish SHL Elitset-72
Gold-72
06German DEL-178
06Swedish SHL Elitset-71

Norgren, Johan
90Swedish Semic Elitserien Stickers-134
91Swedish Semic Elitserien Stickers-185
92Upper Deck-225
92Swedish Semic Elitserien Stickers-204
93Swedish Semic Elitserien-173
94Swedish Leaf-8
97Swedish Collector's Choice-168
98German DEL-115
99German DEL-287
00German DEL-41
02Swedish Malmo Red Hawks-18
02Swedish SHL-232
Parallel-232
03Swedish Elite-240
Silver-240
04Swedish Elitset-86
Gold-86
04Swedish Malmo Red Hawks-16

Noris, Joe
71Penguins Postcards-13
71Toronto Sun-222
73Sabres Postcards-9
76O-Pee-Chee WHA-46
77O-Pee-Chee WHA-5

Norlen, Darryl
96Charlotte Checkers-12

Norman, Brodie
93Quebec Pee-Wee Tournament-1240

Norman, Glen
99Austin Ice Bats-12
01Austin Ice Bats-23

Norman, Todd
93Guelph Storm-12
94Slapshot Promos-4
94Parkhurst SE-SE267
Gold-SE267
94Select-168
Gold-168
94SP-185
Die Cuts-185
94Guelph Storm-19
95Slapshot-99
95Guelph Storm-8
95Classic-85
95Signature Rookies Auto-Phonex-31
95Signature Rook Auto-Phonex Phone Cards-31
96Guelph Storm-15
96Guelph Storm-32
96Guelph Storm Premier Collection-1
97Bowman CHL-28
OPC-28
03St. Francis Xavier X-Men-26

Normand, Dean
91Air Canada SJHL-A1
92Saskatchewan JHL-29

Normandin, Eric
96Rimouski Oceanic-19
96Rimouski Oceanic Quebec Police-18
97Rimouski Oceanic-19
97Bowman CHL-77
OPC-77
98Johnstown Chiefs-23

Normandin, Mathieu
92Quebec Pee-Wee Tournament-211
96Rimouski Oceanic-20
96Rimouski Oceanic Quebec Police-19

Normio, Teemu
01Finnish Cardset-302
04Finnish Cardset-269
05Finnish Cardset -109
06Finnish Cardset-276

Noronen, Mika
97Black Diamond-26
Double Diamond-26
Triple Diamond-26
Quadruple Diamond-26
98UD Choice-278
Prime Choice Reserve-278
Reserve-278
98Finnish Keräilysarja-205
Mad Masks-10
99Finnish Cardset Most Wanted-7
99Finnish Cardset Par Avion-9
00BAP Memorabilia-448
Emerald-448
Ruby-448
Sapphire-448
00BAP Parkhurst 2000-P122
00BAP Signature Series-252
Emerald-252
Ruby-252
Sapphire-252
Autographs-214
Autographs Gold-214
00Private Stock-106
Gold-106
Premiere Date-106
Retail-106
Silver-106
00Stadium Club-238
00Topps Heritage-133
00Topps Premier Plus-92
Blue Ice-92
00Vanguard-106
Pacific Proofs-106
00Rochester Americans-19
01BAP Memorabilia-24
Emerald-24
Ruby-24
Sapphire-24
01Between the Pipes-45
01O-Pee-Chee-272
01O-Pee-Chee Premier Parallel-272
01Parkhurst-280
01Parkhurst Beckett Promos-280
01SP Game Used Authentic Fabric-AFMN
01SP Game Used Authentic Fabric Gold-AFMN
01SPx-97
01Titanium Draft Day Edition-112
01Topps-272
OPC Parallel-272
01Topps Chrome-139
Refractors-139
Black Border Refractors-139
01UD Mask Collection Goalie Jerseys-SYMN
01Upper Deck Victory-364
Gold-364
01Finnish Cardset Haltmeisters-5
02BAP First Edition-71
Jerseys-71
02BAP Signature Series-82
Autographs-82
Autograph Buybacks 2000-214
Autographs Gold-82
02Between the Pipes-73
Gold-73
Silver-73
Emblems-20
Jerseys-20
Numbers-20
Stick and Jerseys-20
Tandems-6
02O-Pee-Chee-299
02O-Pee-Chee Premier Blue Parallel-299
02O-Pee-Chee Premier Red Parallel-299
02O-Pee-Chee Factory Set-299
02Pacific-46
Blue-46
Red-46
02Pacific Calder-58
Silver-58
02Pacific Complete-2
Red-2
02Pacific Exclusive-19
02Parkhurst-174
Bronze-174
Gold-174
Silver-174
02Sabres Team Issue-10
02SP Game Used First Rounder Patches-NO
02Topps-299
OPC Blue Parallel-299
OPC Red Parallel-299
Factory Set-299
02UD Mask Collection-11
02UD Mask Collection-12
02UD Mask Collection Beckett Promos-11
02UD Mask Collection Beckett Promos-12
02UD Top Shelf Dual Player Jerseys-STBN
02UD Top Shelf Stopper Jerseys-SSMN
02Upper Deck Goaltender Threads-MN
02Upper Deck Goaltender Threads Gold-MN
02Upper Deck Vintage-320
02Finnish Cardset-234
03BAP Memorabilia-145
Emerald-145
Gold-145
Ruby-145
Sapphire-145
Deep in the Crease-D13
Future Wave-FW-10
03Beehive Sticks Beige Border-BE21
03ITG Action-62
Jerseys-M59
03Pacific-43
Blue-43
Red-43
03Pacific Calder-12
Silver-12
03Pacific Complete-454
Red-454
03Upper Deck Ice-9
03Upper Deck MVP-62
Gold Script-62
Silver Script-62
Canadian Exclusives-62
03Upper Deck Rookie Update-11
04Pacific-34
Blue-34
Red-34
04SP Authentic-11
Limited-11
Buybacks-146
Buybacks-147
Buybacks-148
Buybacks-149
Buybacks-150
Sign of the Times-SS-FIN
04UD All-World-15
Gold-15
Autographs-15
Dual Autographs-AD-HN
04Ultimate Collection Buybacks-63
04Ultimate Collection Buybacks-64
04Upper Deck-21
Canadian Exclusives-21
HG Glossy Gold-21
HG Glossy Silver-21
04Finnish Cardset-218
Stars of the Game-8
04Swedish Pure Skills-108
Parallel-108
The Wall-MN
04ITG Heroes/Prospects He Shoots/Scores-32
04ITG Heroes and Prospects Net Prospects-31
04ITG Heroes and Prosp Net Prospects Gold-31
05Parkhurst-482
05SP Game Used Authentic Fabrics Dual-BN
05SP Game Used Authentic Fabrics Dual-LN
05SP Game Used Authentic Fabric Dual Auto-LN
05SP Game Used Authentic Fabrics Quad-MNDB
05SP Game Used Authentic Patches Quad -MNDB
05SP Game Used Authentic Fabrics Triple-NKL
05SP Game Used Authentic Patches Dual-BN
05SP Game Used Authentic Patches Dual-LN
05SP Game Used Authentic Patch Dual Autos-LN
05SP Game Used Authentic Patches Triple-NKL
05SP Game Used Auto Draft-AD-NO
05SPx Winning Combos-WC-BN
05SPx Winning Combos Autographs-AWC-BN
05SPx Winning Combos Gold-WC-BN
05SPx Winning Combos Spectrum-WC-BN
05UD Artifacts Auto Facts-AF-NO
05UD Artifacts Auto Facts Blue-AF-NO
05UD Artifacts Auto Facts Copper-AF-NO
05UD Artifacts Auto Facts Pewter-AF-NO
05UD Artifacts Auto Facts Silver-AF-NO
05UD Artifacts Remarkable Artifacts-RA-MN
05UD Artifacts Remarkable Artifacts Dual-RA-MN
05UD PowerPlay Power Marks-PMNO
05Ultra-29
Gold-29
Ice-29
05Upper Deck-23
HG Glossy-23
Jerseys Series II-J2NO
Notable Numbers-N-NO
Patches-P-MN
05Upper Deck MVP-47
Gold-47
Platinum-47
05Upper Deck Toronto Fall Expo-23
05Finnish Cardset -24
Finnish Cardset Super Snatchers-3
06Fleer Fabricology-FNO
06Ultra Fresh Ink-IMN
06Upper Deck MVP-289
Gold Script-289
Super Script-289

Norppa, Timo
92Finnish Jyvas-Hyva Stickers-61
93Finnish Jyvas-Hyva Stickers-117
93Finnish SISU-14
93Swedish Semic World Champ Stickers-70
94Finnish SISU-274
94Finnish Jaa Kiekko-48
95Finnish SISU-296
96Finnish SISU Redline-90

Norrena, Fredrik
94Finnish SISU-97
95Finnish SISU-324
Ghost Goalies-5
95Finnish SISU Limited-1
96Finnish SISU Redline-135
96Finnish SISU Redline Foil Parallels-135
96Finnish SISU Redline Mighty Adversaries-7
98Finnish Keräilysarja-227
Mad Masks-11
99Finnish Cardset-131
00Finnish Cardset-93
01Finnish Cardset-349
01Finnish Cardset Haltmeisters-10
02Finnish Cardset-84
02Swedish SHL-272
02Swedish SHL-294
Masks-9
Parallel-272
Parallel-294
03Swedish Elite-23
03Swedish Elite-210
Signatures-10
Silver-23
Silver-210
04Swedish Elitset-60
Gold-60
In The Crease-6
Signatures Series A-4
04Swedish Pure Skills-41
Parallel-41
The Wall-FN
05Swedish SHL Elitset-69
Catchers-7
Catchers Gold-7
Gold-69
Series Two Jerseys-GWFN
Series Two Signatures-19
Stoppers-8
06Beehive-115
Matte-115
06Black Diamond-162A
Black-162A
Gold-162A
Ruby-162A
06Hot Prospects-109
Red Hot-109
White Hot-109
06O-Pee-Chee-542
06O-Pee-Chee-634
Rainbow-542
Rainbow-634
06SP Authentic-231
Limited-231
06SP Game Used-112
Gold-112
Rainbow-112
Autographs-112
Rookie Exclusives Autographs-RENO
06SPx-157
Spectrum-157
06The Cup-123
Autographed Rookie Masterpiece Pressplates-123
Gold Rainbow Autographed Rookie Patches-123
Masterpiece Pressplates (Bee Hive)-115
Masterpiece Pressplates (Black Diamond)-162
Masterpiece Pressplates (Marquee Rookies)-542
Masterpiece Pressplates (MVP)-317
Masterpiece Pressplates (SP Authentic)-231
Masterpiece Pressplates (SP Game Used)-112
Masterpiece Pressplates (SPx)-157
Masterpiece Pressplates (Sweet Beginnings)-118
Masterpiece Pressplates (Trilogy)-110
Masterpiece Pressplates (Ultimate Collection)-71
Masterpiece Pressplates (Victory)-288
Rookies Black-123
Rookies Platinum-123
06UD Artifacts-239
06Ultimate Collection-71
Ultimate Debut Threads Jerseys-DJ-NO
Ultimate Debut Threads Jerseys Autographs-DJ-NO
Ultimate Debut Threads Patches-DJ-NO
Ultimate Debut Threads Patches Autographs-DJ-NO
06Upper Deck-208
Exclusives Parallel-208
High Gloss Parallel-208
Masterpieces-208
Rookie Materials-RMNO
Rookie Materials Patches-RMNO
06Upper Deck MVP-317
Gold Script-317
Super Script-317
06Upper Deck Sweet Shot-118
Rookie Jerseys Autographs-118
06Upper Deck Trilogy-110
06Upper Deck Victory-288
06Swedish SHL Elitset Goal Patrol-11
06Swedish SHL Elitset In The Crease-6
07Upper Deck Victory-124
Black-124
Gold-124

Norrie, Jason
95Seattle Thunderbirds-19
98Charlotte Checkers-12

Norrie, Shaun
99Calgary Hitmen-20
99Calgary Hitmen Autographs-20
00Calgary Hitmen-20

Norrington, Marc
06Fayetteville FireAntz-11

Norris, Bruce A
83Hall of Fame Postcards-N10
85Hall of Fame-205

Norris, Clayton
907th Inn. Sketch WHL-30
917th Inn. Sketch WHL-318
97St. John's Maple Leafs-18
98Orlando Solar Bears-4
98Orlando Solar Bears II-8
00UK Cardiff Devils-4
00UK Sekonda Superleague-55
01UK Cardiff Devils-1
01UK Nottingham Panthers-3
02UK Cardiff Devils-1

Norris, Dave
75Hamilton Fincups-13
99Fort Wayne Komets Penalty Leaders-6

Norris, Dwayne
92Classic-70
Gold-70
92Classic Four-Sport *-195
Gold-195
Autographs-195A
93Alberta International Team Canada-15
93Donruss-480
93OPC Premier Team Canada-13
93PowerPlay-491
93Ultra-470
93Classic Pro Prospects-66
94Leaf-494
94Score-238
Gold-238
Platinum-238
Team Canada-CT7
95Images-34
Gold-34
96German DEL-351
98German DEL-13
99German DEL-107
00German DEL-130
01German Upper Deck-145
02German DEL City Press-202
03German DEL-101
All-Stars-AS8
04German DEL-112
05German DEL-91
All-Star Jerseys-AS12
Star Attack-ST05
06German DEL-59

Norris, Jack
70Esso Power Players-145
70O-Pee-Chee-165
72 7-Eleven Slurpee Cups WHA-16
75O-Pee-Chee WHA-114
75Phoenix Roadrunners WHA-20

Norris, James
64Beehive Group III Photos-194
69O-Pee-Chee-228
70O-Pee-Chee-257
72Topps-172
83Hall of Fame-145
83Hall of Fame Postcards-D11
83Hall of Fame Postcards-K11
85Hall of Fame-57
85Hall of Fame-145
03BAP Ultimate Memorabilia Memorialized-5
03BAP Ultimate Memorabilia Paper Cuts-27
04Ultimate Collection-56
04Upper Deck-204
Canadian Exclusives-204
HG Glossy Gold-204
HG Glossy Silver-204
05ITG Ultimate Memorabilia Builders Autos-4
06Beehive 5 X 7 Cherry Wood-JNT

Norris, Joe
76San Diego Mariners WHA-8

Norris, Warren
97St. John's Maple Leafs-19
00UK Sekonda Superleague-156
00UK Sheffield Steelers-17
02UK Sheffield Steelers-14

Norrish, Rod
73North Stars Postcards-13

Norrman, Hans-Ove
57Swedish Alfabilder-105

Norrstrom, Rune
69Swedish Hockey-232
71Swedish Hockey-374

Norstebo, Svein Enok
92Norwegian Elite Series-102
93Swedish Semic World Champ Stickers-234
94Finnish Jaa Kiekko-255
95Swedish Globe World Championships-197
95Swedish World Championships Stickers-241
96Swedish Semic Wien-205
99Norwegian National Team-10

Norstrom, Claes
84Swedish Semic Elitserien-125

Norstrom, Hakan
71Swedish Hockey-304
72Swedish Stickers-260

Norstrom, Mattias
91Swedish Semic Elitserien Stickers-12
92Swedish Semic Elitserien Stickers-30
93Donruss-465
93Leaf-426
93OPC Premier-418
Gold-418
93Parkhurst-256
Emerald Ice-256
93Stadium Club-371
Members Only Master Set-371
First Day Issue-371
93Topps/OPC Premier-418
Gold-418
93Ultra-376
93Upper Deck-522
94Leaf-57
94Parkhurst-152
Gold-152
94Pinnacle-489
Artist's Proofs-489
Rink Collection-489
Rookie Team Pinnacle-2
94Select Promos-194
94Select-194
Gold-194
94Ultra-334
94Upper Deck-418
Electric Ice-418
94Binghamton Rangers-15
94Classic-96
Gold-96
94Classic Pro Prospects-5
95Donruss-248
95Leaf-288
95Parkhurst International-143
Emerald Ice-143
95Ultra-106
Gold Medallion-106
96Collector's Choice-130
96SP-76
96Topps Picks-171
OPC Inserts-171
96Ultra-80
Gold Medallion-80
96Upper Deck-277
96Collector's Edge Ice-20
Prism-20
97Be A Player-38
Autographs-38
Autographs Die-Cuts-38

Autographs Prismatic Die-Cuts-38
97Pacific Invincible NHL Regime-94
97Panini Stickers-219
97Upper Deck-82
98OPC Chrome-136
Refractors-136
98Panini Stickers-206
98Topps-136
O-Pee-Chee-136
98Upper Deck-289
Exclusives-289
Exclusives 1 of 1-289
Gold Reserve-289
99BAP Millennium-127
Emerald-127
Ruby-127
Sapphire-127
Signatures-127
Signatures Gold-127
99Pacific-194
Copper-194
Emerald Green-194
Gold-194
Ice Blue-194
Premiere Date-194
Red-194
99Panini Stickers-253
99Stadium Club Promos-PP5
99Stadium Club-133
First Day Issue-133
One of a Kind-133
Printing Plates Black-133
Printing Plates Cyan-133
Printing Plates Magenta-133
Printing Plates Yellow-133
00O-Pee-Chee-259A
00O-Pee-Chee Parallel-259A
00Panini Stickers-170
00Topps/OPC-259A
Parallel-259A
00Upper Deck-310
Exclusives Tier 1-310
Exclusives Tier 2-310
00Upper Deck Vintage-168
01Upper Deck-312
Exclusives-312
02Kings Team Issue-3
02BAP First Edition-173
02BAP Sig Series Auto Buybacks 1999-127
02Kings Game Sheets-25
02Kings Game Sheets-26
02Topps Total-322
02UD Honor Roll-84
02Upper Deck-81
Exclusives-81
02Upper Deck Vintage-116
03ITG Action-236
03Upper Deck-335
Canadian Exclusives-335
HG-335
UD Exclusives-335
03Upper Deck MVP-202
Gold Script-202
Silver Script-202
Canadian Exclusives-202
04Upper Deck-83
Canadian Exclusives-83
HG Glossy Gold-83
HG Glossy Silver-83
04Swedish Alfabilder Alfa Stars-14
04Swedish Alfabilder Alfa Star Golden Ice-11
04Swedish Alfabilder Proof Parallels-14
05Kings Team Issue-11
05Panini Stickers-287
05Parkhurst-231
05Parkhurst-514
Facsimile Auto Parallel-231
Facsimile Auto Parallel-514
05Upper Deck-90
HG Glossy-90
05Upper Deck MVP-182
Gold-182
Platinum-182
05Upper Deck Toronto Fall Expo-90
06Be A Player-73
Autographs-73
Signatures-NO
06O-Pee-Chee-233
Rainbow-233
06Panini Stickers-283
06Upper Deck-342
Exclusives Parallel-342
High Gloss Parallel-342
Masterpieces-342

North, Oliver
93Arizona Icecats-20

Northard, Jason
91British Columbia JHL-80
92British Columbia JHL-114

Northcott, Baldy
33O-Pee-Chee V304B-60
33V129-49
33V252 Canadian Gum-40
33V357 Ice Kings-48
34Beehive Group I Photos-201
34Sweet Caporal-23
36O-Pee-Chee V304D-130
36Triumph Postcards-7
37O-Pee-Chee V304E-166
37V356 Worldwide Gum-22
04ITG Ultimate Mem Marvelous Maroons-2
04ITG Ultimate Memorabilia Paper Cuts-15
05ITG Ultimate Mem Marvelous Maroons Auto-4
06ITG Ultimate Memorabilia Marvelous Maroons Autos-1

Northey, William M
83Hall of Fame Postcards-L12
85Hall of Fame-161

Norton, Brad
99Hamilton Bulldogs-3
00Hamilton Bulldogs-6
01BAP Memorabilia-407
Emerald-407
Ruby-407
Sapphire-407
01SPx-205
01Upper Deck Ice-137
01Hershey Bears-19
05Binghamton Senators-8
05Binghamton Senators Quickway-8

Norton, Chris
88ProCards AHL-187
89ProCards AHL-43
90Moncton Hawks-18
90ProCards AHL/IHL-252
91ProCards-386

Norton, Darcy
86Kamloops Blazers-14
87Kamloops Blazers-15
88ProCards IHL-27
89ProCards IHL-77
90ProCards AHL/IHL-320
91ProCards-321
92Cincinnati Cyclones-19
93Birmingham Bulls Birmingham News-17
93Cincinnati Cyclones-19

Norton, Jeff
89Islanders Team Issue-14
89O-Pee-Chee-120
89Panini Stickers-273
89Topps-120
90Bowman-122
Tiffany-122
90O-Pee-Chee-166
90Panini Stickers-93
90Pro Set-189
90Score-157
Canadian-157
90Score Hottest/Rising Stars-70
90Topps-166
Tiffany-166
90Upper Deck-386
French-386
91Pro Set Platinum-78
91Bowman-225
91O-Pee-Chee-243
91Panini Stickers-248
91Parkhurst-331
French-331
91Pinnacle-172
French-172
91Pro Set-148
French-148
91Score American-222
91Score Canadian Bilingual-222
91Score Canadian English-222
91Score Young Superstars-16
91Stadium Club-98
91Topps-243
91Upper Deck-357
French-357
92Panini Stickers-205
92Panini Stickers French-205
92Parkhurst-337
Emerald Ice-337
92Pinnacle-102
French-102
92Score-56
Canadian-56
92Stadium Club-324
92Topps Gold-526G
92Ultra-349
93Donruss-303
93Leaf-390
93OPC Premier-447
Gold-447
93Panini Stickers-64
93Parkhurst-455
Emerald Ice-455
93Pinnacle-353
Canadian-353
93PowerPlay-223
93Score-69
93Score-522
Gold-522
Canadian-69
Canadian-522
Canadian Gold-522
93Stadium Club-495
Members Only Master Set-495
First Day Issue-495
93Topps/OPC Premier-447
Gold-447
93Ultra-417
93Upper Deck-512
94Be A Player-R57
Signature Cards-90
94Canada Games NHL POGS-218
94Donruss-132
94Flair-168
94Leaf-98
94Pinnacle-99
Artist's Proofs-99
Rink Collection-99
94Stadium Club-86
Members Only Master Set-86
First Day Issue-86
Super Team Winner Cards-86
94Ultra-199
95Canada Games NHL POGS-244
95Collector's Choice-112
Player's Club-112
Player's Club Platinum-112
95Donruss-117
95Leaf-74
95Parkhurst International-349
Emerald Ice-349
95Pinnacle-188
Artist's Proofs-188
Rink Collection-188
95Score-178
Black Ice Artist's Proofs-178
Black Ice-178
95Topps-69
OPC Inserts-69
95Upper Deck-160
Electric Ice-160
Electric Ice Gold-160
96Be A Player-187
Autographs-187
Autographs Silver-187
96Oilers Postcards-6
96Topps Picks-157
OPC Inserts-157
96Ultra-61
Gold Medallion-61
99Upper Deck Victory-255
00Upper Deck-378
Exclusives Tier 1-378
Exclusives Tier 2-378
01Pacific-342
Extreme LTD-342
Hobby LTD-342
Premiere Date-342
Retail LTD-342
01Pacific Arena Exclusives-342

Norton, Steve
92Michigan State Spartans-18
93Michigan State Spartans-15

Norwich, Craig
79Panini Stickers-209
79Jets Postcards-20
80O-Pee-Chee-53
80Topps-53

Norwood, Justin
93Quebec Pee-Wee Tournament-570

Norwood, Lee
80Nordiques Postcards-19
81Capitals Team Issue-12
82Capitals Team Issue-18
87Red Wings Little Caesars-20
88O-Pee-Chee-240
88Red Wings Little Caesars-16
89O-Pee-Chee-75
89O-Pee-Chee Stickers-251
89Panini Stickers-68
89Red Wings Little Caesars-13
89Topps-75
90Devils Team Issue-20
90O-Pee-Chee-285
90Panini Stickers-202
90Pro Set-74
90Score Rookie/Traded-74T
90Topps-285
Tiffany-285
90Upper Deck-78
French-78
91Panini Stickers-214
91Parkhurst-373
French-373
91Score Canadian Bilingual-528
91Score Canadian English-528
91Stadium Club-317

Nose, Virgil
90Rayside-Balfour Jr. Canadians-15
91Rayside-Balfour Jr. Canadians-13

Nosek, David
99Czech OFS-199
99Czech OFS-414
00Czech OFS-220
01Czech OFS-129
02Czech OFS Plus-96
02Czech OFS Plus All-Star Game-H17
02Czech OFS Plus Trios-T17
04Czech OFS-286
05Czech HC Hame Zlin-12
06Czech OFS-236

Nosek, Martin
99Czech Score Blue 2000-70
99Czech Score Red Ice 2000-70
01Czech OFS-151
02Czech OFS Plus-334
03Czech OFS Plus-139

Noseworthy, Dave
897th Inn. Sketch OHL-44

Nosov, Artem
03Russian Under-18 Team-16

Notermann, Jason
03ECHL All-Stars-255
03Johnstown Chiefs-15
03Johnstown Chiefs RBI Sports-222
04Atlantic City Boardwalk Bullies-9
05Rockford Ice Hogs-11
06Rockford IceHogs -19

Nottingham, Mike
84Kamloops Blazers-18
85Kamloops Blazers-17

Nourislamov, Evgueni
01Drummondville Voltigeurs-3
02Drummondville Voltigeurs-2

Novak, Aaron
93Minnesota-Duluth Bulldogs-23
98Wichita Thunder-18
99Wichita Thunder-17
00Wichita Thunder-16

Novak, Brett
01Prince Albert Raiders-15
02Prince Albert Raiders-17
03Prince Albert Raiders-4
04Prince Albert Raiders-16
05Prince Albert Raiders-16

Novak, Eduard
71Finnish Suomi Stickers-34
71Swedish Hockey-57
72Finnish Semic World Championship-37
72Swedish Semic World Championship-37
74Swedish Semic World Champ Stickers-75
94German First League-419
97Czech APS Extraliga-51
99Czech OFS-323
00Czech OFS-107

Novak, Filip
99UD Prospects-52
01Regina Pats-18
02Czech DS-49
02Czech DS-70
02AHL Top Prospects-31
04San Antonio Rampage-5
04ITG Heroes and Prospects-20
Autographs-FN
04ITG Heroes/Prospects Toronto Expo '05-20
04ITG Heroes/Prospects Expo Heroes/Pros-20
05ITG Heroes/Prosp Toronto Expo Parallel -394
05AHL All-Stars-23
05Binghamton Senators-9
05Binghamton Senators Quickway-9
05ITG Heroes and Prospects-394
Autographs Update-A-FN
06Flair Showcase-146
Parallel-146
06Fleer-211
Tiffany-211
06Hot Prospects-110
Red Hot-110
White Hot-110
Hotagraphs-HFN
06O-Pee-Chee-530
Rainbow-530
06SPx-152
Spectrum-152
06The Cup-122
Autographed Rookie Masterpiece Pressplates-122
Gold Rainbow Autographed Rookie Patches-122
Masterpiece Pressplates (Artifacts)-227
Masterpiece Pressplates (Marquee Rookies)-530
Masterpiece Pressplates (MVP)-335
Masterpiece Pressplates (Power Play)-119
Masterpiece Pressplates (SPx)-152
Masterpiece Pressplates (Trilogy)-109
Masterpiece Pressplates (Victory)-211
Rookies Black-122
Rookies Platinum-122
06UD Artifacts-227
Blue-227
Gold-227
Platinum-227
Radiance-227
Red-227
06UD Powerplay-119
Impact Rainbow-119
06Ultimate Collection Ultimate Debut Threads Jerseys-DJ-FN
06Ultimate Collection Ultimate Debut Threads Jerseys Autographs-DJ-FN
06Ultimate Collection Ultimate Debut Threads Patches-DJ-FN
06Ultimate Collection Ultimate Debut Threads Patches Autographs-DJ-FN
06Ultra-219
Gold Medallion-219
Ice Medallion-219
06Upper Deck-209
Exclusives Parallel-209
High Gloss Parallel-209
Masterpieces-209
Rookie Materials-RMFN
Rookie Materials Patches-RMFN
06Upper Deck MVP-335
Gold Script-335
Super Script-335
06Upper Deck Ovation-34
06Upper Deck Trilogy-109
06Upper Deck Victory-211
06Upper Deck Victory Black-211
06Upper Deck Victory Gold-211
06Binghamton Senators 5th Anniversary-20
06Syracuse Crunch-4

Novak, Jack
52Juniors Blue Tint-125

Novak, Jan
97Czech APS Extraliga-156
98Czech OFS-215
99Czech OFS-50
00Czech DS Extraliga-112
00Czech OFS-86
01Czech OFS-274
02Czech OFS Plus-246
03Czech OFS Plus-186
03Czech OFS Plus MS Praha-SE40
04Czech HC Slavia Praha Postcards-14
04Czech OFS-171
Czech/Slovak-10
Defence Points-3
04Czech Zuma-1
04Czech Zuma Stars-Z4
04Czech World Championship Postcards-13
05Czech HC Slavia Praha-11
06Czech LG Hockey Games Postcards-13
06Czech OFS All Stars-3
06Czech OFS Defenders-2

Novak, Jiri
73Finnish Jaakiekko-58
74Swedish Semic World Champ Stickers-65
79Panini Stickers-82

Novak, Lukas
98Czech OFS-309

Novak, Martin
04Belleville Bulls-15

Novak, Richard
89ProCards IHL-106

Novak, Rob
99Des Moines Buccaneers-13

Novak, Vaclav
98Czech OFS-144
99Czech OFS-397
99Czech OFS-399
00Czech OFS-310
01Czech OFS-34
02Czech OFS Plus-162
03Czech OFS Plus-118
04Czech OFS-74
06Czech HC Liberec Postcards-6

Novock, Frank
00Richmond Renegades-14
01Roanoke Express-14
02Roanoke Express-21
02Roanoke Express RBI Sports-200

Novodor, Stephen
93Quebec Pee-Wee Tournament-1256

Novopashin, Vitali
00Russian Hockey League-89

Novoseltsev, Ivan
99BAP Memorabilia-339
Gold-339
Silver-339
99BAP Millennium Calder Candidates Ruby-C48
99BAP Millennium Calder Candidate Emerald-C48
99BAP Millennium Calder Cand Sapphire-C48
99Black Diamond-42
Diamond Cut-42
Final Cut-42
99Crown Royale-61
Limited Series-61
Premiere Date-61
Prospects Parallel-61
99Pacific Dynagon Ice-91
Blue-91
Copper-91
Gold-91
Premiere Date-91
99Pacific Omega-104
Copper-104
Gold-104
Ice Blue-104
Premiere Date-104
99Paramount-258
99SP Authentic-104
99Stadium Club-172
First Day Issue-172
One of a Kind-172
Printing Plates Black-172
Printing Plates Cyan-172
Printing Plates Magenta-172
Printing Plates Yellow-172
99Topps Arena Giveaways-FLO-IN
99Topps Premier Plus-109
Parallel-109
99Ultimate Victory-99
1/1-99
Parallel-99
Parallel 100-99
99Upper Deck Arena Giveaways-FP1
99Upper Deck MVP SC Edition-80
Gold Script-80
Silver Script-80
Super Script-80
99Upper Deck Ovation-28
Standing Ovation-28
99Upper Deck Victory-371
99Wayne Gretzky Hockey-74
99Louisville Panthers-6
99Bowman CHL-150
Gold-150
OPC International-150
00BAP Memorabilia-218
Emerald-218
Ruby-218
Sapphire-218
Promos-218
00BAP Mem Chicago Sportsfest Copper-218
00BAP Memorabilia Chicago Sportsfest Blue-218
00BAP Memorabilia Chicago Sportsfest Gold-218
00BAP Memorabilia Chicago Sportsfest Ruby-218
00BAP Memorabilia Chicago Sun-Times Ruby-218
00BAP Memorabilia Chicago Sun-Times Gold-218
00BAP Mem Chicago Sun-Times Sapphire-218
00BAP Mem Toronto Fall Expo Copper-218
00BAP Memorabilia Toronto Fall Expo Gold-218
00BAP Memorabilia Toronto Fall Expo Ruby-218
00Crown Royale-124
00O-Pee-Chee-282
00O-Pee-Chee Parallel-282
00Pacific-184
Copper-184
Gold-184
Ice Blue-184
Premiere Date-184
00Panthers Team Issue-30
00Paramount-107
Copper-107
Gold-107
Holo-Gold-107
Holo-Silver-107
Ice Blue-107
Premiere Date-107
00SP Authentic-40
BuyBacks-46
Sign of the Times-IN
Sign of the Times-B/N
00Titanium-121
Retail-121
00Titanium Draft Day Edition-121
00Titanium Draft Day Promos-121
00Topps/OPC-282
Parallel-282
00Topps Chrome-177
OPC Refractors-177
Refractors-177
00Upper Deck-79
Exclusives Tier 1-79
Exclusives Tier 2-79
MVP Excellence-ME4
MVP Mark of Excellence-SGHN
MVP ProSign-IV
00Vanguard-122
Pacific Proofs-122
01BAP Memorabilia-213
Emerald-213
Ruby-213
Sapphire-213
01O-Pee-Chee-306
01O-Pee-Chee Premier Parallel-306
01Topps-306
OPC Parallel-306
02BAP First Edition-96
Jerseys-96
02Pacific Complete-346
Red-346
02Topps Total-212
02Upper Deck-324
Exclusives-324
02Upper Deck Beckett UD Promos-324
03Coyotes Postcards-17
03ITG Action-237
03Upper Deck MVP-181
Gold Script-181
Silver Script-181
Canadian Exclusives-181
03Russian World Championship Team 2003-6

Novosjolov, Waldemar
94German DEL-358

Novotny, Andrej
99Czech OFS-95
00Czech OFS-40
01Czech OFS-250
02Czech OFS Plus-223
03Czech OFS Plus-55
03Czech Pardubice Postcards-11
04Czech OFS-126
05Czech HC Pardubice-13
06Czech HC Pardubice Postcards-14
06Czech OFS-122
06Czech OFS-311

Novotny, Ivo
97Czech APS Extraliga-15
98Czech OFS-310

Novotny, Jan
96Czech APS Extraliga-72
97Czech APS Extraliga-193

Novotny, Jiri
95Czech APS Extraliga-241
95Lethbridge Hurricanes-16
96Czech APS Extraliga-70
96Czech APS Extraliga-307
99Czech Score Blue 2000-12
99Czech Score Red Ice 2000-12
00Czech OFS-26
02Czech DS-46
02Czech DS-67
02Rochester Americans-17
03Rochester Americans-19
04Rochester Americans-14
04ITG Heroes and Prospects-4
Autographs-JN
Emblems-1
Emblems Gold-1
Jersey Autographs-1
Jerseys-1
Jerseys Gold-1
Numbers-1
Numbers Gold-1
04ITG Heroes/Prospects Toronto Expo '05-4
04ITG Heroes/Prospects Expo Heroes/Pros-4
05Hot Prospects-109
En Fuego-109
Red Hot-109
White Hot-109
05SP Authentic-253
Limited-253
05SPx-248
05The Cup Masterpiece Pressplates (Ice)-255
05The Cup Master Pressplate Rookie Update-111
05The Cup Masterpiece Pressplates SPA-253
05The Cup Masterpiece Pressplates (SPx)-248
05The Cup Masterpiece Pressplates Trilogy-230
05The Cup Masterpiece Pressplate Ult Coll-196
05Ultimate Collection-196
Gold-196
05Upper Deck Ice-255
05Upper Deck Rookie Update-111
05Upper Deck Trilogy-230
06O-Pee-Chee-52
Rainbow-52
06Upper Deck-274
Exclusives Parallel-274
High Gloss Parallel-274
Masterpieces-274
06Czech OFS Jagr Team-6

Novotny, Marek
94Czech APS Extraliga-162
95Czech APS Extraliga-176
96Czech APS Extraliga-312
97Czech APS Extraliga-291
97Czech DS Extraliga-34
98Czech DS-14
98Czech DS Stickers-107
98Czech OFS-295
99Czech DS-100
99Czech OFS-542
00Czech DS Extraliga-61
00Czech OFS-212
06Czech OFS-320

Novy, Helmut
70Finnish Jaakiekko-91
70Swedish Hockey-370
74Finnish Typotor-63

Novy, Milan
74Swedish Semic World Champ Stickers-59
79Panini Stickers-85
81Swedish Semic Hockey VM Stickers-63
82Capitals Team Issue-19
82Swedish Semic VM Stickers-87
83NHL Key Tags-133
83O-Pee-Chee Stickers-187
83Puffy Stickers-19
83Topps Stickers-187
92Future Trends '76 Canada Cup-155
92Future Trends '76 Canada Cup-186
92Future Trends '76 Canada Cup-198
97Czech APS Extraliga-215
98Czech OFS Legends-11
99Czech OFS-170
01Czech DS Legends-L11

Nowak, Brett
03Providence Bruins-14
04Atlantic City Boardwalk Bullies-27
05Syracuse Crunch-12

Nowak, Daniel
94German DEL-433
95German DEL-392
95German DEL-431
96German DEL-299
98German DEL-211
98German DEL-329
99German DEL-208

Nowak, Derek
93Quebec Pee-Wee Tournament-741

Nowak, Hank
74NHL Action Stamps-93
74NHL Action Stamps Update-2
76O-Pee-Chee NHL-224
76Topps-224

Nowakowski, Jacek
98Danish Hockey League-61
99Danish Hockey League-94

Nowicki, Todd
02Orlando Seals-18

Noye, Tyler
03P.E.I. Rocket-15

Noyers, Mike
06Saint Johns Sea Dogs-2

Noyranen, Pentti
05Finnish Cardset -183
06Finnish Cardset-11

Nuemeier, Troy
04Fort Wayne Komets-12

Nugent, Chris
04Lincoln Stars-13

Numela, Holger
55Swedish Alfabilder-28

Nummela, Tapio
70Finnish Jaakiekko-246

Nummelin, Petteri
93Finnish SISU-32
94Finnish SISU-62
94Finnish SISU-150
94Finnish SISU Magic Numbers-2
94Finnish SISU Specials-3
94Finnish Jaa Kiekko-12
95Finnish SISU Gold Cards-9
95Finnish SISU Limited-3
95Finnish Karjala World Champ Labels-14
95Finnish Semic World Championships-39
95Swedish Leaf-206
95Swedish Upper Deck-209
95Swedish World Championships Stickers-167
96Swedish Semic Wien-3
98Finnish Kerailysarja Leijonat-15
98Swiss Power Play Stickers-60
99Finnish Cardset-187
99Swiss Panini Stickers-61
00BAP Memorabilia-476
Emerald-476
Ruby-476
Sapphire-476
00BAP Signature Series-251
Emerald-251
Ruby-251
Sapphire-251
Autographs-240
Autographs Gold-240
00SP Authentic-142
00SPx-136
00Titanium Draft Day Edition-158
00Titanium Draft Day Promos-158
00Topps Heritage-91
Chrome Parallel-91
00Topps Premier Plus-112
Blue Ice-112
00Topps Stars-122
Blue-122
00Upper Deck-423
Exclusives Tier 1-423
Exclusives Tier 2-423
00Finnish Cardset-234
01Finnish Cardset-161
01Swiss HNL-31
02BAP Sig Series Auto Buybacks 2000-240
02Finnish Cardset-85
02Swiss HNL-280

Nummelin, Timo
66Finnish Jaakiekkosarja-76
70Finnish Jaakiekko-164
71Finnish Suomi Stickers-233
72Finnish Jaakiekko-68
72Finnish Jaakiekko-217
72Finnish Hellas-8
73Finnish Jaakiekko-73
73Finnish Jaakiekko-292
74Finnish Typotor-32
77Finnish Sportscasters-48-1152
78Finnish SM-Liiga-3
78Finnish SM-Liiga-201
79Panini Stickers-165
80Finnish Mallasjuoma-178
81Swedish Semic Hockey VM Stickers-25
82Finnish Skopbank-11
82Swedish Semic VM Stickers-29

Numminen, Kalevi
65Finnish Hellas-160
66Finnish Jaakiekkosarja-148
74Swedish Semic World Champ Stickers-98
77Finnish Sportscasters-75-1800
05Finnish Tappara Legendat-30

Numminen, Reima
71Finnish Suomi Stickers-372

Numminen, Teemu
93Finnish Jyvas-Hyva Stickers-297
93Finnish SISU-71
94Finnish SISU-319
95Finnish SISU-329
97Mississippi Sea Wolves-9
98Phoenix Mustangs-18

Numminen, Teppo
88Jets Police-17
88Jets Postcards-17
89Jets Safeway-22
89Panini Stickers-172
90Bowman-138
Tiffany-138
90Jets IGA-24
90O-Pee-Chee-385
90Panini Stickers-307
90Pro Set-334
90Score-176
Canadian-176
90Topps-385
Tiffany-385
91Pro Set Platinum-248
91Bowman-201
91Jets Panini Team Stickers-18
91Jets IGA-20
91O-Pee-Chee-274
91Panini Stickers-71
91Parkhurst-200
French-200
91Pinnacle-166
French-166
91Pro Set-261
French-261
91Score American-101
91Score Canadian Bilingual-101
91Score Canadian English-101
91Stadium Club-302
91Topps-274
91Upper Deck-240
French-240
91Finnish Semic World Champ Stickers-201
91Swedish Semic World Champ Stickers-201
92Bowman-299
92O-Pee-Chee-4
92Panini Stickers-52
92Panini Stickers French-52
92Parkhurst-438
Emerald Ice-438
92Pinnacle-215
French-215
92Pro Set-210
92Score-102
Canadian-102
92Stadium Club-77
92Topps-339
Gold-339G
92Ultra-243
92Upper Deck-326
92Finnish Semic-5
93Donruss-385
93Jets Readers Club-14
93Jets Ruffles-18
93Leaf-135
93OPC Premier-269
Gold-269
93Panini Stickers-197
93Parkhurst-231
Emerald Ice-231
93Pinnacle-92
Canadian-92
93PowerPlay-272
93Score-132
Canadian-132
93Stadium Club-164
Members Only Master Set-164
OPC-164
First Day Issue-164
First Day Issue OPC-164
93Topps/OPC Premier-269
Gold-269
93Ultra-455
93Upper Deck-53
93Swedish Semic World Champ Stickers-57
94Canada Games NHL POGS-346
94Donruss-267
94EA Sports-146
94Flair-208
94Leaf-233
94OPC Premier-376
Special Effects-376
94Parkhurst-270
Gold-270
SE Euro-Stars-ES10
94Pinnacle-77
Artist's Proofs-77
Rink Collection-77
94Score-91
Gold-91
Platinum-91
94Stadium Club-152
Members Only Master Set-152
First Day Issue-152
Super Team Winner Cards-152
94Topps/OPC Premier-376
Special Effects-376
94Ultra-244
94Upper Deck-113
Electric Ice-113
94Finnish SISU-359
94Finnish SISU Guest Specials-6
94Finnish Jaa Kiekko-10
94Finnish Jaa Kiekko-335
95Be A Player-68
Signatures-S68
Signatures Die Cuts-S68
95Canada Games NHL POGS-294
95Collector's Choice-292
Player's Club-292
Player's Club Platinum-292
95Donruss-261
95Emotion-195
95Finest-167
Refractors-167
95Jets Readers Club-8
95Jets Team Issue-16
95Leaf-247
95Metal-164
95Panini Stickers-220
95Parkhurst International-228
Emerald Ice-228
95Pinnacle-67
Artist's Proofs-67
Rink Collection-67
Global Gold-12
95Playoff One on One-107
95Playoff One on One-328
95Score-139
Black Ice Artist's Proofs-139
Black Ice-139
95SkyBox Impact-183
95Summit-113
Artist's Proofs-113
Ice-113
95Topps-67
OPC Inserts-67
95Ultra-182
Gold Medallion-182
95Upper Deck-275
Electric Ice-275
Electric Ice Gold-275
95Finnish SISU Limited-93
Signed and Sealed-6
95Finnish Semic World Championships-37
95Swedish Globe World Championships-133
96Collector's Choice-209
96Coyotes Coca-Cola-22
96Donruss-126
Press Proofs-126
96Fleer-91
Norris-8
96Fleer Picks-72
96Leaf-113
Press Proofs-113
96Metal Universe-120
96Pinnacle-8
Artist's Proofs-8
Foil-8
Premium Stock-8
Rink Collection-8
96Playoff One on One-350
96Score-5
Artist's Proofs-5
Dealer's Choice Artist's Proofs-5
Special Artist's Proofs-5
Golden Blades-5
96SkyBox Impact-106
NHL on Fox-16
96SP-122
96Summit-55
Artist's Proofs-55
Ice-55
Metal-55
Premium Stock-55
96Ultra-134
Gold Medallion-134
96Upper Deck-131
96Swedish Semic Wien-27
97Collector's Choice-200
97Coyotes Face-Off Luncheon -16
97Pacific-122
Copper-122
Emerald Green-122
Ice Blue-122
Red-122
Silver-122
97Pacific Omega-175
Copper-175
Dark Gray-175
Emerald Green-175
Gold-175
Ice Blue-175
97Panini Stickers-156
97SP Authentic-122
97Upper Deck-336
98Be A Player-106
Press Release-106
98BAP Gold-106
98BAP Autographs-106
98BAP Autographs Gold-106
98BAP Tampa Bay All Star Game-106
98Katch-114
98Kraft Peanut Butter-8
98OPC Chrome-57
Refractors-57
98Pacific-342
Ice Blue-342
Red-342
98Pacific Omega-186
Red-186
Opening Day Issue-186
98Panini Stickers-148
98Paramount-183
Copper-183
Emerald Green-183
Holo-Electric-183
Ice Blue-183
Silver-183
98Topps-57
O-Pee-Chee-57
98UD Choice-157
98UD Choice Preview-157
98UD Choice Prime Choice Reserve-157
98UD Choice Reserve-157
98Upper Deck-155
Exclusives-155
Exclusives 1 of 1-155
Gold Reserve-155
99Aurora-110
Premiere Date-110
99BAP Memorabilia-186
Gold-186
Silver-186
99BAP Millennium-189
Emerald-189
Ruby-189
Sapphire-189
Signatures-189
Signatures Gold-189
99Kraft Peanut Butter-9
99O-Pee-Chee-80
99O-Pee-Chee Chrome-80
99O-Pee-Chee Chrome Refractors-80
99Pacific-323
Copper-323
Emerald Green-323
Gold-323
Ice Blue-323
Premiere Date-323
Red-323
99Pacific Omega-183
Copper-183
Gold-183
Ice Blue-183
Premiere Date-183

99Panini Stickers-280
99Paramount-181
Copper-181
Emerald-181
Gold-181
Holographic Emerald-181
Holographic Gold-181
Holographic Silver-181
Ice Blue-181
Premiere Date-181
Red-181
Silver-181
99Revolution-112
Premiere Date-112
Red-112
Shadow Series-112
99SPx-119
Radiance-119
Spectrum-119
99Stadium Club-41
First Day Issue-41
One of a Kind-41
Printing Plates Black-41
Printing Plates Cyan-41
Printing Plates Magenta-41
Printing Plates Yellow-41
99Topps/OPC-80
99Topps/OPC Chrome-80
Refractors-80
99Upper Deck Victory-233
99Finnish Cardset Aces High-C-3
00BAP Memorabilia-155
Emerald-155
Ruby-155
Sapphire-155
Promos-155
00BAP Mem Chicago Sportsfest Copper-155
00BAP Memorabilia Chicago Sportsfest Blue-155
00BAP Memorabilia Chicago Sportsfest Gold-155
00BAP Memorabilia Chicago Sportsfest Ruby-155
00BAP Memorabilia Chicago Sun-Times Ruby-155
00BAP Memorabilia Chicago Sun-Times Gold-155
00BAP Mem Chicago Sun-Times Sapphire-155
00BAP Mem Toronto Fall Expo Copper-155
00BAP Memorabilia Toronto Fall Expo Gold-155
00BAP Memorabilia Toronto Fall Expo Ruby-155
00BAP Memorabilia Update Teammates-TM30
00BAP Memorabilia Update Teammates-TM33
00BAP Memorabilia Update Teammates Gold-TM30
00BAP Memorabilia Update Teammates Gold-TM33
00BAP Parkhurst 2000-P42
00BAP Sig Ser Department of Defense-DD10
00O-Pee-Chee-79
00O-Pee-Chee Parallel-79
00Pacific-445
Copper-445
Gold-445
Ice Blue-445
Premiere Date-445
00Panini Stickers-189
00Paramount-192
Copper-192
Gold-192
Holo-Gold-192
Holo-Silver-192
Ice Blue-192
Premiere Date-192
00Stadium Club-76
00Titanium Game Gear-43
00Titanium Game Gear-128
00Titanium Game Gear Patches-128
00Topps/OPC-79
Parallel-79
00Topps Chrome-62
OPC Refractors-62
Refractors-62
00Topps Gold Label Bullion-B7
00Topps Gold Label Bullion One to One-B7
00Topps Heritage-186
00Topps Stars-64
Blue-64
00UD Heroes-90
00Upper Deck-135
Exclusives Tier 1-135
Exclusives Tier 2-135
00Upper Deck MVP-136
First Stars-136
Second Stars-136
Third Stars-136
00Upper Deck Vintage-274
01BAP Memorabilia-43
Emerald-43
Ruby-43
Sapphire-43
All-Star Jerseys-ASJ18
All-Star Emblems-ASE18
All-Star Numbers-ASN18
Country of Origin-CO21
01BAP Signature Series-110
Autographs-110
Autographs Gold-110
01Coyotes Team Issue-16
01O-Pee-Chee-123
01O-Pee-Chee Premier Parallel-123
01Pacific-307
Extreme LTD-307
Hobby LTD-307
Premiere Date-307
Retail LTD-307
01Pacific Arena Exclusives-307
01Pacific Heads-Up Quad Jerseys-26
01Parkhurst-53
Gold-53
Silver-53
01Titanium Draft Day Edition-76
01Topps-123
OPC Parallel-123
01Topps Chrome-123
Refractors-123
Black Border Refractors-123
01Upper Deck-366
Exclusives-366
01Upper Deck Victory-275
Gold-275
01Upper Deck Vintage-195
01Upper Deck Vintage-199
01Finnish Cardset Salt Lake City-3
02BAP All-Star Edition-67
Jerseys-67
Jerseys Gold-67
Jerseys Silver-67
02BAP First Edition-40
Jerseys-40
02BAP Sig Series Auto Buybacks 1998-106
02BAP Sig Series Auto Buybacks 1999-189
02BAP Sig Series Auto Buybacks 2001-110
02Coyotes Team Issue-13
02O-Pee-Chee-158
02O-Pee-Chee Premier Blue Parallel-158
02O-Pee-Chee Premier Red Parallel-158
02O-Pee-Chee Factory Set-158
02Pacific-303
Blue-303
Red-303
02Pacific Complete-321
Red-321
02Parkhurst Teammates-TT20
02Parkhurst Retro-117
Minis-117
02Topps-158
OPC Blue Parallel-158
OPC Red Parallel-158
Factory Set-158
02Topps Total-55
02UD Honor Roll-93
02Upper Deck-380
Exclusives-380
02Upper Deck Beckett UD Promos-380
02Upper Deck MVP-144
Gold-144
Classics-144
Golden Classics-144
02Upper Deck Victory-164
Bronze-164
Gold-164
Silver-164
National Pride-NP26
02Upper Deck Vintage-192
02Upper Deck Vintage-283
02Finnish Cardset-235
03Beehive-65
Gold-65
Silver-65
03Black Diamond-94
Black-94
Green-94
Red-94
03NHL Sticker Collection-268
03Pacific-267
Blue-267
Red-267
03Pacific Complete-366
Red-366
03Pacific Exhibit-50
Blue Backs-50
Yellow Backs-50
03Stars Postcards-19
03Upper Deck-306
Canadian Exclusives-306
HG-306
UD Exclusives-306
03Upper Deck MVP-326
Gold Script-326
Silver Script-326
Canadian Exclusives-326
05Panini Stickers-42
05Parkhurst-57
Facsimile Auto Parallel-57
05Upper Deck-265
05Upper Deck MVP-53
Gold-53
Platinum-53
05Finnish Tappara Legendat-10
06O-Pee-Chee-54
Rainbow-54

Nunan, Mark
93Quebec Pee-Wee Tournament-841

Nunweiler, Donavan
97Moose Jaw Warriors-10

Nurmberg, Timo
94Finnish SISU-239
95Finnish SISU-116
96Finnish SISU Redline-130

Nurmi, Heikki
72Finnish Jaakiekko-160
73Finnish Jaakiekko-226

Nurmi, Juha
80Finnish Mallasjuoma-167
83Swedish Semic VM Stickers-42
85Swedish Panini Stickers-169
86Swedish Panini Stickers-178
87Swedish Panini Stickers-179
89Swedish Semic Elitserien Stickers-163

Nurmi, Pertti
70Finnish Jaakiekko-183
71Finnish Suomi Stickers-106
72Finnish Jaakiekko-150
73Finnish Jaakiekko-117

Nurmi, Seppo
66Finnish Jaakiekkosarja-166
70Finnish Jaakiekko-247
71Finnish Suomi Stickers-214
72Finnish Jaakiekko-161
73Finnish Jaakiekko-227

Nurmi, Teemu
04Finnish Cardset-296
05Finnish Cardset -322
06Finnish Cardset-150

Nurminen, Aaro
65Finnish Hellas-107

Nurminen, Jaakko
70Finnish Jaakiekko-199

Nurminen, Jari
72Finnish Jaakiekko-291

Nurminen, Juha
93Finnish SISU-290
94Finnish SISU-243
94Finnish SISU Fire On Ice-17
95Finnish SISU-10

Nurminen, Kai
93Finnish Jyvas-Hyva Stickers-329
93Finnish SISU-48
94Finnish SISU-101
94Finnish SISU-305
94Finnish SISU Fire On Ice-18
94Finnish SISU Horoscopes-13
95Finnish SISU-166
95Finnish SISU Limited-86
95Swedish Leaf-228
95Swedish Upper Deck-90
96Select Certified-91
Artist's Proofs-91
Blue-91
Mirror Blue-91
Mirror Gold-91
Mirror Red-91
Red-91
96SP-181
96Upper Deck-275
96Swedish Semic Wien-36
97Pacific Invincible NHL Regime-95
97Panini Stickers-221
97Swedish Collector's Choice-81
97Swedish Collector's Choice-211
Crash the Game Exchange-C6
Crash the Game Redemption-R6
98Swiss Power Play Stickers-66
99Finnish Cardset-144
Aces High-S-6
00Finnish Cardset Master Blasters-1
00Cleveland Lumberjacks-11
01Finnish Cardset-357
01Finnish Cardset Dueling Aces-3
02Finnish Cardset-86
03Finnish Cardset-165
04Finnish Cardset-178
Parallel-132
05Finnish Cardset -158
06Finnish Cardset-160

Nurminen, Pasi
98Finnish Kerailysarja-51
Mad Masks-3
99Finnish Cardset-203
99Finnish Cardset-258
00Finnish Cardset-38
00Finnish Cardset-351
00Finnish Cardset-NNO
01BAP Memorabilia-358
Emerald-358
Ruby-358
Sapphire-358
01Between the Pipes-151
01Parkhurst-303
01SPx-197
01Titanium Draft Day Edition-106
01UD Mask Collection-133
Gold-133
01UD Premier Collection-89
01UD Top Shelf-122
01Upper Deck Ice-127
01Finnish Cardset-49
01Finnish Cardset-157
01Finnish Cardset Haltmeisters-1
01Chicago Wolves-14
02BAP Signature Series Team Quads-TQ12
02Between the Pipes-94
Gold-94
Silver-94
02O-Pee-Chee-294
02O-Pee-Chee Premier Blue Parallel-294
02O-Pee-Chee Premier Red Parallel-294
02O-Pee-Chee Factory Set-294
02Pacific Complete-233
Red-233
02SPx-101
02Thrashers Postcards-11
02Titanium-6
Blue-6
Red-6
Retail-6
02Topps-294
OPC Blue Parallel-294
OPC Red Parallel-294
Factory Set-294
02UD Foundations-122
02UD Mask Collection-7
02UD Mask Collection Beckett Promos-7
02Upper Deck-197
02Upper Deck-255
Exclusives-197
Exclusives-255
02Upper Deck Beckett UD Promos-255
02Upper Deck MVP-9
Gold-9
Classics-9
Golden Classics-9
02Upper Deck Victory-8
Bronze-8
Gold-8
Silver-8
02Upper Deck Vintage-321
02Finnish Cardset-236
02Finnish Cardset Dynamic Duos-2
02Finnish Cardset Solid Gold-1
03BAP Memorabilia-151
Emerald-151
Gold-151
Ruby-151
Sapphire-151
Deep in the Crease-D1
Masks III-13
Masks III Gold-13
Masks III Silver-13
Masks III Autographs-M-PN
Masks III Memorabilia-13
03BAP Ultimate Memorabilia Autographs-49
Gold-49
03Beehive-8
Gold-8
Silver-8
03Bowman-3
Gold-3
03Bowman Chrome-3
Refractors-3
Gold Refractors-3
Xfractors-3
03Crown Royale-5
Blue-5
Retail-5
Gauntlet of Glory-2
03eTopps-1
03ITG Action-65
Jerseys-M60
03ITG Used Signature Series-81
Gold-81
Autographs-PN
Autographs Gold-PN
03O-Pee-Chee-262
03OPC Blue-262
03OPC Gold-262
03OPC Red-262
03Pacific-19
Blue-19
Red-19
03Pacific Complete-429
Red-429
03Pacific Heads-Up-6
Hobby LTD-6
Retail LTD-6
Stonewallers-2
Stonewallers LTD-2
03Pacific Quest for the Cup-6
Blue-6
03Private Stock Reserve-7
Blue-7
Red-7
Retail-7
03Thrashers Postcards-14
03Titanium-6
Hobby Jersey Number Parallels-6
Retail-6
Retail Jersey Number Parallels-6
03Topps-262
Blue-262
Gold-262
Red-262
03Topps C55-129
Minis-129
Minis American Back-129
Minis American Back Red-129
Minis Bazooka Back-129
Minis Brooklyn Back-129
Minis Hat Trick Back-129
Minis O Canada Back-129
Minis O Canada Back Red-129
Minis Stanley Cup Back-129
03Topps Pristine-68
Gold Refractor Die Cuts-68
Refractors-68
Mini-PM-PN
Press Plates Black-68
Press Plates Cyan-68
Press Plates Magenta-68
Press Plates Yellow-68
03Upper Deck-257
Canadian Exclusives-257
HG-257
UD Exclusives-257
03Upper Deck MVP-26
Gold Script-26
Silver Script-26
Canadian Exclusives-26
SportsNut-SN4
04Pacific-14
Blue-14
Red-14
04Finnish Cardset-124
Stars of the Game-9
04Swedish Malmo Red Hawks-9
04Swedish Pure Skills-134
Parallel-134
05Finnish Cardset -112
Finnish Cardset Super Snatchers-12

Nurminen, Timo
70Finnish Jaakiekko-302
73Finnish Jaakiekko-293

Nurre, Tom
98San Angelo Outlaws-20

Nurro, Kimmo
94Finnish SISU-254

Nurtdinov, Ruslan
00Russian Hockey League-243
02Russian Hockey League-134
03Russian Hockey League-142
03Russian Hockey League-271
03Russian SL-28
05Russian Hockey League RHL-49

Nusbaum, Joel
93Arizona Icecats-9
94Arizona Icecats-11
95Arizona Icecats-9
96Arizona Icecats-14

Nuspliger, Beat
93Swiss HNL-202
95Swiss HNL-363
96Swiss HNL-334

Nussbaum, Andre
02Swiss HNL-190

Nussberger, Stephan
93Swiss HNL-332
95Swiss HNL-478
96Swiss HNL-376

Nussli, Thomas
01Swiss EV Zug Postcards-15
01Swiss HNL-185
02Swiss HNL-317

Nutikka, Veli Pekka
94Finest-135
Super Team Winners-135
Refractors-135
94Parkhurst SE-SE222
Gold-SE222
94SP-159
Die Cuts-159
95Finnish SISU-279
96Finnish SISU Redline-77
98Finnish Kerailysarja-137
99Finnish Cardset-75
00Finnish Cardset-76
01Finnish Cardset-106

Nuutinen, Sami
92Finnish Jyvas-Hyva Stickers-106
93Finnish Jyvas-Hyva Stickers-195
93Finnish SISU-260
93Finnish SISU Autographs-260
93Swedish Semic World Champ Stickers-58
94Finnish SISU-122
95Finnish SISU-85
Double Trouble-6
95Finnish SISU Limited-56
98Finnish Kerailysarja-101
99German DEL-262
00Finnish Cardset-142

Nyberg, Lars
83Swedish Semic Elitserien-164

Nyberg, Patrik
91Swedish Semic Elitserien Stickers-249

Nyc, Oldrich
99Czech Score Blue 2000-79
99Czech Score Red Ice 2000-79

Nycholat, Lawrence
93Quebec Pee-Wee Tournament-175
96Swift Current Broncos-7
97Swift Current Broncos-8
98Swift Current Broncos-13
99Swift Current Broncos-12
03ITG VIP Rookie Debut-109
03Pacific Complete-502
Red-502
03Parkhurst Rookie-104
03Topps Traded-TT127
Blue-TT127
Gold-TT127
Red-TT127
03Upper Deck Rookie Update-167
03Hartford Wolf Pack-18
04AHL All-Stars-30
04Hartford Wolf Pack-19
05ITG Heroes/Prosp Toronto Expo Parallel -71
05AHL All-Stars-24
05Hershey Bears-14
05ITG Heroes and Prospects-71
Autographs-A-LN
Complete Logos-AHL-12
Jerseys-GUJ-44
Jerseys Gold-GUJ-44
Emblems-GUE-44
Emblems Gold-GUE-44
Numbers-GUN-44
Numbers Gold-GUN-44
Nameplates-N-13
Nameplates Gold-N-13
Shooting Stars-AS-2
06ITG Heroes and Prospects Calder Cup Champions-CC09

Nygards, Per
90Swedish Semic Elitserien Stickers-280
91Swedish Semic Elitserien Stickers-63

Nygren, Hakan
64Swedish Coralli ISHockey-146
65Swedish Coralli ISHockey-156
67Swedish Hockey-125
69Swedish Hockey-139
69Swedish Hockey-195
70Swedish Hockey-96
70Swedish Masterserien-39
70Swedish Masterserien-62
71Finnish Suomi Stickers-55
71Swedish Hockey-21
71Swedish Hockey-190
72Finnish Panda Toronto-75
72Finnish Semic World Championship-53
72Swedish Stickers-176
72Swedish Semic World Championship-53
74Swedish Stickers-179
85Swedish Panini Stickers-209
86Swedish Panini Stickers-191
93Swedish Semic Elitserien-293

Nyholm, Bobby
06Kingston Frontenacs-8

Nykoluk, Mike
44Beehive Group II Photos-441
57Parkhurst-T16
81Maple Leafs Postcards-16
82Maple Leafs Postcards-26
83Maple Leafs Postcards-18
94Parkhurst Missing Link-130
98Hershey Bears-38

Nykopp, Timo
92Finnish Jyvas-Hyva Stickers-20
94Finnish SISU-341
95Finnish SISU-150
95Finnish SISU-287
99German Bundesliga 2-59

Nykvist, Hannu
80Finnish Mallasjuoma-63

Nykyforuk, Curtis
88Regina Pats-19
89Victoria Cougars-15

Nylander, Michael
91Swedish Semic Elitserien Stickers-21
91Classic-47
91Star Pics-23
91Ultimate Draft-42
91Ultimate Draft-88
91Ultimate Draft French-42
91Classic Four-Sport *-47
Autographs-47A
92OPC Premier-19
92Parkhurst-294
Emerald Ice-294
92Pinnacle-400
French-400
92Upper Deck-236
92Upper Deck-378
92Upper Deck-520
Euro-Rookies-ER2
92Whalers Dairymart-16
92Swedish Semic Elitserien Stickers-338
92Swedish Semic Elitserien Stickers-339
93Donruss-144
93Donruss-407
93Leaf-94
93OPC Premier-99
Gold-99
93Panini Stickers-128
93Parkhurst-83
Emerald Ice-83
93Pinnacle-166
Canadian-166
93PowerPlay-106
93Score-383
Canadian-383
93Stadium Club-186
Members Only Master Set-186
OPC-186
First Day Issue-186
First Day Issue OPC-186
93Topps/OPC Premier-99
Gold-99
93Ultra-105
Prospects-7
93Upper Deck-70
Hat Tricks-HT13
Next In Line-NL1
SP-62
93Whalers Coke-12
93Swedish Semic World Champ Stickers-40
94Canada Games NHL POGS-57
94Donruss-74
94Leaf-149
94OPC Premier-237
Special Effects-237
94Parkhurst-32
Gold-32
94Pinnacle-142
Artist's Proofs-142
Rink Collection-142
94Score-59
Gold-59
Platinum-59
94Topps/OPC Premier-237
Special Effects-237
94Ultra-32
94Upper Deck-79
94Upper Deck-556
Electric Ice-79
Electric Ice-556
SP Inserts-SP103
SP Inserts Die Cuts-SP103
94Finnish SISU-352
94Finnish SISU Guest Specials-7
95Be A Player-148
Signatures-S148
Signatures Die Cuts-S148
95Canada Games NHL POGS-54
95Collector's Choice-311
Player's Club-311
Player's Club Platinum-311
95Finest-172
Refractors-172
95Metal-22
95Parkhurst International-34
Emerald Ice-34
95Score-289
Black Ice Artist's Proofs-289
Black Ice-289
95SP-20
95Stadium Club-154
Members Only Master Set-154
95Ultra-213
95Upper Deck-454
Electric Ice-454
Electric Ice Gold-454
Special Edition-SE102
Special Edition Gold-SE102
95Finnish SISU Limited-54
Leaf Gallery-3
95Finnish SISU Specials-10
95Swedish Upper Deck-237
95Swedish Globe World Championships-35
96Collector's Choice-38
96Collector's Choice-312
96Leaf-115
Press Proofs-115
96Pinnacle-151
Artist's Proofs-151
Foil-151
Premium Stock-151
Rink Collection-151
96Score-79
Artist's Proofs-79
Dealer's Choice Artist's Proofs-79
Special Artist's Proofs-79
Golden Blades-79
96Upper Deck-27
96Swedish Semic Wien-61
96Swiss HNL-174
97Pacific Omega-33
Copper-33
Dark Gray-33
Emerald Green-33
Gold-33
Ice Blue-33
98Aurora-28
98Finest-63
No Protectors-63
No Protectors Refractors-63
Refractors-63
Promos-PP2
98Pacific-123
Ice Blue-123
Red-123
98Panini Stickers-177
98Paramount-31
Copper-31
Emerald Green-31
Holo-Electric-31
Ice Blue-31
Silver-31
98UD Choice-32
Prime Choice Reserve-32
Reserve-32
99Blackhawks Chicago Sun-Times-8
99Pacific-393
Copper-393
Emerald Green-393
Gold-393
Ice Blue-393
Premiere Date-393
Red-393
99Pacific Omega-54
Copper-54
Gold-54
Ice Blue-54
Premiere Date-54
99Panini Stickers-142
99Upper Deck MVP SC Edition-48
Gold Script-48
Silver Script-48
Super Script-48
99Finnish Cardset Aces High-C-10
00BAP Memorabilia-335
Emerald-335
Ruby-335
Sapphire-335
Promos-335
00BAP Mem Chicago Sportsfest Copper-335
00BAP Memorabilia Chicago Sportsfest Blue-335
00BAP Memorabilia Chicago Sportsfest Gold-335
00BAP Memorabilia Chicago Sportsfest Ruby-335
00BAP Memorabilia Chicago Sun-Times Ruby-335
00BAP Memorabilia Chicago Sun-Times Gold-335
00BAP Mem Chicago Sun-Times Sapphire-335
00BAP Mem Toronto Fall Expo Copper-335
00BAP Memorabilia Toronto Fall Expo Gold-335
00BAP Memorabilia Toronto Fall Expo Ruby-335
00BAP Parkhurst 2000-P178
00O-Pee-Chee-127
00O-Pee-Chee Parallel-127
00Pacific-100
Copper-100
Gold-100
Ice Blue-100
Premiere Date-100
00Panini Stickers-123
00Paramount-52
Copper-52
Gold-52
Holo-Gold-52
Holo-Silver-52
Ice Blue-52
Premiere Date-52
00Titanium Draft Day Edition-19
Patches-19
00Topps/OPC-127
Parallel-127
00Upper Deck-41
Exclusives Tier 1-41
Exclusives Tier 2-41
00Upper Deck MVP-44
First Stars-44
Second Stars-44
Third Stars-44
00Upper Deck Vintage-84
01BAP Memorabilia-117
Emerald-117
Ruby-117
Sapphire-117
01BAP Signature Series-57
Autographs-57
Autographs Gold-57
01O-Pee-Chee-127
01O-Pee-Chee Premier Parallel-127
01Pacific-88
Extreme LTD-88
Hobby LTD-88
Premiere Date-88
Retail LTD-88
01Pacific Adrenaline-40
Blue-40
Premiere Date-40
Red-40
Retail-40
01Pacific Arena Exclusives-88
01Pacific Heads-Up Quad Jerseys-7
01Parkhurst-224
01Private Stock Game Gear-24
01Private Stock Game Gear Patches-24
01Titanium Double-Sided Jerseys-9
01Titanium Double-Sided Patches-9
01Topps-127
OPC Parallel-127
01Upper Deck-39
Exclusives-39
01Upper Deck MVP-41
01Upper Deck Victory-79
Gold-79
01Upper Deck Vintage-56
01Vanguard Memorabilia-7
02BAP First Edition-273
02BAP Sig Series Auto Buybacks 2001-57
02O-Pee-Chee-154
02O-Pee-Chee Premier Blue Parallel-154
02O-Pee-Chee Premier Red Parallel-154
02O-Pee-Chee Factory Set-154
02Pacific Complete-59
Red-59
02Pacific Quest for the Cup-100
Gold-100
02Parkhurst-175
Bronze-175
Gold-175
Silver-175
02Titanium-100
Blue-100
Red-100
Retail-100
02Topps-154
OPC Blue Parallel-154
OPC Red Parallel-154
Factory Set-154
02Topps Total-360
02Upper Deck-35
Exclusives-35
02Upper Deck MVP-39
Gold-39
Classics-39
Golden Classics-39
02Upper Deck Rookie Update-100
02Upper Deck Vintage-55
02Finnish Cardset-237
03ITG Action-549
03O-Pee-Chee-95
03OPC Blue-95
03OPC Gold-95
03OPC Red-95
03Pacific-349
Blue-349
Red-349
03Pacific Complete-173
Red-173
03Pacific Exhibit-150
Blue Backs-150
Yellow Backs-150
03Topps-95
Blue-95
Gold-95
Red-95
03Topps Traded-TT21
Blue-TT21
Gold-TT21
Red-TT21
03Upper Deck-195
Canadian Exclusives-195
HG-195
03Upper Deck MVP-427
Gold Script-427
Silver Script-427
Canadian Exclusives-427
03Upper Deck Victory-197
Bronze-197
Gold-197
Silver-197
04UD All-World-39
Gold-39
04Finnish Cardset-107
Stars of the Game-10
04Swedish Alfabilder Alfa Stars-24
04Swedish Alfabilder Autographs-111
04Swedish Alfabilder Limited Autographs-111
04Swedish Alfabilder Proof Parallels-24
04Swedish Pure Skills-130
Parallel-130
Professional Power-MN
05Beehive Signature Scrapbook-SSNY
05Panini Stickers-104
05Parkhurst-319
Facsimile Auto Parallel-319
05SP Authentic Sign of the Times-NY
05SP Game Used Auto Draft-AD-NY
05SP Game Used SIGnificance-NY
05SP Game Used SIGnificance Gold-S-NY
05SP Game Used Statscriptions-ST-MN
05Upper Deck-128
HG Glossy-128
Notable Numbers-N-MNY
05Upper Deck MVP-258
Gold-258
Platinum-258
05Upper Deck Toronto Fall Expo-128
06Be A Player-72
Autographs-72
Signatures-MN
Signatures 25-78
Signatures Trios-TSNP
06O-Pee-Chee-326
Rainbow-326
06Panini Stickers-107
06Upper Deck Arena Giveaways-NYR5
06Upper Deck-382
Exclusives Parallel-382
High Gloss Parallel-382
Masterpieces-382
06Upper Deck MVP-199
Gold Script-199
Super Script-199
06Upper Deck Ovation-132
06Upper Deck Victory-133
06Upper Deck Victory Black-133
06Upper Deck Victory Gold-133
07Upper Deck Ovation-68
07Upper Deck Victory-24
Black-24
Gold-24

Nylander, Peter
92Swedish Semic Elitserien Stickers-356
95Upper Deck-559
Electric Ice-559
Electric Ice Gold-559
95Signature Rookies-21
Signatures-21
97Swedish Collector's Choice-31
98Swedish UD Choice-43
99Swedish Upper Deck-192
03Swedish Elite-153
Silver-153
04Swedish Elitset-264
Gold-264
Signatures Series B-12
05Finnish Cardset -312
06Swedish SHL Elitset-283

Nylund, Gary
82Maple Leafs Postcards-27
83Maple Leafs Postcards-19
83NHL Key Tags-113
83Vachon-94
84Maple Leafs Postcards-18
84O-Pee-Chee-307
84O-Pee-Chee Stickers-15
84O-Pee-Chee Stickers-16
847-Eleven Discs-46
85Maple Leafs Postcards-23
85O-Pee-Chee-172
85O-Pee-Chee Stickers-14
86Blackhawks Coke-11
86O-Pee-Chee-243
86O-Pee-Chee Stickers-137
87Blackhawks Coke-16
87O-Pee-Chee-82
87O-Pee-Chee Stickers-80
87Panini Stickers-224
87Topps-82
88O-Pee-Chee-15
88Panini Stickers-23
88Topps-15
89Islanders Team Issue-15
89O-Pee-Chee-105
89O-Pee-Chee Stickers-114
89Topps-105
90O-Pee-Chee-233
90Panini Stickers-80
90Pro Set-190
90Score-86
Canadian-86
90Topps-233
Tiffany-233
90Upper Deck-139
French-139
91Bowman-228
91O-Pee-Chee-101
91Panini Stickers-251
91Pinnacle-406
French-406
91Pro Set-150
French-150
91Score American-192
91Score Canadian Bilingual-192
91Score Canadian English-192
91Stadium Club-163
91Topps-101
91Upper Deck-406
French-406
92Score-381
Canadian-381
02Maple Leafs Platinum Collection-87

Nyman, Harri
78Finnish SM-Liiga-115
80Finnish Mallasjuoma-75

Nyman, Jan
83Swedish Semic Elitserien-153

Nyman, Stefan
90Swedish Semic Elitserien Stickers-59
91Swedish Semic Elitserien Stickers-232
93Swedish Semic Elitserien-268
99Danish Hockey League-78

Nyman, Tero
96Finnish SISU Redline-11

Nyman, Tomi
00Finnish Cardset-254

Nyqvist, Mika
98Danish Hockey League-203

Nyren, Giffen
06Moose Jaw Warriors-24

Nyrop, Bill
76Canadiens Postcards-15
76O-Pee-Chee NHL-188
76Topps-188
77Canadiens Postcards-18
77O-Pee-Chee NHL-91
77Topps-91
78O-Pee-Chee-134
78Topps-134
81North Stars Postcards-17
91Knoxville Cherokees-1
92Future Trends '76 Canada Cup-158

Nystrom, Bob
73O-Pee-Chee-202
74NHL Action Stamps-176
74O-Pee-Chee NHL-123
74Topps-123
75O-Pee-Chee NHL-259
75O-Pee-Chee NHL-323
75Topps-259
75Topps-323
76O-Pee-Chee NHL-153
76Topps-153
77O-Pee-Chee NHL-62
77Topps-62
78O-Pee-Chee-153
78Topps-153
79Islanders Transparencies-12
79O-Pee-Chee-217
79Topps-217
80O-Pee-Chee-102
80Topps-102
81O-Pee-Chee-217
82O-Pee-Chee-208
82O-Pee-Chee Stickers-59
82Post Cereal-12
82Topps Stickers-59
83Islanders Team Issue-12
83O-Pee-Chee-14
83O-Pee-Chee Stickers-85
83Topps Stickers-85
84Islanders News-11
84O-Pee-Chee-132
84O-Pee-Chee Stickers-85
84Topps-98
84Kelowna Wings-35
85Islanders News-12
85O-Pee-Chee-11
85O-Pee-Chee Stickers-69
85Topps-11
86Islanders Team Issue-4
86O-Pee-Chee-104
86O-Pee-Chee Stickers-204
86Topps-104
91Upper Deck-641
French-641
93Islanders Chemical Bank Alumni-6

00Upper Deck Legends-84
Legendary Collection Bronze-84
Legendary Collection Gold-84
Legendary Collection Silver-84
Legendary Game Jerseys-JBN
00Upper Deck Vintage Dynasty: A Piece of History-NS
00Upper Deck Vintage Dynasty: A Piece of History Gold-NS
01BAP Ultimate Mem Dynasty Jerseys-9
01BAP Ultimate Mem Dynasty Emblems-9
01BAP Ultimate Mem Dynasty Numbers-9
01Fleer Legacy-10
Ultimate-10
01Greats of the Game-4
Autographs-4
01Parkhurst Autographs-PA57
01UD Stanley Cup Champs-20
02BAP Memorabilia Mini Stanley Cups-21
02BAP Ultimate Memorabilia Numerology-26
02Fleer Throwbacks-59
Gold-59
Platinum-59
Autographs-18
02Parkhurst Vintage Teammates-VT11
02UD Foundations-59
02UD Foundations-121
Classic Greats-GBN
Classic Greats Gold-GBN
Classic Greats Silver-G-BN
Lasting Impressions Sticks-L-BN
Playoff Performers-PBN
Playoff Performers Gold-PBN
Playoff Performers Silver-P-BN
Power Stations-SBN
Power Stations Gold-SBN
Power Stations Silver-S-BN
03Topps Stanley Cup Heroes-BN
03Topps Stanley Cup Heroes Autographs-BN
04ITG Franchises US East-379
Autographs-A-BNY
Double Memorabilia-EDM18
Double Memorabilia Autographs-EDM-BN
Double Memorabilia Gold-EDM18
Memorabilia-ESM28
Memorabilia Autographs-ESM-BN
Memorabilia Gold-ESM28
Original Sticks-EOS10
Original Sticks Autographs-EOS-BN
Original Sticks Gold-EOS10
Teammates-ETM7
Teammates Gold-ETM7
04MasterCard Priceless Moments-3
04UD Legendary Signatures-7
AKA Autographs-AKA-BN
Autographs-BN
04UD Legends Classics-6
Gold-6
Platinum-6
Silver-6
Signature Moments-M48
Signatures-CS46
05ITG Ultimate Mem 3 Star of the Game Jsy-14
05ITG Ult Mem 3 Star of the Game Jsy Gold-14
05SP Authentic Sign of the Times Quads-QTBNP
05SPx Xcitement Legends-XL-BN
05SPx Xcitement Legends Gold-XL-BN
05SPx Xcitement Legends Spectrum-XL-BN
05UD Artifacts-140
Blue-140
Gold-140
Green-140
Pewter-140
Red-140
Auto Facts-AF-NY
Auto Facts Blue-AF-NY
Auto Facts Copper-AF-NY
Auto Facts Pewter-AF-NY
Auto Facts Silver-AF-NY
Gold Autographed-140
06ITG Ultimate Memorabilia Road to the Cup-6
06ITG Ultimate Memorabilia Road to the Cup Gold-6
06SP Game Used SIGnificance-SBN
06UD Artifacts-126
Blue-126
Gold-126
Platinum-126
Radiance-126
Autographed Radiance Parallel-126
Red-126
Auto-Facts-AFBN
Auto-Facts Gold-AFBN
Treasured Patches Blue-TSBN
Treasured Patches Gold-TSBN
Treasured Patches Platinum-TSBN
Treasured Patches Red-TSBN
Treasured Swatches-TSBN
Treasured Swatches Black-TSBN
Treasured Swatches Blue-TSBN
Treasured Swatches Gold-TSBN
Treasured Swatches Platinum-TSBN
Treasured Swatches Red-TSBN
Treasured Swatches Autographed Black-TSBN
Tundra Tandems-TTBN
Tundra Tandems Black-TTBN
Tundra Tandems Blue-TTBN
Tundra Tandems Gold-TTBN
Tundra Tandems Platinum-TTBN
Tundra Tandems Red-TTBN
Tundra Tandems Dual Patches Red-TTBN

Nystrom, Eric
97Quebec Pee-Wee Tournament-820
02BAP Memorabilia Draft Redemptions-10
02Michigan Wolverines-11
03Michigan Wolverines-22
04SP Authentic Rookie Redemptions-RR39
04Michigan Wolverines-18
05ITG Heroes/Prosp Toronto Expo Parallel -79
05ITG Heroes/Prosp Toronto Expo Parallel -366
05Hot Prospects-225
Hot Materials-HMEN
Red Hot-225
White Hot-225
05ITG Ultimate Mem Future Stars Autos-21
05ITG Ultimate Mem Future Star Autos Gold-21
05Parkhurst-613
Facsimile Auto Parallel-613
05SP Authentic-141
Limited-141
Prestigious Pairings-PPPN
Rarefied Rookies-RREN
Rookie Authentics-RAEN
Sign of the Times Triples-TIPN
05SP Game Used-126
Autographs-126
Gold-126
Game Gear-GG-EN
Game Gear Autographs-AG-EN
Rookie Exclusives-EN
Rookie Exclusives Silver-RE-EN
Significant Numbers-SN-EN
05SPx-188
Spectrum-188
Xcitement Rookies-XR-EN
Xcitement Rookies Gold-XR-EN
Xcitement Rookies Spectrum-XR-EN
05The Cup-106
Autographed Rookie Patches Gold Rainbow-106
Black Rainbow Rookies-106
Masterpiece Pressplates (Artifacts)-234
Masterpiece Pressplates (Ice)-121
Masterpiece Pressplates (MVP)-405
Masterpiece Pressplates (Power Play)-151
Masterpiece Pressplates (Power Play)-151
Masterpiece Pressplates (Rookie Update)-200
Masterpiece Pressplates SPA Autos-141
Masterpiece Pressplates (SP Game Used)-126
Masterpiece Pressplates SPx Autos-188
Masterpiece Pressplates (Trilogy)-180
Masterpiece Pressplates Ult Coll Autos-106
Masterpiece Pressplates (Victory)-270
Masterpiece Pressplates Autographs-106
Platinum Rookies-106
05UD Artifacts-234
Gold-RED34
05UD PowerPlay-151
05UD Rookie Class-45
05Ultimate Collection-106
Autographed Patches-106
Ultimate Debut Threads Jerseys-DTJEN
Ultimate Debut Threads Jerseys Autos-DAJEN
Ultimate Debut Threads Patches-DTPEN
Ultimate Debut Threads Patches Autos-DAPEN
Ultimate Signatures-USEN
Ultimate Signatures Pairings-UPIN
05Ultra-265
Gold-265
Fresh Ink-FI-EN
Fresh Ink Blue-FI-EN
Ice-265
Rookie Uniformity Jerseys-RU-EN
Rookie Uniformity Jersey Autographs-ARU-EN
Rookie Uniformity Patches-RUP-EN
Rookie Uniformity Patch Autographs-ARP-EN
05Upper Deck-448
Rookie Ink-RIEN
05Upper Deck Rookie Showcase-RS32
05Upper Deck Rookie Showcase Promos-RS32
05Upper Deck Rookie Threads-RTEN
05Upper Deck Rookie Threads Autographs-ARTEN
05Upper Deck Ice-121
Fresh Ice-FIEN
Fresh Ice Glass-FIEN
Fresh Ice Glass Patches-FIPEN
Glacial Graphs-GGEN
Glacial Graphs Labels-GGEN
Premieres Auto Patches-AIPEN
05Upper Deck MVP-405
Gold-405
Platinum-405
05Upper Deck Rookie Update-200
Inspirations Patch Rookies-200
05Upper Deck Trilogy-180
05Upper Deck Victory-270
Black-270
Gold-270
Silver-270
05AHL Top Prospects-26
05ITG Heroes and Prospects-79
05ITG Heroes and Prospects-366
Autographs-A-EN
Autographs Series II-EN2
Jerseys-GUJ-87
Jerseys Gold-GUJ-87
Emblems-GUE-87
Emblems Gold-GUE-87
Numbers-GUN-87
Numbers Gold-GUN-87
Nameplates-N-68
Nameplates Gold-N-68
06Be A Player Portraits First Exposures-FEEN
06SP Game Used SIGnificance-SEN
06Upper Deck Signatures-SEN
06ITG Heroes and Prospects-156
Autographs-AEN
Making The Bigs-MTB08
Making The Bigs Gold-MTB08
Update Autographs-AEN

Nystrom, Gert
64Swedish Coralli ISHockey-116
67Swedish Hockey-178

Nystrom, Jari
70Finnish Jaakiekko-335
80Finnish Mallasjuoma-213

Nystrom, Karen
94Classic Women of Hockey-W20
97Collector's Choice-295

Nystrom, Lars Frederik
72Swedish Stickers-201
83Swedish Semic Elitserien-186
84Swedish Semic Elitserien-209

Nystrom, Murray
85London Knights-6
86London Knights-14
93London Knights-28

Nystrom, Ove
70Swedish Hockey-218

Nystrom, Seppo
65Finnish Hellas-47
66Finnish Jaakiekkosarja-41

Nyyssonen, Tommi
95Finnish SISU-83
96Finnish SISU Redline-83

O'Brien, Andy
82Kitchener Rangers-26

O'Brien, Bert
99Ottawa 67's-27
00Ottawa 67's-23
01Ottawa 67's-23
02Ottawa 67's-25

O'Brien, Craig
93Quebec Pee-Wee Tournament-557

O'Brien, Dan
89Nashville Knights-16

O'Brien, David
88ProCards AHL-50
89ProCards IHL-19
90ProCards AHL/IHL-92

O'Brien, Dennis
71Toronto Sun-140
73North Stars Action Posters-8
73North Stars Postcards-14
73O-Pee-Chee-88
73Topps-177
74NHL Action Stamps-128
74O-Pee-Chee NHL-96
74Topps-96
75O-Pee-Chee NHL-53
75Topps-53
76O-Pee-Chee NHL-34
76O-Pee-Chee NHL-387
76Topps-34
77O-Pee-Chee NHL-173
77Topps-173
78O-Pee-Chee-104
78Topps-104
79O-Pee-Chee-375
92Toledo Storm Team Issue-29

O'Brien, Doug
00Hull Olympiques-4
Signed-4
01Hull Olympiques-5
02Hull Olympiques-5
03Gatineau Olympiques-16
03Hull Olympiques Memorial Cup-11
04Springfield Falcons-10
04ITG Heroes and Prospects-73
Autographs-DO
04ITG Heroes/Prospects Toronto Expo '05-73
04ITG Heroes/Prospects Expo Heroes/Pros-73
05Hot Prospects-174
En Fuego-174
Red Hot-174
White Hot-174
05SP Authentic-282
Limited-282
05SP Game Used-234
05SPx-286
05The Cup Masterpiece Pressplates (Ice)-262
05The Cup Master Pressplate Rookie Update-184
05The Cup Masterpiece Pressplates SPA-282
05The Cup Masterpiece Pressplates SP GU-234
05The Cup Masterpiece Pressplates (SPx)-286
05The Cup Masterpiece Pressplates Trilogy-310
05The Cup Masterpiece Pressplates Ult Coll-227
05Ultimate Collection-227
Gold-227
05Upper Deck Ice-262
05Upper Deck Rookie Update-184
05Upper Deck Trilogy-310
05Springfield Falcons-7
06Springfield Falcons-2
06ITG Heroes and Prospects-53
Autographs-ADO

O'Brien, Greg
04P.E.I. Rocket-8
05PEI Rocket-9

O'Brien, J.Ambrose
83Hall of Fame-206
83Hall of Fame Postcards-N11
85Hall of Fame-206

O'Brien, Jim
06Minnesota Golden Gophers-15

O'Brien, Keith
00Austin Ice Bats-15

O'Brien, Maurice
90 7th Inn. Sketch OHL-90

O'Brien, Sean
94Richmond Renegades-17
95Anaheim Bullfrogs RHI-14
95Tallahassee Tiger Sharks-7

O'Brien, Shane
00Kingston Frontenacs-14
01Kingston Frontenacs-15
03Cincinnati Mighty Ducks-B10
04Cincinnati Mighty Ducks-6
05Portland Pirates-3
06Beehive-103
Matte-103
06Black Diamond-159A
Black-159A
Gold-159A
Ruby-159A
06Hot Prospects-102
Red Hot-102
White Hot-102
Hot Materials -HMSO
Hot Materials Red Hot-HMSO
Hot Materials White Hot-HMSO
Hotagraphs-HSO
06O-Pee-Chee-536
06O-Pee-Chee-641
Rainbow-536
Rainbow-641
06SP Authentic-162
Limited-162
06SP Game Used-101
Gold-101
Rainbow-101
Autographs-101
Rookie Exclusives Autographs-RESO
06SPx-155
Spectrum-155
06The Cup-109
Autographed Rookie Masterpiece Pressplates-109
Gold Rainbow Autographed Rookie Patches-109
Masterpiece Pressplates (Bee Hive)-103
Masterpiece Pressplates (Black Diamond)-159
Masterpiece Pressplates (Marquee Rookies)-536
Masterpiece Pressplates (MVP)-314
Masterpiece Pressplates (SP Authentic Autographs)-162
Masterpiece Pressplates (SP Game Used)-101
Masterpiece Pressplates (SPx)-155
Masterpiece Pressplates (Sweet Beginnings)-101
Masterpiece Pressplates (Trilogy)-101
Masterpiece Pressplates (Victory)-281
NHL Shields Duals-DSHOS
Rookies Black-109
Rookies Platinum-109
06Ultimate Collection Ultimate Debut Threads Jerseys-DJ-SO
06Ultimate Collection Ultimate Debut Threads Jerseys Autographs-DJ-SO
06Ultimate Collection Ultimate Debut Threads Patches-DJ-SO
06Ultimate Collection Ultimate Debut Threads Patches Autographs-DJ-SO
06Upper Deck-201
Exclusives Parallel-201
High Gloss Parallel-201
Masterpieces-201
Rookie Materials-RMSO
Rookie Materials Patches-RMSO
06Upper Deck MVP-314
Gold Script-314
Super Script-314
06Upper Deck Sweet Shot-101
Rookie Jerseys Autographs-101
06Upper Deck Trilogy-101
06Upper Deck Victory-281
07Upper Deck Rookie Class -42

O'Brien, Steve
96New Hampshire Wildcats-30
97New Hampshire Wildcats-13
98New Hampshire Wildcats-12
99ECHL All-Star Southern Conference-18
00Trenton Titans-6
01Trenton Titans-2-8
02Trenton Titans-B-7
03UK Coventry Blaze-5

O'Brien, Toby
00Johnstown Chiefs-5
02Johnstown Chiefs-11
04Johnstown Chiefs-21

O'Byrne, Ryan
06Hamilton Bulldogs-22

O'Callahan, Jack
80USA Olympic Team Mini Pics-6
83Blackhawks Postcards-17
84O-Pee-Chee-43
84Topps-33
85Blackhawks Team Issue-21
86Blackhawks Coke-12
86O-Pee-Chee-207
88Devils Caretta-22
95Signature Rookies Miracle on Ice-23
95Signature Rookies Miracle on Ice-24
95Signature Rook Miracle on Ice Sigs-23
95Signature Rook Miracle on Ice Sigs-24

O'Connell, Drew
04Waterloo Blackhawks-13

O'Connell, Jack
37V356 Worldwide Gum-107

O'Connell, John
91Minnesota Golden Gophers-20

O'Connell, Keith
97Pensacola Ice Pilots-15
98Pensacola Ice Pilots-8
99Greensboro Generals-7

O'Connell, Mike
79Blackhawks Postcards-16
80O-Pee-Chee-61
80Topps-61
81O-Pee-Chee-6
81Topps-E70
82O-Pee-Chee-17
82O-Pee-Chee Stickers-89
82Post Cereal-1
82Topps Stickers-89
83Bruins Team Issue-13
83NHL Key Tags-4
83O-Pee-Chee-56
83O-Pee-Chee Stickers-52
83Topps Stickers-52
84Bruins Postcards-14
84O-Pee-Chee-12
84O-Pee-Chee Stickers-185
84Topps-9
85O-Pee-Chee-2
85O-Pee-Chee Stickers-161
85Topps-2
86O-Pee-Chee-140
86Topps-140
87O-Pee-Chee-141
87O-Pee-Chee Stickers-107
87Panini Stickers-240
87Red Wings Little Caesars-22
87Topps-141
88O-Pee-Chee-92
88O-Pee-Chee Stickers-248
88Red Wings Little Caesars-18
88Topps-92
89O-Pee-Chee-223
89O-Pee-Chee Stickers-249
89Panini Stickers-69
89Red Wings Little Caesars-14
90O-Pee-Chee-114
90Panini Stickers-215
90Pro Set-75
90Topps-114
Tiffany-114
90ProCards AHL/IHL-296
93St. Cloud State Huskies-20

O'Connell, Pat
97Idaho Steelheads-13

O'Connell, Tim
02Roanoke Express-25
02Roanoke Express RBI Sports-201
03Florida Everblades-14
04Florida Everblades-14
05Missouri River Otters-15
06Stockton Thunder-15b

O'Conner, Mike
93UK Humberside Hawks-17
94UK Sheffield Steelers-9
95UK Sheffield Steelers-8

O'Conner, Patrick
94UK Sheffield Steelers-7
98UK Kingston Hawks-16

O'Connor, Buddy
34Beehive Group I Photos-172
37V356 Worldwide Gum-114
43Parade Sportive *-45
43Parade Sportive *-53
43Parade Sportive *-93
44Beehive Group II Photos-349
45Quaker Oats Photos-102A
45Quaker Oats Photos-102B
05ITG Ultimate Mem Bleu Blanc Rouge Autos-8
05ITG Ultimate Mem Broadway Bluesh Autos-1

O'Connor, Eric
91 7th Inn. Sketch QMJHL-166

O'Connor, Gabriel
06Halifax Mooseheads-18

O'Connor, J.P.
00Jackson Bandits-8
03Gwinnett Gladiators-23

O'Connor, Jeff
93RPI Engineers-19

O'Connor, Mike
94Finnish Jaa Kiekko-315
00UK Sheffield Steelers Centurions-13
01UK Hull Thunder-23
02UK Hull Thunder-25

O'Connor, Myles
89ProCards AHL-206
90Devils Team Issue-21
90ProCards AHL/IHL-576
91O-Pee-Chee-509
91Score American-322
91Score Canadian Bilingual-352
91Score Canadian English-352
91Topps-509
91Upper Deck-485
French-485
91ProCards-425
93OPC Premier Gold-527
93Parkhurst-274
Emerald Ice-274
93Topps/OPC Premier Gold-527G
95Houston Aeros-17
96Cincinnati Cyclones-6

O'Connor, Scott
94Finnish Jaa Kiekko-312

O'Connor, Sean
01Moose Jaw Warriors-9
03Erie Otters-18
03San Antonio Rampage-11
04Cincinnati Mighty Ducks-13
04Erie Otters-8
05Erie Otters-8
05Las Vegas Wranglers-16
06Erie Otters-2
06Plymouth Whalers-17

O'Connor, Terry
52Juniors Blue Tint-161

O'Connor, Tom
93Classic-107
Class of '94-CL7
98ECHL All-Star Northern Conference-1

O'Day, Dan
90Arizona Icecats-9

O'Dette, Matt
93Kitchener Rangers-21
95Slapshot-154
96Roanoke Express-22
00Quebec Citadelles-16
Signed-16
01Quebec Citadelles-17
02Hamilton Bulldogs-10
04Fresno Falcons-13
05Fresno Falcons-15

O'Donnell, Conor
06Brampton Battalion-11

O'Donnell, Fred
73O-Pee-Chee-223
85Kingston Canadians-4
86Kingston Canadians-2

O'Donnell, Mark
91 7th Inn. Sketch OHL-292
96Fort Worth Fire-15
97Fort Worth Brahmas-15

O'Donnell, Sean
88Sudbury Wolves-7
89Sudbury Wolves-17
90 7th Inn. Sketch OHL-390
90Sudbury Wolves-6
91ProCards-10
91Rochester Americans Kodak-20
91Rochester Americans Postcards-16
92Rochester Americans Dunkin' Donuts-12
92Rochester Americans Kodak-15
93Rochester Americans Kodak-18
93Classic Pro Prospects-109
96Be A Player-152
Autographs-152
Autographs Silver-152
97Pacific Invincible NHL Regime-96
98Pacific-242
Ice Blue-242
Red-242
99Pacific-195
Copper-195
Emerald Green-195
Gold-195
Ice Blue-195
Premiere Date-195
Red-195
00BAP Memorabilia-20
Emerald-20
Ruby-20
Sapphire-20
Promos-20
00BAP Mem Chicago Sportsfest Copper-20
00BAP Memorabilia Chicago Sportsfest Blue-20
00BAP Memorabilia Chicago Sportsfest Gold-20
00BAP Memorabilia Chicago Sportsfest Ruby-20
00BAP Memorabilia Chicago Sun-Times Ruby-20
00BAP Memorabilia Chicago Sun-Times Gold-20
00BAP Mem Chicago Sun-Times Sapphire-20
00BAP Mem Toronto Fall Expo Copper-20
00BAP Memorabilia Toronto Fall Expo Gold-20
00BAP Memorabilia Toronto Fall Expo Ruby-20
00Panini Stickers-176
00Paramount-122
Copper-122
Gold-122
Holo-Gold-122
Holo-Silver-122
Ice Blue-122
Premiere Date-122
00Revolution-73
Blue-73
Premiere Date-73
Red-73
00Topps Chrome-238
OPC Refractors-238
Refractors-238
00Upper Deck-317
Exclusives Tier 1-317
Exclusives Tier 2-317
01Parkhurst-242
02Pacific Complete-66
Red-66
02Topps Total-356
03Bruins Team Issue-7
03Parkhurst Original Six Boston-25
06O-Pee-Chee-9
Rainbow-9

O'Donoghue, Don
71O-Pee-Chee-180
71Sargent Promotions Stamps-142
71Toronto Sun-54

O'Driscoll, Alain
00Muskegon Fury-3

O'Drowski, Gerry
63Quebec Aces-19

O'Dwyer, Billy
88Bruins Postcards-15
89ProCards AHL-71
90ProCards AHL/IHL-420
98Bruins Alumni-27
Autographs-27

O'Dwyer, Mike
03Regina Pats-18

O'Flaherty, Gerry
72Canucks Royal Bank-15
72O-Pee-Chee-278
73Canucks Royal Bank-15
73O-Pee-Chee-250
74Canucks Royal Bank-15
74NHL Action Stamps-284
74O-Pee-Chee NHL-71
74Topps-71
75Canucks Royal Bank-16
75O-Pee-Chee NHL-307
75Topps-307
76Canucks Royal Bank-14
76O-Pee-Chee NHL-287
77Canucks Royal Bank-16
77O-Pee-Chee NHL-377
78O-Pee-Chee-365

O'Flaherty, John
34Beehive Group I Photos-245
51Laval Dairy Subset-111
52St. Lawrence Sales-71

O'Flaherty, Kevin
03Las Vegas Wranglers-15
03Las Vegas Wranglers RBI-237

O'Flaherty, Patrick
91British Columbia JHL-114
92British Columbia JHL-179

O'Grady, Mike
95Lethbridge Hurricanes-17
95Classic-51
96Lethbridge Hurricanes-11
98Port Huron Border Cats-2

O'Hagan, Paul
89Oshawa Generals-24
89Oshawa Generals 7th Inning Sketch-14
89 7th Inn. Sketch OHL-14
89 7th Inn. Sketch OHL-194
90 7th Inn. Sketch OHL-344
90 7th Inn. Sketch Memorial Cup-78

O'Hagan, Sean
89Windsor Spitfires-13
90 7th Inn. Sketch OHL-190

O'Handley, P.K.
98Florida Everblades-16
99Florida Everblades-24
00Florida Everblades-21
01Florida Everblades-3

O'Hara, Colin
95Swift Current Broncos-12
96Medicine Hat Tigers-15

O'Hara, Mike
92Fort Worth Fire-14
93Fort Worth Fire-13
93Phoenix Cobras RHI-12

O'Hunter, Pat
28V128-2 Paulin's Candy-43

O'Kane, Kyle
06Lincoln Stars-18
06Lincoln Stars Upper DeckÂ Signature Series -23

O'Keefe, Ryan
96Barrie Colts-19
98Barrie Colts-1
02ECHL All-Star Southern-51
02ECHL Update-U-17

O'Leary, Brian
96Owen Sound Platers-2
97Owen Sound Platers-25
00Owen Sound Attack-13

O'Leary, Geoff
03Elmira Jackals-14

O'Leary, Jamie
01Atlantic City Boardwalk Bullies-17

O'Leary, Kelly
94Classic Women of Hockey-W39

O'Leary, Mark
03Mississauga Ice Dogs-14
04Guelph Storm-12
05Guelph Storm-A-03
06Rio Grande Valley Killer Bees-3

O'Leary, Mickey
24C144 Champ's Cigarettes-46

O'Leary, Pat
98Minnesota Golden Gophers-20
98Sioux City Musketeers-17
99Minnesota Golden Gophers-17
00Minnesota Golden Gophers-17
01Minnesota Golden Gophers-23
03Kalamazoo Wings-17

O'Malley, Brett
00Lethbridge Hurricanes-17
01Lethbridge Hurricanes-15
04Calgary Hitmen-14

O'Malley, Mike
01New Mexico Scorpions-5
02New Mexico Scorpions-11

O'Malley, Terry
69Swedish Hockey-360
70Swedish Masterserien-18

O'Marra, Ryan
03Erie Otters-19
04Erie Otters-17
04Erie Otters-NNO
05ITG Heroes/Prosp Toronto Expo Parallel -118
05Erie Otters-1
05Extreme Top Prospects Signature Edition-S30
05OHL Bell All-Star Classic-34
05ITG Heroes and Prospects-118
Autographs-A-RO
Oh Canada-OC-5
Oh Canada Gold-OC-5
06ITG Heroes and Prospects Jerseys-GUJ45
06ITG Heroes and Prospects Jerseys Gold-GUJ45
06ITG Heroes and Prospects Emblems-GUE45
06ITG Heroes and Prospects Emblems Gold-GUE45
06ITG Heroes and Prospects Numbers-GUN45
06ITG Heroes and Prospects Numbers Gold-GUN45
07ITG Going For Gold World Juniors-19
Autographs-19
Emblems-GUE19
Jerseys-GUJ19
Numbers-GUN19

O'Meara, Cliff
23Crescent Selkirks-1
23V128-1 Paulin's Candy-9
24Crescent Selkirks-10
28V128-2 Paulin's Candy-78

O'Nabigon, Nathan
01Mississauga Ice Dogs-5
03Kitchener Rangers-20
03Kitchener Rangers Memorial Cup-16

O'Neil, Peggy
34Beehive Group I Photos-26
37V356 Worldwide Gum-63

O'Neill, Don
89Peterborough Petes-112
89 7th Inn. Sketch OHL-112
90 7th Inn. Sketch OHL-367
91Peterborough Petes-14
91 7th Inn. Sketch OHL-138

O'Neill, Jeff
93Upper Deck Program of Excellence-E4
93Guelph Storm-2
93Guelph Storm-26
93Classic-108
93Classic-115
Autographs-AU8
Class of '94-CL1
Crash Numbered-N3
Promos-2
94Finest-162
Super Team Winners-162
Refractors-162
94Leaf Limited World Juniors Canada-6
94Pinnacle-534
Artist's Proofs-534
Rink Collection-534
94SP-152
Die Cuts-152
94Guelph Storm-25
94Classic-5
Gold-5
Autographs-5
CHL All-Stars-C7
Draft Day-8
Draft Day-9
Draft Day-10
ROY Sweepstakes-R15
Tri-Cards-T28
94Classic Pro Prospects-205
94Classic Pro Prospects-209
94Assets *-57
94Assets *-82
Phone Cards One Minute/$2-41
94Classic Four-Sport *-119
Gold-119
Autographs-119A
BCs-BC19
High Voltage-HV19
Phone Cards-6
Previews-P1
Printers Proofs-119
Tri-Cards-TC4
95Bashan Super Stickers-55
95Be A Player-166
Signatures-S166
Signatures Die Cuts-S166
95Bowman-118
All-Foil-118
Bowman's Best-BB26
Bowman's Best Refractors-BB26
95Collector's Choice-401
95Donruss-244
Canadian World Junior Team-14
Rated Rookies-4
95Donruss Elite-21
Die Cut Stars-21
Die Cut Uncut-21
Rookies-12
95Finest-96
Refractors-96
95Imperial Stickers-55
95Leaf Limited-63
Rookie Phenoms-8
95Metal-186
95Parkhurst International-259
Emerald Ice-259
95Select Certified-118
Mirror Gold-118
Future-8
95SkyBox Impact-202
NHL On Fox-11
95SP-64
95Stadium Club-192
Members Only Master Set-192
95Summit-183
Artist's Proofs-183
Ice-183
95Topps-285
OPC Inserts-285
Canadian World Juniors-20CJ
SuperSkills Super Rookies-SR3
95Ultra-351
95Upper Deck-264
Electric Ice-264
Electric Ice Gold-264
95Whalers Bob's Stores-20
95Zenith-130
Rookie Roll Call-18
95Images-44
Gold-44
Clear Excitement-CE16
95Images Four-Sport *-98
95Assets Gold *-2
95Assets Gold Phone Cards $2 *-2
96Black Diamond-92
Gold-92
96Collector's Choice-121
96Collector's Choice-343
96Donruss Rated Rookies-5
96Donruss Canadian Ice-82
Gold Press Proofs-82
Red Press Proofs-82
96Donruss Elite-39
Die Cut Stars-39
Aspirations-9
96Fleer Picks-158
96Leaf-209
Press Proofs-209
96Leaf Limited-68
Gold-68
96Leaf Preferred-9
Press Proofs-9
96Metal Universe-69
96Pinnacle-210
Artist's Proofs-210
Foil-210
Premium Stock-210
Rink Collection-210
96Score-250
Artist's Proofs-250
Dealer's Choice Artist's Proofs-250
Special Artist's Proofs-250
Golden Blades-250
96Select Certified-90
Artist's Proofs-90
Blue-90
Mirror Blue-90
Mirror Gold-90
Mirror Red-90
Red-90
96SP-67
96Summit-168
Artist's Proofs-168
Ice-168
Metal-168
Premium Stock-168
96Topps Picks Rookie Stars-RS17
96Topps Picks Rookie Stars OPC-RS17
96Upper Deck-70
96Whalers Kid's Club-6
96Zenith-29
Artist's Proofs-29
96Visions *-93
97Be A Player-130
Autographs-130
Autographs Die-Cuts-130
Autographs Prismatic Die-Cuts-130
97Collector's Choice-117
97Donruss-16
Press Proofs Silver-16
Press Proofs Gold-16
97Donruss Limited-61
Exposure-61
97Donruss Preferred-30
Cut to the Chase-30
97Donruss Priority-125
Stamp of Approval-125
97Hurricanes Team Issue-19
97Pacific-140
Copper-140
Emerald Green-140
Ice Blue-140
Red-140
Silver-140
97Pinnacle-154
Press Plates Back Black-154
Press Plates Back Cyan-154
Press Plates Back Magenta-154
Press Plates Back Yellow-154
Press Plates Front Black-154
Press Plates Front Cyan-154
Press Plates Front Magenta-154
Press Plates Front Yellow-154
97Pinnacle Certified-128
Red-128
Mirror Blue-128
Mirror Gold-128
Mirror Red-128
97Pinnacle Inside-149
97Pinnacle Tot Cert Platinum Blue-128
97Pinnacle Tot Cert Platinum Gold-128
97Pinnacle Totally Certified Platinum Red-128
97Pinnacle Tot Cert Mirror Platinum Gold-128
97Score-147
Artist's Proofs-147
Golden Blades-147
97SP Authentic-28
97Upper Deck-34
98Aurora-36
98Be A Player-175
Press Release-175
98BAP Gold-175
98BAP Autographs-175
98BAP Autographs Gold-175
98Hurricanes Team Issue-24
98Pacific-137
Ice Blue-137
Red-137
98Paramount-40
Copper-40
Emerald Green-40
Holo-Electric-40
Ice Blue-40
Silver-40
98UD Choice-37
98UD Choice Preview-37
98UD Choice Prime Choice Reserve-37
98UD Choice Reserve-37
98Upper Deck-61
Exclusives-61
Exclusives 1 of 1-61
Gold Reserve-61
98Upper Deck MVP-40
Gold Script-40
Silver Script-40
Super Script-40
99BAP Millennium-51
Emerald-51
Ruby-51
Sapphire-51
Signatures-51
Signatures Gold-51
99Crown Royale-29
99O-Pee-Chee-150
99O-Pee-Chee Chrome-150
99O-Pee-Chee Chrome Refractors-150
99Pacific-78
Copper-78
Emerald Green-78
Gold-78
Ice Blue-78
Premiere Date-78
Red-78
99Pacific Omega-48
Copper-48
Gold-48
Ice Blue-48
Premiere Date-48
99Paramount-48
Copper-48
Emerald-48
Gold-48
Holographic Emerald-48
Holographic Gold-48
Holographic Silver-48
Ice Blue-48
Premiere Date-48
Red-48
Silver-48
99Topps/OPC-150
99Topps/OPC Chrome-150
Refractors-150
99Upper Deck-200
Exclusives-200
Exclusives 1 of 1-200
99Upper Deck Arena Giveaways-CH2
99Upper Deck Gold Reserve-200
99Upper Deck MVP SC Edition-37
Gold Script-37
Silver Script-37
Super Script-37
99Upper Deck Victory-62
00BAP Memorabilia-110
Emerald-110
Ruby-110
Sapphire-110
Promos-110
00BAP Mem Chicago Sportsfest Copper-110
00BAP Memorabilia Chicago Sportsfest Blue-110
00BAP Memorabilia Chicago Sportsfest Gold-110
00BAP Memorabilia Chicago Sportsfest Ruby-110
00BAP Memorabilia Chicago Sun-Times Ruby-110
00BAP Memorabilia Chicago Sun-Times Gold-110
00BAP Mem Chicago Sun-Times Sapphire-110
00BAP Mem Toronto Fall Expo Copper-110
00BAP Memorabilia Toronto Fall Expo Gold-110
00BAP Memorabilia Toronto Fall Expo Ruby-110
00BAP Parkhurst 2000-P59
00BAP Signature Series-229
Emerald-229
Ruby-229
Sapphire-229
Autographs-34

Autographs Gold-34
Franchise Players-F6
00Black Diamond-11
Gold-11
00O-Pee-Chee-121
00O-Pee-Chee Parallel-121
00Pacific-88
Copper-88
Gold-88
Ice Blue-88
Premiere Date-88
00Paramount-45
Copper-45
Gold-45
Holo-Gold-45
Holo-Silver-45
Ice Blue-45
Premiere Date-45
00SP Authentic-17
00Stadium Club-142
00Topps/OPC-121
Parallel-121
00Topps Stars-59
Blue-59
00UD Heroes-22
00UD Pros and Prospects-17
00Upper Deck-260
Exclusives Tier 1-260
Exclusives Tier 2-260
00Upper Deck MVP-37
First Stars-37
Second Stars-37
Third Stars-37
00Upper Deck Victory-49
00Upper Deck Vintage-65
00Upper Deck Vintage-73
01Atomic-18
Blue-18
Gold-18
Premiere Date-18
Red-18
Power Play-6
Team Nucleus-3
01BAP Memorabilia-276
Emerald-276
Ruby-276
Sapphire-276
01BAP Signature Series Certified 100-C18
01BAP Signature Series Certified 50-C18
01BAP Signature Series Certified 1 of 1's-C18
01BAP Signature Series Autographs-LJO
01BAP Signature Series Autographs Gold-LJO
01BAP Signature Series Jerseys-GJ-25
01BAP Signature Series Jersey Autographs-GUJO
01BAP Sig Series Jersey and Stick Cards-GSJ-25
01Bowman YoungStars-77
Gold-77
Ice Cubed-77
01Crown Royale-28
Blue-28
Premiere Date-28
Red-28
Retail-28
Jewels of the Crown-5
01O-Pee-Chee-107
01O-Pee-Chee Heritage Parallel-107
01O-Pee-Chee Heritage Parallel Limited-107
01O-Pee-Chee Premier Parallel-107
01Pacific-78
Extreme LTD-78
Hobby LTD-78
Premiere Date-78
Retail LTD-78
01Pacific Adrenaline-36
Blue-36
Premiere Date-36
Red-36
Retail-36
01Pacific Arena Exclusives-78
01Pacific Heads-Up-17
Blue-17
Premiere Date-17
Red-17
Silver-17
01Parkhurst-6
Gold-6
Silver-6
01Private Stock-16
Gold-16
Premiere Date-16
Retail-16
Silver-16
Game Gear-19
01Private Stock Pacific Nights-16
01Private Stock PS-2002-13
01SP Authentic Sign of the Times-JN
01SP Game Used-7
01SPx-162
01Titanium-27
Hobby Parallel-27
Premiere Date-27
Retail-27
Retail Parallel-27
Double-Sided Jerseys-45
Double-Sided Jerseys-62
Double-Sided Patches-62
Double-Sided Patches-45
01Titanium Draft Day Edition-19
01Topps-107
Heritage Parallel-107
Heritage Parallel Limited-107
OPC Parallel-107
01Topps Chrome-107
Refractors-107
Black Border Refractors-107
01Topps Heritage-87
Refractors-87
01Topps Reserve-90
01UD Challenge for the Cup-12
01UD Playmakers-17
01UD Top Shelf-6
01Upper Deck-31
Exclusives-31
01Upper Deck MVP-33
01Upper Deck Victory-63
Gold-63
01Upper Deck Vintage-44
01Upper Deck Vintage-51
01Upper Deck Vintage-52
01Vanguard-17
Blue-17
Red-17
One of Ones-17
Premiere Date-17
Proofs-17
Quebec Tournament Heroes-14
02Atomic-18
Blue-18
Gold-18
Red-18
Cold Fusion-6
Hobby Parallel-18
02BAP First Edition-9
02BAP First Edition-346
02BAP First Edition-412H
Jerseys-9
02BAP Memorabilia-148
Emerald-148
Ruby-148
Sapphire-148
NHL All-Star Game-148
NHL All-Star Game Blue-148
NHL All-Star Game Green-148
NHL All-Star Game Red-148
Stanley Cup Playoffs-SC-24
02BAP Memorabilia Toronto Fall Expo-148
02BAP Signature Series-173
Autographs-173
Autograph Buybacks 1998-175
Autograph Buybacks 1999-51
Autograph Buybacks 2000-34
Autograph Buybacks 2001-LJO
Autographs Gold-173
Golf-GS41
02BAP Ultimate Memorabilia Hat Tricks-4
02Bowman YoungStars-31
Gold-31
Silver-31
02Crown Royale-19
Blue-19
Red-19
Retail-19
02Hurricanes Postcards-5
02ITG Used-6
02ITG Used-106
Franchise Players-F6
Franchise Players Autographs-F6
Franchise Players Gold-F6
02O-Pee-Chee-258
02O-Pee-Chee Premier Blue Parallel-258
02O-Pee-Chee Premier Red Parallel-258
02O-Pee-Chee Factory Set-258
02Pacific-69
Blue-69
Red-69
02Pacific Complete-445
Red-445
02Pacific Exclusive-31
02Pacific Heads-Up-23
Blue-23
Purple-23
Red-23
Quad Jerseys-6
Quad Jerseys Gold-6
02Pacific Quest for the Cup-15
Gold-15
02Parkhurst-120
Bronze-120
Gold-120
Silver-120
Franchise Players-FP6
Jerseys-GJ9
Stick and Jerseys-SJ9
02Parkhurst Retro-41
Minis-41
02Private Stock Reserve-18
Blue-18
Red-18
Retail-18
02SP Game Used-8
02SPx-11
02SPx-81
Spectrum Gold-11
Spectrum Gold-81
Spectrum Silver-11
Spectrum Silver-81
02Stadium Club-32
Silver Decoy Cards-32
Proofs-32
02Titanium-19
Blue-19
Red-19
Retail-19
Jerseys-10
Jerseys Retail-10
Patches-10
02Topps-258
OPC Blue Parallel-258
OPC Red Parallel-258
Factory Set-258
02Topps Chrome-141
Black Border Refractors-141
Refractors-141
02Topps Heritage-84
Chrome Parallel-84
02Topps Total-241
02UD Artistic Impressions-16
Gold-16
02UD Artistic Impressions Beckett Promos-16
02UD Artistic Impressions Retrospectives-R16
02UD Artistic Impress Retrospect Gold-R16
02UD Artistic Impress Retrospect Silver-R16
02UD Honor Roll Team Warriors-TW3
02UD Piece of History-11
02UD Top Shelf-15
02Upper Deck-34
Exclusives-34
Blow-Ups-C5
02Upper Deck Classic Portraits-19
02Upper Deck MVP-35
Gold-35
Classics-35
Golden Classics-35
02Upper Deck Victory-37
Bronze-37
Gold-37
Silver-37
02Upper Deck Vintage-49
02Upper Deck Vintage-266
Green Backs-49
02Vanguard-19
LTD-19
03BAP Memorabilia-38
Emerald-38
Gold-38
Ruby-38
Sapphire-38
03BAP Ultimate Memorabilia Autographs-38
Gold-38
03BAP Ultimate Mem Franch Present Future-6
03Beehive-33
Gold-33
Silver-33
03Black Diamond-96
Black-96
Green-96
Red-96
03Crown Royale-17
Blue-17
Retail-17
03Hurricanes Postcards-14
03ITG Action-141
03ITG Used Signature Series-77
Gold-77
Autographs-JO
Autographs Gold-JO
Franchise-6
Franchise Autographs-6
Franchise Gold-6
03NHL Sticker Collection-37
03O-Pee-Chee-116
03OPC Blue-116
03OPC Gold-116
03OPC Red-116
03Pacific-65
Blue-65
Red-65
03Pacific Complete-268
Red-268
03Pacific Exhibit-29
Blue Backs-29
Yellow Backs-29
03Pacific Invincible-16
Blue-16
Red-16
Retail-16
03Pacific Prism-22
Blue-22
Gold-22
Red-22
03Pacific Supreme-16
Blue-16
Red-16
Retail-16
03Private Stock Reserve-19
Blue-19
Red-19
Retail-19
03SPx-17
Radiance-17
Spectrum-17
03Titanium-21
Hobby Jersey Number Parallels-21
Retail-21
Retail Jersey Number Parallels-21
03Topps-116
Blue-116
Gold-116
Red-116
03Topps C55-73
Minis-73
Minis American Back-73
Minis American Back Red-73
Minis Bazooka Back-73
Minis Brooklyn Back-73
Minis Hat Trick Back-73
Minis O Canada Back-73
Minis O Canada Back Red-73
Minis Stanley Cup Back-73
03Upper Deck-34
Canadian Exclusives-34
HG-34
03Upper Deck Classic Portraits-16
03Upper Deck MVP-77
Gold Script-77
Silver Script-77
Canadian Exclusives-77
SportsNut-SN18
03Upper Deck Trilogy-16
Limited-16
03Upper Deck Victory-32
Bronze-32
Gold-32
Silver-32
03Toronto Star-13
04Pacific-49
Blue-49
Red-49
04Upper Deck-31
Canadian Exclusives-31
HG Glossy Gold-31
HG Glossy Silver-31
05Be A Player Signatures-JO
05Be A Player Signatures Gold-JO
05Beehive Signature Scrapbook-SSJO
05Black Diamond-16
Emerald-16
Gold-16
Onyx-16
Ruby-16
05Panini Stickers-167
05Parkhurst Facsimile Auto Parallel-454
05SP Authentic Sign of the Times-JO
05SP Authentic Sign of the Times Duals-DSO
05SP Authentic Sign of the Times Triples-TBSO
05SP Authentic Sign of the Times Quads-QSSOS
05SP Game Used SIGnificance-JO
05SP Game Used SIGnificance Gold-S-JO
05SP Game Used Significant Numbers-SN-ON
05SP Game Used Statscriptions-ST-JO
05Ultimate Coll Ultimate Achievements-UAON
05Ultimate Collection Ultimate Signatures-USON
05Ultra-182
Gold-182
Fresh Ink-FI-JO
Fresh Ink Blue-FI-JO
Ice-182
05Upper Deck-424
Jerseys Series II-J2ON
Notable Numbers-N-JEO
05Upper Deck Hockey Showcase-HS29
05Upper Deck Showcase Promos-HS29
05Upper Deck MVP-366
Gold-366
Platinum-366
05Upper Deck Victory-33
05Upper Deck Victory-248
Black-33
Black-248
Gold-33
Gold-248
Silver-33
Silver-248
Stars on Ice-SI9
06Black Diamond Gemography-GJO
06Flair Showcase Inks-IJO
06Gatorade-68
06O-Pee-Chee-464
Rainbow-464
06Panini Stickers-167
06Ultra Fresh Ink-IJO
06Upper Deck-432
Exclusives Parallel-432
High Gloss Parallel-432
Masterpieces-432
06Upper Deck MVP-279
Gold Script-279
Super Script-279
07Upper Deck Victory-58
Black-58
Gold-58

O'Neill, Mike

90Moncton Hawks-19
90ProCards AHL/IHL-344
91ProCards-259
92Parkhurst-441
Emerald Ice-441
93Classic Pro Prospects-39
94Parkhurst-268
Gold-268
97Portland Pirates-19
99Long Beach Ice Dogs-4
00UK Sekonda Superleague-143
00UK Sheffield Steelers-18

O'Neill, Ryan

917th Inn. Sketch OHL-180
92Windsor Spitfires-10

O'Neill, Sean

93Quebec Pee-Wee Tournament-744

O'Neill, Wes

04Notre Dame Fighting Irish-1

O'Rear, Hayden

93Knoxville Cherokees-12
94Knoxville Cherokees-7
97Anchorage Aces-15
98Anchorage Aces-4
99Asheville Smoke-11

O'Ree, Willie

44Beehive Group II Photos-53
56Quebec Aces-12
61Union Oil WHL-4
97Beehive-75
Authentic Autographs-75
Golden Portraits-75
98Upper Deck O'Ree Commemorative Card-22
01Greats of the Game Sticks-7
06ITG Ultimate Memorabilia-149
Artist Proof-149
06Parkhurst-87
Autographs-87
06SP Authentic Sign of the Times-STWO
06Upper Deck Sweet Shot Signature Shots/Saves-SSWO
06ITG Heroes and Prospects-6
Autographs-AWO

O'Regan, Tom

84Penguins Heinz Photos-16
94German DEL-59
95German DEL-54
96German DEL-250

O'Reilly, Cal

06AHL Top Prospects-26
06Milwaukee Admirals -12

O'Reilly, Sean

897th Inn. Sketch OHL-90
907th Inn. Sketch OHL-14
917th Inn. Sketch OHL-382
98Wichita Thunder-19
99Wichita Thunder-18
00Wichita Thunder-17

O'Reilly, Terry

73O-Pee-Chee-254
74NHL Action Stamps-22
74O-Pee-Chee NHL-295
75Heroes Stand-Ups-2
75O-Pee-Chee NHL-301
75Topps-301
76O-Pee-Chee NHL-130
76O-Pee-Chee NHL-381
76Topps-130
77O-Pee-Chee NHL-220
77Topps-220
78O-Pee-Chee-40
78O-Pee-Chee-332
78Topps-40
79O-Pee-Chee-238
79Topps-238
80O-Pee-Chee-56
80Topps-56
81O-Pee-Chee-7
81O-Pee-Chee Stickers-50
81Topps-E71
82O-Pee-Chee-18
82O-Pee-Chee Stickers-85
82Post Cereal-1
82Topps Stickers-85
83Bruins Team Issue-14
83Puffy Stickers-12
84Bruins Postcards-15
84O-Pee-Chee-13
84O-Pee-Chee Stickers-162
84Topps-10
88Bruins Sports Action-17
91Pro Set Platinum-289
91Bruins Sports Action Legends-19
98Bruins Alumni-24
Autographs-24
01Fleer Legacy-56
Ultimate-56
01Greats of the Game-80
Autographs-80
01Topps Archives-71
Arena Seats-AST0
Autographs-21
02Fleer Throwbacks-1
Gold-1
Platinum-1
Autographs-1
Squaring Off-4
Squaring Off Memorabilia-4
02Rangers Team Issue-12
02UD Foundations-5
03BAP Ultimate Mem Vintage Jerseys-22
03BAP Ultimate Mem Vintage Jerseys Gold-22
03Parkhurst Original Six Boston-29
03Parkhurst Original Six Boston-78
03Parkhurst Original Six Boston-93
Autographs-12
Memorabilia-BM55
Memorabilia-BM67
03Rangers Team Issue-24
04ITG Franchises US East-315
Autographs-A-TO
Complete Jerseys-ECJ9
Complete Jerseys Gold-ECJ9
Double Memorabilia-EDM16
Double Memorabilia Autographs-EDM-TO
Double Memorabilia Gold-EDM16
Memorabilia-ESM22
Memorabilia Autographs-ESM-TO
Memorabilia Gold-ESM22
Original Sticks-EOS11
Original Sticks Autographs-EOS-TO
Original Sticks Gold-EOS11
Teammates-ETM8
Teammates Gold-ETM8
04ITG Ultimate Memorabilia-107
Gold-107
Autographs-29
Autographs Gold-29
Jersey Autographs-19
Jersey Autographs Gold-19
Original Six-2
Retro Teammates-14
Stick Autographs-22
Stick Autographs Gold-22
04UD Legendary Signatures-83
AKA Autographs-AKA-TO
Autographs-TO
Linemates-SJDMTO
04UD Legends Classics Signature Moments-M7
04UD Legends Classics Signatures-CS7
04UD Legends Classics Signatures-QC5
05Beehive Signature Scrapbook-SSTO
05ITG Tough Customers-TO
Autographs-TO
Complete Jerseys-TO
Double Memorabilia-TO
Famous Battles Autographs-SO
Jerseys-TO
05ITG Ultimate Memorabilia Jersey Autos-35
05ITG Ultimate Mem Jersey Autos Gold-35
05ITG Ultimate Mem Retro Teammate Jerseys-17
05ITG Ult Mem Retro Teammates Jersey Gold-17
05ITG Ultimate Mem 3 Star of the Game Jsy-12
05ITG Ult Mem 3 Star of the Game Jsy Gold-12
05ITG Ultimate Memorabilia Triple Autos-11
05ITG Ultimate Mem Triple Autos Gold-11
05SPx Xcitement Legends-XL-TO
05SPx Xcitement Legends Gold-XL-TO
05SPx Xcitement Legends Spectrum-XL-TO
05UD Artifacts-141
Blue-141
Gold-141
Green-141
Pewter-141
Red-141
Gold Autographed-141
05Upper Deck Notable Numbers-N-TO
06Beehive Signature Scrapbook-SSTO
06Parkhurst-88
06Parkhurst-164
06Parkhurst-244
Autographs-88
Autographs-164
Autographs-244
Autographs Dual-DAOM
06SP Authentic Sign of the Times Triples-ST3COS
06SP Game Used Letter Marks-LMTO
06SP Game Used SIGnificance-STO
06UD Artifacts-127
Blue-127
Gold-127
Platinum-127
Radiance-127
Autographed Radiance Parallel-127
Red-127
06Ultimate Collection Signatures-US-TO
06Upper Deck Sweet Shot Signature Shots/Saves-SSTO
06Upper Deck Trilogy Combo Clearcut Autographs-C3NOB

O'Rourke, Chris

93Flint Generals-5

O'Rourke, Dan

917th Inn. Sketch WHL-311
94Central Hockey League-104
95Louisiana Ice Gators Playoffs-14
95Louisiana Ice Gators Glossy-4
96Louisiana Ice Gators II-13

O'Rourke, Steve

00UK Sekonda Superleague-37
03Mississippi Sea Wolves-8
05Muskegon Fury-13

O'Shea, Dan

93Dayton Bombers-10

O'Shea, Danny

69O-Pee-Chee-131
69Topps-131
70Colgate Stamps-16
70Dad's Cookies-93
70Esso Power Players-167
70Sargent Promotions Stamps-90
71Blues Postcards-14
71O-Pee-Chee-211
71Sargent Promotions Stamps-37
71Toronto Sun-78
72Blues White Border-13
72O-Pee-Chee-201
72Sargent Promotions Stamps-189

O'Shea, Darcy

95Slapshot-251

O'Shea, Kevin

69Swedish Hockey-361
70Sargent Promotions Stamps-25
71Sabres Postcards-85
71Sargent Promotions Stamps-22
71Toronto Sun-35
72O-Pee-Chee-257
72Sargent Promotions Stamps-190

O'Sullivan, Chris

93Donruss Team USA-15
93Pinnacle-484
Canadian-484
93Upper Deck-565
96Black Diamond-19
Gold-19
96Donruss Canadian Ice-133
Gold Press Proofs-133
Red Press Proofs-133
96Leaf Preferred-122
Press Proofs-122
96Select Certified-111
Artist's Proofs-111
Blue-111
Mirror Blue-111
Mirror Gold-111
Mirror Red-111
Red-111
96Upper Deck-230
Generation Next-X4
96Zenith-138
Artist's Proofs-138
97Collector's Choice-35
97Donruss Limited-54
Exposure-54
97Leaf-141
Fractal Matrix-141
Fractal Matrix Die Cuts-141
97Leaf International-141
Universal Ice-141
97Upper Deck-235
97Saint John Flames-19
99AHL All-Stars-7
99Syracuse Crunch-21
01Swiss HNL-59
02Cincinnati Mighty Ducks-A-6

O'Sullivan, Kevin

93Fredericton Canadiens-18
93Classic-71
94Fredericton Canadiens-21

O'Sullivan, Patrick

01Mississauga Ice Dogs-6
02Mississauga Ice Dogs-20
03Mississauga Ice Dogs-15
04Mississauga Ice Dogs-13
04ITG Heroes and Prospects-98
Aspiring-8
Autographs-PO
Combos-11
Emblems-20
Emblems Gold-20
He Shoots-He Scores Prizes-18
Jersey Autographs-20
Jerseys-20
Jerseys Gold-20
National Pride-8
Numbers-20
Numbers Gold-20
04ITG Heroes/Prospects Toronto Expo '05-98
04ITG Heroes/Prospects Expo Heroes/Pros-98
04ITG Heroes/Prosp Toronto Expo Parallel -375
05AHL All-Stars-25
05AHL Top Prospects-27
05Extreme Top Prospects Signature Edition-S18
05ITG Heroes and Prospects-375
Aspiring-ASP3
Autographs Series II-POS
Complete Logos-CHL-22
He Shoots-He Scores Prizes-30
He Shoots-He Scores Prizes-53
Jerseys-GUJ-34
Jerseys Gold-GUJ-34
Emblems-GUE-34
Emblems Gold-GUE-34
Numbers-GUN-34
Numbers Gold-GUN-34
Nameplates-N-2
Nameplates Gold-N-02
06Be A Player-205
Autographs-205
Signatures 10-205
Signatures Trios-TFCO
06Be A Player Portraits-105
06Beehive-126
Blue-126
Gold-126
Matte-126
Red Facsimile Signatures-126
Wood-126
06Black Diamond-199
Black-199
Gold-199
Ruby-199
06Flair Showcase-313
06Hot Prospects-116
Red Hot-116
White Hot-116
Hot Materials -HMOS
Hot Materials Red Hot-HMOS
Hot Materials White Hot-HMOS
Hotagraphs-HPO
06ITG Phenoms Idols Gold-IDJT
06ITG Phenoms Idols Silver-IDJT
06O-Pee-Chee-538
06O-Pee-Chee-627
Rainbow-538
Rainbow-627
06SP Authentic-183
Chirography-PO
Limited-183
06SP Game Used-121
Gold-121
Rainbow-121
Autographs-121
Rookie Exclusives Autographs-REPO
06SPx-188
Spectrum-188
06The Cup-135
Autographed NHL Shields Duals-DASKO
Autographed Rookie Masterpiece Pressplates-135
Gold Rainbow Autographed Rookie Patches-135
Honorable Numbers-HNPO
Masterpiece Pressplates (Be A Player Portraits)-105
Masterpiece Pressplates (Bee Hive)-126
Masterpiece Pressplates (Marquee Rookies)-538
Masterpiece Pressplates (MVP)-298
Masterpiece Pressplates (SP Authentic Autographs)-183
Masterpiece Pressplates (SP Game Used)-121
Masterpiece Pressplates (SPx Autographs)-188
Masterpiece Pressplates (Sweet Beginnings)-131
Masterpiece Pressplates (Trilogy)-117
Masterpiece Pressplates (Ultimate Collection Autographs)-115
Masterpiece Pressplates (Victory)-284
NHL Shields Duals-DSHKO
Rookies Black-135
Rookies Platinum-135
Signature Patches-SPPO
06UD Artifacts-262
06UD Mini Jersey Collection-108
06Ultimate Collection-115
Rookies Autographed NHL Shields-115
Rookies Autographed Patches-115
Ultimate Debut Threads Jerseys-DJ-PO
Ultimate Debut Threads Jerseys Autographs-DJ-PO
Ultimate Debut Threads Patches-DJ-PO
Ultimate Debut Threads Patches Autographs-DJ-PO
06Ultra-246
06Ultra-248
Gold Medallion-246
Ice Medallion-246
06Upper Deck-215
Exclusives Parallel-215
High Gloss Parallel-215
Masterpieces-215
Rookie Game Dated Moments-RGD11
Rookie Headliners-RH1
Rookie Materials-RMPO
Rookie Materials Patches-RMPO
06Upper Deck MVP-298
Gold Script-298
Super Script-298
06Upper Deck Ovation-185
06Upper Deck Sweet Shot-131
Rookie Jerseys Autographs-131
Signature Shots/Saves-SSPO
Signature Shots/Saves Sticks-SSSPO
06Upper Deck Trilogy-117
06Upper Deck Victory-284
06ITG Heroes and Prospects-74
AHL All-Star Jerseys-AJ06
AHL All-Star Jerseys Gold-AJ06
AHL All-Star Emblems-AE06
AHL All-Star Emblems Gold-AE06
AHL All-Star Numbers-AN06
AHL All-Star Numbers Gold-AN06
Autographs-APOS
07Upper Deck Rookie Class -3

O'Toole, John

96OCN Blizzard-18

Oake, Scott

97Pinnacle Hockey Night in Canada-10

Oakley, Ernie

51Laval Dairy QSHL-60

Oates, Adam

87O-Pee-Chee-123
87O-Pee-Chee Stickers-105
87Panini Stickers-248
87Red Wings Little Caesars-21
87Topps-123
88O-Pee-Chee-161
88Panini Stickers-45
88Red Wings Little Caesars-17
88Topps-161
89Blues Kodak-12
89O-Pee-Chee-185
89Topps-185
90Blues Kodak-17
90Bowman-16
Tiffany-16
90O-Pee-Chee-149
90OPC Premier-88
90Panini Stickers-275
90Pro Set-269
90Score-85
Canadian-85
90Score Hottest/Rising Stars-41
90Topps-149
Tiffany-149
90Upper Deck-173
90Upper Deck-483
French-173
French-483
91Pro Set Platinum-113
91Blues Postcards-16
91Bowman-384
91Bowman-406
91Bruins Sports Action-14
91Kraft-5
91O-Pee-Chee-265
91O-Pee-Chee-347
91O-Pee-Chee-448
91OPC Premier-7
91Panini Stickers-31
91Parkhurst-155
91Parkhurst-233
French-155
French-233
91Pinnacle-6
91Pinnacle-378
French-6
French-378
91Pro Set-219
91Pro Set-291
French-219
French-291
CC-CC7
CC French-CC7
Puck Candy-25
St. Louis Midwest-1
91Score American-238
91Score Canadian Bilingual-458
91Score Canadian English-458
91Score Hot Cards-6
91Stadium Club-108
91Topps-265
91Topps-448
91Upper Deck-94
91Upper Deck-252
91Upper Deck-627
French-94
French-252
French-627
91Star Pics-40
92Blues UD Best of the Blues-17
92Bowman-213
92Bowman-258
92Bruins Postcards-7
92McDonald's Upper Deck-11
92O-Pee-Chee-172
92O-Pee-Chee-272
25th Anniv. Inserts-20
92OPC Premier Star Performers-13
92Panini Stickers-136
92Panini Stickers French-136
92Parkhurst-4
Emerald Ice-4
92Pinnacle-40
French-40
92Pro Set-3
92Score-250
Canadian-250
92Seasons Patches-20
92Stadium Club-188
92Stadium Club-245
92Topps-475
Gold-475G
92Ultra-8
92Upper Deck-133
92Upper Deck-455
92Upper Deck-637
93Donruss-18
Special Print-B
93Leaf-235
Hat Trick Artists-8
93McDonald's Upper Deck-21
93OPC Premier-50
93OPC Premier-74
Gold-50
Gold-74
Black Gold-3
93Panini Stickers-2
93Panini Stickers-138
93Parkhurst-11
Emerald Ice-11
93Pinnacle-185
Canadian-185
All-Stars-9
All-Stars Canadian-9
93PowerPlay-23
Point Leaders-11
93Score-125
93Score-478
Canadian-125
Canadian-478
Dream Team-17
Dynamic Duos U.S.-3
93Seasons Patches-13
93Stadium Club-93
Members Only Master Set-93
OPC-93
First Day Issue-93
First Day Issue OPC-93
All-Stars-11
All-Stars Members Only-11
All-Stars OPC-11
Master Photos-11
Master Photos Winners-11
93Topps/OPC Premier-50
93Topps/OPC Premier-74
Gold-50
Gold-74
93Topps Premier Black Gold-5
93Ultra-156
Adam Oates-1
Adam Oates-2
Adam Oates-3
Adam Oates-4
Adam Oates-5
Adam Oates-6
Adam Oates-7
Adam Oates-8
Adam Oates-9
Adam Oates-10
Adam Oates-11
Adam Oates-12
Adam Oates-NNO
All-Stars-7
Premier Pivots-7
93Upper Deck-226
93Upper Deck-286
93Upper Deck-327
Hat Tricks-HT5
Silver Skates-H6
Silver Skates Gold-H6
SP-11
93Upper Deck Locker All-Stars-10
93Classic Pro Prospects-35
BCs-BC18
94SLU Hockey Canadian-9
94Hockey Canadian-9
94SLU Hockey American-15
94Action Packed Mammoth-MM4
94Be A Player-R45
94Canada Games NHL POGS-35
94EA Sports-9
94EA Sports-188
94Finest-67
Super Team Winners-67
Refractors-67
Division's Clear Cut-3
94Flair-12
Hot Numbers-6
94Fleer-16
94Hockey Wit-5
94Kenner Starting Lineup Cards-16
94Kraft-25
94Leaf-305
Gold Stars-14
Limited Inserts-2
94Leaf Limited-104
94OPC Premier-135
94OPC Premier-277
Special Effects-135
Special Effects-277
94Parkhurst-311
Gold-311
Vintage-V46
94Parkhurst SE-SE13
Gold-SE13
94Pinnacle-120
Artist's Proofs-120
Rink Collection-120
94Score-141
Gold-141
Platinum-141
90 Plus Club-3
94Select-58
Gold-58
94SP-8
Die Cuts-8
94Stadium Club Members Only-37
94Stadium Club Super Teams-2
94Stadium Club Super Team MemberOnly Set-2
94Topps/OPC Premier-135
94Topps/OPC Premier-277
Special Effects-135
Special Effects-277
94Ultra-14
Premier Pivots-9
94Upper Deck-11
Electric Ice-11
Predictor Hobby-H20
94Upper Deck Predictor Hobby Exch Gold-H20
94Upper Deck Predictor Hobby Exch Silver-H20
94Upper Deck Predictor Retail-R12
94Upper Deck Predictor Retail-R26
94Upper Deck Predictor Retail-R44
94Upper Deck Predictor Retail Exchange-R12
94Upper Deck Predictor Retail Exchange-R26
94Upper Deck Predictor Retail Exchange-R44
94Upper Deck SP Inserts-SP7
94Upper Deck SP Inserts Die Cuts-SP7
95Bashan Super Stickers-5
95Bashan Super Stickers-8
95Bowman-44
All-Foil-44
95Collector's Choice-197
Player's Club-197
Player's Club Platinum-197

95Donruss-386
Igniters-1
95Donruss Elite-80
Die Cut Stars-80
Die Cut Uncut-80
95Emotion-11
Xcel-1
95Finest-43
Refractors-43
95Hoyle Eastern Playing Cards-48
95Imperial Stickers-8
95Kraft-54
95Leaf-81
95Leaf Limited-108
95Metal-10
Heavy Metal-11
95NHL Aces Playing Cards-10H
95Panini Stickers-3
95Parkhurst International-16
Emerald Ice-16
Parkie's Trophy Picks-PP53
95Pinnacle-3
Artist's Proofs-3
Rink Collection-3
95Pinnacle FANtasy-5
95Playoff One on One-9
95Playoff One on One-121
95Playoff One on One-229
95Pro Magnets-19
95Score-119
Black Ice Artist's Proofs-119
Black Ice-119
95Select Certified-11
Mirror Gold-11
Double Strike-5
Double Strike Gold-5
95SkyBox Impact-12
95SP 7
95Stadium Club Members Only-16
95Stadium Club-40
Members Only Master Set-40
95Summit-4
Artist's Proofs-4
Ice-4
95Topps-180
95Topps-381
OPC Inserts-180
OPC Inserts-381
Marquee Men Power Boosters-381
Power Lines-7PL
95Topps SuperSkills-2
Platinum-2
95Ultra-13
95Ultra-395
Gold Medallion-13
Extra Attackers-16
Premier Pivots-6
Premier Pivots Gold Medallion-6
95Upper Deck-197
Electric Ice-197
Electric Ice Gold-197
95Upper Deck All-Star Game Predictors-28
Redemption Winners-28
95Upper Deck Predictor Retail-R16
95Upper Deck Predictor Retail Exchange-R16
95Upper Deck Special Edition-SE5
95Upper Deck Special Edition Gold-SE5
95Zenith-10
95Swedish Globe World Championships-90
96SLU Hockey American-17
96Black Diamond-152
Gold-152
96Collector's Choice-12
96Collector's Choice-310
MVP-UD15
MVP Gold-UD15
Crash the Game-C21A
Crash the Game-C21B
Crash the Game Gold-C21A
Crash the Game Gold-C21B
Crash the Game Exchange-CR21
Crash the Game Exchange Gold-CR21
96Donruss-41
Press Proofs-41
96Donruss Canadian Ice-8
Gold Press Proofs-8
Red Press Proofs-8
96Donruss Elite-31
Die Cut Stars-31
96Flair-5
Blue Ice-5
96Fleer-6
Art Ross-18
96Fleer Picks-28
Fabulous 50-35
Jagged Edge-15
96Kenner Starting Lineup Cards-17
96Kraft Upper Deck-6
96Kraft Upper Deck-46
96Leaf-112
Press Proofs-112
96Leaf Limited-5
Gold-5
96Leaf Preferred-40
Press Proofs-40
Steel-54
Steel Gold-54
96Maggers-70
96Metal Universe-9
Lethal Weapons-15
Lethal Weapons Super Power-15
96NHL Aces Playing Cards-36
96NHL Pro Stamps-19
96Pinnacle-130
Artist's Proofs-130
Foil-130
Premium Stock-130
Rink Collection-130
96Score-162
Artist's Proofs-162
Dealer's Choice Artist's Proofs-162
Special Artist's Proofs-162
Golden Blades-162
96Select Certified-68
Artist's Proofs-68
Blue-68
Mirror Blue-68
Mirror Gold-68
Mirror Red-68
Red-68
96SkyBox Impact-7
BladeRunners-17
96SP-11
Holoview Collection-HC29
96Summit-15
Artist's Proofs-15
Ice-15
Metal-15
Premium Stock-15
96Team Out-30
96Ultra-10
Gold Medallion-10
Power-14
Power Red Line-6
96Upper Deck-216
Generation Next-X40
96Upper Deck Ice-2
Parallel-2
96Zenith-41
Artist's Proofs-41
96Swedish Semic Wien-100
96Collector's Edge Ice Livin' Large-L3
97Be A Player-5
Autographs-5
Autographs Die-Cuts-5
Autographs Prismatic Die-Cuts-5
97Beehive-38
Golden Portraits-38
97Black Diamond-109
Double Diamond-109
Triple Diamond-109
Quadruple Diamond-109
97Collector's Choice-266
Star Quest-SQ23
Stick'Ums-S28
97Crown Royale-142
Emerald Green-142
Ice Blue-142
Silver-142
97Donruss-25
97Donruss-228
Press Proofs Silver-25
Press Proofs Silver-228
Press Proofs Gold-25
Press Proofs Gold-228
97Donruss Canadian Ice-78
Dominion Series-78
Provincial Series-78
National Pride-7
97Donruss Limited-33
97Donruss Limited-112
97Donruss Limited-162
Exposure-33
Exposure-112
Exposure-162
97Donruss Preferred-100
Cut to the Chase-100
97Donruss Priority-149
Stamp of Approval-149
97Katch-153
Gold-153
Silver-153
97Kraft-8
97Leaf-130
Fractal Matrix-130
Fractal Matrix Die Cuts-130
97Leaf International-130
Universal Ice-130
97NHL Aces Playing Cards-44
97Pacific-37
Copper-37
Emerald Green-37
Ice Blue-37
Red-37
Silver-37
Slap Shots Die-Cuts-12B
97Pacific Dynagon-133
Copper-133
Dark Grey-133
Emerald Green-133
Ice Blue-133
Red-133
Silver-133
Tandems-56
97Pacific Invincible-149
Copper-149
Emerald Green-149
Ice Blue-149
Red-149
Silver-149
97Pacific Omega-243
Copper-243
Dark Gray-243
Emerald Green-243
Gold-243
Ice Blue-243
97Panini Stickers-116
97Paramount-198
Copper-198
Dark Grey-198
Emerald Green-198
Ice Blue-198
Red-198
Silver-198
97Pinnacle-62
Artist's Proofs-62
Rink Collection-62
Press Plates Back Black-62
Press Plates Back Cyan-62
Press Plates Back Magenta-62
Press Plates Back Yellow-62
Press Plates Front Black-62
Press Plates Front Cyan-62
Press Plates Front Magenta-62
Press Plates Front Yellow-62
97Pinnacle Certified-49
Red-49
Mirror Blue-49
Mirror Gold-49
Mirror Red-49
97Pinnacle Inside-28
Coach's Collection-28
Executive Collection-28
97Pinnacle Tot Cert Platinum Blue-49
97Pinnacle Tot Cert Platinum Gold-49
97Pinnacle Totally Certified Platinum Red-49
97Pinnacle Tot Cert Mirror Platinum Gold-49
97Revolution-150
Copper-150
Emerald-150
Ice Blue-150
Silver-150
97Score-117
Artist's Proofs-117
Golden Blades-117
97SP Authentic-162
97SPx-48
Bronze-48
Gold-48
Silver-48
Steel-48
Dimension-SPX12
Grand Finale-48
97Studio-32
Press Proofs Silver-32
Press Proofs Gold-32
97Upper Deck-177
Sixth Sense Masters-SS12
Sixth Sense Wizards-SS12
Smooth Grooves-SG56
Three Star Selects-18A
97Upper Deck Ice-17
Parallel-17
Power Shift-17
97Zenith-32
Z-Gold-32
Z-Silver-32
97Zenith 5 x 7-41
Gold Impulse-41
Silver Impulse-41
98Aurora-199
98Be A Player-296
Press Release-296
98BAP Gold-296
98BAP Autographs-296
98BAP Autographs Gold-296
98BAP AS Milestones-M15
98Bowman's Best-72
Refractors-72
Atomic Refractors-72
98Capitals Kids and Cops-3
98Crown Royale-144
Limited Series-144
98Finest-98
No Protectors-98
No Protectors Refractors-98
Refractors-98
98OPC Chrome-179
Refractors-179
Season's Best-SB23
Season's Best Refractors-SB23
98Pacific-445
Ice Blue-445
Red-445
98Pacific Dynagon Ice-198
Blue-198
Red-198
98Pacific Omega-249
Red-249
Opening Day Issue-249
98Panini Photocards-57
98Panini Stickers-106
98Paramount-249
Copper-249
Emerald Green-249
Holo-Electric-249
Ice Blue-249
Silver-249
98Post-6
98Revolution-149
Ice Shadow-149
Red-149
98SP Authentic-90
Power Shift-90
98Topps-179
O-Pee-Chee-179
Season's Best-SB23
98Topps Gold Label Class 1-80
Black-80
Black One of One-80
One of One-80
Red-80
Red One of One-80
98Topps Gold Label Class 2-80
98Topps Gold Label Class 2 Black-80
98Topps Gold Label Class 2 Black 1 of 1-80
98Topps Gold Label Class 2 One of One-80
98Topps Gold Label Class 2 Red-80
98Topps Gold Label Class 2 Red One of One-80
98Topps Gold Label Class 3-80
98Topps Gold Label Class 3 Black-80
98Topps Gold Label Class 3 Black 1 of 1-80
98Topps Gold Label Class 3 One of One-80
98Topps Gold Label Class 3 Red-80
98Topps Gold Label Class 3 Red One of One-80
98UD Choice-217
98UD Choice Preview-217
98UD Choice Prime Choice Reserve-217
98UD Choice Reserve-217
98Upper Deck-199
Exclusives-199
Exclusives 1 of 1-199
Frozen In Time-FT20
Frozen In Time Quantum 1-FT20
Frozen In Time Quantum 2-FT20
Frozen In Time Quantum 3-FT20
Gold Reserve-199
98Upper Deck MVP-212
Gold Script-212
Silver Script-212
Super Script-212
99Aurora-150
Premiere Date-150
99BAP Memorabilia-75
Gold-75
Silver-75
AS Heritage Ruby-H6
AS Heritage Sapphire-H6
AS Heritage Emerald-H6
99BAP Millennium-248
Emerald-248
Ruby-248
Sapphire-248
Signatures-248
Signatures Gold-248
99Crown Royale-144
Limited Series-144
Premiere Date-144
99O-Pee-Chee-202
99O-Pee-Chee Chrome-202
99O-Pee-Chee Chrome Refractors-202
99Pacific-446
Copper-446
Emerald Green-446
Gold-446
Ice Blue-446
Premiere Date-446
Red-446
99Pacific Dynagon Ice-203
Blue-203
Copper-203
Gold-203
Premiere Date-203
99Pacific Omega-245
Copper-245
Gold-245
Ice Blue-245
Premiere Date-245
99Pacific Prism-150
Holographic Blue-150
Holographic Gold-150
Holographic Mirror-150
Holographic Purple-150
Premiere Date-150
99Panini Stickers-166
99Paramount-248
Copper-248
Emerald-248
Gold-248
Holographic Emerald-248
Holographic Gold-248
Holographic Silver-248
Ice Blue-248
Premiere Date-248
Red-248
Silver-248
99Revolution-150
Premiere Date-150
Red-150
Shadow Series-150
Copper-150
Gold-150
CSC Silver-150
99SP Authentic-89
99SPx-158
Radiance-158
Spectrum-158
99Stadium Club-56
First Day Issue-56
One of a Kind-56
Printing Plates Black-56
Printing Plates Cyan-56
Printing Plates Magenta-56
Printing Plates Yellow-56
99Topps/OPC-202
99Topps/OPC Chrome-202
Refractors-202
99Upper Deck-131
Exclusives-131
Exclusives 1 of 1-131
Headed for the Hall-HOF8
Headed for the Hall Quantum Gold-HOF8
Headed for the Hall Quantum Silver-HOF8
99Upper Deck Gold Reserve-131
99Upper Deck MVP-214
Gold Script-214
Silver Script-214
Super Script-214
99Upper Deck Retro-80
Gold-80
Platinum-80
99Upper Deck Victory-305
99Wayne Gretzky Hockey-175
00SLU Hockey-170
00Aurora-149
Premiere Date-149
00BAP Memorabilia-120
Emerald-120
Ruby-120
Sapphire-120
Promos-120
00BAP Mem Chicago Sportsfest Copper-120
00BAP Memorabilia Chicago Sportsfest Blue-120
00BAP Memorabilia Chicago Sportsfest Gold-120
00BAP Memorabilia Chicago Sportsfest Ruby-120
00BAP Memorabilia Chicago Sun-Times Ruby-120
00BAP Memorabilia Chicago Sun-Times Gold-120
00BAP Mem Chicago Sun-Times Sapphire-120
00BAP Mem Toronto Fall Expo Copper-120
00BAP Memorabilia Toronto Fall Expo Gold-120
00BAP Memorabilia Toronto Fall Expo Ruby-120
00BAP Mem Update Heritage Jersey Cards-H22
00BAP Mem Update Heritage Jersey Gold-H22
00BAP Memorabilia Update Teammates-TM2
00BAP Memorabilia Update Teammates Gold-TM2
00BAP Parkhurst 2000-P45
00BAP Signature Series-179
Emerald-179
Ruby-179
Sapphire-179
Autographs-36
Autographs Gold-36
Jersey Cards-J34
Jersey and Stick Cards-GSJ34
Jersey Cards Autographs-J34
Jersey Emblems-E34
Jersey Numbers-IN34
00BAP Ultimate Memorabilia Autographs-50
Gold-50
00BAP Ultimate Memorabilia Teammates-TM11
00BAP Ultimate Memorabilia Teammates-TM40
00Crown Royale-108
Ice Blue-108
Limited Series-108
Premiere Date-108
Red-108
00O-Pee-Chee-169
00O-Pee-Chee Parallel-169
00Pacific-428
Copper-428
Gold-428
Ice Blue-428
Premiere Date-428
00Panini Stickers-106
00Paramount-248
Copper-248
Gold-248
Holo-Gold-248
Holo-Silver-248
Ice Blue-248
Premiere Date-248
00Private Stock-100
Gold-100
Premiere Date-100
Retail-100
Silver-100
Game Gear-105
00Revolution-149
Blue-149
Premiere Date-149
Red-149
Stat Masters-30
00SP Authentic-90
00SPx-69
Spectrum-69
00Stadium Club-168
00Titanium-100
Blue-100
Gold-100
Premiere Date-100
Red-100
Retail-100
00Topps/OPC-169
Parallel-169
1000 Point Club-PC7
00Topps Chrome-116
OPC Refractors-116
Refractors-116
1000 Point Club Refractors-7
00Topps Gold Label Class 1-25
Gold-25
00Topps Gold Label Class 2-25
00Topps Gold Label Class 2 Gold-25
00Topps Gold Label Class 3-25
00Topps Gold Label Class 3 Gold-25
00Topps Heritage-52
Chrome Parallel-52
00Topps Premier Plus-63
Blue Ice-63
Game-Used Memorabilia-GPAO
Game-Used Memorabilia-GPAOKB
00Topps Stars-55
Blue-55
00UD Heroes-116
00UD Pros and Prospects-86
00Upper Deck-173
Exclusives Tier 1-173
Exclusives Tier 2-173
00Upper Deck Legends-130
Legendary Collection Bronze-130
Legendary Collection Gold-130
Legendary Collection Silver-130
00Upper Deck MVP-178
First Stars-178
Second Stars-178
Third Stars-178
00Upper Deck Victory-235
00Upper Deck Vintage-365
00Upper Deck Vintage-370
00Vanguard-100
Holographic Gold-100
Holographic Purple-100
Pacific Proofs-100
01Atomic-100
Blue-100
Gold-100
Premiere Date-100
Red-100
Team Nucleus-15
01BAP Memorabilia-300
01BAP Memorabilia-455
Emerald-300
Emerald-455
Ruby-300
Ruby-455
Sapphire-300
Sapphire-455
01BAP Signature Series Certified 100-C2
01BAP Signature Series Certified 50-C2
01BAP Signature Series Certified 1 of 1's-C2
01BAP Signature Series Jerseys-GJ-65
01BAP Sig Series Jersey and Stick Cards-GSJ-65
01BAP Signature Series Emblems-GUE-33
01BAP Signature Series Numbers-ITN-33
01BAP Update Heritage-H8
01Bowman YoungStars-32
Gold-32
Ice Cubed-32
01Crown Royale-144
Blue-144
Premiere Date-144
Red-144
Retail-144
01O-Pee-Chee-81
01O-Pee-Chee Heritage Parallel-81
01O-Pee-Chee Heritage Parallel Limited-81
01O-Pee-Chee Premier Parallel-81
01Pacific-398
01Pacific-443
Extreme LTD-398
Gold-443
Hobby LTD-398
Premiere Date-398
Retail LTD-398
01Pacific Adrenaline-200
Blue-200
Premiere Date-200
Red-200
Retail-200
01Pacific Arena Exclusives-398
01Pacific Arena Exclusives-443
01Pacific Heads-Up-100
Blue-100
Premiere Date-100
Red-100
Silver-100
01Parkhurst-85
01Parkhurst-393
Gold-85
Silver-85
Milestones-M34
Milestones-M45
Sticks-PS42
01Private Stock-100
Gold-100
Premiere Date-100
Retail-100
Silver-100
01Private Stock Pacific Nights-100
01Sports Illustrated for Kids III-76
01Stadium Club-60
Award Winners-60
Master Photos-60
Lone Star Signatures-LS6
01Titanium-144
Hobby Parallel-144
Premiere Date-144
Retail-144
Retail Parallel-144
01Topps-81
Heritage Parallel-81
Heritage Parallel Limited-81
OPC Parallel-81
01Topps Chrome-81
Refractors-81
Black Border Refractors-81
01Topps Heritage-92
Refractors-92
Captain's Cloth-CCAO
01Topps Reserve-34
Emblems-AO
Jerseys-AO
Name Plates-AO
Numbers-AO
Patches-AO
01UD Top Shelf-111
01Upper Deck-407
Exclusives-407
01Upper Deck Victory-354
Gold-354
01Czech Stadion-254
02Atomic-3
Blue-3
Gold-3
Red-3
Hobby Parallel-3
Jerseys-1
Jerseys Gold-1
Patches-1
02BAP First Edition-244
02BAP First Edition-373
02BAP Memorabilia-20
02BAP Memorabilia-242
02BAP Memorabilia-262
Emerald-20
Emerald-242
Emerald-262
Ruby-20
Ruby-242
Ruby-262
Sapphire-20
Sapphire-242
Sapphire-262
NHL All-Star Game-20
NHL All-Star Game-242
NHL All-Star Game-262
NHL All-Star Game Blue-20
NHL All-Star Game Blue-242
NHL All-Star Game Blue-262
NHL All-Star Game Green-20
NHL All-Star Game Green-242
NHL All-Star Game Green-262
NHL All-Star Game Red-20
NHL All-Star Game Red-242
NHL All-Star Game Red-262
02BAP Memorabilia Toronto Fall Expo-20
02BAP Memorabilia Toronto Fall Expo-242
02BAP Memorabilia Toronto Fall Expo-262
02BAP Sig Series Auto Buybacks 1998-296
02BAP Sig Series Auto Buybacks 1999-248
02BAP Sig Series Auto Buybacks 2000-36
02BAP Signature Series Golf-GS2
02BAP Signature Series Team Quads-TQ19
02BAP Ultimate Memorabilia Active Eight-2
02BAP Ultimate Memorabilia Active Eight-8
02BAP Ultimate Mem Journey Jerseys-5
02BAP Ultimate Mem Journey Emblems-5
02Crown Royale-3
Blue-3
Red-3
Retail-3
02Ducks Team Issue-1
02ITG Used-1
02ITG Used-101
02McDonald's Pacific Jersey Patch Silver-13
02McDonald's Pacific Jersey Patches Gold-13
02O-Pee-Chee-173
02O-Pee-Chee-173U
02O-Pee-Chee Premier Blue Parallel-173
02O-Pee-Chee Premier Red Parallel-173
02O-Pee-Chee Factory Set-173
02Pacific-284
Blue-284
Red-284
Jerseys-40
Jerseys Holo-Silver-40
02Pacific Complete-114
Red-114
02Pacific Exclusive-3
02Pacific Heads-Up-3
Blue-3
Purple-3
Red-3
Inside the Numbers-1
Quad Jerseys-20
Quad Jerseys Gold-20
02Parkhurst-110
Bronze-110
Gold-110
Silver-110
College Ranks-CR6
College Ranks Jerseys-CRM6
02Parkhurst Retro-11
Minis-11
02Private Stock Reserve-101
Red-101
Retail-101
02SP Authentic-3
Beckett Promos-3
02SPx-77
Spectrum Gold-77
Spectrum Silver-77
02Stadium Club-107
Silver Decoy Cards-107
Proofs-107
02Topps-173
02Topps-173U
OPC Blue Parallel-173
OPC Red Parallel-173
Factory Set-173
02Topps Chrome-100
Black Border Refractors-100
Refractors-100
02Topps Heritage-110
02Topps Heritage-164
02Topps Total-36
02Upper Deck-247
Exclusives-247
02Upper Deck Beckett UD Promos-247
02Upper Deck Rookie Update-2
02Upper Deck Vintage-307
02Vanguard Jerseys-1
02Vanguard Jerseys Gold-1
03BAP Ultimate Memorabilia Autographs-35
Gold-35
03BAP Ultimate Mem Retro Teammates-1
03Beehive-77
Gold-77
Silver-77
03ITG Action-25
Jerseys-M140
03ITG Used Signature Series-86
Gold-86
Autographs-AO
Autographs Gold-AO
03O-Pee-Chee-266
03OPC Blue-266
03OPC Gold-266
03OPC Red-266
03Pacific-7
Blue-7
Red-7
03Pacific Exhibit-3
Blue Backs-3
Yellow Backs-3
03Pacific Prism-3
Blue-3
Gold-3
Red-3
03Parkhurst Original Six Boston-31
Memorabilia-BM34
03Parkhurst Original Six Detroit-34
03SP Authentic-34
Limited-34
03Topps-266
Blue-266
Gold-266
Red-266
Pristine Stick Portions-PPS-AO
Pristine Stick Portion Refractors-PPS-AO
03Topps Traded-TT15
Blue-TT15
Gold-TT15
Red-TT15
03Upper Deck-323
Canadian Exclusives-323
HG-323
UD Exclusives-323
03Upper Deck Ice-33
Gold-33
03Upper Deck Rookie Update-33
03Upper Deck Victory-3
Bronze-3
Gold-3
Silver-3
03Czech Stadion-615
06Parkhurst-85
06Parkhurst-217
Autographs-85
Autographs-217
Autographs Dual-DANO
06The Cup Autographed Foundations-CQAO
06The Cup Autographed Foundations Patches-CQAO
06The Cup Autographed NHL Shields Duals-DASDA
06The Cup Foundations-CQAO
06The Cup Foundations Patches-CQAO
06The Cup Honorable Numbers-HNAO
06The Cup Limited Logos-LLAO
06UD Artifacts Frozen Artifacts-FAAO
06UD Artifacts Frozen Artifacts Black-FAAO
06UD Artifacts Frozen Artifacts Blue-FAAO
06UD Artifacts Frozen Artifacts Gold-FAAO
06UD Artifacts Frozen Artifacts Platinum-FAAO
06UD Artifacts Frozen Artifacts Red-FAAO
06UD Artifacts Frozen Artifacts Patches Black-FAAO
06UD Artifacts Frozen Artifacts Patches Blue-FAAO
06UD Artifacts Frozen Artifacts Patches Gold-FAAO
06UD Artifacts Frozen Artifacts Patches Platinum-FAAO
06UD Artifacts Frozen Artifacts Patches Red-FAAO
06UD Artifacts Tundra Tandems-TTCA
06UD Artifacts Tundra Tandems Black-TTCA
06UD Artifacts Tundra Tandems Blue-TTCA
06UD Artifacts Tundra Tandems Gold-TTCA
06UD Artifacts Tundra Tandems Platinum-TTCA
06UD Artifacts Tundra Tandems Red-TTCA
06UD Artifacts Tundra Tandems Dual Patches Red-TTCA
06Upper Deck Sweet Shot Signature Shots/Saves-SSAO
06Upper Deck Sweet Shot Signature Sticks-STAO

Oates, Matt
94Indianapolis Ice-16
99Tallahassee Tiger Sharks-7
00UK Sekonda Superleague-120
01Idaho Steelheads-10

Oatman, Ed
10Sweet Caporal Postcards-5
11C55-5
12C57-47
23V128-1 Paulin's Candy-61

Obara, Daisuke
03Charlotte Checkers-75

Oberg, Anders
93Swedish Semic Elitserien-87

Oberg, Carl-Goran
56Swedish Alfabilder-42
65Swedish Coralli ISHockey-186
67Swedish Hockey-24
67Swedish Hockey-79
70Swedish Hockey-146
71Swedish Hockey-240
72Swedish Stickers-225
73Swedish Stickers-66
81Swedish Semic Hockey VM Stickers-118

Oberg, Fredrik
92Swedish Semic Elitserien Stickers-195
93Swedish Semic Elitserien-165
95Swedish Leaf-301
Face to Face-12
95Swedish Upper Deck-193
97Swedish Collector's Choice-147
98Swedish UD Choice-196
99Swedish Upper Deck-199
00Swedish Upper Deck-105
01German Upper Deck-30
02German DEL City Press-120
03German DEL City Press-126
All-Stars-AS12
03German DEL-132
04German DEL-156
04German Hannover Scorpions Postcards-21
06Swedish SHL Elitset-275

Oberg, Hans
81Swedish Semic Hockey VM Stickers-122

Oberg, Jan
06Swedish SHL Elitset-97

Oberg, Jan Roger
67Swedish Hockey-212
02Swedish SHL-80
Parallel-80
03Swedish Elite-100
Silver-100
04Swedish Elitset-93
Gold-93
04Swedish MoDo Postcards-29

Oberg, Kjell Sture
67Swedish Hockey-213

Oberg, Lars
71Swedish Hockey-114
72Swedish Stickers-95
73Swedish Stickers-170
74Swedish Stickers-275

Oberg, Peter
02Swedish SHL-84
Parallel-84
03Swedish Elite-108
Silver-108
04Swedish Elitset-246
Gold-246
04Swedish MoDo Postcards-25
05Swedish SHL Elitset-248
06Swedish SHL Elitset-112

Oberg, Stoveln
56Swedish Alfabilder-44

Obermeier, Wolfgang
94German First League-246

Oberrauch, Robert
92Finnish Semic-246
93Swedish Semic World Champ Stickers-211
95Swedish Globe World Championships-228
95Swedish World Championships Stickers-81
96Swedish Semic Wien-176

Oberto, Ben
93Quebec Pee-Wee Tournament-662

Oberwelz, Elger
93Quebec Pee-Wee Tournament-1524

Obloj, Tadeusz
73Finnish Jaakiekko-96
74Finnish Jenkki-101
79Panini Stickers-133

Obresa, Peter
89Swedish Semic World Champ Stickers-119
94German DEL-104
95German DEL-101
99German DEL-99

Obrist, Fabio
95Swiss HNL-306

Obstarczyk, Jonathan
93Quebec Pee-Wee Tournament-806

Obsut, Jaroslav
95Swift Current Broncos-11
96Medicine Hat Tigers-14
98ECHL All-Star Southern Conference-1
00Worcester Icecats-4
01BAP Memorabilia-313
Emerald-313
Ruby-313
Sapphire-313
01Pacific-328
Extreme LTD-328
Hobby LTD-328
Premiere Date-328
Retail LTD-328
01Pacific Arena Exclusives-328
01Parkhurst-310
01SP Authentic-141
Limited-141
Limited Gold-141
01SP Game Used-70
01SPx-102
01UD Challenge for the Cup-101
01Upper Deck-207
Exclusives-207
01Upper Deck MVP-215
01Upper Deck Victory-387
Gold-387
01Upper Deck Vintage-279
01Hershey Bears-20
02Manitoba Moose-11
03Manitoba Moose-21
04Swedish Elitset-217
Gold-217
04Swedish Pure Skills-51
Parallel-51
Signatures-5
05Swedish Lulea Hockey Postcards-25
05Swedish SHL Elitset-85
Gold-85
06Swedish SHL Elitset-216

Obtoj, T.
74Finnish Typotor-90

Obukhov, Dmitri
05Russian Hockey League RHL-51

Ochaba, Martin
93Quebec Pee-Wee Tournament-1546

Ochsner, Marc
95Swiss HNL-11

Ochsner, Sacha
93Swiss HNL-27
95Swiss HNL-533

Oddleifson, Chris
74Canucks Royal Bank-14
74NHL Action Stamps-272
74O-Pee-Chee NHL-108
74Topps-108
75Canucks Royal Bank-15
75O-Pee-Chee NHL-169
75Topps-169
76Canucks Royal Bank-13
76O-Pee-Chee NHL-112
76O-Pee-Chee NHL-395
76Topps-112
77Canucks Canada Dry Cans-11
77Canucks Royal Bank-15
77O-Pee-Chee NHL-209
77Topps-209
78Canucks Royal Bank-18
78O-Pee-Chee-183
78Topps-183
79Canucks Royal Bank-17
79O-Pee-Chee-305
80O-Pee-Chee-295
81O-Pee-Chee Stickers-246

Odelein, Lee
91ProCards-447

Odelein, Lyle
88ProCards IHL-85
89ProCards AHL-185
90Canadiens Postcards-22
90Pro Set-617
91Canadiens Postcards-21
91O-Pee-Chee-350
91Topps-350
91Upper Deck-482
French-482
92Canadiens Postcards-19
92Parkhurst-325
Emerald Ice-325
92Ultra-331
93Canadiens Postcards-17
93Donruss-167
93Leaf-283
93Parkhurst-370
Emerald Ice-370
93Pinnacle-301
Canadian-301
93PowerPlay-132
93Score-283
Canadian-283
93Ultra-354
93Upper Deck-7
94Canada Games NHL POGS-140
94Canadiens Postcards-17

94Donruss-272
94Fleer-105
94Leaf-137
94OPC Premier-43
Special Effects-43
94Parkhurst SE-SE89
Gold-SE89
94Pinnacle-132
Artist's Proofs-132
Rink Collection-132
94Stadium Club-104
Members Only Master Set-104
First Day Issue-104
Super Team Winner Cards-104
94Topps/OPC Premier-43
Special Effects-43
94Ultra-112
95Be A Player-111
Signatures-S111
Signatures Die Cuts-S111
95Canadiens Postcards-10
95Collector's Choice-6
Player's Club-6
Player's Club Platinum-6
95Donruss-281
95Leaf-195
95Parkhurst International-381
Emerald Ice-381
95Pinnacle-196
Artist's Proofs-196
Rink Collection-196
95Playoff One on One-165
95Upper Deck-153
Electric Ice-153
Electric Ice Gold-153
96Be A Player-148
Autographs-148
Autographs Silver-148
96Devils Team Issue-24
96Duracell All-Cherry Team-DC2
96Duracell L'Equipe Beliveau-JB2
96Score-224
Artist's Proofs-224
Dealer's Choice Artist's Proofs-224
Special Artist's Proofs-224
Golden Blades-224
96Upper Deck-289
97Be A Player-17
Autographs-17
Autographs Die-Cuts-17
Autographs Prismatic Die-Cuts-17
97Devils Team Issue-19
97Pacific-143
Copper-143
Emerald Green-143
Ice Blue-143
Red-143
Silver-143
97Score Devils-15
Platinum-15
Premier-15
97Upper Deck-306
98Devils Team Issue-21
98Pacific-267
Ice Blue-267
Red-267
99Devils Team Issue-17
99Pacific-243
Copper-243
Emerald Green-243
Gold-243
Ice Blue-243
Premiere Date-243
Red-243
00BAP Signature Series-159
Emerald-159
Ruby-159
Sapphire-159
Autographs-88
Autographs Gold-88
00Paramount-71
Copper-71
Gold-71
Holo-Gold-71
Holo-Silver-71
Ice Blue-71
Premiere Date-71
00Stadium Club-208
00Titanium Game Gear-80
00Titanium Game Gear Patches-80
00Titanium Draft Day Edition-27
Patches-27
00Topps Chrome-222
OPC Refractors-222
Refractors-222
00Upper Deck Vintage-103
01Atomic Jerseys-15
01Atomic Patches-15
01Blue Jackets Donatos Pizza-15
01Titanium Double-Sided Jerseys-15
01Upper Deck Victory-103
Gold-103
01Vanguard Memorabilia-40
02BAP Sig Series Auto Buybacks 2000-88
02Pacific Complete-386
Red-386
03NHL Sticker Collection-179
03Pacific Complete-312
Red-312
03Panthers Team Issue-14
05Upper Deck MVP-316
Gold-316
Platinum-316
Materials-M-LO
Materials Duals-D-CO

Odelein, Selmar
87Oilers Team Issue-36
88Oilers Tenth Anniversary-26
88ProCards AHL-93

Odeline, Selmar
93UK Sheffield Steelers-13

Oder, Steffen
99German DEL-201

Odgers, Jeff
88Brandon Wheat Kings-12
89Brandon Wheat Kings-20
90Kansas City Blades-2
90ProCards AHL/IHL-600
91Parkhurst-386
French-386
91Upper Deck-597
French-597
92Bowman-397
92O-Pee-Chee-190
92Panini Stickers-130
92Panini Stickers French-130
92Parkhurst-398
Emerald Ice-398
92Stadium Club-142
92Topps-483
Gold-483G
93OPC Premier-497
Gold-497
93Panini Stickers-260
93PowerPlay-224
93Stadium Club-114
Members Only Master Set-114
OPC-114
First Day Issue-114
First Day Issue OPC-114
93Topps/OPC Premier-497
Gold-497
94Leaf-439
94Stadium Club-11
Members Only Master Set-11
First Day Issue-11
Super Team Winner Cards-11
94Ultra-368
96Be A Player-193
Autographs-193
Autographs Silver-193
96Maggers-71
97Pacific-157
Copper-157
Emerald Green-157
Ice Blue-157
Red-157
Silver-157
97Pacific Omega-62
Copper-62
Dark Gray-62
Emerald Green-62
Gold-62
Ice Blue-62
97Panini Stickers-2
97Score Bruins-18
Platinum-18
Premier-18
98Avalanche Team Issue-7
98Pacific-166
Ice Blue-166
Red-166
98Pacific Omega-62
Red-62
Opening Day Issue-62
99Avalanche Team Issue-15
99Pacific-112
Copper-112
Emerald Green-112
Gold-112
Ice Blue-112
Premiere Date-112
Red-112
00BAP Memorabilia Update Tough Materials-T17
00BAP Mem Update Tough Materials Gold-T17
00Paramount-123
Copper-123
Gold-123
Holo-Gold-123
Holo-Silver-123
Ice Blue-123
Premiere Date-123
00Upper Deck NHLPA-PA5
01BAP Update Tough Customers-TC13
01BAP Update Tough Customers-TC17
01BAP Update Tough Customers-TC24
01Pacific-22
01Pacific-402
Extreme LTD-22
Gold-402
Hobby LTD-22
Premiere Date-22
Retail LTD-22
01Pacific Arena Exclusives-22
01Pacific Arena Exclusives-402
01Upper Deck-11
Exclusives-11
02Pacific-19
Blue-19
Red-19
02Pacific Complete-435
Red-435
02Thrashers Postcards-12
03ITG Action-43
03Pacific-20
Blue-20
Red-20
03Upper Deck MVP-25
Gold Script-25
Silver Script-25
Canadian Exclusives-25

Odintsov, Valeri
74Swedish Stickers-70

Odjick, Gino
90Canucks Mohawk-23
90Upper Deck-518
French-518
90ProCards AHL/IHL-334
907th Inn. Sketch Memorial Cup-54
91Bowman-316
91Canucks Autograph Cards-19
91Canucks Team Issue 8x10-19
91O-Pee-Chee-203
91Pro Set-505
French-505
91Score Canadian Bilingual-237
91Score Canadian English-237
91Stadium Club-338
91Topps-203
91Upper Deck-195
French-195
92Canucks Road Trip Art-17
92Parkhurst-422
Emerald Ice-422
92Score-540
Canadian-540
92Ultra-427
93Donruss-346
93Leaf-418
93Parkhurst-485
Emerald Ice-485
93Pinnacle-308
Canadian-308
93PowerPlay-461
93Score-385
Canadian-385
93Ultra-442
94Canada Games NHL POGS-151
94Canucks Program Inserts-17
94Donruss-241
94Fleer-228
94Leaf-200
94Parkhurst SE-SE186
Gold-SE186
94Pinnacle-177
Artist's Proofs-177
Rink Collection-177
94Score-9
Gold-9
Platinum-9
94Ultra-229
94Upper Deck-465
Electric Ice-465
95Be A Player-222
Signatures-S222
Signatures Die Cuts-S222
95Canucks Building the Dream Art-13
95Collector's Choice-290
Player's Club-290
Player's Club Platinum-290
95Upper Deck-338
Electric Ice-338
Electric Ice Gold-338
96Canucks Postcards-29
96Collector's Choice-274
97Collector's Choice-263
97Pacific Dynagon Best Kept Secrets-98
97Score Canucks-16
Platinum-16
Premier-16
97Upper Deck-206
97Upper Deck-379
98Pacific Omega-148
Red-148
Opening Day Issue-148
99BAP Millennium-154
Emerald-154
Ruby-154
Sapphire-154
Signatures-154
Signatures Gold-154
99Panini Stickers-95
99Russian Fetisov Tribute-36
00BAP Memorabilia-319
Emerald-319
Ruby-319
Sapphire-319
Promos-319
00BAP Mem Chicago Sportsfest Copper-319
00BAP Memorabilia Chicago Sportsfest Blue-319
00BAP Memorabilia Chicago Sportsfest Gold-319
00BAP Memorabilia Chicago Sportsfest Ruby-319
00BAP Memorabilia Chicago Sun-Times Ruby-319
00BAP Memorabilia Chicago Sun-Times Gold-319
00BAP Mem Chicago Sun-Times Sapphire-319
00BAP Mem Toronto Fall Expo Copper-319
00BAP Memorabilia Toronto Fall Expo Gold-319
00BAP Memorabilia Toronto Fall Expo Ruby-319
00BAP Memorabilia Update Tough Materials-T22
00BAP Mem Update Tough Materials Gold-T22
00Canadiens Postcards-19
00Pacific-304
Copper-304
Gold-304
Ice Blue-304
Premiere Date-304
01BAP Signature Series-137
Autographs-137
Autographs Gold-137
01BAP Update Tough Customers-TC27
01BAP Update Tough Customers-TC40
01Canadiens Postcards-14
02BAP Sig Series Auto Buybacks 1999-154
02BAP Sig Series Auto Buybacks 2001-137
02Upper Deck-95
Exclusives-95
04ITG Franchises Canadian-127
Autographs-GO
05ITG Tough Customers-GO
Autographs-GO
Emblem and Numbers-GO
Jerseys-GO
Signed Memorabilia-GO

Odling, Sune
73Swedish Stickers-137
74Swedish Stickers-152

Odling, Ulf
93Swedish Semic Elitserien-6

Odmark, Ulf
83Swedish Semic Elitserien-165
86Swedish Panini Stickers-210
87Swedish Panini Stickers-200
89Swedish Semic Elitserien Stickers-184
90Swedish Semic Elitserien Stickers-19
91Swedish Semic Elitserien Stickers-221
92Swedish Semic Elitserien Stickers-241
93Swedish Semic Elitserien-208

Odnokon, Mark
84Minnesota-Duluth Bulldogs-12
85Minnesota-Duluth Bulldogs-17
91Prince Albert Raiders-16
917th Inn. Sketch WHL-263
05Prince Albert Raiders-25

Odnokon, Pat
90Prince Albert Raiders-15

Odrowski, Gerry
44Beehive Group II Photos-198
60Shirriff Coins-58
61Shirriff/Salada Coins-78
62Parkhurst-20
71Blues Postcards-12
72Los Angeles Sharks WHA-11
72O-Pee-Chee-304
74O-Pee-Chee WHA-14

Odut, Mark
04Missouri River Otters-22
05Missouri River Otters-18

Oduya, Fredrik
95Kansas City Blades-15
96Kentucky Thoroughblades-14
97Kentucky Thoroughblades-11
98Orlando Solar Bears II-19

Oduya, Johnny
03Swedish Elite-158
Silver-158
04Swedish Elitset-14
Gold-14
05Swedish SHL Elitset-177
Gold-177
06Beehive-134
Matte-134
06Black Diamond-161A
Black-161A
Gold-161A
Ruby-161A
06Devils Team Set-18
06Hot Prospects-167
Red Hot-167
White Hot-167
06O-Pee-Chee-540
Rainbow-540
06SP Authentic-232
Limited-232
06SP Game Used-131
Gold-131
Rainbow-131
06SPx-156
Spectrum-156
06The Cup-140
Autographed Rookie Masterpiece Pressplates-140
Gold Rainbow Autographed Rookie Patches-140
Masterpiece Pressplates (Bee Hive)-134
Masterpiece Pressplates (Black Diamond)-161
Masterpiece Pressplates (Marquee Rookies)-540
Masterpiece Pressplates (MVP)-316
Masterpiece Pressplates (SP Authentic)-232
Masterpiece Pressplates (SP Game Used)-131
Masterpiece Pressplates (SPx)-156
Masterpiece Pressplates (Trilogy)-127
Masterpiece Pressplates (Ultimate Collection)-82
Masterpiece Pressplates (Victory)-286
Rookies Black-140
Rookies Platinum-140
06Ultimate Collection-82
Ultimate Debut Threads Jerseys-DJ-JO
Ultimate Debut Threads Jerseys Autographs-DJ-JO
Ultimate Debut Threads Patches-DJ-JO
Ultimate Debut Threads Patches Autographs-DJ-JO
06Upper Deck-226
Exclusives Parallel-226
High Gloss Parallel-226
Masterpieces-226
06Upper Deck MVP-316
Gold Script-316
Super Script-316
06Upper Deck Trilogy-127
06Upper Deck Victory-286
06Swedish SHL Elitset-31

Ofukany, Troy
04Kelowna Rockets-22
05Kelowna Rockets-19

Ogilvie, Brian
74NHL Action Stamps-245

Ogilvie, Ryan
95Neepewa Natives-11

Ogorodnikov, Sergei
04Russian Under-18 Team-19

Ogrodnick, John
80O-Pee-Chee-359
81O-Pee-Chee-95
81O-Pee-Chee Stickers-121
81Topps-W95
82O-Pee-Chee-79
82O-Pee-Chee-92
82O-Pee-Chee Stickers-179
82Post Cereal-5
82Topps Stickers-179
83NHL Key Tags-34
83O-Pee-Chee-115
83O-Pee-Chee-128
83O-Pee-Chee Stickers-137
83O-Pee-Chee Stickers-138
83Puffy Stickers-16
83Topps Stickers-137
83Topps Stickers-138
84O-Pee-Chee-62
84O-Pee-Chee-356
84O-Pee-Chee Stickers-34
84O-Pee-Chee Stickers-35
84O-Pee-Chee Stickers-137
84Topps-46
85O-Pee-Chee-70
85O-Pee-Chee Box Bottoms-J
85O-Pee-Chee Stickers-37
85O-Pee-Chee Stickers-119
85Topps-70
85Topps Box Bottoms-J
85Topps Sticker Inserts-1
86Nordiques Team Issue-16
86O-Pee-Chee-87
86O-Pee-Chee Stickers-158
86Topps-87
87O-Pee-Chee-134
87O-Pee-Chee Stickers-218
87Panini Stickers-165
87Red Wings Little Caesars-23
87Topps-134
88O-Pee-Chee-153
88Topps-153
89Panini Stickers-290
89Rangers Marine Midland Bank-25
90Bowman-223
Tiffany-223
90O-Pee-Chee-174
90Panini Stickers-99
90Pro Set-206
90Score-113
Canadian-113
90Topps-174
Tiffany-174
Team Scoring Leaders-18
Team Scoring Leaders Tiffany-18
90Upper Deck-258
French-258
91Pro Set Platinum-204
91Bowman-71
91O-Pee-Chee-365
91Panini Stickers-293
91Parkhurst-115
French-115
91Pinnacle-145
French-145
91Pro Set-169
French-169
91Score American-36
91Score Canadian Bilingual-36
91Score Canadian English-36
91Stadium Club-273
91Topps-365
91Upper Deck-476
French-476
92O-Pee-Chee-351
92Score-329
Canadian-329
92Stadium Club-222
01Greats of the Game-46
Autographs-46
02UD Foundations-24
04ITG Franchises US West-221
Autographs-A-JOG
06Parkhurst-86
Autographs-86
Autographs Dual-DAOL

Oh, David
93Quebec Pee-Wee Tournament-1471

Ohestedt, Martin
98Odessa Jackalopes-18

Ohling, Jens
83Swedish Semic Elitserien-86
84Swedish Semic Elitserien-86
85Swedish Panini Stickers-77
86Swedish Panini Stickers-70
87Swedish Panini Stickers-76
89Swedish Semic Elitserien Stickers-62
90Swedish Semic Elitserien Stickers-286
91Swedish Semic Elitserien Stickers-69
92Swedish Semic Elitserien Stickers-90
93Swedish Semic Elitserien-63
94Swedish Leaf-38
Studio Signatures-3
95Swedish Leaf-33
95Swedish Upper Deck-52
97Swedish Collector's Choice-176

Ohlson, JArl
05Finnish Tappara Legendat-12

Ohlsson, Bengt
92Finnish Semic-26

Ohlsson, Dag
67Swedish Hockey-109

Ohlsson, Eine
67Swedish Hockey-295

Ohlund, Mattias
93Swedish Semic Elitserien-316
94Parkhurst SE-SE243
Gold-SE243
94SP-172
Die Cuts-172
94Upper Deck-520
Electric Ice-520
94Swedish Leaf-288
NHL Draft-1
Rookie Rockets-4
94Signature Rookies Gold Standard *-89
95SP-184
95Swedish Leaf-75
Mega-8
95Swedish Upper Deck-119
95Swedish Upper Deck-229
95Swedish Upper Deck-256
Ticket to North America-NA16
95Swedish Globe World Championships-57
95Signature Rookies-14
Signatures-14
96Swedish Semic Wien-52
96Swedish Semic Wien Coca-Cola Dream Team-5
97Be A Player-215
Autographs-215
Autographs Die-Cuts-215
Autographs Prismatic Die-Cuts-215
97Black Diamond-120
Double Diamond-120
Triple Diamond-120
Quadruple Diamond-120
97Donruss Elite-98
97Donruss Elite-139
Aspirations-98
Aspirations-139
Status-98
Status-139
97Donruss Priority-171
Stamp of Approval-171
97Katch-150
Gold-150
Silver-150
97Pacific Dynagon-NNO
Copper-NNO
Dark Grey-NNO
Emerald Green-NNO
Ice Blue-NNO
Red-NNO
Silver-NNO
97Pacific Omega-234
Copper-234
Dark Gray-234
Emerald Green-234
Gold-234
Ice Blue-234
97Paramount-192
Copper-192
Dark Grey-192
Emerald Green-192
Ice Blue-192
Red-192
Silver-192
97Pinnacle-8
Artist's Proofs-8
Rink Collection-8
Press Plates Back Black-8
Press Plates Back Cyan-8
Press Plates Back Magenta-8
Press Plates Back Yellow-8
Press Plates Front Black-8
Press Plates Front Cyan-8
Press Plates Front Magenta-8
Press Plates Front Yellow-8
97Revolution-144
Copper-144
Emerald-144
Ice Blue-144
Silver-144
97Score-63
Artist's Proofs-63
Golden Blades-63
97Score Canucks-6
Platinum-6
Premier-6
97SP Authentic-196
97Upper Deck-380
97Upper Deck Ice-42
Parallel-42
Power Shift-42
97Zenith-85
Z-Gold-85
Z-Silver-85
97Zenith 5 x 7-73
Gold Impulse-73
Silver Impulse-73
97Zenith Rookie Reign-13
97Zenith Z-Team-11
97Zenith Z-Team Gold-11
98Aurora-191
98Be A Player-142
Press Release-142
98BAP Gold-142
98BAP Autographs-142
98BAP Autographs Gold-142
98BAP Tampa Bay All Star Game-142
98Black Diamond-87
Double Diamond-87
Triple Diamond-87
Quadruple Diamond-87
98Bowman's Best-73
Refractors-73
Atomic Refractors-73
Performers-BP5
Performers Refractors-BP5
Performers Atomic Refractors-BP5
98Crown Royale-138
Limited Series-138
98Finest-38
No Protectors-38
No Protectors Refractors-38
Refractors-38
Centurion-C14
Centurion Refractors-C14
98Katch-148
98McDonald's Upper Deck-22
98OPC Chrome-54
Refractors-54
Board Members-B5
Board Members Refractors-B5
Season's Best-SB11
Season's Best Refractors-SB11
98Pacific-2
Ice Blue-2
Red-2
98Pacific Dynagon Ice-191
Blue-191
Red-191
98Pacific Omega-240
Red-240
Opening Day Issue-240
98Panini Stickers-221
98Paramount-238
Copper-238
Emerald Green-238
Holo-Electric-238
Ice Blue-238
Silver-238
98Revolution-144
Ice Shadow-144
Red-144
All-Star Die Cuts-21
98SP Authentic-84
Power Shift-84
Sign of the Times-MO
Sign of the Times Gold-MO
98SPx Finite-127
Radiance-127
Spectrum-127
98Topps-54
O-Pee-Chee-54
Autographs-A4
Board Members-B5
Ice Age 2000-I12
Season's Best-SB11
98Topps Gold Label Class 1-87
Black-87
Black One of One-87
One of One-87
Red-87
Red One of One-87
98Topps Gold Label Class 2-87
98Topps Gold Label Class 2 Black-87
98Topps Gold Label Class 2 Black 1 of 1-87
98Topps Gold Label Class 2 One of One-87
98Topps Gold Label Class 2 Red-87
98Topps Gold Label Class 2 Red One of One-87
98Topps Gold Label Class 3-87
98Topps Gold Label Class 3 Black-87
98Topps Gold Label Class 3 Black 1 of 1-87
98Topps Gold Label Class 3 One of One-87
98Topps Gold Label Class 3 Red-87
98Topps Gold Label Class 3 Red One of One-87
98UD Choice-206
Prime Choice Reserve-206
Reserve-206
98UD3-14
98UD3-74
98UD3-134
Die-Cuts-14
Die-Cuts-74
Die-Cuts-134
98Upper Deck-197
Exclusives-197
Exclusives 1 of 1-197
Generation Next-GN16
Generation Next Quantum 1-GN16
Generation Next Quantum 2-GN16
Generation Next Quantum 3-GN16
Gold Reserve-197
98Upper Deck MVP-203
Gold Script-203
Silver Script-203
Super Script-203
99Aurora-144
Premiere Date-144
99BAP Memorabilia-19
Gold-19
Silver-19
99BAP Millennium-239
Emerald-239
Ruby-239
Sapphire-239
Signatures-239
Signatures Gold-239
99Kraft Dinner-8
99O-Pee-Chee-76
99O-Pee-Chee Chrome-76
99O-Pee-Chee Chrome Refractors-76
99O-Pee-Chee Now Starring-NS14
99Pacific-430
Copper-430
Emerald Green-430
Gold-430
Ice Blue-430
Premiere Date-430
Red-430
99Panini Stickers-308
99Paramount-239
Copper-239
Emerald-239
Gold-239
Holographic Emerald-239
Holographic Gold-239
Holographic Silver-239
Ice Blue-239
Premiere Date-239
Red-239
Silver-239
99Revolution-145
Premiere Date-145
Red-145
Shadow Series-145
99SPx-152
Radiance-152
Spectrum-152
99Stadium Club-124
First Day Issue-124
One of a Kind-124
Printing Plates Black-124
Printing Plates Cyan-124
Printing Plates Magenta-124
Printing Plates Yellow-124
99Topps/OPC-76
Now Starring-NS14
99Topps/OPC Chrome-76
Refractors-76
99Upper Deck-299
Exclusives-299
Exclusives 1 of 1-299
99Upper Deck Gold Reserve-299
99Upper Deck MVP-207
Gold Script-207
Silver Script-207
Super Script-207
Draw Your Own Trading Card-W22
99Upper Deck Victory-300
00BAP Memorabilia-329
Emerald-329
Ruby-329
Sapphire-329
Promos-329
00BAP Mem Chicago Sportsfest Copper-329
00BAP Memorabilia Chicago Sportsfest Blue-329
00BAP Memorabilia Chicago Sportsfest Gold-329
00BAP Memorabilia Chicago Sportsfest Ruby-329
00BAP Memorabilia Chicago Sun-Times Ruby-329
00BAP Memorabilia Chicago Sun-Times Gold-329
00BAP Mem Chicago Sun-Times Sapphire-329
00BAP Mem Toronto Fall Expo Copper-329
00BAP Memorabilia Toronto Fall Expo Gold-329
00BAP Memorabilia Toronto Fall Expo Ruby-329
00McDonald's Pacific-34
Blue-34
Checklists-8
00O-Pee-Chee-72
00O-Pee-Chee Parallel-72
00Pacific-413
Copper-413
Gold-413
Ice Blue-413
Premiere Date-413
00Panini Stickers-210
00Paramount-241
Copper-241
Gold-241
Holo-Gold-241
Holo-Silver-241
Ice Blue-241
Premiere Date-241
00Stadium Club-58
00Topps/OPC-72
Parallel-72
00Topps Chrome-57
OPC Refractors-57
Refractors-57
00Topps Stars-37
Blue-37
00Upper Deck Vintage-356
01BAP Memorabilia-219
Emerald-219
Ruby-219
Sapphire-219
01O-Pee-Chee-147
01O-Pee-Chee Premier Parallel-147
01Pacific-385
Extreme LTD-385
Hobby LTD-385
Premiere Date-385
Retail LTD-385
01Pacific Arena Exclusives-385
01Topps-147
OPC Parallel-147
02BAP First Edition-44
Jerseys-44
02BAP Sig Series Auto Buybacks 1998-142
02BAP Sig Series Auto Buybacks 1999-239
02BAP Signature Series Defensive Wall-DW10
02BAP Signature Series Golf-GS56
02Canucks Team Issue-12
02NHL Power Play Stickers-166
02O-Pee-Chee-51
02O-Pee-Chee Premier Blue Parallel-51
02O-Pee-Chee Premier Red Parallel-51
02O-Pee-Chee Factory Set-51
02Pacific-382
Blue-382
Red-382
02Pacific Calder-10
Silver-10
02Pacific Complete-57
Red-57
02Topps-51
OPC Blue Parallel-51
OPC Red Parallel-51
Factory Set-51
02Topps Total-60
02Upper Deck-169
02Upper Deck-417
Exclusives-169
Exclusives-417
02Upper Deck Beckett UD Promos-417
03Canucks Postcards-21
03Canucks Sav-on-Foods-10
03Canucks Sav-on-Foods-16
03ITG Action-565
03NHL Sticker Collection-299
03O-Pee-Chee-220
03OPC Blue-220
03OPC Gold-220
03OPC Red-220
03Pacific Complete-262
Red-262
03Topps-220
Blue-220
Gold-220
Red-220
03Upper Deck-434
Canadian Exclusives-434
HG-434
UD Exclusives-434
03Upper Deck MVP-417
Gold Script-417
Silver Script-417
Canadian Exclusives-417
04Pacific-259
Blue-259
Red-259
04Upper Deck World Cup Tribute-NLMO
04Swedish Alfabilder Alfa Stars-2
04Swedish Alfabilder Alfa Star Golden Ice-11
04Swedish Alfabilder Autographs-114
04Swedish Alfabilder Limited Autographs-114
04Swedish Alfabilder Proof Parallels-2
05Be A Player Signatures-MO
05Be A Player Signatures Gold-MO
05Panini Stickers-366
05Parkhurst-475
Facsimile Auto Parallel-475
05Ultimate Coll National Heroes Jersey-NHJMO
05Ultimate Coll National Heroes Patch-NHPMO
05Ultra-193
Gold-193
Ice-193
05Upper Deck-192
Big Playmakers-B-MO
HG Glossy-192
Jerseys-J-MO
Jerseys Series II-J2MO
05Upper Deck MVP-376
Gold-376
Platinum-376
05Upper Deck Toronto Fall Expo-192
06Canucks Postcards-16
06Flair Showcase Stitches-SSOH
06Fleer-191
Tiffany-191
Fabricology-FMO
06Gatorade-84
06O-Pee-Chee-479
Rainbow-479
06Panini Stickers-358
06UD Artifacts Tundra Tandems-TTNO
06UD Artifacts Tundra Tandems Black-TTNO
06UD Artifacts Tundra Tandems Blue-TTNO
06UD Artifacts Tundra Tandems Gold-TTNO
06UD Artifacts Tundra Tandems Platinum-TTNO
06UD Artifacts Tundra Tandems Red-TTNO
06UD Artifacts Tundra Tandems Dual Patches Red-TTNO
06Ultra-191
Gold Medallion-191
Ice Medallion-191
06Upper Deck-190
Exclusives Parallel-190
High Gloss Parallel-190
Masterpieces-190
06Upper Deck MVP-285
Gold Script-285
Super Script-285
06Upper Deck Victory-195
06Upper Deck Victory Black-195
06Upper Deck Victory Gold-195

Ohlzon, Bruno
84Swedish Semic Elitserien-127

Ohman, Jens
89Swedish Semic Elitserien Stickers-183
90Swedish Semic Elitserien Stickers-18
91Swedish Semic Elitserien Stickers-222
98Swedish UD Choice-26

Ohman, Lars
67Swedish Hockey-131
69Swedish Hockey-144
70Swedish Hockey-98
71Swedish Hockey-193

Ohman, Lasse
67Swedish Hockey-25
72Swedish Stickers-179

Ohman, Mats
84Swedish Semic Elitserien-180
86Swedish Panini Stickers-176

Ohman, Robert
83Swedish Semic Elitserien-176

Ohman, Stefan
94Swedish Leaf-228
98Swedish UD Choice-27
00Swedish Upper Deck-164
02Swedish SHL-88
Parallel-88
03Finnish Cardset-153
04Finnish Cardset-164
Parallel-121
04Swedish Pure Skills-138
Parallel-138
05Finnish Cardset -149
06Finnish Cardset-154

Ohman, Tore
67Swedish Hockey-132
69Swedish Hockey-145
70Swedish Hockey-99
71Swedish Hockey-194
72Swedish Stickers-180

Ohmann, Roger
84Swedish Semic Elitserien-179
87Moncton Hawks-18
89Swedish Semic Elitserien Stickers-7
90Swedish Semic Elitserien Stickers-131
91Swedish Semic Elitserien Stickers-182
92Swedish Semic Elitserien Stickers-209
93Swedish Semic Elitserien-179
94Swedish Leaf-272
95Swedish Leaf-88
Goldies-9
95Swedish Upper Deck-139
96German DEL-232
00Swiss Panini Stickers-60
00Swiss Slapshot Mini-Cards-HCCF6
02Swedish SHL-70
Parallel-70

Ohrling, Mattias
03Swedish Elite-267
Silver-267

Ohrlund, Leif
65Swedish Coralli ISHockey-206
67Swedish Hockey-280

Ohrlund, Torbjorn
92Swedish Semic Elitserien Stickers-44

Ohrlund, Uno
56Swedish Alfabilder-49
64Swedish Coralli ISHockey-7
65Swedish Coralli ISHockey-7
67Swedish Hockey-281
69Swedish Hockey-326
71Swedish Hockey-380

Oijennus, Markus
93Finnish SISU-79
94Finnish SISU-114
95Finnish SISU-321

Oijennus, Oiva
72Finnish Jaakiekko-162

73Finnish Jaakiekko-228
78Finnish SM-Liiga-183
80Finnish Mallasjuoma-161

Oikkonen, Pekka
65Finnish Hellas-12

Ojala, Jani
99Bakersfield Condors-13

Ojala, Markus
04Finnish Cardset-308

Ojanen, Janne
88ProCards AHL-346
89Devils Caretta-18
90O-Pee-Chee-30
90Panini Stickers-78
90Pro Set-173
90Topps-30
Tiffany-30
90Upper Deck-290
French-290
91Upper Deck-25
French-25
92OPC Premier-17
92Finnish Semic-21
93OPC Premier-16
Gold-16
93Stadium Club-184
Members Only Master Set-184
OPC-184
First Day Issue-184
First Day Issue OPC-184
93Topps/OPC Premier-16
Gold-16
93Swedish Semic World Champ Stickers-71
94Finnish SISU-208
94Finnish SISU Fire On Ice-19
94Finnish SISU Magic Numbers-4
94Finnish SISU Specials-4
94Finnish Jaa Kiekko-35
95Finnish SISU-322
Gold Cards-19
95Finnish SISU Limited-77
Leaf Gallery-4
95Finnish SISU Specials-6
95Finnish Karjala World Champ Labels-15
95Finnish Semic World Championships-8
95Swedish Globe World Championships-136
95Swedish World Championships Stickers-171
96Finnish SISU Redline Mighty Adversaries-6
96Swedish Semic Wien-8
97Swedish Collector's Choice-141
97Swedish Collector's Choice-214
Crash the Game Exchange-C12
Crash the Game Redemption-R12
Select-UD13
98Finnish Kerailysarja-222
Leijonat-34
99Finnish Cardset-128
99Finnish Cardset-167
Aces High-H-7
00Finnish Cardset-89
01Finnish Cardset-345
01Finnish Cardset Dueling Aces-2
02Finnish Cardset-87
03Finnish Cardset-147
04Finnish Cardset-157
Parallel-116
05Finnish Tappara Legendat-29
05Finnish Cardset -142
06Finnish Cardset-324

Ojanen, Marko
93Finnish SISU-105
94Finnish SISU-132
95Finnish SISU-14
98Finnish Kerailysarja-131
99Finnish Cardset-73
00Finnish Cardset-333
01Finnish Cardset-128
02Finnish Cardset-239
03Finnish Cardset-150
04Finnish Cardset-160
Parallel-119
05Finnish Cardset -144
06Finnish Cardset-327

Ojanen, Reijo
65Finnish Hellas-149

Ojansuu, Jouko
66Finnish Jaakiekkosarja-49

Ojerklint, Ulf
72Swedish Stickers-100

Okabe, Ken
93Quebec Pee-Wee Tournament-156

Okal, Miroslav
94Czech APS Extraliga-194
95Czech APS Extraliga-42
96Czech APS Extraliga-44
97Czech APS Extraliga-67
97Czech DS Stickers-110
98Czech DS-114
98Czech DS Stickers-297
98Czech OFS-30
99Czech DS-8
99Czech OFS-216
00Czech DS Extraliga-55
00Czech OFS-300
01Czech OFS-113
02Czech OFS Plus-36
Trios-T22
03Czech OFS Plus-140
03Czech OFS Plus Insert C-C13
04Czech OFS-287
05Czech HC Hame Zlin-13
06Czech OFS-237

Okal, Zdenek
94Czech APS Extraliga-195
95Czech APS Extraliga-43

Oke, Andrew
03Roanoke Express-315
06Bakersfield Condors-8

Okkonen, Ilkka
71Finnish Suomi Stickers-308

Okposo, Kyle
06Minnesota Golden Gophers-16

Okrzesik, Michael
02Guelph Storm-19
03Guelph Storm-3
04Guelph Storm-4

Oksa, Mika
99Finnish Cardset-205
00Finnish Cardset-4
01Finnish Cardset-2
02Finnish Cardset-88
04Finnish Cardset-2
Parallel-2
05Swedish SHL Elitset-280
Catchers-12
Catchers Gold-12
Gold-280
06Finnish Cardset-209
Between the Pipes-5
06Swedish SHL Elitset Goal Patrol-18

Oksala, Jorma
66Finnish Jaakiekkosarja-154
70Finnish Jaakiekko-218

Oksala, Ossi
70Finnish Jaakiekko-261

Oksanen, Hannu
72Finnish Jaakiekko-313
78Finnish SM-Liiga-60
84Swedish Semic Elitserien-162

Oksanen, Jukka
72Finnish Jaakiekko-349

Oksanen, Lasse
65Finnish Hellas-114
66Finnish Jaakiekkosarja-203
69Swedish Hockey-378
70Finnish Jaakiekko-71
70Finnish Jaakiekko-133
70Swedish Hockey-308
70Swedish Masterserien-13
70Swedish Masterserien-86
70Swedish Masterserien-162
71Finnish Suomi Stickers-72
71Finnish Suomi Stickers-182
71Swedish Hockey-71
72Finnish Jaakiekko-69
72Finnish Jaakiekko-131
72Finnish Hellas-9
72Finnish Panda Toronto-29
72Finnish Panda Toronto-106
72Finnish Semic World Championship-84
72Swedish Stickers-38
72Swedish Semic World Championship-84
73Finnish Jaakiekko-186
74Finnish Typotor-10
74Swedish Stickers-98
74Swedish Semic World Champ Stickers-87
77Finnish Sportscasters-45-1057
78Finnish SM-Liiga-55
80Finnish Mallasjuoma-32
91Finnish Semic World Champ Stickers-229
91Swedish Semic World Champ Stickers-229
96Swedish Semic Wien Hockey Legends-HL14

Oksiuta, Roman
91O-Pee-Chee Inserts-57R
92Russian Stars Red Ace-24
92Russian Stars Red Ace-20
93Donruss-111
Rated Rookies-15
93Leaf-411
93Parkhurst-258
Emerald Ice-258
93Pinnacle-451
Canadian-451
93Upper Deck-509
93Swedish Semic World Champ Stickers-141
93Classic Pro Prospects-11
93Classic Four-Sport *-244
Gold-244
94Finest Bowman's Best-R5
94Finest Bowman's Best Refractors-R5
94Fleer-72
94Cape Breton Oilers-15
95Donruss-66
95Emotion-183
95Finest-94
Refractors-94
95Leaf-77
Studio Rookies-16
95Metal-154
95Panini Stickers-292
95Parkhurst International-211
Emerald Ice-211
95Pinnacle-63
Artist's Proofs-63
Rink Collection-63
95Playoff One on One-210
95Score-285
Black Ice Artist's Proofs-285
Black Ice-285
95SkyBox Impact-172
NHL On Fox-2
95Stadium Club-132
Members Only Master Set-132
95Topps-317
OPC Inserts-317
New To The Game-8NG
95Ultra-171
Gold Medallion-171
All-Rookies-9
All-Rookie Gold Medallion-9
95Upper Deck-476
Electric Ice-476
Electric Ice Gold-476
95Images-35
Gold-35
96Collector's Choice-10
96Donruss-44
Press Proofs-44
96Ducks Team Issue-3
96Metal Universe-4
96Pinnacle-139
Artist's Proofs-139
Foil-139
Premium Stock-139
Rink Collection-139
96Playoff One on One-397
96Score-76
Artist's Proofs-76
Dealer's Choice Artist's Proofs-76
Special Artist's Proofs-76
Golden Blades-76
96SkyBox Impact-3
96Ultra-4
Gold Medallion-4
97Pacific Invincible NHL Regime-164
97Panini Stickers-48
97Score Penguins-13
Platinum-13
Premier-13
00Russian Hockey League-357
01Russian Hockey League-25
03Russian Hockey League-109

Oktyabrev, Arthur
92Russian Stars Red Ace-25
92Russian Stars Red Ace-31
00Russian Hockey League-380
02Russian Hockey League-60
03Russian National Team-32

Okvist, Tore
83Swedish Semic Elitserien-49
84Swedish Semic Elitserien-186

Olafson, Mark
02Kelowna Rockets-24
03Kelowna Rockets Memorial Cup-14
03Kelowna Rockets-15
04Lethbridge Hurricanes-7
05Lethbridge Hurricanes-17

Olaski, Mike
92British Columbia JHL-72

Olausson, Fredrik
84Swedish Semic Elitserien-102
85Swedish Panini Stickers-97
86Jets Postcards-18
87Jets Postcards-16
87O-Pee-Chee-225
87Panini Stickers-361
88Jets Police-18
88Jets Postcards-18
89Jets Safeway-23
89Kraft-51
89Swedish Semic Elitserien Stickers-77
89Swedish Semic World Champ Stickers-10
90Bowman-135
Tiffany-135
90Jets IGA-25
90O-Pee-Chee-242
90Panini Stickers-318
90Pro Set-335A
90Pro Set-335B
90Score-81
Canadian-81
90Topps-242
Tiffany-242
90Upper Deck-237
French-237
91Pro Set Platinum-133
91Bowman 210
91Jets Panini Team Stickers-19
91Jets IGA-21
91O-Pee-Chee-45
91Panini Stickers-67
91Parkhurst-203
French-203
91Pinnacle-74
French-74
91Pro Set-264
French-264
91Score American-18
91Score Canadian Bilingual-18
91Score Canadian English-18
91Stadium Club-185
91Topps-45
91Upper Deck-383
French-383
92Bowman-295
92O-Pee-Chee-121
92Panini Stickers-60
92Panini Stickers French-60
92Parkhurst-212
Emerald Ice-212
92Pinnacle-202
French-202
92Score-13
Canadian-13
92Stadium Club-346
92Topps-120
Gold-120G
92Ultra-244
Imports-18
92Upper Deck-136
92Finnish Semic-59
93Donruss-386
93Donruss-430
93Jets Readers Club-15
93Jets Ruffles-19
93Leaf-124
93OPC Premier-63
Gold-63
93Panini Stickers-198
93Parkhurst-227
Emerald Ice-227
93Pinnacle-392
Canadian-392
93PowerPlay-273
93PowerPlay-342
93Score-79
93Score-645
Gold-645
Canadian-79
Canadian-645
Canadian Gold-645
93Topps/OPC Premier-63
Gold-63
93Ultra-147
93Upper Deck-209
93Swedish Semic World Champ Stickers-26
94Be A Player Signature Cards-8
94Canada Games NHL POGS-103
94Fleer-73
94Leaf-327
94OPC Premier-319
Special Effects-319
94Pinnacle-303
Artist's Proofs-303
Rink Collection-303
94Score-147
Gold-147
Platinum-147
94Stadium Club-198
Members Only Master Set-198
First Day Issue-198
Super Team Winner Cards-198
94Topps/OPC Premier-319
Special Effects-319
94Ultra-74
94Upper Deck-394
Electric Ice-394
95Collector's Choice-98
Player's Club-98
Player's Club Platinum-98
95Swedish Upper Deck-247
95Swedish Globe World Championships-26
96Be A Player-134
Autographs-134
Autographs Silver-134
97Pacific-149
Copper-149
Emerald Green-149
Ice Blue-149
Red-149
Silver-149
97Panini Stickers-54
97Upper Deck-139
98Be A Player-154
Press Release-154
98BAP Gold-154
98BAP Autographs-154
98BAP Autographs Gold-154
98OPC Chrome-150
Refractors-150
98Pacific-356
Ice Blue-356
Red-356
98Pacific Omega-6
Red-6
Opening Day Issue-6
98Panini Stickers-54
98Paramount-195
Copper-195
Emerald Green-195
Holo-Electric-195
Ice Blue-195
Silver-195
98Topps-150
O-Pee-Chee-150
99BAP Memorabilia-165
Gold-165
Silver-165
99O-Pee-Chee-175
99O-Pee-Chee Chrome-175
99O-Pee-Chee Chrome Refractors-175
99Pacific-11
Copper-11
Emerald Green-11
Gold-11
Ice Blue-11
Premiere Date-11
Red-11
99Paramount-5
Copper-5
Emerald-5
Gold-5
Holographic Emerald-5
Holographic Gold-5
Holographic Silver-5
Ice Blue-5
Premiere Date-5
Red-5
Silver-5
99Stadium Club-117
First Day Issue-117
One of a Kind-117
Printing Plates Black-117
Printing Plates Cyan-117
Printing Plates Magenta-117
Printing Plates Yellow-117
99Topps/OPC-175
99Topps/OPC Chrome-175
Refractors-175
99Upper Deck-14
Exclusives-14
Exclusives 1 of 1-14
99Upper Deck Gold Reserve-14
99Upper Deck Victory-8
99Upper Deck Victory-344
00Swiss Slapshot Stickers-35
00Swiss Slapshot Mini-Cards-SCB5
01Upper Deck-295
Exclusives-295
02BAP Sig Series Auto Buybacks 1998-154
02Pacific Complete-350
Red-350
02Upper Deck-249
Exclusives-249
02Upper Deck Beckett UD Promos-249
03Swedish Elite-190
Silver-190
04Swedish Allabilder Alfa Stars-31
04Swedish Allabilder Proof Parallels-31
04Swedish Elitset-48
Dominators-8
Gold-48
04Swedish HV71 Postcards-5
05Swedish SHL Elitset-193
Gold-193
06Swedish SHL Elitset-54

Olausson, Niklas
06Swedish SHL Elitset-210

Olberg, Dan
90Arizona Icecats-10

Olbrich, Michael
94German DEL-175
95German DEL-170

Olczyk, Ed
85Blackhawks Team Issue-24
85O-Pee-Chee-86
85O-Pee-Chee Stickers-26
85Topps-86
86Blackhawks Coke-13
86O-Pee-Chee-82
86O-Pee-Chee Stickers-156
86Topps-82
87Maple Leafs PLAY-9
87Maple Leafs Postcards-14
87Maple Leafs Postcards Oversized-14
87O-Pee-Chee-104
87O-Pee-Chee Stickers-76
87Panini Stickers-230
87Topps-104
88Frito-Lay Stickers-11
88Maple Leafs PLAY-6
88O-Pee-Chee-125
88O-Pee-Chee Box Bottoms-G
88O-Pee-Chee Stickers-181
88Panini Stickers-126
88Topps-125
88Topps Box Bottoms-G
89Kraft-38
89O-Pee-Chee-133
89O-Pee-Chee Stickers-172
89Panini Stickers-132
89Topps-133
89Swedish Semic World Champ Stickers-169
90Bowman-161
Tiffany-161
90Jets IGA-26
90O-Pee-Chee-206
90Panini Stickers-283
90Pro Set-286
90Pro Set-563
90Score-210
Canadian-210
90Score Hottest/Rising Stars-89
90Score Rookie/Traded-51T
90Topps-206
Tiffany-206
90Upper Deck-222
90Upper Deck-431
French-222
French-431
91Pro Set Platinum-134
91Bowman-204
91Jets IGA-22
91Kraft-62
91Maple Leafs Panini Team Stickers-17
91O-Pee-Chee-182
91OPC Premier-196
91Panini Stickers-64
91Parkhurst-204
French-204
91Pinnacle-193
91Pinnacle-386
French-193
French-386
91Pro Set-265
French-265
91Score American-60
91Score Canadian Bilingual-60
91Score Canadian English-60
91Score Kellogg's-18
91Stadium Club-57
91Topps-182
91Upper Deck-99
91Upper Deck-387
French-99
French-387
91Finnish Semic World Champ Stickers-148
91Swedish Semic World Champ Stickers-148
92Bowman-278
92O-Pee-Chee-375
92Panini Stickers-55
92Panini Stickers French-55
92Parkhurst-213
92Parkhurst-350
Emerald Ice-213
Emerald Ice-350
92Pinnacle-145
French-145
92Pro Set-213
92Score-145
Canadian-145
USA Greats-15
92Stadium Club-157
92Topps-17
Gold-17G
92Ultra-245
92Ultra-357
92Upper Deck-211
92Finnish Semic-161
93Leaf-90
93OPC Premier-398
Gold-398
93Parkhurst-402
Emerald Ice-402
93Pinnacle-154
Canadian-154
93PowerPlay-394
93Score-37
Canadian-37
93Stadium Club-197
Members Only Master Set-197
OPC-197
First Day Issue-197
First Day Issue OPC-197
93Topps/OPC Premier-398
Gold-398
93Upper Deck-115
93Swedish Semic World Champ Stickers-184
94Pinnacle-420
Artist's Proofs-420
Rink Collection-420
94Upper Deck-274
Electric Ice-274
94Finnish Jaa Kiekko-115
95Be A Player-141
Signatures-S141
Signatures Die Cuts-S141
95Collector's Choice-106
Player's Club-106
Player's Club Platinum-106
95Jets Team Issue-17
95Score-282
Black Ice Artist's Proofs-282
Black Ice-282
96Leaf-117
Press Proofs-117
96Metal Universe-77
96Score-198
Artist's Proofs-198
Dealer's Choice Artist's Proofs-198
Special Artist's Proofs-198
Golden Blades-198
96SP-75
96Ultra-81
Gold Medallion-81
97Crown Royale-112
Emerald Green-112
Ice Blue-112
Silver-112
97Pacific-92
Copper-92
Emerald Green-92
Ice Blue-92
Red-92
Silver-92
97Pacific Invincible-116
Copper-116
Emerald Green-116
Ice Blue-116
Red-116
Silver-116
97Pacific Omega-188
Copper-188
Dark Gray-188
Emerald Green-188
Gold-188
Ice Blue-188
97Paramount-154
Copper-154
Dark Grey-154
Emerald Green-154
Ice Blue-154
Red-154
Silver-154
97Pinnacle Inside-169
97Score-206
97Score Penguins-7
Platinum-7
Premier-7
98Pacific-357
Ice Blue-357
Red-357
99Pacific-95
Copper-95
Emerald Green-95
Gold-95
Ice Blue-95
Premiere Date-95
Red-95
06ITG International Ice-157
Gold-157
Autographs-AEO
06ITG Ultimate Memorabilia-45
Artist Proof-45

Oldenborger, Jeff
92Quebec Pee-Wee Tournament-1536
94Kamloops Blazers-4
95Kamloops Blazers-17
95Slapshot Memorial Cup-2

Oldis, Ryan
04Chicago Steel-9

Oleinik, Valeri
99Russian Hockey League-268
00Russian Hockey League-341

Oleniuk, Devon
84Saskatoon Blades Stickers-17
86Saskatoon Blades Photos-18
87Kamloops Blazers-16

Olenyn, Jerry
94Las Vegas Thunder-18

Olers, Daniel
99Colorado Gold Kings Taco Bell-17
99Colorado Gold Kings Wendy's-7

Olesehuk, Bill
79Rockies Team Issue-15

Oleson, Cory
90Arizona Icecats-11
91Arizona Icecats-4
91Arizona Icecats-18
92Arizona Icecats-3
92Arizona Icecats-19

Olesz, Rostislav
01Czech OFS Update-316
02Czech OFS Plus-309
03Czech OFS Plus-10
03Czech OFS Plus MS Praha-SE19
04SP Authentic Rookie Redemptions-RR13
04Czech HC Sparta Praha Postcards-14
04Czech OFS-193
05Beehive-105
Beige -105
Blue -105
Gold-105
Red -105
Matte-105
05Black Diamond-202
Emerald-202
Gold-202
Onyx-202
Ruby-202
05Hot Prospects-240
En Fuego-240
Hot Materials-HMRO
Red Hot-240
White Hot-240
05Parkhurst-630
Facsimile Auto Parallel-630
Signatures-RO
True Colors-TCFLA
True Colors-TCFLA
05SP Authentic-158
Limited-158
Prestigious Pairings-PPOS
Rarefied Rookies-RRRO
Rookie Authentics-RARO
05SP Game Used-103
Autographs-103
Gold-103
Rookie Exclusives-RO
Rookie Exclusives Silver-RE-RO
Significant Numbers-SN-RO
05SPx-172
Spectrum-172
Xcitement Rookies-XR-RO
Xcitement Rookies Gold-XR-RO
Xcitement Rookies Spectrum-XR-RO
05The Cup-110
Autographed Rookie Patches Gold Rainbow-110
Black Rainbow Rookies-110
Masterpiece Pressplates (Artifacts)-213
Masterpiece Pressplates (Bee Hive)-105
Masterpiece Pressplates (Black Diamond)-202
Masterpiece Pressplates (Ice)-113
Masterpiece Pressplates (MVP)-416
Masterpiece Pressplates (Power Play)-167
Masterpiece Pressplates Rookie Upd Auto-266
Masterpiece Pressplates SPA Autos-158
Masterpiece Pressplates (SP Game Used)-103
Masterpiece Pressplates SPx Autos-172
Masterpiece Pressplates (Trilogy)-192
Masterpiece Pressplates Ult Coll Autos-117
Masterpiece Pressplates (Victory)-282
Masterpiece Pressplates Autographs-110
Platinum Rookies-110
05UD Artifacts-213
Gold-RED13
05UD PowerPlay-167
05UD Rookie Class-37
05Ultimate Collection-117
Autographed Patches-117
Autographed Shields-117
Ultimate Debut Threads Jerseys-DTJRO
Ultimate Debut Threads Jerseys Autos-DAJRO
Ultimate Debut Threads Patches-DTPRO
Ultimate Debut Threads Patches Autos-DAPRO
Ultimate Signatures-USRO
Ultimate Signatures Pairings-UPHO
05Ultra-268
Gold-268
Fresh Ink-FI-RO
Fresh Ink Blue-FI-RO
Ice-268
Rookie Uniformity Jerseys-RU-RO
Rookie Uniformity Jersey Autographs-ARU-RO
Rookie Uniformity Patches-RUP-RO
Rookie Uniformity Patch Autographs-ARP-RO
05Upper Deck-207
HG Glossy-207
Rookie Ink-RIRO
05Upper Deck Rookie Showcase-RS13
05Upper Deck Rookie Showcase Promos-RS13
05Upper Deck Rookie Threads-RTRO
05Upper Deck Rookie Threads Autographs-ARTRO
05Upper Deck Ice-113
Premieres Auto Patches-AIPRO
05Upper Deck MVP-416
Gold-416
Platinum-416
05Upper Deck Rookie Update-266
05Upper Deck Trilogy-192
05Upper Deck Toronto Fall Expo-207
05Upper Deck Victory-282
Black-282
Gold-282
Silver-282
06Be A Player Portraits First Exposures-FERO
06Be A Player Portraits Signature Portraits-SPRO
06Fleer Signing Day-SDRO
06O-Pee-Chee-211
Rainbow-211
06Panini Stickers-56
06Ultra-88
Gold Medallion-88
Ice Medallion-88
06Upper Deck-85
Exclusives Parallel-85
High Gloss Parallel-85
Masterpieces-85
06Upper Deck MVP-131
Gold Script-131
Super Script-131
06Upper Deck Victory Next In Line-NL24

Olimb, Larry
91Minnesota Golden Gophers-21
92Classic-90
Gold-90

Olinger, Matt
03Wisconsin Badgers-23
04Wisconsin Badgers-2
05Wisconsin Badgers-20

Oliphant, Brett
06Mississauga Ice Dogs-7

Oliphante, Brett
05Mississauga Ice Dogs-15

Oliva, Jiri
99Czech Score Blue 2000-162
99Czech Score Red Ice 2000-162

Oliveira, Mike
95Slapshot-122
98Kingston Frontenacs-15
99Louisiana Ice Gators-2
02ECHL Update-U-18
03New Mexico Scorpions-15
04New Mexico Scorpions-19

Oliveira, Sam
91Cornwall Royals-9
917th Inn. Sketch OHL-7

Oliver, Clark
05Waterloo Blackhawks-16

Oliver, David
91Michigan Wolverines-11
93Michigan Wolverines-17
94Finest Bowman's Best-R6
94Finest Bowman's Best Refractors-R6
94Flair-60
94Fleer-74
94Parkhurst SE-SE60
Gold-SE60
94Pinnacle-490
Artist's Proofs-490
Rink Collection-490
94SP Premier-13
94SP Premier Die-Cuts-13
94Upper Deck-269
Electric Ice-269
SP Inserts-SP117
SP Inserts Die Cuts-SP117
94Cape Breton Oilers-16
94Classic-57
Gold-57
All-Americans-AA6
ROY Sweepstakes-R16
Tri-Cards-T22
95Be A Player-64
Signatures-S64
Signatures Die Cuts-S64
95Canada Games NHL POGS-34
95Canada Games NHL POGS-108
95Collector's Choice-13
Player's Club-13
Player's Club Platinum-13
95Donruss-8
Rookie Team-4
95Emotion-65
95Finest-62
Refractors-62
95Hoyle Western Playing Cards-49
95Leaf-9
Studio Rookies-4
95Leaf Limited-89
95Metal-55
95Panini Stickers-263
95Parkhurst International-76
Emerald Ice-76
95Pinnacle-42
Artist's Proofs-42
Rink Collection-42
95Playoff One on One-38
95Score-60
Black Ice Artist's Proofs-60
Black Ice-60
95SkyBox Impact-63
95SkyBox Impact-231
NHL On Fox-3
95Stadium Club-109
Members Only Master Set-109
95Summit-98
Artist's Proofs-98
Ice-98
95Topps-366
OPC Inserts-366
Hidden Gems-8HG
New To The Game-14NG
95Topps SuperSkills-71
Platinum-71
95Ultra-56
Gold Medallion-56
All-Rookies-10
All-Rookie Gold Medallion-10
95Upper Deck-167
Electric Ice-167
Electric Ice Gold-167
Special Edition-SE120
Special Edition Gold-SE120
95Images-79
Gold-79
Autographs-79A
95Assets Gold *-8
95Assets Gold Phone Cards $2 *-8
96Collector's Choice-96
96Pinnacle-51
Artist's Proofs-51
Foil-51
Premium Stock-51
Rink Collection-51
96Playoff One on One-358
96Score-193
Artist's Proofs-193
Dealer's Choice Artist's Proofs-193
Special Artist's Proofs-193
Golden Blades-193
96Upper Deck-60
96Collector's Edge Ice-35
Crucibles-C7
Prism-35
99Houston Aeros-12
00Upper Deck NHLPA-PA62
00Grand Rapids Griffins-16
01German Upper Deck-187
02Utah Grizzlies-17
03Stars Postcards-20

Oliver, David WPHL
99Huntington Blizzard-12
00Charlotte Checkers-11
02Bossier-Shreveport Mudbugs-14
03Bossier-Shreveport Mudbugs-14

Oliver, Geoff
05Chicoutimi Sagueneens-11

Oliver, Harry
23V128-1 Paulin's Candy-69
33O-Pee-Chee V304A-9
33V129-39
33V357 Ice Kings-23
34Diamond Matchbooks Silver-48
35Diamond Matchbooks Tan 1-52
35Diamond Matchbooks Tan 2-52
35Diamond Matchbooks Tan 3-49
38Bruins Garden Magazine Supplement-5
83Hall of Fame Postcards-K12
85Hall of Fame-146
02BAP Ultimate Mem Paper Cuts Autos-31
03BAP Ultimate Memorabilia Paper Cuts-22
05ITG Ultimate Mem Amazing Amerks Autos-6
05ITG Ultimate Mem Quad Paper Cuts Autos-1

Oliver, John
01Idaho Steelheads-24
04Idaho Steelheads-2

Oliver, Lawrence
92British Columbia JHL-230

Oliver, Matt
98Phoenix Mustangs-17

Oliver, Murray
44Beehive Group II Photos-52
44Beehive Group II Photos-199
60Parkhurst-22
60Shirriff Coins-55
60Topps Stamps-42
61Shirriff/Salada Coins-8
61Topps-14
62Topps-12
Hockey Bucks-19
63Topps-10
64Beehive Group III Photos-20
64Coca-Cola Caps-11
64Topps-79
65Coca-Cola-9
65Topps-34
66Topps-95
67Topps-82
68Maple Leafs White Border-6
68O-Pee-Chee-194
68Post Marbles-16
68Shirriff Coins-167
69Maple Leafs White Border Glossy-24
69O-Pee-Chee-52
69Topps-52
70Dad's Cookies-91
70Esso Power Players-170
70O-Pee-Chee-167
70Sargent Promotions Stamps-86
71O-Pee-Chee-239
71Sargent Promotions Stamps-88
71Toronto Sun-141
72Sargent Promotions Stamps-107
73North Stars Postcards-15
74NHL Action Stamps-130
74O-Pee-Chee NHL-291
75O-Pee-Chee NHL-335
80North Stars Postcards-14
94Parkhurst Tall Boys-2
94Parkhurst Tall Boys-169
95Parkhurst '66-67-9
95Parkhurst '66-67-140
Coins-9

Oliver, Simon
92Saskatchewan JHL-2
96Mississippi Sea Wolves-15

Oliverio, Mike
83Sault Ste. Marie Greyhounds-17
84Sault Ste. Marie Greyhounds-15
87Sault Ste. Marie Greyhounds-17

Oliverius, Michal
99Czech Score Blue 2000-88
99Czech Score Red Ice 2000-88
01Czech OFS-160

Olivestedt, Mattias
93Swedish Semic Elitserien-232

Olivier, Benoit
93Quebec Pee-Wee Tournament-1654

Olivier, Francois
93Quebec Pee-Wee Tournament-229

Olivier, Simon
95Central Hockey League-49
98Oklahoma City Blazers-5
03Thetford Mines Prolab-14
04Thetford Mines Prolab-20

Oliwa, Krzysztof
94Classic Pro Prospects-73
94Signature Rookies Tetrad *-110
Signatures-110
96Albany River Rats-10
97Be A Player-229
Autographs-229
Autographs Die-Cuts-229
Autographs Prismatic Die-Cuts-229
97Devils Team Issue-23
97Pacific Omega-133
Copper-133
Dark Gray-133
Emerald Green-133
Gold-133
Ice Blue-133
97Upper Deck-302
98Devils Team Issue-22
98Pacific-268
Ice Blue-268
Red-268
98Pacific Omega-140
Red-140
Opening Day Issue-140

98Paramount-137
Copper-137
Emerald Green-137
Holo-Electric-137
Ice Blue-137
Silver-137
98Upper Deck-117
Exclusives-117
Exclusives 1 of 1-117
Gold Reserve-117
99Devils Team Issue-22
99Pacific-244
Copper-244
Emerald Green-244
Gold-244
Ice Blue-244
Premiere Date-244
Red-244
99Ultimate Victory-52
1/1-52
Parallel-52
Parallel 100-52
00BAP Memorabilia-333
Emerald-333
Ruby-333
Sapphire-333
Promos-333
00BAP Mem Chicago Sportsfest Copper-333
00BAP Memorabilia Chicago Sportsfest Blue-333
00BAP Memorabilia Chicago Sportsfest Gold-333
00BAP Memorabilia Chicago Sportsfest Ruby-333
00BAP Memorabilia Chicago Sun-Times Ruby-333
00BAP Memorabilia Chicago Sun-Times Gold-333
00BAP Mem Chicago Sun-Times Sapphire-333
00BAP Mem Toronto Fall Expo Copper-333
00BAP Memorabilia Toronto Fall Expo Gold-333
00BAP Memorabilia Toronto Fall Expo Ruby-333
00BAP Memorabilia Update Tough Materials-T13
00BAP Mem Update Tough Materials Gold-T13
00Panini Stickers-141
00Revolution-43
Blue-43
Premiere Date-43
Red-43
00Upper Deck Vintage-104
00Upper Deck Vintage-110
00Czech Stadion-196
01BAP Update Tough Customers-TC12
01BAP Update Tough Customers-TC30
01Pacific-419
Gold-419
01Pacific Arena Exclusives-419
01Topps Reserve Emblems-KO
01Topps Reserve Jerseys-KO
01Topps Reserve Name Plates-KO
01Topps Reserve Numbers-KO
01Topps Reserve Patches-KO
03ITG Action-42
03Pacific Complete-329
Red-329
03Upper Deck Tough Customers-TC-7
03Upper Deck MVP-49
Gold Script-49
Silver Script-49
Canadian Exclusives-49

Olkkonen, Pekka
66Finnish Jaakiekkosarja-206

Ollas, Jesper
05Swedish SHL Elitset-212
Gold-212

Ollikainen, Jarkko
99Finnish Cardset-102
00Finnish Cardset-313
01Finnish Cardset-317

Ollila, Jukka
92Finnish Jyvas-Hyva Stickers-38
93Upper Deck-269
93Finnish Jyvas-Hyva Stickers-80
93Finnish SISU-112
94Finnish SISU-330
95Finnish SISU-313

Ollson, John
81Ottawa 67's-14
82Ottawa 67's-15
83Springfield Indians-5
85Nova Scotia Oilers-9

Olmstead, Bert
44Beehive Group II Photos-132
44Beehive Group II Photos-276
44Beehive Group II Photos-442
45Quaker Oats Photos-103
48Exhibits Canadian-20
51Parkhurst-5
52Parkhurst-93
53Parkhurst-19
54Parkhurst-5
55Parkhurst-42
Quaker Oats-42
57Parkhurst-M19
57Parkhurst-M25
58Parkhurst-27
59Parkhurst-40
60Parkhurst-4
60Shirriff Coins-11
60York Photos-26
61Parkhurst-4
61Shirriff/Salada Coins-52
61York Yellow Backs-19
62Shirriff Coins-11
62Topps-57
63Maple Leafs Team Issue-19
85Hall of Fame-248
93O-Pee-Chee Canadiens Hockey Fest-58
93Parkhurst Parkie Reprints-PR56
94Parkhurst Missing Link-71
94Parkhurst Missing Link-146

Olofson, Jon
98Fort Worth Brahmas-18
99Fort Worth Brahmas-13

Olofsson, Bo
65Swedish Coralli ISHockey-214
67Swedish Hockey-274
69Swedish Hockey-51
70Swedish Hockey-12
71Swedish Hockey-89
72Swedish Stickers-57
73Swedish Stickers-207

Olofsson, Kurt
67Swedish Hockey-226
69Swedish Hockey-342
70Swedish Hockey-258
71Swedish Hockey-318

Olofsson, Stefan
93Swedish Semic Elitserien-16

Olofsson, Thomas
85Swedish Panini Stickers-201

Olofsson, Tony
89Swedish Semic Elitserien Stickers-177
90Swedish Semic Elitserien Stickers-11

Oloriz, Ted
90Fort Saskatchewan Traders-12

Olsen, Atle
92Norwegian Elite Series-10
97Swedish Collector's Choice-65

Olsen, Brad
02Rockford Ice Hogs-19

Olsen, Chance
03Camrose Kodiaks-14
04Camrose Kodiaks-11

Olsen, Christian Seest
05Erie Otters-10

Olsen, Darryl
89ProCards IHL-195
90ProCards AHL/IHL-604
91ProCards-577
99German Bundesliga 2-2
99Corpus Christi IceRays-13
04UK Thommo's Top 10-7

Olsen, Eivind
92Norwegian Elite Series-138

Olsen, Eric
95Slapshot-108

Olsen, Greg
02Indianapolis Ice-13

Olsen, Hasse
99Danish Hockey League-168

Olsen, Jan
64Swedish Corali ISHockey-94
65Swedish Coralli ISHockey-94
67Swedish Hockey-296
69Swedish Hockey-343
70Swedish Hockey-248
71Swedish Hockey-305
72Swedish Stickers-290

Olsen, Michel
99Danish Hockey League-31

Olsen, Oystein
92Finnish Semic-36
92Norwegian Elite Series-9
93Swedish Semic World Champ Stickers-242

Olsen, Rasmus
98Danish Hockey League-81
99Danish Hockey League-36

Olsen, Roger
92Norwegian Elite Series-121

Olsen, Sten
64Swedish Corali ISHockey-153
65Swedish Corali ISHockey-153
67Swedish Hockey-126
69Swedish Hockey-140

Olsen, Stig
92Norwegian Elite Series-231

Olsen, Sven Arild
92Norwegian Elite Series-219

Olsen, Tom Erik
92Norwegian Elite Series-22
93Swedish Semic World Champ Stickers-247
95Swedish World Championships Stickers-243

Olsgard, Chris
98Sioux City Musketeers-18
99Sioux City Musketeers-17
01Ohio State Buckeyes-12
02Ohio State Buckeyes-9
03Ohio State Buckeyes-11

Olson, Bob
91Michigan Tech Huskies-15
01Michigan Tech Huskies-21

Olson, Boyd
95Tri-City Americans-19
96Fredericton Canadiens-15
99Quebec Citadelles-23

Olson, Eddie
51Cleveland Barons-5

Olson, Glenn
03Kootenay Ice-11
04Cleveland Barons-16
05Cleveland Barons-15
05Fresno Falcons-16

Olson, Jarrod
92North Dakota Fighting Sioux-24

Olson, Jon
93Quebec Pee-Wee Tournament-1729

Olson, Josh
03ITG VIP Rookie Debut-138
03Parkhurst Rookie-68
03UD Premier Collection-95
03Upper Deck Rookie Update-179
03San Antonio Rampage-15

Olson, Kelly
98Minnesota Golden Gophers Women-17

Olson, Reilly
03Michigan Wolverines-10
04Michigan Wolverines-19

Olsson, Andreas
94Swedish Leaf-253

Olsson, Bert-Ake
69Swedish Hockey-233

Olsson, Bjorte
92Norwegian Elite Series-90

Olsson, Bo
56Swedish Alfabilder-90
67Swedish Hockey-146
69Swedish Hockey-160
72Swedish Stickers-284

Olsson, Christer
92Swedish Semic Elitserien Stickers-60
93Swedish Semic Elitserien-35
94Swedish Leaf-97
95Swedish Leaf Mega-14
95Swedish World Championships Stickers-145
96Senators Pizza Hut-18
96Swedish Semic Wien-50
All-Stars-AS2
97Pacific Dynagon Best Kept Secrets-66
97Swedish Collector's Choice-69
97Swedish Collector's Choice-203
97Swedish Collector's Choice-223
Crash the Game Exchange-C4
Crash the Game Redemption-R4
Stick'Ums-S3
98Swedish UD Choice-67
Day in the Life-10
00Swedish Upper Deck-33
01Swedish Brynas Tigers-17
02Swedish SHL-134
02Swedish SHL-190
Parallel-134
Parallel-190
Team Captains-5
03Swedish Elite-57
Signatures II-19
Silver-57

Olsson, Dag
65Swedish Corali ISHockey-189
71Swedish Hockey-385

Olsson, Daniel
99Swedish Upper Deck-34

Olsson, Dennis
98Danish Hockey League-88
98Danish Hockey League-127
99Danish Hockey League-221

Olsson, Eine
64Swedish Corali ISHockey-105
65Swedish Corali ISHockey-105

Olsson, Fredrik
90Swedish Semic Elitserien Stickers-218

Olsson, Hakan
67Swedish Hockey-275
69Swedish Hockey-319
70Swedish Hockey-213
84Swedish Semic Elitserien-167

Olsson, Jan
71Swedish Hockey-90
72Swedish Stickers-59
73Swedish Stickers-203
74Swedish Stickers-180

Olsson, Jens
03Swedish Elite-241
Silver-241

Olsson, Johan
01Macon Whoopee-15
05Swedish SHL Elitset-189
Gold-189

Olsson, Jonas
97Swedish Collector's Choice-193
98Swedish UD Choice-195

Olsson, Karl-Erik
56Swedish Alfabilder-51

Olsson, Kent
67Swedish Hockey-92
71Swedish Hockey-117
71Swedish Hockey-141
83Swedish Semic Elitserien-123

Olsson, Leif
71Swedish Hockey-111

Olsson, Mattias
89Swedish Semic Elitserien Stickers-82
90Swedish Semic Elitserien Stickers-255
91Swedish Semic Elitserien Stickers-86
92Swedish Semic Elitserien Stickers-110
93Swedish Semic Elitserien-83
94Swedish Leaf-225
95Swedish Leaf-296
95Swedish Upper Deck-191

Olsson, Nils-Olov
73Swedish Stickers-56
74Swedish Stickers-258
79Panini Stickers-199

Olsson, Olle
69Swedish Hockey-234

Olsson, Ove
82Swedish Semic VM Stickers-20
83Swedish Semic Elitserien-144
83Swedish Semic VM Stickers-20
84Swedish Semic Elitserien-165
85Swedish Panini Stickers-127
85Swedish Panini Stickers-128
85Swedish Panini Stickers-149
86Swedish Panini Stickers-154

Olsson, Per-Erik
71Swedish Hockey-207

Olsson, Peter
95Swedish Upper Deck 1st Division Stars-DS19

Olsson, Roger
65Swedish Corali ISHockey-170
67Swedish Hockey-19
67Swedish Hockey-297
69Swedish Hockey-196
69Swedish Hockey-344
70Finnish Jaakiekko-35
70Swedish Hockey-259
70Swedish Hockey-289
70Swedish Masterserien-108
71Swedish Hockey-319
72Swedish Stickers-299
73Swedish Stickers-142

Olsson, Stefan
89Swedish Semic Elitserien Stickers-231
90Swedish Semic Elitserien Stickers-70
91Swedish Semic Elitserien Stickers-244

Olsson, Sten-Olov
69Swedish Hockey-267

Olsson, Sven-Ove
71Swedish Hockey-153

Olthuis, John
05Vernon Vipers-17

Olund, Tomas
89Swedish Semic Elitserien Stickers-47
90Swedish Semic Elitserien Stickers-195

Olver, Dan
04Northern Michigan Wildcats-16

Olver, John
99Tacoma Sabercats-24

Olvestad, Jimmie
98Black Diamond-111
Double Diamond-111
Triple Diamond-111
Quadruple Diamond-111
98SPx Top Prospects-81
Radiance-81
Spectrum-81
98Swedish UD Choice-65
99Swedish Upper Deck-50
99Swedish Upper Deck-204
00Swedish Upper Deck-55
00Swedish Upper Deck-212
01BAP Signature Series-222
Autographs-222
Autographs Gold-222
01Upper Deck-391
Exclusives-391
02BAP Sig Series Auto Buybacks 2001-222
02O-Pee-Chee-277
02O-Pee-Chee Premier Blue Parallel-277
02O-Pee-Chee Premier Red Parallel-277
02O-Pee-Chee Factory Set-277
02Topps-277
OPC Blue Parallel-277
OPC Red Parallel-277
Factory Set-277
02Topps Total-124
04Swedish Djurgardens Postcards-7
04Swedish Elitset-166
Gold-166
05Swedish SHL Elitset-21
06Swedish SHL Elitset-23

Olympiev, Sergei
93Kitchener Rangers-26
93Phoenix Cobras RHI-13
94Kitchener Rangers-24
96Alaska Gold Kings-12
98Topeka Scarecrows-18

Olympique, Francois
907th Inn. Sketch QMJHL-127

Olynick, Craig
99UD Prospects-41
99UD Prospects-84
01Moose Jaw Warriors-18
03Peoria Rivermen-7

Olynyk, Mike
98Prince George Cougars-16
02Austin Ice Bats-11
03Austin Ice Bats-12
04Austin Ice Bats-9
05Quad City Mallards-11
06Port Huron Flags-4

Olynyk, Nick
03Regina Pats-21

Olynyk, Ryan
00Medicine Hat Tigers-19

Omark, Urban
03Swedish Elite-263
Silver-263

Omicioli, Drew
04German Ingolstadt Panthers-28
05Danbury Trashers-4

Omicioli, Mike
99Hampton Roads Admirals-13
01Columbus Cottonmouths-16
01Roanoke Express-15
04Louisiana Ice Gators-15
05Danbury Trashers-13

Ondraschek, Adam
05German DEL-196

Ondrej, Zdenek
01Idaho Steelheads-11
02Czech OFS Plus-182
03Czech OFS Plus-268
04Czech OFS-298
05Czech HC Znojmo-10
06Czech OFS-123

Ondrejik, Viliam
96Slovakian Quebec Pee-Wee Tournament-20

Ondrejka, Martin
94German DEL-215
95German DEL-214

Ondrik, Cam
97Red Deer Rebels-15

Ondrus, Ben
98Swift Current Broncos-14
99Swift Current Broncos-13
00Swift Current Broncos-14
01Swift Current Broncos-12
02Swift Current Broncos-12
06Flair Showcase-91
06Flair Showcase-163
Parallel-91
Parallel-163
06Fleer-216
Tiffany-216
06Hot Prospects-135
Red Hot-135
White Hot-135
Hot Materials -HMBO
Hot Materials Red Hot-HMBO
Hot Materials White Hot-HMBO
Hotagraphs-HBO
06O-Pee-Chee-518
Rainbow-518
06SP Authentic-230
Limited-230
06SP Game Used-154
Gold-154
Rainbow-154
Autographs-154
Rookie Exclusives Autographs-REBO
06SPx-168
Spectrum-168
06The Cup-162
Autographed Rookie Masterpiece Pressplates-162
Gold Rainbow Autographed Rookie Patches-162
Masterpiece Pressplates (Artifacts)-215
Masterpiece Pressplates (Marquee Rookies)-518
Masterpiece Pressplates (MVP)-323
Masterpiece Pressplates (Power Play)-126
Masterpiece Pressplates (SP Authentic)-230
Masterpiece Pressplates (SP Game Used)-154
Masterpiece Pressplates (SPx Autographs)-168
Masterpiece Pressplates (Trilogy)-154
Masterpiece Pressplates (Victory)-206
Rookies Black-162
Rookies Platinum-162
06UD Artifacts-215
Blue-215
Gold-215
Platinum-215
Radiance-215
Red-215
06UD Powerplay-126
Impact Rainbow-126
06Ultimate Collection Ultimate Debut Threads Jerseys-DJ-ON
06Ultimate Collection Ultimate Debut Threads Jerseys Autographs-DJ-ON
06Ultimate Collection Ultimate Debut Threads Patches-DJ-ON
06Ultimate Collection Ultimate Debut Threads Patches Autographs-DJ-ON
06Ultra-226
Gold Medallion-226
Ice Medallion-226
06Upper Deck-244
Exclusives Parallel-244
High Gloss Parallel-244
Masterpieces-244
Rookie Game Dated Moments-RGD28
Rookie Materials-RMBO
Rookie Materials Patches-RMBO
06Upper Deck MVP-323
Gold Script-323
Super Script-323
06Upper Deck Trilogy-154
06Upper Deck Victory-206
06Upper Deck Victory Black-206
06Upper Deck Victory Gold-206
06Toronto Marlies-21
06ITG Heroes and Prospects-39
Autographs-ABO
07Upper Deck Rookie Class -38

Ondruschka, Florian
04German Weiden Blue Devils-18
05German DEL-367

Onlangs, Van
79Panini Stickers-280

Onofrychuk, Darryl
917th Inn. Sketch WHL-158

Onufrechuk, Chad
97New Hampshire Wildcats-18
98New Hampshire Wildcats-2
99Mobile Mysticks-9
01Johnstown Chiefs-25

Opatovsky, Martin
02Czech OFS Plus-288

Opitz, Gary
93Quebec Pee-Wee Tournament-893

Opp, Darren
91Air Canada SJHL-D19
91Air Canada SJHL All-Stars-39
91Air Canada SJHL All-Stars-47

Oppliger, Charly
02Swiss HNL-495

Oppliger, Patrick
93Swiss HNL-507
95Swiss HNL-385
96Swiss HNL-220
96Swiss HNL-577
98Swiss Power Play Stickers-218
99Swiss Panini Stickers-218
00Swiss Panini Stickers-262
00Swiss Slapshot Mini-Cards-EVZ13
01Swiss EV Zug Postcards-20
01Swiss HNL-186
02Swiss EV Zug Postcards-19
02Swiss HNL-70
03Swiss EV Zug Postcards-17
04Swiss EV Zug Postcards-19

Opsahl, Kevin
03Portland Winter Hawks-22

Opulskis, Juris
94Czech APS Extraliga-127
99German Bundesliga 2-261

Oqvist, Tore
81Swedish Semic Hockey VM Stickers-18
85Swedish Panini Stickers-43
86Swedish Panini Stickers-15
87Swedish Panini Stickers-35

Oravec, Christopher
02German DEL City Press-17
04German DEL-141
04German Hamburg Freezers Postcards-10
05German DEL-116
06German DEL-36

Oravec, Tomas
00Kelowna Rockets-3
01Kelowna Rockets-16

Orban, Bill
67Topps-109

Orct, Zdenek
94Czech APS Extraliga-203
95Czech APS Extraliga-150
96Czech APS Extraliga-167
97Czech APS Extraliga-77
97Czech DS Extraliga-41
97Czech DS Stickers-37
98Czech DS-15
98Czech DS Stickers-87
98Czech OFS-2
99Czech DS-57
Goalies-G5
99Czech OFS-12
99Czech OFS-NNO
99Czech OFS Goalie Die-Cuts-12
00Czech DS Extraliga-37
Goalies-G4
00Czech OFS-135
00Czech OFS Star Emerald-19
00Czech OFS Star Pink-19
00Czech OFS Star Violet-19
01Czech OFS-171
01Czech OFS H Inserts-H3
03Czech OFS Plus-230
03Czech OFS Plus Insert M-M9
03Czech OFS Plus MS Praha-SE14
03Russian Hockey League-237
04Czech OFS-62
Goals-Against Leaders-9
Save Percentage Leaders-3
Team Cards-3
05Czech HC Kladno-9
06Czech HC Kladno Postcards-11
06Czech OFS-261
Stars-16
Team Cards-3

Ordman, Rob
83Brandon Wheat Kings-8

Orekhovski, Oleg
95Classic-65
Autographs-16
95Signature Rookies Future Flash-FF6
95Signature Rook Future Flash Sigs-FF6
99Russian Dynamo Moscow-10
00Russian Dynamo Moscow-6
00Russian Dynamo Moscow Blue-White-3
00Russian Hockey League-338
01Russian Dynamo Moscow-1
01Russian Dynamo Moscow Mentos-10
03Russian Avangard Omsk-22
03Russian SL-8
04Russian Moscow Dynamo-23

Oreskovic, Phil
03Brampton Batallion-16
04Brampton Batallion-6
05Brampton Battalion-2

Oreskovich, Victor
04Notre Dame Fighting Irish-5
05Kitchener Rangers-27
06Kitchener Rangers-20

Organ, Jamie
97UK Guildford Flames-17
99UK Guildford Flames-24

Orimus, Pekka
78Finnish SM-Liiga-58

Orlandi, Philipp
96Swiss HNL-71
98Swiss Power Play Stickers-95
01Swiss HNL-276
02Swiss HNL-90

Orlando, Gaetano
79Montreal Juniors-19
85Sabres Blue Shield-18
85Sabres Blue Shield Small-18
86Sabres Blue Shield-20
86Sabres Blue Shield Small-20
92Finnish Semic-253
93Swedish Semic World Champ Stickers-218
94Finnish Jaa Kiekko-299
95Finnish Semic World Championships-174
95Swedish Globe World Championships-232
95Swedish World Championships Stickers-87
95Swiss HNL-105
96Swedish Semic Wien-180
96Swiss HNL-48
98Swiss Power Play Stickers-173
02Albany River Rats-27
03Albany River Rats-29

Orlando, Jimmy
34Beehive Group I Photos-119
39O-Pee-Chee V301-1-65
76Old Timers-11
04ITG Ultimate Memorabilia Motown Heroes-8
05ITG Ultimate Mem Motown Heroes Autos-1

Orlov, Maxim
00Russian Hockey League-253

Orlov, Vladimir
73Swedish Stickers-126
74Swedish Stickers-91

Ormond, Brett
98Kingston Frontenacs-16

Ormson, Eric
02Arizona Icecats-18

Ornskog, Stefan
89Swedish Semic Elitserien Stickers-115
90Swedish Semic Elitserien Stickers-116
91Swedish Semic Elitserien Stickers-118
92Swedish Semic Elitserien Stickers-140
93Swedish Semic Elitserien-110
94Finnish Jaa Kiekko-71
94Swedish Leaf-28
Gold Cards-22
95Finnish Semic World Championships-71
95Swedish Leaf-57
Champs-11
Goldies-6
95Swedish Upper Deck-83
95Swedish Globe World Championships-39
95Swedish World Championships Stickers-155
97Swedish Collector's Choice-91
97Swedish Collector's Choice-207
97Swedish Collector's Choice-218
Crash the Game Exchange-C23
Crash the Game Redemption-R23
Select-UD8
98Finnish Kerailysarja-138
99Finnish Cardset-76

Oro, Janne
71Finnish Suomi Stickers-316

Orpik, Brooks
01Wilkes-Barre Scranton Penguins-4
02BAP First Edition-431R
02BAP Memorabilia-377
02BAP Ultimate Memorabilia-70
02Pacific Calder-139
Silver-139
02Pacific Complete-584
Red-584
02Pacific Quest for the Cup-139
Gold-139
02Parkhurst-236
Bronze-236
Gold-236
Silver-236
02Parkhurst Retro-238
Minis-238
02SP Authentic-200
02SPx-178
02Titanium-132
Blue-132
Red-132
Retail-132
02UD Artistic Impressions-108
Gold-108
Common Ground-CG11
Common Ground Gold-CG11
Retrospectives-R97
Retrospectives Gold-R97
Retrospectives Signed-R97
Retrospectives Silver-R97
02UD Honor Roll-140
02UD Mask Collection-167
02UD Premier Collection-102
Gold-102
Jerseys Bronze-BO
Jerseys Gold-BO
Jerseys Silver-BO
02Upper Deck Classic Portraits-134
02Upper Deck Rookie Update-151A
02Upper Deck Rookie Update-151B
02Upper Deck Rookie Update-151C
02Wilkes-Barre Scranton Penguins-2
03Beehive-154
Gold-154
Silver-154
03Black Diamond Signature Gems-SG-33
03ITG Action-417
03SPx Big Futures-BF-BO
03SPx Big Futures Limited-BF-BO
03Upper Deck-156
Canadian Exclusives-156
HG-156
03Upper Deck MVP-343
Gold Script-343
Silver Script-343
Canadian Exclusives-343
03Upper Deck Rookie Update YoungStars-YS10
03Upper Deck Trilogy Scripts-S1BO
03Upper Deck Trilogy Scripts Limited-S1BO
03Upper Deck Victory-154
Bronze-154
Gold-154
Silver-154
04Upper Deck Jersey Autographs-GJA-BO
05Be A Player Signatures-OR
05Be A Player Signatures Gold-OR
05Parkhurst-391
Facsimile Auto Parallel-391
05SP Game Used Game Gear-GG-OR
05UD Toronto Fall Expo Priority Signings-PS-BO
05Upper Deck MVP Materials-M-BO
06O-Pee-Chee-395
Rainbow-395

Orr, Billy
75A's 1913 TCMA-12
75Roanoke Valley Rebels-4

Orr, Bobby
66Topps-35
66Topps USA Test-35
67General Mills-5
67Post Cereal Box Backs-9
67Post Cereal Box Backs-10
67Topps-92
67Topps-118
67Topps-128
68Bauer Ads-17
68O-Pee-Chee-2
68O-Pee-Chee-200
68O-Pee-Chee-214
Puck Stickers-4
68Shirriff Coins-5
68Topps-2
69O-Pee-Chee-24
69O-Pee-Chee-209
69O-Pee-Chee-212
Four-in-One-11
Stamps-22
69Topps-24
70Bruins Postcards-16
70Bruins Team Issue-16
70Colgate Stamps-87
70Dad's Cookies-92
70Esso Power Players-56
70O-Pee-Chee-3
70O-Pee-Chee-236
70O-Pee-Chee-246
70O-Pee-Chee-248A
70O-Pee-Chee-248B
70O-Pee-Chee-249
70O-Pee-Chee-252
Deckle-4
70Post Shooters-12
70Sargent Promotions Stamps-1
70Topps-3
Topps/OPC Sticker Stamps-24
71Bazooka-36
71Bruins Postcards-2
71Colgate Heads-8
71Letraset Action Replays-5
71Letraset Action Replays-17
71Mattel Mini-Records-7
71O-Pee-Chee-100
71O-Pee-Chee-245
71O-Pee-Chee-251
O-Pee-Chee/Topps Booklets-24
Posters-1
71Sargent Promotions Stamps-10
71Topps-2
71Topps-3
71Topps-100
71Toronto Sun-15
71Finnish Suomi Stickers-384
71Swedish Hockey-196
72O-Pee-Chee-58
72O-Pee-Chee-129
72O-Pee-Chee-227
72O-Pee-Chee-280
72O-Pee-Chee-283
Player Crests-3
72Sargent Promotions Stamps-17
72Topps-62
72Topps-63
72Topps-100
72Topps-122
72Finnish Semic World Championship-223
72Swedish Stickers-113
72Swedish Semic World Championship-223
73Mac's Milk-19
73O-Pee-Chee-30
73Topps-150
74Lipton Soup-8
74New York News This Day in Sports-1
74NHL Action Stamps-19
74O-Pee-Chee NHL-2
74O-Pee-Chee NHL-28
74O-Pee-Chee NHL-100
74O-Pee-Chee NHL-130
74O-Pee-Chee NHL-248
74Topps-2
74Topps-28
74Topps-100
74Topps-130
74Topps-248
75Heroes Stand-Ups-3
75O-Pee-Chee NHL-100
75O-Pee-Chee NHL-209
75O-Pee-Chee NHL-210
75O-Pee-Chee NHL-288
75O-Pee-Chee NHL-314
75Topps-100
75Topps-209
75Topps-210
75Topps-288
75Topps-314
76O-Pee-Chee NHL-213
76Topps-213
76Topps Glossy Inserts-20
77Coca-Cola-17
77O-Pee-Chee NHL-251
77Sportscasters-102
77Topps-251
77Finnish Sportscasters-04-83
78O-Pee-Chee-300
80Oshawa Generals-25
81TCMA-9
83Hall of Fame-61
83Hall of Fame Postcards-E13
85Hall of Fame-61
88Esso All-Stars-33
89Sports Illustrated for Kids I-317
91BayBank Bobby Orr-1
91BayBank Bobby Orr-2
91BayBank Bobby Orr-3
91BayBank Bobby Orr-NNO
91Bruins Sports Action Legends-20
91Pinnacle-392
French-392
91Score Bobby Orr-1
91Score Bobby Orr-2
91Score Bobby Orr-3
91Score Bobby Orr-4
91Score Bobby Orr-5
91Score Bobby Orr-6
91Score Bobby Orr-AU
91Finnish Semic World Champ Stickers-237
91Swedish Semic World Champ Stickers-237
92Future Trends '76 Canada Cup-104
92Future Trends '76 Canada Cup-126
92Future Trends '76 Canada Cup-184
92Future Trends '76 Canada Cup-196
92Hall of Fame Legends-4
95BayBank Bobby Orr-1
95BayBank Bobby Orr-2
95Parkhurst '66-67-7
95Parkhurst '66-67-SR1
95Parkhurst '66-67-SR2
95Parkhurst '66-67-SR3
95Parkhurst '66-67-SR4
95Parkhurst '66-67-SR5
95Parkhurst '66-67-SRA1
95Parkhurst '66-67-SRA2
95Parkhurst '66-67-SRA3
95Parkhurst '66-67-SRA4
95Parkhurst '66-67-SRA5
Coins-7
Coins-BO1
Coins-BO2
Coins-BO3
Coins-BO4
Coins-BO5
95Pinnacle FANtasy-31
96Pinnacle Bobby Orr Autograph-NNO
97Kenner 12" Specials *-5
97Highland Mint Legends Mint-Cards-3
97Highland Mint Legends Mint-Cards-4
97Highland Mint Mint-Coins-11
98SLU Hockey 12" Figures-3
98Bruins Alumni-4
Autographs-4
99BAP Millennium Pearson-P13
99BAP Millennium Pearson Autographs-P13
99SP Authentic Legendary Heroes-LH2
99SP Authentic Sign of the Times-BO
99SP Authentic Sign of the Times Gold-BO
99Ultimate Victory Legendary Fabrics-BOS
99Ultimate Victory Legendary Fabrics-LFBO
99Ultimate Victory Legendary Fabrics-UFS
99Ultimate Victory Legendary Fabrics-UF
99Ultimate Victory UV Extra-UV4
99Upper Deck Century Legends-2
Century Collection-2
All Century Team-AC4
Century Artifacts-C6
Epic Signatures-BO
Epic Signatures 100-BO
Essence of the Game-E2
99Upper Deck PowerDeck-18
Auxiliary-18
Auxiliary 1 of 1-18
Time Capsule-T4
Time Capsule Auxiliary-T4
Time Capsule Auxiliary 1 of 1-T4
99Upper Deck Retro-81
Gold-81
Platinum-81
Distant Replay-DR10
Distant Replay Level 2-DR10
Generation-G1A
Generation-G4B
Generation Level 2-G1A
Generation Level 2-G4B
Inkredible-BO
Inkredible Level 2-BO
Turn of the Century-TC15
00SP Authentic BuyBacks-1
00SP Authentic Power Skaters-P1
00SP Authentic Sign of the Times-BO
00SP Authentic Sign of the Times-O/B
00SP Authentic Sign of the Times-HOG
00SP Game Used Patch Cards-D-OB
00SP Game Used Patch Cards-P-BO
00UD Heroes-119
Game-Used Twigs-T-BO
Game-Used Twigs Gold-C-BO
Signs of Greatness-BO
00Upper Deck Signs of Greatness-SBO
00Upper Deck Legends-6
Legendary Collection Bronze-6
Legendary Collection Gold-6
Legendary Collection Silver-6
Epic Signatures-BO
Essence of the Game-EG7
Legendary Game Jerseys-JBO
00UD CHL Prospects Autographs-A-BO
01SP Authentic Buybacks-2
01SP Authentic Buybacks-3
01SP Authentic Sign of the Times-BO
01SP Authentic Sign of the Times-GO
01SP Authentic Sign of the Times-BOB
01SPx Signs of Xcellence-BO
01UD Challenge 4 the Cup All-Time Lineup-AT4
01UD Honor Roll-4
01UD Honor Roll-34
Original Six-OS1
01UD Premier Collection-5
Signatures-BO
Signatures Black-BO
01UD Stanley Cup Champs-2
01Upper Deck Legends-1
01Upper Deck Legends-89
Epic Signatures-BO
Fiorentino Collection-FCBO
Sticks-PHBO
01UD Prospects Autographs-A-BO
02SP Authentic Sign of the Times-BO
02SP Authentic Sign of the Times-BB
02SP Authentic Sign of the Times-OB
02SP Authentic Sign of the Times-GHO
02SP Authentic Sign of the Times-OBT
02SP Game Used Signature Style-BO
02SPx-79
Spectrum Gold-79
Spectrum Silver-79
02UD Artistic Impressions-7
Gold-7
02UD Artistic Impressions Beckett Promos-7
02UD Artistic Impressions Great Depiction-GD4
02UD Artistic Impress Great Depiction Gld-GD4
02UD Artistic Impressions Retrospectives-R7
02UD Artistic Impressions Retrospect Gold-R7
02UD Artistic Impress Retrospect Auto-R7
02UD Artistic Impress Retrospect Silver-R7
02UD Chicago National Spokesmen-N9
02Upper Deck Collectors Club-NHL3
02UD Foundations-4
02UD Foundations-103
Lasting Impressions Sticks-L-BO
Signs of Greatness-SGBO
02UD Honor Roll Signature Class-BO
02UD Piece of History-97
02UD Piece of History-115
02UD Piece of History-116
02UD Piece of History-117
Hockey Beginnings-HB1
Marks of Distinction-BO
Simply the Best-SB2
02UD Premier Collection-57A
Signatures Bronze-SBO
Signatures Gold-SBO

Signatures Silver-SBO
02UD Top Shelf Signatures-BO
02Upper Deck-182
Exclusives-182
Gifted Greats-GG2
Classic Portraits Portrait of a Legend-PL1
Classic Portraits Portrait of a Legend-PL2
Classic Portraits Portrait of a Legend-PL3
Classic Portraits Portrait of a Legend-PL4
Classic Portraits Portrait of a Legend-PL5
Classic Portraits Portrait of a Legend-PL6
Classic Portraits Portrait of a Legend-PL7
Classic Portraits Portrait of a Legend-PL8
Classic Portraits Portrait of a Legend-PL9
Classic Portraits Portrait of a Legend-PL10
MVP Prosign-BO
02Upper Deck National Convention *-N9
02Upper Deck Rookie Update-103
Autographs-BO
02UD SuperStars *-36
Gold-36
Magic Moments-MM17
Spokesmen-UD12
Spokesmen-UD27
Spokesmen Black-UD12
Spokesmen Black-UD27
Spokesmen Gold-UD12
Spokesmen Gold-UD27
03BAP Ultimate Memorabilia Autographs-153
Gold-153
03BAP Ultimate Mem Auto Jerseys-153
03BAP Ultimate Mem Auto Emblems-153
03BAP Ultimate Mem Auto Sticks-153
03BAP Ultimate Memorabilia Career Year-7
03BAP Ultimate Memorabilia Cornerstones-5
03BAP Ultimate Memorabilia Emblem Attic-1
03BAP Ultimate Mem Emblem Attic Gold-1
03BAP Ultimate Memorabilia Great Moments-1
03BAP Ultimate Mem Jersey and Emblems-3
03BAP Ultimate Mem Jersey and Emblem Gold-3
03BAP Ultimate Mem Jersey and Numbers-3
03BAP Ultimate Mem Jersey and Number Gold-3
03BAP Ultimate Mem Lifetime Achievers-3
03BAP Ultimate Memorabilia Made to Order-01
03BAP Ultimate Mem Raised to the Rafters-4
03BAP Ultimate Mem Redemption Cards-2
03BAP Ultimate Mem Retro Teammates-5
03BAP Ultimate Mem Retro-Active Trophies-2
03BAP Ultimate Mem Retro-Active Trophies-5
03BAP Ultimate Mem Retro-Active Trophies-11
03BAP Ultimate Mem Seams Unbelievable-4
03BAP Ultimate Memorabilia The Goal-1
03BAP Ultimate Memorabilia The Goal-2
03BAP Ultimate Memorabilia The Goal-5
03BAP Ultimate Memorabilia The Goal-6
03BAP Ultimate Memorabilia The Goal-7
03BAP Ultimate Memorabilia The Goal-8
03BAP Ultimate Memorabilia The Goal-11
03BAP Ultimate Memorabilia The Goal-12
03BAP Ultimate Memorabilia The Goal-13
03BAP Ultimate Memorabilia Triple Threads-13
03BAP Ultimate Mem Ultimate Defenseman-1
03BAP Ultimate Mem Ultimate Defenseman-2
03BAP Ultimate Mem Ultimate Defenseman-3
03BAP Ultimate Mem Ultimate Defenseman-4
03BAP Ultimate Mem Ultimate Defenseman-5
03BAP Ultimate Mem Ultimate Defenseman-6
03BAP Ultimate Mem Ult Defenseman Autos-1
03BAP Ultimate Mem Ult Defenseman Autos-2
03BAP Ultimate Mem Ult Defenseman Autos-3
03BAP Ultimate Mem Ult Defenseman Autos-4
03BAP Ultimate Mem Ult Defenseman Autos-5
03BAP Ultimate Mem Ult Defenseman Autos-6
03BAP Ultimate Mem Vintage Blade of Steel-15
03BAP Ultimate Mem Vint Complete Jersey-1
03BAP Ultimate Mem Vint Comp Jersey Gold-1
03BAP Ultimate Mem Vintage Hat Tricks-1
03BAP Ultimate Mem Vintage Jerseys-2
03BAP Ultimate Mem Vintage Jerseys Gold-2
03Black Diamond Signature Gems-SG-18
03Canada Post-5
03ITG Used Signature Series-115
Gold-115
Autographs-BO
Autographs Gold-BO
Jerseys-4
Jerseys Gold-4
Jersey Autos-4
Emblems-11
Emblems Gold-11
Jersey and Stick-4
Jersey and Stick Gold-4
Norris Trophy-7
Norris Trophy Gold-7
Triple Memorabilia-4
Triple Memorabilia Gold-4
Vintage Memorabilia-1
Vintage Memorabilia Autographs-1
Vintage Memorabilia Gold-1
03Parkhurst Original Six Boston-45
03Parkhurst Original Six Boston-62
03Parkhurst Original Six Boston-81
03Parkhurst Original Six Boston-91
03Parkhurst Original Six Boston-97
Autographs-13
Inserts-B6
Inserts-B11
Memorabilia-BM53
Memorabilia-BM57
Memorabilia-BM58
Memorabilia-BM59
Memorabilia-BM60
03Parkhurst Original Six Chicago-49
03Parkhurst Orig Six He Shoots/Scores-16
03Parkhurst Orig Six He Shoots/Scores-16A
03Parkhurst Orig Six He Shoots/Scores-17
03Parkhurst Orig Six He Shoots/Scores-17A
03Parkhurst Rookie-60
Jerseys-GJ-49
Jerseys Gold-GJ-49
ROYalty-VR-10
ROYalty Autographs-VR-BO
ROYalty Gold-VR-10
03SP Authentic Sign of the Times-BO
03SP Game Used Signers-SPSBO
03SPx-103
Radiance-103
Spectrum-103
03UD Honor Roll Signature Class-SC20
03Upper Deck BuyBacks-26
03Upper Deck BuyBacks-27
03Upper Deck BuyBacks-28
03Upper Deck BuyBacks-29
03Upper Deck BuyBacks-30
03Upper Deck Performers-PS12
03Upper Deck Superstar Spotlight-SS14
03Upper Deck Classic Portraits-115
03Upper Deck Ice Under Glass Autographs-UG-BO
03Upper Deck MVP ProSign-PS-BO
03Upper Deck Trilogy-8
03Upper Deck Trilogy-138
Crest Variations-138
Limited-8
Limited-138
Scripts-S3BO
Scripts Limited-S3BO
Scripts Red-S3BO
03Upper Deck Victory Freshman Flashback-FF47
03Czech Stadion-555
04ITG NHL AS FANtasy AS History Jerseys-SB21
04MasterCard Priceless Moments-2
04UD Legends Classics Jersey Redemptions-JY18
04ITG Heroes and Prospects-171
Autographs-BO
Hero Memorabilia-30
04ITG Heroes/Prospects Toronto Expo '05-171
04ITG Heroes/Prospects Expo Heroes/Pros-171
05NHL Legends Medallions-13
06Beehive-231
5 X 7 Black and White-231
5 X 7 Dark Wood-231
PhotoGraphs-PGBO
Signature Scrapbook-SSBO
06O-Pee-Chee Autographs-A-BO
06Parkhurst-89
Autographs-89
Autographs Dual-DAOB
Autographs Dual-DAOE
06SP Authentic-95
06SP Authentic-105
Limited-95
Limited-105
Sign of the Times-STBO
Sign of the Times Duals-STHO
Sign of the Times Duals-STOB
Sign of the Times Triples-ST3OBE
Sign of the Times Quads-ST4EBOC
Sign of the Times Quads-ST4LOGH
06SP Game Used-10
Gold-10
Rainbow-10
Autographs-10
Letter Marks-LMOR
06The Cup-8
Black Rainbow-8
Enshrinements-EBO
Gold-8
Hardware Heroes-HHBO1
Hardware Heroes-HHBO2
Hardware Heroes-HHBO3
Hardware Heroes-HHBO4
Hardware Heroes-HHBO5
Masterpiece Pressplates-8
Property of-POBO
Stanley Cup Signatures-CSBO
Stanley Cup Titlists-TBO
06Ultimate Collection-5
Signatures-US-OR
Ultimate Achievements-UA-BO
06Upper Deck All-Time Greatest-ATG3
06Upper Deck Sweet Shot-10
Signature Shots/Saves-SSOR
Signature Shots/Saves Ice Signings-SSIBO
Signature Shots/Saves Sticks-SSSOR
Signature Sticks-STBO

Orr, Clint
96Regina Pats-19

Orr, Colton
99Swift Current Broncos-14
00Kamloops Blazers-16
03BAP Memorabilia-218
03ITG Used Signature Series-195
Gold-195
03ITG VIP Rookie Debut-101
03Parkhurst Rookie-90
03Topps Traded-TT157
Blue-TT157
Gold-TT157
Red-TT157
03Upper Deck Rookie Update-145
03Pacific AHL Prospects-68
Gold-68
03Providence Bruins-15
04Providence Bruins-15

Orr, Doug
06Rio Grande Valley Killer Bees-9

Orr, Jamison
02Lincoln Stars-12

Orrgren, Kent
89Swedish Semic Elitserien Stickers-285

Orsagh, Vladimir
99O-Pee-Chee Chrome Refractors-26
99Topps/OPC Chrome Refractors-26

Orskau, Torbjorn
92Norwegian Elite Series-52

Orsolini, Lionel
94Finnish Jaa Kiekko-227
94French National Team-21

Orszagh, Vladimir
99O-Pee-Chee-26
99O-Pee-Chee Chrome-26
99Paramount-145
Copper-145
Emerald-145
Gold-145
Holographic Emerald-145
Holographic Gold-145
Holographic Silver-145
Ice Blue-145
Premiere Date-145
Red-145
Silver-145
99Topps/OPC-26
99Topps/OPC Chrome-26
99Upper Deck MVP SC Edition-115
Gold Script-115
Silver Script-115
Super Script-115
99Lowell Lock Monsters-14
00Upper Deck Victory-266
00Swedish Upper Deck-59
00Swedish Upper Deck-188
SHL Excellence-S1
01Utah Grizzlies-19
02BAP First Edition-281
02O-Pee-Chee-159
02O-Pee-Chee Premier Blue Parallel-159
02O-Pee-Chee Premier Red Parallel-159
02O-Pee-Chee Factory Set-159
02Pacific-213
Blue-213
Red-213
02Pacific Complete-144
Red-144
02Topps-159
OPC Blue Parallel-159
OPC Red Parallel-159
Factory Set-159
02Topps Total-251
02Upper Deck-344
Exclusives-344
02Upper Deck Beckett UD Promos-344
02Slovakian Kvarteto-22
03ITG Action-375
03NHL Sticker Collection-257
03O-Pee-Chee-207
03OPC Blue-207
03OPC Gold-207
03OPC Red-207
03Pacific Complete-205
Red-205
03Topps-207
Blue-207
Gold-207
Red-207
05Swedish Lulea Hockey Postcards-24

Ortiz, Sean
95Dayton Bombers-2
97Toledo Storm-9

Ortmeyer, Jake
02Fort Wayne Komets-13
02Fort Wayne Komets Shoe Carnival-3
03Wheeling Nailers-91
04Louisiana Ice Gators-16

Ortmeyer, Jed
02Michigan Wolverines-6
03ITG Action-635
03ITG Used Signature Series-168
Gold-168
03ITG VIP Rookie Debut-61
03Pacific Complete-570
Red-570
03Parkhurst Original Six New York-24
03Parkhurst Rookie-86
03SP Authentic-133
Limited-133
03Topps Traded-TT126
Blue-TT126
Gold-TT126
Red-TT126
03UD Honor Roll-149
03Upper Deck-469
Canadian Exclusives-469
HG-469
UD Exclusives-469
03Upper Deck Ice-110
Glass Parallel-110
04Hartford Wolf Pack-20
05Parkhurst-331
Facsimile Auto Parallel-331

Osadchy, Alex
95Kansas City Blades-12

Osaer, Phil
93Quebec Pee-Wee Tournament-1308
01Peoria Rivermen-21
02Worcester IceCats-24
03BAP Memorabilia-231
03ITG VIP Rookie Debut-65
03Parkhurst Original Six New York-27
03Parkhurst Rookie-64
03SP Authentic-92
Limited-92
03Hartford Wolf Pack-19
04ITG Heroes and Prospects Net Prospects-29
04ITG Heroes and Prosp Net Prospects Gold-29
05Florida Everblades-9

Osala, Oskar
05Mississauga Ice Dogs-14
06Mississauga Ice Dogs-14
06ITG Heroes and Prospects-105
Autographs-AOO

Osborne, Brad
88Brockville Braves-20

Osborne, Chris
00Mississauga Ice Dogs-19

Osborne, Don
90Michigan Tech Huskies-17
91Michigan Tech Huskies-16
93Thunder Bay Senators-8
94Thunder Bay Senators-19

Osborne, Jeremy
93Quebec Pee-Wee Tournament-799

Osborne, John
01Kitchener Rangers-13

Osborne, Keith
88Niagara Falls Thunder-15
89ProCards IHL-21
90ProCards AHL/IHL-76
91ProCards-341
92Atlanta Knights-7
93Upper Deck-76
93Swiss HNL-483
93Classic Pro Prospects-85
95Peoria Rivermen-15
99Saginaw Gears-4
99UHL All-Stars West-14T

Osborne, Mark
82O-Pee-Chee-93
82O-Pee-Chee Stickers-182
82Post Cereal-5
82Topps Stickers-182
83NHL Key Tags-33
83O-Pee-Chee-252
84O-Pee-Chee-148
84Topps-110
87Maple Leafs PLAY-23
87Maple Leafs Postcards-15
87Maple Leafs Postcards Oversized-15
88Maple Leafs PLAY-23
88O-Pee-Chee-241
88O-Pee-Chee Stickers-168
88Panini Stickers-127
89O-Pee-Chee-274
89O-Pee-Chee Stickers-174
89Panini Stickers-138
90Bowman-156
Tiffany-156
90Jets IGA-27
90O-Pee-Chee-227
90Panini Stickers-278
90Pro Set-287
90Pro Set-564
90Score-104
Canadian-104
90Score Rookie/Traded-28T
90Topps-227
Tiffany-227
90Upper Deck-5
French-5
91Bowman-209
91Jets IGA-23
91Maple Leafs Panini Team Stickers-18
91O-Pee-Chee-345
91Panini Stickers-77
91Pinnacle-96
French-96
91Pro Set-270
French-270
91Score American-39
91Score Canadian Bilingual-39
91Score Canadian English-39
91Stadium Club-21
91Topps-345
91Upper Deck-296
French-296
92Maple Leafs Kodak-18
92Pinnacle-305
French-305
92Score-277
Canadian-277
92Stadium Club-379
92Topps-77
Gold-77G
92Upper Deck-72
93Maple Leafs Score Black's-7
93OPC Premier-268
Gold-268
93Parkhurst-476
Emerald Ice-476
93PowerPlay-452
93Score-316
Canadian-316
93Topps/OPC Premier-268
Gold-268
93Ultra-433
94Be A Player-R113
Signature Cards-18
94Leaf-503
94Maple Leafs Gangsters-14
94Pinnacle-500
Artist's Proofs-500
Rink Collection-500
94Stadium Club-76
Members Only Master Set-76
First Day Issue-76
Super Team Winner Cards-76
94Ultra-335
94Upper Deck-316
Electric Ice-316
95Cleveland Lumberjacks-20
95Cleveland Lumberjacks Postcards-19
96Cleveland Lumberjacks-19
96Cleveland Lumberjacks Multi-Ad-21
97Cleveland Lumberjacks-3
97Cleveland Lumberjacks Postcards-2

Osborne, Matt
94Owen Sound Platers-22
95Slapshot-299
95Upper Deck-515
Electric Ice-515
Electric Ice Gold-515
95Owen Sound Platers-25
95Classic-93
96Owen Sound Platers-9
03Elmira Jackals-15

Osburn, Randy
72Maple Leafs Postcards-22

Oscsner, Sacha
95Swiss HNL-25

Osgood, Chris
907th Inn. Sketch WHL-24
917th Inn. Sketch WHL-196
917th Inn. Sketch Memorial Cup-123
91Classic-43
91Star Pics-55
91Ultimate Draft-38
91Ultimate Draft French-38
91Classic Four-Sport *-43
Autographs-43A
93Donruss-424
93Parkhurst-329
Emerald Ice-329
Calder Candidates-C17
Calder Candidates Gold-C17
93Pinnacle-431
Canadian-431
93PowerPlay-334
Rookie Standouts-9
93Score-609
Gold-609
Canadian-609
Canadian Gold-609
93Stadium Club-350
Members Only Master Set-350
First Day Issue-350
93Ultra-308
Wave of the Future-12
93Upper Deck-267
93Classic Pro Prospects-26
94Donruss-251
94Fleer-63
94Leaf-315
Gold Rookies-10
94Leaf Limited-96
94OPC Premier-87
94OPC Premier-199
94O-Pee-Chee Finest Inserts-8
94OPC Premier Special Effects-87
94OPC Premier Special Effects-199
94Parkhurst-283
Gold-283
94Parkhurst SE-SE54
Gold-SE54
94Pinnacle-199
94Pinnacle-471
Artist's Proofs-199
Artist's Proofs-471
Rink Collection-199
Rink Collection-471
Goaltending Greats-GT16
94Score-256
Gold-256
Platinum-256
94Stadium Club-138
Members Only Master Set-138
First Day Issue-138
Super Teams-7
Super Teams Members Only Master Set-7
Super Team Winner Cards-138
94Topps/OPC Premier-87
94Topps/OPC Premier-199
Special Effects-87
Special Effects-199
94Ultra-64
94Upper Deck-130
Electric Ice-130
94Classic Pro Prospects-28
94Images *-56
95Be A Player-193
Signatures-S193
Signatures Die Cuts-S193
95Bowman-66
All-Foil-66
95Collector's Choice-136
Player's Club-136
Player's Club Platinum-136
95Donruss-23
95Finest-159
Refractors-159
95Leaf-254
95Leaf Limited-61
95Metal-49
95Panini Stickers-187
95Parkhurst International-67
Emerald Ice-67
Parkie's Trophy Picks-PP30
95Pinnacle-160
Artist's Proofs-160
Rink Collection-160
95Score-202
Black Ice Artist's Proofs-202
Black Ice-202
95SkyBox Impact-56
95SP-48
95Stadium Club-135
Members Only Master Set-135
95Summit-122
Artist's Proofs-122
Ice-122
In The Crease-9
95Topps-345
OPC Inserts-345
Young Stars-YS12
95Ultra-236
95Ultra-374
High Speed-13
95Upper Deck-445
Electric Ice-445
Electric Ice Gold-445
NHL All-Stars-AS19
NHL All-Stars Jumbo-AS19
Special Edition-SE116
Special Edition Gold-SE116
95Zenith-80
95Images-71
Gold-71
Platinum Prospects-PR4
96Be A Player Stacking the Pads-2
96Black Diamond-132
Gold-132
96Collector's Choice-84
96Collector's Choice Blow-Ups-84
96Donruss-95
Press Proofs-95
Between the Pipes-5
Dominators-2
96Donruss Canadian Ice-10
Gold Press Proofs-10
Red Press Proofs-10
96Donruss Elite-21
96Donruss Elite-148
Die Cut Stars-21
Die Cut Stars-148
96Flair-29
Blue Ice-29
Hot Gloves-7
96Fleer-33
96Fleer-144
96Fleer-145
96Fleer-146
Vezina-6
96Fleer Picks-10
Fabulous 50-36
Fantasy Force-2
96Kraft Upper Deck-31
96Kraft Upper Deck-51
96Leaf-151
Press Proofs-151
Shut Down-13
The Best Of ...-4
96Leaf Limited-6
Gold-6
96Leaf Preferred-50
Press Proofs-50
Masked Marauders-6
Vanity Plates-3
Vanity Plates Gold-3
96Maggers-72
96McDonald's Pinnacle-7
96Metal Universe-49
Armor Plate-6
Armor Plate Super Power-6
96NHL Aces Playing Cards-37
96Pinnacle-99
Artist's Proofs-99
Foil-99
Premium Stock-99
Rink Collection-99
Team Pinnacle-9
Trophies-6
96Pinnacle Mint-25
Bronze-25
Gold-25
Silver-25
Coins Brass-25
Coins Solid Gold-25
Coins Gold Plated-25
Coins Nickel-25
Coins Silver-25
96Playoff One on One-378
96Score-129
Artist's Proofs-129
Dealer's Choice Artist's Proofs-129
Special Artist's Proofs-129
Golden Blades-129
Net Worth-6
Sudden Death-5
96Select Certified-20
Artist's Proofs-20
Blue-20
Mirror Blue-20
Mirror Gold-20
Mirror Red-20
Red-20
Freezers-10
96SkyBox Impact-38
Zero Heroes-6
96SP-51
Holoview Collection-HC21
SPx Force-3
96SPx-16
Gold-16
96Stadium Club Members Only-21
96Summit-135
Artist's Proofs-135
Ice-135
Metal-135
Premium Stock-135
In The Crease-13
In The Crease Premium Stock-13
Untouchables-13
96Team Out-71
96Topps Picks Fantasy Team-FT2
96Topps Picks Ice D-ID8
96Ultra-54
Gold Medallion-54
96Upper Deck-53
Generation Next-X7
Superstar Showdown-SS30B
96Upper Deck Ice-18
Parallel-18
96Zenith-105
Artist's Proofs-105
Z-Team-18
96Collector's Edge Ice Crucibles-C18
97SLU Hockey One on One-4
97SLU Hockey Canadian-12
97SLU Hockey American-14
97Be A Player-25
Autographs-25
Autographs Die-Cuts-25
Autographs Prismatic Die-Cuts-25
Stacking the Pads-6
97Beehive-37
Golden Portraits-37
97Black Diamond-39
Double Diamond-39
Triple Diamond-39
Quadruple Diamond-39
97Collector's Choice-80
97Crown Royale-49
Emerald Green-49
Ice Blue-49
Silver-49
Freeze Out Die-Cuts-7
97Donruss-13
Press Proofs Silver-13
Press Proofs Gold-13
Between The Pipes-5
97Donruss Canadian Ice-28
Dominion Series-28
Provincial Series-28
National Pride-6
Stanley Cup Scrapbook-5
97Donruss Elite-53
Aspirations-53
Status-53
Craftsmen-7
Master Craftsmen-7
97Donruss Limited-3
97Donruss Limited-115
97Donruss Limited-171
Exposure-3
Exposure-115
Exposure-171
Fabric of the Game-25
97Donruss Preferred-81
Cut to the Chase-81
Color Guard-7
Color Guard Promos-7
97Donruss Priority-81
97Donruss Priority-203
Stamp of Approval-81
Stamp of Approval-203
Postcards-30
Postcards Opening Day Issues-23
Postmaster General-8
Postmaster Generals Promos-8
Stamps-30
Stamps Bronze-30
Stamps Gold-30
Stamps Silver-30
97Highland Mint Mint-Coins-13
97Katch-52
Gold-52
Silver-52
97Kenner Starting Lineup Cards-14
97Leaf-47
Fractal Matrix-47
Fractal Matrix Die Cuts-47
Pipe Dreams-14
97Leaf International-47
Universal Ice-47
97McDonald's Upper Deck-32
97Pacific-137
Copper-137
Emerald Green-137
Ice Blue-137
Red-137
Silver-137
In The Cage Laser Cuts-7
97Pacific Dynagon-43
Copper-43
Dark Grey-43
Emerald Green-43
Ice Blue-43
Red-43
Silver-43
Stonewallers-7
Tandems-12
97Pacific Invincible-50
Copper-50
Emerald Green-50
Ice Blue-50
Red-50
Silver-50
97Pacific Omega-86
Copper-86
Dark Gray-86
Emerald Green-86
Gold-86
Ice Blue-86
No Scoring Zone-4
97Paramount-69
Copper-69
Dark Grey-69
Emerald Green-69
Ice Blue-69
Red-69
Silver-69
Glove Side Laser Cuts-7
97Pinnacle-34
Artist's Proofs-34
Rink Collection-34
Press Plates Back Black-34
Press Plates Back Cyan-34
Press Plates Back Magenta-34
Press Plates Back Yellow-34
Press Plates Front Black-34
Press Plates Front Cyan-34
Press Plates Front Magenta-34
Press Plates Front Yellow-34
Team Pinnacle-10
Team Mirror-10
Team Parallel-10
Team Parallel Mirror-10
97Pinnacle Certified-4
Red-4
Mirror Blue-4
Mirror Gold-4
Mirror Red-4
97Pinnacle Inside-9
Coach's Collection-9
Executive Collection-9
97Pinnacle Tot Cert Platinum Blue-4
97Pinnacle Tot Cert Platinum Gold-4
97Pinnacle Totally Certified Platinum Red-4
97Pinnacle Tot Cert Mirror Platinum Gold-4
97Revolution-50
Copper-50
Emerald-50
Ice Blue-50
Silver-50
Return to Sender Die-Cuts-7
97Score-2
Artist's Proofs-2
Golden Blades-2
Net Worth-4
97Score Red Wings-17
Platinum-17
Premier-17
97SP Authentic-51
97Studio-87
Press Proofs Silver-87
Press Proofs Gold-87
Portraits-36
97Upper Deck-269
97Upper Deck Ice-30
Parallel-30
Power Shift-30
97Zenith-35
Z-Gold-35
Z-Silver-35
97Zenith 5 x 7-17
Gold Impulse-17
Silver Impulse-17
98SLU Hockey-160
98Aurora-67
Championship Fever-18
Championship Fever Copper-18
Championship Fever Ice Blue-18
Championship Fever Red-18
Championship Fever Silver-18
98Be A Player-47
Press Release-47
98BAP Gold-47
98BAP Autographs-47
98BAP Autographs Gold-47
98BAP Playoff Highlights-H13
98BAP Tampa Bay All Star Game-47
98Black Diamond-32
Double Diamond-32
Triple Diamond-32
Quadruple Diamond-32
Winning Formula Gold-WF12
Winning Formula Platinum-WF12
98Bowman's Best-27
Refractors-27
Atomic Refractors-27
Mirror Image Fusion-F20
Mirror Image Fusion Refractors-F20
Mirror Image Fusion Atomic Refractors-F20
Scotty Bowman's Best-SB3
Scotty Refractors-SB3
Scotty Atomic Refractors-SB3
98Crown Royale-47
Limited Series-47
Pivotal Players-9
98Finest-76
No Protectors-76
No Protectors Refractors-76
Refractors-76
Centurion-C3
Centurion Refractors-C3
98Katch-51
98Kenner Starting Lineup Cards-24
98Lunchables Goalie Greats Rounds-5
98Lunchables Goalie Greats Squares-5
98McDonald's Upper Deck-20
98NHL Aces Playing Cards-26
98OPC Chrome-134
Refractors-134
98Pacific-204
Ice Blue-204
Red-204
Gold Crown Die-Cuts-14
Trophy Winners-8
98Pacific Dynagon Ice-67
Blue-67
Red-67
Watchmen-4
98Pacific Omega-86
Red-86
Opening Day Issue-86
98Panini Photocards-58
98Panini Stickers-128
98Paramount-81
Copper-81
Emerald Green-81
Holo-Electric-81
Ice Blue-81
Silver-81
Glove Side Laser Cuts-8
98Revolution-51
Ice Shadow-51
Red-51
Three Pronged Attack-14
Three Pronged Attack Parallel-14
98SP Authentic-30
Power Shift-30
98SPx Top Prospects-24
Radiance-24
Spectrum-24
Winning Materials-CO
98Topps-134
O-Pee-Chee-134
98Topps Gold Label Class 1-76
Black-76
Black One of One-76
One of One-76
Red-76
Red One of One-76
98Topps Gold Label Class 2-76
98Topps Gold Label Class 2 Black-76
98Topps Gold Label Class 2 Black 1 of 1-76
98Topps Gold Label Class 2 One of One-76
98Topps Gold Label Class 2 Red-76
98Topps Gold Label Class 2 Red One of One-76
98Topps Gold Label Class 3-76
98Topps Gold Label Class 3 Black-76
98Topps Gold Label Class 3 Black 1 of 1-76
98Topps Gold Label Class 3 One of One-76
98Topps Gold Label Class 3 Red-76
98Topps Gold Label Class 3 Red One of One-76
98UD Choice-74
98UD Choice-248
Prime Choice Reserve-74
Prime Choice Reserve-248
Reserve-74
Reserve-248
98UD3-51
98UD3-111
98UD3-171
Die-Cuts-51
Die-Cuts-111
Die-Cuts-171
98Upper Deck-263
Exclusives-263
Exclusives 1 of 1-263
Frozen In Time-FT15
Frozen In Time Quantum 1-FT15
Frozen In Time Quantum 2-FT15
Frozen In Time Quantum 3-FT15
Game Jerseys-GJ16
Gold Reserve-263
98Upper Deck MVP-71
Gold Script-71
Silver Script-71
Super Script-71
99SLU Hockey Classic Doubles-4
99SLU Hockey 12" Figures-6
99Aurora-53
Premiere Date-53
Glove Unlimited-8
99BAP Memorabilia-135
Gold-135
Silver-135
99BAP Millennium Goalie Memorabilia-G6
99Black Diamond-37
Diamond Cut-37
Final Cut-37
99Crown Royale-51
Limited Series-51
Premiere Date-51
99Jell-O Partners of Power-10
99McDonald's Upper Deck Signatures-CO
99O-Pee-Chee-84
99O-Pee-Chee Chrome-84
99O-Pee-Chee Chrome Refractors-84
99Pacific-146
Copper-146
Emerald Green-146
Gold-146
Ice Blue-146
Premiere Date-146
Red-146
In the Cage Net-Fusions-7
99Pacific Dynagon Ice-77
Blue-77
Copper-77
Gold-77
Premiere Date-77
99Pacific Omega-84
Copper-84
Gold-84
Ice Blue-84
Premiere Date-84
99Pacific Prism-53
Holographic Blue-53
Holographic Gold-53
Holographic Mirror-53
Holographic Purple-53
Premiere Date-53
99Panini Stickers-239
99Paramount-86
Copper-86
Emerald-86
Gold-86
Holographic Emerald-86
Holographic Gold-86
Holographic Silver-86
Ice Blue-86
Premiere Date-86
Red-86
Silver-86
Glove Side Net Fusions-8
Toronto Fall Expo '99-86
99Revolution-54
Premiere Date-54
Red-54
Shadow Series-54
Copper-54
Gold-54
CSC Silver-54
99SP Authentic-31
99SPx-57
Radiance-57
Spectrum-57
99Stadium Club Promos-PP1
99Stadium Club-89
First Day Issue-89
One of a Kind-89
Printing Plates Black-89
Printing Plates Cyan-89
Printing Plates Magenta-89
Printing Plates Yellow-89
Chrome-31
Chrome Refractors-31
Co-Signers-CS10
Co-Signers-CS11
Lone Star Signatures-LS7
Souvenirs-SCO
99Topps/OPC-84
99Topps Stanley Cup Heroes-SC18
99Topps Stanley Cup Heroes Refractors-SC18
99Topps/OPC Chrome-84
Refractors-84
99Topps Gold Label Class 1-45
Black-45
Black One of One-45
One of One-45
Red-45
Red One of One-45
99Topps Gold Label Class 2-45
99Topps Gold Label Class 2 Black-45

99Topps Gold Label Class 2 Black 1 of 1-45
99Topps Gold Label Class 2 One of One-45
99Topps Gold Label Class 2 Red-45
99Topps Gold Label Class 2 Red One of One-45
99Topps Gold Label Class 3-45
99Topps Gold Label Class 3 Black-45
99Topps Gold Label Class 3 Black 1 of 1-45
99Topps Gold Label Class 3 One of One-45
99Topps Gold Label Class 3 Red-45
99Topps Gold Label Class 3 Red One of One-45
99Topps Premier Plus-10
Parallel-10
99Ultimate Victory-32
1/1-32
Parallel-32
Parallel 100-32
Net Work-NW3
99Upper Deck-221
Exclusives-221
Exclusives 1 of 1-221
Ultimate Defense-UD4
Ultimate Defense Quantum Gold-UD4
Ultimate Defense Quantum Silver-UD4
99Upper Deck Gold Reserve-221
99Upper Deck MVP-71
Gold Script-71
Silver Script-71
Super Script-71
Last Line-LL9
99Upper Deck MVP SC Edition-66
Gold Script-66
Silver Script-66
Super Script-66
Great Combinations-GCYO
Great Combinations Parallel-GCYO
99Upper Deck Ovation-23
Standing Ovation-23
99Upper Deck Victory-105
99Upper Deck Victory-349
99Upper Deck Victory-378
99Wayne Gretzky Hockey-63
Signs of Greatness-CO
99Slovakian Challengers-19
00Aurora-51
Premiere Date-51
00BAP Memorabilia-231
Emerald-231
Ruby-231
Sapphire-231
Promos-231
00BAP Mem Chicago Sportsfest Copper-231
00BAP Memorabilia Chicago Sportsfest Blue-231
00BAP Memorabilia Chicago Sportsfest Gold-231
00BAP Memorabilia Chicago Sportsfest Ruby-231
00BAP Memorabilia Chicago Sun-Times Ruby-231
00BAP Memorabilia Chicago Sun-Times Gold-231
00BAP Mem Chicago Sun-Times Sapphire-231
00BAP Mem Toronto Fall Expo Copper-231
00BAP Memorabilia Toronto Fall Expo Gold-231
00BAP Memorabilia Toronto Fall Expo Ruby-231
00BAP Memorabilia Update Teammates-TM22
00BAP Memorabilia Update Teammates-TM35
00BAP Memorabilia Update Teammates Gold-TM22
00BAP Memorabilia Update Teammates Gold-TM35
00BAP Parkhurst 2000-P73
00BAP Signature Series-235
Emerald-235
Ruby-235
Sapphire-235
Autographs-95
Autographs Gold-95
He Shoots-He Scores Prizes-38
Jersey Cards-J14
Jersey and Stick Cards-GSJ14
Jersey Cards Autographs-J14
Jersey Emblems-E14
Jersey Numbers-IN14
00BAP Ultimate Memorabilia Active Eight-AE7
00BAP Ultimate Mem Dynasty Jerseys-D14
00BAP Ultimate Mem Dynasty Emblems-D14
00BAP Ultimate Mem Game-Used Jerseys-GJ42
00BAP Ultimate Mem Game-Used Emblems-E34
00BAP Ultimate Mem Game-Used Numbers-N34
00BAP Ultimate Mem Game-Used Sticks-GS42
00BAP Ultimate Mem Goalie Memorabilia-GM3
00BAP Ultimate Mem Goalie Memorabilia-GM4
00BAP Ultimate Memorabilia Goalie Sticks-G11
00BAP Ultimate Mem Plante Jersey Cards-PJ5
00BAP Ultimate Mem Plante Skate Cards-PS5
00BAP Ultimate Memorabilia Teammates-TM7
00Black Diamond-22
Gold-22
Game Gear-LOS
00Crown Royale-39
Ice Blue-39
Limited Series-39
Premiere Date-39
Red-39
Game-Worn Jerseys-14
Game-Worn Jersey Patches-14
Premium-Sized Game-Worn Jerseys-14
00McDonald's Pacific-13
Blue-13
Glove Side Net Fusions-3
00O-Pee-Chee-83
00O-Pee-Chee Parallel-83
00Pacific-157
Copper-157
Gold-157
Ice Blue-157
Premiere Date-157
00Paramount-88
Copper-88
Gold-88
Holo-Gold-88
Holo-Silver-88
Ice Blue-88
Premiere Date-88
Game Used Sticks-10
Glove Side Net Fusions-9
Glove Side Net Fusions Platinum-9
00Private Stock-36
Gold-36
Premiere Date-36
Retail-36
Silver-36
Game Gear-46
Game Gear Patches-46
PS-2001 Action-21
00Revolution-53
Blue-53
Premiere Date-53
Red-53
00SP Game Used Tools of the Game-CO
00SP Game Used Tools of the Game Excl-CO
00SP Game Used Tools of the Game Combos-C-OL
00SPx-24
Spectrum-24
Winning Materials-CO
00Stadium Club-42
Glove Save-GS9
00Titanium Game Gear-96
00Titanium Game Gear Patches-96
00Titanium Draft Day Edition-40
Patches-40
00Topps/OPC-83
Parallel-83
Own the Game-OTG18
00Topps Chrome-66
OPC Refractors-66
Refractors-66
00Topps Heritage-141
Original Six Relics-OSJ-CO
Original Six Relics-OSJ
00UD Heroes-44
00UD Reserve Practice Session Jerseys-CO
00UD Reserve Practice Jerseys Autos-CO
00Upper Deck-66
Exclusives Tier 1-66
Exclusives Tier 2-66
e-Cards-EC9
e-Card Prizes-ACO
e-Card Prizes-ECO
e-Card Prizes-SECO
Game Jersey Autographs-HCO
Game Jersey Autographs Exclusives-ESCO
Game Jersey Patches-PCO
Game Jersey Patch Exclusives Series II-ECO
00Upper Deck Ice-17
Immortals-17
Legends-17
Stars-17
Game Jerseys-JCCO
00Upper Deck Legends-45
Legendary Collection Bronze-45
Legendary Collection Gold-45
Legendary Collection Silver-45
00Upper Deck MVP-66
First Stars-66
Masked Men-MM4
Second Stars-66
Third Stars-66
00Upper Deck Victory-90
00Upper Deck Victory-302
00Upper Deck Vintage-128
00Upper Deck Vintage-136
00Upper Deck Vintage-137
Dynasty: A Piece of History-YO
Dynasty: A Piece of History Gold-YO
Great Gloves-GG8
00Vanguard-39
Dual Game-Worn Jerseys-6
Dual Game-Worn Patches-6
Holographic Gold-39
Holographic Purple-39
Pacific Proofs-39
01Atomic Jerseys-24
01Atomic Patches-24
01BAP Memorabilia-37
01BAP Memorabilia-339
Emerald-37
Emerald-339
Ruby-37
Ruby-339
Sapphire-37
Sapphire-339
Goalies Jerseys-GJ8
Goalie Traditions-GT18
Goalie Traditions-GT23
Goalie Traditions-GT24
Goalie Traditions-GT38
01Between the Pipes-72
Double Memorabilia-DM16
Goalie Gear-GG29
Jerseys-GJ8
Record Breakers-RB18
01Bowman YoungStars-39
Gold-39
Ice Cubed-39
01Crown Royale-90
Blue-90
Premiere Date-90
Red-90
Retail-90
01McDonald's Pacific-13
01O-Pee-Chee-85
01O-Pee-Chee-85U
01O-Pee-Chee Heritage Parallel-85
01O-Pee-Chee Heritage Parallel Limited-85
01O-Pee-Chee Premier Parallel-85
01Pacific-148
Extreme LTD-148
Hobby LTD-148
Premiere Date-148
Retail LTD-148
Jerseys-14
Impact Zone-11
01Pacific Adrenaline-121
Blue-121
Premiere Date-121
Red-121
Retail-121
Jerseys-27
01Pacific Arena Exclusives-148
01Pacific Heads-Up-36
Blue-36
Premiere Date-36
Red-36
Silver-36
HD NHL-13
Quad Jerseys-11
Showstoppers-7
01Parkhurst-204
Milestones-M1
01Private Stock-58
Gold-58
Premiere Date-58
Retail-58
Silver-58
Game Gear-64
Game Gear Patches-64
01Private Stock Pacific Nights-58
01SP Authentic-51
Limited-51
Limited Gold-51
01SP Game Used Authentic Fabric-AFCO
01SP Game Used Authentic Fabric-DFYO
01SP Game Used Authentic Fabric-YSFO
01SP Game Used Authentic Fabric Gold-AFCO
01SP Game Used Tools of the Game-TCO
01SPx-182
01Stadium Club Souvenirs-CO
01Titanium-88
Hobby Parallel-88
Premiere Date-88
Retail-88
Retail Parallel-88
Three-Star Selections-6
01Titanium Draft Day Edition-58
01Topps-85
01Topps-85U
Heritage Parallel-85
Heritage Parallel Limited-85
OPC Parallel-85
01Topps Chrome-85
Refractors-85
Black Border Refractors-85
01UD Challenge for the Cup-55
Jerseys-TCO
01UD Mask Collection-119
01UD Mask Collection-182
Gold-119
Gold-182
Goalie Jerseys-CGCO
01UD Playmakers-62
01UD Stanley Cup Champs-61
Pieces of Glory-G-CO
01UD Top Shelf-103
Goalie Gear-SCO
01Upper Deck-343
Exclusives-343
Game Jerseys Series II-FJCO
Goaltender Threads-TTCO
01Upper Deck Ice-103
01Upper Deck MVP Goalie Sticks-G-CO
01Upper Deck Victory-121
01Upper Deck Victory-127
Gold-121
Gold-127
01Vanguard-59
Blue-59
Red-59
One of Ones-59
Premiere Date-59
Proofs-59
Stonewallers-12
V-Team-6
02McFarlane Hockey-60
02McFarlane Hockey-62
02Atomic-63
Blue-63
Gold-63
Red-63
Denied-12
Hobby Parallel-63
02BAP All-Star Edition-68
Jerseys-68
Jerseys Gold-68
Jerseys Silver-68
02BAP First Edition-209
02BAP Memorabilia-87
02BAP Memorabilia-321
Emerald-87
Ruby-87
Sapphire-87
NHL All-Star Game-87
NHL All-Star Game Blue-87
NHL All-Star Game Green-87
NHL All-Star Game Red-87
02BAP Memorabilia Toronto Fall Expo-87
02BAP Signature Series-110
Autographs-110
Autograph Buybacks 1998-47
Autograph Buybacks 2000-95
Autographs Gold-110
Famous Scraps-FS10
Golf-GS22
02BAP Ultimate Memorabilia Cup Duels-18
02BAP Ultimate Mem Dynasty Jerseys-4
02BAP Ultimate Mem Dynasty Emblems-4
02BAP Ultimate Mem Dynasty Numbers-4
02Between the Pipes-50
02Between the Pipes-139
Gold-50
Silver-50
All-Star Stick and Jersey-16
Double Memorabilia-4
Goalie Autographs-17
Pads-9
Tandems-16
02Bowman YoungStars-88
Gold-88
Silver-88
02Crown Royale-60
Blue-60
Red-60
Retail-60
02ITG Used-45
02ITG Used-145
Goalie Pad and Jersey-GP10
Goalie Pad and Jersey Gold-GP10
02O-Pee-Chee-174
02O-Pee-Chee Premier Blue Parallel-174
02O-Pee-Chee Premier Red Parallel-174
02O-Pee-Chee Factory Set-174
02Pacific-240
Blue-240
Red-240
02Pacific Complete-224
Red-224
02Pacific Exclusive-108
02Pacific Heads-Up-73
Blue-73
Purple-73
Red-73
Showstoppers-14
02Parkhurst-13
Bronze-13
Gold-13
Silver-13
02Parkhurst Retro-95
Minis-95
02Private Stock Reserve-63
Blue-63
Red-63
Retail-63
InCrease Security-14
02SP Authentic-57
Beckett Promos-57
02SPx-47
Spectrum Gold-47
Spectrum Silver-47
02Stadium Club-88
Silver Decoy Cards-88
Proofs-88
Puck Stops Here-PSH6
02Topps-174
OPC Blue Parallel-174
OPC Red Parallel-174
Factory Set-174
02Topps Chrome-101
Black Border Refractors-101
Refractors-101
02Topps Heritage-43
Chrome Parallel-43
02Topps Total-199
02UD Artistic Impressions-57
Gold-57
02UD Artistic Impressions Beckett Promos-57
02UD Artistic Impressions Retrospectives-R57
02UD Artistic Impressions Retrospect Gold-R57
02UD Artistic Impress Retrospect Silver-R57
02UD Honor Roll-45
02UD Mask Collection-52
02UD Mask Collection-53
02UD Mask Collection Beckett Promos-52
02UD Mask Collection Beckett Promos-53
02UD Mask Collection Career Wins-CWCO
02UD Mask Collection Masked Marvels-MMCO
02UD Mask Collection Nation's Best-NOBB
02UD Mask Collection Patches-PWCO
02UD Mask Collection Super Stoppers-SSCO
02UD Piece of History-56
02UD Top Shelf-56
02Upper Deck-112
Exclusives-112
Last Line of Defense-LL9
Super Saviors-SA9
02Upper Deck Classic Portraits-63
02Upper Deck MVP-117
Gold-117
Classics-117
Golden Classics-117
Skate Around Jerseys-SDPO
Souvenirs-S-CO
02Upper Deck Rookie Update-85
Jerseys-DCO
Jerseys Gold-DCO
02Upper Deck Victory-135
Bronze-135
Gold-135
Silver-135
02Upper Deck Vintage-162
02Upper Deck Vintage-279
Green Backs-162
Tall Boys-T42
Tall Boys Gold-T42
03BAP Memorabilia-108
Emerald-108
Gold-108
Ruby-108
Sapphire-108
Deep in the Crease-D12
03BAP Ultimate Memorabilia Autographs-8
Gold-8
03BAP Ultimate Memorabilia Triple Threads-5
03Beehive-168
Gold-168
Silver-168
03Black Diamond-89
Black-89
Green-89
Red-89
03Blues Team Set-21
03Bowman-53
Gold-53
03Bowman Chrome-53
Refractors-53
Gold Refractors-53
Xfractors-53
03Crown Royale-81
Blue-81
Retail-81
03ITG Action-582
Jerseys-M235
03ITG Used Signature Series-74
Gold-74
Autographs-CO
Autographs Gold-CO
Goalie Gear-19
Goalie Gear Autographs-19
Goalie Gear Gold-19
03NHL Sticker Collection-80
03O-Pee-Chee-2
03OPC Blue-2
03OPC Gold-2
03OPC Red-2
03Pacific-286
Blue-286
Red-286
03Pacific Calder-83
03Pacific Calder-156
Silver-83
03Pacific Complete-419
Red-419
03Pacific Exhibit-190
03Pacific Exhibit-214
Blue Backs-190
03Pacific Heads-Up-81
Hobby LTD-81
Retail LTD-81
03Pacific Invincible-81
Blue-81
Red-81
Retail-81
Freeze Frame-18
Jerseys-26
03Pacific Luxury Suite-46A
03Pacific Luxury Suite-46B
03Pacific Luxury Suite-46C
03Pacific Prism-139
Blue-139
Patches-139
Red-139
Retail-139
03Parkhurst Original Six Detroit-32
Memorabilia-DM31
Memorabilia-DM56
03Private Stock Reserve-197
Blue-197
Patches-197
Red-197
Retail-197
03SP Authentic-74
Limited-74
03SP Game Used Game Gear-GGCO
03SP Game Used Game Gear Combo-GCCO
03SPx-83
Radiance-83
Spectrum-83
03Titanium-179
Hobby Jersey Number Parallels-179
Patches-179
Retail-179
03Topps-2
Blue-2
Gold-2
Red-2
Pristine Mini-PM-CO
03UD Honor Roll-74
03UD Premier Collection-47
03Upper Deck-170
Canadian Exclusives-170
HG-170
03Upper Deck Classic Portraits-86
Classic Colors-CC-CO
03Upper Deck Ice-75
Gold-75
03Upper Deck MVP-374
Gold Script-374
Silver Script-374
Canadian Exclusives-374
SportsNut-SN75
Threads-TC5
03Upper Deck Rookie Update-74
03Upper Deck Trilogy-86
Limited-86
03Upper Deck Victory-168
Bronze-168
Gold-168
Silver-168
04Pacific-221
Blue-221
Red-221
05Beehive Matted Materials-MMCO
05Beehive Matted Materials Remarkable-RMCO
05McDonalds Upper Deck Goalie Gear-MG11
05Panini Stickers-268
05Parkhurst-178
Facsimile Auto Parallel-178
05SP Authentic Sign of the Times-OS
05SP Authentic Sign of the Times Duals-DLO
05SP Authentic Sign of the Times Triples-TLOH
05SP Game Used SIGnificance-CO
05SP Game Used SIGnificance Gold-S-CO
05SP Game Used Statscriptions-ST-CO
05The Cup Stanley Cup Titlists-TCO
05UD Artifacts Frozen Artifacts-FA-CO
05UD Artifacts Frozen Artifacts Autos-FA-CO
05UD Artifacts Frozen Artifacts Copper-FA-CO
05UD Artifacts Frozen Artifacts Dual-FAD-CO
05UD Artifacts Frozen Artifacts Dual Auto-FAD-CO
05UD Artifact Frozen Artifact Dual Copper-FAD-CO
05UD Artifacts Frozen Artifacts Dual Gold-FAD-CO
05UD Artifact Frozen Artifact Dual Maroon-FAD-CO
05UD Artifact Frozen Artifact Dual Pewter-FAD-CO
05UD Artifact Frozen Artifact Dual Silver-FAD-CO
05UD Artifacts Frozen Artifacts Gold-FA-CO
05UD Artifacts Frozen Artifacts Maroon-FA-CO
05UD Artifacts Frozen Artifacts Pewter-FA-CO
05UD Artifacts Frozen Artifacts Silver-FA-CO
05UD Artifacts Goalie Gear-FG-CO
05UD Artifacts Goalie Gear Autographed-FG-CO
05UD Artifacts Goalie Gear Dual-FPD-CO
05UD Artifacts Goalie Gear Dual Autos-FPD-CO
05UD Artifacts Goalie Gear Pewter-FG-CO
05UD Artifacts Goalie Gear Silver-FG-CO
05Upper Deck-313
Jerseys-J-CO
Jerseys Series II-J2CO
Notable Numbers-N-CO
Patches-P-CO
05Upper Deck Hockey Showcase-HS35
05Upper Deck Showcase Promos-HS35
05Upper Deck Ice Frozen Fabrics-FFCO
05Upper Deck Ice Frozen Fabrics Autos-AFFCO
05Upper Deck Ice Frozen Fabrics Glass-FFCO
05Upper Deck Ice Frozen Fabrics Patches-FFPCO
05Upper Deck Ice Frozen Fabric Patch Auto-FAPCO
05Upper Deck MVP-142
Gold-142
Platinum-142
Materials-M-CO
06Flair Showcase Stitches-SSCO
06Fleer Fabricology-FCO
06O-Pee-Chee-179
Rainbow-179
06SP Game Used Authentic Fabrics Dual-AF2HO
06SP Game Used Authentic Fabrics Dual Patches-AF2HO
06SP Game Used Inked Sweaters Dual-IS2HO
06SP Game Used Inked Sweaters Dual Patches-IS2HO
06The Cup Autographed NHL Shields Duals-DASHO
06UD Artifacts Tundra Tandems-TTHO
06UD Artifacts Tundra Tandems Black-TTHO
06UD Artifacts Tundra Tandems Blue-TTHO
06UD Artifacts Tundra Tandems Gold-TTHO
06UD Artifacts Tundra Tandems Platinum-TTHO
06UD Artifacts Tundra Tandems Red-TTHO
06UD Artifacts Tundra Tandems Dual Patches Red-TTHO
06Ultra-73
Gold Medallion-73
Ice Medallion-73
Fresh Ink-ICO
06Upper Deck-73
Exclusives Parallel-73
High Gloss Parallel-73
Game Jerseys-JCO
Game Patches-PCO
Masterpieces-73
MVP Autographs-OADO
MVP Jerseys-OJOC

Oshie, T.J.
04Sioux Falls Stampede-1-6

Osiecki, Mark
90ProCards AHL/IHL-618
91Flames IGA-14
91Pro Set-528
French-528
91Upper Deck-533
French-533
92Pinnacle-376
French-376
94Minnesota Moose-10

Osiecki, Matt
95Tallahassee Tiger Sharks-13
99Alexandria Warthogs-11

Osinski, Slawomir
94German First League-621

Oslizlo, Lubomir
98Czech OFS-312

Osmak, Corey
93Minnesota-Duluth Bulldogs-24

Ossachuk, Justin
97Spokane Chiefs-6
99Lethbridge Hurricanes-19
04Tulsa Oilers-17

Ossipov, Maxim
99Russian Hockey League-85
00Russian Hockey League-70
01Russian Hockey League-98
04Russian RHL-21

Ossipov, Serguei
92Atlanta Knights-12
98Russian Hockey League-34
99Russian Hockey League-24
99Russian Metallurg Magnetogorsk-42

Ost, Olle
67Swedish Hockey-115

Osterberg, Torsten
56Swedish Alfabilder-99

Osterby, Magnus
03Swedish Elite-239
Silver-239
04Swedish Elitset-84
Gold-84
05Swedish SHL Elitset-205

Osterloh, Sebastian
03German Nuremberg Ice Tigers Postcards-20
04German DEL Update-343
05German DEL-350

Osterlund, Roger
67Swedish Hockey-262
69Swedish Hockey-218

Ostermeier, Andi
94German First League-223

Ostermeier, Max
94German First League-219

Ostler, Karl
94German First League-294
95German DEL-344

Ostling, Jan
67Swedish Hockey-282
69Swedish Hockey-327
70Swedish Hockey-229
71Swedish Hockey-94
72Swedish Stickers-65
73Swedish Stickers-204
74Swedish Stickers-276

Ostling, Stig
67Swedish Hockey-149
69Swedish Hockey-164
70Swedish Hockey-25
71Swedish Hockey-12
71Swedish Hockey-102
72Finnish Jaakiekko-60
72Finnish Hellas-26
72Swedish Stickers-10
72Swedish Stickers-87
73Swedish Stickers-158
74Finnish Jenkki-41
74Swedish Stickers-198
79Panini Stickers-186
83Swedish Semic Elitserien-58

Ostlund, Simon
02Swedish SHL-151
Parallel-151
03Swedish Elite-7
Silver-7

Ostlund, Thomas
84Swedish Semic Elitserien-2
85Swedish Panini Stickers-3
87Swedish Panini Stickers-6
88Swedish Semic Elitserien Stickers-3
90Swedish Semic Elitserien Stickers-75
91Swedish Semic Elitserien Stickers-2
92Swedish Semic Elitserien Stickers-75
93Swedish Semic Elitserien-50
94Swedish Leaf-66
Clean Sweepers-3
95Swedish Leaf-183
Mega-4
Spidermen-3
95Swedish Upper Deck-37
95Swedish Upper Deck-251
95Swedish Globe World Championships-5
95Swedish World Championships Stickers-137
96Swedish Semic Wien-40
96Swiss HNL-203
98Swiss Power Play Stickers-80
99Swiss Panini Stickers-79
00Swiss Panini Stickers-126
00Swiss Slapshot Mini-Cards-HCFG1
02Swedish SHL-135
Parallel-135

Ostrcil, Radim
06Czech OFS-186

Ostroushko, Artem
98Russian Hockey League-134
99Russian Hockey League-254
03Russian Hockey League-64

Ostvang, Borre
92Norwegian Elite Series-222

Oswald, Andreas
94German First League-290

Oswald, Gunter
94German DEL-243
95German DEL-351
95Swedish World Championships Stickers-72
96German DEL-260
98German DEL-47
02German DEL City Press-228
03German DEL-84
04German DEL-93
04German Ingolstadt Panthers-19
05German DEL-153
06German DEL-179

Oswald, Wolfgang
94German First League-55

Otcenas, Ondrej
05Plymouth Whalers-B-04

Otevrel, Jaroslav
92Parkhurst-399
Emerald Ice-399
92Kansas City Blades-9
93Stadium Club-293
Members Only Master Set-293
First Day Issue-293
93Kansas City Blades-6
93Classic Pro Prospects-143
94Finnish SISU-268
94Classic Pro Prospects-126
95Finnish SISU-358
95Finnish SISU-379

Othberg, Kent
70Swedish Hockey-149
71Swedish Hockey-242
73Swedish Stickers-237

Othman, Gery
95Swiss HNL-334
96Swiss HNL-310

Othmann, Robert
01Swiss HNL-475
02Swiss HNL-185

Otis, Jessi
03Huntsville Channel Cats-12

Ott, Andreas
94German DEL-411
95German DEL-225

Ott, Christian
94German First League-95

Ott, Daniel
93Swiss HNL-494
95Swiss HNL-375
02Swiss HNL-168

Ott, Dany
96Swiss HNL-234
01Swiss HNL-405

Ott, Herbert
94German First League-597

Ott, Ralph
93Swiss HNL-443
95Swiss HNL-323
96Swiss HNL-299
98Swiss Power Play Stickers-358
00Swiss Panini Stickers-109
00Swiss Slapshot Mini-Cards-HCD5
01Swiss HNL-106
02Swiss HNL-11

Ott, Steve
00UD CHL Prospects-31
01SPx Rookie Redemption-R18
02BAP First Edition-431H
02BAP Memorabilia-372
02BAP Ultimate Memorabilia-10
02Bowman YoungStars-125
Gold-125
Silver-125
02Crown Royale-111
Blue-111
Purple-111
Red-111
Retail-111
02Pacific Calder-114
Silver-114
02Pacific Complete-518
Red-518
02Pacific Quest for the Cup-115
Gold-115
02Parkhurst-235
Bronze-235
Gold-235
Silver-235
02Parkhurst Retro-210
Minis-210
02SP Authentic-201
02SPx-177
02Titanium-112
Blue-112
Red-112
Retail-112
02UD Artistic Impressions-93
Gold-93
Common Ground-CG19
Common Ground Gold-CG19
Retrospectives-R98
Retrospectives Gold-R98
Retrospectives Signed-R98
Retrospectives Silver-R98
02UD Foundations-167
02UD Honor Roll-139
02UD Premier Collection-100
Gold-100
Jerseys Bronze-SO
Jerseys Gold-SO
Jerseys Silver-SO
02Upper Deck Classic Portraits-133
02Upper Deck Rookie Update-157A
02Upper Deck Rookie Update-157B
02Upper Deck Rookie Update-157C
Autographs-SO
02Vanguard-111
LTD-111
02AHL Top Prospects-32
02Utah Grizzlies-2
03BAP Memorabilia Future of the Game-FG-12
03BAP Ultimate Mem Franch Present Future-10
03Black Diamond-136
Black-136
Green-136
Red-136
Signature Gems-SG-17
03ITG Action-110
03Pacific-109
Blue-109
Red-109
03Pacific Complete-476
Red-476
03Parkhurst Rookie Road to the NHL-RNJ-16
03Parkhurst Rookie Road to the NHL Gold-RTN-16
03Parkhurst Rookie Road to the NHL Emblem-RTNE-16
03Parkhurst Rookie Road NHL Emblem Gold-RTNE-16
03Private Stock Reserve-31
Blue-31
Red-31
Retail-31
03SPx-169
Radiance-169
Spectrum-169
Big Futures-BF-SO
Big Futures Limited-BF-SO
03Stars Postcards-21
03Upper Deck-62
Canadian Exclusives-62
HG-62
Shooting Stars-ST-SO
03Upper Deck MVP-137
Gold Script-137
Silver Script-137
Canadian Exclusives-137
03Upper Deck Trilogy Scripts-S1SO
03Upper Deck Trilogy Scripts-CSSO
03Upper Deck Trilogy Scripts Limited-S1SO
03Upper Deck Trilogy Scripts Red-S1SO
03Upper Deck Victory-60
Bronze-60
Gold-60
Silver-60
04Hamilton Bulldogs-22
05ITG Heroes/Prosp Toronto Expo Parallel -43
05Be A Player Signatures-OT
05Be A Player Signatures Gold-OT
05Parkhurst-155
Facsimile Auto Parallel-155
True Colors-TCDAL
True Colors-TCDAL
05Upper Deck-62
HG Glossy-62
Jerseys-J-SOT
Notable Numbers-N-SO
05Upper Deck MVP-129
Gold-129
Platinum-129
05Upper Deck Toronto Fall Expo-62
05ITG Heroes and Prospects-43
Autographs-A-SO
06Be A Player-71
Autographs-71
Signatures-OT
Signatures Duals-DSO
Signatures Trios-TTLO
06O-Pee-Chee-158
Rainbow-158
Swatches-S-OT
06Stars Team Postcards-17
06UD Artifacts Tundra Tandems-TTDO
06UD Artifacts Tundra Tandems Black-TTDO
06UD Artifacts Tundra Tandems Blue-TTDO
06UD Artifacts Tundra Tandems Gold-TTDO
06UD Artifacts Tundra Tandems Platinum-TTDO
06UD Artifacts Tundra Tandems Red-TTDO
06UD Artifacts Tundra Tandems Dual Patches Red-TTDO
06Upper Deck-66
Exclusives Parallel-66
High Gloss Parallel-66
Masterpieces-66
06Upper Deck MVP-99
Gold Script-99
Super Script-99

Otten, Marc
94German First League-590

Ottila, Rauli
66Finnish Jaakiekkosarja-79
70Finnish Jaakiekko-165
71Finnish Suomi Stickers-234
72Finnish Jaakiekko-218
73Finnish Jaakiekko-194

Ottini, Pietro
01Swiss HNL-428

Ottmann, Brent
04Prince Albert Raiders-11
05Prince Albert Raiders-17
06Prince Albert Raiders-12

Ottmann, Chris
897th Inn. Sketch OHL-169
907th Inn. Sketch OHL-313

Otto, Joel
84Moncton Golden Flames-10
85Flames Red Rooster-19
86Flames Red Rooster-18
86O-Pee-Chee-247
86O-Pee-Chee Stickers-130
87Flames Red Rooster-21
87O-Pee-Chee-212
87O-Pee-Chee Stickers-42
87Panini Stickers-212
88Flames Postcards-8
88O-Pee-Chee-242
88O-Pee-Chee Stickers-83
88Panini Stickers-13
89Kraft-6
89O-Pee-Chee-205
89O-Pee-Chee Stickers-96
90Bowman-99
Tiffany-99
90Flames IGA/McGavin's-19
90O-Pee-Chee-369
90Pro Set-43
90Score-128
Canadian-128
90Topps-369
Tiffany-369
90Upper Deck-141
French-141
91Pro Set Platinum-17
91Bowman-260
91Flames Panini Team Stickers-15
91Flames Panini Team Stickers-G
91Flames IGA-15
91O-Pee-Chee-426
91OPC Premier-102
91Panini Stickers-60
91Parkhurst-253
French-253
91Pinnacle-179
French-179
91Pro Set-37
French-37
91Score American-96
91Score Canadian Bilingual-96
91Score Canadian English-96
91Stadium Club-170
91Topps-428
91Upper Deck-165
French-165
92Bowman-69
92Flames IGA-4
92O-Pee-Chee-82
92Panini Stickers-43
92Panini Stickers French-43
92Parkhurst-259
Emerald Ice-259
92Pinnacle-328
French-328
92Pro Set-28
92Score-332
Canadian-332
92Stadium Club-305
92Topps-471
Gold-471G
92Ultra-26
92Upper Deck-220
92Finnish Semic-167
93Donruss-49
93Leaf-28
93OPC Premier-48
Gold-48
93Panini Stickers-185
93Parkhurst-34
Emerald Ice-34
93Pinnacle-179
Canadian-179
93PowerPlay-40
93Score-74
Canadian-74
93Stadium Club-128
Members Only Master Set-128
OPC-128

First Day Issue-128
First Day Issue OPC-128
93Topps/OPC Premier-48
Gold-48
93Ultra-285
93Upper Deck-124
SP-24
94Be A Player-R2
94Be A Player-R133
Signature Cards-69
94Canada Games NHL POGS-58
94Donruss-102
94Leaf-272
94OPC Premier-508
Special Effects-508
94Parkhurst Vintage-V38
94Parkhurst SE-SE31
Gold-SE31
94Pinnacle-217
Artist's Proofs-217
Rink Collection-217
94Score-18
Gold-18
Platinum-18
94Stadium Club-197
Members Only Master Set-197
First Day Issue-197
Super Team Winner Cards-197
94Topps/OPC Premier-508
Special Effects-508
94Ultra-270
94Upper Deck-43
Electric Ice-43
94Upper Deck NHLPA/Be A Player-34
94Finnish Jaa Kiekko-124
95Canada Games NHL POGS-205
95Collector's Choice-88
Player's Club-88
Player's Club Platinum-88
95Donruss-355
95Panini Stickers-115
95Parkhurst International-162
Emerald Ice-162
95Playoff One on One-295
95Score-186
Black Ice Artist's Proofs-186
Black Ice-186
95SP-111
95Stadium Club-14
Members Only Master Set-14
Nemeses-N8
Nemeses Members Only Master Set-N8
95Topps-236
OPC Inserts-236
95Ultra-27
95Ultra-285
Gold Medallion-27
95Upper Deck-366
Electric Ice-366
Electric Ice Gold-366
Special Edition-SE151
Special Edition Gold-SE151
95Finnish Semic World Championships-115
95Swedish Globe World Championships-113
96Be A Player-76
Autographs-76
Autographs Silver-76
96Black Diamond-29
Gold-29
96Collector's Choice-193
96Flyers Postcards-17
96Upper Deck-124
96Swedish Semic Wien-171
97Flames Collector's Photos-11
97Pacific Invincible NHL Regime-146
97Pacific Omega-169
Copper-169
Dark Gray-169
Emerald Green-169
Gold-169
Ice Blue-169
97Score Flyers-14
Platinum-14
Premier-14
97Upper Deck-333
98Pacific-329
Ice Blue-329
Red-329
98Upper Deck-146
Exclusives-146
Exclusives 1 of 1-146
Gold Reserve-146
04ITG Franchises Canadian-7
Autographs-JOT

Otto, Thomas
94German First League-487

Ottosson, Kristofer
95Swedish Leaf-195
95Swedish Upper Deck-46
00Swedish Upper Deck-51
02Swedish SHL-159
Dynamic Duos-2
Parallel-159
Signatures-4
03Swedish Elite-16
Silver-16
Stars of the Game-1
04Swedish Djurgardens Postcards-8
04Swedish Elitset-141
04Swedish Elitset-162
Gold-141
Gold-162
05Swedish SHL Elitset Autographed Jerseys-GWAKO
05Swedish SHL Elitset Series Two Jerseys-GWKO
06Swedish SHL Elitset-164

Ottosson, Peter
89Swedish Semic Elitserien Stickers-95
90Swedish Semic Elitserien Stickers-268
91Swedish Semic Elitserien Stickers-97
92Finnish Semic-66
92Swedish Semic Elitserien Stickers-119
93Swedish Semic Elitserien-92
94Finnish Jaa Kiekko-65
94Swedish Leaf-99
95Swedish Leaf-46
95Swedish Upper Deck-74
98German DEL-311
99German DEL-255
00Swedish Upper Deck-97

Ouellet, Bryan
93Quebec Pee-Wee Tournament-2

Ouellet, Dean
04Cape Breton Screaming Eagles-13
05Cape Breton Screaming Eagles-8
06Cape Breton Screaming Eagles-7

Ouellet, Georges
51Laval Dairy QSHL-53

Ouellet, Mathieu
93Quebec Pee-Wee Tournament-979

Ouellet, Maxime
92Quebec Pee-Wee Tournament-262
94Quebec Pee-Wee Tournament-1148
95Quebec Pee-Wee Tournament-378
98SP Authentic-115
Power Shift-115
Sign of the Times-MAO
Sign of the Times Gold-MAO
98Upper Deck-392
Exclusives-392
Exclusives 1 of 1-392
Gold Reserve-392
98Quebec Remparts-17
Signed-17
99Black Diamond-101
Diamond Cut-101
Final Cut-101
99SPx-180
Radiance-180
Spectrum-180
99Upper Deck-311
Exclusives-311
Exclusives 1 of 1-311
99Upper Deck Sobey's Memorial Cup-10
99Upper Deck Gold Reserve-311
99Upper Deck MVP SC Ed Game-Used Souvenir-GUMO
99Upper Deck MVP SC Edition ProSign-MO
99Quebec Remparts-18
Signed-18
99Bowman CHL-2
99Bowman CHL-41
99Bowman CHL-163
Gold-2
Gold-41
Gold-163
OPC International-2
OPC International-41
OPC International-163
Autographs-BA22
Autographs Gold-BA22
Autographs Silver-BA22
Scout's Choice-SC4
99UD Prospects-61
Signatures of Tradition-MO
00BAP Memorabilia-434
Emerald-434
Ruby-434
Sapphire-434
00BAP Parkhurst 2000-P250
00BAP Signature Series-277
Emerald-277
Ruby-277
Sapphire-277
Autographs-239
Autographs Gold-239
00Private Stock-135
Gold-135
Premiere Date-135
Retail-135
Silver-135
PS-2001 Rookies-15
00Stadium Club-234
00Topps Heritage-49
Chrome Parallel-49
00Topps Premier Plus-90
Blue Ice-90
Rookies-PR8
Rookies Blue Ice-PR8
00Topps Stars-142
Blue-142
00QMJHL All-Star Program Inserts-2
00Rouyn-Noranda Huskies-16
Signed-16
00UD CHL Prospects-87
CHL Class-CC10
01BAP Memorabilia-20
Emerald-20
Ruby-20
Sapphire-20
01Between the Pipes-9
01O-Pee-Chee-268
01O-Pee-Chee Premier Parallel-268
01Parkhurst-291
01Parkhurst Beckett Promos-291
01SP Game Used Inked Sweaters-DSBO
01SP Game Used Inked Sweaters-DSGO
01Topps-268
OPC Parallel-268
01UD Honor Roll Jerseys-J-MO
01UD Honor Roll Jerseys Gold-J-MO
01UD Playmakers Practice Jerseys-PJMO
01UD Playmakers Practice Jerseys Gold-PJMO
01Upper Deck Game Jerseys-GJMO
01Upper Deck Game Jerseys Series II-GNMO
01Upper Deck Game Jersey Autographs-SJMO
01Upper Deck Victory-383
Gold-383
01Upper Deck Vintage Next In Line-NLCO
02BAP Sig Series Auto Buybacks 2000-239
02Between the Pipes-91
Gold-91
Silver-91
Jerseys-31
Tandems-20
02SP Authentic Sign of the Times-MM
02UD Top Shelf Signatures-MO
02Upper Deck MVP Prosign-MO
02Upper Deck Vintage Jerseys-EEMO
02Upper Deck Vintage Jerseys Gold-EE-MO
02AHL Top Prospects-33
03BAP Memorabilia-142
Emerald-142
Gold-142
Ruby-142
Sapphire-142
03ITG Action-509
03Pacific Complete-494
Red-494
03AHL Top Prospects-26
03Pacific AHL Prospects-66
Gold-66
04Pacific-266
Blue-266
Red-266
04Portland Pirates-17
04ITG Heroes/Prospects He Shoots/Scores-34
04ITG Heroes/Prospects He Shoots/Scores-35
04ITG Heroes and Prospects Net Prospects-30
04ITG Heroes and Prosp Net Prospects Gold-30
05ITG Heroes/Prosp Toronto Expo Parallel -217
05Manitoba Moose-16
05ITG Heroes and Prospects-217
Autographs Series II-MXO
Jerseys-GUJ-92
Jerseys Gold-GUJ-92
Making the Bigs-MTB-10
Measuring Up-MU7
Measuring Up Gold-MU7
Net Prospects Dual-NPD1
Net Prospects Dual Gold-NPD1
06Between The Pipes Emblems-GUE44
06Between The Pipes Emblems Gold-GUE44
06Between The Pipes Jerseys-GUJ44
06Between The Pipes Jerseys Gold-GUJ44
06Between The Pipes Numbers-GUN44
06Between The Pipes Numbers Gold-GUN44
06Between The Pipes Prospect Trios-PT20
06Between The Pipes Prospect Trios Gold-PT20

Ouellet, Michel
96Quebec Pee-Wee Tournament-1144
99Rimouski Oceanic-16
Signed-16
00Rimouski Oceanic-19
Signed-19
01Rimouski Oceanic-17
02Wilkes-Barre Scranton Penguins-5
03Pacific AHL Prospects-96
Gold-96
03Wilkes-Barre Scranton Penguins-19
04AHL All-Stars-31
04AHL Top Prospects-56
04Wilkes-Barre Scranton Penguins-7
04ITG Heroes and Prospects-42
Autographs-MO
Combos-2
Complete Emblems-25
Emblems-12
Emblems Gold-12
Jersey Autographs-12
Jerseys-12
Jerseys Gold-12
Numbers-12
Numbers Gold-12
04ITG Heroes/Prospects Toronto Expo '05-42
04ITG Heroes/Prospects Expo Heroes/Pros-42
05ITG Heroes/Prosp Toronto Expo Parallel -67
05UD Rookie Class-14
05WBS Penguins-21
05ITG Heroes and Prospects-67
Autographs-A-MO
Jerseys-GUJ-21
Jerseys Gold-GUJ-21
Emblems-GUE-21
Emblems Gold-GUE-21
Numbers-GUN-21
Numbers Gold-GUN-21
Shooting Stars-AS-6
06Beehive-147
Matte-147
06Black Diamond-155A
Black-155A
Gold-155A
Ruby-155A
06Fleer-207
Tiffany-207
06Hot Prospects-130
Red Hot-130
White Hot-130
Hotagraphs-HMO
06O-Pee-Chee-524
Rainbow-524
06SP Authentic-199
Limited-199
06SP Game Used-146
Gold-146
Rainbow-146
Autographs-146
Rookie Exclusives Autographs-REMO
06SPx-150
Spectrum-150
06The Cup-149
Autographed Rookie Masterpiece Pressplates-149
Gold Rainbow Autographed Rookie Patches-149
Masterpiece Pressplates (Artifacts)-221
Masterpiece Pressplates (Bee Hive)-147
Masterpiece Pressplates (Black Diamond)-155
Masterpiece Pressplates (Marquee Rookies)-524
Masterpiece Pressplates (MVP)-348
Masterpiece Pressplates (Power Play)-124
Masterpiece Pressplates (SP Authentic Autographs)-199
Masterpiece Pressplates (SP Game Used)-146
Masterpiece Pressplates (SPx)-150
Masterpiece Pressplates (Sweet Beginnings)-144
Masterpiece Pressplates (Trilogy)-146
Masterpiece Pressplates (Ultimate Collection)-89
Masterpiece Pressplates (Victory)-216
NHL Shields Duals-DSHOW
Rookies Black-149
Rookies Platinum-149
06UD Artifacts-221
Blue-221
Gold-221
Platinum-221
Radiance-221
Red-221
06UD Powerplay-124
Impact Rainbow-124
06Ultimate Collection-89
Ultimate Debut Threads Jerseys-DJ-MO
Ultimate Debut Threads Jerseys Autographs-DJ-MO
Ultimate Debut Threads Patches-DJ-MO
Ultimate Debut Threads Patches Autographs-DJ-MO
06Ultra-224
Gold Medallion-224
Ice Medallion-224
06Upper Deck-238
Exclusives Parallel-238
High Gloss Parallel-238
Masterpieces-238
06Upper Deck MVP-348
Gold Script-348
Super Script-348
06Upper Deck Sweet Shot-144
Rookie Jerseys Autographs-144
06Upper Deck Trilogy-146
06Upper Deck Victory-216
06Upper Deck Victory Black-216
06Upper Deck Victory Gold-216

Ouellet, Mike
01OCN Blizzard-23

Ouellet, Robert
98German DEL-40
99German DEL-144

Ouellet, Simon
93Quebec Pee-Wee Tournament-1372

Ouellet-Beaudry, David
00Chicoutimi Sagueneens-17
Signed-17

Ouellete, Denis
93Fredericton Canadiens-19

Ouellette, Adolard
35Diamond Matchbooks Tan 2-53
35Diamond Matchbooks Tan 3-50

Ouellette, Caroline
04Canadian Womens World Championship Team-14
06ITG Going For Gold-6
06ITG Going For Gold Samples-6
06ITG Going For Gold Autographs-AO
06ITG Going For Gold Jerseys-GUJ6

Ouellette, David
93Quebec Pee-Wee Tournament-908

Ouellette, Francois
907th Inn. Sketch QMJHL-157
91ProCards-432
94Erie Panthers-15
95Roller Hockey Magazine RHI-2

Ouellette, Frank
95San Diego Barracudas RHI-5
96Anchorage Aces-11
97Columbus Cottonmouths-13
98Columbus Cottonmouths-11
99Columbus Cottonmouths-18
00Columbus Cottonmouths-11

Ouellette, Pat
04Ottawa 67's-5
05Ottawa 67's-8

Ouellette, Philippe
98Val d'Or Foreurs-S3

Ouimet, Marc
91Michigan Wolverines-13
92Quebec Pee-Wee Tournament-386
93Quebec Pee-Wee Tournament-1339
94Anaheim Bullfrogs RHI-14
95Adirondack Red Wings-18
98Swiss Power Play Stickers-194
99Swiss Panini Stickers-195
00Swiss Panini Stickers-286
01Swiss HNL-19
02Swiss HNL-20

Ouimet, Maxime D.
05Baie-Comeau Drakkar-16

Ouimet, Yan
03Moncton Wildcats-2
04Moncton Wildcats-16
05Quebec Remparts-24
05Quebec Remparts Signature Series-24

Oulahen, Ryan
03Brampton Batallion-17
04Brampton Battalion-24

Ouskun, Brad
05Moncton Wildcats-25
06Moncton Wildcats-19

Ouzas, Michael
02Barrie Colts-18
03St. Michael's Majors-23
04Mississauga Ice Dogs-17
05Extreme Top Prospects Signature Edition-S17

Ovaska, Niko
917th Inn. Sketch WHL-240

Ovcacik, Ctirad
03Czech OFS Plus-394

Ovchinikov, Maxim
00Russian Hockey League-98
04Russian RHL-6

Ovechkin, Alexander
01Russian Dynamo Moscow-15
01Russian Young Lions-3
02Russian Future Stars-1
02Russian Hockey League-198
02Russian Lightnings-1
02Russian SL-28
02Russian Young Lions-2
02Russian Young Lions-NNO
03Russian Hockey League-45
03Russian Hockey League-50
03Russian National Team-24
03Russian SL-9
03Russian Young Lions-3
03Russian Under-18 Team-12
03Russian World Championships Preview-1
04SP Authentic Rookie Redemptions-RR30
04Russian Hope-1
04Russian Moscow Dynamo-22
04Russian World Championship Team-8
04Russian World Junior Team-3
04ITG Heroes and Prospects-116
04ITG Heroes and Prospects-117
04ITG Heroes and Prospects-118
04ITG Heroes and Prospects-119
04ITG Heroes and Prospects-202
04ITG Heroes and Prospects-NNO
Aspiring-2
Aspiring-6
Autographs-A01
Autographs-A02
Autographs-A03
Autographs-A04
Combos-15
Combos-16
Combos-17
Combos-18
Emblems-57
Emblems-59
Emblems Gold-57
Emblems Gold-59
First Overall-1
First Overall-2
First Overall-3
He Shoots-He Scores Prizes-2
He Shoots-He Scores Prizes-6
He Shoots-He Scores Prizes-8
Jersey Autographs-57
Jerseys-57
Jerseys-59
Jerseys Gold-57
Jerseys Gold-59
National Pride-4
Numbers-57
Numbers-59
Numbers Gold-57
Numbers Gold-59
04ITG Heroes/Prospects Toronto Expo '05-116
04ITG Heroes/Prospects Toronto Expo '05-117
04ITG Heroes/Prospects Toronto Expo '05-118
04ITG Heroes/Prospects Toronto Expo '05-119
04ITG Heroes/Prospects Toronto Expo '05-202
04ITG Heroes/Prospects Toronto Expo '05-NNO
04ITG Heroes/Prospects Expo Heroes/Pros-116
04ITG Heroes/Prospects Expo Heroes/Pros-117
04ITG Heroes/Prospects Expo Heroes/Pros-118
04ITG Heroes/Prospects Expo Heroes/Pros-119
05ITG Heroes/Prosp Toronto Expo Parallel -109
05ITG Heroes/Prosp Toronto Expo Parallel -279
05ITG Heroes/Prosp Toronto Expo Parallel -362
05Beehive-102
Beige -102
Blue -102
Gold-102
Red -102
Rookie Jumbos-R2
Matte-102
PhotoGraphs-PGAO
Signature Scrapbook-SSAO
05Black Diamond-191
Emerald-191
Gold-191
Onyx-191
Ruby-191
05Hot Prospects-275
En Fuego-275
Hot Materials-HMAO
Red Hot-275
White Hot-275
05ITG Ultimate Memorabilia Level 1-2
05ITG Ultimate Memorabilia Level 2-2
05ITG Ultimate Memorabilia Level 3-2
05ITG Ultimate Memorabilia Level 4-2
05ITG Ultimate Memorabilia Level 5-2
05ITG Ultimate Mem Alexander The Gr8-1
05ITG Ultimate Mem Alexander The Gr8-2
05ITG Ultimate Mem Alexander The Gr8-3
05ITG Ultimate Mem Alexander The Gr8-4
05ITG Ultimate Mem Alexander The Gr8-5
05ITG Ultimate Mem Alexander The Gr8-6
05ITG Ultimate Mem Alexander The Gr8-7
05ITG Ultimate Mem Alexander The Gr8-8
05ITG Ultimate Mem Alexander The Gr8 Gold-1
05ITG Ultimate Mem Alexander The Gr8 Gold-2
05ITG Ultimate Mem Alexander The Gr8 Gold-3
05ITG Ultimate Mem Alexander The Gr8 Gold-4
05ITG Ultimate Mem Alexander The Gr8 Gold-5
05ITG Ultimate Mem Alexander The Gr8 Gold-6
05ITG Ultimate Mem Alexander The Gr8 Gold-7
05ITG Ultimate Mem Alexander The Gr8 Gold-8
05ITG Ultimate Mem Blades of Steel-1
05ITG Ultimate Mem Blades of Steel Gold-1
05ITG Ultimate Mem Complete Jersey-3
05ITG Ultimate Mem Complete Jersey Gold-3
05ITG Ultimate Mem Complete Package-16
05ITG Ultimate Mem Complete Package Gold-16
05ITG Ultimate Memorabilia Double Autos-12
05ITG Ultimate Mem Double Autos Gold-12
05ITG Ultimate Mem Double Mem-24
05ITG Ultimate Mem Double Mem Autos-1
05ITG Ultimate Mem Double Mem Autos Gold-1
05ITG Ultimate Mem Double Mem Gold-24
05ITG Ultimate Memorabilia Emblems-2
05ITG Ultimate Memorabilia Emblems Gold-2
05ITG Ultimate Mem First Overall Jerseys-8
05ITG Ultimate Mem 1st Overall Jsy Gold-8
05ITG Ultimate Mem First Rounders Jerseys-6
05ITG Ultimate Mem First Rounders Jerseys-10
05ITG Ultimate Mem 1st Round Jersey Gold-6
05ITG Ultimate Mem 1st Round Jersey Gold-10
05ITG Ultimate Mem Future Stars Autos-7
05ITG Ultimate Mem Future Star Autos Gold-7
05ITG Ultimate Mem Future Stars Jerseys-7
05ITG Ultimate Mem Fut Stars Jerseys Gold-7
05ITG Ultimate Mem Future Stars Mem Autos-7
05ITG Ultimate Mem Fut Star Mem Auto Gold-7
05ITG Ultimate Memorabilia Gloves Are Off-2
05ITG Ultimate Mem Gloves Are Off Gold-2
05ITG Ultimate Memorabilia In The Numbers-22
05ITG Ultimate Mem In The Numbers Gold-22
05ITG Ultimate Mem Jersey and Emblem-23
05ITG Ultimate Memorabilia Jersey Autos-36
05ITG Ultimate Mem Jersey Autos Gold-36
05ITG Ultimate Mem Jersey Emblems Gold-23
05ITG Ultimate Memorabilia Jerseys-1
05ITG Ultimate Memorabilia Jerseys Gold-1
05ITG Ultimate Mem Pass the Torch Jerseys-3
05ITG Ultimate Mem Passing Torch Jsy Gold-3
05ITG Ultimate Memorabilia R.O.Y. Autos-20
05ITG Ultimate Mem R.O.Y. Autos Gold-20
05ITG Ultimate Memorabilia R.O.Y. Emblems-9
05ITG Ultimate Mem R.O.Y. Emblems Gold-9
05ITG Ultimate Memorabilia R.O.Y. Jerseys-9
05ITG Ultimate Mem R.O.Y. Jerseys Gold-9
05ITG Ultimate Memorabilia R.O.Y. Numbers-9
05ITG Ultimate Mem R.O.Y. Numbers Gold-9
05ITG Ultimate Mem Seams Unbelievable-11
05ITG Ultimate Mem Seam Unbelievable Gold-11
05ITG Ultimate Memorabilia Sextuple Autos-2
05ITG Ultimate Memorabilia Stick Autos-30
05ITG Ultimate Mem Stick Autos Gold-30
05ITG Ultimate Mem Sticks and Jerseys-6
05ITG Ultimate Mem Stick and Jerseys Gold-6
05ITG Ultimate Mem 3 Star of the Game Jsy-25
05ITG Ult Mem 3 Star of the Game Jsy Gold-25
05ITG Ultimate Memorabilia Trifecta Autos-10
05ITG Ultimate Mem Trifecta Autos Gold-10
05ITG Ultimate Memorabilia Triple Autos-7
05ITG Ultimate Memorabilia Triple Autos-14
05ITG Ultimate Memorabilia Triple Autos-18
05ITG Ultimate Mem Triple Autos Gold-7
05ITG Ultimate Mem Triple Autos Gold-14
05ITG Ultimate Mem Triple Autos Gold-18
05ITG Ultimate Mem Triple Threads Jerseys-1
05ITG Ultimate Mem Triple Thread Jsy Gold-1
05Panini Stickers-2
05Panini Stickers-175
05Parkhurst-588
05Parkhurst-597
05Parkhurst-600
05Parkhurst-669
05Parkhurst-700
Facsimile Auto Parallel-588
Facsimile Auto Parallel-597
Facsimile Auto Parallel-600
Facsimile Auto Parallel-669
Facsimile Auto Parallel-700
Signatures-AO
True Colors-TCWAS
True Colors-TCWAS
05SP Authentic-190
Limited-190
Exquisite Endorsements-EEAO
Marks of Distinction-MDAO
Octographs-OR
Prestigious Pairings-PPPO
Rarefied Rookies-RRAO
Rookie Authentics-RAAO
Sign of the Times Duals-DKO
Sign of the Times Triples-TSOC
Sign of the Times Quads-QSOPC
Sign of the Times Fives-POCLS
Six Star Signatures-SSRO
05SP Game Used-111
Autographs-111
Gold-111
Auto Draft-AD-AO
Game Gear-GG-AO
Game Gear Autographs-AG-AO
Rookie Exclusives-AO
Rookie Exclusives Silver-RE-AO
Significant Numbers-SN-AO
05SPx-190
Spectrum-190
Xcitement Rookies-XR-AO
Xcitement Rookies Gold-XR-AO
Xcitement Rookies Spectrum-XR-AO
05The Cup-179
Autographed Rookie Patches Gold Rainbow-179
Black Rainbow Rookies-179
Dual NHL Shields-DSCO
Dual NHL Shields-DSKO
Dual NHL Shields Autographs-ADSKO
Emblems of Endorsement-EEAO
Honorable Numbers-HNAO
Limited Logos-LLAO
Masterpiece Pressplates (Artifacts)-230
Masterpiece Pressplates (Bee Hive)-102
Masterpiece Pressplates (Black Diamond)-191
Masterpiece Pressplates (Ice)-103
Masterpiece Pressplates (MVP)-394
Masterpiece Pressplates (Power Play)-143
Masterpiece Pressplates (Power Play)-143
Masterpiece Pressplates Rookie Upd Auto-275
Masterpiece Pressplates SPA Autos-190
Masterpiece Pressplates (SP Game Used)-111
Masterpiece Pressplates SPx Autos-190
Masterpiece Pressplates (Trilogy)-220
Masterpiece Pressplates Ult Coll Autos-92
Masterpiece Pressplates (Victory)-264
Masterpiece Pressplates Autographs-179
Noble Numbers Dual-DNNCO
Platinum Rookies-179
Scripted Numbers-SNNO
Scripted Numbers Dual-DSNKO
Scripted Swatches-SSAO
Signature Patches-SPAO
05UD Artifacts-230
Gold-RED30
05UD PowerPlay-143
05UD Rookie Class-2
Commemorative Boxtoppers-CC-2
05Ultimate Collection-92
Autographed Shields-92
Jerseys-JAO
Jerseys Dual-DJOC
Jerseys Triple-TJNOC
Marquee Attractions-MA48
National Heroes Jerseys-NHJAO
National Heroes Patches-NHPAO
Premium Patches-PPAO
Premium Swatches-PSAO
Ultimate Debut Threads Jerseys-DTJAO
Ultimate Debut Threads Patches-DTPAO
Ultimate Patches-PAO
Ultimate Patches Dual-DPOC
Ultimate Patches Triple-TPNOC
Ultimate Signatures-USAO
Ultimate Signatures Foursomes-UFSOBP
Ultimate Signatures Logos-SLAO
Ultimate Signatures Trios-UTSOC
05Ultra-252
Gold-252
Difference Makers-DM9
Difference Makers Jerseys-DMJ-AO
Difference Makers Jersey Autographs-DAJ-AO
Difference Makers Patches-DMP-AO
Difference Makers Patch Autographs-DAP-AO
Fresh Ink-FI-AO
Fresh Ink Blue-FI-AO
Ice-252
Rookie Uniformity Jerseys-RU-AO
Rookie Uniformity Jersey Autographs-ARU-AO
Rookie Uniformity Patches-RUP-AO
Rookie Uniformity Patch Autographs-ARP-AO
Scoring Kings-SK18
Scoring Kings Jerseys-SKJ-AO
Scoring Kings Jersey Autographs-KAJ-AO
Scoring Kings Patches-SKP-AO
Scoring Kings Patch Autographs-KAP-AO
05Upper Deck-443
05Upper Deck-487
Majestic Materials-MMAO
Rookie Ink-RIAO
05Upper Deck Rookie Showcase-RS30
05Upper Deck Rookie Showcase Promos-RS30
05Upper Deck Rookie Threads-RTAO
05Upper Deck Rookie Threads Autographs-ARTAO
05Upper Deck Sportsfest-NHL2
05Upper Deck Stars in the Making-SM2
05Upper Deck Ice-103
Cool Threads-CTAO
Cool Threads Autographs-ACTAO
Cool Threads Glass-CTAO
Cool Threads Patches-CTPAO
Cool Threads Patch Autographs-CAPAO
Glacial Graphs-GGAO
Premieres Auto Patches-AIPAO
Signature Swatches-SSAO
05Upper Deck MVP-394
Gold-394
Platinum-394
Rookie Breakthrough-RB2
05Upper Deck Rookie Update-275
05Upper Deck Trilogy-220
05Upper Deck Victory-264
Black-264
Gold-264
Silver-264
05ITG Heroes and Prospects-109
05ITG Heroes and Prospects-279
05ITG Heroes and Prospects-362
Aspiring-ASP20
Autograph Memorabilia-GA-07
Autograph Memorabilia Gold-GA-07
Autographs-A-AO
Autographs Series II-AO2
Autographs Series II-AO3
Complete Jerseys-CJ-14
Complete Jerseys Gold-CJ-14
Future Teammates-FT14
He Shoots-He Scores Prizes-6
He Shoots-He Scores Prizes-8
He Shoots-He Scores Prizes-19
He Shoots-He Scores Prizes-40
He Shoots-He Scores Prizes-41
He Shoots-He Scores Prizes-51
Jerseys-GUJ-54
Jerseys-GUJ-91
Jerseys Gold-GUJ-54
Jerseys Gold-GUJ-91
Emblems-GUE-54
Emblems-GUE-91
Emblems Gold-GUE-91
Numbers-GUN-54
Numbers-GUN-91
Numbers Gold-GUN-54
Numbers Gold-GUN-91
Making the Bigs-MTB-7
Nameplates-N-32
National Pride-NPR-12
National Pride-NPR-33
06Sports Illustrated for Kids *-33
06Be A Player-70
Autographs-70
Profiles-PP29
Profiles Autographs-PP29
Signatures-AO
Signatures 10-76
Signatures 25-76
Signatures Duals-DOC
Signatures Trios-TOKC
Signatures Foursomes-FOFKF
Up Close and Personal-UC3
Up Close and Personal Autographs-UC3
06Be A Player Portraits-99
Dual Signature Portraits-DSOK
First Exposures-FEAO
Sensational Six-SS1ST
Signature Portraits-SPAO
06Beehive-1
06Beehive-161
Blue-1
Gold-1
Matte-1
Red Facsimile Signatures-1
Wood-1
5 X 7 Black and White-1
5 X 7 Cherry Wood-1
Matted Materials-MMAO
06Black Diamond-168B
Black-168B
Gold-168B
Ruby-168B
Gemography-GAO
Jerseys-JAO
Jerseys Black-JAO
Jerseys Gold-JAO
Jerseys Ruby-JAO
Jerseys Black Autographs -JAO
06Flair Showcase-99
06Flair Showcase-200
06Flair Showcase-269
06Flair Showcase-300
Parallel-99
Parallel-200
Parallel-269
Parallel-300
Hot Numbers-HN42
Hot Numbers Parallel-HN42
Inks-IAO
Stitches-SSAO
Wave of the Future-WF42
06Fleer-195
Oversized-195
Tiffany-195
Fabricology-FAO
Hockey Headliners-HL2
Hockey Headliners-HL14
Hockey Headliners-HL16
Signing Day-SDAO
Speed Machines-SM25
Total O-025
06Hot Prospects-98
Red Hot-98
White Hot-98
Hot Materials -HMAO
Hot Materials Red Hot-HMAO
Hot Materials White Hot-HMAO
06ITG International Ice-59
06ITG International Ice-160
Gold-59
Gold-160
Autographs-AAO
Autographs-AOM
Complete Jersey-CJ08
Complete Jersey Gold-CJ08
Cornerstones-IC02
Cornerstones Gold-IC02
Double Memorabilia-DM04
Double Memorabilia Gold-DM04
Passing The Torch-PTT15
Passing The Torch Gold-PTT15
Quad Patch-QP06
Quad Patch Gold-QP06
Stick and Jersey-SJ07
Stick and Jersey Gold-SJ07
Teammates-IT21
Teammates Gold-IT21
Triple Memorabilia-TM06
Triple Memorabilia Gold-TM06
06ITG Phenoms-AO01
06ITG Phenoms-AO02
06ITG Phenoms-AO03
06ITG Phenoms-AO04
06ITG Phenoms-AO05
06ITG Phenoms-AO06
Autographs-AO01
Autographs-AO02
Autographs-AO03
Autographs-AO04
Autographs-AO05
Autographs-AO06
Double Memorabilia Gold-DMAO
Double Memorabilia Silver-DMAO
Idols Gold-IDAO
Idols Silver-IDAO
Jerseys Gold-GUJAO
Jerseys Gold Dual-DJOC
Jerseys Gold Dual-DJTO
Jerseys Gold Triple-TJCOT
Jerseys Silver-GUJAO
Jerseys Silver Dual-DJOC
Jerseys Silver Dual-DJTO
Jerseys Silver Triple-TJCOT
Patches Gold-GUPAO
Patches Gold Dual-DPOC
Patches Gold Dual-DPTO
Patches Gold Triple-TPCOT
Patches Silver-GUPAO
Patches Silver Dual-DPOC
Patches Silver Dual-DPTO
Patches Silver Triple-TPCOT
Sticks Gold-GUSAO
Sticks Gold Dual-DSOC
Sticks Gold Dual-DSTO
Sticks Gold Triple-TSCOT
Sticks Silver-GUSAO
Sticks Silver Dual-DSOC
Sticks Silver Dual-DSTO
Sticks Silver Triple-TSCOT
Teammates Gold-TMAO
Teammates Silver-TMAO
Triple Memorabilia Gold-TRAO
Triple Memorabilia Silver-TRAO
06ITG Ultimate Memorabilia-5
Artist Proof-5
Autos-50
Autos Gold-50
Autos Dual-7
Autos Dual Gold-7
Autos Triple-7
Autos Triple Gold-7
Complete Jersey-9
Complete Jersey Gold-9
Complete Package-9
Complete Package Gold-9
Cornerstones-1
Cornerstones Gold-1
Double Memorabilia-9
Double Memorabilia Gold-9
Double Memorabilia Autos-8
Double Memorabilia Autos Gold-8
Emblems-2
Emblems Gold-2
First Round Picks-2
First Round Picks Gold-2
Gloves Are Off-1
Gloves Are Off Gold-1
Going For Gold-1
Going For Gold Gold-1
In The Numbers-10
In The Numbers Gold-10
Jerseys-6
Jerseys Gold-6
Jerseys and Emblems-6
Jerseys and Emblems Gold-6
Jerseys Autos-42
Jerseys Autos Gold-42
Passing The Torch-17
Passing The Torch Gold-17
R.O.Y. Autos-10
R.O.Y. Autos Gold-10
R.O.Y. Emblems-10
R.O.Y. Emblems Gold-10
R.O.Y. Jerseys-10
R.O.Y. Jerseys Gold-10
R.O.Y. Numbers-10
R.O.Y. Numbers Gold-10
Stick Rack-17
Stick Rack Gold-17
Sticks Autos-22
Sticks Autos Gold-22
Trifecta Autos-4
Trifecta Autos Gold-4
Triple Thread Jerseys-1
Triple Thread Jerseys Gold-1
06McDonald's Upper Deck-50
Autographs-AAO
Hardware Heroes-HH2
Jerseys-JAO
Patches-PAO
Rookie Review-RR2
06NHL POG-51
06O-Pee-Chee-500
06O-Pee-Chee-615
06O-Pee-Chee-624
06O-Pee-Chee-700
Rainbow-500
Rainbow-615
Rainbow-624
Rainbow-700
Swatches-S-AO
06Panini Stickers-172
06SP Authentic-1
06SP Authentic-103
Limited-1
Limited-103
06SP Game Used-99
Gold-99
Rainbow-99
Authentic Fabrics-AFAO
Authentic Fabrics Parallel-AFAO
Authentic Fabrics Patches-AFAO
Authentic Fabrics Dual-AF2KO
Authentic Fabrics Dual Patches-AF2KO
Authentic Fabrics Triple-AF3WAS
Authentic Fabrics Triple Patches-AF3WAS
Authentic Fabrics Fives-AF51ST
Authentic Fabrics Fives-AF550G
Authentic Fabrics Fives-AP5PTS
Authentic Fabrics Fives-AP5RPT
Authentic Fabrics Fives Patches-AF51ST
Authentic Fabrics Fives Patches-AF550G
Authentic Fabrics Fives Patches-AP5PTS
Authentic Fabrics Fives Patches-AP5RPT
Authentic Fabrics Sevens-AF7CAL
Authentic Fabrics Sevens Patches-AF7CAL
Authentic Fabrics Eights-AF8RUS
Authentic Fabrics Eights Patches-AF8RUS
By The Letter-BLAO
Inked Sweaters-ISAO
Inked Sweaters Patches-ISAO
Inked Sweaters Dual-IS2OK
Inked Sweaters Dual Patches-IS2OK
06SPx-100
Spectrum-100
SPxcitement-X99
SPxcitement Spectrum-X99
Winning Materials-WMAO
Winning Materials Spectrum-WMAO
06Sunkist-7
06The Cup-89
Autographed Foundations-CQOV
Autographed Foundations Patches-CQOV
Autographed NHL Shields Duals-DASMO
Autographed Patches-89
Black Rainbow-89
Foundations-CQOV
Foundations Patches-CQOV
Gold-89
Gold Patches-89
Honorable Numbers-HNOV
Jerseys-89
Limited Logos-LLOV
Masterpiece Pressplates-89
NHL Shields Duals-DSHCO

Scripted Swatches-SSAO
Scripted Swatches Duals-DSOM
Signature Patches-SPAO
06UD Artifacts-1
Blue-1
Gold-1
Platinum-1
Radiance-1
Autographed Radiance Parallel-1
Red-1
Auto-Facts-AFAO
Auto-Facts Gold-AFAO
Treasured Patches Black-TSAO
Treasured Patches Blue-TSAO
Treasured Patches Gold-TSAO
Treasured Patches Platinum-TSAO
Treasured Patches Red-TSAO
Treasured Patches Autographed Black Tag Parallel-TSAO
Treasured Swatches-TSAO
Treasured Swatches Black-TSAO
Treasured Swatches Blue-TSAO
Treasured Swatches Gold-TSAO
Treasured Swatches Platinum-TSAO
Treasured Swatches Red-TSAO
Treasured Swatches Autographed Black-TSAO
Tundra Tandems-TTKO
Tundra Tandems Black-TTKO
Tundra Tandems Blue-TTKO
Tundra Tandems Gold-TTKO
Tundra Tandems Platinum-TTKO
Tundra Tandems Red-TTKO
Tundra Tandems Dual Patches Red-TTKO
06UD Biography of a Season-BOS10
06UD Mini Jersey Collection-100
Jerseys-AO
Jersey Variations-AO
Jersey Autographs-AO
06UD Powerplay-99
Impact Rainbow-99
In Action-IA14
Power Marks-PMAO
Specialists-SAO
Specialists Patches-PAO
06Ultimate Collection-60
Jerseys-UJ-AO
Jerseys Triple-UJ3-OMK
Patches-UJ-AO
Patches Triple-UJ3-OMK
06Ultra-196
Gold Medallion-196
Ice Medallion-196
Action-UA28
Difference Makers-DM27
Fresh Ink-IAO
Scoring Kings-SK2
Uniformity-UAO
Uniformity Patches-UPAO
Uniformity Autographed Jerseys-UAAO
06Upper Deck Arena Giveaways-WSH3
06Upper Deck-442
Exclusives Parallel-442
High Gloss Parallel-442
All-Time Greatest-ATG22
All World-AW30
Award Winners-AW4
Award Winners Canadian Exclusive-OAW1
Century Marks-CM2
Game Dated Moments-GD2
Game Dated Moments-GD18
Game Dated Moments-GD22
Game Jerseys-JAO
Game Patches-PAO
Generations Duals-G2JO
Generations Triples-G3SKO
Generations Patches Dual-G2PJO
Generations Patches Triple-G3PSKO
Goal Rush-GR9
Hometown Heroes-HH42
Masterpieces-442
Oversized Wal-Mart Exclusives-442
Shootout Artists-SA4
Signatures-SAO
Statistical Leaders-SL3
06Upper Deck Rookie Showdown-RS-SCAO
06Upper Deck Entry Draft-DR2
06Upper Deck MVP-292
Gold Script-292
Super Script-292
Clutch Performers-CP10
Gotta Have Hart-HH12
International Icons-II24
Jerseys-OJCO
Jerseys-OJOK
06Upper Deck Ovation-200
06Upper Deck Sweet Shot-100
Sweet Stitches-SSAO
Sweet Stitches Duals-SSAO
Sweet Stitches Triples-SSAO
06Upper Deck Trilogy-99
Frozen In Time-FT1
Honorary Scripted Patches-HSPAO
Honorary Scripted Swatches-HSSAO
Honorary Swatches-HSAO
Ice Scripts-ISAO
Scripts-S1AO
06Upper Deck National NHL-NHL-3
06Upper Deck National NHL VIP-1
06Upper Deck Victory-199
06Upper Deck Victory Black-199
06Upper Deck Victory Gold-199
06Upper Deck Victory GameBreakers-GB50
06Upper Deck Victory Next In Line-NL48
06Upper Deck Victory Oversize Cards-AO
06Russian Sport Collection Olympic Stars-12
06Russian Torino Olympic Team-1
06ITG Heroes and Prospects Making The Bigs-MTB12
06ITG Heroes and Prospects Quad Emblems-QE06
06ITG Heroes and Prospects Quad Emblems Gold-QE06
06ITG Heroes and Prospects Sticks and Jerseys-SJ04
06ITG Heroes and Prospects Sticks and Jerseys Gold-SJ04
06ITG Heroes and Prospects Triple Memorabilia-TM03
06ITG Heroes and Prospects Triple Memorabilia Gold-TM03
07Upper Deck All-Star Game Redemptions-AS10
07Upper Deck Ovation-51
3x5s-XL1
Autographed 3x5s-XLAAO
07Upper Deck Victory-97
Black-97
Gold-97
GameBreakers-GB50
Oversize Cards-OS24
Stars on Ice-SI8

Overton, Shawn
05Vernon Vipers-18

Ovesen, Morten
98Danish Hockey League-212
99Danish Hockey League-187

Oviatt, Steve
93Tacoma Rockets-18

Ovington, Chris
96Red Deer Rebels-11
97Red Deer Rebels-16
98Red Deer Rebels-16
00Spokane Chiefs-20
06Austin Ice Bats-5

Ovtschinnikov, Andrej
94German First League-520

Owchar, Dennis
74Penguins Postcards-16
75O-Pee-Chee NHL-380
76O-Pee-Chee NHL-314
77O-Pee-Chee NHL-391
77Penguins Puck Bucks-25
78O-Pee-Chee-19
78Topps-19

Owen, Bobby
95Waterloo Blackhawks -13

Owen, Gareth
03UK Coventry Blaze-14
06UK Coventry Blaze-14

Owens, Eddie
93Quebec Pee-Wee Tournament-651

Owens, Gareth
02UK Coventry Blaze-16
03UK Coventry Blaze Calendars-11

Owens, Jordan
04Mississauga Ice Dogs-23
05Mississauga Ice Dogs-3
05OHL Bell All-Star Classic-17
06Mississauga Ice Dogs-6

Owens, Mike
06Richmond Renegades-11

Owens, Sean
02Columbia Inferno-107
03Columbia Inferno Update-51

Owsiak, Andrew
06Okotoks Oilers -14

Oxholm, Henrik
98Danish Hockey League-99
99Danish Hockey League-116

Oxholm, Lars
92North Dakota Fighting Sioux-25
98Danish Hockey League-96
99Danish Hockey League-120

Oxtoby, Matt
03Yarmouth Mariners-16

Oystila, Jouko
71Finnish Suomi Stickers-80
71Finnish Suomi Stickers-110
72Finnish Jaakiekko-80
72Finnish Jaakiekko-154
72Finnish Hellas-20
72Finnish Panda Toronto-112
72Finnish Semic World Championship-76
72Swedish Semic World Championship-76
73Finnish Jaakiekko-84
73Finnish Jaakiekko-125
74Finnish Typotor-36
74Swedish Stickers-106
74Swedish Semic World Champ Stickers-82

Oystrick, Nathan
04Northern Michigan Wildcats-17
06AHL Top Prospects-9

Oystrick, Trent
91Rayside-Balfour Jr. Canadians-14

Oystrick, Trevor
90Rayside-Balfour Jr. Canadians-16

Ozarowski, Brent
03Memphis RiverKings-15

Ozellis, Falk
94German DEL-166
95German DEL-166
96German DEL-241
99German Bundesliga 2-241

Ozolin, Vladislav
00Russian Hockey League-249
01Russian Hockey League-65
02Russian Hockey League-228
03Russian Hockey League-152

Ozolinsh, Sandis
91Upper Deck-661
French-661
91Upper Deck Czech World Juniors-22
92OPC Premier-104
92Parkhurst-164
Emerald Ice-164
92Ultra-402
Imports-19
92Upper Deck-568
Euro-Rookies-ER16
92Russian Stars Red Ace-21
93Donruss-312
93Leaf-73
93OPC Premier-168
Gold-168
93Parkhurst-187
Emerald Ice-187
93Pinnacle-142
Canadian-142
93PowerPlay-225
93Score-261
Canadian-261
International Stars-18
International Stars Canadian-18
93Stadium Club-362
Members Only Master Set-362
First Day Issue-362
93Topps/OPC Premier-168
Gold-168
93Ultra-169
93Upper Deck-72
SP-146
94Canada Games NHL POGS-219
94Donruss-120
94Finest-57
Super Team Winners-57
Refractors-57
Division's Clear Cut-17
94Flair-169
94Fleer-200
Franchise Futures-6
94Leaf-169
94Leaf Limited-43
94McDonald's Upper Deck-McD11
94OPC Premier-239
94OPC Premier-430
Special Effects-239
Special Effects-430
94Parkhurst-208
Gold-208
Crash the Game Green-21
Crash the Game Blue-21
Crash the Game Gold-21
Crash the Game Red-21
Vintage-V7
94Pinnacle-22
Artist's Proofs-22
Rink Collection-22
World Edition-WE11
94Score-36
Gold-36
Platinum-36
94Select-63
Gold-63
94SP-108
Die Cuts-108
94Stadium Club Members Only-11
94Stadium Club-177
94Stadium Club-204
Members Only Master Set-177
Members Only Master Set-204
First Day Issue-177
First Day Issue-204
Super Team Winner Cards-177
Super Team Winner Cards-204
94Topps/OPC Premier-239
94Topps/OPC Premier-430
Special Effects-239
Special Effects-430
94Ultra-200
94Upper Deck-490
Electric Ice-490
Predictor Canadian-C27
94Upper Deck Predictor Canadian Exch Gold-C27
94Upper Deck SP Inserts-SP73
94Upper Deck SP Inserts Die Cuts-SP73
95SLU Hockey American-14
95Bashan Super Stickers-29
95Be A Player-183
Signatures-S183
Signatures Die Cuts-S183
95Canada Games NHL POGS-231
95Collector's Choice-9
Player's Club-9
Player's Club Platinum-9
95Donruss-34
95Donruss Elite-93
Die Cut Stars-93
Die Cut Uncut-93
95Emotion-159
95Finest-141
Refractors-141
95Imperial Stickers-29
95Kenner Starting Lineup Cards-16
95Leaf-183
95Leaf Limited-52
95Metal-35
95Panini Stickers-283
95Parkhurst International-185
95Parkhurst International-320
Emerald Ice-185
Emerald Ice-320
All-Stars-2
95Playoff One on One-193
95Score-67
Black Ice Artist's Proofs-67
Black Ice-67
95SkyBox Impact-39
95SP-32
95Summit-137
Artist's Proofs-137
Ice-137
95Ultra-149
95Ultra-224
Gold Medallion-149
95Upper Deck-168
95Upper Deck-470
Electric Ice-168
Electric Ice-470
Electric Ice Gold-168
Electric Ice Gold-470
Special Edition-SE109
Special Edition Gold-SE109
95Zenith-101
96Black Diamond-98
Gold-98
96Collector's Choice-60
MVP-UD35
MVP Gold-UD35
96Donruss-104
Press Proofs-104
96Flair-19
Blue Ice-19
96Fleer-23
Norris-10
Picks Dream Lines-9
Picks Fabulous 50-37
Picks Jagged Edge-8
96Leaf-197
Press Proofs-197
96Maggers-73
96Metal Universe-36
96Pinnacle-159
Artist's Proofs-159
Foil-159
Premium Stock-159
Rink Collection-159
96Playoff One on One-385
96Score-43
Artist's Proofs-43
Dealer's Choice Artist's Proofs-43
Special Artist's Proofs-43
Golden Blades-43
96SkyBox Impact-26
NHL on Fox-17
96Summit-12
Artist's Proofs-12
Ice-12
Metal-12
Premium Stock-12
96Team Out-54
96Topps Picks-21
OPC Inserts-21
96Ultra-38
Gold Medallion-38
96Upper Deck-37
Generation Next-X9
Superstar Showdown-SS20B
96Upper Deck Ice-80
Parallel-80
96Collector's Edge Future Legends-46
97SLU Hockey Canadian-13
97SLU Hockey American-15
97Avalanche Pins-8
97Be A Player-115
Autographs-115
Autographs Die-Cuts-115
Autographs Prismatic Die-Cuts-115
97Black Diamond-27
Double Diamond-27
Triple Diamond-27
Quadruple Diamond-27
97Collector's Choice-60
Star Quest-SQ38
97Donruss-60
Press Proofs Silver-60
Press Proofs Gold-60
Line 2 Line-24
Line 2 Line Die Cut-24
97Donruss Canadian Ice-119
Dominion Series-119
Provincial Series-119
97Donruss Elite-83
Aspirations-83
Status-83
97Donruss Limited-106
97Donruss Limited-145
Exposure-106
Exposure-145
97Donruss Preferred-103
Cut to the Chase-103
97Donruss Priority-45
Stamp of Approval-45
97Katch-40
Gold-40
Silver-40
97Kenner Starting Lineup Cards-15
97Leaf-118
Fractal Matrix-118
Fractal Matrix Die Cuts-118
97Leaf International-118
Universal Ice-118
97NHL Aces Playing Cards-11
97Pacific-75
Copper-75
Emerald Green-75
Ice Blue-75
Red-75
Silver-75
97Pacific Dynagon-32
Copper-32
Dark Grey-32
Emerald Green-32
Ice Blue-32
Red-32
Silver-32
Tandems-41
97Pacific Invincible-37
Copper-37
Emerald Green-37
Ice Blue-37
Red-37
Silver-37
97Pacific Omega-63
Copper-63
Dark Gray-63
Emerald Green-63
Gold-63
Ice Blue-63
97Panini Stickers-206
97Paramount-53
Copper-53
Dark Grey-53
Emerald Green-53
Ice Blue-53
Red-53
Silver-53
97Pinnacle-128
Press Plates Back Black-128
Press Plates Back Cyan-128
Press Plates Back Magenta-128
Press Plates Back Yellow-128
Press Plates Front Black-128
Press Plates Front Cyan-128
Press Plates Front Magenta-128
Press Plates Front Yellow-128
97Pinnacle Certified-89
Red-89
Mirror Blue-89
Mirror Gold-89
Mirror Red-89
97Pinnacle Inside-137
97Pinnacle Tot Cert Platinum Blue-89
97Pinnacle Tot Cert Platinum Gold-89
97Pinnacle Totally Certified Platinum Red-89
97Pinnacle Tot Cert Mirror Platinum Gold-89
97Revolution-37
Copper-37
Emerald-37
Ice Blue-37
Silver-37
97Score-174
97Score Avalanche-6
Platinum-6
Premier-6
97SP Authentic-41
97Studio-82
Press Proofs Silver-82
Press Proofs Gold-82
97Upper Deck-44
Smooth Grooves-SG28
Three Star Selects-20C
97Upper Deck Crash the All-Star Game-10
97Upper Deck Crash the All-Star Game-AR10
97Upper Deck Ice-24
Parallel-24
Power Shift-24
98SLU Hockey One on One-3
98Aurora-50
98Be A Player-188
Press Release-188
98BAP Gold-188
98BAP Autographs-188
98BAP Autographs Gold-188
98Finest-116
No Protectors-116
No Protectors Refractors-116
Refractors-116
98OPC Chrome-121
Refractors-121
Board Members-B10
Board Members Refractors-B10
98Pacific-167
Ice Blue-167
Red-167
98Pacific Omega-63
Red-63
Opening Day Issue-63
98Panini Stickers-190
98Paramount-59
Copper-59
Emerald Green-59
Holo-Electric-59
Ice Blue-59
Silver-59
98Topps-121
O-Pee-Chee-121
Board Members-B10
98UD Choice-60
Prime Choice Reserve-60
Reserve-60
98Upper Deck-250
Exclusives-250
Exclusives 1 of 1-250
Gold Reserve-250
99Avalanche Pins-6
99Avalanche Team Issue-16
99BAP Memorabilia-181
Gold-181
Silver-181
Selects Silver-SL4
Selects Gold-SL4
99BAP Update Teammates Jersey Cards-TM23
99BAP Millennium-68
Emerald-68
Ruby-68
Sapphire-68
Signatures-68
Signatures Gold-68
99O-Pee-Chee-164
99O-Pee-Chee Chrome-164
99O-Pee-Chee Chrome Refractors-164
99Pacific-113
Copper-113
Emerald Green-113
Gold-113
Ice Blue-113
Premiere Date-113
Red-113
99Pacific Omega-64
Copper-64
Gold-64
Ice Blue-64
Premiere Date-64
99Panini Stickers-213
99Paramount-66
Copper-66
Emerald-66
Gold-66
Holographic Emerald-66
Holographic Gold-66
Holographic Silver-66
Ice Blue-66
Premiere Date-66
Red-66
Silver-66
99SPx-44
Radiance-44
Spectrum-44
99Topps/OPC-164
99Topps/OPC Chrome-164
Refractors-164
99Topps Premier Plus-78
Parallel-78
99Upper Deck-213
Exclusives-213
Exclusives 1 of 1-213
All-Star Class-AS17
All-Star Class Quantum Gold-AS17
All-Star Class Quantum Silver-AS17
99Upper Deck Gold Reserve-213
99Upper Deck MVP-56
Gold Script-56
Silver Script-56
Super Script-56
99Upper Deck Victory-83
99Slovakian Challengers-9
00BAP Memorabilia-118
00BAP Memorabilia-409
Emerald-118
Emerald-409
Ruby-118
Ruby-409
Sapphire-118
Sapphire-409
Promos-118
Jersey Cards-J22
Jersey Emblems-E22
Jersey Numbers-N22
Jersey and Stick Cards-JS22
00BAP Mem Chicago Sportsfest Copper-118
00BAP Memorabilia Chicago Sportsfest Blue-118
00BAP Memorabilia Chicago Sportsfest Gold-118
00BAP Memorabilia Chicago Sportsfest Ruby-118
00BAP Memorabilia Chicago Sun-Times Ruby-118
00BAP Memorabilia Chicago Sun-Times Gold-118
00BAP Mem Chicago Sun-Times Sapphire-118
00BAP Mem Toronto Fall Expo Copper-118
00BAP Memorabilia Toronto Fall Expo Gold-118
00BAP Memorabilia Toronto Fall Expo Ruby-118
00BAP Parkhurst 2000-P66
00BAP Parkhurst 2000-P158
00BAP Signature Series-222
Emerald-222
Ruby-222
Sapphire-222
Department of Defense-DD5
00Kraft-11
00O-Pee-Chee-247
00O-Pee-Chee Parallel-247
00Pacific-117
Copper-117
Gold-117
Ice Blue-117
Premiere Date-117
00Panini Stickers-134
00Private Stock Game Gear-14
00SP Authentic-18
00SP Game Used Tools of the Game-SO
00SP Game Used Tools of the Game Excl-SO
00Stadium Club-222
00Titanium Game Gear-4
00Topps/OPC-247
Parallel-247
00Topps Chrome-155
OPC Refractors-155
Refractors-155
00Topps Heritage-211
00UD Heroes-23
00UD Reserve-15
00Upper Deck-264
Exclusives Tier 1-264
Exclusives Tier 2-264
00Upper Deck Victory-66
00Upper Deck Vintage-64
01BAP Memorabilia-72
01BAP Memorabilia-390
Emerald-72
Emerald-390
Ruby-72
Ruby-390
Sapphire-72
Sapphire-390
All-Star Jerseys-ASJ19
All-Star Emblems-ASE19
All-Star Numbers-ASN19
All-Star Starting Lineup-S3
Country of Origin-CO40
01BAP Signature Series-163
Autographs-163
Autographs Gold-163
Department of Defense-DD-10
Jerseys-GJ-86
01Nortel All-Star Game Sheets-6
01O-Pee-Chee-130
01O-Pee-Chee Premier Parallel-130
01Pacific-79
Extreme LTD-79
Hobby LTD-79
Premiere Date-79
Retail LTD-79
01Pacific Arena Exclusives-79
01Parkhurst-177
Sticks-PS45
Teammates-T18
Teammates-T20
01Topps-130
OPC Parallel-130
01UD Mask Collection-41
Gold-41
01UD Stanley Cup Champs-44
01UD Top Shelf Sticks-SSO
01UD Top Shelf Sticks-LOH
01UD Top Shelf Sticks Gold-SSO
01UD Top Shelf Sticks Gold-LOH
01Upper Deck-265
Exclusives-265
01Upper Deck Ice-99
01Upper Deck Victory-64
Gold-64
02BAP All-Star Edition-69
Jerseys-69
Jerseys Gold-69
Jerseys Silver-69
02BAP First Edition-5
02BAP First Edition-312
02BAP First Edition-397
Jerseys-5
02BAP Memorabilia-96
02BAP Memorabilia-254
02BAP Memorabilia-319
Emerald-96
Emerald-254
Ruby-96
Ruby-254
Sapphire-96
Sapphire-254
All-Star Jerseys-ASJ-43
All-Star Starting Lineup-AS-9
NHL All-Star Game-96
NHL All-Star Game-254
NHL All-Star Game Blue-96
NHL All-Star Game Blue-254
NHL All-Star Game Green-96
NHL All-Star Game Green-254
NHL All-Star Game Red-96
NHL All-Star Game Red-254
02BAP Memorabilia Toronto Fall Expo-96
02BAP Memorabilia Toronto Fall Expo-254
02BAP Signature Series-145
Autographs-145
Autograph Buybacks 1998-188
Autograph Buybacks 1999-68
Autograph Buybacks 2001-163
Autographs Gold-145
02Nextel NHL All-Star Game-4
02O-Pee-Chee-215
02O-Pee-Chee Premier Blue Parallel-215
02O-Pee-Chee Premier Red Parallel-215
02O-Pee-Chee Factory Set-215
02Pacific-158
Blue-158
Red-158
02Pacific Complete-77
Red-77
02Pacific Quest for the Cup-3
Gold-3
02Parkhurst-118
Bronze-118
Gold-118
Silver-118
02Parkhurst Retro-108
Minis-108
02Topps-215
OPC Blue Parallel-215
OPC Red Parallel-215
Factory Set-215
02Topps Total-18
02UD Top Shelf-38
02Upper Deck-75
Exclusives-75
All-Star Jerseys-ASSO
All-Star Performers-ASSO
02Upper Deck MVP-80
Gold-80
Classics-80
Golden Classics-80
Overdrive-SO9
02Upper Deck Rookie Update-4
02Upper Deck Victory-91
Bronze-91
Gold-91
Silver-91
02Upper Deck Vintage-110
Green Backs-110
03BAP Memorabilia-81
Emerald-81
Gold-81
Ruby-81
Sapphire-81
All-Star Staring Lineup-3
03Beehive-7
Gold-7
Silver-7
03ITG Action-82
Jerseys-M61
03NHL Sticker Collection-48
03O-Pee-Chee-154
03OPC Blue-154
03OPC Gold-154
03OPC Red-154
03Pacific-8
Blue-8
Red-8
03Pacific Complete-162
Red-162
03Pacific Exhibit-4
Blue Backs-4
Yellow Backs-4
03Topps-154
Blue-154
Gold-154
Red-154
03Upper Deck-3
Canadian Exclusives-3
HG-3
03Upper Deck MVP-5
Gold Script-5
Silver Script-5
Canadian Exclusives-5
04Upper Deck-3
Canadian Exclusives-3
HG Glossy Gold-3
HG Glossy Silver-3
05Ducks Team Issue-15
05Panini Stickers-191
05Parkhurst Facsimile Auto Parallel-11
05Parkhurst True Colors-TCANA
05Parkhurst True Colors-TCANA
05Ultimate Coll National Heroes Jersey-NHJSO
05Ultimate Coll National Heroes Patch-NHPSO
05Ultra-6
Gold-6
Ice-6
05Upper Deck-2
Big Playmakers-B-SO
HG Glossy-2
Jerseys-J-SOZ
Jerseys Series II-J2SO
Patches-P-SO
05Upper Deck MVP-2
Gold-2
Platinum-2
05Upper Deck Toronto Fall Expo-2
05Upper Deck Victory-5
Black-5
Gold-5
Silver-5
06O-Pee-Chee-327
Rainbow-327
Swatches-S-SO
06Upper Deck-131
Exclusives Parallel-131
High Gloss Parallel-131
Game Jerseys-J2SO
Game Patches-P2SO
Masterpieces-131
06Upper Deck MVP-197
Gold Script-197
Super Script-197
Jerseys-OJPO

Ozols, Yuris
00Russian Hockey League-208

Oztekin, Kevin
93Arizona Icecats-14
94Arizona Icecats-6
95Arizona Icecats-5

Paakkarinen, Jyrki
80Finnish Mallasjuoma-140

Paakkarinen, Teemu
05Finnish Cardset -131
06Finnish Cardset-140

Paakkolanvaara, Tommi
05Finnish Cardset -272
06Finnish Cardset-100

Paakkonen, Kalevi
72Finnish Jaakiekko-274

Paananen, Mika
92Finnish Jyvas-Hyva Stickers-83
93Finnish Jyvas-Hyva Stickers-147
93Finnish SISU-148
94Finnish SISU-82
95Finnish SISU-61
96Finnish SISU Redline-62
00Finnish Cardset-173

Paappanen, Tero
03Finnish Cardset-115

Paatero, Orvo
66Finnish Jaakiekkosarja-129

Paavola, Jari
80Finnish Mallasjuoma-196

Pabiska, Lukas
03Czech OFS Plus-120
04Czech OFS-339
05Czech HC Liberec-7
06Czech OFS-97

Pacal, Tomas
94Czech APS Extraliga-32
95Czech APS Extraliga-319
96Czech APS Extraliga-148
97Czech APS Extraliga-249
97Czech DS Stickers-248
98Czech DS Stickers-131
98Czech OFS-149
99Czech DS-74
99Czech OFS-96
00Czech OFS-38
01Czech OFS-249
02Czech OFS Plus-345
03Czech OFS Plus-56
03Czech Pardubice Postcards-12
04Czech OFS-127
05Czech HC Trinec-7
06Czech OFS-163

Pace, Joe
06Richmond Renegades-12

Pachal, Clayton
77Rochester Americans-18

Paciga, Ladislav
04Slovakian Skalica Team Set-18

Packard, Dennis
96Quebec Pee-Wee Tournament-1088
04Johnstown Chiefs-14
04Springfield Falcons-8
05Springfield Falcons-6
06Providence Bruins-12

Packwood, Mark
04Kitchener Rangers-4
05Kitchener Rangers-3
06Kitchener Rangers-15
06Oshawa Generals-23

Paclik, Robert
94German DEL-27

Pacquet, Normand
90 7th Inn. Sketch QMJHL-212

Pacula, Ireneusz
89Swedish Semic World Champ Stickers-149
94German DEL-160
95German DEL-160

Paddock, Cam
99Kelowna Rockets-20
00Kelowna Rockets-24
01Kelowna Rockets-17
02Kelowna Rockets-2
03Kelowna Rockets Memorial Cup-15
03Kelowna Rockets-16
04Wheeling Nailers Riesbeck's-5
04Wilkes-Barre Scranton Penguins-13

Paddock, Gord
83Brandon Wheat Kings-3
88ProCards AHL-127
89ProCards AHL-351
90ProCards AHL/IHL-524

Paddock, John
80Nordiques Postcards-20
80Pepsi-Cola Caps-73
88ProCards AHL-142
90ProCards AHL/IHL-15
91Jets IGA-24
93Jets Ruffles-20
04Binghamton Senators-24

Padelek, Ales
98Czech OFS-303
00Czech OFS-260
02Czech OFS Plus-59
03Czech OFS Plus-16
04Czech OFS-15
06Czech HC Plzen Postcards-2
06Czech OFS-281
Goals Leaders-6

Padelek, Ivan
95Czech APS Extraliga-13
96Czech APS Extraliga-231
97Czech APS Extraliga-37
97Czech DS Stickers-25
98Czech OFS-304
98Czech OFS-486
99Czech OFS-435
00Czech DS Extraliga-168
00Czech OFS-252
01Czech OFS-26
02Czech OFS Plus-60
03Czech OFS Plus-17
03Czech OFS Plus Insert M-M22
04Czech OFS-235

Paden, Kevin
93Classic Four-Sport *-252
Gold-252
94Windsor Spitfires-15
95Tallahassee Tiger Sharks-8
98Huntington Blizzard-15
98Peoria Rivermen-24

Padgett, Trevor
93Quebec Pee-Wee Tournament-1173

Paek, Jim
88ProCards IHL-59
89ProCards IHL-158
90Alberta International Team Canada-7
91Pro Set Platinum-266
91O-Pee-Chee-437
91Parkhurst-133
French-133
91Penguins Coke/Elby's-2
91Penguins Foodland-1
91Pinnacle-344
French-344
91Pro Set-554
French-554
91Topps-437
91Upper Deck-308
French-308
92Bowman-383
92O-Pee-Chee-328
92Parkhurst-375
Emerald Ice-375
92Penguins Coke/Clark-16
92Penguins Foodland-11
92Penguins Foodland Coupon Stickers-9
92Score-537
Canadian-537
92Stadium Club-437
92Topps-243
Gold-243G
92Ultra-168
93OPC Premier-243
Gold-243
93Penguins Foodland-9
93Pinnacle-278
Canadian-278
93Score-334
Canadian-334
93Stadium Club-401
Members Only Master Set-401
First Day Issue-401
93Topps/OPC Premier-243
Gold-243
93Upper Deck-192
94Leaf-512
94OPC Premier-422
Special Effects-422
94Pinnacle-389
Artist's Proofs-389
Rink Collection-389
94Senators Team Issue-25
94Topps/OPC Premier-422
Special Effects-422
95Playoff One on One-288
95Houston Aeros-18
96Cleveland Lumberjacks-20
96Cleveland Lumberjacks Multi-Ad-22
97Cleveland Lumberjacks-21
97Cleveland Lumberjacks Postcards-5
98Cleveland Lumberjacks-16
99Cleveland Lumberjacks-18
00UK Nottingham Panthers-17
00UK Sekonda Superleague-131
02UK Nottingham Panthers-2

Paepke, Christoph
99German DEL-108
00German DEL-131
04German DEL-274

Paetsch, Nathan
01Moose Jaw Warriors-4
01UD Prospects-6
Jerseys-J-NP

Jerseys Gold-J-NP
03Rochester Americans-20
04Rochester Americans-15
05ITG Heroes/Prosp Toronto Expo Parallel -259
05Black Diamond-220
05Hot Prospects-108
En Fuego-108
Red Hot-108
White Hot-108
05SP Authentic-252
Limited-252
05SPx-247
05The Cup Masterpiece Pressplate Artifact-251
05The Cup Master Pressplate Black Diamond-220
05The Cup Masterpiece Pressplates (Ice)-254
05The Cup Master Pressplate Rookie Update-110
05The Cup Masterpiece Pressplates SPA-252
05The Cup Masterpiece Pressplates (SPx)-247
05The Cup Masterpiece Pressplates Trilogy-229
05UD Artifacts-251
05Upper Deck Ice-254
05Upper Deck Rookie Update-110
05Upper Deck Trilogy-229
05AHL All-Stars-26
05AHL Top Prospects-28
05ITG Heroes and Prospects-259
Autographs Series II-NP
06ITG Heroes and Prospects-68
AHL Shooting Stars-AS08
Autographs-ANP

Pafvels, Stig
57Swedish Alfabilder-85

Page, Alexandre
98Val d'Or Foreurs-21

Page, Anthony
97UK Guildford Flames-13
98UK Basingstoke Bison-9

Page, Chris
99Baie-Comeau Drakkar-18
03Tulsa Oilers-14

Page, Etienne
92Quebec Pee-Wee Tournament-715
93Quebec Pee-Wee Tournament-414

Page, Francois
98Mobile Mysticks-22
01Thetford Mines Coyotes-11
02Thetford Mines Coyotes-15
03Thetford Mines Prolab-15
04Thetford Mines Prolab-11

Page, Fred
93Action Packed HOF Induction-9

Page, Margot
94Classic Women of Hockey-W10

Page, Pierre
84Moncton Golden Flames-3
85Flames Red Rooster-20
86Flames Red Rooster-19
87Flames Red Rooster-22
91Nordiques Petro-Canada-22
92Nordiques Petro-Canada-23
93Kraft-46
02German Berlin Polar Bears Postcards-20
03German Berlin Polar Bears Postcards-22
04German Berlin Polar Bears Postcards-22

Page, Pietre
00Swiss Panini Stickers-5

Page, Scott
96Sudbury Wolves-16
96Sudbury Wolves Police-18
97Sudbury Wolves Police-8
99Bowman CHL-127
Gold-127
OPC International-127

Pageau, Cory
907th Inn. Sketch OHL-268

Pageau, Nicholas
05Belleville Bulls-13
06Belleville Bulls-18

Pagee, Lee
05Penticton Vees-14

Pagel, Rico
96Minnesota Golden Gophers-22
97Minnesota Golden Gophers-23
98Minnesota Golden Gophers-16
99Minnesota Golden Gophers-18

Paget, Derek
96Prince Albert Raiders-16
97Prince Albert Raiders-16
98Prince Albert Raiders-19
99Tallahassee Tiger Sharks-2
01Idaho Steelheads-12

Pagnutti, Matt
96Louisiana Ice Gators-12
97Louisiana Ice Gators-4
98Louisiana Ice Gators-13
99Louisiana Ice Gators-3
00Louisiana Ice Gators-19
02Arkansas Riverblades-10
03Florida Everblades-19
04Florida Everblades-3

Pagnutti, Rick
71Rochester Americans-15

Pahlsson, Samuel
95SP-183
95Swedish Leaf-273
95Swedish Upper Deck-168
97Swedish Collector's Choice-161
98Swedish UD Choice-180
Day in the Life-9
99Swedish Upper Deck-182
Lasting Impressions-10
00BAP Memorabilia-399
Emerald-399
Ruby-399
Sapphire-399
00BAP Signature Series-263
Emerald-263
Ruby-263
Sapphire-263
Autographs-225
Autographs Gold-225
00Black Diamond-91
00Crown Royale-109
00Private Stock-102
Gold-102
Premiere Date-102
Retail-102
Silver-102
PS-2001 Rookies-1
00Stadium Club-239
00Titanium-101
Retail-101
00Titanium Draft Day Edition-101
00Titanium Draft Day Promos-101
00Topps Stars-141
Blue-141
00Vanguard-101
Pacific Proofs-101
01Upper Deck Victory-10
Gold-10
02Upper Deck Vintage-3
02Cincinnati Mighty Ducks-A-2
03Upper Deck-251
Canadian Exclusives-251
HG-251
UD Exclusives-251
04Swedish Alfabilder Alfa Stars-26
04Swedish Alfabilder Autographs-125
04Swedish Alfabilder Limited Autographs-125
04Swedish Alfabilder Proof Parallels-26
04Swedish Elitset-176
Gold-176
04Swedish Pure Skills-21
Parallel-21
Professional Power-SP
Signatures-3
05Ducks Team Issue-16
05Parkhurst-8
Facsimile Auto Parallel-8
05Swedish SHL Elitset-33
06O-Pee-Chee-2
Rainbow-2
06Upper Deck-257
Exclusives Parallel-257
High Gloss Parallel-257
Masterpieces-257

Paice, Frank
62Topps-61

Paiement, Adam
00Belleville Bulls-17
01Belleville Bulls-17
02Belleville Bulls-14
03Laredo Bucks-15

Paiement, Jonathan
01Sherbrooke Castors-7
03Lewiston Maineiacs-15

Paiement, Real
81Milwaukee Admirals-2

Paiement, Rosaire
70Canucks Royal Bank-11
70Colgate Stamps-39
70Dad's Cookies-94
70Esso Power Players-48
70O-Pee-Chee-226
70Sargent Promotions Stamps-220
71Canucks Royal Bank-9
71O-Pee-Chee-233
71Sargent Promotions Stamps-218
71Topps-24
71Toronto Sun-285
72Canucks Nalley's-4
72O-Pee-Chee-333
73O-Pee-Chee WHA Posters-5
73Quaker Oats WHA-3
74O-Pee-Chee WHA-7
75O-Pee-Chee WHA-106
76O-Pee-Chee WHA-37
77O-Pee-Chee WHA-36

Paiement, Steven
907th Inn. Sketch QMJHL-126
98Thetford Mines Coyotes-1

Paiement, Wilf
74O-Pee-Chee NHL-292
75O-Pee-Chee NHL-195
75O-Pee-Chee NHL-319
75Topps-195
75Topps-319
76O-Pee-Chee NHL-37
76Rockies Coke Cans-15
76Rockies Puck Bucks-14
76Topps-37
77O-Pee-Chee NHL-130
77Rockies Coke Cans-14
77Topps-130
78O-Pee-Chee-145
78Topps-145
79Panini Stickers-67
79O-Pee-Chee-190
79Topps-190
80Maple Leafs Postcards-19
80O-Pee-Chee-225
80Pepsi-Cola Caps-93
80Topps-225
81Maple Leafs Postcards-17
81O-Pee-Chee-306
81O-Pee-Chee-311
81O-Pee-Chee-326
81O-Pee-Chee Stickers-96
81O-Pee-Chee Stickers-110
81Post Standups-22
81Topps-25
81Topps-63
82Nordiques Postcards-15
82O-Pee-Chee-288
82O-Pee-Chee Stickers-22
82Post Cereal-16
82Topps Stickers-22
83NHL Key Tags-111
83Nordiques Postcards-19
83O-Pee-Chee-298
83Vachon-70
84Nordiques Postcards-19
84O-Pee-Chee-285
84O-Pee-Chee Stickers-175
85Nordiques Provigo-18
85O-Pee-Chee Stickers-152
86Nordiques McDonald's-18
86Sabres Blue Shield-21
86Sabres Blue Shield Small-21
87O-Pee-Chee-180
87Panini Stickers-32
87Topps-180
01Upper Deck Legends-72
02UD Foundations-81
02UD Foundations-93
04ITG Franchises US West-188
04ITG Franchises US West-226
Autographs-A-WP1
Autographs-A-WP2
06Parkhurst-160
06Parkhurst-188
06Parkhurst-247
Autographs-160
Autographs-188
Autographs-247

Paige, Jason
04Notre Dame Fighting Irish-16

Paige, Kyle
04Guelph Storm-17
06Oshawa Generals-10

Paille, Daniel
01Guelph Storm-12
01Guelph Storm Memorial Cup-12
02BAP Memorabilia Draft Redemptions-20
02Guelph Storm-5
03Guelph Storm-13
04Rochester Americans-16
04ITG Heroes and Prospects-67
Autographs-DP
04ITG Heroes/Prospects Toronto Expo '05-67
04ITG Heroes/Prospects Expo Heroes/Pros-67
05Black Diamond-219
05Hot Prospects-223
Hot Materials-HMPA
White Hot-223
05Parkhurst-611
Facsimile Auto Parallel-611
05SP Authentic-198
05SP Game Used-194
05SPx-223
Spectrum-223
05The Cup-169
Autographed Rookie Patches Gold Rainbow-169
Black Rainbow Rookies-169
Masterpiece Pressplates (Artifacts)-253
Masterpiece Pressplates (Black Diamond)-219
Masterpiece Pressplates (Ice)-253
Masterpiece Pressplates (Rookie Update)-242
Masterpiece Pressplates SPA Autos-198
Masterpiece Pressplates (SP Game Used)-194
Masterpiece Pressplates SPx Autos-223
Masterpiece Pressplates (Trilogy)-228
Masterpiece Pressplates Ult Coll-137
Masterpiece Pressplates Autographs-169
Platinum Rookies-169
05UD Artifacts-253
05Ultimate Collection-137
Gold-137
05Upper Deck Ice-253
05Upper Deck Rookie Update-242
05Upper Deck Trilogy-228
06Be A Player Portraits First Exposures-FEDP
06Be A Player Portraits Signature Portraits-SPDP
06Black Diamond Jerseys-JPA
06Black Diamond Jerseys Black-JPA
06Black Diamond Jerseys Gold-JPA
06Black Diamond Jerseys Ruby-JPA
06Rochester Americans-16
06Upper Deck Game Jerseys-JDP
06Upper Deck Game Patches-PDP
06Upper Deck Signatures-SDP
06ITG Heroes and Prospects Jerseys-GUJ28
06ITG Heroes and Prospects Jerseys Gold-GUJ28
06ITG Heroes and Prospects Emblems-GUE28
06ITG Heroes and Prospects Emblems Gold-GUE28
06ITG Heroes and Prospects Numbers-GUN28
06ITG Heroes and Prospects Numbers Gold-GUN28

Paille, Marcel
44Beehive Group II Photos-350
50Quebec Citadelles-16
52Bas Du Fleuve-51
52Juniors Blue Tint-64
64Beehive Group III Photos-145
64Coca-Cola Caps-90
64Topps-92
94Parkhurst Tall Boys-101

Pain, Jason
97Louisville Riverfrogs-4
98Muskegon Fury-2
00Fort Worth Brahmas-12

Pain, Mike
03Saginaw Spirit-15

Painchaud, Chad
03Mississauga Ice Dogs-16
05OHL Bell All-Star Classic-35

Painchaud, Marco
93Quebec Pee-Wee Tournament-43

Painchaud, Olivier
06Chicoutimi Sagueneens-17
06Saint Johns Sea Dogs-15

Paine, Greg
91Ferris State Bulldogs-25
92Ferris State Bulldogs-25

Painter, Glenn
93Memphis RiverKings-11
95Madison Monsters-19
96Fort Worth Fire-8

Paisley, Brooks
97Brandon Wheat Kings-18

Paisley, Jeff
00Mississauga Ice Dogs-20

Paivinen, Matti
66Finnish Jaakiekkosarja-23

Pajala, Jukka
70Finnish Jaakiekko-375

Pajerski, ?
70Swedish Masterserien-200

Pajerski, Sebastien
99Indianapolis Ice-15

Pajic, Rok
06Czech OFS-98

Pajonkowski, Franck
93Swedish Semic World Champ Stickers-264
94Finnish Jaa Kiekko-230
94French National Team-22
95Swedish Globe World Championships-201
96Swedish Semic Wien-190

Pajor, Greg
98BC Icemen-12
98BC Icemen II-13

Pajula, Jari-Pekka
00Finnish Cardset-154
01Finnish Cardset-46

Pakarinen, Sten
72Finnish Jaakiekko-350

Pakaslahti, Petri
98Finnish Kerailysarja-176
99Finnish Cardset-289
00Finnish Cardset-307
01Finnish Cardset-260
02Finnish Cardset-89
03Finnish Cardset-64
04Finnish Cardset-72
Parallel-54
05Finnish Cardset -60
06Finnish Cardset-62

Pakola, Seppo
78Finnish SM-Liiga-23
80Finnish Mallasjuoma-2

Paksal, Reijo
66Finnish Jaakiekkosarja-67
70Finnish Jaakiekko-146
71Finnish Suomi Stickers-196
72Finnish Jaakiekko-234
73Finnish Jaakiekko-268

Palacek, Josef
95Czech APS Extraliga-314
00Czech OFS-29

Paladjev, Evgenij
69Russian National Team Postcards-12
70Finnish Jaakiekko-12
70Russian National Team Postcards-7
70Swedish Hockey-317
70Swedish Masterserien-131
70Swedish Masterserien-137
73Finnish Jaakiekko-12
73Russian National Team-21
74Finnish Jenkki-52

Palahicky, Shane
03Alaska Aces-14
05Bossier-Shreveport Mudbugs-13

Palahnuk, Robb
00Sarnia Sting-20
01Memphis RiverKings-10

Palamar, Ed
52Juniors Blue Tint-9

Palangio, Peter
34Beehive Group I Photos-72

Palaski, Scott
99Sioux City Musketeers-19

Palav, Mathieu
93Quebec Pee-Wee Tournament-1645

Palazzari, Doug
77O-Pee-Chee NHL-354

Palazzo, Justin
05Prince Albert Raiders-18
06Prince Albert Raiders-21

Palecek, Josef
72Finnish Jaakiekko-17
72Finnish Hellas-94
73Finnish Jaakiekko-59
74Finnish Jenkki-80
96Czech APS Extraliga-141
97Czech APS Extraliga-243
99Czech OFS-347
06Czech OFS Coaches-7

Palecek, Lukas
97Czech APS Extraliga-263
99Czech Score Blue 2000-8
99Czech Score Red Ice 2000-8

Paleczny, Larry
95Slapshot-303
95Owen Sound Platers-22
96Owen Sound Platers-20
97Owen Sound Platers-16
97Bowman CHL-29
OPC-29

Palffy, Zigmund
91Upper Deck-16
91Upper Deck-71
French-16
French-71
91Upper Deck Czech World Juniors-97
91Classic-23
91Classic Four-Sport *-23
92Finnish Semic-140
93Donruss-459
93Parkhurst-397
Emerald Ice-397
94Fleer-128
94Leaf-253
94OPC Premier-459
Special Effects-459
94Parkhurst SE-SE107
Gold-SE107
94Pinnacle-256
Artist's Proofs-256
Rink Collection-256
Rookie Team Pinnacle-5
94Score-235
Gold-235
Platinum-235
94Select-196
Gold-196
94Topps/OPC Premier-459
Special Effects-459
94Ultra-329
94Upper Deck-343
94Upper Deck-529
Electric Ice-343
Electric Ice-529
SP Inserts-SP138
SP Inserts Die Cuts-SP138
94Finnish Jaa Kiekko-207
94Classic Pro Prospects-50
95Be A Player-24
Signatures-S24
Signatures Die Cuts-S24
95Canada Games NHL POGS-169
95Collector's Choice-94
Player's Club-94
Player's Club Platinum-94
95Donruss-316
95Donruss Elite-13
Die Cut Stars-13
Die Cut Uncut-13
95Finest-117
Refractors-117
95Metal-92
95Parkhurst International-131
Emerald Ice-131
95Pinnacle-88
Artist's Proofs-88
Rink Collection-88
Global Gold-14
95Playoff One on One-172
95Score-267
Black Ice Artist's Proofs-267
Black Ice-267
95SP-86
95Stadium Club-99
Members Only Master Set-99
95Summit-144
Artist's Proofs-144
Ice-144
95Topps-348
OPC Inserts-348
95Ultra-97
95Ultra-269
Gold Medallion-97
High Speed-14
95Upper Deck-140
Electric Ice-140
Electric Ice Gold-140
Special Edition-SE51
Special Edition Gold-SE51
95Slovakian APS National Team-24
96Be A Player Biscuit In The Basket-15
96Black Diamond-6
Gold-6
96Collector's Choice-156
96Collector's Choice-323
MVP-UD24
MVP Gold-UD24
96Donruss-45
Press Proofs-45
96Donruss Canadian Ice-58
Gold Press Proofs-58
Red Press Proofs-58
96Donruss Elite-52
Die Cut Stars-52
96Flair-56
Blue Ice-56
96Fleer-66
96Fleer Picks-50
Fabulous 50-38
Jagged Edge-20
96Islander Postcards-16
96Kraft Upper Deck-9
96Kraft Upper Deck-38
96Leaf-23
Press Proofs-23
Fire On Ice-7
96Leaf Leather And Laces Promos-P7
96Leaf Leather And Laces-7
96Leaf Limited-57
Gold-57
96Leaf Preferred-103
Press Proofs-103
Steel-32
Steel Gold-32
96Maggers-74
96McDonald's Pinnacle-18
96Metal Universe-95
96Pinnacle-100
Artist's Proofs-100
Foil-100
Premium Stock-100
Rink Collection-100
96Playoff One on One-379
96Score-120
Artist's Proofs-120
Dealer's Choice Artist's Proofs-120
Special Artist's Proofs-120
Golden Blades-120
96Select Certified-23
Artist's Proofs-23
Blue-23
Mirror Blue-23
Mirror Gold-23
Mirror Red-23
Red-23
96SkyBox Impact-77
BladeRunners-18
96SP-97
Holoview Collection-HC28
96SPx-29
Gold-29
96Summit-20
Artist's Proofs-20
Ice-20
Metal-20
Premium Stock-20
96Team Out-15
96Ultra-103
Gold Medallion-103
96Upper Deck-97
Generation Next-X17
Superstar Showdown-SS21A
96Upper Deck Ice-94
Parallel-94
96Zenith-97
Artist's Proofs-97
Assailants-7
96Swedish Semic Wien-234
96Collector's Edge Ice-195
Crucibles-C24
Prism-195
97SLU Hockey Canadian-14
97SLU Hockey American-16
97Be A Player-135
Autographs-135
Autographs Die-Cuts-135
Autographs Prismatic Die-Cuts-135
97Beehive-42
Golden Portraits-42
97Black Diamond-18
Double Diamond-18
Triple Diamond-18
Quadruple Diamond-18
97Collector's Choice-150
Crash the Game-C16A
Crash the Game-C16B
Crash the Game-C16C
Crash the Game Exchange-CR16
Star Quest-SQ66
Stick'Ums-S16
97Crown Royale-79
Emerald Green-79
Ice Blue-79
Silver-79
Hat Tricks Die-Cuts-10
97Donruss-125
Press Proofs Silver-125
Press Proofs Gold-125
Red Alert-8
97Donruss Canadian Ice-33
Dominion Series-33
Provincial Series-33
97Donruss Elite-34
97Donruss Elite-130
Aspirations-34
Aspirations-130
Status-34
Status-130
97Donruss Limited-12
97Donruss Limited-163
97Donruss Limited-181
Exposure-12
Exposure-163
Exposure-181
Fabric of the Game-24
97Donruss Preferred-106
Cut to the Chase-106
97Donruss Priority-58
97Donruss Priority-212
Stamp of Approval-58
Stamp of Approval-212
Direct Deposit-22
Direct Deposit Promos-P22
Postcards-32
Stamps-32
Stamps Bronze-32
Stamps Gold-32
Stamps Silver-32
97Jell-O Juniors To Pros-11
97Katch-90
Gold-90
Silver-90
97Kenner Starting Lineup Cards-16
97Kraft-17
97Leaf-55
Fractal Matrix-55
Fractal Matrix Die Cuts-55
Banner Season-12
97Leaf International-55
Universal Ice-55
97NHL Aces Playing Cards-48
97Pacific-5
Copper-5
Emerald Green-5
Ice Blue-5
Red-5
Silver-5
Team Checklists-15
97Pacific Dynagon-74
Copper-74
Dark Grey-74
Emerald Green-74
Ice Blue-74
Red-74
Silver-74
Best Kept Secrets-57
Dynamic Duos-9B
Tandems-11
97Pacific Invincible-82
Copper-82
Emerald Green-82
Ice Blue-82
Red-82
Silver-82
Attack Zone-13
Feature Performers-20
NHL Regime-119
97Pacific Omega-140
Copper-140
Dark Gray-140
Emerald Green-140
Gold-140
Ice Blue-140
Stick Handle Laser Cuts-12
97Panini Stickers-73
97Paramount-109
Copper-109
Dark Grey-109
Emerald Green-109
Ice Blue-109
Red-109
Silver-109
97Pinnacle-56
Artist's Proofs-56
Rink Collection-56
Press Plates Back Black-56
Press Plates Back Cyan-56
Press Plates Back Magenta-56
Press Plates Back Yellow-56
Press Plates Front Black-56
Press Plates Front Cyan-56
Press Plates Front Magenta-56
Press Plates Front Yellow-56
97Pinnacle Certified-94
Red-94
Mirror Blue-94
Mirror Gold-94
Mirror Red-94
97Pinnacle Inside-14
Coach's Collection-14
Executive Collection-14
Track-22
97Pinnacle Tot Cert Platinum Blue-94
97Pinnacle Tot Certi Platinum Gold-94
97Pinnacle Totally Certified Platinum Red-94
97Pinnacle Tot Cert Mirror Platinum Gold-94
97Revolution-82
Copper-82
Emerald-82
Ice Blue-82
Silver-82
Team Checklist Laser Cuts-15
97Score-106
Artist's Proofs-106
Golden Blades-106
97SP Authentic-91
Icons-I38
Icons Die-Cuts-I38
Icons Embossed-I38
97SPx-28
Bronze-28
Gold-28
Silver-28
Steel-28
Dimension-SPX13
Grand Finale-28
97Studio-46
Press Proofs Silver-46
Press Proofs Gold-46
Hard Hats-13
Portraits-31
97Upper Deck-99
Sixth Sense Masters-SS26
Sixth Sense Wizards-SS26
Smooth Grooves-SG5
The Specialists-22
The Specialists Level 2 Die Cuts-22
97Upper Deck Diamond Vision-21
Signature Moves-21
97Upper Deck Ice-16
Parallel-16
Power Shift-16
97Zenith-30
Z-Gold-30
Z-Silver-30
97Zenith 5 x 7-27
Gold Impulse-27
Silver Impulse-27
98Aurora-117
Championship Fever-29
Championship Fever Copper-29
Championship Fever Ice Blue-29
Championship Fever Red-29
Championship Fever Silver-29
Man Advantage-12
98Be A Player-236
Press Release-236
98BAP Gold-236
98BAP Autographs-236
98BAP Autographs Gold-236
98Black Diamond-53
Double Diamond-53
Triple Diamond-53
Quadruple Diamond-53
Winning Formula Gold-WF17
Winning Formula Platinum-WF17
98Bowman's Best-15
Refractors-15
Atomic Refractors-15
98Crown Royale-84
Limited Series-84
98Finest-40
No Protectors-40
No Protectors Refractors-40
Refractors-40
Centurion-C6
Centurion Refractors-C6
Red Lighters-R20
Red Lighters Refractors-R20
98Islanders Power Play-NYI4
98Katch-88
98OPC Chrome-184
Refractors-184
Season's Best-SB17
Season's Best Refractors-SB17
98Pacific-284
Ice Blue-284
Red-284
Gold Crown Die-Cuts-22
Team Checklists-16
98Pacific Dynagon Ice-116
Blue-116
Red-116
98Pacific Omega-149
Red-149
Opening Day Issue-149
Online-21
98Panini Photocards-59
98Panini Stickers-73
98Paramount-145
Copper-145
Emerald Green-145
Holo-Electric-145
Ice Blue-145
Silver-145
Special Delivery Die-Cuts-11
Team Checklists Die-Cuts-16
98Revolution-89
Ice Shadow-89
Red-89
Showstoppers-22
98SP Authentic-52
Power Shift-52
Snapshots-SS24
98SPx Finite-114
Radiance-114
Spectrum-114
98SPx Top Prospects-36
Radiance-36
Spectrum-36
Highlight Heroes-H19
Lasting Impressions-L29
98Topps-184
O-Pee-Chee-184
Local Legends-L3
Mystery Finest Bronze-M11
Mystery Finest Bronze Refractors-M11
Mystery Finest Gold-M11
Mystery Finest Gold Refractors-M11
Mystery Finest Silver-M11
Mystery Finest Silver Refractors-M11
Season's Best-SB17
98UD Choice-121
Mini Bobbing Head-BH13
98UD Choice Preview-121
98UD Choice Prime Choice Reserve-121
98UD Choice Reserve-121
98UD3-44
98UD3-104
98UD3-164
Die-Cuts-44
Die-Cuts-104
Die-Cuts-164
98Upper Deck-315
Exclusives-315
Exclusives 1 of 1-315
Fantastic Finishers-FF10
Fantastic Finishers Quantum 1-FF10
Fantastic Finishers Quantum 2-FF10
Fantastic Finishers Quantum 3-FF10
Gold Reserve-315
98Upper Deck MVP-125
Gold Script-125
Silver Script-125
Super Script-125
98Slovakian Eurotel-17
99Aurora-69
Striped-69
Premiere Date-69
Premiere Date Striped-69
99BAP Memorabilia-98
Gold-98
Silver-98
99BAP Millennium-120
Emerald-120
Ruby-120
Sapphire-120
Signatures-120
Signatures Gold-120
99Black Diamond-44
Diamond Cut-44
Final Cut-44
Diamonation-D20
99Crown Royale-66
Limited Series-66
Premiere Date-66
International Glory-12
International Glory Parallel-12
99Kings AAA Magnets-2
99O-Pee-Chee-8
99O-Pee-Chee Chrome-8
99O-Pee-Chee Chrome Refractors-8
99Pacific-261
Copper-261
Emerald Green-261
Gold-261
Ice Blue-261
Premiere Date-261
Red-261
Team Leaders-17
99Pacific Dynagon Ice-97
Blue-97
Copper-97
Gold-97
Premiere Date-97
Checkmates American-11
Checkmates American-26
Checkmates Canadian-26
99Pacific Omega-110
Copper-110
Gold-110
Ice Blue-110
Premiere Date-110
99Pacific Prism-68
Holographic Blue-68
Holographic Gold-68
Holographic Mirror-68
Holographic Purple-68
Premiere Date-68
Clear Advantage-11
99Panini Stickers-257
99Paramount-111
Copper-111
Emerald-111
Gold-111
Holographic Emerald-111
Holographic Gold-111
Holographic Silver-111
Ice Blue-111
Premiere Date-111
Red-111
Silver-111
99Revolution-70
Premiere Date-70
Red-70
Shadow Series-70
Copper-70
Gold-70
CSC Silver-70
99SP Authentic-41
Buyback Signatures-43
Buyback Signatures-44
Buyback Signatures-45
Buyback Signatures-46
Buyback Signatures-47
Sign of the Times-ZP
Sign of the Times Gold-ZP
99SPx-76
Radiance-76
Spectrum-76
99Stadium Club-154
First Day Issue-154
One of a Kind-154
Printing Plates Black-154
Printing Plates Cyan-154
Printing Plates Magenta-154
Printing Plates Yellow-154
Chrome-41
Chrome Refractors-41
99Topps/OPC-8
99Topps/OPC Chrome-8
Refractors-8
99Topps Gold Label Class 1-17
Black-17
Black One of One-17
One of One-17
Red-17
Red One of One-17
99Topps Gold Label Class 2-17
99Topps Gold Label Class 2 Black-17
99Topps Gold Label Class 2 Black 1 of 1-17
99Topps Gold Label Class 2 One of One-17
99Topps Gold Label Class 2 Red-17
99Topps Gold Label Class 2 Red One of One-17
99Topps Gold Label Class 3-17
99Topps Gold Label Class 3 Black-17
99Topps Gold Label Class 3 Black 1 of 1-17
99Topps Gold Label Class 3 One of One-17
99Topps Gold Label Class 3 Red-17
99Topps Gold Label Class 3 Red One of One-17
99Topps Gold Label Prime Gold-PG5
99Topps Gold Label Prime Gold One of One -PG5
99Topps Gold Label Prime Gold Black-PG5
99Topps Gold Label Prime Gold Black One of One -PG5
99Topps Gold Label Prime Gold Red-PG5
99Topps Gold Label Prime Gold Red One of One -PG5
99Topps Premier Plus-59
Parallel-59
Code Red-CR3
99Ultimate Victory-42
1/1-42
Parallel-42
Parallel 100-42
99Upper Deck-238
Exclusives-238
Exclusives 1 of 1-238
99Upper Deck Gold Reserve-238
99Upper Deck HoloGrFx-29
Ausome-29
99Upper Deck MVP SC Edition-84
Gold Script-84
Silver Script-84
Super Script-84
Stanley Cup Talent-SC9
99Upper Deck Ovation-30
Standing Ovation-30
Lead Performers-LP13
99Upper Deck Victory-139
99Wayne Gretzky Hockey-80
99Slovakian Challengers-7
00Aurora-67
Premiere Date-67
00BAP Memorabilia-184
Emerald-184
Ruby-184
Sapphire-184
Promos-184
00BAP Mem Chicago Sportsfest Copper-184
00BAP Memorabilia Chicago Sportsfest Blue-184
00BAP Memorabilia Chicago Sportsfest Gold-184
00BAP Memorabilia Chicago Sportsfest Ruby-184
00BAP Memorabilia Chicago Sun-Times Ruby-184
00BAP Memorabilia Chicago Sun-Times Gold-184
00BAP Mem Chicago Sun-Times Sapphire-184
00BAP Mem Toronto Fall Expo Copper-184
00BAP Memorabilia Toronto Fall Expo Gold-184
00BAP Memorabilia Toronto Fall Expo Ruby-184
00BAP Parkhurst 2000-P75
00BAP Signature Series-191
Emerald-191
Ruby-191
Sapphire-191
Autographs-159
Autographs Gold-159
He Shoots-He Scores Points-14
00Crown Royale-49
Ice Blue-49
Limited Series-49
Premiere Date-49
Red-49
00O-Pee-Chee-13
00O-Pee-Chee Parallel-13
00Pacific-200

Copper-200
Gold-200
Ice Blue-200
Premiere Date-200
Reflections-12
00Panini Stickers-167
00Paramount-113
Copper-113
Gold-113
Holo-Gold-113
Holo-Silver-113
Ice Blue-113
Premiere Date-113
00Private Stock-46
Gold-46
Premiere Date-46
Retail-46
Silver-46
Game Gear-55
PS-2001 Action-26
00Revolution-68
Blue-68
Premiere Date-68
Red-68
HD NHL-17
00SP Authentic-42
00SP Game Used-30
00SPx-32
Spectrum-32
00Stadium Club-31
Beam Team-BT27
00Titanium-42
Blue-42
Gold-42
Premiere Date-42
Red-42
Retail-42
All-Stars-6W
Game Gear-22
Game Gear-23
Three-Star Selections-15
00Topps/OPC-13
Parallel-13
00Topps Chrome-13
OPC Refractors-13
Refractors-13
00Topps Gold Label Class 1-16
Gold-16
00Topps Gold Label Class 2-16
00Topps Gold Label Class 2 Gold-16
00Topps Gold Label Class 3-16
00Topps Gold Label Class 3 Gold-16
00Topps Heritage-15
Chrome Parallel-15
00Topps Premier Plus-21
Blue Ice-21
00Topps Stars-8
Blue-8
Game Gear-GGZP
00UD Heroes-56
00UD Pros and Prospects-41
00UD Reserve-40
00Upper Deck-309
Exclusives Tier 1-309
Exclusives Tier 2-309
Skilled Stars-SS12
00Upper Deck Legends-59
Legendary Collection Bronze-59
Legendary Collection Gold-59
Legendary Collection Silver-59
00Upper Deck MVP-89
First Stars-89
Game-Used Souvenirs-GSZP
Second Stars-89
Super Game-Used Souvenirs-GSZP
Talent-M9
Third Stars-89
00Upper Deck Victory-114
00Upper Deck Victory-305
00Upper Deck Vintage-162
00Upper Deck Vintage-172
00Vanguard-48
High Voltage-17
High Voltage Gold-17
High Voltage Green-17
High Voltage Red-17
High Voltage Silver-17
Holographic Gold-48
Holographic Purple-48
Pacific Proofs-48
Press East/West-8
00Czech Stadion-124
01Atomic-47
Blue-47
Gold-47
Premiere Date-47
Red-47
Core Players-7
Power Play-17
Statosphere-15
01BAP Memorabilia-284
Emerald-284
Ruby-284
Sapphire-284
All-Star Jerseys-ASJ3
All-Star Emblems-ASE3
All-Star Numbers-ASN3
All-Star Teammates-AST1
Country of Origin-CO39
Stanley Cup Playoffs-SC11
01BAP Signature Series Certified 100-C50
01BAP Signature Series Certified 50-C50
01BAP Signature Series Certified 1 of 1's-C50
01BAP Signature Series Autographs-LZP
01BAP Signature Series Autographs Gold-LZP
01BAP Signature Series Franchise Jerseys-FP-14
01BAP Sig Series He Shoots/Scores Prizes-31
01BAP Signature Series Jerseys-GJ-30
01BAP Signature Series Jersey Autographs-GUZP
01BAP Sig Series Jersey and Stick Cards-GSJ-30
01BAP Signature Series Teammates-TM-14
01BAP Update He Shoots-He Scores Prizes-18
01Bowman YoungStars-40
Gold-40
Ice Cubed-40
01Crown Royale-69
Blue-69
Premiere Date-69
Red-69
Retail-69
01eTopps-32
01O-Pee-Chee-25
01O-Pee-Chee Heritage Parallel-25
01O-Pee-Chee Heritage Parallel Limited-25
01O-Pee-Chee Premier Parallel-25
01Pacific-184
01Pacific-413
01Pacific-432
Extreme LTD-184
Gold-413
Gold-432
Hobby LTD-184
Premiere Date-184
Retail LTD-184
All-Stars-W5
01Pacific Adrenaline-87
Blue-87
Premiere Date-87
Red-87
Retail-87
World Beaters-8
01Pacific Arena Exclusives-184
01Pacific Arena Exclusives-413
01Pacific Arena Exclusives-432
01Pacific Heads-Up-46
Blue-46
Premiere Date-46
Red-46
Silver-46
All-Star Net-4
Stat Masters-9
01Parkhurst-14
Gold-14
Silver-14
Jerseys-PJ26
Sticks-PS26
World Class Jerseys-WCJ4
World Class Emblems-WCE4
World Class Numbers-WCN4
01Private Stock-45
Gold-45
Premiere Date-45
Retail-45
Silver-45
01Private Stock Pacific Nights-45
01Private Stock PS-2002-36
01Private Stock Reserve-S8
01SP Authentic-39
Limited-39
Limited Gold-39
Sign of the Times-ZP
Sign of the Times-PP
Sign of the Times-PHG
01SP Game Used-26
Authentic Fabric-AFZP
Authentic Fabric-DFPP
Authentic Fabric Gold-AFZP
Inked Sweaters-ISZP
Inked Sweaters-DSGP
Inked Sweaters-DSPB
01SPx-30
01SPx-77
Hidden Treasures-DTPS
01Sports Illustrated for Kids III-36
01Stadium Club-20
Award Winners-20
Master Photos-20
Gallery-G26
Gallery Gold-G26
Perennials-P14
01Titanium-66
Hobby Parallel-66
Premiere Date-66
Retail-66
Retail Parallel-66
All-Stars-11
Double-Sided Jerseys-17
Double-Sided Jerseys-75
Double-Sided Patches-17
Double-Sided Patches-75
01Topps-25
Heritage Parallel-25
Heritage Parallel Limited-25
OPC Parallel-25
Own The Game-OTG10
Shot Masters-SM9
01Topps Chrome-25
Refractors-25
Black Border Refractors-25
01Topps Heritage-13
Refractors-13
01Topps Reserve-27
01UD Challenge for the Cup-40
Jerseys-UCPD
Jersey Autographs-UCAP
01UD Honor Roll-93
01UD Mask Collection-44
Gold-44
Double Patches-DPZP
Jerseys-J-ZP
Jersey and Patch-JPZP
01UD Playmakers-48
Jerseys-J-ZP
Jerseys Gold-J-ZP
01UD Premier Collection Dual Jerseys-DSP
01UD Premier Collection Dual Jersey Black-DSP
01UD Premier Collection Jerseys-BZP
01UD Premier Collection Jerseys Black-B-ZP
01UD Premier Collection Signatures-ZP
01UD Premier Collection Signatures Black-ZP
01UD Top Shelf-20
Sticks-SZP
Sticks Gold-SZP
01Upper Deck-79
01Upper Deck-223
Exclusives-79
Exclusives-223
Crunch Timers-CT7
Fantastic Finishers-FF10
Franchise Cornerstones-FC7
Game Jerseys Series II-PFZP
Shooting Stars-SS9
Skilled Stars-SS10
01Upper Deck Ice-22
01Upper Deck MVP-84
Souvenirs-C-ZP
Souvenirs Gold-C-ZP
Talent-MT11
01Upper Deck Victory-160
01Upper Deck Victory-424
Gold-160
Gold-424
01Upper Deck Vintage-114
01Upper Deck Vintage-121
01Upper Deck Vintage-122
01Vanguard-45
Blue-45
Red-45
Memorabilia-48
One of Ones-45
Premiere Date-45
Proofs-45
01Slovakian Kvarteto-4C
01Utah Grizzlies-12
02Kings Team Issue-2
02Atomic-49
Blue-49
Gold-49
Red-49
Hobby Parallel-49
Power Converters-10
02BAP All-Star Edition-70
Jerseys-70
Jerseys Gold-70
Jerseys Silver-70
02BAP First Edition-17
02BAP First Edition-354
Jerseys-17
02BAP Memorabilia-165
02BAP Memorabilia-214
Emerald-165
Emerald-214
Ruby-165
Ruby-214
Sapphire-165
Sapphire-214
All-Star Jerseys-ASJ-44
Franchise Players-FP-14
NHL All-Star Game-165
NHL All-Star Game-214
NHL All-Star Game Blue-165
NHL All-Star Game Blue-214
NHL All-Star Game Green-165
NHL All-Star Game Green-214
NHL All-Star Game Red-165
NHL All-Star Game Red-214
Teammates-TM-13
02BAP Memorabilia Toronto Fall Expo-165
02BAP Memorabilia Toronto Fall Expo-214
02BAP Signature Series-128
Autographs-128
Autograph Buybacks 1998-236
Autograph Buybacks 1999-120
Autograph Buybacks 2000-159
Autograph Buybacks 2001-LZP
Autographs Gold-128
Jerseys-SGJ44
Jersey Autographs-SGJ44
02Bowman YoungStars-91
Gold-91
Silver-91
02Crown Royale-45
Blue-45
Red-45
Retail-45
Jerseys-8
Jerseys Gold-8
Lords of the Rink-11
02ITG Used-37
02ITG Used-137
Franchise Players-F14
Franchise Players Autographs-F14
Franchise Players Gold-F14
International Experience-IE8
International Experience Gold-IE8
Jerseys-GUJ44
Jersey Autographs-GUJ44
Jerseys Gold-GUJ44
Jersey and Stick-SJ44
Jersey and Stick Gold-SJ44
Teammates-T17
Teammates Gold-T17
02Kings Game Sheets-35
02Kings Game Sheets-36
02O-Pee-Chee-110
02O-Pee-Chee Premier Blue Parallel-110
02O-Pee-Chee Premier Red Parallel-110
02O-Pee-Chee Factory Set-110
02Pacific-171
Blue-171
Red-171
02Pacific Complete-203
Red-203
02Pacific Exclusive-81
02Pacific Heads-Up-57
Blue-57
Purple-57
Red-57
Quad Jerseys-13
Quad Jerseys-34
Quad Jerseys Gold-13
Quad Jerseys Gold-34
02Pacific Quest for the Cup-44
Gold-44
02Parkhurst-123
Bronze-123
Gold-123
Silver-123
Franchise Players-FP14
Jerseys-GJ17
Stick and Jerseys-SJ17
Teammates-TT6
02Parkhurst Retro-27
Minis-27
02Private Stock Reserve-46
Blue-46
Red-46
Retail-46
02SP Authentic-43
Beckett Promos-43
Super Premiums-SPZP
02SP Game Used-23
Authentic Fabrics-AFZP
Authentic Fabrics Gold-AFZP
Authentic Fabrics Rainbow-AFZP
Piece of History-PHZP
Piece of History Gold-PHZP
Piece of History Rainbow-PHZP
02SPx-37
Spectrum Gold-37
Spectrum Silver-37
Winning Materials-WMPA
Winning Materials-WMZP
Winning Materials Gold-PA
Winning Materials Gold-ZP
Winning Materials Silver-PA
Winning Materials Silver-ZP
02Stadium Club-56
Silver Decoy Cards-56
Proofs-56
Passport-12
World Stage-WS12
02Titanium-50
Blue-50
Red-50
Retail-50
02Topps-110
OPC Blue Parallel-110
OPC Red Parallel-110
Factory Set-110
02Topps Chrome All-Star Fantasy-2
02Topps Chrome-70
Black Border Refractors-70
Refractors-70
02Topps Heritage-42
Chrome Parallel-42
02Topps Total-77
02UD Artistic Impressions-42
Gold-42
Artist's Touch-ATZP
Artist's Touch Gold-ATZP
02UD Artistic Impressions Beckett Promos-42
02UD Artistic Impressions Retrospectives-R42
02UD Artistic Impressions Retrospect Gold-R42
02UD Artistic Impress Retrospect Silver-R42
02UD Honor Roll-35
02UD Mask Collection-41
02UD Mask Collection Beckett Promos-41
02UD Mask Collection Instant Offense-IOZP
02UD Mask Collection Patches-PGZP
02UD Piece of History-45
Patches-PHZP
02UD Premier Collection-28
02UD Top Shelf-39
Clutch Performers-CPZP
Dual Player Jerseys-RBZ
Goal Oriented-GOZP
Shooting Stars-SHZP
Signatures-ZP
Sweet Sweaters-SWZP
Triple Jerseys-HTAPS
Triple Jerseys-TSAPP
02Upper Deck-326
Exclusives-326
02Upper Deck Beckett UD Promos-326
02Upper Deck Difference Makers-ZP
02Upper Deck Patchwork-PWZP
02Upper Deck Speed Demons-SDZP
02Upper Deck Classic Portraits-45
Hockey Royalty-DPP
Hockey Royalty Limited-DPP
Starring Cast-CZP
Starring Cast Limited-CZP
02Upper Deck MVP-83
Gold-83
Classics-83
Golden Classics-83
Skate Around Jerseys-SDHP
Skate Around Jerseys-SDPP
Skate Around Jerseys-STDAP
Skate Around Jerseys-STSHP
Souvenirs-S-ZP
02Upper Deck Rookie Update-47
Jerseys-DZP
Jerseys Gold-DZP
02Upper Deck Victory-99
Bronze-99
Gold-99
Silver-99
National Pride-NP41
02Upper Deck Vintage-115
02Upper Deck Vintage-274
Green Backs-115
Tall Boys-T33
Tall Boys Gold-T33
02Vanguard-49
LTD-49
Jerseys-22
Jerseys Gold-22
02Slovakian Kvarteto-3
02UD SuperStars *-123
Gold-123
City All-Stars Dual Jersey-ABZP
Legendary Leaders Dual Jersey-ZPSG
03BAP Memorabilia-100
Emerald-100
Gold-100
Ruby-100
Sapphire-100
03BAP Ultimate Memorabilia Autographs-54
Gold-54
03BAP Ultimate Mem Franch Present Future-14
03BAP Ultimate Memorabilia Nameplates-17
03BAP Ultimate Mem Nameplates Gold-17
03BAP Ultimate Memorabilia Triple Threads-19
03Beehive-93
Variations-93
Gold-93
Silver-93
Jerseys-JT2
Sticks Blue Border-BL2
03Black Diamond-110
Black-110
Green-110
Red-110
03Bowman-73
Gold-73
03Bowman Chrome-73
Refractors-73
Gold Refractors-73
Xfractors-73
03Crown Royale-48
Blue-48
Retail-48
Lords of the Rink-14
03eTopps-20
03ITG Action-265
Jerseys-M141
Jerseys-M254
03ITG Used Signature Series-24
Gold-24
Autographs-ZP
Autographs Gold-ZP
Franchise-14
Franchise Autographs-14
International Experience-22
International Experience Autographs-22
International Experience Emblems Gold-22
International Experience Emblems-22
International Experience Gold-22
Jerseys-46
Jerseys Gold-46
Jersey Autos-46
Emblems-33
Emblems Gold-33
Jersey and Stick-46
Jersey and Stick Gold-46
03NHL Sticker Collection-238
03O-Pee-Chee-260
03OPC Blue-260
03OPC Gold-260
03OPC Red-260
03Pacific-158
Blue-158
Red-158
Jerseys-18
Jerseys Gold-18
03Pacific Calder-50
Silver-50
03Pacific Complete-167
Red-167
03Pacific Exhibit-172
Blue Backs-172
03Pacific Heads-Up-48
Hobby LTD-48
Retail LTD-48
Jerseys-15
03Pacific Invincible-46
Blue-46
Red-46
Retail-46
Featured Performers-14
03Pacific Luxury Suite-11A
03Pacific Luxury Suite-11B
03Pacific Luxury Suite-11C
03Pacific Luxury Suite-11D
03Pacific Luxury Suite-37A
03Pacific Luxury Suite-37B
03Pacific Luxury Suite-37C
03Pacific Prism-122
Blue-122
Patches-122
Red-122
Retail-122
03Pacific Quest for the Cup-51
Blue-51
03Pacific Supreme-46
Blue-46
Red-46
Retail-46
03Parkhurst Rookie-12
03Private Stock Reserve-171
Blue-171
Patches-171
Red-171
Retail-171
03SP Authentic-41
Limited-41
Breakout Seasons-B10
Breakout Seasons Limited-B10
Sign of the Times-ZP
Sign of the Times-PAF
03SP Game Used-22
03SP Game Used-97
Gold-22
Gold-97
Authentic Fabrics-AFZP
Authentic Fabrics-DFBT
Authentic Fabrics-DFPC
Authentic Fabrics Gold-AFZP
Authentic Fabrics Gold-DFBT
Authentic Fabrics Gold-DFPC
Double Threads-DTPF
03SPx-44
03SPx-143
03SPx-188
Radiance-44
Radiance-143
Radiance-188
Spectrum-44
Spectrum-143
Spectrum-188
Origins-O-ZP
Signature Threads-ST-ZP
VIP-VIP-PF
VIP Limited-VIP-PF
03Titanium-160
Hobby Jersey Number Parallels-160
Patches-160
Retail-160
03Topps-260
Blue-260
Gold-260
Red-260
Box Toppers-23
03Topps C55-59
Minis-59
Minis American Back-59
Minis American Back Red-59
Minis Bazooka Back-59
Minis Brooklyn Back-59
Minis Hat Trick Back-59
Minis O Canada Back-59
Minis O Canada Back Red-59
Minis Stanley Cup Back-59
03Topps Pristine-15
Gold Refractor Die Cuts-15
Refractors-15
Jersey Portions-PPJ-ZP
Jersey Portion Refractors-PPJ-ZP
Patches-PP-ZP
Patch Refractors-PP-ZP
Press Plates Black-15
Press Plates Cyan-15
Press Plates Magenta-15
Press Plates Yellow-15
03Topps Traded Franchise Fabrics-FF-ZP
03UD Honor Roll-39
Signature Class-SC21
03UD Premier Collection-26
Signatures-PS-ZP
Signatures Gold-PS-ZP
Teammates-PT-LK
Teammates Patches-PT-LK
03Upper Deck-86
All-Star Class-AS-13
Big Playmakers-BP-ZP
BuyBacks-37
BuyBacks-38
BuyBacks-39
BuyBacks-40
BuyBacks-41
BuyBacks-42
BuyBacks-43
BuyBacks-44
BuyBacks-45
BuyBacks-46
BuyBacks-47
Canadian Exclusives-86
Franchise Fabrics-FF-ZP
HG-86
Jersey Autographs-SJ-ZP
NHL Best-NB-ZP
Three Stars-TS8
03Upper Deck Classic Portraits-43
03Upper Deck Ice-42
Gold-42
Authentics-IA-ZP
Breakers-IB-ZP
Breaker Patches-IB-ZP
Frozen Fabrics-FF-ZP
Frozen Fabric Patches-FF-ZP
03Upper Deck MVP-190
Gold Script-190
Silver Script-190
Canadian Exclusives-190
Souvenirs-S16
SportsNut-SN42
Talent-MT14
03Upper Deck Rookie Update-42
03Upper Deck Rookie Update-157
Skills-SKZP
Super Stars-SSZP
03Upper Deck Trilogy-43
Authentic Patches-AP27
Limited-43
Limited Threads-LT10
Scripts-CSZP
03Upper Deck Victory-83
Bronze-83
Gold-83
Silver-83
Freshman Flashback-FF23
Game Breakers-GB40
03Czech Stadion-544
03Russian World Championship Stars-20
03Toronto Star-45
04Pacific-124
Blue-124
Red-124
04SP Authentic-43
04SP Authentic-117
Limited-43
Limited-117
Buybacks-198
Buybacks-199
Buybacks-200
Sign of the Times-TS-PBF
04UD All-World-6
Gold-6
Autographs-6
Dual Autographs-AD-PS
Five Autographs-AF-YAO
04Ultimate Collection Buybacks-87
04Ultimate Collection Buybacks-88
04Ultimate Collection Buybacks-89
04Ultimate Collection Buybacks-90
04Ultimate Collection Buybacks-91
04Ultimate Collection Buybacks-92
04Ultimate Collection Buybacks-93
04Ultimate Collection Buybacks-94
04Ultimate Collection Buybacks-95
04Ultimate Collection Buybacks-96
04Ultimate Collection Signatures-US-ZP
04Ultimate Collection Signature Logos-ULA-ZP
04Ultimate Collection Signature Patches-SP-ZP
04Czech HC Slavia Praha Postcards-6
04Czech OFS-172
Checklist Cards-8
Stars-18
04Czech Zuma-2
04Czech Zuma Stars-Z3
04Slovakian Skalica Team Set-17
05Be A Player-41
First Period-41
Second Period-41
Third Period-41
Overtime-41
05Beehive-73
Beige -73
Blue -73
Gold-73
Red -73
Matte-73
05Black Diamond-98
Emerald-98
Gold-98
Onyx-98
Ruby-98
05Panini Stickers-142
05SP Authentic-80
Limited-80
Prestigious Pairings-PPRP
05SP Game Used-80
Gold-80
Authentic Fabrics-AF-ZP
Authentic Fabrics Gold-AF-ZP
Authentic Patches Quad -PRLL
Authentic Patches-AP-ZP
Awesome Authentics-AA-ZP
Awesome Authentics Gold-DA-ZP
05SPx-73
Spectrum-73
Winning Combos-WC-PR
Winning Combos Gold-WC-PR
Winning Combos Spectrum-WC-PR
Winning Materials-WM-ZP
Winning Materials Gold-WM-ZP
Winning Materials Spectrum-WM-ZP
05The Cup Honorable Numbers-HNZP
05The Cup Limited Logos-LLZP
05The Cup Scripted Swatches-SSZP
05UD Artifacts Treasured Patches-TP-ZP
05UD Artifacts Treasured Patch Autos-TP-ZP
05UD Artifacts Treasured Patches Dual-TPD-ZP
05UD Artifacts Treasured Patch Dual Autos-TPD-ZP
05UD Artifacts Treasured Patches Pewter-TP-ZP
05UD Artifacts Treasured Patches Silver-TP-ZP
05UD Artifacts Treasured Swatches-TS-ZP
05UD Artifacts Treasured Swatch Autos-TS-ZP
05UD Artifacts Treasured Swatches Blue-TS-ZP
05UD Artifacts Treasured Swatches Copper-TS-ZP
05UD Artifacts Treasured Swatches Dual-TSD-ZP
05UD Artifacts Treasured Swatch Dual Auto-TSD-ZP
05UD Artifacts Treasured Swatch Dual Blue-TSD-ZP
05UD Artifact Treasure Swatch Dual Copper-TSD-ZP
05UD Artifact Treasure Swatch Dual Maroon-TSD-ZP
05UD Artifact Treasure Swatch Dual Pewter-TSD-ZP
05UD Artifact TreasuredSwatch Dual Silver-TSD-ZP
05UD Artifacts Treasured Swatches Maroon-TS-ZP
05UD Artifacts Treasured Swatches Pewter-TS-ZP
05UD Artifacts Treasured Swatches Silver-TS-ZP
05UD PowerPlay-42
Rainbow-42
Power Marks-PMZP
05Ultra-156
Gold-156
Ice-156
05Upper Deck-398
Jerseys Series II-J2ZP
Majestic Materials-MMZP
Patches-P-ZP
Shooting Stars-S-ZP
05Upper Deck Hockey Showcase-HS27
05Upper Deck Showcase Promos-HS27
05Upper Deck Ice-77
Rainbow-77
Frozen Fabrics-FFZP
Frozen Fabrics Autographs-AFFZP
Frozen Fabrics Glass-FFZP
Frozen Fabrics Patches-FFPZP
Frozen Fabrics Patch Autographs-FAPZP
Signature Swatches-SSZP
05Upper Deck MVP-307
Gold-307
Platinum-307
Materials Triples-T-GPD
05Upper Deck Trilogy-71
Honorary Patches-HP-ZP
Honorary Patch Scripts-HSP-ZP
Honorary Swatches-HS-ZP
Honorary Swatch Scripts-HSS-ZP
05Upper Deck Victory-93
Black-93
Gold-93
Silver-93
Game Breakers-GB22
06Parkhurst-159
06UD Artifacts Tundra Tandems-TTLZ
06UD Artifacts Tundra Tandems Black-TTLZ
06UD Artifacts Tundra Tandems Blue-TTLZ
06UD Artifacts Tundra Tandems Gold-TTLZ
06UD Artifacts Tundra Tandems Platinum-TTLZ
06UD Artifacts Tundra Tandems Red-TTLZ
06UD Artifacts Tundra Tandems Dual Patches Red-TTLZ
06Czech NHL ELH Postcards-8

Palichuk, Ed
82Brandon Wheat Kings-13

Palin, Brett
00Kelowna Rockets-14
01Kelowna Rockets-18
02Kelowna Rockets-5
03Kelowna Rockets Memorial Cup-16
03Kelowna Rockets-17
04Kelowna Rockets-7

Palinek, Martin
95Czech APS Extraliga-231
99Czech Score Blue 2000-122
99Czech Score Red Ice 2000-122

Pallante, Rob
92Nashville Knights-19

Pallin, Rob
85Minnesota-Duluth Bulldogs-4
98Las Vegas Coyotes RHI-15

Pallister, Mark
99UK Hull Thunder-13

Palm, Jorgen
71Swedish Hockey-120
72Swedish Stickers-102
73Swedish Stickers-177
74Swedish Stickers-181
85Swedish Panini Stickers-202
86Swedish Panini Stickers-198
89Swedish Semic Elitserien Stickers-271
90Swedish Semic Elitserien Stickers-35
93Swedish Semic Elitserien-292

Palm, Thomas
71Swedish Hockey-128

Palmateer, Mike
76Maple Leafs Postcards-13
77Maple Leafs Postcards-12
77O-Pee-Chee NHL-211
77Topps-211
78Maple Leafs Postcards-17
78O-Pee-Chee-70
78O-Pee-Chee-160
78Topps-70
78Topps-160
79Maple Leafs Postcards-21
79Maple Leafs Postcards-22
79O-Pee-Chee-197
79Topps-197
80O-Pee-Chee-95
80O-Pee-Chee Super-23
80Topps-95
81Capitals Team Issue-13
81O-Pee-Chee-351
81O-Pee-Chee-394
81O-Pee-Chee Stickers-194
81Post Standups-9
81Topps-E121
82Maple Leafs Postcards-28
83Maple Leafs Postcards-20
83NHL Key Tags-119
83O-Pee-Chee-338
83O-Pee-Chee Stickers-39
83Puffy Stickers-5
83Topps Stickers-39
83Vachon-95
84O-Pee-Chee-308
84O-Pee-Chee Stickers-22
02Maple Leafs Platinum Collection-80
02Maple Leafs Platinum Collection-88
Autographs-80
03Parkhurst Original Six Toronto-49
Autographs-14
04ITG Franchises Canadian-98
Autographs-MP
04ITG Franchises US East-449
05Between the Pipes-12
Autographs-A-MP
06Between The Pipes-97
Autographs-AMP
Complete Jersey-CJ09
Complete Jersey Gold-CJ09
Shooting Gallery-SG02
Shooting Gallery Gold-SG02
Stick Work-SW06
Stick Work Gold-SW06

Palmer, Bill
93Quebec Pee-Wee Tournament-674

Palmer, Brad
81North Stars Postcards-19
82O-Pee-Chee-21
82Post Cereal-9
82Victoria Cougars-20
83Bruins Team Issue-15

Palmer, Chris
90ProCards AHL/IHL-565
99UHL All-Stars East-6T

Palmer, Drew
93Seattle Thunderbirds-17
95Seattle Thunderbirds-20

Palmer, Jay
83Brandon Wheat Kings-12

Palmer, Joe
06Ohio State Buckeyes-23

Palmer, Rob
78O-Pee-Chee-298
79O-Pee-Chee-352
80Kings Card Night-10
80O-Pee-Chee-104
80Topps-104

Palmer, Samuel
92Finnish Semic-202

Palmer, Steve
92Clarkson Knights-14
92Quebec Pee-Wee Tournament-301
98German DEL-137
99German DEL-90

Palmer, Tyler
01Columbus Cottonmouths-17
03Muskegon Fury-15

Palmieri, Nick
05Erie Otters-11
06Erie Otters-1

Palmiscno, Tyler
98Sioux City Musketeers-19
99Sioux City Musketeers-18
03North Dakota Fighting Sioux-7
05Dutch Vadeko Flyers -14

Palmqvist, Bjorn
64Swedish Coralli ISHockey-9
64Swedish Coralli ISHockey-157
65Swedish Coralli ISHockey-9
65Swedish Coralli ISHockey-157
67Swedish Hockey-20
67Swedish Hockey-70
69Swedish Hockey-101
69Swedish Hockey-197
70Finnish Jaakiekko-36
70Swedish Hockey-58
70Swedish Hockey-290
70Swedish Masterserien-113
71Finnish Suomi Stickers-56
71Swedish Hockey-22
71Swedish Hockey-129
72Finnish Jaakiekko-54
72Finnish Hellas-36
72Finnish Panda Toronto-76
72Finnish Semic World Championship-60
72Swedish Stickers-19
72Swedish Stickers-106
72Swedish Semic World Championship-60
73Swedish Stickers-214
74Finnish Jenkki-32
74Finnish Typotor-100
74Swedish Stickers-259
74Swedish Semic World Champ Stickers-20

Palmroth, Henri
05Finnish Cardset -328

Palmu, Hannu
72Finnish Jaakiekko-132

Palo, Marko
92Finnish Jyvas-Hyva Stickers-22
93Finnish Jyvas-Hyva Stickers-54
93Finnish SISU-244
93Finnish SISU-379
94Finnish SISU-370
94Finnish Jaa Kiekko-37
94Swedish Leaf-197
95Finnish Beckett Ad Cards-8
95Finnish SISU Gold Cards-20
95Finnish SISU Limited-88
95Finnish Karjala World Champ Labels-16
95Finnish Semic World Championships-13
95Swedish Leaf-268
95Swedish Upper Deck-140
95Swedish World Championships Stickers-175
96Swedish Semic Wien-13
98Finnish Kerailysarja-69
Leijonat-35
99Czech OFS-61
99Finnish Cardset-241
00Finnish Cardset-29
01Finnish Cardset-378
02Finnish Cardset-240

Palo-Oja, Kari
66Finnish Jaakiekkosarja-189
70Finnish Jaakiekko-134
72Finnish Jaakiekko-133
72Finnish Panda Toronto-30
73Finnish Jaakiekko-187

Palomaki, Mikko
05Finnish Cardset -303
06Finnish Cardset-136

Palooja, Kari
65Finnish Hellas-127
71Finnish Suomi Stickers-183

Palov, Rastislav
99Czech OFS-97
03UK Guildford Flames-12
03UK Guildford Flames-28
04UK Guildford Flames-12

Palsola, Sakari
95Finnish SISU-106
96Finnish SISU Redline-102
00Finnish Cardset-58
01Finnish Cardset-288
02Finnish Cardset-241
03Finnish Cardset-98
04Finnish Cardset-104
Parallel-77

Paluch, Scott
88ProCards IHL-76
89ProCards IHL-4

Paluczak, Matt
03Minnesota State Mavericks-16

Pan, Jonathan
02Swiss HNL-355

Pance, Ziga
06Oshawa Generals-14

Panchartek, Frantisek
71Finnish Suomi Stickers-35
71Swedish Hockey-46
72Finnish Panda Toronto-91
72Finnish Semic World Championship-26
72Swedish Semic World Championship-26
74Swedish Semic World Champ Stickers-73

Panchyson, Todd
05Saskatoon Blades-17

Pancoe, Don
88Niagara Falls Thunder-20
89Niagara Falls Thunder-14
897th Inn. Sketch OHL-140

Pandel, Arne
57Swedish Alfabilder-83

Pander, Rasmus
98Danish Hockey League-161
99Danish Hockey League-62

Pandolfo, Jay
93Donruss Team USA-16

93Pinnacle-497
Canadian-497
93Upper Deck-556
96Black Diamond-21
Gold-21
96Devils Team Issue-20
96SP-180
96Albany River Rats-11
97Collector's Choice-145
97Devils Team Issue-15
97Pacific Dynagon Best Kept Secrets-53
97Upper Deck-93
97Albany River Rats-11
98Devils Team Issue-23
98Upper Deck MVP-123
Gold Script-123
Silver Script-123
Super Script-123
99Devils Team Issue-13
99Pacific-245
Copper-245
Emerald Green-245
Gold-245
Ice Blue-245
Premiere Date-245
Red-245
00BAP Signature Series-92
Emerald-92
Ruby-92
Sapphire-92
Autographs-173
Autographs Gold-173
00Devils Team Issue-17
01Devils Team Issue-18
02BAP Sig Series Auto Buybacks 2000-173
02Devils Team Issue-16
03Devils Team Issue-20
03ITG Action-327
03Pacific Complete-297
Red-297
05Devils Team Issue-18
05Parkhurst-296
Facsimile Auto Parallel-296
05Upper Deck MVP-240
Gold-240
Platinum-240
06Devils Team Set-19
06O-Pee-Chee-298
Rainbow-298
06Upper Deck-120
Exclusives Parallel-120
High Gloss Parallel-120
Masterpieces-120

Pandolfo, Mike
02Syracuse Crunch-22
02Syracuse Crunch Sheets-20
03ITG VIP Rookie Debut-148
03Parkhurst Rookie-76
03Upper Deck Rookie Update-189
03Syracuse Crunch-22
04Pacific-281
Blue-281
Red-281
04Syracuse Crunch-23

Pandovski, Bryan
93Quebec Pee-Wee Tournament-488

Panek, Chris
88ProCards AHL-203
89ProCards AHL-19
95German DEL-49

Pang, Darren
82Ottawa 67's-16
83Ottawa 67's-21
87Blackhawks Coke-17
88Blackhawks Coke-15
88O-Pee-Chee-51
88O-Pee-Chee Stickers-8
88O-Pee-Chee Stickers-18
88O-Pee-Chee Stickers-135
88O-Pee-Chee Stickers-151
88Panini Stickers-21
88Topps-51
89O-Pee-Chee-31
89O-Pee-Chee Stickers-10
89Panini Stickers-42
89Topps-31
01Topps Archives-47
02Topps Rookie Reprints-14
02Topps Rookie Reprint Autographs-14
03Parkhurst Original Six Chicago-58
Autographs-13

Panik, Brian
00Sioux City Musketeers-21

Panin, Mikhail
90O-Pee-Chee-492

Pankewicz, Greg
89Regina Pats-15
90 7th Inn. Sketch WHL-180
91Knoxville Cherokees-9
94Classic Pro Prospects-57
97Manitoba Moose-B5
99Houston Aeros-17
03Colorado Eagles-13
04Colorado Eagles-14
05Colorado Eagles-14
06Colorado Eagles -16

Pankewicz, Trent
93Oklahoma City Blazers-11
94Central Hockey League-66
94Oklahoma City Blazers-12

Pankov, Dmitri
95Richmond Renegades-11
00Russian Hockey League-102
03Russian Hockey League-189

Pankov, Vasily
00German DEL-23
01German Upper Deck-12

Pankratz, Joe
94Minnesota Golden Gophers-24

Pannitto, Mark
95North Iowa Huskies-25

Panov, Konstantin
98Kamloops Blazers-19
99Kamloops Blazers-17
00Kamloops Blazers-17
00UD CHL Prospects-69
01Milwaukee Admirals-20
02Milwaukee Admirals-17
02Milwaukee Admirals Postcards-13

Panov, Yuri
98Russian Hockey League-24
99Russian Hockey League-179
00Russian Hockey League-222
03Russian Avangard Omsk-23

Panteleyev, Grigori
92Parkhurst-243
Emerald Ice-243
92Ultra-254
92Upper Deck-492
93Score-337
Canadian-337
93Ultra-179
93Classic Pro Prospects-130
98Orlando Solar Bears-7
98Orlando Solar Bears-14
98Orlando Solar Bears II-9
99German DEL-225

Panzer, Jeff
01Worcester Icecats-4
01Worcester Icecats-28
02Worcester IceCats-20
03Worcester Ice Cats-24
03Worcester Ice Cats 10th Anniversary-15
04Syracuse Crunch-22
06German DEL-47

Paolini, Sam
03Atlantic City Boardwalk Bullies-17
03Atlantic City Boardwalk Bullies RBI-25
03ECHL All-Stars-256
04Atlantic City Boardwalk Bullies Kinko's-13

Paolucci, Dan
90 7th Inn. Sketch QMJHL-144

Paone, Pat
93Peterborough Petes-8

Papa, Loris
95Swiss HNL-423

Papaioannou, Ryan
01Calgary Hitmen-17
01Calgary Hitmen Autographed-17
03Moncton Wildcats-20

Papero, Riley
92Quebec Pee-Wee Tournament-1765
93Quebec Pee-Wee Tournament-177

Papike, Joe
34Beehive Group I Photos-73

Papineau, Justin
94Quebec Pee-Wee Tournament-806
97Upper Deck-415
98Bowman CHL-31
98Bowman CHL-149
Golden Anniversary-31
Golden Anniversary-149
OPC International-31
OPC International-149
Autographs Blue-A1
Autographs Gold-A1
Autographs Silver-A1
98Bowman Chrome CHL-31
98Bowman Chrome CHL-149
Golden Anniversary-31
Golden Anniversary-149
Golden Anniversary Refractors-31
Golden Anniversary Refractors-149
OPC International-31
OPC International-149
OPC International Refractors-31
OPC International Refractors-149
Refractors-31
Refractors-149
99Black Diamond-117
Diamond Cut-117
Final Cut-117
99Upper Deck-331
Exclusives-331
Exclusives 1 of 1-331
99Upper Deck Sobey's Memorial Cup-2
99Upper Deck Gold Reserve-331
99Upper Deck MVP SC Edition-216
Gold Script-216
Silver Script-216
Super Script-216
99Upper Deck Ovation-76
Standing Ovation-76
99Bowman CHL-128
Gold-128
OPC International-128
99UD Prospects-5
CHL Class-C2
00Worcester Icecats-3
01Worcester Icecats-22
01Worcester Icecats-28
02Pacific Calder-92
Silver-92
02Pacific Complete-501
Red-501
02SP Authentic-131
02SPx-122
02AHL Top Prospects-34
02Worcester IceCats-17
03Bowman-95
Gold-95
03Bowman Chrome-95
Refractors-95
Gold Refractors-95
Xfractors-95
03Worcester Ice Cats 10th Anniversary-12

Papineau, Rob
90 7th Inn. Sketch OHL-113

Papista, Costa
85Sudbury Wolves-8
86Sudbury Wolves-3

Papp, Jamie
93Cornell Big Red-20

Papp, Robert
95Swiss HNL-424

Papp, Thomas
95Swiss HNL-32
96Swiss HNL-178
98Swiss Power Play Stickers-227
99Swiss Panini Stickers-228
00Swiss Panini Stickers-270
01Swiss HNL-2
02Swiss HNL-145

Pappas, Perry
90 7th Inn. Sketch OHL-170
91 7th Inn. Sketch OHL-319
91 7th Inn. Sketch Memorial Cup-13
93Sault Ste. Marie Greyhound Memorial Cup-11
96Wheeling Nailers-16

Pappin, Jim
63Rochester Americans-18
64Beehive Group III Photos-177
64Topps-64
64Toronto Star-35
65Maple Leafs White Border-14
65Topps-16
66Topps-76
66Topps USA Test-49
67Post Flip Books-7
67Topps-78
67York Action Octagons-7
67York Action Octagons-8
67York Action Octagons-32
68Blackhawks Team Issue-6
68O-Pee-Chee-21
68Shirriff Coins-33
68Topps-21
69Maple Leafs White Border Glossy-25
69O-Pee-Chee-133
69Topps-73
70Blackhawks Postcards-11
70Colgate Stamps-43
70Esso Power Players-115
70O-Pee-Chee-13
70Sargent Promotions Stamps-41
70Topps-13
71Letraset Action Replays-10
71O-Pee-Chee-98
71Sargent Promotions Stamps-40
71Topps-98
71Toronto Sun-79
72O-Pee-Chee-42
72Sargent Promotions Stamps-64
72Topps-148
73O-Pee-Chee-112
73Topps-112
74Lipton Soup-36
74NHL Action Stamps-76
74O-Pee-Chee NHL-69
74O-Pee-Chee NHL-113
74Topps-69
74Topps-113
75O-Pee-Chee NHL-234
75O-Pee-Chee NHL-317
75Topps-234
75Topps-317
91Ultimate Original Six-62
French-62
94Parkhurst Tall Boys-123
95Parkhurst '66-67-107
Coins-107
02Topps Heritage Reprint Autographs-JP
02Topps Heritage Reprint Relics-JP
02Topps Heritage Reprints-JP
03BAP Ultimate Memorabilia Linemates-5
04ITG Franchises Update Autographs-JPA
06Parkhurst-91
Autographs-91
Autographs Dual-DAHP
07Maple Leafs 1967 Commemorative-19

Paquet, Dave
90 7th Inn. Sketch QMJHL-16
91 7th Inn. Sketch QMJHL-113
91 7th Inn. Sketch Memorial Cup-68

Paquet, Eric
93Quebec Pee-Wee Tournament-280

Paquet, Francois
92Quebec Pee-Wee Tournament-459
92Quebec Pee-Wee Tournament-1310
93Quebec Pee-Wee Tournament-558

Paquet, Jean-Philippe
03Shawinigan Cataractes-19
05ITG Heroes/Prosp Toronto Expo Parallel -148
05Shawinigan Cataractes-5
05ITG Heroes and Prospects-148
Autographs-A-JPP

Paquet, Martin
04Fort Worth Brahmas-13

Paquet, Normand
91 7th Inn. Sketch QMJHL-2
98Thunder Bay Thunder Cats-6
99Rockford IceHogs-15

Paquet, Samuel
01Asheville Smoke-14
02Arkansas Riverblades-11

Paquet, Simon
93Quebec Pee-Wee Tournament-12

Paquette, Andy
85Sudbury Wolves-16
88Sudbury Wolves-20

Paquette, Charles
91 7th Inn. Sketch QMJHL-103
93Sherbrooke Faucons-6
96Providence Bruins-3
97Providence Bruins-13
03St. Jean Mission-19

Paquette, Darryl
90Sudbury Wolves-1
95Hampton Roads Admirals-4
95Portland Pirates-17
96Hampton Roads Admirals-HRA1

Paquette, Francois
91 7th Inn. Sketch QMJHL-199
01Sorel Royaux-17

Paquette, Phil
86Sudbury Wolves-23

Paquette, Real
67Columbus Checkers-10

Paquette, Sacha
93Quebec Pee-Wee Tournament-68

Paquin, Gerard
52Bas Du Fleuve-18

Paquin, Luc
99Cornwall Colts-6

Paquin, Patrice
91 7th Inn. Sketch QMJHL-164
97Mobile Mysticks-13

Para, Kelly
86Kamloops Blazers-15

Paradis, Carl
97New Mexico Scorpions-25
98San Angelo Outlaws-14
99San Angelo Outlaws-13
04St Georges de Beauce Garaga-17

Paradis, Daniel
90 7th Inn. Sketch QMJHL-42
91 7th Inn. Sketch QMJHL-95
91 7th Inn. Sketch Memorial Cup-45

Paradis, David
93Quebec Pee-Wee Tournament-308

Paradis, Dominic
93Quebec Pee-Wee Tournament-258

Paradis, Pascal
93Quebec Pee-Wee Tournament-921

Paradis, Sebastien
93Quebec Pee-Wee Tournament-1198

Paradis, Stephane
91 7th Inn. Sketch QMJHL-140

Paradise, Bob
70Swedish Masterserien-89
70Swedish Masterserien-90
70Swedish Masterserien-183
72Flames Postcards-12
72Sargent Promotions Stamps-11
74NHL Action Stamps-227
74O-Pee-Chee NHL-343
74Penguins Postcards-17
75O-Pee-Chee NHL-21A
75O-Pee-Chee NHL-21B
75Topps-21
76O-Pee-Chee NHL-368
77O-Pee-Chee NHL-203
78O-Pee-Chee-375

Paradise, Chris
02Providence Bruins-11
04Odessa Jackalopes-15

Paradise, Dave
93St. Cloud State Huskies-21
97Peoria Rivermen-17
99Mississippi Sea Wolves-20
03Rockford Ice Hogs-13

Paradise, Dick
72Minnesota Fighting Saints Postcards WHA-17
73Quaker Oats WHA-49

Paradise, Jim
95Tallahassee Tiger Sharks-10
99Tallahassee Tiger Sharks-23

Parco, John
98Hampton Roads Admirals 10th Anniversary-21
99Hampton Roads Admirals-14
00UK Cardiff Devils-6
00UK Sekonda Superleague-65
01UK Cardiff Devils-5
02UK Cardiff Devils-5

Pardavy, Jan
99Czech DS-136
99Czech OFS-443
99Czech OFS-522
All-Star Game Blue-522
All-Star Game Gold-522
All-Star Game Red-522
All-Star Game Silver-522
00Czech DS Extraliga-19
00Czech OFS-333
00Czech OFS Star Emerald-3
00Czech OFS Star Pink-3
00Czech OFS Star Violet-3
01Czech OFS All Stars-22
01Slovakian Kvarteto-5D
02Finnish Cardset-242
02Czech OFS Plus-254
03Czech OFS Plus Insert H-H7
04Czech OFS-299
05Swedish SHL Elitset-251
Gold-251

Pardue, Bill
00Arizona Icecats-19
01Arizona Icecats-18
02Arizona Icecats-19

Pardy, Adam
03Cape Breton Screaming Eagles-2
04Cape Breton Screaming Eagles-14
05Las Vegas Wranglers-17

Pare, Charles
92Quebec Pee-Wee Tournament-1303
93Quebec Pee-Wee Tournament-367

Pare, Francis
93Quebec Pee-Wee Tournament-339
05Shawinigan Cataractes-17

Pare, Frederic
93Quebec Pee-Wee Tournament-391

Pare, Jean-Philippe
98Bowman CHL-94
Golden Anniversary-94
OPC International-94
98Bowman Chrome CHL-94
Golden Anniversary-94
Golden Anniversary Refractors-94
OPC International-94
OPC International Refractors-94
Refractors-94
99Shawinigan Cataractes-10
Signed-10

Pare, Martin
93Quebec Pee-Wee Tournament-1197
99Quebec Remparts-19
Signed-19

Pare, Patrice
79Montreal Juniors-20

Parent, Bernie
64Beehive Group III Photos-21
65Coca-Cola-18
68O-Pee-Chee-89
68Shirriff Coins-122
68Topps-89
69O-Pee-Chee-89
Four-in-One-1
Stamps-23
69Topps-89
70Colgate Stamps-93
70Dad's Cookies-95
70Esso Power Players-216
70O-Pee-Chee-78
70Sargent Promotions Stamps-146
70Topps-78
71Maple Leafs Postcards-14
71O-Pee-Chee-131
71Sargent Promotions Stamps-205
71Topps-131
71Toronto Sun-267
72Philadelphia Blazers-2
72Finnish Semic World Championship-175
72Swedish Semic World Championship-175
73Flyers Linnett-13
73O-Pee-Chee-66
73Topps-66
74Lipton Soup-18
74NHL Action Stamps-202
74O-Pee-Chee NHL-4
74O-Pee-Chee NHL-60
74O-Pee-Chee NHL-138
74O-Pee-Chee NHL-249
74O-Pee-Chee NHL-251
74Topps-4
74Topps-60
74Topps-138
74Topps-249
74Topps-251
75Heroes Stand-Ups-24
75Nabisco Sugar Daddy-15
75O-Pee-Chee NHL-213
75O-Pee-Chee NHL-291
75O-Pee-Chee NHL-300
75Topps-213
75Topps-291
75Topps-300
76O-Pee-Chee NHL-10
76Topps-10
77O-Pee-Chee NHL-8
77O-Pee-Chee NHL-65
77Topps-8
77Topps-65
78O-Pee-Chee-15
78O-Pee-Chee-68
78O-Pee-Chee-70
78Topps-15
78Topps-68
78Topps-70
79O-Pee-Chee-6
79O-Pee-Chee-8
79Topps-6
79Topps-8A
79Topps-8B
85Flyers Postcards-21
85Hall of Fame-246
86Flyers Postcards-19
87Flyers Postcards-8
91Pinnacle-384
French-384
92Flyers Upper Deck Sheets-44
92O-Pee-Chee-217
25th Anniv. Inserts-1
92Parkhurst-470
Emerald Ice-470
93High Liner Greatest Goalies-7
94Parkhurst Tall Boys Future Stars-FS4
95Parkhurst '66-67-14
Coins-14
97SLU Canadian Timeless Legends-6
00BAP Memorabilia Goalie Memorabilia-G11
00BAP Memorabilia Goalie Memorabilia-G12
00BAP Memorabilia Goalie Memorabilia-G30
00BAP Sig Ser Goalie Memorabilia Autos-GLS5
00BAP Ultimate Mem Goalie Memorabilia-GM7
00BAP Ultimate Mem Goalie Memorabilia-GM9
00BAP Ultimate Mem Goalie Memorabilia-GM17
00BAP Ultimate Mem Goalie Mem Autos-UG5
00BAP Ultimate Memorabilia Retro-Active-RA5
00Topps Stanley Cup Heroes-SHBP
00Topps Stanley Cup Heroes Autographs-SHBP
00UD Heroes-135
Signs of Greatness-BP
00Upper Deck Legends-97
Legendary Collection Bronze-97
Legendary Collection Gold-97
Legendary Collection Silver-97
Essence of the Game-EG5
01BAP Ultimate Mem All-Star History-22
01BAP Ultimate Mem Dynasty Jerseys-10
01BAP Ultimate Mem Dynasty Emblems-10
01BAP Ultimate Mem Dynasty Numbers-10
01BAP Ultimate Mem Retired Numbers-17
01BAP Ultimate Memorabilia Retro Trophies-15
01Between the Pipes-118
01Between the Pipes-138
Double Memorabilia-DM26
He Shoots-He Saves Prizes-37
Jersey and Stick Cards-GSJ38
Record Breakers-RB6
Trophy Winners-TW21
Vintage Memorabilia-VM4
01Fleer Legacy-48
Ultimate-48
01Greats of the Game-41
Autographs-41
01Parkhurst Autographs-PA56
01Topps Archives-16
01Topps Chrome Reprints-8
01Topps Chrome Reprint Refractors-8
01Topps Chrome Reprint Autographs-8
01UD Stanley Cup Champs-24
01Upper Deck Legends-54
01Upper Deck Legends-83
02BAP Memorabilia Mini Stanley Cups-13
02BAP NHL All-Star History-22
02BAP Ultimate Memorabilia Conn Smythe-6
02BAP Ultimate Memorabilia Conn Smythe-7
02BAP Ultimate Memorabilia Cup Duels-8
02BAP Ultimate Memorabilia Emblem Attic-2
02BAP Ultimate Memorabilia Numerology-4
02BAP Ultimate Mem Retro Teammates-9
02BAP Ultimate Mem Vintage Jerseys-4
02Between the Pipes Complete Package-CP9
02Between the Pipes Goalie Autographs-27
02Between the Pipes He Shoots/Saves Prize-29
02Between the Pipes Inspirations-I5
02Between the Pipes Record Breakers-10
02Between the Pipes Trappers-GT11
02Between the Pipes Vintage Memorabilia-8
02Between the Pipes Vintage Memorabilia-19
02ITG Used Goalie Pad and Jersey-GP16
02ITG Used Goalie Pad and Jersey Gold-GP16
02Parkhurst Vintage Memorabilia-VM14
02Parkhurst Vintage Teammates-VT13
03BAP Memorabilia Gloves-GUG8
03BAP Memorabilia Vintage Memorabilia-VM-5
03BAP Ultimate Mem Raised to the Rafters-15
03BAP Ultimate Mem Retro Teammates-8
03BAP Ultimate Mem Vint Complete Package-8
03BAP Ultimate Mem Vint Comp Package Gold-8
03ITG Used Signature Series Goalie Gear-25
03ITG Used Sig Series Goalie Gear Autos-25
03ITG Used Sig Series Goalie Gear Gold-25
03ITG Used Sig Series Triple Mem-22
03ITG Used Sig Series Triple Mem Gold-22
03ITG Used Sig Series Vintage Mem -12
03ITG Used Sig Series Vintage Mem Gold-12
03ITG VIP MVP-15
03Parkhurst Original Six Boston-43
Autographs-14
Memorabilia-BM56
04ITG NHL AS FANtasy AS History Jerseys-SB22
04ITG Franchises He Shoots/Scores Prizes-46
04ITG Franchises US East-414
Autographs-A-BPA
Double Memorabilia-EDM5
Double Memorabilia Autographs-EDM-BP
Double Memorabilia Gold-EDM5
Forever Rivals-EFR5
Forever Rivals Gold-EFR5
Goalie Gear-EGG4
Goalie Gear Autographs-EGG-BP
Goalie Gear Gold-EGG4
Memorabilia-ESM29
Memorabilia Autographs-ESM-BP
Memorabilia Gold-ESM29
Original Sticks-EOS16
Original Sticks Autographs-EOS-BP
Original Sticks Gold-EOS16
Triple Memorabilia-ETM2
Triple Memorabilia Autographs-ETP-BP
Triple Memorabilia Gold-ETM2
Trophy Winners-ETW9
Trophy Winners Gold-ETW9
04ITG Ultimate Memorabilia-174
Gold-174
Archives 1st Edition-21
Auto Threads-23
Autographs-40
Autographs Gold-40
Broad Street Bullies Jerseys-3
Broad Street Bullies Jersey Autographs-3
Broad Street Bullies Emblems-3
Broad Street Bullies Emblem Autographs-3
Broad Street Bullies Numbers-3
Broad Street Bullies Number Autographs-3
Complete Package-6
Cornerstones-8
Cornerstones Gold-8
Day In History-30
Day In History-49
Day In History Gold-30
Day In History Gold-49
Goalie Gear-10
Jersey Autographs-13
Jersey Autographs Gold-13
Retro Teammates-11
Stick Autographs-33
Stick Autographs Gold-33
Triple Threads-7
Vezina Trophy-5
04ITG Heroes and Prospects-131
Autographs-BP
04ITG Heroes/Prospects Toronto Expo '05-131
04ITG Heroes/Prospects Expo Heroes/Pros-131
05ITG Heroes/Prosp Toronto Expo Parallel -30
05Between the Pipes-13
Autographs-A-BP
Complete Package-CP-6
Pads-GUP-1
Signed Memorabilia-SM-10
05ITG Ultimate Memorabilia Level 1-7
05ITG Ultimate Memorabilia Level 2-7
05ITG Ultimate Memorabilia Level 3-7
05ITG Ultimate Memorabilia Level 4-7
05ITG Ultimate Memorabilia Level 5-7
05ITG Ultimate Mem Complete Package-17
05ITG Ultimate Mem Complete Package Gold-17
05ITG Ultimate Mem Cornerstones Jerseys-10
05ITG Ultimate Mem Cornerst Jerseys Gold-10
05ITG Ultimate Mem Decades Jerseys-5
05ITG Ultimate Mem Decades Jerseys Gold-5
05ITG Ultimate Memorabilia Double Autos-5
05ITG Ultimate Mem Double Autos Gold-5
05ITG Ultimate Mem Double Mem-10
05ITG Ultimate Mem Double Mem Autos-9
05ITG Ultimate Mem Double Mem Autos-16
05ITG Ultimate Mem Double Mem Autos Gold-9
05ITG Ultimate Mem Double Mem Autos Gold-16
05ITG Ultimate Mem Double Mem Gold-10
05ITG Ultimate Memorabilia Goalie Gear-1
05ITG Ultimate Mem Goalie Gear Gold-1
05ITG Ultimate Memorabilia Jerseys-9
05ITG Ultimate Memorabilia Jerseys Gold-2
05ITG Ultimate Mem Pass the Torch Jerseys-15
05ITG Ultimate Mem Passing Torch Jsy Gold-15
05ITG Ultimate Mem Raised to the Rafters-9
05ITG Ultimate Mem Raised Rafters Gold-9
05ITG Ultimate Mem Record Breaker Jerseys-14
05ITG Ultimate Mem RecBreak Jerseys Gold-14
05ITG Ultimate Mem Retro Teammate Jerseys-8
05ITG Ult Mem Retro Teammate Jersey Gold-8
05ITG Ultimate Memorabilia Stick Autos-21
05ITG Ultimate Mem Stick Autos Gold-21
05ITG Ultimate Memorabilia Trifecta Autos-3
05ITG Ultimate Mem Trifecta Autos Gold-3
05ITG Ultimate Memorabilia Triple Autos-2
05ITG Ultimate Mem Triple Autos Gold-2
05ITG Ultimate Mem Triple Threads Jerseys-9
05ITG Ultimate Mem Triple Thread Jsy Gold-9
05ITG Ultimate Memorabilia Ultimate Autos-14
05ITG Ultimate Mem Ultimate Autos Gold-14
05The Cup-79
Gold-79
Black Rainbow-79
Hardware Heroes-HHBP1
Hardware Heroes-HHBP2
Masterpiece Pressplates-79
05Ultimate Coll Ultimate Achievements-UABP
05Ultimate Collection Ultimate Signatures-USBP
05Ultimate Coll Ultimate Sigs Pairings-UPCP
05Ultimate Coll Ultimate Sigs Trios-UTEHP
05ITG Heroes and Prospects-30
Aspiring-ASP10
Autographs-A-BPA
Hero Memorabilia-HM-31
06Between The Pipes-79
06Between The Pipes-136
06Between The Pipes-145
Autographs-ABP
Complete Package-CP03
Complete Package Gold-CP03
Double Jerseys-DJ03
Double Jerseys Gold-DJ03
Double Memorabilia-DM12
Double Memorabilia Gold-DM12
Pads-GP04
Pads Gold-GP04
Shooting Gallery-SG07
Shooting Gallery Gold-SG07
Stick and Jersey-SJ24
Stick and Jersey Gold-SJ24
Stick and Jersey Autographs-SJ24
Stick Work-SW03
Stick Work Gold-SW03
06ITG Ultimate Memorabilia-13
Artist Proof-13
Autos-66
Autos Gold-66
Complete Package-17
Complete Package Gold-17
Decades-6
Decades Gold-6
Passing The Torch-8
Passing The Torch Gold-8
Retro Teammates-13
Retro Teammates Gold-13
Road to the Cup-9
Road to the Cup Gold-9
Stick Rack-23
Stick Rack Gold-23
Sticks and Jerseys-11
Sticks and Jerseys Gold-11
Triple Thread Jerseys-11
Triple Thread Jerseys Gold-11
06Parkhurst-92
Autographs-92
Autographs Dual-DACP
06SP Authentic Sign of the Times Quads-ST4ECVP
06SP Game Used Letter Marks-LMBP
06The Cup-68
Black Rainbow-68
Gold-68
Masterpiece Pressplates-68
Stanley Cup Signatures-CSBP
06UD Artifacts-128
Blue-128
Gold-128
Platinum-128
Radiance-128
Red-128
06Ultimate Collection Signatures-US-BP
06Ultimate Collection Ultimate Achievements-UA-BP
06Upper Deck Sweet Shot Signature Shots/Saves Sticks-SSSBP
06Upper Deck Sweet Shot Signature Sticks-STBP
06Upper Deck Trilogy Combo Clearcut Autographs-C3CLP
06ITG Heroes and Prospects Triple Memorabilia-TM02
06ITG Heroes and Prospects Triple Memorabilia Gold-TM02

Parent, Frederic
93Quebec Pee-Wee Tournament-266

Parent, Jean-Francois
03Drummondville Voltigeurs-19

Parent, Marc
93Quebec Pee-Wee Tournament-1387

Parent, Michael
00Chicoutimi Sagueneens-16
Signed-16

Parent, Philippe
00Quebec Remparts-15
Signed-15

Parent, Rich
94Muskegon Fury-2
95Muskegon Fury-15
96Detroit Vipers-11
99IHL All-Stars-3
99Utah Grizzlies-2
00SPx-115
Spectrum-115
00Titanium Game Gear-138
00Titanium Game Gear Patches-138
00Upper Deck-193
Exclusives Tier 1-193
Exclusives Tier 2-193
00Wilkes-Barre Scranton Penguins-17
01Between the Pipes-53
01Pacific Heads-Up Quad Jerseys-18
01Pacific Heads-Up Quad Jerseys-29
01Titanium Double-Sided Jerseys-36
01Titanium Draft Day Edition-81
01Vanguard Memorabilia-27
01Vanguard Patches-27
02German DEL City Press-182
03German Berlin Polar Bears Postcards-23
03German DEL-70
04German DEL Update-317
05German DEL-344
Goalies-G11

Parent, Russ
96UK Fife Flyers-3
96St. Louis Vipers RHI-2

Parent, Ryan
03Guelph Storm-6
04Guelph Storm-7
05ITG Heroes/Prosp Toronto Expo Parallel -131
05Guelph Storm-B-02
05OHL Bell All-Star Classic-13
05ITG Heroes and Prospects-131
Autographs-A-RP
Oh Canada-OC-10
Oh Canada Gold-OC-10
06Guelph Storm-20
06ITG Heroes and Prospects-146
Autographs-ARP
07Upper Deck Victory-216
Black-216
Gold-216
07ITG Going For Gold World Juniors-4
Autographs-4
Emblems-GUE4
Jerseys-GUJ4
Numbers-GUN4

Parent, Sebastien
90 7th Inn. Sketch QMJHL-36
91 7th Inn. Sketch QMJHL-91
91 7th Inn. Sketch Memorial Cup-41
97Macon Whoopee-4
97Macon Whoopee Autographs-4
98Idaho Steelheads-12

Parent, Travis
00Brampton Battalion-5A
01Mississauga Ice Dogs-4
02Mississauga Ice Dogs-2

Parent, Vincent
93Quebec Pee-Wee Tournament-84

Parenteau, Pierre-Alexandre
01Chicoutimi Sagueneens-4
03Cincinnati Mighty Ducks-A4
04Cincinnati Mighty Ducks-25
05Portland Pirates-6
06Norfolk Admirals-14
07Upper Deck Victory-243
Black-243
Gold-243

Parfet, Van
93Indianapolis Ice-24
97Las Vegas Thunder-26
98Las Vegas Thunder-27

Pargatzi, Fredy
02Swiss HNL-496

Pargeter, George
51Buffalo Bison-17

Parikka, Pekka
70Finnish Jaakiekko-262

Parikka, Seppo
66Finnish Jaakiekkosarja-55
70Finnish Jaakiekko-147
71Finnish Suomi Stickers-197
72Finnish Jaakiekko-235
73Finnish Jaakiekko-269

Parillo, Nick
02ECHL All-Star Northern-30
03Toledo Storm-6
05Colorado Eagles-15
06Toledo Storm-17

Paris, Benoit
01Drummondville Voltigeurs-15

Paris, Drew
04Quebec Remparts-16
05Quebec Remparts-5
05Quebec Remparts Signature Series-5
05Rimouski Oceanic-27
06Drummondville Voltigeurs-4

Paris, Frederic
93Quebec Pee-Wee Tournament-109

Paris, John
94Atlanta Knights-25
95Atlanta Knights-22
97Macon Whoopee-3
97Macon Whoopee Autographs-3

Paris, Maxime
93Quebec Pee-Wee Tournament-404

Paris, Philippe
99Quebec Remparts-11
Signed-11
00Quebec Remparts-8
Signed-8

Parise, J.P.
68O-Pee-Chee-149
69O-Pee-Chee-127
69Topps-127
70Dad's Cookies-96
70Esso Power Players-171
70North Stars Postcards-6
70O-Pee-Chee-168
70Sargent Promotions Stamps-94
70Topps/OPC Sticker Stamps-24
71O-Pee-Chee-243
71Sargent Promotions Stamps-83
71Toronto Sun-142
72O-Pee-Chee-199
Team Canada-20
72Sargent Promotions Stamps-101
72Finnish Semic World Championship-219
72Swedish Semic World Championship-219
73Mac's Milk-20
73North Stars Action Posters-9
73North Stars Postcards-16
73O-Pee-Chee-46
73Topps-46
74Lipton Soup-4
74NHL Action Stamps-133
74NHL Action Stamps Update-25
74O-Pee-Chee NHL-83
74Topps-83
75O-Pee-Chee NHL-127
75Topps-127
76O-Pee-Chee NHL-182
76Topps-182
77O-Pee-Chee NHL-29
77Topps-29
78North Stars Cloverleaf Dairy-3
78O-Pee-Chee-350
79O-Pee-Chee-118
79Topps-118
80North Stars Postcards-14
91Future Trends Canada '72-99
91Future Trends Canada '72 French-99
04ITG Franchises US East-380
04ITG Franchises US West-245
Autographs-A-JPP
04UD Legendary Signatures-94
Autographs-JP
Summit Stars-CDN7
Summit Stars Autographs-CDN-JP
06Beehive Signature Scrapbook-SSPA
06ITG International Ice-107
Gold-107
Autographs-AJPP
06Parkhurst-128
06Parkhurst-176
Autographs-128
Autographs-176
06SP Authentic Sign of the Times Duals-STPP

Parise, Jordan
03North Dakota Fighting Sioux-21
04North Dakota Fighting Sioux-18
06Between The Pipes-25
Autographs-AJPA

Parise, Zach
03BAP Memorabilia Draft Redemptions-17
03North Dakota Fighting Sioux-11
04SP Authentic Rookie Redemptions-RR18
04AHL All-Stars-32
04AHL Top Prospects-1
04Albany River Rats-16
04ITG Heroes and Prospects-183
Autographs-U-ZP
04ITG Heroes/Prospects Toronto Expo '05-183
05ITG Heroes/Prosp Toronto Expo Parallel -74
05Beehive-107
Beige -107
Blue -107
Gold-107
Red -107
Matte-107
Signature Scrapbook-SSZP
05Black Diamond-192
Emerald-192
Gold-192
Onyx-192
Ruby-192
05Devils Team Issue-25
05Hot Prospects-249
En Fuego-249
Hot Materials-HMZP
Red Hot-249
White Hot-249
05Panini Stickers-90
05Parkhurst-640
Facsimile Auto Parallel-640
Signatures-ZP
True Colors-TCNJD
True Colors-TCNJD
05SP Authentic-167
Limited-167
Rarefied Rookies-RRZP
Rookie Authentics-RAZP
05SP Game Used-142
Autographs-142
Gold-142
Game Gear-GG-ZP
Game Gear Autographs-AG-ZP
Rookie Exclusives-ZP
Rookie Exclusives Silver-RE-ZP
Significant Numbers-SN-ZP
05SPx-163
Spectrum-163
Xcitement Rookies-XR-ZP
Xcitement Rookies Gold-XR-ZP
Xcitement Rookies Spectrum-XR-ZP
05The Cup-113
Autographed Rookie Patches Gold Rainbow-113

Black Rainbow Rookies-113
Masterpiece Pressplates (Artifacts)-218
Masterpiece Pressplates (Bee Hive)-107
Masterpiece Pressplates (Black Diamond)-192
Masterpiece Pressplates (Ice)-115
Masterpiece Pressplates (MVP)-403
Masterpiece Pressplates (Power Play)-155
Masterpiece Pressplates (Power Play)-155
Masterpiece Pressplates (Rookie Update)-216
Masterpiece Pressplates SPA Autos-167
Masterpiece Pressplates (SP Game Used)-142
Masterpiece Pressplates SPx Autos-163
Masterpiece Pressplates (Trilogy)-198
Masterpiece Pressplates Ult Coll Autos-122
Masterpiece Pressplates (Victory)-268
Masterpiece Pressplates Autographs-113
Platinum Rookies-113
05UD Artifacts-218
Gold-RED18
05UD PowerPlay-155
05UD Rookie Class-34
05Ultimate Collection-122
Autographed Patches-122
Autographed Shields-122
Ultimate Debut Threads Jerseys-DTJZP
Ultimate Debut Threads Jerseys Autos-DAJZP
Ultimate Debut Threads Patches-DTPZP
Ultimate Debut Threads Patches Autos-DAPZP
Ultimate Signatures Logos-SLZP
05Ultra-260
Gold-260
Fresh Ink-FI-ZP
Fresh Ink Blue-FI-ZP
Ice-260
Rookie Uniformity Jerseys-RU-ZP
Rookie Uniformity Jersey Autographs-ARU-ZP
Rookie Uniformity Patches-RUP-ZP
Rookie Uniformity Patch Autographs-ARP-ZP
05Upper Deck-206
HG Glossy-206
Rookie Ink-RIZP
05Upper Deck Rookie Showcase-RS18
05Upper Deck Rookie Showcase Promos-RS18
05Upper Deck Rookie Threads-RTZP
05Upper Deck Rookie Threads Autographs-ARTZP
05Upper Deck Stars in the Making-SM13
05Upper Deck Ice-115
Cool Threads-CTZP
Cool Threads Autographs-ACTZP
Cool Threads Glass-CTZP
Cool Threads Patches-CTPZP
Cool Threads Patch Autographs-CAPZP
Fresh Ice-FIZP
Fresh Ice Glass-FIZP
Fresh Ice Glass Patches-FIPZP
Glacial Graphs-GGZP
Glacial Graphs Labels-GGZP
Premieres Auto Patches-AIPZP
05Upper Deck MVP-403
Gold-403
Platinum-403
Rookie Breakthrough-RB7
05Upper Deck Rookie Update-216
Inspirations Patch Rookies-216
05Upper Deck Trilogy-198
05Upper Deck Toronto Fall Expo-206
05Upper Deck Victory-268
Black-268
Gold-268
Silver-268
05ITG Heroes and Prospects-74
Autographs-A-ZP
Autographs-DA-PM
Complete Jerseys-CJ-4
Complete Jerseys Gold-CJ-4
Jerseys-GUJ-58
Jerseys Gold-GUJ-58
Emblems-GUE-58
Emblems Gold-GUE-58
Numbers-GUN-58
Numbers Gold-GUN-58
Nameplates-N-36
Nameplates Gold-N-36
Shooting Stars-AS-10
06Be A Player Portraits First Exposures-FEZP
06Black Diamond-51
Black-51
Gold-51
Ruby-51
06Devils Team Set-20
06Flair Showcase Wave of the Future-WF25
06Fleer-120
Tiffany-120
06O-Pee-Chee-297
06O-Pee-Chee-628
Rainbow-297
Rainbow-628
06Panini Stickers-84
06SP Authentic Sign of the Times Duals-STPP
06The Cup NHL Shields Duals-DSHLE
06UD Biography of a Season-BOS12
06UD Powerplay Power Marks-PMZP
06UD Toronto Fall Expo Priority Signings -PSZP
06Ultra-120
Gold Medallion-120
Ice Medallion-120
06Upper Deck Arena Giveaways-NJD3
06Upper Deck-116
Exclusives Parallel-116
High Gloss Parallel-116
Masterpieces-116
Signatures-SZP
06Upper Deck MVP-174
Gold Script-174
Super Script-174
06Upper Deck Trilogy Combo Clearcut Autographs-C2GP
06Upper Deck Victory-121
06Upper Deck Victory Black-121
06Upper Deck Victory Gold-121
06Upper Deck Victory Next In Line-NL31
07Upper Deck Ovation-72
07Upper Deck Victory-2
Black-2
Gold-2
Stars on Ice-SI46

Parish, Kevin
94UK Guildford Flames-8

Parizeau, Michel
71Blues Postcards-15
71Toronto Sun-242
72Nordiques Postcards-17
72O-Pee-Chee-335
73Nordiques Team Issue-17
73Quaker Oats WHA-43
74O-Pee-Chee WHA-52

Parizek, Jaroslav
98Czech OFS-193
99Czech OFS-277
00Czech OFS-3

Park, Brad
70Dad's Cookies-97
70Esso Power Players-182
70O-Pee-Chee-67
70O-Pee-Chee-239
Deckle-43
70Sargent Promotions Stamps-124
70Topps-67
71Colgate Heads-9
71Letraset Action Replays-20
71O-Pee-Chee-40
71O-Pee-Chee-257
71Sargent Promotions Stamps-116
71Topps-40
71Toronto Sun-178
72O-Pee-Chee-85A
72O-Pee-Chee-85B
72O-Pee-Chee-114
72O-Pee-Chee-227
Player Crests-15
Team Canada-21
72Sargent Promotions Stamps-144
72Topps-30
72Topps-123
72Finnish Semic World Championship-194
72Swedish Stickers-114
72Swedish Semic World Championship-194
73Mac's Milk-21
73O-Pee-Chee-165
73Topps-165
74Lipton Soup-10
74NHL Action Stamps-196
74O-Pee-Chee NHL-50
74O-Pee-Chee NHL-131
74O-Pee-Chee NHL-141
74Topps-50
74Topps-131
74Topps-141
75Heroes Stand-Ups-4
75Nabisco Sugar Daddy-13
75O-Pee-Chee NHL-260A
75O-Pee-Chee NHL-260B
75Topps-260
76O-Pee-Chee NHL-60
76Topps-60
76Topps Glossy Inserts-2
77Coca-Cola-18
77O-Pee-Chee NHL-190
77Sportscasters-717
77Topps-190
77Topps/O-Pee-Chee Glossy-13
Square-13
77Finnish Sportscasters-26-692
78O-Pee-Chee-79
78Topps-79
79O-Pee-Chee-23
79O-Pee-Chee-164
79Topps-23
79Topps-164
80O-Pee-Chee-74
80O-Pee-Chee Super-1
80Topps-74
81O-Pee-Chee-8
81O-Pee-Chee Stickers-48
81Topps-E72
82O-Pee-Chee-19
82O-Pee-Chee Stickers-82
82Post Cereal-1
82Topps Stickers-82
83O-Pee-Chee-129
83O-Pee-Chee Stickers-48
83O-Pee-Chee Stickers-178
83Puffy Stickers-15
83Topps Stickers-48
83Topps Stickers-178
84O-Pee-Chee-63
84O-Pee-Chee-378
84O-Pee-Chee-390
84O-Pee-Chee Stickers-38
84O-Pee-Chee Stickers-231
84Topps-47
88Esso All-Stars-34
91Bruins Sports Action Legends-21
91Future Trends Canada '72-95
91Future Trends Canada '72 French-95
93Zeller's Masters of Hockey-6
93Zeller's Masters of Hockey Signed-6
93Quebec Pee-Wee Tournament Gold-1
94Hockey Wit-10
95Signature Rookies Cool Five-CF2
95Signature Rookies Cool Five Signatures-CF2
98Bruins Alumni-22
Autographs-22
99BAP Memorabilia AS American Hobby-AH9
99BAP Memorabilia AS American Hobby Autos-AH9
99Upper Deck Century Legends Epic Sigs-BP
99Upper Deck Century Legends Epic Sig 100-BP
99Upper Deck Retro-106
Gold-106
Platinum-106
Inkredible-BP
Inkredible Level 2-BP
99Quebec PeeWee Tournament Coll Souv-1
01Fleer Legacy-20
Ultimate-20
Memorabilia-19
01Greats of the Game-77
Autographs-77
Sticks-8
03BAP Ultimate Mem Hometown Heroes-6
03BAP Ultimate Mem Hometown Heroes Gold-6
03Pacific Exhibit-225
03Parkhurst Original Six Boston-38
Autographs-15
Memorabilia-BM65
03Parkhurst Original Six Detroit-53
03Parkhurst Original Six New York-42
03Parkhurst Original Six New York-65
03Parkhurst Original Six New York-80
03Parkhurst Original Six New York-81
03Parkhurst Original Six New York-97
Autographs-12
Inserts-N16
04Canada Post-30
04Canada Post Autographs-6
04ITG Franchises US East-312
04ITG Franchises US East-385
Autographs-A-BP1
Autographs-A-BP2
Complete Jerseys-ECJ6
Complete Jerseys Gold-ECJ6
Forever Rivals-EFR1
Forever Rivals Gold-EFR1
Memorabilia-ESM10
Memorabilia Autographs-ESM-BP
Memorabilia Gold-ESM10
Teammates-ETM5
Teammates Gold-ETM5
04ITG Ultimate Memorabilia-101
04ITG Ultimate Memorabilia-126
04ITG Ultimate Memorabilia-169
Gold-101
Gold-126
Gold-169
Auto Threads-20
Autographs-36
Autographs-42
Autographs Gold-36
Autographs Gold-42
Complete Jerseys-6
Jersey Autographs-16
Jersey Autographs Gold-16
Jersey and Sticks-5
Jersey and Sticks Gold-5
Original Six-8
Original Six-10
Retro Teammates-12
Retro Teammates-14
Stick Autographs-37
Stick Autographs Gold-37
Triple Threads-2
04UD Legendary Signatures-12
Autographs-VP
Summit Stars-CDN5
Summit Stars Autographs-CDN-BP
04UD Legends Classics-9
Gold-9
Platinum-9
Silver-9
Signature Moments-M51
Signature Moments-M60
Signatures-CS49
Signatures-DC10
Signatures-TC8
04ITG Heroes and Prospects-170
Autographs-BPA
04ITG Heroes/Prospects Toronto Expo '05-170
04ITG Heroes/Prospects Expo Heroes/Pros-170
05Beehive Signature Scrapbook-SSBP
05ITG Ultimate Mem Decades Jerseys-1
05ITG Ultimate Mem Decades Jerseys Gold-1
05ITG Ultimate Memorabilia Jersey Autos-32
05ITG Ultimate Mem Jersey Autos Gold-32
05ITG Ultimate Mem Pass the Torch Jerseys-6
05ITG Ultimate Mem Passing Torch Jsy Gold-6
05ITG Ultimate Mem 3 Star of the Game Jsy-12
05ITG Ult Mem 3 Star of the Game Jsy Gold-12
05ITG Ultimate Memorabilia Triple Autos-19
05ITG Ultimate Mem Triple Autos Gold-19
05NHL Legends Medallions-14
05SP Game Used Statscriptions-ST-BP
05SPx Xcitement Legends-XL-BP
05SPx Xcitement Legends Gold-XL-BP
05SPx Xcitement Legends Spectrum-XL-BP
05UD Artifacts-142
Blue-142
Gold-142
Green-142
Pewter-142
Red-142
Gold Autographed-142
05ITG Heroes and Prospects Hero Mem-HM-12
06ITG International Ice-108
Gold-108
Autographs-ABP
06ITG Ultimate Memorabilia-20
Artist Proof-20
Autos-28
Autos Gold-28
Boys Will Be Boys-24
Boys Will Be Boys Gold-24
Decades-7
Decades Gold-7
Jerseys Autos-43
Jerseys Autos Gold-43
Sticks Autos-23
Sticks Autos Gold-23
06Parkhurst-93
06Parkhurst-195
Autographs-93
Autographs-195
Autographs Dual-DABO
06SP Game Used Inked Sweaters Dual-IS2CP
06SP Game Used Inked Sweaters Dual Patches-IS2CP
06The Cup Signature Patches-SPPA
06UD Artifacts Frozen Artifacts-FABP
06UD Artifacts Frozen Artifacts Black-FABP
06UD Artifacts Frozen Artifacts Blue-FABP
06UD Artifacts Frozen Artifacts Gold-FABP
06UD Artifacts Frozen Artifacts Platinum-FABP
06UD Artifacts Frozen Artifacts Red-FABP
06UD Artifacts Frozen Artifacts Patches Black-FABP
06UD Artifacts Frozen Artifacts Patches Blue-FABP
06UD Artifacts Frozen Artifacts Patches Gold-FABP
06UD Artifacts Frozen Artifacts Patches Platinum-FABP
06UD Artifacts Frozen Artifacts Patches Red-FABP
06Ultimate Collection Autographed Jerseys-AJ-BP
06Ultimate Collection Autographed Patches-AJ-BP
06Upper Deck Game Jerseys-J2BP
06Upper Deck Game Patches-P2BP

Park, Greg
04Moose Jaw Warriors-1

Park, Jim
77O-Pee-Chee WHA-56

Park, Richard
93Donruss Team USA-17
93Pinnacle-498
Canadian-498
93Upper Deck-553
94Finest-112
Super Team Winners-112
Refractors-112
94Leaf Limited World Juniors USA-9
94Parkhurst SE-SE249
Gold-SE249
94Score-210
Gold-210
Platinum-210
94SP-175
Die Cuts-175
94Upper Deck-525
Electric Ice-525
95Be A Player-185
Signatures-S185
Signatures Die Cuts-S185
95Bowman-123
All-Foil-123
95Donruss-331
95Finest-89
Refractors-89
95Leaf-221
95Leaf Limited-36
95Metal-187
95Metal Promo Panel-4
95Parkhurst International-169
Emerald Ice-169
95Penguins Foodland-7
95Pinnacle-220
Artist's Proofs-220
Rink Collection-220
95Score-295
Black Ice Artist's Proofs-295
Black Ice-295
95SkyBox Impact-217
95SP-120
95Stadium Club-208
Members Only Master Set-208
95Topps-119
OPC Inserts-119
95Upper Deck-419
Electric Ice-419
Electric Ice Gold-419
95Signature Rookies-12
Signatures-12
96Collector's Choice-217
96Cleveland Lumberjacks-21
96Cleveland Lumberjacks Multi-Ad-23
97Pacific Invincible NHL Regime-6
97Upper Deck-215
99Utah Grizzlies-3
00Cleveland Lumberjacks-19
02Pacific Complete-247
Red-247
02Topps Total-3
02Upper Deck-332
Exclusives-332
02Upper Deck Beckett UD Promos-332
02Upper Deck Vintage-123
02Upper Deck Vintage-275
03ITG Action-284
03Pacific-168
Blue-168
Red-168
03Pacific Complete-272
Red-272
03Wild Law Enforcement Cards-6
04Swedish Malmo Red Hawks-22

Parke, Andre
99Rouyn-Noranda Huskies-24

Parker, Brett
03Prince George Cougars-23

Parker, Derek
99Lethbridge Hurricanes-20

Parker, Jack
03Boston University Terriers-6

Parker, Jeff
88Sabres Blue Shield-17
88Sabres Wonder Bread/Hostess-19
88ProCards AHL-254
89Sabres Blue Shield-14
89Sabres Campbell's-17
90O-Pee-Chee-497

Parker, Jonathan
98Prince George Cougars-17
99Prince George Cougars-12

Parker, Scott
98Pacific Omega-66
Red-66
Opening Day Issue-66
98Hershey Bears-7
99BAP Millennium-64
Emerald-64
Ruby-64
Sapphire-64
Signatures-64
Signatures Gold-64
00Topps Heritage-176
01Avalanche Team Issue-5
01BAP Update Tough Customers-TC23
01BAP Update Tough Customers-TC37
01Pacific-408
Gold-408
01Pacific Arena Exclusives-408
02Avalanche Postcards-3
02BAP Sig Series Auto Buybacks 1999-64
02Pacific-93
Blue-93
Red-93
02Upper Deck-293
Exclusives-293
02Upper Deck Beckett UD Promos-293
03Topps Signs of Toughness-SP
03Topps Tough Materials-GLSP
03Topps Tough Materials Signed-SP
03Topps C55 Relics-TRSP

Parker, Shane
94North Bay Centennials-25
95Slapshot-230

Parker, Stan
52Juniors Blue Tint-86

Parkes, Kyle
04Camrose Kodiaks-9

Parkhomenko, Dmitri
99Russian Hockey League-171
01Russian Hockey League-75

Parkin, Danny
94UK Humberside Hawks-17

Parks, Greg
90OPC Premier-89
91ProCards-462
92Parkhurst-491
Emerald Ice-491
92Swedish Semic Elitserien Stickers-170
93Swedish Semic Elitserien-139
94Score Team Canada-CT11
95Swedish Leaf-175
Face to Face-2
95Swedish Upper Deck-32
96Swiss HNL-335
98Swiss Power Play Stickers-147

Parlatore, Dominic
02UK Hull Thunder-18

Parley, Davis
99Kamloops Blazers-18
00Kamloops Blazers-18
02Kamloops Blazers-12

Parlini, Fred
96UK Guildford Flames-6

Parmstrom, Anders
64Swedish Coralli ISHockey-41
65Swedish Coralli ISHockey-41
67Swedish Hockey-40
69Swedish Hockey-52

Parnell, Greg
90Michigan Tech Huskies-18
91Michigan Tech Huskies-17

Parnham, Brett
06Oshawa Generals-13

Paroshy, Erich
99Hull Olympiques-1
Signed-1

Paroulek, Martin
00Czech OFS-338
01Syracuse Crunch-17
03Czech OFS Plus-158
03Czech OFS Plus-385
04Czech HC Plzen Postcards-13
04Czech OFS-346

Parr, Maurice
51Bas Du Fleuve-53

Parrish, Dwight
91Ferris State Bulldogs-26
92Ferris State Bulldogs-26
96Dayton Bombers-6
98Portland Pirates-23
99Hampton Roads Admirals-15
00UK Sekonda Superleague-56
01UK Cardiff Devils-9
01UK Manchester Storm-5
02UK Cardiff Devils-9
02UK Manchester Storm-7
03UK Manchester Phoenix-4

Parrish, Geno
00Fort Wayne Komets-14
00Fort Wayne Komets Shoe Carnival-10
00Knoxville Speed-20
02ECHL All-Star Northern-31
02Greensboro Generals RBI-15
03Greensboro Generals-188
05Stockton Thunder-16

Parrish, Mark
95Donruss Elite World Juniors-38
97Seattle Thunderbirds-21
98Be A Player-206
Press Release-206
98BAP Gold-206
98BAP Autographs-206
98BAP Autographs Gold-206
98Black Diamond-38
Double Diamond-38
Triple Diamond-38
Quadruple Diamond-38
Myriad-M20
Myriad 2-M20
98Bowman's Best-120
Refractors-120
Atomic Refractors-120
Autographs-A9A
Autographs-A9B
Autographs Refractors-A9A
Autographs Refractors-A9B
Autographs Atomic Refractors-A9A
Autographs Atomic Refractors-A9B
Mirror Image Fusion-F3
Mirror Image Fusion Refractors-F3
Mirror Image Fusion Atomic Refractors-F3
98Crown Royale-61
Limited Series-61
Pivotal Players-12
Rookie Class-3
98Pacific Dynagon Ice-85
Blue-85
Red-85
Rookies-3
98Pacific Omega-106
Red-106
Opening Day Issue-106
Planet Ice-4
Planet Ice Parallel-4
98Panini Photocards-60
98Revolution-64
Ice Shadow-64
Red-64
Showstoppers-19
98SP Authentic-97
Power Shift-97
98SPx Top Prospects-29
Radiance-29
Spectrum-29
98Topps Gold Label Class 1-89
Black-89
Black One of One-89
One of One-89
Red-89
Red One of One-89
98Topps Gold Label Class 2-89
98Topps Gold Label Class 2 Black-89
98Topps Gold Label Class 2 Black 1 of 1-89
98Topps Gold Label Class 2 One of One-89
98Topps Gold Label Class 2 Red-89
98Topps Gold Label Class 2 Red One of One-89
98Topps Gold Label Class 3-89
98Topps Gold Label Class 3 Black-89
98Topps Gold Label Class 3 Black 1 of 1-89
98Topps Gold Label Class 3 One of One-89
98Topps Gold Label Class 3 Red-89
98Topps Gold Label Class 3 Red One of One-89
98Upper Deck-282
Exclusives-282
Exclusives 1 of 1-282
Gold Reserve-282
98Upper Deck MVP-91
Gold Script-91
Silver Script-91
Super Script-91
Power Game-PG12
ProSign-MP
99Aurora-65
Striped-65
Premiere Date-65
Premiere Date Striped-65
99BAP Memorabilia-180
Gold-180
Silver-180
99BAP Millennium-113
Emerald-113
Ruby-113
Sapphire-113
Signatures-113
Signatures Gold-113
99O-Pee-Chee-141
99O-Pee-Chee Chrome-141
99O-Pee-Chee Chrome Refractors-141
99O-Pee-Chee Chrome Ice Futures-IF1
99O-Pee-Chee Chrome Ice Futures Refractor-IF1
99O-Pee-Chee Ice Futures-IF1
99Pacific-180
Copper-180
Emerald Green-180
Gold-180
Ice Blue-180
Premiere Date-180
Red-180
99Pacific Dynagon Ice-92
Blue-92
Copper-92
Gold-92
Premiere Date-92
99Pacific Omega-99
Copper-99
Gold-99
Ice Blue-99
Premiere Date-99
99Pacific Prism-63
Holographic Blue-63
Holographic Gold-63
Holographic Mirror-63
Holographic Purple-63
Premiere Date-63
99Panini Stickers-61
99Paramount-105
Copper-105
Emerald-105
Gold-105
Holographic Emerald-105
Holographic Gold-105
Holographic Silver-105
Ice Blue-105
Premiere Date-105
Red-105
Silver-105
99Revolution-65
Premiere Date-65
Red-65
Shadow Series-65
Showstoppers-20
Copper-65
Gold-65
CSC Silver-65
99SPx-68
Radiance-68
Spectrum-68
99Stadium Club-29
First Day Issue-29
One of a Kind-29
Printing Plates Black-29
Printing Plates Cyan-29
Printing Plates Magenta-29
Printing Plates Yellow-29
Capture the Action-CA4
Capture the Action Game View-CAG4
99Topps/OPC-141
Ice Futures-IF1
99Topps/OPC Chrome-141
Refractors-141
Ice Futures-IF1
Ice Futures Refractors-IF1
99Topps Gold Label Fresh Gold-FG11
99Topps Gold Label Fresh Gold Black-FG11
99Topps Gold Label Fresh Gold Black 1of1-FG11
99Topps Gold Label Fresh Gold One of One-FG11
99Topps Gold Label Fresh Gold Red-FG11
99Topps Gold Label Fresh Gold Red 1 of 1-FG11
99Topps Premier Plus-26
Parallel-26
99Upper Deck-58
Exclusives-58
Exclusives 1 of 1-58
99Upper Deck Arena Giveaways-FP2
99Upper Deck Gold Reserve-58
99Upper Deck HoloGrFx-27
Ausome-27
99Upper Deck MVP-84
Gold Script-84
Silver Script-84
Super Script-84
Draft Report-DR8
99Upper Deck Retro-36
Gold-36
Platinum-36
Generation-G9C
Generation Level 2-G9C
99Upper Deck Victory-121
99Upper Deck Victory-355
99Wayne Gretzky Hockey-73
Signs of Greatness-MP
00Aurora-90
Premiere Date-90
00BAP Memorabilia-482
Emerald-482
Ruby-482
Sapphire-482
00BAP Parkhurst 2000-P37
00O-Pee-Chee-117
00O-Pee-Chee Parallel-117
00Pacific-185
Copper-185
Gold-185
Ice Blue-185
Premiere Date-185
00Topps/OPC-117
Parallel-117
00Topps Chrome-27
OPC Refractors-27
Refractors-27
00Upper Deck-342
Exclusives Tier 1-342
Exclusives Tier 2-342
00Upper Deck Victory-102
00Upper Deck Vintage-232
01Bowman YoungStars-75
Gold-75
Ice Cubed-75
01Crown Royale-91
Blue-91
Premiere Date-91
Red-91
Retail-91
01Pacific-252
Extreme LTD-252
Hobby LTD-252
Premiere Date-252
Retail LTD-252
01Pacific Arena Exclusives-252
01Parkhurst-187
01SP Authentic-53
Limited-53
Limited Gold-53
01Titanium-89
Hobby Parallel-89
Premiere Date-89
Retail-89
Retail Parallel-89
01Topps Chrome-131
Refractors-131
Black Border Refractors-131
01UD Honor Roll-27
01UD Honor Roll-57
01UD Mask Collection-59
Gold-59
01UD Playmakers-63
01UD Top Shelf-104
01Upper Deck-109
Exclusives-109
01Upper Deck Ice-105
01Upper Deck MVP-118
01Upper Deck Victory-226
Gold-226
01Upper Deck Vintage-164
01Vanguard-60
Blue-60
Red-60
One of Ones-60
Premiere Date-60
Proofs-60
02BAP First Edition-221
02BAP Memorabilia-121
Emerald-121
Ruby-121
Sapphire-121
NHL All-Star Game-121
NHL All-Star Game Blue-121
NHL All-Star Game Green-121
NHL All-Star Game Red-121
02BAP Memorabilia Toronto Fall Expo-121
02BAP Signature Series-54
Autographs-54
Autograph Buybacks 1998-206
Autograph Buybacks 1999-113
Autographs Gold-54
Golf-GS50
02Bowman YoungStars-51
Gold-51
Silver-51
02O-Pee-Chee-163
02O-Pee-Chee Premier Blue Parallel-163
02O-Pee-Chee Premier Red Parallel-163
02O-Pee-Chee Factory Set-163
02Pacific-241
Blue-241
Red-241
02Pacific Complete-222
Red-222
02Pacific Exclusive-109
02Pacific Heads-Up-74
Blue-74
Purple-74
Red-74
02Parkhurst-19
Bronze-19
Gold-19
Silver-19
02Parkhurst Retro-49
Minis-49
02Private Stock Reserve-64
Blue-64
Red-64
Retail-64
02Stadium Club-63
Silver Decoy Cards-63
Proofs-63
02Topps-163
OPC Blue Parallel-163
OPC Red Parallel-163
Factory Set-163
02Topps Total-43
02Upper Deck-113
Exclusives-113
02Upper Deck MVP-113
Gold-113
Classics-113
Golden Classics-113
02Upper Deck Rookie Update-62
02Upper Deck Victory-132
Bronze-132
Gold-132
Silver-132
02Upper Deck Vintage-158
02Vanguard-63
LTD-63
03Beehive-123
Gold-123
Silver-123
03ITG Action-306
03NHL Sticker Collection-75
03O-Pee-Chee-79
03OPC Blue-79
03OPC Gold-79
03OPC Red-79
03Pacific-213
Blue-213
Red-213
03Pacific Complete-353
Red-353
03Pacific Exhibit-94
Blue Backs-94
Yellow Backs-94
03Pacific Invincible-61
Blue-61
Red-61
Retail-61
03Pacific Prism-68
Blue-68
Gold-68
Red-68
03Private Stock Reserve-65
Blue-65
Red-65
Retail-65
03SPx Big Futures-BF-MP
03SPx Big Futures Limited-BF-MP
03Topps-79
Blue-79
Gold-79
Red-79
Topps/OPC Idols-UI10
03UD Honor Roll Signature Class-SC32
03Upper Deck-119
Canadian Exclusives-119
HG-119
03Upper Deck MVP-265
Gold Script-265
Silver Script-265
Canadian Exclusives-265
04Pacific-169
Blue-169
Red-169
04SP Authentic Rookie Review-RR-MP
04SP Authentic Sign of the Times-ST-PA
04UD Toronto Fall Expo Priority Signings-MP
04Upper Deck-109
Canadian Exclusives-109
HG Glossy Gold-109
HG Glossy Silver-109
Jersey Autographs-GJA-MP
Jersey Autographs-GJA-PA/MP
05Be A Player Dual Signatures-PP
05Be A Player Signatures-MP
05Be A Player Signatures Gold-MP
05Beehive Matted Materials-MMMP
05Beehive Matted Materials Remarkable-RMMP
05Black Diamond-59
Emerald-59
Gold-59
Onyx-59
Ruby-59
05Panini Stickers-95
05Parkhurst-232
Facsimile Auto Parallel-305
Signatures-MP
True Colors-TCNYI
True Colors-TCNYI
05SP Authentic-64
Limited-64
Prestigious Pairings-PPPH
Sign of the Times Triples-TYPN
05SP Game Used-65
Autographs-65
Gold-65
Authentic Fabrics-AF-MP
Authentic Fabrics Autographs-AAF-MP
Authentic Fabrics Gold-AF-MP
Authentic Fabrics Triple-YSP
Authentic Patches-AP-MP
Authentic Patches Autographs-AAP-MP
Authentic Patches Triple-YSP
Awesome Authentics-AA-MP
SIGnificance-MP
SIGnificance Gold-S-MP
SIGnificance Extra-HP
SIGnificance Extra Gold-HP
05SPx Winning Combos-WC-PS
05SPx Winning Combos Autographs-AWC-PS
05SPx Winning Combos Gold-WC-PS
05SPx Winning Combos Spectrum-WC-PS
05SPx Winning Materials-WM-MP
05SPx Winning Materials Gold-WM-MP
05SPx Winning Materials Spectrum-WM-MP
05SPx Xcitement Superstars-XS-MP
05SPx Xcitement Superstars Gold-XS-MP
05SPx Xcitement Superstars Spectrum-XS-MP
05The Cup Dual NHL Shields-DSYP
05The Cup Dual NHL Shields Autographs-ADSYP
05The Cup Honorable Numbers-HNMP
05The Cup Master Pressplate Rookie Update-223
05The Cup Scripted Swatches-SSMP
05The Cup Signature Patches-SPMP
05UD Artifacts-65
05UD Artifacts-181
Blue-65
Blue-181
Gold-65
Gold-181
Green-65
Green-181
Pewter-65
Pewter-181
Red-65
Red-181
Gold Autographed-65
Gold Autographed-181
05UD PowerPlay-58
Rainbow-58
05UD Toronto Fall Expo Priority Signings-PS-MP
05Ultimate Collection Endorsed Emblems-EEPA
05Ultimate Coll National Heroes Jersey-NHJMP
05Ultimate Coll National Heroes Patch-NHPMP
05Ultra-127
Gold-127
Ice-127
05Upper Deck-120
Big Playmakers-B-MPE
HG Glossy-120
Jerseys-J-MPA
Jerseys Series II-J2PA
Notable Numbers-N-MPH
Patches-P-MPA
Shooting Stars-S-MP
05Upper Deck MVP-248
Gold-248
Platinum-248
Materials-M-MP
05Upper Deck Rookie Update-223
Inspirations Patch Rookies-223
05Upper Deck Trilogy Scripts-SCS-MP
05Upper Deck Toronto Fall Expo-120
05Upper Deck Victory-123
Black-123
Gold-123
Silver-123
06Be A Player-69
Autographs-69
Signatures-PA
Signatures 10-74
Signatures Duals-DBP
Up Close and Personal-UC31
Up Close and Personal Autographs-UC31
06Beehive-54
Matte-54
06Black Diamond-41
Black-41
Gold-41
Ruby-41
Gemography-GMP
06Flair Showcase Inks-IMP
06Flair Showcase Stitches-SSPA
06Fleer-101
Tiffany-101
Fabricology-FMP
06O-Pee-Chee-244
Rainbow-244
06Panini Stickers-294
06SP Authentic Sign of the Times Triples-ST3PGB
06SP Game Used Authentic Fabrics Dual-AF2PB
06SP Game Used Authentic Fabrics Dual Patches-AF2PB
06SP Game Used Inked Sweaters-ISMP
06SP Game Used Inked Sweaters Patches-ISMP
06SP Game Used SIGnificance-SPA
06UD Artifacts Tundra Tandems-TTFP
06UD Artifacts Tundra Tandems Black-TTFP
06UD Artifacts Tundra Tandems Blue-TTFP

06UD Artifacts Tundra Tandems Gold-TTFP
06UD Artifacts Tundra Tandems Platinum-TTFP
06UD Artifacts Tundra Tandems Red-TTFP
06UD Artifacts Tundra Tandems Dual Patches Red-TTFP
06Ultra-98
Gold Medallion-98
Ice Medallion-98
Uniformity-UMP
Uniformity Patches-UPMP
Uniformity Autographed Jerseys-UAMP
06Upper Deck Arena Giveaways-MIN5
06Upper Deck-350
Exclusives Parallel-350
High Gloss Parallel-350
Game Jerseys-J2MP
Game Patches-P2MP
Masterpieces-350
Signature Sensations-SSMP
06Upper Deck MVP-142
Gold Script-142
Super Script-142
Autographs-OABP
06Upper Deck Trilogy Combo Autographed Jerseys-CJGP
06Upper Deck Trilogy Combo Autographed Patches-CJGP
06Upper Deck Trilogy Scripts-TSMP
06Upper Deck Victory-256
06Wild Crime Prevention-4
06Wild Postcards-4

Parro, Dave
77Rochester Americans-19
81Capitals Team Issue-14
82Capitals Team Issue-20
82O-Pee-Chee-371
82O-Pee-Chee Stickers-158
82Topps Stickers-158

Parros, George
03Manchester Monarchs-12
03Manchester Monarchs Team Issue-12
04SP Authentic Rookie Redemptions-RR14
04Manchester Monarchs-9
04Manchester Monarchs Tobacco-10
05Beehive-178
Matte-178
05Black Diamond-249
05Hot Prospects-201
Autographed Patch Variation-201
Autographed Patch Variation Gold-201
Hot Materials-HMGP
Red Hot-201
05Parkhurst-633
Facsimile Auto Parallel-232
Signatures-GP
True Colors-TCLAK
True Colors-TCLAK
05SP Authentic-160
Limited-160
Sign of the Times-GP
05SP Game Used-128
Autographs-128
Gold-128
Rookie Exclusives-GP
Rookie Exclusives Silver-RE-GP
Significant Numbers-SN-GP
05SPx-144
Spectrum-144
05The Cup-187
Black Rainbow Rookies-187
Masterpiece Pressplates (Artifacts)-214
Masterpiece Pressplates (Bee Hive)-178
Masterpiece Pressplates (Black Diamond)-249
Masterpiece Pressplates (Ice)-152
Masterpiece Pressplates (Rookie Update)-139
Masterpiece Pressplates SPA Autos-160
Masterpiece Pressplates (SP Game Used)-128
Masterpiece Pressplates (SPx)-144
Masterpiece Pressplates (SPx)-144
Masterpiece Pressplates Ult Coll-209
Masterpiece Pressplates (Victory)-277
Masterpiece Pressplates Autographs-187
Platinum Rookies-187
05UD Artifacts-214
Gold-RED14
05Ultimate Collection-209
Gold-209
05Ultra-220
Gold-220
Fresh Ink-FI-GP
Fresh Ink Blue-FI-GP
Ice-220
Rookie Uniformity Jerseys-RU-GP
Rookie Uniformity Jersey Autographs-ARU-GP
Rookie Uniformity Patches-RUP-GP
Rookie Uniformity Patch Autographs-ARP-GP
05Upper Deck-218
HG Glossy-218
Rookie Ink-RIGP
05Upper Deck Rookie Showcase-RS14
05Upper Deck Rookie Showcase Promos-RS14
05Upper Deck Rookie Threads-RTGP
05Upper Deck Rookie Threads Autographs-ARTGP
05Upper Deck Ice-152
Fresh Ice-FIGP
Fresh Ice Glass-FIGP
Fresh Ice Glass Patches-FIPGP
Premieres Auto Patches-AIPGP
05Upper Deck Rookie Update-139
05Upper Deck Toronto Fall Expo-218
05Upper Deck Victory-277
Black-277
Gold-277
Silver-277
05Manchester Monarchs-41
06UD Powerplay Last Man Standing-LM3
06Upper Deck-92
Exclusives Parallel-92
High Gloss Parallel-92
Masterpieces-92

Parrott, Jeff
96Detroit Vipers-12
98Manitoba Moose-D3
99Manitoba Moose-6

Parry, Josh
03Arizona Icecats-18
04Arizona Icecats-15

Parse, Scott
02Tri-City Stormfront-14

Parshin, Denis
03Russian Hockey League-217
04Russian Under-18 Team-16

Parson, Mike
90ProCards AHL/IHL-129
94Portland Pirates-19

Parson, Steve
907th Inn. Sketch OHL-291
917th Inn. Sketch OHL-283
93Kingston Frontenacs-20
94Thunder Bay Senators-16
95Thunder Bay Senators-15
96South Carolina Stingrays-18

Parsons, Brad
05South Carolina Stingrays-13

Parsons, Darren
86Regina Pats-23
88Regina Pats-20

Parsons, Don
92Nashville Knights-10
96Louisiana Ice Gators-13
97Louisiana Ice Gators-22
98Las Vegas Coyotes RHI-11
98Louisiana Ice Gators-14
01Memphis RiverKings-13
03Memphis RiverKings-16
04Memphis RiverKings-7
06Quad City Mallards-9

Parsons, George
34Beehive Group I Photos-341
38Quaker Oats Photos-26

Parsons, Steve
01Wilkes-Barre Scranton Penguins-20

Parssinen, Timo
98Finnish Kerailysarja-67
99Finnish Cardset-40
00Finnish Cardset-267
00Finnish Cardset Master Blasters-9
01Atomic-102
Premiere Date-102
01Atomic Toronto Fall Expo-102
01BAP Memorabilia-327
Emerald-327
Ruby-327
Sapphire-327
01BAP Signature Series-224
Autographs-224
Autographs Gold-224
01Bowman YoungStars-129
Gold-129
Ice Cubed-129
01Crown Royale-146
01O-Pee-Chee-337
01Pacific-453
01Pacific Adrenaline-202
Blue-202
Premiere Date-202
Red-202
Retail-202
01Pacific Heads-Up-102
01Parkhurst-279
01Parkhurst Beckett Promos-279
01Private Stock-112
Gold-112
Premiere Date-112
Retail-112
Silver-112
01Private Stock Pacific Nights-112
01Private Stock PS-2002-77
01SP Authentic-132
Limited-132
Limited Gold-132
01SP Game Used-62
01SPx-91
01Stadium Club-127
Award Winners-127
Master Photos-127
01Titanium-146
Retail-146
01Titanium Draft Day Edition-103
01Topps-337
01Topps Chrome-155
Refractors-155
Black Border Refractors-155
01Topps Heritage-144
01Topps Reserve-112
01UD Challenge for the Cup-92
01UD Playmakers-101
01UD Premier Collection-51
01Upper Deck-412
Exclusives-412
01Upper Deck Ice-73
01Upper Deck Vintage-271
01Vanguard-102
Blue-102
Red-102
One of Ones-102
Premiere Date-102
Proofs-102
01Finnish Cardset-174
01Cincinnati Mighty Ducks-16
02BAP Sig Series Auto Buybacks 2001-224
02Upper Deck Bright Futures-PA
02Finnish Cardset-101
03Finnish Cardset-26
04Finnish Cardset-24
Parallel-17
04Swedish Pure Skills-106
Parallel-106
06Swedish SHL Elitset-286
Performers-17

Partanen, Erkki
65Finnish Hellas-135

Partanen, Jarmo
71Finnish Suomi Stickers-350

Parth, Elmar
94Finnish Jaa Kiekko-292

Parthenais, Pat
96Detroit Whalers-13

Partinen, Lalli
65Finnish Hellas-83
66Finnish Jaakiekkosarja-98
69Swedish Hockey-379
70Finnish Jaakiekko-72
70Finnish Jaakiekko-112
70Swedish Hockey-298
71Finnish Suomi Stickers-121
72Finnish Jaakiekko-91
72Finnish Panda Toronto-9
73Finnish Jaakiekko-74
73Finnish Jaakiekko-137
77Finnish Sportscasters-36-845
96Finnish SISU Redline-191

Parviainen, Jari
92Finnish Jyvas-Hyva Stickers-145
93Finnish Jyvas-Hyva Stickers-260
93Finnish SISU-283

Pasanen, Jari
94German First League-622
96German DEL-221

Pascal, Brent
81Regina Pats-19

Pascall, Brad
92Rochester Americans Kodak-16
93Rochester Americans Kodak-19

Paschal, Kevin
92British Columbia JHL-214

Pasche, Cyrill
93Swiss HNL-203
95Swiss HNL-252
96Swiss HNL-401
98Swiss Power Play Stickers-300
99Swiss Panini Stickers-305
01Swiss HNL-315
02Swiss HNL-412

Paschek, Sven
94German First League-386
99German Bundesliga 2-10

Pasco, Ron
93RPI Engineers-20
94Greensboro Monarchs-10
95Tallahassee Tiger Sharks-5
98German DEL-240
99German DEL-180
00German DEL-8
02German DEL City Press-203

Pascual, Ace
96Arizona Icecats-15
97Arizona Icecats-17

Pascucci, Ron
93Hampton Roads Admirals-13
94Hampton Roads Admirals-5
95Hampton Roads Admirals-6
96Portland Pirates-6
98Hampton Roads Admirals 10th Anniversary-26

Pasek, Dusan
82Swedish Semic VM Stickers-93
83Swedish Semic VM Stickers-93
88North Stars ADA-20
89ProCards IHL-82
91Finnish Semic World Champ Stickers-113
91Swedish Semic World Champ Stickers-113
92Finnish Jyvas-Hyva Stickers-101
95Slovakian APS National Team-2
98Czech OFS Legends-20

Pashkov, Alexander
79Russian National Team-5

Pashulka, Steve
92Saskatchewan JHL-43

Pasin, Dave
84Prince Albert Raiders Stickers-20
86O-Pee-Chee-76
86Topps-76
86Moncton Golden Flames-7
88ProCards AHL-221
90ProCards AHL/IHL-425

Pasjkov, Alexander
73Swedish Stickers-120

Paska, Jiri
02Owen Sound Attack-4

Pasko, Brian
04Austin Ice Bats-2

Paslawski, Greg
83Vachon-52
87Blues Kodak-20
87Blues Team Issue-17
87O-Pee-Chee-10
87O-Pee-Chee Stickers-23
87Panini Stickers-314
87Topps-10
88Blues Kodak-17
88Blues Team Issue-17
89Jets Safeway-24
89O-Pee-Chee-268
90Jets IGA-28
90O-Pee-Chee-154
90Panini Stickers-309
90Pro Set-336
90Score-249
Canadian-249
90Topps-154
Tiffany-154
90Upper Deck-239
French-239
91Pro Set Platinum-220
91Jets Panini Team Stickers-20
91Nordiques Petro-Canada-23
91Parkhurst-365
French-365
91Pinnacle-286
French-286
91Pro Set-469
French-469
91Score Canadian Bilingual-579
91Score Canadian English-579
91Score Rookie/Traded-29T
92Bowman-277
92Flyers J.C. Penney-19
92Flyers Upper Deck Sheets-14
92Flyers Upper Deck Sheets-33
92O-Pee-Chee-193
92Parkhurst-132
Emerald Ice-132
92Pinnacle-370
French-370
92Pro Set-155
92Score-175
Canadian-175
Sharpshooters-16
Sharpshooters Canadian-16
92Stadium Club-275
92Topps-33
Gold-33G
92Ultra-375
92Upper Deck-531
93Pinnacle-337
Canadian-337
93Score-290
Canadian-290
95Peoria Rivermen-16
96Collector's Edge Ice-179
Prism-179

Pasma, Rod
907th Inn. Sketch OHL-42
917th Inn. Sketch OHL-234
95Louisiana Ice Gators-12
95Louisiana Ice Gators Playoffs-15

Pasqualotto, Gino
83Swedish Semic VM Stickers-130

Pasquini, Laurent
93Swiss HNL-431
95Swiss HNL-253

Passarelli, Val
90Montreal-Bourassa AAA-17
91Ferris State Bulldogs-27
92Ferris State Bulldogs-27
97Pensacola Ice Pilots-16

Passero, Daniel
96Sault Ste. Marie Greyhounds-15
96Sault Ste. Marie Greyhounds Autographed-15
99Bowman CHL-159
Gold-159
OPC International-159
01Greensboro Generals-1

Passfield, Matt
02Owen Sound Attack-8
03Reading Royals-29
03Reading Royals RBI Sports-299

Passini, Todd
96Madison Monsters-20

Passman, Ken
05German DEL-231

Passmore, Brian
03ECHL Update RBI Sports-130
06Augusta Lynx-14

Passmore, Steve
907th Inn. Sketch WHL-255
917th Inn. Sketch WHL-68
93Kamloops Blazers-19
94Cape Breton Oilers-17
99Pacific-168
Copper-168
Emerald Green-168
Gold-168
Ice Blue-168
Premiere Date-168
Red-168
99SP Authentic-20
99Upper Deck Gold Reserve-340
00Upper Deck NHLPA-PA41
00Lowell Lock Monsters-16
01Between the Pipes-41
Tandems-GT12
01Pacific-89
Extreme LTD-89
Hobby LTD-89
Premiere Date-89
Retail LTD-89
01Pacific Arena Exclusives-89
02BAP First Edition-123
Jerseys-123
02Between the Pipes-16
Gold-16
Silver-16
Tandems-3
02Pacific-80
Blue-80
Red-80
02Pacific Complete-244
Red-244
02UD Mask Collection-19
02UD Mask Collection-20
02UD Mask Collection Beckett Promos-19
02UD Mask Collection Beckett Promos-20
02Upper Deck-284
Exclusives-284
02Upper Deck Beckett UD Promos-284
03BAP Memorabilia Deep in the Crease-D2
03Blackhawks Postcards-18
03Pacific-74
Blue-74
Red-74
03Pacific Complete-468
Red-468
03Parkhurst Original Six Chicago-21
Memorabilia-CM8
03Norfolk Admirals-16
04German Adler Mannheim Eagles Postcards-22
04German DEL Update-285

Pastershank, Corey
03Quebec Remparts-20

Pastika, Michael
94German DEL-421

Pastinsky, Oliver
93Sault Ste. Marie Greyhounds-4
93Sault Ste. Marie Greyhound Memorial Cup-4

Patafie, Brian
81Ottawa 67's-15
83Nova Scotia Voyageurs-18
84Moncton Golden Flames-1
85Moncton Golden Flames-18
86Moncton Golden Flames-6
92Salt Lake Golden Eagles-25

Patch, David
97Dubuque Fighting Saints-6

Patchell, Sean
00Michigan State Spartans-17

Pateman, Jerry
90Pro Set-696

Patenaude, Dave
96OCN Blizzard-3

Patenaude, Rusty
74O-Pee-Chee WHA-51
75O-Pee-Chee WHA-76
76O-Pee-Chee WHA-19

Patera, David
01Czech OFS-183

Patera, Pavel
94Czech APS Extraliga-58
95Czech APS Extraliga-93
95Czech APS Extraliga-371
95Czech APS Extraliga-385
96Czech APS Extraliga-341
96Swedish Semic Wien-114
97Czech APS Extraliga-356
97Swedish Collector's Choice-10
98Czech DS-2
98Czech OFS-107
98Czech OFS-239
98Czech OFS-441
98Czech OFS-480
Olympic Winners-5
98Czech Bonaparte-7C
98Czech Pexeso-24
98Czech Pexeso Series Two-23
99BAP Memorabilia-190
Gold-190
Silver-190
99BAP Millennium-84
Emerald-84
Ruby-84
Sapphire-84
Signatures-84
Signatures Gold-84
99Pacific Dynagon Ice-70
Blue-70
Copper-70
Gold-70
Premiere Date-70
99Panini Stickers-219
99Stadium Club-170
First Day Issue-170
One of a Kind-170
Printing Plates Black-170
Printing Plates Cyan-170
Printing Plates Magenta-170
Printing Plates Yellow-170
99Stars Postcards-21
99Topps Premier Plus-106
Parallel-106
99Upper Deck-219
Exclusives-219
Exclusives 1 of 1-219
99Upper Deck Gold Reserve-219
99Wayne Gretzky Hockey-57
99Czech DS National Stars-NS16
99Czech DS Premium-P9
99Czech OFS-28
99Czech OFS-447
99Czech OFS-481
99Czech OFS-523
All-Star Game Blue-523
All-Star Game Gold-523
All-Star Game Red-523
All-Star Game Silver-523
99Czech OFS Jagr Team Embossed-28
00Panini Stickers-175
00Czech DS Extraliga Team Jagr-JT14
00Czech OFS-390
00Cleveland Lumberjacks-7
01BAP Memorabilia-263
Emerald-263
Ruby-263
Sapphire-263
01Czech DS-37
Ice Heroes-IH3
02BAP Sig Series Auto Buybacks 1999-84
02Czech DS-27
02Czech DS-86
02Czech IQ Sports Blue-18
02Czech IQ Sports Yellow-19
02Czech Stadion Olympics-337
02Russian Hockey League-118
03Czech National Team-4
03Russian Avangard Omsk-13
03Russian Hockey League-222
04Czech OFS-63
06Czech HC Kladno Postcards-9
06Czech OFS-262
Team Cards-3

Paterlini, Thierry
93Swiss HNL-484
95Swiss HNL-307
96Swiss HNL-49
98Swiss Power Play Stickers-48
99Swiss Panini Stickers-46
00Swiss Panini Stickers-118
00Swiss Slapshot Mini-Cards-HCD12
02Swiss HNL-27

Paterson, Cory
88Regina Pats-21
89Regina Pats-16
92Wheeling Thunderbirds-11
93Wheeling Thunderbirds-3
93Wheeling Thunderbirds-PC4
94Wheeling Thunderbirds Photo Album-15
99Tallahassee Tiger Sharks-24

Paterson, Craig
96Richmond Renegades-15
01Kalamazoo K-Wings-13

Paterson, Duncan
99UK Basingstoke Bison-13
00UK Nottingham Panthers-4
00UK Sekonda Superleague-132

Paterson, Joe
85Flyers Postcards-22
86Kings 20th Anniversary Team Issue-17
88ProCards AHL-207
89ProCards IHL-41
90ProCards AHL/IHL-8
91ProCards-203
95Slapshot-380
95Sault Ste. Marie Greyhounds-15
96Sault Ste. Marie Greyhounds-14
96Sault Ste. Marie Greyhounds Autographed-14
99Louisville Panthers-28
00Louisville Panthers-13

Paterson, Mark
81Ottawa 67's-16
82Ottawa 67's-17
83Ottawa 67's-22
86Moncton Golden Flames-17
88ProCards IHL-108

Paterson, Rick
81Blackhawks Borderless Postcards-19
82Blackhawks Postcards-17
82Post Cereal-4
83Blackhawks Postcards-18
83O-Pee-Chee-109
84O-Pee-Chee-44
85Blackhawks Team Issue-8
86Blackhawks Coke-14
93Cleveland Lumberjacks-2
93Cleveland Lumberjacks Postcards-17
94Cleveland Lumberjacks-1
94Cleveland Lumberjacks Postcards-1
95Cleveland Lumberjacks-21
95Cleveland Lumberjacks Postcards-20
96Cleveland Lumberjacks-22
96Cleveland Lumberjacks Multi-Ad-24

Paterson, Ron
81Swedish Semic Hockey VM Stickers-74

Patey, Doug
79O-Pee-Chee-298

Patey, Larry
74NHL Action Stamps-64
75O-Pee-Chee NHL-137
75O-Pee-Chee NHL-316
75Topps-137
75Topps-316
76O-Pee-Chee NHL-320
77O-Pee-Chee NHL-199
77Topps-199
78Blues Postcards-17
78O-Pee-Chee-8
78Topps-8
79O-Pee-Chee-57
79Topps-57
80O-Pee-Chee-310
81O-Pee-Chee-303
82O-Pee-Chee-308
82Post Cereal-17
84O-Pee-Chee-149
84Topps-111

Patoine, Remy
88Richelieu Riverains-20

Patrick, Craig
71O-Pee-Chee-184
72O-Pee-Chee-221
72Sargent Promotions Stamps-55
72Finnish Semic World Championship-130
72Swedish Semic World Championship-130
73O-Pee-Chee-52
73Topps-52
74Lipton Soup-46
74NHL Action Stamps-72
74NHL Action Stamps Update-34
74O-Pee-Chee NHL-262
74Topps-262
75O-Pee-Chee NHL-178
75Topps-178
77O-Pee-Chee NHL-278
95Signature Rookies Miracle on Ice-43
95Signature Rookies Miracle on Ice-44
95Signature Rook Miracle on Ice Sigs-43
95Signature Rook Miracle on Ice Sigs-44

Patrick, Curtiss
04Wheeling Nailers Riesbeck's-7

Patrick, Don
93Quebec Pee-Wee Tournament-677

Patrick, Frank
10C56-1
83Hall of Fame Postcards-B9
85Hall of Fame-23
03BAP Ultimate Memorabilia Paper Cuts-9
03BAP Ultimate Mem Vintage Blade of Steel-5
04ITG Ultimate Mem Blades of Steel-19
06ITG Ultimate Memorabilia Blades of Steel-12
06ITG Ultimate Memorabilia Blades of Steel Gold-12

Patrick, Glen
79Panini Stickers-210
00Wilkes-Barre Scranton Penguins-18
01Wilkes-Barre Scranton Penguins-23
02Wilkes-Barre Scranton Penguins-25

Patrick, Henry
95Swiss HNL-324

Patrick, James
83Canadian National Juniors-11
84O-Pee-Chee-150
84Topps-112
85O-Pee-Chee-15
85O-Pee-Chee Stickers-83
85Topps-15
86O-Pee-Chee-113
86O-Pee-Chee Stickers-220
86Topps-113
87O-Pee-Chee-18
87O-Pee-Chee Stickers-30
87Panini Stickers-107
87Topps-18
88Frito-Lay Stickers-30
88O-Pee-Chee-69
88O-Pee-Chee Stickers-246
88Panini Stickers-303
88Topps-69
89O-Pee-Chee-90
89O-Pee-Chee Stickers-242
89Panini Stickers-289
89Rangers Marine Midland Bank-3
89Topps-90
89Swedish Semic World Champ Stickers-61
90Bowman-225
Tiffany-225
90O-Pee-Chee-101
90O-Pee-Chee-131
90Panini Stickers-97
90Pro Set-207
90Score-194
Canadian-194
90Score Hottest/Rising Stars-84
90Topps-101
90Topps-131
Tiffany-131
90Upper Deck-185
French-185
91Pro Set Platinum-82
91Bowman-66
91O-Pee-Chee-253
91OPC Premier-172
91Panini Stickers-287
91Parkhurst-120
French-120
91Pinnacle-26
French-26
91Pro Set-164
French-164
91Score American-230
91Score Canadian Bilingual-230
91Score Canadian English-230
91Stadium Club-277
91Topps-253
91Upper Deck-275
French-275
92Bowman-127
92O-Pee-Chee-215
92Panini Stickers-240
92Panini Stickers French-240
92Parkhurst-113
Emerald Ice-113
92Pinnacle-140
French-140
92Pro Set-119
92Score-203
Canadian-203
92Stadium Club-394
92Topps-71
Gold-71G
92Ultra-141
92Upper Deck-320
92North Dakota Fighting Sioux-37
93Donruss-213
93Donruss-408
93Leaf-232
93OPC Premier-149
Gold-149
93Parkhurst-360
Emerald Ice-360
93Pinnacle-246
Canadian-246
93PowerPlay-164
93PowerPlay-353
93Score-73
93Score-574
Gold-574
Canadian-73
Canadian-574
Canadian Gold-574
93Stadium Club-302
Members Only Master Set-302
First Day Issue-302
93Topps/OPC Premier-149
Gold-149
93Ultra-336
93Whalers Coke-13
94Be A Player Signature Cards-98
94Canada Games NHL POGS-59
94Donruss-185
94EA Sports-86
94Flair-26
94Fleer-33
94Leaf-271
94OPC Premier-30
Special Effects-30
94Parkhurst-40
Gold-40
94Pinnacle-196
Artist's Proofs-196
Rink Collection-196
94Score-8
Gold-8
Platinum-8
94Topps/OPC Premier-30
Special Effects-30
94Ultra-33
94Upper Deck-424
Electric Ice-424
95Parkhurst International-303
Emerald Ice-303
95Upper Deck-53
Electric Ice-53
Electric Ice Gold-53
96Donruss-158
Press Proofs-158
96Metal Universe-21
96Score-189
Artist's Proofs-189
Dealer's Choice Artist's Proofs-189
Special Artist's Proofs-189
Golden Blades-189
96Topps Picks-165
OPC Inserts-165
97Pacific Dynagon Best Kept Secrets-14
99O-Pee-Chee-123
99O-Pee-Chee Chrome-123
99O-Pee-Chee Chrome Refractors-123
99Topps/OPC-123
99Topps/OPC Chrome-123
Refractors-123
00Upper Deck Vintage-44
02Sabres Team Issue-11
02Upper Deck-268
Exclusives-268
02Upper Deck Beckett UD Promos-268
05German DEL-321

Patrick, Lester
10C56-26
12C57-41
37V356 Worldwide Gum-94
60Topps-1
77Sportscasters-6217
77Finnish Sportscasters-72-1716
83Hall of Fame-40
83Hall of Fame Postcards-C10
85Hall of Fame-40
94Parkhurst Missing Link Pop-Ups-P10
01Upper Deck Legends-48
03BAP Ultimate Memorabilia Memorialized-6
03BAP Ultimate Memorabilia Paper Cuts-47
03Parkhurst Original Six New York-56
04ITG Ultimate Memorabilia-85
Gold-85
Broadway Blueshirts-1
05ITG Ultimate Memorabilia Level 1-63
05ITG Ultimate Memorabilia Level 2-63
05ITG Ultimate Memorabilia Level 3-63
05ITG Ultimate Memorabilia Level 4-63
05ITG Ultimate Memorabilia Level 5-63
05ITG Ultimate Mem Broadway Bluesh Autos-4
05ITG Ultimate Memorabilia Lumbergraphs-8
06ITG Ultimate Memorabilia-88
Artist Proof-88
Broadway Blue Shirts Autos-1

Patrick, Lynn
34Beehive Group I Photos-289
35Diamond Matchbooks Tan 2-54
35Diamond Matchbooks Tan 2-55
35Diamond Matchbooks Tan 3-51
35O-Pee-Chee V304C-79
36O-Pee-Chee V304D-128
37V356 Worldwide Gum-57
39O-Pee-Chee V301-1-36
40O-Pee-Chee V301-2-136
83Hall of Fame-207
83Hall of Fame Postcards-N12
85Hall of Fame-207
03BAP Ultimate Memorabilia Paper Cuts-49
05ITG Ultimate Mem Broadway Bluesh Autos-9
06ITG Ultimate Memorabilia-93
Artist Proof-93
Broadway Blue Shirts Autos-2

Patrick, Murray
34Beehive Group I Photos-290
39O-Pee-Chee V301-1-38
60NHL Ceramic Tiles-31
03BAP Ultimate Memorabilia Paper Cuts-26

Patrick, Ryan
93Quebec Pee-Wee Tournament-770

Patronas, Nik
94Dubuque Fighting Saints-21

Patry, Mario
79Montreal Juniors-21

Patry, Mathieu
93Quebec Pee-Wee Tournament-1068

Patrzek, Fabio
01German Berlin Polar Bears Postcards-18

Patschinski, Rainer
70Finnish Jaakiekko-92
70Swedish Hockey-380
70Swedish Masterserien-176
74Finnish Jenkki-107
04German Berlin Eisbarens 50th Anniv-11

Pattersen, Lars
96Regina Pats-13

Patterson, Brad
01Michigan Tech Huskies-22
03Colorado Eagles-14
05UK Nottingham Panthers-18

Patterson, Brian
99Lethbridge Hurricanes-21
00Lethbridge Hurricanes-18
01Lethbridge Hurricanes-11

Patterson, Colin
83Vachon-15
85Flames Red Rooster-21
86Flames Red Rooster-20
87Flames Red Rooster-23
88Flames Postcards-18
89Kraft-7
89O-Pee-Chee-71
89O-Pee-Chee Stickers-102
89Panini Stickers-36
89Topps-71
90Flames IGA/McGavin's-20
90O-Pee-Chee-420
91Flames Panini Team Stickers-16
91Pro Set-356
French-356
91Sabres Blue Shield-15
91Sabres Pepsi/Campbell's-15
91Score Canadian Bilingual-525
91Score Canadian English-525
92Sabres Blue Shield-16
92Score-312
Canadian-312
92Topps-91
Gold-91G
03Prince George Cougars-21

Patterson, Curtis
05Regina Pats-13

Patterson, Dennis
74NHL Action Stamps-304
75O-Pee-Chee NHL-51
75Topps-51

Patterson, Ed
907th Inn. Sketch WHL-52
907th Inn. Sketch WHL-291
917th Inn. Sketch WHL-94
92Cleveland Lumberjacks-17
93Donruss-474
93Cleveland Lumberjacks-17
93Cleveland Lumberjacks Postcards-18
94Donruss-265
94Leaf-290
94Stadium Club-232
Members Only Master Set-232
First Day Issue-232
Super Team Winner Cards-232
94Cleveland Lumberjacks-19
94Cleveland Lumberjacks Postcards-19
94Classic Pro Prospects-159
95Penguins Foodland-14
96Cleveland Lumberjacks-23
96Cleveland Lumberjacks Multi-Ad-25
97Grand Rapids Griffins-11
98Cincinnati Cyclones-17
98Cincinnati Cyclones 2-3
99Grand Rapids Griffins-16
00Grand Rapids Griffins-17
01German Berlin Polar Bears Postcards-19
02UK London Knights-20
03UK Cardiff Devils-12
05UK Cardiff Devils Challenge Cup-3

Patterson, Gaelan
06Saskatoon Blades-19

Patterson, George
27La Patrie-20
27La Presse Photos-20
33O-Pee-Chee V304A-14
33V357 Ice Kings-35
34Diamond Matchbooks Silver-49

Patterson, James
03Huntsville Channel Cats-13
04Huntsville Havoc-11

Patterson, Josh
01Peterborough Petes-11
02Peterborough Petes-12
03Erie Otters-20

PAtterson, Kent
06Cedar Rapids RoughRiders-12

Patterson, Nevin
97Sudbury Wolves Police-13

Patterson, Pamela
04Ohio State Buckeyes Women-17

Patterson, Phil
81Ottawa 67's-17
82Ottawa 67's-18
83Ottawa 67's-23

Patterson, Ron
91Air Canada SJHL-C30

Pattison, Rob
97Las Vegas Thunder-19
98Albany River Rats-12

Patton, Geoff
01St. Michaels Majors-3
02Guelph Storm-11
03Belleville Bulls-12

Patton, Kirk
95Alaska Gold Kings-14

Patuli, Arduino
93Quebec Pee-Wee Tournament-38

Patzold, Dimitri
01German Upper Deck-255
02German DEL City Press-250
03Cleveland Barons-17
03Johnstown Chiefs RBI Sports-223
04Cleveland Barons-17
05Beehive-170
Matte-170
05Black Diamond-275
05Hot Prospects-210
Autographed Patch Variation-210
Autographed Patch Variation Gold-210
Hot Materials-HMDP
Red Hot-210
05Parkhurst-663
Facsimile Auto Parallel-663
Signatures-DP
05SP Authentic-210
Limited-210
05SP Game Used-182
Gold-182
05SPx-214
Spectrum-214
05The Cup-130
Autographed Rookie Patches Gold Rainbow-130
Black Rainbow Rookies-130
Masterpiece Pressplates (Artifacts)-318
Masterpiece Pressplates (Bee Hive)-170
Masterpiece Pressplates (Black Diamond)-275
Masterpiece Pressplates (Ice)-180
Masterpiece Pressplates (Rookie Update)-244
Masterpiece Pressplates SPA Autos-210
Masterpiece Pressplates (SP Game Used)-182
Masterpiece Pressplates (SPx)-214
Masterpiece Pressplates (Trilogy)-296
Masterpiece Pressplates Ult Coll-166
Masterpiece Pressplates Autographs-130
Platinum Rookies-130

05UD Artifacts-318
05Ultimate Collection-166
  Gold-166
05Upper Deck-465
05Upper Deck Ice-180
05Upper Deck Rookie Update-244
  Inspirations Patch Rookies-244
05Upper Deck Trilogy-296
05Cleveland Barons-16
05ITG Heroes and Prospects-256
  Autographs Series II-DPZ

Pauels, Rodion
94German First League-97

Paukkunen, Markku
00Finnish Cardset-172
01Finnish Cardset-354
04Finnish Cardset-303
05Finnish Cardset -281

Paukner, Andreas
94German First League-229

Paukovich, Geoff
02Tri-City Stormfront-8

Paul, Dustin
97Moose Jaw Warriors-11

Paul, Jeff
95Slapshot-185
98Indianapolis Ice-26
99Cleveland Lumberjacks-16
01SPx Rookie Redemption-R8
01Hershey Bears-21
02BAP Memorabilia-297
  Emerald-297
  Ruby-297
  Sapphire-297
  NHL All-Star Game-297
  NHL All-Star Game Blue-297
  NHL All-Star Game Green-297
  NHL All-Star Game Red-297
02BAP Memorabilia Toronto Fall Expo-297
02BAP Ultimate Memorabilia-27
02SP Authentic-141
02SP Game Used-72
02SPx-174
02Topps Chrome-154
  Black Border Refractors-154
  Refractors-154
02Topps Total-412
02UD Honor Roll-149
02UD Mask Collection-139
02UD Top Shelf-110
02Upper Deck-433
  Exclusives-433
02Upper Deck Classic Portraits-108
02Hershey Bears-16
04Portland Pirates-7
05Hamilton Bulldogs-20

Paul, Jesse
93Quebec Pee-Wee Tournament-851

Paul, John
84Kings Smokey-10
96Detroit Whalers-11

Paul, Kyle
92Saskatchewan JHL-28

Paul, Mathieu
98Halifax Mooseheads-3
98Halifax Mooseheads Second Edition-17
01Kalamazoo K-Wings-7
03Lubbock Cotton Kings-14

Paul, Richard
00Quebec Remparts-3
  Signed-3
00Victoriaville Tigres-17
  Signed-17
03Johnstown Chiefs-17
05Missouri River Otters-3

Paul, Todd
02Drummondville Voltigeurs-3
04Tulsa Oilers-18

Paulhus, Roland
24Anonymous NHL-4
24Anonymous NHL-4

Paulsen, Eirik
92Norwegian Elite Series-141
95Swedish World Championships Stickers-250

Paulsson, Marcus
02Saskatoon Blades-9
03Saskatoon Blades-27
04Swedish Malmo Red Hawks-8
05Finnish Cardset -120
06Swedish SHL Elitset-234

Pauna, Matti
83Swedish Semic Elitserien-39
84Swedish Semic Elitserien-39
85Swedish Panini Stickers-33
86Swedish Panini Stickers-19
87Swedish Panini Stickers-34
90Swedish Semic Elitserien Stickers-138
91Swedish Semic Elitserien Stickers-193

Pavelec, Ondrej
05ITG Heroes/Prosp Toronto Expo Parallel -300
05Cape Breton Screaming Eagles-2
05ITG Heroes and Prospects-300
  Autographs Series II-OP
06Cape Breton Screaming Eagles-23

Pavelec, Stanislav
94Czech APS Extraliga-236
95Czech APS Extraliga-6
96Czech APS Extraliga-55
97Czech APS Extraliga-320
97Czech DS Stickers-231
98Czech DS-117
98Czech DS Stickers-270
98Czech OFS-179

Pavelek, Zdenek
96Czech APS Extraliga-113
97Czech APS Extraliga-119
97Czech DS Stickers-277
98Czech DS Stickers-62
98Czech OFS-124
99Czech DS-180
99Czech OFS-229
99Czech OFS-318
00Czech DS Extraliga-159
00Czech OFS-256
01Czech OFS-27
  All Stars-31
02Czech OFS Plus-97
03Czech OFS Plus-296
03Czech OFS Plus Insert H-H11
03Czech OFS Plus Insert S-S5
03Czech OFS Plus MS Praha-SE21
04Czech OFS-216
  Assist Leaders-6
  Points Leaders-14

Pavelich, Mark
81Swedish Semic Hockey VM Stickers-102
82O-Pee-Chee-231
82O-Pee-Chee Stickers-138
82Post Cereal-13
82Topps Stickers-138
83NHL Key Tags-91
83O-Pee-Chee-238
83O-Pee-Chee-239
83O-Pee-Chee-253
83O-Pee-Chee Stickers-213
83O-Pee-Chee Stickers-214
83Topps Stickers-213
83Topps Stickers-214
84O-Pee-Chee-151
84O-Pee-Chee Stickers-97
84Topps-113
85O-Pee-Chee-69
85O-Pee-Chee Stickers-84
85Topps-69
95Signature Rookies Miracle on Ice-25
95Signature Rookies Miracle on Ice-26
95Signature Rook Miracle on Ice Sigs-25
95Signature Rook Miracle on Ice Sigs-26
04UD Legendary Signatures Miracle Men-USA7
04UD Legendary Sigs Miracle Men Autos-USA-MP

Pavelich, Marty
44Beehive Group II Photos-200
51Parkhurst-54
52Parkhurst-66
53Parkhurst-44
54Parkhurst-43
54Topps-34
76Old Timers-12
80USA Olympic Team Mini Pics-12
94Parkhurst Missing Link-53

Pavelich, Matt
85Hall of Fame-261

Pavels, Stig
64Swedish Coralli ISHockey-53
65Swedish Coralli ISHockey-53

Pavelski, Joe
03Waterloo Blackhawks-2
04Wisconsin Badgers-15
05Wisconsin Badgers-21
06Be A Player-239
06Beehive-149
  Matte-149
06Flair Showcase-326
06Hot Prospects-176
  Red Hot-176
  White Hot-176
06O-Pee-Chee-595
  Rainbow-595
06SP Authentic-219
  Limited-219
06The Cup-152
  Autographed NHL Shields Duals-DASPC
  Autographed Rookie Masterpiece Pressplates-152
  Gold Rainbow Autographed Rookie Patches-152
  Masterpiece Pressplates (Bee Hive)-149
  Masterpiece Pressplates (Marquee Rookies)-595
  Masterpiece Pressplates (SP Authentic)-219
  Masterpiece Pressplates (Sweet Beginnings)-151
  Rookies Black-152
  Rookies Platinum-152
06UD Artifacts-271
06Upper Deck-487
  Exclusives Parallel-487
  High Gloss Parallel-487
  Masterpieces-487
06Upper Deck Sweet Shot-151
  Rookie Jerseys Autographs-151
06AHL Top Prospects-49
06ITG Heroes and Prospects-151
  Autographs-AJPV
  Update Autographs-AJPV
07Upper Deck Ovation-9

Pavese, Jim
80Sault Ste. Marie Greyhounds-18
81Sault Ste. Marie Greyhounds-18
82Post Cereal-16
82Post Cereal-17
87Panini Stickers-310
88Red Wings Little Caesars-19
90ProCards AHL/IHL-423

Pavlas, Ales
06Czech HC Kladno Postcards-1
06Czech OFS-263

Pavlas, Luke
98Sioux City Musketeers-20
99Ohio State Buckeyes-13
00Ohio State Buckeyes-12
01Ohio State Buckeyes-13
02Ohio State Buckeyes-10

Pavlas, Petr
91Finnish Semic World Champ Stickers-108
91Swedish Semic World Champ Stickers-108
94Finnish SISU-205
95Czech APS Extraliga-226
95Finnish Semic World Championships-145
96Czech APS Extraliga-267
97Czech APS Extraliga-222
97Czech DS Extraliga-14
97Czech DS Stickers-171
98Czech DS-26
98Czech DS Stickers-29
98Czech OFS-83
99Czech DS-18
99Czech OFS-140
99Czech OFS-504
  All-Star Game Blue-504
  All-Star Game Gold-504
  All-Star Game Red-504
  All-Star Game Silver-504
00Czech DS Extraliga-149
00Czech OFS-269
01Czech OFS-231
02Czech OFS Plus-139
04Czech OFS Czech/Slovak-37

Pavlicko, Slavomir
04Czech OFS Czech/Slovak-38
04Slovakian Poprad Team Set-17

Pavlik, Karel
95Czech APS Extraliga-223
96Czech APS Extraliga-58

Pavlikovsky, Rastislav
98Cincinnati Cyclones-18
98Cincinnati Cyclones 2-10
99Cincinnati Mighty Ducks-10
00Czech DS Extraliga-156
02Slovakian Kvarteto-14
04Swedish Pure Skills-76
  Parallel-76
05Swedish SHL Elitset-247
  Gold-247

Pavlikovsky, Richard
00Czech OFS-268
02Swedish SHL-38
  Parallel-38
03Swedish Elite-202
  Silver-202
04German DEL-275
05German DEL-230
06German DEL-137

Pavlin, Fabian
79Montreal Juniors-22

Pavlis, Libor
96Czech APS Extraliga-209
97Czech APS Extraliga-137
98Czech DS Stickers-262
98Czech OFS-121
98Czech OFS-327
99Czech OFS-427
01Czech OFS-215
02Czech OFS Plus-289
03Czech OFS Plus-355
04Czech OFS-256

Pavlov, Evgeni
98Russian Hockey League-159

Pavlov, Igor
94German First League-199

Pavlovic, Stanislav
93Quebec Pee-Wee Tournament-1547

Pavlu, Martin
82Swedish Semic VM Stickers-139
83Swedish Semic VM Stickers-139
95Finnish Semic World Championships-176
96Swedish Semic Wien-182

Pavoni, Reto
91Finnish Semic World Champ Stickers-178
91Swedish Semic World Champ Stickers-178
92Finnish Semic-196
93Swiss HNL-8
95Swedish Globe World Championships-208
95Swedish World Championships Stickers-116
95Swiss HNL-6
95Swiss HNL-517
95Swiss HNL-523
95Swiss HNL-529
95Swiss HNL-535
96Swiss HNL-4
96Swiss HNL-516
96Swiss HNL-526
98Swiss Power Play Stickers-103
98Swiss Power Play Stickers-261
99Swiss Panini Stickers-104
99Swiss Panini Stickers-255
00Swiss Panini Stickers-150
00Swiss Slapshot Mini-Cards-EHCK1
01Swiss HNL-52
02Swiss HNL-337
06German DEL-138

Pawlaczyk, Dan
93Detroit Jr. Red Wings-16
94Detroit Jr. Red Wings-19
95Slapshot-63
95Slapshot Memorial Cup-93
96Sarnia Sting-20
96Toledo Storm-28

Pawloski, Jerry
92Harvard Crimson-28

Pawluk, Jeff
917th Inn. Sketch OHL-359

Pawluk, Mike
92British Columbia JHL-148
92British Columbia JHL-245

Pawluk, Ryan
93Kitchener Rangers-12
95Slapshot-314
95Slapshot-426
97Austin Ice Bats-13

Pawlyschyn, Walter
51Laval Dairy Subset-8
52St. Lawrence Sales-35

Payan, Eugene
10Sweet Caporal Postcards-43
11C55-43
12C57-9

Payer, Serge
95Slapshot-138
96Upper Deck-385
96Kitchener Rangers-21
99Kitchener Rangers-3
00Panthers Team Issue-22
00Titanium-122
  Retail-122
00Titanium Draft Day Edition-122
00Titanium Draft Day Promos-122
01Utah Grizzlies-11
03Binghamton Senators-15
04San Antonio Rampage-7
06Binghamton Senators-16
06Binghamton Senators 5th Anniversary-21

Payette, Andre
93Sault Ste. Marie Greyhounds-8
95Slapshot-360
95Sault Ste. Marie Greyhounds-16
95Classic-95
01Manchester Monarchs-5A
04UK Coventry Blaze-12
04UK Coventry Blaze Champions-9

Payette, Daniel
95Halifax Mooseheads-16
00Columbus Cottonmouths-12
01Thetford Mines Coyotes-14
02Thetford Mines Coyotes-16

Payette, Greg
02Utah Grizzlies-30

Payette, Jean
72Nordiques Postcards-18
72O-Pee-Chee-311
73Nordiques Team Issue-18

Payette, Mathieu
01Shawinigan Cataractes-21

Payne, Anthony
93UK Humberside Hawks-15
97UK Kingston Hawks Stickers-9
98UK Kingston Hawks-12
01UK Hull Thunder-11
02UK Hull Thunder-5

Payne, Davis
90Michigan Tech Huskies-19
91Michigan Tech Huskies-18
91Michigan Tech Huskies-34
92Greensboro Monarchs-7
93Greensboro Monarchs-11
94Greensboro Monarchs-9
96Providence Bruins-11
97Pacific Dynagon Best Kept Secrets-7
02ECHL Update-U-19

Payne, Jason
95Slapshot-14
96Flint Generals-15
98Flint Generals-3
99Cincinnati Mighty Ducks-3
06Bloomington PrairieThunder-14

Payne, Mike
01Asheville Smoke-4
02New Mexico Scorpions-19

Payne, Steve
78North Stars Cloverleaf Dairy-7
79North Stars Postcards-11
79O-Pee-Chee-64
79Topps-64
80North Stars Postcards-15
80O-Pee-Chee-139
80O-Pee-Chee-274
80Topps-139
81North Stars Postcards-18
81O-Pee-Chee-166
81O-Pee-Chee Stickers-22
81O-Pee-Chee Stickers-92
81Topps-W110
82North Stars Postcards-18
82O-Pee-Chee-172
82O-Pee-Chee Stickers-191
82Post Cereal-9
82Topps Stickers-191
83NHL Key Tags-62
83North Stars Postcards-22
83O-Pee-Chee-178
83O-Pee-Chee Stickers-121
83Topps Stickers-121
84North Stars 7-Eleven-11
84North Stars Postcards-21
84O-Pee-Chee-106
84O-Pee-Chee Stickers-49
84Topps-80
85North Stars Postcards-23
85O-Pee-Chee-65
85O-Pee-Chee Stickers-42
85Topps-65
86North Stars Postcards-7
86O-Pee-Chee-219
87North Stars Postcards-23
87O-Pee-Chee Stickers-56

Paynter, Gregory
06PEI Rocket-23

Paynter, Kent
82Kitchener Rangers-25
83Kitchener Rangers-12
84Kitchener Rangers-17
85Nova Scotia Oilers-20
88ProCards IHL-109
89ProCards AHL-101
90ProCards AHL/IHL-196
91Jets IGA-25
91Moncton Hawks-21
91ProCards-168
94Milwaukee Admirals-20
95Milwaukee Admirals-14
95Milwaukee Admirals Postcards-2
96Milwaukee Admirals-19

Pazler, Lubos
94Czech APS Extraliga-263

Pazourek, David
99Czech OFS-79
00Czech DS Extraliga-108
00Czech OFS-204
01Czech OFS-101
03Czech OFS Plus-224

Pazourek, Pavel
99Czech OFS-71
00Czech OFS-186

Pazourek, Vaclav
99Asheville Smoke-12
01Missouri River Otters-25

Pchelyakov, Andrei
99Russian Hockey League-139
99Russian Stars Postcards-17
00Russian Hockey League-367
03Russian Hockey League-79

Pchelyakov, Oleg
98Russian Hockey League-139

Peach, Chris
99Alexandria Warthogs-12

Peacock, Richard
95Saskatoon Blades-14
98Anchorage Aces-5

Peacock, Shane
89Lethbridge Hurricanes-16
907th Inn. Sketch WHL-123
917th Inn. Sketch WHL-343
91Classic-48
91Star Pics-33
91Ultimate Draft-43
91Ultimate Draft French-43
91Classic Four-Sport *-48
  Autographs-48A
93Lethbridge Hurricanes-10
96Michigan K-Wings-4
98German DEL-45
99German DEL-338
00German DEL-175
  Profiles-P5
01German Upper Deck-188
  Skilled Stars-SS10
02German DEL City Press-204
03German DEL-114
04German DEL-130
04German Hamburg Freezers Postcards-11
05German DEL-112
  Defender-DF12
  Defender Promos-DF12
06German DEL-60

Peacosh, Gene
71Johnstown Jets Acme-11
73Quaker Oats WHA-24
74O-Pee-Chee WHA-27
74San Diego Mariners WHA-5
75O-Pee-Chee WHA-24
76O-Pee-Chee WHA-60
76O-Pee-Chee WHA-71

Peake, Pat
907th Inn. Sketch OHL-114
91Upper Deck-697
  French-697
91Upper Deck Czech World Juniors-84
917th Inn. Sketch OHL-35
917th Inn. Sketch Memorial Cup-106
91Arena Draft Picks-11
91Arena Draft Picks French-11
91Arena Draft Picks Autographs-11
91Arena Draft Picks Autographs French-11
91Classic-12
91Star Pics-39
91Ultimate Draft-12
91Ultimate Draft-68
91Ultimate Draft French-12
91Classic Four-Sport *-12
  Autographs-12A
93Donruss-361
93Pinnacle-436
  Canadian-436
  Super Rookies-9
  Super Rookies Canadian-9
93PowerPlay-469
  Rookie Standouts-10
93Score-590
  Gold-590
  Canadian-590
  Canadian Gold-590
93Ultra-449
93Upper Deck-518
  SP-172
93Classic-12
93Classic-33
  Autographs-AU9
94Donruss-318
94Flair-203
94Fleer-238
94Leaf-83
  Gold Rookies-12
94OPC Premier-12
  Special Effects-12
94Parkhurst-281
  Gold-281
  Vintage-V63
94Parkhurst SE-SE196
  Gold-SE196
94Pinnacle-136
  Artist's Proofs-136
  Rink Collection-136
94Topps/OPC Premier-12
  Special Effects-12
94Ultra-237
94Upper Deck-125
  Electric Ice-125
  SP Inserts-SP176
  SP Inserts Die Cuts-SP176
94Classic Pro Prospects-29
95Capitals Team Issue-20
95Donruss-230
95Parkhurst International-488
  Emerald Ice-488
95Playoff One on One-214
95Score-181
  Black Ice Artist's Proofs-181
  Black Ice-181
95Stadium Club-136
  Members Only Master Set-136
95Ultra-325
95Upper Deck-163
  Electric Ice-163
  Electric Ice Gold-163
  Special Edition-SE175
  Special Edition Gold-SE175
96Collector's Choice-282
96Score-67
  Artist's Proofs-67
  Dealer's Choice Artist's Proofs-67
  Special Artist's Proofs-67
  Golden Blades-67
96Upper Deck-353
97Be A Player-171
  Autographs-171
  Autographs Die-Cuts-171
  Autographs Prismatic Die-Cuts-171
97Upper Deck-179
02Plymouth Whalers-29

Peal, Allen
52Juniors Blue Tint-113

Pearce, Barcley
97UK Guildford Flames-18
99UK Guildford Flames-25
00UK Guildford Flames-19

Pearce, Frank
51Bas Du Fleuve-9
52Bas Du Fleuve-25

Pearce, Garry
89Regina Pats-17
907th Inn. Sketch WHL-176
917th Inn. Sketch WHL-223

Pearce, Jordan
04Lincoln Stars-1
04Lincoln Stars Update-45

Pearce, Joseph
02Chicago Steel-16

Pearce, Randy
87Kitchener Rangers-23
88Kitchener Rangers-23
89Kitchener Rangers-23
907th Inn. Sketch Memorial Cup-29
91Hampton Roads Admirals-14
93Portland Pirates-1
96Hampton Roads Admirals-HRA13
98Hampton Roads Admirals 10th Anniversary-7

Pearce, Robert
00Quebec Remparts-13
  Signed-13
01Quebec Remparts-8
02Quebec Remparts-7
03Quebec Remparts Memorial Cup-16
03Quebec Remparts-21

Pearn, Perry
93Swiss HNL-134
95Jets Team Issue-4
96Senators Pizza Hut-19
00Senators Team Issue-14
01Senators Team Issue-20
02Senators Team Issue-28
03Senators Postcards-27

Pearpoint, Caine
00Brandon Wheat Kings-18
01Brandon Wheat Kings-17
03Prince Albert Raiders-5
04Prince Albert Raiders-19

Pearsall, Andrew
99Huntington Blizzard-5

Pearson, Andy
85Kingston Canadians-9

Pearson, Kori
95Neepewa Natives-17

Pearson, Lester
03Backcheck: A Hockey Retrospective-13
03BAP Ultimate Memorabilia Memorialized-13

Pearson, Mel
72Minnesota Fighting Saints Postcards WHA-18
02Michigan Wolverines-15
03Michigan Wolverines-25
04Michigan Wolverines-20

Pearson, Rob
897th Inn. Sketch OHL-79
907th Inn. Sketch OHL-15
91Maple Leafs PLAY-24
91OPC Premier-65
91Parkhurst-169
  French-169
91Pinnacle-304
  French-304
91Pro Set-562
  French-562
91Score American-311
91Score Canadian Bilingual-341
91Score Canadian Bilingual-385
91Score Canadian English-341
91Score Canadian English-385
91Upper Deck-598
  French-598
92Bowman-381
92Maple Leafs Kodak-19
92O-Pee-Chee-136
92Panini Stickers-80
92Panini Stickers French-80
92Parkhurst-414
  Emerald Ice-414
92Pinnacle-245
92Pinnacle-287
  French-245
  French-287
  Team 2000-23
  Team 2000 French-23
92Pro Set-191
  Rookie Goal Leaders-9
92Score-333
  Canadian-333
  Young Superstars-18
92Stadium Club-377
92Topps-168
  Gold-168G
92Ultra-423
92Upper Deck-318
93Donruss-339
93Leaf-174
  Maple Leafs Score Black's-6
93OPC Premier-137
  Gold-137
93Parkhurst-474
  Emerald Ice-474
93Pinnacle-89
  Canadian-89
93PowerPlay-453
93Score-96
  Canadian-96
93Stadium Club-498
  Members Only Master Set-498
  First Day Issue-498
93Topps/OPC Premier-137
  Gold-137
93Ultra-434
93Upper Deck-48
94Be A Player Signature Cards-76
94OPC Premier-341
  Special Effects-341
94Pinnacle-375
  Artist's Proofs-375
  Rink Collection-375
94Score-137
  Gold-137
  Platinum-137
94Topps/OPC Premier-341
  Special Effects-341
94Upper Deck-180
  Electric Ice-180
95Upper Deck-212
  Electric Ice-212
  Electric Ice Gold-212
95Portland Pirates-18
97Cleveland Lumberjacks-22
97Cleveland Lumberjacks Postcards-17
01German Upper Deck-83

Pearson, Scott
85Kingston Canadians-15
86Kingston Canadians-11
87Kingston Canadians-22
88Niagara Falls Thunder-11
89ProCards AHL-119
90Maple Leafs Postcards-14
90Nordiques Petro-Canada-35
90O-Pee-Chee-356
90Topps-356
  Tiffany-356
91Bowman-150
91Maple Leafs Panini Team Stickers-19
91O-Pee-Chee-297
91Pro Set-208
  French-208
91Score American-138
91Score Canadian Bilingual-138
91Score Canadian English-138
91Stadium Club-178
91Topps-297
91Upper Deck-336
  French-336
92Nordiques Petro-Canada-24
92Parkhurst-381
  Emerald Ice-381
93Donruss-106
93Leaf-297
93Pinnacle-375
  Canadian-375
93Score-376
93Score-543
  Gold-543
  Canadian-376
  Canadian-543
  Canadian Gold-543
93Upper Deck-389
94Canada Games NHL POGS-100
94Donruss-196
94Leaf-349
94OPC Premier-124
  Special Effects-124
94Parkhurst-78
  Gold-78
94Pinnacle-213
  Artist's Proofs-213
  Rink Collection-213
94Topps/OPC Premier-124
  Special Effects-124
94Ultra-75
94Ultra-250
94Upper Deck-97
  Electric Ice-97
95Parkhurst International-22
  Emerald Ice-22
95Upper Deck-135
  Electric Ice-135
  Electric Ice Gold-135
95Rochester Americans-16
98Chicago Wolves-6
98Chicago Wolves Turner Cup-18
99Chicago Wolves-15
00German DEL-164

Pearson, Ted
84Moncton Golden Flames-14

Pease, James
02UK Coventry Blaze-5
04UK Coventry Blaze-13
04UK Coventry Blaze Champions-8
05UK Coventry Blaze-6
06UK Coventry Blaze-9

Pease, Tom
06UK Coventry Blaze-5

Peat, Stephen
96Red Deer Rebels-8
97Upper Deck-405
97Red Deer Rebels-17
98Red Deer Rebels-17
98Tri-City Americans-19
98Bowman CHL-136
  Golden Anniversary-136
  OPC International-136
  Autographs Blue-A4
  Autographs Gold-A4
  Autographs Silver-A4
98Bowman Chrome CHL-136
  Golden Anniversary-136
  Golden Anniversary Refractors-136
  OPC International-136
  OPC International Refractors-136
  Refractors-136
01BAP Signature Series-249
  Autographs-249
  Autographs Gold-249
01Parkhurst-276
01Parkhurst Beckett Promos-276
01Titanium Draft Day Edition-170
02BAP Signature Series Golf-GS91
02Pacific-398
  Blue-398
  Red-398
02Upper Deck-423
  Exclusives-423
02Upper Deck Beckett UD Promos-423

Peca, David
95Slapshot-40

Peca, Justin
91Michigan Tech Huskies-30
93Michigan Tech Huskies-14
94Erie Panthers-14

Peca, Mike
907th Inn. Sketch OHL-392
90Sudbury Wolves-21
917th Inn. Sketch OHL-247
91Sudbury Wolves-22
92Ottawa 67's-17
92Classic-17
  Gold-17
92Classic Four-Sport *-166
  Gold-166
93Donruss Team Canada-18
93Pinnacle-478
  Canadian-478
93Upper Deck-542
93Classic-25
94Be A Player Signature Cards-165
94Donruss-266
94Finest-59
  Super Team Winners-59
  Refractors-59
94Fleer-229
  Rookie Sensations-8
94Leaf-193
94OPC Premier Special Effects-275
94Parkhurst-245
  Gold-245
94Pinnacle-260
  Artist's Proofs-260
  Rink Collection-260
  Rookie Team Pinnacle-8
94Score-237
  Gold-237
  Platinum-237
94Select-198
  Gold-198
94Topps/OPC Premier Special Effects-275
94Ultra Prospects-6
94Upper Deck-257
94Upper Deck-533
94Upper Deck-547
  Electric Ice-257
  Electric Ice-533
  Electric Ice-547
  Predictor Canadian-C10
94Upper Deck Predictor Canadian Exch Gold-C10
94Upper Deck Predictor Cdn Exch Silver-C10
94Upper Deck SP Inserts-SP173
94Upper Deck SP Inserts Die Cuts-SP173
94Classic-116
  Gold-116
  Tri-Cards-T70
94Classic Pro Prospects-154
95Upper Deck World Junior Alumni-7
95Canada Games NHL POGS-41
95Canucks Building the Dream Art-17
95Donruss-266
95Leaf-114
95Parkhurst International-290
  Emerald Ice-290
95Playoff One on One-128
95Score-157
  Black Ice Artist's Proofs-157
  Black Ice-157
95Topps-350
  OPC Inserts-350
95Ultra-212
95Upper Deck-333
  Electric Ice-333
  Electric Ice Gold-333
96Collector's Choice-32
96Score-209
  Artist's Proofs-209
  Dealer's Choice Artist's Proofs-209
  Special Artist's Proofs-209
  Golden Blades-209
96SkyBox Impact-12
96Upper Deck-21
97Be A Player-44
  Autographs-44
  Autographs Die-Cuts-44
  Autographs Prismatic Die-Cuts-44
97Collector's Choice-26
97Crown Royale-15
  Emerald Green-15
  Ice Blue-15
  Silver-15
  Lamplighters Cel-Fusion Die-Cuts-4
97Donruss-21
  Press Proofs Silver-21
  Press Proofs Gold-21
97Donruss Canadian Ice-89
  Dominion Series-89
  Provincial Series-89
97Donruss Limited-39
  Exposure-39
97Donruss Preferred-34
  Cut to the Chase-34
97Donruss Priority-145
  Stamp of Approval-145
97Katch-16
  Gold-16
  Silver-16
97Leaf-107
  Fractal Matrix-107
  Fractal Matrix Die Cuts-107
97Leaf International-107
  Universal Ice-107
97NHL Aces Playing Cards-27
97Pacific-341
  Copper-341
  Emerald Green-341
  Ice Blue-341
  Red-341
  Silver-341
  Gold Crown Die-Cuts-4
97Pacific Dynagon-12
97Pacific Dynagon-136
  Copper-12
  Copper-136
  Dark Grey-12
  Dark Grey-136
  Emerald Green-12
  Emerald Green-136
  Ice Blue-12
  Ice Blue-136
  Red-12
  Red-136
  Silver-12
  Silver-136
  Best Kept Secrets-105
  Dynamic Duos-3B
  Tandems-21
  Tandems-33
97Pacific Invincible-13
  Copper-13
  Emerald Green-13
  Ice Blue-13
  Red-13
  Silver-13
  Attack Zone-3
  Off The Glass-3
97Pacific Omega-24
  Copper-24
  Dark Gray-24
  Emerald Green-24
  Gold-24
  Ice Blue-24
97Panini Stickers-13
97Panini Stickers-122
97Paramount-21
  Copper-21
  Dark Grey-21
  Emerald Green-21
  Ice Blue-21
  Red-21
  Silver-21
97Pinnacle-101
  Press Plates Back Black-101
  Press Plates Back Cyan-101
  Press Plates Back Magenta-101
  Press Plates Back Yellow-101
  Press Plates Front Black-101
  Press Plates Front Cyan-101
  Press Plates Front Magenta-101
  Press Plates Front Yellow-101
97Pinnacle Certified-99
  Red-99
  Mirror Blue-99
  Mirror Gold-99
  Mirror Red-99
97Pinnacle Inside-128
97Pinnacle Tot Cert Platinum Blue-99
97Pinnacle Tot Certi Platinum Gold-99
97Pinnacle Totally Certified Platinum Red-99
97Pinnacle Tot Cert Mirror Platinum Gold-99
97Revolution-15
  Copper-15
  Emerald-15
  Ice Blue-15
  Silver-15
  Team Checklist Laser Cuts-3
97Score-187
97Score-268
  Check It-14
97Score Sabres-11
  Platinum-11
  Premier-11
97Studio-72
  Press Proofs Silver-72
  Press Proofs Gold-72
97Upper Deck-227
  Game Dated Moments-227
  Three Star Selects-7C
97Sudbury Wolves Anniversary-17
98Aurora-19
  Championship Fever-7
  Championship Fever Copper-7
  Championship Fever Ice Blue-7
  Championship Fever Red-7
  Championship Fever Silver-7
  Man Advantage-4
98Be A Player-12
  Press Release-12
98BAP Gold-12
98BAP Autographs-12
98BAP Autographs Gold-12
98BAP Tampa Bay All Star Game-12
98Bowman's Best-32
  Refractors-32
  Atomic Refractors-32
98Crown Royale-14
  Limited Series-14

Pillars of the Game-3
Pivotal Players-3
98Finest-92
No Protectors-92
No Protectors Refractors-92
Refractors-92
98Katch-15
98OPC Chrome-94
Refractors-94
98Pacific-27
Ice Blue-27
Red-27
Gold Crown Die-Cuts-5
98Pacific Dynagon Ice-20
Blue-20
Red-20
Forward Thinking-3
98Pacific Omega-25
Red-25
Opening Day Issue-25
98Panini Photocards-61
98Panini Stickers-21
98Paramount-21
Copper-21
Emerald Green-21
Holo-Electric-21
Ice Blue-21
Silver-21
98Post-19
98Revolution-15
Ice Shadow-15
Red-15
Showstoppers-5
98SP Authentic-9
Power Shift-9
98SPx Finite-9
Radiance-9
Spectrum-9
98Topps-94
O-Pee-Chee-94
98Topps Gold Label Class 1-91
Black-91
Black One of One-91
One of One-91
Red-91
Red One of One-91
98Topps Gold Label Class 2-91
98Topps Gold Label Class 2 Black-91
98Topps Gold Label Class 2 Black 1 of 1-91
98Topps Gold Label Class 2 One of One-91
98Topps Gold Label Class 2 Red-91
98Topps Gold Label Class 2 Red One of One-91
98Topps Gold Label Class 3-91
98Topps Gold Label Class 3 Black-91
98Topps Gold Label Class 3 Black 1 of 1-91
98Topps Gold Label Class 3 One of One-91
98Topps Gold Label Class 3 Red-91
98Topps Gold Label Class 3 Red One of One-91
98UD Choice-24
Prime Choice Reserve-24
Reserve-24
98Upper Deck-46
Exclusives-46
Exclusives 1 of 1-46
Gold Reserve-46
98Upper Deck MVP-26
Gold Script-26
Silver Script-26
Super Script-26
99Aurora-18
Striped-18
Premiere Date-18
Premiere Date Striped-18
Championship Fever-5
Championship Fever Copper-5
Championship Fever Ice Blue-5
Championship Fever Silver-5
99BAP Memorabilia-131
Gold-131
Silver-131
99BAP Millennium-30
Emerald-30
Ruby-30
Sapphire-30
Signatures-30
Signatures Gold-30
99Black Diamond-12
Diamond Cut-12
Final Cut-12
99Crown Royale-19
Limited Series-19
Premiere Date-19
99Jell-O Partners of Power-4
99Kraft Stanley Cup Moments-5
99McDonald's Upper Deck-MCD13
99McDonald's Upper Deck-MCD13R
99O-Pee-Chee-162
99O-Pee-Chee Chrome-162
99O-Pee-Chee Chrome Refractors-162
99O-Pee-Chee Now Starring-NS3
99Pacific-41
Copper-41
Emerald Green-41
Gold-41
Ice Blue-41
Premiere Date-41
Red-41
Gold Crown Die-Cuts-6
99Pacific Dynagon Ice-32
Blue-32
Copper-32
Gold-32
Premiere Date-32
Checkmates American-8
Checkmates American-23
Checkmates Canadian-8
99Pacific Omega-30
Copper-30
Gold-30
Ice Blue-30
Premiere Date-30
99Pacific Prism-20
Holographic Blue-20
Holographic Gold-20
Holographic Mirror-20
Holographic Purple-20
Premiere Date-20
99Panini Stickers-37
99Paramount-29
Copper-29
Emerald-29
Gold-29
Holographic Emerald-29
Holographic Gold-29
Holographic Silver-29
Ice Blue-29
Premiere Date-29
Red-29
Personal Best-6
99Revolution-19
Premiere Date-19
Red-19
Shadow Series-19
Showstoppers-6
Copper-19
Gold-19
CSC Silver-19
99SP Authentic-9
99SPx-17
Radiance-17
Spectrum-17
99Stadium Club-141
First Day Issue-141
One of a Kind-141
Printing Plates Black-141
Printing Plates Cyan-141
Printing Plates Magenta-141
Printing Plates Yellow-141
99Topps/OPC-162
Now Starring-NS3
99Topps/OPC Chrome-162
Refractors-162
99Topps Gold Label Class 1-5
Black-5
Black One of One-5
One of One-5
Red-5
Red One of One-5
99Topps Gold Label Class 2-5
99Topps Gold Label Class 2 Black-5
99Topps Gold Label Class 2 Black 1 of 1-5
99Topps Gold Label Class 2 One of One-5
99Topps Gold Label Class 2 Red-5
99Topps Gold Label Class 2 Red One of One-5
99Topps Gold Label Class 3-5
99Topps Gold Label Class 3 Black-5
99Topps Gold Label Class 3 Black 1 of 1-5
99Topps Gold Label Class 3 One of One-5
99Topps Gold Label Class 3 Red-5
99Topps Gold Label Class 3 Red One of One-5
99Topps Premier Plus-77
Parallel-77
99Upper Deck-23
Exclusives-23
Exclusives 1 of 1-23
99Upper Deck Gold Reserve-23
99Upper Deck MVP-23
Gold Script-23
Silver Script-23
Super Script-23
99Upper Deck MVP SC Edition-27
Gold Script-27
Silver Script-27
Super Script-27
Great Combinations-GCHP
Great Combinations Parallel-GCHP
99Upper Deck Ovation-7
Standing Ovation-7
99Upper Deck Retro-9
Gold-9
Platinum-9
99Upper Deck Victory-34
99Wayne Gretzky Hockey-27
Elements of the Game-EG2
99Slovakian Challengers-24
00Aurora-20
Premiere Date-20
00BAP Memorabilia-36
Emerald-36
Ruby-36
Sapphire-36
Promos-36
00BAP Mem Chicago Sportsfest Copper-36
00BAP Memorabilia Chicago Sportsfest Blue-36
00BAP Memorabilia Chicago Sportsfest Gold-36
00BAP Memorabilia Chicago Sportsfest Ruby-36
00BAP Memorabilia Chicago Sun-Times Ruby-36
00BAP Memorabilia Chicago Sun-Times Gold-36
00BAP Mem Chicago Sun-Times Sapphire-36
00BAP Mem Toronto Fall Expo Copper-36
00BAP Memorabilia Toronto Fall Expo Gold-36
00BAP Memorabilia Toronto Fall Expo Ruby-36
00BAP Memorabilia Update Teammates-TM6
00BAP Memorabilia Update Teammates Gold-TM6
00BAP Signature Series-9
Emerald-9
Ruby-9
Sapphire-9
Autographs-94
Autographs Gold-94
Jersey Cards-J32
Jersey and Stick Cards-GSJ32
Jersey Cards Autographs-J32
Jersey Emblems-E32
Jersey Numbers-IN32
00BAP Ultimate Memorabilia Autographs-41
Gold-41
00BAP Ultimate Memorabilia Teammates-TM20
00Crown Royale-16
Ice Blue-16
Limited Series-16
Premiere Date-16
Red-16
00O-Pee-Chee-241
00O-Pee-Chee Parallel-241
00Pacific-53
Copper-53
Gold-53
Ice Blue-53
Premiere Date-53
00Panini Stickers-20
00Paramount-31
Copper-31
Gold-31
Holo-Gold-31
Holo-Silver-31
Ice Blue-31
Premiere Date-31
00Revolution-18
Blue-18
Premiere Date-18
Red-18
00SP Game Used Tools of the Game-MP
00SP Game Used Tools of the Game Combos-C-HP
00Stadium Club-90
00Topps/OPC-241
Parallel-241
00Topps Chrome-151
OPC Refractors-151
Refractors-151
00Topps Premier Plus-34
Blue Ice-34
00Topps Stars-68
Blue-68
00Upper Deck Ice-6
Immortals-6
Legends-6
Stars-6
00Upper Deck MVP-26
First Stars-26
Second Stars-26
Third Stars-26
00Upper Deck Victory-27
01Atomic-61
Blue-61
Gold-61
Premiere Date-61
Red-61
Team Nucleus-9
01BAP Memorabilia-377
Emerald-377
Ruby-377
Sapphire-377
01Bowman YoungStars-28
Gold-28
Ice Cubed-28
01Crown Royale-92
Blue-92
Premiere Date-92
Red-92
Retail-92
01Pacific Adrenaline-122
Blue-122
Premiere Date-122
Red-122
Retail-122
01Pacific Heads-Up-61
Blue-61
Premiere Date-61
Red-61
Silver-61
01Parkhurst-32
Gold-32
Silver-32
01Private Stock-59
Gold-59
Premiere Date-59
Retail-59
Silver-59
01Private Stock Pacific Nights-59
01Private Stock PS-2002-45
01SPx-40
01Stadium Club-104
Award Winners-104
Master Photos-104
01Titanium-90
Hobby Parallel-90
Premiere Date-90
Retail-90
Retail Parallel-90
Saturday Knights-13
01Topps Chrome-132
Refractors-132
Black Border Refractors-132
01Topps Heritage-167
01Topps Reserve-81
01UD Challenge for the Cup-56
01UD Honor Roll Defense First-DF6
01UD Mask Collection-60
Gold-60
01UD Top Shelf-102
01Upper Deck-111
01Upper Deck-340
Exclusives-111
Exclusives-340
Leaders of the Pack-LP9
01Upper Deck Vintage-158
01Vanguard-61
Blue-61
Red-61
One of Ones-61
Premiere Date-61
Proofs-61
02Atomic-64
Blue-64
Gold-64
Red-64
Hobby Parallel-64
Super Colliders-9
02BAP First Edition-194
02BAP First Edition-379
02BAP Memorabilia-153
02BAP Memorabilia-248
02BAP Memorabilia-253
Emerald-153
Emerald-248
Emerald-253
Ruby-153
Ruby-248
Ruby-253
Sapphire-153
Sapphire-248
Sapphire-253
NHL All-Star Game-153
NHL All-Star Game-248
NHL All-Star Game-253
NHL All-Star Game Blue-153
NHL All-Star Game Blue-248
NHL All-Star Game Blue-253
NHL All-Star Game Green-153
NHL All-Star Game Green-248
NHL All-Star Game Green-253
NHL All-Star Game Red-153
NHL All-Star Game Red-248
NHL All-Star Game Red-253
02BAP Memorabilia Toronto Fall Expo-153
02BAP Memorabilia Toronto Fall Expo-248
02BAP Memorabilia Toronto Fall Expo-253
02BAP Signature Series-132
Autographs-132
Autograph Buybacks 1998-12
Autograph Buybacks 1999-30
Autograph Buybacks 2000-94
Autographs Gold-132
Franchise Players-FJ19
Golf-GS60
02BAP Ultimate Memorabilia Numerology-27
02BAP Ultimate Memorabilia Retro Trophies-3
02Bowman YoungStars-58
Gold-58
Silver-58
02Crown Royale-61
Blue-61
Red-61
Retail-61
Jerseys-12
Jerseys Gold-12
Dual Patches-15
02eTopps-22
02McDonald's Pacific-24
Salt Lake Gold-9
02O-Pee-Chee-15
02O-Pee-Chee Jumbos-15
02O-Pee-Chee Premier Blue Parallel-15
02O-Pee-Chee Premier Red Parallel-15
02O-Pee-Chee Factory Set-15
02Pacific-242
Blue-242
Red-242
Jerseys-32
Jerseys Holo-Silver-32
02Pacific Complete-26
Red-26
02Pacific Exclusive-110
02Pacific Heads-Up-75
Blue-75
Purple-75
Red-75
Quad Jerseys-18
Quad Jerseys Gold-18
02Pacific Quest for the Cup-61
Gold-61
02Parkhurst-79
Bronze-79
Gold-79
Silver-79
02Parkhurst Retro-62
Minis-62
Franchise Players-RF19
02Private Stock Reserve-131
Red-131
Retail-131
Patches-131
02SP Authentic-58
Beckett Promos-58
02SP Game Used-30
02SPx-48
Spectrum Gold-48
Spectrum Silver-48
02Stadium Club-40
Silver Decoy Cards-40
Proofs-40
02Titanium-66
Blue-66
Red-66
Retail-66
Jerseys-41
Jerseys Retail-41
02Topps-15
OPC Blue Parallel-15
OPC Red Parallel-15
Factory Set-15
02Topps Chrome-15
Black Border Refractors-15
Refractors-15
02Topps Heritage-64
02Topps Heritage-106
Chrome Parallel-64
Autographs-MP
Autographs Black-MP
Autographs Red-MP
02Topps Total-260
Award Winners-AW10
Team Checklists-TTC19
02UD Artistic Impressions-56
Gold-56
02UD Artistic Impressions Beckett Promos-56
02UD Artistic Impressions Retrospectives-R56
02UD Artistic Impress Retrospect Gold-R56
02UD Artistic Impress Retrospect Silver-R56
02UD Honor Roll-46
02UD Honor Roll-89
Team Warriors-TW9
02UD Piece of History-57
02UD Premier Collection-34
02UD Top Shelf-55
02Upper Deck-353
Exclusives-353
02Upper Deck Beckett UD Promos-353
02Upper Deck Classic Portraits-62
02Upper Deck MVP-114
Gold-114
Classics-114
Golden Classics-114
02Upper Deck Rookie Update-156B
02Upper Deck Victory-136
Bronze-136
Gold-136
Silver-136
02Upper Deck Vintage-157
02Upper Deck Vintage-279
02Upper Deck Vintage-311
Green Backs-157
Tall Boys-T41
Tall Boys Gold-T41
02Vanguard-64
LTD-64
Jerseys-28
Jerseys Gold-28
02Ottawa 67's-29
02UD SuperStars *-166
Gold-166
03BAP Memorabilia-54
Emerald-54
Gold-54
Ruby-54
Sapphire-54
03BAP Ultimate Memorabilia Autographs-6
Gold-6
03BAP Ultimate Mem Ultimate Captains-2
03Beehive-125
Gold-125
Silver-125
03Black Diamond-41
Black-41
Green-41
Red-41
03Bowman-72
Gold-72
03Bowman Chrome-72
Refractors-72
Gold Refractors-72
Xfractors-72
03ITG Action-362
Jerseys-M142
03ITG Used Signature Series-71
Gold-71
Autographs-MP
Autographs Gold-MP
Oh Canada-12
Oh Canada Gold-12
Oh Canada Emblems-12
Oh Canada Emblems Gold-12
03McDonald's Pacific-32
03NHL Sticker Collection-76
03O-Pee-Chee-72
03OPC Blue-72
03OPC Gold-72
03OPC Red-72
03Pacific-214
Blue-214
Red-214
Maximum Impact-5
03Pacific Complete-187
Red-187
03Pacific Exhibit-178
Blue Backs-178
03Pacific Invincible-62
Blue-62
Red-62
Retail-62
Featured Performers-19
03Pacific Prism-128
Blue-128
Patches-128
Red-128
Retail-128
03Pacific Supreme-63
Blue-63
Red-63
Retail-63
03Private Stock Reserve-180
Blue-180
Patches-180
Red-180
Retail-180
03SP Authentic-56
Limited-56
03SP Game Used Authentic Fabrics-DFYP
03SP Game Used Authentic Fabrics Gold-DFYP
03SPx-62
Radiance-62
Spectrum-62
03Titanium-168
Hobby Jersey Number Parallels-168
Patches-168
Retail-168
03Topps-72
Blue-72
Gold-72
Red-72
Topps/OPC Idols-CI7
03Topps C55-72
Minis-72
Minis American Back-72
Minis American Back Red-72
Minis Bazooka Back-72
Minis Brooklyn Back-72
Minis Hat Trick Back-72
Minis O Canada Back-72
Minis O Canada Back Red-72
Minis Stanley Cup Back-72
03Topps Pristine-88
Gold Refractor Die Cuts-88
Refractors-88
Press Plates Black-88
Press Plates Cyan-88
Press Plates Magenta-88
Press Plates Yellow-88
03UD Honor Roll-52
03Upper Deck-120
Canadian Exclusives-120
HG-120
Team Essentials-TL-MP
03Upper Deck MVP-267
Gold Script-267
Silver Script-267
Canadian Exclusives-267
03Upper Deck Victory-117
Bronze-117
Gold-117
Silver-117
04Pacific-170
Blue-170
Red-170
04SP Authentic-58
Limited-58
Buybacks-145
Sign of the Times-ST-MP
Sign of the Times-DS-PH
04UD Toronto Fall Expo Priority Signings-PE
04Ultimate Collection-28
Dual Logos-UL2-MD
04Upper Deck-110
Canadian Exclusives-110
HG Glossy Gold-110
HG Glossy Silver-110
Jersey Autographs-GJA-PE
05Be A Player-56
First Period-56
Second Period-56
Third Period-56
Overtime-56
Dual Signatures-MA
Dual Signatures-PP
Outtakes-OT34
Signatures-PE
Signatures Gold-PE
05Beehive Matted Materials-MMPE
05Beehive Matted Materials Remarkable-RMPE
05Beehive Signature Scrapbook-SSMP
05Black Diamond-58
Emerald-58
Gold-58
Onyx-58
Ruby-58
05Panini Stickers-273
05Parkhurst-196
Facsimile Auto Parallel-196
True Colors-TCEDM
True Colors-TCEDM
05SP Authentic-40
Limited-40
Sign of the Times Duals-DPH
05SP Game Used Authentic Fabrics Triple-DLP
05SP Game Used Authentic Patches Triple-DLP
05SP Game Used Significant Numbers-SN-MP
05SPx-115
Winning Combos-WC-PH
Winning Combos Autographs-AWC-PH
Winning Combos Gold-WC-PH
Winning Combos Spectrum-WC-PH
Winning Materials-WM-PE
Winning Materials Autographs-AWM-PE
05The Cup Dual NHL Shields-DSRM
05The Cup Dual NHL Shields Autographs-ADSRM
05The Cup Hardware Heroes-HHMP1
05The Cup Hardware Heroes-HHMP2
05The Cup Honorable Numbers-HNPE
05The Cup Limited Logos-LLMP
05The Cup Master Pressplate Rookie Update-224
05The Cup Scripted Numbers-SNBP
05The Cup Scripted Swatches-SSPE
05UD Artifacts Treasured Patches-TP-MP
05UD Artifacts Treasured Patch Dual Autos-TP-MP
05UD Artifacts Treasured Patches Dual-TPD-MP
05UD Artifacts Treasured Patch Dual Autos-TPD-MP
05UD Artifacts Treasured Patches Pewter-TP-MP
05UD Artifacts Treasured Patches Silver-TP-MP
05UD Artifacts Treasured Swatches-TS-MP
05UD Artifacts Treasured Swatch Autos-TS-MP
05UD Artifacts Treasured Swatches Blue-TS-MP
05UD Artifacts Treasured Swatches Copper-TS-MP
05UD Artifacts Treasured Swatches Dual-TSD-MP
05UD Artifacts Treasured Swatch Dual Auto-TSD-MP
05UD Artifacts Treasured Swatch Dual Blue-TSD-MP
05UD Artifact Treasure Swatch Dual Copper-TSD-MP
05UD Artifact Treasure Swatch Dual Maroon-TSD-MP
05UD Artifact Treasure Swatch Dual Pewter-TSD-MP
05UD Artifacts TreasuredSwatch Dual Silver-TSD-MP
05UD Artifacts Treasured Swatches Maroon-TS-MP
05UD Artifacts Treasured Swatches Pewter-TS-MP
05UD Artifacts Treasured Swatches Silver-TS-MP
05UD PowerPlay-55
Rainbow-55
05UD Toronto Fall Expo Priority Signings-PS-PE
05Ultra-81
Gold-81
Fresh Ink-FI-MP
Fresh Ink Blue-FI-MP
Ice-81
05Upper Deck-323
Big Playmakers-B-MPA
Jerseys-J-MPE
Jerseys Series II-J2MP
Majestic Materials-MMMP
Notable Numbers-N-MP
Patches-P-MPE
Shooting Stars-S-MP
05Upper Deck Hockey Showcase-HS8
05Upper Deck Showcase Promos-HS8
05Upper Deck Ice-39
Rainbow-39
Cool Threads-CTMP
Cool Threads Autographs-ACTMP
Cool Threads Patches-CTPMP
Cool Threads Patch Autographs-CAPMP
Glacial Graphs-GGMP
05Upper Deck MVP-156
Gold-156
Platinum-156
Materials Duals-D-PB
ProSign-P-MP
05Upper Deck Rookie Update-224
Inspirations Patch Rookies-224
05Upper Deck Trilogy Honorary Patches-HP-MP
05Upper Deck Tril Honorary Patch Script-HSP-MP
05Upper Deck Trilogy Honorary Swatches-HS-MP
05Upper Deck Tril Honorary Swatch Scripts-HSS-MP
05Upper Deck Trilogy Scripts-SCS-PE
05Upper Deck Victory-124
Black-124
Gold-124
Silver-124
06Be A Player-68
Autographs-68
Signatures-MP
Signatures 25-73
Signatures Trios-TRPP
Up Close and Personal-UC36
Up Close and Personal Autographs-UC36
06Be A Player Portraits-94
06Beehive-6
06Beehive-164
Matte-6
Matted Materials-MMMP
Remarkable Matted Materials-MMMP
Signature Scrapbook-SSMP
06Black Diamond-126
Black-126
Gold-126
Ruby-126
Jerseys-JMP
Jerseys Black-JMP
Jerseys Gold-JMP
Jerseys Ruby-JMP
Jerseys Black Autographs -JMP
06Flair Showcase Stitches-SSMP
06Fleer-180
Tiffany-180
Fabricology-FPE
06Gatorade-71
06Hot Prospects Hot Materials -HMPE
06Hot Prospects Hot Materials Red Hot-HMPE
06Hot Prospects Hot Materials White Hot-HMPE
06Hot Prospects Hotagraphs-HPE
06McDonald's Upper Deck Autographs-AMP
06O-Pee-Chee-466
Rainbow-466
06Panini Stickers-163
06SP Authentic-7
Chirography-MP
Limited-7
Sign of the Times-STPE
06SP Game Used-95
Gold-95
Rainbow-95
Authentic Fabrics-AFMP
Authentic Fabrics Parallel-AFMP
Authentic Fabrics Patches-AFMP
Authentic Fabrics Dual-AF2PT
Authentic Fabrics Dual Patches-AF2PT
Authentic Fabrics Sixes-AF6SEL
Authentic Fabrics Sixes Patches-AF6SEL
Autographs-95
By The Letter-BLMP
Inked Sweaters-ISPE
Inked Sweaters Patches-ISPE
Inked Sweaters Dual-IS2PT
Inked Sweaters Dual Patches-IS2PT
Letter Marks-LMPE
SIGnificance-SMP
06SPx-94
Spectrum-94
06The Cup Autographed NHL Shields Duals-DASDP
06The Cup Autographed NHL Shields Duals-DASRP
06The Cup NHL Shields Duals-DSHTP
06UD Artifacts-10
Blue-10
Gold-10
Radiance-10
Autographed Radiance Parallel-10
Red-10
Tundra Tandems-TTTO
Tundra Tandems Black-TTTO
Tundra Tandems Blue-TTTO
Tundra Tandems Gold-TTTO
Tundra Tandems Red-TTTO
Tundra Tandems Dual Patches Red-TTTO
06UD Powerplay Specialists-SMP
06UD Powerplay Specialists Patches-PMP
06Ultimate Collection Premium Patches-PS-MP
06Ultimate Collection Premium Swatches-PS-MP
06Ultra-187
Gold Medallion-187
Ice Medallion-187
Uniformity-UPE
Uniformity Patches-UPPD_
Uniformity Autographed Jerseys-UAPE
06Upper Deck Arena Giveaways-TOR5
06Upper Deck-430
Exclusives Parallel-430
High Gloss Parallel-430
Game Jerseys-JMP
Game Patches-PMP
Masterpieces-430
Oversized Wal-Mart Exclusives-430
Signatures-SMP
06Upper Deck MVP-269
Gold Script-269
Super Script-269
Autographs-OAPT
Jerseys-OJDP
06Upper Deck Sweet Shot Signature Shots/Saves-SSMP
06Upper Deck Sweet Shot Signature Shots/Saves Sticks-SSSMP
06Upper Deck Sweet Shot Signature Sticks-STMP
06Upper Deck Trilogy-93
Honorary Scripted Patches-HSPMP
Honorary Scripted Swatches-HSSMP
06Upper Deck Victory-81
06Upper Deck Victory-277
06Upper Deck Victory Black-81
06Upper Deck Victory Gold-81

Pech, Lukas
02Czech OFS Plus-327
04Czech OFS-31
05Czech HC Karlovy Vary-12
06Czech OFS-37

Peck, Jim
74Sioux City Musketeers-15

Peckels, Mallory
04Ohio State Buckeyes Women-18
05Ohio State Buckeyes Women-14
06Ohio State Buckeyes Women-1

Pecker, Cory
02Cincinnati Mighty Ducks-A-11
03Cincinnati Mighty Ducks-A5
04Cincinnati Mighty Ducks-19
04ITG Heroes and Prospects-1
Autographs-CP
04ITG Heroes/Prospects Toronto Expo '05-1
04ITG Heroes/Prospects Expo Heroes/Pros-1
06Binghamton Senators-17
06Binghamton Senators 5th Anniversary-22

Peckham, Theo
04Owen Sound Attack-13
05ITG Heroes/Prosp Toronto Expo Parallel -408
05Owen Sound Attack-18
05ITG Heroes and Prospects-408
Team Cherry-TC5
06Owen Sound Attack-1

Pecora, Jay
99Tupelo T-Rex-4
00Amarillo Rattlers-15

Pecoraro, Joe
01Missouri River Otters-26
02Kalamazoo Wings-10

Peddigrew, Jeff
93Seattle Thunderbirds-18

Peddle, Brad
00Jackson Bandits-18
03Gwinnett Gladiators-3

Pedersen, Allen
82Medicine Hat Tigers-15
83Medicine Hat Tigers-9
85Moncton Golden Flames-4
87O-Pee-Chee-174
87O-Pee-Chee Stickers-132
87Topps-174
88Bruins Sports Action-18
88Bruins Postcards-16
88O-Pee-Chee-103
88Topps-103
89Bruins Sports Action-18
90Bruins Sports Action-19
90O-Pee-Chee-505
90Pro Set-12
90Score-181
Canadian-181
91O-Pee-Chee-128
91Score Canadian Bilingual-599
91Score Canadian English-599
91Topps-128
92Parkhurst-300
Emerald Ice-300
92Whalers Dairymart-17
93OPC Premier-439
Gold-439
93Stadium Club-366
Members Only Master Set-366
First Day Issue-366
93Topps/OPC Premier-439
Gold-439
94Atlanta Knights-6
97Pensacola Ice Pilots-24
98Pensacola Ice Pilots-18
01Colorado Gold Kings-20

Pedersen, Jesper
98Danish Hockey League-9
98Danish Hockey League-140
99Danish Hockey League-91
99Danish Hockey League-106

Pedersen, Kenneth
69Swedish Hockey-287
70Swedish Hockey-184

Pedersen, Kim
93Swiss HNL-403

Pedersen, Kristian
91Swedish Semic Elitserien Stickers-114
92Swedish Semic Elitserien Stickers-130

Pedersen, Lars T.
99Danish Hockey League-11

Pedersen, Michael
99Danish Hockey League-4

Pedersen, Simon
99Danish Hockey League-169

Pedersen, Soren
98Danish Hockey League-153

Pedersen, Thomas
98Danish Hockey League-50
98Danish Hockey League-58
99Danish Hockey League-107

Pederson, Al
96Pensacola Ice Pilots-22

Pederson, Barry
82O-Pee-Chee-20
82O-Pee-Chee Stickers-92
82O-Pee-Chee Stickers-93
82Topps Stickers-92
82Topps Stickers-93
82Victoria Cougars-21
83Bruins Team Issue-16
83NHL Key Tags-3
83O-Pee-Chee-57
83O-Pee-Chee Stickers-49
83O-Pee-Chee Stickers-50
83Puffy Stickers-7
83Topps Stickers-49
83Topps Stickers-50
84Bruins Postcards-16
84O-Pee-Chee-14
84O-Pee-Chee Stickers-187
84Topps-11
85O-Pee-Chee-52
85Topps-52
86Canucks Team Issue-12
86Kraft Drawings-52
86O-Pee-Chee-34
86O-Pee-Chee Stickers-38
86Topps-34
87Canucks Shell Oil-14
87O-Pee-Chee-177
87O-Pee-Chee Stickers-188
87Panini Stickers-346
87Topps-177
88Canucks Mohawk-15
88Frito-Lay Stickers-39
88O-Pee-Chee-32
88O-Pee-Chee Stickers-65
88Panini Stickers-138
88Topps-32
89Canucks Mohawk-14
89O-Pee-Chee-281
89O-Pee-Chee Stickers-60
89Panini Stickers-153
90O-Pee-Chee-134
90Penguins Foodland-4
90Pro Set-238
90Topps-134
Tiffany-134
90Upper Deck-329
French-329
91OPC Premier-124
91Pro Set-351
French-351
91Score Canadian Bilingual-639
91Score Canadian English-639
92Bowman-48
92O-Pee-Chee-295
92Topps-241
Gold-241G

Pederson, Denis
93Prince Albert Raiders-16
93Classic-26
93Classic Four-Sport *-196
Gold-196
94Finest-163
Super Team Winners-163
Refractors-163
94Pinnacle-538
Artist's Proofs-538
Rink Collection-538
94SP-144
Die Cuts-144
94Prince Albert Raiders-15
94Classic-112
Gold-112
Tri-Cards-T37
95Bowman-138
All-Foil-138
95Donruss-257
Canadian World Junior Team-20
95Parkhurst International-395
Emerald Ice-395
95SkyBox Impact-207
95Topps Canadian World Juniors-12CJ
95Ultra-359
95Upper Deck-354
Electric Ice-354
Electric Ice Gold-354
96Be A Player-217
96Be A Player-P217
Autographs-217
Autographs Silver-217
96Devils Team Issue-10
96Leaf-226
Press Proofs-226
96Pinnacle-221
Artist's Proofs-221
Foil-221
Premium Stock-221
Rink Collection-221
96Upper Deck-288
96Albany River Rats-12
97Collector's Choice-149
97Devils Team Issue-8
97Donruss Limited-154
Exposure-154
97Pacific-221
Copper-221
Emerald Green-221
Ice Blue-221
Red-221
Silver-221
97Pacific Invincible-79
Copper-79
Emerald Green-79
Ice Blue-79
Red-79
Silver-79
97Score Devils-11
Platinum-11
Premier-11
97Upper Deck-97
98Devils Team Issue-24
98Finest-144
No Protectors-144
No Protectors Refractors-144
Refractors-144

98OPC Chrome-214
Refractors-214
98Pacific-269
Ice Blue-269
Red-269
98Topps-214
O-Pee-Chee-214
Ice Age 2000-I4
98Upper Deck-312
Exclusives-312
Exclusives 1 of 1-312
Gold Reserve-312
99BAP Millennium-147
Emerald-147
Ruby-147
Sapphire-147
Signatures-147
Signatures Gold-147
99Devils Team Issue-12
00Upper Deck NHLPA-PA87
01Coyotes Team Issue-17
02BAP Sig Series Auto Buybacks 1999-147
03German Berlin Polar Bears Postcards-24
03German DEL-71
04German Berlin Polar Bears Postcards-23
04German DEL-73
05German DEL-37

Pederson, Jody
03Camrose Kodiaks-5
04Camrose Kodiaks-1

Pederson, Mark
85Medicine Hat Tigers-19
88ProCards AHL-280
90Canadiens Postcards-23
90O-Pee-Chee-82
90Pro Set-618
90Score-387
Canadian-387
90Topps-82
Tiffany-82
90Upper Deck-532
French-532
91Bowman-242
91Canadiens Panini Team Stickers-17
91Flyers J.C. Penney-20
91O-Pee-Chee-399
91Parkhurst-345
French-345
91Score Canadian Bilingual-435
91Score Canadian English-435
91Stadium Club-291
91Topps-399
91Upper Deck-363
French-363
92Bowman-390
92O-Pee-Chee-157
92Panini Stickers-188
92Panini Stickers French-188
92Pinnacle-213
French-213
92Score-263
Canadian-263
92Stadium Club-168
92Topps-327
Gold-327G
92Upper Deck-209
98German DEL-32
99German DEL-131
01German Upper Deck-100
05Bakersfield Condors-21

Pederson, Todd
82Medicine Hat Tigers-16

Pederson, Tom
92OPC Premier-33
92Ultra-403
93Parkhurst-184
Emerald Ice-184
93PowerPlay-226
93Upper Deck-92
93Classic Pro Prospects-145
94OPC Premier-142
Special Effects-142
94Pinnacle-448
Artist's Proofs-448
Rink Collection-448
94Topps/OPC Premier-142
Special Effects-142
95Collector's Choice-38
Player's Club-38
Player's Club Platinum-38
97Fort Wayne Komets-15
98German DEL-191
99German DEL-220

Peer, Brit
83Sault Ste. Marie Greyhounds-18
84Sault Ste. Marie Greyhounds-16

Peer, Claudio
95Swiss HNL-430
96Swiss HNL-461

Peer, Daniel
00Swiss Panini Stickers-89
01Swiss HNL-249

Peerless, Blaine
81Milwaukee Admirals-4

Peet, Brandon
03Prince Albert Raiders-2
04Prince Albert Raiders-9

Peet, Shaun
92British Columbia JHL-108
99Kingston Frontenacs-13
01Greensboro Generals-11
02New Mexico Scorpions-12
03New Mexico Scorpions-17

Peeters, Pete
80O-Pee-Chee-279
81O-Pee-Chee-245
81O-Pee-Chee Stickers-177
81Topps-E109
82O-Pee-Chee-22
82O-Pee-Chee Stickers-117
82Post Cereal-14
82Topps Stickers-117
83Bruins Team Issue-17
83NHL Key Tags-1
83O-Pee-Chee-44
83O-Pee-Chee-58
83O-Pee-Chee-209
83O-Pee-Chee-221
83O-Pee-Chee-222
83O-Pee-Chee Stickers-41
83O-Pee-Chee Stickers-42
83O-Pee-Chee Stickers-170
83O-Pee-Chee Stickers-318
83Puffy Stickers-9
83Topps Stickers-41
83Topps Stickers-42
83Topps Stickers-170
83Topps Stickers-318
84Bruins Postcards-17
84O-Pee-Chee-15
84O-Pee-Chee Stickers-144
84O-Pee-Chee Stickers-184
84Topps-12
85O-Pee-Chee-75
85O-Pee-Chee Stickers-160
85Topps-75
86Capitals Kodak-20
86Capitals Police-19
86O-Pee-Chee-77
86Topps-77
87Capitals Kodak-1
87Capitals Team Issue-18
87O-Pee-Chee-44
87Panini Stickers-174
87Topps-44
88Capitals Borderless-16
88Capitals Smokey-17
88O-Pee-Chee-180
88O-Pee-Chee Minis-30
88O-Pee-Chee Stickers-207
88Panini Stickers-364
88Topps-180
89Flyers Postcards-18
89O-Pee-Chee-195
89Topps-195
90Flyers Postcards-19
90O-Pee-Chee-109
90Pro Set-502
90Pro Set Player of the Month-NNO
90Topps-109
Tiffany-109
90Upper Deck-424
French-424
91Bowman-237
91O-Pee-Chee-29
91Pro Set Platinum PC-PC2
91Score Canadian Bilingual-544
91Score Canadian English-544
91Stadium Club-88
91Topps-29
91Upper Deck-642
French-642
04ITG Franchises US East-329
Autographs-A-PPE1
Autographs-A-PPE2
06Parkhurst-96
Autographs-96
Autographs Dual-DAPM

Peeters, Trevor
03Red Deer Rebels-21

Pegg, Jamie
89Peterborough Petes-104
897th Inn. Sketch OHL-104
907th Inn. Sketch OHL-363
99Huntington Blizzard-3

Pehrson, Joakim
85Swedish Panini Stickers-65
86Swedish Panini Stickers-47
87Swedish Panini Stickers-59
89Swedish Semic Elitserien Stickers-43
90Swedish Semic Elitserien Stickers-191
91Swedish Semic Elitserien Stickers-46

Pehu, Sakari
72Finnish Jaakiekko-314

Peintner, Markus
93Quebec Pee-Wee Tournament-1522

Peipmann, Jason
92British Columbia JHL-14

Peirson, John
44Beehive Group II Photos-54A
44Beehive Group II Photos-54B
51Parkhurst-34
52Parkhurst-78
53Parkhurst-88
54Parkhurst-60
55Bruins Photos-14
57Bruins Photos-16
91Bruins Sports Action Legends-22
94Parkhurst Missing Link-5

Peitonen, Esa
79Panini Stickers-170

Peitsomaa, Jukka
80Finnish Mallasjuoma-133

Pejchar, Rudolf
94Czech APS Extraliga-139
95Czech APS Extraliga-244
96Czech APS Extraliga-3
97Czech DS Stickers-113
98Czech DS-12
98Czech OFS-82
99Czech DS-15
Goalies-G2
99Czech OFS-13
99Czech OFS-NNO
99Czech OFS Goalie Die-Cuts-13
03Czech OFS Plus-76
04Czech HC Plzen Postcards-14
04Czech OFS-151

Pekarek, David
907th Inn. Sketch QMJHL-12
917th Inn. Sketch QMJHL-239
917th Inn. Sketch Memorial Cup-66

Pekarik, Pavol
99Czech OFS-299

Pekkala, Jussi
98Finnish Kerailysarja-189
99Finnish Cardset-109
01Swedish Brynas Tigers-18
02Swedish SHL-147
Parallel-147
03Finnish Cardset-129
04Finnish Cardset-137
Parallel-101

Pekkarinen, Veli-Pekka
93Finnish Jyvas-Hyva Stickers-178
93Finnish SISU-170
94Finnish SISU-127
95Finnish SISU-79

Pekki, Semi
94Finnish SISU-70
95Finnish SISU-237
95Finnish SISU Limited-108
96Finnish SISU Redline-40
98Finnish Kerailysarja-66

Pelchat, Patrick
93Amos Les Forestiers-17
98Bowman CHL-88
Golden Anniversary-88
OPC International-88
98Bowman Chrome CHL-88
Golden Anniversary-88
Golden Anniversary Refractors-88
OPC International-88
OPC International Refractors-88
Refractors-88

Pelchat, Rodrigue
51Laval Dairy Lac St. Jean-27

Pelech, Matt
03Sarnia Sting-16
05ITG Heroes/Prosp Toronto Expo Parallel -133
05ITG Heroes and Prospects-133
Autographs-A-MP
06Belleville Bulls-1

Pelech, Michael
05Kitchener Rangers-20

Pelensky, Perry
83Springfield Indians-13

Pelham, Luke
01Moncton Wildcats-24
02Moncton Wildcats-13
03Moncton Wildcats-21
04Gatineau Olympiques-24
04Moncton Wildcats-9

Pelikovsky, Waldemar
06Czech OFS-197

Pelino, Mike
97Spokane Chiefs-28
98Spokane Chiefs-19

Pelkonen, Tommi
04Finnish Cardset-202

Pell, Gordon
897th Inn. Sketch OHL-80
907th Inn. Sketch OHL-213
91Cornwall Royals-4
917th Inn. Sketch OHL-23

Pell, Joey
05Drummondville Voltigeurs-8

Pella, Dean
87Kingston Canadians-18
88Sudbury Wolves-12

Pella, Tyler
87Kingston Canadians-23
88Sudbury Wolves-11

Pellaers, Ryan
917th Inn. Sketch WHL-67

Pellegrims, Mike
96German DEL-167
98German DEL-237
99German DEL-290
00German DEL-227
Profiles-P10
01German Upper Deck-54
02German DEL City Press-56
All-Stars-AS6
03German Deg Metro Stars-15
03German DEL-38
04German DEL-53
All-Stars-AS7
04German Dusseldorf Metro Stars Postcards-15
05German DEL-71
All-Star Jerseys-AS13

Pellegrino, Santino
92Finnish Semic-260
93Swedish Semic World Champ Stickers-228
94Finnish Jaa Kiekko-305

Pellerin, Brian
90Prince Albert Raiders-16
907th Inn. Sketch WHL-266
91ProCards-45
92Peoria Rivermen-18
93Peoria Rivermen-20

Pellerin, Jason
99Odessa Jackalopes-7

Pellerin, Scott
92Maine Black Bears-7
92Classic-81
Gold-81
92Classic Four-Sport *-202
Gold-202
93Leaf-167
93Parkhurst-116
Emerald Ice-116
93Score-373
Canadian-373
93Stadium Club-13
Members Only Master Set-13
OPC-13
First Day Issue-13
First Day Issue OPC-13
93Ultra-142
93Upper Deck-52
93Classic Pro Prospects-18
93Classic Pro Prospects-90
97Be A Player-50
Autographs-50
Autographs Die-Cuts-50
Autographs Prismatic Die-Cuts-50
97Pacific-95
Copper-95
Emerald Green-95
Ice Blue-95
Red-95
Silver-95
97Score Blues-12
Platinum-12
Premier-12
98Pacific-370
Ice Blue-370
Red-370
99Blues Taco Bell-15
99Pacific-361
Copper-361
Emerald Green-361
Gold-361
Ice Blue-361
Premiere Date-361
Red-361
99Panini Stickers-333
00BAP Parkhurst 2000-P233
00Crown Royale-54
Ice Blue-54
Limited Series-54
Premiere Date-54
Red-54
00Kraft-30
00Paramount-124
Copper-124
Gold-124
Holo-Gold-124
Holo-Silver-124
Ice Blue-124
Premiere Date-124
00Stadium Club-201
00Titanium-46
Blue-46
Gold-46
Premiere Date-46
Red-46
Retail-46
00Topps Chrome-233
OPC Refractors-233
Refractors-233
00Topps Stars-93
Blue-93
00UD Heroes-60
00UD Pros and Prospects-43
00Upper Deck-90
00Upper Deck-318
Exclusives Tier 1-90
Exclusives Tier 1-318
Exclusives Tier 2-90
Exclusives Tier 2-318
00Upper Deck Vintage-183
00Upper Deck Vintage-184
01McDonald's Pacific Hometown Pride-3
01Pacific-80
Extreme LTD-80
Hobby LTD-80
Premiere Date-80
Retail LTD-80
01Pacific Arena Exclusives-80
01Upper Deck-246
Exclusives-246
02Coyotes Team Issue-26
02Pacific-117
Blue-117
Red-117
02Pacific Complete-374
Red-374
02Stars Postcards-1
06Manchester Monarchs-23

Pellet, Patrice
96Swiss HNL-267

Pelletier, Chris
04Tulsa Oilers-19

Pelletier, D.J.
03Arizona Icecats-19
04Arizona Icecats-16

Pelletier, Francois
907th Inn. Sketch Memorial Cup-66
92Quebec Pee-Wee Tournament-605

Pelletier, Gaston
52Juniors Blue Tint-77
72Finnish Semic World Championship-155
72Swedish Semic World Championship-155

Pelletier, Jean-Marc
92Quebec Pee-Wee Tournament-612
97Rimouski Oceanic-35
98UD Choice-301
Prime Choice Reserve-301
Reserve-301
99O-Pee-Chee-118
99O-Pee-Chee Chrome-118
99O-Pee-Chee Chrome Refractors-118
99Topps/OPC-118
99Topps/OPC Chrome-118
Refractors-118
99Upper Deck-95
Exclusives-95
Exclusives 1 of 1-95
Crunch Time-CT4
Crunch Time Quantum Gold-CT4
Crunch Time Quantum Silver-CT4
New Ice Age-N11
New Ice Age Quantum Gold-N11
New Ice Age Quantum Silver-N11
99Upper Deck Gold Reserve-95
99Upper Deck MVP-147
Gold Script-147
Silver Script-147
Super Script-147
99Upper Deck Retro Generation-G3C
99Upper Deck Retro Generation Level 2-G3C
99Upper Deck Victory-216
99Quebec PeeWee Tournament Coll Souv-11
00Cincinnati Cyclones-20
02Between the Pipes-78
Gold-78
Silver-78
02UD Mask Collection-66
02UD Mask Collection Beckett Promos-66
02Lowell Lock Monsters-21
03Springfield Falcons Postcards-20
04ITG Heroes and Prospects-29
Autographs-JP
Emblems-23
Emblems Gold-23
He Shoots-He Scores Prizes-37
Jersey Autographs-23
Jerseys-23
Jerseys Gold-23
Net Prospects-18
Net Prospects Gold-18
Numbers-23
Numbers Gold-23
04ITG Heroes/Prospects Toronto Expo '05-29
04ITG Heroes/Prospects Expo Heroes/Pros-29

Pelletier, Jonathan
92Quebec Pee-Wee Tournament-122
99Rouyn-Noranda Huskies-14
00Rimouski Oceanic-20
Signed-20

Pelletier, Lloyd
907th Inn. Sketch WHL-53
917th Inn. Sketch WHL-235

Pelletier, Marcel
51Laval Dairy QSHL-33
52St. Lawrence Sales-90

Pelletier, Mike
02Arizona Icecats-20
04Arizona Icecats-17

Pelletier, Nicolas
00Val d'Or Foreurs-8
Signed-8
01Val d'Or Foreurs-11

Pelletier, Pascal
00Baie-Comeau Drakkar-6
Signed-6
01Baie-Comeau Drakkar-5
02Baie Comeau Drakkar-7
03Shawinigan Cataractes-20
04Louisiana Ice Gators-17
05Providence Bruins-11
06Providence Bruins-13

Pelletier, Pier-Olivier
04Drummondville Voltigeurs-3
04Drummondville Voltigeurs-NNO
05ITG Heroes/Prosp Toronto Expo Parallel -147
05Drummondville Voltigeurs-3
05ITG Heroes and Prospects-147
Autographs-A-POP
06Drummondville Voltigeurs-24

Pelletier, Pierre
03St. Jean Mission-20

Pelletier, Serge
00Swiss Panini Stickers-125
01Swiss HNL-121

Pelletier, Steve
00Val d'Or Foreurs-10
Signed-10
01Val d'Or Foreurs-19
02Quebec Remparts-19
03P.E.I. Rocket-19
05Rockford Ice Hogs-12

Pelletier, Zach
04Ohio State Buckeyes-20
05Ohio State Buckeyes-17
06Ohio State Buckeyes-20

Pelley, Rod
02Ohio State Buckeyes-20
03Ohio State Buckeyes-12
04Ohio State Buckeyes-10
05Ohio State Buckeyes-12

Pellinen, Ossi
04Finnish Cardset-231
05Finnish Cardset -43

Pellinen, Petri
71Finnish Suomi Stickers-332

Pellitier, Nicolas
93Quebec Pee-Wee Tournament-306

Peloffy, Andre
74Capitals White Borders-22
98Swiss Power Play Stickers-78
00Swiss Panini Stickers-245

Peltier, Derek
04Minnesota Golden Gophers-18
05Minnesota Golden Gophers-18
06Minnesota Golden Gophers-17

Peltola, Ari
70Finnish Jaakiekko-336
78Finnish SM-Liiga-232
80Finnish Mallasjuoma-207

Peltola, Juhani
66Finnish Jaakiekkosarja-159

Peltola, Mikko
92Finnish Jyvas-Hyva Stickers-170
93Finnish Jyvas-Hyva Stickers-288
93Finnish SISU-69
94Finnish SISU-324
95Finnish SISU-102
95Finnish Semic World Championships-29
96Finnish SISU Redline-178
97Swedish Collector's Choice-142
98Finnish Kerailysarja-92
99Finnish Cardset-50
01Finnish Cardset-100
02Finnish Cardset-90
02Swiss HNL-318
03Swedish Elite-216
Silver-216
04Swedish Elitset-64
Gold-64
Signatures Series A-5
04Swedish Pure Skills-44
Parallel-44
05Swedish SHL Elitset-74
Gold-74
06Finnish Cardset-229
06Finnish Ilves Team Set-20

Peltola, Pekka
91Finnish Jyvas-Hyva Stickers-10
92Finnish Jyvas-Hyva Stickers-131
93Finnish Jyvas-Hyva Stickers-22
93Finnish SISU-97
94Finnish SISU-68
95Finnish SISU-362

Peltola, Teuvo
66Finnish Jaakiekkosarja-146

Peltomaa, Jussi
06Finnish Porin Assat Pelaajakortit-26

Peltomaa, Timo
91Finnish Semic World Champ Stickers-25
91Finnish Jyvas-Hyva Stickers-15
91Swedish Semic World Champ Stickers-25
92Finnish Jyvas-Hyva Stickers-44
92Finnish Semic-18
93Finnish Jyvas-Hyva Stickers-79
93Finnish SISU-125
93Finnish SISU Promos-NNO
93Swedish Semic World Champ Stickers-72
94Finnish SISU-43
94Finnish SISU-158
94Finnish SISU Horoscopes-8
95Finnish SISU-227
95Finnish SISU Limited-104
95Finnish Semic World Championships-50
96Finnish SISU Redline Sledgehammers-7
96German DEL-63
98Finnish Kerailysarja-93
99Finnish Cardset-288
00Swedish Upper Deck-173
02Finnish Cardset-243
04Finnish Cardset-54
Parallel-40

Peltonen, Esa
69Swedish Hockey-380
70Finnish Jaakiekko-73
70Finnish Jaakiekko-285
70Swedish Hockey-309
70Swedish Masterserien-85
71Finnish Suomi Stickers-73
71Finnish Suomi Stickers-155
71Swedish Hockey-72
72Finnish Jaakiekko-70
72Finnish Jaakiekko-107
72Finnish Hellas-10
72Finnish Panda Toronto-107
72Finnish Semic World Championship-85
72Swedish Semic World Championship-85
73Finnish Jaakiekko-75
73Finnish Jaakiekko-138
74Finnish Jenkki-13
74Finnish Typotor-2
74Finnish Typotor-54
74Swedish Stickers-33
74Swedish Semic World Champ Stickers-88
77Finnish Sportscasters-49-1175
78Finnish SM-Liiga-31
80Finnish Mallasjuoma-5
82Swedish Semic VM Stickers-49

Peltonen, Jari
70Finnish Jaakiekko-337

Peltonen, Jarno
93Finnish Jyvas-Hyva Stickers-83
93Finnish SISU-123
94Finnish SISU-259
95Finnish SISU-235
96Finnish SISU Redline-32
96German DEL-267
98German DEL-250
99German DEL-31
00Finnish Cardset-276
02Swiss HNL-101

Peltonen, Jorma
65Finnish Hellas-126
66Finnish Jaakiekkosarja-197
69Swedish Hockey-381
70Finnish Jaakiekko-74
70Finnish Jaakiekko-135
70Swedish Hockey-310
71Finnish Suomi Stickers-184
72Finnish Jaakiekko-134
72Finnish Panda Toronto-31
73Finnish Jaakiekko-188
74Finnish Typotor-11
74Swedish Stickers-99

Peltonen, Jouni
73Finnish Jaakiekko-314
78Finnish SM-Liiga-157
80Finnish Mallasjuoma-113

Peltonen, Kimmo
99Finnish Cardset-235
00Finnish Cardset-24
01Finnish Cardset-27
02Finnish Cardset-91
03Finnish Cardset-157
04Swedish Elitset-196
Gold-196
Signatures Series B-7
05Finnish Cardset -179
06Finnish Cardset-4

Peltonen, Matti
65Finnish Hellas-148
66Finnish Jaakiekkosarja-162
70Finnish Jaakiekko-219

Peltonen, Pasi
93Finnish SISU-211
94Finnish SISU-103
95Finnish SISU-153
96Finnish SISU Redline-152
98Finnish Kerailysarja-255
99Finnish Cardset-147
00Finnish Cardset-103
01Finnish Cardset-148
02Finnish Cardset-92
03Finnish Cardset-171
04Finnish Cardset-186
Parallel-139
05Finnish Cardset -165
06Finnish Cardset-169
Enforcers-10
06Finnish Porin Assat Pelaajakortit-4

Peltonen, Timo
78Finnish SM-Liiga-158
80Finnish Mallasjuoma-115

Peltonen, Ville
92Upper Deck-616
92Finnish Jyvas-Hyva Stickers-15
93Finnish Jyvas-Hyva Stickers-28
93Finnish SISU-101
93Finnish SISU-365
93Finnish SISU-391
94Finnish SISU-166
94Finnish SISU-216
94Finnish SISU Horoscopes-6
94Finnish Jaa Kiekko-33
94Classic-97
Gold-97
Tri-Cards-T61
95Bowman-133
All-Foil-133
95Parkhurst International-456
95Parkhurst International-521
Emerald Ice-456
Emerald Ice-521
95Upper Deck-384
Electric Ice-384
Electric Ice Gold-384
95Finnish Beckett Ad Cards-3
95Finnish SISU-172
Gold Cards-21
95Finnish SISU Limited-41
95Finnish SISU Painkillers-5
95Finnish Karjala World Champ Labels-17
95Finnish Kellogg's-4
95Finnish Semic World Championships-16
95Finnish Semic World Championships-230
95Swedish World Championships Stickers-178
96Collector's Choice-241
96Donruss-224
Press Proofs-224
96Leaf-144
Press Proofs-144
96Upper Deck-335
96Swedish Semic Wien-16
96Swedish Semic Wien-37
All-Stars-AS6
97Swedish Collector's Choice-79
Crash the Game Exchange-C5
Crash the Game Redemption-R5
Select-UD5
98Predators Team Issue-17
98Finnish Kerailysarja Leijonat-36
99BAP Memorabilia-275
Gold-275
Silver-275
99BAP Millennium-138
Emerald-138
Ruby-138
Sapphire-138
Signatures-138
Signatures Gold-138
99Pacific Dynagon Ice-110
Blue-110
Copper-110
Gold-110
Premiere Date-110
99Panini Stickers-263
99Finnish Cardset-195
Aces High-C-K
00Panini Stickers-181
00Upper Deck NHLPA-PA50
00Finnish Cardset-115
00Milwaukee Admirals Keebler-13
00Milwaukee Admirals Postcards-11
01Finnish Cardset-259
01Finnish Cardset Dueling Aces-2
02BAP Sig Series Auto Buybacks 1999-138
02Finnish Cardset-244
06Russian Sport Collection Olympic Stars-26

Peltoniemi, Ossi
66Finnish Jaakiekkosarja-219

Peltoniemi, Pekka
66Finnish Jaakiekkosarja-121

Pelucha, Petr
97Czech APS Extraliga-101

Peluso, Anthony
05Erie Otters-12
06Erie Otters-18

Peluso, Chris
04Sioux Falls Stampede-2-1
05Sioux Falls Stampede-10

Peluso, Marco
00Lincoln Stars-21
04Minnesota-Duluth Bulldogs-17
05Las Vegas Wranglers-18
06Las Vegas Wranglers-18

Peluso, Mike
89ProCards IHL-57
90Blackhawks Coke-22
90Pro Set-601
91Blackhawks Coke-20
91O-Pee-Chee-293
91Score Canadian Bilingual-529
91Score Canadian English-529
91Topps-293
91Upper Deck-414
French-414
91ProCards-496
92Parkhurst-118
Emerald Ice-118
92Pinnacle-379
French-379
92Pro Set-122
92Score-536
Canadian-536
92Senators Team Issue-12
92Ultra-365
93Leaf-407
93Panini Stickers-116
93Pinnacle-385
Canadian-385
93Score-265
93Score-551
Gold-551
Canadian-265
Canadian-551
Canadian Gold-551
93Stadium Club-497
Members Only Master Set-497
First Day Issue-497
93Omaha Lancers-18
94Leaf-546
94Pinnacle-423
Artist's Proofs-423
Rink Collection-423
95Canada Games NHL POGS-161
95Topps Power Lines-10PL
96Be A Player-136
Autographs-136
Autographs Silver-136
97Flames Collector's Photos-5
97Pacific-306
Copper-306
Emerald Green-306
Ice Blue-306
Red-306
Silver-306
02Fleer Throwbacks-28
Gold-28
Platinum-28

Peluso, Mike A.
98Portland Pirates-15
99Portland Pirates-18
00Worcester Icecats-27
01BAP Memorabilia-322
Emerald-322
Ruby-322
Sapphire-322
01SPx-200
01UD Mask Collection-139
Gold-139
01UD Playmakers-110
01UD Premier Collection-55
01UD Top Shelf-125
01Upper Deck Ice-131
01Norfolk Admirals-14
02Norfolk Admirals-18
03Philadelphia Phantoms-14

Pelyk, Mike
68Maple Leafs White Border-7
68Post Marbles-17
68Shirriff Coins-166
69Maple Leafs White Border Glossy-26
70Dad's Cookies-98
70Esso Power Players-21
70Maple Leafs Postcards-10
70O-Pee-Chee-107
70Sargent Promotions Stamps-203
70Topps-107
71Maple Leafs Postcards-15
71O-Pee-Chee-92
71Sargent Promotions Stamps-197
71Topps-92
71Toronto Sun-268
72Maple Leafs Postcards-23
72O-Pee-Chee-17
72Sargent Promotions Stamps-200
72Topps-107
73Maple Leafs Postcards-21
73O-Pee-Chee-71
73Topps-71
74O-Pee-Chee WHA-19
75Stingers Kahn's-9
76Maple Leafs Postcards-14
76O-Pee-Chee NHL-342

Pelzer, James
91British Columbia JHL-96

Pembroke, Terry
99Fort Wayne Komets Penalty Leaders-8

Pender, Justin
05Halifax Mooseheads-19
06Halifax Mooseheads-16

Penelton, Paul
85Kitchener Rangers-25

Pengelly, Darcy
95Neepawa Natives-16
95Oklahoma Coyotes RHI-13
97New Mexico Scorpions-10

Pengelly, Darren
95Central Hockey League-50

Penicka, Lubomir
81Swedish Semic Hockey VM Stickers-71
82Swedish Semic VM Stickers-94

Penk, Jan
94Czech APS Extraliga-260
95Czech APS Extraliga-133
97Czech APS Extraliga-201
98Czech DS Stickers-233
04German Weiden Blue Devils-19

Penkala, Joe
88Saskatoon Blades-1

Penkoc, Jure
93Quebec Pee-Wee Tournament-1783

Penn, Josh
98Florida Everblades-17

Penn, Shawn
94Toledo Storm-17
95Toledo Storm-19
97Long Beach Ice Dogs-14
98Fort Wayne Komets-26
99Utah Grizzlies-12

Pennanen, Olli
78Finnish SM-Liiga-49

Pennanen, Pentti
66Finnish Jaakiekkosarja-136
70Finnish Jaakiekko-263

Pennell, Fred
87Sudbury Wolves-10

Pennell, Gordie
51Buffalo Bison-18

Pennell, Red
88Sudbury Wolves-10

Penner, Andrew
01Guelph Storm-22
01Guelph Storm Memorial Cup-22
02Guelph Storm-1
03ECHL Update RBI Sports-125
05Hot Prospects-123
En Fuego-123
Red Hot-123
White Hot-123
05SP Authentic-226
Limited-226
05SPx-211
Spectrum-211
05The Cup Masterpiece Pressplates (Ice)-191
05The Cup Master Pressplate Rookie Update-123
05The Cup Masterpiece Pressplates SPA-226
05The Cup Masterpiece Pressplates (SPx)-211
05The Cup Masterpiece Pressplates Trilogy-243
05Upper Deck Ice-191
05Upper Deck Rookie Update-123
05Upper Deck Trilogy-243
05Syracuse Crunch-21
06Between The Pipes-2
Autographs-AAP
Emblems-GUE33
Emblems Gold-GUE33
Emblems Autographs-GUE33
Jerseys-GUJ33
Jerseys Gold-GUJ33
Jerseys Autographs-GUJ33
Numbers-GUN33
Numbers Gold-GUN33
Numbers Autographs-GUN33
06Wilkes-Barre Scranton Penguins-3
06Wilkes-Barre Scranton Penguins Jerseys-2
06ITG Heroes and Prospects-50
Autographs-AAP
Jerseys-GUJ57
Jerseys Gold-GUJ57
Emblems-GUE57
Emblems Gold-GUE57
Numbers-GUN57
Numbers Gold-GUN57

Penner, Dustin
04Cincinnati Mighty Ducks-24
05ITG Heroes/Prosp Toronto Expo Parallel -225
05Beehive-163
Matte-163
05Black Diamond-211
05Hot Prospects-101
En Fuego-101
Red Hot-101
White Hot-101
05Parkhurst-17
Facsimile Auto Parallel-17
05SP Authentic-247
Limited-247
05SP Game Used-192
05SPx-244
05The Cup Masterpiece Pressplate Artifact-243
05The Cup Masterpiece Pressplate Bee Hive-163
05The Cup Masterpiece Pressplate Black Diamond-211
05The Cup Masterpiece Pressplates (Ice)-185
05The Cup Master Pressplate Rookie Update-101
05The Cup Masterpiece Pressplates SPA-247
05The Cup Masterpiece Pressplates SP GU-192
05The Cup Masterpiece Pressplates (SPx)-244
05The Cup Masterpiece Pressplates Trilogy-221
05The Cup Masterpiece Pressplate Ult Coll-193
05UD Artifacts-243
05Ultimate Collection-193
Gold-193
05Upper Deck Ice-185
05Upper Deck Rookie Update-101
05Upper Deck Trilogy-221
05AHL Top Prospects-29
05Portland Pirates-20
05ITG Heroes and Prospects-225
Autographs Series II-DPE
06Be A Player-67
Autographs-67
Signatures-PE
Signatures 25-72
06ITG Ultimate Memorabilia Future Star-15
06ITG Ultimate Memorabilia Future Star Gold-15
06ITG Ultimate Memorabilia Future Star Autos-6
06ITG Ultimate Memorabilia Future Star Autos Gold-6
06ITG Ultimate Memorabilia Future Star Patches Autos-6
06ITG Ultimate Memorabilia Future Star Patches Autos Gold-6
06ITG Ultimate Memorabilia R.O.Y. Autos-7
06ITG Ultimate Memorabilia R.O.Y. Autos Gold-7
06ITG Ultimate Memorabilia R.O.Y. Emblems-7
06ITG Ultimate Memorabilia R.O.Y. Emblems Gold-7
06ITG Ultimate Memorabilia R.O.Y. Jerseys-7
06ITG Ultimate Memorabilia R.O.Y. Jerseys Gold-7
06ITG Ultimate Memorabilia R.O.Y. Numbers-7
06ITG Ultimate Memorabilia R.O.Y. Numbers Gold-7
06O-Pee-Chee-12
Rainbow-12
06ITG Heroes and Prospects-57

Autographs-ADPE
Complete AHL Logos-AHL05
Jerseys-GUJ25
Jerseys Gold-GUJ25
Emblems-GUE25
Emblems Gold-GUE25
Numbers-GUN25
Numbers Gold-GUN25

Penner, Jason
00Sarnia Sting-21
00UD CHL Prospects-25
01Peterborough Petes-7
02Peterborough Petes-13

Penner, Pat
92Fort Worth Fire-15

Penney, Chad
907th Inn. Sketch OHL-314
917th Inn. Sketch OHL-58
93Upper Deck-436
93Sault Ste. Marie Greyhound Memorial Cup-9
94Leaf-241
94OPC Premier-267
Special Effects-267
94Topps/OPC Premier-267
Special Effects-267
94Classic-68
Gold-68
Tri-Cards-T46
94Classic Pro Prospects-65
95PEI Senators-14
97Kentucky Thoroughblades-12
98Colorado Gold Kings-16
98Colorado Gold Kings Postcards-5

Penney, Jackson
90ProCards AHL/IHL-115
92Alberta International Team Canada-15
95German DEL-402
96German DEL-310
98German DEL-232
99Swiss Panini Stickers-47
01German Upper Deck-236
02German DEL City Press-79

Penney, Ryan
95Slapshot-182

Penney, Steve
83Canadiens Postcards-21
83Nova Scotia Voyageurs-15
84Canadiens Postcards-21
84Canadiens Postcards-22
84O-Pee-Chee-269
85Canadiens Placemats-4
85Canadiens Placemats-7
85Canadiens Postcards-25
85Canadiens Provigo-14
85O-Pee-Chee-4
85O-Pee-Chee Stickers-126
85Topps-4
86Jets Postcards-19
86Kraft Drawings-53
86O-Pee-Chee-222
87Moncton Hawks-21

Pennington, Cliff
44Beehive Group II Photos-55A
44Beehive Group II Photos-55B
61Shirriff/Salada Coins-1
61Topps-19
62Topps-14
63Quebec Aces-22
64Beehive Group III Photos-22

Penniston, Don
51Laval Dairy QSHL-58

Pennock, Berkley
93Red Deer Rebels-18

Pennock, Trevor
907th Inn. Sketch WHL-18
91British Columbia JHL-126

Pennoyer, Rob
92British Columbia JHL-128

Penny, Andy
93Quebec Pee-Wee Tournament-1145

Pens, Charlie
06Cape Breton Screaming Eagles-18

Penstock, Byron
90Brandon Wheat Kings-18
907th Inn. Sketch WHL-224
917th Inn. Sketch WHL-302
92Brandon Wheat Kings-18
93Brandon Wheat Kings-1
94Brandon Wheat Kings-15
95Slapshot Memorial Cup-26

Pentikainen, Atte
04Finnish Cardset-313
05Finnish Cardset-342
06Swedish SHL Elitset-184

Penton, Scott
93Owen Sound Platers-22

Penttila, Timo
80Finnish Mallasjuoma-170

Penttinen, Jukka
95Finnish SISU-258
96Finnish SISU Redline-46
98Swedish UD Choice-31

Penzkofer, Christian
94German First League-338

Pepe, Matt
04Kitchener Rangers-19
05Kitchener Rangers-18
06Kitchener Rangers-11

Pepin, Bob
43Parade Sportive *-94
51Laval Dairy Subset-52
52St. Lawrence Sales-83

Pepin, Frederick
93Quebec Pee-Wee Tournament-465

Pepin, Rene
51Laval Dairy QSHL-42
52Bas Du Fleuve-52
52St. Lawrence Sales-82

Peplinski, Jim
80Flames Postcards-15
80Pepsi-Cola Caps-13
81Flames Postcards-15
81O-Pee-Chee-49
82Flames Dollars-5
82O-Pee-Chee-55
82O-Pee-Chee Stickers-216
82Post Cereal-3
82Topps Stickers-216
83Esso-14
83NHL Key Tags-20
83O-Pee-Chee-90
83Vachon-16
84O-Pee-Chee-233
85Flames Red Rooster-22
86Flames Red Rooster-21
86Kraft Drawings-54
86O-Pee-Chee-182
86O-Pee-Chee Stickers-84
86Topps-182
87Flames Red Rooster-24
87O-Pee-Chee-209
87O-Pee-Chee Stickers-46
87Panini Stickers-213
88Flames Postcards-10
88O-Pee-Chee-243
88O-Pee-Chee Stickers-88
88Panini Stickers-14
89O-Pee-Chee-206
89O-Pee-Chee Stickers-99
89Panini Stickers-37
04ITG Franchises Canadian-8
Autographs-JPE
06Parkhurst-94
06Parkhurst-169
Autographs-94
Autographs-169
Autographs Dual-DAPP

Peplinski, Joe
97Arizona Icecats-18

Pepperall, Colin
95Slapshot-197
97Bowman CHL-30
OPC-30
98Bowman CHL-19
Golden Anniversary-19
OPC International-19
98Bowman Chrome CHL-19
Golden Anniversary-19
Golden Anniversary Refractors-19
OPC International-19
OPC International Refractors-19
Refractors-19
99Hampton Roads Admirals-16
01Greenville Grrrowl-12
02UK Manchester Storm-1
02Reading Royals-11
02Reading Royals RBI Sports-178
03Columbus Cottonmouths-17

Pepperall, Ryan
94Kitchener Rangers-16
95Slapshot-147
95Slapshot-NNO
95Classic-46
95Classic-87
96Kitchener Rangers-22
97St. John's Maple Leafs-20
99St. John's Maple Leafs-16
01BC Icemen-16

Perala, Olli-Pekka
71Finnish Suomi Stickers-351

Peralta, Sal
02St. Michaels Majors-23
03St. Michael's Majors-22

Peraoja, Seppo
70Finnish Jaakiekko-185

Perardi, Anthony
95Waterloo Blackhawks -14

Perardi, Eric
93RPI Engineers-21

Percival, Rob
88Brockville Braves-15

Pereira, Joe
03Peoria Rivermen-11
04Peoria Rivermen-20
06Augusta Lynx-15

Pereira, Lenny
94Raleigh Icecaps-14

Pereyaslov, Mikhail
98Russian Hockey League-63
99Russian Hockey League-112

Perez, Bryan
01Michigan Tech Huskies-23
03Roanoke Express-316
04Louisiana Ice Gators-18

Perez, Denis
92Finnish Semic-224
93Swedish Semic World Champ Stickers-255
94Finnish Jaa Kiekko-215
94French National Team-23
95Swedish World Championships Stickers-102
96Swedish Semic Wien-186
98German DEL-242

Perezhogin, Alexander
01BAP Memorabilia Draft Redemptions-25
01Russian Young Lions-9
02Russian Future Stars-7
02Russian Hockey League-122
02Russian Hockey League-201
02Russian Young Lions-13
03Pacific AHL Prospects-29
Gold-29
04SP Authentic Rookie Redemptions-RR16
04Russian Back to Russia-29
05ITG Heroes/Prosp Toronto Expo Parallel -258
05Beehive-108
Beige -108
Blue -108
Gold-108
Red -108
Rookie Jumbos-R4
Matte-108
Signature Scrapbook-SSAP
05Black Diamond-210
Emerald-210
Gold-210
Onyx-210
Ruby-210
05Canadiens Team Issue-15
05Hot Prospects-243
En Fuego-243
Hot Materials-HMAP
Red Hot-243
White Hot-243
05Parkhurst-636
Facsimile Auto Parallel-636
True Colors-TCMTL
True Colors-TCMTL
05SP Authentic-163
Limited-163
Exquisite Endorsements-EEAP
Octographs-OR
Rarefied Rookies-RRAP
Rookie Authentics-RAAP
Sign of the Times Duals-DKP
Sign of the Times Triples-TRRP
05SP Game Used-148
Autographs-148
Gold-148
Auto Draft-AD-AP
Game Gear-GG-AP
Game Gear Autographs-AG-AP
Rookie Exclusives-AP
Rookie Exclusives Silver-RE-AP
Significant Numbers-SN-AP
05SPx-161
Spectrum-161
Xcitement Rookies-XR-AP
Xcitement Rookies Gold-XR-AP
Xcitement Rookies Spectrum-XR-AP
05The Cup-171
Autographed Rookie Patches Gold Rainbow-171
Black Rainbow Rookies-171
Dual NHL Shields-DSPK
Dual NHL Shields Autographs-ADSPK
Masterpiece Pressplates (Artifacts)-216
Masterpiece Pressplates (Bee Hive)-108
Masterpiece Pressplates (Black Diamond)-210
Masterpiece Pressplates (Ice)-114
Masterpiece Pressplates (MVP)-401
Masterpiece Pressplates (Power Play)-154
Masterpiece Pressplates (Power Play)-154
Masterpiece Pressplates Rookie Upd Auto-268
Masterpiece Pressplates SPA Autos-163
Masterpiece Pressplates (SP Game Used)-148
Masterpiece Pressplates SPx Autos-161
Masterpiece Pressplates (Trilogy)-194
Masterpiece Pressplates Ult Coll Autos-99
Masterpiece Pressplates (Victory)-261
Masterpiece Pressplates Autographs-171
Platinum Rookies-171
05UD Artifacts-216
Gold-RED16
05UD PowerPlay-154
05UD Rookie Class-33
05Ultimate Collection-99
Autographed Patches-99
Autographed Shields-99
Jerseys Dual-DJKP
Jerseys Triple-TJKTP
Marquee Attractions-MA26
Marquee Attractions Signatures-SMA26
Premium Patches-PPAP
Premium Swatches-PSAP
Ultimate Debut Threads Jerseys-DTJAP
Ultimate Debut Threads Jerseys Autos-DAJAP
Ultimate Debut Threads Patches-DTPAP
Ultimate Debut Threads Patches Autos-DAPAP
Ultimate Patches Dual-DPKP
Ultimate Patches Triple-TPKTP
Ultimate Signatures-USAP
Ultimate Signatures Logos-SLAP
Ultimate Signatures Pairings-UPKP
Ultimate Signatures Trios-UTRRP
05Ultra-259
Gold-259
Fresh Ink-FI-AP
Fresh Ink Blue-FI-AP
Ice-259
Rookie Uniformity Jerseys-RU-AP
Rookie Uniformity Jersey Autographs-ARU-AP
Rookie Uniformity Patches-RUP-AP
Rookie Uniformity Patch Autographs-ARP-AP
05Upper Deck-226
HG Glossy-226
Majestic Materials-MMAP
Rookie Ink-RIAP
05Upper Deck Rookie Showcase-RS16
05Upper Deck Rookie Showcase Promos-RS16
05Upper Deck Rookie Threads-RTAP
05Upper Deck Rookie Threads Autographs-ARTAP
05Upper Deck Stars in the Making-SM7
05Upper Deck Ice-114
Cool Threads-CTAP
Cool Threads Autographs-ACTAP
Cool Threads Glass-CTAP
Cool Threads Patches-CTPAP
Cool Threads Patch Autographs-CAPAP
Glacial Graphs-GGAP
Premieres Auto Patches-AIPAP
05Upper Deck MVP-401
Gold-401
Platinum-401
Rookie Breakthrough-RB6
05Upper Deck Rookie Update-268
05Upper Deck Trilogy-194
05Upper Deck Toronto Fall Expo-226
05Upper Deck Victory-261
Black-261
Gold-261
Silver-261
05ITG Heroes and Prospects-258
Autographs Series II-APR
Complete Jerseys-CJ-30
Complete Jerseys Gold-CJ-30
Jerseys-GUJ-95
Jerseys Gold-GUJ-95
Nameplates-N-66
Nameplates Gold-N-66
06Be A Player Portraits First Exposures-FEAP
06Canadiens Postcards-16
06Gatorade-40
06O-Pee-Chee-260
Rainbow-260
06Upper Deck-105
Exclusives Parallel-105
High Gloss Parallel-105
Game Jerseys-J2AP
Game Patches-P2AP
Masterpieces-105
Signatures-SAP
06Upper Deck MVP-161
Gold Script-161
Super Script-161
06Upper Deck Victory Next In Line-NL30

Perhomaa, Pentti
70Finnish Jaakiekko-376
80Finnish Mallasjuoma-95

Perhonma, Matti
71Finnish Suomi Stickers-309

Periard, Dominic
99Baie-Comeau Drakkar-19
00Baie-Comeau Drakkar-4
Signed-4
01Austin Ice Bats-11
02Lexington Men O'War-13
03Fresno Falcons-12

Periard, Michel
99Rimouski Oceanic-23
Signed-23
99Bowman CHL-70
Gold-70
OPC International-70
00QMJHL All-Star Program Inserts-9
00Rockford IceHogs-13
01Macon Whoopee-16
03San Antonio Rampage-19
04Portland Pirates-9
05German DEL-274
06German DEL-165

Perillat, Duane
00Prince George Cougars-24

Perkins, Darren
90Prince Albert Raiders-17
907th Inn. Sketch WHL-279
91Prince Albert Raiders-17
917th Inn. Sketch WHL-244
92Anaheim Bullfrogs RHI-14
93Anaheim Bullfrogs RHI-16
93Hampton Roads Admirals-14
93Toledo Storm-12
94Anaheim Bullfrogs RHI-15
94Thunder Bay Senators-2
94Toledo Storm-18
95Anaheim Bullfrogs RHI-5
95Thunder Bay Senators-16
96Anaheim Bullfrogs RHI-20

Perkins, Ian
99Tallahassee Tiger Sharks-12

Perkins, Ross
74O-Pee-Chee WHA-39

Perkins, Terry
86Fredericton Express-20
88Salt Lake Golden Eagles-3

Perkkio, Markku
78Finnish SM-Liiga-150

Perkovic, Steven
93Hampton Roads Admirals-15

Perkovich, Nathan
04Chicago Steel-1

Perlini, Fred
94UK Guildford Flames-4
95UK Guildford Flames-6
95UK Guildford Flames-28
96UK Guildford Flames-29

Perlstrom, Stefan
83Swedish Semic Elitserien-83
84Swedish Semic Elitserien-77
85Swedish Panini Stickers-74
86Swedish Panini Stickers-62

Perna, Dominic
97Bowman CHL-49
OPC-49
98Bowman CHL-83
98Bowman CHL-163
Golden Anniversary-83
Golden Anniversary-163
OPC International-83
OPC International-163
98Bowman Chrome CHL-83
98Bowman Chrome CHL-163
Golden Anniversary-83
Golden Anniversary-163
Golden Anniversary Refractors-83
Golden Anniversary Refractors-163
OPC International-83
OPC International-163
OPC International Refractors-83
OPC International Refractors-163
Refractors-83
Refractors-163

Perna, Mike
93Niagara Falls Thunder-24
95Slapshot-202
98Huntington Blizzard-2
99ECHL All-Star Northern Conference-18
99Huntington Blizzard-2
02UK Manchester Storm-5
03Fort Wayne Komets-16

Pernula, Nick
02Topeka Scarecrows-7

Peroff, Ken
06Brampton Battalion-4

Peron, Mike
98Roanoke Express-11
00Roanoke Express-2
01Roanoke Express-16
02Roanoke Express-22
02Roanoke Express RBI Sports-202
03UK Sheffield Steelers-19
03UK Sheffield Steelers Stickers-3
04UK Sheffield Steelers-10
05UK Sheffield Steelers-2
Gold-2
Silver-2

Peronmaa, Petri
96Finnish SISU Redline-111

Peroutka, Joseph
94German First League-90

Perozhkov, Dmitri
00Russian Hockey League-62

Perpich, John
90Capitals Kodak-19

Perras, J.F.
01Ottawa 67's-1

Perras, Jean-Sebastien
90Montreal-Bourassa AAA-18

Perrault, Jocelyn
88ProCards AHL-121

Perrault, Joel
00Baie-Comeau Drakkar-2
Signed-2
01Baie-Comeau Drakkar-1
02Baie Comeau Drakkar-2
03Cincinnati Mighty Ducks-B11
04Cincinnati Mighty Ducks-10
05Portland Pirates-13
06Black Diamond-149A
Black-149A
Gold-149A
Ruby-149A
06Fleer-220
Tiffany-220
06Hot Prospects-201
06O-Pee-Chee-506
Rainbow-506
06SPx-204
Spectrum-204
06The Cup-99
Autographed Rookie Masterpiece Pressplates-99
Gold Rainbow Autographed Rookies-99
Masterpiece Pressplates (Artifacts)-206
Masterpiece Pressplates (Black Diamond)-149
Masterpiece Pressplates (Marquee Rookies)-506
Masterpiece Pressplates (MVP)-340
Masterpiece Pressplates (Power Play)-122
Masterpiece Pressplates (Trilogy)-143
Masterpiece Pressplates (Victory)-225
Rookies Black-99
Rookies Platinum-99
06UD Artifacts-206
Blue-206
Gold-206
Platinum-206
Radiance-206
Red-206
06UD Powerplay-122
Impact Rainbow-122
06Ultra-222
Gold Medallion-222
Ice Medallion-222
06Upper Deck-235
Exclusives Parallel-235
High Gloss Parallel-235
Masterpieces-235
Rookie Game Dated Moments-RGD20
06Upper Deck MVP-340
Gold Script-340
Super Script-340
06Upper Deck Ovation-88
06Upper Deck Trilogy-143
06Upper Deck Victory-225
06Upper Deck Victory Black-225
06Upper Deck Victory Gold-225

Perrault, Kelly
99ECHL All-Star Southern Conference-13
00Quad-City Mallards-15
02Fort Wayne Komets-14
02Fort Wayne Komets Shoe Carnival-1
03Fort Wayne Komets-17
03Fort Wayne Komets 2003 Champions-2
03Fort Wayne Komets 2003 Champions-12
03Fort Wayne Komets 2003 Champions-18
03Fort Wayne Komets Shoe Carnival-1

Perrault, Kirby
90Michigan Tech Huskies-20
91Michigan Tech Huskies-19
93Michigan Tech Huskies-9

Perreault, Albert
37V356 Worldwide Gum-115

Perreault, Bob
44Beehive Group II Photos-56A
44Beehive Group II Photos-56B
62Topps-2
64Beehive Group III Photos-23

Perreault, Fernand
51Cleveland Barons-14
51Laval Dairy QSHL-98
51Laval Dairy Subset-38

Perreault, Gerry
51Laval Dairy Lac St. Jean-7
83NHL Key Tags-12
84Kellogg's Accordion Discs-3B

Perreault, Gilbert
70Colgate Stamps-28
70Dad's Cookies-99
70Esso Power Players-81
70O-Pee-Chee-131
70Sargent Promotions Stamps-23
70Topps-131
71Bazooka-6
71O-Pee-Chee-60
71O-Pee-Chee-246
O-Pee-Chee/Topps Booklets-8
Posters-14
71Sabres Postcards-80
71Sargent Promotions Stamps-19
71Topps-60
71Toronto Sun-36
72O-Pee-Chee-136
Team Canada-22
72Sabres Pepsi Pinback Buttons-5
72Sabres Pepsi Pinback Buttons-6
72Sabres Pepsi Pinback Buttons-7
72Sabres Postcards-13
72Sargent Promotions Stamps-31
72Topps-120
73O-Pee-Chee-70
73Sabres Bells-4
73Sabres Postcards-10
73Topps-70
74Lipton Soup-2
74NHL Action Stamps-50
74O-Pee-Chee NHL-25
74Sabres Postcards-17
74Topps-25
75O-Pee-Chee NHL-10
75Sabres Linnett-9
75Topps-10
76O-Pee-Chee NHL-2
76O-Pee-Chee NHL-3
76O-Pee-Chee NHL-180
76O-Pee-Chee NHL-214
76O-Pee-Chee NHL-380
76Sabres Glasses-3
76Topps-2
76Topps-3
76Topps-180
76Topps-214
76Topps Glossy Inserts-9
77O-Pee-Chee NHL-7
77O-Pee-Chee NHL-210
77Topps-7
77Topps-210
77Topps/O-Pee-Chee Glossy-14
Square-14
78O-Pee-Chee-130
78Topps-130
79O-Pee-Chee-180
79Sabres Milk Panels-4
79Topps-180
80O-Pee-Chee-80
80O-Pee-Chee Super-2
80Sabres Milk Panels-4
80Topps-80
81O-Pee-Chee-30
81O-Pee-Chee Stickers-60
81Post Standups-2
81Sabres Milk Panels-4
82O-Pee-Chee-25
82O-Pee-Chee-30
82O-Pee-Chee Stickers-118
82Post Cereal-2
83Sabres Milk Panels-7
82Topps Stickers-118
83O-Pee-Chee-67
83O-Pee-Chee Stickers-4
83O-Pee-Chee Stickers-240
83O-Pee-Chee Stickers-241
83Puffy Stickers-8
83Topps Stickers-4
83Topps Stickers-240
83Topps Stickers-241
84Kellogg's Accordion Discs-3A
84O-Pee-Chee-24
84O-Pee-Chee Stickers-201
84O-Pee-Chee Stickers-202
84Sabres Blue Shield-12
847-Eleven Discs-4
84Topps-19
85O-Pee-Chee-160
85O-Pee-Chee Box Bottoms-K
85O-Pee-Chee Stickers-188
85Sabres Blue Shield-19
85Sabres Blue Shield Small-19
857-Eleven Credit Cards-2
85Topps-160
85Topps Box Bottoms-K
86O-Pee-Chee-79
86O-Pee-Chee Stickers-43
86Sabres Blue Shield-22
86Sabres Blue Shield Small-22
86Topps-79
88Esso All-Stars-35
90Score-355
Canadian-355
91Future Trends Canada '72-51
91Future Trends Canada '72 French-51
91Kraft-80
91Pro Set-596
French-596
92Future Trends '76 Canada Cup-162
93Sabres Noco-14
95Zeller's Masters of Hockey Signed-5
99Upper Deck 500 Goal Club-500GP
99Upper Deck 500 Goal Club-500GP
99Upper Deck Century Legends-50
Century Collection-50
00UD Heroes-121
Game-Used Twigs-T-GP
Game-Used Twigs Gold-C-HP
Signs of Greatness-GP
00Upper Deck Legends-14
00Upper Deck Legends-18
Legendary Collection Bronze-14
Legendary Collection Bronze-18
Legendary Collection Gold-14
Legendary Collection Gold-18
Legendary Collection Silver-14
Legendary Collection Silver-18
Enshrined Stars-ES11
Epic Signatures-GP
01BAP Memorabilia 500 Goal Scorers-GS22
01BAP Signature Series 500 Goal Scorers-21
01BAP Sig Series 500 Goal Scorers Autos-21
01BAP Signature Series Vintage Autographs-VA-36
01BAP Ultimate Mem All-Star History-24
01BAP Ultimate Memorabilia Autographs-22
01BAP Ultimate Mem Autographs Gold-22
01BAP Ultimate Memorabilia Calder Trophy-21
01BAP Ultimate Memorabilia Captain's C-10
01BAP Ultimate Mem 500 Goal Scorers-17
01BAP Ultimate Mem 500 Goal Scorers Autos-7
01BAP Ultimate Mem 500 Goal Jerseys/Stick-17
01BAP Ultimate Mem 500 Goal Emblems-17
01BAP Ultimate Mem Retired Numbers-18
01Fleer Legacy-14
Ultimate-14
Memorabilia-20
01Greats of the Game-9
Autographs-9
01Parkhurst Autographs-PA20
01Parkhurst 500 Goal Scorers-PGS22
01Parkhurst Heroes-H14
01SP Game Used Tools of the Game-TGP
01SP Game Used Tools of the Game Signed-STGP
01Upper Deck Legends-7
Epic Signatures-GP
Jerseys-TTGP
Jerseys Platinum-TTGP
Milestones-MGP
Milestones Platinum-MGP
01Upper Deck Vintage Jerseys-SDGP
02BAP NHL All-Star History-24
02BAP Ultimate Memorabilia Numerology-16
02BAP Ultimate Mem Vintage Jerseys-16
02Parkhurst Vintage Memorabilia-VM2
02UD Foundations Signs of Greatness-SGGP
02UD Piece of History Heroes Jerseys-HHGP
02UD Piece of History Mark of Distinction-GP
03BAP Ultimate Mem Jersey and Stick-27
03BAP Ultimate Mem Jersey and Stick Gold-27
03BAP Ultimate Mem Vintage Jerseys-31
03BAP Ultimate Mem Vintage Jerseys Gold-31
03Parkhurst Rookie High Expectations-HE-6
03Parkhurst Rookie High Expectations Gold-HE-6
03Parkhurst Rookie Jerseys-GJ-45
03Parkhurst Rookie Jerseys Gold-GJ-45
03Parkhurst Rookie ROYalty-VR-13
03Parkhurst Rookie ROYalty Gold-VR-13
04ITG NHL AS FANtasy AS History Jerseys-SB24
04ITG Franchises He Shoots/Scores Prizes-47
04ITG Franchises US East-341
Autographs-A-GP
Complete Jerseys-ECJ4
Complete Jerseys Gold-ECJ4
Double Memorabilia-EDM13
Double Memorabilia Autographs-EDM-GP
Double Memorabilia Gold-EDM13
Forever Rivals-EFR3
Forever Rivals Gold-EFR3
Memorabilia-ESM9
Memorabilia Autographs-ESM-GP
Memorabilia Gold-ESM9
04ITG Ultimate Memorabilia-112
Gold-112
Auto Threads-25
Autographs-33
Autographs Gold-33
Calder Trophy-4
Country of Origin-2
Country of Origin Gold-2
Day In History-12
Day In History Gold-12
Jersey Autographs-17
Jersey Autographs Gold-17
Stick Autographs-27
Stick Autographs Gold-27
04SP Authentic Buybacks-59
04SP Authentic Sign of the Times-ST-GI
04SP Authentic Sign of the Times-DS-PR
04SP Authentic Sign of the Times-QS-BDPB
04SP Authentic Sign of the Times-FS-CTR
04UD Legendary Signatures-37
Autographs-GP
HOF Inks-HOF-GP
Linemates-RMGPRR
Summit Stars-CDN9
Summit Stars Autographs-CDN-GP
04UD Legends Classics-24
04UD Legends Classics-73
04UD Legends Classics-85
Gold-24
Gold-73
Gold-85
Platinum-24
Platinum-73
Platinum-85
Silver-24
Silver-73
Silver-85
Signature Moments-M31
Signature Moments-M61
Signatures-CS31
Signatures-DC7
Signatures-DC18
Signatures-TC10
Signatures-QC4
04ITG Heroes and Prospects-125
Aspiring-13
Autographs-GP
Hero Memorabilia-15
04ITG Heroes/Prospects Toronto Expo '05-125
04ITG Heroes/Prospects Expo Heroes/Pros-125
05ITG Heroes/Prosp Toronto Expo Parallel -187
05Beehive-232
Signature Scrapbook-SSGP
05ITG Ultimate Memorabilia Level 1-42
05ITG Ultimate Memorabilia Level 2-42
05ITG Ultimate Memorabilia Level 3-42
05ITG Ultimate Memorabilia Level 4-42
05ITG Ultimate Memorabilia Level 5-42
05ITG Ultimate Mem Double Mem Autos-11
05ITG Ultimate Mem Double Mem Autos Gold-13
05ITG Ultimate Mem First Overall Jerseys-1
05ITG Ultimate Mem 1st Overall Jsy Gold-1
05ITG Ultimate Mem First Rounders Jerseys-1
05ITG Ultimate Mem 1st Round Jersey Gold-1
05ITG Ultimate Memorabilia Jersey Autos-22
05ITG Ultimate Mem Jersey Autos Gold-22
05ITG Ultimate Memorabilia Jerseys-15
05ITG Ultimate Memorabilia Jerseys Gold-15
05ITG Ultimate Mem Pass the Torch Jerseys-20
05ITG Ultimate Mem Passing Torch Jsy Gold-20
05ITG Ultimate Mem R.O.Y. Autos-16
05ITG Ultimate Mem R.O.Y. Autos Gold-16
05ITG Ultimate Memorabilia R.O.Y. Emblems-3
05ITG Ultimate Mem R.O.Y. Emblems Gold-3
05ITG Ultimate Memorabilia R.O.Y. Jerseys-3
05ITG Ultimate Mem R.O.Y. Jerseys Gold-3
05ITG Ultimate Memorabilia R.O.Y. Numbers-3
05ITG Ultimate Mem R.O.Y. Numbers Gold-3
05ITG Ultimate Mem Raised to the Rafters-8
05ITG Ultimate Mem Raised Rafters Gold-8
05ITG Ultimate Memorabilia Stick Autos-22
05ITG Ultimate Mem Stick Autos Gold-22
05ITG Ultimate Mem 3 Star of the Game Jsy-15
05ITG Ult Mem 3 Star of the Game Jsy Gold-15
05ITG Ultimate Mem Triple Threads Jerseys-10
05ITG Ultimate Mem Triple Thread Jsy Gold-10
05ITG Ultimate Memorabilia Ultimate Autos-13
05ITG Ultimate Mem Ultimate Autos Gold-13
05SP Authentic Prestigious Pairings-PPPV
05SP Game Used Authentic Fabrics Dual-SP
05SP Game Used Authentic Patches Dual-SP
05SP Game Used Oldtimer's Challenge-OC-GP
05SP Game Used Oldtimer's Challenge Autos-OCA-GP
05SP Game Used Oldtimer's Challenge Patch-OCP-GP
05SP Game Used Oldtime Chall Patch Autoa-OAP-GP
05SPx-102
Spectrum-102
Xcitement Legends-XL-GP
Xcitement Legends Gold-XL-GP
Xcitement Legends Spectrum-XL-GP
05The Cup-14
Gold-14
Black Rainbow-14
Hardware Heroes-HHGP1
Hardware Heroes-HHGP2
Honorable Numbers-HNGP
Limited Logos-LLGP
Masterpiece Pressplates-14
Noble Numbers-NNPK
Patch Variation-P14
Scripted Swatches-SSGP
Signature Patches-SPGP
05UD Artifacts-143
Blue-143
Gold-143
Green-143
Pewter-143
Red-143
Gold Autographed-143
05Ultimate Coll Ultimate Achievements-UAGP
05Ultimate Collection Ultimate Signatures-USGP
05Ultimate Coll Ultimate Sigs Pairings-UPPV
05Upper Deck All-Time Greatest-8
05Upper Deck All-Time Greatest-64
05Upper Deck Trilogy-157
Crystal-157
Ice Scripts-IS-GP
Legendary Scripts-LEG-GP
Personal Scripts-PER-GP
05ITG Heroes and Prospects-187
Autographs Series II-GP
National Pride-NPR-28
06ITG International Ice-90
06ITG International Ice-103
06ITG International Ice-132
Gold-90
Gold-103
Gold-132
Autographs-AGP
Autographs-AGP2
Autographs-AGP3
Emblem Autographs-GUE20
Emblem Autographs Gold-GUE20
Emblems-GUE20
Emblems Gold-GUE20
Jersey Autographs-GUJ20
Jersey Autographs Gold-GUJ20
Jerseys-GUJ20
Jerseys Gold-GUJ20
My Country My Team-MC8
My Country My Team Gold-MC8
Numbers-GUN20
Numbers Autographs-GUN20
Numbers Autographs Gold-GUN20
Numbers Gold-GUN20
Stick and Jersey-SJ21
Stick and Jersey Gold-SJ21
Teammates-IT04
Teammates Gold-IT04
06ITG Ultimate Memorabilia-56
Artist Proof-56
Autos-29
Autos Gold-29
Blades of Steel-13
Blades of Steel Gold-13
Bowman Factor-9
Bowman Factor Gold-9
Bowman Factor Autos-8
Bowman Factor Autos Gold-8
First Round Picks-24
First Round Picks Gold-24
Jerseys Autos-44
Jerseys Autos Gold-44
Legendary Captains-12
Legendary Captains Gold-12
Sticks and Jerseys-14
Sticks and Jerseys Gold-14
Triple Thread Jerseys-2
Triple Thread Jerseys Gold-2
06Parkhurst-95
06Parkhurst-167
Autographs-95
Autographs-167
Autographs Dual-DAPF
Autographs Dual-DAPG
06SPx-124
Spectrum-124
SPxcitement-X11
SPxcitement Spectrum-X11
SPxcitement Autographs-X11
06The Cup-13
Autographed Foundations-CQGP
Autographed Foundations Patches-CQGP
Autographed Patches-13
Black Rainbow-13
Foundations-CQGP
Foundations Patches-CQGP
Gold-13
Gold Patches-13
Honorable Numbers-HNGP
Jerseys-13
Limited Logos-LLGP
Masterpiece Pressplates-13
Scripted Swatches-SSGP
Signature Patches-SPGP
06UD Artifacts-129
Blue-129
Gold-129
Platinum-129
Radiance-129
Autographed Radiance Parallel-129
Red-129
06Ultimate Collection-9
Autographed Jerseys-AJ-GP
Autographed Patches-AJ-GP
Jerseys-UJ-GP
Jerseys Dual-UJ2-CP
Patches-UJ-GP
Patches Dual-UJ2-CP
Signatures-US-GP
Ultimate Achievements-UA-GP
06Upper Deck All-Time Greatest-ATG4
06Upper Deck All-Time Greatest-ATG26
06Upper Deck Sweet Shot-16
Signature Shots/Saves Sticks-SSSGP
Signature Sticks-STGP
Sweet Stitches-SSGP
Sweet Stitches Duals-SSGP
Sweet Stitches Triples-SSGP

Perreault, Joel
02Baie Comeau Drakkar-2
03Cincinnati Mighty Ducks-B11

Perreault, Mathieu
93Quebec Pee-Wee Tournament-51

Perreault, Maxime
93Quebec Pee-Wee Tournament-1031

Perreault, Nicolas
92Michigan State Spartans-19
93Michigan State Spartans-16
94Saint John Flames-17
95Toledo Storm-2
98Thetford Mines Coyotes-7

Perreault, Yanic
907th Inn. Sketch QMJHL-100
907th Inn. Sketch QMJHL-146
91ProCards-339
917th Inn. Sketch CHL Award Winners-22
917th Inn. Sketch CHL Award Winners-30
917th Inn. Sketch Memorial Cup-115
91Arena Draft Picks-31
91Arena Draft Picks French-31
91Arena Draft Picks Autographs-31
91Arena Draft Picks Autographs French-31
91Classic-39
91Star Pics-22
91Ultimate Draft-34
91Ultimate Draft-54
91Ultimate Draft-87
91Ultimate Draft French-34
91Classic Four-Sport *-39
Autographs-39A
92Score-487
Canadian-487
92Upper Deck-70
92St. John's Maple Leafs-15
93St. John's Maple Leafs-18
94Parkhurst-230
Gold-230
94Classic Pro Prospects-113
95Be A Player-150
Signatures-S150
Signatures Die Cuts-S150
95Donruss-375
95Leaf-249
95Metal-73
95Parkhurst International-372
Emerald Ice-372
95Summit-166
Artist's Proofs-166
Ice-166
95Topps-223
OPC Inserts-223
95Ultra-253
95Upper Deck-28
Electric Ice-28
Electric Ice Gold-28
Special Edition-SE130
Special Edition Gold-SE130
95Zenith-113
96Collector's Choice-126
96Donruss-21
Press Proofs-21
96Donruss Canadian Ice-76

Gold Press Proofs-76
Red Press Proofs-76
96Donruss Elite-76
Die Cut Stars-76
96Kraft Upper Deck-20
96Leaf-7
Press Proofs-7
96Leaf Preferred-107
Press Proofs-107
96Maggers-75
96Pinnacle-42
Artist's Proofs-42
Foil-42
Premium Stock-42
Rink Collection-42
96Score-25
Artist's Proofs-25
Dealer's Choice Artist's Proofs-25
Special Artist's Proofs-25
Golden Blades-25
96Upper Deck-79
96Zenith-86
Artist's Proofs-86
96Collector's Edge Ice-184
Crucibles-C8
Prism-184
QuantumMotion-3
97Beehive-35
Golden Portraits-35
97Black Diamond-127
Double Diamond-127
Triple Diamond-127
Quadruple Diamond-127
97Crown Royale-64
Emerald Green-64
Ice Blue-64
Silver-64
97Donruss Priority-142
Stamp of Approval-142
97Katch-71
Gold-71
Silver-71
97Pacific Invincible NHL Regime-97
97Pacific Omega-111
Copper-111
Dark Gray-111
Emerald Green-111
Gold-111
Ice Blue-111
97Revolution-65
Copper-65
Emerald-65
Ice Blue-65
Silver-65
97SP Authentic-75
Sign of the Times-YP
97Zenith-64
Z-Gold-64
Z-Silver-64
97Zenith 5 x 7-29
Gold Impulse-29
Silver Impulse-29
98Aurora-87
98Be A Player-62
Press Release-62
98BAP Gold-62
98BAP Autographs-62
98BAP Autographs Gold-62
98BAP Tampa Bay All Star Game-62
98Crown Royale-64
Limited Series-64
98Kings Power Play-LAK4
98NHL Game Day Promotion-LAK4
98Pacific-243
Ice Blue-243
Red-243
98Pacific Dynagon Ice-89
Blue-89
Red-89
98Panini Photocards-62
98Paramount-106
Copper-106
Emerald Green-106
Holo-Electric-106
Ice Blue-106
Silver-106
98UD Choice-96
Prime Choice Reserve-96
Reserve-96
98Upper Deck-105
Exclusives-105
Exclusives 1 of 1-105
Gold Reserve-105
99Aurora-137
Premiere Date-137
99BAP Memorabilia-121
Gold-121
Silver-121
99Kraft Face Off Rivals-4
99Maple Leafs Pizza Pizza-19
99Pacific-414
Copper-414
Emerald Green-414
Gold-414
Ice Blue-414
Premiere Date-414
Red-414
99Panini Stickers-158
99Paramount-228
Copper-228
Emerald-228
Gold-228
Holographic Emerald-228
Holographic Gold-228
Holographic Silver-228
Ice Blue-228
Premiere Date-228
Red-228
Silver-228
99Topps Gold Label Class 1-81
Black-81
Black One of One-81
One of One-81
Red-81
Red One of One-81
99Topps Gold Label Class 2-81
99Topps Gold Label Class 2 Black-81
99Topps Gold Label Class 2 Black 1 of 1-81
99Topps Gold Label Class 2 One of One-81
99Topps Gold Label Class 2 Red-81
99Topps Gold Label Class 2 Red One of One-81
99Topps Gold Label Class 3-81
99Topps Gold Label Class 3 Black-81
99Topps Gold Label Class 3 Black 1 of 1-81
99Topps Gold Label Class 3 One of One-81
99Topps Gold Label Class 3 Red-81
99Topps Gold Label Class 3 Red One of One-81
99Upper Deck Victory-290
00BAP Memorabilia-292
Emerald-292
Ruby-292
Sapphire-292
Promos-292
00BAP Mem Chicago Sportsfest Copper-292
00BAP Memorabilia Chicago Sportsfest Blue-292
00BAP Memorabilia Chicago Sportsfest Gold-292
00BAP Memorabilia Chicago Sportsfest Ruby-292
00BAP Memorabilia Chicago Sun-Times Ruby-292
00BAP Memorabilia Chicago Sun-Times Gold-292
00BAP Mem Chicago Sun-Times Sapphire-292
00BAP Mem Toronto Fall Expo Copper-292
00BAP Memorabilia Toronto Fall Expo Gold-292
00BAP Memorabilia Toronto Fall Expo Ruby-292
00O-Pee-Chee-268B
00O-Pee-Chee Parallel-268B
00Pacific-397
Copper-397
Gold-397
Ice Blue-397
Premiere Date-397
00Panini Stickers-100
00Paramount-232
Copper-232
Gold-232
Holo-Gold-232
Holo-Silver-232
Ice Blue-232
Premiere Date-232
00Private Stock Game Gear-97
00Stadium Club-178
00Titanium Game Gear-46
00Topps/OPC-268B
Parallel-268B
00Upper Deck-164
Exclusives Tier 1-164
Exclusives Tier 2-164
00St. John's Maple Leafs-20
01Atomic-52
Blue-52
Gold-52
Premiere Date-52
Red-52
01BAP Memorabilia-141
Emerald-141
Ruby-141
Sapphire-141
01Bowman YoungStars-101
Gold-101
Ice Cubed-101
01Canadiens Postcards-15
01Crown Royale-77
Blue-77
Premiere Date-77
Red-77
Retail-77
01O-Pee-Chee-224
01O-Pee-Chee Premier Parallel-224
01Pacific-370
Extreme LTD-370
Hobby LTD-370
Premiere Date-370
Retail LTD-370
01Pacific Adrenaline-97
Blue-97
Premiere Date-97
Red-97
Retail-97
01Pacific Arena Exclusives-370
01Parkhurst-234
01Private Stock-49
Gold-49
Premiere Date-49
Retail-49
Silver-49
01Private Stock Pacific Nights-49
01Titanium-73
Hobby Parallel-73
Premiere Date-73
Retail-73
Retail Parallel-73
01Topps-224
OPC Parallel-224
01UD Mask Collection-48
Gold-48
01UD Playmakers-52
01Upper Deck-321
Exclusives-321
01Vanguard-50
Blue-50
Red-50
One of Ones-50
Premiere Date-50
Proofs-50
02Atomic-56
Blue-56
Gold-56
Red-56
Hobby Parallel-56
02BAP First Edition-276
02BAP First Edition-386
02BAP Memorabilia-176
Emerald-176
Ruby-176
Sapphire-176
NHL All-Star Game-176
NHL All-Star Game Blue-176
NHL All-Star Game Green-176
NHL All-Star Game Red-176
02BAP Memorabilia Toronto Fall Expo-176
02BAP Signature Series-42
Autographs-42
Autograph Buybacks 1998-62
Autographs Gold-42
02Canadiens Postcards-26
02McDonald's Pacific Jersey Patch Silver-7
02McDonald's Pacific Jersey Patches Gold-7
02NHL Power Play Stickers-63
02O-Pee-Chee-133
02O-Pee-Chee Premier Blue Parallel-133
02O-Pee-Chee Premier Red Parallel-133
02O-Pee-Chee Factory Set-133
02O-Pee-Chee Factory Set Hometown Heroes-HHC17
02Pacific-200
Blue-200
Red-200
Jerseys-26
Jerseys Holo-Silver-26
02Pacific Complete-414
Red-414
02Pacific Exclusive-92
02Pacific Heads-Up-65
Blue-65
Purple-65
Red-65
Quad Jerseys-15
Quad Jerseys Gold-15
02Pacific Quest for the Cup-51
Gold-51
02Parkhurst-176
Bronze-176
Gold-176
Silver-176
02Parkhurst Retro-89
Minis-89
02Private Stock Reserve-54
Blue-54
Red-54
Retail-54
02SP Authentic-49
Beckett Promos-49
02Titanium-56
Blue-56
Red-56
Retail-56
Jerseys-35
Jerseys Retail-35
Patches-35
02Topps-133
OPC Blue Parallel-133
OPC Red Parallel-133
Topps/OPC Hometown Heroes-HHC17
Factory Set-133
02Topps Total-146
02Upper Deck-339
Exclusives-339
02Upper Deck Beckett UD Promos-339
02Upper Deck Classic Portraits-52
02Upper Deck MVP-94
Gold-94
Classics-94
Golden Classics-94
02Upper Deck Victory-112
Bronze-112
Gold-112
Silver-112
02Upper Deck Vintage-131
02Upper Deck Vintage-276
02Vanguard-56
LTD-56
Jerseys-23
Jerseys Gold-23
03Canadiens Postcards-20
03ITG Action-374
Jerseys-M62
03NHL Sticker Collection-57
03O-Pee-Chee-121
03OPC Blue-121
03OPC Gold-121
03OPC Red-121
03Pacific-180
Blue-180
Red-180
03Pacific Complete-273
Red-273
03Pacific Exhibit-78
Blue Backs-78
Yellow Backs-78
03Pacific Montreal International-3
03Pacific Prism-57
Blue-57
Gold-57
Red-57
03Parkhurst Original Six Montreal-23
Memorabilia-MM8
03Private Stock Reserve-54
Blue-54
Red-54
Retail-54
03Topps-121
Blue-121
Gold-121
Red-121
03Topps C55-75
Minis-75
Minis American Back-75
Minis American Back Red-75
Minis Bazooka Back-75
Minis Brooklyn Back-75
Minis Hat Trick Back-75
Minis O Canada Back-75
Minis O Canada Back Red-75
Minis Stanley Cup Back-75
03Upper Deck-348
Canadian Exclusives-348
HG-348
UD Exclusives-348
03Upper Deck MVP-223
Gold Script-223
Silver Script-223
Canadian Exclusives-223
04Pacific-139
Blue-139
Red-139
05Parkhurst-271
Facsimile Auto Parallel-271
05Upper Deck-356
05Upper Deck Victory-108
Black-108
Gold-108
Silver-108
06Be A Player-66
Autographs-66
Signatures-YP
Signatures 10-71
Signatures Trios-TRPP
07Upper Deck Ovation-56

Perrett, Craig
91Air Canada SJHL-C34
98Abilene Aviators-10

Perricone, Eric
99Odessa Jackalopes-8
01Flint Generals-13

Perricone, Joey
04Moose Jaw Warriors-22
05Moose Jaw Warriors-16
06Moose Jaw Warriors-22

Perrier, Bryant
89ProCards IHL-100

Perrin, Eric
97Cleveland Lumberjacks-23
97Cleveland Lumberjacks-28
97Cleveland Lumberjacks Postcards-9
98Kansas City Blades-7
99Kansas City Blades Supercuts-13
00Finnish Cardset-347
01Finnish Cardset-154
02Finnish Cardset-245
03BAP Memorabilia-241
03ITG VIP Rookie Debut-149
03Lightning Team Issue-14
03Parkhurst Rookie-78
03Upper Deck Rookie Update-190
03Finnish Cardset D-Day-DD7
03Hershey Bears-9
03Hershey Bears Patriot News-17
03Pacific AHL Prospects-39
Gold-39
04AHL All-Stars-33
04Hershey Bears Patriot News-21
06Lightning Postcards-13

Perrin, Jesse
06Okotoks Oilers-15

Perron, Jean
84Canadiens Postcards-23
85Canadiens Postcards-26
85Canadiens Provigo-15
86Canadiens Postcards-17
87Canadiens Postcards-22
87Canadiens Vachon Stickers-7
87Canadiens Vachon Stickers-10
88Nordiques Team Issue-41
98Swiss Power Play Stickers-323

Perron, Jonathan
93Quebec Pee-Wee Tournament-62

Perron, Pierre
98Thetford Mines Coyotes-13
01Thetford Mines Coyotes-9

Perrott, Nathan
95Slapshot-236
95Classic-39
96Sault Ste. Marie Greyhounds-16
96Sault Ste. Marie Greyhounds Autographed-16
98Indianapolis Ice-5
99Cleveland Lumberjacks-17
01BAP Memorabilia-442
Emerald-442
Ruby-442
Sapphire-442
01Parkhurst-324
01Titanium Draft Day Edition-144
01UD Premier Collection-68
01Milwaukee Admirals-21
03Parkhurst Original Six Toronto-7

Perry, Adam
05London Knights-9
06London Knights-23
06ITG Heroes and Prospects Complete CHL Logos-CHL15
06ITG Heroes and Prospects Jerseys-GUJ46
06ITG Heroes and Prospects Jerseys Gold-GUJ46
06ITG Heroes and Prospects Emblems-GUE46
06ITG Heroes and Prospects Emblems Gold-GUE46
06ITG Heroes and Prospects Numbers-GUN46
06ITG Heroes and Prospects Numbers Gold-GUN46

Perry, Alan
88ProCards IHL-3
92Oklahoma City Blazers-14
93Oklahoma City Blazers-12
94Central Hockey League-67
94Oklahoma City Blazers-13

Perry, Brian
69O-Pee-Chee-84

Perry, Corey
01London Knights-22
02London Knights-4
03BAP Memorabilia Draft Redemptions-28
03London Knights-2
03London Knights-27
04SP Authentic Rookie Redemptions-RR1
04London Knights-9
04ITG Heroes and Prospects-65
Aspiring-14
Autographs-CPE
Combos-8
Complete Emblems-3
Emblems-3
Emblems Gold-3
He Shoots-He Scores Prizes-10
Jersey Autographs-3
Jerseys-3
Jerseys Gold-3
Numbers-3
Numbers Gold-3
04ITG Heroes/Prospects Toronto Expo '05-65
04ITG Heroes/Prospects Expo Heroes/Pros-65
05ITG Heroes/Prosp Toronto Expo Parallel -154
05ITG Heroes/Prosp Toronto Expo Parallel -332
05ITG Heroes/Prosp Toronto Expo Parallel -377
05Beehive-104
Beige -104
Blue -104
Gold-104
Red -104
Rookie Jumbos-R5
Matte-104
PhotoGraphs-PGCO
Signature Scrapbook-SSCP
05Black Diamond-196
Emerald-196
Gold-196
Onyx-196
Ruby-196
05Ducks Team Issue-17
05Hot Prospects-217
En Fuego-217
Hot Materials-HMCP
Red Hot-217
White Hot-217
05ITG Ultimate Memorabilia Level 1-19
05ITG Ultimate Memorabilia Level 2-19
05ITG Ultimate Memorabilia Level 3-19
05ITG Ultimate Memorabilia Level 4-19
05ITG Ultimate Memorabilia Level 5-19
05ITG Ultimate Mem First Rounders Jerseys-10
05ITG Ultimate Mem 1st Round Jersey Gold-10
05ITG Ultimate Mem Future Stars Jerseys-14
05ITG Ultimate Mem Fut Stars Jerseys Gold-14
05ITG Ultimate Memorabilia Sextuple Autos-2
05Panini Stickers-5
05Parkhurst-602
Facsimile Auto Parallel-602
True Colors-TCANA
True Colors-TCANA
05SP Authentic-132
Limited-132
Exquisite Endorsements-EECP
Octographs-OR
Prestigious Pairings-PPPG
Rarefied Rookies-RRCP
Rookie Authentics-RACP
Sign of the Times Duals-DLP
Sign of the Times Triples-TLPG
Sign of the Times Quads-QSOPC
Six Star Signatures-SSRO
05SP Game Used-134
Autographs-134
Gold-134
Auto Draft-AD-CP
Game Gear-GG-PE
Game Gear Autographs-AG-PE
Rookie Exclusives-CP
Rookie Exclusives Silver-RE-CP
Significant Numbers-SN-CO
05SPx-171
Spectrum-171
Xcitement Rookies-XR-CP
Xcitement Rookies Gold-XR-CP
Xcitement Rookies Spectrum-XR-CP
05The Cup-173
Autographed Rookie Patches Gold Rainbow-173
Black Rainbow Rookies-173
Dual NHL Shields-DSJC
Masterpiece Pressplates (Artifacts)-201
Masterpiece Pressplates (Bee Hive)-104
Masterpiece Pressplates (Black Diamond)-196
Masterpiece Pressplates (Ice)-105
Masterpiece Pressplates (MVP)-415
Masterpiece Pressplates (Power Play)-153
Masterpiece Pressplates (Power Play)-153
Masterpiece Pressplates Rookie Upd Auto-257
Masterpiece Pressplates SPA Autos-132
Masterpiece Pressplates (SP Game Used)-134
Masterpiece Pressplates SPx Autos-171
Masterpiece Pressplates (Trilogy)-171
Masterpiece Pressplates Ult Coll Autos-94
Masterpiece Pressplates (Victory)-281
Masterpiece Pressplates Autographs-173
Noble Numbers-NNNP
Platinum Rookies-173
Scripted Numbers-SNNP
Signature Patches-SPPE
05UD Artifacts-201
Gold-RED1
05UD PowerPlay-153
05UD Rookie Class-32
05Ultimate Collection-94
Autographed Patches-94
Autographed Shields-94
Jerseys-JCO
Jerseys Dual-DJPG
Jerseys Triple-TJPGL
Marquee Attractions-MA1
Marquee Attractions Signatures-SMA1
Premium Patches-PPPE
Premium Swatches-PSPE
Ultimate Debut Threads Jerseys-DTJCP
Ultimate Debut Threads Jerseys Autos-DAJCP
Ultimate Debut Threads Patches-DTPCP
Ultimate Debut Threads Patches Autos-DAPCP
Ultimate Patches-PCO
Ultimate Patches Dual-DPPG
Ultimate Patches Triple-TPPGL
Ultimate Signatures-USPY
Ultimate Signatures Foursomes-UFSOBP
Ultimate Signatures Logos-SLPE
Ultimate Signatures Pairings-UPPG
05Ultra-253
Gold-253
Fresh Ink-FI-CP
Fresh Ink Blue-FI-CP
Ice-253
Rookie Uniformity Jerseys-RU-CP
Rookie Uniformity Jersey Autographs-ARU-CP
Rookie Uniformity Patches-RUP-CP
Rookie Uniformity Patch Autographs-ARP-CP
Scoring Kings-SK29
Scoring Kings Jerseys-SKJ-CP
Scoring Kings Jersey Autographs-KAJ-CP
Scoring Kings Patches-SKP-CP
Scoring Kings Patch Autographs-KAP-CP
05Upper Deck-204
HG Glossy-204
Rookie Ink-RICP
05Upper Deck Rookie Showcase-RS1
05Upper Deck Rookie Showcase Promos-RS1
05Upper Deck Rookie Threads-RTCP
05Upper Deck Rookie Threads Autographs-ARTCP
05Upper Deck Stars in the Making-SM4
05Upper Deck Ice-105
Cool Threads-CTCP
Cool Threads Autographs-ACTCP
Cool Threads Glass-CTCP
Cool Threads Patches-CTPCP
Cool Threads Patch Autographs-CAPCP
Glacial Graphs-GGCP
Premieres Auto Patches-AIPCP
05Upper Deck MVP-415
Gold-415
Platinum-415
Rookie Breakthrough-RB9
05Upper Deck Rookie Update-257
05Upper Deck Trilogy-171
05Upper Deck Toronto Fall Expo-204
05Upper Deck Victory-281
Black-281
Gold-281
Silver-281
05Extreme Top Prospects Signature Edition-S7
05Portland Pirates-7
05ITG Heroes and Prospects-154
05ITG Heroes and Prospects-332
05ITG Heroes and Prospects-377
Autographs-A-CPE
Autographs Series II-CP2
Autographs Series II-CP3
CHL Grads-CG-11
CHL Grads Gold-CG-11
Complete Jerseys-CJ-15
Complete Jerseys Gold-CJ-15
Future Teammates-FT3
He Shoots-He Scores Prizes-16
Jerseys-GUJ-79
Jerseys Gold-GUJ-79
Emblems-GUE-79
Emblems Gold-GUE-79
Numbers-GUN-79
Numbers Gold-GUN-79
Memorial Cup-MC-4
Nameplates-N-59
Nameplates Gold-N-59
National Pride-NPR-37
Spectrum-STM-04
Spectrum Gold-STM-04
06Be A Player Portraits First Exposures-FECP
06Beehive Matted Materials-MMCP
06Beehive Remarkable Matted Materials-MMCP
06Black Diamond-1
Black-1
Gold-1
Ruby-1
Jerseys-JCP
Jerseys Black-JCP
Jerseys Gold-JCP
Jerseys Ruby-JCP
06Flair Showcase-3
06Flair Showcase-103
Parallel-3
Parallel-103
Wave of the Future-WF21
06Fleer-8
Tiffany-8
06Hot Prospects Hot Materials -HMCP
06Hot Prospects Hot Materials Red Hot-HMCP
06Hot Prospects Hot Materials White Hot-HMCP
06ITG International Ice Triple Memorabilia-TM04
06ITG International Ice Triple Memorabilia Gold-TM04
06McDonald's Upper Deck Rookie Review-RR7
06O-Pee-Chee-8
06O-Pee-Chee-643
Rainbow-8
Rainbow-643
06SP Authentic Chirography-CP
06SP Authentic Sign of the Times-STCP
06SP Game Used Authentic Fabrics Dual-AF2SP
06SP Game Used Authentic Fabrics Dual Patches-AF2SP
06The Cup Autographed NHL Shields Duals-DASAN
06UD Artifacts Auto-Facts-AFCP
06UD Artifacts Auto-Facts Gold-AFCP
06UD Artifacts Tundra Tandems-TTSP
06UD Artifacts Tundra Tandems Black-TTSP
06UD Artifacts Tundra Tandems Blue-TTSP
06UD Artifacts Tundra Tandems Gold-TTSP
06UD Artifacts Tundra Tandems Platinum-TTSP
06UD Artifacts Tundra Tandems Red-TTSP
06UD Artifacts Tundra Tandems Dual Patches Red-TTSP
06UD Powerplay Power Marks-PMCP
06Ultra-4
Gold Medallion-4
Ice Medallion-4
06Upper Deck Arena Giveaways-ANA1
06Upper Deck-1
Exclusives Parallel-1
High Gloss Parallel-1
Game Jerseys-JCP
Game Patches-PCP
Masterpieces-1
Signatures-SCP
06Upper Deck MVP-7
Gold Script-7
Super Script-7
Jerseys-OJPJ
06Upper Deck Ovation-101
06Upper Deck Sweet Shot Signature Shots/Saves-SSCP
06Upper Deck Trilogy Combo Clearcut Autographs-C2PG
06Upper Deck Trilogy Honorary Scripted Patches-HSPCO
06Upper Deck Trilogy Honorary Scripted Swatches-HSSCO
06Upper Deck Victory-6
06Upper Deck Victory Black-6
06Upper Deck Victory Gold-6
06Upper Deck Victory Next In Line-NL1
06ITG Heroes and Prospects CHL Top Prospects-TP05
06ITG Heroes and Prospects CHL Top Prospects Gold-TP05
06ITG Heroes and Prospects Complete Jerseys-CJ11
06ITG Heroes and Prospects Complete Jerseys Gold-CJ11
06ITG Heroes and Prospects Quad Emblems-QE07
06ITG Heroes and Prospects Quad Emblems Gold-QE07
06ITG Heroes and Prospects Triple Memorabilia-TM07
06ITG Heroes and Prospects Triple Memorabilia Gold-TM07
07Upper Deck Ovation-100
07Upper Deck Victory-173
Black-173
Gold-173

Perry, Craig
00Spokane Chiefs-21

Perry, Danny
93Quebec Pee-Wee Tournament-732

Perry, Don
78Saginaw Gears-16

Perry, Jeff
907th Inn. Sketch OHL-292
93Quebec Pee-Wee Tournament-647
94Saint John Flames-18
95Saint John Flames-18
96Saint John Flames-23
97Saint John Flames-19
05London Knights-24

Perry, Randy
93Lethbridge Hurricanes-11
95Lethbridge Hurricanes-18
96Seattle Thunderbirds-23
97Bowman CHL-96
OPC-96
98German DEL-221
99German DEL-207
00UK Sekonda Superleague-74
01Louisiana Ice Gators-20
03Bakersfield Condors-22
04Wheeling Nailers Riesbeck's-16
04Wheeling Nailers SGA-8

Perry, Scott
92Quebec Pee-Wee Tournament-1640
01Missouri River Otters-11

Perry, Sean
96Johnstown Chiefs-13

Perry, Ted
02St. Michaels Majors-2
03St. Michael's Majors-2

Perry, Todd
06London Knights-4

Perry, Tom
91Air Canada SJHL-B10
92Saskatchewan JHL-35
97Quad-City Mallards-16
98Colorado Gold Kings-17
98Colorado Gold Kings Postcards-3
98Las Vegas Coyotes RHI-10
99Colorado Gold Kings Taco Bell-3
99Colorado Gold Kings Wendy's-14
01Colorado Gold Kings-16

Perry, Tyler
95Seattle Thunderbirds-21
96Swift Current Broncos-13
99Austin Ice Bats-22
00Austin Ice Bats-16

Pers, Bengt-Ake
86Swedish Panini Stickers-139
87Swedish Panini Stickers-150

Perschau, Dirk
94German DEL-44
95German DEL-32
96German DEL-26
04German Berlin Eisbaren 50th Anniv-40

Pershin, Eduard
98Cleveland Lumberjacks-17
02Charlotte Checkers-90
03Wheeling Nailers-92

Person, Ryan
96OCN Blizzard-24
97OCN Blizzard-23
98OCN Blizzard-22
05Knoxville Ice Bears-13

Person, Todd
92Raleigh Icecaps-10
92Raleigh Icecaps-35

Persson, Bengt
64Swedish Coralli ISHockey-115
65Swedish Coralli ISHockey-115
67Swedish Hockey-260
69Swedish Hockey-306

Persson, Gunnar
83Swedish Semic Elitserien-56
84Swedish Semic Elitserien-56
85Swedish Panini Stickers-53
86Swedish Panini Stickers-35
87Swedish Panini Stickers-28
01Swedish Brynas Tigers-19

Persson, Hakan
87Swedish Panini Stickers-257
92Swedish Semic Elitserien Stickers-256

Persson, Hans Ake
73Swedish Stickers-169

Persson, Ingemar
64Swedish Coralli ISHockey-120
65Swedish Coralli ISHockey-120

Persson, Jerry
91Swedish Semic Elitserien Stickers-294
92Swedish Semic Elitserien Stickers-311
93Swedish Semic Elitserien-278
94Swedish Leaf-257
95Swedish Leaf-199
98Swedish UD Choice-107

Persson, Joakim
90Swedish Semic Elitserien Stickers-274
91Swedish Semic Elitserien Stickers-55
93Swedish Semic Elitserien-42
94Swedish Leaf-192
Rookie Rockets-7
95Swedish Leaf-4
Spidermen-1
95Swedish Upper Deck-1
Ticket to North America-NA1
96German DEL-92
97Swedish Collector's Choice-182

Persson, Jonathan
03P.E.I. Rocket-20

Persson, Kent
65Swedish Coralli ISHockey-204
67Swedish Hockey-276
69Swedish Hockey-320
70Swedish Hockey-224
72Swedish Stickers-281
74Swedish Stickers-260

Persson, Mikael
92Swedish Semic Elitserien Stickers-315

Persson, Niklas
99Swedish Upper Deck-110
99Swedish Upper Deck-209
00Swedish Upper Deck-115
02Swedish SHL-200
Parallel-200
03Swedish Elite-64
Silver-64
05Swedish SHL Elitset-67
Gold-67
Series Two Signatures-16
Teammates-6

Persson, Ola
98Danish Hockey League-1

Persson, Ricard
89Swedish Semic Elitserien Stickers-126
90Swedish Semic Elitserien Stickers-203
91Swedish Semic Elitserien Stickers-132
92Swedish Semic Elitserien Stickers-156
93Swedish Semic Elitserien-178
94Swedish Leaf-55
95Donruss-304
95Stadium Club-225
Members Only Master Set-225
96Be A Player-210
Autographs-210
Autographs Silver-210
97Pacific Invincible NHL Regime-172
99Blues Taco Bell-11
99Paramount-199
Copper-199
Emerald-199
Gold-199
Holographic Emerald-199
Holographic Gold-199
Holographic Silver-199
Ice Blue-199
Premiere Date-199
Red-199
Silver-199
00Senators Team Issue-15
00UD Heroes-83
01Senators Team Issue-21
02German Berlin Polar Bears Postcards-21
02German DEL City Press-35
03German Berlin Polar Bears Postcards-25
03German DEL-72
03Worcester Ice Cats 10th Anniversary-10
04German Berlin Polar Bears Postcards-24
04German DEL-74
All-Stars-AS4

Persson, Stefan
78O-Pee-Chee-144
78Topps-144
79Islanders Transparencies-13
79O-Pee-Chee-32
79Topps-32
80O-Pee-Chee-219
80Topps-219
81O-Pee-Chee-206
81Topps-E92
82O-Pee-Chee-209
82Post Cereal-12
83NHL Key Tags-81
83O-Pee-Chee-15
84Islanders News-20
84O-Pee-Chee-133
84Topps-99
85Islanders News-24
97Swedish Alfabilder Autographs-12
00Upper Deck Vintage Dynasty: A Piece of History-TP
00Upper Deck Vintage Dynasty: A Piece of History Gold-TP

Persson, Stefan (FWD)
83Swedish Semic Elitserien-116
84Swedish Semic Elitserien-116
85Swedish Panini Stickers-105
86Swedish Panini Stickers-103
87Swedish Panini Stickers-101
89Swedish Semic Elitserien Stickers-112
90Swedish Semic Elitserien Stickers-118
01Swedish Alfabilder-12

Persson, Stig-Olof
71Swedish Hockey-338
72Swedish Stickers-150

Persson, Torbjorn
90Swedish Semic Elitserien Stickers-122
91Swedish Semic Elitserien Stickers-123
92Swedish Semic Elitserien Stickers-142
93Swedish Semic Elitserien-112
94Swedish Leaf-132

Perthaler, Christian
93Swedish Semic World Champ Stickers-283
95Austrian National Team-20

Perttula, Antti
70Finnish Jaakiekko-184
71Finnish Suomi Stickers-140
72Finnish Jaakiekko-202
73Finnish Jaakiekko-165

Perttula, Pekka
65Finnish Hellas-142

Peruzzi, Uros
93Quebec Pee-Wee Tournament-1790

Pervukhin, Vasili
79Panini Stickers-143
79Russian National Team-12
81Swedish Semic Hockey VM Stickers-42
82Swedish Semic VM Stickers-55
83Swedish Semic VM Stickers-55
84Russian National Team-15
87Russian National Team-16

Pervyshin, Denis
03Russian Under-18 Team-11

Perzi, Mark
04Arizona Icecats-18

Pesan, Filip
99Czech Score Blue 2000-80
99Czech Score Red Ice 2000-80

Pesat, Ivo
94Czech APS Extraliga-229
95Czech APS Extraliga-4
96Czech APS Extraliga-215
97Czech APS Extraliga-29
98Czech OFS-340
99Czech DS-128
99Czech OFS-544
00Czech DS Extraliga-14
00Czech OFS-321
01Czech OFS-61
01Czech OFS H Inserts-H8
02Czech OFS Plus-37
02Czech OFS Plus Masks-M2
02Czech OFS Plus Trios-T22

Pescheck, Michael
94German First League-143

Peschek, Stefan
94German First League-359

Peschke, Frank
94German DEL-396
95German DEL-417
99German Bundesliga 2-295

Peschke, Raimund
94German First League-443

Pesetti, Ron
87Moncton Hawks-20

Pesjak, Gregor
93Quebec Pee-Wee Tournament-1805

Peska, Jaroslav
94German First League-320

Pesonen, Janne
01Finnish Cardset-286
03Finnish Cardset-95
04Finnish Cardset-101
Parallel-75
05Finnish Cardset -271
06Finnish Cardset-99

Pesonen, Jussi
99Finnish Cardset-278
00Finnish Cardset-50
01Finnish Cardset-262
02Finnish Cardset-246
03Finnish Cardset-65
04Finnish Cardset-58
04Finnish Cardset Signatures-13
05Finnish Cardset -47
06Finnish Cardset-49
06Finnish Ilves Team Set-21

Pesout, Martin
99Czech OFS-131
00Czech OFS-159

Pess, Kyle
02Medicine Hat Tigers-18
04Lethbridge Hurricanes-11

Pestrin, Giovanni
93Swiss HNL-291
96Swiss HNL-514

Pestuka, Ivo
99Czech OFS-287
00Czech OFS-262

Pestunov, Dmitry
02Russian Hockey League-195
02Russian Young Lions-9
03Russian Metallurg Magnitogorsk-6
03Russian Young Lions-5
03Russian Under-18 Team-5
04Russian World Junior Team-4

Pesut, George
75O-Pee-Chee NHL-360

Petajaaho, Sakari
80Finnish Mallasjuoma-57

Petawabano, Rodney
917th Inn. Sketch QMJHL-83
Petendra, Kevin
82Kitchener Rangers-14
Peter, Emanuel
01Swiss HNL-70
02Swiss HNL-127
Peter, Hans
93Quebec Pee-Wee Tournament-1530
Peter, Kristian
93Quebec Pee-Wee Tournament-1713
Peterek, Jan
94Czech APS Extraliga-137
95Czech APS Extraliga-305
97Czech APS Extraliga-331
97Czech DS Stickers-201
98Czech DS Stickers-283
98Czech OFS-186
99Czech OFS-300
99Czech OFS-524
All-Star Game Blue-524
All-Star Game Gold-524
All-Star Game Red-524
All-Star Game Silver-524
99Finnish Cardset-157
00Czech DS Extraliga-155
00Czech OFS-278
02Russian SL-40
04Czech OFS-217
04Czech OFS-411
05Czech HC Trinec-8
06Czech LG Hockey Games Postcards-14
06Czech OFS-164
All Stars-21
Points Leaders-8
Peterik, Yan
02Russian Hockey League-263
03Russian Hockey League-260
Petermann, Felix
03German Nuremberg Ice Tigers Postcards-21
04German DEL-263
04German Nuremburg Ice Tigers Postcards-13
05German DEL-279
Peters, Andrew
98Bowman CHL-150
Golden Anniversary-150
OPC International-150
Autographs Blue-A33
Autographs Gold-A33
Autographs Silver-A33
98Bowman Chrome CHL-150
Golden Anniversary-150
Golden Anniversary Refractors-150
OPC International-150
OPC International Refractors-150
Refractors-150
99Kitchener Rangers-5
00Rochester Americans-20
02Rochester Americans-18
03BAP Ultimate Memorabilia Autographs-93
Gold-93
03Bowman-133
Gold-133
03Bowman Chrome-133
Refractors-133
Gold Refractors-133
Xfractors-133
03ITG Action-656
03ITG Used Signature Series-196
Gold-196
03ITG VIP Rookie Debut-13
03Pacific Complete-556
Red-556
03Pacific Luxury Suite-54
Gold-54
03Pacific Supreme-106
Blue-106
Red-106
Retail-106
03Parkhurst Rookie-164
Rookie Emblems-RE-42
Rookie Emblem Autographs-RE-AP
Rookie Emblems Gold-RE-42
Rookie Jerseys-RJ-42
Rookie Jersey Autographs-RJ-AP
Rookie Jerseys Gold-RJ-42
Rookie Numbers-RN-42
Rookie Number Autographs-RN-AP
Rookie Numbers Gold-RN-42
03Private Stock Reserve-106
Blue-106
Red-106
Retail-106
03SPx-204
Radiance-204
Spectrum-204
03Titanium-104
Hobby Jersey Number Parallels-104
Retail-104
Retail Jersey Number Parallels-104
03Topps C55-132
Minis-132
Minis American Back-132
Minis American Back Red-132
Minis Bazooka Back-132
Minis Brooklyn Back-132
Minis Hat Trick Back-132
Minis O Canada Back-132
Minis O Canada Back Red-132
Minis Stanley Cup Back-132
03Topps Pristine-173
03Topps Pristine-174
03Topps Pristine-175
Gold Refractor Die Cuts-173
Gold Refractor Die Cuts-174
Gold Refractor Die Cuts-175
Refractors-173
Refractors-174
Refractors-175
Press Plates Black-173
Press Plates Black-174
Press Plates Black-175
Press Plates Cyan-173
Press Plates Cyan-174
Press Plates Cyan-175
Press Plates Magenta-173
Press Plates Magenta-174
Press Plates Magenta-175
Press Plates Yellow-173
Press Plates Yellow-174
Press Plates Yellow-175
03Topps Traded-TT89
Blue-TT89
Gold-TT89
Red-TT89
03Upper Deck-239
Canadian Exclusives-239
HG-239
Tough Customers-TC-4
05Panini Stickers-41
06Be A Player-65
Autographs-65
Signatures-AP
Signatures 25-70
Signatures Duals-DPL
Peters, Bill
99Spokane Chiefs-18
00Spokane Chiefs-22
01Spokane Chiefs-24
Peters, Colin
03St. Cloud State Huskies-22
06Idaho Steelheads-19
Peters, Dan
02Philadelphia Phantoms-3
04Atlantic City Boardwalk Bullies-23
Peters, Dietmar
70Finnish Jaakiekko-93
70Swedish Hockey-371
74Finnish Jenkki-104
74Finnish Typotor-64
83Swedish Semic VM Stickers-150
04German Berlin Eisbarens 50th Anniv-24
Peters, Frank
28V128-2 Paulin's Candy-47
Peters, Garrett
05Halifax Mooseheads-8
06Halifax Mooseheads-8
Peters, Garry
65Coca-Cola-88
65Topps-28
68O-Pee-Chee-99
68Topps-99
69O-Pee-Chee-171
70Esso Power Players-210
70Flyers Postcards-10
70O-Pee-Chee-196
70Sargent Promotions Stamps-151
71Bruins Postcards-17
Peters, Geoff
95Bowman Draft Prospects-P26
95Slapshot-190
95Slapshot-440
95Upper Deck-522
Electric Ice-522
Electric Ice Gold-522
95Classic-89
96Visions Signings *-67
Autographs-67A
Autographs Silver-67A
99Cleveland Lumberjacks-18
01Trenton Titans-1-8
02UK Manchester Storm-4
02Reading Royals-21
03Rochester Americans-21
04Rochester Americans-17
06Portland Pirates-1
06Portland Pirates-13
Peters, Jason
89Victoria Cougars-16
90Saskatoon Blades-25
907th Inn. Sketch WHL-251
91British Columbia JHL-134
Peters, Jim
44Beehive Group II Photos-57
44Beehive Group II Photos-133
44Beehive Group II Photos-201
45Quaker Oats Photos-104A
45Quaker Oats Photos-104B
51Parkhurst-41
52Parkhurst-35
53Parkhurst-69
61Hamilton Red Wings-17
76Old Timers-13
81Red Wings Oldtimers-6
Peters, Jim (90s)
91Lake Superior State Lakers-20
92Birmingham Bulls-11
93Birmingham Bulls-11
93Dayton Bombers-5
95Central Hockey League-68
Peters, Jimmy
43Parade Sportive *-95
69O-Pee-Chee-143
70Sargent Promotions Stamps-77
72O-Pee-Chee-224
73O-Pee-Chee-231
Peters, Jon
99Guelph Storm-18
Peters, Jorg
94German First League-280
Peters, Justin
02St. Michaels Majors-1
03St. Michael's Majors-1
04ITG Top Prospects Spring Expo-15
04St. Michael's Majors-1
04ITG Heroes and Prospects-84
Autographs-JPE
Top Prospects-15
04ITG Heroes/Prospects Toronto Expo '05-84
04ITG Heroes/Prospects Expo Heroes/Pros-84
05Plymouth Whalers-B-01
05ITG Heroes and Prospects Oh Canada-OC-14
05ITG Heroes and Prospects Oh Canada Gold-OC-14
06Between The Pipes Prospect Trios-PT08
06Between The Pipes Prospect Trios Gold-PT08
06AHL Top Prospects-2
06Albany River Rats-18
Peters, Ken
98Danish Hockey League-14
Peters, Rob
95Dayton Bombers-19
Peters, Roland
74Finnish Jenkki-103
83Swedish Semic VM Stickers-156
04German Berlin Eisbarens 50th Anniv-4
Peters, Thorsten
94German First League-494
Peters, Tony
92Dayton Bombers-21
93Dayton Bombers-27
Peters, Warren
99UD Prospects-38
00Saskatoon Blades-25
01Saskatoon Blades-12
02Saskatoon Blades-16
04Idaho Steelheads-18
Petersen, Kristian Just
99Danish Hockey League-220
Petersen, Simon
98Danish Hockey League-83
Petersen, Toby
97Black Diamond-135
Double Diamond-135
Triple Diamond-135
Quadruple Diamond-135
98UD Choice-307
Prime Choice Reserve-307
Reserve-307
00Wilkes-Barre Scranton Penguins-19
01BAP Memorabilia-122
Emerald-122
Ruby-122
Sapphire-122
01BAP Signature Series-244
Autographs-244
Autographs Gold-244
01Crown Royale Rookie Royalty-18
01Titanium Draft Day Edition-82
01Upper Deck-372
Exclusives-372
02BAP First Edition-113
Jerseys-113
02Pacific-314
Blue-314
Red-314
Heads-Up Quad Jerseys-22
Heads-Up Quad Jerseys Gold-22
02Titanium Jerseys-55
02Titanium Jerseys Retail-55
02Titanium Patches-55
02Wilkes-Barre Scranton Penguins-12
03Wilkes-Barre Scranton Penguins-20
05Iowa Stars-11
06Iowa Stars-17
Petersen, Vilhelm
38Swedish Liv's Magazine-56
Peterson, Brent
82Sabres Milk Panels-17
83NHL Key Tags-14
83O-Pee-Chee-68
84O-Pee-Chee-25
84Sabres Blue Shield-13
85Canucks Team Issue-18
85O-Pee-Chee-47
85O-Pee-Chee Stickers-178
85Topps-47
86Canucks Team Issue-15
86Kraft Drawings-55
86O-Pee-Chee-251
86O-Pee-Chee Stickers-100
87O-Pee-Chee-263
87O-Pee-Chee Stickers-199
88Whalers Junior Ground Round-12
91Michigan Tech Huskies-30
917th Inn. Sketch WHL-47
93Michigan Tech Huskies-8
93Portland Winter Hawks-18
95Atlanta Knights-15
95Classic-78
Autographs-17
95Classic Five-Sport *-148
Autographs-148
97Milwaukee Admirals-15
97Portland Winter Hawks-25
98Cleveland Lumberjacks-18
99Milwaukee Admirals Keebler-7
01German Upper Deck-133
01German DEL City Press-183
03German DEL-160
Peterson, Brett
03Boston College Eagles-3
04Atlantic City Boardwalk Bullies-24
05Johnstown Chiefs-14
Peterson, Chris
04Gwinnett Gladiators-20
Peterson, Cory
95Central Hockey League-69
95Signature Rookies Auto-Phonex-32
95Signature Rook Auto-Phonex Phone Cards-32
99Asheville Smoke-13
00Asheville Smoke-22
01Asheville Smoke-19
Peterson, Eric
98El Paso Buzzards-20
06Sioux Falls Stampede -9
Peterson, Kyle
93Michigan Tech Huskies-3
97New Orleans Brass-17
Peterson, Ryan
02Topeka Scarecrows-6
04Green Bay Gamblers-14
Peterson, Treavor
03Augusta Lynx-47
Peterzen, Boo
86Swedish Panini Stickers-133
87Swedish Panini Stickers-111
Pethke, Marc
94German DEL-192
95German DEL-171
96German DEL-113
98German DEL-10
99Alexandria Warthogs-13
00German DEL-239
02German DEL City Press-80
Petiot, Richard
05Black Diamond-251
05Hot Prospects-141
En Fuego-141
Red Hot-141
White Hot-141
05SP Authentic-267
Limited-267
05SPx-265
05The Cup Masterpiece Pressplate Artifact-286
05The Cup Masterpiece Pressplate Black Diamond-251
05The Cup Masterpiece Pressplates (Ice)-244
05The Cup Master Pressplate Rookie Update-145
05The Cup Masterpiece Pressplates SPA-267
05The Cup Masterpiece Pressplates (SPx)-265
05The Cup Masterpiece Pressplates Trilogy-266
05The Cup Masterpiece Pressplate Ult Coll-211
05UD Artifacts-286
05Ultimate Collection-211
Gold-211
05Upper Deck Ice-244
05Upper Deck Rookie Update-145
05Upper Deck Trilogy-266
05Manchester Monarchs-13
05Manchester Monarchs-42
Petiquay, Daniel
00Rimouski Oceanic-12
Signed-12
01Rimouski Oceanic-11
02Rimouski Oceanic-12
Petit, Felix
05Quebec Remparts-8
05Quebec Remparts Signature Series-8
06Quebec Remparts-8
Petit, Jerome
93Quebec Pee-Wee Tournament-959
98Val d'Or Foreurs-24
99Baie-Comeau Drakkar-20
Petit, Jonathan
93Quebec Pee-Wee Tournament-1076
Petit, Kevin
03Gatineau Olympiques-17
04Gatineau Olympiques-8
05Gatineau Olympiques-5
06Gatineau Olympiques-9
Petit, Michel
83Canucks Team Issue-16
84Canucks Team Issue-19
85Fredericton Express-16
86Canucks Team Issue-16
87O-Pee-Chee-262
87O-Pee-Chee Stickers-196
87Panini Stickers-342
88Panini Stickers-304
89Nordiques Team Issue-34
89Nordiques General Foods-25
89Nordiques Police-22
89O-Pee-Chee-251
89Panini Stickers-291
90Bowman-170
Tiffany-170
90Maple Leafs Postcards-15
90Nordiques Petro-Canada-20
90Nordiques Team Issue-23
90O-Pee-Chee-271
90Panini Stickers-148
90Pro Set-256A
90Pro Set-256B
90Pro Set-539
90Score-187
Canadian-187
90Score Rookie/Traded-54T
90Topps-271
Tiffany-271
90Upper Deck-181
French-181
91Bowman-158
91Maple Leafs PLAY-25
91O-Pee-Chee-166
91Panini Stickers-98
91Parkhurst-252
French-252
91Pinnacle-49
French-49
91Pro Set-492
French-492
91Score American-103
91Score Canadian Bilingual-103
91Score Canadian English-103
91Stadium Club-311
91Topps-166
91Upper Deck-359
French-359
92Bowman-101
92Durivage Panini-43
92Flames IGA-13
92O-Pee-Chee-185
92Pinnacle-206
French-206
92Score-38
Canadian-38
92Stadium Club-195
92Topps-337
Gold-337G
93OPC Premier-141
Gold-141
93Parkhurst-304
Emerald Ice-304
93PowerPlay-308
93Score-275
Canadian-275
93Stadium Club-232
Members Only Master Set-232
OPC-232
First Day Issue-232
First Day Issue OPC-232
93Topps/OPC Premier-141
Gold-141
93Upper Deck-66
94Leaf-444
94OPC Premier-406
Special Effects-406
94Parkhurst-39
Gold-39
94Topps/OPC Premier-406
Special Effects-406
Petitclerc, Eric
93Quebec Pee-Wee Tournament-49
Petitclerc, Maxime
917th Inn. Sketch QMJHL-291
Petkau, Kenny
04Lethbridge Hurricanes-13
06Chilliwack Bruins-21
Petlak, David
99Czech OFS-80
00Czech OFS-196
Peto, Kyle
06Finnish Cardset-260
Petrakov, Andrei
98Russian Hockey League-131
98Fort Wayne Komets-12
99Russian Hockey League-12
99Russian Metallurg Magnetogorsk-39
00Russian Hockey League-271
Petras, Samuel
02Slovakian Kvarteto-24
Petrasek, David
97Swedish Collector's Choice-87
98Swedish UD Choice-101
99Swedish Upper Deck-87
00Swedish Upper Deck-136
02Swedish Malmo Red Hawks-12
02Swedish SHL-230
Parallel-230
03Swedish Elite-90
Silver-90
04Swedish Elitset-83
Gold-83
04Swedish Malmo Red Hawks-10
04Swedish Pure Skills-57
Parallel-57
05Swedish SHL Elitset-196
Gold-196
06Swedish SHL Elitset-57
Petrash, Ken
94German DEL-231
95German DEL-228
96German DEL-79
Petre, Henrik
97Black Diamond-67
Double Diamond-67
Triple Diamond-67
Quadruple Diamond-67
98UD Choice-292
Prime Choice Reserve-292
Reserve-292
98Swedish UD Choice-217
99Swedish Upper Deck-21
00Swedish Upper Deck-30
01Swedish Brynas Tigers-20
04Swedish Elitset-104
Gold-104
05Swedish SHL Elitset-269
06Finnish Cardset-309
Petrell, Lennart
04Finnish Cardset-26
Parallel-19
05Finnish Cardset -198
06Finnish Cardset-205
Petrenko, Sergei
92Upper Deck-346
92Russian Stars Red Ace-26
93Donruss-43
93Leaf-425
93Parkhurst-292
Emerald Ice-292
93Stadium Club-373
Members Only Master Set-373
First Day Issue-373
93Ultra-275
93Upper Deck-450
93Swedish Semic World Champ Stickers-139
93Rochester Americans Kodak-20
93Classic-91
96Swiss HNL-117
99Czech DS-179
99Czech OFS-230
99Russian Hockey League-201
99Russian Stars of Hockey-8
99Russian Stars Postcards-18
02Russian Transfert-11
Petricig, John
93Quebec Pee-Wee Tournament-608
Petrick, Rico
94German First League-409
Petricko, Matus
06UK Nottingham Panthers-12
Petrilainen, Pasi
95Upper Deck-550
Electric Ice-550
Electric Ice Gold-550
95Finnish SISU-110
96Finnish SISU Redline-127
97Black Diamond-48
Double Diamond-48
Triple Diamond-48
Quadruple Diamond-48
98UD Choice-279
Prime Choice Reserve-279
Reserve-279
98Finnish Kerailysarja-214
99Finnish Cardset-319
00Swedish Upper Deck-166
01Finnish Cardset-352
02Finnish Cardset-247
03Finnish Cardset-145
05Swedish SHL Elitset-272
06Finnish Cardset-228
06Finnish Ilves Team Set-22
Petrin, Mathieu
05Shawinigan Cataractes-18
Petrochinin, Evgeni
99Russian Hockey League-193
99Russian Hockey League-225
99Russian Stars of Hockey-21
00Russian Hockey League-378
02Russian Hockey League-167
Petroni, Pierre
917th Inn. Sketch QMJHL-23
Petrov, Alexei
00Russian Hockey League-294
02Russian Hockey League-6
02Russian Hockey League-264
Petrov, Dmitri
03Russian Under-18 Team-2
Petrov, Oleg
92Canadiens Postcards-20
92OPC Premier-96
92Parkhurst-486
Emerald Ice-486
92Russian Stars Red Ace-27
92Fredericton Canadiens-20
93Donruss-452
93Leaf-260
93O-Pee-Chee Canadiens Hockey Fest-56
93Pinnacle-212
Canadian-212
93PowerPlay-371
93Score-459
Canadian-459
93Upper Deck-84
93Fredericton Canadiens-21
93Classic Pro Prospects-8
94Canada Games NHL POGS-138
94Canadiens Postcards-18
94Donruss-61
94Flair-90
94Leaf-354
94OPC Premier-377
94O-Pee-Chee Finest Inserts-13
94OPC Premier Special Effects-377
94Parkhurst-119
94Parkhurst-291
Gold-119
Gold-291
SE Vintage-40
94Pinnacle-203
Artist's Proofs-203
Rink Collection-203
94Score-260
Gold-260
Platinum-260
94Stadium Club-241
Members Only Master Set-241
First Day Issue-241
Super Team Winner Cards-241
94Topps/OPC Premier-377
Special Effects-377
94Ultra-314
94Upper Deck-137
Electric Ice-137
SP Inserts-SP41
SP Inserts Die Cuts-SP41
94Classic All-Rookie Team-AR4
94Classic Pro Prospects-177
Jumbos-PP9
95Canadiens Postcards-11
95Upper Deck-343
Electric Ice-343
Electric Ice Gold-343
96Swiss HNL-95
98Swiss Power Play Stickers-21
00Canadiens Postcards-21
00Pacific-211
Copper-211
Gold-211
Ice Blue-211
Premiere Date-211
01BAP Signature Series-63
Autographs-63
Autographs Gold-63
01Canadiens Postcards-16
01Pacific-210
Extreme LTD-210
Hobby LTD-210
Premiere Date-210
Retail LTD-210
01Pacific Adrenaline-98
Blue-98
Premiere Date-98
Red-98
Retail-98
01Pacific Arena Exclusives-210
01UD Challenge for the Cup-46
01Upper Deck-92
Exclusives-92
01Upper Deck MVP-98
01Upper Deck Victory-188
Gold-188
01Upper Deck Vintage-132
02BAP First Edition-277
02BAP Sig Series Auto Buybacks 2001-63
02Canadiens Postcards-3
02NHL Power Play Stickers-66
02O-Pee-Chee-84
02O-Pee-Chee Premier Blue Parallel-84
02O-Pee-Chee Premier Red Parallel-84
02O-Pee-Chee Factory Set-84
02Pacific-201
Blue-201
Red-201
02Pacific Complete-323
Red-323
02Pacific Exclusive-93
02Parkhurst Retro-143
Minis-143
02Topps-84
OPC Blue Parallel-84
OPC Red Parallel-84
Factory Set-84
02Topps Total-109
02Upper Deck MVP-97
Gold-97
Classics-97
Golden Classics-97
02Upper Deck Victory-113
Bronze-113
Gold-113
Silver-113
03ITG Action-368
03Pacific-191
Blue-191
Red-191
04Swiss EV Zug Postcards-5
Petrov, Sergei
93Minnesota-Duluth Bulldogs-25
00Knoxville Speed-16
01Rockford IceHogs-21
Petrov, Vladimir
69Russian National Team Postcards-14
69Swedish Hockey-11
70Finnish Jaakiekko-11
70Russian National Team Postcards-16
70Swedish Hockey-328
70Swedish Masterserien-21
70Swedish Masterserien-26
70Swedish Masterserien-70
70Swedish Masterserien-71
70Swedish Masterserien-132
71Finnish Suomi Stickers-12
71Swedish Hockey-39
72Finnish Jaakiekko-31
72Finnish Hellas-75
72Finnish Semic World Championship-16
72Swedish Semic World Championship-16
73Finnish Jaakiekko-13
73Russian National Team-7
73Russian National Team-9
73Swedish Stickers-88
74Finnish Jenkki-53
74Finnish Typotor-71
74Russian National Team-15
74Swedish Stickers-6
74Swedish Semic World Champ Stickers-35
77Finnish Sportscasters-26-673
79Panini Stickers-147
79Russian National Team-14
80USSR Olympic Team Mini Pics-8
91Future Trends Canada '72-52
91Future Trends Canada '72 French-52
95Swedish Globe World Championships-242
99Russian Stars of Hockey-41
03Czech Stadion-556
Petrovicky, Robert
91Upper Deck Czech World Juniors-93
92OPC Premier-36
92Parkhurst-61
Emerald Ice-61
92Pinnacle-402
French-402
92Ultra-302
92Upper Deck-569
Euro-Rookies-ER20
92Whalers Dairymart-18
92Classic-6
Gold-6
92Classic Four-Sport *-156
Gold-156
93Donruss-145
93Leaf-187
93Parkhurst-89
Emerald Ice-89
93PowerPlay-107
93Score-277
Canadian-277
93Ultra-337
93Upper Deck-37
SP-63
93Swedish Semic World Champ Stickers-106
93Classic-144
93Classic Four-Sport *-245
Gold-245
94Be A Player-R84
94Leaf-387
94Parkhurst-94
Gold-94
94Upper Deck-361
Electric Ice-361
94Finnish Jaa Kiekko-210
95Slovakian APS National Team-26
96Swedish Semic Wien-233
97Pacific Dynagon Best Kept Secrets-82
97Panini Stickers-166
97Score Blues-9
Platinum-9
Premier-9
97Upper Deck-350
98Grand Rapids Griffins-14
98IHL All-Star Eastern Conference-16
00Chicago Wolves-20
01Slovakian Kvarteto-6A
01Swiss HNL-231
02Slovakian Kvarteto-15
02Swiss HNL-62
Petrovicky, Ronald
97Regina Pats-11
98Bowman CHL-78
Golden Anniversary-78
OPC International-78
98Bowman Chrome CHL-78
Golden Anniversary-78
Golden Anniversary Refractors-78
OPC International-78
OPC International Refractors-78
Refractors-78
00BAP Memorabilia-478
Emerald-478
Ruby-478
Sapphire-478
00SP Authentic-138
00SPx-133
00Titanium Draft Day Edition-154
00Titanium Draft Day Promos-154
00Topps Premier Plus-140
Blue Ice-140
01BAP Memorabilia-235
Emerald-235
Ruby-235
Sapphire-235
01BAP Signature Series-55
Autographs-55
Autographs Gold-55
01Upper Deck Victory-365
Gold-365
02BAP Sig Series Auto Buybacks 2001-55
03ITG Action-392
03Pacific Complete-396
Red-396
03Thrashers Postcards-15
04Pacific-15
Blue-15
Red-15
04Swedish Pure Skills-6
Parallel-6
06Panini Stickers-140
Petrovka, Vladimir
91Finnish Semic World Champ Stickers-124
91Swedish Semic World Champ Stickers-124
97Czech APS Extraliga-91
98Czech DS-47
98Czech DS Stickers-98
98Czech OFS-9
Petrow, Chris
03Oshawa Generals-4
04Kingston Frontenacs-15
Petruic, Jeff
907th Inn. Sketch WHL-151
917th Inn. Sketch WHL-281
95Dayton Bombers-20
99Idaho Steelheads-12
00San Diego Gulls-15
01Asheville Smoke-21
03Missouri River Otters-6
05Muskegon Fury-14
06Quad City Mallards-10
Petruic, Neil
04Minnesota-Duluth Bulldogs-18
05Binghamton Senators-16
05Binghamton Senators Quickway-16
06Binghamton Senators-18
Petruk, Randy
94Kamloops Blazers-13
95Bowman Draft Prospects-P27
95Upper Deck-524
Electric Ice-524
Electric Ice Gold-524
95Kamloops Blazers-5
95Slapshot Memorial Cup-23
96Kamloops Blazers-17
97Bowman CHL-82
OPC-82
98Florida Everblades-18
98Bowman CHL-42
Golden Anniversary-42
OPC International-42
Scout's Choice-SC10
98Bowman Chrome CHL-42
Golden Anniversary-42
Golden Anniversary Refractors-42
OPC International-42
OPC International Refractors-42
Refractors-42
99Cincinnati Cyclones-16
01Florida Everblades-19
02Lowell Lock Monsters-18
Petrunin, Andrei
92Quebec Pee-Wee Tournament-1774
94SP-190
Die Cuts-190
95SP-178
95Upper Deck-556
Electric Ice-556
Electric Ice Gold-556
95Classic-66
Autographs-18
96Upper Deck Ice-143
98Muskegon Fury-27
99Muskegon Fury-3
00Russian Hockey League-170
02Russian Hockey League-223
03Russian Hockey League-209
04Russian RHL-9
Petruska, Tomas
04Waterloo Blackhawks-2
Petrussek, Gerhard
94German First League-192
Petruzalek, Jakub
03Czech OFS Plus-336
04Ottawa 67's-22
04ITG Heroes and Prospects-221
04ITG Heroes/Prospects Toronto Expo '05-221
06Albany River Rats-19
Petterle, Brian
80Sault Ste. Marie Greyhounds-2
Pettersen, Erik
92Norwegian Elite Series-133
Pettersen, Lars
04Missouri River Otters-21
05Missouri River Otters-8
Pettersson, Anders
89Swedish Semic Elitserien Stickers-132
Pettersson, Daniel
86Swedish Panini Stickers-241
89Swedish Semic Elitserien Stickers-208
Pettersson, Dennis
72Swedish Stickers-276
74Swedish Stickers-182
Pettersson, Erik
56Swedish Allabilder-92
Pettersson, Fredrik
05Calgary Hitmen-14
Pettersson, Hakan
69Swedish Hockey-268
70Swedish Hockey-163
71Finnish Suomi Stickers-57
71Swedish Hockey-23
71Swedish Hockey-258
72Finnish Jaakiekko-55
72Finnish Hellas-40
72Finnish Semic World Championship-66
72Swedish Stickers-238
72Swedish Semic World Championship-66
73Swedish Stickers-242
74Finnish Jenkki-33
74Swedish Stickers-261
Pettersson, Hans
86Swedish Panini Stickers-257
89Swedish Semic Elitserien Stickers-222
90Swedish Semic Elitserien Stickers-58
Pettersson, Henrik
92Swedish Semic Elitserien Stickers-292
Pettersson, Janne
69Swedish Hockey-211
Pettersson, John
87Swedish Panini Stickers-232
Pettersson, Jorgen
81O-Pee-Chee-296
81O-Pee-Chee Stickers-135
81Topps-W121
82O-Pee-Chee-309
82O-Pee-Chee Stickers-202
82Post Cereal-17
82Topps Stickers-202
82Swedish Semic VM Stickers-152
83O-Pee-Chee-318
83O-Pee-Chee Stickers-123
83Puffy Stickers-15
83Topps Stickers-123
84O-Pee-Chee-189
84O-Pee-Chee Stickers-59
85Whalers Junior Wendy's-15
86Capitals Police-20
89Swedish Semic Elitserien Stickers-280
92Blues UD Best of the Blues-18
Pettersson, Kjell-Ronnie
64Swedish Coralli ISHockey-100
65Swedish Coralli ISHockey-100
67Swedish Hockey-298
69Swedish Hockey-345
70Swedish Hockey-260
71Swedish Hockey-320
72Swedish Stickers-300
73Swedish Stickers-144
Pettersson, Lars-Gunnar
83Swedish Semic Elitserien-47
84Swedish Semic Elitserien-47
85Swedish Panini Stickers-41
86Swedish Panini Stickers-20
87Swedish Panini Stickers-182
89Swedish Semic Elitserien Stickers-157
89Swedish Semic World Champ Stickers-25
90Swedish Semic Elitserien Stickers-236
91Swedish Semic Elitserien Stickers-166
92Swedish Semic Elitserien Stickers-191
93Swedish Semic Elitserien-162
Pettersson, Lasse
56Swedish Allabilder-67
Pettersson, Lennart
71Swedish Hockey-82
Pettersson, Martin
83Swedish Semic Elitserien-192
84Swedish Semic Elitserien-215
86Swedish Panini Stickers-231
87Swedish Panini Stickers-226
89Swedish Semic Elitserien Stickers-206
Pettersson, Mattias
96Swedish Brynas Tigers-2
99Swedish Upper Deck-1
01Swedish Brynas Tigers-21
Pettersson, Mikael
86Swedish Panini Stickers-214
89Swedish Semic Elitserien Stickers-237
92Swedish Semic Elitserien Stickers-289
93Swedish Semic Elitserien-256
94Swedish Leaf-239
95Swedish Leaf-134
95Swedish Upper Deck-196
97Swedish Collector's Choice-189
98Swedish UD Choice-175
98Swedish UD Choice-186
99Swedish Upper Deck-177
99Swedish Upper Deck-193
02Swedish SHL-198
Parallel-198
03Swedish Elite-62
Silver-62
05Swedish SHL Elitset-249
Gold-249
06Swedish SHL Elitset-113
Pettersson, Ove
83Swedish Semic Elitserien-132
84Swedish Semic Elitserien-154
85Swedish Panini Stickers-137

86Swedish Panini Stickers-141
87Swedish Panini Stickers-207
89Swedish Semic Elitserien Stickers-176
90Swedish Semic Elitserien Stickers-9

Pettersson, Peter
83Swedish Semic Elitserien-222
95Swedish Upper Deck 1st Division Stars-DS15

Pettersson, Rolf
55Swedish Alfabilder-34

Pettersson, Ronald
64Swedish Coralli ISHockey-14
64Swedish Coralli ISHockey-101
65Swedish Coralli ISHockey-14
65Swedish Coralli ISHockey-101
67Swedish Hockey-299
81Swedish Semic Hockey VM Stickers-126
90Swedish Semic Elitserien Stickers-283
97Swedish Collector's Choice-36
98Swedish UD Choice-51
98Swedish UD Choice-205

Pettersson, Ronnie
02Swedish SHL-13
Parallel-13
03Swedish Elite-13
Silver-13
05Swedish SHL Elitset-14
Gold-14
06Swedish SHL Elitset-14

Pettersson, Stefan
69Swedish Hockey-269
70Swedish Hockey-152
71Swedish Hockey-245
72Swedish Stickers-229
73Swedish Stickers-243
74Swedish Stickers-183
02Swedish SHL-54
Parallel-54
Signatures Series II-1
03Swedish Elite-168
Silver-168
04Swedish Elitset-200
Gold-200
Signatures Series B-9
05Swedish SHL Elitset-60
Gold-60
Series Two Signatures-13
06Swedish SHL Elitset-66

Pettersson, Timmy
02Swedish SHL-180
Parallel-180
03Swedish Elite-48
Silver-48
04Swedish Elitset-270
Gold-270
05Swedish SHL Elitset-123
Gold-123
Teammates-11
06Swedish SHL Elitset-162

Pettersson, Tommy
71Swedish Hockey-270
72Swedish Stickers-246
90Swedish Semic Elitserien Stickers-22
91Swedish Semic Elitserien Stickers-223
99Swedish Upper Deck-181
00Swedish Upper Deck-159
02Swedish SHL-82
Parallel-82
03Swedish Elite-106
Silver-106
04Swedish Elitset-97
Gold-97

Pettersson, Torsten
56Swedish Alfabilder-68

Petterstrom, Pontus
06Swedish SHL Elitset-131

Pettie, Jim
77Rochester Americans-20

Pettinen, Tomi
99Finnish Cardset-249
00Finnish Cardset-33
01Finnish Cardset-39
02BAP All-Star Edition-110
Gold-110
Silver-110
02BAP Memorabilia-376
02Private Stock Reserve Retail-172
02SP Authentic-151
02SPx-169
02Topps Chrome-158
Black Border Refractors-158
Refractors-158
02Topps Total-408
02UD Honor Roll-159
02UD Mask Collection-121
02UD Top Shelf-96
02Finnish Cardset-93
03Bridgeport Sound Tigers-8B
04Finnish Cardset-111
Parallel-82
06Swedish SHL Elitset-175

Pettinger, Gordon
34Beehive Group I Photos-120
37V356 Worldwide Gum-76

Pettinger, Matt
99UD Prospects-43
00Black Diamond-61
Gold-61
00SP Authentic-125
00Topps Gold Label Class 1-114
Gold-114
00Topps Gold Label Class 2-114
00Topps Gold Label Class 2 Gold-114
00Topps Gold Label Class 3-114
00Topps Gold Label Class 3 Gold-114
00Upper Deck-196
Exclusives Tier 1-196
Exclusives Tier 2-196
00Upper Deck Ice-41
00Upper Deck Ice-80
Immortals-41
Legends-41
Stars-41
00Upper Deck MVP-209
First Stars-209
Second Stars-209
Third Stars-209
00Upper Deck Victory-280
00Portland Pirates-18
01BAP Memorabilia-245
Emerald-245
Ruby-245
Sapphire-245
01O-Pee-Chee-299
01O-Pee-Chee Premier Parallel-299
01Parkhurst-202
01Stadium Club Souvenirs-MP
01Titanium Draft Day Edition-171
01Topps-299
OPC Parallel-299
Reserve Emblems-MP
Reserve Jerseys-MP
Reserve Name Plates-MP
Reserve Numbers-MP
Reserve Patches-MP
01Upper Deck Victory-390
Gold-390
02SP Authentic-135
02SP Game Used Future Fabrics-FFMP
02SP Game Used Future Fabrics Gold-FFMP
02SP Game Used Future Fabrics Rainbow-FFMP
02Upper Deck-421
Exclusives-421
02Upper Deck Beckett UD Promos-421
02Upper Deck Bright Futures-MP
04Pacific-267
Blue-267
Red-267
05Parkhurst-486
Facsimile Auto Parallel-486
06O-Pee-Chee-491
Rainbow-491
06Panini Stickers-177
06Ultra-200
Gold Medallion-200
Ice Medallion-200
07Upper Deck Victory-95
Black-95
Gold-95

Petz, Ryan
917th Inn. Sketch WHL-323
96Johnstown Chiefs-14

Peverley, Rich
05Milwaukee Admirals Pepsi-13
06AHL Top Prospects-25
06Milwaukee Admirals -13
07Upper Deck Victory-204
Black-204
Gold-204

Peyton, Chris
95Halifax Mooseheads-8
00Jackson Bandits-13

Pfeiffer, Hans
56Swedish Alfabilder-79

Pfligler, Eric
03Saginaw Spirit-16
04Kitchener Rangers-9

Pfosi, Guido
93Swiss HNL-495
95Swiss HNL-269

Phair, Lyle
88ProCards AHL-214

Phalsson, Samuel
95Collector's Choice-350
Player's Club-350
Player's Club Platinum-350

Phaneuf, Dion
02Red Deer Rebels-3
03BAP Memorabilia Draft Redemptions-9
03Red Deer Rebels-2
04SP Authentic Rookie Redemptions-RR5
04ITG Heroes and Prospects-72
Aspiring-5
Autographs-DPH
Combos-13
Emblems-46
Emblems Gold-46
He Shoots-He Scores Prizes-40
Jersey Autographs-46
Jerseys-46
Jerseys Gold-46
Numbers-46
Numbers Gold-46
04ITG Heroes/Prospects Toronto Expo '05-72
04ITG Heroes/Prospects Expo Heroes/Pros-72
05ITG Heroes/Prosp Toronto Expo Parallel -334
05ITG Heroes/Prosp Toronto Expo Parallel -376
05Beehive-114
Beige -114
Blue -114
Gold-114
Red -114
Matte-114
Signature Scrapbook-SSDP
05Black Diamond-194
Emerald-194
Gold-194
Onyx-194
Ruby-194
05Hot Prospects-274
En Fuego-274
Hot Materials-HMPH
Red Hot-274
White Hot-274
05ITG Ultimate Memorabilia Level 1-25
05ITG Ultimate Memorabilia Level 2-25
05ITG Ultimate Memorabilia Level 3-25
05ITG Ultimate Memorabilia Level 4-25
05ITG Ultimate Memorabilia Level 5-25
05ITG Ultimate Mem Complete Jersey-5
05ITG Ultimate Mem Complete Jersey Gold-5
05ITG Ultimate Memorabilia Double Autos-1
05ITG Ultimate Mem Double Autos Gold-1
05ITG Ultimate Mem Double Mem Autos-4
05ITG Ultimate Mem Double Mem Autos Gold-4
05ITG Ultimate Mem First Rounders Jerseys-7
05ITG Ultimate Mem First Rounders Jerseys-8
05ITG Ultimate Mem 1st Round Jersey Gold-7
05ITG Ultimate Mem 1st Round Jersey Gold-8
05ITG Ultimate Mem Future Stars Autos-12
05ITG Ultimate Mem Future Star Autos Gold-12
05ITG Ultimate Mem Future Stars Jerseys-12
05ITG Ultimate Mem Fut Stars Jerseys Gold-12
05ITG Ultimate Mem Future Stars Mem Autos-12
05ITG Ultimate Mem Fut Star Mem Auto Gold-12
05ITG Ultimate Memorabilia R.O.Y. Autos-5
05ITG Ultimate Mem R.O.Y. Autos Gold-5
05ITG Ultimate Memorabilia R.O.Y. Emblems-12
05ITG Ultimate Mem R.O.Y. Emblems Gold-12
05ITG Ultimate Memorabilia R.O.Y. Jerseys-12
05ITG Ultimate Mem R.O.Y. Jerseys Gold-12
05ITG Ultimate Memorabilia R.O.Y. Numbers-12
05ITG Ultimate Mem R.O.Y. Numbers Gold-12
05ITG Ultimate Memorabilia Sextuple Autos-2
05ITG Ultimate Mem 3 Star of the Game Jsy-25
05ITG Ult Mem 3 Star of the Game Jsy Gold-25
05ITG Ultimate Memorabilia Triple Autos-14
05ITG Ultimate Mem Triple Autos Gold-14
05Panini Stickers-4
05Parkhurst-612
Facsimile Auto Parallel-612
True Colors-TCCGY
True Colors-TCCGY
True Colors-TCEDCA
True Colors-TCEDCA
05SP Authentic-140
Limited-140
Octographs-OR
Prestigious Pairings-PPPN
Prestigious Pairings-PPPO
Rarefied Rookies-RRDP
Rookie Authentics-RADP
Sign of the Times Triples-TIPN
Sign of the Times Fives-POCLS
Six Star Signatures-SSRO
05SP Game Used-130
Autographs-130
Gold-130
Auto Draft-AD-DP
Game Gear-GG-DP
Game Gear Autographs-AG-DP
Rookie Exclusives-DP
Rookie Exclusives Silver-RE-DP
Significant Numbers-SN-DP
05SPx-164
Spectrum-164
Xcitement Rookies-XR-DP
Xcitement Rookies Gold-XR-DP
Xcitement Rookies Spectrum-XR-DP
05The Cup-178
Autographed Rookie Patches Gold Rainbow-178
Black Rainbow Rookies-178
Emblems of Endorsement-EEPH
Honorable Numbers-HNDP
Masterpiece Pressplates (Artifacts)-205
Masterpiece Pressplates (Bee Hive)-114
Masterpiece Pressplates (Black Diamond)-194
Masterpiece Pressplates (Ice)-109
Masterpiece Pressplates (MVP)-404
Masterpiece Pressplates (Power Play)-165
Masterpiece Pressplates Rookie Upd Auto-274
Masterpiece Pressplates SPA Autos-140
Masterpiece Pressplates (SP Game Used)-130
Masterpiece Pressplates SPx Autos-164
Masterpiece Pressplates (Trilogy)-179
Masterpiece Pressplates Ult Coll Autos-105
Masterpiece Pressplates (Victory)-269
Masterpiece Pressplates Autographs-178
Platinum Rookies-178
Scripted Numbers-SNPC
Scripted Swatches-SSDP
Signature Patches-SPDP
05UD Artifacts-205
Gold-RED5
05UD PowerPlay-165
05UD Rookie Class-9
Commemorative Boxtoppers-CC-5
05Ultimate Collection-105
Autographed Patches-105
Autographed Shields-105
Jerseys-JDP
Jerseys Dual-DJPI
Marquee Attractions-MA10
Marquee Attractions Signatures-SMA10
Premium Patches-PPDP
Premium Swatches-PSDP
Ultimate Debut Threads Jerseys-DTJDP
Ultimate Debut Threads Jerseys Autos-DAJDP
Ultimate Debut Threads Patches-DTPDP
Ultimate Debut Threads Patches Autos-DAPDP
Ultimate Patches-PDP
Ultimate Patches Dual-DPPI
05Ultra-261
Gold-261
Fresh Ink-FI-DP
Fresh Ink Blue-FI-DP
Ice-261
Rookie Uniformity Jerseys-RU-DP
Rookie Uniformity Jersey Autographs-ARU-DP
Rookie Uniformity Patches-RUP-DP
Rookie Uniformity Patch Autographs-ARP-DP
05Upper Deck-203
HG Glossy-203
Majestic Materials-MMDP
Rookie Ink-RIDP
05Upper Deck Rookie Showcase-RS5
05Upper Deck Rookie Showcase Promos-RS5
05Upper Deck Rookie Threads-RTDP
05Upper Deck Rookie Threads Autographs-ARTDP
05Upper Deck Stars in the Making-SM8
05Upper Deck Ice-109
Cool Threads-CTDP
Cool Threads Autographs-ACTDP
Cool Threads Glass-CTDP
Cool Threads Patches-CTPDP
Cool Threads Patch Autographs-CAPDP
Glacial Graphs-GGDP
Premieres Auto Patches-AIPDP
05Upper Deck MVP-404
Gold-404
Platinum-404
Rookie Breakthrough-RB8
05Upper Deck Rookie Update-274
05Upper Deck Trilogy-179
05Upper Deck Toronto Fall Expo-203
05Upper Deck Victory-269
Black-269
Gold-269
Silver-269
05ITG Heroes and Prospects-334
05ITG Heroes and Prospects-376
Autograph Memorabilia-GA-01
Autograph Memorabilia Gold-GA-01
Autographs Series II-DP
Autographs Series II-DP2
Autographs Series II-RP
CHL Grads-CG-9
CHL Grads Gold-CG-9
Complete Jerseys-CJ-31
Complete Jerseys Gold-CJ-31
He Shoots-He Scores Prizes-4
He Shoots-He Scores Prizes-22
He Shoots-He Scores Prizes-51
Jerseys-GUJ-109
Jerseys Gold-GUJ-109
Nameplates-N-10
Nameplates Gold-N-10
National Pride-NPR-6
Spectrum-STM-08
Spectrum Gold-STM-08
06Be A Player-64
Autographs-64
Profiles-PP26
Profiles Autographs-PP26
Signatures-DP
Signatures 10-69
Signatures 25-69
Signatures Duals-DIP
Signatures Trios-TIPT
Up Close and Personal-UC15
Up Close and Personal Autographs-UC15
06Be A Player Portraits-18
First Exposures-FEDP
06Beehive-88
06Beehive-223
Blue-88
Gold-88
Matte-88
Red Facsimile Signatures-88
Wood-88
06Black Diamond-130
Black-130
Gold-130
Ruby-130
Gemography-GDP
Jerseys-JDP
Jerseys Black-JDP
Jerseys Gold-JDP
Jerseys Ruby-JDP
Jerseys Black Autographs -JDP
06Flair Showcase-18
06Flair Showcase-113
06Flair Showcase-213
Parallel-18
Parallel-113
Parallel-213
Inks-IDP
Wave of the Future-WF7
06Fleer-32
Tiffany-32
Hockey Headliners-HL19
Signing Day-SDDP
06Gatorade-2
06Hot Prospects-16
Red Hot-16
White Hot-16
Hot Materials -HMDP
Hot Materials Red Hot-HMDP
Hot Materials White Hot-HMDP
06ITG International Ice Teammates-IT10
06ITG International Ice Teammates Gold-IT10
06ITG Ultimate Memorabilia-40
Artist Proof-40
Autos-51
Autos Gold-51
Double Memorabilia Autos-10
Double Memorabilia Autos Gold-10
Emblems-23
Emblems Gold-23
Jerseys Autos-45
Jerseys Autos Gold-45
Stick Rack-17
Stick Rack Gold-17
Sticks Autos-24
Sticks Autos Gold-24
Triple Thread Jerseys-13
Triple Thread Jerseys Gold-13
06McDonald's Upper Deck-7
Autographs-ADP
Rookie Review-RR4
06NHL POG-11
06O-Pee-Chee-70
06O-Pee-Chee-618
Rainbow-70
Rainbow-618
06Panini Stickers-199
06SP Authentic-88
06SP Authentic-109
Limited-88
Limited-109
Sign of the Times-STDP
Sign of the Times Quads-ST4IKPT
06SP Game Used-16
Gold-16
Rainbow-16
Authentic Fabrics-AFDP
Authentic Fabrics Parallel-AFDP
Authentic Fabrics Patches-AFDP
Autographs-16
Inked Sweaters-ISDI
Inked Sweaters Patches-ISDI
06SPx-13
Spectrum-13
SPxcitement-X18
SPxcitement Spectrum-X18
SPxcitement Autographs-X18
Winning Materials-WMDP
Winning Materials Spectrum-WMDP
Winning Materials Autographs-WMDP
06The Cup Autographed Foundations-CQPH
06The Cup Autographed Foundations Patches-CQPH
06The Cup Autographed NHL Shields Duals-DASIP
06The Cup Foundations-CQPH
06The Cup Foundations Patches-CQPH
06The Cup Enshrinements-EDP
06The Cup Honorable Numbers-HNPH
06The Cup Limited Logos-LLPH
06The Cup Scripted Swatches-SSPH
06The Cup Signature Patches-SPDI
06UD Artifacts-86
Blue-86
Gold-86
Platinum-86
Radiance-86
Autographed Radiance Parallel-86
Red-86
Auto-Facts-AFDP
Auto-Facts Gold-AFDP
Tundra Tandems-TTKP
Tundra Tandems Black-TTKP
Tundra Tandems Blue-TTKP
Tundra Tandems Gold-TTKP
Tundra Tandems Platinum-TTKP
Tundra Tandems Red-TTKP
Tundra Tandems Dual Patches Red-TTKP
06UD Mini Jersey Collection-15
Jerseys-DP
Jersey Variations-DP
Jersey Autographs-DP
06UD Powerplay-16
Impact Rainbow-16
Specialists-SDP
Specialists Patches-PDP
06UD Toronto Fall Expo Priority Signings -PSDP
06Ultimate Collection-12
Autographed Jerseys-AJ-PH
Autographed Patches-AJ-PH
Jerseys-UJ-DP
Patches-UJ-DP
06Ultra-33
Gold Medallion-33
Ice Medallion-33
Action-UA3
06Upper Deck Arena Giveaways-CGY2
06Upper Deck-29
Exclusives Parallel-29
High Gloss Parallel-29
Game Dated Moments-GD4
Game Jerseys-J2DP
Game Patches-P2DP
Generations Duals-G2BP
Generations Triples-G3BPB
Generations Patches Dual-G2PBP
Generations Patches Triple-G3PBPB
Hometown Heroes-HH56
Masterpieces-29
Signatures-SPH
Walmart Tins Oversize-29
06Upper Deck MVP-46
Gold Script-46
Super Script-46
Autographs-OAPK
Jerseys-OJPL
Jerseys-OJPN
06Upper Deck Ovation-57
06Upper Deck Sweet Shot-18
Signature Shots/Saves Sticks-SSSDP
Signature Sticks-STDP
Sweet Stitches-SSDP
Sweet Stitches Duals-SSDP
Sweet Stitches Triples-SSDP
06Upper Deck Trilogy-17
Combo Clearcut Autographs-C3IKP
Scripts-S1DP
Scripts-TSDP
06Upper Deck Victory-30
06Upper Deck Victory Black-30
06Upper Deck Victory Gold-30
06Upper Deck Victory Next In Line-NL11
06ITG Heroes and Prospects Quad Emblems-QE03
06ITG Heroes and Prospects Quad Emblems Gold-QE03
06ITG Heroes and Prospects Sticks and Jerseys-SJ16
06ITG Heroes and Prospects Sticks and Jerseys Gold-SJ16
07Upper Deck Ovation-93
3x5s-XL22
Autographed 3x5s-XLADP
07Upper Deck Victory-148
Black-148
Gold-148
EA Sports Face-Off-F06
Stars on Ice-SI3
07ITG Going For Gold World Juniors-26
Autographs-26
Emblems-GUE23
Jerseys-GUJ23

Phelps, Chris
907th Inn. Sketch OHL-115
917th Inn. Sketch OHL-27
94Hampton Roads Admirals-10
95Hampton Roads Admirals-17
96Hampton Roads Admirals-HRA3
97Hampton Roads Admirals-15
98Hampton Roads Admirals-4
98Hampton Roads Admirals 10th Anniversary-6

Phenow, Mark
02Kalamazoo Wings-15
06Bloomington PrairieThunder-15

Philbin, Mick
93Quebec Pee-Wee Tournament-832

Philip, Jochen
74Finnish Jenkki-118

Philipp, Radek
98Czech OFS-118
99Czech OFS-301
99Czech OFS-428
00Czech OFS-246
01Czech DS-8
01Czech OFS-28
02Czech OFS Plus-61
03Finnish Cardset-118
04Czech OFS-236
05Czech HC Vitkovice-12

Philipp, Rainer
72Finnish Semic World Championship-109
72Swedish Semic World Championship-109
79Panini Stickers-108

Philipsen, Jan
99Danish Hockey League-50

Phillip, William
93Quebec Pee-Wee Tournament-713

Phillipoff, Harold
76Nova Scotia Voyageurs-15
78Flames Majik Market-24
79O-Pee-Chee-27
79Topps-27

Phillips, Aaron
01El Paso Buzzards-17
02El Paso Buzzards-5
03Pensacola Ice Pilots-351

Phillips, Bill
28La Presse Photos-11
33O-Pee-Chee V304A-43

Phillips, Brad
99Bakersfield Condors-14

Phillips, Chris
95Bowman Draft Prospects-P28
95Donruss Elite World Juniors-7
95SP-176
95Upper Deck-517
Electric Ice-517
Electric Ice Gold-517
95Prince Albert Raiders-16
96Black Diamond-57
Gold-57
96Upper Deck Ice-137
96Prince Albert Raiders-17
96Coll Edge Future Legends Auto Hot Pick-1
96All-Sport PPF *-72
96All Sport PPF Gold *-72
97Be A Player-219
Autographs-219
Autographs Die-Cuts-219
Autographs Prismatic Die-Cuts-219
97Black Diamond-28
Double Diamond-28
Triple Diamond-28
Quadruple Diamond-28
97Collector's Choice-301
97Crown Royale-92
Emerald Green-92
Ice Blue-92
Silver-92
97Donruss Elite-64
Aspirations-64
Status-64
97Donruss Limited-80
Exposure-80
Fabric of the Game-42
97Donruss Preferred-149
97Donruss Preferred-197
Cut to the Chase-149
Cut to the Chase-197
97Donruss Priority-180
Stamp of Approval-180
97Katch-99
Gold-99
Silver-99
97Leaf-156
97Leaf-198
Fractal Matrix-156
Fractal Matrix-198
Fractal Matrix Die Cuts-156
Fractal Matrix Die Cuts-198
97Leaf International-148
Universal Ice-148
97McDonald's Upper Deck-37
97Pacific Dynagon-NNO
Copper-NNO
Dark Grey-NNO
Emerald Green-NNO
Ice Blue-NNO
Red-NNO
Silver-NNO
97Paramount-127
Copper-127
Dark Grey-127
Emerald Green-127
Ice Blue-127
Red-127
Silver-127
97Pinnacle-5
Artist's Proofs-5
Rink Collection-5
Press Plates Back Black-5
Press Plates Back Cyan-5
Press Plates Back Magenta-5
Press Plates Back Yellow-5
Press Plates Front Black-5
Press Plates Front Cyan-5
Press Plates Front Magenta-5
Press Plates Front Yellow-5
Certified Rookie Redemption-B
Certified Rookie Redemption Gold-B
Certified Rookie Redemption Mirror Gold-B
97Score-71
Artist's Proofs-71
Golden Blades-71
97SP Authentic-187
Icons-I22
Icons Die-Cuts-I22
Icons Embossed-I22
97Studio-103
Press Proofs Silver-103
Press Proofs Gold-103
97Upper Deck-325
Game Dated Moments-325
97Upper Deck Ice-47
Parallel-47
Power Shift-47
97Zenith-89
Z-Gold-89
Z-Silver-89
97Bowman CHL-105
OPC-105
98Aurora-132
98Katch-98
98Pacific-314
Ice Blue-314
Red-314
98Paramount-165
Copper-165
Emerald Green-165
Holo-Electric-165
Ice Blue-165
Silver-165
98Senators Team Issue-15
98UD Choice-143
98UD Choice Preview-143
98UD Choice Prime Choice Reserve-143
98UD Choice Reserve-143
98UD3-13
98UD3-73
98UD3-133
Die-Cuts-13
Die-Cuts-73
Die-Cuts-133
98Upper Deck-22
98Upper Deck-140
Exclusives-22
Exclusives-140
Exclusives 1 of 1-22
Exclusives 1 of 1-140
Gold Reserve-22
Gold Reserve-140
98Upper Deck MVP-144
Gold Script-144
Silver Script-144
Super Script-144
99BAP Millennium-169
Emerald-169
Ruby-169
Sapphire-169
Signatures-169
Signatures Gold-169
99Senators Team Issue-14
99Upper Deck-264
Exclusives-264
Exclusives 1 of 1-264
99Upper Deck Arena Giveaways-OS2
99Upper Deck Gold Reserve-264
99Upper Deck Retro-56
Gold-56
Platinum-56
99Upper Deck Victory-208
00BAP Memorabilia-372
Emerald-372
Ruby-372
Sapphire-372
Promos-372
00BAP Mem Chicago Sportsfest Copper-372
00BAP Memorabilia Chicago Sportsfest Blue-372
00BAP Memorabilia Chicago Sportsfest Gold-372
00BAP Memorabilia Chicago Sportsfest Ruby-372
00BAP Memorabilia Chicago Sun-Times Ruby-372
00BAP Memorabilia Chicago Sun-Times Gold-372
00BAP Mem Chicago Sun-Times Sapphire-372
00BAP Mem Toronto Fall Expo Copper-372
00BAP Memorabilia Toronto Fall Expo Gold-372
00BAP Memorabilia Toronto Fall Expo Ruby-372
00Pacific-284
Copper-284
Gold-284
Ice Blue-284
Premiere Date-284
00Senators Team Issue-16
01BAP Signature Series-7
Autographs-7
Autographs Gold-7
01Pacific-277
Extreme LTD-277
Hobby LTD-277
Premiere Date-277
Retail LTD-277
01Pacific Arena Exclusives-277
01Senators Team Issue-22
02BAP First Edition-100
Jerseys-100
02BAP Sig Series Auto Buybacks 1999-169
02BAP Sig Series Auto Buybacks 2001-7
02BAP Signature Series Defensive Wall-DW8
02BAP Ultimate Memorabilia First Overall-3
02NHL Power Play Stickers-117
02Pacific-271
Blue-271
Red-271
02Pacific Complete-174
Red-174
02Senators Team Issue-12
02Senators Team Issue-2
02Topps Total-76
03ITG Action-487
Jerseys-M63
03NHL Sticker Collection-99
03O-Pee-Chee-92
03OPC Blue-92
03OPC Gold-92
03OPC Red-92
03Pacific Complete-214
Red-214
03Senators Postcards-3
03Topps-92
Blue-92
Gold-92
Red-92
03Upper Deck-381
Canadian Exclusives-381
HG-381
UD Exclusives-381
04Swedish Pure Skills-2
Parallel-2
05Panini Stickers-126
05Parkhurst-348
Facsimile Auto Parallel-348
05Upper Deck-134
HG Glossy-134
05Upper Deck MVP-270
Gold-270
Platinum-270
05Upper Deck Toronto Fall Expo-134
06Beehive Signature Scrapbook-SSCP
06Black Diamond Gemography-GCP
06Fleer Signing Day-SDCP
06Gatorade-58
06Hot Prospects Hotagraphs-HCP
06O-Pee-Chee-347
Rainbow-347
06Panini Stickers-117
06Senators Postcards-10
06SP Game Used SIGnificance-SPH
06Upper Deck Arena Giveaways-OTT2
06Upper Deck-141
Exclusives Parallel-141
High Gloss Parallel-141
Masterpieces-141
Signature Sensations-SSCP

Phillips, David
04UK U-20 Team-12

Phillips, Don
93Quebec Pee-Wee Tournament-871

Phillips, Greg
95Saskatoon Blades-15
96Saskatoon Blades-17
97Saskatoon Blades-16
99Lowell Lock Monsters-15
00Lowell Lock Monsters-25

Phillips, Guy
85Medicine Hat Tigers-4
88ProCards IHL-110
90ProCards AHL/IHL-42
93Richmond Renegades-2
94German First League-434
98German DEL-117

Phillips, Jason
85Brandon Wheat Kings-20

Phillips, Jeff
01Plymouth Whalers-7

Phillips, Jonathan
00UK Cardiff Devils-13
01UK Cardiff Devils-11
02UK Cardiff Devils-11
03UK Cardiff Devils-9
05UK Cardiff Devils Challenge Cup-19

Phillips, Kevin
04UK U-20 Team-2
05UK Hull Stingrays-11

Phillips, Luke
03Huntsville Channel Cats-14
04Huntsville Havoc-20

Phillips, Marshall
92Dayton Bombers-22
93Dayton Bombers-22

Phillips, Rob
91Air Canada SJHL-B5
92Saskatchewan JHL-117
97Peoria Rivermen-7
98Pensacola Ice Pilots-13

Phillips, Ryan
92Tacoma Rockets-15
93Tacoma Rockets-19
98Topeka Scarecrows-19

Phillips, Scott
93Memphis RiverKings-12

Phillips, Steve
02Plymouth Whalers-12

Phillips, Tommy
83Hall of Fame-208
83Hall of Fame Postcards-N13
85Hall of Fame-208

Phillipsen, Jan
98Danish Hockey League-163

Philpott, David
01Moncton Wildcats-15
03Yarmouth Mariners-17

Pianosi, Alexi
06Moncton Wildcats-15

Piatek, Erik
04Slovakian Poprad Team Set-29

Picard, Alexandre (Def)
01Halifax Mooseheads-21
02Halifax Mooseheads-21
03Cape Breton Screaming Eagles-15
04Halifax Mooseheads-1
05Black Diamond-269
05Hot Prospects-159
En Fuego-159
Red Hot-159
White Hot-159
05SP Authentic-274
Limited-274
05SP Game Used-228
05SPx-277
05The Cup Masterpiece Pressplate Artifact-310
05The Cup Master Pressplate Black Diamond-269
05The Cup Masterpiece Pressplates (Ice)-257
05The Cup Master Pressplate Rookie Update-165
05The Cup Masterpiece Pressplates SPA-274
05The Cup Masterpiece Pressplates SP GU-228
05The Cup Masterpiece Pressplates (SPx)-277
05The Cup Masterpiece Pressplates Trilogy-289
05The Cup Masterpiece Pressplate Ult Coll-217
05UD Artifacts-310
05Ultimate Collection-217
Gold-217
05Upper Deck Ice-257
05Upper Deck Rookie Update-165
05Upper Deck Trilogy-289
05Philadelphia Phantoms-16
06Flyers Postcards-19
06Philadelphia Phantoms-20

Picard, Alexandre (Fwd)
03Lewiston Maineiacs-16
04ITG Heroes and Prospects-52
Autographs-AP
Emblems-19
Emblems Gold-19
He Shoots-He Scores Prizes-14
Jersey Autographs-19
Jerseys-19
Jerseys Gold-19
Numbers-19
Numbers Gold-19
Top Prospects-7
04ITG Heroes/Prospects Toronto Expo '05-52
05Black Diamond-232
05Hot Prospects-198
Autographed Patch Variation-198
Autographed Patch Variation Gold-198
Red Hot-198
05Parkhurst-623
Facsimile Auto Parallel-623
Signatures-AP
True Colors-TCCLB
True Colors-TCCLB
05SP Authentic-289
05SP Game Used-204
05SPx-228
05The Cup-167
Autographed Rookie Patches Gold Rainbow-167
Black Rainbow Rookies-167
Masterpiece Pressplates (Artifacts)-266
Masterpiece Pressplates (Black Diamond)-232
Masterpiece Pressplates (Ice)-259
Masterpiece Pressplates (Rookie Update)-240
Masterpiece Pressplates (SP Authentic)-289
Masterpiece Pressplates (SP Game Used)-204
Masterpiece Pressplates SPx Autos-228
Masterpiece Pressplates (Trilogy)-245
Masterpiece Pressplates Ult Coll-144
Masterpiece Pressplates Autographs-167
Platinum Rookies-167
05UD Artifacts-266
05Ultimate Collection-144
Gold-144
05Upper Deck Ice-259
05Upper Deck Rookie Update-240
Inspirations Patch Rookies-240
05Upper Deck Trilogy-245
05AHL Top Prospects-30
05Syracuse Crunch-13
05ITG Heroes and Prospects-203
05ITG Heroes and Prospects-386
Autographs Series II-AP
06UD Artifacts Auto-Facts-AFAP
06UD Artifacts Auto-Facts Gold-AFAP
06Upper Deck-58
Exclusives Parallel-58
High Gloss Parallel-58
Masterpieces-58
MVP Jerseys-OJAB
Trilogy Scripts-TSAP
06Syracuse Crunch-14
06ITG Heroes and Prospects Complete AHL Logos-AHL02
06ITG Heroes and Prospects Jerseys-GUJ27
06ITG Heroes and Prospects Jerseys Gold-GUJ27
06ITG Heroes and Prospects Emblems-GUE27
06ITG Heroes and Prospects Emblems Gold-GUE27
06ITG Heroes and Prospects Numbers-GUN27
06ITG Heroes and Prospects Numbers Gold-GUN27

Picard, Jean-Francois
99Colorado Gold Kings Taco Bell-10
99Colorado Gold Kings Wendy's-1
01Flint Generals-14
01Memphis RiverKings-7
06Austin Ice Bats-20

Picard, Jonathan
92Quebec Pee-Wee Tournament-102
93Quebec Pee-Wee Tournament-219

Picard, Mathieu
06Ohio State Buckeyes-24

Picard, Michel
89ProCards AHL-297
90ProCards AHL/IHL-172
91OPC Premier-20
91Parkhurst-56
French-56
91Pinnacle-327
French-327
91Pro Set-538
French-538
91Score American-317
91Score Canadian Bilingual-347
91Score Canadian English-347
91Upper Deck-48
French-48
91Whalers Jr. 7-Eleven-22
92Bowman-437
92O-Pee-Chee-179
92Stadium Club-119

HG-78
03Upper Deck MVP-168
Gold Script-168
Silver Script-168
Canadian Exclusives-168
03Upper Deck Victory-76
Bronze-76
Gold-76
Silver-76
05Hot Prospects Hot Materials-HMFP
05Parkhurst-195
Facsimile Auto Parallel-195
Signatures-FP
True Colors-TCEDM
True Colors-TCEDM
05Upper Deck Notable Numbers-N-FP
06Black Diamond-34
Black-34
Gold-34
Ruby-34
06Flair Showcase Inks-IFP
06Flair Showcase Stitches-SSFP
06Fleer-82
Tiffany-82
Hockey Headliners-HL13
06Gatorade-24
06Hot Prospects Hotagraphs-HFP
06O-Pee-Chee-192
06O-Pee-Chee-612
Rainbow-192
Rainbow-612
Swatches-S-FP
06Panini Stickers-273
06SP Game Used Authentic Fabrics Dual-AF2TP
06SP Game Used Authentic Fabrics Dual Patches-AF2TP
06SP Game Used Inked Sweaters-ISFP
06SP Game Used Inked Sweaters Patches-ISFP
06SP Game Used Letter Marks-LMFP
06SP Game Used SIGnificance-SFP
06The Cup NHL Shields Duals-DSHPT
06UD Artifacts Auto-Facts-AFFP
06UD Artifacts Auto-Facts Gold-AFFP
06UD Mini Jersey Collection-42
06UD Powerplay Power Marks-PMFP
06Ultra-82
Gold Medallion-82
Ice Medallion-82
Uniformity-UFP
Uniformity Patches-UPFP
Uniformity Autographed Jerseys-UAFP
06Upper Deck Arena Giveaways-EDM2
06Upper Deck-76
Exclusives Parallel-76
High Gloss Parallel-76
Game Dated Moments-GD24
Masterpieces-76
Signatures-SFP
06Upper Deck MVP-114
Gold Script-114
Super Script-114
Jerseys-OJFM
06Upper Deck Ovation-166
06ITG Heroes and Prospects Jerseys-GUJ20
06ITG Heroes and Prospects Jerseys Gold-GUJ20
06ITG Heroes and Prospects Emblems-GUE20
06ITG Heroes and Prospects Emblems Gold-GUE20
06ITG Heroes and Prospects Numbers-GUN20
06ITG Heroes and Prospects Numbers Gold-GUN20

Pisellini, Gino
03Plymouth Whalers-9
05Plymouth Whalers-A-07
06Philadelphia Phantoms-30

Pisiak, Ryan
91Prince Albert Raiders-18
917th Inn. Sketch WHL-259
95Central Hockey League-80
97Louisiana Ice Gators-15
99Austin Ice Bats-4
99Austin Ice Bats-29
01Austin Ice Bats-12
04Thetford Mines Prolab-25

Piskor, Michal
94Czech APS Extraliga-133
95Czech APS Extraliga-233
96Czech APS Extraliga-67
97Czech APS Extraliga-114
97Czech DS Stickers-243
98Czech DS Stickers-58
04German Weiden Blue Devils-20

Piskula, Joe
04Wisconsin Badgers-17
05Wisconsin Badgers-22

Piskunov, Sergei
02Russian Hockey League-245

Pistek, Lubomir
93Quebec Pee-Wee Tournament-1548
98Kelowna Rockets-21
99Kelowna Rockets-1
02Czech OFS Plus-224
03Czech OFS Plus-57
05Czech HC Trinec-9

Pistek, Miroslav
96Slovakian Quebec Pee-Wee Tournament-21

Pistilli, Matthew
05Gatineau Olympiques-26
06Gatineau Olympiques-17

Pistilli, Mike
93Quebec Pee-Wee Tournament-70

Pisto, Jermu
93Finnish SISU-166
94Finnish SISU-287
96Finnish SISU Redline-71
98Finnish Keraliysarja-145
99Finnish Cardset-206
00Finnish Cardset-6
01Finnish Cardset-4
03Finnish Cardset-117
05Finnish Cardset -76
06Finnish Cardset-82

Pistolato, Marco
02Swiss HNL-225

Pither, Luke
05Kingston Frontenacs-9
06Guelph Storm-15

Pitirri, Richard
92Quebec Pee-Wee Tournament-6
95Slapshot-169
99Hampton Roads Admirals-17
00Richmond Renegades-10

Pitkamaki, Juha
00Finnish Cardset-30
01Finnish Cardset-231
02Finnish Cardset-248
03Finnish Cardset-43
04Finnish Cardset-46
Parallel-34
05Finnish Cardset -38
Finnish Cardset Super Snatchers-5
06Swedish SHL Elitset-248

Pitkanen, Joni
01Finnish Cardset-74
02BAP Memorabilia Draft Redemptions-4
02SPx Rookie Redemption-R221
02Finnish Cardset-249
Bound for Glory-6
02Finnish Cardset Dynamic Duos-4
02Finnish Cardset Signatures-6
03BAP Memorabilia-173
Emerald-173
Gold-173
Ruby-173
Sapphire-173
Super Rookies-SR6
Super Rookies Gold-SR6
Super Rookies Silver-SR6
03BAP Ultimate Memorabilia Autographs-113
Gold-113
03BAP Ultimate Mem Auto Jerseys-113
03BAP Ultimate Mem Auto Emblems-113
03BAP Ultimate Mem Auto Numbers-113
03BAP Ultimate Mem Calder Candidates-8
03BAP Ultimate Mem Calder Candidates Gold-8
03BAP Ultimate Mem Franch Present Future-22
03BAP Ultimate Mem Rookie Jersey Emblems-2
03BAP Ultimate Mem Rookie Jsy Emblem Gold-2
03BAP Ultimate Mem Rookie Jersey Numbers-2
03BAP Ultimate Mem Rookie Jsy Number Gold-2
03BAP Ultimate Memorabilia Triple Threads-32
03Beehive-227
Gold-227
Silver-227
Jumbo Variations-21
03Black Diamond-195
Black-195
Green-195
Red-195
03Bowman-156
Gold-156
Premier Performance-PP-JP
Premier Performance Patches-PP-JP
03Bowman Chrome-156
Refractors-156
Gold Refractors-156
Xfractors-156
03Crown Royale-129
Red-129
Retail-129
Royal Portraits-7
03eTopps-52
03Flyers Program Inserts-2
03Flyers Postcards-15
03ITG Action-604
03ITG Toronto Spring Expo Class of 2004-9
03ITG Used Signature Series-133
Autographs Gold-133
03ITG VIP Rookie Debut-14
03Pacific Calder-172
03Pacific Complete-533
Red-533
03Pacific Exhibit-233
03Pacific Heads-Up-128
Hobby LTD-128
Retail LTD-128
Prime Prospects-16
Prime Prospects LTD-16
03Pacific Invincible-120
Blue-120
Red-120
Retail-120
03Pacific Luxury Suite-95
Gold-95
03Pacific Quest for the Cup-129
Calder Contenders-16
03Pacific Supreme-131
03Pacific Supreme-131A
Blue-131
Red-131
Retail-131
03Parkhurst Toronto Expo Rookie Preview-PRP-3
03Parkhurst Rookie-178
All-Rookie-ART-3
All-Rookie Autographs-ART-JP
All-Rookie Gold-ART-3
Calder Candidates-CMC-9
Calder Candidates Gold-CMC-9
Rookie Emblems-RE-15
Rookie Emblem Autographs-RE-JP
Rookie Emblems Gold-RE-15
Rookie Jerseys-RJ-15
Rookie Jersey Autographs-RJ-JP
Rookie Jerseys Gold-RJ-15
Rookie Numbers-RN-15
Rookie Number Autographs-RN-JP
Rookie Numbers Gold-RN-15
Teammates Gold-RT9
Teammates-RT9
03Private Stock Reserve-132
Blue-132
Red-132
Retail-132
Class Act-8
03SP Authentic-149
Limited-149
Sign of the Times-JP
Signed Patches-JP
03SP Game Used-90
Gold-90
Rookie Exclusives-RE7
03SPx-219
Radiance-219
Spectrum-219
03Titanium-130
Hobby Jersey Number Parallels-130
Retail-130
Retail Jersey Number Parallels-130
Right on Target-12
03Topps C55-147
Minis-147
Minis American Back-147
Minis American Back Red-147
Minis Bazooka Back-147
Minis Brooklyn Back-147
Minis Hat Trick Back-147
Minis O Canada Back-147
Minis O Canada Back Red-147
Minis Stanley Cup Back-147
03Topps Pristine-143
03Topps Pristine-144
03Topps Pristine-145
Gold Refractor Die Cuts-143
Gold Refractor Die Cuts-144
Gold Refractor Die Cuts-145
Refractors-143
Refractors-144
Refractors-145
Press Plates Black-143
Press Plates Black-144
Press Plates Black-145
Press Plates Cyan-143
Press Plates Cyan-144
Press Plates Cyan-145
Press Plates Magenta-143
Press Plates Magenta-144
Press Plates Magenta-145
Press Plates Yellow-143
Press Plates Yellow-144
Press Plates Yellow-145
03Topps Traded-TT132
Blue-TT132
Gold-TT132
Red-TT132
Future Phenoms-FP-JP
03UD Honor Roll-179
03UD Premier Collection-110
Teammates-PT-PF2
Teammates Patches-PT-PF2
03Upper Deck-232
Canadian Exclusives-232
HG-232
Rookie Threads-RT-4
03Upper Deck Classic Portraits-173
03Upper Deck Ice-129
Glass Parallel-129
03Upper Deck MVP-443
03Upper Deck Rookie Update-158
YoungStars-YS8
YoungStars-YS8A
03Upper Deck Trilogy-179
Limited-179
03Upper Deck Victory-207
03Finnish Cardset D-Day-DD11
03Finnish Cardset Vintage 1983-V2
04Pacific-196
Blue-196
Red-196
04Pacific Montreal International-7
Gold-7
04Pacific Montreal International Gold-7
04Pacific NHL All-Star FANtasy-7
04Pacific NHL All-Star FANtasy Gold-7
04SP Authentic Octographs-OS-ROK
04SP Authentic Sign of the Times-QS-BPBP
04SP Authentic Sign of the Times-SS-DEE
04SP Authentic Sign of the Times-SS-FIN
04Upper Deck World Cup Tribute-KLJPTR
04Upper Deck All-Star Promos-JP
04AHL All-Stars-34
04AHL All-Stars-47
04AHL Top Prospects-39
04Philadelphia Phantoms-13
05ITG Heroes/Prosp Toronto Expo Parallel -76
05Flyers Team Issue-14
05ITG Ultimate Mem First Rounders Jerseys-8
05ITG Ultimate Mem 1st Round Jersey Gold-8
05Panini Stickers-133
05Parkhurst-355
Facsimile Auto Parallel-355
True Colors-TCPHI
True Colors-TCPHI
True Colors-TCPHPI
True Colors-TCPHPI
05SP Authentic Prestigious Pairings-PPEP
05SP Authentic Scripts to Success-SSJP
05SP Authentic Sign of the Times-JP
05SP Game Used Authentic Fabrics Dual-PE
05SP Game Used Authentic Fabric Dual Auto-PE
05SP Game Used Authentic Patches Dual-PE
05SP Game Used Authentic Patch Dual Autos-PE
05SP Game Used Game Gear-GG-JP
05SP Game Used Game Gear Autographs-AG-JP
05SP Game Used Signature Sticks-SS-JP
05SP Game Used SIGnificance-JP
05SP Game Used SIGnificance Gold-S-JP
05SP Game Used Significant Numbers-SN-JP
05SP Game Used Statscriptions-ST-JP
05The Cup Emblems of Endorsement-EEJP
05The Cup Master Pressplate Rookie Update-222
05The Cup Signature Patches-SPJP
05UD Powerplay Power Marks-PMJP
05Ultimate Collection Endorsed Emblems-EEJP
05Ultimate Coll National Heroes Jersey-NHJJP
05Ultimate Coll National Heroes Patch-NHPJP
05Ultra-144
Gold-144
Ice-144
05Upper Deck-138
Big Playmakers-B-JP
HG Glossy-138
Jerseys-J-JP
Jerseys Series II-J2JP
Notable Numbers-N-JP
Ice Fresh Ice-FIJP
Ice Fresh Ice Glass-FIJP
Ice Fresh Ice Glass Patches-FIPJP
Ice Frozen Fabrics-FFJP
Ice Frozen Fabrics Autographs-AFFJP
Ice Frozen Fabrics Glass-FFJP
Ice Frozen Fabrics Patches-FFPJP
Ice Frozen Fabrics Patch Autographs-FAPJP
05Upper Deck MVP-289
Gold-289
Platinum-289
05Upper Deck Rookie Update-74
05Upper Deck Rookie Update-222
Inspirations Patch Rookies-222
05Upper Deck Trilogy Scripts-SFS-JP
05Upper Deck Toronto Fall Expo-138
05Upper Deck Victory-237
Black-237
Gold-237
Silver-237
05ITG Heroes and Prospects-76
Autographs-A-JPI
Future Teammates-FT2
He Shoots-He Scores Prizes-34
Jerseys-GUJ-11
Jerseys Gold-GUJ-11
Emblems-GUE-11
Emblems Gold-GUE-11
Numbers-GUN-11
Numbers Gold-GUN-11
Nameplates-N-20
Nameplates Gold-N-20
Shooting Stars-AS-9
06Be A Player-63
Autographs-63
Signatures-JP
Signatures 10-68
Portraits Quadruple Signature Portraits-QKKJP
Portraits Signature Portraits-SPJP
06Beehive-30
Matte-30
Signature Scrapbook-SSJP
06Black Diamond-60
Black-60
Gold-60
Ruby-60
Gemography-GJP
06Flair Showcase Inks-IJP
06Flair Showcase Wave of the Future-WF33
06Fleer-146
Tiffany-146
06Flyers Postcards-18
06Hot Prospects Red Hot-72
06Hot Prospects White Hot-72
06Hot Prospects Hot Materials -HMJP
06Hot Prospects Hot Materials Red Hot-HMJP
06Hot Prospects Hot Materials White Hot-HMJP
06Hot Prospects Hotagraphs-HJP
06O-Pee-Chee-358
Rainbow-358
Swatches-S-JP
06Panini Stickers-129
06SP Game Used-75
Gold-75
Rainbow-75
Authentic Fabrics-AFJP
Authentic Fabrics Parallel-AFJP
Authentic Fabrics Patches-AFJP
Authentic Fabrics Eights-AF8FIN
Authentic Fabrics Eights Patches-AF8FIN
Autographs-75
By The Letter-BLJP
Inked Sweaters-ISJP
Inked Sweaters Patches-ISJP
Inked Sweaters Dual-IS2EP
Inked Sweaters Dual Patches-IS2EP
Letter Marks-LMJP
SIGnificance-SJP
06The Cup Autographed NHL Shields Duals-DASGP
06The Cup NHL Shields Duals-DSHPH
06UD Artifacts Tundra Tandems-TTSJ
06UD Artifacts Tundra Tandems Black-TTSJ
06UD Artifacts Tundra Tandems Blue-TTSJ
06UD Artifacts Tundra Tandems Gold-TTSJ
06UD Artifacts Tundra Tandems Platinum-TTSJ
06UD Artifacts Tundra Tandems Red-TTSJ
06UD Artifacts Tundra Tandems Dual Patches Red-TTSJ
06Ultimate Collection Premium Patches-PS-JP
06Ultimate Collection Premium Swatches-PS-JP
06Ultra-142
Gold Medallion-142
Ice Medallion-142
06Upper Deck Arena Giveaways-PHI3
06Upper Deck-145
Exclusives Parallel-145
High Gloss Parallel-145
Game Jerseys-J2JP
Game Patches-P2JP
Generations Duals-G2LP
Generations Patches Dual-G2PLP
Masterpieces-145
Signature Sensations-SSJP
06Upper Deck MVP-212
Gold Script-212
Super Script-212
Jerseys-OJPO
Jerseys-OJPR
06Upper Deck Sweet Shot Signature Shots/Saves-SSJP
06Upper Deck Sweet Shot Signature Sticks-STJP
06Upper Deck Trilogy Honorary Scripted Patches-HSPJP
06Upper Deck Trilogy Honorary Scripted Swatches-HSSJP
06Upper Deck Trilogy Scripts-TSJP
06Upper Deck Victory-146
06Upper Deck Victory Black-146
06Upper Deck Victory Gold-146
06Upper Deck Victory Next In Line-NL39
07Upper Deck Victory-29
Black-29
Gold-29

Pitlick, Lance
90ProCards AHL/IHL-27
95PEI Senators-16
96Senators Pizza Hut-20
97Be A Player-109
Autographs-109
Autographs Die-Cuts-109
Autographs Prismatic Die-Cuts-109
97Pacific Invincible NHL Regime-137
98Senators Team Issue-16
99BAP Millennium-116
Emerald-116
Ruby-116
Sapphire-116
Signatures-116
Signatures Gold-116
00BAP Signature Series-134
Emerald-134
Ruby-134
Sapphire-134
Autographs-89
Autographs Gold-89
00Panthers Team Issue-8
00Upper Deck-76
Exclusives Tier 1-76
Exclusives Tier 2-76
02BAP Sig Series Auto Buybacks 1999-116
02BAP Sig Series Auto Buybacks 2000-89

Pitre, Didier
10C56-23
10Sweet Caporal Postcards-41
11C55-41
12C57-45
27La Patrie-18
83Hall of Fame-130
83Hall of Fame Postcards-I11
85Hall of Fame-130

Pitta, Rick
04Williams Lake Timberwolves-24

Pittet, Matthias
93Swiss HNL-404

Pittis, Domenic
917th Inn. Sketch WHL-347
93Lethbridge Hurricanes-12
94Cleveland Lumberjacks-17
94Cleveland Lumberjacks Postcards-17
95Cleveland Lumberjacks-22
95Cleveland Lumberjacks Postcards-21
97Donruss-212
Press Proofs Silver-212
Press Proofs Gold-212
Rated Rookies-5
Medallist-5
97Donruss Canadian Ice-140
Dominion Series-140
Provincial Series-140
97Score Penguins-20
Platinum-20
Premier-20
98Rochester Americans-20
00Titanium-119
Retail-119
00Titanium Draft Day Edition-119
00Titanium Draft Day Promos-119
00Upper Deck NHLPA-PA36
02Predators Team Issue-4
02Milwaukee Admirals-12
03Rochester Americans-22

Pittis, John
01Michigan Tech Huskies-25

Pittman, Chris
93Kitchener Rangers-11
94Kitchener Rangers-12
95Slapshot-279
96Richmond Renegades-16
02Columbia Inferno-108
02Hartford Wolf Pack-19
03Columbia Inferno-109

Pittman, Mike
93Guelph Storm-13
94Guelph Storm-17
95Slapshot-97
95Guelph Storm-9

Pitton, Bryan
05Brampton Battalion-6
06Between The Pipes-5
Autographs-ABPI
06Brampton Battalion-3

Pitton, Jason
03Sault Ste. Marie Greyhounds-18
04Sault Ste. Marie Greyhounds-13
05Guelph Storm-D-03

Piuhola, Jussi
66Finnish Jaakiekkosarja-134
70Finnish Jaakiekko-264

Piva, Matt
04Oshawa Generals-11
04Oshawa Generals Autographs-11

Pivetz, Mark
92Saskatchewan JHL-140
01Lincoln Stars-26
02Lincoln Stars-26

Pivko, Libor
99Czech DS-47
99Czech OFS-243
00Czech DS Extraliga-152
00Czech OFS-275
01Czech OFS-89
All Stars-30
02Czech DS-38
02Czech OFS Plus-38
03BAP Memorabilia-246
03ITG VIP Rookie Debut-67
03Parkhurst Rookie-63
Rookie Emblems-RE-17
Rookie Emblems Gold-RE-17
Rookie Jerseys-RJ-17
Rookie Jerseys Gold-RJ-17
Rookie Numbers-RN-17
Rookie Numbers Gold-RN-17
03SP Authentic-100
Limited-100
03Upper Deck Rookie Update-208
03Milwaukee Admirals-29
03Milwaukee Admirals Postcards-16
04Milwaukee Admirals-9
05AHL All-Stars-27
05AHL Top Prospects-31
05Milwaukee Admirals Choice-9
05Milwaukee Admirals Pepsi-14
06Czech HC Pardubice Postcards-16
06Czech OFS-315

Pivonka, Michal
86Capitals Kodak-21
86Capitals Police-21
87Capitals Kodak-20
87Capitals Team Issue-19
88Capitals Borderless-17
88Capitals Smokey-18
89Capitals Kodak-20
89Capitals Team Issue-18
90Bowman-68
Tiffany-68
90Capitals Kodak-20
90Capitals Postcards-19
90Capitals Smokey-18
90O-Pee-Chee-68
90Panini Stickers-154
90Pro Set-319
90Score-268
Canadian-268
90Topps-68
Tiffany-68
90Upper Deck-80
French-80
91Pro Set Platinum-132
91Bowman-291
91Bowman-413
91Capitals Junior 5x7-22
91Capitals Kodak-22
91O-Pee-Chee-327
91Panini Stickers-206
91Parkhurst-412
French-412
91Pinnacle-277
French-277
91Pro Set-252
French-252
91Score American-193
91Score Canadian Bilingual-193
91Score Canadian English-193
91Stadium Club-44
91Topps-327
91Upper Deck-229
French-229
91Finnish Semic World Champ Stickers-222
91Swedish Semic World Champ Stickers-222
92Bowman-294
92Capitals Kodak-22
92O-Pee-Chee-30
92Panini Stickers-161
92Panini Stickers French-161
92Parkhurst-432
Emerald Ice-432
92Pinnacle-151
French-151
92Pro Set-201
92Score-253
Canadian-253
92Stadium Club-382
92Topps-107
Gold-107G
92Ultra-237
92Upper Deck-261
92Finnish Semic-138
93Donruss-374
93Leaf-178
93OPC Premier-321
93OPC Premier-360
Gold-321
Gold-360
93Panini Stickers-27
93Parkhurst-487
Emerald Ice-487
93Pinnacle-67
Canadian-67
93PowerPlay-265
93Score-118
Canadian-118
International Stars-15
International Stars Canadian-15
93Stadium Club-405
Members Only Master Set-405
First Day Issue-405
93Topps/OPC Premier-321
93Topps/OPC Premier-360
Gold-321
Gold-360
93Ultra-101
93Upper Deck-154
94Be A Player Signature Cards-160
94Canada Games NHL POGS-248
94Donruss-292
94Leaf-114
94OPC Premier-259
Special Effects-259
94Pinnacle-323
Artist's Proofs-323
Rink Collection-323
94Topps/OPC Premier-259
Special Effects-259
94Ultra-238
94Finnish Jaa Kiekko-178
95Capitals Team Issue-21
95Collector's Choice-260
Player's Club-260
Player's Club Platinum-260
95Donruss-197
95Finest-147
Refractors-147
95Hoyle Eastern Playing Cards-49
95Leaf-162
95Panini Stickers-136
95Parkhurst International-487
Emerald Ice-487
95Score-258
Black Ice Artist's Proofs-258
Black Ice-258
95SkyBox Impact-180
95SP-157
95Summit-147
Artist's Proofs-147
Ice-147
95Topps-330
OPC Inserts-330
95Ultra-177
Gold Medallion-177
95Upper Deck-392
Electric Ice-392
Electric Ice Gold-392
95Swedish Globe World Championships-156
96Be A Player-13
Autographs-13
Autographs Silver-13
96Collector's Choice-280
96Donruss-60
Press Proofs-60
96Donruss Canadian Ice-50
Gold Press Proofs-50
Red Press Proofs-50
96Donruss Elite-35
Die Cut Stars-35
96Fleer-119
96Kraft Upper Deck-12
96Leaf Limited-36
Gold-36
96Leaf Preferred-100
Press Proofs-100
96Maggers-76
96Metal Universe-167
96Pinnacle-173
Artist's Proofs-173
Foil-173
Premium Stock-173
Rink Collection-173
96Score-33
Artist's Proofs-33
Dealer's Choice Artist's Proofs-33
Special Artist's Proofs-33
Golden Blades-33
96Select Certified-52
Artist's Proofs-52
Blue-52
Mirror Blue-52
Mirror Gold-52
Mirror Red-52
Red-52
96SkyBox Impact-142
96Summit-25
Artist's Proofs-25
Ice-25
Metal-25
Premium Stock-25
96Topps Picks-55
OPC Inserts-55
96Ultra-178
Gold Medallion-178
96Upper Deck-355
96Zenith-62
Artist's Proofs-62
96Swedish Semic Wien-126
96Collector's Edge Ice-124
Crucibles-C23
Prism-124
97Pacific-285
Copper-285
Emerald Green-285
Ice Blue-285
Red-285
Silver-285
97Panini Stickers-111
98Be A Player-150
Press Release-150
98BAP Gold-150
98BAP Autographs-150
98BAP Autographs Gold-150
98BAP Tampa Bay All Star Game-150
99Kansas City Blades Supercuts-14
02BAP Sig Series Auto Buybacks 1998-150

Piwowarczyk, Kyle
02London Knights-12

Placatka, Tomas
94Czech APS Extraliga-274
98Danish Hockey League-157
99Danish Hockey League-99

Plachta, Jacek
94German DEL-253
95German DEL-251
96German DEL-140
98German DEL-11
99German DEL-297
00German DEL-218
01German Upper Deck-205
02German DEL City Press-98
03German DEL-115
04German DEL-131
04German Hamburg Freezers Postcards-12
05German DEL-113
06German DEL-74

Plack, Mario
94German First League-594
04German Berlin Eisbarens 50th Anniv-5

Plager, Barclay
68O-Pee-Chee-177
68Shirriff Coins-154
69O-Pee-Chee-176
70Dad's Cookies-101
70Esso Power Players-241
70O-Pee-Chee-99
70Sargent Promotions Stamps-184
70Topps-99
71Blues Postcards-17
71Letraset Action Replays-12
71O-Pee-Chee-66
71Sargent Promotions Stamps-182
71Topps-66
71Toronto Sun-244
72Blues White Border-14
72O-Pee-Chee-35
72Sargent Promotions Stamps-187
72Topps-136
72Finnish Semic World Championship-186
72Swedish Semic World Championship-186
73Blues White Border-13
73O-Pee-Chee-47
73Topps-47
74NHL Action Stamps-241
74O-Pee-Chee NHL-87
74O-Pee-Chee NHL-107
74Topps-87
74Topps-107
75O-Pee-Chee NHL-205
75Topps-205
78Blues Postcards-18
92Blues UD Best of the Blues-24
02Fleer Throwbacks-76
Gold-76
Platinum-76

Plager, Bill
70Sargent Promotions Stamps-187
71Blues Postcards-18
71Sargent Promotions Stamps-190
72Flames Postcards-14
72O-Pee-Chee-122
72Sargent Promotions Stamps-7
72Topps-12
89New Haven Nighthawks-9

Plager, Bob
68O-Pee-Chee-112
68Shirriff Coins-148
68Topps-112
69O-Pee-Chee-13
69Topps-13
70Esso Power Players-238
70O-Pee-Chee-211
70Sargent Promotions Stamps-183
71Blues Postcards-19
71O-Pee-Chee-103
71Sargent Promotions Stamps-189
71Topps-103
71Toronto Sun-245
72Blues White Border-15
72O-Pee-Chee-161
72Sargent Promotions Stamps-186
72Topps-96
73Blues White Border-14
73O-Pee-Chee-148
73Topps-134
74NHL Action Stamps-247
74O-Pee-Chee NHL-107
74Topps-107
75O-Pee-Chee NHL-131
75Topps-131
76O-Pee-Chee NHL-369
77O-Pee-Chee NHL-285
90ProCards AHL/IHL-98
92Blues UD Best of the Blues-7

Plager, Kevin
96St. Louis Vipers RHI-7
97Columbus Cottonmouths-14
98Columbus Cottonmouths-12
99Columbus Cottonmouths-4
00Missouri River Otters-20

Plamondon, Gerry
43Parade Sportive *-64
43Parade Sportive *-96
43Parade Sportive *-97
44Beehive Group II Photos-277
45Quaker Oats Photos-105
51Laval Dairy QSHL-85
51Laval Dairy Subset-85
52Bas Du Fleuve-50
52St. Lawrence Sales-14

Plamondon, Jean
88Richelieu Riverains-21

Plamondon, Justin
98BC Icemen-9
98BC Icemen II-9
01BC Icemen-18

Plamondon, Ray
81Regina Pats-18

Plamondon, Sylvain
93Quebec Pee-Wee Tournament-538
98Quebec Remparts-18
Signed-18
99Quebec Remparts-14
Signed-14

Plampeck, Nicklas
99Danish Hockey League-207

Planche, James
51Laval Dairy QSHL-50

Plandowski, Darryl
93Seattle Thunderbirds-19

Plandowski, Jason
90Fort Saskatchewan Traders-13

Plankers, Jim
84Minnesota-Duluth Bulldogs-11

Planovsky, Antonin
83Swedish Semic VM Stickers-87
94Czech APS Extraliga-120

Plant, Ricky
97UK Guildford Flames-9
99UK Guildford Flames-26
00UK Guildford Flames-20
01UK Guildford Flames-8
02UK Guildford Flames-6
02UK Guildford Flames-27
03UK Guildford Flames-7
03UK Guildford Flames-30
06UK Guildford Flames-8

Plant, Russ
97UK Guildford Flames-20
99UK Guildford Flames-27

Plante, Alexandre
05Calgary Hitmen-15

Plante, Cam
82Brandon Wheat Kings-6
83Brandon Wheat Kings-11
90Kansas City Blades-19
90ProCards AHL/IHL-583

Plante, Dan
93Classic-72
94Donruss-48
94Leaf-214
94OPC Premier-266
Special Effects-266
94Pinnacle-488
Artist's Proofs-488
Rink Collection-488
94Topps/OPC Premier-266
Special Effects-266
94Classic-81
Gold-81
Autographs-NNO
Tri-Cards-T40
94Classic Pro Prospects-95
95SkyBox Impact-210
96Islander Postcards-17
97Pacific Invincible NHL Regime-121
97Upper Deck-309
98Chicago Wolves-2
99Chicago Wolves-19
00Chicago Wolves-21
01Chicago Wolves-16

Plante, Dave
05Rimouski Oceanic-21
06Rimouski Oceanic-11

Plante, Derek
93Donruss-45
93Leaf-258
93OPC Premier-285
Gold-285
93Parkhurst-293
Emerald Ice-293
Calder Candidates-C18
Calder Candidates Gold-C18
93Pinnacle-435
Canadian-435
93PowerPlay-300
Rookie Standouts-11
93Score-589
Gold-589
Canadian-589
Canadian Gold-589
93Stadium Club-491
Members Only Master Set-491
First Day Issue-491
93Topps/OPC Premier-285
Gold-285
93Ultra-276
Wave of the Future-13
93Upper Deck-475
93Minnesota-Duluth Commemorative-2
93Classic-73
94Canada Games NHL POGS-47
94Donruss-78
94Fleer-26
94Leaf-33
Gold Rookies-11
94Leaf Limited-44
94OPC Premier-194
94OPC Premier-501
94O-Pee-Chee Finest Inserts-3
94OPC Premier Special Effects-194
94OPC Premier Special Effects-501
94Parkhurst-277
Gold-277
94Parkhurst SE-SE19
Gold-SE19
Vintage-39
94Pinnacle-95
94Pinnacle-472
Artist's Proofs-95
Artist's Proofs-472
Rink Collection-95
Rink Collection-472
94Score-251
Gold-251
Platinum-251
94Stadium Club Members Only-48
94Stadium Club-30
Members Only Master Set-30
First Day Issue-30
Super Team Winner Cards-30
94Topps/OPC Premier-194
94Topps/OPC Premier-501
Special Effects-194
Special Effects-501
94Ultra-27
All-Rookies-6
All-Rookies Parallel-6
94Upper Deck-142
Electric Ice-142
SP Inserts-SP100
SP Inserts Die Cuts-SP100
94Classic Autographs-NNO
94Classic Pro Prospects-30
Jumbos-PP4

94Images *-43
Sudden Impact-SI8
95Be A Player-16
Signatures-S16
Signatures Die Cuts-S16
95Canada Games NHL POGS-40
95Collector's Choice-51
Player's Club-51
Player's Club Platinum-51
95Donruss-190
95Hoyle Eastern Playing Cards-50
95Leaf-166
95Panini Stickers-16
95Parkhurst International-294
Emerald Ice-294
95Pinnacle-149
Artist's Proofs-149
Rink Collection-149
95Score-213
Black Ice Artist's Proofs-213
Black Ice-213
95SkyBox Impact-18
95Topps-103
OPC Inserts-103
95Upper Deck-409
Electric Ice-409
Electric Ice Gold-409
96Black Diamond-83
Gold-83
96Collector's Choice-27
96Donruss-107
Press Proofs-107
96Metal Universe-16
96Pinnacle-5
Artist's Proofs-5
Foil-5
Premium Stock-5
Rink Collection-5
96Score-174
Artist's Proofs-174
Dealer's Choice Artist's Proofs-174
Special Artist's Proofs-174
Golden Blades-174
96SP-16
96Ultra-19
Gold Medallion-19
96Upper Deck-223
96Upper Deck Ice-7
Parallel-7
97Collector's Choice-24
Star Quest-SQ62
97Donruss-149
Press Proofs Silver-149
Press Proofs Gold-149
97Donruss Canadian Ice-35
Dominion Series-35
Provincial Series-35
97Donruss Elite-82
Aspirations-82
Status-82
97Donruss Limited-49
97Donruss Limited-184
Exposure-49
Exposure-184
97Donruss Preferred-72
Cut to the Chase-72
97Donruss Priority-25
Stamp of Approval-25
97Leaf-112
Fractal Matrix-112
Fractal Matrix Die Cuts-112
97Leaf International-112
Universal Ice-112
97Pacific-262
Copper-262
Emerald Green-262
Ice Blue-262
Red-262
Silver-262
97Pacific Dynagon-13
Copper-13
Dark Grey-13
Emerald Green-13
Ice Blue-13
Red-13
Silver-13
Tandems-28
97Pacific Invincible-14
Copper-14
Emerald Green-14
Ice Blue-14
Red-14
Silver-14
97Pacific Omega-25
Copper-25
Dark Gray-25
Emerald Green-25
Gold-25
Ice Blue-25
97Panini Stickers-12
97Paramount-22
Copper-22
Dark Grey-22
Emerald Green-22
Ice Blue-22
Red-22
Silver-22
97Pinnacle-169
Press Plates Back Black-169
Press Plates Back Cyan-169
Press Plates Back Magenta-169
Press Plates Back Yellow-169
Press Plates Front Black-169
Press Plates Front Cyan-169
Press Plates Front Magenta-169
Press Plates Front Yellow-169
97Pinnacle Certified-110
Red-110
Mirror Blue-110
Mirror Gold-110
Mirror Red-110
97Pinnacle Inside-148
97Pinnacle Tot Cert Platinum Blue-110
97Pinnacle Tot Certi Platinum Gold-110
97Pinnacle Totally Certified Platinum Red-110
97Pinnacle Tot Cert Mirror Platinum Gold-110
97Score-109
Artist's Proofs-109
Golden Blades-109
97Score Sabres-12
Platinum-12
Premier-12
97Studio-36
Press Proofs Silver-36
Press Proofs Gold-36
98Finest-143
No Protectors-143
No Protectors Refractors-143
Refractors-143
98Pacific-107
Ice Blue-107
Red-107
99Pacific-128
Copper-128
Emerald Green-128
Gold-128
Ice Blue-128
Premiere Date-128
Red-128
99Stars Postcards-22
01German Upper Deck-189
02Swiss HNL-273
03German DEL-10
03German Mannheim Eagles Postcards-14
04German Adler Mannheim Eagles Postcards-23
04German DEL-15

Plante, Dominic
02Shawinigan Cataractes-21

Plante, Eric
907th Inn. Sketch QMJHL-4
917th Inn. Sketch QMJHL-285
917th Inn. Sketch Memorial Cup-60
93Drummondville Voltigeurs-15
94Central Hockey League-68
94Oklahoma City Blazers-14

Plante, Jacques
44Beehive Group II Photos-278
44Beehive Group II Photos-351
51Laval Dairy QSHL-92
51Laval Dairy Subset-92
52St. Lawrence Sales-1
54Parkhurst-97
54Parkhurst-98
54Parkhurst-99
55Parkhurst-50
55Parkhurst-71
55Parkhurst-75
Quaker Oats-50
Quaker Oats-71
Quaker Oats-75
57Parkhurst-M15
58Parkhurst-11
58Parkhurst-21
58Parkhurst-22
58Parkhurst-26
58Parkhurst-35
58Parkhurst-39
59Parkhurst-41
60Parkhurst-53
60Shirriff Coins-21
60York Photos-27
61Parkhurst-49
61Shirriff/Salada Coins-113
61York Yellow Backs-23
62Parkhurst-49
62Shirriff Coins-25
62Shirriff Coins-43
62Shirriff Coins-58
62Shirriff Coins-59
62York Iron-On Transfers-2
63Topps-45
64Beehive Group III Photos-146
64Coca-Cola Caps-73
64Topps-68
64Toronto Star-37
680-Pee-Chee-181
Puck Stickers-15
690-Pee-Chee-180
690-Pee-Chee-207
Four-in-One-15
70Dad's Cookies-102
70Esso Power Players-19
70Maple Leafs Postcards-11
700-Pee-Chee-222
70Post Shooters-13
70Sargent Promotions Stamps-199
71Colgate Heads-10
71Frito-Lay-9
71Letraset Action Replays-9
71Maple Leafs Postcards-16
71Mattel Mini-Records-8
710-Pee-Chee-195
710-Pee-Chee-256
O-Pee-Chee/Topps Booklets-4
Posters-15
71Topps-6
71Topps-10
71Toronto Sun-269
72Maple Leafs Postcards-24
72Maple Leafs Postcards-25
720-Pee-Chee-92
72Sargent Promotions Stamps-207
72Topps-24
72Finnish Semic World Championship-169
72Swedish Semic World Championship-169
73Mac's Milk-22
740-Pee-Chee WHA-64
750-Pee-Chee WHA-34
81TCMA-12
83Canadiens Postcards-22
83Hall of Fame-76
83Hall of Fame Postcards-F10
85Hall of Fame-76
91Kraft-6
91Kraft-76
91Pro Set-341
French-341
92Blues UD Best of the Blues-22
92Hall of Fame Legends-11
92Parkhurst Parkie Reprints-PR1
93High Liner Greatest Goalies-10
930-Pee-Chee Canadiens Hockey Fest-32
930-Pee-Chee Canadiens Hockey Fest-40
930-Pee-Chee Canadiens Hockey Fest-59
93Parkhurst Parkie Reprints-PR43
94Hall of Fame Tickets-10
94Parkhurst Missing Link-72
94Parkhurst Missing Link-135
94Parkhurst Missing Link-151
94Parkhurst Missing Link-161
94Parkhurst Missing Link-163
94Parkhurst Tall Boys-100
99Upper Deck Century Legends-9
Century Collection-9
All Century Team-AC6
Century Artifacts-C9
Essence of the Game-E5
99Upper Deck Retro-90
Gold-90
Platinum-90
00BAP Memorabilia Goalie Memorabilia-G15
00BAP Memorabilia Goalie Memorabilia-G23
00BAP Ultimate Memorabilia Captain's C-C8
00BAP Ultimate Mem Goalie Memorabilia-GM1
00BAP Ultimate Mem Goalie Memorabilia-GM10
00BAP Ultimate Mem Goalie Memorabilia-GM14
00BAP Ultimate Mem Goalie Memorabilia-GM16
00BAP Ultimate Mem Goalie Memorabilia-GM17
00BAP Ultimate Mem Plante Jersey Cards-PJ1
00BAP Ultimate Mem Plante Jersey Cards-PJ2
00BAP Ultimate Mem Plante Jersey Cards-PJ3
00BAP Ultimate Mem Plante Jersey Cards-PJ4
00BAP Ultimate Mem Plante Jersey Cards-PJ5
00BAP Ultimate Mem Plante Jersey Cards-PJ6
00BAP Ultimate Mem Plante Jersey Cards-PJ7
00BAP Ultimate Mem Plante Jersey Cards-PJ8
00BAP Ultimate Mem Plante Jersey Cards-PJ9
00BAP Ultimate Mem Plante Jersey Cards-PJ10
00BAP Ultimate Mem Plante Jersey Cards-PJ11
00BAP Ultimate Mem Plante Jersey Cards-PJ12
00BAP Ultimate Mem Plante Jersey Cards-PJ13
00BAP Ultimate Mem Plante Jersey Cards-PJ14
00BAP Ultimate Mem Plante Jersey Cards-PJ15
00BAP Ultimate Mem Plante Skate Cards-PS1
00BAP Ultimate Mem Plante Skate Cards-PS2
00BAP Ultimate Mem Plante Skate Cards-PS3
00BAP Ultimate Mem Plante Skate Cards-PS4
00BAP Ultimate Mem Plante Skate Cards-PS5
00BAP Ultimate Mem Plante Skate Cards-PS6
00BAP Ultimate Mem Plante Skate Cards-PS7
00BAP Ultimate Mem Plante Skate Cards-PS8
00BAP Ultimate Mem Plante Skate Cards-PS9
00BAP Ultimate Mem Plante Skate Cards-PS10
00BAP Ultimate Mem Plante Skate Cards-PS11
00BAP Ultimate Mem Plante Skate Cards-PS12
00BAP Ultimate Mem Plante Skate Cards-PS13
00BAP Ultimate Mem Plante Skate Cards-PS14
00BAP Ultimate Mem Plante Skate Cards-PS15
00BAP Ultimate Memorabilia NHL Records-R4
00BAP Ultimate Memorabilia Retro-Active-RA8
00Upper Deck Legends-66
Legendary Collection Bronze-66
Legendary Collection Gold-66
Legendary Collection Silver-66
of the Cage-LC8
01BAP Memorabilia Goalie Traditions-GT5
01BAP Memorabilia Goalie Traditions-GT28
01BAP Memorabilia Goalie Traditions-GT29
01BAP Memorabilia Goalie Traditions-GT40
01BAP Memorabilia Rocket's Mates-RM1
01BAP Ultimate Mem All-Star History-11
01BAP Ultimate Mem Complete Package-7
01BAP Ultimate Memorabilia Decades-4
01BAP Ultimate Memorabilia Emblem Attic-14
01BAP Ultimate Memorabilia Les Canadiens-18
01BAP Ultimate Mem Prototypical Players-1
01BAP Ultimate Mem Prototypical Players-2
01BAP Ultimate Mem Prototypical Players-3
01BAP Ultimate Mem Retired Numbers-19
01BAP Ultimate Mem Retro Teammates-2
01BAP Ultimate Mem Stanley Cup Winners-7
01Between the Pipes-122
01Between the Pipes-136
He Shoots-He Saves Points-15
Jersey and Stick Cards-GSJ40
Masks-1
Masks Silver-1
Masks Gold-1
Record Breakers-RB2
Record Breakers-RB3
Record Breakers-RB13
Trophy Winners-TW4
Trophy Winners-TW18
Vintage Memorabilia-VM5
01Parkhurst He Shoots-He Scores Points-7
01Parkhurst He Shoots-He Scores Prizes-36
01Parkhurst Heroes-H9
01Parkhurst Reprints-PR10
01Parkhurst Reprints-PR34
01Parkhurst Reprints-PR47
01Parkhurst Reprints-PR66
01Parkhurst Reprints-PR85
01Parkhurst Reprints-PR128
01Parkhurst Reprints-PR138
01Parkhurst Vintage Memorabilia-PV4
01Parkhurst Vintage Memorabilia-PV5
01Parkhurst Vintage Memorabilia-PV6
01Parkhurst Vintage Memorabilia-PV7
01Parkhurst Vintage Memorabilia-PV8
01Topps Archives-6
01UD Stanley Cup Champs-16
Champion Signatures-JP
01Upper Deck Legendary Cut Signatures-LCJP
01Upper Deck Legends-33
01Upper Deck Legends-84
Fiorentino Collection-FCJP
Sticks-PHJP
02BAP Memorabilia-234
Emerald-234
Ruby-234
Sapphire-234
NHL All-Star Game-234
NHL All-Star Game Blue-234
NHL All-Star Game Green-234
NHL All-Star Game Red-234
02BAP Memorabilia Toronto Fall Expo-234
02BAP NHL All-Star History-11
02BAP Ultimate Mem Blades of Steel-6
02BAP Ultimate Mem Complete Package-4
02BAP Ultimate Memorabilia Cup Duels-2
02BAP Ultimate Memorabilia Cup Duels-3
02BAP Ultimate Memorabilia Emblem Attic-11
02BAP Ultimate Memorabilia Great Moments-11
02BAP Ultimate Memorabilia Legend-7
02BAP Ultimate Memorabilia Number Ones-4
02BAP Ultimate Memorabilia Numerology-3
02BAP Ultimate Mem Paper Cuts Autos-24
02BAP Ultimate Mem Retro Teammates-7
02BAP Ultimate Memorabilia Retro Trophies-10
02BAP Ultimate Mem Storied Franchise-5
02BAP Ultimate Mem Vintage Jerseys-21
02Between the Pipes-113
Complete Package-CP4
Double Memorabilia-18
Inspirations-I1
Record Breakers-4
Trappers-GT8
Vintage Memorabilia-10
02ITG Used Vintage Memorabilia-VM2
02ITG Used Vintage Memorabilia Gold-VM2
02Parkhurst Reprints-251
02Parkhurst Retro Nicknames-RN21
02UD Foundations Last Impressions Sticks-L-JP
02UD Mask Collection Mini Masks-JP1
02UD Mask Collection Mini Masks-JP2
03Backcheck: A Hockey Retrospective-16
03BAP Memorabilia Brush with Greatness-8
03BAP Mem Brush with Greatness Contest C-8
03BAP Memorabilia Gloves-GUG6
03BAP Ultimate Memorabilia Cornerstones-1
03BAP Ultimate Memorabilia Cornerstones-2
03BAP Ultimate Memorabilia Emblem Attic-15
03BAP Ultimate Mem Emblem Attic Gold-15
03BAP Ultimate Memorabilia Heroes-8
03BAP Ultimate Mem Jersey and Stick-24
03BAP Ultimate Mem Jersey and Stick Gold-24
03BAP Ultimate Memorabilia Paper Cuts-1
03BAP Ultimate Mem Raised to the Rafters-16
03BAP Ultimate Mem Retro Teammates-2
03BAP Ultimate Mem Retro-Active Trophies-15
03BAP Ultimate Memorabilia Triple Threads-8
03BAP Ultimate Mem Vintage Blade of Steel-12
03BAP Ultimate Mem Vint Complete Jersey-10
03BAP Ultimate Mem Vint Comp Jersey Gold-10
03BAP Ultimate Mem Vint Complete Package-2
03BAP Ultimate Mem Vint Comp Package Gold-2
03BAP Ultimate Mem Vintage Jerseys-5
03BAP Ultimate Mem Vintage Jerseys Gold-5
03BAP Ultimate Memorabilia Vintage Lumber-10
03Canada Post-6
03ITG Toronto Fall Expo Forever Rivals-FR7
03ITG Used Sig Series Triple Mem-23
03ITG Used Sig Series Triple Mem Gold-23
03ITG Used Sig Series Vintage Mem -30
03ITG Used Sig Series Vintage Mem Gold-30
03ITG VIP Collages-28
03ITG VIP MVP-7
03ITG VIP Vintage Memorabilia-12
03Parkhurst Orig Six He Shoots/Scores-12
03Parkhurst Orig Six He Shoots/Scores-12A
03Parkhurst Original Six Montreal-59
03Parkhurst Original Six Montreal-67
03Parkhurst Original Six Montreal-95
Inserts-M1
Inserts-M9
Memorabilia-MM17
Memorabilia-MM34
Memorabilia-MM36
Memorabilia-MM51
Memorabilia-MM63
03Parkhurst Orig Six New York Mem-NM22
03Parkhurst Rookie Before the Mask-BTM-6
03Parkhurst Rookie Before the Mask Gold-BTM-6
04ITG NHL AS FANtasy AS History Jerseys-SB11
04ITG Franchises Canadian-40
Barn Burners-BB7
Barn Burners Gold-BB7
Complete Jerseys-CJ1
Complete Jerseys Gold-CJ1
Double Memorabilia-DM7
Double Memorabilia Gold-DM7
Forever Rivals-FR1
Forever Rivals Gold-FR1
Goalie Gear-GG5
Goalie Gear Gold-GG5
Memorabilia-SM1
Memorabilia Gold-SM1
Original Sticks-OS11
Original Sticks Gold-OS11
Teammates-TM4
Teammates Gold-TM4
Triple Memorabilia-TM4
Triple Memorabilia Gold-TM4
Trophy Winners-TW2
Trophy Winners Gold-TW2
04ITG Franchises He Shoots/Scores Prizes-7
04ITG Franchises Update Goalie Gear-UGG1
04ITG Franchises Update Goalie Gear Gold-UGG1
04ITG Franchises US East-313
04ITG Franchises US West-291
04ITG Ultimate Memorabilia-152
04ITG Ultimate Memorabilia-173
04ITG Ultimate Memorabilia-191
Gold-152
Gold-173
Gold-191
Archives 1st Edition-13
Archives 1st Edition-20
Archives 1st Edition-35
Blades of Steel-4
Bleu Blanc et Rouge-7
Changing the Game-6
Complete Jerseys-12
Complete Package-5
Cornerstones-10
Cornerstones Gold-10
Day In History-11
Day In History Gold-11
Emblem Attic-1
Emblem Attic Gold-1
Goalie Gear-2
Hart Trophy-3
Jersey and Sticks-19
Jersey and Sticks Gold-19
Nicknames-4
Original Six-6
Original Six-14
Paper Cuts Memorabilia-8
Raised to the Rafters-2
Retro Teammates-2
Vezina Trophy-1
Vintage Lumber-14
04UD Legends Classics Jersey Redemptions-JY6
04ITG Heroes and Prospects-164
Aspiring-12
Hero Memorabilia-12
04ITG Heroes/Prospects Toronto Expo '05-164
04ITG Heroes/Prospects Expo Heroes/Pros-164
05Between the Pipes-14
Complete Package-CP-3
Pads-GUP-7
05ITG Ultimate Memorabilia Level 1-52
05ITG Ultimate Memorabilia Level 2-52
05ITG Ultimate Memorabilia Level 3-52
05ITG Ultimate Memorabilia Level 4-52
05ITG Ultimate Memorabilia Level 5-52
05ITG Ultimate Mem Blades of Steel-16
05ITG Ultimate Mem Blades of Steel Gold-16
05ITG Ultimate Mem Bleu Blanc Rouge Autos-1
05ITG Ultimate Mem Complete Package-4
05ITG Ultimate Mem Complete Package Gold-4
05ITG Ultimate Mem Cornerstones Jerseys-3
05ITG Ultimate Mem Cornerst Jerseys Gold-3
05ITG Ultimate Mem Decades Jerseys-3
05ITG Ultimate Mem Decades Jerseys-5
05ITG Ultimate Mem Decades Jerseys Gold-3
05ITG Ultimate Mem Decades Jerseys Gold-5
05ITG Ultimate Mem Double Mem-18
05ITG Ultimate Mem Double Mem Gold-18
05ITG Ultimate Memorabilia Emblem Attic-20
05ITG Ultimate Mem Emblem Attic Gold-20
05ITG Ultimate Memorabilia Gloves Are Off-13
05ITG Ultimate Mem Gloves Are Off Gold-13
05ITG Ultimate Memorabilia Goalie Gear-11
05ITG Ultimate Mem Goalie Gear Gold-11
05ITG Ultimate Memorabilia Jerseys-18
05ITG Ultimate Memorabilia Jerseys Gold-18
05ITG Ultimate Mem Pass the Torch Jerseys-2
05ITG Ultimate Mem Passing Torch Jsy Gold-2
05ITG Ultimate Mem Quad Paper Cuts Autos-4
05ITG Ultimate Mem Sticks and Jerseys-30
05ITG Ultimate Mem Stick and Jerseys Gold-30
05ITG Ultimate Mem 3 Star of the Game Jsy-4
05ITG Ult Mem 3 Star of the Game Jsy Gold-4
05ITG Ultimate Mem Triple Threads Jerseys-8
05ITG Ultimate Mem Triple Thread Jsy Gold-8
05ITG Ultimate Mem Ult Hero Double Jersey-3
05ITG Ult Mem Ult Hero Double Jersey Gold-3
05ITG Ultimate Mem Ult Hero Single Jersey-3
05ITG Ult Mem Ult Hero Single Jersey Gold-3
05ITG Ultimate Mem Ult Hero Triple Jersey-3
05ITG Ult Mem Ult Hero Triple Jersey Gold-3
05ITG Ultimate Memorabilia Vintage Lumber-3
05ITG Ultimate Mem Vintage Lumber Gold-3
05NHL Legends Medallions-15
05The Cup Legendary Cuts-LCJP
05ITG Heroes and Prospects Hero Mem-HM-36
06Between The Pipes-128
06Between The Pipes-141
Complete Package-CP04
Complete Package Gold-CP04
Double Jerseys-DJ13
Double Jerseys Gold-DJ13
Double Memorabilia-DM13
Double Memorabilia Gold-DM13
Gloves-GG15
Gloves Gold-GG15
Pads-GP05
Pads Gold-GP05
Shooting Gallery-SG01
Shooting Gallery-SG09
Shooting Gallery-SG10
Shooting Gallery Gold-SG01
Shooting Gallery Gold-SG09
Shooting Gallery Gold-SG10
Stick and Jersey-SJ25
Stick and Jersey Gold-SJ25
The Mask-M34
The Mask Gold-M34
The Mask Silver-M34
The Mask Game-Used-MGU15
The Mask Game-Used Gold-MGU15
06ITG Ultimate Memorabilia-71
Artist Proof-71
Blades of Steel-17
Blades of Steel Gold-17
Bleu Blanc et Rouge Autos-5
Cornerstones-10
Cornerstones Gold-10
Decades-3
Decades-6
Decades Gold-3
Decades Gold-6
Double Memorabilia-26
Double Memorabilia Gold-26
Emblem Attic-12
Emblem Attic Gold-12
Gloves Are Off-11
Gloves Are Off Gold-11
Passing The Torch-4
Passing The Torch Gold-4
Retro Teammates-4
Retro Teammates Gold-4
Road to the Cup-2
Road to the Cup Gold-2
Stick Rack-2
Stick Rack-4
Stick Rack-20
Stick Rack Gold-2
Stick Rack Gold-4
Stick Rack Gold-20
Triple Thread Jerseys-10
Triple Thread Jerseys Gold-10
06ITG Heroes and Prospects Heroes Memorabilia-HM12
06ITG Heroes and Prospects Heroes Memorabilia Gold-HM12

Plante, Jean-Marc
94Birmingham Bulls-19

Plante, Jean-Marie
50Quebec Citadelles-17
51Laval Dairy Subset-67

Plante, Michel
73Vancouver Blazers-18

Plante, Philippe
92Quebec Pee-Wee Tournament-156
96Rimouski Oceanic-21
96Rimouski Oceanic Quebec Police-20
99Grand Rapids Griffins-18
99Bowman CHL-49
Gold-49
OPC International-49
00Austin Ice Bats-17
02Muskegon Fury-18
04Hamilton Bulldogs-24
05German DEL-92

Plante, Pierre
71Toronto Sun-206
72Blues White Border-16
73Blues White Border-15
730-Pee-Chee-255
74NHL Action Stamps-240
740-Pee-Chee NHL-149
740-Pee-Chee NHL-197
74Topps-149
74Topps-197
750-Pee-Chee NHL-309
75Topps-309
760-Pee-Chee NHL-371
770-Pee-Chee NHL-385
780-Pee-Chee-179
78Topps-179
790-Pee-Chee-275
800-Pee-Chee-369

Plante, Robert
99Alexandria Warthogs-14

Plante, Tyler
04Brandon Wheat Kings-24
05ITG Heroes/Prosp Toronto Expo Parallel -162
05Brandon Wheat Kings-18
05ITG Heroes and Prospects-162
Autographs-A-TPL
06Between The Pipes-51
Autographs-ATP
Prospect Trios-PT10
Prospect Trios Gold-PT10
06ITG Heroes and Prospects Jerseys-GUJ50
06ITG Heroes and Prospects Jerseys Gold-GUJ50
06ITG Heroes and Prospects Emblems-GUE50
06ITG Heroes and Prospects Emblems Gold-GUE50
06ITG Heroes and Prospects Numbers-GUN50
06ITG Heroes and Prospects Numbers Gold-GUN50
06ITG Heroes and Prospects Quad Emblems-QE08
06ITG Heroes and Prospects Quad Emblems Gold-QE08

Plaquin, Ken
90Michigan Tech Huskies-21
91Michigan Tech Huskies-20
91Michigan Tech Huskies-34
94Central Hockey League-84
94San Antonio Iguanas-12
95Central Hockey League-101
99Asheville Smoke-15

Plasek, Karel
96Czech APS Extraliga-164
97Czech APS Extraliga-261
98Czech OFS-159
99Czech DS-195
99Czech OFS-81
00Czech OFS-200
02Czech OFS Plus-114
03Czech OFS Plus-246
04Czech OFS-305
05Czech HC Znojmo-11
06Czech OFS-210

Plass, Martin
06Swedish SHL Elitset-38

Plasse, Michel
72Canadiens Postcards-16
72Dimanche/Derniere Heure *-161
72Dimanche/Derniere Heure *-162
73Canadiens Postcards-17
730-Pee-Chee-252
74NHL Action Stamps-303
74NHL Action Stamps Update-28
740-Pee-Chee NHL-257
74Topps-257
750-Pee-Chee NHL-249
75Topps-249
760-Pee-Chee NHL-172
76Rockies Coke Cans-16
76Rockies Puck Bucks-15
76Topps-172
770-Pee-Chee NHL-92
77Rockies Coke Cans-15
77Topps-92
780-Pee-Chee-36
78Topps-36
790-Pee-Chee-69
79Rockies Team Issue-17
79Topps-69
80Nordiques Postcards-22
80Pepsi-Cola Caps-74
81Nordiques Postcards-13
810-Pee-Chee-281

Plasse, Steve
88Richelieu Riverains-22

Plasszcz, Brian
05Maine Black Bears-20

Plastino, Nicholas
04Barrie Colts-4
06Barrie Colts-6

Plata, Ed
52Juniors Blue Tint-148

Plate, Carsten
94German First League-452

Platil, Jan
00Barrie Colts-19
01Barrie Colts-19
02Barrie Colts-22
03Binghamton Senators-16
04Barrie Colts 10th Anniversary-11
04Binghamton Senators-13
05Binghamton Senators-5
05Binghamton Senators Quickway-5
06Finnish Cardset-286
Enforcers-6
06Binghamton Senators 5th Anniversary-23

Platisha, J.P.
02Topeka Scarecrows-8

Platonov, Denis
02Russian Hockey League-25
03Russian Hockey League-156

Platt, Geoff
03Erie Otters-21
03Saginaw Spirit-17
04Erie Otters-6
04Erie Otters-NNO
05ITG Heroes/Prosp Toronto Expo Parallel -242
05Black Diamond-231
05Hot Prospects-124
En Fuego-124
Red Hot-124
White Hot-124
05SP Authentic-259
Limited-259
05SPx-255
05The Cup Masterpiece Pressplate Artifact-269
05The Cup Master Pressplate Black Diamond-231
05The Cup Masterpiece Pressplates (Ice)-228
05The Cup Master Pressplate Rookie Update-125
05The Cup Masterpiece Pressplates SPA-259
05The Cup Masterpiece Pressplates (SPx)-255
05The Cup Masterpiece Pressplates Trilogy-248
05UD Artifacts-269
05Upper Deck Ice-228
05Upper Deck Rookie Update-125
05Upper Deck Trilogy-248
05AHL Top Prospects-32
05Syracuse Crunch-6
05ITG Heroes and Prospects-242
Autographs Series II-GPL
06Syracuse Crunch-7
06ITG Heroes and Prospects-167
Autographs-AGP
Update Autographs-AGP

Platt, Jason
06Augusta Lynx-16

Platt, Jayme
01Greenville Grrrowl-21
03UK Manchester Phoenix-1
04UK Sheffield Steelers-1
05Danbury Trashers-9

Platt, Spencer
95Neepewa Natives-9

Plattner, Herbert
94German First League-595

Plattner, Toni
94German DEL-285

Plavsic, Adrien
89Blues Kodak-23
89ProCards IHL-14
90Bowman-62
Tiffany-62
90Canucks Mohawk-24
90OPC Premier-90
90Pro Set-644
90Score-394
Canadian-394
91Alberta International Team Canada-17
91Bowman-312
91Canucks Panini Team Stickers-19
91Canucks Autograph Cards-20
91Canucks Team Issue 8x10-20
910-Pee-Chee-162
91Stadium Club-196
91Topps-162
91Upper Deck-424
French-424
92Bowman-363
92Canucks Road Trip Art-18
920-Pee-Chee-156
92Score-531
Canadian-531
Canadian Olympians-11
92Stadium Club-15
92Topps-323
Gold-323G
92Ultra-428
92Upper Deck-519
93OPC Premier-201
Gold-201
93Score-358
Canadian-358
93Stadium Club-201
Members Only Master Set-201
OPC-201
First Day Issue-201
First Day Issue OPC-201
93Topps/OPC Premier-201
Gold-201
94Canucks Program Inserts-18
94Lightning Photo Album-20
94Upper Deck-381
Electric Ice-381
95Collector's Choice-233
Player's Club-233
Player's Club Platinum-233
95Atlanta Knights-16
98Swiss Power Play Stickers-234
99Swiss Panini Stickers-233
00Swiss Panini Stickers-273
00Swiss Slapshot Mini-Cards-ZSCL2
01Swiss HNL-5

Plavucha, Vlastimil
94Finnish Jaa Kiekko-208
95Slovakian APS National Team-15
00Swiss Panini Stickers-191
00Swiss Slapshot Mini-Cards-LT15
01Slovakian Kvarteto-6B

Playfair, Jim
84Nova Scotia Oilers-17
85Nova Scotia Oilers-22
88Oilers Tenth Anniversary-142
89ProCards IHL-62
90ProCards AHL/IHL-398
91ProCards-479
92Indianapolis Ice-20
94Dayton Bombers-20
95Dayton Bombers-1
95Dayton Bombers-25
96Michigan K-Wings-24

Playfair, Larry
800-Pee-Chee-296
81Sabres Milk Panels-10
82Post Cereal-2
82Sabres Milk Panels-10
840-Pee-Chee-26
840-Pee-Chee Stickers-207
84Sabres Blue Shield-14
84Topps-20
84Kelowna Wings-38
850-Pee-Chee-131
85Sabres Blue Shield-20
85Sabres Blue Shield Small-20
85Topps-131
86Kings 20th Anniversary Team Issue-18
860-Pee-Chee-195
86Topps-195
870-Pee-Chee-57
870-Pee-Chee Stickers-211
87Topps-57
88Sabres Blue Shield-18
88Sabres Wonder Bread/Hostess-20
89Sabres Blue Shield-15
89Sabres Campbell's-18
02Fleer Throwbacks-51
Gold-51
Platinum-51
Autographs-15
04ITG Franchises US East-346
Autographs-A-LP

Plch, Jan
02Czech OFS Plus-115

Pleau, Larry
69Canadiens Postcards Color-20
70Sargent Promotions Stamps-107
70Swedish Masterserien-180
71Canadiens Postcards-17
71Sargent Promotions Stamps-100
71Toronto Sun-160
72Whalers New England WHA-12
72Finnish Semic World Championship-229
72Swedish Semic World Championship-229
73Quaker Oats WHA-18
750-Pee-Chee WHA-56
760-Pee-Chee WHA-26

Pleau, Steve
03Worcester Ice Cats-28
04Worcester IceCats-24
05Peoria Rivermen-24

Pleckaitis, Joe
05Ottawa 67's-21
06Barrie Colts-24

Plekanec, Tomas
00Czech OFS-129
01Czech OFS-181
01Czech OFS Red Inserts-RE3D
02Czech DS-48
02Czech DS-69
02Hamilton Bulldogs-7
03BAP Memorabilia-214
03Beehive-207
Gold-207
Silver-207
03ITG Used Signature Series-183
Gold-183
03ITG VIP Rookie Debut-94
03Pacific Complete-540
Red-540
03Parkhurst Original Six Montreal-1
03Parkhurst Rookie-160
03SP Game Used-130
03UD Premier Collection-64
03Upper Deck Classic Portraits-196
03Upper Deck Rookie Update-122
03Pacific AHL Prospects-30
Gold-30
Jerseys-3
04Pacific-286
Blue-286
Red-286
04AHL All-Stars-35
04AHL Top Prospects-16
04Hamilton Bulldogs-23
05ITG Heroes/Prosp Toronto Expo Parallel -263
05Canadiens Team Issue-16
05Parkhurst-259
Facsimile Auto Parallel-259
05Upper Deck-351
05ITG Heroes and Prospects-263
Autographs Series II-TPC
06Canadiens Postcards-17
06Gatorade-44
060-Pee-Chee-268
Rainbow-268
06Czech IIHF World Championship Postcards-15
06Czech OFS Jagr Team-13

Plekhanov, Dmitri
98Russian Hockey League-115
01Russian Hockey League-153

Plenty, Michael
01UK Guildford Flames-3

Plenzich, Mark
03Yarmouth Mariners-18

Pleschberger, Achim
95Swiss HNL-479

Plesh, Mike
83Kingston Canadians-6
84Kingston Canadians-10

Pletka, Vaclav
98Czech OFS-190
99Czech OFS-200
99Czech OFS-483
01BAP Memorabilia-311
Emerald-311
Ruby-311
Sapphire-311
01Bowman YoungStars-121
Gold-121
Ice Cubed-121
01Parkhurst-337
01SP Authentic-168
Limited-168
Limited Gold-168
01SP Game Used-92
01Topps Chrome-180
Refractors-180
Black Border Refractors-180
01UD Challenge for the Cup-127
01UD Premier Collection-77
01Upper Deck Ice-81
02Czech OFS Plus-311
02Czech OFS Plus-364
Trios-T17
Duos-D9
02Czech National Team Postcards-10
03Czech OFS Plus-297
03Czech OFS Plus All-Star Game-H37
03Czech OFS Plus Insert H-H10
04Czech OFS-218
05Czech HC Trinec-10
06Czech CP Cup Postcards-15
06Czech HC Liberec Postcards-7
06Czech OFS-99
06Czech Super Six Postcards-9

Pletsch, Fred
52Juniors Blue Tint-101

Plett, Tim
01Moose Jaw Warriors-11
04Huntsville Havoc-6
04Memphis RiverKings-19

Plett, Willi
770-Pee-Chee NHL-17
77Topps-17
78Flames Majik Market-25
780-Pee-Chee-317
79Flames Postcards-12
79Flames Team Issue-13
790-Pee-Chee-382
80Flames Postcards-14
800-Pee-Chee-320
80Pepsi-Cola Caps-12
81Flames Postcards-16
810-Pee-Chee-35
810-Pee-Chee Stickers-222
81Post Standups-27
81Topps-26
82North Stars Postcards-19
820-Pee-Chee-173
82Post Cereal-3
83NHL Key Tags-62
83North Stars Postcards-23
830-Pee-Chee-179
84North Stars 7-Eleven-2
84North Stars Postcards-22
85North Stars 7-Eleven-7
85North Stars Postcards-24
86North Stars 7-Eleven-3
86North Stars Postcards-6
87Panini Stickers-302
88Bruins Sports Action-19
02Fleer Throwbacks-43
Gold-43
Platinum-43
02UD Foundations-12
Calder Winners-TWP
Calder Winners Gold-TWP
Calder Winners Silver-T-WP
Canadian Heroes-CWP
Canadian Heroes Gold-CWP
Canadian Heroes Silver-C-WP
Power Stations-SWP
Power Stations Gold-SWP
Power Stations Silver-S-WP
04UD Legendary Signatures-72
Autographs-WP
06Parkhurst-98
06Parkhurst-246
Autographs-98
Autographs-246
Autographs Dual-DAPP

Pleva, Jan

00Czech OFS-259
Plihal, Tomas
02Kootenay Ice-3
03Cleveland Barons-18
04Cleveland Barons-18
05Cleveland Barons-17
Plodek, Jan
99Czech Score Blue 2000-78
99Czech Score Red Ice 2000-78
02Czech OFS Plus-163
03Czech OFS Plus-122
04Czech OFS-75
06Czech OFS-100
Team Cards-4
Plodek, Milan
99Czech Score Blue 2000-81
99Czech Score Red Ice 2000-81
Plommer, Tommy
93UK Sheffield Steelers-7
94UK Sheffield Steelers-17
95UK Sheffield Steelers-5
97UK Sheffield Steelers-5
99UK Sheffield Steelers-15
00UK Sheffield Steelers Centurions-2
Plotka, Wolfgang
70Finnish Jaakiekko-94
70Swedish Hockey-372
70Swedish Masterserien-176
04German Berlin Eisbarens 50th Anniv-54
Plotnikov, Alexei
99Russian Hockey League-97
00Russian Hockey League-21
Plouffe, Bertrand Pierre
99Rouyn-Noranda Huskies-15
00Rouyn-Noranda Huskies-6
Signed-6
01Sherbrooke Castors-15
Plouffe, Olivier
03Victoriaville Tigers-19
Plouffe, Sebastien
90Montreal-Bourassa AAA-20
Plouffe, Steve
95Central Hockey League-12
95Fort Worth Fire-18
96Fort Worth Fire-7
97Johnstown Chiefs-11
98Fort Worth Brahmas-2
99Russian Hockey League-124
99Fort Worth Brahmas-14
00Russian Hockey League-4
02Russian Hockey League-28
02Russian Transfert-30
02Russian Ultimate Line-6
Plourde, Alexandre
93Quebec Pee-Wee Tournament-1359
Plourde, Jean-Francois
00Rimouski Oceanic-9
Signed-9
01Rimouski Oceanic-9
03Columbus Cottonmouths-28
03ECHL All-Stars-277
04Atlantic City Boardwalk Bullies-28
05Fresno Falcons-17
Plsek, David
99Czech Score Blue 2000-120
99Czech Score Red Ice 2000-120
Plsek, Lukas
00Czech OFS-322
02Czech OFS Plus-73
02Czech OFS Plus Masks-M5
04Czech OFS-257
Pluck, David
92Windsor Spitfires-7
93Windsor Spitfires-7
94Windsor Spitfires-9
Plumb, Andrew
92British Columbia JHL-152
96Dayton Ice Bandits-13
97Bakersfield Fog-14
Plumb, Randy
81Kingston Canadians-25
Plumb, Ron
72Philadelphia Blazers-3
73Vancouver Blazers-19
74San Diego Mariners WHA-6
75O-Pee-Chee WHA-98
75Stingers Kahn's-10
76O-Pee-Chee WHA-94
76Stingers Kahn's-6
77O-Pee-Chee WHA-24
79O-Pee-Chee-328
Plume, Clay
01Lethbridge Hurricanes-18
Plumhoff, Chris
98Huntington Blizzard-22
00Charlotte Checkers-27
Plumton, Brad
06Westside Warriors-15
Plunkett, Lindsay
97Guelph Storm-13
98Guelph Storm-11
99Guelph Storm-11
00St. Michaels Majors-22
Pluss, Benjamin
93Quebec Pee-Wee Tournament-1627
01Swiss HNL-207
02Swiss HNL-110
Pluss, Martin
96Swiss HNL-23
98Swiss Power Play Stickers-118
98Swiss Power Play Stickers-262
99Swiss Panini Stickers-120
99Swiss Panini Stickers-271
00Swiss Panini Stickers-164
00Swiss Panini Stickers National Team-P29
00Swiss Slapshot Mini-Cards-EHCK12
01Swiss HNL-71
02Swiss HNL-129
02Swiss HNL-246
02Swiss HNL-486
04Swedish Elitset-177
Dominators-7
Gold-177
04Swedish Pure Skills-22
Parallel-22
05Swedish SHL Elitset-34
Pluss, Winners
02Swiss HNL-241
Plyuschev, Alexander
04Russian Under-18 Team-17
Plyustchev, Vladimir
02Russian SL-8
Poapst, Steve
91Hampton Roads Admirals-15
92Hampton Roads Admirals-4
93Portland Pirates-7
94Portland Pirates-20
95Portland Pirates-19
96Portland Pirates-3
96Portland Pirates Shop N' Save-2
97Portland Pirates-20
98Hampton Roads Admirals 10th Anniversary-17
98Portland Pirates-14
99Portland Pirates-19
01Upper Deck Ice-132
02Blackhawks Postcards-2
03Blackhawks Postcards-19
03ITG Action-109
03Parkhurst Original Six Chicago-23
Pobiak, Adam
97Dubuque Fighting Saints-23
Pochipinski, Trevor
91ProCards-378
92Wheeling Thunderbirds-12
Pochon, Steve
96Swiss HNL-361
00Swiss Panini Stickers-70
01Swiss HNL-419
02Swiss HNL-373
Pochyly, Bobby
99Fort Worth Brahmas-15
Pock, Thomas
03BAP Memorabilia-238
03ITG VIP Rookie Debut-145
03Parkhurst Rookie-73
03UD Premier Collection-104
03Upper Deck Rookie Update-186
04Hartford Wolf Pack-21
05ITG Heroes/Prosp Toronto Expo Parallel -272
05AHL All-Stars-28
05Hartford Wolf Pack-17
05ITG Heroes and Prospects-272
Autographs Series II-TPK
Pocock, Steven
93Quebec Pee-Wee Tournament-1169
Podalinski, Alex
98Tacoma Sabercats-17
99Jacksonville Lizard Kings-2
01Russian Hockey League-114
Poddubny, Walt
82Maple Leafs Postcards-29
82Post Cereal-18
83Maple Leafs Postcards-21
83NHL Key Tags-114
83O-Pee-Chee-339
83O-Pee-Chee Stickers-150
83Topps Stickers-150
83Vachon-96A
83Vachon-96B
84Maple Leafs Postcards-19
84O-Pee-Chee-309
85Maple Leafs Postcards-24
87O-Pee-Chee-142
87O-Pee-Chee Box Bottoms-K
87O-Pee-Chee Stickers-32
87Panini Stickers-112
87Topps-142
87Topps Box Bottoms-K
88Nordiques General Foods-30
88Nordiques Team Issue-26
88Oilers Tenth Anniversary-141
88O-Pee-Chee-170
88O-Pee-Chee Stickers-240
88Panini Stickers-309
88Topps-170
89Devils Caretta-19
89O-Pee-Chee-184
89O-Pee-Chee Stickers-85
89Topps-184
90Devils Team Issue-22
90O-Pee-Chee-426
90Pro Set-479
90Score-278
Canadian-278
91Score Canadian Bilingual-400
91Score Canadian English-400
91Stadium Club-177
97Anchorage Aces-2
98Anchorage Aces-11
99Anchorage Aces-21
01Anchorage Aces-19
Poddyakon, Andrei
00Russian Hockey League-87
Podein, Shjon
90ProCards AHL/IHL-229
91ProCards-218
92Oilers Team Issue-13
93Parkhurst-66
Emerald Ice-66
93PowerPlay-84
93Score-424
Canadian-424
93Stadium Club-474
Members Only Master Set-474
First Day Issue-474
93Ultra-140
93Upper Deck-60
93Classic Pro Prospects-9
94Leaf-531
94Parkhurst-81
Gold-81
94Ultra-346
94Upper Deck-356
Electric Ice-356
95Be A Player-77
Signatures-S77
Signatures Die Cuts-S77
95Canada Games NHL POGS-203
95Parkhurst International-426
Emerald Ice-426
95Upper Deck-150
Electric Ice-150
Electric Ice Gold-150
95Swedish World Championships Stickers-224
96Flyers Postcards-18
96Upper Deck-308
97Pacific Invincible NHL Regime-147
97Score Flyers-13
Platinum-13
Premier-13
97Upper Deck-328
98Pacific-330
Ice Blue-330
Red-330
98Upper Deck-337
Exclusives-337
Exclusives 1 of 1-337
Gold Reserve-337
99Avalanche Team Issue-17
99BAP Millennium-71
Emerald-71
Ruby-71
Sapphire-71
Signatures-71
Signatures Gold-71
00Pacific-118
Copper-118
Gold-118
Ice Blue-118
Premiere Date-118
00Upper Deck-48
Exclusives Tier 1-48
Exclusives Tier 2-48
01Avalanche Team Issue-4
01BAP Memorabilia-499
Emerald-499
Ruby-499
Sapphire-499
Stanley Cup Champions-CA5
01Pacific-104
Extreme LTD-104
Hobby LTD-104
Premiere Date-104
Retail LTD-104
01Pacific Arena Exclusives-104
01Parkhurst-362
02BAP Sig Series Auto Buybacks 1999-71
02Blues Team Issue-18
02Pacific Complete-297
Red-297
02Upper Deck Vintage-218
Podesva, Jiri
98Danish Hockey League-47
99Danish Hockey League-88
Podhradsky, Peter
01Cincinnati Mighty Ducks-17
03Czech OFS Plus-64
04Czech OFS-219
06German DEL-61
Podkonicky, Andrej
92Quebec Pee-Wee Tournament-1731
97Portland Winter Hawks-13
98Bowman CHL-56
Golden Anniversary-56
OPC International-56
98Bowman Chrome CHL-56
Golden Anniversary-56
Golden Anniversary Refractors-56
OPC International-56
OPC International Refractors-56
Refractors-56
00Louisville Panthers-17
01BAP Memorabilia-404
Emerald-404
Ruby-404
Sapphire-404
01Pacific-176
Extreme LTD-176
Hobby LTD-176
Premiere Date-176
Retail LTD-176
01Pacific Arena Exclusives-176
01SP Authentic-149
Limited-149
Limited Gold-149
01SPx-107
01UD Top Shelf-55
01UD Top Shelf-55B
01Upper Deck-191
Exclusives-191
01Upper Deck MVP-202
01Upper Deck Victory-373
Gold-373
01Finnish Cardset-209
02German DEL City Press-165
04Czech OFS-76
05Czech HC Liberec-8
06Czech OFS-101
Stars-2
Podlaha, Josef
94Czech APS Extraliga-248
99Czech OFS-141
Podlesak, Martin
00Lethbridge Hurricanes-19
01Lethbridge Hurricanes-9
01UD Prospects-36
Jerseys-J-PO
Jerseys-C-KP
Jerseys Gold-J-PO
Jerseys Gold-C-KP
03Springfield Falcons Postcards-8
04ITG Heroes and Prospects-41
Autographs-MP
Complete Emblems-22
He Shoots-He Scores Prizes-37
04ITG Heroes/Prospects Toronto Expo '05-41
04ITG Heroes/Prospects Expo Heroes/Pros-41
06Czech OFS-76
Podloski, Ray
86Moncton Golden Flames-26
88ProCards AHL-167
99Danish Hockey League-76
Podlubny, David
907th Inn. Sketch WHL-60
Podolka, Michal
95Slapshot-356
95Sault Ste. Marie Greyhounds-17
96Sault Ste. Marie Greyhounds-17
96Sault Ste. Marie Greyhounds Autographed-17
98Topeka Scarecrows-2
98Topeka Scarecrows-21
99Topeka Scarecrows-17
00Czech DS Extraliga-38
00Czech OFS-136
01Czech OFS Update-304
02Czech OFS Plus-203
Trios-T7
03Czech OFS Plus-298
06Czech OFS-150
Podollan, Jason
91British Columbia JHL-104
93Upper Deck Program of Excellence-E2
93Spokane Chiefs-20
94Spokane Chiefs-3
94Classic Tri-Cards-T25
94Signature Rookies Gold Standard *-90
95Donruss Elite World Juniors-20
95SP-172
95Spokane Chiefs-12
95Signature Rookies-13
Signatures-13
96SP-173
96Carolina Monarchs-20
97Collector's Choice-251
97Upper Deck-165
97St. John's Maple Leafs-21
99Lowell Lock Monsters-21
02German DEL City Press-251
03German DEL-11
03German Mannheim Eagles Postcards-13
04German Adler Mannheim Eagles Postcards-24
04German DEL-16
Podolsky, Nelson
51Laval Dairy Subset-59
Podomatski, Egor
99Russian Stars of Hockey-12
99Russian Fetisov Tribute-17
01Russian Ultimate Line-2
02Russian Hockey League-217
02Russian SL-11
02Russian World Championships-1
03Russian Postcards-5
03Russian World Championship Team 2003-2
04Russian Super League All-Stars-1
04Russian World Championship Team-25
Podrasky, Pete
02Cincinnati Mighty Ducks-A-14
Podrezov, Vadim
96Czech APS Extraliga-32
98Muskegon Fury-28
98UHL All-Stars-9
99Muskegon Fury-2
Podsiadlo, Krzysztof
89Swedish Semic World Champ Stickers-140
Podstavek, Albin
02Czech OFS Plus-140
Podwysocki, Bogdan
74Sioux City Musketeers-16
Poeschek, Rudy
84Kamloops Blazers-20
85Kamloops Blazers-19
86Kamloops Blazers-17
89Rangers Marine Midland Bank-29
90ProCards AHL/IHL-18
91Moncton Hawks-22
91ProCards-167
92St. John's Maple Leafs-16
93Lightning Season in Review-22
93Upper Deck-461
94Leaf-75
94Lightning Photo Album-21
94OPC Premier Special Effects-274
94Pinnacle-390
Artist's Proofs-390
Rink Collection-390
95Be A Player-53
Signatures-S53
Signatures Die Cuts-S53
95Lightning Team Issue-14
97Pacific Invincible NHL Regime-186
99Houston Aeros-11
02Fleer Throwbacks-37
Gold-37
Platinum-37
Stickwork-6
Poeta, Tony
52Juniors Blue Tint-110
Pogge, Justin
03Prince George Cougars-2
04Calgary Hitmen-15
05ITG Heroes/Prosp Toronto Expo Parallel -331
05Calgary Hitmen-16
05ITG Heroes and Prospects-331
Autographs Series II-JPG
Autographs Series II-BP
Complete Jerseys-CJ-37
Complete Jerseys Gold-CJ-37
Complete Logos-CHL-24
He Shoots-He Scores Prizes-60
Jerseys-GUJ-67
Jerseys Gold-GUJ-67
Emblems-GUE-67
Emblems Gold-GUE-67
Numbers-GUN-67
Numbers Gold-GUN-67
Measuring Up-MU19
Measuring Up Gold-MU19
Nameplates-N-45
Nameplates Gold-N-45
National Pride-NPR-32
Net Prospects Dual-NPD8
Net Prospects Dual Gold-NPD8
Spectrum-STM-09
Spectrum Gold-STM-09
06Between The Pipes-30
06Between The Pipes-122
Autographs-AJP
Autographs-AJP2
Double Jerseys-DJ15
Double Jerseys Gold-DJ15
Emblems-GUE51
Emblems Gold-GUE51
Emblems Autographs-GUE51
Jerseys-GUJ51
Jerseys Gold-GUJ51
Jerseys Autographs-GUJ51
Numbers-GUN51
Numbers Gold-GUN51
Numbers Autographs-GUN51
Playing For Your Country-PC18
Playing For Your Country Gold-PC18
Prospect Trios-PT18
Prospect Trios Gold-PT18
Shooting Gallery-SG02
Shooting Gallery Gold-SG02
06ITG International Ice-99
Gold-99
Autographs-AJP
Complete Jersey-CJ02
Complete Jersey Gold-CJ02
Goaltending Glory-GG04
Goaltending Glory Gold-GG04
International Rivals-IR19
International Rivals Gold-IR19
Passing The Torch-PTT3
Passing The Torch Gold-PTT3
Triple Memorabilia-TM08
Triple Memorabilia Gold-TM08
06ITG Ultimate Memorabilia Future Star-18
06ITG Ultimate Memorabilia Future Star Gold-18
06ITG Ultimate Memorabilia Future Star Autos-9
06ITG Ultimate Memorabilia Future Star Autos Gold-9
06ITG Ultimate Memorabilia Future Star Patches Autos-9
06ITG Ultimate Memorabilia Future Star Patches Autos Gold-9
06AHL Top Prospects-45
06Toronto Marlies-22
06ITG Heroes and Prospects-140
Autographs-AJP
Complete Jerseys-CJ17
Net Prospects-NPR08
Net Prospects-NPR13
Net Prospects Gold-NPR08
Quad Emblems-QE08
Quad Emblems Gold-QE08
Triple Memorabilia-TM05
Triple Memorabilia Gold-TM05
07ITG Going For Gold World Juniors-29
Autographs-29
Emblems-GUE26
Jerseys-GUJ26
Pogonin, Alexei
99Russian Hockey League-163
01Russian Hockey League-151
Pohanka, Igor
00Prince Albert Raiders-18
00UD CHL Prospects-75
01Prince Albert Raiders-16
02Prince Albert Raiders-18
03Cincinnati Mighty Ducks-B12
04Cincinnati Mighty Ducks-12
05Portland Pirates-17
Pohja, Hannu
70Finnish Jaakiekko-318
Pohja, Tommi
92Finnish Jyvas-Hyva Stickers-159
93Finnish Jyvas-Hyva Stickers-293
93Finnish SISU-77
Pohl, Anton
72Finnish Hellas-49
Pohl, John
98Minnesota Golden Gophers-29
99Minnesota Golden Gophers-19
00Minnesota Golden Gophers-18
01Minnesota Golden Gophers-10
02AHL Top Prospects-35
02Worcester IceCats-5
03BAP Memorabilia-247
03ITG Used Signature Series-164
Gold-164
03ITG VIP Rookie Debut-54
03Pacific Calder-133
Silver-133
03Pacific Complete-591
Red-591
03Pacific Heads-Up-131
Hobby LTD-131
Retail LTD-131
03Pacific Luxury Suite-75
Gold-75
03Pacific Quest for the Cup-133
03Parkhurst Rookie-154
Rookie Emblems-RE-16
Rookie Emblems Gold-RE-16
Rookie Jerseys-RJ-16
Rookie Jerseys Gold-RJ-16
Rookie Numbers-RN-16
Rookie Numbers Gold-RN-16
03SP Authentic-126
Limited-126
03SP Game Used-124
03SPx-230
Radiance-230
Spectrum-230
03Titanium-134
Hobby Jersey Number Parallels-134
Retail-134
Retail Jersey Number Parallels-134
03UD Honor Roll-166
03UD Premier Collection-84
03Upper Deck-461
Canadian Exclusives-461
HG-461
UD Exclusives-461
03Upper Deck Ice-120
Glass Parallel-120
03Upper Deck Rookie Update-102
03AHL Top Prospects-27
03Pacific AHL Prospects-99
Gold-99
03Worcester Ice Cats-8
03Worcester Ice Cats 10th Anniversary-18
04Worcester IceCats-6
04ITG Heroes and Prospects Emblems-28
04ITG Heroes and Prospects Emblems Gold-28
04ITG Heroes/Prospects He Shoots/Scores-28
04ITG Heroes and Prospects Jerseys-28
04ITG Heroes and Prospects Jerseys Gold-28
04ITG Heroes and Prospects Numbers-28
04ITG Heroes and Prospects Numbers Gold-28
05ITG Heroes/Prosp Toronto Expo Parallel -257
05AHL All-Stars-29
05ITG Heroes and Prospects-257
Autographs Series II-JOP
He Shoots-He Scores Prizes-38
06Toronto Marlies-23
06ITG Heroes and Prospects AHL All-Star Jerseys-AJ04
06ITG Heroes and Prospects AHL All-Star Jerseys Gold-AJ04
06ITG Heroes and Prospects AHL All-Star Emblems-AE04
06ITG Heroes and Prospects AHL All-Star Emblems Gold-AE04
06ITG Heroes and Prospects AHL All-Star Numbers-AN04
06ITG Heroes and Prospects AHL All-Star Numbers Gold-AN04
06ITG Heroes and Prospects AHL Shooting Stars-AS05
Pohl, Michael
92Finnish Semic-191
94German DEL-388
95German DEL-379
98German DEL-302
99German DEL-251
Pohl, Petr
03Gatineau Olympiques-18
04Gatineau Olympiques-16
Pohl, Tom
02Tri-City Stormfront-16
02Tri-City Stormfront-16
04Minnesota Golden Gophers-19
05Minnesota Golden Gophers-19
06Minnesota Golden Gophers-18
Pohl, Trevor
86Portland Winter Hawks-17
Pohl, Troy
86Portland Winter Hawks-18
Pohland, Heinz
04German Berlin Eisbarens 50th Anniv-18
Pohling, Jorg
95German DEL-424
Pohorelec, Dusan
94Finnish Jaa Kiekko-209
95Slovakian APS National Team-27
01Czech OFS-242
04UK Guildford Flames-13
Pohtinen, Tapio
71Finnish Suomi Stickers-268
Poikolainen, Juha
71Finnish Suomi Stickers-290
Poikolainen, Jyrki
93Finnish SISU-294
Poikolainen, Pekka
94Finnish SISU-273
95Finnish SISU-264
96Finnish SISU Redline-59
98Finnish Kerailysarja-149
99Finnish Cardset-272
00Finnish Cardset-170
01Finnish Cardset-62
Poile, Bud
34Beehive Group I Photos-342
44Beehive Group II Photos-202
44Beehive Group II Photos-352
45Quaker Oats Photos-43
Poile, David
82Capitals Team Issue-21
86Capitals Police-22
87Capitals Kodak-xx
88Capitals Smokey-19
89Capitals Kodak-xx
90Capitals Kodak-21
Pointek, J.P.
93Quebec Pee-Wee Tournament-850
Poirer, Carl
917th Inn. Sketch QMJHL-258
Poirier, Benoit
93Quebec Pee-Wee Tournament-79
Poirier, Christophe
05Quebec Remparts Signature Series-20
06Quebec Remparts-18
Poirier, Claude
917th Inn. Sketch QMJHL-102
Poirier, Dan
897th Inn. Sketch OHL-64
95Thunder Bay Senators-17
Poirier, Gaetan
96Carolina Monarchs-21
Poirier, Gordon
51Bas Du Fleuve-1
Poirier, Joel
92Sudbury Wolves-24
93Sudbury Wolves-21
93Sudbury Wolves Police-20
93Windsor Spitfires-15
94Windsor Spitfires-17
95Portland Pirates-20
96Hampton Roads Admirals-HRA18
97Hampton Roads Admirals-16
98Hampton Roads Admirals-7
00UK Sekonda Superleague-121
01UK Nottingham Panthers-16
02UK Coventry Blaze-17
03UK Coventry Blaze-15
03UK Coventry Blaze Calendars-10
04UK Coventry Blaze-14
04UK Coventry Blaze Champions-14
05UK Coventry Blaze-14
Poirier, Martin
93Quebec Pee-Wee Tournament-442
Poirier, Nicolas
99Rimouski Oceanic-4
Signed-4
00Rimouski Oceanic-5
Signed-5
00UD CHL Prospects-85
01Rimouski Oceanic-5
04St Georges de Beauce Garaga-4
Poirier, Philippe
95Slapshot-226
05Halifax Mooseheads-13
06Quebec Remparts-19
Poirier, Simon
01Missouri River Otters-24
03Port Huron Beacons-18
Poitras, Conrad
51Bas Du Fleuve-3
Poitras, Martin
96Rimouski Oceanic-22
96Rimouski Oceanic Quebec Police-21
Poitras, Roger
79Montreal Juniors-23
Pojar, Chic
92Raleigh Icecaps-11
92Raleigh Icecaps-36
94Raleigh Icecaps-16
Pojkar, David
01Czech OFS-280
02Czech OFS Plus-322
03Czech OFS Plus-187
04Czech OFS-180
06Czech OFS-300
Pojkar, Vladimir
99Czech OFS-51
Pokorny, Andreas
91Finnish Semic World Champ Stickers-160
91Swedish Semic World Champ Stickers-160
94German DEL-207
95German DEL-201
99German Bundesliga 2-91
00German DEL-230
01German Upper Deck-119
Pokorny, Jan-Hans
94German First League-638
Pokorny, Thomas
94German First League-371
Pokotilo, Vadim
99Russian Hockey League-167
00Russian Hockey League-17
02Russian Hockey League-68
Pokrovski, Valeri
99Russian Hockey League-226
00Russian Hockey League-116
02Russian Hockey League-126
03Russian Hockey League-62
03Russian Hockey League-183
04Russian RHL-17
Polacek, Vladimir
95Slovakian-Quebec Pee-Wee Tournament-22
Polacik, Randy
92British Columbia JHL-137
Polaczek, Aleksander
04German DEL-94
04German Ingolstadt Panthers-20
05German DEL-275
06German DEL-166
Poladiev, Yevgeny
69Swedish Hockey-12
73Swedish Stickers-83
74Swedish Semic World Champ Stickers-31
91Future Trends Canada '72-38
91Future Trends Canada '72 French-38
Polak, Jiri
95Czech APS Extraliga-109
96Czech APS Extraliga-272
97Czech APS Extraliga-226
98Czech DS Stickers-32
98Czech OFS-224
99Czech OFS-319
99Czech Score Blue 2000-123
99Czech Score Red Ice 2000-123
00Czech DS Extraliga-125
00Czech OFS-165
01Czech OFS-57
02Czech OFS Plus-74
03Czech OFS Plus-33
04Czech OFS-38
Polak, Mark
95Medicine Hat Tigers-11
96Medicine Hat Tigers-16
97Pensacola Ice Pilots-17
98Pensacola Ice Pilots-14
Polak, Michal
03Prince Albert Raiders-18
Polak, Roman
04Kootenay Ice-16
06Black Diamond-148A
Black-148A
Gold-148A
Ruby-148A
06Hot Prospects-134
Red Hot-134
White Hot-134
Hotagraphs-HRP
06O-Pee-Chee-557
Rainbow-557
06SP Authentic-203
Limited-203
06SP Game Used-153
Gold-153
Rainbow-153
06SPx-163
Spectrum-163
06The Cup-157
Autographed Rookie Masterpiece Pressplates-157
Gold Rainbow Autographed Rookie Patches-157
Masterpiece Pressplates (Black Diamond)-148
Masterpiece Pressplates (Marquee Rookies)-557
Masterpiece Pressplates (MVP)-322
Masterpiece Pressplates (SP Game Used)-153
Masterpiece Pressplates (SPx)-163
Masterpiece Pressplates (Trilogy)-153
Masterpiece Pressplates (Ultimate Collection)-91
Masterpiece Pressplates (Victory)-303
Rookies Black-157
Rookies Platinum-157
06Ultimate Collection-91
Ultimate Debut Threads Jerseys-DJ-RO
Ultimate Debut Threads Jerseys Autographs-DJ-RO
Ultimate Debut Threads Patches-DJ-RO
Ultimate Debut Threads Patches Autographs-DJ-RO
06Upper Deck-488
Exclusives Parallel-488
High Gloss Parallel-488
Masterpieces-488
Rookie Materials-RMRO
Rookie Materials Patches-RMRO
06Upper Deck MVP-322
Gold Script-322
Super Script-322
06Upper Deck Trilogy-153
06Upper Deck Victory-303
06AHL Top Prospects-32
06Peoria Rivermen-14
Polak, Vojtech
02Czech OFS Plus-326
03Czech OFS Plus-80
04Czech OFS-16
04Czech OFS-383
05Beehive-172
Matte-172
05Black Diamond-235
05Hot Prospects-126
En Fuego-126
Red Hot-126
White Hot-126
05SP Authentic-223
Limited-223
05SP Game Used-178
Gold-178
05SPx-210
Spectrum-210
05The Cup Masterpiece Pressplate Artifact-272
05The Cup Masterpiece Pressplate Bee Hive-172
05The Cup Master Pressplate Black Diamond-235
05The Cup Masterpiece Pressplates (Ice)-181
05The Cup Master Pressplate Rookie Update-128
05The Cup Masterpiece Pressplates SPA-223
05The Cup Masterpiece Pressplates SP GU-178
05The Cup Masterpiece Pressplates (SPx)-210
05The Cup Masterpiece Pressplates Trilogy-251
05The Cup Masterpiece Pressplate Ult Coll-146
05UD Artifacts-272
05Ultimate Collection-146
Gold-146
05Upper Deck Ice-181
05Upper Deck Rookie Update-128
05Upper Deck Trilogy-251
05Iowa Stars-16
06AHL Top Prospects-19
06Iowa Stars-18
Polano, Mike
89Windsor Spitfires-14
907th Inn. Sketch OHL-191
907th Inn. Sketch OHL-250
917th Inn. Sketch OHL-76
Polansky, Jiri
03Czech OFS Plus-299
04Czech OFS-220
05Czech HC Trinec-11
06Czech OFS-165
Stars-15
Polansky, Tomas
99Czech OFS-171
Polasek, Libor
92Hamilton Canucks-24
92Classic-34
Gold-34
92Classic Four-Sport *-181
Gold-181
Autographs-181A
94Classic Pro Prospects-161
95Czech APS Extraliga-340
96Czech APS Extraliga-211
97Czech APS Extraliga-139
97Czech DS Stickers-204
98Czech DS Stickers-259
98Czech OFS-122
98Czech OFS-320
99Czech DS-176
99Czech OFS-429
Polaski, Scott
00Sioux City Musketeers-22
05Colorado Eagles-16
06Colorado EaglesÂ -17
Polcar, Ales
94German DEL-19
95Czech APS Extraliga-21
96Czech APS Extraliga-41
97Czech APS Extraliga-69
97Czech APS Extraliga-311
97Czech DS Stickers-105
98Czech DS-42
98Czech DS Stickers-301
98Czech OFS-299
99Czech Score Blue 2000-46
99Czech Score Red Ice 2000-46
Polera, Jason
98Windsor Spitfires-7
99Kingston Frontenacs-14
Polgase, Clark
95San Diego Barracudas RHI-13
Polglase, Clark
99Bakersfield Condors-15
Policelli, Nick
00Belleville Bulls-3
01Kitchener Rangers-2
Polich, Brandon
00Lincoln Stars-13
Polich, Mike
76Nova Scotia Voyageurs-16
77Nova Scotia Voyageurs-17
78North Stars Cloverleaf Dairy-6
79North Stars Postcards-12
79O-Pee-Chee-333
80North Stars Postcards-16
80O-Pee-Chee-363
81O-Pee-Chee-172
Polikarkin, Vyacheslav
94Erie Panthers-18
95Madison Monsters-11
01Russian Hockey League-26
Polillo, Paul
94Brantford Smoke-6
98Port Huron Border Cats-18
Poliquin, Chad
95Waterloo Blackhawks -15
Polis, Greg
71O-Pee-Chee-41
O-Pee-Chee/Topps Booklets-9
71Penguins Postcards-14
71Sargent Promotions Stamps-172
71Topps-41
71Toronto Sun-223
72O-Pee-Chee-34
72Sargent Promotions Stamps-178
72Topps-43
73O-Pee-Chee-176
73Topps-75
74NHL Action Stamps-187
74O-Pee-Chee NHL-164
74Topps-164
75O-Pee-Chee NHL-201
75Topps-201
76O-Pee-Chee NHL-117
76Topps-117
77O-Pee-Chee NHL-112
77Topps-112
78O-Pee-Chee-246
78Topps-246
79Capitals Team Issue-16
79O-Pee-Chee-273
Poliziani, Danny
52Juniors Blue Tint-23
Polk, Bob
89Nashville Knights-17
Polkovnikov, Oleg
99Russian Hockey League-32
00Russian Dynamo Moscow-8
00Russian Hockey League-238
Poll, Ryan
93Quebec Pee-Wee Tournament-585
Polla, Stefan
94Swedish Leaf-205
95Swedish Leaf-170
95Swedish Upper Deck-31
96Swedish Brynas Tigers-15
Pollak, Marek
96Slovakian Quebec Pee-Wee Tournament-22
Pollanen, Tomi
03Finnish Cardset-179
05Finnish Cardset -261
Pollard, Rick
907th Inn. Sketch OHL-315
Pollock, Brian
02Arizona Icecats-21
03Arizona Icecats-20
Pollock, Jame
95Seattle Thunderbirds-22
96Seattle Thunderbirds-8
97Seattle Thunderbirds-8
00Worcester Icecats-18
01Worcester Icecats-10
02Worcester IceCats-6
03ITG VIP Rookie Debut-105
03Parkhurst Rookie-65
03Topps Traded-TT152
Blue-TT152
Gold-TT152
Red-TT152
03Upper Deck Rookie Update-98
03Worcester Ice Cats-10
05German DEL-276
Defender-DF13
Defender Promos-DF13
06German DEL-167
Pollock, Markus
94German First League-593
Pollock, Sam

83Hall of Fame-147
83Hall of Fame Postcards-K13
85Hall of Fame-147
Polloni, Fabio
82Swedish Semic VM Stickers-131
83Swedish Semic VM Stickers-131
Polman, Rob
81Milwaukee Admirals-13
Polodna, Stanislav
06Erie Otters-6
Poloncic, Gregor
02Czech OFS Plus-98
03Czech OFS Plus-300
Polonic, Tom
69O-Pee-Chee-199
Polonich, Dennis
77O-Pee-Chee NHL-4
77O-Pee-Chee NHL-228
77Topps-4
77Topps-228
78O-Pee-Chee-66
78O-Pee-Chee-106
78Topps-66
78Topps-106
79O-Pee-Chee-224
79Red Wings Postcards-15
79Topps-224
80O-Pee-Chee-54
80Topps-54
Polsky, Gabe
93Quebec Pee-Wee Tournament-1329
Polupanov, Victor
70Finnish Jaakiekko-13
70Russian National Team Postcards-9
70Swedish Hockey-329
70Swedish Masterserien-121
70Swedish Masterserien-129
70Swedish Masterserien-140
Polupanov, Vladimir
73Swedish Stickers-121
Polushin, Alexander
02Russian Hockey League-101
02Russian Hockey League-199
02Russian Lightnings-2
02Russian SL-3
03Russian Young Lions-10
Polyakov, Eduard
99Russian Hockey League-90
Polychronopoulos, Nick
91Prince Albert Raiders-19
917th Inn. Sketch WHL-249
Pomaranski, Joe
05Muskegon Fury-15
Pomerleau, Jacques
77Granby Vics-16
Pomichter, Mike
92Upper Deck-607
94Indianapolis Ice-17
94Classic-58
Gold-58
All-Americans-AA7
Tri-Cards-T13
95Images-94
Gold-94
Autographs-94A
97Springfield Falcons-19
Pominville, Jason
95Quebec Pee-Wee Tournament-1318
96Quebec Pee-Wee Tournament-335
99Shawinigan Cataractes-23
Signed-23
00Shawinigan Cataractes-20
Signed-20
01Shawinigan Cataractes-22
01UD Prospects-19
Jerseys-J-JP
Jerseys Gold-J-JP
02Rochester Americans-19
03Beehive-244
Gold-244
Silver-244
03ITG VIP Rookie Debut-91
03Pacific Calder-103
Silver-103
03Pacific Complete-560
Red-560
03Parkhurst Rookie-61
03SP Authentic-164
03UD Premier Collection-70
03Upper Deck Rookie Update-118
03AHL Top Prospects-29
03Pacific AHL Prospects-71
Gold-71
03Rochester Americans-23
04Rochester Americans-18
05ITG Heroes/Prosp Toronto Expo Parallel -230
05Parkhurst-63
Facsimile Auto Parallel-63
05ITG Heroes and Prospects-230
Autographs Series II-JPO
06O-Pee-Chee-55
Rainbow-55
06Upper Deck Arena Giveaways-BUF4
06Upper Deck-276
Exclusives Parallel-276
High Gloss Parallel-276
Masterpieces-276
06Upper Deck MVP-37
Gold Script-37
Super Script-37
07Upper Deck Ovation-96
07Upper Deck Victory-37
Black-37
Gold-37
Pone, Sarma
98Minnesota Golden Gophers Women-18
Poner, Claude
07th Inn. Sketch QMJHL-92
Poner, Jiri
94Springfield Indians-15
Ponikarovsky, Alexei
99Russian Dynamo Moscow-3
00BAP Memorabilia-521
00Black Diamond-132
00SP Authentic-124
00Upper Deck Ice-101
00St. John's Maple Leafs-21
01O-Pee-Chee-290
01O-Pee-Chee Premier Parallel-290
01Pacific-371
Extreme LTD-371
Hobby LTD-371
Premiere Date-371
Retail LTD-371
01Pacific Arena Exclusives-371
01Titanium Draft Day Edition-168
01Topps-290
OPC Parallel-290
01Upper Deck Victory-389
Gold-389
01St. John's Maple Leafs-19
03O-Pee-Chee-329
03OPC Blue-329
03OPC Gold-329
03OPC Red-329
03Parkhurst Original Six Toronto-20
03Topps-329
Blue-329
Gold-329
Red-329
04Russian Back to Russia-14
05Parkhurst-455
Facsimile Auto Parallel-455
06Gatorade-69
06O-Pee-Chee-469
Rainbow-469
06Upper Deck-431
Exclusives Parallel-431
High Gloss Parallel-431
Masterpieces-431
Ponomarev, Andrei
01Russian Hockey League-27
Pont, Benoit
95Swiss HNL-386
96Swiss HNL-246
98Swiss Power Play Stickers-148
99Swiss Panini Stickers-148
00Swiss Panini Stickers-190
00Swiss Slapshot Mini-Cards-LT16
01Swiss HNL-208
02Swiss HNL-333
Ponte, Randy
97Brandon Wheat Kings-19
98Brandon Wheat Kings-16
99Brandon Wheat Kings-16
00Brandon Wheat Kings-20
01Brandon Wheat Kings-18
02Austin Ice Bats-12
Ponto, Vesa
93Finnish Jyvas-Hyva Stickers-145
93Finnish SISU-143
94Finnish SISU-8
95Finnish SISU-57
99Finnish Cardset-274
Pool, Byron
02Indianapolis Ice-14
Pool, Clayton
96Kamloops Blazers-18
98Kootenay Ice-1
05Muskegon Fury-16
Poole, Nick
95Dayton Bombers-5
03UK Manchester Phoenix-20
04UK Milton Keynes Lightning-19
Pooley, Paul
84Jets Police-17
Pooyak, Dean
91Air Canada SJHL-E6
Pope, Brent
89Peterborough Petes-101
897th Inn. Sketch OHL-101
907th Inn. Sketch OHL-369
917th Inn. Sketch OHL-352
93Wheeling Thunderbirds-12
94Wheeling Thunderbirds-13
94Wheeling Thunderbirds Photo Album-10
95Wheeling Thunderbirds-13
95Wheeling Thunderbirds Series II-11
00Florida Everblades-22
01UK Nottingham Panthers-2
Pope, Ricky
91Arizona Icecats-15
92Arizona Icecats-12
93Arizona Icecats-4
94Arizona Icecats-8
Popeil, Paul
75Houston Aeros WHA-13
Popein, Larry
44Beehive Group II Photos-353
54Topps-55
57Topps-54
58Topps-28
59Topps-21
60Shirriff Coins-84
94Parkhurst Missing Link-95
Poperechny, Vladislav
01Russian Hockey League-152
Popiel, Jan
73Quaker Oats WHA-21
Popiel, Paul
65Topps-40
69O-Pee-Chee-158
70Canucks Royal Bank-12
70Esso Power Players-49
70O-Pee-Chee-122
70Sargent Promotions Stamps-213
70Topps-122
71Canucks Royal Bank-7
71O-Pee-Chee-1
71Sargent Promotions Stamps-212
71Toronto Sun-286
72O-Pee-Chee-67
72Topps-142
74O-Pee-Chee WHA-59
75O-Pee-Chee WHA-68
75O-Pee-Chee WHA-120
76O-Pee-Chee WHA-27
77O-Pee-Chee WHA-63
88Oilers Tenth Anniversary-86
Popiesch, Thomas
94German DEL-330
95German DEL-113
96German DEL-58
99German Bundesliga 2-132
Popikhin, Evgeny
91O-Pee-Chee Inserts-41R
95Swiss HNL-111
96Swiss HNL-102
98Swiss Power Play Stickers-329
99Swiss Panini Stickers-177
00Swiss Panini Stickers-221
01Swiss HNL-145
Poplawski, Derek
02Swift Current Broncos-13
03Portland Winter Hawks-20
Popov, Alexander
99Russian Hockey League-170
00Russian Hockey League-212
01Russian Hockey League-100
03Russian Avangard Omsk-14
Popov, Dmitri
98Russian Hockey League-7
99Russian Hockey League-10
99Russian Metallurg Magnetogorsk-46
01Russian Hockey League-28
Popov, Roman
02Russian Hockey League-88
Popov, Vladimir
73Swedish Stickers-107
02Russian Hockey League-244
04Russian RHL-14
Popovic, Mark
99UD Prospects-85
00St. Michaels Majors-23
00UD CHL Prospects-28
01St. Michaels Majors-8
01UD Prospects-7
Autographs-A-MP
Jersey Autographs-S-MP
Jerseys-J-MP
Jerseys-C-PM
Jerseys Gold-J-MP
Jerseys Gold-C-PM
02Cincinnati Mighty Ducks-B-7
03BAP Memorabilia-215
03BAP Ultimate Mem Rookie Jersey Emblems-38
03BAP Ultimate Mem Rookie Jsy Emblem Gold-38
03BAP Ultimate Mem Rookie Jersey Numbers-38
03BAP Ultimate Mem Rookie Jsy Number Gold-38
03ITG Used Signature Series-157
Gold-157
03ITG VIP Rookie Debut-97
03Parkhurst Rookie-135
Rookie Emblems-RE-29
Rookie Emblems Gold-RE-29
Rookie Jerseys-RJ-29
Rookie Jerseys Gold-RJ-29
Rookie Numbers-RN-29
Rookie Numbers Gold-RN-29
03Upper Deck Rookie Update-126
03AHL Top Prospects-29
03Cincinnati Mighty Ducks-A6
04Cincinnati Mighty Ducks-7
04ITG Heroes and Prospects Emblems-29
04ITG Heroes and Prospects Emblems Gold-29
04ITG Heroes/Prospects He Shoots/Scores-38
04ITG Heroes and Prospects Jerseys-29
04ITG Heroes and Prospects Jerseys Gold-29
04ITG Heroes and Prospects Numbers-29
04ITG Heroes and Prospects Numbers Gold-29
05Black Diamond Gemography-G-MP
05Black Diamond Gemography Emerald-G-MP
05Black Diamond Gemography Gold-G-MP
05Black Diamond Gemography Onyx-G-MP
05Black Diamond Gemography Ruby-G-MP
05UD Artifacts Auto Facts-AF-MP
05UD Artifacts Auto Facts Blue-AF-MP
05UD Artifacts Auto Facts Copper-AF-MP
05UD Artifacts Auto Facts Pewter-AF-MP
05UD Artifacts Auto Facts Silver-AF-MP
05UD Powerplay Power Marks-PMMP
05Ultra Fresh Ink-FI-PE
05Ultra Fresh Ink Blue-FI-PE
05Upper Deck Notable Numbers-N-PO
05Upper Deck MVP ProSign-P-PO
05Chicago Wolves-15
Popovic, Peter
89Swedish Semic Elitserien Stickers-243
90Swedish Semic Elitserien Stickers-154
91Swedish Semic Elitserien Stickers-259
92Swedish Semic Elitserien Stickers-278
93Canadiens Molson-9
93Canadiens Postcards-18
93Donruss-180
93Leaf-417
93OPC Premier-361
Gold-361
93Parkhurst-103
Emerald Ice-103
93PowerPlay-372
93Score-626
Gold-626
Canadian-626
Canadian Gold-626
93Topps/OPC Premier-361
Gold-361
93Upper Deck-445
93Swedish Semic World Champ Stickers-8
94Canada Games NHL POGS-141
94Canadiens Postcards-19
94Donruss-313
94Leaf-176
94OPC Premier-158
Special Effects-158
94Parkhurst SE-SE86
Gold-SE86
94Pinnacle-457
Artist's Proofs-457
Rink Collection-457
94Topps/OPC Premier-158
Special Effects-158
94Ultra-315
94Upper Deck-428
Electric Ice-428
94Finnish Jaa Kiekko-56
94Swedish Leaf-203
Guest Special-7
95Canadiens Postcards-12
95Canadiens Sheets-3
95Parkhurst International-111
Emerald Ice-111
95Upper Deck-192
Electric Ice-192
Electric Ice Gold-192
95Swedish Globe World Championships-19
96Be A Player-6
Autographs-6
Autographs Silver-6
96Canadiens Postcards-19
96Canadiens Sheets-13
97Canadiens Postcards-14
97Pacific Invincible NHL Regime-104
97Panini Stickers-35
98Panini Stickers-36
99Pacific-277
Copper-277
Emerald Green-277
Gold-277
Ice Blue-277
Premiere Date-277
Red-277
00Upper Deck-243
Exclusives Tier 1-243
Exclusives Tier 2-243
02Swedish SHL-92
Parallel-92
02Swedish SHL Promos-TCC9
02Swedish SHL Signatures Series II-10
02Swedish SHL Team Captains-9
03Swedish Elite-114
Signatures-9
Silver-114
04Swedish Elitset-268
Gold-268
High Expectations-9
Jerseys Series 2-PP
04Swedish Pure Skills-83
Parallel-83
Popp, Kevin
93Spokane Chiefs-21
95Seattle Thunderbirds-23
00Fort Wayne Komets-15
01Indianapolis Ice-17
02Indianapolis Ice-15
Popperle, Tomas
03Czech OFS Plus-341
04Czech HC Sparta Praha Postcards-16
04Czech OFS-195
05German DEL-309
Goalies-G12
06Czech LG Hockey Games Postcards-15
06AHL Top Prospects-43
06Syracuse Crunch-1
07Upper Deck Victory-222
Black-222
Gold-222
Poppler, Mats
87Swedish Panini Stickers-262
Porak, Michal
97Czech APS Extraliga-236
99Czech OFS-142
Porco, John
897th Inn. Sketch OHL-81
907th Inn. Sketch OHL-16
94Hampton Roads Admirals-6
96German DEL-127
Porkka, Toni
91ProCards-269
94Finnish SISU-289
95Finnish SISU-97
96Finnish SISU Redline Sledgehammers-6
96German DEL-51
98German DEL-147
99German DEL-84
00German DEL-77
Game Jersey-TP
01German Upper Deck-146
02Finnish Cardset-250
03Finnish Cardset-102
04Finnish Cardset-110
Parallel-81
05Finnish Cardset -101
Port, Andy
94UK Humberside Hawks-22
Porteous, F.
28V128-2 Paulin's Candy-79
Porteous, Ken
80Sault Ste. Marie Greyhounds-1
Porter, Aaron
97OCN Blizzard-14
98OCN Blizzard-13
99Muskegon Fury-19
Porter, Chris
02Lincoln Stars-5
02Lincoln Stars-35
03North Dakota Fighting Sioux-10
04North Dakota Fighting Sioux-19
Porter, J. C.
25Dominion Chocolates-106
27La Presse Photos-19
Porter, Kevin
04Michigan Wolverines-7
Porter, Kris
00Fresno Falcons-15
01Fresno Falcons-14
02Fresno Falcons-21
03Fresno Falcons-13
Porter, Mike
93Quebec Pee-Wee Tournament-1313
Porthen, Jermu
04Finnish Cardset-216
05Finnish Cardset -195
06Finnish Cardset-20
Portland, Jack
34Beehive Group I Photos-175
39O-Pee-Chee V301-1-40
Portner, Phillippe
95Swiss HNL-91
96Swiss HNL-431
01Swiss HNL-346
02Swiss HNL-391
Porvari, Juha-Pekka
71Finnish Suomi Stickers-310
Porvari, Jukka
77Finnish Sportscasters-72-1705
78Finnish SM-Liiga-11
78Finnish SM-Liiga-186
79Panini Stickers-177
80Finnish Mallasjuoma-163
81Rockies Postcards-23
81Swedish Semic Hockey VM Stickers-32
82Finnish Skopbank-12
82Swedish Semic VM Stickers-153
99Finnish Valio World Championships-5
05Finnish Tappara Legendat-4
Porzi, Elko
94German First League-330
Posa, Victor
87Flint Spirits-16
90Richmond Renegades-2
91Michigan Falcons-2
Posillico, Neil
00Barrie Colts-20
03Elmira Jackals-16
Posma, Mike
90ProCards AHL/IHL-563
93Swiss HNL-444
95Swiss HNL-325
96Swiss HNL-300
98Swiss Power Play Stickers-310
Posmyk, Marek
95Upper Deck-542
Electric Ice-542
Electric Ice Gold-542
95Czech APS Extraliga-183
96Czech APS Extraliga-320
97Czech DS Stickers-156
98Bowman CHL-7
Golden Anniversary-7
OPC International-7
98Bowman Chrome CHL-7
Golden Anniversary-7
Golden Anniversary Refractors-7
OPC International-7
OPC International Refractors-7
Refractors-7
99St. John's Maple Leafs-17
00BAP Memorabilia-24
Emerald-24
Ruby-24
Sapphire-24
Promos-24
00BAP Mem Chicago Sportsfest Copper-24
00BAP Memorabilia Chicago Sportsfest Blue-24
00BAP Memorabilia Chicago Sportsfest Gold-24
00BAP Memorabilia Chicago Sportsfest Ruby-24
00BAP Memorabilia Chicago Sun-Times Ruby-24
00BAP Memorabilia Chicago Sun-Times Gold-24
00BAP Mem Chicago Sun-Times Sapphire-24
00BAP Mem Toronto Fall Expo Copper-24
00BAP Memorabilia Toronto Fall Expo Gold-24
00BAP Memorabilia Toronto Fall Expo Ruby-24
00Pacific-383
Copper-383
Gold-383
Ice Blue-383
Premiere Date-383
02Czech OFS Plus-247
03Czech OFS Plus-307
03Czech OFS Plus Insert H-H21
03Czech OFS Plus MS Praha-SE24
05Czech HC Ceski Budejovice-12
06Czech OFS-14
Defenders-7
Posnov, Andrei
00Russian Hockey League-57
Pospisil, David
94Czech APS Extraliga-40
95Czech APS Extraliga-326
96Czech APS Extraliga-154
97Czech APS Extraliga-181
97Czech DS Extraliga-55
97Czech DS Stickers-261
98Czech DS-62
98Czech DS Stickers-157
98Czech OFS-41
98Czech OFS-461
99Czech DS-97
99Czech OFS-371
00Czech DS Extraliga-35
00Czech OFS-71
01Czech OFS-253
02Czech OFS Plus-225
03Czech OFS Plus-210
03Russian Hockey League-185
04Czech HC Plzen Postcards-15
04Czech OFS-152
Pospisil, Frantisek
69Swedish Hockey-36
70Finnish Jaakiekko-56
70Swedish Hockey-350
70Swedish Masterserien-82
71Finnish Suomi Stickers-36
71Swedish Hockey-47
72Finnish Jaakiekko-18
72Finnish Hellas-86
72Finnish Panda Toronto-92
72Finnish Semic World Championship-27
72Swedish Stickers-23
72Swedish Semic World Championship-27
73Finnish Jaakiekko-60
74Finnish Jenkki-81
74Swedish Semic World Champ Stickers-52
95Czech APS Extraliga-394
98Czech OFS Legends-15
01Czech DS Legends-L9
03Czech Stadion-654
Pospisil, Jan
00Czech OFS-111
01Czech OFS-185
01Czech OFS H Inserts-H5
03Czech OFS Plus-225
Pospisil, Robert
97Czech APS Extraliga-253
98Czech OFS-377
99Czech Score Blue 2000-156
99Czech Score Red Ice 2000-156
02Czech OFS Plus-164
Pospisil, Tomas
04Czech OFS-376
06Sarnia Sting-3
Poss, Greg
89ProCards AHL-61
90ProCards AHL/IHL-136
91ProCards-30
99German Bundesliga 2-228
03German Nuremberg Ice Tigers Postcards-22
04German Nuremberg Ice Tigers Postcards-14
Possin, Mike
03New Mexico Scorpions-16
04New Mexico Scorpions-5
06Austin Ice Bats-21
Postma, Marcel
05Dutch Vadeko Flyers -15
Potaichuk, Andrei
92Russian Stars Red Ace-28
94Czech APS Extraliga-92
95Czech APS Extraliga-289
97Czech DS Stickers-74
98Finnish Kerailysarja-265
99Finnish Cardset-154
00Finnish Cardset-299
01Finnish Cardset-83
02Finnish Cardset-98
03Russian Hockey League-74
Potapov, Maxim
00Johnstown Chiefs-13
00QMJHL All-Star Program Inserts-33
04Russian RHL-3
Potapov, Mikhail
00Russian Hockey League-145
Potemkin, Alexei
03Russian Hockey League-229
Pothier, Brian
01BAP Memorabilia-408
Emerald-408
Ruby-408
Sapphire-408
01Crown Royale-148
01Parkhurst-225
01Private Stock-115
Gold-115
Premiere Date-115
Retail-115
Silver-115
01Private Stock Pacific Nights-115
01SP Authentic-134
Limited-134
Limited Gold-134
01SP Game Used-64
01SPx-133
01SPx-133
Rookie Treasures-RTBP
01Titanium-149
Retail-149
01Titanium Draft Day Edition-108
01UD Challenge for the Cup-94
01Upper Deck Vintage-276
01Vanguard-104
Blue-104
Red-104
One of Ones-104
Premiere Date-104
Proofs-104
01Chicago Wolves-17
03Senators Postcards-1
04AHL All-Stars-36
04Binghamton Senators-14
04Binghamton Senators Hess-3
05ITG Heroes/Prosp Toronto Expo Parallel -247
05ITG Heroes and Prospects-247
Autographs Series II-BPO
Jerseys-GUJ-77
Jerseys Gold-GUJ-77
Emblems-GUE-77
Emblems Gold-GUE-77
Numbers-GUN-77
Numbers Gold-GUN-77
Nameplates-N-54
Nameplates Gold-N-54
06O-Pee-Chee-495
Rainbow-495
06Panini Stickers-180
06Ultra-197
Gold Medallion-197
Ice Medallion-197
06Upper Deck-445
Exclusives Parallel-445
High Gloss Parallel-445
Masterpieces-445
06Binghamton Senators 5th Anniversary-24
Poti, Tom
95Donruss Elite World Juniors-31
95Upper Deck-568
Electric Ice-568
Electric Ice Gold-568
95Classic-67
98Black Diamond-36
Double Diamond-36
Triple Diamond-36
Quadruple Diamond-36
98Bowman's Best-111
Refractors-111
Atomic Refractors-111
Mirror Image Fusion-F18
Mirror Image Fusion Refractors-F18
Mirror Image Fusion Atomic Refractors-F18
98Crown Royale-53
Limited Series-53
98Pacific Dynagon Ice-75
Blue-75
Red-75
98Pacific Omega-98
Red-98
Opening Day Issue-98
98SP Authentic-35
Power Shift-35
98SPx Top Prospects-28
Radiance-28
Spectrum-28
98Upper Deck-274
Exclusives-274
Exclusives 1 of 1-274
Generation Next-GN17
Generation Next Quantum 1-GN17
Generation Next Quantum 2-GN17
Generation Next Quantum 3-GN17
Gold Reserve-274
98Upper Deck MVP-79
Gold Script-79
Silver Script-79
Super Script-79
99BAP Memorabilia-228
Gold-228
Silver-228
99BAP Millennium-98
Emerald-98
Ruby-98
Sapphire-98
Signatures-98
Signatures Gold-98
99O-Pee-Chee-70
99O-Pee-Chee Chrome-70
99O-Pee-Chee Chrome Refractors-70
99Pacific-163
Copper-163
Emerald Green-163
Gold-163
Ice Blue-163
Premiere Date-163
Red-163
99Pacific Dynagon Ice-82
Blue-82
Copper-82
Gold-82
Premiere Date-82
99Pacific Omega-91
Copper-91
Gold-91
Ice Blue-91
Premiere Date-91
99Panini Stickers-242
99Paramount-94
Copper-94
Emerald-94
Gold-94
Holographic Emerald-94
Holographic Gold-94
Holographic Silver-94
Ice Blue-94
Premiere Date-94
Red-94
Silver-94
99SPx-66
Radiance-66
Spectrum-66
99Stadium Club-136
First Day Issue-136
One of a Kind-136
Printing Plates Black-136
Printing Plates Cyan-136
Printing Plates Magenta-136
Printing Plates Yellow-136
99Topps/OPC-70
99Topps/OPC Chrome-70
Refractors-70
99Upper Deck-57
Exclusives-57
Exclusives 1 of 1-57
99Upper Deck Gold Reserve-57
99Upper Deck MVP-82
Gold Script-82
Silver Script-82
Super Script-82
Draft Report-DR9
ProSign-TP
99Upper Deck Ovation-26
Standing Ovation-26
99Upper Deck Retro-33
Gold-33
Platinum-33
99Upper Deck Victory-110
99Wayne Gretzky Hockey-71
00BAP Memorabilia-351
Emerald-351
Ruby-351
Sapphire-351
Promos-351
00BAP Mem Chicago Sportsfest Copper-351
00BAP Memorabilia Chicago Sportsfest Blue-351
00BAP Memorabilia Chicago Sportsfest Gold-351
00BAP Memorabilia Chicago Sportsfest Ruby-351
00BAP Memorabilia Chicago Sun-Times Ruby-351
00BAP Memorabilia Chicago Sun-Times Gold-351
00BAP Mem Chicago Sun-Times Sapphire-351
00BAP Mem Toronto Fall Expo Copper-351
00BAP Memorabilia Toronto Fall Expo Gold-351
00BAP Memorabilia Toronto Fall Expo Ruby-351
00BAP Signature Series-26
Emerald-26
Ruby-26
Sapphire-26
Autographs-11
Autographs Gold-11
00O-Pee-Chee-196
00O-Pee-Chee Parallel-196
00Pacific-171
Copper-171
Gold-171
Ice Blue-171
Premiere Date-171
00Paramount-97
Copper-97
Gold-97
Holo-Gold-97
Holo-Silver-97
Ice Blue-97
Premiere Date-97
00Stadium Club-54
00Topps/OPC-196
Parallel-196
00Topps Chrome-130
OPC Refractors-130
Refractors-130
00Upper Deck-299
Exclusives Tier 1-299
Exclusives Tier 2-299
00Upper Deck MVP-72
First Stars-72
Second Stars-72
Third Stars-72
00Upper Deck Victory-94
00Upper Deck Vintage-142
01BAP Memorabilia-494
Emerald-494
Ruby-494
Sapphire-494
01O-Pee-Chee-215
01O-Pee-Chee Premier Parallel-215
01Parkhurst-196
01Parkhurst-391
01SPx-184
01Topps-215
OPC Parallel-215
01Upper Deck-72
Exclusives-72
01Upper Deck MVP-74
01Upper Deck Victory-143
Gold-143
01Upper Deck Vintage-99
01Upper Deck Vintage-105
02BAP Memorabilia-195
Emerald-195
Ruby-195
Sapphire-195
NHL All-Star Game-195
NHL All-Star Game Blue-195
NHL All-Star Game Green-195
NHL All-Star Game Red-195
02BAP Memorabilia Toronto Fall Expo-195
02BAP Sig Series Auto Buybacks 1999-98
02BAP Sig Series Auto Buybacks 2000-11
02BAP Signature Series Golf-GS97
02O-Pee-Chee-64
02O-Pee-Chee Premier Blue Parallel-64
02O-Pee-Chee Premier Red Parallel-64
02O-Pee-Chee Factory Set-64
02Pacific Complete-230
Red-230
02SP Authentic-125
02Titanium-70
Blue-70
Red-70
Retail-70
02Topps-64
OPC Blue Parallel-64
OPC Red Parallel-64
Factory Set-64
02Topps Total-190
02Upper Deck-118
Exclusives-118
02Upper Deck MVP-121
Gold-121
Classics-121
Golden Classics-121
02Upper Deck Victory-143
Bronze-143
Gold-143
Silver-143
02Upper Deck Vintage-164
03ITG Action-381
Jerseys-M64
03O-Pee-Chee-269
03OPC Blue-269
03OPC Gold-269
03OPC Red-269
03Pacific-230
Blue-230
Red-230
03Pacific Complete-76
Red-76
03Pacific Exhibit-100
Blue Backs-100
Yellow Backs-100
03Parkhurst Original Six New York-29
Memorabilia-NM5
03Rangers Team Issue-19
03SP Game Used Authentic Fabrics-DFLP
03SP Game Used Authentic Fabrics Gold-DFLP
03Topps-269
Blue-269
Gold-269
Red-269
03Upper Deck-128
All-Star Class-AS-18
Canadian Exclusives-128
HG-128
03Upper Deck MVP-280
Gold Script-280
Silver Script-280
Canadian Exclusives-280
03Upper Deck Victory-124
Bronze-124
Gold-124
Silver-124
04Pacific-179
Blue-179
Red-179
04Upper Deck-115
Canadian Exclusives-115
HG Glossy Gold-115
HG Glossy Silver-115
05Be A Player Signatures-TP
05Be A Player Signatures Gold-TP
05Panini Stickers-110
05Parkhurst-328
Facsimile Auto Parallel-328
True Colors-TCNYR
True Colors-TCNYR
True Colors-TCNYNY
True Colors-TCNYNY
05SP Authentic Sign of the Times-TP
05SP Game Used Authentic Fabrics-AF-TP
05SP Game Used Authentic Fabrics Autos-AAF-TP
05SP Game Used Authentic Fabrics Gold-AF-TP
05SP Game Used Authentic Patches-AP-TP
05SP Game Used Authentic Patch Autos-AAP-TP
05SP Game Used Auto Draft-AD-TP
05SP Game Used Statscriptions-ST-TP
05SPx-58
Spectrum-58
05UD Artifacts-62
Blue-62
Gold-62
Green-62
Pewter-62
Red-62
Gold Autographed-62
Remarkable Artifacts-RA-TP
Remarkable Artifacts Dual-RA-TP
05Ultra-132
Gold-132
Ice-132
05Upper Deck-125
Big Playmakers-B-TP
HG Glossy-125
Jerseys-J-TP
Jerseys Series II-J2TP
05Upper Deck Ice-64
Rainbow-64
05Upper Deck MVP-254
Gold-254
Platinum-254
Materials-M-TP
ProSign-P-TP
05Upper Deck Trilogy Scripts-SFS-TP
05Upper Deck Toronto Fall Expo-125
05Upper Deck Victory-132
Black-132
Gold-132
Silver-132
06Be A Player-62
Autographs-62
Signatures-TP
Signatures 25-67
Portraits Signature Portraits-SPTP
06Black Diamond Jerseys-JTP
06Black Diamond Jerseys Black-JTP
06Black Diamond Jerseys Gold-JTP
06Black Diamond Jerseys Ruby-JTP
06Fleer Fabricology-FTP
06Hot Prospects Hot Materials -HMTP
06Hot Prospects Hot Materials Red Hot-HMTP
06Hot Prospects Hot Materials White Hot-HMTP
06O-Pee-Chee-309
Rainbow-309
06Upper Deck Game Jerseys-JTP
06Upper Deck Game Patches-PTP
06Upper Deck MVP-183
Gold Script-183
Super Script-183
Potomski, Barry
907th Inn. Sketch OHL-139
917th Inn. Sketch OHL-366
92Anaheim Bullfrogs RHI-7
92Toledo Storm-22
93Toledo Storm-24
95Phoenix Roadrunners-12
96Be A Player-24
Autographs-24
Autographs Silver-24
99San Diego Gulls-12
00Idaho Steelheads-17
Pototschnik, Anthony
03Kitchener Rangers-21
04P.E.I. Rocket-2
Potsma, Paul
05Swift Current Broncos-19
06Swift Current Broncos-17
Potter, Chris
93Roanoke Express-15
94Roanoke Express-3
95Roanoke Express-20
Potter, Corey
06Hartford Wolf Pack-5
Potter, Jeff
00Trenton Titans-20
Pottie, Christopher
02Hull Olympiques-1

Pottie, Steve
98El Paso Buzzards-11

Pottinger, Markus
95German DEL-364
96German DEL-187
99German DEL-270
99German DEL-369
00German DEL-31
01German Upper Deck-23
02German DEL City Press-57
03German Deg Metro Stars-16
04German DEL Update-289
04German Dusseldorf Metro Stars Postcards-16
05German DEL-176

Pottruff, Ryan
03London Knights-24
04London Knights-18
05Guelph Storm-B-01
06Guelph Storm-2

Potts, Stuart
04UK Guildford Flames-7
05UK Guildford Flames-7
06UK Guildford Flames-6

Potuer, Graham
04Everett Silvertips-15
05Everett Silvertips-19

Potulny, Grant
00Minnesota Golden Gophers-19
01Minnesota Golden Gophers-17
02Minnesota Golden Gophers-16
03Minnesota Golden Gophers-22
04Binghamton Senators-15
05Binghamton Senators-11
05Binghamton Senators Quickway-11
06Binghamton Senators-19
06Binghamton Senators 5th Anniversary-25

Potulny, Ryan
01Lincoln Stars-19
02Lincoln Stars-6
02Lincoln Stars-36
02Lincoln Stars-44
03Minnesota Golden Gophers-23
04Minnesota Golden Gophers-20
05Minnesota Golden Gophers-20
06Be A Player-222
06Be A Player Portraits-120
06Beehive-141
Blue-141
Matte-141
Red Facsimile Signatures-141
Wood-141
06Black Diamond-192
Black-192
Gold-192
Ruby-192
06Flair Showcase-74
Parallel-74
06Fleer-228
Tiffany-228
06Hot Prospects-125
Red Hot-125
White Hot-125
Hotagraphs-HRY
06O-Pee-Chee-509
06O-Pee-Chee-633
Rainbow-509
Rainbow-633
06SP Authentic-193
Limited-193
06SP Game Used-139
Gold-139
Rainbow-139
Autographs-139
Letter Marks-LMPO
Rookie Exclusives Autographs-REPO
06SPx-167
Spectrum-167
06The Cup-146
Autographed Rookie Masterpiece Pressplates-146
Gold Rainbow Autographed Rookie Patches-146
Masterpiece Pressplates (Artifacts)-208
Masterpiece Pressplates (Be A Player Portraits)-120
Masterpiece Pressplates (Bee Hive)-141
Masterpiece Pressplates (Marquee Rookies)-509
Masterpiece Pressplates (MVP)-353
Masterpiece Pressplates (Power Play)-120
Masterpiece Pressplates (SP Authentic Autographs)-193
Masterpiece Pressplates (SP Game Used)-139
Masterpiece Pressplates (SPx Autographs)-167
Masterpiece Pressplates (Sweet Beginnings)-142
Masterpiece Pressplates (Trilogy)-140
Masterpiece Pressplates (Ultimate Collection Autographs)-122
Masterpiece Pressplates (Victory)-226
NHL Shields Duals-DSHFP
Rookies Black-146
Rookies Platinum-146
06UD Artifacts-208
Blue-208
Gold-208
Platinum-208
Radiance-208
Red-208
06UD Mini Jersey Collection-120
06UD Powerplay-120
Impact Rainbow-120
06Ultimate Collection-122
Rookies Autographed NHL Shields-122
Rookies Autographed Patches-122
Ultimate Debut Threads Jerseys-DJ-RP
Ultimate Debut Threads Jerseys Autographs-DJ-RP
Ultimate Debut Threads Patches-DJ-RP
Ultimate Debut Threads Patches Autographs-DJ-RP
06Ultra-220
Gold Medallion-220
Ice Medallion-220
06Upper Deck-232
Exclusives Parallel-232
High Gloss Parallel-232
Masterpieces-232
Rookie Game Dated Moments-RGD19
Rookie Headliners-RH8
Rookie Materials-RMRP
Rookie Materials Patches-RMRP
06Upper Deck MVP-353
Gold Script-353
Super Script-353
06Upper Deck Ovation-37
06Upper Deck Sweet Shot-142
Rookie Jerseys Autographs-142
06Upper Deck Trilogy-140
06Upper Deck Victory-226
06Upper Deck Victory Black-226
06Upper Deck Victory Gold-226
06Philadelphia Phantoms-3
07Upper Deck Rookie Class -19

Potvin, Denis
74NHL Action Stamps-179
74O-Pee-Chee NHL-195
74O-Pee-Chee NHL-233
74O-Pee-Chee NHL-252
74Topps-195
74Topps-233
74Topps-252
75Heroes Stand-Ups-16
75O-Pee-Chee NHL-275
75O-Pee-Chee NHL-287
75O-Pee-Chee NHL-323
75Topps-275
75Topps-287
75Topps-323
76O-Pee-Chee NHL-5
76O-Pee-Chee NHL-170
76O-Pee-Chee NHL-389
76Topps-5
76Topps-170
76Topps Glossy Inserts-10
77O-Pee-Chee NHL-10
77Sportscasters-1709
77Topps-10
77Topps/O-Pee-Chee Glossy-15
Square-15
77Finnish Sportscasters-56-1324
78O-Pee-Chee-245
78O-Pee-Chee-334
78Topps-245
79Islanders Transparencies-14
79O-Pee-Chee-70
79Topps-70
80O-Pee-Chee-120
80O-Pee-Chee Super-13
80Topps-120
81O-Pee-Chee-199
81O-Pee-Chee-209
81O-Pee-Chee Stickers-151
81O-Pee-Chee Stickers-159
81Topps-27
81Topps-E130
82McDonald's Stickers-18
82McDonald's Stickers-33
82O-Pee-Chee-210
82O-Pee-Chee Stickers-46
82Post Cereal-12
82Topps Stickers-46
83Islanders Team Issue-13
83NHL Key Tags-81
83O-Pee-Chee-2
83O-Pee-Chee-16
83O-Pee-Chee Stickers-81
83O-Pee-Chee Stickers-82
83O-Pee-Chee Stickers-169
83O-Pee-Chee Stickers-175
83Puffy Stickers-20
83Topps Stickers-81
83Topps Stickers-82
83Topps Stickers-169
83Topps Stickers-175
84Islanders News-21
84O-Pee-Chee-134
84O-Pee-Chee-216
84O-Pee-Chee-389
84O-Pee-Chee Stickers-66
84O-Pee-Chee Stickers-78
84O-Pee-Chee Stickers-79
84O-Pee-Chee Stickers-145
84Topps-100
84Topps-162
85Islanders News-25
85Islanders News-33
85Islanders News Trottier-31
85O-Pee-Chee-25
85O-Pee-Chee Stickers-70
85Topps-25
86Islanders Team Issue-12
86O-Pee-Chee-129
86O-Pee-Chee Stickers-209
86Topps-129
87O-Pee-Chee-1
87O-Pee-Chee Stickers-247
87Panini Stickers-91
87Topps-1
88Esso All-Stars-36
90Pro Set-656
90Upper Deck-515
French-515
91Kraft-61
91Kraft-72
91Pro Set HOF Induction-2
92Future Trends '76 Canada Cup-181
92O-Pee-Chee-57
25th Anniv. Inserts-7
93Islanders Chemical Bank Alumni-7
99Upper Deck Century Legends-15
Century Collection-15
00UD Heroes-132
Signs of Greatness-DP
00Upper Deck Legends-80
Legendary Collection Bronze-80
Legendary Collection Gold-80
Legendary Collection Silver-80
Enshrined Stars-ES6
Epic Signatures-DP
Legendary Game Jerseys-JDP
00Upper Deck Vintage Dynasty: A Piece of History-PR
00Upper Deck Vintage Dynasty: A Piece of History Gold-PR
01BAP Ultimate Mem All-Star History-27
01BAP Ultimate Memorabilia Calder Trophy-20
01BAP Ultimate Memorabilia Captain's C-11
01BAP Ultimate Memorabilia Decades-17
01BAP Ultimate Mem Dynasty Jerseys-11
01BAP Ultimate Mem Dynasty Emblems-11
01BAP Ultimate Mem Dynasty Numbers-11
01BAP Ultimate Memorabilia Emblem Attic-15
01BAP Ultimate Mem Retired Numbers-20
01BAP Ultimate Mem Retro Teammates-5
01BAP Ultimate Mem Stanley Cup Winners-25
01Fleer Legacy-41
Ultimate-41
In the Corners-7
01Greats of the Game-51
Autographs-51
01Parkhurst Autographs-PA48
01Parkhurst He Shoots-He Scores Prizes-11
01Topps Rookie Reprints-1
01Topps Rookie Reprint Autographs-1
01Topps Stanley Cup Heroes-SCHDP
01Topps Stanley Cup Heroes Autographs-SCHADP
01Topps Archives-37
Autographs-3
Autoproofs-3
01Upper Deck Legends-41
Jerseys-TTDP
Jerseys Platinum-TTDP
Milestones-MDP
Milestones Platinum-MDP
Sticks-PHDP
02BAP Memorabilia Mini Stanley Cups-20
02BAP NHL All-Star History-27
02BAP Ultimate Memorabilia Numerology-8
02Fleer Throwbacks-17
Gold-17
Platinum-17
Autographs-8
Squaring Off-5
Squaring Off Memorabilia-5
02Parkhurst Vintage Teammates-VT11
02UD Foundations 1000 Point Club-DP
02UD Foundations 1000 Point Club-PO
02UD Foundations 1000 Point Club Gold-DP
02UD Foundations 1000 Point Club Silver-DP
02UD Foundations Classic Greats-GDP
02UD Foundations Classic Greats Gold-GDP
02UD Foundations Classic Greats Silver-G-DP
02UD Foundations Defense First-DDP
02UD Foundations Defense First Gold-DDP
02UD Foundations Defense First Silver-D-DP
02UD Foundations Milestones-NDP
02UD Foundations Milestones Gold-NDP
02UD Foundations Milestones Silver-N-DP
02UD Foundations Signs of Greatness-SGDP
03BAP Ultimate Memorabilia Cornerstones-8
03BAP Ultimate Mem Hometown Heroes-19
03BAP Ultimate Mem Hometown Heroes Gold-19
03BAP Ultimate Mem Retro Teammates-6
03BAP Ultimate Mem Vintage Jerseys-37
03BAP Ultimate Mem Vintage Jerseys Gold-37
03Canada Post-10
03ITG Used Signature Series Norris Trophy-12
03ITG Used Sig Series Norris Trophy Gold-12
03Parkhurst Rookie High Expectations-HE-7
03Parkhurst Rookie High Expectations Gold-HE-7
03Parkhurst Rookie ROYalty-VR-15
03Parkhurst Rookie ROYalty Gold-VR-15
03Upper Deck Trilogy-135
Crest Variations-135
Limited-135
Scripts-S3DP
Scripts-S3PN
Scripts Limited-S3DP
Scripts Limited-S3PN
Scripts Red-S3DP
04ITG NHL AS FANtasy AS History Jerseys-SB27
04ITG Franchises He Shoots/Scores Prizes-42
04ITG Franchises US East-371
Autographs-A-DP
Barn Burners-EBB3
Barn Burners Gold-EBB3
Complete Jerseys-ECJ7
Complete Jerseys Gold-ECJ7
Double Memorabilia-EDM14
Double Memorabilia Autographs-EDM-DP
Double Memorabilia Gold-EDM14
Forever Rivals-EFR6
Forever Rivals Gold-EFR6
Memorabilia-ESM13
Memorabilia Autographs-ESM-DP
Memorabilia Gold-ESM13
Original Sticks-EOS12
Original Sticks Autographs-EOS-DP
Original Sticks Gold-EOS12
Teammates-ETM7
Teammates Gold-ETM7
Trophy Winners-ETW8
Trophy Winners Gold-ETW8
04ITG Ultimate Memorabilia-49
Gold-49
Auto Threads-21
Autographs-30
Autographs Gold-30
Calder Trophy-8
Cornerstones-9
Cornerstones Gold-9
Country of Origin-16
Country of Origin Gold-16
Day In History-29
Day In History-31
Day In History Gold-29
Day In History Gold-31
Jersey Autographs-33
Jersey Autographs Gold-33
Jersey and Sticks-2
Jersey and Sticks Gold-2
Norris Trophy-6
Retro Teammates-5
Triple Threads-2
04UD Legendary Signatures-25
Autographs-DP
Rearguard Retrospectives-DPKM
04ITG Heroes and Prospects-141
Autographs-DPO
Hero Memorabilia-18
04ITG Heroes/Prospects Toronto Expo '05-141
04ITG Heroes/Prospects Expo Heroes/Pros-141
05ITG Ultimate Memorabilia Level 1-24
05ITG Ultimate Memorabilia Level 2-24
05ITG Ultimate Memorabilia Level 3-24
05ITG Ultimate Memorabilia Level 4-24
05ITG Ultimate Memorabilia Level 5-24
05ITG Ultimate Mem Cornerstones Jerseys-8
05ITG Ultimate Mem Cornerst Jerseys Gold-8
05ITG Ultimate Memorabilia Emblems-28
05ITG Ultimate Memorabilia Emblems Gold-28
05ITG Ultimate Mem First Overall Jerseys-3
05ITG Ultimate Mem 1st Overall Jsy Gold-3
05ITG Ultimate Memorabilia In The Numbers-12
05ITG Ultimate Mem In The Numbers Gold-12
05ITG Ultimate Mem Jersey and Emblem-14
05ITG Ultimate Memorabilia Jersey Autos-33
05ITG Ultimate Mem Jersey Autos Gold-33
05ITG Ultimate Mem Jersey Emblems Gold-14
05ITG Ultimate Memorabilia Jerseys-11
05ITG Ultimate Memorabilia Jerseys Gold-11
05ITG Ultimate Memorabilia R.O.Y. Autos-2
05ITG Ultimate Mem R.O.Y. Autos Gold-2
05ITG Ultimate Mem Raised to the Rafters-10
05ITG Ultimate Mem Raised Rafters Gold-10
05ITG Ultimate Mem Record Breaker Jerseys-20
05ITG Ultimate Mem RecBreak Jerseys Gold-20
05ITG Ultimate Mem Retro Teammate Jerseys-3
05ITG Ult Mem Retro Teammates Jersey Gold-3
05ITG Ultimate Memorabilia Stick Autos-37
05ITG Ultimate Mem Stick Autos Gold-37
05ITG Ultimate Mem Sticks and Jerseys-19
05ITG Ultimate Mem Stick and Jerseys Gold-19
05ITG Ultimate Mem 3 Star of the Game Jsy-20
05ITG Ult Mem 3 Star of the Game Jsy Gold-20
05ITG Ultimate Memorabilia Triple Autos-19
05ITG Ultimate Mem Triple Autos Gold-19
05ITG Ultimate Mem Triple Threads Jerseys-5
05ITG Ultimate Mem Triple Thread Jsy Gold-5
05SP Authentic Sign of the Times Quads-QTBNP
05The Cup-66
Gold-66
Black Rainbow-66
Hardware Heroes-HHDP1
Hardware Heroes-HHDP2
Honorable Numbers-HNPO
Limited Logos-LLDP
Masterpiece Pressplates-66
Noble Numbers-NNPM
Noble Numbers Dual-DNNSP
Patch Variation-P66
Property of-PODP
Scripted Swatches-SSPO
Signature Patches-SPPO
05Ultimate Collection Endorsed Emblems-EEDP
05ITG Heroes and Prospects Hero Mem-HM-53
06ITG International Ice-74
06ITG International Ice-148
Gold-74
Gold-148
Autographs-ADP
Autographs-ADP2
Cornerstones-IC12
Cornerstones Gold-IC12
06ITG Ultimate Memorabilia-39
Artist Proof-39
Autos-36
Autos Gold-36
Boys Will Be Boys-18
Boys Will Be Boys Gold-18
Jerseys Autos-46
Jerseys Autos Gold-46
Retro Teammates-15
Retro Teammates Gold-15
Road to the Cup-6
Road to the Cup Gold-6
Stick Rack-24
Stick Rack Gold-24
06Parkhurst-100
06Parkhurst-191
Autographs-100
Autographs-191
Autographs Dual-DARP
06SP Authentic Sign of the Times Duals-STRP
06SP Game Used Inked Sweaters Dual-IS2BP
06SP Game Used Inked Sweaters Dual Patches-IS2BP
06SP Game Used Letter Marks-LMDP
06SP Game Used SIGnificance-SDP
06The Cup-58
Black Rainbow-58
Gold-58
Gold Patches-58
Masterpiece Pressplates-58
Stanley Cup Signatures-CSDP
06UD Artifacts-130
Blue-130
Gold-130
Platinum-130
Radiance-130
Red-130
06Ultimate Collection Autographed Jerseys-AJ-DP
06Ultimate Collection Autographed Patches-AJ-DP
06Ultimate Collection Jerseys-UJ-PO
06Ultimate Collection Jerseys Dual-UJ2-RP
06Ultimate Collection Jerseys Triple-UJ3-SBG
06Ultimate Collection Signatures-US-PO
06Upper Deck Sweet Shot-69
Signature Shots/Saves-SSDP
Signature Shots/Saves Sticks-SSSDE
Signature Sticks-STPO
Sweet Stitches-SSPO
Sweet Stitches Duals-SSPO
Sweet Stitches Triples-SSPO
06Upper Deck Trilogy Combo Clearcut Autographs-C3BPS
06Upper Deck Trilogy Scripts-TSPO
06ITG Heroes and Prospects-29
Autographs-ADP

Potvin, Felix
90Upper Deck-458
French-458
907th Inn. Sketch QMJHL-35
907th Inn. Sketch QMJHL-159
91Parkhurst-398
French-398
91Pinnacle-345
French-345
91Upper Deck-460
French-460
91ProCards-354
917th Inn. Sketch CHL Award Winners-26
917th Inn. Sketch Memorial Cup-26
917th Inn. Sketch Memorial Cup-72
92Bowman-77
92Maple Leafs Kodak-20
92O-Pee-Chee-73
92OPC Premier-114
Top Rookies-4
92Panini Stickers-G
92Panini Stickers French-G
92Parkhurst-187
92Parkhurst-507
Emerald Ice-187
Emerald Ice-507
92Pinnacle-364
French-364
Team 2000-5
Team 2000 French-5
92Pro Set-242
92Score-472
92Score-501
Canadian-472
Canadian-501
Young Superstars-39
92Sports Illustrated for Kids II-356
92Stadium Club-338
92Topps-3
Gold-3G
92Ultra-213
92Upper Deck-79
Calder Candidates-CC3
93Donruss-343
Elite Inserts-U3
Ice Kings-6
Special Print-W
93Durivage Score-32
93High Liner Greatest Goalies-13
93Kraft-61
93Leaf-409
Gold All-Stars-10
Gold Rookies-4
Painted Warriors-1
Maple Leafs Score Black's-24
93OPC Premier-30
93OPC Premier-111
93OPC Premier-126
93OPC Premier-385
Gold-30
Gold-111
Gold-126
Gold-385
Black Gold-17
93Panini Stickers-139
93Panini Stickers-232
93Parkhurst-202
93Parkhurst-237
Emerald Ice-202
Emerald Ice-237
Cherry's Playoff Heroes-D14
East/West Stars-W9
93Pinnacle-190
Canadian-190
Team 2001-5
Team 2001 Canadian-5
93PowerPlay-246
Gamebreakers-7
Netminders-5
Rising Stars-3
Second Year Stars-8
93Score Samples-5
93Score-5
93Score-484
Canadian-5
Canadian-484
93Seasons Patches-14
93Stadium Club-280
Members Only Master Set-280
First Day Issue-280
Finest-5
Finest Members Only-5
Master Photos-24
Master Photos Winners-24
93Topps/OPC Premier-30
93Topps/OPC Premier-111
93Topps/OPC Premier-126
93Topps/OPC Premier-385
Gold-30
Gold-111
Gold-126
Gold-385
93Topps Premier Black Gold-3
93Ultra-30
93Upper Deck-159
93Upper Deck-285
Future Heroes-28
Next In Line-NL6
NHLPA/Roots-3
SP-160
93Upper Deck Locker All-Stars-58
93Classic-123
Crash Numbered-N9
93Classic Pro Prospects-80
BCs-BC7
94Be A Player Magazine-2
94Be A Player-R81
94Be A Player-R138
94Be A Player-R173
94Canada Games NHL POGS-296
94Donruss-12
Dominators-7
Elite Inserts-8
Masked Marvels-7
94EA Sports-138
94Finest-26
Super Team Winners-26
Refractors-26
94Flair-184
94Fleer-218
Netminders-7
94Hockey Wit-34
94Kraft-49
94Kraft Goalie Masks-5
94Leaf-186
Crease Patrol-4
Gold Stars-13
94Leaf Limited-16
94Maple Leafs Gangsters-15
94Maple Leafs Kodak-21
94Maple Leafs Pin-up Posters-14
94Maple Leafs Postcards-2
94Maple Leafs Postcards-4
94McDonald's Upper Deck-McD14
94OPC Premier-238
94OPC Premier-313
94OPC Premier-355
Special Effects-238
Special Effects-313
Special Effects-355
94Parkhurst-229
Gold-229
SE Vintage-32
94Pinnacle-83
Artist's Proofs-83
Rink Collection-83
Goaltending Greats-GT8
Northern Lights-NL9
Team Pinnacle-TP1
Team Dufex Parallel-TP1
94Post Box Backs-20
94Score-160
Gold-160
Platinum-160
Dream Team-DT2
94Select Promos-90
94Select-90
Gold-90
94SP-117
Die Cuts-117
94Stadium Club Members Only-1
94Stadium Club-15
94Stadium Club-185
Members Only Master Set-15
Members Only Master Set-185
First Day Issue-15
First Day Issue-185
Super Team Winner Cards-15
Super Team Winner Cards-185
94Topps/OPC Premier-238
94Topps/OPC Premier-313
94Topps/OPC Premier-355
Special Effects-238
Special Effects-313
Special Effects-355
94Topps Finest Bronze-18
94Ultra-219
All-Stars-12
Premier Pad Men-4
94Upper Deck-367
Electric Ice-367
Predictor Hobby-H28
94Upper Deck Predictor Hobby Exch Gold-H28
94Upper Deck SP Inserts-SP80
94Upper Deck SP Inserts Die Cuts-SP80
94Upper Deck NHLPA/Be A Player-11
94Classic Pro Prospects-51
Jumbos-PP7
94Images *-121
95SLU Hockey Canadian-11
95SLU Hockey American-15
95Bashan Super Stickers-120
Die-Cut-19
95Be A Player-195
Signatures-S195
Signatures Die Cuts-S195
95Bowman-79
All-Foil-79
95Canada Games NHL POGS-268
95Collector's Choice-114
Player's Club-114
Player's Club Platinum-114
95Donruss-9
Between The Pipes-9
Dominators-8
95Donruss Elite-97
Die Cut Stars-97
Die Cut Uncut-97
Painted Warriors-2
95Emotion-174
95Finest-105
95Finest-135
Refractors-105
Refractors-135
95Hoyle Western Playing Cards-50
95Imperial Stickers-120
Die Cut Superstars-19
95Kenner Starting Lineup Cards-17
95Kraft-23
95Leaf-160
95Leaf Limited-29
Stick Side-3
95McDonald's Pinnacle-MCD-26
95Metal-146
95Metal Promo Panel-1
95NHL Aces Playing Cards-4S
95Panini Stickers-210
95Parkhurst International-204
Emerald Ice-204
Crown Collection Silver Series 1-2
Crown Collection Gold Series 1-2
Goal Patrol-2
95Pinnacle-142
Artist's Proofs-142
Rink Collection-142
Masks-4
Roaring 20s-10
95Pinnacle FANtasy-29
95Playoff One on One-98
95Playoff One on One-204
95Post Upper Deck-22
95Pro Magnets-79
95Score-4
95Score-316
Black Ice Artist's Proofs-4
Black Ice Artist's Proofs-316
Black Ice-4
Black Ice-316
95Select Certified Promos-69
95Select Certified-69
Mirror Gold-69
95SkyBox Impact-164
Deflectors-3
95SP-146
Stars/Etoiles-E27
Stars/Etoiles Gold-E27
95Stadium Club Members Only-40
95Stadium Club-80
Members Only Master Set-80
Extreme North-EN3
Extreme North Members Only Master Set-EN3
95Stadium Club Master Photo Test-7
95Summit-80
Artist's Proofs-80
Ice-80
In The Crease-5
95Topps-315
OPC Inserts-315
Canadian Gold-8CG
Home Grown Canada-HGC18
Mystery Finest-M22
Mystery Finest Refractors-M22
95Topps SuperSkills-85
Platinum-85
95Ultra-162
95Ultra-375
Gold Medallion-162
Premier Pad Men-9
Premier Pad Men Gold Medallion-9
95Upper Deck-48
95Upper Deck-228
Electric Ice-48
Electric Ice-228
Electric Ice Gold-48
Electric Ice Gold-228
NHL All-Stars-AS20
NHL All-Stars Jumbo-AS20
Predictor Hobby-H17
Predictor Hobby Exchange-H17
Special Edition-SE168
Special Edition Gold-SE168
95Zenith-76
Z-Team-17
96Be A Player Stacking the Pads-6
96Black Diamond-129
Gold-129
96Collector's Choice-257
96Collector's Choice-332
MVP-UD20
MVP Gold-UD20
Stick'Ums-S11
96Collector's Choice Blow-Ups-257
96Collector's Choice Blow-Ups Bi-Way-7
96Donruss-96
Press Proofs-96
Between the Pipes-10
96Donruss Canadian Ice-67
Gold Press Proofs-67
Red Press Proofs-67
Les Gardiens-3
96Donruss Elite-5
Die Cut Stars-5
Painted Warriors-6
Painted Warriors Promos-P6
96Duracell L'Equipe Beliveau-JB12
96Flair-91
Blue Ice-91
Hot Gloves-8
96Fleer-109
Vezina-7
96Frosted Flakes Masks-1
96Kraft Upper Deck-61
96Leaf-156
Press Proofs-156
Shut Down-8
96Leaf Limited-80
Gold-80
96Leaf Preferred-36
Press Proofs-36
Masked Marauders-5
Vanity Plates-10
Vanity Plates Gold-10
96Maggers-77
96Maple Leafs Postcards-2
96McDonald's Pinnacle-38
96Metal Universe-152
Armor Plate-7
Armor Plate Super Power-7
96NHL Pro Stamps-79
96Pinnacle-96
Artist's Proofs-96
Foil-96
Premium Stock-96
Rink Collection-96
96Pinnacle Mint-24
Bronze-24
Gold-24
Silver-24
Coins Brass-24
Coins Solid Gold-24
Coins Gold Plated-24
Coins Nickel-24
Coins Silver-24
96Playoff One on One-364
96Post Upper Deck-14
96Score-172
Artist's Proofs-172
Dealer's Choice Artist's Proofs-172
Special Artist's Proofs-172
Golden Blades-172
Sudden Death-12
Superstitions-5
96Select Certified-31
Artist's Proofs-31
Blue-31
Mirror Blue-31
Mirror Gold-31
Mirror Red-31
Red-31
Freezers-8
96SkyBox Impact-129
Zero Heroes-7
96SP-153
Inside Info-IN7
Inside Info Gold-IN7
Game Film-GF7
96SPx-44
Gold-44
96Stadium Club Members Only-13
96Summit-72
Artist's Proofs-72
Ice-72
Metal-72
Premium Stock-72
In The Crease-9
In The Crease Premium Stock-9
Untouchables-17
96Team Out-74
96Topps Picks Ice D-ID14
96Ultra-165
Gold Medallion-165
96Upper Deck-341
96Upper Deck-360
Generation Next-X33
Superstar Showdown-SS11A
96Upper Deck Ice-67
Parallel-67
96Zenith-31
Artist's Proofs-31
Z-Team-16
96Collector's Edge Ice Livin' Large-L7
97Headliners Hockey-19
97Be A Player-4
Autographs-4
Autographs Die-Cuts-4
Autographs Prismatic Die-Cuts-4
Stacking the Pads-3
97Beehive-16
Golden Portraits-16
97Black Diamond-5
Double Diamond-5
Triple Diamond-5
Quadruple Diamond-5
97Collector's Choice-252
Star Quest-SQ29
97Crown Royale-131
Emerald Green-131
Ice Blue-131
Silver-131
Freeze Out Die-Cuts-19
97Donruss-154
Press Proofs Silver-154
Press Proofs Gold-154
Between The Pipes-9
97Donruss Canadian Ice-56
Dominion Series-56
Provincial Series-56
Les Gardiens-2
97Donruss Canadian Ice Les Gardiens Promo-2
97Donruss Elite-100
97Donruss Elite-131
Aspirations-100
Aspirations-131
Status-100
Status-131
Craftsmen-13
Master Craftsmen-13
97Donruss Limited-29
97Donruss Limited-57
97Donruss Limited-77
Exposure-29
Exposure-57
Exposure-77
Fabric of the Game-15
97Donruss Preferred-99
Cut to the Chase-99
Color Guard-5
Color Guard Promos-5
97Donruss Priority-101
97Donruss Priority-198
Stamp of Approval-101
Stamp of Approval-198
Postcards-29
Postcards Opening Day Issues-25
Postmaster General-3
Postmaster Generals Promos-3
Stamps-29
Stamps Bronze-29
Stamps Gold-29
Stamps Silver-29
97Highland Mint Mint-Cards Topps-21
97Highland Mint Mint-Cards Topps-22
97Katch-142
Gold-142
Silver-142
97Leaf-24
97Leaf-P5
Fractal Matrix-24
Fractal Matrix Die Cuts-24
Pipe Dreams-5
97Leaf International-24
Universal Ice-24
97McDonald's Upper Deck-31
97NHL Aces Playing Cards-43
97Pacific-29
Copper-29
Emerald Green-29
Ice Blue-29
Red-29
Silver-29
Card-Supials-19
Card-Supials Minis-19
In The Cage Laser Cuts-20
Team Checklists-24
97Pacific Dynagon-122
Copper-122
Dark Grey-122
Emerald Green-122
Ice Blue-122
Red-122
Silver-122
Best Kept Secrets-92
Stonewallers-20
Tandems-17
97Pacific Invincible-137
Copper-137
Emerald Green-137
Ice Blue-137
Red-137
Silver-137
Feature Performers-33
NHL Regime-195
97Pacific Omega-223
Copper-223
Dark Gray-223
Emerald Green-223
Gold-223
Ice Blue-223
No Scoring Zone-10
Team Leaders-18
97Paramount-183
Copper-183
Dark Grey-183
Emerald Green-183
Ice Blue-183
Red-183
Silver-183
Glove Side Laser Cuts-20
97Pinnacle-95
Artist's Proofs-95
Rink Collection-95
Epix Game Emerald-11
Epix Game Orange-11
Epix Game Purple-11
Epix Moment Emerald-11
Epix Moment Orange-11
Epix Moment Purple-11
Epix Play Emerald-11
Epix Play Orange-11
Epix Play Purple-11
Epix Season Emerald-11
Epix Season Orange-11
Epix Season Purple-11
Press Plates Back Black-95
Press Plates Back Cyan-95
Press Plates Back Magenta-95
Press Plates Back Yellow-95
Press Plates Front Black-95
Press Plates Front Cyan-95
Press Plates Front Magenta-95
Press Plates Front Yellow-95
97Pinnacle Certified-11
Red-11
Mirror Blue-11
Mirror Gold-11
Mirror Red-11
97Pinnacle Inside-46
Coach's Collection-46
Executive Collection-46
Stoppers-21
Track-20
97Pinnacle Tot Cert Platinum Blue-11
97Pinnacle Tot Certi Platinum Gold-11
97Pinnacle Totally Certified Platinum Red-11
97Pinnacle Tot Cert Mirror Platinum Gold-11
97Revolution-136
Copper-136
Emerald-136
Ice Blue-136
Silver-136
Return to Sender Die-Cuts-19
97Score-29
Artist's Proofs-29
Golden Blades-29
Net Worth-16
97Score Maple Leafs-1
Platinum-1
Premier-1
97SP Authentic-151
97Studio-66
Press Proofs Silver-66
Press Proofs Gold-66
Portraits-34
Silhouettes-20
Silhouettes 8x10-20
97Upper Deck-367
97Upper Deck Ice-29
Parallel-29
Power Shift-29
97Zenith-38
Z-Gold-38
Z-Silver-38
97Zenith 5 x 7-42
Gold Impulse-42
Silver Impulse-42
98SLU Hockey-170
98Black Diamond-54
98Finest-70
No Protectors-70
No Protectors Refractors-70
Refractors-70
98Kenner Starting Lineup Cards-25
98NHL Aces Playing Cards-12
98OPC Chrome-29
Refractors-29
98Pacific-29
Ice Blue-29
Red-29
Gold Crown Die-Cuts-31
98Pacific Omega-150
Red-150
Opening Day Issue-150
Online-22
Planet Ice-5
Planet Ice Parallel-5
98Panini Photocards-63
98Panini Stickers-165
98SPx Top Prospects Winning Materials-FP

98Topps-29
O-Pee-Chee-29
98Upper Deck-371
Exclusives-371
Exclusives 1 of 1-371
Gold Reserve-371
98Upper Deck MVP-126
Gold Script-126
Silver Script-126
Super Script-126
99Aurora-91
Striped-91
Premiere Date-91
Premiere Date Striped-91
Glove Unlimited-12
99BAP Memorabilia-139
99BAP Memorabilia-325
Gold-139
Gold-325
Silver-139
Silver-325
99O-Pee-Chee-136
99O-Pee-Chee Chrome-136
99O-Pee-Chee Chrome Refractors-136
99Pacific-263
Copper-263
Emerald Green-263
Gold-263
Ice Blue-263
Premiere Date-263
Red-263
Gold Crown Die-Cuts-22
In the Cage Net-Fusions-11
99Pacific Dynagon Ice-127
Blue-127
Copper-127
Gold-127
Premiere Date-127
99Pacific Omega-237
Copper-237
Gold-237
Ice Blue-237
Premiere Date-237
99Panini Stickers-91
99Panini Stickers-338
99Paramount-146
Copper-146
Emerald-146
Gold-146
Holographic Emerald-146
Holographic Gold-146
Holographic Silver-146
Ice Blue-146
Premiere Date-146
Red-146
Silver-146
Glove Side Net Fusions-12
Ice Alliance-17
Toronto Fall Expo '99-146
99Revolution-93
Premiere Date-93
Red-93
Shadow Series-93
Showstoppers-22
Copper-93
Gold-93
CSC Silver-93
99SPx-91
Radiance-91
Spectrum-91
99Stadium Club-69
First Day Issue-69
One of a Kind-69
Printing Plates Black-69
Printing Plates Cyan-69
Printing Plates Magenta-69
Printing Plates Yellow-69
99Topps/OPC-136
99Topps/OPC Chrome-136
Refractors-136
99Upper Deck-253
Exclusives-253
Exclusives 1 of 1-253
99Upper Deck Gold Reserve-253
99Upper Deck MVP-124
Gold Script-124
Silver Script-124
Super Script-124
Draw Your Own Trading Card-W16
99Upper Deck Victory-184
00Aurora-145
Pinstripes-145
Pinstripes Premiere Date-145
Premiere Date-145
00BAP Memorabilia-45
00BAP Memorabilia-503
Emerald-45
Ruby-45
Sapphire-45
Promos-45
Goalie Memorabilia-G9
Goalie Memorabilia-G20
00BAP Mem Chicago Sportsfest Copper-45
00BAP Memorabilia Chicago Sportsfest Blue-45
00BAP Memorabilia Chicago Sportsfest Gold-45
00BAP Memorabilia Chicago Sportsfest Ruby-45
00BAP Memorabilia Chicago Sun-Times Ruby-45
00BAP Memorabilia Chicago Sun-Times Gold-45
00BAP Mem Chicago Sun-Times Sapphire-45
00BAP Mem Toronto Fall Expo Copper-45
00BAP Memorabilia Toronto Fall Expo Gold-45
00BAP Memorabilia Toronto Fall Expo Ruby-45
00BAP Mem Update Heritage Jersey Cards-H19
00BAP Mem Update Heritage Jersey Gold-H19
00BAP Parkhurst 2000-P79
00BAP Signature Series-90
Emerald-90
Ruby-90
Sapphire-90
Autographs-153
Autographs Gold-153
00BAP Ultimate Mem Game-Used Jerseys-GJ37
00BAP Ultimate Mem Game-Used Sticks-GS37
00BAP Ultimate Mem Goalie Memorabilia-GM4
00BAP Ultimate Memorabilia Goalie Sticks-G29
00BAP Ultimate Mem Plante Jersey Cards-PJ13
00BAP Ultimate Mem Plante Stick Cards-PS13
00BAP Ultimate Mem Journey Jerseys-JJ20
00BAP Ultimate Mem Journey Emblems-JE20
00BAP Ultimate Mem Journey Numbers-JI20
00BAP Ultimate Memorabilia Teammates-TM38
00Black Diamond-58
Gold-58
00Crown Royale-105
Ice Blue-105
Limited Series-105
Premiere Date-105
Red-105
Game-Worn Jerseys-25
Game-Worn Jersey Patches-25
Premium-Sized Game-Worn Jerseys-25

00McDonald's Pacific-35
Blue-35
Checklists-9
00O-Pee-Chee-56
00O-Pee-Chee Parallel-56
00Pacific-414
Copper-414
Gold-414
Ice Blue-414
Premiere Date-414
00Paramount-242
Copper-242
Gold-242
Holo-Gold-242
Holo-Silver-242
Ice Blue-242
Premiere Date-242
Glove Side Net Fusions-19
Glove Side Net Fusions Platinum-19
00Private Stock-97
Gold-97
Premiere Date-97
Retail-97
Silver-97
00Revolution-145
Blue-145
Premiere Date-145
Red-145
00SP Authentic BuyBacks-99
00SP Authentic BuyBacks-100
00SP Authentic BuyBacks-101
00SP Authentic Sign of the Times-FP
00SPx-67
Spectrum-67
Winning Materials-FP
Winning Materials Autographs-SFP
00Stadium Club-75
00Titanium-97
Blue-97
Gold-97
Premiere Date-97
Red-97
Retail-97
Game Gear-49
Game Gear-149
Game Gear Patches-149
Three-Star Selections-9
00Titanium Draft Day Edition-48
00Topps/OPC-56
Parallel-56
00Topps Chrome-44
OPC Refractors-44
Refractors-44
00Topps Heritage-124
00Topps Stars-90
Blue-90
00UD Heroes Signs of Greatness-FP
00Upper Deck-170
Exclusives Tier 1-170
Exclusives Tier 2-170
Game Jersey Doubles-DFP
00Upper Deck MVP-174
First Stars-174
Second Stars-174
Third Stars-174
00Upper Deck Victory-230
00Upper Deck Vintage-357
00Upper Deck Vintage-358
Great Gloves-GG19
00Vanguard-97
Holographic Gold-97
Holographic Purple-97
Pacific Proofs-97
00St. John's Maple Leafs-22
01Atomic-48
Blue-48
Gold-48
Premiere Date-48
Red-48
Jerseys-29
Patches-29
01BAP Memorabilia-78
Emerald-78
Ruby-78
Sapphire-78
Goalies Jerseys-GJ20
01BAP Signature Series Jerseys-GJ-87
01BAP Signature Series Teammates-TM-14
01BAP Ultimate Mem Journey Jerseys-5
01BAP Ultimate Mem Journey Emblems-5
01BAP Ultimate Memorabilia Terry Sawchuk-9
01BAP Update Heritage-H3
01BAP Update Travel Plans-TP13
01Between the Pipes-35
Double Memorabilia-DM1
Goalie Gear-GG1
He Shoots-He Saves Prizes-21
Jerseys-GJ20
Jersey and Stick Cards-GSJ19
Masks-18
Masks Silver-18
Masks Gold-18
01Bowman YoungStars-59
Gold-59
Ice Cubed-59
01Crown Royale-70
Blue-70
Premiere Date-70
Red-70
Retail-70
01McDonald's Pacific-19
01O-Pee-Chee-173
01O-Pee-Chee Premier Parallel-173
01Pacific-185
Extreme LTD-185
Hobby LTD-185
Premiere Date-185
Retail LTD-185
01Pacific Adrenaline-88
Blue-88
Premiere Date-88
Red-88
Retail-88
Creased Lightning-9
Jerseys-20
Power Play-18
01Pacific Arena Exclusives-185
01Pacific Heads-Up-47
Blue-47
Premiere Date-47
Red-47
Silver-47
HD NHL-15
Showstoppers-10
01Pacific Montreal International-4
01Parkhurst-59
Gold-59
Silver-59
01Private Stock-46
Gold-46
Premiere Date-46

Retail-46
Silver-46
Game Gear-52
Game Gear Patches-52
01Private Stock Pacific Nights-46
01Private Stock PS-2002-37
01SP Authentic-40
Limited-40
Limited Gold-40
Sign of the Times-FP
Sign of the Times-PP
Sign of the Times-SDP
01SP Game Used Authentic Fabric-AFFP
01SP Game Used Authentic Fabric-DFPP
01SP Game Used Authentic Fabric-DFPT
01SP Game Used Authentic Fabric Gold-AFFP
01SPx-31
Hidden Treasures-DTTP
01Stadium Club-92
Award Winners-92
Master Photos-92
01Titanium-67
Hobby Parallel-67
Premiere Date-67
Retail-67
Retail Parallel-67
Double-Sided Jerseys-17
Double-Sided Jerseys-20
Double-Sided Patches-17
Double-Sided Patches-20
01Titanium Draft Day Edition-43
01Topps-173
OPC Parallel-173
01Topps Chrome-119
Refractors-119
Black Border Refractors-119
01Topps Heritage-65
Refractors-65
01Topps Reserve-69
01UD Challenge for the Cup-38
Jerseys-TFP
Jersey Autographs-TPO
01UD Mask Collection-114
01UD Mask Collection-179
Gold-114
Gold-179
Double Patches-DPFP
Dual Jerseys-MBFP
Goalie Jerseys-SSFP
Goalie Jerseys-VCFP
Jerseys-J-FP
Jersey and Patch-JPFP
Sticks-SSFP
01UD Playmakers-46
01UD Premier Collection-28
Dual Jerseys-DDP
Dual Jerseys-DJP
Dual Jerseys Black-DDP
Dual Jerseys Black-DJP
Signatures-FP
Signatures Black-FP
01UD Top Shelf-96
01Upper Deck-308
Exclusives-308
Last Line of Defense-LL4
Pride of the Leafs-MLFP
01Upper Deck Ice-101
01Upper Deck MVP Masked Men-MM14
01Upper Deck Victory-158
01Upper Deck Victory-167
Gold-158
Gold-167
01Upper Deck Vintage-115
01Upper Deck Vintage-122
01Vanguard-46
Blue-46
Red-46
One of Ones-46
Premiere Date-46
Proofs-46
Quebec Tournament Heroes-8
02Kings Team Issue-4
02Atomic-50
Blue-50
Gold-50
Red-50
Denied-9
Hobby Parallel-50
02BAP All-Star Edition-71
Jerseys-71
Jerseys Gold-71
Jerseys Silver-71
02BAP First Edition-4
Jerseys-4
02BAP Memorabilia-35
02BAP Memorabilia-259
Emerald-35
Emerald-259
Ruby-35
Ruby-259
Sapphire-35
Sapphire-259
All-Star Jerseys-ASJ-42
NHL All-Star Game-35
NHL All-Star Game-259
NHL All-Star Game Blue-35
NHL All-Star Game Blue-259
NHL All-Star Game Green-35
NHL All-Star Game Green-259
NHL All-Star Game Red-35
NHL All-Star Game Red-259
Stanley Cup Playoffs-SC-11
Teammates-TM-13
02BAP Memorabilia Toronto Fall Expo-35
02BAP Memorabilia Toronto Fall Expo-259
02BAP Signature Series-63
Autographs-63
Autograph Buybacks 2000-153
Autographs Gold-63
Famous Scraps-FS8
Team Quads-TQ10
02Between the Pipes-27
02Between the Pipes-134
Gold-27
Silver-27
All-Star Stick and Jersey-8
Behind the Mask-18
Blockers-4
Emblems-8
Goalie Autographs-18
He Shoots-He Saves Points-8
He Shoots-He Saves Prizes-15
Jerseys-8
Masks II-14
Masks II Gold-14
Masks II Silver-14
Nightmares-GN4
Numbers-8
Stick and Jerseys-8

Tandems-10
02Bowman YoungStars-52
Gold-52
Silver-52
02Crown Royale-46
Blue-46
Red-46
Retail-46
02ITG Used-35
02ITG Used-135
Teammates-T17
Teammates Gold-T17
02Kings Game Sheets-15
02Kings Game Sheets-16
02Maple Leafs Platinum Collection-34
02O-Pee-Chee-172
02O-Pee-Chee Premier Blue Parallel-18
02O-Pee-Chee Premier Red Parallel-18
02O-Pee-Chee Factory Set-18
02Pacific-172
Blue-172
Red-172
02Pacific Complete-368
Red-368
02Pacific Exclusive-82
Advantage-9
02Pacific Heads-Up-58
Blue-58
Purple-58
Red-58
Quad Jerseys-13
Quad Jerseys Gold-13
Showstoppers-11
02Pacific Quest for the Cup-45
Gold-45
02Pacific Toronto Fall Expo-7
Gold-7
02Parkhurst-137
Bronze-137
Gold-137
Silver-137
Teammates-TT6
02Parkhurst Retro-68
Minis-68
Nicknames-RN25
02Private Stock Reserve-125
Red-125
Retail-125
InCrease Security-11
Patches-125
02SP Authentic-42
Beckett Promos-42
02SP Game Used-22
Authentic Fabrics-AFFP
Authentic Fabrics-CFFP
Authentic Fabrics Gold-AFFP
Authentic Fabrics Gold-CFFP
Authentic Fabrics Rainbow-AFFP
Authentic Fabrics Rainbow-CFFP
Piece of History-PHFP
Piece of History Gold-PHFP
Piece of History Rainbow-PHFP
02SPx-36
Spectrum Gold-36
Spectrum Silver-36
Winning Materials-WMFP
Winning Materials Gold-FP
Winning Materials Silver-FP
02Stadium Club-97
Silver Decoy Cards-97
Proofs-97
02Titanium-51
Blue-51
Red-51
Retail-51
02Topps-18
OPC Blue Parallel-18
OPC Red Parallel-18
Factory Set-18
02Topps Chrome-18
Black Border Refractors-18
Refractors-18
02Topps Heritage-83
Chrome Parallel-83
Crease Piece-FP
Crease Piece Patches-FP
02Topps Total-154
02UD Artistic Impressions-43
Gold-43
Artist's Touch-ATFP
Artist's Touch Gold-ATFP
02UD Artistic Impressions Beckett Promos-43
02UD Artistic Impressions Retrospectives-R43
02UD Artistic Impressions Retrospect Gold-R43
02UD Artistic Impress Retrospect Silver-R43
02UD Honor Roll-34
02UD Mask Collection-39
02UD Mask Collection-40
02UD Mask Collection-112
02UD Mask Collection Beckett Promos-39
02UD Mask Collection Beckett Promos-40
02UD Mask Collection Career Wins-CWFP
02UD Mask Collection Great Gloves-GGFP
02UD Mask Collection Masked Marvels-MMFP
02UD Mask Collection Mini Masks-FP
02UD Mask Collection Nation's Best-NRBP
02UD Mask Collection Patches-PWFP
02UD Piece of History-44
Patches-PHFP
02UD Top Shelf-41
Dual Player Jerseys-RPB
Milestones Jerseys-MHPBJ
Stopper Jerseys-SSFP
Sweet Sweaters-SWFP
Triple Jerseys-TSAPP
02Upper Deck-85
Exclusives-85
Blow-Ups-C19
Goaltender Threads-FP
Goaltender Threads Gold-FP
02Upper Deck Classic Portraits-46
Hockey Royalty-BPT
Hockey Royalty-DPP
Hockey Royalty Limited-BPT
Hockey Royalty Limited-DPP
Starring Cast-CFP
Starring Cast Limited-CFP
02Upper Deck MVP-85
Gold-85
Classics-85
Golden Classics-85
Skate Around Jerseys-SAFP
Skate Around Jerseys-SDBP
Skate Around Jerseys-SDPO
Skate Around Jerseys-SDPP
02Upper Deck Rookie Update-48
Jerseys-DFP
Jerseys Gold-DFP

02Upper Deck Victory-96
Bronze-96
Gold-96
Silver-96
02Upper Deck Vintage-119
02Upper Deck Vintage-274
Green Backs-119
Jerseys-EEFP
Jerseys Gold-EE-FP
02Vanguard-50
LTD-50
Stonewallers-5
02UD SuperStars City AS Dual Jersey-FPPL
03BAP Memorabilia-119
Emerald-119
Gold-119
Ruby-119
Sapphire-119
Masks III-16
Masks III Gold-16
Masks III Silver-16
Masks III Autographs-M-FP
Masks III Memorabilia-16
03BAP Ultimate Memorabilia Autographs-36
Gold-36
03BAP Ultimate Memorabilia Triple Threads-1
03Beehive-19
Gold-19
Silver-19
Sticks Beige Border-BE27
Sticks Blue Border-BL14
03Black Diamond-147
Black-147
Green-147
Red-147
03Bruins Team Issue-8
03Crown Royale-8
Blue-8
Retail-8
Gauntlet of Glory-3
03ITG Action-229
Jerseys-M112
03ITG Used Signature Series-48
Gold-48
Autographs-FP
Autographs Gold-FP
Goalie Gear-12
Goalie Gear Autographs-12
Goalie Gear Gold-12
Jerseys-9
Jerseys Gold-9
Jersey Autos-9
Jersey and Stick-9
Jersey and Stick Gold-9
03NHL Sticker Collection-240
03O-Pee-Chee-239
03OPC Blue-239
03OPC Gold-239
03OPC Red-239
03Pacific-159
Blue-159
Red-159
03Pacific Complete-460
Red-460
03Pacific Exhibit-70
Blue Backs-70
Yellow Backs-70
03Pacific Invincible Jerseys-14
03Pacific Prism-50
Blue-50
Gold-50
Red-50
03Parkhurst Original Six Boston-5
Memorabilia-BM51
Memorabilia-BM61
Memorabilia-BM63
03Parkhurst Original Six Toronto-33
03Parkhurst Original Six Toronto-68
Memorabilia-TM59
03Parkhurst Rookie Retro Rookies-RR-18
03Parkhurst Rookie Retro Rookies Gold-RR-18
03Private Stock Reserve-10
Blue-10
Red-10
Retail-10
Increase Security-2
03SP Authentic-6
Limited-6
03SPx-9
Radiance-9
Spectrum-9
03Titanium-10
Hobby Jersey Number Parallels-10
Retail-10
Retail Jersey Number Parallels-10
03Topps-239
Blue-239
Gold-239
Red-239
03Topps C55-43
Minis-43
Minis American Back-43
Minis American Back Red-43
Minis Bazooka Back-43
Minis Brooklyn Back-43
Minis Hat Trick Back-43
Minis O Canada Back-43
Minis O Canada Back Red-43
Minis Stanley Cup Back-43
03Topps Pristine-49
Gold Refractor Die Cuts-49
Refractors-49
Jersey Portions-PPJ-FP
Jersey Portion Refractors-PPJ-FP
Mini-PM-FP
Patches-PP-FP
Patch Refractors-PP-FP
Press Plates Black-49
Press Plates Cyan-49
Press Plates Magenta-49
Press Plates Yellow-49
03Topps Traded-TT1
Blue-TT1
Gold-TT1
Red-TT1
03UD Honor Roll-5
03Upper Deck-264
Canadian Exclusives-264
HG-264
UD Exclusives-264
MVP Souvenirs-S14
04Pacific-23
Blue-23
Red-23
06Between The Pipes-88
Autographs-AFP
Complete Jersey-CJ20
Complete Jersey Gold-CJ20

Double Jerseys-DJ15
Double Jerseys-DJ28
Double Jerseys Gold-DJ15
Double Jerseys Gold-DJ28
Double Memorabilia-DM20
Double Memorabilia Gold-DM20
Emblems-GUE63
Emblems Gold-GUE63
Emblems Autographs-GUE63
Gloves-GG13
Gloves Gold-GG13
Jerseys-GUJ63
Jerseys Gold-GUJ63
Jerseys Autographs-GUJ63
Numbers-GUN63
Numbers Gold-GUN63
Numbers Autographs-GUN63
Shooting Gallery-SG02
Shooting Gallery Gold-SG02
Stick and Jersey-SJ23
Stick and Jersey Gold-SJ23
Stick and Jersey Autographs-SJ23
Stick Work-SW06
Stick Work Gold-SW06
06ITG Ultimate Memorabilia Autos-68
06ITG Ultimate Memorabilia Autos Gold-68
06ITG Ultimate Memorabilia Cornerstones-9
06ITG Ultimate Memorabilia Cornerstones Gold-9
06ITG Ultimate Memorabilia Emblems-20
06ITG Ultimate Memorabilia Emblems Gold-20
06ITG Ultimate Memorabilia Jerseys Autos-66
06ITG Ultimate Memorabilia Jerseys Autos Gold-66
06ITG Ultimate Memorabilia Journey Emblem-18
06ITG Ultimate Memorabilia Journey Emblem Gold-18
06ITG Ultimate Memorabilia Journey Jersey-18
06ITG Ultimate Memorabilia Journey Jersey Gold-18
06ITG Ultimate Memorabilia Retro Teammates-22
06ITG Ultimate Memorabilia Retro Teammates Gold-22
06ITG Ultimate Memorabilia Sticks Autos-31
06ITG Ultimate Memorabilia Sticks Autos Gold-31
06ITG Ultimate Memorabilia Triple Thread Jerseys-5
06ITG Ultimate Memorabilia Triple Thread Jerseys Gold-5

Potvin, Jean
71Toronto Sun-122
74NHL Action Stamps-172
74O-Pee-Chee NHL-101
74Topps-101
75O-Pee-Chee NHL-36
75Topps-36
76O-Pee-Chee NHL-93
76Topps-93
77O-Pee-Chee NHL-144
77Topps-144
78O-Pee-Chee-287
79Islanders Transparencies-15
79O-Pee-Chee-334

Potvin, Marc
90ProCards AHL/IHL-486
91Upper Deck-405
French-405
93Whalers Coke-15
94Leaf-541
94Ultra-259
96Portland Pirates-9
98Chicago Wolves Turner Cup-9
99Mississippi Sea Wolves-2

Potvin, Rick
89Rayside-Balfour Jr. Canadians-17

Potvin, Steve
92Sudbury Wolves-23
93Sudbury Wolves-20
93Sudbury Wolves Police-19
95Classic-89
99German Bundesliga 2-220
00German DEL-114
01Swiss HNL-476
05German DEL-11

Potyok, Shawn
91British Columbia JHL-11

Potz, Jerzy
73Finnish Jaakiekko-97
74Finnish Jenkki-85
79Panini Stickers-124
89Swedish Semic World Champ Stickers-135

Poudrier, Daniel
85Fredericton Express-22
86Fredericton Express-21
87Nordiques General Foods-24
87Nordiques Team Issue-2
94German DEL-75
94German First League-658
95German DEL-34
99German EV Landshut-7
01Thetford Mines Coyotes-18
02Thetford Mines Coyotes-17
03Thetford Mines Prolab-16

Poudrier, Serge
92Finnish Semic-227
93Swedish Semic World Champ Stickers-252
94Finnish Jaa Kiekko-220
94French National Team-25
95Swedish Globe World Championships-204
95Swedish World Championships Stickers-103
96German DEL-6
96Swedish Semic Wien-185
98Swiss Power Play Stickers-333
00Swiss Panini Stickers-310
01Swiss HNL-265
02Swiss HNL-86
04Thetford Mines Prolab-9

Poudrier, Thiery
01Shawinigan Cataractes-14
02Shawinigan Cataractes-12
03Shawinigan Cataractes-21

Pouget, Christian
92Finnish Semic-230
94French National Team-26
95Swedish World Championships Stickers-113
96German DEL-177
96Swedish Semic Wien-189
98German DEL-231
99Swiss Panini Stickers-311

Poukar, Jiri
94Czech APS Extraliga-173
95Czech APS Extraliga-190
96Czech APS Extraliga-325
97Czech APS Extraliga-161
97Czech DS Extraliga-78
97Czech DS Stickers-164
98Czech DS Stickers-198
98Czech OFS-321
98Czech OFS-484
99Czech DS-191
99Czech OFS-82

Poulin, Berthier
93Quebec Pee-Wee Tournament-327

Poulin, Charles
90 7th Inn. Sketch QMJHL-220
91 7th Inn. Sketch QMJHL-12
92Fredericton Canadiens-19
93Quebec Pee-Wee 20th Anniversary-7
93Quebec Pee-Wee 20th Anniversary-9
93Fredericton Canadiens-22
93Classic Pro Prospects-27
98Abilene Aviators-13

Poulin, Daniel
77Kalamazoo Wings-6

Poulin, Dave
83Flyers J.C. Penney-17
84Kellogg's Accordion Discs Singles-28
84O-Pee-Chee-165
84O-Pee-Chee Stickers-110
84Topps-120
85Flyers Postcards-23
85O-Pee-Chee-128
85O-Pee-Chee Stickers-89
85Topps-128
86Flyers Postcards-20
86O-Pee-Chee-71
86O-Pee-Chee Stickers-241
86Topps-71
87Flyers Postcards-20
87O-Pee-Chee-39
87O-Pee-Chee Minis-32
87O-Pee-Chee Stickers-98
87O-Pee-Chee Stickers-179
87Panini Stickers-130
87Panini Stickers-386
87Topps-39
88Flyers Postcards-15
88Frito-Lay Stickers-27
88O-Pee-Chee-100
88Panini Stickers-323
88Topps-100
89Bruins Sports Action Update-7
89Flyers Postcards-19
89O-Pee-Chee-115
89Panini Stickers-305
89Topps-115
90Bowman-36
Tiffany-36
90Bruins Sports Action-20
90O-Pee-Chee-362
90Panini Stickers-4
90Pro Set-13
90Score-217
Canadian-217
90Topps-362
Tiffany-362
90Upper Deck-177
French-177
91Pro Set Platinum-5
91Bowman-359
91Bruins Sports Action-15
91O-Pee-Chee-507
91Pro Set-12
French-12
91Score American-232
91Score Canadian Bilingual-452
91Score Canadian English-452
91Stadium Club-253
91Topps-507
92Bowman-19
92Bruins Postcards-8
92O-Pee-Chee-367
92Panini Stickers-137
92Panini Stickers French-137
92Parkhurst-242
Emerald Ice-242
92Pinnacle-116
French-116
92Pro Set-9
92Score-359
Canadian-359
92Stadium Club-13
92Topps-155
Gold-155G
92Ultra-9
93Donruss-362
93Leaf-332
93OPC Premier-228
Gold-228
93Panini Stickers-4
93Parkhurst-488
Emerald Ice-488
93Pinnacle-229
93Pinnacle-387
Canadian-229
Canadian-387
93PowerPlay-470
93Score-228
93Score-552
Gold-552
Canadian-228
Canadian-552
Canadian Gold-552
93Stadium Club-142
93Stadium Club-301
Members Only Master Set-142
Members Only Master Set-301
OPC-142
First Day Issue-142
First Day Issue-301
93Topps/OPC Premier-228
Gold-228
93Ultra-193
93Ultra-450
Award Winners-5
93Upper Deck-355
Award Winners-AW8
94Be A Player Signature Cards-124
94OPC Premier-236
Special Effects-236
94Parkhurst-253
Gold-253
94Pinnacle-179
Artist's Proofs-179
Rink Collection-179
94Score-38
Gold-38
Platinum-38
94Topps/OPC Premier-236
Special Effects-236
94Ultra-391

Poulin, Dene
00Owen Sound Attack-14
01Sudbury Wolves-12
01Sudbury Wolves Police-22
03Sudbury Wolves-19
04Lakehead University Thunderwolves-22

Poulin, George
10Sweet Caporal Postcards-44

11C55-44
12C57-8

Poulin, Hugo
01Thetford Mines Coyotes-20
02Thetford Mines Coyotes-18
03Thetford Mines Prolab-17
04Thetford Mines Prolab-15

Poulin, Jonathan
93Quebec Pee-Wee Tournament-392

Poulin, Kevin
06Victoriaville Tigres-4

Poulin, Marc
92Quebec Pee-Wee Tournament-741
93Quebec Pee-Wee Tournament-932

Poulin, Mitch
84Nanaimo Clippers-15

Poulin, Pat
80Oshawa Generals-6

Poulin, Patrick
90 7th Inn. Sketch QMJHL-1
90 7th Inn. Sketch QMJHL-152
91Upper Deck-65
French-65
91Upper Deck Czech World Juniors-51
91 7th Inn. Sketch QMJHL-10
91 7th Inn. Sketch Memorial Cup-98
91Arena Draft Picks-7
91Arena Draft Picks French-7
91Arena Draft Picks Autographs-7
91Arena Draft Picks Autographs French-7
91Classic-8
91Ultimate Draft-8
91Ultimate Draft-64
91Ultimate Draft French-8
91Classic Four-Sport *-8
Autographs-8A
92OPC Premier-85
92Parkhurst-60
Emerald Ice-60
92Pinnacle-418
French-418
Team 2000-14
Team 2000 French-14
92Pro Set-227
92Score-478
Canadian-478
Young Superstars-31
92Stadium Club-211
92Topps-328
Gold-328G
92Ultra-304
92Upper Deck-416
92Upper Deck-557
Calder Candidates-CC18
Gordie Howe Selects-G16
92Whalers Dairymart-20
93Blackhawks Coke-10
93Donruss-146
93Durivage Score-50
93Leaf-113
Gold Rookies-10
93Panini Stickers-126
93Parkhurst-307
Emerald Ice-307
93Pinnacle-61
Canadian-61
Team 2001-8
Team 2001 Canadian-8
93PowerPlay-108
93PowerPlay-315
Second Year Stars-9
93Score-202
93Score-571
Gold-571
Canadian-202
Canadian-571
Canadian Gold-571
93Stadium Club-157
Members Only Master Set-157
OPC-157
First Day Issue-157
First Day Issue OPC-157
93Ultra-122
93Ultra-292
93Upper Deck-138
Next In Line-NL2
SP-30
94Be A Player Signature Cards-168
94Blackhawks Coke-10
94Canada Games NHL POGS-69
94Donruss-144
94Fleer-44
94Leaf-390
94OPC Premier-316
Special Effects-316
94Parkhurst SE-SE32
Gold-SE32
94Pinnacle-283
Artist's Proofs-283
Rink Collection-283
94Score Samples-6
94Score-6
Gold-6
Platinum-6
94Stadium Club-13
Members Only Master Set-13
First Day Issue-13
Super Team Winner Cards-13
94Topps/OPC Premier-316
Special Effects-316
94Ultra-43
94Upper Deck-36
Electric Ice-36
95Bashan Super Stickers-25
95Canada Games NHL POGS-67
95Collector's Choice-187
Player's Club-187
Player's Club Platinum-187
95Donruss-269
95Emotion-32
95Imperial Stickers-25
95Leaf-237
95Metal-27
95Panini Stickers-158
95Parkhurst International-42
Emerald Ice-42
95Pinnacle-135
Artist's Proofs-135
Rink Collection-135
95Playoff One on One-133
95Score-158
Black Ice Artist's Proofs-158
Black Ice-158
95SkyBox Impact-32
95Stadium Club-212
Members Only Master Set-212
95Summit-99
Artist's Proofs-99
Ice-99

95Topps-326
OPC Inserts-326
Power Lines-4PL
95Upper Deck-208
Electric Ice-208
Electric Ice Gold-208
Special Edition-SE106
Special Edition Gold-SE106
96Playoff One on One-369
97Collector's Choice-242
97Pacific-230
Copper-230
Emerald Green-230
Ice Blue-230
Red-230
Silver-230
97Upper Deck-366
98Be A Player-69
Press Release-69
98BAP Gold-69
98BAP Autographs-69
98BAP Autographs Gold-69
98BAP Tampa Bay All Star Game-69
98Canadiens Team Issue-14
99Pacific-207
Copper-207
Emerald Green-207
Gold-207
Ice Blue-207
Premiere Date-207
Red-207
99Ultimate Victory-45
1/1-45
Parallel-45
Parallel 100-45
00Canadiens Postcards-20
00Paramount-128
Copper-128
Gold-128
Holo-Gold-128
Holo-Silver-128
Ice Blue-128
Premiere Date-128
00Upper Deck Vintage-192
01Canadiens Postcards-17
02BAP Sig Series Auto Buybacks 1998-69

Poulin, Rick
89Rayside-Balfour Jr. Canadians-18

Poulin, Skinner
10C56-24

Pouliot, Benoit
04Sudbury Wolves-17
04ITG Heroes and Prospects-209
04ITG Heroes/Prospects Toronto Expo '05-209
05ITG Heroes/Prosp Toronto Expo Parallel -134
05Extreme Top Prospects Signature Edition-S15
05OHL Bell All-Star Classic-15
05Sudbury Wolves-26
05ITG Heroes and Prospects-134
Aspiring-ASP17
Autographs-A-BP
Complete Jerseys-CJ-34
Complete Jerseys Gold-CJ-34
Complete Logos-CHL-6
He Shoots-He Scores Prizes-7
He Shoots-He Scores Prizes-46
Jerseys-GUJ-50
Jerseys Gold-GUJ-50
Emblems-GUE-50
Emblems Gold-GUE-50
Numbers-GUN-50
Numbers Gold-GUN-50
Nameplates-N-17
Nameplates Gold-N-17
Oh Canada-OC-8
Oh Canada Gold-OC-8
06Be A Player-226
06Beehive-128
Blue-128
Gold-128
Matte-128
Red Facsimile Signatures-128
Wood-128
06Flair Showcase-315
06Hot Prospects-126
06Hot Prospects-163
Red Hot-126
White Hot-126
Hotagraphs-HBP
06ITG Ultimate Memorabilia Future Star Patches Autos-25
06ITG Ultimate Memorabilia Future Star Patches Autos Gold-25
06O-Pee-Chee-597
Rainbow-597
06SP Authentic-194
06SP Authentic-238
Limited-194
Limited-238
06SP Game Used-123
Gold-123
Rainbow-123
06The Cup-136
Autographed NHL Shields Duals-DASLP
Autographed NHL Shields Duals-DASMN
Autographed Rookie Masterpiece Pressplates-136
Enshrinements-EBP
Gold Rainbow Autographed Rookie Patches-136
Masterpiece Pressplates (Bee Hive)-128
Masterpiece Pressplates (Marquee Rookies)-597
Masterpiece Pressplates (SP Authentic Autographs)-194
Masterpiece Pressplates (SP Authentic)-238
Masterpiece Pressplates (SP Game Used)-123
Masterpiece Pressplates (Sweet Beginnings)-132
Masterpiece Pressplates (Ultimate Collection Autographs)-123
NHL Shields Duals-DSHLP
Rookies Black-136
Rookies Platinum-136
06UD Artifacts-232
06Ultimate Collection-123
Rookies Autographed NHL Shields-123
Rookies Autographed Patches-123
Ultimate Debut Threads Jerseys-DJ-BP
Ultimate Debut Threads Jerseys Autographs-DJ-BP
Ultimate Debut Threads Patches-DJ-BP
Ultimate Debut Threads Patches Autographs-DJ-BP
06Upper Deck-475
Exclusives Parallel-475
High Gloss Parallel-475
Masterpieces-475
06Upper Deck Sweet Shot-132
Rookie Jerseys Autographs-132
06AHL Top Prospects-17
06ITG Heroes and Prospects-155
Autographs-ABP
Complete CHL Logos-CHL09
Complete Jerseys-CJ18
Jerseys-GUJ41
Jerseys Gold-GUJ41
Emblems-GUE41
Emblems Gold-GUE41
Numbers-GUN41
Numbers Gold-GUN41
National Pride-NP12
National Pride Gold-NP12
Quad Emblems-QE07
Quad Emblems-QE11
Quad Emblems Gold-QE07
Triple Memorabilia-TM09
Update Autographs-ABP

Pouliot, Cedric
93Quebec Pee-Wee Tournament-263

Pouliot, James
03Halifax Mooseheads-3
04Halifax Mooseheads-8
05Halifax Mooseheads-7
06Halifax Mooseheads-7

Pouliot, Marc-Antoine
96Quebec Pee-Wee Tournament-1227
01Rimouski Oceanic-23
02Rimouski Oceanic-13
03Rimouski Oceanic-16
03Rimouski Oceanic-NNO
03Rimouski Oceanic Sheets-3
04Rimouski Oceanic-17
04Rimouski Oceanic-LE2
04ITG Heroes and Prospects-90
Autographs-MPO
Combos-7
Emblems-51
Emblems Gold-51
He Shoots-He Scores Prizes-16
Jersey Autographs-51
Jerseys-51
Jerseys Gold-51
Numbers-51
Numbers Gold-51
04ITG Heroes/Prospects Toronto Expo '05-90
04ITG Heroes/Prospects Expo Heroes/Pros-90
05ITG Heroes/Prosp Toronto Expo Parallel -205
05Extreme Top Prospects Signature Edition-S4
05Hamilton Bulldogs-21
05ITG Heroes and Prospects-205
Autographs Series II-MAP
CHL Grads-CG-1
CHL Grads Gold-CG-1
He Shoots-He Scores Prizes-27
Jerseys-GUJ-84
Jerseys Gold-GUJ-84
Emblems-GUE-84
Emblems Gold-GUE-84
Numbers-GUN-84
Numbers Gold-GUN-84
Nameplates-N-49
Nameplates Gold-N-49
06Be A Player-223
06Be A Player Portraits-107
06Beehive-123
Blue-123
Matte-123
Red Facsimile Signatures-123
Wood-123
06Black Diamond-153A
Black-153A
Gold-153A
Ruby-153A
06Flair Showcase-44
06Flair Showcase-128
Parallel-44
Parallel-128
06Fleer-209
Tiffany-209
06Hot Prospects-113
Red Hot-113
White Hot-113
Hot Materials -HMMP
Hot Materials Red Hot-HMMP
Hot Materials White Hot-HMMP
Hotagraphs-HMP
06O-Pee-Chee-522
06O-Pee-Chee-635
Rainbow-522
Rainbow-635
Autographs-A-MP
06SP Authentic-179
Limited-179
06SP Game Used-116
Gold-116
Rainbow-116
Autographs-116
Inked Sweaters-ISPO
Inked Sweaters Patches-ISPO
Rookie Exclusives Autographs-REMP
06SPx-172
Spectrum-172
06The Cup-129
Autographed Rookie Masterpiece Pressplates-129
Gold Rainbow Autographed Rookie Patches-129
Masterpiece Pressplates (Artifacts)-219
Masterpiece Pressplates (Be A Player Portraits)-107
Masterpiece Pressplates (Bee Hive)-123
Masterpiece Pressplates (Black Diamond)-153
Masterpiece Pressplates (Marquee Rookies)-522
Masterpiece Pressplates (MVP)-343
Masterpiece Pressplates (Power Play)-106
Masterpiece Pressplates (SP Game Used)-116
Masterpiece Pressplates (SPx Autographs)-172
Masterpiece Pressplates (Sweet Beginnings)-124
Masterpiece Pressplates (Trilogy)-113
Masterpiece Pressplates (Ultimate Collection Autographs)-113
Masterpiece Pressplates (Victory)-217
Rookies Black-129
Rookies Platinum-129
06UD Artifacts-219
Blue-219
Gold-219
Platinum-219
Radiance-219
Red-219
06UD Mini Jersey Collection-106
06UD Powerplay-106
Impact Rainbow-106
06Ultimate Collection-113
Rookies Autographed NHL Shields-113
Rookies Autographed Patches-113
Ultimate Debut Threads Jerseys-DJ-MP
Ultimate Debut Threads Jerseys Autographs-DJ-MP
Ultimate Debut Threads Patches-DJ-MP
Ultimate Debut Threads Patches Autographs-DJ-MP
06Ultra-207
Gold Medallion-207
Ice Medallion-207
06Upper Deck-212
Exclusives Parallel-212
High Gloss Parallel-212
Masterpieces-212
Rookie Game Dated Moments-RGD10
Rookie Headliners-RH9
Rookie Materials-RMMP
Rookie Materials Patches-RMMP
06Upper Deck MVP-343
Gold Script-343
Super Script-343
06Upper Deck Ovation-21
06Upper Deck Sweet Shot-124
Rookie Jerseys Autographs-124
06Upper Deck Trilogy-113
Honorary Swatches-HSMP
06Upper Deck Victory-217
06Upper Deck Victory Black-217
06Upper Deck Victory Gold-217
06Wilkes-Barre Scranton Penguins-11
06Wilkes-Barre Scranton Penguins Jerseys-19
06ITG Heroes and Prospects-41
Autographs-AMAP
Making The Bigs-MTB11
07Upper Deck Rookie Class -20

Pouliot, Mario
917th Inn. Sketch QMJHL-24

Pouliot, Mathieu
93Quebec Pee-Wee Tournament-925

Poulsen, Marco
93Finnish Jyvas-Hyva Stickers-27
93Finnish SISU-98
94Finnish SISU-346
95Finnish SISU-345
95Finnish SISU Limited-94
98Swiss Power Play Stickers-354
99Danish Hockey League-179

Poulter, Alex
05Red Deer Rebels-14

Pound, Ian
84Kitchener Rangers-12
85Kitchener Rangers-11
86London Knights-17

Pounder, Cheryl
94Classic Women of Hockey-W3
04Canadian Womens World Championship Team-16
06ITG Going For Gold-7
06ITG Going For Gold Samples-7
06ITG Going For Gold Autographs-APO
06ITG Going For Gold Jerseys-GUJ7

Poupard, Rob
96Arizona Icecats-16

Pousaz, Jacques
72Finnish Semic World Championship-148
72Swedish Semic World Championship-148

Pousse, Pierre
92Finnish Semic-240
93Swedish Semic World Champ Stickers-265
94French National Team-27
95Swedish World Championships Stickers-109

Poussu, Pentti
72Finnish Jaakiekko-292

Pouzar, Jaroslav
79Panini Stickers-87
81Swedish Semic Hockey VM Stickers-64
82Oilers Red Rooster-10
83Oilers McDonald's-23
83O-Pee-Chee-41
83O-Pee-Chee Stickers-151
83O-Pee-Chee Stickers-159
83Topps Stickers-151
83Topps Stickers-159
83Vachon-38
84Oilers Red Rooster-10
84Oilers Team Issue-22
84O-Pee-Chee-256
86Oilers Team Issue-20
88Oilers Tenth Anniversary-18
95Czech APS Extraliga-397
98Czech OFS Legends-7
00Czech OFS-5

Poveromo, Rick
93Quebec Pee-Wee Tournament-795

Powderface, Charlie
93Quebec Pee-Wee Tournament-149

Powell, Derek
92Quebec Pee-Wee Tournament-1418
93Quebec Pee-Wee Tournament-760

Powell, Goalie
91Air Canada SJHL-D16
92North Dakota Fighting Sioux-26

Powell, Kevin
92Tacoma Rockets-18
98Wichita Thunder-20
99Wichita Thunder-19
00Wichita Thunder-18

Power, Aaron
00Barrie Colts-21
03South Carolina Stingrays-332
04Barrie Colts 10th Anniversary-14
05South Carolina Stingrays-15
06Las Vegas Wranglers-19

Power, Andrew
93Oshawa Generals-12

Power, Chad
97Ohio State Buckeyes*-1
99Anchorage Aces-6
00Quad-City Mallards-13

Power, Colin
01Guelph Storm-10
01Guelph Storm Memorial Cup-10
02Guelph Storm-14
03St. Michael's Majors-11
04St. Michael's Majors-12

Power, Graham
03St. Francis Xavier X-Men-12
04St. Francis Xavier X-Men-16

Power, Larry
81Ottawa 67's-18
82Ottawa 67's-19

Power, R.
10Sweet Caporal Postcards-40
11C55-40

Power, Richard
00Owen Sound Attack-15
01Owen Sound Attack-13
03Plymouth Whalers-20

Power, Ryan
95Slapshot-229
97Halifax Mooseheads I-15
97Halifax Mooseheads II-14

Powers, Aaron
01Barrie Colts-5

Powers, Andy
94Dubuque Fighting Saints-22
99Columbus Cottonmouths-27
00Columbus Cottonmouths-13
02South Carolina Stingrays-15
02South Carolina Stingrays RBI-218

Powers, Billy
03Michigan Wolverines-30
04Michigan Wolverines-25

Powers, Buddy
93RPI Engineers-23

Powers, Jim
92Raleigh Icecaps-12
92Raleigh Icecaps-23
93Raleigh Icecaps-14
94Raleigh Icecaps-15

Powers, Pat
99Tupelo T-Rex-12
01Bossier-Shreveport Mudbugs-15

Powis, Geoffrey
67Topps-110

Powis, Lynn
73O-Pee-Chee-209
74NHL Action Stamps-296
74O-Pee-Chee NHL-227
74Topps-227
76O-Pee-Chee WHA-86

Poyhia, Harri
80Finnish Mallasjuoma-142

Pozdnyakov, Vladimir
99Russian Hockey League-63
00Russian Hockey League-193

Pozivil, Lukas
01Czech OFS-152
02Czech OFS Plus-204
03Czech OFS Plus-107
04Czech OFS-101
06Czech OFS-143

Poznik, Lukas
98Czech OFS-407
99Czech OFS-172

Pozzo, Kevin
94Brandon Wheat Kings-16
95Slapshot Memorial Cup-30
97New Orleans Brass-12
99Charlotte Checkers-29
00Charlotte Checkers-15

Pozzo, Michael
98Oklahoma City Blazers-13

Pracey, Rick
88Brockville Braves-12
89Sault Ste. Marie Greyhounds-10

Prachar, Dan
94UK Solihull Barons-11
95UK Solihull Barons-9

Prachar, Kamil
92Finnish Semic-127
94Czech APS Extraliga-208
94Finnish Jaa Kiekko-167
95Czech APS Extraliga-152
96Czech APS Extraliga-169

Prada, Martin
94German First League-389

Prajsler, Petr
88ProCards AHL-213
89Kings Smokey-11
90O-Pee-Chee-481
90ProCards AHL/IHL-347
91ProCards-57

Prasek, Branislav
93Quebec Pee-Wee Tournament-1722

Prater, Matt
93Quebec Pee-Wee Tournament-1304

Pratt, Babe
34Beehive Group I Photos-292
34Beehive Group I Photos-343
39O-Pee-Chee V301-1-85
45Quaker Oats Photos-44
55Parkhurst-31
Quaker Oats-31
83Hall of Fame-162
83Hall of Fame Postcards-L13
85Hall of Fame-162
92Hall of Fame Legends-29
94Parkhurst Tall Boys Greats-3
02BAP Ultimate Mem Paper Cuts Autos-25
02Maple Leafs Platinum Collection-60
03BAP Ultimate Mem Maple Leafs Forever-4
03BAP Ultimate Memorabilia Paper Cuts-38
04ITG Ultimate Memorabilia-19
Gold-19
04Ultimate Collection Ultimate Cuts-UC-BP
06ITG Ultimate Memorabilia-11
Artist Proof-11

Pratt, Harlan
95Red Deer Rebels-14
96Prince Albert Raiders-18
97Prince Albert Raiders-17
99Florida Everblades-17
00Cincinnati Cyclones-18
04Springfield Falcons-13
05Springfield Falcons-11

Pratt, Jon
95Peoria Rivermen-17
96Peoria Rivermen-16
96Peoria Rivermen Photo Album-18
97Peoria Rivermen-21

Pratt, Kelly
74Penguins Postcards-18

Pratt, Nolan
93Portland Winter Hawks-19
96Whalers Kid's Club-20
96Springfield Falcons-34
97Hurricanes Team Issue-20
98Hurricanes Team Issue-4
98Upper Deck-239
Exclusives-239
Exclusives 1 of 1-239
Gold Reserve-239
99BAP Millennium-54
Emerald-54
Ruby-54
Sapphire-54
Signatures-54
Signatures Gold-54
00Upper Deck-272
Exclusives Tier 1-272
Exclusives Tier 2-272
02BAP Sig Series Auto Buybacks 1999-54
03ITG Action-591
03Lightning Team Issue-34
05Lightning Team Issue-11
05Parkhurst-443
Facsimile Auto Parallel-443
06Lightning Postcards-14
06O-Pee-Chee-452
Rainbow-452

Pratt, Stan
37V356 Worldwide Gum-126

Pratt, Tom
88ProCards AHL-199

Pratt, Tracy
68Shirriff Coins-119
69O-Pee-Chee-111
69Topps-111
70Dad's Cookies-103
70Esso Power Players-75
70O-Pee-Chee-146
70Sargent Promotions Stamps-19
71Letraset Action Replays-3
71O-Pee-Chee-107
71Sabres Postcards-73
71Sargent Promotions Stamps-25
71Topps-107
71Toronto Sun-37
72O-Pee-Chee-69
72Sabres Postcards-14
72Sargent Promotions Stamps-30
72Topps-84
73O-Pee-Chee-54
73Topps-54
74Canucks Royal Bank-16
74NHL Action Stamps-281
74O-Pee-Chee NHL-41
74Topps-41
75Canucks Royal Bank-17
75O-Pee-Chee NHL-133
75Topps-133
76O-Pee-Chee NHL-275
76Rockies Coke Cans-17
76Rockies Puck Bucks-16

Praught, Devan
05PEI Rocket-12
06PEI Rocket-15

Prawdzik, Wally
00Sudbury Wolves-7

Prazak, Karel
94Czech APS Extraliga-285

Prazma, Marty
86Saskatoon Blades Photos-19

Praznik, Jody
88Saskatoon Blades-6
89Hampton Roads Admirals-18A
89Hampton Roads Admirals-18H
90Hampton Roads Admirals-44
92Tulsa Oilers-13
94Central Hockey League-105
99Corpus Christi IceRays-14
99Corpus Christi IceRays-29
99Corpus Christi IceRays-32

Praznik, Tobin
99Corpus Christi IceRays-15
99Corpus Christi IceRays-32
99Corpus Christi IceRays-34
01Anchorage Aces-12
02New Mexico Scorpions-14

Precechtel, Jaromir
94Czech APS Extraliga-278
95Czech APS Extraliga-100

Prediger, Detlef
01Swiss HNL-358
02Swiss HNL-398

Prefontaine, Brad
91Air Canada SJHL-C2
95Birmingham Bulls-5
97Columbus Cottonmouths-15
98Columbus Cottonmouths-13

Preissing, Tom
03BAP Memorabilia-205
03Black Diamond-149
Black-149
Green-149
Red-149
03Bowman-125
Gold-125
03Bowman Chrome-125
Refractors-125
Gold Refractors-125
Xfractors-125
03Crown Royale-134
Red-134
Retail-134
03ITG Used Signature Series-175
Gold-175
03ITG VIP Rookie Debut-39
03Pacific Complete-525
Red-525
03Pacific Luxury Suite-76
Gold-76
03Pacific Supreme-137
Blue-137
Red-137
Retail-137
03Parkhurst Rookie-119
03Sharks Postcards-13
03SP Authentic-115
Limited-115
03SP Game Used-78
Gold-78
03SPx-197
Radiance-197
Spectrum-197
03Topps Pristine-128
03Topps Pristine-129
03Topps Pristine-130
Gold Refractor Die Cuts-128
Gold Refractor Die Cuts-129
Gold Refractor Die Cuts-130
Refractors-128
Refractors-129
Refractors-130
Press Plates Black-128
Press Plates Black-129
Press Plates Black-130
Press Plates Cyan-128
Press Plates Cyan-129
Press Plates Cyan-130
Press Plates Magenta-128
Press Plates Magenta-129
Press Plates Magenta-130
Press Plates Yellow-128
Press Plates Yellow-129
Press Plates Yellow-130
03Topps Traded-TT139
Blue-TT139
Gold-TT139
Red-TT139
03Upper Deck-240
Canadian Exclusives-240
HG-240
03Upper Deck Rookie Update-210
03Upper Deck Trilogy-167
Limited-167
04German DEL Superstars-SU19
05Parkhurst-405
Facsimile Auto Parallel-405
06O-Pee-Chee-344
Rainbow-344

Premak, Garth
87Kamloops Blazers-18
92Alberta International Team Canada-16

Prendergast, Mike
91Upper Deck Czech World Juniors-69

Prentice, Dean
44Beehive Group II Photos-58
44Beehive Group II Photos-354A
44Beehive Group II Photos-354B
54Parkhurst-74
57Topps-62
58Topps-32
59Topps-17
60Topps-37
Stamps-44
61Shirriff/Salada Coins-84
61Topps-54
62Topps-53
Hockey Bucks-21
63Topps-13
64Beehive Group III Photos-24
64Beehive Group III Photos-91
64Coca-Cola Caps-12
64Topps-19
65Coca-Cola-10
65Topps-102
66Topps-45
66Topps USA Test-45
67Topps-45
68O-Pee-Chee-32
68Shirriff Coins-38
68Topps-32
69O-Pee-Chee-115
69Topps-115
70Dad's Cookies-104
70Esso Power Players-232
70O-Pee-Chee-201
70Sargent Promotions Stamps-165
71Sargent Promotions Stamps-89
71Toronto Sun-143
72O-Pee-Chee-289
72Finnish Semic World Championship-218
72Swedish Semic World Championship-218
73North Stars Postcards-27
91Ultimate Original Six-27
French-27
93Parkhurst Parkie Reprints Case Inserts-9
94Parkhurst Missing Link-91
94Parkhurst Tall Boys-5
95Parkhurst '66-67-51
Coins-51

Prentice, Ryan
99Asheville Smoke-16
04Richmond Riverdogs-9

Presley, Wayne
82Kitchener Rangers-12
83Kitchener Rangers-16
84Kitchener Rangers-20
84Sault Ste. Marie Greyhounds-17
85Nova Scotia Oilers-16
86Blackhawks Coke-15
87Blackhawks Coke-18
87O-Pee-Chee-179
87Panini Stickers-228
87Topps-179
88Blackhawks Coke-16
88O-Pee-Chee-185
88Topps-185
89Blackhawks Coke-20
89O-Pee-Chee-98
89Panini Stickers-52
89Topps-98
90Blackhawks Coke-20
90O-Pee-Chee-456
90Pro Set-434
90Score Rookie/Traded-92T
90Upper Deck-339
French-339
91Pro Set Platinum-228
91Bowman-402
91O-Pee-Chee-385
91OPC Premier-89
91Panini Stickers-19
91Parkhurst-163
French-163
91Pinnacle-68
French-68
91Pro Set-44
91Pro Set-488
French-44
French-488
91Score American-221
91Score Canadian Bilingual-221
91Score Canadian Bilingual-559
91Score Canadian English-221
91Score Canadian English-559
91Score Rookie/Traded-9T
91Sharks Sports Action-18
91Stadium Club-215
91Topps-385
91Upper Deck-371
French-371
92Bowman-76
92Sabres Blue Shield-17
92Sabres Jubilee Foods-11
92Score-213
Canadian-213
92Stadium Club-24
92Topps-424
Gold-424G
93OPC Premier-162
Gold-162
93Panini Stickers-107
93Parkhurst-294
Emerald Ice-294
93Pinnacle-425
Canadian-425
93Score-296
Canadian-296
93Stadium Club-233
Members Only Master Set-233
OPC-233
First Day Issue-233
First Day Issue OPC-233
93Topps/OPC Premier-162
Gold-162
94Leaf-521
94Parkhurst-27
Gold-27
94Pinnacle-321
Artist's Proofs-321
Rink Collection-321
94Stadium Club-196
Members Only Master Set-196
First Day Issue-196
Super Team Winner Cards-196
95Be A Player-45
Signatures-S45
Signatures Die Cuts-S45
95Collector's Choice-179
Player's Club-179
Player's Club Platinum-179
95Score-223
Black Ice Artist's Proofs-223
Black Ice-223
96Detroit Vipers-13

Prest, Trevor
91British Columbia JHL-42

Prestberg, Pelle
97Swedish Collector's Choice-59
98Swedish UD Choice-94
Day in the Life-4
99Swedish Upper Deck-63
00Swedish Upper Deck-67
02Swedish SHL-176
Parallel-176
03Swedish Elite-183
Silver-183
04Swedish Elitset-138
04Swedish Elitset-184
Dominators-1
Gold-138
Gold-184
Signatures-14
04Swedish Pure Skills-28
Parallel-28
05Swedish SHL Elitset-43
Gold-43
Teammates-3
06Swedish SHL Elitset-52

Preston, Brad
98Oklahoma City Blazers-11

Preston, Brian
92British Columbia JHL-23

Preston, Cassidy
04St. Michael's Majors-14

Preston, Dan
917th Inn. Sketch OHL-103
95Slapshot-73
01UK Manchester Storm-2
02UK Manchester Storm-2

Preston, Jordie
02Halifax Mooseheads-14

Preston, Rich
75Houston Aeros WHA-14
76O-Pee-Chee WHA-115
78Jets Postcards-18
79Blackhawks Postcards-17
80Blackhawks Postcards-8
80Blackhawks White Border-10
80O-Pee-Chee-41
80Topps-41
81Blackhawks Borderless Postcards-20
81Blackhawks Brown Background-9
82Blackhawks Postcards-18
82O-Pee-Chee-71
82Post Cereal-4
83Blackhawks Postcards-19
83NHL Key Tags-24
83O-Pee-Chee-110
84Devils Postcards-19
84O-Pee-Chee-118
84Topps-34
85O-Pee-Chee-139
85Topps-139
86Blackhawks Coke-16
86O-Pee-Chee-61
86O-Pee-Chee Stickers-199
86Topps-61
91Blackhawks Coke-21
92Blackhawks Coke-14
93Blackhawks Coke-29
96Regina Pats-23

Preston, Tim
97Seattle Thunderbirds-15
01Saskatoon Blades-13

Preston, Yves
81Milwaukee Admirals-6

Pretty, David
80Quebec Remparts-17

Preucil, Petr
00Quebec Remparts-14
Signed-14
01Quebec Remparts-13
03Baie Comeau Drakkar-22

Preuss, Gunther
94German DEL-143
95German DEL-141

Preuss, Josef
94German First League-370

Prevost, Jordan
03Sudbury Wolves-20

Prevost, Stacy
91Air Canada SJHL-B12
92Saskatchewan JHL-168

Priakin, Sergei
89Kraft-8
90Bowman-103
Tiffany-103
90Flames IGA/McGavin's-21
90Pro Set-594
91Flames Panini Team Stickers-17
93Swiss HNL-178
94Finnish SISU-214
95Finnish SISU-91
95Finnish SISU-380
95Finnish SISU Limited-61
96Finnish SISU Redline-93

Priamo, Tim
06Guelph Storm-18

Priamo, Tom
05Saginaw Spirit-18

Pribil, Frank
94German First League-429

Pribyla, Kamil
94Czech APS Extraliga-125

Price, Carey
04ITG Heroes and Prospects-226
04ITG Heroes/Prospects Toronto Expo '05-226
05ITG Heroes/Prosp Toronto Expo Parallel -157
05ITG Heroes and Prospects-157
Aspiring-ASP1
Autographs-A-CP
Autographs-DA-PR
Complete Jerseys-CJ-10
Complete Jerseys Gold-CJ-10
Complete Logos-CHL-7
He Shoots-He Scores Prizes-10
He Shoots-He Scores Prizes-47
Jerseys-GUJ-36
Jerseys-GUJ-115
Jerseys Gold-GUJ-36
Jerseys Gold-GUJ-115
Emblems-GUE-36
Emblems-GUE-98
Emblems Gold-GUE-36
Emblems Gold-GUE-98
Numbers-GUN-36
Numbers-GUN-98
Numbers Gold-GUN-36
Numbers Gold-GUN-98
Measuring Up-MU17
Measuring Up Gold-MU17
Nameplates-N-6
Nameplates Gold-N-06
Net Prospects-NP-15
Net Prospects Dual-NPD10
Net Prospects Dual Gold-NPD10
Net Prospects Gold-NP-15
Spectrum-STM-01
Spectrum Gold-STM-01
06Between The Pipes-7
06Between The Pipes-107
06Between The Pipes-121
Aspiring-AS05
Aspiring Gold-AS05
Autographs-ACP2
Autographs-ACP
Autographs-ACP3
Double Jerseys-DJ21
Double Jerseys Gold-DJ21
Emblems-GUE48
Emblems Gold-GUE48
Emblems Autographs-GUE48
Jerseys-GUJ48
Jerseys Gold-GUJ48
Jerseys Autographs-GUJ48
Numbers-GUN48
Numbers Gold-GUN48
Numbers Autographs-GUN48
Playing For Your Country-PC11
Playing For Your Country Gold-PC11
Prospect Trios-PT07
Prospect Trios-PT09
Prospect Trios-PT12
Prospect Trios-PT15
Prospect Trios Gold-PT07
Prospect Trios Gold-PT09
Prospect Trios Gold-PT12
Prospect Trios Gold-PT15
Shooting Gallery-SG01
Shooting Gallery Gold-SG01
The Mask-M40
The Mask Gold-M40
The Mask Silver-M40
06ITG Ultimate Memorabilia Double Memorabilia Autos-12
06ITG Ultimate Memorabilia Double Memorabilia Autos Gold-12
06ITG Ultimate Memorabilia Emblems-21
06ITG Ultimate Memorabilia Emblems Gold-21
06ITG Ultimate Memorabilia First Round Picks-6
06ITG Ultimate Memorabilia First Round Picks Gold-6
06ITG Ultimate Memorabilia Future Star-6
06ITG Ultimate Memorabilia Future Star Gold-6
06ITG Ultimate Memorabilia Future Star Autos-20
06ITG Ultimate Memorabilia Future Star Autos Gold-20
06ITG Ultimate Memorabilia Future Star Patches Autos-20
06ITG Ultimate Memorabilia Future Star Patches Autos Gold-20
06ITG Heroes and Prospects CHL Top Prospects-TP16
06ITG Heroes and Prospects CHL Top Prospects Gold-TP16
06ITG Heroes and Prospects Complete CHL Logos-CHL12
06ITG Heroes and Prospects National Pride-NP20
06ITG Heroes and Prospects Net Prospects-NPR09
06ITG Heroes and Prospects Net Prospects Gold-NPR09
06ITG Heroes and Prospects Quad Emblems-QE08
06ITG Heroes and Prospects Quad Emblems-QE15
06ITG Heroes and Prospects Quad Emblems Gold-QE08
06ITG Heroes and Prospects Triple Memorabilia-TM05
06ITG Heroes and Prospects Triple Memorabilia Gold-TM05
07ITG Going For Gold World Juniors-1
Autographs-1
Emblems-GUE1
Jerseys-GUJ1
Numbers-GUN1

Price, Dan
99Austin Ice Bats-10
00Austin Ice Bats-18
01Austin Ice Bats-13
02Austin Ice Bats-13
03Fort Wayne Komets-13
03Fort Wayne Komets Shoe Carnival-13

Price, Derek
03Kootenay Ice-3
04Kootenay Ice-17
05Saskatoon Blades-19
05Swift Current Broncos-3

Price, Gerry
52Juniors Blue Tint-12

Price, Matt
95Slapshot-119
98Kingston Frontenacs-14
03Odessa Jackalopes-15

Price, Noel
52Juniors Blue Tint-149
58Parkhurst-6
59Parkhurst-42
65Quebec Aces-16
68O-Pee-Chee-110
68Shirriff Coins-138
68Topps-110
70Esso Power Players-149
70O-Pee-Chee-163
72Flames Postcards-15
72O-Pee-Chee-163
72Sargent Promotions Stamps-8
73O-Pee-Chee-256
74NHL Action Stamps-17
74O-Pee-Chee NHL-356
75O-Pee-Chee NHL-331
94Parkhurst Missing Link-131

Price, Pat
76O-Pee-Chee NHL-318
77O-Pee-Chee NHL-308
78O-Pee-Chee-368
79Oilers Postcards-19
79O-Pee-Chee-347
80O-Pee-Chee-299
80Pepsi-Cola Caps-37
81O-Pee-Chee-265
82O-Pee-Chee-274
82Post Cereal-15
83Nordiques Postcards-21
83Vachon-71
84Nordiques Postcards-20
84O-Pee-Chee-286
85Nordiques General Foods-20
85Nordiques McDonald's-16
85Nordiques Placemats-4
85Nordiques Placemats-6
85Nordiques Provigo-19
86Nordiques Team Issue-18
86Kraft Drawings-56
86Nordiques General Foods-19
86Nordiques McDonald's-19
86Nordiques Team Issue-18
87North Stars Postcards-24

88Oilers Tenth Anniversary-82
04ITG Franchises Update Autographs-PBR

Priddle, Phil
83Brantford Alexanders-23

Pridham, Colby
06Halifax Mooseheads-19

Priest, Merv
89Brandon Wheat Kings-22
90Brandon Wheat Kings-2
907th Inn. Sketch WHL-220
917th Inn. Sketch WHL-207
95Vancouver VooDoo RHI-19

Priestlay, Brad
03Prince George Cougars-13
04Lakehead University Thunderwolves-27

Priestlay, Craig
99Swift Current Broncos-15
00Swift Current Broncos-15

Priestlay, Ken
84Victoria Cougars-18
87Sabres Blue Shield-19
88ProCards AHL-247
89Sabres Blue Shield-16
89ProCards AHL-257
90Alberta International Team Canada-16
91Parkhurst-359
French-359
91Penguins Coke/Elby's-18
91Pro Set-460
French-460
91Score Canadian Bilingual-658
91Score Canadian English-658
91Upper Deck-525
French-525
92Cleveland Lumberjacks-21
93Swiss HNL-283
95UK Sheffield Steelers-3
97UK Sheffield Steelers-4
00UK Sheffield Steelers Centurions-9

Prieur, Simon
92Quebec Pee-Wee Tournament-907
93Quebec Pee-Wee Tournament-142

Prikryl, Petr
98Czech OFS-362
99Czech DS-142
99Czech OFS-540
00Czech DS Extraliga-2
00Czech OFS-291
01Czech OFS-98
Gold Inserts-G3
02Czech OFS Plus-12
Checklists-C4
02Czech OFS Plus Masks-M8
02Czech OFS Plus Trios-T15
06Czech OFS-74

Prikryl, S.
99Czech OFS-450

Prilepskij, Alexander
74Swedish Stickers-95

Prillo, Eric
907th Inn. Sketch QMJHL-90

Primeau, Eric
84Richelieu Riverains-11

Primeau, Joe
32O'Keefe Maple Leafs-10
33O-Pee-Chee V304A-12
33V129-7
33V288 Hamilton Gum-2
33V357 Ice Kings-40
34Beehive Group I Photos-344
34Sweet Caporal-48
55Parkhurst-24
Quaker Oats-24
83Hall of Fame-131
83Hall of Fame Postcards-I12
85Hall of Fame-131
91Pro Set-338
French-338
02BAP Ultimate Mem Paper Cuts Autos-17
02Maple Leafs Platinum Collection-61
02Parkhurst Reprints-204
03BAP Ultimate Memorabilia Linemates-11
03BAP Ultimate Mem Linemates Autos-4
03BAP Ultimate Mem Maple Leafs Forever-12
03BAP Ultimate Memorabilia Paper Cuts-3
03BAP Ultimate Memorabilia Vintage Lumber-3
04ITG Franchises Canadian-106
04ITG Franchises Update Linemates-ULI1
04ITG Franchises Update Linemates Gold-ULI1
04ITG Ultimate Memorabilia-82
Gold-82
Blades of Steel-15
Maple Leafs Forever-4
Paper Cuts-7
Retro Teammates-10
Vintage Lumber-11
05ITG Ultimate Mem Blades of Steel-4
05ITG Ultimate Mem Blades of Steel Gold-4
05ITG Ultimate Memorabilia Lumbergraphs-5
05ITG Ultimate Memorabilia Vintage Lumber-8
05ITG Ultimate Mem Vintage Lumber Gold-8
06ITG Ultimate Memorabilia Maple Leafs Forever Autos-4
06ITG Ultimate Memorabilia Stick Rack-28
06ITG Ultimate Memorabilia Stick Rack Gold-28
06ITG Ultimate Memorabilia Vintage Lumber-3
06ITG Ultimate Memorabilia Vintage Lumber Gold-3

Primeau, Keith
88Niagara Falls Thunder-4
89Niagara Falls Thunder-15
897th Inn. Sketch OHL-130
897th Inn. Sketch OHL-189
90OPC Premier-91
90Pro Set-606
90Score-436
Canadian-436
90Score Rookie/Traded-90T
90Score Young Superstars-38
90Upper Deck-351
90Upper Deck-354
French-351
French-354
91Bowman-46
91O-Pee-Chee-309
91Red Wings Little Caesars-14
91Score American-144
91Score Canadian Bilingual-144
91Score Canadian English-144
91Stadium Club-305
91Topps-309
91Upper Deck-258
French-258
91ProCards-126
92Panini Stickers-117
92Panini Stickers French-117
92Parkhurst-277
Emerald Ice-277
92Score-316
Canadian-316
92Stadium Club-485
92Topps-99
Gold-99G
92Ultra-286
93Donruss-425
93Leaf-276
93OPC Premier-256
Gold-256
93Panini Stickers-250
93Parkhurst-327
Emerald Ice-327
93Pinnacle-420
Canadian-420
93PowerPlay-75
Rising Stars-4
93Score-364
Canadian-364
93Stadium Club-217
Members Only Master Set-217
OPC-217
First Day Issue-217
First Day Issue OPC-217
93Topps/OPC Premier-256
Gold-256
93Ultra-239
93Upper Deck-413
SP-45
94Canada Games NHL POGS-90
94Donruss-46
94Flair-51
94Fleer-64
94Hockey Wit-67
94Leaf-266
94Leaf Limited-110
94OPC Premier-330
Special Effects-330
94Parkhurst-67
Gold-67
Vintage-V66
94Pinnacle-40
Artist's Proofs-40
Rink Collection-40
94Select-15
Gold-15
94SP-37
Die Cuts-37
94Stadium Club-16
Members Only Master Set-16
First Day Issue-16
Super Team Winner Cards-16
94Topps/OPC Premier-330
Special Effects-330
94Ultra-65
94Upper Deck-337
Electric Ice-337
SP Inserts-SP24
SP Inserts Die Cuts-SP24
95Bashan Super Stickers-40
95Be A Player-115
Signatures-S115
Signatures Die Cuts-S115
95Canada Games NHL POGS-93
95Collector's Choice-161
Player's Club-161
Player's Club Platinum-161
95Donruss-42
95Emotion-57
Ntense Power-2
Xcited-12
95Imperial Stickers-40
95Leaf-170
95Leaf Limited-92
95Metal-50
Iron Warriors-10
95Panini Stickers-181
95Parkhurst International-72
Emerald Ice-72
95Pinnacle-197
Artist's Proofs-197
Rink Collection-197
95Playoff One on One-35
95Score-264
Black Ice Artist's Proofs-264
Black Ice-264
95Select Certified-71
Mirror Gold-71
Double Strike-16
Double Strike Gold-16
95SkyBox Impact-57
95SkyBox Impact-241
95SP-47
95Stadium Club-66
Members Only Master Set-66
Fearless-F3
Fearless Members Only Master Set-F3
95Summit-140
Artist's Proofs-140
Ice-140
95Topps-54
OPC Inserts-54
Home Grown Canada-HGC21
95Topps SuperSkills-47
Platinum-47
95Ultra-48
Gold Medallion-48
Crease Crashers-14
Rising Stars-6
Rising Stars Gold Medallion-6
95Upper Deck-159
95Upper Deck-223
Electric Ice-159
Electric Ice-223
Electric Ice Gold-159
Electric Ice Gold-223
Special Edition-SE27
Special Edition Gold-SE27
95Zenith-83
96Black Diamond-5
Gold-5
96Collector's Choice-87
96Donruss-138
Press Proofs-138
96Donruss Canadian Ice-27
Gold Press Proofs-27
Red Press Proofs-27
96Donruss Elite-73
Die Cut Stars-73
96Flair-43
Blue Ice-43
96Fleer-34
96Leaf-154
Press Proofs-154
96Leaf Preferred-84
Press Proofs-84
96Maggers-78
96Metal Universe-70
96Pinnacle-168
Artist's Proofs-168
Foil-168
Premium Stock-168
Rink Collection-168
96Score-54
Artist's Proofs-54
Dealer's Choice Artist's Proofs-54
Special Artist's Proofs-54
Golden Blades-54
96Select Certified-40
Artist's Proofs-40
Blue-40
Mirror Blue-40
Mirror Gold-40
Mirror Red-40
Red-40
96SkyBox Impact-39
96SP-68
96Summit-16
Artist's Proofs-16
Ice-16
Metal-16
Premium Stock-16
96Topps Picks-109
OPC Inserts-109
96Ultra-75
Gold Medallion-75
96Upper Deck-203
96Upper Deck-271
Generation Next-X34
Power Performers-P4
Superstar Showdown-SS29A
96Upper Deck Ice-27
Parallel-27
96Whalers Kid's Club-5
96Zenith-101
Artist's Proofs-101
96Collector's Edge Ice Livin' Large-L4
97Be A Player Take A Number-15
97Black Diamond-3
Double Diamond-3
Triple Diamond-3
Quadruple Diamond-3
97Collector's Choice-110
Crash the Game-C6A
Crash the Game-C6B
Crash the Game-C6C
Crash the Game Exchange-CR6
Star Quest-SQ55
World Domination-W9
97Crown Royale-25
Emerald Green-25
Ice Blue-25
Silver-25
97Donruss-185
Press Proofs Silver-185
Press Proofs Gold-185
97Donruss Canadian Ice-22
Dominion Series-22
Provincial Series-22
97Donruss Elite-23
Aspirations-23
Status-23
97Donruss Limited-126
Exposure-126
97Donruss Preferred-18
Cut to the Chase-18
97Donruss Priority-38
Stamp of Approval-38
97Esso Olympic Hockey Heroes-19
97Esso Olympic Hockey Heroes French-19
97Hurricanes Team Issue-21
97Katch-29
Gold-29
Silver-29
97Kraft Team Canada-8
97Leaf-119
Fractal Matrix-119
Fractal Matrix Die Cuts-119
97Leaf International-119
Universal Ice-119
97McDonald's Team Canada Coins-10
97Pacific-52
Copper-52
Emerald Green-52
Ice Blue-52
Red-52
Silver-52
Team Checklists-5
97Pacific Dynagon-22
Copper-22
Dark Grey-22
Emerald Green-22
Ice Blue-22
Red-22
Silver-22
Best Kept Secrets-17
Tandems-30
97Pacific Invincible-25
Copper-25
Emerald Green-25
Ice Blue-25
Red-25
Silver-25
97Pacific Omega-44
Copper-44
Dark Gray-44
Emerald Green-44
Gold-44
Ice Blue-44
97Panini Stickers-27
97Paramount-37
Copper-37
Dark Grey-37
Emerald Green-37
Ice Blue-37
Red-37
Silver-37
97Pinnacle-109
Press Plates Back Black-109
Press Plates Back Cyan-109
Press Plates Back Magenta-109
Press Plates Back Yellow-109
Press Plates Front Black-109
Press Plates Front Cyan-109
Press Plates Front Magenta-109
Press Plates Front Yellow-109
97Pinnacle Certified-57
Red-57
Mirror Blue-57
Mirror Gold-57
Mirror Red-57
97Pinnacle Inside-189
97Pinnacle Tot Cert Platinum Blue-57
97Pinnacle Tot Certi Platinum Gold-57
97Pinnacle Totally Certified Platinum Red-57
97Pinnacle Tot Cert Mirror Platinum Gold-57
97Revolution-25
Copper-25
Emerald-25
Ice Blue-25
Silver-25
Team Checklist Laser Cuts-5
97Score-98
Artist's Proofs-98
Golden Blades-98
97SP Authentic-24
97Studio-42
Press Proofs Silver-42
Press Proofs Gold-42
97Upper Deck-29
Smooth Grooves-SG55
97Upper Deck Ice-25
Parallel-25
Power Shift-25
97Zenith-54
Z-Gold-54
Z-Silver-54
97Zenith 5 x 7-13
Gold Impulse-13
Silver Impulse-13
98Aurora-37
Championship Fever-9
Championship Fever Copper-9
Championship Fever Ice Blue-9
Championship Fever Red-9
Championship Fever Silver-9
98Be A Player-23
Press Release-23
98BAP Gold-23
98BAP Autographs-23
98BAP Autographs Gold-23
98BAP Tampa Bay All Star Game-23
98Black Diamond-16
Double Diamond-16
Triple Diamond-16
Quadruple Diamond-16
98Bowman's Best-64
Refractors-64
Atomic Refractors-64
98Crown Royale-26
Limited Series-26
98Finest-42
No Protectors-42
No Protectors Refractors-42
Refractors-42
98Hurricanes Team Issue-23
98Katch-27
98OPC Chrome-124
Refractors-124
98Pacific-138
Ice Blue-138
Red-138
Team Checklists-5
98Pacific Dynagon Ice-37
Blue-37
Red-37
Team Checklists-5
98Pacific Omega-45
Red-45
Opening Day Issue-45
98Panini Photocards-64
98Panini Stickers-30
98Paramount-41
Copper-41
Emerald Green-41
Holo-Electric-41
Ice Blue-41
Silver-41
Team Checklists Die-Cuts-5
98Post-16
98Revolution-26
Ice Shadow-26
Red-26
All-Star Die Cuts-22
98SP Authentic-15
Power Shift-15
98SPx Top Prospects-8
Radiance-8
Spectrum-8
98Topps-124
O-Pee-Chee-124
98Topps Gold Label Class 1-56
Black-56
Black One of One-56
One of One-56
Red-56
Red One of One-56
98Topps Gold Label Class 2-56
98Topps Gold Label Class 2 Black-56
98Topps Gold Label Class 2 Black 1 of 1-56
98Topps Gold Label Class 2 One of One-56
98Topps Gold Label Class 2 Red-56
98Topps Gold Label Class 2 Red One of One-56
98Topps Gold Label Class 3-56
98Topps Gold Label Class 3 Black-56
98Topps Gold Label Class 3 Black 1 of 1-56
98Topps Gold Label Class 3 One of One-56
98Topps Gold Label Class 3 Red-56
98Topps Gold Label Class 3 Red One of One-56
98UD Choice-39
98UD Choice Preview-39
98UD Choice Prime Choice Reserve-39
98UD Choice Reserve-39
98Upper Deck-237
Exclusives-237
Exclusives 1 of 1-237
Gold Reserve-237
98Upper Deck MVP-37
Gold Script-37
Silver Script-37
Super Script-37
Power Game-PG11
99SLU Hockey-14
99Aurora-28
Striped-28
Premiere Date-28
Premiere Date Striped-28
99BAP Memorabilia-261
99BAP Memorabilia-357
Gold-261
Gold-357
Silver-261
Silver-357
99BAP Millennium-48
Emerald-48
Ruby-48
Sapphire-48
Signatures-48
Signatures Gold-48
99Black Diamond-63
Diamond Cut-63
Final Cut-63
99Crown Royale-104
Limited Series-29
Limited Series-104
Premiere Date-29
Premiere Date-104
99Hasbro Starting Lineup Cards-14
99O-Pee-Chee-18
99O-Pee-Chee Chrome-18
99O-Pee-Chee Chrome Refractors-18
99O-Pee-Chee Now Starring-NS12
99Pacific-79
Copper-79
Emerald Green-79
Gold-79
Ice Blue-79
Premiere Date-79
Red-79
99Pacific Dynagon Ice-43
Blue-43
Copper-43
Gold-43
Premiere Date-43
99Pacific Omega-173
Copper-173
Gold-173
Ice Blue-173
Premiere Date-173
99Pacific Prism-31
Holographic Blue-31
Holographic Gold-31
Holographic Mirror-31
Holographic Purple-31
Premiere Date-31
99Paramount-49
Copper-49
Emerald-49
Gold-49
Holographic Emerald-49
Holographic Gold-49
Holographic Silver-49
Ice Blue-49
Premiere Date-49
Red-49
Silver-49
Ice Alliance-6
99Revolution-30
Premiere Date-30
Red-30
Shadow Series-30
99SP Authentic-62
99SPx-29
Radiance-29
Spectrum-29
99Stadium Club-105
First Day Issue-105
One of a Kind-105
Printing Plates Black-105
Printing Plates Cyan-105
Printing Plates Magenta-105
Printing Plates Yellow-105
99Topps/OPC-18
Now Starring-NS12
99Topps/OPC Chrome-18
Refractors-18
99Upper Deck-201
Exclusives-201
Exclusives 1 of 1-201
99Upper Deck Gold Reserve-201
99Upper Deck HoloGrFx-11
Ausome-11
99Upper Deck MVP-38
Gold Script-38
Silver Script-38
Super Script-38
99Upper Deck MVP SC Edition-135
Gold Script-135
Silver Script-135
Super Script-135
99Upper Deck Retro-14
Gold-14
Platinum-14
Inkredible-KP
Inkredible Level 2-KP
99Upper Deck Victory-53
99Upper Deck Victory-57
99Wayne Gretzky Hockey-39
00SLU Hockey-180
00BAP Memorabilia-13
Emerald-13
Ruby-13
Sapphire-13
Promos-13
00BAP Mem Chicago Sportsfest Copper-13
00BAP Memorabilia Chicago Sportsfest Blue-13
00BAP Memorabilia Chicago Sportsfest Gold-13
00BAP Memorabilia Chicago Sportsfest Ruby-13
00BAP Memorabilia Chicago Sun-Times Ruby-13
00BAP Memorabilia Chicago Sun-Times Gold-13
00BAP Mem Chicago Sun-Times Sapphire-13
00BAP Mem Toronto Fall Expo Copper-13
00BAP Memorabilia Toronto Fall Expo Gold-13
00BAP Memorabilia Toronto Fall Expo Ruby-13
00BAP Mem Update Heritage Jersey Cards-H15
00BAP Mem Update Heritage Jersey Gold-H15
00BAP Parkhurst 2000-P125
00BAP Signature Series-132
Emerald-132
Ruby-132
Sapphire-132
Autographs-68
Autographs Gold-68
He Shoots-He Scores Prizes-33
00BAP Ultimate Memorabilia Autographs-33
Gold-33
00O-Pee-Chee-242
00O-Pee-Chee Parallel-242
00Pacific-305
Copper-305
Gold-305
Ice Blue-305
Premiere Date-305
00Paramount-184
Copper-184
Gold-184
Holo-Gold-184
Holo-Silver-184
Ice Blue-184
Premiere Date-184
00SPx-76
Spectrum-76
00Stadium Club-17
00Topps/OPC-242
Parallel-242
00Topps Chrome-152
OPC Refractors-152
Refractors-152
00Topps Gold Label Class 1-23
Gold-23
00Topps Gold Label Class 2-23
00Topps Gold Label Class 2 Gold-23
00Topps Gold Label Class 3-23
00Topps Gold Label Class 3 Gold-23
00Topps Heritage-111
00Topps Premier Plus-81
Blue Ice-81
00UD Heroes-88
00UD Reserve-64
00Upper Deck-356
Exclusives Tier 1-356
Exclusives Tier 2-356
00Upper Deck MVP-126
First Stars-126
Second Stars-126
Third Stars-126
00Upper Deck Victory-170
00Upper Deck Vintage-264
01BAP Memorabilia-99
Emerald-99
Ruby-99
Sapphire-99
He Shoots-He Scores Prizes-24
01BAP Signature Series Jerseys-GJ-51
01BAP Signature Series Jersey Autographs-GUKP
01BAP Sig Series Jersey and Stick Cards-GSJ-51
01BAP Ultimate Mem Journey Emblems-4
01BAP Update Heritage-H18
01Bowman YoungStars-29
Gold-29
Ice Cubed-29
01Flyers Postcards-15
01O-Pee-Chee-13
01O-Pee-Chee Heritage Parallel-13
01O-Pee-Chee Heritage Parallel Limited-13
01O-Pee-Chee Premier Parallel-13
01Pacific-292
01Pacific-437
Extreme LTD-292
Gold-437
Hobby LTD-292
Premiere Date-292
Retail LTD-292
01Pacific Adrenaline-141
Blue-141
Premiere Date-141
Red-141
Retail-141
01Pacific Arena Exclusives-292
01Pacific Arena Exclusives-437
01Parkhurst-52
Gold-52
Silver-52
Jerseys-PJ59
Sticks-PS38
01SP Authentic-62
Limited-62
Limited Gold-62
Jerseys-NNKP
Sign of the Times-KP
01SP Game Used Authentic Fabric-AFKP
01SP Game Used Authentic Fabric-DFPL
01SP Game Used Authentic Fabric-TFLRP
01SP Game Used Authentic Fabric Gold-AFKP
01SP Game Used Patches-PKP
01SP Game Used Patches-CPLP
01SP Game Used Patches-CPPG
01SP Game Used Patches-TPSSP
01SP Game Used Patches Signed-SPKP
01SP Game Used Patches Signed-DSPGP
01SP Game Used Tools of the Game Signed-STKP
01SP Game Used Tools of the Game Signed-SCPS
01SP Game Used Tools of the Game Signed-SCPY
01SPx-48
Hockey Treasures-HTKP
Hockey Treasures Autographed-STKE
Hockey Treasures Autographed-STKP
01Stadium Club-94
Award Winners-94
Master Photos-94
01Topps-13
Heritage Parallel-13
Heritage Parallel Limited-13
OPC Parallel-13
01Topps Chrome-13
Refractors-13
Black Border Refractors-13
01Topps Heritage-36
Refractors-36
01UD Challenge for the Cup-63
Jerseys-TNKP
Jersey Autographs-TNKP
01UD Mask Collection Double Patches-DPKP
01UD Mask Collection Jerseys-J-KP
01UD Mask Collection Jersey and Patch-JPKP
01UD Top Shelf-113
01Upper Deck-127
Exclusives-127
Game Jerseys-CPC
Game Jerseys Series II-PFKP
MVP Morning Skate Jerseys-J-KP
MVP Morning Skate Jersey Autographs-SJ-KP
01Upper Deck Victory-256
01Upper Deck Victory-438
Gold-256
Gold-438
01Upper Deck Vintage-185
01Upper Deck Vintage-191
01Czech Stadion-247
02BAP First Edition-86
Jerseys-86
02BAP Memorabilia-186
02BAP Memorabilia-249
Emerald-186
Emerald-249
Ruby-186
Ruby-249
Sapphire-186
Sapphire-249
NHL All-Star Game-186
NHL All-Star Game-249
NHL All-Star Game Blue-186
NHL All-Star Game Blue-249
NHL All-Star Game Green-186
NHL All-Star Game Green-249
NHL All-Star Game Red-186
NHL All-Star Game Red-249
02BAP Memorabilia Toronto Fall Expo-186
02BAP Memorabilia Toronto Fall Expo-249
02BAP Signature Series-149
Autographs-149
Autograph Buybacks 1998-23
Autograph Buybacks 1999-48
Autograph Buybacks 2000-68
Autographs Gold-149
02Bowman YoungStars-99
Gold-99
Silver-99
02Flyers Postcards-10
02O-Pee-Chee-116
02O-Pee-Chee Premier Blue Parallel-116
02O-Pee-Chee Premier Red Parallel-116
02O-Pee-Chee Factory Set-116
02Pacific-285
Blue-285
Red-285
02Parkhurst-44
Bronze-44
Gold-44
Silver-44
02Parkhurst Retro-93
Minis-93
02SP Game Used Authentic Fabrics-AFKP
02SP Game Used Authentic Fabrics-AFPU
02SP Game Used Authentic Fabrics Gold-AFKP
02SP Game Used Authentic Fabrics Gold-AFPU
02SP Game Used Authentic Fabrics Rainbow-AFKP
02SP Game Used Authentic Fabrics Rainbow-AFPU
02SP Game Used First Rounder Patches-KP
02SP Game Used Piece of History-PHKP
02SP Game Used Piece of History Gold-PHKP
02SP Game Used Piece of History Rainbow-PHKP
02SP Game Used Tools of the Game-KP
02SPx Winning Materials-WMPR
02SPx Winning Materials Gold-PR
02SPx Winning Materials Silver-PR
02SPx Xtreme Talents-KP
02SPx Xtreme Talents Gold-KP
02SPx Xtreme Talents Silver-KP
02Topps-116
OPC Blue Parallel-116
OPC Red Parallel-116
Captain's Cloth-CC2
Captain's Cloth-CC6
Captain's Cloth-CC9
First Round Fabric-KP
First Round Fabric Autographs-KP
Factory Set-116
02Topps Chrome-75
Black Border Refractors-75
Refractors-75
First Round Fabric Patches-KP
02Topps Total-379
02UD Honor Roll-92
Grade A Jerseys-TPRG
02UD Piece of History Patches-PHKP
02UD Top Shelf Dual Player Jerseys-RPT
02UD Top Shelf Dual Player Jerseys-STFP
02UD Top Shelf Sweet Sweaters-SWKP
02Upper Deck-126
Exclusives-126
Blow-Ups-C30
CHL Graduates-CGKP
CHL Graduates Gold-CGKP
Fan Favorites-KP
Good Old Days-GOKP
Number Crunchers-NC10
Patchwork-PWKP
Playbooks Series II-RP
02Upper Deck Classic Portraits-73
Hockey Royalty-PGF
Hockey Royalty Limited-PGF
02Upper Deck MVP-132
Gold-132
Classics-132
Golden Classics-132
Skate Around Jerseys-SAKP
Skate Around Jerseys-SDLP
Skate Around Jerseys-STLPR
02Upper Deck Rookie Update Jerseys-DKP
02Upper Deck Rookie Update Jerseys Gold-DKP
02Upper Deck Victory-159
Bronze-159
Gold-159
Silver-159
02Upper Deck Vintage-186
Green Backs-186
Jerseys-FSKP
Jerseys-SOKP
Jerseys Gold-SO-KP
Jerseys Gold-FS-KP
02UD SuperStars City AS Dual Jersey-KPBA
03Black Diamond Threads-DT-KP
03Black Diamond Threads Green-DT-KP
03Black Diamond Threads Red-DT-KP
03Black Diamond Threads Black-DT-KP
03Flyers Program Inserts-6
03Flyers Postcards-16
03ITG Action-449
Jerseys-M65
03NHL Sticker Collection-105
03O-Pee-Chee-138
03OPC Blue-138
03OPC Gold-138
03OPC Red-138
03Pacific-255
Blue-255
Red-255
03Pacific Complete-68
Red-68
03Pacific Exhibit-111
Blue Backs-111
Yellow Backs-111
03Parkhurst Original Six Detroit-54
Inserts-D-16
Memorabilia-DM32
03Topps-138
Blue-138
Gold-138
Red-138
Pristine Jersey Portions-PPJ-KP
Pristine Jersey Portion Refractors-PPJ-KP
Pristine Patches-PP-KP
Pristine Patch Refractors-PP-KP
Traded Franchise Fabrics-FF-KP
03Upper Deck-140
Canadian Exclusives-140
HG-140
03Upper Deck MVP-308
Gold Script-308
Silver Script-308
Canadian Exclusives-308
Souvenirs-S11
Threads-TC8
03Upper Deck Victory-140
Bronze-140
Gold-140
Silver-140
03Czech Stadion-546
04SP Authentic-134
Limited-134
Buybacks-101
Rookie Review-RR-KP
Sign of the Times-QS-GPRE
Sign of the Times-QS-TPLS
04Ultimate Collection Dual Logos-UL2-LP
04Ultimate Collection Signature Logos-ULA-KP
04Ultimate Collection Signature Patches-SP-KP
04Upper Deck-128
Big Playmakers-BP-KP
Canadian Exclusives-128
Clutch Performers-CP5
HG Glossy Gold-128
HG Glossy Silver-128
05Be A Player-64
First Period-64
Second Period-64
Third Period-64
Overtime-64
Dual Signatures-PE
Dual Signatures-TP
Quad Signatures-IMPL
Quad Signatures-SDPH
Signatures-KP
Signatures Gold-KP
Triple Signatures-PDL
Triple Signatures-PTS
Triple Signatures-TLP
05Beehive-67
05Beehive-206
Beige -67
Blue -67
Gold-67
Red -67
Matte-67
Matted Materials-MMKP
Signature Scrapbook-SSKP
05Black Diamond-140
Emerald-140
Gold-140
Onyx-140
Ruby-140
Jerseys-J-KP
Jerseys Ruby-J-KP
Jersey Duals-DJ-KP
Jersey Triples-TJ-KP
Jersey Quads-QJ-KP
05Flyers Team Issue-15
05Hot Prospects-73
En Fuego-73
Red Hot-73
White Hot-73
05Panini Stickers-130
05Parkhurst-364
05Parkhurst-519
Facsimile Auto Parallel-364
Facsimile Auto Parallel-519
True Colors-TCPHI
True Colors-TCPHI
True Colors-TCPHPI
True Colors-TCPHPI
05SP Authentic-74
Limited-74
Marks of Distinction-MDKP
Sign of the Times-KP
Sign of the Times Duals-DPR
Sign of the Times Triples-TPGC
Sign of the Times Fives-PEGCR
05SP Game Used-73
Autographs-73
Gold-73
Authentic Fabrics-AF-KP
Authentic Fabrics Autographs-AAF-KP
Authentic Fabrics Dual-PG
Authentic Fabrics Dual Autographs-PG
Authentic Fabrics Gold-AF-KP
Authentic Fabrics Quad-GFEP
Authentic Patches Quad -GFEP
Authentic Fabrics Triple-NPJ
Authentic Patches-AP-KP
Authentic Patches Autographs-AAP-KP
Authentic Patches Dual-PG
Authentic Patches Dual Autographs-PG
Authentic Patches Triple-NPJ
Awesome Authentics-AA-KP
Awesome Authentics Gold-DA-KP
Game Gear-GG-KP
Game Gear Autographs-AG-KP
Signature Sticks-SS-KP
SIGnificance-KP
SIGnificance Gold-S-KP
SIGnificance Extra-PE
SIGnificance Extra Gold-PE
Significant Numbers-SN-KP
Statscriptions-ST-KP
05SPx-66
Spectrum-66
Winning Combos-WC-FP
Winning Combos-WC-PE
Winning Combos-WC-PG
Winning Combos Autographs-AWC-PE
Winning Combos Gold-WC-FP
Winning Combos Gold-WC-PE
Winning Combos Gold-WC-PG
Winning Combos Spectrum-WC-FP
Winning Combos Spectrum-WC-PE
Winning Combos Spectrum-WC-PG
Winning Materials-WM-KP
Winning Materials Autographs-AWM-KP
Winning Materials Gold-WM-KP
Winning Materials Spectrum-WM-KP
Xcitement Superstars-XS-KP
Xcitement Superstars Gold-XS-KP
Xcitement Superstars Spectrum-XS-KP
05The Cup-78
Gold-78
Black Rainbow-78
Dual NHL Shields-DSKG
Dual NHL Shields Autographs-ADSKG
Emblems of Endorsement-EEKP
Honorable Numbers-HNKP
Limited Logos-LLKP
Masterpiece Pressplates-78
Masterpiece Pressplates (Rookie Update)-225
Patch Variation-P78
Patch Variation Autographs-AP78
Scripted Numbers Dual-DSNPL
Scripted Swatches-SSKP
Signature Patches-SPKP
05UD Artifacts-74
05UD Artifacts-185
Blue-74
Blue-185
Gold-74
Gold-185
Green-74
Green-185
Pewter-74
Pewter-185
Red-74
Red-185
Gold Autographed-74
Gold Autographed-185
Remarkable Artifacts-RA-KP
Remarkable Artifacts Dual-RA-KP
Treasured Patches-TP-KP
Treasured Patches Autographed-TP-KP
Treasured Patches Dual-TPD-KP
Treasured Patches Dual Autographed-TPD-KP
Treasured Patches Pewter-TP-KP
Treasured Patches Silver-TP-KP
Treasured Swatches-TS-KP
Treasured Swatches Autographed-TS-KP
Treasured Swatches Blue-TS-KP
Treasured Swatches Copper-TS-KP
Treasured Swatches Dual-TSD-KP
Treasured Swatches Dual Autographed-TSD-KP
Treasured Swatches Dual Blue-TSD-KP
Treasured Swatches Dual Copper-TSD-KP
Treasured Swatches Dual Maroon-TSD-KP
Treasured Swatches Dual Pewter-TSD-KP
Treasured Swatches Dual Silver-TSD-KP
Treasured Swatches Maroon-TS-KP
Treasured Swatches Pewter-TS-KP
Treasured Swatches Silver-TS-KP

05UD PowerPlay-65
Rainbow-65
Power Marks-PMKP
Specialists-TSKP
Specialists Patches-SPKP
05Ultimate Collection-68
Gold-68
Endorsed Emblems-EEKP
Jerseys Dual-DJFP
Marquee Attractions-MA37
Marquee Attractions Signatures-SMA37
Ultimate Patches Dual-DPFP
05Ultra-143
Gold-143
Fresh Ink-FI-KP
Fresh Ink Blue-FI-KP
Ice-143
05Upper Deck-139
Big Playmakers-B-KP
HG Glossy-139
Jerseys-J-KP
Jerseys Series II-J2KP
Majestic Materials-MMKP
NHL Generations-TCGP
Notable Numbers-N-KP
Patches-P-KP
Shooting Stars-S-KP
05Upper Deck Ice-72
Rainbow-72
Frozen Fabrics-FFKP
Frozen Fabrics Autographs-AFFKP
Frozen Fabrics Glass-FFKP
Frozen Fabrics Patches-FFPKP
Frozen Fabrics Patch Autographs-FAPKP
05Upper Deck MVP-281
Gold-281
Platinum-281
Materials Duals-D-PD
05Upper Deck Rookie Update-73
05Upper Deck Rookie Update-225
Inspirations Patch Rookies-225
05Upper Deck Trilogy-65
05Upper Deck Trilogy-148
Crystal-148
Honorary Patches-HP-KP
Honorary Patch Scripts-HSP-KP
Honorary Swatches-HS-KP
Honorary Swatch Scripts-HSS-KP
05Upper Deck Toronto Fall Expo-139
05Upper Deck Victory-142
Black-142
Gold-142
Silver-142
Blow-Ups-BU29
Game Breakers-GB32
06Be A Player Portraits Signature Portraits-SPKP
06Flair Showcase-151
Parallel-151
Stitches-SSKP
06Fleer-144
Tiffany-144
Fabricology-FKP
06NHL POG-29
06UD Artifacts Treasured Patches Black-TSKP
06UD Artifacts Treasured Patches Blue-TSKP
06UD Artifacts Treasured Patches Gold-TSKP
06UD Artifacts Treasured Patches Platinum-TSKP
06UD Artifacts Treasured Patches Red-TSKP
06UD Artifacts Treasured Swatches-TSKP
06UD Artifacts Treasured Swatches Black-TSKP
06UD Artifacts Treasured Swatches Blue-TSKP
06UD Artifacts Treasured Swatches Gold-TSKP
06UD Artifacts Treasured Swatches Platinum-TSKP
06UD Artifacts Treasured Swatches Red-TSKP
06UD Powerplay Specialists-SKP
06UD Powerplay Specialists Patches-PKP
06Ultra-144
Gold Medallion-144
Ice Medallion-144
06Upper Deck Game Jerseys-JKP
06Upper Deck Game Patches-PKP
06Upper Deck Generations Duals-G2PG
06Upper Deck Generations Patches Dual-G2PPG
06Upper Deck Signature Sensations-SSKP
06Upper Deck Ovation-138
06Upper Deck Trilogy Combo Clearcut Autographs-C3PGC
06Upper Deck Trilogy Honorary Scripted Patches-HSPKP
06Upper Deck Trilogy Honorary Scripted Swatches-HSSKP
06Upper Deck Trilogy Honorary Swatches-HSKP
06Upper Deck Victory-147
06Upper Deck Victory Black-147
06Upper Deck Victory Gold-147

Primeau, Kevin

80Canucks Silverwood Dairies-19
81Swedish Semic Hockey VM Stickers-90
91Oilers IGA-29
92Oilers IGA-29
99Swiss Panini Stickers-344

Primeau, Reg

99Fort Wayne Komets Points Leaders-7
01Fort Wayne Komets Shoe Carnival-2

Primeau, Wayne

93Upper Deck Program of Excellence-E9
93Owen Sound Platers-23
94Owen Sound Platers-20
94Owen Sound Platers-28
94Owen Sound Platers-29
94Classic-15
Gold-15
CHL Previews-CP1
Tri-Cards-T7
94Classic Four-Sport *-131
Gold-131
Printers Proofs-131
95Bowman-157
All-Foil-157
95Parkhurst International-26
Emerald Ice-26
95SkyBox Impact-191
95Slapshot-240
95Slapshot-301
95Topps-222
OPC Inserts-222
95Upper Deck-433
Electric Ice-433
Electric Ice Gold-433
95Owen Sound Platers-6
95Owen Sound Platers-23
95Owen Sound Platers-32
95Classic-93
95Images-47
Gold-47
95Images Four-Sport *-108
96Black Diamond-76
Gold-76
96Collector's Choice-25
96Fleer-132
96Leaf-231
Press Proofs-231
96Leaf Preferred-131
Press Proofs-131
96Metal Universe-17
96Pinnacle-220
Artist's Proofs-220
Foil-220
Premium Stock-220
Rink Collection-220
96SkyBox Impact-156
96Ultra-20
Gold Medallion-20
Rookies-16
96Upper Deck-20
96Rochester Americans-13
96Collector's Edge Future Legends-36
97Donruss-67
Press Proofs Silver-67
Press Proofs Gold-67
97Donruss Limited-101
Exposure-101
97Donruss Priority-72
Stamp of Approval-72
97Pacific-43
Copper-43
Emerald Green-43
Ice Blue-43
Red-43
Silver-43
97Score Sabres-13
Platinum-13
Premier-13
97Upper Deck-17
98OPC Chrome-146
Refractors-146
98Topps-146
O-Pee-Chee-146
99Upper Deck MVP SC Edition-28
Gold Script-28
Silver Script-28
Super Script-28
00BAP Memorabilia-311
Emerald-311
Ruby-311
Sapphire-311
Promos-311
00BAP Mem Chicago Sportsfest Copper-311
00BAP Memorabilia Chicago Sportsfest Blue-311
00BAP Memorabilia Chicago Sportsfest Gold-311
00BAP Memorabilia Chicago Sportsfest Ruby-311
00BAP Memorabilia Chicago Sun-Times Ruby-311
00BAP Memorabilia Chicago Sun-Times Gold-311
00BAP Mem Chicago Sun-Times Sapphire-311
00BAP Mem Toronto Fall Expo Copper-311
00BAP Memorabilia Toronto Fall Expo Gold-311
00BAP Memorabilia Toronto Fall Expo Ruby-311
00O-Pee-Chee-266B
00O-Pee-Chee Parallel-266B
00Pacific-379
Copper-379
Gold-379
Ice Blue-379
Premiere Date-379
00Titanium Game Gear-139
00Titanium Game Gear Patches-139
00Topps/OPC-266B
Parallel-266B
00Upper Deck-390
Exclusives Tier 1-390
Exclusives Tier 2-390
00Upper Deck Victory-213
01BAP Signature Series-14
Autographs-14
Autographs Gold-14
01Pacific Heads-Up Quad Jerseys-27
01Private Stock Game Gear-82
01Private Stock Game Gear Patches-82
02BAP Sig Series Auto Buybacks 2001-14
02Pacific-315
Blue-315
Red-315
02Pacific Complete-400
Red-400
03ITG Action-403
03NHL Sticker Collection-117
03Pacific Complete-394
Red-394
03Sharks Postcards-14
03Upper Deck-405
Canadian Exclusives-405
HG-405
UD Exclusives-405
05Bruins Boston Globe-9
05Panini Stickers-354
05Parkhurst-39
05Upper Deck-162
HG Glossy-162
05Upper Deck MVP-324
Gold-324
Platinum-324
05Upper Deck Toronto Fall Expo-162
06Be A Player-61
Autographs-61
Signatures-WP
06O-Pee-Chee-48
Rainbow-48
06Upper Deck-271
Exclusives Parallel-271
High Gloss Parallel-271
Masterpieces-271

Prince, Gilles

93Swiss HNL-432

Prince, Guy

91British Columbia JHL-71
92British Columbia JHL-75
93Dayton Bombers-12
95Alaska Gold Kings-15

Prince, Martin

93Quebec Pee-Wee Tournament-46

Princi, Didier

93Swiss HNL-43
95Swiss HNL-36
96Swiss HNL-183

Principato, Anthony

06Lincoln Stars-23

Prindolo, Constant

79Montreal Juniors-24

Printz, David

04Philadelphia Phantoms-14
05Philadelphia Phantoms-17
06Fleer-230
Tiffany-230
06O-Pee-Chee-510
Rainbow-510
06SP Authentic-224
Limited-224
06SPx-147
Spectrum-147
06The Cup-105
Autographed Rookie Masterpiece Pressplates-105
Gold Rainbow Autographed Rookies-105
Masterpiece Pressplates (Artifacts)-209
Masterpiece Pressplates (Marquee Rookies)-510
Masterpiece Pressplates (MVP)-331
Masterpiece Pressplates (Power Play)-111
Masterpiece Pressplates (SP Authentic)-224
Masterpiece Pressplates (SPx)-147
Masterpiece Pressplates (Trilogy)-141
Masterpiece Pressplates (Victory)-315
Rookies Black-105
Rookies Platinum-105
06UD Artifacts-209
Blue-209
Gold-209
Platinum-209
Radiance-209
Red-209
06UD Powerplay-111
Impact Rainbow-111
06Ultimate Collection Ultimate Debut Threads Jerseys-DJ-DP
06Ultimate Collection Ultimate Debut Threads Jerseys Autographs-DJ-DP
06Ultimate Collection Ultimate Debut Threads Patches-DJ-DP
06Ultimate Collection Ultimate Debut Threads Patches Autographs-DJ-DP
06Upper Deck-233
Exclusives Parallel-233
High Gloss Parallel-233
Masterpieces-233
06Upper Deck MVP-331
Gold Script-331
Super Script-331
06Upper Deck Trilogy-141
06Upper Deck Victory-315
06Philadelphia Phantoms-14

Prinz, Cornel

93Quebec Pee-Wee Tournament-1625
99Swiss Panini Stickers-295
02Swiss HNL-447

Priondolo, Constant

83Swedish Semic VM Stickers-133

Prior, Craig

907th Inn. Sketch QMJHL-214

Prior, Dave

91Jets IGA-26
91Moncton Hawks-23
91ProCards-188

Prior, Gary

94German DEL-6
95German DEL-1
96German DEL-1
99German Bundesliga 2-186

Prior, Steve

89Rayside-Balfour Jr. Canadians-19

Prior, Trevor

02UK Sheffield Steelers-15
03ECHL Update RBI Sports-136

Pritchard, Bruce

84Victoria Cougars-19

Pritchard, Robert

04Langley Hornets-14
04Langley Hornets-22

Pritchett, Grant

917th Inn. Sketch OHL-343
93Guelph Storm-24

Prive, Dany

93Quebec Pee-Wee Tournament-1355

Probert, Bob

83Brantford Alexanders-3
84Sault Ste. Marie Greyhounds-18
87Red Wings Little Caesars-24
88Frito-Lay Stickers-41
88O-Pee-Chee-181
88O-Pee-Chee Stickers-247
88Panini Stickers-46
88Red Wings Little Caesars-20
88Topps-181
90Pro Set-76
90Score-143
Canadian-143
90Upper Deck-448
French-448
91Pro Set Platinum-34
91Bowman-55
91O-Pee-Chee-198
91Panini Stickers-146
91Parkhurst-272
French-272
91Pinnacle-183
French-183
91Pro Set-61
French-61
91Red Wings Little Caesars-15
91Score American-73
91Score Canadian Bilingual-73
91Score Canadian English-73
91Stadium Club-59
91Topps-198
91Upper Deck-239
French-239
92Bowman-85
92O-Pee-Chee-252
92Parkhurst-41
Emerald Ice-41
Cherry Picks-CP9
92Pinnacle-56
French-56
92Pro Set-46
92Score-52
Canadian-52
Sharpshooters-17
Sharpshooters Canadian-17
92Seasons Patches-8
92Stadium Club-355
92Topps-63
Gold-63G
92Ultra-53
92Upper Deck-248
93Donruss-104
93Leaf-186
93OPC Premier-177
Gold-177
93Panini Stickers-249
93Parkhurst-333
Emerald Ice-333
93Pinnacle-7
Canadian-7
93PowerPlay-335
93Score-59
Canadian-59
93Stadium Club-137
Members Only Master Set-137
OPC-137
First Day Issue-137
First Day Issue OPC-137
93Topps/OPC Premier-177
Gold-177
93Ultra-309
93Upper Deck-200
SP-46
94Blackhawks Coke-14
94Parkhurst-71
Gold-71
94Pinnacle-404
Artist's Proofs-404
Rink Collection-404
95Be A Player-221
Signatures-S221
Signatures Die Cuts-S221
95Blackhawks Coke-12
95Canada Games NHL POGS-68
95Donruss-247
95Parkhurst International-312
Emerald Ice-312
95Playoff One on One-134
95Stadium Club-152
Members Only Master Set-152
95Topps-299
OPC Inserts-299
95Ultra-218
95Upper Deck-469
Electric Ice-469
Electric Ice Gold-469
Special Edition-SE105
Special Edition Gold-SE105
96Donruss-8
Press Proofs-8
96Pinnacle-84
Artist's Proofs-84
Foil-84
Premium Stock-84
Rink Collection-84
96Score-156
Artist's Proofs-156
Dealer's Choice Artist's Proofs-156
Special Artist's Proofs-156
Golden Blades-156
96Upper Deck-33
Superstar Showdown-SS29B
97Collector's Choice-49
97Katch-36
Gold-36
Silver-36
97Pacific-290
Copper-290
Emerald Green-290
Ice Blue-290
Red-290
Silver-290
97Upper Deck-39
97Upper Deck-197
98Be A Player-181
Press Release-181
98BAP Gold-181
98BAP Autographs-181
98BAP Autographs Gold-181
98Blackhawks Chicago Sun-Times-5
98Katch-34
98OPC Chrome-97
Refractors-97
98Pacific Dynagon Ice-44
Blue-44
Red-44
98Pacific Omega-54
Red-54
Opening Day Issue-54
98Topps-97
O-Pee-Chee-97
98Upper Deck MVP-46
Gold Script-46
Silver Script-46
Super Script-46
99Pacific-96
Copper-96
Emerald Green-96
Gold-96
Ice Blue-96
Premiere Date-96
Red-96
00BAP Memorabilia Update Teammates-TM4
00BAP Memorabilia Update Teammates Gold-TM4
00BAP Memorabilia Update Tough Materials-T1
00BAP Mem Update Tough Materials Gold-T1
00O-Pee-Chee-194
00O-Pee-Chee Parallel-194
00Pacific-101
Copper-101
Gold-101
Ice Blue-101
Premiere Date-101
00Topps/OPC-194
Parallel-194
00Topps Heritage-196
Original Six Relics-OSS-BP
00Upper Deck Vintage-85
00Czech Stadion-197
01BAP Update Tough Customers-TC2
01BAP Update Tough Customers-TC6
01BAP Update Tough Customers-TC34
01O-Pee-Chee-113
01O-Pee-Chee Premier Parallel-113
01Pacific-90
01Pacific-407
Extreme LTD-90
Gold-407
Hobby LTD-90
Premiere Date-90
Retail LTD-90
01Pacific Arena Exclusives-90
01Pacific Arena Exclusives-407
01SP Authentic Jerseys-NNBP
01Topps-113
OPC Parallel-113
02BAP Sig Series Auto Buybacks 1998-181
02BAP Signature Series Famous Scraps-FS2
02BAP Signature Series Famous Scraps-FS9
02Fleer Throwbacks Autographs-11
02Fleer Throwbacks Drop the Gloves-1
02Fleer Throwbacks Squaring Off-1
02Fleer Throwbacks Squaring Off Mem-1
02Fleer Throwbacks Stickwork-13
02Pacific-81
Blue-81
Red-81
02Pacific Complete-91
Red-91
02UD Foundations-15
02Upper Deck-285
Exclusives-285
02Upper Deck Beckett UD Promos-285
02Upper Deck Victory-49
Bronze-49
Gold-49
Silver-49
03Parkhurst Orig Six Chicago Mem -CM61
03Parkhurst Original Six Detroit-31
05ITG Tough Customers-BP
Autographs-BP
Complete Jerseys-BP
Double Memorabilia-BP
Emblem and Numbers-BP
Famous Battles Autographs-GP
Famous Battles Autographs-PC
Jerseys-BP
Signed Memorabilia-BP
Stickwork-BP
05ITG Ultimate Mem Pass the Torch Jerseys-17
05ITG Ultimate Mem Passing Torch Jsy Gold-17
05SP Game Used Oldtimer's Challenge-OC-BP
05SP Game Used Oldtimer's Challenge Autos-OCA-BP
05SP Game Used Oldtimer's Challenge Patch-OCP-BP
05SP Game Used Oldtime Chall Patch Autoa-OAP-BP
06Parkhurst-101
06Parkhurst-233
06Parkhurst-250
Autographs-101
Autographs-233
Autographs-250
Autographs Dual-DAMP
Autographs Dual-DAPK
06SP Game Used Inked Sweaters Dual-IS2WP
06SP Game Used Inked Sweaters Dual Patches-IS2WP
06UD Artifacts-148
Blue-148
Gold-148
Platinum-148
Radiance-148
Autographed Radiance Parallel-148
Red-148
Auto-Facts-AFBP
Auto-Facts Gold-AFBP
Treasured Patches Black-TSBP
Treasured Patches Blue-TSBP
Treasured Patches Gold-TSBP
Treasured Patches Platinum-TSBP
Treasured Patches Red-TSBP
Treasured Patches Autographed Black Tag Parallel-TSBP
Treasured Swatches-TSBP
Treasured Swatches Black-TSBP
Treasured Swatches Blue-TSBP
Treasured Swatches Gold-TSBP
Treasured Swatches Platinum-TSBP
Treasured Swatches Red-TSBP
Treasured Swatches Autographed Black-TSBP
06Upper Deck Game Jerseys-J2PR
06Upper Deck Game Patches-P2PR

Probst, Paul

72Finnish Semic World Championship-151
72Swedish Semic World Championship-151

Probst, Skip

88ProCards IHL-88
91ProCards-450

Probst, Stefan

95Swiss HNL-351

Proceviat, Dick

67Columbus Checkers-11

Proceviat, Steve

90Rayside-Balfour Jr. Canadians-17

Prochazka, Frantisek

93Swedish Semic World Champ Stickers-94
94Finnish Jaa Kiekko-172
95German DEL-410
97Czech APS Extraliga-81
97Czech DS Extraliga-43
98Czech DS Stickers-89
00Czech OFS-405

Prochazka, Libor

94Czech APS Extraliga-52
95Czech APS Extraliga-84
95Czech APS Extraliga-363
96Czech APS Extraliga-78
96Swedish Semic Wien-109
97Czech APS Extraliga-351
97Czech DS Stickers-135
97Swedish Collector's Choice-4
98Czech DS-7
98Czech OFS-235
98Czech OFS-386
98Czech OFS-440
98Czech OFS-471
98Czech Bonaparte-8B
98Czech Pexeso-26
98Czech Pexeso Series Two-22
99Czech DS National Stars-NS11
00Czech DS Extraliga-123
00Czech OFS-163
00Czech OFS Star Emerald-22
00Czech OFS Star Pink-22
00Czech OFS Star Violet-22
01Czech DS-9
01Czech OFS-52
All Stars-11
02Czech OFS Plus-99
Trios-T16
Duos-D8
02Czech IQ Sports Blue-19
02Czech IQ Sports Yellow-21
03Czech OFS Plus-161
03Czech OFS Plus All-Star Game-H33
04Czech HC Sparta Praha Postcards-17
04Czech OFS-196
05Czech HC Kladno-10
06Czech OFS-264
06Swedish SHL Elitset-129

Prochazka, Martin

91Upper Deck Czech World Juniors-96
94Czech APS Extraliga-57
95Czech APS Extraliga-94
95Czech APS Extraliga-370
95Czech APS Extraliga-386
95Finnish Semic World Championships-155
96Swedish Semic Wien-116
97Paramount-184
Copper-184
Dark Grey-184
Emerald Green-184
Ice Blue-184
Red-184
Silver-184
97Score-62
Artist's Proofs-62
Golden Blades-62
97Score Maple Leafs-20
Platinum-20
Premier-20
97Czech APS Extraliga-357
98Pacific-420
Ice Blue-420
Red-420
98Czech DS-3
98Czech OFS-106
98Czech OFS-240
98Czech OFS-442
98Czech OFS-479
Olympic Winners-14
98Czech Bonaparte-1A
98Czech Pexeso-1
98Czech Pexeso Series Two-6
98Czech Pexeso Series Two-19
98Czech Spaghetti-12
99Czech DS National Stars-NS15
99Czech DS Premium-P5
99Czech OFS-29
99Czech OFS-448
99Czech OFS-525
All-Star Game Blue-525
All-Star Game Gold-525
All-Star Game Red-525
All-Star Game Silver-525
99Czech OFS Jagr Team Embossed-29
00Czech DS Extraliga-106
00Czech DS Extraliga-166
Team Jagr-JT8
Top Stars-TS6
00Czech OFS-251
00Czech OFS Star Emerald-27
00Czech OFS Star Pink-27
00Czech OFS Star Violet-27
01Czech DS-19
Best of the Best-BB6
01Czech OFS-46
01Czech OFS Red Inserts-RE6D
02Czech DS-28
02Czech DS-84
02Czech IQ Sports Blue-20
02Czech IQ Sports Yellow-20
02Russian Hockey League-120
03Czech OFS Plus-236
03Czech OFS Plus MS Praha-SE13
04Czech OFS-64
04Czech OFS-412
05Czech HC Kladno-11
06Czech HC Kladno Postcards-5
06Czech OFS-265

Prochazka, Michael

01Czech OFS-232
01Czech OFS-284
03Elmira Jackals-17
03Port Huron Beacons-19

Prochazka, Milan

96Czech APS Extraliga-163
97Czech DS Stickers-263
99Czech DS-196
99Czech OFS-83
00Czech OFS-202
01Czech OFS-261
02Czech OFS Plus-116
03Czech OFS Plus-248
04Czech OFS-32
06Czech OFS-38

Prochazka, Petr

00Saskatoon Blades-26

Prochazka, Radek

96Czech APS Extraliga-279
97Czech APS Extraliga-234
97Czech DS Extraliga-23
97Czech DS Stickers-184
98Czech DS Stickers-41
98Czech OFS-336
99Czech DS-28
99Czech OFS-316
00Czech DS Extraliga-129
00Czech OFS-174
02Czech OFS Plus-141
02Czech OFS Plus-347
05Czech HC Vitkovice-14
06Czech OFS-61

Prochazka, Robert

98Czech OFS-183
99Czech Score Blue 2000-98
99Czech Score Red Ice 2000-98
00Czech OFS-218
03Czech OFS Plus-277

Prochazka, Stanislav

94Czech APS Extraliga-36
95Czech APS Extraliga-328
96Czech APS Extraliga-155
97Czech APS Extraliga-257
97Czech DS Extraliga-71
97Czech DS Stickers-262
98Czech DS-55
98Czech DS Stickers-140
98Czech OFS-155
99Czech DS-83
99Czech OFS-357
00Czech DS Extraliga-95
00Czech OFS-47
01Czech OFS-252
02Czech OFS Plus-165
03Czech OFS Plus-123
04Czech OFS-77
05Czech HC Liberec-9
06Czech OFS-102

Procyshyn, Jeremy

92Saskatchewan JHL-88

Prodgers, Goldie

12C57-37
23V145-1-32
24Anonymous NHL-5
24C144 Champ's Cigarettes-47
04ITG Franchises Canadian-36

Proffitt, Rob

95Alaska Gold Kings-16

Proft, Paris

96German DEL-202

Prokepetz, Jason

98Florida Everblades-19

Prokhorov, Vitali

92OPC Premier-64
92Parkhurst-157
Emerald Ice-157
92Pinnacle-404
French-404
92Ultra-397
92Upper Deck-486
92Finnish Semic-120
92Russian Stars Red Ace-29
92Russian Stars Red Ace-5
92Classic-51
Gold-51
93Donruss-290
93Leaf-326
93OPC Premier-452
Gold-452
93Parkhurst-450
Emerald Ice-450
93PowerPlay-432
93Topps/OPC Premier-452
Gold-452
93Upper Deck-363
93Peoria Rivermen-22
94Canada Games NHL POGS-206
94Donruss-126
94Leaf-295
94Parkhurst-206
Gold-206
94Pinnacle-367
Artist's Proofs-367
Rink Collection-367
94Stadium Club-19
Members Only Master Set-19
First Day Issue-19
Super Team Winner Cards-19
94Ultra-188
94Upper Deck-173
Electric Ice-173
94Classic Pro Prospects-92
Jumbos-PP20
95Swedish Leaf-221
95Swedish Upper Deck-66
99Russian Hockey League-18
99Russian Metallurg Magnetogorsk-51
01Russian Hockey League-29

Prokop, Juraj

03Czech OFS Plus-360

Prokop, Neal

06Moose Jaw Warriors-8

Prokopec, Mike

91Cornwall Royals-17
917th Inn. Sketch OHL-13
93Guelph Storm-16
94Indianapolis Ice-18
95Parkhurst International-308
Emerald Ice-308
95Indianapolis Ice-17
96Zenith-149
Artist's Proofs-149
96Collector's Edge Future Legends-50
98Detroit Vipers-11
98Detroit Vipers Freschetta-9
98IHL All-Star Eastern Conference-11
99IHL All-Stars-7
99Manitoba Moose-5

Prokopetz, Jason

91Air Canada SJHL-E22
92Saskatchewan JHL-82
99Florida Everblades-12

Prokopiev, Alexander

91O-Pee-Chee Inserts-25R
96Czech APS Extraliga-207
97Czech APS Extraliga-135
97Czech DS Extraliga-101
97Czech DS Stickers-200
98Czech DS Stickers-258
99Russian Dynamo Moscow-14
99Russian Stars of Hockey-2
99Russian Stars Postcards-19
00Russian Champions-5
00Russian Hockey League-137
02Russian World Championships-17
03Russian Avangard Omsk-18
03Russian National Team-22
03Russian Postcards-6
04Russian World Championship Team-6

Prokupek, Ladislav

93Parkhurst-514
Emerald Ice-514
94Czech APS Extraliga-176
95Czech APS Extraliga-193
96Czech APS Extraliga-327
97Czech APS Extraliga-306
97Czech DS Stickers-166
98Czech DS Stickers-120
98Czech OFS-94
99Czech OFS-309

Pronger, Chris

91Peterborough Petes-2
917th Inn. Sketch OHL-134
92Upper Deck-591
92Upper Deck-SP3
93Donruss-150
93Donruss-393
Rated Rookies-3
Special Print-J
93Kraft-69
93Leaf-257
Freshman Phenoms-2
93OPC Premier-485
Gold-485
93Parkhurst-249
Emerald Ice-249
Calder Candidates-C2
Calder Candidates Gold-C2
Cherry's Playoff Heroes-D13
93Pinnacle-456
Canadian-456
Super Rookies-2
Super Rookies Canadian-2
93PowerPlay-354
Rookie Standouts-12
93Score-586
Gold-586
Canadian-586
Canadian Gold-586
93Stadium Club-290
Members Only Master Set-290
First Day Issue-290
93Topps/OPC Premier-485
Gold-485
93Ultra-339
Wave of the Future-14
93Upper Deck-190
Silver Skates-H5
Silver Skates Gold-H5
SP-64
93Whalers Coke-16
93Peterborough Petes-29
93Classic-2
Top Ten-DP2
93Classic Four-Sport *-186
Gold-186
Acetates-12
Chromium Draft Stars-DS59
LPs-LP23
Power Pick Bonus-PP19
Tri-Cards-TC4
94Be A Player-R43
94Canada Games NHL POGS-121
94Donruss-215
94Finest-62
Super Team Winners-62
Refractors-62
94Flair-73
94Fleer-88
94Leaf-268
Gold Rookies-9
Limited Inserts-10
94Leaf Limited-22
94OPC Premier-198
94OPC Premier-381
94OPC Premier-484
94O-Pee-Chee Finest Inserts-11
94OPC Premier Special Effects-198
94OPC Premier Special Effects-381
94OPC Premier Special Effects-484
94Parkhurst-274
Gold-274
Vintage-V40
94Parkhurst SE-SE73
Gold-SE73
94Pinnacle-11
94Pinnacle-466
Artist's Proofs-11
Artist's Proofs-466
Rink Collection-11
Rink Collection-466
94Score-252
Gold-252
Platinum-252
94Select-111
Gold-111
94SP-48
Die Cuts-48
94Stadium Club-111
94Stadium Club-235
Members Only Master Set-111
Members Only Master Set-235
First Day Issue-111
First Day Issue-235
Super Team Winner Cards-111
Super Team Winner Cards-235
94Topps/OPC Premier-198
94Topps/OPC Premier-381
94Topps/OPC Premier-484
Special Effects-198
Special Effects-381
Special Effects-484
94Ultra-91
All-Rookies-7
All-Rookies Parallel-7
94Upper Deck-52
Electric Ice-52
SP Inserts-SP33
SP Inserts Die Cuts-SP33
94Upper Deck NHLPA/Be A Player-35
94Classic All-Rookie Team-AR5
94Classic Pro Prospects-31
Autographs-AU6
Jumbos-PP5
94Classic C3 *-19
94Images *-8
94Images *-135
95Bashan Super Stickers-104
95Be A Player-18
Signatures-S18
Signatures Die Cuts-S18
95Bowman-62
All-Foil-62
95Canada Games NHL POGS-243
95Collector's Choice-232
Player's Club-232
Player's Club Platinum-232
95Donruss-63
95Donruss-319
Pro Pointers-17
95Emotion-151
95Hoyle Eastern Playing Cards-51
95Imperial Stickers-104
95Leaf-242
95Leaf Limited-107
95Metal-127
95Panini Stickers-198
95Parkhurst International-175
Emerald Ice-175
95Playoff One on One-309
95Pro Magnets-14
95Score-6
Black Ice Artist's Proofs-6
Black Ice-6
Check It-5
95SkyBox Impact-144
95SP-124
95Stadium Club-69
Members Only Master Set-69
95Summit-30
Artist's Proofs-30
Ice-30
95Topps-308
OPC Inserts-308
Home Grown Canada-HGC15
95Topps SuperSkills-54
Platinum-54
95Ultra-69
95Ultra-302
Gold Medallion-69
95Upper Deck-174
Electric Ice-174
Electric Ice Gold-174
Special Edition-SE160
Special Edition Gold-SE160
95Zenith-28
96Black Diamond-150
Gold-150
96Blues Dispatch 30th Anniversary-4
96Collector's Choice-226
96Donruss-63
Press Proofs-63
96Fleer-99
96Fleer Picks-114
96Leaf-5
Press Proofs-5
96Maggers-79
96Metal Universe-135
96NHL Pro Stamps-14
96Pinnacle-58
Artist's Proofs-58
Foil-58
Premium Stock-58
Rink Collection-58
96Score-166
Artist's Proofs-166
Dealer's Choice Artist's Proofs-166
Special Artist's Proofs-166
Golden Blades-166

96SkyBox Impact-115
96SP-135
Holoview Collection-HC10
96Upper Deck-144
Generation Next-X36
Power Performers-P24
Superstar Showdown-SS27B
96Upper Deck Ice-63
Parallel-63
97Black Diamond-83
Double Diamond-83
Triple Diamond-83
Quadruple Diamond-83
97Collector's Choice-233
World Domination-W14
97Donruss-100
Press Proofs Silver-100
Press Proofs Gold-100
97Donruss Canadian Ice-90
Dominion Series-90
Provincial Series-90
97Donruss Limited-85
Exposure-85
97Donruss Preferred-109
Cut to the Chase-109
97Donruss Priority-91
Stamp of Approval-91
97Esso Olympic Hockey Heroes-15
97Esso Olympic Hockey Heroes French-15
97Gatorade Stickers-4
97Kraft Team Canada-12
97Leaf-90
Fractal Matrix-90
Fractal Matrix Die Cuts-90
97Leaf International-90
Universal Ice-90
97McDonald's Team Canada Coins-4
97Pacific-124
Copper-124
Emerald Green-124
Ice Blue-124
Red-124
Silver-124
97Pacific Omega-196
Copper-196
Dark Gray-196
Emerald Green-196
Gold-196
Ice Blue-196
Team Leaders-17
97Panini Stickers-170
97Pinnacle Inside-175
97Score Blues-7
Platinum-7
Premier-7
97SP Authentic-139
97Upper Deck-142
97Upper Deck-398
98Aurora-163
98Be A Player-123
Press Release-123
98BAP Gold-123
98BAP Autographs-123
98BAP Autographs Gold-123
98BAP Tampa Bay All Star Game-123
98Black Diamond-78
Double Diamond-78
Triple Diamond-78
Quadruple Diamond-78
98Bowman's Best-18
Refractors-18
Atomic Refractors-18
Mirror Image Fusion-F18
Mirror Image Fusion Refractors-F18
Mirror Image Fusion Atomic Refractors-F18
98Crown Royale-116
Limited Series-116
98Finest-22
No Protectors-22
No Protectors Refractors-22
Refractors-22
98Katch-132
98OPC Chrome-181
Refractors-181
Board Members-B1
Board Members Refractors-B1
Season's Best-SB25
Season's Best Refractors-SB25
98Pacific-44
Ice Blue-44
Red-44
98Pacific Dynagon Ice-161
Blue-161
Red-161
98Pacific Omega-205
Red-205
Opening Day Issue-205
98Panini Photocards-65
98Panini Stickers-5
98Panini Stickers-153
98Paramount-206
Copper-206
Emerald Green-206
Holo-Electric-206
Ice Blue-206
Silver-206
98Post-18
98Revolution-124
Ice Shadow-124
Red-124
All-Star Die Cuts-23
98SP Authentic-71
Power Shift-71
98SPx Finite-75
Radiance-75
Spectrum-75
98SPx Top Prospects-52
Radiance-52
Spectrum-52
98Topps-181
O-Pee-Chee-181
Board Members-B1
Ice Age 2000-I7
Season's Best-SB25
98Topps Gold Label Class 1-49
Black-49
Black One of One-49
One of One-49
Red-49
Red One of One-49
98Topps Gold Label Class 2-49
98Topps Gold Label Class 2 Black-49
98Topps Gold Label Class 2 Black 1 of 1-49
98Topps Gold Label Class 2 One of One-49
98Topps Gold Label Class 2 Red-49
98Topps Gold Label Class 2 Red One of One-49
98Topps Gold Label Class 3-49
98Topps Gold Label Class 3 Black-49
98Topps Gold Label Class 3 Black 1 of 1-49
98Topps Gold Label Class 3 One of One-49
98Topps Gold Label Class 3 Red-49
98Topps Gold Label Class 3 Red One of One-49
98UD Choice-185
98UD Choice Preview-185
98UD Choice Prime Choice Reserve-185
98UD Choice Reserve-185
98Upper Deck-174
Exclusives-174
Exclusives 1 of 1-174
Lord Stanley's Heroes-LS20
Lord Stanley's Heroes Quantum 1-LS20
Lord Stanley's Heroes Quantum 2-LS20
Lord Stanley's Heroes Quantum 3-LS20
Gold Reserve-174
98Upper Deck MVP-180
Gold Script-180
Silver Script-180
Super Script-180
99SLU Hockey-15
99Aurora-127
Premiere Date-127
99BAP Memorabilia-89
Gold-89
Silver-89
99BAP Update Teammates Jersey Cards-TM34
99BAP Millennium-202
Emerald-202
Ruby-202
Sapphire-202
Signatures-202
Signatures Gold-202
99Black Diamond-73
Diamond Cut-73
Final Cut-73
99Blues Taco Bell-16
99Crown Royale-119
Limited Series-119
Premiere Date-119
99Hasbro Starting Lineup Cards-15
99Kraft Dinner-9
99McDonald's Upper Deck Game Jerseys-GJCP
99O-Pee-Chee-79
99O-Pee-Chee Chrome-79
99O-Pee-Chee Chrome Refractors-79
99Pacific-362
Copper-362
Emerald Green-362
Gold-362
Ice Blue-362
Premiere Date-362
Red-362
99Pacific Dynagon Ice-167
Blue-167
Copper-167
Gold-167
Premiere Date-167
Checkmates American-4
Checkmates American-19
Checkmates Canadian-4
99Pacific Omega-199
Copper-199
Gold-199
Ice Blue-199
Premiere Date-199
99Pacific Prism-120
Holographic Blue-120
Holographic Gold-120
Holographic Mirror-120
Holographic Purple-120
Premiere Date-120
99Panini Stickers-286
99Paramount-200
Copper-200
Emerald-200
Gold-200
Holographic Emerald-200
Holographic Gold-200
Holographic Silver-200
Ice Blue-200
Premiere Date-200
Red-200
Silver-200
99Revolution-124
Premiere Date-124
Red-124
Shadow Series-124
99SPx-135
Radiance-135
Spectrum-135
99Stadium Club-146
First Day Issue-146
One of a Kind-146
Printing Plates Black-146
Printing Plates Cyan-146
Printing Plates Magenta-146
Printing Plates Yellow-146
99Topps/OPC-79
99Topps/OPC Chrome-79
Refractors-79
99Topps Gold Label Class 1-34
Black-34
Black One of One-34
One of One-34
Red-34
Red One of One-34
99Topps Gold Label Class 2-34
99Topps Gold Label Class 2 Black-34
99Topps Gold Label Class 2 Black 1 of 1-34
99Topps Gold Label Class 2 One of One-34
99Topps Gold Label Class 2 Red-34
99Topps Gold Label Class 2 Red One of One-34
99Topps Gold Label Class 3-34
99Topps Gold Label Class 3 Black-34
99Topps Gold Label Class 3 Black 1 of 1-34
99Topps Gold Label Class 3 One of One-34
99Topps Gold Label Class 3 Red-34
99Topps Gold Label Class 3 Red One of One-34
99Topps Gold Label Quest for the Cup-QC6
99Topps Gold Label Quest for the Cup One of One - QC6
99Topps Gold Label Quest 4 the Cup Black-QC6
99Topps Gold Label Quest for the Cup Black One of One -QC6
99Topps Gold Label Quest for the Cup Red-QC6
99Topps Gold Label Quest for the Cup Red One of One -QC6
99Topps Premier Plus-41
Parallel-41
99Upper Deck-284
Exclusives-284
Exclusives 1 of 1-284
99Upper Deck Gold Reserve-284
99Upper Deck MVP-186
Gold Script-186
Silver Script-186
Super Script-186
99Upper Deck MVP SC Edition-163
Gold Script-163
Silver Script-163
Super Script-163
99Upper Deck Retro-68
Gold-68
Platinum-68
99Upper Deck Victory-263
99Upper Deck Victory-323
99Wayne Gretzky Hockey-147
00Aurora-123
Premiere Date-123
00BAP Memorabilia-220
Emerald-220
Ruby-220
Sapphire-220
Promos-220
Jersey Cards-J7
Jersey Emblems-E7
Jersey Numbers-N7
Jersey and Stick Cards-JS7
00BAP Mem Chicago Sportsfest Copper-220
00BAP Memorabilia Chicago Sportsfest Blue-220
00BAP Memorabilia Chicago Sportsfest Gold-220
00BAP Memorabilia Chicago Sportsfest Ruby-220
00BAP Memorabilia Chicago Sun-Times Ruby-220
00BAP Memorabilia Chicago Sun-Times Gold-220
00BAP Mem Chicago Sun-Times Sapphire-220
00BAP Mem Toronto Fall Expo Copper-220
00BAP Memorabilia Toronto Fall Expo Gold-220
00BAP Memorabilia Toronto Fall Expo Ruby-220
00BAP Parkhurst 2000-P3
00BAP Signature Series-108
Emerald-108
Ruby-108
Sapphire-108
Autographs-80
Autographs Gold-80
Department of Defense-DD19
Franchise Players-F25
He Shoots-He Scores Prizes-26
Jersey Cards-J13
Jersey and Stick Cards-GSJ13
Jersey Cards Autographs-J13
Jersey Emblems-E13
Jersey Numbers-IN13
00BAP Ultimate Memorabilia Autographs-42
Gold-42
00BAP Ultimate Mem Game-Used Jerseys-GJ38
00BAP Ultimate Mem Game-Used Emblems-E31
00BAP Ultimate Mem Game-Used Numbers-N31
00BAP Ultimate Mem Game-Used Sticks-GS38
00BAP Ultimate Memorabilia Hart Trophy-H1
00BAP Ultimate Memorabilia Norris Trophy-N1
00BAP Ultimate Memorabilia Retro-Active-RA1
00Black Diamond-51
Gold-51
00Crown Royale-89
Ice Blue-89
Limited Series-89
Premiere Date-89
Red-89
00Kraft-20
00McDonald's Pacific-28
Blue-28
00O-Pee-Chee-9
00O-Pee-Chee Parallel-9
00Pacific-349
Copper-349
Gold-349
Ice Blue-349
Premiere Date-349
Gold Crown Die Cuts-29
00Panini Stickers-193
00Paramount-208
Copper-208
Gold-208
Holo-Gold-208
Holo-Silver-208
Ice Blue-208
Premiere Date-208
Freeze Frame-30
00Private Stock-84
Gold-84
Premiere Date-84
Retail-84
Silver-84
PS-2001 Action-52
00Revolution-124
Blue-124
Premiere Date-124
Red-124
HD NHL-29
00SP Authentic-77
00SPx-59
00SPx-80
Spectrum-59
Spectrum-80
Highlight Heroes-HH13
00Stadium Club-3
Beam Team-BT30
Capture the Action-CA10
Capture the Action Game View-10
Special Forces-SF2
00Titanium-81
Blue-81
Gold-81
Premiere Date-81
Red-81
Retail-81
00Topps/OPC-9
Parallel-9
Autographs-ACP
Combos-TC6
Combos Jumbos-TC6
00Topps Chrome-9
OPC Refractors-9
Refractors-9
Combos-TC6
Combos Refractors-TC6
00Topps Gold Label Class 1-85
Gold-85
00Topps Gold Label Class 2-85
00Topps Gold Label Class 2 Gold-85
00Topps Gold Label Class 3-85
00Topps Gold Label Class 3 Gold-85
00Topps Gold Label Bullion-B5
00Topps Gold Label Bullion One to One-B5
00Topps Heritage-31
00Topps Heritage-222
00Topps Heritage-228
00Topps Heritage-246
Chrome Parallel-31
00Topps Premier Plus-65
Blue Ice-65
Private Signings-PSCP
Team-PT9
Team Blue Ice-PR9
Trophy Tribute-TT4
World Premier-WP3
00Topps Stars-15
00Topps Stars-135
Blue-15
Blue-135
Autographs-ACP
Game Gear-GGCP
Game Gear-GGCP
Progression-P9
00UD Heroes-102
00UD Pros and Prospects-74
Game Jerseys-CP
Game Jersey Exclusives-CP
00UD Reserve-74
00Upper Deck-151
Exclusives Tier 1-151
Exclusives Tier 2-151
Game Jerseys-CP
Game Jersey Autographs Exclusives-ECP
Number Crunchers-NC9
Triple Threat-TT8
00Upper Deck Ice-34
Immortals-34
Legends-34
Stars-34
00Upper Deck Legends-115
Legendary Collection Bronze-115
Legendary Collection Gold-115
Legendary Collection Silver-115
00Upper Deck MVP-154
First Stars-154
Second Stars-154
Third Stars-154
00Upper Deck Victory-199
00Upper Deck Victory-204
00Upper Deck Victory-257
00Upper Deck Victory-323
00Upper Deck Vintage-309
00Upper Deck Vintage-320
00Upper Deck Vintage-321
All UD Team-UD3
00Vanguard-83
Holographic Gold-83
Holographic Purple-83
Pacific Proofs-83
00Czech Stadion-151
01McFarlane Hockey-100
01McFarlane Hockey-101
01Atomic-82
Blue-82
Gold-82
Premiere Date-82
Red-82
Core Players-16
Power Play-28
01BAP Memorabilia-64
Emerald-64
Ruby-64
Sapphire-64
All-Star Jerseys-ASJ43
All-Star Emblems-ASE43
All-Star Numbers-ASN43
All-Star Jersey Doubles-DASJ25
All-Star Teammates-AST16
All-Star Teammates-AST30
Country of Origin-CO60
He Shoots-He Scores Points-9
He Shoots-He Scores Prizes-13
Patented Power-PP4
Stanley Cup Playoffs-SC19
01BAP Signature Series Certified 100-C10
01BAP Signature Series Certified 50-C10
01BAP Signature Series Certified 1 of 1's-C10
01BAP Signature Series Autographs-LCP
01BAP Signature Series Autographs Gold-LCP
01BAP Sig Series Department of Defense-DD-5
01BAP Signature Series Jerseys-GJ-57
01BAP Signature Series Jersey Autographs-GUCP
01BAP Sig Series Jersey and Stick Cards-GSJ-57
01BAP Signature Series Emblems-GUE-23
01BAP Signature Series Numbers-ITN-23
01BAP Ultimate Memorabilia Captain's C-12
01BAP Ultimate Memorabilia Emblems-26
01BAP Ultimate Memorabilia Jerseys-26
01BAP Ultimate Mem Jerseys and Sticks-26
01BAP Ultimate Memorabilia Numbers-26
01BAP Ultimate Memorabilia Name Plates-34
01BAP Ultimate Mem Prototypical Players-4
01Bowman YoungStars-10
Gold-10
Ice Cubed-10
01Crown Royale-120
Blue-120
Premiere Date-120
Red-120
Retail-120
01EA Sports-6
01McDonald's Pacific-33
01Nortel All-Star Game Sheets-12
01O-Pee-Chee-16
01O-Pee-Chee Heritage Parallel-16
01O-Pee-Chee Heritage Parallel Limited-16
01O-Pee-Chee Premier Parallel-16
01Pacific-329
Extreme LTD-329
Hobby LTD-329
Premiere Date-329
Retail LTD-329
Impact Zone-16
01Pacific Adrenaline-161
Blue-161
Premiere Date-161
Red-161
Retail-161
01Pacific Arena Exclusives-329
01Pacific Heads-Up-80
Blue-80
Premiere Date-80
Red-80
Silver-80
All-Star Net-6
01Parkhurst-86
Gold-86
Silver-86
He Shoots-He Scores Points-8
Heroes-H16
Jerseys-PJ40
Jersey and Stick-PSJ6
Sticks-PS46
Waving the Flag-8
01Private Stock-81
Gold-81
Premiere Date-81
Retail-81
Silver-81
01Private Stock Pacific Nights-81
01Private Stock PS-2002-61
01SP Authentic-78
Limited-78
Limited Gold-78
01SP Game Used-49
01SPx-58
01SPx-90
01Sports Illustrated for Kids III-9
01Stadium Club-3
Award Winners-3
Master Photos-3
Gallery-G36
Gallery Gold-G36
Heart and Soul-HS5
01Titanium-118
Hobby Parallel-118
Premiere Date-118
Retail-118
Retail Parallel-118
All-Stars-15
01Topps-16
Heritage Parallel-16
Heritage Parallel Limited-16
OPC Parallel-16
Captain's Cloth-CC2
01Topps Chrome-16
Refractors-16
Black Border Refractors-16
01Topps Heritage-34
Refractors-34
01Topps Reserve-4
01UD Challenge for the Cup-77
Cornerstones-CR8
01UD Honor Roll-10
01UD Honor Roll-40
Tough Customers-TC6
01UD Mask Collection-84
Gold-84
01UD Playmakers-84
01UD Premier Collection-45
Dual Jerseys-DBP
Dual Jerseys Black-DBP
01UD Top Shelf-38
Sticks-SCP
Sticks-BPR
Sticks Gold-SCP
Sticks Gold-BPR
01Upper Deck-380
Exclusives-380
Gate Attractions-GA15
Leaders of the Pack-LP14
Skilled Stars-SS3
EA Sports Gold-6
01Upper Deck Ice-118
01Upper Deck MVP-162
Talent-MT13
Watch-MW7
01Upper Deck Victory-305
01Upper Deck Victory-393
Gold-305
Gold-393
01Upper Deck Vintage-218
01Upper Deck Vintage-226
01Vanguard-82
Blue-82
Red-82
East Meets West-10
One of Ones-82
Premiere Date-82
Proofs-82
02McFarlane Hockey NHL HITZ 2003-10
02McFarlane Hockey Team Canada-20
02Atomic-83
Blue-83
Gold-83
Red-83
Hobby Parallel-83
National Pride-C10
Super Colliders-12
02BAP All-Star Edition-72
He Shoots-He Score Prizes-22
Jerseys-72
Jerseys Gold-72
Jerseys Silver-72
02BAP First Edition-103
02BAP First Edition-365
02BAP First Edition-385
02BAP First Edition-390
02BAP First Edition-408H
Jerseys-103
02BAP Memorabilia-72
02BAP Memorabilia-225
02BAP Memorabilia-235
Emerald-72
Emerald-225
Emerald-235
Ruby-72
Ruby-225
Ruby-235
Sapphire-72
Sapphire-225
Sapphire-235
All-Star Jerseys-ASJ-45
All-Star Starting Lineup-AS-2
All-Star Teammates-AST-19
Franchise Players-FP-25
He Shoots-He Scores Points-4
He Shoots-He Scores Prizes-17
NHL All-Star Game-72
NHL All-Star Game-225
NHL All-Star Game-235
NHL All-Star Game Blue-72
NHL All-Star Game Blue-225
NHL All-Star Game Blue-235
NHL All-Star Game Green-72
NHL All-Star Game Green-225
NHL All-Star Game Green-235
NHL All-Star Game Red-72
NHL All-Star Game Red-225
NHL All-Star Game Red-235
Teammates-TM-16
02BAP Memorabilia Toronto Fall Expo-72
02BAP Memorabilia Toronto Fall Expo-225
02BAP Memorabilia Toronto Fall Expo-235
02BAP Signature Series-167
Autographs-167
Autograph Buybacks 1998-123
Autograph Buybacks 1999-202
Autograph Buybacks 2000-80
Autograph Buybacks 2001-LCP
Autographs Gold-167
Defensive Wall-DW7
Franchise Players-FJ26
Jerseys-SGJ42
Jersey Autographs-SGJ42
Team Quads-TQ15
02Blues Team Issue-19
02Crown Royale Jerseys-18
02Crown Royale Jerseys Gold-18
02eTopps-27
02ITG Used-67
02ITG Used-167
Franchise Players-F25
Franchise Players Autographs-F25
Franchise Players Gold-F25
Jerseys-GUJ42
Jersey Autographs-GUJ42
Jerseys Gold-GUJ42
Jersey and Stick-SJ42
Jersey and Stick Gold-SJ42
Teammates-T8
Teammates Gold-T8
02McDonald's Pacific-33
Jersey Patches Silver-15
Jersey Patches Gold-15
Salt Lake Gold-3
02Nextel NHL All-Star Game-1
02O-Pee-Chee-6
02O-Pee-Chee Jumbos-21
02O-Pee-Chee Premier Blue Parallel-6
02O-Pee-Chee Premier Red Parallel-6
02O-Pee-Chee Factory Set-6
02Pacific-327
Blue-327
Red-327
02Pacific Chicago National *-8
02Pacific Complete-499
Red-499
02Pacific Exclusive-145
02Pacific Heads-Up-104
Blue-104
Purple-104
Red-104
Quad Jerseys-23
Quad Jerseys-28
Quad Jerseys Gold-23
Quad Jerseys Gold-28
02Parkhurst-72
Bronze-72
Gold-72
Silver-72
Franchise Players-FP25
Heroes-NH9
Jerseys-GJ23
Stick and Jerseys-SJ23
Teammates-TT16
02Parkhurst Retro-113
Minis-113
Franchise Players-RF26
Jerseys-RJ34
Jersey and Sticks-RSJ23
02Private Stock Reserve-139
Red-139
Retail-139
Patches-139
02SP Game Used-43
First Rounder Patches-CP
02SPx-65
Spectrum Gold-65
Spectrum Silver-65
02Stadium Club-69
Silver Decoy Cards-69
Proofs-69
Beam Team-BT7
Lone Star Signatures Blue-LSCP
Lone Star Signatures Red-LSCP
02Titanium Jerseys-58
02Titanium Jerseys Retail-58
02Titanium Patches-58
02Topps-6
OPC Blue Parallel-6
OPC Red Parallel-6
Captain's Cloth-CC4
Captain's Cloth-CC17
Topps/OPC Hometown Heroes-HHU15
Factory Set-6
Factory Set Hometown Heroes-HHU15
02Topps Chrome-6
Black Border Refractors-6
Refractors-6
02Topps Heritage-58
Chrome Parallel-58
02Topps Total-49
02UD Artistic Impressions-76
Gold-76
02UD Artistic Impressions Beckett Promos-76
02UD Artistic Impressions Retrospectives-R76
02UD Artistic Impressions Retrospect Gold-R76
02UD Artistic Impress Retrospect Silver-R76
02Upper Deck Collectors Club-NHL14
02UD Honor Roll-96
02UD Piece of History-78
Awards Collection-AC25
02UD Top Shelf-78
Dual Player Jerseys-RBP
Hardware Heroes-HPMBL
Triple Jerseys-TSDPJ
02Upper Deck-243
02Upper Deck-399
Exclusives-243
Exclusives-399
02Upper Deck Beckett UD Promos-399
02Upper Deck Letters of Note-LNCP
02Upper Deck Letters of Note Gold-LNCP
02Upper Deck Classic Portraits-85
02Upper Deck MVP-162
Gold-162
Classics-162
Golden Classics-162
02Upper Deck Victory-185
Bronze-185
Gold-185
Silver-185
National Pride-NP12
02Upper Deck Vintage-223
02Upper Deck Vintage-286
Green Backs-223
Tall Boys-T57
Tall Boys Gold-T57
03BAP Memorabilia All-Star Emblems-ASE-12
03BAP Memorabilia All-Star Jerseys-ASJ-18
03BAP Memorabilia All-Star Numbers-ASN-12
03BAP Mem He Shoots-He Scores Points-3
03BAP Mem He Shoots-He Scores Prizes-13
03BAP Memorabilia Practice Jerseys-PMP7
03BAP Ultimate Memorabilia Autographs-20
Gold-20
03BAP Ultimate Mem Auto Jerseys-20
03BAP Ultimate Mem Auto Emblems-20
03BAP Ultimate Mem Always An All-Star-18
03BAP Ultimate Mem Always An AS Gold-18
03BAP Ultimate Mem Franch Present Future-25
03BAP Ultimate Memorabilia Jerseys-10
03BAP Ultimate Memorabilia Jerseys Gold-10
03BAP Ultimate Mem Jersey and Emblems-7
03BAP Ultimate Mem Jersey and Emblem Gold-7
03BAP Ultimate Mem Jersey and Numbers-7
03BAP Ultimate Mem Jersey and Number Gold-7
03BAP Ultimate Mem Jersey and Stick-20
03BAP Ultimate Mem Jersey and Stick Gold-20
03BAP Ultimate Memorabilia Nameplates-19
03BAP Ultimate Mem Nameplates Gold-19
03BAP Ultimate Mem Retro-Active Trophies-12
03BAP Ultimate Memorabilia Triple Threads-10
03BAP Ultimate Mem Ultimate Captains-3
03Beehive-166
Gold-166
Silver-166
03Black Diamond-134
Black-134
Green-134
Red-134
Threads-DT-CP
Threads Green-DT-CP
Threads Red-DT-CP
Threads Black-DT-CP
03Blues Team Set-22
03Bowman-36
Gold-36
03Bowman Chrome-36
Refractors-36
Gold Refractors-36
Xfractors-36
03Crown Royale-82
Blue-82
Retail-82
03ITG Action-518
Jerseys-M143
Jerseys-M265
03ITG Used Signature Series-21
Gold-21
Autographs-CP
Autographs Gold-CP
Franchise-26
Franchise Autographs-26
Franchise Gold-26
International Experience-13
International Experience Autographs-13
International Experience Emblems Gold-13
International Experience Emblems-13
International Experience Gold-13
Jerseys-6
Jerseys Gold-6
Jersey Autos-6
Jersey and Stick-6
Jersey and Stick Gold-6
Norris Trophy-2
Norris Trophy Gold-2
03NHL Sticker Collection-278
03O-Pee-Chee-244
03OPC Blue-244
03OPC Gold-244
03OPC Red-244
03Pacific-287
Blue-287
Red-287
03Pacific Complete-384
Red-384
03Pacific Exhibit-123
Blue Backs-123
Yellow Backs-123
03Pacific Heads-Up-82
Hobby LTD-82
Retail LTD-82
03Pacific Luxury Suite-45A
03Pacific Luxury Suite-45B
03Pacific Supreme-82
Blue-82
Red-82
Retail-82
03Parkhurst Rookie-48
Jersey and Sticks-SJ-15
Jersey and Sticks Gold-SJ-15
03Private Stock Reserve-86
Blue-86
Red-86
Retail-86
03SP Authentic Breakout Seasons-B9
03SP Authentic Breakout Seasons Limited-B9
03SP Game Used-42
Gold-42
03SPx-86
Radiance-86
Spectrum-86
03Titanium-84
Hobby Jersey Number Parallels-84
Retail-84
Retail Jersey Number Parallels-84
03Topps-244
Blue-244
Gold-244
Red-244
03Topps C55-81
Minis-81
Minis American Back-81
Minis American Back Red-81
Minis Bazooka Back-81
Minis Brooklyn Back-81
Minis Hat Trick Back-81
Minis O Canada Back-81
Minis O Canada Back Red-81
Minis Stanley Cup Back-81
03Topps Pristine-95
Gold Refractor Die Cuts-95
Refractors-95
Press Plates Black-95
Press Plates Cyan-95
Press Plates Magenta-95
Press Plates Yellow-95
03UD Honor Roll-73
03Upper Deck-169
All-Star Class-AS-25
Canadian Exclusives-169
HG-169
03Upper Deck Classic Portraits-85
03Upper Deck Classic Portraits-160
Classic Stitches-CS-CP
Hockey Royalty-PLB
03Upper Deck MVP-372
Gold Script-372
Silver Script-372
Canadian Exclusives-372
03Upper Deck Trilogy-85
Limited-85
03Upper Deck Victory-167
Bronze-167
Gold-167
Silver-167
Freshman Flashback-FF40
Game Breakers-GB16
03Toronto Star-79
04Pacific-222
Blue-222
Red-222
04SP Authentic-76
04SP Authentic-142
Limited-76
Limited-142
Sign of the Times-ST-CP
Sign of the Times-DS-PW
Sign of the Times-TS-LPJ
Sign of the Times-QS-BPBP
Sign of the Times-SS-DEE
04Ultimate Collection Dual Logos-UL2-MP
04Upper Deck-154
Canadian Exclusives-154
HG Glossy Gold-154
HG Glossy Silver-154
05Be A Player-76
First Period-76
Second Period-76
Third Period-76
Overtime-76
Dual Signatures-KC
Dual Signatures-LP
Outtakes-OT43
Quad Signatures-BLUE
Quad Signatures-GDEF
Signatures-CP
Signatures Gold-CP
Triple Signatures-LBP
Triple Signatures-STL
05Beehive-36
05Beehive-189
Beige -36
Blue -36
Gold-36
Red -36
Matte-36
PhotoGraphs-PGCP
05Black Diamond-114
Emerald-114
Gold-114
Onyx-114
Ruby-114
05Hot Prospects-38
En Fuego-38
Red Hot-38
White Hot-38
05McDonalds Upper Deck-7
05Panini Stickers-272
05Parkhurst-190
05Parkhurst-566
05Parkhurst-682
Facsimile Auto Parallel-190
Facsimile Auto Parallel-566
Facsimile Auto Parallel-682
True Colors-TCEDM
True Colors-TCEDM
True Colors-TCEDCA
True Colors-TCEDCA
05SP Authentic-39
Limited-39
Chirography-SPCP
Marks of Distinction-MDCP
Prestigious Pairings-PPBP
Sign of the Times-CP
Sign of the Times Duals-DPS
Sign of the Times Quads-QPSCW
05SP Game Used-40
Autographs-40
Gold-40
Authentic Fabrics-AF-CP
Authentic Fabrics Autographs-AAF-CP
Authentic Fabrics Dual-PC
Authentic Fabrics Dual Autographs-PC
Authentic Fabrics Gold-AF-CP
Authentic Fabrics Quad-SCPTB
Authentic Patches Quad -SCPTB
Authentic Fabrics Triple-BBP
Authentic Fabrics Triple-CNP
Authentic Fabrics Triple-GNP
Authentic Fabrics Triple-PCS
Authentic Patches-AP-CP
Authentic Patches Autographs-AAP-CP
Authentic Patches Dual-PC
Authentic Patches Dual Autographs-PC
Authentic Patches Triple-BBP
Authentic Patches Triple-CNP
Authentic Patches Triple-GNP
Authentic Patches Triple-PCS
Awesome Authentics-AA-CP
Game Gear-GG-CP
Game Gear Autographs-AG-CP
SIGnificance-CP
SIGnificance Gold-S-CP
Significant Numbers-SN-CP
05SPx-33
Spectrum-33
Winning Combos-WC-BP
Winning Combos-WC-CP
Winning Combos Autographs-AWC-BP
Winning Combos Autographs-AWC-CP
Winning Combos Gold-WC-BP
Winning Combos Gold-WC-CP
Winning Combos Spectrum-WC-BP
Winning Combos Spectrum-WC-CP
Winning Materials-WM-CP
Winning Materials Autographs-AWM-CP
Winning Materials Gold-WM-CP
Winning Materials Spectrum-WM-CP
Xcitement Superstars-XS-CP
Xcitement Superstars Gold-XS-CP
Xcitement Superstars Spectrum-XS-CP
05The Cup-44
Gold-44
Black Rainbow-44
Dual NHL Shields-DSPC
Dual NHL Shields Autographs-ADSPB
Dual NHL Shields Autographs-ADSPC
Emblems of Endorsement-EECP
Hardware Heroes-HHCP
Honorable Numbers-HNCP
Limited Logos-LLCP
Masterpiece Pressplates-44
Masterpiece Pressplates Rookie Upd Auto-274
Noble Numbers-NNPB
Patch Variation-P44
Patch Variation Autographs-AP44
Property of-POCP
Scripted Numbers-SNPB
Scripted Numbers Dual-DSNPB
Scripted Swatches-SSCP
Signature Patches-SPCP
05UD Artifacts Auto Facts-AF-CP
05UD Artifacts Auto Facts Blue-AF-CP
05UD Artifacts Auto Facts Copper-AF-CP
05UD Artifacts Auto Facts Pewter-AF-CP
05UD Artifacts Auto Facts Silver-AF-CP
05UD Artifacts Remarkable Artifacts-RA-CP
05UD Artifacts Remarkable Artifacts Dual-RA-CP
05UD Artifacts Treasured Patches-TP-CP
05UD Artifacts Treasured Patch Autos-TP-CP

05UD Artifacts Treasured Patches Dual-TPD-CP
05UD Artifacts Treasured Patch Dual Autos-TPD-CP
05UD Artifacts Treasured Patches Pewter-TP-CP
05UD Artifacts Treasured Patches Silver-TP-CP
05UD Artifacts Treasured Swatches-TS-CP
05UD Artifacts Treasured Swatch Autos-TS-CP
05UD Artifacts Treasured Swatches Blue-TS-CP
05UD Artifacts Treasured Swatches Copper-TS-CP
05UD Artifacts Treasured Swatches Dual-TSD-CP
05UD Artifacts Treasured Swatch Dual Autos-TSD-CP
05UD Artifacts Treasured Swatch Dual Blue-TSD-CP
05UD Artifact Treasure Swatch Dual Copper-TSD-CP
05UD Artifact Treasure Swatch Dual Maroon-TSD-CP
05UD Artifact Treasure Swatch Dual Pewter-TSD-CP
05UD Artifact TreasuredSwatch Dual Silver-TSD-CP
05UD Artifacts Treasured Swatches Maroon-TS-CP
05UD Artifacts Treasured Swatches Pewter-TS-CP
05UD Artifacts Treasured Swatches Silver-TS-CP
05UD PowerPlay-76
05UD PowerPlay-101
Rainbow-76
05Ultimate Collection-39
Gold-39
Jerseys-JCP
Marquee Attractions-MA22
Marquee Attractions Signatures-SMA22
National Heroes Jerseys-NHJCP
National Heroes Patches-NHPCP
Premium Patches-PPCP
Premium Swatches-PSCP
Ultimate Patches-PCP
Ultimate Signatures Pairings-UPPS
05Ultra-84
Gold-84
Ice-84
05Upper Deck-320
05Upper Deck All-Time Greatest-50
05Upper Deck Big Playmakers-B-CP
05Upper Deck Jerseys-J-CP
05Upper Deck Jerseys Series II-J2CP
05Upper Deck Majestic Materials-MMCP
05Upper Deck Notable Numbers-N-CP
05Upper Deck Patches-P-CP
05Upper Deck School of Hard Knocks-HK2
05Upper Deck Hockey Showcase-HS2
05Upper Deck Showcase Promos-HS2
05Upper Deck Ice-36
Rainbow-36
Frozen Fabrics-FFCP
Frozen Fabrics Autographs-AFFCP
Frozen Fabrics Glass-FFCP
Frozen Fabrics Patches-FFPCP
Frozen Fabrics Patch Autographs-FAPCP
Signature Swatches-SSCP
05Upper Deck MVP-157
Gold-157
Platinum-157
05Upper Deck Rookie Update-39
05Upper Deck Rookie Update-274
05Upper Deck Trilogy-39
05Upper Deck Trilogy-124
Crystal-124
Honorary Patches-HP-CP
Honorary Swatches-HS-CP
05Upper Deck Victory-168
05Upper Deck Victory-218
Black-168
Black-218
Gold-168
Gold-218
Silver-168
Silver-218
Blow-Ups-BU34
06Sports Illustrated for Kids *-90
06Be A Player Portraits-2
06Beehive-99
06Beehive-235
Blue-99
Gold-99
Matte-99
Red Facsimile Signatures-99
Wood-99
06Black Diamond-87
Black-87
Gold-87
Ruby-87
06Flair Showcase-184
06Flair Showcase-233
Parallel-184
Parallel-233
Stitches-SSCP
06Fleer-5
Tiffany-5
Fabricology-FCP
06Hot Prospects-1
Red Hot-1
White Hot-1
06McDonald's Upper Deck Jerseys-JCP
06McDonald's Upper Deck Patches-PCP
06NHL POG-8
06O-Pee-Chee-1
Rainbow-1
Swatches-S-CP
06Panini Stickers-184
06SP Authentic-99
Limited-99
06SP Game Used-1
Gold-1
Rainbow-1
Authentic Fabrics Triple-AF3ANA
Authentic Fabrics Triple Patches-AF3ANA
Authentic Fabrics Quads-AF4BPJM
Authentic Fabrics Quads Patches-AF4BPJM
Authentic Fabrics Fives-AF5DPT
Authentic Fabrics Fives-AP5SCP
Authentic Fabrics Fives Patches-AF5DPT
Authentic Fabrics Fives Patches-AP5SCP
Authentic Fabrics Sixes-AF6NOR
Authentic Fabrics Sixes Patches-AF6NOR
Authentic Fabrics Sevens-AF7MVP
Authentic Fabrics Sevens Patches-AF7MVP
Inked Sweaters-ISCP
Inked Sweaters Patches-ISCP
06SPx-1
Spectrum-1
SPxcitement-X1
SPxcitement Spectrum-X1
SPxcitement Autographs-X1
Winning Materials-WMCP
Winning Materials Spectrum-WMCP
Winning Materials Autographs-WMCP
06The Cup Autographed Foundations-CQCP
06The Cup Autographed Foundations Patches-CQCP
06The Cup Foundations-CQCP
06The Cup Foundations Patches-CQCP
06The Cup NHL Shields Duals-DSHPN
06The Cup NHL Shields Duals-DSHSP
06UD Artifacts-100
06UD Artifacts-170
Blue-100
Blue-170
Gold-100
Gold-170
Platinum-100
Platinum-170
Radiance-100
Radiance-170
Autographed Radiance Parallel-100
Autographed Radiance Parallel-170
Red-100
Red-170
Frozen Artifacts-FACP
Frozen Artifacts Black-FACP
Frozen Artifacts Blue-FACP
Frozen Artifacts Gold-FACP
Frozen Artifacts Platinum-FACP
Frozen Artifacts Red-FACP
Frozen Artifacts Autographed Black-FACP
Frozen Artifacts Patches Black-FACP
Frozen Artifacts Patches Blue-FACP
Frozen Artifacts Patches Gold-FACP
Frozen Artifacts Patches Platinum-FACP
Frozen Artifacts Patches Red-FACP
Frozen Artifacts Patches Autographed Black Tag Parallel-FACP
Tundra Tandems-TTNP
Tundra Tandems Black-TTNP
Tundra Tandems Blue-TTNP
Tundra Tandems Gold-TTNP
Tundra Tandems Platinum-TTNP
Tundra Tandems Red-TTNP
Tundra Tandems Dual Patches Red-TTNP
06UD Biography of a Season-BOS8
06UD Mini Jersey Collection-3
06UD Powerplay-3
Impact Rainbow-3
Specialists-SCP
Specialists Patches-PCP
06Ultra-2
Gold Medallion-2
Ice Medallion-2
Action-UA11
Difference Makers-DM15
Uniformity-UCP
Uniformity Patches-UPCP
Uniformity Autographed Jerseys-UACP
06Upper Deck Arena Giveaways-ANA6
06Upper Deck-251
Exclusives Parallel-251
High Gloss Parallel-251
Game Jerseys-J2CP
Game Patches-P2CP
Masterpieces-251
Oversized Wal-Mart Exclusives-251
Signature Sensations-SSPR
06Upper Deck MVP-1
Gold Script-1
Super Script-1
Clutch Performers-CP15
Gotta Have Hart-HH6
Jerseys-OJPB
06Upper Deck Ovation-19
06Upper Deck Sweet Shot-2
Sweet Stitches-SSCP
Sweet Stitches Duals-SSCP
Sweet Stitches Triples-SSCP
06Upper Deck Trilogy-1
Ice Scripts-ISCP
06Upper Deck Victory-79
06Upper Deck Victory-231
06Upper Deck Victory Black-79
06Upper Deck Victory Gold-79
06Upper Deck Victory Oversize Cards-CP
07Upper Deck Victory-172
Black-172
Gold-172
EA Sports Face-Off-FO5

Pronger, Sean

94Knoxville Cherokees-11
94Classic-93
Gold-93
95Bowman-153
All-Foil-153
96Ducks Team Issue-20
96Pinnacle-223
Artist's Proofs-223
Foil-223
Premium Stock-223
Rink Collection-223
97Be A Player-132
Autographs-132
Autographs Die-Cuts-132
Autographs Prismatic Die-Cuts-132
97Collector's Choice-2
97Donruss-98
Press Proofs Silver-98
Press Proofs Gold-98
97Donruss Limited-101
Exposure-101
97Donruss Preferred-123
Cut to the Chase-123
97Donruss Priority-109
Stamp of Approval-109
97Pacific-156
Copper-156
Emerald Green-156
Ice Blue-156
Red-156
Silver-156
97Score Mighty Ducks-18
Platinum-18
Premier-18
97SP Authentic-2
97Upper Deck-7
00Manitoba Moose-17
01Syracuse Crunch-13
02Pacific Complete-478
Red-478
03ITG Action-137
03Manitoba Moose-13
04German DEL-113

Pronin, Nikolai

98Charlotte Checkers-13
98Thunder Bay Thunder Cats-12
99Russian Hockey League-81
00Russian Hockey League-9
01Russian Hockey League-6
02Russian Hockey League-96
04Russian World Championship Team-3

Pronk, Blake

04Kingston Frontenacs-16
05Kingston Frontenacs-7

Pronovost, Andre

44Beehive Group II Photos-59
44Beehive Group II Photos-203
44Beehive Group II Photos-279
57Parkhurst-M7
58Parkhurst-3
59Parkhurst-35
60Parkhurst-55
60Shirriff Coins-32
60Topps Stamps-45
61Parkhurst-51
61Shirriff/Salada Coins-3
61Topps-5
62Topps-19
62York Iron-On Transfers-30A
63Parkhurst-45
63York White Backs-43
64Beehive Group III Photos-92
94Parkhurst Missing Link-75
94Parkhurst Tall Boys-62

Pronovost, Claude

94Parkhurst Missing Link-15

Pronovost, Jean

60Parkhurst-58
69O-Pee-Chee-155
70Colgate Stamps-50
70Dad's Cookies-105
70Esso Power Players-231
70O-Pee-Chee-202
70Sargent Promotions Stamps-162
71Letraset Action Replays-23
71O-Pee-Chee-118
71Penguins Postcards-15
71Sargent Promotions Stamps-168
71Topps-118
71Toronto Sun-224
72O-Pee-Chee-64
72Sargent Promotions Stamps-176
72Topps-143
72Finnish Semic World Championship-216
72Swedish Semic World Championship-216
73O-Pee-Chee-11
73Topps-11
74NHL Action Stamps-217
74O-Pee-Chee NHL-110
74Penguins Postcards-19
74Topps-110
75O-Pee-Chee NHL-280
75O-Pee-Chee NHL-326
75Topps-280
75Topps-326
76O-Pee-Chee NHL-14
76O-Pee-Chee NHL-218
76Topps-14
76Topps-218
77O-Pee-Chee NHL-261
77Penguins Puck Bucks-19
77Topps-261
78Flames Majik Market-9
78O-Pee-Chee-184
78Topps-184
79Panini Stickers-64
79Flames Postcards-13
79Flames Team Issue-14
79O-Pee-Chee-77
79Topps-77
81O-Pee-Chee-355
81O-Pee-Chee Stickers-196
99Rouyn-Noranda Huskies-25
00Rouyn-Noranda Huskies-26
Signed-26

Pronovost, Marcel

44Beehive Group II Photos-204
51Parkhurst-68
52Parkhurst-61
53Parkhurst-41
54Parkhurst-34
54Topps-27
57Topps-43
58Topps-24
59Topps-44
60NHL Ceramic Tiles-13
60Parkhurst-29
60Shirriff Coins-56
61Parkhurst-29
61Shirriff/Salada Coins-68
62Parkhurst-33
62York Iron-On Transfers-23
63Chex Photos-42
63Parkhurst-46
63Toronto Star-29
63York White Backs-38
64Beehive Group III Photos-93
64Beehive Group III Photos-178A
64Beehive Group III Photos-178B
64Coca-Cola Caps-39
64Topps-39
64Toronto Star-38
65Coca-Cola-92
65Maple Leafs White Border-15
65Topps-80
66Topps-20
66Topps USA Test-20
67Post Flip Books-4
67Topps-81
67York Action Octagons-33
67York Action Octagons-34
68O-Pee-Chee-125
68Post Marbles-19
68Shirriff Coins-171
68Topps-125
69Maple Leafs White Border Glossy-27
76Old Timers-14
81Red Wings Oldtimers-8
83Hall of Fame-148
83Hall of Fame Postcards-K14
85Hall of Fame-148
91Ultimate Original Six-71
French-71
Box Bottoms-3
93Parkhurst Parkie Reprints-PR65
94Parkhurst Missing Link-58
94Parkhurst Tall Boys-55
95Parkhurst '66-67-108
Coins-108
01Greats of the Game-84
Autographs-84
02Maple Leafs Platinum Collection-62
02Parkhurst Reprints-174
02Parkhurst Reprints-179
02Parkhurst Reprints-268
02Parkhurst Reprints-279
02Parkhurst Reprints-291
03Parkhurst Original Six Detroit-51
03Parkhurst Original Six Detroit-65
03Parkhurst Original Six Detroit-86
Autographs-OS-MP
03Parkhurst Original Six Toronto-88
04ITG Franchises Update-495
04ITG Franchises US West-224
Autographs-A-MPR
04ITG Ultimate Memorabilia-55
Gold-55
Autographs-13
Autographs Gold-13
04UD Legends Classics Jersey Redemptions-JY15
06Parkhurst-102
Autographs-102
07Maple Leafs 1967 Commemorative-20

Pronovost, Rene

51Laval Dairy Lac St. Jean-35
52Bas Du Fleuve-47

Propp, Brian

80O-Pee-Chee-39
80Topps-39
81O-Pee-Chee-246
81O-Pee-Chee Stickers-180
81Topps-E110
82O-Pee-Chee-256
82O-Pee-Chee Stickers-111
82Post Cereal-14
82Topps Stickers-111
83Flyers J.C. Penney-18
83NHL Key Tags-94
83O-Pee-Chee-218
83O-Pee-Chee-271
83O-Pee-Chee Stickers-199
83Puffy Stickers-11
83Topps Stickers-199
84O-Pee-Chee-166
84O-Pee-Chee Stickers-112
84Kelowna Wings-34
85Flyers Postcards-24
85O-Pee-Chee-141
85O-Pee-Chee Stickers-90
85Topps-141
86Flyers Postcards-21
86O-Pee-Chee-86
86O-Pee-Chee Stickers-239
86Topps-86
87Flyers Postcards-26
87O-Pee-Chee-158
87O-Pee-Chee Minis-33
87O-Pee-Chee Stickers-97
87Panini Stickers-131
87Panini Stickers-193
87Topps-158
88Flyers Postcards-20
88O-Pee-Chee-168
88O-Pee-Chee Stickers-97
88Panini Stickers-324
88Topps-168
89Bruins Sports Action Update-8
89Flyers Postcards-20
89O-Pee-Chee-139
89O-Pee-Chee Stickers-106
89Panini Stickers-306
89Topps-139
90Bowman-37
Tiffany-37
90O-Pee-Chee-8
90OPC Premier-92
90Panini Stickers-5
90Panini Stickers-325
90Pro Set-14
90Pro Set-360
90Pro Set-460
90Score-269
Canadian-269
90Score Rookie/Traded-34T
90Topps-8
Tiffany-8
90Upper Deck-2
90Upper Deck-409
French-2
French-409
91Pro Set Platinum-187
91Bowman-123
91Bowman-424
91O-Pee-Chee-227
91Panini Stickers-115
91Parkhurst-82
French-82
91Pinnacle-184
French-184
91Pro Set-113
French-113
Platinum PC-PC17
91Score American-223
91Score Canadian Bilingual-223
91Score Canadian English-223
91Stadium Club-237
91Topps-227
91Upper Deck-260
French-260
92Bowman-272
92O-Pee-Chee-350
92Panini Stickers-93
92Panini Stickers French-93
92Pinnacle-178
French-178
92Pro Set-257
92Score-72
Canadian-72
92Stadium Club-374
92Topps-65
Gold-65G
92Upper Deck-177
93Donruss-441
93Panini Stickers-267
93Parkhurst-85
Emerald Ice-85
93Pinnacle-342
Canadian-342
93Score-513
Gold-513
Canadian-513
Canadian Gold-513
93Ultra-340
93Upper Deck-368
93Whalers Coke-17
94Score-247
Gold-247
Platinum-247
94Ultra-92
01Topps Archives-44
02UD Foundations-71
Signs of Greatness-SGBP
04ITG Franchises US East-432
Autographs-A-BPR
04UD Legendary Signatures-48
Autographs-BP

Prorok, Ivo

94Czech APS Extraliga-223
95Czech APS Extraliga-137
96Czech APS Extraliga-15
97Czech APS Extraliga-92
97Czech DS Extraliga-48
97Czech DS Stickers-131
98Czech DS-46
98Czech DS Stickers-99
98Czech OFS-10
98Czech OFS-467
99Czech DS-65
99Czech OFS-156
99Czech OFS-501
All-Star Game Blue-501
All-Star Game Gold-501
All-Star Game Red-501
All-Star Game Silver-501
00Czech OFS-414
02Czech OFS Plus-205
03Czech OFS Plus-108
06Czech IIHF World Championship Postcards-16
06Czech LG Hockey Games Postcards-16
06Czech OFS-144

Prosek, Roman

99Czech OFS-310
00Czech OFS-167
01Czech OFS-198

Proshkin, Vitali

99Russian Dynamo Moscow-8
00Russian Hockey League-126
02Russian Hockey League-206
03Russian Hockey League-154
03Russian World Championship Team 2003-10
04Russian World Championship Team-16

Proske, Frank

83Swedish Semic VM Stickers-157
04German Berlin Eisbarens 50th Anniv-53

Proskurnicki, Andrew

95Slapshot-348
95Sarnia Sting-18
96Sarnia Sting-21

Prosofsky, Garrett

95Saskatoon Blades-16
96Saskatoon Blades-18
97Upper Deck-416
97Saskatoon Blades-18
98Prince Albert Raiders-20
00Prince Albert Raiders-19
03Alaska Aces-15
04Oklahoma City Blazers-12

Prosofsky, Jason

907th Inn. Sketch WHL-31
91Upper Deck-432
French-432
91ProCards-325

Prosofsky, Tyler

92Tacoma Rockets-19
93Tacoma Rockets-22
00Asheville Smoke-9

Prospal, Vaclav

94Classic-29
Gold-29
94Classic Pro Prospects-174
97Be A Player-213
Autographs-213
Autographs Die-Cuts-213
Autographs Prismatic Die-Cuts-213
97Beehive-52
Authentic Autographs-52
Golden Portraits-52
Team-21
Team Gold-21
97Black Diamond Premium Cut-PC21
97Black Diam Premium Cut Double Diam-PC21
97Black Diam Prem Cut Quad Diam Horiz-PC21
97Black Diam Premium Cut Triple Diam-PC21
97Black Diam Premium Cut Quad Diam Vert-PC21
97Collector's Choice-185
97Crown Royale-100
Emerald Green-100
Ice Blue-100
Silver-100
97Donruss-219
Press Proofs Silver-219
Press Proofs Gold-219
Rated Rookies-3
Medallist-3
97Donruss Canadian Ice-135
Dominion Series-135
Provincial Series-135
97Donruss Elite-80
Aspirations-80
Status-80
97Donruss Limited-38
97Donruss Limited-91
97Donruss Limited-100
Exposure-38
Exposure-91
Exposure-100
97Donruss Preferred-105
Cut to the Chase-105
97Donruss Priority-165
97Donruss Priority-190
Stamp of Approval-165
Stamp of Approval-190
97Katch-165
Gold-165
Silver-165
97Leaf-132
97Leaf-165
Fractal Matrix-132
Fractal Matrix-165
Fractal Matrix Die Cuts-132
Fractal Matrix Die Cuts-165
97Leaf International-132
Universal Ice-132
97McDonald's Upper Deck-39
97Paramount-136
Copper-136
Dark Grey-136
Emerald Green-136
Ice Blue-136
Red-136
Silver-136
97Pinnacle-19
Artist's Proofs-19
Rink Collection-19
Press Plates Back Black-19
Press Plates Back Cyan-19
Press Plates Back Magenta-19
Press Plates Back Yellow-19
Press Plates Front Black-19
Press Plates Front Cyan-19
Press Plates Front Magenta-19
Press Plates Front Yellow-19
97Pinnacle Inside-143
97Pinnacle Mint-30
Bronze-30
Gold Team-30
Silver Team-30
Coins Brass-30
Coins Brass Proofs-30
Coins Gold Plated-30
Coins Gold Plated Proofs-30
Coins Nickel Silver-30
Coins Nickel Silver Proofs-30
Coins Solid Gold-30
Coins Solid Silver-30
97Score-51
Artist's Proofs-51
Golden Blades-51
97Score Flyers-18
Platinum-18
Premier-18
97SP Authentic-188
97Upper Deck-125
Smooth Grooves-SG27
97Upper Deck Ice-45
Parallel-45
Lethal Lines-L7C
Lethal Lines 2-L7C
Power Shift-45
97Zenith-91
Z-Gold-91
Z-Silver-91
Rookie Reign-6
Z-Team-13
Z-Team Gold-13
98Finest-49
No Protectors-49
No Protectors Refractors-49
Refractors-49
98Katch-102
98Pacific Dynagon Ice-129
Blue-129
Red-129
98Senators Team Issue-17
98UD Choice-145
Prime Choice Reserve-145
Reserve-145
98Upper Deck-328
Exclusives-328
Exclusives 1 of 1-328
Gold Reserve-328
98Upper Deck MVP-145
Gold Script-145
Silver Script-145
Super Script-145
99BAP Millennium-173
Emerald-173
Ruby-173
Sapphire-173
Signatures-173
Signatures Gold-173
99Pacific-292
Copper-292
Emerald Green-292
Gold-292
Ice Blue-292
Premiere Date-292
Red-292
99Senators Team Issue-15
99Upper Deck Victory-209
99Czech OFS-30
99Czech OFS Jagr Team Embossed-30
00Aurora-103
Premiere Date-103
00BAP Memorabilia-308
Emerald-308
Ruby-308
Sapphire-308
Promos-308
00BAP Mem Chicago Sportsfest Copper-308
00BAP Memorabilia Chicago Sportsfest Blue-308
00BAP Memorabilia Chicago Sportsfest Gold-308
00BAP Memorabilia Chicago Sportsfest Ruby-308
00BAP Memorabilia Chicago Sun-Times Ruby-308
00BAP Memorabilia Chicago Sun-Times Gold-308
00BAP Mem Chicago Sun-Times Sapphire-308
00BAP Mem Toronto Fall Expo Copper-308
00BAP Memorabilia Toronto Fall Expo Gold-308
00BAP Memorabilia Toronto Fall Expo Ruby-308
00O-Pee-Chee-210
00O-Pee-Chee Parallel-210
00Pacific-285
Copper-285
Gold-285
Ice Blue-285
Premiere Date-285
00Panini Stickers-69
00Panthers Team Issue-16
00Paramount-176
Copper-176
Gold-176
Holo-Gold-176
Holo-Silver-176
Ice Blue-176
Premiere Date-176
00Senators Team Issue-17
00Stadium Club-179
00Topps/OPC-210
Parallel-210
00Upper Deck-350
Exclusives Tier 1-350
Exclusives Tier 2-350
00Upper Deck Victory-162
00Upper Deck Vintage-257
00Czech DS Extraliga Team Jagr-JT9
00Czech OFS-389
01Upper Deck-389
Exclusives-389
01Upper Deck Victory-153
Gold-153
01Czech DS-47
02BAP First Edition-269
02BAP Sig Series Auto Buybacks 1999-173
02O-Pee-Chee-109
02O-Pee-Chee Premier Blue Parallel-109
02O-Pee-Chee Premier Red Parallel-109
02O-Pee-Chee Factory Set-109
02Pacific-353
Blue-353
Red-353
02Pacific Complete-69
Red-69
02Parkhurst Retro-200
Minis-200
02Topps-109
OPC Blue Parallel-109
OPC Red Parallel-109
Factory Set-109
02Topps Total-63
02Upper Deck Vintage-227
02Czech DS-51
02Czech DS-65
03BAP Memorabilia-96
Emerald-96
Gold-96
Ruby-96
Sapphire-96
03Beehive-3
Gold-3
Silver-3
03Black Diamond-16
Black-16
Green-16
Red-16
03NHL Sticker Collection-125
03Pacific-310
Blue-310
Red-310
03Pacific Complete-388
Red-388
03Pacific Exhibit-5
Blue Backs-5
Yellow Backs-5
03Private Stock Reserve-3
Blue-3
Red-3
Retail-3
03Upper Deck-246
Canadian Exclusives-246
HG-246
UD Exclusives-246
03Upper Deck Ice-2
Gold-2
03Upper Deck MVP-376
Gold Script-376
Silver Script-376
Canadian Exclusives-376
03Upper Deck Victory-170
Bronze-170
Gold-170
Silver-170
04Pacific-6
Blue-6
Red-6
04Czech World Championship Postcards-14
05Beehive Signature Scrapbook-SSVP
05Hot Prospects-90
En Fuego-90
Red Hot-90
White Hot-90
05Lightning Team Issue-7
05Parkhurst-431
Facsimile Auto Parallel-431
True Colors-TCTBL
True Colors-TCTBL
True Colors-TCFLTB
True Colors-TCFLTB
05SP Authentic Sign of the Times-VP
05SP Game Used Auto Draft-AD-VP
05SP Game Used SIGnificance-VP
05SP Game Used SIGnificance Gold-S-VP
05The Cup Master Pressplate Rookie Update-254
05Upper Deck-418
Jerseys Series II-J2VP
Notable Numbers-N-VP
05Upper Deck MVP-353
Gold-353
Platinum-353
05Upper Deck Rookie Update-90
05Upper Deck Rookie Update-254
Inspirations Patch Rookies-254
05Upper Deck Victory-245
Black-245
Gold-245
Silver-245
05Czech World Champions Postcards-7
05Czech Kvarteto Bonaparte-7a
05Czech Pexeso Mini Blue Set-18
05Czech Pexeso Mini Red Set-23
05Czech Pexeso Mini Red Set-31
06Black Diamond-75
Black-75
Gold-75
Ruby-75
06Fleer-176
Tiffany-176
06Lightning Postcards-15
06NHL POG-43
06O-Pee-Chee-447
Rainbow-447
06Panini Stickers-151
06Ultra-177
Gold Medallion-177
Ice Medallion-177
06Upper Deck Arena Giveaways-TBL2
06Upper Deck-175
Exclusives Parallel-175
High Gloss Parallel-175
Masterpieces-175
06Upper Deck MVP-260
Gold Script-260
Super Script-260
06Upper Deck Ovation-95
06Upper Deck Victory-176
06Upper Deck Victory Black-176
06Upper Deck Victory Gold-176
07Upper Deck Victory-71
Black-71
Gold-71

Prosser, Nate

04Sioux Falls Stampede-1-3
05Sioux Falls Stampede-6

Prosvic, Jaroslav

04Slovakian Skalica Team Set-5

Proteau, Francois

03Cape Breton Screaming Eagles-30

Protivny, Tomas

06Czech HC Sparta Praha Postcards-15
06Czech OFS-75

Protsenko, Boris

95Bowman Draft Prospects-P29
03Fresno Falcons-14

Proud, Joshua

93Quebec Pee-Wee Tournament-1221

Proudley, Mike

06Chilliwack Bruins-24

Proulx, Christian

907th Inn. Sketch QMJHL-218
917th Inn. Sketch QMJHL-167
93Quebec Pee-Wee 20th Anniversary-3
93Quebec Pee-Wee 20th Anniversary-8
93Fredericton Canadiens-23
94Parkhurst-121
Gold-121
94Fredericton Canadiens-23
94Classic Pro Prospects-8
96Milwaukee Admirals-20
97Milwaukee Admirals-16
99German Bundesliga 2-22
03Thetford Mines Prolab-18

Proulx, Gabriel

03Laredo Bucks-16

Proulx, Hugo

917th Inn. Sketch QMJHL-282
917th Inn. Sketch Memorial Cup-57
94Greensboro Monarchs-8
96Quad-City Mallards-9
97Quad-City Mallards-8
98Quad-City Mallards-18
99Quad-City Mallards-9
99UHL All-Stars West-17T
00Quad-City Mallards-11
01Quad-City Mallards-19

Proulx, Oliver

01Drummondville Voltigeurs-10
03ECHL Update RBI Sports-126
05Rockford Ice Hogs-13

Proulx, Steve

01Drummondville Voltigeurs-9

Prout, Daniel

06Sarnia Sting-18

Provaznik, Jiri

94Czech APS Extraliga-46

Provencal, Jacques

88Richelieu Riverains-24

Provencher, Jimmy

96Louisville Riverfrogs-21
00Finnish Cardset-191

Provencher, Maxime

06Chicoutimi Sagueneens-18

Provenzano, Mark

95Slapshot-220

Provost, Claude

44Beehive Group II Photos-280
52Juniors Blue Tint-138
57Parkhurst-M12
58Parkhurst-43
59Parkhurst-18
60NHL Ceramic Tiles-21
60Parkhurst-54
60Parkhurst-58
60Shirriff Coins-33
60York Photos-28
61Parkhurst-50
61Shirriff/Salada Coins-105
61York Yellow Backs-17
62Parkhurst-41
62Shirriff Coins-35
62York Iron-On Transfers-14
63Chex Photos-43
63Parkhurst-36
63Parkhurst-95
63Toronto Star-30
63York White Backs-28
64Beehive Group III Photos-111
64Canadiens Postcards-14
64Coca-Cola Caps-64
64Topps-23
64Toronto Star-39
65Canadiens Steinberg Glasses-6
65Coca-Cola-64
65Topps-8
66Topps-9
66Topps USA Test-9
67Canadiens IGA-14
67Topps-71
67York Action Octagons-4
67York Action Octagons-6
67York Action Octagons-20
67York Action Octagons-36
68Bauer Ads-18
68Canadiens IGA-14
68Canadiens Postcards BW-11
68O-Pee-Chee-163
68O-Pee-Chee-216
68Shirriff Coins-90
69Canadiens Postcards Color-21
69O-Pee-Chee-167
70Canadiens Pins-19
93O-Pee-Chee Canadiens Hockey Fest-43
94Parkhurst Missing Link-73
94Parkhurst Tall Boys-70
Mail-Ins-AS6
Mail-Ins-SL4
95Parkhurst '66-67-61
Coins-61
02Parkhurst Reprints-212
02Parkhurst Reprints-233
02Parkhurst Reprints-257
02Parkhurst Reprints-281

Provost, Paul

51Bas Du Fleuve-37

Prpic, Joel

97Providence Bruins-14
98Providence Bruins-17
99BAP Memorabilia-316
Gold-316
Silver-316
99Upper Deck Gold Reserve-338
99Providence Bruins-20
00Upper Deck Victory-268
00Hershey Bears-11
01Cleveland Barons-18

Prpic, Tony

93Fredericton Canadiens-24
95Wheeling Thunderbirds-12
96Fredericton Canadiens-16
96Pensacola Ice Pilots-17
97Toledo Storm-10
98Idaho Steelheads-14

Prpich, Dave

917th Inn. Sketch OHL-193

Prpich, Mike

03North Dakota Fighting Sioux-5
04North Dakota Fighting Sioux-20
06New Mexico Scorpions-12

Prtt, Stacy

83Brandon Wheat Kings-16

Prucha, Petr

02Czech OFS Plus-226
03Czech OFS Plus-58
03Czech OFS Plus MS Praha-SE12
03Czech Pardubice Postcards-13
04SP Authentic Rookie Redemptions-RR47
04Czech OFS-128
04Czech World Championship Postcards-15
05ITG Heroes/Prosp Toronto Expo Parallel -276
05Beehive-136
Beige -136
Blue -136
Gold -136
Red -136
Matte-136
Signature Scrapbook-SSPP
05Black Diamond-263
05Hot Prospects-152
En Fuego-152
Red Hot-152
White Hot-152
05ITG Ultimate Memorabilia Level 1-80
05ITG Ultimate Memorabilia Level 2-80
05ITG Ultimate Memorabilia Level 3-80
05ITG Ultimate Memorabilia Level 4-80
05ITG Ultimate Memorabilia Level 5-80

05ITG Ultimate Mem Future Stars Autos-18
05ITG Ultimate Mem Future Star Autos Gold-18
05ITG Ultimate Mem Future Stars Jerseys-19
05ITG Ultimate Mem Fut Stars Jerseys Gold-19
05ITG Ultimate Mem Future Stars Mem Autos-18
05ITG Ultimate Mem Fut Star Mem Auto Gold-18
05ITG Ultimate Memorabilia R.O.Y. Autos-9
05ITG Ultimate Mem R.O.Y. Autos Gold-9
05ITG Ultimate Memorabilia R.O.Y. Emblems-13
05ITG Ultimate Mem R.O.Y. Emblems Gold-13
05ITG Ultimate Memorabilia R.O.Y. Jerseys-13
05ITG Ultimate Mem R.O.Y. Jerseys Gold-13
05ITG Ultimate Memorabilia R.O.Y. Numbers-13
05ITG Ultimate Mem R.O.Y. Numbers Gold-13
05ITG Ultimate Memorabilia Stick Autos-19
05ITG Ultimate Mem Stick Autos Gold-19
05Parkhurst-647
Facsimile Auto Parallel-647
Signatures-PP
05SP Authentic-172
Limited-172
Rarefied Rookies-RRPP
05SP Game Used-159
Autographs-159
Gold-159
Rookie Exclusives-PP
Rookie Exclusives Silver-RE-PP
05SPx-174
Spectrum-174
Xcitement Rookies-XR-PP
Xcitement Rookies Gold-XR-PP
Xcitement Rookies Spectrum-XR-PP
05The Cup-135
Autographed Rookie Patches Gold Rainbow-135
Black Rainbow Rookies-135
Dual NHL Shields Autographs-ADSLP
Masterpiece Pressplates (Artifacts)-302
Masterpiece Pressplates (Bee Hive)-136
Masterpiece Pressplates (Black Diamond)-263
Masterpiece Pressplates (Ice)-158
Masterpiece Pressplates (MVP)-419
Masterpiece Pressplates (Power Play)-171
Masterpiece Pressplates (Rookie Update)-255
Masterpiece Pressplates SPA Autos-172
Masterpiece Pressplates (SP Game Used)-159
Masterpiece Pressplates SPx Autos-174
Masterpiece Pressplates (Trilogy)-203
Masterpiece Pressplates Ult Coll Autos-125
Masterpiece Pressplates Autographs-135
Platinum Rookies-135
05UD Artifacts-302
05UD PowerPlay-171
05UD Rookie Class-7
05Ultimate Collection-125
Ultimate Debut Threads Jerseys-DTJPP
Ultimate Debut Threads Patches-DTPPP
Ultimate Debut Threads Patches Autos-DAPPP
05Ultra-230
Gold-230
Ice-230
Rookie Uniformity Jerseys-RU-PP
Rookie Uniformity Jersey Autographs-ARU-PP
Rookie Uniformity Patches-RUP-PP
Rookie Uniformity Patch Autographs-ARP-PP
05Upper Deck Rookie Ink-RIPP
05Upper Deck Rookie Threads-RTPP
05Upper Deck Rookie Threads Autographs-ARTPP
05Upper Deck Ice-158
Fresh Ice-FIPP
Fresh Ice Glass-FIPP
Fresh Ice Glass Patches-FIPPP
Premieres Auto Patches-AIPPP
05Upper Deck MVP-419
Gold-419
Platinum-419
05Upper Deck Rookie Update-255
Inspirations Patch Rookies-255
05Upper Deck Trilogy-203
05Czech Pexeso Mini Blue Set-15
05Czech Pexeso Mini Red Set-5
05ITG Heroes and Prospects-276
Autograph Memorabilia-GA-09
Autograph Memorabilia Gold-GA-09
Autographs Series II-PP
Autographs Series II-PL
Jerseys-GUJ-111
Jerseys Gold-GUJ-111
06Be A Player-60
Autographs-60
Signatures-PP
Signatures 10-65
Signatures Trios-TSNP
Portraits Dual Signature Portraits-DSLP
Portraits First Exposures-FEPP
Portraits Signature Portraits-SPPP
06Beehive Signature Scrapbook-SSPP
06Black Diamond-55
Black-55
Gold-55
Ruby-55
Gemography-GPP
06Flair Showcase Wave of the Future-WF28
06Fleer-131
Tiffany-131
06Hot Prospects Hotagraphs-HPP
06ITG International Ice-46
Gold-46
Autographs-APP
Complete Jersey-CJ12
Cornerstones-IC05
Cornerstones Gold-IC05
06ITG Ultimate Memorabilia Autos-52
06ITG Ultimate Memorabilia Autos Gold-52
06ITG Ultimate Memorabilia Jerseys Autos-47
06ITG Ultimate Memorabilia Jerseys Autos Gold-47
06ITG Ultimate Memorabilia Sticks Autos-15
06ITG Ultimate Memorabilia Sticks Autos Gold-15
06O-Pee-Chee-332
06O-Pee-Chee-625
Rainbow-332
Rainbow-625
Autographs-A-PP
06Panini Stickers-105
06SP Authentic-39
Chirography-PP
Limited-39
Sign of the Times-STPP
06SP Game Used Inked Sweaters-ISPP
06SP Game Used Inked Sweaters Patches-ISPP
06SP Game Used Inked Sweaters Dual-IS2LP
06SP Game Used Inked Sweaters Dual Patches-IS2LP
06SP Game Used Letter Marks-LMPP
06SP Game Used SIGnificance-SPP
06SPx-69
Spectrum-69
Winning Materials-WMPP
Winning Materials Spectrum-WMPP
06UD Artifacts-38
Blue-38
Gold-38
Platinum-38
Radiance-38
Red-38
Tundra Tandems-TTHP
Tundra Tandems Black-TTHP
Tundra Tandems Blue-TTHP
Tundra Tandems Gold-TTHP
Tundra Tandems Platinum-TTHP
Tundra Tandems Red-TTHP
Tundra Tandems Dual Patches Red-TTHP
06Ultra-130
Gold Medallion-130
Ice Medallion-130
Uniformity-UPP
Uniformity Patches-UPPP
Uniformity Autographed Jerseys-UAPP
06Upper Deck Arena Giveaways-NYR2
06Upper Deck-129
Exclusives Parallel-129
High Gloss Parallel-129
Game Jerseys-JPP
Game Patches-PPP
Masterpieces-129
06Upper Deck MVP-195
Gold Script-195
Super Script-195
Jerseys-OJEP
06Upper Deck Ovation-32
06Upper Deck Sweet Shot Signature Shots/Saves-SSPP
06Upper Deck Victory-132
06Upper Deck Victory Black-132
06Upper Deck Victory Gold-132
06Upper Deck Victory Next In Line-NL34
06ITG Heroes and Prospects Quad Emblems-QE06
06ITG Heroes and Prospects Quad Emblems Gold-QE06
06ITG Heroes and Prospects Sticks and Jerseys-SJ13
06ITG Heroes and Prospects Sticks and Jerseys Gold-SJ13

Prud'Homme, Carl
95Slapshot Memorial Cup-58

Prudden, Joshua
03Atlantic City Boardwalk Bullies-18
03Atlantic City Boardwalk Bullies RBI-26
04Atlantic City Boardwalk Bullies Kinko's-15
04Cleveland Barons-19
05Cleveland Barons-18

Pruden, Gregory
94German First League-391

Pruneau, Martial
51Laval Dairy QSHL-13
51Laval Dairy Subset-56
52Bas Du Fleuve-2
52St. Lawrence Sales-79

Prusa, Peter
70Finnish Jaakiekko-95
70Swedish Hockey-381
74Finnish Jenkki-106
74Finnish Typotor-65
04German Berlin Eisbarens 50th Anniv-26

Prusa, Sven
94German DEL-346

Prusek, Martin
95Czech APS Extraliga-293
96Czech APS Extraliga-191
97Czech APS Extraliga-125
97Czech APS Extraliga-344
97Czech DS Extraliga-95
97Czech DS Stickers-189
98Czech DS-23
98Czech DS Stickers-247
98Czech OFS-350
98Czech OFS-419
99Czech DS-169
Goalies-G13
99Czech OFS-14
99Czech OFS-255
99Czech OFS-NNO
99Czech OFS Goalie Die-Cuts-14
00Czech DS Extraliga-157
Goalies-G14
00Czech OFS-239
00Czech OFS Star Emerald-26
00Czech OFS Star Pink-26
00Czech OFS Star Violet-26
01BAP Memorabilia-437
Emerald-437
Ruby-437
Sapphire-437
01Between the Pipes-162
01Parkhurst-333
01UD Mask Collection-156
Gold-156
01Czech DS-52
01Czech OFS All Stars-29
01Grand Rapids Griffins-17
02BAP First Edition-289
02BAP Signature Series-111
Autographs-111
Autographs Gold-111
02Between the Pipes-82
Gold-82
Silver-82
Jerseys-41
Tandems-5
02NHL Power Play Stickers-105
02Pacific Complete-156
Red-156
02Senators Team Issue-13
02Senators Team Issue-21
02SPx-118
02Stadium Club-116
Silver Decoy Cards-116
Proofs-116
02UD Foundations-138
02UD Mask Collection-58
02UD Mask Collection-59
02UD Mask Collection Beckett Promos-58
02UD Mask Collection Beckett Promos-59
02UD Piece of History-141
02Upper Deck-215
Exclusives-215
02Upper Deck MVP-211
Gold-211
Classics-211
Golden Classics-211
02Upper Deck Vintage-342
03BAP Memorabilia-139
Emerald-139
Gold-139
Ruby-139
Sapphire-139
Masks III-10
Masks III Gold-10
Masks III Silver-10
Masks III Memorabilia-10
Tandems-T-2
03BAP Ultimate Memorabilia Autographs-41
Gold-41
03ITG Action-455
03Pacific-240
Blue-240
Red-240
03Pacific Complete-487
Red-487
03Senators Postcards-21
04Czech OFS-238
Stars-30
Team Cards-11
04Czech Zuma-25
04ITG Heroes/Prospects He Shoots/Scores-39
04ITG Heroes and Prospects Net Prospects-25
04ITG Heroes and Prosp Net Prospects Gold-25
05Syracuse Crunch-19

Prust, Brandon
02London Knights-13
03London Knights-25
04London Knights-8
05ITG Heroes and Prospects Memorial Cup-MC-9
06Be A Player-243
06Beehive-110
Matte-110
06Flair Showcase-308
06Hot Prospects-151
Red Hot-151
White Hot-151
06O-Pee-Chee-575
Rainbow-575
06SP Authentic-170
Limited-170
06SP Game Used-142
Gold-142
Rainbow-142
06The Cup-117
Autographed NHL Shields Duals-DASBP
Autographed Rookie Masterpiece Pressplates-117
Gold Rainbow Autographed Rookie Patches-117
Masterpiece Pressplates (Bee Hive)-110
Masterpiece Pressplates (Marquee Rookies)-575
Masterpiece Pressplates (SP Authentic Autographs)-170
Masterpiece Pressplates (SP Game Used)-142
Masterpiece Pressplates (Sweet Beginnings)-112
Masterpiece Pressplates (Ultimate Collection)-68
Masterpiece Pressplates (Victory)-326
NHL Shields Duals-DSHDB
Rookies Black-117
Rookies Platinum-117
06UD Artifacts-268
06Ultimate Collection-68
Ultimate Debut Threads Jerseys-DJ-PR
Ultimate Debut Threads Jerseys Autographs-DJ-PR
Ultimate Debut Threads Patches-DJ-PR
Ultimate Debut Threads Patches Autographs-DJ-PR
06Upper Deck-462
Exclusives Parallel-462
High Gloss Parallel-462
Masterpieces-462
Rookie Headliners-RH20
06Upper Deck Sweet Shot-112
Rookie Jerseys Autographs-112
06Upper Deck Victory-326
07Upper Deck Rookie Class -36

Pryl, Stanislav
70Finnish Jaakiekko-57
70Swedish Hockey-363

Pryor, Chris
84Springfield Indians-16
87North Stars Postcards-25
88ProCards AHL-311
89ProCards AHL-254
90ProCards AHL/IHL-499
91ProCards-475

Prystai, Metro
44Beehive Group II Photos-135
44Beehive Group II Photos-205
51Parkhurst-65
52Parkhurst-60
53Parkhurst-42
54Parkhurst-35
54Topps-24
94Parkhurst Missing Link-57

Przepiorka, Eric
01Sioux Falls Stampede-9

Psenka, Tomas
96Slovakian Quebec Pee-Wee Tournament-23
00Val d'Or Foreurs-7
Signed-7

Psurny, Michal
05Kootenay Ice-18
06Czech OFS-238
Brothers-5

Psurny, Roman
04Medicine Hat Tigers-17
05Medicine Hat Tigers-16
06Czech HC Zlin Hame Postcards-10
06Czech OFS-239
Brothers-5

Pszenyczny, David
03Sarnia Sting-17
04Mississauga Ice Dogs-18

Ptacek, Bohuslav
02Czech OFS Plus-75

Ptacek, Frantisek
94Czech APS Extraliga-77
95Czech APS Extraliga-275
96Czech APS Extraliga-129
97Czech APS Extraliga-5
97Czech DS Stickers-62
98Czech DS-90
98Czech DS Stickers-213
98Czech OFS-131
99Czech OFS-110
00Czech DS Extraliga-5
00Czech OFS-295
01Czech OFS-33
02Czech OFS Plus-13
03Czech OFS Plus-79
03Czech OFS Plus All-Star Game-H31
03Czech OFS Plus MS Praha-SE22
04Czech OFS-33
Checklist Cards-2
Czech/Slovak-11
Defence Points-7
05Czech HC Karlovy Vary-13
06Czech HC Sparta Praha Postcards-5
06Czech OFS-73
All Stars-5
Defenders-15

Pucher, Peter
99Czech DS-192
99Czech OFS-84
00Czech DS Extraliga-103
00Czech OFS-198
01Czech OFS-120
01Slovakian Kvarteto-6C
02Czech OFS Plus-117
Trios-T24
Duos-D13
02Slovakian Kvarteto-28
03Czech OFS Plus-249
03Czech OFS Plus All-Star Game-H44
03Czech OFS Plus Insert M-M20
04Czech OFS-300
Assist Leaders-3
Czech/Slovak-12
Points Leaders-4
05Czech HC Znojmo-12
06Czech OFS-211
Goals Leaders-10
Points Leaders-9

Pucher, Rene
94Finnish Jaa Kiekko-205
95Slovakian APS National Team-18
01Slovakian Kvarteto-6D
02Czech OFS Plus-142
03Czech OFS Plus Insert C-C14

Puchniak, Rob
89Brandon Wheat Kings-16
90Brandon Wheat Kings-19
907th Inn. Sketch WHL-231
917th Inn. Sketch WHL-197

Pudas, Albert
23V128-1 Paulin's Candy-21

Pudlick, Mike
00Lowell Lock Monsters-27
01Manchester Monarchs-8A
02Manchester Monarchs-12
04German Augsburg Panthers Postcards-23
04German DEL-39
05German DEL-356

Puente, Troy
06Texas Tornados-3

Puga, Duane
92British Columbia JHL-79

Pugh, Tyler
06Gatineau Olympiques-28

Pugliese, Billy
02Muskegon Fury-20
03Muskegon Fury-17

Pugliese, MArio
79Panini Stickers-392

Puhakka, Keijo
70Finnish Jaakiekko-286
71Finnish Suomi Stickers-156
72Finnish Jaakiekko-108
73Finnish Jaakiekko-208

Puhakka, Mika
94Finnish SISU-282
95Finnish SISU-226
96Finnish SISU Redline-25
99German Bundesliga 2-274
05German DEL-58

Puhalski, Greg
82Kitchener Rangers-21
83Kitchener Rangers-15
84Kitchener Rangers-19
85London Knights-13
92Toledo Storm-17
92Toledo Storm Team Issue-22
93Toledo Storm-19
94Toledo Storm-19
95Toledo Storm-22
96Toledo Storm-NNO
97Toledo Storm-26
98Port Huron Border Cats-22
00Fort Wayne Komets-23
02Fort Wayne Komets-24
03Fort Wayne Komets 2003 Champions-11

Puistola, Pasi
98Finnish Kerailysarja-81
99Finnish Cardset-44
00Finnish Cardset-344
01Finnish Cardset-338
02Finnish Cardset-99
03Finnish Cardset-144
04Finnish Cardset-154
04Finnish Cardset Signatures-30
05Finnish Cardset -140
06Swedish SHL Elitset-195

Pukka, Mikko
04Finnish Cardset-294
05Finnish Cardset -141
06Finnish Cardset-148

Pulente, Gino
92Lake Superior State Lakers-22

Pulford, Bob
44Beehive Group II Photos-443
57Parkhurst-T4
58Parkhurst-1
58Parkhurst-45
59Parkhurst-28
60Parkhurst-19
60Shirriff Coins-13
60York Photos-29
61Parkhurst-8
61Shirriff/Salada Coins-46
61York Yellow Backs-14
62Parkhurst-11
62Shirriff Coins-6
62York Iron-On Transfers-15
63Chex Photos-44
63Parkhurst-12
63Parkhurst-72
63Toronto Star-31
63York White Backs-18
64Beehive Group III Photos-180A
64Beehive Group III Photos-180B
64Coca-Cola Caps-103
64Topps-60
64Toronto Star-40
65Coca-Cola-102
65Topps-18
66Maple Leafs Hockey Talks-6
66Post Cereal Box Backs-2
66Topps-19
67Post Flip Books-11
67Topps-19
67York Action Octagons-5
67York Action Octagons-6
67York Action Octagons-7
67York Action Octagons-10
67York Action Octagons-15
67York Action Octagons-24
67York Action Octagons-32
68O-Pee-Chee-129
68Post Marbles-20
68Shirriff Coins-162
68Topps-129
69Maple Leafs White Border Glossy-28
69Maple Leafs White Border Glossy-29
69O-Pee-Chee-53
Four-in-One-16
69Topps-53
70Colgate Stamps-2
70Dad's Cookies-106
70Esso Power Players-159
70O-Pee-Chee-36
70Sargent Promotions Stamps-72
70Topps-36
71O-Pee-Chee-94
Posters-2
71Sargent Promotions Stamps-66
71Topps-94
71Toronto Sun-123
72Finnish Semic World Championship-203
72Swedish Semic World Championship-203
74O-Pee-Chee NHL-229
74Topps-229
79Blackhawks Postcards-18
81Blackhawks Borderless Postcards-21
81Blackhawks Brown Background-8
85Blackhawks Team Issue-5
91Pro Set HOF Induction-3
92Blackhawks Coke-17
93Blackhawks Coke-26
94Parkhurst Missing Link-113
94Parkhurst Tall Boys-110
95Parkhurst '66-67-114
Coins-114
99Blackhawks Chicago Sun-Times-10
02Maple Leafs Platinum Collection-63
02Topps Heritage Reprint Autographs-RP
02Topps Heritage Reprint Relics-RP
02Topps Heritage Reprints-RP
04ITG Franchises Canadian-91
Autographs-BPL
04ITG Franchises US West-237
07Maple Leafs 1967 Commemorative-21
Autographs-ABP1
Autographs-ABP2

Pulford, Harvey
83Hall of Fame-24
83Hall of Fame Postcards-B10
85Hall of Fame-24

Pulkki, Simo
04Richmond Riverdogs-5

Pulkkinen, Hannu
72Finnish Jaakiekko-254
73Finnish Jaakiekko-254
78Finnish SM-Liiga-48

Pulkkinen, Petri
92Finnish Jyvas-Hyva Stickers-116
93Finnish Jyvas-Hyva Stickers-200
93Finnish SISU-258

Pulkkinen, Reino
72Finnish Jaakiekko-163
78Finnish SM-Liiga-92

Pulli, Heino
65Finnish Hellas-111
66Finnish Jaakiekkosarja-185

Pulli, Kai
71Finnish Suomi Stickers-374

Pulli, Kalevi
65Finnish Hellas-108

Pulli, Markku
65Finnish Hellas-105
66Finnish Jaakiekkosarja-174
70Finnish Jaakiekko-248

Pulliainen, Jari
91Finnish Jyvas-Hyva Stickers-64
94Finnish SISU-322

Pulliainen, Tuukka
05Finnish Cardset -338
06Finnish Cardset-167
Signature Sensations-31

Pullinen, Reima
78Finnish SM-Liiga-107
80Finnish Mallasjuoma-192

Pullishy, Glen
91British Columbia JHL-33

Pullman, Joel
04Columbus Cottonmouths-3
05Quad City Mallards-13

Pullola, Tommi
91Finnish Jyvas-Hyva Stickers-46
92Finnish Jyvas-Hyva Stickers-135
93Finnish Jyvas-Hyva Stickers-237
93Finnish SISU-196
94Finnish SISU-224
95Finnish SISU-349

Pulpan, Lukas
03Vancouver Giants-23
04Czech OFS-350
06Czech HC Plzen Postcards-7

Pump, Michael
94German First League-287
99German Bundesliga 2-269

Pumple, Rick
72Cleveland Crusaders WHA-12

Puncochar, Ivan
98Czech OFS-328
99Czech OFS-292
00Czech OFS-169

Puncochar, Petr
00Czech OFS-170
02Czech OFS Plus-290
03Czech OFS Plus-376
04Czech OFS-17
06Czech OFS-312

Punsky, Jay
04Arizona Icecats-19

Puntureri, Matt
01Guelph Storm-18
01Guelph Storm Memorial Cup-18
02Guelph Storm-25
03Sault Ste. Marie Greyhounds-19
04Oshawa Generals-12
04Oshawa Generals Autographs-12
04Sault Ste. Marie Greyhounds-18

Puolanne, Lauri
95Finnish SISU-203
96Finnish SISU Redline-6

Pupillo, Daniel
82Swedish Semic VM Stickers-129

Pupkov, Evgeni
98Russian Hockey League-99
99Russian Hockey League-196
00Russian Hockey League-178

Puppa, Daren
85Sabres Blue Shield-21
85Sabres Blue Shield Small-21
86Sabres Blue Shield-23
86Sabres Blue Shield Small-23
87Panini Stickers-23
87Sabres Blue Shield-20
87Sabres Wonder Bread/Hostess-20
88Sabres Blue Shield-19
88Sabres Wonder Bread/Hostess-21
89O-Pee-Chee-200
89Panini Stickers-214
89Sabres Blue Shield-17
89Sabres Campbell's-19
90Bowman-242
Tiffany-242
90Kraft-43
90O-Pee-Chee-204
90O-Pee-Chee-238
90Panini Stickers-31
90Pro Set-27
90Pro Set-365
90Sabres Blue Shield-16
90Sabres Campbell's-19
90Score-60
90Score-318
Canadian-60
Canadian-318
90Score Hottest/Rising Stars-26
90Topps-204
90Topps-238
Tiffany-204
Tiffany-238
90Upper Deck-166
French-166
91Pro Set Platinum-9
91Bowman-37
91O-Pee-Chee-333
91Panini Stickers-298
91Parkhurst-14
French-14
91Pinnacle-137
French-137
91Pro Set-21
French-21
91Sabres Blue Shield-16
91Sabres Pepsi/Campbell's-16
91Score American-106
91Score Canadian Bilingual-106
91Score Canadian English-106
91Stadium Club-231
91Topps-333
91Upper Deck-248
French-248
92Bowman-16
92Maple Leafs Kodak-30
92O-Pee-Chee-53
92Parkhurst-412
Emerald Ice-412
92Pinnacle-327
French-327
92Sabres Blue Shield-18
92Sabres Jubilee Foods-4
92Score-47
Canadian-47
92Sports Illustrated for Kids II-546
92Stadium Club-370
92Topps-457
Gold-457G
92Ultra-261
93Donruss-316
93Leaf-403
93Lightning Season in Review-23
93OPC Premier-364
Gold-364
93Parkhurst-468
Emerald Ice-468
93Pinnacle-361
Canadian-361
93PowerPlay-234
93Score-273
93Score-530
Gold-530
Canadian-273
Canadian-530
Canadian Gold-530
93Stadium Club-275
Members Only Master Set-275
First Day Issue-275
93Topps/OPC Premier-364
Gold-364
93Ultra-427
93Upper Deck-473
94Canada Games NHL POGS-295
94Donruss-100
94Finest-53
Super Team Winners-53
Refractors-53
94Flair-175
94Fleer-209
94Kraft-50
94Leaf-224
94Leaf Limited-109
94Lightning Health Plan-1
94Lightning Photo Album-22
94Lightning Postcards-14
94OPC Premier-410
Special Effects-410
94Parkhurst-225
Gold-225
94Pinnacle-71
Artist's Proofs-71
Rink Collection-71
Goaltending Greats-GT15
94Score-72
Gold-72
Platinum-72
Franchise-TF22
94Select-45
Gold-45
94Stadium Club-162
94Stadium Club-183
Members Only Master Set-162
Members Only Master Set-183
First Day Issue-162
First Day Issue-183
Super Team Winner Cards-162
Super Team Winner Cards-183
94Topps/OPC Premier-410
Special Effects-410
94Ultra-209
94Upper Deck-204
Electric Ice-204
95Be A Player-85
Signatures-S85
Signatures Die Cuts-S85
95Canada Games NHL POGS-256
95Collector's Choice-117
Player's Club-117
Player's Club Platinum-117
95Donruss-84
95Emotion-166
95Finest-11
Refractors-11
95Kraft-29
95Leaf-243
95Leaf Limited-58
95Lightning Team Issue-15
95Metal-139
95Panini Stickers-134
95Parkhurst International-195
Emerald Ice-195
95Pinnacle-105
Artist's Proofs-105
Rink Collection-105
95Playoff One on One-198
95Score-210
Black Ice Artist's Proofs-210
Black Ice-210
95Select Certified-58
Mirror Gold-58
95SkyBox Impact-157
95SP-137
95Stadium Club-6
Members Only Master Set-6
95Summit-85
Artist's Proofs-85
Ice-85
95Topps-226
OPC Inserts-226
95Ultra-155
95Ultra-376
Gold Medallion-155
95Upper Deck-205
Electric Ice-205
Electric Ice Gold-205
Special Edition-SE78
Special Edition Gold-SE78
95Zenith-120
96Collector's Choice-247
96Collector's Choice-331
96Donruss-34
Press Proofs-34
96Donruss Canadian Ice-102
Gold Press Proofs-102
Red Press Proofs-102
96Donruss Elite-114
Die Cut Stars-114
96Fleer-105
96Fleer-146
96Fleer-147
Vezina-8
96Kraft Upper Deck-26
96Leaf-73
Press Proofs-73
Shut Down-15
96Leaf Limited-58
Gold-58
96Leaf Preferred-69
Press Proofs-69
Steel-17
Steel Gold-17
96Maggers-80
96Metal Universe-146
Armor Plate-8
Armor Plate Super Power-8
96NHL Aces Playing Cards-38
96Pinnacle-97
Artist's Proofs-97
Foil-97
Premium Stock-97
Rink Collection-97
96Score-118
Artist's Proofs-118
Dealer's Choice Artist's Proofs-118
Special Artist's Proofs-118
Golden Blades-118
Net Worth-13
Sudden Death-11
96Select Certified-69
Artist's Proofs-69
Blue-69
Mirror Blue-69
Mirror Gold-69
Mirror Red-69
Red-69
Freezers-9
96SkyBox Impact-123
Zero Heroes-8
96Summit-77
Artist's Proofs-77
Ice-77
Metal-77
Premium Stock-77
In The Crease-4
In The Crease Premium Stock-4
96Ultra-159
Gold Medallion-159
96Upper Deck-338
96Zenith-43
Artist's Proofs-43
97SLU Hockey Canadian-15
97SLU Hockey American-17
97Be A Player-76
Autographs-76
Autographs Die-Cuts-76
Autographs Prismatic Die-Cuts-76
Take A Number-16
97Black Diamond-74
Double Diamond-74
Triple Diamond-74
Quadruple Diamond-74
97Collector's Choice-235
97Crown Royale-126
Emerald Green-126
Ice Blue-126
Silver-126
97Donruss-123
Press Proofs Silver-123
Press Proofs Gold-123
97Donruss Canadian Ice-110
Dominion Series-110
Provincial Series-110
97Donruss Elite-79
Aspirations-79
Status-79
97Donruss Limited-170
97Donruss Limited-192
Exposure-170
Exposure-192
97Donruss Preferred-110
Cut to the Chase-110
97Donruss Priority-136
Stamp of Approval-136
97Katch-137
Gold-137
Silver-137
97Kenner Starting Lineup Cards-17
97Leaf-50
Fractal Matrix-50
Fractal Matrix Die Cuts-50
97Leaf International-50
Universal Ice-50
97Pacific Invincible NHL Regime-187
97Pacific Omega-212
Copper-212
Dark Gray-212
Emerald Green-212
Gold-212
Ice Blue-212
97Pinnacle-84
Artist's Proofs-84
Rink Collection-84
Press Plates Back Black-84
Press Plates Back Cyan-84
Press Plates Back Magenta-84
Press Plates Back Yellow-84
Press Plates Front Black-84
Press Plates Front Cyan-84
Press Plates Front Magenta-84
Press Plates Front Yellow-84
97Pinnacle Certified-22
Red-22
Mirror Blue-22
Mirror Gold-22
Mirror Red-22
97Pinnacle Inside-45
Coach's Collection-45
Executive Collection-45
97Pinnacle Tot Cert Platinum Blue-22
97Pinnacle Tot Certi Platinum Gold-22
97Pinnacle Totally Certified Platinum Red-22
97Pinnacle Tot Cert Mirror Platinum Gold-22
97Revolution-129
Copper-129
Emerald-129
Ice Blue-129
Silver-129
97Score-18
Artist's Proofs-18
Golden Blades-18
97SP Authentic-147
97Studio-44
Press Proofs Silver-44
Press Proofs Gold-44
97Upper Deck-362
98SLU Hockey Extended-175
98Be A Player-281
Press Release-281
98BAP Gold-281
98BAP Autographs-281
98BAP Autographs Gold-281
98Kenner Starting Lineup Cards-26
98NHL Aces Playing Cards-23
98Pacific-403
Ice Blue-403
Red-403
98Panini Photocards-66
98Revolution-132
Ice Shadow-132
Red-132
98UD Choice-191
98UD Choice Preview-191
98UD Choice Prime Choice Reserve-191
98UD Choice Reserve-191
98Upper Deck-367
Exclusives-367
Exclusives 1 of 1-367
Gold Reserve-367
98Upper Deck MVP-186
Gold Script-186
Silver Script-186
Super Script-186
99BAP Memorabilia-220
Gold-220
Silver-220
02BAP Sig Series Auto Buybacks 1998-281
03Lightning Team Issue-36
04ITG Franchises US East-440
Autographs-A-DPU

Puppa, Derek
98Huntsville Channel Cats-20

Purcell, Bill
90Newmarket Saints-17

Purcell, Tom
897th Inn. Sketch OHL-164

Purchase, Anthony
93Quebec Pee-Wee Tournament-517

Purdie, Brad
91Air Canada SJHL-D36
92Maine Black Bears-28
93Maine Black Bears-47
96Peoria Rivermen-18
96Peoria Rivermen Photo Album-19
97Manitoba Moose-B6
98Fort Wayne Komets-11
00German DEL-150
01German Upper Deck-162
Skilled Stars-SS3
02German DEL City Press-229
All-Stars-AS13
03German DEL-116
All-Stars-AS12
04German DEL-132
All-Stars-AS18
04German Hamburg Freezers Postcards-13
05German DEL-343
All-Star Jerseys-AS14
06German DEL-112

Purdie, Dennis
897th Inn. Sketch OHL-36
907th Inn. Sketch OHL-140
917th Inn. Sketch OHL-362
917th Inn. Sketch Memorial Cup-120
92Windsor Spitfires-24
93Johnstown Chiefs-12
94Johnstown Chiefs-15
95Toledo Storm-11
96Toledo Storm-19
99San Diego Gulls-13
00San Diego Gulls-16

Purdon, Neal
94Thunder Bay Senators-15
95Thunder Bay Senators-18
98Thunder Bay Thunder Cats-11

Purdy, Brian
89Brandon Wheat Kings-21
90Brandon Wheat Kings-14
907th Inn. Sketch WHL-216A
907th Inn. Sketch WHL-216B
917th Inn. Sketch WHL-202

Purinton, Cal
99Fort Wayne Komets Penalty Leaders-4

Purinton, Dale
96Lethbridge Hurricanes-12
97Charlotte Checkers-17
97Hartford Wolf Pack-14
98Hartford Wolf Pack-14
99Hartford Wolf Pack-17
00BAP Memorabilia-473
Emerald-473
Ruby-473
Sapphire-473
00SP Authentic-155
00Stadium Club-244
00Topps Premier Plus-129
Blue Ice-129
00Topps Stars-118
Blue-118
00Hartford Wolf Pack-21
01BAP Signature Series-95
Autographs-95
Autographs Gold-95
02BAP Sig Series Auto Buybacks 2001-95
03ITG Action-322
03Parkhurst Original Six New York-10
03Rangers Team Issue-20
05Hartford Wolf Pack-18

06Hartford Wolf Pack-18

Purola, Lavi

52Juniors Blue Tint-62

Purontakanen, Mikko

01Finnish Cardset-294
06Finnish Cardset-262

Purpur, Cliff

34Beehive Group I Photos-75

Purschel, Alexander

94German First League-640

Purschel, Dieter

70Finnish Jaakiekko-96
70Swedish Hockey-366

Pursiainen, Juha

00Finnish Cardset-204
01Finnish Cardset-327

Purves, Chris

06Barrie Colts-15

Purves, John

84Belleville Bulls-7
89ProCards AHL-78
90ProCards AHL/IHL-212
91Baltimore Skipjacks-11
91ProCards-551
93Fort Wayne Komets-15
96Kansas City Blades-16
96Collector's Edge Future Legends-37
96Collector's Edge Ice-190
Prism-190
98IHL All-Star Western Conference-19
99IHL All-Stars-5
99Utah Grizzlies-4
00Utah Grizzlies-11
01Utah Grizzlies-9
02UK Nottingham Panthers-13

Puschacher, Michael

95Austrian National Team-21
95Finnish Semic World Championships-183
95Swedish Globe World Championships-182
95Swedish World Championships Stickers-256
96Swedish Semic Wien-211

Puschnig, Andreas

93Swedish Semic World Champ Stickers-284
94Finnish Jaa Kiekko-240
95Austrian National Team-23
95Finnish Semic World Championships-188
95Swedish Globe World Championships-185

Puschnik, Gerhard

93Swedish Semic World Champ Stickers-285
94Finnish Jaa Kiekko-242
95Austrian National Team-22

Pusey, Chris

83Brantford Alexanders-19

Pushkaryov, Konstantin

04Calgary Hitmen-16
05AHL Top Prospects-33
05Manchester Monarchs-14
06Be A Player Portraits-108
06Beehive-127
Matte-127
06Black Diamond-151A
Black-151A
Gold-151A
Ruby-151A
06Flair Showcase-48
06Flair Showcase-131
Parallel-48
Parallel-131
06Fleer-208
Tiffany-208
06Hot Prospects-118
Red Hot-118
White Hot-118
Hot Materials -HMKP
Hot Materials Red Hot-HMKP
Hot Materials White Hot-HMKP
06O-Pee-Chee-517
Rainbow-517
06SP Authentic-185
Limited-185
06SP Game Used-120
Gold-120
Rainbow-120
Autographs-120
Rookie Exclusives Autographs-REKP
06SPx-149
Spectrum-149
06The Cup-134
Autographed Rookie Masterpiece Pressplates-134
Gold Rainbow Autographed Rookie Patches-134
Masterpiece Pressplates (Artifacts)-214
Masterpiece Pressplates (Be A Player Portraits)-108
Masterpiece Pressplates (Bee Hive)-127
Masterpiece Pressplates (Black Diamond)-151
Masterpiece Pressplates (Marquee Rookies)-517
Masterpiece Pressplates (MVP)-342
Masterpiece Pressplates (Power Play)-107
Masterpiece Pressplates (SP Authentic Autographs)-185
Masterpiece Pressplates (SP Game Used)-120
Masterpiece Pressplates (SPx)-149
Masterpiece Pressplates (Sweet Beginnings)-129
Masterpiece Pressplates (Trilogy)-116
Masterpiece Pressplates (Ultimate Collection)-78
Masterpiece Pressplates (Victory)-213
Rookies Black-134
Rookies Platinum-134
06UD Artifacts-214
Blue-214
Gold-214
Platinum-214
Radiance-214
Red-214
06UD Mini Jersey Collection-107
06UD Powerplay-107
Impact Rainbow-107
06Ultimate Collection-78
Ultimate Debut Threads Jerseys-DJ-KP
Ultimate Debut Threads Jerseys Autographs-DJ-KP
Ultimate Debut Threads Patches-DJ-KP
Ultimate Debut Threads Patches Autographs-DJ-KP
06Ultra-208
Gold Medallion-208
Ice Medallion-208
06Upper Deck-217
Exclusives Parallel-217
High Gloss Parallel-217
Masterpieces-217
Rookie Materials-RMKP
Rookie Materials Patches-RMKP
06Upper Deck MVP-342
Gold Script-342
Super Script-342
06Upper Deck Ovation-124
06Upper Deck Sweet Shot-129
Rookie Jerseys Autographs-129
06Upper Deck Trilogy-116
06Upper Deck Victory-213
06Upper Deck Victory Black-213
06Upper Deck Victory Gold-213
06Manchester Monarchs-11
06ITG Heroes and Prospects-42
Autographs-AKP
07Upper Deck Rookie Class -33

Pushkov, Sergei

94Finnish Jaa Kiekko-153
94Swedish Leaf-291

Pushkov, Viktor

69Russian National Team Postcards-19

Pushor, Jamie

907th Inn. Sketch WHL-128
91Upper Deck-63
91Upper Deck-73
French-63
French-73
917th Inn. Sketch WHL-342
917th Inn. Sketch Memorial Cup-122
91Arena Draft Picks-23
91Arena Draft Picks French-23
91Arena Draft Picks Autographs-23
91Arena Draft Picks Autographs French-23
91Classic-28
91Star Pics-3
91Ultimate Draft-24
91Ultimate Draft French-24
91Classic Four-Sport *-28
Autographs-28A
94Leaf-459
94OPC Premier-478
Special Effects-478
94Topps/OPC Premier-478
Special Effects-478
95Bowman-103
All-Foil-103
95Donruss-337
95Stadium Club-224
Members Only Master Set-224
95Adirondack Red Wings-19
96Be A Player-102
Autographs-102
Autographs Silver-102
96Donruss Canadian Ice-118
Gold Press Proofs-118
Red Press Proofs-118
96SkyBox Impact-157
96Summit-196
Artist's Proofs-196
Ice-196
Metal-196
Premium Stock-196
96Upper Deck-54
96Zenith-147
Artist's Proofs-147
97Donruss-52
Press Proofs Silver-52
Press Proofs Gold-52
97Donruss Limited-136
Exposure-136
97Pacific-215
Copper-215
Emerald Green-215
Ice Blue-215
Red-215
Silver-215
97Score Red Wings-19
Platinum-19
Premier-19
98OPC Chrome-51
Refractors-51
98Topps-51
O-Pee-Chee-51
99Stars Postcards-23
99Upper Deck-220
Exclusives-220
Exclusives 1 of 1-220
99Upper Deck Gold Reserve-220
00Topps Chrome-229
OPC Refractors-229
Refractors-229
00Upper Deck-51
Exclusives Tier 1-51
Exclusives Tier 2-51
00Upper Deck Vintage-107
01Blue Jackets Donatos Pizza-23
01UD Mask Collection-77
Gold-77
03Hartford Wolf Pack-20
03Syracuse Crunch-2
04Syracuse Crunch-3
05Syracuse Crunch-15
06Syracuse Crunch-18

Pusie, Jean

35Diamond Matchbooks Tan 1-53
35O-Pee-Chee V304C-91

Puskas, Chris

90Rayside-Balfour Jr. Canadians-18

Pustinen, Juuso

06Kamloops Blazers-17

Pustovalov, Vladislav

00Russian Hockey League-346

Pustulka, Jeff

93Quebec Pee-Wee Tournament-849

Puterman, Leonard

04Cape Breton Screaming Eagles-15

Putilin, Alexei

98Russian Hockey League-147

Putjkov, Victor

69Swedish Hockey-13
70Swedish Masterserien-21
70Swedish Masterserien-22

Putnik, Walter

93Swedish Semic World Champ Stickers-286

Putzi, Michael

95Swiss HNL-431

Puurula, Joni

01Finnish Cardset-214
02Finnish Cardset-100
03Finnish Cardset-29
04Russian Legion-9

Puustinen, Kari

71Finnish Suomi Stickers-269

Pyatanov, Andrei

02Russian SL-32

Pyatt, Nelson

74NHL Action Stamps-96
76O-Pee-Chee NHL-98
76O-Pee-Chee NHL-396
76Rockies Coke Cans-18
76Rockies Puck Bucks-17
76Topps-98
77O-Pee-Chee NHL-252
77Rockies Coke Cans-16
77Topps-252
78O-Pee-Chee-354

Pyatt, Taylor

97Sudbury Wolves Police-11
98SP Authentic-131
Power Shift-131
Sign of the Times-TP
Sign of the Times Gold-TP
98Upper Deck-408
Exclusives-408
Exclusives 1 of 1-408
Gold Reserve-408
98Sudbury Wolves-21
99Black Diamond-98
Diamond Cut-98
Final Cut-98
99SPx-168
Radiance-168
Spectrum-168
99Upper Deck-319
Exclusives-319
Exclusives 1 of 1-319
99Upper Deck Gold Reserve-319
99Upper Deck MVP SC Edition-213
Gold Script-213
Silver Script-213
Super Script-213
Game-Used Souvenirs-GUTP
ProSign-TP
99Upper Deck Ovation-70
Standing Ovation-70
99Sudbury Wolves-10
99Bowman CHL-35
Gold-35
OPC International-35
Autographs-BA6
Autographs Gold-BA6
Autographs Silver-BA6
Scout's Choice-SC8
99UD Prospects Destination the Show-DS6
99UD Prospects Signatures of Tradition-TP
00BAP Memorabilia-423
Emerald-423
Ruby-423
Sapphire-423
00BAP Parkhurst 2000-P167
00BAP Signature Series-254
Emerald-254
Ruby-254
Sapphire-254
Autographs-216
Autographs Gold-216
00Black Diamond-103
00Crown Royale-133
21st Century Rookies-16
00Private Stock-131
Gold-131
Premiere Date-131
Retail-131
Silver-131
00SP Authentic-60
00Stadium Club-235
00Topps Heritage-65
Chrome Parallel-65
00Topps Premier Plus-93
Blue Ice-93
Game-Used Memorabilia-GPTP
Game-Used Memorabilia-GPJVTP
00Vanguard-134
Pacific Proofs-134
01O-Pee-Chee-231
01O-Pee-Chee Premier Parallel-231
01Parkhurst-222
01Topps-231
OPC Parallel-231
01Topps Heritage-182
02BAP First Edition-231
02Bowman YoungStars-105
Gold-105
Silver-105
Autographs-TP
Jerseys-TP
Patches-TP
Double Stuff-TP
Triple Stuff-TP
Rivals-JLTP
Rivals Patches-13
Sticks-TP
02O-Pee-Chee-280
02O-Pee-Chee Premier Blue Parallel-280
02O-Pee-Chee Premier Red Parallel-280
02O-Pee-Chee Factory Set-280
02Pacific Complete-353
Red-353
02Sabres Team Issue-12
02SP Game Used First Rounder Patches-TP
02SP Game Used Future Fabrics-FFTP
02SP Game Used Future Fabrics Gold-FFTP
02SP Game Used Future Fabrics Rainbow-FFTP
02Topps-280
OPC Blue Parallel-280
OPC Red Parallel-280
Factory Set-280
02Topps Total-37
02Upper Deck-21
Exclusives-21
Bright Futures-TP
02Upper Deck Victory-28
Bronze-28
Gold-28
Silver-28
03Crown Royale-12
Blue-12
Retail-12
03ITG Action-94
03Pacific-44
Blue-44
Red-44
03Pacific Complete-66
Red-66
03Upper Deck MVP-56
Gold Script-56
Silver Script-56
Canadian Exclusives-56
06Canucks Postcards-17
06Gatorade-83
06O-Pee-Chee-485
Rainbow-485

Pyatt, Tom

03Saginaw Spirit-18
04Saginaw Spirit-17
05ITG Heroes/Prosp Toronto Expo Parallel -127
05OHL Bell All-Star Classic-36
05Saginaw Spirit-19
05ITG Heroes and Prospects-127
Autographs-A-TP
Jerseys-GUJ-116
Jerseys Gold-GUJ-116
Emblems-GUE-99
Emblems Gold-GUE-99
Numbers-GUN-99
Numbers Gold-GUN-99
06Saginaw Spirit-1
06ITG Heroes and Prospects-150
06ITG Heroes and Prospects-180
Autographs-ATP
Autographs-ATP2
National Pride-NP05
National Pride Gold-NP05
Update Autographs-ATP2
07ITG Going For Gold World Juniors-20
Autographs-20
Emblems-GUE20
Jerseys-GUJ20
Numbers-GUN20

Pycha, Pavel

91Finnish Semic World Champ Stickers-118
91Swedish Semic World Champ Stickers-118
94Czech APS Extraliga-114
95Czech APS Extraliga-66
96Czech APS Extraliga-251
97Czech APS Extraliga-278
97Czech DS Extraliga-33
97Czech DS Stickers-82
98Czech DS Stickers-76

Pye, Bill

92Rochester Americans Dunkin' Donuts-13
92Rochester Americans Kodak-17
98Odessa Jackalopes-17
99Odessa Jackalopes-5

Pyett, Logan

04Regina Pats-6
05Regina Pats-14
06Regina Pats-14

Pyka, Daniel

02German Berlin Polar Bears Postcards-22

Pyka, Nico

98German DEL-166
99German DEL-51
99German DEL-371
00German Berlin Polar Bears Postcards-18
00German DEL-59
01German Berlin Polar Bears Postcards-20
01German Upper Deck-40
02German Berlin Polar Bears Postcards-23
02German DEL City Press-36
03German Mannheim Eagles Postcards-12
04German Adler Mannheim Eagles Postcards-25
04German Berlin Eisbarens 50th Anniv-74
04German DEL-17
05German DEL-379

Pyka, Reemt

94Finnish Jaa Kiekko-285
94German DEL-233
95German DEL-230
95German DEL-432
96German DEL-82
98German DEL-31
98German DEL-317
99German DEL-133
00German DEL-18
01German Upper Deck-13

Pyke, Derrick

95Halifax Mooseheads-12

Pyle, Jeff

94German First League-563
98Mobile Mysticks-19
99Mobile Mysticks-21
03Gwinnett Gladiators-24
04Gwinnett Gladiators-21

Pyliotis, John

93Amos Les Forestiers-18

Pylypow, Kevin

81Regina Pats-17
82Brandon Wheat Kings-2

Pylypuik, Jay

98San Antonio Iguanas-12

Pylypuik, Pat

88Lethbridge Hurricanes-18
89Lethbridge Hurricanes-17
907th Inn. Sketch WHL-139
92Toledo Storm-10
92Toledo Storm Team Issue-17
93Toledo Storm-9

Pyndt, Anders

98Danish Hockey League-175

Pynnonen, Mikka

98UK Kingston Hawks-3

Pynnonen, Pentti

65Finnish Hellas-113
66Finnish Jaakiekkosarja-198

Pyorala, Mika

01Finnish Cardset-283
02Finnish Cardset-251
03Finnish Cardset-94
04Finnish Cardset-100
Parallel-74
05Finnish Cardset -96
06Finnish Cardset-278

Pysz, Patrik

94German DEL-17
95German DEL-280

Pytel, Henryk

79Panini Stickers-130

Pyyhtia, Juhani

65Finnish Hellas-90

Pyykko, Pauli

78Finnish SM-Liiga-98

Pyymaki, Jarkko

04Finnish Cardset-298
05Finnish Cardset -323
06Finnish Cardset-326

Quackenbush, Bill

44Beehive Group II Photos-60
44Beehive Group II Photos-206
51Berk Ross-3
51Parkhurst-26
52Parkhurst-68
53Parkhurst-100
54Parkhurst-51
54Topps-49
55Bruins Photos-13
83Hall of Fame-235
83Hall of Fame Postcards-C11
85Hall of Fame-235
91Bruins Sports Action Legends-23
91Bruins Sports Action Legends-35
02Parkhurst Reprints-186
02Parkhurst Reprints-300
04ITG Franchises Update-452

Quackenbush, Mike

93Quebec Pee-Wee Tournament-518

Quandt, Andy

93Quebec Pee-Wee Tournament-612

Quapp, Vladimir

94German DEL-105

Quebec, Greg

00Columbus Cottonmouths-14

Quenneville, Chad

95Classic-79
Autographs-19
95Classic Five-Sport *-149
Autographs-149
96Pensacola Ice Pilots-8
97Pensacola Ice Pilots-18
98Pensacola Ice Pilots-7

Quenneville, Joel

79Maple Leafs Postcards-23
79O-Pee-Chee-336
79Rockies Team Issue-18
80O-Pee-Chee-19
80Topps-19
81O-Pee-Chee-78
81O-Pee-Chee Stickers-234
81Rockies Postcards-24
81Topps-W83
83NHL Key Tags-72
83O-Pee-Chee-145
83O-Pee-Chee Stickers-225
83Topps Stickers-225
83Whalers Junior Hartford Courant-14
84O-Pee-Chee-77
84Topps-60
84Whalers Junior Wendy's-15
85O-Pee-Chee-103
85O-Pee-Chee Stickers-170
85Topps-103
85Whalers Junior Wendy's-16
86O-Pee-Chee-118
86O-Pee-Chee Stickers-55
86Topps-118
86Whalers Junior Thomas'-18
87Whalers Jr. Burger King/Pepsi-16
88O-Pee-Chee-3
88Topps-3
88Whalers Junior Ground Round-13
89O-Pee-Chee-211
89Whalers Junior Milk-16
90O-Pee-Chee-418
91ProCards-356
92St. John's Maple Leafs-17
01Topps Archives-49
02Maple Leafs Platinum Collection-89

Quenneville, Justin

04Missouri River Otters-24

Quenneville, Yvon

90Rayside-Balfour Jr. Canadians-19

Quesada, Tony

06Austin Ice Bats-6

Quesnel, Alexandre

06Cape Breton Screaming Eagles-14

Quessy, Anthony

98Val d'Or Foreurs-S1
99Shawinigan Cataractes-4
Signed-4
00Shawinigan Cataractes-7
Signed-7

Quessy, Martin

93Quebec Pee-Wee Tournament-204

Quevillon, Monelle

93Quebec Pee-Wee Tournament-64

Quigley, Dave

87Moncton Hawks-19

Quigley, Jim

93Quebec Pee-Wee Tournament-652

Quilty, Johnny

34Beehive Group I Photos-176
40O-Pee-Chee V301-2-106
43Parade Sportive *-69
45Quaker Oats Photos-106

Quincey, Kyle

02London Knights-19
03Mississauga Ice Dogs-17
04Mississauga Ice Dogs-7
05Beehive-167
Matte-167
05Black Diamond-236
05Hot Prospects-200
Autographed Patch Variation-200
Autographed Patch Variation Gold-200
Hot Materials-HMKQ
Red Hot-200
05Parkhurst-626
Facsimile Auto Parallel-626
Signatures-KQ
05SP Authentic-218
05SP Game Used-207
05SPx-229
Spectrum-229
05The Cup-163
Black Rainbow Rookies-163
Masterpiece Pressplates (Artifacts)-274
Masterpiece Pressplates (Bee Hive)-167
Masterpiece Pressplates (Black Diamond)-236
Masterpiece Pressplates (Ice)-221
Masterpiece Pressplates (Rookie Update)-250
Masterpiece Pressplates SPA Autos-218
Masterpiece Pressplates (SP Game Used)-207
Masterpiece Pressplates SPx Autos-229
Masterpiece Pressplates (Trilogy)-252
Masterpiece Pressplates Ult Coll-203
Masterpiece Pressplates Autographs-163
Platinum Rookies-163
05UD Artifacts-274
05Ultimate Collection-203
Gold-203
05Upper Deck Ice-221
05Upper Deck Rookie Update-250
05Upper Deck Trilogy-252
06Upper Deck MVP Autographs-OAFQ

Quinlan, James

94German First League-178

Quinn, Clayton

97OCN Blizzard-6

Quinn, Dan

83Belleville Bulls-3
84O-Pee-Chee-234
85Flames Red Rooster-23
85O-Pee-Chee-176
86O-Pee-Chee-204
86O-Pee-Chee Stickers-87
86Penguins Kodak-18
87O-Pee-Chee-171
87O-Pee-Chee Stickers-173
87Panini Stickers-147
87Penguins Masks-8
87Penguins Kodak-21
87Topps-171
88O-Pee-Chee-41
88O-Pee-Chee Stickers-236
88Panini Stickers-342
88Topps-41
89O-Pee-Chee-152
89O-Pee-Chee Stickers-234
89Panini Stickers-314
89Penguins Foodland-6A
89Topps-152
90Bowman-65
Tiffany-65
90Canucks Mohawk-25
90O-Pee-Chee-272
90OPC Premier-93
90Panini Stickers-305
90Pro Set-303
90Score-55
Canadian-55
90Score Hottest/Rising Stars-24
90Topps-272
Tiffany-272
90Upper Deck-260
French-260
91Pro Set Platinum-209
91Bowman-376
91Canucks Panini Team Stickers-20
91Flyers J.C. Penney-21
91O-Pee-Chee-393
91OPC Premier-27
91Panini Stickers-27
91Parkhurst-351
French-351
91Pinnacle-84
91Pinnacle-408
French-84
French-408
91Pro Set-209
French-209
91Score American-62
91Score Canadian Bilingual-62
91Score Canadian Bilingual-615
91Score Canadian English-62
91Score Canadian English-615
91Score Rookie/Traded-65T
91Stadium Club-243
91Topps-393
91Upper Deck-358
91Upper Deck-563
French-358
French-563
92Bowman-289
92O-Pee-Chee-264
92Stadium Club-22
92Topps-143
Gold-143G
93Swiss HNL-77
94Be A Player Signature Cards-89
94Leaf-61
94Leaf-413
94Pinnacle 504
Artist's Proofs-504
Rink Collection-504
94Ultra-307
95Bashan Super Stickers-85
95Canada Games NHL POGS-192
95Collector's Choice-70
Player's Club-70
Player's Club Platinum-70
95Donruss-240
95Emotion-126
95Imperial Stickers-85
95Leaf-258
95Metal-106
95Panini Stickers-49
95Score-175
Black Ice Artist's Proofs-175
Black Ice-175
95SkyBox Impact-120
95Stadium Club-142
Members Only Master Set-142
95Summit-116
Artist's Proofs-116
Ice-116
95Topps-261
OPC Inserts-261
95Ultra-281
95Upper Deck Special Edition-SE145
95Upper Deck Special Edition Gold-SE145
95Swiss HNL-541
96Collector's Choice-198
96Donruss-92
Press Proofs-92
96Score-228
Artist's Proofs-228
Dealer's Choice Artist's Proofs-228
Special Artist's Proofs-228
Golden Blades-228
97Score Penguins-14
Platinum-14
Premier-14

Quinn, David

92Cleveland Lumberjacks-9

Quinn, Jim

82Kitchener Rangers-16
83Kitchener Rangers-2

Quinn, Kevin

94Johnstown Chiefs-16

Quinn, Matthew

99Rouyn-Noranda Huskies-16
00Rouyn-Noranda Huskies-3
Signed-3

Quinn, Pat

69Maple Leafs White Border Glossy-30
69O-Pee-Chee-186
Four-in-One-8
70Canucks Royal Bank-13
70Colgate Stamps-72
70Dad's Cookies-107
70Esso Power Players-39
70O-Pee-Chee-120
Deckle-1
70Sargent Promotions Stamps-209
70Topps-120
71Canucks Royal Bank-5
71O-Pee-Chee-122
71Sargent Promotions Stamps-219
71Topps-122
71Toronto Sun-287
72Canucks Nalley's-5
72Flames Postcards-16
72O-Pee-Chee-183
Player Crests-1
72Sargent Promotions Stamps-6
73O-Pee-Chee-61
73Topps-61
74NHL Action Stamps-7
74O-Pee-Chee NHL-286
75O-Pee-Chee NHL-172
75Topps-172
76O-Pee-Chee NHL-289
76O-Pee-Chee NHL-379
84Kings Smokey-23
02Maple Leafs Platinum Collection-73
Autographs-73
04ITG Franchises US East-304
Autographs-A-PQ

Quinnell, Bob

91British Columbia JHL-132
92British Columbia JHL-101
99Corpus Christi IceRays-16

Quinney, Ken

85Nordiques Team Issue-19
85Fredericton Express-14
86Nordiques General Foods-20
87Nordiques General Foods-25
87Nordiques Team Issue-30
88ProCards AHL-112
89Halifax Citadels-18
89ProCards AHL-162
90Nordiques Petro-Canada-36
90Halifax Citadels-19
90ProCards AHL/IHL-458
91Upper Deck-419
French-419
91ProCards-127
93Las Vegas Thunder-20
94Las Vegas Thunder-19
95Las Vegas Thunder-15
96Las Vegas Thunder-17
97Las Vegas Thunder-1
98German DEL-152
99German DEL-95
00German DEL-86

Quint, Deron

93Donruss Team USA-18
93Pinnacle-485
Canadian-485
93Upper Deck-561
93Seattle Thunderbirds-20
93Classic-109
Class of '94-CL5
94Finest-116
Super Team Winners-116
Refractors-116
94Leaf Limited World Juniors USA-10
94Parkhurst SE-SE247
Gold-SE247
94Score-208
Gold-208
Platinum-208
94SP-193
Die Cuts-193
94Upper Deck-524
Electric Ice-524
94Classic Tri-Cards-T76
94Classic Pro Prospects-206
95Bowman-107
All-Foil-107
95Donruss-364
95Donruss Elite-89
Die Cut Stars-89
Die Cut Uncut-89
95Finest-101
Refractors-101
95Jets Team Issue-18
95Metal-188
95Parkhurst International-269
Emerald Ice-269
95Select Certified-129
Mirror Gold-129
95SkyBox Impact-227
95SP-165
95Stadium Club-197
Members Only Master Set-197
95Summit-181
Artist's Proofs-181
Ice-181
95Topps-258
OPC Inserts-258
95Ultra-352
95Upper Deck-498
Electric Ice-498
Electric Ice Gold-498
95Images-74
Gold-74
Autographs-74A
95Signature Rookies-26
Signatures-26
96Collector's Choice-206
96Coyotes Coca-Cola-23
96Donruss-225
Press Proofs-225
96Leaf-143
Press Proofs-143
96Upper Deck-128
96Springfield Falcons-4
97Collector's Choice-202
97Coyotes Face-Off Luncheon -17
97Pacific-304
Copper-304
Emerald Green-304
Ice Blue-304
Red-304
Silver-304
99BAP Millennium-192
Emerald-192
Ruby-192
Sapphire-192
Signatures-192
Signatures Gold-192
99Stadium Club-150
First Day Issue-150
One of a Kind-150
Printing Plates Black-150
Printing Plates Cyan-150
Printing Plates Magenta-150
Printing Plates Yellow-150
01Blue Jackets Donatos Pizza-11
01O-Pee-Chee-264
01O-Pee-Chee Premier Parallel-264
01Parkhurst-217
01Topps-264
OPC Parallel-264
02BAP Sig Series Auto Buybacks 1999-192
02Coyotes Team Issue-5
02Pacific-103
Blue-103
Red-103
03Blackhawks Postcards-20
03ITG Action-481
03Pacific Complete-390
Red-390
03Parkhurst Original Six Chicago-3
05German DEL-310
06German DEL-21

Quintal, Stephane

84Richelieu Riverains-12
88Bruins Postcards-17
88ProCards AHL-153
89Bruins Sports Action-19
90Bruins Sports Action-21
90Pro Set-410
91Pro Set-350
French-350
91Score Canadian Bilingual-437
91Score Canadian English-437
92Bowman-337
92Parkhurst-384
Emerald Ice-384
92Score-242
Canadian-242
92Stadium Club-350
92Topps-484
Gold-484G
93Jets Readers Club-16
93Jets Ruffles-21
93Parkhurst-500
Emerald Ice-500
93Pinnacle-326
Canadian-326
93PowerPlay-475
93Score-412
93Score-509
Gold-509
Canadian-412
Canadian-509
Canadian Gold-509
93Stadium Club-242
Members Only Master Set-242
OPC-242
First Day Issue-242
First Day Issue OPC-242
93Ultra-456
93Upper Deck-529
94Canada Games NHL POGS-258
94Fleer-244
94Leaf-293
94OPC Premier-6
Special Effects-6
94Pinnacle-501
Artist's Proofs-501
Rink Collection-501
94Topps/OPC Premier-6
Special Effects-6
94Ultra-245
95Canadiens Postcards-13
95Canadiens Sheets-8
95Collector's Choice-280
Player's Club-280
Player's Club Platinum-280
95Donruss-314
95Emotion-89
95Panini Stickers-45
95Parkhurst International-117
Emerald Ice-117
95Ultra-257
96Canadiens Postcards-20
96Canadiens Sheets-14
96Team Out-87
97Be A Player-94
Autographs-94
Autographs Die-Cuts-94
Autographs Prismatic Die-Cuts-94
97Canadiens Postcards-15
97Pacific-324
Copper-324
Emerald Green-324
Ice Blue-324
Red-324
Silver-324
98Canadiens Team Issue-15
99BAP Memorabilia-188
Gold-188
Silver-188
99Pacific-208
Copper-208
Emerald Green-208
Gold-208
Ice Blue-208
Premiere Date-208
Red-208
99Panini Stickers-105
99Upper Deck Retro-40
Gold-40
Platinum-40
01Canadiens Postcards-18
01Pacific-91
Extreme LTD-91
Hobby LTD-91
Premiere Date-91
Retail LTD-91
01Pacific Arena Exclusives-91
02BAP First Edition-177
02Canadiens Postcards-1
02NHL Power Play Stickers-57
02Pacific Complete-197
Red-197
03Canadiens Postcards-21
03Pacific Complete-362
Red-362
03Parkhurst Orig Six He Shoots/Scores-10
03Parkhurst Orig Six He Shoots/Scores-10A
03Parkhurst Original Six Montreal-26
Memorabilia-MM3
Memorabilia-MM12
03Upper Deck MVP-230
Gold Script-230
Silver Script-230
Canadian Exclusives-230
05Be A Player Signatures-SQ
05Be A Player Signatures Gold-SQ

Quintin, J.F.

89ProCards IHL-97
90ProCards AHL/IHL-117
92OPC Premier-37
92Score-488
Canadian-488
92Upper Deck-483
92Kansas City Blades-14
92Classic-107
Gold-107
93Ultra-192
Prospects-8
93Upper Deck-21
93Kansas City Blades-12
94Parkhurst-212
Gold-212
94Kansas City Blades-14
95Kansas City Blades-16
96Kansas City Blades-17
99German DEL-253
00German DEL-163
01German Upper Deck-55
02German DEL City Press-58

Quiring, Tyler

91British Columbia JHL-116
93Red Deer Rebels-19
98Huntsville Channel Cats-9

Quirk, Stephen

97Halifax Mooseheads II-15

Qvist, Eetu

04Finnish Cardset-142
Parallel-106
05Finnish Cardset -134
06Finnish Cardset-263

Rabbit, Wacey
02Saskatoon Blades-12
03Saskatoon Blades-21
04Saskatoon Blades-20
05ITG Heroes/Prosp Toronto Expo Parallel -324
05Saskatoon Blades-19
05ITG Heroes and Prospects-324
Autographs Series II-WR
06Providence Bruins-14
06ITG Heroes and Prospects National Pride-NP14
06ITG Heroes and Prospects National Pride Gold-NP14
Rabbitt, Kevin
84Nanaimo Clippers-16
Rabbitt, Pat
81Milwaukee Admirals-1
Raboin, Garrett
03Lincoln Stars-7
04Lincoln Stars-7
04Lincoln Stars Update-41
05Lincoln Stars-8
05Lincoln Stars Update Traded-8T
Raby, Mathieu
98Abilene Aviators-5
00Quebec Citadelles-17
Signed-17
Raby, Philippe
93Quebec Pee-Wee Tournament-1070
Rac, Winfried
93Quebec Pee-Wee Tournament-1521
Racette, Jules
51Laval Dairy Lac St. Jean-12
Rachinsky, Yakov
03Russian Hockey League-118
Rachunek, Ivan
98Czech OFS-283
00Czech OFS-369
01Czech OFS-88
02Czech OFS Plus-39
03Czech OFS Plus-369
03Czech OFS Plus-269
04Czech OFS-301
05Czech HC Hame Zlin-14
06Czech CP Cup Postcards-21
06Czech HC Zlin Hame Postcards-11
06Czech OFS-240
All Stars-11
Rachunek, Karel
97Czech APS Extraliga-61
98Czech OFS-275
99Upper Deck Gold Reserve-345
99Grand Rapids Griffins-19
00Private Stock-134
Gold-134
Premiere Date-134
Retail-134
Silver-134
00Senators Team Issue-18
01BAP Memorabilia-162
Emerald-162
Ruby-162
Sapphire-162
01BAP Signature Series-101
Autographs-101
Autographs Gold-101
01Bowman YoungStars-124
Gold-124
Ice Cubed-124
Autographs-KR
Relics-JKR
Relics-SKR
Relics-DSKR
Rivals-R2
01Senators Team Issue-23
01Topps Own The Game-OTG19
01Upper Deck Victory-250
Gold-250
01Czech National Team Postcards-10
02BAP Sig Series Auto Buybacks 2001-101
02Senators Team Issue-15
02Stadium Club YoungStars Relics-S23
02Czech DS-7
03ITG Action-462
03Senators Postcards-16
03Topps Traded-TT3
Blue-TT3
Gold-TT3
Red-TT3
03Upper Deck MVP-297
Gold Script-297
Silver Script-297
Canadian Exclusives-297
04Czech OFS-319
Stars-43
Racicot, Andre
89ProCards AHL-180
90ProCards AHL/IHL-67
91Bowman-337
91Canadiens Postcards-22
91O-Pee-Chee-450
91Score American-395
91Score Canadian Bilingual-285
91Score Canadian English-285
91Stadium Club-377
91Topps-450
91Upper Deck-377
French-377
91ProCards-78
92Canadiens Postcards-21
92Durivage Panini-49
92OPC Premier-11
92Parkhurst-321
Emerald Ice-321
92Ultra-332
92Upper Deck-430
93Canadiens Postcards-19
93Durivage Score-15
93Leaf-294
93OPC Premier-313
Gold-313
93Pinnacle-332
Canadian-332
93Score-437
Canadian-437
93Stadium Club-26
Members Only Master Set-26
OPC-26
First Day Issue-26
First Day Issue OPC-26
93Topps/OPC Premier-313
Gold-313
93Ultra-355
94Portland Pirates-21
95Indianapolis Ice-18
Racicot, Paolo
917th Inn. Sketch QMJHL-105
92Fort Worth Fire-16
Racine, Bruce
88ProCards IHL-61
89ProCards IHL-152
90ProCards AHL/IHL-517
91ProCards-295
92Cleveland Lumberjacks-14
93St. John's Maple Leafs-19
94St. John's Maple Leafs-21
97Fort Wayne Komets-4
98Fort Wayne Komets-20
99Kansas City Blades Supercuts-15
00Finnish Cardset-186
00Finnish Cardset Masquerade-2
01Finnish Cardset-230
02Finnish Cardset-102
Racine, Dany
93Quebec Pee-Wee Tournament-275
Racine, Jean-Francois
96Quebec Pee-Wee Tournament-560
00UD CHL Prospects-78
01Drummondville Voltigeurs-1
03Memphis RiverKings-17
04Memphis RiverKings-8
06Between The Pipes-21
Autographs-AJFR
06Hot Prospects-179
Red Hot-179
White Hot-179
06O-Pee-Chee-583
Rainbow-583
06SP Game Used Rookie Exclusives Autographs-REJF
06The Cup-107
Autographed Rookie Masterpiece Pressplates-107
Gold Rainbow Autographed Rookie Patches-107
Masterpiece Pressplates (Marquee Rookies)-583
Masterpiece Pressplates (Ultimate Collection)-99
Rookies Black-107
Rookies Platinum-107
06Ultimate Collection-99
06Upper Deck-490
Exclusives Parallel-490
High Gloss Parallel-490
Masterpieces-490
06Toronto Marlies-24
Racine, Yves
89ProCards AHL-317
90Bowman-230
Tiffany-230
90O-Pee-Chee-361
90Topps-361
Tiffany-361
90ProCards AHL/IHL-474
91Bowman-44
91O-Pee-Chee-228
91Panini Stickers-141
91Parkhurst-265
French-265
91Pinnacle-233
French-233
91Pro Set-54
French-54
91Score American-158
91Score Canadian Bilingual-158
91Score Canadian English-158
91Score Young Superstars-37
91Stadium Club-198
91Topps-228
91Upper Deck-498
French-498
92Bowman-353
92O-Pee-Chee-297
92Panini Stickers-119
92Panini Stickers French-119
92Pinnacle-332
French-332
92Score-74
Canadian-74
92Stadium Club-6
92Topps-277
Gold-277G
92Ultra-287
92Upper Deck-142
93Donruss-246
93Durivage Score-34
93Flyers J.C. Penney-20
93Flyers Lineup Sheets-26
93Leaf-15
93Parkhurst-422
Emerald Ice-422
93Pinnacle-372
Canadian-372
93PowerPlay-406
93Score-264
93Score-540
Gold-540
Canadian-264
Canadian-540
Canadian Gold-540
93Stadium Club-304
Members Only Master Set-304
First Day Issue-304
93Upper Deck-194
94Canadiens Postcards-20
94Leaf-388
94OPC Premier-67
94OPC Premier-426
Special Effects-67
Special Effects-426
94Parkhurst-168
Gold-168
94Pinnacle-391
Artist's Proofs-391
Rink Collection-391
94Score-162
Gold-162
Platinum-162
94Stadium Club-239
Members Only Master Set-239
First Day Issue-239
Super Team Winner Cards-239
94Topps/OPC Premier-176
94Topps/OPC Premier-426
Special Effects-176
Special Effects-426
94Ultra-316
94Upper Deck-171
Electric Ice-171
95Canada Games NHL POGS-154
95Canadiens Postcards-14
95Pinnacle-178
Artist's Proofs-178
Rink Collection-178
95Score-221
Black Ice Artist's Proofs-221
Black Ice-221
95Topps-138
OPC Inserts-138
95Finnish Semic World Championships-80
95Swedish World Championships Stickers-7
97Be A Player-27
Autographs-27
Autographs Die-Cuts-27
Autographs Prismatic Die-Cuts-27
97Pacific Invincible NHL Regime-30
98Finnish Keraillysarja-102
99German Adler Mannheim Eagles Postcards-14
99German DEL-14
01German Upper Deck-173
02German DEL City Press-252
03German DEL-85
03German Mannheim Eagles Postcards-11
04Thetford Mines Prolab-14
Raczka, Marek
93Quebec Pee-Wee Tournament-1501
Radant, Detlef
83Swedish Semic VM Stickers-153
04German Berlin Eisbaeren 50th Anniv-7
Radbjer, Ulf
84Swedish Semic Elitserien-137
Radchenko, Sergei
97Wheeling Nailers-17
97Wheeling Nailers Photo Pack-17
99Knoxville Speed-12
00Fort Wayne Komets-16
01New Mexico Scorpions-1
Rademaker, Axel
99German DEL-407
Radevic, Radim
94Czech APS Extraliga-17
96Czech APS Extraliga-109
97Czech DS Stickers-281
Radivojevic, Branko
00Belleville Bulls-19
00UD CHL Prospects-44
01BAP Memorabilia-343
Emerald-343
Ruby-343
Sapphire-343
01Parkhurst-339
01SPx-212
01UD Mask Collection-163
Gold-163
01UD Premier Collection-104
01UD Top Shelf-134
02Bowman YoungStars-154
Gold-154
Silver-154
Autographs-BR
Jerseys-BR
Patches-BR
Double Stuff-BR
Triple Stuff-BR
Rivals-BRPB
Rivals Patches-1
Sticks-BR
02Coyotes Team Issue-15
02O-Pee-Chee-273
02O-Pee-Chee Premier Blue Parallel-273
02O-Pee-Chee Premier Red Parallel-273
02O-Pee-Chee Factory Set-273
02SPx-120
02Topps-273
OPC Blue Parallel-273
OPC Red Parallel-273
Factory Set-273
02UD Foundations-139
02UD Piece of History-145
02Upper Deck-219
Exclusives-219
02Upper Deck Vintage-343
03Coyotes Postcards-18
03ITG Action-497
Jerseys-M66
03Pacific Complete-392
Red-392
03Topps C55 Relics-TRBRA
03Upper Deck-394
Canadian Exclusives-394
HG-394
UD Exclusives-394
03Upper Deck MVP-327
Gold Script-327
Silver Script-327
Canadian Exclusives-327
04Czech OFS-258
Stars-36
05Flyers Team Issue-16
Radja, Mike
03Waterloo Blackhawks-9
Radke, Al
91British Columbia JHL-152
Radke, Kyle
04North Dakota Fighting Sioux-21
Radlein, Peter
87Brockville Braves-25
Radmall, Adam
02UK Coventry Blaze-8
03UK Coventry Blaze-7
03UK Coventry Blaze Calendars-11
Radoslovich, Matt
03Boston University Terriers-23
05Quad City Mallards-14
06Quad City Mallards-12
Radulay, Tibor
05Ottawa 67's-22
Radulov, Alexander
04Russian Under-18 Team-22
04Quebec Remparts-10
04ITG Heroes and Prospects-219
05ITG Heroes/Prosp Toronto Expo '05-219
05ITG Heroes/Prosp Toronto Expo Parallel -137
05Extreme Top Prospects Signature Edition-S24
05Quebec Remparts-2
05Quebec Remparts Signature Series-2
05ITG Heroes and Prospects-137
Autographs-A-AR
He Shoots-He Scores Prizes-41
06Be A Player-217
06Beehive-131
Blue-131
Gold-131
Matte-131
Red Facsimile Signatures-131
Wood-131
06Flair Showcase-317
06Hot Prospects-121
Red Hot-121
White Hot-121
Hotagraphs-HRA
06ITG International Ice-70
Gold-70
Autographs-AAR
Quad Patch-QP06
Quad Patch Gold-QP06
06ITG Ultimate Memorabilia Future Star-19
06ITG Ultimate Memorabilia Future Star Gold-19
06ITG Ultimate Memorabilia Future Star Autos-17
06ITG Ultimate Memorabilia Future Star Autos Gold-17
06ITG Ultimate Memorabilia R.O.Y. Autos-4
06ITG Ultimate Memorabilia R.O.Y. Autos Gold-4
06ITG Ultimate Memorabilia R.O.Y. Emblems-4
06ITG Ultimate Memorabilia R.O.Y. Emblems Gold-4
06ITG Ultimate Memorabilia R.O.Y. Jerseys-4
06ITG Ultimate Memorabilia R.O.Y. Jerseys Gold-4
06ITG Ultimate Memorabilia R.O.Y. Numbers-4
06ITG Ultimate Memorabilia R.O.Y. Numbers Gold-4
06ITG Ultimate Memorabilia Triple Thread Jerseys-14
06ITG Ultimate Memorabilia Triple Thread Jerseys Gold-14
06O-Pee-Chee-567
Rainbow-567
06SP Authentic-188
Limited-188
Sign of the Times Duals-STWR
06SP Game Used-127
Gold-127
Rainbow-127
Autographs-127
Rookie Exclusives Autographs-REAR
06SPx-195
Spectrum-195
06The Cup-174
Autographed NHL Shields Duals-DASIA
Autographed NHL Shields Duals-DASMR
Autographed NHL Shields Duals-DASRA
Autographed Rookie Masterpiece Pressplates-174
Enshrinements-ERA
Gold Rainbow Autographed Rookie Patches-174
Honorable Numbers-HNRA
Masterpiece Pressplates (Bee Hive)-131
Masterpiece Pressplates (Marquee Rookies)-567
Masterpiece Pressplates (SP Authentic Autographs)-188
Masterpiece Pressplates (SP Game Used)-127
Masterpiece Pressplates (SPx Autographs)-195
Masterpiece Pressplates (Sweet Beginnings)-136
Masterpiece Pressplates (Ultimate Collection Autographs)-117
Masterpiece Pressplates (Victory)-310
NHL Shields Duals-DSHAM
NHL Shields Duals-DSHKR
NHL Shields Duals-DSHRE
Rookies Black-174
Rookies Platinum-174
Scripted Swatches-SSRA
Signature Patches-SPAR
06UD Artifacts-247
06Ultimate Collection-117
Rookies Autographed NHL Shields-117
Rookies Autographed Patches-117
Signatures-US-RA
Ultimate Debut Threads Jerseys-DJ-AR
Ultimate Debut Threads Jerseys Autographs-DJ-AR
Ultimate Debut Threads Patches-DJ-AR
Ultimate Debut Threads Patches Autographs-DJ-AR
06Ultra-243
06Ultra-245
Gold Medallion-243
Ice Medallion-243
06Upper Deck-476
Exclusives Parallel-476
High Gloss Parallel-476
Masterpieces-476
Rookie Headliners-RH28
06Upper Deck Sweet Shot-136
Rookie Jerseys Autographs-136
Signature Shots/Saves-SSRA
Signature Shots/Saves Ice Signings-SSIAR
Signature Shots/Saves Sticks-SSSRA
06Upper Deck Victory-310
06ITG Heroes and Prospects-125
06ITG Heroes and Prospects-161
Autographs-AAR
Autographs-AAR2
Complete AHL Logos-AHL12
Complete Jerseys-CJ15
Jerseys-GUJ64
Emblems-GUE64
Numbers-GUN64
Memorial Cup Champions-MC11
Quad Emblems-QE11
Triple Memorabilia-TM06
Triple Memorabilia-TM09
Triple Memorabilia Gold-TM06
Update Autographs-AAR2
07Upper Deck All-Star Game Redemptions-AS8
07Upper Deck Rookie Class -18
07Upper Deck Rookie Class C-Card Insert-CC6
Radulov, Igor
01Mississauga Ice Dogs-19
02BAP Memorabilia-342
02BAP Ultimate Memorabilia-82
02Pacific Calder-110
Silver-110
02Pacific Complete-595
Red-595
02SP Authentic-202
02Upper Deck Rookie Update-173
02Norfolk Admirals-19
03Blackhawks Postcards-21
03ITG Action-200
03Parkhurst Original Six Chicago-17
03Private Stock Reserve-21
Blue-21
Red-21
Retail-21
03SPx Big Futures-BF-IR
03SPx Big Futures Limited-BF-IR
03Upper Deck-43
Canadian Exclusives-43
HG-43
03Upper Deck MVP-98
Gold Script-98
Silver Script-98
Canadian Exclusives-98
03Upper Deck Victory-41
Bronze-41
Gold-41
Silver-41
Freshman Flashback-FF11
04Russian Back to Russia-40
04Norfolk Admirals-17
Radums, Nate
04St. Cloud State Huskies-23
Raduns, Nate
03St. Cloud State Huskies-23
05St. Cloud State Huskies-22
06St. Cloud State Huskies-23
Rae, Celena
06Stars Team Postcards-26
Raeder, Cap
88Kings Postcards-23
88Kings Smokey-20
Raemy, Real
99Swiss Panini Stickers-96
01Swiss HNL-457
Raess, Rene
93Swiss HNL-496
Rafalski, Brian
91Upper Deck Czech World Juniors-78
95Swedish Leaf-172
98Finnish Keraillysarja-32
99BAP Memorabilia-67
Gold-67
Silver-67
99BAP Millennium-151
Emerald-151
Ruby-151
Sapphire-151
Signatures-151
Signatures Gold-151
Calder Candidates Ruby-C31
Calder Candidates Emerald-C31
Calder Candidates Sapphire-C31
99Black Diamond-53
Diamond Cut-53
Final Cut-53
99Devils Team Issue-21
99Pacific Dynagon Ice-119
Blue-119
Copper-119
Gold-119
Premiere Date-119
99Pacific Omega-139
Copper-139
Gold-139
Ice Blue-139
Premiere Date-139
99Panini Stickers-82
99Panini Stickers-358
99SP Authentic-106
99Stadium Club-189
First Day Issue-189
One of a Kind-189
Printing Plates Black-189
Printing Plates Cyan-189
Printing Plates Magenta-189
Printing Plates Yellow-189
99Topps Premier Plus-111
Parallel-111
99Ultimate Victory-101
1/1-101
Parallel-101
Parallel 100-101
99Finnish Cardset-161
Aces High-S-4
Par Avion-3
00BAP Memorabilia-312
Emerald-312
Ruby-312
Sapphire-312
Promos-312
00BAP Mem Chicago Sportsfest Copper-312
00BAP Memorabilia Chicago Sportsfest Blue-312
00BAP Memorabilia Chicago Sportsfest Gold-312
00BAP Memorabilia Chicago Sportsfest Ruby-312
00BAP Memorabilia Chicago Sun-Times Ruby-312
00BAP Memorabilia Chicago Sun-Times Gold-312
00BAP Mem Chicago Sun-Times Sapphire-312
00BAP Mem Toronto Fall Expo Copper-312
00BAP Memorabilia Toronto Fall Expo Gold-312
00BAP Memorabilia Toronto Fall Expo Ruby-312
00BAP Parkhurst 2000-P67
00BAP Signature Series-42
Emerald-42
Ruby-42
Sapphire-42
Autographs-175
Autographs Gold-175
00Devils Team Issue-18
00O-Pee-Chee-116
00O-Pee-Chee Parallel-116
00Pacific-242
Copper-242
Gold-242
Ice Blue-242
Premiere Date-242
00Paramount-148
Copper-148
Gold-148
Holo-Gold-148
Holo-Silver-148
Ice Blue-148
Premiere Date-148
00Stadium Club-185
00Topps/OPC-116
Parallel-116
00Topps Chrome-90
OPC Refractors-90
Refractors-90
00Upper Deck-334
Exclusives Tier 1-334
Exclusives Tier 2-334
01BAP Memorabilia-19
Emerald-19
Ruby-19
Sapphire-19
01Devils Team Issue-19
01Parkhurst-78
Gold-78
Silver-78
01UD Mask Collection-58
Gold-58
01Upper Deck-335
Exclusives-335
02BAP First Edition-220
02BAP Signature Series-57
Autographs-57
Autograph Buybacks 1999-151
Autograph Buybacks 2000-175
Autographs Gold-57
02Devils Team Issue-22
02O-Pee-Chee-160
02O-Pee-Chee Premier Blue Parallel-160
02O-Pee-Chee Premier Red Parallel-160
02O-Pee-Chee Factory Set-160
02Pacific-228
Blue-228
Red-228
02Pacific Complete-204
Red-204
02Parkhurst-159
Bronze-159
Gold-159
Silver-159
Hardware-N5
02Topps-160
OPC Blue Parallel-160
OPC Red Parallel-160
Factory Set-160
02Topps Total-359
02Upper Deck-349
Exclusives-349
02Upper Deck Beckett UD Promos-349
02Upper Deck MVP-106
Gold-106
Classics-106
Golden Classics-106
02Upper Deck Vintage-154
02Upper Deck Vintage-278
02Finnish Cardset-103
03Devils Team Issue-28
03ITG Action-317
Jerseys-M67
03O-Pee-Chee-3
03OPC Blue-3
03OPC Gold-3
03OPC Red-3
03Pacific-205
Blue-205
Red-205
03Pacific Complete-7
Red-7
03Topps-3
Blue-3
Gold-3
Red-3
03Upper Deck-361
Canadian Exclusives-361
HG-361
UD Exclusives-361
03Upper Deck MVP-253
Gold Script-253
Silver Script-253
Canadian Exclusives-253
03Czech Stadion-538
04Upper Deck-104
Canadian Exclusives-104
HG Glossy Gold-104
HG Glossy Silver-104
World Cup Tribute-BLBR
05Be A Player Dual Signatures-BS
05Be A Player Signatures-FA
05Be A Player Signatures Gold-FA
05Be A Player Triple Signatures-DEV
05Black Diamond-53
Emerald-53
Gold-53
Onyx-53
Ruby-53
05Devils Team Issue-12
05Panini Stickers-83
05Parkhurst-289
Facsimile Auto Parallel-289
True Colors-TCNJD
True Colors-TCNJD
True Colors-TCNJNY
True Colors-TCNJNY
05SP Authentic Sign of the Times-BR
05SP Authentic Sign of the Times Duals-DBR
05SP Game Used Authentic Fabrics Quad-EMMR
05SP Game Used Authentic Patches Quad -EMMR
05SP Game Used Awesome Authentics-AA-RA
05SP Game Used SIGnificance-RA
05SP Game Used SIGnificance Gold-S-RA
05SP Game Used Significant Numbers-SN-BR
05SP Game Used Statscriptions-ST-RA
05SPx Winning Combos-WC-SR
05SPx Winning Combos Gold-WC-SR
05SPx Winning Combos Spectrum-WC-SR
05The Cup Master Pressplate Rookie Update-202
05Ultimate Coll National Heroes Jersey-NHJRA
05Ultimate Coll National Heroes Patch-NHPRA
05Ultra-120
Gold-120
Ice-120
05Upper Deck-368
Jerseys Series II-J2RK
Notable Numbers-N-BRA
05Upper Deck MVP-236
Gold-236
Platinum-236
05Upper Deck Rookie Update-202
Inspirations Patch Rookies-202
05Upper Deck Victory-118
Black-118
Gold-118
Silver-118
06Be A Player-59
Autographs-59
Signatures-RA
Signatures 10-64
Signatures Duals-DER
06Devils Team Set-21
06Flair Showcase Stitches-SSRA
06Fleer-118
Tiffany-118
06O-Pee-Chee-295
Rainbow-295
06Panini Stickers-80
06The Cup NHL Shields Duals-DSHSR
06Ultra-116
Gold Medallion-116
Ice Medallion-116
06Upper Deck Arena Giveaways-NJD4
06Upper Deck-117
Exclusives Parallel-117
High Gloss Parallel-117
Masterpieces-117
Signature Sensations-SSBR
06Upper Deck MVP-175
Gold Script-175
Super Script-175
Jerseys-OJPR
Jerseys-OJRW
06Upper Deck Ovation-130
06Upper Deck Victory-120
06Upper Deck Victory Black-120
06Upper Deck Victory Gold-120
07Upper Deck Victory-3
Black-3
Gold-3
Raffainer, Raeto
02Swiss HNL-63
Raffl, Thomas
05Swift Current Broncos-4
Raglan, Clare
44Beehive Group II Photos-137
51Parkhurst-36
53Parkhurst-79
Raglan, Herb
84Kingston Canadians-24
87Blues Kodak-21
87Blues Team Issue-18
88Blues Kodak-18
88Blues Team Issue-18
89Blues Kodak-25
90Pro Set-525
91Nordiques Petro-Canada-24
91Pro Set-470
French-470
91Score Canadian Bilingual-536
91Score Canadian English-536
92Nordiques Petro-Canada-25
Ragnarsson, Marcus
89Swedish Semic Elitserien Stickers-59
90Swedish Semic Elitserien Stickers-281
91Swedish Semic Elitserien Stickers-62
92Swedish Semic Elitserien Stickers-80
93Swedish Semic Elitserien-53
94Swedish Leaf-224
95Be A Player-164
Signatures-S164
Signatures Die Cuts-S164
95Bowman-111
All-Foil-111
Bowman's Best-BB29
Bowman's Best Refractors-BB29
95Donruss-264
Rated Rookies-13
95Donruss Elite-38
Die Cut Stars-38
Die Cut Uncut-38
Rookies-7
95Finest-76
Refractors-76
95Leaf Limited-78
Rookie Phenoms-1
95Metal-189
95Parkhurst International-519
95Parkhurst International-531
Emerald Ice-519
Emerald Ice-531
Parkie's Trophy Picks-PP41
95Select Certified-138
Mirror Gold-138
95SkyBox Impact-220
95SP-132
95Stadium Club-148
Members Only Master Set-148
95Summit-195
Artist's Proofs-195
Ice-195
95Topps-287
OPC Inserts-287
95Ultra-353
High Speed-15
95Upper Deck-439
Electric Ice-439
Electric Ice Gold-439
95Zenith-141
Rookie Roll Call-8
95Swedish Globe World Championships-18
95Swedish World Championships Stickers-144
96Collector's Choice-236
96Donruss-234
Press Proofs-234
96Donruss Canadian Ice-83
Gold Press Proofs-83
Red Press Proofs-83
96Fleer-101
Rookie Sensations-8
96Fleer Picks-126
96Leaf-183
Press Proofs-183
96Leaf Limited-42
Gold-42
96Leaf Preferred-52
Press Proofs-52
Steel-13
Steel Gold-13
96Metal Universe-140
96Pinnacle-207
Artist's Proofs-207
Foil-207
Premium Stock-207
Rink Collection-207
96Score-242
Artist's Proofs-242
Dealer's Choice Artist's Proofs-242
Special Artist's Proofs-242
Golden Blades-242
96SkyBox Impact-118
NHL on Fox-18
96Summit-165
Artist's Proofs-165
Ice-165
Metal-165
Premium Stock-165
96Team Out-88
96Topps Picks Rookie Stars-RS7
96Topps Picks Rookie Stars OPC-RS7
96Upper Deck-148
96Zenith-79
Artist's Proofs-79
96Swedish Semic Wien-49
97Collector's Choice-222
97Pacific Dynagon Best Kept Secrets-86
97Panini Stickers-234
97Sharks Fleer All-Star Sheet-6
97Upper Deck-149
98Be A Player-117
Press Release-117
98BAP Gold-117
98BAP Autographs-117
98BAP Autographs Gold-117
98BAP Tampa Bay All Star Game-117
98Panini Stickers-208
98UD Choice-178
Prime Choice Reserve-178
Reserve-178
98Upper Deck-166
Exclusives-166
Exclusives 1 of 1-166
Gold Reserve-166
99BAP Memorabilia-206
Gold-206
Silver-206
99Ultimate Victory-72
1/1-72
Parallel-72
Parallel 100-72
00BAP Memorabilia-305
Emerald-305
Ruby-305
Sapphire-305
Promos-305
00BAP Mem Chicago Sportsfest Copper-305
00BAP Memorabilia Chicago Sportsfest Blue-305
00BAP Memorabilia Chicago Sportsfest Gold-305
00BAP Memorabilia Chicago Sportsfest Ruby-305
00BAP Memorabilia Chicago Sun-Times Ruby-305
00BAP Memorabilia Chicago Sun-Times Gold-305
00BAP Mem Chicago Sun-Times Sapphire-305
00BAP Mem Toronto Fall Expo Copper-305
00BAP Memorabilia Toronto Fall Expo Gold-305
00BAP Memorabilia Toronto Fall Expo Ruby-305
00BAP Parkhurst 2000-P156
00Pacific-446
Copper-446
Gold-446
Ice Blue-446
Premiere Date-446
00Panini Stickers-203
01Parkhurst-197
01Sharks Postcards-11
01Upper Deck Victory-293
Gold-293
02BAP First Edition-193
02BAP Sig Series Auto Buybacks 1998-117
02Pacific Complete-191
Red-191
02Topps Total-294
02Upper Deck Vintage-213
03Flyers Postcards-17
03ITG Action-451
03Pacific Complete-400
Red-400
04Swedish Alfabilder Alfa Stars-17
04Swedish Alfabilder Proof Parallels-17
Ragot, Mike
85Kamloops Blazers-20
Ragulin, Alexander
69Russian National Team Postcards-5
69Swedish Hockey-14
70Finnish Jaakiekko-14
70Russian National Team Postcards-5
70Swedish Hockey-318
70Swedish Masterserien-21
70Swedish Masterserien-23
70Swedish Masterserien-31
70Swedish Masterserien-66
70Swedish Masterserien-126
70Swedish Masterserien-129
71Finnish Suomi Stickers-13
71Swedish Hockey-32
72Finnish Jaakiekko-32
72Finnish Hellas-65
72Finnish Panda Toronto-58
72Finnish Semic World Championship-5
72Swedish Semic World Championship-5
73Finnish Jaakiekko-14
73Russian National Team-12
73Swedish Stickers-79
74Finnish Jenkki-54
74Swedish Semic World Champ Stickers-27
91Future Trends Canada '72-65
91Future Trends Canada '72 French-65
91Finnish Semic World Champ Stickers-242
91Swedish Semic World Champ Stickers-242
03Czech Stadion-651
04Ultimate Collection-49
04Upper Deck-205
Canadian Exclusives-205
HG Glossy Gold-205
HG Glossy Silver-205
Ragusett, Dan
95Waterloo Blackhawks -16
Rahikainen, Riku
01Finnish Cardset-239
03Fresno Falcons-15
06Finnish Cardset-256
Rahkonen, Antti
95Finnish SISU-314
96Finnish SISU Redline-124
Rahm, Niklas
92Swedish Semic Elitserien Stickers-133
93Swedish Semic Elitserien-106
95Swedish Leaf-232
95Swedish Upper Deck-77
98Swedish UD Choice-105
00Swedish Upper Deck-63
Raikkonen, Mikko
66Finnish Jaakiekkosarja-168
70Finnish Jaakiekko-251
71Finnish Suomi Stickers-217
72Finnish Jaakiekko-166
73Finnish Jaakiekko-232
Railio, Seppo
72Finnish Jaakiekko-109
Raimondi, Lenny
93Quebec Pee-Wee Tournament-1281
Rainville, Kevin
01Drummondville Voltigeurs-20
Raisanen, Pertti
71Finnish Suomi Stickers-314
Raiski, Andrei
99Russian Hockey League-NNO
Raissle, David
01Swiss HNL-477
02Swiss HNL-448
Raitanen, Pasi
97UK Kingston Hawks Stickers-17
98UK Kingston Hawks-19
99UK Hull Thunder-15
03UK Sheffield Steelers-20
Raitanen, Rauli
92Finnish Jyvas-Hyva Stickers-203
93Finnish Jyvas-Hyva Stickers-358
93Finnish SISU-229
93Finnish SISU Promos-NNO
93Swedish Semic World Champ Stickers-73
94Finnish SISU-48
94Finnish SISU-381
94Finnish Jaa Kiekko-38
95Finnish SISU-363
95Finnish SISU Limited-21
95Finnish Semic World Championships-51
98Finnish Keraillysarja-266
Raiter, Mark
88Saskatoon Blades-5
90Saskatoon Blades-5
907th Inn. Sketch WHL-84
91Saskatoon Blades-5
917th Inn. Sketch WHL-103
95Birmingham Bulls-6
Rajala, Kari
65Finnish Hellas-76
98Finnish Keraillysarja-37
99Finnish Cardset-224
00Finnish Cardset-25
01Finnish Cardset-201
Rajala, Mika
72Finnish Jaakiekko-315
73Finnish Jaakiekko-116
78Finnish SM-Liiga-162
Rajala, Olli-Pekka
80Finnish Mallasjuoma-127
Rajamaki, Erkki
00Finnish Cardset-261
01Finnish Cardset-221
02Finnish Cardset-252
03Finnish Cardset-52
04Worcester IceCats-11
06Finnish Cardset-9
Signature Sensations-2
Rajamaki, Tommi
94Finest-123
Super Team Winners-123
Refractors-123
94Parkhurst SE-SE226
Gold-SE226
94Upper Deck-512
Electric Ice-512
94Finnish SISU-315
94Finnish SISU NHL Draft-5
95Finnish SISU-355
96Finnish SISU Redline-151
98Finnish Keraillysarja-234
99Finnish Cardset-328
00Finnish Cardset-95

02Swedish SHL-101
Parallel-101
03Swedish Elite-124
Silver-124
04Swedish Elitset-122
Gold-122
Rajaniemi, Vesa
78Finnish SM-Liiga-82
Rajnoha, Pavel
94Czech APS Extraliga-184
95Czech APS Extraliga-184
97Czech APS Extraliga-58
98Czech DS Stickers-292
98Czech OFS-305
Rakhmatullin, Ashkat
02Russian Hockey League-74
Rakos, Daniel
05Swift Current Broncos-6
06Swift Current Broncos-13
Rakovsky, Karl
99Czech Score Blue 2000-96
99Czech Score Red Ice 2000-96
Raleigh, Don
44Beehive Group II Photos-355
51Parkhurst-93
52Parkhurst-99
53Parkhurst-68
54Parkhurst-68
54Topps-53
Rallo, Greg
06Idaho Steelheads-11
Ralph, Brad
99Black Diamond-103
Diamond Cut-103
Final Cut-103
99O-Pee-Chee-275
99O-Pee-Chee Chrome-275
99O-Pee-Chee Chrome Refractors-275
99SP Authentic-135
99Topps/OPC-275
99Topps/OPC Chrome-275
Refractors-275
99Upper Deck MVP SC Edition-207
Gold Script-207
Silver Script-207
Super Script-207
99Bowman CHL-29
Gold-29
OPC International-29
Autographs-BA12
Autographs Gold-BA12
Autographs Silver-BA12
02Augusta Lynx-72
Ralph, Brittny
98Minnesota Golden Gophers Women-19
Ralph, Jason
96Flint Generals-16
01Bakersfield Condors-17
02Bakersfield Condors-13
03Bakersfield Condors-23
05Rockford Ice Hogs-14
06Rockford IceHogs -20
Ralph, Jim
81Ottawa 67's-19
83Springfield Indians-2
85Nova Scotia Oilers-15
88ProCards AHL-224
Ralph, Jon
04Sioux City Musketeers-19
Ralston, Timothy
93Quebec Pee-Wee Tournament-1660
Ram, Jamie
90Michigan Tech Huskies-26
91Michigan Tech Huskies-21
91Michigan Tech Huskies-34
93Michigan Tech Huskies-12
94Binghamton Rangers-16
94Classic-59
Gold-59
All-Americans-AA8
95Binghamton Rangers-18
96Leaf-235
Press Proofs-235
96Kentucky Thoroughblades-15
96Collector's Edge Ice-21
Prism-21
97Kentucky Thoroughblades-13
98Cincinnati Mighty Ducks-12
01Finnish Cardset-247
02Finnish Cardset-104
02Swedish SHL-145
02Swedish SHL-283
Parallel-145
Parallel-283
03Russian Hockey League-145
Ramage, Rob
79Rockies Team Issue-19
80O-Pee-Chee-213
80Topps-213
81O-Pee-Chee-79
81O-Pee-Chee Stickers-154
81O-Pee-Chee Stickers-229
81Post Standups-21
81Rockies Postcards-25
81Topps-W84
82O-Pee-Chee-310
82O-Pee-Chee Stickers-223
82Post Cereal-11
82Topps Stickers-223
83O-Pee-Chee-319
83O-Pee-Chee Stickers-130
83Puffy Stickers-16
83Topps Stickers-130
84O-Pee-Chee-190
84O-Pee-Chee Stickers-62
84O-Pee-Chee Stickers-136
847-Eleven Discs-43
84Topps-134
85O-Pee-Chee-196
857-Eleven Credit Cards-17
86O-Pee-Chee-17
86O-Pee-Chee Stickers-180
86Topps-17
87Blues Kodak-22
87O-Pee-Chee-160
87O-Pee-Chee Stickers-20
87Panini Stickers-306
87Topps-160
88Flames Postcards-1
88O-Pee-Chee-244
88O-Pee-Chee Stickers-84
89Kraft-39
90Bowman-162
Tiffany-162
90Kraft-44
90Maple Leafs Postcards-16
90O-Pee-Chee-317
90Panini Stickers-280
90Pro Set-288
90Score-36
Canadian-36
90Topps-317
Tiffany-317
90Upper Deck-62
French-62
91Bowman-154
91Maple Leafs Panini Team Stickers-20
91O-Pee-Chee-55
91OPC Premier-76
91Panini Stickers-96
91Pinnacle-228
French-228
91Pro Set-232
91Pro Set-407
French-232
French-407
91Score American-233
91Score Canadian Bilingual-573
91Score Canadian English-573
91Score Rookie/Traded-23T
91Stadium Club-239
91Topps-55
92Blues UD Best of the Blues-21
92Parkhurst-175
Emerald Ice-175
92Pinnacle-389
French-389
92Pro Set-177
92Score-351
Canadian-351
92Ultra-413
92Upper Deck-105
93Canadiens Postcards-20
93Flyers J.C. Penney-16
93Flyers Lineup Sheets-27
93PowerPlay-407
93Score-36
93Score-653
Gold-653
Canadian-36
Canadian-653
Canadian Gold-653
93Topps Premier Finest-12
02Fleer Throwbacks-12
Gold-12
Platinum-12
06Parkhurst-103
06Parkhurst-211
06Parkhurst-220
Autographs-103
Autographs-211
Autographs-220
Rambo, Dean
89Saskatoon Blades-24
90Saskatoon Blades-8
907th Inn. Sketch WHL-76
Ramen, Marcus
94Swedish Leaf-167
Ramholt, Arne
95Swiss HNL-294
96Swiss HNL-280
98Swiss Power Play Stickers-315
99Swiss Panini Stickers-110
01Swiss EV Zug Postcards-11
01Swiss HNL-176
02Swiss HNL-265
04Swiss Davos Postcards-23
Ramholt, Tim
01Swiss HNL-6
02Swiss HNL-43
03Cape Breton Screaming Eagles-6
Ramo, Karri
04Finnish Cardset-274
06Be A Player-230
06Flair Showcase-328
06Hot Prospects-193
06SP Authentic-175
Limited-175
06Springfield Falcons-10
06The Cup-158
Autographed Rookie Masterpiece Pressplates-158
Gold Rainbow Autographed Rookie Patches-158
Masterpiece Pressplates (SP Authentic Autographs)-175
Masterpiece Pressplates (Sweet Beginnings)-153
Masterpiece Pressplates (Ultimate Collection)-95
Rookies Black-158
Rookies Platinum-158
06UD Artifacts-257
06Ultimate Collection-95
06Upper Deck-474
Exclusives Parallel-474
High Gloss Parallel-474
Masterpieces-474
06Upper Deck Sweet Shot-153
Rookie Jerseys Autographs-153
06Finnish Cardset-25
Superior Snatchers-9
Superior Snatchers Gold-9
Superior Snatchers Silver-9
06AHL Top Prospects-42
Ramo, Mikko
01Finnish Cardset-308
02Finnish Cardset-257
03Finnish Cardset-113
06Swedish SHL Elitset-249
Ramoser, Roland
91British Columbia JHL-24
96German DEL-326
98German DEL-60
99German DEL-28
Rampa, Pekka
73Finnish Jaakiekko-189
Rampf, Sven
94German First League-583
98German DEL-243
99German DEL-162
00German DEL-15
Rampton, Joey
83Sault Ste. Marie Greyhounds-19
Ramsay, Beattie
25Dominion Chocolates-59
Ramsay, Bruce
92Thunder Bay Thunder Hawks-19
93Thunder Bay Senators-10
94Thunder Bay Senators-18
95Milwaukee Admirals Postcards-10
95Thunder Bay Senators-19
96Grand Rapids Griffins-18
97Grand Rapids Griffins-12
98Grand Rapids Griffins-15
Ramsay, Chad
96OCN Blizzard-19
Ramsay, Craig
72O-Pee-Chee-262
72Sabres Postcards-15
72Sargent Promotions Stamps-38
73O-Pee-Chee-213
74NHL Action Stamps-40
74O-Pee-Chee NHL-305
74Sabres Postcards-18
75O-Pee-Chee NHL-271
75Topps-271
76O-Pee-Chee NHL-78
76Topps-78
77Coca-Cola-19
77O-Pee-Chee NHL-191
77Topps-191
78O-Pee-Chee-9
78Topps-9
79O-Pee-Chee-207
79Sabres Bells-6
79Topps-207
80O-Pee-Chee-13
80Topps-13
81O-Pee-Chee-31
81Sabres Milk Panels-1
82Post Cereal-2
82Sabres Milk Panels-3
83NHL Key Tags-11
83O-Pee-Chee-69
84O-Pee-Chee-27
84O-Pee-Chee Stickers-215
84Sabres Blue Shield-15
84Topps-21
85O-Pee-Chee-32
85O-Pee-Chee Stickers-175
85O-Pee-Chee Stickers-192
85Sabres Blue Shield-22
85Sabres Blue Shield Small-22
85Topps-32
93Sabres Noco-15
96Senators Pizza Hut-21
03Lightning Team Issue-4
05Lightning Team Issue-2
Ramsay, Jed
02Orlando Seals-11
Ramsay, Kyle
06Erie Otters-12
Ramsay, Michael
03Victoriaville Tigers-20
Ramsay, Mike
02Peterborough Petes-16
04Victoriaville Tigres-13
06Odessa Jackalopes-15
Ramsay, Ryan
00UD CHL Prospects-19
01Kitchener Rangers-4
02Plymouth Whalers-10
03Plymouth Whalers-10
04Worcester IceCats-21
05Peoria Rivermen-18
06Peoria Rivermen-15
Ramsey, Mike
80USA Olympic Team Mini Pics-11
80O-Pee-Chee-127
80Topps-127
81Sabres Milk Panels-12
81Swedish Semic Hockey VM Stickers-94
82O-Pee-Chee-32
82Post Cereal-2
82Sabres Milk Panels-15
83NHL Key Tags-9
83O-Pee-Chee-70
83O-Pee-Chee Stickers-243
83Topps Stickers-243
84O-Pee-Chee-28
84O-Pee-Chee Stickers-211
84Sabres Blue Shield-16
84Topps-22
85O-Pee-Chee-77
85O-Pee-Chee Stickers-180
85Sabres Blue Shield-23
85Sabres Blue Shield Small-23
85Topps-77
86O-Pee-Chee-115
86O-Pee-Chee Stickers-44
86Sabres Blue Shield-24
86Sabres Blue Shield Small-24
86Topps-115
87O-Pee-Chee-63
87O-Pee-Chee Stickers-149
87Panini Stickers-25
87Sabres Blue Shield-21
87Sabres Wonder Bread/Hostess-21
87Topps-63
88O-Pee-Chee-133
88O-Pee-Chee Stickers-260
88Panini Stickers-222
88Sabres Blue Shield-20
88Sabres Wonder Bread/Hostess-22
88Topps-133
89O-Pee-Chee-140
89Sabres Blue Shield-18
89Sabres Campbell's-20
89Topps-140
89Swedish Semic World Champ Stickers-158
90O-Pee-Chee-102
90Panini Stickers-24
90Pro Set-28
90Sabres Blue Shield-17
90Sabres Campbell's-20
90Score-23
Canadian-23
90Score Hottest/Rising Stars-13
90Topps-102
Tiffany-102
90Upper Deck-168
French-168
91Pro Set Platinum-13
91Bowman-32
91O-Pee-Chee-236
91Panini Stickers-299
91Parkhurst-19
French-19
91Pinnacle-64
French-64
91Pro Set-25
91Pro Set-568
French-25
French-568
91Sabres Blue Shield-17
91Sabres Pepsi/Campbell's-17
91Score American-61
91Score Canadian Bilingual-61
91Score Canadian English-61
91Stadium Club-135
91Topps-236
92Panini Stickers-253
92Panini Stickers French-253
92Parkhurst-256
Emerald Ice-256
92Pinnacle-21
French-21
92Sabres Blue Shield-19
92Sabres Jubilee Foods-12
92Score-28
Canadian-28
92Stadium Club-386
92Topps-473
Gold-473G
92Ultra-19
93Penguins Foodland-16
93Pinnacle-394
Canadian-394
93Sabres Noco-16
93Score-179
Canadian-179
93Ultra-396
94Leaf-536
94Pinnacle-412
Artist's Proofs-412
Rink Collection-412
95Signature Rookies Miracle on Ice-27
95Signature Rookies Miracle on Ice-28
95Signature Rook Miracle on Ice Sigs-27
95Signature Rook Miracle on Ice Sigs-28
04UD Legendary Signatures-58
Autographs-RA
Miracle Men-USA9
Miracle Men Autographs-USA-RA
Ramsey, Travis
03Salmon Arm Silverbacks-16
04Maine Black Bears-20
05Maine Black Bears-21
Ramsey, Wayne
79Rochester Americans-12
Ramstedt, Johan
95Collector's Choice-341
Player's Club-341
Player's Club Platinum-341
95Swedish Upper Deck 1st Division Stars-DS5
95Signature Rookies Auto-Phonex-33
95Signature Rook Auto-Phonex Phone Cards-33
95Signature Rookies Tetrad Autobilia *-50
98Swedish UD Choice-29
00Swedish Upper Deck-22
06Swedish SHL Elitset-130
Ramstedt, Teemu
06Finnish Cardset-342
Rancourt, Alain
88Richelieu Riverains-25
Rancourt, Fernand
52Bas Du Fleuve-30
Rancourt, Marc
01Belleville Bulls-18
02Belleville Bulls-15
03Belleville Bulls-5
04Belleville Bulls-13
04Belleville Bulls-NNO
Rand, Joe
03St. Michael's Majors-19
04St. Michael's Majors-20
Randall, Bruce
88ProCards AHL-128
Randall, Bryan
95Medicine Hat Tigers-12
96Regina Pats-18
97Regina Pats-15
98Idaho Steelheads-15
99Idaho Steelheads-6
Randall, Greg
04UK Milton Keynes Lightning-16
Randall, Jamie
04UK Milton Keynes Lightning-10
Randall, Ken
23V145-1-34
24C144 Champ's Cigarettes-48
24V130 Maple Crispette-24
24V145-2-12
04ITG Franchises Canadian-86
Randall, Shawn
98Topeka Scarecrows-3
Randell, Lem
03OCN Blizzard-17
Ranford, Bill
86Moncton Golden Flames-5
87O-Pee-Chee-13
87Panini Stickers-5
87Topps-13
88Oilers Tenth Anniversary-60
88Oilers Team Issue-23
89Oilers Team Issue-20
89O-Pee-Chee-233
89O-Pee-Chee Stickers-230
89Panini Stickers-81
90Kraft-45
90Oilers IGA-21
90O-Pee-Chee-226
90O-Pee-Chee-467
90OPC Premier-94
90Panini Stickers-218
90Pro Set-94
90Pro Set-390
90Score-79
90Score-331
90Score-345
90Score-358
90Score-369
Canadian-79
Canadian-345
Canadian-358
90Score Hottest/Rising Stars-39
90Topps-226
Tiffany-226
90Upper Deck-42
90Upper Deck-201
French-42
91Pro Set Platinum-36
91Bowman-101
91Gillette-9
91Kraft-44
91McDonald's Upper Deck-21
91Oilers Panini Team Stickers-17
91Oilers Panini Team Stickers-E
91Oilers Panini Team Stickers-F
91Oilers IGA-17
91Oilers Team Issue-19
91O-Pee-Chee-356
91OPC Premier-18
91Panini Stickers-125
91Parkhurst-53
91Parkhurst-460
French-53
91Pinnacle-170
French-170
B-B7
B French-B7
91Pro Set-70
91Pro Set-283
French-70
French-283
91Score American-30
91Score Canadian Bilingual-30
91Score Canadian English-30
91Stadium Club-249
91Topps-356
91Upper Deck-10
91Upper Deck-117
French-10
French-117
92Bowman-106
92Humpty Dumpty II-18
92Kraft-33
92Oilers IGA-18
92Oilers Team Issue-14
92O-Pee-Chee-137
92OPC Premier Star Performers-19
92Panini Stickers-99
92Panini Stickers French-99
92Parkhurst-50
Emerald Ice-50
92Pinnacle-4
French-4
92Pro Set-51
92Score-236
92Score-424
92Score-495
Canadian-236
Canadian-424
Canadian-495
92Seasons Patches-57
92Stadium Club-66
92Topps-126
Gold-126G
92Ultra-65
92Upper Deck-262
92Finnish Semic-75
93Donruss-117
93Kraft-18
93Kraft Recipes-6
93Kraft Recipes French-6
93Leaf-68
Painted Warriors-10
93OPC Premier-258
Gold-258
93Panini Stickers-U
93Parkhurst-67
Emerald Ice-67
93Pinnacle-81
Canadian-81
93PowerPlay-85
Netminders-6
93Score-155
Canadian-155
Franchise-7
93Stadium Club-131
Members Only Master Set-131
OPC-131
First Day Issue-131
First Day Issue OPC-131
93Topps/OPC Premier-258
Gold-258
93Ultra-158
93Upper Deck-180
SP-52
93Classic Team Canada-TC4
94Be A Player-R28
Signature Cards-16
94Canada Games NHL POGS-279
94Donruss-171
94EA Sports-48
94Finest Ring Leaders-17
94Flair-61
94Fleer-75
94Hockey Wit-76
94Kraft-51
94Leaf-60
Crease Patrol-10
94Leaf Limited-9
94OPC Premier-435
Special Effects-435
94Parkhurst-72
Gold-72
Vintage-V75
94Pinnacle-285
Artist's Proofs-285
Rink Collection-285
Goaltending Greats-GT6
Northern Lights-NL13
94Select-5
Gold-5
94SP-41
Die Cuts-41
94Stadium Club-29
Members Only Master Set-29
First Day Issue-29
Super Teams-8
Super Teams Members Only Master Set-8
Super Team Winner Cards-29
94Topps/OPC Premier-435
Special Effects-435
94Ultra-76
94Upper Deck-21
Electric Ice-21
SP Inserts-SP27
SP Inserts Die Cuts-SP27
94Finnish Jaa Kiekko-79
94Finnish Jaa Kiekko-331
95Bashan Super Stickers-42
95Bashan Super Stickers-45
95Bowman-24
All-Foil-24
95Canada Games NHL POGS-113
95Collector's Choice-246
Player's Club-246
Player's Club Platinum-246
95Donruss-323
95Donruss Elite-12
Die Cut Stars-12
Die Cut Uncut-12
95Emotion-66
95Finest-51
Refractors-51
95Hoyle Western Playing Cards-51
95Imperial Stickers-45
95Kraft-33
95Leaf-86
95Leaf Limited-103
95Metal-56
95NHL Aces Playing Cards-3C
95Parkhurst International-78
95Parkhurst International-282
Emerald Ice-78
Emerald Ice-282
Goal Patrol-9
95Playoff One on One-151
95Playoff One on One-258
95Pro Magnets-84
95Score-239
Black Ice Artist's Proofs-239
Black Ice-239
95Select Certified-55
Mirror Gold-55
95SkyBox Impact-64
95SP-9
95Stadium Club-21
Members Only Master Set-21
Extreme North-EN6
Extreme North Members Only Master Set-EN6
95Summit-71
Artist's Proofs-71
Ice-71
95Topps-241
OPC Inserts-241
Home Grown Canada-HGC8
95Topps SuperSkills-86
Platinum-86
95Ultra-57
Gold Medallion-57
95Upper Deck Special Edition-SE32
95Upper Deck Special Edition Gold-SE32
95Zenith-47
95Finnish Semic World Championships-77
95Finnish Semic World Championships-201
95Finnish Semic World Championships-208
95Swedish Globe World Championships-75
95Swedish World Championships Stickers-1
96Be A Player-16
Autographs-16
Autographs Silver-16
96Black Diamond-80
Gold-80
96Collector's Choice-17
96Donruss-87
Press Proofs-87
96Donruss Canadian Ice-75
Gold Press Proofs-75
Red Press Proofs-75
96Donruss Elite-97
Die Cut Stars-97
96Flair-6
Blue Ice-6
96Fleer-7
96Leaf-2
Press Proofs-2
96Leaf Limited-22
Gold-22
96Leaf Preferred-3
Press Proofs-3
Steel-40
Steel Gold-40
96Maggers-81
96Metal Universe-10
96NHL Pro Stamps-84
96Pinnacle-89
Artist's Proofs-89
Foil-89
Premium Stock-89
Rink Collection-89
96Playoff One on One-374
96Score-40
Artist's Proofs-40
Dealer's Choice Artist's Proofs-40
Special Artist's Proofs-40
Golden Blades-40
Net Worth-15
96SkyBox Impact-8
96SP-9
96Topps Picks-85
OPC Inserts-85
96Ultra-11
Gold Medallion-11
96Upper Deck-8
Superstar Showdown-SS30A
96Upper Deck Ice-3
Parallel-3
96Zenith-72
Artist's Proofs-72
96Swedish Semic Wien-76
96Collector's Edge Ice Livin' Large-L5
97Collector's Choice-267
97Donruss-172
Press Proofs Silver-172
Press Proofs Gold-172
97Donruss Canadian Ice-46
Dominion Series-46
Provincial Series-46
97Donruss Limited-14
Exposure-14
97Donruss Preferred-52
Cut to the Chase-52
97Donruss Priority-55
Stamp of Approval-55
97Katch-154
Gold-154
Silver-154
97Leaf-33
Fractal Matrix-33
Fractal Matrix Die Cuts-33
97Leaf International-33
Universal Ice-33
97Pacific-233
Copper-233
Emerald Green-233
Ice Blue-233
Red-233
Silver-233
97Pacific Dynagon-134
Copper-134
Dark Grey-134
Emerald Green-134
Ice Blue-134
Red-134
Silver-134
Tandems-51
97Pacific Invincible-150
Copper-150
Emerald Green-150
Ice Blue-150
Red-150
Silver-150
97Panini Stickers-110
97Paramount-199
Copper-199
Dark Grey-199
Emerald Green-199
Ice Blue-199
Red-199
Silver-199
97Pinnacle-46
Artist's Proofs-46
Rink Collection-46
Press Plates Back Black-46
Press Plates Back Cyan-46
Press Plates Back Magenta-46
Press Plates Back Yellow-46
Press Plates Front Black-46
Press Plates Front Cyan-46
Press Plates Front Magenta-46
Press Plates Front Yellow-46
97Pinnacle Certified-12
Red-12
Mirror Blue-12
Mirror Gold-12
Mirror Red-12
97Pinnacle Inside-35
Coach's Collection-35
Executive Collection-35
Stoppers-23
97Pinnacle Tot Cert Platinum Blue-12
97Pinnacle Tot Certi Platinum Gold-12
97Pinnacle Totally Certified Platinum Red-12
97Pinnacle Tot Cert Mirror Platinum Gold-12
97Score-13
Artist's Proofs-13
Golden Blades-13
97SP Authentic-165
97Upper Deck-178
98Bowman's Best-87
Refractors-87
Atomic Refractors-87
98Crown Royale-125
Limited Series-125
98NHL Aces Playing Cards-16
98Pacific-446
Ice Blue-446
Red-446
98SP Authentic-78
Power Shift-78
98Upper Deck-364
Exclusives-364
Exclusives 1 of 1-364
Gold Reserve-364
98Upper Deck MVP-188
Gold Script-188
Silver Script-188
Super Script-188
99Kraft Stanley Cup Moments-6
99Pacific-147
Copper-147
Emerald Green-147
Gold-147
Ice Blue-147
Premiere Date-147
Red-147
99Pacific Dynagon Ice-83
Blue-83
Copper-83
Gold-83
Premiere Date-83
99Panini Stickers-250
99SPx-65
Radiance-65
Spectrum-65
99Stadium Club-157
First Day Issue-157
One of a Kind-157
Printing Plates Black-157
Printing Plates Cyan-157
Printing Plates Magenta-157
Printing Plates Yellow-157
00BAP Ultimate Mem Dynasty Jerseys-D5
00BAP Ultimate Mem Dynasty Emblems-D5
01SP Game Used Tools of the Game-TRA
01SP Game Used Tools of the Game-CTRF
01SP Game Used Tools of the Game-TTRFE
01SP Game Used Tools of the Game Signed-STBR
01SP Game Used Tools of the Game Signed-SCRF
01SP Game Used Tools of the Game Signed-SCRH
01UD Stanley Cup Champs-12
Pieces of Glory-G-BR
01Upper Deck Legends-25
01Upper Deck Legends-86
Jerseys-TTBR
Jerseys Platinum-TTBR
02BAP Ultimate Memorabilia Conn Smythe-18
02BAP Ultimate Memorabilia Cup Duels-14
02UD Foundations-2
02UD Foundations-30
Classic Greats-GBR
Classic Greats Gold-GBR
Classic Greats Silver-G-BR
Lasting Impressions Sticks-L-BR
04ITG Franchises Canadian-23
Autographs-BR
Goalie Gear-GG9
Goalie Gear Autographs-GG9
Goalie Gear Gold-GG9
Trophy Winners-TW7
Trophy Winners Gold-TW7
04ITG Ultimate Memorabilia-38
Gold-38
Archives 1st Edition-24
Complete Logo-19
05Between the Pipes-15
Autographs-A-BR
Jerseys-GUJ-11
05SP Game Used Heritage Classic-HC-BR
05SP Game Used Heritage Classic Autos-HCA-BR
05SP Game Used Heritage Classic Patches-HCP-BR
05SP GameUsed Heritage Classic Patch Auto-HAP-BR
05The Cup Noble Numbers Dual-DNNFR
05UD Artifacts Frozen Artifacts-FA-RA
05UD Artifacts Frozen Artifacts Autos-FA-RA
05UD Artifacts Frozen Artifacts Copper-FA-RA
05UD Artifacts Frozen Artifacts Dual-FAD-RA
05UD Artifacts Frozen Artifact Dual Auto-FAD-RA
05UD Artifact Frozen Artifact Dual Copper-FAD-RA
05UD Artifacts Frozen Artifacts Dual Gold-FAD-RA
05UD Artifact Frozen Artifact Dual Maroon-FAD-RA
05UD Artifact Frozen Artifact Dual Pewter-FAD-RA
05UD Artifact Frozen Artifact Dual Silver-FAD-RA
05UD Artifacts Frozen Artifacts Gold-FA-RA
05UD Artifacts Frozen Artifacts Maroon-FA-RA
05UD Artifacts Frozen Artifacts Pewter-FA-RA
05UD Artifacts Frozen Artifacts Silver-FA-RA
05UD Artifacts Goalie Gear-FG-RA
05UD Artifacts Goalie Gear Autographed-FG-RA
05UD Artifacts Goalie Gear Dual-FGD-RA
05UD Artifacts Goalie Gear Dual Autos-FGD-RA
05UD Artifacts Goalie Gear Pewter-FG-RA
05UD Artifacts Goalie Gear Silver-FG-RA
06Between The Pipes-124
Autographs-ABR
Double Jerseys-DJ12
Double Jerseys Gold-DJ12
Emblems-GUE32
Emblems Gold-GUE32
Emblems Autographs-GUE32
Jerseys-GUJ32
Jerseys Gold-GUJ32
Jerseys Autographs-GUJ32
Numbers-GUN32
Numbers Gold-GUN32
Numbers Autographs-GUN32
06ITG International Ice-67
Gold-67
Autographs-ABR
Goaltending Glory-GG11
Goaltending Glory Gold-GG11
International Rivals-IR14
International Rivals Gold-IR14
06SP Authentic Sign of the Times Duals-STRR
06SP Game Used Inked Sweaters Dual-IS2FR
06SP Game Used Letter Marks-LMBR
06SPx-111
Spectrum-111
06The Cup Limited Logos-LLBL
06The Cup Scripted Swatches-SSBR
06The Cup Stanley Cup Signatures-CSBI
06UD Artifacts-131
Blue-131
Gold-131
Platinum-131
Radiance-131
Red-131
Frozen Artifacts-FABR
Frozen Artifacts Black-FABR
Frozen Artifacts Blue-FABR
Frozen Artifacts Gold-FABR
Frozen Artifacts Platinum-FABR
Frozen Artifacts Red-FABR
Frozen Artifacts Autographed Black-FABR
Frozen Artifacts Patches Black-FABR
Frozen Artifacts Patches Blue-FABR
Frozen Artifacts Patches Gold-FABR
Frozen Artifacts Patches Platinum-FABR
Frozen Artifacts Patches Red-FABR
Tundra Tandems-TTFR
Tundra Tandems Black-TTFR
Tundra Tandems Blue-TTFR
Tundra Tandems Gold-TTFR
Tundra Tandems Platinum-TTFR
Tundra Tandems Red-TTFR
Tundra Tandems Dual Patches Red-TTFR
06Upper Deck Sweet Shot Endorsed Equipment-EEBR
06Upper Deck Trilogy Honorary Scripted Patches-HSPBR
06Upper Deck Trilogy Honorary Scripted Swatches-HSSBR
06Upper Deck Trilogy Honorary Swatches-HSBR
Ranger, Joe
85London Knights-2
87Kitchener Rangers-25
Ranger, Nicolas
03Gatineau Olympiques-19
04Gatineau Olympiques-7
Ranger, Paul
03Oshawa Generals-26
03Oshawa Generals-NNO
04Springfield Falcons-22
05Beehive-161
Matte-161
05Black Diamond-284
05Hot Prospects-172
En Fuego-172
Red Hot-172
White Hot-172
05Parkhurst-445
Facsimile Auto Parallel-445
05SP Authentic-238
Limited-238
05SP Game Used-163
Gold-163
05SPx-198
Spectrum-198
05The Cup Masterpiece Pressplate Artifact-330
05The Cup Masterpiece Pressplate Bee Hive-161
05The Cup Master Pressplate Black Diamond-284
05The Cup Masterpiece Pressplates (Ice)-171
05The Cup Master Pressplate Rookie Update-182
05The Cup Masterpiece Pressplates SPA-238
05The Cup Masterpiece Pressplates SP GU-163
05The Cup Masterpiece Pressplates (SPx)-198
05The Cup Masterpiece Pressplates Trilogy-308
05The Cup Masterpiece Pressplate Ult Coll-172
05UD Artifacts-330
05Ultimate Collection-172
Gold-172
05Ultra-248
Gold-248
Ice-248
05Upper Deck Ice-171
05Upper Deck Rookie Update-182
05Upper Deck Trilogy-308
05Springfield Falcons-19
06Black Diamond Gemography-GPR
06Hot Prospects Hotagraphs-HPR
06Lightning Postcards-16
06O-Pee-Chee-445
Rainbow-445
06UD Powerplay Power Marks-PMPR
06Upper Deck-179
Exclusives Parallel-179
High Gloss Parallel-179
Masterpieces-179
06Upper Deck MVP-262
Gold Script-262
Super Script-262
06ITG Heroes and Prospects Jerseys-GUJ26
06ITG Heroes and Prospects Jerseys Gold-GUJ26
06ITG Heroes and Prospects Emblems-GUE26
06ITG Heroes and Prospects Emblems Gold-GUE26
06ITG Heroes and Prospects Numbers-GUN26
06ITG Heroes and Prospects Numbers Gold-GUN26
Rangus, Bob
01Michigan Tech Huskies-26
05Knoxville Ice Bears-14
Ranheim, Paul
89Kraft-9
90Bowman-100
Tiffany-100
90Flames IGA/McGavin's-22
90O-Pee-Chee-20
90Panini Stickers-181
90Panini Stickers-342
90Pro Set-44
90Score-248
Canadian-248
90Topps-20
Tiffany-20
90Upper Deck-104
French-104
91Bowman-251
91Flames Panini Team Stickers-18
91Flames IGA-16
91O-Pee-Chee-15
91Panini Stickers-54
91Parkhurst-249
French-249
91Pinnacle-252
French-252
91Pro Set-31
French-31
91Score American-21
91Score Canadian Bilingual-21
91Score Canadian English-21
91Stadium Club-50
91Topps-15
91Upper Deck-472
French-472
92Bowman-96
92Flames IGA-14
92O-Pee-Chee-36
92Panini Stickers-44
92Panini Stickers French-44
92Parkhurst-260
Emerald Ice-260
92Pinnacle-67
French-67
92Pro Set-29
92Score-149

Canadian-149
92Stadium Club-144
92Topps-486
Gold-486G
92Ultra-27
92Upper Deck-328
93Donruss-50
93Donruss-442
93Leaf-170
93OPC Premier-481
Gold-481
93Panini Stickers-184
93Parkhurst-32
Emerald Ice-32
93Pinnacle-265
Canadian-265
93PowerPlay-309
93Score-165
Canadian-165
93Stadium Club-151
Members Only Master Set-151
OPC-151
First Day Issue-151
First Day Issue OPC-151
93Topps/OPC Premier-481
Gold-481
93Ultra-286
93Upper Deck-131
94Canada Games NHL POGS-116
94Leaf-370
94OPC Premier-96
Special Effects-96
94Pinnacle-138
Artist's Proofs-138
Rink Collection-138
94Topps/OPC Premier-96
Special Effects-96
94Upper Deck-430
Electric Ice-430
95Be A Player-87
Signatures-S87
Signatures Die Cuts-S87
95Canada Games NHL POGS-127
95Collector's Choice-78
Player's Club-78
Player's Club Platinum-78
95Parkhurst International-361
Emerald Ice-361
95Playoff One on One-265
95Topps-232
OPC Inserts-232
95Upper Deck-13
Electric Ice-13
Electric Ice Gold-13
96Whalers Bob's Stores-21
96Whalers Kid's Club-8
97Hurricanes Team Issue-22
98Be A Player-176
Press Release-176
98BAP Gold-176
98BAP Autographs-176
98BAP Autographs Gold-176
98Hurricanes Team Issue-18
98OPC Chrome-102
Refractors-102
98Pacific-139
Ice Blue-139
Red-139
98Topps-102
O-Pee-Chee-102
99Upper Deck-202
Exclusives-202
Exclusives 1 of 1-202
99Upper Deck Gold Reserve-202
00Upper Deck NHLPA-PA65
01Flyers Postcards-16
01Pacific-293
Extreme LTD-293
Hobby LTD-293
Premiere Date-293
Retail LTD-293
01Pacific Arena Exclusives-293
02BAP Sig Series Auto Buybacks 1998-176
02Coyotes Team Issue-27
02Flyers Postcards-7
04ITG Franchises Canadian-9
Autographs-PRA

Raninen, Juha
71Swedish Hockey-382

Rankel, Andre
03German Berlin Polar Bears Postcards-26
04German Berlin Polar Bears Postcards-25
04German DEL Update-293
05German DEL-40
06German DEL-22

Rankin, Evan
03Lincoln Stars-5
03Lincoln Stars Update-45
04Notre Dame Fighting Irish-6

Rankin, Frank
83Hall of Fame-132
83Hall of Fame Postcards-I13
85Hall of Fame-132

Rankin, Rob
01Michigan Tech Huskies-27
02Topeka Scarecrows-19

Rankin, Terry
93Quebec Pee-Wee Tournament-952

Rannard, Fred
98Anchorage Aces-26
99Anchorage Aces-2

Rantala, Mikko
98Finnish Kerailysarja-133

Rantala, Timo
66Finnish Jaakiekkosarja-103

Rantanen, Esko
66Finnish Jaakiekkosarja-169
70Finnish Jaakiekko-249
71Finnish Suomi Stickers-215
72Finnish Jaakiekko-164
73Finnish Jaakiekko-229
99Finnish Cardset-317
00Finnish Cardset-246

Rantanen, Jarmo
65Finnish Hellas-14
66Finnish Jaakiekkosarja-61
70Finnish Jaakiekko-148
71Finnish Suomi Stickers-198
72Finnish Jaakiekko-236
73Finnish Jaakiekko-270
92Finnish Jyvas-Hyva Stickers-81
93Finnish Jyvas-Hyva Stickers-146
93Finnish SISU-145
93Finnish SISU-185B

Rantanen, Kalevi
78Finnish SM-Liiga-110

Rantanen, Kari
70Finnish Jaakiekko-353

Rantanen, Kimmo
71Finnish Suomi Stickers-291

Rantanen, Marko
93Finnish SISU-4
94Finnish SISU-295
95Finnish SISU-247

Rantasila, Juha
65Finnish Hellas-34
66Finnish Jaakiekkosarja-35
69Swedish Hockey-382
70Finnish Jaakiekko-75
70Finnish Jaakiekko-113
70Swedish Hockey-299
70Swedish Masterserien-88
70Swedish Masterserien-166
71Finnish Suomi Stickers-122
72Finnish Jaakiekko-71
72Finnish Jaakiekko-92
72Finnish Panda Toronto-10
72Finnish Semic World Championship-92
72Swedish Semic World Championship-92
73Finnish Jaakiekko-139
74Finnish Typotor-3
74Swedish Stickers-29

Rantasila, Valtonen
70Swedish Masterserien-123

Ranzi, Dominic
93Quebec Pee-Wee Tournament-72

Rapoza, Bobby
96Dayton Ice Bandits-15
98Phoenix Mustangs-19
00Asheville Smoke-10
01Asheville Smoke-10
03Missouri River Otters-8
04Missouri River Otters-18

Rapp, Anders
67Swedish Hockey-243
69Swedish Hockey-288
70Swedish Hockey-185

Rappana, Kevin
92North Dakota Fighting Sioux-27
96Charlotte Checkers-13

Rappl, Daniel
04German Weiden Blue Devils-21

Rappold, Peter
94German First League-128

Rasanen, Erkki
66Finnish Jaakiekkosarja-125
70Finnish Jaakiekko-266

Rasanen, Juhan
71Finnish Suomi Stickers-333

Rasanen, Pekka
80Finnish Mallasjuoma-47

Rasanen, Teijo
72Finnish Jaakiekko-181

Rask, Devin
03Trenton Titans-363

Rask, Jeff
97Central Texas Stampede-12

Rask, Tuukka
04Finnish Cardset-47
04Finnish Cardset Signatures-12
05Finnish Cardset -40
06Between The Pipes-50
06Between The Pipes-116
Autographs-ATR2
Autographs-ATR
06ITG International Ice-54
Gold-54
Autographs-ATR
06Finnish Cardset-39
Between the Pipes-8
Signature Sensations-6
Superior Snatchers-7
Superior Snatchers Gold-7
Superior Snatchers Silver-7
06Finnish Ilves Team Set-23
06ITG Heroes and Prospects-134
Autographs-ATR

Rasmussen, Erik
94Select-152
Gold-152
94Classic Draft Prospects-DP7
95Donruss Elite World Juniors-39
95Minnesota Golden Gophers-24
96Upper Deck Ice-146
96Minnesota Golden Gophers-23
97Be A Player-217
Autographs-217
Autographs Die-Cuts-217
Autographs Prismatic Die-Cuts-217
97Leaf-153
Fractal Matrix-153
Fractal Matrix Die Cuts-153
97Pacific Dynagon-NNO
Copper-NNO
Dark Grey-NNO
Emerald Green-NNO
Ice Blue-NNO
Red-NNO
Silver-NNO
97Paramount-23
Copper-23
Dark Grey-23
Emerald Green-23
Ice Blue-23
Red-23
Silver-23
97Pinnacle-3
Artist's Proofs-3
Rink Collection-3
Press Plates Back Black-3
Press Plates Back Cyan-3
Press Plates Back Magenta-3
Press Plates Back Yellow-3
Press Plates Front Black-3
Press Plates Front Cyan-3
Press Plates Front Magenta-3
Press Plates Front Yellow-3
97Score-58
Artist's Proofs-58
Golden Blades-58
97Score Sabres-16
Platinum-16
Premier-16
97SP Authentic-173
97Upper Deck-226
97Upper Deck Ice-57
Parallel-57
Power Shift-57
97Zenith Rookie Reign-3
97Rochester Americans-2-4
98Finest Futures Finest-F20
98Finest Futures Finest Refractors-F20
98SPx Finite-10
98SPx Finite-142
Radiance-10
Radiance-142
Spectrum-10
Spectrum-142
98UD Choice-25
98UD Choice Preview-25
98UD Choice Prime Choice
Reserve-25
98UD Choice Reserve-25
98Upper Deck-43
Exclusives-43
Exclusives 1 of 1-43
Gold Reserve-43
98Upper Deck MVP-23
Gold Script-23
Silver Script-23
Super Script-23
ProSign-ER
98Rochester Americans-19
99BAP Millennium-31
Emerald-31
Ruby-31
Sapphire-31
Signatures-31
Signatures Gold-31
99Kraft Whiz Kid-7
99O-Pee-Chee-64
99O-Pee-Chee Chrome-64
99O-Pee-Chee Chrome Refractors-64
99Pacific-42
Copper-42
Emerald Green-42
Gold-42
Ice Blue-42
Premiere Date-42
Red-42
99Topps/OPC-64
99Topps/OPC Chrome-64
Refractors-64
00Pacific-54
Copper-54
Gold-54
Ice Blue-54
Premiere Date-54
00Titanium Game Gear-60
00Titanium Game Gear Patches-60
00Titanium Draft Day Edition-12
Patches-12
01Atomic Jerseys-4
01Atomic Patches-4
01Pacific-52
Extreme LTD-52
Hobby LTD-52
Premiere Date-52
Retail LTD-52
01Pacific Arena Exclusives-52
01Pacific Heads-Up Quad Jerseys-23
01Titanium Draft Day Edition-14
02BAP Sig Series Auto Buybacks 1999-31
02Kings Game Sheets-11
02Kings Game Sheets-12
02Pacific Complete-366
Red-366
02Topps Heritage-174
02Upper Deck-330
Exclusives-330
02Upper Deck Beckett UD Promos-330
03Devils Team Issue-10
05Devils Team Issue-24
05Parkhurst-298
Facsimile Auto Parallel-298
05Upper Deck MVP-241
Gold-241
Platinum-241
06Devils Team Set-22
06O-Pee-Chee-304
Rainbow-304

Rasmussen, Morten
98Danish Hockey League-116

Rasolko, Andrei
98Russian Hockey League-148
99Russian Hockey League-164
00Russian Hockey League-371

Raspel, Jan
94German First League-501

Rasten, Marten
98Danish Hockey League-97

Rastio, Jari
78Finnish SM-Liiga-170
80Finnish Mallasjuoma-124

Rastio, Teppo
65Finnish Hellas-20
66Finnish Jaakiekkosarja-13
71Finnish Suomi Stickers-250
77Finnish Sportscasters-50-1199

Raszka, Taylor
02Plymouth Whalers-9
03Saginaw Spirit-19
04Lincoln Stars Update-38
04Saginaw Spirit-14
05Brampton Battalion-19
06Toledo Storm-15

Rataj, Igor
03Czech OFS Plus-253
03Czech OFS Plus All-Star Game-H20
04Czech OFS-78
05Czech HC Liberec-10
06Czech HC Slavia Praha Postcards-11
06Czech OFS-282
Goals Leaders-9

Ratchford, Mike
52Juniors Blue Tint-150

Ratchuk, Peter
95Classic-68
98New Haven Beast-17
98Bowman CHL-99
Golden Anniversary-99
OPC International-99
Scout's Choice-SC14
98Bowman Chrome CHL-99
Golden Anniversary-99
Golden Anniversary Refractors-99
OPC International-99
OPC International Refractors-99
Refractors-99
99Louisville Panthers-10
00Upper Deck-434
Exclusives Tier 1-434
Exclusives Tier 2-434
00Louisville Panthers-6
01Wilkes-Barre Scranton Penguins-18
02Rochester Americans-20
03German DEL-102
04German DEL-114
All-Stars-AS5
05German DEL-251

Ratelle, Jean
44Beehive Group II Photos-356A
44Beehive Group II Photos-356B
60NHL Ceramic Tiles-25
61Shirriff/Salada Coins-98
61Topps-60
62Topps-58
63Topps-63
64Beehive Group III Photos-147
65Coca-Cola-86
65Topps-25
66Topps-29
66Topps USA Test-29
67Topps-31
68O-Pee-Chee-77
68Shirriff Coins-94
68Topps-77
69O-Pee-Chee-42
Four-in-One-17
Stamps-24
69Topps-42
70Colgate Stamps-25
70Dad's Cookies-108
70Esso Power Players-194
70O-Pee-Chee-181
Deckle-40
70Post Shooters-14
70Sargent Promotions Stamps-118
70Topps/OPC Sticker Stamps-26
71Colgate Heads-11
71Letraset Action Replays-14
71O-Pee-Chee-97
Posters-19
71Sargent Promotions Stamps-114
71Topps-97
71Toronto Sun-179
72O-Pee-Chee-12
72O-Pee-Chee-48A
72O-Pee-Chee-48B
72O-Pee-Chee-250
72O-Pee-Chee-280
72O-Pee-Chee-283
Team Canada-23
72Sargent Promotions Stamps-142
72Topps-50
72Topps-62
72Topps-63
72Topps-130
72Finnish Semic World Championship-214
72Swedish Stickers-120
72Swedish Semic World Championship-214
73Mac's Milk-23
73O-Pee-Chee-141
73Topps-73
74NHL Action Stamps-186
74O-Pee-Chee NHL-145
74Topps-145
75Heroes Stand-Ups-5
75O-Pee-Chee NHL-243A
75O-Pee-Chee NHL-243B
75O-Pee-Chee NHL-324
75Topps-243
75Topps-324
76O-Pee-Chee NHL-2
76O-Pee-Chee NHL-80
76O-Pee-Chee NHL-381
76Topps-2
76Topps-80
76Topps Glossy Inserts-22
77O-Pee-Chee NHL-40
77Topps-40
77Topps/O-Pee-Chee Glossy-16
Square-16
78O-Pee-Chee-155
78Topps-155
79O-Pee-Chee-225
79Topps-225
80O-Pee-Chee-6
80Topps-6
85Hall of Fame-249
91Bruins Sports Action Legends-24
91Future Trends Canada '72-66
91Future Trends Canada '72 French-66
93Zeller's Masters of Hockey-7
93Zeller's Masters of Hockey Signed-7
94Parkhurst Tall Boys-89
94Parkhurst Tall Boys-152
95Parkhurst '66-67-88
Coins-88
98Bruins Alumni-10
Autographs-10
99BAP Millennium Pearson-P16
99BAP Millennium Pearson Autographs-P16
01Greats of the Game-27
Autographs-27
01Upper Deck Legends-47
Sticks-PHJR
03Parkhurst Original Six Boston-49
Autographs-16
03Parkhurst Orig Six He Shoots/Scores-24A
03Parkhurst Original Six New York-50
03Parkhurst Original Six New York-66
03Parkhurst Original Six New York-83
03Parkhurst Original Six New York-96
Autographs-13
Inserts-N10
Memorabilia-NM33
Memorabilia-NM54
04ITG Franchises He Shoots/Scores Prizes-39
04ITG Franchises Update-453
04ITG Franchises US East-386
Autographs-A-JR
Barn Burners-EBB1
Barn Burners Gold-EBB1
Memorabilia-ESM30
Memorabilia Autographs-ESM-JR
Memorabilia Gold-ESM30
04ITG Ultimate Memorabilia-5
04ITG Ultimate Memorabilia-67
Gold-5
Gold-67
Auto Threads-22
Autographs-38
Autographs Gold-38
Day In History-41
Day In History Gold-41
Jersey Autographs-29
Jersey Autographs Gold-29
Original Six-7
Original Six-10
Retro Teammates-12
04ITG Heroes and Prospects-127
Autographs-JR
04ITG Heroes/Prospects Toronto Expo '05-127
04ITG Heroes/Prospects Expo Heroes/Pros-127
05ITG Heroes/Prosp Toronto Expo Parallel -29
05ITG Ultimate Mem Retro Teammate Jerseys-21
05ITG Ult Mem Retro Teammates Jersey Gold-21
05ITG Ultimate Mem 3 Star of the Game Jsy-10
05ITG Ult Mem 3 Star of the Game Jsy Gold-10
05ITG Ultimate Memorabilia Ultimate Autos-12
05ITG Ultimate Mem Ultimate Autos Gold-12
05ITG Heroes and Prospects-29
Autographs-A-JR
Hero Memorabilia-HM-33
06ITG Ultimate Memorabilia-76
Artist Proof-76
Cornerstones-6
Cornerstones Gold-6
Jerseys Autos-48
Jerseys Autos Gold-48
Retro Teammates-9
Retro Teammates Gold-9

Rath, Marius
92Finnish Semic-43
92Norwegian Elite Series-12
93Swedish Semic World Champ Stickers-246
94Finnish Jaa Kiekko-266
95Finnish Semic World Championships-182
95Swedish Globe World Championships-195
96Swedish Semic Wien-209

Rathbone, Jason
92Hampton Roads Admirals-10

Rathje, Mike
907th Inn. Sketch WHL-41
917th Inn. Sketch WHL-330
92Upper Deck-589
92Classic-3
92Classic-60
Gold-3
Gold-60
LPs-LP3
92Classic Four-Sport *-153
Gold-153
Autographs-153A
LPs-LP23
93Donruss-314
93Leaf-419
93OPC Premier-427
Gold-427
93Parkhurst-458
Emerald Ice-458
93Pinnacle-442
Canadian-442
93PowerPlay-437
93Score-595
Gold-595
Canadian-595
Canadian Gold-595
93Stadium Club-322
Members Only Master Set-322
First Day Issue-322
93Topps/OPC Premier-427
Gold-427
93Ultra-418
Wave of the Future-15
93Upper Deck-460
SP-147
93Classic-145
C3-22
93Classic Four-Sport *-246
Gold-246
94Donruss-170
94Leaf-139
94Parkhurst SE-SE160
Gold-SE160
94Pinnacle-363
Artist's Proofs-363
Rink Collection-363
94Score-261
Gold-261
Platinum-261
94Stadium Club-215
Members Only Master Set-215
First Day Issue-215
Super Team Winner Cards-215
94Ultra-201
94Upper Deck-168
Electric Ice-168
94Classic Pro Prospects-32
94Images *-92
95Donruss-305
95Emotion-160
95Panini Stickers-285
95Pinnacle-155
Artist's Proofs-155
Rink Collection-155
95SkyBox Impact-151
95Topps-191
OPC Inserts-191
97Pacific Invincible NHL Regime-180
99BAP Millennium-209
Emerald-209
Ruby-209
Sapphire-209
Signatures-209
Signatures Gold-209
99Pacific-379
Copper-379
Emerald Green-379
Gold-379
Ice Blue-379
Premiere Date-379
Red-379
99Upper Deck MVP SC Edition-157
Gold Script-157
Silver Script-157
Super Script-157
00BAP Memorabilia-346
Emerald-346
Ruby-346
Sapphire-346
Promos-346
00BAP Mem Chicago Sportsfest Copper-346
00BAP Memorabilia Chicago Sportsfest Blue-346
00BAP Memorabilia Chicago Sportsfest Gold-346
00BAP Memorabilia Chicago Sportsfest Ruby-346
00BAP Memorabilia Chicago Sun-Times Ruby-346
00BAP Memorabilia Chicago Sun-Times Gold-346
00BAP Mem Chicago Sun-Times Sapphire-346
00BAP Mem Toronto Fall Expo Copper-346
00BAP Memorabilia Toronto Fall Expo Gold-346
00BAP Memorabilia Toronto Fall Expo Ruby-346
01Upper Deck Victory-298
Gold-298
02BAP Sig Series Auto Buybacks 1999-209
02O-Pee-Chee-50
02O-Pee-Chee Premier Blue Parallel-50
02O-Pee-Chee Premier Red Parallel-50
02O-Pee-Chee Factory Set-50
02Pacific Complete-354
Red-354
02Sharks Team Issue-5
02Topps-50
OPC Blue Parallel-50
OPC Red Parallel-50
Factory Set-50
02Topps Total-73
02Upper Deck-146
Exclusives-146
03ITG Action-419
03O-Pee-Chee-81
03OPC Blue-81
03OPC Gold-81
03OPC Red-81
03Pacific Complete-339
Red-339
03Sharks Postcards-15
03Topps-81
Blue-81
Gold-81
Red-81
03Upper Deck-408
Canadian Exclusives-408
HG-408
UD Exclusives-408
05Flyers Team Issue-17
05Parkhurst-358
Facsimile Auto Parallel-358
05Upper Deck-388
05Upper Deck MVP-290
Gold-290
Platinum-290
06Flyers Postcards-2

Rathwell, Derrick
93Quebec Pee-Wee Tournament-586

Ratliff, Elden
92Disney Mighty Ducks Movie-5

Rattray, David
98Amarillo Rattlers-14

Rattray, Donovan
00Red Deer Rebels-15
Signed-15

Ratushny, Dan
91Alberta International Team Canada-18
93Upper Deck-245
95Peoria Rivermen-18
98IHL All-Star Western Conference-8
98Kansas City Blades-3
00Finnish Cardset-265

Raty, Tero
72Finnish Jaakiekko-151

Raty, Tuomo
94Finnish SISU-299

Rau, Daniel
04German Augsburg Panthers Postcards-24
04German DEL-41
05German DEL-12

Rau, Thorsten
94German DEL-180

Raubal, Andreas
94German First League-305
95German DEL-110
02German DEL City Press-230

Raubal, Anton
95German DEL-341
99German Bundesliga 2-82

Raubal, Michael
94German DEL-119
99German Bundesliga 2-277

Raubal, Toni
94German DEL-124

Rauch, Gunther
71Swedish Hockey-375

Rauch, Martin
91Finnish Semic World Champ Stickers-186
91Swedish Semic World Champ Stickers-186
92Finnish Semic-203
93Swiss HNL-66
95Swiss HNL-92
96Swiss HNL-34
98Swiss Power Play Stickers-33
98Swiss Power Play Stickers-263
99Swiss Panini Stickers-34
00Swiss Panini Stickers-134
00Swiss Slapshot Mini-Cards-HCFG6
01Swiss HNL-129
02Swiss HNL-57

Rauhala, Reine
91Swedish Semic Elitserien Stickers-146
92Upper Deck-598
92Swedish Semic Elitserien Stickers-161

Raunio, Matti
95Finnish SISU-304
98Finnish Kerailysarja-174

Raunio, Tapio
65Finnish Hellas-50

Rausse, Errol
79Capitals Team Issue-17

Rautakallio, Pekka
70Finnish Jaakiekko-200
71Finnish Suomi Stickers-90
72Finnish Jaakiekko-72
72Finnish Jaakiekko-255
72Finnish Hellas-11
72Finnish Panda Toronto-42
73Finnish Jaakiekko-76
73Finnish Jaakiekko-255
74Finnish Jenkki-14
74Finnish Typotor-48
74Swedish Semic World Champ Stickers-79
75Phoenix Roadrunners WHA-21
76O-Pee-Chee WHA-116
76Phoenix Roadrunners WHA-15
77Finnish Sportscasters-47-1106
78Finnish SM-Liiga-2
78Finnish SM-Liiga-223
79Panini Stickers-164
79Flames Postcards-14
79Flames Team Issue-15
80Flames Postcards-16
80O-Pee-Chee-356
80Pepsi-Cola Caps-14
81Flames Postcards-17
81O-Pee-Chee-50
81O-Pee-Chee Stickers-223
82O-Pee-Chee Stickers-218
82Post Cereal-3
82Topps Stickers-218
82Swedish Semic VM Stickers-161
83Swedish Semic VM Stickers-29
91Finnish Semic World Champ Stickers-228
91Swedish Semic World Champ Stickers-228
93Swiss HNL-363
95Swiss HNL-213
96Swedish Semic Wien Hockey Legends-HL15
96Swiss HNL-126
99Finnish Valio World Championships-6
99Swiss Panini Stickers-28
00Swiss Panini Stickers-29
02Swiss HNL-261

Rautakallio, Pentti
80Finnish Mallasjuoma-218

Rautakorpi, Jukka
95Finnish SISU-394
05Finnish Tappara Legendat-31

Rautalammi, Tapio
65Finnish Hellas-73
66Finnish Jaakiekkosarja-21
70Finnish Jaakiekko-201

Rautalin, Pentti
65Finnish Hellas-27
66Finnish Jaakiekkosarja-11
70Finnish Jaakiekko-233
71Finnish Suomi Stickers-251

Rautee, Matti
70Finnish Jaakiekko-166
71Finnish Suomi Stickers-235
72Finnish Jaakiekko-219
73Finnish Jaakiekko-295
74Finnish Typotor-33

Rautee, Mikko
99Finnish Cardset-335
00Finnish Cardset-101
01Finnish Cardset-141
05Finnish Cardset -345
06Finnish Cardset-337

Rautee, Pekka
70Finnish Jaakiekko-167
71Finnish Suomi Stickers-236
72Finnish Jaakiekko-220
73Finnish Jaakiekko-296
74Finnish Typotor-34
78Finnish SM-Liiga-207

Rautert, Neville
02German DEL City Press-142
04German DEL-121
05German DEL-93

Rautiainen, Matti
72Finnish Jaakiekko-293
73Finnish Jaakiekko-230
78Finnish SM-Liiga-12
78Finnish SM-Liiga-105
79Panini Stickers-179
80Finnish Mallasjuoma-40

Rautiainen, Tuomo
70Finnish Jaakiekko-220
71Finnish Suomi Stickers-141
72Finnish Jaakiekko-203
73Finnish Jaakiekko-166

Rautio, David
05Swedish SHL Elitset-228
Catchers-8
Catchers Gold-8
Gold-228
Series Two Signatures-21
06Swedish SHL Elitset-82
Goal Patrol-13

Rautio, Jani
93Finnish Jyvas-Hyva Stickers-167
93Finnish SISU-173

Rautio, Kai
92Finnish Jyvas-Hyva Stickers-8
94Finnish SISU-261
95Finnish SISU-72
95Finnish SISU-219
96German DEL-53
98Finnish Kerailysarja-59

Rautio, Mika
91Finnish Jyvas-Hyva Stickers-31
94Finnish SISU-118
94Finnish SISU NHL Phenoms-6
95Finnish SISU-284
95Finnish SISU Limited-55
98Finnish Kerailysarja-243

Rautio, Samuli
93Finnish Jyvas-Hyva Stickers-286
93Finnish SISU-78
94Finnish SISU-126

Ravi, Antti
65Finnish Hellas-94
66Finnish Jaakiekkosarja-100
70Finnish Jaakiekko-287
71Finnish Suomi Stickers-157
72Finnish Jaakiekko-110
73Finnish Jaakiekko-209

Ravlich, Matt
57St. Catherine's Tee Pees-NNO
64Beehive Group III Photos-53
65Coca-Cola-23
65Topps-115
66Topps-58
66Topps USA Test-58
68O-Pee-Chee-152
68Shirriff Coins-29
69O-Pee-Chee-161
70Colgate Stamps-69
70Dad's Cookies-109
70Esso Power Players-160
70O-Pee-Chee-32
70Sargent Promotions Stamps-71
70Topps-32
94Parkhurst Tall Boys-35
95Parkhurst '66-67-22
Coins-22

Rawles, Bill
94UK Guildford Flames-16

Rawlings, Chris
05Salmon Arm Silverbacks-15

Rawlyk, Rory
02Prince Albert Raiders-19
03Charlotte Checkers-76

Rawski, Steven
01St. Michaels Majors-6
02St. Michaels Majors-5
04Lakehead University Thunderwolves-17

Rawson, Geoff
89Niagara Falls Thunder-16
897th Inn. Sketch OHL-129
907th Inn. Sketch OHL-269
917th Inn. Sketch OHL-215

Ray, Chris
03Kelowna Rockets-18
04Kelowna Rockets-9
05Kelowna Rockets-20

Ray, Derek
93Fort Wayne Komets-24
95Fort Wayne Komets-24

Ray, Jean-Michel
84Richelieu Riverains-13

Ray, Martin
907th Inn. Sketch QMJHL-118

Ray, Rob
88ProCards AHL-265
89Sabres Campbell's-21
89ProCards AHL-256
90Pro Set-419
90Sabres Blue Shield-18
90Sabres Campbell's-21
90Upper Deck-516
French-516
90ProCards AHL/IHL-277
91Pro Set-355
French-355
91Sabres Blue Shield-18
91Sabres Pepsi/Campbell's-18
91Score Canadian Bilingual-610
91Score Canadian English-610
91Upper Deck-349
French-349
92Parkhurst-252
Emerald Ice-252
92Sabres Blue Shield-20
92Sabres Jubilee Foods-3
93Score-433
Canadian-433
94Parkhurst-30
Gold-30
94Pinnacle-514
Artist's Proofs-514
Rink Collection-514
95Be A Player-56
Signatures-S56
Signatures Die Cuts-S56
95Collector's Choice-198
Player's Club-198
Player's Club Platinum-198
96Black Diamond-32
Gold-32
96Score-200
Artist's Proofs-200
Dealer's Choice Artist's Proofs-200
Special Artist's Proofs-200
Golden Blades-200
97Collector's Choice-23
97Katch-17
Gold-17
Silver-17
97Pacific Invincible NHL Regime-21
97Score-242
97Score Sabres-14
Platinum-14
Premier-14
97Upper Deck-228
98Be A Player-165
Press Release-165
98BAP Gold-165
98BAP Autographs-165
98BAP Autographs Gold-165
98Pacific-108
Ice Blue-108
Red-108
98Pacific Omega-26
Red-26
Opening Day Issue-26
99Pacific-43
Copper-43
Emerald Green-43
Gold-43
Ice Blue-43
Premiere Date-43
Red-43
00BAP Memorabilia Update Tough Materials-T7
00BAP Mem Update Tough Materials Gold-T7
00Pacific-55
Copper-55
Gold-55
Ice Blue-55
Premiere Date-55
00Titanium Game Gear-61
00Titanium Game Gear Patches-61
00Topps Heritage-166
00Upper Deck NHLPA-PA12
00Upper Deck Vintage-49
01BAP Update Tough Customers-TC8
01BAP Update Tough Customers-TC11
01Pacific-53
01Pacific-404
Extreme LTD-53
Gold-404
Hobby LTD-53
Premiere Date-53
Retail LTD-53
01Pacific Arena Exclusives-53
01Pacific Arena Exclusives-404
01Pacific Heads-Up Quad Jerseys-23
01Private Stock Game Gear-12
01Private Stock Game Gear Patches-12
02BAP Sig Series Auto Buybacks 1998-165
02BAP Signature Series Famous Scraps-FS6
02O-Pee-Chee-136
02O-Pee-Chee Premier Blue Parallel-136
02O-Pee-Chee Premier Red Parallel-136
02O-Pee-Chee Factory Set-136
02Pacific-47
Blue-47
Red-47
02Pacific Complete-84
Red-84
02Sabres Team Issue-13
02Topps-136
OPC Blue Parallel-136
OPC Red Parallel-136
Factory Set-136
03ITG Action-424
03O-Pee-Chee-287
03OPC Blue-287
03OPC Gold-287
03OPC Red-287
03Topps-287
Blue-287
Gold-287
Red-287
Signs of Toughness-RR
Tough Materials-RR
Tough Materials-PSRR
Tough Materials Signed-RR
05SP Game Used Authentic Patches Quad -RBBF
05SPx Winning Combos Autographs-AWC-BB

Ray, Vern
92Thunder Bay Thunder Hawks-18
93Thunder Bay Senators-17
95Central Hockey League-13
95Fort Worth Fire-4
96Fort Worth Fire-13

Raycroft, Andrew
97Sudbury Wolves Police-24
98Sudbury Wolves-25
99Kingston Frontenacs-15
00BAP Memorabilia-485
Emerald-485
Ruby-485
Sapphire-485
00BAP Signature Series-253
Emerald-253
Ruby-253
Sapphire-253
Autographs-215
Autographs Gold-215
00Black Diamond-71
Gold-71
00Crown Royale-111
21st Century Rookies-2
00Private Stock-103
Gold-103
Premiere Date-103
Retail-103
Silver-103
PS-2001 Rookies-2
00SP Authentic-94
00SP Game Used-63
00SPx-121
Spectrum-121
00Stadium Club-251
00Titanium-105
Retail-105
00Titanium Draft Day Edition-105
00Titanium Draft Day Promos-105
00Topps Chrome-250
Blue-250
Red-250

OPC Refractors-250
OPC Refractors Blue-250
OPC Refractors Red-250
Refractors-250
Refractors Blue-250
Refractors Red-250
00Topps Gold Label Class 1-101
Gold-101
00Topps Gold Label Class 2-101
00Topps Gold Label Class 2 Gold-101
00Topps Gold Label Class 3-101
00Topps Gold Label Class 3 Gold-101
00Topps Heritage-93
Chrome Parallel-93
00Topps Premier Plus-115
Blue Ice-115
00Topps Stars-111
Blue-111
00UD Pros and Prospects-94
00UD Reserve-89
00Upper Deck-206
Exclusives Tier 1-206
Exclusives Tier 2-206
00Upper Deck Ice-51
Immortals-51
Legends-51
Stars-51
00Upper Deck MVP-218
First Stars-218
Second Stars-218
Third Stars-218
00Upper Deck Vintage-374
00Vanguard-104
Pacific Proofs-104
01BAP Memorabilia-125
Emerald-125
Ruby-125
Sapphire-125
01Between the Pipes-32
01O-Pee-Chee-304
01O-Pee-Chee Premier Parallel-304
01Parkhurst-271
01Parkhurst Beckett Promos-271
01Topps-304
OPC Parallel-304
01Topps Chrome-147
Refractors-147
Black Border Refractors-147
01Providence Bruins-1
02BAP Sig Series Auto Buybacks 2000-215
02Between the Pipes-84
Gold-84
Silver-84
02O-Pee-Chee-281
02O-Pee-Chee Premier Blue Parallel-281
02O-Pee-Chee Premier Red Parallel-281
02O-Pee-Chee Factory Set-281
02Pacific Calder-56
Silver-56
02Pacific Complete-583
Red-583
02Topps-281
OPC Blue Parallel-281
OPC Red Parallel-281
Factory Set-281
02Providence Bruins-1
03BAP Memorabilia-102
Emerald-102
Gold-102
Ruby-102
Sapphire-102
Future Wave-FW-12
03BAP Ultimate Memorabilia Autographs-9
Gold-9
03BAP Ultimate Mem Calder Candidates-1
03BAP Ultimate Mem Calder Candidates Gold-1
03BAP Ultimate Mem Hometown Heroes-11
03BAP Ultimate Mem Hometown Heroes Gold-11
03BAP Ultimate Memorabilia Jerseys-38
03BAP Ultimate Memorabilia Jerseys Gold-38
03BAP Ultimate Mem Magnificent Prospects-9
03BAP Ultimate Mem Magnif Prospect Autos-9
03BAP Ultimate Mem Nameplates-27
03BAP Ultimate Mem Nameplates Gold-27
03BAP Ultimate Mem Rookie Jersey Emblems-24
03BAP Ultimate Mem Rookie Jsy Emblem Gold-24
03BAP Ultimate Mem Rookie Jersey Numbers-24
03BAP Ultimate Mem Rookie Jsy Number Gold-24
03BAP Ultimate Memorabilia Triple Threads-34
03Beehive-13
Gold-13
Silver-13
03Black Diamond-66
Black-66
Green-66
Red-66
03Bruins Team Issue-9
03eTopps-56
03ITG Action-49
03ITG Used Signature Series-97
Gold-97
Autographs-AR
Autographs Gold-AR
Goalie Gear-33
Goalie Gear Autographs-33
Goalie Gear Gold-33
Triple Memorabilia-29
Triple Memorabilia Gold-29
03Pacific Calder-8
03Pacific Calder-176
Silver-8
Reflections-3
03Pacific Complete-465
Red-465
03Pacific Heads-Up-8
Hobby LTD-8
Retail LTD-8
03Pacific Quest for the Cup-9
Blue-9
Calder Contenders-2
03Parkhurst Original Six Boston-26
Memorabilia-BM62
03Parkhurst Orig Six He Shoots/Scores-14
03Parkhurst Orig Six He Shoots/Scores-14A
03Parkhurst Rookie-5
All-Rookie-ART-1
All-Rookie Autographs-ART-AR
All-Rookie Gold-ART-1
Calder Candidates-CMC-7
Calder Candidate Autographs-CMC-AR
Calder Candidates Gold-CMC-7
Jersey and Sticks-SJ-21
Jersey and Sticks Gold-SJ-21
Rookie Emblems-RE-40
Rookie Emblem Autographs-RE-AR
Rookie Emblems Gold-RE-40
Rookie Jerseys-RJ-40
Rookie Jersey Autographs-RJ-AR
Rookie Jerseys Gold-RJ-40
Rookie Numbers-RN-40
Rookie Number Autographs-RN-AR
Rookie Numbers Gold-RN-40
03Titanium-11
Hobby Jersey Number Parallels-11
Retail-11
Retail Jersey Number Parallels-11
03Topps Traded-TT32
Blue-TT32
Gold-TT32
Red-TT32
03UD Honor Roll-106
03UD Premier Collection-7
03Upper Deck-265
Canadian Exclusives-265
HG-265
UD Exclusives-265
03Upper Deck Ice-6
Gold-6
03Upper Deck MVP-47
Gold Script-47
Silver Script-47
Canadian Exclusives-47
03Upper Deck Rookie Update-8
YoungStars-YS11
YoungStars-YS11A
03Pacific AHL Prospects Crease Lightning-6
04Pacific-24
Blue-24
Red-24
Gold Crown Die-Cuts-2
In The Crease-1
04SP Authentic-7
Limited-7
Buybacks-12
Buybacks-13
Sign of the Times-ST-AR
Sign of the Times-DS-RL
Sign of the Times-DS-RT
Sign of the Times-TS-RBT
Sign of the Times-TS-TRB
Sign of the Times-QS-BTCR
Sign of the Times-FS-BOS
04Ultimate Collection Patch Autographs-UPA-ARJT
04Ultimate Collection Signatures-US-AR
04Ultimate Collection Signature Logos-ULA-AR
04Ultimate Collection Signature Patches-SP-AR
04Upper Deck-18
Canadian Exclusives-18
Hardware Heroes-AW4
HG Glossy Gold-18
HG Glossy Silver-18
Swatch of Six-SS-AR
YoungStars-YS-AR
04Finnish Cardset-292
04Swedish Pure Skills-136
Parallel-136
The Wall-AR
04ITG Heroes/Prospects He Shoots/Scores-11
04ITG Heroes and Prospects Net Prospects-3
04ITG Heroes and Prosp Net Prospects Gold-3
05Be A Player-8
First Period-8
Second Period-8
Third Period-8
Overtime-8
Outtakes-OT5
Quad Signatures-BOST
Signatures-AR
Signatures Gold-AR
Triple Signatures-DRL
Triple Signatures-FGR
Triple Signatures-TGR
05Beehive-9
Matte-9
Matted Materials-MMAR
Signature Scrapbook-SSAR
05Black Diamond-88
Emerald-88
Gold-88
Onyx-88
Ruby-88
05Bruins Boston Globe-19
05Hot Prospects-9
En Fuego-9
Red Hot-9
White Hot-9
05McDonalds Upper Deck-33
Goalie Factory-GF15
Goalie Gear-MG7
05Panini Stickers-27
05Parkhurst-41
Facsimile Auto Parallel-41
True Colors-TCBOS
True Colors-TCBOS
True Colors-TCMOBO
True Colors-TCMOBO
05SP Authentic-10
Limited-10
Chirography-SPAR
Exquisite Endorsements-EEAR
Marks of Distinction-MDAR
Scripts to Success-SSAR
Sign of the Times-AR
Sign of the Times Duals-DRT
Sign of the Times Triples-TRBL
05SP Game Used-10
Autographs-10
Gold-10
Authentic Fabrics-AF-AR
Authentic Fabrics Autographs-AAF-AR
Authentic Fabrics Dual-SR
Authentic Fabrics Dual Autographs-SR
Authentic Fabrics Gold-AF-AR
Authentic Fabrics Quad-TRRK
Authentic Fabrics Quad-TRSB
Authentic Patches Quad -TRRK
Authentic Patches Quad -TRSB
Authentic Fabrics Triple-RLA
Authentic Patches-AP-AR
Authentic Patches Autographs-AAP-AR
Authentic Patches Dual-SR
Authentic Patches Dual Autographs-SR
Authentic Patches Triple-HRR
Authentic Patches Triple-RLA
Awesome Authentics-AA-AR
Awesome Authentics Gold-DA-AR
Game Gear-GG-AR
Game Gear Autographs-AG-AR
Signature Sticks-SS-AR
Statscriptions-ST-AR
05SPx-8
Spectrum-8
Winning Combos-WC-RB
Winning Combos-WC-RL
Winning Combos Autographs-AWC-AK
Winning Combos Autographs-AWC-BO
Winning Combos Gold-WC-RB
Winning Combos Gold-WC-RL
Winning Combos Spectrum-WC-RB
Winning Combos Spectrum-WC-RL
Winning Materials-WM-AR
Winning Materials Autographs-AWM-AR
Winning Materials Gold-WM-AR
Winning Materials Spectrum-WM-AR
05The Cup Dual NHL Shields-DSRT
05The Cup Dual NHL Shields Autographs-ADSRT
05The Cup Emblems of Endorsement-EEAR
05The Cup Hardware Heroes-HHAR
05The Cup Honorable Numbers-HNAR
05The Cup Master Pressplate Rookie Update-199
05The Cup Noble Numbers-NNLR
05The Cup Scripted Numbers-SNLR
05The Cup Scripted Swatches-SSAR
05The Cup Signature Patches-SPAR
05UD Artifacts-7
Blue-7
Gold-7
Green-7
Pewter-7
Red-7
Auto Facts-AF-AR
Auto Facts Blue-AF-AR
Auto Facts Copper-AF-AR
Auto Facts Pewter-AF-AR
Auto Facts Silver-AF-AR
Gold Autographed-7
Remarkable Artifacts-RA-AR
Remarkable Artifacts Dual-RA-AR
05UD PowerPlay-9
05UD PowerPlay-106
05UD PowerPlay-126
Rainbow-9
05UD Toronto Fall Expo Priority Signings-PS-AR
05Ultimate Collection-7
Gold-7
Jerseys Dual-DJBR
Marquee Attractions-MA8
Marquee Attractions Signatures-SMA8
Ultimate Achievements-UAAR
Ultimate Patches Dual-DPBR
Ultimate Signatures-USAR
Ultimate Signatures Pairings-UPRT
05Ultra-15
Gold-15
Difference Makers-DM12
Difference Makers Jerseys-DMJ-AR
Difference Makers Jersey Autographs-DAJ-AR
Difference Makers Patches-DMP-AR
Difference Makers Patch Autographs-DAP-AR
Fresh Ink-FI-AR
Fresh Ink Blue-FI-AR
Ice-15
05Upper Deck-15
05Upper Deck All-Time Greatest-63
05Upper Deck HG Glossy-15
05Upper Deck Jerseys Series II-J2AR
05Upper Deck Majestic Materials-MMAR
05Upper Deck Notable Numbers-N-AR
05Upper Deck Patches-P-AR
05Upper Deck Scrapbooks-HS24
05Upper Deck Ice-8
Rainbow-8
Cool Threads-CTAR
Cool Threads Autographs-ACTAR
Cool Threads Glass-CTAR
Cool Threads Patches-CTPAR
Cool Threads Patch Autographs-CAPAR
Glacial Graphs-GGAR
05Upper Deck MVP-29
Gold-29
Platinum-29
05Upper Deck Rookie Update-7
05Upper Deck Rookie Update-199
05Upper Deck Trilogy-9
05Upper Deck Trilogy-132
Crystal-132
Honorary Patches-HP-AR
Honorary Patch Scripts-HSP-AR
Honorary Swatches-HS-AR
Honorary Swatch Scripts-HSS-AR
Ice Scripts-IS-AR
Scripts-SFS-AR
05Upper Deck Toronto Fall Expo-15
05Upper Deck Victory-15
Black-15
Gold-15
Silver-15
Stars on Ice-SI5
05Finnish Cardset Super Snatchers-14
06Be A Player-58
Autographs-58
Signatures-AR
Signatures 10-63
Signatures 25-63
Signatures Duals-DRT
Signatures Trios-TRPP
Signatures Foursomes-FLTFR
Unmasked Warriors-UM9
Unmasked Warriors Autographs-UM9
Up Close and Personal-UC5
Up Close and Personal Autographs-UC5
06Be A Player Portraits-95
06Beehive-8
Blue-8
Gold-8
Matte-8
Red Facsimile Signatures-8
Wood-8
PhotoGraphs-PGAR
06Between The Pipes Double Jerseys-DJ28
06Between The Pipes Double Jerseys Gold-DJ28
06Between The Pipes Emblems-GUE53
06Between The Pipes Emblems Gold-GUE53
06Between The Pipes Jerseys-GUJ53
06Between The Pipes Jerseys Gold-GUJ53
06Between The Pipes Numbers-GUN53
06Between The Pipes Numbers Gold-GUN53
06Between The Pipes Shooting Gallery-SG02
06Between The Pipes Shooting Gallery Gold-SG02
06Between The Pipes Stick and Jersey-SJ26
06Between The Pipes Stick and Jersey Gold-SJ26
06Between The Pipes The Mask-M06
06Between The Pipes The Mask Gold-M06
06Between The Pipes The Mask Silver-M06
06Between The Pipes The Mask Game-Used-MGU16
06Between The Pipes The Mask Game-Used Gold-MGU16
06Black Diamond-78
Black-78
Gold-78
Ruby-78
06Flair Showcase-198
06Flair Showcase-265
06Flair Showcase-297
Parallel-198
Parallel-265
Parallel-297
Hot Gloves-HG28
Wave of the Future-WF40
06Fleer-184
Tiffany-184
Fabricology-FAR
Netminders-N22
06Gatorade-65
06Hot Prospects-91
Red Hot-91
White Hot-91
Hotagraphs-HAR
06O-Pee-Chee-470
Rainbow-470
Autographs-A-AR
06Panini Stickers-160
06SP Authentic-9
Limited-9
Sign of the Times-STAR
06SP Game Used-94
Gold-94
Rainbow-94
Authentic Fabrics Triple-AF3TOR
Authentic Fabrics Triple Patches-AF3TOR
Authentic Fabrics Sevens-AF7CAL
Authentic Fabrics Sevens Patches-AF7CAL
Autographs-94
Inked Sweaters-ISAR
Inked Sweaters Patches-ISAR
Inked Sweaters Dual-IS2RS
Inked Sweaters Dual Patches-IS2RS
06SPx-93
Spectrum-93
SPxcitement-X94
SPxcitement Spectrum-X94
06The Cup Autographed Foundations-CQAR
06The Cup Autographed Foundations Patches-CQAR
06The Cup Autographed NHL Shields Duals-DASRP
06The Cup Foundations-CQAR
06The Cup Foundations Patches-CQAR
06The Cup Enshrinements-EAR
06The Cup Honorable Numbers-HNAR
06The Cup Limited Logos-LLAR
06The Cup NHL Shields Duals-DSHTO
06The Cup Scripted Swatches-SSAR
06The Cup Signature Patches-SPRA
06UD Artifacts-9
Blue-9
Gold-9
Platinum-9
Radiance-9
Red-9
Tundra Tandems-TTAB
Tundra Tandems Black-TTAB
Tundra Tandems Blue-TTAB
Tundra Tandems Gold-TTAB
Tundra Tandems Platinum-TTAB
Tundra Tandems Red-TTAB
Tundra Tandems Dual Patches Red-TTAB
06UD Mini Jersey Collection-93
06UD Powerplay-94
Impact Rainbow-94
06Ultimate Collection-57
Autographed Jerseys-AJ-AR
Autographed Patches-AJ-AR
Premium Patches-PS-AR
Premium Swatches-PS-AR
Signatures-US-AR
06Ultra-180
Gold Medallion-180
Ice Medallion-180
06Upper Deck Arena Giveaways-TOR4
06Upper Deck-428
Exclusives Parallel-428
High Gloss Parallel-428
Game Jerseys-J2AR
Game Patches-P2AR
Masterpieces-428
Oversized Wal-Mart Exclusives-428
Signatures-SAR
Signature Sensations-SSAR
06Upper Deck MVP-273
Gold Script-273
Super Script-273
Jerseys-OJAR
Last Line of Defense-LL22
06Upper Deck Ovation-197
06Upper Deck Sweet Shot-94
Endorsed Equipment-EEAR
Signature Shots/Saves-SSAR
Signature Shots/Saves Sticks-SSSAR
Sweet Stitches-SSAR
Sweet Stitches Duals-SSAR
Sweet Stitches Triples-SSAR
06Upper Deck Trilogy-92
Honorary Scripted Patches-HSPAR
Honorary Scripted Swatches-HSSAR
Scripts-S3AR
06Upper Deck Victory-19
06Upper Deck Victory-276
06Upper Deck Victory Black-19
06Upper Deck Victory Gold-19
06Upper Deck Victory Next In Line-NL7
07Upper Deck Ovation-55
3x5s-XL4
Autographed 3x5s-XLAAR
07Upper Deck Victory-54
Black-54
Gold-54
GameBreakers-GB41
Oversize Cards-OS16

Raymond, Alain

82North Bay Centennials-18
89Hampton Roads Admirals-19A
89Hampton Roads Admirals-19H
90ProCards AHL/IHL-78
91ProCards-38

Raymond, Eric

90 7th Inn. Sketch QMJHL-73
90 7th Inn. Sketch Memorial Cup-55
91 7th Inn. Sketch QMJHL-241
93Wheeling Thunderbirds-8
95Anaheim Bullfrogs RHI-20

Raymond, Jacques

93O-Pee-Chee Canadiens Hockey Fest-18

Raymond, Marty

05Bakersfield Condors-1

Raymond, Mason

03Camrose Kodiaks-11
04Camrose Kodiaks-13

Raymond, Paul

33V357 Ice Kings-18
35Diamond Matchbooks Tan 1-54
43Parade Sportive *-66

Raymond, Richard

90 7th Inn. Sketch OHL-43
91Cornwall Royals-3
91 7th Inn. Sketch OHL-4

Raymond, Sen. Donat

83Hall of Fame Postcards-E14
85Hall of Fame-73

Raynak, Geoff

92Cornell Big Red-23

Raynak, John

75Roanoke Valley Rebels-2

Rayner, Chuck

34Beehive Group I Photos-246
44Beehive Group II Photos-357
48Exhibits Canadian-51
51Parkhurst-104
52Parkhurst-22
52Royal Desserts-2
53Parkhurst-59
56Adventure R749-63
561956 Adventure Gum-63
83Hall of Fame-163
83Hall of Fame Postcards-L14
85Hall of Fame-163
92Sport-Flash-3
92Sport-Flash Autographs-3
01BAP Memorabilia Goalie Traditions-GT10
01BAP Memorabilia Goalie Traditions-GT34
01BAP Memorabilia Goalie Traditions-GT35
01BAP Memorabilia Goalie Traditions-GT42
01BAP Signature Series Vintage Autographs-VA-14
01BAP Ultimate Mem All-Star History-5
01BAP Ultimate Memorabilia Cornerstones-5
01BAP Ultimate Memorabilia Decades-1
01BAP Update Rocket's Rivals-RR-8
01Between the Pipes-137
01Parkhurst Autographs-PA10
01Parkhurst Reprints-PR36
01Parkhurst Reprints-PR59
01Parkhurst Reprints-PR141
01Parkhurst Vintage Memorabilia-PV24
02BAP NHL All-Star History-5
02Between the Pipes-116
03Parkhurst Original Six New York-53
03Parkhurst Original Six New York-70
03Parkhurst Original Six New York-87
Inserts-N13
Memorabilia-NM25
03Parkhurst Rookie Before the Mask-BTM-15
03Parkhurst Rookie Before the Mask Gold-BTM-15
04ITG NHL AS FANtasy AS History Jerseys-SB5
04ITG Franchises US East-336
04ITG Ultimate Memorabilia-63
Gold-63
Autographs-56
Autographs Gold-56
Broadway Blueshirts-6
Original Six-20
Paper Cuts Memorabilia-19
05ITG Ultimate Mem Decades Jerseys-7
05ITG Ultimate Mem Decades Jerseys Gold-7
05ITG Ultimate Mem Quad Paper Cuts Autos-5
06Between The Pipes Forgotten Franchises-FF01
06ITG Ultimate Memorabilia Decades-4
06ITG Ultimate Memorabilia Decades Gold-4

Razgals, Aigars

98Danish Hockey League-133

Razin, Andrei

98Russian Hockey League-5
99Russian Hockey League-9
99Russian Metallurg Magnetogorsk-36
00Russian Hockey League-336
01Russian Dynamo Moscow-3
01Russian Dynamo Moscow Mentos-12
01Russian Lightnings-4
02Russian SL-1
03Russian Hockey League-10
03Russian SL-10
04Russian Super League All-Stars-10

Razin, Gennady

92Quebec Pee-Wee Tournament-1458
96Kamloops Blazers-19
99Quebec Citadelles-2
00Quebec Citadelles-1
Signed-1
01Quebec Citadelles-1
03Russian Hockey League-15

Razingar, Tomaz

93Quebec Pee-Wee Tournament-1796
99Peoria Rivermen-18
00Peoria Rivermen-19
03Czech OFS Plus-65
03Czech OFS Plus-356
03Czech Pardubice Postcards-14
04Czech OFS-129
06Czech OFS-166
06Czech Super Six Postcards-10

Rdurch, Ingo

94German First League-485

Read, Clayton

99Anchorage Aces-25

Read, Mel

51Laval Dairy QSHL-65

Read, Nathan

97Moose Jaw Warriors-12

Reade, Mark

81Kingston Canadians-4
82Kingston Canadians-12

Reader, Alan

98German DEL-283
99German EHC Straubing-21

Ready, Ryan

95Slapshot-45
99Syracuse Crunch-7
99Bowman CHL-129
Gold-129
OPC International-129
00Kansas City Blades-6
01Manitoba Moose-19
02Manitoba Moose-5
03Manitoba Moose-10
04Philadelphia Phantoms-15
05Hot Prospects-157
En Fuego-157
Red Hot-157
White Hot-157
05The Cup Masterpiece Pressplates (Ice)-226
05The Cup Master Pressplate Rookie Update-164
05Upper Deck Ice-226
05Upper Deck Rookie Update-164
05Philadelphia Phantoms-18

Reagan, Brian

06Texas Tornados-18

Reaney, Brad

04Williams Lake Timberwolves-16

Reaney, Les

03Vernon Vipers-13
04Williams Lake Timberwolves-17

Reardon, Ken

34Beehive Group I Photos-177
40O-Pee-Chee V301-2-116
43Parade Sportive *-72
44Beehive Group II Photos-281
45Quaker Oats Photos-107A
45Quaker Oats Photos-107B
45Quaker Oats Photos-107C
48Exhibits Canadian-21
55Parkhurst-64
Quaker Oats-64
59Parkhurst-22
83Hall of Fame-25
83Hall of Fame Postcards-B11
85Hall of Fame-25
93O-Pee-Chee Canadiens Hockey Fest-42
04ITG Ultimate Memorabilia-86
Gold-86

Reardon, Terry

34Beehive Group I Photos-178

Reasoner, Marty

94Select-150
Gold-150
94Classic Draft Prospects-DP8
95Donruss Elite World Juniors-40
95Upper Deck-566
Electric Ice-566
Electric Ice Gold-566
96Upper Deck Ice-150
98Black Diamond-76
Double Diamond-76
Triple Diamond-76
Quadruple Diamond-76
98Bowman's Best-113
Refractors-113
Atomic Refractors-113
Mirror Image Fusion-F16
Mirror Image Fusion Refractors-F16
Mirror Image Fusion Atomic Refractors-F16
98Pacific Dynagon Ice-162
Blue-162
Red-162
Rookies-7
98Pacific Omega-208
Red-208
Opening Day Issue-208
98SP Authentic-107
Power Shift-107
98Topps Gold Label Class 1-72
Black-72
Black One of One-72
One of One-72
Red-72
Red One of One-72
98Topps Gold Label Class 2-72
98Topps Gold Label Class 2 Black-72
98Topps Gold Label Class 2 Black 1 of 1-72
98Topps Gold Label Class 2 One of One-72
98Topps Gold Label Class 2 Red-72
98Topps Gold Label Class 2 Red One of One-72
98Topps Gold Label Class 3-72
98Topps Gold Label Class 3 Black-72
98Topps Gold Label Class 3 Black 1 of 1-72
98Topps Gold Label Class 3 One of One-72
98Topps Gold Label Class 3 Red-72
98Topps Gold Label Class 3 Red One of One-72
98Upper Deck-419
Exclusives-419
Exclusives 1 of 1-419
Generation Next-GN5
Generation Next Quantum 1-GN5
Generation Next Quantum 2-GN5
Generation Next Quantum 3-GN5
Profiles-P1
Profiles Quantum 1-P1
Profiles Quantum 2-P1
Profiles Quantum 3-P1
Gold Reserve-419
98Upper Deck MVP-178
Gold Script-178
Silver Script-178
Super Script-178
99BAP Memorabilia-253
Gold-253
Silver-253
99O-Pee-Chee-49
99O-Pee-Chee Chrome-49
99O-Pee-Chee Chrome Refractors-49
99Pacific-368
Copper-368
Emerald Green-368
Gold-368
Ice Blue-368
Premiere Date-368
Red-368
99Topps/OPC-49
99Topps/OPC Chrome-49
Refractors-49
00BAP Memorabilia-241
Emerald-241
Ruby-241
Sapphire-241
Promos-241
00BAP Mem Chicago Sportsfest Copper-241
00BAP Memorabilia Chicago Sportsfest Blue-241
00BAP Memorabilia Chicago Sportsfest Gold-241
00BAP Memorabilia Chicago Sportsfest Ruby-241
00BAP Memorabilia Chicago Sun-Times Ruby-241
00BAP Memorabilia Chicago Sun-Times Gold-241
00BAP Mem Chicago Sun-Times Sapphire-241
00BAP Mem Toronto Fall Expo Copper-241
00BAP Memorabilia Toronto Fall Expo Gold-241
00BAP Memorabilia Toronto Fall Expo Ruby-241
00BAP Signature Series-56
Emerald-56
Ruby-56
Sapphire-56
Autographs-61
Autographs Gold-61
00O-Pee-Chee-262A
00O-Pee-Chee Parallel-262A
00Pacific-350
Copper-350
Gold-350
Ice Blue-350
Premiere Date-350
00Topps/OPC-262A
Parallel-262A
00Upper Deck-155
Exclusives Tier 1-155
Exclusives Tier 2-155
00Upper Deck Vintage-311
00Worcester Icecats-22
01Parkhurst-229
02BAP Sig Series Auto Buybacks 2000-61
02NHL Power Play Stickers-38
02Oilers Postcards-7
02Upper Deck-70
Exclusives-70
03ITG Action-285
03Oilers Postcards-14
03Pacific Complete-80
Red-80
03Upper Deck MVP-161
Gold Script-161
Silver Script-161
Canadian Exclusives-161
03Worcester Ice Cats 10th Anniversary-13

Reaugh, Daryl

84Kamloops Blazers-21
85Nova Scotia Oilers-13
87Oilers Team Issue-29
88Oilers Tenth Anniversary-62
88ProCards AHL-80
89ProCards AHL-291
90Upper Deck-541
French-541
90Whalers Jr. 7-Eleven-20
90ProCards AHL/IHL-184
91Bowman-19
91O-Pee-Chee-391
91Stadium Club-326
91Topps-391
91ProCards-93

Reaume, Marc

44Beehive Group II Photos-444
52Juniors Blue Tint-146
55Parkhurst-7
Quaker Oats-7
57Parkhurst-T12
58Parkhurst-20
59Parkhurst-11
60Parkhurst-25
60Shirriff Coins-52
63Chex Photos-45
63Parkhurst-37
63Parkhurst-96
63York White Backs-32
66Tulsa Oilers-9
70Canucks Royal Bank-14
70Esso Power Players-42
70O-Pee-Chee-119
70Topps-119
76Old Timers-15
94Parkhurst Missing Link-114

Reaves, Ryan

04Brandon Wheat Kings-20
05Brandon Wheat Kings-19

Reay, Billy

43Parade Sportive *-67
44Beehive Group II Photos-282
45Quaker Oats Photos-108A
45Quaker Oats Photos-108B
45Quaker Oats Photos-108C
45Quaker Oats Photos-108D
48Exhibits Canadian-22
51Parkhurst-13
52Parkhurst-2
55Parkhurst-66
Quaker Oats-66
57Parkhurst-T25
58Parkhurst-25
63Topps-22
64Topps-38
65Topps-54
66Topps-53
70Blackhawks Postcards-5
74O-Pee-Chee NHL-204
74Topps-204
94Parkhurst Tall Boys-43
02Parkhurst Reprints-152
02Parkhurst Reprints-163
02Parkhurst Reprints-223
02Parkhurst Reprints-230

Rebek, Jeremy

93Owen Sound Platers-24
94Owen Sound Platers-16
95Slapshot-297
95Owen Sound Platers-19
97Toledo Storm-8
99Missouri River Otters-14
99Missouri River Otters Sheet-12
99UHL All-Stars West-8T
00Missouri River Otters-6
02Rockford Ice Hogs-10

Reber, Jorg

93Swiss HNL-67
95Swiss HNL-376
96Swiss HNL-235
98Swiss Power Play Stickers-183
99Swiss Panini Stickers-182
00Swiss Panini Stickers-227
00Swiss Slapshot Mini-Cards-RJ5
01Swiss HNL-306
02Swiss HNL-368

Rebernik, Chris

02St. Michaels Majors-12

Rebolj, Luka

93Quebec Pee-Wee Tournament-1786

Rebolj, Miha

99Czech OFS-111
00Czech OFS-300
03Czech OFS Plus-104

Recchi, Mark

86Kamloops Blazers-18
87Kamloops Blazers-19
88ProCards IHL-62
90Bowman-206
Tiffany-206
90O-Pee-Chee-280
90Panini Stickers-130
90Panini Stickers-341
90Penguins Foodland-6
90Pro Set-239
90Score-186
Canadian-186
90Score Hottest/Rising Stars-81
90Score Young Superstars-35
90Topps-280
Tiffany-280
90Upper Deck-178
90Upper Deck-487
French-178
French-487
91Pro Set Platinum-97
91Pro Set Platinum-144
91Bowman-83
91Kraft-2
91McDonald's Upper Deck-4
91O-Pee-Chee-196
91Panini Stickers-280
91Parkhurst-134
91Parkhurst-347
French-134
French-347
91Penguins Coke/Elby's-8
91Penguins Foodland Coupon Stickers-10
91Pinnacle-151
91Pinnacle-360
French-151
French-360
91Pro Set-184
91Pro Set-313
French-184
French-313
CC-CC8
CC French-CC8
91Score American-145
91Score Canadian Bilingual-145
91Score Canadian English-145
91Score Kellogg's-9
91Score Young Superstars-22
91Stadium Club-256
91Topps-196
Team Scoring Leaders-5
91Upper Deck-92
91Upper Deck-346
French-92
French-346
91Finnish Semic World Champ Stickers-74
91Swedish Semic World Champ Stickers-74
92Bowman-314
92Flyers J.C. Penney-20
92Flyers Upper Deck Sheets-3
92Flyers Upper Deck Sheets-22
92Flyers Upper Deck Sheets-36
92Flyers Upper Deck Sheets-42
92O-Pee-Chee-373
92Panini Stickers-185
92Panini Stickers French-185
92Parkhurst-130
Emerald Ice-130
92Pinnacle Canadian Promo Panels-1
92Pinnacle-80
French-80
92Pro Set-131
92Score-180
Canadian-180
Sharpshooters-18
Sharpshooters Canadian-18
Young Superstars-7
92Seasons Patches-41
92Stadium Club-183
92Topps-267
92Topps-410
Gold-267G
Gold-410G
92Ultra-158
92Upper Deck-327
93Donruss-252
93Flyers J.C. Penney-17
93Flyers Lineup Sheets-28
93Flyers Lineup Sheets-29
93Flyers Lineup Sheets-42
93Leaf-205
93McDonald's Upper Deck-22
93OPC Premier-230
Gold-230
93Panini Stickers-46
93Parkhurst-149
Emerald Ice-149
93Pinnacle-50
Canadian-50
All-Stars-6
All-Stars Canadian-6
Nifty Fifty-13
Team 2001-30
Team 2001 Canadian-30
93PowerPlay-184
Point Leaders-12
93Score-150
93Score-442
Canadian-150
Canadian-442
Dynamic Duos U.S.-1
93Stadium Club-136
Members Only Master Set-136
OPC-136
First Day Issue-136
First Day Issue OPC-136
All-Stars-18
All-Stars Members Only-18
All-Stars OPC-18
93Topps/OPC Premier-230
Gold-230
93Ultra-236
Red Light Specials-8
93Upper Deck-222
93Upper Deck-300
93Upper Deck-350
SP-117
93Upper Deck Locker All-Stars-11
93Swedish Semic World Champ Stickers-205
93Classic Autographs-AU10
93Classic McDonalds-16
93Classic Team Canada-TC5
93Classic Pro Prospects-34
BCs-BC20
94Be A Player-R18-
Signature Cards-7
94Canada Games NHL POGS-195
94Donruss-121
94EA Sports-101
94Finest-109
Super Team Winners-109
Refractors-109
Division's Clear Cut-5
94Flair-130
94Fleer-106
Headliners-9
94Hockey Wit-104
94Kraft-11
94Leaf-89
Gold Stars-15
94Leaf Limited-71
94OPC Premier-90
Special Effects-90
94Parkhurst-165
94Parkhurst-315
Gold-165
Gold-315
SE Vintage-28
94Pinnacle-53
Artist's Proofs-53
Rink Collection-53
94Score-50
Gold-50
Platinum-50
90 Plus Club-7
94Select-30
Gold-30
94SP-62
Die Cuts-62
94Stadium Club Members Only-34
94Stadium Club Super Teams-17
94Stadium Club Super Team MemberOnly Set-17
94Topps/OPC Premier-90
Special Effects-90
94Topps Finest Inserts-21
94Ultra-158
94Upper Deck-94
94Upper Deck-441
Electric Ice-94
Electric Ice-441
SP Inserts-SP58
SP Inserts Die Cuts-SP58
94Finnish Jaa Kiekko-101
94Classic Pro Prospects Intl Heroes-LP24
94Classic Pro Prospects Jumbos-PP13
95Bashan Super Stickers-64
95Bowman-51
All-Foil-51
95Canada Games NHL POGS-150
95Canadiens Postcards-15
95Canadiens Sheets-6
95Collector's Choice-108

Player's Club-108
Player's Club Platinum-108
95Donruss-48
95Donruss Elite-103
Die Cut Stars-103
Die Cut Uncut-103
95Emotion-90
95Finest-119
Refractors-119
95Hoyle Eastern Playing Cards-52
95Imperial Stickers-64
95Kraft-73
95Leaf-65
95Leaf Limited-54
95McDonald's Pinnacle-MCD-24
95Metal-77
95Panini Stickers-41
95Parkhurst International-383
Emerald Ice-383
95Pinnacle-24
Artist's Proofs-24
Rink Collection-24
95Playoff One on One-54
95Post Upper Deck-9
95Pro Magnets-23
95Score Promos-10
95Score-10
Black Ice Artist's Proofs-10
Black Ice-10
Golden Blades-18
95Select Certified-10
Mirror Gold-10
95SkyBox Impact-86
95SP-72
95Stadium Club Members Only-9
95Stadium Club-48
Members Only Master Set-48
95Summit-26
Artist's Proofs-26
Ice-26
95Topps-165
OPC Inserts-165
Home Grown Canada-HGC27
Power Lines-9PL
95Topps SuperSkills-58
Platinum-58
95Ultra-82
Gold Medallion-82
95Upper Deck-490
Special Edition-SE43
Special Edition Gold-SE43
95Zenith-8
95Swedish Globe World Championships-98
95Images Platinum Players-PL6
96Be A Player-20
Autographs-20
Autographs Silver-20
96Black Diamond-149
Gold-149
96Canadiens Postcards-21
96Canadiens Sheets-15
96Collector's Choice-135
96Donruss-27
Press Proofs-27
96Donruss Canadian Ice-23
Gold Press Proofs-23
Red Press Proofs-23
96Donruss Elite-26
Die Cut Stars-26
96Flair-49
Blue Ice-49
96Fleer-55
96Leaf-37
Press Proofs-37
96Leaf Preferred-115
Press Proofs-115
96Metal Universe-81
96NHL Pro Stamps-23
96Pinnacle-64
Artist's Proofs-64
Foil-64
Premium Stock-64
Rink Collection-64
96Post Upper Deck-15
96Score-26
Artist's Proofs-26
Dealer's Choice Artist's Proofs-26
Special Artist's Proofs-26
Golden Blades-26
96SkyBox Impact-63
96SP-85
96Summit-17
Artist's Proofs-17
Ice-17
Metal-17
Premium Stock-17
96Topps Picks-63
OPC Inserts-63
96Ultra-88
Gold Medallion-88
96Upper Deck-87
96Swedish Semic Wien-96
97SLU Hockey Canadian-16
97SLU Hockey American-18
97Beehive-23
Golden Portraits-23
97Black Diamond-23
Double Diamond-23
Triple Diamond-23
Quadruple Diamond-23
97Canadiens Postcards-16
97Collector's Choice-133
Star Quest-SQ75
97Crown Royale-71
Emerald Green-71
Ice Blue-71
Silver-71
97Donruss-136
Press Proofs Silver-136
Press Proofs Gold-136
97Donruss Canadian Ice-53
Dominion Series-53
Provincial Series-53
National Pride-18
97Donruss Limited-52
97Donruss Limited-152
Exposure-52
Exposure-152
97Donruss Preferred-46
Cut to the Chase-46
97Donruss Priority-61
Stamp of Approval-61
97Gatorade Stickers-4
97Katch-77
Gold-77
Silver-77
97Kenner Starting Lineup Cards-18
97Leaf-127
Fractal Matrix-127
Fractal Matrix Die Cuts-127
97Leaf International-127
Universal Ice-127
97NHL Aces Playing Cards-5
97Pacific-298
Copper-298
Emerald Green-298
Ice Blue-298
Red-298
Silver-298
Slap Shots Die-Cuts-4A
97Pacific Dynagon-64
Copper-64
Dark Grey-64
Emerald Green-64
Ice Blue-64
Red-64
Silver-64
Tandems-47
97Pacific Invincible-72
Copper-72
Emerald Green-72
Ice Blue-72
Red-72
Silver-72
97Pacific Omega-121
Copper-121
Dark Gray-121
Emerald Green-121
Gold-121
Ice Blue-121
Team Leaders-12
97Panini Stickers-32
97Paramount-97
Copper-97
Dark Grey-97
Emerald Green-97
Ice Blue-97
Red-97
Silver-97
97Pinnacle-104
Press Plates Back Black-104
Press Plates Back Cyan-104
Press Plates Back Magenta-104
Press Plates Back Yellow-104
Press Plates Front Black-104
Press Plates Front Cyan-104
Press Plates Front Magenta-104
Press Plates Front Yellow-104
97Pinnacle Certified-58
Red-58
Mirror Blue-58
Mirror Gold-58
Mirror Red-58
97Pinnacle Inside-112
97Pinnacle Tot Cert Platinum Blue-58
97Pinnacle Tot Certi Platinum Gold-58
97Pinnacle Totally Certified Platinum Red-58
97Pinnacle Tot Cert Mirror Platinum Gold-58
97Revolution-73
Copper-73
Emerald-73
Ice Blue-73
Silver-73
97Score-130
Artist's Proofs-130
Golden Blades-130
Check It-2
97Score Canadiens-5
Platinum-5
Premier-5
97SP Authentic-79
Icons-I25
Icons Die-Cuts-I25
Icons Embossed-I25
97Studio-57
Press Proofs Silver-57
Press Proofs Gold-57
97Upper Deck-84
Game Dated Moments-84
97Upper Deck Ice-23
Parallel-23
Power Shift-23
97Zenith-36
Z-Gold-36
Z-Silver-36
97Zenith 5 x 7-24
Gold Impulse-24
Silver Impulse-24
98Aurora-95
Championship Fever-25
Championship Fever Copper-25
Championship Fever Ice Blue-25
Championship Fever Red-25
Championship Fever Silver-25
98Be A Player-68
Press Release-68
98BAP Gold-68
98BAP Autographs-68
98BAP Autographs Gold-68
98BAP Tampa Bay All Star Game-68
98Black Diamond-44
Double Diamond-44
Triple Diamond-44
Quadruple Diamond-44
98Bowman's Best-96
Refractors-96
Atomic Refractors-96
98Canadiens Team Issue-16
98Crown Royale-71
Limited Series-71
98Finest-81
No Protectors-81
No Protectors Refractors-81
Refractors-81
98Pacific-256
Ice Blue-256
Red-256
98Pacific Dynagon Ice-97
Blue-97
Red-97
98Pacific Omega-124
Red-124
Opening Day Issue-124
98Panini Photocards-67
98Panini Stickers-34
98Paramount-116
Copper-116
Emerald Green-116
Holo-Electric-116
Ice Blue-116
Silver-116
98Post-7
98Revolution-75
Ice Shadow-75
Red-75
All-Star Die Cuts-24
98SP Authentic-42
Power Shift-42
98SPx Finite-43
Radiance-43
Spectrum-43
98Topps Gold Label Class 1-47
Black-47
Black One of One-47
One of One-47
Red-47
Red One of One-47
98Topps Gold Label Class 2-47
98Topps Gold Label Class 2 Black-47
98Topps Gold Label Class 2 Black 1 of 1-47
98Topps Gold Label Class 2 One of One-47
98Topps Gold Label Class 2 Red-47
98Topps Gold Label Class 2 Red One of One-47
98Topps Gold Label Class 3-47
98Topps Gold Label Class 3 Black-47
98Topps Gold Label Class 3 Black 1 of 1-47
98Topps Gold Label Class 3 One of One-47
98Topps Gold Label Class 3 Red-47
98Topps Gold Label Class 3 Red One of One-47
98UD Choice-109
98UD Choice-231
98UD Choice Preview-109
98UD Choice Prime Choice Reserve-109
98UD Choice Prime Choice Reserve-231
98UD Choice Reserve-109
98UD Choice Reserve-231
98Upper Deck-111
Exclusives-111
Exclusives 1 of 1-111
Fantastic Finishers-FF19
Fantastic Finishers Quantum 1-FF19
Fantastic Finishers Quantum 2-FF19
Fantastic Finishers Quantum 3-FF19
Gold Reserve-111
98Upper Deck MVP-152
Gold Script-152
Silver Script-152
Super Script-152
99Aurora-107
Striped-107
Premiere Date-107
Premiere Date Striped-107
99BAP Memorabilia-13
Gold-13
Silver-13
99BAP Millennium-182
Emerald-182
Ruby-182
Sapphire-182
Signatures-182
Signatures Gold-182
99Crown Royale-105
Limited Series-105
Premiere Date-105
Ice Elite-20
Ice Elite Parallel-20
99O-Pee-Chee-130
99O-Pee-Chee Chrome-130
99O-Pee-Chee Chrome Refractors-130
99Pacific-310
Copper-310
Emerald Green-310
Gold-310
Ice Blue-310
Premiere Date-310
Red-310
Gold Crown Die-Cuts-27
99Pacific Dynagon Ice-149
Blue-149
Copper-149
Gold-149
Premiere Date-149
99Pacific Omega-174
Copper-174
Gold-174
Ice Blue-174
Premiere Date-174
5 Star Talents-22
5 Star Talents Parallel-22
99Pacific Prism-104
Holographic Blue-104
Holographic Gold-104
Holographic Mirror-104
Holographic Purple-104
Premiere Date-104
Clear Advantage-17
99Panini Stickers-126
99Paramount-174
Copper-174
Emerald-174
Gold-174
Holographic Emerald-174
Holographic Gold-174
Holographic Silver-174
Ice Blue-174
Premiere Date-174
Red-174
Silver-174
Personal Best-27
99Revolution-109
Premiere Date-109
Red-109
Shadow Series-109
Top of the Line-28
Copper-109
Gold-109
CSC Silver-109
99SPx-112
Radiance-112
Spectrum-112
99Stadium Club-109
First Day Issue-109
One of a Kind-109
Printing Plates Black-109
Printing Plates Cyan-109
Printing Plates Magenta-109
Printing Plates Yellow-109
99Topps/OPC-130
99Topps/OPC Chrome-130
Refractors-130
99Topps Gold Label Class 1-30
Black-30
Black One of One-30
One of One-30
Red-30
Red One of One-30
99Topps Gold Label Class 2-30
99Topps Gold Label Class 2 Black-30
99Topps Gold Label Class 2 Black 1 of 1-30
99Topps Gold Label Class 2 One of One-30
99Topps Gold Label Class 2 Red-30
99Topps Gold Label Class 2 Red One of One-30
99Topps Gold Label Class 3-30
99Topps Gold Label Class 3 Black-30
99Topps Gold Label Class 3 Black 1 of 1-30
99Topps Gold Label Class 3 One of One-30
99Topps Gold Label Class 3 Red-30
99Topps Gold Label Class 3 Red One of One-30
99Topps Premier Plus-52
Parallel-52
99Upper Deck-97
Exclusives-97
Exclusives 1 of 1-97
99Upper Deck Gold Reserve-97
99Upper Deck MVP-150
Gold Script-150
Silver Script-150
Super Script-150
99Upper Deck MVP SC Edition-134
Gold Script-134
Silver Script-134
Super Script-134
99Upper Deck Retro-59
Gold-59
Platinum-59
99Upper Deck Victory-213
99Wayne Gretzky Hockey-126
00Aurora-109
Pinstripes-109
Pinstripes Premiere Date-109
Premiere Date-109
00BAP Memorabilia-267
Emerald-267
Ruby-267
Sapphire-267
Promos-267
Jersey Cards-J36
Jersey Emblems-E36
Jersey Numbers-N36
Jersey and Stick Cards-JS36
00BAP Mem Chicago Sportsfest Copper-267
00BAP Memorabilia Chicago Sportsfest Blue-267
00BAP Memorabilia Chicago Sportsfest Gold-267
00BAP Memorabilia Chicago Sportsfest Ruby-267
00BAP Memorabilia Chicago Sun-Times Ruby-267
00BAP Memorabilia Chicago Sun-Times Gold-267
00BAP Mem Chicago Sun-Times Sapphire-267
00BAP Mem Toronto Fall Expo Copper-267
00BAP Memorabilia Toronto Fall Expo Gold-267
00BAP Memorabilia Toronto Fall Expo Ruby-267
00BAP Parkhurst 2000-P50
00BAP Signature Series-88
Emerald-88
Ruby-88
Sapphire-88
Autographs-132
Autographs Gold-132
He Shoots-He Scores Prizes-13
00O-Pee-Chee-42
00O-Pee-Chee Parallel-42
00Pacific-306
Copper-306
Gold-306
Ice Blue-306
Premiere Date-306
Gold Crown Die Cuts-25
00Panini Stickers-76
00Paramount-185
Copper-185
Gold-185
Holo-Gold-185
Holo-Silver-185
Ice Blue-185
Premiere Date-185
Freeze Frame-27
00Revolution-111
Blue-111
Premiere Date-111
Red-111
HD NHL-26
Ice Immortals-16
Stat Masters-28
00SP Authentic-66
00Stadium Club-48
Beam Team-BT25
00Topps/OPC-42
Parallel-42
Autographs-AMR
Own the Game-OTG3
00Topps Chrome-34
OPC Refractors-34
Refractors-34
00Topps Gold Label Class 1-3
Gold-3
00Topps Gold Label Class 2-3
00Topps Gold Label Class 2 Gold-3
00Topps Gold Label Class 3-3
00Topps Gold Label Class 3 Gold-3
00Topps Heritage-37
Chrome Parallel-37
00Topps Premier Plus-31
Blue Ice-31
00Topps Stars-29
Blue-29
Game Gear-GGMR
00UD Pros and Prospects-63
00UD Reserve-63
Practice Session Jerseys-MR
Practice Session Jerseys Autographs-MR
00Upper Deck-127
Exclusives Tier 1-127
Exclusives Tier 2-127
00Upper Deck MVP-131
First Stars-131
Second Stars-131
Third Stars-131
00Upper Deck Victory-169
00Upper Deck Vintage-268
01Atomic-73
Blue-73
Gold-73
Premiere Date-73
Red-73
01BAP Memorabilia-292
Emerald-292
Ruby-292
Sapphire-292
Country of Origin-CO55
He Shoots-He Scores Prizes-38
01BAP Signature Series Certified 100-C28
01BAP Signature Series Certified 50-C28
01BAP Signature Series Certified 1 of 1's-C28
01BAP Signature Series Autographs-LMR
01BAP Signature Series Autographs Gold-LMR
01BAP Sig Series He Shoots/Scores Prizes-23
01BAP Signature Series Jerseys-GJ-48
01BAP Sig Series Jersey and Stick Cards-GSJ-48
01BAP Signature Series Emblems-GUE-47
01BAP Signature Series Numbers-ITN-47
01BAP Signature Series Teammates-TM-22
01BAP Ultimate Memorabilia Autographs-6
01BAP Ultimate Mem Autographs Gold-6
01BAP Ultimate Memorabilia Dynamic Duos-10
01BAP Ultimate Memorabilia Les Canadiens-1
01BAP Ultimate Memorabilia Name Plates-6
01BAP Update Heritage-H23
01Bowman YoungStars-108
Gold-108
Ice Cubed-108
01Crown Royale-108
Blue-108
Premiere Date-108
Red-108
Retail-108
01Flyers Postcards-17
01O-Pee-Chee-101
01O-Pee-Chee-322
01O-Pee-Chee Heritage Parallel-101
01O-Pee-Chee Heritage Parallel Limited-101
01O-Pee-Chee Premier Parallel-101
01O-Pee-Chee Premier Parallel-322
01Pacific-294
Extreme LTD-294
Hobby LTD-294
Premiere Date-294
Retail LTD-294
01Pacific Adrenaline-142
Blue-142
Premiere Date-142
Red-142
Retail-142
01Pacific Arena Exclusives-294
01Pacific Heads-Up-73
Blue-73
Premiere Date-73
Red-73
Silver-73
01Parkhurst-22
Gold-22
Silver-22
Jerseys-PJ5
Jersey and Stick-PSJ15
Milestones-M9
Milestones-M30
Sticks-PS5
Teammates-T13
01Private Stock-73
Gold-73
Premiere Date-73
Retail-73
Silver-73
01Private Stock Pacific Nights-73
01SP Authentic-63
Limited-63
Limited Gold-63
Jerseys-NNMR
Sign of the Times-LR
01SP Game Used Authentic Fabric-AFMR
01SP Game Used Authentic Fabric-DFRF
01SP Game Used Authentic Fabric-TFLRP
01SP Game Used Authentic Fabric Gold-AFMR
01Stadium Club-56
Award Winners-56
Master Photos-56
Souvenirs-MR
01Titanium-106
Hobby Parallel-106
Premiere Date-106
Retail-106
Retail Parallel-106
01Topps-101
01Topps-322
Heritage Parallel-101
Heritage Parallel Limited-101
OPC Parallel-101
OPC Parallel-322
01Topps Chrome-101
Refractors-101
Black Border Refractors-101
01Topps Heritage-49
Refractors-49
01Topps Reserve-54
Emblems-MR
Jerseys-MR
Name Plates-MR
Numbers-MR
Patches-MR
01UD Mask Collection-73
Gold-73
01UD Playmakers-72
Combo Jerseys-CJMR
Combo Jerseys Gold-CJMR
Jerseys-J-MR
Jerseys Gold-J-MR
01Upper Deck-128
Exclusives-128
Crunch Timers-CT10
01Upper Deck MVP-141
Morning Skate Jerseys-J-MR
Morning Skate Jersey Autographs-SJ-MR
Souvenirs-S-MR
Souvenirs Gold-S-MR
01Upper Deck Victory-260
01Upper Deck Victory-431
Gold-260
Gold-431
01Upper Deck Vintage-188
01Upper Deck Vintage-190
01Upper Deck Vintage-191
02BAP All-Star Edition-73
He Shoots-He Score Prizes-23
Jerseys-73
Jerseys Gold-73
Jerseys Silver-73
02BAP First Edition-83
02BAP First Edition-311
Jerseys-83
02BAP Memorabilia-182
02BAP Memorabilia-250
Emerald-182
Emerald-250
Ruby-182
Ruby-250
Sapphire-182
Sapphire-250
All-Star Jerseys-ASJ-46
NHL All-Star Game-182
NHL All-Star Game-250
NHL All-Star Game Blue-182
NHL All-Star Game Blue-250
NHL All-Star Game Green-182
NHL All-Star Game Green-250
NHL All-Star Game Red-182
NHL All-Star Game Red-250
Teammates-TM-10
02BAP Memorabilia Toronto Fall Expo-182
02BAP Memorabilia Toronto Fall Expo-250
02BAP Signature Series-158
Autographs-158
Autograph Buybacks 1998-68
Autograph Buybacks 1999-182
Autograph Buybacks 2000-132
Autograph Buybacks 2001-LMR
Autographs Gold-158
Team Quads-TQ3
02BAP Ultimate Memorabilia All-Star MVP-14
02Bowman YoungStars-34
Gold-34
Silver-34
02Flyers Postcards-3
02ITG Used-57
02ITG Used-157
Jerseys-GUJ47
Jersey Autographs-GUJ47
Jerseys Gold-GUJ47
Jersey and Stick-SJ47
Jersey and Stick Gold-SJ47
02O-Pee-Chee-40
02O-Pee-Chee Premier Blue Parallel-40
02O-Pee-Chee Premier Red Parallel-40
02O-Pee-Chee Factory Set-40
02Pacific-286
Blue-286
Red-286
02Pacific Complete-20
02Pacific Complete-213
Red-20
Red-213
02Pacific Exclusive-128
02Pacific Heads-Up-92
Blue-92
Purple-92
Red-92
02Parkhurst-42
Bronze-42
Gold-42
Silver-42
Jerseys-GJ25
Stick and Jerseys-SJ25
Teammates-TT2
02Parkhurst Retro-63
Minis-63
02SP Game Used-60
Authentic Fabrics-AFMR
Authentic Fabrics Gold-AFMR
Authentic Fabrics Rainbow-AFMR
Piece of History-PHMR
Piece of History Gold-PHMR
Piece of History Rainbow-PHMR
02SPx-136
Milestones-MMR
Milestones Gold-MR
Milestones Silver-MR
02Stadium Club-96
Silver Decoy Cards-96
Proofs-96
02Topps-40
OPC Blue Parallel-40
OPC Red Parallel-40
Captain's Cloth-CC2
Factory Set-40
02Topps Chrome-36
Black Border Refractors-36
Refractors-36
02Topps Heritage-67
Chrome Parallel-67
Great Skates-MR
Great Skates Patches-MR
02Topps Total-270
02UD Top Shelf Dual Player Jerseys-STGR
02UD Top Shelf Milestones Jerseys-MBBRR
02UD Top Shelf Triple Jerseys-HTLRR
02Upper Deck-130
Exclusives-130
CHL Graduates-CGMR
CHL Graduates Gold-CGMR
Pinpoint Accuracy-PAMR
Specialists-SMR
Classic Portraits Hockey Royalty-LRR
Classic Portraits Hockey Royalty Limited-LRR
02Upper Deck MVP-134
Gold-134
Classics-134
Golden Classics-134
Skate Around Jerseys-SDKR
Skate Around Jerseys-SDRG
Skate Around Jerseys-STLPR
Souvenirs-S-MR
02Upper Deck Victory-155
Bronze-155
Gold-155
Silver-155
02Upper Deck Vintage-185
02Upper Deck Vintage-302
Green Backs-185
Jerseys-SOMR
Jerseys Gold-SO-MR
03BAP Memorabilia Stanley Cup Playoffs-SCP-15
03BAP Ultimate Memorabilia Autographs-87
Gold-87
03BAP Ultimate Mem Auto Jerseys-87
03Beehive-142
Gold-142
Silver-142
Sticks Blue Border-BL19
03Crown Royale-74
Blue-74
Retail-74
03Flyers Postcards-18
03ITG Action-414
Jerseys-M144
03ITG Used Signature Series-43
Gold-43
Autographs-MR
Autographs Gold-MR
Teammates-2
Teammates Gold-2
03NHL Sticker Collection-106
03O-Pee-Chee-229
03OPC Blue-229
03OPC Gold-229
03OPC Red-229
03Pacific-256
Blue-256
Red-256
03Pacific Calder-74
Silver-74
03Pacific Complete-234
Red-234
03Pacific Exhibit-112
Blue Backs-112
Yellow Backs-112
03Pacific Prism-77
Blue-77
Gold-77
Red-77
03Pacific Quest for the Cup-79
Blue-79
03Parkhurst Original Six Montreal-33
03Private Stock Reserve-77
Blue-77
Red-77
Retail-77
03Titanium-76
Hobby Jersey Number Parallels-76
Retail-76
Retail Jersey Number Parallels-76
03Topps-229
Blue-229
Gold-229
Red-229
03Topps C55-57
Minis-57
Minis American Back-57
Minis American Back Red-57
Minis Bazooka Back-57
Minis Brooklyn Back-57
Minis Hat Trick Back-57
Minis O Canada Back-57
Minis O Canada Back Red-57
Minis Stanley Cup Back-57
03Topps Pristine Popular Demand Relics-PD-MR
03Topps Pristine Popular Demand Relic Ref-PD-MR
03Topps Traded Franchise Fabrics-FF-MR
03UD Premier Collection Stars-ST-MR
03UD Premier Collection Stars Patches-ST-MR
03Upper Deck-138
Canadian Exclusives-138
HG-138
Jerseys-GJ-MR
03Upper Deck MVP-306
Gold Script-306
Silver Script-306
Canadian Exclusives-306
Souvenirs-S12
03Upper Deck Victory-138
Bronze-138
Gold-138
Silver-138
04Pacific-197
Blue-197
Red-197
04SP Authentic-73
04Upper Deck-139
Canadian Exclusives-139
HG Glossy Gold-139
HG Glossy Silver-139
05Be A Player-71
First Period-71
Second Period-71
Third Period-71
Overtime-71
05Beehive-72
Matte-72
05Black Diamond-111
Emerald-111
Gold-111
Onyx-111
Ruby-111
05Hot Prospects-16
En Fuego-16
Red Hot-16
White Hot-16
05Panini Stickers-141
05Parkhurst-98
Facsimile Auto Parallel-383
True Colors-TCPIT
True Colors-TCPIT
05SP Authentic-81
Limited-81
Prestigious Pairings-PPRP
05SP Game Used Authentic Fabrics-AF-MR
05SP Game Used Authentic Fabrics Gold-AF-MR
05SP Game Used Authentic Patches Quad -PRLL
05SP Game Used Authentic Patches-AP-MR
05SP Game Used Auto Draft-AD-RC
05SP Game Used Awesome Authentics-AA-RE
05SPx-74
Spectrum-74
Winning Combos-WC-PR
Winning Combos Gold-WC-PR
Winning Combos Spectrum-WC-PR
05UD Artifacts-82
05UD Artifacts-190
Blue-82
Blue-190
Gold-82
Gold-190
Green-82
Green-190
Pewter-82
Pewter-190
Red-82
Red-190
Frozen Artifacts-FA-RE
Frozen Artifacts Autographed-FA-RE
Frozen Artifacts Copper-FA-RE
Frozen Artifacts Dual-FAD-RE
Frozen Artifacts Dual Autographed-FAD-RE
Frozen Artifacts Dual Copper-FAD-RE
Frozen Artifacts Dual Gold-FAD-RE
Frozen Artifacts Dual Maroon-FAD-RE
Frozen Artifacts Dual Pewter-FAD-RE
Frozen Artifacts Dual Silver-FAD-RE
Frozen Artifacts Gold-FA-RE
Frozen Artifacts Maroon-FA-RE
Frozen Artifacts Patches-FP-RE
Frozen Artifacts Patches Autographed-FP-RE
Frozen Artifacts Patches Dual-FPD-RE
Frozen Artifacts Patches Dual Autos-FPD-RE
Frozen Artifacts Patches Pewter-FP-RE
Frozen Artifacts Patches Silver-FP-RE
Frozen Artifacts Pewter-FA-RE
Frozen Artifacts Silver-FA-RE
Gold Autographed-82
Gold Autographed-190
05UD PowerPlay-72
Rainbow-72
Specialists-TSMR
Specialists Patches-SPMR
05Ultimate Collection Marquee Attractions-MA40
05Ultra-155
Gold-155
Ice-155
05Upper Deck-151
Big Playmakers-B-MRE
HG Glossy-151
Jerseys-J-MR
Majestic Materials-MMRE
Patches-P-MRE
Shooting Stars-S-RE
05Upper Deck Ice-78
Rainbow-78
05Upper Deck MVP-313
Gold-313
Platinum-313
Materials-M-MR
Materials Duals-D-DR
05Upper Deck Trilogy-73
05Upper Deck Toronto Fall Expo-151
05Upper Deck Victory-157
Black-157
Gold-157
Silver-157
06Beehive-20
Matte-20
06Black Diamond-121
Black-121
Gold-121
Ruby-121
Jerseys-JMR
Jerseys Black-JMR
Jerseys Gold-JMR
Jerseys Ruby-JMR
06Flair Showcase-116
Parallel-116
06Hot Prospects-79
Red Hot-79
White Hot-79
Hot Materials -HMMR
Hot Materials Red Hot-HMMR
Hot Materials White Hot-HMMR
06NHL POG-30
06O-Pee-Chee-402
06O-Pee-Chee-666
Rainbow-402
Rainbow-666
Swatches-S-MR
06Panini Stickers-137
06SP Authentic-22
Limited-22
06SP Game Used-83
Gold-83
Rainbow-83
Authentic Fabrics-AFMA
Authentic Fabrics Parallel-AFMA
Authentic Fabrics Patches-AFMA
Authentic Fabrics Dual-AF2RC
Authentic Fabrics Dual Patches-AF2RC
Authentic Fabrics Triple-AF3PIT
Authentic Fabrics Triple Patches-AF3PIT
Authentic Fabrics Fives-AF5ASG
Authentic Fabrics Fives Patches-AF5ASG
By The Letter-BLMR
06SPx-80
06SPx-104
Spectrum-80
Spectrum-104
Winning Materials-WMRE
Winning Materials Spectrum-WMRE
06The Cup NHL Shields Duals-DSHRL
06UD Artifacts-20
Blue-20
Gold-20
Platinum-20
Radiance-20
Red-20
Frozen Artifacts-FAMR
Frozen Artifacts Black-FAMR
Frozen Artifacts Blue-FAMR
Frozen Artifacts Gold-FAMR
Frozen Artifacts Platinum-FAMR
Frozen Artifacts Red-FAMR
Frozen Artifacts Patches Black-FAMR
Frozen Artifacts Patches Blue-FAMR
Frozen Artifacts Patches Gold-FAMR
Frozen Artifacts Patches Platinum-FAMR
Frozen Artifacts Patches Red-FAMR
Treasured Patches Black-TSMR
Treasured Patches Blue-TSMR
Treasured Patches Gold-TSMR
Treasured Patches Platinum-TSMR
Treasured Patches Red-TSMR
Treasured Swatches-TSMR
Treasured Swatches Black-TSMR
Treasured Swatches Blue-TSMR
Treasured Swatches Gold-TSMR
Treasured Swatches Platinum-TSMR
Treasured Swatches Red-TSMR
Tundra Tandems-TTLM
Tundra Tandems-TTRM
Tundra Tandems Black-TTLM
Tundra Tandems Black-TTRM
Tundra Tandems Blue-TTLM
Tundra Tandems Blue-TTRM
Tundra Tandems Gold-TTLM
Tundra Tandems Gold-TTRM
Tundra Tandems Platinum-TTLM
Tundra Tandems Platinum-TTRM
Tundra Tandems Red-TTLM
Tundra Tandems Red-TTRM
Tundra Tandems Dual Patches Red-TTLM
Tundra Tandems Dual Patches Red-TTRM
06UD Biography of a Season-BOS13
06Ultimate Collection Premium Patches-PS-MR
06Ultimate Collection Premium Swatches-PS-MR
06Upper Deck Arena Giveaways-PIT5
06Upper Deck-409
Exclusives Parallel-409
High Gloss Parallel-409
Game Jerseys-JMR
Game Patches-PMR
Masterpieces-409
Oversized Wal-Mart Exclusives-409
06Upper Deck MVP-232
Gold Script-232
Super Script-232
06Upper Deck Sweet Shot Sweet Stitches-SSRE
06Upper Deck Sweet Shot Sweet Stitches Duals-SSRE
06Upper Deck Sweet Shot Sweet Stitches Triples-SSRE
06Upper Deck Trilogy-78
06Upper Deck Victory-36
06Upper Deck Victory-268
06Upper Deck Victory Black-36
06Upper Deck Victory Gold-36
07Upper Deck Ovation-10
07Upper Deck Victory-10
Black-10
Gold-10

Rechlicz, Joel

06Chicoutimi Sagueneens-23

Redden, Wade

93Brandon Wheat Kings-5
94Finest-151
Super Team Winners-151
Refractors-151
94Leaf Limited World Juniors Canada-7
94Parkhurst SE-SE256
Gold-SE256
94Pinnacle-527
Artist's Proofs-527
Rink Collection-527
94Select-160
Gold-160
94SP-139
Die Cuts-139
94Upper Deck-504
Electric Ice-504
94Brandon Wheat Kings-17
94Classic CHL Previews-CP3
95Donruss Canadian World Junior Team-5
95Donruss Elite World Juniors-8
95SP-169
95Topps Canadian World Juniors-1CJ
95Brandon Wheat Kings-15
95Classic-2
95Classic-100
CHL All-Stars-AS2
Ice Breakers-BK2
Ice Breakers Die Cuts-BK2
95Images-5
Gold-5
Clear Excitement-CE5
Platinum Premier Draft Choice-PD2
95Signature Rookies Auto-Phonex-34
95Signature Rook Auto-Phonex Phone Cards-34

95Signature Rookies Auto-Phonex Prodigies-P5
95Slapshot Memorial Cup-31
95Classic Five-Sport *-124
Phone Cards $4-3
Strive For Five-HK1
95Signature Rookies Tetrad Autobilia *-51
95Signature Rookies Tetrad SR Force *-F5
96Be A Player Link to History-9A
96Be A Player Link to History Autographs-9A
96Be A Player Link to History Auto Silver-9A
96Black Diamond-179
Gold-179
96Collector's Choice-362
Jumbos-4
96Donruss Canadian Ice-121
Gold Press Proofs-121
Red Press Proofs-121
96Donruss Elite-140
Die Cut Stars-140
Aspirations-24
96Flair-118
Blue Ice-118
96Leaf Limited Rookies-5
96Leaf Limited Rookies Gold-5
96Leaf Preferred-130
Press Proofs-130
96Metal Universe-190
96Select Certified-100
Artist's Proofs-100
Blue-100
Mirror Blue-100
Mirror Gold-100
Mirror Red-100
Red-100
96Senators Pizza Hut-22
96SP-185
96Ultra-118
Gold Medallion-118
Rookies-17
96Upper Deck-305
Generation Next-X35
96Upper Deck Ice-97
Parallel-97
96Zenith-128
Artist's Proofs-128
96Classic Signings *-71
Blue-71
Die-Cuts-71
Red-71
96Clear Assets Phone Cards $2 *-5
97Black Diamond-50
Double Diamond-50
Triple Diamond-50
Quadruple Diamond-50
97Collector's Choice-176
Star Quest-SQ6
97Donruss-48
Press Proofs Silver-48
Press Proofs Gold-48
Line 2 Line-19
Line 2 Line Die Cut-19
97Donruss Canadian Ice-31
Dominion Series-31
Provincial Series-31
97Donruss Elite-86
Aspirations-86
Status-86
97Donruss Limited-176
97Donruss Limited-189
Exposure-176
Exposure-189
97Donruss Preferred-97
Cut to the Chase-97
97Donruss Priority-131
Stamp of Approval-131
97Katch-100
Gold-100
Silver-100
97Leaf-113
Fractal Matrix-113
Fractal Matrix Die Cuts-113
97Leaf International-113
Universal Ice-113
97McDonald's Upper Deck-6
97Pacific-276
Copper-276
Emerald Green-276
Ice Blue-276
Red-276
Silver-276
97Pacific Dynagon-85
Copper-85
Dark Grey-85
Emerald Green-85
Ice Blue-85
Red-85
Silver-85
Tandems-68
97Pacific Invincible-95
Copper-95
Emerald Green-95
Ice Blue-95
Red-95
Silver-95
97SP Authentic-108
97Studio-97
Press Proofs Silver-97
Press Proofs Gold-97
97Upper Deck-118
Game Dated Moments-118
Smooth Grooves-SG36
Three Star Selects-20B
97Upper Deck Ice-50
Parallel-50
Power Shift-50
98Be A Player-95
Press Release-95
98BAP Gold-95
98BAP Autographs-95
98BAP Autographs Gold-95
98BAP Tampa Bay All Star Game-95
98Black Diamond-60
Double Diamond-60
Triple Diamond-60
Quadruple Diamond-60
98Bowman's Best-85
Refractors-85
Atomic Refractors-85
98Finest-109
No Protectors-109
No Protectors Refractors-109
Refractors-109
Centurion-C9
Centurion Refractors-C9
98Katch-99
98OPC Chrome-61
Refractors-61
Board Members-B15
Board Members Refractors-B15
98Pacific-315
Ice Blue-315
Red-315
98Pacific Omega-167
Red-167
Opening Day Issue-167
98Post-10
98Senators Team Issue-18
98SP Authentic-58
Power Shift-58
98SPx Finite-59
Radiance-59
Spectrum-59
98Topps-61
O-Pee-Chee-61
Board Members-B15
Ice Age 2000-I5
98Topps Gold Label Class 1-88
Black-88
Black One of One-88
One of One-88
Red-88
Red One of One-88
98Topps Gold Label Class 2-88
98Topps Gold Label Class 2 Black-88
98Topps Gold Label Class 2 Black 1 of 1-88
98Topps Gold Label Class 2 One of One-88
98Topps Gold Label Class 2 Red-88
98Topps Gold Label Class 2 Red One of One-88
98Topps Gold Label Class 3-88
98Topps Gold Label Class 3 Black-88
98Topps Gold Label Class 3 Black 1 of 1-88
98Topps Gold Label Class 3 One of One-88
98Topps Gold Label Class 3 Red-88
98Topps Gold Label Class 3 Red One of One-88
98UD Choice-140
Prime Choice Reserve-140
Reserve-140
98Upper Deck-329
Exclusives-329
Exclusives 1 of 1-329
Gold Reserve-329
98Upper Deck MVP-146
Gold Script-146
Silver Script-146
Super Script-146
ProSign-WR
99BAP Memorabilia-105
Gold-105
Silver-105
99O-Pee-Chee-61
99O-Pee-Chee Chrome-61
99O-Pee-Chee Chrome Refractors-61
99O-Pee-Chee Now Starring-NS8
99Pacific-293
Copper-293
Emerald Green-293
Gold-293
Ice Blue-293
Premiere Date-293
Red-293
99Paramount-164
Copper-164
Emerald-164
Gold-164
Holographic Emerald-164
Holographic Gold-164
Holographic Silver-164
Ice Blue-164
Premiere Date-164
Red-164
Silver-164
99Senators Team Issue-16
99Stadium Club-119
First Day Issue-119
One of a Kind-119
Printing Plates Black-119
Printing Plates Cyan-119
Printing Plates Magenta-119
Printing Plates Yellow-119
Co-Signers-CS14
Co-Signers-CS15
Lone Star Signatures-LS6
99Topps/OPC-61
Now Starring-NS8
99Topps/OPC Chrome-61
Refractors-61
99Topps Gold Label Class 1-44
Black-44
Black One of One-44
One of One-44
Red-44
Red One of One-44
99Topps Gold Label Class 2-44
99Topps Gold Label Class 2 Black-44
99Topps Gold Label Class 2 Black 1 of 1-44
99Topps Gold Label Class 2 One of One-44
99Topps Gold Label Class 2 Red-44
99Topps Gold Label Class 2 Red One of One-44
99Topps Gold Label Class 3-44
99Topps Gold Label Class 3 Black-44
99Topps Gold Label Class 3 Black 1 of 1-44
99Topps Gold Label Class 3 One of One-44
99Topps Gold Label Class 3 Red-44
99Topps Gold Label Class 3 Red One of One-44
99Topps Gold Label Fresh Gold-FG3
99Topps Gold Label Fresh Gold Black-FG3
99Topps Gold Label Fresh Gold Black 1of1-FG3
99Topps Gold Label Fresh Gold One of One-FG3
99Topps Gold Label Fresh Gold Red-FG3
99Topps Gold Label Fresh Gold Red 1 of 1-FG3
99Topps Premier Plus-16
Parallel-16
99Upper Deck-267
Exclusives-267
Exclusives 1 of 1-267
99Upper Deck Gold Reserve-267
99Upper Deck MVP-141
Gold Script-141
Silver Script-141
Super Script-141
99Upper Deck Victory-206
99Wayne Gretzky Hockey-119
00BAP Memorabilia-283
Emerald-283
Ruby-283
Sapphire-283
Promos-283
00BAP Mem Chicago Sportsfest Copper-283
00BAP Memorabilia Chicago Sportsfest Blue-283
00BAP Memorabilia Chicago Sportsfest Gold-283
00BAP Memorabilia Chicago Sportsfest Ruby-283
00BAP Memorabilia Chicago Sun-Times Ruby-283
00BAP Memorabilia Chicago Sun-Times Gold-283
00BAP Mem Chicago Sun-Times Sapphire-283
00BAP Mem Toronto Fall Expo Copper-283
00BAP Memorabilia Toronto Fall Expo Gold-283
00BAP Memorabilia Toronto Fall Expo Ruby-283
00O-Pee-Chee-225
00O-Pee-Chee Parallel-225
00Pacific-286
Copper-286
Gold-286
Ice Blue-286
Premiere Date-286
00Senators Team Issue-19
00Stadium Club-101
Souvenirs-SCS1
00Topps/OPC-225
Parallel-225
00Topps Chrome-143
OPC Refractors-143
Refractors-143
00Topps Heritage-184
00Topps Premier Plus-30
Blue Ice-30
00Topps Stars-77
Blue-77
00Upper Deck-124
Exclusives Tier 1-124
Exclusives Tier 2-124
00Upper Deck Victory-165
00Upper Deck Vintage-251
01BAP Memorabilia-138
Emerald-138
Ruby-138
Sapphire-138
01BAP Signature Series-27
Autographs-27
Autographs Gold-27
01McDonald's Pacific Hometown Pride-1
01O-Pee-Chee-117
01O-Pee-Chee Premier Parallel-117
01Pacific-278
Extreme LTD-278
Hobby LTD-278
Premiere Date-278
Retail LTD-278
01Pacific Adrenaline-137
Blue-137
Premiere Date-137
Red-137
Retail-137
01Pacific Arena Exclusives-278
01Parkhurst-148
01Senators Team Issue-24
01Topps-117
OPC Parallel-117
Reserve Emblems-WR
Reserve Jerseys-WR
Reserve Name Plates-WR
Reserve Numbers-WR
Reserve Patches-WR
01Upper Deck-351
Exclusives-351
01Upper Deck MVP-134
01Upper Deck Victory-244
Gold-244
02BAP First Edition-236
02BAP Sig Series Auto Buybacks 1998-95
02BAP Sig Series Auto Buybacks 2001-27
02BAP Signature Series Defensive Wall-DW8
02BAP Signature Series Golf-GS100
02NHL Power Play Stickers-100
02O-Pee-Chee-166
02O-Pee-Chee Premier Blue Parallel-166
02O-Pee-Chee Premier Red Parallel-166
02O-Pee-Chee Factory Set-166
02Pacific-272
Blue-272
Red-272
02Pacific Complete-362
Red-362
02Parkhurst-146
Bronze-146
Gold-146
Silver-146
02Senators Team Issue-14
02Senators Team Issue-3
02Topps-166
OPC Blue Parallel-166
OPC Red Parallel-166
02Topps Promos-PP4
02Topps Factory Set-166
02Topps Chrome-99
Black Border Refractors-99
Refractors-99
02Topps Total-217
02Upper Deck-124
Exclusives-124
02Upper Deck MVP-131
Gold-131
Classics-131
Golden Classics-131
02Upper Deck Victory-151
Bronze-151
Gold-151
Silver-151
02Upper Deck Vintage-174
03ITG Action-404
Jerseys-M68
03NHL Sticker Collection-98
03O-Pee-Chee-228
03OPC Blue-228
03OPC Gold-228
03OPC Red-228
03Pacific-241
Blue-241
Red-241
03Pacific Complete-31
Red-31
03Senators Postcards-4
03Topps-228
Blue-228
Gold-228
Red-228
03Upper Deck-380
Canadian Exclusives-380
HG-380
UD Exclusives-380
03Upper Deck MVP-293
Gold Script-293
Silver Script-293
Canadian Exclusives-293
04Pacific-187
Blue-187
Red-187
04UD Toronto Fall Expo Pride of Canada-10
04Upper Deck World Cup Tribute-WREB
04Upper Deck World Cup Tribute-EBEJWR
05Be A Player Dual Signatures-HR
05Be A Player Quad Signatures-OTWA
05Be A Player Signatures-WR
05Be A Player Signatures Gold-WR
05Black Diamond-61
Emerald-61
Gold-61
Onyx-61
Ruby-61
05McDonalds Upper Deck-11
CHL Graduates-CG3
05Panini Stickers-125
05Parkhurst-337
05Parkhurst-567
Facsimile Auto Parallel-337
Facsimile Auto Parallel-567
True Colors-TCOTT
True Colors-TCOTT
05SP Authentic-69
Limited-69
05SP Game Used Authentic Fabrics Triple-CRH
05SP Game Used Authentic Patches Triple-CRH
05SP Game Used Awesome Authentics-AA-WR
05SPx Winning Combos-WC-RC
05SPx Winning Combos Gold-WC-RC
05SPx Winning Combos Spectrum-WC-RC
05The Cup Emblems of Endorsement-EEWR
05The Cup Masterpiece Pressplate Auto-271
05The Cup Signature Patches-SPWR
05Ultimate Coll National Heroes Jersey-NHJWR
05Ultimate Coll National Heroes Patch-NHPWR
05Ultra-137
Gold-137
Ice-137
05Upper Deck-132
HG Glossy-132
Jerseys Series II-J2WR
NHL Generations-DRB
05Upper Deck MVP-268
Gold-268
Platinum-268
Materials Duals-D-RN
05Upper Deck Rookie Update-69
05Upper Deck Rookie Update-271
05Upper Deck Toronto Fall Expo-132
05Upper Deck Victory-139
Black-139
Gold-139
Silver-139
06Be A Player-57
Autographs-57
Signatures-WR
Signatures 10-62
Signatures Duals-DRM
Signatures Foursomes-FNBRB
Up Close and Personal-UC59
Up Close and Personal Autographs-UC59
06Be A Player Portraits-73
Signature Portraits-SPWR
Triple Signature Portraits-TOTT
06Black Diamond-58
Black-58
Gold-58
Ruby-58
06Flair Showcase Inks-IWR
06Flair Showcase Stitches-SSWR
06Fleer-138
Tiffany-138
06Gatorade-57
06NHL POG-6
06O-Pee-Chee-340
06O-Pee-Chee-603
Rainbow-340
Rainbow-603
Autographs-A-WR
06Panini Stickers-118
06Senators Postcards-14
06SP Authentic Sign of the Times Triples-ST3RHG
06SP Game Used Inked Sweaters-ISWR
06SP Game Used Inked Sweaters Patches-ISWR
06SP Game Used Inked Sweaters Dual-IS2RG
06SP Game Used Inked Sweaters Dual Patches-IS2RG
06SP Game Used SIGnificance-SWR
06The Cup Autographed NHL Shields Duals-DASHR
06UD Artifacts Auto-Facts-AFWR
06UD Artifacts Auto-Facts Gold-AFWR
06UD Artifacts Tundra Tandems-TTWA
06UD Artifacts Tundra Tandems Black-TTWA
06UD Artifacts Tundra Tandems Blue-TTWA
06UD Artifacts Tundra Tandems Gold-TTWA
06UD Artifacts Tundra Tandems Platinum-TTWA
06UD Artifacts Tundra Tandems Red-TTWA
06UD Artifacts Tundra Tandems Dual Patches Red-TTWA
06Ultra-135
Gold Medallion-135
Ice Medallion-135
06Upper Deck Arena Giveaways-OTT4
06Upper Deck-388
Exclusives Parallel-388
High Gloss Parallel-388
Game Jerseys-JWR
Game Patches-PWR
Generations Duals-G2RM
Generations Patches Dual-G2PRM
Masterpieces-388
Signature Sensations-SSWR
Statistical Leaders-SL4
06Upper Deck MVP-203
Gold Script-203
Super Script-203
Jerseys-OJCR
06Upper Deck Ovation-135
06Upper Deck Trilogy Combo Clearcut Autographs-C2RC
06Upper Deck Trilogy Combo Clearcut Autographs-C3RHH
06Upper Deck Trilogy Scripts-TSWR
06Upper Deck Victory-140
06Upper Deck Victory Black-140
06Upper Deck Victory Gold-140
07Upper Deck Victory-44
Black-44
Gold-44

Reddick, Eldon

84Brandon Wheat Kings-20
86Jets Postcards-20
87Jets Postcards-17
87Panini Stickers-357
88Jets Police-19
88Jets Postcards-19
88O-Pee-Chee Stickers-146
89O-Pee-Chee Stickers-137
89ProCards AHL-143
90O-Pee-Chee-452
90Pro Set-445
91Oilers Panini Team Stickers-18
91Oilers Team Issue-20
91ProCards-222
93Cincinnati Cyclones-20
93Classic Four-Sport *-247
Gold-247
94Las Vegas Thunder-20
95Las Vegas Thunder-10
96Grand Rapids Griffins-19
96Collector's Edge Ice-154
Prism-154
QuantumMotion-2
The Wall-TW5
97Grand Rapids Griffins-13
98Fort Wayne Komets-19
99German DEL-98
00German DEL-88
01German Upper Deck-84
Jersey Cards-ER-J
02Fort Wayne Komets-15
02Fort Wayne Komets Shoe Carnival-8
06Parkhurst-105

Reddick, Stan

91Johnstown Chiefs-19
92Raleigh Icecaps-13
92Raleigh Icecaps-28
93Raleigh Icecaps-15

Redding, George

24C144 Champ's Cigarettes-49
24V145-2-28

Reddo, Ronny

94German DEL-204
95German DEL-416
99German Bundesliga 2-294

Reddon, Leslie

94Classic Women of Hockey-W15
97Collector's Choice-278

Reddox, Liam

04Peterborough Petes Postcards-2
04ITG Heroes and Prospects-88
Autographs-LR
04ITG Heroes/Prospects Toronto Expo '05-88
04ITG Heroes/Prospects Expo Heroes/Pros-88
05ITG Heroes/Prosp Toronto Expo Parallel -283
05ITG Heroes and Prospects-283
Autographs Series II-LRD
Oh Canada-OC-1
Oh Canada Gold-OC-1
06Stockton Thunder-12b

Redenbach, Tyler

03Swift Current Broncos-12
04Lethbridge Hurricanes-5
04Swift Current Broncos-15
05ITG Heroes/Prosp Toronto Expo Parallel -223
05AHL Top Prospects-34
05Providence Bruins-12
05ITG Heroes and Prospects-223
Autographs Series II-TR

Rediker, Frank

02Windsor Spitfires-3
04London Knights-10
05London Knights-11
06Stockton Thunder-14b

Redinger, John

93Phoenix Cobras RHI-14

Redlick, Jack

01Vancouver Giants-21

Redlihs, Jakabs

03Boston University Terriers-12
06Syracuse Crunch-22

Redlihs, Krisjanis

02Albany River Rats-13
02Albany River Rats AAP-19
03Albany River Rats-24
03Albany River Rats Kinko's-23
04Albany River Rats-19
05Albany River Rats-19

Redmond, Adam

92Quebec Pee-Wee Tournament-1342
02Medicine Hat Tigers-19
03Indianapolis Ice-15

Redmond, Craig

84Kings Smokey-13
85O-Pee-Chee-121
85Topps-121
88Oilers Tenth Anniversary-161
88Oilers Team Issue-24

Redmond, Dan

89ProCards AHL-82

Redmond, Dick

71Letraset Action Replays-18
71O-Pee-Chee-106
71Sargent Promotions Stamps-144
71Toronto Sun-56
72O-Pee-Chee-151
72Sargent Promotions Stamps-46
72Topps-113
73O-Pee-Chee-12
73Topps-12
74NHL Action Stamps-86
74O-Pee-Chee NHL-186
74Topps-186
75O-Pee-Chee NHL-218
75Topps-218
76O-Pee-Chee NHL-12
76Topps-12
77O-Pee-Chee NHL-213
77Topps-213
78O-Pee-Chee-23
78Topps-23
79O-Pee-Chee-129
79Topps-129
80O-Pee-Chee-36
80Topps-36
81O-Pee-Chee-9
81Topps-E73

Redmond, Eddie

51Laval Dairy QSHL-72

Redmond, Keith

917th Inn. Sketch OHL-122
92Phoenix Roadrunners-18
93Donruss-448
93Phoenix Roadrunners-20
93Classic Pro Prospects-144
94Leaf-15
94Parkhurst-110
Gold-110
94Classic Pro Prospects-76

Redmond, Mickey

64Canadiens Postcards-15
67Canadiens IGA-24
68Canadiens IGA-24
68Canadiens Postcards BW-12
68O-Pee-Chee-64
68Shirriff Coins-92
69Canadiens Postcards Color-22
70Canadiens Pins-20
70Colgate Stamps-44
70Dad's Cookies-110
70Esso Power Players-16
70O-Pee-Chee-175A
70O-Pee-Chee-175B
70Sargent Promotions Stamps-106
71O-Pee-Chee-102
71Sargent Promotions Stamps-52
71Topps-102
71Toronto Sun-101
72O-Pee-Chee-99
Team Canada-24
72Sargent Promotions Stamps-74
72Topps-155
72Finnish Semic World Championship-233
72Swedish Semic World Championship-233
73Mac's Milk-24
73O-Pee-Chee-180
73Red Wings Team Issue-17
73Topps-190
74Nabisco Sugar Daddy-22
74NHL Action Stamps-106
74O-Pee-Chee NHL-6
74O-Pee-Chee NHL-84
74O-Pee-Chee NHL-120
74Topps-6
74Topps-84
74Topps-120
75Nabisco Sugar Daddy-16
75O-Pee-Chee NHL-120
75Topps-120
76Topps-243
81Red Wings Oldtimers-16
89Red Wings Little Caesars-21
89Red Wings Little Caesars-24
91Future Trends Canada '72-18
91Future Trends Canada '72 French-18
99BAP Memorabilia AS Retail-R9
99BAP Memorabilia AS Retail Autographs-R9
03Parkhurst Original Six Detroit-39
03Parkhurst Original Six Detroit-75

Redmond, Tony

98UK Basingstoke Bison-13
99UK Basingstoke Bison-11
01UK Guildford Flames-10
02UK Guildford Flames-7
03UK Guildford Flames-9

Redmond, Zach

06Sioux Falls Stampede -16

Rednicek, Josef

94German DEL-393

Redpath, Oliver

24Crescent Falcon-Tigers-5

Redquest, Greg

75Hamilton Fincups-14

Reed, Bobby

03St. Francis Xavier X-Men-6
04St. Francis Xavier X-Men-17

Reed, Dan

01Plymouth Whalers-26

Reed, Fran

96Madison Monsters-7

Reed, Harrison

06Sarnia Sting-15

Reed, Kelly

907th Inn. Sketch OHL-141
917th Inn. Sketch OHL-368
98UK Kingston Hawks-5

Reed, Tommy

93Quebec Pee-Wee Tournament-622

Reeder, Konrad

03St. Cloud State Huskies-24
04St. Cloud State Huskies-24
05St. Cloud State Huskies-23
05St. Cloud State Huskies-24
06New Mexico Scorpions-11

Reeds, Kyle

05Waterloo Blackhawks-17

Reeds, Mark

88ProCards AHL-65
92Peoria Rivermen-19
93Peoria Rivermen-23
96Peoria Rivermen-19
97Peoria Rivermen-23
98Peoria Rivermen-14
99Missouri River Otters-24
99Missouri River Otters Sheet-23
00Missouri River Otters-18
01Missouri River Otters-13
03Kalamazoo Wings-2
04Kalamazoo Wings-2
05Kalamazoo Wings-2

Reekie, Chad

04UK U-20 Team-10

Reekie, David

04Regina Pats-20
05Regina Pats-15

Reekie, Joe

82North Bay Centennials-19
87Sabres Blue Shield-22
87Sabres Wonder Bread/Hostess-22
88Sabres Blue Shield-21
88Sabres Wonder Bread/Hostess-23
90Bowman-125
Tiffany-125
90Pro Set-487
91Bowman-215
91O-Pee-Chee-144
91Panini Stickers-252
91Parkhurst-328
French-328
91Pinnacle-285
French-285
91Pro Set-429
French-429
91Score American-123
91Score Canadian Bilingual-123
91Score Canadian English-123
91Stadium Club-304
91Topps-144
91Upper Deck-483
French-483
92Bowman-137
92Lightning Sheraton-21
92O-Pee-Chee-224
92OPC Premier-70
92Pinnacle-382
French-382
92Pro Set-179
92Score-397
92Score-510
Canadian-397
Canadian-510
92Stadium Club-264
92Topps-184
Gold-184G
92Upper Deck-106
93Donruss-321
93Leaf-234
93OPC Premier-433
Gold-433
93Parkhurst-460
Emerald Ice-460
93Pinnacle-288
Canadian-288
93Score-167
Canadian-167
93Stadium Club-486
Members Only Master Set-486
First Day Issue-486
93Topps/OPC Premier-433
Gold-433
94Leaf-437
94OPC Premier-167
Special Effects-167
94Pinnacle-351
Artist's Proofs-351
Rink Collection-351
94Topps/OPC Premier-167
Special Effects-167
95Be A Player-66
Signatures-S66
Signatures Die Cuts-S66
95Capitals Team Issue-22
95Emotion-191
97Be A Player-136
Autographs-136
Autographs Die-Cuts-136
Autographs Prismatic Die-Cuts-136
97Pacific Invincible NHL Regime-212
99Stadium Club-59
First Day Issue-59
One of a Kind-59
Printing Plates Black-59
Printing Plates Cyan-59
Printing Plates Magenta-59
Printing Plates Yellow-59
00Upper Deck-405
Exclusives Tier 1-405
Exclusives Tier 2-405

Rees, Mike

98El Paso Buzzards-12
01El Paso Buzzards-9
02Austin Ice Bats-14
06UK Nottingham Panthers-13

Reese, Jason

04Vancouver Giants-5
05Vancouver Giants-17
06Moose Jaw Warriors-19

Reese, Jeff

85London Knights-27
88ProCards AHL-242
90O-Pee-Chee-349
90Panini Stickers-281
90Pro Set-540
90Topps-349
Tiffany-349
91Maple Leafs Panini Team Stickers-21
91Maple Leafs PLAY-26
91O-Pee-Chee-81
91Parkhurst-250
French-250
91Score Canadian Bilingual-410
91Score Canadian English-410
91Topps-81
92Bowman-412
92Flames IGA-9
92O-Pee-Chee-77
92Parkhurst-264
Emerald Ice-264
92Stadium Club-322
92Topps-385
Gold-385G
92Upper Deck-442
93Donruss-443
93OPC Premier-302
Gold-302
93Panini Stickers-187
93PowerPlay-355
93Score-394
93Score-650
Gold-650
Canadian-394
Canadian-650
Canadian Gold-650
93Stadium Club-22
Members Only Master Set-22
OPC-22
First Day Issue-22
First Day Issue OPC-22
93Topps/OPC Premier-302
Gold-302
93Whalers Coke-18
94Leaf-59
94OPC Premier-27
Special Effects-27
94Parkhurst SE-SE74
Gold-SE74
94Topps/OPC Premier-27
Special Effects-27
94Upper Deck-476
Electric Ice-476
95Parkhurst International-460
Emerald Ice-460
96Donruss-31
Press Proofs-31
96Score-213
Artist's Proofs-213
Dealer's Choice Artist's Proofs-213
Special Artist's Proofs-213
Golden Blades-213
96Detroit Vipers-14
97Detroit Vipers-16
03Lightning Team Issue-5
05Lightning Team Issue-3

Reese, Steven

06Sarnia Sting-4

Reesor, Jason

93Niagara Falls Thunder-16
99Bakersfield Condors-16
00Bakersfield Condors-18
02Fort Worth Brahmas-12
03Fort Worth Brahmas-11

Reeve, Jamie

82Regina Pats-3
83Regina Pats-3
93Tacoma Rockets-23

Reeves, Kyle

907th Inn. Sketch WHL-109
91ProCards-39
92Peoria Rivermen-20
93Toledo Storm-26
94Flint Generals-18
95Central Hockey League-14
95Fort Worth Fire-13
00Lubbock Cotton Kings-1

Regan, Brian

98Dayton Bombers-14
98Dayton Bombers EBK-13
99Missouri River Otters-15
99Missouri River Otters Sheet-13
99UHL All-Stars West-6T
01Missouri River Otters-17
03Missouri River Otters-18

Regan, Eric

04Erie Otters-18
06Oshawa Generals-19

Regan, Garrett

03Waterloo Blackhawks-5
04Waterloo Blackhawks-12
05Notre Dame Freshmen-3

Regan, Kevin

03Waterloo Blackhawks-4

Regan, Larry

44Beehive Group II Photos-61
44Beehive Group II Photos-445
52St. Lawrence Sales-103
57Bruins Photos-17
57Topps-6
58Bruins Photos-11
58Topps-10
59Parkhurst-17
60Parkhurst-13
60Shirriff Coins-16
60York Photos-30
94Parkhurst Missing Link-16

Regan, Tim

93RPI Engineers-24
99German Bundesliga 2-272

Regehr, Richie

00Kelowna Rockets-15
03Portland Winter Hawks-5
04Lowell Lock Monsters-17
04Lowell Lock Monsters Photo Album-17
04Portland Winter Hawks-11
04Portland Winter Hawks-NNO
05ITG Heroes/Prosp Toronto Expo Parallel -390
05Hot Prospects-110
En Fuego-110
Red Hot-110
White Hot-110
05SP Authentic-254
Limited-254
05SP Game Used-196
05SPx-249
05The Cup Masterpiece Pressplates (Ice)-238
05The Cup Master Pressplate Rookie Update-113
05The Cup Masterpiece Pressplates SPA-254
05The Cup Masterpiece Pressplates SP GU-196
05The Cup Masterpiece Pressplates (SPx)-249
05The Cup Masterpiece Pressplates Trilogy-231
05The Cup Masterpiece Pressplate Ult Coll-197
05Ultimate Collection-197
Gold-197
05Upper Deck Ice-238
05Upper Deck Rookie Update-113
05Upper Deck Trilogy-231
05AHL All-Stars-30
05ITG Heroes and Prospects-390
Autographs Update-A-RRG
06ITG Heroes and Prospects-61
Autographs-ARRG

Regehr, Robyn

96Kamloops Blazers-20
97Upper Deck-406
98Finest Futures Finest-F15
98Finest Futures Finest Refractors-F15
98Kamloops Blazers-20
98Bowman CHL-137
Golden Anniversary-137
OPC International-137
Autographs Blue-A14
Autographs Gold-A14
Autographs Silver-A14
98Bowman Chrome CHL-137
Golden Anniversary-137
Golden Anniversary Refractors-137
OPC International-137
OPC International Refractors-137
Refractors-137
99BAP Memorabilia-304
Gold-304
Silver-304
99BAP Millennium Calder Candidates Ruby-C44
99BAP Millennium Calder Candidate Emerald-C44
99BAP Millennium Calder Cand Sapphire-C44
99Black Diamond-17
Diamond Cut-17
Final Cut-17
99Crown Royale-24
Limited Series-24
Premiere Date-24
Prospects Parallel-24
99Pacific-453
99Pacific Omega-42
Copper-42
Gold-42
Ice Blue-42
Premiere Date-42
99Topps Arena Giveaways-CAL-RR
99Upper Deck-197
Exclusives-197
Exclusives 1 of 1-197
99Upper Deck Arena Giveaways-CF1
99Upper Deck Gold Reserve-197
99Bowman CHL-119
Gold-119
OPC International-119
00BAP Memorabilia-214
Emerald-214
Ruby-214
Sapphire-214
Promos-214
00BAP Mem Chicago Sportsfest Copper-214
00BAP Memorabilia Chicago Sportsfest Blue-214
00BAP Memorabilia Chicago Sportsfest Gold-214
00BAP Memorabilia Chicago Sportsfest Ruby-214
00BAP Memorabilia Chicago Sun-Times Ruby-214
00BAP Memorabilia Chicago Sun-Times Gold-214
00BAP Mem Chicago Sun-Times Sapphire-214
00BAP Mem Toronto Fall Expo Copper-214
00BAP Memorabilia Toronto Fall Expo Gold-214
00BAP Memorabilia Toronto Fall Expo Ruby-214
00BAP Parkhurst 2000-P88
00BAP Signature Series-65
Emerald-65
Ruby-65
Sapphire-65
Autographs-154
Autographs Gold-154
00O-Pee-Chee-213
00O-Pee-Chee Parallel-213
00Stadium Club-92
00Topps/OPC-213
Parallel-213
00Upper Deck Vintage-59
01Bowman YoungStars-125
Gold-125
Ice Cubed-125
Autographs-RR
Relics-JRR
Relics-SRR
Relics-DSRR
Rivals-R4
01Upper Deck-259
Exclusives-259
01Upper Deck Victory-55
Gold-55
02BAP First Edition-182
02BAP Sig Series Auto Buybacks 2000-154
02NHL Power Play Stickers-9
02O-Pee-Chee-44
02O-Pee-Chee Premier Blue Parallel-44
02O-Pee-Chee Premier Red Parallel-44
02O-Pee-Chee Factory Set-44
02Stadium Club YoungStars Relics-S21
02Topps-44
OPC Blue Parallel-44
OPC Red Parallel-44
Factory Set-44

02Topps Total-192
03ITG Action-78
03O-Pee-Chee-263
03OPC Blue-263
03OPC Gold-263
03OPC Red-263
03Pacific Complete-52
Red-52
03Topps-263
Blue-263
Gold-263
Red-263
Traded Future Phenoms-FP-RR
03Upper Deck-276
Canadian Exclusives-276
HG-276
UD Exclusives-276
04SP Authentic Octographs-OS-CUP
04SP Authentic Sign of the Times-ST-RR
04SP Authentic Sign of the Times-DS-IR
04UD Toronto Fall Expo Pride of Canada-11
04Upper Deck-27
Canadian Exclusives-27
HG Glossy Gold-27
HG Glossy Silver-27
05Be A Player Quad Signatures-SSIR
05Be A Player Signatures-RR
05Be A Player Signatures Gold-RR
05Parkhurst-74
05Parkhurst-568
Facsimile Auto Parallel-74
Facsimile Auto Parallel-568
05The Cup Master Pressplate Rookie Update-250
05Ultra-34
Gold-34
Ice-34
05Upper Deck-27
HG Glossy-27
05Upper Deck MVP-64
Gold-64
Platinum-64
05Upper Deck Rookie Update-250
05Upper Deck Toronto Fall Expo-27
05Czech Stadion-688
06Be A Player-56
Autographs-56
Signatures-RR
Signatures Duals-DRS
06Flair Showcase Stitches-SSRR
06Gatorade-12
06NHL POG-60
06O-Pee-Chee-69
Rainbow-69
06Panini Stickers-201
06Ultra Uniformity-URR
06Ultra Uniformity Patches-UPRR
06Upper Deck-30
Exclusives Parallel-30
High Gloss Parallel-30
Masterpieces-30

Regier, Darcey
81Indianapolis Checkers-16
82Indianapolis Checkers-16

Regier, Steven
02Medicine Hat Tigers-20
06Fleer-218
Tiffany-218
06O-Pee-Chee-512
Rainbow-512
06SPx-197
Spectrum-197
06The Cup Masterpiece Pressplates (Artifacts)-211
06The Cup Masterpiece Pressplates (Marquee Rookies)-512
06The Cup Masterpiece Pressplates (Power Play)-112
06The Cup Masterpiece Pressplates (Trilogy)-130
06The Cup Masterpiece Pressplates (Victory)-220
06UD Artifacts-211
Blue-211
Gold-211
Radiance-211
Red-211
06UD Powerplay-112
Impact Rainbow-112
06Ultra-214
Gold Medallion-214
Ice Medallion-214
06Upper Deck Ovation-181
06Upper Deck Trilogy-130
06Upper Deck Victory-220
06Upper Deck Victory Black-220
06Upper Deck Victory Gold-220

Regin, Peter
05Swedish SHL Elitset-283
Gold-283
06Swedish SHL Elitset-137

Regis, Jean
92Quebec Pee-Wee Tournament-60
93Quebec Pee-Wee Tournament-230

Regnier, Curt
90Prince Albert Raiders-18
907th Inn. Sketch WHL-264
91Prince Albert Raiders-20
917th Inn. Sketch WHL-253
98Danish Hockey League-108
99Danish Hockey League-112

Regnier, Richard
80Finnish Mallasjuoma-85

Regnier, Tom
80Finnish Mallasjuoma-84

Rehak, Dennis
03Prince George Cougars-8

Rehnberg, Henrik
93Swedish Semic Elitserien-315
95Collector's Choice-347
Player's Club-347
Player's Club Platinum-347
95Swedish Upper Deck-61
98Albany River Rats-13
99Swedish Upper Deck-58
00Albany River Rats-17
01Swedish Brynas Tigers-22
02Swedish SHL-4
Parallel-4

Rehnstrom, Kjell
69Swedish Hockey-90

Rehnstrom, Peder
69Swedish Hockey-91

Rehor, Jan
01Czech OFS-146
03Czech OFS Plus-329

Reibel, Earl
44Beehive Group II Photos-62
44Beehive Group II Photos-207
53Parkhurst-36
54Parkhurst-37
54Parkhurst-97
54Topps-52
57Topps-45
58Bruins Photos-12
58Topps-57
94Parkhurst Missing Link-49
94Parkhurst Missing Link-147

Reich, Chad
95Medicine Hat Tigers-13

Reich, Dory
90Fort Saskatchewan Traders-14

Reich, Jeremy
95Seattle Thunderbirds-24
96Upper Deck-386
96Seattle Thunderbirds-15
97Seattle Thunderbirds-13
97Bowman CHL-143
OPC-143
Autographs-23
98Swift Current Broncos-18
99Swift Current Broncos-16
00Syracuse Crunch-12
01Syracuse Crunch-10
02Syracuse Crunch-9
02Syracuse Crunch Sheets-6
03Syracuse Crunch-10
04Syracuse Crunch-9
05Providence Bruins-13
06Providence Bruins-15

Reich, Mike
05Calgary Hitmen-17

Reich, Shawn
90Fort Saskatchewan Traders-15

Reichart, Chris
94Lightning Postcards-15

Reichel, Martin
92Classic-28
Gold-28
92Classic Four-Sport *-177
Gold-177
94German DEL-378
95German DEL-376
95German DEL-439
96German DEL-198
96Swedish Semic Wien-199
98German DEL-251
98German DEL-332
99German DEL-35
00German DEL-190
01German Upper Deck-206
02German DEL City Press-269
03German DEL-103
04German DEL-115
05German DEL-322
06German DEL-62

Reichel, Robert
90Flames IGA/McGavin's-23
90OPC Premier-95
90Pro Set-595
90Score Rookie/Traded-30T
90Score Young Superstars-29
90Upper Deck-533
French-533
91Pro Set Platinum-163
91Bowman-267
91Flames IGA-17
91O-Pee-Chee-411
91Panini Stickers-63
91Panini Stickers-343
91Parkhurst-21
French-21
91Pinnacle-56
French-56
91Pro Set-361
French-361
91Score American-263
91Score Canadian Bilingual-483
91Score Canadian English-483
91Score Young Superstars-24
91Stadium Club-393
91Topps-411
91Upper Deck-223
French-223
91Finnish Semic World Champ Stickers-223
91Swedish Semic World Champ Stickers-223
92Bowman-401
92Flames IGA-5
92O-Pee-Chee-93
92Panini Stickers-42
92Panini Stickers-301
92Panini Stickers French-42
92Panini Stickers French-301
92Parkhurst-26
Emerald Ice-26
92Pinnacle-101
French-101
92Score-106
Canadian-106
92Stadium Club-180
92Topps-157
Gold-157G
92Ultra-28
92Upper Deck-42
92Finnish Semic-142
93Donruss-51
93Leaf-59
93OPC Premier-404
Gold-404
93Panini Stickers-180
93Parkhurst-300
Emerald Ice-300
93Pinnacle-35
Canadian-35
93PowerPlay-41
Rising Stars-5
93Score-204
Canadian-204
International Stars-6
International Stars Canadian-6
93Stadium Club-198
Members Only Master Set-198
OPC-198
First Day Issue-198
First Day Issue OPC-198
93Topps/OPC Premier-404
Gold-404
93Ultra-164
93Upper Deck-313
Hat Tricks-HT4
94Canada Games NHL POGS-60
94Donruss-169
94Flair-27
94Fleer-34
94Kraft-26
94Leaf-243
Limited Inserts-4
94Leaf Limited-39
94OPC Premier-213
Special Effects-213
94Parkhurst-34
Gold-34
Vintage-V47
94Pinnacle-12
Artist's Proofs-12
Rink Collection-12
World Edition-WE13
94Score 90 Plus Club-17
94Select-138
Gold-138
94Topps/OPC Premier-213
Special Effects-213
94Topps Finest Inserts-20
94Ultra-34
94Upper Deck-357
Electric Ice-357
SP Inserts-SP104
SP Inserts Die Cuts-SP104
94Finnish Jaa Kiekko-184
95German DEL-116
95German DEL-445
95Swedish Globe World Championships-159
95Swedish World Championships Stickers-298
96Be A Player-81
Autographs-81
Autographs Silver-81
96Metal Universe-22
96Ultra-26
Gold Medallion-26
96Upper Deck-228
96Czech APS Extraliga-349
96Swedish Semic Wien-128
97Black Diamond-49
Double Diamond-49
Triple Diamond-49
Quadruple Diamond-49
97Collector's Choice-151
97Crown Royale-80
Emerald Green-80
Ice Blue-80
Silver-80
97Pacific-326
Copper-326
Emerald Green-326
Ice Blue-326
Red-326
Silver-326
97Pacific Omega-141
Copper-141
Dark Gray-141
Emerald Green-141
Gold-141
Ice Blue-141
97Panini Stickers-77
97Paramount-110
Copper-110
Dark Grey-110
Emerald Green-110
Ice Blue-110
Red-110
Silver-110
97Revolution-83
Copper-83
Emerald-83
Ice Blue-83
Silver-83
97Score-218
97SP Authentic-97
97Upper Deck-104
97Zenith-70
Z-Gold-70
Z-Silver-70
97Czech APS Extraliga-354
98Aurora-118
98Be A Player-86
Press Release-86
98BAP Gold-86
98BAP Autographs-86
98BAP Autographs Gold-86
98BAP Tampa Bay All Star Game-86
98Bowman's Best-95
Refractors-95
Atomic Refractors-95
98Crown Royale-85
Limited Series-85
96Katch-90
98Pacific-286
Ice Blue-286
Red-286
98Pacific Dynagon Ice-117
Blue-117
Red-117
98Pacific Omega-151
Red-151
Opening Day Issue-151
98Panini Stickers-75
98Paramount-147
Copper-147
Emerald Green-147
Holo-Electric-147
Ice Blue-147
Silver-147
98SP Authentic-54
Power Shift-54
98Topps Gold Label Class 1-19
Black-19
Black One of One-19
One of One-19
Red-19
Red One of One-19
98Topps Gold Label Class 2-19
98Topps Gold Label Class 2 Black-19
98Topps Gold Label Class 2 Black 1 of 1-19
98Topps Gold Label Class 2 One of One-19
98Topps Gold Label Class 2 Red-19
98Topps Gold Label Class 2 Red One of One-19
98Topps Gold Label Class 3-19
98Topps Gold Label Class 3 Black-19
98Topps Gold Label Class 3 Black 1 of 1-19
98Topps Gold Label Class 3 One of One-19
98Topps Gold Label Class 3 Red-19
98Topps Gold Label Class 3 Red One of One-19
98UD Choice-126
Prime Choice Reserve-126
Reserve-126
98Upper Deck MVP-127
Gold Script-127
Silver Script-127
Super Script-127
98Czech OFS-237
Olympic Winners-6
98Czech Bonaparte-18
98Czech Bonaparte Tall-3
98Czech Pexeso-2
98Czech Spaghetti-7
99Pacific-324
Copper-324
Emerald Green-324
Gold-324
Ice Blue-324
Premiere Date-324
Red-324
99Upper Deck-99
Exclusives-99
Exclusives 1 of 1-99
99Upper Deck Gold Reserve-99
99Upper Deck MVP-157
Gold Script-157
Silver Script-157
Super Script-157
99Upper Deck Victory-227
99Czech DS-63
National Stars-NS12
Premium-P11
99Czech OFS-31
99Czech OFS-157
99Czech OFS-266
99Czech OFS-507
All-Star Game Blue-507
All-Star Game Gold-507
All-Star Game Red-507
All-Star Game Silver-507
99Czech OFS Jagr Team Embossed-31
00Czech DS Extraliga-43
National Team-NT5
Top Stars-TS5
Valuable Players-VP4
World Champions-WCH8
00Czech OFS-145
00Czech OFS-409
00Czech OFS Star Emerald-20
00Czech OFS Star Pink-20
00Czech OFS Star Violet-20
01BAP Signature Series-112
Autographs-112
Autographs Gold-112
01Parkhurst-239
01Private Stock Game Gear-96
01Upper Deck-396
Exclusives-396
01Czech DS-42
01Czech DS-59
Best of the Best-BB8
Ice Heroes-IH8
01Czech OFS All Stars-13
02BAP Sig Series Auto Buybacks 1998-86
02BAP Sig Series Auto Buybacks 2001-112
02Maple Leafs Platinum Collection-15
02Maple Leafs Team Issue-9
02NHL Power Play Stickers-134
02Pacific-366
Blue-366
Red-366
02Pacific Complete-78
Red-78
02Topps Total-79
02Upper Deck-408
Exclusives-408
02Upper Deck Beckett UD Promos-408
02Czech DS-53
02Czech DS-67
02Czech DS-91
02Czech IQ Sports Blue-21
02Czech IQ Sports Yellow-21
02Czech Stadion Olympics-342
03ITG Action-552
03Parkhurst Original Six Toronto-21
03Czech National Team Postcards-10
03Russian World Championship Stars-26
04Czech NHL ELH Postcards-11
04Czech OFS-102
Stars-8
04Czech Zuma-14
04Czech Zuma Stars-Z6
05Czech Kvarteto Bonaparte-5c
05Czech Stadion-676
06Czech OFS-145
Team Cards-5

Reichenbach, Richard
06Richmond Renegades-13

Reichenberg, Ronny
86Swedish Panini Stickers-161
89Swedish Semic Elitserien Stickers-139
90Swedish Semic Elitserien Stickers-217

Reichert, Craig
917th Inn. Sketch WHL-18
93Red Deer Rebels-20
98Cincinnati Mighty Ducks-13
99Louisville Panthers-3
00German DEL-48
01Hamilton Bulldogs-8

Reichert, Marc
98Swiss Power Play Stickers-283
98Swiss Panini Stickers-48
99Swiss Panini Stickers-296
00Swiss Panini Stickers-46
01Swiss HNL-92
01Swiss HNL-42
02Swiss HNL-236

Reichmuth, Craig
74San Diego Mariners WHA-7

Reichmuth, Francis
01Swiss HNL-347
02Swiss HNL-418

Reichmuth, Isaac
04Minnesota-Duluth Bulldogs-19

Reid, B.L.
93Quebec Pee-Wee Tournament-822

Reid, Bill
92Saskatchewan JHL-126

Reid, Brandon
95Quebec Pee-Wee Tournament-109
97Halifax Mooseheads I-16
97Halifax Mooseheads II-16
98Halifax Mooseheads-8
98Halifax Mooseheads Second Edition-4
99Halifax Mooseheads-21
00QMJHL All-Star Program Inserts-19
00Val d'Or Foreurs-17
Signed-17
00UD CHL Prospects-88
Future Leaders-FL10
Great Desire-GD5
01Manitoba Moose-20
02BAP Memorabilia-394
02BAP Ultimate Memorabilia-51
02SP Authentic-211
02SPx-180
02Upper Deck Rookie Update-133
02AHL Top Prospects-36
02Manitoba Moose-19
03BAP Memorabilia Future of the Game-FG-9
03ITG Action-532
Jerseys-M69
03O-Pee-Chee-325
03OPC Blue-325
03OPC Gold-325
03OPC Red-325
03Topps-325
Blue-325
Gold-325
Red-325
03Upper Deck-190
Canadian Exclusives-190
HG-190
03Upper Deck MVP-418
Gold Script-418
Silver Script-418
Canadian Exclusives-418
03Manitoba Moose-23
03Pacific AHL Prospects-55
Gold-55
04German DEL-133
04German Hamburg Freezers Postcards-14
04ITG Heroes and Prospects Emblems-39
04ITG Heroes and Prospects Emblems Gold-39
04ITG Heroes/Prospects He Shoots/Scores-30
04ITG Heroes and Prospects Jerseys-39
04ITG Heroes and Prospects Jerseys Gold-39
04ITG Heroes and Prospects Numbers-39
04ITG Heroes and Prospects Numbers Gold-39
06Manitoba Moose-7

Reid, Charlie
23V128-1 Paulin's Candy-68

Reid, Darren
02Medicine Hat Tigers-21
03Medicine Hat Tigers-7
04Springfield Falcons-7
05Black Diamond-285
05Hot Prospects-173
En Fuego-173
Red Hot-173
White Hot-173
05SP Authentic-281
Limited-281
05SP Game Used-235
05SPx-285
05The Cup Masterpiece Pressplate Artifact-331
05The Cup Master Pressplate Black Diamond-285
05The Cup Masterpiece Pressplates (Ice)-245
05The Cup Master Pressplate Rookie Update-183
05The Cup Masterpiece Pressplates SPA-281
05The Cup Masterpiece Pressplates SP GU-235
05The Cup Masterpiece Pressplates (SPx)-285
05The Cup Masterpiece Pressplates Trilogy-309
05The Cup Masterpiece Pressplate Ult Coll-226
05UD Artifacts-331
05Ultimate Collection-226
Gold-226
05Upper Deck Ice-245
05Upper Deck Rookie Update-183
05Upper Deck Trilogy-309
05Springfield Falcons-5
06Springfield Falcons-14
06Philadelphia Phantoms-27

Reid, Dave (00s)
03Atlantic City Boardwalk Bullies-19
03Atlantic City Boardwalk Bullies RBI-27
04Atlantic City Boardwalk Bullies-1
04Atlantic City Boardwalk Bullies Kinko's-7

Reid, Dave (50s)
44Beehive Group II Photos-446

Reid, Dave (80s)
85Moncton Golden Flames-22
86Moncton Golden Flames-24
88Maple Leafs PLAY-24
89O-Pee-Chee Stickers-170
90Maple Leafs Postcards-17
90O-Pee-Chee-290
90Pro Set-541
90Score Rookie/Traded-109T
90Topps-290
Tiffany-290
90Upper Deck-364
French-364
91Bowman-153
91Bruins Sports Action-16
91Maple Leafs Panini Team Stickers-22
91O-Pee-Chee-423
91Panini Stickers-104
91Pro Set Preview-229
91Pro Set-229
91Pro Set-348
French-229
French-348
91Score American-173
91Score Canadian Bilingual-173
91Score Canadian English-173
91Stadium Club-78
91Topps-423
91Upper Deck-217
91Upper Deck-531
French-217
French-531
91ProCards-66
92Parkhurst-249
Emerald Ice-249
92Score-380
Canadian-380
92Topps-521
Gold-521G
93Donruss-403
93OPC Premier-67
Gold-67
93Pinnacle-191
Canadian-191
93PowerPlay-290
93Score-371
Canadian-371
93Stadium Club-100
Members Only Master Set-100
OPC-100
First Day Issue-100
First Day Issue OPC-100
93Topps/OPC Premier-67
Gold-67
93Ultra-269
94Be A Player-R88
Signature Cards-103
94Leaf-501
94OPC Premier-51
Special Effects-51
94Parkhurst SE-SE12
Gold-SE12
94Pinnacle-234
Artist's Proofs-234
Rink Collection-234
94Score-80
Gold-80
Platinum-80
94Topps/OPC Premier-51
Special Effects-51
95Parkhurst International-281
Emerald Ice-281
95Playoff One on One-122
95Topps-76
OPC Inserts-76
96Be A Player-121
Autographs-121
Autographs Silver-121
96Fleer Picks-176
96Pinnacle-182
Artist's Proofs-182
Foil-182
Premium Stock-182
Rink Collection-182
96Playoff One on One-386
96Score-220
Artist's Proofs-220
Dealer's Choice Artist's Proofs-220
Special Artist's Proofs-220
Golden Blades-220
96Stars Postcards-24
96Summit-146
Metal-146
Premium Stock-146
97Collector's Choice-73
97Pacific Invincible NHL Regime-65
97Panini Stickers-141
97Upper Deck-264
99Avalanche Team Issue-18
99O-Pee-Chee-34
99O-Pee-Chee Chrome-34
99O-Pee-Chee Chrome Refractors-34
99Topps/OPC-34
99Topps/OPC Chrome-34
Refractors-34
00BAP Memorabilia-367
Emerald-367
Ruby-367
Sapphire-367
Promos-367
00BAP Mem Chicago Sportsfest Copper-367
00BAP Memorabilia Chicago Sportsfest Blue-367
00BAP Memorabilia Chicago Sportsfest Gold-367
00BAP Memorabilia Chicago Sportsfest Ruby-367
00BAP Memorabilia Chicago Sun-Times Ruby-367
00BAP Memorabilia Chicago Sun-Times Gold-367
00BAP Mem Chicago Sun-Times Sapphire-367
00BAP Mem Toronto Fall Expo Copper-367
00BAP Memorabilia Toronto Fall Expo Gold-367
00BAP Memorabilia Toronto Fall Expo Ruby-367
00Pacific-119
Copper-119
Gold-119
Ice Blue-119
Premiere Date-119
00Titanium Game Gear-77
00Titanium Game Gear Patches-77
00Upper Deck NHLPA-PA24
00Upper Deck Vintage-97
01Atomic Jerseys-12
01Atomic Patches-12
01BAP Memorabilia Stanley Cup Champions-CA13
01Pacific Heads-Up Quad Jerseys-8

Reid, Edward
52Juniors Blue Tint-4

Reid, Elgin
03Ottawa 67's-18
04Ottawa 67's-19
05Ottawa 67's-23

Reid, Grayden
907th Inn. Sketch OHL-293
917th Inn. Sketch OHL-294
91Ultimate Draft-53
91Ultimate Draft French-53

Reid, Isaac
04Calgary Hitmen-17
05Lethbridge Hurricanes-18

Reid, Jarret
907th Inn. Sketch OHL-171
917th Inn. Sketch OHL-324
917th Inn. Sketch Memorial Cup-12
93Sault Ste. Marie Greyhound Memorial Cup-15

Reid, Jason
99Tallahassee Tiger Sharks-3

Reid, Jay
82Medicine Hat Tigers-17

Reid, Jeff
907th Inn. Sketch OHL-44
91Cornwall Royals-22
917th Inn. Sketch OHL-18
93Knoxville Cherokees-13
94Las Vegas Thunder-21

Reid, Jerry
51Cleveland Barons-6

Reid, John
84Belleville Bulls-20
88ProCards IHL-111
89Nashville Knights-18
89Nashville Knights-19
91ProCards-449
96UK Fife Flyers-2

Reid, Kelly
97UK Kingston Hawks Stickers-6

Reid, Kevin
907th Inn. Sketch OHL-172
917th Inn. Sketch OHL-355

Reid, Matt
02Pee Dee Pride RBI-144
03UK Basingstoke Bison-20
03Florence Pride-154
05South Carolina Stingrays-1

Reid, Matt J.
04Johnstown Chiefs-15
05Idaho Steelheads-18

Reid, Reg
24V145-2-55

Reid, Ryan
98San Angelo Outlaws-15
04Atlantic City Boardwalk Bullies-29

Reid, Scott
95Kamloops Blazers-4
06New Mexico Scorpions-6

Reid, Shawn
94Classic-60
Gold-60
All-Americans-AA9
95Binghamton Rangers-19

Reid, Steve
96Sudbury Wolves-17
99OCN Blizzard-18

Reid, Tom
70Esso Power Players-175
70North Stars Postcards-7
70O-Pee-Chee-43
70Sargent Promotions Stamps-85
70Topps-43
71O-Pee-Chee-21
71Sargent Promotions Stamps-82
71Toronto Sun-144
72Sargent Promotions Stamps-99
73North Stars Action Posters-10
73North Stars Postcards-18
73O-Pee-Chee-109
73Topps-109
74NHL Action Stamps-134
74O-Pee-Chee NHL-52
74Topps-52
75O-Pee-Chee NHL-277
75Topps-277
76O-Pee-Chee NHL-123
76Topps-123
77O-Pee-Chee NHL-306
04ITG Franchises Update Autographs-TR

Reid, Tyler
98Halifax Mooseheads-18
98Halifax Mooseheads Second Edition-1
02Hull Olympiques-23
03Hull Olympiques Memorial Cup-12

Reier, Michael
907th Inn. Sketch OHL-214
92Dayton Bombers-23

Reierson, Andy
03Cincinnati Mighty Ducks-A8

Reierson, Dave
88Salt Lake Golden Eagles-9
94German DEL-131
95German DEL-129

Reigle, Ed
51Cleveland Barons-3

Reigstad, Jared
00Missouri River Otters-23
01Rockford IceHogs-11

Reijonen, Esko
65Finnish Hellas-4
66Finnish Jaakiekkosarja-124

Reijonen, Tuomas
95Collector's Choice-336
Player's Club-336
Player's Club Platinum-336
96Finnish SISU Redline-131
99Finnish Cardset-129
00Finnish Cardset-325
01Finnish Cardset-346

Reil, Joachim
82Swedish Semic VM Stickers-107
83Swedish Semic VM Stickers-107
94German DEL-376

Reilly, Blake
04South Surrey Eagles-21
04South Surrey Eagles-22
04Surrey Eagles-18 A

Reilly, Gary
89Lethbridge Hurricanes-18

Reilly, Gene
01Grand Rapids Griffins-25

Reilly, Jason
04UK Guildford Flames-6
05UK Guildford Flames-6

Reimann, Dan
93St. Cloud State Huskies-22
96Johnstown Chiefs-15
97Louisville Riverfrogs-19

Reimann, Tom
03ECHL All-Stars-257
03Greensboro Generals-189
04Atlantic City Boardwalk Bullies-11

Reimari, Jussi-Antti
99Finnish Cardset-93
00Finnish Cardset-194
01Finnish Cardset-310

Reimer, Andrew
917th Inn. Sketch WHL-142

Reimer, James
05Red Deer Rebels-15

Reimer, Mark
88ProCards AHL-8
89ProCards AHL-325
90ProCards AHL/IHL-311
91ProCards-121

Reimer, Oliver
93Quebec Pee-Wee Tournament-1770

Reimer, Patrick
04German DEL Update-290
04German Dusseldorf Metro Stars Postcards-17
05German DEL-79

Reimer, Rob
907th Inn. Sketch WHL-150A
907th Inn. Sketch WHL-150B

Reimola, Pekka
70Finnish Jaakiekko-354

Reindl, Franz
79Panini Stickers-110
82Swedish Semic VM Stickers-118
83Swedish Semic VM Stickers-118

Reindl, Jurgen
94German First League-293

Reiner, Philips
72Finnish Hellas-54

Reinert, Thomas
98Danish Hockey League-149
99Danish Hockey League-164

Reinhard, Alex
96Swiss HNL-30

Reinhard, Francis
72Finnish Semic World Championship-139
72Swedish Semic World Championship-139

Reinhard, Willy
94German First League-489

Reinhart, Alessandro
93Swiss HNL-244
95Swiss HNL-193
96Swiss HNL-85

Reinhart, Derek
03Regina Pats-4
04Regina Pats-5
05Regina Pats-16
06Regina Pats-8

Reinhart, Paul
79Flames Postcards-15
79Flames Team Issue-16
80Flames Postcards-17
80O-Pee-Chee-157
80Pepsi-Cola Caps-15
80Topps-157
81Flames Postcards-18
81O-Pee-Chee-36
81O-Pee-Chee Stickers-224
81Topps-28
82Flames Dollars-6
82O-Pee-Chee-56
82O-Pee-Chee Stickers-219
82Post Cereal-3
82Topps Stickers-219
83Esso-15
83NHL Key Tags-20
83O-Pee-Chee-91
83O-Pee-Chee Stickers-264
83Puffy Stickers-5
83Topps Stickers-264
83Vachon-17
84Kellogg's Accordion Discs-1
84Kellogg's Accordion Discs Singles-29
84O-Pee-Chee-235
847-Eleven Discs-7
85Flames Red Rooster-24
85O-Pee-Chee-48
85O-Pee-Chee Stickers-209
857-Eleven Credit Cards-3
85Topps-48
86Flames Red Rooster-22
86Flames Red Rooster-23
86Kraft Drawings-57
86O-Pee-Chee-205
87Flames Red Rooster-25
87O-Pee-Chee-143
87O-Pee-Chee Minis-34
87O-Pee-Chee Stickers-39
87Panini Stickers-206
87Topps-143
88Canucks Mohawk-16
89Canucks Mohawk-15
89Kraft-44
89Kraft All-Stars Stickers-1
89O-Pee-Chee-148
89O-Pee-Chee Stickers-65
89Topps-148
90Bowman-60
Tiffany-60
90O-Pee-Chee-293
90Panini Stickers-293
90Pro Set-304
90Score-173
Canadian-173
90Topps-293
Tiffany-293
Team Scoring Leaders-5
Team Scoring Leaders Tiffany-5
90Upper Deck-110
French-110
04ITG Franchises Canadian-14
Autographs-PRE

Reinholt, Kevin
03Kelowna Rockets-19
04Kelowna Rockets-28
05Kelowna Rockets-21

Reinholz, Jerrid
99Des Moines Buccaneers-16
02Minnesota Golden Gophers-17
03Minnesota Golden Gophers-24
04Minnesota Golden Gophers-21

Reinig, Dale
94German First League-606

Reinprecht, Steven
00BAP Memorabilia-461
Emerald-461
Ruby-461
Sapphire-461
00BAP Parkhurst 2000-P165
00BAP Signature Series-293
Emerald-293
Ruby-293
Sapphire-293
Autographs-224
Autographs Gold-224
00Black Diamond-78
Gold-78
00Crown Royale-126
21st Century Rookies-11
00Private Stock-122
Gold-122
Premiere Date-122
Retail-122
Silver-122
PS-2001 Rookies-10
00SP Authentic-108
Sign of the Times-SR
00SP Game Used-69
00SPx-97
Spectrum-97
00Stadium Club-253
00Titanium-124
Retail-124
Three-Star Selections-22
00Titanium Draft Day Edition-124
00Titanium Draft Day Promos-124
00Topps Chrome-249
Blue-249
Red-249
OPC Refractors-249
OPC Refractors Blue-249
OPC Refractors Red-249
Refractors-249
Refractors Blue-249
Refractors Red-249
00Topps Gold Label Class 1-107
Gold-107
00Topps Gold Label Class 2-107
00Topps Gold Label Class 2 Gold-107
00Topps Gold Label Class 3-107
00Topps Gold Label Class 3 Gold-107
00Topps Heritage-82
Chrome Parallel-82
00Topps Premier Plus-118
Blue Ice-118
00Topps Stars-115
Blue-115
00UD Heroes-165
00UD Pros and Prospects-107
00UD Reserve-97
00Upper Deck-185
Exclusives Tier 1-185
Exclusives Tier 2-185
00Upper Deck Ice-57
00Upper Deck Ice-67
Immortals-57
Legends-57
Stars-57
00Upper Deck MVP-193
First Stars-193
Second Stars-193
Third Stars-193
00Upper Deck Victory-264
00Vanguard-124
Pacific Proofs-124
01Avalanche Team Issue-18
01BAP Memorabilia-174
Emerald-174
Ruby-174
Sapphire-174
01BAP Signature Series-114
Autographs-114
Autographs Gold-114
01Pacific-105
01Pacific-445
Extreme LTD-105
Hobby LTD-105
Premiere Date-105
Retail LTD-105
01Pacific Arena Exclusives-105
01Parkhurst-168
01SP Authentic-122
Limited-122
Limited Gold-122
01Topps Own The Game-OTG17
01UD Stanley Cup Champs-40
01Upper Deck-48
Exclusives-48
01Upper Deck Victory-94
Gold-94
02Atomic-25
Blue-25
Gold-25

Red-25
Hobby Parallel-25
02Avalanche Postcards-5
02BAP First Edition-6
Jerseys-6
02BAP Memorabilia-2
Emerald-2
Ruby-2
Sapphire-2
NHL All-Star Game-2
NHL All-Star Game Blue-2
NHL All-Star Game Green-2
NHL All-Star Game Red-2
02BAP Memorabilia Toronto Fall Expo-2
02BAP Signature Series-47
Autographs-47
Autograph Buybacks 2000-224
Autograph Buybacks 2001-114
Autographs Gold-47
Golf-GS92
02Pacific-94
Blue-94
Red-94
02Pacific Complete-116
Red-116
02Pacific Exclusive-44
02Parkhurst-119
Bronze-119
Gold-119
Silver-119
College Ranks-CR13
College Ranks Jerseys-CRM13
02Parkhurst Retro-51
Minis-51
02Private Stock Reserve-27
Blue-27
Red-27
Retail-27
02SP Game Used Future Fabrics-FFSR
02SP Game Used Future Fabrics Gold-FFSR
02SP Game Used Future Fabrics Rainbow-FFSR
02Topps Total-173
02UD Artistic Impressions Right Track-RTSR
02UD Artistic Impression Right Track Gold-RTSR
02UD Premier Collection Jerseys Bronze-SR
02UD Premier Collection Jerseys Gold-SR
02UD Premier Collection Jerseys Silver-SR
02UD Top Shelf Dual Player Jerseys-RSR
02UD Top Shelf Goal Oriented-GOSR
02UD Top Shelf Shooting Stars-SHSR
02UD Top Shelf Sweet Sweaters-SWSR
02Upper Deck-287
Exclusives-287
02Upper Deck Beckett UD Promos-287
02Upper Deck On the Rise-ORSR
02Upper Deck Classic Portraits Hockey Royalty-RDF
02Upper Deck Classic Portraits Hockey Royalty Limited-RDF
02Upper Deck Classic Portraits Stitches-CSR
02Upper Deck Classic Portraits Stitches Limited-CSR
02Upper Deck MVP-50
Gold-50
Classics-50
Golden Classics-50
Skate Around Jerseys-SDHR
02Upper Deck Rookie Update-156A
02Upper Deck Vintage-61
Green Backs-61
03Beehive-28
Gold-28
Silver-28
03Black Diamond-3
Black-3
Green-3
Red-3
03ITG Action Jerseys-M70
03O-Pee-Chee-199
03OPC Blue-199
03OPC Gold-199
03OPC Red-199
03Pacific-87
Blue-87
Red-87
03Pacific Complete-323
Red-323
03Pacific Heads-Up-16
Hobby LTD-16
Retail LTD-16
03SPx-15
Radiance-15
Spectrum-15
03Topps-199
Blue-199
Gold-199
Red-199
03Upper Deck-274
Canadian Exclusives-274
HG-274
UD Exclusives-274
03Upper Deck Classic Portraits-13
03Upper Deck MVP-67
Gold Script-67
Silver Script-67
Canadian Exclusives-67
04Pacific-44
Blue-44
Red-44
05Panini Stickers-204
05Parkhurst-374
Facsimile Auto Parallel-374
True Colors-TCPHX
True Colors-TCPHX
05Upper Deck Jerseys-J-STR
06O-Pee-Chee-383
Rainbow-383
06Panini Stickers-324

Reirden, Todd
94Raleigh Icecaps-18
99BAP Memorabilia-313
Gold-313
Silver-313
99Blues Taco Bell-17
99Pacific Omega-200
Copper-200
Gold-200
Ice Blue-200
Premiere Date-200
99Upper Deck MVP SC Edition-165
Gold Script-165
Silver Script-165
Super Script-165
00BAP Signature Series-2
Emerald-2
Ruby-2
Sapphire-2
Autographs-23
Autographs Gold-23
00Upper Deck-153
Exclusives Tier 1-153
Exclusives Tier 2-153
02BAP Sig Series Auto Buybacks 2000-23
02Cincinnati Mighty Ducks-A-4
03Cincinnati Mighty Ducks-A7
04Houston Aeros-14
05German DEL-77

Reis, Matt
05Kingston Frontenacs-6

Reis, Shawn
91Air Canada SJHL-B14

Reise, Leo
23V128-1 Paulin's Candy-36
23V145-1-33
44Beehive Group II Photos-208
44Beehive Group II Photos-358
51Parkhurst-69
52Parkhurst-49
52Royal Desserts-6
53Parkhurst-65
54Parkhurst-67
76Old Timers-16
91Ultimate Original Six-28
French-28

Reiser, Bjorn
05German DEL-59

Reisinger, Ralf
94German DEL-312
95German DEL-211
99German Bundesliga 2-93
01German Upper Deck-56

Reiss, Andy
03Oshawa Generals-14
04German Hannover Scorpions Postcards-22
05German DEL-336

Reiss, Dieter
94German First League-615

Reist, Alain
98Swiss Power Play Stickers-284
98Swiss Power Play Stickers-297
99Swiss Panini Stickers-183
99Swiss Panini Stickers-284
00Swiss Panini Stickers-228
01Swiss HNL-152
02Swiss HNL-37
04Swiss Lausanne HC Postcards-3

Reisweber, Garren
04Green Bay Gamblers-15

Reiter, Jody
91Air Canada SJHL-C4
92Saskatchewan JHL-97

Reiter, Kevin
04Missouri River Otters-20
05Missouri River Otters-20

Reiter, Markus
94German First League-382

Reiter, Peter
94German First League-358

Reitmeir, Thomas
94German First League-258

Reitz, Erik
00Barrie Colts-22
01Barrie Colts-4
03Houston Aeros-17
04Barrie Colts 10th Anniversary-7
04Houston Aeros-15
06Fleer-219
Tiffany-219
06O-Pee-Chee-533
Rainbow-533
06SPx-201
Spectrum-201
06The Cup Masterpiece Pressplates (Artifacts)-229
06The Cup Masterpiece Pressplates (Marquee Rookies)-533
06The Cup Masterpiece Pressplates (MVP)-334
06The Cup Masterpiece Pressplates (Power Play)-108
06The Cup Masterpiece Pressplates (Trilogy)-119
06The Cup Masterpiece Pressplates (Victory)-224
06UD Artifacts-229
Blue-229
Gold-229
Platinum-229
Radiance-229
Red-229
06UD Powerplay-108
Impact Rainbow-108
06Ultra-209
Gold Medallion-209
Ice Medallion-209
06Upper Deck-218
Exclusives Parallel-218
High Gloss Parallel-218
Masterpieces-218
06Upper Deck MVP-334
Gold Script-334
Super Script-334
06Upper Deck Ovation-25
06Upper Deck Trilogy-119
06Upper Deck Victory-224
06Upper Deck Victory Black-224
06Upper Deck Victory Gold-224

Reja, Daniel
93London Knights-14
93London Knights-24
95Slapshot-50
96Louisville Riverfrogs-7
97Louisville Riverfrogs-17
98Bakersfield Condors-18
98Las Vegas Coyotes RHI-16
99Jacksonville Lizard Kings-5

Rejthar, Martin
97Czech APS Extraliga-228
99Czech Score Blue 2000-95
99Czech Score Red Ice 2000-95

Rekis, Arvids
00Peoria Rivermen-18
01Peoria Rivermen-23
02Peoria Rivermen-22
02Peoria Rivermen RBI Sports-164
03German DEL-27
04German Augsburg Panthers Postcards-25
04German DEL-37
05German DEL-13
Defender-DF14
06German DEL-11

Rekomaa, Esko
65Finnish Hellas-143

Relas, Timo
70Finnish Jaakiekko-186
71Finnish Suomi Stickers-107

Relland, Justin
99OCN Blizzard-3

Remackel, Chad
96Grand Rapids Griffins-20
97Mobile Mysticks-21
97Mobile Mysticks Kellogg's-11
98Fayetteville Force-15

Rempel, Brian
02Sault Ste. Marie Greyhounds-11

Rempel, Jon
98Baton Rouge Kingfish-15

Rempel, Nathan
95Saskatoon Blades-17
96Saskatoon Blades-19
97Saskatoon Blades-19
01Louisiana Ice Gators-21
02Louisiana Ice Gators-15
05UK Cardiff Devils-7
Gold-7
Silver-7
05UK Cardiff Devils Challenge Cup-14

Remstam, Mattias
99Swedish Upper Deck-100
00Swedish Upper Deck-104
SHL Signatures-MR
02Swedish SHL-41
Parallel-41
03Swedish Elite-54
Silver-54
04Swedish Elitset-58
Gold-58
05Swedish SHL Elitset-201
Gold-201
Teammates-5
06Swedish SHL Elitset-64

Renard, Jason
91Prince Albert Raiders-21
91 7th Inn. Sketch WHL-246
93Richmond Renegades-9

Renaud, Iannique
97Bakersfield Fog-15
98El Paso Buzzards-13
98Phoenix Mustangs-4
99Quad-City Mallards-1
00Knoxville Speed-17

Renaud, Mark
82Whalers Junior Hartford Courant-15
83NHL Key Tags-46

Renaud, Phil
51Laval Dairy QSHL-18
52St. Lawrence Sales-40

Renaud, Sebastien
93Quebec Pee-Wee Tournament-1351

Renberg, Mikael
90Swedish Semic Elitserien Stickers-241
91Swedish Semic Elitserien Stickers-171
92Upper Deck-233
92Swedish Semic Elitserien Stickers-190
93Donruss-255
Elite Inserts-U1
Rated Rookies-5
93Flyers J.C. Penney-18
93Flyers Lineup Sheets-30
93Flyers Lineup Sheets-40
93Leaf-323
Freshman Phenoms-5
93Parkhurst-251
Emerald Ice-251
Calder Candidates-C12
Calder Candidates Gold-C12
93Pinnacle-454
Canadian-454
Super Rookies-6
Super Rookies Canadian-6
93PowerPlay-408
Global Greats-6
Rookie Standouts-13
93Score-602
Gold-602
Canadian-602
Canadian Gold-602
93Stadium Club-269
Members Only Master Set-269
First Day Issue-269
93Ultra-391
Wave of the Future-16
93Upper Deck-486
SP-118
93Swedish Semic Elitserien-310
93Swedish Semic World Champ Stickers-12
94Be A Player-R74
Signature Cards-24
94Canada Games NHL POGS-181
94Donruss-236
Dominators-4
94Flair-131
94Fleer-158
Franchise Futures-7
94Leaf-54
Gold Rookies-6
Gold Stars-9
94Leaf Limited-48
94McDonald's Upper Deck-McD39
94OPC Premier-191
94OPC Premier-294
94OPC Premier-383
94O-Pee-Chee Finest Inserts-16
94OPC Premier Special Effects-191
94OPC Premier Special Effects-294
94OPC Premier Special Effects-383
94Parkhurst-272
Gold-272
Vintage-V78
94Parkhurst SE-SE129
Gold-SE129
Euro-Stars-ES3
94Pinnacle-79
94Pinnacle-464
Artist's Proofs-79
Artist's Proofs-464
Rink Collection-79
Rink Collection-464
World Edition-WE10
94Score-249
Gold-249
Platinum-249
94Select-61
Gold-61
94SP-83
Die Cuts-83
94Stadium Club Members Only-47
94Stadium Club-145
Members Only Master Set-145
First Day Issue-145
Dynasty and Destiny-4
Dynasty and Destiny Members Only-4
Super Team Winner Cards-145
94Topps/OPC Premier-191
94Topps/OPC Premier-294
94Topps/OPC Premier-383
Special Effects-191
Special Effects-294
Special Effects-383
94Topps Finest Bronze-22
94Ultra-159
All-Rookies-8
All-Rookies Parallel-8
Global Greats-8
Power-7
94Upper Deck-271
94Upper Deck-561
Electric Ice-271
Electric Ice-561
SP Inserts-SP59
SP Inserts Die Cuts-SP59
94Finnish Jaa Kiekko-67
94Swedish Leaf-199
Guest Special-5
94Swedish Olympics Lillehammer*-293
94Classic Pro Prospects-33
Jumbos-PP3
95Bashan Super Stickers-91
95Be A Player-18
Die-Cut-18
95Bowman-83
All-Foil-83
95Collector's Choice-222
Player's Club-222
Player's Club Platinum-222
95Donruss-80
Dominators-2
Elite Inserts-3
95Donruss Elite-94
Die Cut Stars-94
Die Cut Uncut-94
95Emotion-134
Ntense Power-5
95Finest-120
Refractors-120
95Hoyle Eastern Playing Cards-15
95Imperial Stickers-91
Die Cut Superstars-18
95Leaf-128
Fire On Ice-12
Freeze Frame-3
Gold Stars-6
95Leaf Limited-119
95McDonald's Pinnacle-MCD-22
95Metal-113
International Steel-16
95NHL Aces Playing Cards-12C
95Panini Stickers-117
95Parkhurst International-161
95Parkhurst International-243
95Parkhurst International-NNO1
Emerald Ice-161
Emerald Ice-243
All-Stars-6
Crown Collection Silver Series 1-7
Crown Collection Gold Series 1-7
95Pinnacle-41
Artist's Proofs-41
Rink Collection-41
Global Gold-5
Roaring 20s-12
95Playoff One on One-183
95Pro Magnets-55
95Score-35
Black Ice Artist's Proofs-35
Black Ice-35
Lamplighters-8
95Select Certified-31
Mirror Gold-31
Double Strike-12
Double Strike Gold-12
95SkyBox Impact-128
95SkyBox Impact-245
95SP-107
95Stadium Club-110
Members Only Master Set-110
Generation TSC-GT7
Generation TSC Members Only Master Set-GT7
Power Streak-PS5
Power Streak Members Only Master Set-PS5
95Summit-44
Artist's Proofs-44
Ice-44
95Topps-18
95Topps-353
OPC Inserts-18
OPC Inserts-353
Marquee Men Power Boosters-18
Mystery Finest-M12
Mystery Finest Refractors-M12
Power Lines-1PL
Young Stars-YS3
95Topps SuperSkills-8
Platinum-8
95Ultra-120
Gold Medallion-120
High Speed-16
Rising Stars-7
Rising Stars Gold Medallion-7
95Upper Deck-194
Electric Ice-194
Electric Ice Gold-194
Special Edition-SE149
Special Edition Gold-SE149
95Zenith-42
Gifted Grinders-8
95Swedish Upper Deck-235
95Swedish Globe World Championships-29
95Swedish Globe World Championships-259
95Swedish Globe World Championships-260
95Swedish Globe World Championships-261
95Swedish Globe World Championships-268
95Swedish World Championships Stickers-288
96SLU Hockey Canadian-12
96SLU Hockey American-18
96Be A Player-91
96Be A Player-91
Autographs-91
Autographs Silver-91
96Black Diamond-49
Gold-49
96Collector's Choice-189
96Collector's Choice-326
Crash the Game-C25A
Crash the Game-C25B
Crash the Game-C25C
Crash the Game Gold-C25A
Crash the Game Gold-C25B
Crash the Game Gold-C25C
96Donruss-125
Press Proofs-125
96Donruss Canadian Ice-77
Gold Press Proofs-77
Red Press Proofs-77
96Donruss Elite-33
Die Cut Stars-33
96Fleer-83
96Fleer Picks-46
96Flyers Postcards-19
96Kenner Starting Lineup Cards-18
96Leaf-108
Press Proofs-108
96Leaf Limited-79
Gold-79
96Leaf Preferred-58
Press Proofs-58
Steel-58
Steel Gold-58
96Maggers-82
96Metal Universe-115
96NHL Pro Stamps-55
96Pinnacle-55
Artist's Proofs-55
Foil-55
Premium Stock-55
Rink Collection-55
96Score-177
Artist's Proofs-177
Dealer's Choice Artist's Proofs-177
Special Artist's Proofs-177
Golden Blades-177
96SkyBox Impact-98
96SP-115
96Summit-73
Artist's Proofs-73
Ice-73
Metal-73
Premium Stock-73
96Team Out-45
96Ultra-128
Gold Medallion-128
96Upper Deck-307
Power Performers-P2
Superstar Showdown-SS23B
96Upper Deck Ice-46
Parallel-46
96Zenith-109
Artist's Proofs-109
Assailants-4
96Swedish Semic Wien-58
96Swedish Semic Wien-237
96Swedish Semic Wien-238
96Swedish Semic Wien-239
96Swedish Semic Wien-240
96Swedish Semic Wien-NNO
96Swedish Semic Wien Coca-Cola Dream Team-9
97Collector's Choice-184
Star Quest-SQ9
97Donruss-151
Press Proofs Silver-151
Press Proofs Gold-151
97Donruss Canadian Ice-96
Dominion Series-96
Provincial Series-96
97Donruss Limited-64
Exposure-64
97Donruss Preferred-68
Cut to the Chase-68
97Donruss Priority-75
Stamp of Approval-75
97Katch-138
Gold-138
Silver-138
97Kraft-20
97Leaf-38
Fractal Matrix-38
Fractal Matrix Die Cuts-38
97Leaf International-38
Universal Ice-38
97Pacific-59
Copper-59
Emerald Green-59
Ice Blue-59
Red-59
Silver-59
97Pacific Invincible-104
Copper-104
Emerald Green-104
Ice Blue-104
Red-104
Silver-104
97Pacific Omega-213
Copper-213
Dark Gray-213
Emerald Green-213
Gold-213
Ice Blue-213
97Panini Stickers-99
97Paramount-175
Copper-175
Dark Grey-175
Emerald Green-175
Ice Blue-175
Red-175
Silver-175
97Pinnacle-144
Press Plates Back Black-144
Press Plates Back Cyan-144
Press Plates Back Magenta-144
Press Plates Back Yellow-144
Press Plates Front Black-144
Press Plates Front Cyan-144
Press Plates Front Magenta-144
Press Plates Front Yellow-144
97Pinnacle Inside-119
97Revolution-130
Copper-130
Emerald-130
Ice Blue-130
Silver-130
97Score-138
Artist's Proofs-138
Golden Blades-138
97Studio-49
Press Proofs Silver-49
Press Proofs Gold-49
97Upper Deck-119
97Upper Deck-361
97Zenith-45
Z-Gold-45
Z-Silver-45
97Zenith 5 x 7-31
Gold Impulse-31
Silver Impulse-31
98Aurora-174
98Be A Player-131
Press Release-131
98BAP Gold-131
98BAP Autographs-131
98BAP Autographs Gold-131
98BAP Tampa Bay All Star Game-131
98Finest-87
No Protectors-87
No Protectors Refractors-87
Refractors-87
98Katch-137
98OPC Chrome-16
Refractors-16
98Pacific-404
Ice Blue-404
Red-404
98Pacific Omega-178
Red-178
Opening Day Issue-178
98Panini Stickers-98
98Paramount-219
Copper-219
Emerald Green-219
Holo-Electric-219
Ice Blue-219
Silver-219
98Topps-16
O-Pee-Chee-16
98UD Choice-197
98UD Choice Preview-197
98UD Choice Prime Choice Reserve-197
98UD Choice Reserve-197
98Upper Deck-179
Exclusives-179
Exclusives 1 of 1-179
Gold Reserve-179
99BAP Memorabilia-201
Gold-201
Silver-201
99O-Pee-Chee-184
99O-Pee-Chee Chrome-184
99O-Pee-Chee Chrome Refractors-184
99Pacific-311
Copper-311
Emerald Green-311
Gold-311
Ice Blue-311
Premiere Date-311
Red-311
99Pacific Omega-175
Copper-175
Gold-175
Ice Blue-175
Premiere Date-175
99Panini Stickers-122
99Paramount-175
Copper-175
Emerald-175
Gold-175
Holographic Emerald-175
Holographic Gold-175
Holographic Silver-175
Ice Blue-175
Premiere Date-175
Red-175
Silver-175
99Topps/OPC-184
99Topps/OPC Chrome-184
Refractors-184
00BAP Memorabilia-289
Emerald-289
Ruby-289
Sapphire-289
Promos-289
00BAP Mem Chicago Sportsfest Copper-289
00BAP Memorabilia Chicago Sportsfest Blue-289
00BAP Memorabilia Chicago Sportsfest Gold-289
00BAP Memorabilia Chicago Sportsfest Ruby-289
00BAP Memorabilia Chicago Sun-Times Ruby-289
00BAP Memorabilia Chicago Sun-Times Gold-289
00BAP Mem Chicago Sun-Times Sapphire-289
00BAP Mem Toronto Fall Expo Copper-289
00BAP Memorabilia Toronto Fall Expo Gold-289
00BAP Memorabilia Toronto Fall Expo Ruby-289
00Pacific-320
Copper-320
Gold-320
Ice Blue-320
Premiere Date-320
00Swedish Upper Deck-129
00Swedish Upper Deck-200
00Swedish Upper Deck-217
SHL Excellence-S4
SHL Signatures-MN
01BAP Signature Series-136
Autographs-136
Autographs Gold-136
01Parkhurst-208
01Upper Deck-394
Exclusives-394
02BAP First Edition-268
02BAP Sig Series Auto Buybacks 1998-131
02BAP Sig Series Auto Buybacks 2001-136
02Maple Leafs Platinum Collection-16
02Maple Leafs Team Issue-10
02NHL Power Play Stickers-140
02O-Pee-Chee-192
02O-Pee-Chee Premier Blue Parallel-192
02O-Pee-Chee Premier Red Parallel-192
02O-Pee-Chee Factory Set-192
02Pacific-367
Blue-367
Red-367
02Pacific Complete-269
Red-269
02Topps-192
OPC Blue Parallel-192
OPC Red Parallel-192
Factory Set-192
02Topps Total-152
02Upper Deck Victory-202
Bronze-202
Gold-202
Silver-202
03BAP Ultimate Memorabilia Linemates-2
03BAP Ultimate Mem Linemates Autos-8
03ITG Action-555
03Parkhurst Original Six Toronto-22
04Swedish Alfabilder Alfa Stars-6
04Swedish Alfabilder Alfa Star Golden Ice-10
04Swedish Alfabilder Autographs-106
04Swedish Alfabilder Limited Autographs-106
04Swedish Alfabilder Proof Parallels-6
05Swedish Lulea Hockey Postcards-14
05Swedish SHL Elitset-235
Gold-235
Series Two Signatures-22
Teammates-8
06Swedish SHL Elitset-90
Performers-10

Rendall, Bruce
92Thunder Bay Thunder Hawks-17

Rene, Patrice
90 7th Inn. Sketch QMJHL-94

Renfrew, Brian
92Western Michigan Broncos-20
93Western Michigan Broncos-23
95Dayton Bombers-18
96Dayton Ice Bandits-14
97Anchorage Aces-16

Rengert, Chris
04Penticton Vees-16

Renner, Justin
01Owen Sound Attack-14
02Owen Sound Attack-16

Rennette, Tyler
97Bowman CHL-6
97Bowman CHL-131
OPC-6
OPC-131
Autographs-11
00Worcester Icecats-21
01Peoria Rivermen-15
02ECHL All-Star Northern-32
02Peoria Rivermen-13
02Peoria Rivermen Photo Pack-8
02Peoria Rivermen RBI Sports-165
03Peoria Rivermen-23
04Peoria Rivermen-19
05Kalamazoo Wings-12
06Bloomington PrairieThunder-16

Renney, Tom
90 7th Inn. Sketch WHL-287
91 7th Inn. Sketch WHL-75
91 7th Inn. Sketch CHL Award Winners-17
92Alberta International Team Canada-17
93Alberta International Team Canada-16
03Rangers Team Issue-24

Rentz, Ryan
95Waterloo Blackhawks -17

Rentzsch, Marco
92Finnish Semic-176
94German DEL-63
95German DEL-56
96German DEL-253
99German Bundesliga 2-7

Renz, Andreas
94German DEL-438
95German DEL-393
96German DEL-300
98German DEL-223
99German DEL-211
00German DEL-222
01German Upper Deck-147
02German DEL City Press-205
03German DEL-176
04German Cologne Sharks Postcards-22
04German DEL-217
05German DEL-214
05German DEL-286
06German DEL-191

Renzi, Michael
00Belleville Bulls-8
01Belleville Bulls-19
01Belleville Bulls-28
02Arkansas Riverblades-12

Repik, Michal
05Vancouver Giants-18

Repka, Jan
94German First League-89

Repka, Lionel
99Fort Wayne Komets Points Leaders-12
99Fort Wayne Komets Penalty Leaders-14
01Fort Wayne Komets Shoe Carnival-10

Repneev, Vladimir
74Russian National Team-16
00Russian Hockey League-276

Repnjov, Vladimir
74Swedish Stickers-64

Repo, Seppo
70Finnish Jaakiekko-265
71Finnish Suomi Stickers-74
71Finnish Suomi Stickers-292
71Swedish Hockey-121
72Finnish Jaakiekko-73
72Finnish Hellas-12
72Finnish Panda Toronto-108
72Finnish Semic World Championship-86
72Swedish Semic World Championship-86
73Finnish Jaakiekko-77
73Finnish Jaakiekko-210
73Swedish Stickers-38
74Finnish Typotor-35
74Swedish Stickers-73
74Swedish Semic World Champ Stickers-89
76Phoenix Roadrunners WHA-16
77Finnish Sportscasters-74-1760
79Panini Stickers-173
98Danish Hockey League-181

Repp, Carl
89ProCards AHL-8

Repps, Juri
73Swedish Stickers-132

Resare, Bjorn
71Swedish Hockey-386

Resch, Glenn
74NHL Action Stamps-169
74O-Pee-Chee NHL-353
75Heroes Stand-Ups-17
75O-Pee-Chee NHL-145
75Topps-145
76O-Pee-Chee NHL-6
76O-Pee-Chee NHL-250
76Topps-6
76Topps-250
76Topps Glossy Inserts-6
77O-Pee-Chee NHL-6
77O-Pee-Chee NHL-50
77Topps-6
77Topps-50
77Topps/O-Pee-Chee Glossy-17
Square-17
78O-Pee-Chee-105
78Topps-105
79Islanders Transparencies-17
79O-Pee-Chee-6
79O-Pee-Chee-20
79Topps-6
79Topps-20
80O-Pee-Chee-235
80Topps-235
81O-Pee-Chee-80
81O-Pee-Chee-389
81O-Pee-Chee Stickers-230
81Rockies Postcards-26
81Topps-W85
82O-Pee-Chee-145
82O-Pee-Chee-146
82O-Pee-Chee Stickers-222
82Post Cereal-11
82Topps Stickers-222
83Devils Postcards-23
83NHL Key Tags-71
83O-Pee-Chee-236
83O-Pee-Chee Stickers-222
83O-Pee-Chee Stickers-223
83Puffy Stickers-12
83Topps Stickers-222
83Topps Stickers-223
84Devils Postcards-1
84Kellogg's Accordion Discs-6
84O-Pee-Chee-119
84O-Pee-Chee Stickers-68
84O-Pee-Chee Stickers-69
84 7-Eleven Discs-32
84Topps-89
85Devils Postcards-8
85O-Pee-Chee-36
85O-Pee-Chee Box Bottoms-L
85O-Pee-Chee Stickers-61
85 7-Eleven Credit Cards-11
85Topps-36
85Topps Box Bottoms-L
86Flyers Postcards-22
86O-Pee-Chee-158
86O-Pee-Chee Stickers-234
86Topps-158
90Upper Deck-507
French-507
00Upper Deck Legends-85
Legendary Collection Bronze-85
Legendary Collection Gold-85
Legendary Collection Silver-85
Legendary Game Jerseys-JCR
00Upper Deck Vintage Dynasty: A Piece of History-PR
00Upper Deck Vintage Dynasty: A Piece of History Gold-PR
01Greats of the Game-64
Autographs-64
01Topps Archives-54
02Topps Rookie Reprints-15
02Topps Rookie Reprint Autographs-15
02UD Mask Collection Mini Masks-CR
04ITG Franchises US East-357
04ITG Franchises US East-375
Autographs-A-CR2
Autographs-A-CR3
04ITG Franchises US West-186
Autographs-A-CR1
05Between the Pipes-16
Autographs-A-CR
06Between The Pipes-83
06Between The Pipes-137
Autographs-ACR

Reshetnikov, Sergei
99Russian Hockey League-39

Ressmann, Gerald
95Austrian National Team-24
95Swedish World Championships Stickers-273

Retter, Charlie
98Hampton Roads Admirals-16

Rettew, Scott
84Chicoutimi Sagueneens-21

Rettschlag, Adam
91 7th Inn. Sketch WHL-299

Rettschlag, Gus
92British Columbia JHL-3

Retzer, Christian
04German DEL-203
05German DEL-277

Retzer, Hermann
94German First League-601

Retzer, Stephan
94German DEL-255
95German DEL-253
96German DEL-142
02German DEL City Press-184
03German DEL-161
04German DEL-201
05German DEL-252

Reuben, Alexandre
00Quebec Remparts-18
Signed-18

Reuille, Sebastien
99Swiss Panini Stickers-121
00Swiss Panini Stickers-165
00Swiss Slapshot Mini-Cards-EHCK13
01Swiss HNL-164
02Swiss HNL-319

Reunamaki, Matti
65Finnish Hellas-98
66Finnish Jaakiekkosarja-167

Reusse, Wes
92British Columbia JHL-13

Reuta, Viktor
93Guelph Storm-15

Reuter, Christian
94German First League-210

Reuter, Rene
94German DEL-139
95German DEL-139

Reuthie, Christian
71Swedish Hockey-400

Revell, Dan
80Oshawa Generals-4
81Oshawa Generals-5
82Indianapolis Checkers-17

Revelle, Dany
02Mississauga Ice Dogs-21
03Mississauga Ice Dogs-18
04Kingston Frontenacs-17

Revenberg, Jim
89ProCards IHL-180
90ProCards AHL/IHL-339

Revermann, Bob
98Colorado Gold Kings-18
98Colorado Gold Kings Postcards-9

Rexe, Steve
69Swedish Hockey-363

Reymond, Alain
93Swiss HNL-52
95Swiss HNL-254
96Swiss HNL-224

Reynaert, Jeff
93Quebec Pee-Wee Tournament-848
01Western Michigan Broncos-7
02Kalamazoo Wings-23
05Kalamazoo Wings-19
06Bloomington PrairieThunder-17

Reynard, Ryan
95Alaska Gold Kings-17

Reynholds, Greg
93Quebec Pee-Wee Tournament-820

Reynolds, Bobby
89ProCards AHL-126
90Newmarket Saints-18
90ProCards AHL/IHL-152
91Baltimore Skipjacks-4
91ProCards-552
95German DEL-331
96German DEL-105
98Flint Generals-15
00Nebraska Legends-5
01Flint Generals-15

Reynolds, Cody
01OCN Blizzard-7

Reynolds, Derek
03Tulsa Oilers-15
04Lincoln Stars-26
05Lincoln Stars-25

Reynolds, Kurt
04UK U-20 Team-5

Reynolds, Matt
99Brampton Battalion-12
06Rio Grande Valley Killer Bees-2

Reynolds, Peter
98SP Authentic-120
Power Shift-120
Sign of the Times-PRE
98Upper Deck-397
Exclusives-397
Exclusives 1 of 1-397

Gold Reserve-397
99Bowman CHL-17
Gold-17
OPC International-17
Autographs-BA37
Autographs Gold-BA37
Autographs Silver-BA37
01Florida Everblades-15
02Florida Everblades-16
02Florida Everblades RBI-129
03Florida Everblades RBI Sports-172

Reynolds, T.J.
00St. Michaels Majors-24
01Mississauga Ice Dogs-3
03Wheeling Nailers-93
04San Antonio Rampage-3
05Milwaukee Admirals Choice-10
05Milwaukee Admirals Pepsi-15
06Milwaukee Admirals-14

Reynolds, Todd
88Brockville Braves-21

Rezansoff, Jesse
95Swift Current Broncos-17
96Fredericton Canadiens-17
99Louisiana Ice Gators-4

Reznar, Jiri
00Czech OFS-263

Reznicek, Josef
91Finnish Semic World Champ Stickers-107
91Swedish Semic World Champ Stickers-107
95German DEL-411
96Czech APS Extraliga-291
97Czech APS Extraliga-174
97Czech DS Extraliga-50
97Czech DS Stickers-210
98Czech DS-57
98Czech DS Stickers-149
98Czech OFS-35
98Czech OFS-450
99Czech DS-87
99Czech OFS-126
00Czech DS Extraliga-27
00Czech OFS-59
01Czech OFS-205
All Stars-14
02Czech OFS Plus-265
02Czech OFS Plus All-Star Game-H33
02Czech OFS Plus Trios-T10
03Czech OFS Plus-162
04Czech HC Sparta Praha Postcards-18
04Czech OFS-197
Defence Points-6
05Czech HC Karlovy Vary-14
06Czech OFS-39
All Stars-6
Defenders-9

Reznicek, Ladislav
00Sudbury Wolves-11

Rheault, Francis
93Quebec Pee-Wee Tournament-217

Rheaume, Dominic
907th Inn. Sketch QMJHL-232
917th Inn. Sketch QMJHL-128

Rheaume, Herb
24Anonymous NHL-12

Rheaume, Manon
92Sports Illustrated for Kids II-191
92Atlanta Knights-2
92Classic-59
Gold-59
92Classic Manon Rheaume C3 Presidential-1
92Classic Manon Rheaume Promo-NNO
92Classic Four-Sport *-224
Gold-224
Autographs-224A
BCs-BC11
93Bleachers 23K Manon Rheaume-1
93Bleachers 23K Manon Rheaume-2
93Bleachers 23K Manon Rheaume-3
93Bleachers 23K Manon Rheaume-NNO
93Atlanta Knights-22
93Knoxville Cherokees-14
93Quebec Pee-Wee Tournament-NNO
93Quebec Pee-Wee Tournament Gold-2
93Classic-112
93Classic-146
93Classic-149
93Classic-150
93Classic-MR1
Autographs-AU11
Crash Numbered-N8
Manon Rheaume Promo-NNO
McDonalds-17
Previews-HK2
93Classic Pro Prospects-1
93Classic Pro Prospects-2
93Classic Pro Prospects-3
93Classic Pro Prospects-4
93Classic Pro Prospects-5
93Classic Pro Prospects-6
93Classic Pro Prospects-7
93Classic Pro Prospects-100
93Classic Pro Prospects-AU2
BCs-BC10
LPs-LP1
Prototypes-PR2
93Classic C3 *-23
93Classic Four-Sport *-253
Gold-253
McDonald's LPs-LP4
94Santa Fe Hotel/Casino Rheaume Postcard-NNO
94Las Vegas Thunder-22
94Classic-120
94Classic-AU3
Gold-120
Autographs-NNO
Picks-CP15
Previews-HK4
Women of Hockey-W1
Women of Hockey-W21
94Classic Pro Prospects-129
94Classic Pro Prospects-239
94Classic Pro Prospects-250
Autographs-AU7
Jumbos-PP15
94Assets *-21
94Assets *-46
94Assets *-72
94Assets *-97
Die Cuts-DC10
Phone Cards $1000-4
Phone Cards $2000-3
Phone Cards $25-4
Phone Cards $5-14
Phone Cards One Minute/$2-18
Phone Cards One Minute/$2-42
94Images *-111
94Images *-147
Chrome-CC15
95Swedish Globe World Championships-250
95Classic Autographs-NNO
95Images-72
Gold-72
Clear Excitement-CE20
95Images Four-Sport *-118
Clear Excitement-E5
95Assets Gold *-9
95Assets Gold Die Cuts Silver *-SDC13
95Assets Gold Phone Cards $2 *-9
95Assets Gold Phone Cards $5 *-3
96Collector's Edge Future Legends-38
96Collector's Edge Ice-155
Prism-155
96Clear Assets Phone Cards $2 *-11
96Visions *-94
96Visions Signings *-78
99Quebec PeeWee Tournament Coll Souv-3

Rheaume, Pascal
917th Inn. Sketch QMJHL-115
94Classic Pro Prospects-129
94Classic Pro Prospects-145
96Albany River Rats-13
97Be A Player-227
Autographs-227
Autographs Die-Cuts-227
Autographs Prismatic Die-Cuts-227
97Donruss-215
Press Proofs Silver-215
Press Proofs Gold-215
97Donruss Limited-53
97Donruss Limited-66
Exposure-53
Exposure-66
97Pacific Omega-197
Copper-197
Dark Gray-197
Emerald Green-197
Gold-197
Ice Blue-197
98Pacific-371
Ice Blue-371
Red-371
98Upper Deck-175
Exclusives-175
Exclusives 1 of 1-175
Gold Reserve-175
99Blues Taco Bell-22
99Pacific-363
Copper-363
Emerald Green-363
Gold-363
Ice Blue-363
Premiere Date-363
Red-363
00Upper Deck NHLPA-PA77
00Worcester Icecats-7
01BAP Memorabilia-479
Emerald-479
Ruby-479
Sapphire-479
01SPx-155
02Topps Total-86
02Upper Deck MVP-12
Gold-12
Classics-12
Golden Classics-12
02Upper Deck Victory-11
Bronze-11
Gold-11
Silver-11
03Parkhurst Original Six New York-19
04Albany River Rats-20
05Albany River Rats-20

Rhinehart, Dwayne
91Air Canada SJHL-C46
91Air Canada SJHL All-Stars-40

Rhiness, Brad
76San Diego Mariners WHA-10

Rhode, Christian
04German DEL-230

Rhodes, Damian
90Michigan Tech Huskies-22
90Newmarket Saints-19
90ProCards AHL/IHL-167
91ProCards-355
92St. John's Maple Leafs-18
93Leaf-367
93Parkhurst-470
Emerald Ice-470
93PowerPlay-454
93Score-604
Gold-604
Canadian-604
Canadian Gold-604
93Ultra-435
93Upper Deck-364
93St. John's Maple Leafs-20
93Classic Pro Prospects-111
94Maple Leafs Gangsters-16
94Maple Leafs Kodak-22
94Maple Leafs Pin-up Posters-11
94OPC Premier-269
94O-Pee-Chee Finest Inserts-18
94OPC Premier Special Effects-269
94Topps/OPC Premier-269
Special Effects-269
94Upper Deck-154
Electric Ice-154
94Classic Pro Prospects-34
Jumbos-PP21
95Donruss-274
95Parkhurst International-200
95Parkhurst International-417
Emerald Ice-200
Emerald Ice-417
95SP-104
95Upper Deck-337
Electric Ice-337
Electric Ice Gold-337
96Be A Player-202
Autographs-202
Autographs Silver-202
96Black Diamond-71
Gold-71
96Collector's Choice-186
96Collector's Choice-325
96Donruss-156
Press Proofs-156
96Donruss Canadian Ice-16
Gold Press Proofs-16
Red Press Proofs-16
96Donruss Elite-113
Die Cut Stars-113
96Flair-64
Blue Ice-64
96Fleer-76
96Leaf-47
Press Proofs-47
Shut Down-7
96Leaf Limited-55
Gold-55
96Leaf Preferred-109
Press Proofs-109
Steel-50
Steel Gold-50
96McDonald's Pinnacle-39
96Metal Universe-107
Armor Plate-9
Armor Plate Super Power-9
96Pinnacle-150
Artist's Proofs-150
Foil-150
Premium Stock-150
Rink Collection-150
96Score-136
Artist's Proofs-136
Dealer's Choice Artist's Proofs-136
Special Artist's Proofs-136
Golden Blades-136
Net Worth-17
96Select Certified-28
Artist's Proofs-28
Blue-28
Mirror Blue-28
Mirror Gold-28
Mirror Red-28
Red-28
Freezers-15
96Senators Pizza Hut-23
96SkyBox Impact-90
96SP-110
96Summit-21
Artist's Proofs-21
Ice-21
Metal-21
Premium Stock-21
In The Crease-7
In The Crease Premium Stock-7
96Ultra-119
Gold Medallion-119
96Upper Deck-112
96Upper Deck Ice-45
Parallel-45
96Zenith-53
Artist's Proofs-53
97Collector's Choice-178
97Donruss-166
Press Proofs Silver-166
Press Proofs Gold-166
97Donruss Canadian Ice-125
Dominion Series-125
Provincial Series-125
97Donruss Elite-42
Aspirations-42
Status-42
97Donruss Limited-57
97Donruss Limited-186
Exposure-57
Exposure-186
Fabric of the Game-60
97Donruss Preferred-37
Cut to the Chase-37
Color Guard-18
Color Guard-P18
Color Guard Promos-18
97Donruss Priority-57
Stamp of Approval-57
97Katch-101
Gold-101
Silver-101
97Leaf-45
Fractal Matrix-45
Fractal Matrix Die Cuts-45
Pipe Dreams-11
97Leaf International-45
Universal Ice-45
97McDonald's Upper Deck-30
97Pacific-146
Copper-146
Emerald Green-146
Ice Blue-146
Red-146
Silver-146
97Pacific Dynagon-86
Copper-86
Dark Grey-86
Emerald Green-86
Ice Blue-86
Red-86
Silver-86
Tandems-69
97Pacific Omega-157
Copper-157
Dark Gray-157
Emerald Green-157
Gold-157
Ice Blue-157
97Paramount-128
Copper-128
Dark Grey-128
Emerald Green-128
Ice Blue-128
Red-128
Silver-128
97Pinnacle-44
Artist's Proofs-44
Rink Collection-44
Press Plates Back Black-44
Press Plates Back Cyan-44
Press Plates Back Magenta-44
Press Plates Back Yellow-44
Press Plates Front Black-44
Press Plates Front Cyan-44
Press Plates Front Magenta-44
Press Plates Front Yellow-44
97Pinnacle Certified-20
Red-20
Mirror Blue-20
Mirror Gold-20
Mirror Red-20
97Pinnacle Inside-65
Coach's Collection-65
Executive Collection-65
97Pinnacle Tot Cert Platinum Blue-20
97Pinnacle Tot Cert Platinum Gold-20
97Pinnacle Totally Certified Platinum Red-20
97Pinnacle Tot Cert Mirror Platinum Gold-20
97Revolution-94
Copper-94
Emerald-94
Ice Blue-94
Silver-94
97Score-16
Artist's Proofs-16
Golden Blades-16
Net Worth-7
97Studio-71
Press Proofs Silver-71
Press Proofs Gold-71
97Upper Deck-322
98Aurora-133
Championship Fever-33
Championship Fever Copper-33
Championship Fever Ice Blue-33
Championship Fever Red-33
Championship Fever Silver-33
98Be A Player-96
Press Release-96
98BAP Gold-96
98BAP Autographs-96
98BAP Autographs Gold-96
98BAP Tampa Bay All Star Game-96
98Bowman's Best-54
Refractors-54
Atomic Refractors-54
98Crown Royale-95
Limited Series-95
98Finest-146
No Protectors-146
No Protectors Refractors-146
Refractors-146
98Katch-100
98Lunchables Goalie Greats Rounds-6
98Lunchables Goalie Greats Squares-6
98NHL Aces Playing Cards-13
98OPC Chrome-74
Refractors-74
98Pacific-1
Ice Blue-1
Red-1
98Pacific Dynagon Ice-130
Blue-130
Red-130
98Pacific Omega-168
Red-168
Opening Day Issue-168
98Panini Stickers-40
98Paramount-166
Copper-166
Emerald Green-166
Holo-Electric-166
Ice Blue-166
Silver-166
Glove Side Laser Cuts-13
98Revolution-101
Ice Shadow-101
Red-101
98Senators Team Issue-19
98Topps-74
O-Pee-Chee-74
98Topps Gold Label Class 1-97
Black-97
Black One of One-97
One of One-97
Red-97
Red One of One-97
98Topps Gold Label Class 2-97
98Topps Gold Label Class 2 Black-97
98Topps Gold Label Class 2 Black 1 of 1-97
98Topps Gold Label Class 2 One of One-97
98Topps Gold Label Class 2 Red-97
98Topps Gold Label Class 2 Red One of One-97
98Topps Gold Label Class 3-97
98Topps Gold Label Class 3 Black-97
98Topps Gold Label Class 3 Black 1 of 1-97
98Topps Gold Label Class 3 One of One-97
98Topps Gold Label Class 3 Red-97
98Topps Gold Label Class 3 Red One of One-97
98UD Choice-139
98UD Choice Preview-139
98UD Choice Prime Choice Reserve-139
98UD Choice Reserve-139
98Upper Deck-137
Exclusives-137
Exclusives 1 of 1-137
Gold Reserve-137
98Upper Deck MVP-140
Gold Script-140
Silver Script-140
Super Script-140
99Aurora-8
Premiere Date-8
99BAP Memorabilia-234
Gold-234
Silver-234
99BAP Millennium-13
Emerald-13
Ruby-13
Sapphire-13
Signatures-13
Signatures Gold-13
99Black Diamond-4
Diamond Cut-4
Final Cut-4
99Crown Royale-8
Limited Series-8
Premiere Date-8
99O-Pee-Chee-143
99O-Pee-Chee Chrome-143
99O-Pee-Chee Chrome Refractors-143
99Pacific-294
Copper-294
Emerald Green-294
Gold-294
Ice Blue-294
Premiere Date-294
Red-294
99Pacific Dynagon Ice-18
Blue-18
Copper-18
Gold-18
Premiere Date-18
99Pacific Omega-12
Copper-12
Gold-12
Ice Blue-12
Premiere Date-12
99Pacific Prism-8
Holographic Blue-8
Holographic Gold-8
Holographic Mirror-8
Holographic Purple-8
Premiere Date-8
99Panini Stickers-17
99Paramount-14
Copper-14
Emerald-14
Gold-14
Holographic Emerald-14
Holographic Gold-14
Holographic Silver-14
Ice Blue-14
Premiere Date-14
Red-14
Silver-14
Ice Alliance-2
99Revolution-8
Premiere Date-8
Red-8
Shadow Series-8
Copper-8
Gold-8
CSC Silver-8
99SPx-1
Radiance-1
Spectrum-1
99Stadium Club-153
First Day Issue-153
One of a Kind-153
Printing Plates Black-153
Printing Plates Cyan-153
Printing Plates Magenta-153
Printing Plates Yellow-153
99Topps/OPC-143
99Topps/OPC Chrome-143
Refractors-143
99Topps Premier Plus-43
Parallel-43
99Upper Deck-15
99Upper Deck-175
Exclusives-15
Exclusives-175
Exclusives 1 of 1-15
Exclusives 1 of 1-175
99Upper Deck Gold Reserve-15
99Upper Deck Gold Reserve-175
99Upper Deck MVP-2
Gold Script-2
Silver Script-2
Super Script-2
Draft Report-DR1
SC Edition Great Combinations-GCSR
SC Edition Great Combinations Parallel-GCSR
99Upper Deck Victory-11
99Upper Deck Victory-13
99Upper Deck Victory-388
99Wayne Gretzky Hockey-13
00SLU Hockey-190
00Aurora-7
Premiere Date-7
00BAP Memorabilia-33
Emerald-33
Ruby-33
Sapphire-33
Promos-33
00BAP Mem Chicago Sportsfest Copper-33
00BAP Memorabilia Chicago Sportsfest Blue-33
00BAP Memorabilia Chicago Sportsfest Gold-33
00BAP Memorabilia Chicago Sportsfest Ruby-33
00BAP Memorabilia Chicago Sun-Times Ruby-33
00BAP Memorabilia Chicago Sun-Times Gold-33
00BAP Mem Chicago Sun-Times Sapphire-33
00BAP Mem Toronto Fall Expo Copper-33
00BAP Memorabilia Toronto Fall Expo Gold-33
00BAP Memorabilia Toronto Fall Expo Ruby-33
00BAP Parkhurst 2000-P127
00BAP Ultimate Memorabilia Goalie Sticks-G2
00Crown Royale-6
Ice Blue-6
Limited Series-6
Premiere Date-6
Red-6
00O-Pee-Chee-76
00O-Pee-Chee Parallel-76
00Pacific-21
Copper-21
Gold-21
Ice Blue-21
Premiere Date-21
00Paramount-14
Copper-14
Gold-14
Holo-Gold-14
Holo-Silver-14
Ice Blue-14
Premiere Date-14
00Private Stock-5
Gold-5
Premiere Date-5
Retail-5
Silver-5
00Revolution-7
Blue-7
Premiere Date-7
Red-7
00SP Authentic-6
00Stadium Club-15
00Topps/OPC-76
Parallel-76
00Topps Chrome-59
OPC Refractors-59
Refractors-59
00UD Reserve-4
00Upper Deck-11
Exclusives Tier 1-11
Exclusives Tier 2-11
00Upper Deck Legends-5
Legendary Collection Bronze-5
Legendary Collection Gold-5
Legendary Collection Silver-5
00Upper Deck MVP-9
First Stars-9
Second Stars-9
Third Stars-9
00Upper Deck Victory-13
00Upper Deck Vintage-14
00Upper Deck Vintage-23
00Upper Deck Vintage-24
00Vanguard-5
Holographic Gold-5
Holographic Purple-5
Pacific Proofs-5
01BAP Memorabilia-206
Emerald-206
Ruby-206
Sapphire-206
01BAP Signature Series-53
Autographs-53
Autographs Gold-53
01Between the Pipes-24
Double Memorabilia-DM9
Goalie Gear-GG15
He Shoots-He Saves Prizes-36
Jerseys-GJ26
Jersey and Stick Cards-GSJ26
Masks-9
Masks Silver-9
Masks Gold-9
01O-Pee-Chee-112
01O-Pee-Chee Premier Parallel-112
01Pacific-23
Extreme LTD-23
Hobby LTD-23
Premiere Date-23
Retail LTD-23
01Pacific Adrenaline-10
Blue-10
Premiere Date-10
Red-10
Retail-10
01Pacific Arena Exclusives-23
01Parkhurst-231
01Topps-112
OPC Parallel-112
01Upper Deck-241
Exclusives-241
02BAP First Edition-176
02BAP Sig Series Auto Buybacks 1998-96
02BAP Sig Series Auto Buybacks 1999-13
02BAP Sig Series Auto Buybacks 2001-53
02Between the Pipes-65
Gold-65
Silver-65
02Pacific-20
Blue-20
Red-20

Rhodin, Thomas
90Swedish Semic Elitserien Stickers-258
91Swedish Semic Elitserien Stickers-87
92Swedish Semic Elitserien Stickers-109
93Swedish Semic Elitserien-82
94Swedish Leaf-15
95Swedish Leaf-41
95Swedish Upper Deck-60
98German DEL-165
99German DEL-70
00Swedish Upper Deck-79
02Swedish SHL-26
Parallel-26
05Swedish SHL Elitset-184
Gold-184
Series Two Signatures-10
06Swedish SHL Elitset-44

Rhyorchuk, Tyler
02OCN Blizzard-19

Ribbenstrand, Alexander
05Swedish SHL Elitset Rookies-1
06Swedish SHL Elitset-15

Ribble, Jerry
907th Inn. Sketch OHL-45

Ribble, Pat
78Flames Majik Market-3
79O-Pee-Chee-199
79Topps-199
80O-Pee-Chee-393
81O-Pee-Chee-339

Ribeiro, Matt
06Ottawa 67s-10

Ribeiro, Mike
93Quebec Pee-Wee Tournament-1391
97Upper Deck-417
98Bowman's Best-143
Refractors-143
Atomic Refractors-143
98Bowman CHL-85
98Bowman CHL-132
Golden Anniversary-85
Golden Anniversary-132
OPC International-85
OPC International-132
Autographs Blue-A38
Autographs Gold-A38
Autographs Silver-A38
98Bowman Chrome CHL-85
98Bowman Chrome CHL-132
Golden Anniversary-85
Golden Anniversary-132
Golden Anniversary Refractors-85
Golden Anniversary Refractors-132
OPC International-85
OPC International-132
OPC International Refractors-85
OPC International Refractors-132
Refractors-85
Refractors-132
99BAP Memorabilia-348
Gold-348
Silver-348
99BAP Millennium Calder Candidates Ruby-C12
99BAP Millennium Calder Candidate Emerald-C12
99BAP Millennium Calder Cand Sapphire-C12
99Black Diamond-47
Diamond Cut-47
Final Cut-47
99Pacific Dynagon Ice-4
Blue-4
Copper-4
Gold-4
Premiere Date-4
99Pacific Omega-125
Copper-125
Gold-125
Ice Blue-125
Premiere Date-125
99Panini Stickers-71
99SP Authentic-44
Sign of the Times-MRI
Sign of the Times Gold-MRI
99Stadium Club-174
First Day Issue-174
One of a Kind-174
Printing Plates Black-174
Printing Plates Cyan-174
Printing Plates Magenta-174
Printing Plates Yellow-174
99Topps Premier Plus-134
Parallel-134
99Upper Deck-243
Exclusives-243
Exclusives 1 of 1-243
99Upper Deck Arena Giveaways-MC1
99Upper Deck Gold Reserve-243
99Upper Deck HoloGrFx-30
Ausome-30
99Upper Deck Ovation-31
Standing Ovation-31
A Piece Of History-MR
99Upper Deck Victory-370
99Quebec PeeWee Tournament Coll Souv-29
99Quebec Remparts-24
Signed-24
99Rouyn-Noranda Huskies-17
99Bowman CHL-71
Gold-71
OPC International-71
00BAP Memorabilia-258
Emerald-258
Ruby-258
Sapphire-258
Promos-258
00BAP Mem Chicago Sportsfest Copper-258
00BAP Memorabilia Chicago Sportsfest Blue-258
00BAP Memorabilia Chicago Sportsfest Gold-258
00BAP Memorabilia Chicago Sportsfest Ruby-258
00BAP Memorabilia Chicago Sun-Times Ruby-258
00BAP Memorabilia Chicago Sun-Times Gold-258
00BAP Mem Chicago Sun-Times Sapphire-258
00BAP Mem Toronto Fall Expo Copper-258
00BAP Memorabilia Toronto Fall Expo Gold-258
00BAP Memorabilia Toronto Fall Expo Ruby-258
00O-Pee-Chee-315
00O-Pee-Chee Parallel-315
00Paramount-129
Copper-129
Gold-129
Holo-Gold-129
Holo-Silver-129
Ice Blue-129
Premiere Date-129
00SP Authentic BuyBacks-53
00SP Authentic Sign of the Times-RO
00Topps/OPC-315
Parallel-315
00Topps Chrome-210
OPC Refractors-210
Refractors-210
00UD Reserve Buyback Autographs-49
00UD Reserve Buyback Autographs-50
00UD Reserve Buyback Autographs-51
00Upper Deck MVP ProSign-MR
00QMJHL All-Star Program Inserts-10
00Quebec Citadelles-23
Signed-23
01BAP Memorabilia-209
Emerald-209
Ruby-209
Sapphire-209
01BAP Signature Series-237
Autographs-237
Autographs Gold-237
01Bowman YoungStars-120
Gold-120
Ice Cubed-120
Autographs-MR
Relics-JMR
Relics-SMR
Relics-DSMR
Rivals-R7
01Canadiens Postcards-19
01Parkhurst-257
01Parkhurst Beckett Promos-257
01SP Authentic Sign of the Times-MR
01Titanium-74
Hobby Parallel-74
Premiere Date-74
Retail-74
Retail Parallel-74
Rookie Team-7
Three-Star Selections-27
01Titanium Draft Day Edition-140
01Quebec Citadelles-26
02Canadiens Postcards-21
02O-Pee-Chee-76
02O-Pee-Chee Premier Blue Parallel-76
02O-Pee-Chee Premier Red Parallel-76
02O-Pee-Chee Factory Set-76
02Pacific-202
Blue-202
Red-202
Shining Moments-8
02Pacific Complete-171
Red-171
02Pacific Entry Draft-5
02SP Authentic-120
02SP Game Used Future Fabrics-FFMR
02SP Game Used Future Fabrics-FFRI
02SP Game Used Future Fabrics Gold-FFMR
02SP Game Used Future Fabrics Gold-FFRI
02SP Game Used Future Fabrics Rainbow-FFMR
02SP Game Used Future Fabrics Rainbow-FFRI
02Stadium Club YoungStars Relics-S20
02Topps-76
OPC Blue Parallel-76
OPC Red Parallel-76
Factory Set-76
02Upper Deck-93
Exclusives-93
Bright Futures-MR
02Upper Deck Victory-111
Bronze-111
Gold-111
Silver-111
03Beehive-103
Gold-103
Silver-103
03Canadiens Postcards-22
03Crown Royale-55
Blue-55
Retail-55
03ITG Action-361
03Kraft-7
03Pacific-181
Blue-181
Red-181
03Pacific Calder-56
Silver-56
03Pacific Complete-349
Red-349
03Pacific Heads-Up-53
Hobby LTD-53
Retail LTD-53
03Pacific Quest for the Cup-56
Blue-56
03Parkhurst Original Six Montreal-25
03Private Stock Reserve-55
Blue-55
Red-55
Retail-55
03Titanium-55
Hobby Jersey Number Parallels-55
Retail-55
Retail Jersey Number Parallels-55
03Topps Traded Future Phenoms-FP-MR
03UD Premier Collection Stars-ST-MR
03UD Premier Collection Stars Patches-ST-MR
03Upper Deck-343
Canadian Exclusives-343
HG-343
UD Exclusives-343
03Upper Deck Ice-46
Gold-46
03Upper Deck MVP-228
Gold Script-228
Silver Script-228
Canadian Exclusives-228
03Upper Deck Rookie Update-48
04Pacific-140
Blue-140
Red-140
04SP Authentic Buybacks-154
04SP Authentic Buybacks-155
04SP Authentic Buybacks-156
04SP Authentic Sign of the Times-DS-RR
04SP Authentic Sign of the Times-TS-RKR
04SP Authentic Sign of the Times-SS-CNP
04Upper Deck-94
Canadian Exclusives-94
Heritage Classic-CC-MR
HG Glossy Gold-94
HG Glossy Silver-94
04Finnish Cardset-207
04Swedish Pure Skills-99
Parallel-99
05Be A Player Dual Signatures-RR
05Be A Player Dual Signatures-TR
05Be A Player Quad Signatures-MONT
05Be A Player Signatures-RI
05Be A Player Signatures Gold-RI
05Be A Player Triple Signatures-MTL
05Beehive-49
Matte-49
Signature Scrapbook-SSMR
05Black Diamond-100
Emerald-100
Gold-100
Onyx-100
Ruby-100
05Canadiens Team Issue-17
05Hot Prospects-54
En Fuego-54
Red Hot-54
White Hot-54
05McDonalds Upper Deck-27
Top Scorers-TS8
05Panini Stickers-74
05Parkhurst-253
Facsimile Auto Parallel-253
True Colors-TCMTL
True Colors-TCMTL
True Colors-TCMOBO
True Colors-TCMOBO
05SP Authentic-53
Limited-53
Prestigious Pairings-PPRR
Scripts to Success-SSMR
Sign of the Times-MR
Sign of the Times Triples-TRRP
Sign of the Times Quads-QTRRK
05SP Game Used-51
Autographs-51
Gold-51
Authentic Fabrics-AF-MI
Authentic Fabrics Autographs-AAF-MI
Authentic Fabrics Dual-RB
Authentic Fabrics Dual-RR
Authentic Fabrics Dual Autographs-RB
Authentic Fabrics Dual Autographs-RR
Authentic Fabrics Gold-AF-MI
Authentic Patches-AP-MI
Authentic Patches Autographs-AAP-MI
Authentic Patches Dual-RB
Authentic Patches Dual-RR
Authentic Patches Dual Autographs-RB
Authentic Patches Dual Autographs-RR
Auto Draft-AD-MR
Awesome Authentics Gold-DA-MR
Game Gear-GG-MR
Game Gear Autographs-AG-MR
SIGnificance Extra-RR
SIGnificance Extra Gold-RR
Statscriptions-ST-MR
05SPx-46
Spectrum-46
Winning Combos-WC-MP
Winning Combos-WC-RR
Winning Combos-WC-RT
Winning Combos Autographs-AWC-RB
Winning Combos Autographs-AWC-RR
Winning Combos Gold-WC-MP
Winning Combos Gold-WC-RR
Winning Combos Gold-WC-RT
Winning Combos Spectrum-WC-MP
Winning Combos Spectrum-WC-RR
Winning Combos Spectrum-WC-RT
Winning Materials-WM-MR
Winning Materials Autographs-AWM-MR
Winning Materials Gold-WM-MR
Winning Materials Spectrum-WM-MR
05The Cup Dual NHL Shields-DSRR
05UD Artifacts-51
Blue-51
Gold-51
Green-51
Pewter-51
Red-51
Auto Facts-AF-MR
Auto Facts Blue-AF-MR
Auto Facts Copper-AF-MR
Auto Facts Pewter-AF-MR
Auto Facts Silver-AF-MR
Frozen Artifacts-FA-MR
Frozen Artifacts Autographed-FA-MR
Frozen Artifacts Copper-FA-MR
Frozen Artifacts Dual-FAD-MR
Frozen Artifacts Dual Autographed-FAD-MR
Frozen Artifacts Dual Copper-FAD-MR
Frozen Artifacts Dual Gold-FAD-MR
Frozen Artifacts Dual Maroon-FAD-MR
Frozen Artifacts Dual Pewter-FAD-MR
Frozen Artifacts Dual Silver-FAD-MR
Frozen Artifacts Gold-FA-MR
Frozen Artifacts Maroon-FA-MR
Frozen Artifacts Patches-FP-MR
Frozen Artifacts Patches Autographed-FP-MR
Frozen Artifacts Patches Dual-FPD-MR
Frozen Artifacts Patches Dual Autos-FPD-MR
Frozen Artifacts Patches Pewter-FP-MR
Frozen Artifacts Patches Silver-FP-MR
Frozen Artifacts Pewter-FA-MR
Frozen Artifacts Silver-FA-MR
Gold Autographed-51
Remarkable Artifacts-RA-MR
Remarkable Artifacts Dual-RA-MR
05UD PowerPlay-48
Rainbow-48
Power Marks-PMMR
05Ultimate Collection-51
Gold-51
Ultimate Signatures Trios-UTRRP
05Ultra-106
Gold-106
Ice-106
Scoring Kings-SK27
Scoring Kings Jerseys-SKJ-MR
Scoring Kings Jersey Autographs-KAJ-MR
Scoring Kings Patches-SKP-MR
Scoring Kings Patch Autographs-KAP-MR
05Upper Deck-348
Big Playmakers-B-MRI
Jerseys Series II-J2MR
Majestic Materials-MMRO
NHL Generations-DGR
NHL Generations-TLKR
NHL Generations-TSIR
Notable Numbers-N-MR
Shooting Stars-S-MRI
05Upper Deck Ice-52
Rainbow-52
Fresh Ice-FIRI
Fresh Ice Glass-FIRI
Fresh Ice Glass Patches-FIPRI
Glacial Graphs-GGMR
05Upper Deck MVP-207
Gold-207
Platinum-207
ProSign-T-MR

05Upper Deck Rookie Update-53
05Upper Deck Trilogy-45
05Upper Deck Trilogy-162
Crystal-162
Honorary Patches-HP-RI
Honorary Patch Scripts-HSP-RI
Honorary Swatches-HS-RI
Honorary Swatch Scripts-HSS-RI
Scripts-SFS-MR
05Upper Deck Victory-105
Black-105
Gold-105
Silver-105
05Finnish Cardset -8
Finnish Cardset Magicmakers-1
06Be A Player Portraits-57
06Black Diamond-110
Black-110
Gold-110
Ruby-110
Gemography-GMR
06Flair Showcase-55
Parallel-55
Inks-IRI
Stitches-SSMR
06Fleer-106
Tiffany-106
Signing Day-SDMR
06McDonald's Upper Deck-25
06O-Pee-Chee-170
Rainbow-170
Swatches-S-RI
06Panini Stickers-67
06SP Authentic Sign of the Times Duals-STMR
06SP Game Used Authentic Fabrics Eights-AF8CEN
06SP Game Used Authentic Fabrics Eights Patches-AF8CEN
06SP Game Used By The Letter-BLRI
06SP Game Used Inked Sweaters-ISMR
06SP Game Used Inked Sweaters Patches-ISMR
06SP Game Used Letter Marks-LMRI
06SP Game Used SIGnificance-SRI
06SPx-55
Spectrum-55
06Stars Team Postcards-18
06The Cup Autographed NHL Shields Duals-DASMI
06The Cup NHL Shields Duals-DSHEM
06UD Artifacts Auto-Facts-AFRO
06UD Artifacts Auto-Facts Gold-AFRO
06UD Artifacts Tundra Tandems-TTRR
06UD Artifacts Tundra Tandems Black-TTRR
06UD Artifacts Tundra Tandems Blue-TTRR
06UD Artifacts Tundra Tandems Gold-TTRR
06UD Artifacts Tundra Tandems Platinum-TTRR
06UD Artifacts Tundra Tandems Red-TTRR
06UD Artifacts Tundra Tandems Dual Patches Red-TTRR
06Ultra-107
Gold Medallion-107
Ice Medallion-107
06Upper Deck-317
Exclusives Parallel-317
High Gloss Parallel-317
Game Jerseys-J2RI
Game Patches-P2RI
Masterpieces-317
Signatures-SMR
06Upper Deck MVP-155
Gold Script-155
Super Script-155
Autographs-OARK
06Upper Deck Ovation-26
06Upper Deck Trilogy Ice Scripts-ISMR
06Upper Deck Trilogy Scripts-TSMR
06Upper Deck Victory-107
06Upper Deck Victory-243
06Upper Deck Victory Black-107
06Upper Deck Victory Gold-107
07Upper Deck Ovation-32
07Upper Deck Victory-184
Black-184
Gold-184

Ricard, Eric

89ProCards AHL-16
90ProCards AHL/IHL-434
91ProCards-371
94Central Hockey League-31
97New Mexico Scorpions-3
97New Mexico Scorpions II-2
98Florida Everblades-21

Ricci, Mike

89Peterborough Petes-100
897th Inn. Sketch OHL-100
897th Inn. Sketch OHL-183
897th Inn. Sketch OHL-190
90Flyers Postcards-20
90OPC Premier-96
90Pro Set-631
90Score-433
Canadian-433
90Score Rookie/Traded-60T
90Score Young Superstars-39
90Upper Deck-351
90Upper Deck-355
French-351
French-355
91Pro Set Platinum-85
91Bowman-246
91Flyers J.C. Penney-22
91Gillette-32
91Kraft-52
91O-Pee-Chee-13
91O-Pee-Chee-194
91OPC Premier-23
91Panini Stickers-231
91Panini Stickers-338
91Parkhurst-123
French-123
91Pinnacle-32
French-32
91Pro Set-170
French-170
91Score American-28
91Score Canadian Bilingual-28
91Score Canadian English-28
91Score Young Superstars-10
91Stadium Club-386
91Topps-13
91Topps-194
91Upper Deck-143
French-143
91Star Pics-60
92Bowman-406
92Nordiques Petro-Canada-26
92O-Pee-Chee-329
92OPC Premier-91
92Panini Stickers-184
92Panini Stickers French-184
92Parkhurst-146
Emerald Ice-146
92Pinnacle-314
French-314
92Pro Set-133
92Score-84
Canadian-84
92Stadium Club-408
92Topps-86
Gold-86G
92Ultra-178
92Ultra-389
92Upper Deck-477
92Upper Deck-627
93Donruss-280
93Kraft-19
93Kraft Recipes-7
93Kraft Recipes French-7
93Leaf-23
93OPC Premier-62
Gold-62
93Panini Stickers-69
93Parkhurst-439
Emerald Ice-439
93Pinnacle-110
Canadian-110
Team 2001-22
Team 2001 Canadian-22
93PowerPlay-202
93Score-120
Canadian-120
93Stadium Club-176
Members Only Master Set-176
OPC-176
First Day Issue-176
First Day Issue OPC-176
93Topps/OPC Premier-62
Gold-62
93Ultra-168
93Upper Deck-352
NHLPA/Roots-10
SP-129
94Be A Player-R49
94Be A Player-R108
Signature Cards-37
94Canada Games NHL POGS-198
94Donruss-104
94Flair-150
94Fleer-182
94Hockey Wit-79
94Leaf-240
94Nordiques Burger King-20
94OPC Premier-548
Special Effects-548
94Parkhurst-186
Gold-186
Vintage-V52
94Pinnacle-280
Artist's Proofs-280
Rink Collection-280
94Select-114
Gold-114
94SP-98
Die Cuts-98
94Stadium Club-3
Members Only Master Set-3
First Day Issue-3
Super Team Winner Cards-3
94Topps/OPC Premier-548
Special Effects-548
94Ultra-178
94Upper Deck-284
Electric Ice-284
SP Inserts-SP64
SP Inserts Die Cuts-SP64
95Bashan Super Stickers-30
95Canada Games NHL POGS-73
95Collector's Choice-282
Player's Club-282
Player's Club Platinum-282
95Donruss-120
95Emotion-41
95Imperial Stickers-30
95Leaf-156
95Panini Stickers-245
95Parkhurst International-318
Emerald Ice-318
95Pro Magnets-4
95Score-234
Black Ice Artist's Proofs-234
Black Ice-234
Check It-12
95Select Certified Double Strike-6
95Select Certified Double Strike Gold-6
95SkyBox Impact-40
95Stadium Club-71
Members Only Master Set-71
95Summit-109
Artist's Proofs-109
Ice-109
95Ultra-135
Gold Medallion-135
95Upper Deck-457
Electric Ice-457
Electric Ice Gold-457
95Zenith-91
95Finnish Semic World Championships-92
95Swedish World Championships Stickers-14
96Be A Player-116
Autographs-116
Autographs Silver-116
96Black Diamond-109
Gold-109
96Donruss-177
Press Proofs-177
96Donruss Canadian Ice-99
Gold Press Proofs-99
Red Press Proofs-99
96Leaf-141
Press Proofs-141
96Leaf Preferred-78
Press Proofs-78
96Maggers-83
96NHL Pro Stamps-4
96Score-106
Artist's Proofs-106
Dealer's Choice Artist's Proofs-106
Special Artist's Proofs-106
Golden Blades-106
96SP-37
96Summit-70
Artist's Proofs-70
Ice-70
Metal-70
Premium Stock-70
96Upper Deck-36
Power Performers-P25
97Black Diamond-64
Double Diamond-64
Triple Diamond-64
Quadruple Diamond-64
97Collector's Choice-61
97Donruss-180
Press Proofs Silver-180
Press Proofs Gold-180
97Donruss Limited-58
Exposure-58
97Donruss Priority-107
Stamp of Approval-107
97Leaf-65
Fractal Matrix-65
Fractal Matrix Die Cuts-65
97Leaf International-65
Universal Ice-65
97Pacific-109
Copper-109
Emerald Green-109
Ice Blue-109
Red-109
Silver-109
97Score Avalanche-17
Platinum-17
Premier-17
97SP Authentic-136
97Upper Deck-48
98Be A Player-270
Press Release-270
98BAP Gold-270
98BAP Autographs-270
98BAP Autographs Gold-270
98Finest-145
No Protectors-145
No Protectors Refractors-145
Refractors-145
98Pacific-391
Ice Blue-391
Red-391
98Pacific Omega-213
Red-213
Opening Day Issue-213
98UD Choice-180
Prime Choice Reserve-180
Reserve-180
98Upper Deck-170
Exclusives-170
Exclusives 1 of 1-170
Gold Reserve-170
98Upper Deck MVP-177
Gold Script-177
Silver Script-177
Super Script-177
99BAP Memorabilia-296
Gold-296
Silver-296
99BAP Millennium-216
Emerald-216
Ruby-216
Sapphire-216
Signatures-216
Signatures Gold-216
99O-Pee-Chee-37
99O-Pee-Chee Chrome-37
99O-Pee-Chee Chrome Refractors-37
99Pacific-380
Copper-380
Emerald Green-380
Gold-380
Ice Blue-380
Premiere Date-380
Red-380
99Panini Stickers-298
99Paramount-208
Copper-208
Emerald-208
Gold-208
Holographic Emerald-208
Holographic Gold-208
Holographic Silver-208
Ice Blue-208
Premiere Date-208
Red-208
Silver-208
99Stadium Club-111
First Day Issue-111
One of a Kind-111
Printing Plates Black-111
Printing Plates Cyan-111
Printing Plates Magenta-111
Printing Plates Yellow-111
99Topps/OPC-37
99Topps/OPC Chrome-37
Refractors-37
99Upper Deck-111
Exclusives-111
Exclusives 1 of 1-111
99Upper Deck Gold Reserve-111
99Upper Deck MVP-178
Gold Script-178
Silver Script-178
Super Script-178
99Upper Deck Victory-251
00BAP Memorabilia-318
Emerald-318
Ruby-318
Sapphire-318
Promos-318
00BAP Mem Chicago Sportsfest Copper-318
00BAP Memorabilia Chicago Sportsfest Blue-318
00BAP Memorabilia Chicago Sportsfest Gold-318
00BAP Memorabilia Chicago Sportsfest Ruby-318
00BAP Memorabilia Chicago Sun-Times Ruby-318
00BAP Memorabilia Chicago Sun-Times Gold-318
00BAP Mem Chicago Sun-Times Sapphire-318
00BAP Mem Toronto Fall Expo Copper-318
00BAP Memorabilia Toronto Fall Expo Gold-318
00BAP Memorabilia Toronto Fall Expo Ruby-318
00O-Pee-Chee-27
00O-Pee-Chee Parallel-27
00Pacific-364
Copper-364
Gold-364
Ice Blue-364
Premiere Date-364
00Paramount-216
Copper-216
Gold-216
Holo-Gold-216
Holo-Silver-216
Ice Blue-216
Premiere Date-216
00Stadium Club-10
00Topps/OPC-27
Parallel-27
00Topps Heritage-204
00Topps Stars-44
Blue-44
00Upper Deck-374
Exclusives Tier 1-374
Exclusives Tier 2-374
00Upper Deck MVP-149
First Stars-149
Second Stars-149
Third Stars-149
00Upper Deck Victory-196
00Upper Deck Vintage-304
00Czech Stadion-61
01BAP Signature Series-122
Autographs-122
Autographs Gold-122
01O-Pee-Chee-160
01O-Pee-Chee Premier Parallel-160
01Pacific-343
Extreme LTD-343
Hobby LTD-343
Premiere Date-343
Retail LTD-343
01Pacific Adrenaline-169
Blue-169
Premiere Date-169
Red-169
Retail-169
01Pacific Arena Exclusives-343
01Parkhurst-190
01Sharks Postcards-10
01Topps-160
OPC Parallel-160
01Upper Deck-375
Exclusives-375
01Upper Deck MVP-161
01Upper Deck Victory-295
Gold-295
01Upper Deck Vintage-212
02BAP Memorabilia-44
Emerald-44
Ruby-44
Sapphire-44
NHL All-Star Game-44
NHL All-Star Game Blue-44
NHL All-Star Game Green-44
NHL All-Star Game Red-44
02BAP Memorabilia Toronto Fall Expo-44
02BAP Sig Series Auto Buybacks 1998-270
02BAP Sig Series Auto Buybacks 1999-216
02BAP Sig Series Auto Buybacks 2001-122
02BAP Signature Series Golf-GS61
02O-Pee-Chee-107
02O-Pee-Chee Premier Blue Parallel-107
02O-Pee-Chee Premier Red Parallel-107
02O-Pee-Chee Factory Set-107
02Pacific-339
Blue-339
Red-339
02Pacific Complete-70
Red-70
02Parkhurst Retro-92
Minis-92
02Sharks Team Issue-6
02Topps-107
OPC Blue Parallel-107
OPC Red Parallel-107
Factory Set-107
02Topps Chrome-68
Black Border Refractors-68
Refractors-68
02Topps Total-34
02Upper Deck-390
Exclusives-390
02Upper Deck Beckett UD Promos-390
02Upper Deck MVP-155
Gold-155
Classics-155
Golden Classics-155
02Upper Deck Victory-181
Bronze-181
Gold-181
Silver-181
02Upper Deck Vintage-212
02Upper Deck Vintage-285
03Black Diamond-178
Black-178
Green-178
Red-178
03ITG Action-411
03NHL Sticker Collection-289
03Pacific-299
Blue-299
Red-299
03Pacific Complete-56
Red-56
03Sharks Postcards-16
03SPx-82
Radiance-82
Spectrum-82
03Upper Deck-159
Canadian Exclusives-159
HG-159
03Upper Deck Classic Portraits-80
03Upper Deck MVP-347
Gold Script-347
Silver Script-347
Canadian Exclusives-347
03Upper Deck Trilogy-80
Limited-80
05Panini Stickers-323
05Parkhurst-380
Facsimile Auto Parallel-380
05Ultra-151
Gold-151
Ice-151
05Upper Deck Notable Numbers-N-MRI
05Upper Deck MVP-295
Gold-295
Platinum-295
05Upper Deck Victory-153
Black-153
Gold-153
Silver-153
06Upper Deck-152
Exclusives Parallel-152
High Gloss Parallel-152
Masterpieces-152

Ricci, Scott

98BC Icemen-6
98BC Icemen II-3
01Trenton Titans-1-9
03Rochester Americans-24
04UK Nottingham Panthers-16

Ricciardi, Gary

94Thunder Bay Flyers-17
00Fort Wayne Komets-17
00Fort Wayne Komets Shoe Carnival-2
01Roanoke Express-17
02Muskegon Fury-21
03Rockford Ice Hogs-14

Ricciardi, Jeff

897th Inn. Sketch OHL-61
907th Inn. Sketch OHL-91
917th Inn. Sketch OHL-304
93Indianapolis Ice-16
94Indianapolis Ice-19
95Las Vegas Thunder-11
98German DEL-106

Rice, Brad

02Macon Trax-9

Rice, Brian

93Quebec Pee-Wee Tournament-1273

Rice, Jeff

95Arizona Icecats-15

Rice, Mike

99Brampton Battalion-15

Rice, Murray

84Brandon Wheat Kings-10
85Brandon Wheat Kings-10

Rice, Steve

87Kitchener Rangers-16
88Kitchener Rangers-16
89Kitchener Rangers-17
897th Inn. Sketch OHL-181
897th Inn. Sketch OHL-187
90OPC Premier-97
90Pro Set-626
90Score-390
Canadian-390
90Upper Deck-462
90Upper Deck-473
French-462
French-473
90Kitchener Rangers-29
907th Inn. Sketch OHL-249
907th Inn. Sketch Memorial Cup-38
91Oilers IGA-18
91Oilers Team Issue-21
91Pinnacle-334
French-334
91Score Canadian Bilingual-420
91Score Canadian English-420
91Upper Deck-440
91Upper Deck-441
French-440
French-441
91ProCards-227
92Oilers Team Issue-15
92Score-545
Canadian-545
92Upper Deck-98
93Donruss-107
93Parkhurst-72
Emerald Ice-72
93PowerPlay-86
93Stadium Club-446
Members Only Master Set-446
First Day Issue-446
93Ultra-181
93Upper Deck-367
93Classic Pro Prospects-150
94Slapshot Promos-5
94Be A Player Signature Cards-49
94Leaf-324
94Leaf-477
94Pinnacle-154
Artist's Proofs-154
Rink Collection-154
94Stadium Club-54
Members Only Master Set-54
First Day Issue-54
Super Team Winner Cards-54
94Ultra-302
94Upper Deck-294
Electric Ice-294
95Canada Games NHL POGS-128
95Collector's Choice-218
Player's Club-218
Player's Club Platinum-218
95Donruss-81
95Leaf-198
95Panini Stickers-33
95Parkhurst International-95
Emerald Ice-95
95Pinnacle-166
Artist's Proofs-166
Rink Collection-166
95Playoff One on One-156
95Score-167
Black Ice Artist's Proofs-167
Black Ice-167
95Topps-109
OPC Inserts-109
95Upper Deck-210
Electric Ice-210
Electric Ice Gold-210
95Whalers Bob's Stores-22
96Be A Player-8
Autographs-8
Autographs Silver-8
96Whalers Kid's Club-25
96Collector's Edge Ice Crucibles-C13
97Hurricanes Team Issue-23
97Katch-28
Gold-28
Silver-28
97Pacific Dynagon Best Kept Secrets-18
97Paramount-38
Copper-38
Dark Grey-38
Emerald Green-38
Ice Blue-38
Red-38
Silver-38
97Score-76
Artist's Proofs-76
Golden Blades-76
97Upper Deck-32
98Katch-26

Rice, Tyler

91Air Canada SJHL All-Stars-34
91Air Canada SJHL All-Stars-49

Rich, Curtis

98Calgary Hitmen-16
98Calgary Hitmen Autographs-16
99Kelowna Rockets-4

Rich, Dave

95German DEL-325

Rich, Jason

93Quebec Pee-Wee Tournament-1612

Richard, Chad

96Anchorage Aces-12
98Tacoma Sabercats-18
99Anchorage Aces-23
99Tacoma Sabercats-5
01Anchorage Aces-13

Richard, Guillaume

03St. Jean Mission-22

Richard, Henri

44Beehive Group II Photos-283
52Juniors Blue Tint-139
57Parkhurst-M4
58Parkhurst-2
59Parkhurst-39
60NHL Ceramic Tiles-14
60Parkhurst-47
60Parkhurst-57
60Shirriff Coins-34
60York Photos-31
61Parkhurst-43
61Shirriff/Salada Coins-110
61York Yellow Backs-18
62El Producto Discs-6
62Parkhurst-38
62Shirriff Coins-41
62York Iron-On Transfers-10
63Chex Photos-46
63Parkhurst-23
63Parkhurst-82
63Toronto Star-32
63York White Backs-19
64Beehive Group III Photos-112
64Canadiens Postcards-16
64Coca-Cola Caps-66
64Topps-48
64Toronto Star-41
65Canadiens Steinberg Glasses-7
65Coca-Cola-66
65Coca-Cola Booklets-D
65Topps-71
66Topps-8
66Topps USA Test-8
67Canadiens IGA-16
67Post Cereal Box Backs-11
67Post Cereal Box Backs-12
67Post Flip Books-5
67Topps-72
68Canadiens IGA-16
68Canadiens Postcards BW-13
68O-Pee-Chee-165
Puck Stickers-21
68Post Marbles-21
68Shirriff Coins-89
68Topps-64
69Canadiens Postcards Color-23
69O-Pee-Chee-163
Four-in-One-16
69Topps-11
70Canadiens Pins-12
70Colgate Stamps-14
70Dad's Cookies-111
70Esso Power Players-11
70O-Pee-Chee-176
Deckle-24
70Sargent Promotions Stamps-98
71Bazooka-5
71Canadiens Postcards-18
71Frito-Lay-4
71Letraset Action Replays-15
71O-Pee-Chee-120
O-Pee-Chee/Topps Booklets-6
71Sargent Promotions Stamps-103
71Topps-120
71Toronto Sun-161
72Canadiens Postcards-17
72Dimanche/Derniere Heure *-163
72Dimanche/Derniere Heure *-164
72O-Pee-Chee-251
72Sargent Promotions Stamps-119
72Finnish Semic World Championship-198
72Swedish Semic World Championship-198
73Canadiens Postcards-18
73O-Pee-Chee-87
73Topps-87
74Canadiens Postcards-17
74NHL Action Stamps-156
74O-Pee-Chee NHL-243
74O-Pee-Chee NHL-321
74Topps-243
81TCMA-7
82Canadiens Postcards-20
83Hall of Fame-91
83Hall of Fame Postcards-G11
85Hall of Fame-91
91Kraft-88
91Ultimate Original Six-14
91Ultimate Original Six-81
91Ultimate Original Six-95
French-14
French-81
French-95
92Parkhurst Parkie Reprints-PR28
92Sport-Flash-13
92Sport-Flash Autographs-13
93O-Pee-Chee Canadiens Hockey Fest-3
93O-Pee-Chee Canadiens Hockey Fest-61
93O-Pee-Chee Canadiens Panel-1
93Parkhurst Cherry's Playoff Heroes-D18
93Upper Deck Locker All-Stars-47
94Hockey Wit-52
94Parkhurst Missing Link-66
94Parkhurst Tall Boys-67
94Zeller's Masters of Hockey-7
94Zeller's Masters of Hockey Signed-7
95Parkhurst '66-67-58
Coins-58
95Signature Rookies Cool Five-CF5
95Signature Rookies Cool Five Signatures-CF5
99Upper Deck Century Legends-28
Century Collection-28
99Upper Deck Retro-109
Gold-109
Platinum-109
01BAP Memorabilia Rocket's Mates-RM4
01BAP Signature Series Vintage Autographs-VA-20
01BAP Signature Series Vintage Autographs-VA-21
01BAP Ultimate Mem All-Star History-10
01BAP Ultimate Memorabilia Bloodlines-3
01BAP Ultimate Memorabilia Captain's C-13
01BAP Ultimate Memorabilia Emblem Attic-16
01BAP Ultimate Memorabilia Les Canadiens-7
01BAP Ultimate Mem Retired Numbers-21
01BAP Ultimate Mem Retro Teammates-1
01BAP Ultimate Mem Retro Teammates-14
01BAP Ultimate Mem Stanley Cup Winners-1
01Fleer Legacy-15
Ultimate-15
Memorabilia-21
01Greats of the Game-13
Retro Collection-7
Autographs-13
Sticks-9
01Parkhurst Autographs-PA5
01Parkhurst Autographs-PA11
01Parkhurst Heroes-H15
01Parkhurst Reprints-PR35
01Parkhurst Reprints-PR37
01Parkhurst Reprints-PR56
01Parkhurst Reprints-PR74
01Parkhurst Reprints-PR84
01Parkhurst Reprints-PR122
01Parkhurst Reprints-PR142
01Parkhurst Reprints-PR147
01Parkhurst Vintage Memorabilia-PV22
01Parkhurst Vintage Memorabilia-PV23
01Topps Heritage Arena Relics-RHR
01Topps Heritage Arena Relics-RJB/HR
01Topps Heritage Arena Relics-ARHR
01Topps Heritage Arena Relics-ARJB/HR
01Topps Heritage Autographs-AHR
01Topps Heritage Salute-S8
01UD Stanley Cup Champs-18
01Upper Deck Legends-38
02BAP Memorabilia Mini Stanley Cups-7
02BAP NHL All-Star History-10
02BAP Ultimate Memorabilia All-Star MVP-9
02BAP Ultimate Memorabilia Emblem Attic-27
02BAP Ultimate Memorabilia Legend-9
02BAP Ultimate Memorabilia Retro Trophies-4
02BAP Ultimate Mem Storied Franchise-17
02BAP Ultimate Mem Storied Franchise-23
02BAP Ultimate Mem Vintage Jerseys-20
02BAP Ultimate Mem Vintage Jersey Autos-11
02Canadiens AGF-NNO
02Canadiens Molson Export-16
02Parkhurst Vintage Memorabilia-VM11
02Parkhurst Vintage Teammates-VT9
02Parkhurst Retro Nicknames-RN2
03BAP Memorabilia Vintage Memorabilia-VM-11
03BAP Ultimate Memorabilia Autographs-162
Gold-162
03BAP Ultimate Memorabilia Cornerstones-3
03BAP Ultimate Memorabilia Emblem Attic-11
03BAP Ultimate Mem Emblem Attic Gold-11
03BAP Ultimate Memorabilia Great Moments-8
03BAP Ultimate Mem Hometown Heroes-1
03BAP Ultimate Mem Hometown Heroes Gold-1
03BAP Ultimate Mem Retro Teammates-7
03BAP Ultimate Memorabilia Triple Threads-27
03BAP Ultimate Mem Vintage Jerseys-24
03BAP Ultimate Mem Vintage Jerseys Gold-24
03BAP Ultimate Memorabilia Vintage Lumber-2
03ITG Used Sig Series Vintage Mem -15
03ITG Used Sig Series Vintage Mem Autos-15
03ITG Used Sig Series Vintage Mem Gold-15
03Parkhurst Original Six Montreal-43
03Parkhurst Original Six Montreal-65
03Parkhurst Original Six Montreal-74
03Parkhurst Original Six Montreal-90
03Parkhurst Original Six Montreal-91
Autographs-12
Inserts-M5
Memorabilia-MM23
Memorabilia-MM52
04ITG NHL AS FANtasy AS History Jerseys-SB10
04ITG Franchises Canadian-38
Autographs-HR
Barn Burners-BB6
Barn Burners Gold-BB6
Double Memorabilia-DM17
Double Memorabilia Autographs-DM17
Double Memorabilia Gold-DM17
Forever Rivals-FR9
Forever Rivals Gold-FR9
Memorabilia-SM2
Memorabilia Autographs-SM2
Memorabilia Gold-SM2
Teammates-TM9
Teammates Gold-TM9
Trophy Winners-TW10
Trophy Winners Gold-TW10
04ITG Franchises He Shoots/Scores Prizes-5
04ITG Ultimate Memorabilia-53
Gold-53
Auto Threads-15
Autographs-1
Autographs Gold-1
Day In History-1
Day In History Gold-1
Jersey Autographs-47
Jersey Autographs Gold-47
Nicknames-11
Nickname Autographs-15
Original Six-14
Retro Teammates-2
Stick Autographs-11
Stick Autographs Gold-11
Triple Threads-13
04UD Legendary Signatures-44
Autographs-HR
HOF Inks-HOF-HR
04UD Legends Classics Jersey Redemptions-JY1
04ITG Heroes and Prospects-157
Autographs-HR
Hero Memorabilia-13
04ITG Heroes/Prospects Toronto Expo '05-157
04ITG Heroes/Prospects Expo Heroes/Pros-157
05ITG Heroes/Prosp Toronto Expo Parallel -15
05Canada Post-31
05Canada Post Autographs-31
05ITG Ultimate Memorabilia Level 1-47
05ITG Ultimate Memorabilia Level 2-47
05ITG Ultimate Memorabilia Level 3-47
05ITG Ultimate Memorabilia Level 4-47
05ITG Ultimate Memorabilia Level 5-47
05ITG Ultimate Mem Double Mem Autos-15
05ITG Ultimate Mem Double Mem Autos Gold-15
05ITG Ultimate Memorabilia Emblem Attic-2
05ITG Ultimate Mem Emblem Attic Gold-2
05ITG Ultimate Memorabilia Jersey Autos-23
05ITG Ultimate Mem Jersey Autos Gold-23
05ITG Ultimate Memorabilia Jerseys-17
05ITG Ultimate Memorabilia Jerseys Gold-17
05ITG Ultimate Mem Raised to the Rafters-2
05ITG Ultimate Mem Raised Rafters Gold-2
05ITG Ultimate Mem Retro Teammate Jerseys-12
05ITG Ult Mem Retro Teammates Jersey Gold-12
05ITG Ultimate Mem Seams Unbelievable-6
05ITG Ultimate Mem Seam Unbelievable Gold-6
05ITG Ultimate Memorabilia Sextuple Autos-4
05ITG Ultimate Mem 3 Star of the Game Jsy-4
05ITG Ult Mem 3 Star of the Game Jsy Gold-4
05ITG Ultimate Memorabilia Triple Autos-8
05ITG Ultimate Mem Triple Autos Gold-8
05ITG Ultimate Mem Triple Threads Jerseys-7
05ITG Ultimate Mem Triple Thread Jsy Gold-7
05ITG Ultimate Memorabilia Ultimate Autos-11
05ITG Ultimate Mem Ultimate Autos Gold-11
05ITG Ultimate Memorabilia Vintage Lumber-4
05ITG Ultimate Mem Vintage Lumber Gold-4
05ITG Heroes and Prospects-15
Autographs-A-HR
06ITG Ultimate Memorabilia-63
Artist Proof-63
Autos-53
Autos Gold-53
Bloodlines-5
Bloodlines Gold-5
Bowman Factor-7
Bowman Factor Gold-7
Bowman Factor Autos-6
Bowman Factor Autos Gold-6
Legendary Captains-11
Legendary Captains Gold-11
Retro Teammates-6
Retro Teammates Gold-6
Ring Leaders-1
Ring Leaders Gold-1
Road to the Cup-2
Road to the Cup Gold-2

Richard, Jacques

72Flames Postcards-17
72O-Pee-Chee-279
73O-Pee-Chee-169
73Topps-169
74NHL Action Stamps-16
74O-Pee-Chee NHL-14
74O-Pee-Chee NHL-139
74Topps-14
74Topps-139
75O-Pee-Chee NHL-117
75Topps-117
76O-Pee-Chee NHL-8
76Topps-8
77O-Pee-Chee NHL-366
79Rochester Americans-13
80Nordiques Postcards-23
80Pepsi-Cola Caps-75
81Nordiques Postcards-14
81O-Pee-Chee-268
81O-Pee-Chee-285
81O-Pee-Chee Stickers-71
81Topps-29
82Nordiques Postcards-17
82O-Pee-Chee-290
82Post Cereal-16
83Nordiques Postcards-22

Richard, Jason

94Johnstown Chiefs-17

Richard, Jean-Marc

84Chicoutimi Sagueneens-22
88ProCards AHL-115
89Halifax Citadels-19
89ProCards AHL-173
90Halifax Citadels-20
90ProCards AHL/IHL-457
91ProCards-243
93Las Vegas Thunder-21
94Las Vegas Thunder-23
95Las Vegas Thunder-12
98German DEL-148
99German DEL-85
00German DEL-79

Richard, Marcel

95Madison Monsters-23
97Columbus Cottonmouths-16
98Columbus Cottonmouths-14
99Columbus Cottonmouths-8

Richard, Maurice

34Beehive Group I Photos-179
43Parade Sportive *-73
43Parade Sportive *-75
43Parade Sportive *-77
44Beehive Group II Photos-284
45Quaker Oats Photos-109A
45Quaker Oats Photos-109B
45Quaker Oats Photos-109C
45Quaker Oats Photos-109D
48Exhibits Canadian-23
48Exhibits Canadian-24
48Exhibits Canadian-54
48Exhibits Canadian-55
48Exhibits Canadian-60
51Parkhurst-4
52Parkhurst-1
53Parkhurst-24
53Parkhurst-30
54Parkhurst-7
55Parkhurst-37
55Parkhurst-72
55Parkhurst-73
Quaker Oats-37
Quaker Oats-72
Quaker Oats-73
57Parkhurst-M5
58Parkhurst-38
59Parkhurst-2
60Parkhurst-45
60Wonder Bread Labels-4
60Wonder Bread Premium Photos-4
62Wheaties Great Moments in Cdn Sport-12
64Beehive Group III Photos-113
69Equitable Sports Hall of Fame-6
83Hall of Fame-1
83Hall of Fame Postcards-A12
85Hall of Fame-1
91Kraft-6
91Kraft-65
91Pro Set-337
French-337
92Hall of Fame Legends-3
92Score-548C
92Score-549C
Canadian-548C
Canadian-549C
Canadian Olympians-NNO1
Canadian Olympians-NNO2
Canadian Olympians-AU1
92Sport-Flash-9
92Sport-Flash Autographs-9
92Zeller's Masters of Hockey-6
92Zeller's Masters of Hockey Signed-6
93American Licorice Sour Punch Caps-5
93O-Pee-Chee Canadiens Hockey Fest-6
93O-Pee-Chee Canadiens Hockey Fest-29
93O-Pee-Chee Canadiens Hockey Fest-59
93O-Pee-Chee Canadiens Panel-1
93Parkhurst Cherry's Playoff Heroes-D16
93Parkhurst Parkie Reprints-PR36
93Parkhurst Parkie Reprints-PR48
93Parkhurst Parkie Reprints-PR63
93Parkhurst Parkie Reprints Case Inserts-5
94Hockey Wit-16
94Parkhurst Missing Link-65
94Parkhurst Missing Link-139
Autographs-2
94Parkhurst Tall Boys Greats-5
95Signature Rookies Cool Five-CF4
95Signature Rookies Cool Five Signatures-CF4
96SLU Canadian Timeless Legends-6
97SLU Timeless Legends *-6
97Beehive-61
Golden Portraits-61
Golden Originals Autographs-61
99SP Authentic Legendary Heroes-LH4
99SP Authentic Sign of the Times-MRC
99SP Authentic Sign of the Times Gold-MRC
99Topps Stanley Cup Heroes-SC4
99Topps Stanley Cup Heroes Refractors-SC4
99Topps Stanley Cup Heroes Autographs-SCA4
99Upper Deck 500 Goal Club-500MR
99Upper Deck 500 Goal Club-500MR
99Upper Deck Century Legends-5
Century Collection-5
All Century Team-AC8
Epic Signatures-MR
Epic Signatures 100-MR
Essence of the Game-E6
99Upper Deck Retro-84
Gold-84
Platinum-84
Distant Replay-DR14
Distant Replay Level 2-DR14
Generation-G6A
Generation Level 2-G6A

Inkredible-MAR
Inkredible Level 2-MAR
Turn of the Century-TC14
00BAP Ultimate Mem Maurice Richard Autos-R1
00BAP Ultimate Mem Maurice Richard Autos-R2
00BAP Ultimate Mem Maurice Richard Autos-R3
00BAP Ultimate Mem Maurice Richard Autos-R4
00BAP Ultimate Mem Maurice Richard Autos-R5
00Topps Heritage Arena Relics-OSA-MR
00UD Heroes-128
01BAP Memorabilia 500 Goal Scorers-GS17
01BAP Memorabilia Rocket's Mates-RM1
01BAP Memorabilia Rocket's Mates-RM2
01BAP Memorabilia Rocket's Mates-RM3
01BAP Memorabilia Rocket's Mates-RM4
01BAP Memorabilia Rocket's Mates-RM5
01BAP Memorabilia Rocket's Mates-RM6
01BAP Memorabilia Rocket's Mates-RM7
01BAP Memorabilia Rocket's Mates-RM8
01BAP Memorabilia Rocket's Mates-RM9
01BAP Memorabilia Rocket's Mates-RM10
01BAP Signature Series 500 Goal Scorers-27
01BAP Sig Series 500 Goal Scorers Autos-27
01BAP Ultimate Mem All-Star History-4
01BAP Ultimate Memorabilia Bloodlines-3
01BAP Ultimate Memorabilia Cornerstones-2
01BAP Ultimate Memorabilia Emblem Attic-17
01BAP Ultimate Mem 500 Goal Scorers-28
01BAP Ultimate Mem 500 Goal Scorers Autos-22
01BAP Ultimate Mem 500 Goal Jerseys/Stick-28
01BAP Ultimate Mem 500 Goal Emblems-28
01BAP Ultimate Memorabilia Gloves Are Off-1
01BAP Ultimate Memorabilia Les Canadiens-4
01BAP Ultimate Mem Playoff Records-20
01BAP Ultimate Mem Retired Numbers-22
01BAP Ultimate Mem Retro Teammates-1
01BAP Ultimate Mem Retro Teammates-2
01BAP Ultimate Mem Retro Teammates-14
01BAP Ultimate Mem Stanley Cup Winners-5
01BAP Update Passing the Torch-PTT4
01BAP Update Rocket's Rivals-RR-1
01BAP Update Rocket's Rivals-RR-2
01BAP Update Rocket's Rivals-RR-3
01BAP Update Rocket's Rivals-RR-4
01BAP Update Rocket's Rivals-RR-5
01BAP Update Rocket's Rivals-RR-6
01BAP Update Rocket's Rivals-RR-7
01BAP Update Rocket's Rivals-RR-8
01BAP Update Rocket's Rivals-RR-9
01BAP Update Rocket's Rivals-RR-10
01BAP Update Tough Customers-TC31
01Parkhurst 500 Goal Scorers-PGS17
01Parkhurst He Shoots-He Scores Points-20
01Parkhurst Heroes-H4
01Parkhurst Reprints-PR2
01Parkhurst Reprints-PR14
01Parkhurst Reprints-PR42
01Parkhurst Reprints-PR88
01Parkhurst Reprints-PR92
01Parkhurst Reprints-PR108
01Parkhurst Vintage Memorabilia-PV1
01Parkhurst Vintage Memorabilia-PV2
01Parkhurst Vintage Memorabilia-PV3
01UD Stanley Cup Champs-17
01Upper Deck Legends-30
01Upper Deck Legends-94
Fiorentino Collection-FCMR
Sticks-PHMR
02BAP NHL All-Star History-4
02BAP Ultimate Mem Blades of Steel-5
02BAP Ultimate Mem Complete Package-7
02BAP Ultimate Memorabilia Emblem Attic-21
02BAP Ultimate Memorabilia Gloves Are Off-18
02BAP Ultimate Memorabilia Great Moments-3
02BAP Ultimate Memorabilia Great Moments-14
02BAP Ultimate Memorabilia Great Moments-16
02BAP Ultimate Memorabilia Great Moments-18
02BAP Ultimate Memorabilia Legend-1
02BAP Ultimate Memorabilia Legend-2
02BAP Ultimate Memorabilia Legend-3
02BAP Ultimate Memorabilia Legend-4
02BAP Ultimate Memorabilia Legend-5
02BAP Ultimate Memorabilia Legend-6
02BAP Ultimate Memorabilia Legend-7
02BAP Ultimate Memorabilia Legend-8
02BAP Ultimate Memorabilia Legend-9
02BAP Ultimate Memorabilia Legend-10
02BAP Ultimate Memorabilia Numerology-11
02BAP Ultimate Mem Playoff Scorers-13
02BAP Ultimate Mem Retro Teammates-7
02BAP Ultimate Memorabilia Retro Trophies-20
02BAP Ultimate Mem Storied Franchise-8
02BAP Ultimate Mem Vintage Hat Tricks-3
02BAP Ultimate Mem Vintage Jerseys-27
02ITG Used Vintage Memorabilia-VM7
02ITG Used Vintage Memorabilia Gold-VM7
02Parkhurst Reprints-235
02Parkhurst Reprints-264
02Parkhurst Reprints-273
02Parkhurst Reprints-285
02Parkhurst Reprints-295
02Parkhurst Vintage Memorabilia-VM12
02Parkhurst Retro Nicknames-RN17
03Backcheck: A Hockey Retrospective-9
03BAP Memorabilia Brush with Greatness-7
03BAP Mem Brush with Greatness Contest C-7
03BAP Ultimate Memorabilia Vintage Memorabilia-VM-6
03BAP Ultimate Memorabilia Autographs-163
Gold-163
03BAP Ultimate Memorabilia Cornerstones-2
03BAP Ultimate Memorabilia Great Moments-10
03BAP Ultimate Mem Hometown Heroes-1
03BAP Ultimate Mem Hometown Heroes Gold-1
03BAP Ultimate Memorabilia Linemates-10
03BAP Ultimate Mem Linemates Autos-2
03BAP Ultimate Memorabilia Memorialized-3
03BAP Ultimate Memorabilia Paper Cuts-36
03BAP Ultimate Mem Raised to the Rafters-10
03BAP Ultimate Mem Redemption Cards-4
03BAP Ultimate Mem Retro Teammates-2
03BAP Ultimate Mem Retro-Active Trophies-9
03BAP Ultimate Mem Vintage Blade of Steel-3
03BAP Ultimate Mem Vint Comp Package Gold-3
03BAP Ultimate Mem Vint Complete Package-3
03BAP Ultimate Mem Vintage Jerseys-19
03BAP Ultimate Mem Vintage Jerseys Gold-19
03BAP Ultimate Mem Vintage Lumber-6
03Canada Post-3
03ITG Toronto Fall Expo Forever Rivals-FR9
03ITG Used Sig Series Vintage Mem -29
03ITG Used Sig Series Vintage Mem Gold-29
03ITG VIP Collages-33
03ITG VIP MVP-5
03ITG VIP Vintage Memorabilia-15
03Parkhurst Orig Six He Shoots/Scores-11
03Parkhurst Orig Six He Shoots/Scores-11A
03Parkhurst Original Six Montreal-45
03Parkhurst Original Six Montreal-62
03Parkhurst Original Six Montreal-76
03Parkhurst Original Six Montreal-84
03Parkhurst Original Six Montreal-92
03Parkhurst Original Six Montreal-100
Inserts-M4
Memorabilia-MM29
Memorabilia-MM31
Memorabilia-MM37
03Parkhurst Rookie-59
03Czech Stadion-652
04ITG NHL AS FANtasy AS History Jerseys-SB4
04ITG Franchises Canadian-37
Barn Burners-BB8
Barn Burners Gold-BB8
Triple Memorabilia-TM2
Triple Memorabilia Gold-TM2
04ITG Franchises He Shoots/Scores Prizes-4
04ITG Franchises Update Linemates-ULI2
04ITG Franchises Update Linemates Gold-ULI2
04ITG Ultimate Memorabilia-155
Gold-155
Autographs-62
Autographs Gold-62
Blades of Steel-2
Bleu Blanc et Rouge-1
Changing the Game-7
Complete Package-7
Cornerstones-4
Cornerstones Gold-4
Day In History-10
Day In History-14
Day In History-23
Day In History Gold-10
Day In History Gold-14
Day In History Gold-23
Gloves are Off-10
Hart Trophy-2
Jerseys-10
Jerseys Gold-10
Nicknames-2
Original Six-16
Original Six-18
Paper Cuts Memorabilia-3
Retro Teammates-2
Seams Unbelievable-7
Vintage Lumber-8
04UD Legends Classics Jersey Redemptions-JY3
04ITG Heroes and Prospects-166
04ITG Heroes/Prospects Toronto Expo '05-166
04ITG Heroes/Prospects Expo Heroes/Pros-166
05ITG Ultimate Memorabilia Level 1-69
05ITG Ultimate Memorabilia Level 2-69
05ITG Ultimate Memorabilia Level 3-69
05ITG Ultimate Memorabilia Level 4-69
05ITG Ultimate Memorabilia Level 5-69
05ITG Ultimate Mem Blades of Steel-19
05ITG Ultimate Mem Blades of Steel Gold-19
05ITG Ultimate Mem Bleu Blanc Rouge Autos-5
05ITG Ultimate Mem Complete Package-12
05ITG Ultimate Mem Complete Package Gold-12
05ITG Ultimate Mem Cornerstones Jerseys-9
05ITG Ultimate Mem Cornerst Jerseys Gold-9
05ITG Ultimate Mem Decades Jerseys-3
05ITG Ultimate Mem Decades Jerseys Gold-3
05ITG Ultimate Memorabilia Gloves Are Off-5
05ITG Ultimate Mem Gloves Are Off Gold-5
05ITG Ultimate Memorabilia Lumbergraphs-7
05ITG Ultimate Mem Pass the Torch Jerseys-1
05ITG Ultimate Mem Passing Torch Jsy Gold-1
05ITG Ultimate Mem Record Breaker Jerseys-17
05ITG Ultimate Mem RecBreak Jerseys Gold-17
05ITG Ultimate Mem Ult Hero Double Jersey-2
05ITG Ult Mem Ult Hero Double Jersey Gold-2
05ITG Ultimate Mem Ult Hero Single Jersey-2
05ITG Ult Mem Ult Hero Single Jersey Gold-2
05ITG Ultimate Mem Ult Hero Triple Jersey-2
05ITG Ult Mem Ult Hero Triple Jersey Gold-2
05ITG Ultimate Memorabilia Vintage Lumber-5
05ITG Ultimate Mem Vintage Lumber Gold-5
05NHL Legends Medallions-16
05ITG Heroes and Prospects He Shoots-He Scores Prizes-50
06ITG Ultimate Memorabilia-101
Artist Proof-101
Autos-72
Autos Gold-72
Bloodlines-5
Bloodlines Gold-5
Complete Package-11
Complete Package Gold-11
Cornerstones-2
Cornerstones Gold-2
Decades-1
Decades-3
Decades Gold-1
Decades Gold-3
Fire In His Eyes Autos-1
Fire In His Eyes Autos-2
Fire In His Eyes Autos-3
Fire In His Eyes Autos-4
Fire In His Eyes Autos-5
Fire In His Eyes Autos Gold-1
Fire In His Eyes Autos Gold-2
Fire In His Eyes Autos Gold-3
Fire In His Eyes Autos Gold-4
Fire In His Eyes Autos Gold-5
Legendary Captains-1
Legendary Captains Gold-1
Retro Teammates-4
Retro Teammates-17
Retro Teammates Gold-4
Retro Teammates Gold-17
Road to the Cup-2
Road to the Cup Gold-2
Sensational Season-5
Sensational Season Gold-5
Stick Rack-2
Stick Rack-16
Stick Rack-21
Stick Rack Gold-2
Stick Rack Gold-16
Stick Rack Gold-21
Triple Thread Jerseys-8
Triple Thread Jerseys Gold-8
Ultimate Hero Single Jerseys-1
Ultimate Hero Single Jerseys Gold-1
Ultimate Hero Double Jerseys-1
Ultimate Hero Double Jerseys Gold-1
Ultimate Hero Triple Jerseys-1
Ultimate Hero Triple Jerseys Gold-1
Vintage Lumber-2
Vintage Lumber Gold-2

Richard, Mike

88ProCards AHL-44
89ProCards AHL-86
93Swiss HNL-256
95Swiss HNL-228
96Swiss HNL-142
96Swiss HNL-572
98Swiss Power Play Stickers-195
99Swiss Panini Stickers-196
00Swiss Panini Stickers-240
00Swiss Slapshot Mini-Cards-RJ15
01Swiss HNL-165
02Swiss HNL-384

Richard, Rodney

98Bowman CHL-13
Golden Anniversary-13
OPC International-13
98Bowman Chrome CHL-13
Golden Anniversary-13
Golden Anniversary Refractors-13
OPC International-13
OPC International Refractors-13
Refractors-13

Richard, Serge

84Richelieu Riverains-14

Richards, Aaron

01Swift Current Broncos-6
02Swift Current Broncos-14
03Swift Current Broncos-13
05Ultra Scoring Kings-SK30

Richards, Adam

93Quebec Pee-Wee Tournament-1178

Richards, Brad

97Upper Deck-418
97Rimouski Oceanic-39
98Bowman CHL-116
Golden Anniversary-116
OPC International-116
98Bowman Chrome CHL-116
Golden Anniversary-116
Golden Anniversary Refractors-116
OPC International-116
OPC International Refractors-116
Refractors-116
99Rimouski Oceanic-20
Signed-20
99Bowman CHL-57
Gold-57
OPC International-57
00BAP Memorabilia-464
Emerald-464
Ruby-464
Sapphire-464
00BAP Parkhurst 2000-P162
00BAP Signature Series-289
Emerald-289
Ruby-289
Sapphire-289
Autographs-219
Autographs Gold-219
00Black Diamond-109
00Crown Royale-142
21st Century Rookies-23
00Private Stock-146
Gold-146
Premiere Date-146
Retail-146
Silver-146
PS-2001 Rookies-23
00SP Authentic-79
00Titanium-146
Retail-146
Three-Star Selections-28
00Titanium Draft Day Edition-146
00Titanium Draft Day Promos-146
00Topps Gold Label Class 1-87
Gold-87
00Topps Gold Label Class 2-87
00Topps Gold Label Class 2 Gold-87
00Topps Gold Label Class 3-87
00Topps Gold Label Class 3 Gold-87
00Topps Gold Label Autographs-GLA-BR
00Topps Heritage-25
Chrome Parallel-25
00Topps Premier Plus-104
Blue Ice-104
Private Signings-PSBR
Rookies-PR4
Rookies Blue Ice-PR4
00UD Heroes-107
00UD Reserve-78
00Upper Deck Ice-77
00Upper Deck Vintage-324
00Vanguard-147
Pacific Proofs-147
00QMJHL All-Star Program Inserts-41
01Atomic-90
Blue-90
Gold-90
Premiere Date-90
Red-90
01BAP Memorabilia-17
Emerald-17
Ruby-17
Sapphire-17
01BAP Signature Series-26
Autographs-26
Autographs Gold-26
Jerseys-GJ-60
Jersey Autographs-GUBR
Jersey and Stick Cards-GSJ-60
01Bowman YoungStars-162
Gold-162
Ice Cubed-162
Autographs-BR
Relics-JBR
Relics-SBR
Relics-DSBR
Rivals-R2
01Crown Royale Calder Collection Gold Ed-7
01Crown Royale Calder Collection AS Ed-C6
01Crown Royale-129
Blue-129
Premiere Date-129
Red-129
Retail-129
01Crown Royale Toronto Expo Rookie Coll-G8
01McDonald's Pacific Hometown Pride-5
01O-Pee-Chee-64
01O-Pee-Chee Heritage Parallel-64
01O-Pee-Chee Heritage Parallel Limited-64
01O-Pee-Chee Premier Parallel-64
01Pacific-357
01Pacific-451
Extreme LTD-357
Hobby LTD-357
Premiere Date-357
Retail LTD-357
01Pacific Adrenaline-176
Blue-176
Premiere Date-176
Red-176
Retail-176
01Pacific Arena Exclusives-357
01Pacific Heads-Up-88
Blue-88
Premiere Date-88
Red-88
Silver-88
Breaking the Glass-18
Prime Picks-8
Stat Masters-18
01Parkhurst-27
Gold-27
Silver-27
Sticks-PS41
01Private Stock-89
Gold-89
Premiere Date-89
Retail-89
Silver-89
01Private Stock Pacific Nights-89
01Private Stock PS-2002-69
01SP Authentic-79
01SP Authentic-130
Limited-79
Limited-130
Limited Gold-79
Limited Gold-130
01SPx-62
01Stadium Club-75
Award Winners-75
Master Photos-75
01Titanium-127
Hobby Parallel-127
Premiere Date-127
Retail-127
Retail Parallel-127
01Topps-64
Heritage Parallel-64
Heritage Parallel Limited-64
OPC Parallel-64
Own The Game-OTG11
01Topps Chrome-64
Refractors-64
Black Border Refractors-64
01Topps Heritage-26
Refractors-26
01Topps Reserve-96
01UD Challenge for the Cup-80
01UD Mask Collection-88
Gold-88
01UD Playmakers-89
01UD Premier Collection-46
01UD Top Shelf-119
01Upper Deck-156
Exclusives-156
Tandems-T10
01Upper Deck MVP-170
01Upper Deck Victory-316
Gold-316
01Upper Deck Vintage-227
01Upper Deck Vintage-233
01Upper Deck Vintage-234
01Vanguard-90
Blue-90
Red-90
One of Ones-90
Premiere Date-90
Proofs-90
02BAP First Edition-37
Jerseys-37
Scoring Leaders-17
02BAP Memorabilia-10
Emerald-10
Ruby-10
Sapphire-10
Future of the Game-FG-18
NHL All-Star Game-10
NHL All-Star Game Blue-10
NHL All-Star Game Green-10
NHL All-Star Game Red-10
02BAP Memorabilia Toronto Fall Expo-10
02BAP Signature Series-16
Autographs-16
Autograph Buybacks 2000-219
Autograph Buybacks 2001-26
Autographs Gold-16
02Bowman YoungStars-62
Gold-62
Silver-62
02Crown Royale Dual Patches-20
02Lightning Team Issue-10
02O-Pee-Chee-144
02O-Pee-Chee Premier Blue Parallel-144
02O-Pee-Chee Premier Red Parallel-144
02O-Pee-Chee Factory Set-144
02Pacific-354
Blue-354
Red-354
02Pacific Calder-4
Silver-4
02Pacific Complete-308
Red-308
02Pacific Exclusive-157
Jerseys-23
Jerseys Gold-23
02Pacific Heads-Up-113
Blue-113
Purple-113
Red-113
Quad Jerseys-25
Quad Jerseys Gold-25
02Parkhurst-3
Bronze-3
Gold-3
Silver-3
02Parkhurst Retro-57
Minis-57
02Private Stock Reserve-144
Red-144
Retail-144
Patches-144
02SP Authentic-132
02Stadium Club-43
Silver Decoy Cards-43
Proofs-43
Lone Star Signatures Blue-LSBR
Lone Star Signatures Red-LSBR
YoungStars Relics-S10
YoungStars Relics-DS6
02Topps-144
OPC Blue Parallel-144
OPC Red Parallel-144
Factory Set-144
02Topps Chrome-88
Black Border Refractors-88
Refractors-88
Chromographs-CGBR
Chromograph Refractors-CGBR
02Topps Heritage-87
Chrome Parallel-87
02Topps Total-386
02UD Artistic Impressions-79
Gold-79
02UD Artistic Impressions Beckett Promos-79
02UD Artistic Impressions Retrospectives-R79
02UD Artistic Impress Retrospect Gold-R79
02UD Artistic Impress Retrospect Silver-R79
02UD Top Shelf-79
02Upper Deck-156
Exclusives-156
Blow-Ups-C36
02Upper Deck Classic Portraits-88
02Upper Deck MVP-169
Gold-169
Classics-169
Golden Classics-169
02Upper Deck Victory-192
Bronze-192
Gold-192
Silver-192
02Upper Deck Vintage-233
02Upper Deck Vintage-287
Green Backs-233
03BAP Memorabilia-13
Emerald-13
Gold-13
Ruby-13
Sapphire-13
03Beehive-176
Gold-176
Silver-176
03Bowman Future Rivals-RS
03Bowman Future Rivals Patches-RS
03Crown Royale-90
Blue-90
Retail-90
03eTopps-31
03ITG Action-511
Jerseys-M113
03Lightning Team Issue-21
03McDonalds Pacific Hockey Root Checklist-10
03NHL Sticker Collection-126
03O-Pee-Chee-221
03OPC Blue-221
03OPC Gold-221
03OPC Red-221
03Pacific-311
Blue-311
Red-311
03Pacific Complete-40
Red-40
03Pacific Exhibit-132
Blue Backs-132
Yellow Backs-132
03Pacific Prism-91
Blue-91
Gold-91
Red-91
03Private Stock Reserve-202
Blue-202
Patches-202
Red-202
Retail-202
03Topps-221
Blue-221
Gold-221
Red-221
Signs of Youth-BR
03Topps C55-103
Minis-103
Minis American Back-103
Minis American Back Red-103
Minis Bazooka Back-103
Minis Brooklyn Back-103
Minis Hat Trick Back-103
Minis O Canada Back-103
Minis O Canada Back Red-103
Minis Stanley Cup Back-103
Relics-TRBR
03Topps Pristine Jersey Portions-PPJ-BRI
03Topps Pristine Jersey Portion Refractor-PPJ-BRI
03Topps Traded Future Phenoms-FP-BR
03Upper Deck-173
Canadian Exclusives-173
HG-173
03Upper Deck MVP-378
Gold Script-378
Silver Script-378
Canadian Exclusives-378
03Toronto Star-82
04Pacific-241
Blue-241
Red-241
04SP Authentic-79
Limited-79
Octographs-OS-CUP
Sign of the Times-ST-BR
Sign of the Times-QS-LRLK
04UD All-World-25
Gold-25
Six Autographs-AS-RUS
04UD Toronto Fall Expo Pride of Canada-22
04Ultimate Collection Buybacks-3
04Ultimate Collection Patch Autographs-UPA-BR
04Ultimate Collection Patch Autographs-UPA-BRMS
04Ultimate Collection Signatures-US-BR
04Ultimate Collection Signature Logos-ULA-BR
04Ultimate Collection Signature Patches-SP-BR
04Upper Deck-158
Canadian Exclusives-158
Clutch Performers-CP2
Hardware Heroes-AW3
Hardware Heroes-AW8
HG Glossy Gold-158
HG Glossy Silver-158
World Cup Tribute-BR
04Rimouski Oceanic Season Ticket-5
05Be A Player-82
First Period-82
Second Period-82
Third Period-82
Overtime-82
Quad Signatures-SCCH
Signatures-RC
Signatures Gold-RC
Triple Signatures-TBL
05Beehive-82
Matte-82
Matted Materials-MMBR
Matted Materials Remarkable-RMBR
Signature Scrapbook-SSBR
05Black Diamond-116
Emerald-116
Gold-116
Onyx-116
Ruby-116
05Hot Prospects-89
En Fuego-89
Red Hot-89
White Hot-89
05McDonalds Upper Deck-30
05Panini Stickers-152
05Parkhurst-430
05Parkhurst-577
Facsimile Auto Parallel-430
Facsimile Auto Parallel-577
True Colors-TCTBL
True Colors-TCTBL
True Colors-TCFLTB
True Colors-TCFLTB
05SP Authentic-90
Limited-90
Marks of Distinction-MDBR
Prestigious Pairings-PPLR
Sign of the Times-RI
Sign of the Times Triples-TSLR
05SP Game Used-89
Autographs-89
Gold-89
Authentic Fabrics-AF-RI
Authentic Fabrics Autographs-AAF-RI
Authentic Fabrics Gold-AF-RI
Authentic Fabrics Quad-BLSR
Authentic Patches Quad -BLSR
Authentic Fabrics Triple-ARS
Authentic Patches-AP-RI
Authentic Patches Autographs-AAP-RI
Authentic Patches Triple-ARS
Auto Draft-AD-BR
Awesome Authentics-AA-BR
SIGnificance-BR
SIGnificance Gold-S-BR
05SPx-82
Spectrum-82
Winning Combos-WC-GR
Winning Combos-WC-TB
Winning Combos Autographs-AWC-GR
Winning Combos Autographs-AWC-RL
Winning Combos Gold-WC-GR
Winning Combos Gold-WC-TB
Winning Combos Spectrum-WC-GR
Winning Combos Spectrum-WC-TB
Winning Materials-WM-BR
Winning Materials Autographs-AWM-BR
Winning Materials Gold-WM-BR
Winning Materials Spectrum-WM-BR
Xcitement Superstars-XS-BR
Xcitement Superstars Gold-XS-BR
Xcitement Superstars Spectrum-XS-BR
05The Cup-91
Gold-91
Black Rainbow-91
Masterpiece Pressplates-91
Noble Numbers-NNSR
Noble Numbers Dual-DNNLR
Patch Variation-P91
Patch Variation Autographs-AP91
05UD Artifacts-89
Blue-89
Gold-89
Green-89
Pewter-89
Red-89
Auto Facts-AF-BR
Auto Facts Blue-AF-BR
Auto Facts Copper-AF-BR
Auto Facts Pewter-AF-BR
Auto Facts Silver-AF-BR
Frozen Artifacts-FA-BR
Frozen Artifacts Autographed-FA-BR
Frozen Artifacts Copper-FA-BR
Frozen Artifacts Dual-FAD-BR
Frozen Artifacts Dual Autographed-FAD-BR
Frozen Artifacts Dual Copper-FAD-BR
Frozen Artifacts Dual Gold-FAD-BR
Frozen Artifacts Dual Maroon-FAD-BR
Frozen Artifacts Dual Pewter-FAD-BR
Frozen Artifacts Dual Silver-FAD-BR
Frozen Artifacts Gold-FA-BR
Frozen Artifacts Maroon-FA-BR
Frozen Artifacts Patches-FP-BR
Frozen Artifacts Patches Autographed-FP-BR
Frozen Artifacts Patches Dual-FPD-BR
Frozen Artifacts Patches Dual Autos-FPD-BR
Frozen Artifacts Patches Pewter-FP-BR
Frozen Artifacts Patches Silver-FP-BR
Frozen Artifacts Pewter-FA-BR
Frozen Artifacts Silver-FA-BR
Gold Autographed-89
Remarkable Artifacts-RA-BR
Remarkable Artifacts Dual-RA-BR
05UD PowerPlay-79
Rainbow-79
05Ultimate Collection-79
Gold-79
Jerseys Triple-TJLVR
National Heroes Jerseys-NHJRI
National Heroes Patches-NHPRI
Ultimate Patches Triple-TPLVR
Ultimate Signatures-USBR
Ultimate Signatures Trios-UTLLR
05Ultra-174
Gold-174
Ice-174
Scoring Kings-SK16
Scoring Kings Jerseys-SKJ-BR
Scoring Kings Jersey Autographs-KAJ-BR
Scoring Kings Patches-SKP-BR
Scoring Kings Patch Autographs-KAP-BR
05Upper Deck-170
HG Glossy-170
Jerseys Series II-J2BR
Majestic Materials-MMBR
Notable Numbers-N-BR
Patches-P-BR
Shooting Stars-S-BR
05Upper Deck Ice-87
Rainbow-87
05Upper Deck MVP-343
Gold-343
Platinum-343
05Upper Deck Rookie Update-89
05Upper Deck Trilogy-80
05Upper Deck Trilogy-125
Crystal-125
Honorary Patches-HP-BR
Honorary Swatches-HS-BR
05Upper Deck Toronto Fall Expo-170
05Upper Deck Victory-173
Black-173
Gold-173
Silver-173
Game Breakers-GB42
05Czech Stadion-689
05ITG Heroes and Prospects Spectrum-STM-03
05ITG Heroes and Prospects Spectrum Gold-STM-03
06Be A Player-55
Autographs-55
Signatures-BR
Signatures 10-59
Signatures 25-59
Signatures Duals-DRF
Signatures Trios-TLRS
Signatures Foursomes-FMSRS
Up Close and Personal-UC8
Up Close and Personal Autographs-UC8
06Be A Player Portraits-89
06Beehive-10
Blue-10
Matte-10
Red Facsimile Signatures-10
Wood-10
06Black Diamond-124
Black-124
Gold-124
Ruby-124
06Flair Showcase-89
06Flair Showcase-162
06Flair Showcase-264
Parallel-89
Parallel-162
Parallel-264
06Fleer-175
Tiffany-175
06Hot Prospects-88
Red Hot-88
White Hot-88
Hot Materials -HMRI
Hot Materials Red Hot-HMRI
Hot Materials White Hot-HMRI
06Lightning Postcards-17
06McDonald's Upper Deck-41
Jerseys-JSC
Patches-PBR
06NHL POG-18
06O-Pee-Chee-438
Rainbow-438
06Panini Stickers-150
06SP Authentic-12
Limited-12
06SP Game Used-91
Gold-91
Rainbow-91
Authentic Fabrics-AFBR
Authentic Fabrics Parallel-AFBR
Authentic Fabrics Patches-AFBR
Authentic Fabrics Dual-AF2LR
Authentic Fabrics Dual Patches-AF2LR
Authentic Fabrics Triple-AF3TBL
Authentic Fabrics Triple Patches-AF3TBL
Authentic Fabrics Fives-AF5AST
Authentic Fabrics Fives Patches-AF5AST
Authentic Fabrics Sixes-AF6BYN
Authentic Fabrics Sixes Patches-AF6BYN
Authentic Fabrics Sevens-AF7CON
Authentic Fabrics Sevens Patches-AF7CON
06SPx-89
Spectrum-89
SPxcitement-X90
SPxcitement Spectrum-X90
Winning Materials-WMBR
Winning Materials Spectrum-WMBR
06The Cup NHL Shields Duals-DSHLR
06UD Artifacts-11
06UD Artifacts-198
Blue-11
Blue-198
Gold-11
Gold-198
Platinum-11
Platinum-198
Radiance-11
Radiance-198
Red-11
Red-198
Tundra Tandems-TTLR
Tundra Tandems Black-TTLR
Tundra Tandems Blue-TTLR
Tundra Tandems Gold-TTLR
Tundra Tandems Platinum-TTLR
Tundra Tandems Red-TTLR
Tundra Tandems Dual Patches Red-TTLR
06UD Mini Jersey Collection-89
06UD Powerplay-88
Impact Rainbow-88
Specialists-SRI
Specialists Patches-PRI
06Ultimate Collection-53
06Ultra-174
Gold Medallion-174
Ice Medallion-174
Scoring Kings-SK3
06Upper Deck Arena Giveaways-TBL6
06Upper Deck-426
Exclusives Parallel-426
High Gloss Parallel-426
Game Jerseys-JRI
Game Patches-PRI
Masterpieces-426
Oversized Wal-Mart Exclusives-426
Shootout Artists-SA3
06Upper Deck MVP-261
Gold Script-261
Super Script-261
Jerseys-OJRB
06Upper Deck Ovation-94
06Upper Deck Sweet Shot-90
Sweet Stitches-SSRI
Sweet Stitches Duals-SSRI
Sweet Stitches Triples-SSRI
06Upper Deck Trilogy-88
06Upper Deck Victory-180
06Upper Deck Victory Black-180
06Upper Deck Victory Gold-180
06Russian Sport Collection Olympic Stars-38
07Upper Deck Ovation-6
07Upper Deck Victory-70
Black-70
Gold-70

Richards, Chris

00Indianapolis Ice-18
01New Mexico Scorpions-7
02New Mexico Scorpions-15
03New Mexico Scorpions-6
04Austin Ice Bats-6

Richards, Jeff

04Lakehead University Thunderwolves-3
05ITG Heroes/Prospects He Shoots/Scores-35

Richards, Mark

92Toledo Storm-25
95Tallahassee Tiger Sharks-17
95Tallahassee Tiger Sharks-21
99UHL All-Stars East-17T
01Memphis RiverKings-15
03Memphis RiverKings-18
04Memphis RiverKings-12

Richards, Mike

01Kitchener Rangers-11
02Kitchener Rangers Postcards-3
03BAP Memorabilia Draft Redemptions-24
03Kitchener Rangers-22
03Kitchener Rangers Memorial Cup-17
04SP Authentic Rookie Redemptions-RR40
04Kitchener Rangers-2
04ITG Heroes and Prospects-96
Aspiring-7
Autographs-MR
Combos-12
Complete Emblems-6
Emblems-24
Emblems Gold-24
He Shoots-He Scores Prizes-25
Jersey Autographs-24
Jerseys-24
Jerseys Gold-24
National Pride-6
Numbers-24
Numbers Gold-24
04ITG Heroes/Prospects Toronto Expo '05-96
04ITG Heroes/Prospects Expo Heroes/Pros-96
05ITG Heroes/Prosp Toronto Expo Parallel -69
05ITG Heroes/Prosp Toronto Expo Parallel -336
05ITG Heroes/Prosp Toronto Expo Parallel -364
05Beehive-116
Beige -116
Blue -116
Gold-116
Red -116
Matte-116
Signature Scrapbook-SSRI
05Black Diamond-199
Emerald-199
Gold-199
Onyx-199
Ruby-199
05Flyers Team Issue-18
05Hot Prospects-258
En Fuego-258
Hot Materials-HMMR
Red Hot-258
White Hot-258
05ITG Ultimate Memorabilia Level 1-71
05ITG Ultimate Memorabilia Level 2-71
05ITG Ultimate Memorabilia Level 3-71
05ITG Ultimate Memorabilia Level 4-71
05ITG Ultimate Memorabilia Level 5-71
05ITG Ultimate Mem First Rounders Jerseys-10
05ITG Ultimate Mem 1st Round Jersey Gold-10
05ITG Ultimate Mem Future Stars Autos-17
05ITG Ultimate Mem Future Star Autos Gold-17
05ITG Ultimate Mem Future Stars Jerseys-18
05ITG Ultimate Mem Future Stars Jerseys Gold-18
05ITG Ultimate Mem Future Stars Mem Autos-17
05ITG Ultimate Mem Fut Star Mem Auto Gold-17
05ITG Ultimate Memorabilia R.O.Y. Autos-7
05ITG Ultimate Mem R.O.Y. Autos Gold-7
05ITG Ultimate Memorabilia Sextuple Autos-2
05Panini Stickers-3
05Parkhurst-652
Facsimile Auto Parallel-652
Signatures-MR
True Colors-TCPHI
True Colors-TCPHI
05SP Authentic-178
Limited-178
Prestigious Pairings-PPCR
Rarefied Rookies-RRMR
Rookie Authentics-RAMR
Sign of the Times Duals-DPR
Sign of the Times Fives-PEGCR
05SP Game Used-115
Autographs-115
Gold-115
Auto Draft-AD-RI
Game Gear-GG-RI
Game Gear Autographs-AG-RI
Rookie Exclusives-MR
Rookie Exclusives Silver-RE-MR
Significant Numbers-SN-MR
05SPx-165
Spectrum-165
05The Cup-172
Autographed Rookie Patches Gold Rainbow-172
Black Rainbow Rookies-172
Dual NHL Shields-DSJM
Dual NHL Shields Autographs-ADSJM
Masterpiece Pressplates (Artifacts)-235
Masterpiece Pressplates (Bee Hive)-116
Masterpiece Pressplates (Black Diamond)-199
Masterpiece Pressplates (Ice)-117
Masterpiece Pressplates (MVP)-406
Masterpiece Pressplates (Power Play)-156
Masterpiece Pressplates (Power Play)-156
Masterpiece Pressplates Rookie Upd Auto-273
Masterpiece Pressplates SPA Autos-178
Masterpiece Pressplates (SP Game Used)-115
Masterpiece Pressplates SPx Autos-165
Masterpiece Pressplates (Trilogy)-208
Masterpiece Pressplates Ult Coll Autos-129
Masterpiece Pressplates (Victory)-271
Masterpiece Pressplates Autographs-172
Platinum Rookies-172
Signature Patches-SPMR
05UD Artifacts-235
Gold-RED35
05UD PowerPlay-156
05UD Rookie Class-17
05Ultimate Collection-129
Autographed Patches-129
Autographed Shields-129
Jerseys Dual-DJCR
Marquee Attractions-MA36
Marquee Attractions Signatures-SMA36
Premium Patches-PPMR
Premium Swatches-PSMR
Ultimate Debut Threads Jerseys-DTJMR
Ultimate Debut Threads Jerseys Autos-DAJMR
Ultimate Debut Threads Patches-DTPMR
Ultimate Debut Threads Patches Autos-DAPMR
Ultimate Patches Dual-DPCR
Ultimate Signatures Logos-SLMR
Ultimate Signatures Pairings-UPCR
05Ultra-262
Gold-262
Fresh Ink-FI-MR
Fresh Ink Blue-FI-MR
Ice-262
Rookie Uniformity Jerseys-RU-MR
Rookie Uniformity Jersey Autographs-ARU-MR
Rookie Uniformity Patches-RUP-MR
Rookie Uniformity Patch Autographs-ARP-MR
Scoring Kings-SK30
Scoring Kings Jerseys-SKJ-RI
Scoring Kings Jersey Autographs-KAJ-RI
Scoring Kings Patches-SKP-RI
Scoring Kings Patch Autographs-KAP-RI
05Upper Deck-202
HG Glossy-202
Majestic Materials-MMRI
Rookie Ink-RIMR
05Upper Deck Rookie Showcase-RS33
05Upper Deck Rookie Showcase Promos-RS33
05Upper Deck Rookie Threads-RTMR
05Upper Deck Rookie Threads Autographs-ARTMR
05Upper Deck Stars in the Making-SM12
05Upper Deck Ice-117
Cool Threads-CTMR
Cool Threads Autographs-ACTMR
Cool Threads Glass-CTMR
Cool Threads Patches-CTPMR
Cool Threads Patch Autographs-CAPMR
Fresh Ice-FIMR
Fresh Ice Glass-FIMR
Fresh Ice Glass Patches-FIPMR
Glacial Graphs-GGRI

Premieres Auto Patches-AIPMR
05Upper Deck MVP-406
Gold-406
Platinum-406
Rookie Breakthrough-RB13
05Upper Deck Rookie Update-273
05Upper Deck Trilogy-208
05Upper Deck Toronto Fall Expo-202
05Upper Deck Victory-271
Black-271
Gold-271
Silver-271
05Extreme Top Prospects Signature Edition-S28
05ITG Heroes and Prospects-69
05ITG Heroes and Prospects-336
05ITG Heroes and Prospects-364
Autographs-A-MR
Autographs Series II-MR2
Autographs Series II-MR3
CHL Grads-CG-4
CHL Grads Gold-CG-4
Complete Jerseys-CJ-5
Complete Jerseys Gold-CJ-5
He Shoots-He Scores Prizes-35
Jerseys-GUJ-59
Jerseys Gold-GUJ-59
Emblems-GUE-59
Emblems Gold-GUE-59
Numbers-GUN-59
Numbers Gold-GUN-59
Making the Bigs-MTB-14
Nameplates-N-37
Nameplates Gold-N-37
National Pride-NPR-39
06Be A Player-54
Autographs-54
Signatures-RI
Signatures 10-58
Signatures Duals-DRU
Signatures Trios-TGCR
Portraits Dual Signature Portraits-DSRU
Portraits First Exposures-FEMR
Portraits Signature Portraits-SPRD
06Beehive Signature Scrapbook-SSMR
06Black Diamond-61
Black-61
Gold-61
Ruby-61
06Flair Showcase Inks-IMR
06Flair Showcase Wave of the Future-WF34
06Flyers Postcards-8
06O-Pee-Chee-366
06O-Pee-Chee-633
Rainbow-366
Rainbow-633
Autographs-A-MR
06SP Authentic-31
Limited-31
06SP Game Used Inked Sweaters-ISRI
06SP Game Used Inked Sweaters Patches-ISRI
06SP Game Used Letter Marks-LMRM
06SP Game Used SIGnificance-SMR
06UD Artifacts-27
Blue-27
Gold-27
Platinum-27
Radiance-27
Autographed Radiance Parallel-27
Red-27
Auto-Facts-AFMI
Auto-Facts Gold-AFMI
06UD Mini Jersey Collection-72
06UD Toronto Fall Expo Priority Signings -PSMR
06Ultra-147
Gold Medallion-147
Ice Medallion-147
06Upper Deck-146
Exclusives Parallel-146
High Gloss Parallel-146
Masterpieces-146
06Upper Deck MVP-217
Gold Script-217
Super Script-217
Autographs-OACR
06Upper Deck Trilogy-74
06Upper Deck Victory-149
06Upper Deck Victory Black-149
06Upper Deck Victory Gold-149
06Upper Deck Victory Next In Line-NL38
06ITG Heroes and Prospects CHL Top Prospects-TP06
06ITG Heroes and Prospects CHL Top Prospects Gold-TP06
06ITG Heroes and Prospects Quad Emblems-QE10
06ITG Heroes and Prospects Quad Emblems Gold-QE10
07Upper Deck Victory-31
Black-31
Gold-31

Richards, Robin
03Victoriaville Tigers-21

Richards, Steve
95Hampton Roads Admirals-15
00Kitchener Rangers-19
01Val d'Or Foreurs-5

Richards, Todd
89ProCards AHL-183
91Upper Deck-430
French-430
92Topps-79
Gold-79G
93Las Vegas Thunder-22
94Las Vegas Thunder-24
96Collector's Edge Ice-175
Prism-175
98IHL All-Star Eastern Conference-14
98Orlando Solar Bears-8
98Orlando Solar Bears II-10
01Swiss HNL-328
03Milwaukee Admirals-30
04Milwaukee Admirals-25
06Wilkes-Barre Scranton Penguins-24

Richards, Travis
91Minnesota Golden Gophers-22
92Minnesota Golden Gophers-18
93PowerPlay-513
93Stadium Club Team USA-18
93Stadium Club Team USA Members Only-18
93Topps Premier Team USA-7
93Ultra-493
93Classic-74
94Classic Autographs-NNO
95Images-92
Gold-92
96Grand Rapids Griffins-21
97Grand Rapids Griffins-14
98Grand Rapids Griffins-16
99Grand Rapids Griffins-20
00Grand Rapids Griffins-18
01Grand Rapids Griffins-16
02Grand Rapids Griffins-22
03Grand Rapids Griffins-17

Richardson, Bill
51Laval Dairy Subset-113
52St. Lawrence Sales-68

Richardson, Brad
01Owen Sound Attack-15
02Owen Sound Attack-12
03Owen Sound Attack-11
04Upper Deck World Cup Tribute-MSVLBR
04Owen Sound Attack-5
05Beehive-94
Matte-94
05Black Diamond-227
05Hot Prospects-230
En Fuego-230
Hot Materials-HMBR
Red Hot-230
White Hot-230
05Parkhurst-621
Facsimile Auto Parallel-621
05SP Authentic-211
Limited-211
05SP Game Used-202
05SPx-226
Spectrum-226
05The Cup-140
Autographed Rookie Patches Gold Rainbow-140
Black Rainbow Rookies-140
Masterpiece Pressplates (Artifacts)-264
Masterpiece Pressplates (Bee Hive)-94
Masterpiece Pressplates (Black Diamond)-227
Masterpiece Pressplates (Ice)-211
Masterpiece Pressplates (Rookie Update)-206
Masterpiece Pressplates SPA Autos-211
Masterpiece Pressplates (SP Game Used)-202
Masterpiece Pressplates SPx Autos-226
Masterpiece Pressplates (Trilogy)-241
Masterpiece Pressplates Ult Coll-152
Masterpiece Pressplates Autographs-140
Platinum Rookies-140
05UD Artifacts-264
05Ultimate Collection-152
Gold-152
05Upper Deck-485
05Upper Deck Ice-211
05Upper Deck Rookie Update-206
Inspirations Patch Rookies-206
05Upper Deck Trilogy-241
06Avalanche Team Postcards-11
06O-Pee-Chee-136
Rainbow-136
06UD Toronto Fall Expo Priority Signings -PSBR
06Upper Deck MVP-74
Gold Script-74
Super Script-74
Autographs-OARL

Richardson, Bruce
98Hershey Bears-28
98Quad-City Mallards-19
00Louisiana Ice Gators-11
00Manitoba Moose-18
01Cincinnati Mighty Ducks-18
02Louisiana Ice Gators-16
03Hershey Bears-15
03Hershey Bears Patriot News-18
05German DEL-177
06Fort Wayne Komets-15

Richardson, Bryan
93RPI Engineers-25
96Dayton Bombers-15
98Baton Rouge Kingfish-16
00UK Sekonda Superleague-82
02ECHL Update-U-20

Richardson, Dave
62Sudbury Wolves-19
94Parkhurst Tall Boys-94

Richardson, Don
93Quebec Pee-Wee Tournament-1733

Richardson, George
83Hall of Fame-85
83Hall of Fame Postcards-F11
85Hall of Fame-85

Richardson, Glen
75Hamilton Fincups-15

Richardson, Ken
917th Inn. Sketch WHL-230
93Red Deer Rebels-21
98Huntsville Channel Cats-13

Richardson, Lee
02UK Coventry Blaze-19
03UK Coventry Blaze-17
03UK Coventry Blaze Calendars-9
05UK Coventry Blaze-17

Richardson, Luke
87Maple Leafs PLAY-27
87Maple Leafs Postcards-16
87Maple Leafs Postcards Oversized-16
88O-Pee-Chee-245
88O-Pee-Chee Stickers-173
88Panini Stickers-119
89Panini Stickers-142
90Maple Leafs Postcards-18
90O-Pee-Chee-428
90Pro Set-289
90Score-236
Canadian-236
90Upper Deck-362
French-362
91Bowman-167
91Maple Leafs Panini Team Stickers-23
91Oilers IGA-19
91Oilers Team Issue-22
91O-Pee-Chee-351
91OPC Premier-46
91Parkhurst-274
French-274
91Pinnacle-212
French-212
91Pro Set-387
French-387
91Score American-139
91Score Canadian Bilingual-139
91Score Canadian Bilingual-620
91Score Canadian English-139
91Score Canadian English-620
91Score Rookie/Traded-70T
91Stadium Club-172
91Topps-351
91Upper Deck-418
91Upper Deck-522
French-418
French-522
92Bowman-255
92Oilers IGA-19
92Oilers Team Issue-16
92O-Pee-Chee-171
92Pinnacle-41
92Pinnacle-235
French-41
French-235
92Score-62
Canadian-62
92Stadium Club-456
92Topps-409
Gold-409G
92Ultra-297
93Donruss-115
93Pinnacle-139
Canadian-139
93Score-252
Canadian-252
93Ultra-318
94Canada Games NHL POGS-338
94OPC Premier-466
Special Effects-466
94Pinnacle-431
Artist's Proofs-431
Rink Collection-431
94Topps/OPC Premier-466
Special Effects-466
94Upper Deck-215
Electric Ice-215
95Be A Player-70
Signatures-S70
Signatures Die Cuts-S70
95Topps-108
OPC Inserts-108
95Swedish World Championships Stickers-5
96Oilers Postcards-22
96Upper Deck-61
97Collector's Choice-96
97Pacific Invincible NHL Regime-82
97Score Flyers-10
Platinum-10
Premier-10
97Upper Deck-330
98Be A Player-103
Press Release-103
98BAP Gold-103
98BAP Autographs-103
98BAP Autographs Gold-103
98BAP Tampa Bay All Star Game-103
98OPC Chrome-159
Refractors-159
98Topps-159
O-Pee-Chee-159
99Upper Deck MVP SC Edition-138
Gold Script-138
Silver Script-138
Super Script-138
00BAP Memorabilia Update Tough Materials-T16
00BAP Mem Update Tough Materials Gold-T16
00Upper Deck-360
Exclusives Tier 1-360
Exclusives Tier 2-360
01BAP Update Tough Customers-TC13
01BAP Update Tough Customers-TC25
01Flyers Postcards-18
01Upper Deck Ice-111
02BAP First Edition-41
Jerseys-41
02BAP Sig Series Auto Buybacks 1998-103
02Pacific Complete-489
Red-489
02Topps Total-111
02Upper Deck-297
Exclusives-297
02Upper Deck Beckett UD Promos-297
03ITG Action-161
03NHL Sticker Collection-197
04Upper Deck-49
Canadian Exclusives-49
HG Glossy Gold-49
HG Glossy Silver-49
05Parkhurst-463
Facsimile Auto Parallel-149
05Upper Deck MVP-122
Gold-122
Platinum-122
06Lightning Postcards-18

Richardson, Mark
04UK U-20 Team-16
05UK Cardiff Devils Challenge Cup-6

Richardson, Russ
01UK Manchester Storm-18

Richardson, Terry
79O-Pee-Chee-377

Richer, Antoine
92Finnish Semic-237
93Swedish Semic World Champ Stickers-266
94Finnish Jaa Kiekko-224
94French National Team-28
95Finnish Semic World Championships-200
95Swedish Globe World Championships-207
95Swedish World Championships Stickers-114
96Swedish Semic Wien-187

Richer, Stephane JG
88ProCards AHL-296
89ProCards AHL-195
90ProCards AHL/IHL-354
91ProCards-86
93Cincinnati Cyclones-21
95German DEL-270
96German DEL-165
98German DEL-228
99German DEL-12
00German DEL-3
Game Jersey-SR
01German Upper Deck-174
Skilled Stars-SS9
02BAP Sig Series Auto Buybacks 1998-133
02German DEL City Press-81
All-Stars-AS7

Richer, Stephane JJ
84Chicoutimi Sagueneens-23
85Canadiens Postcards-27
85Canadiens Provigo-16
86Canadiens Postcards-18
86Kraft Drawings-58
87Canadiens Postcards-23A
87Canadiens Postcards-23B
87Canadiens Vachon Stickers-51
87Canadiens Vachon Stickers-52
87Canadiens Vachon Stickers-54
87O-Pee-Chee-233
87Panini Stickers-65
88Canadiens Postcards-22
88Frito-Lay Stickers-40
88O-Pee-Chee-5
88O-Pee-Chee Minis-31
88O-Pee-Chee Stickers-49
88Panini Stickers-260
88Topps-5
89Canadiens Kraft-18
89Canadiens Postcards-26
89Canadiens Provigo Figurines-44
89Kraft-24
89O-Pee-Chee-153
89O-Pee-Chee Stickers-51
89Panini Stickers-239
89Topps-153
90Bowman-45
Tiffany-45
90Bowman Hat Tricks-11
Tiffany-11
90Canadiens Postcards-24
90Kraft-46
90Kraft-89
90O-Pee-Chee-186
90OPC Premier-98
90Panini Stickers-53
90Pro Set-156
90Pro Set-370
90Score-75
Canadian-75
90Score Hottest/Rising Stars-38
90Topps-186
Tiffany-186
Team Scoring Leaders-4
Team Scoring Leaders Tiffany-4
90Upper Deck-276
French-276
91Pro Set Platinum-67
91Bowman-330
91Canadiens Panini Team Stickers-18
91Kraft-21
91O-Pee-Chee-298
91O-Pee-Chee-369
91OPC Premier-113
91Panini Stickers-193
91Parkhurst-100
French-100
91Pinnacle-14
French-14
91Pro Set-122
91Pro Set-420
French-122
French-420
91Score American-234
91Score Canadian Bilingual-581
91Score Canadian English-581
91Score Rookie/Traded-31T
91Stadium Club-86
91Topps-369
91Upper Deck-244
91Upper Deck-536
French-244
French-536
92Bowman-46
92Durivage Panini-18
92O-Pee-Chee-76
92OPC Premier Star Performers-18
92Panini Stickers-173
92Panini Stickers French-173
92Parkhurst-91
Emerald Ice-91
92Pinnacle-361
French-361
92Pro Set-93
92Score-140
Canadian-140
92Stadium Club-9
92Topps-160
Gold-160G
92Ultra-117
92Upper Deck-56
93Donruss-190
93Durivage Score-48
93Leaf-138
93OPC Premier-158
93OPC Premier-327
Gold-158
Gold-327
93Panini Stickers-37
93Parkhurst-113
Emerald Ice-113
93Pinnacle-143
Canadian-143
93PowerPlay-141
93Score-34
Canadian-34
93Stadium Club-61
93Stadium Club-347
Members Only Master Set-61
Members Only Master Set-347
OPC-61
First Day Issue-61
First Day Issue-347
First Day Issue OPC-61
93Topps/OPC Premier-158
93Topps/OPC Premier-327
Gold-158
Gold-327
93Ultra-152
93Upper Deck-403
SP-87
94Action Packed Big Picture 24K Gold-9G
94Canada Games NHL POGS-148
94Donruss-79
94EA Sports-76
94Finest-94
Super Team Winners-94
Refractors-94
Division's Clear Cut-10
94Flair-97
94Fleer-116
Slapshot Artists-7
94Leaf-24
94OPC Premier-105
Special Effects-105
94Parkhurst Vintage-V50
94Parkhurst SE-SE100
Gold-SE100
94Pinnacle-166
Artist's Proofs-166
Rink Collection-166
Boomers-BR14
94Select Promos-108
94Select-108
Gold-108
94SP-64
Die Cuts-64
94Topps/OPC Premier-105
Special Effects-105
94Ultra-122
94Upper Deck-388
Electric Ice-388
SP Inserts-SP44
SP Inserts Die Cuts-SP44
95Bashan Super Stickers-69
95Bowman-14
All-Foil-14
95Canada Games NHL POGS-163
95Collector's Choice-250
Player's Club-250
Player's Club Platinum-250
95Donruss-178
95Emotion-101
95Hoyle Eastern Playing Cards-16
95Imperial Stickers-69
95Kraft-71
95Leaf-91
95Leaf Limited-68
95Metal-85
95Panini Stickers-85
95Parkhurst International-118
Emerald Ice-118
95Pinnacle-35
Artist's Proofs-35
Rink Collection-35
95Playoff One on One-60
95Pro Magnets-39
95Score-130
Black Ice Artist's Proofs-130
Black Ice-130
Golden Blades-14
95Select Certified-39
Mirror Gold-39
95SkyBox Impact-96
95SP-85
95Stadium Club-176
Members Only Master Set-176
Power Streak-PS10
Power Streak Members Only Master Set-PS10
95Summit-52
Artist's Proofs-52
Ice-52
95Topps-231
OPC Inserts-231
Home Grown Canada-HGC28
95Topps SuperSkills-41
Platinum-41
95Ultra-91
95Ultra-195
Gold Medallion-91
Gold Medallion-195
95Upper Deck-426
Electric Ice-426
Electric Ice Gold-426
Special Edition-SE47
Special Edition Gold-SE47
95Zenith-39
96SLU Hockey American-19
96Be A Player-50
Autographs-50
Autographs Silver-50
96Canadiens Postcards-22
96Canadiens Sheets-16
96Donruss-108
Press Proofs-108
96Donruss Canadian Ice-98
Gold Press Proofs-98
Red Press Proofs-98
96Donruss Elite-36
Die Cut Stars-36
96Fleer Picks-128
96Kenner Starting Lineup Cards-19
96Leaf-18
Press Proofs-18
96Leaf Preferred-76
Press Proofs-76
96Metal Universe-82
96NHL Pro Stamps-39
96Pinnacle-33
Artist's Proofs-33
Foil-33
Premium Stock-33
Rink Collection-33
96Playoff One on One-342
96Score-232
Artist's Proofs-232
Dealer's Choice Artist's Proofs-232
Special Artist's Proofs-232
Golden Blades-232
96SP-83
96Summit-99
Artist's Proofs-99
Ice-99
Metal-99
Premium Stock-99
96Team Out-35
96Ultra-89
Gold Medallion-89
96Upper Deck-94
96Zenith-42
Artist's Proofs-42
97Canadiens Postcards-17
97Collector's Choice-138
97Crown Royale-72
Emerald Green-72
Ice Blue-72
Silver-72
97Donruss Canadian Ice-104
Dominion Series-104
Provincial Series-104
97Pacific-44
Copper-44
Emerald Green-44
Ice Blue-44
Red-44
Silver-44
Slap Shots Die-Cuts-4C
Team Checklists-13
97Pacific Dynagon-65
Copper-65
Dark Grey-65
Emerald Green-65
Ice Blue-65
Red-65
Silver-65
Best Kept Secrets-50
Tandems-48
97Pacific Invincible-73
Copper-73
Emerald Green-73
Ice Blue-73
Red-73
Silver-73
NHL Regime-105
97Paramount-98
Copper-98
Dark Grey-98
Emerald Green-98
Ice Blue-98
Red-98
Silver-98
97Pinnacle-160
Press Plates Back Black-160
Press Plates Back Cyan-160
Press Plates Back Magenta-160
Press Plates Back Yellow-160
Press Plates Front Black-160
Press Plates Front Cyan-160
Press Plates Front Magenta-160
Press Plates Front Yellow-160
97Score-213
97Score Canadiens-8
Platinum-8
Premier-8
98Aurora-175
98Be A Player-133
Press Release-133
98BAP Gold-133
98BAP Autographs-133
98BAP Autographs Gold-133
98BAP Tampa Bay All Star Game-133
98Crown Royale-126
Limited Series-126
98Pacific-405
Ice Blue-405
Red-405
98Pacific Dynagon Ice-174
Blue-174
Red-174
98Pacific Omega-221
Red-221
Opening Day Issue-221
98Paramount-220
Copper-220
Emerald Green-220
Holo-Electric-220
Ice Blue-220
Silver-220
98Revolution-134
Ice Shadow-134
Red-134
98SPx Finite-78
Radiance-78
Spectrum-78
98UD Choice-193
98UD Choice Preview-193
98UD Choice Prime Choice Reserve-193
98UD Choice Reserve-193
98Upper Deck-183
Exclusives-183
Exclusives 1 of 1-183
Gold Reserve-183
99BAP Memorabilia-85
Gold-85
Silver-85
99Blues Taco Bell-24
99Pacific-394
Copper-394
Emerald Green-394
Gold-394
Ice Blue-394
Premiere Date-394
Red-394
99Panini Stickers-145
99Upper Deck Victory-278
00O-Pee-Chee-226
00O-Pee-Chee Parallel-226
00Pacific-351
Copper-351
Gold-351
Ice Blue-351
Premiere Date-351
00Panini Stickers-198
00Topps/OPC-226
Parallel-226
01BAP Memorabilia-491
Emerald-491
Ruby-491
Sapphire-491
01Parkhurst-356

Richey, Owen
98Prince George Cougars-18

Richey, Steve
81Kingston Canadians-22
82Kingston Canadians-23

Richison, Grant
89ProCards AHL-46
90Moncton Hawks-20
90ProCards AHL/IHL-255
91ProCards-244
93Fort Wayne Komets-16
95Fort Wayne Komets-14
98Kansas City Blades-19
98Muskegon Fury-29
99Kansas City Blades Supercuts-16
00UK Sekonda Superleague-190

Richmond, Danny
98Quebec Pee Wee Tournament-544
02Michigan Wolverines-2
03London Knights-26
04Lowell Lock Monsters-18
04Lowell Lock Monsters Photo Album-18
05ITG Heroes/Prosp Toronto Expo Parallel -384
05Beehive-155
Matte-155
05Black Diamond-223
05Hot Prospects-193
Autographed Patch Variation-193
Hot Materials-HMDR
Red Hot-193
05SP Authentic-199
05SP Game Used-199
05SPx-225
Spectrum-225
05The Cup-128
Autographed Rookie Patches Gold Rainbow-128
Black Rainbow Rookies-128
Masterpiece Pressplates (Artifacts)-258
Masterpiece Pressplates (Bee Hive)-155
Masterpiece Pressplates (Black Diamond)-223
Masterpiece Pressplates (Ice)-189
Masterpiece Pressplates (Rookie Update)-202
Masterpiece Pressplates SPA Autos-199
Masterpiece Pressplates (SP Game Used)-199
Masterpiece Pressplates SPx Autos-225
Masterpiece Pressplates (Trilogy)-236
Masterpiece Pressplates Ult Coll-192
Masterpiece Pressplates Autographs-128
Platinum Rookies-128
05UD Artifacts-258
05Ultimate Collection-192
Gold-192
05Upper Deck-475
05Upper Deck Ice-189
05Upper Deck Rookie Update-202
Inspirations Patch Rookies-202
05Upper Deck Trilogy-236
05ITG Heroes and Prospects-384
Autographs Update-A-DRI
06Black Diamond Gemography-GDR
06Upper Deck Trilogy Scripts-TSDR
06Norfolk Admirals-18

Richmond, Ken
93Quebec Pee-Wee Tournament-1606

Richmond, Steve
86O-Pee-Chee-208
88ProCards AHL-218

Richter, Barry
93PowerPlay-514
93Stadium Club Team USA-19
93Stadium Club Team USA Members Only-19
93Topps Premier Team USA-18
93Ultra-494
93Classic-75
Previews-HK3
94Binghamton Rangers-17
94Classic Autographs-NNO
94Images *-24
95Swedish World Championships Stickers-217
95Binghamton Rangers-20
96Topps Picks-177
OPC Inserts-177
96Upper Deck-219
96Collector's Edge Future Legends-39
97Providence Bruins-15
99Pacific-264
Copper-264
Emerald Green-264
Gold-264
Ice Blue-264
Premiere Date-264
Red-264
99Upper Deck Victory-195
00Quebec Citadelles-18
Signed-18
02Swedish SHL-211
Parallel-211
03Swedish Elite-71
Silver-71
03Swiss EV Zug Postcards-18
04Swiss EV Zug Postcards-4

Richter, Dave
82Birmingham South Stars-9
83North Stars Postcards-24
84North Stars Postcards-23
86Canucks Team Issue-17
87Blues Team Issue-19
87Canucks Shell Oil-15
87O-Pee-Chee-261
87O-Pee-Chee Stickers-190
87Panini Stickers-344
88Blues Kodak-20
88Blues Team Issue-19
90ProCards AHL/IHL-522

Richter, Martin
97Czech APS Extraliga-227
98Czech DS Stickers-33
98Czech OFS-85
98Czech OFS-451
99Czech DS-17
99Czech OFS-143
99Czech OFS-267
00Finnish Cardset-78
01Czech National Team Postcards-11
02Czech DS-20
02Czech OFS Plus-14
Duos-D3
02Finnish Cardset-105
03Czech OFS Plus-323
03Russian Hockey League-215
04Czech HC Sparta Praha Postcards-19
04Czech OFS-198
05Czech HC Liberec-11
06Czech IIHF World Championship Postcards-17
06Czech OFS All Stars-10
06Czech OFS Defenders-4
06Czech OFS Jagr Team-8
06Hartford Wolf Pack-22

Richter, Mike
89Rangers Marine Midland Bank-35
89ProCards IHL-48
90Bowman-218
Tiffany-218
90O-Pee-Chee-330
90Panini Stickers-98
90Panini Stickers-345
90Pro Set-398
90Pro Set-627
90Score-74
Canadian-74
90Score Young Superstars-27
90Topps-330
Tiffany-330
90Upper Deck-32
French-32
91Pro Set Platinum-83
91Pro Set Platinum-279
91Bowman-70
91Gillette-39
91Kraft-88
91O-Pee-Chee-11
91O-Pee-Chee-91
91OPC Premier-78
91Panini Stickers-290
91Parkhurst-117
French-117
91Pinnacle-164
91Pinnacle-384
French-164
French-384
91Pro Set-161
French-161
Awards Special-AC2
91Score American-120
91Score Canadian Bilingual-120
91Score Canadian English-120
91Score Young Superstars-2
91Stadium Club-92
91Topps-11
91Topps-91
91Upper Deck-34
91Upper Deck-175
91Upper Deck-610
91Upper Deck-634
French-34
French-175
French-610
French-634
91Finnish Semic World Champ Stickers-128
91Swedish Semic World Champ Stickers-128
92Bowman-238
92Bowman-354
92McDonald's Upper Deck-25
92O-Pee-Chee-259
92Panini Stickers-231
92Panini Stickers French-231
92Parkhurst-112
Emerald Ice-112
92Pinnacle-75
92Pinnacle-270
French-75
French-270
Team Pinnacle-1
Team French-1
92Pro Set-116
92Score Canadian Promo Sheets-2
92Score-5
Canadian-5
USA Greats-6
Young Superstars-9
92Seasons Patches-29
92Sports Illustrated for Kids II-284
92Stadium Club-242
92Stadium Club-266
92Topps-367
Gold-367G
92Ultra-142
92Upper Deck-34
92Upper Deck-145
92Finnish Semic-148
93Donruss-223
93Leaf-185
93OPC Premier-135
Gold-135
93Panini Stickers-99
93Parkhurst-129
93Parkhurst-132
Emerald Ice-129
Emerald Ice-132
93Pinnacle-242
Canadian-242
93PowerPlay-165
93Score-99
Canadian-99
93Stadium Club-64
Members Only Master Set-64
OPC-64
First Day Issue-64
First Day Issue OPC-64
93Topps/OPC Premier-135
Gold-135
93Ultra-228
93Upper Deck-42
93Swedish Semic World Champ Stickers-170
94Hockey Canadian-10
94SLU Hockey Canadian-10
94SLU Hockey American-16
94Action Packed Big Picture 24K Gold-10G
94Canada Games NHL POGS-288
94Canada Games NHL POGS-337
94Donruss-165
Masked Marvels-8
94EA Sports-90
94Finest-86
Super Team Winners-86
Refractors-86
Bowman's Best-B13
Bowman's Best Refractors-B13
Division's Clear Cut-6
94Flair-117
94Fleer-139
Netminders-8
94Hockey Wit-1
94Kenner Starting Lineup Cards-17
94Kraft-52
94Leaf-18
Crease Patrol-8
Gold Stars-3
94Leaf Limited-17
94McDonald's Upper Deck-NNO
94OPC Premier-70
94OPC Premier-155
94OPC Premier-314
Special Effects-70
Special Effects-155
Special Effects-314
94Parkhurst Vintage-V5
94Parkhurst SE-SE110
Gold-SE110
94Pinnacle-10
Artist's Proofs-10
Rink Collection-10
Goaltending Greats-GT2
Team Pinnacle-TP2
Team Dufex Parallel-TP2
94Score-130
Gold-130
Platinum-130
94Select-133
Gold-133
First Line-FL7
94SP-75
Die Cuts-75
94Stadium Club Members Only-45
94Stadium Club-181
Members Only Master Set-181
First Day Issue-181
Super Teams-15
Super Teams Members Only Master Set-15
Super Team Winner Cards-181
94Topps/OPC Premier-70
94Topps/OPC Premier-155
94Topps/OPC Premier-314
Special Effects-70
Special Effects-155
Special Effects-314
94Ultra-143
Premier Pad Men-5
94Upper Deck-78
Electric Ice-78
Predictor Hobby-H30
94Upper Deck Predictor Hobby Exch Gold-H30
94Upper Deck SP Inserts-SP52
94Upper Deck SP Inserts Die Cuts-SP52
94Finnish Jaa Kiekko-107
94Swedish Olympics Lillehammer*-322
95Bashan Super Stickers-83
95Be A Player-191
Signatures-S191
Signatures Die Cuts-S191
95Canada Games NHL POGS-189
95Collector's Choice-306
Player's Club-306
Player's Club Platinum-306
95Donruss-59
95Emotion-117
95Finest-169
Refractors-169
95Hoyle Eastern Playing Cards-17
95Imperial Stickers-83
95Kraft-22
95Leaf-42
95Metal-98
95Panini Stickers-112
95Parkhurst International-138
Emerald Ice-138
Goal Patrol-12
Parkie's Trophy Picks-PP31
95Pinnacle-47
Artist's Proofs-47
Rink Collection-47
95Playoff One on One-69
95Pro Magnets-99
95Pro Magnets Iron Curtain Insert-4
95Score-140
95Score-321
Black Ice Artist's Proofs-140
Black Ice Artist's Proofs-321
Black Ice-140
Black Ice-321
95Select Certified-73
Mirror Gold-73
95SkyBox Impact-112
95SP-95
95Stadium Club-49
Members Only Master Set-49
Nemeses-N4
Nemeses Members Only Master Set-N4
95Summit-115
Artist's Proofs-115

Ice-115
In The Crease-11
95Topps-212
OPC Inserts-212
Home Grown USA-HGA10
95Topps SuperSkills-74
Platinum-74
95Ultra-276
95Upper Deck-438
Electric Ice-438
Electric Ice Gold-438
Predictor Hobby-H12
Predictor Hobby Exchange-H12
Special Edition-SE58
Special Edition Gold-SE58
95Zenith-53
95Finnish Semic World Championships-218
95Swedish Globe World Championships-100
95Swedish World Championships Stickers-212
96Be A Player Stacking the Pads-10
96Black Diamond-35
Gold-35
96Collector's Choice-167
96Collector's Choice-324
96Donruss-184
Press Proofs-184
96Donruss Canadian Ice-26
Gold Press Proofs-26
Red Press Proofs-26
96Donruss Elite-96
Die Cut Stars-96
Painted Warriors-2
Painted Warriors Promos-P2
96Flair-62
Blue Ice-62
Hot Gloves-9
96Fleer Picks-84
Dream Lines-2
96Kraft Upper Deck-52
96Leaf-178
Press Proofs-178
Shut Down-11
96Leaf Limited-41
Gold-41
96Leaf Preferred-55
Press Proofs-55
Steel-46
Steel Gold-46
Masked Marauders-11
96Maggers-84
96Metal Universe-100
Armor Plate-10
Armor Plate Super Power-10
96NHL Pro Stamps-99
96Pinnacle-112
Artist's Proofs-112
Foil-112
Premium Stock-112
Rink Collection-112
Masks-9
Masks Die Cuts-9
96Pinnacle Fantasy-FC10
96Score-150
Artist's Proofs-150
Dealer's Choice Artist's Proofs-150
Special Artist's Proofs-150
Golden Blades-150
Sudden Death-9
Superstitions-12
96Select Certified-39
Artist's Proofs-39
Blue-39
Mirror Blue-39
Mirror Gold-39
Mirror Red-39
Red-39
Freezers-11
96SkyBox Impact-83
96SP-100
Holoview Collection-HC27
SPx Force-3
96SPx-28
Gold-28
96Summit-145
Artist's Proofs-145
Ice-145
Metal-145
Premium Stock-145
In The Crease-2
In The Crease Premium Stock-2
96Team Out-62
96Topps Picks Ice D-ID13
96Ultra-110
Gold Medallion-110
96Upper Deck-109
96Upper Deck Ice-41
Parallel-41
96Zenith-66
Artist's Proofs-66
Champion Salute-14
Champion Salute Diamond-14
96Swedish Semic Wien-158
97SLU Hockey One on One-6
97Headliners Hockey-20
97Be A Player-37
Autographs-37
Autographs Die-Cuts-37
Autographs Prismatic Die-Cuts-37
Stacking the Pads-10
97Beehive-41
Golden Portraits-41
97Black Diamond-4
Double Diamond-4
Triple Diamond-4
Quadruple Diamond-4
97Collector's Choice-161
Star Quest-SQ30
97Crown Royale-87
Emerald Green-87
Ice Blue-87
Silver-87
Freeze Out Die-Cuts-12
97Donruss-124
Press Proofs Silver-124
Press Proofs Gold-124
97Donruss Canadian Ice-107
Dominion Series-107
Provincial Series-107
Stanley Cup Scrapbook-15
97Donruss Elite-56
Aspirations-56
Status-56
97Donruss Limited-32
97Donruss Limited-134
Exposure-32
Exposure-134
Fabric of the Game-11
97Donruss Preferred-124
Cut to the Chase-124
Color Guard-15
Color Guard Promos-15
97Donruss Priority-143
Stamp of Approval-143
Postmaster General-5
Postmaster Generals Promos-5
97Esso Olympic Hockey Heroes-33
97Esso Olympic Hockey Heroes French-33
97Katch-95
Gold-95
Silver-95
97Leaf-70
Fractal Matrix-70
Fractal Matrix Die Cuts-70
Pipe Dreams-8
97Leaf International-70
Universal Ice-70
97McDonald's Upper Deck-29
97Pacific-197
Copper-197
Emerald Green-197
Ice Blue-197
Red-197
Silver-197
In The Cage Laser Cuts-13
97Pacific Dynagon-82
Copper-82
Dark Grey-82
Emerald Green-82
Ice Blue-82
Red-82
Silver-82
Stonewallers-14
Tandems-70
97Pacific Invincible-90
Copper-90
Emerald Green-90
Ice Blue-90
Red-90
Silver-90
97Pacific Omega-148
Copper-148
Dark Gray-148
Emerald Green-148
Gold-148
Ice Blue-148
No Scoring Zone-8
97Paramount-119
Copper-119
Dark Grey-119
Emerald Green-119
Ice Blue-119
Red-119
Silver-119
Glove Side Laser Cuts-13
97Pinnacle-55
Artist's Proofs-55
Rink Collection-55
Press Plates Back Black-55
Press Plates Back Cyan-55
Press Plates Back Magenta-55
Press Plates Back Yellow-55
Press Plates Front Black-55
Press Plates Front Cyan-55
Press Plates Front Magenta-55
Press Plates Front Yellow-55
Masks-2
Masks Die Cuts-2
Masks Jumbos-2
97Pinnacle Masks Promos-2
97Pinnacle Tins-7
97Pinnacle Certified-13
Red-13
Mirror Blue-13
Mirror Gold-13
Mirror Red-13
97Pinnacle Inside-81
Coach's Collection-81
Executive Collection-81
Stoppers-5
Track-26
Cans-22
Cans Gold-22
97Pinnacle Replica Masks-4
97Pinnacle Tot Cert Platinum Blue-13
97Pinnacle Tot Certi Platinum Gold-13
97Pinnacle Totally Certified Platinum Red-13
97Pinnacle Tot Cert Mirror Platinum Gold-13
97Revolution-90
Copper-90
Emerald-90
Ice Blue-90
Silver-90
Return to Sender Die-Cuts-13
97Score-11
Artist's Proofs-11
Golden Blades-11
Net Worth-6
97Score Rangers-16
Platinum-16
Premier-16
97SP Authentic-101
97SPx-31
Bronze-31
Gold-31
Silver-31
Steel-31
Grand Finale-31
97Studio-59
Press Proofs Silver-59
Press Proofs Gold-59
Portraits-33
97Upper Deck-107
Game Dated Moments-107
Game Jerseys-GJ11
Smooth Grooves-SG53
Three Star Selects-10C
97Upper Deck Ice-3
Parallel-3
Power Shift-3
97Zenith-18
Z-Gold-18
Z-Silver-18
97Zenith 5 x 7-63
Gold Impulse-63
Silver Impulse-63
98Headliners Hockey In the Crease-3
98Headliners Hockey XL-6
98NHL Pro Zone-50
98Aurora-125
Championship Fever-31
Championship Fever Copper-31
Championship Fever Ice Blue-31
Championship Fever Red-31
Championship Fever Silver-31
98Be A Player-89
Press Release-89
98BAP Gold-89
98BAP Autographs-89
98BAP Autographs Gold-89
98BAP Playoff Highlights-H6
98BAP Tampa Bay All Star Game-89
98Black Diamond-58
Double Diamond-58
Triple Diamond-58
Quadruple Diamond-58
98Bowman's Best-43
Refractors-43
Atomic Refractors-43
98Crown Royale-91
Limited Series-91
98Finest-89
No Protectors-89
No Protectors Refractors-89
Refractors-89
98Katch-94
98Lunchables Goalie Greats Rounds-7
98Lunchables Goalie Greats Squares-7
98McDonalds Upper Deck Gretzkys Teammates-T8
98NHL Aces Playing Cards-37
98NHL Game Day Promotion-NYR4
98OPC Chrome-200
Refractors-200
98Pacific-298
Ice Blue-298
Red-298
98Pacific Dynagon Ice-125
Blue-125
Red-125
Watchmen-6
98Pacific Omega-161
Red-161
Opening Day Issue-161
98Panini Photocards-68
98Panini Stickers-82
98Paramount-156
Copper-156
Emerald Green-156
Holo-Electric-156
Ice Blue-156
Silver-156
Glove Side Laser Cuts-12
98Rangers Power Play-NYR4
98Revolution-97
Ice Shadow-97
Red-97
Three Pronged Attack-16
Three Pronged Attack Parallel-16
98SP Authentic-55
Power Shift-55
98SPx Top Prospects Premier Stars-PS7
98SPx Top Prospects Winning Materials-MR
98Topps-200
O-Pee-Chee-200
98Topps Gold Label Class 1-54
Black-54
Black One of One-54
One of One-54
Red-54
Red One of One-54
98Topps Gold Label Class 2-54
98Topps Gold Label Class 2 Black-54
98Topps Gold Label Class 2 Black 1 of 1-54
98Topps Gold Label Class 2 One of One-54
98Topps Gold Label Class 2 Red-54
98Topps Gold Label Class 2 Red One of One-54
98Topps Gold Label Class 3-54
98Topps Gold Label Class 3 Black-54
98Topps Gold Label Class 3 Black 1 of 1-54
98Topps Gold Label Class 3 One of One-54
98Topps Gold Label Class 3 Red-54
98Topps Gold Label Class 3 Red One of One-54
98UD Choice-135
98UD Choice-246
98UD Choice Preview-135
98UD Choice Prime Choice Reserve-135
98UD Choice Prime Choice Reserve-246
98UD Choice Reserve-135
98UD Choice Reserve-246
98Upper Deck-324
Exclusives-324
Exclusives 1 of 1-324
Gold Reserve-324
98Upper Deck MVP-135
Gold Script-135
Silver Script-135
Super Script-135
96Slovakian Eurotel-18
99SLU Hockey Classic Doubles-2
99SLU Hockey Pro Action Deluxe-40
99Aurora-97
Striped-97
Premiere Date-97
Premiere Date Striped-97
Glove Unlimited-13
99BAP Memorabilia-21
Gold-21
Silver-21
99BAP Update Teammates Jersey Cards-TM33
99BAP Millennium-168
Emerald-168
Ruby-168
Sapphire-168
Signatures-168
Signatures Gold-168
99Black Diamond-58
Diamond Cut-58
Final Cut-58
99Crown Royale-92
Limited Series-92
Premiere Date-92
99O-Pee-Chee-59
99O-Pee-Chee Chrome-59
99O-Pee-Chee Chrome Refractors-59
99Pacific-278
Copper-278
Emerald Green-278
Gold-278
Ice Blue-278
Premiere Date-278
Red-278
Gold Crown Die-Cuts-23
In the Cage Net-Fusions-12
Team Leaders-18
99Pacific Dynagon Ice-134
Blue-134
Copper-134
Gold-134
Premiere Date-134
Masks-3
Masks-8
Masks Holographic Blue-3
Masks Holographic Blue-8
Masks Holographic Gold-3
Masks Holographic Gold-8
Masks Holographic Purple-3
Masks Holographic Purple-8
99Pacific Omega-153
Copper-153
Gold-153
Ice Blue-153
Premiere Date-153
Cup Contenders-14
Game-Used Jerseys-5
99Pacific Prism-92
Holographic Blue-92
Holographic Gold-92
Holographic Mirror-92
Holographic Purple-92
Premiere Date-92
99Panini Stickers-101
99Paramount-156
Copper-156
Emerald-156
Gold-156
Holographic Emerald-156
Holographic Gold-156
Holographic Silver-156
Ice Blue-156
Premiere Date-156
Red-156
Silver-156
Glove Side Net Fusions-13
Personal Best-23
99Revolution-100
Premiere Date-100
Red-100
Shadow Series-100
Showstoppers-23
Copper-100
Gold-100
CSC Silver-100
99SP Authentic-55
99SPx-98
Radiance-98
Spectrum-98
99Stadium Club-85
First Day Issue-85
One of a Kind-85
Printing Plates Black-85
Printing Plates Cyan-85
Printing Plates Magenta-85
Printing Plates Yellow-85
Goalie Cam-GC5
99Topps/OPC-59
99Topps Stanley Cup Heroes-SC16
99Topps Stanley Cup Heroes Refractors-SC16
99Topps/OPC Chrome-59
Refractors-59
99Topps Gold Label Class 1-54
Black-54
Black One of One-54
One of One-54
Red-54
Red One of One-54
99Topps Gold Label Class 2-54
99Topps Gold Label Class 2 Black-54
99Topps Gold Label Class 2 Black 1 of 1-54
99Topps Gold Label Class 2 One of One-54
99Topps Gold Label Class 2 Red-54
99Topps Gold Label Class 2 Red One of One-54
99Topps Gold Label Class 3-54
99Topps Gold Label Class 3 Black-54
99Topps Gold Label Class 3 Black 1 of 1-54
99Topps Gold Label Class 3 One of One-54
99Topps Gold Label Class 3 Red-54
99Topps Gold Label Class 3 Red One of One-54
99Topps Premier Plus-76
Parallel-76
Game Pieces-GPMR
Imperial Guard-IG7
99Ultimate Victory-56
1/1-56
Parallel-56
Parallel 100-56
Net Work-NW5
99Upper Deck-87
Exclusives-87
Exclusives 1 of 1-87
Ultimate Defense-UD7
Ultimate Defense Quantum Gold-UD7
Ultimate Defense Quantum Silver-UD7
99Upper Deck Gold Reserve-87
99Upper Deck HoloGrFx-40
Ausome-40
99Upper Deck MVP-133
Gold Script-133
Silver Script-133
Super Script-133
Draw Your Own Trading Card-W2
99Upper Deck MVP SC Edition-118
Gold Script-118
Silver Script-118
Super Script-118
Great Combinations-GCGR
Great Combinations Parallel-GCGR
99Upper Deck Ovation-37
Standing Ovation-37
99Upper Deck Retro-52
Gold-52
Platinum-52
99Upper Deck Victory-189
99Upper Deck Victory-390
99Wayne Gretzky Hockey-115
Tools of Greatness-TGMR
00Aurora-98
Premiere Date-98
00BAP Memorabilia-52
Emerald-52
Ruby-52
Sapphire-52
Promos-52
Goalie Memorabilia-G1
Jersey Cards-J5
Jersey Emblems-E5
Jersey Numbers-N5
Jersey and Stick Cards-JS5
00BAP Mem Chicago Sportsfest Copper-52
00BAP Memorabilia Chicago Sportsfest Blue-52
00BAP Memorabilia Chicago Sportsfest Gold-52
00BAP Memorabilia Chicago Sportsfest Ruby-52
00BAP Memorabilia Chicago Sun-Times Ruby-52
00BAP Memorabilia Chicago Sun-Times Gold-52
00BAP Mem Chicago Sun-Times Sapphire-52
00BAP Mem Toronto Fall Expo Copper-52
00BAP Memorabilia Toronto Fall Expo Gold-52
00BAP Memorabilia Toronto Fall Expo Ruby-52
00BAP Memorabilia Update Teammates-TM19
00BAP Memorabilia Update Teammates-TM32
00BAP Memorabilia Update Teammates Gold-TM19
00BAP Memorabilia Update Teammates Gold-TM32
00BAP Parkhurst 2000-P110
00BAP Signature Series-165
Emerald-165
Ruby-165
Sapphire-165
Autographs-149
Autographs Gold-149
Jersey Cards-J39
Jersey and Stick Cards-GSJ39
Jersey Cards Autographs-J39
Jersey Emblems-E39
Jersey Numbers-IN39
00BAP Ultimate Memorabilia Autographs-34
Gold-34
00BAP Ultimate Mem Game-Used Jerseys-GJ33
00BAP Ultimate Mem Game-Used Emblems-E29
00BAP Ultimate Mem Game-Used Numbers-N29
00BAP Ultimate Mem Game-Used Sticks-GS33
00BAP Ultimate Memorabilia Goalie Memorabilia-GM15
00BAP Ultimate Memorabilia Goalie Sticks-G20
00BAP Ultimate Mem Plante Jersey Cards-PJ8
00BAP Ultimate Mem Plante Skate Cards-PS8
00Crown Royale-72
Ice Blue-72
Limited Series-72
Premiere Date-72
Red-72
Game-Worn Jerseys-17
Game-Worn Jersey Patches-17
Premium-Sized Game-Worn Jerseys-17
00O-Pee-Chee-45
00O-Pee-Chee Parallel-45
00Pacific-269
Copper-269
Gold-269
Ice Blue-269
Premiere Date-269
In the Cage Net-Fusions-8
00Paramount-167
Copper-167
Gold-167
Holo-Gold-167
Holo-Silver-167
Ice Blue-167
Premiere Date-167
Glove Side Net Fusions-13
Glove Side Net Fusions Platinum-13
00Private Stock-67
Gold-67
Premiere Date-67
Retail-67
Silver-67
Game Gear-78
Game Gear-79
Game Gear Patches-78
Game Gear Patches-79
PS-2001 Action-39
00Revolution-99
Blue-99
Premiere Date-99
Red-99
00SP Authentic BuyBacks-75
00SP Authentic BuyBacks-76
00SP Authentic BuyBacks-77
00SP Authentic BuyBacks-78
00SP Authentic BuyBacks-79
00SP Authentic BuyBacks-80
00SP Authentic BuyBacks-81
00SP Authentic Sign of the Times-MR
00SP Game Used-40
Tools of the Game-MR
Tools of the Game Exclusives-MR
Tools of the Game Combos-C-BR
00Stadium Club-9
00Titanium-63
Blue-63
Gold-63
Premiere Date-63
Red-63
Retail-63
Game Gear-118
Game Gear Patches-118
Three-Star Selections-5
00Titanium Draft Day Edition-68
Patches-68
00Topps/OPC-45
Parallel-45
00Topps Chrome-37
OPC Refractors-37
Refractors-37
00Topps Gold Label Class 1-27
Gold-27
00Topps Gold Label Class 2-27
00Topps Gold Label Class 2 Gold-27
00Topps Gold Label Class 3-27
00Topps Gold Label Class 3 Gold-27
00Topps Gold Label Behind the Mask-BTM10
00Topps Gold Label Behind the Mask 1 to 1-BTM10
00Topps Gold Label Bullion-B9
00Topps Gold Label Bullion One to One-B9
00Topps Heritage-102
00Topps Premier Plus-43
Blue Ice-43
Masters of the Break-MB19
00Topps Stars-86
Blue-86
Game Gear-GGMR
00UD Heroes-81
00UD Pros and Prospects-57
00UD Reserve Buyback Autographs-39
00UD Reserve Buyback Autographs-40
00UD Reserve Buyback Autographs-41
00UD Reserve Buyback Autographs-42
00UD Reserve Buyback Autographs-43
00UD Reserve Buyback Autographs-44
00UD Reserve Buyback Autographs-45
00UD Reserve Buyback Autographs-46
00UD Reserve Buyback Autographs-47
00UD Reserve Buyback Autographs-48
00Upper Deck-115
Exclusives Tier 1-115
Exclusives Tier 2-115
e-Cards-EC10
e-Card Prizes-AMR
e-Card Prizes-EMR
e-Card Prizes-SEMR
Game Jersey Autographs-HMR
Game Jersey Autographs Exclusives-ESMR
Legends of the Cage-LC7
00Upper Deck MVP-119
First Stars-119
Game-Used Souvenirs-GSMR
Second Stars-119
Super Game-Used Souvenirs-GSMR
Third Stars-119
00Upper Deck Victory-151
00Upper Deck Vintage-239
00Upper Deck Vintage-246
00Upper Deck Vintage-247
Great Gloves-GG12
00Vanguard-67
Dual Game-Worn Jerseys-9
Holographic Gold-67
Holographic Purple-67
Pacific Proofs-67
00Czech Stadion-152
01Atomic Statosphere-6
01BAP Memorabilia-222
Emerald-222
Ruby-222
Sapphire-222
Goalies Jerseys-GJ14
Goalie Traditions-GT12
Goalie Traditions-GT35
Goalie Traditions-GT36
Goalie Traditions-GT42
01BAP Sig Series International Medals-IS-1
01BAP Signature Series Jerseys-GJ-41
01BAP Signature Series Jersey Autographs-GUMR
01BAP Sig Series Jersey and Stick Cards-GSJ-41
01BAP Signature Series Emblems-GUE-39
01BAP Signature Series Numbers-ITN-39
01BAP Ultimate Mem Legend Terry Sawchuk-8
01Between the Pipes-50
01Between the Pipes-92
All-Star Jerseys-ASJ8
He Shoots-He Saves Prizes-8
Jerseys-GJ14
Jersey and Stick Cards-GSJ13
Masks-22
Masks Silver-22
Masks Gold-22
01Bowman YoungStars-9
Gold-9
Ice Cubed-9
01Crown Royale-98
Blue-98
Premiere Date-98
Red-98
Retail-98
Triple Threads-15
01O-Pee-Chee-187
01O-Pee-Chee Premier Parallel-187
01Pacific-267
Extreme LTD-267
Hobby LTD-267
Premiere Date-267
Retail LTD-267
Jerseys-22
Steel Curtain-13
01Pacific Adrenaline-130
Blue-130
Premiere Date-130
Red-130
Retail-130
Creased Lightning-13
Jerseys-30
Power Play-24
01Pacific Arena Exclusives-267
01Pacific Heads-Up-66
Blue-66
Premiere Date-66
Red-66
Silver-66
HD NHL-18
Quad Jerseys-14
Quad Jerseys-20
Showstoppers-14
01Parkhurst-178
Jerseys-PJ56
Milestones-M42
01Private Stock-65
Gold-65
Premiere Date-65
Retail-65
Silver-65
Game Gear-69
Game Gear Patches-69
01Private Stock Pacific Nights-65
01Titanium-96
Hobby Parallel-96
Premiere Date-96
Retail-96
Retail Parallel-96
Double-Sided Jerseys-29
Double-Sided Patches-29
Three-Star Selections-7
01Titanium Draft Day Edition-63
01Topps-187
OPC Parallel-187
01Topps Chrome-124
Refractors-124
Black Border Refractors-124
01UD Challenge for the Cup Jerseys-TMR
01UD Challenge for the Cup Jersey Autos-TRI
01UD Honor Roll-96
01UD Mask Collection-120
01UD Mask Collection-183
Gold-120
Gold-183
Double Patches-DPMR
Dual Jerseys-MBRD
Goalie Jerseys-CGMR
Jerseys-J-MR
Jersey and Patch-JPMR
01UD Premier Collection Dual Jerseys-DLR
01UD Premier Collection Dual Jerseys-DRJ
01UD Premier Collection Dual Jerseys Black-DLR
01UD Premier Collection Dual Jerseys Black-DRJ
01UD Premier Collection Jerseys-BMR
01UD Premier Collection Jerseys Black-B-MR
01UD Premier Collection Signatures-BR
01UD Premier Collection Signatures Black-BR
01UD Stanley Cup Champs-83
Pieces of Glory-G-MR
Sticks-S-MR
01UD Top Shelf-107
Jerseys-MR
01Upper Deck-344
Exclusives-344
Game Jerseys-GJMR
Goaltender Threads-TTMR
MVP Goalie Sticks-G-MR
01Upper Deck Victory-229
01Upper Deck Victory-237
Gold-229
Gold-237
01Upper Deck Vintage-168
01Upper Deck Vintage-173
01Vanguard-66
Blue-66
Red-66
Memorabilia-20
One of Ones-66
Premiere Date-66
Proofs-66
Stonewallers-13
02McFarlane Hockey-130
02McFarlane Hockey-132
02Atomic-69
Blue-69
Gold-69
Red-69
Denied-13
Hobby Parallel-69
National Pride-U6
02BAP All-Star Edition-74
Jerseys-74
Jerseys Gold-74
Jerseys Silver-74
02BAP First Edition-128
Jerseys-128
02BAP Memorabilia-154
Emerald-154
Ruby-154
Sapphire-154
All-Star Jerseys-ASJ-47
NHL All-Star Game-154
NHL All-Star Game Blue-154
NHL All-Star Game Green-154
NHL All-Star Game Red-154
02BAP Memorabilia Toronto Fall Expo-154
02BAP Sig Series Auto Buybacks 1998-89
02BAP Sig Series Auto Buybacks 1999-168
02BAP Sig Series Auto Buybacks 2000-149
02BAP Ultimate Memorabilia All-Star MVP-17
02Between the Pipes-29
02Between the Pipes-140
Gold-29
Silver-29
All-Star Stick and Jersey-5
Emblems-21
He Shoots-He Saves Points-9
He Shoots-He Saves Prizes-5
Inspirations-I9
Jerseys-21
Masks II-18
Masks II Gold-18
Masks II Silver-18
Nightmares-GN2
Nightmares-GN6
Numbers-21
Stick and Jerseys-21
Tandems-1
02Crown Royale-65
Blue-65
Red-65
Retail-65
Dual Patches-16
Coats of Armor-7
02ITG Used-50
02ITG Used-150
02O-Pee-Chee-128
02O-Pee-Chee Premier Blue Parallel-128
02O-Pee-Chee Premier Red Parallel-128
02O-Pee-Chee Factory Set-128
02Pacific-258
Blue-258
Red-258
02Pacific Complete-21
Red-21
02Pacific Exclusive-118
Advantage-12
02Pacific Heads-Up-83
Blue-83
Purple-83
Red-83
02Pacific Toronto Fall Expo-6
Gold-6
02Parkhurst-33
Bronze-33
Gold-33
Silver-33
College Ranks-CR17
College Ranks Jerseys-CRM17
Hardware-V5
Milestones-MS4
02Parkhurst Retro-177
Minis-177
02Private Stock Reserve-69
Blue-69
Red-69
Retail-69
InCrease Security-15
02Rangers Team Issue-13
02SP Game Used-58
02SPx-50
Spectrum Gold-50
Spectrum Silver-50
02Stadium Club Puck Stops Here-PSH13
02Topps-128
OPC Blue Parallel-128
OPC Red Parallel-128
Factory Set-128
02Topps Chrome-80
Black Border Refractors-80
Refractors-80
02Topps Heritage-54
Chrome Parallel-54
02Topps Total-193
02UD Honor Roll-48
02UD Mask Collection Career Wins-CWMR
02UD Mask Collection Great Gloves-GGMR
02UD Mask Collection Masked Marvels-MMMR
02UD Mask Collection Nation's Best-NRDM
02UD Mask Collection Patches-PWMR
02UD Mask Collection View from the Cage-VMR
02UD Piece of History-59
02UD Piece of History-105
Marks of Distinction-MR
02UD Top Shelf-57
Clutch Performers-CPMR
Dual Player Jerseys-STFR
Milestones Jerseys-MRBRJ
Stopper Jerseys-SSMR
02Upper Deck-365
Exclusives-365
02Upper Deck Beckett UD Promos-365
02Upper Deck MVP Masked Men-MM5
02Upper Deck Victory-145
Bronze-145
Gold-145
Silver-145
National Pride-NP57
02Upper Deck Vintage-280
02Vanguard Stonewallers-8
03BAP Ultimate Memorabilia Heroes-14
03BAP Ultimate Mem Raised to the Rafters-3
03BAP Ultimate Mem Retro Teammates-4
03Duracell-11
03ITG Action-366
Jerseys-M71
03NHL Sticker Collection-90
03Pacific-231
Blue-231
Red-231
Invincible Jerseys-20
03Parkhurst Original Six New York-51
03Parkhurst Original Six New York-94
Memorabilia-NM7
Memorabilia-NM16
03Private Stock Reserve-184
Blue-184
Patches-184
Red-184
Retail-184
04ITG Franchises Update Goalie Gear-UGG3
04ITG Franchises Update Goalie Gear Gold-UGG3
04ITG Franchises US East-401
Barn Burners-EBB10
Barn Burners Gold-EBB10
Double Memorabilia-EDM22
Double Memorabilia Gold-EDM22
Memorabilia-ESM34
Memorabilia Gold-ESM34
04ITG Ultimate Mem Archives 1st Edition-1
04ITG Ultimate Mem Archives 1st Edition-4
04ITG Ultimate Mem Archives 1st Edition-11
04ITG Ultimate Mem Archives 1st Edition-16
04ITG Ultimate Mem Archives 1st Edition-33
04ITG Ultimate Memorabilia Complete Logo-20
04ITG Ultimate Memorabilia Cornerstones-6
04ITG Ultimate Mem Cornerstones Gold-6
04ITG Ultimate Memorabilia Original Six-4
04ITG Ultimate Memorabilia Original Six-5
05Between the Pipes Jerseys-GUJ-7
05Between the Pipes Jersey and Sticks-SJ-7
05ITG Ultimate Memorabilia In The Numbers-24
05ITG Ultimate Mem In The Numbers Gold-24
05ITG Ultimate Mem Pass the Torch Jerseys-9
05ITG Ultimate Mem Passing Torch Jsy Gold-9
05ITG Ultimate Mem Retro Teammate Jerseys-29
05ITG Ult Mem Retro Teammate Jersey Gold-29
05ITG Ultimate Mem 3 Star of the Game Jsy-23
05ITG Ult Mem 3 Star of the Game Jsy Gold-23
06Between The Pipes Double Jerseys-DJ14
06Between The Pipes Double Jerseys-DJ27
06Between The Pipes Double Jerseys Gold-DJ14
06Between The Pipes Double Jerseys Gold-DJ27
06Between The Pipes Emblems-GUE65
06Between The Pipes Emblems Gold-GUE65
06Between The Pipes Jerseys-GUJ65
06Between The Pipes Jerseys Gold-GUJ65
06Between The Pipes Numbers-GUN65
06Between The Pipes Numbers Gold-GUN65
06Between The Pipes Playing For Your Country-PC20
06Between The Pipes Playing For Your Country Gold-PC20
06Between The Pipes Shooting Gallery-SG05
06Between The Pipes Shooting Gallery-SG08
06Between The Pipes Shooting Gallery Gold-SG05
06Between The Pipes Shooting Gallery Gold-SG08
06Between The Pipes Stick and Jersey-SJ27
06Between The Pipes Stick and Jersey Gold-SJ27
06ITG International Ice-35
06ITG International Ice-97
Gold-35
Gold-97
Cornerstones-IC06
Cornerstones-IC08
Cornerstones Gold-IC06
Cornerstones Gold-IC08
Goaltending Glory-GG06
Goaltending Glory Gold-GG06
Greatest Moments-GM09
Greatest Moments Gold-GM09
International Rivals-IR17
International Rivals Gold-IR17
Passing The Torch-PTT4
Passing The Torch Gold-PTT4
Stick and Jersey-SJ12
Stick and Jersey Gold-SJ12
Teammates-IT12
Teammates Gold-IT12
06ITG Ultimate Memorabilia Passing The Torch-20
06ITG Ultimate Memorabilia Passing The Torch Gold-20
06ITG Ultimate Memorabilia Retro Teammates-23
06ITG Ultimate Memorabilia Retro Teammates Gold-23
06ITG Ultimate Memorabilia Stick Rack-25
06ITG Ultimate Memorabilia Stick Rack Gold-25

Richter, Pavel
79Panini Stickers-88
83Swedish Semic VM Stickers-94
94Czech APS Extraliga-299
98Czech OFS-371
99Czech OFS-444
99Czech OFS-101

Richter, Richard
98Czech OFS-95
99Czech Score Blue 2000-63
99Czech Score Red Ice 2000-63

Rickert, Keith
93Quebec Pee-Wee Tournament-185

Rickles, Don
02Arizona Icecats-31
03Arizona Icecats-29

Riddell, Bryan
01Hull Olympiques-2

Ridderwall, Rolf
83Swedish Semic Elitserien-75
84Swedish Semic Elitserien-74
85Swedish Panini Stickers-69
86Swedish Panini Stickers-57
87Swedish Panini Stickers-68
89Swedish Semic Elitserien Stickers-50
89Swedish Semic World Champ Stickers-4
91Finnish Semic World Champ Stickers-28
91Swedish Semic Elitserien Stickers-320
91Swedish Semic Elitserien Stickers-336
91Swedish Semic World Champ Stickers-28
92Swedish Semic Elitserien Stickers-26
94Finnish Jaa Kiekko-53

Riddle, Jake
03Lethbridge Hurricanes-3
04Peoria Rivermen-15

Riddle, Troy
99Des Moines Buccaneers-6
00Minnesota Golden Gophers-20
01Minnesota Golden Gophers-20
02Minnesota Golden Gophers-18
03Minnesota Golden Gophers-25
05Peoria Rivermen-14

Rideout, Scott
93Portland Winter Hawks-20

Ridler, Glenn
00Kingston Frontenacs-15
01Belleville Bulls Update-8
03Cape Fear Fire Antz-11

Ridley, Curt
76Canucks Royal Bank-15
76O-Pee-Chee NHL-197
76Topps-197
77Canucks Canada Dry Cans-12
77Canucks Royal Bank-17
77O-Pee-Chee NHL-395
78O-Pee-Chee-302
79Canucks Royal Bank-18
80Maple Leafs Postcards-21

Ridley, Mike
86Capitals Kodak-22
86O-Pee-Chee-66
86O-Pee-Chee Box Bottoms-L
86O-Pee-Chee Stickers-131
86O-Pee-Chee Stickers-221
86Topps-66
86Topps Box Bottoms-L
87Capitals Kodak-17
87Capitals Team Issue-20
87O-Pee-Chee-8
87O-Pee-Chee Stickers-234
87Panini Stickers-181
87Topps-8
88Capitals Borderless-18
88Capitals Smokey-20

88O-Pee-Chee-104
88O-Pee-Chee Stickers-74
88Panini Stickers-374
88Topps-104
89Capitals Kodak-17
89Capitals Team Issue-19
89O-Pee-Chee-165
89O-Pee-Chee Box Bottoms-B
89O-Pee-Chee Stickers-81
89Panini Stickers-339
89Topps-165
89Topps Box Bottoms-B
90Bowman-77
Tiffany-77
90Capitals Kodak-22
90Capitals Postcards-20
90Capitals Smokey-19
90O-Pee-Chee-327
90Panini Stickers-163
90Pro Set-320A
90Pro Set-320B
90Score-33
Canadian-33
90Topps-327
Tiffany-327
90Upper Deck-97
French-97
91Pro Set Platinum-128
91Bowman-308
91Capitals Junior 5x7-23
91Capitals Kodak-23
91O-Pee-Chee-245
91Panini Stickers-199
91Parkhurst-192
French-192
91Pinnacle-94
French-94
91Pro Set-254
French-254
91Score American-283
91Score Canadian Bilingual-503
91Score Canadian English-503
91Stadium Club-68
91Topps-245
91Upper Deck-112
French-112
92Bowman-360
92Capitals Kodak-23
92O-Pee-Chee-305
92Panini Stickers-162
92Panini Stickers French-162
92Parkhurst-200
Emerald Ice-200
92Pinnacle-170
French-170
92Score-187
Canadian-187
Sharpshooters-6
Sharpshooters Canadian-6
92Stadium Club-200
92Topps-236
Gold-236G
92Ultra-238
92Upper Deck-173
93Donruss-375
93Leaf-102
93OPC Premier-78
Gold-78
93Panini Stickers-25
93Parkhurst-218
Emerald Ice-218
93Pinnacle-135
Canadian-135
93PowerPlay-266
93Score-197
Canadian-197
93Stadium Club-123
Members Only Master Set-123
OPC-123
First Day Issue-123
First Day Issue OPC-123
93Topps/OPC Premier-78
Gold-78
93Ultra-148
93Upper Deck-341
SP-173
94Canada Games NHL POGS-236
94EA Sports-153
94Flair-185
94Fleer-219
94Leaf-374
94Maple Leafs Kodak-23
94Maple Leafs Pin-up Posters-12
94Maple Leafs Postcards-3
94OPC Premier-301
Special Effects-301
94Parkhurst-250
Gold-250
94Parkhurst SE-SE178
Gold-SE178
94Pinnacle-384
Artist's Proofs-384
Rink Collection-384
94Score-199
Gold-199
Platinum-199
94Select-19
Gold-19
94SP-118
Die Cuts-118
94Stadium Club-105
Members Only Master Set-105
First Day Issue-105
Super Team Winner Cards-105
94Topps/OPC Premier-301
Special Effects-301
94Ultra-378
94Upper Deck-177
Electric Ice-177
SP Inserts-SP169
SP Inserts Die Cuts-SP169
95Be A Player-63
Signatures-S63
Signatures Die Cuts-S63
95Canada Games NHL POGS-270
95Collector's Choice-48
Player's Club-48
Player's Club Platinum-48
95Donruss-250
95Emotion-184
95Leaf-212
95Metal-155
95Panini Stickers-289
95Parkhurst International-214
Emerald Ice-214
95Playoff One on One-319
95Score-236
Black Ice Artist's Proofs-236
Black Ice-236
95SkyBox Impact-173
95Stadium Club-51
Members Only Master Set-51
95Ultra-163
95Ultra-318
Gold Medallion-163
95Upper Deck-75
Electric Ice-75
Electric Ice Gold-75
96Black Diamond-125
Gold-125
96Canucks Postcards-17
96Donruss-141
Press Proofs-141
96Pinnacle-172
Artist's Proofs-172
Foil-172
Premium Stock-172
Rink Collection-172
96Score-184
Artist's Proofs-184
Dealer's Choice Artist's Proofs-184
Special Artist's Proofs-184
Golden Blades-184
97Collector's Choice-264
97Pacific-206
Copper-206
Emerald Green-206
Ice Blue-206
Red-206
Silver-206
97Panini Stickers-243
01Upper Deck Legends-66

Ridolf, Charles
00Connecticut Huskies-13

Ridolfi, Brian
96Dayton Bombers-7
98Dayton Bombers-15
98Dayton Bombers EBK-8

Ridpath, Bruce
10C56-34
10Sweet Caporal Postcards-14
11C55-14
12C57-28

Rieciciar, Pavol
01Czech OFS-164

Ried, Joachim
94German First League-197

Riedel, Beau
96Johnstown Chiefs-16

Riedel, Dan
03Lincoln Stars Update-32
04Lincoln Stars-6
04Lincoln Stars Update-40
04Lincoln Stars Update-47

Rieder, Dana
907th Inn. Sketch WHL-32
917th Inn. Sketch WHL-317

Rieder, Kelly
93St. Cloud State Huskies-23
93St. Cloud State Huskies-30

Rieder, Roger
95Swiss HNL-432
96Swiss HNL-464
99Swiss Panini Stickers-316
00Swiss Panini Stickers-90
01Swiss HNL-250
02Swiss HNL-132

Riedmeier, Erwin
72Finnish Semic World Championship-98
72Swedish Semic World Championship-98

Riege, Brad
05Lethbridge Hurricanes-19
06Moose Jaw Warriors-12

Riehl, Jeremy
917th Inn. Sketch WHL-179

Riehl, Kevin
907th Inn. Sketch WHL-33
917th Inn. Sketch WHL-329
93Raleigh Icecaps-16
94Raleigh Icecaps-17
95Signature Rookies Auto-Phonex-35
95Signature Rook Auto-Phonex Phone Cards-35
00UK Sekonda Superleague-25
01UK Belfast Giants-6
03Bakersfield Condors-11

Riekkinen, Antti
98Finnish Keraillysarja-155

Riekkinen, Paavo
70Finnish Jaakiekko-234

Riel, Danick Jasmin
03Rimouski Oceanic Sheets-1

Riel, Guy
80Quebec Remparts-18

Riendeau, Don
92North Dakota Fighting Sioux-28

Riendeau, Vincent
86Sherbrooke Canadiens-22
87Blues Team Issue-20
88Blues Kodak-19
88Blues Team Issue-20
89Blues Kodak-30
89O-Pee-Chee Stickers-146
89O-Pee-Chee Stickers-265
89Panini Stickers-120
90Blues Kodak-18
90Bowman-20
Tiffany-20
90O-Pee-Chee-177
90Panini Stickers-268
90Pro Set-270
90Score-107
Canadian-107
90Topps-177
Tiffany-177
90Upper Deck-152
French-152
91Pro Set Platinum-112
91Bowman-372
91O-Pee-Chee-370
91Pro Set-213
French-213
91Score American-23
91Score Canadian Bilingual-23
91Score Canadian English-23
91Score Rookie/Traded-43T
91Stadium Club-128
91Topps-370
91Upper Deck-220
French-220
92Bowman-262
92Parkhurst-278
Emerald Ice-278
92Pinnacle-177
French-177
92Score-396
Canadian-396
92Stadium Club-172
92Topps-466
Gold-466G
92Ultra-288
93OPC Premier-411
Gold-411
93Pinnacle-312
Canadian-312
93Score-276
Canadian-276
93Topps/OPC Premier-411
Gold-411
94Canada Games NHL POGS-272
94Flair-13
94Kraft-53
94Kraft Goalie Masks-6
94OPC Premier-324
Special Effects-324
94Parkhurst-14
Gold-14
94Pinnacle-212
Artist's Proofs-212
Rink Collection-212
94Stadium Club-43
Members Only Master Set-43
First Day Issue-43
Super Team Winner Cards-43
94Topps/OPC Premier-324
Special Effects-324
94Ultra-15
95German DEL-335

Riendeau, Yanick
01Drummondville Voltigeurs-12
02Drummondville Voltigeurs-11
03Drummondville Voltigeurs-20

Riesen, Daniel
93Swiss HNL-162

Riesen, Michel
95Swiss HNL-282
96Swiss HNL-402
98Swiss Power Play Stickers-285
99Swiss Panini Stickers-297
99Hamilton Bulldogs-21
00BAP Memorabilia-480
Emerald-480
Ruby-480
Sapphire-480
00Black Diamond-119
00SP Authentic-144
Sign of the Times-RI
00Titanium Draft Day Edition-160
00Titanium Draft Day Promos-160
00Topps Heritage-100
Chrome Parallel-100
00Topps Premier Plus-111
Blue Ice-111
00Topps Stars-123
Blue-123
00UD Heroes-164
00UD Pros and Prospects-105
00Upper Deck-412
Exclusives Tier 1-412
Exclusives Tier 2-412
00Upper Deck Vintage-379
00Vanguard-119
Pacific Proofs-119
00Swiss Panini Stickers National Team-P26
00Hamilton Bulldogs-21
01BAP Memorabilia-177
Emerald-177
Ruby-177
Sapphire-177
02Swiss HNL-9
02Swiss HNL-487
04Swiss Davos Postcards-24

Riffel, Kevin
91Air Canada SJHL-89

Riggin, Dennis
52Juniors Blue Tint-1

Riggin, Pat
79Flames Postcards-16
79Flames Team Issue-17
80Flames Postcards-18
80Pepsi-Cola Caps-16
81Flames Postcards-19
81O-Pee-Chee-37
81O-Pee-Chee Stickers-12
81O-Pee-Chee Stickers-221
81Topps-30
82Capitals Team Issue-22
82O-Pee-Chee-372
82Post Cereal-3
83Puffy Stickers-21
84Capitals Pizza Hut-14
84O-Pee-Chee-205
84O-Pee-Chee-218
84O-Pee-Chee-386
84O-Pee-Chee Stickers-65
84O-Pee-Chee Stickers-233
84Topps-148
84Topps-164
85Capitals Pizza Hut-13
85O-Pee-Chee-136
85O-Pee-Chee Stickers-106
85Topps-136
86O-Pee-Chee Stickers-41
87Penguins Kodak-22

Riggin, Travis
93Kitchener Rangers-7
93Kitchener Rangers-29
94Kitchener Rangers-9
95Slapshot-173

Rigolet, Gerald
72Finnish Semic World Championship-158
72Swedish Semic World Championship-158

Riha, Lukas
02Czech OFS Plus-206
03Czech OFS Plus-101
04Czech OFS-103

Riha, Milos
96Czech APS Extraliga-142
97Czech APS Extraliga-242
98Czech OFS-374
99Czech OFS-308
00Czech OFS-287
06Czech OFS Coaches-9

Riihijarvi, Heikki
92Finnish Jyvas-Hyva Stickers-64
93Finnish Jyvas-Hyva Stickers-116
93Finnish SISU-10

Riihijarvi, Juha
92Finnish Jyvas-Hyva Stickers-73
93Finnish SISU-369
93Finnish SISU-369B
93Finnish SISU-384
93Finnish SISU-384B
93Swedish Semic World Champ Stickers-74
93Classic-45
94Finnish SISU-301
94Finnish SISU-382
94Finnish SISU Horoscopes-12
94Finnish Jaa Kiekko-40
94Classic Pro Prospects-48
95Finnish SISU-99
95Finnish SISU Limited-35
95Finnish SISU Spotlights-3
95Finnish Semic World Championships-46
96Finnish SISU Redline-179
96Finnish SISU Redline-NNO
At The Gala-2
96Swedish Semic Wien-34
97Swedish Collector's Choice-146
Crash the Game Exchange-C14
Crash the Game Redemption-R14
98Finnish Keraillysarja Leijonat-37
98Swedish UD Choice-162
99Swedish Upper Deck-164
Lasting Impressions-9
00Swedish Upper Deck-144
Top Playmakers-P7
02Finnish Cardset-106
02Swedish Malmo Red Hawks-10
02Swedish SHL-74
Dynamic Duos-6
Parallel-74
Sharpshooters-SS5
Signatures Series II-12
03Swedish Elite-95
Silver-95
Stars of the Game-7
06Swedish SHL Elitset-98
Performers-12

Riihijarvi, Teemu
95Collector's Choice-331
Player's Club-331
Player's Club Platinum-331
95Upper Deck-548
Electric Ice-548
Electric Ice Gold-548
95Finnish SISU-92
Drafted Dozen-2
95Classic-12
Ice Breakers-BK11
Ice Breakers Die Cuts-BK11
96Finnish SISU Redline-91
98Finnish Keraillysarja-27
99Finnish Cardset-18
99Finnish Cardset-282
Most Wanted-4
00Finnish Cardset-315
01Finnish Cardset-102
02Finnish Cardset-107
04Swedish Elitset-117
Gold-117

Riihimaki, Hannu
80Finnish Mallasjuoma-21

Riihimaki, Markku
70Finnish Jaakiekko-202
71Finnish Suomi Stickers-91
72Finnish Jaakiekko-256
73Finnish Jaakiekko-256

Riihinen, Jani
95Collector's Choice Players Club-330
95Collectors Choice Players Club Platinum-330
98Finnish Keraillysarja-8

Riihiranta, Heikki
70Finnish Jaakiekko-76
70Finnish Jaakiekko-107
70Finnish Jaakiekko-114
70Swedish Hockey-300
70Swedish Masterserien-160
71Finnish Suomi Stickers-123
72Finnish Jaakiekko-74
72Finnish Jaakiekko-93
72Finnish Hellas-13
72Finnish Panda Toronto-11
73Finnish Jaakiekko-78
73Finnish Jaakiekko-140
73Swedish Stickers-34
74O-Pee-Chee WHA-31
74Finnish Typotor-4
74Finnish Typotor-55
74Swedish Stickers-30
74Swedish Semic World Champ Stickers-80
75O-Pee-Chee WHA-125
76O-Pee-Chee WHA-58
78Finnish SM-Liiga-25
80Finnish Mallasjuoma-4

Riihnen, Jani
95Collector's Choice-330

Riitahaara, Pentti
65Finnish Hellas-68
66Finnish Jaakiekkosarja-19

Rikala, Jorma
65Finnish Hellas-49
70Finnish Jaakiekko-115
71Finnish Suomi Stickers-124
72Finnish Jaakiekko-94
72Finnish Panda Toronto-12
73Finnish Jaakiekko-141

Riksman, Juuso
02Swedish SHL-237
Parallel-237
03Swedish Elite-99
Silver-99
Zero Hero-8
04Finnish Cardset-228
04Swedish Pure Skills-112
Parallel-112
05Finnish Cardset -339
06Finnish Cardset-236
Between the Pipes-10
Superior Snatchers-8
Superior Snatchers Gold-8
Superior Snatchers Silver-8
Trophy Winners-4

Rilcof, Kevan
91British Columbia JHL-5
92British Columbia JHL-22

Riley, Bill
77O-Pee-Chee NHL-360
78Capitals Team Issue-12
78O-Pee-Chee-292
79O-Pee-Chee-303
83Nova Scotia Voyageurs-9

Riley, Derek
97Austin Ice Bats-14
97El Paso Buzzards-12

Riley, Jack
34Sweet Caporal-14
35Diamond Matchbooks Tan 1-55

Rimmel, Patrik
94Czech APS Extraliga-10
95Czech APS Extraliga-107
00Czech OFS-270
01Czech OFS-230
03Czech OFS Plus-214
03Czech OFS Plus-350
04Czech OFS-239

Rimroth, Holger
94German First League-430

Rimsky, Dalibor
96Czech APS Extraliga-116

Rinaldo, Niklas
98Danish Hockey League-145
99German Bundesliga 2-169

Rindell, Harri
92Finnish Jyvas-Hyva Stickers-1
93Finnish Jyvas-Hyva Stickers-13
95Finnish SISU-391

Ring, Tomas
91Swedish Semic Elitserien Stickers-138

Ringberg, Victor
05Swedish SHL Elitset-222
Gold-222

Ringler, Tim
81Milwaukee Admirals-15

Ringuet, Christian
92Quebec Pee-Wee Tournament-390
93Quebec Pee-Wee Tournament-1341

Ringuet, Mathieu
93Quebec Pee-Wee Tournament-251

Rink, Tim
03Cape Fear Fire Antz-12

Rinkinen, Juha-Pekka
96Finnish SISU Redline-115

Rinne, Jouni
73Finnish Jaakiekko-315
77Finnish Sportscasters-87-2072
78Finnish SM-Liiga-169

Rinne, Pekka
04Finnish Cardset-257
05ITG Heroes/Prosp Toronto Expo Parallel -233
05Black Diamond-258
05Hot Prospects-146
En Fuego-146
Red Hot-146
White Hot-146
05SP Authentic-271
Limited-271
05SP Game Used-221
05SPx-272
05The Cup Master Pressplate Artifact-295
05The Cup Master Pressplate Black Diamond-258
05The Cup Masterpiece Pressplates (Ice)-251
05The Cup Master Pressplate Rookie Update-153
05The Cup Masterpiece Pressplates SPA-271
05The Cup Masterpiece Pressplates SP GU-221
05The Cup Masterpiece Pressplates (SPx)-272
05The Cup Masterpiece Pressplates Trilogy-276
05The Cup Master Pressplate Ult Coll-214
05UD Artifacts-295
05Ultimate Collection-214
Gold-214
05Upper Deck Ice-251
05Upper Deck Rookie Update-153
05Upper Deck Trilogy-276
05Finnish Cardset -87
05AHL All-Stars-31
05AHL Top Prospects-35
05Milwaukee Admirals Choice-11
05Milwaukee Admirals Pepsi-16
05ITG Heroes and Prospects-233
Autographs Series II-PRI
06Between The Pipes-42
Autographs-APRI
Emblems-GUE31
Emblems Gold-GUE31
Emblems Autographs-GUE31
Jerseys-GUJ31
Jerseys Gold-GUJ31
Jerseys Autographs-GUJ31
Numbers-GUN31
Numbers Gold-GUN31
Numbers Autographs-GUN31
Stick and Jersey-SJ28
Stick and Jersey Gold-SJ28
Stick and Jersey Autographs-SJ28
06Milwaukee Admirals -15
06ITG Heroes and Prospects AHL Shooting Stars-AS01

Rintanen, Kimmo
92Upper Deck-618
93Finnish Jyvas-Hyva Stickers-229
93Finnish SISU-203
93Finnish SISU Autographs-203
94Finnish SISU-257
95Finnish SISU-130
95Finnish Semic World Championships-19
95Finnish Semic World Championships-229
96Finnish SISU Redline-145
Mighty Adversaries-1
96Finnish SISU Redline Promos-11
98Finnish Keraillysarja-109
Leijonat-38
Off Duty-5
99Finnish Cardset-196
99Finnish Cardset-333
00Finnish Cardset-97
00Finnish Cardset-355
01Finnish Cardset-177
01Swiss HNL-72
02Finnish Cardset-108
02Swiss HNL-134

Rintoul, Ryan
99Tupelo T-Rex-19
01Bossier-Shreveport Mudbugs-16

Riopel, Nicola
06Between The Pipes-41
Autographs-ANR
06Moncton Wildcats-1

Riopelle, Howard
43Parade Sportive *-79
44Beehive Group II Photos-285
45Quaker Oats Photos-110A
45Quaker Oats Photos-110B
51Laval Dairy QSHL-101
52St. Lawrence Sales-55

Riou, Kelly
01El Paso Buzzards-5

Rioux, Alexandre
92Quebec Pee-Wee Tournament-23
93Quebec Pee-Wee Tournament-353

Rioux, Daniel
80Quebec Remparts-19

Rioux, Luc
96Detroit Whalers-22

Rioux, Pierre
84Moncton Golden Flames-25
94German DEL-92
96German DEL-271

Rioux, Sebastien
05Saint John's Sea Dogs-21
06Saint Johns Sea Dogs-8

Ripley, Dwayne
95Neepewa Natives-5

Ripley, Vic
33O-Pee-Chee V304B-67
33V357 Ice Kings-54
34Diamond Matchbooks Silver-51
35Diamond Matchbooks Tan 1-56

Riplinger, Brent
92Northern Michigan Wildcats-20
93Northern Michigan Wildcats-23

Risdale, Mike
89Regina Pats-18
907th Inn. Sketch WHL-166
917th Inn. Sketch WHL-238

Risebrough, Doug
74Canadiens Postcards-18
75Canadiens Postcards-14
75Heroes Stand-Ups-12
75O-Pee-Chee NHL-107
75Topps-107
76Canadiens Postcards-16
76O-Pee-Chee NHL-109
76O-Pee-Chee NHL-388
76Topps-109
77Canadiens Postcards-19
77O-Pee-Chee NHL-189
77Topps-189
78Canadiens Postcards-21
78O-Pee-Chee-249
78Topps-249
79Canadiens Postcards-19
79O-Pee-Chee-13
79Topps-13
80Canadiens Postcards-19
80O-Pee-Chee-275
80Pepsi-Cola Caps-55
81Canadiens Postcards-22
81O-Pee-Chee-190
82O-Pee-Chee-57
82Post Cereal-10
83NHL Key Tags-17
83O-Pee-Chee-92
83O-Pee-Chee Stickers-269
83Puffy Stickers-1
83Topps Stickers-269
83Vachon-18
84Kellogg's Accordion Discs-2
84Kellogg's Accordion Discs Singles-31
84O-Pee-Chee-236
84O-Pee-Chee Stickers-241
847-Eleven Discs-8
85Flames Red Rooster-25
85Flames Red Rooster-26
85O-Pee-Chee-243
86Flames Red Rooster-24
86Kraft Drawings-59
86O-Pee-Chee-196
86Topps-196
87Flames Red Rooster-26
88Flames Postcards-26
90Flames IGA/McGavin's-24
90Pro Set-663
91Flames IGA-29

Rishaug, Ryan
95Kamloops Blazers-23

Risidore, Ryan
93Guelph Storm-5
94Guelph Storm-5
94Signature Rookies Tetrad *-112
Signatures-112
95Slapshot-85
95Guelph Storm-20
96Springfield Falcons-28
97Indianapolis Ice-22
98Hartford Wolf Pack-15
99Hamilton Bulldogs-20
00Hamilton Bulldogs-3
02Columbus Cottonmouths-16
03Columbus Cottonmouths-25

Risk, Dave
99Charlotte Checkers-8

Riska, Filip
05Finnish Cardset -247

Risku, Rainer
78Finnish SM-Liiga-85
80Finnish Mallasjuoma-19

Rissling, Gary
84Penguins Heinz Photos-17
02Fleer Throwbacks-85
Gold-85
Platinum-85

Rissling, Jaynen
98Amarillo Rattlers-15

Rissling, Kelly
83Pinebridge Bucks-10

Rissmiller, Pat
02Cleveland Barons-19
03ITG VIP Rookie Debut-60
03Parkhurst Rookie-125
03SP Authentic-120
Limited-120
03UD Honor Roll-139
03Upper Deck-471
Canadian Exclusives-471
HG-471
UD Exclusives-471
03Upper Deck Rookie Update-150
03Cleveland Barons-19
04Cleveland Barons-20
05AHL All-Stars-32
06Cleveland Barons-19

Rita, Jani
98Black Diamond-97
Double Diamond-97
Triple Diamond-97
Quadruple Diamond-97
98SPx Top Prospects-67
Radiance-67
Spectrum-67
98Finnish Keraillysarja-106
99SPx-171
Radiance-171
Spectrum-171
99Finnish Cardset-60
Most Wanted-5
00Finnish Cardset-45
00Finnish Cardset Next Generation-4
01SPx-173
01Hamilton Bulldogs-12
02O-Pee-Chee-287
02O-Pee-Chee Premier Blue Parallel-287
02O-Pee-Chee Premier Red Parallel-287
02O-Pee-Chee Factory Set-287
02Pacific Calder-69
Silver-69
02Pacific Complete-542
Red-542
02SPx-110
02Stadium Club-117
Silver Decoy Cards-117
Proofs-117
02Topps-287
OPC Blue Parallel-287
OPC Red Parallel-287
Factory Set-287
02Topps Chrome-146
Black Border Refractors-146
Refractors-146
02UD Foundations-129
02UD Piece of History-130
02Upper Deck-314
Exclusives-314
02Upper Deck Beckett UD Promos-314
02Upper Deck Vintage-332
02Finnish Cardset-253
02AHL Top Prospects-37
02Hamilton Bulldogs-12
03ITG Action-240
03Upper Deck MVP-172
Gold Script-172
Silver Script-172
Canadian Exclusives-172
03AHL Top Prospects-30
03Pacific AHL Prospects-90
Gold-90
04Finnish Cardset-42
04Finnish Cardset Signatures-11
04Swedish Pure Skills-111
Parallel-111
05Parkhurst-398
Facsimile Auto Parallel-398
05SP Authentic Scripts to Success-SSJR
05SP Authentic Sign of the Times-JA
05Upper Deck-326
Notable Numbers-N-JAR
05Upper Deck MVP-164
Gold-164
Platinum-164
06Finnish Cardset-242

Ritchie, Andrew
93Quebec Pee-Wee Tournament-494

Ritchie, Byron
93Lethbridge Hurricanes-12
95Lethbridge Hurricanes-19
96Lethbridge Hurricanes-13
97Bowman CHL-108
OPC-108
98Hurricanes Team Issue-12
98New Haven Beast-5
99BAP Memorabilia-7
Gold-7
Silver-7
99Pacific-83
Copper-83
Emerald Green-83
Gold-83
Ice Blue-83
Premiere Date-83
Red-83
99Paramount-254
99SP Authentic-95
99Upper Deck MVP SC Edition-41
Gold Script-41
Silver Script-41
Super Script-41
00Upper Deck Victory-274
00Cincinnati Cyclones-4
01BAP Memorabilia-309
Emerald-309
Ruby-309
Sapphire-309
01Parkhurst-357

Ritchie, Darren
92Brandon Wheat Kings-19
93Brandon Wheat Kings-17
94Brandon Wheat Kings-18
95Saint John Flames-19
95South Carolina Stingrays-11
95Slapshot Memorial Cup-40
99German Bundesliga 2-48

Ritchie, Jim
89Sault Ste. Marie Greyhounds-6
91Nashville Knights-20

Ritola, Mattias
05Swedish SHL Elitset Rookies-5

Ritsch, Andreas
93Swiss HNL-117
95Swiss HNL-221
96Swiss HNL-455

Ritson, Joe
01Missouri River Otters-22
03Kalamazoo Wings-25
03Missouri River Otters-17

Ritthaler, Dimitri
94German First League-646

Riutta, Bruce
70Swedish Masterserien-181
72Finnish Semic World Championship-120
72Swedish Semic World Championship-120

Riutta, Topi
99Finnish Cardset-277

Riva, Dan
93Omaha Lancers-20
99Milwaukee Admirals Keebler-16
00Milwaukee Admirals Keebler-14
00Milwaukee Admirals Postcards-12
01Manchester Monarchs-13B
02Manchester Monarchs-25
02Reading Royals-22
02Reading Royals RBI Sports-179
03Trenton Titans-364

Riva, Luigi
93Swiss HNL-144
95Swiss HNL-194
96Swiss HNL-158
98Swiss Power Play Stickers-304
99Swiss Panini Stickers-310

Rivard, Bobby
99Fort Wayne Komets Points Leaders-15

Rivard, Fern
74NHL Action Stamps-142

Rivard, Francois
907th Inn. Sketch QMJHL-102
917th Inn. Sketch QMJHL-130

Rivard, Jean-Francois
917th Inn. Sketch QMJHL-181
98Thunder Bay Thunder Cats-17
98UHL All-Stars-15
99Rockford IceHogs-16
00Rockford IceHogs-14
01Rockford IceHogs-10

Rivard, Ryan
97Owen Sound Platers-11
98Kingston Frontenacs-17
05Florida Seals Team Issue-12

Rivard, Stefan
93North Bay Centennials-12
94North Bay Centennials-14
01Atlantic City Boardwalk Bullies-18
02Atlantic City Boardwalk Bullies-19
03Atlantic City Boardwalk Bullies-20
03Atlantic City Boardwalk Bullies RBI-28
04Atlantic City Boardwalk Bullies Kinko's-19

Rivers, A.J.
97Halifax Mooseheads II-17

Rivers, Andy
84Kingston Canadians-15
86Kingston Canadians-14

Rivers, Daryl
93London Knights-15
95Slapshot-280

Rivers, Gus
36Providence Reds-7

Rivers, Jamie
917th Inn. Sketch OHL-257
91Sudbury Wolves-8
92Sudbury Wolves-9
93Sudbury Wolves-8
93Sudbury Wolves Police-8
94Slapshot Promos-6
94Slapshot Promos-7
94Finest-152
Super Team Winners-152
Refractors-152
94Leaf Limited World Juniors Canada-8
94Pinnacle-526
Artist's Proofs-526
Rink Collection-526
94SP-141
Die Cuts-141
94Upper Deck-501
Electric Ice-501
94Sudbury Wolves-7
94Sudbury Wolves Police-23
95Bowman-132
All-Foil-132
95Donruss-342
Canadian World Junior Team-7
95SkyBox Impact-218
95Topps Canadian World Juniors-21CJ
95Upper Deck-477
Electric Ice-477
Electric Ice Gold-477
95Classic-97
95Signature Rookies-36
Auto-Phonex Beyond 2000-B1
Signatures-36
96Leaf-236
Press Proofs-236
96Pinnacle-216
Artist's Proofs-216
Foil-216
Premium Stock-216
Rink Collection-216
96SkyBox Impact-158
96Upper Deck-145
96Collector's Edge Future Legends-40
96Collector's Edge Ice-95
Prism-95
97Be A Player-231
Autographs-231
Autographs Die-Cuts-231
Autographs Prismatic Die-Cuts-231
97Pacific Omega-198
Copper-198
Dark Gray-198
Emerald Green-198
Gold-198
Ice Blue-198
97Score Blues-13
Platinum-13
Premier-13
97Sudbury Wolves Anniversary-18
98Pacific-372
Ice Blue-372
Red-372
98Upper Deck-359
Exclusives-359
Exclusives 1 of 1-359
Gold Reserve-359
00BAP Memorabilia-384
Emerald-384
Ruby-384
Sapphire-384
Promos-384
00BAP Mem Chicago Sportsfest Copper-384
00BAP Memorabilia Chicago Sportsfest Blue-384
00BAP Memorabilia Chicago Sportsfest Gold-384
00BAP Memorabilia Chicago Sportsfest Ruby-384
00BAP Memorabilia Chicago Sun-Times Ruby-384
00BAP Memorabilia Chicago Sun-Times Gold-384
00BAP Mem Chicago Sun-Times Sapphire-384
00BAP Mem Toronto Fall Expo Copper-384
00BAP Memorabilia Toronto Fall Expo Gold-384
00BAP Memorabilia Toronto Fall Expo Ruby-384
00Senators Team Issue-20
00Upper Deck NHLPA-PA63
01O-Pee-Chee-255
01O-Pee-Chee Premier Parallel-255
01Topps-255
OPC Parallel-255
03Parkhurst Original Six Detroit-14
04Hershey Bears Patriot News-22

Rivers, Korren
93Quebec Pee-Wee Tournament-1098

Rivers, Shawn
907th Inn. Sketch OHL-393
90Sudbury Wolves-18
917th Inn. Sketch OHL-260
91Sudbury Wolves-9
92Atlanta Knights-16
93Score-470
Canadian-470
93Atlanta Knights-16
94Classic Pro Prospects-107
94Signature Rookies Tetrad *-113
Signatures-113
96German DEL-8
96Collector's Edge Ice-108
Prism-108

Rivers, Wayne
61Hamilton Red Wings-16
63Topps-17
64Toronto Star-42
72O-Pee-Chee-315
73Quaker Oats WHA-44
74O-Pee-Chee WHA-13
75O-Pee-Chee WHA-38
76San Diego Mariners WHA-11

Rivet, Adam
99Hull Olympiques-20
Signed-20
00Hull Olympiques-20
Signed-20
00QMJHL All-Star Program Inserts-30

Rivet, Craig
917th Inn. Sketch OHL-235
93Kingston Frontenacs-21
94Fredericton Canadiens-24
95Leaf-310
95Fredericton Canadiens-23
96Canadiens Postcards-23
96Canadiens Sheets-17
96Fredericton Canadiens-18
97Be A Player-102
Autographs-102
Autographs Die-Cuts-102

Autographs Prismatic Die-Cuts-102
97Canadiens Postcards-18
97Pacific Dynagon Best Kept Secrets-51
98Canadiens Team Issue-17
99Stadium Club-76
First Day Issue-76
One of a Kind-76
Printing Plates Black-76
Printing Plates Cyan-76
Printing Plates Magenta-76
Printing Plates Yellow-76
00Canadiens Postcards-22
01Canadiens Postcards-20
02BAP First Edition-179
02Canadiens Postcards-17
02NHL Power Play Stickers-67
02Pacific Complete-314
Red-314
02Parkhurst Teammates-TT7
02Topps Total-326
02Upper Deck-341
Exclusives-341
02Upper Deck Beckett UD Promos-341
02Upper Deck Vintage-136
03Canadiens Postcards-23
03ITG Action-321
03NHL Sticker Collection-58
03Pacific Complete-385
Red-385
03Parkhurst Original Six Montreal-14
Memorabilia-MM6
04Finnish Cardset-304
04Swedish Pure Skills-140
Parallel-140
Professional Power-CR
05Be A Player Signatures-CR
05Be A Player Signatures Gold-CR
05Canadiens Team Issue-18
05Parkhurst-256
Facsimile Auto Parallel-256
05Upper Deck-102
HG Glossy-102
05Upper Deck MVP-214
Gold-214
Platinum-214
05Upper Deck Toronto Fall Expo-102
06Finnish Cardset Magicmakers-17
06Canadiens Postcards-18
06O-Pee-Chee-271
Rainbow-271
06Upper Deck-357
Exclusives Parallel-357
High Gloss Parallel-357
Masterpieces-357

Rizk, Jean-Michel
03Saginaw Spirit-20
03Saginaw Spirit-26
04Saginaw Spirit-3
05Kitchener Rangers-21
06Kitchener Rangers-17

Rizk, Marc-Andre
03Saginaw Spirit-21
03Saginaw Spirit-26

Rizzi, Sandro
98Swiss Power Play Stickers-68
98Swiss Power Play Stickers-286
99Swiss Panini Stickers-71
99Swiss Panini Stickers-272
00Swiss Panini Stickers-119
00Swiss Slapshot Mini-Cards-HCD13
01Swiss HNL-120
02Swiss HNL-260
04Swiss Davos Postcards-25

Rizzi, Tony
04Kingston Frontenacs-22
05Kingston Frontenacs-11

Rjabykin, Dimitri
95Upper Deck-557
Electric Ice-557
Electric Ice Gold-557

Roach, Andy
98UHL All-Star Western Conference-9
98Long Beach Ice Dogs-15
99German DEL-126
01German Upper Deck-175
02German DEL City Press-253
03German DEL-12
All-Stars-AS6
03German Mannheim Eagles Postcards-10
03German Mannheim Eagles Postcards-32
04Swiss Lausanne HC Postcards-5
05Hot Prospects-165
En Fuego-165
Red Hot-165
White Hot-165
05SPx-193
Spectrum-193
05The Cup Masterpiece Pressplates (Ice)-165
05The Cup Master Pressplate Rookie Update-172
05The Cup Masterpiece Pressplates (SPx)-193
05Ultra-246
Gold-246
Ice-246
05Upper Deck Ice-165
05Upper Deck Rookie Update-172
06German DEL-23
New Arrivals-NA8

Roach, Brandon
03Lewiston Maineiacs-17

Roach, Brent
00Hull Olympiques-18
Signed-18
01Hull Olympiques-17
02Hull Olympiques-16
03Hull Olympiques Memorial Cup-14

Roach, Dave
88ProCards AHL-76

Roach, Gary
917th Inn. Sketch OHL-337
93Sault Ste. Marie Greyhounds-13
93Sault Ste. Marie Greyhound Memorial Cup-14
94North Bay Centennials-23
96Louisiana Ice Gators-15
98Louisiana Ice Gators-15
99UHL All-Stars East-8T
01Flint Generals-16

Roach, John
23V145-1-28
24C144 Champ's Cigarettes-50
24V145-2-52
33O-Pee-Chee V304B-53
33V129-18
33V252 Canadian Gum-41
33V357 Ice Kings-67

Roach, Jordan
02Bakersfield Condors-14
03Tulsa Oilers-16

Roach, Mickey
23V145-1-38
24C144 Champ's Cigarettes-51
24V130 Maple Crispette-23
24V145-2-18

Roach, Morgan
98Sioux City Musketeers-21

Roadhouse, Sean
06Texas Tornados-12

Rob, Lubos
93Swedish Semic World Champ Stickers-97
94Czech APS Extraliga-106
95Czech APS Extraliga-67
96Czech APS Extraliga-252
97Czech APS Extraliga-277
97Czech DS Extraliga-32
97Czech DS Stickers-87
98Czech DS Stickers-75
98Czech OFS-418
98Finnish Kerailysarja-161
99Czech DS-39
99Czech OFS-186
00Czech DS Extraliga-80
00Czech OFS-17
01Czech OFS-145
02Czech OFS Plus-183
03Czech OFS Plus-270
03Czech OFS Plus Insert C-C1
03Czech OFS Plus Insert G-G1
03Czech OFS Plus Insert S-S6
06Czech HC Vsetin Postcards-6
06Czech OFS-187

Robazzo, Rino
61Topps-39
63Quebec Aces-20
65Quebec Aces-17

Robb, Doug
81Milwaukee Admirals-12

Robbert, Thomas
99Danish Hockey League-196

Robbins, Adam
95Slapshot-41
96Fort Worth Fire-14
97Fort Worth Brahmas-16
98Port Huron Border Cats-3
00Lubbock Cotton Kings-19

Robbins, Matt
94Classic Pro Prospects-230
96Charlotte Checkers-14

Roberg, Chad
99Minnesota Golden Gophers-20
00Minnesota Golden Gophers-21
01Minnesota Golden Gophers-6
02Minnesota Golden Gophers-19

Roberge, Aaron
03Portland Winter Hawks-8

Roberge, David
93Quebec Pee-Wee Tournament-223

Roberge, Dick
71Johnstown Jets Acme-12

Roberge, Jean
907th Inn. Sketch QMJHL-53
917th Inn. Sketch QMJHL-234
98Thetford Mines Coyotes-20
01Thetford Mines Coyotes-13
02Thetford Mines Coyotes-19
03Thetford Mines Prolab-19

Roberge, Mario
88ProCards AHL-290
89ProCards AHL-187
90ProCards AHL/IHL-57
91Canadiens Postcards-23
91Pro Set-415
French-415
92Canadiens Postcards-22
92Durivage Panini-27
92Parkhurst-322
Emerald Ice-322
93Canadiens Postcards-21
93Durivage Score-16
95Fredericton Canadiens-24
02Fleer Throwbacks-90
Gold-90
Platinum-90

Roberge, Philippe
04Drummondville Voltigeurs-2
04ITG Heroes and Prospects-99
Autographs-PR
04ITG Heroes/Prospects Toronto Expo '05-99
04ITG Heroes/Prospects Expo Heroes/Pros-99
05Rimouski Oceanic-13

Roberge, Roger
51Laval Dairy Subset-44
52St. Lawrence Sales-73

Roberge, Serge
88ProCards AHL-286
89ProCards AHL-200
90Nordiques Petro-Canada-37
90Halifax Citadels-21
90ProCards AHL/IHL-454
91ProCards-538
95Rochester Americans-17
02Fleer Throwbacks-91
Gold-91
Platinum-91

Robert, Claude
51Laval Dairy QSHL-17
52St. Lawrence Sales-47

Robert, Jonathan
00Sherbrooke Castors-9
Signed-9
01Sherbrooke Castors-12
02Rimouski Oceanic-14
06Rio Grande Valley Killer Bees-7

Robert, Maxime
02Cape Breton Screaming Eagles-5
03Gatineau Olympiques-20
03Lewiston Maineiacs-18

Robert, Rene
71Penguins Postcards-16
71Toronto Sun-225
72O-Pee-Chee-2
72Sabres Postcards-16
72Sargent Promotions Stamps-42
72Topps-161
73O-Pee-Chee-139
73Topps-139
74Lipton Soup-24
74NHL Action Stamps-49
74O-Pee-Chee NHL-42
74O-Pee-Chee NHL-142
74Sabres Postcards-19
74Topps-42
74Topps-142
75O-Pee-Chee NHL-46
75O-Pee-Chee NHL-296
75O-Pee-Chee NHL-315
75Sabres Linnett-10
75Topps-46
75Topps-296
75Topps-315
76O-Pee-Chee NHL-42
76O-Pee-Chee NHL-214
76Topps-42
76Topps-214
77O-Pee-Chee NHL-222
77Topps-222
78O-Pee-Chee-188
78Topps-188
79O-Pee-Chee-12
79Rockies Team Issue-20
79Topps-12
80O-Pee-Chee-239
80O-Pee-Chee-259
80Topps-239
80Topps-259
81Maple Leafs Postcards-18
81O-Pee-Chee-322
82O-Pee-Chee-330
93Sabres Noco-17
01Upper Deck Legends-8
04SP Authentic Buybacks-165
04SP Authentic Sign of the Times-DS-PR
04UD Legendary Signatures-69
Autographs-RR
Linemates-RMGPRR
04UD Legends Classics-48
Gold-48
Platinum-48
Silver-48
Signature Moments-M13
Signatures-CS13
Signatures-DC7
Signatures-TC10
05SPx Xcitement Legends-XL-RR
05SPx Xcitement Legends Gold-XL-RR
05SPx Xcitement Legends Spectrum-XL-RR
05UD Artifacts-144
Blue-144
Gold-144
Green-144
Pewter-144
Red-144
Gold Autographed-144
05Upper Deck Trilogy Legendary Scripts-LEG-RR
05Upper Deck Trilogy Personal Scripts-PER-RR

Robert, Ryan
00St. Michaels Majors-25

Robert, Yannick
95Swiss HNL-255

Roberto, Phil
69Canadiens Postcards Color-24
71Blues Postcards-20
71Canadiens Postcards-19
71O-Pee-Chee-228
71Sargent Promotions Stamps-109
71Toronto Sun-162
72Blues White Border-17
72O-Pee-Chee-82
72Topps-52
73Blues White Border-16
73O-Pee-Chee-3
73Topps-151
74NHL Action Stamps-235
74NHL Action Stamps Update-12
74O-Pee-Chee NHL-208
74Topps-208
75O-Pee-Chee NHL-80
75Topps-80
76O-Pee-Chee NHL-345
76Rockies Puck Bucks-18
92Birmingham Bulls-20
93Birmingham Bulls-20
93Birmingham Bulls Birmingham News-1
93Birmingham Bulls Birmingham News-2
94Birmingham Bulls-20
95Birmingham Bulls-2
97Columbus Cottonmouths-21
98Columbus Cottonmouths-21
99Columbus Cottonmouths-10
00Columbus Cottonmouths-22
01Columbus Cottonmouths-21
02Columbus Cottonmouths-20

Roberts, Alex
90ProCards AHL/IHL-408
92Toledo Storm-11
92Toledo Storm Team Issue-18
03Plymouth Whalers-27

Roberts, Alicia
98New Hampshire Wildcats-10

Roberts, Bobby
51Laval Dairy QSHL-103

Roberts, Brad
75HCA Steel City Vacuum-10

Roberts, Chris
75HCA Steel City Vacuum-11

Roberts, Cory
98Owen Sound Platers-26
99Owen Sound Platers-15
00Owen Sound Attack-16
01Owen Sound Attack-16

Roberts, David
91Michigan Wolverines-12
93PowerPlay-515
93Stadium Club Team USA-20
93Stadium Club Team USA Members Only-20
93Topps Premier Team USA-16
93Ultra-495
93Classic-76
94Leaf-478
94Parkhurst-201
Gold-201
94Score-222
Gold-222
Platinum-222
94Finnish Jaa Kiekko-134
94Classic-106
Gold-106
Autographs-106
Tri-Cards-T58
94Classic Four-Sport *-141
Gold-141
Printers Proofs-141
95Emotion-152
95Leaf-13
95Panini Stickers-191
95Parkhurst International-179
Emerald Ice-179
95Pinnacle-157
Artist's Proofs-157
Rink Collection-157
95Score-286
Black Ice Artist's Proofs-286
Black Ice-286
95Topps-43
OPC Inserts-43
95Signature Rookies Auto-Phonex-36
95Signature Rook Auto-Phonex Phone Cards-36
96Be A Player-93
Autographs-93
Autographs Silver-93
96Canucks Postcards-7
96Collector's Edge Ice Crucibles-C1
97Collector's Choice-265
97Donruss Limited-31
Exposure-31
97Pacific Invincible NHL Regime-204
97Panini Stickers-240
97Score Canucks-19
Platinum-19
Premier-19
98Michigan K-Wings-10
99Swiss Panini Stickers-224
00Grand Rapids Griffins-19
01German Berlin Polar Bears Postcards-21
01German Upper Deck-41
02German Berlin Polar Bears Postcards-24
02German DEL City Press-37
Top Scorers-TS8
03German Berlin Polar Bears Postcards-27
03German DEL-73

Roberts, Doug
67Topps-50
68O-Pee-Chee-88
68Topps-88
69O-Pee-Chee-81
69Topps-81
70Esso Power Players-92
70O-Pee-Chee-71
70Sargent Promotions Stamps-138
70Topps-71
71Topps-83
72Sargent Promotions Stamps-26
73O-Pee-Chee-207
73Red Wings McCarthy Postcards-14
74NHL Action Stamps-103
74O-Pee-Chee NHL-312
92Raleigh Icecaps-14
94Central Hockey League-17
94Dallas Freeze-17

Roberts, Gary
82Ottawa 67's-20
83Ottawa 67's-24
84Ottawa 67's-20
86Flames Red Rooster-25
86Moncton Golden Flames-12
87Flames Red Rooster-27
87Panini Stickers-217
88Flames Postcards-19
88Panini Stickers-15
89O-Pee-Chee-202
89O-Pee-Chee Stickers-98
89Panini Stickers-35
90Bowman-95
Tiffany-95
90Flames IGA/McGavin's-25
90O-Pee-Chee-161
90Panini Stickers-179
90Pro Set-45
90Score-106
Canadian-106
90Topps-161
Tiffany-161
90Upper Deck-29
French-29
91Pro Set Platinum-161
91Pro Set Platinum-280
91Bowman-263
91Flames Panini Team Stickers-19
91Flames IGA-18
91O-Pee-Chee-320
91OPC Premier-126
91Panini Stickers-52
91Parkhurst-24
91Parkhurst-436
French-24
French-436
91Pinnacle-37
French-37
91Pro Set-30
French-30
91Score American-199
91Score Canadian Bilingual-199
91Score Canadian English-199
91Stadium Club-126
91Topps-320
91Upper Deck-190
French-190
92Bowman-109
92Bowman-214
92Flames IGA-6
92O-Pee-Chee-72
92OPC Premier Star Performers-14
92Panini Stickers-45
92Panini Stickers French-45
92Parkhurst-22
Emerald Ice-22
Cherry Picks-CP8
92Pinnacle-3
92Pinnacle-242
French-3
French-242
92Pro Set-21
Gold Team Leaders-1
92Score-322
Canadian-322
Sharpshooters-1
Sharpshooters Canadian-1
92Stadium Club-48
92Topps-116
Gold-116G
92Ultra-29
92Upper Deck-289
93Donruss-52
93Leaf-36
93McDonald's Upper Deck-11
93OPC Premier-382
93OPC Premier-510
Gold-382
Gold-510
93Panini Stickers-181
93Parkhurst-302
Emerald Ice-302
93Pinnacle-55
Canadian-55
All-Stars-29
All-Stars Canadian-29
93PowerPlay-42
93Score-241
Canadian-241
Dynamic Duos Canadian-4
93Stadium Club-235
Members Only Master Set-235
OPC-235
First Day Issue-235
First Day Issue OPC-235
All-Stars-16
All-Stars Members Only-16
All-Stars OPC-16
Finest-9
Finest Members Only-9
93Topps/OPC Premier-382
93Topps/OPC Premier-510
Gold-382
Gold-510
93Ultra-187
93Upper Deck-151
Hat Tricks-HT3
SP-25
93Upper Deck Locker All-Stars-32
93Swedish Semic World Champ Stickers-208
94Action Packed Big Picture 24K Gold-11G
94Be A Player Signature Cards-17
94Canada Games NHL POGS-61
94Donruss-143
94EA Sports-22
94Finest-82
Super Team Winners-82
Refractors-82
Division's Clear Cut-19
94Flair-28
94Fleer-35
94Kraft-12
94Leaf-326
94Leaf Limited-114
94OPC Premier-445
Special Effects-445
94Parkhurst Vintage-V29
94Parkhurst SE-SE27
Gold-SE27
94Pinnacle-115
Artist's Proofs-115
Rink Collection-115
Northern Lights-NL16
94Score-186
Gold-186
Platinum-186
Check It-CI12
94Select-147
Gold-147
94Stadium Club-230
Members Only Master Set-230
First Day Issue-230
Super Team Winner Cards-230
94Topps/OPC Premier-445
Special Effects-445
94Topps Finest Inserts-16
94Ultra-35
Red Light Specials-7
94Upper Deck-20
Electric Ice-20
SP Inserts-SP14
SP Inserts Die Cuts-SP14
95Canada Games NHL POGS-55
95Collector's Choice-174
Player's Club-174
Player's Club Platinum-174
95Donruss-372
95Emotion-25
95Hoyle Western Playing Cards-52
95Leaf-277
95Panini Stickers-236
95Parkhurst International-301
Emerald Ice-301
95Pinnacle-137
Artist's Proofs-137
Rink Collection-137
95Playoff One on One-19
95Pro Magnets-49
95Score-97
Black Ice Artist's Proofs-97
Black Ice-97
95Summit-150
Artist's Proofs-150
Ice-150
95Topps-78
OPC Inserts-78
95Ultra-28
Gold Medallion-28
95Upper Deck-19
Electric Ice-19
Electric Ice Gold-19
96Collector's Choice-44
96Maggers-85
96NHL Aces Playing Cards-39
96NHL Pro Stamps-49
97Be A Player-73
Autographs-73
Autographs Die-Cuts-73
Autographs Prismatic Die-Cuts-73
97Black Diamond-86
Double Diamond-86
Triple Diamond-86
Quadruple Diamond-86
97Donruss Preferred-63
Cut to the Chase-63
97Donruss Priority-106
Stamp of Approval-106
97Hurricanes Team Issue-24
97Pacific Omega-45
Copper-45
Dark Gray-45
Emerald Green-45
Gold-45
Ice Blue-45
97Paramount-39
Copper-39
Dark Grey-39
Emerald Green-39
Ice Blue-39
Red-39
Silver-39
97Pinnacle-170
Press Plates Back Black-170
Press Plates Back Cyan-170
Press Plates Back Magenta-170
Press Plates Back Yellow-170
Press Plates Front Black-170
Press Plates Front Cyan-170
Press Plates Front Magenta-170
Press Plates Front Yellow-170
97Revolution-26
Copper-26
Emerald-26
Ice Blue-26
Silver-26
97SP Authentic-26
97Upper Deck-240
Game Dated Moments-240
98Black Diamond-15
Double Diamond-15
Triple Diamond-15
Quadruple Diamond-15
98Hurricanes Team Issue-8
98Katch-29
98Pacific-140
Ice Blue-140
Red-140
98Pacific Omega-46
Red-46
Opening Day Issue-46
98Panini Stickers-28
98Paramount-42
Copper-42
Emerald Green-42
Holo-Electric-42
Ice Blue-42
Silver-42
98UD Choice-36
Prime Choice Reserve-36
Reserve-36
98Upper Deck-236
Exclusives-236
Exclusives 1 of 1-236
Gold Reserve-236
98Upper Deck MVP-41
Gold Script-41
Silver Script-41
Super Script-41
99BAP Memorabilia-153
Gold-153
Silver-153
99BAP Millennium-53
Emerald-53
Ruby-53
Sapphire-53
Signatures-53
Signatures Gold-53
99O-Pee-Chee-50
99O-Pee-Chee Chrome-50
99O-Pee-Chee Chrome Refractors-50
99Pacific-80
Copper-80
Emerald Green-80
Gold-80
Ice Blue-80
Premiere Date-80
Red-80
99Pacific Omega-49
Copper-49
Gold-49
Ice Blue-49
Premiere Date-49
99Panini Stickers-50
99Paramount-50
Copper-50
Emerald-50
Gold-50
Holographic Emerald-50
Holographic Gold-50
Holographic Silver-50
Ice Blue-50
Premiere Date-50
Red-50
Silver-50
99Revolution-31
Premiere Date-31
Red-31
Shadow Series-31
99Stadium Club-102
First Day Issue-102
One of a Kind-102
Printing Plates Black-102
Printing Plates Cyan-102
Printing Plates Magenta-102
Printing Plates Yellow-102
99Topps/OPC-50
99Topps/OPC Chrome-50
Refractors-50
99Upper Deck-33
Exclusives-33
Exclusives 1 of 1-33
99Upper Deck Gold Reserve-33
99Upper Deck MVP-42
Gold Script-42
Silver Script-42
Super Script-42
99Upper Deck Victory-58
00BAP Memorabilia-115
00BAP Memorabilia-400
Emerald-115
Emerald-400
Ruby-115
Ruby-400
Sapphire-115
Sapphire-400
Promos-115
00BAP Mem Chicago Sportsfest Copper-115
00BAP Memorabilia Chicago Sportsfest Blue-115
00BAP Memorabilia Chicago Sportsfest Gold-115
00BAP Memorabilia Chicago Sportsfest Ruby-115
00BAP Memorabilia Chicago Sun-Times Ruby-115
00BAP Memorabilia Chicago Sun-Times Gold-115
00BAP Mem Chicago Sun-Times Sapphire-115
00BAP Mem Toronto Fall Expo Copper-115
00BAP Memorabilia Toronto Fall Expo Gold-115
00BAP Memorabilia Toronto Fall Expo Ruby-115
00BAP Signature Series-249
Emerald-249
Ruby-249
Sapphire-249
00Crown Royale-101
Ice Blue-101
Limited Series-101
Premiere Date-101
Red-101
00O-Pee-Chee-199
00O-Pee-Chee Parallel-199
00Pacific-89
Copper-89
Gold-89
Ice Blue-89
Premiere Date-89
00Private Stock Game Gear-98
00SP Authentic-84
00SPx-148
00Stadium Club-223
00Titanium-92
Blue-92
Gold-92
Premiere Date-92
Red-92
Retail-92
Game Gear-47
00Topps/OPC-199
Parallel-199
00Topps Chrome-133
OPC Refractors-133
Refractors-133
00Topps Heritage-109
00UD Heroes-109
00UD Pros and Prospects-82
00Upper Deck-392
Exclusives Tier 1-392
Exclusives Tier 2-392
00Upper Deck Victory-96
00Upper Deck Vintage-342
01BAP Memorabilia-175
Emerald-175
Ruby-175
Sapphire-175
01BAP Update Heritage-H30
01Bowman YoungStars-94
Gold-94
Ice Cubed-94
01Crown Royale-133
Blue-133
Premiere Date-133
Red-133
Retail-133
01McDonald's Pacific Hometown Pride-10
01O-Pee-Chee-80
01O-Pee-Chee Heritage Parallel-80
01O-Pee-Chee Heritage Parallel Limited-80
01O-Pee-Chee Premier Parallel-80
01Pacific-372
Extreme LTD-372
Hobby LTD-372
Premiere Date-372
Retail LTD-372
01Pacific Adrenaline-184
Blue-184
Premiere Date-184
Red-184
Retail-184
01Pacific Arena Exclusives-372
01Pacific Heads-Up-91
Blue-91
Premiere Date-91
Red-91
Silver-91
01Parkhurst-114
Sticks-PS51
01Stadium Club-85
Award Winners-85
Master Photos-85
01Titanium-131
Hobby Parallel-131
Premiere Date-131
Retail-131
Retail Parallel-131
01Topps-80
Heritage Parallel-80
Heritage Parallel Limited-80
OPC Parallel-80
Autographs-AGR
01Topps Chrome-80
Refractors-80
Black Border Refractors-80
01Topps Heritage-106
Refractors-106
01Upper Deck-161
Exclusives-161
01Upper Deck MVP-174
01Upper Deck Victory-327
Gold-327
01Upper Deck Vintage-240
01Upper Deck Vintage-243
02Atomic-93
Blue-93
Gold-93
Red-93
Hobby Parallel-93
Super Colliders-15
02BAP First Edition-200
02BAP First Edition-427H
02BAP Memorabilia-191
Emerald-191
Ruby-191
Sapphire-191
NHL All-Star Game-191
NHL All-Star Game Blue-191
NHL All-Star Game Green-191
NHL All-Star Game Red-191
Stanley Cup Playoffs-SC-3
02BAP Memorabilia Toronto Fall Expo-191
02BAP Sig Series Auto Buybacks 1999-53
02Maple Leafs Platinum Collection-17
02McDonald's Pacific-37
Jersey Patches Silver-18
Jersey Patches Gold-18
02NHL Power Play Stickers-130
02O-Pee-Chee-88
02O-Pee-Chee Premier Blue Parallel-88
02O-Pee-Chee Premier Red Parallel-88
02O-Pee-Chee Factory Set-88
02Pacific-368
Blue-368
Red-368
02Pacific Complete-468
Red-468
02Pacific Exclusive-162
02Pacific Heads-Up-117
Blue-117
Purple-117
Red-117
Quad Jerseys-26
Quad Jerseys Gold-26
02Pacific Quest for the Cup Jerseys-22
02Parkhurst-32
Bronze-32
Gold-32
Silver-32
Jerseys-GJ10
Stick and Jerseys-SJ10
Teammates-TT3
02Parkhurst Retro-84
Minis-84
02Private Stock Reserve-93
Blue-93
Red-93
Retail-93
02Stadium Club-80
Silver Decoy Cards-80
Proofs-80
02Titanium Jerseys-67
02Titanium Jerseys Retail-67
02Titanium Patches-67
02Topps-88
OPC Blue Parallel-88
OPC Red Parallel-88
Factory Set-88
02Topps Chrome-56
Black Border Refractors-56
Refractors-56
02Topps Total-184
02Upper Deck-162
Exclusives-162
02Upper Deck Classic Portraits-92
02Upper Deck MVP-172
Gold-172
Classics-172
Golden Classics-172
02Upper Deck Victory-201
Bronze-201
Gold-201
Silver-201
02Upper Deck Vintage-238
02Vanguard Jerseys-44
02Vanguard Jerseys Gold-44
03McFarlane Hockey-240
03McFarlane Hockey-242
03BAP Ultimate Memorabilia Autographs-33
Gold-33
03BAP Ultimate Mem Auto Jerseys-33
03Beehive-178
Gold-178
Silver-178
03ITG Action-542
Jerseys-M145
03McDonalds Pacific Hockey Root Checklist-7
03NHL Sticker Collection-137
03Pacific-322
Blue-322
Red-322
03Pacific Calder-94
Silver-94
03Pacific Complete-327
Red-327
03Parkhurst Original Six Toronto-23
Memorabilia-TM2
Memorabilia-TM19
Memorabilia-TM56
03Titanium-185
Hobby Jersey Number Parallels-185
Patches-185
Retail-185
03Upper Deck-183
Canadian Exclusives-183
HG-183
03Upper Deck MVP-402
Gold Script-402
Silver Script-402
Canadian Exclusives-402
03Upper Deck Victory-182
Bronze-182
Gold-182
Silver-182
03Toronto Star-91
04Pacific-250
Blue-250
Red-250
04SP Authentic-86
04Ultimate Collection Dual Logos-UL2-SR
04Upper Deck-164
Canadian Exclusives-164
HG Glossy Gold-164
HG Glossy Silver-164
School of Hard Knocks-SHK3
Swatch of Six-SS-GR
05Be A Player-84
First Period-84
Second Period-84
Third Period-84
Overtime-84
Quad Signatures-MAPL
Signatures-RO
Signatures Gold-RO
05Black Diamond-37
Emerald-37
Gold-37
Onyx-37
Ruby-37
05Panini Stickers-57
05Parkhurst-207
Facsimile Auto Parallel-207
True Colors-TCFLA
True Colors-TCFLA
05UD Artifacts Frozen Artifacts-FA-GR
05UD Artifacts Frozen Artifacts Autos-FA-GR
05UD Artifacts Frozen Artifacts Copper-FA-GR
05UD Artifacts Frozen Artifacts Dual-FAD-GR
05UD Artifacts Frozen Artifact Dual Auto-FAD-GR
05UD Artifact Frozen Artifact Dual Copper-FAD-GR
05UD Artifacts Frozen Artifact Dual Gold-FAD-GR
05UD Artifact Frozen Artifact Dual Maroon-FAD-GR
05UD Artifact Frozen Artifact Dual Pewter-FAD-GR
05UD Artifacts Frozen Artifact Dual Silver-FAD-GR
05UD Artifacts Frozen Artifacts Gold-FA-GR
05UD Artifacts Frozen Artifacts Maroon-FA-GR
05UD Artifacts Frozen Artifacts Patches-FP-GR
05UD Artifact Frozen Artifact Patch Autos-FP-GR
05UD Artifact Frozen Artifact Patch Dual-FPD-GR
05UD Artifacts Frozen Art Patch Dual Auto-FPD-GR
05UD Artifacts Frozen Art Patch Pewter-FP-GR
05UD Artifacts Frozen Art Patch Silver-FP-GR
05UD Artifacts Frozen Artifacts Pewter-FA-GR
05UD Artifacts Frozen Artifacts Silver-FA-GR
05Upper Deck-329
05Upper Deck All-Time Greatest-12
05Upper Deck Jerseys-J-GR
05Upper Deck Hockey Showcase-HS4
05Upper Deck Showcase Promos-HS4
05Upper Deck MVP-173
Gold-173
Platinum-173
05Upper Deck Victory-184
Black-184
Gold-184
Silver-184
06Flair Showcase Stitches-SSGR
06Fleer Fabricology-FGR
06Hot Prospects Hot Materials -HMGR
06Hot Prospects Hot Materials Red Hot-HMGR
06Hot Prospects Hot Materials White Hot-HMGR
06O-Pee-Chee-219
Rainbow-219
Swatches-S-GR
06Panini Stickers-57
06SP Game Used Authentic Fabrics-AFGR
06SP Game Used Authentic Fabrics Parallel-AFGR
06SP Game Used Authentic Fabrics Patches-AFGR
06SP Game Used Authentic Fabrics Sixes-AF6MAS
06SP Game Used Authentic Fabrics Sixes Patches-AF6MAS
06The Cup NHL Shields Duals-DSHNR
06UD Artifacts Tundra Tandems-TTNR
06UD Artifacts Tundra Tandems Black-TTNR
06UD Artifacts Tundra Tandems Blue-TTNR
06UD Artifacts Tundra Tandems Gold-TTNR
06UD Artifacts Tundra Tandems Platinum-TTNR
06UD Artifacts Tundra Tandems Red-TTNR
06UD Artifacts Tundra Tandems Dual Patches Red-TTNR
06Upper Deck-338
Exclusives Parallel-338
High Gloss Parallel-338
Game Jerseys-J2GR
Game Patches-P2GR
Masterpieces-338

Roberts, Gordie
79O-Pee-Chee-265
80O-Pee-Chee-112
80Topps-112
81North Stars Postcards-20
81O-Pee-Chee-167
81Topps-W111
82North Stars Postcards-20
82O-Pee-Chee-174
82Post Cereal-9
83Hall of Fame Postcards-O13
83North Stars Postcards-25
83O-Pee-Chee-180
83O-Pee-Chee Stickers-114
83Topps Stickers-114
83Victoria Cougars-20
84North Stars 7-Eleven-5

84North Stars Postcards-24
84O-Pee-Chee-107
85North Stars Postcards-25
85O-Pee-Chee-28
85O-Pee-Chee Stickers-43
85Topps-28
86North Stars 7-Eleven-10
86North Stars Postcards-8
86O-Pee-Chee-42
86Topps-42
87Blues Team Issue-21
87North Stars Postcards-26
87O-Pee-Chee-41
87O-Pee-Chee Stickers-55
87Topps-41
88Blues Kodak-21
88Blues Team Issue-21
88Panini Stickers-102
89Blues Kodak-4
90O-Pee-Chee-256
90Panini Stickers-269
90Pro Set-271
90Pro Set-510
90Score-245
Canadian-245
90Score Rookie/Traded-83T
90Topps-256
Tiffany-256
91O-Pee-Chee-494
91Penguins Coke/Elby's-28
91Pinnacle-274
French-274
91Pro Set-458
French-458
91Score American-439
91Score Canadian Bilingual-422
91Score Canadian English-422
91Topps-494
92Bowman-197
92Bruins Postcards-9
92O-Pee-Chee-233
92OPC Premier-86
92Pinnacle-312
French-312
92Score-201
Canadian-201
92Stadium Club-185
92Topps-176
Gold-176G
92Ultra-255
93OPC Premier-275
Gold-275
93Pinnacle-319
Canadian-319
93Score-274
Canadian-274
93Stadium Club-41
Members Only Master Set-41
OPC-41
First Day Issue-41
First Day Issue OPC-41
93Topps/OPC Premier-275
Gold-275

Roberts, Gordon
10C56-3
10Sweet Caporal Postcards-33
11C55-33
12C57-23
83Hall of Fame-222
85Hall of Fame-222

Roberts, James Drew
71Letraset Action Replays-14
77O-Pee-Chee NHL-392
78O-Pee-Chee-342

Roberts, James Wilfred
64Beehive Group III Photos-114
64Coca-Cola Caps-72
65Coca-Cola-71
65Topps-74
66Topps-6
68O-Pee-Chee-113
68Shirriff Coins-152
68Topps-113
69Canadiens Postcards Color-25
69O-Pee-Chee-174
Four-in-One-9
69Topps-14
70Dad's Cookies-112
70Esso Power Players-239
70O-Pee-Chee-213
70Sargent Promotions Stamps-179
71Canadiens Postcards-20
71O-Pee-Chee-116
71Sargent Promotions Stamps-181
71Topps-116
71Toronto Sun-246
72Canadiens Postcards-18
72Dimanche/Derniere Heure *-165
72Dimanche/Derniere Heure *-166
72O-Pee-Chee-269
72Sargent Promotions Stamps-126
72Finnish Semic World Championship-182
72Swedish Semic World Championship-182
73Canadiens Postcards-19
73O-Pee-Chee-181
74Canadiens Postcards-19
74NHL Action Stamps-161
74O-Pee-Chee NHL-78
74Topps-78
75Canadiens Postcards-15
75O-Pee-Chee NHL-378
76Canadiens Postcards-17
76O-Pee-Chee NHL-119
76O-Pee-Chee NHL-217
76Topps-119
76Topps-217
77O-Pee-Chee NHL-281
86Penguins Kodak-19
88ProCards AHL-312
89ProCards AHL-253
90ProCards AHL/IHL-182
94Parkhurst Tall Boys-79
95Parkhurst '66-67-72
Coins-72

Roberts, Jason
01Swift Current Broncos-11
02Swift Current Broncos-15

Roberts, Jason AJHL
04Camrose Kodiaks-15

Roberts, Kraig
93Quebec Pee-Wee Tournament-1323

Roberts, Mike
91Johnstown Chiefs-10
93Memphis RiverKings-13

Roberts, Minpy
52Juniors Blue Tint-22

Roberts, Robbie
93Quebec Pee-Wee Tournament-1220

Roberts, Sam
02UK Hull Thunder-20
02Hull Olympiques-6
03Gatineau Olympiques-21
03Hull Olympiques Memorial Cup-13
04Gatineau Olympiques-3

Roberts, Steve
91British Columbia JHL-27
92British Columbia JHL-50
95Dayton Bombers-21
96Dayton Bombers-1
00UK Sekonda Superleague-157
00UK Sekonda Superleague-177
00UK Sheffield Steelers-19
01UK Belfast Giants-31

Roberts, Tim
92Wheeling Thunderbirds-13
93Wheeling Thunderbirds-7
94Wheeling Thunderbirds-5
94Wheeling Thunderbirds Photo Album-4
95Wheeling Thunderbirds Series II-12

Roberts, W.
23V128-1 Paulin's Candy-6
24Crescent Selkirks-5

Robertson, Bob
51Laval Dairy Subset-103
52St. Lawrence Sales-69

Robertson, Brett
04Medicine Hat Tigers-18
05Medicine Hat Tigers-17

Robertson, Chris
88Brandon Wheat Kings-14
95Central Hockey League-70
99Corpus Christi IceRays-17
03Sudbury Wolves-21
06New Mexico Scorpions-4

Robertson, Earl
34Beehive Group I Photos-247
39O-Pee-Chee V301-1-63
06Between The Pipes Forgotten Franchises-FF06
06ITG Ultimate Memorabilia Amazing Amerks Autos-8

Robertson, Fred
32O'Keefe Maple Leafs-18
33V129-15

Robertson, Geordie
79Rochester Americans-14

Robertson, George
44Beehive Group II Photos-286
45Quaker Oats Photos-111

Robertson, Grant
83Belleville Bulls-23
84Belleville Bulls-19

Robertson, Iain
94Finnish Jaa Kiekko-329
01UK Fife Flyers-9

Robertson, James
52Juniors Blue Tint-103

Robertson, Jarrett
06Fayetteville FireAntz-13

Robertson, Kenneth
52Juniors Blue Tint-99

Robertson, Kevin
89Brandon Wheat Kings-11
90Brandon Wheat Kings-9
907th Inn. Sketch WHL-215
91British Columbia JHL-110
92British Columbia JHL-170

Robertson, Matthew
06Prince Albert Raiders-11

Robertson, Peter
03Oklahoma City Blazers-16
04Memphis RiverKings-13

Robertson, Roger
84Belleville Bulls-23

Robertson, Sean
94Prince Albert Raiders-16
97Lethbridge Hurricanes-13
04Colorado Eagles-15
05Colorado Eagles-17
06Colorado EaglesÂ -18

Robertson, Torrie
81Capitals Team Issue-15
83Whalers Junior Hartford Courant-15
84Whalers Junior Wendy's-16
84Victoria Cougars-20
85O-Pee-Chee-218
85Whalers Junior Wendy's-17
86O-Pee-Chee-214
86Whalers Junior Thomas'-19
87Whalers Jr. Burger King/Pepsi-17
88Whalers Junior Ground Round-14
90Pro Set-77
90ProCards AHL/IHL-520

Robertsson, Bert
96Syracuse Crunch-27
99BAP Memorabilia-386
Gold-386
Silver-386
99Pacific Omega-92
Copper-92
Gold-92
Ice Blue-92
Premiere Date-92
00Upper Deck NHLPA-PA59
00Hartford Wolf Pack-22
01Cincinnati Mighty Ducks-19
03Swedish Elite-259
Enforcers-EF7
Silver-259
04Swedish Elitset-110
Gold-110
05Swedish SHL Elitset-119
Gold-119

Robichaud, Andre
92British Columbia JHL-85

Robichaud, Ghislain
93Quebec Pee-Wee Tournament-103

Robichaud, Jason
03Yarmouth Mariners-19

Robichaud, Maxime
06Victoriaville Tigres-11

Robichaud, Ryan
95Slapshot-91
95Guelph Storm-25
96Guelph Storm-10

Robidas, Stephane
97Bowman CHL-65
OPC-65
99BAP Memorabilia-377
Gold-377
Silver-377
99Pacific Omega-124
Copper-124
Gold-124
Ice Blue-124
Premiere Date-124
99Quebec Citadelles-7
00Canadiens Postcards-23
00Upper Deck NHLPA-PA48
01BAP Memorabilia-112
Emerald-112
Ruby-112
Sapphire-112
01Canadiens Postcards-21
02Stars Postcards-4
03ITG Action-185
03Upper Deck MVP-140
Gold Script-140
Silver Script-140
Canadian Exclusives-140
04German DEL-119
Superstars-SU08
06Stars Team Postcards-19

Robidoux, Florent
80Blackhawks Postcards-9
81Blackhawks Brown Background-10
83Springfield Indians-16

Robillard, Andrew
93Quebec Pee-Wee Tournament-475

Robillard, Marc
917th Inn. Sketch OHL-83

Robillard, Nicolas
03Baie Comeau Drakkar-21
04Baie-Comeau Drakkar-16
05Quebec Remparts-17
05Quebec Remparts Signature Series-17

Robin, Jean-Sebastien
98Upper Deck Exclusives-350

Robins, Bobby
06Binghamton Senators-20
06Binghamton Senators 5th Anniversary-26

Robins, Trevor
89Saskatoon Blades-4
90Saskatoon Blades-2
907th Inn. Sketch WHL-88
91Saskatoon Blades-2
917th Inn. Sketch WHL-101
92Brandon Wheat Kings-20
93Kansas City Blades-19
94Kansas City Blades-20
00UK Sekonda Superleague-70
01UK London Knights-20

Robinson, Ben
04Penticton Vees-5
05Penticton Vees-15

Robinson, Bill
51Laval Dairy QSHL-107
52St. Lawrence Sales-58
907th Inn. Sketch OHL-68

Robinson, Brandon
00Mississauga Ice Dogs-21

Robinson, Chad
02Peterborough Petes-15
03Barrie Colts-8
04Barrie Colts-10

Robinson, Chris
03Lincoln Stars Update-35
04Lincoln Stars-19
04Lincoln Stars Update-44

Robinson, Claude C
83Hall of Fame Postcards-J12
85Hall of Fame-192

Robinson, Darcy
97Saskatoon Blades-20
01Wilkes-Barre Scranton Penguins-5
02Wilkes-Barre Scranton Penguins-3
03Wilkes-Barre Scranton Penguins-21
04Wilkes-Barre Scranton Penguins-5

Robinson, Derek
92British Columbia JHL-165

Robinson, Doug
64Coca-Cola Caps-28
64Topps-84
65Coca-Cola-77
65Topps-26
68O-Pee-Chee-160
68Shirriff Coins-61
70Esso Power Players-153
94Parkhurst Tall Boys-34
95Parkhurst '66-67-96
Coins-96

Robinson, Earl
33O-Pee-Chee V304B-55
33V357 Ice Kings-5
34Beehive Group I Photos-180
34Beehive Group I Photos-202
34Sweet Caporal-24
36O-Pee-Chee V304D-115
37O-Pee-Chee V304E-165
37V356 Worldwide Gum-85

Robinson, Garrett
04Moose Jaw Warriors-11
05Moose Jaw Warriors-17
06Moose Jaw Warriors-11

Robinson, Jane
94Classic Women of Hockey-W8

Robinson, Jason
95Slapshot-195
01Greensboro Generals-15
02Pee Dee Pride RBI-145
03UK London Racers-14
04UK London Racers-10
04UK London Racers Playoffs-15
05UK Sheffield Steelers-4
Gold-4
Silver-4

Robinson, Jeremy
95Neepewa Natives-10

Robinson, Jody
92Quebec Pee-Wee Tournament-372
03Bridgeport Sound Tigers-12

Robinson, Justin
94North Bay Centennials-20
95Slapshot-11
95Barrie Colts-23

Robinson, Larry
72Dimanche/Derniere Heure *-167
72Dimanche/Derniere Heure *-168
73Canadiens Postcards-20
73O-Pee-Chee-237
74Canadiens Postcards-20
74NHL Action Stamps-153
74O-Pee-Chee NHL-280
75Canadiens Postcards-16
75Heroes Stand-Ups-13
75O-Pee-Chee NHL-241
75Topps-241
76Canadiens Postcards-18
76O-Pee-Chee NHL-151
76Topps-151
77Canadiens Postcards-20
77Coca-Cola-20
77O-Pee-Chee NHL-2
77O-Pee-Chee NHL-30
77Sportscasters-7301
77Topps-30
77Topps/O-Pee-Chee Glossy-18
Square-18
78Canadiens Postcards-22
78O-Pee-Chee-210
78O-Pee-Chee-329
78Topps-210
79Canadiens Postcards-20
79O-Pee-Chee-50
79Topps-50
80Canadiens Postcards-20
80O-Pee-Chee-84
80O-Pee-Chee-230
80O-Pee-Chee Super-11
80Pepsi-Cola Caps-56
80Topps-84
80Topps-230
81Canadiens Postcards-23
81O-Pee-Chee-179
81O-Pee-Chee-196
81O-Pee-Chee Stickers-31
81O-Pee-Chee Stickers-42
81O-Pee-Chee Stickers-148
81Post Standups-16
81Topps-31
82Canadiens Postcards-21
82Canadiens Steinberg-16
82McDonald's Stickers-17
82McDonald's Stickers-34
82O-Pee-Chee-191
82O-Pee-Chee Stickers-31
82O-Pee-Chee Stickers-169
82Post Cereal-10
82Topps Stickers-31
82Topps Stickers-169
83Canadiens Postcards-23
83Esso-16
83NHL Key Tags-66
83O-Pee-Chee-195
83O-Pee-Chee Stickers-60
83O-Pee-Chee Stickers-61
83Puffy Stickers-2
83Topps Stickers-60
83Topps Stickers-61
83Vachon-53
84Canadiens Postcards-24
84Kellogg's Accordion Discs-2
84Kellogg's Accordion Discs Singles-32
84O-Pee-Chee-270
84O-Pee-Chee Stickers-147
84O-Pee-Chee Stickers-148
847-Eleven Discs-30
84Topps-82
85Canadiens Placemats-5
85Canadiens Placemats-7
85Canadiens Postcards-28
85Canadiens Provigo-17
85O-Pee-Chee-147
85O-Pee-Chee Stickers-140
857-Eleven Credit Cards-10
85Topps-147
86Canadiens Postcards-19
86Kraft Drawings-60
86O-Pee-Chee-62
86O-Pee-Chee Box Bottoms-M
86O-Pee-Chee Stickers-8
86O-Pee-Chee Stickers-123
86Topps-62
86Topps Box Bottoms-M
86Topps Sticker Inserts-12
87Canadiens Kodak-6
87Canadiens Postcards-24
87Canadiens Vachon Stickers-72
87Canadiens Vachon Stickers-73
87O-Pee-Chee-192
87O-Pee-Chee Stickers-16
87Panini Stickers-57
87Pro-Sport All-Stars-1
87Topps-192
88Canadiens Postcards-23
88Esso All-Stars-37
88O-Pee-Chee-246
88O-Pee-Chee Stickers-39
89Kings Smokey-7
89O-Pee-Chee-235
89O-Pee-Chee Stickers-55
89Panini Stickers-245
90Bowman-150
Tiffany-150
90Kings Smokey-9
90Kraft-47
90O-Pee-Chee-261
90Panini Stickers-244
90Pro Set-125
90Score-260
Canadian-260
90Topps-261
Tiffany-261
90Upper Deck-52
French-52
91Bowman-177
91Kraft-79
91Kraft-80
91O-Pee-Chee-458
91Panini Stickers-82
91Parkhurst-74
French-74
91Pinnacle-208
91Pinnacle-403
French-208
French-403
91Pro Set-104
French-104
91Score American-291
91Score Canadian Bilingual-511
91Score Canadian English-511
91Stadium Club-252
91Topps-458
91Upper Deck-499
French-499
92Bowman-215
92Future Trends '76 Canada Cup-182
92O-Pee-Chee-167
25th Anniv. Inserts-6
93O-Pee-Chee Canadiens Hockey Fest-59
93Upper Deck Locker All-Stars-48
94Hockey Wit-92
94Classic Pro Prospects-53
98Kings LA Times Coins-3
99BAP Memorabilia AS Canadian Hobby-CH10
99BAP Memorabilia AS Cdn Hobby Autos-CH10
99Devils Team Issue-27
99Upper Deck Century Legends-25
Century Collection-25
Epic Signatures-LR
Epic Signatures 100-LR
Jerseys of the Century-JC3
99Upper Deck Retro-100
Gold-100
Platinum-100
Turn of the Century-TC11
99Russian Fetisov Tribute-39
00Devils Team Issue-25
00Topps Stanley Cup Heroes-SHLR
00Topps Stanley Cup Heroes Autographs-SHLR
00Topps Stars-98
Blue-98
Autographs-ALR
Progression-P7
Progression-P8
Progression-P9
00Upper Deck Legends-69
Legendary Collection Bronze-69
Legendary Collection Gold-69
Legendary Collection Silver-69
Epic Signatures-LR
Legendary Game Jerseys-JLR
01BAP Ultimate Memorabilia Decades-21
01BAP Ultimate Mem Dynasty Jerseys-12
01BAP Ultimate Mem Dynasty Emblems-12
01BAP Ultimate Mem Dynasty Numbers-12
01BAP Ultimate Memorabilia Emblem Attic-18
01BAP Ultimate Memorabilia Les Canadiens-6
01BAP Ultimate Mem Playoff Records-3
01BAP Ultimate Mem Stanley Cup Winners-10
01Devils Team Issue-20
01Fleer Legacy-46
Ultimate-46
In the Corners-8
Memorabilia-6
01Greats of the Game-44
Autographs-44
Jerseys-5
Patches Gold-5
01Parkhurst Autographs-PA59
01Topps Archives-5
Arena Seats-ASLR
Relics-JLR
01Topps Chrome Reprints-9
01Topps Chrome Reprint Refractors-9
01Topps Chrome Reprint Autographs-9
02BAP Memorabilia Mini Stanley Cups-15
02BAP Ultimate Memorabilia Conn Smythe-10
02BAP Ultimate Memorabilia Numerology-21
02BAP Ultimate Memorabilia Retro Trophies-11
02BAP Ultimate Mem Storied Franchise-4
02BAP Ultimate Mem Vintage Jerseys-25
02Parkhurst Vintage Teammates-VT4
03BAP Ultimate Memorabilia Cornerstones-3
03BAP Ultimate Memorabilia Triple Threads-13
03BAP Ultimate Mem Vintage Jerseys-25
03BAP Ultimate Mem Vintage Jerseys Gold-25
03ITG Toronto Fall Expo Forever Rivals-FR5
03ITG Used Signature Series Norris Trophy-11
03ITG Used Sig Series Norris Trophy Gold-11
03Parkhurst Original Six Montreal-68
03Parkhurst Original Six Montreal-89
03Parkhurst Original Six Montreal-98
Autographs-13
Memorabilia-MM53
04Canada Post-27
04Canada Post Autographs-3
04ITG Franchises Canadian-50
Forever Rivals-FR7
Forever Rivals Gold-FR7
Memorabilia-SM4
Memorabilia Gold-SM4
Original Sticks-OS6
Original Sticks Gold-OS6
Teammates-TM7
Teammates Gold-TM7
Trophy Winners-TW5
Trophy Winners Gold-TW5
04ITG Franchises He Shoots/Scores Prizes-10
04ITG Franchises Update Complete Jerseys-UCJ1
04ITG Franchises Upd Complete Jersey Gold-UCJ1
04ITG Franchises US West-239
Autographs-A-LR1
04ITG Ultimate Memorabilia-143
04ITG Ultimate Memorabilia-154
Gold-143
Gold-154
Auto Threads-5
Autographs-2
Autographs Gold-2
Country of Origin-19
Country of Origin Gold-19
Day In History-30
Day In History Gold-30
Heroes Patrick Roy-4
Jersey Autographs-1
Jersey Autographs Gold-1
Nicknames-9
Nickname Autographs-5
Norris Trophy-2
Original Six-19
Retro Teammates-9
Stick Autographs-12
Stick Autographs Gold-12
Triple Threads-2
04ITG Heroes and Prospects-144
Autographs-LRO
Hero Memorabilia-9
04ITG Heroes/Prospects Toronto Expo '05-144
04ITG Heroes/Prospects Expo Heroes/Pros-144
05ITG Heroes/Prosp Toronto Expo Parallel -191
05Devils Team Issue-5
05ITG Ultimate Memorabilia Level 1-62
05ITG Ultimate Memorabilia Level 2-62
05ITG Ultimate Memorabilia Level 3-62
05ITG Ultimate Memorabilia Level 4-62
05ITG Ultimate Memorabilia Level 5-62
05ITG Ultimate Mem Complete Jersey-17
05ITG Ultimate Mem Complete Jersey Gold-17
05ITG Ultimate Memorabilia Double Autos-11
05ITG Ultimate Mem Double Autos Gold-11
05ITG Ultimate Memorabilia Jersey Autos-24
05ITG Ultimate Mem Jersey Autos Gold-24
05ITG Ultimate Mem Pass the Torch Jerseys-8
05ITG Ultimate Mem Passing Torch Jsy Gold-8
05ITG Ultimate Mem Retro Teammate Jerseys-14
05ITG Ult Mem Retro Teammates Jersey Gold-14
05ITG Ultimate Mem 3 Star of the Game Jsy-18
05ITG Ult Mem 3 Star of the Game Jsy Gold-18
05ITG Ultimate Memorabilia Triple Autos-19
05ITG Ultimate Mem Triple Autos Gold-19
05ITG Ultimate Mem Triple Threads Jerseys-5
05ITG Ultimate Mem Triple Thread Jsy Gold-5
05ITG Ultimate Memorabilia Ultimate Autos-10
05ITG Ultimate Mem Ultimate Autos Gold-10
05NHL Legends Medallions-17
05The Cup Property of-POLR
05Ultimate Coll Ultimate Sigs Trios-UTLBR
05ITG Heroes and Prospects-191
Autographs Series II-LR
Autographs Series II-RP
Hero Memorabilia-HM-54
National Pride-NPR-30
06ITG International Ice-33
06ITG International Ice-48
06ITG International Ice-75
Gold-33
Gold-48
Gold-75
Autographs-ALR
Autographs-ALR2
Autographs-ALR3
Cornerstones-IC12
Cornerstones Gold-IC12
06ITG Ultimate Memorabilia-87
Artist Proof-87
Autos-30
Autos Gold-30
Bowman Factor-6
Bowman Factor Gold-6
Bowman Factor Autos-5
Bowman Factor Autos Gold-5
Boys Will Be Boys-6
Boys Will Be Boys Gold-6
Decades-3
Decades Gold-3
Jerseys Autos-49
Jerseys Autos Gold-49
Retro Teammates-18
Retro Teammates Gold-18
Ring Leaders-8
Ring Leaders Gold-8
Road to the Cup-5
Road to the Cup Gold-5
Stick Rack-10
Stick Rack Gold-10
06Parkhurst-106
Autographs-106
Autographs Dual-DARP
06SP Authentic-120
Limited-120
Sign of the Times Duals-STMC
Sign of the Times Duals-STRP
Sign of the Times Triples-ST3LRS
Sign of the Times Quads-ST4BLSR
06SP Game Used Authentic Fabrics Dual-AF2RL
06SP Game Used Authentic Fabrics Dual Patches-AF2RL
06The Cup-47
Autographed Foundations-CQLR
Autographed Foundations Patches-CQLR
Autographed Patches-47
Black Rainbow-47
Foundations-CQLR
Foundations Patches-CQLR
Enshrinements-ELR
Gold-47
Gold Patches-47
Hardware Heroes Patches-HHLR
Honorable Numbers-HNLR
Jerseys-47
Limited Logos-LLLR
Masterpiece Pressplates-47
Property of-POLR
Scripted Swatches-SSLR
Scripted Swatches Duals-DSLR
Signature Patches-SPLR
Stanley Cup Signatures-CSLR
Stanley Cup Titlists Patches-TLR
06Ultimate Collection Autographed Jerseys-AJ-LR
06Ultimate Collection Autographed Patches-AJ-LR
06Ultimate Collection Jerseys-UJ-LR
06Ultimate Collection Jerseys Dual-UJ2-RP
06Ultimate Collection Jerseys Triple-UJ3-LRS
06Ultimate Collection Patches-UJ-LR
06Ultimate Collection Patches Triple-UJ3-LRS
06Ultimate Collection Signatures-US-LR
06Upper Deck Sweet Shot-59
Signature Shots/Saves Ice Signings-SSILR
Signature Shots/Saves Sticks-SSSRO
Signature Sticks-STRO
Sweet Stitches-SSRO
Sweet Stitches Duals-SSRO
Sweet Stitches Triples-SSRO

Robinson, Mark
04Lakehead University Thunderwolves-26

Robinson, Matt
04Vancouver Giants-6
05Regina Pats-17

Robinson, Michel
03ECHL Update RBI Sports-131
03Greenville Grrrowl-18
05Rockford Ice Hogs-23

Robinson, Moe
77Nova Scotia Voyageurs-18

Robinson, Nathan
00Belleville Bulls-22
01Belleville Bulls-20
02Grand Rapids Griffins-23
03ITG Action-641
03ITG Used Signature Series-174
Gold-174
03ITG VIP Rookie Debut-69
03Pacific Calder-117
Silver-117
03Pacific Complete-537
Red-537
03Pacific Heads-Up-115
Hobby LTD-115
Retail LTD-115
03Pacific Luxury Suite-64
Gold-64
03Pacific Quest for the Cup-116
03Parkhurst Rookie-112
03SP Authentic-106
Limited-106
03Titanium-119
Hobby Jersey Number Parallels-119
Retail-119
Retail Jersey Number Parallels-119
03Topps Traded-TT106
Blue-TT106
Gold-TT106
Red-TT106
03Upper Deck-470
Canadian Exclusives-470
HG-470
UD Exclusives-470
03Upper Deck Rookie Update-143
03Grand Rapids Griffins-18
03Pacific AHL Prospects-27
Gold-27
04AHL Top Prospects-15
05Providence Bruins-14
06German DEL-153
New Arrivals-NA9

Robinson, Nick
93Quebec Pee-Wee Tournament-553
96Sault Ste. Marie Greyhounds-18
96Sault Ste. Marie Greyhounds Autographed-18

Robinson, Rob
89ProCards IHL-22
90ProCards AHL/IHL-79
91Blues Postcards-17
92Topps Gold-527G
92Peoria Rivermen-21
00UK Sekonda Superleague-95

Robinson, Scott
89ProCards IHL-78
90ProCards AHL/IHL-118
91ProCards-153

Robinson, Stephane
84Richelieu Riverains-15

Robinson, Todd
95Upper Deck-508
Electric Ice-508
Electric Ice Gold-508
97Portland Winter Hawks-15
97Bowman CHL-93
OPC-93
98Bowman CHL-52
Golden Anniversary-52
OPC International-52
98Bowman Chrome CHL-52
Golden Anniversary-52
Golden Anniversary Refractors-52
OPC International-52
OPC International Refractors-52
Refractors-52
99Idaho Steelheads-4
00Muskegon Fury-4
02Muskegon Fury-22
03Muskegon Fury-18
05Muskegon Fury-17

Robison, Jeff
92Raleigh Icecaps-15
92Raleigh Icecaps-22
93Raleigh Icecaps-17

Robitaille, Louis
04Portland Pirates-18
05Hot Prospects-186
En Fuego-186
Red Hot-186
White Hot-186
05The Cup Master Pressplate Rookie Update-195
05Upper Deck Rookie Update-195
05Hershey Bears-26

Robitaille, Luc
86Kings 20th Anniversary Team Issue-19
87O-Pee-Chee-42
87O-Pee-Chee Box Bottoms-D
87O-Pee-Chee Minis-35
87O-Pee-Chee Stickers-122
87O-Pee-Chee Stickers-133
87O-Pee-Chee Stickers-177
87O-Pee-Chee Stickers-187
87O-Pee-Chee Stickers-217
87Panini Stickers-277
87Panini Stickers-379
87Topps-42
87Topps Box Bottoms-D
87Topps Sticker Inserts-12
88Esso All-Stars-38
88Frito-Lay Stickers-10
88Kings Postcards-4
88Kings Smokey-21
88O-Pee-Chee-124
88O-Pee-Chee Box Bottoms-P
88O-Pee-Chee Minis-32
88O-Pee-Chee Stickers-114
88O-Pee-Chee Stickers-157
88Panini Stickers-78
88Topps-124
88Topps Box Bottoms-P
88Topps Sticker Inserts-1
89Kings Smokey-8
89O-Pee-Chee-88
89O-Pee-Chee Stickers-148
89Panini Stickers-95
89Panini Stickers-177
89Topps-88
89Swedish Semic World Champ Stickers-68
90Bowman-152
Tiffany-152
90Bowman Hat Tricks-12
Tiffany-12
90Kings Smokey-10
90Kraft-48
90Kraft-75
90O-Pee-Chee-194
90O-Pee-Chee-209
90OPC Premier-99
90Panini Stickers-233
90Panini Stickers-331
90Pro Set-126
90Pro Set-341
90Score-150
90Score-316
Canadian-150
Canadian-316
90Score Hottest/Rising Stars-66
90Topps-194
90Topps-209
Tiffany-194
Tiffany-209
90Upper Deck-73
French-73
91Pro Set Platinum-50
91Pro Set Platinum-142
91Bowman-188
91Gillette-1
91Kraft-70
91McDonald's Upper Deck-14
91O-Pee-Chee-260
91O-Pee-Chee-405
91OPC Premier-34
91Panini Stickers-91
91Panini Stickers-324
91Parkhurst-68
91Parkhurst-224
French-68
French-224
91Pinnacle-17
91Pinnacle-385
French-17
French-385
B-B10
B French-B10
91Pro Set-95
91Pro Set-286
French-95
French-286
Awards Special-AC9
Player of the Month-P6
Puck Candy-12
91Score National-5
91Score Ntnl Candy Wholesalers Convention-5
91Score Fanfest-5
91Score American-3
91Score American-345
91Score Canadian Bilingual-3
91Score Canadian Bilingual-375
91Score Canadian English-3
91Score Canadian English-375
91Stadium Club-159
91Topps-260
91Topps-405
91Upper Deck-145
91Upper Deck-507
91Upper Deck-623
French-145
French-507
French-623
91Finnish Semic World Champ Stickers-70
91Swedish Semic World Champ Stickers-70
92Bowman-70
92Bowman-216
92Durivage Panini-28
92Humpty Dumpty II-19
92Kellogg's Posters-3
92McDonald's Upper Deck-12
92O-Pee-Chee-6
92Panini Stickers-65
92Panini Stickers-288
92Panini Stickers French-65
92Panini Stickers French-288
92Parkhurst-68
92Parkhurst-501
Emerald Ice-68
Emerald Ice-501
92Pinnacle Canadian Promo Panels-3
92Pinnacle-175
92Pinnacle-251
French-175
French-251
92Pro Set-72
92Score-290
92Score-498
Canadian-290
Canadian-498
92Seasons Patches-10
92Sports Illustrated for Kids II-241
92Stadium Club-44
92Stadium Club-247
92Topps-101
92Topps-266
Gold-101G
Gold-266G
92Ultra-87
All-Stars-11
92Upper Deck-8
92Upper Deck-216
Gordie Howe Selects-G2
World Junior Grads-WG20
92Finnish Semic-89
93Donruss-162
93Donruss-395
Special Print-NNO
93Durivage Score-41
93Kraft-20
93Leaf-20
Gold All-Stars-9
93McDonald's Upper Deck-H3
93OPC Premier-90
93OPC Premier-180
Gold-90
Gold-180
93Panini Stickers-201
93Parkhurst-91
Emerald Ice-91
93Pinnacle-145
Canadian-145
All-Stars-37
All-Stars Canadian-37
Nifty Fifty-5
Team Pinnacle-4
Team Canadian-4
93PowerPlay-120
Point Leaders-13
93Score-245
93Score-451
Canadian-245
Canadian-451
Dream Team-24
93Stadium Club-87
Members Only Master Set-87
OPC-87
First Day Issue-87
First Day Issue OPC-87
All-Stars-18
All-Stars Members Only-18
All-Stars OPC-18
Finest-7
Finest Members Only-7
93Topps/OPC Premier-90
93Topps/OPC Premier-180
Gold-90
Gold-180
93Ultra-208
All-Stars-13
Red Light Specials-9
93Upper Deck-231
93Upper Deck-293
93Upper Deck-414
Gretzky's Great Ones-GG8
Hat Tricks-HT17
SP-73
93Upper Deck Locker All-Stars-33
93Swedish Semic World Champ Stickers-204
94Hockey Canadian-11
94SLU Hockey Canadian-11
94SLU Hockey American-17
94Be A Player-R95
Signature Cards-113
94Donruss Ice Masters-9
94EA Sports-64
94EA Sports-200
94Finest-89
Super Team Winners-89
Refractors-89
Division's Clear Cut-4
94Flair-138
Hot Numbers-7
94Fleer-167
94Hockey Wit-96
94Kenner Starting Lineup Cards-18
94Leaf-20
94Leaf-463
94Leaf Limited-88
94NHLPA Phone Cards-5
94OPC Premier-526
94OPC Premier-540
Special Effects-526
Special Effects-540
94Parkhurst Vintage-V67
94Parkhurst SE-SE137
Gold-SE137
94Penguins Foodland-14
94Pinnacle-400
Artist's Proofs-400
Rink Collection-400
Team Pinnacle-TP7
Team Dufex Parallel-TP7
94Post Box Backs-21
94Score Dream Team-DT10
94Select-32
Gold-32
First Line-FL10
94SP-93
Die Cuts-93
94Stadium Club-57
Members Only Master Set-57

First Day Issue-57
Dynasty and Destiny-4
Dynasty and Destiny Members Only-4
Super Team Winner Cards-57
94Topps/OPC Premier-346
94Topps/OPC Premier-526
94Topps/OPC Premier-540
Special Effects-526
Special Effects-540
94Topps Finest Inserts-13
94Ultra-103
94Ultra-350
94Upper Deck-194
Electric Ice-194
SP Inserts-SP152
SP Inserts Die Cuts-SP152
94Upper Deck NHLPA/Be A Player-12
94Finnish Jaa Kiekko-92
94Finnish Jaa Kiekko-353
95SLU Hockey American-16
95Bashan Super Stickers-82
95Bowman-23
All-Foil-23
95Canada Games NHL POGS-183
95Collector's Choice-164
Player's Club-164
Player's Club Platinum-164
95Donruss-104
95Donruss-348
95Donruss Elite-105
Die Cut Stars-105
Die Cut Uncut-105
95Emotion-118
95Finest-24
Refractors-24
95Hoyle Eastern Playing Cards-18
95Imperial Stickers-82
95Kenner Starting Lineup Cards-18
95Leaf-129
95Leaf Limited-91
95Metal-99
95Panini Stickers-61
95Parkhurst International-140
Emerald Ice-140
95Playoff One on One-71
95Playoff One on One-286
95Post Upper Deck-8
95Pro Magnets-100
95Score-54
Black Ice Artist's Proofs-54
Black Ice-54
Lamplighters-9
95Select Certified-53
Mirror Gold-53
95SkyBox Impact-113
Ice Quake-14
95SP-97
95Stadium Club-100
Members Only Master Set-100
95Summit-89
Artist's Proofs-89
Ice-89
Mad Hatters-14
95Topps-40
95Topps-352
95Topps-379
OPC Inserts-40
OPC Inserts-352
OPC Inserts-379
Hidden Gems-2HG
Home Grown Canada-HGC19
Marquee Men Power Boosters-379
95Topps SuperSkills-56
Platinum-56
95Ultra-277
95Upper Deck-8
95Upper Deck-244
Electric Ice-8
Electric Ice-244
Electric Ice Gold-8
Electric Ice Gold-244
Special Edition-SE144
Special Edition Gold-SE144
95Zenith-48
95Finnish Semic World Championships-89
95Swedish Globe World Championships-94
95Swedish Globe World Championships-249
95Swedish World Championships Stickers-21
96Be A Player-12
Autographs-12
Autographs Silver-12
96Collector's Choice-171
96Donruss-7
Press Proofs-7
96Donruss Canadian Ice-64
Gold Press Proofs-64
Red Press Proofs-64
96Donruss Elite-78
Die Cut Stars-78
96Leaf-134
Press Proofs-134
96Leaf Limited-27
Gold-27
96Leaf Preferred-13
Press Proofs-13
96Maggers-86
96Metal Universe-101
96NHL Pro Stamps-100
96Post Upper Deck-16
96Score-113
Artist's Proofs-113
Dealer's Choice Artist's Proofs-113
Special Artist's Proofs-113
Golden Blades-113
96Select Certified-13
Artist's Proofs-13
Blue-13
Mirror Blue-13
Mirror Gold-13
Mirror Red-13
Red-13
96SP-102
96Summit-13
Artist's Proofs-13
Ice-13
Metal-13
Premium Stock-13
96Team Out-2
96Topps Picks-87
OPC Inserts-87
96Ultra-111
Gold Medallion-111
96Zenith-36
Artist's Proofs-36
96Swedish Semic Wien-93
97Beehive-36
Golden Portraits-36
97Black Diamond-76
Double Diamond-76
Triple Diamond-76
Quadruple Diamond-76

97Collector's Choice-170
97Crown Royale-65
Emerald Green-65
Ice Blue-65
Silver-65
97Donruss-90
Press Proofs Silver-90
Press Proofs Gold-90
97Donruss Canadian Ice-68
Dominion Series-68
Provincial Series-68
97Donruss Elite-85
Aspirations-85
Status-85
97Donruss Limited-75
Exposure-75
97Donruss Preferred-121
Cut to the Chase-121
97Donruss Priority-32
Stamp of Approval-32
97Katch-72
Gold-72
Silver-72
97Leaf-121
Fractal Matrix-121
Fractal Matrix Die Cuts-121
97Leaf International-121
Universal Ice-121
97Pacific-145
Copper-145
Emerald Green-145
Ice Blue-145
Red-145
Silver-145
97Pacific Invincible-91
Copper-91
Emerald Green-91
Ice Blue-91
Red-91
Silver-91
97Pacific Omega-112
Copper-112
Dark Gray-112
Emerald Green-112
Gold-112
Ice Blue-112
97Paramount-91
Copper-91
Dark Grey-91
Emerald Green-91
Ice Blue-91
Red-91
Silver-91
97Pinnacle-149
Press Plates Back Black-149
Press Plates Back Cyan-149
Press Plates Back Magenta-149
Press Plates Back Yellow-149
Press Plates Front Black-149
Press Plates Front Cyan-149
Press Plates Front Magenta-149
Press Plates Front Yellow-149
97Pinnacle Certified-92
Red-92
Mirror Blue-92
Mirror Gold-92
Mirror Red-92
97Pinnacle Inside-168
97Pinnacle Tot Cert Platinum Blue-92
97Pinnacle Tot Cert Platinum Gold-92
97Pinnacle Totally Certified Platinum Red-92
97Pinnacle Tot Cert Mirror Platinum Gold-92
97Revolution-66
Copper-66
Emerald-66
Ice Blue-66
Silver-66
97Score-149
Artist's Proofs-149
Golden Blades-149
97SP Authentic-77
Icons-I18
Icons Die-Cuts-I18
Icons Embossed-I18
97Studio-53
Press Proofs Silver-53
Press Proofs Gold-53
97Upper Deck-290
Game Dated Moments-290
97Zenith-41
Z-Gold-41
Z-Silver-41
97Zenith 5 x 7-56
Gold Impulse-56
Silver Impulse-56
98Aurora-88
98Be A Player-61
Press Release-61
98BAP Gold-61
98BAP Autographs-61
98BAP Autographs Gold-61
98BAP AS Milestones-M18
98BAP Tampa Bay All Star Game-61
98Crown Royale-65
Limited Series-65
98Finest-128
No Protectors-128
No Protectors Refractors-128
Refractors-128
98Katch-70
98Kings LA Times Coins-4
98Kings Power Play-LAK3
98McDonalds Upper Deck Gretzkys Teammates-T13
98NHL Game Day Promotion-LAK3
98OPC Chrome-174
Refractors-174
98Pacific-244
Ice Blue-244
Red-244
98Pacific Dynagon Ice-90
Blue-90
Red-90
98Pacific Omega-112
Red-112
Opening Day Issue-112
98Panini Photocards-69
98Paramount-107
Copper-107
Emerald Green-107
Holo-Electric-107
Ice Blue-107
Silver-107
98Revolution-68
Ice Shadow-68
Red-68
98SP Authentic-38
Power Shift-38
98Topps-174
O-Pee-Chee-174
98UD Choice-98
Mini Bobbing Head-BH12

Prime Choice Reserve-98
Reserve-98
98Upper Deck-104
Exclusives-104
Exclusives 1 of 1-104
Gold Reserve-104
98Upper Deck MVP-97
Gold Script-97
Silver Script-97
Super Script-97
99Aurora-70
Striped-70
Premiere Date-70
Premiere Date Striped-70
99BAP Memorabilia-162
Gold-162
Silver-162
99BAP Millennium-122
Emerald-122
Ruby-122
Sapphire-122
Signatures-122
Signatures Gold-122
99Black Diamond-45
Diamond Cut-45
Final Cut-45
99Crown Royale-67
Limited Series-67
Premiere Date-67
Ice Elite-13
Ice Elite Parallel-13
99Kings AAA Magnets-1
99McDonald's Upper Deck Signatures-LR
99O-Pee-Chee-53
99O-Pee-Chee Chrome-53
99O-Pee-Chee Chrome Refractors-53
99Pacific-196
Copper-196
Emerald Green-196
Gold-196
Ice Blue-196
Premiere Date-196
Red-196
Team Leaders-13
99Pacific Dynagon Ice-98
Blue-98
Copper-98
Gold-98
Premiere Date-98
99Pacific Omega-111
Copper-111
Gold-111
Ice Blue-111
Premiere Date-111
99Pacific Prism-69
Holographic Blue-69
Holographic Gold-69
Holographic Mirror-69
Holographic Purple-69
Premiere Date-69
99Panini Stickers-258
99Paramount Ice Alliance-13
99Revolution-71
Premiere Date-71
Red-71
Shadow Series-71
Top of the Line-5
Copper-71
Gold-71
CSC Silver-71
99SP Authentic-40
Buyback Signatures-48
Buyback Signatures-49
Buyback Signatures-50
Buyback Signatures-51
Buyback Signatures-52
Buyback Signatures-53
Jersey Redemption-JLR
Sign of the Times-LR
Sign of the Times Gold-LR
99SPx-75
Radiance-75
Spectrum-75
99Stadium Club-27
First Day Issue-27
One of a Kind-27
Printing Plates Black-27
Printing Plates Cyan-27
Printing Plates Magenta-27
Printing Plates Yellow-27
Chrome-20
Chrome Refractors-20
99Topps/OPC-53
99Topps/OPC Chrome-53
Refractors-53
99Topps Gold Label Class 1-3
Black-3
Black One of One-3
One of One-3
Red-3
Red One of One-3
99Topps Gold Label Class 2-3
99Topps Gold Label Class 2 Black-3
99Topps Gold Label Class 2 Black 1 of 1-3
99Topps Gold Label Class 2 One of One-3
99Topps Gold Label Class 2 Red-3
99Topps Gold Label Class 2 Red One of One-3
99Topps Gold Label Class 3-3
99Topps Gold Label Class 3 Black-3
99Topps Gold Label Class 3 Black 1 of 1-3
99Topps Gold Label Class 3 One of One-3
99Topps Gold Label Class 3 Red-3
99Topps Gold Label Class 3 Red One of One-3
99Topps Premier Plus-11
Parallel-11
99Ultimate Victory-41
1/1-41
Parallel-41
Parallel 100-41
99Upper Deck-234
Exclusives-234
Exclusives 1 of 1-234
500 Goal Club-500LR
500 Goal Club-500LR
Headed for the Hall-HOF12
Headed for the Hall Quantum Gold-HOF12
Headed for the Hall Quantum Silver-HOF12
99Upper Deck Gold Reserve-234
99Upper Deck HoloGrFx-28
Ausome-28
99Upper Deck MVP-96
Gold Script-96
Silver Script-96
Super Script-96
ProSign-LR
99Upper Deck MVP SC Edition-85
Gold Script-85
Silver Script-85
Super Script-85
Clutch Performers-CP5
99Upper Deck Ovation-29

Standing Ovation-29
99Upper Deck Retro-39
Gold-39
Platinum-39
99Upper Deck Victory-134
99Wayne Gretzky Hockey-81
Tools of Greatness-TGLR
99Hull Olympiques-NNO
Signed-NNO
00Aurora-68
Pinstripes-68
Pinstripes Premiere Date-68
Premiere Date-68
00BAP Memorabilia-51
Emerald-51
Ruby-51
Sapphire-51
Promos-51
00BAP Mem Chicago Sportsfest Copper-51
00BAP Memorabilia Chicago Sportsfest Blue-51
00BAP Memorabilia Chicago Sportsfest Gold-51
00BAP Memorabilia Chicago Sportsfest Ruby-51
00BAP Memorabilia Chicago Sun-Times Ruby-51
00BAP Memorabilia Chicago Sun-Times Gold-51
00BAP Mem Chicago Sun-Times Sapphire-51
00BAP Mem Toronto Fall Expo Copper-51
00BAP Memorabilia Toronto Fall Expo Gold-51
00BAP Memorabilia Toronto Fall Expo Ruby-51
00BAP Parkhurst 2000-P213
00BAP Signature Series-204
Emerald-204
Ruby-204
Sapphire-204
Autographs-35
Autographs Gold-35
He Shoots-He Scores Points-15
He Shoots-He Scores Prizes-18
Jersey Cards-J33
Jersey and Stick Cards-GSJ33
Jersey Cards Autographs-J33
Jersey Emblems-E33
Jersey Numbers-IN33
00BAP Ultimate Memorabilia Autographs-44
Gold-44
00BAP Ultimate Mem Game-Used Jerseys-GJ40
00BAP Ultimate Mem Game-Used Emblems-E32
00BAP Ultimate Mem Game-Used Numbers-N32
00BAP Ultimate Mem Game-Used Sticks-GS40
00Black Diamond-29
Gold-29
00Crown Royale-50
Ice Blue-50
Limited Series-50
Premiere Date-50
Red-50
00Kraft-3
00O-Pee-Chee-111
00O-Pee-Chee Parallel-111
00Pacific-201
Copper-201
Gold-201
Ice Blue-201
Premiere Date-201
Gold Crown Die Cuts-17
00Panini Stickers-166
00Paramount-114
Copper-114
Gold-114
Holo-Gold-114
Holo-Silver-114
Ice Blue-114
Premiere Date-114
Freeze Frame-19
Game Used Sticks-12
00Private Stock-47
Gold-47
Premiere Date-47
Retail-47
Silver-47
Extreme Action-10
PS-2001 Action-27
PS-2001 Stars-15
00Revolution-69
Blue-69
Premiere Date-69
Red-69
HD NHL-18
NHL Icons-14
Stat Masters-7
00SP Authentic-43
BuyBacks-47
BuyBacks-48
BuyBacks-49
BuyBacks-50
BuyBacks-51
BuyBacks-52
Sign of the Times-LR
00SP Game Used-29
00SPx-33
Spectrum-33
00Stadium Club-146
00Titanium-43
Blue-43
Gold-43
Premiere Date-43
Red-43
Retail-43
00Topps/OPC-111
Parallel-111
NHL Draft-D14
1000 Point Club-PC10
00Topps Chrome-87
OPC Refractors-87
Refractors-87
Rocket's Flare-RF5
Rocket's Flare Refractors-RF5
1000 Point Club Refractors-10
00Topps Gold Label Class 1-28
Gold-28
00Topps Gold Label Class 2-28
00Topps Gold Label Class 2 Gold-28
00Topps Gold Label Class 3-28
00Topps Gold Label Class 3 Gold-28
00Topps Gold Label Golden Greats-GG12
00Topps Gold Label Golden Greats 1 to 1-GG12
00Topps Heritage-40
Chrome Parallel-40
00Topps Premier Plus-73
Blue Ice-73
Club Signings-CS-5
Club Signings-CSC-3
00Topps Stars-58
Blue-58
00UD Heroes-57
00UD Pros and Prospects-39
00UD Reserve-39
Buyback Autographs-79
Buyback Autographs-80
Buyback Autographs-81
Buyback Autographs-82
Buyback Autographs-83

Buyback Autographs-84
Buyback Autographs-85
Buyback Autographs-86
Buyback Autographs-87
Buyback Autographs-88
Buyback Autographs-89
Buyback Autographs-90
Buyback Autographs-91
Buyback Autographs-92
Buyback Autographs-93
On-Ice Success-OS5
00Upper Deck-80
Exclusives Tier 1-80
Exclusives Tier 2-80
Dignitaries-D7
00Upper Deck Ice-21
Immortals-21
Legends-21
Stars-21
00Upper Deck Legends-60
00Upper Deck Legends-61
Legendary Collection Bronze-60
Legendary Collection Bronze-61
Legendary Collection Gold-60
Legendary Collection Gold-61
Legendary Collection Silver-60
Legendary Collection Silver-61
Supreme Milestones-SM10
00Upper Deck MVP-87
First Stars-87
Second Stars-87
Third Stars-87
00Upper Deck Victory-111
00Upper Deck Vintage-163
00Upper Deck Vintage-173
00Vanguard-49
Holographic Gold-49
Holographic Purple-49
Pacific Proofs-49
01Atomic-38
Blue-38
Gold-38
Premiere Date-38
Red-38
01BAP Memorabilia-95
01BAP Memorabilia-376
Emerald-95
Emerald-376
Ruby-95
Ruby-376
Sapphire-95
Sapphire-376
Country of Origin-CO56
500 Goal Scorers-GS12
Stanley Cup Playoffs-SC18
01BAP Signature Series Certified 100-C23
01BAP Signature Series Certified 50-C23
01BAP Signature Series Certified 1 of 1's-C23
01BAP Signature Series Autographs-LLR
01BAP Signature Series Autographs Gold-LLR
01BAP Signature Series 500 Goal Scorers-11
01BAP Sig Series 500 Goal Scorers Autos-11
01BAP Sig Series He Shoots/Scores Points-8
01BAP Sig Series He Shoots/Scores Prizes-16
01BAP Signature Series Jerseys-GJ-26
01BAP Signature Series Jersey Autographs-GULR
01BAP Sig Series Jersey and Stick Cards-GSJ-26
01BAP Signature Series Emblems-GUE-30
01BAP Signature Series Numbers-ITN-30
01BAP Signature Series Teammates-TM-12
01BAP Ultimate Memorabilia Active Eight-4
01BAP Ultimate Memorabilia Active Eight-6
01BAP Ultimate Mem All-Star History-44
01BAP Ultimate Memorabilia Autographs-15
01BAP Ultimate Mem Autographs Gold-15
01BAP Ultimate Memorabilia Calder Trophy-15
01BAP Ultimate Memorabilia Dynamic Duos-3
01BAP Ultimate Memorabilia Emblems-30
01BAP Ultimate Mem 500 Goal Scorers-21
01BAP Ultimate Mem 500 Goal Scorers Autos-13
01BAP Ultimate Mem 500 Goal Jerseys/Stick-21
01BAP Ultimate Mem 500 Goal Emblems-21
01BAP Ultimate Memorabilia Jerseys-30
01BAP Ultimate Mem Jerseys and Sticks-30
01BAP Ultimate Mem Journey Jerseys-16
01BAP Ultimate Mem Journey Emblems-16
01BAP Ultimate Memorabilia Numbers-30
01BAP Ultimate Memorabilia Name Plates-8
01BAP Ultimate Mem Prototypical Players-10
01BAP Ultimate Mem Retro Teammates-13
01BAP Update He Shoots-He Scores Points-13
01BAP Update He Shoots-He Scores Prizes-4
01BAP Update He Shoots-He Scores Prizes-25
01BAP Update Heritage-H27
01BAP Update Travel Plans-TP8
01Bowman YoungStars-61
Gold-61
Ice Cubed-61
01Crown Royale-55
Blue-55
Premiere Date-55
Red-55
Retail-55
01McDonald's Pacific Hometown Pride-7
01O-Pee-Chee-54
01O-Pee-Chee Heritage Parallel-54
01O-Pee-Chee Heritage Parallel Limited-54
01O-Pee-Chee Premier Parallel-54
01Pacific-186
01Pacific-432
Extreme LTD-186
Gold-432
Hobby LTD-186
Premiere Date-186
Retail LTD-186
All-Stars-NA8
01Pacific Adrenaline-68
Blue-68
Premiere Date-68
Red-68
Retail-68
01Pacific Arena Exclusives-186
01Pacific Arena Exclusives-432
01Pacific Heads-Up-37
Blue-37
Premiere Date-37
Red-37
Silver-37
01Parkhurst-215
500 Goal Scorers-PGS12
Milestones-M7
Milestones-M19U
Sticks-PS61
01Private Stock-36
Gold-36
Premiere Date-36
Retail-36
Silver-36
01Private Stock Pacific Nights-36
01SP Authentic-30
Limited-30

Limited Gold-30
01SP Game Used-21
Authentic Fabric-AFLR
Authentic Fabric Gold-AFLR
01SPx-25
01Titanium-52
Hobby Parallel-52
Premiere Date-52
Retail-52
Retail Parallel-52
01Topps-54
Heritage Parallel-54
Heritage Parallel Limited-54
OPC Parallel-54
01Topps Chrome-54
Refractors-54
Black Border Refractors-54
01Topps Heritage-122
01Topps Heritage-166
01UD Challenge for the Cup-31
Century Men-CM5
Future Famers-FF4
01UD Honor Roll-7
01UD Honor Roll-37
Jerseys-J-LR
Jerseys Gold-J-LR
Playoff Matchups-HS-SR
Playoff Matchups Gold-HS-SR
01UD Playmakers-37
01UD Top Shelf-16
01Upper Deck-65
Exclusives-65
Shooting Stars-SS7
01Upper Deck Ice-96
01Upper Deck MVP-67
Souvenirs-S-LR
Souvenirs Gold-S-LR
01Upper Deck Victory-159
01Upper Deck Victory-423
Gold-159
Gold-423
01Upper Deck Vintage-91
02Atomic Jerseys-9
02Atomic Jerseys Gold-9
02Atomic Patches-9
02Atomic Power Converters-8
02BAP All-Star Edition-75
Jerseys-75
Jerseys Gold-75
Jerseys Silver-75
02BAP First Edition-18
02BAP First Edition-324
Jerseys-18
02BAP Memorabilia-170
Emerald-170
Ruby-170
Sapphire-170
All-Star Jerseys-ASJ-48
All-Star Emblems-ASE-18
All-Star Numbers-ASN-18
NHL All-Star Game-170
NHL All-Star Game Blue-170
NHL All-Star Game Green-170
NHL All-Star Game Red-170
Stanley Cup Champions-SCC-7
Teammates-TM-3
02BAP Memorabilia Toronto Fall Expo-170
02BAP NHL All-Star History-44
02BAP Signature Series-153
Autographs-153
Autograph Buybacks 1998-61
Autograph Buybacks 1999-122
Autograph Buybacks 2000-35
Autograph Buybacks 2001-LLR
Autographs Gold-153
Golf-GS48
Jerseys-SGJ38
Jersey Autographs-SGJ38
02BAP Ultimate Mem Dynasty Jerseys-10
02BAP Ultimate Mem Dynasty Emblems-10
02BAP Ultimate Mem Dynasty Numbers-10
02BAP Ultimate Memorabilia Emblems-23
02BAP Ultimate Mem Lifetime Achievers-16
02BAP Ultimate Memorabilia Numbers-21
02Crown Royale Dual Patches-9
02ITG Used-26
02ITG Used-126
Jerseys-GUJ38
Jersey Autographs-GUJ38
Jerseys Gold-GUJ38
Jersey and Stick-SJ38
Jersey and Stick Gold-SJ38
02O-Pee-Chee-232
02O-Pee-Chee-318
02O-Pee-Chee Premier Blue Parallel-232
02O-Pee-Chee Premier Blue Parallel-318
02O-Pee-Chee Premier Red Parallel-232
02O-Pee-Chee Premier Red Parallel-318
02O-Pee-Chee Factory Set-232
02O-Pee-Chee Factory Set-318
02Pacific-133
Blue-133
Red-133
02Pacific Calder-26
Silver-26
02Pacific Complete-240
Red-240
02Pacific Exclusive-66
02Pacific Heads-Up-46
Blue-46
Purple-46
Red-46
Quad Jerseys-9
Quad Jerseys Gold-9
02Parkhurst-124
Bronze-124
Gold-124
Silver-124
He Shoots-He Scores Prizes-25
Jerseys-GJ18
Stick and Jerseys-SJ18
02Parkhurst Retro-120
Minis-120
02Private Stock Reserve-120
Red-120
Retail-120
02SP Game Used Authentic Fabrics-CFYR
02SP Game Used Authentic Fabrics Gold-CFYR
02SP Game Used Authentic Fabrics Rainbow-CFYR
02SPx-130
02Titanium Jerseys-26
02Titanium Jerseys Retail-26
02Topps-232
02Topps-318
OPC Blue Parallel-232
OPC Blue Parallel-318
OPC Red Parallel-232
OPC Red Parallel-318
Factory Set-232
Factory Set-318
02Topps Chrome-126

Black Border Refractors-126
Refractors-126
02Topps Total-52
02UD Piece of History Awards Collection-AC10
02UD Top Shelf Clutch Performers-CPLR
02UD Top Shelf Hardware Heroes-HSSBR
02UD Top Shelf Milestones Jerseys-MMHYR
02UD Top Shelf Milestones Jerseys-MSYVR
02UD Top Shelf Triple Jerseys-HTSHR
02Upper Deck-66
Exclusives-66
02Upper Deck Victory-80
Bronze-80
Gold-80
Silver-80
02Upper Deck Vintage-92
03McFarlane Hockey-250
03McFarlane Hockey-252
03BAP Memorabilia Jersey and Stick-SJ-13
03BAP Memorabilia Jerseys-GJ-14
03Beehive-91
Variations-91
Gold-91
Silver-91
Sticks Beige Border-BE19
03Black Diamond-97
Black-97
Green-97
Red-97
03Crown Royale-49
Blue-49
Retail-49
03ITG Action Jerseys-M173
03O-Pee-Chee-212
03OPC Blue-212
03OPC Gold-212
03OPC Red-212
03Pacific-124
Blue-124
Red-124
03Pacific Complete-245
Red-245
03Parkhurst Orig Six Detroit Mem-DM4
03Parkhurst Orig Six Detroit Mem-DM16
03Parkhurst Original Six New York-39
03Parkhurst Rookie Records-RRE-3
03Parkhurst Rookie Records Gold-RRE-3
03Parkhurst Rookie ROYalty-VR-23
03Parkhurst Rookie ROYalty Gold-VR-23
03SP Authentic-39
Limited-39
03Titanium-48
Hobby Jersey Number Parallels-48
Retail-48
Retail Jersey Number Parallels-48
03Topps-212
Blue-212
Gold-212
Red-212
03Topps Traded-TT17
Blue-TT17
Gold-TT17
Red-TT17
03UD Premier Collection Stars-ST-LR
03UD Premier Collection Stars Patches-ST-LR
03Upper Deck-88
Canadian Exclusives-88
HG-88
Rookie Update Super Stars-SSLR
03Czech Stadion-545
04ITG NHL AS FANtasy AS History Jerseys-SB44
04Pacific-125
Blue-125
Red-125
Philadelphia-7
04SP Authentic-118
Limited-118
Buybacks-105
Sign of the Times-QS-HRBG
Sign of the Times-SS-AWS
Sign of the Times-SS-RLW
04Ultimate Collection-20
04Upper Deck-81
04Upper Deck-191
Canadian Exclusives-81
Canadian Exclusives-191
HG Glossy Gold-81
HG Glossy Gold-191
HG Glossy Silver-81
HG Glossy Silver-191
05Be A Player-42
First Period-42
Second Period-42
Third Period-42
Overtime-42
Dual Signatures-AR
Dual Signatures-RB
Outtakes-OT25
Signatures-LU
Signatures Gold-LU
05Beehive-41
05Beehive-192
Beige -41
Blue -41
Gold-41
Red -41
Matte-41
Matted Materials-MMLR
Matted Materials Remarkable-RMLR
Signature Scrapbook-SSLR
05Black Diamond-99
Emerald-99
Gold-99
Onyx-99
Ruby-99
Gemography-G-LR
Gemography Emerald-G-LR
Gemography Gold-G-LR
Gemography Onyx-G-LR
Gemography Ruby-G-LR
05Hot Prospects-46
En Fuego-46
Red Hot-46
White Hot-46
05Kings Team Issue-2
05McDonalds Upper Deck-31
05Panini Stickers-283
05Parkhurst-227
05Parkhurst-595
05Parkhurst-684
Facsimile Auto Parallel-227
Facsimile Auto Parallel-595
Facsimile Auto Parallel-684
True Colors-TCLAK
True Colors-TCLAK
True Colors-TCSJLA
True Colors-TCSJLA
05SP Authentic-45
Limited-45
Exquisite Endorsements-EELU
Sign of the Times Duals-DRR

05SP Game Used-46
Autographs-46
Gold-46
Authentic Fabrics Quad-FRRG
Authentic Patches Quad -FRRG
Auto Draft-AD-LR
Significant Numbers-SN-LR
05SPx-39
05SPx-109
Spectrum-39
Spectrum-109
Winning Combos-WC-DR
Winning Combos-WC-LA
Winning Combos Autographs-AWC-DR
Winning Combos Autographs-AWC-LA
Winning Combos Gold-WC-DR
Winning Combos Gold-WC-LA
Winning Combos Spectrum-WC-DR
Winning Combos Spectrum-WC-LA
Winning Materials-WM-LR
Winning Materials Gold-WM-LR
Winning Materials Spectrum-WM-LR
Xcitement Superstars-XS-LR
Xcitement Superstars Gold-XS-LR
Xcitement Superstars Spectrum-XS-LR
05The Cup-50
Gold-50
Black Rainbow-50
Dual NHL Shields-DSRD
Dual NHL Shields Autographs-ADSLA
Emblems of Endorsement-EELR
Hardware Heroes-HHLU
Honorable Numbers-HNLR
Limited Logos-LLLU
Masterpiece Pressplates-50
Masterpiece Pressplates (Rookie Update)-240
Noble Numbers Dual-DNNSR
Patch Variation-P50
Patch Variation Autographs-AP50
Property of-POLU
Scripted Numbers-SNBR
Scripted Numbers Dual-DSNRC
Scripted Swatches-SSLR
Signature Patches-SPLR
Stanley Cup Titlists-TLU
05UD Artifacts-48
05UD Artifacts-170
Blue-48
Blue-170
Gold-48
Gold-170
Green-48
Green-170
Pewter-48
Pewter-170
Red-48
Red-170
Auto Facts-AF-LR
Auto Facts Blue-AF-LR
Auto Facts Copper-AF-LR
Auto Facts Pewter-AF-LR
Auto Facts Silver-AF-LR
Gold Autographed-48
Gold Autographed-170
Remarkable Artifacts-RA-LR
Remarkable Artifacts Dual-RA-LR
05UD PowerPlay-41
Rainbow-41
Power Marks-PMLR
05Ultimate Collection-46
Gold-46
Endorsed Emblems-EELR
Jerseys-JLR
Premium Patches-PPLR
Premium Swatches-PSLR
Ultimate Achievements-UALU
Ultimate Patches-PLR
Ultimate Signatures-USLR
Ultimate Signatures Pairings-UPLA
05Ultra-94
Gold-94
Ice-94
Scoring Kings-SK37
Scoring Kings Jerseys-SKJ-LR
Scoring Kings Patches-SKP-LR
05Upper Deck-86
05Upper Deck All-Time Greatest-28
05Upper Deck All-Time Greatest-74
05Upper Deck Big Playmakers-B-LR
05Upper Deck HG Glossy-86
05Upper Deck Jerseys-J-LR
05Upper Deck Jerseys Series II-J2LR
05Upper Deck Majestic Materials-MMLR
05Upper Deck Notable Numbers-N-LR
05Upper Deck Patches-P-LR
05Upper Deck Shooting Stars-S-LR
05Upper Deck Ice-45
Rainbow-45
Signature Swatches-SSLC
05Upper Deck MVP-178
Gold-178
Platinum-178
05Upper Deck Rookie Update-47
05Upper Deck Rookie Update-240
Inspirations Patch Rookies-240
05Upper Deck Trilogy-42
05Upper Deck Trilogy-141
Crystal-141
Ice Scripts-IS-LR
05Upper Deck Toronto Fall Expo-86
05Upper Deck Victory-91
Black-91
Gold-91
Silver-91
Stars on Ice-SI24
06Beehive-197
06Flair Showcase-132
06Flair Showcase-236
Parallel-132
Parallel-236
Hot Numbers-HN22
Hot Numbers Parallel-HN22
Inks-ILR
06Fleer Hockey Headliners-HL5
06ITG International Ice-44
Gold-44
Autographs-ALRO
06ITG Ultimate Memorabilia-92
Artist Proof-92
Blades of Steel-23
Blades of Steel Gold-23
Captain-C-4
Captain-C Gold-4
Complete Jersey-13
Complete Jersey Gold-13
Emblems-4
Emblems Gold-4
Jerseys-25
Jerseys Gold-25
Jerseys Autos-50
Jerseys Autos Gold-50

Journey Emblem-15
Journey Emblem Gold-15
Journey Jersey-15
Journey Jersey Gold-15
Passing The Torch-3
Passing The Torch Gold-3
R.O.Y. Autos-15
R.O.Y. Autos Gold-15
R.O.Y. Emblems-15
R.O.Y. Emblems Gold-15
R.O.Y. Jerseys-15
R.O.Y. Jerseys Gold-15
R.O.Y. Numbers-15
R.O.Y. Numbers Gold-15
Raised to the Rafters-6
Raised to the Rafters Gold-6
Sticks Autos-16
Sticks Autos Gold-16
Triple Thread Jerseys-15
Triple Thread Jerseys Gold-15
06McDonald's Upper Deck Autographs-ALR
06SP Authentic Sign of the Times-STLR
06SP Authentic Sign of the Times Duals-STRT
06SP Game Used By The Letter-BLLR
06SP Game Used Inked Sweaters-ISLR
06SP Game Used Inked Sweaters Patches-ISLR
06SP Game Used Inked Sweaters Dual-IS2RT
06SP Game Used Inked Sweaters Dual Patches-IS2RT
06SP Game Used Letter Marks-LMLR
06The Cup-40
Autographed Foundations-CQRO
Autographed Foundations Patches-CQRO
Autographed NHL Shields Duals-DASRT
Autographed Patches-40
Black Rainbow-40
Foundations-CQRO
Foundations Patches-CQRO
Gold-40
Gold Patches-40
Honorable Numbers-HNRO
Jerseys-40
Masterpiece Pressplates-40
Scripted Swatches-SSRO
Scripted Swatches Duals-DSDR
Signature Patches-SPRO
06UD Artifacts Tundra Tandems-TTLZ
06UD Artifacts Tundra Tandems Black-TTLZ
06UD Artifacts Tundra Tandems Blue-TTLZ
06UD Artifacts Tundra Tandems Gold-TTLZ
06UD Artifacts Tundra Tandems Platinum-TTLZ
06UD Artifacts Tundra Tandems Red-TTLZ
06UD Artifacts Tundra Tandems Dual Patches Red-TTLZ
06Ultimate Collection Ultimate Achievements-UA-LR
06Ultimate Collection Ultimate Signatures Logos-SL-LR
06Ultra Uniformity-ULR
06Ultra Uniformity Patches-UPLR
06Ultra Uniformity Autographed Jerseys-UALR
06Upper Deck Game Dated Moments-GD3
06Upper Deck Sweet Shot Signature Shots/Saves Sticks-SSSLR
06Upper Deck Sweet Shot Signature Sticks-STLR
06Upper Deck Sweet Shot Sweet Stitches-SSLR
06Upper Deck Sweet Shot Sweet Stitches Duals-SSLR
06Upper Deck Sweet Shot Sweet Stitches Triples-SSLR
06ITG Heroes and Prospects-10
Autographs-ALR
Heroes Memorabilia-HM01
Heroes Memorabilia Gold-HM01

Robitaille, Marc
99St. John's Maple Leafs-18

Robitaille, Mike
71O-Pee-Chee-8
71Sabres Postcards-2
71Sargent Promotions Stamps-29
71Topps-8
71Toronto Sun-38
72Sabres Postcards-17
73O-Pee-Chee-121
73Sabres Postcards-11
73Topps-121
74Canucks Royal Bank-17
74NHL Action Stamps-51
74NHL Action Stamps Update-40
74O-Pee-Chee NHL-159
74Topps-159
75Canucks Royal Bank-18
75O-Pee-Chee NHL-24
75Topps-24
76Canucks Royal Bank-16
76O-Pee-Chee NHL-359

Robitaille, Patrice
92Clarkson Knights-15
95Peoria Rivermen-19
96Milwaukee Admirals-21
98BC Icemen-3
98BC Icemen II-8
98UHL All-Stars-14

Robitaille, Randy
97Score Bruins-12
Platinum-12
Premier-12
97Upper Deck-182
97Providence Bruins-16
98Providence Bruins-18
99BAP Millennium Calder Candidates Ruby-C36
99BAP Millennium Calder Candidate Emerald-C36
99BAP Millennium Calder Cand Sapphire-C36
99Pacific Omega-130
Copper-130
Gold-130
Ice Blue-130
Premiere Date-130
99Upper Deck-246
Exclusives-246
Exclusives 1 of 1-246
99Upper Deck Arena Giveaways-NP2
99Upper Deck Gold Reserve-246
99Upper Deck Victory-18
99Wayne Gretzky Hockey-92
00BAP Memorabilia-175
Emerald-175
Ruby-175
Sapphire-175
Promos-175
00BAP Mem Chicago Sportsfest Copper-175
00BAP Memorabilia Chicago Sportsfest Blue-175
00BAP Memorabilia Chicago Sportsfest Gold-175
00BAP Memorabilia Chicago Sportsfest Ruby-175
00BAP Memorabilia Chicago Sun-Times Ruby-175
00BAP Memorabilia Chicago Sun-Times Gold-175
00BAP Mem Chicago Sun-Times Sapphire-175
00BAP Mem Toronto Fall Expo Copper-175
00BAP Memorabilia Toronto Fall Expo Gold-175
00BAP Memorabilia Toronto Fall Expo Ruby-175
00BAP Signature Series-135
Emerald-135
Ruby-135
Sapphire-135
Autographs-99
Autographs Gold-99
00O-Pee-Chee-155
00O-Pee-Chee Parallel-155
00Topps/OPC-155
Parallel-155
00UD Heroes-67
00Upper Deck-99
Exclusives Tier 1-99
Exclusives Tier 2-99
00Vanguard-55
Holographic Gold-55
Holographic Purple-55
Pacific Proofs-55
01BAP Memorabilia-351
Emerald-351
Ruby-351
Sapphire-351
01Parkhurst-367
01Manchester Monarchs-1A
02BAP Sig Series Auto Buybacks 2000-99
02Pacific-316
Blue-316
Red-316
02Upper Deck-385
Exclusives-385
02Upper Deck Beckett UD Promos-385
03ITG Action-398
03Pacific Complete-408
Red-408
03Thrashers Postcards-16
04Pacific-16
Blue-16
Red-16
05Parkhurst-237
Facsimile Auto Parallel-237
05Upper Deck MVP-224
Gold-224
Platinum-224
06O-Pee-Chee-368
Rainbow-368

Robitaille, Stephane
98German DEL-51
99German DEL-174
00German DEL-118
02German DEL City Press-185
03German DEL-162
05German DEL-49
06German DEL-86

Robson, Blake
99Upper Deck Sobey's Memorial Cup-8
99UD Prospects-34
99UD Prospects-77
03St. Francis Xavier X-Men-7
04St. Francis Xavier X-Men-18

Robson, Bob
91Air Canada SJHL All-Stars-50

Robson, Ryan
95Brandon Wheat Kings-16
95Slapshot Memorial Cup-42
96Brandon Wheat Kings-16
97Brandon Wheat Kings-20
98Brandon Wheat Kings-17

Robus, Rick
95Central Hockey League-32

Rocca, Tony
84Kingston Canadians-22

Roch, Dany
06Victoriaville Tigres-16

Roch, Gaby
04Drummondville Voltigeurs-27
05Drummondville Voltigeurs-16
06Drummondville Voltigeurs-14

Roch, Joel
06Quebec Remparts-20

Roche, Dave
91Peterborough Petes-19
917th Inn. Sketch OHL-139
93Peterborough Petes-3
93Windsor Spitfires-18
93Classic Four-Sport *-211
94Windsor Spitfires-20
95Bowman-144
All-Foil-144
95Donruss-287
95Penguins Foodland-16
95Classic-90
97Pacific-253
Copper-253
Emerald Green-253
Ice Blue-253
Red-253
Silver-253
97Score Penguins-17
Platinum-17
Premier-17
01Cincinnati Mighty Ducks-20
02Albany River Rats-8
02Albany River Rats AAP-20

Roche, Desse
33V357 Ice Kings-70
35Diamond Matchbooks Tan 1-57

Roche, Earl
33V357 Ice Kings-62
35Diamond Matchbooks Tan 1-58

Roche, Ken
03Boston University Terriers-19

Roche, Scott
93North Bay Centennials-21
94North Bay Centennials-2
94Classic Draft Prospects-DP9
95Slapshot-207
95Slapshot-NNO
95Classic-54
95Classic-90
95Signature Rookies Future Flash-FF9
95Signature Rook Future Flash Sigs-FF9
97Peoria Rivermen-19
98Peoria Rivermen-22

Roche, Travis
01BAP Memorabilia-349
Emerald-349
Ruby-349
Sapphire-349
01SP Game Used-82
01UD Challenge for the Cup-113
01UD Premier Collection-67
01Upper Deck-429
Exclusives-429
01Upper Deck Ice-77
04AHL All-Stars-37
04Chicago Wolves-3
05Chicago Wolves-16
05ITG Heroes and Prospects Jerseys-GUJ-42
05ITG Heroes and Prospects Jerseys Gold-GUJ-42
05ITG Heroes and Prospects Emblems-GUE-42
05ITG Heroes and Prospects Emblems Gold-GUE-42
05ITG Heroes and Prospects Numbers-GUN-42
05ITG Heroes and Prospects Numbers Gold-GUN-42

Rocheford, Brian
93Quebec Pee-Wee Tournament-1724

Rochefort, Danny
84Richelieu Riverains-16

Rochefort, Leon
63Quebec Aces-21
64Quebec Aces-15
65Quebec Aces-16
67York Action Octagons-1
68O-Pee-Chee-95
68Shirriff Coins-131
68Topps-95
69O-Pee-Chee-105
Four-in-One-7
69Topps-105
71Canadiens Postcards-21
71O-Pee-Chee-135
71Sargent Promotions Stamps-63
71Toronto Sun-102
72Flames Postcards-18
72O-Pee-Chee-204
72Sargent Promotions Stamps-81
74Canucks Royal Bank-18
75O-Pee-Chee NHL-374
92Sport-Flash-8
92Sport-Flash Autographs-8

Rochefort, Normand
80Nordiques Postcards-24
81Nordiques Postcards-15
82McDonald's Stickers-35
82Nordiques Postcards-18
82O-Pee-Chee-291
82Post Cereal-16
83NHL Key Tags-106
83Nordiques Postcards-23
83O-Pee-Chee-300
83Vachon-72
84Nordiques Postcards-21
84O-Pee-Chee-287
84O-Pee-Chee Stickers-176
85Nordiques General Foods-21
85Nordiques McDonald's-17
85Nordiques Provigo-20
85Nordiques Team Issue-20
85O-Pee-Chee Stickers-148
86Nordiques General Foods-21
86Nordiques McDonald's-20
86Nordiques Team Issue-19
86Nordiques Yum-Yum-8
87Nordiques General Foods-26
87Nordiques Team Issue-4
87Nordiques Yum-Yum-8
87Panini Stickers-161
88O-Pee-Chee Stickers-182
89Rangers Marine Midland Bank-5
90Pro Set-494
90Score-149
Canadian-149
90Upper Deck-437
French-437
91Bowman-73
91Pinnacle-273
French-273
91Score American-171
91Score Canadian Bilingual-171
91Score Canadian English-171
92Durivage Panini-44
92Score-377
Canadian-377
93Atlanta Knights-15
96Kansas City Blades-18
03St. Georges de Beauce Garaga-15

Rochefort, Richard
94Sudbury Wolves-15
94Sudbury Wolves Police-13
95Slapshot-399
95Sudbury Wolves-24
95Sudbury Wolves Police-18
96Sarnia Sting-22
96Sudbury Wolves-18
96Sudbury Wolves Police-19
97Albany River Rats-12
97Sudbury Wolves Anniversary-19
97Bowman CHL-21
OPC-21
98Albany River Rats-14
99Albany River Rats-21
00Albany River Rats-18
01Albany River Rats-11

Rocheleau, Nathan
93Omaha Lancers-21

Rochette, Eric
907th Inn. Sketch QMJHL-22
917th Inn. Sketch Memorial Cup-35

Rochette, Gaeton
77Nova Scotia Voyageurs-19

Rochon, Carl
00Hull Olympiques-14
Signed-14

Rochon, Dylan
01OCN Blizzard-25
02OCN Blizzard-23

Rochon, Frank
75O-Pee-Chee WHA-51

Rochon, Patrick
93RPI Engineers-26
96Mississippi Sea Wolves-16
97Mississippi Sea Wolves-14
98ECHL All-Star Southern Conference-7
99Mississippi Sea Wolves-11
99Mississippi Sea Wolves Kelly Cup-10
03Mississippi Sea Wolves-13

Rock, Aaron
04Saginaw Spirit-20

Rock, Matt
98Guelph Storm-7
99Guelph Storm-6
99Owen Sound Platers-10
00Kitchener Rangers-20

Rockabrand, Ryan
94Arizona Icecats-17
95Arizona Icecats-10

Rockman, Greg
02UK Coventry Blaze-1

Rockstrom, Per
55Swedish Alfabilder-26

Rod, Jean-Luc
93Swiss HNL-508

Rodak, Adam
93St. Cloud State Huskies-24

Rodberg, Steve
03Fort Wayne Komets-23
04Fort Wayne Komets-13
06Bakersfield Condors-3

Rodden, Mike
83Hall of Fame-164
85Hall of Fame-164

Rodden, Milt
83Hall of Fame Postcards-L15

Roddis, Gareth
94UK Solihull Barons-12
95UK Solihull Barons-3

Rodek, Stan
52Juniors Blue Tint-168

Roderick, John
93Peoria Rivermen-24

Rodger, Keith
02Lincoln Stars-20
03Lincoln Stars-19

Rodgers, Alex
06Kamloops Blazers-18

Rodgers, Andrew
97Pensacola Ice Pilots-19
98Pensacola Ice Pilots-11

Rodgers, Marc
917th Inn. Sketch OMJHL-45
92Wheeling Thunderbirds-14
93Knoxville Cherokees-15
93Las Vegas Thunder-23
94Las Vegas Thunder-25
95Las Vegas Thunder-13
98Chicago Wolves Turner Cup-8
99SP Authentic-102
99Topps Premier Plus-91
Parallel-91
99Ultimate Victory-97
1/1-97
Parallel-97
Parallel 100-97
99Manitoba Moose-19

Rodgers, Rob
05Salmon Arm Silverbacks-16

Rodgers, Robbie
04Salmon Arm Silverbacks-4

Rodine, Dimitri
96Flint Generals-17
97Flint Generals-17
01Czech OFS-196
02Czech OFS Plus-291
Trios-T4
03Czech OFS Plus-77

Rodman, Andy
87Brockville Braves-25

Rodman, David
01Val d'Or Foreurs-24
02Val d'Or Foreurs-22

Rodman, Marcel
94Quebec Pee-Wee Tournament-934
00UD CHL Prospects-20

Rodney, Bryan
00Ottawa 67's-18
01Ottawa 67's-20
04London Knights-7
05ITG Heroes and Prospects Memorial Cup-MC-10

Rodrigue, Alex
95Slapshot Memorial Cup-55

Rodrigue, Guillaume
96Rimouski Oceanic Update-7
99Adirondack IceHawks-12
01Sorel Royaux-18

Rodrigue, Jacque
96Dayton Ice Bandits-16
98Odessa Jackalopes-1
99Odessa Jackalopes-16
01Odessa Jackalopes-17

Rodrigue, Marc
98Thetford Mines Coyotes-23

Rodrigue, Sylvain
907th Inn. Sketch QMJHL-20
917th Inn. Sketch QMJHL-96
917th Inn. Sketch Memorial Cup-25

Rodrigues, Mike
00Johnstown Chiefs-26
01Johnstown Chiefs-20
02Johnstown Chiefs-12

Roe, Justin
93Quebec Pee-Wee Tournament-1261

Roe, Zach
01Regina Pats-19

Roed, Peter
97Kentucky Thoroughblades-14
99Kentucky Thoroughblades-23
00German DEL-109
02Kalamazoo Wings-9

Roed, Shawn
06Bloomington PrairieThunder-18

Roeder, Kevin
03Chicago Steel-8

Roedger, Roy
82Swedish Semic VM Stickers-121
83Swedish Semic VM Stickers-121
89Swedish Semic World Champ Stickers-122

Roelofsen, Mike
03Belleville Bulls-19
04Barrie Colts-8
06Sarnia Sting-9

Roemensky, Mike
02Michigan Wolverines-3
03Columbia Inferno Update-52

Roenick, Jeremy
89Blackhawks Coke-6
90Blackhawks Coke-6
90Bowman-1
Tiffany-1
90O-Pee-Chee-7
90OPC Premier-100
90Panini Stickers-201
90Pro Set-58
90Score Promos-179
90Score-179
Canadian-179
90Score Hottest/Rising Stars-31
90Score Young Superstars-24
90Topps-7
Tiffany-7
90Upper Deck-63
90Upper Deck-316
90Upper Deck-481
French-63
French-316
French-481
91Pro Set Platinum-24
91Pro Set Platinum-141
91Blackhawks Coke-22
91Bowman-386
91Bowman-403
91Gillette-13
91Kraft-56
91O-Pee-Chee-106
91OPC Premier-52
91OPC Premier-174
91Panini Stickers-12
91Parkhurst-29
91Parkhurst-439
French-29
French-439
91Pinnacle-120
91Pinnacle-359
French-120
French-359
91Pro Set-40
91Pro Set-280
91Pro Set-605
French-40
French-280
French-605
Puck Candy-6
91Score American-220
91Score American-305
91Score American-418
91Score Canadian Bilingual-220
91Score Canadian Bilingual-309
91Score Canadian Bilingual-334
91Score Canadian English-220
91Score Canadian English-309
91Score Canadian English-334
91Score Hot Cards-10
91Score Kellogg's-5
91Score Young Superstars-21
91Stadium Club-46
91Topps-106
91Upper Deck-36
91Upper Deck-166
91Upper Deck-629
French-36
French-166
French-629
91Finnish Semic World Champ Stickers-149
91Swedish Semic World Champ Stickers-149
92Blackhawks Coke-20
92Bowman-78
92Bowman-217
92Humpty Dumpty II-20
92Kraft-46
92McDonald's Upper Deck-13
92O-Pee-Chee-345
92O-Pee-Chee-383
25th Anniv. Inserts-23
92OPC Premier Star Performers-5
92Panini Stickers-4
92Panini Stickers French-4
92Parkhurst-31
Emerald Ice-31
Cherry Picks-CP2
92Pinnacle-10
92Pinnacle-256
French-10
French-256
Team 2000-27
Team 2000 French-27
92Pro Set-30
92Pro Set-252
Gold Team Leaders-2
92Score-200
92Score-422
92Score-499
Canadian-200
Canadian-422
Canadian-499
Sharpshooters-10
Sharpshooters Canadian-10
USA Greats-3
Young Superstars-10
92Seasons Patches-1
92Sports Illustrated for Kids II-333
92Stadium Club-167
92Stadium Club-255
92Topps-400
Gold-400G
92Ultra-41
92Ultra-NNO
Jeremy Roenick-1
Jeremy Roenick-2
Jeremy Roenick-3
Jeremy Roenick-4
Jeremy Roenick-5
Jeremy Roenick-6
Jeremy Roenick-7
Jeremy Roenick-8
Jeremy Roenick-9
Jeremy Roenick-10
Jeremy Roenick-11
Jeremy Roenick-12
Jeremy Roenick-AU
92Upper Deck-274
Gordie Howe Selects-G8
World Junior Grads-WG19
92Finnish Semic-158
93SLU Hockey Canadian-9
93SLU Hockey American-10
93Blackhawks Coke-8
93Donruss-67
Elite Inserts-6
Special Print-E
93Kenner Starting Lineup Cards-10
93Kraft-47
93Leaf-27
Studio Signature-7
93McDonald's Upper Deck-12
93OPC Premier-450
93OPC Premier-500
Gold-450
Gold-500
93Panini Stickers-M
93Parkhurst-309
Emerald Ice-309
East/West Stars-W6
93Pinnacle-140
Canadian-140
All-Stars-39
All-Stars Canadian-39
Nifty Fifty-15
Team Pinnacle-11
Team Canadian-11
Team 2001-20
Team 2001 Canadian-20
93PowerPlay-54
Gamebreakers-8
Point Leaders-14
93Score-240
Canadian-240
Dynamic Duos U.S.-6
Franchise-4
93Seasons Patches-15
93Stadium Club-190
Members Only Master Set-190
OPC-190
First Day Issue-190
First Day Issue OPC-190
All-Stars-20
All-Stars Members Only-20
All-Stars OPC-20
93Topps/OPC Premier-450
93Topps/OPC Premier-500
Gold-450
Gold-500
93Ultra-186
Premier Pivots-8
93Upper Deck-235
93Upper Deck-289
93Upper Deck-314
Hat Tricks-HT18
NHLPA/Roots-30
Silver Skates-R10
Silver Skates Gold-R10
SP-31
93Upper Deck Locker All-Stars-34
93Swedish Semic World Champ Stickers-180
94SLU Hockey American-18
94Action Packed Big Picture 24K Gold-12G
94Action Packed Big Picture Promos-BP1
94Be A Player-R12
94Be A Player-R144
Signature Cards-12
Up Close and Personal-UC6
94Canada Games NHL POGS-70
94Donruss-222
Dominators-5
Elite Inserts-9
94EA Sports-27
94Finest-73
Super Team Winners-73
Refractors-73
Bowman's Best-B5
Bowman's Best Refractors-B5
94Flair-36
Center Spotlight-10
Scoring Power-9
94Fleer-45
Slapshot Artists-8
94Hockey Wit-103
94Kenner Starting Lineup Cards-19
94Kraft-27
94Leaf-63
Fire on Ice-2
Gold Stars-2
Limited Inserts-5
94Leaf Limited-61
Gold-8
94McDonald's Upper Deck-McD20
94NHLPA Phone Cards-6
94OPC Premier-200
Special Effects-200
94Parkhurst-302
Gold-302
Crash the Game Green-5
Crash the Game Blue-5
Crash the Game Gold-5
Crash the Game Red-5
Vintage-V65
94Parkhurst SE-SE35
Gold-SE35
94Pinnacle-165
Artist's Proofs-165
Rink Collection-165
Gamers-GR14
World Edition-WE3
94Score Check It-CI6
94Score Dream Team-DT18
94Score Franchise-TF5
94Score 90 Plus Club-6
94Select-29
Gold-29
94SP-22
Die Cuts-22
Premier-18
Premier Die-Cuts-18
94Stadium Club Members Only-20
94Stadium Club-59
Members Only Master Set-59
First Day Issue-59
Super Teams-5
Super Teams Members Only Master Set-5
Super Team Winner Cards-59
94Topps/OPC Premier-200
Special Effects-200
94Topps Finest Inserts-11
94Topps/OPC Premier The Go To Guy-8
94Topps Finest Bronze-13
94Ultra-44
Power-8
Speed Merchants-9
94Upper Deck-322
Electric Ice-322
Ice Gallery-IG3
Predictor Canadian-C19
94Upper Deck Predictor Canadian Exch Gold-C19
94Upper Deck Predictor Hobby-H13
94Upper Deck Predictor Hobby Exch Gold-H13
94Upper Deck Predictor Hobby Exch Silver-H13
94Upper Deck Predictor Retail-R8
94Upper Deck Predictor Retail Exchange-R8
94Upper Deck SP Inserts-SP17
94Upper Deck SP Inserts Die Cuts-SP17
94Upper Deck NHLPA/Be A Player-13
94Finnish Jaa Kiekko-122
94Finnish Jaa Kiekko-352
95Bashan Super Stickers-21
Die-Cut-9
95Bowman-20
All-Foil-20
95Canada Games NHL POGS-26
95Canada Games NHL POGS-61
95Collector's Choice-85
Player's Club-85
Player's Club Platinum-85
95Donruss-27
Igniters-7
Pro Pointers-1
95Donruss Elite-47
Die Cut Stars-47
Die Cut Uncut-47
Cutting Edge-14
95Emotion Promo Strip-1
95Emotion-33
95Emotion-NNO
95Emotion-NNO
Xcel-2
Xcited-2
95Finest-25
95Finest-175
Refractors-25
Refractors-175
95Hoyle Western Playing Cards-1
95Imperial Stickers-21
Die Cut Superstars-9
95Leaf-116
95Leaf Limited-80
Stars of the Game-12
95McDonald's Pinnacle-MCD-16
95Metal-28
International Steel-17
95Metal Promo Panel-2
95NHL Aces Playing Cards-5D
95NHL Cool Trade-3
95NHL Cool Trade-RP3
95Panini Stickers-157
95Parkhurst International-307
Emerald Ice-307
95Pinnacle-106
Artist's Proofs-106
Rink Collection-106
Full Contact-4
Roaring 20s-4
95Pinnacle FANtasy-23
95Playoff One on One-24
95Playoff One on One-135
95Playoff One on One-236
95Pro Magnets-10
95Score-55
Black Ice Artist's Proofs-55
Black Ice-55
Border Battle-10
Golden Blades-19
95Select Certified-60
Mirror Gold-60
Double Strike-7
Double Strike Gold-7
95SkyBox Impact Promo Panel-1
95SkyBox Impact-33
95SkyBox Impact-243
95SP-24
Stars/Etoiles-E7
Stars/Etoiles Gold-E7
95Stadium Club Members Only-27
95Stadium Club-166
Members Only Master Set-166
95Summit-82
Artist's Proofs-82
Ice-82
95Topps-3
95Topps-235
OPC Inserts-3
OPC Inserts-235
Home Grown USA-HGA2
Marquee Men Power Boosters-3
Power Lines-4PL
Profiles-PF8
95Topps SuperSkills-65
Platinum-65
95Ultra-35
95Ultra-396
Gold Medallion-35
Crease Crashers-15
Premier Pivots-7
Premier Pivots Gold Medallion-7
Ultraview-8
Ultraview Hot Pack-8
95Upper Deck-227
95Upper Deck-241
95Upper Deck-422
Electric Ice-227
Electric Ice-241
Electric Ice-422
Electric Ice Gold-227
Electric Ice Gold-241
Electric Ice Gold-422
95Upper Deck All-Star Game Predictors-12
Redemption Winners-12
95Upper Deck Freeze Frame-F6
95Upper Deck Freeze Frame Jumbo-F6
95Upper Deck Predictor Retail-R47
95Upper Deck Predictor Retail Exchange-R47
95Upper Deck Special Edition-SE104
95Upper Deck Special Edition Gold-SE104
95Zenith-72
Z-Team-6
95Finnish Semic World Championships-118
95German DEL-446
95Swedish Globe World Championships-117
96Headliners Hockey-14A
96Headliners Hockey-14B
96SLU Hockey American-20
96Be A Player-5
Autographs-5
Autographs Silver-5
96Black Diamond-167
Gold-167
96Collector's Choice-46
96Collector's Choice-297
96Collector's Choice-313
MVP-UD18
MVP Gold-UD18
Stick'Ums-S6
96Coyotes Coca-Cola-24
96Coyotes Coca-Cola-25
96Coyotes Coca-Cola-26
96Donruss-2
Press Proofs-2
Dominators-9
Hit List-4
96Donruss Canadian Ice-57
Gold Press Proofs-57
Red Press Proofs-57
96Donruss Elite-27
Die Cut Stars-27
Status-12
96Flair-72
Blue Ice-72
96Fleer-18
Art Ross-19
Picks Dream Lines-2
Picks Fabulous 50-39
Picks Jagged Edge-10
96Hockey Greats Coins-17
Gold-17
96Kenner Starting Lineup Cards-20
96Leaf-191
Press Proofs-191
Fire On Ice-11
96Leaf Leather And Laces Promos-P13
96Leaf Leather And Laces-13
96Leaf Limited-86
Gold-86
96Leaf Preferred-4
Press Proofs-4
96Maggers-87
96McDonald's Pinnacle-12
96Metal Universe-121
96NHL Aces Playing Cards-4D
96NHL Pro Stamps-10
96Pinnacle-98
Artist's Proofs-98
Foil-98
Premium Stock-98
Rink Collection-98
Team Pinnacle-3
96Pinnacle Mint-15
Bronze-15
Gold-15
Silver-15
Coins Brass-15
Coins Solid Gold-15
Coins Gold Plated-15
Coins Nickel-15
Coins Silver-15
96Post Upper Deck-17
96Score-137
Artist's Proofs-137
Dealer's Choice Artist's Proofs-137
Special Artist's Proofs-137
Check It-5
Golden Blades-137
Sudden Death-5
96Select Certified-77
Artist's Proofs-77
Blue-77
Mirror Blue-77
Mirror Gold-77
Mirror Red-77
Red-77
96SkyBox Impact-108
BladeRunners-19
96SP-119
Clearcut Winner-CW7
96SPx-7
Gold-7
96Summit-138
Artist's Proofs-138
Ice-138
Metal-138
Premium Stock-138
High Voltage-10
High Voltage Mirage-10
96Topps Picks-47
Fantasy Team-FT18
OPC Inserts-47
96Ultra-135
Gold Medallion-135
96Upper Deck-35
96Upper Deck-205
96Upper Deck-312
Generation Next-X12
Hart Hopefuls Bronze-HH17
Hart Hopefuls Gold-HH17
Hart Hopefuls Silver-HH17
Superstar Showdown-SS15A
96Upper Deck Ice-51
Parallel-51
Stanley Cup Foundation-S8
Stanley Cup Foundation Dynasty-S8
96Zenith-30
Artist's Proofs-30
Z-Team-10
96Swedish Semic Wien-167
97SLU Hockey One on One-5
97Headliners Hockey-21
97Be A Player Take A Number-12
97Black Diamond-59
Double Diamond-59
Triple Diamond-59
Quadruple Diamond-59
97Collector's Choice-195
Star Quest-SQ79
Stick'Ums-S13
97Coyotes Face-Off Luncheon -18
97Crown Royale-105
Emerald Green-105
Ice Blue-105
Silver-105
97Donruss-6
Press Proofs Silver-6
Press Proofs Gold-6
97Donruss Canadian Ice-100
Dominion Series-100
Provincial Series-100
Stanley Cup Scrapbook-7
97Donruss Elite-77
Aspirations-77
Status-77
97Donruss Limited-105
97Donruss Limited-120
97Donruss Limited-140
Exposure-105
Exposure-120
Exposure-140
Fabric of the Game-35
97Donruss Preferred-88
Cut to the Chase-88
97Donruss Priority-133
Stamp of Approval-133
Postcards-33
Stamps-33
Stamps Bronze-33
Stamps Gold-33
Stamps Silver-33
97Esso Olympic Hockey Heroes-28
97Esso Olympic Hockey Heroes French-28
97Highland Mint Mint-Cards Pinnacle/Score-13
97Highland Mint Mint-Cards Pinnacle/Score-14
97Katch-112
Gold-112
Silver-112
97Leaf-22
Fractal Matrix-22
Fractal Matrix Die Cuts-22
97Leaf International-22
Universal Ice-22
97NHL Aces Playing Cards-19
97Pacific-97
Copper-97
Emerald Green-97
Ice Blue-97
Red-97
Silver-97
Card-Supials-16
Card-Supials Minis-16
Slap Shots Die-Cuts-7B
Team Checklists-19
97Pacific Dynagon-97
Copper-97
Dark Grey-97
Emerald Green-97
Ice Blue-97
Red-97
Silver-97
Dynamic Duos-12A
Tandems-63
97Pacific Invincible-108
Copper-108
Emerald Green-108
Ice Blue-108
Red-108
Silver-108
Feature Performers-27
97Pacific Omega-176
Copper-176
Dark Gray-176
Emerald Green-176
Gold-176
Ice Blue-176
97Panini Stickers-157
97Paramount-142
Copper-142
Dark Grey-142
Emerald Green-142
Ice Blue-142
Red-142
Silver-142
97Pinnacle-33

97Pinnacle-197
Artist's Proofs-33
Rink Collection-33
Press Plates Back Black-33
Press Plates Back Black-197
Press Plates Back Cyan-33
Press Plates Back Cyan-197
Press Plates Back Magenta-33
Press Plates Back Magenta-197
Press Plates Back Yellow-33
Press Plates Back Yellow-197
Press Plates Front Black-33
Press Plates Front Black-197
Press Plates Front Cyan-33
Press Plates Front Cyan-197
Press Plates Front Magenta-33
Press Plates Front Magenta-197
Press Plates Front Yellow-33
Press Plates Front Yellow-197
97Pinnacle Certified-65
Red-65
Mirror Blue-65
Mirror Gold-65
Mirror Red-65
97Pinnacle Inside-59
Coach's Collection-59
Executive Collection-59
97Pinnacle Tot Cert Platinum Blue-65
97Pinnacle Tot Certi Platinum Gold-65
97Pinnacle Totally Certified Platinum Red-65
97Pinnacle Tot Cert Mirror Platinum Gold-65
97Revolution-108
Copper-108
Emerald-108
Ice Blue-108
Silver-108
97Score-107
Artist's Proofs-107
Golden Blades-107
97SP Authentic-118
97SPx-39
Bronze-39
Gold-39
Silver-39
Steel-39
Dimension-SPX2
Grand Finale-39
97Studio-40
Press Proofs Silver-40
Press Proofs Gold-40
Portraits-30
97Upper Deck-127
Smooth Grooves-SG57
The Specialists-17
The Specialists Level 2 Die Cuts-17
Three Star Selects-16C
97Upper Deck Ice-27
Parallel-27
Power Shift-27
97Zenith-19
Z-Gold-19
Z-Silver-19
97Zenith 5 x 7-22
Gold Impulse-22
Silver Impulse-22
98SLU Hockey-180
98Aurora-146
98Be A Player-107
Press Release-107
98BAP Gold-107
98BAP Autographs-107
98BAP Autographs Gold-107
98BAP AS Game Used Stick Cards-S16
98BAP AS Game Used Jersey Cards-AS17
98BAP Playoff Game Used Jerseys-G3
98BAP Playoff Practice Used Jerseys-P12
98BAP Tampa Bay All Star Game-107
98Black Diamond-68
Double Diamond-68
Triple Diamond-68
Quadruple Diamond-68
98Bowman's Best-55
Refractors-55
Atomic Refractors-55
98Crown Royale-104
Limited Series-104
98Finest-30
No Protectors-30
No Protectors Refractors-30
Refractors-30
98Katch-110
98Kenner Starting Lineup Cards-27
98OPC Chrome-171
Refractors-171
98Pacific-97
Ice Blue-97
Red-97
98Pacific Dynagon Ice-144
Blue-144
Red-144
98Pacific Omega-187
Red-187
Opening Day Issue-187
98Panini Photocards-70
98Panini Stickers-150
98Paramount-184
Copper-184
Emerald Green-184
Holo-Electric-184
Ice Blue-184
Silver-184
98Revolution-111
Ice Shadow-111
Red-111
All-Star Die Cuts-25
Showstoppers-29
98SP Authentic-65
Power Shift-65
Snapshots-SS22
98SPx Top Prospects-47
Radiance-47
Spectrum-47
Highlight Heroes-H24
Lasting Impressions-L20
98Topps-171
O-Pee-Chee-171
98Topps Gold Label Class 1-84
Black-84
Black One of One-84
One of One-84
Red-84
Red One of One-84
98Topps Gold Label Class 2-84
98Topps Gold Label Class 2 Black-84
98Topps Gold Label Class 2 Black 1 of 1-84
98Topps Gold Label Class 2 One of One-84
98Topps Gold Label Class 2 Red-84
98Topps Gold Label Class 2 Red One of One-84
98Topps Gold Label Class 3-84
98Topps Gold Label Class 3 Black-84
98Topps Gold Label Class 3 Black 1 of 1-84
98Topps Gold Label Class 3 One of One-84
98Topps Gold Label Class 3 Red-84
98Topps Gold Label Class 3 Red One of One-84
98UD Choice-158
Prime Choice Reserve-158
Reserve-158
98Upper Deck-339
Exclusives-339
Exclusives 1 of 1-339
Fantastic Finishers-FF22
Fantastic Finishers Quantum 1-FF22
Fantastic Finishers Quantum 2-FF22
Fantastic Finishers Quantum 3-FF22
Gold Reserve-339
98Upper Deck MVP-160
Gold Script-160
Silver Script-160
Super Script-160
Power Game-PG15
99Aurora-111
Striped-111
Premiere Date-111
Premiere Date Striped-111
99BAP Memorabilia-9
Gold-9
Silver-9
AS Heritage Ruby-H3
AS Heritage Sapphire-H3
AS Heritage Emerald-H3
99BAP Update Teammates Jersey Cards-TM1
99BAP Update Teammates Jersey Cards-TM31
99BAP Millennium-190
Emerald-190
Ruby-190
Sapphire-190
Signatures-190
Signatures Gold-190
Jerseys-J29
Jersey Autographs-J29
Jersey and Stick Cards-JS29
Jersey Emblems-E29
Jersey Numbers-N29
99Black Diamond-65
Diamond Cut-65
Final Cut-65
99Crown Royale-109
Limited Series-109
Premiere Date-109
Ice Elite-21
Ice Elite Parallel-21
99Jell-O Pudding Super Skills-6
99O-Pee-Chee-42
99O-Pee-Chee Chrome-42
99O-Pee-Chee Chrome Refractors-42
99Pacific-325
Copper-325
Emerald Green-325
Gold-325
Ice Blue-325
Premiere Date-325
Red-325
Gold Crown Die-Cuts-29
99Pacific Dynagon Ice-153
Blue-153
Copper-153
Gold-153
Premiere Date-153
99Pacific Omega-184
Copper-184
Gold-184
Ice Blue-184
Premiere Date-184
Cup Contenders-16
99Pacific Prism-109
Holographic Blue-109
Holographic Gold-109
Holographic Mirror-109
Holographic Purple-109
Premiere Date-109
99Panini Stickers-281
99Paramount-182
Copper-182
Emerald-182
Gold-182
Holographic Emerald-182
Holographic Gold-182
Holographic Silver-182
Ice Blue-182
Premiere Date-182
Red-182
Silver-182
Personal Best-29
99Revolution-113
Premiere Date-113
Red-113
Shadow Series-113
Showstoppers-28
Copper-113
Gold-113
CSC Silver-113
99SP Authentic-67
Buyback Signatures-54
Buyback Signatures-55
Buyback Signatures-56
Buyback Signatures-57
Buyback Signatures-58
Buyback Signatures-59
Buyback Signatures-60
Buyback Signatures-61
Sign of the Times-JR
Sign of the Times Gold-JR
99SPx-114
Radiance-114
Spectrum-114
Prolifics-P10
99Stadium Club Promos-PP3
99Stadium Club-55
First Day Issue-55
One of a Kind-55
Printing Plates Black-55
Printing Plates Cyan-55
Printing Plates Magenta-55
Printing Plates Yellow-55
Chrome-24
Chrome Refractors-24
99Topps/OPC-42
99Topps/OPC Chrome-42
Refractors-42
99Topps Gold Label Class 1-43
Black-43
Black One of One-43
One of One-43
Red-43
Red One of One-43
99Topps Gold Label Class 2-43
99Topps Gold Label Class 2 Black-43
99Topps Gold Label Class 2 Black 1 of 1-43
99Topps Gold Label Class 2 One of One-43
99Topps Gold Label Class 2 Red-43
99Topps Gold Label Class 2 Red One of One-43
99Topps Gold Label Class 3-43
99Topps Gold Label Class 3
Black-43
99Topps Gold Label Class 3 Black 1 of 1-43
99Topps Gold Label Class 3 One of One-43
99Topps Gold Label Class 3 Red-43
99Topps Gold Label Class 3 Red One of One-43
99Topps Gold Label Prime Gold-PG12
99Topps Gold Label Prime Gold One of One -PG12
99Topps Gold Label Prime Gold Black-PG12
99Topps Gold Label Prime Gold Black One of One -
PG12
99Topps Gold Label Prime Gold Red-PG12
99Topps Gold Label Prime Gold Red One of One -
PG12
99Topps Premier Plus-14
Parallel-14
99Ultimate Victory-68
1/1-68
Parallel-68
Parallel 100-68
99Upper Deck-273
Exclusives-273
Exclusives 1 of 1-273
Game Jerseys Series II-JR
99Upper Deck Gold Reserve-273
99Upper Deck HoloGrFx-46
Ausome-46
99Upper Deck MVP-156
Gold Script-156
Silver Script-156
Super Script-156
Draw Your Own Trading Card-W28
Game-Used Souvenirs-GU25
ProSign-JR
99Upper Deck MVP SC Edition-140
Gold Script-140
Silver Script-140
Super Script-140
Great Combinations-GCTR
Great Combinations Parallel-GCTR
Stanley Cup Talent-SC15
99Upper Deck Ovation-45
Standing Ovation-45
99Upper Deck Retro-60
Gold-60
Platinum-60
99Upper Deck Victory-228
99Wayne Gretzky Hockey-130
Will to Win-W6
00Aurora-112
Pinstripes-112
Pinstripes Premiere Date-112
Premiere Date-112
00BAP Memorabilia-235
Emerald-235
Ruby-235
Sapphire-235
Promos-235
Jersey Cards-J1
Jersey Emblems-E1
Jersey Numbers-N1
Jersey and Stick Cards-JS1
00BAP Memorabilia Chicago Sportsfest Copper-235
00BAP Memorabilia Chicago Sportsfest Blue-235
00BAP Memorabilia Chicago Sportsfest Gold-235
00BAP Memorabilia Chicago Sportsfest Ruby-235
00BAP Memorabilia Chicago Sun-Times Ruby-235
00BAP Memorabilia Chicago Sun-Times Gold-235
00BAP Mem Chicago Sun-Times Sapphire-235
00BAP Mem Toronto Fall Expo Copper-235
00BAP Memorabilia Toronto Fall Expo Gold-235
00BAP Memorabilia Toronto Fall Expo Ruby-235
00BAP Memorabilia Update Teammates-TM5
00BAP Memorabilia Update Teammates-TM38
00BAP Memorabilia Update Teammates Gold-TM5
00BAP Memorabilia Update Teammates Gold-TM38
00BAP Parkhurst 2000-P95
00BAP Signature Series-106
Emerald-106
Ruby-106
Sapphire-106
Autographs-59
Autographs Gold-59
He Shoots-He Scores Prizes-32
Jersey Cards-J29
Jersey and Stick Cards-GSJ29
Jersey Cards Autographs-J29
Jersey Emblems-E29
Jersey Numbers-IN29
00BAP Ultimate Memorabilia Autographs-29
Gold-29
00BAP Ultimate Mem Game-Used Jerseys-GJ29
00BAP Ultimate Mem Game-Used Sticks-GS29
00BAP Ultimate Mem Journey Jerseys-JJ17
00BAP Ultimate Mem Journey Emblems-JE17
00BAP Ultimate Mem Journey Numbers-JI17
00BAP Ultimate Memorabilia Teammates-TM5
00BAP Ultimate Memorabilia Teammates-TM10
00Black Diamond-45
Gold-45
00Crown Royale-84
Ice Blue-84
Limited Series-84
Premiere Date-84
Red-84
Game-Worn Jersey Redemptions-8
00Kraft-23
00O-Pee-Chee-10
00O-Pee-Chee Parallel-10
00Pacific-321
Copper-321
Gold-321
Ice Blue-321
Premiere Date-321
Gold Crown Die Cuts-27
00Panini Stickers-186
00Paramount-193
Copper-193
Gold-193
Holo-Gold-193
Holo-Silver-193
Ice Blue-193
Premiere Date-193
Freeze Frame-29
00Private Stock-76
Gold-76
Premiere Date-76
Retail-76
Silver-76
Artist's Canvas-17
Artist's Canvas Proofs-17
Extreme Action-17
PS-2001 Action-44
PS-2001 Stars-21
00Revolution-114
Blue-114
Premiere Date-114
Red-114
HD NHL-27
Ice Immortals-17
00SP Authentic-67
BuyBacks-91
00SP Game Used-46
Patch Cards-P-JR
Tools of the Game-JR
Tools of the Game Exclusives-JR
Tools of the Game Combos-C-RT
00SPx-52
00SPx-78
Spectrum-52
Spectrum-78
Highlight Heroes-HH11
Winning Materials-JR
Winning Materials-WRE
00Stadium Club-21
Beam Team-BT28
00Titanium-73
Blue-73
Gold-73
Premiere Date-73
Red-73
Retail-73
Game Gear-129
Game Gear Patches-129
00Titanium Draft Day Edition-78
Patches-78
00Topps/OPC-10
Parallel-10
00Topps Chrome-10
OPC Refractors-10
Refractors-10
00Topps Gold Label Class 1-70
Gold-70
00Topps Gold Label Class 2-70
00Topps Gold Label Class 2 Gold-70
00Topps Gold Label Class 3-70
00Topps Gold Label Class 3 Gold-70
00Topps Gold Label Bullion-B7
00Topps Gold Label Bullion One to One-B7
00Topps Gold Label Golden Greats-GG15
00Topps Gold Label Golden Greats 1 to 1-GG15
00Topps Heritage-36
Chrome Parallel-36
00Topps Premier Plus-12
Blue Ice-12
00Topps Stars-16
Blue-16
00UD Heroes-154
Signs of Greatness-JR
00UD Pros and Prospects-65
Game Jersey Autograph Exclusives-S-JR
Game Jersey Autographs-S-JR
NHL Passion-NP6
00UD Reserve-65
00Upper Deck-132
Exclusives Tier 1-132
Exclusives Tier 2-132
e-Cards-EC12
e-Card Prizes-AJR
e-Card Prizes-EJR
e-Card Prizes-SEJR
Frozen in Time-FT6
Game Jersey Autographs-HJR
Game Jersey Autographs Exclusives-ESJR
Number Crunchers-NC6
Skilled Stars-SS16
Triple Threat-TT4
00Upper Deck Ice-31
Immortals-31
Legends-31
Stars-31
00Upper Deck Legends-102
00Upper Deck Legends-104
Legendary Collection Bronze-102
Legendary Collection Bronze-104
Legendary Collection Gold-102
Legendary Collection Gold-104
Legendary Collection Silver-102
Legendary Collection Silver-104
00Upper Deck MVP-134
First Stars-134
Second Stars-134
Talent-M15
Third Stars-134
Top Playmakers-TP10
00Upper Deck Victory-175
00Upper Deck Victory-181
00Upper Deck Victory-255
00Upper Deck Victory-317
00Upper Deck Vintage-273
00Upper Deck Vintage-283
National Heroes-NH18
00Vanguard-76
High Voltage-27
High Voltage Gold-27
High Voltage Green-27
High Voltage Red-27
High Voltage Silver-27
Holographic Gold-76
Holographic Purple-76
Pacific Proofs-76
Press East/West-9
01Atomic-74
Blue-74
Gold-74
Premiere Date-74
Red-74
01BAP Memorabilia-186
01BAP Memorabilia-355
Emerald-186
Emerald-355
Ruby-186
Ruby-355
Sapphire-186
Sapphire-355
All-Star Jersey Doubles-DASJ30
All-Star Teammates-AST17
Country of Origin-CO18
01BAP Signature Series Certified 100-C19
01BAP Signature Series Certified 50-C19
01BAP Signature Series Certified 1 of 1's-C19
01BAP Signature Series Autographs-LJR
01BAP Signature Series Autographs Gold-LJR
01BAP Sig Series He Shoots/Scores Points-9
01BAP Sig Series He Shoots/Scores Prizes-19
01BAP Signature Series Jerseys-GJ-52
01BAP Sig Series Jersey and Stick Cards-GSJ-52
01BAP Signature Series Emblems-GUE-29
01BAP Signature Series Numbers-ITN-29
01BAP Signature Series Teammates-TM-22
01BAP Ultimate Mem All-Star History-42
01BAP Ultimate Memorabilia Autographs-30
01BAP Ultimate Mem Autographs Gold-30
01BAP Ultimate Memorabilia Dynamic Duos-12
01BAP Ultimate Memorabilia Emblems-29
01BAP Ultimate Memorabilia Jerseys-29
01BAP Ultimate Mem Jerseys and Sticks-29
01BAP Ultimate Mem Journey Jerseys-17
01BAP Ultimate Mem Journey Emblems-17
01BAP Ultimate Memorabilia Numbers-29
01BAP Ultimate Memorabilia Name Plates-24
01BAP Update He Shoots-He Scores Prizes-12
01BAP Update Heritage-H22
01BAP Update Travel Plans-TP11
01Bowman YoungStars-49
Gold-49
Ice Cubed-49
01Crown Royale-109
Blue-109
Premiere Date-109
Red-109
Retail-109
Jewels of the Crown-24
01Flyers Postcards-19
01O-Pee-Chee-94
01O-Pee-Chee-94U
01O-Pee-Chee Heritage Parallel-94
01O-Pee-Chee Heritage Parallel Limited-94
01O-Pee-Chee Premier Parallel-94
01Pacific-308
01Pacific-418
01Pacific-438
Extreme LTD-308
Gold-418
Gold-438
Hobby LTD-308
Premiere Date-308
Retail LTD-308
01Pacific Adrenaline-143
Blue-143
Premiere Date-143
Red-143
Retail-143
01Pacific Arena Exclusives-308
01Pacific Arena Exclusives-418
01Pacific Arena Exclusives-438
01Pacific Heads-Up-74
Blue-74
Premiere Date-74
Red-74
Silver-74
Quad Jerseys-16
Stat Masters-13
01Parkhurst-3
Gold-3
Silver-3
He Shoots-He Scores Prizes-30
Milestones-M22
Milestones-M52
Sticks-PS67
Waving the Flag-21
01Private Stock-74
Gold-74
Premiere Date-74
Retail-74
Silver-74
Game Gear Patches-72
01Private Stock Pacific Nights-74
01Private Stock PS-2002-55
01Private Stock Reserve-S14
01SP Authentic-60
01SP Authentic-105
Limited-60
Limited-105
Limited Gold-60
Limited Gold-105
01SP Game Used-39
01SPx-46
01Sports Illustrated for Kids III-139
01Stadium Club-110
Award Winners-110
Master Photos-110
01Titanium-107
Hobby Parallel-107
Premiere Date-107
Retail-107
Retail Parallel-107
Double-Sided Jerseys-50
Double-Sided Jerseys-59
Double-Sided Patches-50
Double-Sided Patches-59
Saturday Knights-17
01Titanium Draft Day Edition-72
01Topps-94
01Topps-94U
Heritage Parallel-94
Heritage Parallel Limited-94
OPC Parallel-94
01Topps Chrome-94
Refractors-94
Black Border Refractors-94
01Topps Heritage-164
01Topps Reserve-95
01UD Challenge for the Cup-62
Century Men-CM1
01UD Honor Roll Tough Customers-TC4
01UD Mask Collection-72
Gold-72
Gloves-GGJR
01UD Playmakers-74
01UD Premier Collection-37
01UD Top Shelf-30
Sticks-SJR
Sticks Gold-SJR
01Upper Deck-131
Exclusives-131
Exclusives-215
Crunch Timers-CT9
Tandems-T7
01Upper Deck Ice-33
Combos-C-JR
Combos Gold-G-JR
First Rounders-F-JR
01Upper Deck MVP-143
Souvenirs-C-JR
Souvenirs Gold-C-JR
01Upper Deck Victory-270
01Upper Deck Victory-425
Gold-270
Gold-425
01Upper Deck Vintage-183
01Vanguard-74
Blue-74
Red-74
Memorabilia-21
One of Ones-74
Patches-21
Premiere Date-74
Proofs-74
Quebec Tournament Heroes-6
02McFarlane Hockey-140
02McFarlane Hockey-142
02Atomic-75
Blue-75
Gold-75
Red-75
Hobby Parallel-75
National Pride-U7
Super Colliders-11
02BAP All-Star Edition-76
Jerseys-76
Jerseys Gold-76
Jerseys Silver-76
02BAP First Edition-149
02BAP First Edition-309
02BAP First Edition-374
02BAP First Edition-402H
He Shoots-He Scores Prizes-27
Jerseys-149
Scoring Leaders-14
02BAP Memorabilia-80
02BAP Memorabilia-252
Emerald-80
Emerald-252
Ruby-80
Ruby-252
Sapphire-80
Sapphire-252
All-Star Jerseys-ASJ-49
All-Star Teammates-AST-2
All-Star Teammates-AST-17
He Shoots-He Scores Points-2
He Shoots-He Scores Prizes-19
NHL All-Star Game-80
NHL All-Star Game-252
NHL All-Star Game Blue-80
NHL All-Star Game Blue-252
NHL All-Star Game Green-80
NHL All-Star Game Green-252
NHL All-Star Game Red-80
NHL All-Star Game Red-252
Teammates-TM-9
02BAP Memorabilia Toronto Fall Expo-80
02BAP Memorabilia Toronto Fall Expo-252
02BAP NHL All-Star History-42
02BAP Signature Series-134
Autographs-134
Autograph Buybacks 1998-107
Autograph Buybacks 1999-190
Autograph Buybacks 2000-59
Autographs Gold-134
Franchise Players-FJ22
Jerseys-SGJ14
Jersey Autographs-SGJ14
Team Quads-TQ3
02BAP Ultimate Memorabilia Emblems-19
02BAP Ultimate Mem Journey Jerseys-15
02BAP Ultimate Mem Journey Emblems-8
02BAP Ultimate Memorabilia Numbers-24
02Bowman YoungStars-77
Gold-77
Silver-77
02Crown Royale-72
Blue-72
Red-72
Retail-72
Jerseys-15
Jerseys Gold-15
02eTopps-50
02Flyers Postcards-21
02ITG Used-55
02ITG Used-155
Jerseys-GUJ14
Jersey Autographs-GUJ14
Jersey Gold-GUJ14
Emblems-E14
Jersey and Stick-SJ14
Jersey and Stick Gold-SJ14
02O-Pee-Chee-87
02O-Pee-Chee-314
02O-Pee-Chee Premier Blue Parallel-87
02O-Pee-Chee Premier Blue Parallel-314
02O-Pee-Chee Premier Red Parallel-87
02O-Pee-Chee Premier Red Parallel-314
02O-Pee-Chee Factory Set-87
02O-Pee-Chee Factory Set-314
02Pacific-287
Blue-287
Red-287
Main Attractions-15
02Pacific Complete-252
Red-252
02Pacific Exclusive-129
02Pacific Heads-Up-93
Blue-93
Purple-93
Red-93
Quad Jerseys-20
Quad Jerseys Gold-20
02Pacific Quest for the Cup-77
Gold-77
Chasing the Cup-14
Jerseys-16
02Parkhurst-104
Bronze-104
Gold-104
Silver-104
He Shoots-He Scores Points-5
He Shoots-He Scores Prizes-10
Jerseys-GJ32
Milestones-MS1
Patented Power-PP4
Stick and Jerseys-SJ32
02Parkhurst Retro-26
Minis-26
Franchise Players-RF22
Jerseys-RJ31
Jersey and Sticks-RSJ29
02Private Stock Reserve-75
Blue-75
Red-75
Retail-75
02SP Authentic-65
Beckett Promos-65
Super Premiums-SPJR
Super Premiums-DPRG
02SP Game Used-37
Authentic Fabrics-AFJR
Authentic Fabrics-AFRO
Authentic Fabrics Gold-AFJR
Authentic Fabrics Gold-AFRO
Authentic Fabrics Rainbow-AFJR
Authentic Fabrics Rainbow-AFRO
First Rounder Patches-JR
Piece of History-PHJR
Piece of History-PHRK
Piece of History Gold-PHJR
Piece of History Gold-PHRK
Piece of History Rainbow-PHJR
Piece of History Rainbow-PHRK
Tools of the Game-JR
02SPx-55
02SPx-138
Spectrum Gold-55
Spectrum Silver-55
Milestones-MJR
Milestones Gold-JR
Milestones Silver-JR
Winning Materials-WMJR
Winning Materials Gold-JR
Winning Materials Silver-JR
02Stadium Club-16
Silver Decoy Cards-16
Proofs-16
World Stage-WS6
02Titanium-76
Blue-76
Red-76
Retail-76
02Topps-87
02Topps-314
OPC Blue Parallel-87
OPC Blue Parallel-314
OPC Red Parallel-87
OPC Red Parallel-314
Topps/OPC Hometown Heroes-HHU10
Factory Set-87
Factory Set-314
Factory Set Hometown Heroes-HHU10
02Topps Chrome-55
Black Border Refractors-55
Refractors-55
02Topps Heritage-20
02Topps Heritage-112
Chrome Parallel-20
02Topps Total-239
Production-TP9
02UD Artistic Impressions-65
Gold-65
Artist's Touch-ATJR
Artist's Touch Gold-ATJR
02UD Artistic Impressions Beckett Promos-65
02UD Artistic Impressions Common Ground-CG17
02UD Artistic Impress Common Ground Gold-CG17
02UD Artistic Impressions Flashbacks-UD10
02UD Artistic Impressions Flashbacks Gold-UD10
02UD Artistic Impressions Retrospectives-R65
02UD Artistic Impress Retrospect Gold-R65
02UD Artistic Impress Retrospect Silver-R65
02UD Foundations-72
02UD Honor Roll-52
Grade A Jerseys-TPRG
Students of the Game-SG23
02UD Mask Collection-62
02UD Mask Collection Beckett Promos-62
02UD Mask Collection Instant Offense-IOJR
02UD Piece of History-65
02UD Premier Collection-40
Jerseys Bronze-JK
Jerseys Bronze-JR
Jerseys Bronze-RG
Jerseys Gold-JK
Jerseys Gold-JR
Jerseys Gold-RG
Jerseys Silver-JK
Jerseys Silver-JR
Jerseys Silver-RG
Patches-PJR
02UD Top Shelf-63
Clutch Performers-CPJR
Milestones Jerseys-MBBRR
Milestones Jerseys-MSFRM
Triple Jerseys-HTLRR
02Upper Deck-127
Exclusives-127
Number Crunchers-NC11
Patch Card Name Plate-JR
Playbooks Series II-RP
Sizzling Scorers-SS12
02Upper Deck Classic Portraits-72
Headliners-RG
Headliners Limited-RG
Hockey Royalty-LRR
Hockey Royalty Limited-LRR
Starring Cast-CJR
Starring Cast Limited-CJR
02Upper Deck MVP-136
Gold-136
Classics-136
Golden Classics-136
Vital Forces-VF11
02Upper Deck Rookie Update-72
02Upper Deck Rookie Update-153C
02Upper Deck Rookie Update-156C
Jerseys-DJR
Jerseys Gold-DJR
02Upper Deck Victory-157
Bronze-157
Gold-157
Silver-157
National Pride-NP58
02Upper Deck Vintage-189
02Upper Deck Vintage-282
02Upper Deck Vintage-301
02Upper Deck Vintage-312
Green Backs-189
Tall Boys-T47
Tall Boys Gold-T47
02Vanguard-75
LTD-75
02UD SuperStars *-190
Gold-190
Leadership Leaders Triple Jersey-ADJ
03McFarlane Hockey 3-Inch Duals-10
03McFarlane Hockey NHL 2-Pack-20
03BAP Memorabilia-40
Emerald-40
Gold-40
Ruby-40
Sapphire-40
All-Star Jerseys-ASJ-36
He Shoots-He Scores Points-2
He Shoots-He Scores Prizes-18
Jersey and Stick-SJ-22
Jerseys-GJ-27
Jersey Autographs-GJ-27
Stanley Cup Playoffs-SCP-22
03BAP Ultimate Memorabilia Autographs-28
Gold-28
03BAP Ultimate Mem Auto Jerseys-28
03BAP Ultimate Mem Auto Emblems-28
03BAP Ultimate Memorabilia Active Eight-7
03BAP Ultimate Memorabilia Dynamic Duos-6
03BAP Ultimate Memorabilia Jerseys-18
03BAP Ultimate Memorabilia Jerseys Gold-18
03BAP Ultimate Mem Jersey and Emblems-16
03BAP Ultimate Mem Jersey and Emblem Gold-16
03BAP Ultimate Mem Jersey and Numbers-16
03BAP Ultimate Mem Jersey and Number Gold-16
03BAP Ultimate Mem Journey Jerseys-9
03BAP Ultimate Mem Journey Jerseys Gold-9
03BAP Ultimate Mem Journey Emblems-9
03BAP Ultimate Mem Journey Emblems Gold-9
03BAP Ultimate Memorabilia Nameplates-18
03BAP Ultimate Mem Nameplates Gold-18
03BAP Ultimate Memorabilia Triple Threads-23
03Beehive-146
Variations-146
Gold-146
Silver-146
Jumbos-21
Jumbo Jerseys-BH1
Jerseys-JT5
Signatures-RF15
Sticks Beige Border-BE22
Sticks Red Border-RE12
03Black Diamond-175
Black-175
Green-175
Red-175
Threads-DT-JR
Threads Green-DT-JR
Threads Red-DT-JR
Threads Black-DT-JR
03Bowman-27
Gold-27
03Bowman Chrome-27
Refractors-27
Gold Refractors-27
Xfractors-27
03Crown Royale-75
Blue-75
Retail-75
Global Conquest-10
Jerseys-19
Patches-19
Lords of the Rink-17
03eTopps-29
03Flyers Program Inserts-1
03Flyers Postcards-19
03ITG Action-469
Jerseys-M174
Jerseys-M262
03ITG Used Signature Series-22
Gold-22
Autographs-JR
Autographs Gold-JR
Franchise-22
Franchise Autographs-22
Franchise Gold-22
Jerseys-15
Jerseys Gold-15
Jersey Autos-15
Emblems-37
Emblems Gold-37
Jersey and Stick-15
Jersey and Stick Gold-15
Teammates-6
Teammates Gold-6
03ITG VIP Jerseys-22
03McDonald's Pacific-39
03NHL Sticker Collection-107
03O-Pee-Chee-110
03OPC Blue-110
03OPC Gold-110
03OPC Red-110
03Pacific-257
Blue-257
Red-257
Jerseys-30
Jerseys Gold-30
Maximum Impact-8
03Pacific Atlantic City National-5
03Pacific Calder-75
Silver-75
03Pacific Complete-208
Red-208
03Pacific Exhibit-186
Blue Backs-186
03Pacific Heads-Up-74
Hobby LTD-74
Retail LTD-74
Fast Forwards-7
Fast Forwards LTD-7
03Pacific Invincible-75
Blue-75
Red-75
Retail-75
Featured Performers-22
03Pacific Luxury Suite-44A
03Pacific Luxury Suite-44B
03Pacific Prism-136
Blue-136
Patches-136
Red-136
Retail-136
03Pacific Quest for the Cup-80
Blue-80
03Pacific Supreme-75
Blue-75
Red-75
Retail-75
Jerseys-20
03Parkhurst Original Six Chicago-33
Inserts-C15
Memorabilia-CM21
Memorabilia-CM36
Memorabilia-CM52
03Parkhurst Rookie-3
Jerseys-GJ-16
Jerseys Gold-GJ-16
Retro Rookies-RR-10
Retro Rookies Gold-RR-10
Teammates Gold-RT9
Teammates-RT9
03Private Stock Reserve-192
Blue-192
Patches-192
Red-192
Retail-192
03SP Authentic-65
Limited-65
Breakout Seasons-B5
Breakout Seasons Limited-B5
Sign of the Times-JR
Sign of the Times-CR
Sign of the Times-CRG
03SP Game Used-35
03SP Game Used-115
Gold-35
Gold-115
Authentic Fabrics-AFJR
Authentic Fabrics-DFRG
Authentic Fabrics-QARGL
Authentic Fabrics Gold-AFJR
Authentic Fabrics Gold-DFRG
Authentic Fabrics Gold-QARGL
Authentic Patches-APJR
Double Threads-DTRA
Premium Patches-PPJR
Signers-SPSJR
Team Threads-TTARL
Top Threads-ARGL
03SPx-73
03SPx-128
03SPx-184
Radiance-73
Radiance-128
Radiance-184
Spectrum-73
Spectrum-128
Spectrum-184
Fantasy Franchise-FF-LRA
Fantasy Franchise Limited-FF-LRA
Origins-O-JR

Signature Threads-ST-JR
Winning Materials-WM-JR
Winning Materials Limited-WM-JR
03Titanium-177
Hobby Jersey Number Parallels-177
Patches-177
Retail-177
03Topps-110
Blue-110
Gold-110
Red-110
Box Toppers-13
Topps/OPC Idols-UI2
Lost Rookies-JR
03Topps C55-27
Minis-27
Minis American Back-27
Minis American Back Red-27
Minis Bazooka Back-27
Minis Brooklyn Back-27
Minis Hat Trick Back-27
Minis O Canada Back-27
Minis O Canada Back Red-27
Minis Stanley Cup Back-27
03Topps Pristine-58
Gold Refractor Die Cuts-58
Refractors-58
Press Plates Black-58
Press Plates Cyan-58
Press Plates Magenta-58
Press Plates Yellow-58
03UD Honor Roll-64
03UD Honor Roll-114
Signature Class-SC22
03UD Premier Collection-41
NHL Shields-SH-JR
NHL Shields-SH-JR2
Signatures-PS-JR
Signatures Gold-PS-JR
Skills-SK-RR
Skills Patches-SK-RR
Teammates-PT-PF1
Teammates-PT-PF2
Teammates Patches-PT-PF1
Teammates Patches-PT-PF2
03Upper Deck-383
All-Star Class-AS-21
Big Playmakers-BP-JR
BuyBacks-139
BuyBacks-140
BuyBacks-141
BuyBacks-142
BuyBacks-143
BuyBacks-144
BuyBacks-145
BuyBacks-146
BuyBacks-147
BuyBacks-148
BuyBacks-149
BuyBacks-150
BuyBacks-151
Canadian Exclusives-383
Fan Favorites-FF1
HG-383
Jersey Autographs-SJ-JR
Memorable Matchups-MM-RR
NHL Best-NB-JR
Patches-LD9
Patches-SP3
Performers-PS4
Power Zone-PZ-3
UD Exclusives-383
03Upper Deck Classic Portraits-70
03Upper Deck Classic Portraits-140
Genuine Greatness-GG-JR
Hockey Royalty-RLA
03Upper Deck Ice-65
Gold-65
Authentics-IA-JR
Breakers-IB-JR
Breaker Patches-IB-JR
Frozen Fabrics-FF-JR
Frozen Fabric Patches-FF-JR
Icons-I-JR
Icons Jerseys-I-JR
Under Glass Autographs-UG-JR
03Upper Deck MVP-305
Gold Script-305
Silver Script-305
Canadian Exclusives-305
Lethal Lineups-LL2
SportsNut-SN65
Winning Formula-WF3
03Upper Deck Rookie Update-65
03Upper Deck Rookie Update-158
Skills-SKJR
Super Stars-SSJR
03Upper Deck Trilogy-70
03Upper Deck Trilogy-111
Authentic Patches-AP14
Crest Variations-111
Limited-70
Limited-111
03Upper Deck Victory-137
Bronze-137
Gold-137
Silver-137
Freshman Flashback-FF35
Game Breakers-GB50
03Toronto Star-69
04ITG NHL AS FANtasy AS History Jerseys-SB42
04Pacific-198
Blue-198
Red-198
Philadelphia-12
04SP Authentic-65
04SP Authentic-133
Limited-65
Limited-133
Buybacks-91
Buybacks-92
Buybacks-93
Rookie Review-RR-JR
Sign of the Times-ST-JR
Sign of the Times-DS-CR
Sign of the Times-TS-CLR
Sign of the Times-TS-GRE
Sign of the Times-QS-GPRE
Sign of the Times-SS-USA
04UD Toronto Fall Expo Priority Signings-JR
04Ultimate Collection-31
Buybacks-29
Buybacks-30
Buybacks-31
Buybacks-32
Dual Logos-UL2-RG
Jerseys-UGJ-JR
Jerseys Gold-UGJ-JR
Jersey Autographs-UGJA-JR
Patches-UP-JR
Patch Autographs-UPA-JR
Signature Logos-ULA-JR
Signature Patches-SP-JR
04Upper Deck-126
04Upper Deck-203
Big Playmakers-BP-JR
Canadian Exclusives-126
Canadian Exclusives-203
HG Glossy Gold-126
HG Glossy Gold-203
HG Glossy Silver-126
HG Glossy Silver-203
Jersey Autographs-GJA-JR
Jersey Autographs-GJA-JR/JL
Patches-GJPA-JR
Patches-GJPL-JR
Patches-GJPN-JR
School of Hard Knocks-SHK4
Three Stars-AS6
05Be A Player Class Action-CA18
05Be A Player Outtakes-OT37
05Beehive-42
05Beehive-191
Beige -42
Blue -42
Gold-42
Red -42
Matte-42
Matted Materials-MMJR
Matted Materials Remarkable-RMJR
Signature Scrapbook-SSJR
05Black Diamond-139
Emerald-139
Gold-139
Onyx-139
Ruby-139
Gemography-G-JR
Gemography Emerald-G-JR
Gemography Gold-G-JR
Gemography Onyx-G-JR
Gemography Ruby-G-JR
Jerseys-J-JR
Jerseys Ruby-J-JR
Jersey Duals-DJ-JR
Jersey Triples-TJ-JR
Jersey Quads-QJ-JR
05Hot Prospects-48
En Fuego-48
Red Hot-48
White Hot-48
05Kings Team Issue-3
05McDonalds Upper Deck-37
Jerseys-MJ15
Patches-MP12
05Panini Stickers-284
05Parkhurst-229
Facsimile Auto Parallel-229
True Colors-TCLAK
True Colors-TCLAK
True Colors-TCSJLA
True Colors-TCSJLA
05SP Authentic-46
05SP Authentic-120
Limited-46
Limited-120
Chirography-SPJR
Exquisite Endorsements-EEJR
Marks of Distinction-MDJR
Sign of the Times-JR
Sign of the Times Duals-DRR
05SP Game Used-45
Autographs-45
Gold-45
Authentic Fabrics-AF-JR
Authentic Fabrics Autographs-AAF-JR
Authentic Fabrics Gold-AF-JR
Authentic Fabrics Quad-FRRG
Authentic Fabrics Quad-TRGL
Authentic Patches Quad -FRRG
Authentic Patches Quad -TRGL
Authentic Fabrics Triple-MLR
Authentic Patches-AP-JR
Authentic Patches Autographs-AAP-JR
Authentic Patches Triple-MLR
Awesome Authentics-AA-JR
Game Gear-GG-JR
Game Gear Autographs-AG-JR
SIGnificance-JR
SIGnificance Gold-S-JR
Significant Numbers-SN-JR
05SPx-38
05SPx-107
Spectrum-38
Spectrum-107
Winning Combos-WC-FR
Winning Combos-WC-LA
Winning Combos Autographs-AWC-LA
Winning Combos Gold-WC-FR
Winning Combos Gold-WC-LA
Winning Combos Spectrum-WC-FR
Winning Combos Spectrum-WC-LA
Winning Materials-WM-JR
Winning Materials Autographs-AWM-JR
Winning Materials Gold-WM-JR
Winning Materials Spectrum-WM-JR
Xcitement Superstars-XS-JR
Xcitement Superstars Gold-XS-JR
Xcitement Superstars Spectrum-XS-JR
05The Cup-49
Gold-49
Black Rainbow-49
Dual NHL Shields Autographs-ADSLA
Masterpiece Pressplates-49
Masterpiece Pressplates (Rookie Update)-216
Noble Numbers Dual-DNNMR
Patch Variation-P49
Patch Variation Autographs-AP49
Property of-POJR
05UD Artifacts Auto Facts-AF-JR
05UD Artifacts Auto Facts Blue-AF-JR
05UD Artifacts Auto Facts Copper-AF-JR
05UD Artifacts Auto Facts Pewter-AF-JR
05UD Artifacts Auto Facts Silver-AF-JR
05UD Artifacts Remarkable Artifacts-RA-JR
05UD Artifacts Remarkable Artifacts Dual-RA-JR
05UD Artifacts Treasured Patches-TP-JR
05UD Artifacts Treasured Patch Autos-TP-JR
05UD Artifacts Treasured Patches Dual-TPD-JR
05UD Artifacts Treasured Patch Dual Autos-TPD-JR
05UD Artifacts Treasured Patches Pewter-TP-JR
05UD Artifacts Treasured Patches Silver-TP-JR
05UD Artifacts Treasured Swatches-TS-JR
05UD Artifacts Treasured Swatch Autos-TS-JR
05UD Artifacts Treasured Swatches Blue-TS-JR
05UD Artifacts Treasured Swatches Copper-TS-JR
05UD Artifacts Treasured Swatches Dual-TSD-JR
05UD Artifacts Treasured Swatch Dual Auto-TSD-JR
05UD Artifacts Treasured Swatch Dual Blue-TSD-JR
05UD Artifact Treasure Swatch Dual Copper-TSD-JR
05UD Artifact Treasure Swatch Dual Maroon-TSD-JR
05UD Artifact Treasure Swatch Dual Pewter-TSD-JR
05UD Artifact TreasuredSwatch Dual Silver-TSD-JR
05UD Artifacts Treasured Swatches Maroon-TS-JR
05UD Artifacts Treasured Swatches Pewter-TS-JR
05UD Artifacts Treasured Swatches Silver-TS-JR
05UD PowerPlay-64
05UD PowerPlay-99
Rainbow-64
05Ultimate Collection-44
Gold-44
Endorsed Emblems-EEJR
Marquee Attractions-MA24
Marquee Attractions Signatures-SMA24
Premium Patches-PPJR
Premium Swatches-PSJR
Ultimate Achievements-UAJR
Ultimate Patches-PJR
Ultimate Signatures Pairings-UPLA
05Ultra-93
Gold-93
Fresh Ink-FI-JR
Fresh Ink Blue-FI-JR
Ice-93
Scoring Kings-SK12
Scoring Kings Jerseys-SKJ-JR
Scoring Kings Jersey Autographs-KAJ-JR
Scoring Kings Patches-SKP-JR
Scoring Kings Patch Autographs-KAP-JR
05Upper Deck-334
Big Playmakers-B-JR
Jerseys-J-JR
Jerseys Series II-J2JR
Majestic Materials-MMJR
Notable Numbers-N-JR
Notable Numbers-N-RO
Patches-P-JR
School of Hard Knocks-HK4
Scrapbooks-HS27
Shooting Stars-S-JR
05Upper Deck Hockey Showcase-HS16
05Upper Deck Showcase Promos-HS16
05Upper Deck Ice-44
Rainbow-44
Frozen Fabrics-FFJR
Frozen Fabrics Autographs-AFFJR
Frozen Fabrics Glass-FFJR
Frozen Fabrics Patches-FFPJR
Frozen Fabrics Patch Autographs-FAPJR
Signature Swatches-SSJR
05Upper Deck MVP-181
Gold-181
Platinum-181
ProSign-P-JR
05Upper Deck Rookie Update-45
05Upper Deck Rookie Update-216
Inspirations Patch Rookies-216
05Upper Deck Trilogy-43
05Upper Deck Trilogy-121
Crystal-121
Crystal Autographs-121
Honorary Patches-HP-JR
Honorary Patch Scripts-HSP-JR
Honorary Swatches-HS-JR
Honorary Swatch Scripts-HSS-JR
05Upper Deck Victory-140
05Upper Deck Victory-222
Black-140
Black-222
Gold-140
Gold-222
Silver-140
Silver-222
Blow-Ups-BU28
Stars on Ice-SI32
06Be A Player Portraits-80
06Beehive-25
06Beehive-172
Blue-25
Gold-25
Matte-25
Red Facsimile Signatures-25
Wood-25
06Black Diamond-120
Black-120
Gold-120
Ruby-120
06Flair Showcase-49
06Flair Showcase-133
06Flair Showcase-237
Parallel-49
Parallel-133
Parallel-237
Hot Numbers-HN21
Hot Numbers Parallel-HN21
Inks-IJR
Stitches-SSJR
06Fleer-152
Tiffany-152
Fabricology-FJR
06Hot Prospects-75
Red Hot-75
White Hot-75
06NHL POG-22
06O-Pee-Chee-384
06O-Pee-Chee-663
Rainbow-384
Rainbow-663
Swatches-S-JR
06Panini Stickers-317
06SP Authentic-25
06SP Authentic-123
Limited-25
Limited-123
06SP Game Used-77
Gold-77
Rainbow-77
Authentic Fabrics Triple-AF3PHX
Authentic Fabrics Triple Patches-AF3PHX
Autographs-77
Inked Sweaters Dual-IS2RD
Inked Sweaters Dual Patches-IS2RD
06SPx-78
Spectrum-78
SPxcitement-X77
SPxcitement Spectrum-X77
SPxcitement Autographs-X77
06The Cup-71
Autographed Foundations-CQJR
Autographed Foundations Patches-CQJR
Autographed Patches-71
Black Rainbow-71
Foundations-CQJR
Foundations Patches-CQJR
Gold-71
Gold Patches-71
Jerseys-71
Limited Logos-LLJR
Masterpiece Pressplates-71
Signature Patches-SPJR
06UD Artifacts-26
Blue-26
Gold-26
Platinum-26
Radiance-26
Autographed Radiance Parallel-26
Red-26
Tundra Tandems-TTRD
Tundra Tandems Black-TTRD
Tundra Tandems Blue-TTRD
Tundra Tandems Gold-TTRD
Tundra Tandems Platinum-TTRD
Tundra Tandems Red-TTRD
Tundra Tandems Dual Patches Red-TTRD
06UD Mini Jersey Collection-78
06UD Powerplay-78
Impact Rainbow-78
06Ultimate Collection Autographed Jerseys-AJ-JR
06Ultimate Collection Autographed Patches-AJ-JR
06Ultimate Collection Jerseys Dual-UJ2-RD
06Ultimate Collection Patches Dual-UJ2-RD
06Ultimate Collection Premium Patches-PS-JR
06Ultimate Collection Premium Swatches-PS-JR
06Ultimate Collection Ultimate Signatures Logos-SL-JR
06Ultra-153
Gold Medallion-153
Ice Medallion-153
06Upper Deck Arena Giveaways-PHX4
06Upper Deck-401
Exclusives Parallel-401
High Gloss Parallel-401
Game Jerseys-J2JR
Game Patches-P2JR
Masterpieces-401
Oversized Wal-Mart Exclusives-401
Signatures-SJR
Signature Sensations-SSJR
06Upper Deck MVP-226
Gold Script-226
Super Script-226
Jerseys-OJRL
06Upper Deck Sweet Shot-79
Signature Shots/Saves Sticks-SSSJR
Signature Sticks-STJR
06Upper Deck Trilogy-77
Combo Autographed Jerseys-CJRD
Combo Autographed Patches-CJRD
Honorary Scripted Patches-HSPJR
Honorary Scripted Swatches-HSSJR
Scripts-S3JR
06Upper Deck Victory-267

Roenick, Trevor
93Maine Black Bears-58
97Las Vegas Thunder-6
98Las Vegas Thunder-17
99Tacoma Sabercats-11
01UK London Knights-6

Roesler, Richard
95Central Hockey League-81

Roest, Stacy
917th Inn. Sketch WHL-326
95Adirondack Red Wings-20
98Pacific Omega-89
Red-89
Opening Day Issue-89
99Upper Deck MVP SC Edition-70
Gold Script-70
Silver Script-70
Super Script-70
00Private Stock-50
Gold-50
Premiere Date-50
Retail-50
Silver-50
00Revolution-74
Blue-74
Premiere Date-74
Red-74
00Topps Chrome-237
OPC Refractors-237
Refractors-237
00Upper Deck-88
Exclusives Tier 1-88
Exclusives Tier 2-88
00Upper Deck NHLPA-PA45
00Upper Deck Vintage-174
01BAP Signature Series-135
Autographs-135
Autographs Gold-135
01Upper Deck-319
Exclusives-319
01Upper Deck MVP-96
01Upper Deck Victory-172
Gold-172
01Wild Team Issue-2
02BAP Sig Series Auto Buybacks 2001-135
02Pacific-186
Blue-186
Red-186
02Grand Rapids Griffins-24

Roff, Paul
85Minnesota-Duluth Bulldogs-11

Rogenmoser, Harry
93Swiss HNL-78
95Swiss HNL-229
96Swiss HNL-143
96Swiss HNL-543
98Swiss Power Play Stickers-196

Roger, Sebastien
98Bowman's Best-148
Refractors-148
Atomic Refractors-148
98Bowman CHL-106
Golden Anniversary-106
OPC International-106
98Bowman Chrome CHL-106
Golden Anniversary-106
Golden Anniversary Refractors-106
OPC International-106
OPC International Refractors-106
Refractors-106
99Bowman CHL-53
Gold-53
OPC International-53
03St. Jean Mission-23

Rogers, Andy
02Calgary Hitmen-21
03Calgary Hitmen-14
04ITG Heroes and Prospects-66
Autographs-AR
04ITG Heroes/Prospects Toronto Expo '05-66
04ITG Heroes/Prospects Expo Heroes/Pros-66
05ITG Heroes/Prosp Toronto Expo Parallel -325
05ITG Heroes and Prospects-325
Autographs Series II-ARG
06Springfield Falcons-18
06ITG Heroes and Prospects Jerseys-GUJ29
06ITG Heroes and Prospects Jerseys Gold-GUJ29
06ITG Heroes and Prospects Emblems-GUE29
06ITG Heroes and Prospects Emblems Gold-GUE29
06ITG Heroes and Prospects Numbers-GUN29
06ITG Heroes and Prospects Numbers Gold-GUN29

Rogers, Brandon
02Michigan Wolverines-16
03Michigan Wolverines-11
06Norfolk Admirals-3

Rogers, Brian
92Quebec Pee-Wee Tournament-1578
01Michigan Tech Huskies-28
02Kalamazoo Wings-22

Rogers, Dan
01Owen Sound Attack-17
02Owen Sound Attack-7
03Belleville Bulls-4

Rogers, Dustin
99OCN Blizzard-14

Rogers, Fred
91Pro Set Platinum-297

Rogers, Kent
91Air Canada SJHL-B17
91Air Canada SJHL All-Stars-7
92Saskatchewan JHL-134

Rogers, Mike
75O-Pee-Chee WHA-8
77O-Pee-Chee WHA-17
79O-Pee-Chee-43
79Topps-43
80O-Pee-Chee-143
80Topps-143
81O-Pee-Chee-127
81O-Pee-Chee-135
81O-Pee-Chee-140
81O-Pee-Chee Stickers-61
81Topps-32
81Topps-53
81Topps-E131
82O-Pee-Chee-232
82O-Pee-Chee Stickers-136
82Post Cereal-13
82Topps Stickers-136
83NHL Key Tags-89
83O-Pee-Chee-254
83O-Pee-Chee Stickers-217
83Topps Stickers-217
84O-Pee-Chee-152
84O-Pee-Chee Stickers-99
84Topps-114
85Oilers Red Rooster-19
85O-Pee-Chee-39
85O-Pee-Chee Stickers-86
85Topps-39
88Oilers Tenth Anniversary-128
06Parkhurst-139
06Parkhurst-223
Autographs-139
Autographs-223

Rogers, Ronny
06Erie Otters-14

Rogers, Scott
91Air Canada SJHL-B32
91Air Canada SJHL-C44
94Classic Pro Prospects-241

Rogerson, Tom
00Sarnia Sting-22

Rogger, Brian
907th Inn. Sketch QMJHL-154

Rogger, Bruno
93Swiss HNL-84

Rogles, Chris
92Clarkson Knights-16
93Indianapolis Ice-18
93Classic-77
94Indianapolis Ice-20
94Classic Autographs-NNO
94Classic Pro Prospects-213
95Las Vegas Thunder-14
96St. Louis Vipers RHI-6
98German DEL-46
99German DEL-188
00German DEL-124
01German Upper Deck-148
Goalies in Action-G5
Jersey Cards-CR-J
02German DEL City Press-206
03German DEL-177
All-Stars-AS3
04German Cologne Sharks Postcards-23
04German DEL-218
05German DEL All-Star Jerseys-AS15

Rogosheske, Alex
03Bowling Green Falcons-3
06Bakersfield Condors-16

Rogov, Alexander
74Swedish Stickers-96

Rogowin, Adam
93Quebec Pee-Wee Tournament-1322

Rohac, Ivan
06Kamloops Blazers-19

Rohde, Christian
01German Upper Deck-242
04German Krefeld Penguins Postcards-18
05German DEL-50

Rohde, Florian
94German First League-251

Rohl, Dieter
70Finnish Jaakiekko-98
70Swedish Hockey-383

Rohlfs, David
03Michigan Wolverines-21
04Michigan Wolverines-1

Rohlicek, Jeff
84Kelowna Wings-15
86Fredericton Express-22
89ProCards IHL-175
90ProCards AHL/IHL-357
91ProCards-397
92Toledo Storm-14
93Toledo Storm-16
95Fort Wayne Komets-15
96Mississippi Sea Wolves-17
97Mississippi Sea Wolves-5

Rohlik, Pavel
94Czech APS Extraliga-249

Rohlin, Leif
89Swedish Semic Elitserien Stickers-245
90Swedish Semic Elitserien Stickers-153
91Swedish Semic Elitserien Stickers-257
92Swedish Semic Elitserien Stickers-281
93Swedish Semic Elitserien-246
94Swedish Leaf-175
Gold Cards-12
Studio Signatures-11
95Donruss-344
95Swedish Globe World Championships-23
95Swedish World Championships Stickers-143
96Canucks Postcards-27
98Swiss Power Play Stickers-10
99Swiss Panini Stickers-11
00Swiss Panini Stickers-12
00Swiss Slapshot Mini-Cards-HCAP6
02Swedish SHL-252
Parallel-252
Signatures Series II-21

Rohloff, Jon
93Minnesota-Duluth Commemorative-4
93Classic-78
94OPC Premier-516
Special Effects-516
94Topps/OPC Premier-516
Special Effects-516
94Ultra-260
94Upper Deck-378
Electric Ice-378
94Classic Autographs-NNO
94Classic Pro Prospects-224
95Donruss-86
95Leaf-322
95Topps-196
OPC Inserts-196
95Upper Deck-127
Electric Ice-127
Electric Ice Gold-127
96Be A Player-207
Autographs-207
Autographs Silver-207
96Collector's Choice-21
96Upper Deck-11
97Pacific Invincible NHL Regime-16
97Providence Bruins-17
99Kansas City Blades Supercuts-17
00Cincinnati Cyclones-14

Rohloff, Todd
98Portland Pirates-12
99Cleveland Lumberjacks-19
00Portland Pirates-6
01BAP Memorabilia-451
Emerald-451
Ruby-451
Sapphire-451
01UD Playmakers-144
03Syracuse Crunch-7
04Rochester Americans-19
05Springfield Falcons-24

Rohrbach, Daniel
93Swiss HNL-271

Rohrbach, Dirk
94German DEL-134
95German DEL-135

Rohrbach, Gabriel
93Swiss HNL-509

Rohrbach, Wilfried
70Finnish Jaakiekko-97
70Swedish Hockey-382
70Swedish Masterserien-175
70Swedish Masterserien-176
04German Berlin Eisbarens 50th Anniv-58

Rohrig, Brad
96Red Deer Rebels-13
97Red Deer Rebels-18
98Swift Current Broncos-17

Rokama, Jouni
91Finnish Jyvas-Hyva Stickers-61
92Finnish Jyvas-Hyva Stickers-172
93Finnish Jyvas-Hyva Stickers-314
93Finnish SISU-29
94Finnish SISU-201
94Finnish SISU NIL Phenoms-4

Roland, Layne
907th Inn. Sketch WHL-331
917th Inn. Sketch WHL-42
93Portland Winter Hawks-21
97Central Texas Stampede-13
99German Bundesliga 2-181
99Corpus Christi IceRays-18

Rolanti, Mike
93RPI Engineers-27

Roles, Scott
92Quebec Pee-Wee Tournament-1355
97Regina Pats-9
98Kootenay Ice-2
99Spokane Chiefs-19

Rolfe, Dale
68O-Pee-Chee-41
68Topps-41
69O-Pee-Chee-100
Four-in-One-18
69Topps-100
70Dad's Cookies-113
70Esso Power Players-129
70O-Pee-Chee-156
70Red Wings Marathon-8
70Sargent Promotions Stamps-55
71O-Pee-Chee-219
71Sargent Promotions Stamps-118
71Toronto Sun-180
72O-Pee-Chee-271
72Sargent Promotions Stamps-146
73O-Pee-Chee-177
74NHL Action Stamps-191
74O-Pee-Chee NHL-341

Rolfe, Dan
91Nashville Knights-7
92Fort Worth Fire-17

Rolinek, Tomas
00Czech OFS-53
01Czech OFS-251
02Czech OFS Plus-227
03Czech OFS Plus-103
03Czech OFS Plus-395
04Czech OFS-130
05Czech HC Pardubice-14
06Czech CP Cup Postcards-16
06Czech HC Pardubice Postcards-17
06Czech IIHF World Championship Postcards-18
06Czech LG Hockey Games Postcards-17
06Czech OFS-124
06Czech Super Six Postcards-11

Rollins, Al
44Beehive Group II Photos-138A
44Beehive Group II Photos-138B
44Beehive Group II Photos-447
45Quaker Oats Photos-45
45Quaker Oats Photos-60C
48Exhibits Canadian-37
51Parkhurst-76
52Parkhurst-31
53Parkhurst-82
54Parkhurst-77
54Topps-26
92Parkhurst Parkie Reprints-PR8
93Parkhurst Parkie Reprints Case Inserts-4
94Parkhurst Missing Link-28
02Parkhurst Reprints-169
02Parkhurst Reprints-197
05ITG Ultimate Mem Quad Paper Cuts Autos-2

Rollins, Jerry
76O-Pee-Chee WHA-43
76Phoenix Roadrunners WHA-17

Roloson, Dwayne
94Saint John Flames-19
94Classic-61
Gold-61
All-Americans-AA10
95Saint John Flames-20
95Images-41
Gold-41
Autographs-41A
96Be A Player-211
Autographs-211
Autographs Silver-211
96Collector's Edge Future Legends-19
96Collector's Edge Ice-73
Prism-73
96Collector's Edge Ice Promos-PR5
96Collector's Edge Ice The Wall-TW8
97Collector's Choice-41
97Donruss-148
Press Proofs Silver-148
Press Proofs Gold-148
97Pacific Invincible NHL Regime-31
97Pacific Omega-34
Copper-34
Dark Gray-34
Emerald Green-34
Gold-34
Ice Blue-34
97Pinnacle-87
Artist's Proofs-87
Rink Collection-87
Press Plates Back Black-87
Press Plates Back Cyan-87
Press Plates Back Magenta-87
Press Plates Back Yellow-87
Press Plates Front Black-87
Press Plates Front Cyan-87
Press Plates Front Magenta-87
Press Plates Front Yellow-87
97Score-38
Artist's Proofs-38
Golden Blades-38
98NHL Aces Playing Cards-4
98Pacific-124
Ice Blue-124
Red-124
00Worcester Icecats-17
01Between the Pipes-83
01Sports Illustrated for Kids III-395
01Titanium-71
Hobby Parallel-71
Premiere Date-71
Retail-71
Retail Parallel-71
02BAP First Edition-264
02BAP Signature Series-4
Autographs-4
Autographs Gold-4
02Between the Pipes-38
Gold-38
Silver-38
Goalie Autographs-19
02O-Pee-Chee-34
02O-Pee-Chee Premier Blue Parallel-34
02O-Pee-Chee Premier Red Parallel-34
02O-Pee-Chee Factory Set-34
02Pacific-187
Blue-187
Red-187
02Pacific Complete-136
Red-136
02Parkhurst Retro-19
Minis-19
02Topps-34
OPC Blue Parallel-34
OPC Red Parallel-34
Factory Set-34
02Topps Total-281
02UD Mask Collection-42
02UD Mask Collection-43
02UD Mask Collection Beckett Promos-42
02UD Mask Collection Beckett Promos-43
02Upper Deck-88
Exclusives-88
02Vanguard-53
LTD-53
03BAP Memorabilia-116
Emerald-116
Gold-116
Ruby-116
Sapphire-116
Deep in the Crease-D11
Stanley Cup Playoffs-SCP-19
Tandems-T-1
03BAP Ultimate Memorabilia Autographs-46
Gold-46
03Beehive-95
Gold-95
Silver-95
03Black Diamond-34
Black-34
Green-34
Red-34
03Bowman-14
Gold-14
03Bowman Chrome-14
Refractors-14
Gold Refractors-14
Xfractors-14
03Crown Royale-52
Blue-52
Retail-52
03Duracell-14
03ITG Action-224
Jerseys-M114
03ITG Used Signature Series-68
Gold-68
Autographs-DR
Autographs Gold-DR
03O-Pee-Chee-43
03OPC Blue-43
03OPC Gold-43
03OPC Red-43
03Pacific-169
Blue-169
Red-169
03Pacific Calder-53
Silver-53
03Pacific Complete-404
Red-404
03Pacific Exhibit-74
Blue Backs-74
Yellow Backs-74
03Pacific Heads-Up-51
Hobby LTD-51
Retail LTD-51
03Pacific Prism-54
Blue-54
Gold-54
Red-54
03Pacific Supreme-49
Blue-49
Red-49
Retail-49
03Parkhurst Rookie-43
03Private Stock Reserve-51
Blue-51
Red-51
Retail-51
03Titanium-53
Hobby Jersey Number Parallels-53
Retail-53
Retail Jersey Number Parallels-53
03Topps-43
Blue-43
Gold-43
Red-43
03Topps Pristine-84
Gold Refractor Die Cuts-84
Refractors-84
Mini-PM-DR
Press Plates Black-84
Press Plates Cyan-84
Press Plates Magenta-84
Press Plates Yellow-84
03Upper Deck-342
Canadian Exclusives-342
HG-342
UD Exclusives-342
03Upper Deck Classic Portraits-49
03Upper Deck MVP-220
Gold Script-220
Silver Script-220
Canadian Exclusives-220
SportsNut-SN43
03Upper Deck Trilogy-49
Limited-49
03Upper Deck Victory-93
Bronze-93
Gold-93
Silver-93
03Wild Law Enforcement Cards-7
03Worcester Ice Cats 10th Anniversary-2
04ITG All-Star FANtasy Hall Minnesota-6
04Pacific-135
Blue-135
Red-135
04SP Authentic Sign of the Times-ST-DR
04Topps NHL All-Star FANtasy-2
04UD All-World-18
Gold-18
Autographs-18
Triple Autographs-AT-TAR
Quad Autographs-AQ-GOL
04Finnish Cardset-108
04Finnish Cardset Signatures-23
04Swedish Pure Skills-131
Parallel-131
05Be A Player-45
First Period-45
Second Period-45
Third Period-45
Overtime-45
Dual Signatures-DR
Signatures-DR
Signatures Gold-DR
05Beehive-45
Matte-45
Matted Materials-MMDR
05Black Diamond-41
Emerald-41
Gold-41
Onyx-41
Ruby-41
05Panini Stickers-296
05Parkhurst-198
Facsimile Auto Parallel-242
Signatures-DW
True Colors-TCMIN
True Colors-TCMIN
05SP Authentic-50
Limited-50
Prestigious Pairings-PPGR
Sign of the Times-RO
05SP Game Used-50
Autographs-50
Gold-50
Authentic Fabrics Dual-RF
Authentic Fabrics Quad-GFRB
Authentic Patches Quad -GFRB
Authentic Fabrics Triple-KRT
Authentic Patches Dual-RF
Authentic Patches Triple-KRT
SIGnificance-DR
SIGnificance Gold-S-DR
05The Cup Honorable Numbers-HNDR
05UD Artifacts-49
Blue-49
Gold-49
Green-49
Pewter-49
Red-49
Gold Autographed-49
05UD PowerPlay-45
Rainbow-45
05Ultimate Collection Endorsed Emblems-EEDR
05Ultra-98
Gold-98
Fresh Ink-FI-DR
Fresh Ink Blue-FI-DR
Ice-98
05Upper Deck-92
05Upper Deck All-Time Greatest-30
05Upper Deck Glossy-92
05Upper Deck Notable Numbers-N-DR
05Upper Deck Ice-48
Rainbow-48
05Upper Deck MVP-197
Gold-197
Platinum-197
05Upper Deck Toronto Fall Expo-92
05Upper Deck Victory-101
Black-101
Gold-101
Silver-101
05Wild Crime Prevention-5
05Finnish Cardset -100
Finnish Cardset Super Snatchers-11
06Be A Player-53
Autographs-53
Signatures-RO
Signatures 10-57
Signatures 25-57
Signatures Duals-DED
Signatures Trios-TRSH
Unmasked Warriors-UM4
Unmasked Warriors Autographs-UM4
Up Close and Personal-UC17
Up Close and Personal Autographs-UC17
Portraits Signature Portraits-SPDR
06Beehive Matted Materials-MMDR
06Beehive Remarkable Matted Materials-MMDR
06Beehive Signature Scrapbook-SSDR
06Between The Pipes-62
Autographs-ADR

Double Jerseys-DJ02
Double Jerseys Gold-DJ02
Emblems-GUE19
Emblems Gold-GUE19
Emblems Autographs-GUE19
Jerseys-GJJ19
Jerseys Gold-GJJ19
Jerseys Autographs-GJJ19
Numbers-GUN19
Numbers Gold-GUN19
Numbers Autographs-GUN19
06Black Diamond-31
Black-31
Gold-31
Ruby-31
06Flair Showcase Hot Gloves-HG12
06Flair Showcase Inks-IDR
06Flair Showcase Stitches-SSDR
06Fleer-78
Tiffany-78
Netminders-N10
Signing Day-SDDR
06Gatorade-19
06Hot Prospects-42
Red Hot-42
White Hot-42
Hotagraphs-HDR
06McDonald's Upper Deck Hot Gloves-HG3
06NHL POG-41
06O-Pee-Chee-194
06O-Pee-Chee-613
Rainbow-194
Rainbow-613
Autographs-A-DR
06Panini Stickers-268
06SP Authentic Chirography-DR
06SP Authentic Sign of the Times-STDR
06SP Authentic Sign of the Times Duals-STRR
06SP Game Used Authentic Fabrics-AFDR
06SP Game Used Authentic Fabrics Parallel-AFDR
06SP Game Used Authentic Fabrics Patches-AFDR
06SP Game Used Authentic Fabrics Triple-AF3EDM
06SP Game Used Authentic Fabrics Triple Patches-AF3EDM
06SP Game Used Inked Sweaters-ISDR
06SP Game Used Inked Sweaters Patches-ISDR
06SP Game Used Inked Sweaters Dual-IS2SR
06SP Game Used Inked Sweaters Dual-IS2WR
06SP Game Used Inked Sweaters Dual Patches-IS2SR
06SP Game Used Inked Sweaters Dual Patches-IS2WR
06SP Game Used Letter Marks-LMDR
06SP Game Used SIGnificance-SDR
06The Cup Autographed NHL Shields Duals-DASAD
06The Cup Limited Logos-LLDR
06UD Artifacts Auto-Facts-AFDR
06UD Artifacts Auto-Facts Gold-AFDR
06UD Mini Jersey Collection-45
06Ultimate Collection Signatures-US-DR
06Ultra-79
Gold Medallion-79
Ice Medallion-79
Fresh Ink-IDR
06Upper Deck Arena Giveaways-EDM6
06Upper Deck-79
Exclusives Parallel-79
High Gloss Parallel-79
Game Jerseys-J2DR
Game Patches-P2DR
Masterpieces-79
Walmart Tins Oversize-79
06Upper Deck MVP-112
Gold Script-112
Super Script-112
Jerseys-OJFR
Last Line of Defense-LL13
06Upper Deck Ovation-70
06Upper Deck Sweet Shot-44
Signature Shots/Saves-SSDR
Signature Shots/Saves Sticks-SSSDR
Signature Sticks-STDR
06Upper Deck Trilogy-42
Honorary Scripted Patches-HSPDR
Honorary Scripted Swatches-HSSDR
Ice Scripts-ISDR
06Upper Deck Victory-80
06Upper Deck Victory Black-80
06Upper Deck Victory Gold-80
07Upper Deck Victory-160
Black-160
Gold-160
Oversize Cards-OS37

Rolston, Brian

91Upper Deck-699
French-699
91Upper Deck Czech World Juniors-86
91Lake Superior State Lakers-21
92Lake Superior State Lakers-23
93PowerPlay-516
93Stadium Club Team USA-21
93Stadium Club Team USA Members Only-21
93Topps Premier Team USA-5
93Ultra-496
93Classic-79
94Be A Player Signature Cards-33
94Finest-4
Super Team Winners-4
Refractors-4
Bowman's Best-R9
Bowman's Best Refractors-R9
94Flair-98
94Fleer-117
94Leaf-441
94Leaf Limited-4
94OPC Premier-438
Special Effects-438
94Parkhurst SE-SE99
Gold-SE99
94Pinnacle-255
94Pinnacle-473
Artist's Proofs-255
Artist's Proofs-473
Rink Collection-255
Rink Collection-473
Rookie Team Pinnacle-8
94Score Top Rookie Redemption-7
94Select-177
Gold-177
Youth Explosion-YE10
94SP Premier-12
94SP Premier Die-Cuts-12
94Topps/OPC Premier-438
Special Effects-438
94Ultra-320
Prospects-7
94Upper Deck-258
Electric Ice-258
Predictor Canadian-C13
94Upper Deck Predictor Canadian Exch Gold-C13
94Upper Deck Predictor Cdn Exch Silver-C13
94Upper Deck SP Inserts-SP135
94Upper Deck SP Inserts Die Cuts-SP135
94Finnish Jaa Kiekko-133
94Classic-76
Gold-76
Autographs-76
Tri-Cards-T37
94Classic Pro Prospects-90
Ice Ambassadors-IA11
International Heroes-LP10
94Classic Four-Sport *-142
Gold-142
Printers Proofs-142
95Collector's Choice-273
95Collector's Choice-366
Player's Club-273
Player's Club-366
Player's Club Platinum-273
Player's Club Platinum-366
95Donruss-286
Pro Pointers-9
95Leaf-294
95Parkhurst International-394
Emerald Ice-394
95Pinnacle-172
Artist's Proofs-172
Rink Collection-172
95Score-80
Black Ice Artist's Proofs-80
Black Ice-80
95Topps-362
OPC Inserts-362
New To The Game-13NG
95Upper Deck-14
Electric Ice-14
Electric Ice Gold-14
95Images-97
Gold-97
96Collector's Choice-151
96Devils Team Issue-14
96Pinnacle-7
Artist's Proofs-7
Foil-7
Premium Stock-7
Rink Collection-7
96Upper Deck-285
96Collector's Edge Ice-8
Prism-8
97Collector's Choice-144
97Pacific Dynagon Best Kept Secrets-54
97Paramount-105
Copper-105
Dark Grey-105
Emerald Green-105
Ice Blue-105
Red-105
Silver-105
97Score-205
97Score Devils-6
Platinum-6
Premier-6
97Upper Deck-92
Smooth Grooves-SG17
98Be A Player-230
Press Release-230
98BAP Gold-230
98BAP Autographs-230
98BAP Autographs Gold-230
98Devils Team Issue-25
98Pacific-270
Ice Blue-270
Red-270
98Pacific Omega-141
Red-141
Opening Day Issue-141
98Upper Deck-123
Exclusives-123
Exclusives 1 of 1-123
Gold Reserve-123
99Avalanche Team Issue-19
99BAP Memorabilia-88
99BAP Memorabilia-320
Gold-88
Gold-320
Silver-88
Silver-320
99O-Pee-Chee-128
99O-Pee-Chee Chrome-128
99O-Pee-Chee Chrome Refractors-128
99Pacific-246
Copper-246
Emerald Green-246
Gold-246
Ice Blue-246
Premiere Date-246
Red-246
99Panini Stickers-334
99Paramount-138
Copper-138
Emerald-138
Gold-138
Holographic Emerald-138
Holographic Gold-138
Holographic Silver-138
Ice Blue-138
Premiere Date-138
Red-138
Silver-138
99Topps/OPC-128
99Topps/OPC Chrome-128
Refractors-128
00BAP Memorabilia-132
Emerald-132
Ruby-132
Sapphire-132
Promos-132
00BAP Mem Chicago Sportsfest Copper-132
00BAP Memorabilia Chicago Sportsfest Blue-132
00BAP Memorabilia Chicago Sportsfest Gold-132
00BAP Memorabilia Chicago Sportsfest Ruby-132
00BAP Memorabilia Chicago Sun-Times Ruby-132
00BAP Memorabilia Chicago Sun-Times Gold-132
00BAP Mem Chicago Sun-Times Sapphire-132
00BAP Mem Toronto Fall Expo Copper-132
00BAP Memorabilia Toronto Fall Expo Gold-132
00BAP Memorabilia Toronto Fall Expo Ruby-132
00BAP Parkhurst 2000-P112
00BAP Signature Series-136
Emerald-136
Ruby-136
Sapphire-136
Autographs-109
Autographs Gold-109
00O-Pee-Chee-75
00O-Pee-Chee Parallel-75
00Pacific-40
Copper-40
Gold-40
Ice Blue-40
Premiere Date-40
00Paramount-20
Copper-20
Gold-20
Holo-Gold-20
Holo-Silver-20
Ice Blue-20
Premiere Date-20
00Stadium Club-151
00Topps/OPC-75
Parallel-75
00Upper Deck-14
Exclusives Tier 1-14
Exclusives Tier 2-14
00Upper Deck MVP-14
First Stars-14
Second Stars-14
Third Stars-14
00Upper Deck Victory-18
00Upper Deck Vintage-26
01BAP Memorabilia-170
Emerald-170
Ruby-170
Sapphire-170
01BAP Sig Series International Medals-IS-8
01Bowman YoungStars-33
Gold-33
Ice Cubed-33
01Crown Royale-11
Blue-11
Premiere Date-11
Red-11
Retail-11
01O-Pee-Chee-129
01O-Pee-Chee Premier Parallel-129
01Pacific-36
Extreme LTD-36
Hobby LTD-36
Premiere Date-36
Retail LTD-36
01Pacific Arena Exclusives-36
01Titanium-9
Hobby Parallel-9
Premiere Date-9
Retail-9
Retail Parallel-9
01Topps-129
OPC Parallel-129
01Topps Chrome-129
Refractors-129
Black Border Refractors-129
01Upper Deck-17
Exclusives-17
01Upper Deck Victory-28
Gold-28
01Upper Deck Vintage-19
02BAP First Edition-19
02BAP First Edition-379
Jerseys-19
02BAP Memorabilia-258
Emerald-258
Ruby-258
Sapphire-258
NHL All-Star Game-258
NHL All-Star Game Blue-258
NHL All-Star Game Green-258
NHL All-Star Game Red-258
02BAP Memorabilia Toronto Fall Expo-258
02BAP Signature Series-78
Autographs-78
Autograph Buybacks 1998-230
Autograph Buybacks 2000-109
Autographs Gold-78
02Bowman YoungStars-45
Gold-45
Silver-45
02Bruins Team Issue-5
02O-Pee-Chee-250
02O-Pee-Chee Premier Blue Parallel-250
02O-Pee-Chee Premier Red Parallel-250
02O-Pee-Chee Factory Set-250
02Pacific-31
Blue-31
Red-31
02Pacific Complete-120
Red-120
02Pacific Exclusive-12
02Pacific Heads-Up-9
Blue-9
Purple-9
Red-9
02Parkhurst-81
Bronze-81
Gold-81
Silver-81
02Parkhurst Retro-69
Minis-69
02Private Stock Reserve-7
Blue-7
Red-7
Retail-7
02Stadium Club-65
Silver Decoy Cards-65
Proofs-65
Passport-14
02Titanium-8
Blue-8
Red-8
Retail-8
02Topps-250
OPC Blue Parallel-250
OPC Red Parallel-250
Factory Set-250
02Topps Total-376
02Upper Deck-12
Exclusives-12
02Upper Deck Classic Portraits-8
02Upper Deck MVP-15
Gold-15
Classics-15
Golden Classics-15
02Upper Deck Victory-20
Bronze-20
Gold-20
Silver-20
02Upper Deck Vintage-25
02Upper Deck Vintage-311
Green Backs-25
02Vanguard-8
LTD-8
03Beehive-15
Gold-15
Silver-15
03ITG Action-12
Jerseys-M72
03NHL Sticker Collection-15
03O-Pee-Chee-204
03OPC Blue-204
03OPC Gold-204
03OPC Red-204
03Pacific-29
Blue-29
Red-29
03Pacific Complete-15
Red-15
03Pacific Exhibit-15
Blue Backs-15
Yellow Backs-15
03Pacific Heads-Up-9
Hobby LTD-9
Retail LTD-9
03Parkhurst Original Six Boston-27
Memorabilia-BM1
03Topps-204
Blue-204
Gold-204
Red-204
Topps/OPC Idols-UI8
03Topps C55-124
Minis-124
Minis American Back-124
Minis American Back Red-124
Minis Bazooka Back-124
Minis Brooklyn Back-124
Minis Hat Trick Back-124
Minis O Canada Back-124
Minis O Canada Back Red-124
Minis Stanley Cup Back-124
03Topps Pristine Jersey Portions-PPJ-BRO
03Topps Pristine Jersey Portion Refractor-PPJ-BRO
03Topps Pristine Patches-PP-BRO
03Topps Pristine Patch Refractors-PP-BRO
03Upper Deck-259
Canadian Exclusives-259
HG-259
UD Exclusives-259
03Upper Deck MVP-34
Gold Script-34
Silver Script-34
Canadian Exclusives-34
04Pacific-25
Blue-25
Red-25
05Be A Player Signatures-BR
05Be A Player Signatures Gold-BR
05Black Diamond-43
Emerald-43
Gold-43
Onyx-43
Ruby-43
05Panini Stickers-298
05Parkhurst-233
Facsimile Auto Parallel-233
True Colors-TCMIN
True Colors-TCMIN
True Colors-TCMIDA
True Colors-TCMIDA
05Ultimate Coll National Heroes Jersey-NHJBR
05Ultimate Coll National Heroes Patch-NHPBR
05Upper Deck-343
Jerseys Series II-J2RO
05Upper Deck MVP-191
Gold-191
Platinum-191
05Upper Deck Victory-99
Black-99
Gold-99
Silver-99
06Be A Player Portraits Signature Portraits-SPBR
06Fleer-96
Tiffany-96
Fabricology-FBR
06O-Pee-Chee-242
Rainbow-242
06Panini Stickers-296
06UD Artifacts Tundra Tandems-TTBR
06UD Artifacts Tundra Tandems Black-TTBR
06UD Artifacts Tundra Tandems Blue-TTBR
06UD Artifacts Tundra Tandems Gold-TTBR
06UD Artifacts Tundra Tandems Platinum-TTBR
06UD Artifacts Tundra Tandems Red-TTBR
06UD Artifacts Tundra Tandems Dual Patches Red-TTBR
06UD Powerplay Specialists-SBR
06UD Powerplay Specialists Patches-PBR
06Ultra-100
Gold Medallion-100
Ice Medallion-100
06Upper Deck Arena Giveaways-MIN3
06Upper Deck-346
Exclusives Parallel-346
High Gloss Parallel-346
Game Jerseys-JBR
Game Patches-PBR
Masterpieces-346
06Upper Deck MVP-146
Gold Script-146
Super Script-146
06Upper Deck Ovation-126
06Upper Deck Victory-98
06Upper Deck Victory Black-98
06Upper Deck Victory Gold-98
06Wild Crime Prevention-5
06Wild Postcards-5
07Upper Deck Victory-139
Black-139
Gold-139

Romaine, Mark

90ProCards AHL/IHL-578
91Cincinnati Cyclones-18
92Birmingham Bulls-18
93Birmingham Bulls-18

Roman, Tom

87Brockville Braves-9

Romanchuk, Tyler

907th Inn. Sketch WHL-34
917th Inn. Sketch WHL-23

Romanchych, Larry

72Flames Postcards-19
72Sargent Promotions Stamps-12
73O-Pee-Chee-185
73Topps-185
74NHL Action Stamps-8
74O-Pee-Chee NHL-157
74Topps-157
75O-Pee-Chee NHL-153
75Topps-153
76O-Pee-Chee NHL-281

Romaniski, Matt

94Dubuque Fighting Saints-23
95North Iowa Huskies-26

Romaniuk, Russ

91Pro Set Platinum-274
91Jets IGA-27
91OPC Premier-162
91Parkhurst-198
French-198
91Pinnacle-324
French-324
91Pro Set-565
French-565
91Score Canadian Bilingual-627
91Score Canadian English-627
91Score Rookie/Traded-77T
91Upper Deck-46
French-46
91UND Fighting Sioux Sports Collectors Card Set - 15
92Bowman-276
92O-Pee-Chee-263
92Panini Stickers-59
92Panini Stickers French-59
92Stadium Club-164
92Topps-390
Gold-390G
92North Dakota Fighting Sioux-38
93Alberta International Team Canada-17
93PowerPlay-492
93Ultra-471
94Parkhurst-265
Gold-265
94Stadium Club-260
Members Only Master Set-260
First Day Issue-260
Super Team Winner Cards-260
94Ultra-394
97Long Beach Ice Dogs-15
97Manitoba Moose-A2
98Las Vegas Thunder-18
99German DEL-36
01UK Manchester Storm-10
03UK Cardiff Devils-7

Romano, Mike

95North Iowa Huskies-27

Romano, Roberto

80Quebec Remparts-20
84Penguins Heinz Photos-18
86O-Pee-Chee-152
86O-Pee-Chee Stickers-229
86Penguins Kodak-20
86Topps-152

Romanov, Alexander

01Russian Hockey League-30

Romanov, Konstantin

04Russian Moscow Dynamo-24

Romanov, Oleg

98Czech OFS-7
99Russian Hockey League-71
00Finnish Cardset-201

Romanov, Stanislav

95Swedish World Championships Stickers-48
96Swedish Semic Wien-150
99Russian Dynamo Moscow-19
00Russian Dynamo Moscow-21

Romashko, Oleg

00Russian Hockey League-343
03Russian Hockey League-12
05Russian Hockey League RHL-41

Rombard, John

93Quebec Pee-Wee Tournament-1735

Rombough, Doug

74NHL Action Stamps-171
74NHL Action Stamps Update-21
74O-Pee-Chee NHL-279
75O-Pee-Chee NHL-161
75Topps-161

Rome, Aaron

00Kootenay Ice-17
02Swift Current Broncos-16
03Swift Current Broncos-14
04Cincinnati Mighty Ducks-3
05Portland Pirates-2
06Portland Pirates-4
07Upper Deck Victory-214
Black-214
Gold-214

Rome, Ashton

05Kamloops Blazers-8

Rome, Brian

82Ottawa 67's-21
84Sault Ste. Marie Greyhounds-19

Rome, Reagan

05Manchester Monarchs-43
05Reading Royals-11
06Reading Royals-4

Rome, Ryan

04Memphis RiverKings-15

Romeiro, R.J.

97Louisville Riverfrogs-24

Romeo, Peter

97Tucson Gila Monsters-4
99UK Basingstoke Bison-5

Romer, Andy

94German DEL-11

Romer, Heinrich

94German DEL-18
95German DEL-17

Romerio, Sunshine

04Swiss Lausanne HC Postcards-9

Romfo, Jeff

93Minnesota-Duluth Bulldogs-26
96South Carolina Stingrays-15

Romic, Jonathon

03OCN Blizzard-18

Rominski, Dale

99Detroit Vipers-13
00SPx-108
Spectrum-108

Romishevski, Igor

69Russian National Team Postcards-6
69Swedish Hockey-15
70Finnish Jaakiekko-15
70Russian National Team Postcards-6
70Swedish Hockey-157
70Swedish Hockey-158
70Swedish Hockey-319
70Swedish Masterserien-21
70Swedish Masterserien-29
70Swedish Masterserien-127
70Swedish Masterserien-132
71Finnish Suomi Stickers-14
71Swedish Hockey-33
72Finnish Jaakiekko-33
72Finnish Hellas-66
72Finnish Panda Toronto-59
72Finnish Semic World Championship-6
72Swedish Stickers-29
72Swedish Semic World Championship-6
74Swedish Semic World Champ Stickers-46

Rommel, Wes

91Air Canada SJHL-B3

Romnes, Doc

34Beehive Group I Photos-77
34Beehive Group I Photos-345
34Diamond Matchbooks Silver-52
35Diamond Matchbooks Tan 1-59

Romy, Kevin

02Swiss HNL-348

Ronan, Dan

00Fort Wayne Komets-18
00Fort Wayne Komets Shoe Carnival-15

Ronan, Ed

91ProCards-90
92Canadiens Postcards-23
92OPC Premier-41
92Parkhurst-88
Emerald Ice-88
92Ultra-333
92Upper Deck-491
93Canadiens Postcards-22
93O-Pee-Chee Canadiens Hockey Fest-45
93Stadium Club-262
Members Only Master Set-262
First Day Issue-262
93Classic Pro Prospects-134
94Canadiens Postcards-21
95Jets Team Issue-19
96Rochester Americans-6

Ronan, John

04Maine Black Bears-7
05Florida Everblades-23
06Austin Ice Bats-7

Ronan, Kyle

95Medicine Hat Tigers-14

Ronan, Skene

10Sweet Caporal Postcards-26
11C55-26
12C57-14

Ronayne, James

04Knoxville Ice Bears-19
05Knoxville Ice Bears-15

Rondeau, Jeremy

95Swift Current Broncos-18
96Swift Current Broncos-19
97Swift Current Broncos-24
98Swift Current Broncos-24

Rondeau, Martin

93Quebec Pee-Wee Tournament-962

Ronkainen, Jarmo

70Finnish Jaakiekko-319

Ronkainen, Vesa

72Finnish Jaakiekko-294

Ronkoske, Jeff

99Des Moines Buccaneers-21

Ronnback, Jimmie

97OCN Blizzard-11
98OCN Blizzard-17

Ronnberg, Joonas

05Finnish Cardset -41
06Finnish Cardset-306

Ronnblom, Anders

64Swedish Coralli ISHockey-141
65Swedish Coralli ISHockey-141

Ronnest, Carsten

99Danish Hockey League-92

Ronning, Cliff

87Blues Kodak-23
88Blues Kodak-22
88ProCards IHL-84
89O-Pee-Chee-45
89O-Pee-Chee Stickers-20
89Panini Stickers-122
89Topps-45
90Blues Kodak-19
90Pro Set-526
90Score Rookie/Traded-81T
91Pro Set Platinum-236
91Bowman-313
91Canucks Autograph Cards-21
91Canucks Molson-7
91Canucks Team Issue 8x10-21
91O-Pee-Chee-59
91Panini Stickers-46
91Parkhurst-182
French-182
91Pinnacle-106
French-106
91Pro Set-241
French-241
91Score American-212
91Score Canadian Bilingual-212
91Score Canadian English-212
91Stadium Club-298
91Topps-59
91Upper Deck-208
French-208
92Bowman-411
92Canucks Road Trip Art-19
92O-Pee-Chee-94
92Panini Stickers-30
92Panini Stickers French-30
92Parkhurst-193
Emerald Ice-193
92Pinnacle-12
French-12
92Pro Set-195
92Score-254
Canadian-254
92Seasons Patches-32
92Stadium Club-373
92Topps-81
Gold-81G
92Ultra-227
92Upper Deck-160
93Donruss-357
93Leaf-183
93OPC Premier-81
Gold-81
93Panini Stickers-168
93Parkhurst-210
Emerald Ice-210
93Pinnacle-69
93Pinnacle-234
Canadian-69
Canadian-234
93PowerPlay-255
93Score-17
93Score-443
Canadian-17
Canadian-443
93Stadium Club-125
Members Only Master Set-125
OPC-125
First Day Issue-125
First Day Issue OPC-125
93Topps/OPC Premier-81
Gold-81
93Ultra-119
93Upper Deck-211
94Canada Games NHL POGS-27
94Canucks Program Inserts-19
94Donruss-278
94EA Sports-141
94Flair-194
94Fleer-230
94Leaf-66
94OPC Premier-291
Special Effects-291
94Parkhurst SE-SE188
Gold-SE188
94Pinnacle-113
Artist's Proofs-113
Rink Collection-113
94Score-86
Gold-86
Platinum-86
94Select-122
Gold-122
94Stadium Club-200
Members Only Master Set-200
First Day Issue-200
Super Team Winner Cards-200
94Topps/OPC Premier-291
Special Effects-291
94Ultra-230
94Upper Deck-358
Electric Ice-358
95Be A Player-91
Signatures-S91
Signatures Die Cuts-S91
95Canada Games NHL POGS-269
95Canucks Building the Dream Art-7
95Collector's Choice-17
Player's Club-17
Player's Club Platinum-17
95Donruss-79
95Panini Stickers-290
95Parkhurst International-479
Emerald Ice-479
95Pinnacle-184
Artist's Proofs-184
Rink Collection-184
95Playoff One on One-211
95Pro Magnets-30
95Score-75
Black Ice Artist's Proofs-75
Black Ice-75
95SP-154
95Stadium Club-128
Members Only Master Set-128
95Topps-99
OPC Inserts-99
95Upper Deck-102
Electric Ice-102
Electric Ice Gold-102
Special Edition-SE174
Special Edition Gold-SE174
96Collector's Choice-270
96Coyotes Coca-Cola-27
96Donruss-47
Press Proofs-47
96Leaf-173
Press Proofs-173
96NHL Pro Stamps-30
96Pinnacle-163
Artist's Proofs-163
Foil-163
Premium Stock-163
Rink Collection-163
96Playoff One on One-398
96Score-163
Artist's Proofs-163
Dealer's Choice Artist's Proofs-163
Special Artist's Proofs-163
Golden Blades-163
96SP-124
96Topps Picks-105
OPC Inserts-105
96Upper Deck-315
96Upper Deck Ice-53
Parallel-53
97Collector's Choice-199
97Coyotes Face-Off Luncheon -19
97Crown Royale-106
Emerald Green-106
Ice Blue-106
Silver-106
97Pacific-200
Copper-200
Emerald Green-200
Ice Blue-200
Red-200
Silver-200
97Paramount-143
Copper-143
Dark Grey-143
Emerald Green-143
Ice Blue-143
Red-143
Silver-143
97Pinnacle Inside-173
97Score-244
97Upper Deck-132
98Aurora-147
98Be A Player-226
Press Release-226
98BAP Gold-226
98BAP Autographs-226
98BAP Autographs Gold-226
98Bowman's Best-61
Refractors-61
Atomic Refractors-61
98Finest-44
No Protectors-44
No Protectors Refractors-44
Refractors-44
98Pacific-343
Ice Blue-343
Red-343
98Pacific Omega-132
Red-132
Opening Day Issue-132
98Panini Stickers-149
98Paramount-185
Copper-185
Emerald Green-185
Holo-Electric-185
Ice Blue-185
Silver-185
98Predators Team Issue-18
98Revolution-80
Ice Shadow-80
Red-80
98Topps Gold Label Class 1-55
Black-55
Black One of One-55
One of One-55
Red-55
Red One of One-55
98Topps Gold Label Class 2-55
98Topps Gold Label Class 2 Black-55
98Topps Gold Label Class 2 Black 1 of 1-55
98Topps Gold Label Class 2 One of One-55
98Topps Gold Label Class 2 Red-55
98Topps Gold Label Class 2 Red One of One-55
98Topps Gold Label Class 3-55
98Topps Gold Label Class 3 Black-55
98Topps Gold Label Class 3 Black 1 of 1-55
98Topps Gold Label Class 3 One of One-55
98Topps Gold Label Class 3 Red-55
98Topps Gold Label Class 3 Red One of One-55
98Upper Deck-156
Exclusives-156
Exclusives 1 of 1-156
Gold Reserve-156
98Upper Deck MVP-112
Gold Script-112
Silver Script-112
Super Script-112
99Aurora-81
Premiere Date-81
99BAP Memorabilia-25
Gold-25
Silver-25
99BAP Millennium-137
Emerald-137
Ruby-137
Sapphire-137
Signatures-137
Signatures Gold-137
99Crown Royale-77
Limited Series-77
Premiere Date-77
99O-Pee-Chee-155
99O-Pee-Chee Chrome-155
99O-Pee-Chee Chrome Refractors-155
99Pacific-231
Copper-231
Emerald Green-231
Gold-231
Ice Blue-231
Premiere Date-231
Red-231
99Pacific Dynagon Ice-111
Blue-111
Copper-111
Gold-111
Premiere Date-111
99Pacific Omega-128
Copper-128
Gold-128
Ice Blue-128
Premiere Date-128
99Pacific Prism-77
Holographic Blue-77
Holographic Gold-77
Holographic Mirror-77
Holographic Purple-77
Premiere Date-77
99Panini Stickers-269
99Paramount-128
Copper-128
Emerald-128
Gold-128
Holographic Emerald-128
Holographic Gold-128
Holographic Silver-128
Ice Blue-128
Premiere Date-128
Red-128
Silver-128
Ice Alliance-15
99Revolution-81
Premiere Date-81
Red-81
Shadow Series-81
99SPx-81
Radiance-81
Spectrum-81
99Stadium Club-103
First Day Issue-103
One of a Kind-103
Printing Plates Black-103
Printing Plates Cyan-103
Printing Plates Magenta-103
Printing Plates Yellow-103
99Topps/OPC-155
99Topps/OPC Chrome-155
Refractors-155
99Topps Gold Label Class 1-78
Black-78
Black One of One-78
One of One-78
Red-78
Red One of One-78
99Topps Gold Label Class 2-78
99Topps Gold Label Class 2 Black-78
99Topps Gold Label Class 2 Black 1 of 1-78
99Topps Gold Label Class 2 One of One-78
99Topps Gold Label Class 2 Red-78
99Topps Gold Label Class 2 Red One of One-78
99Topps Gold Label Class 3-78
99Topps Gold Label Class 3 Black-78
99Topps Gold Label Class 3 Black 1 of 1-78
99Topps Gold Label Class 3 One of One-78
99Topps Gold Label Class 3 Red-78
99Topps Gold Label Class 3 Red One of One-78
99Upper Deck-72
Exclusives-72
Exclusives 1 of 1-72
99Upper Deck Gold Reserve-72
99Upper Deck MVP-108
Gold Script-108
Silver Script-108
Super Script-108
99Upper Deck MVP SC Edition-100
Gold Script-100
Silver Script-100
Super Script-100
99Upper Deck Victory-158
00Aurora-79
Premiere Date-79
00BAP Memorabilia-207
Emerald-207
Ruby-207
Sapphire-207
Promos-207
00BAP Mem Chicago Sportsfest Copper-207
00BAP Memorabilia Chicago Sportsfest Blue-207
00BAP Memorabilia Chicago Sportsfest Gold-207
00BAP Memorabilia Chicago Sportsfest Ruby-207
00BAP Memorabilia Chicago Sun-Times Ruby-207
00BAP Memorabilia Chicago Sun-Times Gold-207
00BAP Mem Chicago Sun-Times Sapphire-207
00BAP Mem Toronto Fall Expo Copper-207
00BAP Memorabilia Toronto Fall Expo Gold-207
00BAP Memorabilia Toronto Fall Expo Ruby-207
00BAP Parkhurst 2000-P57
00BAP Signature Series-242
Emerald-242
Ruby-242
Sapphire-242
Autographs-167
Autographs Gold-167
00Kraft-16
00O-Pee-Chee-90
00O-Pee-Chee Parallel-90
00Pacific-225
Copper-225
Gold-225
Ice Blue-225
Premiere Date-225
00Panini Stickers-182

00Paramount-137
Copper-137
Gold-137
Holo-Gold-137
Holo-Silver-137
Ice Blue-137
Premiere Date-137
00Private Stock Game Gear-62
00Revolution-83
Blue-83
Premiere Date-83
Red-83
00SP Authentic-51
00Stadium Club-61
00Titanium-52
Blue-52
Gold-52
Premiere Date-52
Red-52
Retail-52
00Titanium Draft Day Edition-56
Patches-56
00Topps/OPC-90
Parallel-90
00Topps Chrome-72
OPC Refractors-72
Refractors-72
00Topps Heritage-157
00Topps Stars-85
Blue-85
00UD Heroes-66
00UD Pros and Prospects-49
00UD Reserve-48
00Upper Deck-325
Exclusives Tier 1-325
Exclusives Tier 2-325
00Upper Deck MVP-97
First Stars-97
Second Stars-97
Third Stars-97
00Upper Deck Victory-130
00Upper Deck Vintage-199
00Vanguard Dual Game-Worn Jerseys-11
00Vanguard Dual Game-Worn Patches-11
01BAP Memorabilia-249
01BAP Memorabilia-459
Emerald-249
Emerald-459
Ruby-249
Ruby-459
Sapphire-249
Sapphire-459
01Crown Royale-82
Blue-82
Premiere Date-82
Red-82
Retail-82
Triple Threads-10
01O-Pee-Chee-180
01O-Pee-Chee Premier Parallel-180
01Pacific-221
Extreme LTD-221
Hobby LTD-221
Premiere Date-221
Retail LTD-221
Jerseys-17
01Pacific Adrenaline-107
Blue-107
Premiere Date-107
Red-107
Retail-107
01Pacific Arena Exclusives-221
01Parkhurst-172
01Parkhurst-359
01Private Stock Game Gear-59
01Private Stock Game Gear Patches-59
01Private Stock PS-2002-42
01Titanium-80
Hobby Parallel-80
Premiere Date-80
Retail-80
Retail Parallel-80
Double-Sided Jerseys-22
01Topps-180
OPC Parallel-180
01Topps Reserve-46
01UD Challenge for the Cup-47
01UD Playmakers-57
01Upper Deck-97
Exclusives-97
01Upper Deck MVP-105
01Upper Deck Victory-194
Gold-194
01Upper Deck Vintage-143
01Upper Deck Vintage-147
01Upper Deck Vintage-148
01Vanguard Memorabilia-16
02BAP First Edition-235
02BAP Signature Series-85
Autographs-85
Autograph Buybacks 1998-226
Autograph Buybacks 1999-137
Autograph Buybacks 2000-167
Autographs Gold-85
02Pacific-173
Blue-173
Red-173
Jerseys-23
Jerseys Holo-Silver-23
02Pacific Complete-402
Red-402
02Pacific Exclusive-88
02Pacific Quest for the Cup-49
Gold-49
02Parkhurst-145
Bronze-145
Gold-145
Silver-145
02Private Stock Reserve-50
Blue-50
Red-50
Retail-50
02Titanium-54
Blue-54
Red-54
Retail-54
02Upper Deck Victory-100
Bronze-100
Gold-100
Silver-100
03ITG Action-218
03NHL Sticker Collection-245
03Pacific-170
Blue-170
Red-170
03Pacific Exhibit-75
Blue Backs-75
Yellow Backs-75
03Pacific Prism-55
Blue-55
Gold-55
Red-55
03Topps Traded-TT50
Blue-TT50
Gold-TT50
Red-TT50
03Upper Deck MVP-209
Gold Script-209
Silver Script-209
Canadian Exclusives-209

Ronningen, Jan Tore
92Norwegian Elite Series-20

Ronnkvist, Anders
65Swedish Coralli ISHockey-213

Ronnqvist, Jonas
97Swedish Collector's Choice-125
98Swedish UD Choice-139
99Swedish Upper Deck-141
Hands of Gold-10
Hands of Gold-12
00BAP Memorabilia-427
Emerald-427
Ruby-427
Sapphire-427
00Private Stock-101
Gold-101
Premiere Date-101
Retail-101
Silver-101
00SP Game Used-61
00Titanium Draft Day Edition-152
00Titanium Draft Day Promos-152
00Topps Stars-107
Blue-107
00UD Heroes-159
00UD Pros and Prospects-91
00Upper Deck-416
Exclusives Tier 1-416
Exclusives Tier 2-416
00Upper Deck Vintage-372
00Vanguard-102
01BAP Memorabilia-142
Emerald-142
Ruby-142
Sapphire-142
01BAP Signature Series-52
Autographs-52
Autographs Gold-52
01Cincinnati Mighty Ducks-21
02BAP Sig Series Auto Buybacks 2001-52
02Swiss SCL Tigers-3
03Swedish Elite-229
Silver-229
Stars of the Game-6
04Swedish Elitset-218
Gold-218
High Expectations-7
Limited Signatures-6
Signatures-5
04Swedish Pure Skills-52
Parallel-52
Signatures-6
05Swedish SHL Elitset-86

Ronnqvist, Patrik
03Swedish Elite-152
Silver-152
04Swedish Elitset-7
Gold-7

Ronnqvist, Petter
91Swedish Semic Elitserien Stickers-56
92Swedish Semic Elitserien Stickers-76
93Swedish Semic Elitserien-51
94Swedish Leaf-271
95Swedish Leaf-99
Spidermen-10
95Swedish Upper Deck-152
97Swedish Collector's Choice-149
98Swedish UD Choice-166
99Swiss Panini Stickers-54
00Swiss Panini Stickers-102
05Swedish SHL Elitset-157
06Swedish SHL Elitset-13

Rontti, Mika
91Finnish Cardset-368
04Finnish Cardset-312
06Finnish Cardset-171
06Finnish Porin Assat Pelaajakortit-6

Ronty, Paul
44Beehive Group II Photos-63
44Beehive Group II Photos-359
48Exhibits Canadian-48
51Parkhurst-95
52Parkhurst-24
53Parkhurst-63
54Parkhurst-66
54Topps-15
02Parkhurst Reprints-167
02Parkhurst Reprints-195
05ITG Ultimate Mem Beantown's Best Autos-3

Roodbol, Kees
91British Columbia JHL-112
92British Columbia JHL-166
92British Columbia JHL-212

Rook, Chris
04Columbus Cottonmouths-4

Rooneem, Mark
99Kamloops Blazers-19
00Kamloops Blazers-19
03Calgary Hitmen-15
04Louisiana Ice Gators-19

Rooney, Al
98San Angelo Outlaws-16
99Fort Worth Brahmas-16

Rooney, Brad
02ECHL All-Star Northern-33
02Reading Royals-12
02Reading Royals RBI Sports-180

Rooney, Jesse
01Quad-City Mallards-20

Rooney, Larry
91Richmond Renegades-2
91Richmond Renegades Set 2-16

Rooney, Steve
85Canadiens Postcards-29
85Canadiens Postcards-30
85Canadiens Provigo-18
87Canadiens Postcards-25
87Jets Postcards-18
87O-Pee-Chee-223
88Devils Caretta-23
89ProCards AHL-210
90ProCards AHL/IHL-364

Rooster, Cornelius
92Kellogg's Posters-5

Root, Bill
82Canadiens Postcards-22
82Canadiens Steinberg-17
83Canadiens Postcards-24
83O-Pee-Chee-196
84Maple Leafs Postcards-20
84O-Pee-Chee-271
85Maple Leafs Postcards-25
88ProCards AHL-229
89ProCards AHL-112
90Newmarket Saints-20
90ProCards AHL/IHL-162

Root, Michael
03Barrie Colts-14
04Barrie Colts-15

Rooth, Maria
01Sports Illustrated for Kids III-127

Rorabeck, Ryan
01St. Michaels Majors-15
02St. Michaels Majors-14
03St. Michael's Majors-7
04Belleville Bulls-20
05Belleville Bulls-2

Rosa, Marco
05Milwaukee Admirals Choice-12

Rosa, Mario
96Quebec Pee-Wee Tournament-1193

Rosa, Pavel
97Bowman CHL-51
OPC-51
98Black Diamond-40
Double Diamond-40
Triple Diamond-40
Quadruple Diamond-40
98Pacific Omega-117
Red-117
Opening Day Issue-117
98Revolution-69
Ice Shadow-69
Red-69
98SPx Top Prospects-31
Radiance-31
Spectrum-31
98Long Beach Ice Dogs-16
99BAP Memorabilia-213
Gold-213
Silver-213
99BAP Millennium-125
Emerald-125
Ruby-125
Sapphire-125
Signatures-125
Signatures Gold-125
99O-Pee-Chee-207
99O-Pee-Chee Chrome-207
99O-Pee-Chee Chrome Refractors-207
99Pacific-197
Copper-197
Emerald Green-197
Gold-197
Ice Blue-197
Premiere Date-197
Red-197
99SPx-74
Radiance-74
Spectrum-74
99Topps/OPC-207
99Topps/OPC Chrome-207
Refractors-207
99Upper Deck-63
Exclusives-63
Exclusives 1 of 1-63
99Upper Deck Century Legends-79
Century Collection-79
99Upper Deck Gold Reserve-63
99Upper Deck MVP-93
Gold Script-93
Silver Script-93
Super Script-93
99Upper Deck Retro-38
Gold-38
Platinum-38
99Upper Deck Victory-132
99Long Beach Ice Dogs-2
00Finnish Cardset-148
01Finnish Cardset-264
01Finnish Cardset Dueling Aces-6
02BAP Sig Series Auto Buybacks 1999-125
02Finnish Cardset-109
02Manchester Monarchs-26
03Manchester Monarchs-13
03Manchester Monarchs Team Issue-13
03Pacific AHL Prospects-52
Gold-52
04Russian Legion-1
04Russian Moscow Dynamo-25
06Czech Super Six Postcards-12

Rosa, Stanislav
94Czech APS Extraliga-125

Rosander, Ola
89Swedish Semic Elitserien Stickers-227
90Swedish Semic Elitserien Stickers-69
91Swedish Semic Elitserien Stickers-243

Rosati, Mike
88Niagara Falls Thunder-6
93Swedish Semic World Champ Stickers-210
95Finnish Semic World Championships-171
95Swedish Globe World Championships-226
95Swedish World Championships Stickers-77
96German DEL-159
96Swedish Semic Wien-174
98Portland Pirates-17
99German Adler Mannheim Eagles Postcards-19
99German DEL-18
00German DEL-11
01German Adler Mannheim Eagles Postcards-4
01German Upper Deck-176
Goalies in Action-G7
Jersey Cards-MR-J
02German Adler Mannheim Eagles Postcards-4
02German DEL City Press-254
04German Adler Mannheim Eagles Postcards-27

Rosberg, Jari
70Finnish Jaakiekko-303
71Finnish Suomi Stickers-237
72Finnish Jaakiekko-221
73Finnish Jaakiekko-297

Roscoe, Ron
75Hamilton Fincups-16

Rose, Arthur
51Laval Dairy QSHL-94

Rose, Jarrett
95Slapshot-132

Rose, Jason
97Austin Ice Bats-15
97El Paso Buzzards-4
98Phoenix Mustangs-20
99Muskegon Fury-20

Rose, Jay
90Cincinnati Cyclones-21
91Cincinnati Cyclones-19

Rose, Shaun
97OCN Blizzard-7
98OCN Blizzard-7

Rosebush, Paul
99Bakersfield Condors-17
00Bakersfield Condors-18
01Bakersfield Condors-19
02Bakersfield Condors-15
03Bakersfield Condors-10
04Bakersfield Condors-15
05Bakersfield Condors-5

Rosehill, Jay
06Springfield Falcons-9

Rosen, Anders
71Swedish Hockey-218

Rosen, Daniel
04Green Bay Gamblers-16

Rosen, Johan
93Swedish Semic Elitserien-167
94Swedish Leaf-12
95Swedish Leaf-80
Goldies-8
95Swedish Upper Deck-132
Ticket to North America-NA17
98German DEL-83
99German DEL-335
01German Upper Deck-190
02Swedish SHL-204
Parallel-204
03Swedish Elite-208
Silver-208
05Swedish SHL Elitset-68

Rosen, Roger
95Swedish Leaf-297
Rookies-9
95Swedish Upper Deck-201
97Swedish Collector's Choice-195
97Swedish Collector's Choice-220
Crash the Game Exchange-C30
Crash the Game Redemption-R30
98Swedish UD Choice-197
99Swedish Upper Deck-200

Rosenast, Michael
96Swiss HNL-465
00Swiss Panini Stickers-91
00Swiss Slapshot Mini-Cards-EHCC10

Rosenberg, Edgar
74Swedish Stickers-81

Rosenberg, Hadrian
93Swiss HNL-445

Rosenberg, Kari
93Finnish Jyvas-Hyva Stickers-44
93Finnish SISU-234
94Finnish SISU-34
94Finnish SISU Junior-6
94Finnish SISU NIL Phenoms-5
95Finnish SISU-16
Ghost Goalies-6
95Finnish SISU Limited-82
98Finnish Kerailysarja-52

Rosenblatt, Howie
91ProCards-60
92Cincinnati Cyclones-20
93Classic Pro Prospects-44
94Greensboro Monarchs-7
96Quad-City Mallards-15
97Quad-City Mallards-4
98Quad-City Mallards-20

Rosendahl, Hans Ake
71Swedish Hockey-142
72Swedish Stickers-126
73Swedish Stickers-183

Rosenheck, Jerry
92Clarkson Knights-17

Rosenqvist, Per
92Swedish Semic Elitserien Stickers-212

Rosenstam, Lars
57Swedish Alfabilder-128

Rosol, Petr
89Swedish Semic World Champ Stickers-200
93Swiss HNL-333
94Finnish Jaa Kiekko-187
94Swedish Olympics Lillehammer*-320
95Swiss HNL-480
96Swiss HNL-377
96Swiss HNL-582
98Swiss Power Play Stickers-341
99Czech OFS-346
00Czech DS Extraliga-44
00Czech OFS-146
00Czech OFS-408

Ross, Adam
05Victoriaville Tigres-21
06Victoriaville Tigres-17

Ross, Andy
93Memphis RiverKings-14
94Central Hockey League-106
95Central Hockey League-33
97Austin Ice Bats-16
99Austin Ice Bats-1
99Austin Ice Bats-34
99Corpus Christi IceRays-19
99Memphis RiverKings All-Time-14

Ross, Art
10C56-8
10C56-12
10Sweet Caporal Postcards-31
11C55-31
12C57-20
37V356 Worldwide Gum-96
38Bruins Garden Magazine Supplement-6
60Topps-27
Stamps-46
69O-Pee-Chee-223
70O-Pee-Chee-262
72Topps-170
83Hall of Fame-74
83Hall of Fame Postcards-E15
85Hall of Fame-74
91Bruins Sports Action Legends-25
94Hall of Fame Tickets-4
94Upper Deck Predictor Hobby Exch Silver-H25
03BAP Ultimate Memorabilia Memorialized-8
03SP Authentic Special Cuts-AR
04ITG Franchises Canadian-68
04ITG Ultimate Memorabilia-162
Gold-162
06Beehive 5 X 7 Cherry Wood-ART
06ITG Ultimate Memorabilia-9
Artist Proof-9
Beantown's Best Autos-6

Ross, Brian
83Kitchener Rangers-25

Ross, Chris
99Adirondack IceHawks-7

Ross, Don
72Finnish Semic World Championship-122
72Swedish Semic World Championship-122

Ross, Gordon
917th Inn. Sketch OHL-361
93London Knights-16

Ross, Jared
05Chicago Wolves-17

Ross, John
23V145-1-28
24V145-2-52
83Hall of Fame-102
83Hall of Fame Postcards-G12
85Hall of Fame-102

Ross, Kyle
03Red Deer Rebels-8
04Regina Pats-8
05Regina Pats-18
06Regina Pats-16

Ross, Mike
95South Carolina Stingrays-7
96South Carolina Stingrays-9
98Odessa Jackalopes-7

Ross, Nick
05Regina Pats-19
06Regina Pats-17

Ross, Patrik
89Swedish Semic Elitserien Stickers-116
90Swedish Semic Elitserien Stickers-117
91Swedish Semic Elitserien Stickers-120
92Swedish Semic Elitserien Stickers-141
93Swedish Semic Elitserien-120

Ross, Paul
93Quebec Pee-Wee Tournament-1196

Ross, Philip D
83Hall of Fame Postcards-D12
85Hall of Fame-58

Ross, Tom
93Michigan State Spartans-17

Rossbach, Dirk
94German First League-463

Rossetti, Mike
89Johnstown Chiefs-25
91Johnstown Chiefs-18
91ProCards-56

Rossi, Reijo
72Finnish Jaakiekko-275

Rossi, Rico
92Dallas Freeze-14
02German Adler Mannheim Eagles Postcards-9
03German Mannheim Eagles Postcards-9

Rossignol, Roland
51Bas Du Fleuve-43

Rossiter, Kyle
96Spokane Chiefs-15
97Spokane Chiefs-17
98Spokane Chiefs-20
98Bowman CHL-157
Golden Anniversary-157
OPC International-157
Autographs Blue-A7
Autographs Gold-A7
Autographs Silver-A7
98Bowman Chrome CHL-157
Golden Anniversary-157
Golden Anniversary Refractors-157
OPC International-157
OPC International Refractors-157
Refractors-157
99Spokane Chiefs-20
00Louisville Panthers-9
01BAP Memorabilia-434
Emerald-434
Ruby-434
Sapphire-434
01Parkhurst-316
01Utah Grizzlies-31
02Upper Deck-207
Exclusives-207
02Upper Deck MVP-204
Gold-204
Classics-204
Golden Classics-204
02Upper Deck Vintage-350
03Pacific Complete-532
Red-532
04Chicago Wolves-10

Rosso, Adam
93Quebec Pee-Wee Tournament-1176

Rost, Sonny
54UK A and BC Chewing Gum-37

Rosvall, Kai
70Finnish Jaakiekko-235
71Finnish Suomi Stickers-252
73Finnish Jaakiekko-316

Rota, Blair
95Kamloops Blazers-20
96Kamloops Blazers-21
98San Antonio Iguanas-16
99San Antonio Iguanas-10

Rota, Darcy
74NHL Action Stamps-82
74O-Pee-Chee NHL-269
75O-Pee-Chee NHL-66
75Topps-66
76O-Pee-Chee NHL-47
76Topps-47
77O-Pee-Chee NHL-117
77Topps-117
78O-Pee-Chee-47
78Topps-47
79Flames Team Issue-18
79O-Pee-Chee-360
80Canucks Silverwood Dairies-20
80Canucks Team Issue-18
80O-Pee-Chee-301
80Pepsi-Cola Caps-116
81Canucks Team Issue-18
81O-Pee-Chee-343
82Canucks Team Issue-18
82O-Pee-Chee-355
82Post Cereal-19
83Canucks Team Issue-17
83NHL Key Tags-123
83O-Pee-Chee-344
83O-Pee-Chee-345
83O-Pee-Chee-358
83O-Pee-Chee Stickers-272
83Puffy Stickers-5
83Topps Stickers-272
83Vachon-115
84Canucks Team Issue-20
84O-Pee-Chee-328
84O-Pee-Chee Stickers-280
847-Eleven Discs-50
84Topps-139
04ITG Franchises Canadian-129
Autographs-DRO

Rota, Randy
74NHL Action Stamps-305
74O-Pee-Chee NHL-362
75O-Pee-Chee NHL-237
75Topps-237
76O-Pee-Chee NHL-353

Rotariu, Travis
97Dubuque Fighting Saints-3

Roteliuk, Rob
05Kelowna Rockets-22

Roth, Michael
93Quebec Pee-Wee Tournament-759

Roth, Oliver
93Swiss HNL-230
95Swiss HNL-127
96Swiss HNL-118
98Swiss Power Play Stickers-69
99Swiss Panini Stickers-72
00Swiss Panini Stickers-92
00Swiss Slapshot Mini-Cards-EHCC11
01Swiss HNL-251

Roth, Ryan
99Arizona Icecats-22

Rotheli, Andre
91Finnish Semic World Champ Stickers-195
91Swedish Semic World Champ Stickers-195
92Finnish Semic-213
93Swiss HNL-104
95Swiss HNL-177
96Swiss HNL-72
98Swiss Power Play Stickers-219
99Swiss Panini Stickers-219
00Swiss Panini Stickers-263
00Swiss Slapshot Mini-Cards-EVZ14
01Swiss HNL-46
02Swiss HNL-32

Rothen, Frederic
93Swiss HNL-284
95Swiss HNL-26
96Swiss HNL-24
96Swiss HNL-544
98Swiss Power Play Stickers-119
99Swiss Panini Stickers-73
00Swiss Panini Stickers-120
00Swiss Slapshot Mini-Cards-HCD14
01Swiss EV Zug Postcards-21
01Swiss HNL-187
02Swiss EV Zug Postcards-24
02Swiss HNL-237
03Swiss EV Zug Postcards-19
04Swiss EV Zug Postcards-24

Rothke, Rene
04German DEL-161
04German Hannover Scorpions Postcards-23
05German DEL-139

Rothschild, Sam
24Anonymous NHL-100
24C144 Champ's Cigarettes-52
24V130 Maple Crispette-19
24V145-2-37

Rothwell, Nick
95UK Guildford Flames-10
97UK Guildford Flames-14

Rotkirch, Johann
72Finnish Semic World Championship-114
72Swedish Semic World Championship-114

Rottaris, Mario
93Swiss HNL-53
95Swiss HNL-78
96Swiss HNL-221
98Swiss Power Play Stickers-96
99Swiss Panini Stickers-97
00Swiss Panini Stickers-141
00Swiss Slapshot Mini-Cards-HCFG11
01Swiss HNL-141
02Swiss HNL-167

Rotter, Rafael
05ITG Heroes/Prosp Toronto Expo Parallel -296
05Guelph Storm-C-05
05ITG Heroes and Prospects-296
Autographs Series II-RRO
06Guelph Storm-17

Roubik, Jaroslav
98Czech OFS-372
99Czech Score Blue 2000-4
99Czech Score Red Ice 2000-4

Rouhiainen, Markku
71Finnish Suomi Stickers-270

Rouleau, Alexandre
00Val d'Or Foreurs-14
Signed-14
01Val d'Or Foreurs-13
03Quebec Remparts Memorial Cup-17
03Wheeling Nailers-94
03Wilkes-Barre Scranton Penguins-22
04Wheeling Nailers Riesbeck's-2

Rouleau, Dominic
93Quebec Pee-Wee Tournament-98

Rouleau, Guy
86Sherbrooke Canadiens-23
94German First League-588

Rouleau, Michel
72Nordiques Postcards-19
73Nordiques Team Issue-19
75Roanoke Valley Rebels-5

Rouleau, Tom
97Dubuque Fighting Saints-15
02Reading Royals-20
02Reading Royals RBI Sports-182

Roulette, Allan
98Thunder Bay Thunder Cats-5
99Missouri River Otters-16
99Missouri River Otters Sheet-14

Roulston, Rollie
81Red Wings Oldtimers-21

Roulston, Tom
82Oilers Red Rooster-24
82O-Pee-Chee-118
83O-Pee-Chee-42
83O-Pee-Chee Stickers-103
83Topps Stickers-103
83Vachon-39
84O-Pee-Chee-179
84O-Pee-Chee Stickers-123
84Penguins Heinz Photos-19
88Oilers Tenth Anniversary-15

Roupe, Claes
89Swedish Semic Elitserien Stickers-118

Roupe, Magnus
83Swedish Semic Elitserien-120
84Swedish Semic Elitserien-120
85Swedish Panini Stickers-107
86Swedish Panini Stickers-102
87Flyers Postcards-14
89Swedish Semic Elitserien Stickers-90
90Swedish Semic Elitserien Stickers-263
91Swedish Semic Elitserien Stickers-94
95Swedish Upper Deck 1st Division Stars-DS14
04German Berlin Eisbaeren 50th Anniv-17

Rourke, Alan
96Kitchener Rangers-23
99Kitchener Rangers-20
00St. John's Maple Leafs-23
01St. John's Maple Leafs-20
03ITG VIP Rookie Debut-52
03Parkhurst Rookie-69
03Topps Traded-TT92
Blue-TT92
Gold-TT92
Red-TT92
03UD Honor Roll-165
03Upper Deck-460
Canadian Exclusives-460
HG-460
UD Exclusives-460
03Lowell Lock Monsters-1
03Lowell Lock Monsters Photo Album-11
04Lowell Lock Monsters-19
04Lowell Lock Monsters Photo Album-19

Rouse, Bob
84North Stars Postcards-25
85North Stars Postcards-26
86North Stars 7-Eleven-9
86North Stars Postcards-12
87North Stars Postcards-27
88North Stars ADA-21
89Capitals Kodak-8
89Capitals Team Issue-20
89O-Pee-Chee-26
89Panini Stickers-351
89Topps-26
90Panini Stickers-164
90Pro Set-554
90Score-147
Canadian-147
90Upper Deck-389
French-389
91Maple Leafs PLAY-27
91OPC Premier-151
91Panini Stickers-101
91Parkhurst-176
French-176
91Pro Set-228
French-228
91Score Canadian Bilingual-246
91Score Canadian English-246
92Maple Leafs Kodak-21
92Pinnacle-358
French-358
92Score-130
Canadian-130
92Ultra-214
93Donruss-333
93Leaf-230
Maple Leafs Score Black's-5
93OPC Premier-207
Gold-207
93Pinnacle-289
Canadian-289
93Score-304
Canadian-304
93Stadium Club-353
Members Only Master Set-353
First Day Issue-353
93Topps/OPC Premier-207
Gold-207
94Canada Games NHL POGS-359
94OPC Premier-393
Special Effects-393
94Parkhurst SE-SE51
Gold-SE51
94Pinnacle-374
Artist's Proofs-374
Rink Collection-374
94Stadium Club-238
Members Only Master Set-238
First Day Issue-238
Super Team Winner Cards-238
94Topps/OPC Premier-393
Special Effects-393
94Upper Deck-55
Electric Ice-55
95Be A Player-88
Signatures-S88
Signatures Die Cuts-S88
95Pinnacle-163
Artist's Proofs-163
Rink Collection-163
95Topps-206
OPC Inserts-206
96Score-125
Artist's Proofs-125
Dealer's Choice Artist's Proofs-125
Special Artist's Proofs-125
Golden Blades-125
97Pacific Invincible NHL Regime-72
98Upper Deck MVP-175
Gold Script-175
Silver Script-175
Super Script-175

Rousek, Martin
94Czech APS Extraliga-217
95Czech APS Extraliga-168
96Czech APS Extraliga-181
97Czech APS Extraliga-89
97Czech DS Extraliga-46
97Czech DS Stickers-49
98Czech DS-30
98Czech DS Stickers-96
98Czech OFS-90
99Czech DS-24
99Czech OFS-311
00Czech OFS-178
01Czech OFS Update-309
01Czech OFS-8

Rousseau, Bob
44Beehive Group II Photos-287
60NHL Ceramic Tiles-15
61Shirriff/Salada Coins-117
61York Yellow Backs-35
62Parkhurst-47
62Shirriff Coins-29
62Shirriff Coins-56
62York Iron-On Transfers-18
63Chex Photos-47A
63Chex Photos-47B
63Parkhurst-35
63Parkhurst-94
63York White Backs-25
64Beehive Group III Photos-115
64Canadiens Postcards-17
64Coca-Cola Caps-65
64Topps-80
65Canadiens Steinberg Glasses-8
65Coca-Cola-65
65Topps-70
66Canadiens IGA-6
66Topps-7
66Topps USA Test-7
67Canadiens IGA-15
67Post Flip Books-12
67Topps-68
67York Action Octagons-33
68Canadiens IGA-15
68Canadiens Postcards BW-14
68O-Pee-Chee-65
68Post Marbles-22
68Shirriff Coins-83
68Topps-65
69Canadiens Postcards Color-26
69O-Pee-Chee-9
69Topps-9
70Canadiens Pins-13
70Colgate Stamps-35
70Dad's Cookies-114
70Esso Power Players-173
70North Stars Postcards-8
70O-Pee-Chee-170
Deckle-14
70Sargent Promotions Stamps-96
71O-Pee-Chee-218
71Sargent Promotions Stamps-117
71Toronto Sun-181
72O-Pee-Chee-233
72Sargent Promotions Stamps-145
72Finnish Semic World Championship-200
72Swedish Semic World Championship-200
73O-Pee-Chee-233
74NHL Action Stamps-182
74O-Pee-Chee NHL-326
94Parkhurst Tall Boys-84
95Parkhurst '66-67-77
95Parkhurst '66-67-143
Coins-77

Rousseau, Carl
93Quebec Pee-Wee Tournament-1074

Rousseau, Ghyslain
99Baie-Comeau Drakkar-21
00Baie-Comeau Drakkar-18
Signed-18
01Baie-Comeau Drakkar-15

Rousseau, Guy
52Juniors Blue Tint-142
55Montreal Royals-6
62Quebec Aces-19
64Quebec Aces-16

Rousseau, Maxime
03Gatineau Olympiques-22
04Gatineau Olympiques-12
05Gatineau Olympiques-6

Rousseau, Nicolas
93Quebec Pee-Wee Tournament-420

Rousseau, Rolland
51Laval Dairy QSHL-88
52St. Lawrence Sales-8

Rousseau, Yannick
93Quebec Pee-Wee Tournament-101

Roussel, Antoine
06Chicoutimi Sagueneens-19

Roussel, Dominic
90ProCards AHL/IHL-31
91Parkhurst-450
French-450
91Pinnacle-343
French-343
91Pro Set-552
French-552
91Upper Deck-583
French-583
91ProCards-265
92Bowman-92
92Flyers J.C. Penney-21
92Flyers Upper Deck Sheets-7
92Flyers Upper Deck Sheets-31
92Flyers Upper Deck Sheets-39
92Kraft-27
92O-Pee-Chee-198
92OPC Premier-51
Top Rookies-3
92Panini Stickers-183
92Panini Stickers French-183
92Parkhurst-129
Emerald Ice-129
92Pinnacle-96
French-96
Team 2000-11
Team 2000 French-11
92Pro Set-235
92Score-464
Canadian-464
Young Superstars-36
92Seasons Patches-40
92Stadium Club-315
92Topps-10
92Topps-213
Gold-10G
Gold-213G
92Ultra-159
92Upper Deck-31
Ameri/Can Holograms-6
93Donruss-243
93Durivage Score-39
93Flyers J.C. Penney-19
93Flyers Lineup Sheets-31
93Flyers Lineup Sheets-32
93Kraft-63
93Leaf-244
93OPC Premier-335
Gold-335
93Parkhurst-417
Emerald Ice-417
93Pinnacle-97
Canadian-97
Masks-4
93PowerPlay-409
93Score-82
Canadian-82
93Stadium Club-109
Members Only Master Set-109
OPC-109
First Day Issue-109
First Day Issue OPC-109
93Topps/OPC Premier-335
Gold-335
93Ultra-392
93Upper Deck-336
93Classic McDonalds-18
94Canada Games NHL POGS-290
94Donruss-263
94Leaf-223
94OPC Premier-56
Special Effects-56
94Parkhurst-169
Gold-169
94Pinnacle-208
Artist's Proofs-208
Rink Collection-208
94Score-105
Gold-105
Platinum-105
94Topps/OPC Premier-56
Special Effects-56
94Upper Deck-397
Electric Ice-397
94Classic Pro Prospects-55
Jumbos-PP23
95Be A Player-157
Signatures-S157
Signatures Die Cuts-S157
95Donruss-267
95Score-182
Black Ice Artist's Proofs-182
Black Ice-182
96Donruss Canadian Ice Les Gardiens-7
96Summit-50
Artist's Proofs-50
Ice-50
Metal-50
Premium Stock-50
99BAP Millennium-11
Emerald-11
Ruby-11
Sapphire-11
Signatures-11
Signatures Gold-11
99Pacific-12
Copper-12

Emerald Green-12
Gold-12
Ice Blue-12
Premiere Date-12
Red-12
99Panini Stickers-340
00Pacific-9
Copper-9
Gold-9
Ice Blue-9
Premiere Date-9
01Between the Pipes-75
01Pacific-163
Extreme LTD-163
Hobby LTD-163
Premiere Date-163
Retail LTD-163
01Pacific Arena Exclusives-163
02BAP Sig Series Auto Buybacks 1999-11
02German DEL City Press-82
Roussin, Dany
01Sherbrooke Castors-3
02Rimouski Oceanic-15
03Rimouski Oceanic Sheets-2
04Rimouski Oceanic-3
04ITG Heroes and Prospects-210
Emblems-65
Emblems Gold-65
Jerseys-65
Jerseys Gold-65
Numbers-65
Numbers Gold-65
04ITG Heroes/Prospects Toronto Expo '05-210
05Manchester Monarchs-15
05Manchester Monarchs-44
05Reading Royals-12
05ITG Heroes and Prospects Complete Logos-CHL-13
05ITG Heroes and Prospects Jerseys-GUJ-86
05ITG Heroes and Prospects Jerseys Gold-GUJ-86
05ITG Heroes and Prospects Emblems-GUE-86
05ITG Heroes and Prospects Emblems Gold-GUE-86
05ITG Heroes and Prospects Numbers-GUN-86
05ITG Heroes and Prospects Numbers Gold-GUN-86
05ITG Heroes and Prospects National Pride-NPR-3
06Manchester Monarchs-4
06Reading Royals-11
Rousson, Boris
907th Inn. Sketch QMJHL-64
91ProCards-200
92Binghamton Rangers-21
94Finnish SISU-329
94Classic Pro Prospects-183
95Finnish SISU-95
95Finnish SISU-161
95Finnish SISU-381
Ghost Goalies-2
95Finnish SISU Limited-29
95Finnish SISU Specials-2
96Finnish SISU Redline-95
96Finnish SISU Redline-181
Keeping It Green-3
Mighty Adversaries-2
96Finnish SISU Redline Silver Signatures-3
97Swedish Collector's Choice-50
98German DEL-98
99Finnish Cardset Aces High-H-A
99German DEL-315
00German DEL-236
Profiles-P8
01German Upper Deck-191
02Finnish Cardset-110
02German DEL City Press-99
03German DEL-117
04German DEL-134
04German Hamburg Freezers Postcards-15
05German DEL-114
All-Star Jerseys-AS16
06German DEL-75
Rousu, Miikka
95Finnish SISU-332
96Finnish SISU Redline-142
Rookie Energy-9
00Finnish Cardset-185
Routanen, Arto
83Swedish Semic VM Stickers-36
86Swedish Panini Stickers-115
87Swedish Panini Stickers-112
Routhier, Jean-Marc
88ProCards AHL-111
89Nordiques Police-24
89Halifax Citadels-20
89ProCards AHL-160
Routhier, Stephane
93Drummondville Voltigeurs-2
Rouvali, Simo
95Finnish SISU-132
96Finnish SISU Redline-143
98Finnish Kerailysarja-246
Roux, Jean-Francois
03P.E.I. Rocket-21
Roveda, Reto
95Swiss HNL-392
Rovnianek, Rastislav
06UK Nottingham Panthers-14
Row, Dylan
06Fayetteville FireAntz-14
Row, Todd
96Halifax Mooseheads I-15
96Halifax Mooseheads II-15
97Halifax Mooseheads I-17
Rowan, Chris
99Brampton Battalion-13
00Brampton Battalion-13
Rowatt, Linden
05Regina Pats-20
06Regina Pats-18
Rowbotham, Dave
88ProCards AHL-51
Rowbotham, Ken
897th Inn. Sketch OHL-82
907th Inn. Sketch OHL-17
Rowe, Bobby
10Sweet Caporal Postcards-23
11C55-23
12C57-11
Rowe, Dave
96Madison Monsters-14
Rowe, Jon
92Saskatchewan JHL-99
97Tucson Gila Monsters-1
Rowe, Ken
03Wisconsin Badgers-24
04Wisconsin Badgers-9
Rowe, Randy
00Belleville Bulls-14
01Peoria Rivermen-10
02Peoria Rivermen-9
02Peoria Rivermen RBI Sports-166
03ECHL All-Stars-258
03Peoria Rivermen-19
04Peoria Rivermen-6
05Johnstown Chiefs-15
Rowe, Sean
93Fort Worth Fire-14
94Central Hockey League-32
94Tampa Bay Tritons RHI-17
95Louisiana Ice Gators-13
96Anchorage Aces-13
97Anchorage Aces-17
98Anchorage Aces-6
99Anchorage Aces-16
01BC Icemen-19
Rowe, Tom
78Capitals Team Issue-13
79Capitals Team Issue-18
79O-Pee-Chee-113
79Topps-113
80O-Pee-Chee-214
80Topps-214
81O-Pee-Chee-139
83Moncton Alpines-12
99Lowell Lock Monsters-27
00Lowell Lock Monsters-30
06Albany River Rats-24
Rowell, Ryan
96Halifax Mooseheads I-16
96Halifax Mooseheads II-16
Rowland, Chris
89Spokane Chiefs-15
907th Inn. Sketch WHL-310
917th Inn. Sketch WHL-34
92Thunder Bay Thunder Hawks-20
94Thunder Bay Senators-17
96Louisville Riverfrogs-12
00Lubbock Cotton Kings-7
Rowland, Dean
91British Columbia JHL-85
Rowley, Jordan
06Kamloops Blazers-20
Roworth, Kirk
88Saskatoon Blades-17
Roy, Adam
93Minnesota-Duluth Bulldogs-9
Roy, Allain
92Alberta International Team Canada-18
94Score Team Canada-CT23
94Finnish SISU NHL Phenoms-8
94Swedish Olympics Lillehammer*-316
Roy, Andre
92Quebec Pee-Wee Tournament-1694
96Providence Bruins-49
96Collector's Edge Ice-60
Prism-60
97Charlotte Checkers-18
97Providence Bruins-18
98Fort Wayne Komets-18
99Pacific Omega-166
Copper-166
Gold-166
Ice Blue-166
Premiere Date-166
99Senators Team Issue-17
00BAP Signature Series-210
Emerald-210
Ruby-210
Sapphire-210
Autographs-96
Autographs Gold-96
00Senators Team Issue-21
01BAP Memorabilia-439
Emerald-439
Ruby-439
Sapphire-439
01BAP Update Tough Customers-TC17
01BAP Update Tough Customers-TC18
01BAP Update Tough Customers-TC33
01Pacific-279
01Pacific-417
Extreme LTD-279
Gold-417
Hobby LTD-279
Premiere Date-279
Retail LTD-279
01Pacific Arena Exclusives-279
01Pacific Arena Exclusives-417
01Parkhurst-361
01Senators Team Issue-25
01Upper Deck-353
Exclusives-353
02BAP Sig Series Auto Buybacks 2000-96
02Lightning Team Issue-11
02Pacific Complete-74
Red-74
03ITG Action-504
03Lightning Team Issue-32
03Pacific Complete-158
Red-158
05Parkhurst-397
06Lightning Postcards-19
06O-Pee-Chee-398
Rainbow-398
Roy, Christian
92Quebec Pee-Wee Tournament-399
93Quebec Pee-Wee Tournament-1194
Roy, Claude
52Juniors Blue Tint-34
Roy, Darcy T
81Ottawa 67's-20
82Ottawa 67's-22
83Ottawa 67's-25
Roy, Derek
99Kitchener Rangers-27
00Kitchener Rangers-21
00UD CHL Prospects-9
01Kitchener Rangers-9
01UD Prospects-11
Jerseys-J-DR
Jerseys-C-RT
Jerseys Gold-J-DR
Jerseys Gold-C-RT
02Kitchener Rangers Postcards-4
03BAP Memorabilia-211
03BAP Ultimate Memorabilia Autographs-102
Gold-102
03BAP Ultimate Mem Auto Jerseys-102
03BAP Ultimate Mem Auto Emblems-102
03BAP Ultimate Mem Auto Numbers-102
03BAP Ultimate Mem French Present Future-4
03BAP Ultimate Mem Rookie Jersey Emblems-13
03BAP Ultimate Mem Rookie Jsy Emblem Gold-13
03BAP Ultimate Mem Rookie Jersey Numbers-13
03BAP Ultimate Mem Rookie Jsy Number Gold-13
03ITG Action-609
03ITG Toronto Spring Expo Class of 2004-7
03ITG Used Signature Series-140
Autographs Gold-140
03ITG VIP Rookie Debut-85
03Pacific-361
03Pacific Calder-104
Silver-104
03Pacific Complete-501
Red-501
03Pacific Quest for the Cup-103
03Parkhurst Toronto Expo Rookie Preview-PRP-5
03Parkhurst Rookie-191
Calder Candidates-CMC-15
Calder Candidate Autographs-CMC-DR
Calder Candidates Gold-CMC-15
Road to the NHL-RNJ-11
Road to the NHL Gold-RTN-11
Road to the NHL Emblems-RTNE-11
Road to the NHL Emblems Gold-RTNE-11
Rookie Emblems-RE-31
Rookie Emblem Autographs-RE-DR
Rookie Emblems Gold-RE-31
Rookie Jerseys-RJ-31
Rookie Jersey Autographs-RJ-DR
Rookie Jerseys Gold-RJ-31
Rookie Numbers-RN-31
Rookie Number Autographs-RN-DR
Rookie Numbers Gold-RN-31
03SP Authentic-160
03SPx-238
03Topps Traded-TT90
Blue-TT90
Gold-TT90
Red-TT90
03UD Premier Collection-61
03Upper Deck Classic Portraits-195
03Upper Deck Rookie Update-173
YoungStars-YS6
YoungStars-YS6A
03AHL Top Prospects-31
03Kitchener Rangers Memorial Cup-18
03Rochester Americans-25
03Rochester Americans-26
04Pacific-35
Blue-35
Red-35
04AHL Top Prospects-45
04Rochester Americans-20
04Rochester Americans-28
04ITG Heroes and Prospects-198
Autographs-U-DR
04ITG Heroes/Prospects Toronto Expo '05-198
05ITG Heroes/Prosp Toronto Expo Parallel -48
05Parkhurst-59
Facsimile Auto Parallel-59
True Colors-TCBUF
True Colors-TCBUF
05UD Artifacts Frozen Artifacts-FA-DR
05UD Artifacts Frozen Artifacts Autos-FA-DR
05UD Artifacts Frozen Artifacts Copper-FA-DR
05UD Artifact Frozen Artifact Dual Auto-FAD-DR
05UD Artifact Frozen Artifact Dual Copper-FAD-DR
05UD Artifact Frozen Artifact Dual Gold-FAD-DR
05UD Artifact Frozen Artifact Dual Maroon-FAD-DR
05UD Artifact Frozen Artifact Dual Pewter-FAD-DR
05UD Artifact Frozen Artifact Dual Silver-FAD-DR
05UD Artifacts Frozen Artifacts Gold-FA-DR
05UD Artifacts Frozen Artifacts Maroon-FA-DR
05UD Artifacts Frozen Artifacts Patches-FP-DR
05UD Artifact Frozen Artifact Patch Autos-FP-DR
05UD Artifact Frozen Artifact Patch Dual-FPD-DR
05UD Artifact Frozen Art Patch Dual Auto-FPD-DR
05UD Artifacts Frozen Art Patch Pewter-FP-DR
05UD Artifacts Frozen Art Patch Silver-FP-DR
05UD Artifacts Frozen Artifacts Pewter-FA-DR
05UD Artifacts Frozen Artifacts Silver-FA-DR
05Ultra-26
Gold-26
Ice-26
05Upper Deck-20
HG Glossy-20
05Upper Deck MVP-49
Gold-49
Platinum-49
Materials-M-DR
05Upper Deck Toronto Fall Expo-20
05ITG Heroes and Prospects-48
Autographs-A-DRY
He Shoots-He Scores Prizes-21
Jerseys-GUJ-13
Jerseys Gold-GUJ-13
Emblems-GUE-13
Emblems Gold-GUE-13
Numbers-GUN-13
Numbers Gold-GUN-13
Making the Bigs-MTB-9
Nameplates-N-26
Nameplates Gold-N-26
06Be A Player-52
Autographs-52
Signatures-DR
Signatures 25-56
Signatures Duals-DDR
Signatures Trios-TMAR
06O-Pee-Chee-53
Rainbow-53
06Panini Stickers-34
06Upper Deck-27
Exclusives Parallel-27
High Gloss Parallel-27
Masterpieces-27
06Upper Deck MVP-38
Gold Script-38
Super Script-38
07Upper Deck Victory-39
Black-39
Gold-39
Roy, Eric
93Quebec Pee-Wee Tournament-1195
96Thetford Mines Coyotes-5
01Thetford Mines Coyotes-10
02Thetford Mines Coyotes-20
03Thetford Mines Prolab-20
Roy, Georges
51Laval Dairy QSHL-30
52St. Lawrence Sales-92
Roy, Guy
93Quebec Pee-Wee Tournament-1122
Roy, Jason
93Quebec Pee-Wee Tournament-82
Roy, Jean-Yves
92Binghamton Rangers-17
92Maine Black Bears-14
92Classic-80
Gold-80
92Classic Four-Sport *-203
Gold-203
94Score Team Canada-CT12
94Upper Deck-407
Electric Ice-407
94Binghamton Rangers-18
94Classic Pro Prospects-182
95PEI Senators-17
95Images-96
Gold-96
96Providence Bruins-8
97Collector's Choice-19
97Pacific-313
Copper-313
Emerald Green-313
Ice Blue-313
Red-313
Silver-313
97Score Bruins-11
Platinum-11
Premier-11
97Upper Deck-12
97Providence Bruins-19
99German DEL-114
00Swiss Panini Stickers-142
00Swiss Slapshot Mini-Cards-HCFG12
01Swiss HNL-142
02Swiss HNL-169
03German DEL-178
04German Cologne Sharks Postcards-24
04German DEL-219
05German DEL-215
Roy, Jerome
93Quebec Pee-Wee Tournament-394
Roy, Jimmy
98Manitoba Moose-D6
99Manitoba Moose-19
00Manitoba Moose-19
01Manitoba Moose-21
02Manitoba Moose-9
03Manitoba Moose-15
04Manitoba Moose-11
05AHL All-Stars-33
05Manitoba Moose-17
06German DEL-113
Team Leaders-TL8
05ITG Heroes and Prospects AHL Shooting Stars-AS10
Roy, Joey
93Quebec Pee-Wee Tournament-646
Roy, Jonathan
92Quebec Pee-Wee Tournament-640
93Quebec Pee-Wee Tournament-660
00QMJHL All-Star Program Inserts-12
01Greenville Grrrowl-11
Roy, Lucien
51Laval Dairy Lac St. Jean-22
Roy, Marc Oliver
97Bowman CHL-44
OPC-44
Roy, Marc-Andre
01Baie-Comeau Drakkar-18
02Baie Comeau Drakkar-19
03Columbia Inferno Update-53
04Chicoutimi Sagueneens-13
Roy, Mario
77Granby Vics-17
Roy, Martin
917th Inn. Sketch QMJHL-186
93Quebec Pee-Wee Tournament-368
93Quebec Pee-Wee Tournament-1091
95Richmond Renegades-17
03SPx Style Limited-SPX-RB
05SP Game Used Authentic Fabrics Quad-RBLT
05SP Game Used Authentic Fabrics Triple-BTR
Roy, Mathieu
92Quebec Pee-Wee Tournament-449
00Val d'Or Foreurs-1
Signed-1
01Val d'Or Foreurs-15
02Val d'Or Foreurs-14
03Columbus Cottonmouths-20
05ITG Heroes/Prosp Toronto Expo Parallel -303
05Hot Prospects-132
En Fuego-132
Red Hot-132
White Hot-132
05The Cup Master Pressplate Rookie Update-134
05The Cup Masterpiece Pressplates Trilogy-258
05Upper Deck Rookie Update-134
05Upper Deck Trilogy-258
05Hamilton Bulldogs-22
05ITG Heroes and Prospects-303
Autographs Series II-MRY
06Hamilton Bulldogs-23
07Upper Deck Victory-244
Black-244
Gold-244
Roy, Patrick
85Canadiens Postcards-31
85Canadiens Provigo-19
86Canadiens Postcards-20
86Kraft Drawings-61
86O-Pee-Chee-53
86O-Pee-Chee Stickers-5
86O-Pee-Chee Stickers-19
86O-Pee-Chee Stickers-132
86Topps-53
87Canadiens Postcards-26
87Canadiens Vachon Stickers-23
87Canadiens Vachon Stickers-42
87Canadiens Vachon Stickers-43
87Canadiens Vachon Stickers-69
87Canadiens Vachon Stickers-71
87Canadiens Vachon Stickers-74
87Canadiens Vachon Stickers-76
87O-Pee-Chee-163
87O-Pee-Chee Minis-36
87O-Pee-Chee Stickers-13
87O-Pee-Chee Stickers-185
87Panini Stickers-56
87Panini Stickers-376B
87Topps-163
88Canadiens Postcards-24
88O-Pee-Chee-116
88O-Pee-Chee Minis-33
88O-Pee-Chee Stickers-45
88O-Pee-Chee Stickers-115
88O-Pee-Chee Stickers-214
88Panini Stickers-252
88Panini Stickers-402
88Topps-116
88Topps Sticker Inserts-12
89Canadiens Kraft-19
89Canadiens Postcards-27
89Canadiens Provigo Figurines-33
89Kraft-25
89O-Pee-Chee-17
89O-Pee-Chee-322
89O-Pee-Chee Stickers-14
89O-Pee-Chee Stickers-57
89O-Pee-Chee Stickers-156
89O-Pee-Chee Stickers-170
89O-Pee-Chee Stickers-210
89O-Pee-Chee Stickers-211
89Panini Stickers-235
89Panini Stickers-376
89Panini Stickers-383
89Topps-17
89Topps Sticker Inserts-6
89Swedish Semic World Champ Stickers-54
90Bowman-50
Tiffany-50
90Canadiens Postcards-25
90Kraft-49
90Kraft-90
90O-Pee-Chee-198
90O-Pee-Chee-219
90O-Pee-Chee-512
90O-Pee-Chee Box Bottoms-E
90OPC Premier-101
90Panini Stickers-51
90Panini Stickers-323
90Pro Set-157
90Pro Set-359
90Pro Set-391
90Pro Set-399
90Score Promos-10
90Score-10
90Score-312
90Score-344
90Score-354
90Score-364
Canadian-10
Canadian-312
Canadian-344
Canadian-354
Canadian-364
90Score Hottest/Rising Stars-25
90Topps-198
90Topps-219
Tiffany-198
Tiffany-219
90Topps Box Bottoms-E
90Upper Deck-153
90Upper Deck-207
90Upper Deck-317
90Upper Deck-496
French-153
French-207
French-317
French-496
90Upper Deck Promos-241B
91Pro Set Platinum-61
91Bowman-335
91Canadiens Panini Team Stickers-19
91Canadiens Panini Team Stickers-G
91Canadiens Postcards-24
91Gillette-28
91Kraft-76
91McDonald's Upper Deck-8
91McDonald's Upper Deck-H6
91O-Pee-Chee-270
91O-Pee-Chee-413
91OPC Premier-14
91OPC Premier-170
91Panini Stickers-184
91Panini Stickers-333
91Parkhurst-90
91Parkhurst-220
91Parkhurst-442
91Parkhurst-463
91Parkhurst-470
French-90
French-220
French-442
French-463
French-470
91Pinnacle-175
91Pinnacle-387
French-175
French-387
B-B1
B French-B1
91Pro Set-125
91Pro Set-304
91Pro Set-599
91Pro Set-613
91Pro Set-AU125
91Pro Set-AU599
French-125
French-304
French-599
French-613
French-AU125
French-AU599
CC-CC2
CC French-CC2
Gazette-2
Gazette-SC1
Awards Special-AC3
Puck Candy-14
91Score National-10
91Score Ntnl Candy Wholesalers Convention-10
91Score Fanfest-10
91Score American-75
91Score American-342
91Score American-424
91Score Canadian Bilingual-75
91Score Canadian Bilingual-314
91Score Canadian Bilingual-372
91Score Canadian English-75
91Score Canadian English-314
91Score Canadian English-372
91Score Kellogg's-1
91Stadium Club Members Only-50
91Stadium Club-107
91Topps-270
91Topps-413
91Upper Deck-137
91Upper Deck-614
French-137
French-614
91Finnish Semic World Champ Stickers-52
91Swedish Semic World Champ Stickers-52
92Bowman-74
92Bowman-239
92Canadiens Postcards-24
92Durivage Panini-50
92Durivage Panini-NNO
92Humpty Dumpty I-18
92Kellogg's Posters-4
92Kraft-34
92Kraft-47
92McDonald's Upper Deck-H6
92O-Pee-Chee-111
92O-Pee-Chee-164
25th Anniv. Inserts-19
Trophy Winners-4
92Panini Stickers-147
92Panini Stickers-277
92Panini Stickers French-147
92Panini Stickers French-277
92Parkhurst-84
92Parkhurst-463
92Parkhurst-510
Emerald Ice-84
Emerald Ice-463
Emerald Ice-510
92Pinnacle-130
French-130
92Pro Set-2
92Pro Set-85
Award Winners-CC2
92Score-295
92Score-418
92Score-428
92Score-489
92Score-527
Canadian-295
Canadian-418
Canadian-428
Canadian-489
Canadian-527
92Seasons Patches-21
92Sports Illustrated for Kids II-93
92Sports Illustrated for Kids II-559
92Stadium Club-133
92Stadium Club-252
92Topps-110
92Topps-263
92Topps-491
92Topps-508
Gold-110G
Gold-263G
Gold-491G
Gold-508G
92Ultra-108
All-Stars-3
Award Winners-4
92Upper Deck-149
92Upper Deck-438
92Upper Deck-440
All-World Team-W6
93SLU Hockey Canadian-10
93SLU Hockey American-11
93Canadiens Postcards-23
93Donruss-178
Elite Inserts-9
Ice Kings-1
Special Print-L
93Durivage Score-17
93Durivage Score-NNO
93High Liner Greatest Goalies-1
93Kenner Starting Lineup Cards-11
93Kraft-64
93Kraft-72
93Leaf-33
93Leaf-100
Gold All-Stars-5
Painted Warriors-4
Studio Signature-6
93McDonald's Upper Deck-23
93McDonald's Upper Deck-23L
93O-Pee-Chee Canadiens Hockey Fest-30
93OPC Premier-1
Gold-1
Black Gold-8
93Panini Stickers-B
93Parkhurst-100
Emerald Ice-100
Cherry's Playoff Heroes-D10
East/West Stars-E4
USA/Canada Gold-G9
93Pinnacle-150
93Pinnacle-228
Canadian-150
Canadian-228
All-Stars-18
All-Stars Canadian-18
Team Pinnacle-1
Team Canadian-1
93PowerPlay-133
Gamebreakers-9
Netminders-7
93Score-315
Canadian-315
Dream Team-2
Franchise-10
93Seasons Patches-16
93Stadium Club-231
Members Only Master Set-231
OPC-231
First Day Issue-231
First Day Issue OPC-231
All-Stars-1
All-Stars Members Only-1
All-Stars OPC-1
Finest-11
Finest Members Only-11
Master Photos-7
Master Photos Winners-7
93Topps Premier Promo Sheet-1
93Topps/OPC Premier-1
Gold-1
93Topps Premier Black Gold-22
93Topps Premier Black Gold-B
93Ultra-39
All-Stars-1
93Upper Deck-49
Award Winners-AW4
Next In Line-NL6
NHLPA/Roots-2
SP-81
93Upper Deck Locker All-Stars-12
93Swedish Semic World Champ Stickers-189
93Classic Pro Prospects-33
94Action Packed Badge of Honor Promos-4
94Action Packed Big Picture 24K Gold-13G
94Action Packed Big Picture 24K Gold-14G
94Be A Player-R121
94Be A Player-R179
Up Close and Personal-UC8
94Canada Games NHL POGS-283
94Canadiens Postcards-22
94Donruss-328
Dominators-3
Elite Inserts-10
Masked Marvels-9
94EA Sports-72
94Finest-30
Super Team Winners-30
Refractors-30
Division's Clear Cut-1
Ring Leaders-14
94Flair-91
Hot Numbers-8
94Fleer-107
Netminders-9
94Hockey Wit-3
94Kraft-54
94Kraft Goalie Masks-7
94Leaf-41
Crease Patrol-1
Gold Stars-3
Limited Inserts-12
94Leaf Limited-28
94McDonald's Upper Deck-McD4
94NHLPA Phone Cards-7
94OPC Premier-125
94OPC Premier-310
94OPC Premier-455
Special Effects-125
Special Effects-310
Special Effects-455
94Parkhurst-113
94Parkhurst-312
Gold-113
Gold-312
Crash the Game Green-12
Crash the Game Blue-12
Crash the Game Gold-12
Crash the Game Red-12
SE Vintage-3
94Pinnacle-30
Artist's Proofs-30
Rink Collection-30
Goaltending Greats-GT5
Masks-MA1
Northern Lights-NL1
Team Pinnacle-TP1
Team Dufex Parallel-TP1
94Score Dream Team-DT1
94Score Franchise-TF12
94Select-96
Gold-96
First Line-FL1
94SP-59
Die Cuts-59
94Stadium Club Members Only-23
94Stadium Club-33
94Stadium Club-178
Members Only Master Set-33
Members Only Master Set-178
First Day Issue-33
First Day Issue-178
Finest Inserts-9
Finest Inserts Members Only-9
Super Teams-12
Super Teams Members Only Master Set-12
Super Team Winner Cards-33
Super Team Winner Cards-178
94Topps/OPC Premier-125
94Topps/OPC Premier-310
94Topps/OPC Premier-455
Special Effects-125
Special Effects-310
Special Effects-455
94Topps Finest Bronze-3
94Ultra-113
All-Stars-6
Premier Pad Men-6
94Upper Deck-121
Electric Ice-121
Predictor Hobby-H5
Predictor Hobby-H26
94Upper Deck Predictor Hobby Exch Gold-H5
94Upper Deck Predictor Hobby Exch Gold-H26
94Upper Deck Predictor Hobby Exch Silver-H5
94Upper Deck SP Inserts-SP42
94Upper Deck SP Inserts Die Cuts-SP42
95Bashan Super Stickers-66
Die-Cut-2
95Be A Player-197
Signatures-S197
Signatures Die Cuts-S197
95Bowman-15
All-Foil-15
95Canada Games NHL POGS-5
95Canada Games NHL POGS-27
95Canada Games NHL POGS-155
95Canadiens Postcards-16
95Collector's Choice-95
Player's Club-95
Player's Club Platinum-95
95Donruss-338
Between The Pipes-7
95Donruss Elite-64
Die Cut Stars-64
Die Cut Stars-64U
Die Cut Uncut-64
Die Cut Uncut-64U
Painted Warriors-1
95Emotion-91
95Finest-13
95Finest-145
Refractors-13
Refractors-145
95Hoyle Eastern Playing Cards-27
95Imperial Stickers-66
Die Cut Superstars-2
95Kraft-17
95Leaf-200
95Leaf Limited-66
Stick Side-4
95McDonald's Pinnacle-MCD-25
95Metal-78
95NHL Aces Playing Cards-1S
95NHL Cool Trade-16
95NHL Cool Trade-RP16
95NHL/NHLPA Playing Cards-NNO
95Panini Stickers-46
95Parkhurst International-113
95Parkhurst International-323
Emerald Ice-113
Emerald Ice-323
Crown Collection Silver Series 2-2
Crown Collection Gold Series 2-2
Goal Patrol-3
Parkie's Trophy Picks-PP35
95Pinnacle-169
Artist's Proofs-169
Rink Collection-169
Clear Shots-10
First Strike-4
95Pinnacle FANtasy-10
95Playoff One on One-55
95Playoff One on One-166
95Playoff One on One-274
95Post Upper Deck-10
95Pro Magnets-24
95Score-145
95Score-324
Black Ice Artist's Proofs-145
Black Ice Artist's Proofs-324
Black Ice-145
Black Ice-324
Dream Team-11
95Select Certified-81
Mirror Gold-81
Gold Team-10
95SkyBox Impact-87
Deflectors-8
95SP-30
Stars/Etoiles-E9
Stars/Etoiles Gold-E9
95Stadium Club Members Only-1
95Stadium Club-15
Members Only Master Set-15
Extreme North-EN4
Extreme North Members Only Master Set-EN4
Metalists-M3
Metalists Members Only Master Set-M3
95Summit-149
Artist's Proofs-149
Ice-149
GM's Choice-1
In The Crease-3
95Topps-60
95Topps-377
OPC Inserts-60
OPC Inserts-377
Canadian Gold-1CG
Home Grown Canada-HGC1
Marquee Men Power Boosters-377
Mystery Finest-M20
Mystery Finest Refractors-M20
Profiles-PF3
95Topps SuperSkills-81
Platinum-81
95Ultra-83
95Ultra-351
95Ultra-377
Gold Medallion-83
Premier Pad Men-10
Premier Pad Men Gold Medallion-10
95Upper Deck-39
95Upper Deck-297
Electric Ice-39
Electric Ice-297
Electric Ice Gold-39
Electric Ice Gold-297
Predictor Hobby-H14
Predictor Hobby Exchange-H14
Predictor Retail-R55
Predictor Retail Exchange-R55
Special Edition-SE110
Special Edition-SE131
Special Edition Gold-SE110
95Zenith-117
Z-Team-1
95Swedish Globe World Championships-73
96SLU Hockey Canadian-13
96Headliners Hockey-15A
96Headliners Hockey-15B
96SLU Hockey American-21
96Avalanche Photo Pucks-3
96Be A Player Stacking the Pads-13
96Black Diamond-174
Gold-174
Run for the Cup-RC4
96Collector's Choice-65
96Collector's Choice-307
96Collector's Choice-314
MVP-UD19
MVP Gold-UD19
Stick'Ums-S4
96Donruss-112
Press Proofs-112
Between the Pipes-1
Elite Inserts-10
Elite Inserts Gold-10
96Donruss Canadian Ice-19
Gold Press Proofs-19
Red Press Proofs-19
Les Gardiens-1
96Donruss Elite-66
Die Cut Stars-66
Painted Warriors-1
Painted Warriors Promos-P1
96Duracell All-Cherry Team-DC17
96Duracell L'Equipe Beliveau-JB17
96Flair-20
Blue Ice-20
Hot Gloves-10
Now And Then-2
96Fleer-24
Pearson-9
Vezina-9
Picks Dream Lines-8
Picks Fabulous 50-40
96Hockey Greats Coins-18
Gold-18
96Kenner Starting Lineup Cards-21
96Kraft Upper Deck-17
96Leaf-38
Press Proofs-38
Shut Down-1
Sweaters Away-2
Sweaters Home-2
96Leaf Limited-9
Gold-9
Stubble-1
96Leaf Preferred-1
Press Proofs-1
Steel-36
Steel Gold-36
Masked Marauders-4
96Maggers-88
96McDonald's Pinnacle-30
96Metal Universe-37
Armor Plate-11
Armor Plate Super Power-11
Cool Steel-9
Cool Steel Super Power-9
96NHL Aces Playing Cards-41
96NHL Pro Stamps-24
96Pinnacle-138
Artist's Proofs-138
Foil-138
Premium Stock-138
Rink Collection-138
Masks-1
Masks Die Cuts-1
Team Pinnacle-8
96Pinnacle Fantasy-FC19
96Pinnacle Mint-21
Bronze-21
Gold-21
Silver-21
Coins Brass-21
Coins Solid Gold-21
Coins Gold Plated-21
Coins Nickel-21
Coins Silver-21
96Playoff One on One-431
96Post Upper Deck-18
96Score Samples-1
96Score-1
Artist's Proofs-1
Dealer's Choice Artist's Proofs-1
Special Artist's Proofs-1
Golden Blades-1
Dream Team-12
Net Worth-1
96Select Certified-81
Artist's Proofs-81
Blue-81
Mirror Blue-81
Mirror Gold-81
Mirror Red-81
Red-81
Freezers-2
96SkyBox Impact-27
Countdown to Impact-9
Zero Heroes-9
96SP-35
Clearcut Winner-CW6
Game Film-GF3
96SPx-10
Gold-10
Holoview Heroes-HH2
96Summit-87
Artist's Proofs-87
Ice-87
Metal-87
Premium Stock-87
In The Crease-1
In The Crease Premium Stock-1
Untouchables-15
96Team Out-60
96Topps Picks-11
Fantasy Team-FT1
Ice D-ID7
OPC Inserts-11
96Ultra-39
Gold Medallion-39

Clear the Ice-8
96Upper Deck-38
96Upper Deck-199
96Upper Deck-365
Generation Next-X5
Hart Hopefuls Bronze-HH11
Hart Hopefuls Gold-HH11
Hart Hopefuls Silver-HH11
Lord Stanley's Heroes Finals-LS6
Lord Stanley's Heroes Quarterfinals-LS6
Lord Stanley's Heroes Semifinals-LS6
Superstar Showdown-SS2A
96Upper Deck Ice-107
Parallel-107
Stanley Cup Foundation-S5
Stanley Cup Foundation Dynasty-S5
96Zenith-35
Artist's Proofs-35
Champion Salute-11
Champion Salute Diamond-11
96Swedish Semic Wien Super Goalies-SG7
97SLU Hockey One on One-2
97Headliners Hockey-22
97NHL Pro Zone-50
97Avalanche Pins-3
97Be A Player Stacking the Pads-4
97Be A Player Take A Number-4
97Beehive-19
Golden Portraits-19
Team-15
Team Gold-15
97Black Diamond-41
Double Diamond-41
Triple Diamond-41
Quadruple Diamond-41
Premium Cut-PC2
Premium Cut Double Diamond-PC2
Premium Cut Quadruple Diamond Horiz-PC2
Premium Cut Triple Diamond-PC2
Premium Cut Quadruple Diamond Verticals-PC2
97Collector's Choice-56
97Collector's Choice-316
Magic Men-MM6
Magic Men-MM7
Magic Men-MM8
Magic Men-MM9
Magic Men-MM10
Star Quest-SQ86
Stick'Ums-S23
World Domination-W18
97Crown Royale-37
Emerald Green-37
Ice Blue-37
Silver-37
Blades of Steel Die-Cuts-6
Cramer's Choice Jumbos-5
Cramer's Choice Jumbos Gold-5
Cramer's Choice Jumbos Signed-5
Freeze Out Die-Cuts-5
97Donruss-5
Press Proofs Silver-5
Press Proofs Gold-5
Between The Pipes-1
Elite Inserts-5
97Donruss Canadian Ice-1
Dominion Series-1
Provincial Series-1
Les Gardiens-1
97Donruss Canadian Ice Les Gardiens Promo-1
97Donruss Cdn Ice Stanley Cup Scrapbook-27
97Donruss Elite-14
97Donruss Elite-142
Aspirations-14
Aspirations-142
Status-14
Status-142
Craftsmen-14
Master Craftsmen-14
Prime Numbers-2A
Prime Numbers-2B
Prime Numbers-2C
Prime Numbers Die-Cuts-2A
Prime Numbers Die-Cuts-2B
Prime Numbers Die-Cuts-2C
97Donruss Limited-44
97Donruss Limited-151
97Donruss Limited-198
Exposure-44
Exposure-151
Exposure-198
Fabric of the Game-20
97Donruss Preferred-86
97Donruss Preferred-168
Cut to the Chase-86
Cut to the Chase-168
Color Guard-1
Color Guard Promos-1
Precious Metals-5
97Donruss Priority-1
97Donruss Priority-197
Stamp of Approval-1
Stamp of Approval-197
Postcards-1
Postcards Opening Day Issues-1
Postmaster General-1
Postmaster Generals Promos-1
Stamps-1
Stamps Bronze-1
Stamps Gold-1
Stamps Silver-1
97Esso Olympic Hockey Heroes-17
97Esso Olympic Hockey Heroes French-17
97Gatorade Stickers-6
97Highland Mint Mint-Cards Topps-23
97Highland Mint Mint-Cards Topps-24
97Highland Mint Mint-Coins-14
97Jell-O Juniors To Pros-5
97Katch-41
97Katch-160
Gold-41
Gold-160
Silver-41
Silver-160
97Kraft Team Canada-6
97Leaf-128
97Leaf-187
Fractal Matrix-128
Fractal Matrix-187
Fractal Matrix Die Cuts-128
Fractal Matrix Die Cuts-187
Pipe Dreams-3
97Leaf International-128
Universal Ice-128
97McDonald's Upper Deck-23
Game Film-5
97NHL Aces Playing Cards-13
97Pacific-33
Copper-33
Emerald Green-33
Ice Blue-33
Red-33
Silver-33
Cramer's Choice-5
Gold Crown Die-Cuts-8

In The Cage Laser Cuts-5
Team Checklists-7
97Pacific Dynagon-33
97Pacific Dynagon-138
Copper-33
Copper-138
Dark Grey-33
Dark Grey-138
Emerald Green-33
Emerald Green-138
Ice Blue-33
Ice Blue-138
Red-33
Red-138
Silver-33
Silver-138
Best Kept Secrets-26
Dynamic Duos-6A
Kings of the NHL-3
Stonewallers-6
Tandems-4
Tandems-25
97Pacific Invincible-38
Copper-38
Emerald Green-38
Ice Blue-38
Red-38
Silver-38
Feature Performers-9
NHL Regime-56
NHL Regime-217
97Pacific Omega-64
97Pacific Omega-249
Copper-64
Copper-249
Dark Gray-64
Dark Gray-249
Emerald Green-64
Emerald Green-249
Gold-64
Gold-249
Ice Blue-64
Ice Blue-249
No Scoring Zone-2
Silks-4
Team Leaders-4
97Panini Stickers-127
97Panini Stickers-208
97Paramount-54
Copper-54
Dark Grey-54
Emerald Green-54
Ice Blue-54
Red-54
Silver-54
Big Numbers Die-Cuts-6
Canadian Greats-4
Glove Side Laser Cuts-5
Photoengravings-6
97Pinnacle-29
Artist's Proofs-29
Rink Collection-29
Epix Game Emerald-7
Epix Game Orange-7
Epix Game Purple-7
Epix Moment Emerald-7
Epix Moment Orange-7
Epix Moment Purple-7
Epix Play Emerald-7
Epix Play Orange-7
Epix Play Purple-7
Epix Season Emerald-7
Epix Season Orange-7
Epix Season Purple-7
Press Plates Back Black-29
Press Plates Back Cyan-29
Press Plates Back Magenta-29
Press Plates Back Yellow-29
Press Plates Front Black-29
Press Plates Front Cyan-29
Press Plates Front Magenta-29
Press Plates Front Yellow-29
Masks-5
Masks Die Cuts-5
Masks Jumbos-5
97Pinnacle Masks Promos-5
97Pinnacle Team Pinnacle-1
97Pinnacle Team Pinnacle Mirror-1
97Pinnacle Team Pinnacle Parallel-1
97Pinnacle Team Pinnacle Parallel Mirror-1
97Pinnacle Tins-8
97Pinnacle Certified-2
Red-2
Mirror Blue-2
Mirror Gold-2
Mirror Red-2
Team-2
Gold Team Promo-2
Gold Team-2
97Pinnacle Inside-37
Coach's Collection-37
Executive Collection-37
Stand Up Guys-5A/B
Stand Up Guys-5C/D
Stand Up Guys Promos-5A/B
Stand Up Guys Promos-5C/D
Stoppers-1
Track-2
Cans-12
Cans Gold-12
97Pinnacle Mint-11
Bronze-11
Gold Team-11
Silver Team-11
Coins Brass-11
Coins Brass Proofs-11
Coins Gold Plated-11
Coins Gold Plated Proofs-11
Coins Nickel Silver-11
Coins Nickel Silver Proofs-11
Coins Solid Gold-11
Coins Solid Silver-11
97Pinnacle Power Pack Blow-Ups-5
97Pinnacle Replica Masks-5
97Pinnacle Tot Cert Platinum Blue-2
97Pinnacle Tot Cert Platinum Gold-2
97Pinnacle Totally Certified Platinum Red-2
97Pinnacle Tot Cert Mirror Platinum Gold-2
97Post Pinnacle-2
97Revolution-38
Copper-38
Emerald-38
Ice Blue-38
Silver-38
1998 All-Star Game Die-Cuts-7
NHL Icons-4
Return to Sender Die-Cuts-5
Team Checklist Laser Cuts-7
97Score-33
Artist's Proofs-33
Golden Blades-33
Net Worth-13
97Score Avalanche-1
Platinum-1

Premier-1
97SP Authentic-37
Icons-I24
Icons Die-Cuts-I24
Icons Embossed-I24
Sign of the Times-PR
Tradition-T2
97SPx-10
Bronze-10
Gold-10
Silver-10
Steel-10
DuoView-6
DuoView Autographs-5
Grand Finale-10
Portraits-7
97Studio-7
97Studio-110
Press Proofs Silver-7
Press Proofs Silver-110
Press Proofs Gold-7
Press Proofs Gold-110
Portraits-7
Silhouettes-3
Silhouettes 8x10-3
97Upper Deck-43
97Upper Deck-210
97Upper Deck-420
Blow-Ups 3 x 5-1-6
Blow-Ups 5 x 7-1B
Game Dated Moments-43
Game Jerseys-GJ1
Game Jerseys-GJ2
Game Jerseys-GJ1S
Sixth Sense Masters-SS30
Sixth Sense Wizards-SS30
Smooth Grooves-SG2
The Specialists-2
The Specialists Level 2 Die Cuts-2
Three Star Selects-2B
97Upper Deck Diamond Vision-2
Signature Moves-2
Defining Moments-DM2
97Upper Deck Ice-83
Parallel-83
Champions-IC2
Champions 2 Die Cuts-IC2
Lethal Lines-L10B
Lethal Lines 2-L10B
Power Shift-83
97Zenith-10
Z-Gold-10
Z-Silver-10
97Zenith 5 x 7-3
Gold Impulse-3
Silver Impulse-3
97Zenith Chasing The Cup-1
97Zenith Z-Team-3
97Zenith Z-Team 5x7-3
97Zenith Z-Team Gold-3
97Pinnacle Collector's Club Team Pinnacle-H2
98Headliners Hockey In the Crease-4
98SLU Hockey Classic Doubles-5
98Headliners Hockey XL-7
98SLU Hockey-190
98Aurora-51
Atomic Laser Cuts-6
Championship Fever-12
Championship Fever Copper-12
Championship Fever Ice Blue-12
Championship Fever Red-12
Championship Fever Silver-12
Cubes-5
Front Line Copper-3
Front Line Ice Blue-3
Front Line Red-3
NHL Command-4
98Avalanche Team Issue-8
98Be A Player-34
Press Release-34
98BAP Gold-34
98BAP Autographs-34
98BAP Autographs Gold-34
98BAP AS Game Used Stick Cards-S6
98BAP AS Game Used Jersey Cards-AS6
98BAP Playoff Game Used Jerseys-G8
98BAP Playoff Game Used Jersey Autographs-G8
98BAP Playoff Highlights-H8
98BAP Playoff Practice Used Jerseys-P16
98BAP Tampa Bay All Star Game-34
98Black Diamond-22
Double Diamond-22
Triple Diamond-22
Quadruple Diamond-22
Myriad-M23
Myriad 2-M23
Winning Formula Gold-WF6
Winning Formula Platinum-WF6
98Bowman's Best-28
Refractors-28
Atomic Refractors-28
Mirror Image Fusion-F10
Mirror Image Fusion Refractors-F10
Mirror Image Fusion Atomic Refractors-F10
98Crown Royale-35
Limited Series-35
Cramer's Choice Jumbos-5
Cramer's Choice Jumbos Dark Blue-5
Cramer's Choice Jumbos Green-5
Cramer's Choice Jumbos Red-5
Cramer's Choice Jumbos Light Blue-5
Cramer's Choice Jumbos Gold-5
Cramer's Choice Jumbos Purple-5
Living Legends-5
Master Performers-5
Pillars of the Game-7
98Donruss Elite Promos-16
98Finest-140
No Protectors-140
No Protectors Refractors-140
Refractors-140
Double Sided Mystery Finest-M22
Double Sided Mystery Finest-M25
Double Sided Mystery Finest-M28
Double Sided Mystery Finest-M29
Double Sided Mystery Refractors-M22
Double Sided Mystery Refractors-M25
Double Sided Mystery Refractors-M28
Double Sided Mystery Refractors-M29
98Jell-O Spoons-7
98Katch-159
98Kenner Starting Lineup Cards-28
98Lunchables Goalie Greats Rounds-8
98Lunchables Goalie Greats Squares-8
98McDonald's Upper Deck-15
98NHL Aces Playing Cards-14
98NHL Game Day Promotion-COL1
98OPC Chrome-190
Refractors-190
Blast From the Past-4
Blast From the Past Refractors-4
98Pacific-33
Ice Blue-33
Red-33
Cramer's Choice-4

Dynagon Ice Inserts-6
Titanium Ice-6
Gold Crown Die-Cuts-9
Team Checklists-7
Timelines-4
98Pacific Dynagon Ice-51
Blue-51
Red-51
Adrenaline Rush Bronze-5
Adrenaline Rush Ice Blue-5
Adrenaline Rush Red-5
Adrenaline Rush Silver-5
Watchmen-2
Preeminent Players-4
Team Checklists-7
98Pacific Omega-64
Red-64
Opening Day Issue-64
Championship Spotlight-3
Championship Spotlight Green-3
Championship Spotlight Red-3
Championship Spotlight Gold-3
EO Portraits-5
EO Portraits 1 of 1-5
Face to Face-1
Online-9
Planet Ice-30
Planet Ice Parallel-30
Prism-5
98Panini Photocards-71
98Panini Photocards-106
98Panini Stickers-184
98Paramount-60
Copper-60
Emerald Green-60
Holo-Electric-60
Ice Blue-60
Silver-60
Glove Side Laser Cuts-6
Hall of Fame Bound-4
Hall of Fame Bound Proofs-4
Ice Galaxy-3
Ice Galaxy Gold-3
Ice Galaxy Silver-3
Team Checklists Die-Cuts-7
98Revolution-38
Ice Shadow-38
Red-38
NHL Icons-4
Showstoppers-11
Three Pronged Attack-12
Three Pronged Attack Parallel-12
98SP Authentic-21
Power Shift-21
Authentics-2
Sign of the Times-PR
Sign of the Times Gold-PR
Snapshots-SS2
Stat Masters-S15
98SPx Finite-24
98SPx Finite-119
98SPx Finite-154
98SPx Finite-171
Radiance-24
Radiance-119
Radiance-154
Radiance-171
Spectrum-24
Spectrum-119
Spectrum-154
Spectrum-171
98SPx Top Prospects-14
Radiance-14
Spectrum-14
Highlight Heroes-H9
Lasting Impressions-L23
Premier Stars-PS21
Winning Materials-PR
98Topps-190
O-Pee-Chee-190
Blast From The Past-4
Local Legends-L8
Mystery Finest Bronze-M16
Mystery Finest Bronze Refractors-M16
Mystery Finest Gold-M16
Mystery Finest Gold Refractors-M16
Mystery Finest Silver-M16
Mystery Finest Silver Refractors-M16
98Topps Gold Label Class 1-77
Black-77
Black One of One-77
One of One-77
Red-77
Red One of One-77
98Topps Gold Label Class 2-77
98Topps Gold Label Class 2 Black-77
98Topps Gold Label Class 2 Black 1 of 1-77
98Topps Gold Label Class 2 One of One-77
98Topps Gold Label Class 2 Red-77
98Topps Gold Label Class 2 Red One of One-77
98Topps Gold Label Class 3-77
98Topps Gold Label Class 3 Black-77
98Topps Gold Label Class 3 Black 1 of 1-77
98Topps Gold Label Class 3 One of One-77
98Topps Gold Label Class 3 Red-77
98Topps Gold Label Class 3 Red One of One-77
98UD Choice-54
98UD Choice-232
98UD Choice-243
98UD Choice-309
Blow-Ups-1
Mini Bobbing Head-BH21
Prime Choice Reserve-54
Prime Choice Reserve-232
Prime Choice Reserve-243
Prime Choice Reserve-309
Reserve-54
Reserve-232
Reserve-243
Reserve-309
StarQuest Blue-SQ3
StarQuest Gold-SQ3
StarQuest Green-SQ3
StarQuest Red-SQ3
98UD3-46
98UD3-106
98UD3-166
Die-Cuts-46
Die-Cuts-106
Die-Cuts-166
98Upper Deck-74
98Upper Deck-208
Exclusives-74
Exclusives-208
Exclusives 1 of 1-74
Exclusives 1 of 1-208
Frozen In Time-FT11
Frozen In Time Quantum 1-FT11
Frozen In Time Quantum 2-FT11
Frozen In Time Quantum 3-FT11
Generation Next-GN7
Generation Next-GN8
Generation Next-GN9
Generation Next Quantum 1-GN7

Generation Next Quantum 1-GN8
Generation Next Quantum 1-GN9
Generation Next Quantum 2-GN7
Generation Next Quantum 2-GN8
Generation Next Quantum 2-GN9
Generation Next Quantum 3-GN7
Generation Next Quantum 3-GN8
Generation Next Quantum 3-GN9
Lord Stanley's Heroes-LS10
Lord Stanley's Heroes Quantum 1-LS10
Lord Stanley's Heroes Quantum 2-LS10
Lord Stanley's Heroes Quantum 3-LS10
Profiles-P24
Profiles Quantum 1-P24
Profiles Quantum 2-P24
Profiles Quantum 3-P24
Gold Reserve-74
Gold Reserve-208
98Upper Deck MVP-52
Gold Script-52
Silver Script-52
Super Script-52
Game Souvenirs-PR
OT Heroes-OT2
Special Forces-F13
98Slovakian Eurotel-19
99SLU Hockey Classic Doubles-3
99SLU Hockey 12" Figures-7
99SLU Hockey Pro Action Deluxe-50
99Aurora-41
Striped-41
Premiere Date-41
Premiere Date Striped-41
Canvas Creations-5
Championship Fever-8
Championship Fever Copper-8
Championship Fever Ice Blue-8
Championship Fever Silver-8
Complete Players-5
Complete Players Parallel-5
Complete Players Retail-5
Complete Players Retail Parallel-5
Glove Unlimited-6
Styrotechs-6
99Avalanche Pins-4
99Avalanche Team Issue-20
99BAP Memorabilia-262
Gold-262
Silver-262
Jersey Cards-J6
Jersey Emblems-E6
Jersey Numbers-I6
Jersey and Stick Cards-S6
AS Heritage Ruby-H10
AS Heritage Sapphire-H10
AS Heritage Emerald-H10
99BAP Update Double AS Jersey Cards-D4
99BAP Update Teammates Jersey Cards-TM3
99BAP Update Teammates Jersey Cards-TM21
99BAP Update Teammates Jersey Cards-TM42
99BAP Update Teammates Jersey Cards-TM44
99BAP Millennium-66
Emerald-66
Ruby-66
Sapphire-66
Signatures-66
Signatures Gold-66
Goalie Memorabilia-G2
Jerseys-J23
Jersey Autographs-J23
Jersey and Stick Cards-JS23
Jersey Emblems-E23
Jersey Numbers-N23
Players of the Decade-D3
Players of the Decade Autographs-D3
99Black Diamond-24
Diamond Cut-24
Final Cut-24
A Piece of History-PR
A Piece of History Double-PR
A Piece of History Triple-PR
Diamonation-D5
Diamond Skills-DS3
99Crown Royale-39
Limited Series-39
Premiere Date-39
Card-Supials-7
Card-Supials Minis-7
Cramer's Choice Jumbos-4
Cramer's Choice Jumbos Dark Blue-4
Cramer's Choice Jumbos Gold-4
Cramer's Choice Jumbos Green-4
Cramer's Choice Jumbos Light Blue-4
Cramer's Choice Jumbos Purple-4
Cramer's Choice Jumbos Red-4
Gold Crown Die-Cuts Jumbos-3
Ice Elite-7
Ice Elite Parallel-7
International Glory-7
International Glory Parallel-7
99Jell-O Goalie Collection-5
99Jell-O Partners of Power-9
99McDonald's Upper Deck-MCD15
99McDonald's Upper Deck-MCD15R
99O-Pee-Chee-16
99O-Pee-Chee-284A
99O-Pee-Chee-284B
99O-Pee-Chee-284C
99O-Pee-Chee-284D
99O-Pee-Chee-284E
99O-Pee-Chee Chrome-16
99O-Pee-Chee Chrome-284A
99O-Pee-Chee Chrome-284B
99O-Pee-Chee Chrome-284C
99O-Pee-Chee Chrome-284D
99O-Pee-Chee Chrome-284E
99O-Pee-Chee Chrome Ice Masters-IM18
99O-Pee-Chee Chrome Ice Masters Refractor-IM18
99O-Pee-Chee Chrome Refractors-16
99O-Pee-Chee Chrome Refractors-284A
99O-Pee-Chee Chrome Refractors-284B
99O-Pee-Chee Chrome Refractors-284C
99O-Pee-Chee Chrome Refractors-284D
99O-Pee-Chee Chrome Refractors-284E
99O-Pee-Chee Chrome Postmasters-PM5
99O-Pee-Chee Chrome Postmasters Refractor-PM5
99O-Pee-Chee Ice Masters-IM18
99O-Pee-Chee Post Masters-PM5
99Pacific-114
Copper-114
Emerald Green-114
Gold-114
Ice Blue-114
Premiere Date-114
Red-114
Center Ice-7
Center Ice Proofs-7
Cramer's Choice-4
Gold Crown Die-Cuts-11
Home and Away-5
Home and Away-15
In the Cage Net-Fusions-5
Past and Present-7
Team Leaders-8

99Pacific Dynagon Ice-59
Blue-59
Copper-59
Gold-59
Premiere Date-59
2000 All-Star Preview-5
Lords of the Rink-5
Masks-1
Masks-6
Masks Holographic Blue-1
Masks Holographic Blue-6
Masks Holographic Gold-1
Masks Holographic Gold-6
Masks Holographic Purple-1
Masks Holographic Purple-6
99Pacific Omega-65
Copper-65
Gold-65
Ice Blue-65
Premiere Date-65
Cup Contenders-4
EO Portraits-6
EO Portraits 1/1-6
NHL Generations-4
5 Star Talents-26
5 Star Talents Parallel-26
99Pacific Prism-40
Holographic Blue-40
Holographic Gold-40
Holographic Mirror-40
Holographic Purple-40
Premiere Date-40
Clear Advantage-5
Dial-a-Stats-5
Sno-Globe Die-Cuts-6
99Panini Stickers-211
99Panini Stickers-336
99Paramount-67
Copper-67
Emerald-67
Gold-67
Holographic Emerald-67
Holographic Gold-67
Holographic Silver-67
Ice Blue-67
Premiere Date-67
Red-67
Silver-67
Glove Side Net Fusions-6
Hall of Fame Bound-5
Hall of Fame Bound Proofs-5
Ice Advantage-6
Ice Advantage Proofs-6
Ice Alliance-8
Personal Best-10
Toronto Fall Expo '99-67
99Revolution-42
Premiere Date-42
Red-42
Shadow Series-42
Ice Sculptures-3
NHL Icons-6
Ornaments-7
Showstoppers-10
Copper-42
Gold-42
CSC Silver-42
99SP Authentic-24
Honor Roll-HR2
Special Forces-SF3
99SPx-43
Radiance-43
Spectrum-43
Highlight Heroes-HH5
SPXcitement-X2
SPXtreme-XT5
Starscape-S9
Winning Materials-WM7
99Stadium Club-66
First Day Issue-66
One of a Kind-66
Printing Plates Black-66
Printing Plates Cyan-66
Printing Plates Magenta-66
Printing Plates Yellow-66
Capture the Action-CA23
Capture the Action Game View-CAG23
Chrome-26
Chrome Refractors-26
Chrome Oversized-13
Chrome Oversized Refractors-13
99Topps/OPC-16
99Topps/OPC-284A
99Topps/OPC-284B
99Topps/OPC-284C
99Topps/OPC-284D
99Topps/OPC-284E
Ice Masters-IM18
Postmasters-PM5
99Topps Stanley Cup Heroes-SC9
99Topps Stanley Cup Heroes Refractors-SC9
99Topps/OPC Chrome-16
99Topps/OPC Chrome-284A
99Topps/OPC Chrome-284B
99Topps/OPC Chrome-284C
99Topps/OPC Chrome-284D
99Topps/OPC Chrome-284E
Refractors-16
Refractors-284A
Refractors-284B
Refractors-284C
Refractors-284D
Refractors-284E
Ice Masters-IM18
Ice Masters Refractors-IM18
Postmasters-PM5
Postmasters Refractors-PM5
99Topps Gold Label Class 1-16
Black-16
Black One of One-16
One of One-16
Red-16
Red One of One-16
99Topps Gold Label Class 2-16
99Topps Gold Label Class 2 Black-16
99Topps Gold Label Class 2 Black 1 of 1-16
99Topps Gold Label Class 2 One of One-16
99Topps Gold Label Class 2 Red-16
99Topps Gold Label Class 2 Red One of One-16
99Topps Gold Label Class 3-16
99Topps Gold Label Class 3 Black-16
99Topps Gold Label Class 3 Black 1 of 1-16
99Topps Gold Label Class 3 One of One-16
99Topps Gold Label Class 3 Red-16
99Topps Gold Label Class 3 Red One of One-16
99Topps Gold Label Quest for the Cup-QC4
99Topps Gold Label Quest for the Cup One of One - QC4
99Topps Gold Label Quest 4 the Cup Black-QC4
99Topps Gold Label Quest for the Cup Black One of One -QC4
99Topps Gold Label Quest for the Cup Red-QC4
99Topps Gold Label Quest for the Cup Red One of One -QC4

99Topps Premier Plus-23
Parallel-23
Imperial Guard-IG2
Premier Team-PT8
Premier Team Parallel-PT8
99Ultimate Victory-24
1/1-24
Parallel-24
Parallel 100-24
Net Work-NW2
The Victors-V5
UV Extra-UV2
99Upper Deck-141
99Upper Deck-210
Exclusives-141
Exclusives-210
Exclusives 1 of 1-141
Exclusives 1 of 1-210
All-Star Class-AS2
All-Star Class Quantum Gold-AS2
All-Star Class Quantum Silver-AS2
Crunch Time-CT27
Crunch Time Quantum Gold-CT27
Crunch Time Quantum Silver-CT27
Game Jerseys-PR
Game Jerseys Series II-PR
Game Jersey Patch-PRP
Game Jersey Patch 1 of 1-PRSP
Game Jersey Patch Series II-PRP
Game Jersey Patch Series II 1 of 1-PR-P1
Headed for the Hall-HOF10
Headed for the Hall Quantum Gold-HOF10
Headed for the Hall Quantum Silver-HOF10
Ice Gallery-IG5
Ice Gallery Quantum Gold-IG5
Ice Gallery Quantum Silver-IG5
Marquee Attractions-MA6
Marquee Attractions Quantum Gold-MA6
Marquee Attractions Quantum Silver-MA6
NHL Scrapbook-SB1
NHL Scrapbook Quantum Gold-SB1
NHL Scrapbook Quantum Silver-SB1
PowerDeck Inserts-PD5
Sixth Sense-SS2
Sixth Sense Quantum Gold-SS2
Sixth Sense Quantum Silver-SS2
Ultimate Defense-UD3
Ultimate Defense Quantum Gold-UD3
Ultimate Defense Quantum Silver-UD3
99Upper Deck Century Legends-35
99Upper Deck Century Legends-55
Century Collection-35
Century Collection-55
Essence of the Game-E5
99Upper Deck Gold Reserve-141
99Upper Deck Gold Reserve-210
Game-Used Souvenirs-GRPR
99Upper Deck HoloGrFx-17
Ausome-17
Impact Zone-IZ4
Impact Zone Ausome-IZ4
Pure Skill-PS6
Pure Skill Ausome-PS6
99Upper Deck MVP-55
Gold Script-55
Silver Script-55
Super Script-55
90's Snapshots-S3
Draw Your Own Trading Card-W10
Draw Your Own Trading Card-W19
Last Line-LL3
Talent-MVP7
99Upper Deck MVP SC Edition-51
Gold Script-51
Silver Script-51
Super Script-51
Golden Memories-GM2
Great Combinations-GCRF
Great Combinations Parallel-GCRF
Playoff Heroes-PH3
Stanley Cup Talent-SC5
99Upper Deck Ovation-15
99Upper Deck Ovation-86
Standing Ovation-15
Standing Ovation-86
A Piece Of History-PR
Lead Performers-LP20
Superstar Theater-ST4
99Upper Deck PowerDeck-8
Auxiliary-8
Auxiliary 1 of 1-8
Time Capsule-T3
Time Capsule Auxiliary-T3
Time Capsule Auxiliary 1 of 1-T3
99Upper Deck Retro-20
Gold-20
Platinum-20
Distant Replay-DR7
Distant Replay Level 2-DR7
Generation-G3B
Generation Level 2-G3B
Turn of the Century-TC7
99Upper Deck Victory-78
99Upper Deck Victory-325
99Upper Deck Victory-350
99Upper Deck Victory-376
99Wayne Gretzky Hockey-50
Changing The Game-CG10
Great Heroes-GH5
Tools of Greatness-TGPR
Will to Win-W5
99Quebec PeeWee Tournament Coll Souv-4
00SLU Hockey One On One-40
00McFarlane Hockey-50
00Aurora-40
Pinstripes-40
Pinstripes Premiere Date-40
Premiere Date-40
Canvas Creations-3
Championship Fever-6
Championship Fever Copper-6
Championship Fever Platinum Blue-6
Championship Fever Silver-6
Styrotechs-3B
00BAP Memorabilia-104
Emerald-104
Ruby-104
Sapphire-104
Promos-104
Georges Vezina-V9
Georges Vezina-V11
Georges Vezina-V12
Goalie Memorabilia-G2
Goalie Memorabilia-G15
Goalie Memorabilia-G21
Goalie Memorabilia-G28
Jersey Cards-J34
Jersey Emblems-E34
Jersey Numbers-N34
Jersey and Stick Cards-JS34
00BAP Mem Chicago Sportsfest Copper-104
00BAP Memorabilia Chicago Sportsfest Blue-104
00BAP Memorabilia Chicago Sportsfest Gold-104
00BAP Memorabilia Chicago Sportsfest Ruby-104

00BAP Memorabilia Chicago Sun-Times Ruby-104
00BAP Memorabilia Chicago Sun-Times Gold-104
00BAP Mem Chicago Sun-Times Sapphire-104
00BAP Mem Toronto Fall Expo Copper-104
00BAP Memorabilia Toronto Fall Expo Gold-104
00BAP Memorabilia Toronto Fall Expo Ruby-104
00BAP Mem Update Heritage Jersey Cards-H11
00BAP Mem Update Heritage Jersey Gold-H11
00BAP Memorabilia Update Record Breakers-RB1
00BAP Mem Update Record Breakers Gold-RB1
00BAP Memorabilia Update Teammates-TM18
00BAP Memorabilia Update Teammates-TM28
00BAP Memorabilia Update Teammates Gold-TM18
00BAP Memorabilia Update Teammates Gold-TM28
00BAP Parkhurst 2000-P97
00BAP Signature Series-211
Emerald-211
Ruby-211
Sapphire-211
Autographs-106
Autographs Gold-106
He Shoots-He Scores Points-16
He Shoots-He Scores Prizes-3
Jersey Cards-J23
Jersey and Stick Cards-GSJ23
Jersey Cards Autographs-J23
Jersey Emblems-E23
Jersey Numbers-IN23
00BAP Ultimate Memorabilia Autographs-23
Gold-23
00BAP Ultimate Memorabilia Active Eight-AE5
00BAP Ultimate Memorabilia Active Eight-AE6
00BAP Ultimate Mem Game-Used Jerseys-GJ23
00BAP Ultimate Mem Game-Used Emblems-E21
00BAP Ultimate Mem Game-Used Numbers-N21
00BAP Ultimate Mem Game-Used Sticks-GS23
00BAP Ultimate Mem Goalie Memorabilia-GM1
00BAP Ultimate Mem Goalie Memorabilia-GM2
00BAP Ultimate Mem Goalie Memorabilia-GM11
00BAP Ultimate Mem Goalie Memorabilia-GM20
00BAP Ultimate Memorabilia Goalie Sticks-G8
00BAP Ultimate Mem Plante Jersey Cards-PJ1
00BAP Ultimate Mem Plante Skate Cards-PS1
00BAP Ultimate Mem Journey Jerseys-JJ12
00BAP Ultimate Mem Journey Emblems-JE12
00BAP Ultimate Mem Journey Numbers-JI12
00BAP Ultimate Mem Magnificent Ones-ML5
00BAP Ultimate Mem Magnificent Ones Autos-ML5
00BAP Ultimate Memorabilia NHL Records-R2
00BAP Ultimate Memorabilia Retro-Active-RA2
00BAP Ultimate Memorabilia Retro-Active-RA8
00BAP Ultimate Memorabilia Teammates-TM15
00BAP Ultimate Memorabilia Teammates-TM17
00Black Diamond-14
00Black Diamond-86
Gold-14
Gold-86
Diamonation-IG2
Diamond Skills-IC1
00Crown Royale-30
Ice Blue-30
Limited Series-30
Premiere Date-30
Red-30
Jewels of the Crown-9
Landmarks-4
Now Playing-6
00McDonald's Pacific-9
Blue-9
Glove Side Net Fusions-2
Game Jerseys-3
00O-Pee-Chee-2
00O-Pee-Chee Parallel-2
00Pacific-120
Copper-120
Gold-120
Ice Blue-120
Premiere Date-120
2001: Ice Odyssey-8
Cramer's Choice-4
Jerseys-3
Jersey Patches-3
Gold Crown Die-Cuts-10
In the Cage Net-Fusions-3
North American Stars-3
00Pacific 2001: Ice Odyssey Anaheim Ntnl-8
00Panini Stickers-131
00Paramount-62
Copper-62
Gold-62
Holo-Gold-62
Holo-Silver-62
Ice Blue-62
Premiere Date-62
Epic Scope-6
Freeze Frame-10
Glove Side Net Fusions-7
Glove Side Net Fusions Platinum-7
Hall of Fame Bound-4
Hall of Fame Bound Canvas Proofs-4
Hall of Fame Bound Proofs-4
Sub Zero-3
Sub Zero Gold-3
Sub Zero Red-3
00Private Stock-25
Gold-25
Premiere Date-25
Retail-25
Silver-25
Artist's Canvas-7
Artist's Canvas Proofs-7
Extreme Action-4
Game Gear-28
PS-2001 Action-12
PS-2001 Stars-7
Reserve-6
00Revolution-38
Blue-38
Premiere Date-38
Red-38
HD NHL-11
Ice Immortals-6
NHL Icons-7
Stat Masters-13
00SP Authentic-23
Honor-SP2
Super Stoppers-SS2
00SP Game Used-13
Patch Cards-D-FR
Patch Cards-P-PR
Tools of the Game-PR
Tools of the Game Exclusives-PR
Tools of the Game Combos-C-RF
00SPx-15
00SPx-83
Spectrum-15
Spectrum-83
Winning Materials-PR
Winning Materials-WRO
00Stadium Club-40
Beam Team-BT12
Glove Save-GS3
Special Forces-SF16
00Titanium-22

Blue-22
Gold-22
Premiere Date-22
Red-22
Retail-22
All-Stars-4NA
Game Gear-8
Game Gear-78
Game Gear Patches-78
Three-Star Selections-2
00Titanium Draft Day Edition-25
00Topps/OPC-2
Parallel-2
Combos-TC8
Combos Jumbos-TC8
Hobby Masters-HM9
Own the Game-OTG16
00Topps Chrome-2
OPC Refractors-2
Refractors-2
Combos-TC8
Combos Refractors-TC8
Hobby Masters Refractors-HM9
00Topps Gold Label Class 1-51
Gold-51
00Topps Gold Label Class 2-51
00Topps Gold Label Class 2 Gold-51
00Topps Gold Label Class 3-51
00Topps Gold Label Class 3 Gold-51
00Topps Gold Label Behind the Mask-BTM8
00Topps Gold Label Behind the Mask 1 to 1-BTM8
00Topps Gold Label Bullion-B4
00Topps Gold Label Bullion One to One-B4
00Topps Heritage-24
Chrome Parallel-24
Heroes-HH5
00Topps Premier Plus-8
Blue Ice-8
Masters of the Break-MB12
Trophy Tribute-TT3
World Premier-WP1
00Topps Stars-2
00Topps Stars-136
Blue-2
Blue-136
All-Star Authority-ASA4
Game Gear-GGPR
Progression-P4
Walk of Fame-WF6
00UD Heroes-141
Game-Used Twigs-T-PR
Game-Used Twigs Gold-C-RB
Player Idols-PI2
Second Season Heroes-SS1
Timeless Moments-TM3
00UD Pros and Prospects-23
Championship Rings-CR1
Game Jerseys-PR
Game Jersey Exclusives-PR
Great Skates-GS3
00UD Reserve-22
Golden Goalies-GG3
Power Portfolios-PP1
00Upper Deck-45
Exclusives Tier 1-45
Exclusives Tier 2-45
Dignitaries-D3
Game Jersey Patches-PRP
Game Jersey Patch Autographs Exclusives-PRP
Gate Attractions-GA4
Lord Stanley's Heroes-L1
Skilled Stars-SS5
Triple Threat-TT2
00Upper Deck Ice-10
Immortals-10
Legends-10
Stars-10
Champions-IC1
Gallery-IG2
00Upper Deck Legends-31
00Upper Deck Legends-36
00Upper Deck Legends-73
Legendary Collection Bronze-31
Legendary Collection Bronze-36
Legendary Collection Bronze-73
Legendary Collection Gold-31
Legendary Collection Gold-36
Legendary Collection Gold-73
Legendary Collection Silver-31
Legendary Collection Silver-36
Legendary Collection Silver-73
Essence of the Game-EG4
Legendary Game Jerseys-JPR
of the Cage-LC1
Playoff Heroes-PH1
Supreme Milestones-SM9
00Upper Deck MVP-50
First Stars-50
Game-Used Souvenirs-GSPR
Masked Men-MM2
Second Stars-50
Super Game-Used Souvenirs-GSPR
Talent-M5
Third Stars-50
Valuable Commodities-VC2
00Upper Deck Victory-61
00Upper Deck Victory-244
00Upper Deck Victory-292
00Upper Deck Vintage-87
00Upper Deck Vintage-98
00Upper Deck Vintage-99
All UD Team-UD1
Great Gloves-GG6
National Heroes-NH8
Star Tandems-S2B
00Vanguard-29
Cosmic Force-4
High Voltage-8
High Voltage Gold-8
High Voltage Green-8
High Voltage Red-8
High Voltage Silver-8
Holographic Gold-29
Holographic Purple-29
In Focus-6
Pacific Proofs-29
Press East/West-4
00Czech Stadion-75
00Czech Stadion-120
01McFarlane Hockey Inserts-40
01McFarlane Hockey Inserts-42
01Atomic-26
Blue-26
Gold-26
Premiere Date-26
Red-26
Core Players-3
Jerseys-13
Patches-13
Statosphere-1
Team Nucleus-4
01Avalanche Team Issue-19
01BAP Memorabilia-133
Emerald-133
Ruby-133
Sapphire-133
All-Star Jerseys-ASJ5
All-Star Emblems-ASE5
All-Star Numbers-ASN5
All-Star Jersey Doubles-DASJ2
All-Star Starting Lineup-S7
All-Star Teammates-AST3
All-Star Teammates-AST12
All-Star Teammates-AST35
All-Star Teammates-AST37
All-Star Teammates-AST50
Country of Origin-CO10
Goalies Jerseys-GJ6
Goalie Traditions-GT4
Goalie Traditions-GT28
Goalie Traditions-GT30
Goalie Traditions-GT40
He Shoots-He Scores Points-15
He Shoots-He Scores Prizes-26
Stanley Cup Champions-CA1
Stanley Cup Playoffs-SC17
Stanley Cup Playoffs-SC32
01BAP Signature Series Certified 100-C59
01BAP Signature Series Certified 50-C59
01BAP Signature Series Certified 1 of 1's-C59
01BAP Signature Series Jerseys-GJ-17
01BAP Sig Series Jersey and Stick Cards-GSJ-17
01BAP Signature Series Emblems-GUE-16
01BAP Signature Series Numbers-ITN-16
01BAP Signature Series Teammates-TM-8
01BAP Ultimate Memorabilia Active Eight-2
01BAP Ultimate Mem All-Star History-39
01BAP Ultimate Mem Complete Package-8
01BAP Ultimate Memorabilia Cornerstones-2
01BAP Ultimate Memorabilia Decades-19
01BAP Ultimate Memorabilia Emblems-27
01BAP Ultimate Memorabilia Jerseys-27
01BAP Ultimate Mem Jerseys and Sticks-27
01BAP Ultimate Mem Journey Jerseys-15
01BAP Ultimate Mem Journey Emblems-15
01BAP Ultimate Mem Legend Terry Sawchuk-1
01BAP Ultimate Memorabilia Les Canadiens-10
01BAP Ultimate Memorabilia Numbers-27
01BAP Ultimate Memorabilia Name Plates-11
01BAP Ultimate Mem Playoff Records-1
01BAP Ultimate Mem Playoff Records-2
01BAP Ultimate Mem Prototypical Players-1
01BAP Ultimate Memorabilia Retro Trophies-10
01BAP Ultimate Memorabilia Retro Trophies-14
01BAP Ultimate Memorabilia Retro Trophies-15
01BAP Update He Shoots-He Scores Points-18
01BAP Update He Shoots-He Scores Prizes-40
01BAP Update Heritage-H19
01Between the Pipes-1
01Between the Pipes-94
01Between the Pipes-111
All-Star Jerseys-ASJ9
All-Star Jerseys-ASJ16
Goalie Gear-GG23
He Shoots-He Saves Points-19
He Shoots-He Saves Prizes-27
Jerseys-GJ6
Emblems-GUE3
Jersey and Stick Cards-GSJ6
Masks-13
Masks Silver-13
Masks Gold-13
Record Breakers-RB1
Record Breakers-RB10
Record Breakers-RB11
Record Breakers-RB16
Record Breakers-RB17
Tandems-GT5
Trophy Winners-TW1
01Bowman YoungStars-1
Gold-1
Ice Cubed-1
01Crown Royale-39
Blue-39
Premiere Date-39
Red-39
Retail-39
All-Star Honors-4
Crowning Achievement-12
Jewels of the Crown-7
Legendary Heroes-2
Triple Threads-4
Triple Threads-7
01eTopps-8
01Greats of the Game Jerseys-9
01Greats of the Game Sticks-12
01McDonald's Pacific-6
Glove-Side Net-Fusion-1
Jersey Patches Silver-3
Jersey Patches Gold-3
01Nortel All-Star Game Sheets-11
01O-Pee-Chee-47
01O-Pee-Chee-324
01O-Pee-Chee Heritage Parallel-47
01O-Pee-Chee Heritage Parallel Limited-47
01O-Pee-Chee Premier Parallel-47
01O-Pee-Chee Premier Parallel-324
01O-Pee-Chee Jumbos-5
01Pacific-106
01Pacific-427
Extreme LTD-106
Gold-427
Hobby LTD-106
Premiere Date-106
Retail LTD-106
All-Stars-NA4
Cramer's Choice-3
Gold Crown Die-Cuts-6
Impact Zone-7
Steel Curtain-5
01Pacific Adrenaline-49
Blue-49
Premiere Date-49
Red-49
Retail-49
Blade Runners-2
Creased Lightning-4
Jerseys-9
Power Play-9
01Pacific Arena Exclusives-106
01Pacific Arena Exclusives-427
01Pacific Heads-Up-25
Blue-25
Premiere Date-25
Red-25
Silver-25
Quad Jerseys-9
Quad Jerseys-20
Rink Immortals-2
Showstoppers-4
01Pacific Montreal International-2
01Parkhurst-4
Gold-4
Silver-4
He Shoots-He Scores Points-13
He Shoots-He Scores Prizes-2
Heroes-H3
Jerseys-PJ38
Jersey and Stick-PSJ5
Milestones-M18
Milestones-M37
Milestones-M39
Sticks-PS54
Teammates-T8
Teammates-T22
01Private Stock-23
Gold-23
Premiere Date-23
Retail-23
Silver-23
Game Gear-30
Game Gear Patches-30
01Private Stock Pacific Nights-23
01Private Stock PS-2002-19
01Private Stock Reserve-G2
01SP Authentic-18
01SP Authentic-93
Limited-18
Limited-93
Limited Gold-18
Limited Gold-93
Sign of the Times-PR
01SP Game Used-12
Authentic Fabric-AFPR
Authentic Fabric-DFBR
Authentic Fabric-TFFSR
Authentic Fabric-FSRB
Authentic Fabric Gold-AFPR
Patches-PPR
Patches-CPKR
Patches-CPSR
Tools of the Game-TPR
Tools of the Game-CTFR
Tools of the Game-CTRC
Tools of the Game-CTRF
Tools of the Game-TTDER
Tools of the Game-TTHCR
Tools of the Game-TTRBK
01SPx-17
01SPx-83
Hockey Treasures-HTPR
01Sports Illustrated for Kids III-106
01Stadium Club-87
Award Winners-87
Master Photos-87
Gallery-G29
Gallery Gold-G29
Heart and Soul-HS2
Perennials-P5
Souvenirs-PRMB
Souvenirs-EBMBPR
01Titanium-36
Hobby Parallel-36
Premiere Date-36
Retail-36
Retail Parallel-36
All-Stars-6
Double-Sided Jerseys-13
Double-Sided Patches-13
Three-Star Selections-3
01Topps-47
01Topps-324
Heritage Parallel-47
Heritage Parallel Limited-47
OPC Parallel-47
OPC Parallel-324
Own The Game-OTG22
01Topps Chrome-47
Refractors-47
Black Border Refractors-47
01Topps Heritage-76
01Topps Heritage-128
01Topps Heritage-131
Refractors-76
01Topps Heritage Avalanche NHL AS Game-2
01Topps Reserve-19
Emblems-PR
Jerseys-PR
Name Plates-PR
Numbers-PR
Patches-PR
01UD Challenge for the Cup-20
500 Game Winner-500PR
500 Game Winner-500PRA
All-Time Lineup-AT6
Backstops-BB3
Future Famers-FF2
Jerseys-TPR
Jerseys-TNPR
Jersey Autographs-TPR
01UD Honor Roll-6
01UD Honor Roll-36
Honor Society-HS-RB
Honor Society Gold-HS-RB
Original Six-OS4
Playoff Matchups-HS-RB
Playoff Matchups Gold-HS-RB
Tribute to 500-1
Tribute to 500-2
01UD Mask Collection-108
01UD Mask Collection-175
Gold-108
Gold-175
Double Patches-DPPR
Dual Jerseys-MBPR
Dual Jerseys-PMYR
Goalie Jerseys-SYPR
Goalie Jerseys-VCPR
Goalie Jerseys-CGPR
Goalie Pads-GPPR
Jerseys-J-PR
Jersey and Patch-JPPR
01UD Playmakers-26
Combo Jerseys-CJPR
Combo Jerseys Gold-CJPR
01UD Premier Collection-12
Dual Jerseys-DRB
Dual Jerseys-DSR
Dual Jerseys Black-DRB
Dual Jerseys Black-DSR
Jerseys-BPR
Jerseys-GPR
Jerseys Black-B-PR
Jerseys Black-G-PR
Signatures-PR
Signatures Black-PR
01UD Stanley Cup Champs-38
01UD Stanley Cup Champs-67
Jerseys-T-PR
Jerseys-T-RO
Pieces of Glory-G-PR
Pieces of Glory-G-RO
Sticks-S-PR
Sticks-S-RO
01UD Top Shelf-12
All-Star Nets-NPR
Jerseys-PR
Patches-PPR
Sticks-SPR
Sticks-BPR
Sticks-RSF
Sticks Gold-SPR
Sticks Gold-BPR
Sticks Gold-RSF
01Upper Deck-219
01Upper Deck-276
Exclusives-219
Exclusives-276
Franchise Cornerstones-FC9
Game Jerseys-GJPR
Game Jerseys-CFR
Game Jerseys-FSR
Game Jerseys Series II-FJPR
Game Jerseys Series II-SSPR
Game Jerseys Series II-DJBR
Game Jerseys Series II-TJRBH
Goalies in Action-GL6
Goaltender Threads-TTPR
Last Line of Defense-LL1
Patches-PPR
Patches Series II-PLPR
Patches Series II-PNPR
Patches Series II-NAPR
Pride of a Nation-PNPR
Pride of a Nation-DPRS
Pride of a Nation-TPYRL
Skilled Stars-SS12
01Upper Deck Avalanche NHL All-Star Game-HH1
01Upper Deck Avalanche NHL All-Star Game-PP1
01Upper Deck Ice-8
Combos-C-PR
Combos Gold-G-PR
Jerseys-J-PR
01Upper Deck MVP-49
Goalie Sticks-G-PR
Masked Men-MM3
01Upper Deck Rookie Upd Signs of History-1
01Upper Deck Victory-83
01Upper Deck Victory-92
01Upper Deck Victory-396
Gold-83
Gold-92
Gold-396
01Upper Deck Vintage-68
01Upper Deck Vintage-70
01Upper Deck Vintage-267
01Vanguard-26
Blue-26
Red-26
East Meets West-2
In Focus-1
Memorabilia-10
Memorabilia-43
One of Ones-26
Patches-10
Premiere Date-26
Proofs-26
Quebec Tournament Heroes-3
Stonewallers-5
V-Team-2
02McFarlane Hockey-240
02McFarlane Hockey-242
02Atomic-26
Blue-26
Gold-26
Red-26
Denied-5
Hobby Parallel-26
02BAP All-Star Edition-77
02BAP All-Star Edition-78
02BAP All-Star Edition-79
He Shoots-He Scores Points-16
He Shoots-He Score Prizes-24
Jerseys-77
Jerseys-78
Jerseys-79
Jerseys Gold-77
Jerseys Gold-78
Jerseys Gold-79
Jerseys Silver-77
Jerseys Silver-78
Jerseys Silver-79
02BAP First Edition-147
02BAP First Edition-327
02BAP First Edition-348
02BAP First Edition-376
02BAP First Edition-377
02BAP First Edition-389
Debut Jerseys-2
He Shoots-He Scores Prizes-23
Jerseys-147
02BAP Memorabilia-164
02BAP Memorabilia-208
02BAP Memorabilia-232
Emerald-164
Emerald-208
Emerald-232
Ruby-164
Ruby-208
Ruby-232
Sapphire-164
Sapphire-208
Sapphire-232
All-Star Jerseys-ASJ-50
All-Star Emblems-ASE-19
All-Star Numbers-ASN-19
All-Star Starting Lineup-AS-1
All-Star Teammmates-AST-3
All-Star Teammmates-AST-22
All-Star Teammmates-AST-26
All-Star Triple Jerseys-ASTJ-17
Franchise Players-FP-8
He Shoots-He Scores Points-18
He Shoots-He Scores Prizes-3
Mini Stanley Cups-24
NHL All-Star Game-164
NHL All-Star Game-208
NHL All-Star Game-232
NHL All-Star Game Blue-164
NHL All-Star Game Blue-208
NHL All-Star Game Blue-232
NHL All-Star Game Green-164
NHL All-Star Game Green-208
NHL All-Star Game Green-232
NHL All-Star Game Red-164
NHL All-Star Game Red-208
NHL All-Star Game Red-232
Stanley Cup Playoffs-SC-28
Teammates-TM-5
02BAP Memorabilia Toronto Fall Expo-164
02BAP Memorabilia Toronto Fall Expo-208
02BAP Memorabilia Toronto Fall Expo-232
02BAP NHL All-Star History-39
02BAP Signature Series-160
Autographs-160
Autograph Buybacks 1998-34
Autograph Buybacks 1999-66
Autograph Buybacks 2000-106
Autographs Gold-160
Complete Jersey-CJ2
Defensive Wall-DW1
Famous Scraps-FS10
Golf-GS69
Jerseys-SGJ4
Jersey Autographs-SGJ4
Triple Memorabilia-TM6
02BAP Ultimate Memorabilia Active Eight-3
02BAP Ultimate Memorabilia Active Eight-6
02BAP Ultimate Memorabilia Autographs-15
02BAP Ultimate Mem Autographs Gold-15
02BAP Ultimate Mem Complete Package-8
02BAP Ultimate Memorabilia Conn Smythe-15
02BAP Ultimate Memorabilia Conn Smythe-21
02BAP Ultimate Memorabilia Conn Smythe-29
02BAP Ultimate Memorabilia Cup Duels-10
02BAP Ultimate Memorabilia Cup Duels-13
02BAP Ultimate Memorabilia Cup Duels-17
02BAP Ultimate Memorabilia Cup Duels-20
02BAP Ultimate Memorabilia Emblems-21
02BAP Ultimate Memorabilia Great Moments-10
02BAP Ultimate Memorabilia Jerseys-28
02BAP Ultimate Mem Jersey and Stick-1
02BAP Ultimate Mem Journey Jerseys-1
02BAP Ultimate Mem Journey Emblems-1
02BAP Ultimate Mem Lifetime Achievers-7
02BAP Ultimate Mem Magnificent Ones-1
02BAP Ultimate Mem Magnificent Ones Autos-1
02BAP Ultimate Memorabilia Nameplates-7
02BAP Ultimate Memorabilia Numbers-5
02BAP Ultimate Memorabilia Retro Trophies-2
02BAP Ultimate Mem Storied Franchise-7
02Between the Pipes-1
02Between the Pipes-128
Gold-1
Silver-1
All-Star Stick and Jersey-4
Behind the Mask-3
Complete Package-CP1
Double Memorabilia-7
Emblems-25
He Shoots-He Saves Points-19
He Shoots-He Saves Prizes-1
Inspirations-I1
Inspirations-I3
Inspirations-I4
Inspirations-I8
Jerseys-25
Masks II-8
Masks II Gold-8
Masks II Silver-8
Numbers-25
Pads-2
Record Breakers-2
Record Breakers-5
Record Breakers-12
Record Breakers-15
Stick and Jerseys-25
Tandems-2
Trappers-GT12
02Bowman Toronto Spring Expo-7
02Bowman YoungStars-55
Gold-55
Silver-55
02Crown Royale-25
Blue-25
Red-25
Retail-25
Dual Patches-5
Coats of Armor-1
Royal Portraits-3
02eTopps-3
02ITG Used-15
02ITG Used-115
Franchise Players-F8
Franchise Players Autographs-F8
Franchise Players Gold-F8
Goalie Pad and Jersey-GP2
Goalie Pad and Jersey Gold-GP2
Jerseys-GUJ4
Jersey Autographs-GUJ4
Jerseys Gold-GUJ4
Emblems-E4
Jersey and Stick-SJ4
Jersey and Stick Gold-SJ4
Teammates-T2
Teammates Gold-T2
02McDonald's Pacific-9
Cup Contenders Die-Cuts-2
Glove Side Net-Fusions-1
02Nextel NHL All-Star Game-1
02O-Pee-Chee-1
02O-Pee-Chee-317
02O-Pee-Chee-320
02O-Pee-Chee Jumbos-5
02O-Pee-Chee Premier Blue Parallel-1
02O-Pee-Chee Premier Blue Parallel-317
02O-Pee-Chee Premier Blue Parallel-320
02O-Pee-Chee Premier Red Parallel-1
02O-Pee-Chee Premier Red Parallel-317
02O-Pee-Chee Premier Red Parallel-320
02O-Pee-Chee Factory Set-1
02O-Pee-Chee Factory Set-317
02O-Pee-Chee Factory Set-320
02Pacific-95
Blue-95
Red-95
Cramer's Choice-5
Main Attractions-5
Maximum Impact-2
02Pacific Calder-34
Silver-34
Chasing Glory-3
Hardware Heroes-2
Hart Stoppers-3
02Pacific Complete-165
Red-165
02Pacific Exclusive-45
Advantage-4
Etched in Stone-3
02Pacific Heads-Up-32
Blue-32
Purple-32
Red-32
Etched in Time-7
Inside the Numbers-7
Postseason Picks-4
Showstoppers-6
02Pacific Les Gardiens-3
Gold-3
02Pacific Quest for the Cup-23
Gold-23
Jerseys-6
Raising the Cup-2
02Pacific Toronto Fall Expo-2
Gold-2
02Parkhurst-102
Bronze-102
Gold-102
Silver-102
Franchise Players-FP8
Hardware-V7
He Shoots-He Scores Points-6
He Shoots-He Scores Prizes-16
Jerseys-GJ49
Mario's Mates-MM1
Milestones-MS11
Stick and Jerseys-SJ49
Teammates-TT19
02Parkhurst Retro-18
Minis-18
He Shoots-He Scores Points-19
He Shoots-He Scores Prizes-3
Hopefuls-VH7
Jerseys-RJ1
Jersey and Sticks-RSJ1
Memorabilia-RM6
Nicknames-RN24
02Private Stock Reserve-110
Red-110
Retail-110
Elite-3
InCrease Security-5
02SP Authentic-22
Beckett Promos-22
Sign of the Times-PR
Sign of the Times-BR
Super Premiums-SPPR
Super Premiums-DPFR
Super Premiums-TPRBB
02SP Game Used-13
Authentic Fabrics-AFPR
Authentic Fabrics-AFRY
Authentic Fabrics Gold-AFPR
Authentic Fabrics Gold-AFRY
Authentic Fabrics Rainbow-AFPR
Authentic Fabrics Rainbow-AFRY
Piece of History-PHPR
Piece of History-PHRY
Piece of History Gold-PHPR
Piece of History Gold-PHRY
Piece of History Rainbow-PHPR
Piece of History Rainbow-PHRY
Signature Style-PR
Tools of the Game-PR
02SPx-16
02SPx-84
Spectrum Gold-16
Spectrum Gold-84
Spectrum Silver-16
Spectrum Silver-84
Milestones-MPR
Milestones Gold-PR
Milestones Silver-PR
Winning Materials-WMRO
Winning Materials Gold-RO
Winning Materials Silver-RO
Xtreme Talents-PR
Xtreme Talents Gold-PR
Xtreme Talents Silver-PR
02Stadium Club-73
Silver Decoy Cards-73
Proofs-73
Beam Team-BT3
Puck Stops Here-PSH14
St. Patrick Relics-SAS
St. Patrick Relics-CAJ
St. Patrick Relics-MCJ
St. Patrick Relics-CAJA
St. Patrick Relics-MCJA
St. Patrick Relics-SPS
St. Patrick Relics-CAJP
St. Patrick Relics-MCJP
St. Patrick Relics-CAMCJ
St. Patrick Relics-CAMCJA
St. Patrick Relics-CAMCJS
St. Patrick Relics-CAMCJSA
St. Patrick Relics-CAJPA
St. Patrick Relics-MCJPA
St. Patrick Relics-CAMCJP
St. Patrick Relics-CAMCJPA
02Titanium-26
Blue-26
Red-26
Retail-26
Jerseys-18
Jerseys Retail-18
Saturday Knights-2
Masked Marauders-1
Shadows-3
02Topps-1
02Topps-317
02Topps-320
OPC Blue Parallel-1
OPC Blue Parallel-317
OPC Blue Parallel-320
OPC Red Parallel-1
OPC Red Parallel-317
OPC Red Parallel-320
Topps/OPC Hometown Heroes-HHU19
Patrick Roy Reprints-1
Patrick Roy Reprints-2
Patrick Roy Reprints-3
Patrick Roy Reprints-4
Patrick Roy Reprints-5
Patrick Roy Reprints-6
Patrick Roy Reprints-7
Patrick Roy Reprints-8
Patrick Roy Reprints-9
Patrick Roy Reprints-10
Patrick Roy Reprints-11
Patrick Roy Reprints-12
Patrick Roy Reprints-13
Patrick Roy Reprints-14
Patrick Roy Reprints Autographs-1
Patrick Roy Reprints Autographs-2
Patrick Roy Reprints Autographs-3
Patrick Roy Reprints Autographs-4
Patrick Roy Reprints Autographs-5
Patrick Roy Reprints Autographs-6
Patrick Roy Reprints Autographs-7
Patrick Roy Reprints Autographs-8
Patrick Roy Reprints Autographs-9
Patrick Roy Reprints Autographs-10
Patrick Roy Reprints Autographs-11
Patrick Roy Reprints Autographs-12
Patrick Roy Reprints Autographs-13
Patrick Roy Reprints Autographs-14
Factory Set-1
Factory Set-317
Factory Set-320
Factory Set Hometown Heroes-HHU19
Factory Set Patrick Roy Reprints-1
Factory Set Patrick Roy Reprints-2
Factory Set Patrick Roy Reprints-3
Factory Set Patrick Roy Reprints-4
Factory Set Patrick Roy Reprints-5
Factory Set Patrick Roy Reprints-6
Factory Set Patrick Roy Reprints-7
Factory Set Patrick Roy Reprints-8
Factory Set Patrick Roy Reprints-9
Factory Set Patrick Roy Reprints-10
Factory Set Patrick Roy Reprints-11
Factory Set Patrick Roy Reprints-12
Factory Set Patrick Roy Reprints-13
Factory Set Patrick Roy Reprints-14
02Topps Chrome-1
Black Border Refractors-1
Refractors-1
e-Topps Decoy Cards-3
Patrick Roy Reprints-1
Patrick Roy Reprints-2
Patrick Roy Reprints-3
Patrick Roy Reprints-4
Patrick Roy Reprints-5
Patrick Roy Reprints-6
Patrick Roy Reprints-7
Patrick Roy Reprints-8
Patrick Roy Reprints-9
Patrick Roy Reprints-10
Patrick Roy Reprints-11
Patrick Roy Reprints-12
Patrick Roy Reprints-13
Patrick Roy Reprints-14
Patrick Roy Reprints-15
Patrick Roy Reprints-16
Patrick Roy Reprints-17
Patrick Roy Reprints-18
Patrick Roy Reprints-19
Patrick Roy Reprints-20
Patrick Roy Reprints-21
Patrick Roy Reprints-22
Patrick Roy Reprints-23
Patrick Roy Reprints-24
Patrick Roy Reprints-25
Patrick Roy Reprints Refractors-1
Patrick Roy Reprints Refractors-2
Patrick Roy Reprints Refractors-3
Patrick Roy Reprints Refractors-4
Patrick Roy Reprints Refractors-5
Patrick Roy Reprints Refractors-6
Patrick Roy Reprints Refractors-7
Patrick Roy Reprints Refractors-8
Patrick Roy Reprints Refractors-9
Patrick Roy Reprints Refractors-10
Patrick Roy Reprints Refractors-11
Patrick Roy Reprints Refractors-12
Patrick Roy Reprints Refractors-13
Patrick Roy Reprints Refractors-14
Patrick Roy Reprints Refractors-15
Patrick Roy Reprints Refractors-16
Patrick Roy Reprints Refractors-17
Patrick Roy Reprints Refractors-18
Patrick Roy Reprints Refractors-19
Patrick Roy Reprints Refractors-20
Patrick Roy Reprints Refractors-21
Patrick Roy Reprints Refractors-22
Patrick Roy Reprints Refractors-23
Patrick Roy Reprints Refractors-24
Patrick Roy Reprints Refractors-25
Patrick Roy Reprint Autographs-COA
Patrick Roy Reprint Autographs-CTA
Patrick Roy Reprint Auto Refractors-COA
Patrick Roy Reprint Auto Refractors-CTA
Patrick Roy Reprint Relics-PRJO1
Patrick Roy Reprint Relics-PRJT1
Patrick Roy Reprint Relics-PRP1
Patrick Roy Reprint Relics-PRPT1
02Topps Heritage-27
02Topps Heritage-102
02Topps Heritage-116
02Topps Heritage-117
02Topps Heritage-123
Chrome Parallel-27
USA Test Parallel-27
02Topps Total-11
Award Winners-AW2
Team Checklists-TTC7
Topps-TT2
02UD Artistic Impressions-21
Gold-21
Artist's Touch-ATPR
Artist's Touch Gold-ATPR
02UD Artistic Impressions Beckett Promos-21
02UD Artistic Impressions Common Ground-CG1
02UD Artistic Impress Common Ground Gold-CG1
02UD Artistic Impressions Great Depiction-GD2
02UD Artistic Impress Great Depiction Gld-GD2
02UD Artistic Impressions Performers-SSPR
02UD Artistic Impressions Performers Gold-SSPR
02UD Artistic Impressions Retrospectives-R21
02UD Artistic Impressions Retrospect Gold-R21
02UD Artistic Impress Retrospect Silver-R21
02Upper Deck Collectors Club-NHL6
02UD Foundations-17
02UD Foundations-54
02UD Foundations-112
02UD Foundations-120
02UD Foundations-147
Canadian Heroes-CPR
Canadian Heroes-CRO
Canadian Heroes Gold-CPR
Canadian Heroes Gold-CRO
Canadian Heroes Silver-C-PR
Canadian Heroes Silver-C-RO
Milestones-NPR
Milestones Gold-NPR
Milestones Silver-N-PR
Playoff Performers-PPR
Playoff Performers-PRO
Playoff Performers Gold-PPR
Playoff Performers Gold-PRO
Playoff Performers Silver-P-PR
Playoff Performers Silver-P-RO
02UD Honor Roll-15
Grade A Jerseys-GAPR
Grade A Jerseys-TRFS
Signature Class-PR
Students of the Game-SG7
02UD Mask Collection-21
02UD Mask Collection-22
02UD Mask Collection-23
02UD Mask Collection-92
02UD Mask Collection Beckett Promos-21
02UD Mask Collection Beckett Promos-22
02UD Mask Collection Beckett Promos-23
02UD Mask Collection Career Wins-CWPR
02UD Mask Collection Career Wins-CWRY
02UD Mask Collection Great Gloves-GGPR
02UD Mask Collection Masked Marvels-MMPR
02UD Mask Collection Mini Masks-PR
02UD Mask Collection Mini Masks Autos-PR
02UD Mask Collection Nation's Best-NRBP
02UD Mask Collection Patches-PWPR
02UD Mask Collection Super Stoppers-SSPR
02UD Mask Collection View from the Cage-VPR
02UD Piece of History-24
02UD Piece of History-94
Awards Collection-AC9
Exquisite Combos-ECBR
Hockey Beginnings-HB6
Marks of Distinction-PR
Patches-PHPR
Simply the Best-SB3
02UD Premier Collection-15
Jerseys Bronze-PR
Jerseys Bronze-BR
Jerseys Gold-PR
Jerseys Gold-BR
Jerseys Silver-PR
Jerseys Silver-BR
NHL Patches-PR1
Patches-PPR
Signatures Bronze-SPR
Signatures Bronze-ASPR
Signatures Gold-SPR
Signatures Gold-ASPR
Signatures Silver-SPR
Signatures Silver-ASPR
02UD Top Shelf-21
Clutch Performers-CPPR
Dual Player Jerseys-RRT
Hardware Heroes-HBRBD
Hardware Heroes-HHBRK
Hardware Heroes-HSRBF
Hardware Heroes-HYNLR
Milestones Jerseys-MRBRJ
Signatures-PR
Stopper Jerseys-SSPR
Triple Jerseys-TSTSR
02Upper Deck-43
02Upper Deck-179
02Upper Deck-185
Exclusives-43
Exclusives-179
Exclusives-185
All-Star Performers-ASPR
Blow-Ups-C7
Difference Makers-PR
First Class-UDPR
First Class Gold-UDPR
Game Jersey Autographs-PR
Game Jersey Series II-GJPR
Gifted Greats-GG4
Last Line of Defense-LL3
Patch Card Logo-PR
Patchwork-PWPR
Playbooks-PL4
Playbooks Series II-RT
Saviors Jerseys-SVPR
Super Saviors-SA4
02Upper Deck Classic Portraits-24
Etched in Time-ET3
Genuine Greatness-GG3
Headliners-RA
Headliners Limited-RA
Hockey Royalty-RBT
Hockey Royalty Limited-RBT
Mini-Busts-91
Mini-Busts-92
Mini-Busts-93
Mini-Busts-94
Mini-Busts-95
Mini-Busts-96
Mini-Busts-97
Mini-Busts-98
Mini-Busts-99
Mini-Busts-100
02Upper Deck MVP-44
02Upper Deck MVP-189
Gold-44
Gold-189
Classics-44
Classics-189
Golden Classics-44
Golden Classics-189
Masked Men-MM1
Prosign-PR
Skate Around Jerseys-SAPR
Skate Around Jerseys-SDRA
Skate Around Jerseys-STSFR
Vital Forces-VF5
02Upper Deck Pearson Awards-1
02Upper Deck Rookie Update-27
02Upper Deck Rookie Update-104
02Upper Deck Rookie Update-170
Autographs-PR
Jerseys-DPR
Jerseys-SRS
Jerseys Gold-DPR
Jerseys Gold-SRS
02Upper Deck Victory-50
02Upper Deck Victory-219
Bronze-50
Bronze-219
Gold-50
Gold-219
Silver-50
Silver-219
02Upper Deck Vintage-65
02Upper Deck Vintage-268
02Upper Deck Vintage-292
02Upper Deck Vintage-317
02Upper Deck Vintage-318
02Upper Deck Vintage-319
Tall Boys-T15
Tall Boys Gold-T15
02Vanguard-27
LTD-27
East Meets West-9
Stonewallers-1
V-Team-1
02UD SuperStars *-67
Gold-67
Keys to the City-K6
Legendary Leaders Triple Jersey-LBP
Magic Moments-MM19
03McFarlane Hockey 12-Inch Figures-20
03McFarlane Hockey 12-Inch Figures-22
03McFarlane Hockey 12-Inch Figures-24
03McFarlane Hockey-70
03McFarlane Hockey-72
03McFarlane Hockey-74
03McFarlane Hockey-76
03McFarlane Hockey-78
03BAP Memorabilia-153
Emerald-153
Gold-153
Ruby-153
Sapphire-153
All-Star Complete Jerseys-ASCJ3
All-Star Emblems-ASE-4
All-Star Jerseys-ASJ-8
All-Star Jerseys-ASJ-17
All-Star Jerseys-ASJ-28
All-Star Numbers-ASN-4
All-Star Staring Lineup-7
All-Star Teammates-AST1
All-Star Teammates-AST6
All-Star Teammates-AST8
Brush with Greatness-25
Brush with Greatness Contest Cards-25
Gloves-GUG2
He Shoots-He Scores Points-18
He Shoots-He Scores Prizes-7
Jersey and Stick-SJ-25
Jerseys-GJ-34
Jersey Autographs-GJ-34
03BAP Ultimate Memorabilia Autographs-158
Gold-158
03BAP Ultimate Mem Auto Jerseys-158
03BAP Ultimate Mem Auto Emblems-158
03BAP Ultimate Mem Auto Sticks-158
03BAP Ultimate Mem Always An All-Star-11
03BAP Ultimate Mem Always An AS Gold-11
03BAP Ultimate Memorabilia Career Year-4
03BAP Ultimate Mem Complete Jersey-12
03BAP Ultimate Mem Complete Jersey Gold-12
03BAP Ultimate Memorabilia Cornerstones-1
03BAP Ultimate Memorabilia Great Moments-3
03BAP Ultimate Memorabilia Heroes-8
03BAP Ultimate Memorabilia Heroes-10
03BAP Ultimate Memorabilia Heroes-11

03BAP Ultimate Memorabilia Heroes-13
03BAP Ultimate Mem Heroes Autos-5
03BAP Ultimate Mem Heroes Autos-6
03BAP Ultimate Mem Heroes Autos-7
03BAP Ultimate Mem Jersey and Emblems-31
03BAP Ultimate Mem Jersey and Emblem Gold-31
03BAP Ultimate Mem Jersey and Numbers-31
03BAP Ultimate Mem Jersey and Number Gold-31
03BAP Ultimate Mem Jersey and Stick-21
03BAP Ultimate Mem Jersey and Stick Gold-21
03BAP Ultimate Mem Journey Jerseys-6
03BAP Ultimate Mem Journey Jerseys Gold-6
03BAP Ultimate Mem Journey Emblems-6
03BAP Ultimate Mem Journey Emblems Gold-6
03BAP Ultimate Mem Lifetime Achievers-2
03BAP Ultimate Memorabilia Nameplates-30
03BAP Ultimate Mem Nameplates Gold-30
03BAP Ultimate Memorabilia Numbers-30
03BAP Ultimate Memorabilia Numbers Gold-30
03BAP Ultimate Mem Perennial Power Jersey-1
03BAP Ult Mem Perenn Powerhouse Jsy Stick-1
03BAP Ultimate Mem Perennial Power Emblem-1
03BAP Ultimate Mem Retro-Active Trophies-17
03BAP Ultimate Mem Retro-Active Trophies-19
03BAP Ultimate Mem Seams Unbelievable-2
03BAP Ultimate Memorabilia Triple Threads-7
03BAP Ultimate Mem Vint Complete Package-6
03BAP Ultimate Mem Vint Comp Package Gold-6
03BAP Ultimate Mem Vintage Jerseys-39
03BAP Ultimate Mem Vintage Jerseys Gold-39
03Beehive-51
Variations-51
Gold-51
Silver-51
Signatures-RF2
03Black Diamond Signature Gems-SG-23
03Duracell-13
03ITG Action-116
Highlight Reel-HR2
Jerseys-M195
Jerseys-M215
Jerseys-M227
Jerseys-M248
Oh Canada-OC2
03ITG Toronto Fall Expo Forever Rivals-FR2
03ITG Toronto Fall Expo Jerseys-FE25
03ITG Used Signature Series-117
Gold-117
Autographs-PR
Autographs Gold-PR
Game-Day Jerseys-6
Game-Day Jerseys Gold-6
Goalie Gear-8
Goalie Gear Autographs-8
Goalie Gear Gold-8
Jerseys-33
Jerseys Gold-33
Jersey Autos-33
Emblems-17
Emblems Gold-17
Jersey and Stick-33
Jersey and Stick Gold-33
Retrospectives-1A
Retrospectives-1B
Retrospectives-1C
Retrospectives-1D
Retrospectives-1E
Retrospectives-1F
Retrospectives Gold-1A
Retrospectives Gold-1B
Retrospectives Gold-1C
Retrospectives Gold-1D
Retrospectives Gold-1E
Retrospectives Gold-1F
Teammates-20
Teammates Gold-20
Triple Memorabilia-24
Triple Memorabilia Gold-24
03ITG VIP Brightest Stars-10
03ITG VIP Collages-4
03ITG VIP Jerseys-10
03ITG VIP Jersey and Emblems-8
03ITG VIP Jersey and Numbers-8
03ITG VIP MVP-17
03ITG VIP MVP-18
03ITG VIP Netminders-4
03NHL Sticker Collection-190
03O-Pee-Chee-226
03OPC Blue-226
03OPC Gold-226
03OPC Red-226
03Pacific-88
Blue-88
Red-88
Cramer's Choice-2
In the Crease-3
Jerseys-9
Jerseys Gold-9
Milestones-1
03Pacific Exhibit-162
03Pacific Exhibit-218
Blue Backs-162
Standing on Tradition-3
03Pacific Invincible-24
Blue-24
Red-24
Retail-24
Freeze Frame-4
Jerseys-6
03Pacific Prism-111
Blue-111
Patches-111
Red-111
Retail-111
Crease Police-2
03Pacific Supreme-24
Blue-24
Red-24
Retail-24
Generations-2
Jerseys-10
Standing Guard-3
03Parkhurst Orig Six He Shoots/Scores-9
03Parkhurst Orig Six He Shoots/Scores-9A
03Parkhurst Orig Six He Shoots/Scores-12
03Parkhurst Orig Six He Shoots/Scores-12A
03Parkhurst Original Six Montreal-49
03Parkhurst Original Six Montreal-69
03Parkhurst Original Six Montreal-99
Inserts-M14
Memorabilia-MM15
Memorabilia-MM30
Memorabilia-MM51
03Parkhurst Rookie-56
Jerseys-GJ-41
Jerseys Gold-GJ-41
Jersey and Sticks-SJ-28
Jersey and Sticks Gold-SJ-28
Retro Rookies-RR-4
Retro Rookie Autographs-RR-PR
Retro Rookies Gold-RR-4
03Private Stock Reserve-157
Blue-157
Patches-157
Red-157
Retail-157
03Serious NHL Starz-4
03SP Authentic 10th Anniversary-SP2
03SP Authentic 10th Anniversary Limited-SP2
03SP Authentic Honors-H12
03SP Authentic Honors-H13
03SP Authentic Honors Limited-H12
03SP Authentic Honors Limited-H13
03SP Authentic Sign of the Times-PR
03SP Authentic Sign of the Times-GR
03SP Authentic Sign of the Times-RGB
03SP Game Used Authentic Fabrics-AFPR
03SP Game Used Authentic Fabrics-DFBR
03SP Game Used Authentic Fabrics-DFGR
03SP Game Used Authentic Fabrics-QRGBT
03SP Game Used Authentic Fabrics Gold-AFPR
03SP Game Used Authentic Fabrics Gold-DFBR
03SP Game Used Authentic Fabrics Gold-DFGR
03SP Game Used Authentic Fabrics Gold-QRGBT
03SP Game Used Authentic Patches-APPR
03SP Game Used Double Threads-DTAR
03SP Game Used Double Threads-DTBR
03SP Game Used Game Gear-GGPR
03SP Game Used Game Gear Combo-GCPR
03SP Game Used Limited Threads-LTPR
03SP Game Used Limited Threads Gold-LTPR
03SP Game Used Premium Patches-PPPR
03SP Game Used Signers-SPSPR
03SPx-116
Radiance-116
Spectrum-116
Fantasy Franchise-FF-GRB
Fantasy Franchise Limited-FF-GRB
Hall Pass-HP-PR
Hall Pass Limited-HP-PR
Origins-O-PR
Style-SPX-RB
Style Limited-SPX-RB
Winning Materials-WM-PR
Winning Materials-WM-RY
Winning Materials Limited-WM-PR
Winning Materials Limited-WM-RY
03Topps-226
Blue-226
Gold-226
Red-226
Topps/OPC Idols-CI18
Lost Rookies-PR
Own the Game-OTG14
03Topps All-Star Block Party-1
03Topps Pristine Jersey Portions-PPJ-PR
03Topps Pristine Jersey Portion Refractor-PPJ-PR
03Topps Pristine Patches-PP-PR
03Topps Pristine Patch Refractors-PP-PR
03UD Honor Roll Signature Class-SC23
03UD Premier Collection Legends-PL-PR
03UD Premier Collection Legends Patches-PL-PR
03UD Premier Collection NHL Shields-SH-PR
03UD Premier Collection NHL Shields-SH-ROY
03UD Premier Collection Signatures-PS-PR
03UD Premier Collection Signatures-PS-ROY
03UD Premier Collection Signatures Gold-PS-PR
03UD Premier Collection Signatures Gold-PS-ROY
03UD Toronto Fall Expo Priority Signings-PR
03Upper Deck-52
Big Playmakers-BP-PR
BuyBacks-152
BuyBacks-153
BuyBacks-154
BuyBacks-155
BuyBacks-156
BuyBacks-157
BuyBacks-158
BuyBacks-159
BuyBacks-160
BuyBacks-161
BuyBacks-162
BuyBacks-163
BuyBacks-164
BuyBacks-165
BuyBacks-166
Canadian Exclusives-52
HG-52
Jersey Autographs-SJ-PR
Magic Moments-MM-6
Memorable Matchups-MM-RR
NHL Best-NB-PR
Patches-PLG-PR
Patches-PNM-PR
Patches-PNR-PR
Performers-PS15
Super Saviors-SS-PR
Superstar Spotlight-SS13
03Upper Deck Classic Portraits-116
03Upper Deck Classic Portraits-117
03Upper Deck Classic Portraits-118
03Upper Deck Classic Portraits-119
03Upper Deck Classic Portraits-120
03Upper Deck Classic Portraits-121
03Upper Deck Classic Portraits-122
03Upper Deck Classic Portraits-123
03Upper Deck Classic Portraits-124
03Upper Deck Classic Portraits-125
03Upper Deck Classic Portraits-126
03Upper Deck Classic Portraits-127
03Upper Deck Classic Portraits-128
03Upper Deck Classic Portraits-129
03Upper Deck Classic Portraits-130
03Upper Deck Classic Portraits-131
03Upper Deck Classic Portraits-132
03Upper Deck Classic Portraits-133
03Upper Deck Classic Portraits-134
03Upper Deck Classic Portraits-135
Genuine Greatness-GG-PR
Premium Portraits-PP-PR
Starring Cast-SC-PR
03Upper Deck Ice Authentics-IA-PR
03Upper Deck Ice Breakers-IB-PR
03Upper Deck Ice Breaker Patches-IB-PR
03Upper Deck Ice Clear Cut Winners-CC-PR
03Upper Deck Ice Under Glass Autographs-UG-PR
03Upper Deck MVP-113
Gold Script-113
Silver Script-113
Canadian Exclusives-113
Clutch Performers-CP1
Masked Men-MM2
Souvenirs-S3
Threads-TC9
03Upper Deck Rookie Update-159
Top Draws-TD17
03Upper Deck Trilogy-24
03Upper Deck Trilogy-106
Authentic Patches-AP33
Authentic Patches-AP42
Crest Variations-106
Limited-24
Limited-106
Limited Threads-LT6
Scripts-S2PR
Scripts Limited-S2PR
Scripts Red-S2PR
03Upper Deck Victory-49
Bronze-49
Gold-49
Silver-49
Freshman Flashback-FF14
Game Breakers-GB41
03Toronto Star-23
Foil-30
04ITG NHL AS FANtasy AS History Jerseys-SB39
04ITG Franchises Canadian-59
Autographs-PR2
Complete Jerseys-CJ3
Complete Jerseys Gold-CJ3
Double Memorabilia-DM5
Double Memorabilia Autographs-DM5
Double Memorabilia Gold-DM5
Forever Rivals-FR8
Forever Rivals Gold-FR8
Goalie Gear-GG3
Goalie Gear Autographs-GG3
Goalie Gear Gold-GG3
Memorabilia-SM5
Memorabilia Autographs-SM5
Memorabilia Gold-SM5
Original Sticks-OS8
Original Sticks Autographs-OS8
Original Sticks Gold-OS8
Teammates-TM8
Teammates Gold-TM8
Triple Memorabilia-TM1
Triple Memorabilia Autographs-TM1
Triple Memorabilia Gold-TM1
Trophy Winners-TW4
Trophy Winners Gold-TW4
04ITG Franchises He Shoots/Scores Prizes-12
04ITG Franchises He Shoots/Scores Prizes-22
04ITG Franchises Update Memorabilia-USM1
04ITG Franchises Update Memorabilia Gold-USM1
04ITG Franchises US West-183
Autographs-A-PR1
Barn Burners-WBB5
Barn Burners Gold-WBB5
Complete Jerseys-WCJ6
Complete Jerseys Gold-WCJ6
Double Memorabilia-WDM6
Double Memorabilia Autographs-WDMPR
Double Memorabilia Gold-WDM6
Forever Rivals-WFR1
Forever Rivals Gold-WFR1
Goalie Gear-WGG4
Goalie Gear Autographs-WGGPR
Goalie Gear Gold-WGG4
Memorabilia-WSM9
Memorabilia-WSM29
Memorabilia Autographs-WSMPR1
Memorabilia Autographs-WSMPR2
Memorabilia Gold-WSM9
Memorabilia Gold-WSM29
Original Sticks-WOS1
Original Sticks Autographs-WOSPR
Original Sticks Gold-WOS1
Teammates-WTM4
Teammates Gold-WTM4
Triple Memorabilia Autographs-WTMPR
Triple Memorabilia Gold-WTM4
Trophy Winners-WTW8
Trophy Winners Gold-WTW8
04ITG Ultimate Memorabilia-124
04ITG Ultimate Memorabilia-156
Gold-124
Gold-156
Archives 1st Edition-3
Archives 1st Edition-6
Archives 1st Edition-7
Archives 1st Edition-9
Archives 1st Edition-10
Archives 1st Edition-18
Archives 1st Edition-19
Archives 1st Edition-20
Archives 1st Edition-32
Archives 1st Edition-35
Auto Threads-1
Auto Threads-11
Autographs-7
Autographs-15
Autographs Gold-7
Autographs Gold-15
Changing the Game-2
Complete Jerseys-9
Complete Logo-21
Complete Logo-22
Complete Logo-23
Complete Logo-24
Complete Logo-25
Complete Logo-26
Complete Package-8
Conn Smythe Trophy-2
Cornerstones-10
Cornerstones Gold-10
Country of Origin-8
Country of Origin Gold-8
Day In History-13
Day In History-21
Day In History-36
Day In History Gold-13
Day In History Gold-21
Day In History Gold-36
Gloves are Off-5
Goalie Gear-12
Heroes Patrick Roy-1
Heroes Patrick Roy-2
Heroes Patrick Roy-3
Heroes Patrick Roy-4
Heroes Patrick Roy-5
Heroes Patrick Roy-6
Heroes Patrick Roy-7
Heroes Patrick Roy-8
Heroes Patrick Roy-9
Heroes Patrick Roy-10
Jerseys-2
Jerseys Gold-2
Jersey Autographs-14
Jersey Autographs-21
Jersey Autographs Gold-14
Jersey Autographs Gold-21
Jersey and Sticks-16
Jersey and Sticks Gold-16
Nicknames-25
Nickname Autographs-16
Original Six-5
Original Six-15
Raised to the Rafters-1
Seams Unbelievable-3
Vezina Trophy-6
04SP Authentic-108
Octographs-OS-GOA
Sign of the Times-ST-PR
Sign of the Times-DS-BR
Sign of the Times-TS-RLB
Sign of the Times-QS-FBRE
Sign of the Times-SS-ALS
04UD All-World-93
04UD Legends Classics-41
04UD Legends Classics-62
Gold-41
Gold-62
Platinum-41
Platinum-62
Silver-41
Silver-62
Signature Moments-M52
Signatures-CS50
Signatures-TC1
Signatures-QC1
04UD Toronto Fall Expo Priority Signings-PR
04UD Toronto Fall Expo Priority Signings-RO
04Ultimate Collection-22
Buybacks-71
Buybacks-72
Buybacks-73
Dual Logos-UL2-RB
Dual Logos-UL2-RL
Dual Logos-UL2-TR
Jerseys-UGJ-PR1
Jerseys-UGJ-PR2
Jerseys Gold-UGJ-PR1
Jerseys Gold-UGJ-PR2
Jersey Autographs-UGJA-PR1
Jersey Autographs-UGJA-PR2
Patches-UP-PR1
Patches-UP-PR2
Patch Autographs-UPA-PR
Patch Autographs-UPA-PRJO
Patch Autographs-UPA-PRMB
Signatures-US-PR1
Signature Logos-ULA-PR1
Signature Logos-ULA-PR2
Signature Patches-SP-PR
04Upper Deck-188
1997 Game Jerseys-PR
Canadian Exclusives-188
HG Glossy Gold-188
HG Glossy Silver-188
Jersey Autographs-GJA-PR
Jersey Autographs-GJA-PR/RL
Jersey Autographs-GJA-PR/DA
NHL's Best-NB-PR
Three Stars-AS12
04Upper Deck All-Star Promos-PR
04ITG Heroes and Prospects-174
04ITG Heroes and Prospects-NNO
Aspiring-3
Aspiring-4
Autographs-PRO
He Shoots-He Scores Prizes-3
Hero Memorabilia-6
04ITG Heroes/Prospects Toronto Expo '05-174
04ITG Heroes/Prospects Toronto Expo '05-NNO
04ITG Heroes/Prospects Expo Heroes/Pros-174
04National Trading Card Day *-UD10
05ITG Heroes/Prosp Toronto Expo Parallel -33
05ITG Heroes/Prosp Toronto Expo Parallel -195
05ITG Heroes/Prosp Toronto Expo Parallel -345
05Between the Pipes-17
Autographs-A-PR
Complete Package-CP-2
Double Memorabilia-DM-1
Double Memorabilia-DM-2
Gloves-GUG-2
Jerseys-GUJ-1
Jerseys-GUJ-2
Jersey and Sticks-SJ-1
Jersey and Sticks-SJ-2
Pads-GUP-6
Signed Memorabilia-SM-1
Signed Memorabilia-SM-2
05Black Diamond-187
Emerald-187
Gold-187
Onyx-187
Ruby-187
05ITG Passing the Torch-11
05ITG Passing the Torch-12
05ITG Passing the Torch-13
05ITG Passing the Torch-14
05ITG Passing the Torch-15
05ITG Passing the Torch-16
05ITG Passing the Torch-17
05ITG Passing the Torch-18
05ITG Passing the Torch-19
05ITG Passing the Torch-20
05ITG Passing the Torch-21
05ITG Passing the Torch-22
05ITG Passing the Torch-23
05ITG Passing the Torch-24
05ITG Passing the Torch-25
Autographs-PTT1
Memorabilia-PTT7
Memorabilia-PTT8
Memorabilia-PTT9
Memorabilia-PTT10
Memorabilia-PTT11
Memorabilia-PTT12
Memorabilia-PTT13
Memorabilia-PTT14
Memorabilia-PTT15
Memorabilia-PTT16
Memorabilia-PTT17
Memorabilia-PTT18
Memorabilia-PTT19
Memorabilia-PTT21
Memorabilia-PTT22
Memorabilia-PTT23
Memorabilia-PTT24
Memorabilia-PTT27
Memorabilia-PTT28
Memorabilia-PTT29
Memorabilia-PTT30
Memorabilia Autographs-PTT7A
Memorabilia Autographs-PTT8A
Memorabilia Autographs-PTT9A
Memorabilia Autographs-PTT10A
Memorabilia Autographs-PTT11A
Memorabilia Autographs-PTT12A
Memorabilia Autographs-PTT13A
Memorabilia Autographs-PTT14A
Memorabilia Autographs-PTT21A
Memorabilia Autographs-PTT22A
Memorabilia Autographs-PTT27A
Memorabilia Autographs-PTT28A
Memorabilia Autographs-PTT29A
Memorabilia Autographs-PTT30A
05ITG Ultimate Memorabilia Level 1-76
05ITG Ultimate Memorabilia Level 2-76
05ITG Ultimate Memorabilia Level 3-76
05ITG Ultimate Memorabilia Level 4-76
05ITG Ultimate Memorabilia Level 5-76
05ITG Ultimate Mem Complete Jersey-22
05ITG Ultimate Mem Complete Jersey Gold-22
05ITG Ultimate Mem Complete Package-15
05ITG Ultimate Mem Complete Package Gold-15
05ITG Ultimate Mem Cornerstones Jerseys-3
05ITG Ultimate Mem Cornerst Jerseys Gold-3
05ITG Ultimate Memorabilia Double Autos-2
05ITG Ultimate Memorabilia Double Autos-6
05ITG Ultimate Memorabilia Double Autos-17
05ITG Ultimate Mem Double Autos Gold-2
05ITG Ultimate Mem Double Autos Gold-6
05ITG Ultimate Mem Double Autos Gold-17
05ITG Ultimate Mem Double Mem-4
05ITG Ultimate Mem Double Mem Autos-2
05ITG Ultimate Mem Double Mem Autos Gold-2
05ITG Ultimate Mem Double Mem Gold-4
05ITG Ultimate Memorabilia Emblems-20
05ITG Ultimate Memorabilia Emblems-22
05ITG Ultimate Memorabilia Emblems Gold-20
05ITG Ultimate Memorabilia Emblems Gold-22
05ITG Ultimate Memorabilia Gloves Are Off-8
05ITG Ultimate Mem Gloves Are Off Gold-8
05ITG Ultimate Memorabilia Goalie Gear-14
05ITG Ultimate Memorabilia Goalie Gear-15
05ITG Ultimate Mem Goalie Gear Gold-14
05ITG Ultimate Mem Goalie Gear Gold-15
05ITG Ultimate Memorabilia In The Numbers-18
05ITG Ultimate Memorabilia In The Numbers-19
05ITG Ultimate Mem In The Numbers Gold-18
05ITG Ultimate Mem In The Numbers Gold-19
05ITG Ultimate Mem Jersey and Emblem-8
05ITG Ultimate Mem Jersey and Emblem-9
05ITG Ultimate Memorabilia Jersey Autos-25
05ITG Ultimate Mem Jersey Autos Gold-25
05ITG Ultimate Mem Jersey Emblems Gold-8
05ITG Ultimate Mem Jersey Emblems Gold-9
05ITG Ultimate Memorabilia Jerseys-28
05ITG Ultimate Memorabilia Jerseys Gold-28
05ITG Ultimate Mem Pass the Torch Jerseys-2
05ITG Ultimate Mem Pass the Torch Jerseys-7
05ITG Ultimate Mem Pass the Torch Jerseys-18
05ITG Ultimate Mem Passing Torch Jsy Gold-2
05ITG Ultimate Mem Passing Torch Jsy Gold-7
05ITG Ultimate Mem Passing Torch Jsy Gold-18
05ITG Ultimate Mem Raised to the Rafters-15
05ITG Ultimate Mem Raised Rafters Gold-15
05ITG Ultimate Mem Record Breaker Jerseys-6
05ITG Ultimate Mem Record Breaker Jerseys-12
05ITG Ultimate Mem Record Breaker Jerseys-13
05ITG Ultimate Mem Record Breaker Jerseys-15
05ITG Ultimate Mem RecBreak Jerseys Gold-6
05ITG Ultimate Mem RecBreak Jerseys Gold-12
05ITG Ultimate Mem RecBreak Jerseys Gold-13
05ITG Ultimate Mem RecBreak Jerseys Gold-15
05ITG Ultimate Mem Retro Teammate Jerseys-14
05ITG Ultimate Mem Retro Teammate Jerseys-18
05ITG Ult Mem Retro Teammates Jersey Gold-14
05ITG Ult Mem Retro Teammates Jersey Gold-18
05ITG Ultimate Mem Seams Unbelievable-2
05ITG Ultimate Mem Seam Unbelievable Gold-2
05ITG Ultimate Memorabilia Sextuple Autos-1
05ITG Ultimate Memorabilia Stick Autos-35
05ITG Ultimate Mem Stick Autos Gold-35
05ITG Ultimate Mem Sticks and Jerseys-27
05ITG Ultimate Mem Stick and Jerseys Gold-27
05ITG Ultimate Mem 3 Star of the Game Jsy-18
05ITG Ultimate Mem 3 Star of the Game Jsy-24
05ITG Ult Mem 3 Star of the Game Jsy Gold-18
05ITG Ult Mem 3 Star of the Game Jsy Gold-24
05ITG Ultimate Memorabilia Trifecta Autos-9
05ITG Ultimate Mem Trifecta Autos Gold-9
05ITG Ultimate Memorabilia Triple Autos-9
05ITG Ultimate Mem Triple Autos Gold-9
05ITG Ultimate Mem Triple Threads Jerseys-2
05ITG Ultimate Mem Triple Thread Jsy Gold-2
05ITG Ultimate Memorabilia Ultimate Autos-9
05ITG Ultimate Mem Ultimate Autos Gold-9
05ITG Ultimate Mem Ult Hero Double Jersey-6
05ITG Ult Mem Ult Hero Double Jersey Gold-6
05ITG Ultimate Mem Ult Hero Single Jersey-6
05ITG Ult Mem Ult Hero Single Jersey Gold-6
05ITG Ultimate Mem Ult Hero Triple Jersey-6
05ITG Ult Mem Ult Hero Triple Jersey Gold-6
05SP Authentic Exquisite Endorsements-EEPR
05SP Authentic Immortal Inks-IIPR
05SP Authentic Marks of Distinction-MDPR
05SP Authentic Octographs-OG
05SP Authentic Prestigious Pairings-PPRB
05SP Authentic Sign of the Times Triples-TRTD
05SP Authentic Sign of the Times Quads-QRCEB
05SP Authentic Sign of the Times Fives-LRMMG
05SP Authentic Six Star Signatures-SSGO
05SP Game Used Authentic Fabrics-AF-PR
05SP Game Used Authentic Fabrics Dual-CO
05SP Game Used Authentic Fabric Dual Auto-CO
05SP Game Used Authentic Fabrics Gold-AF-PR
05SP Game Used Authentic Fabrics Quad-RBBF
05SP Game Used Authentic Fabrics Quad-RBLT
05SP Game Used Authentic Patches Quad -RBBF
05SP Game Used Authentic Patches Quad -RBLT
05SP Game Used Authentic Fabrics Triple-BTR
05SP Game Used Authentic Patches-AP-PR
05SP Game Used Authentic Patches Dual-CO
05SP Game Used Authentic Patch Dual Autos-CO
05SP Game Used Authentic Patches Triple-BTR
05SP Game Used Auto Draft-AD-PR
05SP Game Used By the Letter-LM-PR
05SP Game Used Endorsed Equipment-EE-PR
05SP Game Used Game Gear-GG-PR1
05SP Game Used Game Gear-GG-PR2
05SP Game Used Game Gear Autographs-AG-PR1
05SP Game Used SIGnificance-PR
05SP Game Used SIGnificance Gold-S-PR
05SP Game Used Significant Numbers-SN-PR
05SPx Winning Materials Autographs-AWM-PR
05SPx Xcitement Legends-XL-PR
05SPx Xcitement Legends Gold-XL-PR
05SPx Xcitement Legends Spectrum-XL-PR
05The Cup-56
Gold-56
Black Rainbow-56
Dual NHL Shields Autographs-ADSRB
Emblems of Endorsement-EEPR
Hardware Heroes-HHPR1
Hardware Heroes-HHPR2
Hardware Heroes-HHPR3
Honorable Numbers-HNPR
Limited Logos-LLPR
Masterpiece Pressplates-56
Noble Numbers Dual-DNNPR
Noble Numbers Dual-DNNRB
Patch Variation-P56
Patch Variation Autographs-AP56
Scripted Numbers Dual-DSNRB
Scripted Swatches-SSPR1
Scripted Swatches-SSPR2
Signature Patches-SPPR
Stanley Cup Titlists-TPR1
Stanley Cup Titlists-TPR2
05UD PowerPlay-122
05UD PowerPlay-128
05UD Toronto Fall Expo Priority Signings-PS-PR
05UD Toronto Fall Expo Priority Signings-PS-RO
05Ultimate Collection Endorsed Emblems-EEPR
05Ultimate Collection Jerseys-JPR
05Ultimate Collection Jerseys Dual-DJRT
05Ultimate Collection Jerseys Triple-TJRTB
05Ultimate Collection Premium Patches-PPPR
05Ultimate Collection Premium Swatches-PSPR
05Ultimate Coll Ultimate Achievements-UAPR
05Ultimate Collection Ultimate Patches-PPR
05Ultimate Coll Ultimate Patches Dual-DPRT
05Ultimate Coll Ultimate Patches Triple-TPRTB
05Ultimate Collection Ultimate Signatures-USPR
05Ultimate Coll Ultimate Sigs Foursomes-UFRBGL
05Ultimate Coll Ultimate Sigs Logos-SLPR
05Ultimate Coll Ultimate Sigs Pairings-UPBR
05Ultimate Coll Ultimate Sigs Pairings-UPRB
05Ultra Super Six-SS6
05Ultra Super Six-SS8
05Ultra Super Six Jerseys-SSJ-PR1
05Ultra Super Six Jerseys-SSJ-PR2
05Ultra Super Six Jersey Autographs-SAJ-PR1
05Ultra Super Six Jersey Autographs-SAJ-PR2
05Ultra Super Six Patches-SSP-PR1
05Ultra Super Six Patches-SSP-PR2
05Ultra Super Six Patch Autographs-SAP-PR1
05Ultra Super Six Patch Autographs-SAP-PR2
05Upper Deck All-Time Greatest-16
05Upper Deck All-Time Greatest-31
05Upper Deck All-Time Greatest-77
05Upper Deck Big Playmakers-B-PR
05Upper Deck Jerseys-J-PR
05Upper Deck NHL Generations-TRBL
05Upper Deck Patches-P-PR
05Upper Deck Ice Frozen Fabrics-FFPR
05Upper Deck Ice Frozen Fabrics Autos-AFFPR
05Upper Deck Ice Frozen Fabrics Glass-FFPR
05Upper Deck Ice Frozen Fabrics Patches-FFPPR
05Upper Deck Ice Frozen Fabric Patch Auto-FAPPR
05Upper Deck Ice Signature Swatches-SSPR
05Upper Deck Trilogy-103
Crystal-103
05ITG Heroes and Prospects-33
05ITG Heroes and Prospects-195
05ITG Heroes and Prospects-345
AHL Grads-AG-3
AHL Grads Gold-AG-3
Aspiring-ASP1
Autographs-A-PR
Autographs Series II-PR2
Autographs Series II-PR3
Autographs Series II-RT
CHL Grads-CG-6
CHL Grads Gold-CG-6
Future Teammates-FT8
He Shoots-He Scores Prizes-5
He Shoots-He Scores Prizes-44
He Shoots-He Scores Prizes-54
Hero Memorabilia-HM-8
Hero Memorabilia Dual-HDM-4
Measuring Up-MU1
Measuring Up-MU2
Measuring Up-MU3
Measuring Up-MU4
Measuring Up-MU5
Measuring Up-MU6
Measuring Up-MU7
Measuring Up-MU8
Measuring Up-MU9
Measuring Up-MU10
Measuring Up-MU11
Measuring Up-MU12
Measuring Up-MU13
Measuring Up-MU14
Measuring Up-MU15
Measuring Up-MU16
Measuring Up-MU17
Measuring Up-MU18
Measuring Up-MU19
Measuring Up-MU20
Measuring Up Gold-MU1
Measuring Up Gold-MU2
Measuring Up Gold-MU3
Measuring Up Gold-MU4
Measuring Up Gold-MU5
Measuring Up Gold-MU6
Measuring Up Gold-MU7
Measuring Up Gold-MU8
Measuring Up Gold-MU9
Measuring Up Gold-MU10
Measuring Up Gold-MU11
Measuring Up Gold-MU12
Measuring Up Gold-MU13
Measuring Up Gold-MU14
Measuring Up Gold-MU15
Measuring Up Gold-MU16
Measuring Up Gold-MU17
Measuring Up Gold-MU18
Measuring Up Gold-MU19
Measuring Up Gold-MU20
National Pride-NPR-15
Spectrum-STM-01
Spectrum Gold-STM-01
06Beehive-189
5 X 7 Black and White-189
5 X 7 Dark Wood-189
PhotoGraphs-PGPR
Signature Scrapbook-SSPR
06Between The Pipes-98
06Between The Pipes-118
06Between The Pipes-143
Aspiring-AS02
Aspiring-AS05
Aspiring-AS10
Aspiring Gold-AS02
Aspiring Gold-AS05
Aspiring Gold-AS10
Autographs-APR
Autographs-APR2
Complete Jersey-CJ17
Complete Jersey-CJ19
Complete Jersey Gold-CJ17
Complete Jersey Gold-CJ19
Complete Package-CP05
Complete Package-CP06
Complete Package Gold-CP05
Complete Package Gold-CP06
Double Jerseys-DJ05
Double Jerseys-DJ17
Double Jerseys-DJ21
Double Jerseys-DJ22
Double Jerseys-DJ29
Double Jerseys Gold-DJ05
Double Jerseys Gold-DJ17
Double Jerseys Gold-DJ21
Double Jerseys Gold-DJ22
Double Jerseys Gold-DJ29
Double Memorabilia-DM14
Double Memorabilia-DM15
Double Memorabilia Gold-DM14
Double Memorabilia Gold-DM15
Emblems-GUE66
Emblems Gold-GUE66
Emblems Autographs-GUE66
Gloves-GG16
Gloves Gold-GG16
Jerseys-GUJ66
Jerseys Gold-GUJ66
Jerseys Autographs-GUJ66
Numbers-GUN66
Numbers Gold-GUN66
Numbers Autographs-GUN66
Pads-GP06
Pads Gold-GP06
Playing For Your Country-PC21
Playing For Your Country Gold-PC21
Roy vs. Brodeur-RB01
Roy vs. Brodeur-RB02
Roy vs. Brodeur-RB03
Roy vs. Brodeur-RB04
Roy vs. Brodeur-RB05
Roy vs. Brodeur-RB06
Roy vs. Brodeur-RB07
Roy vs. Brodeur-RB08
Roy vs. Brodeur-RB09
Roy vs. Brodeur-RB10
Roy vs. Brodeur Gold-RB01
Roy vs. Brodeur Gold-RB02
Roy vs. Brodeur Gold-RB03
Roy vs. Brodeur Gold-RB04
Roy vs. Brodeur Gold-RB05
Roy vs. Brodeur Gold-RB06
Roy vs. Brodeur Gold-RB07
Roy vs. Brodeur Gold-RB08
Roy vs. Brodeur Gold-RB09
Roy vs. Brodeur Gold-RB10
Shooting Gallery-SG01
Shooting Gallery-SG10
Shooting Gallery Gold-SG01
Shooting Gallery Gold-SG10
Stick and Jersey-SJ29
Stick and Jersey-SJ30
Stick and Jersey Gold-SJ29
Stick and Jersey Gold-SJ30
Stick and Jersey Autographs-SJ29
Stick and Jersey Autographs-SJ30
Stick Work-SW01
Stick Work-SW04
Stick Work Gold-SW01
Stick Work Gold-SW04
The Mask-M22
The Mask Gold-M22
The Mask Silver-M22
The Mask Game-Used-MGU17
The Mask Game-Used Gold-MGU17
06Black Diamond-153B
Gold-153B
Ruby-153B
06Flair Showcase-240
06Flair Showcase-285
Parallel-240
Parallel-285
Hot Numbers-HN24
Hot Numbers Parallel-HN24
06Hot Prospects Hot Materials -HMPR
06Hot Prospects Hot Materials Red Hot-HMPR
06Hot Prospects Hot Materials White Hot-HMPR
06ITG International Ice-128
Gold-128
Autographs-APR
Complete Jersey-CJ17
Complete Jersey Gold-CJ17
Cornerstones-IC09
Cornerstones Gold-IC09
Double Memorabilia-DM02
Double Memorabilia Gold-DM02
Emblem Autographs-GUE38
Emblem Autographs Gold-GUE38
Emblems-GUE38
Emblems Gold-GUE38
Goaltending Glory-GG21
Goaltending Glory Gold-GG21
Jersey Autographs-GUJ38
Jersey Autographs Gold-GUJ38
Jerseys-GUJ38
Jerseys Gold-GUJ38
My Country My Team-MC10
My Country My Team Gold-MC10
Numbers-GUN38
Numbers Autographs-GUN38
Numbers Autographs Gold-GUN38
Numbers Gold-GUN38
Stick and Jersey-SJ08
Stick and Jersey Gold-SJ08
06ITG Ultimate Memorabilia-110
06ITG Ultimate Memorabilia-111
Artist Proof-110
Artist Proof-111
Autos-54
Autos Gold-54
Autos Dual-3
Autos Dual Gold-3
Autos Triple-4
Autos Triple-5
Autos Triple Gold-4
Autos Triple Gold-5
Complete Jersey-5
Complete Jersey-27
Complete Jersey Gold-5
Complete Jersey Gold-27
Complete Package-16
Complete Package Gold-16
Cornerstones-10
Cornerstones Gold-10
Decades-3
Decades-6
Decades Gold-3
Decades Gold-6
Double Memorabilia-2
Double Memorabilia Gold-2
Double Memorabilia Autos-5
Double Memorabilia Autos Gold-5
Emblems-5
Emblems Gold-5
Gloves Are Off-17
Gloves Are Off Gold-17
In The Numbers-2
In The Numbers Gold-2
Jerseys-5
Jerseys Gold-5
Jerseys and Emblems-3
Jerseys and Emblems Gold-3
Jerseys Autos-51
Jerseys Autos Gold-51
Journey Emblem-2
Journey Emblem Gold-2
Journey Jersey-2
Journey Jersey Gold-2
Passing The Torch-4
Passing The Torch Gold-4
Retro Teammates-18
Retro Teammates Gold-18
Ring Leaders-16
Ring Leaders Gold-16
Seams Unbelievable-6
Seams Unbelievable Gold-6
Stick Rack-4
Stick Rack-13
Stick Rack-20
Stick Rack Gold-4
Stick Rack Gold-13
Stick Rack Gold-20
Sticks and Jerseys-1
Sticks and Jerseys Gold-1
Sticks Autos-25
Sticks Autos Gold-25
Trifecta Autos-5
Trifecta Autos Gold-5
Triple Thread Jerseys-5
Triple Thread Jerseys Gold-5
Ultimate Hero Single Jerseys-3
Ultimate Hero Single Jerseys Gold-3
Ultimate Hero Double Jerseys-3
Ultimate Hero Double Jerseys Gold-3
Ultimate Hero Triple Jerseys-3
Ultimate Hero Triple Jerseys Gold-3
06O-Pee-Chee Swatches-S-PR
06Parkhurst-145
Autographs-145
06SP Authentic-144
Limited-144
Sign of the Times Duals-STRB
Sign of the Times Triples-ST3RBW
Sign of the Times Quads-ST4RBLF
06SP Game Used-53
Gold-53
Rainbow-53
Authentic Fabrics Quads-AF4RBTL
Authentic Fabrics Quads Patches-AF4RBTL
Authentic Fabrics Sixes-AF6JEN
Authentic Fabrics Sixes-AF6WIN
Authentic Fabrics Sixes Patches-AF6JEN
Authentic Fabrics Sixes Patches-AF6WIN
Authentic Fabrics Sevens-AF7CON
Authentic Fabrics Sevens-AF7VEZ
Authentic Fabrics Sevens Patches-AF7CON
Authentic Fabrics Sevens Patches-AF7VEZ
Authentic Fabrics Eights-AF8HOF
Authentic Fabrics Eights Patches-AF8HOF
By The Letter-BLPR
Inked Sweaters-ISPR
Inked Sweaters Patches-ISPR
Inked Sweaters Dual-IS2RB
Inked Sweaters Dual Patches-IS2RB
Legendary Fabrics-LFPR
Legendary Fabrics Autographs-LFPR
06SPx-130
Spectrum-130
SPxcitement-X53
SPxcitement Spectrum-X53
SPxcitement Autographs-X53
06The Cup-23
Autographed Foundations-CQPR
Autographed Foundations Patches-CQPR
Autographed NHL Shields Duals-DASLR
Autographed NHL Shields Duals-DASRB
Autographed Patches-23
Black Rainbow-23
Foundations-CQPR
Foundations Patches-CQPR
Enshrinements-EPR
Gold-23
Gold Patches-23
Honorable Numbers-HNPR
Jerseys-23
Limited Logos-LLPR
Masterpiece Pressplates-23
Property of-POPR
Scripted Swatches-SSPR
Scripted Swatches Duals-DSPR
Scripted Swatches Duals-DSRB
Signature Patches-SPPR1
Signature Patches-SPPR2
Stanley Cup Signatures-CSPR
Stanley Cup Signatures-CSRO
06UD Artifacts-142
Blue-142
Gold-142
Platinum-142
Radiance-142
Autographed Radiance Parallel-142
Red-142
Frozen Artifacts-FAPR
Frozen Artifacts Black-FAPR
Frozen Artifacts Blue-FAPR
Frozen Artifacts Gold-FAPR
Frozen Artifacts Platinum-FAPR
Frozen Artifacts Red-FAPR
Frozen Artifacts Autographed Black-FAPR
Frozen Artifacts Patches Black-FAPR
Frozen Artifacts Patches Blue-FAPR
Frozen Artifacts Patches Gold-FAPR
Frozen Artifacts Patches Platinum-FAPR
Frozen Artifacts Patches Red-FAPR
Frozen Artifacts Patches Autographed Black Tag Parallel-FAPR
Tundra Tandems-TTPJ
Tundra Tandems-TTPK
Tundra Tandems-TTRB
Tundra Tandems Black-TTPJ
Tundra Tandems Black-TTPK
Tundra Tandems Black-TTRB
Tundra Tandems Blue-TTPJ
Tundra Tandems Blue-TTPK
Tundra Tandems Blue-TTRB
Tundra Tandems Gold-TTPJ
Tundra Tandems Gold-TTPK
Tundra Tandems Gold-TTRB
Tundra Tandems Platinum-TTPJ
Tundra Tandems Platinum-TTPK
Tundra Tandems Platinum-TTRB
Tundra Tandems Red-TTPJ
Tundra Tandems Red-TTPK
Tundra Tandems Red-TTRB
Tundra Tandems Dual Patches Red-TTPJ
Tundra Tandems Dual Patches Red-TTPK
Tundra Tandems Dual Patches Red-TTRB
06UD Biography of a Season-BOS7
06UD Mini Jersey Collection-56
Jerseys-PR
Jersey Variations-PR
06UD Powerplay Cup Celebrations-CC7
06Ultimate Collection-34
Autographed Jerseys-AJ-PR
Autographed Patches-AJ-PR
Jerseys-UJ-PR
Jerseys Dual-UJ2-RB
Jerseys Triple-UJ3-RBL
Patches-UJ-PR
Patches Dual-UJ2-RB
Patches Triple-UJ3-RBL
Signatures-US-PR
Ultimate Achievements-UA-PR
Ultimate Signatures Logos-SL-PR
06Upper Deck Game Jerseys-J2RO
06Upper Deck Game Patches-P2RO
06Upper Deck Sweet Shot-30
Endorsed Equipment-EEPR
Signature Sticks-STPR
Sweet Stitches-SSPR
Sweet Stitches Duals-SSPR
Sweet Stitches Triples-SSPR
06Upper Deck Trilogy Combo Autographed Jerseys-CJRB
06Upper Deck Trilogy Combo Autographed Patches-CJRB
06Upper Deck Trilogy Combo Clearcut Autographs-C3RBH
06Upper Deck Trilogy Frozen In Time-FT15
06Upper Deck Trilogy Honorary Scripted Patches-HSPPR
06Upper Deck Trilogy Honorary Scripted Swatches-HSSPR
06Upper Deck Trilogy Honorary Swatches-HSPR
06Upper Deck Trilogy Ice Scripts-ISPR
06Upper Deck Trilogy Scripts-S1PR
06Upper Deck Trilogy Scripts-S2PR

06ITG Heroes and Prospects-14
Autographs-APR
Double Memorabilia-DM05
Double Memorabilia Gold-DM05
Heroes Memorabilia-HM06
Heroes Memorabilia Gold-HM06
Memorial Cup Champions-MC12
Quad Emblems-QE14
Triple Memorabilia-TM02
Triple Memorabilia Gold-TM02
Roy, Patrick (minors)
01Sorel Royaux-19
Roy, Philippe
00Muskegon Fury-2
01Johnstown Chiefs-21
02Augusta Lynx-73
02Johnstown Chiefs-13
03UK Basingstoke Bison-5
Roy, Pierre
72Nordiques Postcards-20
73Nordiques Team Issue-20
75O-Pee-Chee WHA-25
76Nordiques Postcards-16
77Nova Scotia Voyageurs-20
Roy, Sebastien
03Lubbock Cotton Kings-15
Roy, Serge
86Swedish Panini Stickers-224
90ProCards AHL/IHL-426
Roy, Simon
90Montreal-Bourassa AAA-21
917th Inn. Sketch QMJHL-61
92Quebec Pee-Wee Tournament-61
93Quebec Pee-Wee Tournament-228
93Quebec Pee-Wee Tournament-1370
95Roller Hockey Magazine RHI-6
Roy, Stephane
88ProCards IHL-33
90Alberta International Team Canada-17
91Alberta International Team Canada-19
92Alberta International Team Canada-19
95Central Hockey League-34
95Signature Rookies-8
Signatures-8
98Abilene Aviators-12
99Quebec Citadelles-11
00UK Sekonda Superleague-47
02Swiss HNL-163
03Worcester Ice Cats 10th Anniversary-16
Roy, Travis
95Pinnacle FANtasy-31
Roy, Vincent
92Quebec Pee-Wee Tournament-643
93Quebec Pee-Wee Tournament-471
Royal, Eric
95Wheeling Thunderbirds-7
95Wheeling Thunderbirds Series II-13
96Wheeling Nailers-17
96Wheeling Nailers Photo Pack-7
Royce, Jason
98Arizona Icecats-23
99Arizona Icecats-23
00Arizona Icecats-20
Royer, Gaetan
98Grand Rapids Griffins-17
99Michigan K-Wings-6
01UD Mask Collection-168
Gold-168
02Upper Deck MVP-216
Gold-216
Classics-216
Golden Classics-216
04Thetford Mines Prolab-27
Royer, Remi
95Bowman Draft Prospects-P30
98Upper Deck-246
Exclusives-246
Exclusives 1 of 1-246
Gold Reserve-246
98Upper Deck MVP-50
Gold Script-50
Silver Script-50
Super Script-50
98Indianapolis Ice-7
98Bowman CHL-87
Golden Anniversary-87
OPC International-87
98Bowman Chrome CHL-87
Golden Anniversary-87
Golden Anniversary Refractors-87
OPC International-87
OPC International Refractors-87
Refractors-87
99BAP Memorabilia-145
Gold-145
Silver-145
99Pacific-99
Copper-99
Emerald Green-99
Gold-99
Ice Blue-99
Premiere Date-99
Red-99
99Upper Deck MVP-49
Gold Script-49
Silver Script-49
Super Script-49
99Upper Deck Victory-70
99Cleveland Lumberjacks-20
00Portland Pirates-10
02Reading Royals RBI Sports-181
03Indianapolis Ice-16
Rozakov, Rail
00Russian Hockey League-192
00Russian Hockey League-290
02Russian Hockey League-50
02Russian Hockey League-268
03Russian Hockey League-203
Rozendal, Scott
01Guelph Storm Memorial Cup-19
Rozin, Sergei
02Russian Hockey League-84
Rozinak, Vaclav
01Czech DS Legends-L4
Rozman, Jure
93Quebec Pee-Wee Tournament-1798
Rozon, Martin
917th Inn. Sketch QMJHL-175
Rozsival, Michal
96Swift Current Broncos-5
97Swift Current Broncos-6
98Bowman CHL-64
Golden Anniversary-64
OPC International-64
Scout's Choice-SC20
98Bowman Chrome CHL-64
Golden Anniversary-64
Golden Anniversary Refractors-64
OPC International-64
OPC International Refractors-64
Refractors-64
99BAP Memorabilia-371
Gold-371
Silver-371
99Pacific Dynagon Ice-162
Blue-162
Copper-162
Gold-162
Premiere Date-162
99Pacific Omega-194
Copper-194
Gold-194
Ice Blue-194
Premiere Date-194
99SP Authentic-112
99Stadium Club-185
First Day Issue-185
One of a Kind-185
Printing Plates Black-185
Printing Plates Cyan-185
Printing Plates Magenta-185
Printing Plates Yellow-185
99Topps Premier Plus-115
Parallel-115
99Upper Deck Arena Giveaways-PP2
00BAP Signature Series-84
Emerald-84
Ruby-84
Sapphire-84
Autographs-91
Autographs Gold-91
00Crown Royale Game-Worn Jerseys-22
00Crown Royale Game-Worn Jersey Patches-22
00Crown Royale Premium-Sized Jerseys-22
00Pacific-335
Copper-335
Gold-335
Ice Blue-335
Premiere Date-335
00Stadium Club-35
00Titanium Game Gear-140
00Titanium Game Gear Patches-140
00Czech OFS-397
01Pacific Heads-Up Quad Jerseys-29
01Private Stock Game Gear-83
01Private Stock Game Gear Patches-83
01Titanium Double-Sided Jerseys-34
01Titanium Double-Sided Patches-34
01Czech DS-29
02BAP First Edition-169
02BAP Sig Series Auto Buybacks 2000-91
02Pacific-317
Blue-317
Red-317
02Pacific Complete-241
Red-241
02Topps Total-387
02Upper Deck-388
Exclusives-388
02Upper Deck Beckett UD Promos-388
03ITG Action-420
03NHL Sticker Collection-118
03Upper Deck-402
Canadian Exclusives-402
HG-402
UD Exclusives-402
04Czech OFS-221
Stars-27
04Czech Zuma-29
05Parkhurst-325
Facsimile Auto Parallel-325
06O-Pee-Chee-325
06O-Pee-Chee-604
Rainbow-325
Rainbow-604
06Panini Stickers-104
06Upper Deck-381
Exclusives Parallel-381
High Gloss Parallel-381
Masterpieces-381
06Czech OFS Jagr Team-11
06Czech NHL ELH Postcards-9
07Upper Deck Ovation-69
Rozsival, Patrik
97Czech APS Extraliga-246
98Czech OFS-380
99Czech OFS-98
02Czech OFS Plus-166
03Czech OFS Plus-124
04Czech OFS-79
Checklist Cards-4
05Czech HC Liberec-12
Rozum, Petr
99Czech Score Blue 2000-107
99Czech Score Red Ice 2000-107
Ruark, Mark
907th Inn. Sketch WHL-203
Ruark, Mike
89Portland Winter Hawks-18
907th Inn. Sketch WHL-311
91ProCards-393
92Phoenix Roadrunners-19
97Manitoba Moose-B8
98Manitoba Moose-C6
99Manitoba Moose-8
00Manitoba Moose-18
Rubachuk, Brad
88Lethbridge Hurricanes-19
89Lethbridge Hurricanes-19
907th Inn. Sketch WHL-127
91ProCards-11
91Rochester Americans Dunkin' Donuts-12
91Rochester Americans Kodak-21
92Rochester Americans Dunkin' Donuts-14
92Rochester Americans Kodak-18
93Rochester Americans Kodak-21
94Binghamton Rangers-19
01UK Manchester Storm Retro-17
Rubic, Robin
84Kitchener Rangers-16
85Sudbury Wolves-9
Rubin, Benjamin
06Quebec Remparts-21
Rubov, Alexei
99Russian Hockey League-223
Rucchin, Lawrence
98German DEL-124
99German DEL-284
Rucchin, Steve
94Ducks Carl's Jr.-19
94Upper Deck-480
Electric Ice-480
95Donruss-140
95Ducks Team Issue-3
95Finest-64
Refractors-64
95Leaf-54
95Metal-4
95Panini Stickers-222
95Parkhurst International-272
Emerald Ice-272
95Pinnacle-58
Artist's Proofs-58
Rink Collection-58
95SP-4
95Stadium Club-214
Members Only Master Set-214
95Topps-33
OPC Inserts-33
95Ultra-202
95Upper Deck-425
Electric Ice-425
Electric Ice Gold-425
Special Edition-SE92
Special Edition Gold-SE92
95Images-56
Gold-57
96Be A Player-186
Autographs-186
Autographs Silver-186
96Black Diamond-20
Gold-20
96Collector's Choice-3
96Ducks Team Issue-11
96Metal Universe-5
96Pinnacle-137
Artist's Proofs-137
Foil-137
Premium Stock-137
Rink Collection-137
96Score-186
Artist's Proofs-186
Dealer's Choice Artist's Proofs-186
Special Artist's Proofs-186
Golden Blades-186
96SP-6
96Upper Deck-214
97Collector's Choice-7
97Crown Royale-3
Emerald Green-3
Ice Blue-3
Silver-3
97Donruss-49
Press Proofs Silver-49
Press Proofs Gold-49
97Donruss Limited-117
Exposure-117
97Donruss Preferred-45
Cut to the Chase-45
97Leaf-101
Fractal Matrix-101
Fractal Matrix Die Cuts-101
97Leaf International-101
Universal Ice-101
97Pacific-104
Copper-104
Emerald Green-104
Ice Blue-104
Red-104
Silver-104
97Pacific Dynagon-4
Copper-4
Dark Grey-4
Emerald Green-4
Ice Blue-4
Red-4
Silver-4
Tandems-30
97Pacific Omega-5
Copper-5
Dark Gray-5
Emerald Green-5
Gold-5
Ice Blue-5
97Panini Stickers-184
97Paramount-5
Copper-5
Dark Grey-5
Emerald Green-5
Ice Blue-5
Red-5
Silver-5
97Pinnacle-151
Press Plates Back Black-151
Press Plates Back Cyan-151
Press Plates Back Magenta-151
Press Plates Back Yellow-151
Press Plates Front Black-151
Press Plates Front Cyan-151
Press Plates Front Magenta-151
Press Plates Front Yellow-151
97Pinnacle Certified-64
Red-64
Mirror Blue-64
Mirror Gold-64
Mirror Red-64
97Pinnacle Inside-188
97Pinnacle Tot Certi Platinum Blue-64
97Pinnacle Tot Certi Platinum Gold-64
97Pinnacle Totally Certified Platinum Red-64
97Pinnacle Tot Cert Mirror Platinum Gold-64
97Score-176
97Score Mighty Ducks-3
Platinum-3
Premier-3
97SP Authentic-5
97Upper Deck-2
98Aurora-4
98Be A Player-151
Press Release-151
98BAP Gold-151
98BAP Autographs-151
98BAP Autographs Gold-151
98Ducks Power Play-ANA2
98Finest-26
No Protectors-26
No Protectors Refractors-26
Refractors-26
98NHL Game Day Promotion-ANA2
98Pacific-62
Ice Blue-62
Red-62
98Pacific Dynagon Ice-4
Blue-4
Red-4
98Pacific Omega-7
Red-7
Opening Day Issue-7
98Panini Stickers-171
98Paramount-5
Copper-5
Emerald Green-5
Holo-Electric-5
Ice Blue-5
Silver-5
98Revolution-4
Ice Shadow-4
Red-4
98UD Choice-6
Prime Choice Reserve-6
Reserve-6
98Upper Deck-214
Exclusives-214
Exclusives 1 of 1-214
Gold Reserve-214
98Upper Deck MVP-8
Gold Script-8
Silver Script-8
Super Script-8
99Aurora-4
Premiere Date-4
99BAP Memorabilia-107
Gold-107
Silver-107
99BAP Millennium-10
Emerald-10
Ruby-10
Sapphire-10
Signatures-10
Signatures Gold-10
99Crown Royale-3
Limited Series-3
Premiere Date-3
99O-Pee-Chee-198
99O-Pee-Chee Chrome-198
99O-Pee-Chee Chrome Refractors-198
99Pacific-13
Copper-13
Emerald Green-13
Gold-13
Ice Blue-13
Premiere Date-13
Red-13
99Pacific Dynagon Ice-11
Blue-11
Copper-11
Gold-11
Premiere Date-11
99Pacific Omega-5
Copper-5
Gold-5
Ice Blue-5
Premiere Date-5
99Pacific Prism-4
Holographic Blue-4
Holographic Gold-4
Holographic Mirror-4
Holographic Purple-4
Premiere Date-4
99Panini Stickers-182
99Paramount-6
Copper-6
Emerald-6
Gold-6
Holographic Emerald-6
Holographic Gold-6
Holographic Silver-6
Ice Blue-6
Premiere Date-6
Red-6
Silver-6
99Revolution-5
Premiere Date-5
Red-5
Shadow Series-5
99SPx-5
Radiance-5
Spectrum-5
99Topps/OPC-198
99Topps/OPC Chrome-198
Refractors-198
99Upper Deck-13
Exclusives-13
Exclusives 1 of 1-13
99Upper Deck Gold Reserve-13
99Upper Deck MVP-8
Gold Script-8
Silver Script-8
Super Script-8
99Upper Deck Victory-5
99Wayne Gretzky Hockey-3
00Aurora-3
Premiere Date-3
00BAP Memorabilia-154
Emerald-154
Ruby-154
Sapphire-154
Promos-154
00BAP Mem Chicago Sportsfest Copper-154
00BAP Memorabilia Chicago Sportsfest Blue-154
00BAP Memorabilia Chicago Sportsfest Gold-154
00BAP Memorabilia Chicago Sportsfest Ruby-154
00BAP Memorabilia Chicago Sun-Times Ruby-154
00BAP Memorabilia Chicago Sun-Times Gold-154
00BAP Mem Chicago Sun-Times Sapphire-154
00BAP Mem Toronto Fall Expo Copper-154
00BAP Memorabilia Toronto Fall Expo Gold-154
00BAP Memorabilia Toronto Fall Expo Ruby-154
00BAP Signature Series-185
Emerald-185
Ruby-185
Sapphire-185
Autographs-97
Autographs Gold-97
00O-Pee-Chee-129
00O-Pee-Chee Parallel-129
00Pacific-10
Copper-10
Gold-10
Ice Blue-10
Premiere Date-10
00Paramount-6
Copper-6
Gold-6
Holo-Gold-6
Holo-Silver-6
Ice Blue-6
Premiere Date-6
00Revolution-3
Blue-3
Premiere Date-3
Red-3
00Stadium Club-162
00Topps/OPC-129
Parallel-129
00Topps Heritage-173
00UD Heroes-1
00UD Reserve-2
00Upper Deck-2
Exclusives Tier 1-2
Exclusives Tier 2-2
00Upper Deck MVP-5
First Stars-5
Second Stars-5
Third Stars-5
00Upper Deck Victory-4
00Upper Deck Vintage-10
01Atomic Jerseys-2
01Atomic Patches-2
01Crown Royale Triple Threads-1
01O-Pee-Chee-185
01O-Pee-Chee Premier Parallel-185
01Pacific-9
Extreme LTD-9
Hobby LTD-9
Premiere Date-9
Retail LTD-9
01Pacific Arena Exclusives-9
01Private Stock Game Gear-4
01Private Stock Game Gear Patches-4
01Titanium Double-Sided Jerseys-1
01Titanium Double-Sided Patches-1
01Topps-185
OPC Parallel-185
01Upper Deck-6
Exclusives-6
01Upper Deck Victory-2
Gold-2
01Upper Deck Vintage-5
02BAP Memorabilia-132
Emerald-132
Ruby-132
Sapphire-132
NHL All-Star Game-132
NHL All-Star Game Blue-132
NHL All-Star Game Green-132
NHL All-Star Game Red-132
02BAP Memorabilia Toronto Fall Expo-132
02BAP Sig Series Auto Buybacks 1998-151
02BAP Sig Series Auto Buybacks 1999-10
02BAP Sig Series Auto Buybacks 2000-97
02BAP Signature Series Golf-GS89
02Bowman YoungStars-79
Gold-79
Silver-79
02Pacific-7
Blue-7
Red-7
02Parkhurst Retro-126
Minis-126
02Topps Total-330
02Upper Deck-3
Exclusives-3
02Vanguard-3
LTD-3
03ITG Action-91
03NHL Sticker Collection-155
03O-Pee-Chee-14
03OPC Blue-14
03OPC Gold-14
03OPC Red-14
03Pacific-9
Blue-9
Red-9
03Pacific Complete-179
Red-179
03Pacific Exhibit-6
Blue Backs-6
Yellow Backs-6
03Pacific Heads-Up-3
Hobby LTD-3
Retail LTD-3
03Titanium-2
Hobby Jersey Number Parallels-2
Retail-2
Retail Jersey Number Parallels-2
03Topps-14
Blue-14
Gold-14
Red-14
03Topps C55-36
Minis-36
Minis American Back-36
Minis American Back Red-36
Minis Bazooka Back-36
Minis Brooklyn Back-36
Minis Hat Trick Back-36
Minis O Canada Back-36
Minis O Canada Back Red-36
Minis Stanley Cup Back-36
03Upper Deck-2
Canadian Exclusives-2
HG-2
03Upper Deck MVP-3
Gold Script-3
Silver Script-3
Canadian Exclusives-3
03Czech Stadion-613
04Pacific-7
Blue-7
Red-7
05Be A Player Signatures-SR
05Be A Player Signatures Gold-SR
05Black Diamond-2
Emerald-2
Gold-2
Onyx-2
Ruby-2
05Panini Stickers-113
05Parkhurst-323
Facsimile Auto Parallel-323
05Ultra-131
Gold-131
Ice-131
05Upper Deck-376
05Upper Deck MVP-260
Gold-260
Platinum-260
05Upper Deck Victory-6
05Upper Deck Victory-232
Black-6
Black-232
Gold-6
Gold-232
Silver-6
Silver-232
06O-Pee-Chee-19
Rainbow-19
06Panini Stickers-11
06Ultra-9
Gold Medallion-9
Ice Medallion-9
06Upper Deck Arena Giveaways-ATL5
06Upper Deck-259
Exclusives Parallel-259
High Gloss Parallel-259
Masterpieces-259
06Upper Deck MVP-18
Ruchar, Milan
94Czech APS Extraliga-67
Ruchty, Matt
91ProCards-410
96Grand Rapids Griffins-22
97Grand Rapids Griffins-15
Rucinski, Mike
86Moncton Golden Flames-25
88ProCards IHL-112
89ProCards IHL-61
93Detroit Jr. Red Wings-6
94Detroit Jr. Red Wings-5
95Slapshot-61
95North Iowa Huskies-28
95Slapshot Memorial Cup-79
96Richmond Renegades-17
98Hurricanes Team Issue-22
98Pacific-46
Ice Blue-46
Red-46
98Upper Deck-235
Exclusives-235
Exclusives 1 of 1-235
Gold Reserve-235
99Charlotte Checkers-12
99Charlotte Checkers-33
99Cincinnati Cyclones-17
00Topps Heritage-207
00Cincinnati Cyclones-9
Rucinsky, Martin
91Oilers Team Issue-23
91Parkhurst-366
French-366
91Upper Deck-19
91Upper Deck-70
French-19
French-70
91ProCards-230
91Classic-17
91Classic Four-Sport *-17
Autographs-17A
92Nordiques Petro-Canada-27
92OPC Premier-124
92Parkhurst-149
Emerald Ice-149
92Pro Set-238
92Score-474
Canadian-474
92Topps-523
Gold-523G
92Ultra-390
92Upper Deck-556
92Finnish Semic-136
93Donruss-281
93Leaf-152
93OPC Premier-367
Gold-367
93Panini Stickers-74
93Parkhurst-170
Emerald Ice-170
93Pinnacle-196
Canadian-196
93PowerPlay-203
93Score-254
Canadian-254
93Stadium Club-11
Members Only Master Set-11
OPC-11
First Day Issue-11
First Day Issue OPC-11
93Topps/OPC Premier-367
Gold-367
93Ultra-191
93Upper Deck-6
94Nordiques Burger King-21
94Parkhurst-191
Gold-191
94Pinnacle-416
Artist's Proofs-416
Rink Collection-416
94Stadium Club-126
Members Only Master Set-126
First Day Issue-126
Super Team Winner Cards-126
94Ultra-179
94Upper Deck-201
Electric Ice-201
94Czech APS Extraliga-221
94Finnish Jaa Kiekko-177
95Parkhurst International-379
Emerald Ice-379
95Upper Deck-485
Electric Ice-485
Electric Ice Gold-485
95Finnish Semic World Championships-152
95Swedish World Championships Stickers-202
96Be A Player-124
Autographs-124
Autographs Silver-124
96Canadiens Postcards-24
96Canadiens Sheets-18
96Collector's Choice-143
96Donruss-123
Press Proofs-123
96Donruss Canadian Ice-81
Gold Press Proofs-81
Red Press Proofs-81
96Flair-50
Blue Ice-50
96Leaf-96
Press Proofs-96
96Pinnacle-63
Artist's Proofs-63
Foil-63
Premium Stock-63
Rink Collection-63
96Score-134
Artist's Proofs-134
Dealer's Choice Artist's Proofs-134
Special Artist's Proofs-134
Golden Blades-134
96SkyBox Impact-64
96Topps Picks-59
OPC Inserts-59
96Upper Deck-280
97Canadiens Postcards-19
97Pacific-220
Copper-220
Emerald Green-220
Ice Blue-220
Red-220
Silver-220
97Pacific Omega-122
Copper-122
Dark Gray-122
Emerald Green-122
Gold-122
Ice Blue-122
97Panini Stickers-36
97Pinnacle-172
Press Plates Back Black-172
Press Plates Back Cyan-172
Press Plates Back Magenta-172
Press Plates Back Yellow-172
Press Plates Front Black-172
Press Plates Front Cyan-172
Press Plates Front Magenta-172
Press Plates Front Yellow-172
97Pinnacle Inside-96
97Score-152
Artist's Proofs-152
Golden Blades-152
97Score Canadiens-9
Platinum-9
Premier-9
97Upper Deck-89
98Aurora-96
98Be A Player-221
Press Release-221
98BAP Gold-221
98BAP Autographs-221
98BAP Autographs Gold-221
98Canadiens Team Issue-18
98OPC Chrome-15
Refractors-15
98Pacific-257
Ice Blue-257
Red-257
98Pacific Omega-125
Red-125
Opening Day Issue-125
98Panini Stickers-37
98Paramount-117
Copper-117
Emerald Green-117
Holo-Electric-117
Ice Blue-117
Silver-117
98Topps-15
O-Pee-Chee-15
98Czech DS-4
98Czech OFS-245
Olympic Winners-7
98Czech Bonaparte-2A
98Czech Pexeso-5
98Czech Pexeso-12
98Czech Pexeso Series Two-9
98Czech Pexeso Series Two-21
98Czech Pexeso Series Two-28
98Czech Spaghetti-8
99Aurora-76
Premiere Date-76
99BAP Memorabilia-119
Gold-119
Silver-119
99BAP Millennium-132
Emerald-132
Ruby-132
Sapphire-132
Signatures-132
Signatures Gold-132
99O-Pee-Chee-166
99O-Pee-Chee Chrome-166
99O-Pee-Chee Chrome Refractors-166
99Pacific-209
Copper-209
Emerald Green-209
Gold-209
Ice Blue-209
Premiere Date-209
Red-209
99Pacific Dynagon Ice-104
Blue-104
Copper-104
Gold-104
Premiere Date-104
99Pacific Omega-121
Copper-121
Gold-121
Ice Blue-121
Premiere Date-121
99Panini Stickers-68
99Paramount-120
Copper-120
Emerald-120
Gold-120
Holographic Emerald-120
Holographic Gold-120
Holographic Silver-120
Ice Blue-120
Premiere Date-120
Red-120
Silver-120
99Revolution-77
Premiere Date-77
Red-77
Shadow Series-77
99Stadium Club-113
First Day Issue-113
One of a Kind-113
Printing Plates Black-113
Printing Plates Cyan-113
Printing Plates Magenta-113
Printing Plates Yellow-113
99Topps/OPC-166
99Topps/OPC Chrome-166
Refractors-166
99Upper Deck MVP-101
Gold Script-101
Silver Script-101
Super Script-101
99Upper Deck Victory-149
99Czech DS National Stars-NS13
99Czech DS Premium-P12
99Czech OFS-32
99Czech OFS Jagr Team Embossed-32
99Slovakian Challengers-12
00Aurora-74
Premiere Date-74
00BAP Memorabilia-197
Emerald-197
Ruby-197
Sapphire-197
Promos-197
00BAP Mem Chicago Sportsfest Copper-197
00BAP Memorabilia Chicago Sportsfest Blue-197
00BAP Memorabilia Chicago Sportsfest Gold-197
00BAP Memorabilia Chicago Sportsfest Ruby-197
00BAP Memorabilia Chicago Sun-Times Ruby-197
00BAP Memorabilia Chicago Sun-Times Gold-197
00BAP Mem Chicago Sun-Times Sapphire-197
00BAP Mem Toronto Fall Expo Copper-197
00BAP Memorabilia Toronto Fall Expo Gold-197
00BAP Memorabilia Toronto Fall Expo Ruby-197
00BAP Parkhurst 2000-P239
00BAP Signature Series-200
Emerald-200
Ruby-200
Sapphire-200
00Canadiens Postcards-24
00Crown Royale-56
Ice Blue-56
Limited Series-56
Premiere Date-56
Red-56
00O-Pee-Chee-95
00O-Pee-Chee Parallel-95
00Pacific-212
Copper-212
Gold-212
Ice Blue-212
Premiere Date-212
00Panini Stickers-43
00Paramount-130
Copper-130
Gold-130
Holo-Gold-130
Holo-Silver-130
Ice Blue-130
Premiere Date-130
00Revolution-78
Blue-78
Premiere Date-78
Red-78
00Stadium Club-165
00Titanium-49
Blue-49
Gold-49
Premiere Date-49
Red-49
Retail-49
00Topps/OPC-95
Parallel-95
00Topps Chrome-75
OPC Refractors-75
Refractors-75
00Topps Stars-81
Blue-81
00UD Heroes-64
00UD Pros and Prospects-46
00Upper Deck-94
Exclusives Tier 1-94
Exclusives Tier 2-94
00Upper Deck MVP-93
First Stars-93
Second Stars-93
Third Stars-93
00Upper Deck Victory-122
00Upper Deck Vintage-195
00Czech DS Extraliga National Team-NT7
00Czech OFS-410
01BAP Memorabilia-248
01BAP Memorabilia-474
Emerald-248
Emerald-474
Ruby-248
Ruby-474
Sapphire-248
Sapphire-474
01BAP Signature Series-117
Autographs-117
Autographs Gold-117
01Canadiens Postcards-22
01EA Sports-5
01O-Pee-Chee-124
01O-Pee-Chee Premier Parallel-124
01Pacific-211
Extreme LTD-211
Hobby LTD-211
Premiere Date-211
Retail LTD-211
01Pacific Adrenaline-99
Blue-99
Premiere Date-99
Red-99
Retail-99
01Pacific Arena Exclusives-211
01Parkhurst-199
01Parkhurst-384
01Stars Postcards-21
01Topps-124
OPC Parallel-124
01Upper Deck-324
Exclusives-324
EA Sports Gold-5
01Upper Deck MVP-102
01Upper Deck Victory-184
Gold-184
01Upper Deck Vintage-133
01Upper Deck Vintage-139
01Czech DS-25
01Czech DS-41
Best of the Best-BB7
Ice Heroes-IH7
02BAP Sig Series Auto Buybacks 1998-221
02BAP Sig Series Auto Buybacks 1999-132
02BAP Sig Series Auto Buybacks 2001-117
02Blues Magnets-2
02Pacific-259
Blue-259
Red-259
02Upper Deck Victory National Pride-NP18
02Czech DS-45
02Czech DS-59
02Czech DS-95
02Czech OFS Plus Trios-T6
02Czech OFS Plus Duos-D21
02Czech IQ Sports Blue-22
02Czech IQ Sports Yellow-23
02Czech Stadion Olympics-341
03ITG Action-564
03Pacific Complete-370
Red-370
03Parkhurst Original Six New York-17
03Rangers Team Issue-21
03Topps Traded-TT80
Blue-TT80
Gold-TT80
Red-TT80
04UD All-World-3
Gold-3
04Czech NHL ELH Postcards-12
04Czech OFS-104
Stars-6
04Czech Zuma-15
04Czech Zuma Stars-27
04Czech World Championship Postcards-16
05Panini Stickers-112
05Parkhurst-320
Facsimile Auto Parallel-320
05Upper Deck-374
05Upper Deck MVP-262
Gold-262
Platinum-262
05Czech World Champions Postcards-13
05Czech Kvarteto Bonaparte-5d
05Czech Pexeso Mini Blue Set-26
05Czech Pexeso Mini Red Set-25
06O-Pee-Chee-434
Rainbow-434
06Panini Stickers-342
06Upper Deck MVP-252
Gold Script-252
Super Script-252
06Czech OFS Jagr Team-20
Ruck, Colin
89Regina Pats-19
907th Inn. Sketch WHL-181
Ruck, Derrick
99Lethbridge Hurricanes-22
00Lethbridge Hurricanes-20
Rud, Eric
98Florida Everblades-22
98Kansas City Blades-5
99Florida Everblades-11
00Idaho Steelheads-18
01Idaho Steelheads-13
05St. Cloud State Huskies-30
06St. Cloud State Huskies-30
Rudberg, Jonas
917th Inn. Sketch OHL-333
Rudby, Lennart
69Swedish Hockey-179
Rudby, Sven Ake
69Swedish Hockey-180
73Swedish Stickers-180
74Swedish Stickers-262
Ruddick, Ken
89Niagara Falls Thunder-17
897th Inn. Sketch OHL-134
907th Inn. Sketch OHL-18
96Louisiana Ice Gators II-14
98Danish Hockey League-229
Ruddock, Ken
91Air Canada SJHL-E16
92Saskatchewan JHL-51
Ruden, Noah
03Michigan Wolverines-20
04Michigan Wolverines-21
06Port Huron Flags-19

Rudenko, Bogdan
95Slapshot-140
96Sarnia Sting-23
97Quad-City Mallards-18
98Colorado Gold Kings-19
98Colorado Gold Kings Postcards-7
99Colorado Gold Kings Taco Bell-5
99Colorado Gold Kings Wendy's-16
00Asheville Smoke-11
03Wheeling Nailers-95
06Fort Wayne Komets-16

Rudisuela, Dan
01Mississauga Ice Dogs-8
02Mississauga Ice Dogs-7
03Mississauga Ice Dogs-19

Rudkowsky, Cody
95Seattle Thunderbirds-25
96Seattle Thunderbirds-30
97Seattle Thunderbirds-23
99Peoria Rivermen-14
99Bowman CHL-122
Gold-122
OPC International-122
00Worcester Icecats-9
01Worcester Icecats-5
02BAP All-Star Edition-106
Gold-106
Silver-106
02BAP Memorabilia-355
02BAP Ultimate Memorabilia-48
02Between the Pipes-89
Gold-89
Silver-89
02Parkhurst-248
Bronze-248
Gold-248
Silver-248
02SP Authentic-159
02SP Game Used-90
02UD Artistic Impressions-120
Gold-120
02UD Honor Roll-127
02UD Mask Collection-117
02UD Premier Collection-66
Gold-66
02UD Top Shelf-120
02Upper Deck-453
Exclusives-453
02Trenton Titans-A-7
03BAP Memorabilia Deep in the Crease-D12
03Reading Royals-27
03Reading Royals RBI Sports-300
05Reading Royals-13

Rudslatt, Daniel
99Swedish Upper Deck-29
00Swedish Upper Deck-41
01Swedish Brynas Tigers-23
02Swedish SHL-161
Parallel-161
03Swedish Elite-17
Signatures II-10
Silver-17
04Swedish Elitset-15
Gold-15
05Swedish SHL Elitset-18

Rudy, Wes
92British Columbia JHL-20

Ruedi, Roland
93Swiss HNL-221
95Swiss HNL-442

Rueger, Brian
93Swiss HNL-322

Rueger, Ronald
93Swiss HNL-389
95Swiss HNL-394
96Swiss HNL-55
98Swiss Power Play Stickers-202
99Swiss Panini Stickers-203
00Swiss Panini Stickers-246
00Swiss Slapshot Mini-Cards-EVZ1
01Swiss EV Zug Postcards-5
01Swiss HNL-168
02Swiss HNL-276

Ruegg, Christian
01Swiss HNL-441
02Swiss HNL-426

Ruel, Claude
68Canadiens Postcards BW-15
69Canadiens Postcards Color-27
70Canadiens Pins-14
76Canadiens Postcards-19
77Canadiens Postcards-21
78Canadiens Postcards-23
79Canadiens Postcards-21
80Canadiens Postcards-21

Ruel, Vincent
92Quebec Pee-Wee Tournament-1062
93Quebec Pee-Wee Tournament-1090

Ruest, Mike
76Saginaw Gears-10

Rueter, Dirk
81Sault Ste. Marie Greyhounds-19

Rueter, Kirk
80Sault Ste. Marie Greyhounds-22

Rufener, Andy
93Swiss HNL-205
95Swiss HNL-230
96Swiss HNL-289
98Swiss Power Play Stickers-120
99Swiss Panini Stickers-122
00Swiss Panini Stickers-166
00Swiss Slapshot Mini-Cards-EHCK14
02Swiss EV Zug Postcards-21
02Swiss HNL-239

Ruff, Jason
88Lethbridge Hurricanes-20
89Lethbridge Hurricanes-20
907th Inn. Sketch WHL-138
91ProCards-46
92Upper Deck-522
92Peoria Rivermen-22
92Classic-109
Gold-109
92Classic Four-Sport *-216
Gold-216
93Atlanta Knights-11
93Classic Pro Prospects-45
94Atlanta Knights-12
95Atlanta Knights-17
98Cleveland Lumberjacks-19
99German DEL-91
00German DEL-80
01UK Belfast Giants-8
02German DEL City Press-143
03UK Belfast Giants-12

Ruff, Lee
02Florida Everblades-17
03Colorado Eagles-15
04Colorado Eagles-16
05Kalamazoo Wings-15

Ruff, Lindy
80O-Pee-Chee-319
82O-Pee-Chee-31
82Post Cereal-2
82Sabres Milk Panels-5
84O-Pee-Chee-29
84O-Pee-Chee Stickers-213
84Sabres Blue Shield-17
84Topps-23
85Sabres Blue Shield-24
85Sabres Blue Shield Small-24
86O-Pee-Chee-4
86Sabres Blue Shield-25
86Sabres Blue Shield Small-25
86Topps-4
87Panini Stickers-35
87Sabres Blue Shield-23
87Sabres Wonder Bread/Hostess-23
88O-Pee-Chee-40
88Sabres Blue Shield-22
88Sabres Wonder Bread/Hostess-24
88Topps-40
89Rangers Marine Midland Bank-44
90O-Pee-Chee-143
90Topps-143
Tiffany-143
91ProCards-6
91Rochester Americans Dunkin' Donuts-13
91Rochester Americans Kodak-22
91Rochester Americans Postcards-17
92San Diego Gulls-22
01Topps Archives-57
06Upper Deck Award Winners Canadian Exclusive-OAW7

Rugg, Stewart
01UK Dundee Stars-13
02UK Dundee Stars-13

Ruggeri, Rosario
01Chicoutimi Sagueneens-21
05ITG Heroes/Prosp Toronto Expo Parallel -358
05ITG Heroes and Prospects-358
Autographs Series II-RR

Ruggiero, Angela
04Tulsa Oilers-21

Ruggiero, Bill
01Moncton Wildcats-1
04Tulsa Oilers-22

Ruggles, Hilton
01UK Manchester Storm Retro-13
02UK Coventry Blaze-18
03UK Coventry Blaze-16
03UK Coventry Blaze History-6

Ruhnke, Kent
95Swiss HNL-460
98Swiss Power Play Stickers-226
99Swiss Panini Stickers-227
02Swiss HNL-247

Ruid, J.C.
98Roanoke Express-14
00Asheville Smoke-12
01Asheville Smoke-22
03Wheeling Nailers-96
06Fort Wayne Komets-17

Ruikka, Ryan
06Lincoln Stars-10

Ruisma, Matti
80Finnish Mallasjuoma-214
84Swedish Semic Elitserien-181

Ruisma, Veli-Matti
78Finnish SM-Liiga-20
78Finnish SM-Liiga-238

Rulik, Radim
96Czech APS Extraliga-287
97Czech APS Extraliga-171
98Czech OFS-33
99Czech OFS-368
00Czech OFS-158
05Czech Pexeso Mini Red Set-16

Rullier, Joe
96Rimouski Oceanic Update-8
97Rimouski Oceanic-7
99Rimouski Oceanic-2
Signed-2
00Lowell Lock Monsters-3
00QMJHL All-Star Program Inserts-4
01Manchester Monarchs-4B
02Manchester Monarchs-13
03Manchester Monarchs-14
03Manchester Monarchs Team Issue-14
04Manchester Monarchs-12
04Manchester Monarchs Tobacco-13
05Hartford Wolf Pack-19
06Manitoba Moose-5

Rumble, Brent
03Kalamazoo Wings-23
05Fort Wayne Komets Choice-8
05Fort Wayne Komets Sprint-15

Rumble, Darren
86Kitchener Rangers-7
87Kitchener Rangers-24
88Kitchener Rangers-28
89ProCards AHL-342
90ProCards AHL/IHL-34
91ProCards-271
92Parkhurst-356
Emerald Ice-356
92Senators Team Issue-13
92Ultra-148
92Upper Deck-110
93OPC Premier-356
Gold-356
93Parkhurst-411
Emerald Ice-411
93PowerPlay-173
93Senators Kraft Sheets-20
93Stadium Club-418
Members Only Master Set-418
First Day Issue-418
93Topps/OPC Premier-356
Gold-356
93Ultra-153
98Grand Rapids Griffins-18
00Worcester Icecats-14
01Pacific-330
Extreme LTD-330
Hobby LTD-330
Premiere Date-330
Retail LTD-330
01Pacific Arena Exclusives-330
01Worcester Icecats-1
02Springfield Falcons-19
03Hershey Bears Patriot News-19
05Springfield Falcons-27
06Springfield Falcons-23

Rummo, Alex
97Central Texas Stampede-14

Rumpel, Jakub
06Medicine Hat Tigers-15

Rumrich, Jurgen
92Finnish Semic-185
94Finnish Jaa Kiekko-286
94German DEL-66
95German DEL-66
95German DEL-434
95Swedish World Championships Stickers-74
96German DEL-262
98German DEL-49
98German DEL-321
99German DEL-181
99German DEL-377
00German DEL-186
Game Jersey-JR
01German Upper Deck-207
02German DEL City Press-270
Top Stars-GT4
03German Nuremberg Ice Tigers Postcards-23
04German DEL-135
04German Hamburg Freezers Postcards-16

Rumrich, Michael
92Finnish Semic-184
93Swedish Semic World Champ Stickers-167
94German DEL-214
95German DEL-213
95Swedish Globe World Championships-220
95Swedish World Championships Stickers-65
99German Bundesliga 2-180

Rumsey, Myles
03Swift Current Broncos-15
04Swift Current Broncos-16
05Swift Current Broncos-21
06Swift Current Broncos-20

Rundqvist, Thomas
82Swedish Semic VM Stickers-17
83Swedish Semic Elitserien-112
83Swedish Semic VM Stickers-17
85Swedish Panini Stickers-100
86Swedish Panini Stickers-96
87Swedish Panini Stickers-97
89Swedish Semic Elitserien Stickers-85
89Swedish Semic World Champ Stickers-18
90Swedish Semic Elitserien Stickers-261
91Finnish Semic World Champ Stickers-39
91Swedish Semic Elitserien Stickers-90
91Swedish Semic Elitserien Stickers-314
91Swedish Semic Elitserien Stickers-324
91Swedish Semic Elitserien Stickers-346
91Swedish Semic World Champ Stickers-39
92Finnish Semic-62
92Swedish Semic Elitserien Stickers-112
93Swedish Semic World Champ Stickers-10
94Finnish Jaa Kiekko-69

Runesson, Benny
69Swedish Hockey-289
70Swedish Hockey-192
71Swedish Hockey-278
72Swedish Stickers-253
74Swedish Stickers-263

Runge, David
93Quebec Pee-Wee Tournament-1472
00Rockford IceHogs-15

Runge, Paul
28V128-2 Paulin's Candy-56
34Beehive Group I Photos-203
35Diamond Matchbooks Tan 2-56
35Diamond Matchbooks Tan 3-52
36O-Pee-Chee V304D-106
37O-Pee-Chee V304E-167
37V356 Worldwide Gum-81

Runyan, Eric
93Omaha Lancers-22

Ruoho, Dan
92Northern Michigan Wildcats-21
95Madison Monsters-7
96Madison Monsters-16

Ruohonen, Juhani
66Finnish Jaakiekkosarja-171
70Finnish Jaakiekko-250
71Finnish Suomi Stickers-216
72Finnish Jaakiekko-165
73Finnish Jaakiekko-231
78Finnish SM-Liiga-89

Ruokonen, Miikka
93Finnish Jyvas-Hyva Stickers-56
94Finnish SISU-298
95Finnish SISU-74
96Finnish SISU Redline-74

Ruokosalmi, Ilpo
71Finnish Suomi Stickers-293

Ruontimo, Kari
66Finnish Jaakiekkosarja-87

Ruotanen, Arto
71Finnish Suomi Stickers-311
80Finnish Mallasjuoma-90
89Swedish Semic Elitserien Stickers-100
90Swedish Semic Elitserien Stickers-102
91Finnish Semic World Champ Stickers-12
91Swedish Semic Elitserien Stickers-110
91Swedish Semic World Champ Stickers-12
93Swedish Semic Elitserien-225
94Swedish Leaf-190
95Swedish Leaf-114
95Swedish Upper Deck-174

Ruotsalainen, Markku
70Finnish Jaakiekko-378

Ruotsalainen, Reijo
70Finnish Jaakiekko-379
71Finnish Suomi Stickers-312
77Finnish Sportscasters-86-2041
78Finnish SM-Liiga-10
78Finnish SM-Liiga-138
80Finnish Mallasjuoma-96
81Swedish Semic Hockey VM Stickers-26
82O-Pee-Chee-233
82Post Cereal-13
82Finnish Skopbank-13
82Swedish Semic VM Stickers-155
83NHL Key Tags-90
83O-Pee-Chee-255
83O-Pee-Chee Stickers-216
83Puffy Stickers-19
83Topps Stickers-216
84O-Pee-Chee-153
84O-Pee-Chee Stickers-101
84Topps-115
85O-Pee-Chee-112
85O-Pee-Chee Box Bottoms-M
85O-Pee-Chee Stickers-81
857-Eleven Credit Cards-13
85Topps-112
85Topps Box Bottoms-M
86O-Pee-Chee-128
86O-Pee-Chee Stickers-225
86Topps-128
87Swedish Panini Stickers-115
88Oilers Tenth Anniversary-22
89Devils Caretta-20
89Finnish Pelimiehen-3
89Swedish Semic World Champ Stickers-30
95Finnish SISU-274
Double Trouble-7
95Finnish SISU Limited-66
95Swiss HNL-524
95Swiss HNL-536
99Finnish Cardset Aces High-S-2
06Parkhurst-107
Autographs-107

Ruotsalainen, Vesa
92Finnish Jyvas-Hyva Stickers-93
93Finnish Jyvas-Hyva Stickers-175
93Finnish SISU-168
96Finnish SISU Redline-112
98Finnish Kerailysarja-191
99Finnish Cardset-111

Rupnow, Mark
95South Carolina Stingrays-24
96Mississippi Sea Wolves-18
97Mississippi Sea Wolves-12
99Mississippi Sea Wolves-25
99Mississippi Sea Wolves Kelly Cup-22
01Bossier-Shreveport Mudbugs-17
02Bossier-Shreveport Mudbugs-15

Ruponen, Pasi
92Finnish Jyvas-Hyva Stickers-140
93Finnish Jyvas-Hyva Stickers-256
93Finnish SISU-288
93Finnish SISU Promos-NNO

Rupp, Duane
67Topps-20
69O-Pee-Chee-153
Four-in-One-8
70Esso Power Players-218
70O-Pee-Chee-89
70Sargent Promotions Stamps-166
70Topps-89
71Toronto Sun-226
72O-Pee-Chee-154
72Sargent Promotions Stamps-180
72Topps-28
75O-Pee-Chee WHA-18
77Rochester Americans-2

Rupp, Michael
98Finest Futures Finest-F8
98Finest Futures Finest Refractors-F8
98OPC Chrome-236
Refractors-236
98Topps-236
O-Pee-Chee-236
98Bowman CHL-151
Golden Anniversary-151
OPC International-151
Autographs Blue-A3
Autographs Gold-A3
Autographs Silver-A3
98Bowman Chrome CHL-151
Golden Anniversary-151
Golden Anniversary Refractors-151
OPC International-151
OPC International Refractors-151
Refractors-151
00Albany River Rats-19
01Albany River Rats-13
02Pacific Calder-80
Silver-80
02Albany River Rats-18
02Albany River Rats AAP-22
03Black Diamond-174
Black-174
Green-174
Red-174
03Bowman-55
Gold-55
03Bowman Chrome-55
Refractors-55
Gold Refractors-55
Xfractors-55
03Devils Team Issue-16
03ITG Action-330
03O-Pee-Chee-322
03OPC Blue-322
03OPC Gold-322
03OPC Red-322
03Topps-322
Blue-322
Gold-322
Red-322
03Topps Traded-TT77
Blue-TT77
Gold-TT77
Red-TT77
03Upper Deck MVP-259
Gold Script-259
Silver Script-259
Canadian Exclusives-259
03Czech Stadion-609

Rupprecht, Derek
97Medicine Hat Tigers-14
98Medicine Hat Tigers-17

Rupprecht, Joel
01Red Deer Rebels-14
02Spokane Chiefs-18

Ruprecht, Tomas
95Czech APS Extraliga-264

Ruprecht, Vaclav
94Czech APS Extraliga-146
95Czech APS Extraliga-252
96Czech APS Extraliga-293

Rush, David
93Quebec Pee-Wee Tournament-1731

Rushforth, Paul
917th Inn. Sketch OHL-67
95South Carolina Stingrays-19
96Rochester Americans-18
97Louisiana Ice Gators-18
99UK London Knights-14
00UK Sekonda Superleague-83
01UK London Knights-27
02UK London Knights-17

Rushmer, Bart
97Lethbridge Hurricanes-14
98SP Authentic-121
Power Shift-121
98Upper Deck-398
Exclusives-398
Exclusives 1 of 1-398
Gold Reserve-398
99Brandon Wheat Kings-17
00Kelowna Rockets-10
01Kelowna Rockets-19
02Columbus Cottonmouths-17

Rushton, Jason
92British Columbia JHL-195
95Central Hockey League-82
98El Paso Buzzards-14
04St Georges de Beauce Garaga-20

Rusin, Jerry
93Quebec Pee-Wee Tournament-1429

Rusk, Mike
93Guelph Storm-6
94Guelph Storm-20
98Topeka Scarecrows-4
99Topeka Scarecrows-15
00Fort Worth Brahmas-13
02Fort Worth Brahmas-13

Ruskowski, Terry
75Houston Aeros WHA-15
76O-Pee-Chee WHA-38
77O-Pee-Chee WHA-37
78Jets Postcards-19
79Blackhawks Postcards-19
79O-Pee-Chee-141
80Blackhawks Postcards-10
80Blackhawks White Border-11
80O-Pee-Chee-119
80Topps-119
81Blackhawks Borderless Postcards-22
81Blackhawks Brown Background-11
81O-Pee-Chee-62
81O-Pee-Chee Stickers-117
81Topps-W74
82O-Pee-Chee-72
82O-Pee-Chee Stickers-178
82Post Cereal-4
82Topps Stickers-178
83O-Pee-Chee-161
83O-Pee-Chee Stickers-291
83Topps Stickers-291
84Kings Smokey-14
84O-Pee-Chee-89
84O-Pee-Chee Stickers-270
84Topps-68
85O-Pee-Chee-33
85O-Pee-Chee Stickers-237
85Topps-33
86O-Pee-Chee-111
86O-Pee-Chee Stickers-226
86Penguins Kodak-21
86Topps-111
87North Stars Postcards-28
87O-Pee-Chee-73
87O-Pee-Chee Stickers-167
87Panini Stickers-150
87Topps-73
88North Stars ADA-22
89Saskatoon Blades-1
90Saskatoon Blades-1
907th Inn. Sketch WHL-92
95Houston Aeros-25
99Knoxville Speed-25
00Knoxville Speed-27
03Laredo Bucks-21

Rusnak, Chad
91Saskatoon Blades-8
917th Inn. Sketch WHL-107
92Saskatchewan JHL-47

Rusnak, Darius
82Swedish Semic VM Stickers-92
83Swedish Semic VM Stickers-92
91Finnish Semic World Champ Stickers-115
91Swedish Semic World Champ Stickers-115
92Finnish Jyvas-Hyva Stickers-91

Rusnak, Stefan
04Slovakian Poprad Team Set-6
04Slovakian Poprad Team Set-26

Russell, Bill HK
97SLU Basketball Classic Doubles-2
97SLU Basketball Classic Doubles-6
99Knoxville Speed-13

Russell, Blaine
95Prince Albert Raiders-17
96Prince Albert Raiders-19
98Huntington Blizzard-20
99Huntington Blizzard-17
00Columbus Cottonmouths-15
01Asheville Smoke-23

Russell, Blair
83Hall of Fame-178
83Hall of Fame Postcards-M14
85Hall of Fame-178

Russell, Bobby
92Quebec Pee-Wee Tournament-1013
97Portland Winter Hawks-8
98Hampton Roads Admirals-9
98Milwaukee Admirals-9
99Hampton Roads Admirals-18
00Jackson Bandits-9
00Jackson Bandits Promos-5
01Norfolk Admirals-3
03Florence Pride-155
03Norfolk Admirals-17
04Idaho Steelheads-16

Russell, Cam
89ProCards IHL-71
90Score-408
Canadian-408
90ProCards AHL/IHL-400
91Upper Deck-352
French-352
91ProCards-486
92Blackhawks Coke-2
93Blackhawks Coke-12
93Stadium Club-286
Members Only Master Set-286
First Day Issue-286
94Blackhawks Coke-15
94Leaf-382
95Be A Player-84
Signatures-S84
Signatures Die Cuts-S84
95Blackhawks Coke-13
97Pacific Invincible NHL Regime-45

Russell, Dustin
99Hull Olympiques-8
Signed-8
03St. Francis Xavier X-Men-14

Russell, Ernest
10C56-20
10Sweet Caporal Postcards-35
11C55-35
12C57-26
83Hall of Fame Postcards-I14
85Hall of Fame-133

Russell, Kerry
91ProCards-105

Russell, Kris
04Medicine Hat Tigers-19
05ITG Heroes/Prosp Toronto Expo Parallel -163
05Medicine Hat Tigers-18
05ITG Heroes and Prospects-163
Autographs-A-KR
06Medicine Hat Tigers-16
06ITG Heroes and Prospects-194
Autographs-AKR
Update Autographs-AKR
07ITG Going For Gold World Juniors-7
Autographs-7
Emblems-GUE7
Jerseys-GUJ7
Numbers-GUN7

Russell, Paul
91ProCards-309

Russell, Phil
73O-Pee-Chee-243
74NHL Action Stamps-89
74O-Pee-Chee NHL-226
74Topps-226
75O-Pee-Chee NHL-102
75O-Pee-Chee NHL-211
75Topps-102
75Topps-211
76O-Pee-Chee NHL-31
76O-Pee-Chee NHL-382
76Topps-31
77O-Pee-Chee NHL-235
77Topps-235
78O-Pee-Chee-12
78Topps-12
79Flames Postcards-17
79Flames Team Issue-19
79O-Pee-Chee-143
79Topps-143
80Flames Postcards-19
80O-Pee-Chee-226
80Pepsi-Cola Caps-17
80Topps-226
81Flames Postcards-20
81O-Pee-Chee-51
81O-Pee-Chee Stickers-226
82O-Pee-Chee-58
82Post Cereal-3
83Devils Postcards-24
83NHL Key Tags-16
83O-Pee-Chee-237
83O-Pee-Chee Stickers-271
83Puffy Stickers-9
83Topps Stickers-271
84Devils Postcards-5
84O-Pee-Chee-120
84O-Pee-Chee Stickers-75
84Kelowna Wings-54
85O-Pee-Chee-30
85O-Pee-Chee Stickers-58
85Topps-30
86O-Pee-Chee-142
86Topps-142
89ProCards IHL-163
90ProCards AHL/IHL-391
92Cleveland Lumberjacks-5
02Fleer Throwbacks-71
Gold-71
Platinum-71
04Springfield Falcons-26
05Springfield Falcons-26

Russell, Ryan
03Kootenay Ice-18
04Kootenay Ice-18
05Kootenay Ice-19

Russell, Scott
97Pinnacle Hockey Night in Canada-11

Russell, Ted
95Dayton Bombers-12
96Johnstown Chiefs-17

Russell-Samways, Dean
94UK Guildford Flames-19
95UK Guildford Flames-16

Russo, Angelo
91Nashville Knights-9

Russo, Joseph
93Omaha Lancers-23
93Quebec Pee-Wee Tournament-689

Russo, Matt
92Saskatchewan JHL-63

Ruston, Ben
95Arizona Icecats-14
96Arizona Icecats-17
97Arizona Icecats-19

Ruthemann, Ivo
95Swiss HNL-128
96Swiss HNL-119
96Swiss HNL-356
96Swiss HNL-556
98Swiss Power Play Stickers-70
98Swiss Power Play Stickers-264
99Swiss Panini Stickers-49
99Swiss Panini Stickers-258
00Swiss Panini Stickers-47
00Swiss Panini Stickers National Team-P23
00Swiss Slapshot Mini-Cards-SCB14
01Swiss HNL-93
02Swiss HNL-279
02Swiss HNL-488

Rutherford, David
04South Surrey Eagles-23
04South Surrey Eagles-24
04Surrey Eagles-19a
04Surrey Eagles-19b
04Surrey Eagles-19
05Vancouver Giants-19

Rutherford, Jim
70Esso Power Players-127
70Red Wings Marathon-9
71Letraset Action Replays-7
71Penguins Postcards-17
71Sargent Promotions Stamps-176
72O-Pee-Chee-15
72Sargent Promotions Stamps-175
72Topps-97
73O-Pee-Chee-59
73Topps-59
74NHL Action Stamps-100
74O-Pee-Chee NHL-225
74Topps-225
75O-Pee-Chee NHL-219
75Topps-219
76O-Pee-Chee NHL-88
76Topps-88
77Coca-Cola-21
77O-Pee-Chee NHL-239
77Topps-239
78O-Pee-Chee-74
78Topps-74
79O-Pee-Chee-122
79Red Wings Postcards-14
79Topps-122
80O-Pee-Chee-125
80Pepsi-Cola Caps-95
80Topps-125
917th Inn. Sketch OHL-47
06Parkhurst-108
Autographs-108

Rutherford, M.
25Dominion Chocolates-58

Rutherford, Paul
91Richmond Renegades-7
91Richmond Renegades Set 2-19

Rutland, Art
81Fredericton Express-21
82Fredericton Express-21

Rutledge, Chris
84Belleville Bulls-28

Rutledge, Wayne
68Shirriff Coins-58
72O-Pee-Chee-329
75Houston Aeros WHA-16
76O-Pee-Chee WHA-6
77O-Pee-Chee WHA-11

Rutschi, Daniel
93Swiss HNL-68
95Swiss HNL-222
96Swiss HNL-281

Ruttan, Jack
83Hall of Fame Postcards-K15
85Hall of Fame-149

Rutter, Mike
01Flint Generals-17
02Odessa Jackalopes-16
03Odessa Jackalopes-16
04Odessa Jackalopes-16
05Odessa Jackalopes-17
06Odessa Jackalopes-16

Rutz, Ryan
04Columbus Cottonmouths-14

Ruuska, Ari
71Finnish Suomi Stickers-352

Ruutti, Matti
71Finnish Suomi Stickers-313

Ruuttu, Christian
86Sabres Blue Shield-26
86Sabres Blue Shield Small-26
87O-Pee-Chee-121
87O-Pee-Chee Minis-37
87O-Pee-Chee Stickers-134
87O-Pee-Chee Stickers-144
87Panini Stickers-28
87Sabres Blue Shield-24
87Sabres Wonder Bread/Hostess-24
87Topps-121
88O-Pee-Chee-18
88O-Pee-Chee Stickers-256
88Panini Stickers-227
88Sabres Blue Shield-23
88Sabres Wonder Bread/Hostess-25
88Topps-18
89O-Pee-Chee-68
89O-Pee-Chee Stickers-255
89Panini Stickers-207
89Sabres Blue Shield-19
89Sabres Campbell's-22
89Topps-68
89Finnish Pelimiehen-4
90Bowman-244
Tiffany-244
90O-Pee-Chee-182
90Panini Stickers-20
90Pro Set-29
90Sabres Blue Shield-19
90Sabres Campbell's-22
90Score-77
Canadian-77
90Topps-182
Tiffany-182
90Upper Deck-170
French-170
91Bowman-25
91Bowman-411
91O-Pee-Chee-115
91Panini Stickers-306
91Parkhurst-242
French-242
91Pinnacle-60
French-60
91Pro Set-22
French-22
91Sabres Blue Shield-19
91Sabres Pepsi/Campbell's-19
91Score American-45
91Score Canadian Bilingual-45
91Score Canadian English-45
91Stadium Club-33
91Topps-115
91Upper Deck-104
French-104
Euro-Stars-11
Euro-Stars French-11
91Finnish Semic World Champ Stickers-205
91Swedish Semic World Champ Stickers-205
92Blackhawks Coke-3
92Bowman-341
92OPC Premier-2
92Panini Stickers-250
92Panini Stickers French-250
92Parkhurst-34
Emerald Ice-34
92Pinnacle-317
French-317
92Score-334
Canadian-334
92Stadium Club-330
92Topps-485
Gold-485G
92Ultra-281
92Upper Deck-446
92Finnish Semic-15
93Blackhawks Coke-17
93Donruss-72
93Leaf-334
93OPC Premier-355
Gold-355
93Parkhurst-39
Emerald Ice-39
93Pinnacle-116
Canadian-116
93Score-84
Canadian-84
93Stadium Club-103
Members Only Master Set-103
OPC-103
First Day Issue-103
First Day Issue OPC-103
93Topps/OPC Premier-355
Gold-355
93Upper Deck-141
93Swedish Semic World Champ Stickers-75
94Canada Games NHL POGS-71
94Parkhurst-42
Gold-42
SE Euro-Stars-ES12
94Pinnacle-434
Artist's Proofs-434
Rink Collection-434
94Stadium Club-131
Members Only Master Set-131
First Day Issue-131
Super Team Winner Cards-131
94Upper Deck-56
Electric Ice-56
94Finnish SISU-234
94Finnish SISU Guest Specials-8
94Finnish Jaa Kiekko-43
95Collector's Choice-278
Player's Club-278
Player's Club Platinum-278
95Playoff One on One-103
95Finnish Jaa Kiekko Lehti Ad Cards-6
95Finnish SISU Limited-42
Signed and Sealed-2
95Finnish Semic World Championships-22
95Swedish Leaf-207
95Swedish Leaf-307
95Swedish Upper Deck-210
95Swedish Upper Deck-233
95Swedish Upper Deck-258
95Swedish Globe World Championships-143
96Swedish Semic Wien-25
96Swiss HNL-290
98Finnish Kerailysarja-16
Leijonat-39
99Finnish Cardset Aces High-S-10
99Russian Fetisov Tribute-34
02Finnish Cardset-111

Ruutu, Jarkko
98Finnish Kerailysarja-49
Leijonat-40
99BAP Memorabilia-347
Gold-347
Silver-347
99Pacific Prism-144
Holographic Blue-144
Holographic Gold-144
Holographic Mirror-144
Holographic Purple-144
Premiere Date-144
99Finnish Cardset Par Avion-12
99Syracuse Crunch-20
00O-Pee-Chee-323
00O-Pee-Chee Parallel-323
00Pacific-417
Copper-417
Gold-417
Ice Blue-417
Premiere Date-417
00Topps/OPC-323
Parallel-323
00Topps Chrome-218
OPC Refractors-218
Refractors-218
00Kansas City Blades-16
01BAP Memorabilia-123
Emerald-123
Ruby-123
Sapphire-123
01BAP Signature Series-97
Autographs-97
Autographs Gold-97
01Finnish Cardset-180
02BAP Sig Series Auto Buybacks 2001-97
02Pacific Complete-462
Red-462
02Finnish Cardset-254
03Canucks Postcards-22
03Canucks Sav-on-Foods-19
03ITG Action-600
03Upper Deck MVP-421
Gold Script-421
Silver Script-421
Canadian Exclusives-421
04UD All-World-12
Gold-12
Autographs-12
Triple Autographs-AT-CWR
04Finnish Cardset-23
Parallel-16
Stars of the Game-11
04Swedish Pure Skills-105
Jerseys-JR
Parallel-105
05Parkhurst-477
Facsimile Auto Parallel-477
05Upper Deck MVP-378
Gold-378
Platinum-378
Materials-M-JR
05Finnish Cardset Magicmakers-4
06O-Pee-Chee-401
Rainbow-401
06Upper Deck-406
Exclusives Parallel-406
High Gloss Parallel-406
Masterpieces-406

Ruutu, Mikko
00Finnish Cardset-284
01Finnish Cardset-57
02Finnish Cardset-255

Ruutu, Tuomo
00Finnish Cardset-165
00Finnish Cardset Next Generation-3
01BAP Memorabilia Draft Redemptions-9
01Finnish Cardset-58
01Finnish Cardset-NNO
02SPx Rookie Redemption-R217
02Finnish Cardset-256
Bound for Glory-7
02Finnish Cardset Dynamic Duos-3
02Finnish Cardset Signatures-7
03BAP Memorabilia-171
Emerald-171
Gold-171
Ruby-171
Sapphire-171
Super Rookies-SR1
Super Rookies Gold-SR1
Super Rookies Silver-SR1
03BAP Ultimate Memorabilia Autographs-99
Gold-99
03BAP Ultimate Mem Auto Jerseys-99
03BAP Ultimate Mem Auto Emblems-99
03BAP Ultimate Mem Auto Numbers-99
03BAP Ultimate Mem Calder Candidates-11
03BAP Ultimate Mem Calder Candidates Gold-11
03BAP Ultimate Mem Franch Present Future-7
03BAP Ultimate Memorabilia Heroes-20
03BAP Ultimate Mem Heroes Autos-10
03BAP Ultimate Mem Magnificent Prospects-6
03BAP Ultimate Mem Magnif Prospect Autos-6
03BAP Ultimate Mem Rookie Jersey Emblems-12
03BAP Ultimate Mem Rookie Jsy Emblem Gold-12
03BAP Ultimate Mem Rookie Jersey Numbers-12
03BAP Ultimate Mem Rookie Jsy Number Gold-12
03BAP Ultimate Memorabilia Triple Threads-31
03Beehive-206
Gold-206
Silver-206
Jumbo Variations-7
03Black Diamond-191
Black-191
Green-191
Red-191
03Blackhawks Postcards-22
03Bowman-113
Gold-113
03Bowman Chrome-113
Refractors-113
Gold Refractors-113
Xfractors-113
03Crown Royale-108
Red-109
Retail-108
Retail-109
03eTopps-47
03ITG Action-603
03ITG Toronto Spring Expo Class of 2004-1
03ITG Used Signature Series-121
Autographs Gold-121
03ITG VIP Rookie Debut-1
03McDonald's Pacific-57
03O-Pee-Chee-337
03O-Pee-Chee-337
03OPC Blue-337
03OPC Gold-337
03OPC Red-337
03Pacific-353
03Pacific Calder-108

Silver-108
03Pacific Complete-546
Red-546
03Pacific Heads-Up-107
Hobby LTD-107
Retail LTD-107
03Pacific Invincible-106
Blue-106
Red-106
Retail-106
03Pacific Luxury Suite-85
Gold-85
03Pacific Quest for the Cup-108
Calder Contenders-5
03Pacific Supreme-111
03Pacific Supreme-111A
Blue-111
Red-111
Retail-111
03Parkhurst Toronto Expo Rookie Preview-PRP-16
03Parkhurst Original Six Chicago-14
03Parkhurst Rookie-190
All-Rookie-ART-10
All-Rookie Autographs-ART-TR
All-Rookie Gold-ART-10
Calder Candidates-CMC-14
Calder Candidates Gold-CMC-14
Rookie Emblems-RE-22
Rookie Emblem Autographs-RE-TR
Rookie Emblems Gold-RE-22
Rookie Jerseys-RJ-22
Rookie Jersey Autographs-RJ-TR
Rookie Jerseys Gold-RJ-22
Rookie Numbers-RN-22
Rookie Number Autographs-RN-TR
Rookie Numbers Gold-RN-22
Teammates Gold-RT22
Teammates-RT22
03Private Stock Reserve-111
Blue-111
Red-111
Retail-111
Class Act-3
03SP Authentic-139
Limited-139
Sign of the Times-TR
Sign of the Times-LFR
Signed Patches-TR
03SP Game Used-85
Gold-85
Rookie Exclusives-RE8
03SPx-225
Radiance-225
Spectrum-225
03Titanium-108
Hobby Jersey Number Parallels-108
Retail-108
Retail Jersey Number Parallels-108
03Topps-337
Blue-337
Gold-337
Red-337
03Topps C55-131
Minis-131
Minis American Back-131
Minis American Back Red-131
Minis Bazooka Back-131
Minis Brooklyn Back-131
Minis Hat Trick Back-131
Minis O Canada Back-131
Minis O Canada Back Red-131
Minis Stanley Cup Back-131
03Topps Pristine-101
03Topps Pristine-102
03Topps Pristine-103
Gold Refractor Die Cuts-101
Gold Refractor Die Cuts-102
Gold Refractor Die Cuts-103
Refractors-101
Refractors-102
Refractors-103
Press Plates Black-101
Press Plates Black-102
Press Plates Black-103
Press Plates Cyan-101
Press Plates Cyan-102
Press Plates Cyan-103
Press Plates Magenta-101
Press Plates Magenta-102
Press Plates Magenta-103
Press Plates Yellow-101
Press Plates Yellow-102
Press Plates Yellow-103
03UD Honor Roll-185
03UD Premier Collection-116
NHL Shields-SH-TR
Signatures-PS-TR
Signatures Gold-PS-TR
Skills-SK-RR
Skills Patches-SK-RR
Stars-ST-TR
Stars Patches-ST-TR
Teammates-PT-CB
Teammates Patches-PT-CB
03Upper Deck-210
Canadian Exclusives-210
HG-210
Rookie Threads-RT-7
03Upper Deck Classic Portraits-176
03Upper Deck Ice-124
Glass Parallel-124
03Upper Deck MVP-452
03Upper Deck Rookie Update-160
YoungStars-YS15
YoungStars-YS15A
03Upper Deck Trilogy-174
Limited-174
03Upper Deck Victory-203
03Finnish Cardset D-Day-DD12
03Finnish Cardset Vintage 1983-V3
04Pacific-62
Blue-62
Red-62
04SP Authentic-20
Limited-20
Sign of the Times-ST-TU
Sign of the Times-TS-LRZ
Sign of the Times-SS-FIN
04Topps NHL All-Star FANtasy-6
04Ultimate Collection-69
04Upper Deck Swatch of Six-SS-TR
04Upper Deck World Cup Tribute-KLJPTR
04Upper Deck YoungStars-YS-TR
05Be A Player-17
First Period-17
Second Period-17
Third Period-17
Overtime-17
Outtakes-OT11
Quad Signatures-HAWK
Quad Signatures-RBSS
Signatures-RU
Signatures Gold-RU
05Beehive-20
Matte-20
05Black Diamond-118
Emerald-118
Gold-118
Onyx-118
Ruby-118
Gemography-G-TR
Gemography Emerald-G-TR
Gemography Gold-G-TR
Gemography Onyx-G-TR
Gemography Ruby-G-TR
05Hot Prospects-22
En Fuego-22
Red Hot-22
White Hot-22
05McDonalds Upper Deck-14
05Panini Stickers-211
05Parkhurst-112
Facsimile Auto Parallel-112
True Colors-TCCHI
True Colors-TCCHI
True Colors-TCCHDE
True Colors-TCCHDE
05SP Authentic-22
Limited-22
Prestigious Pairings-PPRA
Scripts to Success-SSTR
Sign of the Times-TU
Sign of the Times Triples-TKRB
05SP Game Used-21
Autographs-21
Gold-21
Authentic Fabrics-AF-TR
Authentic Fabrics Autographs-AAF-TR
Authentic Fabrics Gold-AF-TR
Authentic Patches-AP-TR
Authentic Patches Autographs-AAP-TR
Awesome Authentics-AA-TR
Statscriptions-ST-TR
05SPx-17
Spectrum-17
Winning Combos-WC-KR
Winning Combos Gold-WC-KR
Winning Combos Spectrum-WC-KR
Winning Materials-WM-TR
Winning Materials Gold-WM-TR
Winning Materials Spectrum-WM-TR
05The Cup Masterpiece Pressplate Auto-265
05The Cup Noble Numbers-NNHR
05UD Artifacts-21
Blue-21
Gold-21
Green-21
Pewter-21
Red-21
Auto Facts-AF-TR
Auto Facts Blue-AF-TR
Auto Facts Copper-AF-TR
Auto Facts Pewter-AF-TR
Auto Facts Silver-AF-TR
Gold Autographed-21
Remarkable Artifacts-RA-TR
Remarkable Artifacts Dual-RA-TR
Treasured Patches-TP-TR
Treasured Patches Autographed-TP-TR
Treasured Patches Dual-TPD-TR
Treasured Patches Dual Autographed-TPD-TR
Treasured Patches Pewter-TP-TR
Treasured Patches Silver-TP-TR
Treasured Swatches-TS-TR
Treasured Swatches Autographed-TS-TR
Treasured Swatches Blue-TS-TR
Treasured Swatches Copper-TS-TR
Treasured Swatches Dual-TSD-TR
Treasured Swatches Dual Autographed-TSD-TR
Treasured Swatches Dual Blue-TSD-TR
Treasured Swatches Dual Copper-TSD-TR
Treasured Swatches Dual Maroon-TSD-TR
Treasured Swatches Dual Pewter-TSD-TR
Treasured Swatches Dual Silver-TSD-TR
Treasured Swatches Maroon-TS-TR
Treasured Swatches Pewter-TS-TR
Treasured Swatches Silver-TS-TR
05UD PowerPlay-20
Rainbow-20
05UD Toronto Fall Expo Priority Signings-PS-TR
05Ultimate Collection-20
Gold-20
Ultimate Signatures-USTR
05Ultra-48
Gold-48
Difference Makers-DM7
Difference Makers Jerseys-DMJ-TR
Difference Makers Jersey Autographs-DAJ-TR
Difference Makers Patches-DMP-TR
Difference Makers Patch Autographs-DAP-TR
Fresh Ink-FI-TR
Fresh Ink Blue-FI-TR
Ice-48
05Upper Deck-38
Big Playmakers-B-TR
HG Glossy-38
Jerseys-J-TRU
Notable Numbers-N-TR
05Upper Deck Ice-21
Rainbow-21
Cool Threads-CTTR
Cool Threads Autographs-ACTTR
Cool Threads Glass-CTTR
Cool Threads Patches-CTPTR
Cool Threads Patch Autographs-CAPTR
05Upper Deck MVP-86
Gold-86
Platinum-86
05Upper Deck Rookie Update-21
05Upper Deck Rookie Update-265
05Upper Deck Trilogy-21
05Upper Deck Trilogy-101
Crystal-101
Crystal Autographs-100
Honorary Patches-HP-TR
Honorary Patch Scripts-HSP-TR
Honorary Swatches-HS-TR
Honorary Swatch Scripts-HSS-TR
Scripts-SCS-TR
05Upper Deck Toronto Fall Expo-38
05Upper Deck Victory-44
Black-44
Gold-44
Silver-44
Game Breakers-GB8
06Be A Player-51
Autographs-51
Signatures-TR
Signatures 10-55
Signatures Duals-DKR
Signatures Trios-TRKS
06Be A Player Portraits-26
Dual Signature Portraits-DSNT
Signature Portraits-SPTR
06Beehive-80
Matte-80
06Black Diamond-94
Black-94
Gold-94
Ruby-94
06Blackhawks Postcards-16
06Flair Showcase-25
06Flair Showcase-118
Parallel-25
Parallel-118
Stitches-SSTR
Wave of the Future-WF9
06Fleer-44
Tiffany-44
Fabricology-FTR
06Hot Prospects-22
Red Hot-22
White Hot-22
06O-Pee-Chee-108
Rainbow-108
Swatches-S-TR
06Panini Stickers-210
06SP Authentic-80
Limited-80
06SP Game Used-23
Gold-23
Rainbow-23
Authentic Fabrics Triple-AF3CHI
Authentic Fabrics Triple Patches-AF3CHI
Autographs-23
06SPx-21
Spectrum-21
SPxcitement-X21
SPxcitement Spectrum-X21
Winning Materials-WMTR
Winning Materials Spectrum-WMTR
Winning Materials Autographs-WMTR
06The Cup NHL Shields Duals-DSHHR
06UD Artifacts-80
Blue-80
Gold-80
Platinum-80
Radiance-80
Red-80
Tundra Tandems-TTRK
Tundra Tandems Black-TTRK
Tundra Tandems Blue-TTRK
Tundra Tandems Gold-TTRK
Tundra Tandems Platinum-TTRK
Tundra Tandems Red-TTRK
Tundra Tandems Dual Patches Red-TTRK
06UD Mini Jersey Collection-23
06UD Powerplay-22
Impact Rainbow-22
Specialists-STR
Specialists Patches-PTR
06Ultra-43
Gold Medallion-43
Ice Medallion-43
06Upper Deck Arena Giveaways-CHI1
06Upper Deck-42
Exclusives Parallel-42
High Gloss Parallel-42
Masterpieces-42
Walmart Tins Oversize-42
06Upper Deck MVP-68
Gold Script-68
Super Script-68
Jerseys-OJKR
06Upper Deck Ovation-11
06Upper Deck Sweet Shot Signature Sticks-STTR
06Upper Deck Trilogy-23
06Upper Deck Victory-41
06Upper Deck Victory Black-41
06Upper Deck Victory Gold-41
06Upper Deck Victory Next In Line-NL14
07Upper Deck Ovation-38
07Upper Deck Victory-120
Black-120
Gold-120

Ruzhenikov, Nikolai
00Russian Hockey League-69

Ruzicka, David
05ITG Heroes/Prosp Toronto Expo Parallel -426
05ITG Ultimate Mem Future Stars Autos-15
05ITG Ultimate Mem Future Star Autos Gold-15
05ITG Ultimate Mem Future Stars Jerseys-16
05ITG Ultimate Mem Fut Stars Jerseys Gold-16
05ITG Ultimate Mem Future Stars Mem Autos-15
05ITG Ultimate Mem Fut Star Mem Auto Gold-15
05ITG Heroes and Prospects-426
Autographs Update-A-DRU
06ITG Heroes and Prospects Jerseys-GUJ02
06ITG Heroes and Prospects Jerseys Gold-GUJ02
06ITG Heroes and Prospects Emblems-GUE02
06ITG Heroes and Prospects Emblems Gold-GUE02
06ITG Heroes and Prospects Numbers-GUN02
06ITG Heroes and Prospects Numbers Gold-GUN02

Ruzicka, Martin
03Everett Silvertips-9
04Lethbridge Hurricanes-9
06Czech OFS-212

Ruzicka, Paul
94German First League-252

Ruzicka, Stefan
03Owen Sound Attack-18
04Owen Sound Attack-12
04ITG Heroes and Prospects-105
Autographs-SR
04ITG Heroes/Prospects Toronto Expo '05-105
04ITG Heroes/Prospects Expo Heroes/Pros-105
05ITG Heroes/Prosp Toronto Expo Parallel -395
05Black Diamond-270
05Hot Prospects-155
En Fuego-155
Red Hot-155
White Hot-155
05SP Game Used-226
05SPx-276
05The Cup Masterpiece Pressplate Artifact-308
05The Cup Master Pressplate Black Diamond-270
05The Cup Master Pressplate Rookie Update-166
05The Cup Masterpiece Pressplates SP GU-226
05The Cup Masterpiece Pressplates (SPx)-276
05The Cup Masterpiece Pressplates Trilogy-290
05The Cup Masterpiece Pressplate Ult Coll-218
05UD Artifacts-308
05Ultimate Collection-218
Gold-218
05Upper Deck Rookie Update-166
05Upper Deck Trilogy-290
05Philadelphia Phantoms-19
05ITG Heroes and Prospects-395
06O-Pee-Chee-369
Rainbow-369
06AHL Top Prospects-34
06Philadelphia Phantoms-22

Ruzicka, Vladimir
89Swedish Semic World Champ Stickers-190
90O-Pee-Chee-393
90Pro Set-588
90Score Rookie/Traded-44T
90Topps-393
Tiffany-393
90Upper Deck-538
French-538
91Pro Set Platinum-152
91Bruins Sports Action-17
91OPC Premier-144
91Parkhurst-3
French-3
91Pinnacle-181
French-181
91Pro Set-353
French-353
91Score Canadian Bilingual-411
91Score Canadian English-411
91Score Rookie/Traded-83T
91Stadium Club-383
91Upper Deck-288
French-288
92Bowman-431
92Bruins Postcards-10
92O-Pee-Chee-228
92Panini Stickers-138
92Panini Stickers French-138
92Parkhurst-5
Emerald Ice-5
92Pinnacle-59
French-59
92Pro Set-5
92Score-208
Canadian-208
92Stadium Club-358
92Topps-333
Gold-333G
92Ultra-10
92Upper Deck-258
Euro-Stars-E4
93Donruss-228
93Leaf-438
93Pinnacle-406
Canadian-406
93PowerPlay-174
93Score-154
93Score-562
Gold-562
Canadian-154
Canadian-562
Canadian Gold-562
93Senators Kraft Sheets-21
93Ultra-383
94Czech APS Extraliga-265
95Czech APS Extraliga-135
96Czech APS Extraliga-20
97Czech APS Extraliga-158
97Czech DS Extraliga-76
97Czech DS Stickers-130
98Czech DS-9
98Czech DS Stickers-195
98Czech OFS-216
98Czech OFS-248
Olympic Winners-8
98Czech Bonaparte-4A
98Czech Bonaparte-8A
99Czech DS-119
National Stars-NS17
99Czech OFS-33
99Czech OFS-52
99Czech OFS Jagr Team Embossed-33
00Czech OFS-407
00Czech OFS-417
02Czech IQ Sports Blue-23
02Czech IQ Sports Blue-24
02Czech IQ Sports Yellow-24
04Czech HC Slavia Praha Postcards-7
05Czech Pexeso Mini Red Set-15
06Czech OFS-301
Coaches-8

Ryabchikov, Evgeny
93Parkhurst-533
Emerald Ice-533
93Pinnacle-508
Canadian-508
94Classic-18
Gold-18
Tri-Cards-T4
94Classic Four-Sport *-123
Printers Proofs-123
95Images-70
Gold-70
95Signature Rookies-9
Signatures-9
96Charlotte Checkers-15
96Dayton Bombers-23
96Collector's Edge Ice-61
Prism-61

Ryabikin, Dmitri
94Signature Rookies Tetrad *-111
Signatures-111
98Russian Hockey League-54
99Russian Hockey League-177
00Russian Hockey League-128
00Russian Hockey League-332
02Russian SL-24
03Russian Avangard Omsk-10
03Russian SL-11

Ryan, Billy
04Maine Black Bears-11
05Maine Black Bears-22

Ryan, Bobby
03Owen Sound Attack-8
04Owen Sound Attack-23
04ITG Heroes and Prospects-55
Autographs-BR
04ITG Heroes/Prospects Toronto Expo '05-55
04ITG Heroes/Prospects Expo Heroes/Pros-55
05ITG Heroes/Prosp Toronto Expo Parallel -112
05ITG Heroes/Prosp Toronto Expo Parallel -372
05Extreme Top Prospects Signature Edition-S20
05OHL Bell All-Star Classic-4
05Owen Sound Attack-1
05ITG Heroes and Prospects-112
Aspiring-ASP8
Autographs-A-BR
Autographs-DA-RL
Autographs Series II-BR2
Complete Jerseys-CJ-18
Complete Jerseys Gold-CJ-18
Complete Logos-CHL-1
He Shoots-He Scores Prizes-18
Jerseys-GUJ-1
Jerseys Gold-GUJ-01
Emblems-GUE-1
Emblems Gold-GUE-01
Numbers-GUN-1
Numbers Gold-GUN-01
Nameplates-N-12
Nameplates Gold-N-12
National Pride-NPR-34
Spectrum-STM-03
Spectrum Gold-STM-03
06ITG International Ice-30
Gold-30
Autographs-ABRY
06ITG Ultimate Memorabilia Future Star-12
06ITG Ultimate Memorabilia Future Star Gold-12
06ITG Ultimate Memorabilia Future Star Autos-3
06ITG Ultimate Memorabilia Future Star Autos Gold-3
06ITG Ultimate Memorabilia Future Star Patches Autos-3
06ITG Ultimate Memorabilia Future Star Patches Autos Gold-3
06Owen Sound Attack-8
06ITG Heroes and Prospects-176
Autographs-ABR
Jerseys-GUJ49
Jerseys-GUJ68
Jerseys Gold-GUJ49
Emblems-GUE49
Emblems-GUE68
Emblems Gold-GUE49
Numbers-GUN49
Numbers-GUN68
Numbers Gold-GUN49
Quad Emblems-QE05
Quad Emblems Gold-QE05
Triple Memorabilia-TM07
Triple Memorabilia Gold-TM07
Update Autographs-ABR

Ryan, Chad
98OCN Blizzard-14

Ryan, Cliff
54UK A and BC Chewing Gum-36

Ryan, D'Arcy
76Saginaw Gears-11

Ryan, Greg
897th Inn. Sketch OHL-33
907th Inn. Sketch OHL-142
917th Inn. Sketch OHL-377
92Ottawa 67's-18

Ryan, Joey
03Quebec Remparts-22
04Quebec Remparts-18
05Quebec Remparts-4
05Quebec Remparts Signature Series-4
06Quebec Remparts-3

Ryan, Jonathan
03Victoriaville Tigers-22

Ryan, Kevin
99German Bundesliga 2-191
01Memphis RiverKings-11

Ryan, Matt
02Guelph Storm-13
03Guelph Storm-18
04Manchester Monarchs-14
04Manchester Monarchs Tobacco-14
05Hot Prospects-139
En Fuego-139
Red Hot-139
White Hot-139
05SP Authentic-265
Limited-265
05SPx-267
05The Cup Masterpiece Pressplates (Ice)-242
05The Cup Master Pressplate Rookie Update-143
05The Cup Masterpiece Pressplates SPA-265
05The Cup Masterpiece Pressplates (SPx)-267
05The Cup Masterpiece Pressplates Trilogy-267
05Upper Deck Ice-242
05Upper Deck Rookie Update-143
05Upper Deck Trilogy-267
05Manchester Monarchs-16
05Manchester Monarchs-45
06Manchester Monarchs-14

Ryan, Michael
94Quebec Pee-Wee Tournament-1256
03Rochester Americans-27
04Rochester Americans-21
06Hot Prospects-150
Red Hot-150
White Hot-150
06O-Pee-Chee-593
Rainbow-593
06Rochester Americans-17
06The Cup Masterpiece Pressplates (Marquee Rookies)-593
06Upper Deck-460
Exclusives Parallel-460
High Gloss Parallel-460
Masterpieces-460

Ryan, Mitch
05Waterloo Blackhawks-18

Ryan, Prestin
04Syracuse Crunch-7
05Hot Prospects-182
En Fuego-182
Red Hot-182
White Hot-182
05The Cup Master Pressplate Rookie Update-191
05Upper Deck Rookie Update-191
05Manitoba Moose-18
06Manitoba Moose-4

Ryan, Sean HK
05Ottawa 67's-9
06Ottawa 67s-16

Ryan, Terry (70s)
72Minnesota Fighting Saints Postcards WHA-19

Ryan, Terry (90s)
92British Columbia JHL-201
94Tri-City Americans-8
95Tri-City Americans-21
95Tri-City Americans-30
95Classic-8
Ice Breakers-BK8
Ice Breakers Die Cuts-BK8
95Images-18
Gold-18
Platinum Premier Draft Choice-PD8
95Signature Rookies Auto-Phonex-37
95Signature Rook Auto-Phonex Beyond 2000-B2
95Signature Rook Auto-Phonex Phone Cards-37
95Classic Five-Sport *-130
95Signature Rookies Tetrad Autobilia *-98
95Signature Rookies Tetrad SR Force *-F10
96Donruss Canadian Ice-142
Gold Press Proofs-142
Red Press Proofs-142
O Canada-16
96Donruss Elite Aspirations-11
96Leaf Preferred-141
Press Proofs-141
96Zenith-144
Artist's Proofs-144
97Donruss-24
Press Proofs Silver-24
Press Proofs Gold-24
97Donruss Canadian Ice-128
Dominion Series-128
Provincial Series-128
97Donruss Limited-123
Exposure-123
97Pinnacle-11
Artist's Proofs-11
Rink Collection-11
Press Plates Back Black-11
Press Plates Back Cyan-11
Press Plates Back Magenta-11
Press Plates Back Yellow-11
Press Plates Front Black-11
Press Plates Front Cyan-11
Press Plates Front Magenta-11
Press Plates Front Yellow-11
97Pinnacle Inside-167
97Score Canadiens-15
Platinum-15
Premier-15
98Black Diamond-45
Double Diamond-45
Triple Diamond-45
Quadruple Diamond-45
98Katch-164
98McDonald's Upper Deck-28
98Upper Deck-294
Exclusives-294
Exclusives 1 of 1-294
Gold Reserve-294
98Upper Deck MVP-103
Gold Script-103
Silver Script-103
Super Script-103
99Pacific-216
Copper-216
Emerald Green-216
Gold-216
Ice Blue-216
Premiere Date-216
Red-216
99St. John's Maple Leafs-19
01Idaho Steelheads-14

Ryasenski, Evgeni
05Russian Hockey League RHL-26

Ryazantsev, Alexander
99Bowman CHL-67
Gold-67
OPC International-67
00Hershey Bears-12
00QMJHL All-Star Program Inserts-27
01Hershey Bears-22
02Hershey Bears-17
03Russian National Team-20
05Russian Hockey League RHL-19B

Ryazantsev, Georgy
03Barrie Colts-19

Rybakov, Alexander
05Russian Hockey League RHL-42

Rybar, Joe
98Peoria Rivermen-20
99Peoria Rivermen-16
00Peoria Rivermen-12
01Peoria Rivermen-18

Rybar, Josef
92British Columbia JHL-76
94Czech APS Extraliga-159
95Czech APS Extraliga-260
96Czech APS Extraliga-305

Rybar, Pavol
99Czech DS-184
Goalies-G14
99Czech OFS-547
01Slovakian Kvarteto-7A
04Czech OFS Czech/Slovak-39
04Czech OFS Czech/Slovak-46

Rybin, Artem
00QMJHL All-Star Program Inserts-39
01Russian Hockey League-149

Rybin, Maxim
99Russian Stars Postcards-20
00Sarnia Sting-23
00UD CHL Prospects-38
01Russian Hockey League-105

Rybovic, Lubomir
94Finnish Jaa Kiekko-195

Rychel, Warren
84Sudbury Wolves-15
88ProCards IHL-113
89ProCards IHL-69
90ProCards AHL/IHL-399
91Moncton Hawks-24
91ProCards-175
92Parkhurst-309
Emerald Ice-309
92Upper Deck-547
93Donruss-156
93Leaf-263
93OPC Premier-266
Gold-266
93Parkhurst-98
Emerald Ice-98
93PowerPlay-362
93Score-640
Gold-640
Canadian-640
Canadian Gold-640
93Stadium Club-258
Members Only Master Set-258
First Day Issue-258
93Topps/OPC Premier-266
Gold-266
93Ultra-346
93Upper Deck-93
94Canada Games NHL POGS-128
94Donruss-240
94Leaf-323
94Maple Leafs Kodak-24
94Maple Leafs Pin-up Posters-15
94Parkhurst SE-SE84
Gold-SE84
94Pinnacle-509
Artist's Proofs-509
Rink Collection-509
96Ducks Team Issue-8
97Be A Player-32
Autographs-32
Autographs Die-Cuts-32
Autographs Prismatic Die-Cuts-32
97Pacific-130
Copper-130
Emerald Green-130
Ice Blue-130
Red-130
Silver-130
97Score Mighty Ducks-13
Platinum-13
Premier-13
98Avalanche Team Issue-9
98Pacific-168
Ice Blue-168
Red-168

Rychley, Marty
97Dubuque Fighting Saints-4

Rycroft, Chad
04Columbus Cottonmouths-5

Rycroft, Jesse
05Quad City Mallards-15

Rycroft, Mark
00SPx Rookie Redemption-RR26
00Worcester Icecats-11
01Atomic-122
Premiere Date-122
01Atomic Toronto Fall Expo-122
01BAP Memorabilia-326
Emerald-326
Ruby-326
Sapphire-326
01BAP Signature Series-246
Autographs-246
Autographs Gold-246
01Bowman YoungStars-119
Gold-119
Ice Cubed-119
01Crown Royale-176
01O-Pee-Chee-352
01Pacific Adrenaline-222
Blue-222
Premiere Date-222
Red-222
Retail-222
01Pacific Heads-Up-117
01Private Stock-138
Gold-138
Premiere Date-138
Retail-138
Silver-138
01Private Stock Pacific Nights-138
01Private Stock PS-2002-87
01SP Authentic-171
Limited-171
Limited Gold-171
01SP Game Used-96
01SPx-126
01Titanium-179
Retail-179
01Titanium Draft Day Edition-162
01Topps-352
01Topps Chrome-170
Refractors-170
Black Border Refractors-170
01UD Challenge for the Cup-131
01UD Honor Roll-87
01UD Playmakers-140
01UD Premier Collection-80
01Upper Deck-439
Exclusives-439
01Upper Deck Ice-68
01Upper Deck Vintage-296
01Vanguard-127
Blue-127
Red-127
One of Ones-127
Premiere Date-127
Proofs-127
01Worcester Icecats-25
02Worcester IceCats-15
03Blues Team Set-23
04Pacific-223
Blue-223
Red-223
05Blues Team Set-14
05Parkhurst-425
Facsimile Auto Parallel-425
05Ultra-168
Gold-168
Ice-168
05Upper Deck-168
HG Glossy-168
Notable Numbers-N-MRY
05Upper Deck MVP-335
Gold-335
Platinum-335
05Upper Deck Toronto Fall Expo-168
06Avalanche Team Postcards-12
06O-Pee-Chee-124
Rainbow-124
06Upper Deck-300
Exclusives Parallel-300
High Gloss Parallel-300
Masterpieces-300

Rycroft, Travis
04Peoria Rivermen-9

Rydberg, Ake
64Swedish Coralli ISHockey-129
65Swedish Coralli ISHockey-129

Ryden, Jorgen
89Swedish Semic Elitserien Stickers-75
90Swedish Semic Elitserien Stickers-249
91Swedish Semic Elitserien Stickers-80

Ryder, Colin
92British Columbia JHL-134
00UK Sekonda Superleague-5
03UK Belfast Giants-13

Ryder, Dan
907th Inn. Sketch OHL-394
90Sudbury Wolves-7
917th Inn. Sketch OHL-255
91Sudbury Wolves-13
93Roanoke Express-16
94Roanoke Express-19
06Plymouth Whalers-18
06ITG Heroes and Prospects-190
Autographs-ADR
Update Autographs-ADR

Ryder, Daniel
04Peterborough Petes Postcards-3
05ITG Heroes/Prosp Toronto Expo Parallel -132
05ITG Heroes and Prospects-132
Autographs-A-DR

Ryder, Michael
93Quebec Pee-Wee Tournament-1417
99Hull Olympiques-19
Signed-19
00Black Diamond-75
Gold-75
00Upper Deck-210
Exclusives Tier 1-210
Exclusives Tier 2-210
00Upper Deck Vintage-396
00QMJHL All-Star Program Inserts-38
00Quebec Citadelles-11
Signed-11
01Quebec Citadelles-13
02Hamilton Bulldogs-15
03BAP Memorabilia-242
03BAP Ultimate Memorabilia Autographs-112
Gold-112
03BAP Ultimate Mem Auto Jerseys-112
03BAP Ultimate Mem Auto Emblems-112
03BAP Ultimate Mem Auto Numbers-112
03BAP Ultimate Mem Calder Candidates-3
03BAP Ultimate Mem Calder Candidates Gold-3
03BAP Ultimate Mem Franch Present Future-16
03BAP Ultimate Mem Magnificent Prospects-4
03BAP Ultimate Mem Magnif Prospect Autos-4
03BAP Ultimate Mem Rookie Jersey Emblems-33
03BAP Ultimate Mem Rookie Jsy Emblem Gold-33
03BAP Ultimate Mem Rookie Jersey Numbers-33
03BAP Ultimate Mem Rookie Jsy Number Gold-33
03BAP Ultimate Memorabilia Triple Threads-33
03Beehive-106
Gold-106
Silver-106
03Canadiens Postcards-24
03ITG Action-633
03ITG Used Signature Series-56
Gold-56
Autographs-MRY
Autographs Gold-MRY
03Pacific Calder-57
Silver-57
Reflections-5
03Pacific Complete-597
Red-597
03Pacific Heads-Up-54
Hobby LTD-54
Retail LTD-54
Prime Prospects-13
Prime Prospects LTD-13
03Pacific Quest for the Cup-57
Blue-57
Calder Contenders-12
03Parkhurst Original Six Montreal-10
03Parkhurst Rookie-24
All-Rookie-ART-5
All-Rookie Autographs-ART-MR
All-Rookie Gold-ART-5
Calder Candidates-CMC-2
Calder Candidate Autographs-CMC-MR
Calder Candidates Gold-CMC-2
Rookie Emblems-RE-46
Rookie Emblem Autographs-RE-MR
Rookie Emblems Gold-RE-46
Rookie Jerseys-RJ-46
Rookie Jersey Autographs-RJ-MR
Rookie Jerseys Gold-RJ-46
Rookie Numbers-RN-46
Rookie Number Autographs-RN-MR
Rookie Numbers Gold-RN-46
Teammates Gold-RT16
Teammates-RT16
03SP Authentic-47
Limited-47
03Titanium-56
Hobby Jersey Number Parallels-56
Retail-56
Retail Jersey Number Parallels-56
Right on Target-9
03Topps Traded-TT47
Blue-TT47
Gold-TT47
Red-TT47
03Upper Deck-345
Canadian Exclusives-345
HG-345
UD Exclusives-345
Rookie Update YoungStars-YS1
03Pacific AHL Prospect Destined Greatness-7
04Pacific-141
Blue-141
Red-141
Gold Crown Die-Cuts-5
04SP Authentic-46
Limited-46
Rookie Review-RR-MR
Sign of the Times-ST-RY
Sign of the Times-DS-MJ
Sign of the Times-DS-PM
Sign of the Times-DS-RR
Sign of the Times-TS-RKR
Sign of the Times-FS-MON
Sign of the Times-FS-NED
04UD All-World-59
Gold-59
Autographs-59
Triple Autographs-AT-RCM
Quad Autographs-AQ-SWE
Six Autographs-AS-SWD
04Ultimate Collection Signatures-US-MR
04Ultimate Collection Signature Logos-ULA-MR
04Ultimate Collection Signature Patches-SP-MR
04Upper Deck-92
Canadian Exclusives-92
Heritage Classic-CC-RY
HG Glossy Gold-92
HG Glossy Silver-92
YoungStars-YS-MR
04ITG Heroes and Prospects Emblems-25
04ITG Heroes and Prospects Emblems Gold-25
04ITG Heroes/Prospects He Shoots/Scores-36
04ITG Heroes and Prospects Jersey Autos-25
04ITG Heroes and Prospects Jerseys-25
04ITG Heroes and Prospects Jerseys Gold-25
04ITG Heroes and Prospects Numbers-25
04ITG Heroes and Prospects Numbers Gold-25
05Be A Player-48
First Period-48
Second Period-48
Third Period-48
Overtime-48
Dual Signatures-RR
Dual Signatures-RT
Dual Signatures-SR
Quad Signatures-MONT
Signatures-RY
Signatures Gold-RY
Triple Signatures-MTL
05Beehive-48
Matte-48
Matted Materials-MMMR
Signature Scrapbook-SSRY
05Black Diamond-101
Emerald-101
Gold-101
Onyx-101
Ruby-101
Gemography-G-MR
Gemography Emerald-G-MR
Gemography Gold-G-MR
Gemography Onyx-G-MR
Gemography Ruby-G-MR
05Canadiens Team Issue-19
05Hot Prospects-53
En Fuego-53
Red Hot-53
White Hot-53
05McDonalds Upper Deck-20
05Panini Stickers-72
05Parkhurst-252
Facsimile Auto Parallel-252
True Colors-TCMTL
True Colors-TCMTL
True Colors-TCMOBO
True Colors-TCMOBO
True Colors-TCTOMO
True Colors-TCTOMO
05SP Authentic-54
Limited-54
Prestigious Pairings-PPRR
Scripts to Success-SSRY
Sign of the Times-RY
Sign of the Times Triples-TRRP
Sign of the Times Quads-QTRRK
05SP Game Used-53
Autographs-53
Gold-53
Authentic Fabrics-AF-RY
Authentic Fabrics Autographs-AAF-RY
Authentic Fabrics Dual-RR
Authentic Fabrics Dual Autographs-RR
Authentic Fabrics Gold-AF-RY

Authentic Fabrics Quad-TRRK
Authentic Patches Quad -TRRK
Authentic Patches-AP-RY
Authentic Patches Autographs-AAP-RY
Authentic Patches Dual-RR
Authentic Patches Dual Autographs-RR
Authentic Patches Triple-HRR
Awesome Authentics-AA-RY
Game Gear-GG-RY
Game Gear Autographs-AG-RY
Signature Sticks-SS-MR
SIGnificance-MR
SIGnificance Gold-S-MR
SIGnificance Extra-CR
SIGnificance Extra-RR
SIGnificance Extra Gold-CR
SIGnificance Extra Gold-RR
Significant Numbers-SN-RY
Statscriptions-ST-RY
05SPx-45
Spectrum-45
Winning Combos-WC-RK
Winning Combos-WC-RR
Winning Combos Autographs-AWC-RR
Winning Combos Gold-WC-RK
Winning Combos Gold-WC-RR
Winning Combos Spectrum-WC-RK
Winning Combos Spectrum-WC-RR
Winning Materials-WM-RY
Winning Materials Autographs-AWM-RY
Winning Materials Gold-WM-RY
Winning Materials Spectrum-WM-RY
05The Cup-59
Gold-59
Black Rainbow-59
Dual NHL Shields-DSRR
Emblems of Endorsement-EERY
Limited Logos-LLRY
Masterpiece Pressplates-59
Patch Variation-P59
Patch Variation Autographs-AP59
Scripted Numbers Dual-DSNBR
Scripted Swatches-SSRY
Signature Patches-SPRY
05UD Artifacts-52
Blue-52
Gold-52
Green-52
Pewter-52
Red-52
Auto Facts-AF-RY
Auto Facts Blue-AF-RY
Auto Facts Copper-AF-RY
Auto Facts Pewter-AF-RY
Auto Facts Silver-AF-RY
Gold Autographed-52
Remarkable Artifacts-RA-RY
Remarkable Artifacts Dual-RA-RY
05UD PowerPlay-46
Rainbow-46
Power Marks-PMRY
05UD Toronto Fall Expo Priority Signings-PS-RY
05Ultimate Collection-49
Gold-49
Endorsed Emblems-EERY
Ultimate Signatures-USRY
Ultimate Signatures Trios-UTRRP
05Ultra-107
Gold-107
Ice-107
05Upper Deck-100
Big Playmakers-B-MRY
HG Glossy-100
Jerseys-J-MRY
Majestic Materials-MMMR
NHL Generations-DAR
Notable Numbers-N-RY
Patches-P-MRY
Shooting Stars-S-MRY
05Upper Deck Ice-51
Rainbow-51
05Upper Deck MVP-202
Gold-202
Platinum-202
05Upper Deck Rookie Update-52
05Upper Deck Trilogy-46
05Upper Deck Trilogy-142
Crystal-142
Honorary Patches-HP-RY
Honorary Patch Scripts-HSP-RY
Honorary Swatches-HS-RY
Honorary Swatch Scripts-HSS-RY
05Upper Deck Toronto Fall Expo-100
05Upper Deck Victory-104
Black-104
Gold-104
Silver-104
Blow-Ups-BU21
Game Breakers-GB24
06Be A Player-50
Autographs-50
Signatures-RD
Signatures 10-54
Signatures 25-54
Signatures Duals-DRH
Signatures Trios-TKRL
Signatures Foursomes-FIBRC
Up Close and Personal-UC37
Up Close and Personal Autographs-UC37
06Be A Player Portraits-59
06Beehive-49
06Beehive-190
Blue-49
Gold-49
Matte-49
Red Facsimile Signatures-49
Wood-49
5 X 7 Black and White-49
PhotoGraphs-PGMR
06Black Diamond-139
Black-139
Gold-139
Ruby-139
Jerseys-JRY
Jerseys Black-JRY
Jerseys Gold-JRY
Jerseys Ruby-JRY
Jerseys Black Autographs -JRY
06Canadiens Postcards-19
06Flair Showcase-54
06Flair Showcase-136
06Flair Showcase-241
Parallel-54
Parallel-136
Parallel-241
Hot Numbers-HN25
Hot Numbers Parallel-HN25
Inks-IRY
Stitches-SSRY
Wave of the Future-WF23
06Fleer-105
Tiffany-105
Signing Day-SDRY
06Gatorade-35
06Hot Prospects-53
Red Hot-53
White Hot-53
Hot Materials -HMRY
Hot Materials Red Hot-HMRY
Hot Materials White Hot-HMRY
Hotagraphs-HMR
06McDonald's Upper Deck-24
Autographs-AMR
Jerseys-JMR
Patches-PMR
06O-Pee-Chee-257
Rainbow-257
Swatches-S-RY
06Panini Stickers-68
06SP Authentic-49
06SP Authentic-138
Limited-49
Limited-138
Sign of the Times-STRY
Sign of the Times Duals-STLR
Sign of the Times Duals-STRL
Sign of the Times Triples-ST3RKH
06SP Game Used-54
Gold-54
Rainbow-54
Authentic Fabrics-AFMR
Authentic Fabrics Parallel-AFMR
Authentic Fabrics Patches-AFMR
Authentic Fabrics Dual-AF2KR
Authentic Fabrics Dual Patches-AF2KR
Authentic Fabrics Triple-AF3MTL
Authentic Fabrics Triple Patches-AF3MTL
Autographs-54
By The Letter-BLRY
Inked Sweaters Dual-IS2KR
Inked Sweaters Dual Patches-IS2KR
Letter Marks-LMMR
SIGnificance-SRY
06SPx-54
Spectrum-54
SPxcitement-X57
SPxcitement Spectrum-X57
SPxcitement Autographs-X57
Winning Materials-WMMR
Winning Materials Spectrum-WMMR
Winning Materials Autographs-WMMR
06The Cup-45
Autographed Foundations-CQMR
Autographed Foundations Patches-CQMR
Autographed NHL Shields Duals-DASKR
Autographed NHL Shields Duals-DASRL
Autographed Patches-45
Black Rainbow-45
Foundations-CQMR
Foundations Patches-CQMR
Enshrinements-EMR
Gold-45
Gold Patches-45
Honorable Numbers-HNMR
Jerseys-45
Limited Logos-LLMR
Masterpiece Pressplates-45
Scripted Swatches-SSMR
Signature Patches-SPMR
06UD Artifacts-49
06UD Artifacts-176
Blue-49
Blue-176
Gold-49
Gold-176
Platinum-49
Platinum-176
Radiance-49
Radiance-176
Autographed Radiance Parallel-49
Autographed Radiance Parallel-176
Red-49
Red-176
Auto-Facts-AFMR
Auto-Facts Gold-AFMR
Treasured Patches Black-TSRY
Treasured Patches Blue-TSRY
Treasured Patches Gold-TSRY
Treasured Patches Platinum-TSRY
Treasured Patches Red-TSRY
Treasured Patches Autographed Black Tag Parallel-TSRY
Treasured Swatches-TSRY
Treasured Swatches Black-TSRY
Treasured Swatches Blue-TSRY
Treasured Swatches Gold-TSRY
Treasured Swatches Platinum-TSRY
Treasured Swatches Red-TSRY
Treasured Swatches Autographed Black-TSRY
Tundra Tandems-TTRR
Tundra Tandems Black-TTRR
Tundra Tandems Blue-TTRR
Tundra Tandems Gold-TTRR
Tundra Tandems Platinum-TTRR
Tundra Tandems Red-TTRR
Tundra Tandems Dual Patches Red-TTRR
06UD Mini Jersey Collection-55
Jerseys-MR
Jersey Variations-MR
Jersey Autographs-MR
06UD Powerplay-55
Impact Rainbow-55
06Ultimate Collection-33
Autographed Jerseys-AJ-RY
Autographed Patches-AJ-RY
Jerseys-UJ-MR
Patches-UJ-MR
Signatures-US-MR
Ultimate Signatures Logos-SL-MR
06Ultra-105
Gold Medallion-105
Ice Medallion-105
Difference Makers-DM17
Fresh Ink-IMR
Scoring Kings-SK20
Uniformity-UMR
Uniformity Patches-UPMR
Uniformity Autographed Jerseys-UAMR
06Upper Deck-352
Exclusives Parallel-352
High Gloss Parallel-352
Game Dated Moments-GD34
Game Jerseys-J2MR
Game Patches-P2MR
Hometown Heroes-HH35
Masterpieces-352
Oversized Wal-Mart Exclusives-352
06Upper Deck MVP-159
Gold Script-159
Super Script-159
Autographs-OARS
Jerseys-OJBR
06Upper Deck Ovation-174
06Upper Deck Sweet Shot-57
Signature Shots/Saves-SSMR
Signature Shots/Saves Ice Signings-SSIMR
Signature Shots/Saves Sticks-SSSMR
Signature Sticks-STMR
Sweet Stitches-SSMR
Sweet Stitches Duals-SSMR
Sweet Stitches Triples-SSMR
06Upper Deck Trilogy-53
Combo Autographed Jerseys-CJKR
Combo Autographed Patches-CJKR
Honorary Scripted Patches-HSPMR
Honorary Scripted Swatches-HSSMR
Honorary Swatches-HSMR
Scripts-TSRY
06Upper Deck Victory-105
06Upper Deck Victory Black-105
06Upper Deck Victory Gold-105
06Upper Deck Victory GameBreakers-GB25
06Upper Deck Victory Oversize Cards-MR
07Upper Deck Victory-51
Black-51
Gold-51
Oversize Cards-OS14
Stars on Ice-SI44

Rydin, Ulf
64Swedish Corall ISHockey-135
65Swedish Corall ISHockey-135
67Swedish Hockey-71
69Swedish Hockey-102
70Swedish Hockey-59
71Swedish Hockey-130

Ryding, Steve
90Knoxville Cherokees-104
91Knoxville Cherokees-5

Rydman, Blaine
72Minnesota Fighting Saints Postcards WHA-20

Rydmark, Daniel
86Swedish Panini Stickers-104
89Swedish Semic Elitserien Stickers-93
90Swedish Semic Elitserien Stickers-141
91Swedish Semic Elitserien Stickers-192
92Finnish Semic-68
92Swedish Semic Elitserien Stickers-214
93Swedish Semic Elitserien-185
94Finnish Jaa Kiekko-66
94Swedish Leaf-91
Gold Cards-5
Top Guns-7
95Swedish Globe World Championships-33
95Swedish World Championships Stickers-151
95Phoenix Roadrunners-13
97Swedish Collector's Choice-144
Stick'Ums-S8
98Swedish UD Choice-191
99Swedish Upper Deck-195
Hands of Gold-14
00Swedish Upper Deck-143
SHL Signatures-DR
02Swedish Malmo Red Hawks-9
02Swedish SHL-73
Parallel-73
03Swedish Elite-94
Signatures II-16
Silver-94
04Swedish Elitset-90
04Swedish Elitset-135
Gold-90
Gold-135

Rygl, Martin
05Czech HC Liberec-13

Ryhanen, Leevi
65Finnish Hellas-86

Ryhanen, Sami
06Finnish Cardset-310

Ryles, Tom
94Dubuque Fighting Saints-24

Rylin, Anders
70Swedish Hockey-52
71Swedish Hockey-121
72Swedish Stickers-98
73Swedish Stickers-216
74Swedish Stickers-184

Rylov, Yakov
04Russian Hope-5
04Russian Moscow Dynamo-26

Ryman, Ake
69Swedish Hockey-291
70Swedish Hockey-194
71Swedish Hockey-279
72Swedish Stickers-254

Ryman, Erik
05Swedish SHL Elitset-161
Gold-161

Ryman, Jonny
69Swedish Hockey-290
70Swedish Hockey-193

Rymsha, Andy
90ProCards AHL/IHL-80
96German DEL-130
98German DEL-210
99German DEL-134

Rymsha, Steve
01Greenville Grrrowl-10
02Reading Royals-19
02Reading Royals RBI Sports-183

Rymut, Cody
04South Surrey Eagles-25

Rymut, Corey
04Surrey Eagles-20
04Surrey Eagles-20

Rynnas, Jussi
05Finnish Cardset -340
06Finnish Cardset-168
06Finnish Porin Assat Pelaajakortit-3

Ryno, Johan
06Swedish SHL Elitset-182

Rypien, Rick
02Regina Pats-8
03Regina Pats-8
04Regina Pats-7
05Hot Prospects-180
En Fuego-180
Red Hot-180
White Hot-180
05SP Authentic-284
Limited-284
05SPx-288
05The Cup Masterpiece Pressplate Artifact-337
05The Cup Masterpiece Pressplates (Ice)-234
05The Cup Master Pressplate Rookie Update-187
05The Cup Masterpiece Pressplates SPA-284
05The Cup Masterpiece Pressplates (SPx)-288
05UD Artifacts-337
05Upper Deck Ice-234
05Upper Deck Rookie Update-187
05Manitoba Moose-19
06ITG Heroes and Prospects-46
Autographs-ARR

Rypien, Wes
01Calgary Hitmen-18
01Calgary Hitmen Autographed-18
02Mississauga Ice Dogs-12
04Fresno Falcons-14

Rysanek, Roman
93Swedish Semic World Champ Stickers-100
94Czech APS Extraliga-138
95Czech APS Extraliga-302
96Czech APS Extraliga-201
97Czech APS Extraliga-133
97Czech DS Extraliga-99
97Czech DS Stickers-206
98Czech DS Stickers-256
99Czech OFS-293

Rytnauer, Ladislav
04Czech OFS-18

Rytz, Simon
02Swiss HNL-364

Ryznar, Jason
02Michigan Wolverines-21
03Michigan Wolverines-6
05Black Diamond-260
05Hot Prospects-148
En Fuego-148
Red Hot-148
White Hot-148
05SP Authentic-272
Limited-272
05SP Game Used-223
05SPx-274
05The Cup Masterpiece Pressplate Artifact-298
05The Cup Master Pressplate Black Diamond-260
05The Cup Masterpiece Pressplates (Ice)-261
05The Cup Master Pressplate Rookie Update-156
05The Cup Masterpiece Pressplates SPA-272
05The Cup Masterpiece Pressplates SP GU-223
05The Cup Masterpiece Pressplates (SPx)-274
05The Cup Masterpiece Pressplates Trilogy-279
05The Cup Masterpiece Pressplate Ult Coll-215
05UD Artifacts-298
05Ultimate Collection-215
Gold-215
05Upper Deck Ice-261
05Upper Deck Rookie Update-156
05Upper Deck Trilogy-279
05Albany River Rats-21

Rziga, Milos
05Russian Hockey League RHL-C1

Saadetin, Ali
66Finnish Jaakiekkosarja-191
70Finnish Jaakiekko-136

Saal, Jason
93Detroit Jr. Red Wings-2
93Classic Four-Sport *-221
Gold-221
94Detroit Jr. Red Wings-16
95St. John's Maple Leafs-17
95Classic-84
95Slapshot Memorial Cup-90
96Peoria Rivermen-20
96Peoria Rivermen Photo Album-20
96St. John's Maple Leafs-21
96Collector's Edge Ice-81
Prism-81
97Hampton Roads Admirals-17
98Hampton Roads Admirals-24
00Louisiana Ice Gators-12
02Arkansas Riverblades-13

Saarela, Ilkka
04Finnish Cardset-267

Saarela, Jari
78Finnish SM-Liiga-117

Saarela, Pasi
93Finnish Jyvas-Hyva Stickers-227
93Finnish SISU-199
94Finnish SISU-277
95Finnish SISU-253
96Finnish SISU Redline-54
Mighty Adversaries-2
98Finnish Kerailysarja-111
99Finnish Cardset-159
99Swedish Upper Deck-78
00Finnish Cardset-192
01Finnish Cardset-305
02Finnish Cardset-112
03Finnish Cardset-112
04Finnish Cardset-123
Parallel-92
05Finnish Cardset -289

Saarelainen, Juhani
71Finnish Suomi Stickers-142

Saarenheimo, Pekka
01Finnish Cardset-282
04Finnish Cardset-99
Parallel-73
05Finnish Cardset -95
06Finnish Cardset-287

Saari, Timo
66Finnish Jaakiekkosarja-196
70Finnish Jaakiekko-137
71Finnish Suomi Stickers-158
72Finnish Jaakiekko-111
72Finnish Hellas-21
73Finnish Jaakiekko-211
74Swedish Stickers-31
80Finnish Mallasjuoma-49

Saarikko, Ilkka
71Finnish Suomi Stickers-253

Saarikko, Kari
78Finnish SM-Liiga-94
80Finnish Mallasjuoma-152

Saarikorpi, Jorma
66Finnish Jaakiekkosarja-177
70Finnish Jaakiekko-252
71Finnish Suomi Stickers-143
72Finnish Jaakiekko-204
73Finnish Jaakiekko-167

Saarikoski, Timo
92Finnish Jyvas-Hyva Stickers-125
93Finnish Jyvas-Hyva Stickers-113
93Finnish SISU-25
93Swedish Semic World Champ Stickers-76
94Finnish SISU-135
94Finnish SISU-380
94Finnish SISU Horoscopes-7
94Finnish Jaa Kiekko-47
95Finnish SISU-54
95Swedish World Championships Stickers-182
98Finnish Kerailysarja-112
99Finnish Cardset-309
00Finnish Cardset-285
01Finnish Cardset-55
02Finnish Cardset-258

Saarinen, Ari
93Finnish Jyvas-Hyva Stickers-354
93Finnish SISU-226
94Finnish SISU-94
95Finnish SISU-160
98Finnish Kerailysarja-197

Saarinen, Jesse
04Finnish Cardset-133
Parallel-98
05Finnish Cardset -123
05Finnish Cardset -344
06Finnish Cardset-127
06Finnish Cardset-336
Signature Sensations-24

Saarinen, Jussi
01Finnish Cardset-314
05Finnish Cardset -299
06Finnish Cardset-128

Saarinen, Olli
78Finnish SM-Liiga-116
80Finnish Mallasjuoma-68

Saarinen, Pasi
95Finnish SISU-233
98Finnish Kerailysarja-82
99Finnish Cardset-45
00Finnish Cardset-161
01Finnish Cardset-250
02Finnish Cardset-259
03Finnish Cardset-20
04Finnish Cardset-19
Parallel-12
05Finnish Cardset -15
06Finnish Cardset-199

Saarinen, Rod
90Kitchener Rangers-27
907th Inn. Sketch OHL-239

Saarinen, Sami
92Finnish Jyvas-Hyva Stickers-190

Saarinen, Simo
89Swedish Semic World Champ Stickers-33
91Finnish Semic World Champ Stickers-7
91Finnish Jyvas-Hyva Stickers-6
91Swedish Semic World Champ Stickers-7
92Finnish Jyvas-Hyva Stickers-3
92Finnish Semic-10
93Finnish Jyvas-Hyva Stickers-15
93Finnish SISU-88
93Finnish SISU Promos-NNO
94Finnish SISU-99
95Finnish SISU-4
95Finnish SISU Limited-39

Saarinen, Toni
95Finnish SISU-228
96Finnish SISU Redline-26
99Finnish Cardset-103
00Finnish Cardset-314
01Finnish Cardset-105
03Finnish Cardset-123
04Finnish Cardset-132
Parallel-97

Saarinen, Veijo
66Finnish Jaakiekkosarja-64
70Finnish Jaakiekko-304
71Finnish Suomi Stickers-199

Saario, Kai
71Finnish Suomi Stickers-353

Saarni, Tarmo
73Finnish Jaakiekko-298

Saarnio, Rauno
72Finnish Jaakiekko-336

Saaronlahti, Jari
71Finnish Suomi Stickers-254
73Finnish Jaakiekko-318

Saavinen, Mikko
05Finnish Cardset -77

Sablik, Lukas
95Czech APS Extraliga-177
97Czech APS Extraliga-292
98Czech DS Stickers-108
98Czech OFS-296
99Czech Score Blue 2000-38
99Czech Score Red Ice 2000-38
03Czech OFS Plus-83
03Czech OFS Plus Insert M-M23
06Czech OFS-40

Sabo, Ed
92Richmond Renegades-14
93Lakeland Ice Warriors-21

Sabo, John
03Atlantic City Boardwalk Bullies-21
04Atlantic City Boardwalk Bullies Kinko's-14

Sabo, Steve
91Air Canada SJHL-E49
92Saskatchewan JHL-163

Sabol, Lubomir
06Czech HC Vsetin Postcards-7
06Czech OFS-188

Sabol, Shaun
88ProCards AHL-134
89ProCards AHL-333
90ProCards AHL/IHL-46
91ProCards-202

Sabourin, Corey
98Sudbury Wolves-16
99Sudbury Wolves-4
00Kingston Frontenacs-16

Sabourin, Dany
00Johnstown Chiefs-23
01Johnstown Chiefs-12
02BAP All-Star Edition-115
Gold-115
Silver-115
02BAP Memorabilia-345
02BAP Ultimate Memorabilia-87
02Between the Pipes-104
Gold-104
Silver-104
02Parkhurst Retro-245
Minis-245
02SP Authentic-172
02UD Honor Roll-106
02UD Mask Collection-130
03Pacific Complete-499
Red-499
03Lowell Lock Monsters-8
03Lowell Lock Monsters Photo Album-24
03Pacific AHL Prospects-43
Gold-43
04Wheeling Nailers Riesbeck's-8
04Wilkes-Barre Scranton Penguins-25
05ITG Heroes/Prosp Toronto Expo Parallel -270
05AHL All-Stars-34
05WBS Penguins-22
05ITG Heroes and Prospects-270
Autographs Series II-DSB
06Canucks Postcards-18
06O-Pee-Chee-481
Rainbow-481
06Upper Deck-435
Exclusives Parallel-435
High Gloss Parallel-435
Masterpieces-435

Sabourin, Gary
68Bauer Ads-19
68O-Pee-Chee-117
68Shirriff Coins-157
68Topps-117
69O-Pee-Chee-19
Four-in-One-3
69Topps-19
70Colgate Stamps-57
70Dad's Cookies-115
70Esso Power Players-244
70O-Pee-Chee-96
Deckle-28
70Sargent Promotions Stamps-186
70Topps-96
71Blues Postcards-21
71Letraset Action Replays-6
71O-Pee-Chee-13
71Sargent Promotions Stamps-177
71Toronto Sun-247
72Blues White Border-18
72O-Pee-Chee-91
72Sargent Promotions Stamps-183
72Topps-163
73Blues White Border-17
73O-Pee-Chee-168
73Topps-184
74Maple Leafs Postcards-17
74NHL Action Stamps-253
74O-Pee-Chee NHL-368
75O-Pee-Chee NHL-299
75Topps-299
76O-Pee-Chee NHL-266
92Blues UD Best of the Blues-15
04ITG Franchises US West-153
Autographs-A-GSB

Sabourin, Ken
82Sault Ste. Marie Greyhounds-18
83Sault Ste. Marie Greyhounds-20
84Sault Ste. Marie Greyhounds-20
86Moncton Golden Flames-13
88Salt Lake Golden Eagles-19
89ProCards IHL-204
90Capitals Kodak-23
90Pro Set-596
90ProCards AHL/IHL-610
91Capitals Junior 5x7-24
91Flames Panini Team Stickers-20
91O-Pee-Chee-43
91Score Canadian Bilingual-398
91Score Canadian English-398
91Stadium Club-396
91Topps-43
91Upper Deck-417
French-417
92Salt Lake Golden Eagles-18
94Milwaukee Admirals-21
95Milwaukee Admirals-15
95Milwaukee Admirals Postcards-21
96Milwaukee Admirals-22
97Milwaukee Admirals-17
98Orlando Solar Bears II-20

Sabroe, Andreas
99Danish Hockey League-182

Sacco, David
93PowerPlay-517
93Stadium Club Team USA-22
93Stadium Club Team USA Members Only-22
93Topps Premier Team USA-13
93Ultra-497
93Classic-80
94Donruss-309
94Ducks Carl's Jr.-20
94Leaf-58
94Score-240
Gold-240
Platinum-240
94Upper Deck-328
Electric Ice-328
94Classic Autographs-NNO
96Leaf-218
Press Proofs-218
96Pinnacle-213
Artist's Proofs-213
Foil-213
Premium Stock-213
Rink Collection-213
96Collector's Edge Ice-14
Prism-14

Sacco, Joe
90Maple Leafs Postcards-19
90Newmarket Saints-21
90ProCards AHL/IHL-156
91Parkhurst-395
French-395
91Score American-319
91Score Canadian Bilingual-349
91Score Canadian English-349
92Bowman-417
92Maple Leafs Kodak-31
92O-Pee-Chee-355
92Parkhurst-185
Emerald Ice-185
92Score-532
Canadian-532
92Stadium Club-398
92Ultra-215
92Upper Deck-266
92Upper Deck-382
92St. John's Maple Leafs-19
93Donruss-2
93OPC Premier-329
Gold-329
93Parkhurst-273
Emerald Ice-273
93PowerPlay-9
93Stadium Club-256
Members Only Master Set-256
First Day Issue-256
93Topps/OPC Premier-329
Gold-329
93Ultra-260
93Upper Deck-36
SP-3
94Be A Player-R87
Signature Cards-79
94Canada Games NHL POGS-29
94Donruss-64
94Ducks Carl's Jr.-21
94Leaf-274
94OPC Premier-309
Special Effects-309
94Parkhurst SE-SE5
Gold-SE5
94Pinnacle-232
Artist's Proofs-232
Rink Collection-232
94Stadium Club-161
Members Only Master Set-161
First Day Issue-161
Super Team Winner Cards-161
94Topps/OPC Premier-309
Special Effects-309
94Ultra-6
94Upper Deck-166
Electric Ice-166
95Collector's Choice-68
Player's Club-68
Player's Club Platinum-68
95Donruss-302
95Hoyle Western Playing Cards-15
95Leaf-164
95Score-68
Black Ice Artist's Proofs-68
Black Ice-68
95Topps-86
OPC Inserts-86
95Upper Deck-43
Electric Ice-43
Electric Ice Gold-43
95Finnish Semic World Championships-112
95Swedish World Championships Stickers-229
96Ducks Team Issue-6
96Upper Deck-4
97Be A Player-39
Autographs-39
Autographs Die-Cuts-39
Autographs Prismatic Die-Cuts-39
97Collector's Choice-5
97Pacific-208
Copper-208
Emerald Green-208
Ice Blue-208
Red-208
Silver-208
97Panini Stickers-186
97Score Mighty Ducks-7
Platinum-7
Premier-7
97SP Authentic-3
97Upper Deck-214
98Pacific-287
Ice Blue-287
Red-287
99Panini Stickers-168
99Wayne Gretzky Hockey-174
00Panini Stickers-104
00Upper Deck NHLPA-PA90
01Upper Deck-405
Exclusives-405
06Albany River Rats-25

Sacharuk, Larry
74NHL Action Stamps-249
75O-Pee-Chee NHL-76
75O-Pee-Chee NHL-327
75Topps-76
75Topps-327

Sachl, Petr
97Czech APS Extraliga-285
98Czech DS Stickers-83
00Milwaukee Admirals Keebler-15
00Milwaukee Admirals Postcards-13
01Milwaukee Admirals-22
03Finnish Cardset-138
04Finnish Cardset-145
Parallel-109
06Czech OFS-104

Sacilotto, Enio
00UK Sekonda Superleague-30

Sacka, Ron
91Michigan Wolverines-14
93Michigan Wolverines-18

Sacratini, Vezio
00UK Cardiff Devils-3
00UK Sekonda Superleague-66
01UK Cardiff Devils-15
01UK London Knights-19
02UK Cardiff Devils-15
02UK London Knights-15
03UK Cardiff Devils-14
04UK EIHL All-Stars-12
05UK Cardiff Devils-4
Gold-4
Silver-4
05UK Cardiff Devils Challenge Cup-4

Sadiki, Ridvan
04Slovakian Poprad Team Set-10

Sadowski, John
94Dubuque Fighting Saints-25
98New Hampshire Wildcats-1
00Roanoke Express-15

Safarik, Michal
97Czech APS Extraliga-46
98Czech OFS-342
99Czech Score Blue 2000-22
99Czech Score Blue 2000-23
99Czech Score Red Ice 2000-22
99Czech Score Red Ice 2000-23
00Czech OFS-331
00Czech OFS-375
04Czech OFS-398

Safarik, Richard
95Slapshot Memorial Cup-62

Saffer, Adam
01Czech OFS-279
02Czech OFS Plus-250
03Czech OFS Plus-190
03Czech OFS Plus-386
04Czech OFS-153
06Czech HC Plzen Postcards-1
06Czech OFS-283

Safin, Vener
99Russian Stars Postcards-21
00Russian Hockey League-246

Safonov, Igor
00Russian Hockey League-96

Safronov, Kirill
98Black Diamond-103
Double Diamond-103
Triple Diamond-103
Quadruple Diamond-103
98SPx Top Prospects-73
Radiance-73
Spectrum-73
99Quebec Remparts-3
Signed-3
00QMJHL All-Star Program Inserts-26
01BAP Memorabilia-472
Emerald-472
Ruby-472
Sapphire-472
02Pacific Complete-596
Red-596
02Chicago Wolves-19
03Milwaukee Admirals-1
03Milwaukee Admirals Postcards-17
04Russian Back to Russia-30

Safronov, Yevgeni
02Russian Hockey League-70
03Russian Hockey League-139

Safsten, Gunnar
67Swedish Hockey-128
69Swedish Hockey-142

Sagala, Patrick
93Quebec Pee-Wee Tournament-45

Saganiuk, Rocky
79Maple Leafs Postcards-24
80Maple Leafs Postcards-22
80O-Pee-Chee-64
80Pepsi-Cola Caps-96
80Topps-64
81Maple Leafs Postcards-19
81O-Pee-Chee-323
82O-Pee-Chee-331
82O-Pee-Chee Stickers-69
82Post Cereal-18
82Topps Stickers-69
84Penguins Heinz Photos-20

Sagat, Martin
03Kootenay Ice-21
04Kootenay Ice-19
06Toronto Marlies-25

Sagert, Kalvin
03Kamloops Blazers-3

Sagissor, Tom
90ProCards AHL/IHL-58
91ProCards-81

Saglo, Rostislav
96Pensacola Ice Pilots-6

Saharchuk, Dennis
89Spokane Chiefs-16
907th Inn. Sketch WHL-199
907th Inn. Sketch WHL-327
917th Inn. Sketch WHL-38

Sahin, Ercan
93Swiss HNL-405

Sahlen, Kenneth
64Swedish Corall ISHockey-165
65Swedish Corall ISHockey-165

Sahlin, Anders
67Swedish Hockey-56

Sahlin, Sven Ake
56Swedish Alfabilder-82

Sahlmann, Jarmo
71Finnish Suomi Stickers-271

Sahlstedt, Kalle
92Finnish Jyvas-Hyva Stickers-134
93Finnish Jyvas-Hyva Stickers-228
93Finnish SISU-195
94Finnish SISU-55
94Finnish SISU Junior-10
95Finnish SISU-103
95Finnish Semic World Championships-21
96Finnish SISU Redline-101
96Finnish SISU Redline Promos-8
98Finnish Kerailysarja-247
99Finnish Cardset-138
00Finnish Cardset-342
00Finnish Cardset Master Blasters-6
02Finnish Cardset-260
02Swedish SHL-44
Parallel-44
Signatures Series II-23
03Swedish Elite-52
Silver-52
04Swedish Elitset-56
Gold-56
05Finnish Cardset -276
06Finnish Cardset-104

Sahlsten, Petter
91Swedish Semic Elitserien Stickers-8

Sahlsten, Tommy
67Swedish Hockey-244

Saifullin, Ramil
98Russian Hockey League-125
99Russian Hockey League-148
00Russian Hockey League-233
01Russian Hockey League-96
02Russian Hockey League-128
03Russian Avangard Omsk-15

Saikkonen, Matti
78Finnish SM-Liiga-132

Sailer, Petr
95Czech APS Extraliga-72
96Czech APS Extraliga-259
97Czech APS Extraliga-283
98Czech DS Stickers-82
98Czech OFS-203
99Czech DS-41
99Czech OFS-187
00Czech OFS-23
01Czech OFS-144
02Czech OFS Plus-184
03Czech OFS Plus-271
04Czech OFS Czech/Slovak-13
05Czech HC Ceski Budejovice-13
06Czech HC Ceske Budejovice Postcards-7
06Czech OFS-15

Sailio, Jari
05Finnish Cardset -207
06Finnish Cardset-32
Playmakers Rookies-11
Playmakers Rookies Gold-11
Playmakers Rookies Silver-11

Sailynoja, Keijo
91Finnish Jyvas-Hyva Stickers-22
92Finnish Jyvas-Hyva Stickers-56
92Finnish Semic-23
93Finnish Jyvas-Hyva Stickers-112
93Finnish SISU-17
94Finnish SISU-124
95Finnish SISU-52
96Finnish SISU Redline-48
98Finnish Kerailysarja-202
99Finnish Cardset-118

Saimo, Simo
65Finnish Hellas-28
66Finnish Jaakiekkosarja-2

Saindon, Paul
51Laval Dairy QSHL-70

Saine, Erkki
65Finnish Hellas-44

Sainomaa, Teemu
00Finnish Cardset-286
01Finnish Cardset-53
02Finnish Cardset-261

Saint James, Susan
91Pro Set Platinum-299

Saittakari, Pekka
06Fayetteville FireAntz-15

Sajdl, Karl
94German First League-206

Sakac, Marcel
71Finnish Suomi Stickers-37
72Finnish Panda Toronto-93
72Finnish Semic World Championship-21
72Swedish Semic World Championship-21
74Swedish Semic World Champ Stickers-72
92British Columbia JHL-118
99German Bundesliga 2-142

Sakala, Mark
91Michigan Wolverines-15
93Michigan Wolverines-19
97El Paso Buzzards-3

Sakarov, Petr
99Czech Score Blue 2000-147
99Czech Score Red Ice 2000-147

Saker, Hans
56Swedish Alfabilder-108

Sakharov, Ivan
01Russian Hockey League-3

Sakic, Brian
907th Inn. Sketch WHL-114A
907th Inn. Sketch WHL-114B
91Upper Deck-461
French-461
917th Inn. Sketch WHL-292
92Upper Deck-36
93Flint Generals-4
94Flint Generals-19
95Flint Generals-21
97Flint Generals-18
97Flint Generals EBK-10

98Flint Generals-8
Sakic, Joe
88Nordiques General Foods-31
88Nordiques Team Issue-27
89Kraft-32
89Nordiques Team Issue-36
89Nordiques General Foods-27
89Nordiques Police-25
89O-Pee-Chee-113
89O-Pee-Chee-313
89O-Pee-Chee Stickers-41
89O-Pee-Chee Stickers-185
89O-Pee-Chee Stickers-187
89Panini Stickers-327
89Topps-113
90Bowman-169
Tiffany-169
90Kraft-50
90Kraft-79
90Nordiques Petro-Canada-21
90O-Pee-Chee-384
90OPC Premier-102
90Panini Stickers-139
90Pro Set-257
90Pro Set-375
90Score-8
Canadian-8
90Score Hottest/Rising Stars-7
90Score Young Superstars-10
90Topps-384
Tiffany-384
Team Scoring Leaders-14
Team Scoring Leaders Tiffany-14
90Upper Deck-164
90Upper Deck-301
90Upper Deck-490
French-164
French-301
French-490
91Pro Set Platinum-102
91Bowman-133
91Gillette-22
91Kraft-41
91McDonald's Upper Deck-5
91Nordiques Panini Team Stickers-18
91Nordiques Petro-Canada-25
91O-Pee-Chee-16
91OPC Premier-70
91Panini Stickers-257
91Panini Stickers-334
91Parkhurst-148
French-148
91Pinnacle-150
91Pinnacle-381
French-150
French-381
91Pro Set-199
91Pro Set-315
French-199
French-315
Awards Special-AC5
Puck Candy-23
91Score American-25
91Score American-336
91Score Canadian Bilingual-25
91Score Canadian Bilingual-366
91Score Canadian English-25
91Score Canadian English-366
91Score Kellogg's-12
91Score Young Superstars-20
91Stadium Club-389
91Topps-16
Topps/Bowman Preview Sheet-3
Team Scoring Leaders-8
91Upper Deck-333
91Upper Deck-616
French-333
French-616
91Finnish Semic World Champ Stickers-75
91Swedish Semic World Champ Stickers-75
92Bowman-240
92Bowman-244
92Humpty Dumpty I-19
92McDonald's Upper Deck-26
92Nordiques Petro-Canada-28
92O-Pee-Chee-54
92O-Pee-Chee-55
25th Anniv. Inserts-22
92OPC Premier Star Performers-11
92Panini Stickers-209
92Panini Stickers French-209
92Parkhurst-147
Emerald Ice-147
92Pinnacle-150
French-150
Team 2000-21
Team 2000 French-21
92Pro Set-150
92Score-240
92Score-434
Canadian-240
Canadian-434
Young Superstars-20
92Seasons Patches-47
92Sports Illustrated for Kids II-499
92Stadium Club-3
92Topps-495
Gold-495G
92Ultra-179
92Upper Deck-36
92Upper Deck-255
World Junior Grads-WG8
93Donruss-282
93Kraft-45
93Kraft-65
93Leaf-87
93McDonald's Upper Deck-24
93OPC Premier-10
Gold-10
Black Gold-15
93Panini Stickers-G
93Parkhurst-169
Emerald Ice-169
East/West Stars-E9
93Pinnacle-290
Canadian-290
All-Stars-13
All-Stars Canadian-13
Captains-19
Captains Canadian-19
Team 2001-25
Team 2001 Canadian-25
93PowerPlay-204
Point Leaders-15
93Score-135
Canadian-135
Dream Team-14
Dynamic Duos Canadian-5
Franchise-17
93Seasons Patches-17
93Stadium Club-32
Members Only Master Set-32
OPC-32
First Day Issue-32
First Day Issue OPC-32
All-Stars-17
All-Stars Members Only-17
All-Stars OPC-17
93Topps/OPC Premier-10
Gold-10
93Ultra-242
93Upper Deck-69
93Upper Deck-223
Next In Line-NL3
NHLPA/Roots-16
Silver Skates-H9
Silver Skates Gold-H9
SP-130
93Upper Deck Locker All-Stars-13
93Swedish Semic World Champ Stickers-206
94Action Packed Big Picture 24K Gold-15G
94Be A Player Magazine-3
94Be A Player-R96
94Canada Games NHL POGS-199
94Donruss-141
94EA Sports-112
94Finest-69
Super Team Winners-69
Refractors-69
Bowman's Best-B18
Bowman's Best-X23
Bowman's Best Refractors-B18
Bowman's Best Refractors-X23
94Flair-151
94Fleer-183
94Hockey Wit-100
94Kraft-28
94Leaf-165
Limited Inserts-19
94Leaf Limited-106
94McDonald's Upper Deck-McD1
94Nordiques Burger King-22
94OPC Premier-480
Special Effects-480
94Parkhurst Crash the Game Green-19
94Parkhurst Crash the Game Blue-19
94Parkhurst Crash the Game Gold-19
94Parkhurst Crash the Game Red-19
94Parkhurst Vintage-V34
94Parkhurst SE-SE147
Gold-SE147
94Pinnacle-50
Artist's Proofs-50
Rink Collection-50
Northern Lights-NL4
94Post Box Backs-22
94Score Franchise-TF19
94Score 90 Plus Club-19
94Select-62
Gold-62
94SP-94
Die Cuts-94
Premier-27
Premier Die-Cuts-27
94Stadium Club Members Only-39
94Stadium Club Super Teams-19
94Stadium Club Super Team MemberOnly Set-19
94Topps/OPC Premier-480
Special Effects-480
The Go To Guy-2
94Ultra-180
94Upper Deck-404
Electric Ice-404
Predictor Hobby-H17
94Upper Deck Predictor Hobby Exch Gold-H17
94Upper Deck Predictor Hobby Exch Silver-H17
94Upper Deck SP Inserts-SP65
94Upper Deck SP Inserts Die Cuts-SP65
94Upper Deck NHLPA/Be A Player-14
95Bashan Super Stickers-27
Die-Cut-4
95Bowman-42
All-Foil-42
Bowman's Best-BB11
Bowman's Best Refractors-BB11
95Canada Games NHL POGS-72
95Collector's Choice-288
95Collector's Choice-362
Player's Club-288
Player's Club-362
Player's Club Platinum-288
Player's Club Platinum-362
Crash The Game-C9A
Crash The Game-C9B
Crash The Game-C9C
Crash The Game Gold-C9A
Crash The Game Gold-C9B
Crash The Game Gold-C9C
Crash the Game Silver Redeemed-C9
Crash the Game Silver Bonus-C9
Crash the Game Gold Redeemed-C9
Crash the Game Gold Bonus-C9
95Donruss-167
Elite Inserts-2
95Donruss Elite-16
Die Cut Stars-16
Die Cut Uncut-16
95Emotion-42
Xcel-9
Xcited-13
95Finest-15
95Finest-80
Refractors-15
Refractors-80
95Hoyle Eastern Playing Cards-14
95Imperial Stickers-27
Die Cut Superstars-4
95Kraft-60
95Leaf-182
95Leaf Limited-64
95McDonald's Pinnacle-NNO
95Metal-36
Heavy Metal-12
International Steel-18
95NHL Aces Playing Cards-13C
95Panini Stickers-246
95Parkhurst International-46
Emerald Ice-46
Parkie's Trophy Picks-PP8
Parkie's Trophy Picks-PP16
95Pinnacle Roaring 20s-17
95Playoff One on One-28
95Playoff One on One-139
95Playoff One on One-242
95Pro Magnets-5
95Score-5
Black Ice Artist's Proofs-5
Black Ice-5
Border Battle-4
Golden Blades-1
95Select Certified-45
Mirror Gold-45
Gold Team-8
95SkyBox Impact-41
95SP-31
Stars/Etoiles-E8
Stars/Etoiles Gold-E8
95Stadium Club Members Only-13
95Stadium Club-167
Members Only Master Set-167
95Summit-61
Artist's Proofs-61
Ice-61
95Topps-266
OPC Inserts-266
Mystery Finest-M6
Mystery Finest Refractors-M6
Profiles-PF20
95Topps SuperSkills-17
Platinum-17
95Ultra-136
95Ultra-397
Gold Medallion-136
Extra Attackers-17
Premier Pivots-8
Premier Pivots Gold Medallion-8
Ultraview-9
Ultraview Hot Pack-9
95Upper Deck-54
95Upper Deck-242
Electric Ice-54
Electric Ice-242
Electric Ice Gold-54
Electric Ice Gold-242
95Upper Deck All-Star Game Predictors-5
Redemption Winners-5
95Upper Deck Predictor Retail-R14
95Upper Deck Predictor Retail-R27
95Upper Deck Predictor Retail-R36
95Upper Deck Predictor Retail-R45
95Upper Deck Predictor Retail Exchange-R14
95Upper Deck Predictor Retail Exchange-R27
95Upper Deck Predictor Retail Exchange-R36
95Upper Deck Predictor Retail Exchange-R45
95Upper Deck Special Edition-SE111
95Upper Deck Special Edition Gold-SE111
95Zenith-64
Z-Team-13
95Finnish Semic World Championships-87
95Swedish World Championships Stickers-20
96SLU Hockey Canadian-14
96Headliners Hockey-16
96SLU Hockey American-22
96Avalanche Photo Pucks-2
96Be A Player Biscuit In The Basket-16
96Black Diamond-169
Gold-169
Run for the Cup-RC10
96Collector's Choice-64
96Collector's Choice-299
96Collector's Choice-314
96Collector's Choice-336
MVP-UD5
MVP Gold-UD5
Crash the Game-C7A
Crash the Game-C7B
Crash the Game Gold-C7A
Crash the Game Gold-C7B
Crash the Game Exchange-CR7
Crash the Game Exchange Gold-CR7
96Donruss-1
Press Proofs-1
Elite Inserts-7
Elite Inserts Gold-7
Go Top Shelf-3
96Donruss Canadian Ice-74
Gold Press Proofs-74
Red Press Proofs-74
O Canada-1
96Donruss Elite-120
Die Cut Stars-120
Status-11
96Duracell All-Cherry Team-DC3
96Duracell L'Equipe Beliveau-JB3
96Flair-21
Blue Ice-21
Center Ice Spotlight-7
96Fleer-25
96Fleer-137
Art Ross-20
Pearson-10
96Fleer Picks-2
Captain's Choice-6
Dream Lines-9
Fabulous 50-41
96Hockey Greats Coins-19
Gold-19
96Kenner Starting Lineup Cards-22
96Kraft Upper Deck-39
96Kraft Upper Deck-47
96Leaf-139
Press Proofs-139
Fire On Ice-3
96Leaf Leather And Laces Promos-P1
96Leaf Leather And Laces-1
96Leaf Limited-56
Gold-56
Stubble-16
96Leaf Preferred-37
Press Proofs-37
Steel-11
Steel Gold-11
Steel Power-1
96Maggers-89
96McDonald's Pinnacle-10
96Metal Universe-38
Ice Carvings-12
Ice Carvings Super Power-12
Lethal Weapons-16
Lethal Weapons Super Power-16
96NHL Aces Playing Cards-42
96NHL Pro Stamps-5
96Pinnacle-201
Artist's Proofs-201
Foil-201
Premium Stock-201
Rink Collection-201
Team Pinnacle-1
Trophies-9
96Pinnacle Fantasy-FC17
96Pinnacle Mint-11
Bronze-11
Gold-11
Silver-11
Coins Brass-11
Coins Solid Gold-11
Coins Gold Plated-11
Coins Nickel-11
Coins Silver-11
96Playoff One on One-432
96Post Upper Deck-19
96Score-9
Artist's Proofs-9
Dealer's Choice Artist's Proofs-9
Special Artist's Proofs-9
Golden Blades-9
Dream Team-3
Sudden Death-11
96Select Certified-16
Artist's Proofs-16
Blue-16
Mirror Blue-16
Mirror Gold-16
Mirror Red-16
Red-16
Cornerstones-9
96SkyBox Impact-28
Countdown to Impact-10
VersaTeam-9
96SP-34
Clearcut Winner-CW19
Inside Info-IN6
Inside Info Gold-IN6
96SPx-9
Gold-9
96Stadium Club Members Only-17
96Summit-1
Artist's Proofs-1
Ice-1
Metal-1
Premium Stock-1
High Voltage-2
High Voltage Mirage-2
Untouchables-3
96Team Out-18
96Topps Picks Fantasy Team-FT20
96Topps Picks Top Shelf-TS12
96Ultra-40
Gold Medallion-40
Power-15
Power Red Line-7
96Upper Deck-204
96Upper Deck-240
Generation Next-X3
Hart Hopefuls Bronze-HH20
Hart Hopefuls Gold-HH20
Hart Hopefuls Silver-HH20
Lord Stanley's Heroes Finals-LS7
Lord Stanley's Heroes Quarterfinals-LS7
Lord Stanley's Heroes Semifinals-LS7
Superstar Showdown-SS16A
96Upper Deck Ice-108
Parallel-108
Stanley Cup Foundation-S5
Stanley Cup Foundation Dynasty-S5
96Zenith-44
Artist's Proofs-44
Champion Salute-8
Champion Salute Diamond-8
96Swedish Semic Wien-95
97SLU Hockey One on One-6
97Headliners Hockey-23
97Avalanche Pins-2
97Be A Player-83
Autographs-83
Autographs Die-Cuts-83
Autographs Prismatic Die-Cuts-83
Take A Number-19
97Beehive-4
Golden Portraits-4
Team-19
Team Gold-19
97Black Diamond-96
Double Diamond-96
Triple Diamond-96
Quadruple Diamond-96
Premium Cut-PC29
Premium Cut Double Diamond-PC29
Premium Cut Quadruple Diamond Horiz-PC29
Premium Cut Triple Diamond-PC29
Premium Cut Quadruple Diamond Verticals-PC29
97Collector's Choice-55
Crash the Game-C18A
Crash the Game-C18B
Crash the Game-C18C
Crash the Game Exchange-CR18
Star Quest-SQ63
Stick'Ums-S19
World Domination-W6
97Crown Royale-38
Emerald Green-38
Ice Blue-38
Silver-38
Hat Tricks Die-Cuts-5
Lamplighters Cel-Fusion Die-Cuts-6
97Donruss-117
Press Proofs Silver-117
Press Proofs Gold-117
Line 2 Line-12
Line 2 Line Die Cut-12
97Donruss Canadian Ice-102
Dominion Series-102
Provincial Series-102
National Pride-17
Stanley Cup Scrapbook-3
97Donruss Elite-49
97Donruss Elite-115
Aspirations-49
Aspirations-115
Status-49
Status-115
Craftsmen-3
Master Craftsmen-3
Prime Numbers-11A
Prime Numbers-11B
Prime Numbers-11C
Prime Numbers Die-Cuts-11A
Prime Numbers Die-Cuts-11C
97Donruss Limited-36
97Donruss Limited-132
97Donruss Limited-190
Exposure-36
Exposure-132
Exposure-190
Fabric of the Game-4
Fabric of the Game-5
97Donruss Preferred-128
97Donruss Preferred-175
Cut to the Chase-128
Cut to the Chase-175
Line of the Times-8A
97Donruss Preferred Line of Times Promos-8A
97Donruss Preferred Precious Metals-11
97Donruss Priority-17
97Donruss Priority-208
Stamp of Approval-17
Stamp of Approval-208
Direct Deposit-11
Postcards-9
Postcards Opening Day Issues-15
Stamps-9
Stamps Bronze-9
Stamps Gold-9
Stamps Silver-9
97Esso Olympic Hockey Heroes-7
97Esso Olympic Hockey Heroes French-7
97Gatorade Stickers-6
97Jell-O Juniors To Pros-6
97Katch-42
Gold-42
Silver-42
97Kraft Team Canada-2
97Leaf-35
Fractal Matrix-35
Fractal Matrix Die Cuts-35
Banner Season-24
Fire On Ice-7
97Leaf International-35
Universal Ice-35
97McDonald's Team Canada Coins-8
97McDonald's Upper Deck-5
97Pacific-38
Copper-38
Emerald Green-38
Ice Blue-38
Red-38
Silver-38
Gold Crown Die-Cuts-9
Slap Shots Die-Cuts-2B
97Pacific Dynagon-34
Copper-34
Dark Grey-34
Emerald Green-34
Ice Blue-34
Red-34
Silver-34
Best Kept Secrets-27
Dynamic Duos-6B
Kings of the NHL-4
Tandems-2
97Pacific Invincible-39
Copper-39
Emerald Green-39
Ice Blue-39
Red-39
Silver-39
Attack Zone-7
Feature Performers-10
NHL Regime-57
Off The Glass-6
97Pacific Omega-65
Copper-65
Dark Gray-65
Emerald Green-65
Gold-65
Ice Blue-65
Game Face-4
Silks-5
Stick Handle Laser Cuts-6
Team Leaders-5
97Panini Stickers-204
97Paramount-55
Copper-55
Dark Grey-55
Emerald Green-55
Ice Blue-55
Red-55
Silver-55
Big Numbers Die-Cuts-7
Canadian Greats-5
Photoengravings-7
97Pinnacle-32
Artist's Proofs-32
Rink Collection-32
Epix Game Emerald-3
Epix Game Orange-3
Epix Game Purple-3
Epix Moment Emerald-3
Epix Moment Orange-3
Epix Moment Purple-3
Epix Play Emerald-3
Epix Play Orange-3
Epix Play Purple-3
Epix Season Emerald-3
Epix Season Orange-3
Epix Season Purple-3
Press Plates Back Black-32
Press Plates Back Cyan-32
Press Plates Back Magenta-32
Press Plates Back Yellow-32
Press Plates Front Black-32
Press Plates Front Cyan-32
Press Plates Front Magenta-32
Press Plates Front Yellow-32
97Pinnacle Certified-50
Red-50
Mirror Blue-50
Mirror Gold-50
Mirror Red-50
97Pinnacle Inside-54
Coach's Collection-54
Executive Collection-54
Track-8
Cans-8
Cans Gold-8
97Pinnacle Mint-12
Bronze-12
Gold Team-12
Silver Team-12
Coins Brass-12
Coins Brass Proofs-12
Coins Gold Plated-12
Coins Gold Plated Proofs-12
Coins Nickel Silver-12
Coins Nickel Silver Proofs-12
Coins Solid Gold-12
Coins Solid Silver-12
97Pinnacle Power Pack Blow-Ups-12
97Pinnacle Tot Cert Platinum Blue-50
97Pinnacle Tot Cert Platinum Gold-50
97Pinnacle Totally Certified Platinum Red-50
97Pinnacle Tot Cert Mirror Platinum Gold-50
97Post Pinnacle-3
97Revolution-39
Copper-39
Emerald-39
Ice Blue-39
Silver-39
1998 All-Star Game Die-Cuts-8
97Score-125
Artist's Proofs-125
Golden Blades-125
97Score Avalanche-18
Platinum-18
Premier-18
97SP Authentic-35
Icons-I4
Icons Die-Cuts-I4
Icons Embossed-I4
97SPx-12
Bronze-12
Gold-12
Silver-12
Steel-12
DuoView-10
Grand Finale-12
97Studio-23
Press Proofs Silver-23
Press Proofs Gold-23
Hard Hats-17
Portraits-23
Silhouettes-12
Silhouettes 8x10-12
97Upper Deck-253
Blow-Ups 3 x 5-2-3
Blow-Ups 5 x 7-3A
Game Dated Moments-253
Game Jerseys-GJ7
Sixth Sense Masters-SS19
Sixth Sense Wizards-SS19
Smooth Grooves-SG35
The Specialists-4
The Specialists Level 2 Die Cuts-4
Three Star Selects-3A
97Upper Deck Diamond Vision-20
Signature Moves-20
Defining Moments-DM5
97Upper Deck Ice-79
Parallel-79
Champions-IC10
Champions 2 Die Cuts-IC10
Power Shift-79
97Zenith-29
Z-Gold-29
Z-Silver-29
97Zenith 5 x 7-7
Gold Impulse-7
Silver Impulse-7
98NHL Pro Zone-60
98SLU Hockey-200
98Aurora-52
Atomic Laser Cuts-7
Championship Fever-13
Championship Fever Copper-13
Championship Fever Ice Blue-13
Championship Fever Red-13
Championship Fever Silver-13
Cubes-6
Front Line Copper-4
Front Line Ice Blue-4
Front Line Red-4
Man Advantage-6
98Avalanche Team Issue-10
98Be A Player-37
Press Release-37
98BAP Gold-37
98BAP Autographs-37
98BAP Autographs Gold-37
98BAP AS Game Used Stick Cards-S12
98BAP AS Game Used Jersey Cards-AS13
98BAP Playoff Game Used Jerseys-G6
98BAP Playoff Game Used Jersey Autographs-G6
98BAP Playoff Highlights-H10
98BAP Playoff Practice Used Jerseys-P15
98BAP Tampa Bay All Star Game-37
98Black Diamond-23
Double Diamond-23
Triple Diamond-23
Quadruple Diamond-23
Myriad-M13
Myriad 2-M13
Winning Formula Gold-WF8
Winning Formula Platinum-WF8
98Bowman's Best-49
Refractors-49
Atomic Refractors-49
98Crown Royale-36
Limited Series-36
Master Performers-6
Pillars of the Game-8
Pivotal Players-5
98Donruss Elite Promos-12
98Finest-91
No Protectors-91
No Protectors Refractors-91
Refractors-91
Double Sided Mystery Finest-M23
Double Sided Mystery Finest-M26
Double Sided Mystery Finest-M28
Double Sided Mystery Finest-M30
Double Sided Mystery Refractors-M23
Double Sided Mystery Refractors-M26
Double Sided Mystery Refractors-M28
Double Sided Mystery Refractors-M30
Red Lighters-R15
Red Lighters Refractors-R15
98Jell-O Spoons-8
98Katch-41
98Kenner Starting Lineup Cards-29
98McDonald's Upper Deck-3
98NHL Game Day Promotion-COL4
98OPC Chrome-68
Refractors-68
98Pacific-169
Ice Blue-169
Red-169
Dynagon Ice Inserts-7
Titanium Ice-7
Gold Crown Die-Cuts-10
Timelines-5
98Pacific Dynagon Ice-52
Blue-52
Red-52
Adrenaline Rush Bronze-6
Adrenaline Rush Ice Blue-6
Adrenaline Rush Red-6
Adrenaline Rush Silver-6
Forward Thinking-6
Montreal Spring Expo '99-52
98Pacific Omega-65
Red-65
Opening Day Issue-65
EO Portraits-6
EO Portraits 1 of 1-6
Face to Face-6
Online-10
Planet Ice-22
Planet Ice Parallel-22
Prism-6
Toronto Spring Expo-65
98Panini Photocards-72
98Panini Stickers-189
98Paramount-61
Copper-61
Emerald Green-61
Holo-Electric-61
Ice Blue-61
Silver-61
Ice Galaxy-4
Ice Galaxy Gold-4
Ice Galaxy Silver-4
Special Delivery Die-Cuts-5
98Post-14
98Revolution-39
Ice Shadow-39
Red-39
Chalk Talk Laser-Cuts-5
Showstoppers-12
Three Pronged Attack-24
Three Pronged Attack Parallel-24
98SP Authentic-22
Power Shift-22
Snapshots-SS19
Stat Masters-S8
98SPx Finite-22
98SPx Finite-92
98SPx Finite-163
Radiance-22
Radiance-92
Radiance-163
Spectrum-22
Spectrum-92
Spectrum-163
98SPx Top Prospects-15
Radiance-15
Spectrum-15
Highlight Heroes-H8
Lasting Impressions-L13
Premier Stars-PS22
Winning Materials-JS
98Topps-68
O-Pee-Chee-68
Local Legends-L10
Mystery Finest Bronze-M20
Mystery Finest Bronze Refractors-M20
Mystery Finest Gold-M20
Mystery Finest Gold Refractors-M20
Mystery Finest Silver-M20
Mystery Finest Silver Refractors-M20
98Topps Gold Label Class 1-65
Black-65
Black One of One-65
One of One-65
Red-65
Red One of One-65
98Topps Gold Label Class 2-65
98Topps Gold Label Class 2 Black-65
98Topps Gold Label Class 2 Black 1 of 1-65
98Topps Gold Label Class 2 One of One-65
98Topps Gold Label Class 2 Red-65
98Topps Gold Label Class 2 Red One of One-65
98Topps Gold Label Class 3-65
98Topps Gold Label Class 3 Black-65
98Topps Gold Label Class 3 Black 1 of 1-65
98Topps Gold Label Class 3 One of One-65
98Topps Gold Label Class 3 Red-65
98Topps Gold Label Class 3 Red One of One-65
98Topps Gold Label Goal Race '99-GR10
98Topps Gold Label Goal Race '99 Black-GR10
98Topps Gold Label Goal '99 Black 1 of 1-GR10
98Topps Gold Label Goal Race 99 1 of 1-GR10
98Topps Gold Label Goal Race '99 Red-GR10
98Topps Gold Label GoalRace 99 Red 1 of 1-GR10
98UD Choice-59
98UD Choice-230
Mini Bobbing Head-BH19
98UD Choice Preview-59
98UD Choice Prime Choice Reserve-59
98UD Choice Prime Choice Reserve-230
98UD Choice Reserve-59
98UD Choice Reserve-230
98UD Choice StarQuest Blue-SQ11
98UD Choice StarQuest Gold-SQ11
98UD Choice StarQuest Green-SQ11
98UD Choice StarQuest Red-SQ11
98UD3-59
98UD3-119
98UD3-179
Die-Cuts-59
Die-Cuts-119
Die-Cuts-179
98Upper Deck-248
Exclusives-248
Exclusives 1 of 1-248
Fantastic Finishers-FF6
Fantastic Finishers Quantum 1-FF6
Fantastic Finishers Quantum 2-FF6
Fantastic Finishers Quantum 3-FF6
Frozen In Time-FT23
Frozen In Time Quantum 1-FT23
Frozen In Time Quantum 2-FT23
Frozen In Time Quantum 3-FT23
Lord Stanley's Heroes-LS2
Lord Stanley's Heroes Quantum 1-LS2
Lord Stanley's Heroes Quantum 2-LS2
Lord Stanley's Heroes Quantum 3-LS2
Gold Reserve-248
98Upper Deck MVP-53
Gold Script-53
Silver Script-53
Super Script-53
OT Heroes-OT15
Snipers-S10
Special Forces-F15
98Slovakian Eurotel-20
99SLU Hockey Classic Doubles-3
99SLU Hockey Pro Action-60
99Aurora-42
Striped-42
Premiere Date-42
Premiere Date Striped-42
Championship Fever-9
Championship Fever Copper-9
Championship Fever Ice Blue-9
Championship Fever Silver-9
99Avalanche Pins-1
99Avalanche Team Issue-21
99BAP Memorabilia-103
Gold-103
Silver-103
99BAP Update Teammates Jersey Cards-TM43
99BAP Update Teammates Jersey Cards-TM44
99BAP Millennium-67
Emerald-67
Ruby-67
Sapphire-67
Signatures-67
Signatures Gold-67
Jerseys-J28
Jersey Autographs-J28
Jersey and Stick Cards-JS28
Jersey Emblems-E28
Jersey Numbers-N28
99Black Diamond-25
Diamond Cut-25
Final Cut-25
A Piece of History-JS
A Piece of History Double-JS
A Piece of History Triple-JS
Myriad-M4
99Crown Royale-40
Limited Series-40
Premiere Date-40
Ice Elite-8
Ice Elite Parallel-8
Team Captain Die-Cuts-3
99Jell-O Partners of Power-9
99Kraft Dinner-10
99O-Pee-Chee-1
99O-Pee-Chee-285A
99O-Pee-Chee-285B
99O-Pee-Chee-285C
99O-Pee-Chee-285D
99O-Pee-Chee-285E
99O-Pee-Chee Chrome-1
99O-Pee-Chee Chrome-285A
99O-Pee-Chee Chrome-285B
99O-Pee-Chee Chrome-285C
99O-Pee-Chee Chrome-285D
99O-Pee-Chee Chrome-285E
99O-Pee-Chee Chrome Ice Masters-IM1
99O-Pee-Chee Chrome Ice Masters Refractor-IM1
99O-Pee-Chee Chrome Refractors-1
99O-Pee-Chee Chrome Refractors-285A
99O-Pee-Chee Chrome Refractors-285B
99O-Pee-Chee Chrome Refractors-285C
99O-Pee-Chee Chrome Refractors-285D
99O-Pee-Chee Chrome Refractors-285E
99O-Pee-Chee Chrome A-Men-AM5
99O-Pee-Chee Chrome A-Men Refractors-AM5
99O-Pee-Chee Chrome Fantastic Finishers-FF6
99OPC Chrome Fantastic Finishers Ref-FF6
99O-Pee-Chee Ice Masters-IM1
99O-Pee-Chee A-Men-AM5
99O-Pee-Chee Fantastic Finishers-FF6
99O-Pee-Chee Top of the World-TW14
99Pacific-115
Copper-115
Emerald Green-115
Gold-115
Ice Blue-115
Premiere Date-115
Red-115
Center Ice-8
Center Ice Proofs-8
Cramer's Choice-5
Gold Crown Die-Cuts-12
Past and Present-8
99Pacific Dynagon Ice-60
Blue-60
Copper-60
Gold-60
Premiere Date-60
2000 All-Star Preview-6
Checkmates American-6
Checkmates American-21
Checkmates Canadian-21
Lamplighter Net-Fusions-4
Lords of the Rink-6
99Pacific Omega-66
Copper-66
Gold-66
Ice Blue-66
Premiere Date-66
Cup Contenders-5
North American All-Stars-3
99Pacific Prism-41
Holographic Blue-41
Holographic Gold-41
Holographic Mirror-41
Holographic Purple-41
Premiere Date-41
Sno-Globe Die-Cuts-7
99Panini Stickers-210
99Panini Stickers-327
99Paramount-68
Copper-68
Emerald-68
Gold-68
Holographic Emerald-68
Holographic Gold-68
Holographic Silver-68
Ice Blue-68
Premiere Date-68
Red-68
Silver-68
Ice Advantage-7
Ice Advantage Proofs-7
Personal Best-11
99Revolution-43
Premiere Date-43
Red-43
Shadow Series-43
Ice Sculptures-4
NHL Icons-7
Showstoppers-11
Top of the Line-13
Copper-43
Gold-43
CSC Silver-43
99SP Authentic-23
Special Forces-SF2
99SPx-39
Radiance-39
Spectrum-39
Prolifics-P4
99Stadium Club-47
First Day Issue-47
One of a Kind-47
Printing Plates Black-47
Printing Plates Cyan-47
Printing Plates Magenta-47
Printing Plates Yellow-47
Chrome-23
Chrome Refractors-23
Chrome Oversized-12
Chrome Oversized Refractors-12
Eyes of the Game-EG5
Eyes of the Game Refractors-EG5
Onyx Extreme-OE6
Onyx Extreme Die-Cut-OE6
99Topps/OPC-1
99Topps/OPC-285A
99Topps/OPC-285B
99Topps/OPC-285C
99Topps/OPC-285D
99Topps/OPC-285E
Autographs-TA1
A-Men-AM5
Fantastic Finishers-FF6
Ice Masters-IM1
99Topps Stanley Cup Heroes-SC10
99Topps Stanley Cup Heroes Refractors-SC10
99Topps/OPC Top of the World-TW14
99Topps/OPC Chrome-1
99Topps/OPC Chrome-285A
99Topps/OPC Chrome-285B
99Topps/OPC Chrome-285C
99Topps/OPC Chrome-285D
99Topps/OPC Chrome-285E
Refractors-1
Refractors-285A
Refractors-285B
Refractors-285C
Refractors-285D
Refractors-285E
A-Men-AM5
A-Men Refractors-AM5
Fantastic Finishers-FF6
Fantastic Finishers Refractors-FF6
Ice Masters-IM1
Ice Masters Refractors-IM1
99Topps Gold Label Class 1-35
Black-35
Black One of One-35
One of One-35
Red-35
Red One of One-35
99Topps Gold Label Class 2-35
99Topps Gold Label Class 2 Black-35
99Topps Gold Label Class 2 Black 1 of 1-35
99Topps Gold Label Class 2 One of One-35
99Topps Gold Label Class 2 Red-35
99Topps Gold Label Class 2 Red One of One-35
99Topps Gold Label Class 3-35
99Topps Gold Label Class 3 Black-35
99Topps Gold Label Class 3 Black 1 of 1-35
99Topps Gold Label Class 3 One of One-35
99Topps Gold Label Class 3 Red-35
99Topps Gold Label Class 3 Red One of One-35
99Topps Gold Label Prime Gold-PG11
99Topps Gold Label Prime Gold One of One -PG11

99Topps Gold Label Prime Gold Black-PG11
99Topps Gold Label Prime Gold Black One of One - PG11
99Topps Gold Label Prime Gold Red-PG11
99Topps Gold Label Prime Gold Red One of One - PG11
99Topps Premier Plus-68
Parallel-68
Feature Presentations-FP1
99Ultimate Victory-23
1/1-23
Parallel-23
Parallel 100-23
Frozen Fury-FF9
Stature-S2
99Upper Deck-159
99Upper Deck-211
Exclusives-159
Exclusives-211
Exclusives 1 of 1-159
Exclusives 1 of 1-211
Crunch Time-CT6
Crunch Time Quantum Gold-CT6
Crunch Time Quantum Silver-CT6
Fantastic Finishers-FF15
Fantastic Finishers Quantum Gold-FF15
Fantastic Finishers Quantum Silver-FF15
Game Jerseys-JS
Game Jersey Patch-JSP
Headed for the Hall-HOF13
Headed for the Hall Quantum Gold-HOF13
Headed for the Hall Quantum Silver-HOF13
99Upper Deck Century Legends-65
Century Collection-65
99Upper Deck Gold Reserve-159
99Upper Deck Gold Reserve-211
99Upper Deck HoloGrFx-15
Ausome-15
99Upper Deck MVP-51
Gold Script-51
Silver Script-51
Super Script-51
Game-Used Souvenirs-GU22
99Upper Deck MVP SC Edition-52
Gold Script-52
Silver Script-52
Super Script-52
Clutch Performers-CP3
Game-Used Souvenirs-GUJS
Stanley Cup Talent-SC4
99Upper Deck Ovation-17
Standing Ovation-17
99Upper Deck Retro-21
Gold-21
Platinum-21
99Upper Deck Victory-79
99Upper Deck Victory-335
99Upper Deck Victory-340
99Wayne Gretzky Hockey-46
Elements of the Game-EG14
Great Heroes-GH3
00SLU Hockey-200
00Aurora-41
Pinstripes-41
Pinstripes Premiere Date-41
Premiere Date-41
Styrotechs-4A
00BAP Memorabilia-233
Emerald-233
Ruby-233
Sapphire-233
Promos-233
Jersey Cards-J24
Jersey Emblems-E24
Jersey Numbers-N24
Jersey and Stick Cards-JS24
00BAP Mem Chicago Sportsfest Copper-233
00BAP Memorabilia Chicago Sportsfest Blue-233
00BAP Memorabilia Chicago Sportsfest Gold-233
00BAP Memorabilia Chicago Sportsfest Ruby-233
00BAP Memorabilia Chicago Sun-Times Ruby-233
00BAP Memorabilia Chicago Sun-Times Gold-233
00BAP Mem Chicago Sun-Times Sapphire-233
00BAP Mem Toronto Fall Expo Copper-233
00BAP Memorabilia Toronto Fall Expo Gold-233
00BAP Memorabilia Toronto Fall Expo Ruby-233
00BAP Memorabilia Update Teammates-TM28
00BAP Memorabilia Update Teammates-TM34
00BAP Memorabilia Update Teammates Gold-TM28
00BAP Memorabilia Update Teammates Gold-TM34
00BAP Parkhurst 2000-P13
00BAP Signature Series-167
Emerald-167
Ruby-167
Sapphire-167
Autographs-170
Autographs Gold-170
He Shoots-He Scores Points-17
He Shoots-He Scores Prizes-22
Jersey Cards-J31
Jersey and Stick Cards-GSJ31
Jersey Cards Autographs-J31
Jersey Emblems-E31
Jersey Numbers-IN31
00BAP Ultimate Memorabilia Autographs-28
Gold-28
00BAP Ultimate Memorabilia Captain's C-C8
00BAP Ultimate Mem Game-Used Jerseys-GJ28
00BAP Ultimate Mem Game-Used Emblems-E25
00BAP Ultimate Mem Game-Used Numbers-N25
00BAP Ultimate Mem Game-Used Sticks-GS28
00BAP Ultimate Memorabilia Teammates-TM16
00BAP Ultimate Memorabilia Teammates-TM17
00Black Diamond Game Gear-GSA
00Crown Royale-31
Ice Blue-31
Limited Series-31
Premiere Date-31
Red-31
Game-Worn Jersey Redemptions-3
Jewels of the Crown-10
00Kraft-22
00McDonald's Pacific-10
Blue-10
00O-Pee-Chee-109
00O-Pee-Chee Parallel-109
00Pacific-121
Copper-121
Gold-121
Ice Blue-121
Premiere Date-121
Jerseys-4
Jersey Patches-4
Gold Crown Die Cuts-9
North American Stars-2
Reflections-6
00Panini Stickers-132
00Paramount-63
Copper-63
Gold-63
Holo-Gold-63
Holo-Silver-63
Ice Blue-63
Premiere Date-63
Epic Scope-7
Freeze Frame-9
Game Used Sticks-5
Jersey and Patches-4
00Private Stock-26
Gold-26
Premiere Date-26
Retail-26
Silver-26
Artist's Canvas-8
Artist's Canvas Proofs-8
Extreme Action-5
Game Gear-29
Game Gear-30
PS-2001 Action-13
PS-2001 Stars-8
Reserve-7
00Revolution-39
Blue-39
Premiere Date-39
Red-39
HD NHL-10
NHL Game Gear-2
NHL Icons-8
Stat Masters-24
00SP Authentic-25
00SP Game Used-14
Patch Cards-P-JS
Tools of the Game-JS
Tools of the Game Exclusives-JS
Tools of the Game Combos-C-SS
00SPx-13
Spectrum-13
SPXcitement-X4
Winning Materials-JS
00Stadium Club-182
Beam Team-BT8
Souvenirs-SCS2
00Titanium-23
Blue-23
Gold-23
Premiere Date-23
Red-23
Retail-23
All-Stars-5NA
Game Gear-9
Game Gear-79
Game Gear-153
Game Gear Patches-79
Three-Star Selections-12
00Titanium Draft Day Edition-26
00Topps/OPC-109
Parallel-109
Own the Game-OTG9
1000 Point Club-PC15
00Topps Chrome-85
OPC Refractors-85
Refractors-85
1000 Point Club Refractors-15
00Topps Gold Label Class 1-65
Gold-65
00Topps Gold Label Class 2-65
00Topps Gold Label Class 2 Gold-65
00Topps Gold Label Class 3-65
00Topps Gold Label Class 3 Gold-65
00Topps Gold Label Golden Greats-GG8
00Topps Gold Label Golden Greats 1 to 1-GG8
00Topps Heritage-54
Chrome Parallel-54
00Topps Premier Plus-19
Blue Ice-19
00Topps Stars-25
00Topps Stars-137
Blue-25
Blue-137
All-Star Authority-ASA9
00UD Heroes-142
NHL Leaders-L3
00UD Reserve-24
Gold Strike-GS2
On-Ice Success-OS3
00Upper Deck-273
Exclusives Tier 1-273
Exclusives Tier 2-273
Game Jerseys-JS
Game Jerseys-JS
Game Jersey Autographs Exclusives-EJS
Game Jersey Doubles-DJS
Game Jersey Patches-JSP
Game Jersey Patch Autographs Exclusives-JSP
Lord Stanley's Heroes-L2
Profiles-P2
Triple Threat-TT5
Legends Legendary Game Jerseys-JJS
Legends Supreme Milestones-SM7
00Upper Deck MVP-48
First Stars-48
Second Stars-48
Talent-M4
Third Stars-48
00Upper Deck Victory-62
00Upper Deck Victory-245
00Upper Deck Victory-293
00Upper Deck Vintage-88
00Upper Deck Vintage-98
00Upper Deck Vintage-99
Star Tandems-S2A
00Vanguard-30
Dual Game-Worn Jerseys-3
Dual Game-Worn Patches-3
High Voltage-9
High Voltage Gold-9
High Voltage Green-9
High Voltage Red-9
High Voltage Silver-9
Holographic Gold-30
Holographic Purple-30
Pacific Proofs-30
00Czech Stadion-192
01Atomic-27
Blue-27
Gold-27
Premiere Date-27
Red-27
Blast-3
Jerseys-14
Patches-14
Power Play-10
Statosphere-12
Team Nucleus-4
01Avalanche Team Issue-15
01BAP Memorabilia-149
Emerald-149
Ruby-149
Sapphire-149
All-Star Jerseys-ASJ12
All-Star Emblems-ASE12
All-Star Numbers-ASN12
All-Star Jersey Doubles-DASJ7
All-Star Starting Lineup-SL12
All-Star Teammates-AST3
All-Star Teammates-AST10
All-Star Teammates-AST35
All-Star Teammates-AST41
Country of Origin-CO5
He Shoots-He Scores Points-16
He Shoots-He Scores Prizes-28
Patented Power-PP5
Stanley Cup Champions-CA10
Stanley Cup Playoffs-SC9
01BAP Signature Series Certified 100-C20
01BAP Signature Series Certified 50-C20
01BAP Signature Series Certified 1 of 1's-C20
01BAP Signature Series Autographs-LJS
01BAP Signature Series Autographs Gold-LJS
01BAP Signature Series Franchise Jerseys-FP-8
01BAP Sig Series He Shoots/Scores Points-19
01BAP Sig Series He Shoots/Scores Prizes-2
01BAP Signature Series Jerseys-GJ-16
01BAP Signature Series Jersey Autographs-GUJS
01BAP Sig Series Jersey and Stick Cards-GSJ-16
01BAP Signature Series Emblems-GUE-15
01BAP Signature Series Numbers-ITN-15
01BAP Signature Series Teammates-TM-8
01BAP Ultimate Memorabilia Active Eight-1
01BAP Ultimate Mem All-Star History-45
01BAP Ultimate Memorabilia Autographs-9
01BAP Ultimate Mem Autographs Gold-9
01BAP Ultimate Memorabilia Dynamic Duos-3
01BAP Ultimate Memorabilia Emblems-15
01BAP Ultimate Memorabilia Gloves Are Off-9
01BAP Ultimate Memorabilia Jerseys-15
01BAP Ultimate Mem Jerseys and Sticks-15
01BAP Ultimate Memorabilia Numbers-12
01BAP Ultimate Memorabilia Name Plates-26
01BAP Ultimate Mem Playoff Records-19
01BAP Ultimate Mem Prototypical Players-9
01BAP Ultimate Memorabilia Retro Trophies-1
01BAP Ultimate Memorabilia Retro Trophies-6
01BAP Ultimate Memorabilia Retro Trophies-20
01Bowman YoungStars-15
Gold-15
Ice Cubed-15
01Crown Royale-40
Blue-40
Premiere Date-40
Red-40
Retail-40
All-Star Honors-5
Crowning Achievement-13
Jewels of the Crown-8
Triple Threads-7
Triple Threads-11
01eTopps-1
01McDonald's Pacific-7
Hockey Greats-2
Jersey Patches Silver-4
Jersey Patches Gold-4
01Nortel All-Star Game Sheets-8
01O-Pee-Chee-27
01O-Pee-Chee-318
01O-Pee-Chee Heritage Parallel-27
01O-Pee-Chee Heritage Parallel Limited-27
01O-Pee-Chee Premier Parallel-27
01O-Pee-Chee Premier Parallel-318
01Pacific-107
01Pacific-408
01Pacific-427
Extreme LTD-107
Gold-408
Gold-427
Hobby LTD-107
Premiere Date-107
Retail LTD-107
All-Stars-NA5
Cramer's Choice-4
Jerseys-9
Gold Crown Die-Cuts-7
01Pacific Adrenaline-50
Blue-50
Premiere Date-50
Red-50
Retail-50
Blade Runners-3
Jerseys-10
World Beaters-3
01Pacific Arena Exclusives-107
01Pacific Arena Exclusives-408
01Pacific Arena Exclusives-427
01Pacific Heads-Up-26
Blue-26
Premiere Date-26
Red-26
Silver-26
HD NHL-3
Quad Jerseys-8
Quad Jerseys-21
Rink Immortals-3
Stat Masters-4
01Parkhurst-26
Gold-26
Silver-26
He Shoots-He Scores Points-14
He Shoots-He Scores Prizes-10
Heroes-H8
Jerseys-PJ15
Jersey and Stick-PSJ13
Milestones-M47
Sticks-PS15
Teammates-T5
Teammates-T22
Waving the Flag-2
01Private Stock-24
Gold-24
Premiere Date-24
Retail-24
Silver-24
Game Gear-31
Game Gear Patches-31
01Private Stock Pacific Nights-24
01Private Stock PS-2002-20
01Private Stock Reserve-S3
01SP Authentic-16
01SP Authentic-94
Limited-16
Limited-94
Limited Gold-16
Limited Gold-94
Jerseys-NNJS
01SP Game Used-10
Authentic Fabric-AFJS
Authentic Fabric-AFSA
Authentic Fabric-DJS
Authentic Fabric-TFFSR
Authentic Fabric-FSRB
Authentic Fabric-GYSL
Authentic Fabric Gold-AFJS
Authentic Fabric Gold-AFSA
Patches-PJS
Patches-CPSR
Patches-TPSSP
01SPx-13
01SPx-81
Hidden Treasures-TTYLS
01Sports Illustrated for Kids III-49
01Sports Illustrated for Kids III-260
01Stadium Club-61
Award Winners-61
Master Photos-61
Gallery-G6
Gallery Gold-G6
NHL Passport-NHLP19
Perennials-P2
Souvenirs-JSCD
Souvenirs-PFJS
Souvenirs-JSCDPF
01Titanium-37
Hobby Parallel-37
Premiere Date-37
Retail-37
Retail Parallel-37
Double-Sided Jerseys-12
Double-Sided Jerseys-42
Double-Sided Patches-12
Double-Sided Patches-42
Three-Star Selections-13
01Titanium Draft Day Edition-27
01Topps-27
01Topps-318
Heritage Parallel-27
Heritage Parallel Limited-27
OPC Parallel-27
OPC Parallel-318
Captain's Cloth-CC1
Own The Game-OTG2
Shot Masters-SM4
Stars of the Game-SG4
01Topps Chrome-27
Refractors-27
Black Border Refractors-27
01Topps Heritage-74
01Topps Heritage-115
01Topps Heritage-123
01Topps Heritage-124
01Topps Heritage-125
01Topps Heritage-130
Refractors-74
01Topps Heritage Avalanche NHL AS Game-4
01Topps Reserve-1
Emblems-JS
Jerseys-JS
Name Plates-JS
Numbers-JS
Patches-JS
01UD Challenge for the Cup-17
Century Men-CM2
Cornerstones-CR3
Future Famers-FF1
Jerseys-TNJS
Jerseys-UCSH
01UD Honor Roll-14
01UD Honor Roll-44
Jerseys-J-JS
Jerseys Gold-J-JS
Playoff Matchups-HS-SR
Playoff Matchups Gold-HS-SR
Student of the Game-SG2
01UD Mask Collection-22
Gold-22
Dual Jerseys-PMSB
01UD Playmakers-23
01UD Premier Collection-11
Dual Jerseys-DKS
Dual Jerseys-DSR
Dual Jerseys Black-DKS
Dual Jerseys Black-DSR
Jerseys-BJS
Jerseys-SJS
Jerseys Black-B-JS
Jerseys Black-S-JS
01UD Stanley Cup Champs-37
Jerseys-T-JS
Pieces of Glory-G-JS
Sticks-S-JS
01UD Top Shelf-8
Jerseys-JS
Sticks-SJS
Sticks-KSF
Sticks-RSF
Sticks Gold-SJS
Sticks Gold-KSF
Sticks Gold-RSF
01Upper Deck-274
Exclusives-274
Crunch Timers-CT1
Fantastic Finishers-FF9
Franchise Cornerstones-FC6
Game Jerseys-AJO
Game Jerseys-FSR
Game Jerseys Series II-FJJS
Game Jerseys Series II-PFJS
Game Jerseys Series II-DJSF
Game Jerseys Series II-TJRBH
Gate Attractions-GA8
Leaders of the Pack-LP3
Patches-PJS
Patches-PSA
Patches Series II-PNJS
Patches Series II-NAJS
Pride of a Nation-PNJS
Pride of a Nation-DPRS
Shooting Stars-SS3
Skilled Stars-SS13
Tandems-T2
01Upper Deck Avalanche NHL All-Star Game-HH3
01Upper Deck Avalanche NHL All-Star Game-PP2
01Upper Deck Ice-90
Combos-C-JS
Combos Gold-C-JS
First Rounders-F-JS
01Upper Deck MVP-43
Morning Skate Jerseys-J-JS
Souvenirs-C-JS
Souvenirs Gold-C-JS
Talent-MT2
Valuable Commodities-VC3
Watch-MW2
01Upper Deck Pearson Awards-3
01Upper Deck Victory-91
01Upper Deck Victory-397
Gold-91
Gold-397
01Upper Deck Vintage-64
01Upper Deck Vintage-69
01Upper Deck Vintage-70
01Upper Deck Vintage-261
01Upper Deck Vintage-263
01Upper Deck Vintage-264
01Upper Deck Vintage-265
Next In Line-NLGS
01Vanguard-27
Blue-27
Red-27
East Meets West-3
In Focus-2
Memorabilia-9
Memorabilia-10
One of Ones-27
Patches-10
Premiere Date-27
Proofs-27
V-Team-12
01Czech Stadion-255
02McFarlane Hockey Team Canada-10
02McFarlane Hockey-70
02McFarlane Hockey-72
02McFarlane Hockey-250
02McFarlane Hockey-252
02Atomic-27
Blue-27
Gold-27
Red-27
Cold Fusion-9
Hobby Parallel-27
National Pride-C4
02Avalanche Postcards-9
02BAP All-Star Edition-80
02BAP All-Star Edition-81
He Shoots-He Scores Points-17
He Shoots-He Score Prizes-25
Jerseys-80
Jerseys-81
Jerseys Gold-80
Jerseys Gold-81
Jerseys Silver-80
Jerseys Silver-81
02BAP First Edition-154
02BAP First Edition-321
02BAP First Edition-429H
Debut Jerseys-20
He Shoots-He Score Points-15
He Shoots-He Score Prizes-6
Jerseys-154
Scoring Leaders-7
02BAP Memorabilia-108
Emerald-108
Ruby-108
Sapphire-108
All-Star Jerseys-ASJ-51
All-Star Emblems-ASE-20
All-Star Numbers-ASN-20
All-Star Teammmates-AST-21
He Shoots-He Scores Points-12
He Shoots-He Scores Prizes-9
Mini Stanley Cups-39
NHL All-Star Game-108
NHL All-Star Game Blue-108
NHL All-Star Game Green-108
NHL All-Star Game Red-108
Teammates-TM-4
02BAP Memorabilia Toronto Fall Expo-108
02BAP NHL All-Star History-45
02BAP Signature Series-141
Autographs-141
Autograph Buybacks 1998-37
Autograph Buybacks 1999-67
Autograph Buybacks 2000-170
Autograph Buybacks 2001-LJS
Autographs Gold-141
Complete Jersey-CJ9
Franchise Players-FJ9
Golf-GS43
Jerseys-SGJ22
Jersey Autographs-SGJ22
Team Quads-TQ1
Triple Memorabilia-TM10
02BAP Ultimate Memorabilia Active Eight-7
02BAP Ultimate Memorabilia Autographs-20
02BAP Ultimate Mem Autographs Gold-20
02BAP Ultimate Memorabilia Captains-8
02BAP Ultimate Memorabilia Conn Smythe-24
02BAP Ultimate Memorabilia Dynamic Duos-7
02BAP Ultimate Memorabilia Emblems-13
02BAP Ultimate Mem 500 Goal Scorers-2
02BAP Ultimate Mem 500 Goal Jersey/Stick-2
02BAP Ultimate Mem 500 Goal Emblems-2
02BAP Ultimate Mem Global Dominators-6
02BAP Ultimate Memorabilia Gloves Are Off-3
02BAP Ultimate Memorabilia Hat Tricks-14
02BAP Ultimate Memorabilia Jerseys-16
02BAP Ultimate Mem Jersey and Stick-20
02BAP Ultimate Mem Lifetime Achievers-20
02BAP Ultimate Mem Magnificent Ones-7
02BAP Ultimate Mem Magnificent Ones Autos-7
02BAP Ultimate Memorabilia Nameplates-14
02BAP Ultimate Memorabilia Numbers-25
02BAP Ultimate Memorabilia Numerology-22
02BAP Ultimate Mem Playoff Scorers-2
02BAP Ultimate Mem Playoff Scorers-7
02BAP Ultimate Memorabilia Retro Trophies-20
02Between the Pipes Nightmares-GN8
02Bowman YoungStars-41
Gold-41
Silver-41
02Crown Royale-26
Blue-26
Red-26
Retail-26
Jerseys-3
Jerseys Gold-3
Dual Patches-6
Lords of the Rink-7
Royal Portraits-4
02eTopps-9
02ITG Used-13
02ITG Used-113
International Experience-IE17
International Experience Gold-IE17
Jerseys-GUJ22
Jersey Autographs-GUJ22
Jerseys Gold-GUJ22
Emblems-E22
Jersey and Stick-SJ22
Jersey and Stick Gold-SJ22
Teammates-T10
Teammates Gold-T10
Triple Memorabilia-TM8
Triple Memorabilia Gold-TM8
02McDonald's Pacific-10
Jersey Patches Silver-4
Jersey Patches Gold-4
Salt Lake Gold-9
02O-Pee-Chee-196
02O-Pee-Chee-330
02O-Pee-Chee Jumbos-6
02O-Pee-Chee Premier Blue Parallel-196
02O-Pee-Chee Premier Blue Parallel-330
02O-Pee-Chee Premier Red Parallel-196
02O-Pee-Chee Premier Red Parallel-330
02O-Pee-Chee Factory Set-196
02O-Pee-Chee Factory Set-330
02Pacific-96
Blue-96
Red-96
Impact Zone-5
Jerseys-11
Jerseys Holo-Silver-11
Lamplighters-6
Maximum Impact-12
02Pacific Calder-35
Silver-35
Hardware Heroes-3
02Pacific Complete-13
Red-13
02Pacific Exclusive-46
Etched in Stone-4
Maximum Overdrive-7
02Pacific Heads-Up-33
Blue-33
Purple-33
Red-33
Etched in Time-8
Inside the Numbers-8
Postseason Picks-5
Quad Jerseys-9
Quad Jerseys Gold-9
Stat Masters-7
02Pacific Quest for the Cup-24
Gold-24
Raising the Cup-3
02Parkhurst-109
Bronze-109
Gold-109
Silver-109
Hardware-A4
Hardware-H4
Hardware-P4
He Shoots-He Scores Points-7
He Shoots-He Scores Prizes-20
Jerseys-GJ34
Mario's Mates-MM8
Patented Power-PP5
Stick and Jerseys-SJ34
Teammates-TT19
02Parkhurst Retro-15
Minis-15
Franchise Players-RF9
He Shoots-He Scores Points-17
He Shoots-He Scores Prizes-9
Jerseys-RJ20
Jersey and Sticks-RSJ13
Memorabilia-RM2
Memorabilia-RM23
02Private Stock Reserve-111
Red-111
Retail-111
02SP Authentic-21
02SP Authentic-94
Beckett Promos-21
Super Premiums-SPJS
Super Premiums-DPDS
02SP Game Used-12
Authentic Fabrics-AFJS
Authentic Fabrics-AFSC
Authentic Fabrics-CFJS
Authentic Fabrics Gold-AFJS
Authentic Fabrics Gold-AFSC
Authentic Fabrics Gold-CFJS
Authentic Fabrics Rainbow-AFJS
Authentic Fabrics Rainbow-AFSC
Authentic Fabrics Rainbow-CFJS
First Rounder Patches-JS
Piece of History-PHJS
Piece of History-PHSC
Piece of History Gold-PHJS
Piece of History Gold-PHSC
Piece of History Rainbow-PHJS
Piece of History Rainbow-PHSC
02SPx-18
02SPx-83
02SPx-131
Spectrum Gold-18
Spectrum Gold-83
Spectrum Silver-18
Spectrum Silver-83
Milestones-MJS
Milestones Gold-JS
Milestones Silver-JS
Smooth Skaters-JS
Smooth Skaters Gold-JS
Smooth Skaters Silver-JS
02Stadium Club-9
Silver Decoy Cards-9
Proofs-9
World Stage-WS4
02Titanium-27
Blue-27
Red-27
Retail-27
Saturday Knights-3
Shadows-4
02Topps-196
02Topps-330
OPC Blue Parallel-196
OPC Blue Parallel-330
OPC Red Parallel-196
OPC Red Parallel-330
Captain's Cloth-CC1
Captain's Cloth-CC7
Captain's Cloth-CC13
Coast to Coast-CD9
Topps/OPC Hometown Heroes-HHU2
Factory Set-196
Factory Set-330
Factory Set Hometown Heroes-HHU2
02Topps Chrome All-Star Fantasy-3
02Topps Chrome-111
Black Border Refractors-111
Refractors-111
02Topps Heritage-34
02Topps Heritage-118
Chrome Parallel-34
02Topps Total-319
Production-TP2
Topps-TT5
02UD Artistic Impressions-22
Gold-22
Artist's Touch-ATJS
Artist's Touch Gold-ATJS
02UD Artistic Impressions Beckett Promos-22
02UD Artistic Impressions Flashbacks-UD1
02UD Artistic Impressions Flashbacks Gold-UD1
02UD Artistic Impressions Retrospectives-R22
02UD Artistic Impressions Retrospect Gold-R22
02UD Artistic Impress Retrospect Silver-R22
02Upper Deck Collectors Club-NHL11
02UD Honor Roll-16
02UD Honor Roll-78
Grade A Jerseys-TRFS
Students of the Game-SG6
02UD Mask Collection-23
02UD Mask Collection Beckett Promos-23
02UD Mask Collection Instant Offense-IOJS
02UD Mask Collection Patches-PGJS
02UD Piece of History-26
02UD Piece of History-104
Awards Collection-AC6
Patches-PHJS
Stellar Stitches-SSJS
02UD Premier Collection-14
Jerseys Bronze-JS
Jerseys Bronze-SR
Jerseys Gold-JS
Jerseys Gold-SR
Jerseys Silver-JS
Jerseys Silver-SR
NHL Patches-JS1
Patches-PJS
02UD Top Shelf-22
All-Stars-ASJS
Clutch Performers-CPJS
Goal Oriented-GOJS
Hardware Heroes-HGKSD
Hardware Heroes-HGSLJ
Hardware Heroes-HSRBF
Sweet Sweaters-SWJS
Triple Jerseys-HTSIG
Triple Jerseys-TSTSR
02Upper Deck-47
02Upper Deck-184
Exclusives-47
Exclusives-184
All-Star Jerseys-ASJS
Blow-Ups-C8
CHL Graduates-CGJS
CHL Graduates Gold-CGJS
First Class-UDJS
First Class Gold-UDJS
Game Jersey Series II-GJJS
Gifted Greats-GG3
Good Old Days-GOJS
Letters of Note-LNJS
Letters of Note Gold-LNJS
Patch Card Numbers-JS
Patchwork-PWJS
Playbooks-PL3
Playbooks Series II-FS
Reaching Fifty-50JS
Reaching Fifty Gold-50JS
Shooting Stars-SS4
Sizzling Scorers-SS5
02Upper Deck Classic Portraits-25
Etched in Time-ET2
Headliners-FS
Headliners Limited-FS
Hockey Royalty-GLS
Hockey Royalty-KSI
Hockey Royalty-TSH
Hockey Royalty Limited-GLS
Hockey Royalty Limited-KSI
Hockey Royalty Limited-TSH
Mini-Busts-66
Mini-Busts-67
Mini-Busts-68
Mini-Busts-69
Mini-Busts-70
Pillars of Strength-PS3
02Upper Deck MVP-49
Gold-49
Classics-49
Golden Classics-49
Skate Around Jerseys-SAJS
Skate Around Jerseys-SDSD
Skate Around Jerseys-STSFR
Vital Forces-VF6
02Upper Deck Rookie Update-25
02Upper Deck Rookie Update-112
Jerseys-DJS
Jerseys-SRS
Jerseys Gold-DJS
Jerseys Gold-SRS
02Upper Deck Victory-53
Bronze-53
Gold-53
Silver-53
National Pride-NP4
02Upper Deck Vintage-67
02Upper Deck Vintage-268
02Upper Deck Vintage-291
02Upper Deck Vintage-307
Tall Boys-T17
Tall Boys Gold-T17
02Vanguard-28
LTD-28
East Meets West-7
In Focus-4
Jerseys-13
Jerseys Gold-13
V-Team-9
02UD SuperStars *-68
Gold-68
City All-Stars Dual Jersey-BGJS
03McFarlane Hockey 3-Inch Duals-20
03Avalanche Team Issue-14
03BAP Memorabilia-41
Emerald-41
Gold-41
Ruby-41
Sapphire-41
All-Star Complete Jerseys-ASCJ8
All-Star Emblems-ASE-16
All-Star Jerseys-ASJ-29
All-Star Numbers-ASN-16
All-Star Teammates-AST10
Brush with Greatness-22
Brush with Greatness Contest Cards-22
He Shoots-He Scores Points-14
He Shoots-He Scores Prizes-17
Jersey and Stick-SJ-26
Jerseys-GJ-35
Jersey Autographs-GJ-35
Stanley Cup Playoffs-SCP-5
03BAP Ultimate Memorabilia Autographs-135
Gold-135
03BAP Ultimate Mem Auto Jerseys-135
03BAP Ultimate Mem Auto Emblems-135
03BAP Ultimate Mem Auto Sticks-135
03BAP Ultimate Memorabilia Active Eight-6
03BAP Ultimate Mem Complete Jersey-6
03BAP Ultimate Mem Complete Jersey Gold-6
03BAP Ultimate Memorabilia Dynamic Duos-4
03BAP Ultimate Memorabilia Emblems-9
03BAP Ultimate Memorabilia Emblems Gold-9
03BAP Ultimate Memorabilia Gloves Are Off-4
03BAP Ultimate Memorabilia Hat Tricks-7
03BAP Ultimate Memorabilia Heroes-16
03BAP Ultimate Memorabilia Jerseys-19
03BAP Ultimate Memorabilia Jerseys Gold-19
03BAP Ultimate Mem Jersey and Emblems-17
03BAP Ultimate Mem Jersey and Emblem Gold-17
03BAP Ultimate Mem Jersey and Numbers-17
03BAP Ultimate Mem Jersey and Number Gold-17
03BAP Ultimate Mem Jersey and Stick-15
03BAP Ultimate Mem Jersey and Stick Gold-15
03BAP Ultimate Memorabilia Numbers-14
03BAP Ultimate Memorabilia Numbers Gold-14
03BAP Ultimate Mem Perennial Power Jersey-2
03BAP Ult Mem Perenn Powerhouse Jsy Stick-2
03BAP Ultimate Mem Perennial Power Emblem-2
03BAP Ultimate Mem Retro-Active Trophies-13
03BAP Ultimate Mem Retro-Active Trophies-19
03BAP Ultimate Memorabilia Triple Threads-21
03Beehive-53
Variations-53
Gold-53
Silver-53
Jumbo Jerseys-BH9
Jerseys-JT31
Sticks Beige Border-BE6
Sticks Red Border-RE15
03Black Diamond-32
Black-32
Green-32
Red-32
03Bowman-19
Gold-19
03Bowman Chrome-19
Refractors-19
Gold Refractors-19
Xfractors-19
03Crown Royale-26
Blue-26
Retail-26
Lords of the Rink-8
03ITG Action-198
Center of Attention-CA3
Highlight Reel-HR6
Jerseys-M196
Jerseys-M216
Oh Canada-OC6
03ITG Toronto Fall Expo Jerseys-FE26
03ITG Used Signature Series-100
Gold-100
Autographs-JSA
Autographs Gold-JSA
Game-Day Jerseys-11
Game-Day Jerseys Gold-11
International Experience-4
International Experience Autographs-4
International Experience Emblems Gold-4
International Experience Emblems-4
International Experience Gold-4
Jerseys-16
Jerseys Gold-16
Jersey Autos-16
Emblems-13
Emblems Gold-13
Jersey and Stick-16
Jersey and Stick Gold-16
Teammates-7
Teammates Gold-7
Triple Memorabilia-25
Triple Memorabilia Gold-25
03ITG VIP Collages-7
03ITG VIP Collage Autographs-7
03ITG VIP International Experience-5
03ITG VIP Jerseys-6
03ITG VIP Jersey Autographs-6
03ITG VIP Jersey and Emblems-4
03ITG VIP Jersey and Numbers-4
03ITG VIP MVP-26
03McDonald's Pacific-13
Etched in Time-2
Patches Silver-7
Patches Gold-7
Patches and Sticks-7
03NHL Sticker Collection-185
03O-Pee-Chee-19
03OPC Blue-19
03OPC Gold-19
03OPC Red-19
03Pacific-89
Blue-89
Red-89
Jerseys-10
Jerseys Gold-10
Milestones-2
View from the Crease-3
03Pacific Calder-25
Silver-25
03Pacific Complete-212
Red-212
03Pacific Exhibit-163
03Pacific Exhibit-225
Blue Backs-163
History Makers-3
03Pacific Heads-Up-26
Hobby LTD-26
Retail LTD-26
In Focus-4
In Focus LTD-4
Rink Immortals-3
Rink Immortals LTD-3
03Pacific Invincible-25
Blue-25
Red-25
Retail-25
Top Line-4
03Pacific Luxury Suite-6A
03Pacific Luxury Suite-6B
03Pacific Luxury Suite-6C
03Pacific Luxury Suite-6D
03Pacific Luxury Suite-28A
03Pacific Luxury Suite-28B
03Pacific Luxury Suite-28C
03Pacific Prism-112
Blue-112
Patches-112
Red-112
Retail-112
03Pacific Quest for the Cup-26
Blue-26
Conquest-2
Jerseys-6
Raising the Cup-5
03Pacific Supreme-25
Blue-25
Red-25
Retail-25
Team-3
03Parkhurst Orig Six Boston Mem -BM43
03Parkhurst Orig Six Chicago Mem -CM43
03Parkhurst Orig Six Detroit Mem-DM43
03Parkhurst Orig Six Montreal Mem-MM43
03Parkhurst Orig Six New York Mem-NM43
03Parkhurst Original Six Shooters-OSM3
03Parkhurst Orig Six Toronto Mem-TM43
03Parkhurst Rookie-2
Emblems-GUE-5
Emblem Autographs-GUE-JS
Emblems Gold-GUE-5
Jerseys-GJ-15
Jersey Autographs-GUJ-JS
Jerseys Gold-GJ-15
Jersey and Sticks-SJ-14
Jersey and Sticks Gold-SJ-14
Retro Rookies-RR-3
Retro Rookie Autographs-RR-JS
Retro Rookies Gold-RR-3
Teammates Gold-RT10
Teammates-RT10
03Private Stock Reserve-158
Blue-158
Patches-158
Red-158
Retail-158
Moments in Time-5
03SP Authentic-20
Limited-20
10th Anniversary-SP6
10th Anniversary Limited-SP6
Foundations-F4
Foundations Limited-F4
03SP Game Used-11
Gold-11
Authentic Fabrics-DFFS
Authentic Fabrics-QFSKS
Authentic Fabrics Gold-DFFS

Authentic Fabrics Gold-QFSKS
Double Threads-DTFS
Premium Patches-PPJSA
Top Threads-FSKS
03SPx-21
03SPx-126
03SPx-180
Radiance-21
Radiance-126
Radiance-180
Spectrum-21
Spectrum-126
Spectrum-180
VIP-VIP-FS
VIP Limited-VIP-FS
Winning Materials-WM-JS
Winning Materials Limited-WM-JS
03Titanium-149
Hobby Jersey Number Parallels-149
Patches-149
Retail-149
Highlight Reels-4
03Topps-19
Blue-19
Gold-19
Red-19
Topps/OPC Idols-CI14
Lost Rookies-JS
03Topps C55-19
Minis-19
Minis American Back-19
Minis American Back Red-19
Minis Bazooka Back-19
Minis Brooklyn Back-19
Minis Hat Trick Back-19
Minis O Canada Back-19
Minis O Canada Back Red-19
Minis Stanley Cup Back-19
03Topps Pristine-74
Gold Refractor Die Cuts-74
Refractors-74
Patches-PP-JS
Patch Refractors-PP-JS
Press Plates Black-74
Press Plates Cyan-74
Press Plates Magenta-74
Press Plates Yellow-74
03Topps Traded Franchise Fabrics-FF-JS
03UD Honor Roll-18
03UD Honor Roll-112
Grade A Jerseys-TCOL
03UD Premier Collection-14
Skills-SK-SY
Skills Patches-SK-SY
Stars-ST-JS
Stars Patches-ST-JS
Teammates-PT-CA1
Teammates Patches-PT-CA1
03Upper Deck-289
500 Goal Club-500-JS
Canadian Exclusives-289
HG-289
Performers-PS11
Team Essentials-TL-JS
UD Exclusives-289
03Upper Deck Classic Portraits-23
03Upper Deck Classic Portraits-109
03Upper Deck Classic Portraits-154
Classic Colors-CC-JS
Hockey Royalty-FSK
03Upper Deck Ice-19
Gold-19
Breakers-IB-JS
Breaker Patches-IB-JS
Clear Cut Winners-CC-JS
Icons-I-JS
03Upper Deck MVP-104
Gold Script-104
Silver Script-104
Canadian Exclusives-104
Lethal Lineups-LL1
Souvenirs-S2
SportsNut-SN23
03Upper Deck Rookie Update-19
All-Star Lineup-AS9
Skills-SKSA
Super Stars-SSJO
03Upper Deck Trilogy-23
Authentic Patches-AP7
Limited-23
Limited Threads-LT17
03Upper Deck Victory-46
Bronze-46
Gold-46
Silver-46
Freshman Flashback-FF13
Game Breakers-GB11
03Toronto Star-21
Foil-28
04ITG NHL AS FANtasy AS History Jerseys-SB45
04Pacific-69
Blue-69
Red-69
All-Stars-3
Cramer's Choice-4
Global Connection-3
Philadelphia-2
04Pacific NHL Draft All-Star Nets-2
04SP Authentic-22
04SP Authentic-107
04UD All-World-99
04UD Toronto Fall Expo Pride of Canada-23
04Ultimate Collection-11
04Ultimate Collection-63
Dual Logos-UL2-FS
Dual Logos-UL2-ST
Dual Logos-UL2-SY
Jerseys-UGJ-JS
Jerseys Gold-UGJ-JS
Patches-UP-JS
04Upper Deck-210
Big Playmakers-BP-JS
Canadian Exclusives-210
Clutch Performers-CP3
HG Glossy Gold-210
HG Glossy Silver-210
Patches-GJPA-JS
Patches-GJPL-JS
Patches-GJPN-JS
Three Stars-AS2
World's Best-WB1
World Cup Tribute-JS
World Cup Tribute-JSMLJI
04Upper Deck Pearson Awards-1
05Be A Player-19
First Period-19
Second Period-19
Third Period-19
Overtime-19
Class Action-CA7
Dual Signatures-SB
Ice Icons-ICE3
Outtakes-OT15
Quad Signatures-COLO
Quad Signatures-HSNT
Quad Signatures-SHSL
Signatures-SA
Signatures Gold-SA
Triple Signatures-AVS
Triple Signatures-SIS
Triple Signatures-STS
World Cup Salute-WCS4
05Beehive-22
05Beehive-181
Beige -22
Blue -22
Gold-22
Red -22
Matte-22
Matted Materials-MMSA
05Black Diamond-172
Emerald-172
Gold-172
Onyx-172
Ruby-172
Jerseys-J-JS
Jerseys Ruby-J-JS
Jersey Duals-DJ-JS
Jersey Triples-TJ-JS
Jersey Quads-QJ-JS
05Hot Prospects-23
En Fuego-23
Red Hot-23
White Hot-23
05McDonalds Upper Deck-24
CHL Graduates-CG1
Top Scorers-TS3
05Panini Stickers-223
05Parkhurst-118
05Parkhurst-508
05Parkhurst-578
05Parkhurst-678
Facsimile Auto Parallel-118
Facsimile Auto Parallel-508
Facsimile Auto Parallel-578
Facsimile Auto Parallel-678
True Colors-TCCOL
True Colors-TCCOL
True Colors-TCDECO
True Colors-TCDECO
05SP Authentic-24
05SP Authentic-102
Limited-24
Limited-102
05SP Game Used-23
Gold-23
Authentic Fabrics-AF-JS
Authentic Fabrics Dual-SB
Authentic Fabrics Gold-AF-JS
Authentic Fabrics Quad-MLYS
Authentic Fabrics Quad-SATH
Authentic Patches Quad -MLYS
Authentic Patches Quad -SATH
Authentic Fabrics Triple-SEL
Authentic Fabrics Triple-TSY
Authentic Patches-AP-JS
Authentic Patches Dual-SB
Authentic Patches Triple-SEL
Authentic Patches Triple-TSY
Awesome Authentics-AA-SA
Awesome Authentics Gold-DA-SA
Game Gear-GG-SA
05SPx-19
Spectrum-19
Winning Combos-WC-FS
Winning Combos-WC-SH
Winning Combos Gold-WC-FS
Winning Combos Gold-WC-SH
Winning Combos Spectrum-WC-FS
Winning Combos Spectrum-WC-SH
Winning Materials-WM-JS
Winning Materials Gold-WM-JS
Winning Materials Spectrum-WM-JS
Xcitement Superstars-XS-JS
Xcitement Superstars Gold-XS-JS
Xcitement Superstars Spectrum-XS-JS
05The Cup-28
Gold-28
Black Rainbow-28
Dual NHL Shields-DSSF
Dual NHL Shields-DSST
Masterpiece Pressplates-28
Masterpiece Pressplates (Rookie Update)-206
Noble Numbers-NNYS
Noble Numbers Dual-DNNJA
Noble Numbers Dual-DNNJJ
Noble Numbers Dual-DNNPJ
Patch Variation-P28
Property of-POJS
05UD Artifacts-24
05UD Artifacts-158
Blue-24
Blue-158
Gold-24
Gold-158
Green-24
Green-158
Pewter-24
Pewter-158
Red-24
Red-158
Gold Autographed-24
Gold Autographed-158
Treasured Patches-TP-JS
Treasured Patches Autographed-TP-JS
Treasured Patches Dual-TPD-JS
Treasured Patches Dual Autographed-TPD-JS
Treasured Patches Pewter-TP-JS
Treasured Patches Silver-TP-JS
Treasured Swatches-TS-JS
Treasured Swatches Autographed-TS-JS
Treasured Swatches Blue-TS-JS
Treasured Swatches Copper-TS-JS
Treasured Swatches Dual-TSD-JS
Treasured Swatches Dual Autographed-TSD-JS
Treasured Swatches Dual Blue-TSD-JS
Treasured Swatches Dual Copper-TSD-JS
Treasured Swatches Dual Maroon-TSD-JS
Treasured Swatches Dual Pewter-TSD-JS
Treasured Swatches Dual Silver-TSD-JS
Treasured Swatches Maroon-TS-JS
Treasured Swatches Pewter-TS-JS
Treasured Swatches Silver-TS-JS
05UD PowerPlay-22
05UD PowerPlay-96
05UD PowerPlay-121
Rainbow-22
05Ultimate Collection-22
Gold-22
Jerseys-JJS
Jerseys Dual-DJSH
National Heroes Jerseys-NHJJS
National Heroes Patches-NHPJS
Premium Patches-PPJS
Premium Swatches-PSJS
Ultimate Patches-PJS
Ultimate Patches Dual-DPSH
05Ultra-55
Gold-55
Ice-55
Scoring Kings-SK8
Scoring Kings Jerseys-SKJ-JS
Scoring Kings Patches-SKP-JS
Super Six-SS5
Super Six Jerseys-SSJ-JS
Super Six Patches-SSP-JS
05Upper Deck-43
05Upper Deck All-Time Greatest-15
05Upper Deck All-Time Greatest-86
05Upper Deck Destined for the Hall-DH3
05Upper Deck Goal Rush-GR5
05Upper Deck HG Glossy-43
05Upper Deck Hometown Heroes-HH1
05Upper Deck Jerseys-J-JS
05Upper Deck Jerseys Series II-J2JS
05Upper Deck Majestic Materials-MMJS
05Upper Deck NHL Generations-TGYS
05Upper Deck NHL Generations-TSHT
05Upper Deck NHL Generations-TSIR
05Upper Deck NHL Generations-TSTP
05Upper Deck Patches-P-JS
05Upper Deck Playoff Performers-PP6
05Upper Deck Scrapbooks-HS20
05Upper Deck Shooting Stars-S-JS
05Upper Deck Ice-22
Rainbow-22
Frozen Fabrics-FFJS
Frozen Fabrics Glass-FFJS
Frozen Fabrics Patches-FFPJS
05Upper Deck MVP-97
05Upper Deck MVP-438
Gold-97
Gold-438
Platinum-97
Platinum-438
Materials Duals-D-SH
Materials Triples-T-SKF
Materials Triples-T-GST
Rising to the Occasion-RO1
05Upper Deck Rookie Update-24
05Upper Deck Rookie Update-206
Inspirations Patch Rookies-206
05Upper Deck Trilogy-23
05Upper Deck Trilogy-102
Crystal-102
Honorary Patches-HP-JS
Honorary Swatches-HS-JS
05Upper Deck Toronto Fall Expo-43
05Upper Deck Victory-45
Black-45
Gold-45
Silver-45
Blow-Ups-BU8
Game Breakers-GB10
Stars on Ice-SI11
06Avalanche Team Postcards-13
06Be A Player-49
Autographs-49
Profiles-PP21
Profiles Autographs-PP21
Signatures-JO
Signatures 10-53
Signatures 25-53
Signatures Duals-DSS
Signatures Trios-TSTS
Signatures Foursomes-FSLST
Up Close and Personal-UC25
Up Close and Personal Autographs-UC25
06Be A Player Portraits-28
Dual Signature Portraits-DSSM
Quadruple Signature Portraits-QSSTS
Sensational Six-SSSJM
Sensational Six-SSSTR
Signature Portraits-SPJS
Triple Signature Portraits-TCOL
Triple Signature Portraits-TSSM
06Beehive-75
06Beehive-213
Blue-75
Gold-75
Matte-75
Red Facsimile Signatures-75
Wood-75
5 X 7 Black and White-75
5 X 7 Cherry Wood-75
Matted Materials-MMJS
06Black Diamond-152B
Black-152B
Gold-152B
Ruby-152B
Jerseys-JJS
Jerseys Black-JJS
Jerseys Gold-JJS
Jerseys Ruby-JJS
06Flair Showcase-177
06Flair Showcase-218
06Flair Showcase-277
Parallel-177
Parallel-218
Parallel-277
Hot Numbers-HN11
Hot Numbers Parallel-HN11
06Fleer-49
Oversized-49
Tiffany-49
Speed Machines-SM8
Total O-05
06Hot Prospects-25
Red Hot-25
White Hot-25
Hot Materials -HMSA
Hot Materials Red Hot-HMSA
Hot Materials White Hot-HMSA
06ITG Ultimate Memorabilia-78
Artist Proof-78
Autos-55
Autos Gold-55
Autos Triple-5
Autos Triple Gold-5
Captain-C-12
Captain-C Gold-12
Complete Jersey-18
Complete Jersey Gold-18
Double Memorabilia-19
Double Memorabilia Gold-19
Emblems-16
Emblems Gold-16
First Round Picks-20
First Round Picks Gold-20
Gloves Are Off-12
Gloves Are Off Gold-12
Going For Gold-29
Going For Gold Gold-29
In The Numbers-8
In The Numbers Gold-8
Jerseys-8
Jerseys Gold-8
Jerseys and Emblems-8
Jerseys and Emblems Gold-8
Jerseys Autos-52
Jerseys Autos Gold-52
Journey Emblem-5
Journey Emblem Gold-5
Journey Jersey-5
Journey Jersey Gold-5
Legendary Captains-13
Legendary Captains Gold-13
Retrospective-11
Retrospective Gold-11
Sticks Autos-26
Sticks Autos Gold-26
Triple Thread Jerseys-16
Triple Thread Jerseys Gold-16
06McDonald's Upper Deck-10
Clear Cut Winners-CC1
Jerseys-JJS
Patches-PJS
06NHL POG-31
06O-Pee-Chee-121
06O-Pee-Chee-647
06O-Pee-Chee-679
Rainbow-121
Rainbow-647
Rainbow-679
Swatches-S-SA
06Panini Stickers-221
06SP Authentic-75
06SP Authentic-124
Limited-75
Limited-124
06SP Game Used-24
Gold-24
Rainbow-24
Authentic Fabrics-AFJS
Authentic Fabrics Parallel-AFJS
Authentic Fabrics Patches-AFJS
Authentic Fabrics Dual-AF2TS
Authentic Fabrics Dual Patches-AF2TS
Authentic Fabrics Triple-AF3COL
Authentic Fabrics Triple Patches-AF3COL
Authentic Fabrics Quads-AF4STSC
Authentic Fabrics Quads Patches-AF4STSC
Authentic Fabrics Fives-AF5ASG
Authentic Fabrics Fives Patches-AF5ASG
Authentic Fabrics Sixes-AF6500
Authentic Fabrics Sixes-AF6BYN
Authentic Fabrics Sixes Patches-AF6500
Authentic Fabrics Sixes Patches-AF6BYN
Authentic Fabrics Sevens-AF7CON
Authentic Fabrics Sevens-AF7LBP
Authentic Fabrics Sevens-AF7MVP
Authentic Fabrics Sevens Patches-AF7CON
Authentic Fabrics Sevens Patches-AF7LBP
Authentic Fabrics Sevens Patches-AF7MVP
Authentic Fabrics Eights-AF8CAN
Authentic Fabrics Eights Patches-AF8CAN
By The Letter-BLJO
06SPx-22
06SPx-106
Spectrum-22
Spectrum-106
SPxcitement-X22
SPxcitement Spectrum-X22
Winning Materials-WMJS
Winning Materials Spectrum-WMJS
06The Cup-22
Black Rainbow-22
Foundations-CQJO
Foundations Patches-CQJO
Gold-22
Gold Patches-22
Jerseys-22
Masterpiece Pressplates-22
NHL Shields Duals-DSHJO
NHL Shields Duals-DSHSF
NHL Shields Duals-DSHSH
NHL Shields Duals-DSHST
06UD Artifacts-74
06UD Artifacts-161
Blue-74
Blue-161
Gold-74
Gold-161
Platinum-74
Platinum-161
Radiance-74
Radiance-161
Red-74
Red-161
Frozen Artifacts-FAJS
Frozen Artifacts Black-FAJS
Frozen Artifacts Blue-FAJS
Frozen Artifacts Gold-FAJS
Frozen Artifacts Platinum-FAJS
Frozen Artifacts Red-FAJS
Frozen Artifacts Patches Black-FAJS
Frozen Artifacts Patches Blue-FAJS
Frozen Artifacts Patches Gold-FAJS
Frozen Artifacts Patches Platinum-FAJS
Frozen Artifacts Patches Red-FAJS
Tundra Tandems-TTPJ
Tundra Tandems-TTST
Tundra Tandems Black-TTPJ
Tundra Tandems Black-TTST
Tundra Tandems Blue-TTPJ
Tundra Tandems Blue-TTST
Tundra Tandems Gold-TTPJ
Tundra Tandems Gold-TTST
Tundra Tandems Platinum-TTPJ
Tundra Tandems Platinum-TTST
Tundra Tandems Red-TTPJ
Tundra Tandems Red-TTST
Tundra Tandems Dual Patches Red-TTPJ
Tundra Tandems Dual Patches Red-TTST
06UD Biography of a Season-BOS14
06UD Mini Jersey Collection-24
Jerseys-JS
Jersey Variations-JS
06UD Powerplay-28
Impact Rainbow-28
In Action-IA2
Specialists-SJS
Specialists Patches-PJS
06Ultimate Collection-17
Jerseys-UJ-JS
Jerseys Dual-UJ2-SS
Jerseys Triple-UJ3-STS
Patches-UJ-JS
Patches Dual-UJ2-SS
Patches Triple-UJ3-STS
06Ultra-49
Gold Medallion-49
Ice Medallion-49
Action-UA5
Scoring Kings-SK13
Uniformity-UJS
Uniformity Patches-UPJS
06Upper Deck Arena Giveaways-COL4
06Upper Deck-54
Exclusives Parallel-54
High Gloss Parallel-54
All-Time Greatest-ATG5
All World-AW23
Game Dated Moments-GD40
Game Jerseys-J2JS
Game Patches-P2JS
Generations Duals-G2SS
Generations Duals-G2PJD
Generations Triples-G3SSC
Generations Patches Dual-G2PJD
Generations Patches Dual-G2PSS
Generations Patches Triple-G3PSSC
Masterpieces-54
06Upper Deck MVP-70
Gold Script-70
Super Script-70
Clutch Performers-CP3
Gotta Have Hart-HH5
Jerseys-OJSM
Jerseys-OJST
06Upper Deck Ovation-161
06Upper Deck Sweet Shot-27
Sweet Stitches-SSJS
Sweet Stitches Duals-SSJS
Sweet Stitches Triples-SSJS
06Upper Deck Trilogy-24
Frozen In Time-FT10
06Upper Deck Victory-47
06Upper Deck Victory Black-47
06Upper Deck Victory Gold-47
06Upper Deck Victory GameBreakers-GB10
06Upper Deck Victory Oversize Cards-JS
06Russian Sport Collection Olympic Stars-39
06ITG Heroes and Prospects Double Memorabilia-DM07
06ITG Heroes and Prospects Heroes Memorabilia-HM21
06ITG Heroes and Prospects Triple Memorabilia-TM10
07Upper Deck All-Star Game Redemptions-AS4
07Upper Deck Victory-159
Black-159
Gold-159
GameBreakers-GB19
Oversize Cards-OS36
Stars on Ice-SI19

Sakmirda, Miroslav
94German First League-474

Sakrajda, Petr
06Czech OFS-189

Saksinen, Esa
05Finnish Cardset -292
06Finnish Cardset-120

Salajko, Jeff
92Ottawa 67's-19
95Slapshot-331
95Sarnia Sting-1

Salamand, Mathieu
92Quebec Pee-Wee Tournament-1199
93Quebec Pee-Wee Tournament-1482

Salaschenko, Alexei
98Sudbury Wolves-3
99Owen Sound Platers-27

Salashcenko, Alexei
99Sudbury Wolves-13

Salcido, Brian
06Portland Pirates-8

Salei, Ruslan
95Las Vegas Thunder-16
96Metal Universe-191
96Select Certified-109
Artist's Proofs-109
Blue-109
Mirror Blue-109
Mirror Gold-109
Mirror Red-109
Red-109
96SP-169
96Ultra-5
Gold Medallion-5
96Upper Deck-215
97Be A Player-124
Autographs-124
Autographs Die-Cuts-124
Autographs Prismatic Die-Cuts-124
97Revolution-4
Copper-4
Emerald-4
Ice Blue-4
Silver-4
98OPC Chrome-99
Refractors-99
98Panini Stickers-174
98Topps-99
O-Pee-Chee-99
99O-Pee-Chee-140
99O-Pee-Chee Chrome-140
99O-Pee-Chee Chrome Refractors-140
99Pacific-14
Copper-14
Emerald Green-14
Gold-14
Ice Blue-14
Premiere Date-14
Red-14
99Paramount-7
Copper-7
Emerald-7
Gold-7
Holographic Emerald-7
Holographic Gold-7
Holographic Silver-7
Ice Blue-7
Premiere Date-7
Red-7
Silver-7
99Topps/OPC-140
99Topps/OPC Chrome-140
Refractors-140
99Cincinnati Mighty Ducks-6
00Panini Stickers-112
00Upper Deck NHLPA-PA2
01Pacific-10
Extreme LTD-10
Hobby LTD-10
Premiere Date-10
Retail LTD-10
01Pacific Arena Exclusives-10
02BAP First Edition-196
02Ducks Team Issue-4
02Pacific Complete-455
Red-455
02Topps Total-85
02Upper Deck-251
Exclusives-251
02Upper Deck Beckett UD Promos-251
02Upper Deck Victory National Pride-NP1
02Upper Deck Vintage-6
03ITG Action-80
03O-Pee-Chee-237
03OPC Blue-237
03OPC Gold-237
03OPC Red-237
03Pacific Complete-319
Red-319
03Topps-237
Blue-237
Gold-237
Red-237
03Upper Deck-252
Canadian Exclusives-252
HG-252
UD Exclusives-252
03Czech Stadion-610
04Russian Back to Russia-37
05Ducks Team Issue-18
05Panini Stickers-188
05Parkhurst-15
Facsimile Auto Parallel-15
05Upper Deck MVP-7
Gold-7
Platinum-7
06O-Pee-Chee-209
Rainbow-209

Saleski, Don
72O-Pee-Chee-213
73Flyers Linnett-14
74NHL Action Stamps-215
74O-Pee-Chee NHL-283
75Flyers Canada Dry Cans-15
75O-Pee-Chee NHL-262
75O-Pee-Chee NHL-337
75Topps-262
76O-Pee-Chee NHL-81
76Topps-81
77Coca-Cola-22
77O-Pee-Chee NHL-233
77Topps-233
78O-Pee-Chee-257
78Topps-257
79Rockies Team Issue-21
04ITG Franchises US East-419
Autographs-A-DOS

Saleva, Henry
72Finnish Jaakiekko-95
73Finnish Jaakiekko-143
78Finnish SM-Liiga-86
80Finnish Mallasjuoma-182
83Swedish Semic Elitserien-170

Salfi, Kent
92Maine Black Bears-13

Salficky, Dusan
94Czech APS Extraliga-25
95Czech APS Extraliga-317
96Czech APS Extraliga-144
97Czech APS Extraliga-173
97Czech DS Extraliga-49
97Czech DS Stickers-246
98Czech DS-17
98Czech DS Stickers-147
98Czech OFS-34
98Czech OFS-447
99Czech DS-85
Goalies-G7
99Czech OFS-15
99Czech OFS-488
99Czech OFS-552
99Czech OFS-NNO
All-Star Game Blue-488
All-Star Game Gold-488
All-Star Game Red-488
All-Star Game Silver-488
99Czech OFS Goalie Die-Cuts-15
00Czech DS Extraliga-25
Goalies-G3
National Team-NT1
World Champions-WCH2
00Czech OFS-57
00Czech OFS Star Emerald-16
00Czech OFS Star Pink-16
00Czech OFS Star Violet-16
01Czech DS-50
01Czech National Team Postcards-12
01Czech OFS All Stars-16
02Czech DS-2
02Czech DS-77
02Russian Hockey League-110
02Russian SL-2
02Russian Ultimate Line-2
03ITG Action-340
03Parkhurst Rookie-70
03Czech National Team-1
03Russian Hockey League-8
04Czech World Championship Postcards-17
04Russian Legion-36
05Russian Hockey League RHL-43
06Czech HC Sparta Praha Postcards-4
06Czech OFS-72
Stars-18
Team Cards-9

Salimov, Marat
03Russian Hockey League-263

Salinger, Dirk
94German First League-361

Salis, Edgar
93Swiss HNL-168
95Swiss HNL-37
96Swiss HNL-184
98Swiss Power Play Stickers-11
98Swiss Power Play Stickers-265
99Swiss Panini Stickers-234
00Swiss Panini Stickers-274
00Swiss Panini Stickers National Team-P7
00Swiss Slapshot Mini-Cards-ZSCL3
01Swiss HNL-7
02Swiss HNL-14

Salisbury, Devin
96OCN Blizzard-8
97OCN Blizzard-17
98OCN Blizzard-16

Sallamaa, Asko
66Finnish Jaakiekkosarja-210

Salle, Johan
90Swedish Semic Elitserien Stickers-130
91Swedish Semic Elitserien Stickers-183
92Swedish Semic Elitserien Stickers-208
93Swedish Semic Elitserien-174
94Swedish Leaf-244
95Swedish Leaf-265
95Swedish Upper Deck-137

Sallin, Hans
85Swedish Panini Stickers-186

Sallinen, Pasi
71Finnish Suomi Stickers-334

Salmela, Anssi
04Finnish Cardset-151
Parallel-113
05Finnish Cardset -138
06Finnish Cardset-296

Salmelainen, Tobias
05Finnish Cardset -197
06Finnish Porin Assat Pelaajakortit-30

Salmelainen, Tommi
71Finnish Suomi Stickers-75
71Finnish Suomi Stickers-125
72Finnish Jaakiekko-96
72Finnish Hellas-14
72Finnish Panda Toronto-13
72Finnish Panda Toronto-109
72Finnish Semic World Championship-87
72Swedish Semic World Championship-87
73Finnish Jaakiekko-142
78Finnish SM-Liiga-33
80Finnish Mallasjuoma-6

Salmelainen, Tony
00Finnish Cardset-138
00Finnish Cardset-277
01Finnish Cardset-241
02Finnish Cardset-262
02Hamilton Bulldogs-4
03Beehive-245
Gold-245
Silver-245
03Bowman-140
Gold-140
03Bowman Chrome-140
Refractors-140
Gold Refractors-140
Xfractors-140
03ITG Action-639
03ITG VIP Rookie Debut-53
03Pacific Complete-508
Red-508
03Pacific Heads-Up-116
Hobby LTD-116
Retail LTD-116
03Pacific Luxury Suite-65
Gold-65
03Pacific Quest for the Cup-117
03Parkhurst Rookie-153
Rookie Emblems-RE-25
Rookie Emblems Gold-RE-25
Rookie Jerseys-RJ-25
Rookie Jerseys Gold-RJ-25
Rookie Numbers-RN-25
Rookie Numbers Gold-RN-25
03SP Authentic-144
Limited-144
Signed Patches-TS
03SPx-229
Radiance-229
03Topps Traded-TT109
Blue-TT109
Gold-TT109
Red-TT109
03UD Honor Roll-154
03UD Premier Collection-86
03Upper Deck-463
03Upper Deck-475
Canadian Exclusives-463
Canadian Exclusives-475
HG-463
HG-475
UD Exclusives-463
UD Exclusives-475
03Upper Deck Ice-107
Glass Parallel-107
03Upper Deck Rookie Update-195
04AHL All-Stars-38
04AHL All-Stars-47
04ITG Heroes and Prospects Emblems-32
04ITG Heroes and Prospects Emblems Gold-32
04ITG Heroes and Prospects Jerseys-32
04ITG Heroes and Prospects Jerseys Gold-32
04ITG Heroes and Prospects Numbers-32
04ITG Heroes and Prospects Numbers Gold-32
05UD Artifacts Auto Facts-AF-TS
05UD Artifacts Auto Facts Blue-AF-TS
05UD Artifacts Auto Facts Copper-AF-TS
05UD Artifacts Auto Facts Pewter-AF-TS
05UD Artifacts Auto Facts Silver-AF-TS
05Upper Deck Notable Numbers-N-TSA
05Upper Deck MVP ProSign-P-TS
05Finnish Cardset -193
06Blackhawks Postcards-5
06Finnish Cardset-18
Trophy Winners-7

Salmi, Jorma
64Swedish Coralli ISHockey-44
65Swedish Coralli ISHockey-96

Salmi, Matti
65Finnish Hellas-41
66Finnish Jaakiekkosarja-52
70Finnish Jaakiekko-203
71Finnish Suomi Stickers-92
72Finnish Jaakiekko-257
72Finnish Panda Toronto-43

Salmik, Peter
94German First League-92

Salminen, Asko
73Finnish Jaakiekko-299

Salminen, Heikki
73Finnish Jaakiekko-190

Salminen, Jussi
95Collector's Choice-339
Player's Club-339
Player's Club Platinum-339
00Finnish Cardset-311

Salminen, Kimmo
94Finnish SISU-73
94Finnish SISU Magic Numbers-9
95Finnish SISU-63
96Finnish SISU Redline-63
98Finnish Kerailysarja-261
00Finnish Cardset-297
01Finnish Cardset-206

Salminen, Mauri
72Finnish Jaakiekko-295

Salminen, Petri
70Finnish Jaakiekko-338

Salminen, Teijo
70Finnish Jaakiekko-355

Salming, Borje
70Swedish Hockey-23
71Swedish Hockey-100
72Finnish Jaakiekko-56
72Finnish Hellas-42
72Swedish Stickers-7
72Swedish Stickers-86
73Maple Leafs Postcards-22
73Finnish Jaakiekko-34
73Swedish Stickers-7
73Swedish Stickers-160
74Lipton Soup-41A
74Lipton Soup-41B
74Maple Leafs Postcards-18
74NHL Action Stamps-269
74O-Pee-Chee NHL-180
74Topps-180
74Swedish Stickers-314
75Heroes Stand-Ups-27
75Maple Leafs Postcards-16
75Maple Leafs Postcards-17
75O-Pee-Chee NHL-283
75O-Pee-Chee NHL-294
75Topps-283
75Topps-294
76Maple Leafs Postcards-15
76O-Pee-Chee NHL-22
76Topps-22
77Maple Leafs Postcards-13
77O-Pee-Chee NHL-2
77O-Pee-Chee NHL-140
77Topps-2
77Topps-140
77Finnish Sportscasters-70-1663
78Maple Leafs Postcards-18
78O-Pee-Chee-240
78O-Pee-Chee-328
78Topps-240
79Maple Leafs Postcards-25
79Maple Leafs Postcards-26
79O-Pee-Chee-40
79Topps-40
80Maple Leafs Postcards-23
80O-Pee-Chee-85
80O-Pee-Chee-210
80O-Pee-Chee Super-19
80Pepsi-Cola Caps-97
80Topps-85
80Topps-210
81Maple Leafs Postcards-20
81O-Pee-Chee-307
81O-Pee-Chee Stickers-98
81O-Pee-Chee Stickers-111
81Post Standups-18
81Topps-33
82Maple Leafs Postcards-30
82Maple Leafs Postcards-31
82O-Pee-Chee-332
82O-Pee-Chee Stickers-75
82O-Pee-Chee Stickers-76
82Post Cereal-18
82Topps Stickers-75
82Topps Stickers-76
82Swedish Semic VM Stickers-143
83Maple Leafs Postcards-22
83NHL Key Tags-117
83O-Pee-Chee-341
83O-Pee-Chee Stickers-33
83O-Pee-Chee Stickers-34
83Puffy Stickers-6
83Topps Stickers-33
83Topps Stickers-34
83Vachon-97
84Kellogg's Accordion Discs-3A
84Kellogg's Accordion Discs-3B
84Kellogg's Accordion Discs Singles-33
84Maple Leafs Postcards-21
84O-Pee-Chee-311
84O-Pee-Chee Stickers-7
84O-Pee-Chee Stickers-8
85Maple Leafs Postcards-26
85O-Pee-Chee-248
85O-Pee-Chee Stickers-12
85 7-Eleven Credit Cards-18
86Kraft Drawings-62
86Maple Leafs Postcards-17
86O-Pee-Chee-169
86O-Pee-Chee Stickers-136
86Topps-169
87Maple Leafs PLAY-8
87Maple Leafs Postcards-17
87Maple Leafs Postcards Oversized-17
87O-Pee-Chee-237
87O-Pee-Chee Stickers-165
87Panini Stickers-326
87Pro-Sport All-Stars-16
88Esso All-Stars-39
88Maple Leafs PLAY-5
88O-Pee-Chee-247
88O-Pee-Chee Stickers-174
88Panini Stickers-120
89O-Pee-Chee-278
89Red Wings Little Caesars-15
90Swedish Semic Elitserien Stickers-77
91Swedish Semic Elitserien Stickers-4
92Future Trends '76 Canada Cup-145
92Future Trends '76 Canada Cup-188
92Future Trends '76 Canada Cup-197
92Finnish Semic-60
92Swedish Semic Elitserien Stickers-36
94Hockey Wit-37
95Swedish Globe World Championships-67
97Swedish Alfabilder Autographs-9
99BAP Memorabilia AS Canadian Hobby-CH1
99BAP Memorabilia AS Cdn Hobby Autos-CH1
01Fleer Legacy-33
Ultimate-33
In the Corners-9
Memorabilia-7
01Greats of the Game-73
Autographs-73
Jerseys-6
Patches Gold-6
01Upper Deck Pride of the Leafs-MLBJ
01Swedish Alfabilder-9
02Maple Leafs Platinum Collection-64
02Maple Leafs Platinum Collection-90
02Maple Leafs Platinum Collection-108
02UD Foundations-21
02UD Foundations-88
Classic Greats-GBS
Classic Greats Gold-GBS
Classic Greats Silver-G-BS
Defense First-DBS
Defense First Gold-DBS
Defense First Silver-D-BS
Playoff Performers-PBS
Playoff Performers Gold-PBS
Playoff Performers Silver-P-BS
02UD Piece of History Heroes Jerseys-HHBS
02UD Piece of History Historical Swatches-HSBS
03BAP Ultimate Mem Retro Teammates-9
03BAP Ultimate Memorabilia Triple Threads-14
03ITG Used Sig Series Vintage Mem -11
03ITG Used Sig Series Vintage Mem Gold-11
03Parkhurst Orig Six He Shoots/Scores-5
03Parkhurst Orig Six He Shoots/Scores-5A
03Parkhurst Original Six Toronto-46
03Parkhurst Original Six Toronto-63
03Parkhurst Original Six Toronto-87
03Parkhurst Original Six Toronto-94
Autographs-16
Memorabilia-TM27
Memorabilia-TM57
04ITG Franchises Canadian-103
Autographs-BS
Forever Rivals-FR4
Forever Rivals Gold-FR4
Memorabilia-SM14
Memorabilia Autographs-SM14
Memorabilia Gold-SM14
04ITG Franchises Update-465
04ITG Ultimate Memorabilia-31
Gold-31
Changing the Game-8
Cornerstones-3
Cornerstones Gold-3
Original Six-3
Retro Teammates-4
04UD All-World-44
04UD All-World-109
Gold-44
Autographs-44
Autographs-109
Dual Autographs-AD-SN
Five Autographs-AF-AST

04UD Legendary Signatures-10
Autographs-BS
Rearguard Retrospectives-BSIT
04Swedish Alfabilder Alfa Stars-47
04Swedish Alfabilder Next In Line-2
04Swedish Alfabilder Proof Parallels-47
05ITG Heroes/Prosp Toronto Expo Parallel -192
05Beehive Signature Scrapbook-SSBS
05ITG Ultimate Memorabilia Level 1-13
05ITG Ultimate Memorabilia Level 2-13
05ITG Ultimate Memorabilia Level 3-13
05ITG Ultimate Memorabilia Level 4-13
05ITG Ultimate Memorabilia Level 5-13
05ITG Ultimate Memorabilia Double Autos-11
05ITG Ultimate Mem Double Autos Gold-11
05ITG Ultimate Mem Double Mem-11
05ITG Ultimate Mem Double Mem Gold-11
05ITG Ultimate Memorabilia Jersey Autos-26
05ITG Ultimate Mem Jersey Autos Gold-26
05ITG Ultimate Mem Pass the Torch Jerseys-16
05ITG Ultimate Mem Passing Torch Jsy Gold-16
05ITG Ultimate Mem Retro Teammate Jerseys-9
05ITG Ult Mem Retro Teammates Jersey Gold-9
05ITG Ultimate Mem Seams Unbelievable-20
05ITG Ultimate Mem Seam Unbelievable Gold-20
05ITG Ultimate Mem 3 Star of the Game Jsy-21
05ITG Ult Mem 3 Star of the Game Jsy Gold-21
05ITG Ultimate Memorabilia Triple Autos-6
05ITG Ultimate Mem Triple Autos Gold-6
05ITG Ultimate Memorabilia Ultimate Autos-8
05ITG Ultimate Mem Ultimate Autos Gold-8
05SP Authentic Exquisite Endorsements-EEBS
05SP Authentic Sign of the Times Fives-SMSMK
05SP Authentic Six Star Signatures-SSTO
05SP Game Used Heritage Classic-HC-BS
05SP Game Used Heritage Classic Autos-HCA-BS
05SP Game Used Heritage Classic Patches-HCP-BS
05SP GameUsed Heritage Classic Patch Auto-HAP-BS
05SPx-94
Spectrum-94
05The Cup Noble Numbers-NNFS
05The Cup Noble Numbers Dual-DNNSS
05UD Artifacts Frozen Artifacts-FA-BS
05UD Artifacts Frozen Artifacts Autos-FA-BS
05UD Artifacts Frozen Artifacts Copper-FA-BS
05UD Artifacts Frozen Artifacts Dual-FAD-BS
05UD Artifacts Frozen Artifact Dual Auto-FAD-BS
05UD Artifact Frozen Artifact Dual Copper-FAD-BS
05UD Artifacts Frozen Artifacts Dual Gold-FAD-BS
05UD Artifact Frozen Artifact Dual Maroon-FAD-BS
05UD Artifact Frozen Artifact Dual Pewter-FAD-BS
05UD Artifact Frozen Artifact Dual Silver-FAD-BS
05UD Artifacts Frozen Artifacts Gold-FA-BS
05UD Artifacts Frozen Artifacts Maroon-FA-BS
05UD Artifacts Frozen Artifacts Patches-FP-BS
05UD Artifact Frozen Artifact Patch Autos-FP-BS
05UD Artifacts Frozen Artifact Patch Dual-FPD-BS
05UD Artifacts Frozen Art Patch Dual Auto-FPD-BS
05UD Artifacts Frozen Art Patch Pewter-FP-BS
05UD Artifacts Frozen Art Patch Silver-FP-BS
05UD Artifacts Frozen Artifacts Pewter-FA-BS
05UD Artifacts Frozen Artifacts Silver-FA-BS
05Upper Deck Notable Numbers-N-BS
05ITG Heroes and Prospects-192
Autographs Series II-BJS
Hero Memorabilia-HM-42
National Pride-NPR-26
06ITG International Ice-24
06ITG International Ice-41
06ITG International Ice-71
Gold-24
Gold-41
Gold-71
Autographs-ABS
Autographs-ABS2
Autographs-ABS3
Cornerstones-IC03
Cornerstones Gold-IC03
Emblem Autographs-GUE25
Emblem Autographs Gold-GUE25
Emblems-GUE25
Emblems Gold-GUE25
Hockey Passport-HP06
Hockey Passport Gold-HP06
International Rivals-IR10
International Rivals Gold-IR10
Jersey Autographs-GUJ25
Jersey Autographs Gold-GUJ25
Jerseys-GUJ25
Jerseys Gold-GUJ25
My Country My Team-MC17
My Country My Team Gold-MC17
Numbers-GUN25
Numbers Autographs-GUN25
Numbers Autographs Gold-GUN25
Numbers Gold-GUN25
Passing The Torch-PTT14
Passing The Torch Gold-PTT14
Teammates-IT15
Teammates Gold-IT15
06ITG Ultimate Memorabilia-19
Artist Proof-19
Complete Jersey-17
Complete Jersey Gold-17
Double Memorabilia-17
Double Memorabilia Gold-17
Jerseys-17
Jerseys Gold-17
Passing The Torch-7
Passing The Torch Gold-7
Retro Teammates-14
Retro Teammates Gold-14
06Parkhurst-109
Autographs-109
06SP Authentic Sign of the Times Duals-STLS
06SP Game Used Inked Sweaters-ISBS
06SP Game Used Inked Sweaters Patches-ISBS
06SP Game Used Inked Sweaters Dual-IS2LS
06SP Game Used Inked Sweaters Dual Patches-IS2LS
06SPx-137
Spectrum-137
SPxcitement-X91
SPxcitement Spectrum-X91
SPxcitement Autographs-X91
Winning Materials-WMSA
Winning Materials Spectrum-WMSA
Winning Materials Autographs-WMSA
06The Cup-86
Autographed Foundations-CQSA
Autographed Foundations Patches-CQSA
Autographed Patches-86
Black Rainbow-86
Foundations-CQSA
Foundations Patches-CQSA
Gold-86
Gold Patches-86
Honorable Numbers-HNSA
Jerseys-86
Limited Logos-LLSA
Masterpiece Pressplates-86
Scripted Swatches-SSBS
Scripted Swatches Duals-DSDB
Signature Patches-SPSA
06UD Artifacts Treasured Patches Black-TSBS
06UD Artifacts Treasured Patches Blue-TSBS
06UD Artifacts Treasured Patches Gold-TSBS
06UD Artifacts Treasured Patches Platinum-TSBS
06UD Artifacts Treasured Patches Red-TSBS
06UD Artifacts Treasured Patches Autographed Black Tag Parallel-TSBS
06UD Artifacts Treasured Swatches-TSBS
06UD Artifacts Treasured Swatches Black-TSBS
06UD Artifacts Treasured Swatches Blue-TSBS
06UD Artifacts Treasured Swatches Gold-TSBS
06UD Artifacts Treasured Swatches Platinum-TSBS
06UD Artifacts Treasured Swatches Red-TSBS
06UD Artifacts Treasured Swatches Autographed Black-TSBS
06UD Artifacts Tundra Tandems-TTDB
06UD Artifacts Tundra Tandems Black-TTDB
06UD Artifacts Tundra Tandems Blue-TTDB
06UD Artifacts Tundra Tandems Gold-TTDB
06UD Artifacts Tundra Tandems Platinum-TTDB
06UD Artifacts Tundra Tandems Red-TTDB
06UD Artifacts Tundra Tandems Dual Patches Red-TTDB
06Ultimate Collection Autographed Jerseys-AJ-SA
06Ultimate Collection Autographed Patches-AJ-SA
06Ultimate Collection Jerseys-UJ-SA
06Ultimate Collection Jerseys Dual-UJ2-DB
06Ultimate Collection Jerseys Triple-UJ3-SSH
06Ultimate Collection Patches-UJ-SA
06Ultimate Collection Patches Dual-UJ2-DB
06Ultimate Collection Patches Triple-UJ3-SSH
06Ultimate Collection Premium Patches-PS-BS
06Ultimate Collection Premium Swatches-PS-BS
06Upper Deck Sweet Shot Signature Shots/Saves Sticks-SSSBS
06Upper Deck Sweet Shot Sweet Stitches-SSSB
06Upper Deck Sweet Shot Sweet Stitches Duals-SSSB
06Upper Deck Sweet Shot Sweet Stitches Triples-SSSB
06Upper Deck Trilogy Combo Clearcut Autographs-C3MSS
06Upper Deck Trilogy Honorary Scripted Patches-HSPBO
06Upper Deck Trilogy Honorary Scripted Swatches-HSSBO
06Upper Deck Trilogy Honorary Swatches-HSBS

Salming, Stig

69Swedish Hockey-71
70Swedish Hockey-24
71Swedish Hockey-101
72Swedish Stickers-85
73Swedish Stickers-161
74Swedish Stickers-185
79Panini Stickers-189
83Swedish Semic Elitserien-74
84Swedish Semic Elitserien-73
85Swedish Panini Stickers-46
86Swedish Panini Stickers-29

Salmon, Tim

83Kingston Canadians-12

Salmond, Scott

91British Columbia JHL-73

Salmonsson, Johannes

03Swedish Elite-164
Silver-164
04Swedish Elitset-164
Gold-164
06Swedish SHL Elitset-153

Salmu, Juha

05Finnish Cardset -244
06Finnish Cardset-72

Salnikov, Roman

98Russian Hockey League-116
00Russian Hockey League-59
03Russian Hockey League-1

Salnikov, Sergei

04Russian Under-18 Team-3

Salo, Ari

90Swedish Semic Elitserien Stickers-5
92Finnish Jyvas-Hyva Stickers-65
93Finnish Jyvas-Hyva Stickers-115
93Finnish SISU-5
94Finnish SISU-119

Salo, Juha

70Finnish Jaakiekko-339
92Finnish Jyvas-Hyva Stickers-63

Salo, Kalevi

65Finnish Hellas-56

Salo, Robert

92Finnish Jyvas-Hyva Stickers-110
93Finnish Jyvas-Hyva Stickers-201
93Finnish SISU-259
94Finnish SISU-93
95Finnish SISU-84
98Finnish Kerailysarja-14

Salo, Sami

94Finnish SISU-236
95Finnish SISU-124
96Finnish SISU Redline-137
Rookie Energy-3
98Pacific Dynagon Ice-131
Blue-131
Red-131
98Pacific Omega-171
Red-171
Opening Day Issue-171
98Senators Team Issue-20
99BAP Memorabilia-56
Gold-56
Silver-56
Selects Silver-SL17
Selects Gold-SL17
99BAP Millennium-174
Emerald-174
Ruby-174
Sapphire-174
Signatures-174
Signatures Gold-174
99O-Pee-Chee-168
99O-Pee-Chee Chrome-168
99O-Pee-Chee Chrome Refractors-168
99Pacific-295
Copper-295
Emerald Green-295
Gold-295
Ice Blue-295
Premiere Date-295
Red-295
99Paramount-165
Copper-165
Emerald-165
Gold-165
Holographic Emerald-165
Holographic Gold-165
Holographic Silver-165
Ice Blue-165
Premiere Date-165
Red-165
Silver-165
99Senators Team Issue-18
99SPx-106
Radiance-106
Spectrum-106
99Topps/OPC-168
99Topps/OPC Chrome-168
Refractors-168
99Upper Deck-91
Exclusives-91
Exclusives 1 of 1-91
99Upper Deck Gold Reserve-91
99Upper Deck MVP-143
Gold Script-143
Silver Script-143
Super Script-143
99Upper Deck Victory-203
99Finnish Cardset Aces High-D-3
00BAP Memorabilia-387
Emerald-387
Ruby-387
Sapphire-387
Promos-387
00BAP Mem Chicago Sportsfest Copper-387
00BAP Memorabilia Chicago Sportsfest Blue-387
00BAP Memorabilia Chicago Sportsfest Gold-387
00BAP Memorabilia Chicago Sportsfest Ruby-387
00BAP Memorabilia Chicago Sun-Times Ruby-387
00BAP Memorabilia Chicago Sun-Times Gold-387
00BAP Mem Chicago Sun-Times Sapphire-387
00BAP Mem Toronto Fall Expo Copper-387
00BAP Memorabilia Toronto Fall Expo Gold-387
00BAP Memorabilia Toronto Fall Expo Ruby-387
00Pacific-287
Copper-287
Gold-287
Ice Blue-287
Premiere Date-287
00Senators Team Issue-22
00Upper Deck Vintage-255
01Senators Team Issue-26
01Upper Deck-354
Exclusives-354
01Upper Deck Victory-251
Gold-251
01Finnish Cardset-163
02BAP First Edition-178
02BAP Sig Series Auto Buybacks 1999-174
02Canucks Team Issue-13
02NHL Power Play Stickers-164
02Pacific-273
Blue-273
Red-273
02Pacific Complete-482
Red-482
02Topps Total-30
02Finnish Cardset-263
Solid Gold-3
03Canucks Postcards-23
03Canucks Sav-on-Foods-24
03ITG Action-561
03Pacific Complete-195
Red-195
04Swedish Pure Skills-17
Parallel-17
Professional Power-SS
05Parkhurst-472
Facsimile Auto Parallel-472
05Upper Deck-191
HG Glossy-191
05Upper Deck MVP-375
Gold-375
Platinum-375
05Upper Deck Toronto Fall Expo-191
05Swedish SHL Elitset-25
Gold-25
06Be A Player-48
Autographs-48
Signatures-SS
Signatures 25-52
06Canucks Postcards-19
06Gatorade-81
06O-Pee-Chee-475
Rainbow-475
06Panini Stickers-359
06Upper Deck-193
Exclusives Parallel-193
High Gloss Parallel-193
Masterpieces-193
06Upper Deck MVP-281
Gold Script-281
Super Script-281
07Upper Deck Victory-135
Black-135
Gold-135

Salo, Tapani

66Finnish Jaakiekkosarja-207

Salo, Tommy

91Swedish Semic Elitserien Stickers-254
92Swedish Semic Elitserien Stickers-275
93Swedish Semic Elitserien-243
94Swedish Leaf Gold Cards-24
95Collector's Choice-235
Player's Club-235
Player's Club Platinum-235
95Donruss-196
95Emotion-107
generatioNext-5
95Leaf-177
95Metal-191
Winners-6
95Panini Stickers-101
95Parkhurst International-128
Emerald Ice-128
95Pinnacle-202
Artist's Proofs-202
Rink Collection-202
95Playoff One on One-282
95Score-314
Black Ice Artist's Proofs-314
Black Ice-314
95Select Certified-112
Mirror Gold-112
95SkyBox Impact-104
95Stadium Club-211
Members Only Master Set-211
95Ultra-98
95Ultra-354
Gold Medallion-98
95Upper Deck-413
Electric Ice-413
Electric Ice Gold-413
95Finnish Semic World Championships-53
95Swedish Upper Deck-246
95Swedish Globe World Championships-3
95Images-3
Gold-3
Clear Excitement-CE3
Platinum Prospects-PR8
96Be A Player-77
Autographs-77
Autographs Silver-77
96Black Diamond-31
Gold-31
96Flair-57
Blue Ice-57
96Islander Postcards-19
96Leaf-221
Press Proofs-221
96Pinnacle-244
Artist's Proofs-244
Foil-244
Premium Stock-244
Rink Collection-244
96Summit-189
Artist's Proofs-189
Ice-189
Metal-189
Premium Stock-189
96Swedish Semic Wien-39
Super Goalies-SG9
96Collector's Edge Future Legends-41
96Collector's Edge Ice-196
Crucibles-C22
Prism-196
96Collector's Edge Ice Promos-PR2
97Be A Player Stacking the Pads-14
97Collector's Choice-158
97Crown Royale-81
Emerald Green-81
Ice Blue-81
Silver-81
97Donruss-33
Press Proofs Silver-33
Press Proofs Gold-33
97Donruss Canadian Ice-106
Dominion Series-106
Provincial Series-106
97Donruss Elite-101
Aspirations-101
Status-101
97Donruss Limited-130
Exposure-130
97Donruss Preferred-32
Cut to the Chase-32
97Donruss Priority-121
Stamp of Approval-121
Postmaster General-15
Postmaster Generals Promos-15
97Pacific-56
Copper-56
Emerald Green-56
Ice Blue-56
Red-56
Silver-56
97Pacific Dynagon-75
Copper-75
Dark Grey-75
Emerald Green-75
Ice Blue-75
Red-75
Silver-75
Stonewallers-13
Tandems-67
97Pacific Invincible-83
Copper-83
Emerald Green-83
Ice Blue-83
Red-83
Silver-83
97Pacific Omega-142
Copper-142
Dark Gray-142
Emerald Green-142
Gold-142
Ice Blue-142
97Panini Stickers-74
97Paramount-111
Copper-111
Dark Grey-111
Emerald Green-111
Ice Blue-111
Red-111
Silver-111
Glove Side Laser Cuts-12
97Pinnacle-59
Artist's Proofs-59
Rink Collection-59
Press Plates Back Black-59
Press Plates Back Cyan-59
Press Plates Back Magenta-59
Press Plates Back Yellow-59
Press Plates Front Black-59
Press Plates Front Cyan-59
Press Plates Front Magenta-59
Press Plates Front Yellow-59
97Pinnacle Certified-24
Red-24
Mirror Blue-24
Mirror Gold-24
Mirror Red-24
97Pinnacle Inside-49
Coach's Collection-49
Executive Collection-49
97Pinnacle Tot Cert Platinum Blue-24
97Pinnacle Tot Certi Platinum Gold-24
97Pinnacle Totally Certified Platinum Red-24
97Pinnacle Tot Cert Mirror Platinum Gold-24
97Revolution-84
Copper-84
Emerald-84
Ice Blue-84
Silver-84
Return to Sender Die-Cuts-12
97Score-9
Artist's Proofs-9
Golden Blades-9
Net Worth-12
97SP Authentic-93
98Aurora-119
98Be A Player-83
Press Release-83
98BAP Gold-83
98BAP Autographs-83
98BAP Autographs Gold-83
98BAP Tampa Bay All Star Game-83
98Crown Royale-86
Limited Series-86
98NHL Aces Playing Cards-38
98OPC Chrome-88
Refractors-88
98Pacific-288
Ice Blue-288
Red-288
98Pacific Dynagon Ice-118
Blue-118
Red-118
98Pacific Omega-152
Red-152
Opening Day Issue-152
98Panini Photocards-73
98Panini Stickers-72
98Paramount-148
Copper-148
Emerald Green-148
Holo-Electric-148
Ice Blue-148
Silver-148
Glove Side Laser Cuts-11
98Revolution-90
Ice Shadow-90
Red-90
98Topps-88
O-Pee-Chee-88
98Upper Deck-317
Exclusives-317
Exclusives 1 of 1-317
Gold Reserve-317
98Upper Deck MVP-129
Gold Script-129
Silver Script-129
Super Script-129
98Slovakian Eurotel-21
99Aurora-58
Premiere Date-58
Glove Unlimited-9
99BAP Memorabilia-39
Gold-39
Silver-39
99BAP Millennium-103
Emerald-103
Ruby-103
Sapphire-103
Signatures-103
Signatures Gold-103
99Crown Royale-55
Limited Series-55
Premiere Date-55
99Jell-O Partners of Power-8
99Pacific-164
Copper-164
Emerald Green-164
Gold-164
Ice Blue-164
Premiere Date-164
Red-164
In the Cage Net-Fusions-8
99Pacific Dynagon Ice-84
Blue-84
Copper-84
Gold-84
Premiere Date-84
99Pacific Omega-93
Copper-93
Gold-93
Ice Blue-93
Premiere Date-93
99Pacific Prism-56
Holographic Blue-56
Holographic Gold-56
Holographic Mirror-56
Holographic Purple-56
Premiere Date-56
99Panini Stickers-241
99Paramount-95
Copper-95
Emerald-95
Gold-95
Holographic Emerald-95
Holographic Gold-95
Holographic Silver-95
Ice Blue-95
Premiere Date-95
Red-95
Silver-95
Glove Side Net Fusions-9
99Revolution-59
Premiere Date-59
Red-59
Shadow Series-59
Copper-59
Gold-59
CSC Silver-59
99SPx-64
Radiance-64
Spectrum-64
99Upper Deck-56
Exclusives-56
Exclusives 1 of 1-56
99Upper Deck Gold Reserve-56
99Upper Deck MVP-80
Gold Script-80
Silver Script-80
Super Script-80
99Upper Deck MVP SC Edition-71
Gold Script-71
Silver Script-71
Super Script-71
99Upper Deck Victory-112
00Aurora-57
Premiere Date-57
00BAP Memorabilia-68
Emerald-68
Ruby-68
Sapphire-68
Promos-68
00BAP Mem Chicago Sportsfest Copper-68
00BAP Memorabilia Chicago Sportsfest Blue-68
00BAP Memorabilia Chicago Sportsfest Gold-68
00BAP Memorabilia Chicago Sportsfest Ruby-68
00BAP Memorabilia Chicago Sun-Times Ruby-68
00BAP Memorabilia Chicago Sun-Times Gold-68
00BAP Mem Chicago Sun-Times Sapphire-68
00BAP Mem Toronto Fall Expo Copper-68
00BAP Memorabilia Toronto Fall Expo Gold-68
00BAP Memorabilia Toronto Fall Expo Ruby-68
00BAP Parkhurst 2000-P224
00BAP Signature Series-157
Emerald-157
Ruby-157
Sapphire-157
Autographs-67
Autographs Gold-67
00BAP Ultimate Memorabilia Goalie Sticks-G12
00BAP Ultimate Mem Plante Jersey Cards-PJ7
00Black Diamond-25
Gold-25
Game Gear-BTS
Game Gear-CTS
00Crown Royale-42
Ice Blue-42
Limited Series-42
Premiere Date-42
Red-42
00O-Pee-Chee-107
00O-Pee-Chee Parallel-107
00Pacific-172
00Pacific-438
Copper-172
Copper-438
Gold-172
Gold-438
Ice Blue-172
Ice Blue-438
Premiere Date-172
Premiere Date-438
Autographs-172
00Paramount-98
Copper-98
Gold-98
Holo-Gold-98
Holo-Silver-98
Ice Blue-98
Premiere Date-98
Glove Side Net Fusions-10
Glove Side Net Fusions Platinum-10
00Private Stock-39
Gold-39
Premiere Date-39
Retail-39
Silver-39
Game Gear-49
00Revolution-58
Blue-58
Premiere Date-58
Red-58
00SP Authentic-37
BuyBacks-37
Sign of the Times-TS
00SP Game Used-26
00SPx-27
Spectrum-27
00Stadium Club-74
00Titanium-36
Blue-36
Gold-36
Premiere Date-36
Red-36
Retail-36
00Topps/OPC-107
Parallel-107
00Topps Chrome-83
OPC Refractors-83
Refractors-83
00Topps Gold Label Class 1-49
Gold-49
00Topps Gold Label Class 2-49
00Topps Gold Label Class 2 Gold-49
00Topps Gold Label Class 3-49
00Topps Gold Label Class 3 Gold-49
00Topps Heritage-66
Chrome Parallel-66
00Topps Premier Plus-77
Blue Ice-77
Masters of the Break-MB20
00Topps Stars-52
Blue-52
00UD Heroes-48
Signs of Greatness-TS
00UD Pros and Prospects-34
00UD Reserve-34
Golden Goalies-GG4
00Upper Deck-70
Exclusives Tier 1-70
Exclusives Tier 2-70
00Upper Deck MVP-77
First Stars-77
Second Stars-77
Third Stars-77
00Upper Deck Victory-96
00Upper Deck Vintage-144
00Upper Deck Vintage-148
00Upper Deck Vintage-149
Great Gloves-GG9
00Vanguard-43
Holographic Gold-43
Holographic Purple-43
Pacific Proofs-43
01McFarlane Hockey-110
01McFarlane Hockey-111
01Atomic-42
Blue-42
Gold-42
Premiere Date-42
Red-42
Team Nucleus-7
01BAP Memorabilia-50
Emerald-50
Ruby-50
Sapphire-50
All-Star Jerseys-ASJ34
All-Star Emblems-ASE34
All-Star Numbers-ASN34
All-Star Teammates-AST18
All-Star Teammates-AST20
Country of Origin-CO29
Stanley Cup Playoffs-SC14
01BAP Signature Series Certified 100-C48
01BAP Signature Series Certified 50-C48
01BAP Signature Series Certified 1 of 1's-C48
01BAP Signature Series Autographs-LTSA
01BAP Signature Series Autographs Gold-LTS
01BAP Signature Series Franchise Jerseys-FP-12
01BAP Signature Series Jerseys-GJ-88
01BAP Ultimate Mem Legend Terry Sawchuk-10
01Between the Pipes-30
01Between the Pipes-169
All-Star Jerseys-ASJ11
He Shoots-He Saves Points-16
He Shoots-He Saves Prizes-10
Jerseys-GJ22
Emblems-GUE8
Jersey and Stick Cards-GSJ21
Masks-16
Masks Silver-16
Masks Gold-16
01Bowman YoungStars-12
Gold-12
Ice Cubed-12
01Crown Royale-61
Blue-61
Premiere Date-61
Red-61
Retail-61
01McDonald's Pacific-16
Glove-Side Net-Fusion-2
01O-Pee-Chee-108
01O-Pee-Chee Heritage Parallel-108
01O-Pee-Chee Heritage Parallel Limited-108
01O-Pee-Chee Premier Parallel-108
01Pacific-164
Extreme LTD-164
Hobby LTD-164
Premiere Date-164
Retail LTD-164
Steel Curtain-8
01Pacific Adrenaline-77
Blue-77
Premiere Date-77
Red-77
Retail-77
Creased Lightning-7
Power Play-15
01Pacific Arena Exclusives-164
01Pacific Heads-Up-41
Blue-41
Premiere Date-41
Red-41
Silver-41
HD NHL-14
Showstoppers-8
01Parkhurst-72
Gold-72
Silver-72
He Shoots-He Scores Prizes-33
Teammates-T26
Waving the Flag-19
01Private Stock-40
Gold-40
Premiere Date-40
Retail-40
Silver-40
01Private Stock Pacific Nights-40
01Private Stock PS-2002-32
01Private Stock Reserve-G5
01SP Authentic-32
Limited-32
Limited Gold-32
Buybacks-35
Buybacks-36
Sign of the Times-TS
Sign of the Times-HS
Sign of the Times-SDP
01SPx-27
01Stadium Club-26
Award Winners-26
Master Photos-26
01Titanium-57
Hobby Parallel-57
Premiere Date-57
Retail-57
Retail Parallel-57
01Topps-108
Heritage Parallel-108
Heritage Parallel Limited-108
OPC Parallel-108
Own The Game-OTG27
Stars of the Game-SG10
01Topps Chrome-108
Refractors-108
Black Border Refractors-108
01Topps Heritage-51
01Topps Heritage-127
Refractors-51
01Topps Reserve-72
01UD Challenge for the Cup-34
Backstops-BB5
01UD Mask Collection-112
01UD Mask Collection-178
Gold-112
Gold-178
Sticks-SSTS
01UD Playmakers-40
01UD Premier Collection-26
Signatures-SA
Signatures Black-SA
01UD Top Shelf-18
01Upper Deck-68
Exclusives-68
Goalies in Action-GL7
01Upper Deck Ice-18
01Upper Deck MVP-75
Goalie Sticks-G-TS
Masked Men-MM5
01Upper Deck Victory-134
01Upper Deck Victory-138
Gold-134
Gold-138
01Upper Deck Vintage-97
01Upper Deck Vintage-105
01Vanguard-40
Blue-40
Red-40
One of Ones-40
Premiere Date-40
Proofs-40
Stonewallers-8
01Utah Grizzlies-5
02McFarlane Hockey Toys-R-Us-20
02McFarlane Hockey-150
02Atomic-43
Blue-43
Gold-43
Red-43
Hobby Parallel-43
02BAP All-Star Edition-82
Jerseys-82
Jerseys Gold-82
Jerseys Silver-82
02BAP First Edition-52
Jerseys-52
02BAP Memorabilia-160
Emerald-160
Ruby-160
Sapphire-160
NHL All-Star Game-160
NHL All-Star Game Blue-160
NHL All-Star Game Green-160
NHL All-Star Game Red-160
02BAP Memorabilia Toronto Fall Expo-160
02BAP Signature Series-105
Autographs-105
Autograph Buybacks 1998-83
Autograph Buybacks 1999-103
Autograph Buybacks 2001-LTSA
Autographs Gold-105
Team Quads-TQ17
02Between the Pipes-5
02Between the Pipes-132
Gold-5
Silver-5
All-Star Stick and Jersey-9
Behind the Mask-5
Blockers-16
Double Memorabilia-8
Emblems-30
Goalie Autographs-20
He Shoots-He Saves Points-16
He Shoots-He Saves Prizes-7
Jerseys-30
Masks II-12
Masks II Gold-12
Masks II Silver-12
Nightmares-GN3
Nightmares-GN7
Numbers-30
Stick and Jerseys-30
Tandems-18
02Bowman YoungStars-89
Gold-89
Silver-89
02Crown Royale-40
Blue-40
Red-40
Retail-40
Dual Patches-10
02ITG Used International Experience-IE24
02ITG Used International Experience Gold-IE24
02McDonalds Pacific Glove Side Net-Fusion-3
02NHL Power Play Stickers-39
02Oilers Postcards-17
02O-Pee-Chee-218
02O-Pee-Chee Premier Blue Parallel-218
02O-Pee-Chee Premier Red Parallel-218
02O-Pee-Chee Factory Set-218
02O-Pee-Chee Factory Set Hometown Heroes-HHC14
02Pacific-148
Blue-148
Red-148
Jerseys-19
Jerseys Holo-Silver-19
02Pacific Complete-254
Red-254
02Pacific Exclusive-71
Jerseys-9
Jerseys Gold-9
02Pacific Heads-Up-50
Blue-50
Purple-50
Red-50
Quad Jerseys-31
Quad Jerseys Gold-31
02Pacific Quest for the Cup-39
Gold-39
02Pacific Toronto Fall Expo-3
Gold-3
02Parkhurst-67
Bronze-67
Gold-67
Silver-67
02Parkhurst Retro-33
Minis-33
02Private Stock Reserve-123
Red-123
Retail-123
InCrease Security-9
Patches-123
02SP Authentic-38
Beckett Promos-38
02SPx-33
Spectrum Gold-33
Spectrum Silver-33
02Stadium Club-81
Silver Decoy Cards-81
Proofs-81
Puck Stops Here-PSH12
02Titanium-43
Blue-43
Red-43
Retail-43
Jerseys-29
Jerseys Retail-29
02Topps-218
OPC Blue Parallel-218
OPC Red Parallel-218
Topps/OPC Hometown Heroes-HHC14
Factory Set-218
02Topps Chrome-121
Black Border Refractors-121
Refractors-121
02Topps Heritage-65
Chrome Parallel-65
02Topps Total-341
Team Checklists-TTC11
02UD Artistic Impressions-38
Gold-38
02UD Artistic Impressions Beckett Promos-38
02UD Artistic Impressions Retrospectives-R38
02UD Artistic Impressions Retrospect Gold-R38
02UD Artistic Impress Retrospect Silver-R38
02UD Honor Roll-31
02UD Mask Collection-34
02UD Mask Collection-35
02UD Mask Collection-36
02UD Mask Collection Beckett Promos-34
02UD Mask Collection Beckett Promos-35
02UD Mask Collection Beckett Promos-36
02UD Mask Collection Career Wins-CWTS
02UD Mask Collection Patches-PWTS
02UD Mask Collection View from the Cage-VTS
02UD Piece of History-39
02UD Top Shelf-34
Signatures-TS
02Upper Deck-71
Exclusives-71
Blow-Ups-C17
Last Line of Defense-LL5
02Upper Deck Classic Portraits-40
02Upper Deck MVP-73
Gold-73
Classics-73
Golden Classics-73
Prosign-TS
02Upper Deck Rookie Update-42
Jerseys-DTS
Jerseys Gold-DTS
02Upper Deck Victory-84
Bronze-84
Gold-84
Silver-84
National Pride-NP46
02Upper Deck Vintage-99
02Upper Deck Vintage-272
Green Backs-99
Tall Boys-T29
Tall Boys Gold-T29
02Vanguard-43
LTD-43
03BAP Memorabilia-167
Emerald-167
Gold-167
Ruby-167
Sapphire-167
03BAP Ultimate Memorabilia Autographs-23
Gold-23
03Beehive-82
Gold-82
Silver-82
Sticks Beige Border-BE38
Sticks Blue Border-BL18
03Black Diamond-44
Black-44
Green-44
Red-44
03Bowman-76
Gold-76
03Bowman Chrome-76
Refractors-76
Gold Refractors-76
Xfractors-76
03Crown Royale-41
Blue-41
Retail-41
03ITG Action-269
Jerseys-M146
Jerseys-M233
03ITG Used Signature Series-75
Gold-75
Autographs-TSA1
Autographs-TSA2
Autographs Gold-TSA1
Autographs Gold-TSA2
Goalie Gear-16
Goalie Gear Autographs-16
Goalie Gear Gold-16
03NHL Sticker Collection-230
03Oilers Postcards-15
03O-Pee-Chee-147
03OPC Blue-147
03OPC Gold-147
03OPC Red-147
03Pacific-137
Blue-137
Red-137
03Pacific Complete-422
Red-422

01SP Game Used Tools of the Game Signed-STSM
01SP Game Used Tools of the Game Signed-SCBS
01SP Game Used Tools of the Game Signed-SCPS
01SPx-3
Hockey Treasures-HTSS
01Stadium Club Souvenirs-SSPB
01Stadium Club Souvenirs-JTJASS
01Titanium-10
Hobby Parallel-10
Premiere Date-10
Retail-10
Retail Parallel-10
Double-Sided Jerseys-3
Double-Sided Patches-3
01Topps-104
Heritage Parallel-104
Heritage Parallel Limited-104
OPC Parallel-104
01Topps Chrome-104
Refractors-104
Black Border Refractors-104
01Topps Heritage-88
Refractors-88
01Topps Reserve Emblems-SS
01Topps Reserve Jerseys-SS
01Topps Reserve Name Plates-SS
01Topps Reserve Numbers-SS
01Topps Reserve Patches-SS
01UD Challenge for the Cup Jersey Autos-UCST
01UD Honor Roll Jerseys-J-SS
01UD Honor Roll Jerseys Gold-J-SS
01UD Mask Collection-7
Gold-7
01UD Playmakers-7
01UD Premier Collection-6
Dual Jerseys-DST
Dual Jerseys Black-DST
Jerseys-BSS
Jerseys Black-B-SS
Signatures-JS
Signatures Black-JS
01UD Top Shelf-78
01Upper Deck-14
Exclusives-14
Tandems-T1
01Upper Deck Ice-3
01Upper Deck MVP-14
Souvenirs-C-SS
Souvenirs Gold-C-SS
01Upper Deck Victory-25
Gold-25
01Upper Deck Vintage-22
01Upper Deck Vintage-26
01Vanguard-7
Blue-7
Red-7
Memorabilia-3
One of Ones-7
Patches-3
Premiere Date-7
Proofs-7
Quebec Tournament Heroes-15
02Atomic-7
Blue-7
Gold-7
Red-7
Hobby Parallel-7
02BAP First Edition-31
02BAP First Edition-418H
Jerseys-31
Scoring Leaders-3
02BAP Memorabilia-169
Emerald-169
Ruby-169
Sapphire-169
NHL All-Star Game-169
NHL All-Star Game Blue-169
NHL All-Star Game Green-169
NHL All-Star Game Red-169
02BAP Memorabilia Toronto Fall Expo-169
02BAP Signature Series-140
Autographs-140
Autograph Buybacks 1998-10
Autograph Buybacks 1999-22
Autograph Buybacks 2000-105
Autograph Buybacks 2001-LSSA
Autographs Gold-140
Jerseys-SGJ31
Jersey Autographs-SGJ31
Team Quads-TQ11
02BAP Ultimate Memorabilia Dynamic Duos-10
02BAP Ultimate Memorabilia Hat Tricks-15
02BAP Ultimate Memorabilia Jerseys-35
02Bowman YoungStars-71
Gold-71
Silver-71
02Bruins Team Issue-6
02Crown Royale-7
Blue-7
Red-7
Retail-7
02ITG Used-8
02ITG Used-108
Jerseys-GUJ31
Jersey Autographs-GUJ31
Jerseys Gold-GUJ31
Jersey and Stick-SJ31
Jersey and Stick Gold-SJ31
Teammates-T3
Teammates Gold-T3
Triple Memorabilia-TM12
Triple Memorabilia Gold-TM12
02O-Pee-Chee-134
02O-Pee-Chee Premier Blue Parallel-134
02O-Pee-Chee Premier Red Parallel-134
02O-Pee-Chee Factory Set-134
02Pacific-32
Blue-32
Red-32
02Pacific Calder-9
Silver-9
02Pacific Complete-403
Red-403
02Pacific Exclusive-13
02Pacific Heads-Up-10
Blue-10
Purple-10
Red-10
Head First-3
Quad Jerseys-3
Quad Jerseys Gold-3
02Parkhurst-132
Bronze-132
Gold-132
Silver-132
Jerseys-GJ31
Stick and Jerseys-SJ31
Teammates-TT8
02Parkhurst Retro-21
Minis-21
Jerseys-RJ30
Jersey and Sticks-RSJ21
02Private Stock Reserve-8
Blue-8
Red-8
Retail-8
02SP Authentic-7
Beckett Promos-7
Sign of the Times-SS
Sign of the Times-ST
Sign of the Times-TSB
Super Premiums-SPSS
Super Premiums-DPST
02SP Game Used-5
Authentic Fabrics-AFSS
Authentic Fabrics-AFSV
Authentic Fabrics-CFTS
Authentic Fabrics Gold-AFSS
Authentic Fabrics Gold-AFSV
Authentic Fabrics Gold-CFTS
Authentic Fabrics Rainbow-AFSS
Authentic Fabrics Rainbow-AFSV
Authentic Fabrics Rainbow-CFTS
First Rounder Patches-SS
Piece of History-PHSS
Piece of History-PHSV
Piece of History Gold-PHSS
Piece of History Gold-PHSV
Piece of History Rainbow-PHSS
Piece of History Rainbow-PHSV
Signature Style-SS
Tools of the Game-SS
02SPx-6
02SPx-78
Spectrum Gold-6
Spectrum Gold-78
Spectrum Silver-6
Spectrum Silver-78
Smooth Skaters-SS
Smooth Skaters Gold-SS
Smooth Skaters Silver-SS
Winning Materials-WMSS
Winning Materials Gold-SS
Winning Materials Silver-SS
Xtreme Talents-SS
Xtreme Talents Gold-SS
Xtreme Talents Silver-SS
02Stadium Club-20
Silver Decoy Cards-20
Proofs-20
Passport-16
02Topps-134
OPC Blue Parallel-134
OPC Red Parallel-134
Factory Set-134
02Topps Chrome-84
Black Border Refractors-84
Refractors-84
02Topps Heritage-35
Chrome Parallel-35
Calder Cloth-SS
Calder Cloth Patches-SS
02Topps Total-207
02UD Artistic Impressions-8
Gold-8
02UD Artistic Impressions Beckett Promos-8
02UD Artistic Impressions Common Ground-CG13
02UD Artistic Impress Common Ground Gold-CG13
02UD Artistic Impressions Retrospectives-R8
02UD Artistic Impressions Retrospect Gold-R8
02UD Artistic Impress Retrospect Silver-R8
02UD Honor Roll-6
Grade A Jerseys-TSTM
02UD Mask Collection Instant Offense-IOSS
02UD Piece of History-6
Awards Collection-AC3
Marks of Distinction-SS
Patches-PHSA
02UD Premier Collection-7
Jerseys Bronze-SS
Jerseys Bronze-ST
Jerseys Gold-SS
Jerseys Gold-ST
Jerseys Silver-SS
Jerseys Silver-ST
Patches-PSS
Signatures Bronze-SSS
Signatures Gold-SSS
Signatures Silver-SSS
02UD Top Shelf-7
Clutch Performers-CPSSA
Dual Player Jerseys-RBS
Goal Oriented-GOSS
Hardware Heroes-HSSBR
Signatures-SS
Sweet Sweaters-SWSS
02Upper Deck-257
Exclusives-257
02Upper Deck Beckett UD Promos-257
02Upper Deck Difference Makers-SS
02Upper Deck Fan Favorites-SS
02Upper Deck Game Jersey Autographs-SS
02Upper Deck Game Jersey Series II-GJSS
02Upper Deck Patch Card Name Plate-SS
02Upper Deck Patchwork-PWSS
02Upper Deck Playbooks Series II-ST
02Upper Deck Specialists-SSS
02Upper Deck Classic Portraits-9
Headliners-ST
Headliners Limited-ST
Stitches-CSS
Stitches Limited-CSS
02Upper Deck MVP-13
Gold-13
Classics-13
Golden Classics-13
02Upper Deck Rookie Update-10
02Upper Deck Rookie Update-157B
02Upper Deck Rookie Update-164
Autographs-SS
Jerseys-DSS
Jerseys-STS
Jerseys Gold-DSS
Jerseys Gold-STS
02Upper Deck Victory-16
Bronze-16
Gold-16
Silver-16
National Pride-NP32
02Upper Deck Vintage-17
02Upper Deck Vintage-263
Green Backs-17
Tall Boys-T6
Tall Boys Gold-T6
02Russian Olympic Team-1
02UD SuperStars City AS Dual Jersey-SSAW
03BAP Memorabilia-87
Emerald-87
Gold-87
Ruby-87
Sapphire-87
Gloves-GUG14
Jersey and Stick-SJ-2
03BAP Ultimate Memorabilia Autographs-56
Gold-56
03BAP Ultimate Mem Auto Jerseys-56
03BAP Ultimate Mem Auto Sticks-56
03BAP Ultimate Memorabilia Gloves Are Off-6
03BAP Ultimate Memorabilia Hat Tricks-13
03BAP Ultimate Mem Jersey and Emblems-38
03BAP Ultimate Mem Jersey and Emblem Gold-38
03BAP Ultimate Mem Jersey and Numbers-38
03BAP Ultimate Mem Jersey and Number Gold-38
03Beehive-21
Variations-21
Gold-21
Silver-21
03Black Diamond-92
Black-92
Green-92
Red-92
Signature Gems-SG-29
03Bowman-35
Gold-35
03Bowman Chrome-35
Refractors-35
Gold Refractors-35
Xfractors-35
03Bruins Team Issue-10
03ITG Action-100
Homeboys-HB14
Jerseys-M175
03ITG Used Signature Series-26
Gold-26
Autographs-SS
Autographs Gold-SSA
Emblems-40
Emblems Gold-40
Jersey and Stick-5
Jersey and Stick Gold-5
03NHL Sticker Collection-16
03Pacific-30
Blue-30
Red-30
03Pacific Complete-142
Red-142
03Pacific Invincible-7
Blue-7
Red-7
Retail-7
03Pacific Luxury Suite-26A
03Pacific Luxury Suite-26B
03Pacific Luxury Suite-26C
03Pacific Luxury Suite-26D
03Pacific Prism-11
Blue-11
Gold-11
Red-11
03Pacific Supreme-7
Blue-7
Red-7
Retail-7
03Parkhurst Original Six Boston-28
Memorabilia-BM2
Memorabilia-BM15
Memorabilia-BM20
03Parkhurst Orig Six He Shoots/Scores-15
03Parkhurst Orig Six He Shoots/Scores-15A
03Parkhurst Rookie ROYalty-VR-6
03Parkhurst Rookie ROYalty Gold-VR-6
03Private Stock Reserve-11
Blue-11
Red-11
Retail-11
03SP Authentic-8
Limited-8
Foundations-F2
Foundations Limited-F2
Sign of the Times-SS
03SP Game Used-6
Gold-6
Double Threads-DTTS
Game Gear-GGSAM
Team Threads-TTTMS
03SPx-7
03SPx-154
Radiance-7
Radiance-154
Spectrum-7
Spectrum-154
Fantasy Franchise-FF-TMS
Fantasy Franchise Limited-FF-TMS
Origins-O-SS
Signature Threads-ST-SS
03Titanium-144
Hobby Jersey Number Parallels-144
Patches-144
Retail-144
03UD Honor Roll-7
Grade A Jerseys-TBOS
Signature Class-SC24
03UD Premier Collection-5
Stars-ST-SS
Stars Patches-ST-SS
Teammates-PT-BB1
Teammates Patches-PT-BB1
03Upper Deck-258
BuyBacks-167
BuyBacks-168
BuyBacks-169
BuyBacks-170
BuyBacks-171
BuyBacks-172
BuyBacks-173
Canadian Exclusives-258
HG-258
Highlight Heroes-HH-SS
Highlight Heroes Jerseys-HH-SS
Jersey Autographs-SJ-SS
UD Exclusives-258
03Upper Deck Classic Portraits-8
03Upper Deck Ice-8
Gold-8
Breakers-IB-SS
Breaker Patches-IB-SS
Frozen Fabrics-FF-SS
Frozen Fabric Patches-FF-SS
03Upper Deck MVP-43
Gold Script-43
Silver Script-43
Canadian Exclusives-43
Lethal Lineups-LL3
SportsNut-SN10
03Upper Deck Rookie Update-6
Super Stars-SSSS
03Upper Deck Trilogy Authentic Patches-AP35
03Upper Deck Trilogy Limited Threads-LT27
03Upper Deck Trilogy Scripts-S2SS
03Upper Deck Trilogy Scripts Limited-S2SS
03Upper Deck Trilogy Scripts Red-S2SS
03Upper Deck Victory-27
Bronze-27
Gold-27
Silver-27
Freshman Flashback-FF6
Game Breakers-GB42
03Toronto Star-8
04Pacific-26
Blue-26
Red-26
Global Connection-2
04Ultimate Collection-74
04Upper Deck-17
Canadian Exclusives-17
HG Glossy Gold-17
HG Glossy Silver-17
World Cup Tribute-AKAYSS
04Russian Back to Russia-38
05Beehive-8
Matte-8
Matted Materials-MMSS
05Black Diamond-89
Emerald-89
Gold-89
Onyx-89
Ruby-89
05Bruins Boston Globe-17
05Panini Stickers-21
05Parkhurst-200
Facsimile Auto Parallel-39
True Colors-TCBOS
True Colors-TCBOS
05SP Authentic-8
Limited-8
05SP Game Used Authentic Fabrics Quad-TRSB
05SP Game Used Authentic Patches Quad -TRSB
05The Cup Dual NHL Shields-DSBS
05UD Artifacts-10
Blue-10
Gold-10
Green-10
Pewter-10
Red-10
Gold Autographed-10
05UD PowerPlay-7
Rainbow-7
05Ultra-21
Gold-21
Ice-21
05Upper Deck-18
Big Playmakers-B-SSA
HG Glossy-18
Jerseys-J-SSA
Jerseys Series II-J2SV
Patches-P-SSV
Shooting Stars-S-SS
Trilogy Honorary Patches-HP-SV
Trilogy Honorary Patch Scripts-HSP-SV
Trilogy Honorary Swatches-HS-SV
Trilogy Honorary Swatch Scripts-HSS-SV
05Upper Deck Toronto Fall Expo-18
05Upper Deck Victory-18
Black-18
Gold-18
Silver-18
06Be A Player-47
Autographs-47
Signatures-SE
Signatures 25-51
Signatures Duals-DKS
06Be A Player Portraits-57
06Beehive Matted Materials-MMSS
06Beehive Remarkable Matted Materials-MMSS
06Beehive Signature Scrapbook-SSSS
06Black Diamond-44
Black-44
Gold-44
Ruby-44
Jerseys-JSS
Jerseys Black-JSS
Jerseys Gold-JSS
Jerseys Ruby-JSS
Jerseys Black Autographs -JSS
06Canadiens Postcards-22
06Flair Showcase Inks-ISS
06Fleer Fabricology-FSS
06Gatorade-43
06Hot Prospects Hot Materials -HMSS
06Hot Prospects Hot Materials Red Hot-HMSS
06Hot Prospects Hot Materials White Hot-HMSS
06NHL POG-45
06O-Pee-Chee-269
Rainbow-269
Swatches-S-SS
06Panini Stickers-69
06SP Game Used Authentic Fabrics-AFSS
06SP Game Used Authentic Fabrics Parallel-AFSS
06SP Game Used Authentic Fabrics Patches-AFSS
06SP Game Used Authentic Fabrics Triple-AF3MTL
06SP Game Used Authentic Fabrics Triple Patches-AF3MTL
06SPx Winning Materials-WMSS
06SPx Winning Materials Spectrum-WMSS
06SPx Winning Materials Autographs-WMSS
06UD Artifacts Tundra Tandems-TTAS
06UD Artifacts Tundra Tandems Black-TTAS
06UD Artifacts Tundra Tandems Blue-TTAS
06UD Artifacts Tundra Tandems Gold-TTAS
06UD Artifacts Tundra Tandems Red-TTAS
06UD Artifacts Tundra Tandems Dual Patches Red-TTAS
06UD Mini Jersey Collection-57
06Ultra Fresh Ink-ISS
06Upper Deck-354
Exclusives Parallel-354
High Gloss Parallel-354
Game Jerseys-JSS
Game Jerseys-J2SS
Game Patches-PSS
Game Patches-J2SS
Masterpieces-354
Signatures-SSS
06Upper Deck MVP-158
Gold Script-158
Super Script-158
Autographs-OARS
Jerseys-OJSA
Jerseys-OJSN
06Upper Deck Sweet Shot Sweet Stitches-SSSS
06Upper Deck Sweet Shot Sweet Stitches Duals-SSSS
06Upper Deck Sweet Shot Sweet Stitches Triples-SSSS
06Upper Deck Trilogy Honorary Scripted Patches-HSPSS
06Upper Deck Trilogy Honorary Scripted Swatches-HSSSS
06Upper Deck Victory-257

Samuel, Andy

96UK Fife Flyers-9
97UK Fife Flyers-12

Samuelsson, Kjell

83Swedish Semic Elitserien-130
84Swedish Semic Elitserien-152
85Swedish Panini Stickers-113
85Swedish Panini Stickers-114
87Flyers Postcards-28
88Flyers Postcards-22
88Panini Stickers-318
89Flyers Postcards-21
89O-Pee-Chee-100
89Topps-100
90Bowman-111
Tiffany-111
90Flyers Postcards-21
90O-Pee-Chee-61
90O-Pee-Chee-80
90Panini Stickers-110
90Pro Set-222
90Score-197
Canadian-197
90Topps-61
90Topps-80
Tiffany-61
90Upper Deck-116
French-116
91Bowman-240
91Flyers J.C. Penney-23
91O-Pee-Chee-211
91O-Pee-Chee-329
91Panini Stickers-239
91Parkhurst-356
French-356
91Pinnacle-149
91Pinnacle-407
French-149
French-407
91Pro Set-181
French-181
91Score American-207
91Score Canadian Bilingual-207
91Score Canadian English-207
91Stadium Club-70
91Topps-211
91Upper Deck-396
French-396
91Swedish Semic Elitserien Stickers-339
92Bowman-165
92O-Pee-Chee-230
92Parkhurst-373
Emerald Ice-373
92Penguins Coke/Clark-17
92Penguins Foodland-14
92Pinnacle-306
French-306
92Score-195
Canadian-195
92Stadium Club-466
92Topps-352
Gold-352G
92Ultra-169
93Donruss-259
93Leaf-274
93OPC Premier-34
Gold-34
93Parkhurst-432
Emerald Ice-432
93Penguins Foodland-18
93Pinnacle-293
Canadian-293
93PowerPlay-414
93Score-184
Canadian-184
93Stadium Club-251
93Stadium Club-426
Members Only Master Set-251
Members Only Master Set-426
First Day Issue-251
First Day Issue-426
93Topps/OPC Premier-34
Gold-34
93Swedish Semic World Champ Stickers-22
94Canada Games NHL POGS-192
94OPC Premier-73
Special Effects-73
94Parkhurst SE-SE138
Gold-SE138
Euro-Stars-ES7
94Penguins Foodland-21
94Pinnacle-277
Artist's Proofs-277
Rink Collection-277
94Topps/OPC Premier-73
Special Effects-73
94Ultra-351
94Upper Deck-128
Electric Ice-128
95Donruss-368
95Parkhurst International-155
Emerald Ice-155
95Playoff One on One-184
95Topps-259
OPC Inserts-259
95Ultra-286
95Upper Deck-350
Electric Ice-350
Electric Ice Gold-350
95Swedish Globe World Championships-27
96Be A Player-189
Autographs-189
Autographs Silver-189
96Flyers Postcards-20
97Pacific-329
Copper-329
Emerald Green-329
Ice Blue-329
Red-329
Silver-329
98OPC Chrome-205
Refractors-205
98Topps-205
O-Pee-Chee-205
06Philadelphia Phantoms-2

Samuelsson, Martin

02BAP Memorabilia-389
02BAP Ultimate Memorabilia-56
02Parkhurst Retro-234
Minis-234
02Providence Bruins-8
03ITG Action-60
03Parkhurst Original Six Boston-13
03Upper Deck MVP-48
Gold Script-48
Silver Script-48
Canadian Exclusives-48
03Providence Bruins-16
04Providence Bruins-16
06Swedish SHL Elitset-209

Samuelsson, Mikael

98Swedish UD Choice-78
00Kentucky Thoroughblades-21
01BAP Memorabilia-295
Emerald-295
Ruby-295
Sapphire-295
01Bowman YoungStars-117
Gold-117
Ice Cubed-117
01O-Pee-Chee-291
01O-Pee-Chee Premier Parallel-291
01Parkhurst-330
01SP Authentic-162
Limited-162
Limited Gold-162
01SPx-144
01SPx-144
Rookie Treasures-RTMS
01Titanium-172
Retail-172
01Titanium Draft Day Edition-153
01Topps-291
OPC Parallel-291
01Topps Chrome-181
Refractors-181
Black Border Refractors-181
01UD Challenge for the Cup-120
01UD Honor Roll-95
01UD Playmakers-130
01UD Premier Collection-73
01UD Top Shelf-46
01UD Top Shelf-46B
01Upper Deck-198
Exclusives-198
01Upper Deck Ice-144
01Upper Deck Victory-386
Gold-386
01Upper Deck Vintage-288
02Pacific Complete-377
Red-377
02Topps Total-67
03Panthers Team Issue-15
03Upper Deck MVP-337
Gold Script-337
Silver Script-337
Canadian Exclusives-337
04Swedish Pure Skills-86
Parallel-86
05Parkhurst-177
Facsimile Auto Parallel-177
05Upper Deck-317
06O-Pee-Chee-181
Rainbow-181
06Upper Deck-69
Exclusives Parallel-69
High Gloss Parallel-69
Masterpieces-69
06Upper Deck MVP-108
Gold Script-108
Super Script-108

Samuelsson, Morgan

89Swedish Semic Elitserien Stickers-159
90Swedish Semic Elitserien Stickers-63
91Swedish Semic Elitserien Stickers-236
92Swedish Semic Elitserien Stickers-49
94Swedish Leaf-172
95Swedish Leaf-12
Face to Face-1
Goldies-1
95Swedish Upper Deck-18
95Swedish World Championships Stickers-146
99Swiss Panini Stickers-353
00Swiss Panini Stickers-319
01Swiss HNL-20
01Swiss HNL-166

Samuelsson, Tommy

81Swedish Semic Hockey VM Stickers-6
82Swedish Semic VM Stickers-10
83Swedish Semic Elitserien-103
84Swedish Semic Elitserien-103
85Swedish Panini Stickers-93
86Swedish Panini Stickers-86
87Swedish Panini Stickers-91
89Swedish Semic Elitserien Stickers-76
89Swedish Semic World Champ Stickers-8
90Swedish Semic Elitserien Stickers-251
91Finnish Semic World Champ Stickers-33
91Swedish Semic Elitserien Stickers-82
91Swedish Semic World Champ Stickers-33
92Swedish Semic Elitserien Stickers-104
93Swedish Semic Elitserien-76
94Swedish Leaf-110
Studio Signatures-4

Samuelsson, Ulf

83Swedish Semic Elitserien-134
84Whalers Junior Wendy's-17
85Whalers Junior Wendy's-18
86Whalers Junior Thomas'-20
87O-Pee-Chee-23
87O-Pee-Chee Stickers-205
87Panini Stickers-41
87Topps-23
87Whalers Jr. Burger King/Pepsi-18
88O-Pee-Chee-136
88O-Pee-Chee Stickers-265
88Panini Stickers-238
88Topps-136
88Whalers Junior Ground Round-15
89O-Pee-Chee-210
89Panini Stickers-228
89Whalers Junior Milk-17
90O-Pee-Chee-511
90Pro Set-109
90Score-152
Canadian-152
90Score Hottest/Rising Stars-64
90Upper Deck-287
French-287
90Whalers Jr. 7-Eleven-21
91Pro Set Platinum-95
91Bowman-88
91Bowman-408
91O-Pee-Chee-323
91Panini Stickers-277
91Parkhurst-361
French-361
91Penguins Coke/Elby's-5
91Penguins Foodland-2
91Penguins Foodland Coupon Stickers-6
91Pinnacle-267
French-267
91Pro Set-459
French-459
91Score American-82
91Score American-304
91Score Canadian Bilingual-82
91Score Canadian Bilingual-308
91Score Canadian English-82
91Score Canadian English-308
91Stadium Club-328
91Topps-323
91Upper Deck-230
French-230
Euro-Stars-17
Euro-Stars French-17
92Bowman-351
92O-Pee-Chee-270
92Panini Stickers-229
92Panini Stickers French-229
92Parkhurst-369
92Parkhurst-446
Emerald Ice-369
Emerald Ice-446
92Penguins Coke/Clark-18
92Penguins Foodland-12
92Penguins Foodland Coupon Stickers-10
92Pinnacle-296
French-296
92Pro Set-143
92Score-90
Canadian-90
92Stadium Club-440
92Topps-127
Gold-127G
92Ultra-170
Imports-20
92Upper Deck-189
92Finnish Semic-58
93Donruss-264
93Leaf-92
93OPC Premier-132
Gold-132
93Panini Stickers-87
93Parkhurst-155
Emerald Ice-155
93Penguins Foodland-3
93Pinnacle-29
Canadian-29
93PowerPlay-194
93Score-161
Canadian-161
93Stadium Club-356
Members Only Master Set-356
First Day Issue-356
93Topps/OPC Premier-132
Gold-132
93Ultra-204
93Upper Deck-142
93Swedish Semic World Champ Stickers-21
94Canada Games NHL POGS-193
94Donruss-296
94EA Sports-104
94Flair-139
94Fleer-168
94Leaf-205
94OPC Premier-391
Special Effects-391
94Parkhurst-183
Gold-183
94Penguins Foodland-5
94Pinnacle-46
Artist's Proofs-46
Rink Collection-46
94Score-156
Gold-156
Platinum-156
Check It-CI7
94Topps/OPC Premier-391
Special Effects-391
94Ultra-169
94Upper Deck-209
Electric Ice-209
95Be A Player-223
Signatures-S223
Signatures Die Cuts-S223
95Canada Games NHL POGS-187
95Collector's Choice-79
Player's Club-79
Player's Club Platinum-79
95Donruss-89
95Donruss-243
95Emotion-119
95Leaf-206
95Metal-100
95Panini Stickers-66
95Parkhurst International-411
Emerald Ice-411
95Playoff One on One-176
95Score-203
Black Ice Artist's Proofs-203
Black Ice-203
95SkyBox Impact-114
95Stadium Club Members Only-17
95Stadium Club-11
Members Only Master Set-11
Fearless-F7
Fearless Members Only Master Set-F7
95Summit-78
Artist's Proofs-78
Ice-78
95Topps-144
OPC Inserts-144
95Ultra-126
95Ultra-278
Gold Medallion-126
95Upper Deck-448
Electric Ice-448
Electric Ice Gold-448
Special Edition-SE142
Special Edition Gold-SE142
95Swedish Globe World Championships-7
95Swedish World Championships Stickers-289
96Penguins Tribune-Review-3
96SkyBox Impact-84
96Upper Deck-104
96Swedish Semic Wien-44
97Be A Player-126
Autographs-126
Autographs Die-Cuts-126
Autographs Prismatic Die-Cuts-126
97Collector's Choice-171
97Pacific-171
Copper-171
Emerald Green-171
Ice Blue-171
Red-171
Silver-171
97Panini Stickers-88
97Score-239
97Score Rangers-15
Platinum-15
Premier-15
97Upper Deck-204
97Upper Deck-313
97Upper Deck-395
98Aurora-126
98Be A Player-93
Press Release-93
98BAP Gold-93
98BAP Autographs-93
98BAP Autographs Gold-93
98BAP Tampa Bay All Star Game-93
98OPC Chrome-127
Refractors-127
98Pacific-299
Ice Blue-299
Red-299
98Panini Stickers-85
98Paramount-157
Copper-157
Emerald Green-157
Holo-Electric-157
Ice Blue-157
Silver-157
98Topps-127
O-Pee-Chee-127
99Pacific-148
Copper-148
Emerald Green-148
Gold-148
Ice Blue-148
Premiere Date-148
Red-148
99Panini Stickers-120
00BAP Ultimate Mem Dynasty Jerseys-D12
00BAP Ultimate Mem Dynasty Emblems-D12
00Panini Stickers-78
01Fleer Legacy-24
Ultimate-24
02BAP Sig Series Auto Buybacks 1998-93
02Fleer Throwbacks-82
Gold-82
Platinum-82
Squaring Off-3
Squaring Off Memorabilia-3
05Hartford Wolf Pack-27

Samuli, Jouni

70Finnish Jaakiekko-168
71Finnish Suomi Stickers-238
72Finnish Jaakiekko-222
73Finnish Jaakiekko-300

Samylin, Vladimir

04Russian Super League All-Stars-14

Sancimino, Mike

92Cornell Big Red-24
93Cornell Big Red-21
96Louisville Riverfrogs-14
97Louisville Riverfrogs-12

Sanda, Dalibor

95Czech APS Extraliga-265
96Czech APS Extraliga-306
97Czech APS Extraliga-187
99Czech Score Blue 2000-11
99Czech Score Red Ice 2000-11

Sandalax, Alex

51Laval Dairy QSHL-38

Sandback, Darrell

93Seattle Thunderbirds-21

Sandbeck, Mike

02Arkansas Riverblades-14
03Fresno Falcons-17

Sandberg, Magnus

04Swedish Elitset-108
Gold-108
05Swedish SHL Elitset-114
Gold-114

Sandberg, Mikael

92Swedish Semic Elitserien Stickers-301
93Swedish Semic Elitserien-267
94Swedish Leaf-290
95Swedish Leaf-198
Spidermen-13
95Swedish Upper Deck-204
97Swedish Collector's Choice-68
98Swedish UD Choice-66
02Swedish SHL-138
02Swedish SHL-206
02Swedish SHL-288
Masks-4
Netminders-NM7
Parallel-138
Parallel-206
Parallel-288
Signatures-8
05Swedish SHL Elitset-171
Gold-171
06Swedish SHL Elitset-26
Goal Patrol-5

Sandelin, Scott

86Canadiens Postcards-21
86Sherbrooke Canadiens-24
87Canadiens Postcards-27
88ProCards AHL-284
89ProCards AHL-332
90ProCards AHL/IHL-41
04Minnesota-Duluth Bulldogs-27

Sandell, Sami

04Brandon Wheat Kings-9
05Brandon Wheat Kings-20
06Finnish Cardset-230
06Finnish Ilves Team Set-24

Sanden, Todd

97Dubuque Fighting Saints-24

Sanders, Frank

72Minnesota Fighting Saints Postcards WHA-21

Sanders, Grant

84Kitchener Rangers-28

Sanderson, Barry

06Mississauga Ice Dogs-10

Sanderson, Derek

67Topps-33
68O-Pee-Chee-6
68O-Pee-Chee-213
68Shirriff Coins-7
68Topps-6
69O-Pee-Chee-201
Four-in-One-8
69Topps-31
70Bruins Postcards-15
70Bruins Team Issue-7
70Colgate Stamps-6
70Dad's Cookies-116
70Esso Power Players-65
70O-Pee-Chee-136
Deckle-5
70Sargent Promotions Stamps-3
70Topps/OPC Sticker Stamps-27
71Bazooka-12
71Bruins Postcards-11
71Colgate Heads-12
71O-Pee-Chee-65
71Sargent Promotions Stamps-4
71Topps-65
71Toronto Sun-16
73O-Pee-Chee-183
73Topps-182
74Nabisco Sugar Daddy-15
74NHL Action Stamps-185
74O-Pee-Chee NHL-290
75O-Pee-Chee NHL-73
75Topps-73
76O-Pee-Chee NHL-20
76Topps-20
77Canucks Canada Dry Cans-13
77O-Pee-Chee NHL-46
77Topps-42
77Topps-46
94Parkhurst Tall Boys Future Stars-FS6
95Parkhurst '66-67-19
Coins-19
98Bruins Alumni-16
Autographs-16
99BAP Memorabilia AS American Hobby-AH3
99BAP Memorabilia AS American Hobby Autos-AH3
01Topps Archives-42
Arena Seats-ASDS
02Topps Stanley Cup Heroes-DS
02Topps Stanley Cup Heroes Autographs-DS
03Parkhurst Original Six Boston-44
Autographs-17
Inserts-B13
04ITG Franchises US East-316
Autographs-A-DSA1
04ITG Franchises US West-287
04ITG Ultimate Memorabilia-103
Gold-103
04UD Legends Classics-17
Gold-17
Platinum-17
Silver-17
Signature Moments-M54

Signatures-CS52
Signatures-DC6
Signatures-DC11
Signatures-TC3
05ITG Heroes/Prosp Toronto Expo Parallel -39
05Beehive Signature Scrapbook-SSDS
05SP Authentic Sign of the Times Quads-QCECS
05SPx Xcitement Legends-XL-SA
05SPx Xcitement Legends Gold-XL-SA
05SPx Xcitement Legends Spectrum-XL-SA
05UD Artifacts-145
Blue-145
Gold-145
Green-145
Pewter-145
Red-145
Gold Autographed-145
05ITG Heroes and Prospects-39
Autographs-A-DSA
06SP Authentic Sign of the Times Triples-ST3COS
06SP Game Used SIGnificance-SDS
06UD Artifacts-132
Blue-132
Gold-132
Platinum-132
Radiance-132
Red-132
06Upper Deck Trilogy Scripts-TSDS

Sanderson, Geoff

907th Inn. Sketch WHL-54
91Pro Set Platinum-256
91Parkhurst-57
French-57
91Pinnacle-309
French-309
91Pro Set-536
French-536
91Score American-324
91Score Canadian Bilingual-354
91Score Canadian English-354
91Upper Deck-588
French-588
91Whalers Jr. 7-Eleven-23
92Bowman-136
92O-Pee-Chee-122
92Panini Stickers-V
92Panini Stickers French-V
92Parkhurst-62
Emerald Ice-62
92Pinnacle-307
French-307
92Pro Set-63
Rookie Goal Leaders-11
92Score-108
Canadian-108
92Stadium Club-111
92Topps-402
Gold-402G
92Ultra-75
92Upper Deck-293
92Whalers Dairymart-21
93Donruss-147
93Kraft-21
93Leaf-77
93OPC Premier-156
Gold-156
93Panini Stickers-L
93Parkhurst-86
Emerald Ice-86
93Pinnacle-9
Canadian-9
93PowerPlay-109
Rising Stars-6
93Score-213
Canadian-213
93Stadium Club-408
Members Only Master Set-408
First Day Issue-408
93Topps Premier Promo Sheet-156
93Topps/OPC Premier-156
Gold-156
93Ultra-151
Speed Merchants-9
93Upper Deck-292
93Upper Deck-316
Hat Tricks-HT2
SP-65
93Whalers Coke-19
93Classic Autographs-AU12
93Classic Team Canada-TC6
94Action Packed Big Picture 24K Gold-16G
94Canada Games NHL POGS-117
94Donruss-77
94EA Sports-58
94Finest-108
Super Team Winners-108
Refractors-108
94Flair-74
94Fleer-89
Slapshot Artists-9
94Hockey Wit-6
94Leaf-219
94Leaf Limited-54
94OPC Premier-205
94OPC Premier-527
Special Effects-205
Special Effects-527
94Parkhurst-95
Gold-95
Crash the Game Green-10
Crash the Game Blue-10
Crash the Game Gold-10
Crash the Game Red-10
Vintage-V49
94Pinnacle-63
Artist's Proofs-63
Rink Collection-63
Boomers-BR8
94Score-144
Gold-144
Platinum-144
Franchise-TF10
94Select-68
Gold-68
94SP-52
Die Cuts-52
94Stadium Club Members Only-36
94Topps/OPC Premier-205
94Topps/OPC Premier-527
Special Effects-205
Special Effects-527
94Topps Finest Inserts-15
94Ultra-93
Speed Merchants-10
94Upper Deck-6
Electric Ice-6
SP Inserts-SP34
SP Inserts Die Cuts-SP34
94Classic Pro Prospects-56
Jumbos-PP16
95Bashan Super Stickers-51
95Bashan Super Stickers-53
95Be A Player-62
Signatures-S62
Signatures Die Cuts-S62
95Bowman-67
All-Foil-67
95Canada Games NHL POGS-125
95Collector's Choice-293
Player's Club-293
Player's Club Platinum-293
Crash The Game-C22A
Crash The Game-C22B
Crash The Game-C22C
Crash The Game Gold-C22A
Crash The Game Gold-C22B
Crash The Game Gold-C22C
Crash the Game Silver Redeemed-C22
Crash the Game Silver Bonus-C22
Crash the Game Gold Redeemed-C22
Crash the Game Gold Bonus-C22
95Donruss-201
95Emotion-77
95Finest-173
Refractors-173
95Hoyle Eastern Playing Cards-19
95Imperial Stickers-53
95Leaf-88
95Metal-66
95NHL Aces Playing Cards-6H
95Panini Stickers-28
95Parkhurst International-91
Emerald Ice-91
95Pinnacle-38
Artist's Proofs-38
Rink Collection-38
95Playoff One on One-266
95Score-111
Black Ice Artist's Proofs-111
Black Ice-111
95Select Certified-26
Mirror Gold-26
95SkyBox Impact-75
95Stadium Club Members Only-8
95Stadium Club-172
Members Only Master Set-172
95Summit-38
Artist's Proofs-38
Ice-38
95Topps-14
95Topps-318
OPC Inserts-14
OPC Inserts-318
Marquee Men Power Boosters-14
95Topps SuperSkills-21
Platinum-21
95Ultra-70
Gold Medallion-70
95Upper Deck-20
Electric Ice-20
Electric Ice Gold-20
Special Edition-SE127
Special Edition Gold-SE127
95Whalers Bob's Stores-23
95Zenith-14
95Swedish World Championships Stickers-12
96Black Diamond-138
Gold-138
96Collector's Choice-113
96Collector's Choice-319
96Donruss-40
Press Proofs-40
96Donruss Canadian Ice-114
Gold Press Proofs-114
Red Press Proofs-114
O Canada-15
96Donruss Elite-127
Die Cut Stars-127
96Flair-44
Blue Ice-44
96Fleer-47
96Kraft Upper Deck-3
96Leaf-105
Press Proofs-105
96Leaf Preferred-86
Press Proofs-86
96Metal Universe-71
96NHL Pro Stamps-128
96Pinnacle-187
Artist's Proofs-187
Foil-187
Premium Stock-187
Rink Collection-187
96Score-119
Artist's Proofs-119
Dealer's Choice Artist's Proofs-119
Special Artist's Proofs-119
Golden Blades-119
96SkyBox Impact-54
96SP-69
96Summit-24
Artist's Proofs-24
Ice-24
Metal-24
Premium Stock-24
96Topps Picks-65
OPC Inserts-65
96Ultra-76
Gold Medallion-76
96Upper Deck-75
96Upper Deck Ice-28
Parallel-28
96Whalers Kid's Club-4
97Be A Player-112
Autographs-112
Autographs Die-Cuts-112
Autographs Prismatic Die-Cuts-112
97Beehive-50
Golden Portraits-50
97Collector's Choice-116
Star Quest-SQ73
97Crown Royale-26
Emerald Green-26
Ice Blue-26
Silver-26
97Donruss-79
Press Proofs Silver-79
Press Proofs Gold-79
97Donruss Canadian Ice-41
Dominion Series-41
Provincial Series-41
National Pride-14
97Donruss Elite-67
Aspirations-67
Status-67
97Donruss Limited-119
97Donruss Limited-135
Exposure-119
Exposure-135
97Donruss Preferred-85
Cut to the Chase-85
97Donruss Priority-50
Stamp of Approval-50
97Hurricanes Team Issue-25
97Katch-30
Gold-30
Silver-30
97Leaf-28
Fractal Matrix-28
Fractal Matrix Die Cuts-28
97Leaf International-28
Universal Ice-28
97NHL Aces Playing Cards-41
97Pacific-270
Copper-270
Emerald Green-270
Ice Blue-270
Red-270
Silver-270
97Pacific Dynagon-23
Copper-23
Dark Grey-23
Emerald Green-23
Ice Blue-23
Red-23
Silver-23
Tandems-38
97Pacific Invincible-26
Copper-26
Emerald Green-26
Ice Blue-26
Red-26
Silver-26
97Panini Stickers-20
97Pinnacle-45
Artist's Proofs-45
Rink Collection-45
Press Plates Back Black-45
Press Plates Back Cyan-45
Press Plates Back Magenta-45
Press Plates Back Yellow-45
Press Plates Front Black-45
Press Plates Front Cyan-45
Press Plates Front Magenta-45
Press Plates Front Yellow-45
97Pinnacle Certified-125
Red-125
Mirror Blue-125
Mirror Gold-125
Mirror Red-125
97Pinnacle Inside-78
Coach's Collection-78
Executive Collection-78
97Pinnacle Tot Cert Platinum Blue-125
97Pinnacle Tot Certi Platinum Gold-125
97Pinnacle Totally Certified Platinum Red-125
97Pinnacle Tot Cert Mirror Platinum Gold-125
97Score-110
Artist's Proofs-110
Golden Blades-110
97SP Authentic-25
97SPx-22
Bronze-22
Gold-22
Silver-22
Steel-22
Grand Finale-22
97Studio-84
Press Proofs Silver-84
Press Proofs Gold-84
97Upper Deck-30
Game Dated Moments-30
Sixth Sense Masters-SS22
Sixth Sense Wizards-SS22
97Upper Deck Ice-8
Parallel-8
Power Shift-8
98Be A Player-163
Press Release-163
98BAP Gold-163
98BAP Autographs-163
98BAP Autographs Gold-163
98Pacific-80
Ice Blue-80
Red-80
98Pacific Omega-27
Red-27
Opening Day Issue-27
98Panini Photocards-75
98UD Choice-27
98UD Choice Preview-27
98UD Choice Prime Choice Reserve-27
98UD Choice Reserve-27
98Upper Deck-45
Exclusives-45
Exclusives 1 of 1-45
Gold Reserve-45
98Upper Deck MVP-24
Gold Script-24
Silver Script-24
Super Script-24
99Pacific-44
Copper-44
Emerald Green-44
Gold-44
Ice Blue-44
Premiere Date-44
Red-44
99Panini Stickers-33
99Paramount-30
Copper-30
Emerald-30
Gold-30
Holographic Emerald-30
Holographic Gold-30
Holographic Silver-30
Ice Blue-30
Premiere Date-30
Red-30
Silver-30
99Ultimate Victory-12
1/1-12
Parallel-12
Parallel 100-12
00BAP Memorabilia-38
Emerald-38
Ruby-38
Sapphire-38
Promos-38
00BAP Mem Chicago Sportsfest Copper-38
00BAP Memorabilia Chicago Sportsfest Blue-38
00BAP Memorabilia Chicago Sportsfest Gold-38
00BAP Memorabilia Chicago Sportsfest Ruby-38
00BAP Memorabilia Chicago Sun-Times Ruby-38
00BAP Memorabilia Chicago Sun-Times Gold-38
00BAP Mem Chicago Sun-Times Sapphire-38
00BAP Mem Toronto Fall Expo Copper-38
00BAP Memorabilia Toronto Fall Expo Gold-38
00BAP Memorabilia Toronto Fall Expo Ruby-38
00BAP Parkhurst 2000-P212
00Crown Royale-32
Ice Blue-32
Limited Series-32
Premiere Date-32
Red-32
00Pacific-56
Copper-56
Gold-56
Ice Blue-56
Premiere Date-56
00Panini Stickers-137
00Private Stock-29
Gold-29
Premiere Date-29
Retail-29
Silver-29
00Revolution-44
Blue-44
Premiere Date-44
Red-44
00SP Authentic-27
00Stadium Club-212
00Titanium-25
Blue-25
Gold-25
Premiere Date-25
Red-25
Retail-25
00Topps Chrome-224
OPC Refractors-224
Refractors-224
00Topps Heritage-195
00Upper Deck-279
Exclusives Tier 1-279
Exclusives Tier 2-279
00Upper Deck Vintage-101
00Upper Deck Vintage-111
00Vanguard-31
Holographic Gold-31
Holographic Purple-31
Pacific Proofs-31
01Atomic-30
Blue-30
Gold-30
Premiere Date-30
Red-30
01BAP Memorabilia-279
Emerald-279
Ruby-279
Sapphire-279
01BAP Signature Series-154
Autographs-154
Autographs Gold-154
01Blue Jackets Donatos Pizza-1
01Blue Jackets Donatos Pizza-18
01Crown Royale-44
Blue-44
Premiere Date-44
Red-44
Retail-44
01McDonald's Pacific Hometown Pride-5
01O-Pee-Chee-242
01O-Pee-Chee Premier Parallel-242
01Pacific-116
Extreme LTD-116
Hobby LTD-116
Premiere Date-116
Retail LTD-116
01Pacific Adrenaline-55
Blue-55
Premiere Date-55
Red-55
Retail-55
01Pacific Arena Exclusives-116
01Pacific Heads-Up-28
Blue-28
Premiere Date-28
Red-28
Silver-28
01Parkhurst-128
01Private Stock PS-2002-22
01SP Authentic-22
Limited-22
Limited Gold-22
01Topps-242
OPC Parallel-242
01Topps Reserve-51
01UD Mask Collection Double Patches-DPGS
01UD Mask Collection Jerseys-J-GS
01UD Mask Collection Jersey and Patch-JPGS
01Upper Deck-51
Exclusives-51
01Upper Deck MVP-51
01Upper Deck Victory-97
Gold-97
01Upper Deck Vintage-72
01Upper Deck Vintage-77
01Upper Deck Vintage-78
02BAP First Edition-263
02BAP Sig Series Auto Buybacks 1998-163
02BAP Sig Series Auto Buybacks 2001-154
02Crown Royale Jerseys-4
02Crown Royale Jerseys Gold-4
02Crown Royale Dual Patches-7
02Pacific-104
Blue-104
Red-104
02Pacific Complete-427
Red-427
02Pacific Heads-Up Quad Jerseys-10
02Pacific Heads-Up Quad Jerseys Gold-10
02Titanium-30
Blue-30
Red-30
Retail-30
Jerseys-20
Jerseys Retail-20
Patches-20
02Topps Total-145
02Upper Deck-294
Exclusives-294
02Upper Deck Beckett UD Promos-294
02Upper Deck Pinpoint Accuracy-PAGS
02Upper Deck Rookie Update-29
02Upper Deck Vintage-78
02Upper Deck Vintage-269
02Vanguard-31
LTD-31
03BAP Memorabilia-28
Emerald-28
Gold-28
Ruby-28
Sapphire-28
03Black Diamond-14
Black-14
Green-14
Red-14
03ITG Action-196
03NHL Sticker Collection-194
03O-Pee-Chee-185
03OPC Blue-185
03OPC Gold-185
03OPC Red-185
03Pacific-97
Blue-97
Red-97
Jerseys-12
Jerseys Gold-12
03Pacific Complete-125
Red-125
03Pacific Exhibit-44
Blue Backs-44
Yellow Backs-44
03Pacific Prism-32
Blue-32
Gold-32
Red-32
03Pacific Supreme-28
Blue-28
Red-28
Retail-28
Generations-3
03Private Stock Reserve-28
Blue-28
Red-28
Retail-28
03Topps-185
Blue-185
Gold-185
Red-185
03Topps C55-104
Minis-104
Minis American Back-104
Minis American Back Red-104
Minis Bazooka Back-104
Minis Brooklyn Back-104
Minis Hat Trick Back-104
Minis O Canada Back-104
Minis O Canada Back Red-104
Minis Stanley Cup Back-104
03Topps Pristine-76
Gold Refractor Die Cuts-76
Refractors-76
Press Plates Black-76
Press Plates Cyan-76
Press Plates Magenta-76
Press Plates Yellow-76
03Topps Traded-TT79
Blue-TT79
Gold-TT79
Red-TT79
03Upper Deck-54
Canadian Exclusives-54
HG-54
03Upper Deck MVP-116
Gold Script-116
Silver Script-116
Canadian Exclusives-116
03Upper Deck Victory-52
Bronze-52
Gold-52
Silver-52
05Be A Player Signatures-SN
05Be A Player Signatures Gold-SN
05Panini Stickers-320
05Parkhurst-373
Facsimile Auto Parallel-373
05UD Artifacts-29
Blue-29
Gold-29
Green-29
Pewter-29
Red-29
Gold Autographed-29
05Upper Deck-57
05Upper Deck-394
Big Playmakers-B-GS
HG Glossy-57
05Upper Deck MVP-293
Gold-293
Platinum-293
05Upper Deck Toronto Fall Expo-57
05Upper Deck Victory-56
05Upper Deck Victory-239
Black-56
Black-239
Gold-56
Gold-239
Silver-56
Silver-239
06Flyers Postcards-4
06O-Pee-Chee-370
Rainbow-370
06Upper Deck-394
Exclusives Parallel-394
High Gloss Parallel-394
Masterpieces-394
06Upper Deck MVP-221
Gold Script-221
Super Script-221
06Upper Deck Victory-155
06Upper Deck Victory-264
06Upper Deck Victory Black-155
06Upper Deck Victory Gold-155

Sanderson, Guy

92Clarkson Knights-19

Sanderson, Mike

92Fort Worth Fire-18
93Fort Worth Fire-15
96Fort Worth Fire-3
97New Mexico Scorpions-7
99Fort Worth Brahmas-17
01Odessa Jackalopes-18

Sandford, Ed

44Beehive Group II Photos-64
51Parkhurst-22
52Parkhurst-69
53Parkhurst-90
54Parkhurst-64
54Topps-48
91Bruins Sports Action Legends-26
98Bruins Alumni-12
Autographs-12
02Parkhurst Reprints-154
02Parkhurst Reprints-185

Sandholm, Ryan

91Air Canada SJHL-A24
92Saskatchewan JHL-103

Sandie, Joel

907th Inn. Sketch OHL-69
917th Inn. Sketch OHL-244
91Sudbury Wolves-10
92Sudbury Wolves-4

Sandilands, Neil

83Kitchener Rangers-6

Sandin, Stefan

84Swedish Semic Elitserien-24
87Swedish Panini Stickers-270

Sandke, Pierre

907th Inn. Sketch QMJHL-58
917th Inn. Sketch QMJHL-275

Sandlak, Jim

85Canucks Team Issue-19
86Canucks Team Issue-19
87Canucks Shell Oil-16
87O-Pee-Chee-264
87O-Pee-Chee Stickers-66A
87O-Pee-Chee Stickers-135
87O-Pee-Chee Stickers-194
87Panini Stickers-352
88Canucks Mohawk-17
88Panini Stickers-139
89Canucks Mohawk-16
89O-Pee-Chee-267
89O-Pee-Chee-316
89Panini Stickers-156
90Bowman-55
Tiffany-55
90Canucks Mohawk-26
90O-Pee-Chee-18
90Panini Stickers-306
90Pro Set-305
90Score-303C
Canadian-303C
90Topps-18
Tiffany-18
91Canucks Panini Team Stickers-21
91Canucks Autograph Cards-22
91Canucks Team Issue 8x10-22
91Parkhurst-405
French-405
91Pinnacle-294
French-294
91Pro Set-497
French-497
91Score Canadian Bilingual-260
91Score Canadian English-260
91Upper Deck-577
French-577
92Canucks Road Trip Art-20
92O-Pee-Chee-168
92Panini Stickers-34
92Panini Stickers French-34
92Pinnacle-210
French-210
92Score-379
Canadian-379
92Stadium Club-175
92Topps-41
Gold-41G
92Ultra-228
92Upper Deck-120
93Donruss-138
93Parkhurst-84
Emerald Ice-84
93Pinnacle-364
Canadian-364
93Score-397
93Score-532
Gold-532
Canadian-397
Canadian-532
Canadian Gold-532
93Upper Deck-393
93Whalers Coke-20
94Canada Games NHL POGS-118
94Parkhurst-91
Gold-91

Sandlin, Tommy

83Swedish Semic Elitserien-50
84Swedish Semic Elitserien-49
85Swedish Panini Stickers-35
89Swedish Semic World Champ Stickers-2
91Swedish Semic Elitserien Stickers-303
92Swedish Semic Elitserien Stickers-325
92Swedish Semic Elitserien Stickers-342
93Swedish Semic Elitserien-290
94Swedish Leaf-296

Sandner, Christopher

94German DEL-317
94German First League-308
95German DEL-354
02German DEL City Press-83

Sandrock, Rob

94Spokane Chiefs-8
96Medicine Hat Tigers-19
97Medicine Hat Tigers-15
98Kelowna Rockets-22
99San Angelo Outlaws-15
01Greensboro Generals-2
03German DEL-149

Sands, Charlie

33V129-16
33V357 Ice Kings-58
34Beehive Group I Photos-29
34Beehive Group I Photos-181
37V356 Worldwide Gum-27
39O-Pee-Chee V301-1-56
40O-Pee-Chee V301-2-102

Sands, Jason

95Slapshot-118
97Sudbury Wolves Police-14

Sands, Mike

83Canadian National Juniors-12
84Springfield Indians-1

Sandstrom, Jan

98Swedish UD Choice-5
99Swedish Upper Deck-5
00Swedish Upper Deck-6
02Swedish SHL-58
Parallel-58
03Swedish Elite-226
Silver-226
04Swedish Elitset-72
Gold-72
05Swedish Lulea Hockey Postcards-5
05Swedish SHL Elitset-84
06Swedish SHL Elitset-85

Sandstrom, Mikael

83Swedish Semic Elitserien-61

Sandstrom, Petter

00Swedish Upper Deck-15
02UK Nottingham Panthers-12

Sandstrom, Ronny

70Swedish Hockey-196
71Swedish Hockey-282

Sandstrom, Tomas

83Swedish Semic Elitserien-72
83Swedish Semic VM Stickers-13
85O-Pee-Chee-123
85Topps-123
86O-Pee-Chee-230
87O-Pee-Chee-28
87O-Pee-Chee Minis-38
87O-Pee-Chee Stickers-35
87Panini Stickers-114
87Topps-28
88O-Pee-Chee-121
88O-Pee-Chee Stickers-242
88Panini Stickers-310
88Topps-121
89O-Pee-Chee-54
89O-Pee-Chee Box Bottoms-C
89O-Pee-Chee Stickers-244
89Panini Stickers-281
89Topps-54
89Topps Box Bottoms-C
90Bowman-141
Tiffany-141
90Bowman Hat Tricks-21
Tiffany-21
90Kings Smokey-6
90O-Pee-Chee-301
90Panini Stickers-243
90Pro Set-127
90Score-183
Canadian-183
90Score Hottest/Rising Stars-79
90Topps-301
Tiffany-301
90Upper Deck-251
French-251
91Pro Set Platinum-53
91Bowman-174
91Bowman-179
91Kraft-63
91O-Pee-Chee-173
91OPC Premier-82
91Panini Stickers-79
91Parkhurst-70
French-70
91Pinnacle-178
French-178
91Pro Set-97
91Pro Set-287
French-97
French-287
91Score American-270
91Score Canadian Bilingual-490
91Score Canadian English-490
91Stadium Club-209
91Topps-173
91Upper Deck-30
91Upper Deck-85
91Upper Deck-141
French-30
French-85
French-141
Euro-Stars-7
Euro-Stars French-7
91Finnish Semic World Champ Stickers-208
91Swedish Semic Elitserien Stickers-319
91Swedish Semic World Champ Stickers-208
92Bowman-22
92O-Pee-Chee-91
92Panini Stickers-67
92Panini Stickers French-67
92Pinnacle-345
French-345
92Score-199
Canadian-199
92Stadium Club-220
92Topps-421
Gold-421G
92Ultra-88
92Upper Deck-424
92Finnish Semic-69
93Donruss-163
93Donruss-475
93Leaf-106
93OPC Premier-434
Gold-434
93Panini Stickers-205
93Parkhurst-362
Emerald Ice-362
93Pinnacle-263
Canadian-263
93PowerPlay-121
93Score-129
Canadian-129
International Stars-21
International Stars Canadian-21
93Stadium Club-25
Members Only Master Set-25
OPC-25
First Day Issue-25
First Day Issue OPC-25
93Topps/OPC Premier-434
Gold-434
93Ultra-246
93Upper Deck-188
93Swedish Semic World Champ Stickers-32
94Canada Games NHL POGS-188
94Donruss-271
94EA Sports-65
94Fleer-169
94Hockey Wit-87
94Leaf-207
94OPC Premier-108
Special Effects-108
94Parkhurst-175
Gold-175
94Penguins Foodland-10
94Pinnacle-313
Artist's Proofs-313
Rink Collection-313
94SP-90
Die Cuts-90
94Topps/OPC Premier-108
Special Effects-108
94Ultra-352
94Upper Deck-461
Electric Ice-461
94Finnish Jaa Kiekko-354
94Swedish Leaf-286
Guest Special-2
95Be A Player-160
Signatures-S160
Signatures Die Cuts-S160
95Bowman-10
All-Foil-10
95Canada Games NHL POGS-214
95Collector's Choice-139
Player's Club-139
Player's Club Platinum-139
95Donruss-118
95Donruss Elite-74
Die Cut Stars-74
Die Cut Uncut-74
95Emotion-141
95Finest-12
Refractors-12
95Leaf-265
95Leaf Limited-60
95Metal-119
95Panini Stickers-62
95Parkhurst International-166
Emerald Ice-166
95Penguins Foodland-15
95Score-279
Black Ice Artist's Proofs-279
Black Ice-279
95Select Certified-107
Mirror Gold-107
95SkyBox Impact-134
95SP-118
95Stadium Club-118
Members Only Master Set-118
95Summit-94
Artist's Proofs-94
Ice-94
95Topps-228
OPC Inserts-228
95Ultra-293
Crease Crashers-16
95Upper Deck-185
Electric Ice-185
Electric Ice Gold-185
Special Edition-SE156
Special Edition Gold-SE156
95Zenith-79
95Swedish Globe World Championships-28
95Swedish World Championships Stickers-290
96Collector's Choice-215
96Donruss-78
Press Proofs-78
96Fleer Picks-66
96Leaf-81
Press Proofs-81
96Maggers-90
96Pinnacle-156
Artist's Proofs-156
Foil-156
Premium Stock-156
Rink Collection-156
96Score-126
Artist's Proofs-126
Dealer's Choice Artist's Proofs-126
Special Artist's Proofs-126
Golden Blades-126
96Summit-81
Artist's Proofs-81
Ice-81
Metal-81
Premium Stock-81
96Upper Deck-137
96Swedish Semic Wien-59
97Crown Royale-4
Emerald Green-4
Ice Blue-4
Silver-4
97Donruss Priority-117
Stamp of Approval-117
97Katch-4
Gold-4
Silver-4
97Pacific-293
Copper-293
Emerald Green-293
Ice Blue-293
Red-293
Silver-293
97Pacific Omega-6
Copper-6
Dark Gray-6
Emerald Green-6
Gold-6
Ice Blue-6
97Panini Stickers-150
97Paramount-6
Copper-6
Dark Grey-6
Emerald Green-6
Ice Blue-6
Red-6
Silver-6
97Pinnacle-180
Press Plates Back Black-180
Press Plates Back Cyan-180
Press Plates Back Magenta-180
Press Plates Back Yellow-180
Press Plates Front Black-180
Press Plates Front Cyan-180
Press Plates Front Magenta-180
Press Plates Front Yellow-180
97Score-258
97Score Mighty Ducks-12
Platinum-12
Premier-12
97SP Authentic-4
98Aurora-5
98Be A Player-153
Press Release-153
98BAP Gold-153
98BAP Autographs-153
98BAP Autographs Gold-153
98Crown Royale-4
Limited Series-4
98OPC Chrome-12
Refractors-12
98Pacific-63
Ice Blue-63
Red-63
98Pacific Dynagon Ice-5
Blue-5
Red-5
98Panini Stickers-172
98Paramount-6
Copper-6
Emerald Green-6
Holo-Electric-6
Ice Blue-6
Silver-6
98Topps-12
O-Pee-Chee-12
98Upper Deck MVP-3
Gold Script-3
Silver Script-3
Super Script-3
99Pacific-15
Copper-15
Emerald Green-15
Gold-15
Ice Blue-15
Premiere Date-15
Red-15
99Swedish Upper Deck-157
SHL Signatures-20
Snapshots-11
00Swedish Upper Deck-147
00Swedish Upper Deck-203
02BAP Sig Series Auto Buybacks 1998-153
02Swedish SHL-140
Parallel-140
04Swedish Alfabilder Alfa Stars-41
04Swedish Alfabilder Autographs-108
04Swedish Alfabilder Limited Autographs-108
04Swedish Alfabilder Proof Parallels-41

Sandstrom, Ulf

86Swedish Panini Stickers-213
87Swedish Panini Stickers-199
89Swedish Semic Elitserien Stickers-179
89Swedish Semic World Champ Stickers-16
90Swedish Semic Elitserien Stickers-235
91Swedish Semic Elitserien Stickers-172
95Swedish Upper Deck 1st Division Stars-DS3

Sandwith, Terran

917th Inn. Sketch WHL-214
93Classic Pro Prospects-114
94Los Angeles Blades RHI-11
98Cincinnati Mighty Ducks-11
99St. John's Maple Leafs-20
00Hamilton Bulldogs-2
01UK Belfast Giants-2

Sanase, Gianni

95Swiss HNL-195
96Swiss HNL-432

Sanford, Curtis

96Owen Sound Platers-3
97Owen Sound Platers-2
98Owen Sound Platers-2
99Owen Sound Platers-6
00Peoria Rivermen-1
01SPx Rookie Redemption-R26
01Peoria Rivermen-3
02BAP All-Star Edition-121
Gold-121
Silver-121
02BAP Memorabilia-362

02BAP Signature Series-178
Autographs-178
Autographs Gold-178
02BAP Ultimate Memorabilia-41
02Between the Pipes-75
Gold-75
Silver-75
Jerseys-35
02Crown Royale-135
Blue-135
Purple-135
Red-135
Retail-135
02ITG Used-197
02Pacific Calder-141
Silver-141
02Pacific Complete-515
Red-515
02Pacific Quest for the Cup-142
Gold-142
02Parkhurst-241
Bronze-241
Gold-241
Silver-241
02Parkhurst Retro-241
Minis-241
02Private Stock Reserve-181
Blue-181
Red-181
Retail-181
02SP Authentic-158
02SP Game Used-92
02Titanium-135
Blue-135
Red-135
Retail-135
02Topps Total-438
02UD Artistic Impressions-109
Gold-109
02UD Honor Roll-126
02UD Mask Collection-125
02UD Premier Collection-67B
Gold-67B
02UD Top Shelf-119
02Upper Deck-452
Exclusives-452
02Vanguard-132
LTD-132
02Worcester IceCats-23
03BAP Memorabilia-112
Emerald-112
Gold-112
Ruby-112
Sapphire-112
Deep in the Crease-D12
03ITG Action-597
03Worcester Ice Cats-2
04Worcester IceCats-1
05ITG Heroes/Prosp Toronto Expo Parallel -221
05Blues Team Set-16
05Parkhurst-418
Facsimile Auto Parallel-418
05Peoria Rivermen-1
05ITG Heroes and Prospects-221
Autographs Series II-CSA
06Flair Showcase Hot Gloves-HG26
06Hot Prospects Hot Materials -HMCS
06Hot Prospects Hot Materials Red Hot-HMCS
06Hot Prospects Hot Materials White Hot-HMCS
06O-Pee-Chee-427
Rainbow-427
06SP Game Used Authentic Fabrics-AFCS
06SP Game Used Authentic Fabrics Parallel-AFCS
06SP Game Used Authentic Fabrics Patches-AFCS
06The Cup NHL Shields Duals-DSHLS
06Ultra-168
Gold Medallion-168
Ice Medallion-168
06Upper Deck-170
Exclusives Parallel-170
High Gloss Parallel-170
Game Jerseys-JCS
Game Patches-PCS
Masterpieces-170
06Upper Deck Ovation-195
06Upper Deck Victory-169
06Upper Deck Victory Black-169
06Upper Deck Victory Gold-169

Sanford, James
00Victoriaville Tigres-1
Signed-1
01Moncton Wildcats-3
02Moncton Wildcats-8
03Moncton Wildcats-1
03Moncton Wildcats-NNO
04Hamilton Bulldogs-25
04Peoria Rivermen-16
05Hamilton Bulldogs-23

Sanford, Jason
91British Columbia JHL-138
92British Columbia JHL-95

Sanger, Jeff
02Reading Royals-29
02Reading Royals RBI Sports-184
03Indianapolis Ice-17

Sanger, Matthias
94German First League-114

Sangermano, Stephen
96Quad-City Mallards-4
98Fayetteville Force-17

Sangl, Reiner
94German First League-275

Sangster, Darryl
92Saskatchewan JHL-104

Sangster, Jack
83Brandon Wheat Kings-18
84Brandon Wheat Kings-18
85Brandon Wheat Kings-18

Sangster, Rob
87Kitchener Rangers-17
88Kitchener Rangers-17
89Kitchener Rangers-18
897th Inn. Sketch OHL-58

Sanguinetti, Bob
04Owen Sound Attack-11
05ITG Heroes/Prosp Toronto Expo Parallel -286
05OHL Bell All-Star Classic-21
05Owen Sound Attack-17
05ITG Heroes and Prospects-286
Autographs Series II-BSG
Team Orr-TO15
06Owen Sound Attack-18
06ITG Heroes and Prospects-89
Autographs-ABSA
CHL Top Prospects-TP07
CHL Top Prospects Gold-TP07
Class of 2006-CL12

Sanipass, Everett
87Blackhawks Coke-19
88Blackhawks Coke-17
88ProCards IHL-114
89Blackhawks Coke-22
89ProCards IHL-63

90Nordiques Petro-Canada-22
90Score-28
Canadian-28
91Bowman-135
91Nordiques Panini Team Stickers-19
91O-Pee-Chee-315
91Panini Stickers-262
91Stadium Club-284
91Topps-315

Sanko, Ron
82Kingston Canadians-16
83North Bay Centennials-21
85Kitchener Rangers-23

Sanley, Robert
06Cape Breton Screaming Eagles-6

Sannitz, Raffaele
01Swiss HNL-47
02Swiss HNL-288
04Syracuse Crunch-19

Sanscartier, Alain
917th Inn. Sketch QMJHL-75

Sansonnens, Alain
98Swiss Power Play Stickers-81
99Swiss Panini Stickers-80
00Swiss Panini Stickers-127

Santala, Seppo
73Finnish Jaakiekko-317

Santala, Tommi
98Black Diamond-100
Double Diamond-100
Triple Diamond-100
Quadruple Diamond-100
98SPx Top Prospects-68
Radiance-68
Spectrum-68
99Finnish Cardset-267
99Columbus Cottonmouths-14
00Finnish Cardset-147
01Finnish Cardset-32
02Finnish Cardset-265
03Finnish Cardset D-Day-DD13
03Chicago Wolves-17
03Pacific AHL Prospects-14
Gold-14
04Chicago Wolves-24
05Finnish Cardset -238
06Canucks Postcards-20
06Finnish Cardset-63
Signature Sensations-11

Santanen, Ari
96Finnish SISU Redline-119
98Finnish Kerailysarja-199
90's Top 12-9
99Finnish Cardset-230

Santanen, Juho
04Finnish Cardset-301
05Finnish Cardset -151
06Finnish Cardset-331
Signature Sensations-29

Santanen, Pekka
78Finnish SM-Liiga-163

Santavuori, Tuomas
04Finnish Cardset-281
05Finnish Cardset -117
06Finnish Cardset-129

Santerre, Gino
93St. Cloud State Huskies-25
96Louisville Riverfrogs-3

Santiago, Chris
06Westside Warriors-7

Santini, Frankie
04Mississauga Ice Dogs-19
05Mississauga Ice Dogs-19
06Mississauga Ice Dogs-17

Santonelli, Ben
93Quebec Pee-Wee Tournament-634

Santorelli, Mark
04Salmon Arm Silverbacks-5
06Chilliwack Bruins-22

Santorelli, Mike
03Vernon Vipers-14
04Northern Michigan Wildcats-18

Santurian, Oleg
93Richmond Renegades-13

Sanza, Nick
82Swedish Semic VM Stickers-123
83Swedish Semic VM Stickers-123

Sapergia, Brent
88ProCards IHL-18
89ProCards IHL-114
90ProCards AHL/IHL-318
91ProCards-331
92Toledo Storm Team Issue-11
93Phoenix Cobras RHI-15
93Wichita Thunder-13
94Central Hockey League-119

Sapin, Benedict
93Swiss HNL-419
96Swiss HNL-369
98Swiss Power Play Stickers-340

Sapisha, Jeff
06Okotoks Oilers -16

Sapjolkin, Alexander
73Swedish Stickers-113

Sapozhnikov, Andrei
93Swedish Semic World Champ Stickers-135
93Classic-92
96German DEL-211
98Russian Hockey League-20
99Russian Hockey League-15
99Russian Metallurg Magnetogorsk-32
00Russian Hockey League-240
02Russian Hockey League-164
03Russian Hockey League-207

Saprykin, Oleg
99BAP Memorabilia-215
Gold-215
Silver-215
99BAP Millennium-41
Emerald-41
Ruby-41
Sapphire-41
Signatures-41
Signatures Gold-41
Calder Candidates Ruby-C23
Calder Candidates Emerald-C23
Calder Candidates Sapphire-C23
99Black Diamond-15
Diamond Cut-15
Final Cut-15
99Crown Royale-25
Limited Series-25
Premiere Date-25
Prospects Parallel-25
99O-Pee-Chee-268
99O-Pee-Chee Chrome-268
99O-Pee-Chee Chrome Refractors-268
99Pacific Dynagon Ice-5
Blue-5
Copper-5
Gold-5

Premiere Date-5
99Pacific Omega-39
Copper-39
Gold-39
Ice Blue-39
Premiere Date-39
99Pacific Prism-25
Holographic Blue-25
Holographic Gold-25
Holographic Mirror-25
Holographic Purple-25
Premiere Date-25
99SP Authentic-98
Sign of the Times-OS
Sign of the Times Gold-OS
99SPx-172
Radiance-172
Spectrum-172
99Stadium Club-186
First Day Issue-186
One of a Kind-186
Printing Plates Black-186
Printing Plates Cyan-186
Printing Plates Magenta-186
Printing Plates Yellow-186
99Topps/OPC-268
99Topps/OPC Chrome-268
Refractors-268
99Topps Premier Plus-99
Parallel-99
99Ultimate Victory-94
1/1-94
Parallel-94
Parallel 100-94
99Upper Deck-169
99Upper Deck-193
Exclusives-169
Exclusives-193
Exclusives 1 of 1-169
Exclusives 1 of 1-193
99Upper Deck Gold Reserve-169
99Upper Deck Gold Reserve-193
99Upper Deck HoloGrFx-9
Ausome-9
99Upper Deck Ovation-9
Standing Ovation-9
99Upper Deck Victory-356
99Wayne Gretzky Hockey-33
99Bowman CHL-13
Gold-13
OPC International-13
Autographs-BA33
Autographs Gold-BA33
Autographs Silver-BA33
99UD Prospects-36
International Stars-IN8
00BAP Memorabilia-228
Emerald-228
Ruby-228
Sapphire-228
Promos-228
00BAP Mem Chicago Sportsfest Copper-228
00BAP Memorabilia Chicago Sportsfest Blue-228
00BAP Memorabilia Chicago Sportsfest Gold-228
00BAP Memorabilia Chicago Sportsfest Ruby-228
00BAP Memorabilia Chicago Sun-Times Ruby-228
00BAP Memorabilia Chicago Sun-Times Gold-228
00BAP Mem Chicago Sun-Times Sapphire-228
00BAP Mem Toronto Fall Expo Copper-228
00BAP Memorabilia Toronto Fall Expo Gold-228
00BAP Memorabilia Toronto Fall Expo Ruby-228
00BAP Parkhurst 2000-P237
00BAP Signature Series-287
Emerald-287
Ruby-287
Sapphire-287
Autographs-232
Autographs Gold-232
00Crown Royale-114
21st Century Rookies-4
00O-Pee-Chee-274
00O-Pee-Chee Parallel-274
00Pacific-72
Copper-72
Gold-72
Ice Blue-72
Premiere Date-72
00Paramount-37
Copper-37
Gold-37
Holo-Gold-37
Holo-Silver-37
Ice Blue-37
Premiere Date-37
00Private Stock-107
Gold-107
Premiere Date-107
Retail-107
Silver-107
PS-2001 New Wave-6
PS-2001 Rookies-4
00Revolution-24
Blue-24
Premiere Date-24
Red-24
00Stadium Club-233
00Titanium-108
Retail-108
00Titanium Draft Day Edition-108
00Titanium Draft Day Promos-108
00Topps/OPC-274
Parallel-274
00Topps Chrome-169
OPC Refractors-169
Refractors-169
00Topps Gold Label Class 1-89
Gold-89
00Topps Gold Label Class 2-89
00Topps Gold Label Class 2 Gold-89
00Topps Gold Label Class 3-89
00Topps Gold Label Class 3 Gold-89
00Topps Heritage-50
Chrome Parallel-50
00Topps Premier Plus-95
Blue Ice-95
Aspirations-PA7
Game-Used Memorabilia-GPOS
Game-Used Memorabilia-GPVBOS
Rookies-PR10
Rookies Blue Ice-PR10
00Topps Stars-148
Blue-148
00UD Pros and Prospects-13
00UD Reserve-13
00Upper Deck-25
Exclusives Tier 1-25
Exclusives Tier 2-25
00Upper Deck Ice-64
00Upper Deck MVP Excellence-ME3
00Upper Deck MVP Mark of Excellence-SGSS
00Upper Deck MVP ProSign-OS
00Vanguard-107
Pacific Proofs-107
01BAP Memorabilia-10

Emerald-10
Ruby-10
Sapphire-10
01BAP Signature Series-128
Autographs-128
Autographs Gold-128
01O-Pee-Chee-137
01O-Pee-Chee Premier Parallel-137
01Pacific-64
Extreme LTD-64
Hobby LTD-64
Premiere Date-64
Retail LTD-64
01Pacific Arena Exclusives-64
01Parkhurst-65
Gold-65
Silver-65
01Topps-137
OPC Parallel-137
Reserve Emblems-OS
Reserve Jerseys-OS
Reserve Name Plates-OS
Reserve Numbers-OS
Reserve Patches-OS
01Upper Deck-29
Exclusives-29
01Upper Deck MVP-29
01Upper Deck Victory-56
Gold-56
01Upper Deck Vintage-39
01Upper Deck Vintage-43
02BAP First Edition-180
02BAP Sig Series Auto Buybacks 1999-41
02BAP Sig Series Auto Buybacks 2000-232
02BAP Sig Series Auto Buybacks 2001-128
02Pacific Complete-441
Red-441
03ITG Action-69
03O-Pee-Chee-146
03OPC Blue-146
03OPC Gold-146
03OPC Red-146
03Pacific Complete-251
Red-251
03Topps-146
Blue-146
Gold-146
Red-146
03Upper Deck-272
Canadian Exclusives-272
HG-272
UD Exclusives-272
03Upper Deck MVP-69
Gold Script-69
Silver Script-69
Canadian Exclusives-69
03Russian World Championship Team 2003-16
04Russian Back to Russia-16
05Panini Stickers-328
05Parkhurst-376
Facsimile Auto Parallel-376
05Upper Deck-396
05Upper Deck MVP-299
Gold-299
Platinum-299
06O-Pee-Chee-381
Rainbow-381
06Upper Deck-153
Exclusives Parallel-153
High Gloss Parallel-153
Masterpieces-153

Saramaa, Erkki
99Swedish Upper Deck-122

Saran, Art
95Central Hockey League-83

Sararcik, Michal
01Czech OFS-71

Sarauer, Andrew
04Northern Michigan Wildcats-19

Sarault, Yves
907th Inn. Sketch QMJHL-175
917th Inn. Sketch QMJHL-105
917th Inn. Sketch Memorial Cup-125
91Classic-49
91Ultimate Draft-44
91Ultimate Draft French-44
91Classic Four-Sport *-49
Autographs-49A
92Fredericton Canadiens-21
93Fredericton Canadiens-25
94Fredericton Canadiens-25
97Score Avalanche-20
Platinum-20
Premier-20
99Grand Rapids Griffins-21
00Upper Deck NHLPA-PA6
01Milwaukee Admirals-23
01Milwaukee Admirals Postcards-3

Saravo, Pekka
00Finnish Cardset-211
01Finnish Cardset-124
03Finnish Cardset-143
04Finnish Cardset-152
04Finnish Cardset Signatures-29
05Swedish Lulea Hockey Postcards-8
05Swedish SHL Elitset-231
Gold-231
06Swedish SHL Elitset-86

Sarazin, Ryan
95Waterloo Blackhawks -18

Sarda, Roger
51Laval Dairy Lac St. Jean-49

Sargant, Shane
87Sault Ste. Marie Greyhounds-27

Sargent, Gary
77O-Pee-Chee NHL-113
77Topps-113
78North Stars Cloverleaf Dairy-1
78O-Pee-Chee-37
78Topps-37
79North Stars Postcards-13
79O-Pee-Chee-52
79Topps-52
80North Stars Postcards-17
80O-Pee-Chee-237
80Topps-237
81North Stars Postcards-21
82North Stars Postcards-21
82Post Cereal-9
92Future Trends Promo Sheet-1

Sarich, Cory
95Bowman Draft Prospects-P31
95Upper Deck-519
Electric Ice-519
Electric Ice Gold-519
95Saskatoon Blades-18
96Upper Deck Ice-132
96Saskatoon Blades-20
97Saskatoon Blades-21
97Bowman CHL-115
OPC-115
98UD Choice-265
Prime Choice Reserve-265

Reserve-265
98Rochester Americans-18
98Bowman CHL-68
Golden Anniversary-68
OPC International-68
98Bowman Chrome CHL-68
Golden Anniversary-68
Golden Anniversary Refractors-68
OPC International-68
OPC International Refractors-68
Refractors-68
99BAP Memorabilia-66
Gold-66
Silver-66
99BAP Millennium-37
Emerald-37
Ruby-37
Sapphire-37
Signatures-37
Signatures Gold-37
99O-Pee-Chee-46
99O-Pee-Chee Chrome-46
99O-Pee-Chee Chrome Refractors-46
99SPx-18
Radiance-18
Spectrum-18
99Topps/OPC-46
99Topps/OPC Chrome-46
Refractors-46
99Upper Deck Arena Giveaways-BS2
99Upper Deck MVP-24
Gold Script-24
Silver Script-24
Super Script-24
99Upper Deck Victory-39
00Pacific-380
Copper-380
Gold-380
Ice Blue-380
Premiere Date-380
00Upper Deck Victory-267
01BAP Signature Series-96
Autographs-96
Autographs Gold-96
02BAP Sig Series Auto Buybacks 1999-37
02BAP Sig Series Auto Buybacks 2001-96
02Pacific Complete-487
Red-487
03ITG Action-516
03Lightning Team Issue-22
03O-Pee-Chee-52
03OPC Blue-52
03OPC Gold-52
03OPC Red-52
03Topps-52
Blue-52
Gold-52
Red-52
05Parkhurst-442
Facsimile Auto Parallel-442
05Upper Deck-420
06Lightning Postcards-20
06O-Pee-Chee-450
Rainbow-450
06Panini Stickers-156

Sarich, Rod
98Calgary Hitmen-5
98Calgary Hitmen Autographs-5
99Calgary Hitmen-21
99Calgary Hitmen Autographs-21
00Calgary Hitmen-21
01Calgary Hitmen-19
01Calgary Hitmen Autographed-19
02ECHL All-Star Southern-52
02ECHL Update-U-21
02Louisiana Ice Gators-17
03Louisiana Ice Gators-18
05UK Sheffield Steelers-13
Gold-13
Silver-13

Sarjeant, Geoff
90Michigan Tech Huskies-23
91Michigan Tech Huskies-22
91Michigan Tech Huskies-23
91Michigan Tech Huskies-34
92Peoria Rivermen-23
93Peoria Rivermen-25
93Classic Pro Prospects-71
94Upper Deck-375
Electric Ice-375
94Classic Four-Sport *-154
Gold-154
Autographs-154A
Printers Proofs-154
95Kansas City Blades-17
96Leaf-228
Press Proofs-228
96Cincinnati Cyclones-31
96Collector's Edge Ice-147
Prism-147
97Cincinnati Cyclones-15
98Detroit Vipers Freschetta-16
00German DEL-166

Sarkijarvi, Hans
83Swedish Semic Elitserien-214
84Swedish Semic Elitserien-238
85Swedish Panini Stickers-237
86Swedish Panini Stickers-258
87Swedish Panini Stickers-244

Sarkilahti, Olli
72Finnish Jaakiekko-353

Sarmatin, Mikhail
98Russian Hockey League-110
02Russian Hockey League-267
03Russian Hockey League-7

Sarnholm, Roland
67Swedish Hockey-300

Sarno, Peter
93Quebec Pee-Wee Tournament-565
98Bowman CHL-16
Golden Anniversary-16
OPC International-16
98Bowman Chrome CHL-16
Golden Anniversary-16
Golden Anniversary Refractors-16
OPC International-16
OPC International Refractors-16
Refractors-16
99Hamilton Bulldogs-12
99Bowman CHL-151
Gold-151
OPC International-151
00Hamilton Bulldogs-12
01Hamilton Bulldogs-7
02Finnish Cardset-266
03BAP Ultimate Memorabilia Autographs-127
Gold-127
03Beehive-249
Gold-249
Silver-249
03Bowman-144
Gold-144
03Bowman Chrome-144

Refractors-144
Gold Refractors-144
Xfractors-144
03ITG Action-616
03ITG VIP Rookie Debut-56
03Pacific Calder-138
Silver-138
03Pacific Complete-569
Red-569
03Pacific Heads-Up-117
Hobby LTD-117
Retail LTD-117
03Pacific Luxury Suite-66
Gold-66
03Parkhurst Rookie-162
03SP Authentic-132
Limited-132
03SPx-234
03Titanium-120
Hobby Jersey Number Parallels-120
Retail-120
Retail Jersey Number Parallels-120
03UD Honor Roll-148
03Upper Deck-468
Canadian Exclusives-468
HG-468
UD Exclusives-468
03Upper Deck Ice-109
Glass Parallel-109
04Manitoba Moose-9
04ITG Heroes and Prospects-196
Autographs-U-PSR
04ITG Heroes/Prospects Toronto Expo '05-196
05Syracuse Crunch-10

Saros, Seppo
71Finnish Suomi Stickers-272

Sarro, Michael
93Quebec Pee-Wee Tournament-736

Sartiala, Timo
72Finnish Jaakiekko-182

Sartjarvi, Pekka
72Finnish Jaakiekko-183

Sarzier, Benoit
93Quebec Pee-Wee Tournament-1496

Saskamoose, Fred
54Parkhurst-82

Sass, Paul
92Lake Superior State Lakers-24

Sasseville, Francois
93Drummondville Voltigeurs-21
96Halifax Mooseheads I-17
96Halifax Mooseheads II-17
99Adirondack IceHawks-11
00Rockford IceHogs-16

Sasso, Tom
90Knoxville Cherokees-109
91ProCards-436

Sasu, Havi
05Czech HC Vsetin-10

Satan, Miroslav
95Bowman-112
All-Foil-112
95Metal-190
95Parkhurst International-348
95Parkhurst International-509
Emerald Ice-348
Emerald Ice-509
95Select Certified-125
Mirror Gold-125
95SkyBox Impact-197
95SP-52
95Stadium Club-122
Members Only Master Set-122
95Topps-283
OPC Inserts-283
95Ultra-355
95Upper Deck-302
Electric Ice-302
Electric Ice Gold-302
95Zenith-150
95Slovakian APS National Team-19
95Classic Autographs-20
95Images-58
Gold-58
96Be A Player-39
Autographs-39
Autographs Silver-39
96Collector's Choice-98
96Donruss-215
Press Proofs-215
96Leaf-189
Press Proofs-189
96Metal Universe-55
96Oilers Postcards-18
96Score-249
Artist's Proofs-249
Dealer's Choice Artist's Proofs-249
Special Artist's Proofs-249
Golden Blades-249
96SkyBox Impact-170
96Summit-166
Artist's Proofs-166
Ice-166
Metal-166
Premium Stock-166
96Topps Picks Rookie Stars-RS12
96Topps Picks Rookie Stars OPC-RS12
96Ultra-62
Gold Medallion-62
96Upper Deck-260
96Swedish Semic Wien-231
97Black Diamond-62
Double Diamond-62
Triple Diamond-62
Quadruple Diamond-62
97Crown Royale-16
Emerald Green-16
Ice Blue-16
Silver-16
97Pacific-132
Copper-132
Emerald Green-132
Ice Blue-132
Red-132
Silver-132
97Pacific Dynagon-14
Copper-14
Dark Grey-14
Emerald Green-14
Ice Blue-14
Red-14
Silver-14
Tandems-21
97Pacific Invincible-15
Copper-15
Emerald Green-15
Ice Blue-15
Red-15
Silver-15
97Pacific Omega-26
Copper-26
Dark Gray-26
Emerald Green-26

Gold-26
Ice Blue-26
97Panini Stickers-18
97Panini Stickers-126
97Paramount-24
Copper-24
Dark Grey-24
Emerald Green-24
Ice Blue-24
Red-24
Silver-24
97Pinnacle-135
Press Plates Back Black-135
Press Plates Back Cyan-135
Press Plates Back Magenta-135
Press Plates Back Yellow-135
Press Plates Front Black-135
Press Plates Front Cyan-135
Press Plates Front Magenta-135
Press Plates Front Yellow-135
97Revolution-16
Copper-16
Emerald-16
Ice Blue-16
Silver-16
97Score-232
97Score Sabres-15
Platinum-15
Premier-15
97SP Authentic-15
97Zenith-51
Z-Gold-51
Z-Silver-51
98Aurora-20
98Be A Player-164
Press Release-164
98BAP Gold-164
98BAP Autographs-164
98BAP Autographs Gold-164
98Black Diamond-8
Double Diamond-8
Triple Diamond-8
Quadruple Diamond-8
98Crown Royale-15
Limited Series-15
98Finest-65
No Protectors-65
No Protectors Refractors-65
Refractors-65
98Pacific-81
Ice Blue-81
Red-81
98Pacific Dynagon Ice-21
Blue-21
Red-21
98Pacific Omega-28
Red-28
Opening Day Issue-28
98Panini Stickers-16
98Paramount-22
Copper-22
Emerald Green-22
Holo-Electric-22
Ice Blue-22
Silver-22
98Revolution-16
Ice Shadow-16
Red-16
98UD Choice-22
Prime Choice Reserve-22
Reserve-22
98Upper Deck-225
Exclusives-225
Exclusives 1 of 1-225
Gold Reserve-225
98Upper Deck MVP-19
Gold Script-19
Silver Script-19
Super Script-19
98Slovakian Eurotel-22
99Aurora-19
Premiere Date-19
99BAP Memorabilia-110
Gold-110
Silver-110
99BAP Millennium-33
Emerald-33
Ruby-33
Sapphire-33
Signatures-33
Signatures Gold-33
99Black Diamond-13
Diamond Cut-13
Final Cut-13
99Crown Royale-20
Limited Series-20
Premiere Date-20
99O-Pee-Chee-244
99O-Pee-Chee Chrome-244
99O-Pee-Chee Chrome Refractors-244
99Pacific-45
Copper-45
Emerald Green-45
Gold-45
Ice Blue-45
Premiere Date-45
Red-45
99Pacific Dynagon Ice-33
Blue-33
Copper-33
Gold-33
Premiere Date-33
99Pacific Omega-31
Copper-31
Gold-31
Ice Blue-31
Premiere Date-31
99Pacific Prism-21
Holographic Blue-21
Holographic Gold-21
Holographic Mirror-21
Holographic Purple-21
Premiere Date-21
99Panini Stickers-38
99Panini Stickers-335
99Paramount-31
Copper-31
Emerald-31
Gold-31
Holographic Emerald-31
Holographic Gold-31
Holographic Silver-31
Ice Blue-31
Premiere Date-31
Red-31
Silver-31
99Revolution-20
Premiere Date-20
Red-20
Shadow Series-20
Top of the Line-22
99SP Authentic-11
99SPx-20
Radiance-20

Spectrum-20
99Stadium Club-80
First Day Issue-80
One of a Kind-80
Printing Plates Black-80
Printing Plates Cyan-80
Printing Plates Magenta-80
Printing Plates Yellow-80
99Topps/OPC-244
99Topps/OPC Chrome-244
Refractors-244
99Topps Gold Label Class 1-57
Black-57
Black One of One-57
One of One-57
Red-57
Red One of One-57
99Topps Gold Label Class 2-57
99Topps Gold Label Class 2 Black-57
99Topps Gold Label Class 2 Black 1 of 1-57
99Topps Gold Label Class 2 One of One-57
99Topps Gold Label Class 2 Red-57
99Topps Gold Label Class 2 Red One of One-57
99Topps Gold Label Class 3-57
99Topps Gold Label Class 3 Black-57
99Topps Gold Label Class 3 Black 1 of 1-57
99Topps Gold Label Class 3 One of One-57
99Topps Gold Label Class 3 Red-57
99Topps Gold Label Class 3 Red One of One-57
99Topps Premier Plus-49
Parallel-49
99Ultimate Victory-11
1/1-11
Parallel-11
Parallel 100-11
99Upper Deck-24
Exclusives-24
Exclusives 1 of 1-24
99Upper Deck Gold Reserve-24
99Upper Deck MVP-26
Gold Script-26
Silver Script-26
Super Script-26
99Upper Deck MVP SC Edition-23
Gold Script-23
Silver Script-23
Super Script-23
99Upper Deck Ovation-8
Standing Ovation-8
99Upper Deck Retro-8
Gold-8
Platinum-8
99Upper Deck Victory-35
99Wayne Gretzky Hockey-22
00SLU Hockey One On One-30
00Aurora-21
Premiere Date-21
00BAP Memorabilia-246
Emerald-246
Ruby-246
Sapphire-246
Promos-246
00BAP Mem Chicago Sportsfest Copper-246
00BAP Memorabilia Chicago Sportsfest Blue-246
00BAP Memorabilia Chicago Sportsfest Gold-246
00BAP Memorabilia Chicago Sportsfest Ruby-246
00BAP Memorabilia Chicago Sun-Times Ruby-246
00BAP Memorabilia Chicago Sun-Times Gold-246
00BAP Mem Chicago Sun-Times Sapphire-246
00BAP Mem Toronto Fall Expo Copper-246
00BAP Memorabilia Toronto Fall Expo Gold-246
00BAP Memorabilia Toronto Fall Expo Ruby-246
00BAP Parkhurst 2000-P56
00BAP Signature Series-234
Emerald-234
Ruby-234
Sapphire-234
Autographs-85
Autographs Gold-85
00O-Pee-Chee-41
00O-Pee-Chee Parallel-41
00Pacific-57
Copper-57
Gold-57
Ice Blue-57
Premiere Date-57
Autographs-57
00Panini Stickers-23
00Paramount-32
Copper-32
Gold-32
Holo-Gold-32
Holo-Silver-32
Ice Blue-32
Premiere Date-32
00Private Stock-13
Gold-13
Premiere Date-13
Retail-13
Silver-13
00Revolution-19
Blue-19
Premiere Date-19
Red-19
00SP Authentic BuyBacks-8
00SP Authentic BuyBacks-9
00SP Authentic BuyBacks-10
00SP Authentic Sign of the Times-MS
00SPx-7
Spectrum-7
Winning Materials-WSA
00Stadium Club-141
00Topps/OPC-41
Parallel-41
00Topps Chrome-33
OPC Refractors-33
Refractors-33
Rocket's Flare-RF9
Rocket's Flare Refractors-RF9
00Topps Gold Label Class 1-75
Gold-75
00Topps Gold Label Class 2-75
00Topps Gold Label Class 2 Gold-75
00Topps Gold Label Class 3-75
00Topps Gold Label Class 3 Gold-75
00Topps Heritage-152
00Topps Premier Plus-52
Blue Ice-52
00Topps Stars-84
Blue-84
00UD Heroes-13
Signs of Greatness-MS
00UD Reserve-11
00Upper Deck-22
Exclusives Tier 1-22
Exclusives Tier 2-22
Ice Game Jerseys-JCMS
00Upper Deck MVP-27
First Stars-27
Second Stars-27
Third Stars-27
00Upper Deck Victory-28
00Upper Deck Vintage-38
00Upper Deck Vintage-49

00Upper Deck Vintage-50
00Vanguard-14
Holographic Gold-14
Holographic Purple-14
Pacific Proofs-14
01BAP Memorabilia-89
Emerald-89
Ruby-89
Sapphire-89
01BAP Signature Series Franchise Jerseys-FP-4
01BAP Signature Series Jerseys-GJ-7
01BAP Signature Series Jersey Autographs-GUMS
01BAP Sig Series Jersey and Stick Cards-GSJ-7
01BAP Signature Series Emblems-GUE-7
01BAP Signature Series Numbers-ITN-7
01BAP Signature Series Teammates-TM-4
01Bowman YoungStars-24
Gold-24
Ice Cubed-24
01Crown Royale-18
Blue-18
Premiere Date-18
Red-18
Retail-18
01O-Pee-Chee-103
01O-Pee-Chee Heritage Parallel-103
01O-Pee-Chee Heritage Parallel Limited-103
01O-Pee-Chee Premier Parallel-103
01Pacific-54
Extreme LTD-54
Hobby LTD-54
Premiere Date-54
Retail LTD-54
01Pacific Adrenaline-24
Blue-24
Premiere Date-24
Red-24
Retail-24
01Pacific Arena Exclusives-54
01Parkhurst-103
Teammates-T11
01Private Stock PS-2002-9
01SP Authentic-8
Limited-8
Limited Gold-8
01SP Game Used-5
Authentic Fabric-AFMS
Authentic Fabric-DFDS
Authentic Fabric Gold-AFMS
Patches-PSA
Patches-CPSK
01SPx-7
Hidden Treasures-DTPS
01Stadium Club-42
Award Winners-42
Master Photos-42
Souvenirs-MIS
01Titanium-16
Hobby Parallel-16
Premiere Date-16
Retail-16
Retail Parallel-16
Double-Sided Jerseys-66
Double-Sided Patches-66
01Topps-103
Heritage Parallel-103
Heritage Parallel Limited-103
OPC Parallel-103
01Topps Chrome-103
Refractors-103
Black Border Refractors-103
01Topps Heritage-31
Refractors-31
Autographs-AMS
01Topps Reserve-26
Emblems-MIS
Jerseys-MIS
Name Plates-MIS
Numbers-MIS
Patches-MIS
01UD Challenge for the Cup-7
01UD Honor Roll Jerseys-J-MS
01UD Honor Roll Jerseys Gold-J-MS
01UD Mask Collection Double Patches-DPMS
01UD Mask Collection Jerseys-J-MS
01UD Mask Collection Jersey and Patch-JPMS
01UD Playmakers-11
Practice Jerseys-PJMS
Practice Jerseys Gold-PJMS
01UD Top Shelf-4
01Upper Deck-19
Exclusives-19
Game Jerseys Series II-FJMS
Game Jerseys Series II-DJSH
01Upper Deck MVP-23
01Upper Deck Victory-38
Gold-38
01Upper Deck Vintage-31
01Upper Deck Vintage-34
01Upper Deck Vintage-35
01Czech Stadion-260
01Slovakian Kvarteto-7B
02Atomic-11
Blue-11
Gold-11
Red-11
Hobby Parallel-11
Power Converters-3
02BAP First Edition-53
02BAP First Edition-344
02BAP First Edition-379
Jerseys-53
02BAP Memorabilia-69
02BAP Memorabilia-204
Emerald-69
Emerald-204
Ruby-69
Ruby-204
Sapphire-69
Sapphire-204
Franchise Players-FP-4
NHL All-Star Game-69
NHL All-Star Game-204
NHL All-Star Game Blue-69
NHL All-Star Game Blue-204
NHL All-Star Game Green-69
NHL All-Star Game Green-204
NHL All-Star Game Red-69
NHL All-Star Game Red-204
02BAP Memorabilia Toronto Fall Expo-69
02BAP Memorabilia Toronto Fall Expo-204
02BAP Signature Series-52
Autographs-52
Autograph Buybacks 1998-164
Autograph Buybacks 1999-33
Autograph Buybacks 2000-85
Autographs Gold-52
Franchise Players-FJ4
Golf-GS63
02Bowman YoungStars-65
Gold-65
Silver-65
02Crown Royale-12
Blue-12
Red-12
Retail-12
02ITG Used Franchise Players-F4
02ITG Used Franchise Players Autographs-F4
02ITG Used Franchise Players Gold-F4
02O-Pee-Chee-20
02O-Pee-Chee Premier Blue Parallel-20
02O-Pee-Chee Premier Red Parallel-20
02O-Pee-Chee Factory Set-20
02Pacific-48
Blue-48
Red-48
Jerseys-4
Jerseys Holo-Silver-4
02Pacific Complete-205
Red-205
02Pacific Exclusive-20
Jerseys-3
Jerseys Gold-3
02Pacific Heads-Up-14
Blue-14
Purple-14
Red-14
Quad Jerseys-4
Quad Jerseys Gold-4
02Pacific Quest for the Cup-10
Gold-10
02Parkhurst-141
Bronze-141
Gold-141
Silver-141
Franchise Players-FP4
Teammates-TT12
02Parkhurst Retro-42
Minis-42
Franchise Players-RF4
02Private Stock Reserve-105
Red-105
Retail-105
Patches-105
02SP Authentic-10
Beckett Promos-10
02SP Game Used Authentic Fabrics-AFSA
02SP Game Used Authentic Fabrics-CFCS
02SP Game Used Authentic Fabrics Gold-AFSA
02SP Game Used Authentic Fabrics Gold-CFCS
02SP Game Used Authentic Fabrics Rainbow-AFSA
02SPx-7
Spectrum Gold-7
Spectrum Silver-7
Smooth Skaters-SA
Smooth Skaters Gold-SA
Smooth Skaters Silver-SA
02Stadium Club-78
Silver Decoy Cards-78
Proofs-78
Passport-10
02Titanium-13
Blue-13
Red-13
Retail-13
02Topps-20
OPC Blue Parallel-20
OPC Red Parallel-20
Factory Set-20
02Topps Chrome-20
Black Border Refractors-20
Refractors-20
02Topps Heritage-18
Chrome Parallel-18
02Topps Total-354
Team Checklists-TTC3
02UD Artistic Impressions-11
Gold-11
02UD Artistic Impressions Beckett Promos-11
02UD Artistic Impressions Retrospectives-R11
02UD Artistic Impressions Retrospect Gold-R11
02UD Artistic Impress Retrospect Silver-R11
02UD Honor Roll-7
Grade A Jerseys-GASA
02UD Mask Collection Instant Offense-IOMS
02UD Piece of History-8
02UD Premier Collection-8
02UD Top Shelf-10
Dual Player Jerseys-RSF
Dual Player Jerseys-RSH
Goal Oriented-GOMS
Shooting Stars-SHMSA
Sweet Sweaters-SWSA
Triple Jerseys-HTBSB
Triple Jerseys-TSASB
02Upper Deck-19
Exclusives-19
Difference Makers-SA
Specialists-SMS
02Upper Deck Classic Portraits-10
Hockey Royalty-SCA
Hockey Royalty Limited-SCA
Starring Cast-CSA
Starring Cast Limited-CSA
02Upper Deck MVP-21
Gold-21
Classics-21
Golden Classics-21
Skate Around Jerseys-STDSB
Skate Around Jerseys-STKFS
Souvenirs-S-MS
02Upper Deck Rookie Update-13
02Upper Deck Victory-27
Bronze-27
Gold-27
Silver-27
National Pride-NP40
02Upper Deck Vintage-29
02Upper Deck Vintage-263
02Upper Deck Vintage-311
Green Backs-29
Tall Boys-T7
Tall Boys Gold-T7
02Slovakian Kvarteto-1
03BAP Memorabilia-60
Emerald-60
Gold-60
Ruby-60
Sapphire-60
03BAP Ultimate Memorabilia Autographs-71
Gold-71
03BAP Ultimate Mem Franch Present Future-4
03Black Diamond-23
Black-23
Green-23
Red-23
03Bowman-71
Gold-71
Goal to Goal-SI
03Bowman Chrome-71
Refractors-71
Gold Refractors-71
Xfractors-71
03ITG Action-66
Jerseys-M73
Jerseys-M244
03ITG Used Signature Series-40
Gold-40
Autographs-MSA
Autographs Gold-MSA
Franchise-4
Franchise Autographs-4
Franchise Gold-4
03NHL Sticker Collection-25
03O-Pee-Chee-66
03OPC Blue-66
03OPC Gold-66
03OPC Red-66
03Pacific-45
Blue-45
Red-45
03Pacific Complete-182
Red-182
03Pacific Exhibit-22
Blue Backs-22
Yellow Backs-22
03Pacific Invincible-11
Blue-11
Red-11
Retail-11
Featured Performers-4
03Pacific Prism-17
Blue-17
Gold-17
Red-17
03Pacific Quest for the Cup-13
Blue-13
03Pacific Supreme Jerseys-5
03Parkhurst Rookie Teammates Gold-RT19
03Parkhurst Rookie Teammates-RT19
03Private Stock Reserve-148
Blue-148
Patches-148
Red-148
Retail-148
03SP Game Used Authentic Fabrics-DFCM
03SP Game Used Authentic Fabrics Gold-DFCM
03SP Game Used Authentic Patches-APMS
03SP Game Used Double Threads-DTDS
03SPx-10
Radiance-10
Spectrum-10
Fantasy Franchise-FF-DSA
Fantasy Franchise Limited-FF-DSA
03Titanium-15
Hobby Jersey Number Parallels-15
Retail-15
Retail Jersey Number Parallels-15
03Topps-66
Blue-66
Gold-66
Red-66
03Topps C55-18
Minis-18
Minis American Back-18
Minis American Back Red-18
Minis Bazooka Back-18
Minis Brooklyn Back-18
Minis Hat Trick Back-18
Minis O Canada Back-18
Minis O Canada Back Red-18
Minis Stanley Cup Back-18
03Topps Pristine-66
Gold Refractor Die Cuts-66
Refractors-66
Jersey Portions-PPJ-MSA
Jersey Portion Refractors-PPJ-MSA
Patches-PP-MSA
Patch Refractors-PP-MSA
Press Plates Black-66
Press Plates Cyan-66
Press Plates Magenta-66
Press Plates Yellow-66
03UD Honor Roll Grade A Jerseys-GAMS
03Upper Deck-268
Canadian Exclusives-268
HG-268
Team Essentials-TP-MS
UD Exclusives-268
03Upper Deck Classic Portraits-9
03Upper Deck MVP-51
Gold Script-51
Silver Script-51
Canadian Exclusives-51
SportsNut-SN12
03Upper Deck Trilogy-9
Limited-9
03Upper Deck Victory-19
Bronze-19
Gold-19
Silver-19
03Russian World Championship Stars-18
03Toronto Star-10
04Pacific-36
Blue-36
Red-36
04SP Authentic-37
04SP Authentic-102
04UD All-World-43
Gold-43
04Upper Deck-20
Canadian Exclusives-20
HG Glossy Gold-20
HG Glossy Silver-20
World Cup Tribute-MGHOMI
05Be A Player-9
First Period-9
Second Period-9
Third Period-9
Overtime-9
05Beehive-56
05Beehive-199
Beige -56
Blue -56
Gold-56
Red -56
Matte-56
Signature Scrapbook-SSMI
05Black Diamond-90
Emerald-90
Gold-90
Onyx-90
Ruby-90
05Hot Prospects-64
En Fuego-64
Red Hot-64
White Hot-64
05Panini Stickers-93
05Parkhurst-302
Facsimile Auto Parallel-302
True Colors-TCNYI
True Colors-TCNYI
True Colors-TCNYNY
True Colors-TCNYNY
05SP Authentic-61
Limited-61
Sign of the Times-SA
Sign of the Times Duals-DYS
05SP Game Used-63
Autographs-63
Gold-63
Authentic Fabrics-AF-SA
Authentic Fabrics Autographs-AAF-SA
Authentic Fabrics Dual-HS
Authentic Fabrics Dual Autographs-HS
Authentic Fabrics Gold-AF-SA
Authentic Fabrics Quad-SDYH
Authentic Fabrics Quad-TBYS
Authentic Patches Quad -SDYH
Authentic Patches Quad -TBYS
Authentic Fabrics Triple-YSP
Authentic Patches-AP-SA
Authentic Patches Autographs-AAP-SA
Authentic Patches Dual-HS
Authentic Patches Dual Autographs-HS
Authentic Patches Triple-YSP
SIGnificance-MS
SIGnificance Gold-S-MS
Significant Numbers-SN-MS
05SPx-56
05SPx-116
Spectrum-56
Spectrum-116
Winning Combos-WC-PS
Winning Combos Autographs-AWC-PS
Winning Combos Gold-WC-PS
Winning Combos Spectrum-WC-PS
Winning Materials-WM-SA
Winning Materials Gold-WM-SA
Winning Materials Spectrum-WM-SA
05The Cup Dual NHL Shields-DSAM
05The Cup Dual NHL Shields Autographs-ADSAM
05The Cup Emblems of Endorsement-EEMS
05The Cup Honorable Numbers-HNSA
05The Cup Limited Logos-LLSA
05The Cup Scripted Numbers Dual-DSNSV
05The Cup Scripted Swatches-SSSA
05The Cup Signature Patches-SPMS
05UD PowerPlay-13
Rainbow-13
05Ultimate Collection-58
Gold-58
Marquee Attractions-MA30
National Heroes Jerseys-NHJSA
National Heroes Patches-NHPSA
Ultimate Signatures-USMS
Ultimate Signatures Pairings-UPYS
05Ultra-124
Gold-124
Fresh Ink-FI-SA
Fresh Ink Blue-FI-SA
Ice-124
05Upper Deck-369
Jerseys Series II-J2MS
Majestic Materials-MMSA
Notable Numbers-N-MSA
Patches-P-MS
05Upper Deck Hockey Showcase-HS23
05Upper Deck Showcase Promos-HS23
05Upper Deck Ice-60
Rainbow-60
05Upper Deck MVP-249
Gold-249
Platinum-249
05Upper Deck Rookie Update-61
05Upper Deck Trilogy-58
05Upper Deck Victory-20
05Upper Deck Victory-230
Black-20
Black-230
Gold-20
Gold-230
Silver-20
Silver-230
Stars on Ice-SI6
06Be A Player Portraits-66
06Beehive-40
06Beehive-184
Blue-40
Gold-40
Matte-40
Red Facsimile Signatures-40
Wood-40
06Black Diamond-114
Black-114
Gold-114
Ruby-114
Gemography-GMS
Jerseys-JSA
Jerseys Black-JSA
Jerseys Gold-JSA
Jerseys Ruby-JSA
Jerseys Black Autographs -JSA
06Flair Showcase-64
06Flair Showcase-143
Parallel-64
Parallel-143
Inks-ISA
Stitches-SSSA
06Fleer-124
Tiffany-124
Speed Machines-SM17
06Hot Prospects-62
Red Hot-62
White Hot-62
06McDonald's Upper Deck-28
06O-Pee-Chee-322
06O-Pee-Chee-689
Rainbow-322
Rainbow-689
Swatches-S-MI
06Panini Stickers-69
06SP Authentic-40
Limited-40
06SP Game Used-64
Gold-64
Rainbow-64
Authentic Fabrics-AFMI
Authentic Fabrics Parallel-AFMI
Authentic Fabrics Patches-AFMI
Authentic Fabrics Dual-AF2SD
Authentic Fabrics Dual Patches-AF2SD
Authentic Fabrics Triple-AF3NYI
Authentic Fabrics Triple Patches-AF3NYI
Autographs-64
By The Letter-BLMI
Inked Sweaters Dual-IS2SY
Inked Sweaters Dual Patches-IS2SY
06SPx-64
Spectrum-64
SPxcitement-X64
SPxcitement Spectrum-X64
SPxcitement Autographs-X64
Winning Materials-WMMS
Winning Materials Spectrum-WMMS
Winning Materials Autographs-WMMS
06The Cup Autographed Foundations-CQSM
06The Cup Autographed Foundations Patches-CQSM
06The Cup Autographed NHL Shields Duals-DASYS
06The Cup Foundations-CQSM
06The Cup Foundations Patches-CQSM
06The Cup Honorable Numbers-HNSM
06The Cup Limited Logos-LLSM
06The Cup NHL Shields Duals-DSHDS
06UD Artifacts-39
06UD Artifacts-182
Blue-39
Blue-182
Gold-39
Gold-182
Platinum-39
Platinum-182
Radiance-39
Radiance-182
Autographed Radiance Parallel-39
Autographed Radiance Parallel-182
Red-39
Red-182
Tundra Tandems-TTMR
Tundra Tandems Black-TTMR
Tundra Tandems Blue-TTMR
Tundra Tandems Gold-TTMR
Tundra Tandems Platinum-TTMR
Tundra Tandems Red-TTMR
Tundra Tandems Dual Patches Red-TTMR
06UD Mini Jersey Collection-63
06UD Powerplay-62
Impact Rainbow-62
06Ultimate Collection Premium Patches-PS-MS
06Ultimate Collection Premium Swatches-PS-MS
06Ultra-123
Gold Medallion-123
Ice Medallion-123
06Upper Deck Arena Giveaways-NYI6
06Upper Deck-121
Exclusives Parallel-121
High Gloss Parallel-121
Game Jerseys-J2SA
Game Patches-P2SA
Generations Duals-G2PSH
Generations Triples-G3HSS
Generations Patches Dual-G2PSH
Generations Patches Triple-G3PHSS
Masterpieces-121
Shootout Artists-SA2
Signature Sensations-SSMS
Walmart Tins Oversize-121
06Upper Deck MVP-181
Gold Script-181
Super Script-181
Autographs-OASC
International Icons-II15
Jerseys-OJES
Jerseys-OJJS
Jerseys-OJSS
06Upper Deck Ovation-30
06Upper Deck Sweet Shot Sweet Stitches-SSSA
06Upper Deck Sweet Shot Sweet Stitches Duals-SSSA
06Upper Deck Sweet Shot Sweet Stitches Triples-SSSA
06Upper Deck Trilogy-61
Honorary Scripted Patches-HSPSA
Honorary Scripted Swatches-HSSSA
Honorary Swatches-HSSA
06Upper Deck Victory-124
06Upper Deck Victory Black-124
06Upper Deck Victory Gold-124
06Russian Sport Collection Olympic Stars-49
07Upper Deck Victory-20
Black-20
Gold-20

Saterdalen, Jeff
92Richmond Renegades-15

Sateri, Esa
93Finnish SISU-242
94Finnish SISU-65

Sather, Glen
67Topps-38
68O-Pee-Chee-134
68Shirriff Coins-15
69O-Pee-Chee-116
69Topps-116
70Dad's Cookies-117
70Esso Power Players-228
70O-Pee-Chee-205
70Sargent Promotions Stamps-167
71O-Pee-Chee-221
71Toronto Sun-182
73Blues White Border-18
74Canadiens Postcards-21
75O-Pee-Chee NHL-222
75Topps-222
76O-Pee-Chee WHA-56
81Oilers Red Rooster-xx
82Oilers Red Rooster-NNO
83Oilers McDonald's-20
84Oilers Red Rooster-NNO
84Oilers Red Rooster-NNO
85Oilers Red Rooster-NNO
86Oilers Red Rooster-NNO
88Oilers Tenth Anniversary-49
88Oilers Tenth Anniversary-117
92Oilers IGA-26
93Upper Deck Locker All-Stars-49
01Greats of the Game Jerseys-7
01Greats of the Game Patches Gold-7
01Topps Archives-67
02Topps Rookie Reprints-11
02Topps Rookie Reprint Autographs-11
03Rangers Team Issue-22
03Rangers Team Issue-23

Sator, Ted
87Sabres Wonder Bread/Hostess-25
88Sabres Wonder Bread/Hostess-26
97New Orleans Brass-18

Satosaari, Tommi
98Finnish Keräilysarja-120
99Finnish Cardset-62
99Finnish Cardset-204
00UK Sekonda Superleague-110
01Finnish Cardset-366
02Finnish Cardset-267
06Finnish Cardset-293

Sattare, Lars
65Swedish Coralli ISHockey-183

Sauer, Billy
04Chicago Steel-5

Sauer, E.J.
91ProCards-440
92Tulsa Oilers-14

Sauer, Jerrid
03Swift Current Broncos-16
04Swift Current Broncos-17
05Medicine Hat Tigers-19
06Medicine Hat Tigers-17

Sauer, Kent
03Pensacola Ice Pilots-352

Sauer, Kurt
99Spokane Chiefs-21
00Spokane Chiefs-23
01Spokane Chiefs-19
02BAP All-Star Edition-117
Gold-117
Silver-117
02BAP Memorabilia-276
Emerald-276
Ruby-276
Sapphire-276
NHL All-Star Game-276
NHL All-Star Game Blue-276
NHL All-Star Game Green-276
NHL All-Star Game Red-276
02BAP Memorabilia Toronto Fall Expo-276
02BAP Ultimate Memorabilia-6
02Bowman YoungStars-119
Gold-119
Silver-119
02Pacific Calder-102
Silver-102
02Pacific Complete-564
Red-564
02Pacific Quest for the Cup-103
Gold-103
02SP Authentic-193
02SP Game Used-69
02SPx-147
02Stadium Club-134
Silver Decoy Cards-134
Proofs-134
02Titanium-103
Blue-103
Red-103
Retail-103
02Topps Chrome-170
Black Border Refractors-170
Refractors-170
02Topps Heritage-145
02Topps Total-415
02UD Honor Roll-103
02UD Mask Collection-126
02UD Top Shelf-106
02Upper Deck-428
Exclusives-428
02Upper Deck Classic Portraits-104
03Black Diamond Signature Gems-SG-34
03ITG Action-52
03Upper Deck MVP-12
Gold Script-12
Silver Script-12
Canadian Exclusives-12
06Avalanche Team Postcards-14

Sauer, Mike
04Portland Winter Hawks-8
05ITG Heroes and Prospects-171
Autographs-A-MSR
06Medicine Hat Tigers-18

Sauffaus, Michael
99Danish Hockey League-131

Sauirol, Claude-Charl
907th Inn. Sketch QMJHL-134

Saulnier, Jules
00Halifax Mooseheads-20

Saulnier, Justin
03Halifax Mooseheads-12
04Halifax Mooseheads-15
05Halifax Mooseheads-12

Saumier, Marc
87Hull Olympiques-16
88ProCards AHL-288
89ProCards AHL-188
91ProCards-392
94Muskegon Fury-10

Saumier, Raymond
89ProCards AHL-284

Saundercock, Paul
90ProCards AHL/IHL-415

Saunders, Dave
87Canucks Shell Oil-17
88O-Pee-Chee-248
88O-Pee-Chee Stickers-61
93Quebec Pee-Wee Tournament-743

Saunders, Derek
93Quebec Pee-Wee Tournament-1297

Saunders, John
00Arizona Icecats-21
01Arizona Icecats-19

Saunders, Ken
67Columbus Checkers-8

Saunders, Lee
92Maine Black Bears-29
93Maine Black Bears-49
96UK Guildford Flames-19

Saunders, Nathan
01Moncton Wildcats-11
02Moncton Wildcats-1
03Moncton Wildcats-10
04Moncton Wildcats-25
05Portland Pirates-14
06Augusta Lynx-17

Saunier, Bruno
92Finnish Semic-225
94Finnish Jaa Kiekko-216

Saunier, Franck
94French National Team-29

Saurdiff, Corwin
92Northern Michigan Wildcats-22
94Hampton Roads Admirals-21
95Hampton Roads Admirals-23
96Columbus Cottonmouths-15
99San Antonio Iguanas-18

Saurette, Kevin
97Regina Pats-5
06Reading Royals-13

Saurio, Matti
65Finnish Hellas-31
66Finnish Jaakiekkosarja-7
70Finnish Jaakiekko-236
71Finnish Suomi Stickers-255
73Finnish Jaakiekko-319

Sauriol, Claude-Charles
87Hull Olympiques-17

Sauter, Cristoph
94German First League-181

Sauter, Doug
83Springfield Indians-25
85Medicine Hat Tigers-8
86Regina Pats-24
87Regina Pats-24
88Brandon Wheat Kings-19
89Brandon Wheat Kings-20
92Wheeling Thunderbirds-22
93Wheeling Thunderbirds-18
94Wheeling Thunderbirds Photo Album-17
95Central Hockey League-54
98Oklahoma City Blazers-18
03Oklahoma City Blazers-22
04Oklahoma City Blazers-19

Sauter, Hardy
89Brandon Wheat Kings-7
90Brandon Wheat Kings-5
907th Inn. Sketch WHL-217
917th Inn. Sketch WHL-2
98Oklahoma City Blazers-15
03Oklahoma City Blazers-13
04Oklahoma City Blazers-5

Sauter, Martin
94German First League-183

Sauve, Bob
76O-Pee-Chee NHL-308
78O-Pee-Chee-265
79O-Pee-Chee-49
79Sabres Bells-7
79Topps-49
80O-Pee-Chee-166
80O-Pee-Chee-266
80Sabres Milk Panels-8
80Topps-166
81O-Pee-Chee-23
81O-Pee-Chee Stickers-56
81Sabres Milk Panels-8
81Topps-E77
82O-Pee-Chee-34
82O-Pee-Chee Stickers-181
82Post Cereal-5
82Sabres Milk Panels-6
82Topps Stickers-181
83O-Pee-Chee-61
83O-Pee-Chee-71
83O-Pee-Chee Stickers-242
83Topps Stickers-242
84O-Pee-Chee-30
84O-Pee-Chee Stickers-208
84Sabres Blue Shield-18
85O-Pee-Chee-174
85O-Pee-Chee Stickers-181
85O-Pee-Chee Stickers-190
86Blackhawks Coke-17
86O-Pee-Chee-124
86O-Pee-Chee Stickers-152
86Topps-124
87O-Pee-Chee-140
87O-Pee-Chee Stickers-75
87Panini Stickers-220
87Topps-140
88Devils Caretta-24

Sauve, Daniel
06Gatineau Olympiques-7

Sauve, J.F.
82O-Pee-Chee-33
82Post Cereal-2
83Nordiques Postcards-24
84Nordiques Postcards-22
85Nordiques General Foods-22
85Nordiques Provigo-21
85O-Pee-Chee Stickers-155
86Nordiques McDonald's-21
86O-Pee-Chee Stickers-23

Sauve, Maxime
06Quebec Remparts-10

Sauve, Philippe
93Quebec Pee-Wee Tournament-1053
94Quebec Pee-Wee Tournament-512
96Rimouski Oceanic-24
96Rimouski Oceanic Quebec Police-22
97Rimouski Oceanic-33
98OPC Chrome-241
Refractors-241
98Topps-241
O-Pee-Chee-241
98Bowman CHL-101
98Bowman CHL-160
Golden Anniversary-101
Golden Anniversary-160
OPC International-101
OPC International-160
Autographs Blue-A23
Autographs Gold-A23
Autographs Silver-A23
98Bowman Chrome CHL-101
98Bowman Chrome CHL-160
Golden Anniversary-101
Golden Anniversary-160
Golden Anniversary Refractors-101
Golden Anniversary Refractors-160
OPC International-101
OPC International-160
OPC International Refractors-101
OPC International Refractors-160
Refractors-101
Refractors-160
99Hull Olympiques-23
Signed-23
99Quebec PeeWee Tournament Coll Souv-19
99UD Prospects-65
00Hershey Bears-13
01Hershey Bears-1
02Between the Pipes-103
Gold-103
Silver-103
02AHL Top Prospects-38
02Hershey Bears-18
03Avalanche Team Issue-15
03Beehive-46
Gold-46
Silver-46
03Black Diamond-95
Black-95
Green-95
Red-95
03Crown Royale-27
Blue-27
Retail-27
03ITG Action-176
03Pacific Calder-26
Silver-26
03Pacific Complete-492
Red-492
03Pacific Heads-Up Prime Prospects-6
03Pacific Heads-Up Prime Prospects LTD-6
03Pacific Quest for the Cup Calder Cont-6
03Parkhurst Rookie All-Rookie-ART-7
03Parkhurst Rookie All-Rookie Gold-ART-7
03Topps Traded-TT38
Blue-TT38
Gold-TT38
Red-TT38
03UD Honor Roll-107
03Upper Deck-294
Canadian Exclusives-294
HG-294
UD Exclusives-294
Rookie Update YoungStars-YS22
03Pacific AHL Prospects Crease Lightning-3
04SP Authentic Rookie Review-RR-PS
04SP Authentic Sign of the Times-ST-PS
04SP Authentic Sign of the Times-QS-TAHS
04Upper Deck YoungStars-YS-PS
04ITG Heroes and Prospects Net Prospects-10
04ITG Heroes and Prosp Net Prospects Gold-10
05Black Diamond-6
Emerald-6
Gold-6
Onyx-6
Ruby-6
05Hot Prospects Hot Materials-HMSA
05Parkhurst Signatures-PS
05Parkhurst True Colors-TCPHX
05Parkhurst True Colors-TCPHX
05SP Authentic Scripts to Success-SSPS
05SP Authentic Sign of the Times-PS
05SP Game Used Authentic Fabrics Dual-SR
05SP Game Used Authentic Fabric Dual Auto-SR
05SP Game Used Authentic Patches Dual-SR
05SP Game Used Authentic Patch Dual Autos-SR
05SP Game Used Auto Draft-AD-PS
05SP Game Used Game Gear-GG-PS
05SP Game Used Game Gear Autographs-AG-PS
05SP Game Used Signature Sticks-SS-PS
05SP Game Used SIGnificance-PS
05SP Game Used SIGnificance Gold-S-PS
05SP Game Used SIGnificance Extra-MS
05SP Game Used SIGnificance Extra Gold-MS
05SP Game Used Statscriptions-ST-SA
05UD Artifacts Auto Facts-AF-PS
05UD Artifacts Auto Facts Blue-AF-PS
05UD Artifacts Auto Facts Copper-AF-PS
05UD Artifacts Auto Facts Pewter-AF-PS
05UD Artifacts Auto Facts Silver-AF-PS
05UD Artifacts Remarkable Artifacts-RA-PS
05UD Artifacts Remarkable Artifacts Dual-RA-PS
05UD Toronto Fall Expo Priority Signings-PS-PS
05Ultra-37
Gold-37
Ice-37
05Upper Deck-273
Jerseys Series II-J2SA
Notable Numbers-N-PHS
Patches-P-PS
Ice Fresh Ice-FIPS
Ice Fresh Ice Glass-FIPS
05Upper Deck MVP-65
Gold-65
Platinum-65
05Upper Deck Trilogy Scripts-SFS-PS
06Between The Pipes-42
Autographs-APS
Emblems-GUE42
Emblems Gold-GUE42
Emblems Autographs-GUE42
Jerseys-GUJ42
Jerseys Gold-GUJ42
Jerseys Autographs-GUJ42
Numbers-GUN42
Numbers Gold-GUN42
Numbers Autographs-GUN42
06Fleer Fabricology-FSA
06Ultra Fresh Ink-IPS
06Upper Deck MVP Autographs-OALS
06Upper Deck Trilogy Scripts-TSPS
06Providence Bruins-17
06ITG Heroes and Prospects AHL All-Star Jerseys-AJ11
06ITG Heroes and Prospects AHL All-Star Jerseys Gold-AJ11
06ITG Heroes and Prospects AHL All-Star Emblems-AE11
06ITG Heroes and Prospects AHL All-Star Emblems Gold-AE11
06ITG Heroes and Prospects AHL All-Star Numbers-AN11
06ITG Heroes and Prospects AHL All-Star Numbers Gold-AN11

Sauve, Simon-Pierre
02Shawinigan Cataractes-20
03Shawinigan Cataractes-22

Sauve, Yann
06Saint John Sea Dogs-24

Savage, Alain
90Montreal-Bourassa AAA-23
917th Inn. Sketch QMJHL-69
96Hampton Roads Admirals-HRA12
97Idaho Steelheads-5
98Idaho Steelheads-16
98Mobile Mysticks-11
00Knoxville Speed-7

Savage, Andre
98Providence Bruins-19
99BAP Memorabilia-341
Gold-341
Silver-341
99Pacific-32
Copper-32
Emerald Green-32
Gold-32
Red-32
99SP Authentic-97
99Providence Bruins-21
00BAP Memorabilia-377
Emerald-377
Ruby-377
Sapphire-377
Promos-377
00BAP Mem Chicago Sportsfest Copper-377
00BAP Memorabilia Chicago Sportsfest Blue-377
00BAP Memorabilia Chicago Sportsfest Gold-377
00BAP Memorabilia Chicago Sportsfest Ruby-377
00BAP Memorabilia Chicago Sun-Times Ruby-377
00BAP Memorabilia Chicago Sun-Times Gold-377
00BAP Mem Chicago Sun-Times Sapphire-377
00BAP Mem Toronto Fall Expo Copper-377
00BAP Memorabilia Toronto Fall Expo Gold-377
00BAP Memorabilia Toronto Fall Expo Ruby-377
00BAP Signature Series-230
Emerald-230
Ruby-230
Sapphire-230
Autographs-44
Autographs Gold-44
00O-Pee-Chee-230
00O-Pee-Chee Parallel-230
00Pacific-42
Copper-42
Gold-42
Ice Blue-42
Premiere Date-42
00Titanium Game Gear-57
00Titanium Game Gear Patches-57
00Topps/OPC-230
Parallel-230
00Upper Deck-18
Exclusives Tier 1-18
Exclusives Tier 2-18
00Upper Deck Victory-262
01Pacific Jerseys-1
01Upper Deck Vintage-139
01Vanguard Memorabilia-40
01Manitoba Moose-22
02BAP Sig Series Auto Buybacks 2000-44
02Philadelphia Phantoms-12
03Providence Bruins-17

Savage, Brian
93Alberta International Team Canada-18
93OPC Premier Team Canada-16
93PowerPlay-493
93Ultra-472
93Classic-81
Team Canada-TC3
94Canadiens Postcards-23
94Donruss-276
94Finest Bowman's Best-R8
94Finest Bowman's Best Refractors-R8
94Fleer-108
94Leaf-292
94OPC Premier-16

Special Effects-16
94Parkhurst SE-SE90
Gold-SE90
94Pinnacle-248
Artist's Proofs-248
Rink Collection-248
Rookie Team Pinnacle-10
94Score-230
Gold-230
Platinum-230
Team Canada-CT8
94Select-192
Gold-192
94Topps/OPC Premier-16
Special Effects-16
94Upper Deck-244
Electric Ice-244
94Classic-34
Gold-34
Autographs-34
Tri-Cards-T34
Pro Prospects International Heroes-LP18
95Be A Player-138
Signatures-S138
Signatures Die Cuts-S138
95Bowman-87
All-Foil-87
95Canada Games NHL POGS-144
95Canadiens Postcards-17
95Canadiens Sheets-9
95Donruss-20
95Donruss Elite-28
Die Cut Stars-28
Die Cut Uncut-28
95Emotion-92
95Finest-23
Refractors-23
95Leaf-175
Studio Rookies-15
95Leaf Limited-82
95Metal-79
Winners-7
95Panini Stickers-36
95Parkhurst International-112
Emerald Ice-112
95Pinnacle-94
Artist's Proofs-94
Rink Collection-94
95Score-76
Black Ice Artist's Proofs-76
Black Ice-76
95SkyBox Impact-88
NHL On Fox-9
95Stadium Club-37
Members Only Master Set-37
95Summit-167
Artist's Proofs-167
Ice-167
95Topps-349
OPC Inserts-349
New To The Game-21NG
95Ultra-84
Gold Medallion-84
High Speed-17
95Upper Deck-36
Electric Ice-36
Electric Ice Gold-36
Special Edition-SE132
Special Edition Gold-SE132
95Zenith-20
96Canadiens Postcards-25
96Canadiens Sheets-19
96Collector's Choice-140
96Donruss-168
Press Proofs-168
96Leaf-111
Press Proofs-111
96Pinnacle-134
Artist's Proofs-134
Foil-134
Premium Stock-134
Rink Collection-134
96Score-147
Artist's Proofs-147
Dealer's Choice Artist's Proofs-147
Special Artist's Proofs-147
Golden Blades-147
96Upper Deck Ice-34
Parallel-34
97Canadiens Postcards-20
97Collector's Choice-131
97Donruss-109
Press Proofs Silver-109
Press Proofs Gold-109
97Donruss Limited-71
Exposure-71
97Donruss Preferred-62
Cut to the Chase-62
97Donruss Priority-128
Stamp of Approval-128
97Leaf-68
Fractal Matrix-68
Fractal Matrix Die Cuts-68
97Leaf International-68
Universal Ice-68
97Pacific-142
Copper-142
Emerald Green-142
Ice Blue-142
Red-142
Silver-142
97Pacific Omega-123
Copper-123
Dark Gray-123
Emerald Green-123
Gold-123
Ice Blue-123
97Panini Stickers-30
97Paramount-99
Copper-99
Dark Grey-99
Emerald Green-99
Ice Blue-99
Red-99
Silver-99
97Pinnacle-152
Press Plates Back Black-152
Press Plates Back Cyan-152
Press Plates Back Magenta-152
Press Plates Back Yellow-152
Press Plates Front Black-152
Press Plates Front Cyan-152
Press Plates Front Magenta-152
Press Plates Front Yellow-152
97Pinnacle Inside-135
97Score-191
97Score Canadiens-6
Platinum-6
Premier-6
97Upper Deck-299
98Aurora-97
98Canadiens Team Issue-19
98Pacific-49
Ice Blue-49
Red-49
98Pacific Omega-126
Red-126
Opening Day Issue-126
98Paramount-118
Copper-118
Emerald Green-118
Holo-Electric-118
Ice Blue-118
Silver-118
98Revolution-76
Ice Shadow-76
Red-76
98UD Choice-111
98UD Choice Preview-111
98UD Choice Prime Choice Reserve-111
98UD Choice Reserve-111
98Upper Deck-115
Exclusives-115
Exclusives 1 of 1-115
Gold Reserve-115
98Upper Deck MVP-108
Gold Script-108
Silver Script-108
Super Script-108
99Aurora-77
Premiere Date-77
99BAP Millennium-133
Emerald-133
Ruby-133
Sapphire-133
Signatures-133
Signatures Gold-133
99Crown Royale-72
Limited Series-72
Premiere Date-72
99Pacific-210
Copper-210
Emerald Green-210
Gold-210
Ice Blue-210
Premiere Date-210
Red-210
99Pacific Dynagon Ice-105
Blue-105
Copper-105
Gold-105
Premiere Date-105
99Pacific Omega-122
Copper-122
Gold-122
Ice Blue-122
Premiere Date-122
99Pacific Prism-74
Holographic Blue-74
Holographic Gold-74
Holographic Mirror-74
Holographic Purple-74
Premiere Date-74
99Panini Stickers-67
99Topps Gold Label Class 1-69
Black-69
Black One of One-69
One of One-69
Red-69
Red One of One-69
99Topps Gold Label Class 2-69
99Topps Gold Label Class 2 Black-69
99Topps Gold Label Class 2 Black 1 of 1-69
99Topps Gold Label Class 2 One of One-69
99Topps Gold Label Class 2 Red-69
99Topps Gold Label Class 2 Red One of One-69
99Topps Gold Label Class 3-69
99Topps Gold Label Class 3 Black-69
99Topps Gold Label Class 3 Black 1 of 1-69
99Topps Gold Label Class 3 One of One-69
99Topps Gold Label Class 3 Red-69
99Topps Gold Label Class 3 Red One of One-69
99Ultimate Victory-46
1/1-46
Parallel-46
Parallel 100-46
99Upper Deck-244
Exclusives-244
Exclusives 1 of 1-244
99Upper Deck Gold Reserve-244
99Upper Deck MVP-107
Gold Script-107
Silver Script-107
Super Script-107
99Upper Deck Victory-150
99Wayne Gretzky Hockey-86
00BAP Memorabilia-170
Emerald-170
Ruby-170
Sapphire-170
Promos-170
00BAP Mem Chicago Sportsfest Copper-170
00BAP Memorabilia Chicago Sportsfest Blue-170
00BAP Memorabilia Chicago Sportsfest Gold-170
00BAP Memorabilia Chicago Sportsfest Ruby-170
00BAP Memorabilia Chicago Sun-Times Ruby-170
00BAP Memorabilia Chicago Sun-Times Gold-170
00BAP Mem Chicago Sun-Times Sapphire-170
00BAP Mem Toronto Fall Expo Copper-170
00BAP Memorabilia Toronto Fall Expo Gold-170
00BAP Memorabilia Toronto Fall Expo Ruby-170
00BAP Parkhurst 2000-P154
00BAP Signature Series-76
Emerald-76
Ruby-76
Sapphire-76
Autographs-9
Autographs Gold-9
00Canadiens Postcards-25
00Crown Royale-57
Ice Blue-57
Limited Series-57
Premiere Date-57
Red-57
00O-Pee-Chee-261B
00O-Pee-Chee Parallel-261B
00Pacific-213
Copper-213
Gold-213
Ice Blue-213
Premiere Date-213
00Paramount-131
Copper-131
Gold-131
Holo-Gold-131
Holo-Silver-131
Ice Blue-131
Premiere Date-131
00Private Stock Game Gear-59
00Stadium Club-199
00Topps/OPC-261B
Parallel-261B
00UD Pros and Prospects-45
00UD Reserve-44
00Upper Deck-93
Exclusives Tier 1-93
Exclusives Tier 2-93
00Upper Deck MVP-90
First Stars-90
Second Stars-90
Third Stars-90
00Upper Deck Victory-123
00Upper Deck Vintage-190
00Czech Stadion-153
01BAP Memorabilia-157
01BAP Memorabilia-458
Emerald-157
Emerald-458
Ruby-157
Ruby-458
Sapphire-157
Sapphire-458
01BAP Signature Series-15
Autographs-15
Autographs Gold-15
Jerseys-GJ-31
Jersey Autographs-GUBSA
Jersey and Stick Cards-GSJ-31
Teammates-TM-16
01Canadiens Postcards-24
01Crown Royale-78
Blue-78
Premiere Date-78
Red-78
Retail-78
01O-Pee-Chee-162
01O-Pee-Chee Premier Parallel-162
01Pacific-212
Extreme LTD-212
Hobby LTD-212
Premiere Date-212
Retail LTD-212
01Pacific Adrenaline-100
Blue-100
Premiere Date-100
Red-100
Retail-100
01Pacific Arena Exclusives-212
01Pacific Heads-Up-51
Blue-51
Premiere Date-51
Red-51
Silver-51
01Parkhurst-147
01Parkhurst-395
01Private Stock-50
Gold-50
Premiere Date-50
Retail-50
Silver-50
01Private Stock Pacific Nights-50
01SP Authentic-44
Limited-44
Limited Gold-44
01SPx-190
01Titanium-75
Hobby Parallel-75
Premiere Date-75
Retail-75
Retail Parallel-75
01Topps-162
OPC Parallel-162
01UD Challenge for the Cup-44
01UD Playmakers-54
01Upper Deck-94
Exclusives-94
01Upper Deck Victory-187
Gold-187
01Upper Deck Vintage-135
01Vanguard-51
Blue-51
Red-51
One of Ones-51
Premiere Date-51
Proofs-51
02BAP Sig Series Auto Buybacks 1999-133
02BAP Sig Series Auto Buybacks 2000-9
02BAP Sig Series Auto Buybacks 2001-15
02BAP Signature Series Golf-GS15
02Coyotes Team Issue-19
02O-Pee-Chee-120
02O-Pee-Chee Premier Blue Parallel-120
02O-Pee-Chee Premier Red Parallel-120
02O-Pee-Chee Factory Set-120
02Pacific-304
Blue-304
Red-304
02Pacific Complete-43
Red-43
02Parkhurst Retro-159
Minis-159
02Topps-120
OPC Blue Parallel-120
OPC Red Parallel-120
Factory Set-120
02Upper Deck-383
Exclusives-383
02Upper Deck Beckett UD Promos-383
03Coyotes Postcards-19
03ITG Action-491
03Pacific Complete-95
Red-95
03Upper Deck-392
Canadian Exclusives-392
HG-392
UD Exclusives-392
05Flyers Team Issue-19
05Parkhurst-362
Facsimile Auto Parallel-362

Savage, David
04UK Guildford Flames-5
05UK Guildford Flames-3
06UK Guildford Flames-3

Savage, Jean-Francois
01Baie-Comeau Drakkar-22

Savage, Joel
89ProCards AHL-263
90ProCards AHL/IHL-266
91Upper Deck-423
French-423
91ProCards-13
91Rochester Americans Dunkin' Donuts-14
91Rochester Americans Kodak-23
91Rochester Americans Postcards-18
92Rochester Americans Kodak-19
95German DEL-381
96German DEL-192
98German DEL-150
99German Adler Mannheim Eagles Postcards-11
99German DEL-11
01Swiss EV Zug Postcards-26
01Swiss HNL-188
02Swiss EV Zug Postcards-25
02Swiss HNL-72
03Swiss EV Zug Postcards-20

Savage, Mike
83Belleville Bulls-11

Savage, Nicolas
93Drummondville Voltigeurs-6

Savage, Reggie
90ProCards AHL/IHL-199
91Score American-320
91Score Canadian Bilingual-350
91Score Canadian English-350
91Baltimore Skipjacks-7
91ProCards-570
92Capitals Kodak-24
92OPC Premier-121
92Parkhurst-426
Emerald Ice-426
92Stadium Club Members Only-48
92Upper Deck-474
93Durivage Score-23
94Nordiques Burger King-23
94Parkhurst-194
Gold-194
95Atlanta Knights-18
96Springfield Falcons-33
96Collector's Edge Ice-102
Prism-102
99Syracuse Crunch-9
00Syracuse Crunch-21
01Swiss HNL-316

Savage, Sebastien
00Ottawa 67's-19

Savage, Stephane
98Owen Sound Platers-10

Savage, Wayne
04St. Michael's Majors-23

Savard, Andre
74NHL Action Stamps-36
74O-Pee-Chee NHL-285
75Heroes Stand-Ups-6
75O-Pee-Chee NHL-155
75Topps-155
76O-Pee-Chee NHL-43
76Topps-43
77O-Pee-Chee NHL-118
77Topps-118
78O-Pee-Chee-253
78Topps-253
79O-Pee-Chee-25
79Topps-25
79Rochester Americans-15
80O-Pee-Chee-375
81O-Pee-Chee-24
81O-Pee-Chee Stickers-54
81Sabres Milk Panels-13
81Topps-E78
82Post Cereal-2
83NHL Key Tags-12
83Nordiques Postcards-25
83Vachon-73
84Nordiques Postcards-23
84O-Pee-Chee-288
84O-Pee-Chee Stickers-170
85Fredericton Express-28
86Fredericton Express-23
87Nordiques General Foods-31
92Nordiques Petro-Canada-29
00Canadiens Postcards-34
04ITG Franchises Canadian-73
Autographs-ASV

Savard, Denis
79Montreal Juniors-25
80Blackhawks Postcards-11
80Blackhawks White Border-12
81Blackhawks Borderless Postcards-23
81Blackhawks Brown Background-12
81O-Pee-Chee-63
81O-Pee-Chee Stickers-112
81Post Standups-3
81Topps-W75
82Blackhawks Postcards-19
82McDonald's Stickers-23
82O-Pee-Chee-73
82O-Pee-Chee Stickers-171
82Post Cereal-4
82Topps Stickers-171
83Blackhawks Postcards-20
83NHL Key Tags-25
83O-Pee-Chee-96
83O-Pee-Chee-111
83O-Pee-Chee Stickers-106
83O-Pee-Chee Stickers-107
83O-Pee-Chee Stickers-153
83Puffy Stickers-18
83Topps Stickers-106
83Topps Stickers-107
83Topps Stickers-153
84O-Pee-Chee-45
84O-Pee-Chee-355
84O-Pee-Chee Stickers-24
84O-Pee-Chee Stickers-25
847-Eleven Discs-9
84Topps-35
85Blackhawks Team Issue-25
85O-Pee-Chee-73
85O-Pee-Chee Stickers-22
857-Eleven Credit Cards-4
85Topps-73
86Blackhawks Coke-18
86O-Pee-Chee-7
86O-Pee-Chee Box Bottoms-N
86O-Pee-Chee Stickers-150
86Topps-7
86Topps Box Bottoms-N
87Blackhawks Coke-20
87O-Pee-Chee-127
87O-Pee-Chee Box Bottoms-N
87O-Pee-Chee Minis-39
87O-Pee-Chee Stickers-78
87Panini Stickers-225
87Topps-127
87Topps Box Bottoms-N
88Blackhawks Coke-18
88Esso All-Stars-40
88Frito-Lay Stickers-6
88O-Pee-Chee-26
88O-Pee-Chee Box Bottoms-H
88O-Pee-Chee Minis-34
88O-Pee-Chee Stickers-13
88Panini Stickers-29
88Topps-26
88Topps Box Bottoms-H
89Blackhawks Coke-1
89O-Pee-Chee-5
89O-Pee-Chee Stickers-16
89Panini Stickers-49
89Sports Illustrated for Kids I-118
89Topps-5
89Swedish Semic World Champ Stickers-66
90Bowman-6
Tiffany-6
90Canadiens Postcards-26
90Kraft-51
90O-Pee-Chee-28
90OPC Premier-103
90Panini Stickers-198
90Pro Set-59A
90Pro Set-59B
90Pro Set-473
90Score-125
Canadian-125
90Score Hottest/Rising Stars-59
90Score Rookie/Traded-1T
90Topps-28
Tiffany-28
90Upper Deck-244
90Upper Deck-426
French-244
French-426
91Pro Set Platinum-64
91Bowman-342
91Canadiens Panini Team Stickers-20
91Canadiens Postcards-25
91Kraft-77
91O-Pee-Chee-330
91OPC Premier-71
91Panini Stickers-187
91Parkhurst-93
91Parkhurst-211
French-93
French-211
91Pinnacle-28
French-28
91Pro Set-128
91Pro Set-305
French-128
French-305
Platinum PC-PC18
91Score American-165
91Score Canadian Bilingual-165
91Score Canadian English-165
91Stadium Club-213
91Topps-330
91Upper Deck-242
French-242
92Bowman-64
92Canadiens Postcards-25
92Durivage Panini-10
92Jofa/Koho-5
92O-Pee-Chee-35
92OPC Premier Star Performers-6
92Panini Stickers-152
92Panini Stickers French-152
92Parkhurst-85
Emerald Ice-85
92Pinnacle American Promo Panel-1
92Pinnacle-61
French-61
92Pro Set-84
92Pro Set-260
92Score-202
Canadian-202
92Seasons Patches-23
92Stadium Club-467
92Topps-414
Gold-414G
92Ultra-109
92Upper Deck-10
92Upper Deck-162
92Upper Deck-638
93Donruss-319
93Durivage Score-25
93Kraft-37
93Leaf-372
93Lightning Season in Review-24
93O-Pee-Chee Canadiens Hockey Fest-50
93OPC Premier-305
Gold-305
93Panini Stickers-17
93Parkhurst-193
Emerald Ice-193
93Pinnacle-391
Canadian-391
93PowerPlay-447
93Score-105
93Score-555
Gold-555
Canadian-105
Canadian-555
Canadian Gold-555
93Stadium Club-297
Members Only Master Set-297
First Day Issue-297
93Topps/OPC Premier-305
Gold-305
93Ultra-428
93Upper Deck-502
Gretzky's Great Ones-GG1
SP-153
94Be A Player Signature Cards-94
94Canada Games NHL POGS-225
94Donruss-284
94Hockey Wit-38
94Leaf-166
94OPC Premier-69
Special Effects-69
94Parkhurst-217
Gold-217
94Pinnacle-340
Artist's Proofs-340
Rink Collection-340
94Stadium Club Super Teams-22
94Stadium Club Super Team MemberOnly Set-22
94Topps/OPC Premier-69
Special Effects-69
94Ultra-373
94Upper Deck-415
Electric Ice-415
SP Inserts-SP76
SP Inserts Die Cuts-SP76
95Blackhawks Coke-14
95Canada Games NHL POGS-62
95Collector's Choice-132
Player's Club-132
Player's Club Platinum-132
95Donruss-233
95Hoyle Western Playing Cards-16
95Leaf-127
95Parkhurst International-40
Emerald Ice-40
95Playoff One on One-237
95Score-281
Black Ice Artist's Proofs-281
Black Ice-281
95Ultra-219
95Upper Deck-434
Electric Ice-434
Electric Ice Gold-434
96Black Diamond-58
Gold-58
96Donruss-51
Press Proofs-51
96Maggers-91
96Score-121
Artist's Proofs-121
Dealer's Choice Artist's Proofs-121
Special Artist's Proofs-121
Golden Blades-121
96Stadium Club Members Only-23
97Pacific-343
Copper-343
Emerald Green-343
Ice Blue-343
Red-343
Silver-343
98Blackhawks Legends-5
99BAP Memorabilia AS Retail-R3
99BAP Memorabilia AS Retail Autographs-R3
99Blackhawks Chicago Sun-Times-10
01Fleer Legacy-45
Ultimate-45
Memorabilia-8
01Greats of the Game-22
Autographs-22
Jerseys-8
Patches Gold-8
02BAP Memorabilia-241
Emerald-241
Ruby-241
Sapphire-241
NHL All-Star Game-241
NHL All-Star Game Blue-241
NHL All-Star Game Green-241
NHL All-Star Game Red-241
02BAP Memorabilia Toronto Fall Expo-241
02UD Foundations-14
02UD Foundations-50
02UD Foundations-111
1000 Point Club-DE
1000 Point Club-SA
1000 Point Club Gold-DE
1000 Point Club Silver-DE
Canadian Heroes-CSA
Canadian Heroes Gold-CSA
Canadian Heroes Silver-C-SA
Classic Greats-GDS
Classic Greats Gold-GDS
Classic Greats Silver-G-DS
Signs of Greatness-SGDS
03Blackhawks Postcards-23
03Parkhurst Original Six Chicago-47
03Parkhurst Original Six Chicago-75
03Parkhurst Original Six Chicago-81
03Parkhurst Original Six Chicago-96
Autographs-15
Inserts-C5
Inserts-C16
Memorabilia-CM62
03Parkhurst Original Six Montreal-54
Autographs-14
04ITG Franchises Canadian Original Sticks-OS10
04ITG Franchises Cdn Original Sticks Gold-OS10
04ITG Franchises Canadian Teammates-TM8
04ITG Franchises Canadian Teammates Gold-TM8
04ITG Franchises He Shoots/Scores Prizes-21
04ITG Franchises Update-492
04ITG Franchises US West-174
Autographs-A-DSV
Original Sticks-WOS12
Original Sticks Autographs-WOSDS
Original Sticks Gold-WOS12
Teammates-WTM7
Teammates Gold-WTM7
04ITG Ultimate Memorabilia-118
04ITG Ultimate Memorabilia-147
Gold-118
Gold-147
Auto Threads-7
Autographs-21
Autographs Gold-21
Cornerstones-2
Cornerstones Gold-2
Jersey Autographs-40
Jersey Autographs Gold-40
Original Six-15
Original Six-19
Retro Teammates-9
Stick Autographs-43
Stick Autographs Gold-43
04UD Legendary Signatures-27
Autographs-DE
Linemates-SLDEMG
05ITG Ultimate Mem First Rounders Jerseys-3
05ITG Ultimate Mem 1st Round Jersey Gold-3
05ITG Ultimate Mem Pass the Torch Jerseys-11
05ITG Ultimate Mem Passing Torch Jsy Gold-11
05ITG Ultimate Mem Retro Teammate Jerseys-23
05ITG Ultimate Mem Retro Teammate Jerseys-26
05ITG Ult Mem Retro Teammates Jersey Gold-23
05ITG Ult Mem Retro Teammates Jersey Gold-26
05ITG Ultimate Mem 3 Star of the Game Jsy-21
05ITG Ult Mem 3 Star of the Game Jsy Gold-21
05SPx Xcitement Legends-XL-DS
05SPx Xcitement Legends Gold-XL-DS
05SPx Xcitement Legends Spectrum-XL-DS
05The Cup-25
Gold-25
Black Rainbow-25
Honorable Numbers-HNDS2
Masterpiece Pressplates-25
Noble Numbers-NNST
Noble Numbers Dual-DNNHS
Patch Variation-P25
05UD Artifacts-146
Blue-146
Gold-146
Green-146
Pewter-146
Red-146
Auto Facts-AF-DS
Auto Facts Blue-AF-DS
Auto Facts Copper-AF-DS
Auto Facts Pewter-AF-DS
Auto Facts Silver-AF-DS
Frozen Artifacts-FA-SA
Frozen Artifacts Autographed-FA-SA
Frozen Artifacts Copper-FA-SA
Frozen Artifacts Dual-FAD-SA
Frozen Artifacts Dual Autographed-FAD-SA
Frozen Artifacts Dual Copper-FAD-SA
Frozen Artifacts Dual Gold-FAD-SA
Frozen Artifacts Dual Maroon-FAD-SA
Frozen Artifacts Dual Pewter-FAD-SA
Frozen Artifacts Dual Silver-FAD-SA
Frozen Artifacts Gold-FA-SA
Frozen Artifacts Maroon-FA-SA
Frozen Artifacts Patches-FP-SA
Frozen Artifacts Patches Autographed-FP-SA
Frozen Artifacts Patches Dual-FPD-SA
Frozen Artifacts Patches Dual Autos-FPD-SA
Frozen Artifacts Patches Pewter-FP-SA
Frozen Artifacts Patches Silver-FP-SA
Frozen Artifacts Pewter-FA-SA
Frozen Artifacts Silver-FA-SA
Gold Autographed-146
05Ultimate Collection Endorsed Emblems-EESV
05Upper Deck Jerseys-J-DSA
05Upper Deck Trilogy-158
Crystal-158
Legendary Scripts-LEG-DS
Personal Scripts-PER-DS
06Blackhawks Postcards-21
06Parkhurst-132
06Parkhurst-172
Autographs-132
Autographs-172
Autographs Dual-DADR
06SP Authentic Sign of the Times-STDS
06SP Authentic Sign of the Times Duals-STDS
06SP Authentic Sign of the Times Quads-ST4EHSW
06SP Game Used Inked Sweaters-ISDS
06SP Game Used Inked Sweaters Patches-ISDS
06SP Game Used Letter Marks-LMDS
06SP Game Used SIGnificance-SDE
06The Cup Autographed Foundations-CQDS
06The Cup Autographed Foundations Patches-CQDS
06The Cup Foundations-CQDS
06The Cup Foundations Patches-CQDS
06The Cup Honorable Numbers-HNDE
06The Cup Limited Logos-LLDE
06The Cup Scripted Swatches-SSDS
06The Cup Signature Patches-SPDS
06UD Artifacts-133
Blue-133
Gold-133
Platinum-133
Radiance-133
Autographed Radiance Parallel-133
Red-133
Auto-Facts-AFDS
Auto-Facts Gold-AFDS
Tundra Tandems-TTWS
Tundra Tandems Black-TTWS
Tundra Tandems Blue-TTWS
Tundra Tandems Gold-TTWS
Tundra Tandems Platinum-TTWS
Tundra Tandems Red-TTWS
Tundra Tandems Dual Patches Red-TTWS
06Ultimate Collection Signatures-US-DS
06Upper Deck Sweet Shot Signature Shots/Saves Sticks-SSSDS
06Upper Deck Sweet Shot Signature Sticks-STSA
06Upper Deck Trilogy Legendary Scripts-LSDS
06Upper Deck Trilogy Scripts-TSSA

Savard, Frederic
88Richelieu Riverains-27

Savard, Marc
93Oshawa Generals-22
94Parkhurst SE-SE263
Gold-SE263
94SP-182
Die Cuts-182
95Slapshot-250
95Classic-91
97Pinnacle-15
Artist's Proofs-15
Rink Collection-15
Press Plates Back Black-15
Press Plates Back Cyan-15
Press Plates Back Magenta-15
Press Plates Back Yellow-15
Press Plates Front Black-15
Press Plates Front Cyan-15
Press Plates Front Magenta-15
Press Plates Front Yellow-15
97Score-67
Artist's Proofs-67
Golden Blades-67
97Score Rangers-19
Platinum-19
Premier-19
97Hartford Wolf Pack-15
97Bowman CHL-7
OPC-7
98Pacific-300
Ice Blue-300
Red-300
98SPx Finite-54
Radiance-54
Spectrum-54
98UD Choice-133
98UD Choice Preview-133
98UD Choice Prime Choice Reserve-133
98UD Choice Reserve-133
98UD3-21
98UD3-81
98UD3-141
Die-Cuts-21
Die-Cuts-81
Die-Cuts-141
98Upper Deck-132
Exclusives-132
Exclusives 1 of 1-132
Gold Reserve-132
98Hartford Wolf Pack-16
99BAP Memorabilia-224
Gold-224
Silver-224
99Pacific-279
Copper-279
Emerald Green-279
Gold-279
Ice Blue-279
Premiere Date-279
Red-279
99Pacific Dynagon Ice-38
Blue-38
Copper-38
Gold-38
Premiere Date-38
99Pacific Omega-40
Copper-40
Gold-40
Ice Blue-40
Premiere Date-40
99Panini Stickers-194
99SP Authentic-14
99SPx-27
Radiance-27
Spectrum-27
99Stadium Club-167
First Day Issue-167
One of a Kind-167
Printing Plates Black-167
Printing Plates Cyan-167
Printing Plates Magenta-167
Printing Plates Yellow-167
99Upper Deck-196
Exclusives-196
Exclusives 1 of 1-196
99Upper Deck Gold Reserve-196
99Upper Deck HoloGrFx-8
Ausome-8
99Upper Deck Victory-52
99Wayne Gretzky Hockey-28
00Aurora-26
Premiere Date-26
00BAP Memorabilia-183
Emerald-183
Ruby-183
Sapphire-183
Promos-183
00BAP Mem Chicago Sportsfest Copper-183
00BAP Memorabilia Chicago Sportsfest Blue-183
00BAP Memorabilia Chicago Sportsfest Gold-183
00BAP Memorabilia Chicago Sportsfest Ruby-183
00BAP Memorabilia Chicago Sun-Times Ruby-183
00BAP Memorabilia Chicago Sun-Times Gold-183
00BAP Mem Chicago Sun-Times Sapphire-183
00BAP Mem Toronto Fall Expo Copper-183
00BAP Memorabilia Toronto Fall Expo Gold-183
00BAP Memorabilia Toronto Fall Expo Ruby-183
00BAP Parkhurst 2000-P6
00BAP Signature Series-17
Emerald-17
Ruby-17
Sapphire-17
Autographs-176
Autographs Gold-176
00Black Diamond-9
Gold-9
00Crown Royale-19
Ice Blue-19
Limited Series-19
Premiere Date-19
Red-19
Game-Worn Jerseys-5
Game-Worn Jersey Patches-5
Premium-Sized Game-Worn Jerseys-5
00O-Pee-Chee-135
00O-Pee-Chee Parallel-135
00Pacific-73
Copper-73
Gold-73
Ice Blue-73
Premiere Date-73
00Panini Stickers-118
00Paramount-38
Copper-38
Gold-38
Holo-Gold-38
Holo-Silver-38
Ice Blue-38
Premiere Date-38
00SP Authentic-14
00Stadium Club-62
00Titanium-12
Blue-12
Gold-12
Premiere Date-12
Red-12
Retail-12
Game Gear-69
Game Gear Patches-69
00Titanium Draft Day Edition-15
Patches-15
00Topps/OPC-135
Parallel-135
00Topps Heritage-129
00UD Heroes-18
00Upper Deck-28
Exclusives Tier 1-28
Exclusives Tier 2-28
00Upper Deck MVP-32
First Stars-32
Second Stars-32
Third Stars-32
00Upper Deck Victory-41
00Upper Deck Vintage-53
00Vanguard-17
Holographic Gold-17
Holographic Purple-17
Pacific Proofs-17
00German DEL-160
Game Jersey-MS
01Atomic-14
Blue-14
Gold-14
Premiere Date-14
Red-14
Jerseys-6
Patches-6
Team Nucleus-2
01BAP Memorabilia-90
Emerald-90
Ruby-90
Sapphire-90
01BAP Signature Series-32
Autographs-32
Autographs Gold-32
01Crown Royale-23
Blue-23
Premiere Date-23
Red-23
Retail-23
Triple Threads-2
01O-Pee-Chee-128
01O-Pee-Chee Premier Parallel-128
01Pacific-65
Extreme LTD-65
Hobby LTD-65
Premiere Date-65
Retail LTD-65
Jerseys-5
01Pacific Adrenaline-28
Blue-28
Premiere Date-28
Red-28
Retail-28
01Pacific Arena Exclusives-65
01Pacific Heads-Up-13
Blue-13
Premiere Date-13
Red-13
Silver-13
Quad Jerseys-5
01Parkhurst-119
01Private Stock-12
Gold-12
Premiere Date-12
Retail-12
Silver-12
Game Gear-16
Game Gear Patches-16
01Private Stock Pacific Nights-12
01SP Game Used Authentic Fabric-AFSV
01SP Game Used Authentic Fabric-DFIS
01SP Game Used Authentic Fabric Gold-AFMS
01SPx-9
01Stadium Club-83
Award Winners-83
Master Photos-83
Souvenirs-MAS
01Titanium-21
Hobby Parallel-21
Premiere Date-21
Retail-21
Retail Parallel-21
Double-Sided Jerseys-5
Double-Sided Jerseys-7
01Titanium Draft Day Edition-16
01Topps-128
OPC Parallel-128
01Topps Chrome-128
Refractors-128
Black Border Refractors-128
01Topps Heritage-97
Refractors-97
01Topps Reserve Emblems-MSA
01Topps Reserve Jerseys-MSA
01Topps Reserve Name Plates-MSA
01Topps Reserve Numbers-MSA
01Topps Reserve Patches-MSA
01UD Mask Collection Double Patches-DPSA
01UD Mask Collection Jerseys-J-SA
01UD Mask Collection Jersey and Patch-JPSA

01UD Playmakers-14
01Upper Deck-28
Exclusives-28
Ice Jerseys-J-MS
01Upper Deck MVP-28
01Upper Deck Victory-50
Gold-50
01Upper Deck Vintage-36
01Upper Deck Vintage-43
01Vanguard-13
Blue-13
Red-13
Memorabilia-4
Memorabilia-41
One of Ones-13
Patches-41
Premiere Date-13
Proofs-13
02BAP First Edition-61
Jerseys-61
02BAP Sig Series Auto Buybacks 2000-176
02BAP Sig Series Auto Buybacks 2001-32
02O-Pee-Chee-72
02O-Pee-Chee Premier Blue Parallel-72
02O-Pee-Chee Premier Red Parallel-72
02O-Pee-Chee Factory Set-72
02Pacific-59
Blue-59
Red-59
02Pacific Complete-407
Red-407
02Pacific Heads-Up Quad Jerseys-5
02Pacific Heads-Up Quad Jerseys Gold-5
02Parkhurst Retro-124
Minis-124
02SP Game Used Piece of History-PHSA
02SP Game Used Piece of History Gold-PHSA
02SP Game Used Piece of History Rainbow-PHSA
02Topps-72
OPC Blue Parallel-72
OPC Red Parallel-72
Factory Set-72
02Topps Total-164
02UD Piece of History-16
02UD Top Shelf Dual Player Jerseys-STIS
02Upper Deck-23
Exclusives-23
Classic Portraits Hockey Royalty-SIT
Classic Portraits Hockey Royalty Limited-SIT
02Upper Deck MVP-28
Gold-28
Classics-28
Golden Classics-28
02Upper Deck Victory-33
Bronze-33
Gold-33
Silver-33
02Upper Deck Vintage-38
02Upper Deck Vintage-265
Green Backs-38
03Beehive-9
Gold-9
Silver-9
03Black Diamond-121
Black-121
Green-121
Red-121
03Crown Royale-6
Blue-6
Retail-6
03ITG Action-55
03O-Pee-Chee-93
03OPC Blue-93
03OPC Gold-93
03OPC Red-93
03Pacific-21
Blue-21
Red-21
03Pacific Calder-5
Silver-5
03Pacific Complete-258
Red-258
03Pacific Prism-7
Blue-7
Gold-7
Red-7
03Private Stock Reserve-8
Blue-8
Red-8
Retail-8
03Thrashers Postcards-17
03Titanium-7
Hobby Jersey Number Parallels-7
Retail-7
Retail Jersey Number Parallels-7
03Topps-93
Blue-93
Gold-93
Red-93
03Upper Deck-253
Canadian Exclusives-253
HG-253
UD Exclusives-253
03Upper Deck MVP-18
Gold Script-18
Silver Script-18
Canadian Exclusives-18
03Upper Deck Victory-8
Bronze-8
Gold-8
Silver-8
04Pacific-17
Blue-17
Red-17
05Black Diamond-5
Emerald-5
Gold-5
Onyx-5
Ruby-5
05Panini Stickers-11
05Parkhurst-19
Facsimile Auto Parallel-19
Signatures-MS
True Colors-TCATL
05SP Game Used Auto Draft-AD-SV
05Ultra-14
Gold-14
Ice-14
05Upper Deck-10
HG Glossy-10
Jerseys Series II-J2SR
05Upper Deck MVP-19
Gold-19
Platinum-19
05Upper Deck Toronto Fall Expo-10
05Upper Deck Victory-11
Black-11
Gold-11
Silver-11
05German DEL-303
06Be A Player-46
Autographs-46
Signatures-MS
Signatures 10-49
Signatures Duals-DBO
Signatures Trios-TBKS
Signatures Foursomes-FMSRS
Up Close and Personal-UC28
Up Close and Personal Autographs-UC28
06Be A Player Portraits-8
06Beehive Matted Materials-MMSA
06Beehive Signature Scrapbook-SSSA
06Black Diamond-7
Black-7
Gold-7
Ruby-7
06Flair Showcase-10
Parallel-10
Inks-IMS
06Fleer-21
Tiffany-21
Signing Day-SDMS
06O-Pee-Chee-38
Rainbow-38
06Panini Stickers-20
06SP Game Used Authentic Fabrics Dual-AF2SB
06SP Game Used Authentic Fabrics Dual Patches-AF2SB
06SP Game Used Authentic Fabrics Fives-AF5AST
06SP Game Used Authentic Fabrics Fives Patches-AF5AST
06SP Game Used Inked Sweaters-ISSA
06SP Game Used Inked Sweaters Patches-ISSA
06SP Game Used Inked Sweaters Dual-IS2MS
06SP Game Used Inked Sweaters Dual Patches-IS2MS
06SP Game Used SIGnificance-SSA
06UD Artifacts-94
Blue-94
Gold-94
Radiance-94
Red-94
Tundra Tandems-TTMS
Tundra Tandems Black-TTMS
Tundra Tandems Blue-TTMS
Tundra Tandems Gold-TTMS
Tundra Tandems Red-TTMS
Tundra Tandems Dual Patches Red-TTMS
06UD Powerplay Specialists-SMS
06UD Powerplay Specialists Patches-PMS
06Ultra-16
Gold Medallion-16
Ice Medallion-16
Fresh Ink-IMS
06Upper Deck Arena Giveaways-BOS5
06Upper Deck-269
Exclusives Parallel-269
High Gloss Parallel-269
Game Jerseys-JMS
Game Patches-PMS
Masterpieces-269
06Upper Deck MVP-27
Gold Script-27
Super Script-27
Jerseys-OJSD
06Upper Deck Ovation-151
06Upper Deck Sweet Shot Signature Shots/Saves-SSMS
06Upper Deck Trilogy Scripts-TSMS
06Upper Deck Victory-10
06Upper Deck Victory-233
06Upper Deck Victory Black-10
06Upper Deck Victory Gold-10
07Upper Deck Ovation-46
07Upper Deck Victory-62
Black-62
Gold-62

Savard, Marc (minors)
907th Inn. Sketch QMJHL-250
917th Inn. Sketch QMJHL-74
917th Inn. Sketch Memorial Cup-64
917th Inn. Sketch Memorial Cup-130
93Dayton Bombers-9
95Slapshot-250
98German DEL-130
99German DEL-358
01Atomic Patches-6
01German Upper Deck-72
02German DEL City Press-271
03German DEL-28
05Black Diamond Ruby-5

Savard, Mike
91Air Canada SJHL-B21
92Saskatchewan JHL-154

Savard, Ray
86Regina Pats-25

Savard, Serge
64Canadiens Postcards-18
67Canadiens IGA-18
68Canadiens IGA-18
68Canadiens Postcards BW-16
68Post Marbles-23
68Shirriff Coins-91
69Canadiens Postcards Color-28
69O-Pee-Chee-4
69O-Pee-Chee-210
Four-in-One-10
69Topps-4
70Canadiens Pins-15
70Colgate Stamps-74
70Dad's Cookies-118
70Esso Power Players-12
70O-Pee-Chee-51
70Sargent Promotions Stamps-110
70Topps-51
71Canadiens Postcards-22
71O-Pee-Chee-143
71Sargent Promotions Stamps-110
71Toronto Sun-163
72Canadiens Postcards-19
72Dimanche/Derniere Heure *-169
72Dimanche/Derniere Heure *-170
72O-Pee-Chee-185
Team Canada-25
72Sargent Promotions Stamps-123
73Canadiens Postcards-21
73Mac's Milk-25
73O-Pee-Chee-24
73Topps-24
74Canadiens Postcards-22
74Lipton Soup-11
74NHL Action Stamps-162
74O-Pee-Chee NHL-53
74Topps-53
75Canadiens Postcards-17
75O-Pee-Chee NHL-144
75Topps-144
76Canadiens Postcards-20
76O-Pee-Chee NHL-205
76Topps-205
77Canadiens Postcards-22
77O-Pee-Chee NHL-45
77Topps-45
78Canadiens Postcards-24
78O-Pee-Chee-190
78O-Pee-Chee-335
78Topps-190
79Canadiens Postcards-22
79O-Pee-Chee-101
79Topps-101
80Canadiens Postcards-22
80O-Pee-Chee-26
80Pepsi-Cola Caps-57
80Topps-26
81Jets Postcards-15
82Jets Postcards-19
82O-Pee-Chee-390
82Post Cereal-21
83NHL Key Tags-137
85Hall of Fame-256
86Canadiens Postcards-26
87Canadiens Postcards-28
88Canadiens Postcards-25
88Esso All-Stars-41
89Canadiens Postcards-28
90Canadiens Postcards-27
90Upper Deck-506
French-506
91Canadiens Postcards-26
91Future Trends Canada '72-53
91Future Trends Canada '72 French-53
91Kraft-77
92Future Trends '76 Canada Cup-117
93O-Pee-Chee Canadiens Hockey Fest-4
93O-Pee-Chee Canadiens Hockey Fest-11
94Hockey Wit-42
95Parkhurst '66-67-74
Coins-74
95Zeller's Masters of Hockey Signed-6
99BAP Memorabilia AS Canadian Hobby-CH12
99BAP Memorabilia AS Cdn Hobby Autos-CH12
99Upper Deck Century Legends-47
Century Collection-47
00Upper Deck Legends-68
Legendary Collection Bronze-68
Legendary Collection Gold-68
Legendary Collection Silver-68
01BAP Ultimate Memorabilia Decades-18
01BAP Ultimate Mem Dynasty Jerseys-13
01BAP Ultimate Mem Dynasty Emblems-13
01BAP Ultimate Mem Dynasty Numbers-13
01BAP Ultimate Memorabilia Les Canadiens-16
01BAP Ultimate Mem Retro Teammates-9
01BAP Ultimate Mem Stanley Cup Winners-6
01Greats of the Game-85
Autographs-85
01Parkhurst Autographs-PA45
01Topps Archives-53
Arena Seats-ASSSA
Autographs-22
01Upper Deck Legends-32
02BAP Memorabilia Mini Stanley Cups-6
02BAP Ultimate Memorabilia Conn Smythe-4
02BAP Ultimate Memorabilia Numerology-20
02BAP Ultimate Mem Retro Teammates-4
02BAP Ultimate Mem Storied Franchise-9
02Parkhurst Vintage Teammates-VT4
03BAP Ultimate Memorabilia Cornerstones-3
03Canada Post-21
03Parkhurst Original Six Montreal-40
03Parkhurst Original Six Montreal-80
Autographs-15
Memorabilia-MM60
03Topps Stanley Cup Heroes-SS
03Topps Stanley Cup Heroes Autographs-SS
04ITG Franchises Canadian-51
Autographs-SSV
Memorabilia-SM11
Memorabilia Autographs-SM11
Memorabilia Gold-SM11
04ITG Franchises Update-500
04ITG Ultimate Memorabilia-158
Gold-158
Triple Threads-1
04ITG Heroes and Prospects-132
Autographs-SS
Hero Memorabilia-23
04ITG Heroes/Prospects Toronto Expo '05-132
04ITG Heroes/Prospects Expo Heroes/Pros-132
05ITG Ultimate Mem Decades Jerseys-4
05ITG Ultimate Mem Decades Jerseys Gold-4
05ITG Ultimate Mem Pass the Torch Jerseys-8
05ITG Ultimate Mem Passing Torch Jsy Gold-8
05ITG Ultimate Mem 3 Star of the Game Jsy-13
05ITG Ult Mem 3 Star of the Game Jsy Gold-13
05NHL Legends Medallions-18
05ITG Heroes and Prospects Hero Mem-HM-50
06ITG International Ice-131
06ITG International Ice-143
Gold-131
Gold-143
Autographs-ASSV
Autographs-ASSV2
06ITG Ultimate Memorabilia-128
Artist Proof-128
Bowman Factor-8
Bowman Factor Gold-8
Bowman Factor Autos-7
Bowman Factor Autos Gold-7
Boys Will Be Boys-16
Boys Will Be Boys Gold-16
Ring Leaders-15
Ring Leaders Gold-15
Road to the Cup-5
Road to the Cup Gold-5
Stick Rack-10
Stick Rack Gold-10

Savaria, Martin
84Richelieu Riverains-17

Savary, Neil
95Slapshot Memorial Cup-74
00Lubbock Cotton Kings-9

Savary, Paul
99Swiss Panini Stickers-341
01Swiss HNL-337
02Swiss HNL-121

Savchenko, Andrei
99Russian Hockey League-83

Savchenkov, Alexander
95Tallahassee Tiger Sharks-15
98Russian Hockey League-29
99Russian Dynamo Moscow-20
00Russian Dynamo Moscow-18
01Russian Dynamo Moscow-21
01Russian Dynamo Moscow Mentos-3
02Russian SL-48
03Russian Hockey League-39
03Russian National Team-35
03Russian SL-39
04Russian Moscow Dynamo-27

Savelli, Ange
75HCA Steel City Vacuum-22

Savenelli, Scott
93Quebec Pee-Wee Tournament-1295

Savenko, Bogdan
93Niagara Falls Thunder-19
94Indianapolis Ice-21
96Syracuse Crunch-25
98Czech OFS-79
99Czech DS-55
99Czech OFS-244

Saviano, Steve
04Florida Everblades-8
05Florida Everblades-10

Savickij, Alexander
94Czech APS Extraliga-145
98Russian Hockey League-109

Saviels, Agris
99Owen Sound Platers-7
99UD Prospects-16
00Owen Sound Attack-17
01Owen Sound Attack-18
02Hershey Bears-19
03Hershey Bears-17
03Hershey Bears Patriot News-20
04Hershey Bears Patriot News-23

Savijoki, Jarkko
96Finnish SISU Redline-22
98Finnish Keralysarja-68
99Finnish Cardset-38
00German DEL-159
01Finnish Cardset-226

Savilahti-Nagander, Per
05Swedish Lulea Hockey Postcards-23
05Swedish SHL Elitset-233
Gold-233
06Swedish SHL Elitset-215

Saville, John
74Sioux City Musketeers-17

Savilov, Gennady
00Russian Hockey League-257

Savoia, Ryan
95Cleveland Lumberjacks-23
95Cleveland Lumberjacks Postcards-22
96Johnstown Chiefs-18
96Collector's Edge Ice-117
Prism-117
00German DEL-27
01Swiss HNL-317
02Swiss HNL-374

Savoie, Claude
907th Inn. Sketch QMJHL-260
917th Inn. Sketch QMJHL-262
93Classic-147
94Classic Pro Prospects-121
95PEI Senators-18
01UK Nottingham Panthers-8
02Thetford Mines Coyotes-21
03Thetford Mines Prolab-21

Savoie, Jeanot
93Quebec Pee-Wee Tournament-1193

Savoie, Michel
917th Inn. Sketch QMJHL-49
92Quebec Pee-Wee Tournament-1693

Savolainen, Hannu
78Finnish SM-Liiga-130

Savolainen, Kari
93Finnish Jyvas-Hyva Stickers-133
95Finnish SISU-390

Savolainen, Matias
66Finnish Jaakiekkosarja-215

Savolainen, Pertti
78Finnish SM-Liiga-69

Savolainen, Raimo
66Finnish Jaakiekkosarja-214

Savolainen, Risto
66Finnish Jaakiekkosarja-216

Savolainen, Veikko
66Finnish Jaakiekkosarja-172
70Finnish Jaakiekko-253
71Finnish Suomi Stickers-219
73Finnish Jaakiekko-234

Savosin, Maxim
00Russian Hockey League-202

Savstrom, Kjell
65Swedish Coralli ISHockey-185
67Swedish Hockey-42
69Swedish Hockey-55
70Swedish Hockey-15

Savunen, Jukka
66Finnish Jaakiekkosarja-4
70Finnish Jaakiekko-237

Sawa, Matt
04Everett Silvertips-16

Sawatske, Tom
03Wisconsin Badgers-25
04Lincoln Stars-17
04Lincoln Stars Update-48

Sawatzky, Cory
99OCN Blizzard-4

Sawchuk, Terry
44Beehive Group II Photos-65
44Beehive Group II Photos-209
48Exhibits Canadian-62
51Parkhurst-61
52Parkhurst-86
53Parkhurst-46
54Parkhurst-33
54Parkhurst-96
54Parkhurst-100
54Topps-58
55Bruins Photos-15
57Topps-35
58Topps-2
59Topps-42
60Parkhurst-31
60Shirriff Coins-41
61Parkhurst-31
61Shirriff/Salada Coins-77
62York Iron-On Transfers-25
63Parkhurst-53
63Toronto Star-33
63York White Backs-37
64Beehive Group III Photos-181
64Coca-Cola Caps-106
64Topps-6
65Coca-Cola-108
65Topps-12
66Topps-13
68O-Pee-Chee-34
Puck Stickers-20
68Topps-34
69O-Pee-Chee-189
70O-Pee-Chee-231
83Hall of Fame-46
83Hall of Fame Postcards-D13
85Hall of Fame-46
91Bruins Sports Action Legends-27
91Bruins Sports Action Legends-35
91Kraft-75
91Parkhurst PHC-PHC9
91Parkhurst PHC French-PHC9
91Pro Set-343
French-343
92Parkhurst Parkie Reprints-PR2
93High Liner Greatest Goalies-11
93Parkhurst Parkie Reprints-PR37
93Parkhurst Parkie Reprints-PR53
94Hall of Fame Tickets-11
94Hockey Wit-83
94Parkhurst Missing Link-17
94Parkhurst Missing Link-153
94Parkhurst Missing Link-167
94Parkhurst Missing Link-168
94Parkhurst Tall Boys-119
94Parkhurst Tall Boys-154
94Parkhurst Tall Boys-156
94Parkhurst Tall Boys-163
94Parkhurst Tall Boys-177
Mail-Ins-TW4
95Parkhurst '66-67-120
Coins-120
99Upper Deck Century Legends-13
Century Collection-13
All Century Team-AC12
Century Artifacts-C10
99Upper Deck Retro-87
Gold-87
Platinum-87
Generation-G10A
Generation Level 2-G10A
00BAP Memorabilia Goalie Memorabilia-G6
00BAP Memorabilia Goalie Memorabilia-G17
00BAP Memorabilia Goalie Memorabilia-G23
00BAP Memorabilia Goalie Memorabilia-G24
00BAP Memorabilia Goalie Memorabilia-G28
00BAP Memorabilia Update Record Breakers-RB1
00BAP Mem Update Record Breakers Gold-RB1
00BAP Ultimate Mem Goalie Memorabilia-GM2
00BAP Ultimate Mem Goalie Memorabilia-GM19
00BAP Ultimate Mem Goalie Memorabilia-GM20
00BAP Ultimate Memorabilia NHL Records-R1
00BAP Ultimate Memorabilia Retro-Active-RA2
00Upper Deck Legends-43
Legendary Collection Bronze-43
Legendary Collection Gold-43
Legendary Collection Silver-43
Essence of the Game-EG4
of the Cage-LC9
01BAP Memorabilia Goalie Traditions-GT16
01BAP Memorabilia Goalie Traditions-GT22
01BAP Memorabilia Goalie Traditions-GT24
01BAP Memorabilia Goalie Traditions-GT38
01BAP Ultimate Mem All-Star History-13
01BAP Ultimate Memorabilia Calder Trophy-24
01BAP Ultimate Mem Complete Package-9
01BAP Ultimate Memorabilia Cornerstones-4
01BAP Ultimate Memorabilia Decades-3
01BAP Ultimate Memorabilia Emblem Attic-19
01BAP Ultimate Mem Retired Numbers-23
01BAP Ultimate Memorabilia Retro Trophies-9
01BAP Ultimate Memorabilia Retro Trophies-11
01BAP Ultimate Mem Retro Teammates-3
01BAP Ultimate Mem Retro Teammates-8
01BAP Ultimate Mem Stanley Cup Winners-24
01BAP Update Rocket's Rivals-RR-4
01Between the Pipes-124
01Between the Pipes-135
Double Memorabilia-DM24
He Shoots-He Saves Points-20
Jersey and Stick Cards-GSJ42
Record Breakers-RB2
Record Breakers-RB5
Record Breakers-RB15
Trophy Winners-TW6
Trophy Winners-TW14
Vintage Memorabilia-VM6
01Fleer Legacy-30
Ultimate-30
Memorabilia-22
01Greats of the Game-36
Retro Collection-11
Sticks-10
01Parkhurst He Shoots-He Scores Points-9
01Parkhurst He Shoots-He Scores Prizes-39
01Parkhurst Heroes-H3
01Parkhurst Reprints-PR5
01Parkhurst Reprints-PR13
01Parkhurst Reprints-PR21
01Parkhurst Reprints-PR45
01Parkhurst Reprints-PR46
01Parkhurst Reprints-PR87
01Parkhurst Reprints-PR112
01Parkhurst Reprints-PR133
01Parkhurst Vintage Memorabilia-PV25
01Parkhurst Vintage Memorabilia-PV26
01Parkhurst Vintage Memorabilia-PV27
01Topps Archives-69
01UD Stanley Cup Champs-8
Champion Signatures-TS
01Upper Deck Legendary Cut Signatures-LCTS
01Upper Deck Legends-16
01Upper Deck Legends-81
Fiorentino Collection-FCTS
02BAP Memorabilia-233
Emerald-233
Ruby-233
Sapphire-233
Mini Stanley Cups-5
NHL All-Star Game-233
NHL All-Star Game Blue-233
NHL All-Star Game Green-233
NHL All-Star Game Red-233
02BAP Memorabilia Toronto Fall Expo-233
02BAP NHL All-Star History-13
02BAP Ultimate Mem Complete Package-9
02BAP Ultimate Memorabilia Cup Duels-2
02BAP Ultimate Memorabilia Cup Duels-4
02BAP Ultimate Memorabilia Cup Duels-5
02BAP Ultimate Memorabilia Emblem Attic-14
02BAP Ultimate Memorabilia Great Moments-19
02BAP Ultimate Memorabilia Number Ones-10
02BAP Ultimate Memorabilia Numerology-2
02BAP Ultimate Mem Paper Cuts Autos-22
02BAP Ultimate Mem Retro Teammates-10
02BAP Ultimate Memorabilia Retro Trophies-2
02BAP Ultimate Mem Vintage Jerseys-36
02Between the Pipes-114
Complete Package-CP3
Double Memorabilia-19
He Shoots-He Saves Prizes-28
Inspirations-I2
Record Breakers-1
Record Breakers-11
Record Breakers-16
Trappers-GT13
Vintage Memorabilia-16
02ITG Used Goalie Pad and Jersey-GP20
02ITG Used Goalie Pad and Jersey Gold-GP20
02ITG Used Vintage Memorabilia-VM18
02ITG Used Vintage Memorabilia Gold-VM18
02Maple Leafs Platinum Collection-65
02Maple Leafs Platinum Collection-105
02Parkhurst Vintage Memorabilia-VM16
02Parkhurst Vintage Teammates-VT6
02Topps Heritage Reprint Relics-TS
02Topps Heritage Reprints-TS
02UD Mask Collection Mini Masks-TS
03BAP Memorabilia Brush with Greatness-19
03BAP Mem Brush with Greatness Contest C-19
03BAP Memorabilia Vintage Memorabilia-VM-7
03BAP Ultimate Memorabilia Cornerstones-7
03BAP Ultimate Memorabilia Emblem Attic-14
03BAP Ultimate Mem Emblem Attic Gold-14
03BAP Ultimate Memorabilia Heroes-9
03BAP Ultimate Mem Hometown Heroes-18
03BAP Ultimate Mem Hometown Heroes Gold-18
03BAP Ultimate Memorabilia Paper Cuts-19
03BAP Ultimate Mem Retro Teammates-3
03BAP Ultimate Mem Retro-Active Trophies-6
03BAP Ultimate Memorabilia Triple Threads-8
03BAP Ultimate Mem Vint Complete Package-1
03BAP Ultimate Mem Vint Comp Package Gold-1
03BAP Ultimate Memorabilia Vintage Lumber-9
03Canada Post-8
03ITG VIP Collages-32
03ITG VIP Vintage Memorabilia-13
03Parkhurst Original Six Boston-54
03Parkhurst Original Six Detroit-35
03Parkhurst Original Six Detroit-61
03Parkhurst Original Six Detroit-87
03Parkhurst Original Six Detroit-94
03Parkhurst Original Six Detroit-95
Inserts-D-1
Inserts-D-7
Memorabilia-DM25
Memorabilia-DM29
Memorabilia-DM34
Memorabilia-DM37
Memorabilia-DM52
03Parkhurst Orig Six He Shoots/Scores-26
03Parkhurst Orig Six He Shoots/Scores-26A
03Parkhurst Orig Six New York Mem-NM21
03Parkhurst Original Six Toronto-35
Inserts-T13
Memorabilia-TM21
03Parkhurst Rookie-58
Before the Mask-BTM-11
Before the Mask Gold-BTM-11
Records-RRE-8
Records Gold-RRE-8
ROYalty-VR-11
ROYalty Gold-VR-11
04ITG NHL AS FANtasy AS History Jerseys-SB13
04ITG Franchises Update-455
04ITG Franchises Update-493
Goalie Gear-UGG2
Goalie Gear Gold-UGG2
Original Sticks-UOS4
Original Sticks Gold-UOS4
04ITG Franchises US East-406
04ITG Franchises US West-213
04ITG Franchises US West-233
Double Memorabilia-WDM15
Double Memorabilia Gold-WDM15
Forever Rivals-WFR5
Forever Rivals Gold-WFR5
Memorabilia-WSM26
Memorabilia Gold-WSM26
Teammates-WTM10
Teammates Gold-WTM10
04ITG Ultimate Memorabilia-79
04ITG Ultimate Memorabilia-111
04ITG Ultimate Memorabilia-194
Gold-79
Gold-111
Gold-194
Calder Trophy-5
Complete Package-2
Cornerstones-1
Cornerstones Gold-1
Day In History-16
Day In History-35
Day In History-45
Day In History Gold-16
Day In History Gold-35
Day In History Gold-45
Goalie Gear-16
Jerseys-8
Jerseys Gold-8
Motown Heroes-5
Nicknames-6
Original Six-1
Original Six-8
Original Six-17
Retro Teammates-6
Vezina Trophy-2
Vintage Lumber-15
04UD Legends Classics Jersey Redemptions-JY9
04UD Legends Classics Jersey Redemptions-JY20
04ITG Heroes and Prospects-165
04ITG Heroes/Prospects Toronto Expo '05-165
04ITG Heroes/Prospects Expo Heroes/Pros-165
05Between the Pipes-18
Complete Package-CP-5
05ITG Ultimate Memorabilia Level 1-92
05ITG Ultimate Memorabilia Level 2-92
05ITG Ultimate Memorabilia Level 3-92
05ITG Ultimate Memorabilia Level 4-92
05ITG Ultimate Memorabilia Level 5-92
05ITG Ultimate Mem Complete Jersey-13
05ITG Ultimate Mem Complete Jersey Gold-13
05ITG Ultimate Mem Complete Package-7
05ITG Ultimate Mem Complete Package Gold-7
05ITG Ultimate Memorabilia Emblem Attic-12
05ITG Ultimate Mem Emblem Attic Gold-12
05ITG Ultimate Memorabilia Jerseys-37
05ITG Ultimate Memorabilia Jerseys Gold-37
05ITG Ultimate Memorabilia Lumbergraphs-3
05ITG Ultimate Mem Pass the Torch Jerseys-4
05ITG Ultimate Mem Passing Torch Jsy Gold-4
05ITG Ultimate Mem Record Breaker Jerseys-11
05ITG Ultimate Mem Record Breaker Jerseys-12
05ITG Ultimate Mem Record Breaker Jerseys-14
05ITG Ultimate Mem RecBreak Jerseys Gold-11
05ITG Ultimate Mem RecBreak Jerseys Gold-12
05ITG Ultimate Mem RecBreak Jerseys Gold-14
05ITG Ultimate Mem Ult Hero Double Jersey-1
05ITG Ult Mem Ult Hero Double Jersey Gold-1
05ITG Ultimate Mem Ult Hero Single Jersey-1
05ITG Ult Mem Ult Hero Single Jersey Gold-1
05ITG Ultimate Mem Ult Hero Triple Jersey-1
05ITG Ult Mem Ult Hero Triple Jersey Gold-1
05ITG Ultimate Memorabilia Vintage Lumber-6
05ITG Ultimate Mem Vintage Lumber Gold-6
05NHL Legends Medallions-19
05ITG Heroes and Prospects He Shoots-He Scores Prizes-49
06Between The Pipes-132
06Between The Pipes-135
06Between The Pipes-144
Complete Package-CP07
Complete Package Gold-CP07
Double Jerseys-DJ07
Double Jerseys-DJ19
Double Jerseys Gold-DJ07
Double Jerseys Gold-DJ19
Double Memorabilia-DM16
Double Memorabilia Gold-DM16
Emblems-GUE49
Emblems Gold-GUE49
Jerseys-GUJ49
Jerseys Gold-GUJ49
Numbers-GUN49
Numbers Gold-GUN49
Shooting Gallery-SG02
Shooting Gallery-SG06
Shooting Gallery-SG09
Shooting Gallery Gold-SG02
Shooting Gallery Gold-SG06
Shooting Gallery Gold-SG09
Stick and Jersey-SJ31
Stick and Jersey Gold-SJ31
06ITG Ultimate Memorabilia-136
Artist Proof-136
Complete Package-7
Complete Package Gold-7
Decades-8
Decades Gold-8
Lumbergraphs-1
Motown Heroes Autos-1
Passing The Torch-11
Passing The Torch Gold-11
Retro Teammates-3
Retro Teammates Gold-3
Road to the Cup-1
Road to the Cup-3
Road to the Cup Gold-1
Road to the Cup Gold-3
Seams Unbelievable-3
Seams Unbelievable Gold-3
Stick Rack-11
Stick Rack Gold-11
Triple Thread Jerseys-10
Triple Thread Jerseys Gold-10
Ultimate Hero Single Jerseys-2
Ultimate Hero Single Jerseys Gold-2
Ultimate Hero Double Jerseys-2
Ultimate Hero Double Jerseys Gold-2
Ultimate Hero Triple Jerseys-2
Ultimate Hero Triple Jerseys Gold-2
Vintage Lumber-4
Vintage Lumber Gold-4
06ITG Heroes and Prospects Heroes Memorabilia-HM19
06ITG Heroes and Prospects Heroes Memorabilia Gold-HM19
07Maple Leafs 1967 Commemorative-22

Sawchuk, Wayne
95Alaska Gold Kings-18

Sawka, Ryan
05Everett Silvertips-20

Sawtell, Drew
88Saskatoon Blades-15
89Saskatoon Blades-14

Sawyer, Dan
94Johnstown Chiefs-18

Sawyer, Jean-Claude
02Cape Breton Screaming Eagles-6
03Cape Breton Screaming Eagles-12
04Cape Breton Screaming Eagles-16
05Cape Breton Screaming Eagles-11
06Cape Breton Screaming Eagles-10

Sawyer, Justin
06Toronto Marlies-26

Sawyer, Kevin
93Spokane Chiefs-22
94Spokane Chiefs-9
96Providence Bruins-25
01BAP Memorabilia-432
Emerald-432
Ruby-432
Sapphire-432
01SP Authentic-133
Limited-133
Limited Gold-133
01SP Game Used-63
01SPx-93
01UD Challenge for the Cup-93
01Upper Deck-414
Exclusives-414
01Upper Deck Vintage-273
02Topps Heritage-114
03ITG Action Jerseys-M74
03Topps Signs of Toughness-KS
03Topps Tough Materials-KS
03Topps Tough Materials-KSRL
03Topps Tough Materials Signed-KS

Saxby, Tony
94UK Humberside Hawks-14

Sayde, Carlos
99Halifax Mooseheads-3

Sayler, Curtis
98Port Huron Border Cats-4
99Missouri River Otters-18
99Missouri River Otters Sheet-16

Sayther, Crystal
04Ohio State Buckeyes Women-7
05Ohio State Buckeyes Women-2

Saywell, Josh
04Kootenay Ice-20

Sbrocca, Christian
90Montreal-Bourassa AAA-24
96Pensacola Ice Pilots-16
03St. Jean Mission-24

Sbrocca, Sandro
00Victoriaville Tigres-12
Signed-12

Scally, Mark
02Johnstown Chiefs-14

Scalzo Jr., Mario
03Victoriaville Tigers-23
03Victoriaville Tigers-NNO
04Victoriaville Tigers-17
05Iowa Stars-23
06Iowa Stars-19

Scalzo, Michael
93Quebec Pee-Wee Tournament-40

Scamurra, Peter
79Capitals Team Issue-19

Scandella, Giulio
00Halifax Mooseheads-21
01Halifax Mooseheads-11

Scanlan, Derek
94Thunder Bay Senators-3

Scanlan, Fred
83Hall of Fame-118
83Hall of Fame Postcards-H13
85Hall of Fame-118

Scantlebury, Stu
90Brandon Wheat Kings-17
907th Inn. Sketch WHL-233
917th Inn. Sketch WHL-211
92Tacoma Rockets-20

Scantlebury, Thomas
96Kamloops Blazers-22
97Lethbridge Hurricanes-15
99Lethbridge Hurricanes-23
00Lethbridge Hurricanes-21

Scanu, Michael
94German First League-549

Scanzano, Jason
92Saskatchewan JHL-142

Scanzano, Shawn
93Quebec Pee-Wee Tournament-31
99Rimouski Oceanic-15
Signed-15
99Rouyn-Noranda Huskies-18
00Rouyn-Noranda Huskies-23
Signed-23
03Tulsa Oilers-17

Scanzano, Wesley
93Quebec Pee-Wee Tournament-30
98Quebec Remparts-19
Signed-19
99Quebec Remparts-7
Signed-7
99Bowman CHL-51
Gold-51
OPC International-51
00QMJHL All-Star Program Inserts-11
00Rouyn-Noranda Huskies-18
Signed-18
03Tulsa Oilers-18

Scaparotti, T.J.
93Quebec Pee-Wee Tournament-649

Scapinello, Marco
92Finnish Semic-257

Scapinello, Ray
90Pro Set-697

Scardocchio, Enrico
917th Inn. Sketch QMJHL-171

Scatch, Clifford
99OCN Blizzard-19
00OCN Blizzard-17

Scatchard, Dave
93Portland Winter Hawks-22
95Signature Rookies-54
Signatures-54
96Syracuse Crunch-21
97Be A Player-234
Autographs-234
Autographs Die-Cuts-234
Autographs Prismatic Die-Cuts-234
97Pacific Omega-235
Copper-235
Dark Gray-235
Emerald Green-235
Gold-235
Ice Blue-235
97SP Authentic-161
98Pacific-433
Ice Blue-433
Red-433
98Paramount-239
Copper-239
Emerald Green-239
Holo-Electric-239
Ice Blue-239
Silver-239
98UD Choice-209
98UD Choice Preview-209
98UD Choice Prime Choice Reserve-209
98UD Choice Reserve-209
99Pacific-431
Copper-431
Emerald Green-431
Gold-431
Ice Blue-431
Premiere Date-431
Red-431
99Upper Deck MVP SC Edition-113
Gold Script-113
Silver Script-113
Super Script-113
00O-Pee-Chee-150
00O-Pee-Chee Parallel-150
00Pacific-255
Copper-255
Gold-255
Ice Blue-255
Premiere Date-255
00Topps/OPC-150
Parallel-150
00Upper Deck-340
Exclusives Tier 1-340
Exclusives Tier 2-340
00Upper Deck MVP-110
First Stars-110
Second Stars-110
Third Stars-110
00Upper Deck Victory-143
01O-Pee-Chee-200
01O-Pee-Chee Premier Parallel-200
01Pacific-253
Extreme LTD-253
Hobby LTD-253
Premiere Date-253
Retail LTD-253
01Pacific Arena Exclusives-253
01Topps-200
OPC Parallel-200
01Upper Deck-341
Exclusives-341
01Upper Deck MVP-122
01Upper Deck Victory-224
Gold-224
01Upper Deck Vintage-162
01Upper Deck Vintage-165
02Pacific Complete-89
Red-89
02Topps Total-373
02Upper Deck-355
Exclusives-355
02Upper Deck Beckett UD Promos-355
02Upper Deck Vintage-161
03ITG Action-365
03O-Pee-Chee-98
03OPC Blue-98
03OPC Gold-98
03OPC Red-98
03Pacific-215
Blue-215
Red-215
03Topps-98
Blue-98
Gold-98
Red-98
03Topps C55-116
Minis-116
Minis American Back-116
Minis American Back Red-116
Minis Bazooka Back-116
Minis Brooklyn Back-116
Minis Hat Trick Back-116
Minis O Canada Back-116
Minis O Canada Back Red-116
Minis Stanley Cup Back-116
03Upper Deck MVP-266
Gold Script-266
Silver Script-266
Canadian Exclusives-266
03Upper Deck Victory-116
Bronze-116
Gold-116
Silver-116
05Parkhurst-375
Facsimile Auto Parallel-375
05Upper Deck MVP-42
Gold-42
Platinum-42
06O-Pee-Chee-376
Rainbow-376

Scatchard, Doug

03Roanoke Express-317
Scerban, Bedrich
89Swedish Semic World Champ Stickers-182
91Finnish Semic World Champ Stickers-105
91Swedish Semic World Champ Stickers-105
92Swedish Semic Elitserien Stickers-53
93Swedish Semic Elitserien-28
93Swedish Semic World Champ Stickers-93
94Finnish Jaa Kiekko-174
94Swedish Leaf-25
95Czech APS Extraliga-358
95Swedish Leaf-17
Face to Face-2
95Swedish Upper Deck-20
95Swedish World Championships Stickers-191
96Czech APS Extraliga-217
97Czech DS Stickers-7
97Czech DS Stickers-24
99German DEL-364
Sceviour, Darin
85Nova Scotia Oilers-19
Schaal, Jurgen
94German DEL-121
95German DEL-121
96German DEL-61
Schachle, Trent
96Dayton Bombers-12
99Adirondack IceHawks-8
Schack, Brian
06Minnesota Golden Gophers-19
Schaden, Mario
93Swedish Semic World Champ Stickers-288
94Finnish Jaa Kiekko-246
95Austrian National Team-25
95Swedish World Championships Stickers-269
Schadler, Herbert
94German First League-58
Schadler, Thomas
94German DEL-422
Schaefer, Jeremy
95Saskatoon Blades-19
98Roanoke Express-16
Schaefer, Nolan
03BAP Memorabilia-217
03ITG Used Signature Series-185
Gold-185
03ITG VIP Rookie Debut-100
03Parkhurst Rookie-89
03Upper Deck Rookie Update-149
03Fresno Falcons-18
04Cleveland Barons-21
05ITG Heroes/Prosp Toronto Expo Parallel -240
05Cleveland Barons-20
05ITG Heroes and Prospects-240
Autographs Series II-NS
Schaefer, Peter
94Brandon Wheat Kings-19
95Brandon Wheat Kings-17
95Classic-14
95Slapshot Memorial Cup-47
96Black Diamond-88
Gold-88
96Upper Deck Ice-135
96Brandon Wheat Kings-15
97Collector's Choice-297
97Donruss Limited-142
Exposure-142
97Bowman CHL-118
OPC-118
98Pacific Omega-242
Red-242
Opening Day Issue-242
98Upper Deck MVP-208
Gold Script-208
Silver Script-208
Super Script-208
99BAP Memorabilia-355
Gold-355
Silver-355
99BAP Millennium Calder Candidates Ruby-C28
99BAP Millennium Calder Candidate Emerald-C28
99BAP Millennium Calder Cand Sapphire-C28
99Crown Royale-139
Limited Series-139
Premiere Date-139
Prospects Parallel-139
99Pacific-432
Copper-432
Emerald Green-432
Gold-432
Ice Blue-432
Premiere Date-432
Red-432
99Pacific Omega-239
Copper-239
Gold-239
Ice Blue-239
Premiere Date-239
99Pacific Prism-145
Holographic Blue-145
Holographic Gold-145
Holographic Mirror-145
Holographic Purple-145
Premiere Date-145
Ice Prospects-10
99Panini Stickers-314
99Panini Stickers-353
99SP Authentic-86
99Topps Gold Label Class 1-90
Black-90
Black One of One-90
One of One-90
Red-90
Red One of One-90
99Topps Gold Label Class 2-90
99Topps Gold Label Class 2 Black-90
99Topps Gold Label Class 2 Black 1 of 1-90
99Topps Gold Label Class 2 One of One-90
99Topps Gold Label Class 2 Red-90
99Topps Gold Label Class 2 Red One of One-90
99Topps Gold Label Class 3-90
99Topps Gold Label Class 3 Black-90
99Topps Gold Label Class 3 Black 1 of 1-90
99Topps Gold Label Class 3 One of One-90
99Topps Gold Label Class 3 Red-90
99Topps Gold Label Class 3 Red One of One-90
99Topps Premier Plus-128
Parallel-128
Premier Rookies-PR3
Premier Rookies Parallel-PR3
Signing Bonus-SB3
99Ultimate Victory-87
1/1-87
Parallel-87
Parallel 100-87
99Upper Deck Arena Giveaways-VC2
99Upper Deck Victory-302
99Wayne Gretzky Hockey-172
00BAP Memorabilia-395
Emerald-395
Ruby-395
Sapphire-395
Promos-395
00BAP Mem Chicago Sportsfest Copper-395
00BAP Memorabilia Chicago Sportsfest Blue-395
00BAP Memorabilia Chicago Sportsfest Gold-395
00BAP Memorabilia Chicago Sportsfest Ruby-395
00BAP Memorabilia Chicago Sun-Times Ruby-395
00BAP Memorabilia Chicago Sun-Times Gold-395
00BAP Mem Chicago Sun-Times Sapphire-395
00BAP Mem Toronto Fall Expo Copper-395
00BAP Memorabilia Toronto Fall Expo Gold-395
00BAP Memorabilia Toronto Fall Expo Ruby-395
000-Pee-Chee-168
000-Pee-Chee Parallel-168
00Pacific-415
Copper-415
Gold-415
Ice Blue-415
Premiere Date-415
00Stadium Club-128
00Topps/OPC-168
Parallel-168
00Upper Deck-397
Exclusives Tier 1-397
Exclusives Tier 2-397
01BAP Signature Series-86
Autographs-86
Autographs Gold-86
010-Pee-Chee-157
010-Pee-Chee Premier Parallel-157
01Pacific-386
Extreme LTD-386
Hobby LTD-386
Premiere Date-386
Retail LTD-386
01Pacific Arena Exclusives-386
01Parkhurst-189
01Topps-157
OPC Parallel-157
01Upper Deck-171
Exclusives-171
01Upper Deck Victory-347
Gold-347
01Upper Deck Vintage-246
01Finnish Cardset-356
02BAP Sig Series Auto Buybacks 2001-86
02NHL Power Play Stickers-107
02Senators Team Issue-9
02Finnish Cardset-113
03ITG Action-441
03Pacific Complete-335
Red-335
03Senators Postcards-10
03Titanium-72
Hobby Jersey Number Parallels-72
Retail-72
Retail Jersey Number Parallels-72
03Upper Deck-134
Canadian Exclusives-134
HG-134
03Upper Deck MVP-298
Gold Script-298
Silver Script-298
Canadian Exclusives-298
05Parkhurst-338
Facsimile Auto Parallel-338
05Upper Deck-382
05Upper Deck MVP-276
Gold-276
Platinum-276
060-Pee-Chee-341
Rainbow-341
06Senators Postcards-12
06Upper Deck-386
Exclusives Parallel-386
High Gloss Parallel-386
Masterpieces-386
06Upper Deck MVP-210
Gold Script-210
Super Script-210
Schaefer, Rik
94German First League-381
Schaeffer, Jeff
95Swift Current Broncos-13
96Swift Current Broncos-9
97Swift Current Broncos-11
Schaeffer, Kevin
03Boston University Terriers-13
Schaeffler, James
91Air Canada SJHL-B2
Schaeufl, Michael
94German First League-202
Schafer, Didier
96Swiss HNL-223
01Swiss HNL-338
02Swiss HNL-462
Schafer, Evan
02Prince Albert Raiders-20
03Prince Albert Raiders-9
04Prince Albert Raiders-4
05Prince Albert Raiders-19
Schafer, Mike
92Western Michigan Broncos-21
Schafer, Paxton
95Medicine Hat Tigers-17
95Classic-41
97Donruss-201
Press Proofs Silver-201
Press Proofs Gold-201
Rated Rookies-2
Medallist-2
97Donruss Canadian Ice-133
Dominion Series-133
Provincial Series-133
97Donruss Limited-142
Exposure-142
97Pacific Dynagon Best Kept Secrets-8
97Upper Deck-183
97Charlotte Checkers-4
Schafer, Stephan
94German First League-420
Schafer, Steven
94German First League-134
Schaffer, Ryan
92British Columbia JHL-169
Schafhauser, Bill
93Swiss HNL-118
95Swiss HNL-168
Schafhauser, Pat
93Swiss HNL-119
95Swiss HNL-141
Schahlin, Anders
69Swedish Hockey-141
Schai, Sylvio
93Swiss HNL-455
Schalker, Haie
94German First League-539
Schaller, Pascal
93Swiss HNL-54
95Swedish World Championships Stickers-132
95Swiss HNL-79
96Swiss HNL-222
98Swiss Power Play Stickers-97
99Swiss Panini Stickers-98
00Swiss Panini Stickers-143
00Swiss Slapshot Mini-Cards-HCFG13
01Swiss HNL-339
02Swiss HNL-349
04Swiss Lausanne HC Postcards-1
Schaltegger, Daniel
93Swiss HNL-129
Schambeck, Thomas
94German First League-339
Schamehorn, Kevin
87Flint Spirits-17
89ProCards IHL-75
Schank, Peter
84Swedish Semic Elitserien-96
Scharf, Chad
03Vancouver Giants-5
04Vancouver Giants-21
Scharf, Chris
917th Inn. Sketch OHL-231
Scharf, Jeff
01Kalamazoo K-Wings-6
03Fort Worth Brahmas-13
Scharf, Marco
94German First League-513
Scharff, Chad
05Vancouver Giants-20
Scharpf, Robert
94German First League-111
Schastlivy, Petr
99BAP Memorabilia-340
Gold-340
Silver-340
99Pacific Omega-162
Copper-162
Gold-162
Ice Blue-162
Premiere Date-162
99Grand Rapids Griffins-22
99IHL All-Stars-8
00BAP Memorabilia-238
Emerald-238
Ruby-238
Sapphire-238
Promos-238
00BAP Mem Chicago Sportsfest Copper-238
00BAP Memorabilia Chicago Sportsfest Blue-238
00BAP Memorabilia Chicago Sportsfest Gold-238
00BAP Memorabilia Chicago Sportsfest Ruby-238
00BAP Memorabilia Chicago Sun-Times Ruby-238
00BAP Memorabilia Chicago Sun-Times Gold-238
00BAP Mem Chicago Sun-Times Sapphire-238
00BAP Mem Toronto Fall Expo Copper-238
00BAP Memorabilia Toronto Fall Expo Gold-238
00BAP Memorabilia Toronto Fall Expo Ruby-238
00BAP Signature Series-267
Emerald-267
Ruby-267
Sapphire-267
Autographs-229
Autographs Gold-229
000-Pee-Chee-311
000-Pee-Chee Parallel-311
00Pacific-291
Copper-291
Gold-291
Ice Blue-291
Premiere Date-291
00Titanium-136
Retail-136
00Titanium Draft Day Edition-136
00Titanium Draft Day Promos-136
00Topps/OPC-311
Parallel-311
00Topps Chrome-206
OPC Refractors-206
Refractors-206
00Upper Deck MVP-200
First Stars-200
Second Stars-200
Third Stars-200
00Upper Deck Victory-276
00Upper Deck Vintage-256
00Grand Rapids Griffins-20
01BAP Memorabilia-120
Emerald-120
Ruby-120
Sapphire-120
010-Pee-Chee-285
010-Pee-Chee Premier Parallel-285
01Topps-285
OPC Parallel-285
01Grand Rapids Griffins-11
02BAP Signature Series-133
Autographs-133
Autograph Buybacks 2000-229
Autographs Gold-133
02NHL Power Play Stickers-111
020-Pee-Chee-301
020-Pee-Chee Premier Blue Parallel-301
020-Pee-Chee Premier Red Parallel-301
020-Pee-Chee Factory Set-301
02Senators Team Issue-12
02SP Authentic-126
02Topps-301
OPC Blue Parallel-301
OPC Red Parallel-301
Factory Set-301
02Upper Deck-368
Exclusives-368
02Upper Deck Beckett UD Promos-368
03ITG Action-434
03Pacific Complete-96
Red-96
03Senators Postcards-13
Schaublin, Jarkko
01Swiss HNL-478
Schaublin, Olivier
01Swiss HNL-468
02Swiss HNL-442
Schauer, Stefan
02German DEL City Press-207
04German DEL-255
04German Nuremburg Ice Tigers Postcards-15
05German DEL-280
06German DEL-168
06German DEL-192
Schefer, Marc
01Swiss HNL-153
02Swiss HNL-311
Scheffelmaier, Brett
97Medicine Hat Tigers-16
98Medicine Hat Tigers-18
99Medicine Hat Tigers-20
99Medicine Hat Tigers-27
00Medicine Hat Tigers-20
02Worcester IceCats-14
03Peoria Rivermen-4
03Worcester Ice Cats-23
Scheidegger, Kim
01Swiss HNL-467
02Swiss HNL-392
Scheidegger, Ueli
93Swiss HNL-364
95Swiss HNL-214
96Swiss HNL-127
Scheidt, Tyler
91Air Canada SJHL-A34
Scheifele, Steve
90ProCards AHL/IHL-44
91Richmond Renegades-15
91Richmond Renegades Set 2-12
Schell, Brad
00Spokane Chiefs-24
01Spokane Chiefs-20
02Spokane Chiefs-19
04Gwinnett Gladiators-22
Schell, Seth
93Quebec Pee-Wee Tournament-773
Schella, John
71Canucks Royal Bank-19
71Toronto Sun-288
727-Eleven Slurpee Cups WHA-17
73Quaker Oats WHA-7
75Houston Aeros WHA-17
750-Pee-Chee WHA-21
760-Pee-Chee WHA-128
Schellenberg, Marco
93Swiss HNL-396
93Swiss HNL-485
95Swiss HNL-308
98Swiss Power Play Stickers-316
Schembri, Andrew
03Ohio State Buckeyes-17
04Ohio State Buckeyes-11
05Ohio State Buckeyes-13
06Ohio State Buckeyes-12
Schenderling, Jeremy
03Kootenay Ice-16
04Swift Current Broncos-18
05Swift Current Broncos-20
06Swift Current Broncos-22
Schenkel, Mathias
93Swiss HNL-105
95Swiss HNL-309
96Swiss HNL-291
98Swiss Power Play Stickers-121
99Swiss Panini Stickers-123
Schenkel, Thomas
02German Adler Mannheim Eagles Postcards-2
05German DEL-311
06German DEL-37
Schenn, Andy
02Spokane Chiefs-20
05Regina Pats-21
Schenn, Luke
05Kelowna Rockets-23
Schepers, Aaron
04Vernon Vipers-16
Scherban, Joel
00London Knights-12
04Lakehead University Thunderwolves-1
Scherer, Matt
02Tri-City Stormfront-12
Scherger, Scott
01Spokane Chiefs-21
02Spokane Chiefs-21
Scherping, Karsten
94German First League-464
Schertz, Jan
94German DEL-48
95German DEL-42
96German DEL-41
01German Berlin Polar Bears Postcards-22
01German Upper Deck-42
Scheucher, Thomas
93Quebec Pee-Wee Tournament-1540
Scheuer, Marc
93Quebec Pee-Wee Tournament-17
Scheuer, Tyson
92British Columbia JHL-225
Schev, Alexander
99Russian Hockey League-134
00Russian Hockey League-270
Schewchuk, Jack
400-Pee-Chee V301-2-126
Schiavo, Jay
93Birmingham Bulls Birmingham News-18
Schichtl, Hans
72Finnish Hellas-59
72Finnish Semic World Championship-97
72Swedish Semic World Championship-97
Schiebel, Brian
91British Columbia JHL-58
92British Columbia JHL-43
Schier, Jan
94German First League-395
Schiestel, Drew
05Mississauga Ice Dogs-4
06Mississauga Ice Dogs-20
Schiff, Ted
93Quebec Pee-Wee Tournament-1743
Schiffel, Heinrich
92Finnish Semic-177
Schiffl, Heinrich
94German DEL-387
95German DEL-368
96German DEL-190
98German DEL-126
99German DEL-282
Schill, Dave
89Kitchener Rangers-10
Schill, Jonathan
98Kingston Frontenacs-18
99Kingston Frontenacs-16
01Syracuse Crunch-23
02Syracuse Crunch-12
Schill, Lee
91British Columbia JHL-137
Schiller, Peter
82Swedish Semic VM Stickers-111
83Swedish Semic VM Stickers-111
Schillgard, Johan
91Swedish Semic Elitserien Stickers-50
Schilling, Paul
72Finnish Semic World Championship-135
72Swedish Semic World Championship-135
Schilstrom, Bo
71Swedish Hockey-368
Schilstrom, Nils-Olov
67Swedish Hockey-192
69Swedish Hockey-250
70Swedish Hockey-144
71Swedish Hockey-238
72Swedish Stickers-215
73Swedish Stickers-70
74Swedish Stickers-186
Schimm, Willi
99German DEL-414
Schindler, Maximilian
94German First League-176
Schinkel, Chris
91Air Canada SJHL-C43
92Saskatchewan JHL-32
Schinkel, Ken
44Beehive Group II Photos-360
52Juniors Blue Tint-26
60Shirriff Coins-96
60Topps-50
61Shirriff/Salada Coins-99
63Topps-62
680-Pee-Chee-106
68Shirriff Coins-135
68Topps-106
690-Pee-Chee-117
Four-in-One-1
69Topps-117
70Colgate Stamps-61
70Dad's Cookies-119
70Esso Power Players-227
700-Pee-Chee-92
70Sargent Promotions Stamps-174
70Topps-92
71Bazooka-33
710-Pee-Chee-64
71Penguins Postcards-18
71Sargent Promotions Stamps-162
71Topps-64
71Toronto Sun-227
720-Pee-Chee-256
72Sargent Promotions Stamps-170
Schinko, Marco
94German DEL-62
Schinko, Thomas
91Finnish Semic World Champ Stickers-170
91Swedish Semic World Champ Stickers-170
92Finnish Semic-188
94Finnish Jaa Kiekko-289
95German DEL-62
96German DEL-258
98German DEL-121
99German DEL-68
02German DEL City Press-272
03German DEL-86
Schinkothe, Jan
94German First League-374
Schioldan, Christian
98Danish Hockey League-138
99Danish Hockey League-165
Schira, Craig
04Regina Pats-23
05Regina Pats-22
06Regina Pats-19
Schistad, Rob
92Norwegian Elite Series-127
93Swedish Semic World Champ Stickers-230
94Finnish Jaa Kiekko-252
95Swedish World Championships Stickers-237
96Czech APS Extraliga-121
96Swedish Semic Wien-201
97Czech DS Stickers-56
98German DEL-222
99German DEL-210
99Norwegian National Team-1
Schlagenhauf, Peter
93Swiss HNL-28
95Swiss HNL-310
96Swiss HNL-292
Schlapfer, Kevin
93Swiss HNL-257
95Swiss HNL-256
96Swiss HNL-336
00Swiss Panini Stickers-298
01Swiss HNL-318
02Swiss HNL-143
Schlegel, Brad
85London Knights-21
86London Knights-8
90Alberta International Team Canada-8
91Alberta International Team Canada-20
91Capitals Kodak-24
91Parkhurst-413
French-413
92OPC Premier-28
92Parkhurst-199
Emerald Ice-199
92Score-477
Canadian-477
Canadian Olympians-9
92Stadium Club-29
92Topps-377
Gold-377G
92Upper Deck-101
94Score Team Canada-CT18
95German DEL-133
95Swedish World Championships Stickers-4
00German DEL-221
02German DEL City Press-208
03German DEL-179
04German Cologne Sharks Postcards-25
04German DEL-220
05German DEL-217
06German DEL-87
Schlemko, David
04Medicine Hat Tigers-20
05Medicine Hat Tigers-20
06Medicine Hat Tigers-19
Schlender, Graham
03UK Coventry Blaze-9
03UK Coventry Blaze Calendars-6
04UK Coventry Blaze-15
04UK Coventry Blaze Champions-11
Schlenker, Chris
01Regina Pats-20
02Regina Pats-15
03Regina Pats-15
04Prince Albert Raiders-20
Schlickenrieder, Josef
89Swedish Semic World Champ Stickers-104
94German DEL-148
95German DEL-126
99German Bundesliga 2-40
Schliebener, Andy
81Fredericton Express-19
82Fredericton Express-19
83Fredericton Express-22
840-Pee-Chee-329
84Fredericton Express-24
85Fredericton Express-18
Schloder, Alois
72Finnish Hellas-52
72Finnish Semic World Championship-107
72Swedish Semic World Championship-107
79Panini Stickers-107
Schlosser, Tomas
93Quebec Pee-Wee Tournament-1703
Schluttenhofer, Ottmar
94German First League-54
Schlyter, Per
98Amarillo Rattlers-16
Schmalz, Kevin
89Brandon Wheat Kings-18
907th Inn. Sketch WHL-236
Schmautz, Bobby
69Seattle Totems-17
71Canucks Royal Bank-12
71Toronto Sun-289
72Canucks Royal Bank-16
720-Pee-Chee-181
72Sargent Promotions Stamps-219
73Canucks Royal Bank-16
730-Pee-Chee-35
73Topps-35
74NHL Action Stamps-25
740-Pee-Chee NHL-27
740-Pee-Chee NHL-117
74Topps-27
74Topps-117
750-Pee-Chee NHL-251
75Topps-251
760-Pee-Chee NHL-189
76Topps-189
770-Pee-Chee NHL-59
77Topps-59
780-Pee-Chee-248
78Topps-248
79Oilers Postcards-21
790-Pee-Chee-144
79Topps-144
80Canucks Silverwood Dairies-23
80Canucks Team Issue-19
80Pepsi-Cola Caps-117
88Oilers Tenth Anniversary-160
Schmautz, Brian
06Okotoks Oilers -17
Schmautz, Cliff
70Esso Power Players-78
700-Pee-Chee-142
70Sargent Promotions Stamps-29
Schmeisser, Egon
04German Berlin Eisbarens 50th Anniv-9
Schmid, Dominik
95Swiss HNL-319
Schmid, Florian
94German First League-220
Schmid, Marcel
95Swiss HNL-326
96Swiss HNL-301
Schmid, Sven
95Swiss HNL-270
96Swiss HNL-389
98Swiss Power Play Stickers-298
99Swiss Panini Stickers-303
00Swiss Panini Stickers-297
01Swiss HNL-307
Schmid, Udo
94German DEL-365
99German Bundesliga 2-97
Schmidgall, Jenny
98Minnesota Golden Gophers Women-20
Schmidt, Andre
94German First League-373
Schmidt, Bryan
06Manchester Monarchs-3
Schmidt, Chris
907th Inn. Sketch WHL-152
917th Inn. Sketch WHL-268
93Seattle Thunderbirds-22
95Seattle Thunderbirds-26
99Mississippi Sea Wolves Kelly Cup-17
00Lowell Lock Monsters-14
01Manchester Monarchs-7A
02BAP Memorabilia-351
02BAP Ultimate Memorabilia-35
02Upper Deck Rookie Update-124
02Manchester Monarchs-27
03Manchester Monarchs-15
03Manchester Monarchs Team Issue-15
04Manchester Monarchs-3
04Manchester Monarchs Tobacco-4
05German DEL-72
Schmidt, Darren
82Brandon Wheat Kings-5
91Air Canada SJHL-E11
92Saskatchewan JHL-31
93Kitchener Rangers-22
Schmidt, Don
84Prince Albert Raiders Stickers-21
85Kamloops Blazers-21
86Kamloops Blazers-19
87Kamloops Blazers-20
88Kamloops Blazers-21
Schmidt, Doug
92Quebec Pee-Wee Tournament-1567
95Waterloo Blackhawks -19
Schmidt, Greg
95Red Deer Rebels-15
96Red Deer Rebels-10
99ECHL All-Star Southern Conference-8
01Colorado Gold Kings-17
02Pee Dee Pride RBI-146
Schmidt, Jack
34Beehive Group I Photos-30
51Laval Dairy QSHL-69
51Laval Dairy Subset-69
52St. Lawrence Sales-17A
Schmidt, Jeff
93St. Cloud State Huskies-26
00Prince Albert Raiders-21
01Prince Albert Raiders-17
03Everett Silvertips-13
Schmidt, Jeff (NCAA)
93St. Cloud State Huskies-26
Schmidt, Joe
51Bas Du Fleuve-7
Schmidt, Kevin
00Indianapolis Ice-19
01Fort Wayne Komets-17
02Fort Wayne Komets-16
02Fort Wayne Komets Shoe Carnival-14
03Fort Wayne Komets-14
03Fort Wayne Komets Shoe Carnival-2
Schmidt, Markus
05German DEL-317
Schmidt, Michael
91Finnish Semic World Champ Stickers-158
91Swedish Semic World Champ Stickers-158
93Swedish Semic World Champ Stickers-152
94German DEL-299
95German DEL-336
04German Hamburg Freezers Postcards-17
Schmidt, Mikkel
98Danish Hockey League-42
99Danish Hockey League-201
Schmidt, Milt
34Beehive Group I Photos-31
36Providence Reds-8
400-Pee-Chee V301-2-132
43Parade Sportive *-3
51Parkhurst-29
52Parkhurst-70
53Parkhurst-92
54Parkhurst-59
54Topps-60
57Bruins Photos-18
60Shirriff Coins-120
63Topps-1
64Topps-70
65Topps-96
74Capitals White Borders-23
83Hall of Fame-165
83Hall of Fame Postcards-L16
85Hall of Fame-165
91Bruins Sports Action Legends-28
91Bruins Sports Action Legends-29
91Bruins Sports Action Legends-36
92Parkhurst Parkie Reprints-PR23
93Parkhurst Parkie Reprints Case Inserts-2
94Hall of Fame Tickets-12
94Kollectorfest-3
94Parkhurst Missing Link-21
94Parkhurst Tall Boys-22
98Bruins Alumni-15
Autographs-15
99Upper Deck Century Legends-26
Century Collection-26
00Topps Heritage Arena Relics-OSA-MS
01BAP Signature Series Vintage Autographs-VA-11
01Parkhurst Autographs-PA7
01Parkhurst Reprints-PR72
01Parkhurst Reprints-PR117
01Parkhurst Reprints-PR123
01Topps Archives-62
02Topps Rookie Reprints-10
02Topps Rookie Reprint Autographs-10
03BAP Ultimate Mem Linemates Autos-3
03Parkhurst Original Six Boston-37
03Parkhurst Original Six Boston-67
03Parkhurst Original Six Boston-76
03Parkhurst Original Six Boston-90
Autographs-18
Inserts-B2
Inserts-B9
04Canada Post-28
04Canada Post Autographs-4
04ITG Franchises US East-309
04ITG Ultimate Memorabilia-96
04ITG Ultimate Memorabilia-105
Gold-96
Gold-105
Autographs-63
Autographs Gold-63
Beantown's Best-2
04ITG Heroes and Prospects-129
Autographs-MSC
04ITG Heroes/Prospects Toronto Expo '05-129
04ITG Heroes/Prospects Expo Heroes/Pros-129
05ITG Heroes/Prosp Toronto Expo Parallel -11
05ITG Ultimate Memorabilia Level 1-72
05ITG Ultimate Memorabilia Level 2-72
05ITG Ultimate Memorabilia Level 3-72
05ITG Ultimate Memorabilia Level 4-72
05ITG Ultimate Memorabilia Level 5-72
05ITG Ultimate Memorabilia Double Autos-16
05ITG Ultimate Mem Double Autos Gold-16
05ITG Ultimate Memorabilia Ultimate Autos-7
05ITG Ultimate Mem Ultimate Autos Gold-7
05ITG Heroes and Prospects-11
Autographs-A-MSH
06ITG Ultimate Memorabilia-106
Artist Proof-106
Complete Jersey-14
Complete Jersey Gold-14
Cornerstones-7
Cornerstones Gold-7
Emblem Attic-1
Emblem Attic Gold-1
In The Numbers-20
In The Numbers Gold-20
Jerseys-12
Jerseys Gold-12
Legendary Captains-16
Legendary Captains Gold-16
Passing The Torch-10
Passing The Torch Gold-10
Raised to the Rafters-8
Raised to the Rafters Gold-8
Retro Teammates-2
Retro Teammates Gold-2
Seams Unbelievable-5
Seams Unbelievable Gold-5
Triple Thread Jerseys-8
Triple Thread Jerseys Gold-8
06Parkhurst-110
06Parkhurst-161
Autographs-110
Autographs-161
Autographs Dual-DASB
06The Cup Hardware Heroes-HHMS
06The Cup Stanley Cup Signatures-CSMS
06The Cup Stanley Cup Titlists-TMS
06ITG Heroes and Prospects-2
Autographs-AMSC
Heroes Memorabilia-HM11
Heroes Memorabilia Gold-HM11
Schmidt, Moritz
94German DEL-40
99German Bundesliga 2-256
Schmidt, Norm
80Oshawa Generals-13
81Oshawa Generals-7
82Oshawa Generals-21
83Penguins Coke-17
86Penguins Kodak-22
Schmidt, Rob
84Nanaimo Clippers-17
94German First League-248
Schmidt, Ryan
95Slapshot-327
Schmiess, Trevor
91Air Canada SJHL-A26
Schmitt, Brandon
99Sioux City Musketeers-20
00Sioux City Musketeers-23
Schmitz, Christian
94German DEL-80
95German DEL-313
96German DEL-96
98German DEL-13
Schmitz, Holger
94German First League-505
Schmitz, Michael
94German First League-421
Schmitz, Patrick
94German First League-552
Schmitz, Sven
94German First League-519
Schmutzler, Jurgen
04German Berlin Eisbarens 50th Anniv-42
Schnabel, Mattias
94German First League-570
Schnabel, Robert
97Red Deer Rebels-19
01BAP Memorabilia-337
Emerald-337
Ruby-337
Sapphire-337
01Parkhurst-326
01SPx-208
01Czech DS-32
01Milwaukee Admirals-24
01Milwaukee Admirals Postcards-1
02Milwaukee Admirals-7
02Milwaukee Admirals Postcards-14
03Pacific Complete-587
Red-587
04Czech HC Sparta Praha Postcards-20
04Czech OFS-199
Stars-49
05Finnish Cardset -189
06Finnish Cardset-196
Enforcers-4
Schnarr, Werner
24C144 Champ's Cigarettes-53
24V145-2-26
Schneeberger, Andre
95Swiss HNL-443
Schneekloth, Aaron
02ECHL All-Star Southern-53
02South Carolina Stingrays-16
02South Carolina Stingrays RBI-219
03Grand Rapids Griffins-19
04New Mexico Scorpions-8
04New Mexico Scorpions-23
06Colorado EaglesA -19
Schnegg, Jean-Luc
93Swiss HNL-489
95Swiss HNL-369
96Swiss HNL-227
Schneidawind, Michael
96German DEL-200
Schneider, Andreas
94German DEL-371
95German DEL-369
95German DEL-437
Schneider, Andrew
907th Inn. Sketch WHL-55
91Upper Deck Czech World Juniors-56
917th Inn. Sketch WHL-174
93Donruss-468
94Swedish Leaf-217
94Classic Pro Prospects-170
98German DEL-212
99German DEL-215
00German DEL-183
00Lincoln Stars-4
01German Upper Deck-192
02German DEL City Press-100
All-Stars-AS14
03German DEL-118
All-Stars-AS17
03North Dakota Fighting Sioux-16
04German DEL-54
04German Dusseldorf Metro Stars Postcards-18
04North Dakota Fighting Sioux-22
05German DEL-73
05WBS Penguins-23
Schneider, Andy
05WBS Penguins-23
Schneider, Bjorn
93Swiss HNL-195
95Swiss HNL-12
96Swiss HNL-12
98Swiss Power Play Stickers-34
01Swiss HNL-308
02Swiss HNL-138
Schneider, Buzz
81Swedish Semic Hockey VM Stickers-106
95Signature Rookies Miracle on Ice-29
95Signature Rookies Miracle on Ice-30
95Signature Rook Miracle on Ice Sigs-29
95Signature Rook Miracle on Ice Sigs-30
04UD Legendary Signatures Miracle Men-USA4
04UD Legendary Sigs Miracle Men Autos-USA-BZ
Schneider, Daniel
95Swiss HNL-271
96Swiss HNL-390
Schneider, David
93Quebec Pee-Wee Tournament-1325
03Finnish Cardset-159
04Finnish Cardset-172
04Finnish Cardset Signatures-35
05Finnish Cardset -202
06Finnish Cardset-27
Schneider, Eric
95Tri-City Americans-22
99Knoxville Speed-14
00Johnstown Chiefs-14
01Johnstown Chiefs-22
03Las Vegas Wranglers-16
03Las Vegas Wranglers RBI-238
06German DEL-88
Schneider, Florian
94German First League-112
Schneider, Geoff
87Kingston Canadians-27
Schneider, Jean-Alain
907th Inn. Sketch OHL-46
91Cornwall Royals-12
917th Inn. Sketch OHL-10
92Birmingham Bulls-14
93Birmingham Bulls-14
93Birmingham Bulls Birmingham News-19
98Columbus Cottonmouths-16
Schneider, Mathieu
89Canadiens Kraft-20
89ProCards AHL-199
90Bowman-52
Tiffany-52
90Canadiens Postcards-28
900-Pee-Chee-372
90Panini Stickers-60
90Pro Set-158
90Score-127
Canadian-127
90Score Young Superstars-18
90Topps-372
Tiffany-372
90Upper Deck-334
French-334
91Bowman-343
91Canadiens Panini Team Stickers-21
91Canadiens Postcards-27
910-Pee-Chee-392
91OPC Premier-181
91Panini Stickers-195
91Parkhurst-88
French-88
91Pinnacle-209
French-209
91Pro Set-119
French-119
91Score American-105
91Score Canadian Bilingual-105
91Score Canadian English-105
91Stadium Club-262
91Topps-392
91Upper Deck-328
French-328
91Finnish Semic World Champ Stickers-137
91Swedish Semic World Champ Stickers-137

92Bowman-190
92Canadiens Postcards-26
92O-Pee-Chee-166
92Panini Stickers-157
92Panini Stickers French-157
92Parkhurst-319
Emerald Ice-319
92Pinnacle-79
French-79
92Pro Set-91
92Score-69
Canadian-69
92Stadium Club-70
92Topps-253
Gold-253G
92Ultra-110
92Upper Deck-545
93Canadiens Molson-10
93Canadiens Postcards-24
93Donruss-179
93Leaf-53
93OPC Premier-163
Gold-163
93Panini Stickers-22
93Parkhurst-373
Emerald Ice-373
93Pinnacle-37
Canadian-37
Team 2001-27
Team 2001 Canadian-27
93PowerPlay-134
93Score-18
Canadian-18
93Stadium Club-391
Members Only Master Set-391
First Day Issue-391
Master Photos-23
Master Photos Winners-23
93Topps/OPC Premier-163
Gold-163
93Ultra-78
93Upper Deck-31
93Swedish Semic World Champ Stickers-177
94Canada Games NHL POGS-142
94Canadiens Postcards-24
94Donruss-233
94EA Sports-68
94Fleer-109
94Leaf-195
94Leaf Limited-101
94OPC Premier-181
Special Effects-181
94Parkhurst Vintage-V32
94Parkhurst SE-SE92
Gold-SE92
94Pinnacle-56
Artist's Proofs-56
Rink Collection-56
94Score-103
Gold-103
Platinum-103
94Select-23
Gold-23
94Topps/OPC Premier-181
Special Effects-181
94Ultra-114
94Upper Deck-101
Electric Ice-101
95Bashan Super Stickers-75
95Be A Player-20
Signatures-S20
Signatures Die Cuts-S20
95Bowman-81
All-Foil-81
95Canada Games NHL POGS-176
95Collector's Choice-322
Player's Club-322
Player's Club Platinum-322
95Donruss-55
95Emotion-108
95Finest-56
Refractors-56
95Imperial Stickers-75
95Leaf-67
95Metal-93
95Panini Stickers-99
95Parkhurst International-130
Emerald Ice-130
95Pinnacle-28
Artist's Proofs-28
Rink Collection-28
95Playoff One on One-64
95Pro Magnets-60
95Score-206
Black Ice Artist's Proofs-206
Black Ice-206
95Select Certified-8
Mirror Gold-8
95SkyBox Impact-105
95SP-89
95Stadium Club-59
Members Only Master Set-59
95Summit-25
Artist's Proofs-25
Ice-25
95Topps-36
OPC Inserts-36
95Topps SuperSkills-6
Platinum-6
95Ultra-99
95Ultra-270
Gold Medallion-99
95Upper Deck-161
Electric Ice-161
Electric Ice Gold-161
95Zenith-21
96Collector's Choice-262
96Donruss-18
Press Proofs-18
96Donruss Canadian Ice-97
Gold Press Proofs-97
Red Press Proofs-97
96Donruss Elite-88
Die Cut Stars-88
96Leaf-190
Press Proofs-190
96Metal Universe-153
96NHL Pro Stamps-60
96Pinnacle-124
Artist's Proofs-124
Foil-124
Premium Stock-124
Rink Collection-124
96Playoff One on One-343
96Post Upper Deck-20
96Score-115
Artist's Proofs-115
Dealer's Choice Artist's Proofs-115
Special Artist's Proofs-115
Golden Blades-115
96SP-155
96Stadium Club Members Only-44
96Summit-30
Artist's Proofs-30
Ice-30
Metal-30
Premium Stock-30
96Team Out-81
96Topps Picks-53
OPC Inserts-53
96Upper Deck-343
97Be A Player-206
Autographs-206
Autographs Die-Cuts-206
Autographs Prismatic Die-Cuts-206
97Donruss Canadian Ice-116
Dominion Series-116
Provincial Series-116
97Donruss Priority-34
Stamp of Approval-34
97Katch-143
Gold-143
Silver-143
97Pacific-179
Copper-179
Emerald Green-179
Ice Blue-179
Red-179
Silver-179
97Pacific Omega-224
Copper-224
Dark Gray-224
Emerald Green-224
Gold-224
Ice Blue-224
97Pinnacle-150
Press Plates Back Black-150
Press Plates Back Cyan-150
Press Plates Back Magenta-150
Press Plates Back Yellow-150
Press Plates Front Black-150
Press Plates Front Cyan-150
Press Plates Front Magenta-150
Press Plates Front Yellow-150
97Score-160
Artist's Proofs-160
Golden Blades-160
97Score Maple Leafs-10
Platinum-10
Premier-10
97Upper Deck-372
98Aurora-184
98Be A Player-239
Press Release-239
98BAP Gold-239
98BAP Autographs-239
98BAP Autographs Gold-239
98Katch-140
98Kraft Peanut Butter-7
98Pacific-72
Ice Blue-72
Red-72
98Paramount-230
Copper-230
Emerald Green-230
Holo-Electric-230
Ice Blue-230
Silver-230
98UD Choice-198
Prime Choice Reserve-198
Reserve-198
99BAP Memorabilia-101
Gold-101
Silver-101
99Pacific-280
Copper-280
Emerald Green-280
Gold-280
Ice Blue-280
Premiere Date-280
Red-280
99Panini Stickers-104
00BAP Memorabilia-431
Emerald-431
Ruby-431
Sapphire-431
00O-Pee-Chee-264A
00O-Pee-Chee Parallel-264A
00Pacific-270
Copper-270
Gold-270
Ice Blue-270
Premiere Date-270
00Topps/OPC-264A
Parallel-264A
01BAP Memorabilia-270
Emerald-270
Ruby-270
Sapphire-270
01BAP Signature Series-159
Autographs-159
Autographs Gold-159
01Pacific-187
Extreme LTD-187
Hobby LTD-187
Premiere Date-187
Retail LTD-187
01Pacific Adrenaline-89
Blue-89
Premiere Date-89
Red-89
Retail-89
01Pacific Arena Exclusives-187
01Upper Deck-310
Exclusives-310
01Upper Deck MVP-87
02BAP First Edition-170
02BAP Memorabilia-327
02BAP Sig Series Auto Buybacks 1998-239
02BAP Sig Series Auto Buybacks 2001-159
02Kings Game Sheets-19
02Kings Game Sheets-20
02Pacific-174
Blue-174
Red-174
02Pacific Complete-139
Red-139
02Topps Total-139
02Upper Deck-329
Exclusives-329
02Upper Deck Beckett UD Promos-329
02Upper Deck MVP-86
Gold-86
Classics-86
Golden Classics-86
02Upper Deck Rookie Update-40
02Upper Deck Victory-101
Bronze-101
Gold-101
Silver-101
02Upper Deck Vintage-117
03ITG Action-252
03NHL Sticker Collection-236
03O-Pee-Chee-112
03OPC Blue-112
03OPC Gold-112
03OPC Red-112
03Pacific-125
Blue-125
Red-125
03Pacific Complete-375
Red-375
03Parkhurst Original Six Detroit-1
03Topps-112
Blue-112
Gold-112
Red-112
03Upper Deck-68
Canadian Exclusives-68
HG-68
03Upper Deck MVP-147
Gold Script-147
Silver Script-147
Canadian Exclusives-147
05Be A Player Signatures-DT
05Be A Player Signatures Gold-DT
05Parkhurst-174
Facsimile Auto Parallel-174
05SP Game Used Authentic Fabrics Quad-FRRG
05Upper Deck-318
05Upper Deck MVP-150
Gold-150
Platinum-150
06O-Pee-Chee-177
Rainbow-177
06Panini Stickers-262
06Upper Deck-322
Exclusives Parallel-322
High Gloss Parallel-322
Masterpieces-322
06Upper Deck MVP-110
Gold Script-110
Super Script-110

Schneider, Patrik
93Quebec Pee-Wee Tournament-1538

Schneider, Raphael
95Swiss HNL-352
96Swiss HNL-325

Schneider, Rato
93Swiss HNL-231

Schneider, Rochus
94German DEL-123
95German DEL-24
96German DEL-21

Schneider, Roland
94German First League-329

Schneider, Sascha
95Swiss HNL-80
98Swiss Power Play Stickers-220
99Swiss Panini Stickers-220
00Swiss Panini Stickers-264
00Swiss Slapshot Mini-Cards-EVZ15
02Swiss HNL-334

Schneider, Scott
87Moncton Hawks-22
88ProCards AHL-177
89ProCards AHL-52
90Moncton Hawks-21
90ProCards AHL/IHL-260
91ProCards-362

Schneider, Stephan
95Swiss HNL-243
96Swiss HNL-456
98Swiss Power Play Stickers-35

Schneider, Tim
03Memphis RiverKings-19
06Bloomington PrairieThunder-19

Schneider, Wes
96Lethbridge Hurricanes-18

Schneitberger, Otto
72Finnish Hellas-44
72Finnish Semic World Championship-105
72Swedish Semic World Championship-105

Schnelle, Tim
00German DEL-231

Schnetz, Richard
94German First League-105

Schnitzer, Florian
04German DEL-238
04German Krefeld Penguins Postcards-19
05German DEL-330
06German DEL-76

Schnitzler, Armin
94German First League-496

Schnobrich, Tim
94German DEL-22
95German DEL-182

Schnoz, Roger
93Swiss HNL-296

Schnuriger, Ronald
93Quebec Pee-Wee Tournament-1624

Schnyder, Daniel
02Swiss HNL-380

Schnyder, Fabian
04Swiss EV Zug Postcards-21

Schnyder, Stefan
01Swiss HNL-21

Schocher, Mario
92Quebec Pee-Wee Tournament-1626
96Swiss HNL-120
96Swiss HNL-491
98Swiss Power Play Stickers-71
98Swiss Power Play Stickers-287
99Swiss Panini Stickers-74
00Swiss Panini Stickers-121
00Swiss Slapshot Mini-Cards-HCD15
01Swiss HNL-340

Schock, Harold
93Michigan Wolverines-20

Schock, Ron
64Beehive Group III Photos-25
64Coca-Cola Caps-17
65Topps-36
66Topps-100
68O-Pee-Chee-118
68Shirriff Coins-147
68Topps-118
69O-Pee-Chee-120
Four-in-One-13
69Topps-120
70Colgate Stamps-42
70Esso Power Players-229
70O-Pee-Chee-91
Deckle-9
70Sargent Promotions Stamps-170
70Topps-91
Topps/OPC Sticker Stamps-29
71Letraset Action Replays-23
71O-Pee-Chee-56
71Penguins Postcards-19
71Sargent Promotions Stamps-170
71Topps-56
71Toronto Sun-228
72O-Pee-Chee-81
72Sargent Promotions Stamps-179
72Topps-59
73O-Pee-Chee-200
73Topps-113
74Lipton Soup-43
74NHL Action Stamps-226
74O-Pee-Chee NHL-167
74Penguins Postcards-20
74Topps-167
75O-Pee-Chee NHL-75
75O-Pee-Chee NHL-326
75Topps-75
75Topps-326
76O-Pee-Chee NHL-248
76O-Pee-Chee NHL-392
76Topps-248
77O-Pee-Chee NHL-51
77Topps-51
78O-Pee-Chee-384
79Rochester Americans-16
94Parkhurst Tall Boys-21
95Parkhurst '66-67-13
Coins-13

Schockenmaier, Chad
99Kamloops Blazers-20
00Kamloops Blazers-20

Schockey, Parry
94Spokane Chiefs-27

Schoder, Matthias
01Swiss HNL-383
02Swiss HNL-35

Schoen, Brian
93Toledo Storm-28
94Central Hockey League-33
95Louisiana Ice Gators-14
01BC Icemen-21

Schoenfeld, Jim
72O-Pee-Chee-220
72Sabres Pepsi Pinback Buttons-8
72Sabres Postcards-18
72Sargent Promotions Stamps-41
73O-Pee-Chee-86
73O-Pee-Chee-137
73Sabres Postcards-12
73Topps-5
73Topps-86
74NHL Action Stamps-37
74O-Pee-Chee NHL-121
74Sabres Postcards-20
74Topps-121
75O-Pee-Chee NHL-138
75Sabres Linnett-11
75Topps-138
76O-Pee-Chee NHL-241
76Sabres Glasses-4
76Topps-241
77O-Pee-Chee NHL-108
77Topps-108
78O-Pee-Chee-178
78Topps-178
79O-Pee-Chee-171
79Sabres Bells-8
79Topps-171
80O-Pee-Chee-96
80Topps-96
81Sabres Milk Panels-6
82O-Pee-Chee-94
82O-Pee-Chee Stickers-183
82Post Cereal-5
82Topps Stickers-183
83NHL Key Tags-29
83O-Pee-Chee-59
83O-Pee-Chee Stickers-136
83Puffy Stickers-8
83Topps Stickers-136
85Sabres Blue Shield-25
85Sabres Blue Shield Small-25
88Devils Caretta-25
90Upper Deck-505
French-505
93Sabres Noco-19
95Capitals Team Issue-23
02Fleer Throwbacks-13
Gold-13
Platinum-13
Autographs-7
Squaring Off-4
Squaring Off Memorabilia-4
02Rangers Team Issue-14
05Hartford Wolf Pack-25
06Parkhurst-111
06Parkhurst-165
Autographs-111
Autographs-165

Schoenroth, Todd
91Air Canada SJHL-E42

Schofield, Dave
88ProCards IHL-42

Schofield, Dwight
84O-Pee-Chee-191

Scholz, Dirk
94German First League-512

Scholz, Kris
98Minnesota Golden Gophers Women-21

Scholz, Norbert
94German First League-390

Scholz, Olaf
94German DEL-108
95German DEL-330
96German DEL-108
99German Bundesliga 2-18

Schoneck, Drew
917th Inn. Sketch WHL-161
92Tacoma Rockets-21
00Columbus Cottonmouths-16
01Prince Albert Raiders-18
02Fresno Falcons-15
03Fresno Falcons-19
04Las Vegas Wranglers-21

Schoneck, Scott
97Moose Jaw Warriors-13
05Las Vegas Wranglers-19
06Las Vegas Wranglers-20

Schonenberger, Lovis
01Swiss HNL-479
02Swiss EV Zug Postcards-15
02Swiss HNL-242
03Swiss EV Zug Postcards-21
04Swiss Lausanne HC Postcards-21

Schonfeld, Marc
94German First League-83

Schonfelder, Paul
03Rockford Ice Hogs-15

Schonhaar, Marcel
93Swiss HNL-397

Schonmoser, Christian
95German DEL-342
99German DEL-43
01German Upper Deck-208
02German DEL City Press-273
03German Nuremberg Ice Tigers Postcards-24

Schooley, Derek
92Western Michigan Broncos-22
93Western Michigan Broncos-25
94Huntington Blizzard-18

Schoop, Raphael
02Swiss HNL-431

Schopf, Patrick
93Swedish Semic World Champ Stickers-110
93Swiss HNL-111
95Swiss HNL-160
96Swiss HNL-54
98Swiss Power Play Stickers-203
99Swiss Panini Stickers-204
00Swiss Panini Stickers-247
00Swiss Slapshot Mini-Cards-EVZ2
01Swiss EV Zug Postcards-4
01Swiss HNL-169
02Swiss EV Zug Postcards-6
02Swiss HNL-214
03Swiss EV Zug Postcards-22

Schopper, Benedikt
04German DEL-162
04German Hannover Scorpions Postcards-24
05German DEL-337

Schork, Eric
93Quebec Pee-Wee Tournament-774

Schraeder, Chad
91British Columbia JHL-14
92British Columbia JHL-203

Schramm, Dietmar
94German First League-542

Schramm, Josef
72Finnish Semic World Championship-94
72Swedish Semic World Championship-94

Schraner, Patrick
93Quebec Pee-Wee Tournament-1623

Schrapp, Dennis
94German DEL-30
95German DEL-3

Schraven, Tobias
95German DEL-373

Schreiber, Wally
81Regina Pats-16
94Score Team Canada-CT22
94German DEL-261
95German DEL-258
96German DEL-146
98German DEL-66
99German DEL-230
00German DEL-93
Profiles-P4
01German Upper Deck-101
02German DEL City Press-121
02German DEL City Press-122
03German DEL All-Stars-AS14
05German DEL-338

Schremp, Rob
00Quebec Pee Wee Tournament-1347
02Mississauga Ice Dogs-16
03London Knights-1
04London Knights-4
04ITG Heroes and Prospects-100
Autographs-RSC
Emblems-62
Emblems Gold-62
Jerseys-62
Jerseys Gold-62
Numbers-62
Numbers Gold-62
Top Prospects-11
04ITG Heroes/Prospects Toronto Expo '05-100
04ITG Heroes/Prospects Expo Heroes/Pros-100
05Extreme Top Prospects Signature Edition-S8
05London Knights-1
05OHL Bell All-Star Classic-37
05ITG Heroes and Prospects-115
Aspiring-ASP7
Autographs-A-RSC
Complete Jerseys-CJ-11
Complete Jerseys Gold-CJ-11
Complete Logos-CHL-20
He Shoots-He Scores Prizes-27
Jerseys-GUJ-38
Jerseys Gold-GUJ-38
Emblems-GUE-38
Emblems Gold-GUE-38
Numbers-GUN-38
Numbers Gold-GUN-38
Memorial Cup-MC-2
Nameplates-N-14
Nameplates Gold-N-14
Spectrum-STM-04
Spectrum Gold-STM-04
06ITG International Ice-138
Gold-138
Autographs-ARS
06ITG Ultimate Memorabilia Future Star-13
06ITG Ultimate Memorabilia Future Star Gold-13
06ITG Ultimate Memorabilia Future Star Autos-4
06ITG Ultimate Memorabilia Future Star Autos Gold-4
06ITG Ultimate Memorabilia Future Star Patches Autos-4
06ITG Ultimate Memorabilia Future Star Patches Autos Gold-4
06AHL Top Prospects-47
06Wilkes-Barre Scranton Penguins-16
06Wilkes-Barre Scranton Penguins Jerseys-22
06ITG Heroes and Prospects-173
Autographs-ARSC
Complete AHL Logos-AHL14
Jerseys-GUJ72
Emblems-GUE72
Numbers-GUN72
Quad Emblems-QE07
Quad Emblems-QE11
Quad Emblems Gold-QE07
Update Autographs-ARSC
07Upper Deck Ovation-29
07Upper Deck Victory-210
Black-210
Gold-210

Schremp, Tyler
06Richmond Renegades-14

Schrepfer, Rolf
93Swiss HNL-456
95Swiss HNL-335
96Swiss HNL-311
98Swiss Power Play Stickers-244
99Swiss Panini Stickers-246
00Swiss Panini Stickers-287
00Swiss Slapshot Mini-Cards-ZSCL15
01Swiss HNL-94
02Swiss HNL-82

Schriefer, R.J.
95North Iowa Huskies-29

Schriner, Dave
34Beehive Group I Photos-249
34Beehive Group I Photos-346
35Diamond Matchbooks Tan 1-60
35Diamond Matchbooks Tan 2-57
35Diamond Matchbooks Tan 3-53
36Champion Postcards-4
36O-Pee-Chee V304D-98
37V356 Worldwide Gum-58
39O-Pee-Chee V301-1-14
40O-Pee-Chee V301-2-122
45Quaker Oats Photos-46
55Parkhurst-27
Quaker Oats-27
83Hall of Fame Postcards-J13
85Hall of Fame-236
02BAP Ultimate Mem Paper Cuts Autos-11
02Maple Leafs Platinum Collection-66
03BAP Ultimate Mem Maple Leafs Forever-18
03BAP Ultimate Memorabilia Paper Cuts-33
04ITG Franchises US East-368
04ITG Ultimate Memorabilia-97
Gold-97
Paper Cuts-3
05ITG Ultimate Mem Amazing Amerks Autos-5
06ITG Ultimate Memorabilia Amazing Amerks Autos-3

Schriner, Marty
91Upper Deck Czech World Juniors-68
91UND Fighting Sioux Sports Collectors Card Set -14
92North Dakota Fighting Sioux-29
94Roanoke Express-9
95Roanoke Express-7

Schroder, Gilbert
94German First League-516

Schroder, Klaus
83Swedish Semic VM Stickers-149
94German DEL-33

Schroder, Markus
04German DEL Update-301
04German Ingolstadt Panthers-21

Schroder, Stefan
04German DEL Update-334

Schubert, Andreas
94German DEL-56
95German DEL-58
96German DEL-206

Schubert, Christoph
99German EV Landshut-5
00German DEL-176
01German Upper Deck-263
03Binghamton Senators-17
04Binghamton Senators-16
04Binghamton Senators Hess-4
05Beehive-169
Matte-169
05Black Diamond-265
05Hot Prospects-208
Autographed Patch Variation-208
Autographed Patch Variation Gold-208
Hot Materials-HMCS
Red Hot-208
05Parkhurst-651
Facsimile Auto Parallel-651
Signatures-CS
05SP Authentic-204
Limited-204
05SP Game Used-184
Gold-184
05SPx-215
Spectrum-215
05The Cup-124
Autographed Rookie Patches Gold Rainbow-124
Black Rainbow Rookies-124
Masterpiece Pressplates (Artifacts)-306
Masterpiece Pressplates (Bee Hive)-169
Masterpiece Pressplates (Black Diamond)-265
Masterpiece Pressplates (Ice)-178
Masterpiece Pressplates (Rookie Update)-222
Masterpiece Pressplates SPA Autos-204
Masterpiece Pressplates (SP Game Used)-184
Masterpiece Pressplates (SPx)-215
Masterpiece Pressplates (Trilogy)-285
Masterpiece Pressplates Ult Coll-160
Masterpiece Pressplates (Victory)-294
Masterpiece Pressplates Autographs-124
Platinum Rookies-124
05UD Artifacts-306
05Ultimate Collection-160
Gold-160
Ultimate Debut Threads Jerseys-DTJCS
05Upper Deck-460
05Upper Deck Ice-178
05Upper Deck Rookie Update-222
Inspirations Patch Rookies-222
05Upper Deck Trilogy-285
05Upper Deck Victory-294
Black-294
Gold-294
Silver-294
05German DEL-285
06Senators Postcards-13
06Binghamton Senators 5th Anniversary-27

Schubert, Sven
94German First League-52

Schubert, Thomas
91Upper Deck-681
French-681
91Upper Deck Czech World Juniors-44
94German DEL-397
95German DEL-412

Schuchuk, Gary
91ProCards-132

Schueller, Doug
01Macon Whoopee-17
02Roanoke Express-23
02Roanoke Express RBI Sports-203
03UK Basingstoke Bison-6
04UK Coventry Blaze-16
04UK Coventry Blaze Champions-5
05Sioux Falls Stampede-23

Schuler, Alan
92Richmond Renegades-16
93Richmond Renegades-4
00UK Cardiff Devils-2
00UK Sekonda Superleague-57
01UK Cardiff Devils-3
02UK Cardiff Devils-3

Schuler, Beat
04Swiss EV Zug Postcards-25

Schuler, Laura
97Collector's Choice-294

Schullstrom, Jan
67Swedish Hockey-193
69Swedish Hockey-251
70Swedish Hockey-136
71Swedish Hockey-228
72Swedish Stickers-216
73Swedish Stickers-72

Schulte, Paxton
917th Inn. Sketch WHL-13
94Classic Pro Prospects-124
96Saint John Flames-17
97Saint John Flames-20
00UK Sekonda Superleague-26
01UK Belfast Giants-16
03UK Belfast Giants-15

Schultz, Andreas
93Swedish Semic Elitserien-103
94Swedish Leaf-165

Schultz, Brian
98Danish Hockey League-122
99Danish Hockey League-37

Schultz, Dave
73Flyers Linnett-15
73O-Pee-Chee-137
73O-Pee-Chee-166
73Topps-5
73Topps-149
74Lipton Soup-30
74NHL Action Stamps-206
74O-Pee-Chee NHL-5
74O-Pee-Chee NHL-154
74O-Pee-Chee NHL-196
74Topps-5
74Topps-154
74Topps-196
75Flyers Canada Dry Cans-16
75Heroes Stand-Ups-25
75O-Pee-Chee NHL-147
75O-Pee-Chee NHL-211
75Topps-147
75Topps-211
76O-Pee-Chee NHL-4
76O-Pee-Chee NHL-150
76O-Pee-Chee NHL-391
76Topps-4
76Topps-150
77O-Pee-Chee NHL-353
78O-Pee-Chee-66
78O-Pee-Chee-225
78Topps-66
78Topps-225
79O-Pee-Chee-4
79O-Pee-Chee-134
79Topps-4
79Topps-134
79Rochester Americans-17
81Topps Thirst Break-44
92Parkhurst-473
Emerald Ice-473
96Madison Monsters-2
98SLU Hockey Classic Doubles-6
01BAP Ultimate Mem Dynasty Jerseys-14
01BAP Ultimate Mem Dynasty Emblems-14
01BAP Ultimate Mem Dynasty Numbers-14
01BAP Ultimate Mem Retro Teammates-6
01BAP Update Tough Customers-TC1
01Fleer Legacy-55
Ultimate-55
01Greats of the Game-45
Autographs-45
01Parkhurst Autographs-PA43
01Topps Archives-66
Autographs-18
02BAP Signature Series Famous Scraps-FS1
02BAP Ultimate Mem Retro Teammates-9
02Fleer Throwbacks-67
Gold-67
Platinum-67
Autographs-22
Squaring Off-2
Squaring Off-8
Squaring Off Memorabilia-2
Squaring Off Memorabilia-8
02Parkhurst Vintage Teammates-VT13
03Topps Stanley Cup Heroes-DS
03Topps Stanley Cup Heroes Autographs-DS
04ITG Franchises US East-412
Autographs-A-DSC1
Memorabilia-ESM12
Memorabilia Autographs-ESM-DS
Memorabilia Gold-ESM12
Teammates-ETM6
Teammates Gold-ETM6
04ITG Franchises US West-276
04ITG Ultimate Mem Broad St Bullie Jersey-4
04ITG Ult Mem Broad St Bullie Jersey Auto-4
04ITG Ultimate Mem Broad St Bullie Emblem-4
04ITG Ult Mem Broad St Bullie Emblem Auto-4
04ITG Ultimate Mem Broad St Bullie Number-4
04ITG Ult Mem Broad St Bullie Number Auto-4
04ITG Ultimate Memorabilia Triple Threads-10
04UD Legendary Signatures-22
AKA Autographs-AKA-HS
Autographs-HS
04UD Legends Classics-15
Gold-15
Platinum-15
Silver-15
Jersey Redemptions-JY29
Signature Moments-M39
Signature Moments-M59
Signatures-CS37
Signatures-DC15
05ITG Tough Customers-DS
Autographs-DS
Famous Battles Autographs-SO
Famous Battles Autographs-WS
Jerseys-DS
Signed Memorabilia-DS
05ITG Ultimate Mem Pass the Torch Jerseys-17
05ITG Ultimate Mem Passing Torch Jsy Gold-17
05ITG Ultimate Mem Record Breaker Jerseys-19
05ITG Ultimate Mem RecBreak Jerseys Gold-19
05UD Artifacts Auto Facts-AF-SC
05UD Artifacts Auto Facts Blue-AF-SC
05UD Artifacts Auto Facts Copper-AF-SC
05UD Artifacts Auto Facts Pewter-AF-SC
05UD Artifacts Auto Facts Silver-AF-SC
06ITG Ultimate Memorabilia-38
Artist Proof-38
Road to the Cup-9
Road to the Cup Gold-9
06Parkhurst-112
06Parkhurst-235
Autographs-112
Autographs-235
Autographs Dual-DASD

Schultz, Derrick
00Kitchener Rangers-22

Schultz, Igor
94German DEL-117
95German DEL-118
96German DEL-64

Schultz, Jeff
03Calgary Hitmen-16
04ITG Top Prospects Spring Expo-6
04Calgary Hitmen-18
04ITG Heroes and Prospects-81
Autographs-JS
Top Prospects-6
04ITG Heroes/Prospects Toronto Expo '05-81
04ITG Heroes/Prospects Expo Heroes/Pros-81
05ITG Heroes/Prosp Toronto Expo Parallel -311
05Calgary Hitmen-18
05ITG Heroes and Prospects-311
Autographs Series II-JSC
Jerseys-GUJ-110
Jerseys Gold-GUJ-110
Emblems-GUE-94
Emblems Gold-GUE-94
Numbers-GUN-94
Numbers Gold-GUN-94
06AHL Top Prospects-16
06ITG Heroes and Prospects Calder Cup Champions-CC12
06ITG Heroes and Prospects National Pride-NP13
06ITG Heroes and Prospects National Pride Gold-NP13
07Upper Deck Victory-223
Black-223
Gold-223

Schultz, Jesse
01Prince Albert Raiders-19
02Kelowna Rockets-14
03Columbia Inferno Update-54
03Kelowna Rockets Memorial Cup-17
04Manitoba Moose-12
05Manitoba Moose-20
06Be A Player-237
06Beehive-157
Blue-157
Gold-157
Matte-157
Red Facsimile Signatures-157
Wood-157
06Flair Showcase-330
06Hot Prospects-184
Red Hot-184
White Hot-184
06O-Pee-Chee-598
Rainbow-598
06SP Authentic-206
Limited-206
06The Cup-166
Autographed Rookie Masterpiece Pressplates-166
Gold Rainbow Autographed Rookie Patches-166
Masterpiece Pressplates (Bee Hive)-157
Masterpiece Pressplates (Marquee Rookies)-598
Masterpiece Pressplates (SP Authentic Autographs)-206
Masterpiece Pressplates (SP Authentic)-214
Masterpiece Pressplates (Sweet Beginnings)-158
Masterpiece Pressplates (Ultimate Collection)-100
Rookies Black-166
Rookies Platinum-166
06UD Artifacts-265
06Ultimate Collection-100
06Upper Deck-492
Exclusives Parallel-492
High Gloss Parallel-492
Masterpieces-492
06Upper Deck Sweet Shot-158
Rookie Jerseys Autographs-158
06Manitoba Moose-15

Schultz, Jurgen
94German First League-500

Schultz, Ken
51Cleveland Barons-13

Schultz, Kris
00Columbus Cottonmouths-17
00Wichita Thunder-19
01Asheville Smoke-15

Schultz, Lacey
04Ohio State Buckeyes Women-12
05Ohio State Buckeyes Women-6
06Ohio State Buckeyes Women-15

Schultz, Lasse
80Finnish Mallasjuoma-155

Schultz, Martin
94German DEL-118
95German DEL-119

Schultz, Mike
98Huntington Blizzard-16
98Peoria Rivermen-26
99Knoxville Speed-15
00Knoxville Speed-8

Schultz, Nick
98Prince Albert Raiders-21
99UD Prospects-51
99UD Prospects-86
00SPx Rookie Redemption-RR15
00Prince Albert Raiders-22
01BAP Memorabilia-383
Emerald-383
Ruby-383
Sapphire-383
01BAP Signature Series-214
Autographs-214
Autographs Gold-214
01Bowman YoungStars-128
Gold-128
Ice Cubed-128
01Crown Royale-166
01O-Pee-Chee-339
01Pacific Adrenaline-212
Blue-212
Premiere Date-212
Red-212
Retail-212
01Parkhurst-296
01Parkhurst Beckett Promos-296
01Private Stock-126
Gold-126
Gold-126
Premiere Date-126
Premiere Date-126
Retail-126
Retail-126
Silver-126
01Private Stock Pacific Nights-126
01SP Game Used-81
01Titanium-165
Retail-165
01Titanium Draft Day Edition-137
01Topps-339
01Topps Chrome-157
Refractors-157
Black Border Refractors-157
01Topps Reserve-107
01UD Challenge for the Cup-112
01UD Honor Roll-75
01UD Premier Collection-66
01Upper Deck-428
Exclusives-428
01Upper Deck Ice-57
01Vanguard-117
Blue-117
Red-117
One of Ones-117
Premiere Date-117
Proofs-117
01Wild Crime Prevention-24
02BAP Sig Series Auto Buybacks 2001-214
02Bowman YoungStars-136
Gold-136
Silver-136
Autographs-NS
Jerseys-NS
Patches-NS
Double Stuff-NS
Triple Stuff-NS
Rivals-NSNH
Rivals Patches-14
Sticks-NS
02O-Pee-Chee-293
02O-Pee-Chee Premier Blue Parallel-293
02O-Pee-Chee Premier Red Parallel-293
02O-Pee-Chee Factory Set-293
02Pacific Complete-49

Red-49
02Topps-293
OPC Blue Parallel-293
OPC Red Parallel-293
Factory Set-293
02Topps Total-16
02Upper Deck Vintage-124
03Bowman-78
Gold-78
03Bowman Chrome-78
Refractors-78
Gold Refractors-78
Xfractors-78
03ITG Action-274
Jerseys-M75
03O-Pee-Chee-67
03OPC Blue-67
03OPC Gold-67
03OPC Red-67
03Pacific Complete-308
Red-308
03Parkhurst Rookie Road to the NHL-RNJ-1
03Parkhurst Rookie Road to the NHL Gold-RTN-1
03Parkhurst Rookie Road to the NHL Emblem-RTNE-1
03Parkhurst Rookie Road NHL Emblem Gold-RTNE-1
03Topps-67
Blue-67
Gold-67
Red-67
03Topps C55-83
Minis-83
Minis American Back-83
Minis American Back Red-83
Minis Bazooka Back-83
Minis Brooklyn Back-83
Minis Hat Trick Back-83
Minis O Canada Back-83
Minis O Canada Back Red-83
Minis Stanley Cup Back-83
Relics-TRNS
03Wild Law Enforcement Cards-8
04German DEL-200
Superstars-SU18
05Parkhurst-244
Facsimile Auto Parallel-244
05Upper Deck-345
Notable Numbers-N-NS
05Upper Deck MVP-199
Gold-199
Platinum-199
05Wild Crime Prevention-7
06Be A Player-45
Autographs-45
Signatures-NS
06O-Pee-Chee-248
Rainbow-248
06Upper Deck-97
Exclusives Parallel-97
High Gloss Parallel-97
Masterpieces-97

Schultz, Ray
99Kansas City Blades Supercuts-18
00Cleveland Lumberjacks-22
02Atomic-119
Blue-119
Gold-119
Red-119
Hobby Parallel-119
02BAP Memorabilia-328
02Crown Royale-126
Blue-126
Purple-126
Red-126
Retail-126
02Pacific Heads-Up-141
02Private Stock Reserve-171
Blue-171
Red-171
Retail-171
02SP Authentic-150
02UD Foundations-136
02UD Mask Collection-133
02UD Piece of History-139
02UD Top Shelf-95
02Upper Deck-214
Exclusives-214
02Upper Deck MVP-210
Gold-210
Classics-210
Golden Classics-210
02Upper Deck Victory-131
Bronze-131
Gold-131
Silver-131
02Upper Deck Vintage-340
03Milwaukee Admirals-26
03Milwaukee Admirals Postcards-18
04Albany River Rats-21
05Albany River Rats-22

Schultz, Stephen
06Lincoln Stars-9
06Lincoln Stars Traded-16T
06Lincoln Stars Upper DeckÂ Signature Series -24

Schultz, Torben
98Danish Hockey League-128
99Danish Hockey League-3

Schulz, David
02Swift Current Broncos-17
03Swift Current Broncos-17
04Swift Current Broncos-19
05Saskatoon Blades-20

Schulz, Karsten
94German DEL-439
95German DEL-400

Schumacher, Fabio
01Swiss EV Zug Postcards-9
01Swiss HNL-177
02Swiss EV Zug Postcards-12
03Swiss EV Zug Postcards-23

Schumacher, Philip
92Quebec Pee-Wee Tournament-1679
99German DEL-19
01German Upper Deck-249

Schumacher, Robert
94German First League-187

Schumperli, Bernhard
91Upper Deck-667
French-667
91Upper Deck Czech World Juniors-28
93Swiss HNL-206
95Swiss HNL-283
96Swiss HNL-247
98Swiss Power Play Stickers-197
99Swiss Panini Stickers-197
00Swiss Panini Stickers-241
00Swiss Slapshot Mini-Cards-RJ16
01Swiss HNL-209
02Swiss HNL-112

Schupbach, Marco
01Swiss HNL-348
02Swiss HNL-158

Schupbach, Martin
02Swiss HNL-406

Schur, Hartwig
74Finnish Jenkki-117

Schurch, Reto
95Swiss HNL-86
98Swiss Power Play Stickers-30
01Swiss HNL-260
02Swiss HNL-287

Schure, Peter
91Cincinnati Cyclones-22

Schury, Daniel
94German First League-207

Schushack, Chris
917th Inn. Sketch OHL-XXX

Schussler, Kyle
06Okotoks Oilers -18

Schust, Ben
95Slapshot-364
95Sault Ste. Marie Greyhounds-18
96Sault Ste. Marie Greyhounds-19
96Sault Ste. Marie Greyhounds Autographed-19
98Roanoke Express-15
00Roanoke Express-6

Schuster, Alexander
94German DEL-286
99German Bundesliga 2-168

Schuster, Christian
93Swiss HNL-245
96Swiss HNL-302
01Swiss HNL-406
02Swiss HNL-405

Schuster, Manfred
89Swedish Semic World Champ Stickers-110
94German First League-161

Schuster, Michael
94German First League-368

Schuster, Rainer
94German First League-341

Schutt, Rod
76Nova Scotia Voyageurs-17
77Nova Scotia Voyageurs-23
79O-Pee-Chee-234
79Topps-234
80O-Pee-Chee-307
81O-Pee-Chee-259
81O-Pee-Chee Stickers-186
81Topps-E116
97Sudbury Wolves Anniversary-20

Schutte, Kyle
01Val d'Or Foreurs-18

Schutte, Michael
02Springfield Falcons-20
03Springfield Falcons Postcards-25
05Providence Bruins-15

Schutz, Derek
95Spokane Chiefs-20
96Spokane Chiefs-16
97Spokane Chiefs-18
97Bowman CHL-97
97Bowman CHL-127
OPC-97
OPC-127
Autographs-127
98Spokane Chiefs-21
99Spokane Chiefs-23
00Richmond Renegades-13

Schutz, Felix
05Saint John's Sea Dogs-8
06Saint Johns Sea Dogs-4
06ITG Heroes and Prospects-186
Autographs-AFS
Update Autographs-AFS

Schutz, Marco
03German Mannheim Eagles Postcards-3
04German Adler Mannheim Eagles Postcards-28
05German DEL-255

Schutz, Richard
99German DEL-413

Schutz, Robert
94German First League-560

Schwab, Corey
907th Inn. Sketch WHL-19
91ProCards-416
94Classic Enforcers-E5
95Bowman-164
All-Foil-164
95Parkhurst International-389
Emerald Ice-389
96Be A Player-104
Autographs-104
Autographs Silver-104
96Donruss Elite-128
Die Cut Stars-128
96Leaf Preferred-126
Press Proofs-126
96Collector's Edge Ice-9
Prism-9
QuantumMotion-12
97Collector's Choice-244
97Donruss-77
Press Proofs Silver-77
Press Proofs Gold-77
97Donruss Limited-130
Exposure-130
97Leaf-96
Fractal Matrix-96
Fractal Matrix Die Cuts-96
97Leaf International-96
Universal Ice-96
97Pacific-126
Copper-126
Emerald Green-126
Ice Blue-126
Red-126
Silver-126
97Upper Deck-153
98NHL Aces Playing Cards-3
98Cleveland Lumberjacks-20
99Pacific-395
Copper-395
Emerald Green-395
Gold-395
Ice Blue-395
Premiere Date-395
Red-395
00Kansas City Blades-21
01Between the Pipes-81
02BAP First Edition-239
02BAP Memorabilia-97
Emerald-97
Ruby-97
Sapphire-97
NHL All-Star Game-97
NHL All-Star Game Blue-97
NHL All-Star Game Green-97
NHL All-Star Game Red-97
02BAP Memorabilia Toronto Fall Expo-97
02Between the Pipes-62
Gold-62
Silver-62
02Devils Team Issue-24
02Pacific-369
Blue-369
Red-369
02Pacific Complete-426
Red-426
02UD Mask Collection-50
02UD Mask Collection-51
02UD Mask Collection Beckett Promos-50
02UD Mask Collection Beckett Promos-51
03BAP Memorabilia-110
Emerald-110
Gold-110
Ruby-110
Sapphire-110
Deep in the Crease-D4
Stanley Cup Champions-SCC-10
Tandems-T-5
03Devils Team Issue-35
03ITG Action-320
03Pacific Complete-423
Red-423
03Upper Deck-362
Canadian Exclusives-362
HG-362
UD Exclusives-362
03Upper Deck MVP-261
Gold Script-261
Silver Script-261
Canadian Exclusives-261

Schwab, Tobias
04German DEL Update-319
05German DEL-179

Schwabe, Evan
04Minnesota-Duluth Bulldogs-21

Schwabe, Jens
91Upper Deck-680
French-680
91Upper Deck Czech World Juniors-43
94German DEL-395

Schwalb, Mike
89Nashville Knights-21

Schwamberger, Mark
02Lincoln Stars-31

Schwan, Jake
03Waterloo Blackhawks-15

Schwanz, Erik
03Brampton Batallion-18

Schwark, Bob
91Air Canada SJHL-D10

Schwartz, Brandon
00Sioux City Musketeers-24

Schwartz, Darren
89Johnstown Chiefs-30
92Wheeling Thunderbirds-15
93Wheeling Thunderbirds-2
93Wheeling Thunderbirds-PC2
93Wheeling Thunderbirds-UD8
94Classic Pro Prospects-247
95Tallahassee Tiger Sharks-9

Schwartz, Dustin
96Medicine Hat Tigers-20
98Red Deer Rebels-18

Schwartz, Justin
97Medicine Hat Tigers-17
98Medicine Hat Tigers-19

Schwarz, Evan
00Connecticut Huskies-14

Schwarz, Ingo
94German First League-378
99German Bundesliga 2-13

Schwarz, Marek
03Czech OFS Plus-163
03Czech OFS Plus-278
03Czech OFS Plus MS Praha-SE42
04Vancouver Giants-22
04ITG Heroes and Prospects-229
04ITG Heroes/Prospects Toronto Expo '05-229
05ITG Heroes/Prosp Toronto Expo Parallel -427
05ITG Ultimate Mem Future Stars Autos-14
05ITG Ultimate Mem Future Star Autos Gold-14
05ITG Ultimate Mem Future Stars Jerseys-15
05ITG Ultimate Mem Fut Stars Jerseys Gold-15
05ITG Ultimate Mem Future Stars Mem Autos-14
05ITG Ultimate Mem Fut Star Mem Auto Gold-14
05ITG Heroes and Prospects-427
Autographs Update-A-MSZ
He Shoots-He Scores Prizes-57
06Be A Player-221
06Beehive-152
Matte-152
06Between The Pipes-36
06Between The Pipes-113
Aspiring-AS06
Aspiring Gold-AS06
Autographs-AMS2
Autographs-AMS
Emblems-GUE59
Emblems Gold-GUE59
Emblems Autographs-GUE59
Jerseys-GUJ59
Jerseys Gold-GUJ59
Jerseys Autographs-GUJ59
Numbers-GUN59
Numbers Gold-GUN59
Numbers Autographs-GUN59
Playing For Your Country-PC22
Playing For Your Country Gold-PC22
Prospect Trios-PT16
Prospect Trios Gold-PT16
The Mask-M21
The Mask Gold-M21
The Mask Silver-M21
06Flair Showcase-327
06Hot Prospects-133
Red Hot-133
White Hot-133
06ITG International Ice-9
Gold-9
Autographs-AMS
Passing The Torch-PTT7
Passing The Torch Gold-PTT7
06ITG Ultimate Memorabilia Future Star-5
06ITG Ultimate Memorabilia Future Star Gold-5
06ITG Ultimate Memorabilia Future Star Autos-19
06ITG Ultimate Memorabilia Future Star Autos Gold-19
06ITG Ultimate Memorabilia Future Star Patches Autos-19
06ITG Ultimate Memorabilia Future Star Patches Autos Gold-19
06SP Authentic-217
Limited-217
06The Cup-156
Autographed Rookie Masterpiece Pressplates-156
Gold Rainbow Autographed Rookie Patches-156
Masterpiece Pressplates (Bee Hive)-152
Masterpiece Pressplates (SP Authentic)-217
Masterpiece Pressplates (Sweet Beginnings)-152
Masterpiece Pressplates (Ultimate Collection)-92
Rookies Black-156
Rookies Platinum-156
06UD Artifacts-256
06Ultimate Collection-92
06Upper Deck Sweet Shot-152
Rookie Jerseys Autographs-152
06Czech OFS Jagr Team-1
06AHL Top Prospects-33
06Peoria Rivermen-16
06ITG Heroes and Prospects Complete Jerseys-CJ04
06ITG Heroes and Prospects Complete Jerseys Gold-CJ04
06ITG Heroes and Prospects Jerseys-GUJ01
06ITG Heroes and Prospects Jerseys Gold-GUJ01
06ITG Heroes and Prospects Emblems-GUE01
06ITG Heroes and Prospects Emblems Gold-GUE01
06ITG Heroes and Prospects Numbers-GUN01
06ITG Heroes and Prospects Numbers Gold-GUN01
06ITG Heroes and Prospects Net Prospects-NPR02
06ITG Heroes and Prospects Net Prospects Gold-NPR02

Schwarz, Oliver
94German DEL-355

Schwarz, Tassilo
02Swiss HNL-473

Schwarz, Ueli
95Swiss HNL-85
98Swiss Power Play Stickers-28
99Swiss Panini Stickers-78

Schwarz, Zeno
02Swiss HNL-474

Schwefel, Harry
01Kalamazoo K-Wings-10

Schweitzer, Aaron
99Colorado Gold Kings Taco Bell-15
99Colorado Gold Kings Wendy's-18

Schweizer, Andreas
01Swiss HNL-77
02Swiss HNL-465

Schwele, Sebastian
95German DEL-192

Schweyer, Rob
93Owen Sound Platers-25
94Owen Sound Platers-13
00Columbus Cottonmouths-18

Schwindt, Garry
94German First League-611

Schyadilov, Igor
03Russian Hockey League-34

Schymainski, Martin
04German DEL Update-336
05German DEL-51

Sciacca, Jonathan
06Kingston Frontenacs-19

Sciba, Josh
04Notre Dame Fighting Irish-14

Scissons, Jeff
00Kansas City Blades-15

Scissons, Scott
88Saskatoon Blades-19
89Saskatoon Blades-20
90Score-432
Canadian-432
90Upper Deck-357
French-357
90Saskatoon Blades-19
907th Inn. Sketch WHL-77
91Alberta International Team Canada-21
91Upper Deck-428
French-428
93Donruss-210
93Leaf-243
93Parkhurst-121
Emerald Ice-121
93Upper Deck-511

Sclisizzi, Enio
52Parkhurst-32

Scollan, Mark
91Air Canada SJHL All-Stars-11
91Air Canada SJHL All-Stars-47
92Cornell Big Red-25
93Cornell Big Red-22

Scoran, Kory
06Idaho Steelheads-20

Scorsone, Anthony
93Quebec Pee-Wee Tournament-870

Scorsune, Matthew
00Hershey Bears-14
01Hershey Bears-24

Scotland, Colin
97Sudbury Wolves Police-15
98Kingston Frontenacs-19

Scott, Blair
89Victoria Cougars-17
917th Inn. Sketch OHL-101
94Classic Pro Prospects-148
00UK Sekonda Superleague-96
01UK Manchester Storm Retro-12

Scott, Brad
907th Inn. Sketch WHL-173
94German First League-448
99German Bundesliga 2-178

Scott, Brent
97El Paso Buzzards-2
99Tupelo T-Rex-1

Scott, Brian
93Kingston Frontenacs-8
94Parkhurst SE-SE268
Gold-SE268
94SP-186
Die Cuts-186
94Kitchener Rangers Update-31
95Slapshot-396
95Signature Rookies Auto-Phonex-38
95Signature Rook Auto-Phonex Phone Cards-38
96Sudbury Wolves-19
96Sudbury Wolves Police-20
97Johnstown Chiefs-21

Scott, Chubby
23V128-1 Paulin's Candy-52

Scott, Clark
93Quebec Pee-Wee Tournament-195

Scott, Daniel
03UK Nottingham Panthers-15
04UK Nottingham Panthers-17
05UK Nottingham Panthers-13

Scott, Dennis
897th Inn. Sketch OHL-137

Scott, Fred
96Dayton Ice Bandits-17

Scott, Ganton
24C144 Champ's Cigarettes-54
24V130 Maple Crispette-29
24V145-2-38

Scott, Greg
917th Inn. Sketch OHL-206
93Huntington Blizzard-22

Scott, Irvin
52Juniors Blue Tint-49

Scott, Jerry
84Ottawa 67's-21

Scott, Justin
04Moose Jaw Warriors-8
05Red Deer Rebels-16
06Regina Pats-20

Scott, Kevin
91Cincinnati Cyclones-21

Scott, Laurie
23V128-1 Paulin's Candy-40

Scott, Mark
99Columbus Cottonmouths-16
02Arkansas Riverblades-15
03UK London Racers-15
05Roanoke Valley Vipers-10

Scott, Peter
93Arizona Icecats-13
94Arizona Icecats-14
95Arizona Icecats-8
96Arizona Icecats-18

Scott, Richard
99Charlotte Checkers-14
00Charlotte Checkers-29
00Hartford Wolf Pack-23
01BAP Memorabilia-370
Emerald-370
Ruby-370
Sapphire-370
01Topps Chrome-178
Refractors-178
Black Border Refractors-178
01UD Challenge for the Cup-122
01UD Honor Roll-82
02Hartford Wolf Pack-20
03Hartford Wolf Pack-21

Scott, Ron
89New Haven Nighthawks-10
89ProCards AHL-5
90ProCards AHL/IHL-424

Scott, Topher
02Chicago Steel-17

Scott, Travis
93Windsor Spitfires-3
94Windsor Spitfires-3
95Slapshot-231
99Lowell Lock Monsters-18
99Mississippi Sea Wolves Kelly Cup-21
00Black Diamond-121
00SP Authentic-146
00Lowell Lock Monsters-19
01Between the Pipes-38
01Upper Deck Victory-374
Gold-374
01Manchester Monarchs-2B
02Between the Pipes-37
Gold-37
Silver-37
02Manchester Monarchs-14
03BAP Memorabilia Deep in the Crease-D14
03San Antonio Rampage-23
04San Antonio Rampage-21
05Russian Hockey League RHL-28

Scott, Tyler
93Quebec Pee-Wee Tournament-1274
06Bakersfield Condors-17

Scott, Vince
03Erie Otters-22
04Erie Otters-9
05Erie Otters-9

Scoville, Darrel
99BAP Memorabilia-338
Gold-338
Silver-338
01Syracuse Crunch-18
02Syracuse Crunch-15
02Syracuse Crunch Sheets-10
03Syracuse Crunch-4

Scremin, Claudio
90Kansas City Blades-1
90ProCards AHL/IHL-597
91Kansas City Blades-14
91ProCards-508
92Kansas City Blades-19
94Kansas City Blades-15
95Kansas City Blades-18
96Kansas City Blades-19
97Kansas City Blades Magnets-1
98German DEL-195
99UK London Knights-15
04UK Thommo's Top 10-3

Scruderi, Ken
00Lincoln Stars-2

Scruton, Howie
81Kingston Canadians-19

Scuderi, Ken
06Augusta Lynx-18

Scuderi, Robert
01Wilkes-Barre Scranton Penguins-2
02Wilkes-Barre Scranton Penguins-1
03ITG VIP Rookie Debut-119
03Parkhurst Rookie-88
03Topps Traded-TT147
Blue-TT147
Gold-TT147
Red-TT147
03Upper Deck Rookie Update-207
03Wilkes-Barre Scranton Penguins-23
04Wilkes-Barre Scranton Penguins-2

Scullion, Bert
51Bas Du Fleuve-49

Scully, Barry
99Fort Wayne Komets Points Leaders-9

Scully, Sean
00Ottawa 67's-10
01Ottawa 67's-12
02Ottawa 67's-13

Seaborg, Justin
99OCN Blizzard-5
01OCN Blizzard-18

Seabrook, Brent
01Lethbridge Hurricanes-20
03BAP Memorabilia Draft Redemptions-14
03Lethbridge Hurricanes-4
04SP Authentic Rookie Redemptions-RR7
04Lethbridge Hurricanes-4
04ITG Heroes and Prospects-58
Autographs-BS
Combos-5
Complete Emblems-7
Emblems-45
Emblems Gold-45
He Shoots-He Scores Prizes-12
Jersey Autographs-45
Jerseys-45
Jerseys Gold-45
Numbers-45
Numbers Gold-45
04ITG Heroes/Prospects Toronto Expo '05-58
04ITG Heroes/Prospects Expo Heroes/Pros-58
05Beehive-122
Beige -122
Blue -122
Gold-122
Red -122
Matte-122
Signature Scrapbook-SSSE
05Black Diamond-151
Emerald-151
Gold-151
Onyx-151
Ruby-151
05Hot Prospects-229
En Fuego-229
Hot Materials-HMBS
Red Hot-229
White Hot-229
05Parkhurst-616
Facsimile Auto Parallel-616
Signatures-BS
True Colors-TCCHI
True Colors-TCCHI
05SP Authentic-145
Limited-145
Rarefied Rookies-RRBS
Rookie Authentics-RABS
Sign of the Times Duals-DBS
05SP Game Used-122
Autographs-122
Gold-122
Rookie Exclusives-BS
Rookie Exclusives Silver-RE-BS
Significant Numbers-SN-BS
05SPx-184
Spectrum-184
Xcitement Rookies-XR-BS
Xcitement Rookies Gold-XR-BS
Xcitement Rookies Spectrum-XR-BS
05The Cup-105
Autographed Rookie Patches Gold Rainbow-105
Black Rainbow Rookies-105
Masterpiece Pressplates (Artifacts)-207
Masterpiece Pressplates (Bee Hive)-122
Masterpiece Pressplates (Black Diamond)-151
Masterpiece Pressplates (Ice)-123
Masterpiece Pressplates (MVP)-431
Masterpiece Pressplates (Power Play)-140
Masterpiece Pressplates (Rookie Update)-203
Masterpiece Pressplates SPA Autos-145
Masterpiece Pressplates (SP Game Used)-122
Masterpiece Pressplates SPx Autos-184
Masterpiece Pressplates (Trilogy)-182
Masterpiece Pressplates Ult Coll Autos-109
Masterpiece Pressplates (Victory)-253
Masterpiece Pressplates Autographs-105
Platinum Rookies-105
05UD Artifacts-207
Gold-RED7
05UD PowerPlay-140
05UD Rookie Class-29
05Ultimate Collection-109
Autographed Patches-109
Autographed Shields-109
Jerseys Dual-DJSB
Ultimate Debut Threads Jerseys-DTJBS
Ultimate Debut Threads Jerseys Autos-DAJBS
Ultimate Debut Threads Patches-DTPBS
Ultimate Debut Threads Patches Autos-DAPBS
Ultimate Patches Dual-DPSB
05Ultra-209
Gold-209
Ice-209
Rookie Uniformity Jerseys-RU-BS
Rookie Uniformity Jersey Autographs-ARU-BS
Rookie Uniformity Patches-RUP-BS
Rookie Uniformity Patch Autographs-ARP-BS
05Upper Deck-209
HG Glossy-209
Rookie Ink-RIBS
05Upper Deck Rookie Showcase-RS7
05Upper Deck Rookie Showcase Promos-RS7
05Upper Deck Rookie Threads-RTBS
05Upper Deck Rookie Threads Autographs-ARTBS
05Upper Deck Ice-123
Cool Threads-CTBS
Cool Threads Autographs-ACTBS
Cool Threads Glass-CTBS
Cool Threads Patches-CTPBS
Cool Threads Patch Autographs-CAPBS
Fresh Ice-FIBS
Fresh Ice Glass-FIBS
Fresh Ice Glass Patches-FIPBS
Premieres Auto Patches-AIPBS
05Upper Deck MVP-431
Gold-431
Platinum-431
05Upper Deck Rookie Update-203
Inspirations Patch Rookies-203
05Upper Deck Trilogy-182
05Upper Deck Toronto Fall Expo-209
05Upper Deck Victory-253
Black-253
Gold-253
Silver-253
05ITG Heroes/Prospects He Shoots/Scores-24
06Be A Player-44
Autographs-44
Signatures-SK
Signatures 25-47
Signatures Duals-DCH
Signatures Trios-TRKS
Portraits Signature Portraits-SPBS
06Black Diamond-19
Black-19
Gold-19
Ruby-19
06Blackhawks Postcards-10
06Fleer-48
Tiffany-48
Signing Day-SDBS
06O-Pee-Chee-117
06O-Pee-Chee-645
Rainbow-117
Rainbow-645
06UD Toronto Fall Expo Priority Signings -PSBS
06Upper Deck Arena Giveaways-CHI3
06Upper Deck-293
Exclusives Parallel-293
High Gloss Parallel-293
Masterpieces-293
06Upper Deck Ovation-160
06Upper Deck Victory-44
06Upper Deck Victory Black-44
06Upper Deck Victory Gold-44

Seabrooke, Glen
88ProCards AHL-129
89ProCards AHL-336

Seale, Travis
91Michigan Tech Huskies-30
93Michigan Tech Huskies-11

Searle, Doug
89Peterborough Petes-119
897th Inn. Sketch OHL-119
907th Inn. Sketch OHL-371
91Peterborough Petes-9
917th Inn. Sketch OHL-140
93Knoxville Cherokees-16
94Knoxville Cherokees-6
96Roanoke Express-14
98Roanoke Express-8
99Knoxville Speed-16
99UHL All-Stars East-20T
00UK Sekonda Superleague-178
01UK Belfast Giants-28
05Knoxville Ice Bears-16

Searles, Steve
907th Inn. Sketch QMJHL-173
917th Inn. Sketch QMJHL-119

Searles, Yannick
00Quebec Remparts-10
Signed-10
01Quebec Remparts-9
02Moncton Wildcats-22

Sears, Sverre
93Greensboro Monarchs-13
94Greensboro Monarchs-6
95Flint Generals-3

Seaton, Bryant
81Victoria Cougars-13

Seaton, Mike
89Victoria Cougars-18
907th Inn. Sketch WHL-8
91Nashville Knights-21
92Nashville Knights-14

Sebald, Andreas
94German First League-375

Sebastian, Jeff
88Regina Pats-22
89Portland Winter Hawks-19
907th Inn. Sketch WHL-313
917th Inn. Sketch WHL-136
98German DEL-6
99German DEL-305
00UK Sekonda Superleague-146
00UK Sheffield Steelers-20
01UK Sheffield Steelers-18
03UK Manchester Phoenix-19
05UK Nottingham Panthers-16

Sebek, Venci
94German DEL-385
95German DEL-150

Sebesta, Pavel
95Czech APS Extraliga-308
97Czech APS Extraliga-107
98Czech DS Stickers-60
99Czech Score Blue 2000-103
99Czech Score Red Ice 2000-103
03Czech OFS Plus-357

Sebestu, Richard
95Czech APS Extraliga-211

Sebor, Jan
98Czech OFS-258

Seca, Dylan
94Kitchener Rangers Update-34

Secemski, Krystof
94Sudbury Wolves-16
94Sudbury Wolves Police-14

Sechny, Richard
04Czech OFS Czech/Slovak-41

Seck, Bruno
00Swiss Panini Stickers-276

Seckler, Roland
94German First League-144

Secord, Al
80Blackhawks Postcards-12
80O-Pee-Chee-129
80Topps-129
81Blackhawks Borderless Postcards-24
81Blackhawks Brown Background-13
81O-Pee-Chee-72
82Blackhawks Postcards-20
82O-Pee-Chee-60
82O-Pee-Chee-74
82O-Pee-Chee Stickers-175
82Post Cereal-4
82Topps Stickers-175
83Blackhawks Postcards-21
83NHL Key Tags-25
83O-Pee-Chee-95
83O-Pee-Chee-112
83O-Pee-Chee-219
83O-Pee-Chee Stickers-111
83O-Pee-Chee Stickers-156
83O-Pee-Chee Stickers-160
83Puffy Stickers-16
83Topps Stickers-111
83Topps Stickers-156
83Topps Stickers-160
84O-Pee-Chee-46
847-Eleven Discs-10
85Blackhawks Team Issue-9
86Blackhawks Coke-19
86O-Pee-Chee-100
86O-Pee-Chee Stickers-155
86Topps-100
87Maple Leafs PLAY-14
87Maple Leafs Postcards-18
87Maple Leafs Postcards Oversized-18
87O-Pee-Chee-111
87O-Pee-Chee Stickers-74
87Panini Stickers-229
87Topps-111
88Maple Leafs PLAY-14
88O-Pee-Chee-249
88O-Pee-Chee Stickers-179
89Blackhawks Coke-18
90Bowman-12
Tiffany-12
90Pro Set-60A
90Pro Set-60B
91Upper Deck-635
French-635
94Arizona Icecats-23
95Images-89
Gold-89
01Upper Deck Legends-10
02UD Foundations-13
Signs of Greatness-SGAS

Secord, Brian
95Slapshot-370
95Classic-83
96Pensacola Ice Pilots-14
96Richmond Renegades-18
98Dayton Bombers-16
98Dayton Bombers EBK-3

Seda, Michael
06Czech HC Pardubice Postcards-18
06Czech OFS-127

Seder, Conlan
00Kamloops Blazers-21
03Kamloops Blazers-15
04Vancouver Giants-23

Sedevie, Layne
01Sioux Falls Stampede-10
02Topeka Scarecrows-1

Sedin, Daniel
97Black Diamond-114
Double Diamond-114
Triple Diamond-114
Quadruple Diamond-114
97Swedish Collector's Choice-159
Crash the Game Exchange-C15
Crash the Game Redemption-R15
Select-UD2
Stick'Ums-S11
98Black Diamond-109
Double Diamond-109
Triple Diamond-109
Quadruple Diamond-109
98SPx Top Prospects-79
Radiance-79
Spectrum-79
98UD Choice-294
Prime Choice Reserve-294
Reserve-294
98Swedish UD Choice-177
98Swedish UD Choice-219
98Swedish UD Choice-GJ1
98Swedish UD Choice-GJA1
99Black Diamond-119
Diamond Cut-119
Final Cut-119
99SPx-164
Radiance-164
Spectrum-164
99Upper Deck-165
99Upper Deck-307
Exclusives-165
Exclusives-307
Exclusives 1 of 1-165
Exclusives 1 of 1-307
99Upper Deck Gold Reserve-165
99Upper Deck Gold Reserve-307
99Upper Deck MVP SC Edition-217
Gold Script-217
Silver Script-217
Super Script-217
99Upper Deck Ovation-62
Standing Ovation-62
99Upper Deck Victory-368
99Swedish Upper Deck-179
99Swedish Upper Deck-217
Hands of Gold-2
Hands of Gold-12
PowerDeck-2
SHL Signatures-15
99UD Prospects-66
Destination the Show-DS4
International Stars-IN1
Signatures of Tradition-DS
00SP Authentic Autographed Replica Jersey-5
00BAP Memorabilia-397
Emerald-397
Ruby-397
Sapphire-397
00BAP Parkhurst 2000-P101
00BAP Signature Series-280
Emerald-280
Ruby-280
Sapphire-280
Autographs-242
Autographs Gold-242
Franchise Players-F29
00BAP Ultimate Memorabilia Autographs-47
Gold-47
00Black Diamond-110
00Crown Royale-143
21st Century Rookies-24
Now Playing-19
00Paramount-251
Copper-251
Gold-251
Holo-Gold-251
Holo-Silver-251
Ice Blue-251
Premiere Date-251
00Private Stock-148
Gold-148
Premiere Date-148
Retail-148
Silver-148
PS-2001 Rookies-24
00SP Authentic-85
Sign of the Times-DS
Sign of the Times-S/S
00SP Game Used-57
00SPx-149
00Stadium Club-232
00Titanium-148
Retail-148
Three-Star Selections-29
00Titanium Draft Day Edition-148
00Titanium Draft Day Promos-148
00Topps Chrome-171
OPC Refractors-171
Refractors-171
00Topps Gold Label Class 1-68
Gold-68
00Topps Gold Label Class 2-68
00Topps Gold Label Class 2 Gold-68
00Topps Gold Label Class 3-68
00Topps Gold Label Class 3 Gold-68
00Topps Gold Label Bullion-B10
00Topps Gold Label Bullion One to One-B10
00Topps Gold Label New Generation-NG11
00Topps Gold Label New Generation 1 to 1-NG11
00Topps Heritage-33
Chrome Parallel-33
New Tradition-NT2
00Topps Premier Plus-97
Blue Ice-97
Private Signings-PSDS
Rookies-PR7
Rookies Blue Ice-PR7
00Topps Stars-145
Blue-145
00UD Heroes-114
00UD Pros and Prospects-84
Now Appearing-NA7
00UD Reserve-84
Buyback Autographs-128
Buyback Autographs-129
Buyback Autographs-130
Buyback Autographs-131
00Upper Deck-400
Exclusives Tier 1-400
Exclusives Tier 2-400
00Upper Deck Ice-79
00Upper Deck MVP Excellence-ME7
00Upper Deck MVP Mark of Excellence-SGSE
00Upper Deck Vintage-353
00Vanguard-149
High Voltage-34
High Voltage Gold-34
High Voltage Green-34
High Voltage Red-34
High Voltage Silver-34
In Focus-19
Pacific Proofs-149
00Swedish Upper Deck Game Jerseys-DS
01Atomic-95
Blue-95
Gold-95
Premiere Date-95
Red-95
Power Play-33

Team Nucleus-14
01BAP Memorabilia-6
Emerald-6
Ruby-6
Sapphire-6
He Shoots-He Scores Prizes-1
Stanley Cup Playoffs-SC10
01BAP Signature Series-51
Autographs-51
Autographs Gold-51
Jerseys-GJ-63
Jersey Autographs-GUDS
Jersey and Stick Cards-GSJ-63
Teammates-TM-29
01Crown Royale Calder Collection Gold Ed-2
01Crown Royale Calder Collection AS Ed-C7
01Crown Royale-139
Blue-139
Premiere Date-139
Red-139
Retail-139
01McDonald's Pacific Future Legends-5
01O-Pee-Chee-63
01O-Pee-Chee Heritage Parallel-63
01O-Pee-Chee Heritage Parallel Limited-63
01O-Pee-Chee Premier Parallel-63
01Pacific-387
Extreme LTD-387
Hobby LTD-387
Premiere Date-387
Retail LTD-387
01Pacific Adrenaline-192
Blue-192
Premiere Date-192
Red-192
Retail-192
Playmakers-9
01Pacific Arena Exclusives-387
01Pacific Heads-Up-95
Blue-95
Premiere Date-95
Red-95
Silver-95
Breaking the Glass-19
Prime Picks-9
01Parkhurst-89
Gold-89
Silver-89
Jerseys-PJ12
Sticks-PS12
Teammates-T17
01Private Stock-95
Gold-95
Premiere Date-95
Retail-95
Silver-95
01Private Stock Pacific Nights-95
01SP Authentic-86
Limited-86
Limited Gold-86
Sign of the Times-DS
Sign of the Times-SS
Sign of the Times-SSN
01SP Game Used-57
01SPx-67
01Stadium Club-17
Award Winners-17
Master Photos-17
Gallery-G38
Gallery Gold-G38
01Titanium-138
Hobby Parallel-138
Premiere Date-138
Retail-138
Retail Parallel-138
Double-Sided Jerseys-54
Double-Sided Patches-54
01Titanium Draft Day Edition-97
01Topps-63
Heritage Parallel-63
Heritage Parallel Limited-63
OPC Parallel-63
Own The Game-OTG18
01Topps Chrome-63
Refractors-63
Black Border Refractors-63
01Topps Heritage-48
Refractors-48
01Topps Reserve-67
01UD Top Shelf-44
Jerseys-DS
Jersey Autographs-DS
01Upper Deck-168
Exclusives-168
Game Jerseys-NGDS
Game Jerseys-CSS
Game Jersey Autographs-SDS
Ice Autographs-DS
01Upper Deck MVP-182
01Upper Deck Victory-344
Gold-344
01Upper Deck Vintage-245
01Upper Deck Vintage-251
01Vanguard Prime Prospects-19
02BAP First Edition-39
02BAP First Edition-430R
Jerseys-39
02BAP Memorabilia-66
Emerald-66
Ruby-66
Sapphire-66
NHL All-Star Game-66
NHL All-Star Game Blue-66
NHL All-Star Game Green-66
NHL All-Star Game Red-66
02BAP Memorabilia Toronto Fall Expo-66
02BAP Signature Series-55
Autographs-55
Autograph Buybacks 2000-242
Autograph Buybacks 2001-51
Autographs Gold-55
Golf-GS25
Team Quads-TQ14
02Canucks Team Issue-14
02Crown Royale Dual Patches-22
02ITG Used-73
02ITG Used-173
02NHL Power Play Stickers-160
02O-Pee-Chee-58
02O-Pee-Chee Premier Blue Parallel-58
02O-Pee-Chee Premier Red Parallel-58
02O-Pee-Chee Factory Set-58
02Pacific-383
Blue-383
Red-383
02Pacific Complete-130
Red-130
02Pacific Heads-Up Head First-15
02Pacific Heads-Up Quad Jerseys-27
02Pacific Heads-Up Quad Jerseys Gold-27
02Parkhurst-167
Bronze-167
Gold-167
Silver-167
02Titanium Jerseys-71
02Titanium Jerseys Retail-71
02Topps-58
OPC Blue Parallel-58
OPC Red Parallel-58
Factory Set-58
02Topps Total-309
02UD Piece of History Mark of Distinction-DS
02UD Top Shelf Signatures-DS
02Upper Deck-167
Exclusives-167
02Upper Deck MVP-181
Gold-181
Classics-181
Golden Classics-181
Prosign-DS
02Upper Deck Vintage-249
Green Backs-249
03Beehive-185
Gold-185
Silver-185
03Canucks Postcards-24
03Canucks Sav-on-Foods-6
03Canucks Sav-on-Foods-20
03ITG Action-550
Jerseys-M76
03O-Pee-Chee-218
03OPC Blue-218
03OPC Gold-218
03OPC Red-218
03Pacific-335
Blue-335
Red-335
03Pacific Complete-46
Red-46
03Pacific Exhibit-144
Blue Backs-144
Yellow Backs-144
03Pacific Prism-96
Blue-96
Gold-96
Red-96
03Pacific Supreme Generations-12
03Titanium-96
Hobby Jersey Number Parallels-96
Retail-96
Retail Jersey Number Parallels-96
03Topps-218
Blue-218
Gold-218
Red-218
03Upper Deck-430
Canadian Exclusives-430
HG-430
UD Exclusives-430
03Upper Deck MVP-416
Gold Script-416
Silver Script-416
Canadian Exclusives-416
03Upper Deck Victory-193
Bronze-193
Gold-193
Silver-193
04Pacific-260
Blue-260
Red-260
04UD All-World-64
Gold-64
04Swedish Alfabilder Alfa Stars-12
04Swedish Alfabilder Proof Parallels-12
04Swedish Elitset-243
Dominators-9
Gold-243
04Swedish MoDo Postcards-3
04Swedish Pure Skills-65
Parallel-65
Professional Power-DS
Signatures-10
05Panini Stickers-364
05Parkhurst-466
Facsimile Auto Parallel-466
05Upper Deck-431
Jerseys-J-DSE
Patches-P-DS
05Upper Deck MVP-374
Gold-374
Platinum-374
05Swedish SHL Elitset-97
Gold-97
Playmakers-8
06Black Diamond-80
Black-80
Gold-80
Ruby-80
06Canucks Postcards-21
06Fleer-189
Tiffany-189
Fabricology-FDS
06Gatorade-78
06Hot Prospects-96
Red Hot-96
White Hot-96
06O-Pee-Chee-478
Rainbow-478
06Panini Stickers-356
06SP Game Used Authentic Fabrics-AFDS
06SP Game Used Authentic Fabrics Parallel-AFDS
06SP Game Used Authentic Fabrics Patches-AFDS
06SP Game Used Authentic Fabrics Triple-AF3VAN
06SP Game Used Authentic Fabrics Triple Patches-AF3VAN
06The Cup NHL Shields Duals-DSHHD
06UD Artifacts Tundra Tandems-TTHD
06UD Artifacts Tundra Tandems Black-TTHD
06UD Artifacts Tundra Tandems Blue-TTHD
06UD Artifacts Tundra Tandems Gold-TTHD
06UD Artifacts Tundra Tandems Platinum-TTHD
06UD Artifacts Tundra Tandems Red-TTHD
06UD Artifacts Tundra Tandems Dual Patches Red-TTHD
06Ultra-194
Gold Medallion-194
Ice Medallion-194
06Upper Deck Arena Giveaways-VAN6
06Upper Deck-191
Exclusives Parallel-191
High Gloss Parallel-191
Game Jerseys-J2DS
Game Patches-P2DS
Masterpieces-191
06Upper Deck MVP-284
Gold Script-284
Super Script-284
06Upper Deck Ovation-149
06Upper Deck Trilogy-98
06Upper Deck Victory-196
06Upper Deck Victory Black-196
06Upper Deck Victory Gold-196
07Upper Deck Ovation-2
07Upper Deck Victory-132
Black-132
Gold-132

Sedin, Henrik
97Black Diamond-136
Double Diamond-136
Triple Diamond-136
Quadruple Diamond-136
97Swedish Collector's Choice-160
Crash the Game Exchange-C16
Crash the Game Redemption-R16
Select-UD9
Stick'Ums-S10
98Black Diamond-110
Double Diamond-110
Triple Diamond-110
Quadruple Diamond-110
98SPx Top Prospects-80
Radiance-80
Spectrum-80
98UD Choice-295
Prime Choice Reserve-295
Reserve-295
98Swedish UD Choice-178
98Swedish UD Choice-220
98Swedish UD Choice-GJ1
98Swedish UD Choice-GJA1
99Black Diamond-120
Diamond Cut-120
Final Cut-120
99SPx-165
Radiance-165
Spectrum-165
99Upper Deck-166
99Upper Deck-308
Exclusives-166
Exclusives-308
Exclusives 1 of 1-166
Exclusives 1 of 1-308
99Upper Deck Gold Reserve-166
99Upper Deck Gold Reserve-308
99Upper Deck MVP SC Edition-218
Gold Script-218
Silver Script-218
Super Script-218
99Upper Deck Ovation-63
Standing Ovation-63
99Upper Deck Victory-369
99Swedish Upper Deck-180
99Swedish Upper Deck-220
Hands of Gold-3
Hands of Gold-13
PowerDeck-2
SHL Signatures-16
99UD Prospects-67
Destination the Show-DS3
International Stars-IN2
Signatures of Tradition-HS
00SP Authentic Autographed Replica Jersey-6
00BAP Memorabilia-496
Emerald-496
Ruby-496
Sapphire-496
00BAP Parkhurst 2000-P207
00BAP Signature Series-281
Emerald-281
Ruby-281
Sapphire-281
Autographs-243
Autographs Gold-243
00Black Diamond-111
00Crown Royale-144
21st Century Rookies-25
Now Playing-20
00Paramount-252
Copper-252
Gold-252
Holo-Gold-252
Holo-Silver-252
Ice Blue-252
Premiere Date-252
00Private Stock-149
Gold-149
Premiere Date-149
Retail-149
Silver-149
PS-2001 Rookies-25
00SP Authentic-86
Sign of the Times-HS
Sign of the Times-S/S
00SP Game Used-58
00SPx-150
00Stadium Club-231
00Titanium-149
Retail-149
Three-Star Selections-30
00Titanium Draft Day Edition-149
00Titanium Draft Day Promos-149
00Topps Chrome-209
OPC Refractors-209
Refractors-209
00Topps Gold Label Class 1-77
Gold-77
00Topps Gold Label Class 2-77
00Topps Gold Label Class 2 Gold-77
00Topps Gold Label Class 3-77
00Topps Gold Label Class 3 Gold-77
00Topps Gold Label Bullion-B10
00Topps Gold Label Bullion One to One-B10
00Topps Gold Label New Generation-NG7
00Topps Gold Label New Generation 1 to 1-NG7
00Topps Heritage-19
Chrome Parallel-19
New Tradition-NT9
00Topps Premier Plus-87
Blue Ice-87
Private Signings-PSHS
Rookies-PR2
Rookies Blue Ice-PR2
00Topps Stars-144
Blue-144
00UD Heroes-113
00UD Pros and Prospects-85
Now Appearing-NA8
00UD Reserve-85
Buyback Autographs-113
Buyback Autographs-114
Buyback Autographs-115
Buyback Autographs-116
Buyback Autographs-117
00Upper Deck-402
Exclusives Tier 1-402
Exclusives Tier 2-402
Triple Threat-TT3
00Upper Deck Ice-78
00Upper Deck MVP Excellence-ME7
00Upper Deck MVP Mark of Excellence-SGSE
00Upper Deck Vintage-355
00Vanguard-150
High Voltage-35
High Voltage Gold-35
High Voltage Green-35
High Voltage Red-35
High Voltage Silver-35
In Focus-20
Pacific Proofs-150
00Swedish Upper Deck Game Jerseys-HS
01Atomic-96
Blue-96
Gold-96
Premiere Date-96
Red-96
Power Play-34
Team Nucleus-14
01BAP Memorabilia-46
Emerald-46
Ruby-46
Sapphire-46
01BAP Signature Series-72
Autographs-72
Autographs Gold-72
Jerseys-GJ-13
Jersey Autographs-GUHS
Jersey and Stick Cards-GSJ-13
01Crown Royale Calder Collection Gold Ed-3
01Crown Royale Calder Collection AS Ed-C8
01Crown Royale-140
Blue-140
Premiere Date-140
Red-140
Retail-140
01McDonald's Pacific Future Legends-6
01O-Pee-Chee-45
01O-Pee-Chee Heritage Parallel-45
01O-Pee-Chee Heritage Parallel Limited-45
01O-Pee-Chee Premier Parallel-45
01Pacific-388
Extreme LTD-388
Hobby LTD-388
Premiere Date-388
Retail LTD-388
01Pacific Adrenaline-193
Blue-193
Premiere Date-193
Red-193
Retail-193
Playmakers-10
01Pacific Arena Exclusives-388
01Pacific Heads-Up-96
Blue-96
Premiere Date-96
Red-96
Silver-96
Breaking the Glass-20
Prime Picks-10
01Parkhurst-75
Gold-75
Silver-75
01Private Stock-96
Gold-96
Premiere Date-96
Retail-96
Silver-96
01Private Stock Pacific Nights-96
01SP Authentic-87
Limited-87
Limited Gold-87
Sign of the Times-HS
Sign of the Times-SS
Sign of the Times-SSN
01SP Game Used Inked Sweaters-ISHS
01Stadium Club-43
Award Winners-43
Master Photos-43
Gallery-G15
Gallery Gold-G15
01Titanium-139
Hobby Parallel-139
Premiere Date-139
Retail-139
Retail Parallel-139
Double-Sided Jerseys-54
Double-Sided Patches-54
01Titanium Draft Day Edition-98
01Topps-45
Heritage Parallel-45
Heritage Parallel Limited-45
OPC Parallel-45
01Topps Chrome-45
Refractors-45
Black Border Refractors-45
01Topps Heritage-27
Refractors-27
01Topps Reserve-23
01UD Top Shelf Jerseys-HS
01UD Top Shelf Jersey Autographs-HS
01Upper Deck-169
Exclusives-169
Game Jerseys-NGHS
Game Jerseys-CSS
Game Jersey Autographs-SHS
Ice Autographs-HS
01Upper Deck Victory-345
Gold-345
01Upper Deck Vintage-251
01Vanguard Prime Prospects-20
02BAP First Edition-27
02BAP First Edition-430R
Jerseys-27
02BAP Memorabilia-173
Emerald-173
Ruby-173
Sapphire-173
NHL All-Star Game-173
NHL All-Star Game Blue-173
NHL All-Star Game Green-173
NHL All-Star Game Red-173
02BAP Memorabilia Toronto Fall Expo-173
02BAP Signature Series-17
Autographs-17
Autograph Buybacks 2000-243
Autograph Buybacks 2001-72
Autographs Gold-17
Team Quads-TQ14
02Canucks Team Issue-15
02Crown Royale Dual Patches-22
02ITG Used-74
02ITG Used-174
02NHL Power Play Stickers-167
02O-Pee-Chee-213
02O-Pee-Chee Premier Blue Parallel-213
02O-Pee-Chee Premier Red Parallel-213
02O-Pee-Chee Factory Set-213
02Pacific-384
Blue-384
Red-384
02Pacific Complete-235
Red-235
02Pacific Heads-Up Head First-16
02Pacific Heads-Up Quad Jerseys-27
02Pacific Heads-Up Quad Jerseys Gold-27
02Parkhurst-165
Bronze-165
Gold-165
Silver-165
02Parkhurst Retro-169
Minis-169
02Titanium Jerseys-72
02Titanium Jerseys Retail-72
02Titanium Patches-72
02Topps-213
OPC Blue Parallel-213
OPC Red Parallel-213
Factory Set-213
02Topps Total-12
02UD Piece of History Mark of Distinction-HS
02UD Top Shelf Signatures-HS
02Upper Deck-413
Exclusives-413
02Upper Deck Beckett UD Promos-413
02Upper Deck MVP-182
Gold-182
Classics-182
Golden Classics-182
Prosign-HS
02Upper Deck Vintage-247
Green Backs-247
03Beehive-188
Gold-188
Silver-188
03Canucks Postcards-25
03Canucks Sav-on-Foods-14
03Canucks Sav-on-Foods-20
03ITG Action-544
Jerseys-M77
03NHL Sticker Collection-297
03O-Pee-Chee-20
03OPC Blue-20
03OPC Gold-20
03OPC Red-20
03Pacific-336
Blue-336
Red-336
03Pacific Complete-44
Red-44
03Pacific Exhibit-145
Blue Backs-145
Yellow Backs-145
03Pacific Prism-97
Blue-97
Gold-97
Red-97
03Titanium-97
Hobby Jersey Number Parallels-97
Retail-97
Retail Jersey Number Parallels-97
03Topps-20
Blue-20
Gold-20
Red-20
03Upper Deck-189
Canadian Exclusives-189
HG-189
03Upper Deck MVP-414
Gold Script-414
Silver Script-414
Canadian Exclusives-414
03Upper Deck Victory-192
Bronze-192
Gold-192
Silver-192
04Pacific-261
Blue-261
Red-261
04UD All-World-65
Gold-65
04Swedish Alfabilder Alfa Stars-20
04Swedish Alfabilder Autographs-105
04Swedish Alfabilder Limited Autographs-105
04Swedish Alfabilder Proof Parallels-20
04Swedish Elitset-247
Dominators-9
Gold-247
04Swedish MoDo Postcards-2
04Swedish Pure Skills-68
Parallel-68
Professional Power-HS
Signatures-11
05Beehive Matted Materials-MMHS
05Panini Stickers-365
05Parkhurst-467
Facsimile Auto Parallel-467
05Upper Deck-430
Jerseys-J-HSE
Patches-P-HS
05Upper Deck MVP-377
Gold-377
Platinum-377
05Swedish SHL Elitset-101
Gold-101
Playmakers-9
06Be A Player-43
Autographs-43
Signatures-HS
Signatures 10-46
Up Close and Personal-UC20
Up Close and Personal Autographs-UC20
06Black Diamond-81
Black-81
Gold-81
Ruby-81
06Canucks Postcards-22
06Fleer-190
Tiffany-190
06Gatorade-79
06Hot Prospects-97
Red Hot-97
White Hot-97
Hot Materials -HMHS
Hot Materials Red Hot-HMHS
Hot Materials White Hot-HMHS
06O-Pee-Chee-477
Rainbow-477
Swatches-S-HS
06Panini Stickers-357
06SP Game Used Authentic Fabrics-AFHS
06SP Game Used Authentic Fabrics Parallel-AFHS
06SP Game Used Authentic Fabrics Patches-AFHS
06SP Game Used Authentic Fabrics Triple-AF3VAN
06SP Game Used Authentic Fabrics Triple Patches-AF3VAN
06SP Game Used Authentic Fabrics Quads-AF4SFSZ
06SP Game Used Authentic Fabrics Quads Patches-AF4SFSZ
06The Cup NHL Shields Duals-DSHHD
06UD Artifacts Tundra Tandems-TTHD
06UD Artifacts Tundra Tandems Black-TTHD
06UD Artifacts Tundra Tandems Blue-TTHD
06UD Artifacts Tundra Tandems Gold-TTHD
06UD Artifacts Tundra Tandems Platinum-TTHD
06UD Artifacts Tundra Tandems Red-TTHD
06UD Artifacts Tundra Tandems Dual Patches Red-TTHD
06UD Mini Jersey Collection-97
06UD Powerplay-98
Impact Rainbow-98
06Ultra-190
Gold Medallion-190
Ice Medallion-190
06Upper Deck Arena Giveaways-VAN2
06Upper Deck-189
Exclusives Parallel-189
High Gloss Parallel-189
Game Jerseys-J2HS
Game Patches-P2HS
Masterpieces-189
06Upper Deck MVP-287
Gold Script-287
Super Script-287
06Upper Deck Ovation-198
06Upper Deck Trilogy-97
06Upper Deck Victory-190
06Upper Deck Victory Black-190
06Upper Deck Victory Gold-190
07Upper Deck Ovation-3
07Upper Deck Victory-134
Black-134
Gold-134

Sedlacek, Lukas
03Tulsa Oilers-19

Sedlacek, Miroslav
99Czech Score Blue 2000-62
99Czech Score Red Ice 2000-62

Sedlak, Premysl
98Czech OFS-402
99Czech Score Blue 2000-69
99Czech Score Red Ice 2000-69
00Czech OFS-128
01Czech OFS-266

Sedlak, Zdenek
94Czech APS Extraliga-201
95Czech APS Extraliga-49
96Czech APS Extraliga-38
97Czech APS Extraliga-68
98Czech DS Stickers-302
98Czech OFS-80
99Czech DS-93
99Czech OFS-376
00Finnish Cardset-291
01Czech OFS-220
02Czech DS-29
02Swiss HNL-207
03Czech OFS Plus-215
03Czech OFS Plus-342

Sedlar, Dalibor
06Czech OFS-241

Sedlbauer, Ron
75Canucks Royal Bank-19
76Canucks Royal Bank-17
76O-Pee-Chee NHL-271
77Canucks Royal Bank-18
77O-Pee-Chee NHL-368
78Canucks Royal Bank-19
78O-Pee-Chee-139
78Topps-139
79Canucks Royal Bank-19
79O-Pee-Chee-19
79Topps-19
80Blackhawks Postcards-13
80O-Pee-Chee-134
80Topps-134
81Blackhawks Brown Background-14
81O-Pee-Chee-324

Sedy, Petr
94Czech APS Extraliga-98
95Czech APS Extraliga-59
96Czech APS Extraliga-245

Seeberger, Christian
94German DEL-177
95German DEL-173
99German Bundesliga 2-17

Seegmiller, Matt
06Oshawa Generals-17

Seeholzer, Marco
93Swiss HNL-382
95Swiss HNL-51
96Swiss HNL-268
01Swiss HNL-458
02Swiss HNL-205

Seeley, Richard
96Lethbridge Hurricanes-15
97Prince Albert Raiders-18
98Prince Albert Raiders-22
99Lowell Lock Monsters-3
99Bowman CHL-98
Gold-98
OPC International-98
00Lowell Lock Monsters-17
01Manchester Monarchs-8B
02Manchester Monarchs-15
03Manchester Monarchs-16
03Manchester Monarchs Team Issue-16
05Manchester Monarchs-17

Seesvuori, Risto
70Finnish Jaakiekko-222
71Finnish Suomi Stickers-144

Sefcik, Karel
98Czech OFS-284
99Czech Score Blue 2000-163
99Czech Score Red Ice 2000-163

Seftel, Steve
85Kingston Canadians-8
86Kingston Canadians-20
87Kingston Canadians-20
88ProCards AHL-42
89ProCards AHL-90
90ProCards AHL/IHL-203
91Baltimore Skipjacks-12
91ProCards-556

Segal, Brandon
99Calgary Hitmen-22
99Calgary Hitmen Autographs-22
00Calgary Hitmen-22
01Calgary Hitmen-20
01Calgary Hitmen Autographed-20
02Calgary Hitmen-18
03Calgary Hitmen-17
03Milwaukee Admirals-19
04Milwaukee Admirals-14
05Milwaukee Admirals Choice-13
05Milwaukee Admirals Pepsi-17
06Milwaukee Admirals -16

Segal, Corey
93Quebec Pee-Wee Tournament-1264

Seger, Mathias
96Swiss HNL-135
98Swiss Power Play Stickers-184
98Swiss Power Play Stickers-266
99Swiss Panini Stickers-235
99Swiss Panini Stickers-259
00Swiss Panini Stickers-275
00Swiss Panini Stickers National Team-P11
00Swiss Slapshot Mini-Cards-ZSCL4
01Swiss HNL-8
02Swiss HNL-238
02Swiss HNL-266

Segerberg, Hans
84Swedish Semic Elitserien-138
85Swedish Panini Stickers-21
87Swedish Panini Stickers-19

Segerman, Gunnar
56Swedish Alfabilder-66

Segersten, Jan
84Swedish Semic Elitserien-159
85Swedish Panini Stickers-142

Segla, Michal
04Czech OFS Czech/Slovak-40

Segstro, Trevor
03Elmira Jackals-18

Seguin, Brett
897th Inn. Sketch OHL-49
907th Inn. Sketch OHL-92
917th Inn. Sketch OHL-301
93Muskegon Fury-5
94Muskegon Fury-8
95Muskegon Fury-4
97Austin Ice Bats-17
98Topeka Scarecrows-5
99Topeka Scarecrows-18
00Austin Ice Bats-19
01Austin Ice Bats-14
02Austin Ice Bats-15
03Austin Ice Bats-13

Seguin, Cody
93Quebec Pee-Wee Tournament-153

Seguin, Ian
01Moncton Wildcats-8

Seguin, J.F.
99Kingston Frontenacs-17
00Kingston Frontenacs-17
01Sudbury Wolves-13
01Sudbury Wolves Police-8

Seguin, Philippe
01Val d'Or Foreurs-1

Seguin, Samuel
98Halifax Mooseheads-4
98Halifax Mooseheads Second Edition-13

Seguin, Steve
81Kingston Canadians-13
82Kingston Canadians-10
84Kings Smokey-21

Seher, Kurt
907th Inn. Sketch WHL-61
917th Inn. Sketch WHL-133
96Anaheim Bullfrogs RHI-6
96Charlotte Checkers-16
97Charlotte Checkers-5
97Charlotte Checkers-25
98Charlotte Checkers-14
99Charlotte Checkers-4
00Charlotte Checkers-7
02Charlotte Checkers-91

Sehlstedt, Christer
69Swedish Hockey-103
72Swedish Stickers-226
73Swedish Stickers-226
74Swedish Stickers-149

Seib, Jirko
94German First League-616

Seibel, Chad
88Lethbridge Hurricanes-21
90Prince Albert Raiders-19
907th Inn. Sketch WHL-280
917th Inn. Sketch WHL-40
94Greensboro Monarchs-5

Seibel, Kevin
99Prince George Cougars-6
00Swift Current Broncos-16
01Swift Current Broncos-3

Seibert, Earl
34Beehive Group I Photos-78
35Diamond Matchbooks Tan 1-61
35Diamond Matchbooks Tan 4-12
35Diamond Matchbooks Tan 5-10
37Diamond Matchbooks Tan 6-10
39O-Pee-Chee V301-1-76
83Hall of Fame Postcards-K16
85Hall of Fame-150
92Hall of Fame Legends-27
94Parkhurst Missing Link Pop-Ups-P12
04ITG Ultimate Mem Chitown Immortals-7
05ITG Ultimate Mem Quad Paper Cuts Autos-2
06ITG Ultimate Memorabilia Lumbergraphs-12
06ITG Ultimate Memorabilia Paper Cuts Autos-6

Seibert, Oliver
83Hall of Fame Postcards-J14
85Hall of Fame-193

Seidel, Mike
06Cedar Rapids RoughRiders-13

Seidenberg, Dennis
99German DEL-23
01German Upper Deck-261
02Atomic-121
Blue-121
Gold-121
Red-121
Hobby Parallel-121
02BAP All-Star Edition-125
Gold-125
Silver-125
02BAP Memorabilia-273
Emerald-273
Ruby-273
Sapphire-273
NHL All-Star Game-273
NHL All-Star Game Blue-273
NHL All-Star Game Green-273
NHL All-Star Game Red-273
02BAP Memorabilia Toronto Fall Expo-273
02BAP Signature Series-180
All-Rookie-AR3
Autographs-180
Autographs Gold-180
Defensive Wall-DW3
Jerseys-SGJ65
Jersey Autographs-SGJ65
02BAP Ultimate Memorabilia-3
Calder Candidates-8
02Bowman YoungStars-147
Gold-147
Silver-147
Autographs-DS
Jerseys-DS
Patches-DS
Double Stuff-DS
Triple Stuff-DS
Rivals-BJDS
Rivals Patches-9
Sticks-DS
02Crown Royale-129
Blue-129
Purple-129
Red-129
Retail-129
02Flyers Postcards-15
02ITG Used-83
Calder Jerseys-C13
Calder Jerseys Gold-C13
02Pacific Calder-135
Silver-135
02Pacific Complete-538
Red-538
02Pacific Exclusive-187
Blue-187
Gold-187
02Pacific Heads-Up-143
02Pacific Quest for the Cup-135
Gold-135
02Parkhurst-203
Bronze-203
Gold-203
Silver-203
02Parkhurst Retro-203
Minis-203
02Private Stock Reserve-175
Blue-175
Red-175
Retail-175
02SP Authentic-153
02SP Game Used-87
02Stadium Club-137
Silver Decoy Cards-137
Proofs-137
02Titanium-128
Blue-128
Red-128
Retail-128
02Topps Chrome-172
Black Border Refractors-172
Refractors-172
02Topps Heritage-143
02Topps Total-427
02UD Honor Roll-122
02UD Mask Collection-142
02UD Piece of History-144
02UD Premier Collection-63
Gold-63
02UD Top Shelf-99
02Upper Deck-445
Exclusives-445
02Upper Deck Classic Portraits-123
02Vanguard-126
LTD-126
03ITG Action-482
03O-Pee-Chee-194
03OPC Blue-194
03OPC Gold-194
03OPC Red-194
03Topps-194
Blue-194
Gold-194
Red-194
03Philadelphia Phantoms-6
04German DEL Global Players-GP5
04Philadelphia Phantoms-16
05Flyers Team Issue-20
05German DEL-288
05Philadelphia Phantoms All-Decade Team-11

Seidenberg, Yannic
02German Adler Mannheim Eagles Postcards-8
02German DEL City Press-255
03German Mannheim Eagles Postcards-5
03Medicine Hat Tigers-8
04German Cologne Sharks Postcards-26
04German DEL-222
05German DEL-160
06German DEL-100

Seiker, Shane
907th Inn. Sketch WHL-328

Seikola, Markus
00Finnish Cardset-337
01Finnish Cardset-138
02Finnish Cardset-114
04Finnish Cardset-171
Parallel-126
05Finnish Cardset -330
06Swedish SHL Elitset-173

Seiler, Daniel
93Quebec Pee-Wee Tournament-1622

Seiling, Ric
75Hamilton Fincups-17
78O-Pee-Chee-242
78Topps-242
79O-Pee-Chee-119
79Sabres Milk Panels-2
79Topps-119
80O-Pee-Chee-159
80Sabres Milk Panels-4
80Topps-159
81O-Pee-Chee-32
81Sabres Milk Panels-15
82O-Pee-Chee-35
82O-Pee-Chee Stickers-123
82Post Cereal-2
82Sabres Milk Panels-8
82Topps Stickers-123
83NHL Key Tags-13
83O-Pee-Chee-72
84O-Pee-Chee-31
84O-Pee-Chee Stickers-216
84Sabres Blue Shield-19
85O-Pee-Chee Stickers-182
85Sabres Blue Shield-26
85Sabres Blue Shield Small-26
86O-Pee-Chee-201
95Owen Sound Platers-2

Seiling, Rod
64Beehive Group III Photos-148
64Coca-Cola Caps-85
64Topps-57
65Topps-23
66Topps-22
66Topps USA Test-22
67Topps-27
68O-Pee-Chee-71
68Shirriff Coins-93
68Topps-71
69O-Pee-Chee-36
Four-in-One-13
69Topps-36
70Dad's Cookies-120
70Esso Power Players-191
70O-Pee-Chee-184
70Sargent Promotions Stamps-128
71O-Pee-Chee-53
71Sargent Promotions Stamps-119
71Topps-53
71Toronto Sun-183
72O-Pee-Chee-194
Team Canada-26
72Sargent Promotions Stamps-148
72Topps-149
73O-Pee-Chee-9
73Topps-9
74Maple Leafs Postcards-19
74NHL Action Stamps-190
74NHL Action Stamps Update-37
74O-Pee-Chee NHL-102
74Topps-102
75Maple Leafs Postcards-18
75O-Pee-Chee NHL-229
75Topps-229
76O-Pee-Chee NHL-280
77O-Pee-Chee NHL-226
77Topps-226
78Flames Majik Market-15
78O-Pee-Chee-394
91Future Trends Canada '72-21
91Future Trends Canada '72 French-21
94Parkhurst Tall Boys-93
95Parkhurst '66-67-95
Coins-95
04UD Legendary Signatures-73
Autographs-RS

Summit Stars-CDN18
Summit Stars Autographs-CDN-RS

Seiling, Scott

94Owen Sound Platers-15
95Slapshot-254
95Slapshot-296
95Owen Sound Platers-18

Seils, Jason

94Minnesota Golden Gophers-25
95Minnesota Golden Gophers-25

Seistamo, Jouni

65Finnish Hellas-152
66Finnish Jaakiekkosarja-156
05Finnish Tappara Legendat-20

Seitsonen, Aki

03Prince Albert Raiders-1
04Prince Albert Raiders-14
05Prince Albert Raiders-20
06Las Vegas Wranglers-21

Seitz, David

92Clarkson Knights-20
96South Carolina Stingrays-14
98ECHL All-Star Southern Conference-9
01South Carolina Stingrays-15
02South Carolina Stingrays-17
02South Carolina Stingrays RBI-220
03South Carolina Stingrays-333

Seitz, Thomas

95Swiss HNL-336
96Swiss HNL-442

Seivo, Jyrki

73Finnish Jaakiekko-118

Sejba, Jiri

89Swedish Semic World Champ Stickers-196
90Sabres Blue Shield-21
90Sabres Campbell's-23
90ProCards AHL/IHL-286
91Upper Deck-362
French-362
91ProCards-5
91Rochester Americans Dunkin' Donuts-15
91Rochester Americans Kodak-24
91Rochester Americans Postcards-19
92Finnish Jyvas-Hyva Stickers-58
94Czech APS Extraliga-37
98Czech OFS Legends-4
99German DEL-356

Sejejs, Normunds

95Czech APS Extraliga-156
96Czech APS Extraliga-175
97Czech DS Stickers-39
98Czech OFS-334
00Czech DS Extraliga-124
00Czech OFS-166
03Czech OFS Plus All-Star Game-H2

Sejna, Peter

93Quebec Pee-Wee Tournament-1715
99Des Moines Buccaneers-9
02SPx Rookie Redemption-R210
03BAP Memorabilia-174
Emerald-174
Gold-174
Ruby-174
Sapphire-174
03BAP Ultimate Mem Rookie Jersey Emblems-32
03BAP Ultimate Mem Rookie Jsy Emblem Gold-32
03BAP Ultimate Mem Rookie Jersey Numbers-32
03BAP Ultimate Mem Rookie Jsy Number Gold-32
03Beehive-233
Gold-233
Silver-233
03Black Diamond-196
Black-196
Green-196
Red-196
03Blues Team Set-25
03Bowman-148
Gold-148
Premier Performance-PP-PS
Premier Performance Patches-PP-PS
Signs of the Future-SOF-PS
03Bowman Chrome-148
Refractors-148
Gold Refractors-148
Xfractors-148
03Crown Royale-132
Red-132
Retail-132
03eTopps-42
03ITG Action-548
03ITG Used Signature Series-167
Gold-167
03McDonald's Pacific-43
03O-Pee-Chee-316
03OPC Blue-316
03OPC Gold-316
03OPC Red-316
03Pacific-288
Blue-288
Red-288
03Pacific Calder-173
03Pacific Complete-535
Red-535
03Pacific Exhibit-124
Blue Backs-124
Yellow Backs-124
03Pacific Heads-Up-132
Hobby LTD-132
Retail LTD-132
03Pacific Invincible-122
Blue-122
Red-122
Retail-122
03Pacific Luxury Suite-97
Gold-97
03Pacific Prism-85
Blue-85
Gold-85
Red-85
03Pacific Quest for the Cup-134
03Pacific Supreme-135
03Pacific Supreme-135A
Blue-135
Red-135
Retail-135
03Parkhurst Rookie-139
Rookie Emblems-RE-30
Rookie Emblems Gold-RE-30
Rookie Jerseys-RJ-30
Rookie Jerseys Gold-RJ-30
Rookie Numbers-RN-30
Rookie Numbers Gold-RN-30
Teammates Gold-RT14
Teammates-RT14
03Private Stock Reserve-136
Blue-136
Red-136
Retail-136
Class Act-10
03SP Authentic-156
Limited-156
Signed Patches-PS
03SP Game Used-79
Gold-79
Authentic Fabrics-AFPS
Authentic Fabrics Gold-AFPS
03SPx-208
Radiance-208
Spectrum-208
03Titanium-135
Hobby Jersey Number Parallels-135
Retail-135
Retail Jersey Number Parallels-135
03Topps-316
Blue-316
Gold-316
Red-316
03Topps C55-141
Minis-141
Minis American Back-141
Minis American Back Red-141
Minis Bazooka Back-141
Minis Brooklyn Back-141
Minis Hat Trick Back-141
Minis O Canada Back-141
Minis O Canada Back Red-141
Minis Stanley Cup Back-141
03Topps Pristine-134
03Topps Pristine-135
03Topps Pristine-136
Gold Refractor Die Cuts-134
Gold Refractor Die Cuts-135
Gold Refractor Die Cuts-136
Refractors-134
Refractors-135
Refractors-136
Mini-PM-PS
Press Plates Black-134
Press Plates Black-135
Press Plates Black-136
Press Plates Cyan-134
Press Plates Cyan-135
Press Plates Cyan-136
Press Plates Magenta-134
Press Plates Magenta-135
Press Plates Magenta-136
Press Plates Yellow-134
Press Plates Yellow-135
Press Plates Yellow-136
03Topps Traded Future Phenoms-FP-PS
03UD Honor Roll-168
03UD Premier Collection-106
03Upper Deck-241
Canadian Exclusives-241
HG-241
Rookie Threads-RT-5
03Upper Deck Classic Portraits-165
03Upper Deck Ice-100
Glass Parallel-100
03Upper Deck MVP-375
Gold Script-375
Silver Script-375
Canadian Exclusives-375
03Upper Deck Rookie Update-137
03Upper Deck Trilogy-168
Limited-168
03Upper Deck Victory-162
Bronze-162
Gold-162
Silver-162
03Pacific AHL Prospects-100
Gold-100
Destined for Greatness-10
04Pacific NHL All-Star FANtasy-9
04Pacific NHL All-Star FANtasy Gold-9
04AHL Top Prospects-60
04Worcester IceCats-16
05ITG Heroes/Prosp Toronto Expo Parallel -245
05UD Powerplay Power Marks-PMPS
05AHL Top Prospects-36
05Peoria Rivermen-16
05ITG Heroes and Prospects-245
Autographs Series II-PSJ
06Peoria Rivermen-17

Sekera, Andrej

04Owen Sound Attack-16
05OHL Bell All-Star Classic-9
05Owen Sound Attack-3
06Hot Prospects-197
06Rochester Americans-18
06The Cup Masterpiece Pressplates (Ultimate Collection)-64
06Ultimate Collection-64

Sekera, Martin

94Czech APS Extraliga-44
97Czech APS Extraliga-122

Sekeras, Lubomir

94Finnish Jaa Kiekko-192
95Czech APS Extraliga-227
95Slovakian APS National Team-9
96Czech APS Extraliga-53
96Swedish Semic Wien-222
97Czech APS Extraliga-317
97Czech DS Extraliga-5
97Czech DS Stickers-229
98Czech DS-115
98Czech DS Stickers-268
98Czech OFS-385
99Czech DS-104
99Czech OFS-409
00BAP Memorabilia-491
Emerald-491
Ruby-491
Sapphire-491
00BAP Parkhurst 2000-P219
00BAP Signature Series-271
Emerald-271
Ruby-271
Sapphire-271
Autographs-233
Autographs Gold-233
00SP Authentic-147
00SPx-179
00Stadium Club-256
00Topps Premier Plus-108
Blue Ice-108
00Upper Deck-432
Exclusives Tier 1-432
Exclusives Tier 2-432
00Upper Deck Ice-113
00Czech OFS-402
01Pacific-200
Extreme LTD-200
Hobby LTD-200
Premiere Date-200
Retail LTD-200
01Pacific Adrenaline-94
Blue-94
Premiere Date-94
Red-94
Retail-94
01Pacific Arena Exclusives-200
01Upper Deck-86
Exclusives-86
01Upper Deck MVP-92
01Upper Deck Victory-174
Gold-174
01Upper Deck Vintage-126
01Upper Deck Vintage-130
01Slovakian Kvarteto-7C
02Pacific Complete-359
Red-359
02Topps Total-348
03ITG Action-244
03Russian Hockey League-261
04German DEL-256
06Czech HC Zlin Hame Postcards-13
06Czech OFS-242

Selanne, Teemu

91Upper Deck-21
French-21
91Finnish Semic World Champ Stickers-21
91Finnish Jyvas-Hyva Stickers-21
91Swedish Semic World Champ Stickers-21
92OPC Premier-68
92Parkhurst-209
92Parkhurst-217
92Parkhurst-500
Emerald Ice-209
Emerald Ice-217
Emerald Ice-500
92Pinnacle Canadian Promo Panels-3
92Pinnacle-406
French-406
92Sports Illustrated for Kids II-200
92Sports Illustrated for Kids II-710
92Stadium Club Members Only-49
92Stadium Club Members Only-50
92Ultra-444
92Ultra-450
Imports-21
92Upper Deck-574
Calder Candidates-CC10
Euro-Rookies-ER6
Gordie Howe Selects-G15
92Finnish Semic-11
93Donruss-387
93Donruss-394
Elite Inserts-3
Ice Kings-10
Special Print-Z
93Jets Readers Club-17
93Jets Ruffles-22
93Kraft-22
93Leaf-13
93Leaf-110
Gold All-Stars-3
Gold Rookies-1
Hat Trick Artists-3
93McDonald's Upper Deck-H2
93OPC Premier-92
93OPC Premier-130
93OPC Premier-148
93OPC Premier-483
Gold-92
Gold-130
Gold-148
Gold-483
Black Gold-20
93Panini Stickers-142
93Panini Stickers-Q
93Parkhurst-233
93Parkhurst-235
Emerald Ice-233
Emerald Ice-235
East/West Stars-W3
USA/Canada Gold-G8
93Pinnacle I Samples-5
93Pinnacle-4
93Pinnacle-222
Canadian-4
Canadian-222
All-Stars-32
All-Stars Canadian-32
Nifty Fifty-3
Team Pinnacle-12
Team Canadian-12
Team 2001-10
Team 2001 Canadian-10
93PowerPlay-274
Global Greats-7
Point Leaders-16
Second Year Stars-10
Slapshot Artists-9
93Score-331
93Score-477
Canadian-331
Canadian-477
Dream Team-21
Dynamic Duos Canadian-2
Franchise-24
International Stars-2
International Stars Canadian-2
93Seasons Patches-18
93Stadium Club-141
93Stadium Club-210
Members Only Master Set-141
Members Only Master Set-210
OPC-141
OPC-210
First Day Issue-141
First Day Issue-210
First Day Issue OPC-141
First Day Issue OPC-210
All-Stars-22
All-Stars Members Only-22
All-Stars OPC-22
Master Photos-4
Master Photos Winners-4
93Topps/OPC Premier-92
93Topps/OPC Premier-130
93Topps/OPC Premier-148
93Topps/OPC Premier-483
Gold-92
Gold-130
Gold-148
Gold-483
93Topps Premier Black Gold-1
93Topps Premier Black Gold-A
93Ultra-48
93Ultra-250
All-Stars-11
Award Winners-6
Red Light Specials-10
Speed Merchants-10
93Upper Deck-281
93Upper Deck-309
93Upper Deck-448
93Upper Deck-SP4
Award Winners-AW2
Future Heroes-32
NHLPA/Roots-17
Silver Skates-R2
Silver Skates Gold-R2
SP-177
93Upper Deck Locker All-Stars-35
93Swedish Semic World Champ Stickers-77
93Classic-124
Crash Numbered-N5
McDonalds-19
Previews-HK4
94SLU Hockey Canadian-12
94Hockey Canadian-12
94SLU Hockey American-19
94Be A Player Magazine-4
94Be A Player-R11
Signature Cards-11
Up Close and Personal-UC4
94Canada Games NHL POGS-253
94Donruss-210
Dominators-8
94EA Sports-149
94Finest-76
Super Team Winners-76
Refractors-76
Bowman's Best-B14
Bowman's Best Refractors-B14
94Flair-209
94Fleer-245
94Hockey Wit-55
94Kenner Starting Lineup Cards-20
94Leaf-362
Fire on Ice-12
Limited Inserts-26
94Leaf Limited-68
94McDonald's Upper Deck-McD25
94OPC Premier-95
94OPC Premier-243
94OPC Premier-416
Special Effects-95
Special Effects-243
Special Effects-416
94Parkhurst-300
Gold-300
Crash the Game Green-26
Crash the Game Blue-26
Crash the Game Gold-26
Crash the Game Red-26
Vintage-V81
94Parkhurst SE-SE201
Gold-SE201
Euro-Stars-ES13
94Pinnacle-25
Artist's Proofs-25
Rink Collection-25
Boomers-BR15
Gamers-GR1
Northern Lights-NL11
World Edition-WE1
94Post Box Backs-23
94Score-178
Gold-178
Platinum-178
Franchise-TF26
94Select-74
Gold-74
94SP-131
Die Cuts-131
Premier-22
Premier Die-Cuts-22
94Stadium Club Members Only-10
94Stadium Club Super Teams-26
94Stadium Club Super Team MemberOnly Set-26
94Topps/OPC Premier-95
94Topps/OPC Premier-243
94Topps/OPC Premier-416
Special Effects-95
Special Effects-243
Special Effects-416
94Topps Finest Bronze-5
94Ultra-246
Global Greats-9
Red Light Specials-8
94Upper Deck-90
94Upper Deck-557
Electric Ice-90
Electric Ice-557
Ice Gallery-IG13
Predictor Retail-R3
94Upper Deck Predictor Retail Exchange-R3
94Upper Deck SP Inserts-SP88
94Upper Deck SP Inserts Die Cuts-SP88
94Upper Deck NHLPA/Be A Player-15
94Finnish SISU-263
94Finnish SISU Guest Specials-9
94Finnish Jaa Kiekko-20
94Finnish Jaa Kiekko-345
94Classic Pro Prospects Intl Heroes-LP23
94Classic Pro Prospects Jumbos-PP10
95Bashan Super Stickers-133
95Bashan Super Stickers-134
95Bowman-75
All-Foil-75
Bowman's Best-BB2
Bowman's Best Refractors-BB2
95Canada Games NHL POGS-292
95Collector's Choice-244
Player's Club-244
Player's Club Platinum-244
95Donruss-100
95Donruss Elite-73
Die Cut Stars-73
Die Cut Uncut-73
Cutting Edge-15
95Emotion-196
95Finest-35
95Finest-155
Refractors-35
Refractors-155
95Hoyle Western Playing Cards-17
95Imperial Stickers-134
95Jets Readers Club-9
95Jets Team Issue-20
95Kraft-3
95Leaf-137
95Leaf Limited-44
Stars of the Game-7
95McDonald's Pinnacle-MCD-19
95Metal-165
International Steel-19
95NHL Aces Playing Cards-8C
95Panini Stickers-217
95Parkhurst International-232
95Parkhurst International-250
95Parkhurst International-275
95Parkhurst International-NNO2
Emerald Ice-232
Emerald Ice-250
Emerald Ice-275
All-Stars-5
Crown Collection Silver Series 1-9
Crown Collection Gold Series 1-9
Parkie's Trophy Picks-PP17
Parkie's Trophy Picks-PP51
95Pinnacle Roaring 20s-19
95Pinnacle FANtasy-15
95Playoff One on One-108
95Playoff One on One-219
95Playoff One on One-329
95Pro Magnets-63
95Score-7
Black Ice Artist's Proofs-7
Black Ice-7
Golden Blades-2
Lamplighters-14
95Select Certified-76
Mirror Gold-76
95SkyBox Impact-184
Ice Quake-15
95SP-2
Holoviews-FX1
Holoviews Special FX-FX1
Stars/Etoiles-E2
Stars/Etoiles Gold-E2
95Stadium Club Members Only-43
95Stadium Club-188
Members Only Master Set-188
Extreme North-EN2
Extreme North Members Only Master Set-EN2
Generation TSC-GT2
Generation TSC Members Only Master Set-GT2
95Summit-54
Artist's Proofs-54
Ice-54
95Topps-195
OPC Inserts-195
Canadian Gold-9CG
Mystery Finest-M9
Mystery Finest Refractors-M9
Power Lines-2PL
Profiles-PF18
Young Stars-YS11
95Topps SuperSkills-31
Platinum-31
95Ultra-183
Gold Medallion-183
95Upper Deck-171
95Upper Deck-253
Electric Ice-171
Electric Ice-253
Electric Ice Gold-171
Electric Ice Gold-253
Electric Ice Gold-J-171
95Upper Deck All-Star Game Predictors-7
Redemption Winners-7
95Upper Deck NHL All-Stars-AS12
95Upper Deck NHL All-Stars Jumbo-AS12
95Upper Deck Predictor Retail-R49
95Upper Deck Predictor Retail Exchange-R49
95Upper Deck Special Edition-SE89
95Upper Deck Special Edition Gold-SE89
95Zenith-102
95Finnish Jaa Kiekko Lehti Ad Cards-4
95Finnish SISU Limited-15
Signed and Sealed-3
95Finnish Semic World Championships-41
95Swedish Globe World Championships-140
95Swedish World Championships Stickers-294
96Headliners Hockey-17
96Be A Player Biscuit In The Basket-11
96Be A Player Link to History-1B
96Be A Player Link to History Autographs-1B
96Be A Player Link to History Auto Silver-1B
96Black Diamond-146
Gold-146
Run for the Cup-RC18
96Collector's Choice-2
96Collector's Choice-309
96Collector's Choice-336
MVP-UD7
MVP Gold-UD7
Stick'Ums-S13
Crash the Game-C19A
Crash the Game-C19B
Crash the Game-C19C
Crash the Game Gold-C19A
Crash the Game Gold-C19B
Crash the Game Gold-C19C
Crash the Game Exchange-CR19
Crash the Game Exchange Gold-CR19
96Donruss-157
Press Proofs-157
Dominators-8
Go Top Shelf-2
96Donruss Canadian Ice-85
Gold Press Proofs-85
Red Press Proofs-85
96Donruss Elite-59
Die Cut Stars-59
Status-10
96Ducks Team Issue-24
96Flair-3
Blue Ice-3
Center Ice Spotlight-8
96Fleer-3
Art Ross-21
Picks Dream Lines-5
Picks Fabulous 50-42
96Kraft Upper Deck-60
96Leaf-52
96Leaf-238
Press Proofs-52
Press Proofs-238
Fire On Ice-9
96Leaf Limited-64
Gold-64
96Leaf Preferred-56
Press Proofs-56
Steel Power-10
Vanity Plates-11
Vanity Plates Gold-11
96Maggers-92
96McDonald's Pinnacle-2
96Metal Universe-6
Lethal Weapons-17
Lethal Weapons Super Power-17
96NHL Aces Playing Cards-43
96NHL Pro Stamps-63
96Pinnacle-155
96Pinnacle-250
Artist's Proofs-155
Artist's Proofs-250
Foil-155
Foil-250
Premium Stock-155
Premium Stock-250
Rink Collection-155
Rink Collection-250
By The Numbers-1
By The Numbers-P1
By The Numbers Premium-1
96Pinnacle Mint-13
Bronze-13
Gold-13
Silver-13
Coins Brass-13
Coins Solid Gold-13
Coins Gold Plated-13
Coins Nickel-13
Coins Silver-13
96Playoff One on One-428
96Score-145
Artist's Proofs-145
Dealer's Choice Artist's Proofs-145
Special Artist's Proofs-145
Golden Blades-145
Sudden Death-15
Superstitions-1
96Select Certified-32
Artist's Proofs-32
Blue-32
Mirror Blue-32
Mirror Gold-32
Mirror Red-32
Red-32
Cornerstones-12
96SkyBox Impact-4
BladeRunners-20
VersaTeam-10
96SP-2
Inside Info-IN4
Inside Info Gold-IN4
SPx Force-2
96SPx-2
Gold-2
96Stadium Club Members Only-14
96Summit-133
Artist's Proofs-133
Ice-133
Metal-133
Premium Stock-133
High Voltage-12
High Voltage Mirage-12
Untouchables-8
96Team Out-34
96Topps Picks-7
Fantasy Team-FT21
OPC Inserts-7
Top Shelf-TS8
96Ultra-6
Gold Medallion-6
Power-16
Power Red Line-8
96Upper Deck-211
Generation Next-X16
Hart Hopefuls Bronze-HH15
Hart Hopefuls Gold-HH15
Hart Hopefuls Silver-HH15
Lord Stanley's Heroes Finals-LS16
Lord Stanley's Heroes Quarterfinals-LS16
Lord Stanley's Heroes Semifinals-LS16
Superstar Showdown-SS10A
96Upper Deck Ice-77
Parallel-77
Stanley Cup Foundation-S6
Stanley Cup Foundation Dynasty-S6
96Zenith-28
Artist's Proofs-28
Z-Team-3
96Swedish Semic Wien-31
Nordic Stars-NS2
97SLU Hockey Canadian-17
97SLU Hockey American-19
97Headliners Hockey-24
97Be A Player One Timers-8
97Beehive-2
Golden Portraits-2
Team-11
Team Gold-11
97Black Diamond-95
Double Diamond-95
Triple Diamond-95
Quadruple Diamond-95
Premium Cut-PC15
Premium Cut Double Diamond-PC15
Premium Cut Quadruple Diamond Horiz-PC15
Premium Cut Triple Diamond-PC15
Premium Cut Quadruple Diamond Verticals-PC15
97Collector's Choice-8
Crash the Game-C8A
Crash the Game-C8B
Crash the Game-C8C
Crash the Game Exchange-CR8
Star Quest-SQ80
Stick'Ums-S18
97Crown Royale-5
Emerald Green-5
Ice Blue-5
Silver-5
Blades of Steel Die-Cuts-2
Cramer's Choice Jumbos-2
Cramer's Choice Jumbos Gold-2
Cramer's Choice Jumbos Signed-2
Hat Tricks Die-Cuts-2
Lamplighters Cel-Fusion Die-Cuts-2
97Donruss-159
Press Proofs Silver-159
Press Proofs Gold-159
Elite Inserts-12
Line 2 Line-2
Line 2 Line Die Cut-2
97Donruss Canadian Ice-74
Dominion Series-74
Provincial Series-74
Stanley Cup Scrapbook-8
97Donruss Elite-17
97Donruss Elite-120
97Donruss Elite-149
Aspirations-17
Aspirations-120
Aspirations-149
Status-17
Status-120
Status-149
Back to the Future-3
Back to the Future Autographs-3
Craftsmen-15
Master Craftsmen-15
Prime Numbers-7A
Prime Numbers-7B
Prime Numbers-7C
Prime Numbers Die-Cuts-7A
Prime Numbers Die-Cuts-7B
Prime Numbers Die-Cuts-7C
97Donruss Limited-11
97Donruss Limited-56
97Donruss Limited-143
Exposure-11
Exposure-56
Exposure-143
Fabric of the Game-43
97Donruss Preferred-95
97Donruss Preferred-178
Cut to the Chase-95
Cut to the Chase-178
Line of the Times-5B
97Donruss Preferred Line of Times Promos-5B
97Donruss Preferred Precious Metals-9
97Donruss Priority-6
97Donruss Priority-187
Stamp of Approval-6
Stamp of Approval-187
Direct Deposit-15
Postcards-14
Postcards Opening Day Issues-6
Stamps-14
Stamps Bronze-14
Stamps Gold-14
Stamps Silver-14
97Esso Olympic Hockey Heroes-50
97Esso Olympic Hockey Heroes French-50
97Gatorade Stickers-6
97Highland Mint Mint-Cards Topps-25
97Highland Mint Mint-Cards Topps-26
97Highland Mint Mint-Coins-15
97Katch-5
Gold-5
Silver-5
97Kenner Starting Lineup Cards-19
97Kraft-12
97Leaf-18
97Leaf-182
Fractal Matrix-18
Fractal Matrix-182
Fractal Matrix Die Cuts-18
Fractal Matrix Die Cuts-182
Banner Season-8
Fire On Ice-10
97Leaf International-18
Universal Ice-18
97McDonald's Upper Deck-11
97NHL Aces Playing Cards-50
97Pacific-8
Copper-8
Emerald Green-8
Ice Blue-8
Red-8
Silver-8
Card-Supials-2
Card-Supials Minis-2
Gold Crown Die-Cuts-2
Slap Shots Die-Cuts-1C
Team Checklists-1
97Pacific Dynagon-5
97Pacific Dynagon-135
Copper-5
Copper-135
Dark Grey-5
Dark Grey-135
Emerald Green-5
Emerald Green-135
Ice Blue-5
Ice Blue-135
Red-5
Red-135
Silver-5
Silver-135
Best Kept Secrets-4
Dynamic Duos-1B
Tandems-7
Tandems-24
97Pacific Invincible-4
Copper-4
Emerald Green-4
Ice Blue-4
Red-4
Silver-4
Attack Zone-2
Feature Performers-2
NHL Regime-7
Off The Glass-2
97Pacific Omega-7
97Pacific Omega-247
Copper-7
Copper-247
Dark Gray-247
Emerald Green-7
Emerald Green-247
Gold-7
Gold-247
Ice Blue-7
Ice Blue-247
Game Face-2
Silks-2
Stick Handle Laser Cuts-2
97Panini Stickers-188
97Paramount-7
Copper-7
Dark Grey-7
Emerald Green-7
Ice Blue-7
Red-7
Silver-7
Big Numbers Die-Cuts-2
Photoengravings-2
97Pinnacle-86
Artist's Proofs-86
Rink Collection-86
Epix Game Emerald-15
Epix Game Orange-15
Epix Game Purple-15
Epix Moment Emerald-15
Epix Moment Orange-15
Epix Moment Purple-15
Epix Play Emerald-15
Epix Play Orange-15
Epix Play Purple-15
Epix Season Emerald-15
Epix Season Orange-15
Epix Season Purple-15
Press Plates Back Black-86
Press Plates Back Cyan-86
Press Plates Back Magenta-86
Press Plates Back Yellow-86
Press Plates Front Black-86
Press Plates Front Cyan-86
Press Plates Front Magenta-86
Press Plates Front Yellow-86
97Pinnacle Certified-39
Red-39
Mirror Blue-39
Mirror Gold-39
Mirror Red-39
Team-16
Gold Team Promo-16
Gold Team-16
97Pinnacle Inside-38
Coach's Collection-38
Executive Collection-38
Track-11
Cans-19
Cans Gold-19
97Pinnacle Mint-7
Bronze-7
Gold Team-7
Silver Team-7
Coins Brass-7
Coins Brass Proofs-7
Coins Gold Plated-7
Coins Gold Plated Proofs-7
Coins Nickel Silver-7
Coins Nickel Silver Proofs-7
Coins Solid Gold-7
Coins Solid Silver-7
Minternational-4
Minternational Coins-4
97Pinnacle Power Pack Blow-Ups-24
97Pinnacle Tot Cert Platinum Blue-39
97Pinnacle Tot Cert Platinum Gold-39
97Pinnacle Totally Certified Platinum Red-39
97Pinnacle Tot Cert Mirror Platinum Gold-39
97Post Pinnacle-19
97Revolution-5
Copper-5
Emerald-5
Ice Blue-5
Silver-5
1998 All-Star Game Die-Cuts-1
NHL Icons-2
97Score-113
Artist's Proofs-113
Golden Blades-113
97Score Mighty Ducks-2
Platinum-2
Premier-2
97SP Authentic-1
Icons-I19
Icons Die-Cuts-I19
Icons Embossed-I19
97SPx-2
Bronze-2
Gold-2
Silver-2
Steel-2
Dimension-SPX18
Grand Finale-2
97Studio-18
97Studio-107
Press Proofs Silver-18
Press Proofs Silver-107
Press Proofs Gold-18
Press Proofs Gold-107
Hard Hats-11
Portraits-18
Silhouettes-17
Silhouettes 8x10-17
97Upper Deck-1
Blow-Ups 3 x 5-1-7
Blow-Ups 5 x 7-2B
Game Dated Moments-1
Sixth Sense Masters-SS8
Sixth Sense Wizards-SS8
Smooth Grooves-SG8
The Specialists-8
The Specialists Level 2 Die Cuts-8
Three Star Selects-5A
97Upper Deck Crash the All-Star Game-4
97Upper Deck Crash the All-Star Game-AR4
97Upper Deck Diamond Vision-16
Signature Moves-16
97Upper Deck Ice-80
Parallel-80
Champions-IC8
Champions 2 Die Cuts-IC8
Lethal Lines-L9C
Lethal Lines 2-L9C
Power Shift-80
97Zenith-24
Z-Gold-24
Z-Silver-24
97Zenith 5 x 7-6
Gold Impulse-6
Silver Impulse-6
97Zenith Z-Team-1
97Zenith Z-Team 5x7-1
97Zenith Z-Team Gold-1
98Aurora-6
Atomic Laser Cuts-2
Championship Fever-2
Championship Fever Copper-2
Championship Fever Ice Blue-2
Championship Fever Red-2
Championship Fever Silver-2
Cubes-2
Man Advantage-2
NHL Command-1
98Be A Player-3
Press Release-3
98BAP Gold-3
98BAP Autographs-3
98BAP Autographs Gold-3
98BAP AS Game Used Stick Cards-S3
98BAP AS Game Used Jersey Cards-AS3
98BAP Playoff Game Used Jerseys-G11
98BAP Playoff Game Used Jersey Autographs-G11
98BAP Playoff Practice Used Jerseys-P9
98BAP Tampa Bay All Star Game-3
98Black Diamond-2
Double Diamond-2
Triple Diamond-2
Quadruple Diamond-2
Myriad-M7
Myriad 2-M7
Winning Formula Gold-WF2
Winning Formula Platinum-WF2
98Bowman's Best-45
Refractors-45
Atomic Refractors-45
Mirror Image Fusion-F4
Mirror Image Fusion Refractors-F4
Mirror Image Fusion Atomic Refractors-F4
98Crown Royale-5
Limited Series-5
Cramer's Choice Jumbos-2
Cramer's Choice Jumbos Dark Blue-2
Cramer's Choice Jumbos Green-2
Cramer's Choice Jumbos Red-2
Cramer's Choice Jumbos Light Blue-2
Cramer's Choice Jumbos Gold-2
Cramer's Choice Jumbos Purple-2
Living Legends-2
Master Performers-2
Pillars of the Game-1
98Donruss Elite Promos-6
98Ducks Power Play-ANA4
98Finest-1
No Protectors-1
No Protectors Refractors-1
Refractors-1
Centurion-C15
Centurion Refractors-C15
Double Sided Mystery Finest-M11
Double Sided Mystery Finest-M15
Double Sided Mystery Finest-M16
Double Sided Mystery Finest-M17
Double Sided Mystery Refractors-M11
Double Sided Mystery Refractors-M15
Double Sided Mystery Refractors-M16
Double Sided Mystery Refractors-M17
Oversize-1
Oversize Refractors-1
Red Lighters-R8
Red Lighters Refractors-R8
98Katch-3
98NHL Game Day Promotion-ANA4
98OPC Chrome-109
Refractors-109
Season's Best-SB13
Season's Best Refractors-SB13
98Pacific-8
Ice Blue-8
Red-8
Dynagon Ice Inserts-2
Titanium Ice-2
Gold Crown Die-Cuts-2
Timelines-1
98Pacific Dynagon Ice-6
Blue-6
Red-6
Adrenaline Rush Bronze-2
Adrenaline Rush Ice Blue-2

Adrenaline Rush Red-2
Adrenaline Rush Silver-2
Forward Thinking-2
98Pacific Omega-8
Red-8
Opening Day Issue-8
EO Portraits-2
EO Portraits 1 of 1-2
Face to Face-7
Online-2
Planet Ice-23
Planet Ice Parallel-23
Prism-2
Toronto Spring Expo-8
98Panini Photocards-76
98Panini Photocards-107
98Panini Stickers-1
98Panini Stickers-169
98Paramount-7
Copper-7
Emerald Green-7
Holo-Electric-7
Ice Blue-7
Silver-7
Hall of Fame Bound-1
Hall of Fame Bound Proofs-1
Special Delivery Die-Cuts-2
Team Checklists Die-Cuts-1
98Revolution-5
Ice Shadow-5
Red-5
All-Star Die Cuts-26
Chalk Talk Laser-Cuts-2
Showstoppers-2
Three Pronged Attack-22
Three Pronged Attack Parallel-22
98SP Authentic-2
Power Shift-2
Snapshots-SS10
Stat Masters-S26
98SPx Finite-1
98SPx Finite-104
98SPx Finite-157
Radiance-1
Radiance-104
Radiance-157
Spectrum-1
Spectrum-104
Spectrum-157
98SPx Top Prospects-2
Radiance-2
Spectrum-2
Highlight Heroes-H2
Lasting Impressions-L7
Premier Stars-PS17
98Topps-109
O-Pee-Chee-109
Local Legends-L15
Mystery Finest Bronze-M1
Mystery Finest Bronze Refractors-M1
Mystery Finest Gold-M1
Mystery Finest Gold Refractors-M1
Mystery Finest Silver-M1
Mystery Finest Silver Refractors-M1
Season's Best-SB13
98Topps Gold Label Class 1-7
Black-7
Black One of One-7
One of One-7
Red-7
Red One of One-7
98Topps Gold Label Class 2-7
98Topps Gold Label Class 2 Black-7
98Topps Gold Label Class 2 Black 1 of 1-7
98Topps Gold Label Class 2 One of One-7
98Topps Gold Label Class 2 Red-7
98Topps Gold Label Class 2 Red One of One-7
98Topps Gold Label Class 3-7
98Topps Gold Label Class 3 Black-7
98Topps Gold Label Class 3 Black 1 of 1-7
98Topps Gold Label Class 3 One of One-7
98Topps Gold Label Class 3 Red-7
98Topps Gold Label Class 3 Red One of One-7
98Topps Gold Label Goal Race '99-GR3
98Topps Gold Label Goal Race '99 Black-GR3
98Topps Gold Label Goal '99 Black 1 of 1-GR3
98Topps Gold Label Goal Race 99 1 of 1-GR3
98Topps Gold Label Goal Race '99 Red-GR3
98Topps Gold Label GoalRace 99 Red 1 of 1-GR3
98UD Choice-8
98UD Choice-242
Mini Bobbing Head-BH15
Prime Choice Reserve-8
Prime Choice Reserve-242
Reserve-8
Reserve-242
StarQuest Blue-SQ5
StarQuest Gold-SQ5
StarQuest Green-SQ5
StarQuest Red-SQ5
98UD3-58
98UD3-118
98UD3-178
Die-Cuts-58
Die-Cuts-118
Die-Cuts-178
98Upper Deck-16
98Upper Deck-34
Exclusives-16
Exclusives-34
Exclusives 1 of 1-16
Exclusives 1 of 1-34
Fantastic Finishers-FF23
Fantastic Finishers Quantum 1-FF23
Fantastic Finishers Quantum 2-FF23
Fantastic Finishers Quantum 3-FF23
Frozen In Time-FT28
Frozen In Time Quantum 1-FT28
Frozen In Time Quantum 2-FT28
Frozen In Time Quantum 3-FT28
Lord Stanley's Heroes-LS30
Lord Stanley's Heroes Quantum 1-LS30
Lord Stanley's Heroes Quantum 2-LS30
Lord Stanley's Heroes Quantum 3-LS30
Profiles-P8
Profiles Quantum 1-P8
Profiles Quantum 2-P8
Profiles Quantum 3-P8
Gold Reserve-16
Gold Reserve-34
98Upper Deck MVP-2
Gold Script-2
Silver Script-2
Super Script-2
Snipers-S4
Special Forces-F10
98Finnish Keràilysarja 90's Top 12-5
98Finnish Keràilysarja Dream Team-7
98Slovakian Eurotel-23
99Aurora-5
Striped-5
Premiere Date-5
Premiere Date Striped-5
Canvas Creations-2
Championship Fever-2
Championship Fever Copper-2
Championship Fever Ice Blue-2
Championship Fever Silver-2
Complete Players-2
Complete Players Parallel-2
Complete Players Retail-2
Complete Players Retail Parallel-2
Styrotechs-2
99BAP Memorabilia-171
Gold-171
Silver-171
Jersey Cards-J3
Jersey Emblems-E3
Jersey Numbers-I3
Jersey and Stick Cards-S3
AS Heritage Ruby-H7
AS Heritage Sapphire-H7
AS Heritage Emerald-H7
99BAP Update Double AS Jersey Cards-D10
99BAP Update Teammates Jersey Cards-TM4
99BAP Update Teammates Jersey Cards-TM12
99BAP Update Teammates Jersey Cards-TM28
99BAP Update Teammates Jersey Cards-TM45
99BAP Millennium Prototypes-1
99BAP Millennium-2
Emerald-2
Ruby-2
Sapphire-2
Signatures-2
Signatures Gold-2
Jerseys-J8
Jersey Autographs-J8
Jersey and Stick Cards-JS8
Jersey Emblems-E8
Jersey Numbers-N8
99Black Diamond-2
Diamond Cut-2
Final Cut-2
A Piece of History-TS
A Piece of History Double-TS
A Piece of History Triple-TS
Diamonation-D4
Diamond Might-DM7
Diamond Skills-DS1
Myriad-M2
99Crown Royale-4
Limited Series-4
Premiere Date-4
Card-Supials-2
Card-Supials Minis-2
Cramer's Choice Jumbos-2
Cramer's Choice Jumbos Dark Blue-2
Cramer's Choice Jumbos Gold-2
Cramer's Choice Jumbos Green-2
Cramer's Choice Jumbos Light Blue-2
Cramer's Choice Jumbos Purple-2
Cramer's Choice Jumbos Red-2
Gold Crown Die-Cuts Jumbos-1
Ice Elite-2
Ice Elite Parallel-2
International Glory-1
International Glory Parallel-1
99Kraft Peanut Butter-10
99O-Pee-Chee-17
99O-Pee-Chee All-Topps-AT14
99O-Pee-Chee Chrome-17
99O-Pee-Chee Chrome All Topps-AT14
99O-Pee-Chee Chrome All-Topps Refractors-AT14
99O-Pee-Chee Chrome Ice Masters-IM20
99O-Pee-Chee Chrome Ice Masters Refractor-IM20
99O-Pee-Chee Chrome Refractors-17
99O-Pee-Chee Chrome A-Men-AM4
99O-Pee-Chee Chrome A-Men Refractors-AM4
99O-Pee-Chee Chrome Fantastic Finishers-FF1
99OPC Chrome Fantastic Finishers Ref-FF1
99O-Pee-Chee Ice Masters-IM20
99O-Pee-Chee A-Men-AM4
99O-Pee-Chee Fantastic Finishers-FF1
99O-Pee-Chee Top of the World-TW1
99Pacific-16
Copper-16
Emerald Green-16
Gold-16
Ice Blue-16
Premiere Date-16
Red-16
Center Ice-2
Center Ice Proofs-2
Gold Crown Die-Cuts-2
Home and Away-2
Home and Away-12
Past and Present-2
99Pacific Dynagon Ice-12
Blue-12
Copper-12
Gold-12
Premiere Date-12
2000 All-Star Preview-2
Checkmates American-2
Checkmates American-17
Checkmates Canadian-17
Lamplighter Net-Fusions-2
Lords of the Rink-2
99Pacific Omega-6
Copper-6
Gold-6
Ice Blue-6
Premiere Date-6
EO Portraits-2
EO Portraits 1/1-2
Game-Used Jerseys-1
NHL Generations-2
5 Star Talents-14
5 Star Talents Parallel-14
World All-Stars-1
99Pacific Prism-5
Holographic Blue-5
Holographic Gold-5
Holographic Mirror-5
Holographic Purple-5
Premiere Date-5
Clear Advantage-2
Dial-a-Stats-2
Sno-Globe Die-Cuts-2
99Panini Stickers-176
99Panini Stickers-318
99Paramount-8
Copper-8
Emerald-8
Gold-8
Holographic Emerald-8
Holographic Gold-8
Holographic Silver-8
Ice Blue-8
Premiere Date-8
Red-8
Silver-8
Ice Advantage-2
Ice Advantage Proofs-2
Personal Best-2
Toronto Fall Expo '99-8
99Revolution-4
Premiere Date-4
Red-4
Shadow Series-4
NHL Icons-1
Ornaments-2
Showstoppers-2
Top of the Line-21
Copper-4
Gold-4
CSC Silver-4
99SP Authentic-2
Supreme Skill-SS2
99SPx Highlight Heroes-HH10
99SPx SPXcitement-X20
99SPx SPXtreme-XT4
99SPx Starscape-S8
99Stadium Club-40
First Day Issue-40
One of a Kind-40
Printing Plates Black-40
Printing Plates Cyan-40
Printing Plates Magenta-40
Printing Plates Yellow-40
Capture the Action-CA15
Capture the Action Game View-CAG15
Chrome-22
Chrome Refractors-22
Chrome Oversized-11
Chrome Oversized Refractors-11
Eyes of the Game-EG4
Eyes of the Game Refractors-EG4
Onyx Extreme-OE8
Onyx Extreme Die-Cut-OE8
99Topps/OPC-17
All-Topps-AT14
A-Men-AM4
Fantastic Finishers-FF1
Ice Masters-IM20
Top of the World-TW1
99Topps/OPC Chrome-17
Refractors-17
All-Topps-AT14
All-Topps Refractors-AT14
A-Men-AM4
A-Men Refractors-AM4
Fantastic Finishers-FF1
Fantastic Finishers Refractors-FF1
Ice Masters-IM20
Ice Masters Refractors-IM20
99Topps Gold Label Class 1-23
Black-23
Black One of One-23
One of One-23
Red-23
Red One of One-23
99Topps Gold Label Class 2-23
99Topps Gold Label Class 2 Black-23
99Topps Gold Label Class 2 Black 1 of 1-23
99Topps Gold Label Class 2 One of One-23
99Topps Gold Label Class 2 Red-23
99Topps Gold Label Class 2 Red One of One-23
99Topps Gold Label Class 3-23
99Topps Gold Label Class 3 Black-23
99Topps Gold Label Class 3 Black 1 of 1-23
99Topps Gold Label Class 3 One of One-23
99Topps Gold Label Class 3 Red-23
99Topps Gold Label Class 3 Red One of One-23
99Topps Gold Label Prime Gold-PG7
99Topps Gold Label Prime Gold One of One -PG7
99Topps Gold Label Prime Gold Black-PG7
99Topps Gold Label Prime Gold Black One of One - PG7
99Topps Gold Label Prime Gold Red-PG7
99Topps Gold Label Prime Gold Red One of One - PG7
99Topps Premier Plus-17
Parallel-17
Calling All Calders-CAC6
Code Red-CR2
99Ultimate Victory-2
1/1-2
Parallel-2
Parallel 100-2
Smokin Guns-SG12
99Upper Deck-153
99Upper Deck-174
Exclusives-153
Exclusives-174
Exclusives 1 of 1-153
Exclusives 1 of 1-174
All-Star Class-AS5
All-Star Class Quantum Gold-AS5
All-Star Class Quantum Silver-AS5
Crunch Time-CT21
Crunch Time Quantum Gold-CT21
Crunch Time Quantum Silver-CT21
Fantastic Finishers-FF6
Fantastic Finishers Quantum Gold-FF6
Fantastic Finishers Quantum Silver-FF6
Game Jerseys-TS
Game Jerseys Series II-TS
Game Jersey Patch-TSP
Game Jersey Patch 1 of 1-TSSP
Ice Gallery-IG6
Ice Gallery Quantum Gold-IG6
Ice Gallery Quantum Silver-IG6
Marquee Attractions-MA12
Marquee Attractions Quantum Gold-MA12
Marquee Attractions Quantum Silver-MA12
New Ice Age-N6
New Ice Age Quantum Gold-N6
New Ice Age Quantum Silver-N6
NHL Scrapbook-SB11
NHL Scrapbook Quantum Gold-SB11
NHL Scrapbook Quantum Silver-SB11
99Upper Deck Century Legends-59
Century Collection-59
99Upper Deck Gold Reserve-153
99Upper Deck Gold Reserve-174
99Upper Deck HoloGrFx-1
Ausome-1
Pure Skill-PS5
Pure Skill Ausome-PS5
99Upper Deck MVP-5
Gold Script-5
Silver Script-5
Super Script-5
90's Snapshots-S8
Game-Used Souvenirs-GU2
Game-Used Souvenirs-GU16
Hands of Gold-H4
99Upper Deck MVP SC Edition-1
Gold Script-1
Silver Script-1
Super Script-1
Game-Used Souvenirs-GUTS
Great Combinations-GCKS
Great Combinations Parallel-GCKS
Second Season Snipers-SS1
Stanley Cup Talent-SC2
99Upper Deck Ovation-2
Standing Ovation-2
Lead Performers-LP12
Superstar Theater-ST10
99Upper Deck PowerDeck-2
Auxiliary-2
Auxiliary 1 of 1-2
99Upper Deck Retro-2
Gold-2
Platinum-2
Generation-G8B
Generation Level 2-G8B
99Upper Deck Victory-3
99Upper Deck Victory-321
99Upper Deck Victory-326
99Upper Deck Victory-334
99Upper Deck Victory-337
99Wayne Gretzky Hockey-4
Elements of the Game-EG1
Great Heroes-GH9
Tools of Greatness-TGTS
99Finnish Cardset-197
99Finnish Cardset-NNO
Aces High-J2
Blazing Patriots-4
Most Wanted-3
99Slovakian Challengers-17
00Aurora-4
Pinstripes-4
Pinstripes Premiere Date-4
Premiere Date-4
Championship Fever-2
Championship Fever Copper-2
Championship Fever Platinum Blue-2
Championship Fever Silver-2
Scouting Reports-2
Styrotechs-1B
00BAP Memorabilia-272
00BAP Memorabilia-498
Emerald-272
Ruby-272
Sapphire-272
Promos-272
Jersey Cards-J15
Jersey Emblems-E15
Jersey Numbers-N15
Jersey and Stick Cards-JS15
Patent Power Jerseys-PP5
00BAP Mem Chicago Sportsfest Copper-272
00BAP Memorabilia Chicago Sportsfest Blue-272
00BAP Memorabilia Chicago Sportsfest Gold-272
00BAP Memorabilia Chicago Sportsfest Ruby-272
00BAP Memorabilia Chicago Sun-Times Ruby-272
00BAP Memorabilia Chicago Sun-Times Gold-272
00BAP Mem Chicago Sun-Times Sapphire-272
00BAP Mem Toronto Fall Expo Copper-272
00BAP Memorabilia Toronto Fall Expo Gold-272
00BAP Memorabilia Toronto Fall Expo Ruby-272
00BAP Mem Update Heritage Jersey Cards-H9
00BAP Mem Update Heritage Jersey Gold-H9
00BAP Memorabilia Update Teammates-TM26
00BAP Memorabilia Update Teammates-TM39
00BAP Memorabilia Update Teammates Gold-TM26
00BAP Memorabilia Update Teammates Gold-TM39
00BAP Parkhurst 2000-P33
00BAP Signature Series-41
Emerald-41
Ruby-41
Sapphire-41
Autographs-165
Autographs Gold-165
Jersey Cards-J8
Jersey and Stick Cards-GSJ8
Jersey Cards Autographs-J8
Jersey Emblems-E8
Jersey Numbers-IN8
00BAP Ultimate Memorabilia Autographs-8
Gold-8
00BAP Ultimate Mem Game-Used Jerseys-GJ8
00BAP Ultimate Mem Game-Used Emblems-E6
00BAP Ultimate Mem Game-Used Numbers-N6
00BAP Ultimate Mem Game-Used Sticks-GS8
00BAP Ultimate Mem Journey Jerseys-JJ10
00BAP Ultimate Mem Journey Emblems-JE10
00BAP Ultimate Mem Journey Numbers-JI10
00BAP Ultimate Memorabilia NHL Records-R6
00BAP Ultimate Memorabilia Teammates-TM21
00BAP Ultimate Memorabilia Teammates-TM22
00BAP Ultimate Memorabilia Teammates-TM33
00Black Diamond-2
Gold-2
Diamond Might-FP1
Game Gear-GTS
00Crown Royale-3
Ice Blue-3
Limited Series-3
Premiere Date-3
Red-3
Jewels of the Crown-2
Now Playing-2
00McDonald's Pacific-2
Blue-2
Game Jerseys-1
00O-Pee-Chee-64
00O-Pee-Chee Parallel-64
00Pacific-11
00Pacific-432
Copper-11
Copper-432
Gold-11
Gold-432
Ice Blue-11
Ice Blue-432
Premiere Date-11
Premiere Date-432
2001: Ice Odyssey-2
Cramer's Choice-2
Euro-Stars-1
Gold Crown Die Cuts-2
Reflections-2
00Pacific 2001: Ice Odyssey Anaheim Ntnl-2
00Panini Stickers-111
00Paramount-7
Copper-7
Gold-7
Holo-Gold-7
Holo-Silver-7
Ice Blue-7
Premiere Date-7
Epic Scope-2
Freeze Frame-2
00Private Stock-3
Gold-3
Premiere Date-3
Retail-3
Silver-3
Artist's Canvas-2
Artist's Canvas Proofs-2
Extreme Action-2
Game Gear-3
Game Gear Patches-3
PS-2001 Action-2
PS-2001 Stars-2
Reserve-2
00Revolution-4
Blue-4
Premiere Date-4
Red-4
HD NHL-2
Ice Immortals-2
NHL Icons-2
Stat Masters-1
00SP Authentic Special Forces-SF1
00SP Game Used-2
Patch Cards-P-TS
Tools of the Game-TS
Tools of the Game Exclusives-TS
Tools of the Game Combos-C-KS
00SPx-2
Spectrum-2
SPXcitement-X1
Winning Materials-TS
Winning Materials-WSE
00Stadium Club-13
Beam Team-BT10
Capture the Action-CA12
Capture the Action Game View-12
00Titanium-2
Blue-2
Gold-2
Premiere Date-2
Red-2
Retail-2
Game Gear-54
Game Gear Patches-54
00Titanium Draft Day Edition-92
Patches-92
00Topps/OPC-64
Parallel-64
Combos-TC2
Combos Jumbos-TC2
Own the Game-OTG5
00Topps Chrome-52
OPC Refractors-52
Refractors-52
Combos-TC2
Combos Refractors-TC2
Rocket's Flare-RF10
Rocket's Flare Refractors-RF10
00Topps Gold Label Class 1-82
Gold-82
00Topps Gold Label Class 2-82
00Topps Gold Label Class 2 Gold-82
00Topps Gold Label Class 3-82
00Topps Gold Label Class 3 Gold-82
00Topps Gold Label Golden Greats-GG10
00Topps Gold Label Golden Greats 1 to 1-GG10
00Topps Heritage-28
Chrome Parallel-28
Heroes-HH10
00Topps Premier Plus-35
Blue Ice-35
Game-Used Memorabilia-GPTS
Game-Used Memorabilia-GPTSMB
Masters of the Break-MB2
Team-PT10
Team Blue Ice-PR10
Trophy Tribute-TT14
World Premier-WP18
00Topps Stars-35
00Topps Stars-138
Blue-35
Blue-138
All-Star Authority-ASA7
Game Gear-GGTS
00UD Heroes-140
Game-Used Twigs-T-TS
Game-Used Twigs Gold-C-KS
Timeless Moments-TM1
00UD Pros and Prospects-2
Game Jerseys-TS
Game Jersey Exclusives-TS
ProMotion-PM1
00UD Reserve-3
Gold Strike-GS1
Practice Session Jerseys-TS
Practice Session Jerseys Autographs-TS
00Upper Deck-231
Exclusives Tier 1-231
Exclusives Tier 2-231
All-Star Class-A1
Fantastic Finishers-FF2
Game Jerseys-TS
Game Jerseys-TS
Game Jersey Autographs Exclusives-ETS
Game Jersey Combos-DSK
Game Jersey Doubles-DTS
Game Jersey Patches-PTS
Game Jersey Patches-TSP
Game Jersey Patch Autographs Exclusives-TSP
Game Jersey Patch Exclusives Series II-ETS
Skilled Stars-SS2
Triple Threat-TT9
UD Flashback-UD1
00Upper Deck Ice-2
Immortals-2
Legends-2
Stars-2
Gallery-IG1
Game Jerseys-JCTS
00Upper Deck Legends-2
00Upper Deck Legends-3
Legendary Collection Bronze-2
Legendary Collection Bronze-3
Legendary Collection Gold-2
Legendary Collection Gold-3
Legendary Collection Silver-2
Legendary Collection Silver-3
Legendary Game Jerseys-JTS
00Upper Deck MVP-6
First Stars-6
Game-Used Souvenirs-GSTS
Second Stars-6
Super Game-Used Souvenirs-GSTS
Talent-M2
Third Stars-6
Top Draws-TD1
00Upper Deck Victory-7
00Upper Deck Victory-281
00Upper Deck Vintage-2
00Upper Deck Vintage-11
National Heroes-NH2
Star Tandems-S1B
00Vanguard-3
High Voltage-2
High Voltage Gold-2
High Voltage Green-2
High Voltage Red-2
High Voltage Silver-2
Holographic Gold-3
Holographic Purple-3
In Focus-2
Pacific Proofs-3
Press East/West-2
00Finnish Cardset-117
01Atomic-87
Blue-87
Gold-87
Premiere Date-87
Red-87
Core Players-17
Jerseys-47
Patches-47
Power Play-30
Team Nucleus-12
01BAP Memorabilia-265
Emerald-265
Ruby-265
Sapphire-265
All-Star Jerseys-ASJ48
All-Star Emblems-ASE48
All-Star Numbers-ASN48
All-Star Jersey Doubles-DASJ27
All-Star Teammates-AST26
All-Star Teammates-AST45
Country of Origin-CO22
He Shoots-He Scores Points-20
He Shoots-He Scores Prizes-9
01BAP Signature Series Certified 100-C47
01BAP Signature Series Certified 50-C47
01BAP Signature Series Certified 1 of 1's-C47
01BAP Signature Series Autographs-LTS
01BAP Signature Series Autographs Gold-LTSE
01BAP Sig Series He Shoots/Scores Points-10
01BAP Sig Series He Shoots/Scores Prizes-12
01BAP Signature Series Jerseys-GJ-8
01BAP Signature Series Jersey Autographs-GUTS
01BAP Sig Series Jersey and Stick Cards-GSJ-8
01BAP Signature Series Emblems-GUE-8
01BAP Signature Series Numbers-ITN-8
01BAP Signature Series Teammates-TM-25
01BAP Ultimate Memorabilia Active Eight-6
01BAP Ultimate Memorabilia Calder Trophy-9
01BAP Ultimate Memorabilia Dynamic Duos-8
01BAP Ultimate Memorabilia Emblems-23
01BAP Ultimate Memorabilia Jerseys-23
01BAP Ultimate Mem Jerseys and Sticks-23
01BAP Ultimate Mem Journey Jerseys-13
01BAP Ultimate Mem Journey Emblems-13
01BAP Ultimate Memorabilia Numbers-23
01BAP Ultimate Memorabilia Name Plates-13
01BAP Ultimate Mem Scoring Leaders-12
01BAP Ultimate Mem Scoring Leaders-17
01BAP Ultimate Mem Scoring Leaders-18
01BAP Update Heritage-H7
01BAP Update Travel Plans-TP4
01Bowman YoungStars-17
Gold-17
Ice Cubed-17
01Crown Royale-126
Blue-126
Premiere Date-126
Red-126
Retail-126
Jewels of the Crown-27
01eTopps-11
01McDonald's Pacific-36
Cosmic Force-4
Jersey Patches Silver-16
Jersey Patches Gold-16
01O-Pee-Chee-11
01O-Pee-Chee Heritage Parallel-11
01O-Pee-Chee Heritage Parallel Limited-11
01O-Pee-Chee Premier Parallel-11
01Pacific-344
01Pacific-421
01Pacific-441
Extreme LTD-344
Gold-421
Gold-441
Hobby LTD-344
Premiere Date-344
Retail LTD-344
Jerseys-34
01Pacific Adrenaline-170
Blue-170
Premiere Date-170
Red-170
Retail-170
Jerseys-43
Playmakers-8
World Beaters-18
01Pacific Arena Exclusives-344
01Pacific Arena Exclusives-421
01Pacific Arena Exclusives-441
01Pacific Heads-Up-85
Blue-85
Premiere Date-85
Red-85
Silver-85
HD NHL-8
Quad Jerseys-1
Stat Masters-16
01Parkhurst-25
Gold-25
Silver-25
He Shoots-He Scores Prizes-9
Milestones-M32
Sticks-PS34
Teammates-T25
World Class Jerseys-WCJ2
World Class Emblems-WCE2
World Class Numbers-WCN2
Waving the Flag-13
01Private Stock-87
Gold-87
Premiere Date-87
Retail-87
Silver-87
Game Gear-92
Game Gear Patches-92
01Private Stock Pacific Nights-87
01Private Stock PS-2002-66
01Private Stock Reserve-S17
01Sharks Postcards-16
01SP Authentic-71
01SP Authentic-107
Limited-71
Limited-107
Limited Gold-71
Limited Gold-107
Buybacks-37
Buybacks-38
Buybacks-39
Sign of the Times-TS
01SP Game Used-46
Authentic Fabric-AFTS
Authentic Fabric Gold-AFTS
Patches Signed-SPTS
Tools of the Game Signed-STTS
01SPx-56
Hidden Treasures-TTBSS
Hockey Treasures-HTTS
01Stadium Club-40
Award Winners-40
Master Photos-40
Gallery-G14
Gallery Gold-G14
NHL Passport-NHLP8
01Titanium-124
Hobby Parallel-124
Premiere Date-124
Retail-124
Retail Parallel-124
All-Stars-17
Double-Sided Jerseys-39
01Topps-11
Heritage Parallel-11
Heritage Parallel Limited-11
OPC Parallel-11
Shot Masters-SM17
01Topps Chrome-11
Refractors-11
Black Border Refractors-11
01Topps Heritage-18
Refractors-18
01Topps Reserve-77
01UD Challenge for the Cup-73
01UD Honor Roll-21
01UD Honor Roll-51
01UD Mask Collection-82
Gold-82
Double Patches-DPTS
Jerseys-J-TS
Jersey and Patch-JPTS
01UD Playmakers-82
Jerseys-J-TS
Jerseys Gold-J-TS
01UD Premier Collection-43
Dual Jerseys-DSN
Dual Jerseys-DSP
Dual Jerseys Black-DSN
Dual Jerseys Black-DSP
Jerseys-BTS
Jerseys Black-B-TS
Signatures-TS
Signatures Black-TS
01UD Top Shelf-37
Jerseys-TS
Jersey Autographs-TS
01Upper Deck-145
Exclusives-145
Crunch Timers-CT11
Fantastic Finishers-FF8
Franchise Cornerstones-FC13
Game Jerseys-ATS
Game Jerseys-CKS
Gate Attractions-GA11
Patches-PTS
Pride of a Nation-PNTS
Pride of a Nation-DPSK
Shooting Stars-SS16
Skilled Stars-SS4
Tandems-T8
01Upper Deck Ice-115
01Upper Deck MVP-159
Souvenirs-S-TS
Souvenirs Gold-S-TS
Talent-MT9
01Upper Deck Victory-290
Gold-290
01Upper Deck Vintage-210
01Upper Deck Vintage-217
01Vanguard-88
Blue-88
Red-88
East Meets West-6
Memorabilia-15
One of Ones-88
Premiere Date-88
Proofs-88
V-Team-18
01Finnish Cardset Salt Lake City-7
01Finnish Cardset Teemu Selanne-NNO
02Atomic-88
Blue-88
Gold-88
Red-88
Cold Fusion-21
Hobby Parallel-88
02BAP All-Star Edition-83
He Shoots-He Scores Points-5
He Shoots-He Score Prizes-26
Jerseys-83
Jerseys Gold-83
Jerseys Silver-83
02BAP First Edition-135
02BAP First Edition-306
02BAP First Edition-400
02BAP First Edition-429R
Debut Jerseys-6
He Shoots-He Score Points-7
He Shoots-He Scores Prizes-19
Jerseys-135
02BAP Memorabilia-162
Emerald-162
Ruby-162
Sapphire-162
All-Star Jerseys-ASJ-52
All-Star Emblems-ASE-21
All-Star Numbers-ASN-21
All-Star Starting Lineup-AS-12
All-Star Teammmates-AST-1
All-Star Teammmates-AST-15
All-Star Teammmates-AST-30
All-Star Triple Jerseys-ASTJ-18
He Shoots-He Scores Prizes-30
NHL All-Star Game-162
NHL All-Star Game Blue-162
NHL All-Star Game Green-162
NHL All-Star Game Red-162
Stanley Cup Playoffs-SC-17
Teammates-TM-18
02BAP Memorabilia Toronto Fall Expo-162
02BAP Signature Series-116
Autographs-116
Autograph Buybacks 1998-3
Autograph Buybacks 1999-2
Autograph Buybacks 2000-165
Autographs Gold-116
Complete Jersey-CJ10
Franchise Players-FJ25
Golf-GS93
Jerseys-SGJ24
Jersey Autographs-SGJ24
Team Quads-TQ18
02BAP Ultimate Memorabilia All-Star MVP-22
02BAP Ultimate Memorabilia Dynamic Duos-8
02BAP Ultimate Memorabilia Great Moments-8
02BAP Ultimate Memorabilia Jerseys-37
02BAP Ultimate Mem Jersey and Stick-30
02Bowman YoungStars-101
Gold-101
Silver-101
02Crown Royale-86
Blue-86
Red-86
Retail-86
Lords of the Rink-17
02eTopps-30
02ITG Used-65
02ITG Used-165
International Experience-IE10
International Experience Gold-IE10
Jerseys-GUJ24
Jersey Autographs-GUJ24
Jerseys Gold-GUJ24
Emblems-E24
Jersey and Stick-SJ24
Jersey and Stick Gold-SJ24
Teammates-T16
Teammates Gold-T16
02McDonald's Pacific-35
02Nextel NHL All-Star Game-3
02O-Pee-Chee-105
02O-Pee-Chee Premier Blue Parallel-105
02O-Pee-Chee Premier Red Parallel-105
02O-Pee-Chee Factory Set-105
02Pacific-340
Blue-340
Red-340
Impact Zone-10
02Pacific Calder-18
Silver-18
02Pacific Complete-436
Red-436
02Pacific Exclusive-152
Maximum Overdrive-17
02Pacific Heads-Up-110
Blue-110
Purple-110
Red-110
Quad Jerseys-33
Quad Jerseys Gold-33
02Pacific Quest for the Cup-87
Gold-87
Chasing the Cup-15
02Parkhurst-25
Bronze-25
Gold-25
Silver-25
He Shoots-He Scores Prizes-21
Jerseys-GJ13
Patented Power-PP3
Stick and Jerseys-SJ13
Teammates-TT15
02Parkhurst Retro-97
Minis-97
Franchise Players-RF25
He Shoots-He Scores Prizes-30
Jerseys-RJ40
Nicknames-RN26
02Private Stock Reserve-88
Blue-88
Red-88
Retail-88
02Sharks Team Issue-7
02SP Authentic-76
Beckett Promos-76
Sign of the Times-TS
Sign of the Times-SN
02SP Game Used-61
First Rounder Patches-TS
Piece of History-PHTS
Piece of History Gold-PHTS
Piece of History Rainbow-PHTS
Signature Style-TS
Tools of the Game-TS
02SPx-142
Milestones-MTS
Milestones Gold-TS
Milestones Silver-TS
02Stadium Club-91
Silver Decoy Cards-91
Proofs-91
World Stage-WS14
02Titanium-88
Blue-88
Red-88
Retail-88
02Topps-105
OPC Blue Parallel-105
OPC Red Parallel-105
Factory Set-105
02Topps Chrome-66
Black Border Refractors-66
Refractors-66
02Topps Heritage-21
Chrome Parallel-21
02Topps Total-250
Production-TP11
02UD Artistic Impressions-73
Gold-73
02UD Artistic Impressions Beckett Promos-73
02UD Artistic Impressions Retrospectives-R73
02UD Artistic Impressions Retrospect Gold-R73
02UD Artistic Impress Retrospect Silver-R73
02Upper Deck Collectors Club-NHL13
02UD Honor Roll Signature Class-TS
02UD Honor Roll Students of the Game-SG26
02UD Piece of History-100
Awards Collection-AC24
Marks of Distinction-TS
Patches-PHTS
02UD Premier Collection Patches-PTS
02UD Top Shelf-75
All-Stars-ASTS
Clutch Performers-CPTS
Goal Oriented-GOTS
Hardware Heroes-HSSBR
Milestones Jerseys-MBMBS
Shooting Stars-SHTS
Sweet Sweaters-SWTS
Triple Jerseys-HTAPS
Triple Jerseys-HTJHS
02Upper Deck-195
02Upper Deck-392
Exclusives-195
Exclusives-392
All-Star Jerseys-ASTS
All-Star Performers-ASTS
02Upper Deck Beckett UD Promos-392
02Upper Deck Good Old Days-GOTS
02Upper Deck Playbooks-PL11
02Upper Deck Shooting Stars-SS13
02Upper Deck Classic Portraits-82
Etched in Time-ET14
Hockey Royalty-SLN
Hockey Royalty Limited-SLN
Pillars of Strength-PS9
02Upper Deck MVP-157
Gold-157
Classics-157
Golden Classics-157
Prosign-SE
Skate Around Jerseys-SDMS
Skate Around Jerseys-STSHP
Skate Around Jerseys-STSMJ
Souvenirs-S-TS
Vital Forces-VF13
02Upper Deck Rookie Update-86
02Upper Deck Victory National Pride-NP27
02Upper Deck Vintage-304
02Vanguard-87
LTD-87
02Finnish Cardset-115
02Finnish Cardset Dynamic Duos-10
02Finnish Cardset Solid Gold-6
02UD SuperStars *-216
Gold-216
03McFarlane Hockey-80
03McFarlane Hockey-82
03McFarlane Hockey-84
03McFarlane Hockey-85
03McFarlane Hockey-86

03McFarlane Hockey-88
03Avalanche Team Issue-16
03BAP Memorabilia-93
Emerald-93
Gold-93
Ruby-93
Sapphire-93
All-Star Jerseys-ASJ-7
All-Star Staring Lineup-12
He Shoots-He Scores Points-13
He Shoots-He Scores Prizes-6
Jerseys-GJ-48
Jersey Autographs-GJ-48
03BAP Ultimate Memorabilia Autographs-88
Gold-88
03BAP Ultimate Mem Auto Jerseys-88
03BAP Ultimate Mem Always An All-Star-8
03BAP Ultimate Mem Always An AS Gold-8
03BAP Ultimate Memorabilia Dynamic Duos-1
03BAP Ultimate Memorabilia Heroes-15
03BAP Ultimate Memorabilia Jerseys-2
03BAP Ultimate Memorabilia Jerseys Gold-2
03BAP Ultimate Mem Jersey and Emblems-40
03BAP Ultimate Mem Jersey and Emblem Gold-40
03BAP Ultimate Mem Jersey and Numbers-40
03BAP Ultimate Mem Jersey and Number Gold-40
03BAP Ultimate Mem Journey Jerseys-3
03BAP Ultimate Mem Journey Jerseys Gold-3
03BAP Ultimate Mem Journey Emblems-3
03BAP Ultimate Mem Journey Emblems Gold-3
03BAP Ultimate Memorabilia Nameplates-9
03BAP Ultimate Mem Nameplates Gold-9
03BAP Ultimate Mem Perennial Power Jersey-10
03BAP Ult Mem Perenn Powerhouse Jsy Stick-10
03BAP Ultimate Mem Perennial Power Emblem-10
03BAP Ultimate Memorabilia Triple Threads-20
03Beehive-47
Gold-47
Silver-47
Jerseys-JT38
Sticks Beige Border-BE13
03Black Diamond-107
Black-107
Green-107
Red-107
03Crown Royale Global Conquest-3
03Crown Royale Jerseys-7
03Crown Royale Patches-7
03eTopps-40
03ITG Action-172
03ITG Used Signature Series-13
Gold-13
Autographs-TS
Autographs Gold-TS
International Experience-16
International Experience Autographs-16
International Experience Emblems Gold-16
International Experience Emblems-16
International Experience Gold-16
Jerseys-44
Jerseys Gold-44
Jersey Autos-44
Emblems-7
Emblems Gold-7
Jersey and Stick-44
Jersey and Stick Gold-44
Teammates-1
Teammates Gold-1
03NHL Sticker Collection-287
03O-Pee-Chee-35
03OPC Blue-35
03OPC Gold-35
03OPC Red-35
03Pacific-300
Blue-300
Red-300
Main Attractions-13
03Pacific Complete-126
Red-126
03Pacific Exhibit-39
Blue Backs-39
Yellow Backs-39
03Pacific Invincible-26
Blue-26
Red-26
Retail-26
Afterburners-3
03Pacific Luxury Suite-29A
03Pacific Luxury Suite-29B
03Pacific Luxury Suite-29C
03Pacific Luxury Suite-31A
03Pacific Luxury Suite-31B
03Pacific Prism-89
Blue-89
Gold-89
Red-89
03Pacific Quest for the Cup-27
Blue-27
03Parkhurst Orig Six Boston Mem -BM47
03Parkhurst Orig Six Chicago Mem -CM47
03Parkhurst Orig Six Detroit Mem-DM47
03Parkhurst Orig Six Montreal Mem-MM47
03Parkhurst Orig Six New York Mem-NM47
03Parkhurst Original Six Shooters-OSM7
03Parkhurst Orig Six Toronto Mem-TM47
03Parkhurst Rookie Jerseys-GJ-27
03Parkhurst Rookie Jerseys Gold-GJ-27
03Parkhurst Rookie Jersey and Sticks-SJ-30
03Parkhurst Rookie Jersey and Sticks Gold-SJ-30
03Parkhurst Rookie Records-RRE-1
03Parkhurst Rookie Records-RRE-2
03Parkhurst Rookie Records Gold-RRE-1
03Parkhurst Rookie Records Gold-RRE-2
03Parkhurst Rookie Retro Rookies-RR-20
03Parkhurst Rookie Retro Rookies Gold-RR-20
03Parkhurst Rookie ROYalty-VR-5
03Parkhurst Rookie ROYalty Gold-VR-5
03Private Stock Reserve-159
Blue-159
Patches-159
Red-159
Retail-159
03SP Authentic 10th Anniversary-SP5
03SP Authentic 10th Anniversary Limited-SP5
03SP Authentic Breakout Seasons-B22
03SP Authentic Breakout Seasons Limited-B22
03SP Authentic Foundations-F3
03SP Authentic Foundations Limited-F3
03SP Game Used Authentic Fabrics-DFKS
03SP Game Used Authentic Fabrics-QFSKS
03SP Game Used Authentic Fabrics Gold-DFKS
03SP Game Used Authentic Fabrics Gold-QFSKS
03SP Game Used Double Threads-DTKS
03SP Game Used Game Gear-GGTS
03SP Game Used Limited Threads-LTTS
03SP Game Used Limited Threads Gold-LTTS
03SP Game Used Premium Patches-PPTS
03SP Game Used Team Threads-TTFSK
03SP Game Used Top Threads-FSKS
03SPx-22
03SPx-153
Radiance-22
Radiance-153
Spectrum-22
Spectrum-153
Fantasy Franchise-FF-KSF
Fantasy Franchise Limited-FF-KSF
Origins-O-TS
VIP-VIP-SK
VIP Limited-VIP-SK
Winning Materials-WM-TS
Winning Materials Limited-WM-TS
03Titanium-150
Hobby Jersey Number Parallels-150
Retail-150
03Topps-35
Blue-35
Gold-35
Red-35
Topps/OPC Idols-II15
03Topps C55-28
Minis-28
Minis American Back-28
Minis American Back Red-28
Minis Bazooka Back-28
Minis Brooklyn Back-28
Minis Hat Trick Back-28
Minis O Canada Back-28
Minis O Canada Back Red-28
Minis Stanley Cup Back-28
03Topps Traded-TT9
Blue-TT9
Gold-TT9
Red-TT9
03UD Honor Roll-115
03UD Premier Collection Teammates-PT-CA2
03UD Premier Collection Teammates Patches-PT-CA2
03Upper Deck-50
All-Star Class-AS-6
Big Playmakers-BP-TS
Canadian Exclusives-50
HG-50
Highlight Heroes-HH-TS
Highlight Heroes Jerseys-HH-TS
03Upper Deck Classic Portraits-20
Classic Colors-CC-TS
03Upper Deck MVP-110
Gold Script-110
Silver Script-110
Canadian Exclusives-110
03Upper Deck Rookie Update Top Draws-TD2
03Upper Deck Trilogy-20
Authentic Patches-AP25
Limited-20
03Upper Deck Victory-155
Bronze-155
Gold-155
Silver-155
Freshman Flashback-FF37
Game Breakers-GB25
04Pacific-71
Blue-71
Red-71
Global Connection-4
04UD All-World-17
04UD All-World-107
Gold-17
04Ultimate Collection-70
Dual Logos-UL2-KS
04Upper Deck-47
Canadian Exclusives-47
HG Glossy Gold-47
HG Glossy Silver-47
World's Best-WB14
World Cup Tribute-OJSKTS
05Beehive-1
05Beehive-243
Matte-1
05Black Diamond Jerseys-J-TS
05Black Diamond Jerseys Ruby-J-TS
05Black Diamond Jersey Duals-DJ-TS
05Black Diamond Jersey Triples-TJ-TS
05Black Diamond Jersey Quads-QJ-TS
05Ducks Team Issue-19
05Hot Prospects-3
En Fuego-3
Red Hot-3
White Hot-3
05Panini Stickers-192
05Parkhurst-2
05Parkhurst-592
Facsimile Auto Parallel-2
Facsimile Auto Parallel-592
True Colors-TCANA
True Colors-TCANA
05SP Authentic-3
Limited-3
05SP Game Used-2
Gold-2
Authentic Fabrics Dual-GS
Authentic Fabrics Quad-SGLC
Authentic Patches Quad -SGLC
Authentic Fabrics Triple-KSK
Authentic Patches Dual-GS
Authentic Patches Triple-KSK
Awesome Authentics-AA-TS
Awesome Authentics Gold-DA-TS
05SPx Winning Combos-WC-AN
05SPx Winning Combos Gold-WC-AN
05SPx Winning Combos Spectrum-WC-AN
05SPx Winning Materials-WM-TS
05SPx Winning Materials Gold-WM-TS
05SPx Winning Materials Spectrum-WM-TS
05The Cup-2
Gold-2
Black Rainbow-2
Dual NHL Shields-DSGS
Dual NHL Shields-DSKS
Masterpiece Pressplates-2
Noble Numbers-NNSS
Noble Numbers Dual-DNNFI
Noble Numbers Dual-DNNGS
Noble Numbers Dual-DNNKS
Patch Variation-P2
05UD Artifacts Treasured Patches-TP-TS
05UD Artifacts Treasured Patch Autos-TP-TS
05UD Artifacts Treasured Patches Dual-TPD-TS
05UD Artifacts Treasured Patch Dual Autos-TPD-TS
05UD Artifacts Treasured Patches Pewter-TP-TS
05UD Artifacts Treasured Patches Silver-TP-TS
05UD Artifacts Treasured Swatches-TS-TS
05UD Artifacts Treasured Swatch Autos-TS-TS
05UD Artifacts Treasured Swatches Blue-TS-TS
05UD Artifacts Treasured Swatches Copper-TS-TS
05UD Artifacts Treasured Swatches Dual-TSD-TS
05UD Artifacts Treasured Swatch Dual Auto-TSD-TS
05UD Artifacts Treasured Swatch Dual Blue-TSD-TS
05UD Artifact Treasure Swatch Dual Copper-TSD-TS
05UD Artifact Treasure Swatch Dual Maroon-TSD-TS
05UD Artifact Treasure Swatch Dual Pewter-TSD-TS
05UD Artifact TreasuredSwatch Dual Silver-TSD-TS
05UD Artifacts Treasured Swatches Maroon-TS-TS
05UD Artifacts Treasured Swatches Pewter-TS-TS
05UD Artifacts Treasured Swatches Silver-TS-TS
05UD Powerplay Specialists-TSTS
05UD Powerplay Specialists Patches-SPTS
05Ultimate Collection-1
Gold-1
Jerseys-JTS
Jerseys Dual-DJLS
National Heroes Jerseys-NHJTS
National Heroes Patches-NHPTS
Premium Patches-PPTS
Premium Swatches-PSTS
Ultimate Patches-PTS
Ultimate Patches Dual-DPLS
05Ultra-2
Gold-2
Ice-2
05Upper Deck-243
05Upper Deck All-Time Greatest-90
05Upper Deck Jerseys-J-TSE
05Upper Deck Jerseys Series II-J2TS
05Upper Deck Majestic Materials-MMTS
05Upper Deck NHL Generations-DKS
05Upper Deck NHL Generations-TSKJ
05Upper Deck Patches-P-TS
05Upper Deck Hockey Showcase-HS24
05Upper Deck Showcase Promos-HS24
05Upper Deck Ice-4
Rainbow-4
05Upper Deck MVP-5
Gold-5
Platinum-5
05Upper Deck Rookie Update-2
05Upper Deck Victory-53
05Upper Deck Victory-201
Black-53
Black-201
Gold-53
Gold-201
Silver-53
Silver-201
05Czech Stadion-681
06Sports Illustrated for Kids *-81
06Be A Player-42
Autographs-42
Profiles-PP3
Profiles Autographs-PP3
Signatures-TS
Signatures 10-45
Signatures 25-45
Signatures Duals-DSK
Signatures Duals-DSN
Signatures Foursomes-FSKJL
Up Close and Personal-UC56
Up Close and Personal Autographs-UC56
06Be A Player Portraits-3
06Beehive-98
06Beehive-234
Blue-98
Gold-98
Matte-98
Red Facsimile Signatures-98
Wood-98
5 X 7 Black and White-98
06Black Diamond-85
Black-85
Gold-85
Ruby-85
06Flair Showcase-2
06Flair Showcase-101
06Flair Showcase-202
Parallel-2
Parallel-101
Parallel-202
Hot Numbers-HN1
Hot Numbers Parallel-HN1
Stitches-SSTS
06Fleer-3
Tiffany-3
Fabricology-FTS
Hockey Headliners-HL3
Speed Machines-SM2
06Hot Prospects-3
Red Hot-3
White Hot-3
Hot Materials -HMTS
Hot Materials Red Hot-HMTS
Hot Materials White Hot-HMTS
06McDonald's Upper Deck-1
06NHL POG-47
06O-Pee-Chee-5
06O-Pee-Chee-646
06O-Pee-Chee-671
Rainbow-5
Rainbow-646
Rainbow-671
Swatches-S-TS
06Panini Stickers-187
06SP Authentic-100
06SP Authentic-157
Limited-100
Limited-157
06SP Game Used-2
Gold-2
Rainbow-2
Authentic Fabrics-AFTS
Authentic Fabrics Parallel-AFTS
Authentic Fabrics Patches-AFTS
Authentic Fabrics Dual-AF2SP
Authentic Fabrics Dual Patches-AF2SP
Authentic Fabrics Triple-AF3ANA
Authentic Fabrics Triple Patches-AF3ANA
Authentic Fabrics Fives-AF5ASG
Authentic Fabrics Fives Patches-AF5ASG
Authentic Fabrics Sixes-AF6MAS
Authentic Fabrics Sixes-AF6MRT
Authentic Fabrics Sixes Patches-AF6MAS
Authentic Fabrics Sixes Patches-AF6MRT
Authentic Fabrics Eights-AF8FIN
Authentic Fabrics Eights Patches-AF8FIN
By The Letter-BLTS
06SPx-2
06SPx-101
Spectrum-2
Spectrum-101
SPxcitement-X2
SPxcitement Spectrum-X2
Winning Materials-WMTS
Winning Materials Spectrum-WMTS
06The Cup-1
Black Rainbow-1
Foundations-CQTS
Foundations Patches-CQTS
Gold-1
Gold Patches-1
Jerseys-1
Masterpiece Pressplates-1
NHL Shields Duals-DSHSG
NHL Shields Duals-DSHSK
NHL Shields Duals-DSHSP
06UD Artifacts-98
06UD Artifacts-151
Blue-98
Blue-151
Gold-98
Gold-151
Platinum-98
Platinum-151
Radiance-98
Radiance-151
Red-98
Red-151
Frozen Artifacts-FATS
Frozen Artifacts Black-FATS
Frozen Artifacts Blue-FATS
Frozen Artifacts Gold-FATS
Frozen Artifacts Platinum-FATS
Frozen Artifacts Red-FATS
Frozen Artifacts Patches Black-FATS
Frozen Artifacts Patches Blue-FATS
Frozen Artifacts Patches Gold-FATS
Frozen Artifacts Patches Platinum-FATS
Frozen Artifacts Patches Red-FATS
Tundra Tandems-TTSP
Tundra Tandems Black-TTSP
Tundra Tandems Blue-TTSP
Tundra Tandems Gold-TTSP
Tundra Tandems Platinum-TTSP
Tundra Tandems Red-TTSP
Tundra Tandems Dual Patches Red-TTSP
06UD Mini Jersey Collection-1
06UD Powerplay-2
Impact Rainbow-2
Specialists-STS
Specialists Patches-PTS
06Ultimate Collection-1
Jerseys-UJ-TS
Jerseys Dual-UJ2-KS
Patches-UJ-TS
Patches Dual-UJ2-KS
06Ultra-5
Gold Medallion-5
Ice Medallion-5
Uniformity-UTS
Uniformity Patches-UPTS
06Upper Deck Arena Giveaways-ANA2
06Upper Deck-3
Exclusives Parallel-3
High Gloss Parallel-3
All-Time Greatest-ATG1
All World-AW4
Award Winners Canadian Exclusive-OAW14
Game Dated Moments-GD13
Game Jerseys-J2TS
Game Patches-P2TS
Generations Triples-G3SKO
Generations Patches Triple-G3PSKO
Goal Rush-GR12
Hometown Heroes-HH29
Masterpieces-3
Walmart Tins Oversize-3
06Upper Deck MVP-4
Gold Script-4
Super Script-4
International Icons-II1
Jerseys-OJCS
Jerseys-OJSF
06Upper Deck Ovation-2
06Upper Deck Sweet Shot-1
Sweet Stitches-SSTS
Sweet Stitches Duals-SSTS
Sweet Stitches Triples-SSTS
06Upper Deck Trilogy-2
06Upper Deck Victory-3
06Upper Deck Victory Black-3
06Upper Deck Victory Gold-3
06Russian Sport Collection Olympic Stars-27
07Upper Deck Victory-174
Black-174
Gold-174
GameBreakers-GB25
Stars on Ice-SI13

Selby, Brit
64Beehive Group III Photos-182
65Coca-Cola-97
66Maple Leafs Hockey Talks-7
66Topps-18
68O-Pee-Chee-96
68Shirriff Coins-129
68Topps-96
69Maple Leafs White Border Glossy-31
69O-Pee-Chee-48
69Topps-48
70Colgate Stamps-37
70Dad's Cookies-121
70Esso Power Players-248
70O-Pee-Chee-111A
70O-Pee-Chee-111B
70Sargent Promotions Stamps-202
70Topps-111
71O-Pee-Chee-226
71Sargent Promotions Stamps-183
73Quaker Oats WHA-39
94Parkhurst Tall Boys-121
95Parkhurst '66-67-111
95Parkhurst '66-67-132
Coins-111
02Maple Leafs Platinum Collection-91
07Maple Leafs 1967 Commemorative-23

Selby, Matt
93Quebec Pee-Wee Tournament-1473

Selden, Bobby
04Northern Michigan Wildcats-20

Self, Andrew
05Belleville Bulls-24
06Sudbury Wolves-2

Self, Brad
01Peterborough Petes-13

Self, Mike
02Windsor Spitfires-29
04Lakehead University Thunderwolves-15

Self, Scott
93Quebec Pee-Wee Tournament-547

Selig, Scott
04Oklahoma City Blazers-9

Seliger, Marc
91Upper Deck-683
French-683
91Upper Deck Czech World Juniors-46
94German DEL-384
95German DEL-103
95Signature Rookies-30
Signatures-30
96Swedish Semic Wien-193
96Hampton Roads Admirals-HRA19
98German DEL-2
99German DEL-40
00German DEL-195
01German Upper Deck Goalies in Action-G9
02German DEL City Press-274
Top Stars-GT1
03German DEL-13
03German Mannheim Eagles Postcards-2
04German DEL-276

Selinder, Lennart
64Swedish Coralli ISHockey-42
65Swedish Coralli ISHockey-42
67Swedish Hockey-41
69Swedish Hockey-53
70Swedish Hockey-13
71Swedish Hockey-91
72Swedish Stickers-60
73Swedish Stickers-201

Selinger, Pavel
02Czech OFS Plus-297
03Czech OFS Plus-39

Selingr, Pavel
98Czech OFS-75
99Czech OFS-201
00Czech OFS-258
01Czech OFS-45
04Czech OFS-259
06Czech OFS-213

Seliutin, Sergei
99Russian Hockey League-209
00Russian Hockey League-211
01Russian Hockey League-31

Selivanov, Alexander
94Finest-79
Super Team Winners-79
Refractors-79
Bowman's Best-R17
Bowman's Best Refractors-R17
94Fleer-210
94Lightning Photo Album-23
94Lightning Postcards-16
94SP-113
Die Cuts-113
94Upper Deck-425
94Upper Deck-532
Electric Ice-425
Electric Ice-532
SP Inserts-SP165
SP Inserts Die Cuts-SP165
95Be A Player-145
Signatures-S145
Signatures Die Cuts-S145
95Bowman-73
All-Foil-73
95Canada Games NHL POGS-252
95Collector's Choice-165
Player's Club-165
Player's Club Platinum-165
95Donruss-90
95Donruss Elite-84
Die Cut Stars-84
Die Cut Uncut-84
95Finest-32
Refractors-32
95Leaf-49
95Lightning Team Issue-16
95Metal-140
95Panini Stickers-132
95Parkhurst International-194
Emerald Ice-194
95Pinnacle-116
Artist's Proofs-116
Rink Collection-116
Global Gold-17
95Playoff One on One-199
95SP-140
95Stadium Club-111
Members Only Master Set-111
95Topps-367
OPC Inserts-367
New To The Game-11NG
95Ultra-310
95Upper Deck-316
Electric Ice-316
Electric Ice Gold-316
Special Edition-SE77
Special Edition Gold-SE77
95Images-16
Gold-16
95Signature Rookies Auto-Phonex-39
95Signature Rook Auto-Phonex Phone Cards-39
96Collector's Choice-253
96Donruss-32
Press Proofs-32
96Donruss Elite-95
Die Cut Stars-95
96Fleer-106
96Leaf-62
Press Proofs-62
96Leaf Limited-45
Gold-45
96Leaf Preferred-43
Press Proofs-43
96Metal Universe-147
96Pinnacle-77
Artist's Proofs-77
Foil-77
Premium Stock-77
Rink Collection-77
96Playoff One on One-390
96Score-27
Artist's Proofs-27
Dealer's Choice Artist's Proofs-27
Special Artist's Proofs-27
Golden Blades-27
Superstitions-10
96SkyBox Impact-124
96SP-148
96Summit-58
Artist's Proofs-58
Ice-58
Metal-58
Premium Stock-58
96Topps Picks-123
OPC Inserts-123
96Ultra-160
Gold Medallion-160
96Upper Deck-339
96Zenith-21
Artist's Proofs-21
97Black Diamond-121
Double Diamond-121
Triple Diamond-121
Quadruple Diamond-121
97Collector's Choice-241
97Pacific Dynagon Best Kept Secrets-89
97Pacific Omega-214
Copper-214
Dark Gray-214
Emerald Green-214
Gold-214
Ice Blue-214
97Panini Stickers-102
97Paramount-176
Copper-176
Dark Grey-176
Emerald Green-176
Ice Blue-176
Red-176
Silver-176
97Score-245
97SP Authentic-146
97Upper Deck-156
98Aurora-176
98Be A Player-130
Press Release-130
98BAP Gold-130
98BAP Autographs-130
98BAP Autographs Gold-130
98BAP Tampa Bay All Star Game-130
98OPC Chrome-85
Refractors-85
98Pacific-406
Ice Blue-406
Red-406
98Panini Stickers-97
98Paramount-221
Copper-221
Emerald Green-221
Holo-Electric-221
Ice Blue-221
Silver-221
98SP Authentic Sign of the Times-AS
98SP Authentic Sign of the Times Gold-AS
98SPx Finite-80
Radiance-80
Spectrum-80
98Topps-85
O-Pee-Chee-85
98UD Choice-195
98UD Choice Preview-195
98UD Choice Prime Choice Reserve-195
98UD Choice Reserve-195
98Upper Deck-182
Exclusives-182
Exclusives 1 of 1-182
Gold Reserve-182
99Crown Royale-56
Limited Series-56
Premiere Date-56
99Pacific-165
Copper-165
Emerald Green-165
Gold-165
Ice Blue-165
Premiere Date-165
Red-165
99Pacific Omega-94
Copper-94
Gold-94
Ice Blue-94
Premiere Date-94
99Pacific Prism-57
Holographic Blue-57
Holographic Gold-57
Holographic Mirror-57
Holographic Purple-57
Premiere Date-57
99SP Authentic-36
99Stadium Club-116
First Day Issue-116
One of a Kind-116
Printing Plates Black-116
Printing Plates Cyan-116
Printing Plates Magenta-116
Printing Plates Yellow-116
99Topps Gold Label Class 1-76
Black-76
Black One of One-76
One of One-76
Red-76
Red One of One-76
99Topps Gold Label Class 2-76
99Topps Gold Label Class 2 Black-76
99Topps Gold Label Class 2 Black 1 of 1-76
99Topps Gold Label Class 2 One of One-76
99Topps Gold Label Class 2 Red-76
99Topps Gold Label Class 2 Red One of One-76
99Topps Gold Label Class 3-76
99Topps Gold Label Class 3 Black-76
99Topps Gold Label Class 3 Black 1 of 1-76
99Topps Gold Label Class 3 One of One-76
99Topps Gold Label Class 3 Red-76
99Topps Gold Label Class 3 Red One of One-76
99Ultimate Victory-37
1/1-37
Parallel-37
Parallel 100-37
99Upper Deck MVP SC Edition-73
Gold Script-73
Silver Script-73
Super Script-73
00BAP Memorabilia-310
Emerald-310
Ruby-310
Sapphire-310
Promos-310
00BAP Mem Chicago Sportsfest Copper-310
00BAP Memorabilia Chicago Sportsfest Blue-310
00BAP Memorabilia Chicago Sportsfest Gold-310
00BAP Memorabilia Chicago Sportsfest Ruby-310
00BAP Memorabilia Chicago Sun-Times Ruby-310
00BAP Memorabilia Chicago Sun-Times Gold-310
00BAP Mem Chicago Sun-Times Sapphire-310
00BAP Mem Toronto Fall Expo Copper-310
00BAP Memorabilia Toronto Fall Expo Gold-310
00BAP Memorabilia Toronto Fall Expo Ruby-310
00O-Pee-Chee-233
00O-Pee-Chee Parallel-233
00Pacific-173
Copper-173
Gold-173
Ice Blue-173
Premiere Date-173
00Panini Stickers-163
00Paramount-99
Copper-99
Gold-99
Holo-Gold-99
Holo-Silver-99
Ice Blue-99
Premiere Date-99
00Topps/OPC-233
Parallel-233
00Upper Deck Victory-99
01German Upper Deck-86
Gate Attractions-GA5
02BAP Sig Series Auto Buybacks 1998-130
02Russian SL-20
02Russian Transfert-18
03German DEL-191
04German DEL-239
All-Stars-AS16
04German Krefeld Penguins Postcards-20
05German DEL-232
All-Star Jerseys-AS17
06German DEL-140

Selke, Frank
55Parkhurst-68
Quaker Oats-68
59Parkhurst-47
81Maple Leafs Postcards-26
83Hall of Fame-41
83Hall of Fame Postcards-C12
85Hall of Fame-41
87Panini Stickers-385
90Upper Deck French-208
94Parkhurst Missing Link-85
01Upper Deck Legends-62
02Parkhurst Reprints-244
03BAP Ultimate Memorabilia Paper Cuts-14
04ITG Ultimate Mem Bleu Blanc et Rouge-9
04ITG Ultimate Memorabilia Paper Cuts-13
05ITG Ultimate Memorabilia Builders Autos-1
05The Cup Legendary Cuts-LCFS
06The Cup Legendary Cuts-LCFS

Selkirk, Jason
91Air Canada SJHL-A5

Sellan, Mike
00St. Michaels Majors-26

Sellars, Luke
95Quebec Pee-Wee Tournament-834
99Black Diamond-112
Diamond Cut-112
Final Cut-112
99O-Pee-Chee-274
99O-Pee-Chee Chrome-274
99O-Pee-Chee Chrome Refractors-274
99SP Authentic-134
99Topps/OPC-274
99Topps/OPC Chrome-274
Refractors-274
99Upper Deck MVP SC Edition-206
Gold Script-206
Silver Script-206
Super Script-206
99Ottawa 67's-20
99Bowman CHL-28
Gold-28
OPC International-28
Autographs-BA13
Autographs Gold-BA13
Autographs Silver-BA13
00Ottawa 67's-14
01Chicago Wolves-18
02Chicago Wolves-20
03Chicago Wolves-18

Selleke, Jason
99Ohio State Buckeyes-14
00Indianapolis Ice-20
01Indianapolis Ice-18
02Fort Wayne Komets-17
03Indianapolis Ice-18

Sellers, Luke
05Danbury Trashers-14

Sellitto, Alessandro
01Swiss HNL-449

Selman, Brent
93Lakeland Ice Warriors-22

Selmser, Sean
93Red Deer Rebels-22
95Hampton Roads Admirals-19
98Fort Wayne Komets-17
99Hamilton Bulldogs-19
00Syracuse Crunch-19
01SP Authentic-147
Limited-147
Limited Gold-147
01SPx-139
01SPx-139
Rookie Treasures-RTSS
01Upper Deck-189
Exclusives-189
01Hamilton Bulldogs-15

Selthun, David
98Kelowna Rockets-23
99Kelowna Rockets-22
00Kelowna Rockets-16
01Lethbridge Hurricanes-17
01Vancouver Giants-22

Seluyanov, Alexander
00Russian Hockey League-305
03Russian Hockey League-129

Seluyanov, Viacheslav
04Russian Hope-6

Selvek, Jan
95Slovakian APS National Team-4

Selwood, Brad
70Maple Leafs Postcards-12
71Maple Leafs Postcards-17
71Sargent Promotions Stamps-207
71Toronto Sun-270
72Whalers New England WHA-13
74Team Canada L'Equipe WHA-19
75O-Pee-Chee WHA-82

Selyanin, Sergei
91O-Pee-Chee Inserts-58R
94Finnish Jaa Kiekko-141

Semak, Alexander
91O-Pee-Chee Inserts-42R
91Parkhurst-323
French-323
91Upper Deck-4
French-4
91Finnish Semic World Champ Stickers-94
91Swedish Semic World Champ Stickers-94
92Bowman-164
92Panini Stickers-176
92Panini Stickers-296
92Panini Stickers French-176
92Panini Stickers French-296
92Parkhurst-329
Emerald Ice-329
92Score-451
Canadian-451
92Stadium Club-444
92Topps-419
Gold-419G
92Ultra-341
92Upper Deck-45
Euro-Rookie Team-ERT5
92Finnish Semic-113
92Russian Stars Red Ace-30
93Donruss-191
93Leaf-35
93OPC Premier-102
Gold-102
93Panini Stickers-36
93Parkhurst-109
Emerald Ice-109
93Pinnacle-47
Canadian-47
93PowerPlay-142
93Score-284
Canadian-284
International Stars-14
International Stars Canadian-14
93Stadium Club-365
Members Only Master Set-365
First Day Issue-365
93Topps/OPC Premier-102
Gold-102
93Ultra-166
93Upper Deck-178
SP-88
94Be A Player Signature Cards-4
94EA Sports-75
94Flair-99
94Fleer-118
94Leaf-543
94Lightning Photo Album-24
94Pinnacle-362
Artist's Proofs-362
Rink Collection-362
94Stadium Club-245
Members Only Master Set-245
First Day Issue-245
Super Team Winner Cards-245
94Ultra-321
94Upper Deck-219
Electric Ice-219
94Finnish Jaa Kiekko-158
95Collector's Choice-56
Player's Club-56
Player's Club Platinum-56
95Emotion-109
95Panini Stickers-127
95Parkhurst International-135
Emerald Ice-135
95Topps-97
OPC Inserts-97
95Ultra-271
95Upper Deck-40
Electric Ice-40
Electric Ice Gold-40
96Canucks Postcards-20
96Collector's Choice-163
96Donruss-26
Press Proofs-26
96Pinnacle-188
Artist's Proofs-188
Foil-188
Premium Stock-188
Rink Collection-188
96Score-212
Artist's Proofs-212
Dealer's Choice Artist's Proofs-212
Special Artist's Proofs-212
Golden Blades-212
96Upper Deck-98
98Albany River Rats-15
98Chicago Wolves Turner Cup-22
99German Bundesliga 2-108
00Russian Hockey League-146
01Russian Hockey League-60
01Russian Hockey League-171
02Russian Hockey League-218
02Russian Transfert-27
03Russian Hockey League-148
04Russian Super League All-Stars-7

Seman, Daniel
99Czech OFS-231
00Czech OFS-248
01Czech OFS Update-310
03Czech OFS Plus-22
04Czech OFS-355

Seman, Filip
06Czech OFS-62

Semandel, Kurt
90Kansas City Blades-15
90ProCards AHL/IHL-598

Semchuk, Brandy
90ProCards AHL/IHL-430
92Phoenix Roadrunners-20
95Central Hockey League-102

Semenchenko, Vitali
03Russian Avangard Omsk-26

Semeniuk, Darrin
94Anchorage Aces-6

Semeniuk, Trevor
83Medicine Hat Tigers-10
84Victoria Cougars-21

Semenko, Dave
79Oilers Postcards-20
79O-Pee-Chee-371
80O-Pee-Chee-360
80Pepsi-Cola Caps-38
81Oilers Red Rooster-27
81O-Pee-Chee-121
82Oilers Red Rooster-27
82O-Pee-Chee-119
82Post Cereal-6
83NHL Key Tags-41
83Oilers Dollars-H19
83Oilers McDonald's-2
83Vachon-40
84Oilers Red Rooster-27
84Oilers Team Issue-23
85Oilers Red Rooster-27
87Maple Leafs PLAY-26
87Maple Leafs Postcards-19
87Maple Leafs Postcards Oversized-19
88Oilers Tenth Anniversary-6
01Fleer Legacy-28
Ultimate-28
02Fleer Throwbacks-29
Gold-29
Platinum-29
04ITG Franchises Canadian-21
Autographs-DSE
05ITG Tough Customers-DSE
Stickwork-DS
06Parkhurst-113
06Parkhurst-240
Autographs-113
Autographs-240
Autographs Dual-DAWS

Semenov, Alexei
99Sudbury Wolves-12
00Sudbury Wolves-12
00UD CHL Prospects-27
01Hamilton Bulldogs-18
02BAP Memorabilia-381
02BAP Ultimate Memorabilia-88
02Parkhurst Retro-221
Minis-221
02SP Authentic-203
02SPx-192
02UD Artistic Impressions-131
Gold-131
02UD Honor Roll-133
02UD Premier Collection-60A
Gold-60A
Jerseys Bronze-AX
Jerseys Gold-AX
Jerseys Silver-AX
02Hamilton Bulldogs-19
03ITG Action-251
03Oilers Postcards-16
03O-Pee-Chee-330
03OPC Blue-330
03OPC Gold-330
03OPC Red-330
03Topps-330
Blue-330
Gold-330
Red-330
03Upper Deck MVP-170
Gold Script-170
Silver Script-170
Canadian Exclusives-170
03Upper Deck Rookie Update YoungStars-YS21
05UD Powerplay Specialists-TSAS
05UD Powerplay Specialists Patches-SPAS
05Upper Deck MVP-161
Gold-161
Platinum-161

Semenov, Anatoli
89Swedish Semic World Champ Stickers-99

90Oilers IGA-22
90O-Pee-Chee-468
90OPC Premier-104
90Pro Set-608
90Score Rookie/Traded-39T
90Upper Deck-405
French-405
91Bowman-113
91Oilers Panini Team Stickers-19
91Oilers IGA-20
91Oilers Team Issue-24
91O-Pee-Chee-390
91Panini Stickers-127
91Parkhurst-279
French-279
91Score Canadian Bilingual-258
91Score Canadian English-258
91Stadium Club-366
91Topps-390
91Upper Deck-269
French-269
Euro-Stars-4
Euro-Stars French-4
91Russian Stars Red Ace-16
91Russian Tri-Globe Semenov-11
91Russian Tri-Globe Semenov-12
91Russian Tri-Globe Semenov-13
91Russian Tri-Globe Semenov-14
91Russian Tri-Globe Semenov-15
92Bowman-423
92O-Pee-Chee-83
92Parkhurst-420
Emerald Ice-420
92Pinnacle-386
French-386
92Score-336
Canadian-336
Sharpshooters-28
Sharpshooters Canadian-28
92Stadium Club-143
92Topps-68
Gold-68G
92Ultra-429
92Upper Deck-20
92Upper Deck-535
93Donruss-3
93Leaf-338
93OPC Premier-506
Gold-506
93Panini Stickers-174
93Parkhurst-3
Emerald Ice-3
93Pinnacle-368
Canadian-368
93PowerPlay-10
93Score-93
93Score-536
Gold-536
Canadian-93
Canadian-536
Canadian Gold-536
93Stadium Club-368
Members Only Master Set-368
First Day Issue-368
93Topps/OPC Premier-506
Gold-506
93Ultra-261
93Upper Deck-46
SP-4
94Canada Games NHL POGS-347
94Donruss-326
94EA Sports-5
94Flair-5
94Leaf-303
94OPC Premier-524
Special Effects-524
94Parkhurst-1
Gold-1
94Pinnacle-322
Artist's Proofs-322
Rink Collection-322
94Score-16
Gold-16
Platinum-16
94Topps/OPC Premier-524
Special Effects-524
94Ultra-7
94Upper Deck-105
Electric Ice-105
95Donruss-312
95Leaf-238
95Parkhurst International-429
Emerald Ice-429
96Collector's Choice-7
97Pacific-106
Copper-106
Emerald Green-106
Ice Blue-106
Red-106
Silver-106

Semenov, Denis
06Westside Warriors-8

Semenov, Dmitri
00Russian Dynamo Moscow-32
01Russian Dynamo Moscow-14

Semenov, Maxim
03Russian Hockey League-117

Semin, Alexander
02BAP Memorabilia Draft Redemptions-13
02Russian Hockey League-48
02Russian Transfert-1
02Russian Young Lions-4
03BAP Memorabilia-193
Emerald-193
Gold-193
Ruby-193
Sapphire-193
Super Rookies-SR19
Super Rookies Gold-SR19
Super Rookies Silver-SR19
03BAP Ultimate Memorabilia Autographs-94
Gold-94
03BAP Ultimate Mem Auto Jerseys-94
03BAP Ultimate Mem Auto Emblems-94
03BAP Ultimate Mem Auto Numbers-94
03BAP Ultimate Mem Franch Present Future-30
03BAP Ultimate Mem Rookie Jersey Emblems-27
03BAP Ultimate Mem Rookie Jsy Emblem Gold-27
03BAP Ultimate Mem Rookie Jersey Numbers-27
03BAP Ultimate Mem Rookie Jsy Number Gold-27
03BAP Ultimate Memorabilia Triple Threads-31
03Beehive-236
Gold-236
Silver-236
03Black Diamond-159
Black-159
Green-159
Red-159
03Bowman-137
Gold-137
03Bowman Chrome-137
Refractors-137
Gold Refractors-137
Xfractors-137
03ITG Action-606
03ITG Used Signature Series-145
Autographs Gold-145
03ITG VIP Rookie Debut-42
03Pacific Calder-139
Silver-139
03Pacific Complete-541
Red-541
03Pacific Heads-Up-136
Hobby LTD-136
Retail LTD-136
03Pacific Luxury Suite-79
Gold-79
03Pacific Quest for the Cup-139
03Parkhurst Toronto Expo Rookie Preview-PRP-20
03Parkhurst Rookie-196
Rookie Emblems-RE-41
Rookie Emblem Autographs-RE-AS
Rookie Emblems Gold-RE-41
Rookie Jerseys-RJ-41
Rookie Jersey Autographs-RJ-AS
Rookie Jerseys Gold-RJ-41
Rookie Numbers-RN-41
Rookie Number Autographs-RN-AS
Rookie Numbers Gold-RN-41
03SP Authentic-158
Limited-158
Signed Patches-AS
03SP Game Used-77
Gold-77
03SPx-216
Radiance-216
Spectrum-216
03Titanium-139
Hobby Jersey Number Parallels-139
Retail-139
Retail Jersey Number Parallels-139
03Topps C55-139
Minis-139
Minis American Back-139
Minis American Back Red-139
Minis Bazooka Back-139
Minis Brooklyn Back-139
Minis Hat Trick Back-139
Minis O Canada Back-139
Minis O Canada Back Red-139
Minis Stanley Cup Back-139
03Topps Pristine-167
03Topps Pristine-168
03Topps Pristine-169
Gold Refractor Die Cuts-167
Gold Refractor Die Cuts-168
Gold Refractor Die Cuts-169
Refractors-167
Refractors-168
Refractors-169
Press Plates Black-167
Press Plates Black-168
Press Plates Black-169
Press Plates Cyan-167
Press Plates Cyan-168
Press Plates Cyan-169
Press Plates Magenta-167
Press Plates Magenta-168
Press Plates Magenta-169
Press Plates Yellow-167
Press Plates Yellow-168
Press Plates Yellow-169
03Topps Traded-TT144
Blue-TT144
Gold-TT144
Red-TT144
03UD Honor Roll-176
03UD Premier Collection-80
03Upper Deck-219
Canadian Exclusives-219
HG-219
03Upper Deck Classic Portraits-189
03Upper Deck Ice-103
Glass Parallel-103
03Upper Deck MVP-451
03Upper Deck Rookie Update-154
03Upper Deck Trilogy-166
Limited-166
03Russian Young Lions-2
03Russian World Championship Team 2003-4
04Pacific-299
Blue-299
Red-299
04Russian Back to Russia-11
04Russian World Junior Team-20
05Upper Deck-197
HG Glossy-197
05Upper Deck MVP-388
Gold-388
Platinum-388
05Upper Deck Toronto Fall Expo-197
05Upper Deck Victory-198
Black-198
Gold-198
Silver-198
05Russian Hockey League RHL-24
06Hot Prospects-100
06Upper Deck Arena Giveaways-WSH2
06Upper Deck-198
Exclusives Parallel-198
High Gloss Parallel-198
Masterpieces-198
Victory-280
07Upper Deck Victory-93
Black-93
Gold-93

Semin, Dmitri
02Russian Future Stars-14
02Russian Hockey League-12

Semin, Nikolai
92Upper Deck-610
99Russian Hockey League-42
02Russian Hockey League-105
03Russian Hockey League-153
03Russian National Team-10

Semin, Sergei
00Russian Hockey League-330
01Russian Hockey League-137
03Russian Hockey League-61

Semjonovs, Aleksandrs
98Swedish UD Choice-32
00Swedish Upper Deck-25
SHL Signatures-AS

Senden, Stuart
97Minnesota Golden Gophers-25
98Minnesota Golden Gophers-17
99Minnesota Golden Gophers-22
00Minnesota Golden Gophers-23

Senderovitz, Michael
98Danish Hockey League-206
99Danish Hockey League-130

Sendrey, Rastislav
95Slovakian-Quebec Pee-Wee Tournament-23

Sendt, Thorsten
94German DEL-217

Senecal, Mario
51Bas Du Fleuve-56
52Bas Du Fleuve-49

Senecal, Sylvain
84Richelieu Riverains-18

Senechal, Claude
50Quebec Citadelles-18

Senff, Danny
95Neepewa Natives-23

Senft, Ryan
01Saskatoon Blades-26

Senftleben, Helmut
04German Berlin Eisbarens 50th Anniv-25

Senger, Patrick
98German DEL-200
99German DEL-278
01German Upper Deck-24
02German DEL City Press-122

Senins, Sergejs
98Danish Hockey League-152
99Danish Hockey League-167

Senkow, Derek
95Medicine Hat Tigers-18

Senn, Trevor
92Wheeling Thunderbirds-16
95Richmond Renegades-15
96Richmond Renegades-19
04Richmond Riverdogs-15

Senseman, Michael
05Regina Pats-23

Sentner, Peter
90ProCards AHL/IHL-361
91Greensboro Monarchs-12

Sepanski, Jeff
93Quebec Pee-Wee Tournament-1266

Sepkowski, Todd
84Sudbury Wolves-8

Sepovalov, Vladimir
74Finnish Jenkki-63

Seppa, Jyrki
72Finnish Jaakiekko-351
80Finnish Mallasjuoma-36

Seppanen, Leo
70Finnish Jaakiekko-254
71Finnish Suomi Stickers-220
72Finnish Jaakiekko-168
72Finnish Hellas-15
73Finnish Jaakiekko-235
74Finnish Jenkki-15
74Swedish Semic World Champ Stickers-93
78Finnish SM-Liiga-87

Seppanen, Teemu
05Finnish Cardset -314

Seppanen, Veikko
73Finnish Jaakiekko-236

Seppo, Jukka
91Finnish Jyvas-Hyva Stickers-2
92Finnish Jyvas-Hyva Stickers-11
93Finnish SISU-253
93Swedish Semic World Champ Stickers-78
94Finnish SISU-246
94Finnish SISU Horoscopes-2
95Finnish SISU-343
95Finnish SISU Limited-95
95Finnish SISU Specials-9
96German DEL-239
98Finnish Kerailysarja Leijonat-41
98German DEL-48
99Czech OFS-62
99Finnish Cardset Most Wanted-9
99German DEL-357

Serafini, Ron
75Phoenix Roadrunners WHA-22

Serdachny, Dean
97Swift Current Broncos-16
98Swift Current Broncos-5
99Swift Current Broncos-17
00Swift Current Broncos-17

Serena, Christian
95Swiss HNL-495
96Swiss HNL-412
98Swiss Power Play Stickers-322
99Swiss Panini Stickers-339

Sereno, Dominick
93Quebec Pee-Wee Tournament-676

Sergeant, Peter
04Erie Otters-15

Sergeev, Dmitri
01Russian Hockey League-9

Sergeyev, Dennis
01Calgary Hitmen-21
01Calgary Hitmen Autographed-21
02Swift Current Broncos-18

Sergievsky, Alexei
01Russian Hockey League-142

Sergott, Keith
91Ferris State Bulldogs-28
92Ferris State Bulldogs-28

Serikow, Alexander
95German DEL-279
96German DEL-176
98German DEL-235
98German DEL-333
99German DEL-331
99German DEL-379
00German DEL-178
02German DEL City Press-186
03German DEL-163
04German DEL-196
04German DEL Update-313
04German Hannover Scorpions Postcards-25
05German DEL-189

Serle, Doug
01UK London Knights-2
04Knoxville Ice Bears-9

Sernjajev, Vladimir
74Swedish Stickers-77

Seroski, Joe
95Slapshot-362
96Sault Ste. Marie Greyhounds-20
96Sault Ste. Marie Greyhounds Autographed-20
97New Orleans Brass-9
02Orlando Seals-19

Serov, Vladislav
92Quebec Pee-Wee Tournament-1467
99Manitoba Moose-3
00Quad-City Mallards-5
01Greensboro Generals-4
04Bakersfield Condors-16

Serowik, Jeff
90ProCards AHL/IHL-154
91ProCards-337
92St. John's Maple Leafs-20
93Cincinnati Cyclones-22
95Indianapolis Ice-19
96Las Vegas Thunder-18

Serratorre, Frank
94Minnesota Moose-8
95Minnesota Moose-15

Sersen, Michal
03Rimouski Oceanic-17
03Rimouski Oceanic Sheets-2
04Rimouski Oceanic-18
05Quebec Remparts-6
05Quebec Remparts Signature Series-6
06ITG Heroes and Prospects Memorial Cup Champions-MC08

Sershen, Katie
04Ohio State Buckeyes Women-8
05Ohio State Buckeyes Women-3

Sertich, Andrew
02Minnesota Golden Gophers-20
03Minnesota Golden Gophers-26
04Minnesota Golden Gophers-22
05Minnesota Golden Gophers-21

Sertich, Marty
01Sioux Falls Stampede-11
06Iowa Stars-20

Sertich, Mike
84Minnesota-Duluth Bulldogs-30
85Minnesota-Duluth Bulldogs-33
93Minnesota-Duluth Bulldogs-27
01Michigan Tech Huskies-29

Servant, Frederick
93Amos Les Forestiers-20

Servatius, Darren
89Johnstown Chiefs-22

Servatius, Ron
89Nashville Knights-22

Serviss, Tom
72Los Angeles Sharks WHA-12

Sesito, Tom
06Wilkes-Barre Scranton Penguins Jerseys-14

Sessa, Jason
99Louisiana Ice Gators-17
01South Carolina Stingrays-16
02UK Sheffield Steelers-16

Sestito, Tim
01Plymouth Whalers-17
02Plymouth Whalers-17
03Plymouth Whalers-11
06Stockton Thunder-8

Sestito, Tom
05Plymouth Whalers-A-06
06Plymouth Whalers-19

Sethereng, Morten
74Finnish Typotor-80

Setikovsky, Jindrich
94Czech APS Extraliga-290
95Czech APS Extraliga-243

Setoguchi, Devin
03Saskatoon Blades-22
04Saskatoon Blades-15
04ITG Heroes and Prospects-225
04ITG Heroes/Prospects Toronto Expo '05-225
05ITG Heroes/Prosp Toronto Expo Parallel -160
05Saskatoon Blades-21
05ITG Heroes and Prospects-160
Autographs-A-DSE
Complete Logos-CHL-3
Jerseys-GUJ-25
Jerseys Gold-GUJ-25
Emblems-GUE-25
Emblems Gold-GUE-25
Numbers-GUN-25
Numbers Gold-GUN-25
06ITG Heroes and Prospects-177
Autographs-ADSE
National Pride-NP11
National Pride Gold-NP11
Update Autographs-ADSE

Setz, Christian
94German First League-347

Setzinger, Oliver
97Quebec Pee-Wee Tournament-1113
00Finnish Cardset-275
01Finnish Cardset-41
02Finnish Cardset-116
Bound for Glory-8
Signatures-8
03Finnish Cardset-126
04Finnish Cardset-45
Parallel-33
05Finnish Cardset -37

Seuthe, Jorn
94German First League-33

Seva, Janne
92Finnish Jyvas-Hyva Stickers-43
93Finnish Jyvas-Hyva Stickers-87
93Finnish SISU-131
94Finnish SISU-347
95Finnish SISU-35
98Finnish Kerailysarja-177
99Finnish Cardset-88
01Finnish Cardset-191

Sevastyanov, Mikhail
00Russian Hockey League-198

Sevastyanov, Sergei
00Russian Hockey League-196

Sevc, Martin
04Czech OFS-65
06Czech CP Cup Postcards-20
06Czech HC Kladno Postcards-6
06Czech LG Hockey Games Postcards-18
06Czech OFS-266
Defenders-8

Sevcik, Frantisek
69Swedish Hockey-37
70Finnish Jaakiekko-58
70Swedish Hockey-364
94Czech APS Extraliga-111
95Czech APS Extraliga-209
96Czech APS Extraliga-258
97Czech DS Stickers-92
99Czech Score Blue 2000-158
99Czech Score Red Ice 2000-158

Sevcik, Jaroslav
88ProCards AHL-109
89Halifax Citadels-21
89ProCards AHL-176
90Halifax Citadels-22
90ProCards AHL/IHL-460
95German DEL-332

Sevecek, Rene
95Czech APS Extraliga-299
96Czech APS Extraliga-198
97Czech DS Stickers-194
98Czech DS-104
98Czech DS Stickers-252
98Czech OFS-115

Severin, Goczi
93Quebec Pee-Wee Tournament-1705

Severson, Cam
94Kamloops Blazers-23
96Lethbridge Hurricanes-16
97Prince Albert Raiders-19
98Spokane Chiefs-22
00Quad-City Mallards-22
01Hartford Wolf Pack-19
02BAP Memorabilia-310
02BAP Ultimate Memorabilia-93
02Upper Deck Rookie Update-176
02Cincinnati Mighty Ducks-A-13
03Upper Deck MVP-4
Gold Script-4
Silver Script-4
Canadian Exclusives-4
03Cincinnati Mighty Ducks-A9
04Milwaukee Admirals-4
06German DEL-180

Severson, Ryan
01Fort Wayne Komets-18
02Fort Wayne Komets-18
02Fort Wayne Komets Shoe Carnival-7
03Fort Wayne Komets-6
03Fort Wayne Komets Shoe Carnival-15

Severyn, Brent
84Brandon Wheat Kings-24
88ProCards AHL-106
89Halifax Citadels-22
89ProCards AHL-171
90Halifax Citadels-23
90ProCards AHL/IHL-456
91ProCards-408
93OPC Premier-392
Gold-392
93Panthers Team Issue-8
93Parkhurst-77
Emerald Ice-77
93Score-652
Gold-652
Canadian-652
Canadian Gold-652
93Topps/OPC Premier-392
Gold-392
93Ultra-331
93Upper Deck-453
94Leaf-342
94OPC Premier-334
Special Effects-334
94Parkhurst-90
Gold-90
94Topps/OPC Premier-334
Special Effects-334
95Topps-243
OPC Inserts-243
96Be A Player-185
Autographs-185
Autographs Silver-185
97Pacific Invincible NHL Regime-58
00German DEL-144
Star Attractions-S10
02Fleer Throwbacks-77
Gold-77
Platinum-77

Sevidov, Alexander
73Swedish Stickers-134

Sevigny, Louis Phillippe
94Parkhurst SE-SE259
Gold-SE259
94SP-180
Die Cuts-180

Sevigny, Marco
98Thetford Mines Coyotes-2

Sevigny, Pierre
90Upper Deck-456
French-456
907th Inn. Sketch QMJHL-226
91ProCards-88
92Fredericton Canadiens-22
93Canadiens Postcards-25
93Donruss-169
93Durivage Score-2
93Leaf-392
93Parkhurst-106
Emerald Ice-106
Calder Candidates-C7
Calder Candidates Gold-C7
93Score-634
Gold-634
Canadian-634
Canadian Gold-634
93Upper Deck-455
SP-82
93Classic Pro Prospects-51
94Canadiens Postcards-25
94Donruss-195
94Leaf-309
94Parkhurst-117
Gold-117
94Stadium Club-193
Members Only Master Set-193
First Day Issue-193
Super Team Winner Cards-193
94Upper Deck-402
Electric Ice-402
95Fredericton Canadiens-25
96Fredericton Canadiens-19
97Hartford Wolf Pack-16
98Orlando Solar Bears II-21
99Quebec Citadelles-13
00Quebec Citadelles-10
Signed-10
01Quebec Citadelles-12
03Thetford Mines Prolab-22

Sevigny, Pierre (80s)
84Chicoutimi Sagueneens-24

Sevigny, Richard
79Canadiens Postcards-23
80Canadiens Postcards-23
80O-Pee-Chee-385
81Canadiens Postcards-24
81O-Pee-Chee-191
81O-Pee-Chee-387
81O-Pee-Chee Stickers-40
81O-Pee-Chee Stickers-256
82Canadiens Postcards-23
82Canadiens Steinberg-18
82Post Cereal-10
83Canadiens Postcards-25
83NHL Key Tags-70
83O-Pee-Chee-197
83Vachon-54
84Nordiques Postcards-24
84O-Pee-Chee-289
85Nordiques General Foods-23
85Nordiques McDonald's-18
85Nordiques Provigo-22
85Nordiques Team Issue-21
86Nordiques General Foods-22
86Nordiques McDonald's-22
86Nordiques Team Issue-20
87Nordiques General Foods-27
87Nordiques Team Issue-1
02Canadiens Molson Export-33

Sevigny, Tommy
93Quebec Pee-Wee Tournament-112

Sevon, Jorma
78Finnish SM-Liiga-192
82Swedish Semic VM Stickers-42

Sevon, Seppo
72Finnish Jaakiekko-276
78Finnish SM-Liiga-101
80Finnish Mallasjuoma-42

Sevostjanov, Mikhail
02Russian Hockey League-47
03Russian Hockey League-135
03Russian Hockey League-270

Sevostjanov, Sergei
02Russian Hockey League-41
03Russian Hockey League-137
03Russian Hockey League-269

Sewell, Joey
03Port Huron Beacons-20

Sewell, Rich
91Michigan Falcons-5

Sexsmith, Dean
84Brandon Wheat Kings-5
85Brandon Wheat Kings-5

Sexsmith, Tyson
05Vancouver Giants-21
06Between The Pipes-52
Autographs-ATS

Sexton, Dan
83Victoria Cougars-21
84Victoria Cougars-22
87Regina Pats-23
06Sioux Falls Stampede -19

Sexton, William
52Juniors Blue Tint-108

Seydoux, Philippe
06Finnish Cardset-213

Seymour, Dean
91Air Canada SJHL-A47
91Air Canada SJHL All-Stars-26
93Northern Michigan Wildcats-24
96Louisiana Ice Gators II-15
96Louisville Riverfrogs-15
99Danish Hockey League-113
01Swiss HNL-395

Seymour, Glen
86Portland Winter Hawks-19

Seymour, Jay
96OCN Blizzard-15

Seymour, John
03Brampton Batallion-19
04Brampton Battalion-18
05Brampton Battalion-17
06Brampton Battalion-19

Seymour, Matt
01St. Michaels Majors-21
02St. Michaels Majors-20

Seymour, Ryan
06Halifax Mooseheads-6

Sgroi, Mike
01Rockford IceHogs-16
02Lexington Men O'War-23
04Wilkes-Barre Scranton Penguins-17
05Albany River Rats-23

Sgualdo, Rene
72Finnish Semic World Championship-153
72Swedish Semic World Championship-153

Shabanov, Sergei
00Russian Hockey League-172

Shack, Eddie
44Beehive Group II Photos-361
44Beehive Group II Photos-448A
58Topps-30
59Topps-57
60Shirriff Coins-87
60Topps-7
60York Photos-32
61Parkhurst-7
61Shirriff/Salada Coins-48
61York Yellow Backs-25
62Parkhurst-14
62Shirriff Coins-8
62York Iron-On Transfers-32
63Chex Photos-48
63Maple Leafs Team Issue-20
63Parkhurst-9
63Parkhurst-69
63Toronto Star-34
63York White Backs-4
64Beehive Group III Photos-183
64Coca-Cola Caps-105
64Topps-71
65Coca-Cola-104
65Maple Leafs White Border-16
66Maple Leafs Hockey Talks-8
66Topps-17
67Topps-34
68O-Pee-Chee-137
68Shirriff Coins-1
69O-Pee-Chee-139
Four-in-One-16
69Topps-106
70Colgate Stamps-41
70Dad's Cookies-122
70Esso Power Players-89
70O-Pee-Chee-35
Deckle-2
70Sargent Promotions Stamps-69
70Topps-35
71O-Pee-Chee-96
71Sabres Postcards-89
71Sargent Promotions Stamps-20
71Topps-96
71Toronto Sun-39
72O-Pee-Chee-186
72O-Pee-Chee-274
Player Crests-17
73Maple Leafs Postcards-23
73O-Pee-Chee-242
74Maple Leafs Postcards-20
91Ultimate Original Six-41
French-41
Box Bottoms-4
94Parkhurst Missing Link Future Stars-FS4
94Parkhurst Tall Boys-117
94Parkhurst Tall Boys-164
95Parkhurst '66-67-113
Coins-113
00Upper Deck Legends-123
Legendary Collection Bronze-123
Legendary Collection Gold-123
Legendary Collection Silver-123
02Maple Leafs Platinum Collection-35
02Topps Heritage Reprint Autographs-ES
02Topps Heritage Reprint Relics-ES
02Topps Heritage Reprints-ES
03Parkhurst Orig Six Toronto Autos-8
04UD Legends Classics Jersey Redemptions-JY13
05ITG Tough Customers-ES
Autographs-ES
05ITG Ultimate Memorabilia Level 1-30
05ITG Ultimate Memorabilia Level 2-30
05ITG Ultimate Memorabilia Level 3-30
05ITG Ultimate Memorabilia Level 4-30
05ITG Ultimate Memorabilia Level 5-30
06Parkhurst-114
Autographs-114
Autographs Dual-DAES
07Maple Leafs 1967 Commemorative-24
Autographs-AES1
Autographs-AES2
Jerseys-JES

Shack, Joe
54UK A and BC Chewing Gum-75

Shadilov, Igor
99Russian Dynamo Moscow-2
01Russian Hockey League-56
02Russian Hockey League-177
02Russian Hockey League-215
04Russian Moscow Dynamo-35

Shadrin, Vladimir
70Finnish Jaakiekko-16
70Russian National Team Postcards-19
70Swedish Hockey-330
71Finnish Suomi Stickers-15
72Finnish Jaakiekko-34
72Finnish Hellas-78
72Finnish Panda Toronto-60
72Finnish Semic World Championship-19
72Swedish Semic World Championship-19
73Finnish Jaakiekko-15
73Russian National Team-18
73Swedish Stickers-90
74Finnish Jenkki-55
74Finnish Typotor-72
74Russian National Team-17
74Swedish Semic World Champ Stickers-37
91Future Trends Canada '72-54
91Future Trends Canada '72 French-54

Shaffer, Chris
04Lakehead University Thunderwolves-2

Shafigulin, Grigory
03Russian Under-18 Team-1
04Russian World Junior Team-13

Shafikov, Ruslan
99Russian Hockey League-246
03Russian Hockey League-179

Shafronov, Konstantin
95Fort Wayne Komets-16
97Fort Wayne Komets-14
98Russian Hockey League-11
99Russian Metallurg Magnetogorsk-53
01Russian Hockey League-115

Shaidullin, Vadim
94Finnish SISU-300

Shakhraichuk, Vadim
98German DEL-260
99German DEL-27
00Russian Hockey League-224
03Russian Hockey League-38
04Russian Legion-11

Shakotko, Darren
95Lethbridge Hurricanes-21
96Lethbridge Hurricanes-17
97Lethbridge Hurricanes-16
03Bakersfield Condors-18

Shalamai, Sergei
98Russian Hockey League-102
99Russian Hockey League-241
00Russian Hockey League-175
01Russian Hockey League-63
02Russian Hockey League-159
03Russian Hockey League-4
03Russian SL-25

Shalawylo, Bill
92Michigan State Spartans-20

Shaldybin, Yevgeny
96Providence Bruins-23
97Providence Bruins-20
99UHL All-Stars East-1T

Shalimov, Viktor
82Swedish Semic VM Stickers-65
83Swedish Semic VM Stickers-65

Shalnov, Stanislav
00Russian Hockey League-252
01Russian Hockey League-93
03Russian Avangard Omsk-8

Shamolin, Dmitri
99Swiss Panini Stickers-347
01Swiss HNL-277
02Swiss HNL-303

Shanahan, Brendan
85London Knights-9
86London Knights-6
88Devils Caretta-26
88O-Pee-Chee-122
88Panini Stickers-276
88Topps-122
89Devils Caretta-21
89O-Pee-Chee-147
89O-Pee-Chee Stickers-89
89Panini Stickers-255
89Topps-147
90Bowman-85
Tiffany-85
90Devils Team Issue-23
90O-Pee-Chee-259
90OPC Premier-105
90Panini Stickers-64
90Pro Set-174
90Score-146
Canadian-146
90Score Young Superstars-23
90Topps-259
Tiffany-259
90Upper Deck-269
French-269
91Pro Set Platinum-111
91Blues Postcards-18
91Bowman-288
91Kraft-7
91O-Pee-Chee-140
91OPC Premier-130
91Panini Stickers-222
91Parkhurst-153
French-153
91Pinnacle-41
French-41
91Pro Set-131
91Pro Set-475
French-131
French-475
91Score American-286
91Score Canadian Bilingual-588
91Score Canadian English-588
91Score Rookie/Traded-38T
91Stadium Club-199
91Topps-140
91Upper Deck-561
French-561
92Bowman-183
92Humpty Dumpty I-20
92O-Pee-Chee-244
92Panini Stickers-17
92Panini Stickers French-17
92Parkhurst-156
Emerald Ice-156
Cherry Picks-CP10
92Pinnacle-114
92Pinnacle-248
French-114
French-248
92Pro Set-163
92Score-392
Canadian-392
92Seasons Patches-15
92Sports Illustrated for Kids II-465
92Stadium Club-371
92Topps-295
Gold-295G
92Ultra-189
92Upper Deck-122
93Donruss-299
93Kraft-23
93Leaf-30
Gold All-Stars-9
93OPC Premier-247
Gold-247
93Panini Stickers-158
93Parkhurst-172
Emerald Ice-172
93Pinnacle-205
Canadian-205
Nifty Fifty-14
Team 2001-29
Team 2001 Canadian-29
93PowerPlay-216
Slapshot Artists-10
93Score-238
Canadian-238
93Stadium Club-389
Members Only Master Set-389
First Day Issue-389
93Topps/OPC Premier-247
Gold-247
93Ultra-245
93Upper Deck SP-140
94Be A Player-R86
94Be A Player-R104
94Be A Player-R137
Signature Cards-86
94Canada Games NHL POGS-207
94Canada Games NHL POGS-265
94Donruss-174
94EA Sports-124
94Finest-92
Super Team Winners-92
Refractors-92
Division's Clear Cut-14
94Flair-158
Hot Numbers-9
94Fleer-191
Headliners-10
94Hockey Wit-29
94Kraft-71
94Leaf-113
Limited Inserts-20
94Leaf Limited-97
94McDonald's Upper Deck-McD30
94OPC Premier-215
94OPC Premier-529
Special Effects-215
Special Effects-529
94Parkhurst-196
94Parkhurst-298
Gold-196
Gold-298
94Pinnacle-32
Artist's Proofs-32
Rink Collection-32
Boomers-BR6
Gamers-GR10
Team Pinnacle-TP6
Team Dufex Parallel-TP6
94Score-155
Gold-155
Platinum-155
Check It-CI5
90 Plus Club-8
94Select-129
Gold-129
First Line-FL4
94SP-101
Die Cuts-101
94Stadium Club Members Only-16
94Stadium Club Super Teams-20
94Stadium Club Super Team MemberOnly Set-20
94Topps/OPC Premier-215
94Topps/OPC Premier-529
Special Effects-215
Special Effects-529
94Topps Finest Inserts-5
94Ultra-189
Power-9
Red Light Specials-9
94Upper Deck-292
Electric Ice-292
Ice Gallery-IG4
Predictor Retail-R7
94Upper Deck Predictor Retail Exchange-R7
94Upper Deck SP Inserts-SP69
94Upper Deck SP Inserts Die Cuts-SP69
94Upper Deck NHLPA/Be A Player-16
94Finnish Jaa Kiekko-100
95SLU Hockey Canadian-12
95SLU Hockey American-17
95Bashan Super Stickers-52
Die-Cut-22
95Be A Player Lethal Lines-LL13
95Bowman-28
All-Foil-28
95Canada Games NHL POGS-126
95Collector's Choice-4
Player's Club-4
Player's Club Platinum-4
95Donruss-180
95Donruss-377
Marksmen-8
95Donruss Elite-3
Die Cut Stars-3
Die Cut Uncut-3
95Emotion-78
Ntense Power-7
95Finest-39
95Finest-65
Refractors-39
Refractors-65
95Hoyle Western Playing Cards-18
95Imperial Stickers-52
Die Cut Superstars-22
95Kenner Starting Lineup Cards-19
95Leaf-121
95Leaf Limited-94
95Metal-67
Iron Warriors-11
Iron Warriors-13
95Panini Stickers-31
95Parkhurst International-97
Emerald Ice-97
NHL All-Stars-3
95Pinnacle Full Contact-5
95Pinnacle Roaring 20s-18
95Pinnacle FANtasy-6
95Playoff One on One-47
95Playoff One on One-157
95Post Upper Deck-11
95Pro Magnets-129
95Score-20
Black Ice Artist's Proofs-20

Black Ice-20
Golden Blades-17
95Select Certified-64
Mirror Gold-64
Double Strike-9
Double Strike Gold-9
95SkyBox Impact-76
95SP-62
Stars/Etoiles-E16
Stars/Etoiles Gold-E16
95Stadium Club-25
Members Only Master Set-25
Fearless-F1
Fearless Members Only Master Set-F1
95Summit-124
Artist's Proofs-124
Ice-124
GM's Choice-20
95Topps-16
95Topps-370
OPC Inserts-16
OPC Inserts-370
Home Grown Canada-HGC10
Marquee Men Power Boosters-16
Mystery Finest-M10
Mystery Finest Refractors-M10
95Topps SuperSkills-55
Platinum-55
95Ultra-142
95Ultra-247
Gold Medallion-142
Crease Crashers-17
95Upper Deck-184
Electric Ice-184
Electric Ice Gold-184
95Upper Deck All-Star Game Predictors-20
Redemption Winners-20
95Upper Deck NHL All-Stars-AS4
95Upper Deck NHL All-Stars Jumbo-AS4
95Upper Deck Predictor Retail-R4
95Upper Deck Predictor Retail Exchange-R4
95Upper Deck Special Edition-SE125
95Upper Deck Special Edition Gold-SE125
95Whalers Bob's Stores-24
95Zenith-86
Z-Team-16
95Finnish Semic World Championships-88
95German DEL-447
95Swedish Globe World Championships-86
95Swedish World Championships Stickers-16
96Headliners Hockey-18
96SLU Hockey American-23
96Be A Player Biscuit In The Basket-10
96Be A Player Link to History-3B
96Be A Player Link to History Autographs-3B
96Be A Player Link to History Auto Silver-3B
96Black Diamond-114
Gold-114
96Collector's Choice-112
96Collector's Choice-319
MVP-UD26
MVP Gold-UD26
Stick'Ums-S12
Crash the Game-C14A
Crash the Game-C14B
Crash the Game-C14C
Crash the Game Gold-C14A
Crash the Game Gold-C14B
Crash the Game Gold-C14C
Crash the Game Exchange-CR14
Crash the Game Exchange Gold-CR14
96Donruss-178
Press Proofs-178
Elite Inserts-6
Elite Inserts Gold-6
Hit List-7
96Donruss Canadian Ice-101
Gold Press Proofs-101
Red Press Proofs-101
O Canada-12
96Donruss Elite-126
Die Cut Stars-126
Perspective-7
96Duracell All-Cherry Team-DC12
96Flair-30
Blue Ice-30
96Fleer-48
96Fleer Picks-40
Captain's Choice-10
Dream Lines-7
Fabulous 50-43
96Kenner Starting Lineup Cards-23
96Kraft Upper Deck-57
96Leaf-146
Press Proofs-146
96Leaf Leather And Laces Promos-P17
96Leaf Leather And Laces-17
96Leaf Sweaters Away-10
96Leaf Sweaters Home-10
96Leaf Limited-2
Gold-2
96Leaf Limited Bash the Boards Promos-P9
96Leaf Limited Bash The Boards-9
96Leaf Limited Bash The Boards Ltd Ed-9
96Leaf Preferred-31
Press Proofs-31
Steel-29
Steel Gold-29
96Maggers-93
96Metal Universe-50
Cool Steel-10
Cool Steel Super Power-10
Lethal Weapons-18
Lethal Weapons Super Power-18
96NHL Aces Playing Cards-44
96NHL Pro Stamps-129
96Pinnacle-56
Artist's Proofs-56
Foil-56
Premium Stock-56
Rink Collection-56
By The Numbers-2
By The Numbers Premium-2
Team Pinnacle-5
96Pinnacle Fantasy-FC8
96Pinnacle Mint-18
Bronze-18
Gold-18
Silver-18
Coins Brass-18
Coins Solid Gold-18
Coins Gold Plated-18
Coins Nickel-18
Coins Silver-18
96Post Upper Deck-21
96Score-2
Artist's Proofs-2
Dealer's Choice Artist's Proofs-2
Special Artist's Proofs-2
Check It-6
Golden Blades-2
Sudden Death-3
96Select Certified-72
Artist's Proofs-72
Blue-72
Mirror Blue-72
Mirror Gold-72
Mirror Red-72
Red-72
96SkyBox Impact-55
BladeRunners-21
96SP-50
Clearcut Winner-CW8
Inside Info-IN3
Inside Info Gold-IN3
96SPx-19
Gold-19
96Stadium Club Members Only-26
96Summit-139
Artist's Proofs-139
Ice-139
Metal-139
Premium Stock-139
96Ultra-55
Gold Medallion-55
Clear the Ice-9
96Upper Deck-252
Generation Next-X14
Power Performers-P1
Superstar Showdown-SS6B
96Upper Deck Ice-85
Parallel-85
Stanley Cup Foundation-S2
Stanley Cup Foundation Dynasty-S2
96Zenith-77
Artist's Proofs-77
Z-Team-4
96Swedish Semic Wien-90
97Headliners Hockey-25
97Be A Player One Timers-4
97Beehive-3
Golden Portraits-3
Team-4
Team Gold-4
97Black Diamond-149
Double Diamond-149
Triple Diamond-149
Quadruple Diamond-149
Premium Cut-PC3
Premium Cut Double Diamond-PC3
Premium Cut Quadruple Diamond Horiz-PC3
Premium Cut Triple Diamond-PC3
Premium Cut Quadruple Diamond Verticals-PC3
97Collector's Choice-76
Crash the Game-C4A
Crash the Game-C4B
Crash the Game-C4C
Crash the Game Exchange-CR4
Star Quest-SQ74
Stick'Ums-S14
World Domination-W4
97Crown Royale-50
Emerald Green-50
Ice Blue-50
Silver-50
Blades of Steel Die-Cuts-9
Hat Tricks Die-Cuts-7
Lamplighters Cel-Fusion Die-Cuts-8
97Donruss-181
Press Proofs Silver-181
Press Proofs Gold-181
Elite Inserts-9
Line 2 Line-10
Line 2 Line Die Cut-10
97Donruss Canadian Ice-67
Dominion Series-67
Provincial Series-67
National Pride-5
Stanley Cup Scrapbook-33
97Donruss Elite-18
97Donruss Elite-133
Aspirations-18
Aspirations-133
Status-18
Status-133
Craftsmen-27
Master Craftsmen-27
Prime Numbers-9A
Prime Numbers-9B
Prime Numbers-9C
Prime Numbers Die-Cuts-9A
Prime Numbers Die-Cuts-9B
Prime Numbers Die-Cuts-9C
97Donruss Limited-1
97Donruss Limited-38
97Donruss Limited-169
Exposure-1
Exposure-38
Exposure-169
Fabric of the Game-13
Fabric of the Game-53
97Donruss Preferred-3
97Donruss Preferred-184
Cut to the Chase-3
Cut to the Chase-184
Line of the Times-2C
97Donruss Preferred Line of Times Promos-2C
97Donruss Preferred Precious Metals-1
97Donruss Priority-19
97Donruss Priority-186
Stamp of Approval-19
Stamp of Approval-186
Direct Deposit-1
Postcards-2
Postcards Opening Day Issues-17
Stamps-2
Stamps Bronze-2
Stamps Gold-2
Stamps Silver-2
97Esso Olympic Hockey Heroes-10
97Esso Olympic Hockey Heroes French-10
97Katch-53
Gold-53
Silver-53
97Kraft Team Canada-11
97Leaf-12
97Leaf-179
Fractal Matrix-12
Fractal Matrix-179
Fractal Matrix Die Cuts-12
Fractal Matrix Die Cuts-179
Banner Season-6
Fire On Ice-5
97Leaf International-12
Universal Ice-12
97McDonald's Team Canada Coins-5
97McDonald's Upper Deck-14
97NHL Aces Playing Cards-10
97Pacific-14
Copper-14
Emerald Green-14
Ice Blue-14
Red-14
Silver-14
Gold Crown Die-Cuts-10
Slap Shots Die-Cuts-3A
97Pacific Dynagon-44
97Pacific Dynagon-139
Copper-44
Copper-139
Dark Grey-44
Dark Grey-139
Emerald Green-44
Emerald Green-139
Ice Blue-44
Ice Blue-139
Red-44
Red-139
Silver-44
Silver-139
Best Kept Secrets-34
Dynamic Duos-8A
Tandems-6
Tandems-26
97Pacific Invincible-51
Copper-51
Emerald Green-51
Ice Blue-51
Red-51
Silver-51
Attack Zone-10
Feature Performers-14
NHL Regime-73
Off The Glass-8
97Pacific Omega-87
Copper-87
Dark Gray-87
Emerald Green-87
Gold-87
Ice Blue-87
Game Face-7
Stick Handle Laser Cuts-8
Team Leaders-8
97Panini Stickers-154
97Paramount-70
Copper-70
Dark Grey-70
Emerald Green-70
Ice Blue-70
Red-70
Silver-70
Big Numbers Die-Cuts-9
Canadian Greats-6
Photoengravings-9
97Pinnacle-80
Artist's Proofs-80
Rink Collection-80
Epix Game Emerald-16
Epix Game Orange-16
Epix Game Purple-16
Epix Moment Emerald-16
Epix Moment Orange-16
Epix Moment Purple-16
Epix Play Emerald-16
Epix Play Orange-16
Epix Play Purple-16
Epix Season Emerald-16
Epix Season Orange-16
Epix Season Purple-16
Press Plates Back Black-80
Press Plates Back Cyan-80
Press Plates Back Magenta-80
Press Plates Back Yellow-80
Press Plates Front Black-80
Press Plates Front Cyan-80
Press Plates Front Magenta-80
Press Plates Front Yellow-80
Team Pinnacle-8
Team Mirror-8
Team Parallel-8
Team Parallel Mirror-8
97Pinnacle Certified-61
Red-61
Mirror Blue-61
Mirror Gold-61
Mirror Red-61
Team-17
Gold Team Promo-17
Gold Team-17
97Pinnacle Inside-1
Coach's Collection-1
Executive Collection-1
Track-14
Cans-1
Cans Gold-1
Promos-1
97Pinnacle Mint-6
Bronze-6
Gold Team-6
Silver Team-6
Coins Brass-6
Coins Brass Proofs-6
Coins Gold Plated-6
Coins Gold Plated Proofs-6
Coins Nickel Silver-6
Coins Nickel Silver Proofs-6
Coins Solid Gold-6
Coins Solid Silver-6
97Pinnacle Power Pack Blow-Ups-20
97Pinnacle Tot Cert Platinum Blue-61
97Pinnacle Tot Certi Platinum Gold-61
97Pinnacle Totally Certified Platinum Red-61
97Pinnacle Tot Cert Mirror Platinum Gold-61
97Revolution-51
Copper-51
Emerald-51
Ice Blue-51
Silver-51
1998 All-Star Game Die-Cuts-11
97Score-80
Artist's Proofs-80
Golden Blades-80
Check It-3
97Score Red Wings-1
Platinum-1
Premier-1
97SP Authentic-55
Icons-I10
Icons Die-Cuts-I10
Icons Embossed-I10
97SPx-16
Bronze-16
Gold-16
Silver-16
Steel-16
Dimension-SPX7
Grand Finale-16
97Studio-6
97Studio-105
Press Proofs Silver-6
Press Proofs Silver-105
Press Proofs Gold-6
Press Proofs Gold-105
Hard Hats-9
Portraits-6
Silhouettes-11
Silhouettes 8x10-11
97Upper Deck-268
Game Dated Moments-268
Game Jerseys-GJ13
Sixth Sense Masters-SS14
Sixth Sense Wizards-SS14
Smooth Grooves-SG14
The Specialists-14
The Specialists Level 2 Die Cuts-14
Three Star Selects-6B
97Upper Deck Crash the All-Star Game-9
97Upper Deck Crash the All-Star Game-AR9
97Upper Deck Diamond Vision-11
Signature Moves-11
Defining Moments-DM6
97Upper Deck Ice-84
Parallel-84
Champions-IC14
Champions 2 Die Cuts-IC14
Lethal Lines-L2A
Lethal Lines 2-L2A
Power Shift-84
97Zenith-3
Z-Gold-3
Z-Silver-3
97Zenith 5 x 7-9
Gold Impulse-9
Silver Impulse-9
97Zenith Chasing The Cup-6
97Zenith Z-Team-9
97Zenith Z-Team 5x7-9
97Zenith Z-Team Gold-9
98SLU Hockey One on One-5
98SLU Hockey Extended-205
98Aurora-68
Atomic Laser Cuts-10
Championship Fever-19
Championship Fever Copper-19
Championship Fever Ice Blue-19
Championship Fever Red-19
Championship Fever Silver-19
Cubes-9
Man Advantage-9
98Be A Player-195
Press Release-195
98BAP Gold-195
98BAP Autographs-195
98BAP Autographs Gold-195
98BAP AS Game Used Stick Cards-S21
98BAP AS Game Used Jersey Cards-AS23
98BAP Playoff Game Used Jerseys-G14
98BAP Playoff Game Used Jersey Autographs-G14
98BAP Playoff Practice Used Jerseys-P21
98Black Diamond-33
Double Diamond-33
Triple Diamond-33
Quadruple Diamond-33
Myriad-M9
Myriad 2-M9
Winning Formula Gold-WF10
Winning Formula Platinum-WF10
98Bowman's Best-52
Refractors-52
Atomic Refractors-52
98Crown Royale-48
Limited Series-48
Master Performers-10
Pillars of the Game-13
Pivotal Players-10
98Donruss Elite Promos-9
98Finest-123
No Protectors-123
No Protectors Refractors-123
Refractors-123
Double Sided Mystery Finest-M33
Double Sided Mystery Finest-M36
Double Sided Mystery Finest-M38
Double Sided Mystery Finest-M40
Double Sided Mystery Refractors-M33
Double Sided Mystery Refractors-M36
Double Sided Mystery Refractors-M38
Double Sided Mystery Refractors-M40
Promos-PP3
Red Lighters-R10
Red Lighters Refractors-R10
98Katch-52
98Kenner Starting Lineup Cards-30
98Kraft Fearless Forwards-9
98McDonald's Upper Deck-5
98OPC Chrome-216
Refractors-216
98Pacific-14
Ice Blue-14
Red-14
Gold Crown Die-Cuts-15
Timelines-7
Trophy Winners-9
98Pacific Dynagon Ice-68
Blue-68
Red-68
Forward Thinking-10
98Pacific Omega-87
Red-87
Opening Day Issue-87
EO Portraits-10
EO Portraits 1 of 1-10
Face to Face-5
Online-15
Planet Ice-17
Planet Ice Parallel-17
Prism-9
98Panini Photocards-77
98Panini Stickers-133
98Paramount-82
Copper-82
Emerald Green-82
Holo-Electric-82
Ice Blue-82
Silver-82
Special Delivery Die-Cuts-8
98Revolution-52
Ice Shadow-52
Red-52
All-Star Die Cuts-27
Chalk Talk Laser-Cuts-9
Showstoppers-17
Three Pronged Attack-5
Three Pronged Attack Parallel-5
98SP Authentic-29
Power Shift-29
Snapshots-SS14
Stat Masters-S1
98SPx Finite-32
98SPx Finite-96
98SPx Finite-158
Radiance-32
Radiance-96
Radiance-158
Spectrum-32
Spectrum-96
Spectrum-158
98SPx Top Prospects-22
Radiance-22
Spectrum-22
Highlight Heroes-H13
Lasting Impressions-L9
Premier Stars-PS27
98Topps-216
O-Pee-Chee-216
98Topps Gold Label Class 1-1
Black-1
Black One of One-1
One of One-1
Red-1
Red One of One-1
98Topps Gold Label Class 2-1
98Topps Gold Label Class 2 Black-1
98Topps Gold Label Class 2 Black 1 of 1-1
98Topps Gold Label Class 2 One of One-1
98Topps Gold Label Class 2 Red-1
98Topps Gold Label Class 2 Red One of One-1
98Topps Gold Label Class 3-1
98Topps Gold Label Class 3 Black-1
98Topps Gold Label Class 3 Black 1 of 1-1
98Topps Gold Label Class 3 One of One-1
98Topps Gold Label Class 3 Red-1
98Topps Gold Label Class 3 Red One of One-1
98Topps Gold Label Goal Race '99-GR8
98Topps Gold Label Goal Race '99 Black-GR8
98Topps Gold Label Goal '99 Black 1 of 1-GR8
98Topps Gold Label Goal Race 99 1 of 1-GR8
98Topps Gold Label Goal Race '99 Red-GR8
98Topps Gold Label GoalRace 99 Red 1 of 1-GR8
98UD Choice-76
Mini Bobbing Head-BH24
Prime Choice Reserve-76
Reserve-76
StarQuest Blue-SQ9
StarQuest Gold-SQ9
StarQuest Green-SQ9
StarQuest Red-SQ9
98UD3-47
98UD3-107
98UD3-167
Die-Cuts-47
Die-Cuts-107
Die-Cuts-167
98Upper Deck-87
Exclusives-87
Exclusives 1 of 1-87
Fantastic Finishers-FF5
Fantastic Finishers Quantum 1-FF5
Fantastic Finishers Quantum 2-FF5
Fantastic Finishers Quantum 3-FF5
Frozen In Time-FT22
Frozen In Time Quantum 1-FT22
Frozen In Time Quantum 2-FT22
Frozen In Time Quantum 3-FT22
Game Jerseys-GJ15
Generation Next-GN13
Generation Next-GN14
Generation Next-GN15
Generation Next Quantum 1-GN13
Generation Next Quantum 1-GN14
Generation Next Quantum 1-GN15
Generation Next Quantum 2-GN13
Generation Next Quantum 2-GN14
Generation Next Quantum 2-GN15
Generation Next Quantum 3-GN13
Generation Next Quantum 3-GN14
Generation Next Quantum 3-GN15
Lord Stanley's Heroes-LS4
Lord Stanley's Heroes Quantum 1-LS4
Lord Stanley's Heroes Quantum 2-LS4
Lord Stanley's Heroes Quantum 3-LS4
Profiles-P14
Profiles Quantum 1-P14
Profiles Quantum 2-P14
Profiles Quantum 3-P14
Gold Reserve-87
98Upper Deck MVP-72
Gold Script-72
Silver Script-72
Super Script-72
Game Souvenirs-BS
OT Heroes-OT13
Power Game-PG1
Special Forces-F8
99Aurora-54
Striped-54
Premiere Date-54
Premiere Date Striped-54
Championship Fever-12
Championship Fever Copper-12
Championship Fever Ice Blue-12
Championship Fever Silver-12
Styrotechs-9
99BAP Memorabilia-231
Gold-231
Silver-231
Jersey Cards-J23
Jersey Emblems-E23
Jersey Numbers-I23
Jersey and Stick Cards-S23
AS Heritage Ruby-H1
AS Heritage Sapphire-H1
AS Heritage Emerald-H1
99BAP Update Double AS Jersey Cards-D11
99BAP Update Teammates Jersey Cards-TM5
99BAP Update Teammates Jersey Cards-TM9
99BAP Update Teammates Jersey Cards-TM35
99BAP Update Teammates Jersey Cards-TM38
99BAP Update Teammates Jersey Cards-TM40
99BAP Millennium-90
Emerald-90
Ruby-90
Sapphire-90
Signatures-90
Signatures Gold-90
Jerseys-J2
Jersey Autographs-J2
Jersey and Stick Cards-JS2
Jersey Emblems-E2
Jersey Numbers-N2
99Black Diamond-35
Diamond Cut-35
Final Cut-35
Diamond Might-DM2
99Crown Royale-52
Limited Series-52
Premiere Date-52
Card-Supials-10
Card-Supials Minis-10
Ice Elite-11
Ice Elite Parallel-11
International Glory-10
International Glory Parallel-10
99Kraft Dinner-11
99Kraft Peanut Butter-11
99O-Pee-Chee-196
99O-Pee-Chee Chrome-196
99O-Pee-Chee Chrome Refractors-196
99Pacific-149
Copper-149
Emerald Green-149
Gold-149
Ice Blue-149
Premiere Date-149
Red-149
Center Ice-10
Center Ice Proofs-10
Gold Crown Die-Cuts-17
Past and Present-12
99Pacific Dynagon Ice-78
Blue-78
Copper-78
Gold-78
Premiere Date-78
Checkmates American-2
Checkmates American-17
Checkmates Canadian-2
99Pacific Omega-85
Copper-85
Gold-85
Ice Blue-85
Premiere Date-85
Cup Contenders-9
EO Portraits-8
EO Portraits 1/1-8
North American All-Stars-5
5 Star Talents-7
5 Star Talents Parallel-7
99Pacific Prism-48
Holographic Blue-48
Holographic Gold-48
Holographic Mirror-48
Holographic Purple-48
Premiere Date-48
Clear Advantage-8
Sno-Globe Die-Cuts-10
99Panini Stickers-234
99Paramount-87
Copper-87
Emerald-87
Gold-87
Holographic Emerald-87
Holographic Gold-87
Holographic Silver-87
Ice Blue-87
Premiere Date-87
Red-87
Silver-87
Ice Advantage-9
Ice Advantage Proofs-9
Personal Best-17
99Revolution-55
Premiere Date-55
Red-55
Shadow Series-55
NHL Icons-10
Ornaments-10
Showstoppers-17
Top of the Line-3
Copper-55
Gold-55
CSC Silver-55
99SP Authentic-32
99SPx-56
Radiance-56
Spectrum-56
Prolifics-P7
SPXcitement-X17
SPXtreme-XT7
99Stadium Club-106
First Day Issue-106
One of a Kind-106
Printing Plates Black-106
Printing Plates Cyan-106
Printing Plates Magenta-106
Printing Plates Yellow-106
Chrome-34
Chrome Refractors-34
99Topps/OPC-196
99Topps/OPC Chrome-196
Refractors-196
99Topps Gold Label Class 1-55
Black-55
Black One of One-55
One of One-55
Red-55
Red One of One-55
99Topps Gold Label Class 2-55
99Topps Gold Label Class 2 Black-55
99Topps Gold Label Class 2 Black 1 of 1-55
99Topps Gold Label Class 2 One of One-55
99Topps Gold Label Class 2 Red-55
99Topps Gold Label Class 2 Red One of One-55
99Topps Gold Label Class 3-55
99Topps Gold Label Class 3 Black-55
99Topps Gold Label Class 3 Black 1 of 1-55
99Topps Gold Label Class 3 One of One-55
99Topps Gold Label Class 3 Red-55
99Topps Gold Label Class 3 Red One of One-55
99Topps Premier Plus-58
Parallel-58
99Ultimate Victory-33
1/1-33
Parallel-33
Parallel 100-33
Stature-S5
99Upper Deck-50
99Upper Deck-155
Exclusives-50
Exclusives-155
Exclusives 1 of 1-50
Exclusives 1 of 1-155
Crunch Time-CT5
Crunch Time Quantum Gold-CT5
Crunch Time Quantum Silver-CT5
Fantastic Finishers-FF11
Fantastic Finishers Quantum Gold-FF11
Fantastic Finishers Quantum Silver-FF11
NHL Scrapbook-SB12
NHL Scrapbook Quantum Gold-SB12
NHL Scrapbook Quantum Silver-SB12
Sixth Sense-SS14
Sixth Sense Quantum Gold-SS14
Sixth Sense Quantum Silver-SS14
99Upper Deck Century Legends-70
Century Collection-70
99Upper Deck Gold Reserve-50
99Upper Deck Gold Reserve-155
99Upper Deck HoloGrFx-22
Ausome-22
99Upper Deck MVP-70
Gold Script-70
Silver Script-70
Super Script-70
90's Snapshots-S5
Game-Used Souvenirs-GU7
Game-Used Souvenirs-GU21
99Upper Deck MVP SC Edition-67
Gold Script-67
Silver Script-67
Super Script-67
Great Combinations-GCSF
Great Combinations Parallel-GCSF
Second Season Snipers-SS4
99Upper Deck Ovation Lead Performers-LP18
99Upper Deck Retro-29
Gold-29
Platinum-29
Generation-G9B
Generation Level 2-G9B
99Upper Deck Victory-97
99Wayne Gretzky Hockey-62
Tools of Greatness-TGBS
99Slovakian Challengers-20
00Aurora-52
Pinstripes-52
Pinstripes Premiere Date-52
Premiere Date-52
Championship Fever-11
Championship Fever Copper-11
Championship Fever Platinum Blue-11
Championship Fever Silver-11
Dual Game-Worn Jerseys-3
Game-Worn Jerseys-2
Game-Worn Jersey Patches-2
Scouting Reports-10
Styrotechs-6A
00BAP Memorabilia-165
Emerald-165
Ruby-165
Sapphire-165
Promos-165
Jersey Cards-J6
Jersey Emblems-E6
Jersey Numbers-N6
Jersey and Stick Cards-JS6
Patent Power Jerseys-PP6
00BAP Mem Chicago Sportsfest Copper-165
00BAP Memorabilia Chicago Sportsfest Blue-165
00BAP Memorabilia Chicago Sportsfest Gold-165
00BAP Memorabilia Chicago Sportsfest Ruby-165
00BAP Memorabilia Chicago Sun-Times Ruby-165
00BAP Memorabilia Chicago Sun-Times Gold-165
00BAP Mem Chicago Sun-Times Sapphire-165
00BAP Mem Toronto Fall Expo Copper-165
00BAP Memorabilia Toronto Fall Expo Gold-165
00BAP Memorabilia Toronto Fall Expo Ruby-165
00BAP Mem Update Heritage Jersey Cards-H17
00BAP Mem Update Heritage Jersey Gold-H17
00BAP Memorabilia Update Teammates-TM16
00BAP Memorabilia Update Teammates-TM22
00BAP Memorabilia Update Teammates Gold-TM16
00BAP Memorabilia Update Teammates Gold-TM22
00BAP Parkhurst 2000-P10
00BAP Signature Series-206
Emerald-206
Ruby-206
Sapphire-206
Autographs-55
Autographs Gold-55
He Shoots-He Scores Points-18
He Shoots-He Scores Prizes-28
Jersey Cards-J2
Jersey and Stick Cards-GSJ2
Jersey Cards Autographs-J2
Jersey Emblems-E2
Jersey Numbers-IN2
00BAP Ultimate Memorabilia Autographs-2
Gold-2
00BAP Ultimate Mem Dynasty Jerseys-D17
00BAP Ultimate Mem Dynasty Emblems-D17
00BAP Ultimate Mem Game-Used Jerseys-GJ2
00BAP Ultimate Mem Game-Used Emblems-E1
00BAP Ultimate Mem Game-Used Numbers-N1
00BAP Ultimate Mem Game-Used Sticks-GS2
00BAP Ultimate Mem Journey Jerseys-JJ18
00BAP Ultimate Mem Journey Emblems-JE18
00BAP Ultimate Mem Journey Numbers-JI18
00BAP Ultimate Memorabilia Teammates-TM2
00BAP Ultimate Memorabilia Teammates-TM4
00BAP Ultimate Memorabilia Teammates-TM8
00Black Diamond-21
Gold-21
Diamond Might-FP5
00Crown Royale-40
Ice Blue-40
Limited Series-40
Premiere Date-40
Red-40
Game-Worn Jerseys-15
Game-Worn Jersey Patches-15
Premium-Sized Game-Worn Jerseys-15
Jewels of the Crown-13
00McDonald's Pacific-14
Blue-14
00O-Pee-Chee-115
00O-Pee-Chee Parallel-115
00Pacific-158
Copper-158
Gold-158
Ice Blue-158
Premiere Date-158
Jerseys-7
Jersey Patches-7
Gold Crown Die Cuts-14
North American Stars-5
Reflections-9
00Panini Stickers-152
00Paramount-89
Copper-89
Gold-89
Holo-Gold-89
Holo-Silver-89
Ice Blue-89
Premiere Date-89
Epic Scope-10
Freeze Frame-15
Sub Zero-4
Sub Zero Gold-4
Sub Zero Red-4
00Private Stock-37
Gold-37
Premiere Date-37
Retail-37
Silver-37
Artist's Canvas-11
Artist's Canvas Proofs-11
Game Gear-47
Game Gear Patches-47
PS-2001 Action-22
PS-2001 Stars-12
Reserve-9
00Revolution-54
Blue-54
Premiere Date-54
Red-54
HD NHL-15
Ice Immortals-10
NHL Icons-11
Stat Masters-5
00SP Authentic-32
Special Forces-SF3
00SP Game Used-22
Tools of the Game Combos-C-SH
00SPx-23
00SPx-72
Spectrum-23
Spectrum-72
Highlight Heroes-HH7
Winning Materials-BS
00Stadium Club-2
Special Forces-SF12
00Titanium-34
Blue-34
Gold-34
Premiere Date-34
Red-34
Retail-34
Game Gear-97
Game Gear Patches-97
00Titanium Draft Day Edition-41
Patches-41
00Topps/OPC-115
Parallel-115
00Topps Chrome-89
OPC Refractors-89
Refractors-89
00Topps Gold Label Class 1-2
Gold-2
00Topps Gold Label Class 2-2
00Topps Gold Label Class 2 Gold-2
00Topps Gold Label Class 3-2
00Topps Gold Label Class 3 Gold-2
00Topps Gold Label Bullion-B3
00Topps Gold Label Bullion One to One-B3
00Topps Gold Label Golden Greats-GG14
00Topps Gold Label Golden Greats 1 to 1-GG14
00Topps Heritage-27
00Topps Heritage-219
Chrome Parallel-27
Heroes-HH18
00Topps Premier Plus-50
Blue Ice-50
World Premier-WP12
00Topps Stars-26
Blue-26
00UD Heroes-147
Player Idols-PI1
Today's Snipers-TS2
00UD Pros and Prospects-30
Championship Rings-CR2
Game Jerseys-BS
Game Jersey Exclusives-BS
Great Skates-GS4
00UD Reserve-30
00Upper Deck-62
Exclusives Tier 1-62
Exclusives Tier 2-62
Game Jerseys-BS
Game Jerseys-BS
Game Jersey Autographs Exclusives-EBS
Game Jersey Combos-DYS
Game Jersey Doubles-DBS
Game Jersey Patches-BSP
Game Jersey Patches-PBS
Game Jersey Patch Autographs Exclusives-BSP
Game Jersey Patch Exclusives Series II-EBS
Lord Stanley's Heroes-L5
Number Crunchers-NC2
Profiles-P4
Skilled Stars-SS10
Triple Threat-TT6
00Upper Deck Ice-16
Immortals-16
Legends-16
Stars-16
Gallery-IG3
Game Jerseys-JCBS
00Upper Deck Legends-44
Legendary Collection Bronze-44
Legendary Collection Gold-44
Legendary Collection Silver-44
Essence of the Game-EG6
00Upper Deck MVP-64
First Stars-64
Game-Used Souvenirs-GSBS
Second Stars-64
Super Game-Used Souvenirs-GSBS
Third Stars-64
Top Draws-TD4
00Upper Deck Victory-82
00Upper Deck Victory-248
00Upper Deck Victory-299
00Upper Deck Vintage-129
00Upper Deck Vintage-136
Star Tandems-S3B
00Vanguard-40
Dual Game-Worn Jerseys-5
Dual Game-Worn Patches-5
High Voltage-13
High Voltage Gold-13
High Voltage Green-13
High Voltage Red-13
High Voltage Silver-13
Holographic Gold-40
Holographic Purple-40
Pacific Proofs-40
01Atomic-39
Blue-39
Gold-39
Premiere Date-39
Red-39
Jerseys-25
Power Play-13
Team Nucleus-6
01BAP Memorabilia-161
Emerald-161
Ruby-161
Sapphire-161
All-Star Jersey Doubles-DASJ19
All-Star Teammates-AST19
Country of Origin-CO53
He Shoots-He Scores Prizes-29
01BAP Signature Series Certified 100-C6
01BAP Signature Series Certified 50-C6
01BAP Signature Series Certified 1 of 1's-C6
01BAP Signature Series Autographs-LBS
01BAP Signature Series Autographs Gold-LBS
01BAP Signature Series 500 Goal Scorers-29
01BAP Sig Series He Shoots/Scores Points-17
01BAP Sig Series He Shoots/Scores Prizes-6
01BAP Signature Series Jerseys-GJ-27
01BAP Signature Series Jersey Autographs-GUBS
01BAP Sig Series Jersey and Stick Cards-GSJ-27
01BAP Signature Series Emblems-GUE-18
01BAP Signature Series Numbers-ITN-18
01BAP Signature Series Teammates-TM-11
01BAP Ultimate Memorabilia Autographs-13
01BAP Ultimate Mem Autographs Gold-13
01BAP Ultimate Memorabilia Dynamic Duos-8
01BAP Ultimate Memorabilia Emblems-17
01BAP Ultimate Mem 500 Goal Scorers-30
01BAP Ultimate Mem 500 Goal Jerseys/Stick-30
01BAP Ultimate Mem 500 Goal Emblems-30
01BAP Ultimate Memorabilia Jerseys-17
01BAP Ultimate Mem Jerseys and Sticks-17
01BAP Ultimate Mem Journey Jerseys-12
01BAP Ultimate Mem Journey Emblems-12
01BAP Ultimate Memorabilia Numbers-18
01BAP Ultimate Mem Prototypical Players-12
01BAP Update Heritage-H14
01Bowman YoungStars-50
Gold-50
Ice Cubed-50
01Crown Royale-56
Blue-56
Premiere Date-56
Red-56
Retail-56
All-Star Honors-9
Jewels of the Crown-11
01eTopps-4

01McDonald's Pacific-14
Jersey Patches Silver-10
Jersey Patches Gold-10
01O-Pee-Chee-69
01O-Pee-Chee Heritage Parallel-69
01O-Pee-Chee Heritage Parallel Limited-69
01O-Pee-Chee Premier Parallel-69
01Pacific-149
Extreme LTD-149
Hobby LTD-149
Premiere Date-149
Retail LTD-149
01Pacific Adrenaline-69
Blue-69
Premiere Date-69
Red-69
Retail-69
01Pacific Arena Exclusives-149
01Pacific Heads-Up-38
Blue-38
Premiere Date-38
Red-38
Silver-38
Quad Jerseys-11
01Parkhurst-11
Gold-11
Silver-11
He Shoots-He Scores Prizes-5
Jerseys-PJ39
Milestones-M25
Milestones-M51
Sticks-PS53
Teammates-T1
Teammates-T23
01Private Stock-37
Gold-37
Premiere Date-37
Retail-37
Silver-37
Game Gear-44
01Private Stock Pacific Nights-37
01Private Stock PS-2002-29
01Private Stock Reserve-S4
01SP Authentic-31
Limited-31
Limited Gold-31
Jerseys-NNBS
01SP Game Used-17
Authentic Fabric-AFBS
Authentic Fabric-DFFS
Authentic Fabric-TFYSF
Authentic Fabric-YSFO
Authentic Fabric Gold-AFBS
Patches-PBS
Patches-CPSB
Patches-CPSY
Patches-TPSLS
01SPx-23
Hidden Treasures-TTFSD
01Sports Illustrated for Kids III-135
01Stadium Club-8
Award Winners-8
Master Photos-8
Gallery-G2
Gallery Gold-G2
Heart and Soul-HS10
01Stadium Club Toronto Fall Expo-5
01Titanium-53
Hobby Parallel-53
Premiere Date-53
Retail-53
Retail Parallel-53
All-Stars-10
Saturday Knights-6
Three-Star Selections-14
01Topps-69
Heritage Parallel-69
Heritage Parallel Limited-69
OPC Parallel-69
01Topps Chrome-69
Refractors-69
Black Border Refractors-69
01Topps Heritage-24
Refractors-24
01Topps Reserve-75
01UD Challenge for the Cup-29
Jerseys-TNBS
Jerseys-UCSY
01UD Honor Roll-19
01UD Honor Roll-49
01UD Honor Roll-94
Jerseys-J-BS
Jerseys Gold-J-BS
01UD Mask Collection-32
Gold-32
Double Patches-DPBS
Gloves-GGBS
Jerseys-J-BS
Jersey and Patch-JPBS
01UD Playmakers-36
01UD Premier Collection-20
Dual Jerseys-DSY
Dual Jerseys Black-DSY
Jerseys-BBS
Jerseys Black-B-BS
01UD Stanley Cup Champs-64
Jerseys-T-BS
Pieces of Glory-G-BS
Sticks-S-BS
01UD Top Shelf-91
Jerseys-BS
Sticks-SBS
Sticks Gold-SBS
01Upper Deck-290
Exclusives-290
Game Jerseys-YSF
Game Jerseys Series II-FJBS
Game Jerseys Series II-PFBS
Game Jerseys Series II-DJFS
Game Jerseys Series II-TJYFS
Gate Attractions-GA13
Patches-PBS
Patches Series II-PNBS
Patches Series II-NABS
Pride of a Nation-DPYS
Shooting Stars-SS6
Tandems-T3
01Upper Deck Ice-97
01Upper Deck MVP-65
Souvenirs-S-BS
Souvenirs Gold-S-BS
01Upper Deck Victory-132
01Upper Deck Victory-439
Gold-132
Gold-439
01Upper Deck Vintage-89
01Upper Deck Vintage-95
01Upper Deck Vintage-96
01Vanguard-37
Blue-37
Red-37
East Meets West-8
In Focus-4
One of Ones-37
Premiere Date-37
Proofs-37
Quebec Tournament Heroes-7
V-Team-13
02McFarlane Hockey-160
02McFarlane Hockey-162
02Atomic-40
Blue-40
Gold-40
Red-40
Cold Fusion-11
Hobby Parallel-40
National Pride-C6
Super Colliders-6
02BAP All-Star Edition-84
02BAP All-Star Edition-85
02BAP All-Star Edition-86
He Shoots-He Scores Points-6
He Shoots-He Score Prizes-27
Jerseys-84
Jerseys-85
Jerseys-86
Jerseys Gold-84
Jerseys Gold-85
Jerseys Gold-86
Jerseys Silver-84
Jerseys Silver-85
Jerseys Silver-86
02BAP First Edition-139
02BAP First Edition-319
02BAP First Edition-394
02BAP First Edition-428H
He Shoots-He Scores Prizes-21
Jerseys-139
Scoring Leaders-9
02BAP Memorabilia-23
02BAP Memorabilia-235
02BAP Memorabilia-249
Emerald-23
Emerald-235
Emerald-249
Ruby-23
Ruby-235
Ruby-249
Sapphire-23
Sapphire-235
Sapphire-249
All-Star Jerseys-ASJ-53
All-Star Emblems-ASE-22
All-Star Numbers-ASN-22
All-Star Starting Lineup-AS-6
All-Star Teammmates-AST-5
All-Star Teammmates-AST-27
All-Star Triple Jerseys-ASTJ-19
He Shoots-He Scores Points-7
He Shoots-He Scores Prizes-14
NHL All-Star Game-23
NHL All-Star Game-235
NHL All-Star Game-249
NHL All-Star Game Blue-23
NHL All-Star Game Blue-235
NHL All-Star Game Blue-249
NHL All-Star Game Green-23
NHL All-Star Game Green-235
NHL All-Star Game Green-249
NHL All-Star Game Red-23
NHL All-Star Game Red-235
NHL All-Star Game Red-249
Stanley Cup Champions-SCC-6
Teammates-TM-2
02BAP Memorabilia Toronto Fall Expo-23
02BAP Memorabilia Toronto Fall Expo-235
02BAP Memorabilia Toronto Fall Expo-249
02BAP Signature Series-126
Autographs-126
Autograph Buybacks 1998-195
Autograph Buybacks 1999-90
Autograph Buybacks 2000-55
Autograph Buybacks 2001-LBS
Autographs Gold-126
Jerseys-SGJ20
Jersey Autographs-SGJ20
02BAP Ultimate Memorabilia Dynamic Duos-6
02BAP Ultimate Mem Dynasty Jerseys-1
02BAP Ultimate Mem Dynasty Emblems-1
02BAP Ultimate Mem Dynasty Numbers-1
02BAP Ultimate Memorabilia Emblems-10
02BAP Ultimate Mem Global Dominators-10
02BAP Ultimate Memorabilia Jerseys-6
02BAP Ultimate Mem Jersey and Stick-17
02BAP Ultimate Mem Lifetime Achievers-3
02BAP Ultimate Mem Magnificent Ones-10
02BAP Ultimate Mem Magnificent Ones Autos-10
02BAP Ultimate Memorabilia Numbers-9
02Bowman YoungStars-104
Gold-104
Silver-104
02Crown Royale-36
Blue-36
Red-36
Retail-36
Lords of the Rink-9
02eTopps-31
02ITG Used-23
02ITG Used-123
Jerseys-GUJ20
Jersey Autographs-GUJ20
Jerseys Gold-GUJ20
Emblems-E20
Jersey and Stick-SJ20
Jersey and Stick Gold-SJ20
Teammates-T9
Teammates Gold-T9
02McDonald's Pacific-12
Salt Lake Gold-5
02Nextel NHL All-Star Game-2
02O-Pee-Chee-263
02O-Pee-Chee-316
02O-Pee-Chee-326
02O-Pee-Chee Jumbos-8
02O-Pee-Chee Premier Blue Parallel-263
02O-Pee-Chee Premier Blue Parallel-316
02O-Pee-Chee Premier Blue Parallel-326
02O-Pee-Chee Premier Red Parallel-263
02O-Pee-Chee Premier Red Parallel-316
02O-Pee-Chee Premier Red Parallel-326
02O-Pee-Chee Factory Set-263
02O-Pee-Chee Factory Set-316
02O-Pee-Chee Factory Set-326
02Pacific-134
Blue-134
Red-134
Impact Zone-6
02Pacific Calder-39
Silver-39
02Pacific Complete-483
Red-483
02Pacific Exclusive-67
02Pacific Heads-Up-47
Blue-47
Purple-47
Red-47
Bobble Heads-10
Inside the Numbers-11
Postseason Picks-7
02Pacific Quest for the Cup-36
Gold-36
Raising the Cup-7
02Parkhurst-94
Bronze-94
Gold-94
Silver-94
He Shoots-He Scores Points-8
He Shoots-He Scores Prizes-18
Jerseys-GJ41
Patented Power-PP1
Stick and Jerseys-SJ41
Teammates-TT4
02Parkhurst Retro-16
Minis-16
He Shoots-He Scores Points-6
He Shoots-He Scores Prizes-14
Jerseys-RJ17
Jersey and Sticks-RSJ26
Memorabilia-RM18
02Private Stock Reserve-37
Blue-37
Red-37
Retail-37
02SP Authentic-31
02SP Authentic-97
Beckett Promos-31
Super Premiums-SPBS
Super Premiums-DPYS
02SP Game Used-18
Authentic Fabrics-AFBS
Authentic Fabrics-AFSN
Authentic Fabrics-CFSH
Authentic Fabrics Gold-AFBS
Authentic Fabrics Gold-AFSN
Authentic Fabrics Gold-CFSH
Authentic Fabrics Rainbow-AFBS
Authentic Fabrics Rainbow-AFSN
Authentic Fabrics Rainbow-CFSH
First Rounder Patches-BS
Piece of History-PHBS
Piece of History-PHSH
Piece of History Gold-PHBS
Piece of History Gold-PHSH
Piece of History Rainbow-PHBS
Piece of History Rainbow-PHSH
Tools of the Game-BS
02SPx-31
02SPx-137
Spectrum Gold-31
Spectrum Silver-31
Milestones-MBS
Milestones-MSH
Milestones Gold-BS
Milestones Gold-SH
Milestones Silver-BS
Milestones Silver-SH
Xtreme Talents-BS
Xtreme Talents Gold-BS
Xtreme Talents Silver-BS
02Stadium Club-95
Silver Decoy Cards-95
Proofs-95
Beam Team-BT6
02Titanium-39
Blue-39
Red-39
Retail-39
02Topps-263
02Topps-316
02Topps-326
OPC Blue Parallel-263
OPC Blue Parallel-316
OPC Blue Parallel-326
OPC Red Parallel-263
OPC Red Parallel-316
OPC Red Parallel-326
Topps/OPC Hometown Heroes-HHU12
Factory Set-263
Factory Set-316
Factory Set-326
Factory Set Hometown Heroes-HHU12
02Topps Chrome-144
Black Border Refractors-144
Refractors-144
02Topps Heritage-80
02Topps Heritage-126
Chrome Parallel-80
02Topps Total-369
Production-TP6
02UD Artistic Impressions-35
Gold-35
Artist's Touch-ATBS
Artist's Touch Gold-ATBS
02UD Artistic Impressions Beckett Promos-35
02UD Artistic Impressions Retrospectives-R35
02UD Artistic Impressions Retrospect Gold-R35
02UD Artistic Impress Retrospect Silver-R35
02UD Honor Roll-29
Grade A Jerseys-TYFS
Team Warriors-TW6
02UD Mask Collection-33
02UD Mask Collection Beckett Promos-33
02UD Mask Collection Instant Offense-IOBS
02UD Mask Collection Patches-PGBS
02UD Piece of History-37
Patches-PHBS
02UD Premier Collection-23
Jerseys Bronze-BS
Jerseys Bronze-SY
Jerseys Gold-BS
Jerseys Gold-SY
Jerseys Silver-BS
Jerseys Silver-SY
Patches-PBS
02UD Top Shelf-32
Clutch Performers-CPBS
Dual Player Jerseys-STYS
Milestones Jerseys-MSFRM
Milestones Jerseys-MSYVR
Shooting Stars-SHBS
Triple Jerseys-HTSHR
Triple Jerseys-TSSYH
02Upper Deck-233
02Upper Deck-306
Exclusives-233
Exclusives-306
02Upper Deck Beckett UD Promos-306
02Upper Deck Difference Makers-BS
02Upper Deck Good Old Days-GOBS
02Upper Deck Number Crunchers-NC5
02Upper Deck Patch Card Logo-BS
02Upper Deck Patchwork-PWBS
02Upper Deck Pinpoint Accuracy-PABS
02Upper Deck Playbooks-PL5
02Upper Deck Playbooks Series II-SL
02Upper Deck Sizzling Scorers-SS7
02Upper Deck Classic Portraits-37
Etched in Time-ET6
Hockey Royalty-SYL
Hockey Royalty Limited-SYL
Mini-Busts-1
Mini-Busts-2
Mini-Busts-3
Mini-Busts-4
Pillars of Strength-PS5
Starring Cast-CBS
Starring Cast Limited-CBS
02Upper Deck MVP-64
Gold-64
Classics-64
Golden Classics-64
Highlight Nights-HN4
02Upper Deck Rookie Update-35
02Upper Deck Rookie Update-149A
Jerseys-DBS
Jerseys-SYS
Jerseys Gold-DBS
Jerseys Gold-SYS
02Upper Deck Victory-73
Bronze-73
Gold-73
Silver-73
National Pride-NP7
02Upper Deck Vintage-97
02Upper Deck Vintage-271
02Upper Deck Vintage-294
Green Backs-97
Tall Boys-T25
Tall Boys Gold-T25
02Vanguard-39
LTD-39
03McFarlane Hockey Toys-R-Us-10
03McFarlane Hockey NHL 2-Pack-20
03BAP Memorabilia-15
Emerald-15
Gold-15
Ruby-15
Sapphire-15
All-Star Emblems-ASE-11
All-Star Jerseys-ASJ-16
All-Star Jerseys-ASJ-37
All-Star Numbers-ASN-11
All-Star Teammates-AST7
He Shoots-He Scores Points-12
He Shoots-He Scores Prizes-12
Jersey and Stick-SJ-38
Jerseys-GJ-31
Jersey Autographs-GJ-31
Practice Jerseys-PMP12
03BAP Ultimate Mem Always An All-Star-17
03BAP Ultimate Mem Always An AS Gold-17
03BAP Ultimate Mem Complete Jersey-18
03BAP Ultimate Mem Complete Jersey Gold-18
03BAP Ultimate Memorabilia Dynamic Duos-4
03BAP Ultimate Mem Jersey and Emblems-4
03BAP Ultimate Mem Jersey and Emblem Gold-4
03BAP Ultimate Mem Jersey and Numbers-4
03BAP Ultimate Mem Jersey and Number Gold-4
03BAP Ultimate Mem Jersey and Stick-18
03BAP Ultimate Mem Jersey and Stick Gold-18
03BAP Ultimate Memorabilia Nameplates-22
03BAP Ultimate Mem Nameplates Gold-22
03BAP Ultimate Memorabilia Triple Threads-24
03Beehive-70
Gold-70
Silver-70
Jerseys-JT13
Sticks Beige Border-BE10
Sticks Red Border-RE9
03Black Diamond-77
Black-77
Green-77
Red-77
Threads-DT-BS
Threads Green-DT-BS
Threads Red-DT-BS
Threads Black-DT-BS
03Crown Royale-37
Blue-37
Retail-37
03ITG Action-215
Jerseys-M176
Oh Canada-OC13
03ITG Toronto Fall Expo Jerseys-FE8
03ITG Used Signature Series-102
Gold-102
Autographs-BS
Autographs Gold-BS
Game-Day Jerseys-10
Game-Day Jerseys Gold-10
Jersey and Stick-13
Jersey and Stick Gold-13
Oh Canada-13
Oh Canada Gold-13
Oh Canada Emblems-13
Oh Canada Emblems Gold-13
03ITG VIP Jerseys-24
03ITG VIP Jersey Autographs-24
03McDonald's Pacific Patches Silver-10
03McDonald's Pacific Patches Gold-10
03McDonald's Pacific Patches and Sticks-10
03NHL Sticker Collection-215
03O-Pee-Chee-257
03OPC Blue-257
03OPC Gold-257
03OPC Red-257
03Pacific-126
Blue-126
Red-126
Jerseys-15
Jerseys Gold-15
Maximum Impact-4
03Pacific Calder-40
Silver-40
03Pacific Complete-34
Red-34
03Pacific Exhibit-55
Blue Backs-55
Yellow Backs-55
03Pacific Heads-Up-37
Hobby LTD-37
Retail LTD-37
03Pacific Invincible-35
Blue-35
Red-35
Retail-35
03Pacific Luxury Suite-33A
03Pacific Luxury Suite-33B
03Pacific Luxury Suite-33C
03Pacific Prism-117
Blue-117
Patches-117
Red-117
Retail-117
03Pacific Quest for the Cup-40
Blue-40
Raising the Cup-10
03Parkhurst Original Six Detroit-23
03Parkhurst Original Six Detroit-69
Memorabilia-DM2
Memorabilia-DM17
Memorabilia-DM54
03Parkhurst Rookie Jerseys-GJ-33
03Parkhurst Rookie Jerseys Gold-GJ-33
03Parkhurst Rookie Jersey and Sticks-SJ-16
03Parkhurst Rookie Jersey and Sticks Gold-SJ-16
03SPx-33
03SPx-127
Radiance-33
Radiance-127
Spectrum-33
Spectrum-127
Fantasy Franchise-FF-HYS
Fantasy Franchise Limited-FF-HYS
Origins-O-BS
Style-SPX-BS
Style Limited-SPX-BS
VIP-VIP-YS
VIP Limited-VIP-YS
03Titanium-153
Hobby Jersey Number Parallels-153
Retail-153
03Topps-257
Blue-257
Gold-257
Red-257
Topps/OPC Idols-CI17
Lost Rookies-BS
C55 Award Winners-5
03UD Honor Roll-111
03Upper Deck-309
500 Goal Club-500-BS
Canadian Exclusives-309
HG-309
Power Zone-PZ-4
UD Exclusives-309
03Upper Deck Classic Portraits-31
Classic Colors-CC-BS
Hockey Royalty-YHS
03Upper Deck Ice Breakers-IB-BS
03Upper Deck Ice Breaker Patches-IB-BS
03Upper Deck Ice Clear Cut Winners-CC-BS
03Upper Deck MVP-144
Gold Script-144
Silver Script-144
Canadian Exclusives-144
Lethal Lineups-LL6
Threads-TC3
03Upper Deck Trilogy-31
Limited-31
03Upper Deck Victory-64
Bronze-64
Gold-64
Silver-64
Freshman Flashback-FF19
Game Breakers-GB45
03Toronto Star-29
04Pacific-98
Blue-98
Red-98
04SP Authentic-33
04SP Authentic-114
04Ultimate Collection Dual Logos-UL2-SL
04Ultimate Collection Patches-UP-BS
04Upper Deck-63
04Upper Deck-206
1997 Game Jerseys-BS
Canadian Exclusives-63
Canadian Exclusives-206
HG Glossy Gold-63
HG Glossy Gold-206
HG Glossy Silver-63
HG Glossy Silver-206
School of Hard Knocks-SHK1
Swatch of Six-SS-BS
05Be A Player-30
First Period-30
Second Period-30
Third Period-30
Overtime-30
Outtakes-OT21
Signatures-BS
Signatures Gold-BS
05Beehive-32
05Beehive-188
Beige -32
Blue -32
Gold-32
Red -32
Matte-32
05Black Diamond-135
Emerald-135
Gold-135
Onyx-135
Ruby-135
Jerseys-J-BS
Jersey Ruby-J-BS
Jersey Duals-DJ-BS
Jersey Triples-TJ-BS
Jersey Quads-QJ-BS
05Hot Prospects-34
En Fuego-34
Red Hot-34
White Hot-34
05McDonalds Upper Deck-17
05Panini Stickers-260
05Parkhurst-171
Facsimile Auto Parallel-171
True Colors-TCDET
True Colors-TCDET
True Colors-TCDECO
True Colors-TCDECO
05SP Authentic-34
05SP Authentic-122
Limited-34
Limited-122
05SP Game Used-34
Gold-34
Authentic Fabrics-AF-BS
Authentic Fabrics Dual-YS
Authentic Fabrics Gold-AF-BS
Authentic Fabrics Quad-YDSL
Authentic Patches Quad -YDSL
Authentic Fabrics Triple-ISL
Authentic Patches-AP-BS
Authentic Patches Dual-YS
Authentic Patches Triple-ISL
Awesome Authentics-AA-BS
By the Letter-LM-BS
Game Gear-GG-SH
05SPx-29
Spectrum-29
Winning Combos-WC-SY
Winning Combos Gold-WC-SY
Winning Combos Spectrum-WC-SY
Winning Materials-WM-BS
Winning Materials Gold-WM-BS
Winning Materials Spectrum-WM-BS
Xcitement Superstars-XS-BS
Xcitement Superstars Gold-XS-BS
Xcitement Superstars Spectrum-XS-BS
05The Cup-40
Gold-40
Black Rainbow-40
Masterpiece Pressplates-40
Masterpiece Pressplates (Rookie Update)-217
Noble Numbers-NNSC
Noble Numbers Dual-DNNSR
Noble Numbers Dual-DNNYS
Patch Variation-P40
05UD Artifacts-38
05UD Artifacts-166
Blue-38
Blue-166
Gold-38
Gold-166
Green-38
Green-166
Pewter-38
Pewter-166
Red-38
Red-166
Gold Autographed-38
Gold Autographed-166
Treasured Patches-TP-BS
Treasured Patches Autographed-TP-BS
Treasured Patches Dual-TPD-BS
Treasured Patches Dual Autographed-TPD-BS
Treasured Patches Pewter-TP-BS
Treasured Patches Silver-TP-BS
Treasured Swatches-TS-BS
Treasured Swatches Autographed-TS-BS
Treasured Swatches Blue-TS-BS
Treasured Swatches Copper-TS-BS
Treasured Swatches Dual-TSD-BS
Treasured Swatches Dual Autographed-TSD-BS
Treasured Swatches Dual Blue-TSD-BS
Treasured Swatches Dual Copper-TSD-BS
Treasured Swatches Dual Maroon-TSD-BS
Treasured Swatches Dual Pewter-TSD-BS
Treasured Swatches Dual Silver-TSD-BS
Treasured Swatches Maroon-TS-BS
Treasured Swatches Pewter-TS-BS
Treasured Swatches Silver-TS-BS
05UD PowerPlay-33
Rainbow-33
Specialists-TSBS
Specialists Patches-SPBS
05Ultimate Collection-35
Gold-35
Premium Patches-PPBS
Premium Swatches-PSBS
Ultimate Patches-PBS
Ultimate Patches Dual-DPSY
05Ultra-75
Gold-75
Ice-75
Scoring Kings-SK34
Scoring Kings Jerseys-SKJ-BS
Scoring Kings Patches-SKP-BS
05Upper Deck-312
Big Playmakers-B-BS
Destined for the Hall-DH7
Jerseys Series II-J2BS
Majestic Materials-MMBS
NHL Generations-DST
NHL Generations-TMST
NHL Generations-TNSN
Patches-P-BS
School of Hard Knocks-HK7
Scrapbooks-HS28
Shooting Stars-S-BS
05Upper Deck Ice-33
Rainbow-33
Frozen Fabrics-FFBS
Frozen Fabrics Glass-FFBS
Frozen Fabrics Patches-FFPBS
05Upper Deck MVP-146
Gold-146
Platinum-146
05Upper Deck Rookie Update-36
05Upper Deck Trilogy-34
05Upper Deck Trilogy-138
Crystal-138
05Upper Deck Victory-68
Black-68
Gold-68
Silver-68
Blow-Ups-BU15
Game Breakers-GB16
06Be A Player Portraits-70
06Beehive-36
06Beehive-180
Blue-36
Gold-36
Matte-36
Red Facsimile Signatures-36
Wood-36
5 X 7 Black and White-36
5 X 7 Dark Wood-36
06Black Diamond-141
Black-141
Gold-141
Ruby-141
Jerseys-JSN
Jerseys Black-JSN
Jerseys Gold-JSN
Jerseys Ruby-JSN
06Flair Showcase-183
06Flair Showcase-230
Parallel-183
Parallel-230
Hot Numbers-HN18
Hot Numbers Parallel-HN18
06Fleer-130
Tiffany-130
06Hot Prospects-64
Red Hot-64
White Hot-64
Hot Materials -HMBS
Hot Materials Red Hot-HMBS
Hot Materials White Hot-HMBS
06McDonald's Upper Deck-16
Jerseys-JBS
Patches-PBS
06NHL POG-37
06O-Pee-Chee-329
06O-Pee-Chee-660
Rainbow-329
Rainbow-660
Swatches-S-SH
06Panini Stickers-101
06SP Authentic-37
06SP Authentic-106
Limited-37
Limited-106
06SP Game Used-65
Gold-65
Rainbow-65
Authentic Fabrics-AFBS
Authentic Fabrics Parallel-AFBS
Authentic Fabrics Patches-AFBS
Authentic Fabrics Dual-AF2SJ
Authentic Fabrics Dual Patches-AF2SJ
Authentic Fabrics Triple-AF3NYR
Authentic Fabrics Triple Patches-AF3NYR
Authentic Fabrics Quads-AF4SKGN
Authentic Fabrics Quads Patches-AF4SKGN
Authentic Fabrics Sixes-AF6500
Authentic Fabrics Sixes Patches-AF6500
Authentic Fabrics Eights-AF8CAN
Authentic Fabrics Eights Patches-AF8CAN
06SPx-66
06SPx-109
Spectrum-66
Spectrum-109
SPxcitement-X68
SPxcitement Spectrum-X68
06The Cup-60
Black Rainbow-60
Foundations-CQSH
Foundations Patches-CQSH
Gold-60
Gold Patches-60
Jerseys-60
Masterpiece Pressplates-60
NHL Shields Duals-DSHJB
NHL Shields Duals-DSHSD
06UD Artifacts-35
06UD Artifacts-168
Blue-35
Blue-168
Gold-35
Gold-168
Platinum-35
Platinum-168
Radiance-35
Radiance-168
Red-35
Red-168
Tundra Tandems-TTBJ
Tundra Tandems Black-TTBJ
Tundra Tandems Blue-TTBJ
Tundra Tandems Gold-TTBJ
Tundra Tandems Platinum-TTBJ
Tundra Tandems Red-TTBJ
Tundra Tandems Dual Patches Red-TTBJ
06UD Biography of a Season-BOS2
06UD Mini Jersey Collection-67
06UD Powerplay-67
Impact Rainbow-67
Specialists-SBS
Specialists Patches-PBS
06Ultimate Collection-41
Jerseys-UJ-BS
Patches-UJ-BS
06Ultra-131
Gold Medallion-131
Ice Medallion-131
Action-UA10
Scoring Kings-SK4
06Upper Deck Arena Giveaways-NYR6
06Upper Deck-383
Exclusives Parallel-383
High Gloss Parallel-383
Game Jerseys-JSH
Game Patches-PSH
Generations Duals-G2SN
Generations Patches Dual-G2PSN
Goal Rush-GR13
Masterpieces-383
Oversized Wal-Mart Exclusives-383
06Upper Deck MVP-192
Gold Script-192
Super Script-192
Jerseys-OJSG
Jerseys-OJSL
06Upper Deck Ovation-16
06Upper Deck Sweet Shot-72
Sweet Stitches-SSBR
Sweet Stitches Duals-SSBR
Sweet Stitches Triples-SSBR
06Upper Deck Trilogy-66
Frozen In Time-FT3
06Upper Deck Victory-70
06Upper Deck Victory-260
06Upper Deck Victory Black-70
06Upper Deck Victory Gold-70
06Upper Deck Victory GameBreakers-GB18
07Upper Deck Ovation-16
07Upper Deck Victory-23
Black-23
Gold-23
Oversize Cards-OS7
Stars on Ice-SI43

Shanahan, Chris
96Sudbury Wolves-20
96Sudbury Wolves Police-21

Shanahan, Ryan
92Sudbury Wolves-12
93Sudbury Wolves-10
93Sudbury Wolves Police-11
94Sudbury Wolves-9
94Sudbury Wolves Police-15
95Slapshot-392
95Sudbury Wolves-6
95Sudbury Wolves Police-19
96Louisiana Ice Gators-16
96Louisiana Ice Gators II-16
98Louisiana Ice Gators-16
99Louisiana Ice Gators-8
00Louisiana Ice Gators-5
01Louisiana Ice Gators-22

Shanahan, Sean
76Rockies Coke Cans-19
76Rockies Puck Bucks-19
77Rochester Americans-21

Shand, Dave
77O-Pee-Chee NHL-355
78Flames Majik Market-8
78O-Pee-Chee-356
79Panini Stickers-57
79Flames Postcards-18
79Flames Team Issue-20
79O-Pee-Chee-394
80Maple Leafs Postcards-24
80O-Pee-Chee-282
80Pepsi-Cola Caps-98

Shandurov, Dmitri
99Russian Hockey League-62
99Russian Hockey League-99

Shaneberger, Gray
03Florida Everblades-21
03Florida Everblades RBI Sports-173
04Kalamazoo Wings-18
05Roanoke Valley Vipers-5

Shange, Ntsika
98Danish Hockey League-107
99Danish Hockey League-117

Shank, Daniel
87Hull Olympiques-18
88ProCards AHL-23
90Bowman-235
Tiffany-235
90O-Pee-Chee-34
90Pro Set-78
90Score-377
Canadian-377
90Topps-34
Tiffany-34
90Upper Deck-99
French-99
90ProCards AHL/IHL-489
91ProCards-119
92San Diego Gulls-23
93Phoenix Cobras RHI-16
93San Diego Gulls-18
94Anaheim Bullfrogs RHI-16
94Detroit Vipers Pogs-5
94Minnesota Moose-5
95Las Vegas Thunder-18
98Phoenix Mustangs-6

Shannon, Darrin
89ProCards AHL-275
90O-Pee-Chee-310
90Pro Set-592
90Sabres Campbell's-24
90Score-410
Canadian-410
90Topps-310
Tiffany-310
90ProCards AHL/IHL-278
91Pro Set Platinum-246
91Bowman-24
91Jets IGA-28
91O-Pee-Chee-214
91OPC Premier-146
91Parkhurst-201
French-201
91Pinnacle-243
French-243
91Pro Set-14
91Pro Set-515
French-14
French-515
91Score Canadian Bilingual-438
91Score Canadian English-438
91Score Rookie/Traded-107T
91Stadium Club-361
91Topps-214
91Upper Deck-322
91Upper Deck-581
French-322
French-581
92Bowman-385
92O-Pee-Chee-332
92Panini Stickers-58
92Panini Stickers French-58
92Parkhurst-436
Emerald Ice-436
92Pinnacle-106
French-106
92Pro Set-218
92Score-36
Canadian-36
92Stadium Club-55
92Topps-167
Gold-167G
92Ultra-246
92Upper Deck-132
93Donruss-388
93Jets Readers Club-18
93Jets Ruffles-23
93Leaf-194
93OPC Premier-261
Gold-261
93Panini Stickers-192
93Parkhurst-499
Emerald Ice-499
93Pinnacle-266
Canadian-266
93Score-280
Canadian-280
93Stadium Club-191
Members Only Master Set-191
OPC-191
First Day Issue-191
First Day Issue OPC-191
93Topps/OPC Premier-261
Gold-261
94Canada Games NHL POGS-254
94Donruss-139
94Flair-210
94Leaf-251
94OPC Premier-254
Special Effects-254
94Parkhurst SE-SE204
Gold-SE204
94Pinnacle-279
Artist's Proofs-279
Rink Collection-279
94Topps/OPC Premier-254
Special Effects-254
94Ultra-395
94Upper Deck-483
Electric Ice-483
95Jets Readers Club-10
95Jets Team Issue-21
95Pinnacle-69
Artist's Proofs-69
Rink Collection-69
95Score-103
Black Ice Artist's Proofs-103
Black Ice-103
96Be A Player-183
Autographs-183
Autographs Silver-183
96Coyotes Coca-Cola-28
97Coyotes Face-Off Luncheon -20
97Pacific Invincible NHL Regime-154
99St. John's Maple Leafs-21
04ITG Franchises Canadian-142
Autographs-DSH
04ITG Franchises US West-266

Shannon, Darryl
88ProCards AHL-243
90Newmarket Saints-22
90ProCards AHL/IHL-151
91Maple Leafs PLAY-28
91Parkhurst-390
French-390
91Pro Set-490
French-490
91Upper Deck-493
French-493
92Maple Leafs Kodak-32
95Jets Team Issue-22
95Upper Deck-282
Electric Ice-282
Electric Ice Gold-282
96Be A Player-90
Autographs-90
Autographs Silver-90
97Pacific-72
Copper-72
Emerald Green-72
Ice Blue-72
Red-72
Silver-72
97Panini Stickers-14
97Score Sabres-19
Platinum-19
Premier-19
98Pacific-109
Ice Blue-109
Red-109
99Pacific-46
Copper-46
Emerald Green-46
Gold-46
Ice Blue-46

Premiere Date-46
Red-46
00UD Heroes-65
02German DEL City Press-231
03German Berlin Polar Bears Postcards-28

Shannon, Gerry
34Beehive Group I Photos-204
35Diamond Matchbooks Tan 1-62
36Providence Reds-9
37O-Pee-Chee V304E-179

Shannon, John
97Pinnacle Hockey Night in Canada-12

Shannon, Matt
03Cape Fear Fire Antz-13

Shannon, Ryan
96Quebec Pee-Wee Tournament-32
98Calgary Hitmen-2
98Calgary Hitmen Autographs-2
98Bowman CHL-63
Golden Anniversary-63
OPC International-63
98Bowman Chrome CHL-63
Golden Anniversary-63
Golden Anniversary Refractors-63
OPC International-63
OPC International Refractors-63
Refractors-63
99Syracuse Crunch-22
00Fort Worth Brahmas-14
05ITG Heroes/Prosp Toronto Expo Parallel -208
05AHL All-Stars-35
05AHL Top Prospects-37
05Portland Pirates-12
05ITG Heroes and Prospects-208
Autographs Series II-RSH
06Be A Player Portraits-121
06Beehive-102
Matte-102
06Black Diamond-160A
Black-160A
Gold-160A
Ruby-160A
06Flair Showcase-301
06Hot Prospects-101
Red Hot-101
White Hot-101
Hotagraphs-HRS
06O-Pee-Chee-537
06O-Pee-Chee-632
Rainbow-537
Rainbow-632
06SP Authentic-161
Limited-161
06SP Game Used-102
Gold-102
Rainbow-102
Autographs-102
Rookie Exclusives Autographs-RERS
06SPx-178
Spectrum-178
06The Cup-110
Autographed Rookie Masterpiece Pressplates-110
Gold Rainbow Autographed Rookie Patches-110
Masterpiece Pressplates (Be A Player Portraits)-121
Masterpiece Pressplates (Bee Hive)-102
Masterpiece Pressplates (Black Diamond)-160
Masterpiece Pressplates (Marquee Rookies)-537
Masterpiece Pressplates (MVP)-315
Masterpiece Pressplates (SP Authentic Autographs)-161
Masterpiece Pressplates (SP Game Used)-102
Masterpiece Pressplates (SPx Autographs)-178
Masterpiece Pressplates (Sweet Beginnings)-102
Masterpiece Pressplates (Trilogy)-102
Masterpiece Pressplates (Ultimate Collection)-62
Masterpiece Pressplates (Victory)-283
NHL Shields Duals-DSHOS
Rookies Black-110
Rookies Platinum-110
06UD Artifacts-231
06UD Mini Jersey Collection-104
06Ultimate Collection-62
Ultimate Debut Threads Jerseys-DJ-RS
Ultimate Debut Threads Jerseys Autographs-DJ-RS
Ultimate Debut Threads Patches-DJ-RS
Ultimate Debut Threads Patches Autographs-DJ-RS
06Ultra-232
Gold Medallion-232
Ice Medallion-232
06Upper Deck-202
Exclusives Parallel-202
High Gloss Parallel-202
Masterpieces-202
Rookie Game Dated Moments-RGD1
Rookie Materials-RMRS
Rookie Materials Patches-RMRS
06Upper Deck MVP-315
Gold Script-315
Super Script-315
06Upper Deck Sweet Shot-102
Rookie Jerseys Autographs-102
06Upper Deck Trilogy-102
06Upper Deck Victory-283
06AHL Top Prospects-35
06ITG Heroes and Prospects-79
Autographs-ARS
07Upper Deck Rookie Class -41

Shantz, Brian
88Kamloops Blazers-22
89Kamloops Blazers-19
907th Inn. Sketch Memorial Cup-11
94Central Hockey League-85
94San Antonio Iguanas-13
95Central Hockey League-104
98San Antonio Iguanas-3
99San Antonio Iguanas-7

Shantz, David
03Mississauga Ice Dogs-20
04ITG Top Prospects Spring Expo-2
04Mississauga Ice Dogs-5
04ITG Heroes and Prospects-69
Autographs-DS
Top Prospects-2
04ITG Heroes/Prospects Toronto Expo '05-69
04ITG Heroes/Prospects Expo Heroes/Pros-69

Shantz, Jeff
907th Inn. Sketch WHL-174
917th Inn. Sketch WHL-219
92Classic-15
Gold-15
92Classic Four-Sport *-164
Gold-164
93Blackhawks Coke-5
93Donruss-75
93Leaf-405
93Parkhurst-314
Emerald Ice-314
93Pinnacle-428
Canadian-428
93PowerPlay-316
93Score-605
Gold-605
Canadian-605
Canadian Gold-605
93Stadium Club-348
Members Only Master Set-348
First Day Issue-348
93Upper Deck-258
93Upper Deck-451
SP-32
93Classic-27
94Blackhawks Coke-16
94Donruss-247
94Leaf-196
94OPC Premier-342
94O-Pee-Chee Finest Inserts-23
94OPC Premier Special Effects-342
94Parkhurst-46
94Parkhurst-289
Gold-46
Gold-289
94Pinnacle-458
Artist's Proofs-458
Rink Collection-458
94Stadium Club-92
Members Only Master Set-92
First Day Issue-92
Super Team Winner Cards-92
94Topps/OPC Premier-342
Special Effects-342
94Upper Deck-379
Electric Ice-379
94Indianapolis Ice-22
95Blackhawks Coke-15
95Collector's Choice-124
Player's Club-124
Player's Club Platinum-124
95Donruss-209
95Leaf-252
95Topps-179
OPC Inserts-179
95Upper Deck-182
Electric Ice-182
Electric Ice Gold-182
96Collector's Choice-53
97Be A Player-173
Autographs-173
Autographs Die-Cuts-173
Autographs Prismatic Die-Cuts-173
97Pacific Invincible NHL Regime-46
97Upper Deck-248
98Aurora-43
98Be A Player-31
Press Release-31
98BAP Gold-31
98BAP Autographs-31
98BAP Autographs Gold-31
98BAP Tampa Bay All Star Game-31
98Pacific-151
Ice Blue-151
Red-151
98Upper Deck MVP-33
Gold Script-33
Silver Script-33
Super Script-33
99Pacific-60
Copper-60
Emerald Green-60
Gold-60
Ice Blue-60
Premiere Date-60
Red-60
99Upper Deck MVP SC Edition-35
Gold Script-35
Silver Script-35
Super Script-35
00BAP Signature Series-169
Emerald-169
Ruby-169
Sapphire-169
Autographs-190
Autographs Gold-190
00Pacific-74
Copper-74
Gold-74
Ice Blue-74
Premiere Date-74
00Titanium Game Gear-70
00Titanium Game Gear Patches-70
00Upper Deck-258
Exclusives Tier 1-258
Exclusives Tier 2-258
01Atomic Jerseys-7
01Atomic Patches-7
01Upper Deck Vintage-40
02Avalanche Postcards-14
02BAP Sig Series Auto Buybacks 1998-31
05German DEL-253

Shantz, Paul
03St. Georges de Beauce Garaga-16
04St Georges de Beauce Garaga-3

Shapley, Larry
99Manitoba Moose-17
99Tallahassee Tiger Sharks-14

Shapovalov, Vladimir
70Swedish Masterserien-138
72Finnish Jaakiekko-35

Sharapov, Andrei
00Russian Hockey League-84

Shargorodsky, Oleg
98Fort Wayne Komets-16
99Russian Hockey League-208
99Russian Stars of Hockey-23
00Russian Hockey League-138
01Russian Hockey League-91
02Russian Hockey League-154

Sharifijanov, Maxim
99Kitchener Rangers-8

Sharifijanov, Vadim
92Upper Deck-612
93Parkhurst-527
Emerald Ice-527
93Pinnacle-503
93Upper Deck-574
93Classic-110
Class of '94-CL6
94Score-212
Gold-212
Platinum-212
94Classic-21
Gold-21
Tri-Cards-T37
94Classic Pro Prospects-207
94Classic Four-Sport *-138
Printers Proofs-138
94Signature Rookies Gold Standard *-91
94Signature Rookies Tetrad *-114
Signatures-114
95Images Four-Sport *-112
96Albany River Rats-14
97Donruss-204
Press Proofs Silver-204
Press Proofs Gold-204
97Donruss Canadian Ice-134
Dominion Series-134
Provincial Series-134
97Donruss Limited-78
Exposure-78
97Leaf-163
Fractal Matrix-163
Fractal Matrix Die Cuts-163
97Pinnacle Inside-183
97Score-56
Artist's Proofs-56
Golden Blades-56
97Score Devils-17
Platinum-17
Premier-17
97Albany River Rats-13
98Devils Team Issue-26
98Pacific Omega-142
Red-142
Opening Day Issue-142
98Upper Deck-309
Exclusives-309
Exclusives 1 of 1-309
Generation Next-GN28
Generation Next Quantum 1-GN28
Generation Next Quantum 2-GN28
Generation Next Quantum 3-GN28
Gold Reserve-309
99BAP Memorabilia-123
Gold-123
Silver-123
99BAP Millennium-146
Emerald-146
Ruby-146
Sapphire-146
Signatures-146
Signatures Gold-146
99Devils Team Issue-5
99O-Pee-Chee-160
99O-Pee-Chee Chrome-160
99O-Pee-Chee Chrome Refractors-160
99Pacific-247
Copper-247
Emerald Green-247
Gold-247
Ice Blue-247
Premiere Date-247
Red-247
99SPx-89
Radiance-89
Spectrum-89
99Topps/OPC-160
99Topps/OPC Chrome-160
Refractors-160
99Upper Deck-80
Exclusives-80
Exclusives 1 of 1-80
New Ice Age-N4
New Ice Age Quantum Gold-N4
New Ice Age Quantum Silver-N4
99Upper Deck Gold Reserve-80
99Upper Deck HoloGrFx-34
Ausome-34
99Upper Deck MVP-121
Gold Script-121
Silver Script-121
Super Script-121
99Upper Deck Retro-48
Gold-48
Platinum-48
99Upper Deck Victory-168
99Wayne Gretzky Hockey Signs of Greatness-VS
00Kansas City Blades-11
01Russian Hockey League-51
02BAP Sig Series Auto Buybacks 1999-146
03Russian Hockey League-184

Sharipov, Azhat
00Russian Hockey League-148

Sharnin, Alexei
00Russian Hockey League-142

Sharp, Derek
00OCN Blizzard-13

Sharp, MacGregor
03Camrose Kodiaks-3
04Camrose Kodiaks-10

Sharp, Patrick
02Atomic-122
Blue-122
Gold-122
Red-122
Hobby Parallel-122
02BAP All-Star Edition-150
Gold-150
Silver-150
02BAP Memorabilia-282
Emerald-282
Ruby-282
Sapphire-282
NHL All-Star Game-282
NHL All-Star Game Blue-282
NHL All-Star Game Green-282
NHL All-Star Game Red-282
02BAP Memorabilia Toronto Fall Expo-282
02BAP Ultimate Memorabilia-12
02Bowman YoungStars-163
Gold-163
Silver-163
02Crown Royale-130
Blue-130
Purple-130
Red-130
Retail-130
02Pacific Exclusive-188
Blue-188
Gold-188
02Parkhurst-212
Bronze-212
Gold-212
Silver-212
02Private Stock Reserve-176
Blue-176
Red-176
Retail-176
02SP Authentic-155
02SP Game Used-88
02SPx-173
02Stadium Club-138
Silver Decoy Cards-138
Proofs-138
02Topps Chrome-165
Black Border Refractors-165
Refractors-165
02Topps Heritage-150
02Topps Total-417
02UD Artistic Impressions-125
Gold-125
02UD Mask Collection-128
02UD Piece of History-143
02UD Premier Collection-62
Gold-62
02UD Top Shelf-101
02Upper Deck-447
Exclusives-447
02Upper Deck Classic Portraits-124
02Upper Deck Rookie Update-156A
02Upper Deck Rookie Update-156B
02Upper Deck Rookie Update-156C
02Vanguard-127
LTD-127
02Philadelphia Phantoms-9
03AHL Top Prospects-32
03Philadelphia Phantoms-19
04AHL All-Stars-39
04Philadelphia Phantoms-17
05ITG Heroes/Prosp Toronto Expo Parallel -100
05Flyers Team Issue-21
05Upper Deck-390
Jerseys Series II-J2PS
05Philadelphia Phantoms All-Decade Team-1
05ITG Heroes and Prospects-100
Autographs-A-PS
06Blackhawks Postcards-8
06Fleer Fabricology-FPS
06O-Pee-Chee-116
Rainbow-116
06Panini Stickers-214
06Upper Deck-47
Exclusives Parallel-47
High Gloss Parallel-47
Masterpieces-47

Sharp, Ryan
00Owen Sound Attack-18
01Owen Sound Attack-19
02Barrie Colts-7

Sharples, Jeff
84Kelowna Wings-4
86Portland Winter Hawks-20
87Red Wings Little Caesars-25
88O-Pee-Chee-48
88O-Pee-Chee Stickers-74
88O-Pee-Chee Stickers-205
88O-Pee-Chee Stickers-249
88Panini Stickers-38
88Red Wings Little Caesars-21
88Topps-48
89O-Pee-Chee-42
89Panini Stickers-66
89Topps-42
90ProCards AHL/IHL-559
92Kansas City Blades-4
93Las Vegas Thunder-24
94Las Vegas Thunder-26
95Las Vegas Thunder-17
96Collector's Edge Ice-156
Prism-156
99IHL All-Stars-17
99Utah Grizzlies-31
04Las Vegas Wranglers-23

Sharples, Scott
92St. John's Maple Leafs-21

Sharples, Warren
90ProCards AHL/IHL-625
91ProCards-591

Sharpley, Glen
77O-Pee-Chee NHL-158
77Topps-158
78North Stars Cloverleaf Dairy-7
78O-Pee-Chee-175
78Topps-175
79Panini Stickers-63
79North Stars Postcards-14
79O-Pee-Chee-93
79Topps-93
80Blackhawks Postcards-14
80North Stars Postcards-18
80O-Pee-Chee-218
80Topps-218
81Blackhawks Borderless Postcards-25
81Blackhawks Brown Background-15
81O-Pee-Chee-64
81O-Pee-Chee Stickers-116
81Topps-W76
82O-Pee-Chee-75

Sharrers, Matt
92British Columbia JHL-155

Sharron, Eric
84Richelieu Riverains-19

Sharrow, Jimmy
02Halifax Mooseheads-20
03Halifax Mooseheads-1
03Halifax Mooseheads-NNO
04Halifax Mooseheads-13

Sharuga, Matt
99Austin Ice Bats-22
02Austin Ice Bats-16

Shasby, Matt
03Columbus Cottonmouths-19
03ECHL Update RBI Sports-118
04Hamilton Bulldogs-26

Shashov, Vladimir
90O-Pee-Chee-506

Shastin, Evgeny
Red Army-6R

Shastin, Igor
00Russian Hockey League-130
00Russian Hockey League-288
01Russian Hockey League-69
02Swiss HNL-209
03Russian Hockey League-170

Shatalov, Yuri
74Russian National Team-18
91Future Trends Canada '72-29
91Future Trends Canada '72 French-29

Shattock, Tyler
06Kamloops Blazers-21

Shaunessy, Scott
88ProCards AHL-108
89ProCards IHL-124
90ProCards AHL/IHL-385
91ProCards-247
92Cincinnati Cyclones-21
93Cincinnati Cyclones-23
98Fort Worth Brahmas-4

Shaunessy, Steve
90Cincinnati Cyclones-20
91Cincinnati Cyclones-23
93Memphis RiverKings-15

Shaver, Al
93Action Packed HOF Induction-6

Shaver, Ryan
95Slapshot-427
96Barrie Colts-21

Shaw, Brad
81Ottawa 67's-21
82Ottawa 67's-23
83Ottawa 67's-26
89Whalers Junior Milk-18
90Bowman-260
Tiffany-260
90O-Pee-Chee-144
90O-Pee-Chee-279
90Panini Stickers-48
90Panini Stickers-344
90Pro Set-110
90Score-99
90Score-325
Canadian-99
Canadian-325
90Topps-144
90Topps-279
Tiffany-279
90Upper Deck-90
90Upper Deck-327
French-90
French-327
90Whalers Jr. 7-Eleven-22
91Pro Set Platinum-45
91Bowman-8
91O-Pee-Chee-442
91Panini Stickers-311
91Parkhurst-62
French-62
91Pinnacle-88
French-88
91Pro Set-87
French-87
91Score American-289
91Score Canadian Bilingual-509
91Score Canadian English-509
91Stadium Club-83
91Topps-442
91Upper Deck-297
French-297
91Whalers Jr. 7-Eleven-24
92Bowman-111
92Panini Stickers-265
92Panini Stickers French-265
92Parkhurst-352
Emerald Ice-352
92Pinnacle-372
French-372
92Pro Set-124
92Score-85
Canadian-85
92Senators Team Issue-14
92Stadium Club-65
92Topps-89
Gold-89G
92Ultra-366
92Upper Deck-109
93Donruss-234
93Kraft-35
93Kraft Recipes-8
93Kraft Recipes French-8
93Leaf-11
93Panini Stickers-120
93Pinnacle-271
Canadian-271
93PowerPlay-175
93Score-15
Canadian-15
93Senators Kraft Sheets-22
93Ultra-167
94Canada Games NHL POGS-176
94EA Sports-92
94EA Sports-203
94OPC Premier-161
Special Effects-161
94Parkhurst SE-SE122
Gold-SE122
94Pinnacle-162
Artist's Proofs-162
Rink Collection-162
94Score-76
Gold-76
Platinum-76
94Topps/OPC Premier-161
Special Effects-161
94Ultra-151
96Detroit Vipers-16
97Detroit Vipers-7
98Detroit Vipers-2
98Detroit Vipers Freschetta-11
98IHL All-Star Eastern Conference-8
02Cincinnati Mighty Ducks-B-3
03Cincinnati Mighty Ducks-B13
04Cincinnati Mighty Ducks-1

Shaw, Brian
06Erie Otters-19

Shaw, Chris
05Bossier-Shreveport Mudbugs-14

Shaw, Dave
82Kitchener Rangers-9
83Kitchener Rangers-27
84Fredericton Express-2
85Nordiques General Foods-24
85Nordiques McDonald's-19
85Nordiques Provigo-23
85Nordiques Team Issue-22
86Nordiques General Foods-23
86Nordiques McDonald's-23
86Nordiques Team Issue-21
86O-Pee-Chee-236
86O-Pee-Chee Stickers-31
86O-Pee-Chee Stickers-133
87O-Pee-Chee-252
87O-Pee-Chee Stickers-223
88O-Pee-Chee-57
88O-Pee-Chee Stickers-243
88Topps-57
89O-Pee-Chee-39
89Rangers Marine Midland Bank-21
89Topps-39
90O-Pee-Chee-403
90Pro Set-495
90Score-98
Canadian-98
90Upper Deck-15
French-15
91Bowman-64
91Oilers IGA-21
91O-Pee-Chee-306
91Panini Stickers-294
91Pinnacle-251
French-251
91Score American-161
91Score Canadian Bilingual-161
91Score Canadian English-161
91Stadium Club-306
91Topps-306
91Upper Deck-409
French-409
92Bowman-141
92Pinnacle-343
French-343
92Score-183
Canadian-183
92Stadium Club-162
92Topps-420
Gold-420G
92Ultra-256
93Leaf-249
93OPC Premier-179
Gold-179
93Pinnacle-124
Canadian-124
93Score-205
Canadian-205
93Stadium Club-229
Members Only Master Set-229
OPC-229
First Day Issue-229
First Day Issue OPC-229
93Topps/OPC Premier-179
Gold-179
94Be A Player Signature Cards-136
94Lightning Postcards-17
94OPC Premier-358
Special Effects-358
94Pinnacle-435
Artist's Proofs-435
Rink Collection-435
94Topps/OPC Premier-358
Special Effects-358
95Lightning Team Issue-17
97Pacific Invincible NHL Regime-188

Shaw, Dean
84Brandon Wheat Kings-4

Shaw, Evan
03Quebec Remparts Memorial Cup-18
03Quebec Remparts-23
04Quebec Remparts-25

Shaw, Harry
66Tulsa Oilers-10

Shaw, Jeff
01Sudbury Wolves-14
01Sudbury Wolves Police-12

Shaw, Jim
75O-Pee-Chee WHA-55

Shaw, Jordan
99Knoxville Speed-17

Shaw, Lloyd
93Seattle Thunderbirds-23
95Seattle Thunderbirds-27
96Red Deer Rebels-23
98Cincinnati Mighty Ducks-20
00Hamilton Bulldogs-19

Shaw, Matt
97Mobile Mysticks-3
97Mobile Mysticks Kellogg's-8

Shawana, Willis
93Quebec Pee-Wee Tournament-497

Shawara, Mitch
93Prince Albert Raiders-17
94Prince Albert Raiders-17
95Prince Albert Raiders-18
99San Antonio Iguanas-19

Shayakhmetov, Nail
00Russian Hockey League-248

Shea, Dan
04UK Coventry Blaze-17
04UK Coventry Blaze Champions-2
05UK Coventry Blaze-2

Shea, James
907th Inn. Sketch OHL-117
917th Inn. Sketch OHL-45

Shea, Michael
93Swedish Semic World Champ Stickers-271
94Finnish Jaa Kiekko-236
94Central Hockey League-107
95Austrian National Team-26
95Finnish Semic World Championships-185
95Swedish Globe World Championships-189

Sheahan, Brock
04Notre Dame Fighting Irish-7

Sheahan, Brodie
04Salmon Arm Silverbacks-6
05Salmon Arm Silverbacks-17

Shean, Tim
92Cornell Big Red-26
93Cornell Big Red-23

Sheane, Blake
98El Paso Buzzards-15
00Columbus Cottonmouths-19

Shearer, Danny
75Hamilton Fincups-18

Shearer, Rob
93Windsor Spitfires-14
94Windsor Spitfires-16
95Slapshot-419
98Hershey Bears-9
00Black Diamond-94
00Hershey Bears-15
01Upper Deck Victory-367
Gold-367
01Finnish Cardset-363
02German Berlin Polar Bears Postcards-25
02German DEL City Press-38
03German Berlin Polar Bears Postcards-29
03German DEL-74
04German Berlin Polar Bears Postcards-26
04German DEL-75

Sheblanov, Alexei
99Russian Hockey League-69

Shedden, Darryl
95Louisiana Ice Gators-15
95Louisiana Ice Gators Playoffs-16
96Hampton Roads Admirals-HRA8
96Louisiana Ice Gators II-17

Shedden, Doug
80Sault Ste. Marie Greyhounds-5
82Post Cereal-15
83NHL Key Tags-102
83O-Pee-Chee-285
83O-Pee-Chee Stickers-228
83Penguins Heinz Photos-20
83Topps Stickers-228
84O-Pee-Chee Stickers-120
84Penguins Heinz Photos-21
85O-Pee-Chee-247
85O-Pee-Chee Stickers-102
86Nordiques Team Issue-22
86O-Pee-Chee-153
86O-Pee-Chee Stickers-164
86Topps-153
87O-Pee-Chee-249
87O-Pee-Chee Stickers-226
88ProCards AHL-238
89ProCards AHL-125
90Maple Leafs Postcards-20
90Pro Set-542
90Newmarket Saints-23
90ProCards AHL/IHL-158
93Wichita Thunder-18
94Central Hockey League-120
95Louisiana Ice Gators-16
95Louisiana Ice Gators Playoffs-17
96Louisiana Ice Gators-22
96Louisiana Ice Gators II-22
97Louisiana Ice Gators-21
98Louisiana Ice Gators-17
01Memphis RiverKings-21

Sheehan, Bob
98Charlotte Checkers-15

Sheehan, Bobby
71O-Pee-Chee-177
71Toronto Sun-57
72O-Pee-Chee-297
73Quaker Oats WHA-20
76Topps-183
77O-Pee-Chee WHA-47
78O-Pee-Chee-311
89New Haven Nighthawks-11
98Charlotte Checkers-15

Sheehan, James
907th Inn. Sketch OHL-118
917th Inn. Sketch OHL-65
03Elmira Jackals-19

Sheehan, Kevin
90Arizona Icecats-2
90Arizona Icecats-12

Sheehan, Murray
94Detroit Jr. Red Wings-6
95Slapshot-68
95Slapshot Memorial Cup-80

Sheehy, Neil
84Moncton Golden Flames-4
85Flames Red Rooster-27
86Flames Red Rooster-26
87O-Pee-Chee-213
87O-Pee-Chee Stickers-38
87Panini Stickers-209
88Capitals Borderless-19
88Capitals Smokey-21
89Capitals Kodak-15
89Capitals Team Issue-21
90Capitals Postcards-21
90Capitals Smokey-20
90O-Pee-Chee-188
90Topps-188
Tiffany-188
91Flames IGA-19
91O-Pee-Chee-407
91Score Canadian Bilingual-636
91Score Canadian English-636
91Score Rookie/Traded-86T
91Topps-407

Sheehy, Tim
70Swedish Masterserien-91
72Whalers New England WHA-14
72Finnish Semic World Championship-128
72Swedish Semic World Championship-128
76O-Pee-Chee WHA-33

Sheen, Elliott
06Okotoks Oilers -19

Sheen, Everett
06Okotoks Oilers -20

Sheen, Kyle
03Kamloops Blazers-11

Sheenan, Gary
95Swiss HNL-486

Shefchyk, Mark
01Calgary Hitmen-22
01Calgary Hitmen Autographed-22
02Calgary Hitmen-7
03Brandon Wheat Kings-20

Shefer, Andrei
99Black Diamond-115
Diamond Cut-115
Final Cut-115
99SP Authentic-129
99Upper Deck-329
Exclusives-329
Exclusives 1 of 1-329
99Upper Deck Sobey's Memorial Cup-6
99Upper Deck Gold Reserve-329
99Upper Deck MVP SC Edition-202
Gold Script-202
Silver Script-202
Super Script-202
99UD Prospects-63
00Russian Hockey League-304
00QMJHL All-Star Program Inserts-40
02Russian Hockey League-176

Sheflo, Alec
87Kamloops Blazers-21

Shekny, Richard
02Russian Hockey League-44

Shelley, Jody
95Halifax Mooseheads-15
96Halifax Mooseheads I-18
96Halifax Mooseheads II-18
97Bowman CHL-76
OPC-76
98Johnstown Chiefs-9
99Johnstown Chiefs-18
00Syracuse Crunch-9
01BAP Memorabilia-428
Emerald-428
Ruby-428
Sapphire-428
01Crown Royale-154
01SP Authentic-142
Limited-142
Limited Gold-142
01SPx-135
01SPx-135
Rookie Treasures-RTJS
01Titanium Draft Day Edition-121
01Upper Deck-185
Exclusives-185
01Upper Deck Victory-371
Gold-371
01Syracuse Crunch-7
02Pacific-105
Blue-105
Red-105
02Topps Total-385
02Upper Deck-299
Exclusives-299
02Upper Deck Beckett UD Promos-299
02Upper Deck Vintage-76
02Upper Deck Vintage-269
03ITG Action-144
03O-Pee-Chee-284
03OPC Blue-284
03OPC Gold-284
03OPC Red-284
03Pacific Complete-387
Red-387
03SP Game Used Authentic Fabrics-DFDS
03SP Game Used Authentic Fabrics Gold-DFDS
03SP Game Used Team Threads-TTDSS
03SPx Style-SPX-DS
03SPx Style Limited-SPX-DS
03Topps-284
Blue-284
Gold-284
Red-284
Own the Game-OTG16
03Upper Deck-57
Canadian Exclusives-57
HG-57
Tough Customers-TC-1
03Upper Deck MVP-124
Gold Script-124
Silver Script-124
Canadian Exclusives-124
04Finnish Cardset-256
04Swedish Pure Skills-125
Parallel-125
05Be A Player Signatures-JD
05Be A Player Signatures Gold-JD
05Parkhurst-149
05Upper Deck-53
HG Glossy-53
05Upper Deck MVP-124
Gold-124
Platinum-124
05Upper Deck Toronto Fall Expo-53
06Be A Player-41
Autographs-41
Signatures-SH
Signatures 25-44
Signatures Duals-DMS
Signatures Duals-DSO
06Black Diamond Jerseys-JSH
06Black Diamond Jerseys Black-JSH
06Black Diamond Jerseys Gold-JSH
06Black Diamond Jerseys Ruby-JSH
06O-Pee-Chee-145
Rainbow-145
06UD Powerplay Last Man Standing-LM1
06Upper Deck-312
Exclusives Parallel-312
High Gloss Parallel-312
Game Jerseys-J2SH
Game Patches-P2SH
Masterpieces-312
06Upper Deck MVP-91
Gold Script-91
Super Script-91

Shelley, Ryan
04Maine Black Bears-26
05Maine Black Bears-23

Shelton, Doug
67Topps-53

Shemko, Mike
907th Inn. Sketch WHL-240

Shendelev, Sergei
94Finnish Jaa Kiekko-142
94German DEL-306
95Finnish Semic World Championships-127
95German DEL-107
96German DEL-52

Shenkar, Alexander
00Russian Hockey League-79

Shennan, Andrew
01Barrie Colts-12
02Barrie Colts-3
03Barrie Colts-5
04Barrie Colts-6
04Erie Otters-19

Shepard, Bradley
907th Inn. Sketch OHL-316
917th Inn. Sketch OHL-55

Shepard, Ken
91Oshawa Generals-5
93Oshawa Generals-3
96Binghamton Rangers-17
98San Antonio Iguanas-1

Shepelev, Sergei
82Swedish Semic VM Stickers-61
83Swedish Semic VM Stickers-61
84Russian National Team-16

Shepheard, Brent
04Maine Black Bears-22
05Maine Black Bears-24

Shepherd, Craig
92Tulsa Oilers-15

Shepherd, Doug
00Amarillo Rattlers-16

Shepherd, Jim
98Mobile Mysticks-20
99Austin Ice Bats-19
01Johnstown Chiefs-23
02Augusta Lynx-75
03Lubbock Cotton Kings-16

Shepley, Zack
05Plymouth Whalers-B-07
06Plymouth Whalers-20

Sheppard, Brent
91Air Canada SJHL-D40

Sheppard, Doug
00Roanoke Express-20
03Oklahoma City Blazers-19

Sheppard, Graham
04Langley Hornets-15

Sheppard, Gregg
72O-Pee-Chee-240
73O-Pee-Chee-8
73Topps-8
74Lipton Soup-29
74NHL Action Stamps-35
74O-Pee-Chee NHL-184
74Topps-184
75Heroes Stand-Ups-7
75O-Pee-Chee NHL-235
75Topps-235
76O-Pee-Chee NHL-155
76Topps-155
77O-Pee-Chee NHL-95
77Topps-95
78O-Pee-Chee-18
78Topps-18
79O-Pee-Chee-172
79Topps-172
80O-Pee-Chee-325
82Post Cereal-15

Sheppard, James
04Cape Breton Screaming Eagles-17
05ITG Heroes/Prosp Toronto Expo Parallel -143
05Cape Breton Screaming Eagles-1
05Extreme Top Prospects Signature Edition-S13
05ITG Heroes and Prospects-143
Autographs-A-JSH
Team Orr-TO16
06Cape Breton Screaming Eagles-1
06ITG Heroes and Prospects-87
Autographs-AJSH
CHL Top Prospects-TP09
CHL Top Prospects Gold-TP09
Class of 2006-CL05
Complete CHL Logos-CHL04
Jerseys-GUJ47
Jerseys Gold-GUJ47
Emblems-GUE47
Emblems Gold-GUE47
Numbers-GUN47
Numbers Gold-GUN47

Sheppard, Johnny
23V128-1 Paulin's Candy-47
24Anonymous NHL-129
33O-Pee-Chee V304A-30
33V252 Canadian Gum-42
34Diamond Matchbooks Silver-53

Sheppard, Kenzie
03Halifax Mooseheads-24
04Halifax Mooseheads-16
05Quebec Remparts-16
05Quebec Remparts Signature Series-16
06Quebec Remparts-22

Sheppard, Ray
87Sabres Blue Shield-25
87Sabres Wonder Bread/Hostess-26

88O-Pee-Chee-55
88O-Pee-Chee Minis-35
88O-Pee-Chee Stickers-126
88O-Pee-Chee Stickers-161
88O-Pee-Chee Stickers-262
88Panini Stickers-228
88Sabres Blue Shield-25
88Sabres Wonder Bread/Hostess-27
88Topps-55
89O-Pee-Chee-119
89O-Pee-Chee Stickers-259
89Panini Stickers-211
89Sabres Blue Shield-20
89Sabres Campbell's-23
89Topps-119
90O-Pee-Chee-446
90OPC Premier-106
90Pro Set-496
90Score Rookie/Traded-97T
90Upper Deck-420
French-420
91Pro Set Platinum-169
91Bowman-63
91O-Pee-Chee-289
91OPC Premier-2
91Panini Stickers-286
91Parkhurst-41
French-41
91Pinnacle-155
French-155
91Pro Set-162
91Pro Set-380
French-162
French-380
91Score American-213
91Score Canadian Bilingual-213
91Score Canadian Bilingual-586
91Score Canadian English-213
91Score Canadian English-586
91Score Rookie/Traded-36T
91Stadium Club-381
91Topps-289
91Upper Deck-390
91Upper Deck-573
French-390
French-573
92Bowman-25
92O-Pee-Chee-154
92Panini Stickers-121
92Panini Stickers French-121
92Parkhurst-280
Emerald Ice-280
92Pinnacle-119
French-119
92Pro Set-47
92Score-163
Canadian-163
Sharpshooters-20
Sharpshooters Canadian-20
92Stadium Club-85
92Topps-257
Gold-257G
92Ultra-289
92Upper Deck-296
93Donruss-105
93Leaf-44
93Panini Stickers-247
93Parkhurst-330
Emerald Ice-330
93Pinnacle-153
Canadian-153
93PowerPlay-76
93Score-83
Canadian-83
93Ultra-310
93Upper Deck-398
94Be A Player-R54
94Canada Games NHL POGS-91
94Donruss-293
94Finest-50
Super Team Winners-50
Refractors-50
94Flair-52
94Fleer-65
94Leaf-107
94Leaf Limited-26
94OPC Premier-429
Special Effects-429
94Parkhurst SE-SE49
Gold-SE49
94Pinnacle-14
Artist's Proofs-14
Rink Collection-14
94Score-175
Gold-175
Platinum-175
90 Plus Club-15
94Select-56
Gold-56
94SP-38
Die Cuts-38
94Stadium Club-40
Members Only Master Set-40
First Day Issue-40
Super Team Winner Cards-40
94Topps/OPC Premier-429
Special Effects-429
94Topps Finest Inserts-6
94Ultra-66
94Upper Deck-152
Electric Ice-152
95Be A Player-60
Signatures-S60
Signatures Die Cuts-S60
95Canada Games NHL POGS-98
95Collector's Choice-177
Player's Club-177
Player's Club Platinum-177
95Donruss-198
95Donruss-276
Marksmen-4
95Donruss Elite-102
Die Cut Stars-102
Die Cut Uncut-102
95Emotion-58
95Finest-16
Refractors-16
95Hoyle Western Playing Cards-19
95Leaf-118
95Leaf Limited-106
95Metal-134
95Panini Stickers-183
95Parkhurst International-457
Emerald Ice-457
95Playoff One on One-36
95Pro Magnets-104
95Score-127
Black Ice Artist's Proofs-127
Black Ice-127
95SkyBox Impact-152
95SP-130
95Stadium Club-215
Members Only Master Set-215
95Summit-77
Artist's Proofs-77
Ice-77
95Ultra-49
95Ultra-305
Gold Medallion-49
Red Light Specials-9
Red Light Specials Gold Medallion-9
95Upper Deck-254
95Upper Deck-348
Electric Ice-254
Electric Ice-348
Electric Ice Gold-254
Electric Ice Gold-348
Special Edition-SE161
Special Edition Gold-SE161
95Zenith-92
96Black Diamond-66
Gold-66
96Collector's Choice-111
96Donruss-210
Press Proofs-210
96Flair-38
Blue Ice-38
96Fleer-42
96Leaf-114
Press Proofs-114
96Leaf Preferred-92
Press Proofs-92
96Metal Universe-62
96NHL Pro Stamps-104
96Playoff One on One-338
96Score-112
Artist's Proofs-112
Dealer's Choice Artist's Proofs-112
Special Artist's Proofs-112
Golden Blades-112
96SkyBox Impact-48
96SP-66
96Summit-88
Artist's Proofs-88
Ice-88
Metal-88
Premium Stock-88
96Topps Picks-129
OPC Inserts-129
96Ultra-68
Gold Medallion-68
96Upper Deck-263
96Upper Deck Ice-23
Parallel-23
97Be A Player-46
Autographs-46
Autographs Die-Cuts-46
Autographs Prismatic Die-Cuts-46
97Collector's Choice-99
Crash the Game-C5A
Crash the Game-C5B
Crash the Game-C5C
Crash the Game Exchange-CR5
Star Quest-SQ60
97Donruss-101
Press Proofs Silver-101
Press Proofs Gold-101
97Donruss Canadian Ice-29
Dominion Series-29
Provincial Series-29
97Donruss Limited-141
Exposure-141
97Donruss Preferred-36
Cut to the Chase-36
97Donruss Priority-114
Stamp of Approval-114
97Katch-65
Gold-65
Silver-65
97Leaf-115
Fractal Matrix-115
Fractal Matrix Die Cuts-115
97Leaf International-115
Universal Ice-115
97Pacific-80
Copper-80
Emerald Green-80
Ice Blue-80
Red-80
Silver-80
97Pacific Dynagon-55
Copper-55
Dark Grey-55
Emerald Green-55
Ice Blue-55
Red-55
Silver-55
Tandems-52
97Pacific Invincible-63
Copper-63
Emerald Green-63
Ice Blue-63
Red-63
Silver-63
97Panini Stickers-61
97Paramount-84
Copper-84
Dark Grey-84
Emerald Green-84
Ice Blue-84
Red-84
Silver-84
97Pinnacle-164
Press Plates Back Black-164
Press Plates Back Cyan-164
Press Plates Back Magenta-164
Press Plates Back Yellow-164
Press Plates Front Black-164
Press Plates Front Cyan-164
Press Plates Front Magenta-164
Press Plates Front Yellow-164
97Pinnacle Certified-90
Red-90
Mirror Blue-90
Mirror Gold-90
Mirror Red-90
97Pinnacle Inside-139
97Pinnacle Tot Cert Platinum Blue-90
97Pinnacle Tot Certi Platinum Gold-90
97Pinnacle Totally Certified Platinum Red-90
97Pinnacle Tot Cert Mirror Platinum Gold-90
97Score-121
Artist's Proofs-121
Golden Blades-121
97Upper Deck-280
98Hurricanes Team Issue-17
98Katch-28
98Pacific Omega-47
Red-47
Opening Day Issue-47
98Revolution-27
Ice Shadow-27
Red-27
98Upper Deck-240
Exclusives-240
Exclusives 1 of 1-240
Gold Reserve-240
99Aurora-29
Premiere Date-29
99O-Pee-Chee-243
99O-Pee-Chee Chrome-243
99O-Pee-Chee Chrome Refractors-243
99Pacific-81
Copper-81
Emerald Green-81
Gold-81
Ice Blue-81
Premiere Date-81
Red-81
99Topps/OPC-243
99Topps/OPC Chrome-243
Refractors-243
99Upper Deck MVP SC Edition-83
Gold Script-83
Silver Script-83
Super Script-83

Sheppard, Scott
00Kitchener Rangers-23
01Kingston Frontenacs-16
02Ottawa 67's-11
03London Knights-12
05Bossier-Shreveport Mudbugs-15

Sheptak, Curtis
00Finnish Cardset-224
01Finnish Cardset-149
02German DEL City Press-293
04Fresno Falcons-15

Sherban, Trevor
89Saskatoon Blades-8
90Saskatoon Blades-6
907th Inn. Sketch WHL-85
917th Inn. Sketch WHL-297
94Tampa Bay Tritons RHI-10
95Oklahoma Coyotes RHI-14
98Kansas City Blades-4
99Missouri River Otters-19
99Missouri River Otters Sheet-17
00Missouri River Otters-7

Sherdahl, Quinn
97Swift Current Broncos-18
98Swift Current Broncos-3

Sherevtsov, Sergei
00Russian Hockey League-184

Sherf, John
34Beehive Group I Photos-121

Sheridan, John
75O-Pee-Chee WHA-107

Shermerhorn, Dan
92British Columbia JHL-193
92British Columbia JHL-206
93Maine Black Bears-48
97Las Vegas Thunder-20
98Baton Rouge Kingfish-17
00Idaho Steelheads-19
01Idaho Steelheads-15

Shero, Fred
44Beehive Group II Photos-362
51Cleveland Barons-2
74O-Pee-Chee NHL-21
74Topps-21
92Parkhurst-480
Emerald Ice-480
04ITG Franchises US East-407
04ITG Ultimate Memorabilia-177
Gold-177
Paper Cuts-20

Sherry, Simon
93Sudbury Wolves-19
93Sudbury Wolves Police-18
94Sudbury Wolves-19
94Sudbury Wolves Police-16
95Slapshot-401
95Sudbury Wolves-7
95Sudbury Wolves Police-20

Sherstenka, Dan
907th Inn. Sketch WHL-115
917th Inn. Sketch WHL-183

Sherven, Gord
83Canadian National Juniors-13
84North Stars Postcards-26
85North Stars Postcards-27
85Oilers Red Rooster-8
88Oilers Tenth Anniversary-12
94German DEL-302
95German DEL-89
96German DEL-278
98German DEL-295
99German DEL-248

Shevalier, Jeff
917th Inn. Sketch OHL-68
93North Bay Centennials-20
95Phoenix Roadrunners-14
97Collector's Choice-127
97Pacific Invincible NHL Regime-98
97Springfield Falcons-20
98Cincinnati Cyclones-19
98Cincinnati Cyclones 2-11
99Detroit Vipers-6
99Quebec Citadelles-21
01Idaho Steelheads-16

Shevchenko, Alexander
02Windsor Spitfires-21

Sheviev, Maxim
01Russian Young Lions-11
03Russian Hockey League-101
03Russian Young Lions-4

Shevtsov, Igor
00Russian Hockey League-100

Shevtsov, Oleg
00Russian Dynamo Moscow-2
00Russian Goalkeepers-5
00Russian Hockey League-322

Shewan, Mike
03UK Coventry Blaze History-17

Shewchuk, Jack
34Beehive Group I Photos-32

Shibicky, Alex
34Beehive Group I Photos-293
36O-Pee-Chee V304D-109
37V356 Worldwide Gum-90
39O-Pee-Chee V301-1-88
74Sioux City Musketeers-18
05ITG Ultimate Mem Broadway Bluesh Autos-3
06ITG Ultimate Memorabilia Broadway Blue Shirts
Autos-5

Shick, Rob
90Pro Set-698

Shields, Allan
33V357-2 Ice Kings Premiums-5
34Beehive Group I Photos-250
35O-Pee-Chee V304C-89
37O-Pee-Chee V304E-162
37V356 Worldwide Gum-60

Shields, Colin
04Atlantic City Boardwalk Bullies-5

Shields, Jordan
96Dayton Bombers-4
97New Mexico Scorpions-13

Shields, Kelly
03Fort Wayne Komets-20

Shields, Steve
91Michigan Wolverines-16
93Michigan Wolverines-21
94Classic-62
Gold-62
Tri-Cards-T7
95Rochester Americans-18
96Rochester Americans-17
97Be A Player-233
Autographs-233
Autographs Die-Cuts-233
Autographs Prismatic Die-Cuts-233
97Donruss-51
Press Proofs Silver-51
Press Proofs Gold-51
97Donruss Canadian Ice-132
Dominion Series-132
Provincial Series-132
Stanley Cup Scrapbook-12
97Donruss Limited-23
97Donruss Limited-63
Exposure-23
Exposure-63
97Donruss Preferred-80
Cut to the Chase-80
97Donruss Priority-115
Stamp of Approval-115
97Leaf-86
Fractal Matrix-86
Fractal Matrix Die Cuts-86
97Leaf International-86
Universal Ice-86
97Pacific Invincible NHL Regime-22
97Pacific Omega-27
Copper-27
Dark Gray-27
Emerald Green-27
Gold-27
Ice Blue-27
97Pinnacle-97
Artist's Proofs-97
Rink Collection-97
Press Plates Back Black-97
Press Plates Back Cyan-97
Press Plates Back Magenta-97
Press Plates Back Yellow-97
Press Plates Front Black-97
Press Plates Front Cyan-97
Press Plates Front Magenta-97
Press Plates Front Yellow-97
97Pinnacle Certified-7
Red-7
Mirror Blue-7
Mirror Gold-7
Mirror Red-7
97Pinnacle Inside-77
Coach's Collection-77
Executive Collection-77
Stoppers-19
97Pinnacle Tot Cert Platinum Blue-7
97Pinnacle Tot Certi Platinum Gold-7
97Pinnacle Totally Certified Platinum Red-7
97Pinnacle Tot Cert Mirror Platinum Gold-7
97Score-44
Artist's Proofs-44
Golden Blades-44
97Score Sabres-2
Platinum-2
Premier-2
97Studio-79
Press Proofs Silver-79
Press Proofs Gold-79
97Upper Deck-18
98Be A Player-269
Press Release-269
98BAP Gold-269
98BAP Autographs-269
98BAP Autographs Gold-269
98NHL Aces Playing Cards-44
98Pacific-110
Ice Blue-110
Red-110
98Pacific Omega-214
Red-214
Opening Day Issue-214
99Aurora-122
Premiere Date-122
Glove Unlimited-18
99BAP Memorabilia-288
Gold-288
Silver-288
99BAP Millennium-213
Emerald-213
Ruby-213
Sapphire-213
Signatures-213
Signatures Gold-213
99Black Diamond-77
Diamond Cut-77
Final Cut-77
99Crown Royale-126
Limited Series-126
Premiere Date-126
99Pacific-381
Copper-381
Emerald Green-381
Gold-381
Ice Blue-381
Premiere Date-381
Red-381
99Pacific Dynagon Ice-175
Blue-175
Copper-175
Gold-175
Premiere Date-175
99Pacific Omega-210
Copper-210
Gold-210
Ice Blue-210
Premiere Date-210
99Pacific Prism-127
Holographic Blue-127
Holographic Gold-127
Holographic Mirror-127
Holographic Purple-127
Premiere Date-127
99Paramount-209
Copper-209
Emerald-209
Gold-209
Holographic Emerald-209
Holographic Gold-209
Holographic Silver-209
Ice Blue-209
Premiere Date-209
Red-209
Silver-209
99Revolution-129
Premiere Date-129
Red-129
Shadow Series-129
99SP Authentic-72
99Stadium Club-137
First Day Issue-137
One of a Kind-137
Printing Plates Black-137
Printing Plates Cyan-137
Printing Plates Magenta-137
Printing Plates Yellow-137
99Ultimate Victory-73
1/1-73
Parallel-73
Parallel 100-73
Net Work-NW7
99Upper Deck-278
Exclusives-278
Exclusives 1 of 1-278
99Upper Deck Gold Reserve-278
99Upper Deck MVP SC Edition-155
Gold Script-155
Silver Script-155
Super Script-155
Stanley Cup Talent-SC17
99Upper Deck Ovation-52
Standing Ovation-52
99Upper Deck Victory-256
99Wayne Gretzky Hockey-150
00Aurora-130
Premiere Date-130
00BAP Memorabilia-182
Emerald-182
Ruby-182
Sapphire-182
Promos-182
00BAP Mem Chicago Sportsfest Copper-182
00BAP Memorabilia Chicago Sportsfest Blue-182
00BAP Memorabilia Chicago Sportsfest Gold-182
00BAP Memorabilia Chicago Sportsfest Ruby-182
00BAP Memorabilia Chicago Sun-Times Ruby-182
00BAP Memorabilia Chicago Sun-Times Gold-182
00BAP Mem Chicago Sun-Times Sapphire-182
00BAP Mem Toronto Fall Expo Copper-182
00BAP Memorabilia Toronto Fall Expo Gold-182
00BAP Memorabilia Toronto Fall Expo Ruby-182
00BAP Parkhurst 2000-P150
00BAP Signature Series-250
Emerald-250
Ruby-250
Sapphire-250
00BAP Ultimate Memorabilia Goalie Sticks-G26
00Black Diamond-49
Gold-49
Game Gear-LSS
00Crown Royale-95
Ice Blue-95
Limited Series-95
Premiere Date-95
Red-95
00O-Pee-Chee-161
00O-Pee-Chee Parallel-161
00Pacific-365
Copper-365
Gold-365
Ice Blue-365
Premiere Date-365
00Paramount-217
Copper-217
Gold-217
Holo-Gold-217
Holo-Silver-217
Ice Blue-217
Premiere Date-217
Glove Side Net Fusions-17
Glove Side Net Fusions Platinum-17
00Revolution-131
Blue-131
Premiere Date-131
Red-131
00SP Authentic BuyBacks-95
00SP Authentic Sign of the Times-SS
00SP Game Used-50
00SPx-57
Spectrum-57
00Stadium Club-68
00Titanium-87
Blue-87
Gold-87
Premiere Date-87
Red-87
Retail-87
00Topps/OPC-161
Parallel-161
Own the Game-OTG20
00Topps Chrome-112
OPC Refractors-112
Refractors-112
00UD Heroes-99
00Upper Deck-148
Exclusives Tier 1-148
Exclusives Tier 2-148
00Upper Deck Ice-33
Immortals-33
Legends-33
Stars-33
00Upper Deck Legends-111
Legendary Collection Bronze-111
Legendary Collection Gold-111
Legendary Collection Silver-111
00Upper Deck MVP-151
First Stars-151
Masked Men-MM7
Second Stars-151
Third Stars-151
00Upper Deck Victory-198
00Upper Deck Vintage-306
00Upper Deck Vintage-307
00Upper Deck Vintage-308
Great Gloves-GG15
01Atomic-2
Blue-2
Gold-2
Premiere Date-2
Red-2
01BAP Signature Series-173
Autographs-173
Autographs Gold-173
01Between the Pipes-52
He Shoots-He Saves Prizes-29
Jerseys-GJ35
Jersey and Stick Cards-GSJ33
Masks-8
Masks Silver-8
Masks Gold-8
Tandems-GT6
01Pacific-11
Extreme LTD-11
Hobby LTD-11
Premiere Date-11
Retail LTD-11
97-98 Subset-355
97-98 Subset Gold Parallel-355
Steel Curtain-1
01Pacific Adrenaline-5
Blue-5
Premiere Date-5
Red-5
Retail-5
Power Play-2
01Pacific Arena Exclusives-11
01Pacific Heads-Up-2
Blue-2
Premiere Date-2
Red-2
Silver-2
Showstoppers-1
01Private Stock PS-2002-2
01UD Playmakers-1
01UD Top Shelf Goalie Gear-LPSS
01Upper Deck-233
Exclusives-233
02BAP First Edition-91
Jerseys-91
02BAP Memorabilia-57
Emerald-57
Ruby-57
Sapphire-57
NHL All-Star Game-57
NHL All-Star Game Blue-57
NHL All-Star Game Green-57
NHL All-Star Game Red-57
02BAP Memorabilia Toronto Fall Expo-57
02BAP Signature Series-73
Autographs-73
Autograph Buybacks 1998-269
Autograph Buybacks 1999-213
Autograph Buybacks 2001-173
Autographs Gold-73
Jerseys-SGJ51
Jersey Autographs-SGJ51
Team Quads-TQ11
02Between the Pipes-52
02Between the Pipes-123
Gold-52
Silver-52
Behind the Mask-20
Goalie Autographs-21
Jerseys-37
Masks II-3
Masks II Gold-3
Masks II Silver-3
Pads-12
Tandems-17
02Crown Royale-8
Blue-8
Red-8
Retail-8
02Pacific-8
Blue-8
Red-8
02Pacific Complete-481
Red-481
02Pacific Exclusive-14
02Parkhurst-144
Bronze-144
Gold-144
Silver-144
02Private Stock Reserve-9
Blue-9
Red-9
Retail-9
02SP Authentic-8
Beckett Promos-8
02SP Game Used Authentic Fabrics-AFSH
02SP Game Used Authentic Fabrics Gold-AFSH
02SP Game Used Authentic Fabrics Rainbow-AFSH
02SP Game Used Tools of the Game-SH
02Titanium-9
Blue-9
Red-9
Retail-9
02Topps Heritage-176
02Topps Total-292
02UD Mask Collection-9
02UD Mask Collection-100
02UD Mask Collection Beckett Promos-9
02UD Top Shelf Stopper Jerseys-SSSS
02Upper Deck-258
Exclusives-258
02Upper Deck Beckett UD Promos-258
02Upper Deck Goaltender Threads-SS
02Upper Deck Goaltender Threads Gold-SS
02Vanguard-9
LTD-9
03BAP Memorabilia-165
Emerald-165
Gold-165
Ruby-165
Sapphire-165
Deep in the Crease-D14
03Beehive-83
Gold-83
Silver-83
03Bowman-104
Gold-104
03Bowman Chrome-104
Refractors-104
Gold Refractors-104
Xfractors-104
03ITG Action-92
03NHL Sticker Collection-20
03O-Pee-Chee-64
03OPC Blue-64
03OPC Gold-64
03OPC Red-64
03Pacific-31
Blue-31
Red-31
03Pacific Complete-472
Red-472
03Pacific Prism-12
Blue-12
Gold-12
Red-12
03Parkhurst Orig Six Boston Mem -BM9
03Parkhurst Orig Six Boston Mem -BM18
03SP Game Used Game Gear-GGSS
03Topps-64
Blue-64
Gold-64
Red-64
03Topps Pristine-3
Gold Refractor Die Cuts-3
Refractors-3
Press Plates Black-3
Press Plates Cyan-3
Press Plates Magenta-3
Press Plates Yellow-3
03Topps Traded-TT65
Blue-TT65
Gold-TT65
Red-TT65
03Upper Deck-20
03Upper Deck-329
Canadian Exclusives-20
Canadian Exclusives-329
HG-20
HG-329
UD Exclusives-329
03Upper Deck MVP-50
Gold Script-50
Silver Script-50
Canadian Exclusives-50
03Upper Deck Victory-18
Bronze-18
Gold-18
Silver-18
05Be A Player Signatures-SI
05Be A Player Signatures Gold-SI
05Upper Deck-255

Shier, Andrew
94Richmond Renegades-1
94Classic-44
Gold-44
95Milwaukee Admirals-16
95Milwaukee Admirals Postcards-14
96Richmond Renegades-21

Shier, Luke
04Langley Hornets-16

Shierreffs, Steve
00Finnish Cardset-294
03Finnish Cardset-170

Shikhanov, Sergei
00Russian Hockey League-150
01Russian Hockey League-47

Shill, Aaron
93Quebec Pee-Wee Tournament-548

Shill, Jack
34Beehive Group I Photos-347
36O-Pee-Chee V304D-99
37V356 Worldwide Gum-39

Shilov, Sergei
99Russian Hockey League-58

Shilov, Valeri
98Danish Hockey League-70

Shilton, Rob
01Sudbury Wolves-15
01Sudbury Wolves Police-14

Shim, Kyuin
92Northern Michigan Wildcats-23
95Central Hockey League-71

Shimkovski, Sergei
98Russian Hockey League-138

Shine, Jordan
04Barrie Colts-22
06London Knights-16

Shinin, Alexander
02Russian Hockey League-170
02Russian Hockey League-180

Shinkar, Alexander
02Russian Hockey League-174

Shinkar, Sergei
03Russian Hockey League-279

Shinske, Rick
78Blues Postcards-19

Shipley, Blake
92Saskatchewan JHL-41

Shipley, Bruce
75HCA Steel City Vacuum-12

Shipulin, Roman
98Russian Hockey League-66

Shipulski, Jay
98New Hampshire Wildcats-14
00Roanoke Express-19

Shires, Jim
71Blues Postcards-22
71Toronto Sun-248

Shirjaev, Valeri
89Russian National Team-22
89Swedish Semic World Champ Stickers-84
90O-Pee-Chee Red Army-13R
91O-Pee-Chee Inserts-59R
93Swiss HNL-497
95Swiss HNL-377
96Swiss HNL-109
98Swiss Power Play Stickers-303
99Russian Fetisov Tribute-32
99Swiss Panini Stickers-310
00Swiss Panini Stickers-61
00Swiss Slapshot Mini-Cards-HCCF4
01Swiss HNL-288
02Swiss HNL-354

Shirokov, Sergei
04Russian Under-18 Team-8

Shirreffs, Steve
99Portland Pirates-20
02Finnish Cardset-268
02Reading Royals-26

Shiryaev, Dennis
99Corpus Christi IceRays-20
99Fort Worth Brahmas-18
01Louisiana Ice Gators-19
02Louisiana Ice Gators-18
03Louisiana Ice Gators-19
04Bakersfield Condors-17
05Bakersfield Condors-11

Shishkanov, Timofei
99Russian Hockey League-242
02Russian Hockey League-187
02Russian Hockey League-249
02Quebec Remparts-9
03Beehive-208
Gold-208
Silver-208
03ITG Action-651
03ITG Used Signature Series-163
Gold-163
03ITG VIP Rookie Debut-90
03Pacific Calder-123
Silver-123
03Pacific Complete-521
Red-521
03Parkhurst Rookie-171
03SP Authentic-163
03UD Premier Collection-63
03Upper Deck Classic Portraits-190
03Upper Deck Rookie Update-114
03Upper Deck Trilogy-187
03Milwaukee Admirals-12
03Milwaukee Admirals Postcards-19
03Pacific AHL Prospects-59
Gold-59
03Quebec Remparts Memorial Cup-19
04Pacific-287
Blue-287
Red-287
04AHL Top Prospects-33
04Milwaukee Admirals-27
04ITG Heroes and Prospects-12
Autographs-TS
Emblems-42
Emblems Gold-42
He Shoots-He Scores Prizes-20
Jersey Autographs-42
Jerseys-42
Jerseys Gold-42
Numbers-42
Numbers Gold-42
04ITG Heroes/Prospects Toronto Expo '05-12
04ITG Heroes/Prospects Expo Heroes/Pros-12
05Black Diamond Gemography-G-TS
05Black Diamond Gemography Emerald-G-TS
05Black Diamond Gemography Gold-G-TS
05Black Diamond Gemography Onyx-G-TS
05Black Diamond Gemography Ruby-G-TS
05Parkhurst Signatures-TS
05SP Game Used Auto Draft-AD-TS
05Ultra Fresh Ink-FI-TS
05Ultra Fresh Ink Blue-FI-TS
05Milwaukee Admirals Choice-14

Shishkovich, Alexanders
99Danish Hockey League-90

Shitikov, Dmitri
02Russian Future Stars-13
03Russian Under-18 Team-22
04Russian Under-18 Team-5
05Russian Hockey League RHL-10

Shitkovski, Sergei
99Russian Hockey League-146
00Russian Hockey League-384

Shkotov, Alexei
02Russian SL-51
03Quebec Remparts-24
04Russian World Junior Team-5
04Worcester IceCats-15
05Russian Hockey League RHL-16

Shmyr, Dean
91British Columbia JHL-127
92Dallas Freeze-15
93Dallas Freeze-14
94Central Hockey League-86
94San Antonio Iguanas-14
99Greensboro Generals-11
00Knoxville Speed-9
03Greensboro Generals-190

Shmyr, Jason
97Anchorage Aces-18
99Portland Pirates-21
00Portland Pirates-19
02Manitoba Moose-26

Shmyr, Paul
70Blackhawks Postcards-13
71O-Pee-Chee-6
71Sargent Promotions Stamps-140
71Toronto Sun-58
72Cleveland Crusaders WHA-13
75O-Pee-Chee WHA-5
76O-Pee-Chee WHA-69
76San Diego Mariners WHA-12
77O-Pee-Chee WHA-59
79North Stars Postcards-15
80North Stars Postcards-19
80O-Pee-Chee-66
80Topps-66
82Post Cereal-7

Shmyr, Ryan
00Lubbock Cotton Kings-12
06UK Nottingham Panthers-15

Shmyrko, Gord
82Medicine Hat Tigers-18
83Medicine Hat Tigers-22

Shoaf, Trevor
93Spokane Chiefs-23
01BC Icemen-22

Shockey, John
95Spokane Chiefs-24
98Idaho Steelheads-17
00Cleveland Lumberjacks-14
00Jackson Bandits-6
02Reading Royals-10
03Las Vegas Wranglers-17
03Las Vegas Wranglers RBI-239

Shockey, Parry
96Lethbridge Hurricanes-19

Shoebottom, Bruce
88ProCards AHL-166
89ProCards AHL-63
90Pro Set-411
90ProCards AHL/IHL-130
91ProCards-36
92Rochester Americans Dunkin' Donuts-15
92Rochester Americans Kodak-20
93Oklahoma City Blazers-14

Shold, Terry
85Minnesota-Duluth Bulldogs-2

Sholl, Brad
94Los Angeles Blades RHI-12

Shore, Eddie
27La Presse Photos-17
33Sport Kings R338 *-19
33O-Pee-Chee V304A-3
33Sport Kings R338 *-19
33V129-37
34Beehive Group I Photos-33
34Diamond Matchbooks Silver-54
34Sweet Caporal-29
36O-Pee-Chee V304D-118
36Triumph Postcards-8
37V356 Worldwide Gum-5
38Bruins Garden Magazine Supplement-7
39O-Pee-Chee V301-1-100
60Topps-20
83Hall of Fame-223
83Hall of Fame Postcards-O14
85Hall of Fame-223
91Bruins Sports Action Legends-30
94Parkhurst Missing Link Pop-Ups-P7
99Upper Deck Century Legends-10
Century Collection-10
All Century Team-AC10
99Upper Deck Retro-88
Gold-88
Platinum-88
Generation-G4A
Generation Level 2-G4A
00Upper Deck Legends-10
Legendary Collection Bronze-10
Legendary Collection Gold-10
Legendary Collection Silver-10
01Upper Deck Legendary Cut Signatures-LCES
01Upper Deck Legends-2
02BAP Ultimate Memorabilia Gloves Are Off-10
02BAP Ultimate Memorabilia Great Moments-2
02BAP Ultimate Mem Vintage Hat Tricks-1
02ITG Used Vintage Memorabilia-VM10
02ITG Used Vintage Memorabilia Gold-VM10
02Parkhurst Vintage Teammates-VT19
03BAP Memorabilia Gloves-GUG20
03BAP Memorabilia Vintage Memorabilia-VM-16
03BAP Ultimate Memorabilia Cornerstones-5
03BAP Ultimate Memorabilia Gloves Are Off-20
03BAP Ultimate Memorabilia Paper Cuts-39
03BAP Ultimate Mem Raised to the Rafters-20
03BAP Ultimate Mem Retro Teammates-10
03BAP Ultimate Mem Retro-Active Trophies-8
03BAP Ultimate Mem Vintage Blade of Steel-11
03BAP Ultimate Mem Vintage Hat Tricks-4
03Canada Post-9
03ITG Used Sig Series Triple Mem-5
03ITG Used Sig Series Triple Mem Gold-5
03ITG Used Sig Series Vintage Mem -24
03ITG Used Sig Series Vintage Mem Gold-24
03ITG VIP MVP-3
03Parkhurst Original Six Boston-47
03Parkhurst Original Six Boston-63

03Parkhurst Original Six Boston-89
Inserts-B1
Inserts-B7
Memorabilia-BM24
Memorabilia-BM25
Memorabilia-BM39
03Parkhurst Orig Six He Shoots/Scores-16
03Parkhurst Orig Six He Shoots/Scores-16A
04ITG Franchises US East-323
Double Memorabilia-EDM1
Double Memorabilia Gold-EDM1
Memorabilia-ESM1
Memorabilia Gold-ESM1
Teammates-ETM1
Teammates Gold-ETM1
Triple Memorabilia-ETM3
Triple Memorabilia Gold-ETM3
Trophy Winners-ETW1
Trophy Winners Gold-ETW1
04ITG Ultimate Memorabilia-83
Gold-83
Beantown's Best-6
Blades of Steel-7
Changing the Game-11
Cornerstones-5
Cornerstones Gold-5
Original Six-4
Original Six-20
Paper Cuts-12
Paper Cuts Memorabilia-4
Retro Teammates-7
05ITG Ultimate Memorabilia Level 1-31
05ITG Ultimate Memorabilia Level 2-31
05ITG Ultimate Memorabilia Level 3-31
05ITG Ultimate Memorabilia Level 4-31
05ITG Ultimate Memorabilia Level 5-31
05ITG Ultimate Mem Beantown's Best Autos-2
05ITG Ultimate Mem Blades of Steel-13
05ITG Ultimate Mem Blades of Steel Gold-13
05ITG Ultimate Mem Complete Package-5
05ITG Ultimate Mem Complete Package Gold-5
05ITG Ultimate Mem Cornerstones Jerseys-2
05ITG Ultimate Mem Cornerst Jerseys Gold-2
05ITG Ultimate Mem Decades Jerseys-1
05ITG Ultimate Mem Decades Jerseys-4
05ITG Ultimate Mem Decades Jerseys Gold-1
05ITG Ultimate Mem Decades Jerseys Gold-4
05ITG Ultimate Mem Double Mem-19
05ITG Ultimate Mem Double Mem Gold-19
05ITG Ultimate Memorabilia Gloves Are Off-18
05ITG Ultimate Mem Gloves Are Off Gold-18
05ITG Ultimate Mem Pass the Torch Jerseys-6
05ITG Ultimate Mem Passing Torch Jsy Gold-6
05ITG Ultimate Mem Retro Teammate Jerseys-2
05ITG Ult Mem Retro Teammates Jersey Gold-2
05ITG Ultimate Mem 3 Star of the Game Jsy-1
05ITG Ult Mem 3 Star of the Game Jsy Gold-1
05The Cup Legendary Cuts-LCES
05ITG Heroes and Prospects Hero Mem-HM-30
06ITG Ultimate Memorabilia-46
Artist Proof-46
Beantown's Best Autos-3
Blades of Steel-9
Blades of Steel Gold-9
Complete Package-6
Complete Package Gold-6
Cornerstones-7
Cornerstones Gold-7
Decades-7
Decades Gold-7
Double Memorabilia-29
Double Memorabilia Gold-29
Gloves Are Off-9
Gloves Are Off Gold-9
Passing The Torch-6
Passing The Torch Gold-6
Retro Teammates-2
Retro Teammates Gold-2

Shore, Hamby
10Sweet Caporal Postcards-12
11C55-12
12C57-30

Shorkey, Andrew
06Owen Sound Attack-5

Short, Kayle
907th Inn. Sketch OHL-215
917th Inn. Sketch OHL-349
92Sudbury Wolves-19
93Guelph Storm-4
97Hampton Roads Admirals-18
97Portland Pirates-21
99UK Sheffield Steelers-16
00UK Sekonda Superleague-147
00UK Sheffield Steelers-21
00UK Sheffield Steelers Centurions-12
01UK Manchester Storm-15
02Fresno Falcons-19
03Las Vegas Wranglers-18

Short, Steve
83Brantford Alexanders-16

Shotkov, Alexei
02Russian Hockey League-114

Shouneyia, John
02Michigan Wolverines-12

Showalter, Chris
94Dubuque Fighting Saints-26

Shpakovski, Dmitri
98Russian Hockey League-67

Shrieves, Aaron
03Cape Fear Fire Antz-14

Shrum, Steve
96Kamloops Blazers-23
98Kamloops Blazers-21
99Kamloops Blazers-21
06Odessa Jackalopes-17

Shtaiger, Evgeny
03Russian Hockey League-195

Shtalenkov, Mikhail
91O-Pee-Chee Inserts-43R
91Finnish Semic World Champ Stickers-79
91Swedish Semic World Champ Stickers-79
92Finnish Semic-100
92Russian Stars Red Ace-19
93Classic-148
93Classic Pro Prospects-94
93Classic Four-Sport *-219
Gold-219
94Donruss-314
94Ducks Carl's Jr.-22
94Fleer-7
94Leaf-209
94OPC Premier-3
Special Effects-3
94Parkhurst-4
Gold-4
94Pinnacle-331
Artist's Proofs-331
Rink Collection-331
94Topps/OPC Premier-3
Special Effects-3
94Ultra-252
94Upper Deck-462
Electric Ice-462
94Classic Pro Prospects-49
95Be A Player-69
Signatures-S69
Signatures Die Cuts-S69
95Collector's Choice-227
Player's Club-227
Player's Club Platinum-227
95Ducks Team Issue-4
95Parkhurst International-6
Emerald Ice-6
95Pinnacle-145
Artist's Proofs-145
Rink Collection-145
95Topps-344
OPC Inserts-344
95Upper Deck-91
Electric Ice-91
Electric Ice Gold-91
95Finnish Semic World Championships-121
95Finnish Semic World Championships-211
95Swedish Globe World Championships-164
95Swedish World Championships Stickers-27
96Collector's Choice-4
96Ducks Team Issue-1
96Upper Deck-7
97Be A Player-66
Autographs-66
Autographs Die-Cuts-66
Autographs Prismatic Die-Cuts-66
97Pacific Invincible NHL Regime-8
97Pacific Omega-8
Copper-8
Dark Gray-8
Emerald Green-8
Gold-8
Ice Blue-8
97Score-21
Artist's Proofs-21
Golden Blades-21
97Score Mighty Ducks-16
Platinum-16
Premier-16
98Aurora-104
98Be A Player-204
Press Release-204
98BAP Gold-204
98BAP Autographs-204
98BAP Autographs Gold-204
98NHL Aces Playing Cards-22
98Pacific-65
Ice Blue-65
Red-65
98Pacific Omega-95
Red-95
Opening Day Issue-95
98Paramount-127
Copper-127
Emerald Green-127
Holo-Electric-127
Ice Blue-127
Silver-127
98Revolution-56
Ice Shadow-56
Red-56
98UD Choice-2
Prime Choice Reserve-2
Reserve-2
98Slovakian Eurotel-24
99Pacific-326
Copper-326
Emerald Green-326
Gold-326
Ice Blue-326
Premiere Date-326
Red-326
99Pacific Dynagon Ice-154
Blue-154
Copper-154
Gold-154
Premiere Date-154
99Pacific Omega-100
Copper-100
Gold-100
Ice Blue-100
Premiere Date-100
00Pacific-186
Copper-186
Gold-186
Ice Blue-186
Premiere Date-186
00Russian Dynamo Moscow-4
00Russian Dynamo Moscow Blue-White-1
00Russian Goalkeepers-2
00Russian Hockey League-317
01Russian Dynamo Moscow-17
01Russian Dynamo Moscow Mentos-6
02BAP Sig Series Auto Buybacks 1998-204

Shtepa, Evgeny
99Russian Stars Postcards-22

Shuchuk, Gary
91Score American-315
91Score Canadian Bilingual-345
91Score Canadian English-345
91Upper Deck-376
French-376
92Parkhurst-484
Emerald Ice-484
93Donruss-157
93Leaf-222
93OPC Premier-499
Gold-499
93Parkhurst-95
Emerald Ice-95
93Stadium Club-351
Members Only Master Set-351
First Day Issue-351
93Topps/OPC Premier-499
Gold-499
93Ultra-12
Prospects-9
93Upper Deck-13
94Be A Player Signature Cards-36
94Parkhurst SE-SE85
Gold-SE85
94Stadium Club-47
Members Only Master Set-47
First Day Issue-47
Super Team Winner Cards-47
95Phoenix Roadrunners-15
00German DEL-44
01German Upper Deck-163
02German DEL City Press-232
03Springfield Falcons Postcards-15

Shudo, Chris
03Salmon Arm Silverbacks-17

Shudra, Ron
85Kamloops Blazers-22
86Kamloops Blazers-20
88Oilers Tenth Anniversary-11
88ProCards AHL-91
89ProCards IHL-128
93UK Sheffield Steelers-14
94UK Sheffield Steelers-15
95UK Sheffield Steelers-2
97UK Sheffield Steelers-19
99UK Hull Thunder-14
00UK Sheffield Steelers Centurions-5
00UK Sheffield Steelers Centurions-18
01UK Sheffield Steelers-19
02UK Coventry Blaze-9
03UK Coventry Blaze History-18
03UK Sheffield Steelers-21
03UK Sheffield Steelers Stickers-9
04UK Ron Shudra Testimonial-1
04UK Ron Shudra Testimonial-2
04UK Ron Shudra Testimonial-3
04UK Ron Shudra Testimonial-4
04UK Ron Shudra Testimonial-5
04UK Ron Shudra Testimonial-6
04UK Ron Shudra Testimonial-7
04UK Ron Shudra Testimonial-8
04UK Ron Shudra Testimonial-9
04UK Ron Shudra Testimonial-10
04UK Ron Shudra Testimonial-11
04UK Ron Shudra Testimonial-12
04UK Ron Shudra Testimonial-13
04UK Ron Shudra Testimonial-14
04UK Ron Shudra Testimonial-15
04UK Ron Shudra Testimonial-16
04UK Sheffield Steelers-6
05UK Sheffield Steelers-3
Gold-3
Silver-3

Shukaev, Mikhail
00Russian Hockey League-131
03Russian Hockey League-265
03Russian SL-31

Shulakov, Dmitri
98Russian Hockey League-68
99Russian Hockey League-115
00Russian Hockey League-23

Shulakov, Vitali
03Russian Hockey League-18

Shulga, Dmitri
00Russian Hockey League-215

Shulmistra, Richard
94Classic-31
Gold-31
96Albany River Rats-15
98IHL All-Star Western Conference-1
98Manitoba Moose-D5
99Louisville Panthers-18
01German Berlin Polar Bears Postcards-23
01German Upper Deck-43
Jersey Cards-RS-J
02German Berlin Polar Bears Postcards-26
02German DEL City Press-39
03German DEL-14
03German Mannheim Eagles Postcards-1

Shultz, Tanner
02Saskatoon Blades-24
03Saskatoon Blades-20

Shumykin, Sergei
00Russian Hockey League-342

Shupe, Jack
81Victoria Cougars-14

Shurupov, Andrei
95Slapshot-54
03Russian Hockey League-92

Shute, Dave
907th Inn. Sketch WHL-35
91Knoxville Cherokees-10
93Raleigh Icecaps-18
95Central Hockey League-103

Shutron, Ben
04Kingston Frontenacs-18
05ITG Heroes/Prosp Toronto Expo Parallel -399
05Kingston Frontenacs-3
05ITG Heroes and Prospects-399
Autographs Update-A-BSH
Team Orr-TO17
06Kingston Frontenacs-16
06ITG Heroes and Prospects-184
Autographs-ABSH
CHL Top Prospects-TP01
CHL Top Prospects Gold-TP01
Jerseys-GUJ44
Jerseys Gold-GUJ44
Emblems-GUE44
Emblems Gold-GUE44
Numbers-GUN44
Numbers Gold-GUN44
Update Autographs-ABSH

Shutt, Steve
72Canadiens Postcards-20
72Canadiens Great West Life Prints-6
72Dimanche/Derniere Heure *-171
72Dimanche/Derniere Heure *-172
73Canadiens Postcards-22
74Canadiens Postcards-23
74NHL Action Stamps-151
74O-Pee-Chee NHL-316
75Canadiens Postcards-18
75O-Pee-Chee NHL-181
75Topps-181
76Canadiens Postcards-21
76O-Pee-Chee NHL-59
76Topps-59
77Canadiens Postcards-23
77Coca-Cola-23
77O-Pee-Chee NHL-1
77O-Pee-Chee NHL-3
77O-Pee-Chee NHL-7
77O-Pee-Chee NHL-120
77O-Pee-Chee NHL-217
77Sportscasters-4513
77Topps-1
77Topps-3
77Topps-7
77Topps-120
77Topps-217
77Topps/O-Pee-Chee Glossy-19
Square-19
77Finnish Sportscasters-50-1178
78Canadiens Postcards-25
78O-Pee-Chee-63
78O-Pee-Chee-67
78O-Pee-Chee-170
78O-Pee-Chee-333
78Topps-63
78Topps-67
78Topps-170
79Canadiens Postcards-24
79O-Pee-Chee-90
79Topps-90
80Canadiens Postcards-24
80O-Pee-Chee-89
80O-Pee-Chee-180
80Pepsi-Cola Caps-58
80Topps-89
80Topps-180
81Canadiens Postcards-25
81O-Pee-Chee-180
81O-Pee-Chee-197
81O-Pee-Chee Stickers-32
81O-Pee-Chee Stickers-44
81Topps-34
81Topps-56
82Canadiens Postcards-24
82Canadiens Steinberg-19
82O-Pee-Chee-192
82O-Pee-Chee Stickers-32
82O-Pee-Chee Stickers-33
82Post Cereal-10
82Topps Stickers-32
82Topps Stickers-33
83Canadiens Postcards-26
83NHL Key Tags-67
83O-Pee-Chee-198
83O-Pee-Chee Stickers-6
83O-Pee-Chee Stickers-57
83Puffy Stickers-6
83Topps Stickers-6
83Topps Stickers-57
83Vachon-55
84O-Pee-Chee-272
88Esso All-Stars-42
92Future Trends '76 Canada Cup-183
93Action Packed HOF Induction-4
95Zeller's Masters of Hockey Signed-7
96Canadiens Postcards-26
01BAP Ultimate Mem Dynasty Jerseys-15
01BAP Ultimate Mem Dynasty Emblems-15
01BAP Ultimate Mem Dynasty Numbers-15
01BAP Ultimate Memorabilia Les Canadiens-3
01BAP Ultimate Mem Stanley Cup Winners-22
01Greats of the Game-12
Autographs-12
01Parkhurst Autographs-PA51
01Topps Archives-32
Arena Seats-ASSSH
01Upper Deck Legends-36
Jerseys-TTSS
Jerseys-TTSL
Jerseys Platinum-TTSS
Jerseys Platinum-TTSL
Milestones-MSS
Milestones Platinum-MSS
01Upper Deck Vintage Sweaters of Honor-SHSS
02BAP Memorabilia Mini Stanley Cups-14
02BAP Ultimate Mem Storied Franchise-21
02Canadiens AGF-NNO
02Topps Stanley Cup Heroes-SS
02Topps Stanley Cup Heroes Autographs-SS
03BAP Ultimate Memorabilia Linemates-8
03Parkhurst Original Six Montreal-57
03Parkhurst Original Six Montreal-96
Autographs-16
Memorabilia-MM61
04ITG Franchises Canadian-55
Autographs-SSH
Forever Rivals-FR10
Forever Rivals Gold-FR10
Memorabilia-SM17
Memorabilia Autographs-SM17
Memorabilia Gold-SM17
Original Sticks-OS7
Original Sticks Autographs-OS7
Original Sticks Gold-OS7
04ITG Franchises Update-471
Linemates-ULI4
Linemates Gold-ULI4
04ITG Ultimate Memorabilia-47
Gold-47
Retro Teammates-9
04UD Legendary Signatures-80
Autographs-SC
Linemates-SCPMGL
04Upper Deck Heritage Classic-CC-SS
04ITG Heroes and Prospects-146
Autographs-SSH
04ITG Heroes/Prospects Toronto Expo '05-146
04ITG Heroes/Prospects Expo Heroes/Pros-146
05ITG Ultimate Mem Record Breaker Jerseys-7
05ITG Ultimate Mem RecBreak Jerseys Gold-7
05ITG Ultimate Mem Retro Teammate Jerseys-16
05ITG Ult Mem Retro Teammates Jersey Gold-16
05ITG Ultimate Mem Sticks and Jerseys-20
05ITG Ultimate Mem Stick and Jerseys Gold-20
05ITG Ultimate Mem 3 Star of the Game Jsy-11
05ITG Ult Mem 3 Star of the Game Jsy Gold-11
05NHL Legends Medallions-20
05SP Authentic Six Star Signatures-SSMO
05SP Game Used Heritage Classic-HC-SS
05SP Game Used Heritage Classic Autos-HCA-SS
05SP Game Used Heritage Classic Patches-HCP-SS
05SP GameUsed Heritage Classic Patch Auto-HAP-SS
05SP Game Used Oldtimer's Challenge-OC-SS
05SP Game Used Oldtimer's Challenge Autos-OCA-SS
05SP Game Used Oldtimer's Challenge Patch-OCP-SS
05SP Game Used Oldtime Chall Patch Autoa-OAP-SS
05The Cup-55
Gold-55
Black Rainbow-55
Emblems of Endorsement-EESS
Limited Logos-LLSS
Masterpiece Pressplates-55
Noble Numbers-NNBS
Patch Variation-P55
Patch Variation Autographs-AP55
Scripted Numbers-SNBS
Scripted Numbers Dual-DSNLS
Signature Patches-SPSH
05ITG Heroes and Prospects Hero Mem-HM-37
06ITG International Ice-47
Gold-47
Autographs-ASS
My Country My Team-MC7
My Country My Team Gold-MC7
06ITG Ultimate Memorabilia-131
Artist Proof-131
Bowman Factor-5
Bowman Factor Gold-5
Boys Will Be Boys-14
Boys Will Be Boys Gold-14
Retro Teammates-12
Retro Teammates Gold-12
Road to the Cup-5
Road to the Cup Gold-5
06SP Authentic Sign of the Times Triples-ST3LRS
06SP Authentic Sign of the Times Quads-ST4BLSR
06SPx-139
Spectrum-139
06The Cup Autographed Foundations-CQST
06The Cup Autographed Foundations Patches-CQST
06The Cup Foundations-CQST
06The Cup Foundations Patches-CQST
06The Cup Enshrinements-ESS
06The Cup Honorable Numbers-HNSH
06The Cup Limited Logos-LLSH
06The Cup Scripted Swatches-SSSH
06The Cup Signature Patches-SPSS
06The Cup Stanley Cup Signatures-CSSH
06UD Artifacts-134
Blue-134
Gold-134
Platinum-134
Radiance-134
Autographed Radiance Parallel-134
Red-134
Auto-Facts-AFSS
Auto-Facts Gold-AFSS
Frozen Artifacts-FASS
Frozen Artifacts Black-FASS
Frozen Artifacts Blue-FASS
Frozen Artifacts Gold-FASS
Frozen Artifacts Platinum-FASS
Frozen Artifacts Red-FASS
Frozen Artifacts Autographed Black-FASS
Frozen Artifacts Patches Black-FASS
Frozen Artifacts Patches Blue-FASS
Frozen Artifacts Patches Gold-FASS
Frozen Artifacts Patches Platinum-FASS
Frozen Artifacts Patches Red-FASS
Frozen Artifacts Patches Autographed Black Tag Parallel-FASS
Tundra Tandems-TTLS
Tundra Tandems Black-TTLS
Tundra Tandems Blue-TTLS
Tundra Tandems Gold-TTLS
Tundra Tandems Platinum-TTLS
Tundra Tandems Red-TTLS
Tundra Tandems Dual Patches Red-TTLS
06Ultimate Collection Jerseys Triple-UJ3-LRS
06Ultimate Collection Patches Triple-UJ3-LRS
06Upper Deck Sweet Shot Sweet Stitches-SSSH
06Upper Deck Sweet Shot Sweet Stitches Duals-SSSH
06Upper Deck Sweet Shot Sweet Stitches Triples-SSSH
06Upper Deck Trilogy Combo Clearcut Autographs-C3BLS
06Upper Deck Trilogy Scripts-TSSS

Shutter, Walter
86Saskatoon Blades Photos-21

Shutz, Derek
04Richmond Riverdogs-19

Shvetsov, Oleg
01Russian Hockey League-133

Shvidki, Denis
97Black Diamond-116
Double Diamond-116
Triple Diamond-116
Quadruple Diamond-116
98Black Diamond-107
Double Diamond-107
Triple Diamond-107
Quadruple Diamond-107
98SPx Top Prospects-74
Radiance-74
Spectrum-74
98UD Choice-286
Prime Choice Reserve-286
Reserve-286
98Barrie Colts-20
99Black Diamond-99
Diamond Cut-99
Final Cut-99
99SPx-170
Radiance-170
Spectrum-170
99Upper Deck-170
99Upper Deck-315
Exclusives-170
Exclusives-315
Exclusives 1 of 1-170
Exclusives 1 of 1-315
99Upper Deck Gold Reserve-170
99Upper Deck Gold Reserve-315
99Upper Deck MVP SC Edition-212
Gold Script-212
Silver Script-212
Super Script-212
Game-Used Souvenirs-GUDS
Game-Used Souvenirs-SGDS
ProSign-DS
99Upper Deck Ovation-68
Standing Ovation-68
99Bowman CHL-24
99Bowman CHL-130
Gold-24
Gold-130
OPC International-24
OPC International-130
Autographs-BA17
Autographs Gold-BA17
Autographs Silver-BA17
Scout's Choice-SC6
99UD Prospects-6
CHL Class-C6
Destination the Show-DS9
International Stars-IN5
Signatures of Tradition-DSH
00BAP Memorabilia-421
Emerald-421
Ruby-421
Sapphire-421
00BAP Signature Series-283
Emerald-283
Ruby-283
Sapphire-283
Autographs-245
Autographs Gold-245
00Crown Royale-125
00Private Stock-120
Gold-120
Premiere Date-120
Retail-120
Silver-120
00Titanium-123
Retail-123
00Titanium Draft Day Edition-123
00Titanium Draft Day Promos-123
00Topps Heritage-158
00Topps Premier Plus-100
Blue Ice-100
00UD Heroes-54
00Louisville Panthers-11
01BAP Memorabilia-109
Emerald-109
Ruby-109
Sapphire-109
01Upper Deck-304
Exclusives-304
01Upper Deck MVP-83
01Upper Deck Victory-155
Gold-155
01Upper Deck Vintage-109
02O-Pee-Chee-304
02O-Pee-Chee Premier Blue Parallel-304
02O-Pee-Chee Premier Red Parallel-304
02O-Pee-Chee Factory Set-304
02Topps-304
OPC Blue Parallel-304
OPC Red Parallel-304
Factory Set-304
03ITG Action-206
03Upper Deck MVP-185
Gold Script-185
Silver Script-185
Canadian Exclusives-185
03Pacific AHL Prospects-75
Gold-75
Jerseys-4
03San Antonio Rampage-14
04Barrie Colts 10th Anniversary-12
04ITG Heroes and Prospects Emblems-35
04ITG Heroes and Prospects Emblems Gold-35
04ITG Heroes and Prospects Jerseys-35
04ITG Heroes and Prospects Jerseys Gold-35
04ITG Heroes and Prospects Numbers-35
04ITG Heroes and Prospects Numbers Gold-35
06ITG Heroes and Prospects AHL All-Star Jerseys-AJ09
06ITG Heroes and Prospects AHL All-Star Jerseys Gold-AJ09
06ITG Heroes and Prospects AHL All-Star Emblems-AE09
06ITG Heroes and Prospects AHL All-Star Emblems Gold-AE09
06ITG Heroes and Prospects AHL All-Star Numbers-AN09
06ITG Heroes and Prospects AHL All-Star Numbers Gold-AN09

Shybunka, Derek
97New Mexico Scorpions-20

Shybunka, Tyler
96Swift Current Broncos-10
97Swift Current Broncos-12

Shyiak, Brock
92Thunder Bay Thunder Hawks-24

Shyiak, Dave
92Northern Michigan Wildcats-31

Sibbald, Mark
04Vernon Vipers-3

Sibbald, Mike
03Vernon Vipers-15

Sibr, Drew
91Arizona Icecats-5

Sicak, Vladimir
98Czech OFS-200
99Medicine Hat Tigers-22
99Medicine Hat Tigers-29
01Finnish Cardset-215
02Finnish Cardset-117
03Finnish Cardset-31
04Finnish Cardset-31
04Finnish Cardset Signatures-8
05Swedish SHL Elitset-243
Gold-243
06Finnish Cardset-335

Sich, Rob
06Fayetteville FireAntz-16

Siciliano, Dave
99Owen Sound Platers-2
00Sioux City Musketeers-25
04Sioux City Musketeers-27

Siciliano, Pete
91Hampton Roads Admirals-16

Sicinski, Bob
73Quaker Oats WHA-12

Siddall, Matt
04Northern Michigan Wildcats-21

Sidelnikov, Alexander
73Finnish Jaakiekko-16
73Russian National Team-3
73Swedish Stickers-78
74Finnish Jenkki-56
74Russian National Team-19
74Swedish Stickers-52
91Future Trends Canada '72-28
91Future Trends Canada '72 French-28

Sideroff, Dean
91Air Canada SJHL-A35

Sidikov, Rustan
03Russian Under-18 Team-9

Sidorenko, Kirill
02Russian Hockey League-78

Sidorkiewicz, Peter
80Oshawa Generals-21
81Oshawa Generals-3
82Oshawa Generals-3
83Oshawa Generals-1
89O-Pee-Chee-11
89O-Pee-Chee Stickers-42
89O-Pee-Chee Stickers-118
89Panini Stickers-220
89Topps-11
89Whalers Junior Milk-19
90Bowman-255
Tiffany-255
90O-Pee-Chee-14
90Panini Stickers-38
90Pro Set-451
90Score-46
Canadian-46
90Score Young Superstars-4
90Topps-14
Tiffany-14
90Upper Deck-69
French-69
90Whalers Jr. 7-Eleven-23
91Bowman-13
91O-Pee-Chee-296
91Panini Stickers-310
91Parkhurst-286
French-286
91Pinnacle-234
French-234
91Pro Set-90
French-90
91Score American-203
91Score Canadian Bilingual-203
91Score Canadian English-203
91Stadium Club-125
91Topps-296
91Upper Deck-325
French-325
91Whalers Jr. 7-Eleven-25
92Bowman-162
92Kraft-35
92O-Pee-Chee-175
92OPC Premier-112
92Parkhurst-120
92Parkhurst-450
Emerald Ice-120
Emerald Ice-450
92Pinnacle-371
French-371
92Pro Set-125
92Score-41
92Score-515
Canadian-41
Canadian-515
92Stadium Club-27
92Topps-332
Gold-332G
92Ultra-150
92Ultra-367
92Upper Deck-14
92Upper Deck-480
93Panini Stickers-121
93Pinnacle-381
Canadian-381
All-Stars-17
All-Stars Canadian-17
Masks-10
93Score-102
Canadian-102
Franchise-14
93Stadium Club All-Stars-13
93Stadium Club All-Stars Members Only-13
93Stadium Club All-Stars OPC-13
94EA Sports-96
94EA Sports-206
96Albany River Rats-16
97Albany River Rats-14
04Erie Otters-24

Sidorov, Ivan
03Russian Metallurg Magnitogorsk-7

Sidorovski, Alexander
00Russian Hockey League-237

Sidoruk, Kendall
00Idaho Steelheads-20

Sidyakin, Andrei
00Russian Hockey League-149
02Russian Hockey League-135

Siebert, Babe
28La Presse Photos-12
33O-Pee-Chee V304B-49
33V129-28
33V252 Canadian Gum-43
33V357 Ice Kings-8
34Beehive Group I Photos-182
34Sweet Caporal-30
37O-Pee-Chee V304E-150
37V356 Worldwide Gum-3
38Quaker Oats Photos-27
55Parkhurst-62
Quaker Oats-62
83Hall of Fame-59
83Hall of Fame Postcards-D14
85Hall of Fame-59
02Parkhurst Reprints-210
03BAP Ultimate Memorabilia Paper Cuts-34
04ITG Ultimate Memorabilia-100
Gold-100
Marvelous Maroons-3
05ITG Ultimate Memorabilia Lumbergraphs-12
06ITG Ultimate Memorabilia Bleu Blanc et Rouge Autos-1

Siegel, Marc
96Johnstown Chiefs-19

Siegert, Riccardo
94German First League-488

Siegmund, Ulf
94German First League-349

Siegwart, Patrick
95Swiss HNL-456
96Swiss HNL-443
01Swiss HNL-378
02Swiss HNL-425

Siekkinen, Ari-Pekka
91Finnish Jyvas-Hyva Stickers-25
92Finnish Jyvas-Hyva Stickers-70
93Finnish Jyvas-Hyva Stickers-134
93Finnish SISU-136
94Finnish SISU-50
94Finnish SISU NIL Phenoms-7
95Finnish SISU-56
Ghost Goalies-7
95Finnish SISU Limited-46
96Finnish SISU Redline Mighty Adversaries-9
98Finnish Kerailysarja-7
Mad Masks-1
99Finnish Cardset-7
Puck Stoppers-2
00Finnish Cardset-287
02Finnish Cardset-118

Siekris, Billy
06Oshawa Generals-20

Sievert, Pasqual
01Swiss HNL-443
02Swiss HNL-427

Sievert, Tyson
04Saskatoon Blades-5
05Regina Pats-24

Sifers, Jamie
06Toronto Marlies-27

Sigalet, Jonathan
05Providence Bruins-16
06Providence Bruins-16
07Upper Deck Victory-225
Black-225
Gold-225

Sigalet, Jordan
03Bowling Green Falcons-9
05Beehive-149
Beige -149
Blue -149
Gold-149
Red -149
Matte-149
05Black Diamond-215
05Hot Prospects-189
Autographed Patch Variation-189
Autographed Patch Variation Gold-189
Hot Materials-HMSI
Red Hot-189
05Parkhurst-608
Facsimile Auto Parallel-608
Signatures-JS
05SP Authentic-206
Limited-206
05SP Game Used-180
Gold-180
05SPx-212
Spectrum-212
05The Cup-127
Autographed Rookie Patches Gold Rainbow-127
Black Rainbow Rookies-127
Masterpiece Pressplates (Artifacts)-250
Masterpiece Pressplates (Bee Hive)-149
Masterpiece Pressplates (Black Diamond)-215
Masterpiece Pressplates (Ice)-184
Masterpiece Pressplates (Rookie Update)-199
Masterpiece Pressplates SPA Autos-206
Masterpiece Pressplates (SP Game Used)-180
Masterpiece Pressplates (SPx)-212
Masterpiece Pressplates (Trilogy)-225
Masterpiece Pressplates Ult Coll-138
Masterpiece Pressplates Autographs-127
Platinum Rookies-127
05UD Artifacts-250
05Ultimate Collection-138
Gold-138
Ultimate Debut Threads Jerseys-DTJSI
Ultimate Debut Threads Jerseys Autos-DAJSI
Ultimate Debut Threads Patches-DTPSI
Ultimate Debut Threads Patches Autos-DAPSI
05Upper Deck-463
05Upper Deck Ice-184
05Upper Deck Rookie Update-199
05Upper Deck Trilogy-225
05Providence Bruins-17
06Providence Bruins-17

Sigel, Marc
97New Mexico Scorpions-22

Sigg, Daniel
93Swiss HNL-16
95Swiss HNL-13
96Swiss HNL-110
98Swiss Power Play Stickers-185
99Swiss Panini Stickers-184
01Swiss HNL-450
02Swiss HNL-432

Sigg, Roger
93Swiss HNL-222
95Swiss HNL-223
96Swiss HNL-136
98Swiss Power Play Stickers-186
99Swiss Panini Stickers-185
00Swiss Panini Stickers-229
00Swiss Slapshot Mini-Cards-RJ4
01Swiss HNL-266

Sigmansky, Jorn
94German First League-490

Signer, Marco
01Swiss HNL-319
02Swiss HNL-195

Signorell, Riccardo
93Swiss HNL-310
95Swiss HNL-433
96Swiss HNL-466
98Swiss Power Play Stickers-318
99Swiss Panini Stickers-323
01Swiss HNL-396
02Swiss HNL-151

Signoretti, Andre
99Ohio State Buckeyes-15
00Charlotte Checkers-24
00Ohio State Buckeyes-1

Sigouin, Michael
92British Columbia JHL-21

Sigouin, Nicolas
05Drummondville Voltigeurs-13

Sigrist, Christian
93Swiss HNL-169

Sihvonen, Kari
05Finnish Cardset -296
06Finnish Cardset-301

Sihvonen, Petteri
70Finnish Jaakiekko-255
92Finnish Jyvas-Hyva Stickers-141

Sihvonen, Toni
92Finnish Jyvas-Hyva Stickers-142
93Finnish Jyvas-Hyva Stickers-327
93Finnish SISU-45
94Finnish SISU-136
95Finnish SISU-211
96Finnish SISU Redline-12
98Finnish Kerailysarja-45
Off Duty-2
99Finnish Cardset-198
99Finnish Cardset-230
00Finnish Cardset-16
00Finnish Cardset-237
01Finnish Cardset-176
02Finnish Cardset-119
04Finnish Cardset-103
04Swedish Pure Skills Signatures-16
05Finnish Cardset -118
06Finnish Cardset-300

Siimes, Rauli
70Finnish Jaakiekko-341

Siisala, Arto
71Finnish Suomi Stickers-294

Siissala, Arto
73Finnish Jaakiekko-212

Siitarinen, Jorma
70Finnish Jaakiekko-223
71Finnish Suomi Stickers-145
72Finnish Jaakiekko-205
73Finnish Jaakiekko-119

Siivonen, Hannu
70Finnish Jaakiekko-238
71Finnish Suomi Stickers-256
74Finnish Typotor-23
78Finnish SM-Liiga-153

Siivonen, Janne
00Finnish Cardset-304
01Finnish Cardset-94
04Finnish Cardset-270

Sikela, Lubos
92Norwegian Elite Series-217

Sikich, Zach
00Sioux Falls Stampede-16
06Quad City Mallards-13

Sikkula, Timo
98Finnish Kerailysarja-157

Sikl, Zdenek
96Flint Generals-18

Siklenka, Mike
99Hampton Roads Admirals-19
00Richmond Renegades-16
02BAP Memorabilia-384
02BAP Ultimate Memorabilia-81
02Upper Deck Rookie Update-147
02Philadelphia Phantoms-14
03Philadelphia Phantoms-15

Silander, Jukka
72Finnish Jaakiekko-337

Silfver, Claes-Henrik
83Swedish Semic Elitserien-119
84Swedish Semic Elitserien-119
85Swedish Panini Stickers-106
86Swedish Panini Stickers-101
87Swedish Panini Stickers-103

Silfverberg, Conny
81Swedish Semic Hockey VM Stickers-10
83Swedish Semic Elitserien-66
84Swedish Semic Elitserien-66
85Swedish Panini Stickers-60
86Swedish Panini Stickers-42
87Swedish Panini Stickers-55

Silfverberg, Jan-Erik
72Swedish Stickers-41
72Swedish Stickers-82
73Swedish Stickers-157
74Swedish Stickers-187

Silfwerplatz, Johan
98Swedish UD Choice-6
99German Bundesliga 2-77
00UK Sekonda Superleague-10

Silietti, Fabrizio
95Swiss HNL-481
96Swiss HNL-378
01Swiss HNL-438

Silius, Kari
72Finnish Jaakiekko-296

Silk, Dave
80USA Olympic Team Mini Pics-10
81Swedish Semic Hockey VM Stickers-98
84O-Pee-Chee-16
85Jets Police-17
95Signature Rookies Miracle on Ice-31

95Signature Rookies Miracle on Ice-32
95Signature Rook Miracle on Ice Sigs-31
95Signature Rook Miracle on Ice Sigs-32
04UD Legendary Signatures Miracle Men-USA15
04UD Legendary Sigs Miracle Men Autos-USA-SI

Sillanpaa, Kari
65Finnish Hellas-13
66Finnish Jaakiekkosarja-25

Sillanpaa, Olli
01Finnish Cardset-222

Sillanpaa, Teemu
92Finnish Jyvas-Hyva Stickers-105
93Finnish Jyvas-Hyva Stickers-196
93Finnish SISU-261
94Finnish SISU-56
95Finnish SISU-286
98German DEL-306
99German DEL-246

Sillers, Gerry
71Rochester Americans-16

Sillgren, Harri
93Finnish Jyvas-Hyva Stickers-328
93Finnish SISU-49
94Finnish SISU-112
95Finnish SISU-133
Painkillers-6
97Swedish Collector's Choice-197
98Finnish Keraillysarja-178
99Finnish Cardset-90
00Finnish Cardset-308
01Finnish Cardset-275
02Finnish Cardset-269

Silling, Christian
93Swiss HNL-246

Sillinger, Mike
87Regina Pats-24
88Regina Pats-23
89Regina Pats-20
90OPC Premier-107
90Upper Deck-452
French-452
907th Inn. Sketch WHL-186
91O-Pee-Chee-337
91Score American-327
91Score Canadian Bilingual-357
91Score Canadian English-357
91Topps-337
91Upper Deck-457
French-457
91ProCards-130
92Parkhurst-38
Emerald Ice-38
92Ultra-290
92Upper Deck-524
93Donruss-92
93Leaf-306
93Parkhurst-331
Emerald Ice-331
93PowerPlay-336
93Score-651
Gold-651
Canadian-651
Canadian Gold-651
93Ultra-311
94Be A Player Signature Cards-171
94Leaf-394
94OPC Premier-171
Special Effects-171
94Topps/OPC Premier-171
Special Effects-171
94Upper Deck-200
Electric Ice-200
95Donruss-219
95Parkhurst International-274
Emerald Ice-274
95Playoff One on One-3
95Playoff One on One-225
95Ultra-203
95Upper Deck-72
Electric Ice-72
Electric Ice Gold-72
Special Edition-SE91
Special Edition Gold-SE91
96Canucks Postcards-26
96Playoff One on One-331
96Upper Deck-349
97Be A Player-16
Autographs-16
Autographs Die-Cuts-16
Autographs Prismatic Die-Cuts-16
97Collector's Choice-260
97Pacific-336
Copper-336
Emerald Green-336
Ice Blue-336
Red-336
Silver-336
97Upper Deck-170
98Finest-28
No Protectors-28
No Protectors Refractors-28
Refractors-28
98Pacific-331
Ice Blue-331
Red-331
98Upper Deck-147
Exclusives-147
Exclusives 1 of 1-147
Gold Reserve-147
99BAP Millennium-223
Emerald-223
Ruby-223
Sapphire-223
Signatures-223
Signatures Gold-223
99Crown Royale-130
Limited Series-130
Premiere Date-130
99Pacific-396
Copper-396
Emerald Green-396
Gold-396
Ice Blue-396
Premiere Date-396
Red-396
99Pacific Omega-219
Copper-219
Gold-219
Ice Blue-219
Premiere Date-219
99Upper Deck MVP SC Edition-171
Gold Script-171
Silver Script-171
Super Script-171
00BAP Memorabilia-250
Emerald-250
Ruby-250
Sapphire-250
Promos-250
00BAP Mem Chicago Sportsfest Copper-250
00BAP Memorabilia Chicago Sportsfest Blue-250
00BAP Memorabilia Chicago Sportsfest Gold-250
00BAP Memorabilia Chicago Sportsfest Ruby-250
00BAP Memorabilia Chicago Sun-Times Ruby-250
00BAP Memorabilia Chicago Sun-Times Gold-250
00BAP Mem Chicago Sun-Times Sapphire-250
00BAP Mem Toronto Fall Expo Copper-250
00BAP Memorabilia Toronto Fall Expo Gold-250
00BAP Memorabilia Toronto Fall Expo Ruby-250
00O-Pee-Chee-173
00O-Pee-Chee Parallel-173
00Panthers Team Issue-19
00Stadium Club-82
00Topps/OPC-173
Parallel-173
00Upper Deck-307
Exclusives Tier 1-307
Exclusives Tier 2-307
00Upper Deck Vintage-159
01Blue Jackets Donatos Pizza-21
01O-Pee-Chee-194
01O-Pee-Chee Premier Parallel-194
01Pacific-280
Extreme LTD-280
Hobby LTD-280
Premiere Date-280
Retail LTD-280
01Pacific Arena Exclusives-280
01Parkhurst-374
01Topps-194
OPC Parallel-194
01UD Mask Collection-25
Gold-25
01Upper Deck-282
Exclusives-282
02BAP First Edition-275
02BAP Signature Series-32
Autographs-32
Autograph Buybacks 1999-223
Autographs Gold-32
02O-Pee-Chee-193
02O-Pee-Chee Premier Blue Parallel-193
02O-Pee-Chee Premier Red Parallel-193
02O-Pee-Chee Factory Set-193
02Pacific-106
Blue-106
Red-106
02Pacific Complete-228
Red-228
02Topps-193
OPC Blue Parallel-193
OPC Red Parallel-193
Factory Set-193
02Topps Total-158
02Upper Deck-54
Exclusives-54
02Upper Deck Victory-63
Bronze-63
Gold-63
Silver-63
03Coyotes Postcards-20
03NHL Sticker Collection-199
03Pacific-98
Blue-98
Red-98
03Upper Deck-398
Canadian Exclusives-398
HG-398
UD Exclusives-398
03Upper Deck MVP-119
Gold Script-119
Silver Script-119
Canadian Exclusives-119
05Be A Player Dual Signatures-ST
05Be A Player Quad Signatures-BLUE
05Be A Player Signatures-SG
05Be A Player Signatures Gold-SG
05Blues Team Set-17
05Parkhurst-272
Facsimile Auto Parallel-272
05UD Artifacts-86
Blue-86
Gold-86
Green-86
Pewter-86
Red-86
Gold Autographed-86
05Upper Deck MVP-338
Gold-338
Platinum-338
06Be A Player-40
Autographs-40
Signatures-SI
Signatures Duals-DSH
Signatures Trios-TYSS
06Fleer-126
Tiffany-126
06O-Pee-Chee-315
Rainbow-315
06Panini Stickers-95
06Ultra-126
Gold Medallion-126
Ice Medallion-126
06Upper Deck-372
Exclusives Parallel-372
High Gloss Parallel-372
Masterpieces-372
06Upper Deck MVP-182
Gold Script-182
Super Script-182
06Upper Deck Ovation-177
06Upper Deck Victory-259

Sillman, Tuomo
71Finnish Suomi Stickers-185
72Finnish Jaakiekko-135
73Finnish Jaakiekko-191

Sills, Francois
94German DEL-238
95German DEL-114
96German DEL-59

Siltala, Mike
81Kingston Canadians-18
82Kingston Canadians-8

Siltanen, Risto
72Finnish Jaakiekko-316
77Finnish Sportscasters-75-1796
78Finnish SM-Liiga-5
78Finnish SM-Liiga-51
79Panini Stickers-166
79Oilers Postcards-22
80O-Pee-Chee-315
80Pepsi-Cola Caps-39
81Oilers Red Rooster-8
81Oilers West Edmonton Mall-8
81O-Pee-Chee-122
81O-Pee-Chee Stickers-214
82O-Pee-Chee-129
82Post Cereal-6
82Whalers Junior Hartford Courant-16
82Swedish Semic VM Stickers-157
83NHL Key Tags-50
83O-Pee-Chee-146
83O-Pee-Chee Stickers-257
83Puffy Stickers-14
83Topps Stickers-257
83Whalers Junior Hartford Courant-16
84O-Pee-Chee-78
84Topps-61
84Whalers Junior Wendy's-18
85Nordiques McDonald's-20
85Nordiques Team Issue-23
85Whalers Junior Wendy's-19
86Nordiques General Foods-24
86Nordiques Team Issue-23
86O-Pee-Chee-187
86O-Pee-Chee Stickers-29
86Topps-187
87Panini Stickers-159
88Oilers Tenth Anniversary-48
91Finnish Jyvas-Hyva Stickers-18
94Finnish SISU-250
95Finnish SISU-140
95Finnish SISU Limited-92
99Finnish Cardset Aces High-C-5

Siltavirta, Sami
01Finnish Cardset-269

Silva, Eric
93Quebec Pee-Wee Tournament-637

Silvasti, Mikko
70Finnish Jaakiekko-320

Silvennoinen, Juha
71Finnish Suomi Stickers-273
73Finnish Jaakiekko-160
74Finnish Jenkki-16
80Finnish Mallasjuoma-81

Silvennoinen, Mikko
05Finnish Cardset -136

Silver, Chad
88Regina Pats-24
93Swiss HNL-55
95Swiss HNL-178
96Swiss HNL-73
98Swiss Power Play Stickers-245

Silver, Harry
71Finnish Suomi Stickers-239
72Finnish Jaakiekko-223

Silver, Maury
92Anaheim Bullfrogs RHI-2

Silver, Shawn
93Sudbury Wolves-1
93Sudbury Wolves Police-21
93Windsor Spitfires-2
94Owen Sound Platers-1
99UK Sheffield Steelers-17
00UK Sekonda Superleague-71
01UK Fife Flyers-1
02Indianapolis Ice-16

Silver, Stuart
92Anaheim Bullfrogs RHI-3
93Phoenix Cobras RHI-3

Silverio, Matt
93Quebec Pee-Wee Tournament-1673

Silverman, Andy
92Maine Black Bears-3
93Maine Black Bears-38
95Binghamton Rangers-21
96Binghamton Rangers-18

Silverson, Jamie
04Salmon Arm Silverbacks-1

Silverstone, David
00Belleville Bulls-13
01Belleville Bulls-21
02Roanoke Express-24
02Roanoke Express RBI Sports-204

Silverthorn, Steve
05Idaho Steelheads-19
06Idaho Steelheads-23

Silvia, Rob
93Quebec Pee-Wee Tournament-1575

Sim, Jonathan
95Slapshot-340
95Sarnia Sting-10
96Sarnia Sting-24
97Bowman CHL-31
OPC-31
98IHL All-Star Eastern Conference-7
98Michigan K-Wings-11
98Bowman CHL-15
Golden Anniversary-15
OPC International-15
98Bowman Chrome CHL-15
Golden Anniversary-15
Golden Anniversary Refractors-15
OPC International-15
OPC International Refractors-15
Refractors-15
99BAP Memorabilia-65
Gold-65
Silver-65
99Black Diamond-32
Diamond Cut-32
Final Cut-32
99Pacific-133
Copper-133
Emerald Green-133
Gold-133
Ice Blue-133
Premiere Date-133
Red-133
99SP Authentic-101
99Topps Arena Giveaways-DAL-JS
99Ultimate Victory-96
1/1-96
Parallel-96
Parallel 100-96
99Upper Deck-47
Exclusives-47
Exclusives 1 of 1-47
99Upper Deck Gold Reserve-47
99Upper Deck MVP-66
Gold Script-66
Silver Script-66
Super Script-66
99Upper Deck Victory-92
99Michigan K-Wings-4
00O-Pee-Chee-324
00O-Pee-Chee Parallel-324
00Stars Postcards-21
00Topps/OPC-324
Parallel-324
00Topps Chrome-219
OPC Refractors-219
Refractors-219
01Utah Grizzlies-4
02Utah Grizzlies-1
03ITG Action-262
04Philadelphia Phantoms-18
05Flyers Team Issue-22
05Parkhurst-214
Facsimile Auto Parallel-214

Sim, Mike
95Slapshot-263
00Quad-City Mallards-12

Sim, Trevor
89Kamloops Blazers-20
90ProCards AHL/IHL-230
907th Inn. Sketch Memorial Cup-20
92Alberta International Team Canada-20
93Alberta International Team Canada-19
93OPC Premier Team Canada-11
93PowerPlay-494
93Ultra-473
94Milwaukee Admirals-22

Sim, Zach
04Everett Silvertips-10
05Everett Silvertips-21

Sima, Jaroslav
74Swedish Stickers-112

Simakov, Alexei
00Russian Hockey League-353
02Russian Hockey League-140

Simanek, Jiri
99Czech OFS-188
00Czech DS Extraliga-82
00Czech OFS-21
01Czech OFS-183
02Czech OFS Plus-186
03Czech OFS Plus-272
06Czech HC Ceske Budejovice Postcards-8
06Czech OFS-16

Simard, Charles
02Swiss EV Zug Postcards-10
02Swiss HNL-222
04Fresno Falcons-16

Simard, Martin
88Salt Lake Golden Eagles-11
90ProCards AHL/IHL-616
91Flames IGA-20
91Pro Set-526
French-526
94Milwaukee Admirals-23
96Providence Bruins-13
97Springfield Falcons-21

Simard, Mathieu
00Rimouski Oceanic-17
Signed-17
01Val d'Or Foreurs-22

Simard, Olivier
93Quebec Pee-Wee Tournament-473

Simard, Patrick
04Baie-Comeau Drakkar-17
05Baie-Comeau Drakkar-3

Simard, Sebastien
96Rimouski Oceanic-25

Simaro, Patrick
03Baie Comeau Drakkar-2

Simchuk, Konstantin
98Las Vegas Coyotes RHI-1
98Las Vegas Thunder-19
98Port Huron Border Cats-25
99Knoxville Speed-18
00Fort Wayne Komets-19
02Russian Hockey League-158
03Russian SL-12
04Russian Super League All-Stars-17

Simcik, Jan
917th Inn. Sketch QMJHL-141

Simek, Martin
94Czech APS Extraliga-81

Simeon, Ivo
01Swiss HNL-252

Simicek, Radek
01Czech OFS-23

Simicek, Robert
94Czech APS Extraliga-130

Simicek, Roman
95Czech APS Extraliga-306
96Czech APS Extraliga-202
97Czech APS Extraliga-132
97Czech APS Extraliga-363
97Czech DS Extraliga-10
97Czech DS Stickers-196
98Czech DS Stickers-255
98Czech Pexeso Series Two-25
98Finnish Keraillysarja-65
99Czech OFS-268
99Finnish Cardset-34
99Finnish Cardset-163
00BAP Memorabilia-404
Emerald-404
Ruby-404
Sapphire-404
00BAP Signature Series-268
Emerald-268
Ruby-268
Sapphire-268
Autographs-230
Autographs Gold-230
00Black Diamond-99
00SP Authentic-121
00SP Game Used-80
00SPx-170
00Stadium Club-246
00Titanium Draft Day Edition-162
00Titanium Draft Day Promos-162
00Topps Premier Plus-110
Blue Ice-110
00UD Heroes-176
00UD Pros and Prospects-121
00Upper Deck-426
Exclusives Tier 1-426
Exclusives Tier 2-426
00Upper Deck Vintage-391
01O-Pee-Chee-219
01O-Pee-Chee Premier Parallel-219
01Topps-219
OPC Parallel-219
01Upper Deck-89
Exclusives-89
01Upper Deck MVP-95
01Upper Deck Victory-178
Gold-178
02BAP Sig Series Auto Buybacks 2000-230
02Czech IQ Sports Blue-11
02Finnish Cardset-270
03Czech OFS Plus-344
03Czech OFS Plus MS Praha-SE2
04Czech OFS-356
Stars II-13
05Czech HC Vitkovice-15
06Czech OFS-63

Simich, Darrell
05Cape Breton Screaming Eagles-5

Simioni, Mario
84Moncton Golden Flames-15
92Finnish Semic-262
99Danish Hockey League-114
04German Krefeld Penguins Postcards-21

Simmen, Rolf
93Swiss HNL-163

Simmer, Charlie
79O-Pee-Chee-191
79Topps-191
80Kings Card Night-11
80O-Pee-Chee-4
80O-Pee-Chee-83
80O-Pee-Chee-161
80O-Pee-Chee-165
80O-Pee-Chee-171
80O-Pee-Chee-240
80Topps-4
80Topps-83
80Topps-161
80Topps-165
80Topps-171
80Topps-240
81O-Pee-Chee-142
81O-Pee-Chee-151
81O-Pee-Chee-391
81O-Pee-Chee Stickers-144
81O-Pee-Chee Stickers-236
81O-Pee-Chee Stickers-266
81Topps-35
81Topps-W130
82O-Pee-Chee-159
82O-Pee-Chee Stickers-237
82Post Cereal-8
82Topps Stickers-237
83NHL Key Tags-53
83O-Pee-Chee-162
83O-Pee-Chee Stickers-290
83Puffy Stickers-8
83Topps Stickers-290
84Bruins Postcards-18
84O-Pee-Chee-90
84O-Pee-Chee-358
84O-Pee-Chee Stickers-266
84Topps-69
85O-Pee-Chee-87
85O-Pee-Chee Stickers-158
85Topps-87
86O-Pee-Chee-145
86O-Pee-Chee Stickers-36
86Topps-145
87O-Pee-Chee-52
87O-Pee-Chee Stickers-137
87Panini Stickers-11
87Penguins Kodak-23
87Topps-52
88O-Pee-Chee-250
90ProCards AHL/IHL-300
91ProCards-333
02Coyotes Team Issue-30
02UD Foundations-40
Signs of Greatness-SGCS
03BAP Ultimate Memorabilia Linemates-6
04ITG Franchises Update Teammates-UTM2
04ITG Franchises Update Teammates Gold-UTM2
04ITG Franchises US West-231
Autographs-A-CS
Original Sticks-WOS15
Original Sticks Gold-WOS15
04UD Legendary Signatures-17
Autographs-CS
Linemates-CSMDDT

Simmonds, Wayne
06Owen Sound Attack-13

Simmons, Don
44Beehive Group II Photos-66A
44Beehive Group II Photos-66B
44Beehive Group II Photos-449
57Topps-14
58Bruins Photos-13
58Topps-44
59Topps-11
60Shirriff Coins-101
60Topps-43
62Shirriff Coins-22
63Chex Photos-49
63Maple Leafs Team Issue-21
63Parkhurst-2
63Parkhurst-62
63York White Backs-15
64Beehive Group III Photos-184
65Coca-Cola-90
65Topps-88

Simmons, Gary
74NHL Action Stamps Update-8
74O-Pee-Chee NHL-371
75O-Pee-Chee NHL-29
75Topps-29
76O-Pee-Chee NHL-176
76Topps-176
78O-Pee-Chee-385

Simmons, Stuart
03Brampton Batallion-20
04Brampton Battalion-5

Simms, Brad
92Quebec Pee-Wee Tournament-1114
95Slapshot-345
95Sarnia Sting-15
96Sarnia Sting-25
97Sudbury Wolves Police-22

Simoes, Stefan
907th Inn. Sketch QMJHL-148
917th Inn. Sketch QMJHL-197
93Quebec Pee-Wee Tournament-419
94Flint Generals-20
95Central Hockey League-84
03Laredo Bucks-17
06UK Nottingham Panthers-16

Simola, Jari
72Finnish Jaakiekko-352

Simon, Ben
01BAP Memorabilia-321
Emerald-321
Ruby-321
Sapphire-321
01UD Honor Roll-64
01UD Premier Collection-52
01Upper Deck-420
Exclusives-420
01Chicago Wolves-19
02Chicago Wolves-21
03Thrashers Postcards-18
04Chicago Wolves-13
05Syracuse Crunch-5
06Syracuse Crunch-9

Simon, Chris
897th Inn. Sketch OHL-56
917th Inn. Sketch OHL-313
92Nordiques Petro-Canada-30
93Leaf-416
93Parkhurst-171
Emerald Ice-171
Calder Candidates-C13
Calder Candidates Gold-C13
93Pinnacle-219
Canadian-219
93Score-473
Canadian-473
93Ultra-224
All-Rookies-7
93Upper Deck-243
SP-131
93Classic Four-Sport *-217
Gold-217
94Be A Player Signature Cards-58
94Leaf-339
94Nordiques Burger King-24
94Pinnacle-506
Artist's Proofs-506
Rink Collection-506
94Upper Deck-299
Electric Ice-299
96Black Diamond-67
Gold-67
96Collector's Choice-66
96Flair-100
Blue Ice-100
96Score-190
Artist's Proofs-190
Dealer's Choice Artist's Proofs-190
Special Artist's Proofs-190
Golden Blades-190
96Upper Deck Ice-73
Parallel-73
97Be A Player-65
Autographs-65
Autographs Die-Cuts-65
Autographs Prismatic Die-Cuts-65
97Collector's Choice-269
97Pacific Invincible NHL Regime-213
97Upper Deck-205
97Upper Deck-387
98Finest-99
No Protectors-99
No Protectors Refractors-99
Refractors-99
99Pacific Dynagon Ice-204
Blue-204
Copper-204
Gold-204
Premiere Date-204
99Panini Stickers-171
00Aurora-150
Premiere Date-150
00BAP Memorabilia-172
Emerald-172
Ruby-172
Sapphire-172
Promos-172
00BAP Mem Chicago Sportsfest Copper-172
00BAP Memorabilia Chicago Sportsfest Blue-172
00BAP Memorabilia Chicago Sportsfest Gold-172
00BAP Memorabilia Chicago Sportsfest Ruby-172
00BAP Memorabilia Chicago Sun-Times Ruby-172
00BAP Memorabilia Chicago Sun-Times Gold-172
00BAP Mem Chicago Sun-Times Sapphire-172
00BAP Mem Toronto Fall Expo Copper-172
00BAP Memorabilia Toronto Fall Expo Gold-172
00BAP Memorabilia Toronto Fall Expo Ruby-172
00BAP Parkhurst 2000-P63
00BAP Signature Series-49
Emerald-49
Ruby-49
Sapphire-49
00O-Pee-Chee-93
00O-Pee-Chee Parallel-93
00Pacific-429
Copper-429
Gold-429
Ice Blue-429
Premiere Date-429
00Paramount-249
Copper-249
Gold-249
Holo-Gold-249
Holo-Silver-249
Ice Blue-249
Premiere Date-249
00Revolution-150
Blue-150
Premiere Date-150
Red-150
00SP Game Used-60
00Stadium Club-70
00Topps/OPC-93
Parallel-93
00Topps Chrome-74
OPC Refractors-74
Refractors-74
00Topps Heritage-168
00Topps Premier Plus-38
Blue Ice-38
00UD Reserve-86
00Upper Deck-174
Exclusives Tier 1-174
Exclusives Tier 2-174
00Upper Deck MVP-179
First Stars-179
Second Stars-179
Third Stars-179
00Upper Deck Victory-240
00Upper Deck Vintage-359
00Upper Deck Vintage-369
01BAP Update Tough Customers-TC21
01BAP Update Tough Customers-TC27
01O-Pee-Chee-225
01O-Pee-Chee Premier Parallel-225
01Pacific-399
01Pacific-425
Extreme LTD-399
Gold-425
Hobby LTD-399
Premiere Date-399
Retail LTD-399
01Pacific Arena Exclusives-399
01Pacific Arena Exclusives-425
01Topps-225
OPC Parallel-225
01Upper Deck Victory-353
Gold-353
02BAP Memorabilia-4
Emerald-4
Ruby-4
Sapphire-4
NHL All-Star Game-4
NHL All-Star Game Blue-4
NHL All-Star Game Green-4
NHL All-Star Game Red-4
02BAP Memorabilia Toronto Fall Expo-4
02BAP Signature Series Gold-GS23
02O-Pee-Chee-198
02O-Pee-Chee Premier Blue Parallel-198
02O-Pee-Chee Premier Red Parallel-198
02O-Pee-Chee Factory Set-198
02Pacific-399
Blue-399
Red-399
02Pacific Complete-495
Red-495
02Topps-198
OPC Blue Parallel-198
OPC Red Parallel-198
Factory Set-198
02Topps Total-82
02Upper Deck-177
Exclusives-177
03ITG Action-642
03Pacific-75
Blue-75
Red-75
03Pacific Complete-326
Red-326
03Parkhurst Original Six New York-22
03Rangers Team Issue-23
03Upper Deck MVP-96
Gold Script-96
Silver Script-96
Canadian Exclusives-96
04Pacific-45
Blue-45
Red-45
04Upper Deck-25
Canadian Exclusives-25
HG Glossy Gold-25
HG Glossy Silver-25
05Parkhurst-78
Facsimile Auto Parallel-78
05SP Game Used Authentic Fabrics Triple-DBS
05SP Game Used Authentic Patches Triple-DBS
05Upper Deck-276
Big Playmakers-B-CS
Patches-P-CS
School of Hard Knocks-HK3
05Upper Deck MVP-59
Gold-59
Platinum-59
Materials-M-CS
05Upper Deck Victory-31
Black-31
Gold-31
Silver-31
06Be A Player-39
Autographs-39
Signatures-CS
Signatures Duals-DAS
06O-Pee-Chee-312
Rainbow-312
06UD Powerplay Last Man Standing-LM6

Simon, Darcy
91ProCards-71
92Fredericton Canadiens-23
95PEI Senators-19
96Grand Rapids Griffins-23
97Grand Rapids Griffins-16

Simon, Dieter
74Finnish Jenkki-116
83Swedish Semic VM Stickers-151

Simon, Eric
93Quebec Pee-Wee Tournament-1369

Simon, Jason
86London Knights-11
89Nashville Knights-23
89ProCards AHL-203
90ProCards AHL/IHL-569
91ProCards-442
96Las Vegas Thunder-19
98Colorado Gold Kings-20
98Colorado Gold Kings Postcards-1
04Huntsville Havoc-15

Simon, Joey
87Sudbury Wolves-11
93Muskegon Fury-11
94Brantford Smoke-9

Simon, Jurgen
94German DEL-194
95German DEL-178
96German DEL-118

Simon, Marc
93Quebec Pee-Wee Tournament-44

Simon, Regg
02Tri-City Stormfront-25

Simon, Robert
94German First League-545

Simon, Todd
907th Inn. Sketch OHL-270
917th Inn. Sketch OHL-211
92Rochester Americans Dunkin' Donuts-16
92Rochester Americans Kodak-21
93Rochester Americans Kodak-22
94Donruss-16
94OPC Premier-469
Special Effects-469
94Pinnacle-491
Artist's Proofs-491
Rink Collection-491
94Score-234
Gold-234
Platinum-234
94Select-195
Gold-195
94Stadium Club-221
Members Only Master Set-221
First Day Issue-221
Super Team Winner Cards-221
94Topps/OPC Premier-469
Special Effects-469
94Upper Deck-456
Electric Ice-456
94Classic Pro Prospects-228
95Las Vegas Thunder-19
96Detroit Vipers-17
96Collector's Edge Ice-157
Prism-157
97Cincinnati Cyclones-16
98Cincinnati Cyclones-20
98Cincinnati Cyclones 2-6
99Cincinnati Cyclones-18
00German DEL-162
01German Upper Deck-73
Skilled Stars-SS4
04German DEL-277

Simonen, Sami
93Finnish SISU-177
94Finnish SISU-33
95Finnish SISU-77
96Finnish SISU Redline-75
98Finnish Keraillysarja-158
Off Duty-7
99Danish Hockey League-77

Simonet, Roland
93Swiss HNL-297
95Swiss HNL-244
96Swiss HNL-457

Simonetti, Frank
98Bruins Alumni-32
Autographs-32

Simoni, Steve
83Ottawa 67's-27
84Ottawa 67's-23
92Oklahoma City Blazers-15
93Oklahoma City Blazers-15
94Central Hockey League-70
94Oklahoma City Blazers-15
95Central Hockey League-51

Simonovic, Miroslav
01Czech OFS-203
Gold Inserts-G10
02Slovakian Kvarteto-31
03Czech OFS Plus All-Star Game-H1

Simons, Mikael
04Swedish Elitset-263
Gold-263
Signatures Series B-11
05Swedish SHL Elitset-117
Gold-117
06Swedish SHL Elitset-128

Simonson, Derek
91Air Canada SJHL-B32
91Air Canada SJHL-E17
92Saskatchewan JHL-50

Simonson, Morgan
03Lincoln Stars-2

Simonton, Reid
98German DEL-238
99Swedish Upper Deck-76
00UK Sekonda Superleague-38
01German Upper Deck-14
02German DEL City Press-18
06UK Coventry Blaze-3

Simpson, Blair
97Medicine Hat Tigers-18
98Medicine Hat Tigers-20

Simpson, Bobby
77O-Pee-Chee NHL-310
78O-Pee-Chee-372

Simpson, Cole
04Moose Jaw Warriors-3
05Moose Jaw Warriors-18

Simpson, Craig
86Penguins Kodak-23
87Oilers Team Issue-18
87O-Pee-Chee-80
87O-Pee-Chee Stickers-166
87Panini Stickers-149
87Penguins Masks-9
87Topps-80
88Oilers Tenth Anniversary-93
88Oilers Team Issue-25
88O-Pee-Chee-27
88O-Pee-Chee Minis-36
88O-Pee-Chee Stickers-123
88O-Pee-Chee Stickers-228
88Panini Stickers-62
88Topps-27
89Kraft-16
89Oilers Team Issue-21
89O-Pee-Chee-99
89O-Pee-Chee Stickers-217
89Panini Stickers-75
89Topps-99
90Bowman-201
Tiffany-201
90Kraft-52
90Oilers IGA-23
90O-Pee-Chee-240
90Panini Stickers-229
90Pro Set-95
90Score-58
Canadian-58
90Score Hottest/Rising Stars-2
90Topps-240
Tiffany-240
90Upper Deck-129
French-129
91Pro Set Platinum-40
91Bowman-107
91Kraft-81
91Oilers Panini Team Stickers-20
91Oilers IGA-22
91Oilers Team Issue-25
91O-Pee-Chee-460
91Panini Stickers-130
91Parkhurst-54
French-54
91Pinnacle-196
French-196
91Pro Set-69
French-69
Puck Candy-9
91Score American-255
91Score Canadian Bilingual-475
91Score Canadian English-475
91Stadium Club-137
91Topps-460
91Upper Deck-286
French-286
92Bowman-150
92Oilers IGA-20
92Oilers Team Issue-17
92O-Pee-Chee-225
92Panini Stickers-102
92Panini Stickers French-102
92Parkhurst-51
Emerald Ice-51
92Pinnacle-321
French-321
92Pro Set-56
92Score-260
Canadian-260
Sharpshooters-30
Sharpshooters Canadian-30
92Stadium Club-473
92Topps-356
Gold-356G
92Ultra-66
92Upper Deck-309
93Donruss-31
93Leaf-344
93OPC Premier-231
93OPC Premier-333
Gold-231
Gold-333
93Panini Stickers-237
93Parkhurst-19
Emerald Ice-19
93Pinnacle-396
Canadian-396
93PowerPlay-301
93Score-139
93Score-557
Gold-557
Canadian-139
Canadian-557
Canadian Gold-557
93Stadium Club-305
Members Only Master Set-305
First Day Issue-305
93Topps/OPC Premier-231
93Topps/OPC Premier-333
Gold-231
Gold-333
93Ultra-277
93Upper Deck-430
SP-19
94Be A Player-R77
94Be A Player-R120
Signature Cards-122
94Donruss-112
94Finest Ring Leaders-7
94Leaf-198
94OPC Premier-349
Special Effects-349
94Parkhurst Vintage-V11
94Parkhurst SE-SE22
Gold-SE22
94Pinnacle-294
Artist's Proofs-294
Rink Collection-294
94Score-54
Gold-54

Platinum-54
94Topps/OPC Premier-349
Special Effects-349
94Ultra-266
94Upper Deck-50
Electric Ice-50
95Collector's Choice-231
Player's Club-231
Player's Club Platinum-231
Simpson, Dave
82Indianapolis Checkers-18
Simpson, Geoff
92Northern Michigan Wildcats-24
93Huntington Blizzard-23
Simpson, Joe
23V128-1 Paulin's Candy-41
24Anonymous NHL-82
24Anonymous NHL-82
83Hall of Fame Postcards-B12
85Hall of Fame-26
04ITG Franchises Update-480
04ITG Ultimate Memorabilia Paper Cuts-23
05ITG Ultimate Mem Amazing Amerks Autos-1
05ITG Ultimate Mem Paper Cut Autos-5
06ITG Ultimate Memorabilia Paper Cuts Autos-12
Simpson, Kent
98Johnstown Chiefs-20
00UK Sekonda Superleague-158
00UK Sekonda Superleague-202
00UK Sheffield Steelers-23
01German Upper Deck-237
02UK Sheffield Steelers-17
05UK Sheffield Steelers-12
Gold-12
Silver-12
Simpson, Paul
93UK Humberside Hawks-6
94UK Humberside Hawks-6
97UK Kingston Hawks Stickers-5
Simpson, Regan
91Air Canada SJHL-E27
92Saskatchewan JHL-86
Simpson, Reid
89ProCards AHL-354
90ProCards AHL/IHL-29
91ProCards-272
96Devils Team Issue-33
97Be A Player-47
Autographs-47
Autographs Die-Cuts-47
Autographs Prismatic Die-Cuts-47
97Devils Team Issue-26
99O-Pee-Chee-87
99O-Pee-Chee Chrome-87
99O-Pee-Chee Chrome Refractors-87
99Topps/OPC-87
99Topps/OPC Chrome-87
Refractors-87
99Cleveland Lumberjacks-21
00Upper Deck NHLPA-PA78
01Canadiens Postcards-25
01O-Pee-Chee-262
01O-Pee-Chee Premier Parallel-262
01Topps-262
OPC Parallel-262
02Milwaukee Admirals-9
03Wilkes-Barre Scranton Penguins-24
Simpson, Sean
93Swiss HNL-110
98Swiss Power Play Stickers-201
03Swiss EV Zug Postcards-24
04Swiss EV Zug Postcards-26
Simpson, Shawn
87Sault Ste. Marie Greyhounds-13
88ProCards AHL-28
89ProCards AHL-98
90ProCards AHL/IHL-215
Simpson, Terry
86Islanders Team Issue-29
90Jets IGA-29
91Jets IGA-29
95Jets Team Issue-4
Simpson, Todd
93Saskatoon Blades-18
94Saint John Flames-20
95Saint John Flames-21
96Be A Player-105
Autographs-105
Autographs Silver-105
97Collector's Choice-36
97Flames Collector's Photos-12
97Pacific-73
Copper-73
Emerald Green-73
Ice Blue-73
Red-73
Silver-73
97Upper Deck-238
99O-Pee-Chee-174
99O-Pee-Chee Chrome-174
99O-Pee-Chee Chrome Refractors-174
99Pacific-61
Copper-61
Emerald Green-61
Gold-61
Ice Blue-61
Premiere Date-61
Red-61
99Topps/OPC-174
99Topps/OPC Chrome-174
Refractors-174
99Upper Deck Retro-10
Gold-10
Platinum-10
00BAP Memorabilia-375
Emerald-375
Ruby-375
Sapphire-375
Promos-375
00BAP Mem Chicago Sportsfest Copper-375
00BAP Memorabilia Chicago Sportsfest Blue-375
00BAP Memorabilia Chicago Sportsfest Gold-375
00BAP Memorabilia Chicago Sportsfest Ruby-375
00BAP Memorabilia Chicago Sun-Times Ruby-375
00BAP Memorabilia Chicago Sun-Times Gold-375
00BAP Mem Chicago Sun-Times Sapphire-375
00BAP Mem Toronto Fall Expo Copper-375
00BAP Memorabilia Toronto Fall Expo Gold-375
00BAP Memorabilia Toronto Fall Expo Ruby-375
00BAP Memorabilia Update Tough Materials-T12
00BAP Mem Update Tough Materials Gold-T12
00BAP Signature Series-93
Emerald-93
Ruby-93
Sapphire-93
Autographs-183
Autographs Gold-183
00Panthers Team Issue-23
01Coyotes Team Issue-18
01O-Pee-Chee-261
01O-Pee-Chee Premier Parallel-261
01Topps-261
OPC Parallel-261
02BAP Sig Series Auto Buybacks 2000-183
02Coyotes Team Issue-2
Simpson, Tom
74O-Pee-Chee WHA-16
75O-Pee-Chee WHA-81
Simpson, Wade
89Oshawa Generals-10
89Oshawa Generals 7th Inning Sketch-8
897th Inn. Sketch OHL-8
907th Inn. Sketch OHL-345
907th Inn. Sketch Memorial Cup-83
91Oshawa Generals-4
91Oshawa Generals Sheet-4
917th Inn. Sketch OHL-167
92Oshawa Generals Sheet-1
Sims, Al
74NHL Action Stamps-20
74O-Pee-Chee NHL-333
75O-Pee-Chee NHL-136
75Topps-136
77Rochester Americans-22
79O-Pee-Chee-272
80O-Pee-Chee-233
80Topps-233
81O-Pee-Chee-131
81O-Pee-Chee Stickers-66
81Topps-E85
89ProCards IHL-138
90ProCards AHL/IHL-539
91ProCards-261
97Milwaukee Admirals-22
98Milwaukee Admirals-1
99IHL All-Stars-22
99Milwaukee Admirals Keebler-19
03Fort Worth Brahmas-19
04Fort Worth Brahmas-19
05WBS Penguins-29
Sims, Dan
94Thunder Bay Flyers-18
Simurda, Dave
82Kingston Canadians-19
83Kingston Canadians-23
Simurda, Marcel
04Czech OFS Czech/Slovak-42
Sinagl, Petr
00Czech OFS-183
02Czech OFS Plus-294
Sinasac, Tim
00Rimouski Oceanic-2
Signed-2
Sincinski, John
97Columbus Cottonmouths-17
Sinclair, Alan
91Michigan Wolverines-17
93Michigan Wolverines-22
Sinclair, Colin
98Kootenay Ice-20
00Kootenay Ice-19
Sinclair, Darren
93Spokane Chiefs-24
94Spokane Chiefs-19
96Syracuse Crunch-10
Sinclair, Doug
91Johnstown Chiefs-5
92Dallas Freeze-16
95Spokane Chiefs-6
Sinclair, Reg
44Beehive Group II Photos-363
51Parkhurst-103
52Parkhurst-104
Sinclair, Robbie
98Columbus Cottonmouths-17
Sindel, Jakub
03Czech OFS Plus-155
04Czech HC Sparta Praha Postcards-21
04Czech OFS-200
04Brandon Wheat Kings-16
05Czech HC Sparta Praha-9
06Czech OFS-284
Sindel, Jaromir
81Swedish Semic Hockey VM Stickers-56
82Swedish Semic VM Stickers-78
83Swedish Semic VM Stickers-78
89Swedish Semic World Champ Stickers-179
91Finnish Jyvas-Hyva Stickers-49
92Finnish Jyvas-Hyva Stickers-155
93Finnish SISU-58
94Czech APS Extraliga-70
98Czech OFS Legends-18
00Czech OFS-81
Sindel, Roman
85Minnesota-Duluth Bulldogs-21
95Czech APS Extraliga-228
Sindelar, Filip
99Czech Score Blue 2000-50
99Czech Score Red Ice 2000-50
06Czech HC Liberec Postcards-8
Sindelar, Roman
94German First League-596
Sindelar, Rudolf
94German First League-313
Sinden, Harry
52Juniors Blue Tint-85
66Topps-31
85Hall of Fame-241
91Bruins Sports Action Legends-31
91Future Trends Canada '72-94
91Future Trends Canada '72 French-94
92Hall of Fame Legends-33
98Bruins Alumni-2
Autographs-2
Sinding Olsen, Ulrick
98Danish Hockey League-226
99Danish Hockey League-148
Sindler, Zdenek
98Czech OFS-161
Sinfeld, Garrett
05Saginaw Spirit-20
Sinfield, Garrett
05Saginaw Spirit-20
06Saginaw Spirit-3
Singbush, Alex
34Beehive Group I Photos-183
40O-Pee-Chee V301-2-114
Singer, Josh
01Michigan Tech Huskies-30
04St. Cloud State Huskies-25
05St. Cloud State Huskies-18
05St. Cloud State Huskies-25
Sinisalo, Ilkka
78Finnish SM-Liiga-40
80Finnish Mallasjuoma-15
82Post Cereal-14
82Swedish Semic VM Stickers-158
83Flyers J.C. Penney-19
83NHL Key Tags-94
84O-Pee-Chee-167
85Flyers Postcards-25
85O-Pee-Chee-188
86Flyers Postcards-23
86O-Pee-Chee-36
86O-Pee-Chee Stickers-238
86Topps-36
87Flyers Postcards-23
87Panini Stickers-136
88Flyers Postcards-18
88O-Pee-Chee-111
88Panini Stickers-325
88Topps-111
89Flyers Postcards-22
90Bowman-112
Tiffany-112
90O-Pee-Chee-152
90OPC Premier-108
90Panini Stickers-123
90Pro Set-223
90Pro Set-461
90Score-286
Canadian-286
90Score Rookie/Traded-93T
90Topps-152
Tiffany-152
90Upper Deck-120
French-120
91O-Pee-Chee-510
91Topps-510
91Finnish Semic World Champ Stickers-206
91Swedish Semic World Champ Stickers-206
94Finnish SISU-90
95Finnish SISU-293
95Finnish SISU Limited-59
99Finnish Cardset Aces High-C-9
99Russian Fetisov Tribute-31
Sinisalo, Tomas
06Finnish Cardset-187
Sinkewich, Russ
04Lincoln Stars Update-34
Sinkkonen, Janne
00Finnish Cardset-197
Sinkkonen, Keijo
66Finnish Jaakiekkosarja-99
72Finnish Jaakiekko-184
Sinkkonen, Martti
65Finnish Hellas-96
66Finnish Jaakiekkosarja-101
72Finnish Jaakiekko-185
Sinkkonen, Olli
01Finnish Cardset-315
Sinner, Stephan
94German DEL-71
95German DEL-57
96German DEL-207
99German Bundesliga 2-58
Sinopoli, Chris
93Quebec Pee-Wee Tournament-1474
Sip, Radek
907th Inn. Sketch WHL-141
917th Inn. Sketch WHL-341
94Czech APS Extraliga-216
95Czech APS Extraliga-167
96Czech APS Extraliga-276
97Czech DS Stickers-187
99Czech Score Blue 2000-35
99Czech Score Red Ice 2000-35
Sipchenko, Igor
00Russian Hockey League-115
Sipilainen, Olli
00Finnish Cardset-324
01Finnish Cardset-118
06Finnish Cardset-255
Sipmeier, Achim
94German First League-337
Sipotz, Brian
04Chicago Wolves-14
05AHL Top Prospects-38
05Chicago Wolves-18
Siren, Esa
71Finnish Suomi Stickers-159
72Finnish Jaakiekko-112
93Swiss HNL-462
Siren, Ismo
03Finnish Cardset-46
Siren, Jaakko
65Finnish Hellas-131
66Finnish Jaakiekkosarja-105
71Finnish Suomi Stickers-186
Siren, Jorma
72Finnish Jaakiekko-277
73Finnish Jaakiekko-169
Siren, Niki
00Finnish Cardset-212
01Finnish Cardset-319
02Swiss HNL-320
Siren, Teemu
99Finnish Cardset-215
00Finnish Cardset-9
01Finnish Cardset-9
Siren, Ville
86Penguins Kodak-24
87Penguins Masks-10
87Penguins Kodak-24
88Panini Stickers-335
90O-Pee-Chee-383
90Pro Set-144
90Topps-383
Tiffany-383
91Finnish Semic World Champ Stickers-9
91Finnish Jyvas-Hyva Stickers-17
91Swedish Semic World Champ Stickers-9
92Finnish Semic-8
92Swedish Semic Elitserien Stickers-181
93Swedish Semic Elitserien-152
93Swedish Semic World Champ Stickers-59
94Finnish SISU-371
94Finnish Jaa Kiekko-15
94Swedish Leaf-246
95Swiss HNL-446
96Swiss HNL-35
98Finnish Kerailysarja-30
99Finnish Cardset Most Wanted-12
Siritsa, Oleg
02Swiss HNL-216
Sirkka, Jeff
85Kingston Canadians-14
86Kingston Canadians-23
87Kingston Canadians-12
89ProCards AHL-59
90ProCards AHL/IHL-406
91ProCards-477
92Rochester Americans Dunkin' Donuts-17
92Rochester Americans Kodak-22
93Portland Pirates-19
97Cincinnati Cyclones-17
98Colorado Gold Kings-21
98Colorado Gold Kings Postcards-4
Sirkkola, Risto
72Finnish Jaakiekko-278
Sirman, Matt
93Quebec Pee-Wee Tournament-564
Siro, Jarmo
72Finnish Jaakiekko-317
Siro, Jukka
72Finnish Jaakiekko-318
Sirois, Allan
98ECHL All-Star Southern Conference-12
02Pee Dee Pride RBI-147
03Florence Pride-156
04Rimouski Oceanic Season Ticket-6
Sirois, Bob
76O-Pee-Chee NHL-323
77O-Pee-Chee NHL-351
78Capitals Team Issue-14
78O-Pee-Chee-96
78Topps-96
79O-Pee-Chee-29
79Topps-29
80O-Pee-Chee-313
Sirota, Jason
91British Columbia JHL-64
Sirvio, Arto
80Finnish Mallasjuoma-12
89Swedish Semic Elitserien Stickers-278
90Swedish Semic Elitserien Stickers-41
92Finnish Jyvas-Hyva Stickers-92
93Finnish Jyvas-Hyva Stickers-179
93Finnish SISU-175
94Finnish SISU-92
95Finnish SISU-292
96Finnish SISU Redline-78
Sisca, Daniel
99Owen Sound Platers-19
00Owen Sound Attack-19
01Mississauga Ice Dogs-22
01Owen Sound Attack-20
02Mississauga Ice Dogs-23
03Sarnia Sting-18
05Florida Everblades-14
Siska, Randy
83Victoria Cougars-22
84Victoria Cougars-23
85Medicine Hat Tigers-21
Sissillan, Patric
907th Inn. Sketch QMJHL-34
Sistonen, Teemu
70Finnish Jaakiekko-224
Sitko, Jon
06Toledo Storm-7
Sittler, Darryl
70Esso Power Players-35
70Maple Leafs Postcards-13
70O-Pee-Chee-218
71Maple Leafs Postcards-18
71O-Pee-Chee-193
71Sargent Promotions Stamps-204
71Toronto Sun-271
72Maple Leafs Postcards-26
72Maple Leafs Postcards-27
72O-Pee-Chee-188
72Sargent Promotions Stamps-204
73Mac's Milk-26
73Maple Leafs Postcards-24
73Maple Leafs Postcards-25
73O-Pee-Chee-132
73Topps-132
74Lipton Soup-3
74Maple Leafs Postcards-21
74NHL Action Stamps-257
74O-Pee-Chee NHL-40
74O-Pee-Chee NHL-219
74Topps-40
74Topps-219
75Heroes Stand-Ups-28
75Maple Leafs Postcards-19
75Maple Leafs Postcards-20
75O-Pee-Chee NHL-150
75O-Pee-Chee NHL-328
75Topps-150
75Topps-328
76Maple Leafs Postcards-16
76O-Pee-Chee NHL-66
76O-Pee-Chee NHL-207
76O-Pee-Chee NHL-394
76Topps-66
76Topps-207
76Topps Glossy Inserts-8
77Coca-Cola-24
77Maple Leafs Postcards-14
77O-Pee-Chee NHL-38
77Sportscasters-4718
77Topps-38
77Topps/O-Pee-Chee Glossy-20
Square-20
77Finnish Sportscasters-53-1265
78Maple Leafs Postcards-19
78O-Pee-Chee-4
78O-Pee-Chee-30
78O-Pee-Chee-64
78O-Pee-Chee-65
78O-Pee-Chee-69
78O-Pee-Chee-331
78Topps-4
78Topps-30
78Topps-64
78Topps-65
78Topps-69
79Maple Leafs Postcards-27
79Maple Leafs Postcards-28
79O-Pee-Chee-120
79Topps-120
80Maple Leafs Postcards-25
80Maple Leafs Postcards-26
80O-Pee-Chee-50
80O-Pee-Chee-165
80O-Pee-Chee-193
80O-Pee-Chee Super-20
80Topps-50
80Topps-165
80Topps-193
81Maple Leafs Postcards-21
81O-Pee-Chee-308
81O-Pee-Chee-312
81O-Pee-Chee Stickers-97
81O-Pee-Chee Stickers-109
81Topps-36
82O-Pee-Chee-257
82O-Pee-Chee Stickers-114
82Post Cereal-14
82Topps Stickers-114
83Flyers J.C. Penney-20
83NHL Key Tags-93
83O-Pee-Chee-257
83O-Pee-Chee-258
83O-Pee-Chee-272
83O-Pee-Chee Stickers-3
83O-Pee-Chee Stickers-191
83Puffy Stickers-10
83Topps Stickers-3
83Topps Stickers-191
84Kellogg's Accordion Discs-6
84O-Pee-Chee-168
84O-Pee-Chee Stickers-108
847-Eleven Discs-38
84Topps-121
85O-Pee-Chee Stickers-36
88Esso All-Stars-43
90Pro Set-404
90Upper Deck-504
French-504
91Kraft-40
92Future Trends '76 Canada Cup-116
92Future Trends '76 Canada Cup-173
92Future Trends '76 Canada Cup-175
92Future Trends '76 Canada Cup-199
92O-Pee-Chee-191
25th Anniv. Inserts-8
92Pinnacle-248
French-248
94Hockey Wit-73
95Zeller's Masters of Hockey Signed-8
99BAP Memorabilia AS Canadian Hobby-CH3
99BAP Memorabilia AS Cdn Hobby Autos-CH3
00Topps AS Sittler-1
00Upper Deck AS Sittler-1
01Fleer Legacy-62
Ultimate-62
In the Corners-10
Memorabilia-23
Memorabilia Autographs-7
01Greats of the Game-52
Autographs-52
Sticks-11
01Topps Archives-39
Arena Seats-ASDSI
Autographs-17
01Upper Deck Legends-59
Sticks-PHDS
02BAP Signature Series Golf-GS28
02BAP Ultimate Memorabilia Great Moments-5
02BAP Ultimate Mem Retro Teammates-1
02Maple Leafs Platinum Collection-67
02Maple Leafs Platinum Collection-92
02Maple Leafs Platinum Collection-101
03BAP Ultimate Mem Retro Teammates-9
03ITG Toronto Fall Expo Forever Rivals-FR6
03Pacific Exhibit-222
03Parkhurst Orig Six He Shoots/Scores-2
03Parkhurst Orig Six He Shoots/Scores-2A
03Parkhurst Original Six Toronto-43
03Parkhurst Original Six Toronto-65
03Parkhurst Original Six Toronto-79
03Parkhurst Original Six Toronto-91
03Parkhurst Original Six Toronto-93
Autographs-9
Inserts-T15
Memorabilia-TM55
04ITG Franchises Canadian-102
Autographs-DS2
Barn Burners-BB2
Barn Burners Gold-BB2
Forever Rivals-FR7
Forever Rivals Gold-FR7
Teammates-TM5
Teammates Gold-TM5
04ITG Franchises He Shoots/Scores Prizes-16
04ITG Franchises Update-487
04ITG Franchises US West-220
Autographs-A-DS1
04ITG Ultimate Memorabilia-127
04ITG Ultimate Memorabilia-189
Gold-127
Gold-189
Cornerstones-7
Cornerstones Gold-7
Day In History-20
Day In History-25
Day In History-28
Day In History Gold-20
Day In History Gold-25
Day In History Gold-28
Heroes Steve Yzerman-4
Jersey Autographs-39
Jersey Autographs Gold-39
Original Six-10
Original Six-11
Retro Teammates-4
Seams Unbelievable-8
Stick Autographs-45
Stick Autographs Gold-45
Triple Threads-12
04UD Legendary Signatures-20
Autographs-DS
HOF Inks-HOF-DS
Linemates-ETDSLM
04UD Legends Classics-55
04UD Legends Classics-59
04UD Legends Classics-86
Gold-55
Gold-59
Gold-86
Platinum-55
Platinum-59
Platinum-86
Silver-55
Silver-59
Silver-86
05ITG Heroes/Prosp Toronto Expo Parallel -32
05ITG Ultimate Memorabilia Level 1-22
05ITG Ultimate Memorabilia Level 2-22
05ITG Ultimate Memorabilia Level 3-22
05ITG Ultimate Memorabilia Level 4-22
05ITG Ultimate Memorabilia Level 5-22
05ITG Ultimate Mem Complete Jersey-14
05ITG Ultimate Mem Complete Jersey Gold-14
05ITG Ultimate Mem Cornerstones Jerseys-5
05ITG Ultimate Mem Cornerst Jerseys Gold-5
05ITG Ultimate Mem Decades Jerseys-6
05ITG Ultimate Mem Decades Jerseys Gold-6
05ITG Ultimate Mem Double Mem Autos-14
05ITG Ultimate Mem Double Mem Autos Gold-14
05ITG Ultimate Memorabilia Emblems-5
05ITG Ultimate Memorabilia Emblems Gold-5
05ITG Ultimate Mem First Rounders Jerseys-4
05ITG Ultimate Mem 1st Round Jersey Gold-4
05ITG Ultimate Memorabilia In The Numbers-5
05ITG Ultimate Mem In The Numbers Gold-5
05ITG Ultimate Mem Jersey and Emblem-26
05ITG Ultimate Mem Jersey Emblems Gold-26
05ITG Ultimate Memorabilia Jerseys-9
05ITG Ultimate Memorabilia Jerseys Gold-9
05ITG Ultimate Mem Raised to the Rafters-5
05ITG Ultimate Mem Raised Rafters Gold-5
05ITG Ultimate Mem Record Breaker Jerseys-10
05ITG Ultimate Mem RecBreak Jerseys Gold-10
05ITG Ultimate Mem Retro Teammate Jerseys-9
05ITG Ult Mem Retro Teammates Jersey Gold-9
05ITG Ultimate Memorabilia Sextuple Autos-5
05ITG Ultimate Mem 3 Star of the Game Jsy-13
05ITG Ult Mem 3 Star of the Game Jsy Gold-13
05ITG Ultimate Memorabilia Triple Autos-6
05ITG Ultimate Mem Triple Autos Gold-6
05ITG Ultimate Memorabilia Ultimate Autos-5
05ITG Ultimate Mem Ultimate Autos Gold-5
05NHL Legends Medallions-21
05SP Authentic Exquisite Endorsements-EEDS
05SP Authentic Sign of the Times Fives-SMSMK
05SP Authentic Six Star Signatures-SSTO
05SP Game Used Authentic Fabrics Dual-SP
05SP Game Used Authentic Patches Dual-SP
05SP Game Used Heritage Classic-HC-DS
05SP Game Used Heritage Classic Autos-HCA-DS
05SP Game Used Heritage Classic Patches-HCP-DS
05SP GameUsed Heritage Classic Patch Auto-HAP-DS
05SP Game Used Oldtimer's Challenge-OC-DS
05SP Game Used Oldtimer's Challenge Autos-OCA-DS
05SP Game Used Oldtimer's Challenge Patch-OCP-DS
05The Cup-93
Gold-93
Black Rainbow-93
Emblems of Endorsement-EEDS
Honorable Numbers-HNDS
Limited Logos-LLDS
Masterpiece Pressplates-93
Noble Numbers-NNMS
Noble Numbers Dual-DNNMS
Noble Numbers Dual-DNNSS
Patch Variation-P93
Patch Variation Autographs-AP93
Scripted Numbers-SNMS
Scripted Numbers Dual-DSNSM
05UD Artifacts Frozen Artifacts-FA-DS
05UD Artifacts Frozen Artifacts Autos-FA-DS
05UD Artifacts Frozen Artifacts Copper-FA-DS
05UD Artifacts Frozen Artifacts Dual-FAD-DS
05UD Artifacts Frozen Artifact Dual Auto-FAD-DS
05UD Artifact Frozen Artifact Dual Copper-FAD-DS
05UD Artifacts Frozen Artifacts Dual Gold-FAD-DS
05UD Artifact Frozen Artifact Dual Maroon-FAD-DS
05UD Artifact Frozen Artifact Dual Pewter-FAD-DS
05UD Artifact Frozen Artifact Dual Silver-FAD-DS
05UD Artifacts Frozen Artifacts Gold-FA-DS
05UD Artifacts Frozen Artifacts Maroon-FA-DS
05UD Artifacts Frozen Artifacts Patches-FP-DS
05UD Artifact Frozen Artifact Patch Autos-FP-DS
05UD Artifacts Frozen Artifact Patch Dual-FPD-DS
05UD Artifacts Frozen Art Patch Dual Auto-FPD-DS
05UD Artifacts Frozen Art Patch Pewter-FP-DS
05UD Artifacts Frozen Art Patch Silver-FP-DS
05UD Artifacts Frozen Artifacts Pewter-FA-DS
05UD Artifacts Frozen Artifacts Silver-FA-DS
05Ultimate Collection Endorsed Emblems-EEDS
05Upper Deck All-Time Greatest-56
05Upper Deck Notable Numbers-N-DS
05ITG Heroes and Prospects-32
Aspiring-ASP15
Autographs-A-DS
Hero Memorabilia-HM-35
National Pride-NPR-14
06Beehive Signature Scrapbook-SSDS
06ITG International Ice-22
Gold-22
Autographs-ADS
Canadian Dream Team-DT06
Canadian Dream Team Gold-DT06
Emblem Autographs-GUE35
Emblem Autographs Gold-GUE35
Emblems-GUE35
Emblems Gold-GUE35
Greatest Moments-GM05
Greatest Moments Gold-GM05
International Rivals-IR05
International Rivals Gold-IR05
Jersey Autographs-GUJ35
Jersey Autographs Gold-GUJ35
Jerseys-GUJ35
Jerseys Gold-GUJ35
My Country My Team-MC24
My Country My Team Gold-MC24
Numbers-GUN35
Numbers Autographs-GUN35
Numbers Autographs Gold-GUN35
Numbers Gold-GUN35
Teammates-IT03
Teammates Gold-IT03
Triple Memorabilia-TM01
Triple Memorabilia Gold-TM01
06ITG Ultimate Memorabilia-36
Artist Proof-36
Autos-31
Autos Gold-31
Autos Triple-9
Autos Triple Gold-9
Blades of Steel-5
Blades of Steel Gold-5
Captain-C-9
Captain-C Gold-9
Cornerstones-3
Cornerstones Gold-3
Decades-2
Decades Gold-2
Jerseys Autos-53
Jerseys Autos Gold-53
Legendary Captains-9
Legendary Captains Gold-9
Passing The Torch-2
Passing The Torch Gold-2
Retro Teammates-14
Retro Teammates Gold-14
Stick Rack-9
Stick Rack-22
Stick Rack Gold-9
Stick Rack Gold-22
Sticks Autos-27
Sticks Autos Gold-27
06Parkhurst-116
06Parkhurst-209
Autographs-116
Autographs-209
Autographs Dual-DASV
06SP Authentic Sign of the Times Quads-ST4BCTS
06SP Game Used Authentic Fabrics Quads-AF4NMBT
06SP Game Used Authentic Fabrics Quads Patches-AF4NMBT
06SPx-138
Spectrum-138
SPxcitement-X92
SPxcitement Spectrum-X92
SPxcitement Autographs-X92
06The Cup-84
Autographed Patches-84
Black Rainbow-84
Gold-84
Gold Patches-84
Honorable Numbers-HNDS
Jerseys-84
Limited Logos-LLDS
Masterpiece Pressplates-84
Scripted Swatches Duals-DSDB
06UD Artifacts-135
Blue-135
Gold-135
Platinum-135
Radiance-135
Autographed Radiance Parallel-135
Red-135
Frozen Artifacts-FADS
Frozen Artifacts Black-FADS
Frozen Artifacts Blue-FADS
Frozen Artifacts Gold-FADS
Frozen Artifacts Platinum-FADS
Frozen Artifacts Red-FADS
Frozen Artifacts Autographed Black-FADS
Frozen Artifacts Patches Black-FADS
Frozen Artifacts Patches Blue-FADS
Frozen Artifacts Patches Gold-FADS
Frozen Artifacts Patches Platinum-FADS
Frozen Artifacts Patches Red-FADS
Frozen Artifacts Patches Autographed Black Tag Parallel-FADS
Tundra Tandems-TTDB
Tundra Tandems-TTSV
Tundra Tandems Black-TTDB
Tundra Tandems Black-TTSV
Tundra Tandems Blue-TTDB
Tundra Tandems Blue-TTSV
Tundra Tandems Gold-TTDB
Tundra Tandems Gold-TTSV
Tundra Tandems Platinum-TTDB
Tundra Tandems Platinum-TTSV
Tundra Tandems Red-TTDB
Tundra Tandems Red-TTSV
Tundra Tandems Dual Patches Red-TTDB
Tundra Tandems Dual Patches Red-TTSV
06Ultimate Collection Jerseys Dual-UJ2-DB
06Ultimate Collection Jerseys Triple-UJ3-SSH
06Ultimate Collection Patches Dual-UJ2-DB
06Ultimate Collection Patches Triple-UJ3-SSH
06Upper Deck All-Time Greatest-ATG21
06Upper Deck Sweet Shot-97
Signature Shots/Saves Sticks-SSSSI
Sweet Stitches-SSDS
Sweet Stitches Duals-SSDS
Sweet Stitches Triples-SSDS
06Upper Deck Trilogy Combo Clearcut Autographs-C3MSS
06Upper Deck Trilogy Honorary Scripted Patches-HSPDS
06Upper Deck Trilogy Honorary Scripted Swatches-HSSDS
06Upper Deck Trilogy Honorary Swatches-HSDS
06Upper Deck Trilogy Scripts-S2DS
Sittler, Ryan
91Upper Deck-695
French-695
91Upper Deck Czech World Juniors-82
93Donruss Team USA-19
93Pinnacle-499
Canadian-499
93Upper Deck-551
93Michigan Wolverines-23
95Images-65
Gold-65
98Charlotte Checkers-16
06ITG International Ice Greatest Moments Gold-GM05
Sittlow, Chris
93Minnesota-Duluth Bulldogs-28
Sivek, Michal
97Czech APS Extraliga-17
98Czech OFS-369
99Black Diamond-116
Diamond Cut-116
Final Cut-116
99SP Authentic-133
99Upper Deck MVP SC Edition-205
Gold Script-205
Silver Script-205
Super Script-205
99UD Prospects-59
00Czech OFS-312
02Wilkes-Barre Scranton Penguins-14
03ITG Action-485
03Pacific AHL Prospects-97
Gold-97
03Wilkes-Barre Scranton Penguins-25
04Czech HC Sparta Praha Postcards-22
04Czech OFS-201
Stars-50
05Czech HC Sparta Praha-10
06Czech CP Cup Postcards-17
06Czech HC Sparta Praha Postcards-10
06Czech OFS-71
Sivertson, Daryn
84Kelowna Wings-6
Sivertsson, Lars-Ake
64Swedish Coralli ISHockey-22
64Swedish Coralli ISHockey-84
65Swedish Coralli ISHockey-22
65Swedish Coralli ISHockey-84
67Swedish Hockey-57
69Swedish Hockey-72
70Swedish Hockey-34
71Swedish Hockey-112
Sives, Dean
90Arizona Icecats-13
91Arizona Icecats-11
Sivic, Mitja
93Quebec Pee-Wee Tournament-1784
Sivonen, Heikki
66Finnish Jaakiekkosarja-173
Sivonen, Mikko
00Knoxville Speed-18
Sivov, Alexander
99Russian Hockey League-243
Siwiec, Stephen
03Boston University Terriers-2
Sjalin, Kent
65Swedish Coralli ISHockey-180
Sjalin, Tommy
83Swedish Semic Elitserien-160
Sjatavalov, Juri
74Swedish Stickers-57
Sjerven, Grant
93St. Cloud State Huskies-27
94Richmond Renegades-13
95Richmond Renegades-19
96Richmond Renegades-20
99UK Sheffield Steelers-18
Sjilov, Viktor
73Swedish Stickers-135
Sjoberg, Christer
71Swedish Hockey-339
Sjoberg, Goran
83Swedish Semic Elitserien-68
89Swedish Semic Elitserien Stickers-251
90Swedish Semic Elitserien Stickers-161
96Swedish Brynas Tigers-26
Sjoberg, Hans
64Swedish Coralli ISHockey-86
65Swedish Coralli ISHockey-86
67Swedish Hockey-58
Sjoberg, Jarl
56Swedish Alfabilder-52
Sjoberg, Lars-Erik
64Swedish Coralli ISHockey-47
65Swedish Coralli ISHockey-47
67Swedish Hockey-72
69Swedish Hockey-124
69Swedish Hockey-198
70Finnish Jaakiekko-37
70Swedish Hockey-249
70Swedish Hockey-280
70Swedish Masterserien-42
70Swedish Masterserien-54
70Swedish Masterserien-55
70Swedish Masterserien-111
71Swedish Hockey-11
71Swedish Hockey-306
72Finnish Jaakiekko-57
72Finnish Hellas-27
72Finnish Semic World Championship-45
72Swedish Stickers-8
72Swedish Stickers-291
72Swedish Semic World Championship-45
73Finnish Jaakiekko-35
73Swedish Stickers-4
73Swedish Stickers-138
74O-Pee-Chee WHA-66
74Finnish Jenkki-34
74Swedish Stickers-20
74Swedish Stickers-188
74Swedish Semic World Champ Stickers-4
75O-Pee-Chee WHA-109
76O-Pee-Chee WHA-30
76O-Pee-Chee WHA-63
77O-Pee-Chee WHA-21
78Jets Postcards-20
79Jets Postcards-21
79O-Pee-Chee-396
Sjodin, Tommy
86Swedish Panini Stickers-41
89Swedish Semic Elitserien Stickers-30
90Swedish Semic Elitserien Stickers-177
91Swedish Semic Elitserien Stickers-31
92OPC Premier-109
92Parkhurst-79
92Parkhurst-224
Emerald Ice-79
Emerald Ice-224
92Pinnacle-401
French-401
92Ultra-323
92Upper Deck-528
92Swedish Semic Elitserien Stickers-336
92Swedish Semic Elitserien Stickers-344
93PowerPlay-65
93Score-248
Canadian-248
93Stadium Club-106
Members Only Master Set-106
OPC-106
First Day Issue-106
First Day Issue OPC-106
93Ultra-233
93Swedish Semic World Champ Stickers-24
94EA Sports-32
95Finnish Semic World Championships-61
95Swedish Globe World Championships-16
95Swedish World Championships Stickers-139
95Swiss HNL-142
95Swiss HNL-512
95Swiss HNL-525
96Swedish Semic Wien-48
All-Stars-AS3
96Swiss HNL-159
98Swiss Power Play Stickers-110
99Swedish Upper Deck-19
SHL Signatures-18
00Swedish Upper Deck-32
00Swedish Upper Deck-184
01Swedish Brynas Tigers-24
02Swedish SHL-3
Dynamic Duos-1
Parallel-3
02Swedish SHL Promos-TCC1
03Swedish Elite-3
Signatures-2
Silver-3
04Swedish Elitset-3
Gold-3
04Swedish Pure Skills-3
Parallel-3
05Swedish SHL Elitset-4
06Swedish SHL Elitset-3
Sjogren, Christian
01Finnish Cardset-342
03Swedish Elite-131
Enforcers-EF10
Silver-131
04Swedish Elitset-131
Gold-131
Sjogren, Olle
64Swedish Coralli ISHockey-59
65Swedish Coralli ISHockey-59
67Swedish Hockey-110
69Swedish Hockey-125
70Swedish Hockey-79
71Swedish Hockey-170
72Swedish Stickers-158
Sjogren, Soren
71Swedish Hockey-92
72Swedish Stickers-58
73Swedish Stickers-197
Sjogren, Thomas
89Swedish Semic Elitserien Stickers-229
90ProCards AHL/IHL-204
91Swedish Semic Elitserien Stickers-296
92Swedish Semic Elitserien Stickers-323
93Swedish Semic Elitserien-276
94Swedish Leaf-46
95Finnish SISU-265
95Finnish SISU-382
95Finnish SISU Limited-52
95Finnish SISU Spotlights-5
96Finnish SISU Redline-65
Mighty Adversaries-5
96Finnish SISU Redline Promos-5
98Swedish UD Choice-140
99German DEL-273
00German DEL-32
Sjoholm, Bengt
71Swedish Hockey-307
73Swedish Stickers-139
Sjokvist, Gosta
67Swedish Hockey-227
69Swedish Hockey-270
Sjokvist, Niklas
97Swedish Collector's Choice-54
98Swedish UD Choice-91
99Swedish Upper Deck-60
Sjolander, Par
83Swedish Semic Elitserien-33
Sjolund, Andreas
95Collector's Choice-340
Player's Club-340
Player's Club Platinum-340
97Idaho Steelheads-12
98Idaho Steelheads-18
99Idaho Steelheads-20
Sjoman, Ari
73Finnish Jaakiekko-320
Sjoo, Hasse
83Swedish Semic Elitserien-238
87Swedish Panini Stickers-123
89Swedish Semic Elitserien Stickers-107

Sjoqvist, Bernt
56Swedish Alfabilder-107
Sjoroos, Rauno
80Finnish Mallasjuoma-194
Sjostedt, Bo
71Finnish Suomi Stickers-295
Sjostrom, Bo
69Swedish Hockey-212
Sjostrom, Dick
69Swedish Hockey-213
Sjostrom, Fredrik
01BAP Memorabilia Draft Redemptions-11
01Calgary Hitmen-23
01Calgary Hitmen Autographed-23
02Calgary Hitmen-11
03BAP Memorabilia-209
03BAP Ultimate Memorabilia Autographs-121
Gold-121
03Beehive-218
Gold-218
Silver-218
03Coyotes Postcards-21
03ITG Used Signature Series-137
Autographs Gold-137
03ITG VIP Rookie Debut-70
03Pacific-366
03Pacific Calder-129
Silver-129
03Pacific Complete-542
Red-542
03Pacific Heads-Up-129
Hobby LTD-129
Retail LTD-129
03Pacific Luxury Suite-73
Gold-73
03Pacific Quest for the Cup-130
03Parkhurst Rookie-156
03SP Authentic-116
Limited-116
03SP Game Used-126
03SPx-237
03Titanium-131
Hobby Jersey Number Parallels-131
Retail-131
Retail Jersey Number Parallels-131
03Topps Traded-TT135
Blue-TT135
Gold-TT135
Red-TT135
03UD Premier Collection-105
03Upper Deck-455
Canadian Exclusives-455
HG-455
UD Exclusives-455
03Upper Deck Classic Portraits-193
03Upper Deck Ice-127
Glass Parallel-127
03Upper Deck Rookie Update-164
Top Draws-TD20
03Upper Deck Trilogy-185
03Pacific AHL Prospects-78
Gold-78
03Springfield Falcons Postcards-10
04Pacific-206
Blue-206
Red-206
04SP Authentic Sign of the Times-ST-FS
04SP Authentic Sign of the Times-DS-DS
04Upper Deck All-Star Promos-FS
04Swedish Alfabilder Alfa Stars-37
04Swedish Alfabilder Proof Parallels-37
04ITG Heroes and Prospects-112
Autographs-FS
04ITG Heroes/Prospects Toronto Expo '05-112
04ITG Heroes/Prospects Expo Heroes/Pros-112
05Black Diamond Gemography-G-FS
05Black Diamond Gemography Emerald-G-FS
05Black Diamond Gemography Gold-G-FS
05Black Diamond Gemography Onyx-G-FS
05Black Diamond Gemography Ruby-G-FS
05Parkhurst-379
Facsimile Auto Parallel-379
05UD Powerplay Power Marks-PMFS
05Upper Deck Trilogy Scripts-SFS-FS
06O-Pee-Chee-387
Rainbow-387
06UD Toronto Fall Expo Priority Signings -PSFS
06Upper Deck Signature Sensations-SSFS
Sjostrom, Lasse
69Swedish Hockey-214
70Swedish Hockey-210
71Swedish Hockey-299
Sjtjegolev, Stanislav
73Swedish Stickers-127
Skaarberg, Tommy
92Norwegian Elite Series-86
Skaare, Bjorn
92Norwegian Elite Series-197
Skabelka, Andrei
98Russian Hockey League-74
00Russian Hockey League-164
04Russian Super League All-Stars-27
Skadra, Martin
04Slovakian Skalica Team Set-28
Skalde, Jarrod
89Oshawa Generals-18
89Oshawa Generals 7th Inning Sketch-2
897th Inn. Sketch OHL-2
897th Inn. Sketch OHL-193
907th Inn. Sketch OHL-346
907th Inn. Sketch Memorial Cup-91
91Score American-392
91Score Canadian Bilingual-282
91Score Canadian English-282
91Upper Deck-446
French-446
91ProCards-411
92Pro Set-231
92Stadium Club-189
92Topps-84
Gold-84G
92Upper Deck-91
93Leaf-333
93PowerPlay-11
93Upper Deck-12
93San Diego Gulls-19
94Las Vegas Thunder-27
94Classic Pro Prospects-192
95Saint John Flames-22
96Saint John Flames-18
96Collector's Edge Ice-15
Prism-15
97Be A Player-198
Autographs-198
Autographs Die-Cuts-198
Autographs Prismatic Die-Cuts-198
98Kentucky Thoroughblades-18
99IHL All-Stars-19
99Utah Grizzlies-5
00Topps Heritage-213
01Chicago Wolves-20
02Swiss HNL-304
Skaleski, Ryan
99Ohio State Buckeyes-16
00Richmond Renegades-12
Skar, T.
74Finnish Typotor-81
Skarda, Krysta
04Ohio State Buckeyes Women-13
05Ohio State Buckeyes Women-7
06Ohio State Buckeyes Women-10
Skarda, Randy
90ProCards AHL/IHL-81
Skarica, Pasko
05Waterloo Blackhawks-19
Skarin, Hans-Gunnar
72Swedish Stickers-202
Skarm, Roland
57Swedish Alfabilder-127
Skarp, Lennart
57Swedish Alfabilder-119
Skarperud, Tim
98Sioux City Musketeers-22
02Grand Rapids Griffins-25
03Grand Rapids Griffins-20
Skaug, Eric
01Ohio State Buckeyes-14
02Ohio State Buckeyes-11
Skazyk, Eddy
93Cornell Big Red-24
97Bakersfield Fog-16
99Corpus Christi IceRays-21
Skellett, Jason
897th Inn. Sketch OHL-91
907th Inn. Sketch OHL-216
Skellett, Jordan
05Mississauga Ice Dogs-11
06Mississauga Ice Dogs-11
Skene, Dan
92British Columbia JHL-234
Skene, Ricky
02UK Guildford Flames-17
06UK Guildford Flames-21
Skiehar, Shawn
02Louisiana Ice Gators-19
03South Carolina Stingrays-334
04Louisiana Ice Gators-20
Skille, Jack
05Wisconsin Badgers-23
06ITG Ultimate Memorabilia Future Star-25
06ITG Ultimate Memorabilia Future Star Gold-25
06ITG Ultimate Memorabilia Future Star Autos-12
06ITG Ultimate Memorabilia Future Star Autos Gold-12
06ITG Ultimate Memorabilia Future Star Patches Autos-12
06ITG Ultimate Memorabilia Future Star Patches Autos Gold-12
Skillgard, Johan
90Brandon Wheat Kings-16
907th Inn. Sketch WHL-223
Skilliter, Willie
917th Inn. Sketch OHL-275
93Owen Sound Platers-26
94Owen Sound Platers-6
Skilnick, Jason
95Brandon Wheat Kings-18
Skime, Larry
70Swedish Masterserien-178
Skinnari, Mikko
04UK Milton Keynes Lightning-13
Skinnari, Ville
93Finnish SISU-285
93Finnish SISU-293B
Skinner, Alf
24C144 Champ's Cigarettes-55
24V130 Maple Crispette-5
24V145-2-27
Skinner, Brett
05Manitoba Moose-21
06Portland Pirates-14
Skinner, Danny
93Quebec Pee-Wee Tournament-636
Skinner, Jim
94Parkhurst Missing Link-63
Skinner, Larry
76Rockies Puck Bucks-20
Skinner, Peder
05Kingston Frontenacs-20
06Kingston Frontenacs-5
Skinner, Robert
05Penticton Vees-16
06Penticton Vees-18
Skinner, Tom
01German Berlin Polar Bears Postcards-24
Skinns, Dean
03UK Basingstoke Bison-2
Skjodt, Charlie
81Indianapolis Checkers-17
Skladany, Frantisek
96Slovakian Quebec Pee-Wee Tournament-25
03Boston University Terriers-26
04Hershey Bears Patriot News-24
06Czech OFS-41
Sklenar, Jakub
06Czech OFS-302
Sklenar, Jaroslav
02Czech OFS Plus-118
02Czech OFS Plus-314
Sklenicka, Zbynek
04Czech OFS-105
06Czech OFS-146
Skoda, Vladimir
03Czech OFS Plus-273
06Czech HC Vsetin Postcards-8
06Czech OFS-192
Skogland, Mike
95North Iowa Huskies-30
Skoglund, Emil
92Swedish Semic Elitserien Stickers-162
Skoglund, Ulf
83Swedish Semic Elitserien-143
84Swedish Semic Elitserien-164
85Swedish Panini Stickers-148
86Swedish Panini Stickers-151
87Swedish Panini Stickers-165
Skogs, Borje
71Swedish Hockey-219
72Swedish Stickers-195
Skogs, Thomas
05Swedish SHL Elitset-259
Gold-259
06Swedish SHL Elitset-119
Skokan, Ales
99Czech Score Blue 2000-58
99Czech Score Red Ice 2000-58
Skokan, David
06Rimouski Oceanic-7
Skold, Joakim
91Swedish Semic Elitserien Stickers-250
Skold, Leif
64Swedish Coralli ISHockey-126
Skolney, Shawn
96Seattle Thunderbirds-24
97Moose Jaw Warriors-14
Skolney, Wade
97Brandon Wheat Kings-21
98Brandon Wheat Kings-18
99Brandon Wheat Kings-18
00Brandon Wheat Kings-22
01Brandon Wheat Kings-19
02Philadelphia Phantoms-20
03Philadelphia Phantoms-23
04Philadelphia Phantoms-19
05Hot Prospects-156
En Fuego-156
Red Hot-156
White Hot-156
05SP Game Used-165
Gold-165
05SPx-196
Spectrum-196
05The Cup Masterpiece Pressplates (Ice)-161
05The Cup Master Pressplate Rookie Update-162
05The Cup Masterpiece Pressplates SP GU-165
05The Cup Masterpiece Pressplates (SPx)-196
05Ultra-237
Gold-237
Ice-237
05Upper Deck Ice-161
05Upper Deck Rookie Update-162
05Philadelphia Phantoms-20
06Wilkes-Barre Scranton Penguins-22
06Wilkes-Barre Scranton Penguins Jerseys-20
Skonberg, Alf
57Swedish Alfabilder-78
Skoog, Borje
70Swedish Hockey-127
Skoog, Robert
84Swedish Semic Elitserien-171
85Swedish Panini Stickers-156
86Swedish Panini Stickers-166
87Swedish Panini Stickers-171
89Swedish Semic Elitserien Stickers-146
90Swedish Semic Elitserien Stickers-224
91Swedish Semic Elitserien Stickers-152
92Swedish Semic Elitserien Stickers-175
93Swedish Semic Elitserien-146
Skoog, Simon
03Swedish Elite-191
Silver-191
04Swedish HV71 Postcards-3
05Swedish SHL Elitset-54
Gold-54
06Swedish SHL Elitset-229
Skopac, Tony
92Swedish Semic Elitserien Stickers-89
94Swedish Leaf-230
95Swedish Upper Deck 1st Division Stars-DS10
Skopintsev, Andrei
95German DEL-10
95Swedish World Championships Stickers-31
96Swedish Semic Wien-140
98Cleveland Lumberjacks-21
00BAP Memorabilia-251
Emerald-251
Ruby-251
Sapphire-251
Promos-251
00BAP Mem Chicago Sportsfest Copper-251
00BAP Memorabilia Chicago Sportsfest Blue-251
00BAP Memorabilia Chicago Sportsfest Gold-251
00BAP Memorabilia Chicago Sportsfest Ruby-251
00BAP Memorabilia Chicago Sun-Times Ruby-251
00BAP Memorabilia Chicago Sun-Times Gold-251
00BAP Mem Chicago Sun-Times Sapphire-251
00BAP Mem Toronto Fall Expo Copper-251
00BAP Memorabilia Toronto Fall Expo Gold-251
00BAP Memorabilia Toronto Fall Expo Ruby-251
01Russian Dynamo Moscow-5
01Russian Dynamo Moscow Mentos-11
02Russian SL-7
03Russian Hockey League-35
04Russian Moscow Dynamo-28
04Russian World Championship Team-5
Skoptsov, Alexander
00Russian Hockey League-328
01Russian Hockey League-150
Skordaker, Lennart
67Swedish Hockey-164
Skorepa, Zdenek
94Czech APS Extraliga-214
95Slapshot-120
96Albany River Rats-17
97Albany River Rats-15
98Czech OFS-271
99Czech DS-68
99Czech OFS-158
99Czech OFS-390
00Czech DS Extraliga-120
00Czech OFS-98
01Czech OFS-63
02Czech OFS Plus-335
03Czech OFS Plus-279
03Czech OFS Plus Insert M-M14
03Russian Hockey League-199
04Czech OFS-222
06Czech OFS-167
Skorodenski, Warren
85Blackhawks Team Issue-16
85O-Pee-Chee-255
85O-Pee-Chee-264
85Nova Scotia Oilers-11
87Oilers Team Issue-30
88Oilers Tenth Anniversary-131
Skorohod, Alexander
01Mississauga Ice Dogs-14
Skorvaga, Norbert
95Slovakian-Quebec Pee-Wee Tournament-24
Skoryna, Chris
917th Inn. Sketch OHL-36
93Guelph Storm-18
96St. Louis Vipers RHI-5
00Fresno Falcons-16
01Fresno Falcons-15
02Bakersfield Condors-16
Skosyrev, Sergei
90O-Pee-Chee-496
Skoula, Martin
96Barrie Colts-22
98Finest Futures Finest-F14
98Finest Futures Finest Refractors-F14
98Barrie Colts-7
98Bowman CHL-22
98Bowman CHL-158
Golden Anniversary-22
Golden Anniversary-158
OPC International-22
OPC International-158
Autographs Blue-A39
Autographs Gold-A39
Autographs Silver-A39
98Bowman Chrome CHL-22
98Bowman Chrome CHL-158
Golden Anniversary-22
Golden Anniversary-158
Golden Anniversary Refractors-22
Golden Anniversary Refractors-158
OPC International-22
OPC International-158
OPC International Refractors-22
OPC International Refractors-158
Refractors-22
Refractors-158
99Avalanche Team Issue-22
99BAP Memorabilia-314
Gold-314
Silver-314
99BAP Millennium Calder Candidates Ruby-C14
99BAP Millennium Calder Candidate Emerald-C14
99BAP Millennium Calder Cand Sapphire-C14
99Pacific Dynagon Ice-61
Blue-61
Copper-61
Gold-61
Premiere Date-61
99Pacific Omega-68
Copper-68
Gold-68
Ice Blue-68
Premiere Date-68
99Stadium Club-187
First Day Issue-187
One of a Kind-187
Printing Plates Black-187
Printing Plates Cyan-187
Printing Plates Magenta-187
Printing Plates Yellow-187
99Topps Premier Plus-132
Parallel-132
99Bowman CHL-140
Gold-140
OPC International-140
00BAP Memorabilia-29
Emerald-29
Ruby-29
Sapphire-29
Promos-29
00BAP Mem Chicago Sportsfest Copper-29
00BAP Memorabilia Chicago Sportsfest Blue-29
00BAP Memorabilia Chicago Sportsfest Gold-29
00BAP Memorabilia Chicago Sportsfest Ruby-29
00BAP Memorabilia Chicago Sun-Times Ruby-29
00BAP Memorabilia Chicago Sun-Times Gold-29
00BAP Mem Chicago Sun-Times Sapphire-29
00BAP Mem Toronto Fall Expo Copper-29
00BAP Memorabilia Toronto Fall Expo Gold-29
00BAP Memorabilia Toronto Fall Expo Ruby-29
00BAP Signature Series-109
Emerald-109
Ruby-109
Sapphire-109
Autographs-90
Autographs Gold-90
00O-Pee-Chee-48
00O-Pee-Chee Parallel-48
00Pacific-122
Copper-122
Gold-122
Ice Blue-122
Premiere Date-122
00Paramount-64
Copper-64
Gold-64
Holo-Gold-64
Holo-Silver-64
Ice Blue-64
Premiere Date-64
Game Used Sticks-6
00Private Stock Game Gear-31
00Topps/OPC-48
Parallel-48
00Topps Chrome-39
OPC Refractors-39
Refractors-39
00Topps Stars Progression-P9
00Upper Deck-47
Exclusives Tier 1-47
Exclusives Tier 2-47
01Avalanche Team Issue-17
01BAP Memorabilia-283
Emerald-283
Ruby-283
Sapphire-283
Stanley Cup Champions-CA4
01BAP Signature Series-106
Autographs-106
Autographs Gold-106
01O-Pee-Chee-151
01O-Pee-Chee Premier Parallel-151
01Topps-151
OPC Parallel-151
01Czech Stadion-224
02Avalanche Postcards-10
02BAP First Edition-50
Jerseys-50
02BAP Sig Series Auto Buybacks 2000-90
02BAP Sig Series Auto Buybacks 2001-106
02BAP Signature Series Golf-GS53
02Pacific Complete-76
Red-76
02Topps Total-299
02Czech Stadion Olympics-350
03ITG Action-156
03O-Pee-Chee-141
03OPC Blue-141
03OPC Gold-141
03OPC Red-141
03Pacific Complete-30
Red-30
03Topps-141
Blue-141
Gold-141
Red-141
03Topps Traded-TT70
Blue-TT70
Gold-TT70
Red-TT70
04Pacific-8
Blue-8
Red-8
04Czech OFS-106
Checklist Cards-5
Stars-7
04Czech Zuma-16
04Barrie Colts 10th Anniversary-4
05Parkhurst-242
Facsimile Auto Parallel-154
05Upper Deck MVP-138
Gold-138
Platinum-138
05Czech Kvarteto Bonaparte-2b
06Panini Stickers-300
06Czech IIHF World Championship Postcards-19
06Czech LG Hockey Games Postcards-19
Skov, Anders
99Danish Hockey League-15
Skov, Elmer
52Juniors Blue Tint-10
Skov, Glen
44Beehive Group II Photos-210
51Parkhurst-57
52Parkhurst-63
53Parkhurst-48
54Parkhurst-40
54Topps-16
57Topps-30
58Topps-3
59Topps-12
76Old Timers-17
81Red Wings Oldtimers-19
94Parkhurst Missing Link-23
Skov, Jesper
98Danish Hockey League-3
Skovby, Casper
99Danish Hockey League-192
Skovira, Miroslav
95Czech APS Extraliga-237
03Czech OFS Plus All-Star Game-H10
04Slovakian Poprad Team Set-16
Skraem, Peter
98Danish Hockey League-105
99Danish Hockey League-110
Skrastins, Karlis
95Finnish SISU-326
95Finnish SISU-383
98Milwaukee Admirals-15
99BAP Memorabilia-379
Gold-379
Silver-379
99Pacific Omega-131
Copper-131
Gold-131
Ice Blue-131
Premiere Date-131
99Upper Deck Gold Reserve-344
00O-Pee-Chee-212
00O-Pee-Chee Parallel-212
00Topps/OPC-212
Parallel-212
01UD Mask Collection-52
Gold-52
03Avalanche Team Issue-17
03Pacific Complete-307
Red-307
05Parkhurst-130
Facsimile Auto Parallel-130
05Upper Deck MVP-111
Gold-111
Platinum-111
06Avalanche Team Postcards-15
06O-Pee-Chee-135
Rainbow-135
Skrbek, Pavel
95Czech APS Extraliga-348
96Czech APS Extraliga-82
97Czech APS Extraliga-200
97Czech DS Extraliga-91
98Czech DS Stickers-232
99Czech OFS-34
99Czech OFS Jagr Team Embossed-34
00Milwaukee Admirals Keebler-16
00Milwaukee Admirals Postcards-14
01BAP Memorabilia-354
Emerald-354
Ruby-354
Sapphire-354
01Parkhurst-325
01SP Authentic-156
Limited-156
Limited Gold-156
01UD Challenge for the Cup-116
01Upper Deck Ice-78
01Upper Deck Victory-378
Gold-378
01Czech OFS Update-295
02Swedish SHL-218
Parallel-218
02Swiss SCL Tigers-2
03Swedish Elite-81
Silver-81
04Swedish Elitset-254
Gold-254
04Swedish Pure Skills-74
Parallel-74
05Swedish Lulea Hockey Postcards-9
05Swedish SHL Elitset-232
Gold-232
06Swedish SHL Elitset-213
Skriko, Petri
83Swedish Semic VM Stickers-41
84Canucks Team Issue-21
85Canucks Team Issue-20
86Canucks Team Issue-11
86Kraft Drawings-63
86O-Pee-Chee-252
86O-Pee-Chee Stickers-103
87Canucks Shell Oil-18
87O-Pee-Chee-255
87O-Pee-Chee Minis-40
87O-Pee-Chee Stickers-192
87Panini Stickers-347
88Canucks Mohawk-18
88O-Pee-Chee-137
88O-Pee-Chee Stickers-64
88Panini Stickers-140
88Topps-137
89Canucks Mohawk-17
89O-Pee-Chee-33
89O-Pee-Chee Box Bottoms-D
89O-Pee-Chee Stickers-70
89Panini Stickers-147
89Topps-33
89Topps Box Bottoms-D
89Swedish Semic World Champ Stickers-44
90Bowman-54
Tiffany-54
90O-Pee-Chee-316
90Panini Stickers-298
90Pro Set-306
90Score-154
Canadian-154
90Topps-316
Tiffany-316
90Upper Deck-147
90Upper Deck-302
French-147
French-302
91Bowman-364
91Canucks Panini Team Stickers-22
91O-Pee-Chee-30
91Pro Set-8
91Pro Set-517
French-8
French-517
91Score American-188
91Score Canadian Bilingual-188
91Score Canadian English-188
91Score Rookie/Traded-72T
91Stadium Club-315
91Topps-30
91Upper Deck-334
French-334
91Finnish Semic World Champ Stickers-204
91Swedish Semic World Champ Stickers-204
92Finnish Semic-12
93Finnish SISU Promos-NNO
93Swedish Semic World Champ Stickers-79
98Danish Hockey League-167
Skrlac, Rob
95Kamloops Blazers-14
96Kamloops Blazers-24
97Albany River Rats-16
98Albany River Rats-16
99Albany River Rats-22
00Albany River Rats-20
02Albany River Rats-20
02Albany River Rats AAP-23
03ITG VIP Rookie Debut-84
03Parkhurst Rookie-95
03Upper Deck Rookie Update-97
03Albany River Rats-25
03Albany River Rats Kinko's-24
04Albany River Rats-22
Skroder, Per-Age
99Norwegian National Team-13
02Swedish SHL Sharpshooters-SS4
02Swedish SHL Signatures Series II-24
03Swedish Elite-195
Global Impact-GI5
Silver-195
04Swedish Elitset-52
Gold-52
05Swedish SHL Elitset-273
06Swedish SHL Elitset-242
Skrudland, Brian
81Saskatoon Blades-10
83Nova Scotia Voyageurs-11
85Canadiens Postcards-32
85Canadiens Provigo-20
86Canadiens Postcards-22
86Kraft Drawings-64
87Canadiens Postcards-29
87Canadiens Vachon Stickers-32
87Canadiens Vachon Stickers-34
87Canadiens Vachon Stickers-36
87O-Pee-Chee-235
87Panini Stickers-67
88Canadiens Postcards-26
89Canadiens Kraft-21
89Canadiens Postcards-29
89Canadiens Provigo Figurines-39
90Bowman-49
Tiffany-49
90Canadiens Postcards-29
90O-Pee-Chee-270
90Panini Stickers-55
90Pro Set-159
90Score-238
Canadian-238
90Topps-270
Tiffany-270
90Upper Deck-93
French-93
91Bowman-331
91Canadiens Panini Team Stickers-22
91Canadiens Postcards-28
91O-Pee-Chee-349
91Panini Stickers-194
91Parkhurst-314
French-314
91Pinnacle-160
French-160
91Pro Set-127
91Pro Set-306
French-127
French-306
91Score American-294
91Score Canadian Bilingual-514
91Score Canadian English-514
91Stadium Club-129
91Topps-349
91Upper Deck-422
French-422
92Canadiens Postcards-27
92O-Pee-Chee-45
92Parkhurst-266
Emerald Ice-266
92Pinnacle-347
French-347
92Score-136
Canadian-136
92Stadium Club-114
92Topps-408
Gold-408G
92Ultra-111
93Donruss-124
93Kraft-48
93Leaf-325
93OPC Premier-26
93OPC Premier-508
Gold-26
Gold-508
93Parkhurst-75
Emerald Ice-75
93Pinnacle-188
Canadian-188
Captains-9
Captains Canadian-9
Expansion-5
93PowerPlay-100
93Score-258
93Score-505
Gold-505
Canadian-258
Canadian-505
Canadian Gold-505
93Stadium Club-177
93Stadium Club-349
Members Only Master Set-177
Members Only Master Set-349
OPC-177
First Day Issue-177
First Day Issue-349
First Day Issue OPC-177
93Topps/OPC Premier-26
93Topps/OPC Premier-508
Gold-26
Gold-508
93Ultra-332
93Upper Deck-96
SP-59
94Canada Games NHL POGS-110
94Donruss-130
94EA Sports-51
94Flair-68
94Leaf-177
94OPC Premier-265
Special Effects-265
94Panthers Pop-ups-1
94Parkhurst SE-SE63
Gold-SE63
94Pinnacle-21
Artist's Proofs-21
Rink Collection-21
94Score-53
Gold-53
Platinum-53
94Select-126
Gold-126
94Stadium Club-36
Members Only Master Set-36
First Day Issue-36
Super Team Winner Cards-36
94Topps/OPC Premier-265
Special Effects-265
94Ultra-85
94Upper Deck-331
Electric Ice-331
95Panini Stickers-72
95Parkhurst International-358
Emerald Ice-358
95Playoff One on One-43
95Score-74
Black Ice Artist's Proofs-74
Black Ice-74
95Summit-136
Artist's Proofs-136
Ice-136
95Ultra-63
Gold Medallion-63
95Upper Deck-276
Electric Ice-276
Electric Ice Gold-276
96Be A Player-205
Autographs-205
Autographs Silver-205
96Black Diamond-64
Gold-64
96Donruss-118
Press Proofs-118
96Kraft Upper Deck-39
96Leaf-69
Press Proofs-69
96Score-133
Artist's Proofs-133
Dealer's Choice Artist's Proofs-133
Special Artist's Proofs-133
Golden Blades-133
96SP-64
96Summit-39
Artist's Proofs-39
Ice-39
Metal-39
Premium Stock-39
96Saskatoon Blades-21
97Pacific-295
Copper-295
Emerald Green-295
Ice Blue-295
Red-295
Silver-295
97Paramount-120
Copper-120
Dark Grey-120
Emerald Green-120
Ice Blue-120
Red-120
Silver-120
98Pacific-182
Ice Blue-182
Red-182
99Stars Postcards-24
Skrudland, Scott
05Kamloops Blazers-12
Skrypec, Gerry
907th Inn. Sketch OHL-94
917th Inn. Sketch OHL-296
92Ottawa 67's-20
93Detroit Jr. Red Wings-19
93Niagara Falls Thunder-4
Skudra, Peter
94Greensboro Monarchs-4
95Oklahoma Coyotes RHI-15
97Revolution-114
Copper-114
Emerald-114
Ice Blue-114
Silver-114
97SP Authentic-130
98Be A Player-110
Press Release-110
98BAP Gold-110
98BAP Autographs-110
98BAP Autographs Gold-110
98BAP Tampa Bay All Star Game-110
98NHL Aces Playing Cards-30
98Pacific-358
Ice Blue-358
Red-358
98UD Choice-170
Prime Choice Reserve-170
Reserve-170
98Upper Deck-165
Exclusives-165
Exclusives 1 of 1-165
Gold Reserve-165
99Pacific-345
Copper-345
Emerald Green-345
Gold-345
Ice Blue-345
Premiere Date-345
Red-345
99Wayne Gretzky Hockey-141
01Between the Pipes-89
01Canucks Postcards-11
01Pacific-38
Extreme LTD-38
Hobby LTD-38
Premiere Date-38
Retail LTD-38
01Pacific Arena Exclusives-38
02BAP Sig Series Auto Buybacks 1998-110
02Between the Pipes-54
Gold-54
Silver-54
02NHL Power Play Stickers-155
02Pacific-385
Blue-385
Red-385
02Pacific Complete-335
Red-335
02UD Mask Collection-85
02UD Mask Collection-86
02UD Mask Collection Beckett Promos-85
02UD Mask Collection Beckett Promos-86
03Pacific-337
Blue-337
Red-337
03Russian Hockey League-104
03Russian Hockey League-250
03Russian SL-23
Skugarev, Alexander
99Russian Hockey League-111
03Russian Hockey League-136
03Russian National Team-12
04Russian World Championship Team-11
Skuhravy, Vaclav
00Czech OFS-131
01Czech OFS-179
02Czech OFS Plus-292
02Czech OFS Plus All-Star Game-H34
03Czech OFS Plus-78
03Czech OFS Plus-364
04Czech OFS-34
05Czech HC Karlovy Vary-15
06Czech CP Cup Postcards-18
06Czech OFS-42
Skuhrovec, Radim
99Czech OFS-332
01Czech OFS-180
03Czech OFS Plus-367
04Czech OFS-107
06Czech OFS-147
Skuta, Vitezslav
94Czech APS Extraliga-122
95Czech APS Extraliga-341
96Czech APS Extraliga-196
97Czech APS Extraliga-128
97Czech DS Extraliga-97
97Czech DS Stickers-192
98Czech DS-65
98Czech DS Stickers-15
98Czech DS Stickers-249
98Czech OFS-116
98Czech OFS-319
99Czech DS-115
99Czech OFS-391
00Czech DS Extraliga-160
00Czech OFS-242
01Czech OFS-40
Skvaridlo, Tomas
99Kingston Frontenacs-18
00Kingston Frontenacs-18
Skvorstsov, Alexander
81Swedish Semic Hockey VM Stickers-53
84Russian National Team-17
Skwarchuk, Sam
00Kitchener Rangers-24
01Sudbury Wolves-16
01Sudbury Wolves Police-21
Skygge, Martin
98Danish Hockey League-218
99Danish Hockey League-149
Skyllqvist, Roddy
71Swedish Hockey-340
72Swedish Stickers-146
Skytta, Mika
98Finnish Kerallysarja-200
99Finnish Cardset-116
00Finnish Cardset-82
01Finnish Cardset-331
03UK Manchester Phoenix-18
04Finnish Cardset-290
05Finnish Cardset -132
Slabon, Damian
93Quebec Pee-Wee Tournament-1509
Slaby, Lukas
99Czech OFS-63
Slaby, Vaclav
95Czech APS Extraliga-229
97Czech APS Extraliga-110
Slade, Dustin
04South Surrey Eagles-26
04Surrey Eagles-21
04Regina Pats-22
04Surrey Eagles-21
05ITG Heroes/Prosp Toronto Expo Parallel -424
05Vancouver Giants-22
05ITG Heroes and Prospects-424
Sladok, Jozef
06Plymouth Whalers-21
Sladovnik, Jeremy
97Flint Generals-19
97Flint Generals EBK-14
98Flint Generals-4
Slais, Eric
02Chicago Steel-18
04Chicago Steel-4
Slanec, Josef
99Czech OFS-400
00Czech OFS-315
01Czech OFS-213
Slaney, Darryl
93Quebec Pee-Wee Tournament-567
Slaney, John
897th Inn. Sketch OHL-185
90Upper Deck-360
90Upper Deck-457
French-360
French-457
907th Inn. Sketch OHL-47
91Upper Deck Czech World Juniors-54
91Cornwall Royals-24
917th Inn. Sketch OHL-1
93Parkhurst-494
Emerald Ice-494
93Score-636
Gold-636
Canadian-636
Canadian Gold-636
93Portland Pirates-20
94Donruss-298
94Leaf-96
94OPC Premier-402
Special Effects-402
94Parkhurst-257
Gold-257
94Pinnacle-214
Artist's Proofs-214
Rink Collection-214
94Score-262
Gold-262
Platinum-262
94Stadium Club-39
94Stadium Club-113
Members Only Master Set-39
Members Only Master Set-113
First Day Issue-39
First Day Issue-113
Super Team Winner Cards-39
Super Team Winner Cards-113
94Topps/OPC Premier-402
Special Effects-402
94Upper Deck-39
Electric Ice-39
95Parkhurst International-47
Emerald Ice-47
96Be A Player-100
Autographs-100
Autographs Silver-100
96Fleer Picks-154
96Upper Deck-81
97Las Vegas Thunder-9
98Predators Team Issue-19
99Wayne Gretzky Hockey-142
00Paramount-201
Copper-201
Gold-201

Holo-Gold-201
Holo-Silver-201
Ice Blue-201
Premiere Date-201
00Wilkes-Barre Scranton Penguins-20
02Philadelphia Phantoms-17
03Philadelphia Phantoms-11
04Philadelphia Phantoms-20
05AHL All-Stars-36
05Philadelphia Phantoms-21
05Philadelphia Phantoms All-Decade Team-4
06Philadelphia Phantoms-8
06ITG Heroes and Prospects AHL Shooting Stars-AS09

Slaney, Robert
05Cape Breton Screaming Eagles-7

Slanina, Peter
82Swedish Semic VM Stickers-99
83Swedish Semic VM Stickers-88
89Swedish Semic World Champ Stickers-183
91Finnish Semic World Champ Stickers-109
91Swedish Semic World Champ Stickers-109

Slaninak, Jozef
04Slovakian Poprad Team Set-24

Slansky, Vaclav
93Red Deer Rebels-23

Slapke, Peter
70Finnish Jaakiekko-99
70Swedish Hockey-373
70Swedish Masterserien-169
74Finnish Jenkki-120
74Finnish Typotor-66
99German DEL-415

Slater, Chris
93Michigan State Spartans-18
02UK London Knights-10
03UK Basingstoke Bison-18

Slater, Ian
06Cedar Rapids RoughRiders-14

Slater, Jim
96Quebec Pee-Wee Tournament-678
02BAP Memorabilia Draft Redemptions-30
04SP Authentic Rookie Redemptions-RR51
05Beehive-147
Beige -147
Blue -147
Gold-147
Red -147
Matte-147
05Black Diamond-213
05Hot Prospects-187
Autographed Patch Variation-187
Autographed Patch Variation Gold-187
Hot Materials-HMJS
Red Hot-187
05Parkhurst-604
Facsimile Auto Parallel-604
Signatures-JS
05SP Authentic-134
Limited-134
Rarefied Rookies-RRJS
Sign of the Times-JS
05SP Game Used-137
Autographs-137
Gold-137
Auto Draft-AD-JS
Rookie Exclusives-JS
Rookie Exclusives Silver-RE-JS
05SPx-143
Spectrum-143
Xcitement Rookies-XR-JS
Xcitement Rookies Gold-XR-JS
Xcitement Rookies Spectrum-XR-JS
05The Cup-134
Autographed Rookie Patches Gold Rainbow-134
Black Rainbow Rookies-134
Masterpiece Pressplates (Artifacts)-242
Masterpiece Pressplates (Bee Hive)-147
Masterpiece Pressplates (Black Diamond)-213
Masterpiece Pressplates (Ice)-143
Masterpiece Pressplates (MVP)-428
Masterpiece Pressplates (Rookie Update)-197
Masterpiece Pressplates SPA Autos-134
Masterpiece Pressplates (SP Game Used)-137
Masterpiece Pressplates (SPx)-143
Masterpiece Pressplates (SPx)-143
Masterpiece Pressplates (Trilogy)-174
Masterpiece Pressplates Ult Coll-135
Masterpiece Pressplates Autographs-134
Platinum Rookies-134
05UD Artifacts-242
Gold-RED42
05Ultimate Collection-135
Gold-135
Ultimate Debut Threads Jerseys-DTJJS
Ultimate Debut Threads Jerseys Autos-DAJJS
Ultimate Debut Threads Patches-DTPJS
Ultimate Debut Threads Patches Autos-DAPJS
05Ultra-202
Gold-202
Ice-202
Rookie Uniformity Jerseys-RU-JS
Rookie Uniformity Jersey Autographs-ARU-JS
Rookie Uniformity Patches-RUP-JS
Rookie Uniformity Patch Autographs-ARP-JS
05Upper Deck-222
HG Glossy-222
Rookie Ink-RIJS
Rookie Threads-RTJS
Rookie Threads Autographs-ARTJS
05Upper Deck Ice-143
Premieres Auto Patches-AIPJS
05Upper Deck MVP-428
Gold-428
Platinum-428
05Upper Deck Rookie Update-197
Inspirations Patch Rookies-197
05Upper Deck Trilogy-174
05Upper Deck Toronto Fall Expo-222
06Black Diamond-5
Black-5
Gold-5
Ruby-5
Gemography-GJS
06Fleer-9
Tiffany-9
06O-Pee-Chee-24
Rainbow-24
06Upper Deck-11
Exclusives Parallel-11
High Gloss Parallel-11
Masterpieces-11
06Upper Deck MVP-12
Gold Script-12
Super Script-12

Slater, Ken
83Kingston Canadians-27
84Kingston Canadians-4

Slater, Mark
97UK Fife Flyers-5

Slater, Peter
72Los Angeles Sharks WHA-13

Slaughter, Sgt.
99Arizona Icecats-24
04Arizona Icecats-27
05Topps Heritage Autographs-16
05Topps Heritage-86

Slavetinsky, Lukas
05German DEL-331

Slavik, Jan
96Peoria Rivermen-21
96Peoria Rivermen Photo Album-21
98Huntington Blizzard-6
99Czech OFS-53
00Czech OFS-92
01Czech OFS-53

Slavik, Michal
94Czech APS Extraliga-11
95Czech APS Extraliga-111
96Czech APS Extraliga-274
97Czech DS Stickers-186
98Czech OFS-259
99Czech Score Blue 2000-140
99Czech Score Red Ice 2000-140

Slavik, Robert
94Czech APS Extraliga-95
95Czech APS Extraliga-54
96Czech APS Extraliga-240
97Czech APS Extraliga-267
99Czech Score Blue 2000-109
99Czech Score Red Ice 2000-109
03Czech OFS Plus-250
04Czech OFS-309
Team Cards-14

Slawson, Randy
82Brandon Wheat Kings-17

Sleaver, John
52Juniors Blue Tint-177

Sledzik, Jacek
93Quebec Pee-Wee Tournament-1503

Slegr, Jiri
91Upper Deck-18
French-18
91Finnish Semic World Champ Stickers-106
91Swedish Semic World Champ Stickers-106
91Star Pics-29
92Canucks Road Trip Art-21
92OPC Premier-54
92Parkhurst-196
Emerald Ice-196
92Ultra-430
92Upper Deck-515
Euro-Rookies-ER9
92Finnish Semic-131
93Donruss-358
93Leaf-31
93OPC Premier-164
Gold-164
93Parkhurst-214
Emerald Ice-214
93Pinnacle-417
Canadian-417
93PowerPlay-256
93Score-378
Canadian-378
93Stadium Club-42
Members Only Master Set-42
OPC-42
First Day Issue-42
First Day Issue OPC-42
93Topps/OPC Premier-164
Gold-164
93Ultra-136
93Upper Deck-18
SP-166
93Classic Four-Sport *-249
Gold-249
94Be A Player-R123
Signature Cards-119
94Canucks Program Inserts-20
94Donruss-294
94Leaf-520
94OPC Premier-543
Special Effects-543
94Parkhurst Vintage-V27
94Parkhurst SE-SE189
Gold-SE189
94Topps/OPC Premier-543
Special Effects-543
94Ultra-385
94Upper Deck-95
Electric Ice-95
94Czech APS Extraliga-209
94Finnish Jaa Kiekko-182
94Finnish Jaa Kiekko-343
95Canada Games NHL POGS-110
95Canucks Building the Dream Art-11
95Collector's Choice-144
Player's Club-144
Player's Club Platinum-144
95Parkhurst International-344
Emerald Ice-344
95Upper Deck-42
Electric Ice-42
Electric Ice Gold-42
95Swedish Globe World Championships-151
96Swedish Semic Wien-113
97Czech APS Extraliga-346
98Finest-46
No Protectors-46
No Protectors Refractors-46
Refractors-46
98Pacific-71
Ice Blue-71
Red-71
98Pacific Dynagon Ice-153
Blue-153
Red-153
98Paramount-196
Copper-196
Emerald Green-196
Holo-Electric-196
Ice Blue-196
Silver-196
98Czech OFS-233
Olympic Winners-9
98Czech Bonaparte-3D
98Czech Bonaparte-7A
98Czech Pexeso-13
98Czech Pexeso-22
98Czech Spaghetti-9
99BAP Memorabilia-62
Gold-62
Silver-62
99Pacific-346
Copper-346
Emerald Green-346
Gold-346
Ice Blue-346
Premiere Date-346
Red-346
99Panini Stickers-132
99Czech DS National Stars-NS4
99Czech DS Premium-P7
99Czech OFS-35
99Czech OFS Jagr Team Embossed-35
00BAP Memorabilia-123
Emerald-123
Ruby-123
Sapphire-123
Promos-123
00BAP Mem Chicago Sportsfest Copper-123
00BAP Memorabilia Chicago Sportsfest Blue-123
00BAP Memorabilia Chicago Sportsfest Gold-123
00BAP Memorabilia Chicago Sportsfest Ruby-123
00BAP Memorabilia Chicago Sun-Times Ruby-123
00BAP Memorabilia Chicago Sun-Times Gold-123
00BAP Mem Chicago Sun-Times Sapphire-123
00BAP Mem Toronto Fall Expo Copper-123
00BAP Memorabilia Toronto Fall Expo Gold-123
00BAP Memorabilia Toronto Fall Expo Ruby-123
00BAP Parkhurst 2000-P145
00BAP Signature Series-110
Emerald-110
Ruby-110
Sapphire-110
Autographs-100
Autographs Gold-100
00Pacific-336
Copper-336
Gold-336
Ice Blue-336
Premiere Date-336
00Upper Deck-143
Exclusives Tier 1-143
Exclusives Tier 2-143
00Czech Stadion-113
01BAP Memorabilia-169
01BAP Memorabilia-447
Emerald-169
Emerald-447
Ruby-169
Ruby-447
Sapphire-169
Sapphire-447
01Pacific-24
Extreme LTD-24
Hobby LTD-24
Premiere Date-24
Retail LTD-24
01Pacific Arena Exclusives-24
01Upper Deck-10
Exclusives-10
01Upper Deck MVP-9
01Upper Deck Victory-16
Gold-16
02BAP Sig Series Auto Buybacks 2000-100
02Pacific-135
Blue-135
Red-135
02Czech OFS Plus-208
Trios-T6
Duos-D21
02Czech IQ Sports Blue-25
02Czech IQ Sports Yellow-25
02Czech IQ Sports Yellow-26
02Czech Stadion Cup Finals-491
02Russian SL-25
03Canucks Postcards-26
04Czech NHL ELH Postcards-13
04Czech OFS-108
Stars-9
04Czech Zuma-17
04Czech World Championship Postcards-18
05Panini Stickers-28
05Upper Deck-259
05Upper Deck MVP-38
Gold-38
Platinum-38
05Czech World Champions Postcards-2
05Czech Kvarteto Bonaparte-4a
05Czech Pexeso Mini Blue Set-8
05Czech Pexeso Mini Red Set-2
05Czech Pexeso Mini Red Set-29
06Czech OFS-148

Slehofer, Robert
93Swiss HNL-457
95Swiss HNL-337
96Swiss HNL-269
98Swiss Power Play Stickers-98
99Swiss Panini Stickers-99
00Swiss Panini Stickers-144
00Swiss Slapshot Mini-Cards-HCFG14
01Swiss HNL-143
02Swiss HNL-53
04Swiss Lausanne HC Postcards-2

Sleigher, Louis
82Nordiques Postcards-19
83Nordiques Postcards-26
83O-Pee-Chee-301
83Vachon-74
84Bruins Postcards-19
84O-Pee-Chee-290

Sleigher, Pierre-Luc
00Victoriaville Tigres-11
Signed-11
03Atlantic City Boardwalk Bullies-22
03Atlantic City Boardwalk Bullies RBI-29
04Atlantic City Boardwalk Bullies Kinko's-9

Slemko, Ryan
907th Inn. Sketch WHL-322

Sletner, Frode
92Norwegian Elite Series-173

Slettvoll, John
93Swiss HNL-83
95Swiss HNL-134
99Swiss Panini Stickers-276

Slezak, Roman
94German First League-632

Slifka, Dave
94Central Hockey League-69
94Oklahoma City Blazers-16

Slinde, Jeff
04Wisconsin Badgers-25
05Wisconsin Badgers-24

Sliva, Craig
93Quebec Pee-Wee Tournament-1284

Slivchenko, Vadim
93Wheeling Thunderbirds-15
93Wheeling Thunderbirds-UD9
94Wheeling Thunderbirds-4
94Wheeling Thunderbirds-PC2
94Wheeling Thunderbirds Photo Album-5
95Houston Aeros-19
00German DEL-217
01German Upper Deck-87
02German DEL City Press-294
Top Scorers-TS2
03German DEL-57
04German DEL Update-337

Sliwinski, Max
04Arizona Icecats-20

Sliz, Greg
84Ottawa 67's-24

Slizek, Ladislav
94Czech APS Extraliga-268
96Czech APS Extraliga-21
97Czech APS Extraliga-147
97Czech DS Stickers-127
98Czech OFS-250
98Czech OFS-293
99Czech Score Blue 2000-3
99Czech Score Red Ice 2000-3

Sloan, Blake
93Donruss Team USA-20
93Pinnacle-486
Canadian-486
93Michigan Wolverines-24
99BAP Memorabilia-166
Gold-166
Silver-166
99BAP Millennium-74
Emerald-74
Ruby-74
Sapphire-74
Signatures-74
Signatures Gold-74
Calder Candidates Ruby-C9
Calder Candidates Emerald-C9
Calder Candidates Sapphire-C9
99O-Pee-Chee-124
99O-Pee-Chee Chrome-124
99O-Pee-Chee Chrome Refractors-124
99Pacific-133
Copper-133
Emerald Green-133
Gold-133
Ice Blue-133
Premiere Date-133
Red-133
99Stars Postcards-25
99Topps/OPC-124
99Topps/OPC Chrome-124
Refractors-124
99Ultimate Victory-30
1/1-30
Parallel-30
Parallel 100-30
00Pacific-140
Copper-140
Gold-140
Ice Blue-140
Premiere Date-140
00Stars Postcards-22
00Titanium Game Gear-91
00Titanium Game Gear Patches-91
01BAP Memorabilia-452
Emerald-452
Ruby-452
Sapphire-452
01Blue Jackets Donatos Pizza-5
01Pacific Heads-Up Quad Jerseys-24
01Private Stock Game Gear-33
01Private Stock Game Gear Patches-33
01Upper Deck Victory-105
Gold-105
02BAP Sig Series Auto Buybacks 1999-74
02NHL Power Play Stickers-14
02Pacific Complete-408
Red-408
03ITG Action-83
03Stars Postcards-22

Sloan, Tod
44Beehive Group II Photos-139
44Beehive Group II Photos-450
45Quaker Oats Photos-47A
45Quaker Oats Photos-47B
48Exhibits Canadian-39
51Parkhurst-87
52Parkhurst-48
53Parkhurst-5
54Parkhurst-30
54Parkhurst-98
55Parkhurst-10
55Parkhurst-77
Quaker Oats-10
Quaker Oats-77
57Parkhurst-T5
58Topps-42
59Topps-13
60Shirriff Coins-64
60Topps-51
91Ultimate Original Six-42
French-42
94Parkhurst Missing Link-112
94Parkhurst Missing Link-144
94Parkhurst Missing Link-174
01Parkhurst Reprints-PR85
05ITG Heroes/Prosp Toronto Expo Parallel -199
05ITG Ultimate Memorabilia Ultimate Autos-6
05ITG Ultimate Mem Ultimate Autos Gold-6
05ITG Heroes and Prospects-199
Autographs Series II-TS

Sloan, Tyler
00Kamloops Blazers-22
02Syracuse Crunch-3
03Syracuse Crunch-18
05Las Vegas Wranglers-20

Sloboda, Karol
01Ottawa 67's-3
02Ottawa 67's-2
04Czech OFS-361

Sloboda, Radovan
03Czech OFS Plus-324
03Czech OFS Plus Insert H-H22
04Slovakian Skalica Team Set-20

Slobodian, Colin
01Swift Current Broncos-18

Slobodzian, Pete
34Beehive Group I Photos-252

Slominski, Laura
98Minnesota Golden Gophers Women-22

Slonina, Steve
03Gwinnett Gladiators-8
03Gwinnett Gladiators RBI Sports-207
05Stockton Thunder-17
06Stockton Thunder-11b

Slota, Kevin
93London Knights-17
95Slapshot-176

Sloth, Rene
98Danish Hockey League-131
99Danish Hockey League-40

Slotte, Ulf
66Finnish Jaakiekkosarja-213

Slovak, Juraj
99Greensboro Generals-12
01Colorado Gold Kings-18
02Greensboro Generals RBI-16

Slovak, Martin
02Cape Breton Screaming Eagles-9

Slovak, Tomas
01Kelowna Rockets-20
02Kelowna Rockets-19
03Hershey Bears-5
03Hershey Bears Patriot News-21
03Kelowna Rockets Memorial Cup-18
03Reading Royals-6
03Reading Royals RBI Sports-301
06Swedish SHL Elitset-250

Slowakiewicz, Andrzej
73Finnish Jaakiekko-98
74Finnish Jenkki-86
79Panini Stickers-122

Slowakiewicz, Josef
73Finnish Jaakiekko-99
74Finnish Jenkki-87

Slowakiewicz, Pawel
93Quebec Pee-Wee Tournament-1514

Slowakiewicz, T.
79Panini Stickers-119

Slowinski, Ed
44Beehive Group II Photos-364
51Parkhurst-102
52Parkhurst-19

Slukynsky, Fred
00Fort Wayne Komets-20

Slukynsky, Tim
91Air Canada SJHL-C27
92Saskatchewan JHL-166

Slupina, Roman
96Czech APS Extraliga-99

Slusar, Bobbi-Jo
04Wisconsin Badgers Women-19

Sly, Darryl
63Rochester Americans-19
68Maple Leafs White Border-9
70Canucks Royal Bank-15
70Esso Power Players-41
70O-Pee-Chee-115
70Sargent Promotions Stamps-221
70Topps-115

Sly, Ryan
95Slapshot-386
95Sudbury Wolves-19
95Sudbury Wolves Police-21
96Sudbury Wolves-21
96Sudbury Wolves Police-22

Smaagaard, Garrett
01Minnesota Golden Gophers-16
02Minnesota Golden Gophers-21
03Minnesota Golden Gophers-27
04Minnesota Golden Gophers-23

Smaby, Matt
03North Dakota Fighting Sioux-20
04North Dakota Fighting Sioux-23
06Springfield Falcons-19

Smach, Ondrej
04Czech OFS-407
06Czech OFS-215

Smadis, Darren
93Spokane Chiefs-25

Smagin, Alexander
00Russian Hockey League-386

Smagin, Vladimir
74Swedish Stickers-92

Smail, Doug
80Jets Postcards-19
80Pepsi-Cola Caps-136
81Jets Postcards-16
82Jets Postcards-20
82O-Pee-Chee-388
83Jets Postcards-20
83O-Pee-Chee-390
83O-Pee-Chee Stickers-287
83Topps Stickers-287
83Vachon-136
84Jets Police-18
84O-Pee-Chee-346
85Jets Police-18
85O-Pee-Chee-175
85O-Pee-Chee Stickers-255
86Jets Postcards-21
86O-Pee-Chee-256
87Jets Postcards-19
87O-Pee-Chee-181
87O-Pee-Chee Stickers-254
87Panini Stickers-367
87Topps-181
88Jets Police-20
88Jets Postcards-20
88O-Pee-Chee-251
88O-Pee-Chee Stickers-137
88Panini Stickers-158
89Jets Safeway-25
89O-Pee-Chee-294
89O-Pee-Chee Stickers-141
89Panini Stickers-171
90Bowman-134
Tiffany-134
90O-Pee-Chee-268
90Panini Stickers-308
90Pro Set-462
90Score-196
Canadian-196
90Score Rookie/Traded-69T
90Topps-268
Tiffany-268
90Upper Deck-105
French-105
91Bowman-118
91Jets Panini Team Stickers-21
91Nordiques Petro-Canada-26
91O-Pee-Chee-334
91Panini Stickers-111
91Pro Set-117
91Pro Set-466
French-117
French-466
91Score American-12
91Score Canadian Bilingual-12
91Score Canadian Bilingual-592
91Score Canadian English-12
91Score Canadian English-592
91Stadium Club-255
91Topps-334
92Bowman-362
92O-Pee-Chee-196
92Pinnacle-377
French-377
92Score-197
Canadian-197
92Stadium Club-334
92Topps-459
Gold-459G
92Upper Deck-124
04ITG Franchises Canadian-143
Autographs-DSM

Smaill, Walter
10Sweet Caporal Postcards-27
11C55-27A
11C55-27B
12C57-22

Smale, Andrew
01Mississauga Ice Dogs-16
06New Mexico Scorpions-8

Small, Brent
03St. Michael's Majors-13

Small, Brian
81Ottawa 67's-22
83Belleville Bulls-10

Small, Sami Jo
04Canadian Womens World Championship Team-17
06ITG Going For Gold-21
06ITG Going For Gold Samples-21
06ITG Going For Gold Autographs-ASM
06ITG Going For Gold Jerseys-GUJ21

Small, Steve
02UK Coventry Blaze-22
04UK Coventry Blaze-23

Small, Todd
91Air Canada SJHL-A30

Smarda, Jan
98Czech OFS-311

Smart, Cadrin
917th Inn. Sketch WHL-344
95Kamloops Blazers-30

Smart, Jason
88Saskatoon Blades-20
89Saskatoon Blades-21
91ProCards-305
92Cleveland Lumberjacks-20
95Toledo Storm-17

Smart, Kelly
94Brandon Wheat Kings-20
95Brandon Wheat Kings-19
95Slapshot Memorial Cup-35
96Brandon Wheat Kings-14
97Brandon Wheat Kings-22
97Bowman CHL-106
OPC-106
99Austin Ice Bats-18
00Austin Ice Bats-20
01Austin Ice Bats-15
02Austin Ice Bats-17
03Austin Ice Bats-14
04Austin Ice Bats-3

Smazal, Heiko
95German DEL-292
96German DEL-319
98German DEL-259
99German DEL-319
99German DEL-385
01German Upper Deck-194
02German DEL City Press-101
03German DEL-119
04German DEL-136
05German DEL-115

Smazal, Mike
94German DEL-252
04German Hamburg Freezers Postcards-18

Smeaton, Cooper
83Hall of Fame Postcards-C13
85Hall of Fame-42

Smedberg, Peter
86Swedish Panini Stickers-215

Smedsmo, Dave
75Stingers Kahn's-11

Smegal, Ray
06Austin Ice Bats-8

Smehlik, Richard
92OPC Premier-90
92Parkhurst-14
Emerald Ice-14
92Pinnacle-393
French-393
92Sabres Blue Shield-21
92Sabres Jubilee Foods-13
92Ultra-262
Imports-22
92Upper Deck-564
Euro-Rookies-ER1
92Finnish Semic-129
92Classic-40
Gold-40
93Donruss-40
93Leaf-188
93OPC Premier-521
Gold-521
93Panini Stickers-110
93Parkhurst-20
Emerald Ice-20
93Pinnacle-152
Canadian-152
93PowerPlay-33
93Score-249
Canadian-249
93Stadium Club-107
Members Only Master Set-107
OPC-107
First Day Issue-107
First Day Issue OPC-107
93Topps/OPC Premier-521
Gold-521
93Ultra-200
93Upper Deck-169
94Canada Games NHL POGS-52
94Donruss-136
94Flair-22
94Fleer-27
94Leaf-306
94OPC Premier-93
Special Effects-93
94Parkhurst-28
Gold-28
94Pinnacle-17
Artist's Proofs-17
Rink Collection-17
94Score-129
Gold-129
Platinum-129
94Topps/OPC Premier-93
Special Effects-93
94Ultra-28
94Upper Deck-181
Electric Ice-181
94Czech APS Extraliga-128
94Finnish Jaa Kiekko-168
95Donruss-76
95Leaf-276
95Panini Stickers-22
95Pinnacle-187
Artist's Proofs-187
Rink Collection-187
95Topps-168
OPC Inserts-168
95Swedish Globe World Championships-147
96Upper Deck Ice-6
Parallel-6
97Be A Player-74
Autographs-74
Autographs Die-Cuts-74
Autographs Prismatic Die-Cuts-74
97Pacific Invincible NHL Regime-23
98Pacific-42
Ice Blue-42
Red-42
98Panini Stickers-20
98Czech OFS-230
Olympic Winners-12
98Czech Bonaparte-2C
98Czech Pexeso-6
98Czech Spaghetti-11
99Panini Stickers-34
00Stadium Club-29
00Titanium Game Gear-62
00Titanium Game Gear Patches-62
01Crown Royale Triple Threads-5
01Pacific Heads-Up Quad Jerseys-23
01Private Stock Game Gear-13
01Private Stock Game Gear Patches-13
02Czech IQ Sports Blue-26
02Czech IQ Sports Yellow-27
02Czech Stadion Olympics-349

Smelle, Carl
51Laval Dairy Subset-81
52St. Lawrence Sales-34

Smelle, Tom
51Laval Dairy Subset-84
52St. Lawrence Sales-21

Smerciak, Marian
94Finnish Jaa Kiekko-193
95Slovakian APS National Team-12
96Swedish Semic Wien-223
03UK Guildford Flames-4
03UK Guildford Flames-28
04UK Guildford Flames-4
05UK Guildford Flames-2
06UK Guildford Flames-2

Smetak, Martin
94Czech APS Extraliga-9
95Czech APS Extraliga-339
96Czech APS Extraliga-203
97Czech DS Stickers-207

Smicek, Jiri
94German DEL-349

Smid, Karel
94Czech APS Extraliga-142
95Czech APS Extraliga-246
96Czech APS Extraliga-292
97Czech DS Extraliga-21
97Czech DS Stickers-209
98Czech DS Stickers-52
98Danish Hockey League-139
99Danish Hockey League-158

Smid, Ladislav
03Czech OFS Plus-127
04Czech OFS-80
05ITG Heroes/Prosp Toronto Expo Parallel -220
05Portland Pirates-16
05ITG Heroes and Prospects-220
Autographs Series II-LS
06Be A Player-214
06Be A Player Portraits-124
06Beehive-121
Blue-121
Matte-121
Red Facsimile Signatures-121
Wood-121
06Black Diamond-208
Black-208
Gold-208
Ruby-208
06Flair Showcase-312
06Gatorade-28
06Hot Prospects-114
Red Hot-114
White Hot-114
Hot Materials -HMLS
Hot Materials Red Hot-HMLS
Hot Materials White Hot-HMLS
Hotagraphs-HLS
06ITG International Ice-151
Gold-151
Autographs-ALS
06O-Pee-Chee-553
06O-Pee-Chee-626
Rainbow-553
Rainbow-626
06SP Authentic-178
Limited-178
06SP Game Used-118
Gold-118
Rainbow-118
Autographs-118
Rookie Exclusives Autographs-RELS
06SPx-184
Spectrum-184
06The Cup-130
Autographed Rookie Masterpiece Pressplates-130
Gold Rainbow Autographed Rookie Patches-130
Masterpiece Pressplates (Be A Player Portraits)-124
Masterpiece Pressplates (Bee Hive)-121
Masterpiece Pressplates (Marquee Rookies)-553
Masterpiece Pressplates (MVP)-312
Masterpiece Pressplates (SP Authentic Autographs)-178
Masterpiece Pressplates (SP Game Used)-118
Masterpiece Pressplates (SPx Autographs)-184
Masterpiece Pressplates (Sweet Beginnings)-125
Masterpiece Pressplates (Trilogy)-115
Masterpiece Pressplates (Ultimate Collection Autographs)-111
Masterpiece Pressplates (Victory)-299
NHL Shields Duals-DSHPL
Rookies Black-130
Rookies Platinum-130
06UD Artifacts-242
06UD Mini Jersey Collection-114
06Ultimate Collection-111
Rookies Autographed NHL Shields-111
Rookies Autographed Patches-111
Ultimate Debut Threads Jerseys-DJ-LS
Ultimate Debut Threads Jerseys Autographs-DJ-LS
Ultimate Debut Threads Patches-DJ-LS
Ultimate Debut Threads Patches Autographs-DJ-LS
06Ultra-239
06Ultra-240
Gold Medallion-240
Ice Medallion-240
06Upper Deck-213
Exclusives Parallel-213
High Gloss Parallel-213
Masterpieces-213
Rookie Game Dated Moments-RGD9
Rookie Headliners-RH7
Rookie Materials-RMLS
Rookie Materials Patches-RMLS
06Upper Deck MVP-312
Gold Script-312
Super Script-312
06Upper Deck Sweet Shot-125
Rookie Jerseys Autographs-125
06Upper Deck Trilogy-115
06Upper Deck Victory-299
06ITG Heroes and Prospects-65
Autographs-ALS
07Upper Deck Rookie Class -17

Smid, Zdenek
99Czech DS-16
99Czech OFS-532
00Czech DS Extraliga-122
Goalies-G11
00Czech OFS-161
01Finnish Cardset-212
02Czech OFS Plus-332
03Czech OFS Plus-209
04Czech HC Slavia Praha Postcards-21
04Czech OFS-35
Team Cards-2

Smieja, Dustin
02Minnesota Golden Gophers-22
03Minnesota Golden Gophers-6

Smift, Michael
05Mississauga Ice Dogs-5

Smillie, Rob
92British Columbia JHL-176

Smillie, Steve
917th Inn. Sketch OHL-367
97UK Kingston Hawks Stickers-11
98UK Basingstoke Bison-4
99German Bundesliga 2-140
01UK Hull Thunder-18
02UK Hull Thunder-17

Smirko, Rastislav
04North Dakota Fighting Sioux-24

Smirnov, Alexander
90O-Pee-Chee-499
91O-Pee-Chee Inserts-60R
92Finnish Jyvas-Hyva Stickers-179
93Finnish Jyvas-Hyva Stickers-326
93Finnish SISU-39
94Finnish SISU-77
94Finnish Jaa Kiekko-139
94Swedish Olympics Lillehammer*-283
95Finnish Semic World Championships-125
95Swedish Globe World Championships-170
96Swedish Semic Wien-139
01Russian Hockey League-32

Smirnov, Alexei
00Russian Dynamo Moscow-19
00Russian Hockey League-315
02Atomic-103
Blue-103
Gold-103
Red-103
Hobby Parallel-103
02BAP All-Star Edition-127
Gold-127
Silver-127
02BAP First Edition-433H
02BAP Memorabilia-300
Emerald-300
Ruby-300
Sapphire-300
NHL All-Star Game-300
NHL All-Star Game Blue-300
NHL All-Star Game Green-300
NHL All-Star Game Red-300
02BAP Memorabilia Toronto Fall Expo-300
02BAP Signature Series-184
Autographs-184
Autographs Gold-184
Jerseys-SGJ56
Jersey Autographs-SGJ56
02BAP Ultimate Memorabilia-30
Autographs-2
Autographs Gold-2
Calder Candidates-10
02Bowman YoungStars-151
Gold-151
Silver-151
02Crown Royale-103
Blue-103
Purple-103
Red-103
Retail-103
Rookie Royalty-3
02eTopps-44
02ITG Used-196
Calder Jerseys-C11
Calder Jerseys Gold-C11
02Pacific-402
02Pacific Calder-103
Silver-103
02Pacific Complete-582
Red-582
02Pacific Exclusive-194
Blue-194
Gold-194
02Pacific Heads-Up-128
02Pacific Quest for the Cup-104
Gold-104
02Parkhurst-230
Bronze-230
Gold-230
Silver-230
02Parkhurst Retro-230
Minis-230
02Private Stock Reserve-153
Blue-153
Red-153
Retail-153
Class Act-2
02SP Authentic-181
Signed Patches-PSM
02SP Game Used-66
02SPx-146
02Stadium Club-124
Silver Decoy Cards-124
Proofs-124
02Titanium-104
Blue-104
Red-104
Retail-104
02Topps Chrome-178
Black Border Refractors-178
Refractors-178
02Topps Heritage-134
02Topps Total-418
02UD Artistic Impressions-99
Gold-99
02UD Foundations-144
02UD Honor Roll-101
02UD Mask Collection-177
02UD Piece of History-122
02UD Premier Collection-71B
Gold-71B
Signatures Bronze-SAS
Signatures Gold-SAS
Signatures Silver-SAS
02UD Top Shelf-122
02Upper Deck-227
Exclusives-227
02Upper Deck Classic Portraits-101
02Upper Deck Rookie Update-150A
02Upper Deck Rookie Update-150B
02Upper Deck Rookie Update-150C
02Vanguard-103
LTD-103
Prime Prospects-2
02Cincinnati Mighty Ducks-B-14
03BAP Memorabilia Future of the Game-FG-11
03ITG Action-37
Jerseys-M78
03O-Pee-Chee-172
03OPC Blue-172
03OPC Gold-172
03OPC Red-172
03SP Authentic Sign of the Times-AS

03Topps-172
Blue-172
Gold-172
Red-172
03Upper Deck Shooting Stars-ST-SV
03Upper Deck MVP-11
Gold Script-11
Silver Script-11
Canadian Exclusives-11
03Cincinnati Mighty Ducks-A10
04Cincinnati Mighty Ducks-22

Smirnov, Andrei
89Swedish Semic World Champ Stickers-83
99Russian Hockey League-198

Smirnov, Oleg
99Russian Hockey League-35
00Russian Dynamo Moscow-20

Smirnov, Pavel
99Tallahassee Tiger Sharks-20

Smirnov, Sergei
99Russian Hockey League-56

Smirnov, Vasili
00Russian Hockey League-88

Smit, Richard
97Louisiana Ice Gators-5

Smital, Lukas
96Johnstown Chiefs-20
97Johnstown Chiefs-10
98Johnstown Chiefs-12
01Johnstown Chiefs-13
02Johnstown Chiefs-15

Smith , Mike (CIAU)
01Kingston Frontenacs-17
03St. Francis Xavier X-Men-10
04St. Francis Xavier X-Men-19

Smith, Aaron
04Reading Royals-10

Smith, Adam
91British Columbia JHL-32
92Tacoma Rockets-22
93Upper Deck Program of Excellence-E1
93Tacoma Rockets-24
96Binghamton Rangers-19
97Hartford Wolf Pack-17
98Hartford Wolf Pack-17
00UK Sekonda Superleague-148
00UK Sheffield Steelers-24

Smith, Adrian
68Partridge Meats *-19
00Fresno Falcons-17
01Fresno Falcons-16

Smith, Al
69Maple Leafs White Border Glossy-32
70Esso Power Players-217
70O-Pee-Chee-87
70Sargent Promotions Stamps-161
70Topps-87
71Letraset Action Replays-19
71O-Pee-Chee-27
71Sargent Promotions Stamps-61
71Topps-27
71Toronto Sun-103
72Whalers New England WHA-15
73O-Pee-Chee WHA Posters-1
73Quaker Oats WHA-2
76O-Pee-Chee NHL-152
76Topps-152
77O-Pee-Chee WHA-49
79O-Pee-Chee-300
80O-Pee-Chee-252
80Topps-252

Smith, Alex
24Anonymous NHL-22
24Anonymous NHL-22
33O-Pee-Chee V304B-69
33V129-47
33V252 Canadian Gum-44
35Diamond Matchbooks Tan 1-63

Smith, Alfred
83Hall of Fame Postcards-J15
85Hall of Fame-194

Smith, Andy
06Prince Albert Raiders-18

Smith, Barry (C/CO)
77Rochester Americans-23
79Rockies Team Issue-22
93Knoxville Cherokees-17
94Erie Panthers-3
94Knoxville Cherokees-2
96Knoxville Cherokees-2
98Baton Rouge Kingfish-20
99Syracuse Crunch-16
00Kansas City Blades-24

Smith, Barry (CO)
87Sabres Wonder Bread/Hostess-27
88Sabres Wonder Bread/Hostess-28

Smith, Barry (D/CO)
94Erie Panthers-3
98Baton Rouge Kingfish-20
99Syracuse Crunch-16
00Kansas City Blades-24

Smith, Billy
73O-Pee-Chee-142
73Topps-162
74NHL Action Stamps-178
74O-Pee-Chee NHL-82
74Topps-82
75O-Pee-Chee NHL-372
76O-Pee-Chee NHL-46
76Topps-46
77Coca-Cola-25
77O-Pee-Chee NHL-229
77Topps-229
78O-Pee-Chee-62
78Topps-62
79Islanders Transparencies-18
79O-Pee-Chee-242
79Topps-242
80O-Pee-Chee-5
80O-Pee-Chee-60
80Topps-5
80Topps-60
81O-Pee-Chee-207
81O-Pee-Chee Stickers-161
81Topps-E93
82McDonald's Stickers-4
82McDonald's Stickers-16
82O-Pee-Chee-211
82O-Pee-Chee Stickers-60
82O-Pee-Chee Stickers-61
82O-Pee-Chee Stickers-251
82Post Cereal-12
82Topps Stickers-60
82Topps Stickers-61
82Topps Stickers-251
83Islanders Team Issue-14
83NHL Key Tags-82
83O-Pee-Chee-17
83O-Pee-Chee Stickers-16
83O-Pee-Chee Stickers-86
83O-Pee-Chee Stickers-316
83Puffy Stickers-19
83Topps Stickers-16
83Topps Stickers-86
83Topps Stickers-316
84Islanders News-23
84Islanders News-36
84O-Pee-Chee-135
84O-Pee-Chee Stickers-91
84Topps-101
85Islanders News-27
85Islanders News-34
85O-Pee-Chee Stickers-76
86Islanders Team Issue-3
86O-Pee-Chee-228
86O-Pee-Chee Stickers-213
87Panini Stickers-89
88Esso All-Stars-44
88O-Pee-Chee-17
88Topps-17
917th Inn. Sketch OHL-96
93Action Packed HOF Induction-3
93Islanders Chemical Bank Alumni-8
94Hockey Wit-95
97SP Authentic Mark of a Legend-M2
97SP Authentic Tradition-T2
00Panthers Team Issue-6
00Topps Premier Plus Club Signings-CS-1
00Topps Premier Plus Club Signings-CSC-1
00Topps Stars-99
Blue-99
Autographs-ABSM
Progression-P4
Progression-P5
Progression-P6
01BAP Ultimate Mem Dynasty Jerseys-16
01BAP Ultimate Mem Dynasty Emblems-16
01BAP Ultimate Mem Dynasty Numbers-16
01BAP Ultimate Mem Retired Numbers-24
01BAP Ultimate Mem Stanley Cup Winners-27
01Between the Pipes-117
He Shoots-He Saves Prizes-38
Trophy Winners-TW8
Trophy Winners-TW20
Vintage Memorabilia-VM11
01Fleer Legacy-23
Ultimate-23
In the Corners-11
01Greats of the Game-17
Autographs-17
01Topps Archives-20
Autographs-20
Relics-JBIS
01Topps Chrome Reprints-1
01Topps Chrome Reprint Refractors-1
01Topps Chrome Reprint Autographs-1
01Upper Deck Legends-45
01Upper Deck Legends-87
Jerseys-TTBS
Jerseys-TTST
Jerseys Platinum-TTBS
Jerseys Platinum-TTST
Sticks-PHBS
01Upper Deck Vintage Jerseys-GGBS
01Upper Deck Vintage Jerseys-SCBS
01Upper Deck Vintage Next In Line-NLSC
02BAP Ultimate Memorabilia Conn Smythe-13
02BAP Ultimate Memorabilia Cup Duels-9
02Fleer Throwbacks-54
Gold-54
Platinum-54
Autographs-17
Squaring Off-9
02UD Foundations Signs of Greatness-SGBS
03BAP Ultimate Memorabilia Cornerstones-8
03Topps Stanley Cup Heroes-BS
03Topps Stanley Cup Heroes Autographs-BS
04ITG Franchises He Shoots/Scores Prizes-43
04ITG Franchises Update-472
Double Memorabilia-UDM4
Double Memorabilia Gold-UDM4
04ITG Franchises US East-370
Autographs-A-BSM
Barn Burners-EBB7
Barn Burners Gold-EBB7
Goalie Gear-EGG2
Goalie Gear Autographs-EGG-BS
Goalie Gear Gold-EGG2
Memorabilia-ESM11
Memorabilia Autographs-ESM-BS
Memorabilia Gold-ESM11
04ITG Ultimate Memorabilia-16
Gold-16
Autographs-41
Autographs Gold-41
Cornerstones-9
Cornerstones Gold-9
Day In History-5
Day In History-19
Day In History Gold-5
Day In History Gold-19
Goalie Gear-19
Jersey Autographs-35
Jersey Autographs Gold-35
Retro Teammates-5
Stick Autographs-41
Stick Autographs Gold-41
Triple Threads-7
04UD Legendary Signatures-21
Autographs-BI
HOF Inks-HOF-BI
05Between the Pipes-19
Autographs-A-BS
Jerseys-GUJ-9
05ITG Ultimate Memorabilia Level 1-10
05ITG Ultimate Memorabilia Level 2-10
05ITG Ultimate Memorabilia Level 3-10
05ITG Ultimate Memorabilia Level 4-10
05ITG Ultimate Memorabilia Level 5-10
05ITG Ultimate Mem Cornerstones Jerseys-8
05ITG Ultimate Mem Cornerst Jerseys Gold-8
05ITG Ultimate Memorabilia Goalie Gear-3
05ITG Ultimate Mem Goalie Gear Gold-3
05ITG Ultimate Mem Retro Teammate Jerseys-3
05ITG Ult Mem Retro Teammates Jersey Gold-3
05ITG Ultimate Mem 3 Star of the Game Jsy-16
05ITG Ult Mem 3 Star of the Game Jsy Gold-16
05ITG Ultimate Mem Triple Threads Jerseys-4
05ITG Ultimate Mem Triple Thread Jsy Gold-4
05SP Game Used Game Gear-GG-BS
05The Cup Emblems of Endorsement-EEBS
05The Cup Hardware Heroes-HHBS
05The Cup Limited Logos-LLBS
05The Cup Noble Numbers Dual-DNNSP
05The Cup Signature Patches-SPBS
05The Cup Stanley Cup Titlists-TBS
06Beehive-183
5 X 7 Black and White-183
06Between The Pipes-80
06Between The Pipes-137
Autographs-ABS
Double Jerseys-DJ24
Double Jerseys Gold-DJ24
Emblems-GUE12
Emblems Gold-GUE12
Emblems Autographs-GUE12
Jerseys-GUJ12
Jerseys Gold-GUJ12
Jerseys Autographs-GUJ12
Numbers-GUN12
Numbers Gold-GUN12
Numbers Autographs-GUN12
Stick and Jersey-SJ32
Stick and Jersey Gold-SJ32
Stick and Jersey Autographs-SJ32
06ITG Ultimate Memorabilia Boys Will Be Boys-17
06ITG Ultimate Memorabilia Boys Will Be Boys Gold-17
06ITG Ultimate Memorabilia Road to the Cup-6
06ITG Ultimate Memorabilia Road to the Cup Gold-6
06SP Game Used Authentic Fabrics Quads-AF4FCSW
06SP Game Used Authentic Fabrics Quads Patches-AF4FCSW
06SPx-142
Spectrum-142
Winning Materials-WMBS
Winning Materials Spectrum-WMBS
Winning Materials Autographs-WMBS
06The Cup-57
Autographed Foundations-CQBS
Autographed Foundations Patches-CQBS
Autographed Patches-57
Black Rainbow-57
Foundations-CQBS
Foundations Patches-CQBS
Gold-57
Gold Patches-57
Honorable Numbers-HNBS
Jerseys-57
Limited Logos-LLBS
Masterpiece Pressplates-57
Signature Patches-SPBS
Stanley Cup Signatures-CSBS
06UD Artifacts-136
Blue-136
Gold-136
Radiance-136
Autographed Radiance Parallel-136
Red-136
Auto-Facts-AFBS
Auto-Facts Gold-AFBS
06Ultimate Collection Autographed Jerseys-AJ-BS
06Ultimate Collection Autographed Patches-AJ-BS
06Ultimate Collection Jerseys-UJ-BI
06Ultimate Collection Jerseys Triple-UJ3-SBG
06Ultimate Collection Patches-UJ-BI
06Upper Deck Sweet Shot-68
Signature Sticks-STBS
Sweet Stitches-SSBS
Sweet Stitches Duals-SSBS
Sweet Stitches Triples-SSBS
06Upper Deck Trilogy Combo Autographed Jerseys-CJBS
06Upper Deck Trilogy Combo Autographed Patches-CJBS
06Upper Deck Trilogy Combo Clearcut Autographs-C2SH
06Upper Deck Trilogy Combo Clearcut Autographs-C3BPS
06Upper Deck Trilogy Honorary Scripted Patches-HSPBS
06Upper Deck Trilogy Honorary Scripted Swatches-HSSBS
06Upper Deck Trilogy Honorary Swatches-HSSM
06Upper Deck Trilogy Legendary Scripts-LSBS
06Upper Deck Trilogy Scripts-TSBS
06ITG Heroes and Prospects-20
Autographs-ABSM
Heroes Memorabilia-HM02
Heroes Memorabilia Gold-HM02

Smith, Billy USHL
04Green Bay Gamblers-17
06SP Game Used Authentic Fabrics Quads-AF4FCSW
06SP Game Used Authentic Fabrics Quads Patches-AF4FCSW

Smith, Bobby
78North Stars Cloverleaf Dairy-5
79North Stars Postcards-16
79O-Pee-Chee-206
79Topps-206
80North Stars Postcards-20
80O-Pee-Chee-17
80Topps-17
81North Stars Postcards-22
81O-Pee-Chee-157
81O-Pee-Chee-170
81O-Pee-Chee-174
81O-Pee-Chee Stickers-88
81Post Standups-5
81Topps-37
81Topps-55
81Topps-W131
82North Stars Postcards-22
82O-Pee-Chee-175
82O-Pee-Chee-176
82O-Pee-Chee Stickers-188
82Post Cereal-9
82Topps Stickers-188
83Canadiens Postcards-27
83NHL Key Tags-60
83O-Pee-Chee-181
83O-Pee-Chee Stickers-116
83Puffy Stickers-14
83Topps Stickers-116
83Vachon-56
84Canadiens Postcards-25
84O-Pee-Chee-273
84O-Pee-Chee Stickers-151
84O-Pee-Chee Stickers-152
84Topps-83
85Canadiens Placemats-6
85Canadiens Placemats-7
85Canadiens Postcards-33
85Canadiens Postcards-34
85Canadiens Provigo-21
85O-Pee-Chee-181
85O-Pee-Chee Stickers-132
86Canadiens Postcards-23
86Kraft Drawings-65
86O-Pee-Chee-188
86O-Pee-Chee Stickers-13
86Topps-188
87Canadiens Kodak-7
87Canadiens Postcards-30
87Canadiens Vachon Stickers-26
87Canadiens Vachon Stickers-28
87Canadiens Vachon Stickers-30
87Canadiens Vachon Stickers-41
87Canadiens Vachon Stickers-86
87O-Pee-Chee-48
87O-Pee-Chee Stickers-10
87Panini Stickers-62
87Topps-48
88Canadiens Postcards-27
88O-Pee-Chee-88
88O-Pee-Chee Box Bottoms-D
88O-Pee-Chee Stickers-46
88Panini Stickers-261
88Topps-88
88Topps Box Bottoms-D
89Canadiens Kraft-22
89Canadiens Postcards-30
89Canadiens Provigo Figurines-15
89Kraft-26
89O-Pee-Chee-188
89O-Pee-Chee Stickers-47
89Panini Stickers-236
89Topps-188
90Bowman-51
Tiffany-51
90Kraft-53
90O-Pee-Chee-287
90OPC Premier-109
90Panini Stickers-52
90Pro Set-160
90Pro Set-463
90Score-61
Canadian-61
90Score Rookie/Traded-75T
90Topps-287
Tiffany-287
90Upper Deck-72
90Upper Deck-406
French-72
French-406
91Bowman-117
91Kraft-82
91O-Pee-Chee-398
91Panini Stickers-113
91Parkhurst-83
91Parkhurst-217
French-83
French-217
91Pinnacle-210
French-210
91Pro Set-115
91Pro Set-289
French-115
French-289
Platinum PC-PC13
91Score American-32
91Score Canadian Bilingual-32
91Score Canadian English-32
91Stadium Club-25
91Topps-398
91Upper Deck-293
French-293
92Bowman-54
92O-Pee-Chee-396
92Panini Stickers-96
92Panini Stickers French-96
92Pinnacle-142
French-142
92Pro Set-81
92Pro Set-259
92Score-205
92Score-446
Canadian-205
Canadian-446
92Stadium Club-427
92Topps-388
Gold-388G
92Ultra-97
01Greats of the Game-50
Autographs-50
01Topps Archives-77
Arena Seats-ASBS
Relics-JBOS
04ITG Franchises US West-244
Autographs-A-BSH
06Parkhurst-118
Autographs-118

Smith, Brad
80Flames Postcards-20
80Pepsi-Cola Caps-18
81O-Pee-Chee-103
86Maple Leafs Postcards-18
87Maple Leafs PLAY-22
87Panini Stickers-335
89Windsor Spitfires-16
907th Inn. Sketch OHL-200
03Parkhurst Original Six Detroit-49
Autographs-OS-BS
05Moncton Wildcats-26
06Moncton Wildcats-16

Smith, Brad (QMJHL)
05Moncton Wildcats-26
06Moncton Wildcats-16

Smith, Brandon
89Portland Winter Hawks-20
907th Inn. Sketch WHL-314
917th Inn. Sketch WHL-27
93Portland Winter Hawks-23
94Dayton Bombers-17
95Adirondack Red Wings-21
98Providence Bruins-20
99Providence Bruins-22
00SPx-93
Spectrum-93
00Upper Deck-219
Exclusives Tier 1-219
Exclusives Tier 2-219
00Upper Deck MVP-187
First Stars-187
Second Stars-187
Third Stars-187
00Upper Deck Victory-262
00Providence Bruins-17
01Cleveland Barons-19
03Bridgeport Sound Tigers-9
04Rochester Americans-22
06Rochester Americans-19

Smith, Brian
60Parkhurst-27
68Bauer Ads-20

Smith, Bryan
00Sioux City Musketeers-26

Smith, Buddy
99ECHL All-Star Southern Conference-3
02Arkansas Riverblades-16
02ECHL All-Star Southern-54
02ECHL Update-U-22

Smith, Carter
04Moose Jaw Warriors-21
05Moose Jaw Warriors-19

Smith, Chris
80Oshawa Generals-20
81Oshawa Generals-2
83Moncton Alpines-2

Smith, Chris (MSU)
92Michigan State Spartans-21
93Michigan State Spartans-19

Smith, Clint
34Beehive Group I Photos-294
39O-Pee-Chee V301-1-35
91Pro Set HOF Induction-6
04ITG Ultimate Mem Chitown Immortals-2
05ITG Ultimate Mem Broadway Bluesh Autos-10
06Parkhurst-119
06Parkhurst-221
Autographs-119
Autographs-221
06The Cup Stanley Cup Signatures-CSCS

Smith, Corey
01Bossier-Shreveport Mudbugs-18
02Macon Trax-1

Smith, Dallas
60Shirriff Coins-116
60Topps Stamps-47
61Shirriff/Salada Coins-2
61Topps-4
62Topps-9
66Topps-101
66Topps USA Test-3
67Topps-41
68O-Pee-Chee-136
68Shirriff Coins-13
69O-Pee-Chee-25
69Topps-25
70Bruins Postcards-17
70Bruins Team Issue-8
70Esso Power Players-69
70O-Pee-Chee-137
70Sargent Promotions Stamps-16
71Bruins Postcards-15
71Letraset Action Replays-5
71O-Pee-Chee-170
71Sargent Promotions Stamps-11
71Toronto Sun-17
72O-Pee-Chee-21
72O-Pee-Chee-135
72Sargent Promotions Stamps-19
72Topps-45
73O-Pee-Chee-167
73Topps-42
74NHL Action Stamps-33
74O-Pee-Chee NHL-146
74Topps-146
75O-Pee-Chee NHL-118
75Topps-118
76O-Pee-Chee NHL-105
76Topps-105
98Bruins Alumni-20
Autographs-20

Smith, Damian
94Finnish Jaa Kiekko-319
96UK Guildford Flames-12

Smith, Dan
95Tri-City Americans-23
98Hershey Bears-22
99BAP Memorabilia-279
Gold-279
Silver-279
00Hershey Bears-16
02Springfield Falcons-21
05Hamilton Bulldogs-24

Smith, Daniel
06Halifax Mooseheads-11

Smith, Darcy
93Seattle Thunderbirds-25
95Medicine Hat Tigers-19
96Kamloops Blazers-25
97Peoria Rivermen-9
98Peoria Rivermen-11

Smith, Darin
85London Knights-12
88ProCards IHL-87
89ProCards IHL-9
90Kansas City Blades-8
90ProCards AHL/IHL-591
91ProCards-248
93Fort Wayne Komets-17
95Fort Wayne Komets-17

Smith, Darren
90Fort Saskatchewan Traders-16

Smith, Darryl
04Guelph Storm-21
05Gatineau Olympiques-24
06Gatineau Olympiques-18

Smith, Dave
93Fort Wayne Komets-18
94Binghamton Rangers-20

Smith, David
97UK Fife Flyers-20
00UK Guildford Flames-23
01UK Guildford Flames-17

Smith, Dean
94UK Sheffield Steelers-8

Smith, Denis
51Laval Dairy Subset-12
52Bas Du Fleuve-6
52St. Lawrence Sales-42
94Windsor Spitfires-7
95Slapshot-410
95Classic-36
95Classic-98
95Classic Five-Sport *-155
Autographs-155
97Donruss-206
Press Proofs Silver-206
Press Proofs Gold-206
97Donruss Canadian Ice-142
Dominion Series-142
Provincial Series-142
97Donruss Limited-37
Exposure-37
97Upper Deck-194
97St. John's Maple Leafs-22
97Bowman CHL-37
OPC-37
99St. John's Maple Leafs-22
00Pacific-398
Copper-398
Gold-398
Ice Blue-398
Premiere Date-398
00St. John's Maple Leafs-24
01St. John's Maple Leafs-21
03Hershey Bears-3
03Hershey Bears Patriot News-22

Smith, Denis (50s)
51Laval Dairy Subset-12
52Bas Du Fleuve-6

Smith, Dennis
81Kingston Canadians-21
82Kingston Canadians-2
83Kingston Canadians-2
88ProCards AHL-9
89ProCards AHL-96
91ProCards-54
96Michigan K-Wings-2

Smith, Derek
78O-Pee-Chee-222
78Topps-222
79O-Pee-Chee-89
79Topps-89
80O-Pee-Chee-199
80Topps-199
81O-Pee-Chee-25
81O-Pee-Chee Stickers-59
81Sabres Milk Panels-14
81Topps-E79
82O-Pee-Chee-95
82Post Cereal-5
88Flyers Postcards-19
98Huntington Blizzard-10
01Notre Dame Fighting Irish-16
03Notre Dame Fighting Irish-2

Smith, Derek (Minors)
98Huntington Blizzard-10

Smith, Derek (ND)
01Notre Dame Fighting Irish-16
03Notre Dame Fighting Irish-2

Smith, Derrick
85Flyers Postcards-26
86Flyers Postcards-24
87Flyers Postcards-24
87Panini Stickers-135
89Flyers Postcards-23
89Panini Stickers-304
90Flyers Postcards-22
90O-Pee-Chee-463
90Pro Set-503
91Bowman-245
91O-Pee-Chee-486
91Panini Stickers-232
91Pro Set-174
French-174
91Score Canadian Bilingual-444
91Score Canadian English-444
91Topps-486
92O-Pee-Chee-363
96Michigan K-Wings-15
96Collector's Edge Ice-142
Prism-142
00Brampton Battalion-27

Smith, Des
34Beehive Group I Photos-206
37O-Pee-Chee V304E-148
39O-Pee-Chee V301-1-77

Smith, Don
10Sweet Caporal Postcards-19
11C55-19
12C57-12
01Florida Everblades-13
02Florida Everblades-18
02Florida Everblades RBI-130
03Elmira Jackals-20

Smith, Don (Vintage)
10Sweet Caporal Postcards-19
11C55-19
12C57-12

Smith, Doug
82O-Pee-Chee-160
82Post Cereal-8
84Kings Smokey-15
84O-Pee-Chee-91
86O-Pee-Chee-202
86Sabres Blue Shield-27
86Sabres Blue Shield Small-27
87Sabres Blue Shield-26
87Sabres Wonder Bread/Hostess-28
88Oilers Tenth Anniversary-69
89Canucks Mohawk-18

Smith, Doug (Minors)
91Ferris State Bulldogs-29
92Ferris State Bulldogs-29
97Central Texas Stampede-15

Smith, Ed
84Sudbury Wolves-16

Smith, Evan
06Penticton Vees-19

Smith, Fiona
97Collector's Choice-293

Smith, Floyd
44Beehive Group II Photos-211
63Parkhurst-57
63York White Backs-42
64Beehive Group III Photos-94A
64Beehive Group III Photos-94B
64Beehive Group III Photos-94C
64Coca-Cola Caps-50
64Topps-42
64Toronto Star-43
65Coca-Cola-49
65Topps-109
66Topps-106
67Topps-52
68Maple Leafs White Border-10
68O-Pee-Chee-130
68Post Marbles-24
68Shirriff Coins-170
68Topps-130
69Maple Leafs White Border Glossy-33
69O-Pee-Chee-49
69Topps-49
70Dad's Cookies-123
70Esso Power Players-85
70O-Pee-Chee-140
70Sargent Promotions Stamps-30
71O-Pee-Chee-158
71Sabres Postcards-84
74O-Pee-Chee NHL-176
74Topps-176
79Maple Leafs Postcards-29
94Parkhurst Tall Boys-45
95Parkhurst '66-67-52
Coins-52

Smith, Frank D
83Hall of Fame Postcards-G13
85Hall of Fame-103

Smith, Gairin
897th Inn. Sketch OHL-65
907th Inn. Sketch OHL-217
917th Inn. Sketch OHL-100
93Roanoke Express-17
94Wheeling Thunderbirds-11
94Wheeling Thunderbirds Photo Album-9
95Wheeling Thunderbirds-11
95Wheeling Thunderbirds Series II-14
96Carolina Monarchs-22

Smith, Gary
67Seals Team Issue-17
68O-Pee-Chee-176
68Shirriff Coins-115
69O-Pee-Chee-78
69Topps-78
70Colgate Stamps-90
70Esso Power Players-91
70O-Pee-Chee-69
70Sargent Promotions Stamps-129
70Topps-69
71O-Pee-Chee/Topps Booklets-22
71Sargent Promotions Stamps-43
71Topps-124
71Toronto Sun-80
72O-Pee-Chee-117
72Sargent Promotions Stamps-61
72Topps-114
72Finnish Semic World Championship-171
72Swedish Semic World Championship-171
73Canucks Royal Bank-17
73O-Pee-Chee-126
73Topps-126
74Canucks Royal Bank-19
74Lipton Soup-15
74NHL Action Stamps-274
74O-Pee-Chee NHL-22
74Topps-22
75Canucks Royal Bank-20
75O-Pee-Chee NHL-115
75Topps-115
76O-Pee-Chee NHL-317
77O-Pee-Chee NHL-184
77Topps-184
79Jets Postcards-22
79O-Pee-Chee-103
79Topps-103
04ITG Franchises Canadian-126
04ITG Franchises US West-155
Autographs-A-GAS

Smith, Geoff
89Oilers Team Issue-22
90Bowman-192
Tiffany-192
90Oilers IGA-24
90O-Pee-Chee-33
90Pro Set-446
90Score-326
90Score-373
Canadian-326
Canadian-373
90Topps-33
Tiffany-33
90Upper Deck-326
French-326
91Bowman-112
91Oilers Panini Team Stickers-21
91Oilers IGA-23
91Oilers Team Issue-26
91O-Pee-Chee-301
91Pinnacle-283
French-283
91Pro Set-384
French-384
91Score American-87
91Score Canadian Bilingual-87
91Score Canadian English-87
91Stadium Club-42
91Topps-301
92Bowman-95
92Oilers IGA-21
92Oilers Team Issue-18
92O-Pee-Chee-338
92Pinnacle-192
French-192
92Score-192
Canadian-192
92Stadium Club-84
92Topps-275
Gold-275G
93Donruss-112
93Donruss-435
93Leaf-302
93Pinnacle-416
Canadian-416
93Score-306
93Score-646
Gold-646
Canadian-306
Canadian-646
Canadian Gold-646
94Leaf-366
94Parkhurst-82
Gold-82
94Pinnacle-354
Artist's Proofs-354
Rink Collection-354
94Upper Deck-109
Electric Ice-109
96Carolina Monarchs-23
97Hartford Wolf Pack-18
98Cincinnati Cyclones-21
98Cincinnati Cyclones 2-17

Smith, Gord
74Capitals White Borders-24
76O-Pee-Chee NHL-303
77O-Pee-Chee NHL-387
78Capitals Team Issue-15
78O-Pee-Chee-347
79Jets Postcards-23
79O-Pee-Chee-285
82Brandon Wheat Kings-18

Smith, Gord (WHL)
82Brandon Wheat Kings-18

Smith, Greg
92Dallas Freeze-17
93Dallas Freeze-15
94Central Hockey League-121
95Central Hockey League-85
97Central Texas Stampede-16
98Wichita Thunder-21
99Wichita Thunder-20
00Wichita Thunder-20

Smith, Greg (Minors)
92Dallas Freeze-17
93Dallas Freeze-15
94Central Hockey League-121
95Central Hockey League-85
97Central Texas Stampede-16
98Wichita Thunder-21
99Wichita Thunder-20
00Wichita Thunder-20

Smith, Greg (NHL)
77O-Pee-Chee NHL-269
78North Stars Cloverleaf Dairy-3
78O-Pee-Chee-303
79North Stars Postcards-17
79O-Pee-Chee-11
79Topps-11
80North Stars Postcards-21
81O-Pee-Chee-168
81Topps-W112
82O-Pee-Chee-96
82Post Cereal-5
83NHL Key Tags-30
83O-Pee-Chee-130
83O-Pee-Chee Stickers-140
83Topps Stickers-140
84O-Pee-Chee-64
86Capitals Kodak-24
86Capitals Police-23
87Capitals Kodak-19
87Capitals Team Issue-21
87Red Wings Little Caesars-26
04ITG Franchises US West-180
Autographs-A-GRS

Smith, Ian
97Johnstown Chiefs-28

Smith, Jarrett
97Bowman CHL-122
OPC-122
Autographs-2
Bowman's Best-15
Bowman's Best Atomic Refractors-15
Bowman's Best Refractor-15
98Prince George Cougars-19
01Cincinnati Mighty Ducks-22
02Cincinnati Mighty Ducks-A-7

Smith, Jason
907th Inn. Sketch WHL-62
917th Inn. Sketch WHL-226
917th Inn. Sketch WHL-309
92Classic-10
Gold-10
92Classic Four-Sport *-159
Autographs-159A
93Donruss-182
93Leaf-389
93Parkhurst-379
Emerald Ice-379
93Pinnacle-433
Canadian-433
93PowerPlay-381
93Score-613
Gold-613
Canadian-613
Canadian Gold-613
93Ultra-363
Wave of the Future-17
93Upper Deck-252
94Donruss-256
94Leaf-245
94OPC Premier-344
Special Effects-344
94Parkhurst-130
Gold-130
94Pinnacle-417
Artist's Proofs-417
Rink Collection-417
94Stadium Club-83
Members Only Master Set-83
First Day Issue-83
Super Team Winner Cards-83
94Topps/OPC Premier-344
Special Effects-344
94Ultra-322
94Erie Panthers-13
94Classic Pro Prospects-135
95Donruss-279
96Devils Team Issue-26
96Saint John Flames-19
97Be A Player-191
Autographs-191
Autographs Die-Cuts-191
Autographs Prismatic Die-Cuts-191
97Pacific Invincible NHL Regime-196
98Be A Player-139
Press Release-139
98BAP Gold-139
98BAP Autographs-139
98BAP Autographs Gold-139
98BAP Tampa Bay All Star Game-139
98Pacific-421
Ice Blue-421
Red-421
99Wayne Gretzky Hockey-70
00O-Pee-Chee-258B
00O-Pee-Chee Parallel-258B
00Topps/OPC-258B
Parallel-258B
01O-Pee-Chee-182
01O-Pee-Chee Premier Parallel-182
01Pacific-165
Extreme LTD-165
Hobby LTD-165
Premiere Date-165
Retail LTD-165
01Pacific Arena Exclusives-165
01Topps-182
OPC Parallel-182
01Topps Chrome-121
Refractors-121
Black Border Refractors-121
02BAP First Edition-280
02BAP Sig Series Auto Buybacks 1998-139
02Oilers Postcards-8
02O-Pee-Chee-75
02O-Pee-Chee Premier Blue Parallel-75
02O-Pee-Chee Premier Red Parallel-75
02O-Pee-Chee Factory Set-75
02Pacific Complete-281
Red-281
02Pacific Exclusive-72
02Parkhurst-168
Bronze-168
Gold-168
Silver-168
02Topps-75
OPC Blue Parallel-75
OPC Red Parallel-75
Factory Set-75
02Topps Total-247
02UD Honor Roll-82
02Upper Deck-319
Exclusives-319
02Upper Deck Beckett UD Promos-319
03ITG Action-201
03NHL Sticker Collection-228
03Oilers Postcards-17
03Pacific Complete-87
Red-87
03Upper Deck-321
Canadian Exclusives-321
HG-321
UD Exclusives-321
04SP Authentic-36
04Upper Deck-69
Canadian Exclusives-69
HG Glossy Gold-69
HG Glossy Silver-69
05Be A Player-36
First Period-36
Second Period-36
Third Period-36
Overtime-36
Dual Signatures-SS
Quad Signatures-SSIR
Signatures-JS
Signatures Gold-JS
05Black Diamond-33
Emerald-33
Gold-33
Onyx-33
Ruby-33
05McDonalds Upper Deck-13
05Panini Stickers-280
05Parkhurst-197
05Parkhurst-512
Facsimile Auto Parallel-197
Facsimile Auto Parallel-512
True Colors-TCEDM
True Colors-TCEDM
05Upper Deck-76
Big Playmakers-B-JS
HG Glossy-76
Jerseys-J-JS
05Upper Deck MVP-154
Gold-154
Platinum-154
05Upper Deck Toronto Fall Expo-76
05Upper Deck Victory-81

Black-81
Gold-81
Silver-81
06Be A Player-38
Autographs-38
Signatures-JA
Signatures 25-41
Signatures Duals-DED
06Gatorade-27
06McDonald's Upper Deck-56
06O-Pee-Chee-196
Rainbow-196
06Panini Stickers-270
06Upper Deck-329
Exclusives Parallel-329
High Gloss Parallel-329
Masterpieces-329
06Upper Deck MVP-117
Gold Script-117
Super Script-117

Smith, Jeff
907th Inn. Sketch OHL-218
917th Inn. Sketch OHL-290
98Red Deer Rebels-19
99San Angelo Outlaws-23
00Red Deer Rebels-16
Signed-16
01Red Deer Rebels-15
02Hull Olympiques-2
02Trenton Titans-B-9
03Hull Olympiques Memorial Cup-15
03Trenton Titans-365
04Philadelphia Phantoms-21

Smith, Jeff (80s)
83Springfield Indians-17

Smith, Jeff (Goon)
98Red Deer Rebels-19
00Red Deer Rebels-16
Signed-16
01Red Deer Rebels-15
02Trenton Titans-B-9
03Trenton Titans-365
04Philadelphia Phantoms-21

Smith, Jeff (OHL)
907th Inn. Sketch OHL-218
917th Inn. Sketch OHL-290

Smith, Jeff (QMJHL)
02Hull Olympiques-2
03Hull Olympiques Memorial Cup-15

Smith, Jerad
97Portland Winter Hawks-6

Smith, Jeremy
01Sioux Falls Stampede-12
05Plymouth Whalers-B-03
06Plymouth Whalers-22

Smith, Jeremy (Goalie)
05Plymouth Whalers-B-03
06Plymouth Whalers-22

Smith, Jerrod
01St. Michaels Majors-12

Smith, Jim
87Sudbury Wolves-9
88Sudbury Wolves-9

Smith, Joel
82North Bay Centennials-20

Smith, John
51Laval Dairy QSHL-44

Smith, Jonathon
05Red Deer Rebels-17

Smith, Jordan
02Sault Ste. Marie Greyhounds-15
03Sault Ste. Marie Greyhounds-20
04Sault Ste. Marie Greyhounds-15
05Portland Pirates-9

Smith, Julian
96Detroit Whalers-14
06Austin Ice Bats-9

Smith, Kenny
44Beehive Group II Photos-67
05Portland Pirates-10

Smith, Kenny (00s)
05Portland Pirates-10

Smith, Kenton
98Calgary Hitmen-4
98Calgary Hitmen Autographs-4
99Calgary Hitmen-23
99Calgary Hitmen Autographs-23
03Columbus Cottonmouths-23

Smith, Kyle
03Camrose Kodiaks-8

Smith, Marcus
00Kitchener Rangers-25
01Kitchener Rangers-15
03Kitchener Rangers-23
03Kitchener Rangers Memorial Cup-19

Smith, Mark
95Lethbridge Hurricanes-22
95Saskatoon Blades-20
96Lethbridge Hurricanes-20
97Lethbridge Hurricanes-17
98Kentucky Thoroughblades-19
98Bowman CHL-70
Golden Anniversary-70
OPC International-70
98Bowman Chrome CHL-70
Golden Anniversary-70
Golden Anniversary Refractors-70
OPC International-70
OPC International Refractors-70
Refractors-70
99Kentucky Thoroughblades-24
99Odessa Jackalopes-12
00BAP Memorabilia-425
Emerald-425
Ruby-425
Sapphire-425
00SP Authentic-122
00SP Game Used-81
00SPx-171
00Titanium Draft Day Edition-173
00Titanium Draft Day Promos-173
00UD Pros and Prospects-122
00UD Reserve-112
00Upper Deck-419
Exclusives Tier 1-419
Exclusives Tier 2-419
00Upper Deck Ice-121
00Kentucky Thoroughblades-22
01Odessa Jackalopes-19
02Lexington Men O'War-9
03ITG Action-447
05Parkhurst-414
Facsimile Auto Parallel-414
05Fort Wayne Komets Choice-15
06O-Pee-Chee-415
Rainbow-415

Smith, Mark (Minors)
95Saskatoon Blades-20
99Odessa Jackalopes-12
01Odessa Jackalopes-19
02Lexington Men O'War-9
03Alaska Aces-16
05Fort Wayne Komets Choice-15

Smith, Martin
91Air Canada SJHL-B29
91Air Canada SJHL-D15
91Air Canada SJHL All-Stars-4
92Richmond Renegades-17

Smith, Matt
917th Inn. Sketch WHL-63
99Peoria Rivermen-17
00Finnish Cardset-153
01Finnish Cardset-40

Smith, Matthew
06Quebec Remparts-23

Smith, Michael 90's
91Lake Superior State Lakers-22
92Lake Superior State Lakers-25
93Roanoke Express-18
93Classic-82
94Roanoke Express-5
94Classic Pro Prospects-244
95Roanoke Express-5
96Roanoke Express-5

Smith, Mike
01Arizona Icecats-20
02Arizona Icecats-22
03Arizona Icecats-21
04Arizona Icecats-21

Smith, Mike (Goalie)
99Kingston Frontenacs-19
00Sudbury Wolves-24
01Kingston Frontenacs-17
01Sudbury Wolves-17
01Sudbury Wolves Police-24
02ECHL All-Star Northern-34
02Lexington Men O'War-4
02Utah Grizzlies-27
03BAP Memorabilia-219
03Beehive-216
Gold-216
Silver-216
03ITG Used Signature Series-188
Gold-188
03ITG VIP Rookie Debut-102
03Parkhurst Rookie-114
03Stars Postcards-23
03UD Premier Collection-67
03Upper Deck Rookie Update-138
04Houston Aeros-16
06Between The Pipes-40
Autographs-AMSM
Emblems-GUE13
Emblems Gold-GUE13
Emblems Autographs-GUE13
Jerseys-GUJ13
Jerseys Gold-GUJ13
Jerseys Autographs-GUJ13
Numbers-GUN13
Numbers Gold-GUN13
Numbers Autographs-GUN13
06Stars Team Postcards-20
06ITG Heroes and Prospects Net Prospects-NPR14

Smith, Nathan
98Swift Current Broncos-11
99Swift Current Broncos-18
00Swift Current Broncos-18
00UD CHL Prospects-68
Future Leaders-FL8
01Swift Current Broncos-8
02Manitoba Moose-16
03Beehive-250
Gold-250
Silver-250
03ITG VIP Rookie Debut-62
03Parkhurst Rookie-122
03SP Authentic-134
Limited-134
03Topps Traded-TT142
Blue-TT142
Gold-TT142
Red-TT142
03UD Honor Roll-144
03Upper Deck-457
Canadian Exclusives-457
HG-457
UD Exclusives-457
03Upper Deck Ice-111
Glass Parallel-111
03Upper Deck Rookie Update-131
03Manitoba Moose-9
04SP Authentic Rookie Review-RR-NS
04SP Authentic Sign of the Times-ST-NS
04SP Authentic Sign of the Times-FS-VAN
04Manitoba Moose-10
05UD Powerplay Power Marks-PMNS
05Upper Deck Jerseys-J-NS
05Upper Deck Trilogy Scripts-SFS-NS
05Manitoba Moose-22
06Manitoba Moose-13

Smith, Neil
92Western Michigan Broncos-23
01Belleville Bulls Update-4
02Belleville Bulls-16
03Cape Breton Screaming Eagles-20
04Cape Breton Screaming Eagles-18

Smith, Neil (GM)
92Western Michigan Broncos-23

Smith, Nick
96Barrie Colts-23
97Barrie Colts-20
98Barrie Colts-18
99Louisville Panthers-22
01BAP Memorabilia-359
Emerald-359
Ruby-359
Sapphire-359
01UD Honor Roll-74
01Upper Deck Ice-138
02Pacific-159
Blue-159
Red-159
02Cincinnati Mighty Ducks-A-12
03Cincinnati Mighty Ducks-A11

Smith, Normie
34Beehive Group I Photos-123
37V356 Worldwide Gum-74
04ITG Franchises Update-467
06ITG Ultimate Memorabilia Motown Heroes Autos-4

Smith, Randy
83Saskatoon Blades-12
88ProCards IHL-34
89ProCards IHL-87
90Alberta International Team Canada-18
91Alberta International Team Canada-22
92Score Canadian Olympians-4
93Las Vegas Thunder-25

Smith, Reginald
24Anonymous NHL-21
24C144 Champ's Cigarettes-56
24V-122-47
24V145-2-5
25Dominion Chocolates-69
33V357 Ice Kings-31
33V357-2 Ice Kings Premiums-6
34Beehive Group I Photos-207
34Sweet Caporal-25
35O-Pee-Chee V304C-76
36Champion Postcards-3
36O-Pee-Chee V304D-132
37V356 Worldwide Gum-20
39O-Pee-Chee V301-1-17
83Hall of Fame Postcards-C14
85Hall of Fame-43
03BAP Ultimate Memorabilia Paper Cuts-32
04ITG Franchises Canadian-67
04ITG Ultimate Mem Marvelous Maroons-1
05ITG Ultimate Mem Marvelous Maroons Auto-9
06ITG Ultimate Memorabilia Amazing Amerks Autos-6
06ITG Ultimate Memorabilia Marvelous Maroons Autos-6
06ITG Ultimate Memorabilia Paper Cuts Autos-11
06ITG Ultimate Memorabilia Sensational Sens Autos-6

Smith, Rick 70's
70Bruins Postcards-18
70Bruins Team Issue-17
70Esso Power Players-61
70O-Pee-Chee-135
70Sargent Promotions Stamps-11
71Bruins Postcards-7
71O-Pee-Chee-174
71Sargent Promotions Stamps-5
72O-Pee-Chee-23
72O-Pee-Chee-284
72Topps-34
74Minnesota Fighting Saints WHA-20
74Team Canada L'Equipe WHA-20
75O-Pee-Chee WHA-41
76O-Pee-Chee NHL-269
77O-Pee-Chee NHL-104
77Topps-104
78O-Pee-Chee-164
78Topps-164
79O-Pee-Chee-59
79Topps-59

Smith, Rick 80's
83Saskatoon Blades-21

Smith, Rob
01Calgary Hitmen-24
01Calgary Hitmen Autographed-24
02Calgary Hitmen-6
03Brampton Batallion-21

Smith, Ron
91ProCards-212
92Quebec Pee-Wee Tournament-1590
93Quebec Pee-Wee Tournament-797
95Cincinnati Cyclones-24
96Cincinnati Cyclones-NNO
97Cincinnati Cyclones-20
98Cincinnati Cyclones-28
98Cincinnati Cyclones 2-24
99Cincinnati Cyclones-25
00Cincinnati Cyclones-23

Smith, Ron (PW)
93Quebec Pee-Wee Tournament-797

Smith, Russell
96Rimouski Oceanic Update-9

Smith, Ryan
907th Inn. Sketch WHL-131
91Air Canada SJHL-C11
917th Inn. Sketch WHL-205
92Brandon Wheat Kings-21
93Lethbridge Hurricanes-15
99Ohio State Buckeyes-17
00Ohio State Buckeyes-10
01Ohio State Buckeyes-15
03Russian World Championship Stars-33
04Ultimate Collection Dual Logos-UL2-IS
05SP Authentic Sign of the Times-RS

Smith, Ryan (Center)
91Air Canada SJHL-C11

Smith, Ryan (OSU)
99Ohio State Buckeyes-17
00Ohio State Buckeyes-10
01Ohio State Buckeyes-15

Smith, Sandy
90ProCards AHL/IHL-373
91ProCards-299
92Cleveland Lumberjacks-19
95Minnesota Moose-3
98Swiss Power Play Stickers-324
99German DEL-60
00German Berlin Polar Bears Postcards-19

Smith, Scooter
03Reading Royals RBI Sports-302
06Toledo Storm-11

Smith, Scott
92Northern Michigan Wildcats-25
93Northern Michigan Wildcats-25
94Owen Sound Platers-12
98Sudbury Wolves-22

Smith, Shawn
98Thunder Bay Thunder Cats-16
99Rockford IceHogs-17
00Rockford IceHogs-17

Smith, Sid
44Beehive Group II Photos-451
45Quaker Oats Photos-48A
45Quaker Oats Photos-48B
48Exhibits Canadian-38
51Parkhurst-84
52Parkhurst-45
53Parkhurst-2
54Parkhurst-2
55Parkhurst-2
55Parkhurst-75
Quaker Oats-2
Quaker Oats-75
57Parkhurst-T10
91Ultimate Original Six-43
French-43
94Parkhurst Missing Link-109
02Maple Leafs Platinum Collection-36
02Maple Leafs Platinum Collection-104
03Parkhurst Original Six Toronto-53
03Parkhurst Original Six Toronto-70
03Parkhurst Original Six Toronto-80
Autographs-10
04ITG Franchises Canadian-93

Smith, Simon
97UK Guildford Flames-19

Smith, Steve
83Moncton Alpines-10
84Nova Scotia Oilers-11
85Oilers Red Rooster-5
86Oilers Red Rooster-5
86Oilers Team Issue-5
87Oilers Team Issue-5
87Panini Stickers-269
88Oilers Tenth Anniversary-121
88Oilers Team Issue-26
88O-Pee-Chee-252
88O-Pee-Chee Stickers-225
88Panini Stickers-55
88ProCards AHL-249
88Salt Lake Golden Eagles-7
89Kraft-17
89Oilers Team Issue-23
89O-Pee-Chee-228
89O-Pee-Chee Stickers-223
89Panini Stickers-83
89Kitchener Rangers-28
89ProCards AHL-272
90Bowman-200
Tiffany-200
90Oilers IGA-25
90O-Pee-Chee-368
90Panini Stickers-226
90Pro Set-96
90Score-129
Canadian-129
90Topps-368
Tiffany-368
90Upper Deck-148
French-148
90Kitchener Rangers-9
90ProCards AHL/IHL-287
907th Inn. Sketch OHL-199
907th Inn. Sketch OHL-240
907th Inn. Sketch Memorial Cup-37
91Pro Set Platinum-27
91Blackhawks Coke-23
91Bowman-106
91Bowman-417
91Kraft-85
91Oilers Panini Team Stickers-22
91O-Pee-Chee-21
91OPC Premier-136
91Panini Stickers-121
91Parkhurst-31
French-31
91Pinnacle-18
French-18
91Pro Set-73
91Pro Set-284
91Pro Set-370
French-73
French-284
French-370
91Score American-11
91Score Canadian Bilingual-11
91Score Canadian Bilingual-623
91Score Canadian English-11
91Score Canadian English-623
91Score Rookie/Traded-73T
91Stadium Club-230
91Topps-21
91Upper Deck-350
French-350
917th Inn. Sketch OHL-187
92Bowman-24
92O-Pee-Chee-108
92Panini Stickers-12
92Panini Stickers French-12
92Parkhurst-32
92Parkhurst-444
Emerald Ice-32
Emerald Ice-444
92Pinnacle-57
French-57
92Pro Set-37
92Score-48
Canadian-48
92Stadium Club-383
92Topps-315
Gold-315G
92Ultra-42
92Finnish Semic-79
93Blackhawks Coke-20
93Donruss-68
93Leaf-95
93OPC Premier-39
Gold-39
93Panini Stickers-154
93Parkhurst-310
Emerald Ice-310
93Pinnacle-70
Canadian-70
93PowerPlay-55
93Score-192
Canadian-192
93Stadium Club-218
Members Only Master Set-218
OPC-218
First Day Issue-218
First Day Issue OPC-218
93Topps/OPC Premier-39
Gold-39
93Ultra-231
94Be A Player-R62
94Blackhawks Coke-17
94Canada Games NHL POGS-74
94Donruss-183
94EA Sports-26
94Finest Ring Leaders-12
94Flair-37
94Fleer-46
94Leaf-257
94OPC Premier-133
Special Effects-133
94Pinnacle-211
Artist's Proofs-211
Rink Collection-211
94Score-121
Gold-121
Platinum-121
94Topps/OPC Premier-133
Special Effects-133
94Ultra-45
94Finnish Jaa Kiekko-85
95Be A Player-123
Signatures-S123
Signatures Die Cuts-S123
95Blackhawks Coke-16
95Donruss-179
95Leaf-194
95Parkhurst International-43
Emerald Ice-43
95Pinnacle-191
Artist's Proofs-191
Rink Collection-191
95Score-27
Black Ice Artist's Proofs-27
Black Ice-27
95Topps-205
OPC Inserts-205
95Finnish Semic World Championships-81
95Swedish Globe World Championships-78
97Pacific Dynagon Best Kept Secrets-22
99O-Pee-Chee-62
99O-Pee-Chee Chrome-62
99O-Pee-Chee Chrome Refractors-62
99Panini Stickers-188
99Paramount-42
Copper-42
Emerald-42
Gold-42
Holographic Emerald-42
Holographic Gold-42
Holographic Silver-42
Ice Blue-42
Premiere Date-42
Red-42
99Topps/OPC-62
99Topps/OPC Chrome-62
Refractors-62
02Fleer Throwbacks-14
Gold-14
Platinum-14
02Peterborough Petes-2

Smith, Steve (Center)
89Kitchener Rangers-28
90Kitchener Rangers-9
907th Inn. Sketch OHL-199
907th Inn. Sketch OHL-240
907th Inn. Sketch Memorial Cup-37
917th Inn. Sketch OHL-187

Smith, Steve (Minors)
80Sault Ste. Marie Greyhounds-8
81Sault Ste. Marie Greyhounds-20
82Sault Ste. Marie Greyhounds-19
83Springfield Indians-22

Smith, Stuart
82Whalers Junior Hartford Courant-17

Smith, Thomas J
85Hall of Fame-237

Smith, Tim
98Spokane Chiefs-23
99Spokane Chiefs-24
00Spokane Chiefs-25
01Swift Current Broncos-9
02Columbia Inferno-109
03Columbia Inferno-110

Smith, Todd
82Oshawa Generals-6
04Minnesota-Duluth Bulldogs-22

Smith, Todd (80s)
82Oshawa Generals-6

Smith, Tommy
83Hall of Fame Postcards-H14
91Arizona Icecats-9
92Arizona Icecats-4

Smith, Tommy (HOF)
83Hall of Fame Postcards-H14

Smith, Travis
91Air Canada SJHL-C48
92Saskatchewan JHL-152
96Denver University Pioneers-1
98Roanoke Express-13
00Roanoke Express-14
01Roanoke Express-18
05Roanoke Valley Vipers-11

Smith, Trevor
87Kingston Canadians-29

Smith, Troy
95Slapshot-60
96Detroit Whalers-15
03St. Francis Xavier X-Men-9
04Louisiana Ice Gators-21
05Danbury Trashers-15
07Topps Chrome Printing Plates Black-TC169

Smith, Vern
84Springfield Indians-7
88ProCards AHL-313
89ProCards AHL-293
90ProCards AHL/IHL-533
91ProCards-387

Smith, Warren
96Denver University Pioneers-9

Smith, Wayne
85Minnesota-Duluth Bulldogs-6

Smith, Wyatt
94Select-156
Gold-156
95Donruss Elite World Juniors-41
95Minnesota Golden Gophers-26
96Minnesota Golden Gophers-24
97Minnesota Golden Gophers-21
98Minnesota Golden Gophers-23
00Pacific-323
Copper-323
Gold-323
Ice Blue-323
Premiere Date-323
00Private Stock-138
Gold-138
Premiere Date-138
Retail-138
Silver-138
PS-2001 Rookies-17
00Vanguard-140
Pacific Proofs-140
02Milwaukee Admirals-3
03Milwaukee Admirals-24
03Milwaukee Admirals Postcards-20
04Milwaukee Admirals-24
06O-Pee-Chee-253
Rainbow-253

Smith, Zack
05Swift Current Broncos-24
06Swift Current Broncos-19

Smithson, Jerred
98Calgary Hitmen-19
98Calgary Hitmen Autographs-19
99Calgary Hitmen-24
99Calgary Hitmen Autographs-24
01Manchester Monarchs-11A
02BAP Memorabilia-303
02BAP Ultimate Memorabilia-90
02Pacific Complete-597
Red-597
02UD Artistic Impressions-118
Gold-118
02UD Honor Roll-132
02UD Premier Collection-88
Gold-88
02Manchester Monarchs-28
03Manchester Monarchs-17
03Manchester Monarchs Team Issue-17
04Milwaukee Admirals-11

Smithurst, Michael
92Norwegian Elite Series-155

Smolenak, Radek
04Kingston Frontenacs-9
05ITG Heroes/Prosp Toronto Expo Parallel -124
05Kingston Frontenacs-8
05ITG Heroes and Prospects-124
Autographs-A-RS

Smolik, Jaroslav
95Czech APS Extraliga-218
95Czech APS Extraliga-343
99Czech Score Blue 2000-136
99Czech Score Red Ice 2000-136

Smolinski, Bryan
92Parkhurst-481
Emerald Ice-481
92Michigan State Spartans-22
93Donruss-30
93Leaf-204
93OPC Premier-466
Gold-466
93Parkhurst-259
Emerald Ice-259
93Pinnacle-217
Canadian-217
93PowerPlay-291
Rookie Standouts-14
93Score-472
Canadian-472
93Stadium Club-274
Members Only Master Set-274
First Day Issue-274
93Topps/OPC Premier-466
Gold-466
93Ultra-232
All-Rookies-6
93Upper Deck-242
SP-12
93Michigan State Spartans-20
94Be A Player Signature Cards-47
94Canada Games NHL POGS-38
94Donruss-21
94Fleer-17
94Leaf-130
Gold Rookies-14
94Leaf Limited-57
94OPC Premier-196
94OPC Premier-479
94O-Pee-Chee Finest Inserts-2
94OPC Premier Special Effects-196
94OPC Premier Special Effects-479
94Parkhurst-12
94Parkhurst-276
Gold-12
Gold-276
SE Vintage-26
94Pinnacle-13
94Pinnacle-470
Artist's Proofs-13
Artist's Proofs-470
Rink Collection-13
Rink Collection-470
94Select-132
Gold-132
94SP-11
Die Cuts-11
94Stadium Club-103
Members Only Master Set-103
First Day Issue-103
Super Team Winner Cards-103
94Topps/OPC Premier-196
94Topps/OPC Premier-479
Special Effects-196
Special Effects-479
94Ultra-16
All-Rookies-9
All-Rookies Parallel-9
94Upper Deck-399
Electric Ice-399
SP Inserts-SP96
SP Inserts Die Cuts-SP96
95Canada Games NHL POGS-213
95Collector's Choice-178
Player's Club-178
Player's Club Platinum-178
95Donruss-138
95Donruss-327
95Emotion-142
95Hoyle Eastern Playing Cards-20
95Leaf-239
95Metal-120
95Panini Stickers-60
95Parkhurst International-168
Emerald Ice-168
95Penguins Foodland-24
95Playoff One on One-188
95Pro Magnets-94
95Score-43
Black Ice Artist's Proofs-43
Black Ice-43
95SkyBox Impact-135
95Stadium Club-210
Members Only Master Set-210
95Summit-156
Artist's Proofs-156
Ice-156
95Ultra-14
95Ultra-294
Gold Medallion-14
95Upper Deck-494
Electric Ice-494
Electric Ice Gold-494
96Be A Player-132
Autographs-132
Autographs Silver-132
96Black Diamond-120
Gold-120
96Collector's Choice-218
96Donruss-99
Press Proofs-99
96Flair-58
Blue Ice-58
96Fleer-89
96Fleer Picks-132
96Islander Postcards-20
96NHL Pro Stamps-94
96Pinnacle-125
Artist's Proofs-125
Foil-125
Premium Stock-125
Rink Collection-125
96Playoff One on One-389
96Score-88
Artist's Proofs-88
Dealer's Choice Artist's Proofs-88
Special Artist's Proofs-88
Golden Blades-88
96SkyBox Impact-104
96Upper Deck-322
96Upper Deck Ice-39
Parallel-39
97Collector's Choice-152
97Crown Royale-82
Emerald Green-82
Ice Blue-82
Silver-82
97Pacific-196
Copper-196
Emerald Green-196
Ice Blue-196
Red-196
Silver-196
97Pacific Dynagon-76
Copper-76
Dark Grey-76
Emerald Green-76
Ice Blue-76
Red-76
Silver-76
Tandems-68
97Pacific Invincible-84
Copper-84
Emerald Green-84
Ice Blue-84
Red-84
Silver-84
97Pacific Omega-143
Copper-143
Dark Gray-143
Emerald Green-143
Gold-143
Ice Blue-143
97Panini Stickers-81
97Paramount-112
Copper-112
Dark Grey-112
Emerald Green-112
Ice Blue-112
Red-112
Silver-112
97Pinnacle Certified-108
Red-108
Mirror Blue-108
Mirror Gold-108
Mirror Red-108
97Pinnacle Inside-178
97Pinnacle Tot Cert Platinum Blue-108
97Pinnacle Tot Cert Platinum Gold-108
97Pinnacle Totally Certified Platinum Red-108
97Pinnacle Tot Cert Mirror Platinum Gold-108
97Score-241
97Upper Deck-310
98Aurora-120
98Be A Player-233
Press Release-233
98BAP Gold-233
98BAP Autographs-233
98BAP Autographs Gold-233
98Islanders Power Play-NYI2
98OPC Chrome-38
Refractors-38
98Pacific-289
Ice Blue-289
Red-289
98Pacific Dynagon Ice-119
Blue-119
Red-119
98Panini Stickers-74
98Paramount-149
Copper-149
Emerald Green-149
Holo-Electric-149
Ice Blue-149
Silver-149
98Topps-38
O-Pee-Chee-38
98UD Choice-127
98UD Choice Preview-127
98UD Choice Prime Choice Reserve-127
98UD Choice Reserve-127
98Upper Deck-128
Exclusives-128
Exclusives 1 of 1-128
Gold Reserve-128
99Crown Royale-68
Limited Series-68
Premiere Date-68
99Pacific-265
Copper-265
Emerald Green-265
Gold-265
Ice Blue-265
Premiere Date-265
Red-265
99Pacific Omega-112
Copper-112
Gold-112
Ice Blue-112
Premiere Date-112
99Panini Stickers-255
99Upper Deck-236
Exclusives-236
Exclusives 1 of 1-236
99Upper Deck Gold Reserve-236
99Upper Deck MVP SC Edition-86
Gold Script-86
Silver Script-86
Super Script-86
99Upper Deck Victory-140
00BAP Memorabilia-69
Emerald-69
Ruby-69
Sapphire-69
Promos-69
00BAP Mem Chicago Sportsfest Copper-69
00BAP Memorabilia Chicago Sportsfest Blue-69
00BAP Memorabilia Chicago Sportsfest Gold-69
00BAP Memorabilia Chicago Sportsfest Ruby-69
00BAP Memorabilia Chicago Sun-Times Ruby-69
00BAP Memorabilia Chicago Sun-Times Gold-69
00BAP Mem Chicago Sun-Times Sapphire-69
00BAP Mem Toronto Fall Expo Copper-69
00BAP Memorabilia Toronto Fall Expo Gold-69
00BAP Memorabilia Toronto Fall Expo Ruby-69
00BAP Parkhurst 2000-P199
00O-Pee-Chee-110
00O-Pee-Chee Parallel-110
00Pacific-202
Copper-202
Gold-202
Ice Blue-202
Premiere Date-202
00Paramount-115
Copper-115
Gold-115
Holo-Gold-115
Holo-Silver-115
Ice Blue-115
Premiere Date-115
00Stadium Club-177
00Titanium Game Gear-24
00Topps/OPC-110
Parallel-110
00Topps Chrome-86
OPC Refractors-86
Refractors-86
00Upper Deck-311
Exclusives Tier 1-311
Exclusives Tier 2-311
00Upper Deck MVP-84
First Stars-84
Second Stars-84
Third Stars-84
00Upper Deck Victory-115
00Upper Deck Vintage-166
01BAP Memorabilia-152
Emerald-152
Ruby-152
Sapphire-152
01BAP Signature Series-134
Autographs-134
Autographs Gold-134
01O-Pee-Chee-163
01O-Pee-Chee Premier Parallel-163
01Pacific-188
Extreme LTD-188
Hobby LTD-188
Premiere Date-188
Retail LTD-188
01Pacific Adrenaline-90
Blue-90
Premiere Date-90
Red-90
Retail-90
01Pacific Arena Exclusives-188
01Parkhurst-162
01Titanium Double-Sided Jerseys-18
01Titanium Double-Sided Patches-18
01Topps-163
OPC Parallel-163
01Upper Deck-82
Exclusives-82
01Upper Deck MVP-88
01Upper Deck Victory-162
Gold-162
02Kings Team Issue-5
02BAP Sig Series Auto Buybacks 1998-233
02BAP Sig Series Auto Buybacks 2001-134
02Crown Royale Dual Patches-12
02Kings Game Sheets-1
02Kings Game Sheets-2
02O-Pee-Chee-231
02O-Pee-Chee Premier Blue Parallel-231
02O-Pee-Chee Premier Red Parallel-231
02O-Pee-Chee Factory Set-231
02Pacific-175
Blue-175
Red-175
02Pacific Complete-133
Red-133
02Pacific Exclusive-83
Jerseys-12
Jerseys Gold-12
02Pacific Heads-Up Quad Jerseys-13
02Pacific Heads-Up Quad Jerseys Gold-13
02Private Stock Reserve-47
Blue-47
Red-47
Retail-47
02Topps-231
OPC Blue Parallel-231
OPC Red Parallel-231
Factory Set-231
02Topps Total-284
02Upper Deck-328
Exclusives-328
02Upper Deck Beckett UD Promos-328
02Upper Deck MVP-87
Gold-87
Classics-87
Golden Classics-87
02Upper Deck Vintage-120
03ITG Action-489
03NHL Sticker Collection-235
03O-Pee-Chee-152
03OPC Blue-152
03OPC Gold-152
03OPC Red-152
03Pacific-242
Blue-242
Red-242
03Pacific Complete-67
Red-67
03Pacific Exhibit-105
Blue Backs-105
Yellow Backs-105
03Private Stock Reserve-188
Blue-188
Patches-188
Red-188
Retail-188
03Senators Postcards-14
03Topps-152
Blue-152
Gold-152
Red-152
03Upper Deck-378
Canadian Exclusives-378
HG-378
UD Exclusives-378
04Pacific-188
Blue-188
Red-188
05Parkhurst-339
Facsimile Auto Parallel-339
05Upper Deck-383
05Upper Deck MVP-271
Gold-271
Platinum-271
06Blackhawks Postcards-19
06O-Pee-Chee-112
Rainbow-112
06Panini Stickers-213
06Upper Deck Arena Giveaways-CHI5
06Upper Deck-296
Exclusives Parallel-296
High Gloss Parallel-296
Masterpieces-296
06Upper Deck MVP-67
Gold Script-67
Super Script-67

Smolka, Lukas
99Czech OFS-232
00Czech OFS-241
01Czech OFS-39
01Czech OFS H Inserts-H6
02Czech OFS Plus-313

Smreczynski, Robert
93Quebec Pee-Wee Tournament-1504

Smrek, Peter
93Quebec Pee-Wee Tournament-1706
00Worcester Icecats-26
01BAP Memorabilia-200
Emerald-200
Ruby-200
Sapphire-200
01O-Pee-Chee-269
01O-Pee-Chee Premier Parallel-269
01Private Stock-132
Gold-132
Premiere Date-132
Retail-132
Silver-132
01Private Stock Pacific Nights-132
01SP Authentic-161
Limited-161
Limited Gold-161
01SP Game Used-89
01SPx-143
01SPx-143
Rookie Treasures-RTPS
01Stadium Club-122
Award Winners-122
Master Photos-122
01Topps-269
OPC Parallel-269
01Topps Heritage-149
01Topps Reserve-118
01Upper Deck-199
Exclusives-199
01Upper Deck MVP-208
01Upper Deck Victory-381

Gold-381
01Upper Deck Vintage-289
01Hartford Wolf Pack-20
02Slovakian Kvarteto-9
02Milwaukee Admirals-18
03Binghamton Senators-18
04German DEL-278
05Swedish SHL Elitset-254
Gold-254

Smrke, John
78Blues Postcards-20
79O-Pee-Chee-340

Smrke, Lou
51Laval Dairy QSHL-24
52St. Lawrence Sales-94

Smrke, Stan
51Laval Dairy QSHL-23
52St. Lawrence Sales-97
63Rochester Americans-20

Smuk, Cody
06Chilliwack Bruins-23

Smulders, Brad
05Dutch Vadeko Flyers -16

Smyke, Jesse
05Everett Silvertips-22

Smyl, Stan
78Canucks Royal Bank-20
79Canucks Royal Bank-20
80Canucks Silverwood Dairies-21
80Canucks Team Issue-20
80O-Pee-Chee-128
80O-Pee-Chee-208
80Pepsi-Cola Caps-118
80Topps-128
80Topps-208
81Canucks Team Issue-19
81O-Pee-Chee-328
81Post Standups-25
81Topps-38
82Canucks Team Issue-19
82O-Pee-Chee-356
82O-Pee-Chee Stickers-242
82Post Cereal-19
82Topps Stickers-242
83Canucks Team Issue-18
83NHL Key Tags-123
83O-Pee-Chee-359
83O-Pee-Chee Stickers-274
83Puffy Stickers-2
83Topps Stickers-274
83Vachon-116
84Canucks Team Issue-22
84Kellogg's Accordion Discs-4
84Kellogg's Accordion Discs Singles-35
84O-Pee-Chee-330
84O-Pee-Chee Stickers-281
84 7-Eleven Discs-51
84Topps-140
84Kelowna Wings-28
85Canucks Team Issue-21
85O-Pee-Chee-68
85O-Pee-Chee Stickers-247
85 7-Eleven Credit Cards-19
85Topps-68
86Canucks Team Issue-18
86Kraft Drawings-66
86O-Pee-Chee-50
86O-Pee-Chee Stickers-96
86Topps-50
87Canucks Shell Oil-19
87O-Pee-Chee-4
87O-Pee-Chee Stickers-198
87Panini Stickers-349
87Topps-4
88Canucks Mohawk-19
88O-Pee-Chee-253
88O-Pee-Chee Stickers-60
88Panini Stickers-141
89Canucks Mohawk-19
89O-Pee-Chee-283
89O-Pee-Chee Stickers-68
89Panini Stickers-159
90Canucks Mohawk-27
90Panini Stickers-292
90Pro Set-548
90Score-374
Canadian-374
90Upper Deck-299
French-299
91Canucks Panini Team Stickers-23
99Syracuse Crunch-17
00Kansas City Blades-23
02Fleer Throwbacks-21
Gold-21
Platinum-21
04ITG Franchises Canadian-120
Autographs-SSM
04UD Legendary Signatures Autographs-SS
04UD Legendary Signatures Linemates-TISSTT

Smyth, Adam
00Ottawa 67's-8
01Ottawa 67's-8
02Ottawa 67's-7
03Owen Sound Attack-21
04Gwinnett Gladiators-23

Smyth, Brad
90 7th Inn. Sketch OHL-143
93Birmingham Bulls Birmingham News-20
93Cincinnati Cyclones-24
94Birmingham Bulls-21
96Select Certified-113
Artist's Proofs-113
Blue-113
Mirror Blue-113
Mirror Gold-113
Mirror Red-113
Red-113
96Zenith-150
Artist's Proofs-150
96Collector's Edge Future Legends-20
97Pacific Invincible NHL Regime-99
97Hartford Wolf Pack-19
98Be A Player-75
Press Release-75
98BAP Gold-75
98BAP Autographs-75
98BAP Autographs Gold-75
98BAP Tampa Bay All Star Game-75
98Milwaukee Admirals Postcards-2
99Hartford Wolf Pack-18
00Hartford Wolf Pack-24
01Hartford Wolf Pack-21
02BAP Sig Series Auto Buybacks 1998-75
02Senators Team Issue-23
04Manchester Monarchs-2
04Manchester Monarchs Tobacco-3
05Manchester Monarchs-18
06German DEL-77
06Binghamton Senators 5th Anniversary-28

Smyth, Greg
88Nordiques General Foods-32
88Nordiques Team Issue-28
89Halifax Citadels-23
89ProCards AHL-177
90Halifax Citadels-25
90ProCards AHL/IHL-453
91Nordiques Petro-Canada-27
91Pro Set-465
French-465
92Flames IGA-7
93OPC Premier-306
Gold-306
93Topps/OPC Premier-306
Gold-306
94Blackhawks Coke-18
96St. John's Maple Leafs-22
97St. John's Maple Leafs-23

Smyth, Jared
93Quebec Pee-Wee Tournament-154
96Spokane Chiefs-10
97Spokane Chiefs-12
98Spokane Chiefs-24
01Columbus Cottonmouths-18
02Lexington Men O'War-6

Smyth, Kevin
90 7th Inn. Sketch WHL-155
91 7th Inn. Sketch WHL-279
92Classic-24
Gold-24
92Classic Four-Sport *-173
Gold-173
93Donruss-444
94Donruss-59
94Leaf-320
94OPC Premier-68
Special Effects-68
94Parkhurst-99
Gold-99
94Score-225
Gold-225
Platinum-225
94Topps/OPC Premier-68
Special Effects-68
94Classic-47
Gold-47
Tri-Cards-T28
94Classic Pro Prospects-225
95Panini Stickers-30
95Ultra-71
Gold Medallion-71
95Upper Deck-181
Electric Ice-181
Electric Ice Gold-181
95Whalers Bob's Stores-25
98Tacoma Sabercats-19
01Idaho Steelheads-17

Smyth, Matt
04Owen Sound Attack-10
05Belleville Bulls-5
05Brampton Battalion-11
06Brampton Battalion-12

Smyth, Matthew
85London Knights-17
03Owen Sound Attack-2

Smyth, Ryan
94Finest-165
Super Team Winners-165
Refractors-165
94Leaf Limited World Juniors Canada-9
94Pinnacle-535
Artist's Proofs-535
Rink Collection-535
94SP-142
Die Cuts-142
94Upper Deck-443
Electric Ice-443
SP Inserts-SP118
SP Inserts Die Cuts-SP118
94Classic-6
Gold-6
CHL All-Stars-C8
94Classic Four-Sport *-120
Gold-120
Printers Proofs-120
94Signature Rookies Gold Standard *-92
Signatures-GS18
95Donruss-321
Canadian World Junior Team-22
95Leaf-196
95Pinnacle-204
Artist's Proofs-204
Rink Collection-204
95Score-304
Black Ice Artist's Proofs-304
Black Ice-304
95Select Certified-121
Mirror Gold-121
95SkyBox Impact-198
95Summit-176
Artist's Proofs-176
Ice-176
95Topps Canadian World Juniors-8CJ
95Zenith-137
95Images Four-Sport *-99
95Signature Rookies-31
Auto-Phonex Beyond 2000-B3
Signatures-31
95Signature Rookies Tetrad Autobilia *-99
96Be A Player-198
Autographs-198
Autographs Silver-198
96Donruss-223
Press Proofs-223
96Donruss Canadian Ice-89
Gold Press Proofs-89
Red Press Proofs-89
96Donruss Elite-124
Die Cut Stars-124
96Flair-35
Blue Ice-35
96Leaf-171
Press Proofs-171
96Leaf Preferred-72
Press Proofs-72
96Oilers Postcards-94
96SP-56
96Team Out-10
96Upper Deck-258
96Zenith-104
Artist's Proofs-104
97Collector's Choice-92
97Crown Royale-54
Emerald Green-54
Ice Blue-54
Silver-54
Blades of Steel Die-Cuts-11
Hat Tricks Die-Cuts-9
97Donruss-158
Press Proofs Silver-158
Press Proofs Gold-158
Line 2 Line-22
Line 2 Line Die Cut-22
Red Alert-2
97Donruss Canadian Ice-52
Dominion Series-52
Provincial Series-52
National Pride-10
Stanley Cup Scrapbook-17
97Donruss Elite-70
97Donruss Elite-140
Aspirations-70
Aspirations-140
Status-70
Status-140
Craftsmen-21
Master Craftsmen-21
97Donruss Limited-26
97Donruss Limited-65
97Donruss Limited-99
Exposure-26
Exposure-65
Exposure-99
Fabric of the Game-50
97Donruss Preferred-119
97Donruss Preferred-189
Cut to the Chase-119
Cut to the Chase-189
Line of the Times-1A
97Donruss Preferred Line of Times Promos-1A
97Donruss Priority-24
97Donruss Priority-201
Stamp of Approval-24
Stamp of Approval-201
Direct Deposit-5
Postcards-19
Postcards Opening Day Issues-18
Stamps-19
Stamps Bronze-19
Stamps Gold-19
Stamps Silver-19
97Katch-59
Gold-59
Silver-59
97Leaf-49
97Leaf-184
Fractal Matrix-49
Fractal Matrix-184
Fractal Matrix Die Cuts-49
Fractal Matrix Die Cuts-184
Banner Season-10
Fire On Ice-9
97Leaf International-49
Universal Ice-49
97NHL Aces Playing Cards-16
97Pacific-94
Copper-94
Emerald Green-94
Ice Blue-94
Red-94
Silver-94
Gold Crown Die-Cuts-12
97Pacific Dynagon-51
Copper-51
Dark Grey-51
Emerald Green-51
Ice Blue-51
Red-51
Silver-51
Best Kept Secrets-39
Tandems-47
97Pacific Invincible-58
Copper-58
Emerald Green-58
Ice Blue-58
Red-58
Silver-58
NHL Regime-83
97Pacific Omega-95
Copper-95
Dark Gray-95
Emerald Green-95
Gold-95
Ice Blue-95
Game Face-9
Team Leaders-10
97Panini Stickers-212
97Paramount-77
Copper-77
Dark Grey-77
Emerald Green-77
Ice Blue-77
Red-77
Silver-77
Canadian Greats-8
97Pinnacle Certified-79
Red-79
Mirror Blue-79
Mirror Gold-79
Mirror Red-79
97Pinnacle Tot Cert Platinum Blue-79
97Pinnacle Tot Cert Platinum Gold-79
97Pinnacle Totally Certified Platinum Red-79
97Pinnacle Tot Cert Mirror Platinum Gold-79
97Revolution-56
Copper-56
Emerald-56
Ice Blue-56
Silver-56
Team Checklist Laser Cuts-10
97Score-120
Artist's Proofs-120
Golden Blades-120
Check It-8
97SP Authentic-61
97Studio-16
Press Proofs Silver-16
Press Proofs Gold-16
Hard Hats-8
Portraits-16
Portraits-NNO
Silhouettes-21
Silhouettes 8x10-21
97Upper Deck-274
Game Dated Moments-274
97Upper Deck Ice-6
Parallel-6
Lethal Lines-L5A
Lethal Lines 2-L5A
Power Shift-6
97Zenith-71
Z-Gold-71
Z-Silver-71
97Zenith 5 x 7-16
Gold Impulse-16
Silver Impulse-16
98Aurora-76
98Bowman's Best-69
Refractors-69
Atomic Refractors-69
98Crown Royale-54
Limited Series-54
Pivotal Players-11
98OPC Chrome-40
Refractors-40
98Pacific-94
Ice Blue-94
Red-94
Team Checklists-10
98Pacific Dynagon Ice-76
Blue-76
Red-76
Team Checklists-10
98Pacific Omega-96
Red-96
Opening Day Issue-96
98Panini Photocards-78
98Paramount-92
Copper-92
Emerald Green-92
Holo-Electric-92
Ice Blue-92
Silver-92
Team Checklists Die-Cuts-10
98Revolution-57
Ice Shadow-57
Red-57
98SP Authentic Sign of the Times-RS
98SP Authentic Sign of the Times Gold-RS
98Topps-40
O-Pee-Chee-40
98Topps Gold Label Class 1-32
Black-32
Black One of One-32
One of One-32
Red-32
Red One of One-32
98Topps Gold Label Class 2-32
98Topps Gold Label Class 2 Black-32
98Topps Gold Label Class 2 Black 1 of 1-32
98Topps Gold Label Class 2 One of One-32
98Topps Gold Label Class 2 Red-32
98Topps Gold Label Class 2 Red One of One-32
98Topps Gold Label Class 3-32
98Topps Gold Label Class 3 Black-32
98Topps Gold Label Class 3 Black 1 of 1-32
98Topps Gold Label Class 3 One of One-32
98Topps Gold Label Class 3 Red-32
98Topps Gold Label Class 3 Red One of One-32
98UD Choice-82
Prime Choice Reserve-82
Reserve-82
98Upper Deck-272
Exclusives-272
Exclusives 1 of 1-272
Gold Reserve-272
98Upper Deck MVP-82
Gold Script-82
Silver Script-82
Super Script-82
99Aurora-59
Premiere Date-59
99BAP Memorabilia-219
Gold-219
Silver-219
99Crown Royale-57
Limited Series-57
Premiere Date-57
99O-Pee-Chee-32
99O-Pee-Chee Chrome-32
99O-Pee-Chee Chrome Refractors-32
99Pacific-166
Copper-166
Emerald Green-166
Gold-166
Ice Blue-166
Premiere Date-166
Red-166
99Pacific Dynagon Ice-85
Blue-85
Copper-85
Gold-85
Premiere Date-85
99Pacific Omega-95
Copper-95
Gold-95
Ice Blue-95
Premiere Date-95
99Pacific Prism-58
Holographic Blue-58
Holographic Gold-58
Holographic Mirror-58
Holographic Purple-58
Premiere Date-58
99Panini Stickers-244
99Paramount-96
Copper-96
Emerald-96
Gold-96
Holographic Emerald-96
Holographic Gold-96
Holographic Silver-96
Ice Blue-96
Premiere Date-96
Red-96
Silver-96
99Revolution-60
Premiere Date-60
Red-60
Shadow Series-60
99Topps/OPC-32
99Topps/OPC Chrome-32
Refractors-32
99Upper Deck MVP SC Edition-74
Gold Script-74
Silver Script-74
Super Script-74
99Wayne Gretzky Hockey-69
00Aurora-58
Premiere Date-58
00BAP Memorabilia-113
Emerald-113
Ruby-113
Sapphire-113
Promos-113
00BAP Mem Chicago Sportsfest Copper-113
00BAP Memorabilia Chicago Sportsfest Blue-113
00BAP Memorabilia Chicago Sportsfest Gold-113
00BAP Memorabilia Chicago Sportsfest Ruby-113
00BAP Memorabilia Chicago Sun-Times Ruby-113
00BAP Memorabilia Chicago Sun-Times Gold-113
00BAP Mem Chicago Sun-Times Sapphire-113
00BAP Mem Toronto Fall Expo Copper-113
00BAP Memorabilia Toronto Fall Expo Gold-113
00BAP Memorabilia Toronto Fall Expo Ruby-113
00BAP Parkhurst 2000-P68
00BAP Signature Series-153
Emerald-153
Ruby-153
Sapphire-153
Autographs-27
Autographs Gold-27
00Crown Royale-43
Ice Blue-43
Limited Series-43
Premiere Date-43
Red-43
00O-Pee-Chee-112
00O-Pee-Chee Parallel-112
00Pacific-174
Copper-174
Gold-174
Ice Blue-174
Premiere Date-174
00Panini Stickers-162
00Paramount-100
Copper-100
Gold-100
Holo-Gold-100
Holo-Silver-100
Ice Blue-100
Premiere Date-100
00Private Stock-40
Gold-40
Premiere Date-40
Retail-40
Silver-40
00Revolution-59
Blue-59
Premiere Date-59
Red-59
00SP Authentic-36
00Stadium Club-45
00Titanium-37
Blue-37
Gold-37
Premiere Date-37
Red-37
Retail-37
00Titanium Draft Day Edition-44
Patches-44
00Topps/OPC-112
Parallel-112
00Topps Stars-73
Blue-73
00UD Heroes-49
00UD Pros and Prospects-33
00UD Reserve-33
00Upper Deck-68
Exclusives Tier 1-68
Exclusives Tier 2-68
00Upper Deck MVP-76
First Stars-76
Second Stars-76
Third Stars-76
00Upper Deck Victory-98
00Upper Deck Vintage-143
00Vanguard Dual Game-Worn Jerseys-7
00Vanguard Dual Game-Worn Patches-7
01Atomic-43
Blue-43
Gold-43
Premiere Date-43
Red-43
Team Nucleus-7
01BAP Memorabilia-94
Emerald-94
Ruby-94
Sapphire-94
01BAP Signature Series-115
Autographs-115
Autographs Gold-115
01Bowman YoungStars-64
Gold-64
Ice Cubed-64
01Crown Royale-62
Blue-62
Premiere Date-62
Red-62
Retail-62
Jewels of the Crown-13
01McDonald's Pacific-17
01O-Pee-Chee-235
01O-Pee-Chee Premier Parallel-235
01Pacific-166
01Pacific-411
01Pacific-430
Extreme LTD-166
Gold-411
Gold-430
Hobby LTD-166
Premiere Date-166
Retail LTD-166
01Pacific Adrenaline-78
Blue-78
Premiere Date-78
Red-78
Retail-78
01Pacific Arena Exclusives-166
01Pacific Arena Exclusives-411
01Pacific Arena Exclusives-430
01Pacific Heads-Up-42
Blue-42
Premiere Date-42
Red-42
Silver-42
01Parkhurst-49
Gold-49
Silver-49
01Private Stock-41
Gold-41
Premiere Date-41
Retail-41
Silver-41
Game Gear-48
Game Gear Patches-48
01Private Stock Pacific Nights-41
01Private Stock PS-2002-33
01SP Authentic-33
Limited-33
Limited Gold-33
01Stadium Club-86
Award Winners-86
Master Photos-86
01Titanium-58
Hobby Parallel-58
Premiere Date-58
Retail-58
Retail Parallel-58
01Topps-235
OPC Parallel-235
01Topps Chrome-43
Refractors-43
Black Border Refractors-43
01Topps Heritage-95
Refractors-95
01UD Challenge for the Cup-33
01UD Mask Collection-37
Gold-37
01UD Playmakers-41
01Upper Deck-71
Exclusives-71
01Upper Deck MVP-72
01Upper Deck Victory-137
Gold-137
01Upper Deck Vintage-102
01Upper Deck Vintage-104
01Upper Deck Vintage-105
01Vanguard-41
Blue-41
Red-41
One of Ones-41
Premiere Date-41
Proofs-41
02McFarlane Hockey-170
02McFarlane Hockey-172
02Atomic-44
Blue-44
Gold-44
Red-44
Hobby Parallel-44
Jerseys-10
Jerseys Gold-10
Patches-10
Super Colliders-7
02BAP First Edition-195
02BAP First Edition-412R
02BAP Memorabilia-135
Emerald-135
Ruby-135
Sapphire-135
NHL All-Star Game-135
NHL All-Star Game Blue-135
NHL All-Star Game Green-135
NHL All-Star Game Red-135
02BAP Memorabilia Toronto Fall Expo-135
02BAP Signature Series-46
Autographs-46
Autograph Buybacks 2000-27
Autograph Buybacks 2001-115
Autographs Gold-46
Golf-GS81
02Bowman YoungStars-18
Gold-18
Silver-18
02Crown Royale-41
Blue-41
Red-41
Retail-41
Dual Patches-10
02McDonald's Pacific-16
Salt Lake Gold-4
02NHL Power Play Stickers-31
02Oilers Postcards-22
02O-Pee-Chee-67
02O-Pee-Chee Jumbos-10
02O-Pee-Chee Premier Blue Parallel-67
02O-Pee-Chee Premier Red Parallel-67
02O-Pee-Chee Factory Set-67
02O-Pee-Chee Factory Set Hometown Heroes-HHC3
02Pacific-149
Blue-149
Red-149
02Pacific Complete-32
Red-32
02Pacific Exclusive-73
02Pacific Heads-Up-51
Blue-51
Purple-51
Red-51
Quad Jerseys-5
Quad Jerseys Gold-5
02Pacific Quest for the Cup-40
Gold-40
02Parkhurst-80
Bronze-80
Gold-80
Silver-80
02Parkhurst Retro-39
Minis-39
02Private Stock Reserve-39
Blue-39
Red-39
Retail-39
02Stadium Club-22
Silver Decoy Cards-22
Proofs-22
02Titanium-44
Blue-44
Red-44
Retail-44
Jerseys-30
Jerseys Retail-30
Patches-30
02Topps-67
OPC Blue Parallel-67
OPC Red Parallel-67
Topps/OPC Hometown Heroes-HHC3
Factory Set-67
02Topps Chrome-45
Black Border Refractors-45
Refractors-45
02Topps Heritage-47
Chrome Parallel-47
02Topps Total-268
02UD Piece of History-40
02UD Top Shelf-33
02Upper Deck-72
Exclusives-72
02Upper Deck Classic Portraits-41
02Upper Deck MVP-70
Gold-70
Classics-70
Golden Classics-70
02Upper Deck Victory-83
Bronze-83
Gold-83
Silver-83
02Upper Deck Vintage-100
02Upper Deck Vintage-272
Green Backs-100
02Vanguard Jerseys-20
02Vanguard Jerseys Gold-20
03BAP Memorabilia-79
Emerald-79
Gold-79
Ruby-79
Sapphire-79
Practice Jerseys-PMP14
03BAP Ultimate Memorabilia Autographs-15
Gold-15
03BAP Ultimate Mem Franch Present Future-12
03Beehive-78
Gold-78
Silver-78
Jerseys-JT20
03Black Diamond-25
Black-25
Green-25
Red-25
03Crown Royale-42
Blue-42
Retail-42
03ITG Action-216
Jerseys-M79
03ITG Used Signature Series-39
Gold-39
Autographs-RS
Autographs Gold-RS
Franchise-12
Franchise Autographs-12
Franchise Gold-12
Oh Canada-14
Oh Canada Gold-14
Oh Canada Emblems-14
Oh Canada Emblems Gold-14
03Kraft-8
03McDonald's Pacific-23
Patches Silver-13
Patches Gold-13
Patches and Sticks-13
Saturday Night Rivals-2
03NHL Sticker Collection-225
03Oilers Postcards-18
03O-Pee-Chee-267
03OPC Blue-267
03OPC Gold-267
03OPC Red-267
03Pacific-138
Blue-138
Red-138
Jerseys-17
Jerseys Gold-17
03Pacific Calder-42
Silver-42
03Pacific Complete-102
Red-102
03Pacific Exhibit-170
Blue Backs-170
03Pacific Heads-Up-42
Hobby LTD-42
Retail LTD-42
03Pacific Invincible-40
Blue-40
Red-40
Retail-40
03Pacific Luxury Suite-35A
03Pacific Luxury Suite-35B
03Pacific Luxury Suite-35C
03Pacific Prism-42
Blue-42
Gold-42
Red-42
03Pacific Quest for the Cup-43
Blue-43
Jerseys-10
03Pacific Supreme-40
Blue-40
Red-40
Retail-40
Jerseys-14
03Pacific Toronto Fall Expo-3
03Private Stock Reserve-168
Blue-168
Patches-168
Red-168
Retail-168
03SPx-36
Radiance-36
Spectrum-36
03Titanium-155
Hobby Jersey Number Parallels-155
Patches-155
Retail-155
03Topps-267
Blue-267
Gold-267
Red-267
03Topps C55-117
Minis-117
Minis American Back-117
Minis American Back Red-117
Minis Bazooka Back-117
Minis Brooklyn Back-117
Minis Hat Trick Back-117
Minis O Canada Back-117
Minis O Canada Back Red-117
Minis Stanley Cup Back-117
03Upper Deck-74
Canadian Exclusives-74
Franchise Fabrics-FF-RS
HG-74
03Upper Deck Classic Portraits-35
03Upper Deck MVP-160
Gold Script-160
Silver Script-160
Canadian Exclusives-160
SportsNut-SN36
03Upper Deck Trilogy-35
Limited-35
03Upper Deck Victory-71
Bronze-71
Gold-71
Silver-71
03Russian World Championship Stars-33
03Toronto Star-38
04Pacific-106
Blue-106
Red-106
04SP Authentic-37
Limited-37
Buybacks-174
Rookie Review-RR-RS
Sign of the Times-ST-RS
Sign of the Times-DS-RA
Sign of the Times-SS-CNP
04UD Toronto Fall Expo Pride of Canada-25
04Ultimate Collection-18
Dual Logos-UL2-IS
04Upper Deck-68
Canadian Exclusives-68
Heritage Classic-CC-RS
HG Glossy Gold-68
HG Glossy Silver-68
World Cup Tribute-SGTHRS
05Be A Player-35
First Period-35
Second Period-35
Third Period-35
Overtime-35
Dual Signatures-SS
Outtakes-OT23
Quad Signatures-SDPH
Quad Signatures-SSIR
Signatures-RS
Signatures Gold-RS
05Beehive-37
Matte-37
Signature Scrapbook-SSRS
05Black Diamond-32
Emerald-32
Gold-32
Onyx-32
Ruby-32
05Hot Prospects-40
En Fuego-40
Red Hot-40
White Hot-40
05McDonalds Upper Deck-44
05Panini Stickers-271
05Parkhurst-189
05Parkhurst-579
Facsimile Auto Parallel-189
Facsimile Auto Parallel-579
Signatures-RS
True Colors-TCEDM
True Colors-TCEDM
True Colors-TCEDCA
True Colors-TCEDCA
05SP Authentic-41
Limited-41
Sign of the Times-RS
Sign of the Times Duals-DPS
Sign of the Times Quads-QPSCW
05SP Game Used-39
Autographs-39
Gold-39
Authentic Fabrics-AF-RS
Authentic Fabrics Autographs-AAF-RS
Authentic Fabrics Dual-SC
Authentic Fabrics Gold-AF-RS
Authentic Fabrics Quad-SCPTB
Authentic Patches Quad -SCPTB
Authentic Fabrics Triple-PCS
Authentic Patches-AP-RS
Authentic Patches Autographs-AAP-RS
Authentic Patches Dual-SC
Authentic Patches Triple-PCS
Awesome Authentics-AA-RS
SIGnificance-RS
SIGnificance Gold-S-RS
SIGnificance Extra-SC
SIGnificance Extra Gold-SC
Significant Numbers-SN-RS
Statscriptions-ST-RS
05SPx-34
Spectrum-34
Winning Combos-WC-ED
Winning Combos-WC-SC
Winning Combos Autographs-AWC-SC
Winning Combos Autographs-AWC-SH
Winning Combos Gold-WC-ED
Winning Combos Gold-WC-SC
Winning Combos Spectrum-WC-ED
Winning Combos Spectrum-WC-SC
Winning Materials-WM-RS
Winning Materials Autographs-AWM-RS
Winning Materials Gold-WM-RS
Winning Materials Spectrum-WM-RS
05The Cup Dual NHL Shields-DSRM
05The Cup Dual NHL Shields Autographs-ADSAR
05The Cup Dual NHL Shields Autographs-ADSRM
05The Cup Emblems of Endorsement-EERS
05The Cup Limited Logos-LLRS
05The Cup Masterpiece Pressplate Auto-263
05UD Artifacts-42
Blue-42
Gold-42
Green-42
Pewter-42
Red-42
Auto Facts-AF-RS
Auto Facts Blue-AF-RS
Auto Facts Copper-AF-RS
Auto Facts Pewter-AF-RS
Auto Facts Silver-AF-RS
Gold Autographed-42
Remarkable Artifacts-RA-RS
Remarkable Artifacts Dual-RA-RS
Treasured Patches-TP-RS
Treasured Patches Autographed-TP-RS
Treasured Patches Dual-TPD-RS
Treasured Patches Dual Autographed-TPD-RS
Treasured Patches Pewter-TP-RS
Treasured Patches Silver-TP-RS
Treasured Swatches-TS-RS
Treasured Swatches Autographed-TS-RS
Treasured Swatches Blue-TS-RS
Treasured Swatches Copper-TS-RS
Treasured Swatches Dual-TSD-RS
Treasured Swatches Dual Autographed-TSD-RS
Treasured Swatches Dual Blue-TSD-RS
Treasured Swatches Dual Copper-TSD-RS
Treasured Swatches Dual Maroon-TSD-RS
Treasured Swatches Dual Pewter-TSD-RS
Treasured Swatches Dual Silver-TSD-RS
Treasured Swatches Maroon-TS-RS
Treasured Swatches Pewter-TS-RS
Treasured Swatches Silver-TS-RS
05UD PowerPlay-37
Rainbow-37
05Ultimate Collection-38
Gold-38
Endorsed Emblems-EERS
National Heroes Jerseys-NHJRS
National Heroes Patches-NHPRS
Ultimate Achievements-UARS
Ultimate Signatures-USSM
Ultimate Signatures Pairings-UPPS
05Ultra-82
Gold-82
Fresh Ink-FI-RS
Fresh Ink Blue-FI-RS
Ice-82
05Upper Deck-319
Big Playmakers-B-RS
Jerseys Series II-J2RS
Majestic Materials-MMRS
Notable Numbers-N-RS
Patches-P-RS
Shooting Stars-S-RS
05Upper Deck Ice-38
Rainbow-38
Frozen Fabrics-FFRS
Frozen Fabrics Autographs-AFFRS
Frozen Fabrics Glass-FFRS
Frozen Fabrics Patches-FFPRS
Frozen Fabrics Patch Autographs-FAPRS
05Upper Deck MVP-153
Gold-153
Platinum-153
ProSign-P-RS
05Upper Deck Rookie Update-38
05Upper Deck Rookie Update-263
05Upper Deck Trilogy-38
05Upper Deck Trilogy-139
Crystal-139
Honorary Patches-HP-RS
Honorary Swatches-HS-RS
Ice Scripts-IS-RS
Scripts-SCS-RS
05Upper Deck Victory-80
Black-80
Gold-80
Silver-80
Blow-Ups-BU17
Game Breakers-GB20
06Be A Player-37
Autographs-37
Profiles-PP8
Profiles Autographs-PP8
Signatures-RS
Signatures 10-40
Signatures 25-40
Signatures Duals-DSY
Signatures Trios-TYSS
Up Close and Personal-UC50
Up Close and Personal Autographs-UC50
06Be A Player Portraits-44
06Beehive-62
06Beehive-201
Blue-62
Gold-62
Matte-62
Red Facsimile Signatures-62
Wood-62
Matted Materials-MMRS
Remarkable Matted Materials-MMRS
06Black Diamond-104
Black-104

Gold-104
Ruby-104
06Flair Showcase Inks-IRS
06Fleer-79
Tiffany-79
06Gatorade-20
06Hot Prospects-40
Red Hot-40
White Hot-40
06McDonald's Upper Deck-19
Autographs-ARS
Clear Cut Winners-CC10
Hardware Heroes-HH9
06O-Pee-Chee-206
06O-Pee-Chee-682
Rainbow-206
Rainbow-682
Autographs-A-RS
Swatches-S-RS
06Panini Stickers-269
06SP Authentic-61
Limited-61
Sign of the Times Duals-STAS
Sign of the Times Triples-ST3SSH
06SP Game Used-40
Gold-40
Rainbow-40
Authentic Fabrics-AFRS
Authentic Fabrics Parallel-AFRS
Authentic Fabrics Patches-AFRS
Authentic Fabrics Triple-AF3EDM
Authentic Fabrics Triple Patches-AF3EDM
Autographs-40
By The Letter-BLRS
Inked Sweaters-ISRS
Inked Sweaters Patches-ISRS
Inked Sweaters Dual-IS2SR
Inked Sweaters Dual Patches-IS2SR
Letter Marks-LMSM
SIGnificance-SRS
06SPx-38
Spectrum-38
SPxcitement-X41
SPxcitement Spectrum-X41
SPxcitement Autographs-X41
Winning Materials-WMRS
Winning Materials Spectrum-WMRS
Winning Materials Autographs-WMRS
06Sunkist-5
06The Cup Autographed Foundations-CQRS
06The Cup Autographed Foundations Patches-CQRS
06The Cup Autographed NHL Shields Duals-DASEO
06The Cup Foundations-CQRS
06The Cup Foundations Patches-CQRS
06The Cup Enshrinements-ERS
06The Cup Honorable Numbers-HNRS
06The Cup Limited Logos-LLRS
06The Cup NHL Shields Duals-DSHRP
06The Cup Scripted Swatches-SSRS
06The Cup Scripted Swatches Duals-DSAR
06The Cup Signature Patches-SPRS
06UD Artifacts-62
Blue-62
Gold-62
Platinum-62
Radiance-62
Autographed Radiance Parallel-62
Red-62
Auto-Facts-AFRS
Auto-Facts Gold-AFRS
Frozen Artifacts-FARS
Frozen Artifacts Black-FARS
Frozen Artifacts Blue-FARS
Frozen Artifacts Gold-FARS
Frozen Artifacts Platinum-FARS
Frozen Artifacts Red-FARS
Frozen Artifacts Autographed Black-FARS
Frozen Artifacts Patches Black-FARS
Frozen Artifacts Patches Blue-FARS
Frozen Artifacts Patches Gold-FARS
Frozen Artifacts Patches Platinum-FARS
Frozen Artifacts Patches Red-FARS
Frozen Artifacts Patches Autographed Black Tag Parallel-FARS
Tundra Tandems-TTRS
Tundra Tandems Black-TTRS
Tundra Tandems Blue-TTRS
Tundra Tandems Gold-TTRS
Tundra Tandems Platinum-TTRS
Tundra Tandems Red-TTRS
Tundra Tandems Dual Patches Red-TTRS
06UD Mini Jersey Collection-44
06UD Powerplay-42
Impact Rainbow-42
Power Marks-PMRS
06Ultimate Collection Jerseys Dual-UJ2-HS
06Ultimate Collection Patches Dual-UJ2-HS
06Ultimate Collection Premium Patches-PS-RS
06Ultimate Collection Premium Swatches-PS-RS
06Ultimate Collection Signatures-US-RS
06Ultimate Collection Ultimate Signatures Logos-SL-RS
06Ultra-80
Gold Medallion-80
Ice Medallion-80
Fresh Ink-IRS
Scoring Kings-SK16
06Upper Deck Arena Giveaways-EDM4
06Upper Deck-325
Exclusives Parallel-325
High Gloss Parallel-325
Game Dated Moments-GD25
Game Jerseys-J2RS
Game Patches-P2RS
Masterpieces-325
Oversized Wal-Mart Exclusives-325
Signature Sensations-SSRS
06Upper Deck MVP-118
Gold Script-118
Super Script-118
Clutch Performers-CP14
Jerseys-OJER
Jerseys-OJIS
06Upper Deck Ovation-120
06Upper Deck Sweet Shot Signature Shots/Saves-SSRS
06Upper Deck Sweet Shot Signature Shots/Saves Sticks-SSSRS
06Upper Deck Sweet Shot Sweet Stitches-SSRS
06Upper Deck Sweet Shot Sweet Stitches Duals-SSRS
06Upper Deck Sweet Shot Sweet Stitches Triples-SSRS
06Upper Deck Trilogy-39
Combo Clearcut Autographs-C2AR
Honorary Scripted Patches-HSPRS
Honorary Scripted Swatches-HSSRS
Honorary Swatches-HSRS
06Upper Deck Victory-76
06Upper Deck Victory Black-76
06Upper Deck Victory Gold-76
07Upper Deck Victory-18
Black-18
Gold-18
Stars on Ice-SI29

Smyth, Sean
05Kitchener Rangers-8
05Shawinigan Cataractes-23

Smythe, Conn
320'Keefe Maple Leafs-19
37V356 Worldwide Gum-95
69O-Pee-Chee-229
70O-Pee-Chee-256
83Hall of Fame-27
83Hall of Fame Postcards-B13
85Hall of Fame-27
90Upper Deck French-201
92Hall of Fame Legends-2
01Upper Deck Legends-63
03BAP Ultimate Memorabilia Memorialized-4
04ITG Ultimate Mem Maple Leafs Forever-6
05ITG Ultimate Memorabilia Builders Autos-5
06Beehive 5 X 7 Cherry Wood-CST
06ITG Ultimate Memorabilia-32
Artist Proof-32
Builders Autos-2
Lumbergraphs-11

Smythe, Stafford
59Parkhurst-36

Snecinski, Joe
93Quebec Pee-Wee Tournament-1296

Snedden, Dennis
91ProCards-615
93Toledo Storm-13

Sneddon, Bob
70Esso Power Players-108

Snee, Brandon
02Muskegon Fury-24

Snell, Chris
897th Inn. Sketch OHL-51
90Upper Deck-468
French-468
907th Inn. Sketch OHL-95
91ProCards-7
91Rochester Americans Dunkin' Donuts-16
91Rochester Americans Kodak-25
91Rochester Americans Postcards-20
917th Inn. Sketch CHL Award Winners-4
917th Inn. Sketch Memorial Cup-21
92Rochester Americans Dunkin' Donuts-18
92Rochester Americans Kodak-23
93Minnesota-Duluth Bulldogs-20
93St. John's Maple Leafs-21
94Classic Pro Prospects-93
95Phoenix Roadrunners-16
96Collector's Edge Ice-185
Prism-185
98German DEL-133
99German DEL-97
00German DEL-100
00St. John's Maple Leafs-25
01German Upper Deck-88
02German DEL City Press-84
All-Stars-AS8

Snell, Ted
74NHL Action Stamps-294
74NHL Action Stamps Update-13
95Swiss HNL-31

Snell, Wes
98Swiss Power Play Stickers-134
99Swiss Panini Stickers-357
01Swiss HNL-407
02Swiss HNL-116

Snellman, Niko
06Regina Pats-21

Snellman, Ville
03Finnish Cardset-50
04Finnish Cardset-117
Parallel-87
05Finnish Cardset -106
06Finnish Cardset-316

Snepsts, Harold
75Canucks Royal Bank-21
75O-Pee-Chee NHL-396
76Canucks Royal Bank-18
76O-Pee-Chee NHL-366
76O-Pee-Chee NHL-395
77Canucks Canada Dry Cans-14
77Canucks Royal Bank-19
77O-Pee-Chee NHL-295
78Canucks Royal Bank-21
78O-Pee-Chee-380
79Canucks Royal Bank-21
79O-Pee-Chee-186
79Topps-186
80Canucks Silverwood Dairies-22
80Canucks Team Issue-21
80O-Pee-Chee-312
80Pepsi-Cola Caps-119
81O-Pee-Chee-344
81O-Pee-Chee Stickers-250
82Canucks Team Issue-20
82O-Pee-Chee-357
82O-Pee-Chee Stickers-243
82Post Cereal-19
82Topps Stickers-243
83Canucks Team Issue-19
83Esso-18
83NHL Key Tags-125
83O-Pee-Chee-360
83Vachon-117
84North Stars Postcards-27
84O-Pee-Chee-108
847-Eleven Discs-28
84Kelowna Wings-47
85O-Pee-Chee-232
85O-Pee-Chee Stickers-44
87O-Pee-Chee Stickers-110
87Panini Stickers-241
88Canucks Mohawk-20
89Canucks Mohawk-20
89O-Pee-Chee-286
90Blues Kodak-20
90Pro Set-527
90Score Rookie/Traded-61T
91ProCards-35
93San Diego Gulls-20
02Fleer Throwbacks-15
Gold-15
Platinum-15
02UD Foundations-94
Canadian Heroes-CHS
Canadian Heroes Gold-CHS
Canadian Heroes Silver-C-HS
Defense First-DHS
Defense First Gold-DHS
Defense First Silver-D-HS
Power Stations-SHS
Power Stations Gold-SHS
Power Stations Silver-S-HS
04ITG Franchises Canadian-118
Autographs-HS
04UD Legendary Signatures-99
Autographs-SN

Snesar, Shawn
88Saskatoon Blades-8
89Saskatoon Blades-7
91Hampton Roads Admirals-17
92Hampton Roads Admirals-1
93Hampton Roads Admirals-16
94Richmond Renegades-3
98Hampton Roads Admirals 10th Anniversary-28

Snesrud, Mat
95North Iowa Huskies-31
02Manchester Monarchs-29
02Reading Royals-4
02Reading Royals RBI Sports-185
03Reading Royals-4
03Reading Royals RBI Sports-303
04Missouri River Otters-10

Snetsinger, Bradley
04Mississauga Ice Dogs-2

Snider, Ed
92Flyers Upper Deck Sheets-44

Snider, Shawn
99Owen Sound Platers-22
00Owen Sound Attack-20
01Sudbury Wolves-18
01Sudbury Wolves Police-11
03St. Francis Xavier X-Men-23
04St. Francis Xavier X-Men-20

Sniderman, Jhase
03Erie Otters-23
04Erie Otters-5
05Moncton Wildcats-27
06Moncton Wildcats-13

Snis, Ingemar
70Swedish Hockey-80
71Swedish Hockey-171
72Swedish Stickers-270

Snita, Marcin
95Slapshot-353
95Sarnia Sting-23
96Sarnia Sting-26

Snitowsky, Greg
03Huntsville Channel Cats-15
05Port Huron Flags-26

Snopek, Jan
93Oshawa Generals-4
95Slapshot-248
98Czech OFS-86
99Czech DS-20
99Czech OFS-144
00Czech DS Extraliga-114
00Czech OFS-88
01Czech OFS-278
02Czech OFS Plus-119
Trios-T24
03Czech OFS Plus-247
03Czech OFS Plus Insert H-H8
03Czech OFS Plus MS Praha-SE17
04Czech OFS-131
05Czech HC Pardubice-15
06Czech HC Pardubice Postcards-19
06Czech OFS-125

Snow, Aaron
04Brampton Battalion-11
05Brampton Battalion-10
06Belleville Bulls-11

Snow, Garth
92Maine Black Bears-15
92Maine Black Bears-33
93Donruss-481
93PowerPlay-425
93Score-628
Gold-628
Canadian-628
Canadian Gold-628
93Classic-58
94Leaf-180
94Classic-84
Gold-84
ROY Sweepstakes-R17
Tri-Cards-T55
94Classic Pro Prospects-35
94Classic Four-Sport *-143
Gold-143
Autographs-143A
Printers Proofs-143
94Images *-21
95Be A Player-57
Signatures-S57
Signatures Die Cuts-S57
95Parkhurst International-425
Emerald Ice-425
95SkyBox Impact-215
95Ultra-287
95Upper Deck-289
Electric Ice-289
Electric Ice Gold-289
96Donruss-207
Press Proofs-207
96Flyers Postcards-21
96Leaf-97
Press Proofs-97
96Score-204
Artist's Proofs-204
Dealer's Choice Artist's Proofs-204
Special Artist's Proofs-204
Golden Blades-204
97Be A Player-77
Autographs-77
Autographs Die-Cuts-77
Autographs Prismatic Die-Cuts-77
Stacking the Pads-12
97Crown Royale Freeze Out Die-Cuts-14
97Donruss-11
Press Proofs Silver-11
Press Proofs Gold-11
Between The Pipes-7
97Donruss Canadian Ice-38
Dominion Series-38
Provincial Series-38
Stanley Cup Scrapbook-10
97Donruss Limited-170
Exposure-170
97Donruss Preferred-111
Cut to the Chase-111
97Donruss Priority-138
Stamp of Approval-138
Postmaster General-16
Postmaster General-P16
Postmaster Generals Promos-16
97Pacific-147
Copper-147
Emerald Green-147
Ice Blue-147
Red-147
Silver-147
In The Cage Laser Cuts-15
97Pacific Dynagon-93
Copper-93
Dark Grey-93
Emerald Green-93
Ice Blue-93
Red-93
Silver-93
Stonewallers-16
Tandems-54
97Pacific Omega-170
Copper-170
Dark Gray-170
Emerald Green-170
Gold-170
Ice Blue-170
97Paramount-137
Copper-137
Dark Grey-137
Emerald Green-137
Ice Blue-137
Red-137
Silver-137
Glove Side Laser Cuts-15
97Pinnacle-63
Artist's Proofs-63
Rink Collection-63
Press Plates Back Black-63
Press Plates Back Cyan-63
Press Plates Back Magenta-63
Press Plates Back Yellow-63
Press Plates Front Black-63
Press Plates Front Cyan-63
Press Plates Front Magenta-63
Press Plates Front Yellow-63
Masks-8
Masks Die Cuts-8
Masks Jumbos-8
97Pinnacle Masks Promos-8
97Pinnacle Tins-9
97Pinnacle Certified-28
Red-28
Mirror Blue-28
Mirror Gold-28
Mirror Red-28
97Pinnacle Inside-68
Coach's Collection-68
Executive Collection-68
Stand Up Guys-4A/B
Stand Up Guys-4C/D
Stand Up Guys Promos-4A/B
Stand Up Guys Promos-4C/D
Stoppers-17
97Pinnacle Tot Cert Platinum Blue-28
97Pinnacle Tot Certi Platinum Gold-28
97Pinnacle Totally Certified Platinum Red-28
97Pinnacle Tot Cert Mirror Platinum Gold-28
97Score-3
Artist's Proofs-3
Golden Blades-3
Net Worth-8
97Score Flyers-2
Platinum-2
Premier-2
98Aurora-192
98Be A Player-144
Press Release-144
98BAP Gold-144
98BAP Autographs-144
98BAP Autographs Gold-144
98BAP Tampa Bay All Star Game-144
98Crown Royale-139
Limited Series-139
98NHL Aces Playing Cards-45
98OPC Chrome-122
Refractors-122
98Pacific-434
Ice Blue-434
Red-434
98Pacific Dynagon Ice-192
Blue-192
Red-192
98Pacific Omega-241
Red-241
Opening Day Issue-241
98Panini Photocards-79
98Paramount-240
Copper-240
Emerald Green-240
Holo-Electric-240
Ice Blue-240
Silver-240
98Revolution-145
Ice Shadow-145
Red-145
98SPx Finite-86
Radiance-86
Spectrum-86
98Topps-122
O-Pee-Chee-122
98UD Choice-207
98UD Choice Preview-207
98UD Choice Prime Choice Reserve-207
98UD Choice Reserve-207
98Upper Deck-198
Exclusives-198
Exclusives 1 of 1-198
Gold Reserve-198
99Aurora-145
Premiere Date-145
99BAP Millennium Goalie Memorabilia-G4
99Crown Royale-140
Limited Series-140
Premiere Date-140
99O-Pee-Chee-116
99O-Pee-Chee Chrome-116
99O-Pee-Chee Chrome Refractors-116
99Pacific-433
Copper-433
Emerald Green-433
Gold-433
Ice Blue-433
Premiere Date-433
Red-433
99Panini Stickers-316
99Paramount-240
Copper-240
Emerald-240
Gold-240
Holographic Emerald-240
Holographic Gold-240
Holographic Silver-240
Ice Blue-240
Premiere Date-240
Red-240
Silver-240
99Revolution-146
Premiere Date-146
Red-146
Shadow Series-146
99Topps/OPC-116
99Topps/OPC Chrome-116
Refractors-116
99Upper Deck-295
Exclusives-295
Exclusives 1 of 1-295
99Upper Deck Gold Reserve-295
99Wayne Gretzky Hockey-169
00Pacific-416
Copper-416
Gold-416
Ice Blue-416
Premiere Date-416
00Titanium-78
Blue-78
Gold-78
Premiere Date-78
Red-78
Retail-78
01Between the Pipes-68
01O-Pee-Chee-179
01O-Pee-Chee Premier Parallel-179
01Pacific-317
Extreme LTD-317
Hobby LTD-317
Premiere Date-317
Retail LTD-317
01Pacific Arena Exclusives-317
01Topps-179
OPC Parallel-179
02BAP Sig Series Auto Buybacks 1998-144
02Between the Pipes-57
Gold-57
Silver-57
02Pacific-243
Blue-243
Red-243
02Pacific Complete-477
Red-477
02UD Mask Collection-52
02UD Mask Collection-53
02UD Mask Collection Beckett Promos-52
02UD Mask Collection Beckett Promos-53
03BAP Memorabilia-121
Emerald-121
Gold-121
Ruby-121
Sapphire-121
03ITG Action-338
Jerseys-M80
03O-Pee-Chee-245
03OPC Blue-245
03OPC Gold-245
03OPC Red-245
03Pacific-216
Blue-216
Red-216
03Pacific Complete-415
Red-415
03Pacific Invincible Freeze Frame-14
03Private Stock Reserve-66
Blue-66
Red-66
Retail-66
03Titanium-66
Hobby Jersey Number Parallels-66
Retail-66
Retail Jersey Number Parallels-66
03Topps-245
Blue-245
Gold-245
Red-245
03Upper Deck-370
Canadian Exclusives-370
HG-370
UD Exclusives-370
03Upper Deck MVP-274
Gold Script-274
Silver Script-274
Canadian Exclusives-274
SportsNut-SN53
03Upper Deck Victory-120
Bronze-120
Gold-120
Silver-120
05Be A Player Signatures-GS
05Be A Player Signatures Gold-GS
05Panini Stickers-102
05Parkhurst-314
Facsimile Auto Parallel-314
05Upper Deck-121
HG Glossy-121
05Upper Deck MVP-251
Gold-251
Platinum-251
05Upper Deck Toronto Fall Expo-121

Snow, Jason
89Windsor Spitfires-15
907th Inn. Sketch OHL-96

Snowball, Robert
03Roanoke Express-318
06Port Huron Flags-7

Snowden, John
00Lincoln Stars-8
01Lincoln Stars-20
02Lincoln Stars-10
02Lincoln Stars-38
02Lincoln Stars-46
03ECHL All-Stars-278
06Reading Royals-9

Snowie, Nathan
05PEI Rocket-5

Snuggerud, Dave
89Sabres Blue Shield-21
89Sabres Campbell's-24
90Bowman-249
Tiffany-249
90O-Pee-Chee-340
90Panini Stickers-19
90Pro Set-30
90Sabres Blue Shield-22
90Sabres Campbell's-25
90Score Rookie/Traded-48T
90Topps-340
Tiffany-340
90Upper Deck-189
French-189
91Bowman-29
91O-Pee-Chee-441
91Panini Stickers-308
91Pinnacle-223
French-223
91Pro Set-18
French-18
91Sabres Blue Shield-20
91Sabres Pepsi/Campbell's-20
91Score American-206
91Score Canadian Bilingual-206
91Score Canadian English-206
91Stadium Club-320
91Topps-441
91Upper Deck-194
French-194
92Bowman-309
92Pinnacle-183
French-183
92Score-182
Canadian-182
94Minnesota Moose-9

Snusz, Jason
93Quebec Pee-Wee Tournament-807

Snyder, Dan
95Slapshot-294
95Owen Sound Platers-16
96Owen Sound Platers-16
97Owen Sound Platers-13
98Owen Sound Platers-13
99Bowman CHL-152
Gold-152
OPC International-152
01BAP Memorabilia-413
Emerald-413
Ruby-413
Sapphire-413
01SPx-134
01SPx-134
Rookie Treasures-RTDS
01UD Top Shelf-47
01UD Top Shelf-47B
01Upper Deck-181
Exclusives-181
01Upper Deck MVP-190
01Upper Deck Victory-362
Gold-362
01Chicago Wolves-21
02Pacific Calder-53
Silver-53
02Pacific Complete-519
Red-519
02Thrashers Postcards-14
03ITG Action-21

Snyder, Gerry
93Quebec Pee-Wee Tournament-869

Snyder, Jeff
99Kitchener Rangers-12
00Kitchener Rangers-26

Snyder, Matt
93Quebec Pee-Wee Tournament-715

Soares, Josh
04Maine Black Bears-15
05Maine Black Bears-25

Sobchuk, Dennis
74O-Pee-Chee WHA-56
74Phoenix Roadrunners WHA Pins-8
75O-Pee-Chee WHA-115
75Stingers Kahn's-12
76O-Pee-Chee WHA-29
76Stingers Kahn's-7
77O-Pee-Chee WHA-53
86Regina Pats-26
87Regina Pats-25

Sobchuk, Gene
71Rochester Americans-17
75Stingers Kahn's-13

Sobek, Jeanine
94Classic Women of Hockey-W35

Soberlak, Peter
85Kamloops Blazers-23
89ProCards AHL-134
90ProCards AHL/IHL-226
91ProCards-229

Soboczynski, Anthony
05Saginaw Spirit-21

Sobotka, Vladimir
04Czech OFS-182
06Czech HC Slavia Praha Postcards-12
06Czech OFS-303

Sobottka, Dirk
94German First League-403

Sobush, Shawn
94Thunder Bay Flyers-19
95Sudbury Wolves Police-22

Soccio, Len
94German First League-613
95Buffalo Stampedes RHI-20
96German DEL-218
98German DEL-181
99German DEL-227
00German DEL-229
Game Jersey-LE
01German Upper Deck-102
Gate Attractions-GA6
02German DEL City Press-123
02German DEL City Press-124
Top Scorers-TS5
03German DEL-133
04German DEL-157
04German Hannover Scorpions Postcards-26

Sochor, Jan
97Czech APS Extraliga-169
98Czech OFS-256
99Czech OFS-54
00Czech DS Extraliga-21
00Czech OFS-337
01Czech OFS Update-321
02Czech OFS Plus-76
03Czech OFS Plus-35

Sochorec, Ales
97Czech APS Extraliga-310
99Czech Score Blue 2000-20
99Czech Score Red Ice 2000-20

Sochorek, Dalibor
03Czech OFS Plus-358

Soderberg, Ake
69Swedish Hockey-272
70Swedish Hockey-164
71Swedish Hockey-259
72Finnish Semic World Championship-70
72Swedish Stickers-239
72Swedish Semic World Championship-70
73Swedish Stickers-239
74Swedish Stickers-265

Soderberg, Anders
91Swedish Semic Elitserien Stickers-333
93Swedish Semic Elitserien-205
94Parkhurst SE-SE234
Gold-SE234
94SP-169
Die Cuts-169
94Upper Deck-521
Electric Ice-521
94Swedish Leaf-220
95Swedish Leaf-103
Goldies-10
95Swedish Upper Deck-161
95Swedish Upper Deck-221
97Swedish Collector's Choice-158
98Swedish UD Choice-181
99Swedish Upper Deck-183
00Swedish Upper Deck-158
02Swedish SHL-243
Parallel-243
03Swedish Elite-105
Silver-105
04Swedish Elitset-96
Gold-96
06Swedish SHL Elitset-272
Performers-16

Soderberg, Carl
04Swedish Elitset-231
Future Stars-1
Gold-231
04Swedish Malmo Red Hawks-12
04Swedish Pure Skills-60
Parallel-60
Signatures-7

Soderberg, Lars-Erik
55Swedish Alfabilder-25

Soderberg, Lennart
64Swedish Coralli ISHockey-39
65Swedish Coralli ISHockey-39

Soderblom, Lars
57Swedish Alfabilder-81

Sodergren, Hakan
83Swedish Semic Elitserien-95
83Swedish Semic VM Stickers-21
84Swedish Semic Elitserien-88
85Swedish Panini Stickers-84
86Swedish Panini Stickers-69
87Swedish Panini Stickers-80
89Swedish Semic Elitserien Stickers-60
89Swedish Semic World Champ Stickers-23
90Swedish Semic Elitserien Stickers-290

Soderholm, Patrik
89Swedish Semic Elitserien Stickers-190

Soderholm, Toni
03Finnish Cardset-19
04Finnish Cardset-18
Parallel-11

Soderling, Benny
64Swedish Coralli ISHockey-40
65Swedish Coralli ISHockey-40

Soderlund, Cenneth
86Swedish Panini Stickers-159
89Swedish Semic Elitserien Stickers-140
90Swedish Semic Elitserien Stickers-215
91Swedish Semic Elitserien Stickers-143
92Swedish Semic Elitserien Stickers-172

Soderlund, Kent
71Swedish Hockey-123

Soderstrom, Christian
02Swedish SHL-267
Parallel-267
03Swedish Elite-127
Silver-127
04Swedish Elitset-127
Gold-127
05Swedish SHL Elitset-137
Series Two Signatures-27
06Swedish SHL Elitset-189

Soderstrom, Dan
67Swedish Hockey-112
69Swedish Hockey-126
70Swedish Hockey-81
71Swedish Hockey-172
72Finnish Semic World Championship-68
72Swedish Stickers-164
72Swedish Semic World Championship-68
73Finnish Jaakiekko-38
73Swedish Stickers-15
73Swedish Stickers-51
74Finnish Typotor-101
74Swedish Stickers-25
74Swedish Stickers-266
74Swedish Semic World Champ Stickers-10
81Swedish Semic Hockey VM Stickers-16
84Swedish Semic Elitserien-169
85Swedish Panini Stickers-132

Soderstrom, Hans
64Swedish Coralli ISHockey-69

Soderstrom, Mathias
02UK Coventry Blaze-7
03UK Coventry Blaze-2
03UK Coventry Blaze Calendars-1
03UK Coventry Blaze History-3

Soderstrom, Runar
56Swedish Alfabilder-39

Soderstrom, Tommy
89Swedish Semic Elitserien Stickers-51
90Swedish Semic Elitserien Stickers-273
91Finnish Semic World Champ Stickers-29
91Swedish Semic Elitserien Stickers-54
91Swedish Semic Elitserien Stickers-316
91Swedish Semic Elitserien Stickers-338
91Swedish Semic World Champ Stickers-29
92Flyers Upper Deck Sheets-28
92Flyers Upper Deck Sheets-31
92Parkhurst-367
92Parkhurst-448
Emerald Ice-367
Emerald Ice-448
92Ultra-160
Imports-23
92Upper Deck-377
92Upper Deck-475
92Finnish Semic-51
92Swedish Semic Elitserien Stickers-343
93Donruss-253
93Flyers J.C. Penney-21
93Leaf-37
Gold Rookies-12
93OPC Premier-55
93OPC Premier-122
Gold-55
Gold-122
93Panini Stickers-55
93Parkhurst-150
Emerald Ice-150
93Pinnacle-19
Canadian-19
93PowerPlay-185
Netminders-8
Second Year Stars-11
93Score-336
Canadian-336
International Stars-5
International Stars Canadian-5
93Stadium Club-340
93Stadium Club-430
Members Only Master Set-340
Members Only Master Set-430
First Day Issue-340
First Day Issue-430
93Topps/OPC Premier-55
93Topps/OPC Premier-122
Gold-55
Gold-122
93Ultra-217
93Upper Deck-182
93Swedish Semic World Champ Stickers-19
93Classic-125
McDonalds-20
93Classic Pro Prospects-91
BCs-BC8
94EA Sports-102
94Leaf-184
94Pinnacle-309
Artist's Proofs-309
Rink Collection-309
94Stadium Club-24
Members Only Master Set-24
First Day Issue-24
Super Team Winner Cards-24
94Ultra-160
94Upper Deck-474
Electric Ice-474
94Finnish Jaa Kiekko-52
94Finnish Jaa Kiekko-334
94Swedish Olympics Lillehammer*-294
95Collector's Choice-28
Player's Club-28
Player's Club Platinum-28
95Kraft-34
95Parkhurst International-127
95Parkhurst International-240
Emerald Ice-127
Emerald Ice-240
95Pinnacle-90
Artist's Proofs-90
Rink Collection-90
Global Gold-15
95Score-215
Black Ice Artist's Proofs-215
Black Ice-215
95Summit-46
Artist's Proofs-46
Ice-46
95Topps-334
OPC Inserts-334
95Ultra-100
Gold Medallion-100
95Upper Deck-313
Electric Ice-313
Electric Ice Gold-313
Special Edition-SE140
Special Edition Gold-SE140
95Finnish Semic World Championships-54
95Finnish Semic World Championships-212
95Swedish Upper Deck-238
95Swedish Globe World Championships-1
96Donruss-72
Press Proofs-72
96Leaf-51
Press Proofs-51
96Score-82
Artist's Proofs-82
Dealer's Choice Artist's Proofs-82
Special Artist's Proofs-82
Golden Blades-82
96Swedish Semic Wien-38
96Swedish Semic Wien Coca-Cola Dream Team-1
96Swedish Semic Wien Super Goalies-SG4
97Swedish Collector's Choice-33
97Swedish Collector's Choice-199
98Swedish UD Choice-49
Day in the Life-3
99Swedish Upper Deck-35
99Swedish Upper Deck-219
SHL Signatures-19
Snapshots-4

Soderstrom, Ulf
99Swedish Upper Deck-127
Hands of Gold-11
SHL Signatures-12
00Swedish Upper Deck-84
02Swedish SHL-171
Parallel-171
Signatures Series II-5
03Swedish Elite-184
Silver-184
04Swedish Elitset-208
Gold-208
05Swedish SHL Elitset-75
Series One Signatures-1
06Swedish SHL Elitset-75

Sodervik, Juhani
66Finnish Jaakiekkosarja-144
70Finnish Jaakiekko-267

Sodke, Sonny
82Brandon Wheat Kings-4

Soetaert, Doug
80O-Pee-Chee-324
81Jets Postcards-17
82Jets Postcards-21
82O-Pee-Chee-389
82O-Pee-Chee Stickers-211
82Topps Stickers-211
83Jets Postcards-21
83O-Pee-Chee-391
83O-Pee-Chee Stickers-288
83Topps Stickers-288
83Vachon-137
84Canadiens Postcards-26
84O-Pee-Chee-347
85Canadiens Postcards-35
85Canadiens Postcards-36
85Canadiens Provigo-22
85O-Pee-Chee Stickers-136
86O-Pee-Chee Stickers-16
89New Haven Nighthawks-12
03Everett Silvertips-25
04Everett Silvertips-5

Sofan, Udo
94German First League-436

Sogaard, Kim
92Finnish Semic-31
92Norwegian Elite Series-74
93Swedish Semic World Champ Stickers-236

Soghomonian, J. Marc
94French National Team-30

Soguel, Sergio
93Swiss HNL-232
95Swiss HNL-231
96Swiss HNL-144

Sohlin, Stefan
87Swedish Panini Stickers-255

Sohlman, Rauli
78Finnish SM-Liiga-88
80Finnish Mallasjuoma-45
83Swedish Semic VM Stickers-27

Sohrman, Richard
93Swedish Semic Elitserien-272

Soin, Sergei
00Russian Hockey League-54
02Russian Future Stars-18
02Russian Hockey League-209
02Russian SL-26
02Russian Young Lions-6
03Russian World Championship Team 2003-11

Soini, Voitto
66Finnish Jaakiekkosarja-70
70Finnish Jaakiekko-150
71Finnish Suomi Stickers-201

Soke, Carlos
99Rockford IceHogs-18

Soke, Craig
03Bossier-Shreveport Mudbugs-15

Sokka, Mikko
96Finnish SISU Redline-139
98Finnish Kerailysarja-254

Sokkanen, Juha
80Finnish Mallasjuoma-144

Sokol, Matt
05Medicine Hat Tigers-21

Sokolov, Andrei
98Russian Hockey League-9
99Russian Hockey League-8
99Russian Metallurg Magnetogorsk-47

Sokolov, Denis
00Russian Hockey League-216

Sokolov, Maxim
99Russian Hockey League-247
99Russian Stars of Hockey-31
99Russian Fetisov Tribute-9
00Russian Goalkeepers-1

00Russian Hockey League-376
01Russian Hockey League-59
01Russian Hockey League-122
02Russian Hockey League-119
02Russian Hockey League-129
02Russian SL-19
02Russian Transfert-20
02Russian Transfert Promos-6
02Russian World Championships-4
03Russian Avangard Omsk-1
03Russian Hockey League-226
03Russian Postcards-7
03Russian World Championship Stars-31
03Russian World Championship Team 2003-1
04Russian World Championship Team-18
06Russian Sport Collection Olympic Stars-13
06Russian Torino Olympic Team-3

Sokolovski, Alexander
74Swedish Stickers-73

Sokolsky, Jamie
95Slapshot-37
96Owen Sound Platers-10
97Owen Sound Platers-7
97Bowman CHL-38
OPC-38
98Huntington Blizzard-4
99Huntington Blizzard-4

Solari, Kelvin
93Peterborough Petes-23
01Missouri River Otters-12

Solbach, Carsten
94German DEL-429
95German DEL-385
96German DEL-292
99German Bundesliga 2-158

Solberg, Chad
02Chicago Steel-19

Solberg, J-E
74Finnish Typotor-82

Solberg, Lars Erik
92Norwegian Elite Series-156

Solderer, Erich
93Swedish Semic World Champ Stickers-275
94Finnish Jaa Kiekko-238

Soldt, Van
79Panini Stickers-277

Solei, Brent
04Minnesota Golden Gophers-24
05Minnesota Golden Gophers-22
06Minnesota Golden Gophers-20

Soler, Jeremy
93Quebec Pee-Wee Tournament-58

Solesky, Aaron
93Quebec Pee-Wee Tournament-811

Soleway, Jay
80Flames Postcards-21

Solf, Patrick
94German DEL-50
95German DEL-33

Solheim, Ken
82North Stars Postcards-23
83O-Pee-Chee-131
84North Stars Postcards-28
85Nova Scotia Oilers-6
88Oilers Tenth Anniversary-8

Solimine, E.J.
03Boston University Terriers-9

Soling, Jonas
96Sudbury Wolves-22
96Sudbury Wolves Police-23
97Sudbury Wolves Police-9
98ECHL All-Star Southern Conference-5
01Swedish Brynas Tigers-25
02Swedish SHL-11
Parallel-11
Signatures-1
03Swedish Elite-6
Silver-6
04Swedish Elitset-150
Gold-150
High Expectations-1
05Swedish SHL Elitset-224
Gold-224
06Swedish SHL Elitset-74

Solinger, Bob
44Beehive Group II Photos-452
45Quaker Oats Photos-49
51Parkhurst-88
52Parkhurst-50
53Parkhurst-16
61Union Oil WHL-8

Solinski, Jacek
89Swedish Semic World Champ Stickers-144

Solly, Jim
92Oklahoma City Blazers-16
93Oklahoma City Blazers-16
94Huntington Blizzard-19

Solnik, Adam
00Mississauga Ice Dogs-22
03Rockford Ice Hogs-16

Solodukhin, Vyacheslav
72Finnish Jaakiekko-36
91Future Trends Canada '72-28
91Future Trends Canada '72 French-28

Solomatov, Sergei
98Danish Hockey League-225

Solomon, Trevor
03Sarnia Sting-19

Soloviev, Maxim
00Russian Hockey League-134
01Russian Hockey League-138

Soloviev, Nikolai
03Russian Hockey League-196

Soltys, Erik
04Maine Black Bears-30

Soltys, Roman
04Slovakian Poprad Team Set-30

Solvennoinen, Juha
78Finnish SM-Liiga-189

Solway, David
06Sioux Falls Stampede -8

Somers, Art
24Holland Creameries-3
28V128-2 Paulin's Candy-49
33O-Pee-Chee V304A-17
34Diamond Matchbooks Silver-55
35Diamond Matchbooks Tan 2-58

Somers, Chris
86London Knights-29

Somerville, Brant
93Quebec Pee-Wee Tournament-572

Somerville, Cory
93Quebec Pee-Wee Tournament-1475

Somerville, Darryl
93Quebec Pee-Wee Tournament-571

Somerville, Ross
25Dominion Chocolates-113

Somervuori, Eero
95Finnish SISU-256
97Black Diamond-139
Double Diamond-139
Triple Diamond-139
Quadruple Diamond-139
98UD Choice-281
Prime Choice Reserve-281
Reserve-281
98Finnish Kerailysarja-113
99Finnish Cardset-64
00Finnish Cardset-149
01Finnish Cardset-29
02Finnish Cardset-271
03Finnish Cardset D-Day-DD14
03Pacific AHL Prospects-31
Gold-31
04Finnish Cardset-106
Parallel-79

Somik, Radovan
00Czech OFS-370
01SPx Rookie Redemption-R22
01Czech OFS-87
02Atomic-129
02BAP All-Star Edition-123
Gold-123
Silver-123
02BAP Memorabilia-306
02BAP Signature Series All-Rookie-AR6
02BAP Ultimate Memorabilia-33
02Bowman YoungStars-121
Gold-121
Silver-121
02Crown Royale-131
Blue-131
Purple-131
Red-131
Retail-131
02Flyers Postcards-8
02ITG Used-90
Calder Jerseys-C18
Calder Jerseys Gold-C18
02Pacific Calder-136
Silver-136
02Pacific Complete-550
Red-550
02Pacific Quest for the Cup-136
Gold-136
02Parkhurst-233
Bronze-233
Gold-233
Silver-233
02Private Stock Reserve-177
Blue-177
Red-177
Retail-177
02SP Authentic-154
02SPx-172
02Titanium-129
Blue-129
Red-129
Retail-129
02Topps Chrome-159
Black Border Refractors-159
Refractors-159
02Topps Heritage-153
02Topps Total-423
02UD Honor Roll-162
02UD Mask Collection-120
02UD Top Shelf-100
02Upper Deck-446
Exclusives-446
02Vanguard-128
LTD-128
02Slovakian Kvarteto-17
03Flyers Postcards-20
03ITG Action-440
Jerseys-M81
04Czech OFS-266
Stars-37

Sommer, Lars
02Swiss HNL-470

Sommer, Marcel
99Swiss Panini Stickers-198
01Swiss HNL-480
02Swiss HNL-449

Sommer, Pascal
95Swiss HNL-93
96Swiss HNL-236
98Swiss Power Play Stickers-36
99Swiss Panini Stickers-35
01Swiss HNL-309

Sommer, Roy
88Oilers Tenth Anniversary-110
92Richmond Renegades-18
93Richmond Renegades-11
94Richmond Renegades-20
95Richmond Renegades-24
98Kentucky Thoroughblades-23
00Kentucky Thoroughblades-25
01Cleveland Barons-23
02Cleveland Barons-20
03Cleveland Barons-23
04Cleveland Barons-25
05Cleveland Barons-26

Sommerfeld, Marcus
04German DEL Update-298

Sommerfeld, Matt
99Swift Current Broncos-19
00Swift Current Broncos-19
01Swift Current Broncos-21

Sommers, Darb
23V128-1 Paulin's Candy-58

Sondell, Daniel
06Swedish SHL Elitset-265

Sonderby, Jannik
98Danish Hockey League-224
99Danish Hockey League-139

Songin, Tim
06Toledo Storm-4

Songin, Tom
98Bruins Alumni-29
Autographs-29

Sonier, Federick
03Halifax Mooseheads-17

Sonier, Grant
93Anaheim Bullfrogs RHI-17
94Anaheim Bullfrogs RHI-17
95Anaheim Bullfrogs RHI-2
98Fort Wayne Komets-24

Sonmez, Jim
88Sudbury Wolves-18
89Sudbury Wolves-13
907th Inn. Sketch OHL-19

Sonmor, Glen
72Minnesota Fighting Saints Postcards WHA-22
79North Stars Postcards-18
80North Stars Postcards-14
81North Stars Postcards-23

Sonne, Brennan
05Everett Silvertips-23

Sonne, Brett
05Calgary Hitmen-19

Sonne, Kiel
03Salmon Arm Silverbacks-18
04Salmon Arm Silverbacks-15

Sonnenberg, Eric
99Lethbridge Hurricanes-24
01Regina Pats-21

Sonnenberg, Kyle
04Belleville Bulls-11
04Brampton Battalion-25
05Brampton Battalion-23
06Brampton Battalion-10

Sonnenberg, Martin
95Saskatoon Blades-21
96Saskatoon Blades-22
97Saskatoon Blades-22
98Bowman CHL-69
Golden Anniversary-69
OPC International-69
98Bowman Chrome CHL-69
Golden Anniversary-69
Golden Anniversary Refractors-69
OPC International-69
OPC International Refractors-69
Refractors-69
99BAP Millennium-200
Emerald-200
Ruby-200
Sapphire-200
Signatures-200
Signatures Gold-200
99Upper Deck Gold Reserve-347
99Upper Deck MVP SC Edition-149
Gold Script-149
Silver Script-149
Super Script-149
00Wilkes-Barre Scranton Penguins-21
01Wilkes-Barre Scranton Penguins-9
02BAP Sig Series Auto Buybacks 1999-200
03Lowell Lock Monsters-14
03Lowell Lock Monsters Photo Album-10
05Hartford Wolf Pack-20
06Finnish Cardset-265

Sopanen, Vili
06Finnish Cardset-298

Sopel, Brent
95Swift Current Broncos-14
96Swift Current Broncos-6
99Syracuse Crunch-14
00BAP Memorabilia-34
Emerald-34
Ruby-34
Sapphire-34
Promos-34
00BAP Mem Chicago Sportsfest Copper-34
00BAP Memorabilia Chicago Sportsfest Blue-34
00BAP Memorabilia Chicago Sportsfest Gold-34
00BAP Memorabilia Chicago Sportsfest Ruby-34
00BAP Memorabilia Chicago Sun-Times Ruby-34
00BAP Memorabilia Chicago Sun-Times Gold-34
00BAP Mem Chicago Sun-Times Sapphire-34
00BAP Mem Toronto Fall Expo Copper-34
00BAP Memorabilia Toronto Fall Expo Gold-34
00BAP Memorabilia Toronto Fall Expo Ruby-34
00BAP Signature Series-262
Emerald-262
Ruby-262
Sapphire-262
Autographs-15
Autographs Gold-15
00O-Pee-Chee-302
00O-Pee-Chee Parallel-302
00SP Authentic-165
00Topps/OPC-302
Parallel-302
00Topps Chrome-197
OPC Refractors-197
Refractors-197
00Upper Deck-195
Exclusives Tier 1-195
Exclusives Tier 2-195
00Upper Deck MVP-208
First Stars-208
Second Stars-208
Third Stars-208
00Upper Deck Victory-271
00Upper Deck Vintage-393
01O-Pee-Chee-260
01O-Pee-Chee Premier Parallel-260
01SP Authentic Sign of the Times-BS
01Topps-260
OPC Parallel-260
02BAP Sig Series Auto Buybacks 2000-15
02NHL Power Play Stickers-168
02Pacific-386
Blue-386
Red-386
02Pacific Complete-457
Red-457
02Topps Total-28
02Upper Deck Victory-206
Bronze-206
Gold-206
Silver-206
03Canucks Postcards-27
03Canucks Sav-on-Foods-15
03ITG Action-517
03Pacific-338
Blue-338
Red-338
03Pacific Complete-342
Red-342
03Upper Deck MVP-415
Gold Script-415
Silver Script-415
Canadian Exclusives-415
05Be A Player Signatures-BT
05Be A Player Signatures Gold-BT
05Be A Player Triple Signatures-NMS
05Parkhurst Facsimile Auto Parallel-308
05Ultra-126
Gold-126
Ice-126
05Upper Deck-373
05Upper Deck MVP-245
Gold-245
Platinum-245
05Upper Deck Victory-194
Black-194
Gold-194
Silver-194
06O-Pee-Chee-229
Rainbow-229

Soracreppa, Martino
92Finnish Semic-264

Sorensen, Anders
93Swiss HNL-436
99Mobile Mysticks-16

Sorensen, Bjornar
92Norwegian Elite Series-235

Sorensen, Blake
03UK Basingstoke Bison-14

Sorensen, Christopher
02Rimouski Oceanic-17

Sorensen, Dana
03Minnesota State Mavericks-17

Sorensen, Kasper
98Danish Hockey League-55

Sorensen, Magnus
98Danish Hockey League-13
99Danish Hockey League-141

Sorensen, Martin
98Danish Hockey League-214

Sorensen, Ronnie
99Danish Hockey League-97

Sorenson, Kelly
92Hampton Roads Admirals-5
93Hampton Roads Admirals-17
94Hampton Roads Admirals-15
98Hampton Roads Admirals 10th Anniversary-10

Sorg, Jonathan
97Johnstown Chiefs-12
98Johnstown Chiefs-13
01Indianapolis Ice-19
02Bakersfield Condors-17

Sorli, Oyvind
92Norwegian Elite Series-122
99Norwegian National Team-22

Sorlie, Bard
99Norwegian National Team-23

Sormunen, Pasi
92Finnish Jyvas-Hyva Stickers-13
93Finnish Jyvas-Hyva Stickers-21
93Finnish SISU-89
93Swedish Semic World Champ Stickers-60
94Finnish SISU-238
94Finnish Jaa Kiekko-11
95Finnish SISU-45
95Finnish Semic World Championships-6
96Finnish SISU Redline-44
Sledgehammers-3
98Finnish Kerailysarja-13
99German DEL-42
00Swiss Panini Stickers-83
00Swiss Slapshot Mini-Cards-EHCC6

Sorochan, Aaron
00Prince Albert Raiders-23
01Prince Albert Raiders-20
02Prince Albert Raiders-21
03Vancouver Giants-3
04Lethbridge Hurricanes-22

Sorochan, Jason
907th Inn. Sketch WHL-135
917th Inn. Sketch WHL-350

Sorochan, Lee
917th Inn. Sketch WHL-338
93Lethbridge Hurricanes-16
94Finest-153
Super Team Winners-153
Refractors-153
94Pinnacle-528
Artist's Proofs-528
Rink Collection-528
94SP-147
Die Cuts-147
95Donruss Canadian World Junior Team-9
95Topps Canadian World Juniors-9CJ
95Binghamton Rangers-22
96Binghamton Rangers-20
97Hartford Wolf Pack-20
98Fort Wayne Komets-23
98Hartford Wolf Pack-18
00Finnish Cardset-281
01German Berlin Polar Bears Postcards-25
01German Upper Deck-44

Sorokin, Oleg
03Finnish Cardset-172
04Finnish Cardset-187
04Finnish Cardset Signatures-37

Sorokin, Sergei
91O-Pee-Chee Inserts-44R
92Upper Deck-343
93Swedish Semic World Champ Stickers-134
93Classic-93
94Finnish Jaa Kiekko-144
94Swedish Olympics Lillehammer*-282
95German DEL-85
96German DEL-274
00German DEL-50
01Russian Hockey League-33

Sorokin, Vladimir
74Swedish Stickers-76

Sorrell, John
33O-Pee-Chee V304A-42
33V252 Canadian Gum-45
34Beehive Group I Photos-124
37V356 Worldwide Gum-25
39O-Pee-Chee V301-1-60

Soryal, Justin
04Peterborough Petes Postcards-17

Soskin, Barry
92Toledo Storm-4
92Toledo Storm Team Issue-4
95Toledo Storm-21
95Waterloo Blackhawks -24
96Toledo Storm-NNO
97Toledo Storm-27
06Toledo Storm-25

Soso, Brian
06Kitchener Rangers-22

Sostorics, Colleen
04Canadian Womens World Championship Team-18
06ITG Going For Gold-8
06ITG Going For Gold Samples-8
06ITG Going For Gold Autographs-AS
06ITG Going For Gold Jerseys-GUJ8

Sotiropolous, Chris
98Swift Current Broncos-20

Sotropa, J.
91Air Canada SJHL-D37
92Saskatchewan JHL-139

Souch, Mark
90Fort Saskatchewan Traders-17

Souchotte, Kurtise
91Air Canada SJHL-B49
92Saskatchewan JHL-72

Soucy, Alfred
52Juniors Blue Tint-42

Soucy, Christian
93Indianapolis Ice-20
94Parkhurst SE-SE33
Gold-SE33
94Ultra-276
94Upper Deck-223
Electric Ice-223
94Indianapolis Ice-23
94Classic Pro Prospects-75
95Indianapolis Ice-20
97Austin Ice Bats-18

Soucy, Dominic
03P.E.I. Rocket-22
04P.E.I. Rocket-7

Soucy, Jean-Francois
01UD Prospects-12
Jerseys-J-JF
Jerseys Gold-J-JF
03ECHL Update RBI Sports-143

Soucy, Jean-Philippe
92Quebec Pee-Wee Tournament-109
99Jacksonville Lizard Kings-1
00Wilkes-Barre Scranton Penguins-22
04St Georges de Beauce Garaga-15

Soucy, Patrick
93Quebec Pee-Wee Tournament-136

Soudek, Karel
95Czech APS Extraliga-58
96Czech APS Extraliga-242
97Czech APS Extraliga-269
97Czech DS Extraliga-29
97Czech DS Stickers-76
98Czech DS Stickers-69
99Czech DS-187
99Czech OFS-470
99Czech OFS-526
All-Star Game Blue-526
All-Star Game Gold-526
All-Star Game Red-526
All-Star Game Silver-526
00Czech DS Extraliga-102
00Czech OFS-193
01Czech OFS-104
02Czech OFS Plus-120
02Czech OFS Plus All-Star Game-H18
02Czech OFS Plus Trios-T25

Soukoroff, Phil
93Johnstown Chiefs-9

Soulard, Dominic
92Quebec Pee-Wee Tournament-1365
93Quebec Pee-Wee Tournament-344

Soule, Russ
83Belleville Bulls-28

Soules, Jason
88Niagara Falls Thunder-9
90Upper Deck-75
French-75
907th Inn. Sketch OHL-219
91ProCards-219

Soules, Nate
91Arizona Icecats-16
92Arizona Icecats-13
93Arizona Icecats-15
94Arizona Icecats-4

Soulier, Mathieu
93Quebec Pee-Wee Tournament-27

Soulliere, Stephane
92Oshawa Generals Sheet-15
93Oshawa Generals-11
94Sarnia Sting-11
96Knoxville Cherokees-16
97Charlotte Checkers-6

Souray, Sheldon
95Signature Rookies-27
Signatures-27
96Albany River Rats-18
97Devils Team Issue-2
98Devils Team Issue-27
98Pacific-271
Ice Blue-271
Red-271
98Paramount-138
Copper-138
Emerald Green-138
Holo-Electric-138
Ice Blue-138
Silver-138
98Upper Deck-122
Exclusives-122
Exclusives 1 of 1-122
Gold Reserve-122
99Devils Team Issue-2
99Upper Deck Arena Giveaways-ND2
99Wayne Gretzky Hockey-97
00Canadiens Postcards-26
00O-Pee-Chee-262B
00O-Pee-Chee Parallel-262B
00Pacific-214
Copper-214
Gold-214
Ice Blue-214
Premiere Date-214
00Topps/OPC-262B
Parallel-262B
01BAP Signature Series-92
Autographs-92
Autographs Gold-92
01Canadiens Postcards-26
02BAP Sig Series Auto Buybacks 2001-92
02Canadiens Postcards-16
02NHL Power Play Stickers-69
02Upper Deck-337
Exclusives-337
02Upper Deck Beckett UD Promos-337
03Canadiens Postcards-25
03Pacific Complete-224
Red-224
03Pacific Quest for the Cup-58
Blue-58
03Parkhurst Original Six Montreal-19
03Titanium-57
Hobby Jersey Number Parallels-57
Retail-57
Retail Jersey Number Parallels-57
04Pacific-142
Blue-142
Red-142
04UD All-World-53
Gold-53
Autographs-53
Dual Autographs-AD-SC
04Upper Deck-96
Canadian Exclusives-96
HG Glossy Gold-96
HG Glossy Silver-96
04Swedish Pure Skills-27
Parallel-27
05Be A Player Quad Signatures-MONT
05Be A Player Signatures-SS
05Be A Player Signatures Gold-SS
05Black Diamond-46
Emerald-46
Gold-46
Onyx-46
Ruby-46
Gemography-G-SS
Gemography Emerald-G-SS
Gemography Gold-G-SS
Gemography Onyx-G-SS
Gemography Ruby-G-SS
05Canadiens Team Issue-20
05Panini Stickers-75
05Parkhurst-258
Facsimile Auto Parallel-258
05SP Authentic Sign of the Times-SS
05SP Game Used Auto Draft-AD-SH
05SP Game Used SIGnificance-SS
05SP Game Used SIGnificance Gold-S-SS
05UD Powerplay Power Marks-PMSS
05Ultra-108
Gold-108
Fresh Ink-FI-SS
Fresh Ink Blue-FI-SS
Ice-108
05Upper Deck-101
HG Glossy-101
Notable Numbers-N-SS
05Upper Deck MVP-210
Gold-210
Platinum-210
ProSign-P-SS
05Upper Deck Toronto Fall Expo-101
05Upper Deck Victory-106
Black-106
Gold-106
Silver-106
06Be A Player-36
Autographs-36
Signatures-SO
Signatures 10-39
Signatures Duals-DSM
06Canadiens Postcards-21
06Gatorade-33
06O-Pee-Chee-261
Rainbow-261
06Panini Stickers-71
06Upper Deck-355
Exclusives Parallel-355
High Gloss Parallel-355
Masterpieces-355
06Upper Deck MVP-160
Gold Script-160
Super Script-160
07Upper Deck Victory-50
Black-50
Gold-50

Sousa, Steve
93Quebec Pee-Wee Tournament-1388

Southern, Bruce
88Jets Police-23

Southern, Dirk
01Lincoln Stars-21
04Northern Michigan Wildcats-22
06Augusta Lynx-20

Southorn, Jordon
06PEI Rocket-7

Soutokorva, Osmo
89Swedish Semic Elitserien Stickers-150
90Swedish Semic Elitserien Stickers-231
91Swedish Semic Elitserien Stickers-208
97Swedish Collector's Choice-121
98Swedish UD Choice-135

Soutukorvo, Osmo
99Swedish Upper Deck-137
00Swedish Upper Deck-123
02Russian Transfert-12
02Russian Transfert Promos-2

Souza, Mike
98New Hampshire Wildcats-17
01Norfolk Admirals-15
04Hershey Bears Patriot News-25
04Reading Royals-15

Sova, Joe
05Waterloo Blackhawks-20

Sova, Tommi
94Finest-138
Super Team Winners-138
Refractors-138
94Parkhurst SE-SE224
Gold-SE224
95Finnish SISU-49
98Finnish Kerailysarja-192
99Finnish Cardset-112
00UK Sekonda Superleague-123

Sozinov, Vadim
00Ottawa 67's-16

Spaan, Christian
94German First League-568
99German Bundesliga 2-254

Spaccucci, Nicola
96Rimouski Oceanic Quebec Police-23

Spacek, Jaroslav
94Czech APS Extraliga-148
95Czech APS Extraliga-249
96Czech APS Extraliga-294
97Czech APS Extraliga-352
97Czech DS Stickers-211
97Swedish Collector's Choice-55
98Upper Deck-281
Exclusives-281
Exclusives 1 of 1-281
Gold Reserve-281
98Upper Deck MVP-86
Gold Script-86
Silver Script-86
Super Script-86
98Czech OFS-236
Olympic Winners-13
98Czech Bonaparte-3B
98Czech Pexeso-9
98Czech Pexeso Series Two-8
99BAP Memorabilia-352
Gold-352
Silver-352
99Pacific-181
Copper-181
Emerald Green-181
Gold-181
Ice Blue-181
Premiere Date-181
Red-181
99Panini Stickers-57
99Ultimate Victory-39
1/1-39
Parallel-39
Parallel 100-39
99Czech DS National Stars-NS5
99Czech DS Premium-P8
99Czech OFS-36
99Czech OFS Jagr Team Embossed-36
00BAP Memorabilia-276
Emerald-276
Ruby-276
Sapphire-276
Promos-276
00BAP Mem Chicago Sportsfest Copper-276
00BAP Memorabilia Chicago Sportsfest Blue-276
00BAP Memorabilia Chicago Sportsfest Gold-276
00BAP Memorabilia Chicago Sportsfest Ruby-276
00BAP Memorabilia Chicago Sun-Times Ruby-276
00BAP Memorabilia Chicago Sun-Times Gold-276
00BAP Mem Chicago Sun-Times Sapphire-276
00BAP Mem Toronto Fall Expo Copper-276
00BAP Memorabilia Toronto Fall Expo Gold-276
00BAP Memorabilia Toronto Fall Expo Ruby-276
00BAP Signature Series-244
Emerald-244
Ruby-244
Sapphire-244
Autographs-187
Autographs Gold-187
00O-Pee-Chee-258A
00O-Pee-Chee Parallel-258A
00Panini Stickers-34
00Stadium Club-175
00Topps/OPC-258A
Parallel-258A
00Czech OFS-404
01Upper Deck-269
Exclusives-269
01Upper Deck MVP-39
01Upper Deck Victory-77
Gold-77
01Upper Deck Vintage-55
02BAP First Edition-249
02Pacific Complete-255
Red-255
02Upper Deck MVP-52
Gold-52
Classics-52
Golden Classics-52
02Czech DS-18
02Czech DS-43
02Czech DS-57
02Czech DS-93
02Czech IQ Sports Blue-27
02Czech IQ Sports Yellow-28
02Czech National Team Postcards-11
02Czech Stadion Olympics-348
03ITG Action-169
03Pacific Complete-165
Red-165
03Upper Deck-300
Canadian Exclusives-300
HG-300
UD Exclusives-300
03Upper Deck MVP-118
Gold Script-118
Silver Script-118
Canadian Exclusives-118
04Czech HC Plzen Postcards-16
04Czech HC Slavia Praha Postcards-18
04Czech NHL ELH Postcards-14
04Czech OFS-154
04Czech OFS-390
Checklist Cards-7
Stars-16
04Czech Zuma-23
04Czech World Championship Postcards-19
05Parkhurst-191
Facsimile Auto Parallel-191
05Upper Deck-291
05Upper Deck MVP-93
Gold-93
Platinum-93
05Czech World Champions Postcards-22
05Czech Kvarteto Bonaparte-2d
05Czech Pexeso Mini Blue Set-6
05Czech Pexeso Mini Red Set-26
06Fleer-28
Tiffany-28
06O-Pee-Chee-65
Rainbow-65
06Upper Deck-278
Exclusives Parallel-278
High Gloss Parallel-278
Masterpieces-278
06Upper Deck MVP-35
Gold Script-35
Super Script-35
06Czech NHL ELH Postcards-10

Spadafora, Paul
99Hull Olympiques-17
Signed-17
00Trenton Titans-21
01Florida Everblades-16
02Atlantic City Boardwalk Bullies-20

Spadafore, Tim
93RPI Engineers-28

Spadaro, Gene
93Quebec Pee-Wee Tournament-758

Spade, Steve
03Barrie Colts-2
04Belleville Bulls-23
05Belleville Bulls-16

Spady, Erik
05Salmon Arm Silverbacks-18

Spalding, Jason
93Quebec Pee-Wee Tournament-1443

Spaling, Nathan
03Guelph Storm-11

Spaling, Nick
05Kitchener Rangers-15
06Kitchener Rangers-3

Spallone, Jordon
93Quebec Pee-Wee Tournament-757

Spang, Dan
03Boston University Terriers-21

Spangler, Ken
88Flint Spirits-18
89ProCards IHL-118
91ProCards-446
93Flint Generals-12
94Flint Generals-21
96Flint Generals-19
97Flint Generals-20
97Flint Generals EBK-3

Spanhel, Martin
97Czech APS Extraliga-71
98Czech OFS-48
99Czech DS-91
99Czech OFS-372
99Czech OFS-484
99Czech OFS-509
All-Star Game Blue-509
All-Star Game Gold-509
All-Star Game Red-509
All-Star Game Silver-509
00SPx Rookie Redemption-RR9
00Syracuse Crunch-14
01BAP Memorabilia-253
Emerald-253
Ruby-253
Sapphire-253
01Crown Royale-155
01O-Pee-Chee-296
01O-Pee-Chee Premier Parallel-296
01Pacific-117
Extreme LTD-117
Hobby LTD-117
Premiere Date-117
Retail LTD-117
01Pacific Arena Exclusives-117
01Parkhurst-312
01SPx-136
01SPx-136
Rookie Treasures-RTMS
01Titanium Draft Day Edition-122
01Topps-296
OPC Parallel-296
01UD Challenge for the Cup-103
01UD Honor Roll-91
01UD Premier Collection-57
01UD Top Shelf-52
01UD Top Shelf-52B
01Upper Deck-186
Exclusives-186
01Upper Deck Ice-51
01Upper Deck MVP-196
01Upper Deck Victory-371
Gold-371
01Syracuse Crunch-11
02Czech OFS Plus-16
03Finnish Cardset-28
05Czech HC Sparta Praha-11

Spantig, Ingolf
83Swedish Semic VM Stickers-144

Sparkes, Brad
85Kitchener Rangers-28

Sparks, Andy
94UK Guildford Flames-5
95UK Guildford Flames-8
02UK Guildford Flames-29

Sparks, Ron
84Nanaimo Clippers-18

Sparks, Todd
907th Inn. Sketch QMJHL-131
917th Inn. Sketch QMJHL-215
95Richmond Renegades-4
96Fredericton Canadiens-20
98Danish Hockey League-198
99Danish Hockey League-7
99German Bundesliga 2-170

Sparling, Ryan
05Saint John's Sea Dogs-20
06Saint Johns Sea Dogs-3

Sparre, Daniel
03Halifax Mooseheads-6
03Victoriaville Tigers-24
04Halifax Mooseheads-3
05Hartford Wolf Pack-21

Sparre, Kris
06Barrie Colts-18

Sparrow, Spunk
23V128-1 Paulin's Candy-49

Spaulding, Ryan
04Chicoutimi Sagueneens-21

Speck, Fred
71Sargent Promotions Stamps-220
71Toronto Sun-290
72Minnesota Fighting Saints Postcards WHA-23
72O-Pee-Chee-331

Spector, Lee
02Ohio State Buckeyes-12
03Ohio State Buckeyes-13
04Ohio State Buckeyes-12

Speer, Dan
01Sudbury Wolves-19
01Sudbury Wolves Police-19
02Barrie Colts-21
03Barrie Colts-20
04Barrie Colts-7

Speer, Michael
907th Inn. Sketch OHL-185
907th Inn. Sketch OHL-294
91ProCards-487
92Indianapolis Ice-22
93Indianapolis Ice-21
94Brantford Smoke-20
94Classic Pro Prospects-168

Spehar, Dave
96Minnesota Golden Gophers-25
97Minnesota Golden Gophers-19
98Minnesota Golden Gophers-19
99Minnesota Golden Gophers-23

Speight, Jason
03Erie Otters-24
04Erie Otters-20

Speirs, Pete
23Crescent Selkirks-3
23V128-1 Paulin's Candy-2
24Crescent Selkirks-12

Spelda, Jaroslav
94Czech APS Extraliga-28
99Czech OFS-373
00Czech OFS-63
02Czech OFS Plus-267
04Czech OFS-66
05Czech HC Kladno-12

Spence, Daniel
04Calgary Hitmen-19
05Calgary Hitmen-20

Spence, Jason
99Johnstown Chiefs-6
00Johnstown Chiefs-15
01Johnstown Chiefs-17
02Johnstown Chiefs-16
03Laredo Bucks-18
04Las Vegas Wranglers-17
05Johnstown Chiefs-16

Spence, Joe
61Sudbury Wolves-16
62Sudbury Wolves-20

Spence, Mark
98Phoenix Mustangs-5
99Huntington Blizzard-14
00Charlotte Checkers-21

Spence, Russell
01OCN Blizzard-15
03ECHL Update RBI Sports-132
03Greenville Grrrowl-19

Spence, Wally
92Saskatchewan JHL-21

Spencer, Brian
69Maple Leafs White Border Matte-5
71Maple Leafs Postcards-19
71O-Pee-Chee-198
71Toronto Sun-272
72O-Pee-Chee-61
72Sargent Promotions Stamps-132
72Topps-53
73O-Pee-Chee-83
73Topps-83
74NHL Action Stamps-38
74O-Pee-Chee NHL-328
74Sabres Postcards-21
75O-Pee-Chee NHL-384
76O-Pee-Chee NHL-191
76Topps-191
77O-Pee-Chee NHL-9
77Topps-9
78O-Pee-Chee-137
78Topps-137

Spencer, Irv
60Shirriff Coins-88
61Shirriff/Salada Coins-86
61Topps-47
62Topps-17
73Vancouver Blazers-21

Spencer, Joe
02Orlando Seals-12

Spencer, Sean
907th Inn. Sketch OHL-97
917th Inn. Sketch OHL-295
92Ottawa 67's-21

Spencer, Steven
01Swift Current Broncos-1
02Swift Current Broncos-19
03South Carolina Stingrays-335

Spencer, Tim
05Moncton Wildcats-12

Spenrath, Greg
91ProCards-145
93Las Vegas Thunder-26
00Fresno Falcons-18
01Fresno Falcons-17
02Fresno Falcons-23
03Fresno Falcons-20
04Fresno Falcons-17

Sperger, Zdenek
94Czech APS Extraliga-107
95Czech APS Extraliga-74

Spero, Kevin
91Oshawa Generals-10
91Oshawa Generals Sheet-20
917th Inn. Sketch OHL-168
92Oshawa Generals Sheet-11

Sperrle, Daniel
03Swedish Elite-209
Silver-209
04Swedish Elitset-201
Gold-201
05Swedish SHL Elitset-252
Gold-252
06Swedish SHL Elitset-146
Goal Patrol-15

Spets, Lars-Erik
05Swedish SHL Elitset-155
Gold-155
06Swedish SHL Elitset-11

Speyers, Chris
24C144 Champ's Cigarettes-57
34Diamond Matchbooks Silver-56

Spezia, Alex
02Chicago Steel-20
03Chicago Steel-17

Spezza, Jason
99Brampton Battalion-27
99Bowman CHL-153
Gold-153
OPC International-153
Scout's Choice-SC11
99UD Prospects-2
99UD Prospects-81
CHL Class-C1
Destination the Show-DS1
Signatures of Tradition-JS
00Upper Deck Jason Spezza Giveaways-1
00Upper Deck Jason Spezza Giveaways-2
00Mississauga Ice Dogs-23
00UD CHL Prospects-11
00UD CHL Prospects-89
00UD CHL Prospects-99
Autographs-A-JS
CHL Class-CC3
Destination the Show-D1
Future Leaders-FL1
Game Jersey Autographs-S-JA
Game Jersey Autographs-S-JS
Game Jerseys-JA
Game Jerseys-JS
Game Jerseys-S-B
Game Jerseys-S-L
Game Jerseys-S-S
Game Jerseys-S-T
Game Jerseys-S-Z
Great Desire-GD1
Supremacy-CS1
01BAP Memorabilia Draft Redemptions-2
01SPx Rookie Redemption-R21
01UD Top Shelf Rookie Redemption-TS4
01Belleville Bulls Update-5
01Belleville Bulls Update-6
01Belleville Bulls Update-7
01UD Prospects-1
01UD Prospects-41
01UD Prospects-42
01UD Prospects-43
01UD Prospects-44
Autographs-A-JS
Jersey Autographs-S-JS
Jersey Autographs-S-WA
Jersey Autographs-S-WH
Jerseys-J-JS
Jerseys-J-WA
Jerseys-J-WH
Jerseys-C-BS
Jerseys-C-SA
Jerseys-C-SB
Jerseys-C-SH
Jerseys-C-SM
Jerseys-C-SS
Jerseys-C-SW
Jerseys Gold-J-JS
Jerseys Gold-J-WA
Jerseys Gold-J-WH
Jerseys Gold-C-BS
Jerseys Gold-C-SA
Jerseys Gold-C-SB
Jerseys Gold-C-SH
Jerseys Gold-C-SM
Jerseys Gold-C-SS
Jerseys Gold-C-SW
02Atomic-128
02BAP All-Star Edition-138
Gold-138
Silver-138
02BAP First Edition-435R
02BAP Memorabilia-295
Emerald-295
Ruby-295
Sapphire-295
Future of the Game-FG-21
NHL All-Star Game-295
NHL All-Star Game Blue-295
NHL All-Star Game Green-295
NHL All-Star Game Red-295
02BAP Memorabilia Toronto Fall Expo-295
02BAP Signature Series Jerseys-SGJ54
02BAP Signature Series Jersey Autographs-SGJ54
02BAP Signature Series Team Quads-TQ20
02BAP Ultimate Memorabilia-47
Calder Candidates-4
Jerseys-13
Nameplates-6
02Bowman YoungStars-126
Gold-126
Silver-126
02Crown Royale-127
Blue-127
Purple-127
Red-127
Retail-127
Rookie Royalty-17
Royal Portraits-8
02eTopps-47
02ITG Used-200
Calder Jerseys-C1
Calder Jerseys Gold-C1
Emblems-E40
02O-Pee-Chee-335
02O-Pee-Chee Premier Blue Parallel-335
02O-Pee-Chee Premier Red Parallel-335
02O-Pee-Chee Factory Set-335
02Pacific Calder-133
Silver-133
Reflections-18
02Pacific Complete-577
Red-577
02Pacific Exclusive-179B
Blue-179B
Gold-179B
02Pacific Quest for the Cup-133
Gold-133
Calder Contenders-10
Jerseys-14
02Parkhurst-247
Bronze-247
Gold-247
Silver-247
Jerseys-GJ52
02Parkhurst Retro-247
Minis-247
Jerseys-RJ13
Jersey and Sticks-RSJ9
Memorabilia-RM15
02Private Stock Reserve-173
Blue-173
Red-173
Retail-173
02Senators Team Issue-24
02SP Authentic-191
Sign of the Times-SP
Sign of the Times-SZ
Sign of the Times-SZB
Signed Patches-PJS
02SP Game Used-82
Signature Style-SP
02SPx-175
02Stadium Club-133
Silver Decoy Cards-133
Proofs-133
02Titanium-126
Blue-126
Red-126
Retail-126
Right on Target-17
02Topps-335
OPC Blue Parallel-335
OPC Red Parallel-335
Factory Set-335
02Topps Chrome-151
Black Border Refractors-151
Refractors-151
02Topps Heritage-147
02Topps Total-411
02UD Artistic Impressions-97
Gold-97
Common Ground-CG3
Common Ground Gold-CG3
Retrospectives-R91
Retrospectives Gold-R91
Retrospectives Signed-R91
Retrospectives Silver-R91
02UD Foundations-164
02UD Honor Roll-160
Signature Class-JS
Students of the Game-SG22
02UD Mask Collection-171
02UD Premier Collection-83
Gold-83
Jerseys Bronze-JR
Jerseys Gold-JR
Jerseys Silver-JR
Signatures Bronze-SSP
Signatures Gold-SSP
Signatures Silver-SSP
02UD Top Shelf-133
02Upper Deck-443
Exclusives-443
02Upper Deck Classic Portraits-126
Mini-Busts-56
Mini-Busts-57
Mini-Busts-58
Mini-Busts-59
Mini-Busts-60
Mini-Busts-61
Mini-Busts-62
Mini-Busts-63
Mini-Busts-64
Mini-Busts-65
02Upper Deck Rookie Update-163
Autographs-JA
02Vanguard-124
LTD-124
In Focus-8
Prime Prospects-18
02AHL Top Prospects-39
03BAP Memorabilia-36
Emerald-36
Gold-36
Ruby-36
Sapphire-36
Brush with Greatness-6
Brush with Greatness Contest Cards-6
Future of the Game-FG-14
Jerseys-GJ-13
Stanley Cup Playoffs-SCP-27
03BAP Ultimate Memorabilia Autographs-31
Gold-31
03BAP Ultimate Mem Auto Jerseys-31
03BAP Ultimate Mem Auto Emblems-31
03BAP Ultimate Memorabilia Dynamic Duos-10
03BAP Ultimate Memorabilia Emblems-8
03BAP Ultimate Memorabilia Emblems Gold-8
03BAP Ultimate Mem Franch Present Future-21
03BAP Ultimate Memorabilia Jerseys-16
03BAP Ultimate Memorabilia Jerseys Gold-16
03BAP Ultimate Mem Jersey and Emblems-15
03BAP Ultimate Mem Jersey and Emblem Gold-15
03BAP Ultimate Mem Jersey and Numbers-15
03BAP Ultimate Mem Jersey and Number Gold-15
03BAP Ultimate Mem Jersey and Stick-1
03BAP Ultimate Mem Jersey and Stick Gold-1
03BAP Ultimate Memorabilia Numbers-13
03BAP Ultimate Memorabilia Numbers Gold-13
03Beehive-136
Variations-136
Gold-136
Silver-136
Jumbos-19
Jumbo Variations-19
Jumbo Jerseys-BH21
Jerseys-JT3
Signatures-RF3
03Black Diamond-28
Black-28
Green-28
Red-28
Signature Gems-SG-27
Threads-DT-JS
Threads Green-DT-JS
Threads Red-DT-JS
Threads Black-DT-JS
03Bowman-74
Gold-74
Future Fabrics-FF-JS
Future Fabric Patches-JS
Future Rivals-SH
Future Rivals Patches-SH
Goal to Goal-SG
03Bowman Chrome-74
Refractors-74
Gold Refractors-74
Xfractors-74
03Crown Royale-72
Blue-72
Retail-72
Jerseys-17
Patches-17
Lords of the Rink-16
03ITG Action-479
Center of Attention-CA9
Jerseys-M177
Oh Canada-OC9
03ITG Toronto Fall Expo Jerseys-FE9
03ITG Used Signature Series-47
Gold-47
Autographs-JS
Autographs Gold-JS
International Experience-7
International Experience Autographs-7
International Experience Emblems Gold-7
International Experience Emblems-7
International Experience Gold-7
Jerseys-14
Jerseys Gold-14
Jersey Autos-14
Emblems-23
Emblems Gold-23
Jersey and Stick-14
Jersey and Stick Gold-14
Teammates-3
Teammates Gold-3
03ITG VIP Brightest Stars-5
03ITG VIP Collages-21
03ITG VIP International Experience-3
03ITG VIP Jerseys-29
03ITG VIP Jersey and Emblems-7
03ITG VIP Jersey and Numbers-7
03ITG VIP Making the Bigs-4
03ITG VIP Sophomores-7
03McDonald's Pacific Canadian Pride-5
03McDonald's Pacific Patches Silver-19
03McDonald's Pacific Patches Gold-19
03McDonald's Pacific Patches and Sticks-19
03NHL Sticker Collection-94
03Pacific-243
Blue-243
Red-243
Jerseys-28
Jerseys Gold-28
03Pacific Atlantic City National-5
03Pacific Calder Contenders Entry Draft-10
03Pacific Calder-73
Silver-73
03Pacific Calder Collection NHL All-Star Block Party
Gold-9
03Pacific Complete-119
Red-119
03Pacific Exhibit-106
Blue Backs-106
Yellow Backs-106
Pursuing Prominence-10
03Pacific Heads-Up-71
Hobby LTD-71
Retail LTD-71
In Focus-9
In Focus LTD-9
Jerseys-20
03Pacific Invincible-71
Blue-71
Red-71
Retail-71
Featured Performers-21
New Sensations-18
03Pacific Luxury Suite-14A
03Pacific Luxury Suite-14B
03Pacific Luxury Suite-14C
03Pacific Luxury Suite-14D
03Pacific Montreal Olympic Stadium Show-8
Gold-8
03Pacific Prism-134
Blue-134
Patches-134
Red-134
Retail-134
Paramount Prodigies-18
Rookie Revolution-11
03Pacific Quest for the Cup-77
Blue-77
Chasing the Cup-7
03Pacific Supreme-72
Blue-72
Red-72
Retail-72
Generations-6
03Pacific Toronto Spring Expo-7
Gold-7
03Parkhurst Rookie-47
Jerseys-GJ-5
Jersey Autographs-GUJ-JS
Jerseys Gold-GJ-5
Jersey and Sticks-SJ-19
Jersey and Sticks Gold-SJ-19
Road to the NHL-RNJ-2
Road to the NHL Gold-RTN-2
Road to the NHL Emblems-RTNE-2
Road to the NHL Emblems Gold-RTNE-2
Teammates Gold-RT8
Teammates-RT8
03Private Stock Reserve-189
Blue-189
Patches-189
Red-189
Retail-189
Rising Stock-11
03Senators Postcards-23
03SP Authentic-61
Limited-61
10th Anniversary-SP11
10th Anniversary Limited-SP11
Honors-H18
Honors Limited-H18
Sign of the Times-JS
Sign of the Times-HS
Sign of the Times-GTS
Sign of the Times-NSZ
03SP Game Used-33
Gold-33
Authentic Fabrics-AFJS
Authentic Fabrics-DFGS
Authentic Fabrics-DFSH
Authentic Fabrics-QSAHL
Authentic Fabrics-QSNZH
Authentic Fabrics Gold-AFJS
Authentic Fabrics Gold-DFGS
Authentic Fabrics Gold-DFSH
Authentic Fabrics Gold-QSAHL
Authentic Fabrics Gold-QSNZH
Double Threads-DTSH
Limited Threads-LTJS
Limited Threads Gold-LTJS
Premium Patches-PPJS
Signers-SPSJS
Team Threads-TTSHL
Top Threads-SAHL
03SPx-69
03SPx-149
03SPx-163
Radiance-69
Radiance-149
Radiance-163
Spectrum-69
Spectrum-149
Spectrum-163
Big Futures-BF-JS
Big Futures Limited-BF-JS
Fantasy Franchise-FF-HSL
Fantasy Franchise-FF-NSZ
Fantasy Franchise Limited-FF-HSL
Fantasy Franchise Limited-FF-NSZ
Origins-O-JS
Signature Threads-ST-JS
Style-SPX-GS
Style Limited-SPX-GS
Winning Materials-WM-JZ
Winning Materials-WM-SA
Winning Materials Limited-WM-JZ
Winning Materials Limited-WM-SA
03Titanium-175
Hobby Jersey Number Parallels-175
Patches-175
Retail-175
Right on Target-11
03Topps First Round Fabrics-JP
03Topps First Round Fabrics-JSJB
03Topps C55 Relics-TRJS
03Topps Pristine Popular Demand Relics-PD-JSP
03Topps Pristine Popular Demand Relic Ref-PD-JSP
03Topps Traded-TT72
Blue-TT72
Gold-TT72
Red-TT72
03UD Honor Roll-59
03UD Honor Roll-110
Signature Class-SC30
03UD Premier Collection-38
NHL Shields-SH-JS
Signatures-PS-JS
Signatures Gold-PS-JS
Super Stars-SS-JS
Super Stars Patches-SS-JS
Teammates-PT-OS
Teammates Patches-PT-OS
03UD Toronto Fall Expo Priority Signings-JS
03Upper Deck-136
03Upper Deck-445
All-Star Class-AS-19
All-Star Lineup-AS6
BuyBacks-48
BuyBacks-49
Canadian Exclusives-136
Canadian Exclusives-445
HG-136
HG-445
Highlight Heroes-HH-JS
Highlight Heroes Jerseys-HH-JS
Jersey Autographs-SJ-JS
Magic Moments-MM-3
Patches-PLG-JS
Patches-PNM-JS
Patches-PNR-JS
Shooting Stars-ST-JS
Superstar Spotlight-SS7
UD Exclusives-445
03Upper Deck All-Star Promos-S3
03Upper Deck All-Star Promos-AS7
03Upper Deck Classic Portraits-68
03Upper Deck Classic Portraits-159
Classic Colors-CC-JS
Genuine Greatness-GG-JS
03Upper Deck Ice-62
Gold-62
Authentics-IA-JS
Breakers-IB-SP
Breaker Patches-IB-SP
Frozen Fabrics-FF-JS
Frozen Fabric Patches-FF-JS
Under Glass Autographs-UG-JS
03Upper Deck MVP-299
Gold Script-299
Silver Script-299
Canadian Exclusives-299
SportsNut-SN63
Winning Formula-WF5
03Upper Deck Rookie Update-61
Skills-SKJS
Super Stars-SSJS
Top Draws-TD6
03Upper Deck Trilogy-68
03Upper Deck Trilogy-121
Crest Variations-121
Limited-68
Limited-121
Limited Threads-LT14
Scripts-S1JS
Scripts Limited-S1JS
03Upper Deck Victory-134
Bronze-134
Gold-134
Silver-134
Freshman Flashback-FF31
Game Breakers-GB49
03Pacific AHL Prospect Destined Greatness-1
03Toronto Star-65
Foil-22
04Upper Deck National Convention *-TN17
04Pacific-189
Blue-189
Red-189
Gold Crown Die-Cuts-7
04SP Authentic-62
Limited-62
Buybacks-73
Buybacks-74
Buybacks-75
Buybacks-76
Buybacks-77
Rookie Review-RR-SP
Sign of the Times-ST-SP
Sign of the Times-DS-HS
Sign of the Times-DS-SH
Sign of the Times-TS-NSS
Sign of the Times-FS-NED
Sign of the Times-FS-SEN
Sign of the Times-SS-CNP
04UD Toronto Fall Expo Priority Signings-JS
04Ultimate Collection-30
Buybacks-26
Dual Logos-UL2-SH
Jerseys-UGJ-SP
Jerseys Gold-UGJ-SP
Jersey Autographs-UGJA-SP
Patches-UP-SP
Patch Autographs-UPA-SP
Signatures-US-SP
Signature Logos-ULA-SP
Signature Patches-SP-SP
04Upper Deck-124
1997 Game Jerseys-JS
Canadian Exclusives-124
HG Glossy Gold-124
HG Glossy Silver-124
Jersey Autographs-GJA-JS
Jersey Autographs-GJA-JS/AY
04Upper Deck All-Star Promos-JS
04AHL All-Stars-40
04AHL Top Prospects-3
04Binghamton Senators-17
04Binghamton Senators Hess-12
04ITG Heroes and Prospects-115
Emblems-33
Emblems Gold-33
He Shoots-He Scores Prizes-24
Jerseys-33
Jerseys Gold-33
National Pride-3
Numbers-33
Numbers Gold-33
04ITG Heroes/Prospects Toronto Expo '05-115
04ITG Heroes/Prospects Expo Heroes/Pros-115
05ITG Heroes/Prosp Toronto Expo Parallel -46
05ITG Heroes/Prosp Toronto Expo Parallel -344
05Be A Player-62
First Period-62
Second Period-62
Third Period-62
Overtime-62
Dual Signatures-JE
Dual Signatures-SR
Outtakes-OT36
Signatures-SP
Signatures Gold-SP
Triple Signatures-BSH
Triple Signatures-STS
05Beehive-63
05Beehive-204
Matte-63
Matted Materials-MMJS
Matted Materials Remarkable-RMJS
PhotoGraphs-PGJS
Signature Scrapbook-SSJS
05Black Diamond-138
Emerald-138
Gold-138
Onyx-138
Ruby-138
Gemography-G-SP
Gemography Emerald-G-SP
Gemography Gold-G-SP
Gemography Onyx-G-SP
Gemography Ruby-G-SP
05Hot Prospects-67
En Fuego-67
Red Hot-67
White Hot-67
05McDonalds Upper Deck Chasing the Cup-CC5
05McDonalds Upper Deck Jerseys-MJ12
05Panini Stickers-116
05Parkhurst-336
Facsimile Auto Parallel-336
True Colors-TCOTT
True Colors-TCOTT
True Colors-TCOTTO
True Colors-TCOTTO
05SP Authentic-72
Limited-72
Exquisite Endorsements-EEJS
Marks of Distinction-MDJS
Sign of the Times-SP
Sign of the Times Duals-DSH
Sign of the Times Triples-THAS
Sign of the Times Quads-QSHAH
05SP Game Used-70
Autographs-70
Gold-70
Authentic Fabrics-AF-SP
Authentic Fabrics Autographs-AAF-SP
Authentic Fabrics Dual-DJ
Authentic Fabrics Dual-SA
Authentic Fabrics Dual Autographs-DJ
Authentic Fabrics Dual Autographs-SA
Authentic Fabrics Gold-AF-SP
Authentic Fabrics Quad-NSZB
Authentic Fabrics Quad-SAHH
Authentic Patches Quad -NSZB
Authentic Patches Quad -SAHH
Authentic Patches-AP-SP
Authentic Patches Autographs-AAP-SP
Authentic Patches Dual-DJ
Authentic Patches Dual-SA
Authentic Patches Dual Autographs-DJ
Authentic Patches Dual Autographs-SA
Auto Draft-AD-SP
Awesome Authentics-AA-JS
By the Letter-LM-SP
Game Gear-GG-JS
Game Gear Autographs-AG-JS
SIGnificance-JS
SIGnificance Gold-S-JS
Significant Numbers-SN-JS
Statscriptions-ST-JS
05SPx-64
Spectrum-64
Winning Combos-WC-SA
Winning Combos-WC-SB
Winning Combos Autographs-AWC-OT
Winning Combos Gold-WC-SA
Winning Combos Gold-WC-SB
Winning Combos Spectrum-WC-SA
Winning Combos Spectrum-WC-SB
Winning Materials-WM-SP
Winning Materials Autographs-AWM-JS
Winning Materials Gold-WM-SP
Winning Materials Spectrum-WM-SP
05The Cup-72
Gold-72
Black Rainbow-72
Dual NHL Shields-DSHS
Masterpiece Pressplates-72
Masterpiece Pressplates Rookie Upd Auto-256
Noble Numbers-NNJS
Noble Numbers-NNSR
Noble Numbers-NNTS
Patch Variation-P72
Property of-POSP
05UD Artifacts-71
Blue-71
Gold-71
Green-71
Pewter-71
Red-71
Auto Facts-AF-JS
Auto Facts Blue-AF-JS
Auto Facts Copper-AF-JS
Auto Facts Pewter-AF-JS
Auto Facts Silver-AF-JS
Gold Autographed-71
Remarkable Artifacts-RA-JS
Remarkable Artifacts Dual-RA-JS
Treasured Patches-TP-SP
Treasured Patches Autographed-TP-SP
Treasured Patches Dual-TPD-SP
Treasured Patches Dual Autographed-TPD-SP
Treasured Patches Pewter-TP-SP
Treasured Patches Silver-TP-SP
Treasured Swatches-TS-SP
Treasured Swatches Autographed-TS-SP
Treasured Swatches Blue-TS-SP
Treasured Swatches Copper-TS-SP
Treasured Swatches Dual-TSD-SP
Treasured Swatches Dual Autographed-TSD-SP
Treasured Swatches Dual Blue-TSD-SP
Treasured Swatches Dual Copper-TSD-SP
Treasured Swatches Dual Maroon-TSD-SP
Treasured Swatches Dual Pewter-TSD-SP
Treasured Swatches Dual Silver-TSD-SP
Treasured Swatches Maroon-TS-SP
Treasured Swatches Pewter-TS-SP
Treasured Swatches Silver-TS-SP
05UD PowerPlay-62
05UD PowerPlay-113
Rainbow-62
Specialists-TSSP
Specialists Patches-SPSP
05UD Toronto Fall Expo Priority Signings-PS-JS
05Ultimate Collection-62
Gold-62
Endorsed Emblems-EESP
Jerseys-JSP
Jerseys Dual-DJJD
Jerseys Triple-TJHSH
Marquee Attractions-MA34
Premium Patches-PPPS
Premium Swatches-PSPS
Ultimate Patches-PSP
Ultimate Patches Dual-DPJD
Ultimate Patches Triple-TPHSH
Ultimate Signatures Foursomes-UFHHSH
Ultimate Signatures Pairings-UPHS
Ultimate Signatures Trios-UTHAS
05Ultra-134
Gold-134
Fresh Ink-FI-JS
Fresh Ink Blue-FI-JS
Ice-134
Scoring Kings-SK13
Scoring Kings Jerseys-SKJ-JS
Scoring Kings Jersey Autographs-KAJ-JS
Scoring Kings Patches-SKP-JS
Scoring Kings Patch Autographs-KAP-JS
05Upper Deck-133
05Upper Deck All-Time Greatest-42
05Upper Deck Big Playmakers-B-SP
05Upper Deck HG Glossy-133
05Upper Deck Jerseys-J-SP
05Upper Deck Jerseys Series II-J2SP
05Upper Deck Majestic Materials-MMSP
05Upper Deck NHL Generations-DYS
05Upper Deck NHL Generations-TSTP
05Upper Deck Notable Numbers-N-JS
05Upper Deck Patches-P-SP
05Upper Deck Ice-68
Rainbow-68
Frozen Fabrics-FFSP
Frozen Fabrics Autographs-AFFSP
Frozen Fabrics Glass-FFSP
Frozen Fabrics Patches-FFPSP
Frozen Fabrics Patch Autographs-FAPSP
Signature Swatches-SSJS
05Upper Deck MVP-269
Gold-269
Platinum-269
05Upper Deck Rookie Update-68
05Upper Deck Rookie Update-256
05Upper Deck Trilogy-62
05Upper Deck Trilogy-120
Crystal-120
Crystal Autographs-120
Honorary Patches-HP-SP
Honorary Patch Scripts-HSP-SP
Honorary Swatches-HS-SP
Honorary Swatch Scripts-HSS-SP
Personal Scripts-PER-SP
Scripts-SCS-JS
05Upper Deck Toronto Fall Expo-133
05Upper Deck Victory-136
Black-136
Gold-136
Silver-136
Blow-Ups-BU27
Stars on Ice-SI31
05ITG Heroes and Prospects-46
05ITG Heroes and Prospects-344
AHL Grads-AG-1
AHL Grads Gold-AG-1
Aspiring-ASP16
Complete Jerseys-CJ-19
Complete Jerseys Gold-CJ-19
Future Teammates-FT5
He Shoots-He Scores Prizes-33
Jerseys-GUJ-15
Jerseys Gold-GUJ-15
Emblems-GUE-15
Emblems Gold-GUE-15
Numbers-GUN-15
Numbers Gold-GUN-15
Making the Bigs-MTB-2
Nameplates-N-15
Nameplates Gold-N-15
National Pride-NPR-4
Shooting Stars-AS-4
Spectrum-STM-02
Spectrum Gold-STM-02
06Be A Player-35
Autographs-35
Signatures-SP
Signatures 10-38
Signatures 25-38
Signatures Duals-DHS
Signatures Duals-DSA
Signatures Trios-TSAH
Signatures Foursomes-FMSRS
Up Close and Personal-UC22
Up Close and Personal Autographs-UC22
06Be A Player Portraits-72
Dual Signature Portraits-DSDJ
Quadruple Signature Portraits-QSSTS
Sensational Six-SSCDN
Signature Portraits-SPSP
Timeless Tens-TTCAN
Triple Signature Portraits-TNSS
Triple Signature Portraits-TOTT
06Beehive-31
06Beehive-177
Blue-31
Gold-31
Matte-31
Red Facsimile Signatures-31
Wood-31
5 X 7 Black and White-31
5 X 7 Dark Wood-31
06Black Diamond-162B
Black-159B
Gold-162B
Ruby-162B
06Flair Showcase-69
06Flair Showcase-189
06Flair Showcase-251
06Flair Showcase-291
Parallel-69
Parallel-189
Parallel-251
Parallel-291
Stitches-SSJS
Wave of the Future-WF29
06Fleer-136
Tiffany-136
Fabricology-FJS
Total O-018
06Gatorade-46
06Hot Prospects-67
Red Hot-67
White Hot-67
Hot Materials -HMSP
Hot Materials Red Hot-HMSP
Hot Materials White Hot-HMSP
06ITG International Ice-146
Gold-146
Autographs-AJS
Cornerstones-IC11
Cornerstones Gold-IC11
Emblem Autographs-GUE09
Emblem Autographs Gold-GUE09
Emblems-GUE09
Emblems Gold-GUE09
Jersey Autographs-GUJ09
Jersey Autographs Gold-GUJ09
Jerseys-GUJ09
Jerseys Gold-GUJ09
My Country My Team-MC11
My Country My Team Gold-MC11
Numbers-GUN09
Numbers Autographs-GUN09
Numbers Autographs Gold-GUN09
Numbers Gold-GUN09
Stick and Jersey-SJ17
Stick and Jersey Gold-SJ17
06ITG Ultimate Memorabilia-74
Artist Proof-74
Autos-69
Autos Gold-69
Complete Jersey-28
Complete Jersey Gold-28
Emblems-17
Emblems Gold-17
First Round Picks-26
First Round Picks Gold-26
Going For Gold-14
Going For Gold Gold-14
In The Numbers-15
In The Numbers Gold-15
Jerseys-22
Jerseys Gold-22
Jerseys Autos-54
Jerseys Autos Gold-54
Triple Thread Jerseys-13
Triple Thread Jerseys Gold-13
06McDonald's Upper Deck-31
Jerseys-JSP
Patches-PSP
06NHL POG-23
06O-Pee-Chee-355
Rainbow-355
Swatches-S-JS
06Panini Stickers-113
06Senators Postcards-11
06SP Authentic-32
06SP Authentic-121
Limited-32
Limited-121
06SP Game Used-71
Gold-71
Rainbow-71
Authentic Fabrics-AFSP
Authentic Fabrics Parallel-AFSP
Authentic Fabrics Patches-AFSP
Authentic Fabrics Dual-AF2SH
Authentic Fabrics Dual Patches-AF2SH
Authentic Fabrics Triple-AF3OTT
Authentic Fabrics Triple Patches-AF3OTT
Authentic Fabrics Quads-AF4LMSB
Authentic Fabrics Quads Patches-AF4LMSB
Authentic Fabrics Fives-AF5AST
Authentic Fabrics Fives Patches-AF5AST
Authentic Fabrics Eights-AF8CEN
Authentic Fabrics Eights Patches-AF8CEN
Inked Sweaters Dual-IS2SS
Inked Sweaters Dual Patches-IS2SS
06SPx-71
Spectrum-71
SPxcitement-X70
SPxcitement Spectrum-X70
Winning Materials-WMSP
Winning Materials Spectrum-WMSP
06Sunkist-2
06The Cup-64
Autographed Foundations-CQSP
Autographed Foundations Patches-CQSP
Autographed NHL Shields Duals-DASDJ
Autographed Patches-64
Black Rainbow-64
Foundations-CQSP
Foundations Patches-CQSP
Gold-64
Gold Patches-64
Honorable Numbers-HNJS
Jerseys-64
Masterpiece Pressplates-64
NHL Shields Duals-DSHAS
NHL Shields Duals-DSHJD
Scripted Swatches-SSJS
Scripted Swatches Duals-DSHS
Signature Patches-SPJS
06UD Artifacts-31
06UD Artifacts-187
Blue-31
Blue-187
Gold-31
Gold-187
Platinum-31
Platinum-187
Radiance-31
Radiance-187
Red-31
Red-187
Frozen Artifacts-FASP
Frozen Artifacts Black-FASP
Frozen Artifacts Blue-FASP
Frozen Artifacts Gold-FASP
Frozen Artifacts Platinum-FASP
Frozen Artifacts Red-FASP
Frozen Artifacts Patches Black-FASP
Frozen Artifacts Patches Blue-FASP
Frozen Artifacts Patches Gold-FASP
Frozen Artifacts Patches Platinum-FASP
Frozen Artifacts Patches Red-FASP
Tundra Tandems-TTJH
Tundra Tandems Black-TTJH
Tundra Tandems Blue-TTJH
Tundra Tandems Gold-TTJH
Tundra Tandems Platinum-TTJH
Tundra Tandems Red-TTJH
Tundra Tandems Dual Patches Red-TTJH
06UD Mini Jersey Collection-69
06UD Powerplay-69
Impact Rainbow-69
Specialists-SSP
Specialists Patches-PSP
06UD Toronto Fall Expo Priority Signings -PSJS
06Ultimate Collection-44
Jerseys-UJ-SP
Jerseys Dual-UJ2-SH
Patches-UJ-SP
Patches Dual-UJ2-SH
06Ultra-134
Gold Medallion-134
Ice Medallion-134
Difference Makers-DM25
Scoring Kings-SK12
06Upper Deck Arena Giveaways-OTT1
06Upper Deck-135
Exclusives Parallel-135
High Gloss Parallel-135
Game Jerseys-JJS
Game Patches-PJS
Generations Duals-G2SS
Generations Triples-G3SSC
Generations Patches Dual-G2PSS
Generations Patches Triple-G3PSSC
Hometown Heroes-HH37
Masterpieces-135
Walmart Tins Oversize-135
06Upper Deck MVP-201
Gold Script-201
Super Script-201
Jerseys-OJKS
Jerseys-OJOT
06Upper Deck Ovation-33
06Upper Deck Ovation-83
06Upper Deck Sweet Shot-74
Sweet Stitches-SSSP
Sweet Stitches Duals-SSSP
Sweet Stitches Triples-SSSP
06Upper Deck Trilogy-68
Honorary Scripted Patches-HSPJS
Honorary Scripted Swatches-HSSJS
Honorary Swatches-HSJS
06Upper Deck Victory-135
06Upper Deck Victory Black-135
06Upper Deck Victory Gold-135
06Upper Deck Victory GameBreakers-GB32
06Upper Deck Victory Next In Line-NL35
06Upper Deck Victory Oversize Cards-SP
06Binghamton Senators 5th Anniversary-29
06ITG Heroes and Prospects-27
Autographs-AJS
Sticks and Jerseys-SJ12
Sticks and Jerseys Gold-SJ12
07Sports Illustrated for Kids *-178
07Upper Deck Ovation-14
3x5s-XL10
07Upper Deck Victory-42
Black-42
Gold-42
GameBreakers-GB26
Oversize Cards-OS12
Stars on Ice-SI9
07ITG Going For Gold World Juniors-25
Autographs-25
Emblems-GUE25
Jerseys-GUJ25

Spicer, Chris
04Sioux City Musketeers-20

Spicer, Cody
01Peterborough Petes-1

Spicer, Justin
93Quebec Pee-Wee Tournament-798

Spiegel, Josh
93Quebec Pee-Wee Tournament-1572

Spiers, Pete
28V128-2 Paulin's Candy-76

Spiewak, Kevin
93Quebec Pee-Wee Tournament-710
03ECHL All-Stars-259
03South Carolina Stingrays-336

Spila, Pavol
93Quebec Pee-Wee Tournament-1543

Spila, Tomas
01Quebec Remparts-11
06Czech OFS-305

Spilar, Gabriel
03Czech OFS Plus-321

Spiler, Roman
99Czech Score Blue 2000-49
99Czech Score Red Ice 2000-49

Spiller, Matthew
00UD CHL Prospects-63
01UD Prospects-5
Jerseys-J-MS
Jerseys Gold-J-MS
02SPx Rookie Redemption-R208
03BAP Ultimate Memorabilia Autographs-105
Gold-105
03Bowman-122
Gold-122
03Bowman Chrome-122
Refractors-122
Gold Refractors-122
Xfractors-122
03Coyotes Postcards-22
03Crown Royale-130
Red-130
Retail-130
03ITG VIP Rookie Debut-36
03Pacific Complete-553
Red-553
03Pacific Supreme-132
Blue-132
Red-132
Retail-132
03Parkhurst Rookie-168
03Private Stock Reserve-133
Blue-133
Red-133
Retail-133
03SP Authentic-108
Limited-108
03SP Game Used-74
Gold-74
03SPx-203
Radiance-203
Spectrum-203
03Topps Traded-TT134
Blue-TT134
Gold-TT134
Red-TT134
03UD Honor Roll-143

03Upper Deck-233
Canadian Exclusives-233
HG-233
03Upper Deck MVP-460
03Upper Deck Rookie Update-214
03Upper Deck Trilogy-163
Limited-163
06ITG Heroes and Prospects-77
Autographs-AMSP

Spina, David
06Springfield Falcons-15

Spina, Steve
93Sault Ste. Marie Greyhounds-27

Spink, Lonnie
85Kamloops Blazers-24

Spiridonov, Andrei
03Russian Hockey League-65
04Russian World Junior Team-7

Spiridonov, Maxim
98Grand Rapids Griffins-19
98IHL All-Star Eastern Conference-15
99Tallahassee Tiger Sharks-19
00Hamilton Bulldogs-7
02Russian Hockey League-67
03Russian National Team-7

Spirin, Dmitri
01Russian Hockey League-1

Spitzer, Zbynek
99Czech OFS-449
00Czech OFS-330
02Czech OFS Plus-366

Spitzer, Zdenek
05Czech HC Vsetin-11

Spitzig, Tim
917th Inn. Sketch OHL-79
93Kitchener Rangers-1
93Kitchener Rangers-9
94Kitchener Rangers-10

Splawinski, Dave
99OCN Blizzard-17
00OCN Blizzard-25
01OCN Blizzard-27

Splett, Jamie
88Regina Pats-25
89Regina Pats-21
907th Inn. Sketch WHL-178

Spojcar, Petr
99Czech Score Blue 2000-67
99Czech Score Red Ice 2000-67

Spoltore, Fred
95Louisiana Ice Gators-17

Spoltore, John
897th Inn. Sketch OHL-149
907th Inn. Sketch OHL-317
917th Inn. Sketch OHL-66
94Tampa Bay Tritons RHI-4
95Louisiana Ice Gators Playoffs-18
95San Diego Barracudas RHI-8
96Louisiana Ice Gators-17
97Louisiana Ice Gators-16
98Louisiana Ice Gators-18
99ECHL All-Star Southern Conference-12
99Louisiana Ice Gators-14
00Louisiana Ice Gators-15
06Bloomington PrairieThunder-6

Spooner, Doug
94Anchorage Aces-18

Spott, Steve
90Richmond Renegades-5

Sprague, Jay
03Chicago Steel-5

Spratt, Jimmy
04Sioux City Musketeers-21

Spratt, Len
84Kingston Canadians-9

Sprenger, Jim
84Minnesota-Duluth Bulldogs-13
85Minnesota-Duluth Bulldogs-22

Spring, Corey
95Atlanta Knights-19
98Cleveland Lumberjacks-22
00UK Sekonda Superleague-105

Spring, Don
80Jets Postcards-20
80Pepsi-Cola Caps-137
81Jets Postcards-18
81O-Pee-Chee-375
81Swedish Semic Hockey VM Stickers-80
82Jets Postcards-22
82O-Pee-Chee-392
82Post Cereal-21
83NHL Key Tags-138
83O-Pee-Chee-392

Spring, Frank
75O-Pee-Chee NHL-341

Spring, Jesse
23V145-1-36
24C144 Champ's Cigarettes-58
24V145-2-20

Sproat, Jeff
00Roanoke Express-18
01Roanoke Express-19

Sprott, Jim
86London Knights-12
90Halifax Citadels-26
90ProCards AHL/IHL-464
91ProCards-377
95Central Hockey League-105
01Bossier-Shreveport Mudbugs-19
02Bossier-Shreveport Mudbugs-16
03Bossier-Shreveport Mudbugs-16

Sproxton, Dennis
907th Inn. Sketch WHL-70
94Tampa Bay Tritons RHI-7

Spruce, Andy
76Canucks Royal Bank-19
77Rockies Coke Cans-17
78O-Pee-Chee-378
84Sudbury Wolves-1

Sprukts, Janis
05Finnish Cardset -211
06Hot Prospects-160
Red Hot-160
White Hot-160
06O-Pee-Chee-566
Rainbow-566
06Rochester Americans-20
06SP Authentic-182
Limited-182
06SP Game Used-119
Gold-119
Rainbow-119
Autographs-119
Rookie Exclusives Autographs-RESP
06SPx-206
Spectrum-206
06The Cup-131
Autographed Rookie Masterpiece Pressplates-131
Gold Rainbow Autographed Rookie Patches-131
Masterpiece Pressplates (Marquee Rookies)-566
Masterpiece Pressplates (SP Authentic
Autographs)-182
Masterpiece Pressplates (SP Game Used)-119
Masterpiece Pressplates (Sweet Beginnings)-126
Masterpiece Pressplates (Ultimate Collection)-76
Masterpiece Pressplates (Victory)-309
Rookies Black-131
Rookies Platinum-131
06UD Artifacts-243
06Ultimate Collection-76
06Upper Deck Sweet Shot-126
Rookie Jerseys Autographs-126
06Upper Deck Victory-309
06ITG Heroes and Prospects-174
Autographs-AJSP
Update Autographs-AJSP
07Upper Deck Rookie Class -40

Spry, Brad
907th Inn. Sketch OHL-98

Spry, Earl
94German DEL-227
95German DEL-224
96German DEL-75

Spurgeon, Tyler
02Kelowna Rockets-8
03Kelowna Rockets Memorial Cup-19
03Kelowna Rockets-20
04Kelowna Rockets-16
05Kelowna Rockets-24
06Stockton Thunder-9

Spurr, Chad
96Sault Ste. Marie Greyhounds-21
96Sault Ste. Marie Greyhounds Autographed-21
02Bossier-Shreveport Mudbugs-17
03Bossier-Shreveport Mudbugs-17
05Bossier-Shreveport Mudbugs-17

Spurr, Kyle
01St. Michaels Majors-14
02St. Michaels Majors-13
03Guelph Storm-20
04Guelph Storm-23

Spurrell, Douglas
93Quebec Pee-Wee Tournament-196

Srdinko, Jan
94Czech APS Extraliga-237
95Czech APS Extraliga-7
96Czech APS Extraliga-220
97Czech APS Extraliga-49
97Czech DS Stickers-22
98Czech DS-78
98Czech DS Stickers-169
98Czech OFS-102
98Czech OFS-425
98Czech OFS-474
99Czech DS-129
99Czech OFS-269
99Czech OFS-444
99Czech OFS-527
All-Star Game Blue-527
All-Star Game Gold-527
All-Star Game Red-527
All-Star Game Silver-527
00Czech DS Extraliga-15
00Czech OFS-323
01Czech OFS-31
All Stars-28
02Czech OFS Plus-15
02Czech OFS Plus All-Star Game-H35
02Czech OFS Plus Trios-T15
03Czech OFS Plus-164
04Czech OFS Czech/Slovak-14
05Swedish SHL Elitset-207
Gold-207

Srek, Pavel
94Czech APS Extraliga-80
95Czech APS Extraliga-274
97Czech APS Extraliga-178
98Czech DS Stickers-154
98Czech OFS-135
99Czech OFS-112
00Czech OFS-297
01Czech OFS-29
02Czech OFS Plus-17
03Czech OFS Plus-320
04Czech HC Plzen Postcards-17

Srochenski, Darren
93Wichita Thunder-14
94Central Hockey League-34

Srsen, Tomas
90ProCards AHL/IHL-237
91ProCards-234
92Swedish Semic Elitserien Stickers-166
93Swedish Semic Elitserien-234
94Swedish Leaf-45
Top Guns-1
95Czech APS Extraliga-17
95Czech APS Extraliga-368
95Finnish Semic World Championships-156
96Czech APS Extraliga-228
97Czech APS Extraliga-38
97Czech DS Extraliga-60
97Czech DS Stickers-34
98Czech DS-83
98Czech DS Stickers-176
98Czech OFS-343
99German DEL-363
00Czech DS Extraliga-150
00Czech OFS-273
00Czech OFS Star Emerald-31
00Czech OFS Star Pink-31
00Czech OFS Star Violet-31
02Czech OFS Plus-143
Duos-D24

Sryubko, Andrei
97Toledo Storm-6
98Las Vegas Thunder-20
98Port Huron Border Cats-17
99Grand Rapids Griffins-23
00Syracuse Crunch-3
01Syracuse Crunch-2

St-Denis, Frederic
04Drummondville Voltigeurs-11
05Drummondville Voltigeurs-18

St-Onge, David
96Rimouski Oceanic-26
96Rimouski Oceanic Quebec Police-24
97Rimouski Oceanic-25

St-Pierre, Kim
01Blizzak Kim St-Pierre-NNO
04Canadian Womens World Championship Team-19

St-Pierre, Simon
00Victoriaville Tigres-6
Signed-6
03Victoriaville Tigers-25

St. Amour, Martin
90ProCards AHL/IHL-70
91Cincinnati Cyclones-20
99San Diego Gulls-14

St. Amour, Stephane
917th Inn. Sketch QMJHL-161
93Drummondville Voltigeurs-12
95San Diego Barracudas RHI-11
98Bakersfield Condors-19
99San Diego Gulls-15

St. Aubin, Joey
88Kitchener Rangers-14
89Kitchener Rangers-15
90Kitchener Rangers-13
907th Inn. Sketch OHL-241
907th Inn. Sketch Memorial Cup-47

St. Croix, Chris
95Kamloops Blazers-16
96Kamloops Blazers-26
98Kamloops Blazers-22
99Bowman CHL-120
Gold-120
OPC International-120
01Hartford Wolf Pack-22
02Columbia Inferno-110
03Columbia Inferno-111

St. Croix, Rick
81O-Pee-Chee-252
82Maple Leafs Postcards-32
82O-Pee-Chee-258
83Maple Leafs Postcards-24
83O-Pee-Chee-340
83O-Pee-Chee Stickers-36
83Topps Stickers-36
83Vachon-98
84O-Pee-Chee-310
85O-Pee-Chee Stickers-8
88Jets Police-23

St. Cyr, Gerry
907th Inn. Sketch WHL-249
917th Inn. Sketch WHL-64
92Thunder Bay Thunder Hawks-12
93Thunder Bay Senators-18
94Toledo Storm-21
95Flint Generals-17
98Las Vegas Coyotes RHI-13

St. Cyr, Raymond
52Juniors Blue Tint-44

St. Denis, Frederic
03Drummondville Voltigeurs-21
06Drummondville Voltigeurs-16

St. Germain, Carl
01Sorel Royaux-20

St. Germain, David
93Quebec Pee-Wee Tournament-409
98Val d'Or Foreurs-14
00Baie-Comeau Drakkar-19
Signed-19
01Trenton Titans-1-10
02Trenton Titans-B-8
03Charlotte Checkers-77

St. Germain, Francois
88Richelieu Riverains-26

St. Germain, Luc
93Amos Les Forestiers-19

St. Germain, Matt
91Peterborough Petes-18
917th Inn. Sketch OHL-137
93Peterborough Petes-12

St. Hilaire, Alain
99Missouri River Otters-17
99Missouri River Otters Sheet-15
00Trenton Titans-7
01Trenton Titans-2-9

St. Hilaire, Irene
51Laval Dairy Subset-55
52Bas Du Fleuve-19
52St. Lawrence Sales-87

St. Jacques, Bruno
99Baie-Comeau Drakkar-22
01BAP Memorabilia-318
Emerald-318
Ruby-318
Sapphire-318
01Titanium-175
Retail-175
01Titanium Draft Day Edition-157
01UD Honor Roll-84
01UD Playmakers-133
01UD Premier Collection-75
02O-Pee-Chee-292
02O-Pee-Chee Premier Blue Parallel-292
02O-Pee-Chee Premier Red Parallel-292
02O-Pee-Chee Factory Set-292
02SPx-119
02Topps-292
OPC Blue Parallel-292
OPC Red Parallel-292
Factory Set-292
02Upper Deck-218
Exclusives-218
02Philadelphia Phantoms-2
03Hurricanes Postcards-16
03O-Pee-Chee-306
03OPC Blue-306
03OPC Gold-306
03OPC Red-306
03Topps-306
Blue-306
Gold-306
Red-306
04Lowell Lock Monsters-21
04Lowell Lock Monsters Photo Album-20
05Portland Pirates-19
06Norfolk Admirals-6

St. Jacques, Chris
99Medicine Hat Tigers-10
00Medicine Hat Tigers-21
02Medicine Hat Tigers-23
06Toronto Marlies-28

St. Jacques, Cody
06Guelph Storm-23

St. Jacques, Kevin
89Lethbridge Hurricanes-21
907th Inn. Sketch WHL-134
917th Inn. Sketch WHL-352
92Indianapolis Ice-21
93Indianapolis Ice-19
93Classic Pro Prospects-136
02Indianapolis Ice-17
02Indianapolis Ice-18
04Bakersfield Condors-18
05Bakersfield Condors-12
06Bakersfield Condors-20

St. Jacques, Michel
907th Inn. Sketch QMJHL-33
917th Inn. Sketch QMJHL-82
917th Inn. Sketch Memorial Cup-30
94Central Hockey League-71

St. James, Tom
82Kitchener Rangers-7

St. Jean, Marc
03Atlantic City Boardwalk Bullies-23
03Charlotte Checkers-78
04Atlantic City Boardwalk Bullies Kinko's-18

St. Jean, Maurice
51Laval Dairy Lac St. Jean-25
52Bas Du Fleuve-24

St. John, Jimi
02Arkansas Riverblades-17

St. John, Mike
897th Inn. Sketch OHL-143

St. Laurent, Andre
75O-Pee-Chee NHL-387
76O-Pee-Chee NHL-29
76Topps-29
77O-Pee-Chee NHL-171
77Topps-171
78O-Pee-Chee-32
78Topps-32
79O-Pee-Chee-73
79Topps-73
80O-Pee-Chee-316
83NHL Key Tags-105
83O-Pee-Chee-286
83Penguins Heinz Photos-21

St. Laurent, Dollard
44Beehive Group II Photos-140
44Beehive Group II Photos-288
45Quaker Oats Photos-112
48Exhibits Canadian-25
52Parkhurst-52
53Parkhurst-23
55Parkhurst-48
Quaker Oats-48
57Parkhurst-M10
58Topps-5
59Topps-43
60Shirriff Coins-74
61Shirriff/Salada Coins-35
61Topps-31
61Topps-44
62Topps-30
62Quebec Aces-20
64Beehive Group III Photos-54
91Ultimate Original Six-15
French-15
93Parkhurst Parkie Reprints-PR68
94Parkhurst Missing Link-69
01BAP Memorabilia Rocket's Mates-RM6
01BAP Signature Series Vintage Autographs-VA-23
01Parkhurst Autographs-PA15
01Parkhurst Reprints-PR20
01Parkhurst Reprints-PR52
01Parkhurst Reprints-PR68
01Parkhurst Reprints-PR114
03Parkhurst Original Six Montreal-55

St. Laurent, Sam
88ProCards AHL-7
89ProCards AHL-315
90ProCards AHL/IHL-9
91ProCards-193

St. Louis, France
94Classic Women of Hockey-W2
97Collector's Choice-284
06ITG Going For Gold-23
06ITG Going For Gold Samples-23
06ITG Going For Gold Autographs-ASTL

St. Louis, Jonathan
97Rimouski Oceanic-36
99Halifax Mooseheads-11
01New Mexico Scorpions-9

St. Louis, Josh
95Swift Current Broncos-15
96Swift Current Broncos-11
02Augusta Lynx-74
03Austin Ice Bats-15

St. Louis, Martin
97Cleveland Lumberjacks-24
97Cleveland Lumberjacks-28
97Cleveland Lumberjacks Postcards-7
98Crown Royale-20
Limited Series-20
98Pacific Dynagon Ice-28
Blue-28
Red-28
98Pacific Omega-38
Red-38
Opening Day Issue-38
98Upper Deck-234
Exclusives-234
Exclusives 1 of 1-234
Gold Reserve-234
99AHL All-Stars-8
00Topps Premier Plus-85
Blue Ice-85
01BAP Signature Series-49
Autographs-49
Autographs Gold-49
01Crown Royale-130
Blue-130
Premiere Date-130
Red-130
Retail-130
01Pacific-358
Extreme LTD-358
Hobby LTD-358
Premiere Date-358
Retail LTD-358
01Pacific Adrenaline-177
Blue-177
Premiere Date-177
Red-177
Retail-177
01Pacific Arena Exclusives-358
01Sports Illustrated for Kids III-403
01Titanium-128
Hobby Parallel-128
Premiere Date-128
Retail-128
Retail Parallel-128
01Upper Deck-158
Exclusives-158
01Upper Deck Victory-322
Gold-322
01Upper Deck Vintage-231
01Vanguard-91
Blue-91
Red-91
One of Ones-91
Premiere Date-91
Proofs-91
02BAP Signature Series-91
Autographs-91
Autograph Buybacks 2001-49
Autographs Gold-91
02Bowman YoungStars-100
Gold-100
Silver-100
02Crown Royale-89
Blue-89
Red-89
Retail-89
02eTopps-55
02Lightning Team Issue-12
02O-Pee-Chee-37
02O-Pee-Chee Premier Blue Parallel-37
02O-Pee-Chee Premier Red Parallel-37
02O-Pee-Chee Factory Set-37
02Pacific-355
Blue-355
Red-355
02Pacific Complete-393
Red-393
02Pacific Quest for the Cup-90
Gold-90
Jerseys-20
02Parkhurst-134
Bronze-134
Gold-134
Silver-134
02Parkhurst Retro-193
Minis-193
02Titanium-91
Blue-91
Red-91
Retail-91
02Topps-37
OPC Red Parallel-37
Factory Set-37
02Topps Total-132
02Upper Deck-159
Exclusives-159
02Upper Deck MVP-167
Gold-167
Classics-167
Golden Classics-167
02Upper Deck Rookie Update-89
02Upper Deck Victory-194
Bronze-194
Gold-194
Silver-194
02Upper Deck Vintage-231
02Vanguard-90
LTD-90
03BAP Memorabilia-52
Emerald-52
Gold-52
Ruby-52
Sapphire-52
Stanley Cup Playoffs-SCP-13
03BAP Ultimate Memorabilia Autographs-81
Gold-81
03BAP Ultimate Mem Auto Jerseys-81
03BAP Ultimate Mem Auto Emblems-81
03BAP Ultimate Memorabilia Heroes-19
03BAP Ultimate Mem Heroes Autos-9
03BAP Ultimate Mem Hometown Heroes-12
03BAP Ultimate Mem Hometown Heroes Gold-12
03BAP Ultimate Memorabilia Jerseys-39
03BAP Ultimate Memorabilia Jerseys Gold-39
03BAP Ultimate Mem Jersey and Emblems-25
03BAP Ultimate Mem Jersey and Emblem Gold-25
03BAP Ultimate Mem Jersey and Numbers-25
03BAP Ultimate Mem Jersey and Number Gold-25
03BAP Ultimate Mem Redemption Cards-3
03BAP Ultimate Memorabilia Triple Threads-17
03Beehive-173
Gold-173
Silver-173
03Black Diamond-119
Black-119
Green-119
Red-119
03Bowman-98
Gold-98
03Bowman Chrome-98
Refractors-98
Gold Refractors-98
Xfractors-98
03Crown Royale-91
Blue-91
Retail-91
03ITG Action-562
First Time All-Star-FT9
Jerseys-M147
03ITG Used Signature Series-20
Gold-20
Autographs-MS
Autographs Gold-MS
03Lightning Team Issue-26
03McDonald's Pacific-45
03NHL Sticker Collection-127
03O-Pee-Chee-249
03OPC Blue-249
03OPC Gold-249
03OPC Red-249
03Pacific-312
Blue-312
Red-312
03Pacific Calder-91
Silver-91
03Pacific Complete-29
Red-29
03Pacific Exhibit-133
Blue Backs-133
Yellow Backs-133
03Pacific Heads-Up-88
Hobby LTD-88
Retail LTD-88
03Pacific Invincible-88
Blue-88
Red-88
Retail-88
Afterburners-9
03Pacific Prism-143
Blue-143
Patches-143
Red-143
Retail-143
03Pacific Quest for the Cup-93
Blue-93
03Pacific Supreme-89
Blue-89
Red-89
Retail-89
03Parkhurst Rookie-26
Jerseys-GJ-10
Jersey Autographs-GUJ-MS
Jerseys Gold-GJ-10
03Private Stock Reserve-203
Blue-203
Patches-203
Red-203
Retail-203
03SP Game Used-96
Gold-96
Double Threads-DTLS
03SPx-88
Radiance-88
Spectrum-88
VIP-VIP-LS
VIP Limited-VIP-LS
03Titanium-183
Hobby Jersey Number Parallels-183
Patches-183
Retail-183
03Topps-249
Blue-249
Gold-249
Red-249
Box Toppers-20
03Topps C55-80
Minis-80
Minis American Back-80
Minis American Back Red-80
Minis Bazooka Back-80
Minis Brooklyn Back-80
Minis Hat Trick Back-80
Minis O Canada Back-80
Minis O Canada Back Red-80
Minis Stanley Cup Back-80
03Topps Pristine-96
Gold Refractor Die Cuts-96
Refractors-96
Autographs-PE-MS
Autographs Gold-PE-MS
Press Plates Black-96
Press Plates Cyan-96
Press Plates Magenta-96
Press Plates Yellow-96
03Upper Deck-419
Canadian Exclusives-419
HG-419
Jerseys-GJ-MS
Jerseys-UD-MS
UD Exclusives-419
03Upper Deck Classic Portraits-88
03Upper Deck MVP-379
Gold Script-379
Silver Script-379
Canadian Exclusives-379
SportsNut-SN80
03Upper Deck Rookie Update Super Stars-SSMSL
03Upper Deck Trilogy-88
Limited-88
03Upper Deck Victory-172
Bronze-172
Gold-172
Silver-172
03Toronto Star-85
04Pacific-242
Blue-242
Red-242
All-Stars-12
Cramer's Choice-9
04Pacific NHL Draft All-Star Nets-2
04SP Authentic-81
04SP Authentic-115
Limited-81
Limited-115
Buybacks-134
Octographs-OS-CUP
Octographs-OS-ART
Sign of the Times-ST-ST
Sign of the Times-DS-LK
Sign of the Times-DS-LL
Sign of the Times-TS-ILN
Sign of the Times-QS-HINS
Sign of the Times-QS-LKSN
Sign of the Times-QS-LRLK
Sign of the Times-SS-CAN
04UD All-World-80
04UD All-World-103
Gold-80
Autographs-80
Autographs-103
Six Autographs-AS-SWT
04UD Toronto Fall Expo Pride of Canada-24
04Ultimate Collection-38
Buybacks-58
Buybacks-59
Dual Logos-UL2-LL
Jerseys-UGJ-MS
Jerseys Gold-UGJ-MS
Jersey Autographs-UGJA-MS
Patches-UP-MS
Patch Autographs-UPA-MS
Patch Autographs-UPA-BRMS
Signatures-US-MS
Signature Logos-ULA-MS
Signature Patches-SP-MS
04Upper Deck 1997 Game Jerseys-MS
04Upper Deck Big Playmakers-BP-MS
04Upper Deck Hardware Heroes-AW2
04Upper Deck Hardware Heroes-AW7
04Upper Deck Patches-GJPA-MS
04Upper Deck Patches-GJPL-MS
04Upper Deck Patches-GJPN-MS
04Upper Deck World's Best-WB3
04Upper Deck World Cup Tribute-ML
04Upper Deck World Cup Tribute-MSVLBR
04Upper Deck Pearson Awards-2
04Swiss Lausanne HC Postcards-13
05Be A Player-79
First Period-79
Second Period-79
Third Period-79
Overtime-79
Class Action-CA12
Dual Signatures-LI
Dual Signatures-LL
Outtakes-OT45
Quad Signatures-IMPL
Quad Signatures-SCCH
Quad Signatures-SHSL
Signatures-SL
Signatures Gold-SL
Triple Signatures-TBL
05Beehive-80
05Beehive-214
Beige -80
Blue -80
Gold-80
Red -80
Matte-80
Matted Materials-MMSL
Matted Materials Remarkable-RMSL
PhotoGraphs-PGSL
Signature Scrapbook-SSSL
05Black Diamond-182
Emerald-182
Gold-182
Onyx-182
Ruby-182
Gemography-G-SL
Gemography Emerald-G-SL
Gemography Gold-G-SL
Gemography Onyx-G-SL
Gemography Ruby-G-SL
Jerseys-J-SL
Jerseys Ruby-J-SL
Jersey Duals-DJ-SL
Jersey Triples-TJ-SL
Jersey Quads-QJ-SL
05Hot Prospects-91
En Fuego-91
Red Hot-91
White Hot-91
05Lightning Team Issue-9
05McDonalds Upper Deck-38
Top Scorers-TS2
05Panini Stickers-153
05Parkhurst-434
05Parkhurst-580
Facsimile Auto Parallel-434
Facsimile Auto Parallel-580
True Colors-TCTBL
True Colors-TCTBL
True Colors-TCFLTB
True Colors-TCFLTB
05SP Authentic-88
05SP Authentic-111
Limited-88
Limited-111
Chirography-SPSL
Exquisite Endorsements-EESL
Marks of Distinction-MDSL
Octographs-OF
Prestigious Pairings-PPIS
Sign of the Times-SL
Sign of the Times Duals-DSL
Sign of the Times Triples-TSLR
Sign of the Times Fives-ISNKN
05SP Game Used-87
Autographs-87
Gold-87
Authentic Fabrics Autographs-AAF-MS
Authentic Fabrics Dual-IS
Authentic Fabrics Dual-LS
Authentic Fabrics Dual Autographs-IS
Authentic Fabrics Dual Autographs-LS
Authentic Fabrics Gold-AF-MS
Authentic Fabrics Quad-BLSR
Authentic Patches Quad -BLSR
Authentic Fabrics Triple-BIS
Authentic Fabrics Triple-SFI
Authentic Fabrics Triple-SHA
Authentic Fabrics Triple-SNI
Authentic Patches-AP-MS
Authentic Patches Autographs-AAP-MS
Authentic Patches Dual-LS
Authentic Patches Dual Autographs-IS
Authentic Patches Dual Autographs-LS
Authentic Patches Triple-SFI
Authentic Patches Triple-SHA
Authentic Patches Triple-SNI
Awesome Authentics-AA-SL
SIGnificance-SL
SIGnificance Gold-S-SL
SIGnificance Extra-SF
SIGnificance Extra Gold-SF
Significant Numbers-SN-SL
Statscriptions-ST-SL
05SPx-83
Spectrum-83
Winning Combos-WC-SF
Winning Combos-WC-SL
Winning Combos Autographs-AWC-SF
Winning Combos Autographs-AWC-SL
Winning Combos Gold-WC-SF
Winning Combos Gold-WC-SL
Winning Combos Spectrum-WC-SF
Winning Combos Spectrum-WC-SL
Winning Materials-WM-SL
Winning Materials Autographs-AWM-SL
Winning Materials Gold-WM-SL
Winning Materials Spectrum-WM-SL
Xcitement Superstars-XS-SL
Xcitement Superstars Gold-XS-SL
Xcitement Superstars Spectrum-XS-SL
05The Cup-89
Gold-89
Black Rainbow-89
Dual NHL Shields-DSIL
Dual NHL Shields Autographs-ADSLL
Emblems of Endorsement-EESL
Hardware Heroes-HHSL1
Hardware Heroes-HHSL2
Hardware Heroes-HHSL3
Honorable Numbers-HNSL
Limited Logos-LLSL
Masterpiece Pressplates-89
Masterpiece Pressplates (Rookie Update)-212
Noble Numbers-NNSL
Noble Numbers Dual-DNNLG
Noble Numbers Dual-DNNLL
Patch Variation-P89
Patch Variation Autographs-AP89
Property of-POSL
Scripted Swatches-SSSL
Signature Patches-SPSL
05UD Artifacts-91
05UD Artifacts-193
Blue-91
Blue-193
Gold-91
Gold-193
Green-91
Green-193
Pewter-91
Pewter-193
Red-91
Red-193
Auto Facts-AF-SL
Auto Facts Blue-AF-SL
Auto Facts Copper-AF-SL
Auto Facts Pewter-AF-SL
Auto Facts Silver-AF-SL
Frozen Artifacts-FA-SL
Frozen Artifacts Autographed-FA-SL
Frozen Artifacts Copper-FA-SL
Frozen Artifacts Dual-FAD-SL
Frozen Artifacts Dual Autographed-FAD-SL
Frozen Artifacts Dual Copper-FAD-SL
Frozen Artifacts Dual Gold-FAD-SL
Frozen Artifacts Dual Maroon-FAD-SL
Frozen Artifacts Dual Pewter-FAD-SL
Frozen Artifacts Dual Silver-FAD-SL
Frozen Artifacts Gold-FA-SL
Frozen Artifacts Maroon-FA-SL
Frozen Artifacts Patches-FP-SL
Frozen Artifacts Patches Autographed-FP-SL
Frozen Artifacts Patches Dual-FPD-SL
Frozen Artifacts Patches Dual Autos-FPD-SL
Frozen Artifacts Patches Pewter-FP-SL
Frozen Artifacts Patches Silver-FP-SL
Frozen Artifacts Pewter-FA-SL
Frozen Artifacts Silver-FA-SL
Gold Autographed-91
Gold Autographed-193
Remarkable Artifacts-RA-SL
Remarkable Artifacts Dual-RA-SL
Treasured Patches-TP-SL
Treasured Patches Autographed-TP-SL
Treasured Patches Dual-TPD-SL
Treasured Patches Dual Autographed-TPD-SL
Treasured Patches Pewter-TP-SL
Treasured Patches Silver-TP-SL
Treasured Swatches-TS-SL
Treasured Swatches Autographed-TS-SL
Treasured Swatches Blue-TS-SL
Treasured Swatches Copper-TS-SL
Treasured Swatches Dual-TSD-SL
Treasured Swatches Dual Autographed-TSD-SL
Treasured Swatches Dual Blue-TSD-SL
Treasured Swatches Dual Copper-TSD-SL
Treasured Swatches Dual Maroon-TSD-SL
Treasured Swatches Dual Pewter-TSD-SL
Treasured Swatches Dual Silver-TSD-SL
Treasured Swatches Maroon-TS-SL
Treasured Swatches Pewter-TS-SL
Treasured Swatches Silver-TS-SL
05UD PowerPlay-81
05UD PowerPlay-103
Rainbow-81
Power Marks-PMMS
05UD Toronto Fall Expo Priority Signings-PS-SL
05Ultimate Collection-80
Gold-80
Endorsed Emblems-EESL
Jerseys-JMA
Jerseys Dual-DJSL
Jerseys Triple-TJLVR
Marquee Attractions-MA42
Marquee Attractions Signatures-SMA42
National Heroes Patches-NHPSL
Premium Swatches-PSSL
Ultimate Achievements-UASL
Ultimate Patches-PMA
Ultimate Patches Dual-DPSL
Ultimate Patches Triple-TPLVR
Ultimate Signatures-USSL
Ultimate Signatures Foursomes-UFINNL
Ultimate Signatures Logos-SLSL
Ultimate Signatures Pairings-UPSL
Ultimate Signatures Trios-UTILN
Ultimate Signatures Trios-UTLLR
05Ultra-172
Gold-172
Difference Makers-DM10
Difference Makers Jerseys-DMJ-SL
Difference Makers Jersey Autographs-DAJ-SL
Difference Makers Patches-DMP-SL
Difference Makers Patch Autographs-DAP-SL
Ice-172
Scoring Kings-SK2
Scoring Kings Jerseys-SKJ-SL
Scoring Kings Jersey Autographs-KAJ-SL
Scoring Kings Patches-SKP-SL
Scoring Kings Patch Autographs-KAP-SL
05Upper Deck-172
05Upper Deck All-Time Greatest-53
05Upper Deck Big Playmakers-B-MST
05Upper Deck Goal Celebrations-GC5
05Upper Deck Goal Rush-GR2
05Upper Deck HG Glossy-172
05Upper Deck Hometown Heroes-HH11
05Upper Deck Jerseys Series II-J2SL
05Upper Deck Majestic Materials-MMMS
05Upper Deck Notable Numbers-N-MS
05Upper Deck Patches-P-MST
05Upper Deck Playoff Performers-PP2
05Upper Deck Scrapbooks-HS26
05Upper Deck Shooting Stars-S-MS
05Upper Deck Ice-86
Rainbow-86
Frozen Fabrics-FFSL
Frozen Fabrics Autographs-AFFSL
Frozen Fabrics Glass-FFSL
Frozen Fabrics Patches-FFPSL
Frozen Fabrics Patch Autographs-FAPSL
Signature Swatches-SSMS
05Upper Deck MVP-345
05Upper Deck MVP-445
Gold-345
Gold-445
Platinum-345
Platinum-445
Materials Triples-T-LKF
ProSign-P-SL
Rising to the Occasion-RO3
05Upper Deck Rookie Update-88
05Upper Deck Rookie Update-212
05Upper Deck Trilogy-82
05Upper Deck Trilogy-126
Crystal-126
Crystal Autographs-126
Honorary Patches-HP-SL
Honorary Patch Scripts-HSP-SL
Honorary Swatch Scripts-HSS-SL
Ice Scripts-IS-SL
05Upper Deck Toronto Fall Expo-172
05Upper Deck Victory-179
Black-179
Gold-179
Silver-179
Blow-Ups-BU35
Game Breakers-GB40
Stars on Ice-SI39
05Czech Stadion-690
06Be A Player-34
Autographs-34
Signatures-SL
Signatures 10-37
Signatures 25-37
Signatures Duals-DLS
Signatures Trios-TLRS
Up Close and Personal-UC33
Up Close and Personal Autographs-UC33
06Be A Player Portraits-91
06Beehive-11
Blue-11
Gold-11
Matte-11
Red Facsimile Signatures-11
Wood-11
06Black Diamond-77
Black-77
Gold-77
Ruby-77
06Flair Showcase-88
06Flair Showcase-196
06Flair Showcase-263
Parallel-88
Parallel-196
Parallel-263
Hot Numbers-HN37
Hot Numbers Parallel-HN37
06Fleer-173
Tiffany-173
Speed Machines-SM22
06Hot Prospects-89
Red Hot-89
White Hot-89
06Lightning Postcards-21
06McDonald's Upper Deck-42
06O-Pee-Chee-449
Rainbow-449
Swatches-S-MS
06Panini Stickers-153
06SP Authentic-11
06SP Authentic-136
Limited-11
Limited-136
06SP Game Used-90
Gold-90
Rainbow-90
Authentic Fabrics-AFSM
Authentic Fabrics Parallel-AFSM
Authentic Fabrics Patches-AFSM
Authentic Fabrics Triple-AF3TBL
Authentic Fabrics Triple Patches-AF3TBL
Authentic Fabrics Sevens-AF7ART
Authentic Fabrics Sevens-AF7LBP
Authentic Fabrics Sevens-AF7MVP
Authentic Fabrics Sevens Patches-AF7ART
Authentic Fabrics Sevens Patches-AF7LBP
Authentic Fabrics Sevens Patches-AF7MVP
Autographs-90

By The Letter-BLMS
Inked Sweaters Dual-IS2SD
Inked Sweaters Dual Patches-IS2SD
06SPx-91
Spectrum-91
SPxcitement-X89
SPxcitement Spectrum-X89
Winning Materials-WMST
Winning Materials Spectrum-WMST
06The Cup Autographed Foundations-CQMS
06The Cup Autographed Foundations Patches-CQMS
06The Cup Autographed NHL Shields Duals-DASGS
06The Cup Autographed NHL Shields Duals-DASSL
06The Cup Foundations-CQMS
06The Cup Foundations Patches-CQMS
06The Cup Honorable Numbers-HNMS
06The Cup Limited Logos-LLST
06The Cup Scripted Swatches-SSMS
06The Cup Scripted Swatches Duals-DSLS
06The Cup Signature Patches-SPMS
06The Cup Stanley Cup Signatures-CSST
06UD Artifacts-13
06UD Artifacts-196
Blue-13
Blue-196
Gold-13
Gold-196
Radiance-13
Radiance-196
Red-13
Red-196
Tundra Tandems-TTSF
Tundra Tandems Black-TTSF
Tundra Tandems Blue-TTSF
Tundra Tandems Gold-TTSF
Tundra Tandems Red-TTSF
Tundra Tandems Dual Patches Red-TTSF
06UD Mini Jersey Collection-88
06UD Powerplay-89
Impact Rainbow-89
06Ultimate Collection-55
Jerseys-UJ-ST
Jerseys Dual-UJ2-LS
Patches-UJ-ST
Patches Dual-UJ2-LS
06Ultra-175
Gold Medallion-175
Ice Medallion-175
Action-UA26
06Upper Deck Arena Giveaways-TBL1
06Upper Deck-174
Exclusives Parallel-174
High Gloss Parallel-174
All-Time Greatest-ATG20
Game Jerseys-J2MA
Masterpieces-174
Signatures-SMS
06Upper Deck MVP-258
06Upper Deck MVP-359
Gold Script-258
Gold Script-359
Super Script-258
Super Script-359
Clutch Performers-CP13
Gotta Have Hart-HH3
Jerseys-OJMS
Jerseys-OJSH
06Upper Deck Ovation-44
06Upper Deck Sweet Shot-92
Signature Sticks-STMS
Sweet Stitches-SSST
Sweet Stitches Duals-SSST
Sweet Stitches Triples-SSST
06Upper Deck Trilogy-90
Combo Clearcut Autographs-C2LS
Honorary Scripted Patches-HSPST
Honorary Scripted Swatches-HSSST
Honorary Swatches-HSST
06Upper Deck Victory-177
06Upper Deck Victory Black-177
06Upper Deck Victory Gold-177
06Upper Deck Victory GameBreakers-GB45
06Upper Deck Victory Oversize Cards-MS
07Upper Deck Victory-73
Black-73
Gold-73
GameBreakers-GB42
Oversize Cards-OS20
Stars on Ice-SI26

St. Louis, Todd
95Slapshot-175
97Fort Worth Brahmas-17

St. Marseille, Derrick
77Nova Scotia Voyageurs-22

St. Marseille, Frank
690-Pee-Chee-177
70Colgate Stamps-22
70Dad's Cookies-126
70Esso Power Players-242
700-Pee-Chee-214
Deckle-26
70Sargent Promotions Stamps-180
70Topps/OPC Sticker Stamps-28
71Bazooka-17
71Blues Postcards-23
710-Pee-Chee-38
O-Pee-Chee/Topps Booklets-15
71Sargent Promotions Stamps-184
71Topps-38
71Toronto Sun-249
720-Pee-Chee-65
72Sargent Promotions Stamps-188
72Topps-71
730-Pee-Chee-262
74NHL Action Stamps-110
740-Pee-Chee NHL-98
740-Pee-Chee NHL-374
74Topps-98
750-Pee-Chee NHL-15
75Topps-15
760-Pee-Chee NHL-276
77Nova Scotia Voyageurs-21
92Blues UD Best of the Blues-19

St. Martin, Blair
95Medicine Hat Tigers-16
96Medicine Hat Tigers-18
97Medicine Hat Tigers-19

St. Pierre , Kim
01Blizzak Kim St-Pierre-NNO
06ITG Going For Gold-2
Autographs-AST
Jerseys-GUJ2

St. Pierre, David
907th Inn. Sketch QMJHL-236
91Upper Deck Czech World Juniors-49
917th Inn. Sketch QMJHL-145
92Salt Lake Golden Eagles-19
93Classic Pro Prospects-108
95Hampton Roads Admirals-14
99German Bundesliga 2-33

St. Pierre, Karl
99UD Prospects-87
00Chicoutimi Sagueneens-15
Signed-15
02Quebec Remparts-13
03Quebec Remparts Memorial Cup-20

St. Pierre, Kevin
02Bakersfield Condors-18
03Fort Wayne Komets-21
03Fort Wayne Komets Shoe Carnival-9
04Fort Wayne Komets-14
04Fort Wayne Komets Shoe Carnival-12
05Fort Wayne Komets Choice-1
05Fort Wayne Komets Sprint-16
06Fort Wayne Komets-18

St. Pierre, Marcel
51Bas Du Fleuve-35

St. Pierre, Martin
01Guelph Storm-7
01Guelph Storm Memorial Cup-7
02Guelph Storm-2
03Guelph Storm-8
04ITG Heroes and Prospects-92
Autographs-MSP
04ITG Heroes/Prospects Toronto Expo '05-92
04ITG Heroes/Prospects Expo Heroes/Pros-92
05Hot Prospects-117
En Fuego-117
Red Hot-117
White Hot-117
05SP Authentic-224
Limited-224
05SP Game Used-200
05SPx-251
05The Cup Masterpiece Pressplate Artifact-261
05The Cup Masterpiece Pressplates (Ice)-190
05The Cup Master Pressplate Rookie Update-119
05The Cup Masterpiece Pressplates SPA-224
05The Cup Masterpiece Pressplates SP GU-200
05The Cup Masterpiece Pressplates (SPx)-251
05The Cup Masterpiece Pressplates Trilogy-237
05UD Artifacts-261
05Upper Deck Ice-190
05Upper Deck Rookie Update-119
05Upper Deck Trilogy-237
05AHL All-Stars-37
05AHL Top Prospects-39
05Norfolk Admirals-7
05ITG Heroes and Prospects-227
Autographs Series II-MSP
06Norfolk Admirals-21
06ITG Heroes and Prospects-54
AHL All-Star Jerseys Gold-AJ02
AHL All-Star Emblems-AE02
AHL All-Star Emblems Gold-AE02
AHL All-Star Numbers-AN02
AHL All-Star Numbers Gold-AN02
Autographs-AMST

St. Pierre, Samuel
99Detroit Vipers-15
99QMJHL All-Star Game Program Inserts-1
99Bowman CHL-75
Gold-75
OPC International-75
02Johnstown Chiefs-17
04German Weiden Blue Devils-22

St. Pierre, Yan
917th Inn. Sketch QMJHL-243
93Drummondville Voltigeurs-8

St. Sauveur, Claude
730-Pee-Chee WHA Posters-18
73Vancouver Blazers-20
740-Pee-Chee WHA-62
750-Pee-Chee WHA-124
760-Pee-Chee WHA-90
770-Pee-Chee WHA-7

St. Vincent, Guy
04New Mexico Scorpions-9
04New Mexico Scorpions-24

Staal, Eric
01Peterborough Petes-10
02SPx Rookie Redemption-R216
02Peterborough Petes-10
03BAP Memorabilia-176
Emerald-176
Gold-176
Ruby-176
Sapphire-176
Draft Redemptions-2
Future of the Game-FG-19
Super Rookies-SR9
Super Rookies Gold-SR9
Super Rookies Silver-SR9
03BAP Ultimate Memorabilia Autographs-91
Gold-91
03BAP Ultimate Mem Auto Jerseys-91
03BAP Ultimate Mem Auto Emblems-91
03BAP Ultimate Mem Auto Numbers-91
03BAP Ultimate Mem Calder Candidates-2
03BAP Ultimate Mem Calder Candidates Gold-2
03BAP Ultimate Mem Franch Present Future-6
03BAP Ultimate Mem Hometown Heroes-8
03BAP Ultimate Mem Hometown Heroes Gold-8
03BAP Ultimate Mem Magnificent Prospects-2
03BAP Ultimate Mem Magnif Prospect Autos-2
03BAP Ultimate Mem Rookie Jersey Emblems-23
03BAP Ultimate Mem Rookie Jsy Emblem Gold-23
03BAP Ultimate Mem Rookie Jersey Numbers-23
03BAP Ultimate Mem Rookie Jsy Number Gold-23
03BAP Ultimate Memorabilia Triple Threads-33
03Beehive-204
Gold-204
Silver-204
Jumbo Variations-6
03Black Diamond-190
Black-190
Green-190
Red-190
03Bowman-120
Gold-120
Signs of the Future-SOF-ES
03Bowman Chrome-120
Refractors-120
Gold Refractors-120
Xfractors-120
03Crown Royale-107
Red-108
Retail-107
Retail-108
Lords of the Rink-4
Royal Portraits-3
03eTopps-44
03Hurricanes Postcards-15
03ITG Action-602
03ITG Toronto Spring Expo Class of 2004-1
03ITG Used Signature Series-136
Autographs Gold-136
03ITG VIP Rookie Debut-18
03McDonald's Pacific-56
030-Pee-Chee-334
03OPC Blue-334
03OPC Gold-334
03OPC Red-334
03Pacific-352
03Pacific Calder-106
Silver-106
Reflections-4
03Pacific Complete-522
Red-522
03Pacific Exhibit-229
03Pacific Heads-Up-106
Hobby LTD-106
Retail LTD-106
In Focus-3
In Focus LTD-3
Prime Prospects-5
Prime Prospects LTD-5
03Pacific Invincible-105
Blue-105
Red-105
Retail-105
03Pacific Luxury Suite-84
Gold-84
03Pacific Prism-154
03Pacific Quest for the Cup-106
Calder Contenders-4
03Pacific Supreme-109
03Pacific Supreme-109A
Blue-108
Red-108
Retail-109
03Parkhurst Toronto Expo Rookie Preview-PRP-7
03Parkhurst Rookie-176
All-Rookie-ART-4
All-Rookie Autographs-ART-ES
All-Rookie Gold-ART-4
Calder Candidates-CMC-1
Calder Candidate Autographs-CMC-ES
Calder Candidates Gold-CMC-1
Road to the NHL-RNJ-9
Road to the NHL Gold-RTN-9
Road to the NHL Emblems-RTNE-9
Road to the NHL Emblems Gold-RTNE-9
Rookie Emblems-RE-48
Rookie Emblem Autographs-RE-ES
Rookie Emblems Gold-RE-48
Rookie Jerseys-RJ-48
Rookie Jersey Autographs-RJ-ES
Rookie Jerseys Gold-RJ-48
Rookie Numbers-RN-48
Rookie Number Autographs-RN-ES
Rookie Numbers Gold-RN-48
03Private Stock Reserve-108
Blue-108
Red-108
Retail-108
Class Act-2
03SP Authentic-137
Limited-137
Sign of the Times-KL
Sign of the Times-FS
Sign of the Times-LFR
Signed Patches-ES
03SP Game Used-84
Gold-84
Rookie Exclusives-RE9
03SPx-227
Radiance-227
Spectrum-227
03Titanium-106
Hobby Jersey Number Parallels-106
Retail-106
Retail Jersey Number Parallels-106
Right on Target-3
03Topps-334
Blue-334
Gold-334
Red-334
03Topps C55-149
Minis-149
Minis American Back-149
Minis American Back Red-149
Minis Bazooka Back-149
Minis Brooklyn Back-149
Minis Hat Trick Back-149
Minis O Canada Back-149
Minis O Canada Back Red-149
Minis Stanley Cup Back-149
03Topps Pristine-149
03Topps Pristine-150
03Topps Pristine-151
Gold Refractor Die Cuts-149
Gold Refractor Die Cuts-150
Gold Refractor Die Cuts-151
Refractors-149
Refractors-150
Refractors-151
Mini-PM-ES
Press Plates Black-149
Press Plates Black-150
Press Plates Black-151
Press Plates Cyan-149
Press Plates Cyan-150
Press Plates Cyan-151
Press Plates Magenta-149
Press Plates Magenta-150
Press Plates Magenta-151
Press Plates Yellow-149
Press Plates Yellow-150
Press Plates Yellow-151
03UD Honor Roll-187
03UD Premier Collection-114
NHL Shields-SH-ES
Signatures-PS-ES
Signatures Gold-PS-ES
Stars-ST-ES
Stars Patches-ST-ES
Teammates-PT-CH
Teammates Patches-PT-CH
03Upper Deck-206
Canadian Exclusives-206
HG-206
Rookie Threads-RT-6
03Upper Deck Classic Portraits-169
03Upper Deck Ice-123
Glass Parallel-123
03Upper Deck MVP-441
03Upper Deck Rookie Update-161
YoungStars-YS2
YoungStars-YS2A
03Upper Deck Trilogy-173
Limited-173
03Upper Deck Victory-202
04Pacific-50
Blue-50
Red-50
Gold Crown Die-Cuts-3
04Pacific Montreal International-2
Gold-2
04Pacific Montreal International Gold-2
04Pacific NHL All-Star FANtasy-3
04Pacific NHL All-Star FANtasy Gold-3
04Pacific Toronto Spring Expo-2
Gold-2
04SP Authentic-17
Limited-17
Octographs-OS-ROK
Sign of the Times-ST-ES
Sign of the Times-DS-ST
Sign of the Times-TS-NSS
Sign of the Times-TS-SHZ
Sign of the Times-QS-FSHZ
Sign of the Times-QS-TPLS
04Topps NHL All-Star FANtasy-5
04Ultimate Collection-8
Buybacks-10
Signatures-US-ES
Signature Logos-ULA-ES
Signature Patches-SP-ES
04Upper Deck-35
Canadian Exclusives-35
HG Glossy Gold-35
HG Glossy Silver-35
YoungStars-YS-ES
04Upper Deck All-Star Promos-ES
04AHL All-Stars-41
04AHL Top Prospects-24
04Lowell Lock Monsters-20
04Lowell Lock Monsters Photo Album-21
04ITG Heroes and Prospects-193
Autographs-U-ES
04ITG Heroes/Prospects Toronto Expo '05-193
05ITG Heroes/Prosp Toronto Expo Parallel -82
05ITG Heroes/Prosp Toronto Expo Parallel -370
05Be A Player-16
First Period-16
Second Period-16
Third Period-16
Overtime-16
Dual Signatures-JE
Outtakes-OT10
Quad Signatures-RBSS
Signatures-EI
Signatures Gold-EI
05Beehive-18
Matte-18
PhotoGraphs-PGES
05Black Diamond-15
Emerald-15
Gold-15
Onyx-15
Ruby-15
05Hot Prospects-17
En Fuego-17
Red Hot-17
White Hot-17
05McDonalds Upper Deck-34
05Panini Stickers-44
05Parkhurst-84
05Parkhurst-676
Facsimile Auto Parallel-84
Facsimile Auto Parallel-676
True Colors-TCCAR
True Colors-TCCAR
05SP Authentic-20
Limited-20
Scripts to Success-SSES
Sign of the Times-ES
Sign of the Times Duals-DCS
05SP Game Used-19
Autographs-19
Gold-19
Authentic Fabrics Dual-SS
Authentic Fabrics Dual Autographs-SS
Authentic Patches Dual-SS
Authentic Patches Dual Autographs-SS
Awesome Authentics-AA-ES
Game Gear-GG-ES
Game Gear Autographs-AG-ES
Signature Sticks-SS-ES
SIGnificance-ES
SIGnificance Gold-S-ES
Statscriptions-ST-ES
05SPx-16
Spectrum-16
Winning Combos-WC-EJ
Winning Combos Autographs-AWC-SW
Winning Combos Gold-WC-EJ
Winning Combos Spectrum-WC-EJ
Winning Materials Gold-WM-ES
Winning Materials Spectrum-WM-ES
05The Cup-21
Gold-21
Black Rainbow-21
Dual NHL Shields Autographs-ADSSG
Emblems of Endorsement-EEES
Honorable Numbers-HNER
Limited Logos-LLES
Masterpiece Pressplates-21
Masterpiece Pressplates (Rookie Update)-243
Noble Numbers-NNSI
Noble Numbers-NNSM
Noble Numbers Dual-DNNST
Patch Variation-P21
Patch Variation Autographs-AP21
Property of-POES
Scripted Numbers-SNSI
Scripted Numbers-SNSM
Scripted Numbers Dual-DSNNS
Scripted Numbers Dual-DSNSW
Scripted Swatches-SSER
Signature Patches-SPES
05UD Artifacts-18
Blue-18
Gold-18
Green-18
Pewter-18
Red-18
Auto Facts-AF-ES
Auto Facts Blue-AF-ES
Auto Facts Copper-AF-ES
Auto Facts Pewter-AF-ES
Auto Facts Silver-AF-ES
Gold Autographed-18
Remarkable Artifacts-RA-ES
Remarkable Artifacts Dual-RA-ES
05UD PowerPlay-17
Rainbow-17
05UD Toronto Fall Expo Priority Signings-PS-ES
05Ultimate Collection-18
Gold-18
Endorsed Emblems-EEES
Jerseys-JES
Marquee Attractions-MA12
Marquee Attractions Signatures-SMA12
Premium Patches-PPES
Premium Swatches-PSES
Ultimate Achievements-UAES
Ultimate Patches-PES
Ultimate Signatures-USES
Ultimate Signatures Logos-SLES
Ultimate Signatures Pairings-UPSC
05Ultra-40
Gold-40
Fresh Ink-FI-ES
Fresh Ink Blue-FI-ES
Ice-40
05Upper Deck-280
Big Playmakers-B-ES
Jerseys Series II-J2ES
Majestic Materials-MMES
Notable Numbers-N-ES
Patches-P-ES
05Upper Deck Ice-19
Rainbow-19
05Upper Deck MVP-78
Gold-78
Platinum-78
05Upper Deck Rookie Update-16
05Upper Deck Rookie Update-243
Inspirations Patch Rookies-243
05Upper Deck Trilogy-18
05Upper Deck Trilogy-100
Crystal-100
05Upper Deck Victory-37
Black-37
Gold-37
Silver-37
05ITG Heroes and Prospects-82
05ITG Heroes and Prospects-370
Aspiring-ASP15
Autographs-A-ES
Autographs-DA-SY
Autographs Series II-ES2
Complete Jerseys-CJ-26
Complete Jerseys Gold-CJ-26
Complete Logos-CHL-11
Future Teammates-FT6
He Shoots-He Scores Prizes-13
He Shoots-He Scores Prizes-23
Jerseys-GUJ-16
Jerseys Gold-GUJ-16
Emblems-GUE-16
Emblems Gold-GUE-16
Numbers-GUN-16
Numbers Gold-GUN-16
Making the Bigs-MTB-5
Nameplates-N-25
Nameplates Gold-N-25
Spectrum-STM-07
Spectrum Gold-STM-07
06Sports Illustrated for Kids *-62
06Be A Player-33
Autographs-33
Profiles-PP25
Profiles Autographs-PP25
Signatures-ES
Signatures 10-36
Signatures 25-36
Signatures Duals-DSB
Signatures Trios-TSBC
Signatures Foursomes-FSLST
Up Close and Personal-UC18
Up Close and Personal Autographs-UC18
06Be A Player Portraits-22
Dual Signature Portraits-DSWS
Quadruple Signature Portraits-QSSTS
Sensational Six-SSCDN
Signature Portraits-SPST
Timeless Tens-TTCAN
Triple Signature Portraits-TNSS
06Beehive-82
06Beehive-221
Blue-82
Gold-82
Matte-82
Red Facsimile Signatures-82
Wood-82
5 X 7 Black and White-82
5 X 7 Dark Wood-82
Matted Materials-MMES
PhotoGraphs-PGES
Remarkable Matted Materials-MMES
Signature Scrapbook-SSES
06Black Diamond-131
Black-131
Black-151B
Gold-131
Ruby-131
06Flair Showcase-19
06Flair Showcase-176
06Flair Showcase-214
06Flair Showcase-276
Parallel-19
Parallel-176
Parallel-214
Parallel-276
Hot Numbers-HN7
Hot Numbers Parallel-HN7
Stitches-SSES
Wave of the Future-WF8
06Fleer-35
Oversized-35
Tiffany-35
Total 0-04
06Hot Prospects-19
Red Hot-19
White Hot-19
Hot Materials -HMES
Hot Materials Red Hot-HMES
Hot Materials White Hot-HMES
Hotagraphs-HES
06Hurricanes Postcards-20
06ITG Ultimate Memorabilia-47
Artist Proof-47
Autos-56
Autos Gold-56
Autos Dual-4
Autos Dual Gold-4
Autos Triple-6
Autos Triple Gold-6
Bloodlines-2
Bloodlines Gold-2
Bloodlines Autos-2
Bloodlines Autos-4
Bloodlines Autos Gold-2
Bloodlines Autos Gold-4
Complete Jersey-29
Complete Jersey Gold-29
Double Memorabilia Autos-1
Double Memorabilia Autos Gold-1
Emblems-6
Emblems Gold-6
First Round Picks-8
First Round Picks Gold-8
Going For Gold-7
Going For Gold Gold-7
In The Numbers-16
In The Numbers Gold-16
Jerseys-24
Jerseys Gold-24
Jerseys Autos-55
Jerseys Autos Gold-55
Stick Rack-17
Stick Rack Gold-17
Sticks and Jerseys-8
Sticks and Jerseys Gold-8
Sticks Autos-28
Sticks Autos Gold-28
Triple Thread Jerseys-13
Triple Thread Jerseys Gold-13
06McDonald's Upper Deck-8
Autographs-AES
Clear Cut Winners-CC4
Hardware Heroes-HH8
Jerseys-JES
Patches-PES
06NHL POG-24
06O-Pee-Chee-94
06O-Pee-Chee-611
06O-Pee-Chee-676
Rainbow-94
Rainbow-611
Rainbow-676
Swatches-S-ES
06Panini Stickers-43
06SP Authentic-82
06SP Authentic-113
Chirography-ES
Limited-82
Limited-113
Sign of the Times-STES
Sign of the Times Duals-STSS
Sign of the Times Duals-STSW
Sign of the Times Triples-ST3HNS
Sign of the Times Triples-ST3WSW
06SP Game Used-17
Gold-17
Rainbow-17
Authentic Fabrics-AFES
Authentic Fabrics Parallel-AFES
Authentic Fabrics Patches-AFES
Authentic Fabrics Dual-AF2SW
Authentic Fabrics Dual Patches-AF2SW
Authentic Fabrics Triple-AF3CAR
Authentic Fabrics Triple Patches-AF3CAR
Authentic Fabrics Quads-AF4STSC
Authentic Fabrics Quads Patches-AF4STSC
Authentic Fabrics Fives-AP5SCP
Authentic Fabrics Fives Patches-AP5SCP
Authentic Fabrics Eights-AF8CEN
Authentic Fabrics Eights Patches-AF8CEN
Autographs-17
By The Letter-BLES
Inked Sweaters-ISES
Inked Sweaters Patches-ISES
Inked Sweaters Dual-IS2SS
Inked Sweaters Dual-IS2SW
Inked Sweaters Dual Patches-IS2SS
Inked Sweaters Dual Patches-IS2SW
Letter Marks-LMES
SIGnificance-SES
06SPx-16
06SPx-105
Spectrum-16
Spectrum-105
Winning Materials-WMES
Winning Materials Spectrum-WMES
Winning Materials Autographs-WMES
06The Cup-17
Autographed Foundations-CQES
Autographed Foundations Patches-CQES
Autographed NHL Shields Duals-DASEC
Autographed NHL Shields Duals-DASSC
Autographed NHL Shields Duals-DASST
Autographed NHL Shields Duals-DASSW
Autographed Patches-17
Black Rainbow-17
Foundations-CQES
Foundations Patches-CQES
Enshrinements-EES
Gold-17
Gold Patches-17
Honorable Numbers-HNES
Jerseys-17
Limited Logos-LLES
Masterpiece Pressplates-17
Property of-POES
Scripted Swatches-SSES
Scripted Swatches Duals-DSSS
Signature Patches-SPES
Stanley Cup Signatures-CSES
Stanley Cup Titlists Patches-TES
06UD Artifacts-81
06UD Artifacts-159
Blue-81
Blue-159
Gold-81
Gold-159
Platinum-81
Platinum-159
Radiance-81
Radiance-159
Red-81
Red-159
Frozen Artifacts-FAES
Frozen Artifacts Black-FAES
Frozen Artifacts Blue-FAES
Frozen Artifacts Gold-FAES
Frozen Artifacts Platinum-FAES
Frozen Artifacts Red-FAES
Frozen Artifacts Patches Black-FAES
Frozen Artifacts Patches Blue-FAES
Frozen Artifacts Patches Gold-FAES
Frozen Artifacts Patches Platinum-FAES
Frozen Artifacts Patches Red-FAES
Tundra Tandems-TTSW
Tundra Tandems Black-TTSW
Tundra Tandems Blue-TTSW
Tundra Tandems Gold-TTSW
Tundra Tandems Platinum-TTSW
Tundra Tandems Red-TTSW
Tundra Tandems Dual Patches Red-TTSW
06UD Biography of a Season-BOS1
06UD Mini Jersey Collection-17
Jerseys-ES
Jersey Variations-ES
Jersey Autographs-ES
06UD Powerplay-18
Impact Rainbow-18
Cup Celebrations-CC1
Specialists-SES
Specialists Patches-PES
06Ultimate Collection-13
Autographed Jerseys-AJ-ES
Autographed Patches-AJ-ES
Jerseys-UJ-ES
Jerseys Dual-UJ2-SW
Jerseys Triple-UJ3-STS
Patches-UJ-ES
Patches Dual-UJ2-SW
Patches Triple-UJ3-STS
Premium Patches-PS-ES
Premium Swatches-PS-ES
Signatures-US-ES
Ultimate Achievements-UA-ES
Ultimate Signatures Logos-SL-ES
06Ultra-37
Gold Medallion-37
Ice Medallion-37
Action-UA4
Difference Makers-DM7
Scoring Kings-SK7
Uniformity-UES
Uniformity Patches-UPES
06Upper Deck Arena Giveaways-CAR1
06Upper Deck-35
Exclusives Parallel-35
High Gloss Parallel-35
All World-AW8
Century Marks-CM6
Game Jerseys-J2ES
Game Patches-P2ES
Generations Duals-G2TS
Generations Triples-G3LTS
Generations Patches Dual-G2PTS
Generations Patches Triple-G3PLTS
Goal Rush-GR11
Hometown Heroes-HH33
Masterpieces-35
Signatures-SES
Walmart Tins Oversize-35
06Upper Deck MVP-56
Gold Script-56
Super Script-56
Clutch Performers-CP11
Gotta Have Hart-HH15
Jerseys-OJER
Jerseys-OJEV
06Upper Deck Ovation-111
06Upper Deck Sweet Shot-22
Signature Shots/Saves-SSES
Signature Shots/Saves Ice Signings-SSIES
Signature Shots/Saves Sticks-SSSES
Signature Sticks-STES
Sweet Stitches-SSES
Sweet Stitches Duals-SSES
Sweet Stitches Triples-SSES
06Upper Deck Trilogy-18
Combo Clearcut Autographs-C3CGS
Honorary Scripted Patches-HSPES
Honorary Scripted Swatches-HSSES
Honorary Swatches-HSES
Scripts-S2ES
Scripts-S3ES
06Upper Deck Victory-35
06Upper Deck Victory Black-35
06Upper Deck Victory Gold-35
06Upper Deck Victory GameBreakers-GB7
06Upper Deck Victory Next In Line-NL12
06Upper Deck Victory Oversize Cards-ES
06ITG Heroes and Prospects CHL Top Prospects-TP19
06ITG Heroes and Prospects CHL Top Prospects Gold-TP19
06ITG Heroes and Prospects Making The Bigs-MTB10
06ITG Heroes and Prospects Making The Bigs Gold-MTB10
06ITG Heroes and Prospects Quad Emblems-QE10
06ITG Heroes and Prospects Quad Emblems Gold-QE10
06ITG Heroes and Prospects Sticks and Jerseys-SJ01
06ITG Heroes and Prospects Sticks and Jerseys Gold-SJ01
06ITG Heroes and Prospects Triple Memorabilia-TM08
06ITG Heroes and Prospects Triple Memorabilia Gold-TM08
07Upper Deck Ovation-92
3x5s-XL20
07Upper Deck Victory-85
Black-85
Gold-85
EA Sports Face-Off-F03
GameBreakers-GB39
Oversize Cards-OS23
Stars on Ice-SI12

Staal, Jared
06Sudbury Wolves-11
06ITG Heroes and Prospects-94
Autographs-AJAS

Staal, Jordan
04Peterborough Petes Postcards-1
04ITG Heroes and Prospects-215
04ITG Heroes/Prospects Toronto Expo '05-215
05ITG Heroes/Prosp Toronto Expo Parallel -116
05OHL Bell All-Star Classic-38
05ITG Heroes and Prospects-116
Autographs-A-JST
He Shoots-He Scores Prizes-52
Team Orr-TO18
06Be A Player-216
Profiles-PP18
Profiles Autographs-PP18
Signatures 10-216
Signatures 25-216
Signatures Duals-DFS
Signatures Trios-TFSM
Signatures Foursomes-FSSLK
Up Close and Personal-UC57
Up Close and Personal Autographs-UC57
06Be A Player Portraits-113
06Beehive-146
Blue-146
Gold-146
Matte-146
Red Facsimile Signatures-146
Wood-146
5 X 7 Black and White-146
5 X 7 Dark Wood-146
06Black Diamond-205
Black-205
Gold-205
Ruby-205
06Flair Showcase-323
06Hot Prospects-140
Red Hot-140
White Hot-140
Hot Materials -HMST
Hot Materials Red Hot-HMST
Hot Materials White Hot-HMST
Hotagraphs-HST
06ITG Ultimate Memorabilia-83
Artist Proof-83
Autos Dual-4
Autos Dual Gold-4
Autos Triple-6
Autos Triple Gold-6
Bloodlines-2
Bloodlines Gold-2
Bloodlines Autos-2
Bloodlines Autos-7
Bloodlines Autos Gold-2
Bloodlines Autos Gold-7
Complete Jersey-30
Complete Jersey Gold-30
Double Memorabilia-28
Double Memorabilia Gold-28
Double Memorabilia Autos-1
Double Memorabilia Autos Gold-1
First Round Picks-25
First Round Picks Gold-25
Future Star-8
Future Star Gold-8
Future Star Autos-22
Future Star Autos Gold-22
Future Star Patches Autos-22
Future Star Patches Autos Gold-22
Jerseys and Emblems-20
Jerseys and Emblems Gold-20
R.O.Y. Autos-6
R.O.Y. Autos Gold-6
R.O.Y. Emblems-6
R.O.Y. Emblems Gold-6
R.O.Y. Jerseys-6
R.O.Y. Jerseys Gold-6
R.O.Y. Numbers-6
R.O.Y. Numbers Gold-6
Triple Thread Jerseys-14
Triple Thread Jerseys Gold-14
06O-Pee-Chee-546
06O-Pee-Chee-643
Rainbow-546
Rainbow-643
Autographs-A-JS
06SP Authentic-198
Chirography-JS
Limited-198
Sign of the Times Duals-STSA
Sign of the Times Duals-STSS
Sign of the Times Quads-ST4MKSL
06SP Game Used-147
Gold-147
Rainbow-147
Autographs-147
Rookie Exclusives Autographs-REJS
06SPx-191
Spectrum-191
06The Cup-169
Autographed Foundations-CQJS
Autographed Foundations Patches-CQJS
Autographed NHL Shields Duals-DASMS
Autographed NHL Shields Duals-DASSK
Autographed NHL Shields Duals-DASST
Autographed Rookie Masterpiece Pressplates-169
Foundations-CQJS
Foundations Patches-CQJS
Enshrinements-EJS
Gold Rainbow Autographed Rookie Patches-169
Honorable Numbers-HNJR
Limited Logos-LLJS
Masterpiece Pressplates (Be A Player Portraits)-113
Masterpiece Pressplates (Bee Hive)-146
Masterpiece Pressplates (Marquee Rookies)-546
Masterpiece Pressplates (MVP)-301
Masterpiece Pressplates (SP Authentic Autographs)-198
Masterpiece Pressplates (SP Game Used)-147
Masterpiece Pressplates (SPx Autographs)-191
Masterpiece Pressplates (Sweet Beginnings)-145
Masterpiece Pressplates (Trilogy)-147
Masterpiece Pressplates (Ultimate Collection Autographs)-127
Masterpiece Pressplates (Victory)-292
NHL Shields Duals-DSHJA
NHL Shields Duals-DSHJK
NHL Shields Duals-DSHPJ
Property of-POST
Rookies Black-169
Rookies Platinum-169
Scripted Swatches-SSST
Scripted Swatches Duals-DSSS
Signature Patches-SPJO
06UD Artifacts-261
06UD Mini Jersey Collection-124
06Ultimate Collection-127
Autographed Jerseys-AJ-JS
Autographed Patches-AJ-JS
Jerseys Triple-UJ3-CMS
Patches Triple-UJ3-CMS
Rookies Autographed NHL Shields-127
Rookies Autographed Patches-127
Signatures-US-ST
Ultimate Debut Threads Jerseys-DJ-ST
Ultimate Debut Threads Jerseys Autographs-DJ-ST
Ultimate Debut Threads Patches-DJ-ST
Ultimate Debut Threads Patches Autographs-DJ-ST
06Ultra-247
06Ultra-249
Gold Medallion-247
Ice Medallion-247
06Upper Deck-239
Exclusives Parallel-239
High Gloss Parallel-239
Masterpieces-239
Rookie Game Dated Moments-RGD22
Rookie Headliners-RH23
Rookie Materials-RMJS
Rookie Materials Patches-RMJS
Signatures-SJS
06Upper Deck MVP-301
Gold Script-301
Super Script-301
06Upper Deck Ovation-191
06Upper Deck Sweet Shot-145
Rookie Jerseys Autographs-145
Signature Shots/Saves-SSST
Signature Shots/Saves Ice Signings-SSIST
Signature Shots/Saves Sticks-SSSJS
Signature Sticks-STST
06Upper Deck Trilogy-147
06Upper Deck Victory-292
06ITG Heroes and Prospects-83
Autographs-AJST
CHL Top Prospects-TP11
CHL Top Prospects Gold-TP11
Class of 2006-CL01
Complete CHL Logos-CHL01
Complete Jerseys-CJ07
Complete Jerseys Gold-CJ07
Double Memorabilia-DM01
Double Memorabilia Gold-DM01
Quad Emblems-QE01
Quad Emblems-QE16
Quad Emblems Gold-QE01
Triple Memorabilia-TM08
Triple Memorabilia Gold-TM08
07Upper Deck All-Star Game Redemptions-AS5
07Upper Deck Ovation-63
07Upper Deck Rookie Class -16
07Upper Deck Rookie Class C-Card Insert-CC3
07Upper Deck Victory-11
Black-11
Gold-11
Stars on Ice-SI31

Staal, Kim
99Swedish Upper Deck-158
99Swedish Upper Deck-212
00Swedish Upper Deck-148
03Swedish Elite-246
Silver-246
04Swedish Elitset-92
Gold-92
Signatures Series A-2
04Swedish Malmo Red Hawks-7
06Milwaukee Admirals -17

Staal, Marc
03Sudbury Wolves-22
04Sudbury Wolves-4
04ITG Heroes and Prospects-89
Autographs-MS
04ITG Heroes/Prospects Toronto Expo '05-89
04ITG Heroes/Prospects Expo Heroes/Pros-89
05ITG Heroes/Prosp Toronto Expo Parallel -125
05Extreme Top Prospects Signature Edition-S14

05OHL Bell All-Star Classic-10
05Sudbury Wolves-1
05ITG Heroes and Prospects-125
Autographs-A-MST
Complete Jerseys-CJ-33
Complete Jerseys Gold-CJ-33
Complete Logos-CHL-10
He Shoots-He Scores Prizes-13
He Shoots-He Scores Prizes-56
Jerseys-GUJ-52
Jerseys Gold-GUJ-52
Emblems-GUE-52
Emblems Gold-GUE-52
Numbers-GUN-52
Numbers Gold-GUN-52
Nameplates-N-19
Nameplates Gold-N-19
06ITG Ultimate Memorabilia Autos Triple-6
06ITG Ultimate Memorabilia Autos Triple Gold-6
06ITG Ultimate Memorabilia Bloodlines-2
06ITG Ultimate Memorabilia Bloodlines Gold-2
06ITG Ultimate Memorabilia Bloodlines Autos-4
06ITG Ultimate Memorabilia Bloodlines Autos-7
06ITG Ultimate Memorabilia Bloodlines Autos Gold-4
06ITG Ultimate Memorabilia Bloodlines Autos Gold-7
06ITG Ultimate Memorabilia First Round Picks-22
06ITG Ultimate Memorabilia First Round Picks Gold-22
06ITG Ultimate Memorabilia Future Star-22
06ITG Ultimate Memorabilia Future Star Gold-22
06Sudbury Wolves-1
06ITG Heroes and Prospects-130
06ITG Heroes and Prospects-148
Autographs-AMS1
Autographs-AMS2
Complete CHL Logos-CHL08
Complete Jerseys-CJ14
Jerseys-GUJ40
Jerseys Gold-GUJ40
Emblems-GUE40
Emblems Gold-GUE40
Numbers-GUN40
Numbers Gold-GUN40
National Pride-NP08
National Pride-NP21
National Pride Gold-NP08
Quad Emblems-QE03
Quad Emblems Gold-QE03
Triple Memorabilia-TM08
Triple Memorabilia Gold-TM08
07ITG Going For Gold World Juniors-8
Autographs-8
Emblems-GUE8
Jerseys-GUJ8
Numbers-GUN8

Stabl, Lukas
99Czech Score Blue 2000-37
99Czech Score Red Ice 2000-37

Stacchi, Mike
95Roanoke Express-5

Stacey, Brian
917th Inn. Sketch OHL-373
93London Knights-18
95Slapshot-372
95Sault Ste. Marie Greyhounds-19
96Kansas City Blades-20

Stacey, Michael
01Drummondville Voltigeurs-13

Stacey, Travis
06Gatineau Olympiques-19

Stach, Lubomir
03Czech OFS Plus-42
04Belleville Bulls-12
06Czech HC Vsetin Postcards-9
06Czech OFS-193

Stachniak, Pat
93Quebec Pee-Wee Tournament-1142
03Odessa Jackalopes-17

Stackhouse, Ron
70Esso Power Players-106
710-Pee-Chee-83
71Sargent Promotions Stamps-64
71Toronto Sun-59
720-Pee-Chee-287
72Sargent Promotions Stamps-77
730-Pee-Chee-236
73Red Wings Team Issue-18
73Red Wings McCarthy Postcards-15
74NHL Action Stamps-228
740-Pee-Chee NHL-188
74Penguins Postcards-21
74Topps-188
750-Pee-Chee NHL-111
75Topps-111
760-Pee-Chee NHL-72
76Topps-72
770-Pee-Chee NHL-157
77Penguins Puck Bucks-3
77Topps-157
780-Pee-Chee-72
78Topps-72
790-Pee-Chee-154
79Topps-154
800-Pee-Chee-228
80Topps-228
810-Pee-Chee-266
810-Pee-Chee Stickers-188
820-Pee-Chee-275
82Post Cereal-15

Stadey, Ben
93Waterloo Black Hawks-22

Stadier, Uli
94German First League-236

Stadler, Roland
95Swiss HNL-NNO

Stadler, Walter
72Finnish Semic World Championship-95
72Swedish Semic World Championship-95

Stady, John
93Quebec Pee-Wee Tournament-178

Staeger, Julien
93Quebec Pee-Wee Tournament-1487

Stafford, Ben
01Trenton Titans-2-10
02Philadelphia Phantoms-16
03Philadelphia Phantoms-3
04Philadelphia Phantoms-22

Stafford, Drew
03North Dakota Fighting Sioux-12
04North Dakota Fighting Sioux-25
06Be A Player-218
06Beehive-109
Blue-109
Gold-109
Matte-109
Red Facsimile Signatures-109
Wood-109
06Flair Showcase-305
06Hot Prospects-105
Red Hot-105
White Hot-105
Hot Materials -HMDS
Hot Materials Red Hot-HMDS
Hot Materials White Hot-HMDS
060-Pee-Chee-578
060-Pee-Chee-638
Rainbow-578
Rainbow-638
06Rochester Americans-21
06SP Authentic-168
Limited-168
06SP Game Used-133
Gold-133
Rainbow-133
Autographs-133
Rookie Exclusives Autographs-REDS
06SPx-144
Spectrum-144
06The Cup-114
Autographed NHL Shields Duals-DASDS
Autographed NHL Shields Duals-DASSM
Autographed Rookie Masterpiece Pressplates-114
Enshrinements-EDS
Gold Rainbow Autographed Rookie Patches-114
Masterpiece Pressplates (Bee Hive)-109
Masterpiece Pressplates (Marquee Rookies)-578
Masterpiece Pressplates (SP Authentic Autographs)-168
Masterpiece Pressplates (SP Game Used)-133
Masterpiece Pressplates (SPx Autographs)-144
Masterpiece Pressplates (Sweet Beginnings)-109
Masterpiece Pressplates (Ultimate Collection Autographs)-131
Masterpiece Pressplates (Victory)-328
NHL Shields Duals-DSHLY
Rookies Black-114
Rookies Platinum-114
06UD Artifacts-234
06Ultimate Collection-131
Rookies Autographed NHL Shields-131
Rookies Autographed Patches-131
Ultimate Debut Threads Jerseys-DJ-DS
Ultimate Debut Threads Jerseys Autographs-DJ-DS
Ultimate Debut Threads Patches-DJ-DS
Ultimate Debut Threads Patches Autographs-DJ-DS
06Upper Deck-456
Exclusives Parallel-456
High Gloss Parallel-456
Masterpieces-456
Rookie Headliners-RH30
06Upper Deck Sweet Shot-109
Rookie Jerseys Autographs-109
Signature Shots/Saves-SSDS
06Upper Deck Victory-328
06AHL Top Prospects-39
06ITG Heroes and Prospects-170
Autographs-ADS
Complete AHL Logos-AHL13
Complete Jerseys-CJ16
Jerseys-GUJ63
Emblems-GUE63
Numbers-GUN63
Quad Emblems-QE11
Triple Memorabilia-TM09
Update Autographs-ADS
07Upper Deck Rookie Class -45
07Upper Deck Victory-36
Black-36
Gold-36

Stafford, Garrett
93Quebec Pee-Wee Tournament-1254
03Pacific AHL Prospects-22
Gold-22
04Cleveland Barons-22
04ITG Heroes and Prospects-44
Autographs-GS
Combos-5
Complete Emblems-26
Emblems-11
Emblems Gold-11
He Shoots-He Scores Prizes-27
Jersey Autographs-11
Jerseys-11
Jerseys Gold-11
Numbers-11
Numbers Gold-11
04ITG Heroes/Prospects Toronto Expo '05-44
04ITG Heroes/Prospects Expo Heroes/Pros-44
05Cleveland Barons-21

Stagg, Brian
917th Inn. Sketch OHL-232

Stagma, Borek
01Czech OFS-272

Stahan, Butch
51Laval Dairy QSHL-105
52St. Lawrence Sales-72

Stahl, Christer
72Swedish Stickers-271
74Swedish Stickers-151

Stahl, Craig
95Tri-City Americans-24
99Austin Ice Bats-3
00Columbus Cottonmouths-20
01Greensboro Generals-17
02New Mexico Scorpions-16
03New Mexico Scorpions-19
04Columbus Cottonmouths-15

Stahl, Mikael
86Swedish Panini Stickers-216
87Swedish Panini Stickers-206
89Swedish Semic Elitserien Stickers-185
90Swedish Semic Elitserien Stickers-20

Stahl, Paul
64Swedish Coralli ISHockey-164
65Swedish Coralli ISHockey-164
67Swedish Hockey-127

Stahlhammer, Tomi
06Cedar Rapids RoughRiders-15

Staios, Steve
907th Inn. Sketch OHL-271
917th Inn. Sketch OHL-219
917th Inn. Sketch Memorial Cup-107
91Arena Draft Picks-20
91Arena Draft Picks French-20
91Arena Draft Picks Autographs-20
91Arena Draft Picks Autographs French-20
91Classic-24
91Star Pics-51
91Ultimate Draft-22
91Ultimate Draft French-22
91Classic Four-Sport *-24
Autographs-24A
92Sudbury Wolves-27
93Peoria Rivermen-26
94Classic Pro Prospects-149
96Leaf-223
Press Proofs-223
96Pinnacle-231
Artist's Proofs-231
Foil-231
Premium Stock-231
Rink Collection-231
96Upper Deck-218
97Be A Player-161
Autographs-161
Autographs Die-Cuts-161
Autographs Prismatic Die-Cuts-161
99Paramount-15
Copper-15
Emerald-15
Gold-15
Holographic Emerald-15
Holographic Gold-15
Holographic Silver-15
Ice Blue-15
Premiere Date-15
Red-15
Silver-15
00Topps Heritage-199
00Upper Deck-241
Exclusives Tier 1-241
Exclusives Tier 2-241
01Upper Deck Victory-18
Gold-18
02NHL Power Play Stickers-45
02Oilers Postcards-10
02Pacific Complete-451
Red-451
03ITG Action-204
03Oilers Postcards-19
03Pacific Complete-305
Red-305
05Be A Player Signatures-SO
05Be A Player Signatures Gold-SO
05Panini Stickers-281
06Gatorade-29
060-Pee-Chee-205
Rainbow-205
06Upper Deck-326
Exclusives Parallel-326
High Gloss Parallel-326
Masterpieces-326

Stait, Bill
92Saskatchewan JHL-54

Stajan, Matt
00Belleville Bulls-11
01Belleville Bulls-22
02SPx Rookie Redemption-R212
02Belleville Bulls-17
02Belleville Bulls-26
03BAP Memorabilia-192
Emerald-192
Gold-192
Ruby-192
Sapphire-192
03BAP Ultimate Memorabilia Autographs-126
Gold-126
03BAP Ultimate Mem Auto Jerseys-126
03BAP Ultimate Mem Auto Emblems-126
03BAP Ultimate Mem Auto Numbers-126
03BAP Ultimate Mem Franch Present Future-28
03BAP Ultimate Mem Rookie Jersey Emblems-18
03BAP Ultimate Mem Rookie Jsy Emblem Gold-18
03BAP Ultimate Mem Rookie Jersey Numbers-18
03BAP Ultimate Mem Rookie Jsy Number Gold-18
03Beehive-234
Gold-234
Silver-234
03Black Diamond-187
Black-187
Green-187
Red-187
03Bowman-147
Gold-147
Premier Performance-PP-MST0
Premier Performance Patches-PP-MST0
Signs of the Future-SOF-MS
03Bowman Chrome-147
Refractors-147
Gold Refractors-147
Xfractors-147
03Crown Royale-135
Red-135
Retail-135
Royal Portraits-10
03eTopps-43
03ITG Action-503
03ITG Toronto Spring Expo Class of 2004-4
03ITG Used Signature Series-149
Autographs Gold-149
03McDonald's Pacific-49
030-Pee-Chee-317
03OPC Blue-317
03OPC Gold-317
03OPC Red-317
03Pacific-323
Blue-323
Red-323
03Pacific Calder-174
03Pacific Complete-514
Red-514
03Pacific Exhibit-138
Blue Backs-138
Yellow Backs-138
03Pacific Heads-Up-134
Hobby LTD-134
Retail LTD-134
Prime Prospects-19
Prime Prospects LTD-19
03Pacific Invincible-124
Blue-124
Red-124
Retail-124
03Pacific Luxury Suite-99
Gold-99
03Pacific Prism-94
Blue-94
Gold-94
Red-94
03Pacific Quest for the Cup-136
Calder Contenders-19
03Pacific Supreme-139
03Pacific Supreme-139A
Blue-139
Red-139
Retail-139
03Parkhurst Toronto Expo Rookie Preview-PRP-13
03Parkhurst Original Six Toronto-9
03Parkhurst Rookie-198
Calder Candidates-CMC-12
Calder Candidate Autographs-CMC-MS
Calder Candidates Gold-CMC-12
Rookie Emblems-RE-44
Rookie Emblem Autographs-RE-MST
Rookie Emblems Gold-RE-44
Rookie Jerseys-RJ-44
Rookie Jersey Autographs-RJ-MST
Rookie Jerseys Gold-RJ-44
Rookie Numbers-RN-44
Rookie Number Autographs-RN-MST
Rookie Numbers Gold-RN-44
Teammates Gold-RT3
Teammates-RT3
03Private Stock Reserve-139
Blue-139
Red-139
Retail-139
Class Act-12
03SP Authentic-157
Limited-157
Signed Patches-MS
03SP Game Used-81
Gold-81
03SPx-209
Radiance-209
Spectrum-209
03Titanium-214
Patches-214
Right on Target-15
03Topps-317
Blue-317
Gold-317
Red-317
03Topps C55-142
Minis-142
Minis American Back-142
Minis American Back Red-142
Minis Bazooka Back-142
Minis Brooklyn Back-142
Minis Hat Trick Back-142
Minis O Canada Back-142
Minis O Canada Back Red-142
Minis Stanley Cup Back-142
03Topps Pristine-137
03Topps Pristine-138
03Topps Pristine-139
Gold Refractor Die Cuts-137
Gold Refractor Die Cuts-138
Gold Refractor Die Cuts-139
Refractors-137
Refractors-138
Refractors-139
Mini-PM-MS0
Press Plates Black-137
Press Plates Black-138
Press Plates Black-139
Press Plates Cyan-137
Press Plates Cyan-138
Press Plates Cyan-139
Press Plates Magenta-137
Press Plates Magenta-138
Press Plates Magenta-139
Press Plates Yellow-137
Press Plates Yellow-138
Press Plates Yellow-139
03Topps Traded Future Phenoms-FP-MS
03UD Honor Roll-169
03UD Premier Collection-107
03Upper Deck-242
Canadian Exclusives-242
HG-242
03Upper Deck Classic Portraits-166
03Upper Deck Ice-101
Glass Parallel-101
03Upper Deck MVP-407
Gold Script-407
Silver Script-407
Canadian Exclusives-407
03Upper Deck Rookie Update-175
YoungStars-YS7
YoungStars-YS7A
03Upper Deck Trilogy-170
Limited-170
03Upper Deck Victory-175
Bronze-175
Gold-175
Silver-175
04Pacific-298
Blue-298
Red-298
04Pacific NHL All-Star FANtasy-10
04Pacific NHL All-Star FANtasy Gold-10
04Pacific Toronto Spring Expo-8
Gold-8
04SP Authentic Sign of the Times-ST-MJ
04SP Authentic Sign of the Times-FS-NED
04Upper Deck YoungStars-YS-MS
04AHL Top Prospects-52
05Be A Player Quad Signatures-MAPL
05Be A Player Quad Signatures-RBSS
05Be A Player Signatures-MS
05Be A Player Signatures Gold-MS
05Beehive Matted Materials-MMST
05Panini Stickers-174
05Parkhurst-461
Facsimile Auto Parallel-461
05SP Authentic-95
Limited-95
Scripts to Success-SSMS
Sign of the Times-MS
Sign of the Times Duals-DAS
Sign of the Times Triples-TSAS
Sign of the Times Quads-QSSOS
05SP Game Used Authentic Fabrics-AF-ST
05SP Game Used Authentic Fabrics Autos-AAF-ST
05SP Game Used Authentic Fabrics Dual-SS
05SP Game Used Authentic Fabric Dual Auto-SS
05SP Game Used Authentic Fabrics Gold-AF-ST
05SP Game Used Authentic Fabrics Quad-SNSA
05SP Game Used Authentic Patches Quad -SNSA
05SP Game Used Authentic Patches-AP-ST
05SP Game Used Authentic Patch Autos-AAP-ST
05SP Game Used Authentic Patches Dual-SS
05SP Game Used Authentic Patch Dual Autos-SS
05SP Game Used Auto Draft-AD-MS
05SP Game Used Awesome Authentics-AA-MS
05SP Game Used Awesome Authentics Gold-DA-MS
05SP Game Used Statscriptions-ST-MS
05SPx Winning Combos-WC-SW
05SPx Winning Combos Autographs-AWC-SA
05SPx Winning Combos Gold-WC-SW
05SPx Winning Combos Spectrum-WC-SW
05SPx Winning Materials-WM-ST
05SPx Winning Materials Gold-WM-ST
05SPx Winning Materials Spectrum-WM-ST
05The Cup Honorable Numbers-HNST
05The Cup Scripted Swatches-SSST
05UD Artifacts Auto Facts-AF-ST
05UD Artifacts Auto Facts Blue-AF-ST
05UD Artifacts Auto Facts Copper-AF-ST
05UD Artifacts Auto Facts Pewter-AF-ST
05UD Artifacts Auto Facts Silver-AF-ST
05UD Artifacts Remarkable Artifacts-RA-MS
05UD Artifacts Remarkable Artifacts Dual-RA-MS
05UD Artifacts Treasured Patches-TP-ST
05UD Artifacts Treasured Patch Autos-TP-ST
05UD Artifacts Treasured Patches Dual-TPD-ST
05UD Artifacts Treasured Patch Dual Autos-TPD-ST
05UD Artifacts Treasured Patches Pewter-TP-ST
05UD Artifacts Treasured Patches Silver-TP-ST
05UD Artifacts Treasured Swatches-TS-ST
05UD Artifacts Treasured Swatch Autos-TS-ST
05UD Artifacts Treasured Swatches Blue-TS-ST
05UD Artifacts Treasured Swatches Copper-TS-ST
05UD Artifacts Treasured Swatches Dual-TSD-ST
05UD Artifacts Treasured Swatch Dual Auto-TSD-ST
05UD Artifacts Treasured Swatch Dual Blue-TSD-ST
05UD Artifact Treasure Swatch Dual Copper-TSD-ST
05UD Artifact Treasure Swatch Dual Maroon-TSD-ST
05UD Artifact Treasure Swatch Dual Pewter-TSD-ST
05UD Artifact TreasuredSwatch Dual Silver-TSD-ST
05UD Artifacts Treasured Swatches Maroon-TS-ST
05UD Artifacts Treasured Swatches Pewter-TS-ST
05UD Artifacts Treasured Swatches Silver-TS-ST
05UD Toronto Fall Expo Priority Signings-PS-ST
05Ultimate Collection Endorsed Emblems-EEMS
05Ultra-185
Gold-185
Fresh Ink-FI-MS
Fresh Ink Blue-FI-MS
Ice-185
05Upper Deck-178
HG Glossy-178
Jerseys-J-MST
Majestic Materials-MMST
Notable Numbers-N-MJ
Ice Glacial Graphs-GGMS
Ice Glacial Graphs Labels-GGMS
05Upper Deck MVP-363
Gold-363
Platinum-363
05Upper Deck Trilogy Scripts-SFS-MS
05Upper Deck Toronto Fall Expo-178
06Be A Player-32
Autographs-32
Signatures-SJ
Signatures 10-35
Signatures Duals-DWS
Signatures Trios-TTWS
Portraits Signature Portraits-SPSJ
06Black Diamond Jerseys-JST
06Black Diamond Jerseys Black-JST
06Black Diamond Jerseys Gold-JST
06Black Diamond Jerseys Ruby-JST
06Flair Showcase Stitches-SSSM
06Fleer Fabricology-FST
06Gatorade-74
060-Pee-Chee-461
Rainbow-461
06SP Game Used Authentic Fabrics-AFSJ
06SP Game Used Authentic Fabrics Parallel-AFSJ
06SP Game Used Authentic Fabrics Patches-AFSJ
06UD Artifacts Tundra Tandems-TTAM
06UD Artifacts Tundra Tandems Black-TTAM
06UD Artifacts Tundra Tandems Blue-TTAM
06UD Artifacts Tundra Tandems Gold-TTAM
06UD Artifacts Tundra Tandems Platinum-TTAM
06UD Artifacts Tundra Tandems Red-TTAM
06UD Artifacts Tundra Tandems Dual Patches Red-TTAM
06Upper Deck-434
Exclusives Parallel-434
High Gloss Parallel-434
Game Jerseys-JSM
Game Patches-PST
Masterpieces-434
Signatures-SST
06Upper Deck MVP-278
Gold Script-278
Super Script-278
06Upper Deck Victory Next In Line-NL44

Stajan, Thomas
06Brampton Battalion-13
06Owen Sound Attack-12

Stajduhar, Nick
907th Inn. Sketch OHL-144
917th Inn. Sketch OHL-380
93Donruss Team Canada-19
93Parkhurst-507
Emerald Ice-507
93Pinnacle-463
Canadian-463
93Upper Deck-543
93London Knights-19
93London Knights-25
93Classic-28
93Classic Four-Sport *-199
Gold-199
94Cape Breton Oilers-18
94Classic-83
Gold-83
96Upper Deck-194
96Pensacola Ice Pilots-19
97Pensacola Ice Pilots-20
98Pensacola Ice Pilots-2
99UHL All-Stars East-3T

Stalberg, Lars
67Swedish Hockey-93

Stalnacke, Erik
84Swedish Semic Elitserien-182
85Swedish Panini Stickers-170
86Swedish Panini Stickers-177
87Swedish Panini Stickers-177

Stals, Juris
03Hartford Wolf Pack-22

Stambaugh, Matt
93Quebec Pee-Wee Tournament-152

Stambert, Orvar
83Swedish Semic Elitserien-80
84Swedish Semic Elitserien-80
85Swedish Panini Stickers-71
86Swedish Panini Stickers-60
87Swedish Panini Stickers-70
89Swedish Semic Elitserien Stickers-54
90Swedish Semic Elitserien Stickers-279
91Swedish Semic Elitserien Stickers-60

Stamkos, Steve
06Sarnia Sting-1
06ITG Heroes and Prospects-80
Autographs-ASS

Stamler, Lorne
78Maple Leafs Postcards-20
780-Pee-Chee-301
79Jets Postcards-24
81Indianapolis Checkers-18
82Indianapolis Checkers-19

Stamoulis, Dinos
00Sioux Falls Stampede-17

Stamp, Eric
917th Inn. Sketch OHL-195

Stana, Rastislav
00Richmond Renegades-18
02Slovakian Kvarteto-5
03BAP Memorabilia-206
03BAP Ultimate Mem Rookie Jersey Emblems-40
03BAP Ultimate Mem Rookie Jsy Emblem Gold-40
03BAP Ultimate Mem Rookie Jersey Numbers-40
03BAP Ultimate Mem Rookie Jsy Number Gold-40
03Beehive-246
Gold-246
Silver-246
03ITG Used Signature Series-166
Gold-166
03ITG VIP Rookie Debut-57
03Pacific Calder-140
Silver-140
03Pacific Complete-484
Red-484
03Pacific Luxury Suite-80
Gold-80
03Pacific Quest for the Cup-140
03Parkhurst Toronto Expo Rookie Preview-PRP-12
03Parkhurst Rookie-144
Rookie Emblems-RE-39
Rookie Emblems Gold-RE-39
Rookie Jerseys-RJ-39
Rookie Jerseys Gold-RJ-39
Rookie Numbers-RN-39
Rookie Numbers Gold-RN-39
03SP Authentic-128
Limited-128
03Titanium-140
Hobby Jersey Number Parallels-140
Retail-140
Retail Jersey Number Parallels-140
03Topps Traded-TT145
Blue-TT145
Gold-TT145
Red-TT145
03UD Honor Roll-158
03Upper Deck-464
Canadian Exclusives-464
HG-464
UD Exclusives-464
03Upper Deck Ice-108
Glass Parallel-108
03Upper Deck Rookie Update-146
03Pacific AHL Prospects Crease Lightning-5
04Swedish Elitset-265
Gold-265
Masks-7
04Swedish Pure Skills-81
Parallel-81
04ITG Heroes and Prospects-37
Autographs-U-RS
He Shoots-He Scores Prizes-34
Net Prospects-9
Net Prospects Gold-9
04ITG Heroes/Prospects Toronto Expo '05-37
04ITG Heroes/Prospects Expo Heroes/Pros-37
05Upper Deck Victory-199
Black-199
Gold-199
Silver-199
05Swedish SHL Elitset-267
Catchers-11
Catchers Gold-11
Gold-267
Stoppers-11
06Swedish SHL Elitset-225

Stancok, Robert
03UK Nottingham Panthers-6

Standbrook, Grant
05Maine Black Bears-31

Standish, Bobby
91Air Canada SJHL-D3

Standish, Marty
97Portland Winter Hawks-20
99Missouri River Otters-20
99Missouri River Otters Sheet-18
99Bowman CHL-114
Gold-114
OPC International-114
03Oklahoma City Blazers-20

Standling, David
94UK Humberside Hawks-NNO

Stanek, Ales
02Czech OFS Plus-144

Stanek, Ed
93Waterloo Black Hawks-23

Stanek, Ondrej
03Czech OFS Plus-188

Stanfield, Fred
64Beehive Group III Photos-55A
64Beehive Group III Photos-55B
64Coca-Cola Caps-23
65Coca-Cola-24
65Topps-63
66Topps-56
67Topps-36
680-Pee-Chee-10
68Shirriff Coins-9
68Topps-10
690-Pee-Chee-32
69Topps-32
70Bruins Postcards-14
70Bruins Team Issue-18
70Dad's Cookies-124
70Esso Power Players-66
700-Pee-Chee-5
Deckle-7
70Sargent Promotions Stamps-12
70Topps-5
71Bruins Postcards-12
710-Pee-Chee-7
71Sargent Promotions Stamps-1
71Topps-7
71Toronto Sun-19
720-Pee-Chee-150
72Sargent Promotions Stamps-15
72Topps-135
73North Stars Postcards-19
74NHL Action Stamps-132
74NHL Action Stamps Update-5
740-Pee-Chee NHL-31
74Topps-31
750-Pee-Chee NHL-332
75Sabres Linnett-12
760-Pee-Chee NHL-58
76Topps-58
770-Pee-Chee NHL-161
77Topps-161
780-Pee-Chee-352
91Ultimate Original Six-54
French-54
94Parkhurst Tall Boys-37
95Parkhurst '66-67-25
Coins-25
98Bruins Alumni-17
Autographs-17

Stanfield, Jim
72Sargent Promotions Stamps-86

Stanfield, Rob
95Slapshot-134
96Kitchener Rangers-24
98Huntington Blizzard-14
01Atlantic City Boardwalk Bullies-19

Stangby, Shane
907th Inn. Sketch WHL-252
91Air Canada SJHL-E47

Stangle, Frank
37V356 Worldwide Gum-110

Staniforth, Kent
907th Inn. Sketch WHL-144
917th Inn. Sketch WHL-272

Staniowski, Ed
760-Pee-Chee NHL-104
76Topps-104
770-Pee-Chee NHL-54
77Topps-54
78Blues Postcards-21
790-Pee-Chee-327
800-Pee-Chee-328
81Jets Postcards-19
82Jets Postcards-23
820-Pee-Chee-393
820-Pee-Chee Stickers-210
82Post Cereal-21
82Topps Stickers-210
83NHL Key Tags-139

Stanislav, Simo
93Quebec Pee-Wee Tournament-1711

Stankiewicz, Brian
93Swedish Semic World Champ Stickers-269
94Finnish Jaa Kiekko-232

Stankovic, Peter
94German First League-163

Stanley, Allan
44Beehive Group II Photos-365
44Beehive Group II Photos-453A
44Beehive Group II Photos-453B
51Parkhurst-94
52Parkhurst-21
53Parkhurst-64
54Topps-41
57Topps-15
58Parkhurst-23
59Parkhurst-44
60Parkhurst-16
60Shirriff Coins-6
60York Photos-33
61Parkhurst-16
61Shirriff/Salada Coins-42
61York Yellow Backs-9
62Parkhurst-9
62Shirriff Coins-2
63Chex Photos-50
63Maple Leafs Team Issue-22
63Parkhurst-1
63Parkhurst-61
63Toronto Star-35
63York White Backs-14
64Beehive Group III Photos-185
64Coca-Cola Caps-107
64Topps-104
64Toronto Star-44
65Coca-Cola-106
65Maple Leafs White Border-17
66Topps-16
66Topps-128
66Topps USA Test-16
67Topps-13
67York Action Octagons-1
67York Action Octagons-26
680-Pee-Chee-183
Puck Stickers-16
68Shirriff Coins-125
69Maple Leafs White Border Glossy-34
83Hall of Fame-238
83Hall of Fame Postcards-G14
85Hall of Fame-238
91Ultimate Original Six-44
91Ultimate Original Six-75
French-44
French-75
92Parkhurst Parkie Reprints-PR11
94Parkhurst Missing Link-20
94Parkhurst Tall Boys-115
95Parkhurst '66-67-110
Coins-110
02Maple Leafs Platinum Collection-68
02Parkhurst Reprints-166
02Parkhurst Reprints-184
02Parkhurst Reprints-229
02Parkhurst Reprints-250
02Parkhurst Reprints-263
02Parkhurst Reprints-274
02Parkhurst Reprints-283
02Parkhurst Reprints-293
03Parkhurst Original Six Boston-42
03Parkhurst Orig Six New York Autos-14
04ITG Franchises Canadian Autographs-AS2
04ITG Franchises US East-396
04ITG Ultimate Memorabilia-60
04ITG Ultimate Memorabilia-94
Gold-60
Gold-94
05Canada Post-33
05Canada Post Autographs-33
06Parkhurst-156
06Parkhurst-193
Autographs-156
Autographs-193
07Maple Leafs 1967 Commemorative-25

Stanley, Barney
23V128-1 Paulin's Candy-30
83Hall of Fame Postcards-A13

Stanley, Chris
99Bowman CHL-131
Gold-131
OPC International-131
04Las Vegas Wranglers-7
05Las Vegas Wranglers-21

Stanley, Daryl
81Saskatoon Blades-2
83Springfield Indians-23
86Flyers Postcards-25
87Canucks Shell Oil-20
89Canucks Mohawk-21

Stanley, Graham
89ProCards AHL-18
90ProCards AHL/IHL-353

Stanley, Joe
84Nanaimo Clippers-19

Stanley, Lord
83Hall of Fame-13
83Hall of Fame Postcards-A14
85Hall of Fame-13
92Hall of Fame Legends-18
01SP Game Used Signs of Tradition-LCLS
01Upper Deck Legendary Cut Signatures-LCLS
04ITG Ultimate Memorabilia-71
Gold-71
Holy Grail-1
Paper Cuts-1
04Ultimate Collection-55
04Upper Deck-207
Canadian Exclusives-207
HG Glossy Gold-207
HG Glossy Silver-207
05ITG Ultimate Memorabilia Level 1-65
05ITG Ultimate Memorabilia Level 2-65
05ITG Ultimate Memorabilia Level 3-65
05ITG Ultimate Memorabilia Level 4-65
05ITG Ultimate Memorabilia Level 5-65
05ITG Ultimate Mem The Holy Grail Auto-1
06ITG Ultimate Memorabilia-91
Artist Proof-91

Stanley, Russell
83Hall of Fame-12
85Hall of Fame-12

Stanowski, Wally
34Beehive Group I Photos-348
390-Pee-Chee V301-1-11
400-Pee-Chee V301-2-103
44Beehive Group II Photos-366
44Beehive Group II Photos-454
45Quaker Oats Photos-50A
45Quaker Oats Photos-50B

Stansfield, Sean
88Sudbury Wolves-16

Stansik, Chris
04Green Bay Gamblers-18
05Lincoln Stars Update Traded-2T
06Lincoln Stars-6
06Lincoln Stars Traded-9T
06Lincoln Stars Upper DeckÂ Signature Series -25

Stantien, Roman
94Czech APS Extraliga-242
95Czech APS Extraliga-22
96Czech APS Extraliga-229
97Czech APS Extraliga-50
98Czech DS-86
98Czech OFS-112
99Czech DS-137
99Czech OFS-64
00Czech OFS-336
01Czech OFS All Stars-27
01Slovakian Kvarteto-7D
01Slovakian Kvarteto-8A
02Czech OFS Plus-77
03Czech OFS Plus-34
03Czech OFS Plus Insert H-H12
04Czech OFS-260
05Czech HC Vsetin-12
06Czech HC Vsetin Postcards-10
06Czech OFS-190
Team Cards-12

Stanton, Paul
89ProCards IHL-156
90OPC Premier-110
90Pro Set-633
90Score Rookie/Traded-27T
90Upper Deck-404
French-404
91Bowman-91
910-Pee-Chee-339
91Panini Stickers-274
91Penguins Coke/Elby's-22
91Penguins Foodland-13
91Pro Set-457
French-457
91Score American-366
91Score Canadian Bilingual-406
91Score Canadian English-406
91Stadium Club-380
91Topps-339
91Upper Deck-203
French-203
92Bowman-284
920-Pee-Chee-361
92Penguins Coke/Clark-19
92Penguins Foodland-13
92Pinnacle-308
French-308
92Score-135
Canadian-135
92Stadium Club-52
92Topps-460
Gold-460G
92Ultra-381
92Upper Deck-100
93OPC Premier-5
Gold-5
93Parkhurst-288
Emerald Ice-288
93Pinnacle-330
Canadian-330
93Score-321
93Score-510
Gold-510
Canadian-321
Canadian-510
Canadian Gold-510
93Stadium Club-52
Members Only Master Set-52
OPC-52
First Day Issue-52
First Day Issue OPC-52
93Topps/OPC Premier-5
Gold-5
95German DEL-267
96German DEL-161
98German DEL-229
99German Adler Mannheim Eagles Postcards-2
99German DEL-3
00German DEL-197
Star Attractions-S8
01German Upper Deck Skilled Stars-SS11
02German DEL City Press-85
All-Stars-AS15
03German DEL-104
All-Stars-AS5

Stanton, Ryan
06Moose Jaw Warriors-3

Staples, Jeff
92Brandon Wheat Kings-22
93Brandon Wheat Kings-3
94Brandon Wheat Kings-21
95Slapshot Memorial Cup-28
98Milwaukee Admirals-23
98Milwaukee Admirals Postcards-3

Stapleton, Mike
86Blackhawks Coke-20
87Blackhawks Coke-21
88ProCards IHL-115
90ProCards AHL/IHL-402
91Blackhawks Coke-24
92Penguins Coke/Clark-20
93Penguins Foodland-21
93Score-638
Gold-638
Canadian-638
Canadian Gold-638
94Leaf-147
94Pinnacle-228
Artist's Proofs-228
Rink Collection-228
95Jets Team Issue-23
95Playoff One on One-39
96Be A Player-92
Autographs-92
Autographs Silver-92
96Coyotes Coca-Cola-29
97Coyotes Face-Off Luncheon -21
97Pacific Invincible NHL Regime-155
99Pacific-327
Copper-327
Emerald Green-327
Gold-327
Ice Blue-327
Premiere Date-327
Red-327
00Pacific-22
Copper-22
Gold-22
Ice Blue-22
Premiere Date-22
02Finnish Cardset-123

02Swedish SHL-194
Parallel-194
Stapleton, Pat
44Beehive Group II Photos-68A
44Beehive Group II Photos-68B
61Shirriff/Salada Coins-13
61Topps-18
62Topps-8
64Beehive Group III Photos-26
64Beehive Group III Photos-56
65Topps-120
66Topps-57
66Topps-129
66Topps USA Test-57
67Topps-61
68Blackhawks Team Issue-7
68O-Pee-Chee-15
68Shirriff Coins-18
68Topps-15
69O-Pee-Chee-69
Four-in-One-17
69Topps-69
70Colgate Stamps-77
70Dad's Cookies-125
70Esso Power Players-119
70O-Pee-Chee-17
70Sargent Promotions Stamps-44
70Topps-17
71Letraset Action Replays-13
71O-Pee-Chee-25
71O-Pee-Chee-258
71Sargent Promotions Stamps-45
71Topps-25
71Toronto Sun-81
72O-Pee-Chee-4
72O-Pee-Chee-249
Team Canada-27
72Sargent Promotions Stamps-69
72Topps-70
72Topps-129
73Mac's Milk-27
73O-Pee-Chee WHA Posters-4
74O-Pee-Chee WHA-35
74Team Canada L'Equipe WHA-21
91Future Trends Canada '72-9
91Future Trends Canada '72 French-9
91Kraft-68
91Kraft-69
95Parkhurst '66-67-38
Coins-38
03Parkhurst Original Six Chicago-41
04ITG Franchises US West-164
Autographs-A-PS
04UD Legendary Signatures-60
Autographs-PS
Summit Stars-CDN19
Summit Stars Autographs-CDN-PS
Stapleton, Tim
04Minnesota-Duluth Bulldogs-23
06Finnish Cardset-240
Starck, Lars
67Swedish Hockey-73
69Swedish Hockey-104
71Swedish Hockey-357
Starenky, Dave
04Gatineau Olympiques-20
Starikov, Sergei
81Swedish Semic Hockey VM Stickers-43
82Swedish Semic VM Stickers-59
83Swedish Semic VM Stickers-59
84Russian National Team-18
87Russian National Team-17
89Devils Caretta-22
90ProCards AHL/IHL-557
91ProCards-327
92San Diego Gulls-24
Stark, Jay
86Portland Winter Hawks-21
Stark, Ralf
02German DEL City Press-295
Starke, Joe
35Diamond Matchbooks Tan 1-64
Starke, Matthias
94German First League-437
Starke, Robert
00Missouri River Otters-16
Starke, Sean
04Kalamazoo Wings-20
06Quad City Mallards-14
Starkhov, Juri
94German First League-100
Starkov, Kirill
05Swedish SHL Elitset-179
Gold-179
06Swedish SHL Elitset-34
Starkov, Oleg
98Danish Hockey League-10
99Danish Hockey League-12
Starling, Chad
98Kamloops Blazers-23
99Kamloops Blazers-22
00Sudbury Wolves-13
01Peoria Rivermen-5
03Peoria Rivermen-5
04Peoria Rivermen-1
Starnyski, Aaron
94Sudbury Wolves-22
Starosta, Tomas
03Czech OFS Plus All-Star Game-H18
04Czech OFS Czech/Slovak-43
Starostenko, Dmitri
92Russian Stars Red Ace-31
92Russian Stars Red Ace-25
94Binghamton Rangers-21
94Classic Pro Prospects-118
95Binghamton Rangers-23
99Russian Stars Postcards-23
00Russian Hockey League-269
01Russian Dynamo Moscow-4
01Russian Dynamo Moscow Mentos-7
01Russian Legions-2
03Russian Hockey League-48
Starr, Aaron
00Saskatoon Blades-22
01OCN Blizzard-9
02OCN Blizzard-8
03OCN Blizzard-19
Starr, Harold
35Diamond Matchbooks Tan 2-59
35Diamond Matchbooks Tan 3-54
05The Cup Legendary Cuts-LCHS
Starrett, Mike
93Quebec Pee-Wee Tournament-1143
Starshinov, Vyatcheslav
69Russian National Team Postcards-8
69Swedish Hockey-16
70Finnish Jaakiekko-17
70Russian National Team Postcards-8
70Swedish Hockey-331
70Swedish Masterserien-35
70Swedish Masterserien-65
70Swedish Masterserien-72
70Swedish Masterserien-121
70Swedish Masterserien-129
70Swedish Masterserien-136
71Finnish Suomi Stickers-16
71Swedish Hockey-40
72Finnish Panda Toronto-61
72Finnish Semic World Championship-8
72Swedish Semic World Championship-8
74Swedish Semic World Champ Stickers-44
91Future Trends Canada '72-38
Startup, James
91Saskatoon Blades-23
917th Inn. Sketch WHL-106
Stary, Jan
06Czech HC Pardubice Postcards-23
06Czech OFS-313
Stas, Sergei
94Erie Panthers-7
95Fort Wayne Komets-18
98German DEL-252
99German DEL-306
00German DEL-21
01German Upper Deck-164
02German DEL City Press-233
03German DEL-58
Stasche, Joachim
74Finnish Jenkki-102
04German Berlin Eisbaren 50th Anniv-6
Stasiuk, Jeremy
93Spokane Chiefs-26
94Spokane Chiefs-17
95Dayton Bombers-27
Stasiuk, Vic
44Beehive Group II Photos-69
44Beehive Group II Photos-212A
44Beehive Group II Photos-212B
44Beehive Group II Photos-212C
51Parkhurst-62
52Parkhurst-90
53Parkhurst-39
55Bruins Photos-16
57Bruins Photos-19
57Topps-11
58Bruins Photos-14
58Topps-9
59Topps-14
60Shirriff Coins-103
60Topps-66
61Parkhurst-32
61Shirriff/Salada Coins-63
62Parkhurst-22
62York Iron-On Transfers-30B
63Parkhurst-58
70Flyers Postcards-11
93Parkhurst Parkie Reprints-PR64
94Parkhurst Missing Link-9
94Parkhurst Missing Link-169
03BAP Ultimate Mem Linemates Autos-9
03BAP Ultimate Mem Linemates Autos-10
Stastny, Anton
80Nordiques Postcards-25
80Pepsi-Cola Caps-76
81Nordiques Postcards-16
81O-Pee-Chee-282
81O-Pee-Chee Stickers-70
82Nordiques Postcards-20
82O-Pee-Chee-294
82O-Pee-Chee Stickers-24
82Topps Stickers-24
83NHL Key Tags-109
83Nordiques Postcards-27
83O-Pee-Chee-302
83O-Pee-Chee Stickers-252
83Puffy Stickers-14
83Topps Stickers-252
83Vachon-75
84Nordiques Postcards-25
84O-Pee-Chee-291
84O-Pee-Chee Stickers-178
85Nordiques General Foods-25
85Nordiques McDonald's-21
85Nordiques Placemats-6
85Nordiques Provigo-24
85Nordiques Team Issue-24
85O-Pee-Chee-78
85O-Pee-Chee Stickers-147
85Topps-78
86Kraft Drawings-67
86Nordiques General Foods-25
86Nordiques McDonald's-24
86Nordiques Team Issue-24
86Nordiques Yum-Yum-9
86O-Pee-Chee-125
86O-Pee-Chee Stickers-27
86Topps-125
87Nordiques General Foods-28
87Nordiques Team Issue-15
87Nordiques Yum-Yum-9
87O-Pee-Chee-185
87O-Pee-Chee Stickers-228
87Panini Stickers-166
87Topps-185
88Nordiques General Foods-33
88Nordiques Team Issue-29
88O-Pee-Chee-98
88O-Pee-Chee Stickers-194
88Panini Stickers-357
88Topps-98
94Finnish Jaa Kiekko-202
02UD Foundations-76
04ITG Franchises Canadian-83
06ITG Ultimate Memorabilia Stick Rack-18
06ITG Ultimate Memorabilia Stick Rack Gold-18
06Parkhurst-120
Autographs-120
Autographs Dual-DAST1
06SP Authentic Sign of the Times Quads-ST4SSSS
Stastny, Bohuslav
71Finnish Suomi Stickers-38
71Swedish Hockey-58
72Finnish Jaakiekko-19
72Finnish Hellas-91
72Finnish Panda Toronto-94
72Finnish Semic World Championship-32
72Swedish Semic World Championship-32
73Finnish Jaakiekko-61
74Finnish Jenkki-82
74Finnish Typotor-120
74Swedish Stickers-16
74Swedish Semic World Champ Stickers-64
Stastny, Marian
79Panini Stickers-90
81Nordiques Postcards-18
82McDonald's Stickers-10
82Nordiques Postcards-21
82O-Pee-Chee-295
82O-Pee-Chee Stickers-20
82Post Cereal-16
82Topps Stickers-20
83NHL Key Tags-108
83Nordiques Postcards-28
83O-Pee-Chee-303
83O-Pee-Chee Stickers-168
83O-Pee-Chee Stickers-251
83Puffy Stickers-16
83Topps Stickers-168
83Topps Stickers-251
83Vachon-76
84Nordiques Postcards-26
84O-Pee-Chee-292
84O-Pee-Chee Stickers-177
85Maple Leafs Postcards-27
86O-Pee-Chee Stickers-144
04ITG Franchises Canadian-74
Autographs-MST
06ITG Ultimate Memorabilia Stick Rack-18
06ITG Ultimate Memorabilia Stick Rack Gold-18
06Parkhurst-121
Autographs-121
Autographs Dual-DAST2
Stastny, Martin
95Swiss HNL-505
Stastny, Michal
99Missouri River Otters-21
99Missouri River Otters Sheet-19
01Memphis RiverKings-6
Stastny, Paul
06Avalanche Team Postcards-16
06Be A Player-219
Profiles-PP12
Profiles Autographs-PP12
Signatures 10-219
Signatures 25-219
Signatures Duals-DSS
Signatures Trios-TSTS
Signatures Foursomes-FSSLK
Up Close and Personal-UC45
Up Close and Personal Autographs-UC45
06Be A Player Portraits-114
06Beehive-114
Blue-114
Gold-114
Matte-114
Red Facsimile Signatures-114
Wood-114
06Black Diamond-206
Black-206
Gold-206
Ruby-206
06Flair Showcase-310
06Hot Prospects-108
Red Hot-108
White Hot-108
Hot Materials -HMPS
Hot Materials Red Hot-HMPS
Hot Materials White Hot-HMPS
Hotagraphs-HPS
06ITG Ultimate Memorabilia Bloodlines-1
06ITG Ultimate Memorabilia Bloodlines Gold-1
06ITG Ultimate Memorabilia Bloodlines Autos-1
06ITG Ultimate Memorabilia Bloodlines Autos Gold-1
06ITG Ultimate Memorabilia Future Star-14
06ITG Ultimate Memorabilia Future Star Gold-14
06ITG Ultimate Memorabilia Future Star Autos-5
06ITG Ultimate Memorabilia Future Star Autos Gold-5
06ITG Ultimate Memorabilia Future Star Patches Autos-5
06ITG Ultimate Memorabilia Future Star Patches Autos Gold-5
06ITG Ultimate Memorabilia R.O.Y. Autos-8
06ITG Ultimate Memorabilia R.O.Y. Autos Gold-8
06ITG Ultimate Memorabilia R.O.Y. Emblems-8
06ITG Ultimate Memorabilia R.O.Y. Emblems Gold-8
06ITG Ultimate Memorabilia R.O.Y. Jerseys-8
06ITG Ultimate Memorabilia R.O.Y. Jerseys Gold-8
06ITG Ultimate Memorabilia R.O.Y. Numbers-8
06ITG Ultimate Memorabilia R.O.Y. Numbers Gold-8
06O-Pee-Chee-548
06O-Pee-Chee-620
Rainbow-548
Rainbow-620
Autographs-A-PS
06SP Authentic-174
Limited-174
Sign of the Times Duals-STQC
Sign of the Times Triples-ST3SSS
Sign of the Times Quads-ST4SSSS
06SP Game Used-111
Gold-111
Rainbow-111
Autographs-111
Rookie Exclusives Autographs-REPS
06SPx-186
Spectrum-186
06The Cup-172
Autographed NHL Shields Duals-DASSS
Autographed NHL Shields Duals-DASSV
Autographed Rookie Masterpiece Pressplates-172
Enshrinements-EPS
Gold Rainbow Autographed Rookie Patches-172
Honorable Numbers-HNPS
Masterpiece Pressplates (Be A Player Portraits)-114
Masterpiece Pressplates (Bee Hive)-114
Masterpiece Pressplates (Marquee Rookies)-548
Masterpiece Pressplates (MVP)-302
Masterpiece Pressplates (SP Authentic Autographs)-174
Masterpiece Pressplates (SP Game Used)-111
Masterpiece Pressplates (SPx Autographs)-186
Masterpiece Pressplates (Sweet Beginnings)-117
Masterpiece Pressplates (Trilogy)-108
Masterpiece Pressplates (Ultimate Collection Autographs)-108
Masterpiece Pressplates (Victory)-294
NHL Shields Duals-DSHPJ
NHL Shields Duals-DSHTS
Rookies Black-172
Rookies Platinum-172
Scripted Swatches Duals-DSPP
Signature Patches-SPPS
06UD Artifacts-238
06Ultimate Collection-108
Rookies Autographed NHL Shields-108
Rookies Autographed Patches-108
Signatures-US-PS
Ultimate Debut Threads Jerseys-DJ-PS
Ultimate Debut Threads Jerseys Autographs-DJ-PS
Ultimate Debut Threads Patches-DJ-PS
Ultimate Debut Threads Patches Autographs-DJ-PS
06Ultra-248
Gold Medallion-248
Ice Medallion-248
06Upper Deck-207
Exclusives Parallel-207
High Gloss Parallel-207
Masterpieces-207
Rookie Game Dated Moments-RGD5
Rookie Headliners-RH27
Rookie Materials-RMPS
Rookie Materials Patches-RMPS
06Upper Deck MVP-302
Gold Script-302
Super Script-302
06Upper Deck Ovation-163
06Upper Deck Sweet Shot-117
Rookie Jerseys Autographs-117
Signature Shots/Saves-SSPS
Signature Shots/Saves Sticks-SSSPS
06Upper Deck Trilogy-108
06Upper Deck Victory-294
07Upper Deck Ovation-36
07Upper Deck Rookie Class -22
07Upper Deck Victory-153
Black-153
Gold-153
GameBreakers-GB36
Stastny, Peter
79Panini Stickers-84
80Nordiques Postcards-26
80Pepsi-Cola Caps-77
81Nordiques Postcards-17
81O-Pee-Chee-269
81O-Pee-Chee-286
81O-Pee-Chee-287
81O-Pee-Chee-395
81O-Pee-Chee Stickers-69
81O-Pee-Chee Stickers-263
81Topps-39
81Topps-61
82McDonald's Stickers-24
82Nordiques Postcards-22
82O-Pee-Chee-276
82O-Pee-Chee-292
82O-Pee-Chee-293
82O-Pee-Chee Stickers-15
82O-Pee-Chee Stickers-19
82O-Pee-Chee Stickers-167
82Topps Stickers-15
82Topps Stickers-19
82Topps Stickers-167
83NHL Key Tags-110
83Nordiques Postcards-29
83O-Pee-Chee-304
83O-Pee-Chee Stickers-167
83O-Pee-Chee Stickers-253
83Puffy Stickers-13
83Topps Stickers-167
83Topps Stickers-253
83Vachon-77
84Kellogg's Accordion Discs-2
84Kellogg's Accordion Discs Singles-36
84Nordiques Postcards-27
84O-Pee-Chee-293
84O-Pee-Chee Stickers-141
84O-Pee-Chee Stickers-164
84O-Pee-Chee Stickers-165
847-Eleven Discs-41
84Topps-130
85Nordiques General Foods-26
85Nordiques McDonald's-22
85Nordiques Placemats-5
85Nordiques Placemats-6
85Nordiques Provigo-25
85Nordiques Team Issue-25
85O-Pee-Chee-31
85O-Pee-Chee Stickers-156
857-Eleven Credit Cards-16
85Topps-31
86Kraft Drawings-68
86Nordiques General Foods-26
86Nordiques McDonald's-25
86Nordiques Team Issue-25
86Nordiques Yum-Yum-10
86O-Pee-Chee-20
86O-Pee-Chee Stickers-26
86Topps-20
87Nordiques General Foods-29
87Nordiques Team Issue-21
87Nordiques Yum-Yum-10
87O-Pee-Chee-21
87O-Pee-Chee Stickers-222
87Panini Stickers-164
87Pro-Sport All-Stars-12
87Topps-21
88Frito-Lay Stickers-21
88Nordiques General Foods-34
88Nordiques Team Issue-30
88O-Pee-Chee-22
88O-Pee-Chee Minis-37
88O-Pee-Chee Stickers-189
88Panini Stickers-358
88Topps-22
89Kraft-33
89Nordiques Team Issue-37
89Nordiques General Foods-28
89Nordiques Police-26
89O-Pee-Chee-143
89O-Pee-Chee Stickers-182
89Panini Stickers-324
89Topps-143
90Bowman-86
Tiffany-86
90Devils Team Issue-24
90Kraft-54
90Nordiques Team Issue-24
90O-Pee-Chee-334
90Panini Stickers-70
90Pro Set-175A
90Pro Set-175B
90Score-96
Canadian-96
90Score Hottest/Rising Stars-48
90Topps-334
Tiffany-334
90Upper Deck-163
French-163
91Pro Set Platinum-194
91Bowman-287
91Kraft-83
91O-Pee-Chee-191
91O-Pee-Chee-275
91Panini Stickers-220
91Parkhurst-103
91Parkhurst-209
French-103
French-209
91Pinnacle-266
French-266
91Pro Set-143
French-143
Puck Candy-16
91Score American-66
91Score Canadian Bilingual-66
91Score Canadian English-66
91Stadium Club-263
91Topps-275
91Upper Deck-113
French-113
92Bowman-249
92Future Trends '76 Canada Cup-131
92O-Pee-Chee-216
92Panini Stickers-174
92Panini Stickers French-174
92Pinnacle-359
French-359
92Pro Set-100
92Score-291
Canadian-291
92Stadium Club-140
92Topps-469
Gold-469G
92Ultra-118
Imports-24
93Donruss-487
93Panini Stickers-41
93Score-22
Canadian-22
94Canada Games NHL POGS-208
94Donruss-191
94Flair-159
94Hockey Wit-70
94OPC Premier-182
Special Effects-182
94Parkhurst-203
Gold-203
94Pinnacle-134
Artist's Proofs-134
Rink Collection-134
94Topps/OPC Premier-182
Special Effects-182
94Ultra-190
94Upper Deck-60
Electric Ice-60
94Finnish Jaa Kiekko-200
95Slovakian APS National Team-22
96Swedish Semic Wien-227
98Hall of Fame Medallions-2
98Czech OFS Legends-3
99Upper Deck Century Legends-36
Century Collection-36
00Upper Deck Legends-109
Legendary Collection Bronze-109
Legendary Collection Gold-109
Legendary Collection Silver-109
01Greats of the Game-11
Retro Collection-6
Autographs-11
Board Certified-5
01Topps Archives-21
Autographs-26
01Upper Deck Legends-76
02UD Foundations Signs of Greatness-SGPS
02UD Piece of History Heroes Jerseys-HHPS
02UD Piece of History Mark of Distinction-PS
02Slovakian Kvarteto-23
04ITG Franchises Canadian-76
04UD All-World-7
04UD All-World-114
Gold-7
Autographs-7
Autographs-114
Dual Autographs-AD-PS
Triple Autographs-AT-KSN
Triple Autographs-AT-SHH
Quad Autographs-AQ-OAS
Five Autographs-AF-YAO
Five Autographs-AF-AST
05SP Game Used Heritage Classic-HC-PS
05SP Game Used Heritage Classic Autos-HCA-PS
05SP Game Used Heritage Classic Patches-HCP-PS
05SP GameUsed Heritage Classic Patch Auto-HAP-PS
05SP Game Used Statscriptions-ST-PS
05SPx-118
Spectrum-118
Xcitement Legends-XL-PS
Xcitement Legends Gold-XL-PS
Xcitement Legends Spectrum-XL-PS
05The Cup Noble Numbers-NNSE
05The Cup Noble Numbers-NNSL
05UD Artifacts-147
Blue-147
Gold-147
Green-147
Pewter-147
Red-147
Gold Autographed-147
05Upper Deck All-Time Greatest-88
06Beehive Signature Scrapbook-SSPS
06ITG International Ice-92
06ITG International Ice-115
Gold-92
Gold-115
Autographs-APS
Autographs-APS2
Cornerstones-IC05
Cornerstones Gold-IC05
Emblem Autographs-GUE30
Emblem Autographs Gold-GUE30
Emblems-GUE30
Emblems Gold-GUE30
International Rivals-IR06
Jersey Autographs-GUJ30
Jersey Autographs Gold-GUJ30
Jerseys-GUJ30
Jerseys Gold-GUJ30
Numbers-GUN30
Numbers Autographs-GUN30
Numbers Autographs Gold-GUN30
Numbers Gold-GUN30
Passing The Torch-PTT11
Passing The Torch Gold-PTT11
Stick and Jersey-SJ11
Stick and Jersey Gold-SJ11
Teammates-IT20
Teammates Gold-IT20
06ITG Ultimate Memorabilia-115
Artist Proof-115
Bloodlines-1
Bloodlines Gold-1
Bloodlines Autos-1
Bloodlines Autos Gold-1
Boys Will Be Boys-21
Boys Will Be Boys Gold-21
Stick Rack-18
Stick Rack Gold-18
Sticks and Jerseys-9
Sticks and Jerseys Gold-9
06O-Pee-Chee Swatches-S-PS
06Parkhurst-122
06Parkhurst-175
Autographs-122
Autographs-175
Autographs Dual-DAST1
Autographs Dual-DAST2
06SP Authentic Sign of the Times Duals-STQC
06SP Authentic Sign of the Times Triples-ST3SSS
06SP Authentic Sign of the Times Quads-ST4SSSS
06SP Game Used By The Letter-BLPS
06SPx-118
Spectrum-118
06The Cup-76
Autographed Foundations-CQPS
Autographed Foundations Patches-CQPS
Autographed Patches-76
Black Rainbow-76
Foundations-CQPS
Foundations Patches-CQPS
Gold-76
Gold Patches-76
Honorable Numbers-HNST
Jerseys-76
Limited Logos-LLPS
Masterpiece Pressplates-76
Scripted Swatches Duals-DSPP
Signature Patches-SPST
06UD Artifacts-115
Blue-115
Gold-115
Platinum-115
Radiance-115
Red-115
Frozen Artifacts-FAPS
Frozen Artifacts Black-FAPS
Frozen Artifacts Blue-FAPS
Frozen Artifacts Gold-FAPS
Frozen Artifacts Platinum-FAPS
Frozen Artifacts Red-FAPS
Frozen Artifacts Autographed Black-FAPS
Frozen Artifacts Patches Black-FAPS
Frozen Artifacts Patches Blue-FAPS
Frozen Artifacts Patches Gold-FAPS
Frozen Artifacts Patches Platinum-FAPS
Frozen Artifacts Patches Red-FAPS
Frozen Artifacts Patches Autographed Black Tag Parallel-FAPS
Tundra Tandems-TTGP
Tundra Tandems Black-TTGP
Tundra Tandems Blue-TTGP
Tundra Tandems Gold-TTGP
Tundra Tandems Platinum-TTGP
Tundra Tandems Red-TTGP
Tundra Tandems Dual Patches Red-TTGP
06Ultimate Collection Jerseys-UJ-PS
06Ultimate Collection Jerseys Dual-UJ2-SS
06Ultimate Collection Patches-UJ-PS
06Ultimate Collection Patches Dual-UJ2-SS
06Ultimate Collection Signatures-US-SP
06Ultimate Collection Ultimate Achievements-UA-PS
06Upper Deck Game Jerseys-J2PS
06Upper Deck Game Patches-P2PS
06Upper Deck Sweet Shot-85
Signature Shots/Saves Sticks-SSSST
Sweet Stitches-SSPS
Sweet Stitches Duals-SSPS
Sweet Stitches Triples-SSPS
06ITG Heroes and Prospects-4
Autographs-APS
Stastny, Vladimir
02Slovakian Kvarteto-30
Stastny, Yan
03German DEL-209
04German DEL-257
04German Nuremburg Ice Tigers Postcards-16
05ITG Heroes/Prosp Toronto Expo Parallel -218
05German DEL All-Star Jerseys-AS18
05German DEL Star Attack-ST06
05AHL Top Prospects-40
05Iowa Stars-25
05ITG Heroes and Prospects-218
Autographs Series II-YS
Complete Logos-AHL-20
Jerseys-GUJ-71
Jerseys Gold-GUJ-71
Emblems-GUE-71
Emblems Gold-GUE-71
Numbers-GUN-71
Numbers Gold-GUN-71
06Be A Player Portraits-101
06Beehive-107
Matte-107
06Black Diamond-150A
Black-150A
Gold-150A
Ruby-150A
06Flair Showcase-106
Parallel-106
06Fleer-215
Tiffany-215
06Hot Prospects-103
Red Hot-103
White Hot-103
Hotagraphs-HYS
06ITG International Ice-111
Gold-111
Autographs-AYS
06ITG Ultimate Memorabilia Bloodlines-1
06ITG Ultimate Memorabilia Bloodlines Gold-1
06O-Pee-Chee-502
Rainbow-502
06SP Authentic-166
Limited-166
Sign of the Times Triples-ST3SSS
Sign of the Times Quads-ST4SSSS
06SP Game Used-103
Gold-103
Rainbow-103
Autographs-103
Rookie Exclusives Autographs-REYS
06SPx-164
Spectrum-164
06The Cup-155
Autographed NHL Shields Duals-DASSS
Autographed Rookie Masterpiece Pressplates-155
Gold Rainbow Autographed Rookie Patches-155
Masterpiece Pressplates (Artifacts)-202
Masterpiece Pressplates (Be A Player Portraits)-101
Masterpiece Pressplates (Bee Hive)-107
Masterpiece Pressplates (Black Diamond)-150
Masterpiece Pressplates (Marquee Rookies)-502
Masterpiece Pressplates (MVP)-357
Masterpiece Pressplates (Power Play)-101
Masterpiece Pressplates (SP Authentic Autographs)-166
Masterpiece Pressplates (SP Game Used)-103
Masterpiece Pressplates (SPx Autographs)-164
Masterpiece Pressplates (Sweet Beginnings)-105
Masterpiece Pressplates (Trilogy)-103
Masterpiece Pressplates (Ultimate Collection)-90
Masterpiece Pressplates (Victory)-204
NHL Shields Duals-DSHPY
Rookies Black-155
Rookies Platinum-155
06UD Artifacts-202
Blue-202
Gold-202
Platinum-202
Radiance-202
Red-202
06UD Mini Jersey Collection-101
06UD Powerplay-101
Impact Rainbow-101
06Ultimate Collection-90
Ultimate Debut Threads Jerseys-DJ-YS
Ultimate Debut Threads Jerseys Autographs-DJ-YS
Ultimate Debut Threads Patches-DJ-YS
Ultimate Debut Threads Patches Autographs-DJ-YS
06Ultra-201
Gold Medallion-201
Ice Medallion-201
06Upper Deck-203
Exclusives Parallel-203
High Gloss Parallel-203
Masterpieces-203
Rookie Game Dated Moments-RGD4
Rookie Materials-RMYS
Rookie Materials Patches-RMYS
06Upper Deck MVP-357
Gold Script-357
Super Script-357
Autographs-OABS
06Upper Deck Sweet Shot-105
Rookie Jerseys Autographs-105
06Upper Deck Trilogy-103
06Upper Deck Victory-204
06Upper Deck Victory Black-204
06Upper Deck Victory Gold-204
06Providence Bruins-18
07Upper Deck Rookie Class -47
State, Jeff
03Charlotte Checkers-79
03Hartford Wolf Pack-23
05Reading Royals-14
Stathopoulos, Mike
00London Knights-27
01London Knights-7
02London Knights-5
04Gwinnett Gladiators-24
Stathos, Dave
02Finnish Cardset-272
02Finnish Cardset-297
03Finnish Cardset-15
04Finnish Cardset-14
Parallel-10
06Swedish SHL Elitset-261
Statkus, Joe
01Rockford IceHogs-15
02Rockford Ice Hogs-16
Stauber, Pete
91ProCards-129
Stauber, Robb
90O-Pee-Chee-181
90Topps-181
Tiffany-181
90Upper Deck-165
French-165
90ProCards AHL/IHL-418
92OPC Premier-115
92Parkhurst-303
Emerald Ice-303
92Ultra-311
92Upper Deck-495
93OPC Premier-109
Gold-109
93Pinnacle-338
Canadian-338
Masks-3
93PowerPlay-363
93Score-346
Canadian-346
93Stadium Club-327
Members Only Master Set-327
First Day Issue-327
93Topps/OPC Premier-109
Gold-109
93Ultra-347
94Be A Player-R59
94OPC Premier-248
Special Effects-248
94Parkhurst-109
Gold-109
94Topps/OPC Premier-248
Special Effects-248
95Parkhurst International-25
Emerald Ice-25
95Rochester Americans-19
96Portland Pirates-1
96Portland Pirates Shop N' Save-1
97Hartford Wolf Pack-21
Staubitz, Brad
02Sault Ste. Marie Greyhounds-21
03Sault Ste. Marie Greyhounds-21
04Ottawa 67's-15
04Sault Ste. Marie Greyhounds-21
05Cleveland Barons-22
Stauder, Alois
94German First League-364
Stauffacher, Luke
04Minnesota-Duluth Bulldogs-24
06Quad City Mallards-15
Stauffer, Zach
93Quebec Pee-Wee Tournament-778
Staunton, Matt
98UK Kingston Hawks-18
Stauss, Judd
01Greenville Grrrowl-4
Stavensky, Stanislav
99Czech Score Blue 2000-33
99Czech Score Red Ice 2000-33
00Czech OFS-152
02Czech OFS Plus-207
Stavert, Jonathan
93Quebec Pee-Wee Tournament-1219
Stavjana, Antonin
89Swedish Semic World Champ Stickers-181
91Finnish Semic World Champ Stickers-111
91Finnish Jyvas-Hyva Stickers-41
91Swedish Semic World Champ Stickers-111
92Swedish Semic Elitserien Stickers-127
93Swedish Semic Elitserien-100
94Czech APS Extraliga-230
94Finnish Jaa Kiekko-173
95Czech APS Extraliga-8
95Czech APS Extraliga-357
95Czech APS Extraliga-389
95Swedish Globe World Championships-150
95Swedish World Championships Stickers-194
96Czech APS Extraliga-216
96Swedish Semic Wien-105
97Czech APS Extraliga-31
97Czech APS Extraliga-373
97Czech DS Extraliga-57
97Czech DS Stickers-6
97Czech DS Stickers-19
98Czech DS Stickers-10
98Czech DS Stickers-168
98Czech OFS-273
Legends-17
99Czech OFS-206
00Czech OFS-347
00Czech OFS-406
Stavjana, Miroslav
94Czech APS Extraliga-240
98Czech DS Stickers-123
Stay, Tim
93Quebec Pee-Wee Tournament-679
01Odessa Jackalopes-20
Stayzer, Blair
98Windsor Spitfires-8
01Johnstown Chiefs-19
03Roanoke Express-319
Stchadilov, Igor
00Russian Dynamo Moscow-7
Ste-Marie, Mathieu
04Drummondville Voltigeurs-7
Ste. Marie, Roger
51Bas Du Fleuve-28
52Bas Du Fleuve-62
Stead, Nick
93Quebec Pee-Wee Tournament-831
Steadman, Rick
01London Knights-15
02London Knights-9
03London Knights-15
04London Knights-2
Stearns, Cal
60Cleveland Barons-16
Steber, Jan
03Halifax Mooseheads-11
04Halifax Mooseheads-9
Steblecki, Roman
89Swedish Semic World Champ Stickers-145
Steblyk, Brent
82Medicine Hat Tigers-19
83Medicine Hat Tigers-12
Stebnicki, Marek
94German DEL-241
95German DEL-235
96German DEL-86
98German DEL-26
99German DEL-137
00German DEL-206
Star Attractions-S3
Stecher, Dino
91Finnish Semic World Champ Stickers-179
91Swedish Semic World Champ Stickers-179
93Swiss HNL-34
95Swiss HNL-33
Steciuk, Lucasz
05PEI Rocket-16
Steck, Bruno
93Swiss HNL-323
95Swiss HNL-38
96Swiss HNL-185
98Swiss Power Play Stickers-12
99Swiss Panini Stickers-12
01Swiss HNL-9
04Swiss Lausanne HC Postcards-4
Steckel, Dave
00Ohio State Buckeyes-16
01BAP Memorabilia Draft Redemptions-30
01Ohio State Buckeyes-16
02Ohio State Buckeyes-13
03Ohio State Buckeyes-14
04Manchester Monarchs-5
04Manchester Monarchs Tobacco-6
05Hot Prospects-184
En Fuego-184
Red Hot-184
White Hot-184
05SP Authentic-286
Limited-286
05SPx-291
05The Cup Masterpiece Pressplates (Ice)-236
05The Cup Master Pressplate Rookie Update-192
05The Cup Masterpiece Pressplates SPA-286
05The Cup Masterpiece Pressplates (SPx)-291
05The Cup Masterpiece Pressplates Trilogy-319
05Upper Deck Ice-236
05Upper Deck Rookie Update-192
05Upper Deck Trilogy-319
05Hershey Bears-15
06ITG Heroes and Prospects Calder Cup Champions-CC08
Stecksen, Ulf
69Swedish Hockey-215
Steege, Brandon
91Minnesota Golden Gophers-23
92Minnesota Golden Gophers-19
93Minnesota Golden Gophers-24
94Minnesota Golden Gophers-26
Steel, Andy
93UK Humberside Hawks-19
97UK Kingston Hawks Stickers-12
98UK Kingston Hawks-15
Steel, Greg
78Saginaw Gears-17
Steele, Mark
93Quebec Pee-Wee Tournament-198
Steele, Ryan
93Quebec Pee-Wee Tournament-1694
Steelers, Sheffield
93UK Sheffield Steelers-18
94UK Sheffield Steelers-5
95UK Sheffield Steelers-14
97UK Sheffield Steelers-14
00UK Sekonda Superleague-169
Steen, Alexander
02BAP Memorabilia Draft Redemptions-24
02Swedish SHL-279
Dynamic Duos-9
Parallel-279
Signatures-18
03Swedish Elite-174
Hot Numbers-HN4
Rookies-4
Silver-174
04SP Authentic Rookie Redemptions-RR28
04Swedish Alfabilder Alfa Stars-39
04Swedish Alfabilder Proof Parallels-39
04Swedish Elitset-28
04Swedish Elitset-249
Dominators-4
Future Stars-8
Gold-28
Gold-249
04Swedish MoDo Postcards-8
04Swedish Pure Skills-70
Parallel-70
05Beehive-112
Beige -112
Blue -112
Gold-112
Red -112
Matte-112
Signature Scrapbook-SSST
05Black Diamond-201
Emerald-201
Gold-201
Onyx-201
Ruby-201
05Hot Prospects-270
En Fuego-270
Hot Materials-HMST
Red Hot-270
White Hot-270
05Parkhurst-667
Facsimile Auto Parallel-667
True Colors-TCTOR
True Colors-TCTOR
True Colors-TCTOMO
True Colors-TCTOMO
05SP Authentic-188
Limited-188
Exquisite Endorsements-EEAS

Octographs-OR
Rarefied Rookies-RRAL
Rookie Authentics-RAAS
Sign of the Times Duals-DSS
Sign of the Times Triples-TSAS
Sign of the Times Triples-TSOC
Sign of the Times Quads-QSOPC
Sign of the Times Quads-QSSOS
05SP Game Used-136
Autographs-136
Gold-136
Auto Draft-AD-AS
Game Gear-GG-AS
Game Gear Autographs-AG-AS
Rookie Exclusives-AS
Rookie Exclusives Silver-RE-AS
Significant Numbers-SN-AS
05SPx-169
Spectrum-169
Xcitement Rookies-XR-AS
Xcitement Rookies Gold-XR-AS
Xcitement Rookies Spectrum-XR-AS
05The Cup-174
Autographed Rookie Patches Gold Rainbow-174
Black Rainbow Rookies-174
Dual NHL Shields-DSMA
Masterpiece Pressplates (Artifacts)-228
Masterpiece Pressplates (Bee Hive)-112
Masterpiece Pressplates (Black Diamond)-201
Masterpiece Pressplates (Ice)-118
Masterpiece Pressplates (MVP)-413
Masterpiece Pressplates (Power Play)-136
Masterpiece Pressplates Rookie Upd Auto-260
Masterpiece Pressplates SPA Autos-188
Masterpiece Pressplates (SP Game Used)-136
Masterpiece Pressplates SPx Autos-169
Masterpiece Pressplates (Trilogy)-218
Masterpiece Pressplates Ult Coll Autos-96
Masterpiece Pressplates (Victory)-279
Masterpiece Pressplates Autographs-174
Platinum Rookies-174
Scripted Swatches-SSAS
05UD Artifacts-228
Gold-RED28
05UD PowerPlay-136
05UD Rookie Class-10
Commemorative Boxtoppers-CC-6
05Ultimate Collection-96
Autographed Patches-96
Autographed Shields-96
Jerseys-JAS
Marquee Attractions-MA44
Marquee Attractions Signatures-SMA44
Premium Patches-PPAS
Premium Swatches-PSAS
Ultimate Debut Threads Jerseys-DTJAS
Ultimate Debut Threads Jerseys Autos-DAJAS
Ultimate Debut Threads Patches-DTPAS
Ultimate Debut Threads Patches Autos-DAPAS
Ultimate Patches-PAS
Ultimate Signatures-USST
Ultimate Signatures Foursomes-UFSOBP
Ultimate Signatures Logos-SLAS
Ultimate Signatures Trios-UTSOC
05Ultra-266
Gold-266
Fresh Ink-FI-AS
Fresh Ink Blue-FI-AS
Ice-266
Rookie Uniformity Jerseys-RU-AS
Rookie Uniformity Jersey Autographs-ARU-AS
Rookie Uniformity Patches-RUP-AS
Rookie Uniformity Patch Autographs-ARP-AS
05Upper Deck-205
HG Glossy-205
Majestic Materials-MMAS
Rookie Ink-RIST
05Upper Deck Rookie Showcase-RS28
05Upper Deck Rookie Showcase Promos-RS28
05Upper Deck Rookie Threads-RTST
05Upper Deck Rookie Threads Autographs-ARTST
05Upper Deck Stars in the Making-SM10
05Upper Deck Ice-118
Cool Threads-CTAS
Cool Threads Autographs-ACTAS
Cool Threads Glass-CTAS
Cool Threads Patches-CTPAS
Cool Threads Patch Autographs-CAPAS
Glacial Graphs-GGST
Premieres Auto Patches-AIPAS
Signature Swatches-SSAS
05Upper Deck MVP-413
Gold-413
Platinum-413
Rookie Breakthrough-RB10
05Upper Deck Rookie Update-260
05Upper Deck Trilogy-218
05Upper Deck Toronto Fall Expo-205
05Upper Deck Victory-279
Black-279
Gold-279
Silver-279
06Be A Player Portraits-93
First Exposures-FEAS
06Beehive-7
Matte-7
Matted Materials-MMAS
06Black Diamond-125
Black-125
Gold-125
Ruby-125
Jerseys-JAS
Jerseys Black-JAS
Jerseys Gold-JAS
Jerseys Ruby-JAS
06Flair Showcase-93
Parallel-93
Wave of the Future-WF38
06Fleer-183
Tiffany-183
06Gatorade-62
06Hot Prospects-92
Red Hot-92
White Hot-92
Hot Materials -HMAS
Hot Materials Red Hot-HMAS
Hot Materials White Hot-HMAS
06McDonald's Upper Deck-46
Rookie Review-RR5
06O-Pee-Chee-462
06O-Pee-Chee-644
Rainbow-462
Rainbow-644
Swatches-S-AS
06Panini Stickers-168
06SP Authentic-8
06SP Authentic-104
Limited-8
Limited-104
06SP Game Used-92
Gold-92
Rainbow-92
Authentic Fabrics-AFAS
Authentic Fabrics Parallel-AFAS
Authentic Fabrics Patches-AFAS
Authentic Fabrics Dual-AF2SS
Authentic Fabrics Dual Patches-AF2SS
Authentic Fabrics Triple-AF3TOR
Authentic Fabrics Triple Patches-AF3TOR
Authentic Fabrics Eights-AF8CEN
Authentic Fabrics Eights Patches-AF8CEN
Inked Sweaters Dual-IS2RS
Inked Sweaters Dual Patches-IS2RS
06SPx-95
Spectrum-95
SPxcitement-X95
SPxcitement Spectrum-X95
Winning Materials-WMAS
Winning Materials Spectrum-WMAS
06The Cup NHL Shields Duals-DSHSS
06UD Artifacts-8
Blue-8
Gold-8
Platinum-8
Radiance-8
Red-8
Tundra Tandems-TTAM
Tundra Tandems Black-TTAM
Tundra Tandems Blue-TTAM
Tundra Tandems Gold-TTAM
Tundra Tandems Platinum-TTAM
Tundra Tandems Red-TTAM
Tundra Tandems Dual Patches Red-TTAM
06UD Mini Jersey Collection-91
06UD Powerplay-92
Impact Rainbow-92
06UD Toronto Fall Expo Priority Signings -PSAS
06Ultimate Collection Premium Patches-PS-AS
06Ultimate Collection Premium Swatches-PS-AS
06Ultra-183
Gold Medallion-183
Ice Medallion-183
06Upper Deck Arena Giveaways-TOR3
06Upper Deck-183
Exclusives Parallel-183
High Gloss Parallel-183
Game Jerseys-J2AS
Game Patches-P2AS
Generations Duals-G2FS
Generations Triples-G3NZS
Generations Patches Dual-G2PFS
Generations Patches Triple-G3PNZS
Hometown Heroes-HH53
Masterpieces-183
Signature Sensations-SSAS
Walmart Tins Oversize-183
06Upper Deck MVP-270
Gold Script-270
Super Script-270
Jerseys-OJHS
06Upper Deck Ovation-47
06Upper Deck Ovation-147
06Upper Deck Sweet Shot Sweet Stitches-SSAS
06Upper Deck Sweet Shot Sweet Stitches Duals-SSAS
06Upper Deck Sweet Shot Sweet Stitches Triples-SSAS
06Upper Deck Trilogy-94
06Upper Deck Victory-187
06Upper Deck Victory Black-187
06Upper Deck Victory Gold-187
06Upper Deck Victory Next In Line-NL45
07Upper Deck Ovation-4
07Upper Deck Victory-55
Black-55
Gold-55

Steen, Anders
80Jets Postcards-21
80Pepsi-Cola Caps-138
83Swedish Semic Elitserien-118

Steen, Calle
03Swedish Elite-188
Silver-188
04Swedish Elitset-191
Gold-191

Steen, Oscar
05Swedish SHL Elitset-215
Gold-215
06Swedish SHL Elitset-243

Steen, Thomas
81Jets Postcards-20
82Jets Postcards-24
82O-Pee-Chee-391
82Swedish Semic VM Stickers-150
83Jets Postcards-22
83O-Pee-Chee-393
83O-Pee-Chee Stickers-289
83Topps Stickers-289
83Vachon-138
84Jets Police-19
84O-Pee-Chee-348
84O-Pee-Chee Stickers-292
85Jets Police-19
85O-Pee-Chee-206
85O-Pee-Chee Stickers-253
86Jets Postcards-22
86Kraft Drawings-69
86O-Pee-Chee-257
86O-Pee-Chee Stickers-110
87Jets Postcards-20
87O-Pee-Chee-221
87Panini Stickers-365
88Jets Police-21
88Jets Postcards-21
88O-Pee-Chee-254
88O-Pee-Chee Stickers-138
88Panini Stickers-159
89Jets Safeway-26
89O-Pee-Chee-290
89O-Pee-Chee Stickers-144
89Panini Stickers-163
89Swedish Semic World Champ Stickers-15
90Bowman-133
Tiffany-133
90Jets IGA-30
90Kraft-55
90O-Pee-Chee-283
90Panini Stickers-316
90Pro Set-356
90Pro Set-565
90Score-14
Canadian-14
90Score Hottest/Rising Stars-8
90Topps-283
Tiffany-283
90Upper Deck-94
90Upper Deck-313
French-94
French-313
91Pro Set Platinum-138
91Bowman-200
91Jets Panini Team Stickers-22
91Jets IGA-30
91O-Pee-Chee-218
91Panini Stickers-68
91Pinnacle-275
French-275
91Pro Set-271
French-271
91Score American-198
91Score Canadian Bilingual-198
91Score Canadian English-198
91Stadium Club-207
91Topps-218
91Upper Deck-181
French-181
91Finnish Semic World Champ Stickers-209
91Swedish Semic World Champ Stickers-209
92Bowman-312
92O-Pee-Chee-385
92Panini Stickers-53
92Panini Stickers French-53
92Parkhurst-214
Emerald Ice-214
92Pinnacle-29
French-29
92Pro Set-217
92Score-80
Canadian-80
92Topps-141
Gold-141G
92Ultra-247
92Upper Deck-154
92Finnish Semic-70
93Donruss-389
93Jets Readers Club-19
93Jets Ruffles-24
93Leaf-165
93OPC Premier-11
Gold-11
93Panini Stickers-191
93Parkhurst-502
Emerald Ice-502
93Pinnacle-159
Canadian-159
93PowerPlay-275
93PowerPlay-476
93Score-71
Canadian-71
93Stadium Club-282
Members Only Master Set-282
First Day Issue-282
93Topps/OPC Premier-11
Gold-11
93Ultra-69
93Upper Deck-166
93Swedish Semic World Champ Stickers-36
94Be A Player Signature Cards-159
94Canada Games NHL POGS-255
94Donruss-154
94EA Sports-148
94Leaf-376
94OPC Premier-471
Special Effects-471
94Parkhurst-263
Gold-263
94Pinnacle-171
Artist's Proofs-171
Rink Collection-171
94Score-65
Gold-65
Platinum-65
94Stadium Club-176
Members Only Master Set-176
First Day Issue-176
Super Team Winner Cards-176
94Topps/OPC Premier-471
Special Effects-471
94Ultra-396
94Upper Deck-192
Electric Ice-192
95Swedish Globe World Championships-40
95Swedish World Championships Stickers-291
96German DEL-33
98German DEL-162
04ITG Franchises Canadian-141
04ITG Franchises Update Autographs-TS
04UD All-World-56
04UD All-World-115
Gold-56
Autographs-56
Autographs-115
Dual Autographs-AD-LS
Triple Autographs-AT-SLN
Quad Autographs-AQ-SWE
Five Autographs-AF-YAO
04German Berlin Eisbarens 50th Anniv-71
05SP Authentic Sign of the Times Duals-DSS
05UD Artifacts-148
Blue-148
Gold-148
Green-148
Pewter-148
Red-148
Gold Autographed-148
06ITG International Ice-73
Gold-73
Autographs-ATS
06Parkhurst-123
06Parkhurst-203
Autographs-123
Autographs-203
Autographs Dual-DAHS
06UD Artifacts-137
Blue-137
Gold-137
Radiance-137
Autographed Radiance Parallel-137
Red-137
Auto-Facts-AFTS
Auto-Facts Gold-AFTS

Steenbergen, Lyle
96Saskatoon Blades-23
98Calgary Hitmen-15
98Calgary Hitmen Autographs-15

Steer, Franz
94German First League-53
04German Berlin Eisbarens 50th Anniv-12

Steer, Jamie
90Michigan Tech Huskies-24
91Michigan Tech Huskies-24
91Michigan Tech Huskies-25
91Michigan Tech Huskies-34
92Greensboro Monarchs-16
94Dayton Bombers-8
94Dayton Bombers-22
94Classic Pro Prospects-240

Steeves, Ryan
04Hershey Bears Patriot News-26

Steeves, Tom
72Johnstown Jets-4

Stefan, Greg
80Oshawa Generals-22
84O-Pee-Chee-65
84O-Pee-Chee Stickers-41
84Topps-48
85O-Pee-Chee-157
85O-Pee-Chee Stickers-31
85Topps-157
86O-Pee-Chee-51
86O-Pee-Chee Stickers-165
86Topps-51
87O-Pee-Chee-186
87Panini Stickers-237
87Red Wings Little Caesars-27
87Topps-186
88O-Pee-Chee-68
88O-Pee-Chee Minis-38
88O-Pee-Chee Stickers-252
88Panini Stickers-37
88Red Wings Little Caesars-22
88Topps-68
89O-Pee-Chee-23
89O-Pee-Chee Stickers-248
89Panini Stickers-59
89Red Wings Little Caesars-16
89Topps-23

Stefan, Joe
90ProCards AHL/IHL-519

Stefan, Leo
94Finnish Jaa Kiekko-290
94German DEL-206
95German DEL-208
95Swedish Globe World Championships-223
95Swedish World Championships Stickers-75
96German DEL-290
96Swedish Semic Wien-200
98German DEL-324
99German Bundesliga 2-89
00German DEL-54
Game Jersey-LS
01German Upper Deck-57
03German DEL-180
04German DEL-221

Stefan, Patrik
97Czech APS Extraliga-20
97Czech DS Extraliga-87
98Czech DS Stickers-222
98Long Beach Ice Dogs-17
98Long Beach Ice Dogs Promo-NNO
99BAP Memorabilia-1
Gold-1
Silver-1
99BAP Millennium-12
Emerald-12
Ruby-12
Sapphire-12
Signatures-12
Signatures Gold-12
Calder Candidates Ruby-C7
Calder Candidates Emerald-C7
Calder Candidates Sapphire-C7
99Black Diamond-5
Diamond Cut-5
Final Cut-5
Diamonation-D2
Myriad-M1
99Crown Royale-9
Limited Series-9
Premiere Date-9
Card-Supials-3
Card-Supials Minis-3
Century 21-2
International Glory-2
International Glory Parallel-2
99O-Pee-Chee Chrome-293
99O-Pee-Chee Chrome Refractors-293
99Pacific Dynagon Ice-6
Blue-6
Copper-6
Gold-6
Premiere Date-6
Checkmates American-3
Checkmates American-18
Checkmates Canadian-18
Lamplighter Net-Fusions-3
99Pacific Omega-13
Copper-13
Gold-13
Ice Blue-13
Premiere Date-13
EO Portraits-3
EO Portraits 1/1-3
NHL Generations-10
5 Star Talents-1
5 Star Talents Parallel-1
99Pacific Prism-9
Holographic Blue-9
Holographic Gold-9
Holographic Mirror-9
Holographic Purple-9
Premiere Date-9
Ice Prospects-1
99Panini Stickers-15
99Paramount-251
Copper-251
Emerald-251
Gold-251
Holographic Emerald-251
Holographic Gold-251
Holographic Silver-251
Ice Blue-251
Premiere Date-251
Red-251
Silver-251
Toronto Fall Expo '99-251
99SP Authentic-91
Jersey Redemption-JPS
Sign of the Times-PS
Sign of the Times Gold-PS
Tomorrow's Headliners-TH1
99SPx-163
Radiance-163
Spectrum-163
SPXcitement-X8
99Stadium Club-181
First Day Issue-181
One of a Kind-181
Printing Plates Black-181
Printing Plates Cyan-181
Printing Plates Magenta-181
Printing Plates Yellow-181
Chrome-43
Chrome Refractors-43
Chrome Oversized-18
Chrome Oversized Refractors-18
99Topps Arena Giveaways-ATL-PS
99Topps/OPC Chrome-293
Refractors-293
99Topps Gold Label Class 1-97
Black-97
Black One of One-97
One of One-97
Red-97
Red One of One-97
99Topps Gold Label Class 2-97
99Topps Gold Label Class 2 Black-97
99Topps Gold Label Class 2 Black 1 of 1-97
99Topps Gold Label Class 2 One of One-97
99Topps Gold Label Class 2 Red-97
99Topps Gold Label Class 2 Red One of One-97
99Topps Gold Label Class 3-97
99Topps Gold Label Class 3 Black-97
99Topps Gold Label Class 3 Black 1 of 1-97
99Topps Gold Label Class 3 One of One-97
99Topps Gold Label Class 3 Red-97
99Topps Gold Label Class 3 Red One of One-97
99Topps Gold Label Fresh Gold-FG6
99Topps Gold Label Fresh Gold Black-FG6
99Topps Gold Label Fresh Gold Black 1of1-FG6
99Topps Gold Label Fresh Gold One of One-FG6
99Topps Gold Label Fresh Gold Red-FG6
99Topps Gold Label Fresh Gold Red 1 of 1-FG6
99Topps Premier Plus-101
Parallel-101
Premier Rookies-PR5
Premier Rookies Parallel-PR5
Signing Bonus-SB4
The Next Ones-TNO7
99Ultimate Victory-91
1/1-91
Parallel-91
Parallel 100-91
Frozen Fury-FF6
Smokin Guns-SG8
99Upper Deck-161
99Upper Deck-181
Exclusives-161
Exclusives-181
Exclusives 1 of 1-161
Exclusives 1 of 1-181
All-Star Class-AS20
All-Star Class Quantum Gold-AS20
All-Star Class Quantum Silver-AS20
Ice Gallery-IG8
Ice Gallery Quantum Gold-IG8
Ice Gallery Quantum Silver-IG8
NHL Scrapbook-SB15
NHL Scrapbook Quantum Gold-SB15
NHL Scrapbook Quantum Silver-SB15
Sixth Sense-SS7
Sixth Sense Quantum Gold-SS7
Sixth Sense Quantum Silver-SS7
99Upper Deck Arena Giveaways-AT1
99Upper Deck Gold Reserve-161
99Upper Deck Gold Reserve-181
UD Authentics-PS
99Upper Deck HoloGrFx-3
Ausome-3
UD Authentics-PS
99Upper Deck MVP SC Edition-13
Gold Script-13
Silver Script-13
Super Script-13
Cup Contenders-CC1
Great Combinations-GCSR
Great Combinations Parallel-GCSR
ProSign-PS
99Upper Deck Ovation-3
99Upper Deck Ovation-90
Standing Ovation-3
Standing Ovation-90
A Piece Of History-PS
A Piece Of History-PSS
Lead Performers-LP9
99Upper Deck PowerDeck-3
Auxiliary-3
Auxiliary 1 of 1-3
99Upper Deck Victory-357
99Wayne Gretzky Hockey-8
Great Heroes-GH8
Signs of Greatness-PS
00Aurora-8
Pinstripes-8
Pinstripes Premiere Date-8
Premiere Date-8
Scouting Reports-3
00BAP Memorabilia-268
Emerald-268
Ruby-268
Sapphire-268
Promos-268
00BAP Mem Chicago Sportsfest Copper-268
00BAP Memorabilia Chicago Sportsfest Blue-268
00BAP Memorabilia Chicago Sportsfest Gold-268
00BAP Memorabilia Chicago Sportsfest Ruby-268
00BAP Memorabilia Chicago Sun-Times Ruby-268
00BAP Memorabilia Chicago Sun-Times Gold-268
00BAP Mem Chicago Sun-Times Sapphire-268
00BAP Mem Toronto Fall Expo Copper-268
00BAP Memorabilia Toronto Fall Expo Gold-268
00BAP Memorabilia Toronto Fall Expo Ruby-268
00BAP Parkhurst 2000-P70
00BAP Signature Series-214
Emerald-214
Ruby-214
Sapphire-214
Autographs-137
Autographs Gold-137
Franchise Players-F2
He Shoots-He Scores Prizes-16
00BAP Ultimate Memorabilia Autographs-35
Gold-35
00BAP Ultimate Mem Game-Used Jerseys-GJ34
00BAP Ultimate Mem Game-Used Emblems-E30
00BAP Ultimate Mem Game-Used Numbers-N30
00BAP Ultimate Mem Game-Used Sticks-GS34
00Black Diamond-3
Gold-3
00Crown Royale-7
Ice Blue-7
Limited Series-7
Premiere Date-7
Red-7
Jewels of the Crown-3
00McDonald's Pacific-3
Blue-3
Gold Crown Die Cuts-1
00O-Pee-Chee-14
00O-Pee-Chee Parallel-14
00Pacific-23
Copper-23
Gold-23
Ice Blue-23
Premiere Date-23
00Panini Stickers-5
00Paramount-15
Copper-15
Gold-15
Holo-Gold-15
Holo-Silver-15
Ice Blue-15
Premiere Date-15
00Private Stock-6
Gold-6
Premiere Date-6
Retail-6
Silver-6
PS-2001 New Wave-1
Reserve-3
00Revolution-8
Blue-8
Premiere Date-8
Red-8
HD NHL-3
00SP Authentic-4
00SP Game Used-3
00SPx-3
Spectrum-3
Highlight Heroes-HH2
00Stadium Club-117
Capture the Action-CA13
Capture the Action Game View-13
00Topps/OPC-14
Parallel-14
NHL Draft-D5
00Topps Chrome-14
OPC Refracters-14
Refractors-14
00Topps Gold Label Class 1-19
Gold-19
00Topps Gold Label Class 2-19
00Topps Gold Label Class 2 Gold-19
00Topps Gold Label Class 3-19
00Topps Gold Label Class 3 Gold-19
00Topps Gold Label New Generation-NG12
00Topps Gold Label New Generation 1 to 1-NG12
00Topps Heritage-11
Chrome Parallel-11
00Topps Premier Plus-3
Blue Ice-3
00Topps Stars-13
Blue-13
Progression-P2
00UD Heroes-5
00UD Pros and Prospects-6
00UD Reserve-5
00Upper Deck-12
Exclusives Tier 1-12
Exclusives Tier 2-12
Prospects In Depth-P1
00Upper Deck Ice-3
Immortals-3
Legends-3
Stars-3
Clear Cut Autographs-PS
00Upper Deck Legends-4
00Upper Deck Legends-5
Legendary Collection Bronze-4
Legendary Collection Bronze-5
Legendary Collection Gold-4
Legendary Collection Gold-5
Legendary Collection Silver-4
Legendary Collection Silver-5
Epic Signatures-PS
00Upper Deck MVP-12
Excellence-ME8
First Stars-12
Mark of Excellence-SGSL
ProSign-PS
Second Stars-12
Third Stars-12
00Upper Deck Victory-9
00Upper Deck Victory-11
00Upper Deck Victory-283
00Upper Deck Vintage-13
00Upper Deck Vintage-23
00Upper Deck Vintage-24
National Heroes-NH3
00Vanguard-6
Holographic Gold-6
Holographic Purple-6
Pacific Proofs-6
00Czech Stadion-91
01Atomic-4
Blue-4
Gold-4
Premiere Date-4
Red-4
Power Play-2
01BAP Memorabilia-69
Emerald-69
Ruby-69
Sapphire-69
He Shoots-He Scores Prizes-16
01BAP Signature Series-2
Autographs-2
Autographs Gold-2
Teammates-TM-2
01Crown Royale-8
Blue-8
Premiere Date-8
Red-8
Retail-8
01O-Pee-Chee-75
01O-Pee-Chee Heritage Parallel-75
01O-Pee-Chee Heritage Parallel Limited-75
01O-Pee-Chee Premier Parallel-75
01Pacific-25
Extreme LTD-25
Hobby LTD-25
Premiere Date-25
Retail LTD-25
Top Draft Picks-2
01Pacific Top Draft Picks Draft Day Promo-2
01Pacific Adrenaline-11
Blue-11
Premiere Date-11
Red-11
Retail-11
01Pacific Arena Exclusives-25
01Pacific Heads-Up-5
Blue-5
Premiere Date-5
Red-5
Silver-5
Breaking the Glass-2
01Parkhurst-2
Gold-2
Silver-2
Jerseys-PJ17
Sticks-PS17
01Private Stock-4
Gold-4
Premiere Date-4
Retail-4
Silver-4
01Private Stock Pacific Nights-4
01SP Authentic-121
Limited-121
Limited Gold-121
Sign of the Times-PS
01SP Game Used Patches-PPS
01SP Game Used Patches-TPSSP
01SP Game Used Patches Signed-SPPS
01SPx-2
01Stadium Club-74
Award Winners-74
Master Photos-74
01Titanium-6
Hobby Parallel-6
Premiere Date-6
Retail-6
Retail Parallel-6
01Titanium Draft Day Edition-8
01Topps-75
Heritage Parallel-75
Heritage Parallel Limited-75
OPC Parallel-75
01Topps Reserve-17
01UD Top Shelf-2
Jerseys-PS
Jersey Autographs-PS
01Upper Deck-9
Exclusives-9
Game Jerseys-NGPS
Ice First Rounders-F-PS
01Upper Deck MVP-7
Souvenirs-S-PS
Souvenirs Gold-S-PS
01Upper Deck Victory-13
Gold-13
01Upper Deck Vintage-10
01Upper Deck Vintage-17
02BAP First Edition-65
Jerseys-65
02BAP Memorabilia-143
Emerald-143
Ruby-143
Sapphire-143
NHL All-Star Game-143
NHL All-Star Game Blue-143
NHL All-Star Game Green-143
NHL All-Star Game Red-143
02BAP Memorabilia Toronto Fall Expo-143
02BAP Signature Series-61
Autographs-61
Autograph Buybacks 1999-12
Autograph Buybacks 2000-137
Autograph Buybacks 2001-2
Autographs Gold-61
Phenoms-YP5
Team Quads-TQ12
02BAP Ultimate Memorabilia First Overall-11
02O-Pee-Chee-138
02O-Pee-Chee Premier Blue Parallel-138
02O-Pee-Chee Premier Red Parallel-138
02O-Pee-Chee Factory Set-138
02Pacific-21
Blue-21
Red-21
02Pacific Complete-466
Red-466
02Pacific Exclusive-9
02Pacific Heads-Up Quad Jerseys-2
02Pacific Heads-Up Quad Jerseys Gold-2
02Parkhurst-17
Bronze-17
Gold-17
Silver-17
Teammates-TT9
02Parkhurst Retro-185
Minis-185
02Private Stock Reserve-5
Blue-5
Red-5
Retail-5
02SP Game Used First Rounder Patches-PS
02Thrashers Postcards-15
02Titanium Jerseys-4
02Titanium Jerseys Retail-4
02Titanium Patches-4
02Topps-138
OPC Blue Parallel-138
OPC Red Parallel-138
Factory Set-138
02Topps Total-46
02Upper Deck-10
Exclusives-10
Bright Futures-PS
02Upper Deck MVP-11
Gold-11
Classics-11
Golden Classics-11
02Upper Deck Rookie Update-7
02Upper Deck Vintage-9
02Upper Deck Vintage-262
02Vanguard Jerseys-4
02Vanguard Jerseys Gold-4
02Czech DS-60
02Czech DS-74
03BAP Memorabilia-67
Emerald-67
Gold-67
Ruby-67
Sapphire-67
03Beehive Sticks Beige Border-BE15
03Beehive Sticks Blue Border-BL16
03ITG Action-73
Jerseys-M115
03NHL Sticker Collection-5
03O-Pee-Chee-118
03OPC Blue-118
03OPC Gold-118
03OPC Red-118
03Pacific-22
Blue-22
Red-22
03Pacific Complete-265
Red-265
03Pacific Exhibit-11
Blue Backs-11
Yellow Backs-11
03Pacific Prism-8
Blue-8
Gold-8
Red-8
03Thrashers Postcards-19
03Topps-118
Blue-118
Gold-118
Red-118
Pristine Stick Portions-PPS-PS
Pristine Stick Portion Refractors-PPS-PS
03Upper Deck-10
Canadian Exclusives-10
HG-10
03Upper Deck MVP-19
Gold Script-19
Silver Script-19
Canadian Exclusives-19
03Upper Deck Victory-9
Bronze-9
Gold-9
Silver-9
04Pacific-18
Blue-18
Red-18
04Upper Deck-9
Canadian Exclusives-9
HG Glossy Gold-9
HG Glossy Silver-9
04Finnish Cardset-57
Parallel-43
Stars of the Game-12
04Swedish Pure Skills-115
Parallel-115
Professional Power-PS
05Hot Prospects Hot Materials-HMPS
05Panini Stickers-18
05Parkhurst-26
Facsimile Auto Parallel-26
True Colors-TCATL
True Colors-TCATL
05SP Game Used Authentic Fabrics Quad-KHLS
05SP Game Used Authentic Patches Quad -KHLS
05Ultra-12
Gold-12
Ice-12
05Upper Deck-8
HG Glossy-8
Jerseys-J-PAS
05Upper Deck MVP-14
Gold-14
Platinum-14
05Upper Deck Toronto Fall Expo-8
05Upper Deck Victory-12
Black-12
Gold-12
Silver-12
05Finnish Cardset -46
Finnish Cardset Magicmakers-8
06Fleer Fabricology-FPA
06O-Pee-Chee-160
Rainbow-160
06SP Game Used Authentic Fabrics-AFPS
06SP Game Used Authentic Fabrics Parallel-AFPS
06SP Game Used Authentic Fabrics Patches-AFPS
06Stars Team Postcards-21
06Upper Deck-316
Exclusives Parallel-316
High Gloss Parallel-316
Masterpieces-316
Victory-245
06Czech IIHF World Championship Postcards-20
06Czech LG Hockey Games Postcards-20

Stefaniak, Josef
70Swedish Masterserien-197

Stefanka, Filip
97Czech APS Extraliga-324
99Czech OFS-304
02Czech OFS Plus-146
Trios-T2
03Czech OFS Plus-280
04Czech OFS-223
05Czech HC Vsetin-13

Stefanka, Juraj
01Czech OFS-211
02Czech OFS Plus-268
03Czech OFS Plus-237
03Czech OFS Plus-351
04Czech OFS-357

Stefanski, Bud
00Barrie Colts-23

Stefanski, Sean
01Kingston Frontenacs-18
01Owen Sound Attack-21
02Sault Ste. Marie Greyhounds-14
03Sudbury Wolves-23
04Lakehead University Thunderwolves-19
05Florida Everblades-16

Steffen, Franz
93Swiss HNL-130
95Swiss HNL-179
96Swiss HNL-74
98Swiss Power Play Stickers-22
98Swiss Power Play Stickers-267
99Swiss Panini Stickers-24
00Swiss Panini Stickers-48
00Swiss Slapshot Mini-Cards-SCB15
01Swiss HNL-95

Steffen, Jeff
81Oshawa Generals-22
82Oshawa Generals-8
83Oshawa Generals-25

Steffen, Todd
82Kitchener Rangers-23

Steffensen, Michael
98Danish Hockey League-64

Stefishen, Adam
00Prince George Cougars-18
03Fresno Falcons-21

Stefl, Martin
06Czech HC Vsetin Postcards-11
06Czech OFS-194
Stars-21
Team Cards-12

Steger, Thomas
93Swiss HNL-458

Stehlik, Richard
03Lewiston Maineiacs-19
04Slovakian Skalica Team Set-24

Stehlin, Laurent
93Swiss HNL-383
95Swiss HNL-387
96Swiss HNL-270

Steidl, Christian
94German First League-255

Steidl, Florian
94German First League-260

Steiger, Alan
93Quebec Pee-Wee Tournament-1737

Steiger, Ewald
94German DEL-310

Steiger, Helmut
82Swedish Semic VM Stickers-119
83Swedish Semic VM Stickers-119
89Swedish Semic World Champ Stickers-116
91Finnish Semic World Champ Stickers-174
91Swedish Semic World Champ Stickers-174
94German DEL-267
95German DEL-260
96German DEL-148

Steiger, Nicholas
95Swiss HNL-39
96Swiss HNL-186

Steil, Todd
03Camrose Kodiaks-21
04Camrose Kodiaks-7

Stein, Phil
34Beehive Group I Photos-349

Steinberg, Thomas
94German First League-88

Steinbock, Stefan
94German DEL-325
95German DEL-301
96German DEL-328

Steinburg, Trevor
85Nordiques General Foods-27
86Fredericton Express-25
88Nordiques General Foods-35
88Nordiques Team Issue-31
89Halifax Citadels-24
89ProCards AHL-154
90Halifax Citadels-27
90ProCards AHL/IHL-462
91ProCards-372

Steinecker, Stefan
92Finnish Semic-178
94German DEL-57
95German DEL-52

Steinegger, Martin
93Swiss HNL-196
95Swedish World Championships Stickers-123
95Swiss HNL-94
96Swiss HNL-36
98Swiss Power Play Stickers-37
98Swiss Power Play Stickers-268

99Swiss Panini Stickers-36
99Swiss Panini Stickers-260
00Swiss Panini Stickers-36
00Swiss Panini Stickers National Team-P6
00Swiss Slapshot Mini-Cards-SCB6
01Swiss HNL-83
02Swiss HNL-77
02Swiss HNL-489

Steiner, Daniel
00Swiss Panini Stickers-192
01Swiss HNL-210
02Swiss HNL-335

Steiner, Ondrej
92Upper Deck-604
92Classic-37
Gold-37
94Czech APS Extraliga-158
95Czech APS Extraliga-255
97Czech APS Extraliga-231
98Czech DS-27
98Czech DS Stickers-38
98Czech OFS-91
99Finnish Cardset-345
01Czech OFS-208
02Czech OFS Plus-248
03Russian Hockey League-107
05Czech HC Vsetin-14

Steingraber, Christian
06Sarnia Sting-19

Steingrog, Bastian
04German DEL Update-312
05German DEL-340

Steingross, Bastian
03German DEL-59
04German Hannover Scorpions Postcards-27

Steinmann, Janick
05Kamloops Blazers-9

Steinmann, Robert
94German First League-353

Steinmetz, Todd
93Waterloo Black Hawks-24

Stejskal, Jiri
04Czech OFS-335
06Czech OFS-103
Stars-1
Team Cards-4

Stejskal, Michael
94German First League-153

Stejskal, Patrik
02Czech OFS Plus-363

Steklac, Peter
96Slovakian Quebec Pee-Wee Tournament-26

Stelcich, Martin
94Czech APS Extraliga-213
99Czech Score Blue 2000-34
99Czech Score Red Ice 2000-34

Stelljes, Matt
92Minnesota Golden Gophers-20

Stelmak, Jamie
91Air Canada SJHL-B36
92Saskatchewan JHL-137

Stelnov, Alexei
99Russian Metallurg Magnetogorsk-50

Stelnov, Igor
87Russian National Team-18
89Swedish Semic World Champ Stickers-85
91O-Pee-Chee Inserts-26R
92Swedish Semic Elitserien Stickers-260

Stemkowski, Pete
64Beehive Group III Photos-186
65Coca-Cola-98
65Topps-84
66Topps-15
66Topps USA Test-15
67Post Flip Books-10
67Topps-12
67York Action Octagons-8
67York Action Octagons-9
67York Action Octagons-12
67York Action Octagons-14
68O-Pee-Chee-33
68Shirriff Coins-43
68Topps-33
69O-Pee-Chee-65
69Topps-65
70Esso Power Players-196
70O-Pee-Chee-25
70O-Pee-Chee-182
70Sargent Promotions Stamps-50
70Topps-25
71O-Pee-Chee-217
71Sargent Promotions Stamps-115
71Toronto Sun-184
72O-Pee-Chee-78
72Sargent Promotions Stamps-143
73O-Pee-Chee-217
74Lipton Soup-42
74NHL Action Stamps-193
74O-Pee-Chee NHL-77
74Topps-77
75O-Pee-Chee NHL-303
75Topps-303
76O-Pee-Chee NHL-166
76Topps-166
77O-Pee-Chee NHL-272
77Sportscasters-6416
77Finnish Sportscasters-68-1623
78O-Pee-Chee-290
94Parkhurst Tall Boys-113
95Parkhurst '66-67-112
Coins-112
07Maple Leafs 1967 Commemorative-26

Stempfle, Ryan
00Saskatoon Blades-9
01Saskatoon Blades-22
02Medicine Hat Tigers-24

Stempniak, Lee
04SP Authentic Rookie Redemptions-RR34
05Beehive-97
Matte-97
Signature Scrapbook-SSLS
05Black Diamond-279
05Blues Team Set-18
05Hot Prospects-214
Autographed Patch Variation-214
Hot Materials-HMLS
Red Hot-214
05Parkhurst-664
Facsimile Auto Parallel-664
Signatures-LS
True Colors-TCSTL
True Colors-TCSTL
05SP Authentic-212
Limited-212
05SP Game Used-129
Autographs-129
Gold-129
Rookie Exclusives-LS
Rookie Exclusives Silver-RE-LS
05SPx-192
Spectrum-192
05The Cup-152
Autographed Rookie Patches Gold Rainbow-152
Black Rainbow Rookies-152
Masterpiece Pressplates (Artifacts)-326
Masterpiece Pressplates (Bee Hive)-97
Masterpiece Pressplates (Black Diamond)-279
Masterpiece Pressplates (Ice)-168
Masterpiece Pressplates (MVP)-432
Masterpiece Pressplates (Power Play)-162
Masterpiece Pressplates (Power Play)-162
Masterpiece Pressplates (Rookie Update)-233
Masterpiece Pressplates SPA Autos-212
Masterpiece Pressplates (SP Game Used)-129
Masterpiece Pressplates (SPx)-192
Masterpiece Pressplates (Trilogy)-216
Masterpiece Pressplates Ult Coll-169
Masterpiece Pressplates Autographs-152
Platinum Rookies-152
05UD Artifacts-326
05UD PowerPlay-162
05Ultimate Collection-169
Gold-169
05Ultra-245
Gold-245
Ice-245
05Upper Deck Ice-168
05Upper Deck MVP-432
Gold-432
Platinum-432
05Upper Deck Rookie Update-233
Inspirations Patch Rookies-233
05Upper Deck Trilogy-216
06Be A Player-31
Autographs-31
Signatures-LS
Signatures 10-34
Signatures Trios-TWBS
Up Close and Personal-UC27
Up Close and Personal Autographs-UC27
Portraits Signature Portraits-SPLS
06Fleer-170
Tiffany-170
06O-Pee-Chee-424
Rainbow-424
06UD Artifacts Auto-Facts-AFLS
06UD Artifacts Auto-Facts Gold-AFLS
06Ultra-171
Gold Medallion-171
Ice Medallion-171
06Upper Deck Arena Giveaways-STL3
06Upper Deck-171
Exclusives Parallel-171
High Gloss Parallel-171
Masterpieces-171
06Upper Deck MVP-254
Gold Script-254
Super Script-254
06Upper Deck Trilogy Scripts-TSLS
06Upper Deck Victory-170
06Upper Deck Victory Black-170
06Upper Deck Victory Gold-170
07Upper Deck Victory-115
Black-115
Gold-115

Sten, Marko
92Finnish Jyvas-Hyva Stickers-191
93Finnish SISU-210

Stenar, Olle
57Swedish Alfabilder-138
64Swedish Coralli ISHockey-66
65Swedish Coralli ISHockey-66

Stenfors, Pekka
78Finnish SM-Liiga-231

Stengaard, Mathies
98Danish Hockey League-222

Stengler, Blair
04Swift Current Broncos-20

Stenlund, Bernt-Ola
57Swedish Alfabilder-117

Stenlund, Ola
83Swedish Semic Elitserien-178
84Swedish Semic Elitserien-201
86Swedish Panini Stickers-223
87Swedish Panini Stickers-216
89Swedish Semic Elitserien Stickers-197

Stenlund, Ove
64Swedish Coralli ISHockey-150
65Swedish Coralli ISHockey-150
67Swedish Hockey-277
69Swedish Hockey-321
70Swedish Hockey-225
72Swedish Stickers-283

Stensrud, Evan
97Dubuque Fighting Saints-7

Stenvall, Heikko
65Finnish Hellas-19
66Finnish Jaakiekkosarja-12
70Finnish Jaakiekko-239

Stenvall, Lars
73Swedish Stickers-40

Stepan, Brad
87Sault Ste. Marie Greyhounds-25

Stepanek, Dan
94Dubuque Fighting Saints-27

Stepanek, Jakub
06Czech OFS-64

Stepanek, Martin
94Czech APS Extraliga-65
95Czech APS Extraliga-85
96Czech APS Extraliga-173
97Czech APS Extraliga-84
97Czech DS Extraliga-44
97Czech DS Stickers-5
97Czech DS Stickers-97
98Czech DS-44
98Czech DS Stickers-14
98Czech DS Stickers-91
98Czech OFS-5
98Czech OFS-424
98Czech OFS-454
99Czech OFS-270
99Finnish Cardset-284
00Czech DS Extraliga National Team-NT3
00Czech DS Extraliga World Champions-WCH4
00Finnish Cardset-256
01Swiss HNL-220
02Swiss HNL-187
03Finnish Cardset-88
03Finnish Cardset Globetrotters-GR6
05Czech HC Plzen-10
06Czech OFS-267

Stepanishev, Anatoli
98Russian Hockey League-118

Stepanov, Alexander
98Russian Hockey League-132
99Russian Dynamo Moscow-23
99Russian Hockey League-6
00Russian Dynamo Moscow-25
00Russian Hockey League-326
01Russian Dynamo Moscow Mentos-4
01Russian Hockey League-10
02Russian Lightnings-3
03Russian Hockey League-44
03Russian Hockey League-49
03Russian National Team-9
04Russian Moscow Dynamo-29

Stepanov, Anatoli
01Russian Hockey League-5
01Russian Hockey League-10

Stepanov, Igor
98Russian Hockey League-111
99Russian Hockey League-75

Stepanov, Maxim
99Russian Hockey League-29
99Russian Stars Postcards-24

Stephan, Fabian
99Swiss Panini Stickers-37
00Swiss Panini Stickers-37
01Swiss HNL-154
02Swiss HNL-312

Stephan, Greg
95Slapshot-79

Stephan, Joe
89ProCards IHL-127

Stephan, Tobias
97Quebec Pee-Wee Tournament-1126
01Swiss HNL-235
02Swiss HNL-103
06Between The Pipes-47
Autographs-ATST
06Iowa Stars-21
07Upper Deck Victory-221
Black-221
Gold-221

Stephens, B.J.
02Orlando Seals-1
06Fayetteville FireAntz-17

Stephens, Charlie
97Beehive-72
Authentic Autographs-72
Golden Portraits-72
98SP Authentic-132
Power Shift-132
Sign of the Times-CS
Sign of the Times Gold-CS
98Upper Deck-409
Exclusives-409
Exclusives 1 of 1-409
Gold Reserve-409
98Guelph Storm-16
99Guelph Storm-14
99Bowman CHL-31
Gold-31
OPC International-31
Autographs-BA10
Autographs Gold-BA10
Autographs Silver-BA10
01London Knights-10
02AHL Top Prospects-40
02Hershey Bears-20
03ITG Action-134
03AHL Top Prospects-33
03Hershey Bears-18
03Hershey Bears Patriot News-23
04Binghamton Senators-18
05Binghamton Senators-6
05Binghamton Senators Quickway-6
06German DEL-48
06Binghamton Senators 5th Anniversary-30

Stephens, Evan
04Sioux Falls Stampede-3-1
06Cedar Rapids RoughRiders-16

Stephens, Kelly
98Madison Monsters-5

Stephens, Matt
92Quebec Pee-Wee Tournament-1599
93Quebec Pee-Wee Tournament-519

Stephens, Scott
97Johnstown Chiefs-22
00Topps Chrome-161
OPC Refractors-161
Refractors-161

Stephens, Troy
89Peterborough Petes-98
897th Inn. Sketch OHL-98
907th Inn. Sketch OHL-372
93Phoenix Cobras RHI-17
95Central Hockey League-15
95Fort Worth Fire-10

Stephenson Sr., Wayne
51Bas Du Fleuve-10

Stephenson, Bob
79Maple Leafs Postcards-30
79O-Pee-Chee-391

Stephenson, Dave
97Owen Sound Platers-9
98Owen Sound Platers-8
99Owen Sound Platers-18

Stephenson, Ken
69Swedish Hockey-364

Stephenson, Logan
05ITG Heroes/Prosp Toronto Expo Parallel -327
05ITG Heroes and Prospects-327
Autographs Series II-LST
06ITG Heroes and Prospects National Pride-NP01
06ITG Heroes and Prospects National Pride Gold-NP01

Stephenson, Matt
04St. Cloud State Huskies-26
05St. Cloud State Huskies-8
06St. Cloud State Huskies-26

Stephenson, Ryan
05Plymouth Whalers-B-13

Stephenson, Scott
99UK Hull Thunder-9

Stephenson, Shay
00Red Deer Rebels-17
Signed-17
01Red Deer Rebels-16
02Red Deer Rebels-21
03Red Deer Rebels-16
05Reading Royals-15
06Manchester Monarchs-20

Stephenson, Slade
917th Inn. Sketch WHL-356

Stephenson, Wayne
69Swedish Hockey-365
70Swedish Masterserien-188
72Blues White Border-19
72O-Pee-Chee-275
72Sargent Promotions Stamps-191
73Blues White Border-19
73O-Pee-Chee-31
73Topps-31
74O-Pee-Chee NHL-218
74Topps-218
75Flyers Canada Dry Cans-17
75O-Pee-Chee NHL-355
76O-Pee-Chee NHL-190
76Topps-190
77O-Pee-Chee NHL-142
77Topps-142
78O-Pee-Chee-223
78Topps-223
79Capitals Team Issue-21
79O-Pee-Chee-38
79Topps-38
80O-Pee-Chee-121
80Topps-121
81Swedish Semic Hockey VM Stickers-73

Stepp, Joel
00Red Deer Rebels-18
Signed-18
01Red Deer Rebels-17
01UD Prospects-28
Jerseys-J-ST
Jerseys Gold-J-ST
02Red Deer Rebels-9
03Cincinnati Mighty Ducks-A12
04Cincinnati Mighty Ducks-16

Sterbak, Jan
99Czech OFS-417

Sterflinger, Robert
94German DEL-99
95German DEL-86
96German DEL-275

Sterflinger, Thomas
94German DEL-336
95German DEL-294
96German DEL-323

Sterling, Brett
06ITG Heroes and Prospects-165
Autographs-ABST

Sterling, Larry
04Fort Worth Brahmas-14

Stern, Mike
81Oshawa Generals-13
82Oshawa Generals-17
83Oshawa Generals-20

Stern, Ron
97Flames Collector's Photos-8

Stern, Ronnie
87Flint Spirits-18
88Canucks Mohawk-21
89ProCards IHL-179
90Canucks Mohawk-28
90Pro Set-549
91Canucks Panini Team Stickers-24
91Flames IGA-21
91Pro Set-362
French-362
91Score Canadian Bilingual-408
91Score Canadian English-408
92Flames IGA-25
92Parkhurst-265
Emerald Ice-265
92Pinnacle-217
French-217
92Score-237
Canadian-237
92Ultra-271
93Durivage Score-28
93Leaf-261
93OPC Premier-341
Gold-341
93Parkhurst-303
Emerald Ice-303
93PowerPlay-43
93Score-409
Canadian-409
93Stadium Club-68
Members Only Master Set-68
OPC-68
First Day Issue-68
First Day Issue OPC-68
93Topps/OPC Premier-341
Gold-341
94Be A Player-R122
94Leaf-399
94OPC Premier-71
Special Effects-71
94Topps/OPC Premier-71
Special Effects-71
94Upper Deck-27
Electric Ice-27
95Be A Player-79
Signatures-S79
Signatures Die Cuts-S79
95Canada Games NHL POGS-59
95Leaf-204
95Panini Stickers-238
95Playoff One on One-131
95Topps-181
OPC Inserts-181
95Upper Deck-368
Electric Ice-368
Electric Ice Gold-368
96Upper Deck-28
97Pacific-346
Copper-346
Emerald Green-346
Ice Blue-346
Red-346
Silver-346
99Pacific-382
Copper-382
Emerald Green-382
Gold-382
Ice Blue-382
Premiere Date-382
Red-382
02Fleer Throwbacks-60
Gold-60
Platinum-60

Sterner, Krister
70Swedish Hockey-67
71Swedish Hockey-156
72Swedish Stickers-39
73Swedish Stickers-152
74Swedish Stickers-150

Sterner, Ove
65Swedish Coralli ISHockey-104

Sterner, Ulf
64Swedish Coralli ISHockey-4
64Swedish Coralli ISHockey-97
65Swedish Coralli ISHockey-4
65Swedish Coralli ISHockey-97
67Swedish Hockey-165
69Swedish Hockey-199
69Swedish Hockey-346
70Finnish Jaakiekko-38
70Swedish Hockey-291
70Swedish Masterserien-41
70Swedish Masterserien-48
70Swedish Masterserien-57
70Swedish Masterserien-58
70Swedish Masterserien-115
71Finnish Suomi Stickers-58
71Swedish Hockey-24
71Swedish Hockey-154
72Finnish Panda Toronto-77
72Finnish Semic World Championship-56
72Swedish Semic World Championship-56
73Finnish Jaakiekko-36
73Swedish Stickers-9
73Swedish Stickers-179
74Finnish Jenkki-35
74Swedish Stickers-317
81Swedish Semic Hockey VM Stickers-115
91Finnish Semic World Champ Stickers-234
91Swedish Semic World Champ Stickers-234
95Swedish Globe World Championships-69
97Swedish Alfabilder Autographs-6
98Swedish UD Choice-200
01Swedish Alfabilder-6
04Swedish Alfabilder Alfa Stars-49
04Swedish Alfabilder Next In Line-4
04Swedish Alfabilder Proof Parallels-49

Sterz, Peter
94German First League-38

Stetter, Hans-Jorg
94German First League-117

Stettler, Olivier
93Quebec Pee-Wee Tournament-1620

Stevens, Bart
02Fort Wayne Komets-19

Stevens, Cam
06Chilliwack Bruins-9

Stevens, Chris
05Medicine Hat Tigers-22
06Medicine Hat Tigers-20

Stevens, Christopher
06Rimouski Oceanic-19

Stevens, John
83Oshawa Generals-26
88ProCards AHL-123
89ProCards AHL-346
90ProCards AHL/IHL-189
91ProCards-108
02Philadelphia Phantoms-23
03Philadelphia Phantoms-24
05Philadelphia Phantoms All-Decade Team-5

Stevens, Judd
01Minnesota Golden Gophers-11
02Minnesota Golden Gophers-23
03Minnesota Golden Gophers-28
04Minnesota Golden Gophers-25

Stevens, Kevin
89Panini Stickers-321
89Penguins Coke/Elby's-4
89Penguins Foodland-7
90Bowman-208
Tiffany-208
90O-Pee-Chee-360
90OPC Premier-111
90Panini Stickers-131
90Penguins Foodland-9
90Pro Set-240
90Score-53
Canadian-53
90Score Young Superstars-17
90Topps-360
Tiffany-360
90Upper Deck-14
French-14
91Pro Set Platinum-93
91Bowman-92
91Bowman-418
91Bowman-421
91Bowman-422
91McDonald's Upper Deck-3
91O-Pee-Chee-267
91O-Pee-Chee-421
91OPC Premier-26
91Panini Stickers-269
91Parkhurst-135
91Parkhurst-473
French-135
French-473
91Penguins Coke/Elby's-25
91Penguins Foodland-8
91Penguins Foodland Coupon Stickers-9
91Pinnacle-191
French-191
B-B4
B French-B4
91Pro Set-185
91Pro Set-314
French-185
French-314
Player of the Month-P2
91Score American-248
91Score Canadian Bilingual-468
91Score Canadian English-468
91Stadium Club-234
91Topps-267
91Topps-421
91Upper Deck-154
91Upper Deck-613
French-154
French-613
91Finnish Semic World Champ Stickers-145
91Swedish Semic World Champ Stickers-145
92Bowman-241
92Bowman-366
92Humpty Dumpty I-21
92McDonald's Upper Deck-H3
92O-Pee-Chee-29
92Panini Stickers-221
92Panini Stickers-281
92Panini Stickers French-221
92Panini Stickers French-281
92Parkhurst-138
92Parkhurst-466
Emerald Ice-138
Emerald Ice-466
92Penguins Coke/Clark-21
92Penguins Foodland-15
92Penguins Foodland Coupon Stickers-11
92Pinnacle Canadian Promo Panels-2
92Pinnacle-288
French-288
Team Pinnacle-4
Team French-4
92Pro Set-140
92Score Canadian Promo Sheets-1
92Score Canadian Promo Sheets-2
92Score-25
92Score-492
92Score-518
Canadian-25
Canadian-492
USA Greats-10
92Seasons Patches-66
92Stadium Club-110
92Stadium Club-257
92Topps-259
92Topps-343
92Topps-429
Gold-259G
Gold-343G
Gold-429G
92Ultra-171
All-Stars-5
92Upper Deck-275
92Upper Deck-454
92Upper Deck-630
Gordie Howe Selects-G4
93Donruss-265
93Leaf-69
Gold All-Stars-4
Hat Trick Artists-9
93McDonald's Upper Deck-25
93OPC Premier-170
93OPC Premier-370
Gold-170
Gold-370
93Panini Stickers-79
93Parkhurst-158
Emerald Ice-158
93Penguins Foodland-17
93Pinnacle-149
Canadian-149
All-Stars-15
All-Stars Canadian-15
Nifty Fifty-9
Team Pinnacle-4
Team Canadian-4
93PowerPlay-195
Point Leaders-17
93Score-325
Canadian-325
Dream Team-23
Dynamic Duos Canadian-8
93Seasons Patches-19
93Stadium Club-158
93Stadium Club-457
Members Only Master Set-158
Members Only Master Set-457
OPC-158
First Day Issue-158
First Day Issue-457
First Day Issue OPC-158
All-Stars-6
All-Stars Members Only-6
All-Stars OPC-6
93Topps/OPC Premier-170
93Topps/OPC Premier-370
Gold-170
Gold-370
93Ultra-229
All-Stars-6
93Upper Deck-126
93Upper Deck-230
Hat Tricks-HT19
SP-124
93Upper Deck Locker All-Stars-14
93Swedish Semic World Champ Stickers-179
93Classic Pro Prospects-31
94Be A Player-R82
94Canada Games NHL POGS-189
94Donruss-229
94EA Sports-106
94Finest-80
Super Team Winners-80
Refractors-80
Ring Leaders-13
94Flair-140
94Fleer-170
94Hockey Wit-20
94Leaf-356
94Leaf Limited-46
94OPC Premier-290
Special Effects-290
94Parkhurst-177
Gold-177
SE Vintage-9
94Penguins Foodland-19
94Pinnacle-299
Artist's Proofs-299
Rink Collection-299
Team Pinnacle-TP7
Team Dufex Parallel-TP7
94Score-182
Gold-182
Platinum-182
Check It-CI4
94Select-106
Gold-106
94Topps/OPC Premier-290
Special Effects-290
94Topps Finest Inserts-17
94Ultra-170
Red Light Specials-10
94Upper Deck-390
Electric Ice-390
SP Inserts-SP62
SP Inserts Die Cuts-SP62
95Bashan Super Stickers-9
95Be A Player-12
Signatures-S12
Signatures Die Cuts-S12
95Bowman-59
All-Foil-59
95Collector's Choice-219
Player's Club-219
Player's Club Platinum-219
95Donruss-221
95Donruss Elite-95
Die Cut Stars-95
Die Cut Uncut-95
95Emotion-12
Ntense Power-8
95Hoyle Eastern Playing Cards-21
95Imperial Stickers-9
95Leaf-216
95Leaf Limited-96
95Metal-11
95Panini Stickers-7
95Parkhurst International-10
95Parkhurst International-370
Emerald Ice-10
Emerald Ice-370
95Pinnacle FANtasy-28
95Playoff One on One-10
95Playoff One on One-123
95Pro Magnets-20
95Score-44
Black Ice Artist's Proofs-44
Black Ice-44
95Select Certified-46
Mirror Gold-46
95SkyBox Impact-13
95Stadium Club-50
Members Only Master Set-50
Fearless-F6
Fearless Members Only Master Set-F6
95Summit-67
Artist's Proofs-67
Ice-67
95Topps-282
OPC Inserts-282
Hidden Gems-11HG
Power Lines-5PL
95Topps SuperSkills-61
Platinum-61
95Ultra-127
95Ultra-207
Gold Medallion-127
Crease Crashers-18
95Upper Deck-96
Electric Ice-96
Electric Ice Gold-96
Special Edition-SE96
Special Edition Gold-SE96
95Zenith-52
Gifted Grinders-2
95Swedish Globe World Championships-122
96Collector's Choice-124
96Maggers-94
96NHL Pro Stamps-20
96Penguins Tribune-Review-6
96Playoff One on One-333
96SP-73
96Team Out-12
96Topps Picks-81
OPC Inserts-81
96Upper Deck-78
Generation Next-X34
96Collector's Edge Ice Livin' Large-L10
97Donruss Priority-42
Stamp of Approval-42
97Katch-96
Gold-96
Silver-96
97Pacific-115
Copper-115
Emerald Green-115
Ice Blue-115
Red-115
Silver-115
97Pacific Omega-149
Copper-149
Dark Gray-149
Emerald Green-149
Gold-149
Ice Blue-149
97Panini Stickers-225
97Paramount-121
Copper-121
Dark Grey-121
Emerald Green-121
Ice Blue-121
Red-121
Silver-121
97Pinnacle-143
Press Plates Back Black-143
Press Plates Back Cyan-143
Press Plates Back Magenta-143
Press Plates Back Yellow-143
Press Plates Front Black-143
Press Plates Front Cyan-143
Press Plates Front Magenta-143
Press Plates Front Yellow-143
97Pinnacle Inside-153
97Revolution-91
Copper-91
Emerald-91
Ice Blue-91
Silver-91
97Score-159
Artist's Proofs-159
Golden Blades-159
97Score Rangers-6
Platinum-6
Premier-6
98Aurora-127
98Be A Player-88
Press Release-88
98BAP Gold-88
98BAP Autographs-88
98BAP Autographs Gold-88
98BAP Tampa Bay All Star Game-88
98Finest-56
No Protectors-56
No Protectors Refractors-56
Refractors-56
98Katch-95
98Pacific-301
Ice Blue-301
Red-301
98Paramount-158
Copper-158
Emerald Green-158
Holo-Electric-158
Ice Blue-158
Silver-158
98Upper Deck-130
Exclusives-130
Exclusives 1 of 1-130
Gold Reserve-130
99BAP Memorabilia-294
Gold-294
Silver-294
99Pacific-281
Copper-281
Emerald Green-281
Gold-281
Ice Blue-281
Premiere Date-281
Red-281
99Panini Stickers-103
99Paramount-157
Copper-157
Emerald-157
Gold-157
Holographic Emerald-157
Holographic Gold-157
Holographic Silver-157
Ice Blue-157
Premiere Date-157
Red-157
Silver-157
99Upper Deck Victory-198
00Titanium Game Gear-141
00Titanium Game Gear Patches-141
00Titanium Draft Day Edition-87
Patches-87
01Atomic Patches-46
01BAP Signature Series-143
Autographs-143
Autographs Gold-143
01Pacific-318
Extreme LTD-318
Hobby LTD-318
Premiere Date-318
Retail LTD-318
01Pacific Arena Exclusives-318
01Pacific Heads-Up Quad Jerseys-15
01Private Stock Game Gear-84
01Upper Deck-141
Exclusives-141
01Upper Deck Vintage-206
02BAP Sig Series Auto Buybacks 1998-88
02BAP Sig Series Auto Buybacks 2001-143
03SP Game Used Team Threads-TTBSG
04ITG Franchises US West-274
Autographs-A-KS

Stevens, Mike
83Kitchener Rangers-21
84Kitchener Rangers-25
85Fredericton Express-5
86Fredericton Express-24
88ProCards AHL-301
89ProCards AHL-240
90Newmarket Saints-24
90ProCards AHL/IHL-146
91ProCards-345
92Binghamton Rangers-7
95Cleveland Lumberjacks-24
95Cleveland Lumberjacks Postcards-23
96Collector's Edge Ice-118
Prism-118
98German DEL-236
99German Adler Mannheim Eagles Postcards-16
99German DEL-15
01German Upper Deck-177
02German DEL City Press-102

Stevens, Minors
98Amarillo Rattlers-17

Stevens, P.C.
23V128-1 Paulin's Candy-33

Stevens, Peter
06Kingston Frontenacs-14

Stevens, Randy
91Michigan Tech Huskies-30
93Michigan Tech Huskies-7
95Classic-80
Autographs-21
96Louisville Riverfrogs-11

Stevens, Rod
917th Inn. Sketch WHL-82
93Kamloops Blazers-20
96Syracuse Crunch-38
00UK Sekonda Superleague-179
01UK Belfast Giants-15
06UK Nottingham Panthers-17

Stevens, Scott
82Capitals Team Issue-23
83O-Pee-Chee-376
83O-Pee-Chee Stickers-188
83Topps Stickers-188
84Capitals Pizza Hut-15
84O-Pee-Chee-206
84Topps-149
85Capitals Pizza Hut-14
85O-Pee-Chee-62
85O-Pee-Chee Stickers-107
85Topps-62
86Capitals Kodak-25
86Capitals Police-24
86O-Pee-Chee-126
86O-Pee-Chee Stickers-254
86Topps-126
87Capitals Kodak-3
87Capitals Team Issue-22
87O-Pee-Chee-25
87O-Pee-Chee Stickers-233
87Panini Stickers-177
87Topps-25
88Capitals Borderless-20
88Capitals Smokey-22
88Frito-Lay Stickers-15
88O-Pee-Chee-60
88O-Pee-Chee Minis-39
88O-Pee-Chee Stickers-68
88Panini Stickers-358
88Topps-60
88Topps Sticker Inserts-4
89Capitals Kodak-3
89Capitals Team Issue-22
89O-Pee-Chee-93
89O-Pee-Chee Stickers-76
89Panini Stickers-341
89Topps-93
89Swedish Semic World Champ Stickers-58
90Blues Kodak-21
90Kraft-56
90O-Pee-Chee-211
90O-Pee-Chee-394
90OPC Premier-112
90Panini Stickers-155
90Pro Set-321
90Pro Set-528
90Score-188
90Score-341
Canadian-188
Canadian-341
90Score Hottest/Rising Stars-82
90Score Rookie/Traded-40T
90Topps-211
90Topps-394
Tiffany-211
90Upper Deck-236
90Upper Deck-436
90Upper Deck-482
French-236
French-436
French-482
91Pro Set Platinum-72
91Pro Set Platinum-281
91Bowman-369
91Kraft-53
91McDonald's Upper Deck-24
91O-Pee-Chee-481
91OPC Premier-84
91Panini Stickers-26
91Parkhurst-102
French-102
91Pinnacle-81
French-81
91Pro Set-216
91Pro Set-292
91Pro Set-423
French-216
French-292
French-423
91Score American-40
91Score American-303
91Score Canadian Bilingual-40
91Score Canadian Bilingual-307
91Score Canadian Bilingual-595
91Score Canadian English-40
91Score Canadian English-307
91Score Canadian English-595
91Score Rookie/Traded-45T
91Stadium Club-265
91Topps-481
91Upper Deck-132
91Upper Deck-539
French-132
French-539
91Finnish Semic World Champ Stickers-56
91Swedish Semic World Champ Stickers-56
92Blues UD Best of the Blues-20
92Bowman-160
92Bowman-242
92Humpty Dumpty I-22
92McDonald's Upper Deck-27
92O-Pee-Chee-251
92O-Pee-Chee-336
25th Anniv. Inserts-16
92Panini Stickers-181
92Panini Stickers French-181
92Parkhurst-92
Emerald Ice-92
Cherry Picks-CP18
92Pinnacle Canadian Promo Panels-1
92Pinnacle-280
French-280
92Pro Set-95

92Score-75
92Score-429
Canadian-429
92Seasons Patches-50
92Sports Illustrated for Kids II-366
92Stadium Club-151
92Topps-156
92Topps-269
Gold-156G
Gold-269G
92Ultra-119
92Upper Deck-297
92Finnish Semic-78
93Donruss-192
93Kraft-49
93Leaf-60
93McDonald's Upper Deck-26
93OPC Premier-80
Gold-80
93Panini Stickers-43
93Parkhurst-114
Emerald Ice-114
93Pinnacle-25
Canadian-25
All-Stars-4
All-Stars Canadian-4
Captains-13
Captains Canadian-13
Team Pinnacle-3
Team Canadian-3
93PowerPlay-143
93Score-111
Canadian-111
Dream Team-5
Franchise-11
93Stadium Club-383
Members Only Master Set-383
First Day Issue-383
All-Stars-9
All-Stars Members Only-9
All-Stars OPC-9
93Topps/OPC Premier-80
Gold-80
93Ultra-189
93Upper Deck-119
SP-89
93Upper Deck Locker All-Stars-15
93Swedish Semic World Champ Stickers-196
94Be A Player-R146
94Canada Games NHL POGS-152
94Canada Games NHL POGS-262
94Canada Games NHL POGS-345
94Donruss-262
Dominators-2
94EA Sports-73
94Finest-18
Super Team Winners-18
Refractors-18
Division's Clear Cut-7
94Flair-100
94Fleer-119
94Hockey Wit-65
94Kraft-72
94Leaf-363
Gold Stars-12
94Leaf Limited-85
94McDonald's Upper Deck-McD7
94OPC Premier-126
94OPC Premier-153
94OPC Premier-370
94OPC Premier-451
94OPC Premier-494
Special Effects-126
Special Effects-153
Special Effects-370
Special Effects-451
Special Effects-494
94Parkhurst Crash the Game Green-13
94Parkhurst Crash the Game Blue-13
94Parkhurst Crash the Game Gold-13
94Parkhurst Crash the Game Red-13
94Parkhurst Vintage-V41
94Parkhurst SE-SE97
Gold-SE97
94Pinnacle-310
Artist's Proofs-310
Rink Collection-310
Team Pinnacle-TP5
Team Dufex Parallel-TP5
94Score-193
Gold-193
Platinum-193
Check It-CI2
Dream Team-DT5
Franchise-TF13
94Select-82
Gold-82
First Line-FL8
94SP-66
Die Cuts-66
94Stadium Club Members Only-30
94Stadium Club-4
Members Only Master Set-4
First Day Issue-4
Super Team Winner Cards-4
94Topps/OPC Premier-126
94Topps/OPC Premier-153
94Topps/OPC Premier-370
94Topps/OPC Premier-451
94Topps/OPC Premier-494
Special Effects-126
Special Effects-153
Special Effects-370
Special Effects-451
Special Effects-494
94Ultra-123
94Upper Deck-73
Electric Ice-73
Ice Gallery-IG5
Predictor Canadian-C30
94Upper Deck Predictor Canadian Exch Gold-C30
94Upper Deck Predictor Retail-R48
94Upper Deck Predictor Retail Exchange-R48
94Upper Deck SP Inserts-SP45
94Upper Deck SP Inserts Die Cuts-SP45
94Upper Deck NHLPA/Be A Player-36
94Finnish Jaa Kiekko-83
95SLU Hockey Canadian-13
95SLU Hockey American-18
95Bashan Super Stickers-68
95Bashan Super Stickers-72
95Be A Player-219
Signatures-S219
Signatures Die Cuts-S219
95Bowman-50
All-Foil-50
Bowman's Best-BB4
Bowman's Best Refractors-BB4
95Canada Games NHL POGS-165
95Collector's Choice-223
Player's Club-223
Player's Club Platinum-223
95Donruss-163
95Donruss Elite-70
Die Cut Stars-70
Die Cut Uncut-70
95Emotion-102
95Finest-33
95Finest-152
Refractors-33
Refractors-152
95Hoyle Eastern Playing Cards-22
95Imperial Stickers-72
95Kenner Starting Lineup Cards-20
95Kraft-6
95Leaf-124
95Metal-86
Iron Warriors-12
95NHL Aces Playing Cards-2C
95Panini Stickers-89
95Parkhurst International-121
Emerald Ice-121
NHL All-Stars-4
95Pinnacle-86
Artist's Proofs-86
Rink Collection-86
Full Contact-2
95Playoff One on One-61
95Playoff One on One-167
95Post Upper Deck-12
95Pro Magnets-40
95Score-160
Black Ice Artist's Proofs-160
Black Ice-160
95Select Certified-66
Mirror Gold-66
Double Strike-18
Double Strike Gold-18
95SkyBox Impact-97
95SP-81
Holoviews-FX13
Holoviews Special FX-FX13
95Stadium Club Members Only-10
95Stadium Club-45
Members Only Master Set-45
Fearless-F4
Fearless Members Only Master Set-F4
Nemeses-N1
Nemeses Members Only Master Set-N1
95Summit-134
Artist's Proofs-134
Ice-134
GM's Choice-8
95Topps-275
OPC Inserts-275
Mystery Finest-M17
Mystery Finest Refractors-M17
Profiles-PF13
Rink Leaders-6RL
95Topps SuperSkills-7
Platinum-7
95Ultra-92
95Ultra-196
Gold Medallion-92
Gold Medallion-196
95Upper Deck-482
Electric Ice-482
Electric Ice Gold-482
95Upper Deck All-Star Game Predictors-27
Redemption Winners-27
95Upper Deck NHL All-Stars-AS2
95Upper Deck NHL All-Stars Jumbo-AS2
95Upper Deck Predictor Hobby-H35
95Upper Deck Predictor Hobby Exchange-H35
95Upper Deck Special Edition-SE49
95Upper Deck Special Edition Gold-SE49
95Zenith-89
95Swedish Globe World Championships-81
96Black Diamond-124
Gold-124
96Collector's Choice-148
96Collector's Choice-305
96Collector's Choice-322
MVP-UD36
MVP Gold-UD36
96Devils Team Issue-4
96Donruss-57
Press Proofs-57
Hit List-9
96Donruss Canadian Ice-103
Gold Press Proofs-103
Red Press Proofs-103
96Donruss Elite-30
Die Cut Stars-30
96Duracell All-Cherry Team-DC16
96Duracell L'Equipe Beliveau-JB16
96Flair-54
Blue Ice-54
96Fleer-61
96Kraft Upper Deck-38
96Leaf-175
Press Proofs-175
96Leaf Limited-23
Gold-23
96Leaf Preferred-38
Press Proofs-38
96Maggers-95
96Metal Universe-88
96NHL Pro Stamps-40
96Pinnacle-4
Artist's Proofs-4
Foil-4
Premium Stock-4
Rink Collection-4
96Post Upper Deck-22
96Score-138
Artist's Proofs-138
Dealer's Choice Artist's Proofs-138
Special Artist's Proofs-138
Golden Blades-138
96Select Certified-54
Artist's Proofs-54
Blue-54
Mirror Blue-54
Mirror Gold-54
Mirror Red-54
Red-54
96SkyBox Impact-71
96SP-89
96SPx-24
Gold-24
96Stadium Club Members Only-27
96Summit-9
Artist's Proofs-9
Ice-9
Metal-9
Premium Stock-9
96Team Out-48
96Topps Picks-115
Ice D-ID4
OPC Inserts-115
96Ultra-95
Gold Medallion-95
96Upper Deck-286
Generation Next-X36
Power Performers-P9
Superstar Showdown-SS9B
96Zenith-73
Artist's Proofs-73
96Swedish Semic Wien-80
97Black Diamond-17
Double Diamond-17
Triple Diamond-17
Quadruple Diamond-17
97Collector's Choice-140
World Domination-W17
97Crown Royale-77
Emerald Green-77
Ice Blue-77
Silver-77
97Devils Team Issue-4
97Donruss-194
Press Proofs Silver-194
Press Proofs Gold-194
97Donruss Canadian Ice-114
Dominion Series-114
Provincial Series-114
97Donruss Limited-176
Exposure-176
97Katch-84
Gold-84
Silver-84
97Kraft Team Canada-10
97McDonald's Team Canada Coins-12
97Pacific-273
Copper-273
Emerald Green-273
Ice Blue-273
Red-273
Silver-273
97Pacific Omega-134
Copper-134
Dark Gray-134
Emerald Green-134
Gold-134
Ice Blue-134
97Pinnacle-158
Press Plates Back Black-158
Press Plates Back Cyan-158
Press Plates Back Magenta-158
Press Plates Back Yellow-158
Press Plates Front Black-158
Press Plates Front Cyan-158
Press Plates Front Magenta-158
Press Plates Front Yellow-158
97Pinnacle Certified-115
Red-115
Mirror Blue-115
Mirror Gold-115
Mirror Red-115
97Pinnacle Inside-154
97Pinnacle Tot Cert Platinum Blue-115
97Pinnacle Tot Certi Platinum Gold-115
97Pinnacle Totally Certified Platinum Red-115
97Pinnacle Tot Cert Mirror Platinum Gold-115
97Score-224
97Score Devils-8
Platinum-8
Premier-8
97SP Authentic-85
Icons-I35
Icons Die-Cuts-I35
Icons Embossed-I35
97SPx-26
Bronze-26
Gold-26
Silver-26
Steel-26
Grand Finale-26
97Upper Deck-95
97Upper Deck-396
Three Star Selects-11C
98SLU Hockey Classic Doubles-1
98Aurora-113
98Black Diamond-49
Double Diamond-49
Triple Diamond-49
Quadruple Diamond-49
98Devils Power Play-NJD2
98Devils Team Issue-28
98Finest-132
No Protectors-132
No Protectors Refractors-132
Refractors-132
Promos-PP1
98Katch-81
98OPC Chrome-23
Refractors-23
Board Members-B12
Board Members Refractors-B12
98Pacific-272
Ice Blue-272
Red-272
98Pacific Dynagon Ice-112
Blue-112
Red-112
98Pacific Omega-143
Red-143
Opening Day Issue-143
98Paramount-139
Copper-139
Emerald Green-139
Holo-Electric-139
Ice Blue-139
Silver-139
98SP Authentic-49
Power Shift-49
98Topps-23
O-Pee-Chee-23
Board Members-B12
98Topps Gold Label Class 1-100
Black-100
Black One of One-100
One of One-100
Red-100
Red One of One-100
98Topps Gold Label Class 2-100
98Topps Gold Label Class 2 Black-100
98Topps Gold Label Class 2 Black 1 of 1-100
98Topps Gold Label Class 2 One of One-100
98Topps Gold Label Class 2 Red-100
98Topps Gold Label Class 2 Red One of One-100
98Topps Gold Label Class 3-100
98Topps Gold Label Class 3 Black-100
98Topps Gold Label Class 3 Black 1 of 1-100
98Topps Gold Label Class 3 One of One-100
98Topps Gold Label Class 3 Red-100
98Topps Gold Label Class 3 Red One of One-100
98UD Choice-113
98UD Choice-239
98UD Choice Preview-113
98UD Choice Prime Choice Reserve-113
98UD Choice Prime Choice Reserve-239
98UD Choice Reserve-113
98UD Choice Reserve-239
98Upper Deck-121
Exclusives-121
Exclusives 1 of 1-121
Gold Reserve-121
98Upper Deck MVP-116
Gold Script-116
Silver Script-116
Super Script-116
99BAP Memorabilia-52
Gold-52
Silver-52
99BAP Update Teammates Jersey Cards-TM31
99Devils Team Issue-1
99Jell-O Partners of Power-1
99Kraft Dinner-12
99McDonald's Upper Deck Game Jerseys-GJSS
99O-Pee-Chee-167
99O-Pee-Chee Chrome-167
99O-Pee-Chee Chrome Refractors-167
99Pacific-250
Copper-250
Emerald Green-250
Gold-250
Ice Blue-250
Premiere Date-250
Red-250
99Panini Stickers-76
99SPx-84
Radiance-84
Spectrum-84
99Stadium Club-132
First Day Issue-132
One of a Kind-132
Printing Plates Black-132
Printing Plates Cyan-132
Printing Plates Magenta-132
Printing Plates Yellow-132
99Topps/OPC-167
99Topps/OPC Chrome-167
Refractors-167
99Topps Gold Label Class 1-72
Black-72
Black One of One-72
One of One-72
Red-72
Red One of One-72
99Topps Gold Label Class 2-72
99Topps Gold Label Class 2 Black-72
99Topps Gold Label Class 2 Black 1 of 1-72
99Topps Gold Label Class 2 One of One-72
99Topps Gold Label Class 2 Red-72
99Topps Gold Label Class 2 Red One of One-72
99Topps Gold Label Class 3-72
99Topps Gold Label Class 3 Black-72
99Topps Gold Label Class 3 Black 1 of 1-72
99Topps Gold Label Class 3 One of One-72
99Topps Gold Label Class 3 Red-72
99Topps Gold Label Class 3 Red One of One-72
99Topps Premier Plus-46
Parallel-46
99Ultimate Victory-51
1/1-51
Parallel-51
Parallel 100-51
99Upper Deck-250
Exclusives-250
Exclusives 1 of 1-250
99Upper Deck Gold Reserve-250
99Upper Deck MVP-114
Gold Script-114
Silver Script-114
Super Script-114
99Upper Deck MVP SC Edition-105
Gold Script-105
Silver Script-105
Super Script-105
99Upper Deck Retro-46
Gold-46
Platinum-46
99Upper Deck Victory-170
99Wayne Gretzky Hockey-96
99Russian Fetisov Tribute-24
00Aurora-85
Premiere Date-85
00BAP Memorabilia-59
Emerald-59
Ruby-59
Sapphire-59
Promos-59
Jersey Cards-J12
Jersey Emblems-E12
Jersey Numbers-N12
Jersey and Stick Cards-JS12
00BAP Mem Chicago Sportsfest Copper-59
00BAP Memorabilia Chicago Sportsfest Blue-59
00BAP Memorabilia Chicago Sportsfest Gold-59
00BAP Memorabilia Chicago Sportsfest Ruby-59
00BAP Memorabilia Chicago Sun-Times Ruby-59
00BAP Memorabilia Chicago Sun-Times Gold-59
00BAP Mem Chicago Sun-Times Sapphire-59
00BAP Mem Toronto Fall Expo Copper-59
00BAP Memorabilia Toronto Fall Expo Gold-59
00BAP Memorabilia Toronto Fall Expo Ruby-59
00BAP Mem Update Heritage Jersey Cards-H21
00BAP Mem Update Heritage Jersey Gold-H21
00BAP Memorabilia Update Teammates-TM21
00BAP Memorabilia Update Teammates-TM31
00BAP Memorabilia Update Teammates Gold-TM21
00BAP Memorabilia Update Teammates Gold-TM31
00BAP Parkhurst 2000-P144
00BAP Signature Series-115
Emerald-115
Ruby-115
Sapphire-115
Autographs-152
Autographs Gold-152
Department of Defense-DD6
Jersey Cards-J17
Jersey and Stick Cards-GSJ17
Jersey Cards Autographs-J17
Jersey Emblems-E17
Jersey Numbers-IN17
00BAP Ultimate Memorabilia Autographs-36
Gold-36
00BAP Ultimate Mem Game-Used Jerseys-GJ39
00BAP Ultimate Mem Game-Used Sticks-GS39
00Black Diamond-35
Gold-35
00Devils Team Issue-19
00Kraft-4
00McDonald's Pacific-22
Blue-22
00O-Pee-Chee-28
00O-Pee-Chee Parallel-28
00Pacific-243
Copper-243
Gold-243
Ice Blue-243
Premiere Date-243
00Paramount-149
Copper-149
Gold-149
Holo-Gold-149
Holo-Silver-149
Ice Blue-149
Premiere Date-149
00Revolution-88
Blue-88
Premiere Date-88
Red-88
00SPx-40
00SPx-73
Spectrum-40
Spectrum-73
00Stadium Club-33
Special Forces-SF1
00Topps/OPC-28
Parallel-28
00Topps Chrome-26
OPC Refractors-26
Refractors-26
00Topps Gold Label Class 1-40
Gold-40
00Topps Gold Label Class 2-40
00Topps Gold Label Class 2 Gold-40
00Topps Gold Label Class 3-40
00Topps Gold Label Class 3 Gold-40
00Topps Heritage-59
00Topps Heritage-228
00Topps Heritage-239
Chrome Parallel-59
Heroes-HH9
00Topps Premier Plus-71
Blue Ice-71
World Premier-WP5
00Topps Stars-48
Blue-48
Progression-P7
00UD Heroes-73
00UD Pros and Prospects-51
Championship Rings-CR5
00Upper Deck-108
Exclusives Tier 1-108
Exclusives Tier 2-108
00Upper Deck Legends-78
00Upper Deck Legends-79
Legendary Collection Bronze-78
Legendary Collection Bronze-79
Legendary Collection Gold-78
Legendary Collection Gold-79
Legendary Collection Silver-78
Legendary Collection Silver-79
00Upper Deck MVP-109
First Stars-109
Second Stars-109
Third Stars-109
00Upper Deck Victory-139
00Upper Deck Vintage-210
00Upper Deck Vintage-221
00Czech Stadion-95
01BAP Memorabilia-26
Emerald-26
Ruby-26
Sapphire-26
All-Star Teammates-AST15
He Shoots-He Scores Prizes-5
Stanley Cup Playoffs-SC3
01BAP Signature Series Certified 100-C43
01BAP Signature Series Certified 50-C43
01BAP Signature Series Certified 1 of 1's-C43
01BAP Signature Series Autographs-LSST
01BAP Signature Series Autographs Gold-LSST
01BAP Signature Series Jerseys-GJ-33
01BAP Signature Series Jersey Autographs-GUSS
01BAP Sig Series Jersey and Stick Cards-GSJ-33
01BAP Signature Series Teammates-TM-18
01BAP Ultimate Memorabilia Active Eight-7
01BAP Ultimate Memorabilia Autographs-8
01BAP Ultimate Mem Autographs Gold-8
01Bowman YoungStars-96
Gold-96
Ice Cubed-96
01Crown Royale-87
Blue-87
Premiere Date-87
Red-87
Retail-87
01Devils Team Issue-22
01O-Pee-Chee-41
01O-Pee-Chee Heritage Parallel-41
01O-Pee-Chee Heritage Parallel Limited-41
01O-Pee-Chee Premier Parallel-41
01Pacific-238
Extreme LTD-238
Hobby LTD-238
Premiere Date-238
Retail LTD-238
01Pacific Adrenaline-117
Blue-117
Premiere Date-117
Red-117
Retail-117
01Pacific Arena Exclusives-238
01Pacific Heads-Up-58
Blue-58
Premiere Date-58
Red-58
Silver-58
01Parkhurst-165
Heroes-H12
Jerseys-PJ28
Milestones-M13
Sticks-PS28
Teammates-T14
01SP Authentic-50
Limited-50
Limited Gold-50
Jerseys-NNSS
01SP Game Used Authentic Fabric-AFSS
01SP Game Used Authentic Fabric Gold-AFSS
01Sports Illustrated for Kids III-307
01Stadium Club Gallery-G9
01Stadium Club Gallery Gold-G9
01Stadium Club Heart and Soul-HS6
01Titanium-85
Hobby Parallel-85
Premiere Date-85
Retail-85
Retail Parallel-85
Double-Sided Jerseys-21
Double-Sided Patches-21
01Titanium Draft Day Edition-55
01Topps-41
Heritage Parallel-41
Heritage Parallel Limited-41
OPC Parallel-41
01Topps Chrome-41
Refractors-41
Black Border Refractors-41
01Topps Heritage-91
01Topps Heritage-118
Refractors-91
01UD Honor Roll-23
01UD Honor Roll-53
Playoff Matchups-HS-SS
Playoff Matchups Gold-HS-SS
Pucks-P-SS
Pucks Gold-P-SS
Tough Customers-TC3
01UD Stanley Cup Champs-69
01Upper Deck-106
Exclusives-106
Game Jerseys Series II-FJSS
Game Jerseys Series II-DJSB
Leaders of the Pack-LP7
Pride of a Nation-DPSB
01Upper Deck MVP-111
01Upper Deck Victory-206
01Upper Deck Victory-434
Gold-206
Gold-434
01Upper Deck Vintage-155
01Upper Deck Vintage-157
01Upper Deck Vintage-265
02McFarlane Hockey-80
02McFarlane Hockey-82
02BAP All-Star Edition-87
Jerseys-87
Jerseys Gold-87
Jerseys Silver-87
02BAP First Edition-12
02BAP First Edition-329
Jerseys-12
02BAP Memorabilia-171
Emerald-171
Ruby-171
Sapphire-171
Mini Stanley Cups-38
NHL All-Star Game-171
NHL All-Star Game Blue-171
NHL All-Star Game Green-171
NHL All-Star Game Red-171
02BAP Memorabilia Toronto Fall Expo-171
02BAP Signature Series-147
Autographs-147
Autograph Buybacks 2000-152
Autograph Buybacks 2001-LSST
Autographs Gold-147
Defensive Wall-DW6
Golf-GS84
Team Quads-TQ7
02BAP Ultimate Memorabilia Conn Smythe-28
02Bowman YoungStars-33
Gold-33
Silver-33
02Devils Team Issue-2
02O-Pee-Chee-82
02O-Pee-Chee Premier Blue Parallel-82
02O-Pee-Chee Premier Red Parallel-82
02O-Pee-Chee Factory Set-82
02Pacific-229
Blue-229
Red-229
02Pacific Complete-467
Red-467
02Pacific Heads-Up Quad Jerseys-17
02Pacific Heads-Up Quad Jerseys Gold-17
02Parkhurst-15
Bronze-15
Gold-15
Silver-15
Teammates-TT5
02Parkhurst Retro-125
Minis-125
02Stadium Club-53
Silver Decoy Cards-53
Proofs-53
02Titanium Jerseys-40
02Titanium Jerseys Retail-40
02Titanium Patches-40
02Topps-82
OPC Blue Parallel-82
OPC Red Parallel-82
Factory Set-82
02Topps Chrome-51
Black Border Refractors-51
Refractors-51
02Topps Heritage-66
Chrome Parallel-66
02Topps Total-53
02UD Honor Roll-88
02UD Top Shelf All-Stars-ASSS
02UD Top Shelf Dual Player Jerseys-STBS
02Upper Deck-102
Exclusives-102
Blow-Ups-C24
Letters of Note-LNSS
Letters of Note Gold-LNSS
02Upper Deck MVP-109
Gold-109
Classics-109
Golden Classics-109
02Upper Deck Rookie Update-151C
02Upper Deck Rookie Update-161B
02Upper Deck Victory-124
Bronze-124
Gold-124
Silver-124
02Upper Deck Vintage-148
02Upper Deck Vintage-278
03BAP Memorabilia Stanley Cup Champions-SCC-8
03BAP Memorabilia Stanley Cup Playoffs-SCP-31
03BAP Ultimate Memorabilia Autographs-45
Gold-45
03BAP Ultimate Mem Auto Sticks-45
03BAP Ultimate Memorabilia Active Eight-6
03BAP Ultimate Mem Ultimate Captains-4
03Beehive-118
Gold-118
Silver-118
03Black Diamond-133
Black-133
Green-133
Red-133
03Bowman-79
Gold-79
03Bowman Chrome-79
Refractors-79
Gold Refractors-79
Xfractors-79
03Devils Team Issue-4
03ITG Action-364
Jerseys-M116
03ITG Used Signature Series-33
Gold-33
Autographs-SST
Autographs Gold-SST
Teammates-16
Teammates Gold-16
03McDonald's Pacific-31
03NHL Sticker Collection-68
03O-Pee-Chee-128
03O-Pee-Chee-280
03O-Pee-Chee-299
03OPC Blue-128
03OPC Blue-280
03OPC Blue-299
03OPC Gold-128
03OPC Gold-280
03OPC Gold-299
03OPC Red-128
03OPC Red-280
03OPC Red-299
03Pacific-206
Blue-206
Red-206
03Pacific Atlantic City National-4
03Pacific Complete-130
Red-130
03Pacific Exhibit-90
Blue Backs-90
Yellow Backs-90
03Pacific Invincible-59
Blue-59
Red-59
Retail-59
03Pacific Prism-65
Blue-65
Gold-65
Red-65
03Pacific Quest for the Cup-65
Blue-65
Connquest-5
Raising the Cup-13
03Parkhurst Rookie Teammates Gold-RT15
03Parkhurst Rookie Teammates-RT15
03Private Stock Reserve-62
Blue-62
Red-62
Retail-62
03SP Authentic-54
Limited-54
Foundations-F8
Foundations Limited-F8
03SPx-56
03SPx-123
Radiance-56
Radiance-123
Spectrum-56
Spectrum-123
Fantasy Franchise-FF-SBJ
Fantasy Franchise Limited-FF-SBJ
VIP-VIP-SB
VIP Limited-VIP-SB
03Topps-128
03Topps-280
03Topps-299
Blue-128
Blue-280
Blue-299
Gold-128
Gold-280
Gold-299
Red-128
Red-280
Red-299
03Topps C55-4
Minis-4
Minis American Back-4
Minis American Back Red-4
Minis Bazooka Back-4
Minis Brooklyn Back-4
Minis Hat Trick Back-4
Minis O Canada Back-4
Minis O Canada Back Red-4
Minis Stanley Cup Back-4
03Topps Pristine-87
Gold Refractor Die Cuts-87
Refractors-87
Press Plates Black-87
Press Plates Cyan-87
Press Plates Magenta-87
Press Plates Yellow-87
03UD Honor Roll-50
03UD Premier Collection-31
Teammates-PT-ND
Teammates Patches-PT-ND
03Upper Deck-116
Canadian Exclusives-116
HG-116
Magic Moments-MM-2
Memorable Matchups-MM-LS
Performers-PS2
Team Essentials-TL-SS
03Upper Deck Classic Portraits-58
03Upper Deck Ice-53
Gold-53
Breakers-IB-ST
Breaker Patches-IB-ST
Clear Cut Winners-CC-SS
03Upper Deck MVP-257
Gold Script-257
Silver Script-257
Canadian Exclusives-257
03Upper Deck Rookie Update-54
03Upper Deck Trilogy-58
Limited-58
Limited Threads-LT2
Limited Threads-LT15
03Upper Deck Victory-112
Bronze-112
Gold-112
Silver-112
03Czech Stadion-601
03Toronto Star-54
04Pacific-162
Blue-162
Red-162
04SP Authentic-54
04SP Authentic-124
04Upper Deck-106
04Upper Deck-209
Canadian Exclusives-106
Canadian Exclusives-209
HG Glossy Gold-106
HG Glossy Gold-209
HG Glossy Silver-106
HG Glossy Silver-209
School of Hard Knocks-SHK2
05SPx Winning Combos-WC-SR
05SPx Winning Combos Gold-WC-SR
05SPx Winning Combos Spectrum-WC-SR
05UD Artifacts Treasured Patches-TP-SS
05UD Artifacts Treasured Patch Autos-TP-SS
05UD Artifacts Treasured Patches Dual-TPD-SS
05UD Artifacts Treasured Patch Dual Autos-TPD-SS
05UD Artifacts Treasured Patches Pewter-TP-SS
05UD Artifacts Treasured Patches Silver-TP-SS
05UD Artifacts Treasured Swatches-TS-SS
05UD Artifacts Treasured Swatch Autos-TS-SS
05UD Artifacts Treasured Swatches Blue-TS-SS
05UD Artifacts Treasured Swatches Copper-TS-SS
05UD Artifacts Treasured Swatches Dual-TSD-SS
05UD Artifacts Treasured Swatch Dual Auto-TSD-SS
05UD Artifacts Treasured Swatch Dual Blue-TSD-SS
05UD Artifact Treasure Swatch Dual Copper-TSD-SS
05UD Artifact Treasure Swatch Dual Maroon-TSD-SS
05UD Artifact Treasure Swatch Dual Pewter-TSD-SS
05UD Artifact TreasuredSwatch Dual Silver-TSD-SS
05UD Artifacts Treasured Swatches Maroon-TS-SS
05UD Artifacts Treasured Swatches Pewter-TS-SS
05UD Artifacts Treasured Swatches Silver-TS-SS
05Upper Deck-113
Big Playmakers-B-SST
HG Glossy-113
Jerseys-J-SST
NHL Generations-DSC
Patches-P-SST
School of Hard Knocks-HK1
MVP Materials-M-SS
Trilogy Honorary Patches-HP-SS
Trilogy Honorary Patch Scripts-HSP-SS
Trilogy Honorary Swatches-HS-SS
Trilogy Honorary Swatch Scripts-HSS-SS
05Upper Deck Toronto Fall Expo-113
05Upper Deck Victory-116
Black-116
Gold-116
Silver-116
Stars on Ice-SI27
06Devils Team Set-39
06Devils Team Set-41
06Parkhurst-124
06Parkhurst-189
06Parkhurst-208
Autographs-124
Autographs-189
Autographs-208
06SP Authentic-134
Limited-134
06The Cup-53
Autographed Foundations-CQSS
Autographed Foundations Patches-CQSS
Autographed NHL Shields Duals-DASBS
Autographed NHL Shields Duals-DASNJ
Autographed Patches-53
Black Rainbow-53
Foundations-CQSS
Foundations Patches-CQSS
Enshrinements-EST
Gold-53
Gold Patches-53
Honorable Numbers-HNSS
Jerseys-53
Limited Logos-LLSS
Masterpiece Pressplates-53
NHL Shields Duals-DSHSR
Scripted Swatches-SSSS
Signature Patches-SPSE
Stanley Cup Signatures-CSSS
Stanley Cup Titlists Patches-TSS
06Ultimate Collection Jerseys-UJ-SS
06Ultimate Collection Patches-UJ-SS
06Ultimate Collection Premium Patches-PS-SS
06Ultimate Collection Premium Swatches-PS-SS
06Ultimate Collection Signatures-US-SS

Stevens, Troy
96Dayton Ice Bandits-18

Stevenson, G.
75HCA Steel City Vacuum-13

Stevenson, Garnet
96Red Deer Rebels-22

Stevenson, Grant
03Cleveland Barons-20
04Cleveland Barons-23
04ITG Heroes and Prospects-50
Autographs-GST
Complete Emblems-27
Emblems-10
Emblems Gold-10
He Shoots-He Scores Prizes-27
Jersey Autographs-10
Jerseys-10
Jerseys Gold-10
Numbers-10
Numbers Gold-10
04ITG Heroes/Prospects Toronto Expo '05-50
04ITG Heroes/Prospects Expo Heroes/Pros-50
05Black Diamond-278
05Hot Prospects-163
En Fuego-163
Red Hot-163
White Hot-163
05Parkhurst-412
Facsimile Auto Parallel-412
05SP Authentic-276
Limited-276
05SP Game Used-232
05SPx-281
05The Cup Masterpiece Pressplate Artifact-320
05The Cup Master Pressplate Black Diamond-278
05The Cup Masterpiece Pressplates (Ice)-225
05The Cup Master Pressplate Rookie Update-170
05The Cup Masterpiece Pressplates SPA-276
05The Cup Masterpiece Pressplates SP GU-232
05The Cup Masterpiece Pressplates (SPx)-281
05The Cup Masterpiece Pressplates Trilogy-297
05The Cup Masterpiece Pressplate Ult Coll-222
05UD Artifacts-320
05Ultimate Collection-222
Gold-222
05Upper Deck Ice-225
05Upper Deck Rookie Update-170
05Upper Deck Trilogy-297
05Cleveland Barons-23
05ITG Heroes and Prospects Jerseys-GUJ-105
05ITG Heroes and Prospects Jerseys Gold-GUJ-105

Stevenson, Jason
917th Inn. Sketch OHL-90

Stevenson, Jeremy
907th Inn. Sketch OHL-48
91Cornwall Royals-10
917th Inn. Sketch OHL-8
93Sault Ste. Marie Greyhounds-25
94Greensboro Monarchs-2
98Cincinnati Mighty Ducks-17
99Cincinnati Mighty Ducks-24
00SPx-111
Spectrum-111
00Upper Deck Victory-272
00Milwaukee Admirals Keebler-17
01Milwaukee Admirals-25

Stevenson, Mike
96OCN Blizzard-12

Stevenson, Shayne
86London Knights-15
88Kitchener Rangers-20
89Kitchener Rangers-21
897th Inn. Sketch OHL-182
90Score-405
Canadian-405
90ProCards AHL/IHL-123
907th Inn. Sketch Memorial Cup-49
91O-Pee-Chee-121
91Topps-121
91Upper Deck-332
French-332
92Atlanta Knights-13
93Fort Wayne Komets-19
98San Angelo Outlaws-17
00UK Sekonda Superleague-106

Stevenson, Travis
917th Inn. Sketch WHL-273

Stevenson, Turner
90Score-426
Canadian-426
907th Inn. Sketch WHL-9
91Upper Deck-691
French-691
91Upper Deck Czech World Juniors-65
917th Inn. Sketch WHL-125
92Fredericton Canadiens-24
93Upper Deck-248
93Fredericton Canadiens-26
94Canadiens Postcards-26

94Fleer-110
94Leaf-492
94OPC Premier-392
Special Effects-392
94Topps/OPC Premier-392
Special Effects-392
94Ultra-317
94Upper Deck-221
Electric Ice-221
SP Inserts-SP132
SP Inserts Die Cuts-SP132
94Fredericton Canadiens-26
95Upper Deck World Junior Alumni-6
95Canadiens Postcards-18
95Canadiens Sheets-5
95Collector's Choice-167
Player's Club-167
Player's Club Platinum-167
95Donruss-218
95Leaf-285
95Parkhurst International-385
Emerald Ice-385
95Pinnacle-115
Artist's Proofs-115
Rink Collection-115
95Topps-34
OPC Inserts-34
95Upper Deck-202
Electric Ice-202
Electric Ice Gold-202
96Canadiens Postcards-27
96Canadiens Sheets-20
96Upper Deck-85
97Be A Player-181
Autographs-181
Autographs Die-Cuts-181
Autographs Prismatic Die-Cuts-181
97Canadiens Postcards-21
97Pacific Invincible NHL Regime-106
97Upper Deck-297
98Be A Player-71
Press Release-71
98BAP Gold-71
98BAP Autographs-71
98BAP Autographs Gold-71
98BAP Tampa Bay All Star Game-71
98Canadiens Team Issue-20
99Pacific-211
Copper-211
Emerald Green-211
Gold-211
Ice Blue-211
Premiere Date-211
Red-211
00BAP Memorabilia-462
Emerald-462
Ruby-462
Sapphire-462
00Devils Team Issue-20
01Devils Team Issue-23
02BAP Sig Series Auto Buybacks 1998-71
02Devils Team Issue-18
03Devils Team Issue-24
03ITG Action-378
05Flyers Team Issue-23

Steward, Dallas
04Tulsa Oilers-23

Stewart, Adam
96Prince Albert Raiders-20

Stewart, Alan
88ProCards AHL-334
90Devils Team Issue-25
90OPC Premier-113
90Pro Set-480

Stewart, Andy
94Central Hockey League-35

Stewart, Anthony
01Kingston Frontenacs-19
03BAP Memorabilia Draft Redemptions-25
04ITG Top Prospects Spring Expo-19
04Kingston Frontenacs-2
04ITG Heroes and Prospects-54
Autographs-AS
Complete Emblems-9
Emblems-56
Emblems Gold-56
He Shoots-He Scores Prizes-17
Jersey Autographs-56
Jerseys-56
Jerseys Gold-56
Numbers-56
Numbers Gold-56
Top Prospects-19
04ITG Heroes/Prospects Toronto Expo '05-54
04ITG Heroes/Prospects Expo Heroes/Pros-54
05Beehive-142
Beige -142
Blue -142
Gold-142
Red -142
Matte-142
Signature Scrapbook-SSAS
05Black Diamond-244
05Hot Prospects-239
En Fuego-239
Hot Materials-HMAS
Red Hot-239
White Hot-239
05Parkhurst-631
Facsimile Auto Parallel-631
Signatures-AS
True Colors-TCFLA
True Colors-TCFLA
05SP Authentic-159
Limited-159
Prestigious Pairings-PPOS
Rarefied Rookies-RRAS
Rookie Authentics-RAST
05SP Game Used-161
Autographs-161
Gold-161
Game Gear-GG-ST
Game Gear Autographs-AG-ST
Rookie Exclusives-ST
Rookie Exclusives Silver-RE-ST
Significant Numbers-SN-ST
05SPx-187
Spectrum-187
Xcitement Rookies-XR-ST
Xcitement Rookies Gold-XR-ST
Xcitement Rookies Spectrum-XR-ST
05The Cup-189
Black Rainbow Rookies-189
Masterpiece Pressplates (Artifacts)-280
Masterpiece Pressplates (Bee Hive)-142
Masterpiece Pressplates (Black Diamond)-244
Masterpiece Pressplates (Ice)-130
Masterpiece Pressplates (Rookie Update)-211
Masterpiece Pressplates SPA Autos-159
Masterpiece Pressplates (SP Game Used)-161
Masterpiece Pressplates SPx Autos-187
Masterpiece Pressplates (Trilogy)-193
Masterpiece Pressplates Ult Coll Autos-118
Masterpiece Pressplates (Victory)-283
Masterpiece Pressplates Autographs-189
Platinum Rookies-189
05UD Artifacts-280
05UD Rookie Class-43
05Ultimate Collection-118
05Ultra-250
Gold-250
Fresh Ink-FI-ST
Fresh Ink Blue-FI-ST
Ice-250
Rookie Uniformity Jerseys-RU-ST
Rookie Uniformity Jersey Autographs-ARU-ST
Rookie Uniformity Patches-RUP-ST
Rookie Uniformity Patch Autographs-ARP-ST
05Upper Deck-453
Rookie Ink-RIAS
Rookie Threads-RTAS
Rookie Threads Autographs-ARTAS
05Upper Deck Ice-130
Fresh Ice-FIAS
Fresh Ice Glass-FIAS
Fresh Ice Glass Patches-FIPAS
Premieres Auto Patches-AIPST
05Upper Deck Rookie Update-211
Inspirations Patch Rookies-211
05Upper Deck Trilogy-193
05Upper Deck Victory-283
Black-283
Gold-283
Silver-283
05Extreme Top Prospects Signature Edition-S16
05ITG Heroes/Prospects He Shoots/Scores-28
05ITG Heroes and Prospects Jerseys-GUJ-80
05ITG Heroes and Prospects Jerseys Gold-GUJ-80
05ITG Heroes and Prospects Emblems-GUE-80
05ITG Heroes and Prospects Emblems Gold-GUE-80
05ITG Heroes and Prospects Numbers-GUN-80
05ITG Heroes and Prospects Numbers Gold-GUN-80
05ITG Heroes and Prospects National Pride-NPR-41
06Rochester Americans-22
06UD Powerplay Power Marks-PMAS

Stewart, Bill
79O-Pee-Chee-313
79Rochester Americans-19
83Maple Leafs Postcards-23
84Maple Leafs Postcards-22
93Swedish Semic World Champ Stickers-213
95Swedish Globe World Championships-230
97Saint John Flames-24
99Danish Hockey League-23
03German Mannheim Eagles Postcards-6
04Swiss Lausanne HC Postcards-24

Stewart, Bill (30s)
35Diamond Matchbooks Tan 5-11
37Diamond Matchbooks Tan 6-11
37V356 Worldwide Gum-135

Stewart, Bill (50s)
52Juniors Blue Tint-94

Stewart, Blair
78O-Pee-Chee-355
79O-Pee-Chee-332

Stewart, Blake
06Quad City Mallards-16

Stewart, Bob
72Sargent Promotions Stamps-56
73O-Pee-Chee-188
73Topps-159
74NHL Action Stamps-71
74O-Pee-Chee NHL-92
74Topps-92
75O-Pee-Chee NHL-47
75Topps-47
76O-Pee-Chee NHL-291
77Coca-Cola-26
77O-Pee-Chee NHL-299
78Blues Postcards-22
78O-Pee-Chee-46
78Topps-46
79O-Pee-Chee-297
04ITG Franchises US West-156
Autographs-A-BST

Stewart, Bobby
99ECHL All-Star Southern Conference-1
99Mobile Mysticks-5
01Idaho Steelheads-18
02Fort Wayne Komets-20
02Fort Wayne Komets Shoe Carnival-6
03Fort Wayne Komets-1
03Fort Wayne Komets Shoe Carnival-8

Stewart, Brett
94German First League-307
95German DEL-353

Stewart, Brian
95Slapshot-376
95Sault Ste. Marie Greyhounds-20
96Sault Ste. Marie Greyhounds-22
96Sault Ste. Marie Greyhounds Autographed-22

Stewart, Bryan
90Fort Saskatchewan Traders-18

Stewart, Cam
91Michigan Wolverines-18
93Donruss-20
93Leaf-337
93Parkhurst-284
Emerald Ice-284
93Pinnacle-434
Canadian-434
93PowerPlay-292
93Score-588
Gold-588
Canadian-588
Canadian Gold-588
93Stadium Club-440
Members Only Master Set-440
First Day Issue-440
93Ultra-270
93Upper Deck-464
94Donruss-316
94Leaf-281
94OPC Premier-111
Special Effects-111
94Topps/OPC Premier-111
Special Effects-111
94Upper Deck-487
Electric Ice-487
94Classic Autographs-NNO
94Classic Pro Prospects-36
98IHL All-Star Western Conference-16
00BAP Signature Series-140
Emerald-140
Ruby-140
Sapphire-140
Autographs-151
Autographs Gold-151
00Stadium Club-202
00Upper Deck Vintage-182
02BAP Sig Series Auto Buybacks 2000-151
06Houston Aeros RetroA -3

Stewart, Charles
24Anonymous NHL-39

Stewart, Chris
98Huntsville Channel Cats-1
99San Antonio Iguanas-20
03Colorado Eagles-21
04Colorado Eagles-17
04Kingston Frontenacs-4
05ITG Heroes/Prosp Toronto Expo Parallel -281
05Colorado Eagles-20
05Kingston Frontenacs-2
05OHL Bell All-Star Classic-11
05ITG Heroes and Prospects-281
Autographs Series II-CS
Team Cherry-TC3
06Kingston Frontenacs-1
06ITG Heroes and Prospects-110
Autographs-ACS
Class of 2006-CL11
Quad Emblems-QE01
Quad Emblems Gold-QE01
07Finest Refractors Black-166

Stewart, Chris CO
03Colorado Eagles-21
04Colorado Eagles-17
05Colorado Eagles-20

Stewart, Dan
03Fort Wayne Komets-5
03Fort Wayne Komets Shoe Carnival-14
04Fort Wayne Komets Shoe Carnival-13

Stewart, Danny
05Danbury Trashers-5
06UK Coventry Blaze-16

Stewart, Dany
01Rimouski Oceanic-3
02Rimouski Oceanic-18
03Rimouski Oceanic-18
03Rimouski Oceanic Sheets-5
04Fort Wayne Komets-15
04Rimouski Oceanic-19
05PEI Rocket-29

Stewart, Dave
907th Inn. Sketch OHL-71
917th Inn. Sketch OHL-236
92Phoenix Roadrunners-21
93Phoenix Roadrunners-21
93Quebec Pee-Wee Tournament-1607
94Roanoke Express-4
95Roanoke Express-2
96Roanoke Express-2
00Jackson Bandits-17
00Jackson Bandits Promos-6
03Reading Royals-22
05Missouri River Otters-4

Stewart, Doug
81Ottawa 67's-12
81Ottawa 67's-23
82Ottawa 67's-24
83Brantford Alexanders-11
91British Columbia JHL-63

Stewart, Doug (BC)
91British Columbia JHL-63

Stewart, Ernie
04Salmon Arm Silverbacks-14
05Salmon Arm Silverbacks-19

Stewart, Gary
88ProCards IHL-5

Stewart, Gaye
34Beehive Group I Photos-350A
34Beehive Group I Photos-350B
43Parade Sportive *-80
44Beehive Group II Photos-141
44Beehive Group II Photos-213
45Quaker Oats Photos-51A
45Quaker Oats Photos-51B
51Parkhurst-99
52Parkhurst-25
91Ultimate Original Six-45
French-45
02Parkhurst Reprints-168
06ITG Ultimate Memorabilia Chi-Town Immortals Autos-6

Stewart, Glenn
94Greensboro Monarchs-3
95Anaheim Bullfrogs RHI-17
96Anaheim Bullfrogs RHI-13
96Quad-City Mallards-11
97Quad-City Mallards-1
98Quad-City Mallards-23
98UHL All-Stars-22
99Quad-City Mallards-17
99UHL All-Stars West-18T

Stewart, Greg
04Peterborough Petes Postcards-22

Stewart, Jack
34Beehive Group I Photos-125
40O-Pee-Chee V301-2-124
44Beehive Group II Photos-142
44Beehive Group II Photos-214
51Berk Ross-4
51Parkhurst-53
76Old Timers-18
83Hall of Fame Postcards-N15
85Hall of Fame-210
02BAP Ultimate Mem Paper Cuts Autos-14
02Parkhurst Reprints-158
04ITG Franchises US West-219
04ITG Ultimate Memorabilia-88
Gold-88
Motown Heroes-6
Paper Cuts-8
05ITG Ultimate Mem Quad Paper Cuts Autos-3
06ITG Ultimate Memorabilia Motown Heroes Autos-3

Stewart, Jamie
91Michigan Falcons-18

Stewart, Jason
99Missouri River Otters Sheet-20

Stewart, John
72Flames Postcards-20
74O-Pee-Chee NHL-175
74Topps-175
92Quebec Pee-Wee Tournament-1845

Stewart, John (PW)
92Quebec Pee-Wee Tournament-1845

Stewart, Jon
91Rayside-Balfour Jr. Canadians-15

Stewart, Justin
00Quebec Remparts-9
Signed-9

Stewart, Karl
01Plymouth Whalers-13
02Plymouth Whalers-3
03ITG Action-634
03ITG VIP Rookie Debut-58
03Pacific Complete-576
Red-576
03Parkhurst Rookie-116
03Topps Traded-TT86
Blue-TT86
Gold-TT86
Red-TT86
03UD Honor Roll-159
03Upper Deck-465
Canadian Exclusives-465
HG-465
UD Exclusives-465
03Chicago Wolves-19
03Pacific AHL Prospects-15
Gold-15
04AHL Top Prospects-8
04Chicago Wolves-21
05Chicago Wolves-19
06Blackhawks Postcards Glossy-4

Stewart, Michael
92Binghamton Rangers-3
92Classic-71
Gold-71
92Classic Four-Sport *-197
Gold-197
94Binghamton Rangers-22
94Classic Four-Sport *-147
Gold-147
Printers Proofs-147
97Manitoba Moose-B3
98Manitoba Moose-C7
99Manitoba Moose-2

Stewart, Nels
24Anonymous NHL-97
28La Presse Photos-13
33O-Pee-Chee V304A-6
33V252 Canadian Gum-46
33V357 Ice Kings-12
34Beehive Group I Photos-255
34Diamond Matchbooks Silver-57
34Sweet Caporal-31
35Diamond Matchbooks Tan 1-65
35Diamond Matchbooks Tan 2-60
35Diamond Matchbooks Tan 3-55
38Bruins Garden Magazine Supplement-8
60Topps-5
Stamps-48
83Hall of Fame-86
83Hall of Fame Postcards-F12
85Hall of Fame-86
02BAP Ultimate Mem Blades of Steel-1
03BAP Ultimate Mem Retro Teammates-10
03BAP Ultimate Mem Vintage Blade of Steel-18
04ITG Franchises Canadian-65
04ITG Ultimate Mem Blades of Steel-8
04ITG Ultimate Memorabilia Nicknames-17
04ITG Ultimate Mem Paper Cuts Mem-24
04ITG Ultimate Mem Retro Teammates-7
05ITG Ultimate Memorabilia Level 1-73
05ITG Ultimate Memorabilia Level 2-73
05ITG Ultimate Memorabilia Level 3-73
05ITG Ultimate Memorabilia Level 4-73
05ITG Ultimate Memorabilia Level 5-73
05ITG Ultimate Mem Blades of Steel-7
05ITG Ultimate Mem Blades of Steel Gold-7
05ITG Ultimate Mem Record Breaker Jerseys-17
05ITG Ultimate Mem RecBreak Jerseys Gold-17
06ITG Ultimate Memorabilia Amazing Amerks Autos-1
06ITG Ultimate Memorabilia Blades of Steel-25
06ITG Ultimate Memorabilia Blades of Steel Gold-25
06ITG Ultimate Memorabilia Lumbergraphs-4
06ITG Ultimate Memorabilia Marvelous Maroons Autos-2
06ITG Ultimate Memorabilia Paper Cuts Autos-2

Stewart, Paul
90Pro Set-699

Stewart, Ralph
64Coca-Cola Caps-98
74NHL Action Stamps-167
74O-Pee-Chee NHL-158
74O-Pee-Chee NHL-233
74Topps-158
74Topps-233
75O-Pee-Chee NHL-182
75Topps-182
76Canucks Royal Bank-20
76O-Pee-Chee NHL-229
76Topps-229
77O-Pee-Chee NHL-386

Stewart, Rob
95Vancouver VooDoo RHI-13
00UK Sekonda Superleague-180
01UK Belfast Giants-7
03UK Belfast Giants-16
04UK Sheffield Steelers-12

Stewart, Ron
44Beehive Group II Photos-455
45Quaker Oats Photos-52
52Parkhurst-94
53Parkhurst-9
54Parkhurst-23
54Parkhurst-92
55Parkhurst-5
Quaker Oats-5
57Parkhurst-T7
58Parkhurst-14
59Parkhurst-26
60Parkhurst-6
60Shirriff Coins-10
60York Photos-34
61Parkhurst-6
61York Yellow Backs-20
62Parkhurst-6
62Shirriff Coins-21
63Chex Photos-51
63Parkhurst-14
63Parkhurst-74
63Toronto Star-36
63York White Backs-3
64Beehive Group III Photos-27
64Beehive Group III Photos-187A
64Beehive Group III Photos-187B
64Topps-99
64Toronto Star-45
65Coca-Cola-4
65Topps-103
66Topps-94
68O-Pee-Chee-168
68Shirriff Coins-108
69O-Pee-Chee-41
69Topps-41
70Esso Power Players-189
70O-Pee-Chee-64
70Sargent Promotions Stamps-120
70Topps-64
71O-Pee-Chee-236
94Parkhurst Missing Link-110
94Parkhurst Tall Boys-128
95Parkhurst '66-67-2
Coins-2
02Maple Leafs Platinum Collection-37
02Parkhurst Reprints-177
02Parkhurst Reprints-190
02Parkhurst Reprints-200
02Parkhurst Reprints-220
02Parkhurst Reprints-240
02Parkhurst Reprints-246
02Parkhurst Reprints-258
02Parkhurst Reprints-296
03Parkhurst Orig Six Toronto Autos-11

Stewart, Ryan
84Kamloops Blazers-22
87Moncton Hawks-23
93Windsor Spitfires-19
01Greenville Grrrowl-16
02UK Manchester Storm-13
02Florida Everblades-19
03Greenville Grrrowl-20
06Blackhawks Postcards Glossy-5

Stewart, Scott
91Air Canada SJHL-B24

Stewart, Tom
98Columbus Cottonmouths-18
98Topeka Scarecrows-6
99Indianapolis Ice-16
02Macon Trax-5

Stich, David
04Czech OFS-344
06Saint Johns Sea Dogs-16

Stickle, Leon
90Pro Set-700

Stickney, Brent
93Flint Generals-2

Stieler, David
06Swift Current Broncos-3

Stiles, Tony
84Moncton Golden Flames-24
85Moncton Golden Flames-12

Still, Alastair
88Sudbury Wolves-17
89Sudbury Wolves-2
907th Inn. Sketch OHL-395
90Sudbury Wolves-17
917th Inn. Sketch OHL-230

Stillhardt, Ron
96Swiss HNL-478
96Swiss HNL-493

Stillman, Cory
907th Inn. Sketch OHL-192
917th Inn. Sketch OHL-175
917th Inn. Sketch CHL Award Winners-5
92Windsor Spitfires-31
92Classic-5
92Classic-8
Gold-5
Gold-8
LPs-LP5
92Classic Four-Sport *-155
Autographs-155A
93Classic-29
94OPC Premier-515
Special Effects-515
94Parkhurst SE-SE29
Gold-SE29
94Pinnacle-494
Artist's Proofs-494
Rink Collection-494
94Topps/OPC Premier-515
Special Effects-515
94Upper Deck-268
Electric Ice-268
94Saint John Flames-22
94Classic-49
Gold-49
Tri-Cards-T10
94Classic Pro Prospects-190
94Classic Four-Sport *-144
Autographs-144A
Printers Proofs-144
95Be A Player-132
Signatures-S132
Signatures Die Cuts-S132
95Bowman-131
All-Foil-131
Bowman's Best-BB27
Bowman's Best Refractors-BB27
95Canada Games NHL POGS-51
95Collector's Choice-111
Player's Club-111
Player's Club Platinum-111
95Donruss-152
Rated Rookies-12
95Finest-61
Refractors-61
95Leaf-5
95Parkhurst International-299
Emerald Ice-299
95Pinnacle-212
Artist's Proofs-212
Rink Collection-212
95Score-300
Black Ice Artist's Proofs-300
Black Ice-300
95Select Certified-128
Mirror Gold-128
95SP-17
95Topps-332
OPC Inserts-332
SuperSkills Super Rookies-SR4
95Ultra-214
95Upper Deck-283
Electric Ice-283
Electric Ice Gold-283
95Zenith-123
Rookie Roll Call-16
95Images-38
Gold-38
96Collector's Choice-40
96Donruss-231
Press Proofs-231
96Donruss Elite-106
Die Cut Stars-106
96Leaf-138
Press Proofs-138
96Leaf Preferred-15
Press Proofs-15
96Score-243
Artist's Proofs-243
Dealer's Choice Artist's Proofs-243
Special Artist's Proofs-243
Golden Blades-243
96Select Certified-58
Artist's Proofs-58
Blue-58
Mirror Blue-58
Mirror Gold-58
Mirror Red-58
Red-58
96SkyBox Impact-172
96Topps Picks-145
OPC Inserts-145
Rookie Stars-RS9
Rookie Stars OPC-RS9
96Upper Deck-229
96Zenith-113
Artist's Proofs-113
96Collector's Edge Ice-74
Prism-74
97Be A Player-24
Autographs-24
Autographs Die-Cuts-24
Autographs Prismatic Die-Cuts-24
97Crown Royale-21
Emerald Green-21
Ice Blue-21
Silver-21
97Donruss Priority-88
Stamp of Approval-88
97Katch-24
Gold-24
Silver-24
97Pacific-211
Copper-211
Emerald Green-211
Ice Blue-211
Red-211
Silver-211
97Pacific Omega-35
Copper-35
Dark Gray-35
Emerald Green-35
Gold-35
Ice Blue-35
97Pinnacle Inside-164
97Revolution-20
Copper-20
Emerald-20
Ice Blue-20
Silver-20
97Score-225
97SP Authentic-19
97Zenith-52
Z-Gold-52
Z-Silver-52
98Aurora-29
98Katch-24
98Kraft Fearless Forwards-10
98OPC Chrome-191
Refractors-191
98Pacific-125
Ice Blue-125
Red-125
98Pacific Omega-35
Red-35
Opening Day Issue-35
98Panini Photocards-80
98Panini Stickers-180
98Paramount-32
Copper-32
Emerald Green-32
Holo-Electric-32
Ice Blue-32
Silver-32
98Revolution-22
Ice Shadow-22
Red-22
98Topps-191
O-Pee-Chee-191
98UD Choice-33
98UD Choice Preview-33
98UD Choice Prime Choice Reserve-33
98UD Choice Reserve-33
98Upper Deck-54
Exclusives-54
Exclusives 1 of 1-54
Gold Reserve-54
99Aurora-24
Premiere Date-24
99BAP Memorabilia-57
Gold-57
Silver-57
99BAP Millennium-43
Emerald-43
Ruby-43
Sapphire-43
Signatures-43
Signatures Gold-43
99O-Pee-Chee-57
99O-Pee-Chee Chrome-57
99O-Pee-Chee Chrome Refractors-57
99Pacific-62
Copper-62
Emerald Green-62
Gold-62
Ice Blue-62
Premiere Date-62
Red-62
99Pacific Dynagon Ice-39
Blue-39
Copper-39
Gold-39
Premiere Date-39
99Pacific Omega-41
Copper-41
Gold-41
Ice Blue-41
Premiere Date-41
99Pacific Prism-26
Holographic Blue-26
Holographic Gold-26
Holographic Mirror-26
Holographic Purple-26
Premiere Date-26
99Panini Stickers-191
99Paramount-43
Copper-43
Emerald-43
Gold-43
Holographic Emerald-43
Holographic Gold-43
Holographic Silver-43
Ice Blue-43
Premiere Date-43
Red-43
99Revolution-26
Premiere Date-26
Red-26
Shadow Series-26
99Stadium Club-97
First Day Issue-97
One of a Kind-97
Printing Plates Black-97
Printing Plates Cyan-97
Printing Plates Magenta-97
Printing Plates Yellow-97
99Topps/OPC-57
99Topps/OPC Chrome-57
Refractors-57
99Ultimate Victory-15
1/1-15
Parallel-15
Parallel 100-15
99Upper Deck MVP SC Edition-31
Gold Script-31
Silver Script-31
Super Script-31
99Wayne Gretzky Hockey-32
00BAP Memorabilia-167
Emerald-167
Ruby-167
Sapphire-167
Promos-167
00BAP Mem Chicago Sportsfest Copper-167
00BAP Memorabilia Chicago Sportsfest Blue-167
00BAP Memorabilia Chicago Sportsfest Gold-167
00BAP Memorabilia Chicago Sportsfest Ruby-167
00BAP Memorabilia Chicago Sun-Times Ruby-167
00BAP Memorabilia Chicago Sun-Times Gold-167
00BAP Mem Chicago Sun-Times Sapphire-167
00BAP Mem Toronto Fall Expo Copper-167
00BAP Memorabilia Toronto Fall Expo Gold-167
00BAP Memorabilia Toronto Fall Expo Ruby-167
00BAP Parkhurst 2000-P231
00O-Pee-Chee-253B
00O-Pee-Chee Parallel-253B
00Pacific-75
Copper-75
Gold-75
Ice Blue-75
Premiere Date-75
00Paramount-39
Copper-39
Gold-39
Holo-Gold-39
Holo-Silver-39
Ice Blue-39
Premiere Date-39
00Titanium Game Gear-71
00Titanium Game Gear Patches-71
00Titanium Draft Day Edition-90
Patches-90
00Topps/OPC-253B
Parallel-253B
00UD Heroes-19
00Upper Deck-256
Exclusives Tier 1-256
Exclusives Tier 2-256
00Upper Deck Victory-40
00Upper Deck Vintage-57
00Vanguard Dual Game-Worn Jerseys-10
00Vanguard Dual Game-Worn Patches-10
01BAP Memorabilia-243
Emerald-243
Ruby-243
Sapphire-243
01BAP Signature Series-123
Autographs-123
Autographs Gold-123
01Crown Royale Triple Threads-19
01O-Pee-Chee-241
01O-Pee-Chee Premier Parallel-241
01Pacific-331
Extreme LTD-331
Hobby LTD-331
Premiere Date-331
Retail LTD-331
Jerseys-32
01Pacific Adrenaline-162
Blue-162
Premiere Date-162
Red-162
Retail-162
Jerseys-40
01Pacific Arena Exclusives-331
01Private Stock Game Gear-88
01Private Stock Game Gear Patches-88
01Topps-241
OPC Parallel-241
01Upper Deck-154
Exclusives-154
01Upper Deck MVP-168
01Upper Deck Victory-304
Gold-304
01Upper Deck Vintage-222
01Vanguard Memorabilia-6
01Vanguard Patches-6
02BAP First Edition-252
02BAP Signature Series-117
Autographs-117
Autograph Buybacks 1999-43
Autograph Buybacks 2001-123
Autographs Gold-117
02Blues Team Issue-21
02O-Pee-Chee-145
02O-Pee-Chee Premier Blue Parallel-145
02O-Pee-Chee Premier Red Parallel-145
02O-Pee-Chee Factory Set-145
02Pacific-328
Blue-328
Red-328
02Pacific Complete-320
Red-320
02Pacific Quest for the Cup-83
Gold-83
02Titanium-84
Blue-84
Red-84
Retail-84
02Topps-145
OPC Blue Parallel-145
OPC Red Parallel-145
Factory Set-145
02Topps Total-93
02Upper Deck-155
Exclusives-155
02Upper Deck Victory-190
Bronze-190
Gold-190
Silver-190
02Upper Deck Vintage-222
02Vanguard-83
LTD-83
03BAP Memorabilia-220
03Lightning Team Issue-35
03NHL Sticker Collection-274
03O-Pee-Chee-45
03OPC Blue-45
03OPC Gold-45
03OPC Red-45
03Pacific-289
Blue-289
Red-289
03Pacific Complete-261
Red-261
03Pacific Heads-Up-89
Hobby LTD-89
Retail LTD-89
03Private Stock Reserve-204
Blue-204
Patches-204
Red-204
Retail-204
03Titanium-92
Hobby Jersey Number Parallels-92
Retail-92
Retail Jersey Number Parallels-92
03Topps-45
Blue-45
Gold-45
Red-45
03Topps Traded-TT28
Blue-TT28
Gold-TT28
Red-TT28
03Upper Deck-417
Canadian Exclusives-417
HG-417
UD Exclusives-417
04Pacific-243
Blue-243
Red-243
05Be A Player Quad Signatures-SCCH
05Be A Player Signatures-CS
05Be A Player Signatures Gold-CS
05Beehive Signature Scrapbook-SSCS
05Parkhurst-85
Facsimile Auto Parallel-85
True Colors-TCCAR
True Colors-TCCAR
05SP Game Used Authentic Fabrics Triple-KNS
05SP Game Used Authentic Patches Triple-KNS
05SP Game Used SIGnificance-CS
05SP Game Used SIGnificance Gold-S-CS
05The Cup Master Pressplate Rookie Update-242
05Ultra-45
Gold-45
Ice-45
05Upper Deck-282
Jerseys Series II-J2CS
Notable Numbers-N-CS
05Upper Deck Hockey Showcase-HS39
05Upper Deck Showcase Promos-HS39
05Upper Deck MVP-84
Gold-84
Platinum-84
05Upper Deck Rookie Update-242
05Upper Deck Victory-178
Black-178
Gold-178
Silver-178
06Beehive Matted Materials-MMCS
06Beehive Remarkable Matted Materials-MMCS
06Black Diamond Gemography-GCS
06Fleer-38
Tiffany-38
06Hurricanes Postcards-21
06O-Pee-Chee-88
Rainbow-88
Autographs-A-CS
06Panini Stickers-44
06SP Game Used Authentic Fabrics Fives-AP5SCP
06SP Game Used Authentic Fabrics Fives Patches-AP5SCP
06Upper Deck-40
Exclusives Parallel-40
High Gloss Parallel-40
Masterpieces-40
Signatures-SCS
06Upper Deck MVP-57
Gold Script-57
Super Script-57
07Upper Deck Victory-83
Black-83
Gold-83

Stillman, Cory A.
99Kingston Frontenacs-20
00Kingston Frontenacs-19
00UD CHL Prospects-8
01Kingston Frontenacs-20
01UD Prospects-30
Autographs-A-CS
Jersey Autographs-S-CS
Jerseys-J-CS
Jerseys-C-MS
Jerseys Gold-J-CS
Jerseys Gold-C-MS
03Barrie Colts-21
04Barrie Colts 10th Anniversary-19

Stillman, Fredrik
85Swedish Panini Stickers-183
86Swedish Panini Stickers-119
87Swedish Panini Stickers-114
89Swedish Semic Elitserien Stickers-101
90Swedish Semic Elitserien Stickers-103
91Finnish Semic World Champ Stickers-34
91Swedish Semic Elitserien Stickers-107
91Swedish Semic Elitserien Stickers-345
91Swedish Semic World Champ Stickers-34
92Swedish Semic Elitserien Stickers-135
93Swedish Semic Elitserien-107
93Swedish Semic Elitserien-309
93Swedish Semic World Champ Stickers-6
94Finnish Jaa Kiekko-57
94Swedish Leaf-216
Gold Cards-6
Studio Signatures-5
95Finnish Semic World Championships-56
95German DEL-55
95Swedish Globe World Championships-17
95Swedish World Championships Stickers-140
97Swedish Collector's Choice-89
Stick'Ums-S5
98Swedish UD Choice-104
99German DEL-268
00Swedish Upper Deck-95

Stingh, Harkie
95Slapshot-35

Stinziani, Michael
05Gatineau Olympiques-14
06Gatineau Olympiques-20

Stirling, Brett
06AHL Top Prospects-8

Stirling, Scott
00Trenton Titans-8
01Atlantic City Boardwalk Bullies-20
02Atlantic City Boardwalk Bullies-21
02ECHL All-Star Northern-35
03Atlantic City Boardwalk Bullies-24
03Atlantic City Boardwalk Bullies RBI-30
03ECHL All-Stars-260
04Atlantic City Boardwalk Bullies Kinko's-27

Stirling, Steve
99Lowell Lock Monsters-26
06Springfield Falcons-22

Stirnimann, Reto
95Swiss HNL-129
96Swiss HNL-121
98Swiss Power Play Stickers-72
99Swiss Panini Stickers-247
00Swiss Panini Stickers-288
01Swiss HNL-22
02Swiss HNL-21

Stitt, Mark
95Anaheim Bullfrogs RHI-16
95Toledo Storm-10
96Anaheim Bullfrogs RHI-14
00San Diego Gulls-17

Stiver, Dan
91Michigan Wolverines-19
93St. John's Maple Leafs-22
94Classic Pro Prospects-99

Stoa, Ryan
05Minnesota Golden Gophers-23
06Minnesota Golden Gophers-21

Stocco, Regan
93Guelph Storm-7
94Guelph Storm-8
95Slapshot-81
95Guelph Storm-19
99Alexandria Warthogs-15
01UK Guildford Flames-5

Stock, Corey
907th Inn. Sketch WHL-309
917th Inn. Sketch WHL-162
92Tacoma Rockets-23
93Tacoma Rockets-25

Stock, Dean

97Halifax Mooseheads I-18
97Halifax Mooseheads II-18
02Arkansas Riverblades-18
Stock, P.J.
97Hartford Wolf Pack-22
98Upper Deck-131
Exclusives-131
Exclusives 1 of 1-131
Gold Reserve-131
98Hartford Wolf Pack-19
99Hartford Wolf Pack-19
00Upper Deck NHLPA-PA66
01BAP Signature Series-175
Autographs-175
Autographs Gold-175
01BAP Update Tough Customers-TC14
01BAP Update Tough Customers-TC36
01Parkhurst-370
01UD Mask Collection-10
Gold-10
02BAP First Edition-224
02BAP Sig Series Auto Buybacks 2001-175
02Bruins Team Issue-7
02Pacific-33
Blue-33
Red-33
02Pacific Complete-397
Red-397
02Topps Total-70
02Upper Deck Victory-17
Bronze-17
Gold-17
Silver-17
02Upper Deck Vintage-18
03Black Diamond-181
Black-181
Green-181
Red-181
03ITG Action-71
03O-Pee-Chee-34
03OPC Blue-34
03OPC Gold-34
03OPC Red-34
03Pacific-32
Blue-32
Red-32
03Parkhurst Original Six Boston-24
03SPx Style-SPX-DS
03SPx Style Limited-SPX-DS
03Topps-34
Blue-34
Gold-34
Red-34
Signs of Toughness-PJS
Tough Materials-PJS
Tough Materials-PSRR
Tough Materials Signed-PJS
03Upper Deck-18
Canadian Exclusives-18
Fan Favorites-FF8
HG-18
Tough Customers-TC-8
Classic Portraits Hockey Royalty-DSB
03Upper Deck MVP-44
Gold Script-44
Silver Script-44
Canadian Exclusives-44
03Upper Deck Victory-16
Bronze-16
Gold-16
Silver-16
03Philadelphia Phantoms-18
Stockdale, Mark
04Green Bay Gamblers-19
Stocker, Marcel
93Swiss HNL-446
Stockham, Darryl
95Brandon Wheat Kings-20
95Slapshot Memorial Cup-46
96Brandon Wheat Kings-4
Stockwell, Tanner
03Regina Pats-6
Stoddard, Jack
52Parkhurst-97
53Parkhurst-60
Stoffel, Andri
01Swiss HNL-388
02Swiss HNL-148
Stoffel, Ivo
93Swiss HNL-298
95Swiss HNL-245
96Swiss HNL-257
00Swiss Panini Stickers-82
00Swiss Slapshot Mini-Cards-EHCC4
01Swiss HNL-241
Stojanov, Alek
907th Inn. Sketch OHL-220
917th Inn. Sketch Memorial Cup-110
91Arena Draft Picks-5
91Arena Draft Picks French-5
91Arena Draft Picks Autographs-5
91Arena Draft Picks Autographs French-5
91Classic-6
91Star Pics-46
91Ultimate Draft-6
91Ultimate Draft-62
91Ultimate Draft French-6
91Ultimate Draft Promos-2
91Classic Four-Sport *-6
Autographs-6A
95Bowman-141
All-Foil-141
95Donruss-329
95Leaf-297
95Topps-368
OPC Inserts-368
95Upper Deck-195
Electric Ice-195
Electric Ice Gold-195
96Be A Player-80
Autographs-80
Autographs Silver-80
99Detroit Vipers-8
01New Mexico Scorpions-11
Stokan, David
05Rimouski Oceanic-14
Stokes, Ryan
01Barrie Colts-2
02Mississauga Ice Dogs-19
03Mississauga Ice Dogs-21
Stokke, Jesse
01Sioux Falls Stampede-13
Stoic, Miroslav
02Spokane Chiefs-22
04Slovakian Poprad Team Set-27
Stolec, Randy
93Quebec Pee-Wee Tournament-1693
Stolk, Darren
89ProCards IHL-157
90ProCards AHL/IHL-384
91ProCards-579
92Salt Lake Golden Eagles-20

95Oklahoma Coyotes RHI-16
Stoll, Jarret
98Kootenay Ice-14
99UD Prospects-35
99UD Prospects-78
00Kootenay Ice-20
02BAP Memorabilia-305
02BAP Ultimate Memorabilia-72
02SP Authentic-216
02SPx-184
02UD Premier Collection-72A
Gold-72A
02Upper Deck Rookie Update-160A
02Upper Deck Rookie Update-160B
02Upper Deck Rookie Update-160C
02Hamilton Bulldogs-9
03ITG Action-282
03Oilers Postcards-20
03Pacific Complete-574
Red-574
03Upper Deck MVP-173
Gold Script-173
Silver Script-173
Canadian Exclusives-173
05Parkhurst-188
Facsimile Auto Parallel-188
05Upper Deck-325
06Be A Player-30
Autographs-30
Signatures-JS
Signatures 25-33
Signatures Duals-DJS
Signatures Trios-TRSH
06Black Diamond-61
Matte-61
Matted Materials-MMST
Remarkable Matted Materials-MMST
Signature Scrapbook-SSJS
06Black Diamond-32
Black-32
Gold-32
Ruby-32
06Flair Showcase Wave of the Future-WF15
06Fleer-80
Tiffany-80
06Gatorade-21
06Hot Prospects Hot Materials -HMJS
06Hot Prospects Hot Materials Red Hot-HMJS
06Hot Prospects Hot Materials White Hot-HMJS
06Hot Prospects Hotagraphs-HJS
06McDonald's Upper Deck-17
06O-Pee-Chee-198
Rainbow-198
06Panini Stickers-276
06SP Authentic Sign of the Times-STJS
06SP Authentic Sign of the Times Triples-ST3SSH
06SP Game Used Authentic Fabrics-AFST
06SP Game Used Authentic Fabrics Parallel-AFST
06SP Game Used Authentic Fabrics Patches-AFST
06SP Game Used Authentic Fabrics Eights-AF8CEN
06SP Game Used Authentic Fabrics Eights Patches-AF8CEN
06SP Game Used Inked Sweaters-ISJS
06SP Game Used Inked Sweaters Patches-ISJS
06SP Game Used Inked Sweaters Dual-IS2HS
06SP Game Used Inked Sweaters Dual Patches-IS2HS
06SP Game Used SIGnificance-SJS
06The Cup Autographed NHL Shields Duals-DASLS
06UD Artifacts Tundra Tandems-TTJJ
06UD Artifacts Tundra Tandems Black-TTJJ
06UD Artifacts Tundra Tandems Blue-TTJJ
06UD Artifacts Tundra Tandems Gold-TTJJ
06UD Artifacts Tundra Tandems Platinum-TTJJ
06UD Artifacts Tundra Tandems Red-TTJJ
06UD Artifacts Tundra Tandems Dual Patches Red-TTJJ
06Ultra-77
Gold Medallion-77
Ice Medallion-77
06Upper Deck Arena Giveaways-EDM3
06Upper Deck-77
Exclusives Parallel-77
High Gloss Parallel-77
Game Jerseys-J2ST
Game Patches-P2ST
Masterpieces-77
06Upper Deck MVP-116
Gold Script-116
Super Script-116
Jerseys-OJCJ
Jerseys-OJJJ
Jerseys-OJJM
06Upper Deck Ovation-20
06Upper Deck Sweet Shot Signature Shots/Saves-SSJS
06Upper Deck Sweet Shot Signature Shots/Saves Ice Signings-SSIJS
06Upper Deck Sweet Shot Signature Shots/Saves Sticks-SSSSJ
06Upper Deck Trilogy Honorary Scripted Patches-HSPJA
06Upper Deck Trilogy Honorary Scripted Swatches-HSSJA
06Upper Deck Victory Next In Line-NL22
07Upper Deck Victory-162
Black-162
Gold-162
Stoller, Pascal
95Swiss HNL-353
96Swiss HNL-326
98Swiss Power Play Stickers-235
99Swiss Panini Stickers-236
00Swiss Panini Stickers-181
00Swiss Slapshot Mini-Cards-LT8
01Swiss HNL-199
02Swiss HNL-106
Stolp, Jeff
91Minnesota Golden Gophers-24
93Dayton Bombers-17
94Dayton Bombers-19
94Dayton Bombers-24
Stolpe, Jan
67Swedish Hockey-228
69Swedish Hockey-271
Stoltz, Roland
64Swedish Coralli ISHockey-29
64Swedish Coralli ISHockey-124
65Swedish Coralli ISHockey-29
65Swedish Coralli ISHockey-124
67Swedish Hockey-74
69Swedish Hockey-105
81Swedish Semic Hockey VM Stickers-111
83Swedish Semic Elitserien-191
84Swedish Semic Elitserien-214
86Swedish Panini Stickers-230
97Swedish Alfabilder Autographs-2
98Swedish UD Choice-198
98Swedish UD Choice-208
01Swedish Alfabilder-2
Stone, Colin
02Swift Current Broncos-20
03Swift Current Broncos-18

04Swift Current Broncos-21
Stone, Derek
03Austin Ice Bats-16
Stone, Jason
00UK Guildford Flames-22
00Kelowna Rockets-13
03UK Cardiff Devils-4
05UK Cardiff Devils Challenge Cup-12
Stone, Justin
93Quebec Pee-Wee Tournament-638
Stone, Matt
907th Inn. Sketch OHL-99
917th Inn. Sketch OHL-311
Stone, Mike
91Michigan Wolverines-20
93Michigan Wolverines-25
94Huntington Blizzard-20
Stone, Ryan
01Brandon Wheat Kings-20
02Brandon Wheat Kings-13
03Brandon Wheat Kings-12
04Brandon Wheat Kings-13
04ITG Heroes and Prospects-214
04ITG Heroes/Prospects Toronto Expo '05-214
05ITG Heroes/Prosp Toronto Expo Parallel -237
06WBS Penguins-24
05ITG Heroes and Prospects-237
Autographs Series II-RST
06Wilkes-Barre Scranton Penguins-18
06Wilkes-Barre Scranton Penguins Jerseys-18
Stone, Shawn
917th Inn. Sketch WHL-31
Stoneman, Kevin
98OCN Blizzard-10
Stonier, Troy
95Slapshot-271
00Austin Ice Bats-21
Stopar, Rob
897th Inn. Sketch OHL-94
90Kitchener Rangers-10
907th Inn. Sketch OHL-242
Stopfgeshoff, Jonas
96Swedish Brynas Tigers-14
02German DEL City Press-86
05German DEL-94
Storey, Ben
00Hershey Bears-17
02Lexington Men O'War-8
03ECHL All-Stars-279
03Louisiana Ice Gators-20
Storey, Red
83Hall of Fame Postcards-B14
85Hall of Fame-28
Storf, Florian
94German DEL-106
95German DEL-104
96German DEL-49
99German Bundesliga 2-287
Stork, Dean
92British Columbia JHL-12
99Hampton Roads Admirals-20
02Arkansas Riverblades-19
05Stockton Thunder-18
Stork, Rastislav
04Czech OFS Czech/Slovak-44
Storm, Jay
93Michigan Tech Huskies-4
Storm, Jim
90Michigan Tech Huskies-16
91Michigan Tech Huskies-26
91Michigan Tech Huskies-34
93Donruss-445
93Parkhurst-354
Emerald Ice-354
93PowerPlay-356
93Score-610
Gold-610
Canadian-610
Canadian Gold-610
93Stadium Club Team USA-23
93Stadium Club Team USA Members Only-23
93Topps Premier Team USA-22
93Whalers Coke-21
94Donruss-280
94Leaf-213
94Pinnacle-237
Artist's Proofs-237
Rink Collection-237
94Stadium Club-26
Members Only Master Set-26
First Day Issue-26
Super Team Winner Cards-26
94Classic Autographs-NNO
94Classic Pro Prospects-37
96Michigan K-Wings-19
Stormqvist, Jan-Erik
89Swedish Semic Elitserien Stickers-34
90Swedish Semic Elitserien Stickers-182
Storr, Jamie
917th Inn. Sketch OHL-270
93Donruss Team Canada-20
93Parkhurst-508
Emerald Ice-508
93Pinnacle-458
Canadian-458
93Upper Deck-538
93Owen Sound Platers-27
93Owen Sound Platers-28
93Owen Sound Platers-29
93Owen Sound Platers-30
94Be A Player-R157
94Finest-12
94Finest-146
Super Team Winners-12
Super Team Winners-146
Refractors-12
Refractors-146
Bowman's Best-R7
Bowman's Best Refractors-R7
94Fleer-99
Rookie Sensations-9
94Leaf Phenoms-1
94Leaf Limited World Juniors Canada-10
94OPC Premier-437
Special Effects-437
94Parkhurst SE-SE80
Gold-SE80
94Pinnacle-254
94Pinnacle-475
94Pinnacle-521
Artist's Proofs-254
Artist's Proofs-475
Rink Collection-254
Rink Collection-475
Rookie Team Pinnacle-1
94Score-201
Gold-201
Platinum-201
Top Rookie Redemption-5
94Select Promos-YE1
94Select-170
Gold-170

Youth Explosion-YE1
94SP-137
Die Cuts-137
94Topps/OPC Premier-437
Special Effects-437
94Ultra Prospects-8
94Upper Deck-236
94Upper Deck-531
94Upper Deck-568
Electric Ice-236
Electric Ice-531
Electric Ice-568
SP Inserts-SP128
SP Inserts Die Cuts-SP128
94Owen Sound Platers-26
94Owen Sound Platers-27
94Owen Sound Platers-28
94Windsor Spitfires-2
94Classic-7
Gold-7
CHL All-Stars-C9
ROY Sweepstakes-R18
Tri-Cards-T31
94Classic Four-Sport *-121
Gold-121
Printers Proofs-121
95Upper Deck World Junior Alumni-15
95Bowman-128
All-Foil-128
95Collector's Choice-213
Player's Club-213
Player's Club Platinum-213
95Donruss-67
Canadian World Junior Team-1
Pro Pointers-15
95Emotion-84
generationNext-4
95Leaf-12
Studio Rookies-13
95Leaf Limited-101
95Metal-192
95Parkhurst International-104
Emerald Ice-104
95Playoff One on One-52
95Pro Magnets-69
95Select Certified-136
Mirror Gold-136
95SkyBox Impact-204
95Topps-363
OPC Inserts-363
Canadian World Juniors-2CJ
95Ultra-77
95Ultra-356
Gold Medallion-77
95Upper Deck-47
Electric Ice-47
Electric Ice Gold-47
96Phoenix Roadrunners-17
95Images-75
Gold-75
95Images Four-Sport *-100
96Fleer-133
Calder Candidates-8
96Metal Universe-192
96NHL Pro Stamps-69
96SkyBox Impact-159
96Ultra-82
Gold Medallion-82
Rookies-18
96Collector's Edge Future Legends-42
96Collector's Edge Ice Platinum Club-8
97Donruss-31
Press Proofs Silver-31
Press Proofs Gold-31
97Donruss Limited-76
Exposure-76
97Donruss Preferred-27
Cut to the Chase-27
97Donruss Priority-153
Stamp of Approval-153
97Leaf-138
Fractal Matrix-138
Fractal Matrix Die Cuts-138
97Leaf International-138
Universal Ice-138
97Pacific Omega-113
Copper-113
Dark Gray-113
Emerald Green-113
Gold-113
Ice Blue-113
97Pinnacle-82
Artist's Proofs-82
Rink Collection-82
Press Plates Back Black-82
Press Plates Back Cyan-82
Press Plates Back Magenta-82
Press Plates Back Yellow-82
Press Plates Front Black-82
Press Plates Front Cyan-82
Press Plates Front Magenta-82
Press Plates Front Yellow-82
97Score-46
Artist's Proofs-46
Golden Blades-46
97Upper Deck-287
97Upper Deck Ice-34
Parallel-34
Power Shift-34
98Aurora-89
98Bowman's Best Mirror Image Fusion-F20
98Bowmans Best Mirror Im Fusion Ref-F20
98Bowmans Best Mirror Im Fusion Atom Ref-F20
98NHL Aces Playing Cards-17
98OPC Chrome-24
Refractors-24
98Pacific-245
Ice Blue-245
Red-245
98Pacific Omega-113
Red-113
Opening Day Issue-113
98Paramount-108
Copper-108
Emerald Green-108
Holo-Electric-108
Ice Blue-108
Silver-108
98Topps-24
O-Pee-Chee-24
98UD3-6
98UD3-66
98UD3-126
Die-Cuts-6
Die-Cuts-66
Die-Cuts-126
98Upper Deck-107
Exclusives-107
Exclusives 1 of 1-107
Gold Reserve-107
99Aurora-71
Premiere Date-71
99BAP Memorabilia-95

Gold-95
Silver-95
99BAP Millennium-123
Emerald-123
Ruby-123
Sapphire-123
Signatures-123
Signatures Gold-123
99O-Pee-Chee-102
99O-Pee-Chee Chrome-102
99O-Pee-Chee Chrome Refractors-102
99Pacific-198
Copper-198
Emerald Green-198
Gold-198
Ice Blue-198
Premiere Date-198
Red-198
99Pacific Omega-113
Copper-113
Gold-113
Ice Blue-113
Premiere Date-113
99Paramount-112
Copper-112
Emerald-112
Gold-112
Holographic Emerald-112
Holographic Gold-112
Holographic Silver-112
Ice Blue-112
Premiere Date-112
Red-112
Silver-112
99Revolution-72
Premiere Date-72
Red-72
Shadow Series-72
99Topps Arena Giveaways-LA-JS
99Topps/OPC-102
99Topps/OPC Chrome-102
Refractors-102
99Upper Deck MVP-94
Gold Script-94
Silver Script-94
Super Script-94
99Upper Deck Victory-141
00Aurora-69
Premiere Date-69
00BAP Memorabilia-76
Emerald-76
Ruby-76
Sapphire-76
Promos-76
00BAP Mem Chicago Sportsfest Copper-76
00BAP Memorabilia Chicago Sportsfest Blue-76
00BAP Memorabilia Chicago Sportsfest Gold-76
00BAP Memorabilia Chicago Sportsfest Ruby-76
00BAP Memorabilia Chicago Sun-Times Ruby-76
00BAP Memorabilia Chicago Sun-Times Gold-76
00BAP Mem Chicago Sun-Times Sapphire-76
00BAP Mem Toronto Fall Expo Copper-76
00BAP Memorabilia Toronto Fall Expo Gold-76
00BAP Memorabilia Toronto Fall Expo Ruby-76
00BAP Parkhurst 2000-P249
00BAP Signature Series-40
Emerald-40
Ruby-40
Sapphire-40
Autographs-155
Autographs Gold-155
00BAP Ultimate Memorabilia Goalie Sticks-G14
00Crown Royale-51
Ice Blue-51
Limited Series-51
Premiere Date-51
Red-51
00Pacific-203
Copper-203
Gold-203
Ice Blue-203
Premiere Date-203
00Paramount-116
Copper-116
Gold-116
Holo-Gold-116
Holo-Silver-116
Ice Blue-116
Premiere Date-116
00Revolution-70
Blue-70
Premiere Date-70
Red-70
00Titanium-44
Blue-44
Gold-44
Premiere Date-44
Red-44
Retail-44
00Topps Heritage-119
00UD Reserve-41
00Upper Deck-312
Exclusives Tier 1-312
Exclusives Tier 2-312
00Upper Deck Vintage-169
00Upper Deck Vintage-172
01Between the Pipes-60
01Pacific-189
Extreme LTD-189
Hobby LTD-189
Premiere Date-189
Retail LTD-189
01Pacific Arena Exclusives-189
02BAP First Edition-127
Jerseys-127
02BAP Signature Series-33
Autographs-33
Autograph Buybacks 1999-123
Autograph Buybacks 2000-155
Autographs Gold-33
02Between the Pipes-24
Gold-24
Silver-24
Jerseys-43
Tandems-10
02Kings Game Sheets-27
02Kings Game Sheets-28
02Pacific-176
Blue-176
Red-176
02Pacific Complete-99
Red-99
02Parkhurst-164
Bronze-164
Gold-164
Silver-164
02UD Mask Collection-39
02UD Mask Collection-40
02UD Mask Collection Beckett Promos-39
02UD Mask Collection Beckett Promos-40
02Upper Deck-327
Exclusives-327
02Upper Deck Beckett UD Promos-327
03Beehive-37

Gold-37
Silver-37
03Hurricanes Postcards-17
03ITG Action-238
03Pacific-160
Blue-160
Red-160
03Pacific Complete-433
Red-433
03SP Authentic-14
Limited-14
03UD Honor Roll-12
03Upper Deck-283
Canadian Exclusives-283
HG-283
UD Exclusives-283
03Upper Deck Victory-87
Bronze-87
Gold-87
Silver-87
04Springfield Falcons-14
05Philadelphia Phantoms-22
06German DEL-49
New Arrivals-NA10
Stortini, Zack
01Sudbury Wolves-20
01Sudbury Wolves Police-18
03Sudbury Wolves-24
04Sudbury Wolves-7
05Milwaukee Admirals Pepsi-18
06Hamilton Bulldogs-24
07Upper Deck Victory-235
Black-235
Gold-235
Storykh, Anton
05PEI Rocket-15
Stos, Jason
89Windsor Spitfires-17
907th Inn. Sketch OHL-193
917th Inn. Sketch OHL-183
92Toledo Storm Team Issue-21
Stos, Jon
89Windsor Spitfires-18
907th Inn. Sketch OHL-119
91Rayside-Balfour Jr. Canadians-16
Stothers, Mike
81Kingston Canadians-20
88ProCards AHL-130
89ProCards AHL-343
90ProCards AHL/IHL-39
91ProCards-270
Stoughton, Blaine
74Maple Leafs Postcards-22
74O-Pee-Chee NHL-348
75Maple Leafs Postcards-21
75O-Pee-Chee NHL-265
75Topps-265
77O-Pee-Chee WHA-6
79O-Pee-Chee-356
80O-Pee-Chee-30
80O-Pee-Chee-59
80O-Pee-Chee-161
80O-Pee-Chee-167
80Topps-30
80Topps-59
80Topps-161
80Topps-167
81O-Pee-Chee-132
81O-Pee-Chee Stickers-63
81Topps-E86
82O-Pee-Chee-122
82O-Pee-Chee-130
82O-Pee-Chee-131
82O-Pee-Chee Stickers-126
82Post Cereal-7
82Topps Stickers-126
82Whalers Junior Hartford Courant-18
83NHL Key Tags-47
83O-Pee-Chee-135
83O-Pee-Chee-136
83O-Pee-Chee-147
83O-Pee-Chee Stickers-258
83O-Pee-Chee Stickers-259
83Puffy Stickers-15
83Topps Stickers-258
83Topps Stickers-259
83Whalers Junior Hartford Courant-17
84O-Pee-Chee-154
91Cincinnati Cyclones-24
92Cincinnati Cyclones-25
Stowards, Blain
00Prince Albert Raiders-24
Stowe, Mark
90Prince Albert Raiders-20
907th Inn. Sketch WHL-263
Stoyanovich, Dave
83Nova Scotia Voyageurs-17
Stoyanovich, Steve
81Indianapolis Checkers-19
82Indianapolis Checkers-20
83Whalers Junior Hartford Courant-18
93London Knights-27
Strachan, Al
93Action Packed HOF Induction-10
Strachan, Rick
98UK Basingstoke Bison-1
99UK Basingstoke Bison-1
00UK Cardiff Devils-5
00UK Sekonda Superleague-58
01UK Cardiff Devils-2
02UK Cardiff Devils-2
05UK Hull Stingrays-2
Strachan, Tyson
03Ohio State Buckeyes-19
04Ohio State Buckeyes-13
05Ohio State Buckeyes-14
06Ohio State Buckeyes-13
Strachan, Wayne
91Lake Superior State Lakers-23
92Lake Superior State Lakers-26
98Thunder Bay Thunder Cats-7
98UHL All-Stars-17
99Rockford IceHogs-19
Strader, Dave
89Red Wings Little Caesars-24
Strain, Craig
06Colorado EaglesA -20
Strain, Ryan
90Saskatoon Blades-24
907th Inn. Sketch WHL-90
917th Inn. Sketch WHL-163
Straka, Josef
95Czech APS Extraliga-165
96Czech APS Extraliga-186
97Czech APS Extraliga-95
97Czech DS Stickers-54
98Czech DS-49
98Czech OFS-12
99Czech DS-69
99Czech OFS-159
99Czech OFS-379
00Czech OFS-72

01Czech OFS-229
02Czech OFS Plus-266
02Czech OFS Plus All-Star Game-H36
02Czech OFS Plus Trios-T11
03Czech OFS Plus-204
03Czech OFS Plus Insert M-M1
04Czech HC Plzen Postcards-18
04Czech OFS-144
04Czech OFS-408
Assist Leaders-4
Czech/Slovak-15
Goals Leaders-4
Points Leaders-3
05Czech HC Plzen-11
05Czech HC Sparta Praha-12
06Finnish Cardset-292
Straka, Martin
91Upper Deck Czech World Juniors-99
92OPC Premier-21
92Parkhurst-140
Emerald Ice-140
92Penguins Coke/Clark-22
92Penguins Foodland-17
92Ultra-382
92Upper Deck-559
Euro-Rookies-ER19
92Classic-33
Gold-33
92Classic Four-Sport *-180
Gold-180
93Donruss-266
93Leaf-220
93OPC Premier-155
Gold-155
93Parkhurst-156
Emerald Ice-156
93Penguins Foodland-8
93Pinnacle-204
Canadian-204
93PowerPlay-415
Rising Stars-7
93Score-375
Canadian-375
93Stadium Club-415
Members Only Master Set-415
First Day Issue-415
93Topps/OPC Premier-155
Gold-155
93Ultra-244
93Upper Deck-40
SP-125
94Canada Games NHL POGS-190
94Donruss-224
94Flair-141
94Fleer-171
94Leaf-36
94Leaf Limited-62
94OPC Premier-164
Special Effects-164
94Parkhurst Vintage-V16
94Parkhurst SE-SE134
Gold-SE134
94Penguins Foodland-25
94Pinnacle-352
Artist's Proofs-352
Rink Collection-352
94Score-82
Gold-82
Platinum-82
94Select-36
Gold-36
94Stadium Club-34
Members Only Master Set-34
First Day Issue-34
Super Team Winner Cards-34
94Topps/OPC Premier-164
Special Effects-164
94Ultra-171
94Upper Deck-289
Electric Ice-289
SP Inserts-SP153
SP Inserts Die Cuts-SP153
94Czech APS Extraliga-155
95Be A Player-106
Signatures-S106
Signatures Die Cuts-S106
95Bowman-72
All-Foil-72
95Canada Games NHL POGS-193
95Emotion-127
95Finest-92
Refractors-92
95Leaf-253
95Metal-107
95Parkhurst International-145
95Parkhurst International-397
Emerald Ice-145
Emerald Ice-397
95Playoff One on One-289
95Pro Magnets-115
95Score-132
Black Ice Artist's Proofs-132
Black Ice-132
95Senators Team Issue-21
95SkyBox Impact-121
95Stadium Club-87
Members Only Master Set-87
95Topps-246
OPC Inserts-246
95Ultra-282
95Upper Deck-427
Electric Ice-427
Electric Ice Gold-427
Special Edition-SE146
Special Edition Gold-SE146
95Finnish Semic World Championships-160
95Swedish World Championships Stickers-207
96NHL Pro Stamps-115
96Playoff One on One-410
96Upper Deck-267
96Upper Deck Ice-24
Parallel-24
97Pacific-139
Copper-139
Emerald Green-139
Ice Blue-139
Red-139
Silver-139
97Panini Stickers-57
97Revolution-115
Copper-115
Emerald-115
Ice Blue-115
Silver-115
97SP Authentic-129
98Aurora-157
98Be A Player-115
Press Release-115
98BAP Gold-115
98BAP Autographs-115
98BAP Autographs Gold-115
98BAP Tampa Bay All Star Game-115
98OPC Chrome-45
Refractors-45

98Pacific-82
Ice Blue-82
Red-82
98Pacific Dynagon Ice-154
Blue-154
Red-154
98Pacific Omega-199
Red-199
Opening Day Issue-199
98Panini Stickers-52
98Paramount-197
Copper-197
Emerald Green-197
Holo-Electric-197
Ice Blue-197
Silver-197
98Revolution-120
Ice Shadow-120
Red-120
98SP Authentic-69
Power Shift-69
98Topps-45
O-Pee-Chee-45
98Upper Deck-349
Exclusives-349
Exclusives 1 of 1-349
Gold Reserve-349
98Upper Deck MVP-168
Gold Script-168
Silver Script-168
Super Script-168
98Czech OFS-246
Olympic Winners-20
98Czech Bonaparte-7B
98Czech Pexeso-23
98Czech Spaghetti-6
98Slovakian Eurotel-25
99Aurora-118
Premiere Date-118
99BAP Memorabilia-177
Gold-177
Silver-177
99BAP Millennium-198
Emerald-198
Ruby-198
Sapphire-198
Signatures-198
Signatures Gold-198
99Black Diamond-69
Diamond Cut-69
Final Cut-69
99O-Pee-Chee-91
99O-Pee-Chee Chrome-91
99O-Pee-Chee Chrome Refractors-91
99Pacific-347
Copper-347
Emerald Green-347
Gold-347
Ice Blue-347
Premiere Date-347
Red-347
99Pacific Dynagon Ice-163
Blue-163
Copper-163
Gold-163
Premiere Date-163
99Pacific Omega-191
Copper-191
Gold-191
Ice Blue-191
Premiere Date-191
99Pacific Prism-116
Holographic Blue-116
Holographic Gold-116
Holographic Mirror-116
Holographic Purple-116
Premiere Date-116
99Panini Stickers-138
99Paramount-192
Copper-192
Emerald-192
Gold-192
Holographic Emerald-192
Holographic Gold-192
Holographic Silver-192
Ice Blue-192
Premiere Date-192
Red-192
Silver-192
99Revolution-120
Premiere Date-120
Red-120
Shadow Series-120
99SP Authentic-70
99SPx-121
Radiance-121
Spectrum-121
99Stadium Club-62
First Day Issue-62
One of a Kind-62
Printing Plates Black-62
Printing Plates Cyan-62
Printing Plates Magenta-62
Printing Plates Yellow-62
99Topps/OPC-91
99Topps/OPC Chrome-91
Refractors-91
99Ultimate Victory-70
1/1-70
Parallel-70
Parallel 100-70
99Upper Deck-276
Exclusives-276
Exclusives 1 of 1-276
99Upper Deck Gold Reserve-276
99Upper Deck MVP-166
Gold Script-166
Silver Script-166
Super Script-166
SC Edition Great Combinations-GCJS
SC Edition Great Combinations Parallel-GCJS
99Upper Deck Retro-65
Gold-65
Platinum-65
99Upper Deck Victory-239
99Wayne Gretzky Hockey-137
99Czech DS National Stars-NS14
99Czech OFS-37
99Czech OFS Jagr Team Embossed-37
00Aurora-118
Premiere Date-118
00BAP Memorabilia-261
Emerald-261
Ruby-261
Sapphire-261
Promos-261
00BAP Mem Chicago Sportsfest Copper-261
00BAP Memorabilia Chicago Sportsfest Blue-261
00BAP Memorabilia Chicago Sportsfest Gold-261
00BAP Memorabilia Chicago Sportsfest Ruby-261
00BAP Memorabilia Chicago Sun-Times Ruby-261
00BAP Memorabilia Chicago Sun-Times Gold-261
00BAP Mem Chicago Sun-Times Sapphire-261
00BAP Mem Toronto Fall Expo Copper-261

00BAP Memorabilia Toronto Fall Expo Gold-261
00BAP Memorabilia Toronto Fall Expo Ruby-261
00BAP Memorabilia Update Teammates-TM20
00BAP Memorabilia Update Teammates Gold-TM20
00BAP Parkhurst 2000-P140
00BAP Signature Series-199
Emerald-199
Ruby-199
Sapphire-199
00Black Diamond-48
Gold-48
00Crown Royale-88
Ice Blue-88
Limited Series-88
Premiere Date-88
Red-88
Game-Worn Jerseys-23
Game-Worn Jersey Patches-23
Premium-Sized Game-Worn Jerseys-23
00O-Pee-Chee-165
00O-Pee-Chee Parallel-165
00Pacific-337
Copper-337
Gold-337
Ice Blue-337
Premiere Date-337
00Panini Stickers-82
00Paramount-202
Copper-202
Gold-202
Holo-Gold-202
Holo-Silver-202
Ice Blue-202
Premiere Date-202
00Private Stock-81
Gold-81
Premiere Date-81
Retail-81
Silver-81
PS-2001 Action-48
00Revolution-120
Blue-120
Premiere Date-120
Red-120
00Titanium-79
Blue-79
Gold-79
Premiere Date-79
Red-79
Retail-79
Game Gear-142
Game Gear-155
Game Gear Patches-142
00Titanium Draft Day Edition-88
Patches-88
00Topps/OPC-165
Parallel-165
00Topps Chrome-114
OPC Refractors-114
Refractors-114
00Topps Heritage-155
00UD Heroes-97
00Upper Deck-367
Exclusives Tier 1-367
Exclusives Tier 2-367
00Upper Deck MVP-145
First Stars-145
Second Stars-145
Third Stars-145
00Upper Deck Victory-188
00Upper Deck Vintage-294
00Vanguard-81
Holographic Gold-81
Holographic Purple-81
Pacific Proofs-81
00Czech DS Extraliga Team Jagr-JT5
00Czech DS Extraliga Team Jagr Parallel-JT5
00Czech OFS-393
00Czech Stadion-77
01Atomic-80
Blue-80
Gold-80
Premiere Date-80
Red-80
Statosphere-19
01BAP Memorabilia-164
Emerald-164
Ruby-164
Sapphire-164
He Shoots-He Scores Prizes-30
Stanley Cup Playoffs-SC5
01BAP Signature Series Jerseys-GJ-89
01Crown Royale Triple Threads-17
01Crown Royale Triple Threads-20
01O-Pee-Chee-60
01O-Pee-Chee Heritage Parallel-60
01O-Pee-Chee Heritage Parallel Limited-60
01O-Pee-Chee Premier Parallel-60
01Pacific-319
Extreme LTD-319
Hobby LTD-319
Premiere Date-319
Retail LTD-319
Jerseys-31
01Pacific Adrenaline-156
Blue-156
Premiere Date-156
Red-156
Retail-156
01Pacific Arena Exclusives-319
01Pacific Heads-Up Quad Jerseys-18
01Pacific Heads-Up Quad Jerseys-28
01Parkhurst-63
Gold-63
Silver-63
Jerseys-PJ41
01Private Stock-79
Gold-79
Premiere Date-79
Retail-79
Silver-79
Game Gear-85
Game Gear Patches-85
01Private Stock Pacific Nights-79
01Stadium Club-71
Award Winners-71
Master Photos-71
01Titanium Double-Sided Jerseys-34
01Titanium Double-Sided Patches-34
01Topps-60
Heritage Parallel-60
Heritage Parallel Limited-60
OPC Parallel-60
Own The Game-OTG6
01Topps Chrome-60
Refractors-60
Black Border Refractors-60
01Topps Heritage-99
Refractors-99
Jerseys-JMS
01Topps Reserve-64
Emblems-MST
Jerseys-MST
Name Plates-MST
Numbers-MST
Patches-MST
01UD Challenge for the Cup-70
01Upper Deck-368
Exclusives-368
01Upper Deck MVP-155
01Upper Deck Victory-283
01Upper Deck Victory-436
Gold-283
Gold-436
01Upper Deck Vintage-204
01Upper Deck Vintage-208
01Vanguard Memorabilia-23
01Vanguard Memorabilia-27
01Vanguard Patches-23
01Vanguard Patches-27
01Czech DS-39
Ice Heroes-IH5
01Czech Stadion-258
02BAP First Edition-59
Jerseys-59
02BAP Memorabilia-147
Emerald-147
Ruby-147
Sapphire-147
NHL All-Star Game-147
NHL All-Star Game Blue-147
NHL All-Star Game Green-147
NHL All-Star Game Red-147
02BAP Memorabilia Toronto Fall Expo-147
02BAP Signature Series-28
Autographs-28
Autograph Buybacks 1998-115
Autograph Buybacks 1999-198
Autographs Gold-28
Team Quads-TQ8
02Crown Royale Dual Patches-18
02O-Pee-Chee-70
02O-Pee-Chee Premier Blue Parallel-70
02O-Pee-Chee Premier Red Parallel-70
02O-Pee-Chee Factory Set-70
02Pacific-318
Blue-318
Red-318
02Pacific Complete-29
Red-29
02Pacific Exclusive-140
02Parkhurst-151
Bronze-151
Gold-151
Silver-151
02Parkhurst Retro-88
Minis-88
02Topps-70
OPC Blue Parallel-70
OPC Red Parallel-70
Factory Set-70
02Topps Chrome-47
Black Border Refractors-47
Refractors-47
02Topps Total-196
02Upper Deck-139
Exclusives-139
02Upper Deck MVP-149
Gold-149
Classics-149
Golden Classics-149
02Upper Deck Rookie Update-80
02Upper Deck Victory-171
Bronze-171
Gold-171
Silver-171
02Upper Deck Vintage-201
Green Backs-201
02Czech IQ Sports Blue-28
03Beehive-159
Gold-159
Silver-159
03Black Diamond-74
Black-74
Green-74
Red-74
03ITG Action-452
Jerseys-M82
03O-Pee-Chee-70
03OPC Blue-70
03OPC Gold-70
03OPC Red-70
03Pacific-276
Blue-276
Red-276
03Pacific Complete-49
Red-49
03Pacific Exhibit-119
Blue Backs-119
Yellow Backs-119
03Pacific Prism-81
Blue-81
Gold-81
Red-81
03Private Stock Reserve-195
Blue-195
Patches-195
Red-195
Retail-195
03SP Authentic-70
Limited-70
03SPx-77
Radiance-77
Spectrum-77
03Topps-70
Blue-70
Gold-70
Red-70
03Topps C55-123
Minis-123
Minis American Back-123
Minis American Back Red-123
Minis Bazooka Back-123
Minis Brooklyn Back-123
Minis Hat Trick Back-123
Minis O Canada Back-123
Minis O Canada Back Red-123
Minis Stanley Cup Back-123
03Topps Pristine-93
Gold Refractor Die Cuts-93
Refractors-93
Popular Demand Relics-PD-MSK
Popular Demand Relic Refractors-PD-MSK
Press Plates Black-93
Press Plates Cyan-93
Press Plates Magenta-93
Press Plates Yellow-93
03Topps Traded-TT19
Blue-TT19
Gold-TT19
Red-TT19
03UD Honor Roll-69
03UD Premier Collection Stars-ST-MS
03UD Premier Collection Stars Patches-ST-MS
03Upper Deck-337
Canadian Exclusives-337
HG-337
UD Exclusives-337
03Upper Deck Classic Portraits-78
03Upper Deck Ice-40
Gold-40
03Upper Deck MVP-334
Gold Script-334
Silver Script-334
Canadian Exclusives-334
SportsNut-SN72
03Upper Deck Rookie Update-40
03Upper Deck Trilogy-78
Limited-78
03Upper Deck Victory-150
Bronze-150
Gold-150
Silver-150
03Czech National Team Postcards-11
03Russian World Championship Stars-27
04Upper Deck-82
Canadian Exclusives-82
HG Glossy Gold-82
HG Glossy Silver-82
World Cup Tribute-MHSKTV
04Czech HC Plzen Postcards-19
04Czech NHL ELH Postcards-15
04Czech OFS-147
Stars-15
04Czech Zuma-22
04Czech World Championship Postcards-20
05Hot Prospects-66
En Fuego-66
Red Hot-66
White Hot-66
05Panini Stickers-105
05Parkhurst-318
Facsimile Auto Parallel-318
True Colors-TCNYR
True Colors-TCNYR
True Colors-TCNJNY
True Colors-TCNJNY
True Colors-TCNYNY
True Colors-TCNYNY
05SP Authentic-66
Limited-66
05The Cup Master Pressplate Rookie Update-255
05Ultimate Coll National Heroes Jersey-NHJMS
05Ultimate Coll National Heroes Patch-NHPMS
05Upper Deck-375
Big Playmakers-B-MS
Notable Numbers-N-MST
05Upper Deck Hockey Showcase-HS34
05Upper Deck Showcase Promos-HS34
05Upper Deck MVP-255
Gold-255
Platinum-255
Materials-M-MS
05Upper Deck Rookie Update-64
05Upper Deck Rookie Update-255
Inspirations Patch Rookies-255
05Czech World Champions Postcards-14
05Czech Kvarteto Bonaparte-5b
05Czech Pexeso Mini Blue Set-28
05Czech Pexeso Mini Red Set-24
06Be A Player-29
Autographs-29
Signatures-ST
Signatures 10-32
Signatures Duals-DHM
Signatures Trios-TSNP
Up Close and Personal-UC34
Up Close and Personal Autographs-UC34
06Black Diamond-56
Black-56
Gold-56
Ruby-56
06Flair Showcase Stitches-SSST
06Fleer-129
Tiffany-129
Fabricology-FMS
06O-Pee-Chee-333
Rainbow-333
Swatches-S-ST
06Panini Stickers-106
06The Cup NHL Shields Duals-DSHJS
06Ultra-128
Gold Medallion-128
Ice Medallion-128
Uniformity-UST
Uniformity Patches-UPST
06Upper Deck Arena Giveaways-NYR3
06Upper Deck-134
Exclusives Parallel-134
High Gloss Parallel-134
Masterpieces-134
06Upper Deck MVP-193
Gold Script-193
Super Script-193
Jerseys-OJSS
06Upper Deck Ovation-183
06Upper Deck Victory-131
06Upper Deck Victory Black-131
06Upper Deck Victory Gold-131
06Czech OFS Jagr Team-19
06Russian Sport Collection Olympic Stars-30
07Upper Deck Ovation-15
07Upper Deck Victory-22
Black-22
Gold-22

Straka, Michal
94Czech APS Extraliga-156
94Cleveland Lumberjacks-22
95Czech APS Extraliga-254
96Czech APS Extraliga-303
97Czech APS Extraliga-184
97Czech DS Stickers-222
98Czech DS-61
98Czech DS Stickers-160
98Czech OFS-44
99Czech DS-92
99Czech OFS-374
00Czech DS Extraliga-34
00Czech OFS-70
01Czech OFS-227
02Czech OFS Plus-167
03Czech OFS Plus-125
03Czech OFS Plus-377
03Czech OFS Plus-387
03Czech OFS Plus Insert C-C4
04Czech HC Plzen Postcards-20
04Czech OFS-149
05Czech HC Plzen-12

Strakhov, Alexei
99Russian Hockey League-114

Strakhov, Andrej
99German Bundesliga 2-117
01German Upper Deck-264
02German DEL City Press-19
03German DEL-29
04German DEL-116
05German DEL-323

Strakhov, Yuri
90O-Pee-Chee-484

Stralman, Anton
05Swedish SHL Elitset Rookies-9
06Swedish SHL Elitset-135

Stramkowski, Jens
98German DEL-217
99German DEL-202
00German DEL-215
02German DEL City Press-296

Stranberg, Dan
92Quebec Pee-Wee Tournament-930
93Quebec Pee-Wee Tournament-582

Strand, Jan Roger
71Swedish Hockey-280
72Swedish Stickers-255
74Swedish Stickers-264

Strand, Luke
98Madison Monsters-9
04Green Bay Gamblers-20

Strand, Paul
90Fort Saskatchewan Traders-19

Strandberg, Tomas
89Swedish Semic Elitserien Stickers-254
90Swedish Semic Elitserien Stickers-167
91Swedish Semic Elitserien Stickers-17
92Swedish Semic Elitserien Stickers-39
94Swedish Leaf-48
95Swedish Leaf-156
Face to Face-1
95Swedish Upper Deck-13
97Swedish Collector's Choice-7
99Swiss Panini Stickers-124
02Swedish SHL-16
Parallel-16

Strander, Pekka
78Finnish SM-Liiga-174
80Finnish Mallasjuoma-116

Stranka, Gerhard
94German First League-286
95German DEL-334

Stransky, Vladimir
95Czech APS Extraliga-291

Strasser, Aaron
94German First League-98

Strasser, Christian
02Swiss HNL-437

Stratton, Art
63York White Backs-44
69Seattle Totems-6

Straub, Brian
91ProCards-323
94Atlanta Knights-18
95Fort Wayne Komets-19

Straub, Josef
94Czech APS Extraliga-199
95Czech APS Extraliga-39
96Czech APS Extraliga-62
97Czech APS Extraliga-333
97Czech DS Extraliga-116
97Czech DS Stickers-244
98Czech DS-113
98Czech DS Stickers-278
98Czech OFS-27
99Czech DS-9
99Czech OFS-455
00Czech DS Extraliga-167
00Czech OFS-253
00Czech OFS Star Emerald-28
00Czech OFS Star Pink-28
00Czech OFS Star Violet-28
01Czech OFS-41
02Czech OFS Plus-251
03Czech OFS Plus Insert C-C12

Straube, Chris
94German DEL-319
95German DEL-284
98German DEL-258
99German Adler Mannheim Eagles Postcards-24
99German DEL-22
00German DEL-12
01German Adler Mannheim Eagles Postcards-5
02German DEL City Press-20
05German SC Bietigheim-Bissingen Steelers-20

Strauss, Frank
94German First League-401

Strauss, Thomas
93Quebec Pee-Wee Tournament-1537

Strauss, Wolfgang
95Austrian National Team-27

Strautman, Tyler
04Brandon Wheat Kings-10
05Brandon Wheat Kings-21

Strba, Martin
95Czech APS Extraliga-73
97Czech APS Extraliga-284
98Czech OFS-204
99Czech DS-40
99Czech OFS-285
00Czech OFS-22
01Czech OFS-147
02Czech OFS Plus-187
03Czech OFS Plus-330
04Czech OFS-343
06Czech HC Sparta Praha Postcards-13
06Czech OFS Points Leaders-14

Strbak, Martin
99Czech OFS-160
00Czech DS Extraliga-17
00Czech OFS-325
01Czech OFS-76
02Slovakian Kvarteto-10
03ITG VIP Rookie Debut-33
03Parkhurst Rookie-106
03UD Honor Roll-156
04Russian Legion-4

Street, Ben
03Salmon Arm Silverbacks-19
04Salmon Arm Silverbacks-7
05Wisconsin Badgers-25

Street, Keith
89ProCards IHL-171
94Anchorage Aces-21
96Anchorage Aces-14
97Anchorage Aces-19
98Anchorage Aces-14
99Anchorage Aces-13

Streit, Flavio
01Swiss HNL-323
02Swiss HNL-439

Streit, Karl
94German First League-119

Streit, Mark
95Swiss HNL-69
96Swiss HNL-111
98Swiss Power Play Stickers-61
98Swiss Power Play Stickers-269
99Swiss Panini Stickers-261
00Swiss Panini Stickers National Team-P8
00Swiss Slapshot Mini-Cards-ZSCL5
01Swiss HNL-10
01Swiss HNL-192
02Swiss HNL-47
02Swiss HNL-104
02Swiss HNL-490
02Swiss HNL-494
05Canadiens Team Issue-21
05Hot Prospects-143
En Fuego-143
Red Hot-143
White Hot-143
05SP Authentic-268
Limited-268
05SP Game Used-157
Gold-157
05SPx-195
Spectrum-195
05The Cup Masterpiece Pressplates (Ice)-154
05The Cup Master Pressplate Rookie Update-149
05The Cup Masterpiece Pressplates SPA-268
05The Cup Masterpiece Pressplates SP GU-157
05The Cup Masterpiece Pressplates (SPx)-195
05The Cup Masterpiece Pressplates Trilogy-196
05The Cup Masterpiece Pressplate Ult Coll-153
05Ultimate Collection-153
Gold-153
05Ultra-224
Gold-224
Ice-224
05Upper Deck Ice-154
05Upper Deck Rookie Update-149
05Upper Deck Trilogy-196
06Canadiens Postcards-20

Streit, Martin
97Czech APS Extraliga-233
97Czech DS Stickers-177
98Czech DS Stickers-40
99Czech DS-26
99Czech OFS-145
99Czech OFS-436
00Czech OFS-284
01Czech OFS-72
02Czech OFS Plus-78

Strelkov, Mikhail
01Russian Hockey League-34

Strelow, Warren
90Devils Team Issue-26

Stretch, C.J.
05Kamloops Blazers-10
06Kamloops Blazers-22

Streu, Craig
94Tampa Bay Tritons RHI-6
96German DEL-15
99German Bundesliga 2-242

Strgacic, Anton
93Quebec Pee-Wee Tournament-498

Striar, Rob
93Fort Worth Fire-16

Strida, Florian
94German First League-238
95Czech APS Extraliga-315

Strida, Martin
94German First League-245

Stridh, Jonny
83Swedish Semic Elitserien-67
84Swedish Semic Elitserien-67
85Swedish Panini Stickers-61
86Swedish Panini Stickers-48
87Swedish Panini Stickers-56

Striemitzer, Klaus
94German DEL-354

Stringer, Rejean
91Air Canada SJHL-A9
92Saskatchewan JHL-122
00Fresno Falcons-19
02Columbia Inferno-111
02ECHL All-Star Southern-55
04Peoria Rivermen-21
05UK Cardiff Devils Challenge Cup-5

Stripp, Wayne
89Hampton Roads Admirals-20A
89Hampton Roads Admirals-20H

Stritesky, Matej
06Czech OFS-191

Strobel, Eric
80USA Olympic Team Mini Pics-9
81Swedish Semic Hockey VM Stickers-103
95Signature Rookies Miracle on Ice-35
95Signature Rookies Miracle on Ice-36
95Signature Rook Miracle on Ice Sigs-35
95Signature Rook Miracle on Ice Sigs-36
04UD Legendary Signatures Miracle Men-USA17
04UD Legendary Sigs Miracle Men Autos-USA-ES

Strobel, Mark
96Albany River Rats-19

Strobl, Klaus
94German First League-256

Strohack, Mark
907th Inn. Sketch OHL-295
96Fort Worth Fire-9
97Fort Worth Brahmas-18
98Fort Worth Brahmas-11
00Wichita Thunder-21

Strohm, Lennart
69Swedish Hockey-216
71Swedish Hockey-347

Stroka, Rafal
92Finnish Semic-274

Strom, Daniel
04German Weiden Blue Devils-23

Strom, Dennis
90Swedish Semic Elitserien Stickers-119
91Swedish Semic Elitserien Stickers-122
92Swedish Semic Elitserien Stickers-144

Strom, Ingemar
83Swedish Semic Elitserien-166
85Swedish Panini Stickers-214
89Swedish Semic Elitserien Stickers-187
90Swedish Semic Elitserien Stickers-21
91Swedish Semic Elitserien Stickers-220

Strom, Peter
93Swedish Semic Elitserien-280
94Parkhurst SE-SE242
Gold-SE242
94Swedish Leaf-233
NHL Draft-8
95Swedish Leaf-148
Goldies-4
95Swedish Upper Deck-212
97Swedish Collector's Choice-83
98Swedish UD Choice-79
99Swedish Upper Deck-83
00Swedish Upper Deck-72
02Swedish SHL-121
Parallel-121
03Swedish Elite-32
Silver-32
04Swedish Elitset-32
Gold-32
05Swedish SHL Elitset-286
Series Two Signatures-26
06Swedish SHL Elitset-143

Stromback, Doug
84Kitchener Rangers-13
93Huntington Blizzard-24
95Central Hockey League-35
99Memphis RiverKings All-Time-2

Stromberg, Hans
69Swedish Hockey-54
70Swedish Hockey-14
71Swedish Hockey-93

Stromberg, Mika
91Finnish Jyvas-Hyva Stickers-23
92Finnish Jyvas-Hyva Stickers-55
93Finnish Jyvas-Hyva Stickers-111
93Finnish SISU-9
93Swedish Semic World Champ Stickers-61
94Finnish SISU-313
94Finnish SISU-387
94Finnish SISU Junior-9
94Finnish Jaa Kiekko-14
94Signature Rookies Tetrad *-115
Signatures-115
95Finnish Beckett Ad Cards-7
95Finnish SISU-47
95Finnish SISU-168
Double Trouble-2
Gold Cards-10
95Finnish SISU Limited-12
95Finnish Karjala World Champ Labels-18
95Finnish Semic World Championships-26
95Swedish World Championships Stickers-163
96Finnish SISU Redline-42
96Finnish SISU Redline-183
At The Gala-6
96Swedish Semic Wien-18
98Finnish Kerailysarja-104
Leijonat-16
99Swiss Panini Stickers-86
00Swiss Panini Stickers-84
00Swiss Slapshot Mini-Cards-EHCC5
01Swiss HNL-242
02Finnish Cardset-273
03Swedish Elite-159
Silver-159
04Swedish Djurgardens Postcards-9
04Swedish Elitset-157
Gold-157
06Finnish Cardset-214

Stromberg, Mikko
01Finnish Cardset-195
05Finnish Cardset -301
06Finnish Cardset-133
Between the Pipes-18
Signature Sensations-25

Strome, Anders
05Florida Everblades-15

Strompf, Ladislav
94German DEL-110
95German DEL-105
99German Bundesliga 2-234

Stromqvist, Hakan
89Swedish Semic Elitserien Stickers-172

Stromsoe, Ulf
69Swedish Hockey-307
70Swedish Hockey-212

Stromvall, Johan
84Swedish Semic Elitserien-191
85Swedish Panini Stickers-168
86Swedish Panini Stickers-184
87Swedish Panini Stickers-178
89Swedish Semic Elitserien Stickers-156
90Swedish Semic Elitserien Stickers-234
91Swedish Semic Elitserien Stickers-163
92Swedish Semic Elitserien Stickers-187
93Swedish Semic Elitserien-158
94Swedish Leaf-30
Studio Signatures-7
95Swedish Leaf-249
95Swedish Upper Deck-125

Stronach, Matthew
93Quebec Pee-Wee Tournament-1438

Strong, Dean
04Vernon Vipers-4

Strong, Ken
95Swedish Globe World Championships-183

Stroshein, Garret
04SP Authentic-95
04Ultimate Collection-47
04Portland Pirates-19
05Providence Bruins-18

Strot, Brett
90Knoxville Cherokees-114
91Michigan Falcons-12
93Flint Generals-3
96Quad-City Mallards-12

Strozynski, Sebastian
00Rouyn-Noranda Huskies-5
Signed-5
02Moncton Wildcats-21

Struch, David
88Saskatoon Blades-12
89Saskatoon Blades-12
90Saskatoon Blades-10
907th Inn. Sketch WHL-78
91Saskatoon Blades-10
94Saint John Flames-23
95Saint John Flames-23
00UK Nottingham Panthers-6
00UK Sekonda Superleague-139
01UK London Knights-7
03UK Nottingham Panthers-5

Strudwick, Jason
93Kamloops Blazers-21
94Kamloops Blazers-14
95Slapshot Memorial Cup-21
96Kentucky Thoroughblades-17
96Collector's Edge Ice-96
Prism-96
97Kentucky Thoroughblades-15
98Upper Deck MVP-202
Gold Script-202
Silver Script-202
Super Script-202
99Upper Deck-296
Exclusives-296
Exclusives 1 of 1-296
99Upper Deck Gold Reserve-296
00BAP Memorabilia-321
Emerald-321
Ruby-321
Sapphire-321
Promos-321
00BAP Mem Chicago Sportsfest Copper-321
00BAP Memorabilia Chicago Sportsfest Blue-321
00BAP Memorabilia Chicago Sportsfest Gold-321
00BAP Memorabilia Chicago Sportsfest Ruby-321
00BAP Memorabilia Chicago Sun-Times Ruby-321
00BAP Memorabilia Chicago Sun-Times Gold-321
00BAP Mem Chicago Sun-Times Sapphire-321
00BAP Mem Toronto Fall Expo Copper-321
00BAP Memorabilia Toronto Fall Expo Gold-321
00BAP Memorabilia Toronto Fall Expo Ruby-321
01BAP Signature Series-66
Autographs-66
Autographs Gold-66
02BAP Sig Series Auto Buybacks 2001-66
02Blackhawks Postcards-3
03Blackhawks Postcards-24
03ITG Action-140
03Parkhurst Original Six Chicago-7
03Upper Deck Tough Customers-TC-14

Strueby, Nathan
96Swift Current Broncos-15

Strueby, Todd
81Saskatoon Blades-16
83Moncton Alpines-20
84Nova Scotia Oilers-10
88Oilers Tenth Anniversary-132
90Alberta International Team Canada-19
91ProCards-585

Struger, Gerhard
93Quebec Pee-Wee Tournament-1534

Strumm, Bob
97Las Vegas Thunder-11
98Las Vegas Thunder-24

Strunk, Steve
95PEI Senators-20
96Milwaukee Admirals-23

Struzinski, Martin
98Danish Hockey League-63
99Danish Hockey League-59

Stryncl, Tomas
04Brampton Battalion-9
05Brampton Battalion-8
06Brampton Battalion-7

Stuart, Brad
96Regina Pats-4
97Regina Pats-24
98Bowman's Best-137
Refractors-137
Atomic Refractors-137
98Finest Futures Finest-F4
98Finest Futures Finest Refractors-F4
98OPC Chrome-228
Refractors-228
98Topps-228
O-Pee-Chee-228
98Bowman CHL-66
98Bowman CHL-138
Golden Anniversary-66
Golden Anniversary-138
OPC International-66
OPC International-138
Autographs Blue-A22
Autographs Gold-A22
Autographs Silver-A22
Scout's Choice-SC8
98Bowman Chrome CHL-66
98Bowman Chrome CHL-138
Golden Anniversary-66
Golden Anniversary-138
Golden Anniversary Refractors-66
Golden Anniversary Refractors-138
OPC International-66
OPC International-138
OPC International Refractors-66
OPC International Refractors-138
Refractors-66
Refractors-138
99BAP Memorabilia-242
Gold-242
Silver-242
99BAP Millennium-214
Emerald-214
Ruby-214
Sapphire-214
Signatures-214
Signatures Gold-214
Calder Candidates Ruby-C41
Calder Candidates Emerald-C41
Calder Candidates Sapphire-C41
99O-Pee-Chee Chrome-288
99O-Pee-Chee Chrome Refractors-288
99Pacific-463
99Pacific Dynagon Ice-176
Blue-176
Copper-176
Gold-176
Premiere Date-176
99Pacific Omega-212
Copper-212
Gold-212
Ice Blue-212
Premiere Date-212
99Pacific Prism-128
Holographic Blue-128
Holographic Gold-128
Holographic Mirror-128
Holographic Purple-128
Premiere Date-128
Ice Prospects-7
99Panini Stickers-304
99SP Authentic-71
Sign of the Times-BS
Sign of the Times Gold-BS
99Stadium Club-195
First Day Issue-195
One of a Kind-195
Printing Plates Black-195
Printing Plates Cyan-195
Printing Plates Magenta-195
Printing Plates Yellow-195
99Topps Arena Giveaways-SJ-BS
99Topps/OPC Chrome-288
Refractors-288
99Topps Gold Label Class 1-89
Black-89
Black One of One-89
One of One-89
Red-89
Red One of One-89
99Topps Gold Label Class 2-89
99Topps Gold Label Class 2 Black-89
99Topps Gold Label Class 2 Black 1 of 1-89
99Topps Gold Label Class 2 One of One-89
99Topps Gold Label Class 2 Red-89
99Topps Gold Label Class 2 Red One of One-89
99Topps Gold Label Class 3-89
99Topps Gold Label Class 3 Black-89
99Topps Gold Label Class 3 Black 1 of 1-89
99Topps Gold Label Class 3 One of One-89
99Topps Gold Label Class 3 Red-89
99Topps Gold Label Class 3 Red One of One-89
99Topps Premier Plus-125
Parallel-125
Premier Rookies-PR2
Premier Rookies Parallel-PR2
99Upper Deck-167
99Upper Deck-281
Exclusives-167
Exclusives-281
Exclusives 1 of 1-167
Exclusives 1 of 1-281
99Upper Deck Arena Giveaways-SS1
99Upper Deck Gold Reserve-167
99Upper Deck Gold Reserve-281
99Upper Deck HoloGrFx-50
Ausome-50
99Upper Deck Ovation-51
Standing Ovation-51
99Upper Deck Victory-365
99Wayne Gretzky Hockey-154
99Bowman CHL-99
Gold-99
OPC International-99
Scout's Choice-SC15
00BAP Memorabilia-19
Emerald-19
Ruby-19
Sapphire-19
Promos-19
00BAP Mem Chicago Sportsfest Copper-19
00BAP Memorabilia Chicago Sportsfest Blue-19
00BAP Memorabilia Chicago Sportsfest Gold-19
00BAP Memorabilia Chicago Sportsfest Ruby-19
00BAP Memorabilia Chicago Sun-Times Ruby-19
00BAP Memorabilia Chicago Sun-Times Gold-19
00BAP Mem Chicago Sun-Times Sapphire-19
00BAP Mem Toronto Fall Expo Copper-19
00BAP Memorabilia Toronto Fall Expo Gold-19
00BAP Memorabilia Toronto Fall Expo Ruby-19
00BAP Parkhurst 2000-P81
00BAP Signature Series-8
Emerald-8
Ruby-8
Sapphire-8
Autographs-84
Autographs Gold-84
00BAP Ultimate Memorabilia Autographs-49
Gold-49
00O-Pee-Chee-237
00O-Pee-Chee Parallel-237
00Pacific-366
Copper-366
Gold-366
Ice Blue-366
Premiere Date-366
00Paramount-218
Copper-218
Gold-218
Holo-Gold-218
Holo-Silver-218
Ice Blue-218
Premiere Date-218
00SPx-58
Spectrum-58
00Stadium Club-155
Lone Star Signatures-LS10
11 X 14 Autographs-BS
00Topps/OPC-237
Parallel-237
Own the Game-OTG27
00Topps Chrome-147
OPC Refractors-147
Refractors-147
00Topps Gold Label New Generation-NG6
00Topps Gold Label New Generation 1 to 1-NG6
00Topps Heritage-108
00Topps Premier Plus-47
Blue Ice-47
Private Signings-PSBS
00Topps Stars-30
Blue-30
Autographs-ABST
Progression-P8
00UD Heroes-100
00Upper Deck-147
Exclusives Tier 1-147
Exclusives Tier 2-147
00Upper Deck MVP-147
First Stars-147
Second Stars-147
Third Stars-147
00Upper Deck Victory-194
00Upper Deck Vintage-301
01BAP Memorabilia-22
Emerald-22
Ruby-22
Sapphire-22
01BAP Signature Series-76
Autographs-76
Autographs Gold-76
01O-Pee-Chee-118
01O-Pee-Chee Premier Parallel-118
01Pacific-345
Extreme LTD-345
Hobby LTD-345
Premiere Date-345
Retail LTD-345
01Pacific Arena Exclusives-345
01Parkhurst-131
01Sharks Postcards-4
01SP Authentic-125
Limited-125
Limited Gold-125
01Topps-118
OPC Parallel-118
01UD Honor Roll-29
01UD Honor Roll-59
01Upper Deck-376
Exclusives-376
01Upper Deck MVP-158
01Upper Deck Victory-294
Gold-294
01Upper Deck Vintage-215
01Upper Deck Vintage-217
02BAP First Edition-204
02BAP Sig Series Auto Buybacks 1999-214
02BAP Sig Series Auto Buybacks 2000-84
02BAP Sig Series Auto Buybacks 2001-76
02BAP Signature Series Phenoms-YP6
02Pacific-341
Blue-341
Red-341
02Pacific Calder-6
Silver-6
02Pacific Complete-145
Red-145
02Parkhurst-90
Bronze-90
Gold-90
Silver-90
02Topps Total-225
02Upper Deck Victory-180
Bronze-180
Gold-180
Silver-180
02Upper Deck Vintage-216
03BAP Memorabilia-14
Emerald-14
Gold-14
Ruby-14
Sapphire-14
03ITG Action-496
03O-Pee-Chee-241
03OPC Blue-241
03OPC Gold-241
03OPC Red-241
03Pacific Complete-269
Red-269
03Sharks Postcards-17
03Topps-241
Blue-241
Gold-241

Red-241
03Upper Deck-409
Canadian Exclusives-409
HG-409
UD Exclusives-409
03Upper Deck MVP-353
Gold Script-353
Silver Script-353
Canadian Exclusives-353
05Black Diamond-72
Emerald-72
Gold-72
Onyx-72
Ruby-72
05Bruins Boston Globe-10
05Panini Stickers-346
05Parkhurst-40
Facsimile Auto Parallel-40
05The Cup Master Pressplate Rookie Update-253
05Ultra-164
Gold-164
Ice-164
05Upper Deck-161
05Upper Deck-263
HG Glossy-161
05Upper Deck MVP-323
Gold-323
Platinum-323
05Upper Deck Rookie Update-253
Inspirations Patch Rookies-253
05Upper Deck Toronto Fall Expo-161
06Be A Player-28
Autographs-28
Signatures-BS
Signatures 25-31
Signatures Duals-DRS
06Black Diamond Jerseys-JBS
06Black Diamond Jerseys Black-JBS
06Black Diamond Jerseys Gold-JBS
06Black Diamond Jerseys Ruby-JBS
06Flair Showcase Stitches-SSBS
06Fleer Fabricology-FBS
06O-Pee-Chee-41
Rainbow-41
Swatches-S-BS
06Panini Stickers-23
06SP Game Used Authentic Fabrics Dual-AF2SC
06SP Game Used Authentic Fabrics Dual Patches-AF2SC
06UD Artifacts Frozen Artifacts-FABS
06UD Artifacts Frozen Artifacts Black-FABS
06UD Artifacts Frozen Artifacts Blue-FABS
06UD Artifacts Frozen Artifacts Gold-FABS
06UD Artifacts Frozen Artifacts Platinum-FABS
06UD Artifacts Frozen Artifacts Red-FABS
06UD Artifacts Frozen Artifacts Patches Black-FABS
06UD Artifacts Frozen Artifacts Patches Blue-FABS
06UD Artifacts Frozen Artifacts Patches Gold-FABS
06UD Artifacts Frozen Artifacts Patches Platinum-FABS
06UD Artifacts Frozen Artifacts Patches Red-FABS
06Ultra-17
Gold Medallion-17
Ice Medallion-17
Uniformity-UBS
Uniformity Patches-UPBS
06Upper Deck-16
Exclusives Parallel-16
High Gloss Parallel-16
Game Jerseys-JBS
Game Patches-PBS
Masterpieces-16
06Upper Deck MVP-26
Gold Script-26
Super Script-26
06Upper Deck Victory-18
06Upper Deck Victory Black-18
06Upper Deck Victory Gold-18

Stuart, Bruce
10C56-17
10Sweet Caporal Postcards-15
11C55-15
83Hall of Fame-224
83Hall of Fame Postcards-015
85Hall of Fame-224

Stuart, Colin
04Chicago Wolves-9
05Chicago Wolves-20

Stuart, Hod
83Hall of Fame Postcards-F13
85Hall of Fame-87

Stuart, Ira
28V128-2 Paulin's Candy-61

Stuart, Mark
03BAP Memorabilia Draft Redemptions-21
05ITG Heroes/Prosp Toronto Expo Parallel -393
05Providence Bruins-19
05ITG Heroes and Prospects-393
Autographs Update-A-MKS
06Be A Player-210
06Be A Player Portraits-102
06Beehive-106
Matte-106
06Black Diamond-190
Black-190
Gold-190
Ruby-190
06Flair Showcase-12
Parallel-12
06Fleer-204
Tiffany-204
06Hot Prospects-104
Red Hot-104
White Hot-104
Hot Materials -HMMS
Hot Materials Red Hot-HMMS
Hot Materials White Hot-HMMS
Hotagraphs-HMA
06O-Pee-Chee-503
06O-Pee-Chee-637
Rainbow-503
Rainbow-637
06SP Authentic-164
Limited-164
06SP Game Used-104
Gold-104
Rainbow-104
Autographs-104
Rookie Exclusives Autographs-REMS
06SPx-165
Spectrum-165
06The Cup-112
Autographed Rookie Masterpiece Pressplates-112
Gold Rainbow Autographed Rookie Patches-112
Masterpiece Pressplates (Artifacts)-203
Masterpiece Pressplates (Be A Player Portraits)-102
Masterpiece Pressplates (Bee Hive)-106
Masterpiece Pressplates (Marquee Rookies)-503
Masterpiece Pressplates (MVP)-344
Masterpiece Pressplates (Power Play)-102
Masterpiece Pressplates (SP Authentic Autographs)-164
Masterpiece Pressplates (SP Game Used)-104
Masterpiece Pressplates (SPx Autographs)-165
Masterpiece Pressplates (Sweet Beginnings)-106
Masterpiece Pressplates (Trilogy)-104
Masterpiece Pressplates (Ultimate Collection Autographs)-105
Masterpiece Pressplates (Victory)-221
NHL Shields Duals-DSHSL
Rookies Black-112
Rookies Platinum-112
06UD Artifacts-203
Blue-203
Gold-203
Platinum-203
Radiance-203
Red-203
06UD Mini Jersey Collection-102
06UD Powerplay-102
Impact Rainbow-102
06Ultimate Collection-105
Rookies Autographed NHL Shields-105
Rookies Autographed Patches-105
Ultimate Debut Threads Jerseys-DJ-MS
Ultimate Debut Threads Jerseys Autographs-DJ-MS
Ultimate Debut Threads Patches-DJ-MS
Ultimate Debut Threads Patches Autographs-DJ-MS
06Ultra-202
Gold Medallion-202
Ice Medallion-202
06Upper Deck-452
Exclusives Parallel-452
High Gloss Parallel-452
Masterpieces-452
Rookie Game Dated Moments-RGD3
Rookie Materials-RMMS
Rookie Materials Patches-RMMS
06Upper Deck MVP-344
Gold Script-344
Super Script-344
Autographs-OACS
06Upper Deck Ovation-106
06Upper Deck Sweet Shot-106
Rookie Jerseys Autographs-106
06Upper Deck Trilogy-104
06Upper Deck Victory-221
06Upper Deck Victory Black-221 *
06Upper Deck Victory Gold-221
06Providence Bruins-19
07Upper Deck Rookie Class -11

Stuart, Mike
03ITG VIP Rookie Debut-48
03Parkhurst Rookie-115
03UD Honor Roll-162
03Upper Deck-450
Canadian Exclusives-450
HG-450
UD Exclusives-450
03Upper Deck Rookie Update-123
03Worcester Ice Cats-12
04Worcester IceCats-8
05Peoria Rivermen-9
06Peoria Rivermen-18

Stuart, Red
23V145-1-22
24Anonymous NHL-40
24V145-2-31

Stubel, Chris
01Vancouver Giants-23

Stuchlik, Martin
05Bossier-Shreveport Mudbugs-18

Stuck, Dan
88ProCards AHL-144
89ProCards AHL-358
98Hershey Bears-34

Stuckey, Mark
94German DEL-248

Stucki, Richard
93Swiss HNL-247
95Swiss HNL-444
96Swiss HNL-434
98Swiss Power Play Stickers-345
99Swiss Panini Stickers-334
00Swiss Panini Stickers-313
01Swiss HNL-369
02Swiss HNL-180

Studeny, Vaclav
02Czech OFS Plus-145

Studer, Markus
93Swiss HNL-154
95Swiss HNL-311

Studer, Martin
93Swiss HNL-438

Studer, Nicolas
96Swiss HNL-413
01Swiss HNL-329
02Swiss HNL-341

Studer, Thomas
93Swiss HNL-406
95Swiss HNL-445
96Swiss HNL-435
01Swiss HNL-267
02Swiss HNL-297

Stumpel, Jozef
91Parkhurst-231
French-231
91Classic-34
91Classic Four-Sport *-34
92Pinnacle-412
French-412
92Upper Deck-485
93Donruss-23
93Leaf-404
93OPC Premier-416
Gold-416
93Parkhurst-15
Emerald Ice-15
93PowerPlay-293
93Stadium Club-488
Members Only Master Set-488
First Day Issue-488
93Topps/OPC Premier-416
Gold-416
93Ultra-212
All-Rookies-9
93Upper Deck-379
93Classic Pro Prospects-83
BCs-BC16
94Donruss-322
94Leaf-143
94OPC Premier-214
Special Effects-214
94Parkhurst-19
94Parkhurst-293
Gold-19
Gold-293
94Pinnacle-418
Artist's Proofs-418
Rink Collection-418
94Topps/OPC Premier-214
Special Effects-214
Special Effects-274
94Ultra-261
94Upper Deck-155
Electric Ice-155
95Be A Player-208
Signatures-S208
Signatures Die Cuts-S208
95Collector's Choice-308
Player's Club-308
Player's Club Platinum-308
95Donruss-195
95Leaf-223
95Parkhurst International-13
Emerald Ice-13
95Upper Deck-157
Electric Ice-157
Electric Ice Gold-157
95German DEL-448
95Slovakian APS National Team-28
96Black Diamond-60
Gold-60
96Flair-7
Blue Ice-7
96Leaf-116
Press Proofs-116
96Score-187
Artist's Proofs-187
Dealer's Choice Artist's Proofs-187
Special Artist's Proofs-187
Golden Blades-187
96Upper Deck-12
96Swedish Semic Wien-230
97Collector's Choice-18
Star Quest-SQ17
97Crown Royale-66
Emerald Green-66
Ice Blue-66
Silver-66
97Donruss-134
Press Proofs Silver-134
Press Proofs Gold-134
97Donruss Canadian Ice-43
Dominion Series-43
Provincial Series-43
97Donruss Elite-26
Aspirations-26
Status-26
97Donruss Limited-96
Exposure-96
97Donruss Preferred-55
Cut to the Chase-55
97Donruss Priority-60
Stamp of Approval-60
97Kraft-18
97Leaf-40
Fractal Matrix-40
Fractal Matrix Die Cuts-40
97Leaf International-40
Universal Ice-40
97Pacific-71
Copper-71
Emerald Green-71
Ice Blue-71
Red-71
Silver-71
97Pacific Dynagon-9
Copper-9
Dark Grey-9
Emerald Green-9
Ice Blue-9
Red-9
Silver-9
Tandems-31
97Pacific Invincible-10
Copper-10
Emerald Green-10
Ice Blue-10
Red-10
Silver-10
97Pacific Omega-114
Copper-114
Dark Gray-114
Emerald Green-114
Gold-114
Ice Blue-114
97Panini Stickers-3
97Paramount-92
Copper-92
Dark Grey-92
Emerald Green-92
Ice Blue-92
Red-92
Silver-92
97Pinnacle-138
Press Plates Back Black-138
Press Plates Back Cyan-138
Press Plates Back Magenta-138
Press Plates Back Yellow-138
Press Plates Front Black-138
Press Plates Front Cyan-138
Press Plates Front Magenta-138
Press Plates Front Yellow-138
97Pinnacle Certified-97
Red-97
Mirror Blue-97
Mirror Gold-97
Mirror Red-97
97Pinnacle Inside-127
97Pinnacle Tot Cert Platinum Blue-97
97Pinnacle Tot Certi Platinum Gold-97
97Pinnacle Totally Certified Platinum Red-97
97Pinnacle Tot Cert Mirror Platinum Gold-97
97Revolution-67
Copper-67
Emerald-67
Ice Blue-67
Silver-67
Team Checklist Laser Cuts-12
97Score-122
Artist's Proofs-122
Golden Blades-122
97SP Authentic-71
97Zenith-28
Z-Gold-28
Z-Silver-28
97Zenith 5 x 7-23
Gold Impulse-23
Silver Impulse-23
98Aurora-90
98Be A Player-63
Press Release-63
98BAP Gold-63
98BAP Autographs-63
98BAP Autographs Gold-63
98BAP Tampa Bay All Star Game-63
98Bowman's Best-91
Refractors-91
Atomic Refractors-91
98Crown Royale-66
Limited Series-66
98Finest-67
No Protectors-67
No Protectors Refractors-67
Refractors-67
98Kings Power Play-LAK2
98NHL Game Day Promotion-LAK2
98OPC Chrome-132
Refractors-132
Season's Best-SB24
Season's Best Refractors-SB24
98Pacific-246
Ice Blue-246
Red-246
Team Checklists-12
98Pacific Dynagon Ice-91
Blue-91
Red-91
98Pacific Omega-114
Red-114
Opening Day Issue-114
98Panini Stickers-201
98Paramount-109
Copper-109
Emerald Green-109
Holo-Electric-109
Ice Blue-109
Silver-109
98Revolution-70
Ice Shadow-70
Red-70
98SP Authentic Sign of the Times-JS
98SP Authentic Sign of the Times Gold-JS
98SPx Finite-41
Radiance-41
Spectrum-41
98Topps-132
O-Pee-Chee-132
Season's Best-SB24
98UD Choice-100
Prime Choice Reserve-100
Reserve-100
98Upper Deck-103
Exclusives-103
Exclusives 1 of 1-103
Gold Reserve-103
99Aurora-72
Premiere Date-72
99BAP Memorabilia-241
Gold-241
Silver-241
99O-Pee-Chee-41
99O-Pee-Chee Chrome-41
99O-Pee-Chee Chrome Refractors-41
99Pacific-199
Copper-199
Emerald Green-199
Gold-199
Ice Blue-199
Premiere Date-199
Red-199
99Pacific Dynagon Ice-99
Blue-99
Copper-99
Gold-99
Premiere Date-99
99Panini Stickers-259
99Paramount-113
Copper-113
Emerald-113
Gold-113
Holographic Emerald-113
Holographic Gold-113
Holographic Silver-113
Ice Blue-113
Premiere Date-113
Red-113
Silver-113
99SP Authentic Sign of the Times-JST
99SP Authentic Sign of the Times Gold-JST
99Stadium Club-37
First Day Issue-37
One of a Kind-37
Printing Plates Black-37
Printing Plates Cyan-37
Printing Plates Magenta-37
Printing Plates Yellow-37
99Topps/OPC-41
99Topps/OPC Chrome-41
Refractors-41
99Topps Gold Label Class 1-83
Black-83
Black One of One-83
One of One-83
Red-83
Red One of One-83
99Topps Gold Label Class 2-83
99Topps Gold Label Class 2 Black-83
99Topps Gold Label Class 2 Black 1 of 1-83
99Topps Gold Label Class 2 One of One-83
99Topps Gold Label Class 2 Red-83
99Topps Gold Label Class 2 Red One of One-83
99Topps Gold Label Class 3-83
99Topps Gold Label Class 3 Black-83
99Topps Gold Label Class 3 Black 1 of 1-83
99Topps Gold Label Class 3 One of One-83
99Topps Gold Label Class 3 Red-83
99Topps Gold Label Class 3 Red One of One-83
99Upper Deck-237
Exclusives-237
Exclusives 1 of 1-237
99Upper Deck Gold Reserve-237
99Upper Deck MVP-97
Gold Script-97
Silver Script-97
Super Script-97
SC Edition ProSign-JS
99Upper Deck Victory-136
99Wayne Gretzky Hockey-82
00Aurora-70
Pinstripes-70
Pinstripes Premiere Date-70
Premiere Date-70
00BAP Memorabilia-168
Emerald-168
Ruby-168
Sapphire-168
Promos-168
00BAP Mem Chicago Sportsfest Copper-168
00BAP Memorabilia Chicago Sportsfest Blue-168
00BAP Memorabilia Chicago Sportsfest Gold-168
00BAP Memorabilia Chicago Sportsfest Ruby-168
00BAP Memorabilia Chicago Sun-Times Ruby-168
00BAP Memorabilia Chicago Sun-Times Gold-168
00BAP Mem Chicago Sun-Times Sapphire-168
00BAP Mem Toronto Fall Expo Copper-168
00BAP Memorabilia Toronto Fall Expo Gold-168
00BAP Memorabilia Toronto Fall Expo Ruby-168
00BAP Parkhurst 2000-P15
00BAP Signature Series-174
Emerald-174
Ruby-174
Sapphire-174
00O-Pee-Chee-177
00O-Pee-Chee Parallel-177
00Pacific-204
Copper-204
Gold-204
Ice Blue-204
Premiere Date-204
00Panini Stickers-168
00Paramount-117
Copper-117
Gold-117
Holo-Gold-117
Holo-Silver-117
Ice Blue-117
Premiere Date-117
00Stadium Club-112
00Titanium Game Gear-25
00Topps/OPC-177
Parallel-177
00Topps Chrome-118
OPC Refractors-118
Refractors-118
00Upper Deck-83
Exclusives Tier 1-83
Exclusives Tier 2-83
00Upper Deck MVP-86
First Stars-86
Second Stars-86
Third Stars-86
00Upper Deck Victory-112
01BAP Memorabilia-110
01BAP Memorabilia-469
Emerald-110
Emerald-469
Ruby-110
Ruby-469
Sapphire-110
Sapphire-469
01BAP Signature Series-116
Autographs-116
Autographs Gold-116
01O-Pee-Chee-207
01O-Pee-Chee Premier Parallel-207
01Pacific-190
Extreme LTD-190
Hobby LTD-190
Premiere Date-190
Retail LTD-190
01Pacific Adrenaline-16
Blue-16
Premiere Date-16
Red-16
Retail-16
01Pacific Arena Exclusives-190
01Parkhurst-198
01Parkhurst-369
01SPx-157
01Topps-207
OPC Parallel-207
01Upper Deck-83
01Upper Deck-248
Exclusives-83
Exclusives-248
01Upper Deck Ice-87
01Upper Deck MVP-85
01Upper Deck Victory-161
Gold-161
01Upper Deck Vintage-120
01Upper Deck Vintage-122
01Slovakian Kvarteto-8B
02BAP Memorabilia-163
Emerald-163
Ruby-163
Sapphire-163
NHL All-Star Game-163
NHL All-Star Game Blue-163
NHL All-Star Game Green-163
NHL All-Star Game Red-163
02BAP Memorabilia Toronto Fall Expo-163
02BAP Sig Series Auto Buybacks 1998-63
02BAP Sig Series Auto Buybacks 2001-116
02O-Pee-Chee-201
02O-Pee-Chee Premier Blue Parallel-201
02O-Pee-Chee Premier Red Parallel-201
02O-Pee-Chee Factory Set-201
02Pacific-34
Blue-34
Red-34
02Pacific Complete-218
Red-218
02Parkhurst Retro-78
Minis-78
02Topps-201
OPC Blue Parallel-201
OPC Red Parallel-201
Factory Set-201
02Topps Total-153
02Upper Deck-260
Exclusives-260
02Upper Deck Beckett UD Promos-260
02Upper Deck MVP-18
Gold-18
Classics-18
Golden Classics-18
02Upper Deck Victory-15
Bronze-15
Gold-15
Silver-15
02Upper Deck Vintage-21
02Slovakian Kvarteto-16
03NHL Sticker Collection-18
03O-Pee-Chee-254
03OPC Blue-254
03OPC Gold-254
03OPC Red-254
03Pacific-33
Blue-33
Red-33
03Pacific Complete-344
Red-344
03Topps-254
Blue-254
Gold-254
Red-254
03Topps Traded-TT16
Blue-TT16
Gold-TT16
Red-TT16
03Upper Deck-333
Canadian Exclusives-333
HG-333
UD Exclusives-333
03Upper Deck MVP-204
Gold Script-204
Silver Script-204
Canadian Exclusives-204
03Czech Stadion-539
04Pacific-126
Blue-126
Red-126
04Czech HC Slavia Praha Postcards-8
04Czech OFS-173
Stars-19
04Czech Zuma-3
04Czech Zuma Stars-Z5
05Panini Stickers-66
05Parkhurst-205
Facsimile Auto Parallel-205
05Upper Deck MVP-177
Gold-177
Platinum-177
06Fleer Tiffany-88
06O-Pee-Chee-213
Rainbow-213
06Panini Stickers-58
06Upper Deck-335
Exclusives Parallel-335
High Gloss Parallel-335
Masterpieces-335
06Czech NHL ELH Postcards-11
07Upper Deck Victory-90
Black-90
Gold-90

Stumpf, Juri
94German DEL-35
95German DEL-28
99German Bundesliga 2-230

Sturch, David
92Salt Lake Golden Eagles-21

Sturgeon, Adam
01Belleville Bulls-23
01Mississauga Ice Dogs-12
03Saginaw Spirit-22

Sturgeon, Mike
82Brandon Wheat Kings-19

Sturgeon, Peter
75O-Pee-Chee NHL-393

Sturges, Dan
03Waterloo Blackhawks-7
04Green Bay Gamblers-21
04Green Bay Gamblers-25

Sturm, Marco
95German DEL-261
96German DEL-149
97Be A Player-243
Autographs-243
Autographs Die-Cuts-243
Autographs Prismatic Die-Cuts-243
One Timers-19
97Beehive Team-25
97Beehive Team Gold-25
97Black Diamond-71
Double Diamond-71
Triple Diamond-71
Quadruple Diamond-71
Premium Cut-PC12
Premium Cut Double Diamond-PC12
Premium Cut Quadruple Diamond Horiz-PC12
Premium Cut Triple Diamond-PC12
Premium Cut Quadruple Diamond Verticals-PC12
97Crown Royale-122
Emerald Green-122
Ice Blue-122
Silver-122
97Donruss Priority-168
Stamp of Approval-168
97Katch-125
Gold-125
Silver-125
97Pacific Omega-206
Copper-206
Dark Gray-206
Emerald Green-206
Gold-206
Ice Blue-206
97Revolution-127
Copper-127
Emerald-127
Ice Blue-127
Silver-127
97SP Authentic-192
Icons-I40
Icons Die-Cuts-I40
Icons Embossed-I40
97Upper Deck-355
97Upper Deck Ice-52
Parallel-52
Power Shift-52
97Zenith-87
Z-Gold-87
Z-Silver-87
97Zenith 5 x 7-68
Gold Impulse-68
Silver Impulse-68
97Zenith Rookie Reign-9
97Zenith Z-Team-15
97Zenith Z-Team Gold-15
98Aurora-171
98Be A Player-119
Press Release-119
98BAP Gold-119
98BAP Autographs-119
98BAP Autographs Gold-119
98BAP Tampa Bay All Star Game-119
98Bowman's Best-83
Refractors-83
Atomic Refractors-83
98Crown Royale-121
Limited Series-121
98Finest-147
No Protectors-147
No Protectors Refractors-147
Refractors-147
98Katch-124
98OPC Chrome-17
Refractors-17
Season's Best-SB12
Season's Best Refractors-SB12
98Pacific-392
Ice Blue-392
Red-392
98Pacific Dynagon Ice-169
Blue-169
Red-169
98Pacific Omega-215
Red-215
Opening Day Issue-215
98Panini Stickers-214
98Paramount-215
Copper-215
Emerald Green-215
Holo-Electric-215
Ice Blue-215
Silver-215
98Revolution-129
Ice Shadow-129
Red-129
98SPx Finite-72
98SPx Finite-150
Radiance-72
Radiance-150
Spectrum-72
Spectrum-150
98Topps-17
O-Pee-Chee-17
Ice Age 2000-I2
Season's Best-SB12
98Topps Gold Label Class 1-71
Black-71
Black One of One-71
One of One-71
Red-71
Red One of One-71
98Topps Gold Label Class 2-71
98Topps Gold Label Class 2 Black-71
98Topps Gold Label Class 2 Black 1 of 1-71
98Topps Gold Label Class 2 One of One-71
98Topps Gold Label Class 2 Red-71
98Topps Gold Label Class 2 Red One of One-71
98Topps Gold Label Class 3-71
98Topps Gold Label Class 3 Black-71
98Topps Gold Label Class 3 Black 1 of 1-71
98Topps Gold Label Class 3 One of One-71
98Topps Gold Label Class 3 Red-71
98Topps Gold Label Class 3 Red One of One-71
98UD Choice-181
98UD Choice Preview-181
98UD Choice Prime Choice Reserve-181
98UD Choice Reserve-181
98UD3-27
98UD3-87
98UD3-147
Die-Cuts-27
Die-Cuts-87
Die-Cuts-147
98Upper Deck-169
Exclusives-169
Exclusives 1 of 1-169
Gold Reserve-169
98Upper Deck MVP-172
Gold Script-172
Silver Script-172
Super Script-172
99BAP Memorabilia-248
Gold-248
Silver-248
99O-Pee-Chee-114
99O-Pee-Chee Chrome-114
99O-Pee-Chee Chrome Refractors-114
99O-Pee-Chee Top of the World-TW20
99Pacific-383
Copper-383
Emerald Green-383
Gold-383
Ice Blue-383
Premiere Date-383
Red-383
99Panini Stickers-302
99Paramount-210
Copper-210
Emerald-210
Gold-210
Holographic Emerald-210
Holographic Gold-210
Holographic Silver-210
Ice Blue-210
Premiere Date-210
Red-210
Silver-210
99SPx-130
Radiance-130
Spectrum-130
99Topps Arena Giveaways-SJ-MS
99Topps/OPC-114
Top of the World-TW20
99Topps/OPC Chrome-114
Refractors-114
99Upper Deck-279
Exclusives-279
Exclusives 1 of 1-279
99Upper Deck Gold Reserve-279
99Upper Deck MVP-177
Gold Script-177
Silver Script-177
Super Script-177
99Upper Deck Victory-253
99Wayne Gretzky Hockey-153
00BAP Memorabilia-16
Emerald-16
Ruby-16
Sapphire-16
Promos-16
00BAP Mem Chicago Sportsfest Copper-16
00BAP Memorabilia Chicago Sportsfest Blue-16
00BAP Memorabilia Chicago Sportsfest Gold-16
00BAP Memorabilia Chicago Sportsfest Ruby-16
00BAP Memorabilia Chicago Sun-Times Ruby-16
00BAP Memorabilia Chicago Sun-Times Gold-16
00BAP Mem Chicago Sun-Times Sapphire-16
00BAP Mem Toronto Fall Expo Copper-16
00BAP Memorabilia Toronto Fall Expo Gold-16
00BAP Memorabilia Toronto Fall Expo Ruby-16
00Pacific-367
Copper-367
Gold-367
Ice Blue-367
Premiere Date-367
00Upper Deck-377
Exclusives Tier 1-377
Exclusives Tier 2-377
00Upper Deck Vintage-302
01Bowman YoungStars-109
Gold-109
Ice Cubed-109
01O-Pee-Chee-97
01O-Pee-Chee Heritage Parallel-97
01O-Pee-Chee Heritage Parallel Limited-97
01O-Pee-Chee Premier Parallel-97
01Pacific-346
Extreme LTD-346
Hobby LTD-346
Premiere Date-346
Retail LTD-346
01Pacific Adrenaline-171
Blue-171
Premiere Date-171
Red-171
Retail-171
01Pacific Arena Exclusives-346
01Sharks Postcards-9
01Topps-97
Heritage Parallel-97
Heritage Parallel Limited-97
OPC Parallel-97
01Topps Chrome-97
Refractors-97
Black Border Refractors-97
01Upper Deck Victory-299
Gold-299
02BAP Sig Series Auto Buybacks 1998-119
02Bowman YoungStars-75
Gold-75
Silver-75
02O-Pee-Chee-253
02O-Pee-Chee Premier Blue Parallel-253
02O-Pee-Chee Premier Red Parallel-253
02O-Pee-Chee Factory Set-253
02Pacific-342
Blue-342
Red-342
02Sharks Team Issue-8
02Stadium Club-83
Silver Decoy Cards-83
Proofs-83
Passport-17
02Topps-253
OPC Blue Parallel-253
OPC Red Parallel-253
Factory Set-253
02Topps Chrome-136
Black Border Refractors-136
Refractors-136
02Topps Heritage Great Skates-MS
02Topps Heritage Great Skates Patches-MS
02Topps Total-108
02Upper Deck-148
Exclusives-148
Victory National Pride-NP29
02Upper Deck Vintage-214
03Black Diamond-65
Black-65
Green-65
Red-65
03Crown Royale Global Conquest-4
03ITG Action-461
03NHL Sticker Collection-288
03O-Pee-Chee-268
03OPC Blue-268
03OPC Gold-268
03OPC Red-268
03Pacific-301
Blue-301
Red-301
03Pacific Complete-9
Red-9
03Pacific Heads-Up-85
Hobby LTD-85
Retail LTD-85
03Pacific Supreme-86
Blue-86
Red-86
Retail-86
03Sharks Postcards-18
03Titanium-90
Hobby Jersey Number Parallels-90
Retail-90
Retail Jersey Number Parallels-90
03Topps-268
Blue-268
Gold-268
Red-268
Pristine Patches-PP-MST
Pristine Patch Refractors-PP-MST
Pristine Popular Demand Relics-PD-MST
Pristine Popular Demand Relic Refractor-PD-MST
03Upper Deck-158
Canadian Exclusives-158
HG-158
03Upper Deck MVP-346
Gold Script-346
Silver Script-346
Canadian Exclusives-346
03Czech Stadion-540
04Pacific-233
Blue-233
Red-233
04UD All-World-21
Gold-21
04Ultimate Collection-71
04Upper Deck-145
Canadian Exclusives-145
HG Glossy Gold-145
HG Glossy Silver-145
04German DEL-95
Global Players-GP4
Superstars-SU11
04German Ingolstadt Panthers-22
05Beehive Signature Scrapbook-SSMS
05Black Diamond-71
Emerald-71
Gold-71
Onyx-71
Ruby-71
05Bruins Boston Globe-14
05Panini Stickers-345
05Parkhurst-38
Facsimile Auto Parallel-38
05SP Authentic Sign of the Times-ST
05SP Game Used Statscriptions-ST-ST
05Ultra-163
Gold-163
Ice-163
05Upper Deck-157
05Upper Deck-262
HG Glossy-157
Notable Numbers-N-MAS
05Upper Deck MVP-319
Gold-319
Platinum-319
05Upper Deck Toronto Fall Expo-157
05Upper Deck Victory-164
Black-164
Gold-164
Silver-164
05German DEL-291
DEB-Jerseys-TR04
06Fleer-19
Tiffany-19
06O-Pee-Chee-43
Rainbow-43
06Panini Stickers-21
06Ultra-18
Gold Medallion-18
Ice Medallion-18
06Upper Deck-18
Exclusives Parallel-18
High Gloss Parallel-18
Masterpieces-18
06Upper Deck MVP-24
Gold Script-24
Super Script-24
International Icons-II4
06Upper Deck Ovation-55
06Upper Deck Victory-17
06Upper Deck Victory Black-17
06Upper Deck Victory Gold-17
06German DEL-193
07Upper Deck Victory-63
Black-63
Gold-63

Sturz, Christian
93Quebec Pee-Wee Tournament-751

Stussi, Rene
92Quebec Pee-Wee Tournament-1630
95Swiss HNL-338
96Swiss HNL-312
98Swiss Power Play Stickers-122
98Swiss Power Play Stickers-288
99Swiss Panini Stickers-221
00Swiss Panini Stickers-93
01Swiss HNL-253
02Swiss HNL-450

Stutzel, Mike
03ITG VIP Rookie Debut-142
03Parkhurst Rookie-72
03UD Premier Collection-99
03Upper Deck Rookie Update-183
03Springfield Falcons Postcards-13
04Pacific-295
Blue-295
Red-295
05Idaho Steelheads-20

Styblo, Ludek
93Quebec Pee-Wee Tournament-1541
Styf, Par
02Swedish SHL-265
Parallel-265
03Swedish Elite-126
Enforcers-EF6
Signatures II-5
Silver-126
04Swedish Elitset-126
Gold-126
05Swedish SHL Elitset-281
06Swedish SHL Elitset-281
Subban, P.K.
05Belleville Bulls-6
06Belleville Bulls-19
Subbotin, Andrei
98Russian Hockey League-40
99Russian Stars Postcards-25
01Russian Hockey League-95
02Russian Hockey League-124
02Russian Hockey League-210
03Russian SL-13
Subbotin, Dmitri
00Russian Dynamo Moscow-28
00Russian Dynamo Moscow Blue-White-5
00Russian Hockey League-320
03Russian Avangard Omsk-9
Subr, Bohuslav
97Guelph Storm-16
98Guelph Storm-10
99Guelph Storm-10
Suchan, Greg
89Niagara Falls Thunder-18
897th Inn. Sketch OHL-133
Suchan, Jaroslav
98Czech OFS-50
04Czech OFS-19
Team Cards-1
Suchan, Rainer
94German First League-357
99German Bundesliga 2-184
02German DEL City Press-144
04German DEL-279
05German DEL-14
06German DEL-12
Suchanek, Kamil
99Czech OFS-246
Suchanek, Karel
95Czech APS Extraliga-220
96Czech APS Extraliga-96
Suchanek, Pavel
91British Columbia JHL-30
92British Columbia JHL-68
Suchanek, Petr
97Czech APS Extraliga-111
98Czech OFS-318
99Czech OFS-245
00Czech OFS-272
01Idaho Steelheads-19
03Muskegon Fury-19
04Idaho Steelheads-6
Suchanek, Rudolf
94Czech APS Extraliga-103
95Czech APS Extraliga-55
96Czech APS Extraliga-241
97Czech APS Extraliga-268
97Czech DS Extraliga-28
97Czech DS Stickers-81
98Czech DS-33
98Czech DS Stickers-68
98Czech OFS-195
99Czech DS-33
99Czech OFS-189
00Czech DS Extraliga-76
00Czech OFS-9
00Czech OFS Star Emerald-14
00Czech OFS Star Pink-14
00Czech OFS Star Violet-14
01Czech OFS-132
All Stars-18
01Czech OFS Red Inserts-RE9D
02Czech OFS Plus-185
Trios-T1
03Czech OFS Plus-274
Suchy, Jan
69Swedish Hockey-38
70Finnish Jaakiekko-59
70Swedish Hockey-351
70Swedish Masterserien-12
70Swedish Masterserien-77
70Swedish Masterserien-143
70Swedish Masterserien-156
71Finnish Suomi Stickers-39
71Swedish Hockey-48
72Finnish Semic World Championship-36
72Swedish Semic World Championship-36
74Swedish Stickers-117
74Swedish Semic World Champ Stickers-67
91Finnish Semic World Champ Stickers-247
91Swedish Semic World Champ Stickers-247
96Swedish Semic Wien Hockey Legends-HL17
Suchy, Jiri
05Halifax Mooseheads-4
06Halifax Mooseheads-4
Suchy, Petr
98Czech OFS-347
99Czech OFS-65
99Czech Score Blue 2000-149
99Czech Score Red Ice 2000-149
00Czech OFS-144
Suchy, Radoslav
97Las Vegas Thunder-23
97Bowman CHL-64
OPC-64
99BAP Memorabilia-315
Gold-315
Silver-315
99Pacific Omega-186
Copper-186
Gold-186
Ice Blue-186
Premiere Date-186
99Topps Arena Giveaways-PHO-RS
00Panini Stickers-191
00Private Stock Game Gear-88
00Private Stock Game Gear Patches-88
00Titanium Draft Day Edition-79
Patches-79
00Upper Deck-364
Exclusives Tier 1-364
Exclusives Tier 2-364
01Coyotes Team Issue-19
01Pacific Heads-Up Quad Jerseys-26
02BAP First Edition-291
02Coyotes Team Issue-8
03Coyotes Postcards-23
03ITG Action-402
03O-Pee-Chee-174
03OPC Blue-174
03OPC Gold-174
03OPC Red-174
03Pacific Complete-88
Red-88
03Topps-174
Blue-174
Gold-174
Red-174
04Slovakian Poprad Team Set-12
Suda, Justin
01Kingston Frontenacs-21
04Kingston Frontenacs-20
Suderman, Joe
98Kelowna Rockets-24
99Kelowna Rockets-7
00Kelowna Rockets-19
01Prince Albert Raiders-21
Suderman, Matt
00Saskatoon Blades-7
01Saskatoon Blades-23
02Saskatoon Blades-3
05Missouri River Otters-23
Suer, Chad
06Moose Jaw Warriors-4
Sugden, Brandon
92Quebec Pee-Wee Tournament-500
95Slapshot-160
96Barrie Colts-24
98Dayton Bombers EBK-18
03Syracuse Crunch-19
04Syracuse Crunch-18
05Syracuse Crunch-18
Suggitt, Jeff
99Knoxville Speed-19
Suggs, Mike
03Saginaw Spirit-23
Suglobov, Aleksander
02Russian Hockey League-207
03Beehive-228
Gold-228
Silver-228
03ITG Action-654
03ITG Used Signature Series-169
Gold-169
03ITG VIP Rookie Debut-99
03Pacific Complete-557
Red-557
03Parkhurst Rookie-105
03SP Authentic-165
03Topps Traded-TT123
Blue-TT123
Gold-TT123
Red-TT123
03UD Premier Collection-65
03Upper Deck Rookie Update-132
03Russian World Championship Team 2003-12
03AHL Top Prospects-34
03Albany River Rats-26
03Albany River Rats Kinko's-25
03Pacific AHL Prospects-4
Gold-4
04Pacific-290
Blue-290
Red-290
04AHL Top Prospects-2
04Albany River Rats-24
05AHL All-Stars-38
05Albany River Rats-24
06Toronto Marlies-29
06ITG Heroes and Prospects-51
Autographs-AAS
Suhonen, Alpo
66Finnish Jaakiekkosarja-44
70Finnish Jaakiekko-187
89Jets Safeway-29
93Finnish Jyvas-Hyva Stickers-103
93Finnish SISU-2
95Swiss HNL-3
96Swiss HNL-176
Suhonen, Samuli
05Finnish Cardset -78
06Finnish Cardset-186
Suhrada, Jiri
95Czech APS Extraliga-217
Suhy, Andy
92Toledo Storm-9
92Toledo Storm Team Issue-20
93Toledo Storm-8
Suikkanen, Kai
78Finnish SM-Liiga-148
80Finnish Mallasjuoma-105
Suk, Joe
87Hull Olympiques-19
Suk, Steve
92Michigan State Spartans-23
93Michigan State Spartans-23
97Mobile Mysticks-17
97Mobile Mysticks Kellogg's-10
Sukovic, Mil
917th Inn. Sketch QMJHL-8
Sulak, Alexej
94German First League-262
Sulander, Ari
93Finnish Jyvas-Hyva Stickers-104
93Finnish SISU-3
94Finnish SISU-41
94Finnish SISU-388
94Finnish SISU NIL Phenoms-3
94Finnish SISU Specials-8
95Finnish SISU-43
95Finnish SISU-167
Ghost Goalies-3
Gold Cards-3
95Finnish SISU Limited-10
95Finnish Karjala World Champ Labels-19
96Finnish SISU Redline-41
96Finnish SISU Redline-175
At The Gala-8
96Finnish SISU Redline Foil Parallels-41
96Finnish SISU Redline Keeping It Green-1
96Finnish SISU Redline Mighty Adversaries-4
96Finnish SISU Redline Silver Signatures-4
96Swedish Semic Wien-10
98Finnish Kerailysarja Dream Team-2
98Swiss Power Play Stickers-228
99Finnish Cardset-179
99Swiss Panini Stickers-229
00Finnish Cardset-231
00Swiss Panini Stickers-271
00Swiss Slapshot Mini-Cards-ZSCL1
01Finnish Cardset Haltmeisters-7
01Swiss HNL-3
02Finnish Cardset-121
02Swiss HNL-12
Sulc, Jan
98Owen Sound Platers-14
00Johnstown Chiefs-22
01Czech OFS-163
02Czech OFS Plus-209
Sulkovsky, David
99German DEL-238
02German DEL City Press-103
04German DEL-117
05German DEL-95
06German DEL-114
Sulku, Sebastian
93Finnish SISU-7
94Finnish SISU-275
95Finnish SISU-137
98Finnish Kerailysarja-146
99Finnish Cardset-236
00Finnish Cardset-25
01Finnish Cardset-217
02Finnish Cardset-122
03Finnish Cardset-3
04Swedish Elitset-149
Gold-149
05Swedish SHL Elitset-5
Gold-5
Sullamaa, Petri
92Finnish Jyvas-Hyva Stickers-51
Sulliman, Doug
80O-Pee-Chee-306
82O-Pee-Chee-132
82O-Pee-Chee Stickers-128
82Post Cereal-7
82Topps Stickers-128
82Whalers Junior Hartford Courant-19
83NHL Key Tags-47
83O-Pee-Chee-148
83O-Pee-Chee Stickers-256
83Topps Stickers-256
83Whalers Junior Hartford Courant-19
84Devils Postcards-22
85O-Pee-Chee-234
86Devils Police-17
86O-Pee-Chee-121
86Topps-121
87O-Pee-Chee-116
87O-Pee-Chee Stickers-59
87Panini Stickers-82
87Topps-116
88Flyers Postcards-12
88O-Pee-Chee-172
88Topps-172
89Flyers Postcards-24
90Bowman-110
Tiffany-110
90Devils Team Issue-27
90O-Pee-Chee-473
Sullivan, Andy
93St. John's Maple Leafs-23
Sullivan, Bob
82Whalers Junior Hartford Courant-20
83NHL Key Tags-48
83O-Pee-Chee-149
83O-Pee-Chee Stickers-189
83Topps Stickers-189
Sullivan, Brad
01Michigan Tech Huskies-31
Sullivan, Brent
98Owen Sound Platers-24
99Owen Sound Platers-26
00Barrie Colts-24
05Port Huron Flags-18
Sullivan, Brian
91ProCards-412
93Classic Pro Prospects-77
97Grand Rapids Griffins-17
Sullivan, Chris
92Michigan State Spartans-24
93Michigan State Spartans-22
96Dayton Bombers-2
97Donruss Limited-46
Exposure-46
Sullivan, Dale
00Hull Olympiques-19
Signed-19
01Hull Olympiques-20
02Hull Olympiques-19
03Hull Olympiques Memorial Cup-16
Sullivan, Dan
00Mississauga Ice Dogs-24
00Owen Sound Attack-21
01Owen Sound Attack-22
02Roanoke Express-3
03Lowell Lock Monsters-9
03Lowell Lock Monsters Photo Album-14
Sullivan, George
44Beehive Group II Photos-70
44Beehive Group II Photos-367
51Parkhurst-27
52Parkhurst-79
54Topps-42
57Topps-56
58Topps-48
59Topps-59
60Shirriff Coins-82
60Topps-18
61Shirriff/Salada Coins-91
61Topps-48
63Topps-44
64Beehive Group III Photos-149
64Topps-29
65Topps-87
91Ultimate Original Six-29
French-29
94Parkhurst Missing Link-86
94Parkhurst Missing Link-170
94Parkhurst Tall Boys-108
04ITG Franchises US East-404
Autographs-A-RSU
Sullivan, Jeffrey
96Halifax Mooseheads I-19
96Halifax Mooseheads II-19
97Halifax Mooseheads I-19
97Halifax Mooseheads II-19
98Halifax Mooseheads-12
98Halifax Mooseheads Second Edition-5
99Johnstown Chiefs-8
00Johnstown Chiefs-20
01Johnstown Chiefs-5
02Johnstown Chiefs-18
03Johnstown Chiefs-2
04Johnstown Chiefs-16
Sullivan, Jerry
65Finnish Hellas-137
Sullivan, Kelly
93Quebec Pee-Wee Tournament-549
01Sioux Falls Stampede-14
Sullivan, Kevin
90Kansas City Blades-6
90ProCards AHL/IHL-595
91Nashville Knights-14
Sullivan, Michael
90ProCards AHL/IHL-307
90Rayside-Balfour Jr. Canadians-20
91Parkhurst-383
French-383
92Bowman-116
92O-Pee-Chee-144
92Parkhurst-395
Emerald Ice-395
92Score-533
Canadian-533
92Stadium Club-262
92Topps-282
Gold-282G
92Upper Deck-46
93OPC Premier-21
Gold-21
93Panini Stickers-262
93Parkhurst-454
Emerald Ice-454
93Pinnacle-287
Canadian-287
93Score-390
Canadian-390
93Stadium Club-139
Members Only Master Set-139
OPC-139
First Day Issue-139
First Day Issue OPC-139
93Topps/OPC Premier-21
Gold-21
94Be A Player Signature Cards-75
95Donruss-211
95Leaf-167
95Parkhurst International-300
Emerald Ice-300
96Toledo Storm-14
97Be A Player-179
Autographs-179
Autographs Die-Cuts-179
Autographs Prismatic Die-Cuts-179
97Pacific Invincible NHL Regime-32
97Pensacola Ice Pilots-21
98Pensacola Ice Pilots-25
99Paramount-183
Copper-183
Emerald-183
Gold-183
Holographic Emerald-183
Holographic Gold-183
Holographic Silver-183
Ice Blue-183
Premiere Date-183
Red-183
99German DEL-296
00Upper Deck-137
Exclusives Tier 1-137
Exclusives Tier 2-137
01Coyotes Team Issue-20
03Bruins Team Issue-11
Sullivan, Patrick
93Quebec Pee-Wee Tournament-535
Sullivan, Peter
76O-Pee-Chee WHA-42
77O-Pee-Chee WHA-27
78Jets Postcards-21
79Jets Postcards-25
79O-Pee-Chee-378
80Jets Postcards-22
80O-Pee-Chee-29
80Pepsi-Cola Caps-139
80Topps-29
Sullivan, Sean
03Boston University Terriers-15
Sullivan, Steve
93Sault Ste. Marie Greyhounds-24
93Sault Ste. Marie Greyhound Memorial Cup-16
96Be A Player-209
Autographs-209
Autographs Silver-209
96Devils Team Issue-11
96Donruss-229
Press Proofs-229
96Leaf Gold Rookies-10
96Leaf Preferred-143
Press Proofs-143
96Pinnacle-226
Artist's Proofs-226
Foil-226
Premium Stock-226
Rink Collection-226
96SkyBox Impact-160
96Summit-180
Artist's Proofs-180
Ice-180
Metal-180
Premium Stock-180
96Upper Deck-185
96Zenith-140
Artist's Proofs-140
96Albany River Rats-20
96Collector's Edge Future Legends-21
96Collector's Edge Ice Platinum Club-4
97Collector's Choice-248
Star Quest-SQ4
97Donruss-39
Press Proofs Silver-39
Press Proofs Gold-39
97Donruss Canadian Ice-94
Dominion Series-94
Provincial Series-94
97Donruss Limited-116
Exposure-116
97Donruss Preferred-131
Cut to the Chase-131
97Donruss Priority-92
Stamp of Approval-92
97Leaf-84
Fractal Matrix-84
Fractal Matrix Die Cuts-84
97Leaf International-84
Universal Ice-84
97Pacific-283
Copper-283
Emerald Green-283
Ice Blue-283
Red-283
Silver-283
97Pacific Dynagon-123
Copper-123
Dark Grey-123
Emerald Green-123
Ice Blue-123
Red-123
Silver-123
Tandems-52
97Pacific Invincible-138
Copper-138
Emerald Green-138
Ice Blue-138
Red-138
Silver-138
97Panini Stickers-175
97Pinnacle-134
Press Plates Back Black-134
Press Plates Back Cyan-134
Press Plates Back Magenta-134
Press Plates Back Yellow-134
Press Plates Front Black-134
Press Plates Front Cyan-134
Press Plates Front Magenta-134
Press Plates Front Yellow-134
97Pinnacle Certified-83
Red-83
Mirror Blue-83
Mirror Gold-83
Mirror Red-83
97Pinnacle Inside-102
97Pinnacle Tot Cert Platinum Blue-83
97Pinnacle Tot Certi Platinum Gold-83
97Pinnacle Totally Certified Platinum Red-83
97Pinnacle Tot Cert Mirror Platinum Gold-83
97Score-185
97Score Maple Leafs-7
Platinum-7
Premier-7
97SP Authentic-154
97Upper Deck-160
98Be A Player-286
Press Release-286
98BAP Gold-286
98BAP Autographs-286
98BAP Autographs Gold-286
98Pacific-422
Ice Blue-422
Red-422
99Blackhawks Lineup Cards-8
99Pacific-415
Copper-415
Emerald Green-415
Gold-415
Ice Blue-415
Premiere Date-415
Red-415
99Pacific Omega-55
Copper-55
Gold-55
Ice Blue-55
Premiere Date-55
99Paramount-229
Copper-229
Emerald-229
Gold-229
Holographic Emerald-229
Holographic Gold-229
Holographic Silver-229
Ice Blue-229
Premiere Date-229
Red-229
Silver-229
99Ultimate Victory-20
1/1-20
Parallel-20
Parallel 100-20
99Slovakian Challengers-4
00Aurora-33
Premiere Date-33
00BAP Memorabilia-57
Emerald-57
Ruby-57
Sapphire-57
Promos-57
00BAP Mem Chicago Sportsfest Copper-57
00BAP Memorabilia Chicago Sportsfest Blue-57
00BAP Memorabilia Chicago Sportsfest Gold-57
00BAP Memorabilia Chicago Sportsfest Ruby-57
00BAP Memorabilia Chicago Sun-Times Ruby-57
00BAP Memorabilia Chicago Sun-Times Gold-57
00BAP Mem Chicago Sun-Times Sapphire-57
00BAP Mem Toronto Fall Expo Copper-57
00BAP Memorabilia Toronto Fall Expo Gold-57
00BAP Memorabilia Toronto Fall Expo Ruby-57
00BAP Parkhurst 2000-P172
00BAP Signature Series-160
Emerald-160
Ruby-160
Sapphire-160
Autographs-98
Autographs Gold-98
00O-Pee-Chee-232
00O-Pee-Chee Parallel-232
00Pacific-102
Copper-102
Gold-102
Ice Blue-102
Premiere Date-102
00Panini Stickers-128
00Paramount-53
Copper-53
Gold-53
Holo-Gold-53
Holo-Silver-53
Ice Blue-53
Premiere Date-53
00Revolution-31
Blue-31
Premiere Date-31
Red-31
00SP Authentic-19
00SP Game Used-12
00Stadium Club-143
00Titanium-17
Blue-17
Gold-17
Premiere Date-17
Red-17
Retail-17
00Titanium Draft Day Edition-20
Patches-20
00Topps/OPC-232
Parallel-232
00Topps Heritage-192
00UD Heroes-27
00UD Pros and Prospects-19
00UD Reserve-18
00Upper Deck-38
Exclusives Tier 1-38
Exclusives Tier 2-38
00Upper Deck MVP-45
First Stars-45
Second Stars-45
Third Stars-45
00Upper Deck Victory-52
00Upper Deck Vintage-76
01Atomic-20
Blue-20
Gold-20
Premiere Date-20
Red-20
01BAP Memorabilia-277
Emerald-277
Ruby-277
Sapphire-277
01BAP Signature Series-83
Autographs-83
Autographs Gold-83
01Bowman YoungStars-85
Gold-85
Ice Cubed-85
01Crown Royale-33
Blue-33
Premiere Date-33
Red-33
Retail-33
01O-Pee-Chee-72
01O-Pee-Chee Heritage Parallel-72
01O-Pee-Chee Heritage Parallel Limited-72
01O-Pee-Chee Premier Parallel-72
01Pacific-92
01Pacific-407
Extreme LTD-92
Gold-407
Hobby LTD-92
Premiere Date-92
Retail LTD-92
01Pacific Adrenaline-41
Blue-41
Premiere Date-41
Red-41
Retail-41
01Pacific Arena Exclusives-92
01Pacific Arena Exclusives-407
01Pacific Heads-Up-19
Blue-19
Premiere Date-19
Red-19
Silver-19
Quad Jerseys-7
01Parkhurst-151
01Private Stock-18
Gold-18
Premiere Date-18
Retail-18
Silver-18
Game Gear-25
Game Gear Patches-25
01Private Stock Pacific Nights-18
01SP Authentic-15
Limited-15
Limited Gold-15
01SPx-12
Hidden Treasures-DTSG
Hidden Treasures-TTDSA
01Stadium Club-55
Award Winners-55
Master Photos-55
01Titanium Double-Sided Jerseys-10
01Titanium Double-Sided Jerseys-73
01Titanium Double-Sided Patches-73
01Titanium Draft Day Edition-24
01Topps-72
Heritage Parallel-72
Heritage Parallel Limited-72
OPC Parallel-72
01Topps Chrome-72
Refractors-72
Black Border Refractors-72
01Topps Heritage-53
Refractors-53
01Topps Reserve-97
01UD Challenge for the Cup-15
01UD Mask Collection-19
Gold-19
Double Patches-DPSS
Jerseys-J-SS
Jersey and Patch-JPSS
01UD Playmakers-20
01UD Top Shelf-84
01Upper Deck-37
Exclusives-37
01Upper Deck MVP-37
01Upper Deck Victory-72
01Upper Deck Victory-435
Gold-72
Gold-435
01Upper Deck Vintage-58
01Upper Deck Vintage-60
01Upper Deck Vintage-61
01Vanguard Memorabilia-8
02BAP First Edition-112
Jerseys-112
02BAP Memorabilia-138
Emerald-138
Ruby-138
Sapphire-138
NHL All-Star Game-138
NHL All-Star Game Blue-138
NHL All-Star Game Green-138
NHL All-Star Game Red-138
02BAP Memorabilia Toronto Fall Expo-138
02BAP Signature Series-100
Autographs-100
Autograph Buybacks 1998-286
Autograph Buybacks 2000-98
Autograph Buybacks 2001-83
Autographs Gold-100
02Bowman YoungStars-54
Gold-54
Silver-54
02Crown Royale Dual Patches-4
02O-Pee-Chee-179
02O-Pee-Chee Premier Blue Parallel-179
02O-Pee-Chee Premier Red Parallel-179
02O-Pee-Chee Factory Set-179
02Pacific-82
Blue-82
Red-82
Jerseys-8
Jerseys Holo-Silver-8
02Pacific Complete-211
Red-211
02Pacific Heads-Up Quad Jerseys-7
02Pacific Heads-Up Quad Jerseys Gold-7
02Parkhurst-83
Bronze-83
Gold-83
Silver-83
02Parkhurst Retro-59
Minis-59
02SP Game Used Authentic Fabrics-AFSU
02SP Game Used Authentic Fabrics Gold-AFSU
02SP Game Used Authentic Fabrics Rainbow-AFSU
02SPx Smooth Skaters-SU
02SPx Smooth Skaters Gold-SU
02SPx Smooth Skaters Silver-SU
02Stadium Club-48
Silver Decoy Cards-48
Proofs-48
02Titanium Jerseys-15
02Titanium Jerseys Retail-15
02Titanium Patches-15
02Topps-179
OPC Blue Parallel-179
OPC Red Parallel-179
Factory Set-179
02Topps Chrome-104
Black Border Refractors-104
Refractors-104
02Topps Total-17
02UD Piece of History-19
Patches-PHSS
02UD Top Shelf Clutch Performers-CPSSU
02UD Top Shelf Dual Player Jerseys-RSR
02UD Top Shelf Dual Player Jerseys-STSM
02UD Top Shelf Goal Oriented-GOSU
02UD Top Shelf Shooting Stars-SHSS
02UD Top Shelf Sweet Sweaters-SWSU
02UD Top Shelf Triple Jerseys-TSSAT
02Upper Deck-40
Exclusives-40
CHL Graduates-CGSS
CHL Graduates Gold-CGSS
Speed Demons-SDSS
02Upper Deck MVP-40
Gold-40
Classics-40
Golden Classics-40
02Upper Deck Victory-46
Bronze-46
Gold-46
Silver-46
02Upper Deck Vintage-53
Green Backs-53
03Blackhawks Postcards-25
03ITG Action-107
03ITG Action-645
03NHL Sticker Collection-174
03O-Pee-Chee-42
03OPC Blue-42
03OPC Gold-42
03OPC Red-42
03Pacific-76
Blue-76
Red-76
03Pacific Complete-180
Red-180
03Pacific Supreme-19
Blue-19
Red-19
Retail-19
03Parkhurst Original Six Chicago-27
Memorabilia-CM2
Memorabilia-CM11
Memorabilia-CM56
03Parkhurst Rookie-25
03Topps-42
Blue-42
Gold-42
Red-42
03Topps Traded-TT22
Blue-TT22
Gold-TT22
Red-TT22
03Upper Deck-285
Canadian Exclusives-285
HG-285
UD Exclusives-285
03Upper Deck MVP-90
Gold Script-90
Silver Script-90
Canadian Exclusives-90
03Upper Deck Rookie Update-49
03Upper Deck Victory-37
Bronze-37
Gold-37
Silver-37
04Pacific-149
Blue-149
Red-149
04SP Authentic-49
Limited-49
Buybacks-190
Buybacks-191
Buybacks-192
Buybacks-193
Sign of the Times-ST-SU
04Upper Deck-98
Canadian Exclusives-98
HG Glossy Gold-98
HG Glossy Silver-98
05Be A Player-50
First Period-50
Second Period-50
Third Period-50
Overtime-50
Outtakes-OT30
Signatures-SE
Signatures Gold-SE
05Black Diamond-47
Emerald-47
Gold-47
Onyx-47
Ruby-47
05Hot Prospects-57
En Fuego-57
Red Hot-57
White Hot-57
05Panini Stickers-308
05Parkhurst-270
Facsimile Auto Parallel-270
Signatures-SS
05SP Game Used-56
Autographs-56
Gold-56
Auto Draft-AD-SS
05UD Artifacts-55
Blue-55
Gold-55
Green-55
Pewter-55
Red-55
Auto Facts-AF-SS
Auto Facts Blue-AF-SS
Auto Facts Copper-AF-SS
Auto Facts Pewter-AF-SS
Auto Facts Silver-AF-SS
Gold Autographed-55
Remarkable Artifacts-RA-SS
Remarkable Artifacts Dual-RA-SS
05UD PowerPlay-49
Rainbow-49
05Ultra-112
Gold-112
Ice-112
05Upper Deck-107
05Upper Deck All-Time Greatest-33
05Upper Deck HG Glossy-107
05Upper Deck Jerseys Series II-J2SS
05Upper Deck Majestic Materials-MMSS
05Upper Deck Notable Numbers-N-TV
05Upper Deck Patches-P-SSU
05Upper Deck Ice-53
Rainbow-53
05Upper Deck MVP-217
Gold-217
Platinum-217
ProSign-P-SU
05Upper Deck Trilogy-50
05Upper Deck Toronto Fall Expo-107
05Upper Deck Victory-112
Black-112
Gold-112
Silver-112
Game Breakers-GB26
06Be A Player-27
Autographs-27
Signatures-SU
Signatures 25-30
Signatures Duals-DNA
Signatures Trios-TFLS
Portraits Signature Portraits-SPSS
06Black Diamond-47
Black-47
Gold-47
Ruby-47
06Fleer-110
Tiffany-110
06O-Pee-Chee-285
Rainbow-285
06Panini Stickers-306
06SP Game Used Authentic Fabrics-AFSU
06SP Game Used Authentic Fabrics Parallel-AFSU
06SP Game Used Authentic Fabrics Patches-AFSU
06SP Game Used Authentic Fabrics Dual-AF2AS
06SP Game Used Authentic Fabrics Dual Patches-AF2AS
06SP Game Used Inked Sweaters Dual-IS2AS
06SP Game Used Inked Sweaters Dual Patches-IS2AS
06The Cup Autographed NHL Shields Duals-DASVS
06The Cup NHL Shields Duals-DSHKS
06UD Artifacts Frozen Artifacts-FASU
06UD Artifacts Frozen Artifacts Black-FASU
06UD Artifacts Frozen Artifacts Blue-FASU
06UD Artifacts Frozen Artifacts Gold-FASU
06UD Artifacts Frozen Artifacts Platinum-FASU
06UD Artifacts Frozen Artifacts Red-FASU
06UD Artifacts Frozen Artifacts Patches Black-FASU
06UD Artifacts Frozen Artifacts Patches Blue-FASU
06UD Artifacts Frozen Artifacts Patches Gold-FASU
06UD Artifacts Frozen Artifacts Patches Platinum-FASU
06UD Artifacts Frozen Artifacts Patches Red-FASU
06UD Powerplay-56
Impact Rainbow-56
06Ultra-110
Gold Medallion-110
Ice Medallion-110
06Upper Deck Arena Giveaways-NSH6
06Upper Deck-107
Exclusives Parallel-107
High Gloss Parallel-107
Game Jerseys-JST
Game Patches-PSU
Masterpieces-107
Signature Sensations-SSSS
06Upper Deck MVP-166
Gold Script-166
Super Script-166
Jerseys-OJLS
Jerseys-OJSC
06Upper Deck Ovation-77
06Upper Deck Trilogy Combo Clearcut Autographs-C2VS
06Upper Deck Trilogy Honorary Scripted Patches-HSPSU
06Upper Deck Trilogy Honorary Scripted Swatches-HSSSU
06Upper Deck Victory-111
06Upper Deck Victory Black-111
06Upper Deck Victory Gold-111
07Upper Deck Victory-110
Black-110
Gold-110
Sullivan, Steve (Minors)
91ProCards-443
92Nashville Knights-11
96Collector's Edge Ice-10
Prism-10
Sullivan, Todd
95South Carolina Stingrays-21
Sullivan, Tom
907th Inn. Sketch OHL-120
917th Inn. Sketch OHL-186
Sulzer, Alexander
03German Deg Metro Stars-17
04German DEL-61
04German Dusseldorf Metro Stars Postcards-19
05German DEL-80
05German DEL-376
06German DEL-50
06German DEL-194
Summanen, Arto
72Finnish Jaakiekko-186
Summanen, Raimo
83Oilers McDonald's-4
83Swedish Semic VM Stickers-37
84Nova Scotia Oilers-16
85Oilers Red Rooster-25
86Oilers Red Rooster-25
86Oilers Team Issue-25
88Oilers Tenth Anniversary-3
89Swedish Semic World Champ Stickers-40
91Finnish Semic World Champ Stickers-20
91Finnish Jyvas-Hyva Stickers-16
91Swedish Semic World Champ Stickers-20
92Finnish Jyvas-Hyva Stickers-182
92Finnish Semic-16
93Finnish SISU-377
94Finnish SISU-252
94Finnish SISU Horoscopes-15
95Finnish SISU Gold Cards-22
95Finnish SISU Limited-7
95Finnish Karjala World Champ Labels-20
96Swedish Semic Wien-7
98Finnish Kerailysarja Leijonat-42
99Finnish Cardset Aces High-S-8
02Finnish Cardset-274
Summerfelt, Pete
03Trenton Titans-366
Summerfield, Garrett
05Fort Wayne Komets Choice-11
Summerhill, Bill
34Beehive Group I Photos-184
Summermatter, Paul
93Swiss HNL-347
Summers, Matt
03OCN Blizzard-20
Summers, Mike
93Quebec Pee-Wee Tournament-897
Summers, Rod
84Nanaimo Clippers-20
Sumner, Rob
89Victoria Cougars-19
96Seattle Thunderbirds-NNO
97Seattle Thunderbirds-26
Sumner, Steve
89ProCards AHL-310
99Houston Aeros-NNO
Sundberg, Alexander
98Danish Hockey League-80
99Danish Hockey League-218
Sundberg, Niklas
02ECHL Update-U-23
03UK Nottingham Panthers-1
Sundberg, Ola
86Swedish Panini Stickers-160
Sundberg, Reino
86Swedish Panini Stickers-247
87Swedish Panini Stickers-233
89Swedish Semic Elitserien Stickers-217
90Swedish Semic Elitserien Stickers-51
91Swedish Semic Elitserien Stickers-226
Sundblad, Erling
69Swedish Hockey-161
70Swedish Hockey-128
Sundblad, Niklas
90Swedish Semic Elitserien Stickers-96
91Swedish Semic Elitserien Stickers-23
91Arena Draft Picks-15

91Arena Draft Picks French-15
91Arena Draft Picks Autographs-15
91Arena Draft Picks Autographs French-15
91Classic-16
91Star Pics-8
91Ultimate Draft-16
91Ultimate Draft-72
91Ultimate Draft-85
91Ultimate Draft French-16
91Classic Four-Sport *-16
Autographs-16A
92Upper Deck-227
92Swedish Semic Elitserien Stickers-46
94Saint John Flames-24
94Classic Pro Prospects-143
95Saint John Flames-24
96Leaf-234
Press Proofs-234
96Pinnacle-230
Artist's Proofs-230
Foil-230
Premium Stock-230
Rink Collection-230
96Summit-176
Artist's Proofs-176
Ice-176
Premium Stock-176
98Swedish UD Choice-164
99Swedish Upper Deck-166
00German DEL-49
01German Upper Deck-149
02German DEL City Press-209
03Swedish Elite-244
Enforcers-EF11
Silver-244
05German DEL-52

Sundelin, Erkki

71Finnish Suomi Stickers-257
73Finnish Jaakiekko-321

Sunderland, Mathieu

93Drummondville Voltigeurs-23
95Classic-23
96Rimouski Oceanic-27

Sunderman, Stephen

01Kelowna Rockets-21
02Kelowna Rockets-7
03OCN Blizzard-21
03Saginaw Spirit-24

Sundh, Oscar

06Swedish SHL Elitset-282

Sundin, Andreas

03Swedish Elite-220
Silver-220

Sundin, Fredrik

03Swedish Elite-275
Silver-275
04Swedish Elitset-132
Gold-132

Sundin, Mats

89Swedish Semic Elitserien Stickers-72
90Kraft-42
90Nordiques Petro-Canada-23
90OPC Premier-114
90Pro Set-636
90Score-398
Canadian-398
90Score Rookie/Traded-100T
90Score Young Superstars-7
90Upper Deck-365
French-365
91Pro Set Platinum-99
91Bowman-137
91Kraft-4
91Nordiques Panini Team Stickers-20
91Nordiques Panini Team Stickers-H
91Nordiques Petro-Canada-28
91O-Pee-Chee-12
91O-Pee-Chee-219
91Panini Stickers-255
91Parkhurst-144
French-144
91Pinnacle-10
91Pinnacle-389
French-10
French-389
91Pro Set-197
French-197
91Score American-130
91Score Canadian Bilingual-130
91Score Canadian English-130
91Score Young Superstars-3
91Stadium Club-300
91Topps-12
91Topps-219
91Upper Deck-31
91Upper Deck-93
91Upper Deck-134
French-31
French-93
French-134
Euro-Stars-13
Euro-Stars French-13
91Finnish Semic World Champ Stickers-211
91Swedish Semic Elitserien Stickers-323
91Swedish Semic Elitserien Stickers-357
91Swedish Semic World Champ Stickers-211
91Star Pics-50
92Bowman-344
92Humpty Dumpty II-21
92Jofa/Koho-6
92Nordiques Petro-Canada-31
92O-Pee-Chee-110
92Panini Stickers-212
92Panini Stickers-302
92Panini Stickers French-212
92Panini Stickers French-302
92Parkhurst-148
92Parkhurst-221
Emerald Ice-148
Emerald Ice-221
92Pinnacle-90
French-90
Team 2000-7
Team 2000 French-7
92Pro Set-149
92Score-153
Canadian-153
Young Superstars-3
92Sports Illustrated for Kids II-601
92Stadium Club-478
92Topps-415
Gold-415G
92Ultra-180
Imports-25
92Upper Deck-121
92Upper Deck-374
Euro-Stars-E18
World Junior Grads-WG17
92Finnish Semic-72
92Swedish Semic Elitserien Stickers-348
93Donruss-283
Special Print-S
93Leaf-136
93OPC Premier-460
Gold-460
Black Gold-6
93Panini Stickers-68
93Parkhurst-435
Emerald Ice-435
First Overall-F5
93Pinnacle I Samples-6
93Pinnacle-2
Canadian-2
Team 2001-15
Team 2001 Canadian-15
93PowerPlay-205
Global Greats-8
Point Leaders-18
93Score-9
Canadian-9
Dynamic Duos Canadian-5
International Stars-10
International Stars Canadian-10
93Stadium Club-370
93Stadium Club-425
Members Only Master Set-370
Members Only Master Set-425
First Day Issue-370
First Day Issue-425
93Topps/OPC Premier-460
Gold-460
93Topps Premier Finest-5
93Ultra-137
93Upper Deck-220
93Upper Deck-228
93Upper Deck-302
93Upper Deck-419
Hat Tricks-HT20
SP-132
93Upper Deck Locker All-Stars-59
93Swedish Semic Elitserien-306
93Swedish Semic World Champ Stickers-33
94Be A Player-R76
94Canada Games NHL POGS-237
94EA Sports-111
94Finest-110
Super Team Winners-110
Refractors-110
94Flair-186
94Fleer-220
94Hockey Wit-51
94Kraft-13
94Leaf-530
94Leaf Limited-42
94Maple Leafs Kodak-25
94Maple Leafs Pin-up Posters-1
94Maple Leafs Postcards-1
94Maple Leafs Postcards-2
94Maple Leafs Postcards-3
94OPC Premier-160
94OPC Premier-345
94OPC Premier-412
Special Effects-160
Special Effects-345
Special Effects-412
94Parkhurst-185
Gold-185
94Parkhurst SE-SE175
Gold-SE175
Euro-Stars-ES2
Vintage-37
94Pinnacle-386
Artist's Proofs-386
Rink Collection-386
Northern Lights-NL10
94Score-89
Gold-89
Platinum-89
94Select-21
Gold-21
94SP-116
Die Cuts-116
94Stadium Club-90
Members Only Master Set-90
First Day Issue-90
Super Team Winner Cards-90
94Topps/OPC Premier-160
94Topps/OPC Premier-345
94Topps/OPC Premier-412
Special Effects-160
Special Effects-345
Special Effects-412
94Topps Finest Bronze-11
94Ultra-220
94Ultra-379
94Upper Deck-51
94Upper Deck-548
Electric Ice-51
Electric Ice-548
SP Inserts-SP170
SP Inserts Die Cuts-SP170
94Finnish Jaa Kiekko-74
94Swedish Leaf-232
Guest Special-1
94Swedish Olympics Lillehammer*-292
95Bashan Super Stickers-118
95Be A Player-203
Signatures-S203
Signatures Die Cuts-S203
95Bowman-49
All-Foil-49
95Canada Games NHL POGS-259
95Collector's Choice-90
Player's Club-90
Player's Club Platinum-90
Crash The Game-C30A
Crash The Game-C30B
Crash The Game-C30C
Crash The Game Gold-C30A
Crash The Game Gold-C30B
Crash The Game Gold-C30C
Crash the Game Silver Redeemed-C30
Crash the Game Silver Bonus-C30
Crash the Game Gold Redeemed-C30
Crash the Game Gold Bonus-C30
95Donruss-176
95Donruss Elite-72
Die Cut Stars-72
Die Cut Uncut-72
Cutting Edge-11
95Emotion-175
95Finest-177
Refractors-177
95Hoyle Western Playing Cards-20
95Imperial Stickers-118
95Kraft-75
95Leaf-244
Fire On Ice-8
95Leaf Limited-120
Stars of the Game-9
95McDonald's Pinnacle-MCD-18
95Metal-147
International Steel-20
95NHL Aces Playing Cards-10D
95Panini Stickers-201
95Parkhurst International-201
95Parkhurst International-247
Emerald Ice-201
Emerald Ice-247
All-Stars-6
Crown Collection Silver Series 2-8
Crown Collection Gold Series 2-8
95Pinnacle-19
Artist's Proofs-19
Rink Collection-19
Global Gold-3
Roaring 20s-7
95Playoff One on One-99
95Pro Magnets-80
95Score-56
Black Ice Artist's Proofs-56
Black Ice-56
Border Battle-15
Golden Blades-16
95Select Certified-7
Mirror Gold-7
95SkyBox Impact-165
95SP-141
Stars/Etoiles-E26
Stars/Etoiles Gold-E26
95Stadium Club Members Only-26
95Stadium Club-75
Members Only Master Set-75
95Stadium Club Master Photo Test-8
95Summit-9
Artist's Proofs-9
Ice-9
95Topps-19
95Topps-150
OPC Inserts-19
OPC Inserts-150
Canadian Gold-10CG
Marquee Men Power Boosters-19
95Topps SuperSkills-32
Platinum-32
95Ultra-164
Gold Medallion-164
Extra Attackers-19
Premier Pivots-9
Premier Pivots Gold Medallion-9
95Upper Deck-147
95Upper Deck-219
Electric Ice-147
Electric Ice-219
Electric Ice Gold-147
Electric Ice Gold-219
NHL All-Stars-AS18
NHL All-Stars Jumbo-AS18
Special Edition-SE169
Special Edition Gold-SE169
95Zenith-19
95Finnish Semic World Championships-62
95Swedish Upper Deck-236
95Swedish Globe World Championships-13
95Swedish Globe World Championships-251
95Swedish Globe World Championships-256
95Swedish Globe World Championships-257
95Swedish Globe World Championships-258
95Swedish Globe World Championships-269
95Swedish World Championships Stickers-292
96SLU Hockey Canadian-15
96Headliners Hockey-19
96SLU Hockey American-24
96Be A Player Biscuit In The Basket-12
96Black Diamond-163
Gold-163
Run for the Cup-RC13
96Collector's Choice-255
96Collector's Choice-332
Jumbos-5
MVP-UD44
MVP Gold-UD44
Crash the Game-C29A
Crash the Game-C29B
Crash the Game-C29C
Crash the Game Gold-C29A
Crash the Game Gold-C29B
Crash the Game Gold-C29C
Crash the Game Exchange-CR29
Crash the Game Exchange Gold-CR29
96Donruss-30
Press Proofs-30
96Donruss Canadian Ice-12
Gold Press Proofs-12
Red Press Proofs-12
96Donruss Elite-55
Die Cut Stars-55
96Duracell L'Equipe Beliveau-JB13
96Flair-92
Blue Ice-92
Center Ice Spotlight-9
96Fleer-110
96Kenner Starting Lineup Cards-24
96Kraft Upper Deck-7
96Kraft Upper Deck-70
96Leaf-53
Press Proofs-53
96Leaf Limited-28
Gold-28
96Leaf Preferred-14
Press Proofs-14
Steel-33
Steel Gold-33
96Maggers-96
96Maple Leafs Postcards-1
96Metal Universe-154
96NHL Aces Playing Cards-45
96NHL Pro Stamps-80
96Pinnacle-144
Artist's Proofs-144
Foil-144
Premium Stock-144
Rink Collection-144
96Pinnacle Mint-17
Bronze-17
Gold-17
Silver-17
Coins Brass-17
Coins Solid Gold-17
Coins Gold Plated-17
Coins Nickel-17
Coins Silver-17
96Score-160
Artist's Proofs-160
Dealer's Choice Artist's Proofs-160
Special Artist's Proofs-160
Golden Blades-160
Superstitions-3
96Select Certified-85
Artist's Proofs-85
Blue-85
Mirror Blue-85
Mirror Gold-85
Mirror Red-85
Red-85
96SkyBox Impact-130
96SP-151
Clearcut Winner-CW12
Holoview Collection-HC20
96SPx-43
Gold-43
96Stadium Club Members Only-18
96Summit-51
Artist's Proofs-51
Ice-51
Metal-51
Premium Stock-51
96Team Out-41
96Topps Picks-43
OPC Inserts-43
Top Shelf-TS13
96Ultra-166
Gold Medallion-166
Mr. Momentum-9
96Upper Deck-160
Game Jerseys-GJ13
Generation Next-X38
Lord Stanley's Heroes Finals-LS19
Lord Stanley's Heroes Quarterfinals-LS19
Lord Stanley's Heroes Semifinals-LS19
Power Performers-P28
Superstar Showdown-SS23A
96Zenith-64
Artist's Proofs-64
96Swedish Semic Wien-56
96Swedish Semic Wien Coca-Cola Dream Team-7
96Swedish Semic Wien Nordic Stars-NS3
97SLU Hockey One on One-7
97Headliners Hockey-26
97Beehive-39
Golden Portraits-39
97Black Diamond-77
Double Diamond-77
Triple Diamond-77
Quadruple Diamond-77
Premium Cut-PC30
Premium Cut Double Diamond-PC30
Premium Cut Quadruple Diamond Horiz-PC30
Premium Cut Triple Diamond-PC30
Premium Cut Quadruple Diamond Verticals-PC30
97Collector's Choice-245
97Collector's Choice-320
Crash the Game-C23A
Crash the Game-C23B
Crash the Game-C23C
Crash the Game Exchange-CR23
Star Quest-SQ83
Stick'Ums-S17
97Crown Royale-132
Emerald Green-132
Ice Blue-132
Silver-132
Hat Tricks Die-Cuts-17
97Donruss-139
Press Proofs Silver-139
Press Proofs Gold-139
Red Alert-9
97Donruss Canadian Ice-40
Dominion Series-40
Provincial Series-40
97Donruss Elite-58
Aspirations-58
Status-58
97Donruss Limited-9
97Donruss Limited-13
97Donruss Limited-128
Exposure-9
Exposure-13
Exposure-128
Fabric of the Game-16
Fabric of the Game-26
97Donruss Preferred-38
Cut to the Chase-38
97Donruss Priority-56
Stamp of Approval-56
97Esso Olympic Hockey Heroes-42
97Esso Olympic Hockey Heroes French-42
97Jell-O Juniors To Pros-12
97Katch-144
Gold-144
Silver-144
97Kraft-21
97Kraft 3-D World's Best-2
97Leaf-142
Fractal Matrix-142
Fractal Matrix Die Cuts-142
Banner Season-19
97Leaf International-142
Universal Ice-142
97McDonald's Upper Deck-13
Game Film-10
97NHL Aces Playing Cards-35
97Pacific-205
Copper-205
Emerald Green-205
Ice Blue-205
Red-205
Silver-205
Slap Shots Die-Cuts-10B
97Pacific Dynagon-124
97Pacific Dynagon-144
Copper-124
Copper-144
Dark Grey-124
Dark Grey-144
Emerald Green-124
Emerald Green-144
Ice Blue-124
Ice Blue-144
Red-124
Red-144
Silver-124
Silver-144
Best Kept Secrets-93
Tandems-16
Tandems-27
97Pacific Invincible-139
Copper-139
Emerald Green-139
Ice Blue-139
Red-139
Silver-139
Feature Performers-34
97Pacific Omega-225
Copper-225
Dark Gray-225
Emerald Green-225
Gold-225
Ice Blue-225
Stick Handle Laser Cuts-18
97Panini Stickers-179
97Paramount-185
Copper-185
Dark Grey-185
Emerald Green-185
Ice Blue-185
Red-185
Silver-185
97Pinnacle-50
Artist's Proofs-50
Rink Collection-50
Press Plates Back Black-50
Press Plates Back Cyan-50
Press Plates Back Magenta-50
Press Plates Back Yellow-50
Press Plates Front Black-50
Press Plates Front Cyan-50
Press Plates Front Magenta-50
Press Plates Front Yellow-50
97Pinnacle Certified-53
Red-53
Mirror Blue-53
Mirror Gold-53
Mirror Red-53
Team-15
Gold Team Promo-15
Gold Team-15
97Pinnacle Inside-21
Coach's Collection-21
Executive Collection-21
Track-23
Cans-4
Cans Gold-4
97Pinnacle Mint-10
Bronze-10
Gold Team-10
Silver Team-10
Coins Brass-10
Coins Brass Proofs-10
Coins Gold Plated-10
Coins Gold Plated Proofs-10
Coins Nickel Silver-10
Coins Nickel Silver Proofs-10
Coins Solid Gold-10
Coins Solid Silver-10
97Pinnacle Power Pack Blow-Ups-16
97Pinnacle Tot Cert Platinum Blue-53
97Pinnacle Tot Cert Platinum Gold-53
97Pinnacle Totally Certified Platinum Red-53
97Pinnacle Tot Cert Mirror Platinum Gold-53
97Revolution-137
Copper-137
Emerald-137
Ice Blue-137
Silver-137
Team Checklist Laser Cuts-24
97Score-95
Artist's Proofs-95
Golden Blades-95
97Score Maple Leafs-4
Platinum-4
Premier-4
97SP Authentic-150
Icons-I33
Icons Die-Cuts-I33
Icons Embossed-I33
Sign of the Times-MS
97SPx-46
Bronze-46
Gold-46
Silver-46
Steel-46
Dimension-SPX17
Grand Finale-46
97Studio-67
Press Proofs Silver-67
Press Proofs Gold-67
Hard Hats-24
97Upper Deck-369
Game Dated Moments-369
Sixth Sense Masters-SS13
Sixth Sense Wizards-SS13
Smooth Grooves-SG13
The Specialists-13
The Specialists Level 2 Die Cuts-13
Three Star Selects-14B
97Upper Deck Crash the All-Star Game-7
97Upper Deck Crash the All-Star Game-AR7
97Upper Deck Diamond Vision-17
Signature Moves-17
97Upper Deck Ice-73
Parallel-73
Champions-IC13
Champions 2 Die Cuts-IC13
Lethal Lines-L4C
Lethal Lines 2-L4C
Power Shift-73
97Zenith-48
Z-Gold-48
Z-Silver-48
97Zenith 5 x 7-52
Gold Impulse-52
Silver Impulse-52
98Aurora-185
Atomic Laser Cuts-17
Championship Fever-46
Championship Fever Copper-46
Championship Fever Ice Blue-46
Championship Fever Red-46
Championship Fever Silver-46
Cubes-16
Man Advantage-17
98Be A Player-136
Press Release-136
98BAP Gold-136
98BAP Autographs-136
98BAP Autographs Gold-136
98BAP AS Game Used Stick Cards-S5
98BAP AS Game Used Jersey Cards-AS5
98BAP Playoff Game Used Jerseys-G2
98BAP Playoff Game Used Jersey Autographs-G2
98BAP Playoff Practice Used Jerseys-P20
98BAP Tampa Bay All Star Game-136
98Black Diamond-84
Double Diamond-84
Triple Diamond-84
Quadruple Diamond-84
Winning Formula Gold-WF27
Winning Formula Platinum-WF27
98Bowman's Best-39
Refractors-39
Atomic Refractors-39
98Crown Royale-132
Limited Series-132
Master Performers-18
Pillars of the Game-23
Pivotal Players-22
98Finest-106
No Protectors-106
No Protectors Refractors-106
Refractors-106
Red Lighters-R19
Red Lighters Refractors-R19
98Katch-141
98Kraft Fearless Forwards-11
98McDonald's Upper Deck-12
98OPC Chrome-71
Refractors-71
98Pacific-13
Ice Blue-13
Red-13
Gold Crown Die-Cuts-32
Team Checklists-25
Timelines-18
98Pacific Dynagon Ice-184
Blue-184
Red-184
Forward Thinking-18
Team Checklists-25
98Pacific Omega-231
Red-231
Opening Day Issue-231
EO Portraits-19
EO Portraits 1 of 1-19
Face to Face-8
Online-33
Planet Ice-11
Planet Ice Parallel-11
Prism-19
98Panini Photocards-81
98Panini Photocards-108
98Panini Stickers-164
98Paramount-231
Copper-231
Emerald Green-231
Holo-Electric-231
Ice Blue-231
Silver-231
Special Delivery Die-Cuts-17
Team Checklists Die-Cuts-25
98Revolution-140
Ice Shadow-140
Red-140
All-Star Die Cuts-28
Chalk Talk Laser-Cuts-18
Showstoppers-34
98SP Authentic-83
Power Shift-83
Sign of the Times-MS
Sign of the Times Gold-MS
Snapshots-SS23
98SPx Finite-82
98SPx Finite-118
98SPx Finite-162
Radiance-82
Radiance-118
Radiance-162
Spectrum-82
Spectrum-118
Spectrum-162
98SPx Top Prospects-55
Radiance-55
Spectrum-55
Highlight Heroes-H27
Lasting Impressions-L8
Premier Stars-PS13
Winning Materials-MS
98Topps-71
O-Pee-Chee-71
Local Legends-L2
98Topps Gold Label Class 1-53
Black-53
Black One of One-53
One of One-53
Red-53
Red One of One-53
98Topps Gold Label Class 2-53
98Topps Gold Label Class 2 Black-53
98Topps Gold Label Class 2 Black 1 of 1-53
98Topps Gold Label Class 2 One of One-53
98Topps Gold Label Class 2 Red-53
98Topps Gold Label Class 2 Red One of One-53
98Topps Gold Label Class 3-53
98Topps Gold Label Class 3 Black-53
98Topps Gold Label Class 3 Black 1 of 1-53
98Topps Gold Label Class 3 One of One-53
98Topps Gold Label Class 3 Red-53
98Topps Gold Label Class 3 Red One of One-53
98UD Choice-203
Mini Bobbing Head-BH17
98UD Choice Preview-203
98UD Choice Prime Choice Reserve-203
98UD Choice Reserve-203
98UD Choice StarQuest Blue-SQ19
98UD Choice StarQuest Gold-SQ19
98UD Choice StarQuest Green-SQ19
98UD Choice StarQuest Red-SQ19
98UD3-48
98UD3-108
98UD3-168
Die-Cuts-48
Die-Cuts-108
Die-Cuts-168
98Upper Deck-370
Exclusives-370
Exclusives 1 of 1-370
Fantastic Finishers-FF14
Fantastic Finishers Quantum 1-FF14
Fantastic Finishers Quantum 2-FF14
Fantastic Finishers Quantum 3-FF14
Game Jerseys-GJ19
Lord Stanley's Heroes-LS24
Lord Stanley's Heroes Quantum 1-LS24
Lord Stanley's Heroes Quantum 2-LS24
Lord Stanley's Heroes Quantum 3-LS24
Profiles-P28
Profiles Quantum 1-P28
Profiles Quantum 2-P28
Profiles Quantum 3-P28
Gold Reserve-370
98Upper Deck MVP-195
Gold Script-195
Silver Script-195
Super Script-195
Power Game-PG8
98Slovakian Eurotel-26
99Aurora-138
Striped-138
Premiere Date-138
Premiere Date Striped-138
Championship Fever-20
Championship Fever Copper-20
Championship Fever Ice Blue-20
Championship Fever Silver-20
Styrotechs-19
99BAP Memorabilia-233
Gold-233
Silver-233
Jersey Cards-J5
Jersey Emblems-E5
Jersey Numbers-I5
Jersey and Stick Cards-S5
AS Heritage Ruby-H21
AS Heritage Sapphire-H21
AS Heritage Emerald-H21
99BAP Update Double AS Jersey Cards-D6
99BAP Update Teammates Jersey Cards-TM25
99BAP Update Teammates Jersey Cards-TM30
99BAP Update Teammates Jersey Cards-TM41
99BAP Millennium-226
Emerald-226
Ruby-226
Sapphire-226
Signatures-226
Signatures Gold-226
Jerseys-J15
Jersey Autographs-J15
Jersey and Stick Cards-JS15
Jersey Emblems-E15
Jersey Numbers-N15
99Black Diamond-82
Diamond Cut-82
Final Cut-82
Diamonation-D15
Diamond Might-DM8
99Crown Royale-135
Limited Series-135
Premiere Date-135
Card-Supials-19
Card-Supials Minis-19
International Glory-25
International Glory Parallel-25
Team Captain Die-Cuts-9
99Jell-O Partners of Power-6
99Kraft Dinner-13
99Kraft Face Off Rivals-1
99Maple Leafs Pizza Pizza-20
99McDonald's Upper Deck-MCD9
99McDonald's Upper Deck-MCD9R
99O-Pee-Chee-15
99O-Pee-Chee Autographs-TA5
99O-Pee-Chee Chrome-15
99O-Pee-Chee Chrome Ice Masters-IM6
99O-Pee-Chee Chrome Ice Masters Refractor-IM6
99O-Pee-Chee Chrome Refractors-15
99O-Pee-Chee Ice Masters-IM6
99O-Pee-Chee Top of the World-TW5
99Oscar Mayer Lunchables-11
99Pacific-416
Copper-416
Emerald Green-416
Gold-416
Ice Blue-416
Premiere Date-416
Red-416
Center Ice-19
Center Ice Proofs-19
Gold Crown Die-Cuts-25
99Pacific Dynagon Ice-190
Blue-190
Copper-190
Gold-190
Premiere Date-190
2000 All-Star Preview-19
Checkmates American-15
Checkmates American-30
Checkmates Canadian-30
99Pacific Omega-228
Copper-228
Gold-228
Ice Blue-228
Premiere Date-228
EO Portraits-19
EO Portraits 1/1-19
Game-Used Jerseys-10
5 Star Talents-24
5 Star Talents Parallel-24
World All-Stars-9
99Pacific Prism-139
Holographic Blue-139
Holographic Gold-139
Holographic Mirror-139
Holographic Purple-139
Premiere Date-139
Clear Advantage-20
99Panini Stickers-153
99Paramount-230
Copper-230
Emerald-230
Gold-230
Holographic Emerald-230
Holographic Gold-230
Holographic Silver-230
Ice Blue-230
Premiere Date-230
Red-230
Silver-230
Ice Advantage-19
Ice Advantage Proofs-19
Personal Best-35
Toronto Fall Expo '99-230
99Revolution-140
Premiere Date-140
Red-140
Shadow Series-140
NHL Icons-19
Ornaments-19
Showstoppers-34
Top of the Line-19
Copper-140
Gold-140
CSC Silver-140
99SP Authentic-81
99SPx-143
Radiance-143
Spectrum-143
SPXtreme-XT13
99Stadium Club-2
First Day Issue-2
One of a Kind-2
Printing Plates Black-2
Printing Plates Cyan-2
Printing Plates Magenta-2
Printing Plates Yellow-2
Capture the Action-CA17
Capture the Action Game View-CAG17
Chrome-2
Chrome Refractors-2
Chrome Oversized-2
Chrome Oversized Refractors-2
Co-Signers-CS4
Co-Signers-CS7
Co-Signers-CS8
Eyes of the Game-EG8
Eyes of the Game Refractors-EG8
Lone Star Signatures-LS3
Souvenirs-SMS
99Topps/OPC-15
Autographs-TA5
Ice Masters-IM6
Top of the World-TW5
99Topps/OPC Chrome-15
Refractors-15
Ice Masters-IM6
Ice Masters Refractors-IM6
99Topps Gold Label Class 1-56
Black-56
Black One of One-56
One of One-56
Red-56
Red One of One-56
99Topps Gold Label Class 2-56
99Topps Gold Label Class 2 Black-56
99Topps Gold Label Class 2 Black 1 of 1-56
99Topps Gold Label Class 2 One of One-56
99Topps Gold Label Class 2 Red-56
99Topps Gold Label Class 2 Red One of One-56
99Topps Gold Label Class 3-56
99Topps Gold Label Class 3 Black-56
99Topps Gold Label Class 3 Black 1 of 1-56
99Topps Gold Label Class 3 One of One-56
99Topps Gold Label Class 3 Red-56
99Topps Gold Label Class 3 Red One of One-56
99Topps Gold Label Quest for the Cup-QC10
99Topps Gold Label Quest for the Cup One of One - QC10
99Topps Gold Label Quest 4 the Cup Black-QC10
99Topps Gold Label Quest for the Cup Black One of One -QC10
99Topps Gold Label Quest for the Cup Red-QC10
99Topps Gold Label Quest for the Cup Red One of One -QC10
99Topps Premier Plus-54
Parallel-54
Premier Team-PT5
Premier Team Parallel-PT5
99Ultimate Victory-82
1/1-82
Parallel-82
Parallel 100-82
99Upper Deck-121
Exclusives-121
Exclusives 1 of 1-121
All-Star Class-AS9
All-Star Class Quantum Gold-AS9
All-Star Class Quantum Silver-AS9
Crunch Time-CT13
Crunch Time Quantum Gold-CT13
Crunch Time Quantum Silver-CT13
Marquee Attractions-MA8
Marquee Attractions Quantum Gold-MA8
Marquee Attractions Quantum Silver-MA8
Sixth Sense-SS17
Sixth Sense Quantum Gold-SS17
Sixth Sense Quantum Silver-SS17
99Upper Deck Century Legends-66
Century Collection-66
99Upper Deck Gold Reserve-121
99Upper Deck HoloGrFx-55
Ausome-55
99Upper Deck MVP-196
Gold Script-196
Silver Script-196
Super Script-196
99Upper Deck MVP SC Edition-173
Gold Script-173
Silver Script-173
Super Script-173
Great Combinations-GCSJ
Great Combinations Parallel-GCSJ
Second Season Snipers-SS11
Stanley Cup Talent-SC18
99Upper Deck Ovation-56
Standing Ovation-56
99Upper Deck Retro-74
Gold-74
Platinum-74
99Upper Deck Victory-280
99Upper Deck Victory-281
99Wayne Gretzky Hockey-160
Tools of Greatness-TGMS
Will to Win-W9
00Aurora-140
Pinstripes-140
Pinstripes Premiere Date-140
Premiere Date-140
Scouting Reports-20
Styrotechs-10B
00BAP Memorabilia-296
Emerald-296
Ruby-296
Sapphire-296
Promos-296
Jersey Cards-J2
Jersey Emblems-E2
Jersey Numbers-N2
Jersey and Stick Cards-JS2
Patent Power Jerseys-PP4
00BAP Mem Chicago Sportsfest Copper-296
00BAP Memorabilia Chicago Sportsfest Blue-296
00BAP Memorabilia Chicago Sportsfest Gold-296
00BAP Memorabilia Chicago Sportsfest Ruby-296
00BAP Memorabilia Chicago Sun-Times Ruby-296
00BAP Memorabilia Chicago Sun-Times Gold-296
00BAP Mem Chicago Sun-Times Sapphire-296
00BAP Mem Toronto Fall Expo Copper-296
00BAP Memorabilia Toronto Fall Expo Gold-296
00BAP Memorabilia Toronto Fall Expo Ruby-296
00BAP Mem Update Heritage Jersey Cards-H4
00BAP Mem Update Heritage Jersey Gold-H4
00BAP Memorabilia Update Teammates-TM9
00BAP Memorabilia Update Teammates-TM24
00BAP Memorabilia Update Teammates Gold-TM9
00BAP Memorabilia Update Teammates Gold-TM24
00BAP Parkhurst 2000-P126
00BAP Signature Series-34
Emerald-34
Ruby-34
Sapphire-34
Autographs-93
Autographs Gold-93
He Shoots-He Scores Points-19
He Shoots-He Scores Prizes-37
Jersey Cards-J15
Jersey and Stick Cards-GSJ15
Jersey Cards Autographs-J15
Jersey Emblems-E15
Jersey Numbers-IN15
00BAP Ultimate Memorabilia Autographs-15
Gold-15
00BAP Ultimate Memorabilia Captain's C-C3
00BAP Ultimate Mem Game-Used Jerseys-GJ15
00BAP Ultimate Mem Game-Used Emblems-E13
00BAP Ultimate Mem Game-Used Numbers-N13
00BAP Ultimate Mem Game-Used Sticks-GS15
00BAP Ultimate Mem Journey Jerseys-JJ5
00BAP Ultimate Mem Journey Emblems-JE5
00BAP Ultimate Mem Journey Numbers-JI5
00BAP Ultimate Memorabilia Teammates-TM12
00BAP Ultimate Memorabilia Teammates-TM14
00BAP Ultimate Memorabilia Teammates-TM34
00BAP Ultimate Memorabilia Teammates-TM38
00Black Diamond-56
Gold-56
00Crown Royale-102
Ice Blue-102
Limited Series-102
Premiere Date-102
Red-102
Game-Worn Jersey-24
Game-Worn Jersey Patches-24
Jewels of the Crown-25
Now Playing-18
00Kraft-27
00McDonald's Pacific-33
Blue-33
Checklists-7
Dial-A-Stats-6
Game Jerseys-10
00O-Pee-Chee-4
00O-Pee-Chee Parallel-4
00Pacific-399
00Pacific-448
Copper-399
Copper-448
Gold-399
Gold-448
Ice Blue-399
Ice Blue-448
Premiere Date-399
Premiere Date-448

2001: Ice Odyssey-20
Cramer's Choice-10
Euro-Stars-9
Gold Crown Die Cuts-33
Reflections-19
00Pacific 2001: Ice Odyssey Anaheim Ntnl-20
00Panini Stickers-95
00Paramount-233
Copper-233
Gold-233
Holo-Gold-233
Holo-Silver-233
Ice Blue-233
Premiere Date-233
Epic Scope-20
Freeze Frame-34
Sub Zero-10
Sub Zero Gold-10
Sub Zero Red-10
00Private Stock-94
Gold-94
Premiere Date-94
Retail-94
Silver-94
Game Gear-99
Game Gear Patches-99
PS-2001 Action-56
PS-2001 Stars-25
00Revolution-140
Blue-140
Premiere Date-140
Red-140
HD NHL-34
NHL Icons-19
Stat Masters-29
00SP Authentic-82
00SP Game Used-56
Patch Cards-P-MS
Tools of the Game-MS
Tools of the Game Exclusives-MS
Tools of the Game Combos-C-GS
00SPx-66
Spectrum-66
SPXcitement-X14
Winning Materials-WSU
00Stadium Club-150
Special Forces-SF10
00Titanium-93
Blue-93
Gold-93
Premiere Date-93
Red-93
Retail-93
All-Stars-9W
Three-Star Selections-20
00Titanium Draft Day Edition-97
00Topps/OPC-4
Parallel-4
NHL Draft-D6
00Topps Chrome-4
OPC Refractors-4
Refractors-4
00Topps Gold Label Class 1-24
Gold-24
00Topps Gold Label Class 2-24
00Topps Gold Label Class 2 Gold-24
00Topps Gold Label Class 3-24
00Topps Gold Label Class 3 Gold-24
00Topps Gold Label Bullion-B6
00Topps Gold Label Bullion One to One-B6
00Topps Heritage-13
Chrome Parallel-13
Arena Relics-OSA-MS
Original Six Relics-OSS-MS
00Topps Premier Plus-74
Blue Ice-74
00Topps Stars-10
Blue-10
00UD Heroes-111
Game-Used Twigs-T-MS
Game-Used Twigs Gold-C-JS
Today's Snipers-TS6
00UD Pros and Prospects-81
00UD Reserve-81
Gold Strike-GS9
00Upper Deck-391
Exclusives Tier 1-391
Exclusives Tier 2-391
Fantastic Finishers-FF11
Game Jerseys-MS
Game Jerseys-MS
Game Jersey Autographs Exclusives-EMS
Game Jersey Combos-DSJ
Profiles-P9
Skilled Stars-SS19
Triple Threat-TT3
00Upper Deck Ice-38
Immortals-38
Legends-38
Stars-38
00Upper Deck Legends-125
Legendary Collection Bronze-125
Legendary Collection Gold-125
Legendary Collection Silver-125
Legendary Game Jerseys-JMS
00Upper Deck MVP-167
First Stars-167
Second Stars-167
Third Stars-167
00Upper Deck Victory-216
00Upper Deck Victory-217
00Upper Deck Vintage-334
00Upper Deck Vintage-345
00Upper Deck Vintage-346
National Heroes-NH20
00Vanguard-94
Dual Game-Worn Jerseys-2
Dual Game-Worn Patches-2
High Voltage-33
High Voltage Gold-33
High Voltage Green-33
High Voltage Red-33
High Voltage Silver-33
Holographic Gold-94
Holographic Purple-94
In Focus-18
Pacific Proofs-94
00Czech Stadion-81
01McFarlane Hockey-50
01Atomic-93
Blue-93
Gold-93
Premiere Date-93
Red-93
Jerseys-48
Patches-48
Power Play-32
Team Nucleus-13
01BAP Memorabilia-298
Emerald-298
Ruby-298
Sapphire-298
All-Star Jerseys-ASJ38
All-Star Emblems-ASE38
All-Star Numbers-ASN38
All-Star Jersey Doubles-DASJ13
All-Star Teammates-AST20
All-Star Teammates-AST29
All-Star Teammates-AST43
All-Star Teammates-AST45
Country of Origin-CO54
He Shoots-He Scores Points-10
He Shoots-He Scores Prizes-39
Patented Power-PP1
Stanley Cup Playoffs-SC1
01BAP Signature Series Certified 100-C29
01BAP Signature Series Certified 50-C29
01BAP Signature Series Certified 1 of 1's-C29
01BAP Signature Series Franchise Jerseys-FP-28
01BAP Sig Series He Shoots/Scores Points-11
01BAP Sig Series He Shoots/Scores Prizes-11
01BAP Signature Series Jerseys-GJ-62
01BAP Sig Series Jersey and Stick Cards-GSJ-62
01BAP Signature Series Emblems-GUE-40
01BAP Signature Series Numbers-ITN-40
01BAP Signature Series Teammates-TM-28
01BAP Ultimate Memorabilia Active Eight-8
01BAP Ultimate Mem All-Star History-52
01BAP Ultimate Memorabilia Captain's C-14
01BAP Ultimate Mem Complete Package-10
01BAP Ultimate Memorabilia Cornerstones-1
01BAP Ultimate Memorabilia Dynamic Duos-6
01BAP Ultimate Memorabilia Emblems-11
01BAP Ultimate Memorabilia Gloves Are Off-13
01BAP Ultimate Memorabilia Jerseys-11
01BAP Ultimate Mem Jerseys and Sticks-11
01BAP Ultimate Mem Journey Jerseys-8
01BAP Ultimate Mem Journey Emblems-8
01BAP Ultimate Memorabilia Numbers-10
01BAP Ultimate Memorabilia Name Plates-5
01BAP Update Heritage-H10
01BAP Update Passing the Torch-PTT6
01Bowman YoungStars-5
Gold-5
Ice Cubed-5
01Crown Royale-134
Blue-134
Premiere Date-134
Red-134
Retail-134
All-Star Honors-20
Jewels of the Crown-29
Triple Threads-12
01eTopps-20
01McDonald's Pacific-39
Cosmic Force-5
Jersey Patches Silver-19
Jersey Patches Gold-19
01O-Pee-Chee-19
01O-Pee-Chee Heritage Parallel-19
01O-Pee-Chee Heritage Parallel Limited-19
01O-Pee-Chee Premier Parallel-19
01Pacific-373
01Pacific-423
01Pacific-442
Extreme LTD-373
Gold-423
Gold-442
Hobby LTD-373
Premiere Date-373
Retail LTD-373
All-Stars-W10
Jerseys-35
Impact Zone-19
Top Draft Picks-7
01Pacific Top Draft Picks Draft Day Promo-7
01Pacific Adrenaline-185
Blue-185
Premiere Date-185
Red-185
Retail-185
Jerseys-47
World Beaters-19
01Pacific Arena Exclusives-373
01Pacific Arena Exclusives-423
01Pacific Arena Exclusives-442
01Pacific Heads-Up-92
Blue-92
Premiere Date-92
Red-92
Silver-92
All-Star Net-5
HD NHL-9
Stat Masters-19
01Parkhurst-20
Gold-20
Silver-20
He Shoots-He Scores Points-10
He Shoots-He Scores Prizes-7
Jerseys-PJ4
Jersey and Stick-PSJ3
Milestones-M29
Sticks-PS4
Teammates-T7
Teammates-T26
Waving the Flag-17
01Private Stock-92
Gold-92
Premiere Date-92
Retail-92
Silver-92
Game Gear-97
Game Gear Patches-97
01Private Stock Pacific Nights-92
01Private Stock PS-2002-71
01Private Stock Reserve-S19
01SP Authentic-83
Limited-83
Limited Gold-83
01SP Game Used-55
Patches-PMS
Patches-CPSJ
01SPx-65
Hidden Treasures-DTSF
Hidden Treasures-TTBSS
01Sports Illustrated for Kids III-214
01Stadium Club-50
Award Winners-50
Master Photos-50
Gallery-G3
Gallery Gold-G3
NHL Passport-NHLP3
01Titanium-132
Hobby Parallel-132
Premiere Date-132
Retail-132
Retail Parallel-132
All-Stars-19
Double-Sided Jerseys-30
Double-Sided Jerseys-42
Double-Sided Patches-30
Double-Sided Patches-42
Saturday Knights-20
Three-Star Selections-19
01Titanium Draft Day Edition-90
01Topps-19
Heritage Parallel-19
Heritage Parallel Limited-19
OPC Parallel-19
01Topps Chrome-19
Refractors-19
Black Border Refractors-19
01Topps Heritage-6
Refractors-6
01Topps Reserve-43
01UD Challenge for the Cup-84
Cornerstones-CR9
Jerseys-UCSJ
01UD Honor Roll Jerseys-J-SU
01UD Honor Roll Jerseys Gold-J-SU
01UD Honor Roll Playoff Matchups-HS-SS
01UD Honor Roll Playoff Matchups Gold-HS-SS
01UD Honor Roll Pucks-P-MS
01UD Honor Roll Pucks Gold-P-MS
01UD Honor Roll Student of the Game-SG6
01UD Mask Collection-92
Gold-92
Double Patches-DPMS
Jerseys-J-MS
Jersey and Patch-JPMS
01UD Playmakers-93
01UD Premier Collection-48
Jerseys-BMS
Jerseys Black-B-MS
01UD Top Shelf-42
01Upper Deck-164
Exclusives-164
Franchise Cornerstones-FC15
Game Jerseys-AMS
Leaders of the Pack-LP15
Patches-PMS
Pride of a Nation-DPFS
Pride of a Nation-TPFSL
Pride of the Leafs-MLMS
01Upper Deck Ice-122
01Upper Deck MVP-173
01Upper Deck Victory-326
01Upper Deck Victory-426
Gold-326
Gold-426
01Upper Deck Vintage-236
01Upper Deck Vintage-242
01Upper Deck Vintage-243
01Vanguard-94
Blue-94
Red-94
East Meets West-9
In Focus-9
Memorabilia-34
Memorabilia-44
One of Ones-94
Premiere Date-94
Proofs-94
V-Team-19
02McFarlane Hockey Maple Leafs-10
02Atomic-94
Blue-94
Gold-94
Red-94
Cold Fusion-22
Hobby Parallel-94
02BAP All-Star Edition-88
02BAP All-Star Edition-89
He Shoots-He Scores Points-7
He Shoots-He Score Prizes-28
Jerseys-88
Jerseys-89
Jerseys Gold-88
Jerseys Gold-89
Jerseys Silver-88
Jerseys Silver-89
02BAP First Edition-137
02BAP First Edition-305
02BAP First Edition-368
02BAP First Edition-372
02BAP First Edition-378
02BAP First Edition-402R
Debut Jerseys-4
He Shoots-He Score Points-19
He Shoots-He Scores Prizes-3
Jerseys-137
Scoring Leaders-18
02BAP Memorabilia-198
02BAP Memorabilia-228
Emerald-198
Emerald-228
Ruby-198
Ruby-228
Sapphire-198
Sapphire-228
All-Star Jerseys-ASJ-54
All-Star Emblems-ASE-23
All-Star Numbers-ASN-23
All-Star Teammates-AST-8
All-Star Teammmates-AST-16
All-Star Triple Jerseys-ASTJ-20
Franchise Players-FP-28
He Shoots-He Scores Prizes-26
NHL All-Star Game-198
NHL All-Star Game-228
NHL All-Star Game Blue-198
NHL All-Star Game Blue-228
NHL All-Star Game Green-198
NHL All-Star Game Green-228
NHL All-Star Game Red-198
NHL All-Star Game Red-228
Teammates-TM-8
02BAP Memorabilia Toronto Fall Expo-198
02BAP Memorabilia Toronto Fall Expo-228
02BAP NHL All-Star History-52
02BAP Signature Series-119
Autographs-119
Autograph Buybacks 1998-136
Autograph Buybacks 1999-226
Autograph Buybacks 2000-93
Autographs Gold-119
Franchise Players-FJ28
Goll-GS54
Jerseys-SGJ16
Jersey Autographs-SGJ16
Team Quads-TQ2
Triple Memorabilia-TM2
02BAP Ultimate Memorabilia Captains-6
02BAP Ultimate Mem Complete Package-6
02BAP Ultimate Memorabilia Dynamic Duos-2
02BAP Ultimate Memorabilia Emblems-1
02BAP Ultimate Memorabilia First Overall-8
02BAP Ultimate Memorabilia Gloves Are Off-13
02BAP Ultimate Memorabilia Hat Tricks-19
02BAP Ultimate Memorabilia Jerseys-24
02BAP Ultimate Mem Jersey and Stick-21
02BAP Ultimate Memorabilia Numbers-29
02Between the Pipes Nightmares-GN10
02Bowman Toronto Spring Expo-10
02Bowman YoungStars-12
Gold-12
Silver-12
02Crown Royale-93
Blue-93
Red-93
Retail-93
Lords of the Rink-19
02eTopps-4
02ITG Used-72
02ITG Used-172
Franchise Players-F28
Franchise Players Autographs-F28
Franchise Players Gold-F28
International Experience-IE3
International Experience Gold-IE3
Jerseys-GUJ16
Jersey Autographs-GUJ16
Jerseys Gold-GUJ16
Emblems-E16
Jersey and Stick-SJ16
Jersey and Stick Gold-SJ16
Teammates-T12
Teammates Gold-T12
Triple Memorabilia-TM3
Triple Memorabilia Gold-TM3
02Maple Leafs Platinum Collection-18
02Maple Leafs Team Issue-11
02McDonald's Pacific-38
Atomic-5
Cup Contenders Die-Cuts-6
02NHL Power Play Stickers-123
02O-Pee-Chee-29
02O-Pee-Chee-329
02O-Pee-Chee Jumbos-22
02O-Pee-Chee Premier Blue Parallel-29
02O-Pee-Chee Premier Blue Parallel-329
02O-Pee-Chee Premier Red Parallel-29
02O-Pee-Chee Premier Red Parallel-329
02O-Pee-Chee Factory Set-29
02O-Pee-Chee Factory Set-329
02O-Pee-Chee Factory Set Hometown Heroes-HHC5
02Pacific-370
Blue-370
Red-370
Cramer's Choice-10
Lamplighters-12
Main Attractions-18
Maximum Impact-16
02Pacific Calder-50
Silver-50
02Pacific Complete-304
Red-304
02Pacific Exclusive-163
Jerseys-24
Jerseys Gold-24
Maximum Overdrive-18
02Pacific Heads-Up-118
Blue-118
Purple-118
Red-118
Bobble Heads-11
Etched in Time-14
Inside the Numbers-21
Postseason Picks-10
Quad Jerseys-31
Quad Jerseys Gold-31
Stat Masters-13
02Pacific Quest for the Cup-93
Gold-93
Chasing the Cup-17
02Parkhurst-92
Bronze-92
Gold-92
Silver-92
Franchise Players-FP28
Hardware-A9
Hardware-P9
Heroes-NH6
He Shoots-He Scores Points-9
He Shoots-He Scores Prizes-12
Jerseys-GJ47
Mario's Mates-MM7
Milestones-MS8
Patented Power-PP2
Stick and Jerseys-SJ47
Teammates-TT3
02Parkhurst Retro-23
Minis-23
Franchise Players-RF28
He Shoots-He Scores Prizes-26
Hopefuls-RR3
Jerseys-RJ21
Jersey and Sticks-RSJ14
Memorabilia-RM24
02Private Stock Reserve-146
Red-146
Retail-146
02SP Authentic-84
Beckett Promos-84
Super Premiums-SPMS
02SP Game Used-46
Authentic Fabrics-AFMS
Authentic Fabrics-AFMT
Authentic Fabrics Gold-AFMS
Authentic Fabrics Gold-AFMT
Authentic Fabrics Rainbow-AFMS
Authentic Fabrics Rainbow-AFMT
First Rounder Patches-MS
Piece of History-PHMS
Piece of History-PHSU
Piece of History Gold-PHMS
Piece of History Gold-PHSU
Piece of History Rainbow-PHMS
Piece of History Rainbow-PHSU
Tools of the Game-MS
02SPx-70
02SPx-99
02SPx-140
Spectrum Gold-70
Spectrum Gold-99
Spectrum Silver-70
Spectrum Silver-99
Smooth Skaters-MS
Smooth Skaters Gold-MS
Smooth Skaters Silver-MS
Xtreme Talents-MS
Xtreme Talents Gold-MS
Xtreme Talents Silver-MS
02Stadium Club-14
Silver Decoy Cards-14
Proofs-14
Passport-4
World Stage-WS19
02Titanium-94
Blue-94
Red-94
Retail-94
Saturday Knights-9
02Topps-29
02Topps-329
OPC Blue Parallel-29
OPC Blue Parallel-329
OPC Red Parallel-29
OPC Red Parallel-329
Captain's Cloth-CC5
Captain's Cloth-CC6
Captain's Cloth-CC11
Coast to Coast-CC4
First Round Fabric-MS
First Round Fabric Autographs-MS
Topps/OPC Hometown Heroes-HHC5
Own The Game-OTG4
Own The Game-OTG7
Factory Set-29
Factory Set-329
02Topps Chrome-29
Black Border Refractors-29
Refractors-29
e-Topps Decoy Cards-4
First Round Fabric Patches-MS
02Topps Heritage-13
02Topps Heritage-108
02Topps Heritage-109
02Topps Heritage-124
Chrome Parallel-13
USA Test Parallel-13
02Topps Total-280
Production-TP3
Team Checklists-TTC28
Topps-TT6
02UD Artistic Impressions-82
Gold-82
Artist's Touch-ATMS
Artist's Touch Gold-ATMS
02UD Artistic Impressions Beckett Promos-82
02UD Artistic Impress Common Ground-CG12
02UD Artistic Impress Common Ground Gold-CG12
02UD Artistic Impressions Retrospectives-R82
02UD Artistic Impress Retrospect Gold-R82
02UD Artistic Impress Retrospect Silver-R82
02UD Foundations-89
02UD Foundations-161
02UD Honor Roll-65
02UD Honor Roll-98
Grade A Jerseys-GAMS
Students of the Game-SG29
Team Warriors-TW14
02UD Mask Collection-84
02UD Mask Collection Beckett Promos-84
02UD Mask Collection Instant Offense-IOSU
02UD Mask Collection Patches-PGMS
02UD Piece of History-83
Patches-PHMS
Stellar Stitches-SSMS
02UD Premier Collection-50
Jerseys Bronze-MS
Jerseys Gold-MS
Jerseys Silver-MS
NHL Patches-MS1
Patches-PMS
02UD Top Shelf-83
All-Stars-ASMS
Clutch Performers-CPMS
Goal Oriented-GOMA
Shooting Stars-SHMSU
Sweet Sweaters-SWMS
02Upper Deck-164
02Upper Deck-244
Exclusives-164
Exclusives-244
Blow-Ups-C38
Difference Makers-MS
Good Old Days-GOMS
Letters of Note-LNMS
Letters of Note Gold-LNMS
Patch Card Logo-MS
Patchwork-PWMS
Playbooks-PL14
Sizzling Scorers-SS13
02Upper Deck Classic Portraits-91
Etched in Time-ET15
Hockey Royalty-SNL
Hockey Royalty Limited-SNL
Starring Cast-CMS
Starring Cast Limited-CMS
02Upper Deck MVP-175
Gold-175
Classics-175
Golden Classics-175
02Upper Deck Rookie Update-92
02Upper Deck Rookie Update-113
Jerseys-DMS
Jerseys Gold-DMS
02Upper Deck Victory-200
Bronze-200
Gold-200
Silver-200
National Pride-NP49
02Upper Deck Vintage-237
02Upper Deck Vintage-288
02Upper Deck Vintage-306
Jerseys-OSMS
Tall Boys-T60
Tall Boys Gold-T60
02Vanguard-93
LTD-93
East Meets West-6
02UD SuperStars *-244
Gold-244
City All-Stars Dual Jersey-CDMS
03McFarlane Hockey 3-Inch Duals-50
03BAP Memorabilia-53
Emerald-53
Gold-53
Ruby-53
Sapphire-53
All-Star Jerseys-ASJ-38
Brush with Greatness-18
Brush with Greatness Contest Cards-18
He Shoots-He Scores Points-11
He Shoots-He Scores Prizes-19
Jersey and Stick-SJ-6
Jerseys-GJ-6
Jersey Autographs-GJ-6
03BAP Ultimate Memorabilia Autographs-148
Gold-148
03BAP Ultimate Mem Auto Jerseys-148
03BAP Ultimate Mem Auto Emblems-148
03BAP Ultimate Memorabilia Active Eight-4
03BAP Ultimate Mem Always An All-Star-20
03BAP Ultimate Mem Always An AS Gold-20
03BAP Ultimate Mem Complete Package-6
03BAP Ultimate Mem Complete Package Gold-6
03BAP Ultimate Memorabilia Dynamic Duos-2
03BAP Ultimate Memorabilia Emblems-17
03BAP Ultimate Memorabilia Emblems Gold-17
03BAP Ultimate Mem Franch Present Future-28
03BAP Ultimate Memorabilia Gloves Are Off-7
03BAP Ultimate Memorabilia Hat Tricks-4
03BAP Ultimate Memorabilia Heroes-6
03BAP Ultimate Mem Heroes Autos-3
03BAP Ultimate Memorabilia Jerseys-11
03BAP Ultimate Memorabilia Jerseys Gold-11
03BAP Ultimate Mem Jersey and Emblems-27
03BAP Ultimate Mem Jersey and Emblem Gold-27
03BAP Ultimate Mem Jersey and Numbers-27
03BAP Ultimate Mem Jersey and Number Gold-27
03BAP Ultimate Mem Jersey and Stick-5
03BAP Ultimate Mem Jersey and Stick Gold-5
03BAP Ultimate Memorabilia Nameplates-21
03BAP Ultimate Mem Nameplates Gold-21
03BAP Ultimate Memorabilia Numbers-8
03BAP Ultimate Memorabilia Numbers Gold-8
03BAP Ultimate Memorabilia Triple Threads-15
03Beehive-183
Variations-183
Gold-183
Silver-183
Jumbo Jerseys-BH11
Jerseys-JT36
Sticks Beige Border-BE9
Sticks Red Border-RE8
03Black Diamond-88
Black-88
Green-88
Red-88
Threads-DT-MS
Threads Green-DT-MS
Threads Red-DT-MS
Threads Black-DT-MS
03Bowman-105
Gold-105
03Bowman Chrome-105
Refractors-105
Gold Refractors-105
Xfractors-105
03Crown Royale-95
Blue-95
Retail-95
Lords of the Rink-21
03ITG Action-599
Center of Attention-CA10
Jerseys-M178
Jerseys-M268
03ITG Toronto Fall Expo Forever Rivals-FR1
03ITG Toronto Fall Expo Jerseys-FE10
03ITG Used Signature Series-109
Gold-109
Autographs-MSU
Autographs Gold-MSU
Franchise-28
Franchise Autographs-28
Franchise Gold-28
Game-Day Jerseys-1
Game-Day Jerseys Gold-1
International Experience-25
International Experience Autographs-25
International Experience Emblems Gold-25
International Experience Emblems-25
International Experience Gold-25
Jerseys-27
Jerseys Gold-27
Jersey Autos-27
Emblems-25
Emblems Gold-25
Jersey and Stick-27
Jersey and Stick Gold-27
Retrospectives-5A
Retrospectives-5B
Retrospectives-5C
Retrospectives-5D
Retrospectives-5E
Retrospectives-5F
Retrospectives Gold-5A
Retrospectives Gold-5B
Retrospectives Gold-5C
Retrospectives Gold-5D
Retrospectives Gold-5E
Retrospectives Gold-5F
Teammates-15
Teammates Gold-15
Triple Memorabilia-2
Triple Memorabilia Gold-2
03ITG VIP International Experience-8
03ITG VIP Jerseys-3
03ITG VIP Jersey Autographs-3
03McDonald's Pacific-50
Patches Silver-23
Patches Gold-23
Patches and Sticks-23
Saturday Night Rivals-4
03NHL Sticker Collection-133
03O-Pee-Chee-140
03OPC Blue-140
03OPC Gold-140
03OPC Red-140
03Pacific-324
Blue-324
Red-324
Main Attractions-14
Milestones-7
03Pacific Calder-95
Silver-95
03Pacific Complete-4
Red-4
03Pacific Exhibit-196
Blue Backs-196
03Pacific Heads-Up-93
Hobby LTD-93
Retail LTD-93
03Pacific Invincible-92
Blue-92
Red-92
Retail-92
Featured Performers-28
03Pacific Luxury Suite-20A
03Pacific Luxury Suite-20B
03Pacific Luxury Suite-20C
03Pacific Luxury Suite-20D
03Pacific Luxury Suite-48A
03Pacific Luxury Suite-48B
03Pacific Luxury Suite-48C
03Pacific Prism-145
Blue-145
Patches-145
Red-145
Retail-145
03Pacific Quest for the Cup-96
Blue-96
Chasing the Cup-8
03Pacific Supreme-93
Blue-93
Red-93
Retail-93
Generations-11
Jerseys-23
03Parkhurst Orig Six He Shoots/Scores-2
03Parkhurst Orig Six He Shoots/Scores-2A
03Parkhurst Original Six Toronto-24
03Parkhurst Original Six Toronto-61
03Parkhurst Original Six Toronto-71
Memorabilia-TM1
Memorabilia-TM14
Memorabilia-TM36
Memorabilia-TM55
03Parkhurst Rookie-55
High Expectations-HE-9
High Expectations Gold-HE-9
Jerseys-GJ-18
Jerseys Gold-GJ-18
Jersey and Sticks-SJ-10
Jersey and Sticks Gold-SJ-10
Retro Rookies-RR-11
Retro Rookies Gold-RR-11
Teammates Gold-RT3
Teammates-RT3
03Private Stock Reserve-206
Blue-206
Patches-206
Red-206
Retail-206
03SP Authentic-82
Limited-82
Breakout Seasons-B17
Breakout Seasons Limited-B17
Foundations-F9
Foundations Limited-F9
03SP Game Used-47
Gold-47
Authentic Fabrics-QSNBM
Authentic Fabrics Gold-QSNBM
Double Threads-DTSB
Double Threads-DTSN
Game Gear-GGMS
Game Gear Combo-GCMS
Limited Threads-LTMS
Limited Threads Gold-LTMS
Premium Patches-PPMS
Team Threads-TTSNB
03SPx-93
03SPx-130
03SPx-181
Radiance-93
Radiance-130
Radiance-181
Spectrum-93
Spectrum-130
Spectrum-181
Fantasy Franchise-FF-NSM
Fantasy Franchise Limited-FF-NSM
Origins-O-MS
Style-SPX-NZ
Style Limited-SPX-NZ
Winning Materials-WM-MS
Winning Materials Limited-WM-MS
03Titanium-186
Hobby Jersey Number Parallels-186
Patches-186
Retail-186
03Topps-140
Blue-140
Gold-140
Red-140
First Overall Fabrics-MS
First Overall Fabrics-MMMS
First Overall Fabrics-MSEL
Topps/OPC Idols-II20
03Topps C55-13
Minis-13
Minis American Back-13
Minis American Back Red-13
Minis Bazooka Back-13
Minis Brooklyn Back-13
Minis Hat Trick Back-13
Minis O Canada Back-13
Minis O Canada Back Red-13
Minis Stanley Cup Back-13
Relics-TRMS
03Topps Pristine-65
Gold Refractor Die Cuts-65
Refractors-65
Jersey Portions-PPJ-MSU
Jersey Portion Refractors-PPJ-MSU
Patches-PP-MSU
Patch Refractors-PP-MSU
Press Plates Black-65
Press Plates Cyan-65
Press Plates Magenta-65
Press Plates Yellow-65
Stick Portions-PPS-MS
Stick Portion Refractors-PPS-MS
03Topps Traded Franchise Fabrics-FF-MS
03UD Honor Roll-82
03UD Honor Roll-116
Grade A Jerseys-TTOR
03UD Premier Collection-51
Teammates-PT-TM1
Teammates-PT-TM2
Teammates Patches-PT-TM1
Teammates Patches-PT-TM2
03Upper Deck-423
All-Star Class-AS-27
Big Playmakers-BP-MS
Canadian Exclusives-423
Franchise Fabrics-FF-MS
HG-423
Patches-LD4
Team Essentials-TL-MS
Three Stars-TS10
UD Exclusives-423
03Upper Deck Classic Portraits-91
Hockey Royalty-BSM
03Upper Deck Ice-81
Gold-81
Breakers-IB-MS
Breaker Patches-IB-MS
Frozen Fabrics-FF-MS
Frozen Fabric Patches-FF-MS
03Upper Deck MVP-391
Gold Script-391
Silver Script-391
Canadian Exclusives-391
SportsNut-SN82
03Upper Deck Rookie Update-80
Skills-SKMS
Super Stars-SSMS
03Upper Deck Trilogy-91
03Upper Deck Trilogy-113
Authentic Patches-AP12
Crest Variations-113
Limited-91
Limited-113
Limited Threads-LT8
03Upper Deck Victory-177
Bronze-177
Gold-177
Silver-177
Freshman Flashback-FF44
Game Breakers-GB23
03Russian World Championship Stars-9
03Toronto Star-92
Foil-25
04ITG NHL AS FANtasy AS History Jerseys-SB52
04Pacific-251
Blue-251
Red-251
Global Connection-8
04SP Authentic-85
04SP Authentic-145
04Ultimate Collection-39
04Ultimate Collection-78
Dual Logos-UL2-BS
Dual Logos-UL2-SR
Jerseys-UGJ-SU
Jerseys Gold-UGJ-SU
Patches-UP-SU
04Upper Deck 1997 Game Jerseys-SU
04Upper Deck Big Playmakers-BP-SU
04Upper Deck Three Stars-AS3
04Upper Deck World's Best-WB24
04Upper Deck World Cup Tribute-MS
04Upper Deck World Cup Tribute-PFSUDA
04Swedish Alfabilder Alfa Stars-13
04Swedish Alfabilder Proof Parallels-13
05Be A Player-85
First Period-85
Second Period-85
Third Period-85
Overtime-85
Class Action-CA11
Outtakes-OT46
Quad Signatures-MAPL
Quad Signatures-SHSL
Signatures-SU
Signatures Gold-SU
Triple Signatures-HSN
Triple Signatures-PTS
Triple Signatures-SIS
Triple Signatures-SNL
05Beehive-83
05Beehive-216
Beige -83
Blue -83
Gold-83
Red -83
Matte-83
Matted Materials-MMMS
Matted Materials Remarkable-RMMS
05Black Diamond-183
Emerald-183
Gold-183
Onyx-183
Ruby-183
Jerseys-J-SU
Jerseys Ruby-J-SU
Jersey Duals-DJ-SU
Jersey Triples-TJ-SU
Jersey Quads-QJ-SU
05Hot Prospects-92
En Fuego-92
Red Hot-92
White Hot-92
05McDonalds Upper Deck-12
Autographs-MA9
Chasing the Cup-CC6
Jerseys-MJ3
Patches-MP3
Top Scorers-TS9
05Panini Stickers-163
05Parkhurst-447
05Parkhurst-523
05Parkhurst-698
Facsimile Auto Parallel-447
Facsimile Auto Parallel-523
Facsimile Auto Parallel-698
True Colors-TCTOR
True Colors-TCTOR
True Colors-TCTOTO
True Colors-TCTOTO
True Colors-TCTOMO
True Colors-TCTOMO
05SP Authentic-93
05SP Authentic-114
Limited-93
Limited-114
Exquisite Endorsements-EEMS
Marks of Distinction-MDMS
Prestigious Pairings-PPBS
Sign of the Times Duals-DSO
Sign of the Times Triples-TBSO
Sign of the Times Quads-QSSOS
Six Star Signatures-SSTO
05SP Game Used-91
Autographs-91
Gold-91
Authentic Fabrics-AF-SU
Authentic Fabrics Dual-MO
Authentic Fabrics Dual Autographs-MO
Authentic Fabrics Gold-AF-SU
Authentic Fabrics Quad-SNSA
Authentic Patches Quad -SNSA
Authentic Fabrics Triple-NSL
Authentic Fabrics Triple-SFN
Authentic Patches-AP-SU
Authentic Patches Dual-MO
Authentic Patches Dual Autographs-MO
Authentic Patches Triple-NSL
Authentic Patches Triple-SFN
Auto Draft-AD-SU
Awesome Authentics-AA-SU
Awesome Authentics Gold-DA-SU
Game Gear-GG-SU
Game Gear Autographs-AG-SU
SIGnificance-SU
SIGnificance Gold-S-SU
SIGnificance Extra-SA
SIGnificance Extra Gold-SA
Significant Numbers-SN-SU
05SPx-84
05SPx-112
Spectrum-84
Spectrum-112
Winning Combos-WC-SN
Winning Combos-WC-TO
Winning Combos Gold-WC-LS
Winning Combos Gold-WC-SN
Winning Combos Gold-WC-TO
Winning Combos Spectrum-WC-LS
Winning Combos Spectrum-WC-SN
Winning Combos Spectrum-WC-TO
Winning Materials-WM-SU
Winning Materials Gold-WM-SU
Winning Materials Spectrum-WM-SU
Xcitement Superstars-XS-MS
Xcitement Superstars Gold-XS-MS
Xcitement Superstars Spectrum-XS-MS
05The Cup-94
Gold-94
Black Rainbow-94
Dual NHL Shields-DSMA
Dual NHL Shields-DSME
Dual NHL Shields-DSPM
Dual NHL Shields-DSSA
Dual NHL Shields-DSSB
Masterpiece Pressplates-94
Masterpiece Pressplates Rookie Upd Auto-260
Noble Numbers-NNSD
Noble Numbers-NNSS
Noble Numbers Dual-DNNFS
Noble Numbers Dual-DNNSL
Patch Variation-P94
Property of-POSU
05UD Artifacts-95
05UD Artifacts-196
Blue-95
Blue-196
Gold-95
Gold-196
Green-95
Green-196
Pewter-95
Pewter-196
Red-95
Red-196

Auto Facts-AF-SU
Auto Facts Blue-AF-SU
Auto Facts Copper-AF-SU
Auto Facts Pewter-AF-SU
Auto Facts Silver-AF-SU
Gold Autographed-95
Gold Autographed-196
Remarkable Artifacts-RA-SU
Remarkable Artifacts Dual-RA-SU
Treasured Patches-TP-SU
Treasured Patches Autographed-TP-SU
Treasured Patches Dual-TPD-SU
Treasured Patches Dual Autographed-TPD-SU
Treasured Patches Pewter-TP-SU
Treasured Patches Silver-TP-SU
Treasured Swatches-TS-SU
Treasured Swatches Autographed-TS-SU
Treasured Swatches Blue-TS-SU
Treasured Swatches Copper-TS-SU
Treasured Swatches Dual-TSD-SU
Treasured Swatches Dual Autographed-TSD-SU
Treasured Swatches Dual Blue-TSD-SU
Treasured Swatches Dual Copper-TSD-SU
Treasured Swatches Dual Maroon-TSD-SU
Treasured Swatches Dual Pewter-TSD-SU
Treasured Swatches Dual Silver-TSD-SU
Treasured Swatches Maroon-TS-SU
Treasured Swatches Pewter-TS-SU
Treasured Swatches Silver-TS-SU
05UD PowerPlay-85
05UD PowerPlay-104
Rainbow-85
05Ultimate Collection-85
Gold-85
Jerseys-JMS
Jerseys Triple-TJSLA
Marquee Attractions-MA45
National Heroes Jerseys-NHJSU
National Heroes Patches-NHPSU
Premium Patches-PPMS
Premium Swatches-PSMS
Ultimate Patches-PMS
Ultimate Patches Triple-TPSLA
05Ultra-180
Gold-180
Ice-180
Scoring Kings-SK4
Scoring Kings Jerseys-SKJ-MS
Scoring Kings Jersey Autographs-KAJ-MS
Scoring Kings Patches-SKP-MS
Scoring Kings Patch Autographs-KAP-MS
05Upper Deck-177
05Upper Deck All-Time Greatest-55
05Upper Deck Big Playmakers-B-MSU
05Upper Deck Goal Celebrations-GC7
05Upper Deck HG Glossy-177
05Upper Deck Hometown Heroes-HH5
05Upper Deck Jerseys-J-MS
05Upper Deck Jerseys Series II-J2SU
05Upper Deck Majestic Materials-MMSU
05Upper Deck NHL Generations-TSFZ
05Upper Deck Notable Numbers-N-SU
05Upper Deck Patches-P-MSU
05Upper Deck Scrapbooks-HS18
05Upper Deck Shooting Stars-S-MS
05Upper Deck Ice-90
Rainbow-90
Frozen Fabrics-FFMS
Frozen Fabrics Autographs-AFFMS
Frozen Fabrics Glass-FFMS
Frozen Fabrics Patches-FFPMS
Frozen Fabrics Patch Autographs-FAPMS
Signature Swatches-SSSU
05Upper Deck MVP-354
Gold-354
Platinum-354
05Upper Deck Rookie Update-91
05Upper Deck Rookie Update-260
05Upper Deck Trilogy-85
05Upper Deck Trilogy-129
Crystal-129
Crystal Autographs-129
Honorary Patches-HP-MS
Honorary Patch Scripts-HSP-MS
Honorary Swatches-HS-MS
Honorary Swatch Scripts-HSS-MS
Ice Scripts-IS-MS
05Upper Deck Toronto Fall Expo-177
05Upper Deck Victory-181
Black-181
Gold-181
Silver-181
Blow-Ups-BU39
Game Breakers-GB44
Stars on Ice-SI43
06Be A Player Portraits-92
Sensational Six-SS1ST
Sensational Six-SSSJM
Sensational Six-SSSTR
Signature Portraits-SPSM
Triple Signature Portraits-TSSM
06Beehive-5
06Beehive-165
Blue-5
Gold-5
Matte-5
Red Facsimile Signatures-5
Wood-5
5 X 7 Black and White-5
Matted Materials-MMMS
06Black Diamond-167B
Black-166B
Gold-167B
Ruby-167B
Jerseys-JSM
Jerseys Black-JSM
Jerseys Gold-JSM
Jerseys Ruby-JSM
06Flair Showcase-197
06Flair Showcase-266
06Flair Showcase-298
Parallel-197
Parallel-266
Parallel-298
Hot Numbers-HN38
Hot Numbers Parallel-HN38
Stitches-SSSU
06Fleer-179
Oversized-179
Tiffany-179
Speed Machines-SM23
Total 0-023
06Gatorade-61
06Hot Prospects-90
Red Hot-90
White Hot-90
Hot Materials -HMSU
Hot Materials Red Hot-HMSU
Hot Materials White Hot-HMSU
06McDonald's Upper Deck-45
06McDonald's Upper Deck-52
Clear Cut Winners-CC9
Jerseys-JMS
Patches-PMS

060-Pee-Chee-454
060-Pee-Chee-669
060-Pee-Chee-698
Rainbow-454
Rainbow-669
Rainbow-698
Swatches-S-SU
06Panini Stickers-161
06SP Authentic-6
06SP Authentic-137
Limited-6
Limited-137
06SP Game Used-93
Gold-93
Rainbow-93
Authentic Fabrics-AFMS
Authentic Fabrics Parallel-AFMS
Authentic Fabrics Patches-AFMS
Authentic Fabrics Dual-AF2SS
Authentic Fabrics Dual Patches-AF2SS
Authentic Fabrics Triple-AF3TOR
Authentic Fabrics Triple Patches-AF3TOR
Authentic Fabrics Quads-AF4SFSZ
Authentic Fabrics Quads Patches-AF4SFSZ
Authentic Fabrics Sixes-AF6500
Authentic Fabrics Sixes Patches-AF6500
Authentic Fabrics Eights-AF8SWE
Authentic Fabrics Eights Patches-AF8SWE
By The Letter-BLMA
06SPx-92
06SPx-110
Spectrum-92
Spectrum-110
SPxcitement-X93
SPxcitement Spectrum-X93
06Sunkist-3
06The Cup-82
Black Rainbow-82
Foundations-CQSU
Foundations Patches-CQSU
Gold-82
Gold Patches-82
Jerseys-82
Masterpiece Pressplates-82
NHL Shields Duals-DSHSA
NHL Shields Duals-DSHSS
NHL Shields Duals-DSHTO
06UD Artifacts-6
06UD Artifacts-199
Blue-6
Blue-199
Gold-6
Gold-199
Platinum-6
Platinum-199
Radiance-6
Radiance-199
Red-6
Red-199
Tundra Tandems-TTTO
Tundra Tandems Black-TTTO
Tundra Tandems Blue-TTTO
Tundra Tandems Gold-TTTO
Tundra Tandems Red-TTTO
Tundra Tandems Dual Patches Red-TTTO
06UD Biography of a Season-BOS3
06UD Mini Jersey Collection-90
Jerseys-MS
Jersey Variations-MS
06UD Powerplay-91
Impact Rainbow-91
In Action-IA12
06Ultimate Collection-56
Jerseys-UJ-MS
Jerseys Triple-UJ3-SFL
Patches-UJ-MS
Patches Triple-UJ3-SFL
06Ultra-181
Gold Medallion-181
Ice Medallion-181
Action-UA29
Difference Makers-DM19
Scoring Kings-SK19
Uniformity-USU
Uniformity Patches-UPSU
06Upper Deck Arena Giveaways-TOR1
06Upper Deck-181
Exclusives Parallel-181
High Gloss Parallel-181
All World-AW29
Game Jerseys-J2SU
Game Patches-P2SU
Masterpieces-181
Walmart Tins Oversize-181
06Upper Deck MVP-268
Gold Script-268
Super Script-268
Clutch Performers-CP7
Gotta Have Hart-HH23
International Icons-II22
Jerseys-OJOT
Jerseys-OJSK
06Upper Deck Ovation-145
06Upper Deck Sweet Shot-93
Sweet Stitches-SSSU
Sweet Stitches Duals-SSSU
Sweet Stitches Triples-SSSU
06Upper Deck Trilogy-91
Frozen In Time-FT12
06Upper Deck Victory-183
06Upper Deck Victory Black-183
06Upper Deck Victory Gold-183
06Upper Deck Victory GameBreakers-GB48
06Upper Deck Victory Oversize Cards-SU
06Russian Sport Collection Olympic Stars-20
07Upper Deck Victory-60
Black-60
Gold-60
GameBreakers-GB22
Oversize Cards-OS17
Stars on Ice-SI28

Sundin, Ronnie
92Swedish Semic Elitserien Stickers-307
93Swedish Semic Elitserien-274
94Swedish Leaf-24
95Swedish Leaf-141
95Swedish Upper Deck-207
97Hartford Wolf Pack-23
98Swedish UD Choice-70
99Swedish Upper Deck-72
00Swedish Upper Deck-64
02Swedish SHL-114
Parallel-114
03Swedish Elite-25
Silver-25
04Swedish Elitset-26
Gold-26
05Swedish SHL Elitset-176
Gold-176
06Swedish SHL Elitset-174

Sundin, Sture
64Swedish Coralli ISHockey-112
65Swedish Coralli ISHockey-112

Sundkvist, Hjalle
57Swedish Alfabilder-120

Sundkvist, Kent
70Swedish Hockey-129
71Swedish Hockey-220

Sundlov, Michael
87Swedish Panini Stickers-48
89Swedish Semic Elitserien Stickers-28
90Swedish Semic Elitserien Stickers-175
91Swedish Semic Elitserien Stickers-28
92Swedish Semic Elitserien Stickers-51
93Swedish Semic Elitserien-26
93Swedish Semic Elitserien-307
94Swedish Leaf-126
Clean Sweepers-2
Gold Cards-15
95Swedish Leaf-15
Champs-12
Mega-1
Spidermen-2
95Swedish Upper Deck-19
96Swedish Brynas Tigers-3
97Swedish Collector's Choice-17
97Swedish Collector's Choice-216

Sundquist, Carl
72Finnish Jaakiekko-58
72Finnish Hellas-28

Sundquist, Christer
67Swedish Hockey-94

Sundquist, Magnus
98Danish Hockey League-211
99Danish Hockey League-145

Sundquist, Rod
04Missouri River Otters-26

Sundqvist, Hjalle
56Swedish Alfabilder-63

Sundqvist, Jurgen
05Swedish SHL Elitset-148
06Swedish SHL Elitset-4

Sundqvist, Karl-Johan
71Swedish Hockey-143
72Swedish Stickers-9
72Swedish Stickers-122
73Finnish Jaakiekko-37
73Swedish Stickers-8
73Swedish Stickers-184
74Finnish Jenkki-36
74Swedish Stickers-189
74Swedish Semic World Champ Stickers-7

Sundqvist, Sven-Erik
56Swedish Alfabilder-83

Sundstrom, Billy
69Swedish Hockey-106
70Swedish Hockey-53
71Swedish Hockey-122
72Swedish Stickers-97
73Swedish Stickers-210

Sundstrom, Kjell
67Swedish Hockey-21
67Swedish Hockey-261
69Swedish Hockey-308
70Swedish Hockey-211
71Swedish Hockey-300
72Swedish Stickers-73

Sundstrom, Niklas
91Swedish Semic Elitserien Stickers-331
92Upper Deck-597
92Swedish Semic Elitserien Stickers-244
93Parkhurst-506
Emerald Ice-506
93Swedish Semic Elitserien-212
93Classic-8
Top Ten-DP8
93Classic Four-Sport *-192
Gold-192
94Parkhurst SE-SE237
Gold-SE237
94SP-168
Die Cuts-168
94Swedish Leaf-284
94Classic-79
Gold-79
Tri-Cards-T43
95Be A Player-177
Signatures-S177
Signatures Die Cuts-S177
95Bowman-113
All-Foil-113
Bowman's Best-BB21
Bowman's Best Refractors-BB21
95Collector's Choice-408
95Donruss-382
Rated Rookies-3
95Donruss Elite-60
Die Cut Stars-60
Die Cut Uncut-60
Rookies-14
95Finest-59
Refractors-59
95Leaf Limited-104
Rookie Phenoms-4
95Metal-193
International Steel-21
95Parkhurst International-261
95Parkhurst International-514
Emerald Ice-261
Emerald Ice-514
95Select Certified-135
Mirror Gold-135
95SkyBox Impact-213
NHL On Fox-16
95SP-96
95Stadium Club-205
Members Only Master Set-205
95Summit-187
Artist's Proofs-187
Ice-187
95Topps-341
OPC Inserts-341
SuperSkills Super Rookies-SR14
95Ultra-357
Extra Attackers-18
95Upper Deck-261
Electric Ice-261
Electric Ice Gold-261
Predictor Hobby-H28
Predictor Hobby Exchange-H28
95Zenith-128
Rookie Roll Call-14
95Swedish Globe World Championships-60
96Collector's Choice-168
96Donruss-237
Press Proofs-237
96Donruss Elite-47
Die Cut Stars-47
96Fleer-72
96Leaf-172
Press Proofs-172
96Metal Universe-102
96Score-269
Artist's Proofs-269
Dealer's Choice Artist's Proofs-269
Special Artist's Proofs-269
Golden Blades-269

96SkyBox Impact-85
96SP Holoview Collection-HC26
96Topps Picks Rookie Stars-RS18
96Topps Picks Rookie Stars OPC-RS18
96Ultra-112
Gold Medallion-112
96Upper Deck-107
Generation Next-X24
97Collector's Choice-165
Star Quest-SQ41
97Crown Royale-88
Emerald Green-88
Ice Blue-88
Silver-88
97Donruss-178
Press Proofs Silver-178
Press Proofs Gold-178
97Donruss Limited-64
Exposure-64
97Donruss Priority-67
Stamp of Approval-67
97Leaf-36
Fractal Matrix-36
Fractal Matrix Die Cuts-36
97Leaf International-36
Universal Ice-36
97Pacific-86
Copper-86
Emerald Green-86
Ice Blue-86
Red-86
Silver-86
97Pacific Omega-150
Copper-150
Dark Gray-150
Emerald Green-150
Gold-150
Ice Blue-150
97Panini Stickers-89
97Pinnacle Inside-155
97Score-194
97Score Rangers-5
Platinum-5
Premier-5
97SP Authentic-104
97Upper Deck-106
Three Star Selects-7B
98Be A Player-240
Press Release-240
98BAP Gold-240
98BAP Autographs-240
98BAP Autographs Gold-240
98Finest-121
No Protectors-121
No Protectors Refractors-121
Refractors-121
98OPC Chrome-197
Refractors-197
98Pacific-302
Ice Blue-302
Red-302
98Panini Stickers-86
98Paramount-159
Copper-159
Emerald Green-159
Holo-Electric-159
Ice Blue-159
Silver-159
98Topps-197
O-Pee-Chee-197
98UD Choice-132
Prime Choice Reserve-132
Reserve-132
98Upper Deck-136
Exclusives-136
Exclusives 1 of 1-136
Generation Next-GN26
Generation Next Quantum 1-GN26
Generation Next Quantum 2-GN26
Generation Next Quantum 3-GN26
Gold Reserve-136
98Upper Deck MVP-137
Gold Script-137
Silver Script-137
Super Script-137
99BAP Memorabilia-112
Gold-112
Silver-112
99BAP Millennium-212
Emerald-212
Ruby-212
Sapphire-212
Signatures-212
Signatures Gold-212
99Pacific-282
Copper-282
Emerald Green-282
Gold-282
Ice Blue-282
Premiere Date-282
Red-282
99Pacific Dynagon Ice-177
Blue-177
Copper-177
Gold-177
Premiere Date-177
99Panini Stickers-297
99Stadium Club-152
First Day Issue-152
One of a Kind-152
Printing Plates Black-152
Printing Plates Cyan-152
Printing Plates Magenta-152
Printing Plates Yellow-152
99Upper Deck-280
Exclusives-280
Exclusives 1 of 1-280
99Upper Deck Gold Reserve-280
99Upper Deck HoloGrFx-48
Ausome-48
99Upper Deck Victory-279
00SLU Hockey-210
00BAP Memorabilia-256
Emerald-256
Ruby-256
Sapphire-256
Promos-256
00BAP Mem Chicago Sportsfest Copper-256
00BAP Memorabilia Chicago Sportsfest Blue-256
00BAP Memorabilia Chicago Sportsfest Gold-256
00BAP Memorabilia Chicago Sportsfest Ruby-256
00BAP Memorabilia Chicago Sun-Times Ruby-256
00BAP Memorabilia Chicago Sun-Times Gold-256
00BAP Mem Chicago Sun-Times Sapphire-256
00BAP Mem Toronto Fall Expo Copper-256
00BAP Memorabilia Toronto Fall Expo Gold-256
00BAP Memorabilia Toronto Fall Expo Ruby-256
000-Pee-Chee-34
000-Pee-Chee Parallel-34
00Pacific-447
Copper-447
Gold-447
Ice Blue-447
Premiere Date-447

00Panini Stickers-201
00Topps/OPC-34
Parallel-34
00Upper Deck-376
Exclusives Tier 1-376
Exclusives Tier 2-376
00Upper Deck Vintage-297
010-Pee-Chee-232
010-Pee-Chee Premier Parallel-232
01Pacific-347
Extreme LTD-347
Hobby LTD-347
Premiere Date-347
Retail LTD-347
01Pacific Arena Exclusives-347
01Parkhurst-185
01Sharks Postcards-8
01Topps-232
OPC Parallel-232
02BAP First Edition-77
Jerseys-77
02BAP Sig Series Auto Buybacks 1998-240
02BAP Sig Series Auto Buybacks 1999-212
020-Pee-Chee-114
020-Pee-Chee Premier Blue Parallel-114
020-Pee-Chee Premier Red Parallel-114
020-Pee-Chee Factory Set-114
02Pacific Complete-137
Red-137
02Topps-114
OPC Blue Parallel-114
OPC Red Parallel-114
Factory Set-114
02Topps Total-181
03Canadiens Postcards-26
03ITG Action-367
03Pacific-182
Blue-182
Red-182
03Pacific Complete-47
Red-47
03Parkhurst Original Six Montreal-6
Memorabilia-MM2
03Topps Traded-TT46
Blue-TT46
Gold-TT46
Red-TT46
03Upper Deck MVP-226
Gold Script-226
Silver Script-226
Canadian Exclusives-226
04Swedish Alfabilder Alfa Stars-34
04Swedish Alfabilder Alfa Star Golden Ice-10
04Swedish Alfabilder Autographs-119
04Swedish Alfabilder Limited Autographs-119
04Swedish Alfabilder Proof Parallels-34
05Canadiens Team Issue-22
05Parkhurst-265
Facsimile Auto Parallel-265
05Upper Deck MVP-211
Gold-211
Platinum-211
06Swedish SHL Elitset-244

Sundstrom, Olie
89Swedish Semic Elitserien Stickers-122
90Swedish Semic Elitserien Stickers-199
91Swedish Semic Elitserien Stickers-129
92Nashville Knights-23
93Cleveland Lumberjacks-24
93Cleveland Lumberjacks Postcards-19
94Cleveland Lumberjacks-24
94Cleveland Lumberjacks Postcards-23
96Johnstown Chiefs-21
97Wheeling Nailers-13
97Wheeling Nailers Photo Pack-13
98Port Huron Border Cats-5
01Anchorage Aces-14

Sundstrom, Patrik
82Canucks Team Issue-21
82Swedish Semic VM Stickers-15
83Canucks Team Issue-20
830-Pee-Chee-361
830-Pee-Chee Stickers-152
83Topps Stickers-152
83Vachon-118
84Canucks Team Issue-23
840-Pee-Chee-331
840-Pee-Chee Stickers-279
85Canucks Team Issue-22
850-Pee-Chee-115
850-Pee-Chee Stickers-241
857-Eleven Credit Cards-19
85Topps-115
86Canucks Team Issue-20
86Kraft Drawings-70
860-Pee-Chee-156
860-Pee-Chee Stickers-101
86Topps-156
870-Pee-Chee-34
870-Pee-Chee Stickers-201
87Panini Stickers-348
87Topps-34
88Devils Caretta-27
880-Pee-Chee-67
88Panini Stickers-277
88Topps-67
89Devils Caretta-23
890-Pee-Chee-56
890-Pee-Chee Stickers-82
89Panini Stickers-250
89Topps-56
89Swedish Semic World Champ Stickers-21
90Bowman-89
Tiffany-89
90Devils Team Issue-28
900-Pee-Chee-306
90Panini Stickers-65
90Pro Set-176A
90Pro Set-176B
90Score-19
Canadian-19
90Score Hottest/Rising Stars-10
90Topps-306
Tiffany-306
90Upper Deck-288
French-288
91Pro Set Platinum-71
91Bowman-279
910-Pee-Chee-451
91Panini Stickers-217
91Pinnacle-290
French-290
91Pro Set-141
French-141
91Score American-117
91Score Canadian Bilingual-117
91Score Canadian English-117
91Stadium Club-229
91Topps-451
91Upper Deck-369
French-369
93Swedish Semic Elitserien-19

Sundstrom, Peter
82Swedish Semic VM Stickers-16
83Swedish Semic VM Stickers-16
840-Pee-Chee-155
84Topps-116
86Swedish Panini Stickers-23
87Capitals Kodak-12
87Capitals Team Issue-23
88Capitals Borderless-21
88Capitals Smokey-23
89Devils Caretta-24
90Swedish Semic Elitserien Stickers-136
91Swedish Semic Elitserien Stickers-191
92Swedish Semic Elitserien Stickers-219
93Swedish Semic Elitserien-190
94Swedish Leaf-127

Sundt, Robert
92Norwegian Elite Series-62

Sunesson, Ake
67Swedish Hockey-111

Suni, Erkki
70Finnish Jaakiekko-288
71Finnish Suomi Stickers-160
72Finnish Jaakiekko-187

Sunohara, Vicky
97Collector's Choice-280
04Canadian Womens World Championship Team-20
06ITG Going For Gold-17
06ITG Going For Gold Samples-17
06ITG Going For Gold Autographs-ASU
06ITG Going For Gold Jerseys-GUJ17

Suokas, Jari
70Finnish Jaakiekko-321

Suokko, Erkki
65Finnish Hellas-110

Suokko, Jorma
65Finnish Hellas-109
66Finnish Jaakiekkosarja-184

Suoknuuti, Simo
70Finnish Jaakiekko-305
71Finnish Suomi Stickers-258

Suomalainen, Jaakko
04Finnish Cardset-273
06Finnish Cardset-268
Between the Pipes-14

Suomalainen, Jukka
94Finnish SISU-280
95Finnish SISU-138

Suominen, Tapani
65Finnish Hellas-77
66Finnish Jaakiekkosarja-31

Suominen, Tuomas
06Finnish Cardset-340

Suominen, Veikko
70Finnish Jaakiekko-306
71Finnish Suomi Stickers-187
72Finnish Jaakiekko-136
72Finnish Panda Toronto-32
73Finnish Jaakiekko-192
78Finnish SM-Liiga-62

Suoniemi, Raimo
71Finnish Suomi Stickers-146
72Finnish Jaakiekko-206
73Finnish Jaakiekko-170
74Finnish Jenkki-17
74Finnish Typotor-30
74Swedish Semic World Champ Stickers-90

Suoniemi, Tomi
00Finnish Cardset-145

Suoraniemi, Kari
80Finnish Mallasjuoma-92
87Swedish Panini Stickers-218
89Swedish Semic Elitserien Stickers-194
89Swedish Semic World Champ Stickers-37
92Swedish Semic Elitserien Stickers-255
93Swedish Semic Elitserien-221
94Finnish SISU-372
94Swedish Leaf-116

Suoraniemi, Seppo
71Finnish Suomi Stickers-161
72Finnish Jaakiekko-113
72Finnish Hellas-22
73Finnish Jaakiekko-120
74Finnish Jenkki-18
74Finnish Typotor-15
74Swedish Stickers-101
74Swedish Semic World Champ Stickers-81
77Finnish Sportscasters-85-2017
78Finnish SM-Liiga-202
80Finnish Mallasjuoma-179
81Swedish Semic Hockey VM Stickers-23
82Finnish Skopbank-14
82Swedish Semic VM Stickers-32

Suorsa, Jari
96Finnish SISU Redline-38

Sup, Michal
91British Columbia JHL-16
917th Inn. Sketch WHL-90
94Czech APS Extraliga-88
95Czech APS Extraliga-139
96Czech APS Extraliga-23
97Czech APS Extraliga-163
98Czech DS-74
98Czech DS Stickers-200
98Czech OFS-219
99Czech DS-121
99Czech OFS-55
99Czech OFS-510
All-Star Game Blue-510
All-Star Game Gold-510
All-Star Game Red-510
All-Star Game Silver-510
00Czech OFS-99
00Czech OFS-413
01Czech OFS-277
02Czech OFS Plus-249
03Czech OFS Plus-189
03Czech OFS Plus All-Star Game-H29
03Czech OFS Plus Insert G-G2
03Czech OFS Plus Insert H-H24
03Czech OFS Plus MS Praha-SE46
04Czech HC Slavia Praha Postcards-17
04Czech OFS-174
Czech/Slovak-16
Goals Leaders-2
Points Leaders-11
04Czech World Championship Postcards-21
05Czech HC Slavia Praha-12
06Czech HC Slavia Praha Postcards-13
06Czech OFS-304
Goals Leaders-2
Points Leaders-15

Sup, Radek
03Czech National Team Postcards-12
04Czech HC Slavia Praha Postcards-9

Supler, Julius
97Portland Winter Hawks-27
98Czech OFS-129

Supuka, Jan
93Quebec Pee-Wee Tournament-1719

Sura, Tapani
72Finnish Jaakiekko-238
73Finnish Jaakiekko-273

Surette, Brian
95Halifax Mooseheads-17

Surma, Damian
95Quebec Pee-Wee Tournament-764
00SP Authentic-127
00SP Game Used-90
00SPx-128
Spectrum-128
00UD Pros and Prospects-132
00Upper Deck-439
Exclusives Tier 1-439
Exclusives Tier 2-439
01Plymouth Whalers-5
02Lowell Lock Monsters-14
03Florida Everblades RBI Sports-174
03Lowell Lock Monsters-7
03Lowell Lock Monsters Photo Album-8
04Florida Everblades-20
05Kalamazoo Wings-9
05Missouri River Otters-21

Surois, Bob
79Capitals Team Issue-20

Surovy, Tomas
95Slovakian-Quebec Pee-Wee Tournament-25
01Wilkes-Barre Scranton Penguins-15
02BAP Memorabilia-387
02BAP Ultimate Memorabilia-64
02Pacific Calder-140
Silver-140
02Pacific Complete-522
Red-522
02Pacific Quest for the Cup-140
Gold-140
02SP Authentic-205
02Upper Deck Rookie Update-134
02Wilkes-Barre Scranton Penguins-18
03ITG Action-409
03Pacific-277
Blue-277
Red-277
03Pacific Complete-204
Red-204
03AHL Top Prospects-35
03Wilkes-Barre Scranton Penguins-26
04Wilkes-Barre Scranton Penguins-20
05Parkhurst-396
Facsimile Auto Parallel-396
05WBS Penguins-25
06Swedish SHL Elitset-224

Sushinski, Maxim
93Pinnacle-510
Canadian-510
98Russian Hockey League-23
99Russian Hockey League-169
99Russian Stars of Hockey-6
00BAP Memorabilia-412
Emerald-412
Ruby-412
Sapphire-412
00BAP Parkhurst 2000-P185
00BAP Signature Series-273
Emerald-273
Autographs-235
Autographs Gold-235
00Private Stock-127
Gold-127
Premiere Date-127
Retail-127
Silver-127
00Topps Gold Label Class 1-33
Gold-33
00Topps Gold Label Class 2-33
00Topps Gold Label Class 2 Gold-33
00Topps Gold Label Class 3-33
00Topps Gold Label Class 3 Gold-33
00Topps Heritage-131
00UD Heroes-61
01Russian Lightnings-1
02BAP Sig Series Auto Buybacks 2000-235
02Russian World Championships-3
03Russian Avangard Omsk-3
03Russian National Team-21
03Russian Postcards-8
04Russian World Championship Team-9
05Russian Hockey League RHL-30
06Czech Super Six Postcards-13
06Russian Torino Olympic Team-7

Susi, Timo
77Finnish Sportscasters-90-2169
78Finnish SM-Liiga-185
80Finnish Mallasjuoma-162
81Swedish Semic Hockey VM Stickers-31
82Finnish Skopbank-15
82Swedish Semic VM Stickers-48
83Swedish Semic VM Stickers-48
05Finnish Tappara Legendat-13

Suter, Bob
80USA Olympic Team Mini Pics-8
81Swedish Semic Hockey VM Stickers-92
95Signature Rookies Miracle on Ice-33
95Signature Rookies Miracle on Ice-34
95Signature Rook Miracle on Ice Sigs-33
95Signature Rook Miracle on Ice Sigs-34
04UD Legendary Signatures Miracle Men-USA18
04UD Legendary Sigs Miracle Men Autos-USA-OB

Suter, Curtis
96Spokane Chiefs-21
97Spokane Chiefs-22
98Spokane Chiefs-25

Suter, Garrett
04Green Bay Gamblers-22
04Green Bay Gamblers-25

Suter, Gary
85Flames Red Rooster-28
86Flames Red Rooster-27
86Kraft Drawings-71
860-Pee-Chee-189
860-Pee-Chee Stickers-134
860-Pee-Chee Stickers-192
86Topps-189
87Flames Red Rooster-28
870-Pee-Chee-176
870-Pee-Chee Stickers-49
87Panini Stickers-207
87Topps-176
88Flames Postcards-13
880-Pee-Chee-43
880-Pee-Chee Minis-40
880-Pee-Chee Stickers-89
880-Pee-Chee Stickers-113
88Panini Stickers-7
88Topps-43
88Topps Sticker Inserts-11
89Kraft-61
890-Pee-Chee-108
890-Pee-Chee Stickers-100
89Panini Stickers-30
89Topps-108
89Swedish Semic World Champ Stickers-155
90Bowman-101
Tiffany-101
90Flames IGA/McGavin's-26
900-Pee-Chee-205

90Panini Stickers-177
90Pro Set-46
90Score-88
Canadian-88
90Topps-205
Tiffany-205
90Upper Deck-273
French-273
91Pro Set Platinum-20
91Bowman-254
91Flames Panini Team Stickers-21
91Flames Panini Team Stickers-H
91Flames IGA-22
91Kraft-72
910-Pee-Chee-151
91Panini Stickers-57
91Parkhurst-25
French-25
91Pinnacle-11
91Pinnacle-392
French-11
French-392
91Pro Set-32
91Pro Set-276
French-32
French-276
91Score American-244
91Score Canadian Bilingual-464
91Score Canadian English-464
91Stadium Club-143
91Topps-151
91Upper Deck-341
91Upper Deck-510
French-341
French-510
91Finnish Semic World Champ Stickers-132
91Swedish Semic World Champ Stickers-132
92Bowman-55
92Flames IGA-8
920-Pee-Chee-278
92Panini Stickers-48
92Panini Stickers French-48
92Parkhurst-23
Emerald Ice-23
92Pinnacle-195
French-195
92Pro Set-27
92Score-17
Canadian-17
92Stadium Club-423
92Topps-308
Gold-308G
92Ultra-30
92Upper Deck-249
92Finnish Semic-152
93Donruss-53
93Donruss-415
93Leaf-140
93OPC Premier-178
Gold-178
93Panini Stickers-186
93Parkhurst-299
Emerald Ice-299
93Pinnacle-14
Canadian-14
93PowerPlay-44
93Score-13
Canadian-13
93Stadium Club-228
Members Only Master Set-228
OPC-228
First Day Issue-228
First Day Issue OPC-228
93Topps/OPC Premier-178
Gold-178
93Topps Premier Black Gold-10
93Ultra-226
93Upper Deck-357
93Swedish Semic World Champ Stickers-176
94Be A Player-R94
Signature Cards-112
94Blackhawks Coke-19
94Canada Games NHL POGS-75
94Donruss-217
94EA Sports-19
94Flair-38
94Fleer-47
94Hockey Wit-41
94Leaf-317
94OPC Premier-168
Special Effects-168
94Parkhurst-47
Gold-47
Vintage-V74
94Pinnacle-137
Artist's Proofs-137
Rink Collection-137
94Score-44
Gold-44
Platinum-44
94Topps/OPC Premier-168
Special Effects-168
94Ultra-46
94Upper Deck-74
Electric Ice-74
SP Inserts-SP107
SP Inserts Die Cuts-SP107
94Finnish Jaa Kiekko-121
95Blackhawks Coke-17
95Canada Games NHL POGS-69
95Collector's Choice-8
Player's Club-8
Player's Club Platinum-8
95Donruss-99
95Donruss Elite-11
Die Cut Stars-11
Die Cut Uncut-11
95Emotion-34
95Finest-126
Refractors-126
95Leaf-219
95Metal-29
95Panini Stickers-165
95Parkhurst International-39
Emerald Ice-39
Parkie's Trophy Picks-PP26
95Pinnacle-68
Artist's Proofs-68
Rink Collection-68
95Playoff One on One-238
95Score-82
Black Ice Artist's Proofs-82
Black Ice-82
95SkyBox Impact-34
95SP-25
95Stadium Club-124
Members Only Master Set-124
95Summit-59
Artist's Proofs-59
Ice-59
95Topps-156
OPC Inserts-156
Hidden Gems-9HG
95Ultra-36

Gold Medallion-36
95Upper Deck-284
Electric Ice-284
Electric Ice Gold-284
NHL All-Stars-AS8
NHL All-Stars Jumbo-AS8
Special Edition-SE107
Special Edition Gold-SE107
95Zenith-73
95Swedish Globe World Championships-104
95Swedish World Championships Stickers-219
96Be A Player-180
Autographs-180
Autographs Silver-180
96Collector's Choice-52
96Donruss-130
Press Proofs-130
96Fleer-19
96Leaf-32
Press Proofs-32
96Maggers-97
96Metal Universe-28
96Pinnacle-195
Artist's Proofs-195
Foil-195
Premium Stock-195
Rink Collection-195
96Score-182
Artist's Proofs-182
Dealer's Choice Artist's Proofs-182
Special Artist's Proofs-182
Golden Blades-182
96SkyBox Impact-20
96SP-29
96Team Out-82
96Topps Picks-41
OPC Inserts-41
96Ultra-33
Gold Medallion-33
96Upper Deck-235
Generation Next-X37
96Swedish Semic Wien-162
97Collector's Choice-45
97Pacific-212
Copper-212
Emerald Green-212
Ice Blue-212
Red-212
Silver-212
98OPC Chrome-26
Refractors-26
98Pacific-152
Ice Blue-152
Red-152
98Panini Stickers-116
98Topps-26
O-Pee-Chee-26
98UD Choice-47
98UD Choice Preview-47
98UD Choice Prime Choice Reserve-47
98UD Choice Reserve-47
99BAP Memorabilia-33
Gold-33
Silver-33
99Pacific Omega-211
Copper-211
Gold-211
Ice Blue-211
Premiere Date-211
99Panini Stickers-299
99Upper Deck MVP-179
Gold Script-179
Silver Script-179
Super Script-179
99Upper Deck Victory-254
00BAP Memorabilia-294
Emerald-294
Ruby-294
Sapphire-294
Promos-294
00BAP Mem Chicago Sportsfest Copper-294
00BAP Memorabilia Chicago Sportsfest Blue-294
00BAP Memorabilia Chicago Sportsfest Gold-294
00BAP Memorabilia Chicago Sportsfest Ruby-294
00BAP Memorabilia Chicago Sun-Times Ruby-294
00BAP Memorabilia Chicago Sun-Times Gold-294
00BAP Mem Chicago Sun-Times Sapphire-294
00BAP Mem Toronto Fall Expo Copper-294
00BAP Memorabilia Toronto Fall Expo Gold-294
00BAP Memorabilia Toronto Fall Expo Ruby-294
00Pacific-368
Copper-368
Gold-368
Ice Blue-368
Premiere Date-368
01O-Pee-Chee-146
01O-Pee-Chee Premier Parallel-146
01Sharks Postcards-7
01Topps-146
OPC Parallel-146
02Pacific-343
Blue-343
Red-343
04ITG Franchises Canadian-15
Autographs-GS

Suter, Markus

93Swiss HNL-407

Suter, Ryan

03BAP Memorabilia Draft Redemptions-7
03Wisconsin Badgers-26
04SP Authentic Rookie Redemptions-RR17
04Milwaukee Admirals-13
05ITG Heroes/Prosp Toronto Expo Parallel -101
05Beehive-115
Beige -115
Blue -115
Gold-115
Red -115
Matte-115
05Black Diamond-204
Emerald-204
Gold-204
Onyx-204
Ruby-204
05Hot Prospects-247
En Fuego-247
Hot Materials-HMRS
Red Hot-247
White Hot-247
05Parkhurst-639
Facsimile Auto Parallel-639
True Colors-TCNSH
True Colors-TCNSH
05SP Authentic-166
Limited-166
Rarefied Rookies-RRRS
Rookie Authentics-RARS
05SP Game Used-138
Autographs-138
Gold-138
Rookie Exclusives-RS
Rookie Exclusives Silver-RE-RS
Significant Numbers-SN-SM
05SPx-182
Spectrum-182
Xcitement Rookies-XR-RS
Xcitement Rookies Gold-XR-RS
Xcitement Rookies Spectrum-XR-RS
05The Cup-111
Autographed Rookie Patches Gold Rainbow-111
Black Rainbow Rookies-111
Masterpiece Pressplates (Artifacts)-217
Masterpiece Pressplates (Bee Hive)-115
Masterpiece Pressplates (Black Diamond)-204
Masterpiece Pressplates (Ice)-133
Masterpiece Pressplates (MVP)-417
Masterpiece Pressplates (Power Play)-147
Masterpiece Pressplates (Power Play)-147
Masterpiece Pressplates (Rookie Update)-215
Masterpiece Pressplates SPA Autos-166
Masterpiece Pressplates (SP Game Used)-138
Masterpiece Pressplates SPx Autos-182
Masterpiece Pressplates (Trilogy)-197
Masterpiece Pressplates Ult Coll Autos-121
Masterpiece Pressplates (Victory)-287
Masterpiece Pressplates Autographs-111
Platinum Rookies-111
05UD Artifacts-217
Gold-RED17
05UD PowerPlay-147
05UD Rookie Class-41
05Ultimate Collection-121
Autographed Patches-121
Autographed Shields-121
Ultimate Debut Threads Jerseys-DTJRS
Ultimate Debut Threads Jerseys Autos-DAJRS
Ultimate Debut Threads Patches-DTPRS
Ultimate Debut Threads Patches Autos-DAPRS
Ultimate Signatures-USRS
05Ultra-226
Gold-226
Fresh Ink-FI-SU
Fresh Ink Blue-FI-SU
Ice-226
Rookie Uniformity Jerseys-RU-RS
Rookie Uniformity Jersey Autographs-ARU-RS
Rookie Uniformity Patches-RUP-RS
Rookie Uniformity Patch Autographs-ARP-RS
05Upper Deck-454
Rookie Ink-RIRS
05Upper Deck Rookie Showcase-RS17
05Upper Deck Rookie Showcase Promos-RS17
05Upper Deck Rookie Threads-RTRS
05Upper Deck Rookie Threads Autographs-ARTRS
05Upper Deck Ice-133
Cool Threads-CTRS
Cool Threads Autographs-ACTRS
Cool Threads Glass-CTRS
Cool Threads Patches-CTPRS
Cool Threads Patch Autographs-CAPRS
Fresh Ice-FIRS
Fresh Ice Glass-FIRS
Fresh Ice Glass Patches-FIPRS
Premieres Auto Patches-AIPRS
05Upper Deck MVP-417
Gold-417
Platinum-417
05Upper Deck Rookie Update-215
Inspirations Patch Rookies-215
05Upper Deck Trilogy-197
05Upper Deck Victory-287
Black-287
Gold-287
Silver-287
05ITG Heroes and Prospects-101
Autographs-A-RSU
06Be A Player Portraits First Exposures-FERS
06Be A Player Portraits Signature Portraits-SPSR
06Fleer Signing Day-SDRS
06O-Pee-Chee-280
06O-Pee-Chee-630
Rainbow-280
Rainbow-630
06Ultra Fresh Ink-ISU
06Upper Deck-112
Exclusives Parallel-112
High Gloss Parallel-112
Masterpieces-112

Sutherby, Brian

00SPx Rookie Redemption-RR30
01Atomic-125
Premiere Date-125
01Atomic Toronto Fall Expo-125
01BAP Memorabilia-307
Emerald-307
Ruby-307
Sapphire-307
01BAP Signature Series-223
Autographs-223
Autographs Gold-223
01Bowman YoungStars-123
Gold-123
Ice Cubed-123
01Crown Royale-180
01O-Pee-Chee-345
01Pacific Adrenaline-225
Blue-225
Premiere Date-225
Red-225
Retail-225
Rookie Report-20
01Pacific Heads-Up-120
01Parkhurst-262
01Parkhurst Beckett Promos-262
01Private Stock-140
Gold-140
Premiere Date-140
Retail-140
Silver-140
01Private Stock Pacific Nights-140
01Private Stock PS-2002-92
01SP Game Used-100
01SPx-132
01Stadium Club-138
Award Winners-138
Master Photos-138
01Titanium-184
Retail-184
01Titanium Draft Day Edition-172
01Topps-345
01Topps Chrome-163
Refractors-163
Black Border Refractors-163
01Topps Heritage-140
01Topps Reserve-103
01UD Challenge for the Cup-134
01UD Mask Collection-170
Gold-170
01UD Playmakers-145
01UD Premier Collection-108
01UD Top Shelf-76
01Upper Deck-231
Exclusives-231
01Upper Deck Ice-72
01Upper Deck MVP-232
01Upper Deck Victory-452
01Upper Deck Vintage-300
01Vanguard-130
Blue-130
Red-130
One of Ones-130
Premiere Date-130
Proofs-130
01Moose Jaw Warriors-10
02BAP Sig Series Auto Buybacks 2001-223
02Bowman YoungStars-130
Gold-130
Silver-130
Autographs-BS
Jerseys-BS
Patches-BS
Double Stuff-BS
Triple Stuff-BS
MVP Puck Relic-1
Rivals-TABS
Rivals Patches-4
Sticks-BS
02O-Pee-Chee-291
02O-Pee-Chee Premier Blue Parallel-291
02O-Pee-Chee Premier Red Parallel-291
02O-Pee-Chee Factory Set-291
02Pacific Calder-100
Silver-100
02Pacific Complete-559
Red-559
02Topps-291
OPC Blue Parallel-291
OPC Red Parallel-291
Factory Set-291
02Upper Deck-424
Exclusives-424
02Upper Deck Beckett UD Promos-424
02Upper Deck Victory-217
Bronze-217
Gold-217
Silver-217
03Bowman-24
Gold-24
Future Fabrics-FF-BS
Future Fabric Patches-BS
Future Rivals-RS
Future Rivals Patches-RS
03Bowman Chrome-24
Refractors-24
Gold Refractors-24
Xfractors-24
03ITG Action-514
03O-Pee-Chee-17
03OPC Blue-17
03OPC Gold-17
03OPC Red-17
03Pacific Complete-380
Red-380
03Topps-17
Blue-17
Gold-17
Red-17
04Portland Pirates-2
05Panini Stickers-177
05Parkhurst-491
Facsimile Auto Parallel-491
05ITG Heroes and Prospects Complete Logos-AHL-5
05ITG Heroes and Prospects Jerseys-GUJ-2
05ITG Heroes and Prospects Jerseys Gold-GUJ-02
05ITG Heroes and Prospects Emblems-GUE-2
05ITG Heroes and Prospects Emblems Gold-GUE-02
05ITG Heroes and Prospects Numbers-GUN-2
05ITG Heroes and Prospects Numbers Gold-GUN-02
05ITG Heroes and Prospects Making the Big-MTB-4
06O-Pee-Chee-496
Rainbow-496
06Panini Stickers-179
06Upper Deck MVP-290
Gold Script-290
Super Script-290

Sutherland, Bill

60Cleveland Barons-17
62Quebec Aces-21
64Quebec Aces-17
65Quebec Aces-19
68Maple Leafs White Border-11
68O-Pee-Chee-196
69O-Pee-Chee-172
70O-Pee-Chee-83
70Topps-83
71O-Pee-Chee-141
71Sargent Promotions Stamps-188
71Toronto Sun-250
79Jets Postcards-26
81Jets Postcards-21
82Jets Postcards-25
84Jets Police-23
85Jets Police-23
86Jets Postcards-3
88Jets Police-23
89ProCards AHL-75

Sutherland, Capt.J.T.

83Hall of Fame-44
83Hall of Fame Postcards-C15
85Hall of Fame-44

Sutherland, Jeff

92Quebec Pee-Wee Tournament-1607
93Quebec Pee-Wee Tournament-520

Sutherland, Robbie

99Halifax Mooseheads-14
00Halifax Mooseheads-22
01Halifax Mooseheads-14

Sutherland, Steve

72Los Angeles Sharks WHA-14
76Nordiques Marie Antoinette-13
76Nordiques Postcards-17
76O-Pee-Chee WHA-127

Sutherlin, Taylor

03Portland Winter Hawks-3

Sutinen, Timo

71Finnish Suomi Stickers-108
72Finnish Jaakiekko-152
73Finnish Jaakiekko-79
73Finnish Jaakiekko-121
74Finnish Jenkki-19
74Finnish Typotor-16
74Finnish Typotor-56
74Swedish Stickers-102
74Swedish Semic World Champ Stickers-91
96German DEL-134

Sutter, Brandon

05ITG Heroes/Prosp Toronto Expo Parallel -314
05Red Deer Rebels-18
05ITG Heroes and Prospects-314
Autographs Series II-BSU
06ITG Heroes and Prospects-118
06ITG Heroes and Prospects-142
Autographs-ABS1
Autographs-ABS2
Quad Emblems-QE02
Quad Emblems Gold-QE02

Sutter, Brent

82O-Pee-Chee-216
82O-Pee-Chee Stickers-56
82Topps Stickers-56
83Islanders Team Issue-15
83NHL Key Tags-79
83O-Pee-Chee-18
84Islanders News-12
84O-Pee-Chee-136
84O-Pee-Chee Stickers-88
84Topps-102
84Kelowna Wings-29
85Islanders News-13
85O-Pee-Chee-107
85O-Pee-Chee Stickers-71
85O-Pee-Chee Stickers-117
85Topps-107
86Islanders Team Issue-7
86O-Pee-Chee-117
86O-Pee-Chee Stickers-211
86Topps-117
87O-Pee-Chee-27
87O-Pee-Chee Stickers-241
87Panini Stickers-99
87Topps-27
88O-Pee-Chee-7
88O-Pee-Chee Stickers-105
88Panini Stickers-292
88Topps-7
89Islanders Team Issue-17
89O-Pee-Chee-14
89O-Pee-Chee Stickers-115
89Panini Stickers-266
89Topps-14
90Bowman-126
Tiffany-126
90Kraft-57
90O-Pee-Chee-258
90OPC Premier-115
90Panini Stickers-90
90Pro Set-191
90Score-39
Canadian-39
90Score Hottest/Rising Stars-19
90Topps-258
Tiffany-258
90Upper Deck-249
French-249
91Pro Set Platinum-74
91Pro Set Platinum-164
91Blackhawks Coke-25
91Bowman-226
91Kraft-43
91O-Pee-Chee-165
91OPC Premier-156
91Panini Stickers-246
91Parkhurst-35
91Parkhurst-460
French-35
91Pinnacle-79
French-79
91Pro Set-154
91Pro Set-374
French-154
French-374
91Score American-243
91Score Canadian Bilingual-463
91Score Canadian English-463
91Score Rookie/Traded-103T
91Stadium Club-180
91Topps-165
91Upper Deck-140
91Upper Deck-645
French-140
French-645
92Blackhawks Coke-5
92Bowman-147
92O-Pee-Chee-60
92Parkhurst-33
Emerald Ice-33
Cherry Picks-CP3
92Pinnacle-39
French-39
92Pro Set-36
92Score-112
Canadian-112
92Stadium Club-428
92Topps-75
Gold-75G
92Ultra-43
92Upper Deck-199
92Finnish Semic-92
93Blackhawks Coke-11
93Donruss-69
93Leaf-142
93OPC Premier-147
Gold-147
93Panini Stickers-151
93Parkhurst-308
Emerald Ice-308
93Pinnacle-91
Canadian-91
93PowerPlay-56
93Score-44
Canadian-44
93Stadium Club-211
Members Only Master Set-211
OPC-211
First Day Issue-211
First Day Issue OPC-211
93Topps/OPC Premier-147
Gold-147
93Ultra-206
94Blackhawks Coke-20
94Canada Games NHL POGS-72
94Donruss-290
94Leaf-30
94Pinnacle-117
Artist's Proofs-117
Rink Collection-117
94Score-32
Gold-32
Platinum-32
94Stadium Club-218
Members Only Master Set-218
First Day Issue-218
Super Team Winner Cards-218
94Ultra-47
94Finnish Jaa Kiekko-91
95Be A Player-140
Signatures-S140
Signatures Die Cuts-S140
95Blackhawks Coke-18
95Score-272
Black Ice Artist's Proofs-272
Black Ice-272
97Pacific-186
Copper-186
Emerald Green-186
Ice Blue-186
Red-186
Silver-186
00Upper Deck Vintage Dynasty: A Piece of History-NS
00Upper Deck Vintage Dynasty: A Piece of History Gold-NS
01Fleer Legacy-54
Ultimate-54
01Upper Deck Legends Milestones-MBS
01Upper Deck Legends Milestones Platinum-MBS
03Blackhawks Postcards-26
03Red Deer Rebels-23
06Parkhurst-125
06Parkhurst-192
Autographs-125
Autographs-192
Autographs Dual-DALS
Autographs Dual-DASU2
06SP Authentic Sign of the Times Triples-ST3SUT1
06The Cup Signature Patches-SPSU
06Upper Deck Sweet Shot Signature Shots/Saves Sticks-SSSBR

Sutter, Brett

03Kootenay Ice-22
04Kootenay Ice-21
05ITG Heroes/Prosp Toronto Expo Parallel -158
05Red Deer Rebels-19
05ITG Heroes and Prospects-158
Autographs-A-BS
Jerseys-GUJ-70
Jerseys Gold-GUJ-70
Emblems-GUE-70
Emblems Gold-GUE-70
Numbers-GUN-70
Numbers Gold-GUN-70
Nameplates-N-48
Nameplates Gold-N-48
06ITG Heroes and Prospects-123
Autographs-ABRS

Sutter, Brian

78Blues Postcards-23
78O-Pee-Chee-319
79O-Pee-Chee-84
79Topps-84
80O-Pee-Chee-244
80Topps-244
81O-Pee-Chee-297
81O-Pee-Chee Stickers-133
81Topps-W122
82O-Pee-Chee-298
82O-Pee-Chee-311
82O-Pee-Chee Stickers-198
82Post Cereal-17
82Topps Stickers-198
83O-Pee-Chee-308
83O-Pee-Chee-320
83O-Pee-Chee Stickers-127
83O-Pee-Chee Stickers-128
83Puffy Stickers-17
83Topps Stickers-127
83Topps Stickers-128
84O-Pee-Chee-192
84O-Pee-Chee Stickers-56
84Topps-135
85O-Pee-Chee-135
85O-Pee-Chee Box Bottoms-N
85O-Pee-Chee Stickers-46
857-Eleven Credit Cards-17
85Topps-135
85Topps Box Bottoms-N
86O-Pee-Chee-72
86O-Pee-Chee Box Bottoms-O
86O-Pee-Chee Stickers-175
86Topps-72
86Topps Box Bottoms-O
87Blues Kodak-24
87Blues Team Issue-22
88Blues Team Issue-22
88O-Pee-Chee Stickers-15
88Panini Stickers-111
89Blues Kodak-NNO
90Blues Kodak-22
90Pro Set-676
91Score American-378
91Score Canadian Bilingual-268
91Score Canadian English-268
91Upper Deck-645
French-645
92Blues UD Best of the Blues-25
97Flames Collector's Photos-7
01Greats of the Game-69
Autographs-69
02Blackhawks Postcards-4
04ITG Franchises Update-491
04UD Legendary Signatures-14
Autographs-BR
Linemates-BRBFWB
06Parkhurst-130
06Parkhurst-206
Autographs-130
Autographs-206
Autographs Dual-DASU2
06SP Authentic Sign of the Times Triples-ST3SUT2
06Upper Deck Sweet Shot Signature Shots/Saves Sticks-SSSSU

Sutter, Darryl

80Blackhawks Postcards-15
80Blackhawks White Border-13
81Blackhawks Borderless Postcards-26
81Blackhawks Brown Background-16
81O-Pee-Chee-65
81Topps-W77
82Blackhawks Postcards-21
82O-Pee-Chee-76
83Blackhawks Postcards-22
83NHL Key Tags-27
83O-Pee-Chee-113
83O-Pee-Chee Stickers-105
83Topps Stickers-105
84O-Pee-Chee-47
84O-Pee-Chee Stickers-30
84Topps-36
85Blackhawks Team Issue-11
85O-Pee-Chee-100
85Topps-100
86Blackhawks Coke-21
86O-Pee-Chee-49
86O-Pee-Chee Stickers-151
86Topps-49
87Blackhawks Coke-22
87Panini Stickers-234
88ProCards IHL-116
89ProCards IHL-58
90Blackhawks Coke-26
91Blackhawks Coke-26
91Upper Deck-645
French-645
92Blackhawks Coke-15
93Blackhawks Coke-27
06Parkhurst-127
06Parkhurst-171
Autographs-127
Autographs-171
Autographs Dual-DASU1
06SP Authentic Sign of the Times Triples-ST3SUT1

Sutter, Doug

94Wheeling Thunderbirds-20

Sutter, Duane

81O-Pee-Chee-211
82O-Pee-Chee-212
82O-Pee-Chee Stickers-52
82Topps Stickers-52
83Islanders Team Issue-16
83O-Pee-Chee-19
84Islanders News-13
84O-Pee-Chee-137
84Kelowna Wings-48
85Islanders News-14
85O-Pee-Chee-227
85O-Pee-Chee Stickers-72
86Islanders Team Issue-13
86O-Pee-Chee-39
86O-Pee-Chee Stickers-210
86Topps-39
87Blackhawks Coke-23
87O-Pee-Chee-43
87Panini Stickers-102
87Topps-43
88Blackhawks Coke-19
89Blackhawks Coke-7
89O-Pee-Chee-221
90Bowman-12
Tiffany-12
90O-Pee-Chee-466
90Pro Set-61A
90Pro Set-61B
91Upper Deck-645
French-645
93Indianapolis Ice-23
94Indianapolis Ice-24
00Panthers Team Issue-3
06Parkhurst-126
Autographs-126
Autographs Dual-DASU1
06SP Authentic Sign of the Times Triples-ST3SUT1

Sutter, Fabian

01Swiss HNL-96
02Swiss HNL-31
04Swiss Davos Postcards-26

Sutter, Jock

06Moose Jaw Warriors-1

Sutter, Patrick

93Swiss HNL-94
95Swiss HNL-143
96Swiss HNL-62
98Swiss Power Play Stickers-211
98Swiss Power Play Stickers-270
99Swiss Panini Stickers-212
99Swiss Panini Stickers-262
00Swiss Panini Stickers-254
00Swiss Panini Stickers National Team-P10
00Swiss Slapshot Mini-Cards-EVZ7
01Swiss HNL-32
02Swiss HNL-79
02Swiss HNL-240

Sutter, Rich

83Flyers J.C. Penney-21
83Penguins Heinz Photos-22
84O-Pee-Chee-169
84O-Pee-Chee Stickers-111
84Kelowna Wings-24
85Flyers Postcards-27
85O-Pee-Chee-208
86Canucks Team Issue-21
86O-Pee-Chee-29
86O-Pee-Chee Stickers-242
86Topps-29
87Canucks Shell Oil-21
87O-Pee-Chee-258
87O-Pee-Chee Stickers-193
87Panini Stickers-350
88Canucks Mohawk-22
88O-Pee-Chee-255
88O-Pee-Chee Stickers-57
88Panini Stickers-142
89Canucks Mohawk-22
89O-Pee-Chee-282
89O-Pee-Chee Stickers-62
89Panini Stickers-157
90Blues Kodak-23
90O-Pee-Chee-405
90Pro Set-272
90Score-281
Canadian-281
90Upper Deck-328
French-328
91Pro Set Platinum-108
91Blues Postcards-19
91Bowman-370
91O-Pee-Chee-143
91Panini Stickers-33
91Parkhurst-372
French-372
91Pinnacle-268
French-268
91Pro Set-217
French-217
91Score American-63
91Score American-378
91Score Canadian Bilingual-63
91Score Canadian Bilingual-268
91Score Canadian English-63
91Score Canadian English-268
91Stadium Club-192
91Topps-143
91Upper Deck-317
91Upper Deck-645
French-317
French-645
92Bowman-256
92Panini Stickers-19
92Panini Stickers French-19
92Score-327
Canadian-327
92Stadium Club-389
92Stadium Club-488
92Topps-434
Gold-434G
92Ultra-398
92Upper Deck-143
93Blackhawks Coke-3
93Panini Stickers-160
93Pinnacle-108
Canadian-108
93PowerPlay-317
93Score-323
93Score-498
Gold-498
Canadian-323
Canadian-498
Canadian Gold-498
93Stadium Club-46
Members Only Master Set-46
OPC-46
First Day Issue-46
First Day Issue OPC-46
93Ultra-293
94Maple Leafs Kodak-26
94Maple Leafs Pin-up Posters-26
94Pinnacle-235
Artist's Proofs-235
Rink Collection-235
06SP Authentic Sign of the Times Triples-ST3SUT2

Sutter, Ron

83Flyers J.C. Penney-22
84O-Pee-Chee-170
84O-Pee-Chee Stickers-107
84Topps-122
84Kelowna Wings-40
85Flyers Postcards-28
85O-Pee-Chee-6
85Topps-6
86Flyers Postcards-26
86O-Pee-Chee-109
86O-Pee-Chee Stickers-243
86Topps-109
87Flyers Postcards-16
87O-Pee-Chee-113
87O-Pee-Chee Stickers-102
87Panini Stickers-137
87Topps-113
88Flyers Postcards-11
88O-Pee-Chee-126
88Topps-126
89Flyers Postcards-25
89O-Pee-Chee-173
89O-Pee-Chee Stickers-107
89Panini Stickers-299
89Topps-173
90Flyers Postcards-23
90O-Pee-Chee-45
90Panini Stickers-109
90Pro Set-224
90Score-153
Canadian-153
90Topps-45
Tiffany-45
90Upper Deck-68
French-68
91Pro Set Platinum-222
91Blues Postcards-20
91Bowman-238
91O-Pee-Chee-232
91OPC Premier-95
91Panini Stickers-233
91Parkhurst-158
French-158
91Pinnacle-95
French-95
91Pro Set-178
91Pro Set-476
French-178
French-476
91Score American-298
91Score American-378
91Score Canadian Bilingual-268
91Score Canadian Bilingual-619
91Score Canadian English-268
91Score Canadian English-619
91Score Rookie/Traded-69T
91Stadium Club-49
91Topps-232
91Upper Deck-309
91Upper Deck-645
French-309
French-645
92Bowman-175
92O-Pee-Chee-362
92Panini Stickers-20
92Panini Stickers French-20
92Parkhurst-389
Emerald Ice-389
92Pro Set-162
92Score-86
Canadian-86
92Stadium Club-36
92Stadium Club-488
92Topps-371
Gold-371G
92Ultra-190
92Upper Deck-184
93Donruss-288
93Donruss-482
93Leaf-275
93OPC Premier-103
Gold-103
93Panini Stickers-161
93Pinnacle-95
Canadian-95
93Score-39
Canadian-39
93Stadium Club-86
Members Only Master Set-86
OPC-86
First Day Issue-86
First Day Issue OPC-86
93Topps/OPC Premier-103
Gold-103
93Upper Deck-33
94Leaf-351
94OPC Premier-428
Special Effects-428
94Parkhurst-192
Gold-192
94Pinnacle-383
Artist's Proofs-383
Rink Collection-383
94Score-177
Gold-177
Platinum-177
94Topps/OPC Premier-428
Special Effects-428
95Score-113
Black Ice Artist's Proofs-113
Black Ice-113
97Be A Player-106
Autographs-106
Autographs Die-Cuts-106
Autographs Prismatic Die-Cuts-106
97Pacific Invincible NHL Regime-181
99BAP Millennium-208
Emerald-208
Ruby-208
Sapphire-208
Signatures-208
Signatures Gold-208
99Paramount-211
Copper-211
Emerald-211
Gold-211
Holographic Emerald-211
Holographic Gold-211
Holographic Silver-211
Ice Blue-211
Premiere Date-211
Red-211
Silver-211
01O-Pee-Chee-249
01O-Pee-Chee Premier Parallel-249
01Topps-249
OPC Parallel-249
02BAP Sig Series Auto Buybacks 1999-208
06Parkhurst-129
06Parkhurst-201
06SP Authentic Sign of the Times Triples-ST3SUT2

Sutter, Shaun

93Quebec Pee-Wee Tournament-836
97Lethbridge Hurricanes-18
99Medicine Hat Tigers-17
00Calgary Hitmen-23
03Florence Pride-158
04Fresno Falcons-18
05UK Nottingham Panthers-7

Sutton, Allen

04UK Milton Keynes Lightning-14

Sutton, Andy

98Be A Player-268
Press Release-268
98BAP Gold-268
98BAP Autographs-268
98BAP Autographs Gold-268
99Upper Deck MVP-181
Gold Script-181
Silver Script-181
Super Script-181
00Upper Deck-89
Exclusives Tier 1-89
Exclusives Tier 2-89
01O-Pee-Chee-116
01O-Pee-Chee Premier Parallel-116
01Topps-116
OPC Parallel-116
01Upper Deck Victory-181
Gold-181
02BAP Sig Series Auto Buybacks 1998-268
02Pacific Complete-276
Red-276
02Thrashers Postcards-16
03Pacific Complete-24
Red-24
03Thrashers Postcards-20
03Upper Deck MVP-23
Gold Script-23
Silver Script-23
Canadian Exclusives-23
05Parkhurst-28
Facsimile Auto Parallel-28
05Upper Deck-11
HG Glossy-11
05Upper Deck MVP-17
Gold-17
Platinum-17
05Upper Deck Toronto Fall Expo-11
06O-Pee-Chee-18
Rainbow-18
06Panini Stickers-12
06Thrashers Postcards-2
06Upper Deck-263
Exclusives Parallel-263
High Gloss Parallel-263
Masterpieces-263

Sutton, Blake

91Air Canada SJHL-E29

Sutton, Boyd

91Greensboro Monarchs-13
92Oklahoma City Blazers-17
93Phoenix Cobras RHI-18

Sutton, Dave

91Rayside-Balfour Jr. Canadians-17

Sutton, Ken

88Saskatoon Blades-7
89ProCards AHL-260
90ProCards AHL/IHL-271
91Parkhurst-239
French-239
91Pinnacle-325
French-325
91Sabres Blue Shield-21
91Sabres Pepsi/Campbell's-21
91Score American-393
91Score Canadian Bilingual-283
91Score Canadian English-283
91Upper Deck-458
French-458
92Bowman-422
92O-Pee-Chee-165
92Parkhurst-254
Emerald Ice-254
92Pinnacle-216
French-216
92Sabres Blue Shield-22
92Sabres Jubilee Foods-10
92Score-292
Canadian-292
92Stadium Club-292
92Topps-59
Gold-59G
92Ultra-20
93Leaf-295
93OPC Premier-89
Gold-89
93Pinnacle-336
Canadian-336
93Score-410
Canadian-410
93Stadium Club-219
Members Only Master Set-219
OPC-219
First Day Issue-219
First Day Issue OPC-219
93Topps/OPC Premier-89
Gold-89
94Leaf-498
94Pinnacle-437
Artist's Proofs-437
Rink Collection-437
97Devils Team Issue-5
97Albany River Rats-17
98Albany River Rats-17
99Albany River Rats-23
00Devils Team Issue-21
00Upper Deck Vintage-219
01Topps Heritage-186
02Albany River Rats-14
02Albany River Rats AAP-24
03German DEL-87
04German DEL-96
04German Ingolstadt Panthers-23
05German DEL-155

Sutton, Pat

02Owen Sound Attack-3
03Owen Sound Attack-4
04Belleville Bulls-18
06Port Huron Flags-3

Sutton, Scott

89Rayside-Balfour Jr. Canadians-20
91Rayside-Balfour Jr. Canadians-18

Sutyla, Ken

67Columbus Checkers-13

Suur, Dmitrij

04Czech OFS-36

Suursoo, Toivo

98Swedish UD Choice-165
99Swedish Upper Deck-167
02Swedish Malmo Red Hawks-14
02Swedish SHL-236
Parallel-236
03Russian Hockey League-262
03Swedish Elite-97
Global Impact-GI9
Silver-97

Suutarinen, Harri
01Finnish Cardset-225
Suvanto, Esa
70Finnish Jaakiekko-342
Suvanto, Harri
92Finnish Jyvas-Hyva Stickers-124
93Finnish SISU-192
94Finnish SISU-100
95Finnish SISU-134
99Finnish Cardset-85
Suvanto, Mikko
99Danish Hockey League-14
03Finnish Cardset-54
04Finnish Cardset-236
Suwek, Richard
79Rochester Americans-20
Suzor, Mark
77Rockies Coke Cans-18
78O-Pee-Chee-307
78Saginaw Gears-18
Suzuki, Takahito
02Charlotte Checkers-92
02ECHL All-Star Northern-36
Svacina, Vladimir
04Mississauga Ice Dogs-12
05Mississauga Ice Dogs-2
Svagrovsky, David
04Colorado Eagles-18
Svanberg, Bo
86Swedish Panini Stickers-105
87Swedish Panini Stickers-102
90Swedish Semic Elitserien Stickers-145
91Swedish Semic Elitserien Stickers-197
92Swedish Semic Elitserien Stickers-213
93Swedish Semic Elitserien-184
94Swedish Leaf-79
95Swedish Leaf-95
95Swedish Upper Deck-145
Svanberg, Ola
05Swedish SHL Elitset-55
Gold-55
Series One Signatures-8
Star Potential-8
06Swedish SHL Elitset-56
Svangstu, Lee
96Medicine Hat Tigers-21
97Idaho Steelheads-10
00Asheville Smoke-13
Svard, Bertil
56Swedish Alfabilder-72
Svard, Sven
56Swedish Alfabilder-69
Svarny, Ivan
02Belleville Bulls-18
03Belleville Bulls-14
04New Mexico Scorpions-15
Svartvadet, Per
93Swedish Semic Elitserien-210
94Parkhurst SE-SE235
Gold-SE235
94Swedish Leaf-245
95Swedish Leaf-107
95Swedish Upper Deck-166
97Swedish Collector's Choice-162
97Swedish Collector's Choice-204
97Swedish Collector's Choice-215
98Swedish UD Choice-176
99BAP Memorabilia-334
Gold-334
Silver-334
99BAP Millennium Calder Candidates Ruby-C45
99BAP Millennium Calder Candidate Emerald-C45
99BAP Millennium Calder Cand Sapphire-C45
99O-Pee-Chee Chrome-295
99O-Pee-Chee Chrome Refractors-295
99Pacific Dynagon Ice-19
Blue-19
Copper-19
Gold-19
Premiere Date-19
99Panini Stickers-16
99Topps/OPC Chrome-295
Refractors-295
99Topps Premier Plus-123
Parallel-123
99Upper Deck-177
Exclusives-177
Exclusives 1 of 1-177
99Upper Deck Gold Reserve-177
00Pacific-24
Copper-24
Gold-24
Ice Blue-24
Premiere Date-24
00Upper Deck-238
Exclusives Tier 1-238
Exclusives Tier 2-238
02Pacific Complete-367
Red-367
02Thrashers Postcards-16
03Swedish Elite-255
Hot Numbers-HN12
Silver-255
04Swedish Elitset-250
Gold-250
Signatures-7
04Swedish MoDo Postcards-7
04Swedish Pure Skills-71
Jerseys-PS
Parallel-71
05Swedish SHL Elitset-104
Gold-104
Series One Jerseys-2
Teammates-7
Teammates-9
06Swedish SHL Elitset-114
Performers-13
Svatos, Marek
00Kootenay Ice-21
02SPx Rookie Redemption-R196
02Hershey Bears-21
03Avalanche Team Issue-18
03BAP Memorabilia-190
Emerald-190
Gold-190
Ruby-190
Sapphire-190
03Black Diamond-157
Black-157
Green-157
Red-157
03Bowman-115
Gold-115
Premier Performance-PP-MS
Premier Performance Patches-PP-MS
03Bowman Chrome-115
Refractors-115
Gold Refractors-115
Xfractors-115
03ITG Action-652
03ITG Used Signature Series-191
Gold-191
03ITG VIP Rookie Debut-31
03Parkhurst Rookie-150
Rookie Emblems-RE-18
Rookie Emblems Gold-RE-18
Rookie Jerseys-RJ-18
Rookie Jerseys Gold-RJ-18
Rookie Numbers-RN-18
Rookie Numbers Gold-RN-18
Teammates Gold-RT12
Teammates-RT12
03SP Authentic-104
Limited-104
03SP Game Used-57
Gold-57
03SPx-199
Radiance-199
Spectrum-199
03Topps Pristine-131
03Topps Pristine-132
03Topps Pristine-133
Gold Refractor Die Cuts-131
Gold Refractor Die Cuts-132
Gold Refractor Die Cuts-133
Refractors-131
Refractors-132
Refractors-133
Press Plates Black-131
Press Plates Black-132
Press Plates Black-133
Press Plates Cyan-131
Press Plates Cyan-132
Press Plates Cyan-133
Press Plates Magenta-131
Press Plates Magenta-132
Press Plates Magenta-133
Press Plates Yellow-131
Press Plates Yellow-132
Press Plates Yellow-133
03Topps Traded-TT97
Blue-TT97
Gold-TT97
Red-TT97
03UD Honor Roll-140
03Upper Deck-213
Canadian Exclusives-213
HG-213
03Upper Deck Classic Portraits-186
03Upper Deck MVP-463
03Upper Deck Rookie Update-194
03Upper Deck Trilogy-147
Limited-147
04Pacific-278
Blue-278
Red-278
04Hershey Bears Patriot News-27
05ITG Heroes/Prosp Toronto Expo Parallel -85
05ITG Heroes/Prosp Toronto Expo Parallel -363
05Hot Prospects-24
En Fuego-24
Red Hot-24
White Hot-24
05ITG Ultimate Mem Future Star Autos-3
05ITG Ultimate Mem Future Star Autos Gold-3
05ITG Ultimate Mem Future Stars Jerseys-3
05ITG Ultimate Mem Fut Stars Jerseys Gold-3
05ITG Ultimate Mem Future Stars Mem Autos-3
05ITG Ultimate Mem Fut Star Mem Auto Gold-3
05ITG Ultimate Memorabilia Jersey Autos-39
05ITG Ultimate Mem Jersey Auto Gold-39
05ITG Ultimate Memorabilia R.O.Y. Autos-15
05ITG Ultimate Mem R.O.Y. Auto Gold-15
05ITG Ultimate Memorabilia R.O.Y. Emblems-14
05ITG Ultimate Mem R.O.Y. Emblems Gold-14
05ITG Ultimate Memorabilia R.O.Y. Jerseys-14
05ITG Ultimate Mem R.O.Y. Jerseys Gold-14
05ITG Ultimate Memorabilia R.O.Y. Numbers-14
05ITG Ultimate Mem R.O.Y. Numbers Gold-14
05ITG Ultimate Memorabilia Stick Autos-26
05ITG Ultimate Mem Stick Autos Gold-26
05ITG Ultimate Memorabilia Triple Autos-14
05ITG Ultimate Mem Triple Autos Gold-14
05Parkhurst-119
Facsimile Auto Parallel-119
True Colors-TCCOL
True Colors-TCCOL
05The Cup-32
Gold-32
Black Rainbow-32
Emblems of Endorsement-EESV
Honorable Numbers-HNMS
Masterpiece Pressplates-32
Noble Numbers-NNZS
Patch Variation-P32
Patch Variation Autographs-AP32
Scripted Numbers-SNZS
Scripted Numbers Dual-DSNCZ
Signature Patches-SPSV
05UD Rookie Class-4
05Ultimate Collection-21
Gold-21
National Heroes Jerseys-NHJSV
National Heroes Patches-NHPSV
Ultimate Signatures-USSV
Ultimate Signatures Trios-UTTHS
05Upper Deck-295
05Upper Deck Rookie Update-25
05ITG Heroes and Prospects-85
05ITG Heroes and Prospects-363
Autograph Memorabilia-GA-06
Autograph Memorabilia Gold-GA-06
Autographs-A-MSV
Autographs Series II-MSV2
He Shoots-He Scores Prizes-25
Jerseys-GUJ-100
Jerseys Gold-GUJ-100
Spectrum-STM-10
Spectrum Gold-STM-10
06Avalanche Team Postcards-17
06Be A Player Portraits-27
Dual Signature Portraits-DSHS
Signature Portraits-SPMS
Triple Signature Portraits-TCOL
06Beehive-78
Matte-78
Matted Materials-MMSV
Remarkable Matted Materials-MMSV
Signature Scrapbook-SSMS
06Black Diamond-97
Black-97
Gold-97
Ruby-97
Jerseys-JMS
Jerseys Black-JMS
Jerseys Gold-JMS
Jerseys Ruby-JMS
Jerseys Black Autographs -JMS
06Flair Showcase-30
06Flair Showcase-121
06Flair Showcase-222
Parallel-30
Parallel-121
Parallel-222
Inks-ISV
Stitches-SSMS
Wave of the Future-WF10
06Fleer-52
Tiffany-52
Hockey Headliners-HL25
06Hot Prospects-28
Red Hot-28
White Hot-28
Hotagraphs-HMS
06ITG Ultimate Memorabilia Jerseys Autos-56
06ITG Ultimate Memorabilia Jerseys Autos Gold-56
06ITG Ultimate Memorabilia Stick Rack-13
06ITG Ultimate Memorabilia Stick Rack Gold-13
06McDonald's Upper Deck Rookie Review-RR12
06O-Pee-Chee-130
06O-Pee-Chee-620
Rainbow-130
Rainbow-620
Autographs-A-MS
06Panini Stickers-223
06SP Authentic-78
Chirography-MS
Limited-78
Sign of the Times-STSV
Sign of the Times Duals-STHS
Sign of the Times Triples-ST3HTS
06SP Game Used-27
Gold-27
Rainbow-27
Authentic Fabrics Dual-AF2HS
Authentic Fabrics Dual Patches-AF2HS
Authentic Fabrics Fives-AF5GWG
Authentic Fabrics Fives-AP5RPT
Authentic Fabrics Fives Patches-AF5GWG
Authentic Fabrics Fives Patches-AP5RPT
Autographs-27
Inked Sweaters-ISSV
Inked Sweaters Patches-ISSV
Letter Marks-LMSV
SIGnificance-SSV
06SPx-23
Spectrum-23
SPxcitement-X25
SPxcitement Spectrum-X25
SPxcitement Autographs-X25
06The Cup Autographed NHL Shields Duals-DASCO
06The Cup Autographed NHL Shields Duals-DASHS
06The Cup Autographed NHL Shields Duals-DASSV
06The Cup Enshrinements-EMS
06The Cup Honorable Numbers-HNSV
06The Cup Limited Logos-LLMS
06The Cup Signature Patches-SPSV
06UD Artifacts-77
Blue-77
Gold-77
Platinum-77
Radiance-77
Autographed Radiance Parallel-77
Red-77
Auto-Facts-AFMS
Auto-Facts Gold-AFMS
Tundra Tandems-TTHS
Tundra Tandems Black-TTHS
Tundra Tandems Blue-TTHS
Tundra Tandems Gold-TTHS
Tundra Tandems Platinum-TTHS
Tundra Tandems Red-TTHS
Tundra Tandems Dual Patches Red-TTHS
06UD Mini Jersey Collection-25
06UD Powerplay-26
Impact Rainbow-26
06Ultimate Collection Signatures-US-MS
06Ultimate Collection Ultimate Signatures Logos-SL-MS
06Ultra-52
Gold Medallion-52
Ice Medallion-52
Action-UA6
Uniformity-UMS
Uniformity Patches-UPMS
06Upper Deck Arena Giveaways-COL5
06Upper Deck-299
Exclusives Parallel-299
High Gloss Parallel-299
Game Dated Moments-GD39
Game Jerseys-J2MS
Game Patches-P2MS
Generations Duals-G2HS
Generations Triples-G3HSS
Generations Patches Dual-G2PHS
Generations Patches Triple-G3PHSS
Masterpieces-299
Oversized Wal-Mart Exclusives-299
06Upper Deck MVP-73
Gold Script-73
Super Script-73
Jerseys-OJJM
Jerseys-OJSV
06Upper Deck Ovation-162
06Upper Deck Sweet Shot Signature Shots/Saves-SSSV
06Upper Deck Sweet Shot Signature Shots/Saves Ice Signings-SSIMS
06Upper Deck Sweet Shot Signature Shots/Saves Sticks-SSSMS
06Upper Deck Sweet Shot Signature Sticks-STSV
06Upper Deck Sweet Shot Sweet Stitches-SSMS
06Upper Deck Sweet Shot Sweet Stitches Duals-SSMS
06Upper Deck Sweet Shot Sweet Stitches Triples-SSMS
06Upper Deck Trilogy-27
Combo Clearcut Autographs-C2HS
Honorary Scripted Patches-HSPMS
Honorary Scripted Swatches-HSSMS
Honorary Swatches-HSMS
Ice Scripts-ISMS
Scripts-S2MS
06Upper Deck Victory-49
06Upper Deck Victory Black-49
06Upper Deck Victory Gold-49
06Upper Deck Victory GameBreakers-GB12
06Upper Deck Victory Next In Line-NL15
06ITG Heroes and Prospects Quad Emblems-QE09
06ITG Heroes and Prospects Quad Emblems Gold-QE09
06ITG Heroes and Prospects Sticks and Jerseys-SJ17
06ITG Heroes and Prospects Sticks and Jerseys Gold-SJ17
07Upper Deck Ovation-37
07Upper Deck Victory-157
Black-157
Gold-157
Svec, David
99Czech Score Blue 2000-127
99Czech Score Red Ice 2000-127
Svedberg, Hans
64Swedish Coralli ISHockey-13
64Swedish Coralli ISHockey-139
65Swedish Coralli ISHockey-13
65Swedish Coralli ISHockey-139
Svedberg, Johan
04Swedish Elitset-279
Gold-279
05Swedish SHL Elitset-132
Gold-132
Svedberg, Lennart
64Swedish Coralli ISHockey-21
64Swedish Coralli ISHockey-79
65Swedish Coralli ISHockey-21
65Swedish Coralli ISHockey-79
67Swedish Hockey-22
67Swedish Hockey-147
67Swedish Hockey-162
69Swedish Hockey-200
70Finnish Jaakiekko-39
70Swedish Hockey-118
70Swedish Hockey-147
70Swedish Hockey-153
70Swedish Hockey-281
70Swedish Masterserien-46
70Swedish Masterserien-50
70Swedish Masterserien-105
71Finnish Suomi Stickers-59
71Swedish Hockey-10
71Swedish Hockey-247
72Finnish Panda Toronto-78
72Finnish Semic World Championship-46
72Swedish Semic World Championship-46
81Swedish Semic Hockey VM Stickers-114
91Finnish Semic World Champ Stickers-232
91Swedish Semic World Champ Stickers-232
95Swedish Globe World Championships-66
98Swedish UD Choice-207
98Swedish UD Choice-210
Svedberg, Mathias
90Swedish Semic Elitserien Stickers-107
91Swedish Semic Elitserien Stickers-113
92Swedish Semic Elitserien Stickers-132
93Swedish Semic Elitserien-105
94Swedish Leaf-111
98Swedish UD Choice-3
99Swedish Upper Deck-3
02German DEL City Press-297
Svedman, Jan
69Swedish Hockey-235
Svee, David
02Swedish SHL-255
Parallel-255
Svehla, Robert
92Swedish Semic Elitserien Stickers-207
93Swedish Semic Elitserien-177
93Swedish Semic World Champ Stickers-102
94Swedish Leaf-43
Top Guns-6
95Be A Player-169
Signatures-S169
Signatures Die Cuts-S169
95Donruss-370
95Finest-183
Refractors-183
95Leaf-230
95Metal-194
95Parkhurst International-84
Emerald Ice-84
95Select Certified-115
Mirror Gold-115
95Stadium Club-216
Members Only Master Set-216
95Summit-196
Artist's Proofs-196
Ice-196
95Topps-257
OPC Inserts-257
95Ultra-358
High Speed-18
95Upper Deck-172
Electric Ice-172
Electric Ice Gold-172
95Zenith-148
95Slovakian APS National Team-13
96Collector's Choice-104
96Donruss-77
Press Proofs-77
96Flair-39
Blue Ice-39
96Fleer-43
96Fleer Picks-42
96Leaf-77
Press Proofs-77
96Metal Universe-63
96Pinnacle-38
Artist's Proofs-38
Foil-38
Premium Stock-38
Rink Collection-38
96Score-83
Artist's Proofs-83
Dealer's Choice Artist's Proofs-83
Special Artist's Proofs-83
Golden Blades-83
96SkyBox Impact-49
96SP-63
96Summit-52
Artist's Proofs-52
Ice-52
Metal-52
Premium Stock-52
96Team Out-56
96Ultra-69
Gold Medallion-69
96Upper Deck-67
96Swedish Semic Wien-221
97Collector's Choice-104
Star Quest-SQ2
97Pacific-243
Copper-243
Emerald Green-243
Ice Blue-243
Red-243
Silver-243
97Pacific Dynagon-56
Copper-56
Dark Grey-56
Emerald Green-56
Ice Blue-56
Red-56
Silver-56
Tandems-51
97Pacific Omega-101
Copper-101
Dark Gray-101
Emerald Green-101
Gold-101
Ice Blue-101
97Panini Stickers-55
97Pinnacle-141
Press Plates Back Black-141
Press Plates Back Cyan-141
Press Plates Back Magenta-141
Press Plates Back Yellow-141
Press Plates Front Black-141
Press Plates Front Cyan-141
Press Plates Front Magenta-141
Press Plates Front Yellow-141
97Pinnacle Inside-159
97Score-189
97Upper Deck-73
98Be A Player-59
Press Release-59
98BAP Gold-59
98BAP Autographs-59
98BAP Autographs Gold-59
98BAP Tampa Bay All Star Game-59
98Finest-77
No Protectors-77
No Protectors Refractors-77
Refractors-77
98Kraft Peanut Butter-2
98Pacific-228
Ice Blue-228
Red-228
98Panini Stickers-57
98Paramount-100
Copper-100
Emerald Green-100
Holo-Electric-100
Ice Blue-100
Silver-100
98SPx Finite-38
Radiance-38
Spectrum-38
98UD Choice-88
Prime Choice Reserve-88
Reserve-88
98Upper Deck-278
Exclusives-278
Exclusives 1 of 1-278
Gold Reserve-278
98Upper Deck MVP-88
Gold Script-88
Silver Script-88
Super Script-88
99BAP Memorabilia-8
Gold-8
Silver-8
99O-Pee-Chee-154
99O-Pee-Chee Chrome-154
99O-Pee-Chee Chrome Refractors-154
99Pacific-182
Copper-182
Emerald Green-182
Gold-182
Ice Blue-182
Premiere Date-182
Red-182
99Pacific Omega-101
Copper-101
Gold-101
Ice Blue-101
Premiere Date-101
99Panini Stickers-95
99Topps/OPC-154
99Topps/OPC Chrome-154
Refractors-154
99Upper Deck MVP Draw Your Own-W20
99Upper Deck Victory-128
99Slovakian Challengers-2
00BAP Memorabilia-208
Emerald-208
Ruby-208
Sapphire-208
Promos-208
00BAP Mem Chicago Sportsfest Copper-208
00BAP Memorabilia Chicago Sportsfest Blue-208
00BAP Memorabilia Chicago Sportsfest Gold-208
00BAP Memorabilia Chicago Sportsfest Ruby-208
00BAP Memorabilia Chicago Sun-Times Ruby-208
00BAP Memorabilia Chicago Sun-Times Gold-208
00BAP Mem Chicago Sun-Times Sapphire-208
00BAP Mem Toronto Fall Expo Copper-208
00BAP Memorabilia Toronto Fall Expo Gold-208
00BAP Memorabilia Toronto Fall Expo Ruby-208
00BAP Parkhurst 2000-P179
00O-Pee-Chee-47
00O-Pee-Chee Parallel-47
00Pacific-187
Copper-187
Gold-187
Ice Blue-187
Premiere Date-187
00Panini Stickers-36
00Panthers Team Issue-24
00Paramount-108
Copper-108
Gold-108
Holo-Gold-108
Holo-Silver-108
Ice Blue-108
Premiere Date-108
00Stadium Club-196
00Titanium Game Gear-99
00Titanium Game Gear Patches-99
00Titanium Draft Day Edition-47
Patches-47
00Topps/OPC-47
Parallel-47
00Topps Stars-62
Blue-62
00Upper Deck-306
Exclusives Tier 1-306
Exclusives Tier 2-306
00Upper Deck Vintage-157
01BAP Signature Series-158
Autographs-158
Autographs Gold-158
01Pacific-177
Extreme LTD-177
Hobby LTD-177
Premiere Date-177
Retail LTD-177
Adrenaline Jerseys-19
01Pacific Arena Exclusives-177
01Private Stock Game Gear-50
01Private Stock Game Gear Patches-50
01Upper Deck-78
Exclusives-78
01Upper Deck Victory-150
Gold-150
01Slovakian Kvarteto-8C
02BAP First Edition-290
02BAP First Edition-381
02BAP Memorabilia-244
Emerald-244
Ruby-244
Sapphire-244
NHL All-Star Game-244
NHL All-Star Game Blue-244
NHL All-Star Game Green-244
NHL All-Star Game Red-244
02BAP Memorabilia Toronto Fall Expo-244
02BAP Sig Series Auto Buybacks 1998-59
02BAP Sig Series Auto Buybacks 2001-158
02Maple Leafs Platinum Collection-19
02Maple Leafs Team Issue-12
02Pacific-160
Blue-160
Red-160
02Pacific Complete-83
Red-83
02Parkhurst Retro-184
Minis-184
02Upper Deck-409
Exclusives-409
02Upper Deck Beckett UD Promos-409
03ITG Action-573
03Pacific-325
Blue-325
Red-325
03Parkhurst Orig Six Toronto Mem-TM12
03Russian World Championship Stars-21
Svejkovsky, Jaroslav
95Bowman Draft Prospects-P32
95Tri-City Americans-25
96Flair-125
Blue Ice-125
96Portland Pirates-15
96Portland Pirates Shop N' Save-6
97Be A Player-242
Autographs-242
Autographs Die-Cuts-242
Autographs Prismatic Die-Cuts-242
97Collector's Choice-272
97Crown Royale-143
Emerald Green-143
Ice Blue-143
Silver-143
97Donruss-220
Press Proofs Silver-220
Press Proofs Gold-220
Rated Rookies-9
Medallist-9
97Donruss Canadian Ice-143
Dominion Series-143
Provincial Series-143
97Donruss Elite-22
97Donruss Elite-141
Aspirations-22
Aspirations-141
Status-22
Status-141
Craftsmen-5
Master Craftsmen-5
97Donruss Limited-33
97Donruss Limited-96
97Donruss Limited-143
Exposure-33
Exposure-96
Exposure-143
Fabric of the Game-32
97Donruss Preferred-146
97Donruss Preferred-167
Cut to the Chase-146
Cut to the Chase-167
Line of the Times-8B
97Donruss Preferred Line of Times Promos-8B
97Donruss Priority-167
97Donruss Priority-219
Stamp of Approval-167
Stamp of Approval-219
Direct Deposit-19
97Katch-155
Gold-155
Silver-155
97Leaf-67
97Leaf-167
Fractal Matrix-67
Fractal Matrix-167
Fractal Matrix Die Cuts-67
Fractal Matrix Die Cuts-167
97Leaf International-67
Universal Ice-67
97McDonald's Upper Deck-35
97Paramount-200
Copper-200
Dark Grey-200
Emerald Green-200
Ice Blue-200
Red-200
Silver-200
97Pinnacle-25
Artist's Proofs-25
Rink Collection-25
Press Plates Back Black-25
Press Plates Back Cyan-25
Press Plates Back Magenta-25
Press Plates Back Yellow-25
Press Plates Front Black-25
Press Plates Front Cyan-25
Press Plates Front Magenta-25
Press Plates Front Yellow-25
97Pinnacle Inside-125
97Pinnacle Mint-25
Bronze-25
Gold Team-25
Silver Team-25
Coins Brass-25
Coins Brass Proofs-25
Coins Gold Plated-25
Coins Gold Plated Proofs-25
Coins Nickel Silver-25
Coins Nickel Silver Proofs-25
Coins Solid Gold-25
Coins Solid Silver-25
97Score-53
Artist's Proofs-53
Golden Blades-53
97SP Authentic Sign of the Times-JS
97Studio-47
Press Proofs Silver-47
Press Proofs Gold-47
Portraits-32
97Upper Deck-195
Smooth Grooves-SG52
97Upper Deck Ice-40
Parallel-40
Power Shift-40
98Pacific-447
Ice Blue-447
Red-447
98Pacific Dynagon Ice-199
Blue-199
Red-199
98Upper Deck-384
Exclusives-384
Exclusives 1 of 1-384
Gold Reserve-384
98Upper Deck MVP-217
Gold Script-217
Silver Script-217
Super Script-217
99O-Pee-Chee-161
99O-Pee-Chee Chrome-161
99O-Pee-Chee Chrome Refractors-161
99Pacific-447
Copper-447
Emerald Green-447
Gold-447
Ice Blue-447
Premiere Date-447
Red-447
99SPx-157
Radiance-157
Spectrum-157
99Topps/OPC-161
99Topps/OPC Chrome-161
Refractors-161
99Upper Deck-130
Exclusives-130
Exclusives 1 of 1-130
99Upper Deck Gold Reserve-130
99Upper Deck MVP-213
Gold Script-213
Silver Script-213
Super Script-213
99Upper Deck Victory-307
00Panini Stickers-90
Svendsberget, Geir
92Norwegian Elite Series-170
92Norwegian Elite Series-210
99Norwegian National Team-2
Svensson, Anders
84Swedish Semic Elitserien-104
90Swedish Semic Elitserien Stickers-132
91Swedish Semic Elitserien Stickers-184
92Swedish Semic Elitserien Stickers-202
Svensson, Bjorn
03Saskatoon Blades-14
04Saskatoon Blades-22
05Moose Jaw Warriors-20
Svensson, Curt
69Swedish Hockey-181
Svensson, Fredrik
97Wheeling Nailers-15
97Wheeling Nailers Photo Pack-15
02Swedish SHL-221
Parallel-221
06Finnish Cardset-215
Svensson, Goran
65Swedish Coralli ISHockey-173
Svensson, Gunnar
56Swedish Alfabilder-118
84Swedish Semic Elitserien-98
85Swedish Panini Stickers-79
Svensson, Henry
64Swedish Coralli ISHockey-159
65Swedish Coralli ISHockey-159
67Swedish Hockey-75
69Swedish Hockey-107
71Swedish Hockey-360
Svensson, Jan-Olov
72Swedish Stickers-84
73Swedish Stickers-156
74Swedish Stickers-190
Svensson, Kjell
64Swedish Coralli ISHockey-61
65Swedish Coralli ISHockey-61
67Swedish Hockey-194
69Swedish Hockey-252
81Swedish Semic Hockey VM Stickers-110
Svensson, Kurt
64Swedish Coralli ISHockey-132
65Swedish Coralli ISHockey-132
Svensson, Lasse
55Swedish Alfabilder-35
Svensson, Leif
71Swedish Hockey-358
73Swedish Stickers-62
74Swedish Stickers-191
78Capitals Team Issue-16
79Capitals Team Issue-22
79O-Pee-Chee-374
Svensson, Magnus
83Swedish Semic Elitserien-131
84Swedish Semic Elitserien-153
85Swedish Panini Stickers-136
86Swedish Panini Stickers-140
87Swedish Panini Stickers-151
89Swedish Semic Elitserien Stickers-125
91Swedish Semic Elitserien Stickers-133
92Swedish Semic Elitserien Stickers-158
93Swedish Semic Elitserien-128
94Finnish Jaa Kiekko-58
94Swedish Leaf Gold Cards-13
95Donruss-251
95Emotion-71
95Leaf-10
95Panini Stickers-78
95Parkhurst International-83
Emerald Ice-83
95SkyBox Impact-69
95Finnish Semic World Championships-55
95Finnish Semic World Championships-203
95Swedish Upper Deck-243
95Swedish Globe World Championships-12
95Swedish World Championships Stickers-138
96Swedish Semic Wien-46
97Swedish Collector's Choice-97
97Swedish Collector's Choice-104
Crash the Game Exchange-C11
Crash the Game Redemption-R11
98Swedish UD Choice-123
99Swiss Panini Stickers-186
00Swedish Upper Deck-107
SHL Signatures-MS
04Swedish Alfabilder Alfa Stars-44
04Swedish Alfabilder Autographs-123
04Swedish Alfabilder Limited Autographs-123
04Swedish Alfabilder Proof Parallels-44
Svensson, Nils-Goran
85Swedish Panini Stickers-179
Svensson, Nils-Gunnar
86Swedish Panini Stickers-118
89Swedish Semic Elitserien Stickers-103
Svensson, Ove
69Swedish Hockey-108
70Swedish Hockey-60
71Swedish Hockey-131
73Swedish Stickers-224
Svensson, Pelle
92Swedish Semic Elitserien Stickers-265
93Swedish Semic Elitserien-235
95Swedish Upper Deck-182
96German DEL-40
98German DEL-173
99German DEL-327
04German Berlin Eisbarens 50th Anniv-8
Svensson, Per-Johan
94Swedish Leaf-57
95Swedish Leaf-120
Svensson, Stefan
83Swedish Semic Elitserien-127
84Swedish Semic Elitserien-150
86Swedish Panini Stickers-227
87Swedish Panini Stickers-217
Svensson, Tord
71Swedish Hockey-208
72Swedish Stickers-185
74Swedish Stickers-192
Sverztov, Alexander
91Upper Deck Czech World Juniors-8
Svetlik, Martin
907th Inn. Sketch WHL-101
99Czech Score Blue 2000-15
99Czech Score Red Ice 2000-15
Svetlov, Sergei
82Swedish Semic VM Stickers-69
87Russian National Team-19
94German First League-481
Svik, Jan
01Czech OFS-225
02Czech OFS Plus-269
03Czech OFS Plus-206
Svitov, Alexander
99Russian Hockey League-176
00Russian Hockey League-229
00Russian Hockey League-309
01BAP Memorabilia Draft Redemptions-3
01SPx Rookie Redemption-R27
01Russian Hockey League-98
01Russian Young Lions-2
02Atomic-124
Blue-124
Gold-124
Red-124
Hobby Parallel-124
02BAP All-Star Edition-136
Gold-136
Silver-136
02BAP First Edition-436H
02BAP Memorabilia-299
Emerald-299
Ruby-299
Sapphire-299
NHL All-Star Game-299
NHL All-Star Game Blue-299
NHL All-Star Game Green-299
NHL All-Star Game Red-299
02BAP Memorabilia Toronto Fall Expo-299
02BAP Ultimate Memorabilia-29
Autographs-26
Calder Candidates-18
02Bowman YoungStars-115
Gold-115
Silver-115
Autographs-AS
Jerseys-AS
Patches-AS
Double Stuff-AS
Triple Stuff-AS
Rivals-AFAS
Rivals Patches-12
Sticks-AS
02Crown Royale-137
Blue-137
Purple-137
Red-137
Retail-137
Rookie Royalty-20
02eTopps-48
02ITG Used-195
Calder Jerseys-C7
Calder Jerseys Gold-C7
02O-Pee-Chee-334
02O-Pee-Chee Premier Blue Parallel-334
02O-Pee-Chee Premier Red Parallel-334
02O-Pee-Chee Factory Set-334
02Pacific-410
02Pacific Calder-146
Silver-146
02Pacific Complete-563
Red-563
02Pacific Exclusive-200
Blue-200
Gold-200
02Pacific Heads-Up-144
02Pacific Quest for the Cup-147
Gold-147
02Parkhurst-229
Bronze-229
Gold-229
Silver-229
Hardware-C3
02Parkhurst Retro-229
Minis-229
02Private Stock Reserve-182
Blue-182
Red-182
Retail-182
Moments in Time-8
02SP Authentic-190
Signed Patches-PAS
02SP Game Used-93
02SPx-159
02Stadium Club-122
Silver Decoy Cards-122
Proofs-122
02Titanium-137
Blue-137
Red-137
Retail-137
02Topps-334
OPC Blue Parallel-334
OPC Red Parallel-334
Factory Set-334
02Topps Chrome-179
Black Border Refractors-179
Refractors-179
02Topps Heritage-136
02Topps Total-435
02UD Artistic Impressions-122
Gold-122
Common Ground-CG16
Common Ground Gold-CG16
Retrospectives-R100
Retrospectives Gold-R100
Retrospectives Signed-R100
Retrospectives Silver-R100
02UD Foundations-162
02UD Honor Roll-164
Signature Class-AS
02UD Mask Collection-163
02UD Piece of History-147
02UD Premier Collection-84
Gold-84
Jerseys Bronze-AS
Jerseys Gold-AS
Jerseys Silver-AS
Signatures Bronze-SSV
Signatures Gold-SSV
Signatures Silver-SSV
02UD Top Shelf-135
02Upper Deck-245
Exclusives-245
02Upper Deck Classic Portraits-128
02Upper Deck Rookie Update-149A
02Upper Deck Rookie Update-149B
02Upper Deck Rookie Update-149C
02Vanguard-134
LTD-134
03Black Diamond-59
Black-59
Green-59
Red-59
Signature Gems-SG-15
Threads-DT-AS
Threads Green-DT-AS
Threads Red-DT-AS
Threads Black-DT-AS
03Bowman-28

Gold-28
Future Fabrics-FF-AS
Future Fabric Patches-AS
03Bowman Chrome-28
Refractors-28
Gold Refractors-28
Xfractors-28
03ITG Action-521
Jerseys-M83
03Lightning Team Issue-19
03O-Pee-Chee-155
03OPC Blue-155
03OPC Gold-155
03OPC Red-155
03Pacific-313
Blue-313
Red-313
03Pacific Calder Collection NHL All-Star Block Party
Gold-10
03SPx Big Futures-BF-AS
03SPx Big Futures Limited-BF-AS
03Topps-155
Blue-155
Gold-155
Red-155
C55 Relics-TRAS
03Topps Traded-TT68
Blue-TT68
Gold-TT68
Red-TT68
03Upper Deck-175
Canadian Exclusives-175
HG-175
Shooting Stars-ST-AS
03Upper Deck All-Star Promos-AS10
03Upper Deck MVP-384
Gold Script-384
Silver Script-384
Canadian Exclusives-384
03Upper Deck Rookie Update Top Draws-TD19
03Upper Deck Victory-173
Bronze-173
Gold-173
Silver-173
04Upper Deck Jersey Autographs-GJA-AS
04AHL All-Stars-42
04AHL Top Prospects-54
04Syracuse Crunch-12
04ITG Heroes and Prospects-113
04ITG Heroes/Prospects Toronto Expo '05-113
04ITG Heroes/Prospects Expo Heroes/Pros-113
05ITG Heroes/Prosp Toronto Expo Parallel -106
05ITG Heroes and Prospects-106
Autographs-A-AS

Svoboda, Adam
97Czech APS Extraliga-245
98Czech DS Stickers-128
98Czech OFS-146
99Czech DS-72
99Czech OFS-548
00Czech DS Extraliga-86
Goalies-G8
00Czech OFS-32
00Czech OFS Star Emerald-11
00Czech OFS Star Pink-11
00Czech OFS Star Violet-11
01Czech OFS-228
01Czech OFS H Inserts-H13
02Czech DS-4
02Czech DS-82
02Czech OFS Plus-229
02Czech OFS Plus All-Star Game-H37
02Czech OFS Plus Checklists-C7
02Czech OFS Plus Masks-M16
02Czech OFS Plus Trios-T8
02Czech OFS Plus Duos-D10
03Czech OFS Plus-59
03Czech OFS Plus All-Star Game-H23
03Czech OFS Plus All-Star Game-H45
03Czech OFS Plus Checklists-3
03Czech OFS Plus Insert B-B3
03Czech OFS Plus Insert H-H17
03Czech OFS Plus Insert P-P4
03Czech OFS Plus MS Praha-SE9
03Czech Pardubice Postcards-15
04Czech OFS Czech/Slovak-17
04Czech OFS Czech/Slovak-45
04Czech OFS Goals-Against Leaders-2
04Czech OFS Save Percentage Leaders-7
04German DEL-258
04German Nuremburg Ice Tigers Postcards-17
05Czech Pexeso Mini Red Set-9
06Czech HC Pardubice Postcards-20
06Czech HC Slavia Praha Postcards-14
06Czech IIHF World Championship Postcards-21
06Czech LG Hockey Games Postcards-21

Svoboda, Dalimil
99Czech Score Blue 2000-13
99Czech Score Red Ice 2000-13

Svoboda, Jaroslav
98Kootenay Ice-12
00Black Diamond-69
Gold-69
00Upper Deck-204
Exclusives Tier 1-204
Exclusives Tier 2-204
00Upper Deck Ice-49
Immortals-49
Legends-49
Stars-49
00Upper Deck Victory-279
00Cincinnati Cyclones-19
01SPx Rookie Redemption-R6
02BAP Memorabilia-113
Emerald-113
Ruby-113
Sapphire-113
NHL All-Star Game-113
NHL All-Star Game Blue-113
NHL All-Star Game Green-113
NHL All-Star Game Red-113
02BAP Memorabilia Toronto Fall Expo-113
02BAP Signature Series Golf-GS40
02Bowman YoungStars-139
Gold-139
Silver-139
02Pacific Calder-62
Silver-62
02Pacific Complete-37
Red-37
02Pacific Exclusive-32
02SP Authentic-111
02SPx-105
02Stadium Club-114
Silver Decoy Cards-114
Proofs-114
02Upper Deck-31
Exclusives-31
02Upper Deck Vintage-325
02Czech Stadion Cup Finals-490
03Hurricanes Postcards-18
03ITG Action-168
03Upper Deck-278
Canadian Exclusives-278
HG-278
UD Exclusives-278
03Upper Deck MVP-85
Gold Script-85
Silver Script-85
Canadian Exclusives-85
05Upper Deck-61
HG Glossy-61
05Upper Deck MVP-134
Gold-134
Platinum-134
05Upper Deck Toronto Fall Expo-61
06Czech OFS-214
Jagr Team-22

Svoboda, Karel
86Sherbrooke Canadiens-25

Svoboda, Ladislav
95Czech APS Extraliga-146
96Czech APS Extraliga-87
97Czech APS Extraliga-208
97Czech DS Extraliga-94
97Czech DS Stickers-145
98Czech DS-98
98Czech DS Stickers-240
98Czech OFS-169
99Czech DS-162
99Czech OFS-173
00Czech DS Extraliga-139
00Czech OFS-120
01Czech OFS-168
All Stars-20
02Czech OFS Plus-293
02Czech OFS Plus All-Star Game-H38
03Czech OFS Plus-81
03Czech OFS Plus-343
03Czech OFS Plus Insert C-C2

Svoboda, Oldrich
92Finnish Semic-123
93Finnish Jyvas-Hyva Stickers-254
93Finnish SISU-280
94Finnish Jaa Kiekko-164
95Czech APS Extraliga-53
96Czech APS Extraliga-239
97Czech APS Extraliga-266
97Czech DS Extraliga-27
97Czech DS Stickers-75
98Czech DS-13
98Czech DS Stickers-67
98Czech OFS-410
99German DEL-341
00Czech DS Extraliga-97
Goalies-G9
00Czech OFS-187
00Czech OFS Star Emerald-33
00Czech OFS Star Pink-33
00Czech OFS Star Violet-33
01Czech OFS-110
All Stars-3
Gold Inserts-G7
02Czech OFS Plus-121
Duos-D12
03Czech OFS Plus-126
03Czech OFS Plus Checklists-6
03Czech OFS Plus MS Praha-SE26
04Czech OFS Goals-Against Leaders-13

Svoboda, Petr
84Canadiens Postcards-27
85Canadiens Placemats-3
85Canadiens Placemats-7
85Canadiens Postcards-37
85Canadiens Provigo-23
85O-Pee-Chee Stickers-139
86Canadiens Postcards-24
86Kraft Drawings-72
86O-Pee-Chee Stickers-17
86O-Pee-Chee Stickers-160
87Canadiens Postcards-31
87Canadiens Vachon Stickers-75
87Canadiens Vachon Stickers-77
87O-Pee-Chee Stickers-18
88Canadiens Postcards-28
88O-Pee-Chee-256
88O-Pee-Chee Minis-41
88O-Pee-Chee Stickers-44
88Panini Stickers-255
89Canadiens Kraft-23
89Canadiens Postcards-31
89Canadiens Provigo Figurines-25
89Kraft-27
89O-Pee-Chee-238
89O-Pee-Chee Stickers-54
89Panini Stickers-244
90Bowman-46
Tiffany-46
90Canadiens Postcards-30
90O-Pee-Chee-246
90Panini Stickers-50
90Pro Set-161
90Score-191
Canadian-191
90Topps-246
Tiffany-246 .
90Upper Deck-193
French-193
91Pro Set Platinum-65
91Bowman-341
91Canadiens Panini Team Stickers-23
91Canadiens Postcards-29
91O-Pee-Chee-76
91OPC Premier-168
91Panini Stickers-185
91Parkhurst-237
French-237
91Pinnacle-197
French-197
91Pro Set-123
French-123
91Score American-95
91Score Canadian Bilingual-95
91Score Canadian English-95
91Stadium Club-127
91Topps-76
91Upper Deck-285
French-285
92Bowman-47
92O-Pee-Chee-109
92Pinnacle-117
French-117
92Pro Set-16
92Sabres Blue Shield-23
92Sabres Jubilee Foods-14
92Score-114
Canadian-114
92Stadium Club-227
92Topps-312
Gold-312G
92Ultra-263
93Donruss-41
93Leaf-131
93OPC Premier-308
93OPC Premier-324
Gold-308
Gold-324
93Pinnacle-32
Canadian-32
93Score-110
Canadian-110
93Stadium Club-132
Members Only Master Set-132
OPC-132
First Day Issue-132
First Day Issue OPC-132
93Topps/OPC Premier-308
93Topps/OPC Premier-324
Gold-308
Gold-324
93Upper Deck-465
94EA Sports-14
94Leaf-393
94Parkhurst SE-SE21
Gold-SE21
94Pinnacle-424
Artist's Proofs-424
Rink Collection-424
94Czech APS Extraliga-205
95Canada Games NHL POGS-208
95Collector's Choice-93
Player's Club-93
Player's Club Platinum-93
95Donruss-306
95Leaf-180
95Parkhurst International-427
Emerald Ice-427
95Pinnacle-168
Artist's Proofs-168
Rink Collection-168
Global Gold-21
95Score-287
Black Ice Artist's Proofs-287
Black Ice-287
95Upper Deck-76
Electric Ice-76
Electric Ice Gold-76
96Be A Player-56
Autographs-56
Autographs Silver-56
96Flyers Postcards-22
96SP-111
97Pacific-277
Copper-277
Emerald Green-277
Ice Blue-277
Red-277
Silver-277
97Panini Stickers-97
97Score Flyers-17
Platinum-17
Premier-17
98Be A Player-104
Press Release-104
98BAP Gold-104
98BAP Autographs-104
98BAP Autographs Gold-104
98BAP Tampa Bay All Star Game-104
98Panini Stickers-89
98Czech OFS-54
98Czech OFS-231
Olympic Winners-10
98Czech Bonaparte-5D
98Czech Bonaparte-6A
98Czech Pexeso-19
98Czech Spaghetti-10
99O-Pee-Chee-208
99O-Pee-Chee Chrome-208
99O-Pee-Chee Chrome Refractors-208
99Pacific-397
Copper-397
Emerald Green-397
Gold-397
Ice Blue-397
Premiere Date-397
Red-397
99Panini Stickers-144
99Topps/OPC-208
99Topps/OPC Chrome-208
Refractors-208
99Upper Deck MVP SC Edition-172
Gold Script-172
Silver Script-172
Super Script-172
Great Combinations-GCLS
Great Combinations Parallel-GCLS
99Czech DS National Stars-NS8
00BAP Memorabilia-39
Emerald-39
Ruby-39
Sapphire-39
Promos-39
00BAP Mem Chicago Sportsfest Copper-39
00BAP Memorabilia Chicago Sportsfest Blue-39
00BAP Memorabilia Chicago Sportsfest Gold-39
00BAP Memorabilia Chicago Sportsfest Ruby-39
00BAP Memorabilia Chicago Sun-Times Ruby-39
00BAP Memorabilia Chicago Sun-Times Gold-39
00BAP Mem Chicago Sun-Times Sapphire-39
00BAP Mem Toronto Fall Expo Copper-39
00BAP Memorabilia Toronto Fall Expo Gold-39
00BAP Memorabilia Toronto Fall Expo Ruby-39
00O-Pee-Chee-162
00O-Pee-Chee Parallel-162
00Pacific-381
Copper-381
Gold-381
Ice Blue-381
Premiere Date-381
00Panini Stickers-93
00Paramount-224
Copper-224
Gold-224
Holo-Gold-224
Holo-Silver-224
Ice Blue-224
Premiere Date-224
00Revolution Game-Worn Jerseys-10
00Revolution Game-Worn Jersey Patches-10
00Topps/OPC-162
Parallel-162
00Topps Heritage Chrome Parallel-84
00Upper Deck MVP-164
First Stars-164
Second Stars-164
Third Stars-164
00Upper Deck Vintage-331
00Upper Deck Vintage-332
00Czech Stadion-76
01O-Pee-Chee Premier Parallel-292
01Titanium Double-Sided Jerseys-40
01Titanium Double-Sided Patches-40
01Topps OPC Parallel-292
02BAP Sig Series Auto Buybacks 1998-104
02BAP Sig Series Auto Buybacks 2000-228
02Czech IQ Sports Blue-29
02Czech IQ Sports Yellow-29

Svoboda, Petr (Prospect)
99Czech OFS-202
00BAP Memorabilia-456
Emerald-456
Ruby-456
Sapphire-456
00BAP Signature Series-266
Emerald-266
Ruby-266
Sapphire-266
Autographs-228
Autographs Gold-228
00Private Stock-147
Gold-147
Premiere Date-147
Retail-147
Silver-147
Game Gear-94
Game Gear Patches-94
00SP Authentic-164
00Stadium Club-242
00Topps Heritage-84
00Topps Premier Plus-131
Blue Ice-131
00Topps Stars-120
Blue-120
00Vanguard-148
Pacific Proofs-148
01O-Pee-Chee-292
01Topps-292
01St. John's Maple Leafs-22
02Czech OFS Plus-338
Trios-T24

Svoboda, Radek
96Czech APS Extraliga-280
97Czech APS Extraliga-235
97Czech DS Stickers-182
98Czech DS Stickers-42
98Czech OFS-337
99Czech OFS-127

Svoboda, Radoslav
81Swedish Semic Hockey VM Stickers-61
83Swedish Semic VM Stickers-85

Svoboda, Tomas
05Drummondville Voltigeurs-15
06Drummondville Voltigeurs-13

Svoboda, Valeri
95Slapshot-424

Svozil, Ladislav
81Swedish Semic Hockey VM Stickers-67
94German First League-156
95Czech APS Extraliga-292
96Czech APS Extraliga-190
97Czech APS Extraliga-124
98Czech OFS-113
04Slovakian Poprad Team Set-1

Svrbik, Richard
96Slovakian Quebec Pee-Wee Tournament-27

Swain, Brad
92British Columbia JHL-19

Swain, Garry
76O-Pee-Chee WHA-91

Swain, Matt
01Fort Wayne Komets-19

Swallow, Kevin
04Chicago Steel-3

Swan, Bryce
04Halifax Mooseheads-2
05ITG Heroes/Prosp Toronto Expo Parallel -310
05Halifax Mooseheads-10
05ITG Heroes and Prospects-310
Autographs Series II-BSW
06Halifax Mooseheads-12

Swan, Jim
86Portland Winter Hawks-22

Swanjord, Scott
93Waterloo Black Hawks-25

Swanson, Alan
04Northern Michigan Wildcats-23

Swanson, Brad
93Portland Winter Hawks-24
96Seattle Thunderbirds-5
97Prince Albert Raiders-20

Swanson, Brian
93Omaha Lancers-24
95Donruss Elite World Juniors-42
99Hamilton Bulldogs-10
00BAP Memorabilia-470
Emerald-470
Ruby-470
Sapphire-470
00Private Stock-119
Gold-119
Premiere Date-119
Retail-119
Silver-119
00SP Authentic-143
00SPx-178
00Topps Premier Plus-105
Blue Ice-105
00UD Pros and Prospects-104
00Upper Deck-422
Exclusives Tier 1-422
Exclusives Tier 2-422
00Upper Deck Ice-112
00Vanguard-120
Pacific Proofs-120
00Hamilton Bulldogs-15
01Hamilton Bulldogs-11
02NHL Power Play Stickers-32
02Oilers Postcards-18
03Chicago Wolves-20
04German DEL-197
05German DEL-278

Swanson, Jeremy
01Barrie Colts-13
02Barrie Colts-14
03Barrie Colts-13
04Barrie Colts 10th Anniversary-8
05Florida Everblades-24

Swanson, John
03Lincoln Stars Update-36
04Lincoln Stars-20
05St. Cloud State Huskies-7
05St. Cloud State Huskies-27

Swanson, Kevin
98Kelowna Rockets-25
98Prince George Cougars-20
99Kelowna Rockets-8
00Kelowna Rockets-20

Swanson, Matt
99Houston Aeros-3

Swanson, Ryan
01Lincoln Stars-22
04Minnesota-Duluth Bulldogs-25

Swanson, Scott
93Omaha Lancers-25
01Idaho Steelheads-20
03Colorado Eagles-16

Swarbrick, George
67Seals Team Issue-18
68O-Pee-Chee-174
68Shirriff Coins-113
70Flyers Postcards-12
70O-Pee-Chee-82
70Topps-82

Swardh, Magnus
93Swedish Semic Elitserien-219
94Swedish Leaf-89
95Swedish Leaf-113
Spidermen-11
95Swedish Upper Deck-170

Swartz, Tim
95Slapshot-383
95Sudbury Wolves-15
96Sudbury Wolves Police-24

Sweatt, Lee
02Chicago Steel-21

Sweeney, Bob
86Moncton Golden Flames-21
88Bruins Sports Action-20
88Bruins Postcards-18
88O-Pee-Chee-134
88O-Pee-Chee Stickers-28
88O-Pee-Chee Stickers-68
88O-Pee-Chee Stickers-130
88Panini Stickers-214
88Topps-134
89Bruins Sports Action-20
89O-Pee-Chee-135
89Topps-135
90Bowman-28
Tiffany-28
90Bruins Sports Action-22
90O-Pee-Chee-99
90Panini Stickers-15
90Pro Set-15
90Score-235
Canadian-235
90Topps-99
Tiffany-99
90Upper Deck-198
French-198
91Bowman-357
91Bruins Sports Action-18
91O-Pee-Chee-99
91Panini Stickers-177
91Pinnacle-222
French-222
91Pro Set-6
French-6
91Score American-176
91Score Canadian Bilingual-176
91Score Canadian English-176
91Stadium Club-75
91Topps-99
91Upper Deck-391
French-391
92Bowman-5
92Bowman-402
92O-Pee-Chee-21
92OPC Premier-110
92Parkhurst-251
Emerald Ice-251
92Sabres Blue Shield-24
92Sabres Jubilee Foods-15
92Score-317
Canadian-317
92Stadium Club-455
92Topps-111
Gold-111G
92Ultra-264
92Upper Deck-47
92Upper Deck-449
93OPC Premier-431
Gold-431
93Panini Stickers-104
93Parkhurst-290
Emerald Ice-290
93Pinnacle-118
Canadian-118
93PowerPlay-34
93Score-146
Canadian-146
93Stadium Club-63
Members Only Master Set-63
OPC-63
First Day Issue-63
First Day Issue OPC-63
93Topps/OPC Premier-431
Gold-431
93Ultra-278
93Upper Deck-312
94Leaf-417
94Parkhurst SE-SE17
Gold-SE17
94Pinnacle-411
Artist's Proofs-411
Rink Collection-411
94Upper Deck-445
Electric Ice-445
95Be A Player-26
Signatures-S26
Signatures Die Cuts-S26
95Playoff One on One-232
95Upper Deck-443
Electric Ice-443
Electric Ice Gold-443
96Collector's Choice-37
00German DEL Star Attractions-S7

Sweeney, Don
89Bruins Sports Action Update-9
89ProCards AHL-58
90Bruins Sports Action-23
90Pro Set-412
90Score-51A
90Score-51B
Canadian-51A
Canadian-51B
91Pro Set Platinum-153
91Bowman-365
91Bruins Sports Action-19
91O-Pee-Chee-319
91Panini Stickers-180
91Parkhurst-228
French-228
91Pinnacle-419
French-419
91Score American-146
91Score Canadian Bilingual-146
91Score Canadian English-146
91Stadium Club-370
91Topps-319
91Upper Deck-338
French-338
92Bowman-5
92Bowman-402
92Bruins Postcards-11
92O-Pee-Chee-40
92Parkhurst-244
Emerald Ice-244
92Pinnacle-179
French-179
92Score-186
Canadian-186
92Stadium Club-337
92Topps-417
Gold-417G
92Ultra-257
92Upper Deck-391
93Donruss-21
93Leaf-281
93OPC Premier-334
Gold-334
93Panini Stickers-11
93Parkhurst-13
Emerald Ice-13
93Pinnacle-269
Canadian-269
93PowerPlay-24
93Score-169
Canadian-169
93Stadium Club-117
Members Only Master Set-117
OPC-117
First Day Issue-117
First Day Issue OPC-117
93Topps/OPC Premier-334
Gold-334
93Ultra-271
93Upper Deck-101
94Be A Player Signature Cards-60
94Canada Games NHL POGS-40
94Donruss-281
94EA Sports-8
94Flair-14
94Fleer-18
94Leaf-518
94OPC Premier-262
Special Effects-262
94Parkhurst SE-SE15
Gold-SE15
94Pinnacle-91
Artist's Proofs-91
Rink Collection-91
94Score-101
Gold-101
Platinum-101
94Topps/OPC Premier-262
Special Effects-262
94Ultra-17
94Upper Deck-446
Electric Ice-446
95Collector's Choice-91
Player's Club-91
Player's Club Platinum-91
95Donruss-101
95Emotion-13
95Leaf-191
95Panini Stickers-11
95Parkhurst International-283
Emerald Ice-283
95Pinnacle-141
Artist's Proofs-141
Rink Collection-141
95Score-163
Black Ice Artist's Proofs-163
Black Ice-163
95SP-11
95Stadium Club-146
Members Only Master Set-146
95Topps-127
OPC Inserts-127
95Topps SuperSkills-26
Platinum-26
95Ultra-208
95Upper Deck-35
Electric Ice-35
Electric Ice Gold-35
96Be A Player-97
Autographs-97
Autographs Silver-97
96Collector's Choice-14
96SP-10
96Upper Deck-217
97Pacific Invincible NHL Regime-17
97Panini Stickers-7
97Score Bruins-20
Platinum-20
Premier-20
97Upper Deck-14
98OPC Chrome-141
Refractors-141
98Topps-141
O-Pee-Chee-141
98Upper Deck-40
Exclusives-40
Exclusives 1 of 1-40
Gold Reserve-40
99Upper Deck Victory-31
00Paramount-22
Copper-22
Gold-22
Holo-Gold-22
Holo-Silver-22
Ice Blue-22
Premiere Date-22
00Titanium Draft Day Edition-7
00Upper Deck Vintage-35
00Vanguard Dual Game-Worn Jerseys-14
00Vanguard Dual Game-Worn Patches-14
01McDonald's Pacific Hometown Pride-3
01Pacific-39
Extreme LTD-39
Hobby LTD-39
Premiere Date-39
Retail LTD-39
01Pacific Arena Exclusives-39
01Pacific Heads-Up Quad Jerseys-3
01Vanguard Memorabilia-3
01Vanguard Patches-3
02BAP First Edition-163
02Pacific Heads-Up Quad Jerseys-3
02Pacific Heads-Up Quad Jerseys Gold-3
03Parkhurst Orig Six Boston Mem -BM4
03Stars Postcards-24
03Upper Deck MVP-136
Gold Script-136
Silver Script-136
Canadian Exclusives-136

Sweeney, Michael
93Quebec Pee-Wee Tournament-733

Sweeney, Patrick
03Brampton Batallion-22
04Brampton Battalion-19

Sweeney, Tim
89ProCards IHL-203
90Flames IGA/McGavin's-27
90OPC Premier-116
90Pro Set-597
90Score Rookie/Traded-13T
90Upper Deck-531
French-531
91Bowman-261
91Flames Panini Team Stickers-22
91Flames IGA-23
91Pro Set-364
French-364
91Stadium Club-394
91Upper Deck-375
French-375
92Upper Deck-95
93Donruss-11
93Ducks Milk Caps-1
93OPC Premier-426
Gold-426
93Parkhurst-7
Emerald Ice-7
93PowerPlay-12
93Stadium Club-473
Members Only Master Set-473
First Day Issue-473
93Topps/OPC Premier-426
Gold-426
93Ultra-262
93Upper Deck-385
94Canada Games NHL POGS-34
94Donruss-214
94Flair-6
94Leaf-21
94OPC Premier-147
Special Effects-147
94Parkhurst-9
Gold-9
94Pinnacle-93
Artist's Proofs-93
Rink Collection-93
94Topps/OPC Premier-147
Special Effects-147
94Ultra-8
94Upper Deck-38
Electric Ice-38
95Finnish Semic World Championships-108
95Swedish World Championships Stickers-226
96Providence Bruins-21
97Be A Player-156
Autographs-156
Autographs Die-Cuts-156
Autographs Prismatic Die-Cuts-156
97Pacific-183
Copper-183
Emerald Green-183
Ice Blue-183
Red-183
Silver-183
97Pacific Omega-151
Copper-151
Dark Gray-151
Emerald Green-151
Gold-151
Ice Blue-151
97Hartford Wolf Pack-24
98Pacific-303
Ice Blue-303
Red-303

Sweet, Troy
907th Inn. Sketch OHL-347
91Oshawa Generals Sheet-8
917th Inn. Sketch OHL-159

Sweezey, Richard
93Quebec Pee-Wee Tournament-94

Sweitzer, Jason
95Slapshot-252
96Visions Signings *-70
Autographs-70A
Autographs Silver-70A

Swenson, Barkley
91Prince Albert Raiders-22
917th Inn. Sketch WHL-257
92Tacoma Rockets-24
95Central Hockey League-52

Swenson, Greg
92Cornell Big Red-27

Swerhone, Matt
04Vernon Vipers-15
05Vernon Vipers-19

Swett, Jesse
93Quebec Pee-Wee Tournament-1233

Swiatek, Andrezej
89Swedish Semic World Champ Stickers-136

Swibenko, Marco
94German DEL-41
95German DEL-38

Swibenko, Thomas
04German Berlin Eisbarens 50th Anniv-27

Swick, Michael
06Sudbury Wolves-24

Swider, Kevin
04Knoxville Ice Bears-3
05Knoxville Ice Bears-17

Swift, Michael
04Mississauga Ice Dogs-8
06Mississauga Ice Dogs-8

Swiniarski, Brian
06Odessa Jackalopes-18

Swinson, Wes
93Kitchener Rangers-20
94Kitchener Rangers-22
95Slapshot-127
99Greensboro Generals-20
01Augusta Lynx-6

Swistak, J.J.
02Michigan Wolverines-27

Swistak, Mike
93Quebec Pee-Wee Tournament-1299

Swit, Jason
05Cape Breton Screaming Eagles-3
06Cape Breton Screaming Eagles-3

Switek, Anthony
92Quebec Pee-Wee Tournament-1424
93Quebec Pee-Wee Tournament-1573

Switzer, Craig
03Salmon Arm Silverbacks-20

Switzer, Derek
897th Inn. Sketch OHL-150
907th Inn. Sketch OHL-318

Switzer, Jason
91British Columbia JHL-23
92British Columbia JHL-199

Swystun, Tyler
06Medicine Hat Tigers-21

Sychev, Roman
04Russian RHL-4

Sychra, Martin
93Kingston Frontenacs-14
94Fredericton Canadiens-27
95Wheeling Thunderbirds-14
97Czech APS Extraliga-118
98Czech DS Stickers-61
98Charlotte Checkers-17
99German DEL-347
00German DEL-156
01German Upper Deck-69
02German DEL City Press-275
04German DEL-198
05German DEL-190

Sydor, Darryl
88Kamloops Blazers-23
89Kamloops Blazers-21
90Score-425
Canadian-425
90Upper Deck-358
French-358
907th Inn. Sketch WHL-307
907th Inn. Sketch Memorial Cup-12
91OPC Premier-90
91Pinnacle-321
French-321
91Pro Set-542
French-542
91Score Canadian Bilingual-631
91Score Canadian English-631
91Score Rookie/Traded-81T
91Upper Deck-549
French-549
917th Inn. Sketch CHL Award Winners-14
92Bowman-321
92O-Pee-Chee-11
92OPC Premier-16
92Panini Stickers-F
92Panini Stickers French-F
92Parkhurst-69
Emerald Ice-69
92Pro Set-228
92Score-410
Canadian-410
92Stadium Club-72
92Topps-39
Gold-39G
92Ultra-312
92Upper Deck-63
93Donruss-164
93Leaf-206
Gold Rookies-15
93OPC Premier-226
Gold-226
93Parkhurst-96
Emerald Ice-96
93Pinnacle-113
Canadian-113
93PowerPlay-122
93Score-311
Canadian-311
93Stadium Club-225
Members Only Master Set-225
OPC-225
First Day Issue-225
First Day Issue OPC-225
93Topps/OPC Premier-226
Gold-226
93Ultra-60
93Upper Deck-83
SP-74
94Be A Player-R90
Signature Cards-26
94Donruss-70
94Leaf-136
94OPC Premier-86
Special Effects-86
94Parkhurst SE-SE82
Gold-SE82
94Pinnacle-328
Artist's Proofs-328
Rink Collection-328
94Score-97
Gold-97
Platinum-97
94Stadium Club-164
Members Only Master Set-164
First Day Issue-164
Super Teams-11
Super Teams Members Only Master Set-11
Super Team Winner Cards-164
94Topps/OPC Premier-86
Special Effects-86
94Ultra-308
94Upper Deck-104
Electric Ice-104
95Canada Games NHL POGS-141
95Collector's Choice-83
Player's Club-83
Player's Club Platinum-83
95Donruss-73
95Emotion-85
95Leaf-199
95Panini Stickers-275
95Parkhurst International-371
Emerald Ice-371
95Pinnacle-96
Artist's Proofs-96
Rink Collection-96
95Playoff One on One-160
95Score-26
Black Ice Artist's Proofs-26
Black Ice-26
95SkyBox Impact-82
95Ultra-78
Gold Medallion-78
95Upper Deck-5
Electric Ice-5
Electric Ice Gold-5
95Swedish World Championships Stickers-6
96Be A Player-176
96Be A Player-P176
Autographs-176
Autographs Silver-176
96Playoff One on One-375
96Stars Postcards-25
96Summit-33
Artist's Proofs-33
Ice-33
Metal-33
Premium Stock-33
97Collector's Choice-72
97Donruss Limited-6
Exposure-6
97Katch-48
Gold-48
Silver-48
97Pacific-48
Copper-48
Emerald Green-48
Ice Blue-48
Red-48
Silver-48
97Pacific Dynagon-39
Copper-39
Dark Grey-39
Emerald Green-39
Ice Blue-39
Red-39
Silver-39
Tandems-34
97Pacific Omega-75
Copper-75
Dark Gray-75
Emerald Green-75
Gold-75
Ice Blue-75
97Panini Stickers-140
97Paramount-62
Copper-62
Dark Grey-62
Emerald Green-62
Ice Blue-62
Red-62
Silver-62
97Pinnacle-139
Press Plates Back Black-139
Press Plates Back Cyan-139

ress Plates Back Magenta-139
ress Plates Back Yellow-139
ress Plates Front Black-139
ress Plates Front Cyan-139
ress Plates Front Magenta-139
ress Plates Front Yellow-139
Score-238
Upper Deck-54
Aurora-60
Be A Player-191
ress Release-191
BAP Gold-191
BAP Autographs-191
BAP Autographs Gold-191
Black Diamond-28
Double Diamond-28
Triple Diamond-28
Quadruple Diamond-28
Crown Royale-43
Limited Series-43
Finest-148
No Protectors-148
No Protectors Refractors-148
Refractors-148
Katch-48
Kraft Peanut Butter-4
Pacific-183
Ice Blue-183
Red-183
Pacific Omega-75
Red-75
Opening Day Issue-75
Panini Stickers-125
Paramount-70
Copper-70
Emerald Green-70
Holo-Electric-70
Ice Blue-70
Silver-70
Revolution-46
Ice Shadow-46
Red-46
UD Choice-67
UD Choice Preview-67
UD Choice Prime Choice Reserve-67
UD Choice Reserve-67
Upper Deck-79
Exclusives-79
Exclusives 1 of 1-79
Game Jerseys-GJ20
Gold Reserve-79
Upper Deck MVP-62
Gold Script-62
Silver Script-62
Super Script-62
BAP Memorabilia-271
Gold-271
Silver-271
BAP Update Teammates Jersey Cards-TM29
BAP Millennium-85
Emerald-85
Ruby-85
Sapphire-85
Signatures-85
Signatures Gold-85
McDonald's Upper Deck Game Jerseys-GJDS
O-Pee-Chee-240
O-Pee-Chee Chrome-240
O-Pee-Chee Chrome Refractors-240
Pacific-129
Copper-129
Emerald Green-129
Gold-129
Ice Blue-129
Premiere Date-129
Red-129
Panini Stickers-223
Paramount-77
Copper-77
Emerald-77
Gold-77
Holographic Emerald-77
Holographic Gold-77
Holographic Silver-77
Ice Blue-77
Premiere Date-77
Red-77
Silver-77
SPx-49
Radiance-49
Spectrum-49
Stars Postcards-26
Topps/OPC-240
Topps/OPC Chrome-240
Refractors-240
Upper Deck-217
Exclusives-217
Exclusives 1 of 1-217
Upper Deck Gold Reserve-217
Upper Deck MVP-61
Gold Script-61
Silver Script-61
Super Script-61
Upper Deck Victory-94
BAP Memorabilia-112
Emerald-112
Ruby-112
Sapphire-112
Promos-112
Jersey Cards-J19
Jersey Emblems-E19
Jersey Numbers-N19
Jersey and Stick Cards-JS19
BAP Mem Chicago Sportsfest Copper-112
BAP Memorabilia Chicago Sportsfest Blue-112
BAP Memorabilia Chicago Sportsfest Gold-112
BAP Memorabilia Chicago Sportsfest Ruby-112
BAP Memorabilia Chicago Sun-Times Ruby-112
BAP Memorabilia Chicago Sun-Times Gold-112
BAP Mem Chicago Sun-Times Sapphire-112
BAP Mem Toronto Fall Expo Copper-112
BAP Memorabilia Toronto Fall Expo Gold-112
BAP Memorabilia Toronto Fall Expo Ruby-112
BAP Memorabilia Update Teammates-TM14
BAP Memorabilia Update Teammates Gold-TM14
BAP Parkhurst 2000-P64
BAP Signature Series-223
Emerald-223
Ruby-223
Sapphire-223
BAP Ultimate Memorabilia Teammates-TM28
0O-Pee-Chee-256A
0O-Pee-Chee Parallel-256A
Pacific-141
Copper-141
Gold-141
Ice Blue-141
Premiere Date-141
Jerseys-6
Jersey Patches-6
Paramount Jersey and Patches-5
Private Stock Game Gear-40
Private Stock Game Gear-41
Private Stock Game Gear Patches-40
00Private Stock Game Gear Patches-41
00Stars Postcards-23
00Titanium Game Gear-92
00Titanium Game Gear Patches-92
00Titanium Draft Day Edition-35
Patches-35
00Topps/OPC-256A
Parallel-256A
00Upper Deck-58
Exclusives Tier 1-58
Exclusives Tier 2-58
00Upper Deck Vintage-120
01BAP Memorabilia-176
Emerald-176
Ruby-176
Sapphire-176
01BAP Signature Series-182
Autographs-182
Autographs Gold-182
01Pacific-135
Extreme LTD-135
Hobby LTD-135
Premiere Date-135
Retail LTD-135
01Pacific Arena Exclusives-135
01Pacific Heads-Up Quad Jerseys-10
01Parkhurst-145
Teammates-T12
01Private Stock Game Gear-39
01Private Stock Game Gear Patches-39
01Stars Postcards-22
01UD Stanley Cup Champs-55
01Upper Deck-287
Exclusives-287
01Upper Deck Victory-120
Gold-120
01Vanguard Memorabilia-12
01Vanguard Patches-12
02BAP All-Star Edition-90
Jerseys-90
Jerseys Gold-90
Jerseys Silver-90
02BAP First Edition-111
Jerseys-111
02BAP Memorabilia-21
Emerald-21
Ruby-21
Sapphire-21
NHL All-Star Game-21
NHL All-Star Game Blue-21
NHL All-Star Game Green-21
NHL All-Star Game Red-21
02BAP Memorabilia Toronto Fall Expo-21
02BAP Signature Series-161
Autographs-161
Autograph Buybacks 1998-191
Autograph Buybacks 1999-85
Autograph Buybacks 2001-182
Autographs Gold-161
02Pacific-118
Blue-118
Red-118
02Pacific Complete-340
Red-340
02Stars Postcards-21
02Topps Total-253
03BAP Memorabilia-239
03Beehive-56
Gold-56
Silver-56
03ITG Action Jerseys-M84
03NHL Sticker Collection-209
03O-Pee-Chee-151
03OPC Blue-151
03OPC Gold-151
03OPC Red-151
03Pacific Complete-220
Red-220
03Topps-151
Blue-151
Gold-151
Red-151
03Topps Traded-TT11
Blue-TT11
Gold-TT11
Red-TT11
03Upper Deck-299
Canadian Exclusives-299
HG-299
UD Exclusives-299
03Upper Deck MVP-134
Gold Script-134
Silver Script-134
Canadian Exclusives-134
05Be A Player Signatures-DY
05Be A Player Signatures Gold-DY
05Lightning Team Issue-5
05Parkhurst-439
Facsimile Auto Parallel-439
05Upper Deck-174
HG Glossy-174
05Upper Deck MVP-352
Gold-352
Platinum-352
05Upper Deck Toronto Fall Expo-174
06O-Pee-Chee-165
Rainbow-165
06Stars Team Postcards-22

Sykes, Phil
84Kings Smokey-22
86Kings 20th Anniversary Team Issue-20
86O-Pee-Chee-216
87Panini Stickers-285
88ProCards AHL-197
89ProCards AHL-4
90Jets IGA-31
91Bowman-194
91Jets Panini Team Stickers-23
91Jets IGA-31
91O-Pee-Chee-189
91Score Canadian Bilingual-534
91Score Canadian English-534
91Stadium Club-271
91Topps-189

Sykko, Tomi
04Finnish Cardset-305
05Finnish Cardset -331
06Finnish Cardset-159

Sykora, Marek
94Czech APS Extraliga-279
96Czech APS Extraliga-1
97Czech APS Extraliga-170
98Czech OFS-285
98Czech OFS-445
99Czech OFS-116
00Czech OFS-56
06Czech OFS Coaches-10

Sykora, Michal
917th Inn. Sketch WHL-164
92Tacoma Rockets-25
92Tacoma Rockets-29
93Donruss-307
93Leaf-431
93Parkhurst-257
Emerald Ice-257
93Pinnacle-452
Canadian-452
93Score-600
Gold-600
Canadian-600
Canadian Gold-600
93Upper Deck-489
93Classic-30
94Donruss-204
94Fleer-201
94Leaf-122
94OPC Premier-362
Special Effects-362
94Topps/OPC Premier-362
Special Effects-362
94Ultra-369
94Upper Deck-195
Electric Ice-195
94Kansas City Blades-3
94Classic Pro Prospects-38
95Canada Games NHL POGS-230
95Panini Stickers-286
95Parkhurst International-181
Emerald Ice-181
95Topps-105
OPC Inserts-105
96Be A Player-113
Autographs-113
Autographs Silver-113
96Upper Deck-151
96Czech APS Extraliga-345
97Pacific Invincible NHL Regime-47
97Panini Stickers-132
97Indianapolis Ice-23
98Czech DS Stickers-129
98Czech OFS-373
99Czech DS-145
99Czech OFS-401
99Czech OFS-506
All-Star Game Blue-506
All-Star Game Gold-506
All-Star Game Red-506
All-Star Game Silver-506
00Czech DS Extraliga Valuable Players-VP3
00Czech DS Extraliga World Champions-WCH6
01Czech DS-10
Best of the Best-BB3
01Czech National Team Postcards-13
01Czech OFS-248
01Czech OFS Red Inserts-RE11D
02Czech DS-19
02Czech OFS Plus-230
02Czech OFS Plus All-Star Game-H39
02Czech OFS Plus Trios-T8
02Czech OFS Plus Duos-D11
02Czech Stadion Olympics-351
03Czech OFS Plus-61
03Czech OFS Plus All-Star Game-H24
03Czech OFS Plus All-Star Game-H45
03Czech OFS Plus Insert H-H18
03Czech OFS Plus MS Praha-SE7
03Czech Pardubice Postcards-16
04Czech OFS Czech/Slovak-18
04Czech OFS Defence Points-5

Sykora, Michal (PW)
96Slovakian Quebec Pee-Wee Tournament-28
02Czech OFS Plus All-Star Game-H39

Sykora, Otto
94German DEL-341
95German DEL-307
96German DEL-334
03German Nuremberg Ice Tigers Postcards-25
04German Nuremburg Ice Tigers Postcards-18

Sykora, Petr
94Classic Draft Prospects-DP10
94Assets *-60
94Assets *-85
Phone Cards One Minute/$2-48
95Bowman-116
All-Foil-116
95Donruss Rated Rookies-16
95Finest-134
Refractors-134
95Metal-195
95Parkhurst International-512
95Parkhurst International-523
Emerald Ice-512
Emerald Ice-523
Parkie's Trophy Picks-PP43
95Select Certified-144
Mirror Gold-144
95SP-83
95Upper Deck-318
Electric Ice-318
Electric Ice Gold-318
95Classic-18
Autographs-22
Ice Breakers-BK16
Ice Breakers Die Cuts-BK16
95Images-81
Gold-81
Autographs-81A
Clear Excitement-CE11
95Images Four-Sport *-117
95Images Platinum Premier Draft Choice-PD4
95Assets Gold *-7
95Assets Gold Phone Cards $2 *-7
95Classic Five-Sport *-137
Autographs-137A
Autographs-137B
Fast Track-FT14
Strive For Five-HK7
96Classic Assets Phone Cards $2 Hot Print-27
96Collector's Choice-147
96Collector's Choice-339
96Devils Team Issue-17
96Donruss Rated Rookies-2
96Donruss Canadian Ice-72
Gold Press Proofs-72
Red Press Proofs-72
96Donruss Elite-122
Die Cut Stars-122
Aspirations-3
96Fleer Rookie Sensations-9
96Fleer Picks-74
96Leaf-206
Press Proofs-206
96Leaf Limited-54
Gold-54
96Leaf Preferred-21
Press Proofs-21
Steel-12
Steel Gold-12
96Metal Universe-89
96Score-237
Artist's Proofs-237
Dealer's Choice Artist's Proofs-237
Special Artist's Proofs-237
Golden Blades-237
96SkyBox Impact-72
96SkyBox Impact-171
NHL on Fox-19
96SP-88
96SPx-23
Gold-23
96Stadium Club Members Only-49
96Summit-170
Artist's Proofs-170
Ice-170
Metal-170
Premium Stock-170
96Topps Picks Rookie Stars-RS6
96Topps Picks Rookie Stars OPC-RS6
96Ultra-96
Gold Medallion-96
96Upper Deck-93
Generation Next-X26
Superstar Showdown-SS21B
96Zenith-56
Artist's Proofs-56
96Collector's Edge Future Legends-22
96Assets *-45
Hot Prints-45
96Assets Phone Cards $2 *-27
Hot Prints-27
96Classic Signings Freshly Inked *-FS25
96Clear Assets *-57
Phone Cards $2-22
Phone Cards $5-16
96Visions *-91
96Visions *-123
96Visions Signings *-76
Artistry-6
97Be A Player-134
Autographs-134
Autographs Die-Cuts-134
Autographs Prismatic Die-Cuts-134
97Devils Team Issue-12
97Pacific Omega-135
Copper-135
Dark Gray-135
Emerald Green-135
Gold-135
Ice Blue-135
97Panini Stickers-68
97Score Devils-14
Platinum-14
Premier-14
97SP Authentic-90
98Devils Team Issue-29
98OPC Chrome-2
Refractors-2
98Pacific-273
Ice Blue-273
Red-273
98Pacific Omega-144
Red-144
Opening Day Issue-144
98Panini Stickers-64
98Topps-2
O-Pee-Chee-2
98UD Choice-112
Prime Choice Reserve-112
Reserve-112
98Upper Deck-310
Exclusives-310
Exclusives 1 of 1-310
Gold Reserve-310
98Czech Pexeso Series Two-11
98Czech Pexeso Series Two-24
99Aurora-88
Premiere Date-88
99BAP Memorabilia-281
Gold-281
Silver-281
Selects Silver-SL13
Selects Gold-SL13
99BAP Millennium-145
Emerald-145
Ruby-145
Sapphire-145
Signatures-145
Signatures Gold-145
99Crown Royale-83
Limited Series-83
Premiere Date-83
99Devils Team Issue-10
99O-Pee-Chee-100
99O-Pee-Chee Chrome-100
99O-Pee-Chee Chrome Refractors-100
99O-Pee-Chee Now Starring-NS5
99Pacific-248
Copper-248
Emerald Green-248
Gold-248
Ice Blue-248
Premiere Date-248
Red-248
99Pacific Dynagon Ice-120
Blue-120
Copper-120
Gold-120
Premiere Date-120
99Pacific Omega-138
Copper-138
Gold-138
Ice Blue-138
Premiere Date-138
99Pacific Prism-84
Holographic Blue-84
Holographic Gold-84
Holographic Mirror-84
Holographic Purple-84
Premiere Date-84
99Panini Stickers-78
99Paramount-139
Copper-139
Emerald-139
Gold-139
Holographic Emerald-139
Holographic Gold-139
Holographic Silver-139
Ice Blue-139
Premiere Date-139
Red-139
Silver-139
99Revolution-89
Premiere Date-89
Red-89
Shadow Series-89
99Stadium Club-63
First Day Issue-63
One of a Kind-63
Printing Plates Black-63
Printing Plates Cyan-63
Printing Plates Magenta-63
Printing Plates Yellow-63
99Topps/OPC-100
Now Starring-NS5
99Topps/OPC Chrome-100
Refractors-100
99Topps Gold Label Class 1-51
Black-51
Black One of One-51
One of One-51
Red-51
Red One of One-51
99Topps Gold Label Class 2-51
99Topps Gold Label Class 2 Black-51
99Topps Gold Label Class 2 Black 1 of 1-51
99Topps Gold Label Class 2 One of One-51
99Topps Gold Label Class 2 Red-51
99Topps Gold Label Class 2 Red One of One-51
99Topps Gold Label Class 3-51
99Topps Gold Label Class 3 Black-51
99Topps Gold Label Class 3 Black 1 of 1-51
99Topps Gold Label Class 3 One of One-51
99Topps Gold Label Class 3 Red-51
99Topps Gold Label Class 3 Red One of One-51
99Topps Gold Label Fresh Gold-FG5
99Topps Gold Label Fresh Gold Black-FG5
99Topps Gold Label Fresh Gold Black 1of1-FG5
99Topps Gold Label Fresh Gold One of One-FG5
99Topps Gold Label Fresh Gold Red-FG5
99Topps Gold Label Fresh Gold Red 1 of 1-FG5
99Topps Premier Plus-72
Parallel-72
99Upper Deck-79
Exclusives-79
Exclusives 1 of 1-79
99Upper Deck Gold Reserve-79
99Upper Deck MVP-119
Gold Script-119
Silver Script-119
Super Script-119
99Upper Deck Victory-171
99Wayne Gretzky Hockey-98
99Czech DS National Stars-NS23
00Aurora-86
Premiere Date-86
Dual Game-Worn Jerseys-1
Game-Worn Jerseys-8
Game-Worn Jersey Patches-8
00BAP Memorabilia-128
Emerald-128
Ruby-128
Sapphire-128
Promos-128
00BAP Mem Chicago Sportsfest Copper-128
00BAP Memorabilia Chicago Sportsfest Blue-128
00BAP Memorabilia Chicago Sportsfest Gold-128
00BAP Memorabilia Chicago Sportsfest Ruby-128
00BAP Memorabilia Chicago Sun-Times Ruby-128
00BAP Memorabilia Chicago Sun-Times Gold-128
00BAP Mem Chicago Sun-Times Sapphire-128
00BAP Mem Toronto Fall Expo Copper-128
00BAP Memorabilia Toronto Fall Expo Gold-128
00BAP Memorabilia Toronto Fall Expo Ruby-128
00BAP Memorabilia Update Teammates-TM1
00BAP Memorabilia Update Teammates-TM27
00BAP Memorabilia Update Teammates Gold-TM1
00BAP Memorabilia Update Teammates Gold-TM27
00BAP Parkhurst 2000-P180
00BAP Signature Series-233
Emerald-233
Ruby-233
Sapphire-233
Autographs-75
Autographs Gold-75
00Devils Team Issue-22
00O-Pee-Chee-156
00O-Pee-Chee Parallel-156
00Pacific-244
Copper-244
Gold-244
Ice Blue-244
Premiere Date-244
00Panini Stickers-47
00Paramount-150
Copper-150
Gold-150
Holo-Gold-150
Holo-Silver-150
Ice Blue-150
Premiere Date-150
00Private Stock-60
Gold-60
Premiere Date-60
Retail-60
Silver-60
Extreme Action-12
Game Gear-65
Game Gear Patches-65
PS-2001 Action-34
00Revolution-89
Blue-89
Premiere Date-89
Red-89
00SP Authentic Sign of the Times-PS
00SP Authentic Sign of the Times-B/S
00Stadium Club-170
00Topps/OPC-156
Parallel-156
00Topps Chrome-110
OPC Refractors-110
Refractors-110
00Upper Deck-103
Exclusives Tier 1-103
Exclusives Tier 2-103
00Upper Deck Vintage-218
00Czech DS Extraliga Team Jagr-JT3
00Czech DS Extraliga Team Jagr Parallel-JT3
00Czech OFS-391
01BAP Memorabilia-79
Emerald-79
Ruby-79
Sapphire-79
01BAP Signature Series-138
Autographs-138
Autographs Gold-138
Jerseys-GJ-74
01Bowman YoungStars-93
Gold-93
Ice Cubed-93
01Crown Royale-88
Blue-88
Premiere Date-88
Red-88
Retail-88
01Devils Team Issue-24
01O-Pee-Chee-109
01O-Pee-Chee Heritage Parallel-109
01O-Pee-Chee Heritage Parallel Limited-109
01O-Pee-Chee Premier Parallel-109
01Pacific-239
Extreme LTD-239
Hobby LTD-239
Premiere Date-239
Retail LTD-239
Adrenaline Jerseys-26
01Pacific Arena Exclusives-239
01Parkhurst-48
Gold-48
Silver-48
01SP Authentic Sign of the Times-HHS
01Stadium Club-72
Award Winners-72
Master Photos-72
NHL Passport-NHLP12
01Topps-109
Heritage Parallel-109
Heritage Parallel Limited-109
OPC Parallel-109
01Topps Chrome-109
Refractors-109
Black Border Refractors-109
01Topps Heritage-60
Refractors-60
01Topps Reserve-23
01UD Stanley Cup Champs-74
01Upper Deck-334
Exclusives-334
Ice Autographs-PS
01Upper Deck MVP-114
01Upper Deck Victory-211
Gold-211
01Upper Deck Vintage-153
01Czech DS-49
01Czech Stadion-223
02BAP First Edition-129
02BAP First Edition-415H
Jerseys-129
02BAP Memorabilia-269
Emerald-269
Ruby-269
Sapphire-269
NHL All-Star Game-269
NHL All-Star Game Blue-269
NHL All-Star Game Green-269
NHL All-Star Game Red-269
02BAP Memorabilia Toronto Fall Expo-269
02BAP Signature Series-121
Autographs-121
Autograph Buybacks 1999-145
Autograph Buybacks 2000-75
Autograph Buybacks 2001-138
Autographs Gold-121
Golf-GS73
02Bowman YoungStars-66
Gold-66
Silver-66
02Ducks Team Issue-5
02ITG Used-3
02ITG Used-103
02O-Pee-Chee-164
02O-Pee-Chee-164U
02O-Pee-Chee Premier Blue Parallel-164
02O-Pee-Chee Premier Red Parallel-164
02O-Pee-Chee Factory Set-164
02Pacific-230
Blue-230
Red-230
02Pacific Complete-313
Red-313
02Pacific Exclusive-4
02Parkhurst Retro-100
Minis-100
02Private Stock Reserve-3
Blue-3
Red-3
Retail-3
02Stadium Club-105
Silver Decoy Cards-105
Proofs-105
02Titanium-3
Blue-3
Red-3
Retail-3
02Topps-164
02Topps-164U
OPC Blue Parallel-164
OPC Red Parallel-164
Factory Set-164
02Topps Chrome-98
Black Border Refractors-98
Refractors-98
02Topps Heritage-159
02Topps Total-340
02Upper Deck-248
Exclusives-248
02Upper Deck Beckett UD Promos-248
02Upper Deck Victory-123
Bronze-123
Gold-123
Silver-123
National Pride-NP17
02Czech Stadion Olympics-340
03BAP Memorabilia-73
Emerald-73
Gold-73
Ruby-73
Sapphire-73
03Beehive-1
Gold-1
Silver-1
03Black Diamond-50
Black-50
Green-50
Red-50
03Bowman-42
Gold-42
03Bowman Chrome-42
Refractors-42
Gold Refractors-42
Xfractors-42
03ITG Action-75
03ITG Used Signature Series Autographs-PS
03ITG Used Sig Series Autographs Gold-PS
03NHL Sticker Collection-157
03O-Pee-Chee-18
03OPC Blue-18
03OPC Gold-18
03OPC Red-18
03Pacific-10
Blue-10
Red-10
03Pacific Complete-263
Red-263
03Pacific Prism-4
Blue-4
Gold-4
Red-4
03Pacific Supreme-3
Blue-3
Red-3
Retail-3
03Private Stock Reserve-4
Blue-4
Red-4
Retail-4
03Titanium-3
Hobby Jersey Number Parallels-3
Retail-3
Retail Jersey Number Parallels-3
03Topps-18
Blue-18
Gold-18
Red-18
03Topps C55-52
Minis-52
Minis American Back-52
Minis American Back Red-52
Minis Bazooka Back-52
Minis Brooklyn Back-52
Minis Hat Trick Back-52
Minis O Canada Back-52
Minis O Canada Back Red-52
Minis Stanley Cup Back-52
03Topps Pristine-83
Gold Refractor Die Cuts-83
Refractors-83
Press Plates Black-83
Press Plates Cyan-83
Press Plates Magenta-83
Press Plates Yellow-83
03Upper Deck-1
Canadian Exclusives-1
HG-1
03Upper Deck MVP-2
Gold Script-2
Silver Script-2
Canadian Exclusives-2
SportsNut-SN3
03Upper Deck Rookie Update-1
03Upper Deck Victory-2
Bronze-2
Gold-2
Silver-2
03Czech OFS Plus-62
03Czech Stadion-612
03Toronto Star-2
04Pacific-9
Blue-9
Red-9
04UD All-World-37
Gold-37
04Upper Deck-1
Canadian Exclusives-1
HG Glossy Gold-1
HG Glossy Silver-1
04Czech OFS-132
Assist Leaders-15
Czech/Slovak-19
04Russian Legion-27
05Ducks Team Issue-20
05Panini Stickers-197
05Parkhurst-322
Facsimile Auto Parallel-322
True Colors-TCNYR
True Colors-TCNYR
05Ultra-3
Gold-3
Ice-3
05Upper Deck-248
Jerseys-J-PSY
Notable Numbers-N-PSY
05Upper Deck MVP-12
Gold-12
Platinum-12
05Czech World Champions Postcards-18
05Czech Kvarteto Bonaparte-6b
05Czech Pexeso Mini Blue Set-20
05Czech Pexeso Mini Red Set-14
06Gatorade-16
06O-Pee-Chee-203
Rainbow-203
06Upper Deck-331
Exclusives Parallel-331
High Gloss Parallel-331
Masterpieces-331
Victory-249
06Czech CP Cup Postcards-19
06Czech HC Pardubice Postcards-21
06Czech OFS-126
All Stars-13
Stars-11
Team Cards-6
07Upper Deck Victory-165
Black-165
Gold-165

Sykora, Petr (Prospect)
96Czech APS Extraliga-162
96Collector's Edge Ice-11
Prism-11
97Czech APS Extraliga-262
98Milwaukee Admirals-22
98Milwaukee Admirals Postcards-5
99Czech OFS-294
99Czech OFS-358
00Czech OFS-52
01Czech DS-20
01Czech OFS-259
All Stars-38
02Czech OFS Plus-231
Trios-T8
02Czech IQ Sports Yellow-15
03Czech OFS Plus All-Star Game-H25
03Czech OFS Plus Insert M-M4
03Czech OFS Plus MS Praha-SE8
04Czech OFS Goals Leaders-6
04Czech OFS Points Leaders-10

Sykora, Tomas
99Czech OFS-305
00Czech OFS-283

Sykora, Vaclav
93Finnish Jyvas-Hyva Stickers-223
93Finnish SISU-182
94Finnish SISU-396
95Finnish SISU-388
96Czech APS Extraliga-120
97Czech APS Extraliga-2
98Czech OFS-272
99Czech OFS-146
00Czech OFS-133
06Czech OFS Coaches-11

Sylvegard, Patrik
92Swedish Semic Elitserien Stickers-215
93Swedish Semic Elitserien-186
94Swedish Leaf-103
95Swedish Leaf-90
95Swedish Upper Deck-146
97Swedish Collector's Choice-145
98Swedish UD Choice-161

Sylvester, Dean
96Kansas City Blades-21
98Rochester Americans-17
99Black Diamond-6
Diamond Cut-6
Final Cut-6
99Pacific Omega-14
Copper-14
Gold-14
Ice Blue-14
Premiere Date-14
99SP Authentic-92
99Upper Deck MVP SC Edition-11
Gold Script-11
Silver Script-11
Super Script-11
00O-Pee-Chee-251A
00O-Pee-Chee Parallel-251A
00Pacific-25
Copper-25
Gold-25
Ice Blue-25
Premiere Date-25
00Topps/OPC-251A
Parallel-251A
00Upper Deck-7
Exclusives Tier 1-7
Exclusives Tier 2-7
00Upper Deck MVP-10
First Stars-10
Second Stars-10
Third Stars-10
00Upper Deck Victory-15
00Upper Deck Vintage-18

Sylvester, Derek
93Niagara Falls Thunder-21

Sylvester, Dustin
05Kootenay Ice-20

Sylvester, Gary
04Kelowna Rockets-21
05Penticton Vees-17
06Penticton Vees-20

Sylvia, Mike
95Donruss Elite World Juniors-43
95Upper Deck-565
Electric Ice-565
Electric Ice Gold-565

Symes, Brad
93Portland Winter Hawks-25
95Signature Rookies-64A
95Signature Rookies-64B
Signatures-45
96Wheeling Nailers-18
96Wheeling Nailers Photo Pack-9
97New Orleans Brass-5

Symington, Jeremy
03Lubbock Cotton Kings-17
05Port Huron Flags-21
06Rio Grande Valley Killer Bees-10

Synish, Doug
897th Inn. Sketch OHL-42

Synkov, Oleg
01UK Hull Thunder-17

Synowietz, Heinrich
94German First League-618
96German DEL-208

Synowietz, Paul
94German First League-619
96German DEL-209

Syposz, Janusz
92Finnish Semic-270

Syroczynski, Matt
06Fort Wayne Komets-19

Syrtsov, Nikolai
98Port Huron Border Cats-21
03Russian Hockey League-67

Sysela, Robert
96Czech APS Extraliga-339

Syvasalmi, Kari
93Finnish SISU-227
95Finnish SISU-365

Syversen, Arild
92Norwegian Elite Series-226

Syversen, Lase
92Norwegian Elite Series-73

Syversne, Petter
92Norwegian Elite Series-174

Syvret, Corey
05London Knights-18
06Guelph Storm-21
06London Knights-22
06ITG Heroes and Prospects-121
Autographs-ACSV

Syvret, Danny
02London Knights-17
03London Knights-4
04London Knights-11
04ITG Heroes and Prospects-212
Emblems-64
Emblems Gold-64
Jerseys-64
Jerseys Gold-64
Numbers-64
Numbers Gold-64
04ITG Heroes/Prospects Toronto Expo '05-212
05Black Diamond-241
05Hot Prospects-129
En Fuego-129
Red Hot-129
White Hot-129
05SP Authentic-227
Limited-227
05SP Game Used-209
05SPx-257
05The Cup Masterpiece Pressplate Artifact-276
05The Cup Master Pressplate Black Diamond-241
05The Cup Masterpiece Pressplates (Ice)-195
05The Cup Master Pressplate Rookie Update-131
05The Cup Masterpiece Pressplates SPA-227
05The Cup Masterpiece Pressplates SP GU-209
05The Cup Masterpiece Pressplates (SPx)-257
05The Cup Masterpiece Pressplates Trilogy-259
05The Cup Masterpiece Pressplate Ult Coll-204
05UD Artifacts-276
05Ultimate Collection-204
Gold-204
05Upper Deck Ice-195
05Upper Deck Rookie Update-131
05Upper Deck Trilogy-259
05Extreme Top Prospects Signature Edition-S9
05Hamilton Bulldogs-25
05ITG Heroes/Prospects He Shoots/Scores-15
05ITG Heroes and Prospects Memorial Cup-MC-1
06ITG Heroes and Prospects-48
Autographs-ADSV

Szabo, Dave
917th Inn. Sketch OHL-64
99Tupelo T-Rex-6

Szabo, Peter
03St. Cloud State Huskies-25
04St. Cloud State Huskies-27

Szabo, Tony
93Roanoke Express-19

Szadkowski, Nick
96Seattle Thunderbirds-19

Szatmary, Rob
92British Columbia JHL-82

Szczachor, Michael
03Swift Current Broncos-19
04Swift Current Broncos-22

Szczepaniec, Oskar
95Swiss HNL-196
96Swiss HNL-86
98Swiss Power Play Stickers-135
99Swiss Panini Stickers-111
00Swiss Panini Stickers-156
00Swiss Slapshot Mini-Cards-EHCK5

Szczygiel, Darrin
98Thunder Bay Thunder Cats-4

Szeja, Jan
73Finnish Jaakiekko-100
74Finnish Typotor-91

Szeryk, Jeff
89Sault Ste. Marie Greyhounds-25
90Kitchener Rangers-16

Szoke, Mark

907th Inn. Sketch WHL-213
917th Inn. Sketch WHL-6
917th Inn. Sketch Memorial Cup-81
93Lethbridge Hurricanes-17
Szopinski, Robert
89Swedish Semic World Champ Stickers-134
92Finnish Semic-271
Szturm, Pat
94Thunder Bay Senators-4
95Thunder Bay Senators-20
Szuper, Levente
99Ottawa 67's-24
02BAP All-Star Edition-107
Gold-107
Silver-107
02BAP Memorabilia-392
02BAP Ultimate Memorabilia-74
02Between the Pipes-102
Gold-102
Silver-102
02ITG Used-99
02Parkhurst-246
Bronze-246
Gold-246
Silver-246
02Parkhurst Retro-227
Minis-227
02SP Authentic-167
02SP Game Used-98
02UD Artistic Impressions-107
Gold-107
Common Ground-CG5
Common Ground Gold-CG5
02UD Honor Roll-107
02UD Mask Collection-141
02UD Premier Collection-49B
Gold-49
02Upper Deck-431
Exclusives-431
03Peoria Rivermen-14
06German DEL-39
New Arrivals-NA11
Szura, Joe
67Seals Team Issue-19
68O-Pee-Chee-175
70O-Pee-Chee-73
70Topps-73
72Los Angeles Sharks WHA-15
72O-Pee-Chee-313
Szwez, Jeff
01Kitchener Rangers-20
03Florence Pride-157
06Syracuse Crunch-16
Szysky, Chris
95Swift Current Broncos-16
96Swift Current Broncos-12
99Grand Rapids Griffins-24
00Grand Rapids Griffins-21
01Grand Rapids Griffins-10
02UK Sheffield Steelers-18
Taavola, Ulf
86Swedish Panini Stickers-188
Tabacek, Jan
02Cincinnati Mighty Ducks-B-6
06Czech OFS-70
Tabara, Zdislav
94Czech APS Extraliga-298
95Czech APS Extraliga-2
96Czech APS Extraliga-213
97Czech APS Extraliga-27
98Czech OFS-97
98Czech OFS-468
99Czech OFS-56
00Czech OFS-318
Tabaracci, Rick
89ProCards AHL-45
90Jets IGA-32
90Pro Set-649
90Upper Deck-520
French-520
90Moncton Hawks-23
90ProCards AHL/IHL-343
91Bowman-207
91Jets IGA-32
91Jets Panini Team Stickers-24
91O-Pee-Chee-158
91O-Pee-Chee-375
91Score Canadian Bilingual-244
91Score Canadian English-244
91Stadium Club-395
91Topps-375
91Upper Deck-339
French-339
91Moncton Hawks-26
91ProCards-185
92Bowman-324
92Score-529
Canadian-529
92Stadium Club-135
92Topps-453
Gold-453G
92Ultra-445
92Upper Deck-58
92Upper Deck-358
93Donruss-363
93Leaf-241
93OPC Premier-239
Gold-239
93Pinnacle-299
Canadian-299
93PowerPlay-267
93Score-403
Canadian-403
93Stadium Club-378
Members Only Master Set-378
First Day Issue-378
Master Photos-19
Master Photos Winners-19
93Topps/OPC Premier-239
Gold-239
94Canada Games NHL POGS-299
94Donruss-49
94Flair-204
94OPC Premier-367
Special Effects-367
94Parkhurst-255
Gold-255
94Pinnacle-444
Artist's Proofs-444
Rink Collection-444
Masks-MA5
94Stadium Club-74
Members Only Master Set-74
First Day Issue-74
Super Team Winner Cards-74
94Topps/OPC Premier-367
Special Effects-367
94Ultra-239
94Upper Deck-187
Electric Ice-187
95Donruss-214
95Parkhurst International-32
Emerald Ice-32
95Stadium Club-119
Members Only Master Set-119
95Upper Deck-196
Electric Ice-196
Electric Ice Gold-196
Special Edition-SE103
Special Edition Gold-SE103
96Be A Player-164
Autographs-164
Autographs Silver-164
96Donruss-10
Press Proofs-10
96Leaf-149
Press Proofs-149
96Pinnacle-66
Artist's Proofs-66
Foil-66
Premium Stock-66
Rink Collection-66
96Score-23
Artist's Proofs-23
Dealer's Choice Artist's Proofs-23
Special Artist's Proofs-23
Golden Blades-23
97Donruss Priority-105
Stamp of Approval-105
97Pacific-256
Copper-256
Emerald Green-256
Ice Blue-256
Red-256
Silver-256
97Pacific Omega-36
Copper-36
Dark Gray-36
Emerald Green-36
Gold-36
Ice Blue-36
97Paramount-31
Copper-31
Dark Grey-31
Emerald Green-31
Ice Blue-31
Red-31
Silver-31
97Revolution-21
Copper-21
Emerald-21
Ice Blue-21
Silver-21
97Score-28
Artist's Proofs-28
Golden Blades-28
97Upper Deck-236
98NHL Aces Playing Cards-8
98OPC Chrome-77
Refractors-77
98Pacific-126
Ice Blue-126
Red-126
98Panini Stickers-179
98Paramount-33
Copper-33
Emerald Green-33
Holo-Electric-33
Ice Blue-33
Silver-33
98Topps-77
O-Pee-Chee-77
99Pacific-448
Copper-448
Emerald Green-448
Gold-448
Ice Blue-448
Premiere Date-448
Red-448
00Utah Grizzlies-16
Tabobondung, Barry
80Oshawa Generals-8
Tabor, Heiko
94German First League-637
Tabor, Jan
94German DEL-404
95German DEL-423
Taborsky, Martin
98Czech OFS-399
99Czech OFS-333
00Czech OFS-118
Taborsky, Pavel
94Czech APS Extraliga-78
95Czech APS Extraliga-9
98Czech OFS-165
Tabuchie, Nick
56Quebec Aces-13
Tacchini, Eammanuel
01Swiss HNL-429
Taccoz, Gabriel
93Swiss HNL-334
95Swiss HNL-257
96Swiss HNL-396
99Swiss Panini Stickers-359
00Swiss Panini Stickers-322
01Swiss HNL-359
Taffe, Jeff
99Minnesota Golden Gophers-24
00Minnesota Golden Gophers-24
01SPx Rookie Redemption-R23
01Minnesota Golden Gophers-21
02Atomic-130
02BAP All-Star Edition-131
Gold-131
Silver-131
02BAP First Edition-435H
02BAP Memorabilia-279
Emerald-279
Ruby-279
Sapphire-279
NHL All-Star Game-279
NHL All-Star Game Blue-279
NHL All-Star Game Green-279
NHL All-Star Game Red-279
02BAP Memorabilia Toronto Fall Expo-279
02BAP Ultimate Memorabilia-31
02Crown Royale-132
Blue-132
Purple-132
Red-132
Retail-132
02ITG Used-190
02Pacific Calder-138
Silver-138
02Pacific Complete-578
Red-578
02Pacific Quest for the Cup-138
Gold-138
02Parkhurst-231
Bronze-231
Gold-231
Silver-231
02Parkhurst Retro-231
Minis-231
02Private Stock Reserve-178
Blue-178
Red-178
Retail-178
02SP Authentic-192
02SP Game Used-89
02SPx-157
02Titanium-130
Blue-130
Red-130
Retail-130
02Topps Chrome-171
Black Border Refractors-171
Refractors-171
02Topps Total-428
02UD Artistic Impressions-119
Gold-119
Common Ground-CG20
Common Ground Gold-CG20
02UD Honor Roll-123
02UD Mask Collection-174
02UD Premier Collection-76
Gold-76
Signatures Bronze-STA
Signatures Gold-STA
Signatures Silver-STA
02UD Top Shelf-134
02Upper Deck-448
Exclusives-448
02Upper Deck Classic Portraits-125
02Upper Deck Rookie Update-153A
02Upper Deck Rookie Update-153B
02Upper Deck Rookie Update-153C
02Vanguard-129
LTD-129
02AHL Top Prospects-41
02Springfield Falcons-22
03Black Diamond Signature Gems-SG-37
03Coyotes Postcards-24
03ITG Action-470
03Pacific-268
Blue-268
Red-268
03Upper Deck MVP-330
Gold Script-330
Silver Script-330
Canadian Exclusives-330
03AHL Top Prospects-36
03Pacific AHL Prospects-79
Gold-79
04Pacific-207
Blue-207
Red-207
06ITG Heroes and Prospects-166
Autographs-AJTF
Update Autographs-AJTF
Taglianetti, Peter
86Sherbrooke Canadiens-26
87Jets Postcards-21
88Jets Police-22
88Jets Postcards-23
88O-Pee-Chee-257
88Panini Stickers-152
89Jets Safeway-27
89O-Pee-Chee-297
89O-Pee-Chee Stickers-146
89Panini Stickers-174
90O-Pee-Chee-435
90OPC Premier-117
90Pro Set-505
90Score Rookie/Traded-16T
91Penguins Coke/Elby's-32
91Penguins Foodland-14
91Score Canadian Bilingual-448
91Score Canadian English-448
92Pinnacle-383
French-383
92Ultra-204
93OPC Premier-248
Gold-248
93Parkhurst-430
Emerald Ice-430
93Penguins Foodland-22
93Score-295
Canadian-295
93Stadium Club-243
Members Only Master Set-243
OPC-243
First Day Issue-243
First Day Issue OPC-243
93Topps/OPC Premier-248
Gold-248
93Ultra-397
93Upper Deck-100
94Donruss-89
94Parkhurst SE-SE141
Gold-SE141
94Penguins Foodland-18
94Pinnacle-505
Artist's Proofs-505
Rink Collection-505
Tahkapaa, Matti
01Finnish Cardset-350
Tahtinen, Markku
99Finnish Cardset-346
00Finnish Cardset-131
01Finnish Cardset-155
02Finnish Cardset-113
03Finnish Cardset-110
04Finnish Cardset-122
Parallel-91
05Finnish Cardset -110
06Swedish SHL Elitset-274
Tahtisalo, Petri
99Finnish Cardset-331
06Finnish Cardset-282
Taillefer, Pete
51Laval Dairy Subset-26
Taillefer, Terry
88ProCards AHL-148
Taillens, Reto
72Finnish Semic World Championship-162
72Swedish Semic World Championship-162
Taimio, Tomi
78Finnish SM-Liiga-41
Tait, Ashley
97UK Kingston Hawks Stickers-13
98UK Kingston Hawks-17
00UK Nottingham Panthers-15
00UK Sekonda Superleague-140
01UK Nottingham Panthers-11
02UK Coventry Blaze-15
03UK Coventry Blaze-13
03UK Coventry Blaze Calendars-2
04UK Coventry Blaze-18
04UK Coventry Blaze Champions-13
05UK Coventry Blaze-12
06UK Coventry Blaze-8
Tait, Terry
80Sault Ste. Marie Greyhounds-6
81Sault Ste. Marie Greyhounds-21
82Sault Ste. Marie Greyhounds-20
84Springfield Indians-11
Tait, Warren
03UK London Racers-17
05UK Sheffield Steelers-9
Gold-9
Silver-9
Tajcnar, Rudolf
72Finnish Jaakiekko-20
72Finnish Hellas-85
72Finnish Panda Toronto-95
72Finnish Semic World Championship-25
72Swedish Semic World Championship-25
74Finnish Jenkki-83
74Swedish Semic World Champ Stickers-69
Takac, Roman
99Prince George Cougars-14
Takala, Markku
93Finnish SISU-276
Takala, Tuomas
05Finnish Cardset -347
06Finnish Cardset-178
06Finnish Porin Assat Pelaajakortit-21
Takhar, Daljit
92British Columbia JHL-218
Takko, Kari
80Finnish Mallasjuoma-220
83Swedish Semic VM Stickers-28
86North Stars Postcards-14
87North Stars Postcards-29
87Panini Stickers-288
88North Stars ADA-23
88Panini Stickers-85
89Panini Stickers-102
89Finnish Pelimiehen-5
90Oilers IGA-26
90Upper Deck-543
French-543
90ProCards AHL/IHL-106
91Finnish Jyvas-Hyva Stickers-67
92Finnish Jyvas-Hyva Stickers-189
93Finnish Jyvas-Hyva Stickers-344
93Finnish SISU-208
94Finnish SISU-27
94Finnish SISU-151
94Finnish SISU NHL Phenoms-2
94Finnish SISU Specials-6
95Finnish SISU-149
Ghost Goalies-4
95Finnish SISU Limited-19
Leaf Gallery-6
96Finnish SISU Redline-149
96Finnish SISU Redline-NNO
96Finnish SISU Redline Foil Parallels-149
96Finnish SISU Redline Mighty Adversaries-1
97Swedish Collector's Choice-84
98Finnish Kerailysarja 90's Top 12-12
98Swedish UD Choice-100
99Finnish Cardset Aces High-S-A
99Swedish Upper Deck-86
Lasting Impressions-5
01Finnish Cardset-232
02Finnish Cardset-123
Tala, Hannu
00Finnish Cardset-110
Talafous, Dean
75O-Pee-Chee NHL-197
75Topps-197
76O-Pee-Chee NHL-103
76Topps-103
77O-Pee-Chee NHL-49
77Topps-49
78O-Pee-Chee-149
78Topps-149
79O-Pee-Chee-54
79Topps-54
80O-Pee-Chee-132
80Topps-132
81O-Pee-Chee-235
95AHCA-8
Talafous, Pete
03Wisconsin Badgers-27
04Wisconsin Badgers-5
Talakowski, Ron
93Thunder Bay Senators-13
Talbot, Eric
93Quebec Pee-Wee Tournament-920
Talbot, Jean-Guy
44Beehive Group II Photos-289
55Parkhurst-53
Quaker Oats-53
57Parkhurst-M9
58Parkhurst-41
59Parkhurst-49
60NHL Ceramic Tiles-23
60Parkhurst-52
60Shirriff Coins-35
60York Photos-35
61Parkhurst-48
61Shirriff/Salada Coins-109
61York Yellow Backs-12
62Parkhurst-51
62Shirriff Coins-39
62Shirriff Coins-44
62York Iron-On Transfers-4
63Chex Photos-52
63Parkhurst-23
63Parkhurst-81
63Toronto Star-37
63York White Backs-23
64Beehive Group III Photos-116
64Coca-Cola Caps-67
64Topps-52
65Canadiens Steinberg Glasses-9
65Coca-Cola-67
65Topps-4
66Topps-3
67Topps-104
68O-Pee-Chee-179
69O-Pee-Chee-15
69Topps-15
70O-Pee-Chee-100
70Sargent Promotions Stamps-189
70Topps-100
72Blues White Border-20
73Blues White Border-20
91Ultimate Original Six-16
French-16
93O-Pee-Chee Canadiens Hockey Fest-53
93Parkhurst Parkie Reprints-PR52
94Parkhurst Missing Link-80
94Parkhurst Missing Link-88
94Parkhurst Tall Boys-76
95Parkhurst '66-67-68
Coins-68
01BAP Memorabilia Rocket's Mates-RM10
01BAP Signature Series Vintage Autographs-VA-25
01Parkhurst Autographs-PA17
01Parkhurst Reprints-PR11
01Parkhurst Reprints-PR44
01Parkhurst Reprints-PR111
01Parkhurst Reprints-PR129
03Parkhurst Original Six Montreal-56
Autographs-17
04ITG Ultimate Memorabilia-57
Gold-57
Talbot, Joe
99Ottawa 67's-11
00Ottawa 67's-1
03ECHL All-Stars-280
03ECHL Update RBI Sports-49
Talbot, Julian
02Ottawa 67's-19
03Ottawa 67's-19
04Ottawa 67's-9
05Ottawa 67's-1
Talbot, Maxime
00Hull Olympiques-16
Signed-16
00Rouyn-Noranda Huskies-7
Signed-7
01Hull Olympiques-18
02Hull Olympiques-17
03Gatineau Olympiques-23
03Hull Olympiques Memorial Cup-17
04SP Authentic Rookie Redemptions-RR46
04Wilkes-Barre Scranton Penguins-18
05Beehive-141
Beige -141
Blue -141
Gold-141
Red -141
Matte-141
05Black Diamond-162
Emerald-162
Gold-162
Onyx-162
Ruby-162
05Hot Prospects-262
En Fuego-262
Hot Materials-HMMT
Red Hot-262
White Hot-262
05Parkhurst-658
Facsimile Auto Parallel-658
True Colors-TCPIT
True Colors-TCPIT
05SP Authentic-182
Limited-182
Rarefied Rookies-RRMT
Sign of the Times-MT
05SP Game Used-123
Autographs-123
Gold-123
Rookie Exclusives-MT
Rookie Exclusives Silver-RE-MT
05SPx-139
Spectrum-139
Xcitement Rookies-XR-MT
Xcitement Rookies Gold-XR-MT
Xcitement Rookies Spectrum-XR-MT
05The Cup-126
Autographed Rookie Patches Gold Rainbow-126
Black Rainbow Rookies-126
Masterpiece Pressplates (Artifacts)-313
Masterpiece Pressplates (Bee Hive)-141
Masterpiece Pressplates (Black Diamond)-162
Masterpiece Pressplates (Ice)-162
Masterpiece Pressplates (Rookie Update)-228
Masterpiece Pressplates SPA Autos-182
Masterpiece Pressplates (SP Game Used)-123
Masterpiece Pressplates (SPx)-139
Masterpiece Pressplates (SPx)-139
Masterpiece Pressplates (Trilogy)-212
Masterpiece Pressplates Ult Coll-164
Masterpiece Pressplates (Victory)-286
Masterpiece Pressplates Autographs-126
Platinum Rookies-126
05UD Artifacts-313
05Ultimate Collection-164
Gold-164
Ultimate Debut Threads Jerseys-DTJMT
Ultimate Debut Threads Jerseys Autos-DAJMT
Ultimate Debut Threads Patches-DTPMT
Ultimate Debut Threads Patches Autos-DAPMT
05Ultra-240
Gold-240
Ice-240
Rookie Uniformity Jerseys-RU-MT
Rookie Uniformity Jersey Autographs-ARU-MT
Rookie Uniformity Patches-RUP-MT
Rookie Uniformity Patch Autographs-ARP-MT
05Upper Deck-236
HG Glossy-236
Rookie Ink-RIMT
Rookie Threads-RTMT
Rookie Threads Autographs-ARTMT
05Upper Deck Ice-162
Fresh Ice-FIMT
Fresh Ice Glass-FIMT
Fresh Ice Glass Patches-FIPMT
Premieres Auto Patches-AIPMT
05Upper Deck Rookie Update-228
Inspirations Patch Rookies-228
05Upper Deck Trilogy-212
05Upper Deck Toronto Fall Expo-236
05Upper Deck Victory-286
Black-286
Gold-286
Silver-286
06UD Powerplay Power Marks-PMMT
06Wilkes-Barre Scranton Penguins-13
06Wilkes-Barre Scranton Penguins Jerseys-16
06ITG Heroes and Prospects Jerseys-GUJ13
06ITG Heroes and Prospects Jerseys Gold-GUJ13
06ITG Heroes and Prospects Emblems-GUE13
06ITG Heroes and Prospects Emblems Gold-GUE13
06ITG Heroes and Prospects Numbers-GUN13
06ITG Heroes and Prospects Numbers Gold-GUN13
Taliercio, Chris
02Louisiana Ice Gators-20
03Columbus Stars-5
Tallackson, Barry
01Minnesota Golden Gophers-25
02Minnesota Golden Gophers-24
03Minnesota Golden Gophers-1
04Minnesota Golden Gophers-26
05Beehive-153
Matte-153
05Black Diamond-259
05Hot Prospects-248
En Fuego-248
Hot Materials-HMBT
Red Hot-248
White Hot-248
05Parkhurst-641
Facsimile Auto Parallel-641
Signatures-BT
True Colors-TCNJD
True Colors-TCNJD
05SP Authentic-201
Limited-201
05SP Game Used-222
05SPx-235
Spectrum-235
05The Cup-145
Autographed Rookie Patches Gold Rainbow-145
Black Rainbow Rookies-145
Masterpiece Pressplates (Artifacts)-296
Masterpiece Pressplates (Bee Hive)-153
Masterpiece Pressplates (Black Diamond)-259
Masterpiece Pressplates (Ice)-200
Masterpiece Pressplates (Rookie Update)-217
Masterpiece Pressplates SPA Autos-201
Masterpiece Pressplates (SP Game Used)-222
Masterpiece Pressplates SPx Autos-235
Masterpiece Pressplates (Trilogy)-277
Masterpiece Pressplates Ult Coll-189
Masterpiece Pressplates Autographs-145
Platinum Rookies-145
05UD Artifacts-296
05Ultimate Collection-189
Gold-189
Ultimate Debut Threads Jerseys-DTJBT
Ultimate Debut Threads Jerseys Autos-DAJBT
Ultimate Debut Threads Patches-DTPBT
Ultimate Debut Threads Patches Autos-DAPBT
05Upper Deck-472
05Upper Deck Ice-200
Premieres Auto Patches-AIPBT
05Upper Deck Rookie Update-217
Inspirations Patch Rookies-217
05Upper Deck Trilogy-277
05AHL Top Prospects-41
05Albany River Rats-25
06Devils Team Set-24
06Fleer Fabricology-FBT
06Hot Prospects Hotagraphs-HBT
06Upper Deck Game Jerseys-JBT
06Upper Deck Game Patches-PBT
Tallackson, Trevor
94Dubuque Fighting Saints-28
Tallaire, Gerald
91Air Canada SJHL-B19
91Air Canada SJHL All-Stars-35
91Air Canada SJHL All-Stars-48
92Saskatchewan JHL-3
01Austin Ice Bats-16
02Austin Ice Bats-18
03Austin Ice Bats-17
Tallaire, Sean
91Air Canada SJHL-C18
92Lake Superior State Lakers-27
97Grand Rapids Griffins-18
99Utah Grizzlies-10
00Kansas City Blades-5
01German Upper Deck-120
02German DEL City Press-145
Top Scorers-TS7
03German DEL-88
04German DEL-259
05German DEL-156
06German DEL-129
Tallari, Joe
04Johnstown Chiefs-17
05Johnstown Chiefs-17
06Las Vegas Wranglers-22
Tallarini, Alain
02Swiss HNL-189
Tallas, Rob
91British Columbia JHL-106
91British Columbia JHL-119
917th Inn. Sketch WHL-126
93Seattle Thunderbirds-26
96Providence Bruins-29
97Score Bruins-3
Platinum-3
Premier-3
97Upper Deck-223
97Providence Bruins-1
98Be A Player-158
Press Release-158
98BAP Gold-158
98BAP Autographs-158
98BAP Autographs Gold-158
98NHL Aces Playing Cards-28
98Pacific-100
Ice Blue-100
Red-100
98Pacific Omega-18
Red-18
Opening Day Issue-18
99Pacific-29
Copper-29
Emerald Green-29
Gold-29
Ice Blue-29
Premiere Date-29
Red-29
00Upper Deck NHLPA-PA21
01Wilkes-Barre Scranton Penguins-1
02BAP Sig Series Auto Buybacks 1998-158
02Wilkes-Barre Scranton Penguins-22
03Finnish Cardset-30
Tallberg, Gunnar
65Swedish Coralli ISHockey-70
67Swedish Hockey-195
69Swedish Hockey-251
Tallberg, Thomas
86Swedish Panini Stickers-107
91Swedish Semic Elitserien Stickers-44
92Swedish Semic Elitserien Stickers-62
93Swedish Semic Elitserien-36
94Swedish Leaf-1
95Swedish Leaf-22
Tallinder, Henrik
98Swedish UD Choice-7
99Swedish Upper Deck-7
99Swedish Upper Deck-201
00Finnish Cardset-216
01Parkhurst-322
01SPx Rookie Redemption-R4
01Finnish Cardset-137
02Bowman YoungStars-107
Gold-107
Silver-107
Autographs-HT
Jerseys-HT
Patches-HT
Double Stuff-HT
Triple Stuff-HT
Rivals-DVHT
Rivals Patches-5
Sticks-HT
02Pacific Calder-59
Silver-59
02Pacific Complete-562
Red-562
02SPx-104
02UD Foundations-124
02UD Piece of History-123
02Upper Deck-198
Exclusives-198
02Upper Deck MVP-196
Gold-196
Classics-196
Golden Classics-196
02Upper Deck Vintage-323
02Finnish Cardset-275
03ITG Action-33
04Swedish Elitset-203
Dominators-6
Gold-203
05Parkhurst-66
Facsimile Auto Parallel-66
06O-Pee-Chee-56
Rainbow-56
06Upper Deck-24
Exclusives Parallel-24
High Gloss Parallel-24
Masterpieces-24
Tallon, Dale
70Canucks Royal Bank-16
70Colgate Stamps-81
70Dad's Cookies-127
70Esso Power Players-50
70O-Pee-Chee-225
70Post Shooters-15
70Sargent Promotions Stamps-215
71Canucks Royal Bank-11
71Colgate Heads-13
71Letraset Action Replays-20
71O-Pee-Chee-234
O-Pee-Chee/Topps Booklets-3
Posters-5
71Sargent Promotions Stamps-209
71Topps-95
71Toronto Sun-291
72Canucks Royal Bank-17
72O-Pee-Chee-121
Player Crests-21
72Sargent Promotions Stamps-211
72Topps-15
72Finnish Semic World Championship-222
72Swedish Semic World Championship-222
73Mac's Milk-28
73O-Pee-Chee-211
73Topps-129
74Lipton Soup-22
74NHL Action Stamps-74
74O-Pee-Chee NHL-360
75O-Pee-Chee NHL-351
76O-Pee-Chee NHL-89
76O-Pee-Chee NHL-382
76Topps-89
77O-Pee-Chee NHL-124
77Topps-124
78O-Pee-Chee-146
78Topps-146
91Future Trends Canada '72-22
91Future Trends Canada '72 French-22
91Pro Set-595
French-595
04ITG Franchises Canadian-133
Autographs-DTL
Tambellini, Jeff
02Michigan Wolverines-7
03BAP Memorabilia Draft Redemptions-27
03Michigan Wolverines-1
04Michigan Wolverines-22
05ITG Heroes/Prosp Toronto Expo Parallel -204
05Beehive-159
Matte-159
05Black Diamond-247
05Hot Prospects-241
En Fuego-241
Hot Materials-HMJT
Red Hot-241
White Hot-241
05Parkhurst-642
Facsimile Auto Parallel-633
Signatures-JT
05SP Authentic-217
Limited-217
05SP Game Used-215
05SPx-231
Spectrum-231
05The Cup-150
Black Rainbow Rookies-150
Masterpiece Pressplates (Artifacts)-284
Masterpiece Pressplates (Bee Hive)-159
Masterpiece Pressplates (Black Diamond)-247
Masterpiece Pressplates (Ice)-219
Masterpiece Pressplates (Rookie Update)-212
Masterpiece Pressplates SPA Autos-217
Masterpiece Pressplates (SP Game Used)-215
Masterpiece Pressplates SPx Autos-231
Masterpiece Pressplates (Trilogy)-263
Masterpiece Pressplates Ult Coll-190
Masterpiece Pressplates Autographs-150
Platinum Rookies-150
05UD Artifacts-284
05Ultimate Collection-190
Gold-190
Ultimate Debut Threads Jerseys-DTJJT
Ultimate Debut Threads Patches-DTPJT
05Upper Deck-486
05Upper Deck Ice-219
05Upper Deck Rookie Update-212
05Upper Deck Trilogy-263
05AHL All-Stars-39
05AHL Top Prospects-42
05Manchester Monarchs-19
05Manchester Monarchs-16
05ITG Heroes and Prospects-204
Autographs Series II-JTA
Complete Jerseys-CJ-39
Complete Jerseys Gold-CJ-39
Complete Logos-AHL-18
Jerseys-GUJ-61
Jerseys Gold-GUJ-61
Emblems-GUE-61
Emblems Gold-GUE-61
Numbers-GUN-61
Numbers Gold-GUN-61
Nameplates-N-39
Nameplates Gold-N-39
06Be A Player Portraits First Exposures-FEJT
06Fleer Signing Day-SDTA
06O-Pee-Chee-317
Rainbow-317
06UD Toronto Fall Expo Priority Signings -PSJT
06Upper Deck Arena Giveaways-NYI2
06Upper Deck-124
Exclusives Parallel-124
High Gloss Parallel-124
Masterpieces-124
Signatures-SJT
06Upper Deck MVP-190
Gold Script-190
Super Script-190
06Upper Deck Trilogy Scripts-TSTA
06AHL Top Prospects-5
06ITG Heroes and Prospects-75
AHL All-Star Jerseys-AJ01
AHL All-Star Jerseys Gold-AJ01
AHL All-Star Emblems-AE01
AHL All-Star Emblems Gold-AE01
AHL All-Star Numbers-AN01
AHL All-Star Numbers Gold-AN01
Autographs-AJTA
Tambellini, Steve
79Islanders Transparencies-19
80O-Pee-Chee-365
81O-Pee-Chee-81
81Rockies Postcards-27
81Topps-W86
82O-Pee-Chee-134
82O-Pee-Chee-147
82O-Pee-Chee Stickers-226
82Post Cereal-11
82Topps Stickers-226
83NHL Key Tags-75
83O-Pee-Chee-93
83O-Pee-Chee-223
83O-Pee-Chee Stickers-219
83Puffy Stickers-4
83Topps Stickers-219
83Vachon-19
84O-Pee-Chee-237
84O-Pee-Chee Stickers-239
85Canucks Team Issue-23
86Canucks Team Issue-22
86Canucks Shell Oil-22
87O-Pee-Chee-259
87Panini Stickers-351
88O-Pee-Chee-258
88O-Pee-Chee Stickers-62
Tambijevs, Leonids
98Finnish Kerailysarja-179
99Finnish Cardset-91
99Finnish Cardset-165
03Russian World Championship Stars-2
Tamburro, Mike
93RPI Engineers-29
96Cleveland Lumberjacks-24
96Cleveland Lumberjacks Multi-Ad-26
97Cleveland Lumberjacks-25
97Cleveland Lumberjacks Postcards-24
00Jackson Bandits-1
00Jackson Bandits Promos-7
Tamer, Chris
91Michigan Wolverines-21
93Cleveland Lumberjacks-7
93Cleveland Lumberjacks Postcards-20
93Classic-83
94Leaf-513
94OPC Premier-224
Special Effects-224
94Penguins Foodland-12
94Pinnacle-259
Artist's Proofs-259
Rink Collection-259
Rookie Team Pinnacle-4
94Topps/OPC Premier-224
Special Effects-224
94Upper Deck-318
Electric Ice-318
94Cleveland Lumberjacks-6
94Cleveland Lumberjacks Postcards-6
94Classic-94
Gold-94
Autographs-94
94Classic Pro Prospects-119
95Parkhurst International-436
Emerald Ice-436
95Penguins Foodland-18
95Topps-169
OPC Inserts-169
96Be A Player-182
Autographs-182
Autographs Silver-182
96Collector's Edge Ice-119
Prism-119
97Pacific Invincible NHL Regime-165
97Upper Deck-345
98Pacific-359
Ice Blue-359
Red-359
00Stadium Club-174
01Upper Deck Vintage-12
02Thrashers Postcards-17
03Thrashers Postcards-21
Tamer, John
84Belleville Bulls-25
Tammelin, Rauli
70Finnish Jaakiekko-169
71Finnish Suomi Stickers-240
72Finnish Jaakiekko-224
73Finnish Jaakiekko-301
78Finnish SM-Liiga-213
80Finnish Mallasjuoma-186
Tammi, Jukka
89Swedish Semic World Champ Stickers-28
91Finnish Semic World Champ Stickers-4
91Finnish Jyvas-Hyva Stickers-13
91Swedish Semic World Champ Stickers-4
92Finnish Jyvas-Hyva Stickers-36
93Finnish Jyvas-Hyva Stickers-74
93Finnish SISU-109
94Finnish SISU-38
94Finnish SISU Magic Numbers-10
94Finnish Jaa Kiekko-3
95Finnish SISU-339
Ghost Goalies-8
Gold Cards-4
95Finnish SISU Limited-91
95Finnish Karjala World Champ Labels-21
95Finnish Semic World Championships-30
95Finnish Semic World Championships-216
95Swedish World Championships Stickers-162
96German DEL-47
96Swedish Semic Wien-12
98Finnish Kerailysarja 90's Top 12-4
98Finnish Kerailysarja Leijonat-3
98German DEL-132
Tammi, Veli-Matti
70Finnish Jaakiekko-356
Tamminen, Joe
93Minnesota-Duluth Bulldogs-29
Tamminen, Juhani
65Finnish Hellas-102
70Finnish Jaakiekko-77
70Finnish Jaakiekko-170
70Finnish Jaakiekko-357
70Swedish Hockey-311
71Finnish Suomi Stickers-76
71Finnish Suomi Stickers-162
71Swedish Hockey-73
72Finnish Jaakiekko-114
72Finnish Hellas-16
72Finnish Semic World Championship-88
72Swedish Semic World Championship-88
73Finnish Jaakiekko-80
73Finnish Jaakiekko-144
74Finnish Jenkki-20
74Finnish Typotor-5
74Finnish Typotor-57
74Swedish Stickers-34
74Swedish Semic World Champ Stickers-92
76Phoenix Roadrunners WHA-18
77Finnish Sportscasters-46-1084
78Finnish SM-Liiga-16
78Finnish SM-Liiga-208
79Panini Stickers-176
80Finnish Mallasjuoma-161
81Swedish Semic Hockey VM Stickers-34
82Finnish Skopbank-16
82Swedish Semic VM Stickers-50
92Finnish Semic-194

94French National Team-31
96Finnish SISU Redline-198

Tamminen, Kauko
71Finnish Suomi Stickers-335

Tamminen, Mikko
98Finnish Keräilysarja-209

Tamminen, Teemu
93Finnish SISU-252

Tamminen, Tiny
51Laval Dairy Lac St. Jean-37

Tanabe, David
98Black Diamond-120
Double Diamond-120
Triple Diamond-120
Quadruple Diamond-120
98SPx Top Prospects-90
Radiance-90
Spectrum-90
99BAP Memorabilia-359
Gold-359
Silver-359
99BAP Millennium Calder Candidates Ruby-C5
99BAP Millennium Calder Candidate Emerald-C5
99BAP Millennium Calder Cand Sapphire-C5
99Black Diamond-18
Diamond Cut-18
Final Cut-18
99Pacific-454
99Pacific Dynagon Ice-44
Blue-44
Copper-44
Gold-44
Premiere Date-44
99Pacific Omega-50
Copper-50
Gold-50
Ice Blue-50
Premiere Date-50
99SP Authentic Sign of the Times-DT
99SP Authentic Sign of the Times Gold-DT
99SPx-178
Radiance-178
Spectrum-178
99Stadium Club-178
First Day Issue-178
One of a Kind-178
Printing Plates Black-178
Printing Plates Cyan-178
Printing Plates Magenta-178
Printing Plates Yellow-178
99Topps Arena Giveaways-CAR-DT
99Topps Gold Label Class 1-93
Black-93
Black One of One-93
One of One-93
Red-93
Red One of One-93
99Topps Gold Label Class 2-93
99Topps Gold Label Class 2 Black-93
99Topps Gold Label Class 2 Black 1 of 1-93
99Topps Gold Label Class 2 One of One-93
99Topps Gold Label Class 2 Red-93
99Topps Gold Label Class 2 Red One of One-93
99Topps Gold Label Class 3-93
99Topps Gold Label Class 3 Black-93
99Topps Gold Label Class 3 Black 1 of 1-93
99Topps Gold Label Class 3 One of One-93
99Topps Gold Label Class 3 Red-93
99Topps Gold Label Class 3 Red One of One-93
99Topps Premier Plus-124
Parallel-124
99Upper Deck Arena Giveaways-CH1
99Upper Deck Ovation-12
Standing Ovation-12
99Wayne Gretzky Hockey-36
00BAP Memorabilia-47
Emerald-47
Ruby-47
Sapphire-47
Promos-47
00BAP Mem Chicago Sportsfest Copper-47
00BAP Memorabilia Chicago Sportsfest Blue-47
00BAP Memorabilia Chicago Sportsfest Gold-47
00BAP Memorabilia Chicago Sportsfest Ruby-47
00BAP Memorabilia Chicago Sun-Times Ruby-47
00BAP Memorabilia Chicago Sun-Times Gold-47
00BAP Mem Chicago Sun-Times Sapphire-47
00BAP Mem Toronto Fall Expo Copper-47
00BAP Memorabilia Toronto Fall Expo Gold-47
00BAP Memorabilia Toronto Fall Expo Ruby-47
00BAP Parkhurst 2000-P223
00BAP Signature Series-116
Emerald-116
Ruby-116
Sapphire-116
Autographs-162
Autographs Gold-162
00O-Pee-Chee-279
00O-Pee-Chee Parallel-279
00Pacific-90
Copper-90
Gold-90
Ice Blue-90
Premiere Date-90
00Paramount-46
Copper-46
Gold-46
Holo-Gold-46
Holo-Silver-46
Ice Blue-46
Premiere Date-46
00Topps/OPC-279
Parallel-279
00Topps Chrome-174
OPC Refractors-174
Refractors-174
00Upper Deck-35
Exclusives Tier 1-35
Exclusives Tier 2-35
00Upper Deck MVP-36
First Stars-36
Second Stars-36
Third Stars-36
00Upper Deck Victory-274
00Upper Deck Vintage-70
01BAP Memorabilia-48
Emerald-48
Ruby-48
Sapphire-48
01BAP Signature Series-113
Autographs-113
Autographs Gold-113
01Bowman YoungStars-133
Gold-133
Ice Cubed-133
Autographs-DT
Relics-JDT
Relics-SDT
Relics-DSDT
Rivals-R3
01O-Pee-Chee-196
01O-Pee-Chee Premier Parallel-196
01Parkhurst-51
Gold-51
Silver-51
01Topps-196
OPC Parallel-196
01Upper Deck-34
Exclusives-34
01Upper Deck MVP-36
01Upper Deck Victory-66
Gold-66
01Upper Deck Vintage-47
02BAP Sig Series Auto Buybacks 2000-162
02BAP Sig Series Auto Buybacks 2001-113
02O-Pee-Chee-119
02O-Pee-Chee Premier Blue Parallel-119
02O-Pee-Chee Premier Red Parallel-119
02O-Pee-Chee Factory Set-119
02Pacific-70
Blue-70
Red-70
02Pacific Complete-82
Red-82
02Stadium Club YoungStars Relics-S13
02Topps-119
OPC Blue Parallel-119
OPC Red Parallel-119
Factory Set-119
02Topps Total-242
02Upper Deck Vintage-51
03Beehive-150
Gold-150
Silver-150
03Coyotes Postcards-7
03Coyotes Postcards-25
03Pacific Complete-381
Red-381
03Upper Deck-396
Canadian Exclusives-396
HG-396
UD Exclusives-396
05Bruins Boston Globe-8
05Parkhurst-45
Facsimile Auto Parallel-45
06Hurricanes Postcards-22

Tanaka, Cory
05Belleville Bulls-22
05Plymouth Whalers-A-05
06Belleville Bulls-12

Tanberg, T.J.
99Greensboro Generals-6

Tancill, Chris
90ProCards AHL/IHL-179
91Pro Set-539
French-539
91Upper Deck-455
French-455
91ProCards-104
93Donruss-84
93OPC Premier-429
Gold-429
93Parkhurst-318
Emerald Ice-318
93Topps/OPC Premier-429
Gold-429
93Classic Pro Prospects-20
94Kansas City Blades-6
95Kansas City Blades-19
96Pinnacle-71
Artist's Proofs-71
Foil-71
Premium Stock-71
Rink Collection-71
96Kentucky Thoroughblades-16
98Swiss Power Play Stickers-123
99Swiss Panini Stickers-222
00Swiss Panini Stickers-265
00Swiss Slapshot Mini-Cards-EVZ16
01Swiss EV Zug Postcards-24
01Swiss HNL-189
02Swiss EV Zug Postcards-3
02Swiss HNL-167
03Swiss EV Zug Postcards-25

Tanel, Matt
01Mississauga Ice Dogs-2

Tanevski, Dan
907th Inn. Sketch OHL-221
917th Inn. Sketch OHL-347B
93Sault Ste. Marie Greyhound Memorial Cup-2

Tangradi, Eric
06Belleville Bulls-13

Tanguay, Alex
92Quebec Pee-Wee Tournament-1252
93Quebec Pee-Wee Tournament-523
96Halifax Mooseheads I-20
96Halifax Mooseheads II-20
97Black Diamond-105
Double Diamond-105
Triple Diamond-105
Quadruple Diamond-105
97Zenith-99
Z-Gold-99
Z-Silver-99
97Zenith 5 x 7-79
Gold Impulse-79
Silver Impulse-79
97Halifax Mooseheads I-20
97Halifax Mooseheads II-20
97Halifax Mooseheads II-27
98Finest Futures Finest-F10
98Finest Futures Finest Refractors-F10
98OPC Chrome-237
Refractors-237
98Topps-237
O-Pee-Chee-237
98UD Choice-257
Prime Choice Reserve-257
Reserve-257
98Upper Deck Game Jerseys-GJ14
98Halifax Mooseheads-7
98Halifax Mooseheads-27
98Halifax Mooseheads Second Edition-21
98Bowman CHL-108
98Bowman CHL-152
Golden Anniversary-108
Golden Anniversary-152
OPC International-108
OPC International-152
Autographs Blue-A35
Autographs Gold-A35
Autographs Silver-A35
Scout's Choice-SC15
98Bowman Chrome CHL-108
98Bowman Chrome CHL-152
Golden Anniversary-108
Golden Anniversary-152
Golden Anniversary Refractors-108
Golden Anniversary Refractors-152
OPC International-108
OPC International-152
OPC International Refractors-108
OPC International Refractors-152
Refractors-108
Refractors-152
99Avalanche Team Issue-23
99BAP Memorabilia-79
Gold-79
Silver-79
99BAP Millennium-73
Emerald-73
Ruby-73
Sapphire-73
Signatures-73
Signatures Gold-73
Calder Candidates Ruby-C1
Calder Candidates Emerald-C1
Calder Candidates Sapphire-C1
99Crown Royale-41
Limited Series-41
Premiere Date-41
Prospects Parallel-41
Card-Supials-8
Card-Supials Minis-8
99O-Pee-Chee Chrome-287
99O-Pee-Chee Chrome Refractors-287
99Pacific Dynagon Ice-62
Blue-62
Copper-62
Gold-62
Premiere Date-62
99Pacific Omega-67
Copper-67
Gold-67
Ice Blue-67
Premiere Date-67
5 Star Talents-2
5 Star Talents Parallel-2
99Pacific Prism-42
Holographic Blue-42
Holographic Gold-42
Holographic Mirror-42
Holographic Purple-42
Premiere Date-42
Clear Advantage-6
Ice Prospects-3
99Panini Stickers-216
99Panini Stickers-355
99Paramount-255
99SP Authentic Sign of the Times-AT
99SP Authentic Sign of the Times Gold-AT
99SPx-41
Radiance-41
Spectrum-41
SPXcitement-X13
99Stadium Club-194
First Day Issue-194
One of a Kind-194
Printing Plates Black-194
Printing Plates Cyan-194
Printing Plates Magenta-194
Printing Plates Yellow-194
Chrome-46
Chrome Refractors-46
99Topps Arena Giveaways-COL-AT
99Topps/OPC Chrome-287
Refractors-287
99Topps Gold Label Class 1-91
Black-91
Black One of One-91
One of One-91
Red-91
Red One of One-91
99Topps Gold Label Class 2-91
99Topps Gold Label Class 2 Black-91
99Topps Gold Label Class 2 Black 1 of 1-91
99Topps Gold Label Class 2 One of One-91
99Topps Gold Label Class 2 Red-91
99Topps Gold Label Class 2 Red One of One-91
99Topps Gold Label Class 3-91
99Topps Gold Label Class 3 Black-91
99Topps Gold Label Class 3 Black 1 of 1-91
99Topps Gold Label Class 3 One of One-91
99Topps Gold Label Class 3 Red-91
99Topps Gold Label Class 3 Red One of One-91
99Topps Gold Label Fresh Gold-FG9
99Topps Gold Label Fresh Gold Black-FG9
99Topps Gold Label Fresh Gold Black 1of1-FG9
99Topps Gold Label Fresh Gold One of One-FG9
99Topps Gold Label Fresh Gold Red-FG9
99Topps Gold Label Fresh Gold Red 1 of 1-FG9
99Topps Premier Plus-133
Parallel-133
Premier Rookies-PR1
Premier Rookies Parallel-PR1
Signing Bonus-SB5
99Upper Deck-212
Exclusives-212
Exclusives 1 of 1-212
99Upper Deck Arena Giveaways-CA1
99Upper Deck Gold Reserve-212
99Upper Deck MVP SC Edition ProSign-AT
99Upper Deck Ovation-16
Standing Ovation-16
99Upper Deck Victory-364
99Wayne Gretzky Hockey-52
99Quebec PeeWee Tournament Coll Souv-10
99Bowman CHL-55
Gold-55
OPC International-55
Scout's Choice-SC18
00Aurora-42
Pinstripes-42
Pinstripes Premiere Date-42
Premiere Date-42
Autographs-42
00BAP Memorabilia-25
Emerald-25
Ruby-25
Sapphire-25
Promos-25
00BAP Mem Chicago Sportsfest Copper-25
00BAP Memorabilia Chicago Sportsfest Blue-25
00BAP Memorabilia Chicago Sportsfest Gold-25
00BAP Memorabilia Chicago Sportsfest Ruby-25
00BAP Memorabilia Chicago Sun-Times Ruby-25
00BAP Memorabilia Chicago Sun-Times Gold-25
00BAP Mem Chicago Sun-Times Sapphire-25
00BAP Mem Toronto Fall Expo Copper-25
00BAP Memorabilia Toronto Fall Expo Gold-25
00BAP Memorabilia Toronto Fall Expo Ruby-25
00BAP Parkhurst 2000-P38
00BAP Signature Series-137
Emerald-137
Ruby-137
Sapphire-137
Autographs-120
Autographs Gold-120
00McDonald's Pacific Gold Crown Die Cuts-2
00O-Pee-Chee-229
00O-Pee-Chee Parallel-229
00Pacific-123
Copper-123
Gold-123
Ice Blue-123
Premiere Date-123
Autographs-123
00Paramount-65
Copper-65
Gold-65
Holo-Gold-65
Holo-Silver-65
Ice Blue-65
Premiere Date-65
Game Used Sticks-7
00Private Stock Game Gear-32
00Private Stock PS-2001 Action-14
00Revolution-40
Blue-40
Premiere Date-40
Red-40
00Stadium Club-161
00Titanium-24
Blue-24
Gold-24
Premiere Date-24
Red-24
Retail-24
00Topps/OPC-229
Parallel-229
Own the Game-OTG22
00Topps Chrome-144
OPC Refractors-144
Refractors-144
00Topps Gold Label New Generation-NG4
00Topps Gold Label New Generation 1 to 1-NG4
00Topps Heritage-139
00Topps Heritage-229
00UD Heroes-30
00Upper Deck-275
Exclusives Tier 1-275
Exclusives Tier 2-275
Prospects In Depth-P3
00Upper Deck MVP-54
First Stars-54
Second Stars-54
Third Stars-54
00Upper Deck Victory-67
00Upper Deck Vintage-95
01Atomic-28
Blue-28
Gold-28
Premiere Date-28
Red-28
01Avalanche Team Issue-12
01BAP Memorabilia-13
Emerald-13
Ruby-13
Sapphire-13
He Shoots-He Scores Prizes-3
Stanley Cup Champions-CA6
01BAP Signature Series-103
Autographs-103
Autographs Gold-103
Jerseys-GJ-14
Jersey Autographs-GUAT
Jersey and Stick Cards-GSJ-14
01BAP Update He Shoots-He Scores Prizes-37
01Bowman YoungStars-113
Gold-113
Ice Cubed-113
01Crown Royale-41
Blue-41
Premiere Date-41
Red-41
Retail-41
01O-Pee-Chee-12
01O-Pee-Chee Heritage Parallel-12
01O-Pee-Chee Heritage Parallel Limited-12
01O-Pee-Chee Premier Parallel-12
01Pacific-108
Extreme LTD-108
Hobby LTD-108
Premiere Date-108
Retail LTD-108
01Pacific Adrenaline-51
Blue-51
Premiere Date-51
Red-51
Retail-51
01Pacific Arena Exclusives-108
01Pacific Heads-Up Breaking the Glass-7
01Parkhurst-68
Gold-68
Silver-68
He Shoots-He Scores Prizes-22
Jerseys-PJ54
Sticks-PS37
01Private Stock-25
Gold-25
Premiere Date-25
Retail-25
Silver-25
01Private Stock Pacific Nights-25
01SP Authentic-116
Limited-116
Limited Gold-116
01SPx-167
Hidden Treasures-TTTHN
01Sports Illustrated for Kids III-358
01Stadium Club-68
Award Winners-68
Master Photos-68
01Titanium Double-Sided Jerseys-12
01Titanium Double-Sided Jerseys-14
01Titanium Double-Sided Patches-12
01Titanium Double-Sided Patches-14
01Titanium Draft Day Edition-28
01Topps-12
Heritage Parallel-12
Heritage Parallel Limited-12
OPC Parallel-12
01Topps Chrome-12
Refractors-12
Black Border Refractors-12
01Topps Heritage-56
Refractors-56
01Topps Reserve-98
01UD Honor Roll Playoff Matchups-HS-TM
01UD Honor Roll Playoff Matchups Gold-HS-TM
01UD Mask Collection-24
Gold-24
Double Patches-DPAT
Jerseys-J-AT
Jersey and Patch-JPAT
01UD Stanley Cup Champs-33
Sticks-S-AT
01UD Top Shelf-87
01Upper Deck-44
Exclusives-44
Game Jerseys Series II-DJTD
01Upper Deck Avalanche NHL All-Star Game-CA4
01Upper Deck MVP-50
01Upper Deck Victory-87
Gold-87
01Vanguard-28
Blue-28
Red-28
One of Ones-28
Premiere Date-28
Proofs-28
Quebec Tournament Heroes-16
01Czech Stadion-225
02BAP First Edition-87
02BAP First Edition-420H
Jerseys-87
02BAP Memorabilia-17
Emerald-17
Ruby-17
Sapphire-17
Future of the Game-FG-17
NHL All-Star Game-17
NHL All-Star Game Blue-17
NHL All-Star Game Green-17
NHL All-Star Game Red-17
02BAP Memorabilia Toronto Fall Expo-17
02BAP Signature Series-41
Autographs-41
Autograph Buybacks 1999-73
Autograph Buybacks 2001-103
Autographs Gold-41
Golf-GS4
Phenoms-YP7
02Crown Royale Dual Patches-6
02ITG Used-12
02ITG Used-112
02O-Pee-Chee-95
02O-Pee-Chee Premier Blue Parallel-95
02O-Pee-Chee Premier Red Parallel-95
02O-Pee-Chee Factory Set-95
02Pacific-97
Blue-97
Red-97
02Pacific Complete-279
Red-279
02Pacific Exclusive-47
02Pacific Heads-Up Quad Jerseys-8
02Pacific Heads-Up Quad Jerseys Gold-8
02Parkhurst-45
Bronze-45
Gold-45
Silver-45
Jerseys-GJ27
Stick and Jerseys-SJ27
02Parkhurst Retro-98
Minis-98
02Private Stock Reserve-28
Blue-28
Red-28
Retail-28
02SP Game Used Authentic Fabrics-AFAT
02SP Game Used Authentic Fabrics-AFTA
02SP Game Used Authentic Fabrics Gold-AFAT
02SP Game Used Authentic Fabrics Gold-AFTA
02SP Game Used Authentic Fabrics Rainbow-AFAT
02SP Game Used Authentic Fabrics Rainbow-AFTA
02SP Game Used First Rounder Patches-AT
02SP Game Used Future Fabrics-FFAT
02SP Game Used Future Fabrics Gold-FFAT
02SP Game Used Future Fabrics Rainbow-FFAT
02SP Game Used Piece of History-PHAT
02SP Game Used Piece of History-PHTA
02SP Game Used Piece of History Gold-PHAT
02SP Game Used Piece of History Gold-PHTA
02SP Game Used Piece of History Rainbow-PHAT
02SP Game Used Piece of History Rainbow-PHTA
02Stadium Club Champions Fabric-FC3
02Stadium Club Champions Patches-PC-3
02Topps-95
OPC Blue Parallel-95
OPC Red Parallel-95
Factory Set-95
02Topps Chrome-60
Black Border Refractors-60
Refractors-60
02Topps Heritage Great Skates-AT
02Topps Heritage Great Skates Patches-AT
02Topps Total-215
02UD Piece of History-28
02UD Top Shelf Goal Oriented-GOAT
02UD Top Shelf Shooting Stars-SHAT
02UD Top Shelf Sweet Sweaters-SWAT
02UD Top Shelf Triple Jerseys-TSTSR
02Upper Deck-286
Exclusives-286
02Upper Deck Beckett UD Promos-286
02Upper Deck CHL Graduates-CGAT
02Upper Deck CHL Graduates Gold-CGAT
02Upper Deck Pinpoint Accuracy-PAAT
02Upper Deck Playbooks Series II-RT
02Upper Deck Classic Portraits Hockey Royalty-GTD
02Upper Deck Classic Portraits Hockey Royalty-TSH
02Upper Deck Classic Portraits Hockey Royalty
Limited-GTD
02Upper Deck Classic Portraits Hockey Royalty
Limited-TSH
02Upper Deck Classic Portraits Starring Cast-CAT
02Upper Deck Classic Portraits Starring Cast
Limited-CAT
02Upper Deck MVP Skate Around Jerseys-SDTBL
02Upper Deck MVP Skate Around Jerseys-STTDH
02Upper Deck MVP Souvenirs-S-AT
02Upper Deck Victory-55
Bronze-55
Gold-55
Silver-55
02Upper Deck Vintage-70
Green Backs-70
Tall Boys-T19
Tall Boys Gold-T19
03Avalanche Team Issue-19
03BAP Ultimate Memorabilia Heroes-16
03BAP Ultimate Mem Perennial Power Jersey-6
03BAP Ult Mem Perenn Powerhouse Jsy Stick-6
03BAP Ultimate Mem Perennial Power Emblem-6
03Beehive-48
Gold-48
Silver-48
03Black Diamond-46
Black-46
Green-46
Red-46
Threads-DT-AT
Threads Green-DT-AT
Threads Red-DT-AT
Threads Black-DT-AT
03ITG Action-145
Jerseys-M117
03NHL Sticker Collection-186
03O-Pee-Chee-195
03OPC Blue-195
03OPC Gold-195
03OPC Red-195
03Pacific-90
Blue-90
Red-90
Jerseys-11
Jerseys Gold-11
03Pacific Calder-27
Silver-27
03Pacific Complete-60
Red-60
03Pacific Exhibit-40
Blue Backs-40
Yellow Backs-40
03Pacific Heads-Up-27
Hobby LTD-27
Retail LTD-27
In Focus-5
In Focus LTD-5
03Pacific Prism-28
Blue-28
Gold-28
Red-28
03Pacific Quest for the Cup-28
Blue-28
03Parkhurst Rookie-40
03Titanium-29
Hobby Jersey Number Parallels-29
Retail-29
Retail Jersey Number Parallels-29
03Topps-195
Blue-195
Gold-195
Red-195
03Topps C55-95
Minis-95
Minis American Back-95
Minis American Back Red-95
Minis Bazooka Back-95
Minis Brooklyn Back-95
Minis Hat Trick Back-95
Minis O Canada Back-95
Minis O Canada Back Red-95
Minis Stanley Cup Back-95
03Topps Pristine Patches-PP-AT
03Topps Pristine Patch Refractors-PP-AT
03Topps Traded Future Phenoms-FP-AT
03Upper Deck-46
Canadian Exclusives-46
HG-46
03Upper Deck MVP-103
Gold Script-103
Silver Script-103
Canadian Exclusives-103
03Upper Deck Victory-45
Bronze-45
Gold-45
Silver-45
03Toronto Star-20
04Pacific-72
Blue-72
Red-72
04SP Authentic-25
Limited-25
Buybacks-4
Buybacks-5
Buybacks-6
Buybacks-7
Buybacks-8
Buybacks-9
Sign of the Times-ST-AT
Sign of the Times-TS-HTA
Sign of the Times-QS-TAHS
04UD All-World-81
Gold-81
Autographs-81
Dual Autographs-AD-JA
Six Autographs-AS-SWT
04Ultimate Collection Buybacks-1
04Ultimate Collection Jerseys-UGJ-AT
04Ultimate Collection Jerseys Gold-UGJ-AT
04Ultimate Collection Jersey Autographs-UGJA-AT
04Ultimate Collection Patch Autographs-UPA-AT
04Ultimate Collection Patch Autographs-UPA-ATMH
04Ultimate Collection Signatures-US-AT
04Ultimate Collection Signature Logos-ULA-AT
04Ultimate Collection Signature Patches-SP-AT
04Upper Deck-43
Big Playmakers-BP-AT
Canadian Exclusives-43
HG Glossy Gold-43
HG Glossy Silver-43
05Be A Player-23
First Period-23
Second Period-23
Third Period-23
Overtime-23
Dual Signatures-PA
Outtakes-OT14
Quad Signatures-COLO
Signatures-AT
Signatures Gold-AT
Triple Signatures-AVS
05Beehive-24
05Beehive-182
Beige -24
Blue -24
Gold-24
Red -24
Matte-24
05Black Diamond-130
Emerald-130
Gold-130
Onyx-130
Ruby-130
05Hot Prospects-26
En Fuego-26
Red Hot-26
White Hot-26
05Panini Stickers-226
05Parkhurst-117
Facsimile Auto Parallel-117
True Colors-TCCOL
True Colors-TCCOL
True Colors-TCDECO
True Colors-TCDECO
05SP Authentic-25
05SP Authentic-118
Limited-25
Limited-118
Chirography-SPAT
Marks of Distinction-MDAT
Sign of the Times Triples-TTHW
05SP Game Used-25
Autographs-25
Gold-25
Authentic Fabrics-AF-AT
Authentic Fabrics Autographs-AAF-AT
Authentic Fabrics Dual-TH
Authentic Fabrics Dual Autographs-TH
Authentic Fabrics Gold-AF-AT
Authentic Fabrics Quad-SATH
Authentic Patches Quad -SATH
Authentic Patches-AP-AT
Authentic Patches Autographs-AAP-AT
Authentic Patches Dual-TH
Authentic Patches Dual Autographs-TH
Awesome Authentics-AA-AT
Awesome Authentics Gold-DA-AT
Game Gear-GG-AT
Game Gear Autographs-AG-AT
Signature Sticks-SS-AT
05SPx-22
Spectrum-22
Winning Combos-WC-TH
Winning Combos Autographs-AWC-TH
Winning Combos Gold-WC-TH
Winning Combos Spectrum-WC-TH
Winning Materials-WM-AT
Winning Materials Autographs-AWM-AT
Winning Materials Gold-WM-AT
Winning Materials Spectrum-WM-AT
Xcitement Superstars-XS-AT
Xcitement Superstars Gold-XS-AT
Xcitement Superstars Spectrum-XS-AT
05The Cup-29
Gold-29
Black Rainbow-29
Dual NHL Shields-DSST
Emblems of Endorsement-EEAT
Honorable Numbers-HNAT
Limited Logos-LLAT
Masterpiece Pressplates-29
Masterpiece Pressplates Rookie Upd Auto-257
Noble Numbers-NNST
Noble Numbers Dual-DNNJA
Patch Variation-P29
Patch Variation Autographs-AP29
Property of-POAT
Scripted Numbers-SNTH
Scripted Numbers Dual-DSNCO
Scripted Numbers Dual-DSNTH
Scripted Swatches-SSAT
Signature Patches-SPAT
Stanley Cup Titlists-TAT
05UD Artifacts-28
05UD Artifacts-161
Blue-28
Blue-161
Gold-28
Gold-161
Green-28
Green-161
Pewter-28
Pewter-161
Red-28
Red-161
Auto Facts-AF-AT
Auto Facts Blue-AF-AT
Auto Facts Copper-AF-AT
Auto Facts Pewter-AF-AT
Auto Facts Silver-AF-AT
Gold Autographed-28
Gold Autographed-161
Remarkable Artifacts-RA-AT
Remarkable Artifacts Dual-RA-AT
Treasured Patches-TP-AT
Treasured Patches Autographed-TP-AT
Treasured Patches Dual-TPD-AT
Treasured Patches Dual Autographed-TPD-AT
Treasured Patches Pewter-TP-AT
Treasured Patches Silver-TP-AT
Treasured Swatches-TS-AT
Treasured Swatches Autographed-TS-AT
Treasured Swatches Blue-TS-AT
Treasured Swatches Copper-TS-AT
Treasured Swatches Dual-TSD-AT
Treasured Swatches Dual Autographed-TSD-AT
Treasured Swatches Dual Blue-TSD-AT
Treasured Swatches Dual Copper-TSD-AT
Treasured Swatches Dual Maroon-TSD-AT
Treasured Swatches Dual Pewter-TSD-AT
Treasured Swatches Dual Silver-TSD-AT
Treasured Swatches Maroon-TS-AT
Treasured Swatches Pewter-TS-AT
Treasured Swatches Silver-TS-AT
05UD PowerPlay-23
Rainbow-23
05Ultimate Collection-25
Gold-25
Endorsed Emblems-EEAT
Marquee Attractions-MA14
Marquee Attractions Signatures-SMA14
Ultimate Achievements-UAAT
Ultimate Signatures-USAT
Ultimate Signatures Pairings-UPTH
Ultimate Signatures Trios-UTTHS
05Ultra-57
Gold-57
Fresh Ink-FI-AT
Fresh Ink Blue-FI-AT
Ice-57
Scoring Kings-SK9
Scoring Kings Jerseys-SKJ-AT
Scoring Kings Jersey Autographs-KAJ-AT
Scoring Kings Patches-SKP-AT
Scoring Kings Patch Autographs-KAP-AT
05Upper Deck-45
Big Playmakers-B-AT
HG Glossy-45
Majestic Series II-J2AT
Majestic Materials-MMAT
NHL Generations-TSHT
Notable Numbers-N-AT
Patches-P-AT
05Upper Deck Ice-24
Rainbow-24
Frozen Fabrics-FFAT
Frozen Fabrics Autographs-AFFAT
Frozen Fabrics Glass-FFAT
Frozen Fabrics Patches-FFPAT
Frozen Fabrics Patch Autographs-FAPAT
Signature Swatches-SSAT
05Upper Deck MVP-99
Gold-99
Platinum-99
05Upper Deck Rookie Update-23
05Upper Deck Rookie Update-257
05Upper Deck Trilogy-26
05Upper Deck Trilogy-134
Crystal-134
Honorary Patches-HP-AT
Honorary Patch Scripts-HSP-AT
Honorary Swatches-HS-AT
Honorary Swatch Scripts-HSS-AT
Ice Scripts-IS-AT
05Upper Deck Toronto Fall Expo-45
05Upper Deck Victory-50
Black-50
Gold-50
Silver-50
Stars on Ice-SI13
06Be A Player-26
Autographs-26
Signatures-AT
Signatures 10-28
Signatures 25-28
Signatures Duals-DCA
Signatures Trios-TIPT
Up Close and Personal-UC1
Up Close and Personal Autographs-UC1
06Be A Player Portraits-19
Dual Signature Portraits-DSIT
Signature Portraits-SPAT
Timeless Tens-TTCAN
Triple Signature Portraits-TCGY
06Beehive-87
06Beehive-225
Blue-87
Matte-87
Red Facsimile Signatures-87
Wood-87
Matted Materials-MMAT
06Black Diamond-92
Black-92
Gold-92
Ruby-92
Jerseys-JAT
Jerseys Black-JAT
Jerseys Gold-JAT
Jerseys Ruby-JAT
Jerseys Black Autographs -JAT
06Flair Showcase-28
06Flair Showcase-179
06Flair Showcase-219
Parallel-28
Parallel-179
Parallel-219
Hot Numbers-HN9
Hot Numbers Parallel-HN9
Stitches-SSAT
06Fleer-34
Tiffany-34
Speed Machines-SM7
06Gatorade-4
06Hot Prospects-17
Red Hot-17
White Hot-17
06McDonald's Upper Deck Autographs-AAT
06McDonald's Upper Deck Jerseys-JAT
06McDonald's Upper Deck Patches-PAT
06NHL POG-19
06O-Pee-Chee-83
Rainbow-83
Swatches-S-AT
06Panini Stickers-198
06SP Authentic-86
Limited-86
Sign of the Times Duals-STIT
Sign of the Times Triples-ST3ITK
Sign of the Times Quads-ST4IKPT
06SP Game Used-15
Gold-15
Rainbow-15
Authentic Fabrics-AFAT
Authentic Fabrics Parallel-AFAT
Authentic Fabrics Patches-AFAT
Authentic Fabrics Dual-AF2TK
Authentic Fabrics Dual Patches-AF2TK
Authentic Fabrics Triple-AF3CGY
Authentic Fabrics Triple Patches-AF3CGY
Inked Sweaters Dual-IS2IT
Inked Sweaters Dual Patches-IS2IT
06SPx-12
Spectrum-12
SPxcitement-X17
SPxcitement Spectrum-X17
SPxcitement Autographs-X17
Winning Materials-WMAT
Winning Materials Spectrum-WMAT
Winning Materials Autographs-WMAT
06The Cup Autographed NHL Shields Duals-DASIT
06The Cup Limited Logos-LLAT
06The Cup Scripted Swatches-SSAT
06The Cup Scripted Swatches Duals-DSTI
06The Cup Signature Patches-SPAT
06The Cup Stanley Cup Signatures-CSAT
06UD Artifacts-87
06UD Artifacts-162
Blue-87
Blue-162
Gold-87
Gold-162
Platinum-87
Platinum-162
Radiance-87
Radiance-162
Red-87
Red-162
Frozen Artifacts-FAAT
Frozen Artifacts Black-FAAT
Frozen Artifacts Blue-FAAT
Frozen Artifacts Gold-FAAT
Frozen Artifacts Platinum-FAAT
Frozen Artifacts Red-FAAT
Frozen Artifacts Patches Black-FAAT
Frozen Artifacts Patches Blue-FAAT
Frozen Artifacts Patches Gold-FAAT
Frozen Artifacts Patches Platinum-FAAT
Frozen Artifacts Patches Red-FAAT
Tundra Tandems-TTIT
Tundra Tandems Black-TTIT
Tundra Tandems Blue-TTIT
Tundra Tandems Gold-TTIT
Tundra Tandems Platinum-TTIT
Tundra Tandems Red-TTIT
Tundra Tandems Dual Patches Red-TTIT
06UD Mini Jersey Collection-13
06UD Powerplay-17
Impact Rainbow-17
Specialists-SAT
Specialists Patches-PAT
06Ultimate Collection Premium Patches-PS-AT
06Ultimate Collection Premium Swatches-PS-AT
06Ultimate Collection Signatures-US-AT
06Ultra-34
Gold Medallion-34
Ice Medallion-34
Difference Makers-DM9
Scoring Kings-SK1
06Upper Deck Arena Giveaways-CGY4
06Upper Deck-279
Exclusives Parallel-279
High Gloss Parallel-279
Game Jerseys-JAT
Game Patches-PAT
Masterpieces-279
Oversized Wal-Mart Exclusives-279
Signatures-SAT
Signature Sensations-SSAT
06Upper Deck MVP-42
Gold Script-42
Super Script-42
Jerseys-OJTN
06Upper Deck Ovation-12
06Upper Deck Sweet Shot-17
Signature Shots/Saves-SSAT
Sweet Stitches-SSAT
Sweet Stitches Duals-SSAT
Sweet Stitches Triples-SSAT
06Upper Deck Trilogy-16
Combo Autographed Jerseys-CJIT
Combo Autographed Patches-CJIT
Combo Clearcut Autographs-C3HTT
Honorary Scripted Patches-HSPAT
Honorary Scripted Swatches-HSSAT
06Upper Deck Victory-51
06Upper Deck Victory-235
06Upper Deck Victory Black-51
06Upper Deck Victory Gold-51
06Upper Deck Victory GameBreakers-GB11
06Upper Deck Victory Oversize Cards-AT
07Upper Deck Victory-149
Black-149
Gold-149

Tanguay, Charles
04Moncton Wildcats-8

Tanguay, Christian
81Fredericton Express-20

82Fredericton Express-20
83Fredericton Express-10
Tanguay, Francois
93Quebec Pee-Wee Tournament-1595
Tanguay, Luc
93Quebec Pee-Wee Tournament-330
Tanguay, Martin
88Richelieu Riverains-28
917th Inn. Sketch QMJHL-135
92Quebec Pee-Wee Tournament-97
93Atlanta Knights-13
93Knoxville Cherokees-18
93Quebec Pee-Wee Tournament-224
94Classic Pro Prospects-132
96Knoxville Cherokees-12
Tanguay, Mathieu
93Quebec Pee-Wee Tournament-1075
Tanguay, Maxime
05Chicoutimi Sagueneens-15
05Rimouski Oceanic-29
06Rimouski Oceanic-2
Tannahill, Don
72Canucks Royal Bank-18
72O-Pee-Chee-238
73Canucks Royal Bank-18
73O-Pee-Chee-69
73Topps-69
74O-Pee-Chee NHL-117
74Topps-117
Tanner, John
897th Inn. Sketch OHL-38
90Nordiques Petro-Canada-24
90OPC Premier-118
90Pro Set-637
907th Inn. Sketch OHL-145
907th Inn. Sketch OHL-377
91Nordiques Panini Team Stickers-21
91Upper Deck-119
French-119
91ProCards-366
92Nordiques Petro-Canada-32
92Score-452
Canadian-452
96Wheeling Nailers-19
Tanner, Marco
95Swiss HNL-411
96Swiss HNL-479
Tanner, Ralph
93Swiss HNL-272
Tannhof, Lars
94German First League-431
Tano, Lars-Goran
69Swedish Hockey-73
Tano, Patrik
02Swedish SHL-223
Parallel-223
Tansowny, Steve
92Saskatchewan JHL-53
Tanti, Tony
80Oshawa Generals-16
81Blackhawks Borderless Postcards-27
81Oshawa Generals-18
82Oshawa Generals-11
83Canadian National Juniors-14
83Canucks Team Issue-21
83O-Pee-Chee-362
83Vachon-119
84Canucks Team Issue-24
84O-Pee-Chee-332
84O-Pee-Chee-369
84O-Pee-Chee Stickers-274
84O-Pee-Chee Stickers-275
847-Eleven Discs-52
84Topps-141
85Canucks Team Issue-24
85O-Pee-Chee-153
85O-Pee-Chee Stickers-245
85Topps-153
86Canucks Team Issue-23
86Kraft Drawings-73
86O-Pee-Chee-120
86O-Pee-Chee Stickers-99
86Topps-120
87Canucks Shell Oil-23
87O-Pee-Chee-97
87O-Pee-Chee Stickers-195
87Panini Stickers-345
87Pro-Sport All-Stars-15
87Topps-97
88Canucks Mohawk-23
88Frito-Lay Stickers-42
88O-Pee-Chee-82
88O-Pee-Chee Stickers-59
88Panini Stickers-143
88Topps-82
89Canucks Mohawk-23
89Kraft-45
89O-Pee-Chee-280
89O-Pee-Chee Stickers-71
89Panini Stickers-149
90Bowman-213
Tiffany-213
90O-Pee-Chee-157
90Panini Stickers-124
90Penguins Foodland-14
90Pro Set-241
90Score-137
Canadian-137
90Topps-157
Tiffany-157
90Upper Deck-197
French-197
91Bowman-34
91O-Pee-Chee-133
91Parkhurst-236
French-236
91Sabres Blue Shield-22
91Sabres Pepsi/Campbell's-22
91Score American-49
91Score Canadian Bilingual-49
91Score Canadian English-49
91Stadium Club-285
91Topps-133
92Bowman-172
92O-Pee-Chee-34
92Score-116
Canadian-116
92Stadium Club-312
92Topps-235
Gold-235G
92Upper Deck-182
94German DEL-54
95German DEL-59
96German DEL-256
01Upper Deck Legends-65
02UD Foundations-96
04UD Legendary Signatures-85
Autographs-TT
Linemates-TISSTT
Tapp, Jason
03Columbus Cottonmouths-8
04Missouri River Otters-3

05Quad City Mallards-16
06Quad City Mallards-17
Tapper, Brad
92Quebec Pee-Wee Tournament-491
00BAP Memorabilia-437
Emerald-437
Ruby-437
Sapphire-437
00SP Authentic-93
00Stadium Club-247
00Titanium-104
Retail-104
00Titanium Draft Day Edition-104
00Titanium Draft Day Promos-104
00Topps Heritage-83
Chrome Parallel-83
00Topps Premier Plus-113
Blue Ice-113
00Upper Deck Ice-105
01BAP Memorabilia-221
Emerald-221
Ruby-221
Sapphire-221
01BAP Signature Series-217
Autographs-217
Autographs Gold-217
01O-Pee-Chee-302
01O-Pee-Chee Premier Parallel-302
01Topps-302
OPC Parallel-302
01Upper Deck Victory-362
Gold-362
01Chicago Wolves-22
02BAP Sig Series Auto Buybacks 2001-217
02Pacific Complete-429
Red-429
02Thrashers Postcards-18
03ITG Action-10
03Pacific Complete-57
Red-57
04German DEL-260
04German Nuremburg Ice Tigers Postcards-19
05German DEL-135
Star Attack-ST07
Tarabrin, Dimitri
94Signature Rookies Gold Standard *-93
95Signature Rookies-32
Signatures-32
97Wheeling Nailers-4
97Wheeling Nailers Photo Pack-4
99Johnstown Chiefs-11
00Johnstown Chiefs-25
02Johnstown Chiefs-19
03Johnstown Chiefs-3
03Johnstown Chiefs RBI Sports-224
04Johnstown Chiefs-18
05Johnstown Chiefs-18
Tarala, Jeff
97Dubuque Fighting Saints-11
Tarasenko, Andrei
95Swedish World Championships Stickers-40
00Russian Hockey League-160
02Russian Hockey League-75
Tarasov, Anatoli V
69Russian National Team Postcards-21
83Hall of Fame Postcards-D15
85Hall of Fame-239
91Future Trends Canada '72-4
91Future Trends Canada '72 French-4
Tarasov, Dmitri
99Russian Hockey League-166
00Russian Hockey League-11
03Russian Hockey League-17
Tarasov, Vadim
98Russian Hockey League-103
99Russian Hockey League-197
99Russian Stars Postcards-26
00Russian Hockey League-173
00Russian Hockey League-300
01Quebec Citadelles-15
02Russian Hockey League-90
02Russian Transfert-16
02Russian Ultimate Line-11
03Russian Hockey League-194
03Russian SL-17
Tarasov, Vladimir
98Russian Hockey League-137
99Russian Hockey League-184
Tarasov, Yevgeny
96Swedish Semic Wien-131
98Russian Hockey League-42
Tarasuk, Allan
82Brandon Wheat Kings-15
83Brandon Wheat Kings-21
Tarasuk, Rick
917th Inn. Sketch OHL-269
Tarasuk, Steve
06Kitchener Rangers-2
Taratukhin, Andrei
02Russian Future Stars-10
02Russian Hockey League-193
02Russian SL-45
04Russian RHL-5
06Russian Torino Olympic Team-22
Tardif, Christian
907th Inn. Sketch QMJHL-71
917th Inn. Sketch QMJHL-33
Tardif, Jamie
01Peterborough Petes-17
02Peterborough Petes-20
04Peterborough Petes Postcards-4
05OHL Bell All-Star Classic-40
06Toledo Storm-2
Tardif, Jean-Pierre
98Thetford Mines Coyotes-4
Tardif, Marc
69Canadiens Postcards Color-29
70Colgate Stamps-17
70Esso Power Players-8
70O-Pee-Chee-179
71Canadiens Postcards-23
71O-Pee-Chee-29
71Sargent Promotions Stamps-111
71Topps-29
71Toronto Sun-164
72Canadiens Postcards-21
72Dimanche/Derniere Heure *-173
72O-Pee-Chee-11
72Sargent Promotions Stamps-118
72Topps-105
73O-Pee-Chee WHA Posters-20
74O-Pee-Chee WHA-43
74Team Canada L'Equipe WHA-22
75O-Pee-Chee WHA-30
75O-Pee-Chee WHA-71
76Nordiques Marie Antoinette-11
76Nordiques Postcards-18
76O-Pee-Chee WHA-1
76O-Pee-Chee WHA-2
76O-Pee-Chee WHA-3
76O-Pee-Chee WHA-5
76O-Pee-Chee WHA-118

77O-Pee-Chee WHA-20
79O-Pee-Chee-108
79Topps-108
80Nordiques Postcards-27
80O-Pee-Chee-256
80O-Pee-Chee Super-17
80Pepsi-Cola Caps-78
80Topps-256
81Nordiques Postcards-19
81O-Pee-Chee-283
81O-Pee-Chee Stickers-76
82Nordiques Postcards-23
82O-Pee-Chee-296
82O-Pee-Chee Stickers-21
82Post Cereal-16
82Topps Stickers-21
83Esso-19
83Nordiques Postcards-30
83O-Pee-Chee-305
83O-Pee-Chee Stickers-247
83Topps Stickers-247
04ITG Franchises Canadian-75
Autographs-MT
06Parkhurst-157
06Parkhurst-174
Autographs-157
Autographs-174
Tardif, Marc (Minors)
907th Inn. Sketch QMJHL-109
917th Inn. Sketch OHL-207
917th Inn. Sketch QMJHL-73
93Atlanta Knights-7
94Classic Pro Prospects-223
95South Carolina Stingrays-13
96South Carolina Stingrays-17
Tardif, Patrice
92Maine Black Bears-10
93Maine Black Bears-46
94Fleer-192
94Upper Deck-470
Electric Ice-470
94Classic Tri-Cards-T58
95Donruss-87
95Leaf-22
95Score-88
Black Ice Artist's Proofs-88
Black Ice-88
95Topps-172
OPC Inserts-172
95Images-27
Gold-27
Clear Excitement-CE14
96Detroit Vipers-18
96Collector's Edge Ice-97
Prism-97
97Rochester Americans-3-3
98Manitoba Moose-D8
99Manitoba Moose-14
99Quebec Citadelles-12
00German DEL-121
01Thetford Mines Coyotes-21
02Thetford Mines Coyotes-22
03Thetford Mines Prolab-23
04Thetford Mines Prolab-5
Tardif, Steve
93Drummondville Voltigeurs-22
97Indianapolis Ice-24
98Florida Everblades-23
99Florida Everblades-20
03St. Georges de Beauce Garaga-17
04St Georges de Beauce Garaga-1
Tardy, Weston
06Augusta Lynx-21
Tarini, Nick
06Sudbury Wolves-7
Tarkiainen, Juhani
66Finnish Jaakiekkosarja-211
Tarkir, Chris
03Lincoln Stars-18
Tarkir, Zach
04Northern Michigan Wildcats-24
Tarkki, Tuomas
04Northern Michigan Wildcats-25
05Chicago Wolves-21
06Finnish Cardset-269
Between the Pipes-15
Tarko, Kari-Pekka
72Finnish Jaakiekko-354
Tarnasky, Nick
02Kelowna Rockets-25
03Lethbridge Hurricanes-5
04Springfield Falcons-19
05Hot Prospects-171
En Fuego-171
Red Hot-171
White Hot-171
05SP Authentic-244
Limited-244
05SP Game Used-172
Gold-172
05SPx-203
Spectrum-203
05The Cup Masterpiece Pressplate Artifact-329
05The Cup Masterpiece Pressplates (Ice)-207
05The Cup Master Pressplate Rookie Update-180
05The Cup Masterpiece Pressplates SPA-244
05The Cup Masterpiece Pressplates SP GU-172
05The Cup Masterpiece Pressplates (SPx)-203
05The Cup Masterpiece Pressplates Trilogy-307
05The Cup Masterpiece Pressplate Ult Coll-229
05UD Artifacts-329
05Ultimate Collection-229
Gold-229
05Upper Deck Ice-207
05Upper Deck Rookie Update-180
05Upper Deck Trilogy-307
05Springfield Falcons-17
06Lightning Postcards-22
Tarnowski, Chris
84Victoria Cougars-24
85Kamloops Blazers-25
86Kamloops Blazers-21
86Regina Pats-27
Tarnstrom, Dick
92Swedish Semic Elitserien Stickers-31
94Parkhurst SE-SE239
Gold-SE239
94Swedish Leaf-211
NHL Draft-10
95Swedish Leaf-9
95Swedish Upper Deck-3
Ticket to North America-NA2
97Swedish Collector's Choice-5
98Swedish UD Choice-4
99Swedish Upper Deck-4
00Swedish Upper Deck-3
02Atomic-123
Blue-123
Gold-123
Red-123
Hobby Parallel-123
02BAP All-Star Edition-122
Gold-122

Silver-122
02BAP Memorabilia-334
02BAP Ultimate Memorabilia-36
02Crown Royale-133
Blue-133
Purple-133
Red-133
Retail-133
02ITG Used-95
02Pacific Complete-599
Red-599
02Pacific Quest for the Cup-141
Gold-141
02Parkhurst-234
Bronze-234
Gold-234
Silver-234
02Parkhurst Retro-250
Minis-250
02Private Stock Reserve-179
Blue-179
Red-179
Retail-179
02SP Authentic-180
02Titanium-133
Blue-133
Red-133
Retail-133
02UD Artistic Impressions-98
Gold-98
02UD Honor Roll-124
02UD Mask Collection-138
02UD Premier Collection-70A
Gold-70A
02Vanguard-130
LTD-130
03ITG Action-499
03NHL Sticker Collection-119
03O-Pee-Chee-274
03OPC Blue-274
03OPC Gold-274
03OPC Red-274
03Pacific-278
Blue-278
Red-278
03Pacific Complete-176
Red-176
03Pacific Exhibit-120
Blue Backs-120
Yellow Backs-120
03Titanium-82
Hobby Jersey Number Parallels-82
Retail-82
Retail Jersey Number Parallels-82
03Topps-274
Blue-274
Gold-274
Red-274
03Topps C55-82
Minis-82
Minis American Back-82
Minis American Back Red-82
Minis Bazooka Back-82
Minis Brooklyn Back-82
Minis Hat Trick Back-82
Minis O Canada Back-82
Minis O Canada Back Red-82
Minis Stanley Cup Back-82
03Upper Deck-154
Canadian Exclusives-154
HG-154
03Upper Deck MVP-335
Gold Script-335
Silver Script-335
Canadian Exclusives-335
04Pacific-216
Blue-216
Red-216
04UD All-World-73
Gold-73
04Upper Deck-141
Canadian Exclusives-141
HG Glossy Gold-141
HG Glossy Silver-141
04Swedish Alfabilder Alfa Stars-28
04Swedish Alfabilder Autographs-118
04Swedish Alfabilder Limited Autographs-118
04Swedish Alfabilder Proof Parallels-28
04Swedish Elitset-267
Dominators-8
Gold-267
Signatures Series B-13
04Swedish Pure Skills-82
Parallel-82
Professional Power-DT
05Panini Stickers-150
05Upper Deck-155
HG Glossy-155
05Upper Deck MVP-317
Gold-317
Platinum-317
05Upper Deck Toronto Fall Expo-155
05Upper Deck Victory-158
Black-158
Gold-158
Silver-158
05Swedish SHL Elitset-121
Tarrant, Jerry
89ProCards IHL-27
91ProCards-373
Tartaglione, Tommy
05Vancouver Giants-23
Tartari, Stephan
907th Inn. Sketch QMJHL-115
Tarvainen, Jussi
93Finnish SISU-180
94Finest-142
Super Team Winners-142
Refractors-142
94Parkhurst SE-SE225
Gold-SE225
94Finnish SISU-71
94Finnish SISU Junior-8
94Finnish SISU NHL Draft-3
95Finnish SISU-75
96Finnish SISU Redline-81
98Finnish Kerailysarja-134
99Finnish Cardset-177
99Finnish Cardset-323
00Finnish Cardset-88
01Finnish Cardset-127
02Finnish Cardset-124
03Swedish Elite-221
Silver-221
04Swedish Elitset-67
Gold-67
05Swedish SHL Elitset-80
Gold-80
06Swedish SHL Elitset-79
Tasala, Lasse
80Finnish Mallasjuoma-33
Tashjian, Gary
93Quebec Pee-Wee Tournament-729

Tasker, Michael
97UK Kingston Hawks Stickers-20
98UK Kingston Hawks-23
02UK Coventry Blaze-20
03UK Coventry Blaze-18
03UK Coventry Blaze Calendars-8
03UK Coventry Blaze History-4
Tasku, Petteri
05Finnish Cardset -350
06Finnish Porin Assat Pelaajakortit-23
Taskula, Keijo
80Finnish Mallasjuoma-135
Tassone, Joe
97Central Texas Stampede-17
Tassone, Lyle
04Vernon Vipers-14
Tassone, Matt
06Swift Current Broncos-16
Tatarinov, Mikhail
90Capitals Kodak-24
90Capitals Smokey-21
90Pro Set-647
90Score Rookie/Traded-53T
90Upper Deck-401
French-401
91Pro Set Platinum-218
91Bowman-298
91Nordiques Petro-Canada-29
91O-Pee-Chee-465
91OPC Premier-62
91Panini Stickers-210
91Parkhurst-145
French-145
91Pinnacle-97
French-97
91Pro Set-462
French-462
91Score American-37
91Score Canadian Bilingual-37
91Score Canadian Bilingual-562
91Score Canadian English-37
91Score Canadian English-562
91Score Rookie/Traded-12T
91Stadium Club-390
91Topps-465
91Finnish Semic World Champ Stickers-215
91Russian Stars Red Ace-17
91Russian Sports Unite Hearts-9
91Russian Stars in NHL-9
91Swedish Semic World Champ Stickers-215
92Bowman-395
92Nordiques Petro-Canada-33
92O-Pee-Chee-253
92Panini Stickers-208
92Panini Stickers French-208
92Pinnacle-35
French-35
92Score-107
Canadian-107
92Stadium Club-47
92Topps-180
Gold-180G
92Ultra-181
92Upper Deck-183
92Finnish Semic-102
93Leaf-342
93Score-328
Canadian-328
93Upper Deck-386
94Finnish Jaa Kiekko-336
Tatarintsev, Konstantin
99Russian Hockey League-91
Tatarnic, Jason
99UK Hull Thunder-12
Tataryn, Josh
99Ottawa 67's-12
03Port Huron Beacons-21
06Fayetteville FireAntz-18
Taticek, Petr
94German First League-354
02BAP Memorabilia Draft Redemptions-9
02Sault Ste. Marie Greyhounds-12
03AHL Top Prospects-37
03Pacific AHL Prospects-76
Gold-76
03San Antonio Rampage-18
04San Antonio Rampage-17
04ITG Heroes and Prospects-19
Autographs-PT
04ITG Heroes/Prospects Toronto Expo '05-19
04ITG Heroes/Prospects Expo Heroes/Pros-19
05ITG Heroes/Prosp Toronto Expo Parallel -219
05Black Diamond-246
05Hot Prospects-133
En Fuego-133
Red Hot-133
White Hot-133
05SP Authentic-263
Limited-263
05The Cup Masterpiece Pressplate Artifact-282
05The Cup Master Pressplate Black Diamond-246
05The Cup Masterpiece Pressplates (Ice)-256
05The Cup Master Pressplate Rookie Update-137
05The Cup Masterpiece Pressplates SPA-263
05The Cup Masterpiece Pressplates Trilogy-262
05The Cup Masterpiece Pressplate Ult Coll-207
05UD Artifacts-282
05Ultimate Collection-207
Gold-207
05Upper Deck Ice-256
05Upper Deck Rookie Update-137
05Upper Deck Trilogy-262
05ITG Heroes and Prospects-219
Autographs Series II-PT
06Czech OFS Jagr Team-4
06ITG Heroes and Prospects Jerseys-GUJ55
06ITG Heroes and Prospects Jerseys Gold-GUJ55
06ITG Heroes and Prospects Emblems-GUE55
06ITG Heroes and Prospects Emblems Gold-GUE55
06ITG Heroes and Prospects Numbers-GUN55
06ITG Heroes and Prospects Numbers Gold-GUN55
Tattner, Michael
94German DEL-373
Taubert, Kristian
92Finnish Jyvas-Hyva Stickers-47
94Finnish SISU-353
00Finnish Cardset-178
01Finnish Cardset-76
02UK Nottingham Panthers-9
03UK Nottingham Panthers-9
Taugher, Johnny
37V356 Worldwide Gum-116
Tauriainen, Jarmo
70Finnish Jaakiekko-380
80Finnish Mallasjuoma-109
Tauson, Claus
98Danish Hockey League-87
Tavares, John
05ITG Heroes/Prosp Toronto Expo Parallel -111
05ITG Heroes/Prosp Toronto Expo Parallel -371
05ITG Heroes and Prospects-111
05ITG Heroes and Prospects-371

Autograph Memorabilia-GA-02
Autograph Memorabilia Gold-GA-02
Autographs-A-JT
Autographs Series II-JT2
Autographs Series II-LT2
Autographs Update-DA-ET
Complete Jerseys-CJ-9
Complete Jerseys Gold-CJ-9
Complete Logos-CHL-16
He Shoots-He Scores Prizes-43
He Shoots-He Scores Prizes-50
Jerseys-GUJ-65
Jerseys Gold-GUJ-65
Emblems-GUE-65
Emblems Gold-GUE-65
Numbers-GUN-65
Numbers Gold-GUN-65
Nameplates-N-43
Nameplates Gold-N-43
Spectrum-STM-02
Spectrum Gold-STM-02
06ITG International Ice-53
Gold-53
Autographs-AJT
Canadian Dream Team-DT12
Canadian Dream Team Gold-DT12
Complete Jersey-CJ01
Complete Jersey Gold-CJ01
Cornerstones-IC11
Cornerstones Gold-IC11
Emblem Autographs-GUE11
Emblem Autographs Gold-GUE11
Emblems-GUE11
Emblems Gold-GUE11
Jersey Autographs-GUJ11
Jersey Autographs Gold-GUJ11
Jerseys-GUJ11
Jerseys Gold-GUJ11
My Country My Team-MC25
My Country My Team Gold-MC25
Numbers-GUN11
Numbers Autographs-GUN11
Numbers Autographs Gold-GUN11
Numbers Gold-GUN11
06ITG Phenoms-JT01
06ITG Phenoms-JT02
06ITG Phenoms-JT03
06ITG Phenoms-JT04
06ITG Phenoms-JT05
06ITG Phenoms-JT06
Autographs-JT01
Autographs-JT02
Autographs-JT03
Autographs-JT04
Autographs-JT05
Autographs-JT06
Double Memorabilia Gold-DMJT
Double Memorabilia Silver-DMJT
Idols Gold-IDJT
Idols Silver-IDJT
Jerseys Gold-GUJJT
Jerseys Gold Dual-DJCT
Jerseys Gold Dual-DJTO
Jerseys Gold Triple-TJCOT
Jerseys Silver-GUJJT
Jerseys Silver Dual-DJCT
Jerseys Silver Dual-DJTO
Jerseys Silver Triple-TJCOT
Patches Gold-GUPJT
Patches Gold Dual-DPCT
Patches Gold Dual-DPTO
Patches Gold Triple-TPCOT
Patches Silver-GUPJT
Patches Silver Dual-DPCT
Patches Silver Dual-DPTO
Patches Silver Triple-TPCOT
Sticks Gold-GUSJT
Sticks Gold Dual-DSCT
Sticks Gold Dual-DSTO
Sticks Gold Triple-TSCOT
Sticks Silver-GUSJT
Sticks Silver Dual-DSCT
Sticks Silver Dual-DSTO
Sticks Silver Triple-TSCOT
06ITG Ultimate Memorabilia-81
Artist Proof-81
Autos-57
Autos Gold-57
Autos Dual-8
Autos Dual Gold-8
Autos Triple-10
Autos Triple Gold-10
Complete Jersey-8
Complete Jersey Gold-8
Double Memorabilia-6
Double Memorabilia Gold-6
Double Memorabilia Autos-9
Double Memorabilia Autos Gold-9
Emblems-18
Emblems Gold-18
Future Star-2
Future Star Gold-2
Future Star Autos-16
Future Star Autos Gold-16
Future Star Patches Autos-16
Future Star Patches Autos Gold-16
Going For Gold-30
Going For Gold Gold-30
In The Numbers-6
In The Numbers Gold-6
Jerseys-26
Jerseys Gold-26
Jerseys and Emblems-19
Jerseys and Emblems Gold-19
Jerseys Autos-57
Jerseys Autos Gold-57
Passing The Torch-19
Passing The Torch Gold-19
Seams Unbelievable-2
Seams Unbelievable Gold-2
Sensational Season-7
Sensational Season Gold-7
Sticks Autos-29
Sticks Autos Gold-29
Triple Thread Jerseys-12
Triple Thread Jerseys Gold-12
06Oshawa Generals-1
06ITG Heroes and Prospects-82
06ITG Heroes and Prospects-139
Autographs-AJT1
Autographs-AJT2
Complete CHL Logos-CHL11
Complete Jerseys-CJ02
Complete Jerseys Gold-CJ02
Double Memorabilia-DM08
Jerseys-GUJ34
Jerseys Gold-GUJ34
Emblems-GUE34
Emblems Gold-GUE34
Numbers-GUN34
Numbers Gold-GUN34
Quad Emblems-QE02
Quad Emblems-QE15
Quad Emblems Gold-QE02

Record Breaking Season-RS01
Record Breaking Season-RS02
Record Breaking Season-RS03
Record Breaking Season-RS04
Record Breaking Season-RS05
Record Breaking Season-RS06
Record Breaking Season-RS07
Record Breaking Season-RS08
Record Breaking Season-RS09
Record Breaking Season-RS10
Record Breaking Season Autographs-RS01
Record Breaking Season Autographs-RS02
Record Breaking Season Autographs-RS03
Record Breaking Season Autographs-RS04
Record Breaking Season Autographs-RS05
Record Breaking Season Autographs-RS06
Record Breaking Season Autographs-RS07
Record Breaking Season Autographs-RS08
Record Breaking Season Autographs-RS09
Record Breaking Season Autographs-RS10
Sticks and Jerseys-SJ02
Sticks and Jerseys Gold-SJ02
Tavi, Mikko
92Clarkson Knights-21
93Finnish Jyvas-Hyva Stickers-176
93Finnish SISU-165
Taylor, Adam
00Kootenay Ice-22
02Kootenay Ice-4
03Kootenay Ice-13
04Kootenay Ice-22
Taylor, Andrew
93Kitchener Rangers-18
93Kitchener Rangers-29
93Quebec Pee-Wee Tournament-500
94Detroit Jr. Red Wings-13
94Kitchener Rangers-20
95Slapshot-70
95Signature Rookies-65
Signatures-65
95Slapshot Memorial Cup-87
96Detroit Whalers-16
98Florida Everblades-24
02Indianapolis Ice-19
Taylor, Bart
91British Columbia JHL-121
92British Columbia JHL-172
Taylor, Billy
34Beehive Group I Photos-351
39O-Pee-Chee V301-1-15
40O-Pee-Chee V301-2-107
45Quaker Oats Photos-54
Taylor, Bobby
73O-Pee-Chee-238
75Flyers Canada Dry Cans-18
92Parkhurst-475
Emerald Ice-475
04ITG Franchises US East-423
Autographs-A-BTA
Taylor, Chris
897th Inn. Sketch OHL-26
907th Inn. Sketch OHL-146
91Upper Deck-454
French-454
917th Inn. Sketch OHL-370
93Classic Pro Prospects-113
95Score-303
Black Ice Artist's Proofs-303
Black Ice-303
00Rochester Americans-21
02Rochester Americans-21
04Rochester Americans-23
06German DEL-63
New Arrivals-NA12
Taylor, Cyclone
10C56-15
10Sweet Caporal Postcards-20
11C55-20
12C57-43
60Topps-46
Stamps-49
83Hall of Fame Postcards-A15
85Hall of Fame-14
03BAP Ultimate Mem Vintage Blade of Steel-4
03ITG VIP Vintage Memorabilia-1
04ITG Ultimate Memorabilia-26
Gold-26
Blades of Steel-3
Nicknames-26
05ITG Ultimate Memorabilia Level 1-20
05ITG Ultimate Memorabilia Level 2-20
05ITG Ultimate Memorabilia Level 3-20
05ITG Ultimate Memorabilia Level 4-20
05ITG Ultimate Memorabilia Level 5-20
05ITG Ultimate Mem Blades of Steel-17
05ITG Ultimate Mem Blades of Steel Gold-17
06ITG Ultimate Memorabilia-34
Artist Proof-34
Taylor, Danny
03Guelph Storm-2
04Guelph Storm-1
05Kingston Frontenacs-22
06Bakersfield Condors-11
Taylor, Dave
78O-Pee-Chee-353
79O-Pee-Chee-232
79Topps-232
80Kings Card Night-12
80O-Pee-Chee-137
80Topps-137
81O-Pee-Chee-143
81O-Pee-Chee-152
81O-Pee-Chee-391
81O-Pee-Chee Stickers-149
81O-Pee-Chee Stickers-237
81O-Pee-Chee Stickers-268
81Topps-40
81Topps-W132
82O-Pee-Chee-161
82O-Pee-Chee Stickers-164
82O-Pee-Chee Stickers-231
82Post Cereal-8
82Topps Stickers-164
82Topps Stickers-231
83O-Pee-Chee-163
83Puffy Stickers-12
84Kings Smokey-16
84O-Pee-Chee-92
84O-Pee-Chee Stickers-267
847-Eleven Discs-25
85O-Pee-Chee-214
85O-Pee-Chee Stickers-238
857-Eleven Credit Cards-8
86Kings 20th Anniversary Team Issue-21
86O-Pee-Chee-63
86O-Pee-Chee Stickers-90
86Topps-63
87O-Pee-Chee-118
87O-Pee-Chee Stickers-215
87Panini Stickers-280
87Topps-118
88Kings Postcards-2
88Kings Smokey-22

88O-Pee-Chee-46
88O-Pee-Chee Stickers-155
88Panini Stickers-79
88Topps-46
89Kings Smokey-6
89O-Pee-Chee-58
89O-Pee-Chee Stickers-151
89Panini Stickers-98
89Topps-58
90Bowman-149
Tiffany-149
90Bowman Hat Tricks-22
Tiffany-22
90Kings Smokey-8
90O-Pee-Chee-314
90Panini Stickers-236
90Pro Set-128
90Score-166
Canadian-166
90Topps-314
Tiffany-314
90Upper Deck-214
French-214
91Bowman-186
91O-Pee-Chee-138
91Panini Stickers-89
91Parkhurst-67
91Parkhurst-214
French-67
French-214
91Pinnacle-249
91Pinnacle-373
French-249
French-373
91Pro Set-103
91Pro Set-325
French-103
French-325
Awards Special-AC16
91Score American-214
91Score American-374
91Score American-435
91Score Canadian Bilingual-214
91Score Canadian Bilingual-264
91Score Canadian Bilingual-325
91Score Canadian English-214
91Score Canadian English-264
91Score Canadian English-325
91Stadium Club-232
91Topps-138
91Upper Deck-270
French-270
92Bowman-37
92Parkhurst-307
Emerald Ice-307
92Pinnacle-367
French-367
92Pro Set-258
92Score-49
Canadian-49
92Stadium Club-234
92Topps-446
Gold-446G
92Ultra-313
93Leaf-374
93Panini Stickers-206
93Parkhurst-367
Emerald Ice-367
93Pinnacle-412
Canadian-412
93PowerPlay-364
93Score-389
Canadian-389
93Ultra-348
94Hockey Wit-21
94Stadium Club Members Only-14
95Lethbridge Hurricanes-23
96Lethbridge Hurricanes-21
97Moose Jaw Warriors-15
98Kings LA Times Coins-5
01Greats of the Game-61
Autographs-61
03BAP Ultimate Memorabilia Linemates-6
04ITG Franchises US West-232
Autographs-A-DTA
04UD Legendary Signatures-23
Autographs-DT
Linemates-CSMDDT
04UD Legends Classics-16
Gold-16
Platinum-16
Silver-16
Signature Moments-M34
Signature Moments-M41
Signature Moments-M65
Signatures-CS39
Signatures-DC16
Signatures-DC17
05Beehive Signature Scrapbook-SSDT
05SP Authentic Exquisite Endorsements-EEDT
05SP Authentic Prestigious Pairings-PPDT
05SP Authentic Sign of the Times Quads-QGTVD
05SP Game Used Statscriptions-ST-DT
05SPx Xcitement Legends-XL-DT
05SPx Xcitement Legends Gold-XL-DT
05SPx Xcitement Legends Spectrum-XL-DT
05The Cup Hardware Heroes-HHDT
05The Cup Scripted Swatches-SSDT
05UD Artifacts-149
Blue-149
Gold-149
Green-149
Pewter-149
Red-149
Auto Facts-AF-OK
Auto Facts Blue-AF-OK
Auto Facts Copper-AF-OK
Auto Facts Pewter-AF-OK
Auto Facts Silver-AF-OK
Gold Autographed-149
06SP Authentic Sign of the Times Duals-STRT
06SP Authentic Sign of the Times Quads-ST4BCTS
06SP Game Used Authentic Fabrics Quads-AF4NMBT
06SP Game Used Authentic Fabrics Quads Patches-AF4NMBT
06SP Game Used Inked Sweaters Dual-IS2RT
06SP Game Used Inked Sweaters Dual Patches-IS2RT
06SP Game Used SIGnificance-SDT
06The Cup Autographed NHL Shields Duals-DASRT
06The Cup Property of-PODT
06The Cup Scripted Swatches-SSDT
06The Cup Signature Patches-SPDT
06Ultimate Collection Autographed Jerseys-AJ-DT
06Ultimate Collection Autographed Patches-AJ-DT
06Ultimate Collection Jerseys-UJ-DT
06Ultimate Collection Patches-UJ-DT
06Upper Deck Sweet Shot Signature Shots/Saves Sticks-SSSDT
06Upper Deck Trilogy Scripts-TSDT
Taylor, Dylan
95Slapshot-124
01Indianapolis Ice-20

Taylor, Eric
79Montreal Juniors-26
Taylor, Gary
907th Inn. Sketch OHL-222
Taylor, Grant
03UK Belfast Giants-17
Taylor, Greg
91Air Canada SJHL-D28
97Columbus Cottonmouths-18
Taylor, Harry
44Beehive Group II Photos-456
45Quaker Oats Photos-53
Taylor, Jack
51Laval Dairy QSHL-67
Taylor, Jake
03Minnesota Golden Gophers-2
04Hartford Wolf Pack-22
05Hartford Wolf Pack-22
06Hartford Wolf Pack-16
Taylor, Jason
92Dallas Freeze-18
93Dallas Freeze-16
94Central Hockey League-18
94Dallas Freeze-18
97Central Texas Stampede-18
00Utah Grizzlies-13
Taylor, Jim
89ProCards AHL-80
Taylor, Justin
99Medicine Hat Tigers-21
99Medicine Hat Tigers-28
03Camrose Kodiaks-18
03Red Deer Rebels-12
04Langley Hornets-17
04Lowell Lock Monsters-22
04Lowell Lock Monsters Photo Album-22
05Salmon Arm Silverbacks-24
Taylor, Justin (BCHL)
04Langley Hornets-17
05Salmon Arm Silverbacks-20
Taylor, Karl
897th Inn. Sketch OHL-45
907th Inn. Sketch OHL-319
06Reading Royals-18
Taylor, Keith
75HCA Steel City Vacuum-14
Taylor, Mark
83O-Pee-Chee-273
83O-Pee-Chee Stickers-190
83Penguins Coke-18
83Topps Stickers-190
84O-Pee-Chee Stickers-121
84Penguins Heinz Photos-22
84Topps-127
92Cornell Big Red-30
93Cornell Big Red-30
Taylor, Matt
84Belleville Bulls-29
Taylor, Mike
94Richmond Renegades-16
95Richmond Renegades-2
96Richmond Renegades-22
00San Diego Gulls-18
Taylor, Paul
91British Columbia JHL-49
92Northern Michigan Wildcats-26
93Northern Michigan Wildcats-26
94Dayton Bombers-2
95Peoria Rivermen-20
98Tacoma Sabercats-20
Taylor, Randy
88ProCards IHL-6
89ProCards IHL-151
Taylor, Rod
92Hampton Roads Admirals-11
93Hampton Roads Admirals-18
94Hampton Roads Admirals-8
95Hampton Roads Admirals-12
96Hampton Roads Admirals-HRA10
97Hampton Roads Admirals-19
98Hampton Roads Admirals-13
98Hampton Roads Admirals 10th Anniversary-2
99Hampton Roads Admirals-21
00Richmond Renegades-9
02Peoria Rivermen RBI Sports-167
02South Carolina Stingrays-18
02South Carolina Stingrays RBI-221
Taylor, Ryan
95Slapshot-184
Taylor, Scott
85Kitchener Rangers-13
86Kitchener Rangers-12
89Hampton Roads Admirals-21
91Nashville Knights-18
Taylor, Shayne
06Erie Otters-10
Taylor, Ted
61Sudbury Wolves-17
62Sudbury Wolves-21
65Topps-95
70Canucks Royal Bank-17
71Canucks Royal Bank-17
71Sargent Promotions Stamps-223
72O-Pee-Chee-312
73Quaker Oats WHA-28
75Houston Aeros WHA-18
Taylor, Tim
90ProCards AHL/IHL-211
91Baltimore Skipjacks-1
91ProCards-563
92Finnish Semic-146
94Ultra-286
94Upper Deck-325
Electric Ice-325
94Signature Rookies Tetrad *-116
Previews-T2
Signatures-116
95Be A Player-101
Signatures-S101
Signatures Die Cuts-S101
95Donruss-349
95Topps-132
OPC Inserts-132
95Upper Deck-295
Electric Ice-295
Electric Ice Gold-295
97Be A Player-114
Autographs-114
Autographs Die-Cuts-114
Autographs Prismatic Die-Cuts-114
97Pacific Dynagon Best Kept Secrets-35
97SP Authentic-9
98Pacific-101
Ice Blue-101
Red-101
98Upper Deck-37
Exclusives-37
Exclusives 1 of 1-37
Gold Reserve-37
99Ultimate Victory-58
1/1-58
Parallel-58
Parallel 100-58
00Upper Deck Vintage-245
02BAP First Edition-167
03ITG Action-574
03Lightning Team Issue-27
03Pacific Complete-316
Red-316
03Upper Deck MVP-389
Gold Script-389
Silver Script-389
Canadian Exclusives-389
05Be A Player Signatures-TT
05Be A Player Signatures Gold-TT
05Lightning Team Issue-10
05Parkhurst-441
Facsimile Auto Parallel-441
05Upper Deck-176
HG Glossy-176
05Upper Deck MVP-349
Gold-349
Platinum-349
05Upper Deck Toronto Fall Expo-176
06Be A Player-25
Autographs-25
Signatures-TT
06Lightning Postcards-23
06O-Pee-Chee-448
Rainbow-448
06Upper Deck-425
Exclusives Parallel-425
High Gloss Parallel-425
Masterpieces-425
Taylor, Tyler
06Oshawa Generals-3
Teal, Gordon
28V128-2 Paulin's Candy-65
56Quebec Aces-14
Teal, Jeff
83Nova Scotia Voyageurs-22
Tebbutt, Greg
83Penguins Coke-19
Tedenby, Robert
86Swedish Panini Stickers-211
Teevens, Mark
88ProCards IHL-4
94German DEL-69
95German DEL-70
96German DEL-265
Teichmann, Brad
907th Inn. Sketch OHL-20
917th Inn. Sketch OHL-46
Teijonmaa, Olli
71Finnish Suomi Stickers-336
Teimonen, Miikka
95Finnish SISU-288
Tejchma, Jeremy
05Waterloo Blackhawks-21
Tejkl, Petr
94Czech APS Extraliga-4
95Czech APS Extraliga-105
96Czech APS Extraliga-101
97Czech DS Stickers-269
99Czech OFS-247
Telfer, Craig
93Quebec Pee-Wee Tournament-496
Teljukin, Andrei
01German Upper Deck-223
02German DEL City Press-187
03German DEL-134
04German DEL-158
04German Hannover Scorpions Postcards-28
05German DEL-53
Tellqvist, Mikael
00Swedish Upper Deck-44
00Swedish Upper Deck-186
Masked Men-M2
SHL Signatures-ME
Top Draws-T3
01St. John's Maple Leafs-23
02BAP All-Star Edition-114
Gold-114
Silver-114
02BAP Memorabilia-280
Emerald-280
Ruby-280
Sapphire-280
NHL All-Star Game-280
NHL All-Star Game Blue-280
NHL All-Star Game Green-280
NHL All-Star Game Red-280
02BAP Memorabilia Toronto Fall Expo-280
02BAP Ultimate Memorabilia-32
02Between the Pipes-77
Gold-77
Silver-77
02Bowman YoungStars-146
Gold-146
Silver-146
02ITG Used-191
02Maple Leafs Team Issue-13
02Pacific Calder-148
Silver-148
02Pacific Complete-594
Red-594
02Pacific Quest for the Cup-149
Gold-149
02Parkhurst-232
Bronze-232
Gold-232
Silver-232
02Parkhurst Retro-232
Minis-232
02SP Authentic-195
02SP Game Used-103
02SPx-158
02Titanium-139
Blue-139
Red-139
Retail-139
02Topps Chrome-157
Black Border Refractors-157
Refractors-157
02Topps Total-421
02UD Artistic Impressions-115
Gold-115
02UD Honor Roll-165
02UD Mask Collection-179
02UD Premier Collection-77
Gold-77
Signatures Bronze-SMT
Signatures Gold-SMT
Signatures Silver-SMT
02UD Top Shelf-103
02Upper Deck-455
Exclusives-455
02Upper Deck Rookie Update-171
Autographs-MT
02St. John's Maple Leafs Aliant-3
03BAP Memorabilia-146
Emerald-146
Gold-146
Ruby-146
Sapphire-146
Deep in the Crease-D9
Future Wave-FW-11
03Maple Leafs Team Issue-2
03Pacific Complete-418
Red-418
03Parkhurst Original Six Toronto-25
03SP Authentic Sign of the Times-MT
03Topps Traded-TT62
Blue-TT62
Gold-TT62
Red-TT62
03Upper Deck-428
Canadian Exclusives-428
HG-428
UD Exclusives-428
03Upper Deck MVP-405
Gold Script-405
Silver Script-405
Canadian Exclusives-405
03Russian World Championship Stars-11
03Pacific AHL Prospects-82
Gold-82
04Swedish Alfabilder Alfa Stars-32
04Swedish Alfabilder Autographs-112
04Swedish Alfabilder Limited Autographs-112
04Swedish Alfabilder Proof Parallels-32
04ITG Heroes/Prospects He Shoots/Scores-29
04ITG Heroes and Prospects Net Prospects-27
04ITG Heroes and Prosp Net Prospects Gold-27
05Be A Player Signatures-TE
05Be A Player Signatures Gold-TE
05Parkhurst-458
Facsimile Auto Parallel-458
Signatures-MT
05Upper Deck-428
06Between The Pipes-39
Emblems-GUE30
Emblems Gold-GUE30
Jerseys-GUJ30
Jerseys Gold-GUJ30
Numbers-GUN30
Numbers Gold-GUN30
The Mask-M33
The Mask Gold-M33
The Mask Silver-M33
06Flair Showcase Inks-ITE
06Fleer Signing Day-SDMT
06UD Artifacts Auto-Facts-AFMT
06UD Artifacts Auto-Facts Gold-AFMT
06Ultra Fresh Ink-IMT
06Upper Deck-184
Exclusives Parallel-184
High Gloss Parallel-184
Masterpieces-184
06Upper Deck MVP-276
Gold Script-276
Super Script-276
Autographs-OAAT
06Upper Deck Trilogy Scripts-TSMT
07Upper Deck Victory-199
Black-199
Gold-199
Tellstrom, Johan
03Swedish Elite-235
Silver-235
04Swedish Elitset-80
Gold-80
Teltscher, Michael
94German First League-351
99German Bundesliga 2-23
Temple, Jeff
95Brandon Wheat Kings-21
96Medicine Hat Tigers-22
97Medicine Hat Tigers-20
Templeton, Bert
82North Bay Centennials-21
83North Bay Centennials-25
897th Inn. Sketch OHL-173
907th Inn. Sketch OHL-323
917th Inn. Sketch OHL-72
93North Bay Centennials-23
95Slapshot-6
95Barrie Colts-20
96Barrie Colts-25
97Barrie Colts-21
98Barrie Colts-23
99Sudbury Wolves-22
00Sudbury Wolves-20
01Sudbury Wolves-21
01Sudbury Wolves Police-2
Tendler, Blaine
06Prince Albert Raiders-6
Tenhunen, Seppo
78Finnish SM-Liiga-139
80Finnish Mallasjuoma-97
Tenisi, Guido
82Swedish Semic VM Stickers-124
83Swedish Semic VM Stickers-124
Tenkanen, Valtteri
05Finnish Cardset -249
06Finnish Cardset-251
Tenkrat, Petr
96Czech APS Extraliga-93
97Czech APS Extraliga-211
98Czech DS Stickers-243
98Czech OFS-171
98Czech OFS-459
99Czech OFS-271
99Finnish Cardset-243
00BAP Memorabilia-507
00BAP Parkhurst 2000-P157
00Black Diamond-112
00SP Authentic-91
00Titanium Draft Day Edition-153
00Titanium Draft Day Promos-153
00Upper Deck Ice-104
00Finnish Cardset Master Blasters-3
01BAP Memorabilia-412
Emerald-412
Ruby-412
Sapphire-412
01Parkhurst-365
01Upper Deck Victory-8
Gold-8
01Czech DS-35
Ice Heroes-IH10
02Czech National Team Postcards-12
02Finnish Cardset-276
04Finnish Cardset-105
Parallel-78
04Swedish Pure Skills-129
Parallel-129
05Finnish Cardset -98
06Czech IIHF World Championship Postcards-22
06Czech LG Hockey Games Postcards-22
06Czech OFS Jagr Team-12
06Czech Super Six Postcards-14
Tennant, Ken
52Juniors Blue Tint-126
Tennant, Nathan
98Kingston Frontenacs-20
99Kingston Frontenacs-21
00Kingston Frontenacs-20
01Kingston Frontenacs-22
01Plymouth Whalers-4
Tenute, Joey
00Barrie Colts-25
01Barrie Colts-8
03Sarnia Sting-20
04Barrie Colts 10th Anniversary-13
05ITG Heroes/Prosp Toronto Expo Parallel -216
05Hot Prospects-185
En Fuego-185
Red Hot-185
White Hot-185
05SPx-293
05The Cup Master Pressplate Rookie Update-194
05The Cup Masterpiece Pressplates (SPx)-293
05The Cup Masterpiece Pressplates Trilogy-320
05Upper Deck Rookie Update-194
05Upper Deck Trilogy-320
05Hershey Bears-16
05ITG Heroes and Prospects-216
Autographs Series II-JTE
06ITG Heroes and Prospects Calder Cup Champions-CC11
Teplyakov, Dmitri
99Russian Hockey League-190
00Russian Hockey League-67
Tepper, Stephen
93Roanoke Express-20
94Central Hockey League-36
Terbenche, Paul
67Topps-58
70O-Pee-Chee-123
70Topps-123
72Sabres Postcards-19
73O-Pee-Chee-229
73Sabres Postcards-13
75O-Pee-Chee WHA-112
78Jets Postcards-22
Terechin, Juri
74Swedish Stickers-55
Terekhov, Alexander
95Czech APS Extraliga-323
98Russian Hockey League-25
Terekhov, Vladimir
00Russian Hockey League-282
Tereshenko, Alexei
99Russian Dynamo Moscow-1
00Russian Dynamo Moscow-24
02Russian SL-50
03Russian Hockey League-43
04Russian Moscow Dynamo-30
Terglav, Edo
93Quebec Pee-Wee Tournament-1794
00QMJHL All-Star Program Inserts-32
Terkelsen, Jens
98Danish Hockey League-27
Ternavski, Artem
02Russian Hockey League-82
Terreri, Chris
88ProCards AHL-344
89Devils Caretta-25
90Devils Team Issue-29
90O-Pee-Chee-284
90O-Pee-Chee-375
90Panini Stickers-68
90Pro Set-481
90Score-239
Canadian-239
90Topps-284
90Topps-375
Tiffany-375
90Upper Deck-183
French-183
91Pro Set Platinum-68
91Pro Set Platinum-288
91Bowman-283
91Gillette-38
91O-Pee-Chee-422
91OPC Premier-197
91Panini Stickers-221
91Parkhurst-98
French-98
91Pinnacle-247
French-247
91Pro Set-137
French-137
91Score American-151
91Score Canadian Bilingual-151
91Score Canadian English-151
91Score Young Superstars-15
91Stadium Club-297
91Topps-422
91Upper Deck-115
French-115
91Finnish Semic World Champ Stickers-129
91Swedish Semic World Champ Stickers-129
92Bowman-386
92Humpty Dumpty II-22
92Kraft-30
92O-Pee-Chee-282
92Panini Stickers-171
92Panini Stickers French-171
92Parkhurst-93
Emerald Ice-93
92Pinnacle-274
French-274
92Pro Set-97
92Score-270
Canadian-270
92Seasons Patches-51
92Stadium Club-74
92Topps-303
Gold-303G
92Ultra-120
92Upper Deck-43
93Donruss-194
93Leaf-430
93OPC Premier-213
Gold-213
93Panini Stickers-D
93Parkhurst-112
Emerald Ice-112
93Pinnacle-267
Canadian-267
93PowerPlay-144
93Score-237
Canadian-237
93Stadium Club-328
Members Only Master Set-328
First Day Issue-328
93Topps/OPC Premier-213
Gold-213
93Ultra-209
93Upper Deck-110
94Canada Games NHL POGS-285
94Donruss-285
94EA Sports-78
94Hockey Wit-31
94Leaf-134
94OPC Premier-13
94OPC Premier-83
Special Effects-13
94Parkhurst SE-SE94
Gold-SE94
94Pinnacle-335
Artist's Proofs-335
Rink Collection-335
94Topps/OPC Premier-13
94Topps/OPC Premier-83
Special Effects-13
94Ultra-323
95Be A Player-27
Signatures-S27
Signatures Die Cuts-S27
95Finest-149
Refractors-149
95Parkhurst International-451
Emerald Ice-451
95Score-243
Black Ice Artist's Proofs-243
Black Ice-243
95SP-131
95Ultra-306
95Upper Deck-450
Electric Ice-450
Electric Ice Gold-450
96Collector's Choice-239
96Collector's Choice-330
96Donruss-38
Press Proofs-38
96Fleer-102
96Leaf-94
Press Proofs-94
96Maggers-98
96Pinnacle-103
Artist's Proofs-103
Foil-103
Premium Stock-103
Rink Collection-103
96Score Artist's Proofs-28
96Score Dealer's Choice Artist's Proofs-28
96Score Special Artist's Proofs-28
96Score Golden Blades-28
96SkyBox Impact-119
96Summit-89
Artist's Proofs-89
Ice-89
Metal-89
Premium Stock-89
96Upper Deck-147
97Be A Player-30
Autographs-30
Autographs Die-Cuts-30
Autographs Prismatic Die-Cuts-30
97Crown Royale-31
Emerald Green-31
Ice Blue-31
Silver-31
97Pacific Invincible NHL Regime-48
97Score-48
Artist's Proofs-48
Golden Blades-48
97Sharks Fleer All-Star Sheet-7
97SP Authentic-33
97Upper Deck-40
98Devils Team Issue-30
98NHL Aces Playing Cards-18
98Pacific-40
Ice Blue-40
Red-40
98Upper Deck-307
Exclusives-307
Exclusives 1 of 1-307
Gold Reserve-307
99Devils Team Issue-24
99Pacific-249
Copper-249
Emerald Green-249
Gold-249
Ice Blue-249
Premiere Date-249
Red-249
00Devils Team Issue-23
00Pacific-245
Copper-245
Gold-245
Ice Blue-245
Premiere Date-245
00Private Stock Game Gear-66
00Private Stock Game Gear Patches-66
00Titanium Game Gear-107
00Titanium Game Gear Patches-107
00Titanium Draft Day Edition-64
Patches-64
00Vanguard Dual Game-Worn Jerseys-19
00Vanguard Dual Game-Worn Patches-19
01Atomic Jerseys-39
01Atomic Patches-39
01Crown Royale Triple Threads-13
01Pacific-254
Extreme LTD-254
Hobby LTD-254
Premiere Date-254
Retail LTD-254
Jerseys-20
01Pacific Arena Exclusives-254
04ITG Franchises US East-360
Autographs-A-CT
Terrien, Benoit
907th Inn. Sketch QMJHL-68
Terrion, Greg
81O-Pee-Chee-155
82Maple Leafs Postcards-33
82Maple Leafs Postcards-34
82O-Pee-Chee-333
82O-Pee-Chee Stickers-234
82Topps Stickers-234
83Maple Leafs Postcards-23
83NHL Key Tags-114
83O-Pee-Chee-342
83O-Pee-Chee Stickers-37
83Topps Stickers-37
83Vachon-99
84Maple Leafs Postcards-23
84O-Pee-Chee-312
84O-Pee-Chee Stickers-19
85Maple Leafs Postcards-28
85O-Pee-Chee Stickers-18
86Kraft Drawings-74
86Maple Leafs Postcards-19
86O-Pee-Chee-244
86O-Pee-Chee Stickers-147
87Maple Leafs PLAY-21
87O-Pee-Chee-241
87O-Pee-Chee Stickers-153
88ProCards AHL-240
Terris, Marc
96Peoria Rivermen-22
96Peoria Rivermen Photo Album-22
97Peoria Rivermen-15
Terry, Chris
05Plymouth Whalers-B-11
06Plymouth Whalers-23
Tertyshny, Alexei
99Russian Hockey League-126
00Russian Hockey League-41
02Russian Hockey League-144
03Russian SL-30
Tertyshny, Dimitri
98Bowman's Best-118
Refractors-118
Atomic Refractors-118
98Pacific Omega-179
Red-179
Opening Day Issue-179
98Upper Deck-336
Exclusives-336
Exclusives 1 of 1-336
Gold Reserve-336
99BAP Memorabilia-DT5
Gold-DT5
Tertyshny, Sergei
94Portland Pirates-22
95Portland Pirates-21
98Russian Hockey League-14
99Russian Hockey League-21
99Russian Metallurg Magnetogorsk-29
99Russian Stars of Hockey-10
00Russian Hockey League-158
01Russian Hockey League-99
Tervo, Heimo
65Finnish Hellas-78
Tervonen, Kai
92Finnish Jyvas-Hyva Stickers-14
93Finnish Jyvas-Hyva Stickers-25
93Finnish SISU-93
Terzo, Anthony
96Detroit Whalers-17
99Huntington Blizzard-11
Tesarek, Tomas
00Prince George Cougars-16
Tesarik, Daniel
96Czech APS Extraliga-235
Tesarik, Radim
94Czech APS Extraliga-187
95Czech APS Extraliga-36
96Czech APS Extraliga-31
97Czech APS Extraliga-30
97Czech DS Extraliga-58
97Czech DS Stickers-99
98Czech DS-79
98Czech DS Stickers-170
98Czech OFS-101
99Czech DS-132
99Czech OFS-66
99Czech OFS-485
99Czech OFS-528
All-Star Game Blue-528
All-Star Game Gold-528
All-Star Game Red-528
All-Star Game Silver-528
00Czech DS Extraliga-18
00Czech OFS-326
01Czech OFS All Stars-4
02Czech OFS Plus-298
Trios-T18
02Czech National Team Postcards-13
02Russian Hockey League-241
03Czech OFS Plus-142
03Czech OFS Plus-359
03Czech OFS Plus MS Praha-SE32
04Czech OFS-288
Defence Points-13
05Czech HC Trinec-12
06Czech OFS-168
All Stars-7
Defenders-12
Tesch, Willi
94German First League-415
Tesi, Mike
96Arizona Icecats-19
97Arizona Icecats-20
98Arizona Icecats-24
Tesikov, Alex
99BAP Millennium Calder Candidates Ruby-C29
99BAP Millennium Calder Candidate Emerald-C29
99BAP Millennium Calder Cand Sapphire-C29
Tesink, Brad
05Gatineau Olympiques-13
06Gatineau Olympiques-8
Teskey, Doug
94Thunder Bay Flyers-20
00Fort Wayne Komets-21
00Fort Wayne Komets Shoe Carnival-6
01Fort Wayne Komets-1
01Fort Wayne Komets Shoe Carnival-13
03ECHL Update RBI Sports-64
03Toledo Storm-2
Tesliuk, Roman
03Kamloops Blazers-2
05Kamloops Blazers-3
Tessier, Brian
86Kingston Canadians-6
Tessier, Dan
99Ottawa 67's-13
99Bowman CHL-132
Gold-132
OPC International-132
00Louisiana Ice Gators-18
03Columbus Cottonmouths-27
04Fresno Falcons-19
05UK Nottingham Panthers-8
Tessier, Dave
93Quebec Pee-Wee Tournament-1089
Tessier, J.P.
00Jackson Bandits-22
Tessier, Jason
99Rouyn-Noranda Huskies-19
01El Paso Buzzards-12
Tessier, Kelsey
06Quebec Remparts-5
Tessier, Michael
03Cape Breton Screaming Eagles-21
04Quebec Remparts-23
Tessier, Orval
52Juniors Blue Tint-104
56Quebec Aces-15
60Shirriff Coins-114
82Blackhawks Postcards-22
83Blackhawks Postcards-23
Tessier, Patrick
917th Inn. Sketch QMJHL-34
01Chicoutimi Sagueneens-7
Tessier, Tommy
93Quebec Pee-Wee Tournament-50
Testa, Andrew R
93Quebec Pee-Wee Tournament-1675
Testwuide, Jon-Paul
03Waterloo Blackhawks-17
Testwuide, Mike
04Waterloo Blackhawks-9
05Waterloo Blackhawks-22
Tetarenko, Joey
95Upper Deck-523
Electric Ice-523
Electric Ice Gold-523
97Portland Winter Hawks-24
97Bowman CHL-86
OPC-86
98New Haven Beast-18
99Louisville Panthers-20
00Louisville Panthers-5
01BAP Signature Series-133
Autographs-133
Autographs Gold-133
01BAP Update Tough Customers-TC10
02BAP Sig Series Auto Buybacks 2001-133
03Lowell Lock Monsters-12
03Lowell Lock Monsters Photo Album-16
Tetrault, Alain
77Granby Vics-18
Tetrault, Daniel
95Brandon Wheat Kings-22
96Upper Deck-376
96Brandon Wheat Kings-2
97Brandon Wheat Kings-23
97Bowman CHL-134
OPC-134
Autographs-14
98Brandon Wheat Kings-19
99Brandon Wheat Kings-19
00Austin Ice Bats-22
01Austin Ice Bats-17
02Trenton Titans-B-10
03Austin Ice Bats-18
04New Mexico Scorpions-20
Tetrault, Eric
01Chicoutimi Sagueneens-12
Tetrault, Justin
00OCN Blizzard-20
01OCN Blizzard-22
Tetzlaff, Jeff
95Slapshot-25
95Barrie Colts-21
96Barrie Colts-26
97Barrie Colts-22
98Barrie Colts-14
04Barrie Colts 10th Anniversary-20
Teubert, Colten
06Regina Pats-22
Teui, Mikko
94Finnish SISU-113
Texeira, Chuck
92Maine Black Bears-31
93Maine Black Bears-51
Tezikov, Alexei
98Bowman CHL-118
Golden Anniversary-118
OPC International-118
98Bowman Chrome CHL-118
Golden Anniversary-118
Golden Anniversary Refractors-118
OPC International-118
OPC International Refractors-118
Refractors-118
99BAP Memorabilia-81
Gold-81
Silver-81
99Pacific-450
Copper-450
Emerald Green-450
Gold-450
Ice Blue-450
Premiere Date-450
Red-450
99Pacific Omega-247
Copper-247
Gold-247
Ice Blue-247
Premiere Date-247
99Paramount-249
Copper-249
Emerald-249
Gold-249
Holographic Emerald-249
Holographic Gold-249
Holographic Silver-249
Ice Blue-249
Premiere Date-249
Red-249
Silver-249
99Upper Deck-302
Exclusives-302
Exclusives 1 of 1-302
99Upper Deck Arena Giveaways-WC2
99Upper Deck Gold Reserve-302
99Portland Pirates-2
00O-Pee-Chee-313
00O-Pee-Chee Parallel-313
00Topps/OPC-313
Parallel-313
00Topps Chrome-208
OPC Refractors-208
Refractors-208
00Portland Pirates-14
Thacker, Rod
87Sault Ste. Marie Greyhounds-32
Thake, Matte
93Quebec Pee-Wee Tournament-576
Thaler, Alexander
94Finnish Jaa Kiekko-297
95Swedish World Championships Stickers-83
Thaler, Chris
00Mississauga Ice Dogs-25
Thalmann, Philippe
01Swiss HNL-300
02Swiss HNL-361
Thang, Ryan
04Sioux Falls Stampede-1-5
05Sioux Falls Stampede-9
Thanner, Rudolf
72Finnish Hellas-46
Tharp, Ben
99Minnesota Golden Gophers-25
00Minnesota Golden Gophers-25
Thau, Steffen
94German First League-573
Thawley, Mark
92Arizona Icecats-15
93Arizona Icecats-18
94Arizona Icecats-15
95Arizona Icecats-6
Theander, Bo
71Swedish Hockey-173
73Swedish Stickers-58
Theberge, Edouard
51Bas Du Fleuve-23
Theberge, Gerry
51Laval Dairy Lac St. Jean-14
Theberge, Greg
81Capitals Team Issue-16
82Post Cereal-20
Theel, Justin
93Omaha Lancers-26
Thelander, Anders
71Swedish Hockey-328
Thelen, A.J.
05ITG Heroes/Prosp Toronto Expo Parallel -313
05Prince Albert Raiders-21
05ITG Heroes and Prospects-313
Autographs Series II-AJT
06Prince Albert Raiders-5
Theler, Yannick
93Swiss HNL-433
95Swiss HNL-482
96Swiss HNL-379
Thelin, Goran
65Swedish Coralli ISHockey-205
67Swedish Hockey-278
69Swedish Hockey-322
70Swedish Hockey-226
Thelin, Mats
82Swedish Semic VM Stickers-8
83Swedish Semic Elitserien-3
83Swedish Semic VM Stickers-8
84Bruins Postcards-20
87Swedish Panini Stickers-11
89Swedish Semic Elitserien Stickers-4
90Swedish Semic Elitserien Stickers-78
91Swedish Semic Elitserien Stickers-6
92Swedish Semic Elitserien Stickers-29
Thelin, Ove
67Swedish Hockey-279
69Swedish Hockey-323
70Swedish Hockey-227
72Swedish Stickers-277
Thelven, Michael
83Swedish Semic Elitserien-84
83Swedish Semic VM Stickers-9
84Swedish Semic Elitserien-76
85Swedish Panini Stickers-123
85Swedish Panini Stickers-124
87O-Pee-Chee-24
87Panini Stickers-9
87Topps-24
88Bruins Sports Action-21
88Bruins Postcards-19
88Panini Stickers-206
89Bruins Sports Action-21
Themens, Jean
93Quebec Pee-Wee Tournament-1395
Theodore, Jose
95Donruss Elite World Juniors-2
95Upper Deck-530
Electric Ice-530
Electric Ice Gold-530
95Signature Rookies-10
Auto-Phonex Beyond 2000-B5
Signatures-10
95Slapshot Memorial Cup-73
96Black Diamond-116
Gold-116
96Canadiens Postcards-28
96Canadiens Sheets-21
96Collector's Choice-351
Jumbos-3
96Donruss-227
Press Proofs-227
Canadian Ice Les Gardiens-10
96Donruss Elite-139
Die Cut Stars-139
96Flair-112
Blue Ice-112
96Fleer-134
Calder Candidates-9
96Leaf Gold Rookies-3
96Pinnacle-217
Artist's Proofs-217
Foil-217
Premium Stock-217
Rink Collection-217
96Score-267
Artist's Proofs-267
Dealer's Choice Artist's Proofs-267
Special Artist's Proofs-267
Golden Blades-267
96SkyBox Impact-161
96SP-174
96Summit-182
Artist's Proofs-182
Ice-182
Metal-182
Premium Stock-182
96Upper Deck-279
96Upper Deck Ice-90
Parallel-90
96Fredericton Canadiens-21
97Collector's Choice-135
97Donruss-81
Press Proofs Silver-81
Press Proofs Gold-81
Between The Pipes-6
Canadian Ice Les Gardiens-6
97Donruss Canadian Ice Les Gardiens Promo-6
97Donruss Cdn Ice Stanley Cup Scrapbook-14
97Donruss Limited-81
97Donruss Limited-151
97Donruss Limited-152
Exposure-81
Exposure-151
Exposure-152
Fabric of the Game-71
97Donruss Preferred-102
Cut to the Chase-102
Color Guard-11
Color Guard Promos-11
97Gatorade Stickers-3
97Leaf-122
Fractal Matrix-122
Fractal Matrix Die Cuts-122
Pipe Dreams-9
97Leaf International-122
Universal Ice-122
97Pacific Invincible NHL Regime-107
97Pinnacle Inside-56
Coach's Collection-56
Executive Collection-56
Stoppers-14
97Score-42
Artist's Proofs-42
Golden Blades-42
97Score Canadiens-3
Platinum-3
Premier-3
97SP Authentic Sign of the Times-JTH
97Studio-24
Press Proofs Silver-24
Press Proofs Gold-24
97Upper Deck-85
Game Dated Moments-85
Smooth Grooves-SG60
Three Star Selects-12C
97Upper Deck Ice-36
Parallel-36
Power Shift-36
98Be A Player-219
Press Release-219
98BAP Gold-219
98BAP Autographs-219
98BAP Autographs Gold-219

98Bowman's Best Mirror Image Fusion-F19
98Bowmans Best Mirror Im Fusion Ref-F19
98Bowmans Best Mirror Im Fusion Atom Ref-F19
98Canadiens Team Issue-21
98NHL Aces Playing Cards-9
98Upper Deck-114
Exclusives-114
Exclusives 1 of 1-114
Generation Next-GN8
Generation Next Quantum 1-GN8
Generation Next Quantum 2-GN8
Generation Next Quantum 3-GN8
Gold Reserve-114
MVP ProSign-JT
99Crown Royale-73
Limited Series-73
Premiere Date-73
99McDonald's Upper Deck-MCD16
Signatures-JT
99O-Pee-Chee-195
99O-Pee-Chee Chrome-195
99O-Pee-Chee Chrome Refractors-195
99Pacific-212
Copper-212
Emerald Green-212
Gold-212
Ice Blue-212
Premiere Date-212
Red-212
99Pacific Omega-123
Copper-123
Gold-123
Ice Blue-123
Premiere Date-123
99SP Authentic-45
99Stadium Club-144
First Day Issue-144
One of a Kind-144
Printing Plates Black-144
Printing Plates Cyan-144
Printing Plates Magenta-144
Printing Plates Yellow-144
99Topps/OPC-195
99Topps/OPC Chrome-195
Refractors-195
99Upper Deck MVP SC Edition-93
Gold Script-93
Silver Script-93
Super Script-93
99Upper Deck Victory-153
00Aurora-75
Pinstripes-75
Pinstripes Premiere Date-75
Premiere Date-75
Autographs-75
00BAP Memorabilia-287
Emerald-287
Ruby-287
Sapphire-287
Promos-287
00BAP Mem Chicago Sportsfest Copper-287
00BAP Memorabilia Chicago Sportsfest Blue-287
00BAP Memorabilia Chicago Sportsfest Gold-287
00BAP Memorabilia Chicago Sportsfest Ruby-287
00BAP Memorabilia Chicago Sun-Times Ruby-287
00BAP Memorabilia Chicago Sun-Times Gold-287
00BAP Mem Chicago Sun-Times Sapphire-287
00BAP Mem Toronto Fall Expo Copper-287
00BAP Memorabilia Toronto Fall Expo Gold-287
00BAP Memorabilia Toronto Fall Expo Ruby-287
00BAP Parkhurst 2000-P94
00BAP Signature Series-44
Emerald-44
Ruby-44
Sapphire-44
Autographs-195
Autographs Gold-195
00Black Diamond-30
Gold-30
00Canadiens Postcards-8
00Crown Royale-58
Ice Blue-58
Limited Series-58
Premiere Date-58
Red-58
00O-Pee-Chee-25
00O-Pee-Chee Parallel-25
00Pacific-215
Copper-215
Gold-215
Ice Blue-215
Premiere Date-215
2001: Ice Odyssey-11
Autographs-215
00Pacific 2001: Ice Odyssey Anaheim Ntnl-11
00Paramount-132
Copper-132
Gold-132
Holo-Gold-132
Holo-Silver-132
Ice Blue-132
Premiere Date-132
Glove Side Net Fusions-11
Glove Side Net Fusions Platinum-11
00Private Stock-53
Gold-53
Premiere Date-53
Retail-53
Silver-53
PS-2001 Action-29
PS-2001 New Wave-11
00Revolution-79
Blue-79
Premiere Date-79
Red-79
Stat Masters-15
00SP Authentic-46
Sign of the Times-JT
00SP Game Used-32
00Stadium Club Lone Star Signatures-LS6
00Stadium Club 11 X 14 Autographs-JT
00Titanium-50
Blue-50
Gold-50
Premiere Date-50
Red-50
Retail-50
00Topps/OPC-25
Parallel-25
Autographs-AJT
00Topps Chrome-24
OPC Refractors-24
Refractors-24
00Topps Heritage-162
00Topps Heritage-233
00UD Heroes-63
00UD Pros and Prospects-44
00UD Reserve-45
Buyback Autographs-101
Buyback Autographs-102
Buyback Autographs-103
Golden Goalies-GG5
00Upper Deck-96
Exclusives Tier 1-96
Exclusives Tier 2-96
Game Jersey Autographs Canadian-CJT
Rise to Prominence-RP3
00Upper Deck Ice-22
Immortals-22
Legends-22
Stars-22
00Upper Deck Legends-72
Legendary Collection Bronze-72
Legendary Collection Gold-72
Legendary Collection Silver-72
00Upper Deck MVP-92
First Stars-92
Second Stars-92
Third Stars-92
00Upper Deck Victory-121
00Upper Deck Vintage-193
00Upper Deck Vintage-196
00Upper Deck Vintage-197
Great Gloves-GG11
Original 6: A Piece of History-OJT
Original 6: A Piece of History Gold-OJT
00Vanguard-53
Holographic Gold-53
Holographic Purple-53
Pacific Proofs-53
01McFarlane Hockey-60
01McFarlane Hockey-62
01Atomic-53
Blue-53
Gold-53
Premiere Date-53
Red-53
01BAP Memorabilia Country of Origin-C052
01BAP Memorabilia Goalies Jerseys-GJ11
01BAP Memorabilia Goalie Traditions-GT6
01BAP Memorabilia Goalie Traditions-GT29
01BAP Memorabilia Goalie Traditions-GT30
01BAP Memorabilia Goalie Traditions-GT40
01BAP Signature Series Franchise Jerseys-FP-16
01BAP Signature Series Jerseys-GJ-85
01BAP Signature Series Teammates-TM-16
01BAP Ultimate Mem Legend Terry Sawchuk-13
01BAP Ultimate Memorabilia Les Canadiens-8
01BAP Ultimate Memorabilia MVP-1
01BAP Ultimate Memorabilia Vezina Winner-1
01BAP Update He Shoots-He Scores Points-14
01BAP Update He Shoots-He Scores Prizes-3
01BAP Update He Shoots-He Scores Prizes-31
01Between the Pipes-44
01Between the Pipes-170
Double Memorabilia-DM14
Goalie Gear-GG6
He Shoots-He Saves Points-8
He Shoots-He Saves Prizes-18
Jerseys-GJ11
Jersey and Stick Cards-GSJ10
Masks-20
Masks Silver-20
Masks Gold-20
Tandems-GT3
01Bowman YoungStars-26
Gold-26
Ice Cubed-26
01Canadiens Postcards-23
01Crown Royale-79
Blue-79
Premiere Date-79
Red-79
Retail-79
Triple Threads-4
01McDonald's Pacific-22
Glove-Side Net-Fusion-3
01O-Pee-Chee-98
01O-Pee-Chee Heritage Parallel-98
01O-Pee-Chee Heritage Parallel Limited-98
01O-Pee-Chee Premier Parallel-98
01Pacific-213
Extreme LTD-213
Hobby LTD-213
Premiere Date-213
Retail LTD-213
Steel Curtain-10
01Pacific Adrenaline-101
Blue-101
Premiere Date-101
Red-101
Retail-101
Creased Lightning-10
Power Play-20
01Pacific Arena Exclusives-213
01Pacific Heads-Up-52
Blue-52
Premiere Date-52
Red-52
Silver-52
HD NHL-16
Showstoppers-11
01Pacific Montreal International-5
01Parkhurst-74
Gold-74
Silver-74
01Private Stock-51
Gold-51
Premiere Date-51
Retail-51
Silver-51
Game Gear-55
Game Gear Patches-55
01Private Stock Pacific Nights-51
01SP Authentic-43
Limited-43
Limited Gold-43
01SP Game Used-28
Authentic Fabric-AFJO
Authentic Fabric-DFPT
Authentic Fabric Gold-AFJO
Inked Sweaters-DSJT
Patches Signed-SPTH
Tools of the Game-TTH
Tools of the Game-CTKT
Tools of the Game-CTTD
Tools of the Game Signed-STJT
01SPx Hidden Treasures-DTTT
01SPx Hidden Treasures-TTBTT
01Sports Illustrated for Kids III-204
01Stadium Club-38
Award Winners-38
Master Photos-38
01Titanium-76
Hobby Parallel-76
Premiere Date-76
Retail-76
Retail Parallel-76
All-Stars-12
Double-Sided Jerseys-20
Double-Sided Patches-20
Saturday Knights-11
01Topps-98
Heritage Parallel-98
Heritage Parallel Limited-98
OPC Parallel-98
01Topps Chrome-98
Refractors-98
Black Border Refractors-98
01Topps Heritage-41
Refractors-41
01Topps Reserve-76
01UD Mask Collection-116
Gold-116
Double Patches-DPTH
Dual Jerseys-MBBT
Goalie Jerseys-SSTH
Goalie Pads-GPJT
Jerseys-J-TH
Jersey and Patch-JPTH
Sticks-SSJT
01UD Playmakers-53
01UD Premier Collection-30
Dual Jerseys-DBTE
Dual Jerseys Black-DBTE
Jerseys-BJT
Jerseys Black-B-JT
Signatures-JT
Signatures Black-JT
01UD Top Shelf-98
Goalie Gear-LPJT
Jerseys-JO
Jersey Autographs-JO
01Upper Deck-320
Exclusives-320
Goaltender Threads-TTJO
01Upper Deck Ice-25
01Upper Deck MVP-100
Goalie Sticks-G-JT
01Upper Deck Victory-182
01Upper Deck Victory-186
Gold-182
Gold-186
01Upper Deck Vintage-134
01Upper Deck Vintage-139
01Vanguard-52
Blue-52
Red-52
Memorabilia-32
Memorabilia-43
One of Ones-52
Premiere Date-52
Proofs-52
Stonewallers-10
02McFarlane Hockey Toys-R-Us-10
02Atomic-57
Blue-57
Gold-57
Red-57
Denied-10
Hobby Parallel-57
Jerseys-11
Jerseys Gold-11
Patches-11
02BAP All-Star Edition-91
Jerseys-91
Jerseys Gold-91
Jerseys Silver-91
02BAP First Edition-138
02BAP First Edition-314
02BAP First Edition-356
02BAP First Edition-377
He Shoots-He Scores Prizes-25
Jerseys-138
02BAP Memorabilia-93
02BAP Memorabilia-216
Emerald-93
Emerald-216
Ruby-93
Ruby-216
Sapphire-93
Sapphire-216
All-Star Jerseys-ASJ-55
All-Star Emblems-ASE-24
All-Star Numbers-ASN-24
All-Star Teammmates-AST-26
Franchise Players-FP-16
Future of the Game-FG-6
He Shoots-He Scores Points-6
He Shoots-He Scores Prizes-15
NHL All-Star Game-93
NHL All-Star Game-216
NHL All-Star Game Blue-93
NHL All-Star Game Blue-216
NHL All-Star Game Green-93
NHL All-Star Game Green-216
NHL All-Star Game Red-93
NHL All-Star Game Red-216
Stanley Cup Playoffs-SC-6
Teammates-TM-12
02BAP Memorabilia Toronto Fall Expo-93
02BAP Memorabilia Toronto Fall Expo-216
02BAP Signature Series-65
Autographs-65
Autograph Buybacks 1998-219
Autograph Buybacks 2000-195
Autographs Gold-65
Franchise Players-FJ16
Jerseys-SGJ13
Jersey Autographs-SGJ13
Team Quads-TQ6
02BAP Ultimate Memorabilia Autographs-22
02BAP Ultimate Mem Autographs Gold-22
02BAP Ultimate Memorabilia Jerseys-3
02BAP Ultimate Mem Jersey and Stick-24
02BAP Ultimate Memorabilia Retro Trophies-10
02Between the Pipes-2
02Between the Pipes-136
Gold-2
Silver-2
All-Star Stick and Jersey-10
Behind the Mask-11
Double Memorabilia-5
Emblems-14
Future Wave-2
Goalie Autographs-22
He Shoots-He Saves Points-20
He Shoots-He Saves Prizes-20
Inspirations-I3
Jerseys-14
Masks II-16
Masks II Gold-16
Masks II Silver-16
Numbers-14
Pads-6
Stick and Jerseys-14
Tandems-9
02Bowman Toronto Spring Expo-4
02Bowman YoungStars-72
Gold-72
Silver-72
02Canadiens Postcards-19
02Crown Royale-52
Blue-52
Red-52
Retail-52
Jerseys-9
Jerseys Gold-9
Coats of Armor-5
02eTopps-7
02ITG Used-39
02ITG Used-139
Franchise Players-F16
Franchise Players Autographs-F16
Franchise Players Gold-F16
Goalie Pad and Jersey-GP1
Goalie Pad and Jersey Gold-GP1
Jerseys-GUJ13
Jersey Autographs-GUJ13
Jerseys Gold-GUJ13
Emblems-E13
Jersey and Stick-SJ13
Jersey and Stick Gold-SJ13
Teammates-T6
Teammates Gold-T6
02McDonald's Pacific-22
Glove Side Net-Fusions-4
Jersey Patches Silver-8
Jersey Patches Gold-8
02NHL Power Play Stickers-62
02O-Pee-Chee-190
02O-Pee-Chee-319
02O-Pee-Chee Jumbos-12
02O-Pee-Chee Premier Blue Parallel-190
02O-Pee-Chee Premier Blue Parallel-319
02O-Pee-Chee Premier Red Parallel-190
02O-Pee-Chee Premier Red Parallel-319
02O-Pee-Chee Factory Set-190
02O-Pee-Chee Factory Set-319
02O-Pee-Chee Factory Set Hometown Heroes-HHC9
02Pacific-203
Blue-203
Red-203
Jerseys-27
Jerseys Holo-Silver-27
Main Attractions-10
Maximum Impact-4
02Pacific Calder-43
Silver-43
Hardware Heroes-7
02Pacific Complete-412
Red-412
02Pacific Exclusive-94
Advantage-10
02Pacific Heads-Up-66
Blue-66
Purple-66
Red-66
Bobble Heads-12
Inside the Numbers-12
Postseason Picks-9
Quad Jerseys-15
Quad Jerseys Gold-15
Showstoppers-12
02Pacific Les Gardiens-5
Gold-5
02Pacific Quest for the Cup-52
Gold-52
Chasing the Cup-8
02Pacific Toronto Fall Expo-2
Gold-2
02Parkhurst-93
Bronze-93
Gold-93
Silver-93
Franchise Players-FP16
Hardware-H5
Hardware-V3
He Shoots-He Scores Points-10
He Shoots-He Scores Prizes-9
Jerseys-GJ2
Mario's Mates-MM10
Stick and Jerseys-SJ2
Teammates-TT7
02Parkhurst Retro-135
Minis-135
Franchise Players-RF16
He Shoots-He Scores Prizes-22
Jerseys-RJ24
Jersey and Sticks-RSJ17
Memorabilia-RM7
02Private Stock Reserve-127
Red-127
Retail-127
InCrease Security-12
Patches-127
02SP Authentic-47
Beckett Promos-47
Super Premiums-SPTH
Super Premiums-DPTK
02SP Game Used-25
Authentic Fabrics-AFTH
Authentic Fabrics-CFTK
Authentic Fabrics Gold-AFTH
Authentic Fabrics Gold-CFTK
Authentic Fabrics Rainbow-AFTH
Authentic Fabrics Rainbow-CFTK
Piece of History-PHTH
Piece of History Gold-PHTH
Piece of History Rainbow-PHTH
Tools of the Game-TH
02SPx-40
02SPx-92
Spectrum Gold-40
Spectrum Gold-92
Spectrum Silver-40
Spectrum Silver-92
Winning Materials-WMTH
Winning Materials Gold-TH
Winning Materials Silver-TH
Xtreme Talents-TH
Xtreme Talents Gold-TH
Xtreme Talents Silver-TH
02Stadium Club-1
Silver Decoy Cards-1
Proofs-1
Beam Team-BT5
Lone Star Signatures Blue-LSJT
Lone Star Signatures Red-LSJTH
Puck Stops Here-PSH4
02Titanium-57
Blue-57
Red-57
Retail-57
Jerseys-36
Jerseys Retail-36
Patches-36
Saturday Knights-5
Masked Marauders-4
02Topps-190
02Topps-319
OPC Blue Parallel-190
OPC Blue Parallel-319
OPC Red Parallel-190
OPC Red Parallel-319
Topps/OPC Hometown Heroes-HHC9
Factory Set-190
Factory Set-319
02Topps Chrome-109
Black Border Refractors-109
Refractors-109
02Topps Heritage-3
02Topps Heritage-105
02Topps Heritage-116
02Topps Heritage-129
Chrome Parallel-3
USA Test Parallel-3
02Topps Total-31
Award Winners-AW4
Team Checklists-TTC16
Topps-TT4
02UD Artistic Impressions-49
Gold-49
Artist's Touch-ATTH
Artist's Touch Gold-ATTH
02UD Artistic Impressions Beckett Promos-49
02UD Artistic Impressions Retrospectives-R49
02UD Artistic Impressions Retrospect Gold-R49
02UD Artistic Impress Retrospect Auto-R49
02UD Artistic Impress Retrospect Silver-R49
02UD Honor Roll-38
02UD Mask Collection-45
02UD Mask Collection-46
02UD Mask Collection-47
02UD Mask Collection-97
02UD Mask Collection Beckett Promos-45
02UD Mask Collection Beckett Promos-46
02UD Mask Collection Beckett Promos-47
02UD Mask Collection Great Gloves-GGJT
02UD Mask Collection Masked Marvels-MMTH
02UD Mask Collection Mini Masks-JT
02UD Mask Collection Mini Masks Autos-JT
02UD Mask Collection Nation's Best-NLBT
02UD Mask Collection Patches-PWTH
02UD Mask Collection Super Stoppers-SSJT
02UD Mask Collection View from the Cage-VTH
02UD Piece of History-48
Patches-PHJT
Threads-TTJT
02UD Premier Collection-31
Jerseys Bronze-JT
Jerseys Bronze-TK
Jerseys Gold-JT
Jerseys Gold-TK
Jerseys Silver-JT
Jerseys Silver-TK
Patches-PJT
02UD Top Shelf-45
Dual Player Jerseys-RRT
Dual Player Jerseys-STKT
Signatures-TH
Stopper Jerseys-SSTH
Sweet Sweaters-SWTH
02Upper Deck-92
Exclusives-92
All-Star Jerseys-ASJT
All-Star Performers-ASJT
Blow-Ups-C21
Difference Makers-JT
First Class-UDJT
First Class Gold-UDJT
Goaltender Threads-JT
Goaltender Threads Gold-JT
Last Line of Defense-LL7
Patch Card Numbers-JT
Patchwork-PWTH
Playbooks-PL10
Playbooks Series II-KT
Saviors Jerseys-SVJT
Super Saviors-SA7
02Upper Deck Classic Portraits-53
Etched in Time-ET9
Headliners-TK
Headliners Limited-TK
Hockey Royalty-RBT
Hockey Royalty Limited-RBT
Stitches-CTH
Stitches Limited-CTH
02Upper Deck MVP-96
Gold-96
Classics-96
Golden Classics-96
Masked Men-MM3
02Upper Deck Rookie Update-54
Jerseys-DTH
Jerseys Gold-DTH
02Upper Deck Victory-109
Bronze-109
Gold-109
Silver-109
02Upper Deck Vintage-134
02Upper Deck Vintage-276
02Upper Deck Vintage-318
02Upper Deck Vintage-319
Jerseys-OSJT
Tall Boys-T35
Tall Boys Gold-T35
02Vanguard-57
LTD-57
Jerseys-24
Jerseys Gold-24
Stonewallers-6
V-Team-4
02UD SuperStars *-138
Gold-138
03BAP Memorabilia-129
Emerald-129
Gold-129
Ruby-129
Sapphire-129
All-Star Complete Jerseys-ASCJ7
All-Star Emblems-ASE-13
All-Star Jerseys-ASJ-15
All-Star Numbers-ASN-13
All-Star Teammates-AST6
Brush with Greatness-15
Brush with Greatness Contest Cards-15
Deep in the Crease-D3
He Shoots-He Scores Points-1
He Shoots-He Scores Prizes-11
Jersey and Stick-SJ-32
Jerseys-GJ-41
Tandems-T-8
03BAP Ultimate Memorabilia Autographs-146
Gold-146
03BAP Ultimate Mem Auto Jerseys-146
03BAP Ultimate Mem Auto Emblems-146
03BAP Ultimate Mem Complete Package-10
03BAP Ultimate Mem Complete Package Gold-10
03BAP Ultimate Memorabilia Cornerstones-1
03BAP Ultimate Memorabilia Emblems-11
03BAP Ultimate Memorabilia Emblems Gold-11
03BAP Ultimate Mem Franch Present Future-16
03BAP Ultimate Memorabilia Great Moments-5
03BAP Ultimate Memorabilia Heroes-10
03BAP Ultimate Mem Heroes Autos-5
03BAP Ultimate Mem Hometown Heroes-12
03BAP Ultimate Mem Hometown Heroes Gold-12
03BAP Ultimate Memorabilia Jerseys-21
03BAP Ultimate Memorabilia Jerseys Gold-21
03BAP Ultimate Mem Jersey and Emblems-19
03BAP Ultimate Mem Jersey and Emblem Gold-19
03BAP Ultimate Mem Jersey and Numbers-19
03BAP Ultimate Mem Jersey and Number Gold-19
03BAP Ultimate Memorabilia Nameplates-24
03BAP Ultimate Mem Nameplates Gold-24
03BAP Ultimate Memorabilia Numbers-16
03BAP Ultimate Memorabilia Numbers Gold-16
03BAP Ultimate Mem Retro-Active Trophies-17
03BAP Ultimate Memorabilia Triple Threads-5
03Beehive-104
Variations-104
Gold-104
Silver-104
Jumbo Jerseys-BH8
Jerseys-JT15
Signatures-RF6
Sticks Beige Border-BE40
Sticks Red Border-RE4
03Black Diamond-33
Black-33
Green-33
Red-33
Signature Gems-SG-30
Threads-DT-TE
Threads Green-DT-TE
Threads Red-DT-TE
Threads Black-DT-TE
03Bowman-49
Gold-49
Future Rivals-LT
Future Rivals Patches-LT
03Bowman Chrome-49
Refractors-49
Gold Refractors-49
Xfractors-49
03Canadiens Postcards-27
03Crown Royale-56
Blue-56
Retail-56
Gauntlet of Glory-11
03Duracell-8
03ITG Action-348
Jerseys-M198
Jerseys-M218
Jerseys-M240
Jerseys-M256
03ITG Toronto Fall Expo Jerseys-FE15
03ITG Used Signature Series-59
Gold-59
Autographs-JTHE
Autographs Gold-JTHE
Franchise-16
Franchise Autographs-16
Franchise Gold-16
Goalie Gear-7
Goalie Gear Autographs-7
Goalie Gear Gold-7
Jerseys-19
Jerseys Gold-19
Jersey Autos-19
Jersey and Stick-19
Jersey and Stick Gold-19
03ITG VIP Collages-20
03ITG VIP Netminders-12
03Jose Theodore Mike's Postcards-1
03Jose Theodore Mike's Postcards-2
03Jose Theodore Mike's Postcards-3
03McDonald's Pacific-29
Patches Silver-15
Patches Gold-15
Patches and Sticks-15
Net Fusions-4
03NHL Sticker Collection-60
03O-Pee-Chee-120
03OPC Blue-120
03OPC Gold-120
03OPC Red-120
03Pacific-183
Blue-183
Red-183
In the Crease-6
Jerseys-21
Jerseys Gold-21
03Pacific Calder-58
Silver-58
03Pacific Complete-436
Red-436
03Pacific Exhibit-175
03Pacific Exhibit-222
Blue Backs-175
Standing on Tradition-7
03Pacific Heads-Up-55
Hobby LTD-55
Retail LTD-55
Stonewallers-6
Stonewallers LTD-6
03Pacific Invincible-51
Blue-51
Red-51
Retail-51
Featured Performers-16
Freeze Frame-10
Jerseys-16
03Pacific Luxury Suite-12A
03Pacific Luxury Suite-12B
03Pacific Luxury Suite-12C
03Pacific Luxury Suite-12D
03Pacific Luxury Suite-38A
03Pacific Luxury Suite-38B
03Pacific Luxury Suite-38C
03Pacific Montreal International-2
03Pacific Prism-124
Blue-124
Patches-124
Red-124
Retail-124
Crease Police-5
03Pacific Quest for the Cup-59
Blue-59
03Pacific Supreme-52
Blue-52
Red-52
Retail-52
Jerseys-16
Standing Guard-8
03Pacific Toronto Fall Expo-4
03Parkhurst Orig Six He Shoots/Scores-9
03Parkhurst Orig Six He Shoots/Scores-9A
03Parkhurst Original Six Montreal-2
Memorabilia-MM1
Memorabilia-MM11
Memorabilia-MM14
Memorabilia-MM54
03Parkhurst Rookie-38
Jerseys-GJ-24
Jersey Autographs-GUJ-JTHE
Jerseys Gold-GJ-24
Jersey and Sticks-SJ-22
Jersey and Sticks Gold-SJ-22
Road to the NHL-RNJ-6
Road to the NHL Gold-RTN-6
Road to the NHL Emblems-RTNE-6
Road to the NHL Emblems Gold-RTNE-6
Teammates Gold-RT16
Teammates-RT16
03Private Stock Reserve-174
Blue-174
Patches-174
Red-174
Retail-174
Increase Security-8
03SP Authentic-45
Limited-45
Breakout Seasons-B12
Breakout Seasons Limited-B12
Foundations-F10
Foundations Limited-F10
Sign of the Times-JT
Sign of the Times-TK
03SP Game Used-24
Gold-24
Authentic Fabrics-DFTK
Authentic Fabrics-QKTHK
Authentic Fabrics Gold-DFTK
Authentic Fabrics Gold-QKTHK
Authentic Patches-APJTH
Game Gear-GGJT
Game Gear Combo-GCJT
Team Threads-TTKTH
03SPx-50
Radiance-50
Spectrum-50
Signature Threads-ST-JT
Winning Materials-WM-TH
Winning Materials Limited-WM-TH
03Titanium-162
Hobby Jersey Number Parallels-162
Patches-162
Retail-162
Masked Marauders-5
03Topps-120
Blue-120
Gold-120
Red-120
Topps/OPC Idols-CI12
03Topps C55-130
Minis-130
Minis American Back-130
Minis American Back Red-130
Minis Bazooka Back-130
Minis Brooklyn Back-130
Minis Hat Trick Back-130
Minis O Canada Back-130
Minis O Canada Back Red-130
Minis Stanley Cup Back-130
Relics-TRJT
03Topps Pristine-85
Gold Refractor Die Cuts-85
Refractors-85
Mini-PM-JTH
Popular Demand Relics-PD-JTH
Popular Demand Relic Refractors-PD-JTH
Press Plates Black-85
Press Plates Cyan-85
Press Plates Magenta-85
Press Plates Yellow-85
03Topps Traded Franchise Fabrics-FF-JTH
03UD Honor Roll-43
Signature Class-SC25
03UD Premier Collection-28
NHL Shields-SH-TH
Signatures-PS-JTH
Signatures Gold-PS-JTH
Teammates-PT-MC
Teammates Patches-PT-MC
03Upper Deck-347
03Upper Deck-473
BuyBacks-174
BuyBacks-175
BuyBacks-176
BuyBacks-177
BuyBacks-178
Canadian Exclusives-347
Canadian Exclusives-473
Franchise Fabrics-FF-JT
HG-347
HG-473
Memorable Matchups-MM-TH
Memorable Matchups-MM-TT
Performers-PS6
UD Exclusives-347
UD Exclusives-473
03Upper Deck Classic Portraits-52
Hockey Royalty-KTH
03Upper Deck Ice-48
Gold-48
Authentics-IA-TH
Breakers-IB-TH
Breaker Patches-IB-TH
Frozen Fabrics-FF-TH
Frozen Fabric Patches-FF-TH
03Upper Deck MVP-231
Gold Script-231
Silver Script-231
Canadian Exclusives-231
SportsNut-SN46
03Upper Deck Rookie Update-46
Skills-SKJT
03Upper Deck Trilogy-52
03Upper Deck Trilogy-119
Authentic Patches-AP6
Crest Variations-119
Limited-52
Limited-119
Scripts-S2JT
Scripts Limited-S2JT
03Upper Deck Victory-98
Bronze-98
Gold-98
Silver-98
03Toronto Star-48
Foil-13
04Pacific-143
Blue-143
Red-143
All-Stars-9
In The Crease-7
04SP Authentic-47
04SP Authentic-121
Limited-47
Limited-121
Buybacks-100
Octographs-OS-GOA
Sign of the Times-ST-JO
Sign of the Times-DS-MJ
Sign of the Times-FS-GOL
Sign of the Times-FS-MON
Sign of the Times-SS-CAN
04UD All-World-48
04UD All-World-105
Gold-48
Autographs-48
Triple Autographs-AT-TAR
Quad Autographs-AQ-GOL
04UD Toronto Fall Expo Pride of Canada-3
04Ultimate Collection-23
Buybacks-43
Buybacks-44
Buybacks-45
Buybacks-46
Buybacks-47
Buybacks-48
Buybacks-49
Dual Logos-UL2-KT
Dual Logos-UL2-TR
Jerseys-UGJ-JO
Jerseys Gold-UGJ-JO
Jersey Autographs-UGJA-JO
Patches-UP-JO
Patch Autographs-UPA-JO
Patch Autographs-UPA-PRJO
Signatures-US-JO
Signature Logos-ULA-JO
Signature Patches-SP-JO
04Upper Deck-95
Canadian Exclusives-95
Heritage Classic-CC-JT
HG Glossy Gold-95
HG Glossy Silver-95
NHL's Best-NB-JT
Swatch of Six-SS-JT
World Cup Tribute-MBRLJT
04Swedish Pure Skills-8
Parallel-8
The Wall-JT
05ITG Heroes/Prosp Toronto Expo Parallel -12
05ITG Heroes/Prosp Toronto Expo Parallel -342
05Be A Player-47
First Period-47
Second Period-47
Third Period-47
Overtime-47
Class Action-CA13
Dual Signatures-RT
Dual Signatures-TR
Outtakes-OT28
Quad Signatures-BLTG
Quad Signatures-GOAL
Quad Signatures-MONT
Signatures-TH
Signatures Gold-TH
Triple Signatures-MTL
05Beehive-47
05Beehive-195
Beige -47
Blue -47
Gold-47
Red -47
Matte-47
Matted Materials-MMJO
Matted Materials Remarkable-RMJO
05Between the Pipes-20
Autographs-A-JT
Complete Package-CP-7
Double Memorabilia-DM-8
Gloves-GUG-5
Jerseys-GUJ-8
Jersey and Sticks-SJ-9
Pads-GUP-8
Signed Memorabilia-SM-8
05Black Diamond-177
Emerald-177
Gold-177
Onyx-177
Ruby-177
Jerseys-J-JO
Jerseys Ruby-J-JO
Jersey Duals-DJ-JO
Jersey Triples-TJ-JO
Jersey Quads-QJ-JO
05Canadiens Team Issue-23
05Hot Prospects-27
En Fuego-27
Red Hot-27
White Hot-27
05ITG Ultimate Memorabilia Level 1-59
05ITG Ultimate Memorabilia Level 2-59
05ITG Ultimate Memorabilia Level 3-59
05ITG Ultimate Memorabilia Level 4-59
05ITG Ultimate Memorabilia Level 5-59
05ITG Ultimate Mem Complete Jersey-8
05ITG Ultimate Mem Complete Jersey Gold-8
05ITG Ultimate Mem Complete Package-9
05ITG Ultimate Mem Complete Package Gold-9
05ITG Ultimate Mem Cornerstones Jerseys-3
05ITG Ultimate Mem Cornerst Jerseys Gold-3
05ITG Ultimate Mem Double Mem-12
05ITG Ultimate Mem Double Mem Gold-12
05ITG Ultimate Memorabilia Emblems-26
05ITG Ultimate Memorabilia Emblems Gold-26
05ITG Ultimate Memorabilia Goalie Gear-17
05ITG Ultimate Mem Goalie Gear Gold-17
05ITG Ultimate Memorabilia In The Numbers-14
05ITG Ultimate Mem In The Numbers Gold-14
05ITG Ultimate Mem Jersey and Emblem-4
05ITG Ultimate Memorabilia Jersey Autos-27
05ITG Ultimate Mem Jersey Autos Gold-27
05ITG Ultimate Mem Jersey Emblems Gold-4
05ITG Ultimate Memorabilia Jerseys-21
05ITG Ultimate Memorabilia Jerseys Gold-21
05ITG Ultimate Mem Pass the Torch Jerseys-2
05ITG Ultimate Mem Passing Torch Jsy Gold-2
05ITG Ultimate Memorabilia Stick Autos-23
05ITG Ultimate Mem Stick Autos Gold-23
05ITG Ultimate Memorabilia Triple Autos-9
05ITG Ultimate Mem Triple Autos Gold-9
05McDonalds Upper Deck-35
Autographs-MA8
Chasing the Cup-CC2
Goalie Factory-GF9
Goalie Gear-MG6
Jerseys-MJ9
Patches-MP9
05Panini Stickers-69
05Parkhurst-120
Facsimile Auto Parallel-250
True Colors-TCMTL
True Colors-TCMTL
True Colors-TCMOBO
True Colors-TCMOBO
True Colors-TCTOMO
True Colors-TCTOMO
05SP Authentic-51
05SP Authentic-123
Limited-51
Limited-123
Chirography-SPJT
Exquisite Endorsements-EEJT
Marks of Distinction-MDJT
Octographs-OG
Sign of the Times Duals-DTD
Sign of the Times Triples-TRTD
Sign of the Times Quads-QTRRK
Six Star Signatures-SSGO
05SP Game Used-52
Autographs-52
Gold-52
Authentic Fabrics-AF-TH
Authentic Fabrics Autographs-AAF-TH
Authentic Fabrics Dual-KT
Authentic Fabrics Dual Autographs-KT
Authentic Fabrics Gold-AF-TH
Authentic Fabrics Quad-RBLT
Authentic Fabrics Quad-TRRK
Authentic Patches Quad -RBLT
Authentic Patches Quad -TRRK
Authentic Fabrics Triple-BTR
Authentic Patches-AP-TH
Authentic Patches Autographs-AAP-TH
Authentic Patches Dual-KT
Authentic Patches Dual Autographs-KT

Theoret, Luc

Theriault, Francois

Theriault, Joel

Theriault, Michel

Theriault, Patrice

Theriault, Patrick

Theriault, Paul

Theriault, Yannick

Therien, Chris

Therkildsen, Peter

Thermell, Tobias

Therrien, Benoit

Therrien, Gaston

Therrien, Mario

Therrien, Mathieu

Therrien, Michel

Therrien, Pierre-Luc

Theus, Marcus

Thibaudeau, Gilles

Thibault, Alexandre

Thibault, Daniel

Thibault, Etienne

Thibault, Frederic

Thibault, Gilles

Thibault, Gyslain

Thibault, Jasmin

Thibault, Jocelyn

Blue-21
Gold-21
Premiere Date-21
Red-21
Jerseys-10
Patches-10
01BAP Memorabilia-12
Emerald-12
Ruby-12
Sapphire-12
Goalies Jerseys-GJ5
Goalie Traditions-GT9
Goalie Traditions-GT25
Goalie Traditions-GT27
Goalie Traditions-GT39
01BAP Signature Series Jerseys-GJ-90
01BAP Ultimate Mem Legend Terry Sawchuk-14
01Between the Pipes-18
01Between the Pipes-102
Double Memorabilia-DM19
Goalie Gear-GG21
He Shoots-He Saves Points-9
He Shoots-He Saves Prizes-19
Jerseys-GJ5
Emblems-GUE2
Jersey and Stick Cards-GSJ5
Masks-35
Masks Silver-35
Masks Gold-35
Tandems-GT12
01Bowman YoungStars-41
Gold-41
Ice Cubed-41
01Crown Royale-34
Blue-34
Premiere Date-34
Red-34
Retail-34
01O-Pee-Chee-209
01O-Pee-Chee Premier Parallel-209
01Pacific-93
Extreme LTD-93
Hobby LTD-93
Premiere Date-93
Retail LTD-93
Steel Curtain-4
01Pacific Adrenaline-42
Blue-42
Premiere Date-42
Red-42
Retail-42
Creased Lightning-3
Power Play-8
01Pacific Arena Exclusives-93
01Pacific Heads-Up-20
Blue-20
Premiere Date-20
Red-20
Silver-20
Quad Jerseys-6
01Parkhurst-121
Teammates-T9
01Private Stock-19
Gold-19
Premiere Date-19
Retail-19
Silver-19
Game Gear-26
Game Gear Patches-26
01Private Stock Pacific Nights-19
01Private Stock PS-2002-15
01SPx-164
Hidden Treasures-DTTP
Hidden Treasures-DTTT
Hidden Treasures-TTBTT
01Titanium-32
Hobby Parallel-32
Premiere Date-32
Retail-32
Retail Parallel-32
01Topps-209
OPC Parallel-209
01Topps Chrome-126
Refractors-126
Black Border Refractors-126
01UD Mask Collection-107
Gold-107
Double Patches-DPJT
Dual Jerseys-MBTB
Dual Jerseys-PMFT
Goalie Jerseys-MMJT
Goalie Jerseys-SSJT
Jerseys-J-JT
Jersey and Patch-JPJT
01UD Playmakers-21
01UD Premier Collection-10
Dual Jerseys-DAT
Dual Jerseys-DTB
Dual Jerseys Black-DAT
Dual Jerseys Black-DTB
01Upper Deck-41
Exclusives-41
Game Jerseys-GJJT
Goaltender Threads-TTJT
MVP Masked Men-MM4
01Upper Deck Victory-71
01Upper Deck Victory-78
Gold-71
Gold-78
01Vanguard-22
Blue-22
Red-22
One of Ones-22
Premiere Date-22
Proofs-22
Quebec Tournament Heroes-11
02McFarlane Hockey-180
02McFarlane Hockey-182
02Atomic-21
Blue-21
Gold-21
Red-21
Denied-4
Hobby Parallel-21
02BAP First Edition-14
02BAP First Edition-409R
Jerseys-14
02BAP Memorabilia-75
02BAP Memorabilia-232
Emerald-75
Emerald-232
Ruby-75
Ruby-232
Sapphire-75
Sapphire-232
NHL All-Star Game-75
NHL All-Star Game-232
NHL All-Star Game Blue-75
NHL All-Star Game Blue-232
NHL All-Star Game Green-75
NHL All-Star Game Green-232
NHL All-Star Game Red-75
NHL All-Star Game Red-232
02BAP Memorabilia Toronto Fall Expo-75
02BAP Memorabilia Toronto Fall Expo-232
02BAP Signature Series-43
Autographs-43
Autograph Buybacks 1998-66
Autograph Buybacks 1999-61
Autograph Buybacks 2000-138
Autographs Gold-43
Franchise Players-FJ7
02Between the Pipes-21
02Between the Pipes-127
Gold-21
Silver-21
Behind the Mask-10
Blockers-6
Complete Package-CP8
Double Memorabilia-13
Emblems-13
Goalie Autographs-23
He Shoots-He Saves Points-17
He Shoots-He Saves Prizes-18
Jerseys-13
Masks II-7
Masks II Gold-7
Masks II Silver-7
Numbers-13
Pads-14
Stick and Jerseys-13
Tandems-3
Trappers-GT14
02Blackhawks Postcards-5
02Bowman YoungStars-23
Gold-23
Silver-23
02Crown Royale-21
Blue-21
Red-21
Retail-21
02eTopps-56
02ITG Used-11
02ITG Used-111
Goalie Pad and Jersey-GP4
Goalie Pad and Jersey Gold-GP4
02O-Pee-Chee-222
02O-Pee-Chee Premier Blue Parallel-222
02O-Pee-Chee Premier Red Parallel-222
02O-Pee-Chee Factory Set-222
02Pacific-83
Blue-83
Red-83
02Pacific Complete-411
Red-411
02Pacific Exclusive-37
02Pacific Heads-Up-26
Blue-26
Purple-26
Red-26
Showstoppers-5
02Pacific Les Gardiens-2
Gold-2
02Pacific Quest for the Cup-18
Gold-18
02Pacific Toronto Fall Expo-9
Gold-9
02Parkhurst-63
Bronze-63
Gold-63
Silver-63
Teammates-TT13
02Parkhurst Retro-132
Minis-132
Franchise Players-RF7
Hopefuls-VH6
Jerseys-RJ38
Jersey and Sticks-RSJ30
02Private Stock Reserve-21
Blue-21
Red-21
Retail-21
InCrease Security-4
02SP Authentic-19
Beckett Promos-19
02SP Game Used Authentic Fabrics-AFTT
02SP Game Used Authentic Fabrics-CFTB
02SP Game Used Authentic Fabrics Gold-AFTT
02SP Game Used Authentic Fabrics Gold-CFTB
02SP Game Used Authentic Fabrics Rainbow-AFTT
02SP Game Used Authentic Fabrics Rainbow-CFTB
02SP Game Used Piece of History-PHJO
02SP Game Used Piece of History-PHTT
02SP Game Used Piece of History Gold-PHJO
02SP Game Used Piece of History Gold-PHTT
02SP Game Used Piece of History Rainbow-PHJO
02SP Game Used Piece of History Rainbow-PHTT
02SPx-15
Spectrum Gold-15
Spectrum Silver-15
02Stadium Club-90
Silver Decoy Cards-90
Proofs-90
02Titanium-23
Blue-23
Red-23
Retail-23
02Topps-222
OPC Blue Parallel-222
OPC Red Parallel-222
Factory Set-222
02Topps Chrome-122
Black Border Refractors-122
Refractors-122
02Topps Heritage-61
Chrome Parallel-61
02Topps Total-24
Team Checklists-TTC6
02UD Artistic Impressions-19
Gold-19
02UD Artistic Impressions Beckett Promos-19
02UD Artistic Impressions Retrospectives-R19
02UD Artistic Impressions Retrospect Gold-R19
02UD Artistic Impress Retrospect Silver-R19
02UD Honor Roll-14
02UD Mask Collection-19
02UD Mask Collection-20
02UD Mask Collection-96
02UD Mask Collection Beckett Promos-19
02UD Mask Collection Beckett Promos-20
02UD Mask Collection Career Wins-CWJT
02UD Mask Collection Masked Marvels-MMJT
02UD Mask Collection Patches-PWJT
02UD Mask Collection View from the Cage-VJT
02UD Piece of History-20
02UD Premier Collection-12
02UD Top Shelf-18
Dual Player Jerseys-STDT
Stopper Jerseys-SSJT0
Sweet Sweaters-SWJT
Triple Jerseys-TSSAT
02Upper Deck Goaltender Threads-TH
02Upper Deck Goaltender Threads Gold-TH
02Upper Deck Saviors Jerseys-SVTH
02Upper Deck Classic Portraits-22
Hockey Royalty-BPT
Hockey Royalty-DZT
Hockey Royalty Limited-BPT
Hockey Royalty Limited-DZT
02Upper Deck MVP-41
Gold-41
Classics-41
Golden Classics-41
02Upper Deck Rookie Update-23
02Upper Deck Victory-44
Bronze-44
Gold-44
Silver-44
02Upper Deck Vintage-58
02Upper Deck Vintage-267
Green Backs-58
Tall Boys-T14
Tall Boys Gold-T14
02Vanguard-24
LTD-24
03BAP Memorabilia-126
Emerald-126
Gold-126
Ruby-126
Sapphire-126
Deep in the Crease-D2
Jersey and Stick-SJ-5
Masks III-20
Masks III Gold-20
Masks III Silver-20
Masks III Autographs-M-JT
Masks III Memorabilia-20
03BAP Ultimate Memorabilia Autographs-17
Gold-17
03BAP Ultimate Mem Auto Jerseys-17
03BAP Ultimate Mem Franch Present Future-7
03Beehive-44
Variations-44
Gold-44
Silver-44
Jumbos-7
Jerseys-JT39
Sticks Beige Border-BE4
03Black Diamond-105
Black-105
Green-105
Red-105
Threads-DT-TH
Threads Green-DT-TH
Threads Red-DT-TH
Threads Black-DT-TH
03Blackhawks Postcards-27
03Bowman-108
Gold-108
03Bowman Chrome-108
Refractors-108
Gold Refractors-108
Xfractors-108
03Crown Royale-21
Blue-21
Retail-21
Gauntlet of Glory-5
03ITG Action-197
First Time All-Star-FT10
Jerseys-M179
Jerseys-M231
Jerseys-M247
03ITG Used Signature Series-54
Gold-54
Autographs-JTH
Autographs Gold-JTH
Goalie Gear-9
Goalie Gear Autographs-9
Goalie Gear Gold-9
Triple Memorabilia-11
Triple Memorabilia Gold-11
03McDonald's Pacific-9
03NHL Sticker Collection-180
03O-Pee-Chee-137
03OPC Blue-137
03OPC Gold-137
03OPC Red-137
03Pacific-77
Blue-77
Red-77
In the Crease-2
03Pacific Complete-420
Red-420
03Pacific Exhibit-159
Blue Backs-159
Standing on Tradition-2
03Pacific Heads-Up-22
Hobby LTD-22
Retail LTD-22
03Pacific Invincible-18
Blue-18
Red-18
Retail-18
Featured Performers-7
Freeze Frame-3
03Pacific Prism-25
Blue-25
Gold-25
Red-25
03Pacific Quest for the Cup Jerseys-4
03Pacific Supreme-20
Blue-20
Red-20
Retail-20
Standing Guard-2
03Parkhurst Original Six Chicago-28
Memorabilia-CM1
Memorabilia-CM10
Memorabilia-CM14
Memorabilia-CM54
03Parkhurst Orig Six He Shoots/Scores-19
03Parkhurst Orig Six He Shoots/Scores-19A
03Parkhurst Rookie Teammates Gold-RT22
03Parkhurst Rookie Teammates-RT22
03Private Stock Reserve-22
Blue-22
Red-22
Retail-22
Increase Security-4
03SP Authentic-17
Limited-17
Breakout Seasons-B23
Breakout Seasons Limited-B23
03SP Game Used-10
Gold-10
Authentic Fabrics-DFZT
Authentic Fabrics Gold-DFZT
Double Threads-DTZT
Limited Threads-LTJTH
Limited Threads Gold-LTJTH
Premium Patches-PPJT
03SPx-19
Radiance-19
Spectrum-19
03Titanium-26
Hobby Jersey Number Parallels-26
Retail-26
Retail Jersey Number Parallels-26
03Topps-137
Blue-137
Gold-137
Red-137
Topps/OPC Idols-CI20
03Topps C55-61
Minis-61
Minis American Back-61
Minis American Back Red-61
Minis Bazooka Back-61
Minis Brooklyn Back-61
Minis Hat Trick Back-61
Minis O Canada Back-61
Minis O Canada Back Red-61
Minis Stanley Cup Back-61
03Topps Pristine-78
Gold Refractor Die Cuts-78
Refractors-78
Mini-PM-JT
Press Plates Black-78
Press Plates Cyan-78
Press Plates Magenta-78
Press Plates Yellow-78
03UD Honor Roll-15
03UD Premier Collection-11
Teammates-PT-CB
Teammates Patches-PT-CB
03Upper Deck-44
Big Playmakers-BP-TH
Canadian Exclusives-44
HG-44
Highlight Heroes-HH-JT
Highlight Heroes Jerseys-HH-JT
Patches-SV6
03Upper Deck Classic Portraits-19
03Upper Deck Classic Portraits-149
Classic Stitches-CS-TH
03Upper Deck Ice-18
Gold-18
03Upper Deck MVP-100
Gold Script-100
Silver Script-100
Canadian Exclusives-100
Masked Men-MM4
SportsNut-SN19
03Upper Deck Rookie Update-16
03Upper Deck Trilogy-19
03Upper Deck Trilogy-118
Crest Variations-118
Limited-19
Limited-118
Limited Threads-LT16
03Upper Deck Victory-42
Bronze-42
Gold-42
Silver-42
Freshman Flashback-FF10
Game Breakers-GB48
03Toronto Star-19
04Pacific-63
Blue-63
Red-63
04Ultimate Collection-9
04Upper Deck-41
Canadian Exclusives-41
HG Glossy Gold-41
HG Glossy Silver-41
Swatch of Six-SS-JO
05Be A Player Dual Signatures-DT
05Be A Player Quad Signatures-HAWK
05Be A Player Signatures-JT
05Be A Player Signatures Gold-JT
05Black Diamond-19
Emerald-19
Gold-19
Onyx-19
Ruby-19
05McDonalds Upper Deck Goalie Gear-MG2
05Parkhurst-395
Facsimile Auto Parallel-395
True Colors-TCPIT
True Colors-TCPIT
05SP Authentic Prestigious Pairings-PPTF
05SP Game Used Awesome Authentics-AA-JT
05SP Game Used SIGnificance-JN
05SP Game Used SIGnificance Gold-S-JN
05SP Game Used Statscriptions-ST-JT
05UD Artifacts Frozen Artifacts-FA-JT
05UD Artifacts Frozen Artifacts Autos-FA-JT
05UD Artifacts Frozen Artifacts Copper-FA-JT
05UD Artifacts Frozen Artifacts Dual-FAD-JT
05UD Artifacts Frozen Artifact Dual Auto-FAD-JT
05UD Artifact Frozen Artifact Dual Copper-FAD-JT
05UD Artifacts Frozen Artifacts Dual Gold-FAD-JT
05UD Artifact Frozen Artifact Dual Maroon-FAD-JT
05UD Artifact Frozen Artifact Dual Pewter-FAD-JT
05UD Artifact Frozen Artifact Dual Silver-FAD-JT
05UD Artifacts Frozen Artifacts Gold-FA-JT
05UD Artifacts Frozen Artifacts Maroon-FA-JT
05UD Artifacts Frozen Artifacts Pewter-FA-JT
05UD Artifacts Frozen Artifacts Silver-FA-JT
05UD Artifacts Goalie Gear-FG-JT
05UD Artifacts Goalie Gear Autographed-FG-JT
05UD Artifacts Goalie Gear Dual-FGD-JT
05UD Artifacts Goalie Gear Dual Autos-FGD-JT
05UD Artifacts Goalie Gear Pewter-FG-JT
05UD Artifacts Goalie Gear Silver-FG-JT
05UD PowerPlay-21
Rainbow-21
Specialists-TSTH
Specialists Patches-SPTH
05Ultra-153
Gold-153
Fresh Ink-FI-JN
Fresh Ink Blue-FI-JN
Ice-153
05Upper Deck-402
Notable Numbers-N-JTH
Patches-P-JTH
Patches-P-TI
05Upper Deck Hockey Showcase-HS17
05Upper Deck Showcase Promos-HS17
05Upper Deck Ice Frozen Fabrics-FFJT
05Upper Deck Ice Frozen Fabrics Autos-AFFJT
05Upper Deck Ice Frozen Fabrics Glass-FFJT
05Upper Deck Ice Frozen Fabrics Patches-FFPJT
05Upper Deck Ice Frozen Fabric Patch Auto-FAPJT
05Upper Deck MVP-314
Gold-314
Platinum-314
05Upper Deck Victory-41
Black-41
Gold-41
Silver-41
Stars on Ice-SI10
06O-Pee-Chee-397
Rainbow-397

Thibault, Larry
52Juniors Blue Tint-102

Thibault, Tommy
93Quebec Pee-Wee Tournament-1114

Thibeault, David
92Quebec Pee-Wee Tournament-839
97Bowman CHL-78
OPC-78
98Bowman CHL-96
Golden Anniversary-96
OPC International-96
98Bowman Chrome CHL-96
Golden Anniversary-96
Golden Anniversary Refractors-96
OPC International-96
OPC International Refractors-96
Refractors-96
99Tallahassee Tiger Sharks-6
99Bowman CHL-80
Gold-80
OPC International-80
01Thetford Mines Coyotes-23
02Thetford Mines Coyotes-23
03Thetford Mines Prolab-24
04Thetford Mines Prolab-1

Thibeault, Marc
917th Inn. Sketch QMJHL-254

Thibert, Benoit
99Indianapolis Ice-17
00Missouri River Otters-13

Thibert, Paul
77Granby Vics-19

Thibodeau, Mathieu
00Sherbrooke Castors-17
Signed-17

Thiel, Rob
87Kitchener Rangers-9
88Kitchener Rangers-9

Thiele, Georg
94Anchorage Aces-22

Thierren, Mario
98Idaho Steelheads-19

Thiessen, Brad
04Penticton Vees-21

Thiessen, Garrett
05Kamloops Blazers-4

Thiessen, Kelly
89Brandon Wheat Kings-3
907th Inn. Sketch WHL-64

Thiessen, Stewart
01Lethbridge Hurricanes-3
04South Surrey Eagles-27
04Surrey Eagles-22
04Surrey Eagles-22
04Vancouver Giants-4

Thiessen, Travis
907th Inn. Sketch WHL-145
917th Inn. Sketch WHL-277
92Cleveland Lumberjacks-4
93Cleveland Lumberjacks-5
93Cleveland Lumberjacks Postcards-21
94Indianapolis Ice-25
95Peoria Rivermen-21
99Colorado Gold Kings Taco Bell-1
99Colorado Gold Kings Wendy's-6
01Colorado Gold Kings-19
02Muskegon Fury-25

Thietke, Mark
83Saskatoon Blades-24
84Kamloops Blazers-23

Thiffault, Charles
81Nordiques Postcards-20
82Nordiques Postcards-24
85Nordiques Team Issue-26
86Nordiques General Foods-27
90Canadiens Postcards-31
91Canadiens Postcards-30

Thiffault, Maurice
51Laval Dairy Lac St. Jean-33

Thimm, Norman
93Quebec Pee-Wee Tournament-1778

Thinel, Marc-Andre
95Quebec Pee-Wee Tournament-448
99Bowman CHL-27
99Bowman CHL-76
99Bowman CHL-164
Gold-27
Gold-76
Gold-164
OPC International-27
OPC International-76
OPC International-164
Autographs-BA14
Autographs Gold-BA14
Autographs Silver-BA14
00Black Diamond-68
Gold-68
00SP Authentic-128
00SP Game Used-85
00SPx-127
Spectrum-127
00UD Pros and Prospects-127
00UD Reserve-115
00Upper Deck-203
Exclusives Tier 1-203
Exclusives Tier 2-203
00Upper Deck Ice-48
Immortals-48
Legends-48
Stars-48
00Upper Deck Vintage-394
00QMJHL All-Star Program Inserts-17
00Victoriaville Tigres-9
Signed-9
01Quebec Citadelles-7
02Lexington Men O'War-5
02Utah Grizzlies-14
03Columbus Cottonmouths-10
03ECHL Update RBI Sports-119
04Hamilton Bulldogs-27

Thinel, Sebastien
00Victoriaville Tigres-22
Signed-22
01Quebec Remparts-23
02Odessa Jackalopes-17
03Odessa Jackalopes-18
04Odessa Jackalopes-17
05Odessa Jackalopes-18

Thivierge, Sebastien
93Quebec Pee-Wee Tournament-1060
95German DEL-286

Thivierge, Stephane
01Thetford Mines Coyotes-4

Tholsson, Staffan
92Norwegian Elite Series-72

Thom, Henry
94German First League-569

Thoma, Bryce
00Red Deer Rebels-19
Signed-19
01Red Deer Rebels-18
02Red Deer Rebels-4
06Las Vegas Wranglers-23

Thoma, Peter
95Swiss HNL-434

Thomas, Ambria
98Minnesota Golden Gophers Women-23

Thomas, Andrew
03Waterloo Blackhawks-11

Thomas, Bill
90Hampton Roads Admirals-52
02Tri-City Stormfront-13
06Fleer-221
Tiffany-221
06Hot Prospects-174
Red Hot-174
White Hot-174
06O-Pee-Chee-505
Rainbow-505
06SP Authentic-221
Limited-221
06SPx-213
Spectrum-213
06The Cup Masterpiece Pressplates (Artifacts)-205
06The Cup Masterpiece Pressplates (Marquee Rookies)-505
06The Cup Masterpiece Pressplates (MVP)-324
06The Cup Masterpiece Pressplates (Power Play)-121
06The Cup Masterpiece Pressplates (SP Authentic)-221
06The Cup Masterpiece Pressplates (Trilogy)-142
06The Cup Masterpiece Pressplates (Victory)-222
06UD Artifacts-205
Blue-205
Gold-205
Platinum-205
Radiance-205
Red-205
06UD Powerplay-121
Impact Rainbow-121
06Ultra-221
Gold Medallion-221
Ice Medallion-221
06Upper Deck-234
Exclusives Parallel-234
High Gloss Parallel-234
Masterpieces-234
06Upper Deck MVP-324
Gold Script-324
Super Script-324
06Upper Deck Ovation-39
06Upper Deck Trilogy-142
06Upper Deck Victory-222
06Upper Deck Victory Black-222
06Upper Deck Victory Gold-222
06AHL Top Prospects-40
06ITG Heroes and Prospects-153
Autographs-ABT
Update Autographs-ABT

Thomas, Conrade
94Central Hockey League-122

Thomas, Cy
45Quaker Oats Photos-55

Thomas, David
93Quebec Pee-Wee Tournament-785

Thomas, Gary
93Lakeland Ice Warriors-23

Thomas, Kahlil
97Flint Generals-21
97Flint Generals EBK-2
98Flint Generals-22
01Memphis RiverKings-2
04Oklahoma City Blazers-17

Thomas, Mark
03UK Manchester Phoenix-6
04UK London Racers-13
04UK London Racers Playoffs-16
05UK Sheffield Steelers-7
Gold-7
Silver-7

Thomas, Matt
03Atlantic City Boardwalk Bullies-28
04Atlantic City Boardwalk Bullies-17
04Atlantic City Boardwalk Bullies Kinko's-29
05Fresno Falcons-25

Thomas, Matthew
93Quebec Pee-Wee Tournament-1692
03Atlantic City Boardwalk Bullies-28

Thomas, Mike
06Saint Johns Sea Dogs-10

Thomas, Reg
76O-Pee-Chee WHA-82
77O-Pee-Chee WHA-29
00Sarnia Sting-24
03Sault Ste. Marie Greyhounds-22
04Sault Ste. Marie Greyhounds-24

Thomas, Ryan
01Vancouver Giants-24

Thomas, Scott
907th Inn. Sketch WHL-143
917th Inn. Sketch WHL-165
92Rochester Americans Dunkin' Donuts-19
92Rochester Americans Kodak-24
92Classic-74
Gold-74
92Classic Four-Sport *-198
Gold-198
93Leaf-360
93OPC Premier-336
Gold-336
93Parkhurst-25
Emerald Ice-25
93PowerPlay-302
93Score-469
Canadian-469
93Stadium Club-471
Members Only Master Set-471
First Day Issue-471
93Topps/OPC Premier-336
Gold-336
93Upper Deck-247
93Rochester Americans Kodak-23
93Classic Pro Prospects-19
93Classic Pro Prospects-125
95Cincinnati Cyclones-17
96Cincinnati Cyclones-19
97Detroit Vipers-10
98IHL All-Star Western Conference-20
98Manitoba Moose-C8
99Long Beach Ice Dogs-7
00Upper Deck NHLPA-PA42
00Manitoba Moose-21
01Manchester Monarchs-14B
02Cleveland Barons-21

Thomas, Steve
85Maple Leafs Postcards-29
86Kraft Drawings-75
86Maple Leafs Postcards-20
86O-Pee-Chee-245
86O-Pee-Chee Stickers-135
86O-Pee-Chee Stickers-140
87Blackhawks Coke-24
87O-Pee-Chee-188
87O-Pee-Chee Stickers-154
87Panini Stickers-329
87Topps-188
88Blackhawks Coke-20
88O-Pee-Chee-259
88Panini Stickers-30
89Blackhawks Coke-13
89O-Pee-Chee-82
89O-Pee-Chee Stickers-15
89Panini Stickers-50
89Topps-82
90Blackhawks Coke-7
90Bowman-4
Tiffany-4
90Bowman Hat Tricks-13
Tiffany-13
90O-Pee-Chee-92
90Pro Set-62
90Score-66
Canadian-66
90Score Hottest/Rising Stars-30
90Topps-92
Tiffany-92
90Upper Deck-221
French-221
91Pro Set Platinum-203
91Bowman-391
91O-Pee-Chee-210
91OPC Premier-195
91Panini Stickers-14
91Parkhurst-105
French-105
91Pinnacle-116
French-116
91Pro Set-45
91Pro Set-438
French-45
French-438
91Score American-94
91Score Canadian Bilingual-94
91Score Canadian English-94
91Score Rookie/Traded-51T
91Stadium Club-109
91Topps-210
91Upper Deck-162
91Upper Deck-534
French-162
French-534
92Bowman-117
92Humpty Dumpty II-23
92O-Pee-Chee-395
92Panini Stickers-203
92Panini Stickers French-203
92Parkhurst-338
92Parkhurst-454
Emerald Ice-338
Emerald Ice-454
92Pinnacle-128
French-128
92Pro Set-106
92Score-12
Canadian-12
92Stadium Club-369
92Topps-222
Gold-222G
92Ultra-131
92Upper Deck-171
93American Licorice Sour Punch Caps-6
93Donruss-208
93Leaf-81
93OPC Premier-300
Gold-300
93Panini Stickers-57
93Parkhurst-124
Emerald Ice-124
93Pinnacle-173
Canadian-173
93PowerPlay-154
93Score-141
Canadian-141
93Stadium Club-195
Members Only Master Set-195
OPC-195
First Day Issue-195
First Day Issue OPC-195
93Topps/OPC Premier-300
Gold-300
93Ultra-216
93Upper Deck-122
SP-95
94Be A Player-R171
Signature Cards-145
94Canada Games NHL POGS-159
94Donruss-142
94EA Sports-82
94Finest-37
Super Team Winners-37
Refractors-37
94Flair-108
94Fleer-129
Slapshot Artists-10
94Leaf-67
94Leaf Limited-6
94OPC Premier-495
Special Effects-495
94Parkhurst Vintage-V68
94Parkhurst SE-SE102
Gold-SE102
94Pinnacle-52
Artist's Proofs-52
Rink Collection-52
Boomers-BR11
94Score-37
Gold-37
Platinum-37
94Select-105
Gold-105
94SP-71
Die Cuts-71
94Stadium Club-80
Members Only Master Set-80
First Day Issue-80
Super Team Winner Cards-80
94Topps/OPC Premier-495
Special Effects-495
94Topps Finest Inserts-14
94Ultra-132
94Upper Deck-275
Electric Ice-275
SP Inserts-SP139
SP Inserts Die Cuts-SP139
95Bowman-19
All-Foil-19
95Canada Games NHL POGS-158
95Collector's Choice-248
Player's Club-248
Player's Club Platinum-248
95Donruss-32
95Donruss-363
95Donruss Elite-71
Die Cut Stars-71
Die Cut Uncut-71
95Finest-14
Refractors-14
95Hoyle Eastern Playing Cards-23
95Leaf-125
95Leaf Limited-84
95Metal-87
95Panini Stickers-95
95Parkhurst International-390
Emerald Ice-390
95Playoff One on One-169
95Score-226
Black Ice Artist's Proofs-226
Black Ice-226
95SkyBox Impact-98
95SP-80
95Stadium Club-16
Members Only Master Set-16
95Summit-161
Artist's Proofs-161
Ice-161
95Topps-256
OPC Inserts-256
95Ultra-263
95Upper Deck-472
Electric Ice-472
Electric Ice Gold-472
Special Edition-SE136
Special Edition Gold-SE136
95Zenith-114
Gifted Grinders-18
95Swedish Globe World Championships-248
95Swedish World Championships Stickers-22
96Collector's Choice-145
96Collector's Choice-322
Crash the Game-C16A
Crash the Game-C16B
Crash the Game-C16C
Crash the Game Gold-C16A
Crash the Game Gold-C16B
Crash the Game Gold-C16C
Crash the Game Exchange-CR16
Crash the Game Exchange Gold-CR16
96Devils Team Issue-32
96Donruss-193
Press Proofs-193
96Fleer-62
96Leaf-25
Press Proofs-25
96Metal Universe-90
96Pinnacle-53
Artist's Proofs-53
Foil-53
Premium Stock-53
Rink Collection-53
96Score-64
Artist's Proofs-64
Dealer's Choice Artist's Proofs-64
Special Artist's Proofs-64
Golden Blades-64
96SkyBox Impact-73
96Summit-31
Artist's Proofs-31
Ice-31
Metal-31
Premium Stock-31
96Topps Picks-75
OPC Inserts-75
96Ultra-97
Gold Medallion-97
96Upper Deck-284
96Upper Deck Ice-37
Parallel-37
96Zenith-33
Artist's Proofs-33
97Be A Player-71
Autographs-71
Autographs Die-Cuts-71
Autographs Prismatic Die-Cuts-71
97Devils Team Issue-25
97Pacific-195
Copper-195
Emerald Green-195
Ice Blue-195
Red-195
Silver-195
97Score Devils-10
Platinum-10
Premier-10
98Pacific-274
Ice Blue-274
Red-274
98Pacific Omega-232
Red-232
Opening Day Issue-232
98Upper Deck-374
Exclusives-374
Exclusives 1 of 1-374
Gold Reserve-374
98Upper Deck MVP-196
Gold Script-196
Silver Script-196
Super Script-196
99Aurora-139
Premiere Date-139
99BAP Memorabilia-148
Gold-148
Silver-148
99Maple Leafs Pizza Pizza-10
99McDonald's Upper Deck Signatures-ST
99O-Pee-Chee-115
99O-Pee-Chee Chrome-115
99O-Pee-Chee Chrome Refractors-115
99Pacific-417
Copper-417
Emerald Green-417
Gold-417
Ice Blue-417
Premiere Date-417
Red-417
99Pacific Dynagon Ice-191
Blue-191
Copper-191
Gold-191
Premiere Date-191
99Pacific Omega-229
Copper-229
Gold-229
Ice Blue-229
Premiere Date-229
99Panini Stickers-154
99Paramount-231
Copper-231
Emerald-231
Gold-231
Holographic Emerald-231
Holographic Gold-231
Holographic Silver-231
Ice Blue-231
Premiere Date-231
Red-231
Silver-231
99Revolution-141
Premiere Date-141
Red-141
Shadow Series-141
Copper-141
Gold-141
CSC Silver-141
99Topps/OPC-115
99Topps/OPC Chrome-115
Refractors-115
99Upper Deck-124
Exclusives-124
Exclusives 1 of 1-124
99Upper Deck Gold Reserve-124
99Upper Deck MVP-200
Gold Script-200

Silver Script-200
Super Script-200
99Upper Deck Victory-287
99Wayne Gretzky Hockey-161
00Aurora-141
Premiere Date-141
00BAP Memorabilia-42
Emerald-42
Ruby-42
Sapphire-42
Promos-42
00BAP Mem Chicago Sportsfest Copper-42
00BAP Memorabilia Chicago Sportsfest Blue-42
00BAP Memorabilia Chicago Sportsfest Gold-42
00BAP Memorabilia Chicago Sportsfest Ruby-42
00BAP Memorabilia Chicago Sun-Times Ruby-42
00BAP Memorabilia Chicago Sun-Times Gold-42
00BAP Mem Chicago Sun-Times Sapphire-42
00BAP Mem Toronto Fall Expo Copper-42
00BAP Memorabilia Toronto Fall Expo Gold-42
00BAP Memorabilia Toronto Fall Expo Ruby-42
00BAP Parkhurst 2000-P131
00BAP Signature Series-152
Emerald-152
Ruby-152
Sapphire-152
Autographs-17
Autographs Gold-17
000-Pee-Chee-191
000-Pee-Chee Parallel-191
00Pacific-400
Copper-400
Gold-400
Ice Blue-400
Premiere Date-400
00Panini Stickers-97
00Paramount-234
Copper-234
Gold-234
Holo-Gold-234
Holo-Silver-234
Ice Blue-234
Premiere Date-234
00Topps/OPC-191
Parallel-191
00Topps Chrome-127
OPC Refractors-127
Refractors-127
00Topps Stars-89
Blue-89
00Upper Deck-162
Exclusives Tier 1-162
Exclusives Tier 2-162
00Upper Deck MVP-170
First Stars-170
Second Stars-170
Third Stars-170
00Upper Deck Victory-223
00Upper Deck Vintage-337
01BAP Memorabilia-492
Emerald-492
Ruby-492
Sapphire-492
01McDonald's Pacific Hometown Pride-10
010-Pee-Chee-134
010-Pee-Chee Premier Parallel-134
01Pacific-374
Extreme LTD-374
Hobby LTD-374
Premiere Date-374
Retail LTD-374
01Pacific Arena Exclusives-374
01Parkhurst-372
01Topps-134
OPC Parallel-134
01Upper Deck-271
Exclusives-271
02BAP Memorabilia-346
02BAP Sig Series Auto Buybacks 2000-17
02Pacific-84
Blue-84
Red-84
02Pacific Complete-142
Red-142
02Topps Total-375
03ITG Action-93
03Pacific-11
Blue-11
Red-11
03Pacific Complete-497
Red-497
03Pacific Exhibit-7
Blue Backs-7
Yellow Backs-7
03Parkhurst Original Six Detroit-17
03Upper Deck MVP-6
Gold Script-6
Silver Script-6
Canadian Exclusives-6
03Czech Stadion-617
05Be A Player Signatures-TO
05Be A Player Signatures Gold-TO

Thomas, Tim
99Detroit Vipers-12
00Swedish Upper Deck-1
Masked Men-M1
01SPx Rookie Redemption-R3
02BAP All-Star Edition-116
Gold-116
Silver-116
02BAP Memorabilia-383
02BAP Ultimate Memorabilia-45
02Between the Pipes-63
Gold-63
Silver-63
Jerseys-38
02Crown Royale-104
Blue-104
Purple-104
Red-104
Retail-104
02Pacific Quest for the Cup-106
Gold-106
02Parkhurst-244
Bronze-244
Gold-244
Silver-244
02Private Stock Reserve-154
Blue-154
Red-154
Retail-154
02SP Authentic-137
02Titanium-106
Blue-106
Red-106
Retail-106
02Topps Chrome-162
Black Border Refractors-162
Refractors-162
02UD Honor Roll-104
02UD Mask Collection-143
02UD Premier Collection-45B
Gold-45
02UD Top Shelf-91
02Upper Deck-429
Exclusives-429
02Vanguard-104
LTD-104
02Finnish Cardset-277
02Providence Bruins-20
03Providence Bruins-18
04Finnish Cardset-63
Parallel-46
Stars of the Game-13
04Swedish Pure Skills-117
Parallel-117
The Wall-TT
04ITG Heroes and Prospects Net Prospects-16
04ITG Heroes and Prosp Net Prospects Gold-16
05Bruins Boston Globe-20
05Parkhurst-36
Facsimile Auto Parallel-36
05Finnish Cardset -51
Finnish Cardset Super Snatchers-7
05Providence Bruins-20
05ITG Heroes and Prospects Jerseys-GUJ-66
05ITG Heroes and Prospects Jerseys Gold-GUJ-66
05ITG Heroes and Prospects Emblems-GUE-66
05ITG Heroes and Prospects Emblems Gold-GUE-66
05ITG Heroes and Prospects Numbers-GUN-66
05ITG Heroes and Prospects Numbers Gold-GUN-66
05ITG Heroes and Prospects Nameplates-N-44
05ITG Heroes and Prospects Nameplate Gold-N-44
06Between The Pipes-77
Autographs-ATT
Double Jerseys-DJ10
Double Jerseys Gold-DJ10
Emblems-GUE50
Emblems Gold-GUE50
Emblems Autographs-GUE50
Jerseys-GUJ50
Jerseys Gold-GUJ50
Jerseys Autographs-GUJ50
Numbers-GUN50
Numbers Gold-GUN50
Numbers Autographs-GUN50
Prospect Trios-PT01
Prospect Trios Gold-PT01
Shooting Gallery-SG03
Shooting Gallery Gold-SG03
Stick and Jersey-SJ34
Stick and Jersey Gold-SJ34
Stick and Jersey Autographs-SJ34
06Hot Prospects Hot Materials -HMTT
06Hot Prospects Hot Materials Red Hot-HMTT
06Hot Prospects Hot Materials White Hot-HMTT
060-Pee-Chee-37
Rainbow-37
06SP Game Used Authentic Fabrics-AFTT
06SP Game Used Authentic Fabrics Parallel-AFTT
06SP Game Used Authentic Fabrics Patches-AFTT
06SP Game Used Authentic Fabrics Dual-AF2TT
06SP Game Used Authentic Fabrics Dual Patches-AF2TT
06The Cup NHL Shields Duals-DSHTT
06Upper Deck-17
Exclusives Parallel-17
High Gloss Parallel-17
Game Jerseys-J2TT
Game Patches-J2TT
Masterpieces-17
06Upper Deck MVP-23
Gold Script-23
Super Script-23
06Upper Deck Ovation-105
06Upper Deck Victory-13
06Upper Deck Victory Black-13
06Upper Deck Victory Gold-13
06ITG Heroes and Prospects-16
Autographs-ATT
Jerseys-GUJ35
Jerseys Gold-GUJ35
Emblems-GUE35
Emblems Gold-GUE35
Numbers-GUN35
Numbers Gold-GUN35
07Upper Deck Victory-61
Black-61
Gold-61

Thomas, Wayne
72Dimanche/Derniere Heure *-174
72Dimanche/Derniere Heure *-175
73Canadiens Postcards-23
730-Pee-Chee-221
74Canadiens Postcards-24
74NHL Action Stamps Update-23
75Heroes Stand-Ups-29
75Maple Leafs Postcards-22
75Maple Leafs Postcards-23
750-Pee-Chee NHL-347
76Maple Leafs Postcards-17
760-Pee-Chee NHL-84
76Topps-84
770-Pee-Chee NHL-19
77Topps-19
780-Pee-Chee-166
78Topps-166
790-Pee-Chee-126
79Topps-126
87Blackhawks Coke-25
88ProCards IHL-73
89ProCards IHL-23

Thomas, Werner
04German Berlin Eisbarens 50th Anniv-31

Thomas, Zakary
93Quebec Pee-Wee Tournament-1267

Thomassen, Ronni
98Danish Hockey League-120
99Danish Hockey League-42

Thomassian, Eric
03Boston University Terriers-18

Thomassin, Michael
93Quebec Pee-Wee Tournament-290

Thomasson, Stefan
00Arizona Icecats-22

Thomerson, Bob
74Sioux City Musketeers-19

Thomlinson, Dave
83Brandon Wheat Kings-10
84Brandon Wheat Kings-22
85Brandon Wheat Kings-22
88ProCards IHL-78
89Blues Kodak-40
89ProCards IHL-15
90Bowman-21
Tiffany-21
90ProCards AHL/IHL-82
91Upper Deck-557
French-557
91ProCards-53
92Binghamton Rangers-6
93Phoenix Roadrunners-22
95Phoenix Roadrunners-18
97Manitoba Moose-A4

Thommen, Gregor
98Swiss Power Play Stickers-38
99Swiss Panini Stickers-38
99Swiss Panini Stickers-285
01Swiss HNL-60
02Swiss HNL-295

Thompson, Adam
91Air Canada SJHL-D17
92Lake Superior State Lakers-28
94Central Hockey League-87

Thompson, Adam (80s)
81Saskatoon Blades-8

Thompson, Andy
00Kootenay Ice-23

Thompson, Ben
98Medicine Hat Tigers-21
99Medicine Hat Tigers-12
00Medicine Hat Tigers-22

Thompson, Billy
99Prince George Cougars-23
00Prince George Cougars-2
03Binghamton Senators-19
04Binghamton Senators-19
05Binghamton Senators-10
05Binghamton Senators Quickway-10
06Between The Pipes Prospect Trios-PT19
06Between The Pipes Prospect Trios Gold-PT19
06Flair Showcase-145
Parallel-145
06Fleer-213
Tiffany-213
06Hot Prospects Hot Materials -HMBT
06Hot Prospects Hot Materials Red Hot-HMBT
06Hot Prospects Hot Materials White Hot-HMBT
060-Pee-Chee-529
Rainbow-529
06SPx-151
Spectrum-151
06The Cup-103
Autographed Rookie Masterpiece Pressplates-103
Gold Rainbow Autographed Rookies-103
Masterpiece Pressplates (Artifacts)-226
Masterpiece Pressplates (Marquee Rookies)-529
Masterpiece Pressplates (MVP)-325
Masterpiece Pressplates (SPx)-151
Masterpiece Pressplates (Victory)-202
Rookies Black-103
Rookies Platinum-103
06UD Artifacts-226
Blue-226
Gold-226
Platinum-226
Radiance-226
Red-226
06Ultimate Collection Ultimate Debut Threads Jerseys-DJ-BT
06Ultimate Collection Ultimate Debut Threads Jerseys Autographs-DJ-BT
06Ultimate Collection Ultimate Debut Threads Patches-DJ-BT
06Ultimate Collection Ultimate Debut Threads Patches Autographs-DJ-BT
06Ultra-218
Gold Medallion-218
Ice Medallion-218
06Upper Deck Rookie Materials-RMBT
06Upper Deck Rookie Materials Patches-RMBT
06Upper Deck MVP-325
Gold Script-325
Super Script-325
06Upper Deck Ovation-136
06Upper Deck Victory-202
06Upper Deck Victory Black-202
06Upper Deck Victory Gold-202
06Binghamton Senators 5th Anniversary-31
06ITG Heroes and Prospects Jerseys-GUJ22
06ITG Heroes and Prospects Jerseys Gold-GUJ22
06ITG Heroes and Prospects Emblems-GUE22
06ITG Heroes and Prospects Emblems Gold-GUE22
06ITG Heroes and Prospects Numbers-GUN22
06ITG Heroes and Prospects Numbers Gold-GUN22

Thompson, Brad
03Grand Rapids Griffins-24
03Minnesota State Mavericks-18
05Idaho Steelheads-21
06Bloomington PrairieThunder-21

Thompson, Brent
907th Inn. Sketch WHL-43
91Upper Deck-608
French-608
91ProCards-402
92Score-455
Canadian-455
92Stadium Club-92
92Topps-161
Gold-161G
93OPC Premier-406
Gold-406
93Stadium Club-489
Members Only Master Set-489
First Day Issue-489
93Topps/OPC Premier-406
Gold-406
96Springfield Falcons-3
97Hartford Wolf Pack-25
98Hartford Wolf Pack-20
99Louisville Panthers-2
00Louisville Panthers-2
01Hershey Bears-25
02Hershey Bears-22
03Colorado Eagles-17
04Providence Bruins-17

Thompson, Brett
92Quebec Pee-Wee Tournament-1333
95Slapshot-83
95Guelph Storm-24
96Guelph Storm-2
96Guelph Storm Premier Collection-4

Thompson, Briane
917th Inn. Sketch OHL-317
93Sault Ste. Marie Greyhounds-19
93Sault Ste. Marie Greyhound Memorial Cup-21
98Bakersfield Condors-20
99Bakersfield Condors-18
01Florida Everblades-11
02UK Nottingham Panthers-7
03UK Nottingham Panthers-7

Thompson, Bryan
01London Knights-5
01Plymouth Whalers-27

Thompson, Cecil
330-Pee-Chee V304B-68
33V357 Ice Kings-57
34Beehive Group I Photos-35
34Diamond Matchbooks Silver-58
34Sweet Caporal-32
37V356 Worldwide Gum-12
38Bruins Garden Magazine Supplement-9
390-Pee-Chee V301-1-75
60Topps-55
83Hall of Fame Postcards-A16
85Hall of Fame-15
91Bruins Sports Action Legends-32
94Parkhurst Tall Boys Greats-9
01Between the Pipes-129
01Between the Pipes-134
Trophy-Winners-TW11
Vintage Memorabilia-VM19
02BAP Ultimate Memorabilia Cup Duels-1
02BAP Ultimate Mem Paper Cuts Autos-5
02Between the Pipes-111
Vintage Memorabilia-14
02ITG Used Vintage Memorabilia-VM4
02ITG Used Vintage Memorabilia Gold-VM4
02Parkhurst Vintage Memorabilia-VM13
02Parkhurst Vintage Teammates-VT19
03BAP Memorabilia Vintage Memorabilia-VM-1
03BAP Ultimate Mem Retro Teammates-10
03ITG Used Sig Series Vintage Mem -22
03ITG Used Sig Series Vintage Mem Gold-22
03Parkhurst Original Six Boston-46
Inserts-B14
Memorabilia-BM21
03Parkhurst Rookie Before the Mask-BTM-7
03Parkhurst Rookie Before the Mask Gold-BTM-7
04ITG Franchises US East-331
Double Memorabilia-EDM6
Double Memorabilia Gold-EDM6
Goalie Gear-EGG3
Goalie Gear Gold-EGG3
Memorabilia-ESM15
Memorabilia Gold-ESM15
Teammates-ETM1
Teammates Gold-ETM1
04ITG Ultimate Memorabilia-108
04ITG Ultimate Memorabilia-132
Gold-108
Gold-132
Beantown's Best-5
Goalie Gear-4
Original Six-6
Original Six-19
Retro Teammates-7
05Between the Pipes-21
05ITG Ultimate Memorabilia Level 1-94
05ITG Ultimate Memorabilia Level 2-94
05ITG Ultimate Memorabilia Level 3-94
05ITG Ultimate Memorabilia Level 4-94
05ITG Ultimate Memorabilia Level 5-94
05ITG Ultimate Memorabilia Goalie Gear-19
05ITG Ultimate Mem Goalie Gear Gold-19
05ITG Ultimate Mem Pass the Torch Jerseys-5
05ITG Ultimate Mem Passing Torch Jsy Gold-5
05ITG Ult Mem 3 Star of the Game Jsy Gold-1
06Between The Pipes-133
Double Memorabilia-DM17
Double Memorabilia Gold-DM17
Pads-GP07
Pads Gold-GP07
Shooting Gallery-SG03
Shooting Gallery Gold-SG03
06ITG Ultimate Memorabilia-139
Artist Proof-139
Beantown's Best Autos-2
Decades-8
Decades Gold-8
Retro Teammates-2
Retro Teammates Gold-2

Thompson, Chad
91Knoxville Cherokees-7

Thompson, Chad (OHL)
91Knoxville Cherokees-7
01London Knights-14
03Barrie Colts-6
04Oshawa Generals-18
04Oshawa Generals Autographs-18

Thompson, Chris
95Slapshot-8
95Barrie Colts-22
95Seattle Thunderbirds-28
96Seattle Thunderbirds-11
97Barrie Colts-23
97Guelph Storm-2
97Seattle Thunderbirds-7
98Albany River Rats-18
02Augusta Lynx-76
03Florida Everblades-23
04Louisiana Ice Gators-22

Thompson, Clark
04Camrose Kodiaks-3

Thompson, Corey
91Air Canada SJHL-B4

Thompson, Dallas
92Tacoma Rockets-26
93Tacoma Rockets-26
99Prince George Cougars-21

Thompson, Danny
94UK Humberside Hawks-20

Thompson, David
03Camrose Kodiaks-23
04Camrose Kodiaks-12

Thompson, Derek
87Sudbury Wolves-23
88Sudbury Wolves-14

Thompson, Dewar
51Laval Dairy Subset-53
52St. Lawrence Sales-88

Thompson, Errol
72Maple Leafs Postcards-28
73Maple Leafs Postcards-26
74Maple Leafs Postcards-23
74NHL Action Stamps-266
75Heroes Stand-Ups-30
75Maple Leafs Postcards-24
750-Pee-Chee NHL-114
75Topps-114
76Maple Leafs Postcards-18
760-Pee-Chee NHL-259
760-Pee-Chee NHL-394
76Topps-259
77Maple Leafs Postcards-15
770-Pee-Chee NHL-293
780-Pee-Chee-57
78Topps-57
790-Pee-Chee-106
79Red Wings Postcards-16
79Topps-106
800-Pee-Chee-234
80Topps-234
04UD Legendary Signatures-34
Autographs-ET
Linemates-ETDSLM

Thompson, Jamie
92Maine Black Bears-36
93Omaha Lancers-27
97El Paso Buzzards-1
98ECHL All-Star Northern Conference-7
98Peoria Rivermen-7
98Peoria Rivermen-28
99UK Guildford Flames-29
00Worcester Icecats-13
01Worcester Icecats-13
03Elmira Jackals-21
05Danbury Trashers-20

Thompson, Jarrett
01Greensboro Generals-5

Thompson, Jean-Guy
51Laval Dairy Lac St. Jean-54

Thompson, Jeremy
95Tri-City Americans-26
97Austin Ice Bats-19
98Johnstown Chiefs-10
99Knoxville Speed-20

Thompson, Mark
97Regina Pats-19
98Kootenay Ice-6
00Johnstown Chiefs-27
02Augusta Lynx-77

Thompson, Michael
93Quebec Pee-Wee Tournament-1476

Thompson, Mike
99Johnstown Chiefs-23
99Tallahassee Tiger Sharks-10
03Elmira Jackals-9
06SP Authentic Sign of the Times Dual-PT

Thompson, Nate
05Providence Bruins-21
06Hot Prospects-146
Red Hot-146
White Hot-146
060-Pee-Chee-565
Rainbow-565
06SP Authentic-167
Limited-167
06SP Game Used-105
Gold-105
Rainbow-105
06SPx-205
Spectrum-205
06The Cup-91
Autographed Rookie Masterpiece Pressplates-91
Gold Rainbow Autographed Rookies-91
Masterpiece Pressplates (Marquee Rookies)-565
Masterpiece Pressplates (SP Authentic Autographs)-167
Masterpiece Pressplates (SP Game Used)-105
Masterpiece Pressplates (Victory)-308
Rookies Black-91
Rookies Platinum-91
06Upper Deck-455
Exclusives Parallel-455
High Gloss Parallel-455
Masterpieces-455
Victory-308
06Providence Bruins-21
07Upper Deck Rookie Class -49

Thompson, Paul
33V129-50
34Beehive Group I Photos-81
35Diamond Matchbooks Tan 1-66
35Diamond Matchbooks Tan 2-61
35Diamond Matchbooks Tan 3-56
35Diamond Matchbooks Tan 4-13
35Diamond Matchbooks Tan 5-12
36Triumph Postcards-9
37Diamond Matchbooks Tan 6-12
37V356 Worldwide Gum-6
94UK Guildford Flames-15
95UK Guildford Flames-9
95UK Guildford Flames-27
96UK Guildford Flames-7
97UK Guildford Flames-8
99UK Hull Thunder-11
02UK Coventry Blaze-21
03UK Coventry Blaze History-8
04UK Coventry Blaze-19
04UK Coventry Blaze Champions-20
06UK Coventry Blaze-20

Thompson, Rhys
34Beehive Group I Photos-352
91Air Canada SJHL-D17

Thompson, Rocky
95Medicine Hat Tigers-20
96Medicine Hat Tigers-23
97Saint John Flames-21
00Louisville Panthers-10
01BAP Memorabilia-444
Emerald-444
Ruby-444
Sapphire-444
01BAP Update Tough Customers-TC20
01BAP Update Tough Customers-TC36
01Upper Deck Victory-373
Gold-373
01Hershey Bears-26
05Peoria Rivermen-3
06Peoria Rivermen-19

Thompson, Ryan
92Quebec Pee-Wee Tournament-1331
01Guelph Storm-14
01Guelph Storm Memorial Cup-14
02Guelph Storm-4

Thompson, Scott
98Quad-City Mallards-21
99Brampton Battalion-25
00Brampton Battalion-22

Thompson, Sean
02Plymouth Whalers-6
03Plymouth Whalers-12

Thompson, Shaun
03UK Basingstoke Bison-15
04UK U-20 Team-4

Thompson, Shawn
91Air Canada SJHL-B15
98Spokane Chiefs-26
99Spokane Chiefs-25
00Spokane Chiefs-26

Thompson, Tim
93Niagara Falls Thunder-6
02Parkhurst Vintage Teammates-VT19

Thompson, Tom
96Arizona Icecats-20
97Arizona Icecats-21
98Arizona Icecats-25
99Arizona Icecats-25

Thompson, Tyler
06Cedar Rapids RoughRiders-17

Thompson, Wayne
83Nova Scotia Voyageurs-20

Thoms, Bill
320'Keefe Maple Leafs-NNO
33V129-10
33V288 Hamilton Gum-7
33V357 Ice Kings-50
34Beehive Group I Photos-353
350-Pee-Chee V304C-85
370-Pee-Chee V304E-143
38Quaker Oats Photos-28
390-Pee-Chee V301-1-48

Thomsen, Anders
98Danish Hockey League-151
99Danish Hockey League-155

Thomsen, Jens Sonny
99Danish Hockey League-89

Thomsen, Michael
98Danish Hockey League-48
98Danish Hockey League-220
99Danish Hockey League-140

Thomsen, Ulrick
98Danish Hockey League-166

Thomson, Ben
02Medicine Hat Tigers-25

Thomson, Bruce
82Brandon Wheat Kings-8

Thomson, Darryl
98Kingston Frontenacs-21
99Kingston Frontenacs-22
00Kingston Frontenacs-21

Thomson, Floyd
71Blues Postcards-24
72Blues White Border-21
73Blues White Border-21
74NHL Action Stamps-236
740-Pee-Chee NHL-298
750-Pee-Chee NHL-149
75Topps-149
760-Pee-Chee NHL-356
770-Pee-Chee NHL-358

Thomson, Greg
94German DEL-232
95German DEL-106
96German DEL-50

Thomson, Jed
93Quebec Pee-Wee Tournament-578

Thomson, Jim
44Beehive Group II Photos-457
45Quaker Oats Photos-56A
45Quaker Oats Photos-56B
45Quaker Oats Photos-56C
45Quaker Oats Photos-56D
48Exhibits Canadian-41
51Parkhurst-82
52Parkhurst-43
53Parkhurst-8
54Parkhurst-32
55Parkhurst-11
Quaker Oats-11
57Topps-23
89ProCards AHL-225
90ProCards AHL/IHL-422
92Topps-67
Gold-67G
94Ducks Carl's Jr.-23
94Parkhurst Missing Link-119

Thomson, Kelly
04London Knights-19

Thomson, Matt
05Kitchener Rangers-12

Thomson, Tom
91Air Canada SJHL-C32
91Air Canada SJHL-E23
92Saskatchewan JHL-131

Thony, Roger
93Swedish Semic World Champ Stickers-126
93Swiss HNL-179
95Swiss HNL-233
96Swiss HNL-146

Thorburn, Chris
00UD CHL Prospects-14
01UD Prospects-31
Autographs-A-CT
Jersey Autographs-S-CT
Jerseys-J-CT
Jerseys-C-MT
Jerseys Gold-J-CT
Jerseys Gold-C-MT
02Plymouth Whalers-20
02Saginaw Spirit-2
03Rochester Americans-29
04Rochester Americans-24
05Beehive-168
Matte-168
05Black Diamond-218
05Hot Prospects-191
Autographed Patch Variation-191
Hot Materials-HMCT
Red Hot-191
05Parkhurst Signatures-CT
05SP Authentic-290
05SP Game Used-195
05SPx-222
Spectrum-222
05The Cup-158
Black Rainbow Rookies-158
Masterpiece Pressplates (Artifacts)-252
Masterpiece Pressplates (Bee Hive)-168
Masterpiece Pressplates (Black Diamond)-218
Masterpiece Pressplates (Ice)-222
Masterpiece Pressplates (Rookie Update)-251
Masterpiece Pressplates (SP Authentic)-290
Masterpiece Pressplates (SP Game Used)-195
Masterpiece Pressplates SPx Autos-222
Masterpiece Pressplates (Trilogy)-227
Masterpiece Pressplates Ult Coll-195
Masterpiece Pressplates Autographs-158
Platinum Rookies-158
05UD Artifacts-252
05Ultimate Collection-195
Gold-195
05Upper Deck Ice-222
05Upper Deck Rookie Update-251
Inspirations Patch Rookies-251
05Upper Deck Trilogy-227
05AHL Top Prospects-43
06Upper Deck Signatures-SCT

Thoresen, Jan Erik
92Norwegian Elite Series-75

Thoresen, Patrick
01Moncton Wildcats-20
02Baie Comeau Drakkar-20
05Swedish SHL Elitset-22
Gold-22
Series Two Signatures-4
Teammates-2
06Be A Player-233
Autographs-233
Signatures 25-233
06Be A Player Portraits-104
06Beehive-122
Matte-122
06Black Diamond-166A
Black-166A
Gold-166A
Ruby-166A
06Gatorade-22
06Hot Prospects-115
Red Hot-115
White Hot-115
Hot Materials -HMPA
Hot Materials Red Hot-HMPA
Hot Materials White Hot-HMPA
060-Pee-Chee-552
060-Pee-Chee-644
Rainbow-552
Rainbow-644
06SP Authentic-181
Limited-181
06SP Game Used-117
Gold-117
Rainbow-117
Autographs-117
Rookie Exclusives Autographs-REPT
06SPx-160
Spectrum-160
06The Cup-128
Autographed Rookie Masterpiece Pressplates-128
Gold Rainbow Autographed Rookie Patches-128
Masterpiece Pressplates (Be A Player Portraits)-104
Masterpiece Pressplates (Bee Hive)-122
Masterpiece Pressplates (Black Diamond)-166
Masterpiece Pressplates (Marquee Rookies)-552
Masterpiece Pressplates (MVP)-311
Masterpiece Pressplates (SP Authentic Autographs)-181
Masterpiece Pressplates (SP Game Used)-117
Masterpiece Pressplates (SPx)-160
Masterpiece Pressplates (Sweet Beginnings)-123
Masterpiece Pressplates (Trilogy)-114
Masterpiece Pressplates (Ultimate Collection Autographs)-112
Masterpiece Pressplates (Victory)-298
NHL Shields Duals-DSHPL
NHL Shields Duals-DSHRP
Rookies Black-128
Rookies Platinum-128
06UD Artifacts-263
06UD Mini Jersey Collection-122
06Ultimate Collection-112
Rookies Autographed NHL Shields-112
Rookies Autographed Patches-112
Ultimate Debut Threads Jerseys-DJ-PT
Ultimate Debut Threads Jerseys Autographs-DJ-PT
Ultimate Debut Threads Patches-DJ-PT
Ultimate Debut Threads Patches Autographs-DJ-PT
06Upper Deck-214
Exclusives Parallel-214
High Gloss Parallel-214
Masterpieces-214
Rookie Game Dated Moments-RGD8
Rookie Headliners-RH13
Rookie Materials-RMPT
Rookie Materials Patches-RMPT
06Upper Deck MVP-311
Gold Script-311
Super Script-311
06Upper Deck Sweet Shot-123
Rookie Jerseys Autographs-123
06Upper Deck Trilogy-114
06Upper Deck Victory-298
06Swedish SHL Elitset-24
07Upper Deck Rookie Class -43

Thoresen, Petter
92Finnish Semic-44
92Norwegian Elite Series-32
93Swedish Semic World Champ Stickers-239
94Finnish Jaa Kiekko-270
95Swedish World Championships Stickers-252

Thoreson, Patrick
06Ultra-231
Gold Medallion-231
Ice Medallion-231

Thoreus, Lars
71Swedish Hockey-387
72Swedish Stickers-261

Thoring, Clay
99Swift Current Broncos-20
00Swift Current Broncos-20
01Vancouver Giants-25

Thoring, Cody
03Everett Silvertips-14
04Everett Silvertips-7
05Everett Silvertips-24
06Moose Jaw Warriors-20

Thorkildsen, K.
74Finnish Typotor-83

Thorlakson, Kevin
84Nanaimo Clippers-21

Thorn, Christopher
03Swedish Elite-161
Silver-161
05Swedish SHL Elitset-16
Series One Signatures-15
Star Potential-4

Thorn, H.
95German DEL-311

Thornberg, Martin
03Swedish Elite-196
Silver-196
04Swedish Elitset-54
Gold-54
05Swedish SHL Elitset-197
06Swedish SHL Elitset-59

Thornberg, Ove
86Swedish Panini Stickers-127
87Swedish Panini Stickers-126
89Swedish Semic Elitserien Stickers-109
90Swedish Semic Elitserien Stickers-113
91Swedish Semic Elitserien Stickers-117
92Swedish Semic Elitserien Stickers-137
93Swedish Semic Elitserien-108
94Swedish Leaf-76
Top Guns-8

Thornbury, Tom
84Fredericton Express-21
94Central Hockey League-72
94Oklahoma City Blazers-18

Thorne, Curtis
03Yarmouth Mariners-20

Thorne, Gary
04Upper Deck-208

Thornson, Len
99Fort Wayne Komets Points Leaders-2
01Fort Wayne Komets Shoe Carnival-6

Thornton, Andrew
04UK U-20 Team-19
05UK Hull Stingrays-4

Thornton, Bob
93North Bay Centennials-18
00Richmond Renegades-5

Thornton, Cody
02Belleville Bulls-19
03Belleville Bulls-2
04Belleville Bulls-3

Thornton, Erin
907th Inn. Sketch WHL-187
91British Columbia JHL-129
92British Columbia JHL-35

Thornton, Joe
95Slapshot-363
95Sault Ste. Marie Greyhounds-21
95Classic-95
96Black Diamond-160
Gold-160
96Upper Deck-370
96Upper Deck Ice-116
96Sault Ste. Marie Greyhounds-23
96Sault Ste. Marie Greyhounds-24
96Sault Ste. Marie Greyhounds Autographed-23
96Sault Ste. Marie Greyhounds Autographed-24
96All-Sport PPF *-171
96All Sport PPF Gold *-171
97Be A Player-232
Autographs-232
Autographs Die-Cuts-232
Autographs Prismatic Die-Cuts-232
One Timers-20
97Beehive-51
Authentic Autographs-51
Golden Portraits-51
Team-22
Team Gold-22
97Black Diamond-112
Double Diamond-112
Triple Diamond-112
Quadruple Diamond-112
Premium Cut-PC17
Premium Cut Double Diamond-PC17
Premium Cut Quadruple Diamond Horiz-PC17
Premium Cut Triple Diamond-PC17
Premium Cut Quadruple Diamond Verticals-PC17
97Collector's Choice-296
97Crown Royale-11
Emerald Green-11
Ice Blue-11
Silver-11
Blades of Steel Die-Cuts-3
Cramer's Choice Jumbos-3
Cramer's Choice Jumbos Gold-3
Cramer's Choice Jumbos Signed-3
Hat Tricks Die-Cuts-3
Lamplighters Cel-Fusion Die-Cuts-3
97Donruss Elite-6
97Donruss Elite-138
97Donruss Elite-148
Aspirations-6
Aspirations-138
Aspirations-148
Status-6
Status-138
Status-148
Back to the Future-1
Back to the Future Autographs-1
Craftsmen-24
Master Craftsmen-24
97Donruss Limited-92
97Donruss Limited-187
Exposure-92
Exposure-187
97Donruss Preferred-151
97Donruss Preferred-200
Cut to the Chase-151
Cut to the Chase-200
Line of the Times-2B
97Donruss Preferred Line of Times Promos-2B
97Donruss Preferred Precious Metals-2
97Donruss Priority-173
97Donruss Priority-207
97Donruss Priority-215
Stamp of Approval-173
Stamp of Approval-207
Stamp of Approval-215
Direct Deposit-25
Postcards-16
Postcards Opening Day Issues-28
Stamps-16
Stamps Bronze-16
Stamps Gold-16
Stamps Silver-16
97Katch-164
Gold-164
Silver-164
97Leaf-41
97Leaf-150
Fractal Matrix-41
Fractal Matrix-150
Fractal Matrix Die Cuts-41
Fractal Matrix Die Cuts-150
Fire On Ice-14
97Leaf International-41
Universal Ice-41
97McDonald's Upper Deck-33
97Pacific Dynagon-NNO
Copper-NNO
Dark Grey-NNO
Emerald Green-NNO
Ice Blue-NNO
Red-NNO
Silver-NNO
97Pacific Omega-19
Copper-19
Dark Gray-19
Emerald Green-19
Gold-19
Ice Blue-19
97Paramount-16
Copper-16
Dark Grey-16
Emerald Green-16
Ice Blue-16
Red-16
Silver-16
Big Numbers Die-Cuts-3
Canadian Greats-2
Photoengravings-3
97Pinnacle-23
Artist's Proofs-23
Rink Collection-23
Press Plates Back Black-23
Press Plates Back Cyan-23
Press Plates Back Magenta-23
Press Plates Back Yellow-23
Press Plates Front Black-23
Press Plates Front Cyan-23
Press Plates Front Magenta-23
Press Plates Front Yellow-23
Certified Rookie Redemption-A
Certified Rookie Redemption Gold-A
Certified Rookie Redemption Mirror Gold-A
97Pinnacle Mint-29
Bronze-29
Gold Team-29
Silver Team-29
Coins Brass-29
Coins Brass Proofs-29
Coins Gold Plated-29
Coins Gold Plated Proofs-29
Coins Nickel Silver-29
Coins Nickel Silver Proofs-29
Coins Solid Gold-29
Coins Solid Silver-29
97Pinnacle Power Pack Blow-Ups-3
97Revolution-11
Copper-11
Emerald-11
Ice Blue-11
Silver-11
Team Checklist Laser Cuts-2
97Score-54
Artist's Proofs-54
Golden Blades-54
97Score Bruins-17
Platinum-17
Premier-17
97SP Authentic-171
Icons-I9
Icons Die-Cuts-I9
Icons Embossed-I9

Sign of the Times-JT
Tradition-T3
97Studio-54
Press Proofs Silver-54
Press Proofs Gold-54
Portraits-22
97Upper Deck-218
Blow-Ups 3 x 5-2-2
Game Dated Moments-218
Sixth Sense Masters-SS6
Sixth Sense Wizards-SS6
Smooth Grooves-SG6
97Upper Deck Ice-46
Parallel-46
Champions-IC6
Champions 2 Die Cuts-IC6
Lethal Lines-L1C
Lethal Lines 2-L1C
Power Shift-46
97Zenith-92
Z-Gold-92
Z-Silver-92
97Zenith 5 x 7-74
Gold Impulse-74
Silver Impulse-74
97Zenith Rookie Reign-2
97Zenith Z-Team-10
97Zenith Z-Team Gold-10
97Bowman CHL-32
97Bowman CHL-125
OPC-32
OPC-125
Autographs-125
Bowman's Best-1
Bowman's Best Atomic Refractors-1
Bowman's Best Refractor-1
97Autographed Collection *-45
Autographs-45
Autographs Gold-45
Game Breakers-GB29
97Players Club #1 Die-Cuts *-D4
97Players Club *-22
97Talk N' Sports *-50
Phone Cards $1-50
97Visions Signings *-41
Autographs-55
98SLU Hockey-210
98Be A Player-9
Press Release-9
98BAP Gold-9
98BAP Autographs-9
98BAP Autographs Gold-9
98BAP Tampa Bay All Star Game-9
98Black Diamond-7
Double Diamond-7
Triple Diamond-7
Quadruple Diamond-7
98Bowman's Best-84
Refractors-84
Atomic Refractors-84
98Donruss Elite Promos-11
98Finest Centurion-C17
98Finest Centurion Refractors-C17
98Kenner Starting Lineup Cards-31
98OPC Chrome-112
Refractors-112
98Pacific-102
Ice Blue-102
Red-102
98Pacific Dynagon Ice-15
Blue-15
Red-15
98Pacific Omega-19
Red-19
Opening Day Issue-19
98Panini Photocards-83
98SP Authentic-5
Power Shift-5
Sign of the Times-JT
Sign of the Times Gold-JT
98SPx Finite-133
Radiance-133
Spectrum-133
98SPx Top Prospects-5
Radiance-5
Spectrum-5
98Topps-112
O-Pee-Chee-112
Ice Age 2000-I13
98Topps Gold Label Class 1-81
Black-81
Black One of One-81
One of One-81
Red-81
Red One of One-81
98Topps Gold Label Class 2-81
98Topps Gold Label Class 2 Black-81
98Topps Gold Label Class 2 Black 1 of 1-81
98Topps Gold Label Class 2 One of One-81
98Topps Gold Label Class 2 Red-81
98Topps Gold Label Class 2 Red One of One-81
98Topps Gold Label Class 3-81
98Topps Gold Label Class 3 Black-81
98Topps Gold Label Class 3 Black 1 of 1-81
98Topps Gold Label Class 3 One of One-81
98Topps Gold Label Class 3 Red-81
98Topps Gold Label Class 3 Red One of One-81
98UD Choice-19
98UD Choice Preview-19
98UD Choice Prime Choice Reserve-19
98UD Choice Reserve-19
98UD3-15
98UD3-75
98UD3-135
Die-Cuts-15
Die-Cuts-75
Die-Cuts-135
98Upper Deck-19
98Upper Deck-218
Exclusives-19
Exclusives-218
Exclusives 1 of 1-19
Exclusives 1 of 1-218
Generation Next-GN12
Generation Next Quantum 1-GN12
Generation Next Quantum 2-GN12
Generation Next Quantum 3-GN12
Gold Reserve-19
Gold Reserve-218
98Upper Deck MVP-12
Gold Script-12
Silver Script-12
Super Script-12
98Autographed Collection *-4
Parallel-4
Athletic Excellence-AE2
Blue Ribbon Autographs-14
Sports City USA-SC9
99Aurora-14
Premiere Date-14
99BAP Memorabilia-35
Gold-35
Silver-35
99BAP Millennium-24
Emerald-24
Ruby-24
Sapphire-24
Signatures-24
Signatures Gold-24
99Black Diamond-10
Diamond Cut-10
Final Cut-10
99Bruins Season Ticket Offer-1
99Crown Royale-15
Limited Series-15
Premiere Date-15
Card-Supials-4
Card-Supials Minis-4
Ice Elite-3
Ice Elite Parallel-3
99O-Pee-Chee-21
99O-Pee-Chee Autographs-TA10
99O-Pee-Chee Chrome-21
99O-Pee-Chee Chrome Refractors-21
99Pacific-30
Copper-30
Emerald Green-30
Gold-30
Ice Blue-30
Premiere Date-30
Red-30
99Pacific Dynagon Ice-26
Blue-26
Copper-26
Gold-26
Premiere Date-26
99Pacific Omega-22
Copper-22
Gold-22
Ice Blue-22
Premiere Date-22
99Pacific Prism-15
Holographic Blue-15
Holographic Gold-15
Holographic Mirror-15
Holographic Purple-15
Premiere Date-15
99Panini Stickers-26
99Paramount-24
Copper-24
Emerald-24
Gold-24
Holographic Emerald-24
Holographic Gold-24
Holographic Silver-24
Ice Blue-24
Premiere Date-24
Red-24
Silver-24
99Revolution-15
Premiere Date-15
Red-15
Shadow Series-15
Copper-15
Gold-15
CSC Silver-15
99SP Authentic-6
Tomorrow's Headliners-TH2
99SPx-11
Radiance-11
Spectrum-11
99Stadium Club-75
First Day Issue-75
One of a Kind-75
Printing Plates Black-75
Printing Plates Cyan-75
Printing Plates Magenta-75
Printing Plates Yellow-75
Chrome-27
Chrome Refractors-27
99Topps Arena Giveaways-BOS-JT
99Topps/OPC-21
Autographs-TA10
99Topps/OPC Chrome-21
Refractors-21
99Topps Gold Label Class 1-40
Black-40
Black One of One-40
One of One-40
Red-40
Red One of One-40
99Topps Gold Label Class 2-40
99Topps Gold Label Class 2 Black-40
99Topps Gold Label Class 2 Black 1 of 1-40
99Topps Gold Label Class 2 One of One-40
99Topps Gold Label Class 2 Red-40
99Topps Gold Label Class 2 Red One of One-40
99Topps Gold Label Class 3-40
99Topps Gold Label Class 3 Black-40
99Topps Gold Label Class 3 Black 1 of 1-40
99Topps Gold Label Class 3 One of One-40
99Topps Gold Label Class 3 Red-40
99Topps Gold Label Class 3 Red One of One-40
99Topps Gold Label Fresh Gold-FG2
99Topps Gold Label Fresh Gold Black-FG2
99Topps Gold Label Fresh Gold Black 1of1-FG2
99Topps Gold Label Fresh Gold One of One-FG2
99Topps Gold Label Fresh Gold Red-FG2
99Topps Gold Label Fresh Gold Red 1 of 1-FG2
99Topps Premier Plus-79
Parallel-79
The Next Ones-TNO4
99Upper Deck-18
Exclusives-18
Exclusives 1 of 1-18
Game Jerseys Series II-JT
Game Jersey Patch Series II-JTP
New Ice Age-N19
New Ice Age Quantum Gold-N19
New Ice Age Quantum Silver-N19
99Upper Deck Century Legends-78
Century Collection-78
99Upper Deck Gold Reserve-18
99Upper Deck MVP-13
Gold Script-13
Silver Script-13
Super Script-13
ProSign-JT
99Upper Deck MVP SC Edition-16
Gold Script-16
Silver Script-16
Super Script-16
Great Combinations-GCTS
Great Combinations Parallel-GCTS
Second Season Snipers-SS2
99Upper Deck Retro-6
Gold-6
Platinum-6
99Upper Deck Victory-23
99Wayne Gretzky Hockey-16
00Aurora-15
Pinstripes-15
Pinstripes Premiere Date-15
Premiere Date-15
Scouting Reports-4
00BAP Memorabilia-127
Emerald-127
Ruby-127
Sapphire-127
Promos-127
00BAP Mem Chicago Sportsfest Copper-127
00BAP Memorabilia Chicago Sportsfest Blue-127
00BAP Memorabilia Chicago Sportsfest Gold-127
00BAP Memorabilia Chicago Sportsfest Ruby-127
00BAP Memorabilia Chicago Sun-Times Ruby-127
00BAP Memorabilia Chicago Sun-Times Gold-127
00BAP Mem Chicago Sun-Times Sapphire-127
00BAP Mem Toronto Fall Expo Copper-127
00BAP Memorabilia Toronto Fall Expo Gold-127
00BAP Memorabilia Toronto Fall Expo Ruby-127
00BAP Parkhurst 2000-P26
00BAP Signature Series-36
Emerald-36
Ruby-36
Sapphire-36
Autographs-113
Autographs Gold-113
Franchise Players-F3
00BAP Ultimate Memorabilia Autographs-45
Gold-45
00Black Diamond-4
Gold-4
Game Gear-GTH
00Crown Royale-12
Ice Blue-12
Limited Series-12
Premiere Date-12
Red-12
Jewels of the Crown-5
00Kraft-13
00McDonald's Pacific-4
Blue-4
00O-Pee-Chee-16
00O-Pee-Chee Parallel-16
00Pacific-43
Copper-43
Gold-43
Ice Blue-43
Premiere Date-43
Gold Crown Die Cuts-3
00Panini Stickers-16
00Paramount-23
Copper-23
Gold-23
Holo-Gold-23
Holo-Silver-23
Ice Blue-23
Premiere Date-23
00Private Stock-9
Gold-9
Premiere Date-9
Retail-9
Silver-9
Artist's Canvas-3
Artist's Canvas Proofs-3
PS-2001 Action-4
PS-2001 New Wave-2
00Revolution-13
Blue-13
Premiere Date-13
Red-13
HD NHL-4
00SP Authentic-7
Parents' Scrapbook-PS2
00SP Game Used-5
00SPx Highlight Heroes-HH3
00SPx Winning Materials-WTH
00Stadium Club-89
Beam Team-BT15
00Titanium-7
Blue-7
Gold-7
Premiere Date-7
Red-7
Retail-7
00Titanium Draft Day Edition-8
Patches-8
00Topps/OPC-16
Parallel-16
Combos-TC7
Combos Jumbos-TC7
NHL Draft-D7
00Topps Chrome-16
OPC Refractors-16
Refractors-16
Combos-TC7
Combos Refractors-TC7
00Topps Gold Label Class 1-7
Gold-7
00Topps Gold Label Class 2-7
00Topps Gold Label Class 2 Gold-7
00Topps Gold Label Class 3-7
00Topps Gold Label Class 3 Gold-7
00Topps Gold Label New Generation-NG3
00Topps Gold Label New Generation 1 to 1-NG3
00Topps Heritage-12
Chrome Parallel-12
Arena Relics-OSA-JT
Autographs-HA-JT
New Tradition-NT5
Original Six Relics-OSJ-JT
Original Six Relics-OSJ
Original Six Relics-OSJA-JT
00Topps Premier Plus-9
Blue Ice-9
Aspirations-PA5
00Topps Stars-51
Blue-51
00UD Heroes-10
00UD Pros and Prospects-7
00UD Reserve-8
Practice Session Jerseys-JT
Practice Session Jerseys Autographs-JT
00Upper Deck-13
Exclusives Tier 1-13
Exclusives Tier 2-13
Game Jerseys-JT
Game Jersey Autographs-HJT
Game Jersey Autographs Exclusives-EJT
Game Jersey Autographs Exclusives-ESJT
Game Jersey Combos-DTS
Game Jersey Patches-JTP
Game Jersey Patch Autographs Exclusives-JTP
00Upper Deck Ice-4
Immortals-4
Legends-4
Stars-4
00Upper Deck Legends-11
00Upper Deck Legends-13
Legendary Collection Bronze-11
Legendary Collection Bronze-13
Legendary Collection Gold-11
Legendary Collection Gold-13
Legendary Collection Silver-11
Legendary Collection Silver-13
Epic Signatures-JT
00Upper Deck MVP-17
First Stars-17
Second Stars-17
Third Stars-17
00Upper Deck Victory-17
00Upper Deck Victory-20
00Upper Deck Victory-285
00Upper Deck Vintage-25
00Upper Deck Vintage-36
00Upper Deck Vintage-37
00Vanguard-10
Dual Game-Worn Jerseys-1
Dual Game-Worn Patches-1
High Voltage-3
High Voltage Gold-3
High Voltage Green-3
High Voltage Red-3
High Voltage Silver-3
Holographic Gold-10
Holographic Purple-10
Pacific Proofs-10
Press East/West-11
01McFarlane Hockey-120
01McFarlane Hockey-121
01Atomic-9
Blue-9
Gold-9
Premiere Date-9
Red-9
Core Players-2
Power Play-4
Team Nucleus-1
01BAP Memorabilia-8
Emerald-8
Ruby-8
Sapphire-8
Country of Origin-CO50
01BAP Signature Series Certified 100-C21
01BAP Signature Series Certified 50-C21
01BAP Signature Series Certified 1 of 1's-C21
01BAP Signature Series Autographs-LJT
01BAP Signature Series Autographs Gold-LJT
01BAP Signature Series Franchise Jerseys-FP-3
01BAP Sig Series He Shoots/Scores Prizes-21
01BAP Signature Series Jerseys-GJ-3
01BAP Signature Series Jersey Autographs-GUJT
01BAP Sig Series Jersey and Stick Cards-GSJ-3
01BAP Signature Series Emblems-GUE-3
01BAP Signature Series Numbers-ITN-3
01BAP Ultimate Memorabilia Cornerstones-6
01BAP Ultimate Memorabilia Name Plates-21
01BAP Update He Shoots-He Scores Prizes-26
01BAP Update Passing the Torch-PTT1
01Bowman YoungStars-14
Gold-14
Ice Cubed-14
01Crown Royale-13
Blue-13
Premiere Date-13
Red-13
Retail-13
Jewels of the Crown-2
01McDonald's Pacific-2
01O-Pee-Chee-88
01O-Pee-Chee Heritage Parallel-88
01O-Pee-Chee Heritage Parallel Limited-88
01O-Pee-Chee Premier Parallel-88
01Pacific-40
01Pacific-426
Extreme LTD-40
Gold-426
Hobby LTD-40
Premiere Date-40
Retail LTD-40
Gold Crown Die-Cuts-2
97-98 Subset-354
97-98 Subset Gold Parallel-354
Top Draft Picks-4
01Pacific Top Draft Picks Draft Day Promo-4
01Pacific Adrenaline-17
Blue-17
Premiere Date-17
Red-17
Retail-17
Playmakers-1
01Pacific Arena Exclusives-40
01Pacific Arena Exclusives-426
01Pacific Heads-Up-10
Blue-10
Premiere Date-10
Red-10
Silver-10
Quad Jerseys-2
Stat Masters-2
01Parkhurst-79
Gold-79
Silver-79
Heroes-H5
Jerseys-PJ21
Jersey and Stick-PSJ20
Sticks-PS21
Teammates-T4
Teammates-T19
01Private Stock-7
Gold-7
Premiere Date-7
Retail-7
Silver-7
01Private Stock Pacific Nights-7
01Private Stock PS-2002-6
01Private Stock Reserve-S2
01SP Authentic-6
Limited-6
Limited Gold-6
Sign of the Times-JT
Sign of the Times-ET
Sign of the Times-HT
Sign of the Times-TL
01SP Game Used-3
Authentic Fabric-AFJT
Authentic Fabric-DFTG
Authentic Fabric Gold-AFJT
Inked Sweaters-ISJT
Inked Sweaters-DSST
Patches-PJT
Patches Signed-SPJT
Patches Signed-DSPTB
Tools of the Game-TJT
Tools of the Game Signed-STJT
Tools of the Game Signed-SCLT
Tools of the Game Signed-SCTY
01SPx-4
01Sports Illustrated for Kids III-316
01Stadium Club-91
Award Winners-91
Master Photos-91
Souvenirs-JT
Souvenirs-JTJASS
01Titanium-11
Hobby Parallel-11
Premiere Date-11
Retail-11
Retail Parallel-11
All-Stars-1
Double-Sided Jerseys-74
Saturday Knights-2
01Titanium Draft Day Edition-11
01Topps-88
Heritage Parallel-88
Heritage Parallel Limited-88
OPC Parallel-88
01Topps Chrome-88
Refractors-88
Black Border Refractors-88
01Topps Heritage-57
Refractors-57
Jerseys-JJT
01Topps Reserve-49
Emblems-JT
Jerseys-JT
Name Plates-JT
Numbers-JT
Patches-JT
01UD Challenge for the Cup-5
Jersey Autographs-UCST
01UD Honor Roll-26
01UD Honor Roll-56
Jerseys-J-JT
Jerseys Gold-J-JT
01UD Mask Collection-8
Gold-8
01UD Playmakers-8
01UD Premier Collection-3
Dual Jerseys-DST
Dual Jerseys-DTN
Dual Jerseys-DBTO
Dual Jerseys Black-DST
Dual Jerseys Black-DTN
Dual Jerseys Black-DBTO
Jerseys-SJT
Jerseys Black-S-JT
Signatures-JS
Signatures Black-JS
01UD Top Shelf-3
Jerseys-JT
Jersey Autographs-JT
01Upper Deck-13
Exclusives-13
Tandems-T1
01Upper Deck Ice-2
01Upper Deck MVP-12
01Upper Deck Victory-26
Gold-26
01Upper Deck Vintage-23
01Upper Deck Vintage-25
01Upper Deck Vintage-26
01Vanguard-8
Blue-8
Red-8
One of Ones-8
Premiere Date-8
Proofs-8
02McFarlane Hockey Toys-R-Us-10
02Atomic-8
Blue-8
Gold-8
Red-8
Cold Fusion-4
Hobby Parallel-8
Super Colliders-2
02BAP All-Star Edition-92
Jerseys-92
Jerseys Gold-92
Jerseys Silver-92
02BAP First Edition-159
02BAP First Edition-333
02BAP First Edition-343
02BAP First Edition-416R
Debut Jerseys-17
He Shoots-He Score Points-11
He Shoots-He Scores Prizes-15
Jerseys-159
02BAP Memorabilia-122
02BAP Memorabilia-203
Emerald-122
Emerald-203
Ruby-122
Ruby-203
Sapphire-122
Sapphire-203
All-Star Jerseys-ASJ-56
Franchise Players-FP-3
Future of the Game-FG-10
NHL All-Star Game-122
NHL All-Star Game-203
NHL All-Star Game Blue-122
NHL All-Star Game Blue-203
NHL All-Star Game Green-122
NHL All-Star Game Green-203
NHL All-Star Game Red-122
NHL All-Star Game Red-203
Stanley Cup Playoffs-SC-5
02BAP Memorabilia Toronto Fall Expo-122
02BAP Memorabilia Toronto Fall Expo-203
02BAP Signature Series-122
Autographs-122
Autograph Buybacks 1998-9
Autograph Buybacks 1999-24
Autograph Buybacks 2000-113
Autograph Buybacks 2001-LJT
Autographs Gold-122
Franchise Players-FJ3
Jerseys-SGJ12
Jersey Autographs-SGJ12
Team Quads-TQ11
Triple Memorabilia-TM4
02BAP Ultimate Memorabilia Autographs-21
02BAP Ultimate Mem Autographs Gold-21
02BAP Ultimate Memorabilia Captains-3
02BAP Ultimate Memorabilia Dynamic Duos-1
02BAP Ultimate Memorabilia Emblems-2
02BAP Ultimate Memorabilia First Overall-7
02BAP Ultimate Memorabilia Gloves Are Off-17
02BAP Ultimate Memorabilia Hat Tricks-6
02BAP Ultimate Memorabilia Jerseys-17
02BAP Ultimate Mem Jersey and Stick-7
02BAP Ultimate Memorabilia Nameplates-3
02BAP Ultimate Memorabilia Numbers-28
02Bowman YoungStars-5
Gold-5
Silver-5
02Bruins Team Issue-8
02Crown Royale-9
Blue-9
Red-9
Retail-9
Lords of the Rink-4
02eTopps-37
02ITG Used-7
02ITG Used-107
Franchise Players-F3
Franchise Players Autographs-F3
Franchise Players Gold-F3
Jerseys-GUJ12
Jersey Autographs-GUJ12
Jerseys Gold-GUJ12
Emblems-E12
Jersey and Stick-SJ12
Jersey and Stick Gold-SJ12
Teammates-T3
Teammates Gold-T3
Triple Memorabilia-TM1
Triple Memorabilia Gold-TM1
02McDonald's Pacific-4
Cup Contenders Die-Cuts-1
02O-Pee-Chee-10
02O-Pee-Chee Jumbos-1
02O-Pee-Chee Premier Blue Parallel-10
02O-Pee-Chee Premier Red Parallel-10
02O-Pee-Chee Factory Set-10
02Pacific-35
Blue-35
Red-35
Cramer's Choice-3
Impact Zone-3
Jerseys-3
Jerseys Holo-Silver-3
Lamplighters-3
Main Attractions-3
Maximum Impact-10
02Pacific Calder-31
Silver-31
Chasing Glory-1
Hart Stoppers-1
02Pacific Chicago National *-2
02Pacific Complete-492
Red-492
02Pacific Exclusive-15
Jerseys-2
Jerseys Gold-2
Maximum Overdrive-4
02Pacific Heads-Up-11
Blue-11
Purple-11
Red-11
Bobble Heads-13
Etched in Time-3
Head First-4
Inside the Numbers-4
Quad Jerseys-3
Quad Jerseys Gold-3
Stat Masters-4
02Pacific Quest for the Cup-8
Gold-8
Chasing the Cup-4
Jerseys-3
02Parkhurst-114
Bronze-114
Gold-114
Silver-114
Franchise Players-FP3
Heroes-NH2
He Shoots-He Scores Points-11
He Shoots-He Scores Prizes-8
Jerseys-GJ40
Patented Power-PP10
Stick and Jerseys-SJ40
Teammates-TT8
02Parkhurst Retro-6
Minis-6
Franchise Players-RF3
He Shoots-He Scores Points-7
He Shoots-He Scores Prizes-16
Hopefuls-HH2
Hopefuls-RR7
Jerseys-RJ7
Jersey and Sticks-RSJ7
Memorabilia-RM3
Memorabilia-RM19
02Private Stock Reserve-104
Red-104
Retail-104
Patches-104
02SP Authentic-6
02SP Authentic-92
Beckett Promos-6
Sign of the Times-JT
Sign of the Times-ST
Sign of the Times-DBT
Sign of the Times-TSB
Super Premiums-SPJT
Super Premiums-DPST
Super Premiums-TPTBN
02SP Game Used-4
Authentic Fabrics-AFJT
Authentic Fabrics-CFTS
Authentic Fabrics Gold-AFJT
Authentic Fabrics Gold-CFTS
Authentic Fabrics Rainbow-AFJT
Authentic Fabrics Rainbow-CFTS
First Rounder Patches-JT
Piece of History-PHJT
Piece of History Gold-PHJT
Piece of History Rainbow-PHJT
Signature Style-JT
Tools of the Game-JT
02SPx-5
02SPx-80
Spectrum Gold-5
Spectrum Gold-80
Spectrum Silver-5
Spectrum Silver-80
Smooth Skaters-JT
Smooth Skaters Gold-JT
Smooth Skaters Silver-JT
Winning Materials-WMJT
Winning Materials Gold-JT
Winning Materials Silver-JT
Xtreme Talents-JT
Xtreme Talents Gold-JT
Xtreme Talents Silver-JT
02Stadium Club-74
Silver Decoy Cards-74
Proofs-74
Beam Team-BT9
02Titanium-10
Blue-10
Red-10
Retail-10
Jerseys-5
Jerseys Retail-5
Patches-5
Shadows-2
02Topps-10
OPC Blue Parallel-10
OPC Red Parallel-10
Coast to Coast-CC7
Topps/OPC Hometown Heroes-HHU18
Factory Set-10
Factory Set Hometown Heroes-HHU18
02Topps Chrome-10
Black Border Refractors-10
Refractors-10
02Topps Heritage-5
Chrome Parallel-5
02Topps Total-211
Team Checklists-TTC2
Topps-TT8
02UD Artistic Impressions-6
Gold-6
Artist's Touch-ATJT
Artist's Touch Gold-ATJT
02UD Artistic Impressions Beckett Promos-6
02UD Artistic Impressions Great Depiction-GD12
02UD Artistic Impress Great Depiction Gld-GD12
02UD Artistic Impressions Retrospectives-R6
02UD Artistic Impressions Retrospect Gold-R6
02UD Artistic Impress Retrospect Auto-R6
02UD Artistic Impress Retrospect Silver-R6
02UD Foundations-145
02UD Honor Roll-5
02UD Honor Roll-73
Grade A Jerseys-TSTM
Students of the Game-SG3
Team Warriors-TW1
02UD Mask Collection-10
02UD Mask Collection Beckett Promos-10
02UD Mask Collection Instant Offense-IOJT
02UD Piece of History-5
Marks of Distinction-JT
Patches-PHTH
Stellar Stitches-SSJT
02UD Premier Collection-5
Jerseys Bronze-TH
Jerseys Bronze-ST
Jerseys Gold-TH
Jerseys Gold-ST
Jerseys Silver-TH
Jerseys Silver-ST
Patches-PTH
Signatures Bronze-SJT
Signatures Bronze-AS-JT
Signatures Gold-SJT
Signatures Gold-AS-JT
Signatures Silver-SJT
Signatures Silver-AS-JT
02UD Top Shelf-6
Clutch Performers-CPJT
Dual Player Jerseys-RPT
Dual Player Jerseys-STBT
Dual Player Jerseys-STST
Goal Oriented-GOJT
Sweet Sweaters-SWJO
Triple Jerseys-HTLJT
Triple Jerseys-HTNTH
Triple Jerseys-TSGTD
02Upper Deck-11
02Upper Deck-425
Exclusives-11
Exclusives-425
02Upper Deck Beckett UD Promos-425
02Upper Deck Blow-Ups-C3
02Upper Deck CHL Graduates-CGJT
02Upper Deck CHL Graduates Gold-CGJT
02Upper Deck Difference Makers-JT
02Upper Deck Game Jersey Autographs-JT
02Upper Deck Game Jersey Series II-GJJT
02Upper Deck Number Crunchers-NC1
02Upper Deck Patch Card Numbers-JT
02Upper Deck Patchwork-PWJT
02Upper Deck Pinpoint Accuracy-PAJT
02Upper Deck Playbooks Series II-ST
02Upper Deck Shooting Stars-SS3
02Upper Deck Sizzling Scorers-SS2
02Upper Deck Classic Portraits-7
Headliners-ST
Headliners Limited-ST
Hockey Royalty-GTM
Hockey Royalty-LLT
Hockey Royalty Limited-GTM
Hockey Royalty Limited-LLT
Mini-Busts-71
Mini-Busts-72
Mini-Busts-73
Mini-Busts-74
Mini-Busts-75
Mini-Busts-76
Mini-Busts-77
Mini-Busts-78
Mini-Busts-79
Mini-Busts-80
Stitches-CJT
Stitches Limited-CJT
02Upper Deck MVP-14
Gold-14
Classics-14
Golden Classics-14
Highlight Nights-HN2
Skate Around Jerseys-SAJT
Skate Around Jerseys-STLNT
Skate Around Jerseys-STMMT
Skate Around Jerseys-STTDG
Vital Forces-VF3
02Upper Deck Rookie Update-9
02Upper Deck Rookie Update-106
02Upper Deck Rookie Update-172
Jerseys-DJT
Jerseys-STS
Jerseys Gold-DJT
Jerseys Gold-STS
02Upper Deck Victory-18
Bronze-18
Gold-18
Silver-18
02Upper Deck Vintage-23
02Upper Deck Vintage-263
Tall Boys-T5
Tall Boys Gold-T5
02Vanguard-10
LTD-10
East Meets West-2
Jerseys-5
Jerseys Gold-5
V-Team-8
03McFarlane Hockey 3-Inch Duals-30
03BAP Memorabilia-42
Emerald-42
Gold-42
Ruby-42
Sapphire-42
All-Star Complete Jerseys-ASCJ6
All-Star Emblems-ASE-10
All-Star Jerseys-ASJ-14
All-Star Numbers-ASN-10
All-Star Teammates-AST5
Brush with Greatness-20
Brush with Greatness Contest Cards-20
He Shoots-He Scores Points-10
He Shoots-He Scores Prizes-10
Jersey and Stick-SJ-1
Jerseys-GJ-1
Jersey Autographs-GJ-1
03BAP Ultimate Memorabilia Autographs-134
Gold-134
03BAP Ultimate Mem Auto Jerseys-134
03BAP Ultimate Mem Auto Emblems-134
03BAP Ultimate Mem Auto Sticks-134
03BAP Ultimate Mem Complete Jersey-1
03BAP Ultimate Mem Complete Jersey Gold-1
03BAP Ultimate Memorabilia Cornerstones-5
03BAP Ultimate Memorabilia Dynamic Duos-8
03BAP Ultimate Memorabilia Emblems-10
03BAP Ultimate Memorabilia Emblems Gold-10
03BAP Ultimate Mem Franch Present Future-3
03BAP Ultimate Memorabilia Gloves Are Off-1
03BAP Ultimate Memorabilia Hat Tricks-5
03BAP Ultimate Memorabilia Heroes-2
03BAP Ultimate Mem Heroes Autos-1
03BAP Ultimate Mem Hometown Heroes-13
03BAP Ultimate Mem Hometown Heroes Gold-13
03BAP Ultimate Memorabilia Jerseys-6
03BAP Ultimate Memorabilia Jerseys Gold-6
03BAP Ultimate Mem Jersey and Emblems-18
03BAP Ultimate Mem Jersey and Emblem Gold-18
03BAP Ultimate Mem Jersey and Numbers-18
03BAP Ultimate Mem Jersey and Number Gold-18
03BAP Ultimate Mem Jersey and Stick-11
03BAP Ultimate Mem Jersey and Stick Gold-11
03BAP Ultimate Memorabilia Nameplates-12
03BAP Ultimate Mem Nameplates Gold-12
03BAP Ultimate Memorabilia Numbers-5
03BAP Ultimate Memorabilia Numbers Gold-5
03BAP Ultimate Memorabilia Triple Threads-18
03Beehive-20
Variations-20
Gold-20
Silver-20
Jumbos-4
Jumbo Variations-4
Jumbo Jerseys-BH17
Jerseys-JT25
Signatures-RF11
03Black Diamond-144
Black-144
Green-144
Red-144
Signature Gems-SG-19
Threads-DT-JT
Threads Green-DT-JT
Threads Red-DT-JT
Threads Black-DT-JT
03Bowman-10
Gold-10
Goal to Goal-TK
03Bowman Chrome-10
Refractors-10
Gold Refractors-10
Xfractors-10
03Bruins Team Issue-12
03Crown Royale-9
Blue-9
Retail-9
Jerseys-3
Patches-3
Lords of the Rink-3
03eTopps-32
03ITG Action-1
Center of Attention-CA6
Homeboys-HB7
Jerseys-M199
Jerseys-M219
Jerseys-M243
Oh Canada-OC14
03ITG Toronto Fall Expo Jerseys-FE16
03ITG Used Signature Series-35
Gold-35
Autographs-JT
Autographs Gold-JT
Franchise-3
Franchise Autographs-3
Franchise Gold-3
Jerseys-17
Jerseys Gold-17
Jersey Autos-17
Emblems-15
Emblems Gold-15
Teammates-17
Teammates Gold-17
Triple Memorabilia-26
Triple Memorabilia Gold-26
03ITG VIP Collages-14
03ITG VIP Collage Autographs-14
03ITG VIP Jerseys-1
03ITG VIP Jersey Autographs-1
03ITG VIP Jersey and Emblems-1
03ITG VIP Jersey and Numbers-1
03Kraft-9
03McDonald's Pacific-4
Canadian Pride-2
Hockey Roots Checklists-9
Patches Silver-3
Patches Gold-3
Patches and Sticks-3
03NHL Sticker Collection-17
03O-Pee-Chee-1
03OPC Blue-1
03OPC Gold-1
03OPC Red-1
03Pacific-34
Blue-34
Red-34
Jerseys-5
Jerseys Gold-5
Main Attractions-3
Maximum Impact-1
View from the Crease-2
03Pacific Calder-9
03Pacific Calder-143
Silver-9
03Pacific Complete-242
Red-242
03Pacific Exhibit-155
Blue Backs-155
Pursuing Prominence-3
03Pacific Heads-Up-10
Hobby LTD-10
Retail LTD-10
Jerseys-3
Mini Sweaters-3
Rink Immortals-1
Rink Immortals LTD-1
03Pacific Invincible-8
Blue-8
Red-8
Retail-8
Featured Performers-3
03Pacific Luxury Suite-26A
03Pacific Luxury Suite-26B
03Pacific Luxury Suite-26C
03Pacific Luxury Suite-26D
03Pacific Prism-105
Blue-105
Patches-105
Red-105
Retail-105
Stat Masters-2
03Pacific Quest for the Cup-10
Blue-10
Chasing the Cup-3
Jerseys-2
03Pacific Supreme-8
Blue-8
Red-8
Retail-8
Jerseys-3
Team-1
03Parkhurst Original Six Boston-7
03Parkhurst Original Six Boston-71
Inserts-B16
Memorabilia-BM6
Memorabilia-BM16
Memorabilia-BM19
Memorabilia-BM52
03Parkhurst Orig Six He Shoots/Scores-13
03Parkhurst Orig Six He Shoots/Scores-13A
03Parkhurst Rookie-9

Emblems-GUE-8
Emblem Autographs-GUE-JT
Emblems Gold-GUE-8
High Expectations-HE-10
High Expectations Gold-HE-10
Jerseys-GJ-3
Jersey Autographs-GUJ-JT
Jerseys Gold-GJ-3
Teammates Gold-RT11
Teammates-RT11
03Private Stock Reserve-145
Blue-145
Patches-145
Red-145
Retail-145
Moments in Time-2
03SP Authentic-7
Limited-7
10th Anniversary-SP12
10th Anniversary Limited-SP12
Breakout Seasons-B4
Breakout Seasons Limited-B4
Foundations-F2
Foundations Limited-F2
Honors-H25
Honors Limited-H25
Sign of the Times-JTH
Sign of the Times-ET
Sign of the Times-GTS
03SP Game Used-5
03SP Game Used-93
Gold-5
Gold-93
Authentic Fabrics-AFJT
Authentic Fabrics-DFTM
Authentic Fabrics Gold-AFJT
Authentic Fabrics Gold-DFTM
Authentic Patches-APJT
Double Threads-DTTM
Double Threads-DTTS
Limited Threads-LTJT
Limited Threads Gold-LTJT
Premium Patches-PPTH
Signers-SPSJT
03SPx-6
03SPx-129
03SPx-133
03SPx-159
03SPx-177
Radiance-6
Radiance-129
Radiance-133
Radiance-159
Radiance-177
Spectrum-6
Spectrum-129
Spectrum-133
Spectrum-159
Spectrum-177
Big Futures-BF-JT
Big Futures Limited-BF-JT
Fantasy Franchise-FF-KTH
Fantasy Franchise-FF-TMS
Fantasy Franchise Limited-FF-KTH
Fantasy Franchise Limited-FF-TMS
Origins-O-JT
Signature Threads-ST-JT
Style-SPX-GS
Style-SPX-HT
Style Limited-SPX-GS
Style Limited-SPX-HT
VIP-VIP-TM
VIP Limited-VIP-TM
03Titanium-193
Patches-193
Highlight Reels-2
03Topps-1
Blue-1
Gold-1
Red-1
Box Toppers-1
First Overall Fabrics-JT
First Overall Fabrics-JTIK
First Overall Fabrics-JTVL
Topps/OPC Idols-CI5
Own the Game-OTG3
03Topps C55-100
03Topps C55-100B
Minis-100
Minis American Back-100
Minis American Back Red-100
Minis Bazooka Back-100
Minis Brooklyn Back-100
Minis Hat Trick Back-100
Minis O Canada Back-100
Minis O Canada Back Red-100
Minis Stanley Cup Back-100
Relics-TRJTH
03Topps Pristine-40
Gold Refractor Die Cuts-40
Refractors-40
Popular Demand Relics-PD-JT
Popular Demand Relic Refractors-PD-JT
Press Plates Black-40
Press Plates Cyan-40
Press Plates Magenta-40
Press Plates Yellow-40
03Topps Traded Franchise Fabrics-FF-JT
03UD Honor Roll-6
03UD Honor Roll-92
03UD Honor Roll-128
Grade A Jerseys-GAJT
Grade A Jerseys-TBOS
Signature Class-SC26
03UD Premier Collection-6
NHL Shields-SH-JT
Signatures-PS-JT
Signatures Gold-PS-JT
Skills-SK-FT
Skills-SK-LT
Skills Patches-SK-FT
Skills Patches-SK-LT
Super Stars-SS-JT
Super Stars Patches-SS-JT
Teammates-PT-BB1
Teammates-PT-BB2
Teammates Patches-PT-BB1
Teammates Patches-PT-BB2
03UD Toronto Fall Expo Priority Signings-JT
03Upper Deck-14
03Upper Deck-199
All-Star Class-AS-3
All-Star Lineup-AS3
Big Playmakers-BP-JT
BuyBacks-1
BuyBacks-2
BuyBacks-3
BuyBacks-4
BuyBacks-5
BuyBacks-6
BuyBacks-7
Canadian Exclusives-14
Canadian Exclusives-199
Franchise Fabrics-FF-JT
Gifted Greats-GG3
HG-14
HG-199
Jersey Autographs-SJ-JT
Magic Moments-MM-7
Memorable Matchups-MM-TT
Patches-LD5
Patches-PLG-JT
Patches-PNM-JT
Patches-PNR-JT
Power Zone-PZ-1
Superstar Spotlight-SS2
Team Essentials-TL-JT
Team Essentials-TP-JT
Three Stars-TS15
03Upper Deck All-Star Promos-AS1
03Upper Deck Classic Portraits-6
03Upper Deck Classic Portraits-102
03Upper Deck Classic Portraits-152
Classic Stitches-CS-JT
Genuine Greatness-GG-JT
Headliners-HH-JT
Premium Portraits-PP-JT
03Upper Deck Ice-7
Gold-7
Authentics-IA-JT
Breakers-IB-JT
Breaker Patches-IB-JT
Frozen Fabrics-FF-JT
Frozen Fabric Patches-FF-JT
Under Glass Autographs-UG-JT
03Upper Deck MVP-31
03Upper Deck MVP-437
Gold Script-31
Gold Script-437
Silver Script-31
Silver Script-437
Canadian Exclusives-31
Canadian Exclusives-437
Clutch Performers-CP4
Lethal Lineups-LL3
ProSign-PS-JT
SportsNut-SN8
Talent-MT6
03Upper Deck Rookie Update-7
03Upper Deck Rookie Update-151
All-Star Lineup-AS3
Skills-SKTH
Super Stars-SSJT
03Upper Deck Trilogy-6
03Upper Deck Trilogy-101
Authentic Patches-AP19
Crest Variations-101
Limited-6
Limited-101
Limited Threads-LT19
Scripts-S2JT
Scripts Limited-S2JT
Scripts Red-S2JT
03Upper Deck Victory-12
Bronze-12
Gold-12
Silver-12
Freshman Flashback-FF5
Game Breakers-GB32
03Toronto Star-7
Foil-6
04Upper Deck Sportsfest *-SF4
04Upper Deck National Convention *-TN15
04Pacific-27
Blue-27
Red-27
All-Stars-2
Cramer's Choice-2
Global Connection-2
04Pacific NHL All-Star Nets-1
Gold-1
04Pacific National Convention-2
04SP Authentic-8
04SP Authentic-99
Limited-8
Limited-99
Buybacks-94
Buybacks-95
Buybacks-96
Buybacks-97
Octographs-OS-CAP
Rookie Review-RR-JT
Sign of the Times-ST-JT
Sign of the Times-DS-RT
Sign of the Times-DS-ST
Sign of the Times-DS-TN
Sign of the Times-TS-BNT
Sign of the Times-TS-TRB
Sign of the Times-QS-BTCR
Sign of the Times-QS-GTDC
Sign of the Times-QS-TPLS
Sign of the Times-FS-BOS
Sign of the Times-SS-ALS
04SP Game Used Hawaii Conference Patch-PP11
04UD All-World-78
04UD All-World-94
Gold-78
Autographs-78
Autographs-94
Dual Autographs-AD-JA
Dual Autographs-AD-NT
Quad Autographs-AQ-GSC
Six Autographs-AS-SWT
04UD Toronto Fall Expo Pride of Canada-26
04Ultimate Collection-4
04Ultimate Collection-60
Buybacks-33
Buybacks-34
Buybacks-35
Buybacks-36
Buybacks-37
Buybacks-38
Buybacks-39
Buybacks-40
Buybacks-41
Buybacks-42
Dual Logos-UL2-NT
Dual Logos-UL2-ST
Dual Logos-UL2-TL
Jerseys-UGJ-JT
Jerseys Gold-UGJ-JT
Jersey Autographs-UGJA-JT
Patches-UP-JT
Patch Autographs-UPA-JT
Patch Autographs-UPA-ARJT
Signatures-US-JT
Signature Logos-ULA-JT
Signature Patches-SP-JT
04Upper Deck-13
1997 Game Jerseys-BB
Big Playmakers-BP-TH
Canadian Exclusives-13
Clutch Performers-CP4
HG Glossy Gold-13
HG Glossy Silver-13
Jersey Autographs-GJA-TH
Patches-GJPA-BB
Patches-GJPL-BB
Patches-GJPN-BB
Swatch of Six-SS-TH
World's Best-WB6
World Cup Tribute-BB
World Cup Tribute-SGTHRS
04Upper Deck All-Star Promos-JT
04Swiss Davos Postcards-27
04Upper Deck Sportsfest *-SF4
05Be A Player-7
First Period-7
Second Period-7
Third Period-7
Overtime-7
Class Action-CA4
Dual Signatures-HT
Dual Signatures-NT
Dual Signatures-TM
Dual Signatures-TP
Outtakes-OT6
Quad Signatures-BOST
Quad Signatures-HSNT
Signatures-SJ
Signatures Gold-SJ
Triple Signatures-PTS
Triple Signatures-STS
Triple Signatures-TLP
World Cup Salute-WCS7
05Beehive-74
05Beehive-247
Beige -74
Blue -74
Gold-74
Red -74
Matte-74
Matted Materials-MMJT
Matted Materials Remarkable-RMJT
PhotoGraphs-PGJT
Signature Scrapbook-SSJT
05Black Diamond-170
Emerald-170
Gold-170
Onyx-170
Ruby-170
Gemography-G-JT
Gemography Emerald-G-JT
Gemography Gold-G-JT
Gemography Onyx-G-JT
Gemography Ruby-G-JT
Jerseys-J-JT
Jerseys Ruby-J-JT
Jersey Duals-DJ-JT
Jersey Triples-TJ-JT
Jersey Quads-QJ-JT
05Hot Prospects-82
En Fuego-82
Red Hot-82
White Hot-82
05McDonalds Upper Deck-8
Autographs-MA3
Chasing the Cup-CC7
CHL Graduates-CG5
Jerseys-MJ2
Patches-MP2
Top Scorers-TS15
05Panini Stickers-19
05Parkhurst-400
05Parkhurst-581
05Parkhurst-591
05Parkhurst-695
Facsimile Auto Parallel-400
Facsimile Auto Parallel-581
Facsimile Auto Parallel-591
Facsimile Auto Parallel-695
True Colors-TCSJS
True Colors-TCSJS
True Colors-TCSJLA
True Colors-TCSJLA
05SP Authentic-85
05SP Authentic-109
Limited-85
Limited-109
Chirography-SPJO
Exquisite Endorsements-EEJO
Marks of Distinction-MDJO
Prestigious Pairings-PPTC
Sign of the Times Quads-QTNBB
Sign of the Times Fives-TNCMC
05SP Game Used-81
Autographs-81
Gold-81
Authentic Fabrics-AF-JT
Authentic Fabrics Autographs-AAF-JT
Authentic Fabrics Dual-NT
Authentic Fabrics Dual-PB
Authentic Fabrics Dual Autographs-NT
Authentic Fabrics Dual Autographs-PB
Authentic Fabrics Gold-AF-JT
Authentic Fabrics Quad-TRSB
Authentic Patches Quad -TRSB
Authentic Fabrics Triple-TBM
Authentic Fabrics Triple-TSY
Authentic Patches-AP-JT
Authentic Patches Autographs-AAP-JT
Authentic Patches Dual-NT
Authentic Patches Dual-PB
Authentic Patches Dual Autographs-NT
Authentic Patches Dual Autographs-PB
Authentic Patches Triple-TBM
Authentic Patches Triple-TSY
Auto Draft-AD-JO
Awesome Authentics-AA-JO
Game Gear-GG-JO
SIGnificance-JT
SIGnificance Gold-S-JT
SIGnificance Extra-TB
SIGnificance Extra Gold-TB
Significant Numbers-SN-JO
05SPx-7
Spectrum-7
Winning Combos-WC-BO
Winning Combos-WC-JP
Winning Combos Autographs-AWC-TB
Winning Combos Gold-WC-BO
Winning Combos Gold-WC-JP
Winning Combos Spectrum-WC-BO
Winning Combos Spectrum-WC-JP
Winning Materials-WM-JT
Winning Materials Autographs-AWM-JO
Winning Materials Gold-WM-JT
Winning Materials Spectrum-WM-JT
Xcitement Superstars-XS-JO
Xcitement Superstars Gold-XS-JO
Xcitement Superstars Spectrum-XS-JO
05The Cup-86
Gold-86
Black Rainbow-86
Dual NHL Shields Autographs-ADSTC
Emblems of Endorsement-EEJO
Honorable Numbers-HNJO
Limited Logos-LLJO
Masterpiece Pressplates-86
Masterpiece Pressplates Rookie Upd Auto-272
Noble Numbers-NNTN
Noble Numbers-NNTS
Noble Numbers-NNYT
Noble Numbers Dual-DNNJJ
Noble Numbers Dual-DNNST
Patch Variation-P86
Patch Variation Autographs-AP86
Property of-POJO
Scripted Numbers-SNTN
Scripted Numbers Dual-DSNTM
Scripted Swatches-SSJO
Signature Patches-SPJO
05UD Artifacts-8
05UD Artifacts-154
Blue-8
Blue-154
Gold-8
Gold-154
Green-8
Green-154
Pewter-8
Pewter-154
Red-8
Red-154
Auto Facts-AF-JT
Auto Facts Blue-AF-JT
Auto Facts Copper-AF-JT
Auto Facts Pewter-AF-JT
Auto Facts Silver-AF-JT
Gold Autographed-8
Gold Autographed-154
Remarkable Artifacts-RA-JT
Remarkable Artifacts Dual-RA-JT
Treasured Patches-TP-JT
Treasured Patches Autographed-TP-JT
Treasured Patches Dual-TPD-JT
Treasured Patches Dual Autographed-TPD-JT
Treasured Patches Pewter-TP-JT
Treasured Patches Silver-TP-JT
Treasured Swatches-TS-JT
Treasured Swatches Autographed-TS-JT
Treasured Swatches Blue-TS-JT
Treasured Swatches Copper-TS-JT
Treasured Swatches Dual-TSD-JT
Treasured Swatches Dual Autographed-TSD-JT
Treasured Swatches Dual Blue-TSD-JT
Treasured Swatches Dual Copper-TSD-JT
Treasured Swatches Dual Maroon-TSD-JT
Treasured Swatches Dual Pewter-TSD-JT
Treasured Swatches Dual Silver-TSD-JT
Treasured Swatches Maroon-TS-JT
Treasured Swatches Pewter-TS-JT
Treasured Swatches Silver-TS-JT
05UD PowerPlay-8
05UD PowerPlay-93
Rainbow-8
Power Marks-PMJT
Specialists-TSJT
Specialists Patches-SPJT
05UD Toronto Fall Expo Priority Signings-PS-JT
05Ultimate Collection-74
Gold-74
Endorsed Emblems-EEJO
Jerseys-JJO
Marquee Attractions-MA41
Marquee Attractions Signatures-SMA41
National Heroes Jerseys-NHJJO
National Heroes Patches-NHPJO
Premium Patches-PPJO
Premium Swatches-PSJO
Ultimate Achievements-UAJO
Ultimate Patches-PJO
Ultimate Signatures-USJO
Ultimate Signatures Logos-SLJO
Ultimate Signatures Pairings-UPTC
Ultimate Signatures Trios-UTTNC
05Ultra-17
Gold-17
Fresh Ink-FI-JT
Fresh Ink Blue-FI-JT
Ice-17
Scoring Kings-SK3
Scoring Kings Jerseys-SKJ-JT
Scoring Kings Jersey Autographs-KAJ-JT
Scoring Kings Patches-SKP-JT
Scoring Kings Patch Autographs-KAP-JT
Super Six-SS2
Super Six Jerseys-SSJ-JT
Super Six Jersey Autographs-SAJ-JT
Super Six Patches-SSP-JT
Super Six Patch Autographs-SAP-JT
05Upper Deck-14
05Upper Deck-199
05Upper Deck-407
05Upper Deck All-Time Greatest-5
05Upper Deck Big Playmakers-B-JT
05Upper Deck HG Glossy-14
05Upper Deck HG Glossy-199
05Upper Deck Hometown Heroes-HH3
05Upper Deck Jerseys-J-JT
05Upper Deck Majestic Materials-MMJT
05Upper Deck NHL Generations-DST
05Upper Deck NHL Generations-TBTN
05Upper Deck NHL Generations-TMST
05Upper Deck NHL Generations-TSTP
05Upper Deck Notable Numbers-N-JT
05Upper Deck Patches-P-JT
05Upper Deck Scrapbooks-HS3
05Upper Deck Shooting Stars-S-JT
05Upper Deck Ice-80
Rainbow-80
Cool Threads-CTJT
Cool Threads Autographs-ACTJT
Cool Threads Glass-CTJT
Cool Threads Patches-CTPJT
Cool Threads Patch Autographs-CAPJT
Signature Swatches-SSJT
05Upper Deck MVP-28
05Upper Deck MVP-439
Gold-28
Gold-439
Platinum-28
Platinum-439
Materials Triples-T-GST
ProSign-P-JT
05Upper Deck Rookie Update-81
05Upper Deck Rookie Update-272
05Upper Deck Trilogy-8
05Upper Deck Trilogy-95
Crystal-95
Crystal Autographs-95
Honorary Patches-HP-JT
Honorary Patch Scripts-HSP-JT
Honorary Swatches-HS-JT
Honorary Swatch Scripts-HSS-JT
Ice Scripts-IS-JT
Scripts-SSS-JT
05Upper Deck Toronto Fall Expo-14
05Upper Deck Toronto Fall Expo-199
05Upper Deck Victory-19
Black-19
Gold-19
Silver-19
Blow-Ups-BU5
Game Breakers-GB5
Stars on Ice-SI4
06Sports Illustrated for Kids *-96
06Be A Player-23
Profiles-PP20
Signatures-JT
Signatures Trios-TTCM
Signatures Foursomes-FSLST
Up Close and Personal-UC26
06Be A Player Portraits-84
Dual Signature Portraits-DSCT
Quadruple Signature Portraits-QSSTS
Sensational Six-SS1ST
Sensational Six-SSSJM
Signature Portraits-SPJO
Timeless Tens-TTCAN
Triple Signature Portraits-TSJS
06Beehive-15
06Beehive-167
Blue-15
Gold-15
Matte-15
Red Facsimile Signatures-15
Wood-15
5 X 7 Black and White-15
5 X 7 Cherry Wood-15
Matted Materials-MMJT
PhotoGraphs-PGJT
Remarkable Matted Materials-MMJT
06Black Diamond-166B
Black-163B
Gold-166B
Ruby-166B
Jerseys-JJT
Jerseys Black-JJT
Jerseys Gold-JJT
Jerseys Ruby-JJT
Jerseys Black Autographs -JJT
06Flair Showcase-194
06Flair Showcase-260
06Flair Showcase-295
Parallel-194
Parallel-260
Parallel-295
Hot Numbers-HN35
Hot Numbers Parallel-HN35
Inks-ITH
Stitches-SSJO
06Fleer-163
Oversized-163
Tiffany-163
Fabricology-FJT
Hockey Headliners-HL7
Signing Day-SDTH
Total O-021
06Hot Prospects-83
Red Hot-83
White Hot-83
Hot Materials -HMJT
Hot Materials Red Hot-HMJT
Hot Materials White Hot-HMJT
Hotagraphs-HJT
06ITG Ultimate Memorabilia-79
Artist Proof-79
Autos-58
Autos Gold-58
Autos Dual-7
Autos Dual Gold-7
Autos Triple-1
Autos Triple Gold-1
Blades of Steel-19
Blades of Steel Gold-19
Complete Jersey-2
Complete Jersey Gold-2
Complete Package-12
Complete Package Gold-12
Cornerstones-7
Cornerstones Gold-7
Decades-7
Decades Gold-7
Double Memorabilia-7
Double Memorabilia Gold-7
Double Memorabilia Autos-7
Double Memorabilia Autos Gold-7
First Round Picks-5
First Round Picks Gold-5
Gloves Are Off-13
Gloves Are Off Gold-13
Going For Gold-15
Going For Gold Gold-15
Jerseys-2
Jerseys Gold-2
Jerseys and Emblems-2
Jerseys and Emblems Gold-2
Jerseys Autos-58
Jerseys Autos Gold-58
Passing The Torch-10
Passing The Torch Gold-10
Seams Unbelievable-10
Seams Unbelievable Gold-10
Triple Thread Jerseys-16
Triple Thread Jerseys Gold-16
06McDonald's Upper Deck-38
Autographs-AJT
Clear Cut Winners-CC8
Hardware Heroes-HH1
Hardware Heroes-HH4
Jerseys-JJT
Patches-PJT
06NHL POG-20
06O-Pee-Chee-421
06O-Pee-Chee-601
Rainbow-421
Rainbow-601
Autographs-A-JT
06Panini Stickers-330
06SP Authentic-16
06SP Authentic-125
Limited-16
Limited-125
Sign of the Times Duals-STLT
Sign of the Times Triples-ST3MTC
06SP Game Used-84
Gold-84
Rainbow-84
Authentic Fabrics-AFJT
Authentic Fabrics Parallel-AFJT
Authentic Fabrics Patches-AFJT
Authentic Fabrics Dual-AF2MT
Authentic Fabrics Dual Patches-AF2MT
Authentic Fabrics Triple-AF3SJS
Authentic Fabrics Triple Patches-AF3SJS
Authentic Fabrics Quads-AF4STSC
Authentic Fabrics Quads Patches-AF4STSC
Authentic Fabrics Fives-AF5AST
Authentic Fabrics Fives-AP5PTS
Authentic Fabrics Fives Patches-AF5AST
Authentic Fabrics Fives Patches-AP5PTS
Authentic Fabrics Sevens-AF7ART
Authentic Fabrics Sevens-AF7MVP
Authentic Fabrics Sevens Patches-AF7ART
Authentic Fabrics Sevens Patches-AF7MVP
Authentic Fabrics Eights-AF8CAN
Authentic Fabrics Eights Patches-AF8CAN
By The Letter-BLJT
Inked Sweaters-ISJT
Inked Sweaters Patches-ISJT
06SPx-85
Spectrum-85
SPxcitement-X82
SPxcitement Spectrum-X82
SPxcitement Autographs-X82
Winning Materials-WMTH
Winning Materials Spectrum-WMTH
Winning Materials Autographs-WMTH
06Sunkist-9
06The Cup-77
Autographed Foundations-CQJT
Autographed Foundations Patches-CQJT
Autographed NHL Shields Duals-DASTB
Autographed NHL Shields Duals-DASTC
Autographed NHL Shields Duals-DASTM
Autographed Patches-77
Black Rainbow-77
Foundations-CQJT
Foundations Patches-CQJT
Enshrinements-EJT
Gold-77
Gold Patches-77
Hardware Heroes Patches-HHJT
Honorable Numbers-HNJT
Jerseys-77
Limited Logos-LLJT
Masterpiece Pressplates-77
NHL Shields Duals-DSHJO
Scripted Swatches-SSJT
Scripted Swatches Duals-DSTC
Signature Patches-SPJT
06UD Artifacts-17
06UD Artifacts-193
Blue-17
Blue-193
Gold-17
Gold-193
Platinum-17
Platinum-193
Radiance-17
Radiance-193
Autographed Radiance Parallel-17
Autographed Radiance Parallel-193
Red-17
Red-193
Auto-Facts-AFTH
Auto-Facts Gold-AFTH
Treasured Patches Black-TSJT
Treasured Patches Blue-TSJT
Treasured Patches Gold-TSJT
Treasured Patches Platinum-TSJT
Treasured Patches Red-TSJT
Treasured Patches Autographed Black Tag
Parallel-TSJT
Treasured Swatches-TSJT
Treasured Swatches Black-TSJT
Treasured Swatches Blue-TSJT
Treasured Swatches Gold-TSJT
Treasured Swatches Platinum-TSJT
Treasured Swatches Red-TSJT
Treasured Swatches Autographed Black-TSJT
Tundra Tandems-TTTC
Tundra Tandems Black-TTTC
Tundra Tandems Blue-TTTC
Tundra Tandems Gold-TTTC
Tundra Tandems Platinum-TTTC
Tundra Tandems Red-TTTC
Tundra Tandems Dual Patches Red-TTTC
06UD Mini Jersey Collection-85
Jerseys-JT
Jersey Variations-JT
Jersey Autographs-JT
06UD Powerplay-82
Impact Rainbow-82
In Action-IA11
Power Marks-PMJT
Specialists-SJT
Specialists Patches-PJT
06Ultimate Collection-50
Autographed Jerseys-AJ-JT
Autographed Patches-AJ-JT
Jerseys-UJ-JT
Jerseys Dual-UJ2-TC
Jerseys Triple-UJ3-STS
Patches-UJ-JT
Patches Dual-UJ2-TC
Patches Triple-UJ3-STS
Premium Patches-PS-JT
Premium Swatches-PS-JT
Signatures-US-TH
Ultimate Achievements-UA-JT
Ultimate Signatures Logos-SL-JT
06Ultra-161
Gold Medallion-161
Ice Medallion-161
Action-UA24
Difference Makers-DM29
Scoring Kings-SK14
Uniformity-UJT
Uniformity Patches-UPJT
Uniformity Autographed Jerseys-UAJT
06Upper Deck Arena Giveaways-SJS1
06Upper Deck-161
Exclusives Parallel-161
High Gloss Parallel-161
All World-AW3
Award Winners-AW1
Award Winners Canadian Exclusive-OAW4
Award Winners Canadian Exclusive-OAW5
Century Marks-CM1
Game Dated Moments-GD15
Game Dated Moments-GD23
Game Jerseys-JJT
Game Patches-PJT
Generations Duals-G2TS
Generations Triples-G3LTS
Generations Patches Dual-G2PTS
Generations Patches Triple-G3PLTS
Masterpieces-161
Statistical Leaders-SL1
Walmart Tins Oversize-161
06Upper Deck Entry Draft-DR6
06Upper Deck MVP-240
06Upper Deck MVP-358
Gold Script-240
Gold Script-358
Super Script-240
Super Script-358
Autographs-OATM
Gotta Have Hart-HH1
Jerseys-OJST
06Upper Deck Ovation-90
06Upper Deck Sweet Shot-86
Signature Shots/Saves-SSJT
Signature Shots/Saves Ice Signings-SSIJT
Signature Shots/Saves Sticks-SSSTH
Signature Sticks-STJT
Sweet Stitches-SSTH
Sweet Stitches Duals-SSTH
Sweet Stitches Triples-SSTH
06Upper Deck Trilogy-81
Combo Autographed Jerseys-CJTC
Combo Autographed Patches-CJTC
Combo Clearcut Autographs-C3MTC
Honorary Scripted Patches-HSPJT
Honorary Scripted Swatches-HSSJT
Honorary Swatches-HSJT
Ice Scripts-ISJO
Scripts-S2TH
Scripts-S3JT
06Upper Deck Victory-163
06Upper Deck Victory Black-163
06Upper Deck Victory Gold-163
06Upper Deck Victory GameBreakers-GB42
06Upper Deck Victory Oversize Cards-JT
06Russian Sport Collection Olympic Stars-40
06ITG Heroes and Prospects Heroes Memorabilia-HM23
06ITG Heroes and Prospects Triple Memorabilia-TM10
07Upper Deck Victory-181
Black-181
Gold-181
GameBreakers-GB3
Oversize Cards-OS40
Stars on Ice-SI2
07ITG Going For Gold World Juniors-28
Autographs-28

Thornton, Michelle

98New Hampshire Wildcats-6

Thornton, Mike

96Dayton Ice Bandits-20
98BC Icemen-20
98BC Icemen II-23

Thornton, Scott

897th Inn. Sketch OHL-83
90Maple Leafs Postcards-21
90Pro Set-640
90Upper Deck-459
French-459
91Bowman-168
91Oilers IGA-24
91Oilers Team Issue-27
91Score Canadian Bilingual-605
91Score Canadian English-605
91Score Rookie/Traded-55T
91Stadium Club-378
91Upper Deck-353
91Upper Deck-521
French-353
French-521
94Leaf-431
94Parkhurst-73
Gold-73
94Upper Deck-426
Electric Ice-426
95Canada Games NHL POGS-112
95Donruss-262
95Panini Stickers-258
95Pinnacle-162
Artist's Proofs-162
Rink Collection-162
95Topps-82
OPC Inserts-82
96Be A Player-153
Autographs-153
Autographs Silver-153
96Canadiens Postcards-30
96Canadiens Sheets-23
97Canadiens Postcards-23
98Canadiens Team Issue-22
98Finest-93
No Protectors-93
No Protectors Refractors-93
Refractors-93
99BAP Millennium-135
Emerald-135
Ruby-135
Sapphire-135
Signatures-135
Signatures Gold-135
99Panini Stickers-70
00BAP Memorabilia-353
Emerald-353
Ruby-353
Sapphire-353
Promos-353
00BAP Mem Chicago Sportsfest Copper-353
00BAP Memorabilia Chicago Sportsfest Blue-353
00BAP Memorabilia Chicago Sportsfest Gold-353
00BAP Memorabilia Chicago Sportsfest Ruby-353
00BAP Memorabilia Chicago Sun-Times Ruby-353
00BAP Memorabilia Chicago Sun-Times Gold-353
00BAP Mem Chicago Sun-Times Sapphire-353
00BAP Mem Toronto Fall Expo Copper-353
00BAP Memorabilia Toronto Fall Expo Gold-353
00BAP Memorabilia Toronto Fall Expo Ruby-353
00O-Pee-Chee-144
00O-Pee-Chee Parallel-144
00Pacific-142
Copper-142
Gold-142
Ice Blue-142
Premiere Date-142
00Stadium Club-225
00Topps/OPC-144
Parallel-144
00Topps Heritage-182
00Upper Deck-375
Exclusives Tier 1-375
Exclusives Tier 2-375
01Pacific-348
Extreme LTD-348
Hobby LTD-348
Premiere Date-348
Retail LTD-348
01Pacific Arena Exclusives-348
01Sharks Postcards-12
01Upper Deck-146
Exclusives-146
01Upper Deck Victory-297
Gold-297
01Upper Deck Vintage-213
02BAP Sig Series Auto Buybacks 1999-135
02Pacific-344
Blue-344
Red-344
02Pacific Complete-325
Red-325
02Pacific Exclusive-153
02Private Stock Reserve-89
Blue-89
Red-89
Retail-89
02Topps Total-295
02Upper Deck-394
Exclusives-394
02Upper Deck Beckett UD Promos-394
02Upper Deck Victory-182
Bronze-182
Gold-182
Silver-182
02Upper Deck Vintage-209
03ITG Action-435
03Pacific Complete-136
Red-136
03Sharks Postcards-19
03Upper Deck-410
Canadian Exclusives-410
HG-410
UD Exclusives-410
04Swedish Pure Skills-87
Parallel-87
05Parkhurst-408
Facsimile Auto Parallel-408
05Upper Deck MVP-326
Gold-326
Platinum-326
05Swedish SHL Elitset Playmakers-11
06O-Pee-Chee-232
Rainbow-232

Thornton, Shawn

95Slapshot-316
97St. John's Maple Leafs-24
99St. John's Maple Leafs-23
00St. John's Maple Leafs-26
01SPx Rookie Redemption-R7
01Norfolk Admirals-20
02BAP All-Star Edition-120
Gold-120
Silver-120
02BAP Memorabilia-291
Emerald-291
Ruby-291
Sapphire-291
NHL All-Star Game-291
NHL All-Star Game Blue-291
NHL All-Star Game Green-291
NHL All-Star Game Red-291
02BAP Memorabilia Toronto Fall Expo-291
02Bowman YoungStars-150
Gold-150
Silver-150
02ITG Used-194
02SP Authentic-139
02Topps Chrome-153
Black Border Refractors-153
Refractors-153
02Topps Heritage-142
02UD Honor Roll-108
02UD Mask Collection-118
02UD Top Shelf-108
02Upper Deck-432
Exclusives-432
02Upper Deck Classic Portraits-107
02Norfolk Admirals-20
03Parkhurst Original Six Chicago-25
03Norfolk Admirals-18
04Norfolk Admirals-18
05Norfolk Admirals-24
06Portland Pirates-17

Thornton, Steven

95Peoria Rivermen-22
96German DEL-180
00UK Cardiff Devils-8
00UK Sekonda Superleague-67
01UK Cardiff Devils-8
01UK London Knights-11
02UK Cardiff Devils-8

Thorp, Ernie

01Rockford IceHogs-6

Thorpe, Matt

66Columbus Checkers-14

Thorpe, Robert

907th Inn. Sketch OHL-122
917th Inn. Sketch OHL-69
96Toledo Storm-33
97Toledo Storm-2

Thorpe, Ryan

98Kamloops Blazers-24
99Spokane Chiefs-26
00Spokane Chiefs-27

Thorpe, Steve

99Memphis RiverKings All-Time-10

Thors, Ulf

71Swedish Hockey-191
72Swedish Stickers-177

Thorsheim, Tai

98Minnesota Golden Gophers Women-24

Thortsen, Mitch

00Sioux City Musketeers-27

Thorwalls, Ola

03Swedish Elite-47
Silver-47
04Swedish Elitset-49
Gold-49

Thrussell, Ryan

97Portland Winter Hawks-19

Thudium, Calvin

87Portland Winter Hawks-20
88Portland Winter Hawks-20
907th Inn. Sketch WHL-212
917th Inn. Sketch Memorial Cup-91

Thulin, Kurt

64Swedish Coralli ISHockey-30
64Swedish Coralli ISHockey-128
65Swedish Coralli ISHockey-30
65Swedish Coralli ISHockey-128
67Swedish Hockey-76

Thun, Christer

65Finnish Hellas-144

Thunderchild, Lenny

04Lethbridge Hurricanes-20

Thunman, Sven

55Swedish Alfabilder-17

Thuot, Francois

03Val d'Or Foreurs-13
04Barrie Colts-18
05Saginaw Spirit-22

Thur, Lubos

94German First League-365

Thuresson, Andreas

06Swedish SHL Elitset-230

Thuresson, Marcus

89Swedish Semic Elitserien Stickers-142
90Swedish Semic Elitserien Stickers-213
91Swedish Semic Elitserien Stickers-140
92Swedish Semic Elitserien Stickers-164
93Swedish Semic Elitserien-133
94Swedish Leaf-29
95Swedish Leaf-226
95Swedish Upper Deck-92
98Swedish UD Choice-158
Day in the Life-8
99Swedish Upper Deck-161
Hands of Gold-11
Hands of Gold-13
00Swedish Upper Deck-142
00Swedish Upper Deck-204
SHL Signatures-MT
02Swedish Malmo Red Hawks-7
02Swedish SHL-72
Parallel-72
Signatures Series II-14
03German DEL-39

Thurier, Fred

34Beehive Group I Photos-256
51Cleveland Barons-7

Thurlby, Tom

61Union Oil WHL-12
Thurner, Michael
94German First League-149
99German DEL-235
Thurstan, Trevor
91Air Canada SJHL-A19
Thurston, Brent
907th Inn. Sketch WHL-204
917th Inn. Sketch Memorial Cup-78
95Vancouver VooDoo RHI-7
Thurston, Brett
98Brandon Wheat Kings-20
99Brandon Wheat Kings-20
00Brandon Wheat Kings-5
01Brandon Wheat Kings-21
02Brandon Wheat Kings-3
Thurston, Eric
81Victoria Cougars-15
82Victoria Cougars-22
83Victoria Cougars-23
Thusberg, Jorma
70Finnish Jaakiekko-116
71Finnish Suomi Stickers-126
72Finnish Jaakiekko-97
72Finnish Panda Toronto-14
73Finnish Jaakiekko-145
Thuss, Chuck
95Louisiana Ice Gators Playoffs-19
95Louisiana Ice Gators Glossy-5
97Mobile Mysticks-1
99Mississippi Sea Wolves-23
99Mississippi Sea Wolves Kelly Cup-24
Thyer, Mario
89ProCards IHL-85
90Score-382
Canadian-382
90ProCards AHL/IHL-119
91ProCards-160
92Cincinnati Cyclones-22
Tiainen, Raimo
66Finnish Jaakiekkosarja-9
Tiainen, Tero
95Finnish SISU-289
96Finnish SISU Redline-87
98Finnish Kerailysarja-26
99Finnish Cardset-16
Tiala, Harri
84Swedish Semic Elitserien-16
Tibbatts, Derek
89Saskatoon Blades-13
90Saskatoon Blades-12
907th Inn. Sketch WHL-79
91Saskatoon Blades-12
917th Inn. Sketch WHL-111
93Saskatoon Blades-19
93Saskatoon Blades-20
Tibbatts, Trent
92Saskatchewan JHL-96
Tibbetts, Bill
93London Knights-20
00SPx Rookie Redemption-RR24
00Wilkes-Barre Scranton Penguins-23
01BAP Memorabilia-242
Emerald-242
Ruby-242
Sapphire-242
01Crown Royale-175
01SPx-122
01Titanium-178
Retail-178
01Titanium Draft Day Edition-158
01UD Top Shelf-63
01UD Top Shelf-63B
01Upper Deck-205
Exclusives-205
01Upper Deck Ice-66
01Upper Deck MVP-213
01Upper Deck Victory-385
Gold-385
02Pacific-288
Blue-288
Red-288
02Hartford Wolf Pack-21
04Idaho Steelheads-7
05Chicago Wolves-22
05Rockford Ice Hogs-15
Tice, Dan
01Sorel Royaux-22
03St. Jean Mission-25
Tichkin, Alexander
00Russian Hockey League-5
Tichy, Marek
94Czech APS Extraliga-235
96Czech APS Extraliga-269
97Czech DS Stickers-175
Tichy, Milan
91ProCards-485
92Indianapolis Ice-23
93PowerPlay-101
93Score-461
Canadian-461
93Ultra-247
All-Rookies-10
93Classic Pro Prospects-25
Tidball, Brandon
03Quebec Remparts-25
04Quebec Remparts-11
Tidball, Curtis
02Quebec Remparts-11
03Quebec Remparts Memorial Cup-21
Tidey, Alex
88Oilers Tenth Anniversary-163
Tidsbury, Shane
92British Columbia JHL-175
Tie, Jussi
95Collector's Choice-325
Player's Club-325
Player's Club Platinum-325
Tiegermann, Pascal
01Swiss HNL-397
02Swiss HNL-385
Tiemonen, Markku
98Danish Hockey League-85
Tiemstra, Darren
01Columbus Cottonmouths-19
02Columbus Cottonmouths-18
Tieranta, Anssi
06Finnish Cardset-347
06Finnish Porin Assat Pelaajakortit-10
Tiesling, Patrick
06Sioux Falls Stampede -2
Tietzen, Dave
98Swiss Power Play Stickers-317
Tifu, Yannick
05Rockford Ice Hogs-16
Tigay, David
93Quebec Pee-Wee Tournament-1306
Tiihonen, Matti
05Finnish Cardset -264
Tiilikainen, Jarno
00Finnish Cardset-289
Tiilikainen, Jukka
93Finnish Jyvas-Hyva Stickers-199
93Finnish SISU-265
94Finnish SISU-227
95Finnish SISU-129
95Finnish Semic World Championships-228
98Finnish Kerailysarja-114
99Finnish Cardset-65
00Finnish Cardset-247
02Swedish SHL-95
Parallel-95
03Finnish Cardset-9
04Finnish Cardset-234
05Swedish SHL Elitset-217
Gold-217
Tiinus, Markku
92Finnish Jyvas-Hyva Stickers-114
Tikhomirov, Vladimir
00Russian Hockey League-275
00Russian Hockey League-297
02Russian Hockey League-156
Tikhonov, Sergei
99Russian Hockey League-233
Tikhonov, Vasily
92Finnish Jyvas-Hyva Stickers-188
95Kansas City Blades-23
01Swiss HNL-190
02Russian Hockey League-162
Tikhonov, Viktor
74Swedish Stickers-80
79Russian National Team-2
84Russian National Team-19
87Russian National Team-20
89Russian National Team-23
89Swedish Semic World Champ Stickers-77
900-Pee-Chee Red Army-17R
92Finnish Semic-98
99Russian Fetisov Tribute-40
02Russian Hockey League-163
02Russian SL-34
03Russian National Team-25
Tikkanen, Esa
85Oilers Red Rooster-10
86Oilers Red Rooster-10
86Oilers Team Issue-10
87Oilers Team Issue-10
870-Pee-Chee-7
870-Pee-Chee Stickers-83
87Panini Stickers-264
87Topps-7
88Oilers Tenth Anniversary-29
88Oilers Team Issue-27
880-Pee-Chee-260
880-Pee-Chee Stickers-220
88Panini Stickers-63
89Kraft-18
89Oilers Team Issue-24
890-Pee-Chee-12
890-Pee-Chee-328
890-Pee-Chee Stickers-219
89Topps-12
89Finnish Pelimiehen-6
90Bowman-194
Tiffany-194
90Oilers IGA-27
900-Pee-Chee-156
90Panini Stickers-223
90Pro Set-97
90Score-13
90Score-342
Canadian-13
Canadian-342
90Score Hottest/Rising Stars-6
90Topps-156
Tiffany-156
90Upper Deck-167
French-167
91Pro Set Platinum-39
91Bowman-98
91Gillette-2
91Oilers Panini Team Stickers-23
91Oilers IGA-25
91Oilers Team Issue-28
910-Pee-Chee-378
91OPC Premier-121
91Panini Stickers-123
91Parkhurst-55
French-55
91Pinnacle-24
French-24
91Pro Set-71
French-71
Awards Special-AC14
91Score American-241
91Score Canadian Bilingual-461
91Score Canadian English-461
91Stadium Club-69
91Topps-378
Team Scoring Leaders-6
91Upper Deck-83
91Upper Deck-182
French-83
French-182
Euro-Stars-10
Euro-Stars French-10
91Finnish Semic World Champ Stickers-203
91Swedish Semic World Champ Stickers-203
92Bowman-144
92Oilers IGA-23
920-Pee-Chee-319
92Panini Stickers-103
92Panini Stickers French-103
92Parkhurst-46
Emerald Ice-46
92Pinnacle-336
French-336
92Pro Set-53
92Score Canadian Promo Sheets-1
92Score-16
Canadian-16
92Stadium Club-104
92Topps-476
Gold-476G
92Ultra-67
92Upper Deck-188
92Finnish Semic-14
93Donruss-215
93Leaf-288
93OPC Premier-282
Gold-282
93Panini Stickers-95
93Parkhurst-135
Emerald Ice-135
93Pinnacle-279
Canadian-279
93PowerPlay-395
Global Greats-9
93Score-97
Canadian-97
93Stadium Club-477
Members Only Master Set-477
First Day Issue-477
Master Photos-13
Master Photos Winners-13
93Topps/OPC Premier-282
Gold-282
93Ultra-377
93Upper Deck-457
SP-104
93Swedish Semic World Champ Stickers-80
94Canada Games NHL POGS-209
94Flair-160
94Fleer-193
94OPC Premier-504
94OPC Premier-528
Special Effects-504
Special Effects-528
94Parkhurst SE-SE157
Gold-SE157
Euro-Stars-ES11
94Pinnacle-174
Artist's Proofs-174
Rink Collection-174
94Score-136
Gold-136
Platinum-136
94SP-103
Die Cuts-103
94Stadium Club-258
Members Only Master Set-258
First Day Issue-258
Super Team Winner Cards-258
94Topps/OPC Premier-504
94Topps/OPC Premier-528
Special Effects-504
Special Effects-528
94Ultra-191
94Upper Deck-42
Electric Ice-42
SP Inserts-SP160
SP Inserts Die Cuts-SP160
94Finnish SISU-276
94Finnish SISU Guest Specials-10
94Finnish Jaa Kiekko-34
94Finnish Jaa Kiekko-349
94Swedish Olympics Lillehammer*-303
95Canada Games NHL POGS-239
95Collector's Choice-268
Player's Club-268
Player's Club Platinum-268
95Donruss-17
95Emotion-153
95Hoyle Western Playing Cards-21
95Leaf-319
95Metal-88
95Panini Stickers-192
95Parkhurst International-173
95Parkhurst International-235
95Parkhurst International-478
Emerald Ice-173
Emerald Ice-235
Emerald Ice-478
95Pinnacle-57
Artist's Proofs-57
Rink Collection-57
Global Gold-10
95Playoff One on One-196
95Pro Magnets-15
95Score-123
Black Ice Artist's Proofs-123
Black Ice-123
95SkyBox Impact-145
95SP-153
95Ultra-143
95Ultra-264
Gold Medallion-143
95Upper Deck-126
Electric Ice-126
Electric Ice Gold-126
Special Edition-SE70
Special Edition-SE137
Special Edition Gold-SE70
Special Edition Gold-SE137
95Finnish Jaa Kiekko Lehti Ad Cards-5
95Finnish SISU Limited-40
Signed and Sealed-8
95Finnish Semic World Championships-43
95Swedish Globe World Championships-138
95Swedish World Championships Stickers-295
96Be A Player-31
Autographs-31
Autographs Silver-31
96Canucks Postcards-10
96Collector's Choice-273
96Maggers-100
96Metal Universe-160
96NHL Pro Stamps-15
96Pinnacle-46
Artist's Proofs-46
Foil-46
Premium Stock-46
Rink Collection-46
96Playoff One on One-392
96Team Out-7
96Ultra-171
Gold Medallion-171
96Upper Deck-352
96Swedish Semic Wien-28
Nordic Stars-NS6
97Esso Olympic Hockey Heroes-49
97Esso Olympic Hockey Heroes French-49
97Pacific-249
Copper-249
Emerald Green-249
Ice Blue-249
Red-249
Silver-249
97Panini Stickers-86
97Paramount-85
Copper-85
Dark Grey-85
Emerald Green-85
Ice Blue-85
Red-85
Silver-85
97Score-236
97Upper Deck-111
98McDonalds Upper Deck Gretzkys Teammates-T6
98Pacific-448
Ice Blue-448
Red-448
98Pacific Omega-162
Red-162
Opening Day Issue-162
98Panini Stickers-109
98Finnish Kerailysarja Leijonat-43
99Finnish Cardset-265
Aces High-S-K
00Finnish Cardset-240
00German DEL-170
Star Attractions-S6
02Finnish Cardset-125
04ITG Franchises Canadian-20
04ITG Franchises Update Autographs-ET
06ITG International Ice-86
06ITG International Ice-141
Gold-86
Gold-141
Autographs-AET
Autographs-AET2
Cornerstones-IC04
Cornerstones Gold-IC04
Tikkanen, Harri
98Finnish Kerailysarja-186
99Finnish Cardset-107
00Finnish Cardset-321
01Finnish Cardset-108
02Finnish Cardset-126
04Finnish Cardset-284
05Finnish Cardset -125
06Finnish Cardset-135
Tiley, Brad
89Sault Ste. Marie Greyhounds-20
907th Inn. Sketch OHL-173
91ProCards-61
917th Inn. Sketch Memorial Cup-6
92Phoenix Roadrunners-22
93Phoenix Roadrunners-23
93Classic Pro Prospects-129
94Anaheim Bullfrogs RHI-18
94Detroit Vipers Pogs-3
97Springfield Falcons-22
99AHL All-Stars-9
02Philadelphia Phantoms-19
03Milwaukee Admirals-11
03Milwaukee Admirals Postcards-21
04AHL All-Stars-43
04Milwaukee Admirals-3
05Springfield Falcons-3
06German DEL-115
New Arrivals-NA13
Tillander, Kurt
69Swedish Hockey-217
Tilley, Steve
03P.E.I. Rocket-23
Tilley, Tom
87Blues Team Issue-23
88Blues Kodak-23
88Blues Team Issue-23
89Blues Kodak-20
89Panini Stickers-128
900-Pee-Chee-498
90ProCards AHL/IHL-83
91Bowman-377
93Parkhurst-442
Emerald Ice-442
93Upper Deck-491
95Milwaukee Admirals-17
96Milwaukee Admirals-24
96Collector's Edge Future Legends-43
98Chicago Wolves-22
98Chicago Wolves Turner Cup-17
98IHL All-Star Western Conference-7
99Chicago Wolves-14
00Chicago Wolves-22
Tilson, Michael
92Quebec Pee-Wee Tournament-1111
95Slapshot-110
97Sudbury Wolves Police-19
99Fort Worth Brahmas-19
00Fort Worth Brahmas-15
01Fort Worth Brahmas-15
Tiltgen, Dean
907th Inn. Sketch WHL-104
917th Inn. Sketch WHL-289
Timakov, Stanislav
00Russian Hockey League-204
01Russian Hockey League-35
Timander, Mattias
92Swedish Semic Elitserien Stickers-233
93Swedish Semic Elitserien-197
94Swedish Leaf-179
95Swedish Leaf-101
Face to Face-10
95Swedish Upper Deck-153
Ticket to North America-NA19
96Black Diamond-47
Gold-47
96Donruss Canadian Ice-138
Gold Press Proofs-138
Red Press Proofs-138
96Donruss Elite-135
Die Cut Stars-135
96Flair-101
Blue Ice-101
96Leaf Preferred-120
Press Proofs-120
96Select Certified-99
Artist's Proofs-99
Blue-99
Mirror Blue-99
Mirror Gold-99
Mirror Red-99
Red-99
96SP-170
96Upper Deck-220
96Zenith-134
Artist's Proofs-134
97Be A Player-151
Autographs-151
Autographs Die-Cuts-151
Autographs Prismatic Die-Cuts-151
97Pacific-235
Copper-235
Emerald Green-235
Ice Blue-235
Red-235
Silver-235
97Panini Stickers-5
97Upper Deck-224
98Providence Bruins-21
00BAP Signature Series-117
Emerald-117
Ruby-117
Sapphire-117
Autographs-172
Autographs Gold-172
00Panini Stickers-140
01Blue Jackets Donatos Pizza-6
02Upper Deck-358
Exclusives-358
02Upper Deck Beckett UD Promos-358
03Pacific Complete-89
Red-89
04Swedish Elitset-237
Gold-237
04Swedish MoDo Postcards-6
04Swedish Pure Skills-63
Parallel-63
05Be A Player Signatures-TI
05Be A Player Signatures Gold-TI
05Swedish SHL Elitset-242
Gold-242
06Swedish SHL Elitset-103
Timchenko, Oleg
98Bowman CHL-105
Golden Anniversary-105
OPC International-105
98Bowman Chrome CHL-105
Golden Anniversary-105
Golden Anniversary Refractors-105
OPC International-105
OPC International Refractors-105
Refractors-105
99Greensboro Generals-4
Timchenko, Vyacheslav
98Russian Hockey League-117
Timewell, Jason
91British Columbia JHL-67
Timgren, Ray
44Beehive Group II Photos-458
45Quaker Oats Photos-57A
45Quaker Oats Photos-57B
48Exhibits Canadian-40
51Parkhurst-78
54Topps-13
02Parkhurst Reprints-161
Timmer, Bernd
94German First League-641
Timmins, Scott
06Kitchener Rangers-4
Timmins, Sean
91Air Canada SJHL-D26
Timmons, Brad
98Minnesota Golden Gophers-24
Timmons, K.C.
98Tri-City Americans-14
00Hershey Bears-18
01Hershey Bears-27
02Hershey Bears-23
Timms, Michael
01UK Guildford Flames-19
03UK Guildford Flames-8
Timofeev, Boris
95Swedish World Championships Stickers-37
Timofeev, Denis
99Providence Bruins-23
Timofeev, Dmitri
01Russian Hockey League-36
Timonen, Jussi
02Finnish Cardset Bound for Glory-9
02Finnish Cardset Signatures-9
04Finnish Cardset-138
Parallel-102
05Finnish Cardset -124
06Hot Prospects-171
Red Hot-171
White Hot-171
060-Pee-Chee-591
Rainbow-591
06SP Authentic-225
Limited-225
06The Cup-147
Autographed Rookie Masterpiece Pressplates-147
Gold Rainbow Autographed Rookie Patches-147
Masterpiece Pressplates (Marquee Rookies)-591
Masterpiece Pressplates (SP Authentic)-225
Masterpiece Pressplates (Sweet Beginnings)-141
Masterpiece Pressplates (Ultimate Collection)-87
Rookies Black-147
Rookies Platinum-147
06Ultimate Collection-87
06Upper Deck-480
Exclusives Parallel-480
High Gloss Parallel-480
Masterpieces-480
06Upper Deck Sweet Shot-141
Rookie Jerseys Autographs-141
06Finnish Cardset-134
06Philadelphia Phantoms-26
Timonen, Kimmo
93Upper Deck-268
93Finnish Jyvas-Hyva Stickers-165
93Finnish SISU-163
93Finnish SISU-396
94Finest-129
Super Team Winners-129
Refractors-129
94Parkhurst SE-SE218
Gold-SE218
94SP-160
Die Cuts-160
94Upper Deck-510
Electric Ice-510
94Finnish SISU-304
95Finnish SISU-123
Double Trouble-1
95Finnish SISU Limited-65
95Finnish Semic World Championships-10
95Finnish Semic World Championships-233
96Finnish SISU Redline-182
98Pacific Omega-134
Red-134
Opening Day Issue-134
98Predators Team Issue-20
98Finnish Kerailysarja Leijonat-17
98IHL All-Star Western Conference-13
98Milwaukee Admirals Postcards-9
99BAP Memorabilia-397
Gold-397
Silver-397
99Panini Stickers-265
99Upper Deck-74
Exclusives-74
Exclusives 1 of 1-74
99Upper Deck Gold Reserve-74
99Upper Deck MVP-111
Gold Script-111
Silver Script-111
Super Script-111
99Upper Deck Victory-159
99Wayne Gretzky Hockey-93
99Finnish Cardset-188
Aces High-S-5
Blazing Patriots-3
00BAP Memorabilia-56
Emerald-56
Ruby-56
Sapphire-56
Promos-56
00BAP Mem Chicago Sportsfest Copper-56
00BAP Memorabilia Chicago Sportsfest Blue-56
00BAP Memorabilia Chicago Sportsfest Gold-56
00BAP Memorabilia Chicago Sportsfest Ruby-56
00BAP Memorabilia Chicago Sun-Times Ruby-56
00BAP Memorabilia Chicago Sun-Times Gold-56
00BAP Mem Chicago Sun-Times Sapphire-56
00BAP Mem Toronto Fall Expo Copper-56
00BAP Memorabilia Toronto Fall Expo Gold-56
00BAP Memorabilia Toronto Fall Expo Ruby-56
00BAP Parkhurst 2000-P5
00BAP Signature Series-35
Emerald-35
Ruby-35
Sapphire-35
Autographs-103
Autographs Gold-103
00Pacific-226
Copper-226
Gold-226
Ice Blue-226
Premiere Date-226
00Panini Stickers-184
00Stadium Club-197
00Titanium Draft Day Edition-57
00Topps Stars-63
Blue-63
00Upper Deck-101
Exclusives Tier 1-101
Exclusives Tier 2-101
00Upper Deck Victory-131
00Upper Deck Vintage-206
00Vanguard Dual Game-Worn Jerseys-12
00Vanguard Dual Game-Worn Patches-12
00Finnish Cardset-352
01Pacific Adrenaline Jerseys-24
01Upper Deck-100
Exclusives-100
01Upper Deck MVP-107
01Upper Deck Victory-197
Gold-197
01Finnish Cardset-162
01Finnish Cardset Salt Lake City-4
02BAP Signature Series-34
Autographs-34
Autograph Buybacks 2000-103
Autographs Gold-34
020-Pee-Chee-252
020-Pee-Chee Premier Blue Parallel-252
020-Pee-Chee Premier Red Parallel-252
020-Pee-Chee Factory Set-252
02Pacific-214
Blue-214
Red-214
02Pacific Complete-41
Red-41
02Predators Team Issue-5
02Topps-252
OPC Blue Parallel-252
OPC Red Parallel-252
Factory Set-252
02Topps Total-331
02Upper Deck-345
Exclusives-345
02Upper Deck Beckett UD Promos-345
02Upper Deck MVP-100
Gold-100
Classics-100
Golden Classics-100
02Upper Deck Victory-120
Bronze-120
Gold-120
Silver-120
02Upper Deck Vintage-143
02Finnish Cardset-278
03ITG Action-346
03NHL Sticker Collection-259
030-Pee-Chee-161
03OPC Blue-161
03OPC Gold-161
03OPC Red-161
03Pacific-192
Blue-192
Red-192
03Pacific Complete-27
Red-27
03Topps-161
Blue-161
Gold-161
Red-161
03Upper Deck-354
Canadian Exclusives-354
HG-354
UD Exclusives-354
03Upper Deck MVP-236
Gold Script-236
Silver Script-236
Canadian Exclusives-236
05Be A Player World Cup Salute-WCS6
05Panini Stickers-310
05Parkhurst-273
Facsimile Auto Parallel-273
05SP Game Used Statscriptions-ST-KT
05Ultra-114
Gold-114
Ice-114
05Upper Deck-358
Notable Numbers-N-KT
05Upper Deck MVP-225
Gold-225
Platinum-225
05Upper Deck Victory-113
Black-113
Gold-113
Silver-113
06Be A Player-22
Autographs-22
Signatures-KT
Signatures 25-24
Up Close and Personal-UC55
Up Close and Personal Autographs-UC55
06Black Diamond Gemography-GKT
060-Pee-Chee-283
Rainbow-283
06Panini Stickers-311
06Ultra-114
Gold Medallion-114
Ice Medallion-114
06Upper Deck Arena Giveaways-NSH3
06Upper Deck-111
Exclusives Parallel-111
High Gloss Parallel-111
Masterpieces-111
Signature Sensations-SSKT
Victory-113
Victory Black-113
Victory Gold-113
07Upper Deck Ovation-20
07Upper Deck Victory-108
Black-108
Gold-108
Timosaari, Ari
70Finnish Jaakiekko-381
71Finnish Suomi Stickers-315
80Finnish Mallasjuoma-108
Timoschuk, Roland
94German DEL-186
95German DEL-186
96German DEL-125
99German Bundesliga 2-205
Tinordi, Mark
90Pro Set-145
90Score-304A
Canadian-304A
91Pro Set Platinum-58
91Bowman-124
91Kraft-22
910-Pee-Chee-308
91Panini Stickers-109
91Parkhurst-304
French-304
91Pinnacle-199
French-199
91Pro Set-107
91Pro Set-575
French-107
French-575
91Score American-93
91Score Canadian Bilingual-93
91Score Canadian English-93
91Score Young Superstars-18
91Stadium Club-392
91Topps-308
91Upper Deck-295
French-295
92Bowman-218
92Bowman-399
92Humpty Dumpty I-23
920-Pee-Chee-17
92Panini Stickers-97
92Panini Stickers French-97
92Parkhurst-76
Emerald Ice-76
92Pinnacle-18
92Pinnacle-252
French-18
French-252
92Pro Set-78
92Score-7
Canadian-7
92Stadium Club-435
92Topps-4
Gold-4G
92Ultra-98
92Upper Deck-73
92Finnish Semic-83
93Donruss-79
93Kraft-40
93Leaf-146
93OPC Premier-24
Gold-24
93Panini Stickers-275
93Parkhurst-320
Emerald Ice-320
93Pinnacle-16
Canadian-16
Captains-6
Captains Canadian-6
93PowerPlay-66
93Score-53
Canadian-53
93Stadium Club-384
Members Only Master Set-384
First Day Issue-384
93Topps/OPC Premier-24
Gold-24
93Ultra-213
93Upper Deck-89
94Canada Games NHL POGS-85
94Donruss-206
94EA Sports-31
94Finest-25
Super Team Winners-25
Refractors-25
94Flair-45
94Fleer-239
94Leaf-91
94OPC Premier-24
94OPC Premier-452
Special Effects-24
Special Effects-452
94Parkhurst-59
Gold-59
94Pinnacle-29
Artist's Proofs-29
Rink Collection-29
94Score-68
Gold-68
Platinum-68
94Stars HockeyKaps-23
94Stars Score Sheet-68
94Topps/OPC Premier-24
94Topps/OPC Premier-452
Special Effects-24
Special Effects-452
94Ultra-57
94Upper Deck-369
Electric Ice-369
SP Inserts-SP177
SP Inserts Die Cuts-SP177
94Finnish Jaa Kiekko-82
95Be A Player-220
Signatures-S220
Signatures Die Cuts-S220
95Canada Games NHL POGS-284
95Capitals Team Issue-26
95Collector's Choice-141
Player's Club-141
Player's Club Platinum-141
95Donruss-255
95Panini Stickers-144
95Parkhurst International-224
Emerald Ice-224
95Pinnacle Full Contact-10
95Playoff One on One-215
95Score-144
Black Ice Artist's Proofs-144
Black Ice-144
95Stadium Club Members Only-21
95Stadium Club-67
Members Only Master Set-67
95Summit-93
Artist's Proofs-93
Ice-93
95Topps-198
OPC Inserts-198
95Ultra-178
Gold Medallion-178
95Upper Deck-94
Electric Ice-94
Electric Ice Gold-94
95Finnish Semic World Championships-84
95Swedish Globe World Championships-80
96Donruss-153
Press Proofs-153
96Leaf-31
Press Proofs-31
96Score-11
Artist's Proofs-11
Dealer's Choice Artist's Proofs-11
Special Artist's Proofs-11
Golden Blades-11
96Upper Deck Ice-74
Parallel-74
97Pacific-181
Copper-181
Emerald Green-181
Ice Blue-181
Red-181
Silver-181
97Upper Deck-385
98OPC Chrome-157
Refractors-157
98Pacific-449
Ice Blue-449
Red-449
98Topps-157
O-Pee-Chee-157
04UD Legendary Signatures-98
Autographs-MT
Rearguard Retrospectives-CHMT
Tipler, Curtis
95Bowman Draft Prospects-P33
96Regina Pats-2
98Prince George Cougars-21
99Rockford IceHogs-20
Tipler, Travis
98Wichita Thunder-22
99Wichita Thunder-21
Tipoff, Matthew
06Belleville Bulls-14
Tipper, Kevin
05Prince Albert Raiders-22
Tippett, Brad
907th Inn. Sketch WHL-182
917th Inn. Sketch WHL-241
Tippett, Dave
84Whalers Junior Wendy's-19
85Whalers Junior Wendy's-20
860-Pee-Chee-148
86Topps-148
86Whalers Junior Thomas'-21
870-Pee-Chee-86
87Panini Stickers-51
87Topps-86
87Whalers Jr. Burger King/Pepsi-19
880-Pee-Chee-85
88Panini Stickers-244
88Topps-85
88Whalers Junior Ground Round-16
890-Pee-Chee-134
890-Pee-Chee Stickers-268
89Panini Stickers-226
89Topps-134
89Whalers Junior Milk-20
90Capitals Kodak-25
90Capitals Postcards-22
90Capitals Smokey-22
900-Pee-Chee-183
90OPC Premier-119
90Panini Stickers-37
90Pro Set-111
90Pro Set-555
90Score-192
Canadian-192
90Score Rookie/Traded-29T
90Topps-183
Tiffany-183
90Upper Deck-270
French-270
91Capitals Junior 5x7-25
91Capitals Kodak-25
91Score American-437
91Score Canadian Bilingual-409
91Score Canadian English-409
91Upper Deck-480
French-480
92Parkhurst-372
Emerald Ice-372
92Penguins Coke/Clark-23
92Penguins Foodland-16
93Flyers J.C. Penney-22
93Flyers Lineup Sheets-33
93Leaf-349
93OPC Premier-387
Gold-387
93Panini Stickers-85
93PowerPlay-410
93Score-584
Gold-584
Canadian-584
Canadian Gold-584
93Stadium Club-124
Members Only Master Set-124
OPC-124
First Day Issue-124
First Day Issue OPC-124
93Topps/OPC Premier-387
Gold-387
95Houston Aeros-24
98IHL All-Star Western Conference-22
06Stars Team Postcards-25
06Houston Aeros RetroÂ -10
Tirkkonen, Antti
95Finnish SISU-342
Tirkkonen, Heikki
70Finnish Jaakiekko-268
Tirkkonen, Paavo
66Finnish Jaakiekkosarja-128
70Finnish Jaakiekko-269
Tirkkonen, Pekka
91Finnish Jyvas-Hyva Stickers-32
92Finnish Jyvas-Hyva Stickers-96
93Finnish Jyvas-Hyva Stickers-168
93Finnish SISU-178
93Finnish SISU Autographs-178
93Finnish SISU Promos-NNO
94Finnish SISU-40
94Finnish SISU-171
94Finnish Jaa Kiekko-25
95Finnish SISU-80
95Finnish SISU Limited-70
96German DEL-197
98Finnish Kerailysarja-151
99Finnish Cardset-310
00Finnish Cardset-79
01Finnish Cardset-115
02Finnish Cardset-279
03Swedish Elite-218
Silver-218
Tisdale, Dory
01El Paso Buzzards-13
Tisdale, Tim
89ProCards AHL-142
90ProCards AHL/IHL-227
92Wheeling Thunderbirds-17
93Wheeling Thunderbirds-PC3
93Wheeling Thunderbirds-UD2
94Fredericton Canadiens-28
94Wheeling Thunderbirds-2
94Wheeling Thunderbirds Photo Album-13
95Wheeling Thunderbirds-21
95Wheeling Thunderbirds Series II-16
Titov, Alexander
99Russian Hockey League-119
03Russian Hockey League-141
Titov, German
92Finnish Jyvas-Hyva Stickers-185
93Donruss-56
93Leaf-309
93Parkhurst-255
Emerald Ice-255
93PowerPlay-310
93Score-614
Gold-614
Canadian-614
Canadian Gold-614
93Stadium Club-364
Members Only Master Set-364
First Day Issue-364
93Upper Deck-476
93Finnish SISU-376
93Finnish SISU Promos-NNO
93Classic-94

94Donruss-228
94Finest-75
Super Team Winners-75
Refractors-75
94Flair-29
94Fleer-36
94Leaf-261
94OPC Premier-9
Special Effects-9
94Parkhurst SE-SE26
Gold-SE26
94Pinnacle-167
Artist's Proofs-167
Rink Collection-167
94Score-95
Gold-95
Platinum-95
94SP-18
Die Cuts-18
94Topps/OPC Premier-9
Special Effects-9
94Ultra-36
94Upper Deck-2
Electric Ice-2
94Finnish SISU-361
94Finnish SISU Guest Specials-11
95Canada Games NHL POGS-50
95Collector's Choice-15
Player's Club-15
Player's Club Platinum-15
95Donruss-229
95Donruss Elite-41
Die Cut Stars-41
Die Cut Uncut-41
95Hoyle Western Playing Cards-22
95Leaf-31
95Panini Stickers-234
95Parkhurst International-28
Emerald Ice-28
95Pinnacle-52
Artist's Proofs-52
Rink Collection-52
Global Gold-9
95Playoff One on One-20
95Pro Magnets-50
95Score-71
Black Ice Artist's Proofs-71
Black Ice-71
95SkyBox Impact-25
95SP-18
95Upper Deck-207
Electric Ice-207
Electric Ice Gold-207
Special Edition-SE14
Special Edition Gold-SE14
96Be A Player-49
Autographs-49
Autographs Silver-49
96Collector's Choice-39
96Donruss-58
Press Proofs-58
96Fleer-14
96Fleer Picks-106
96Maggers-101
96Metal Universe-23
96NHL Pro Stamps-50
96Pinnacle-36
Artist's Proofs-36
Foil-36
Premium Stock-36
Rink Collection-36
96Playoff One on One-354
96Score-165
Artist's Proofs-165
Dealer's Choice Artist's Proofs-165
Special Artist's Proofs-165
Golden Blades-165
96SkyBox Impact-15
96SP-24
96Summit-108
Artist's Proofs-108
Ice-108
Metal-108
Premium Stock-108
96Ultra-27
Gold Medallion-27
96Upper Deck-227
96Swedish Semic Wien-154
97Collector's Choice-39
97Pacific-263
Copper-263
Emerald Green-263
Ice Blue-263
Red-263
Silver-263
97Pacific Dynagon-19
Copper-19
Dark Grey-19
Emerald Green-19
Ice Blue-19
Red-19
Silver-19
Tandems-34
97Pacific Invincible-21
Copper-21
Emerald Green-21
Ice Blue-21
Red-21
Silver-21
97Pacific Omega-37
Copper-37
Dark Gray-37
Emerald Green-37
Gold-37
Ice Blue-37
97Panini Stickers-192
97Paramount-32
Copper-32
Dark Grey-32
Emerald Green-32
Ice Blue-32
Red-32
Silver-32
97Pinnacle Certified-88
Red-88
Mirror Blue-88
Mirror Gold-88
Mirror Red-88
97Pinnacle Tot Cert Platinum Blue-88
97Pinnacle Tot Certi Platinum Gold-88
97Pinnacle Totally Certified Platinum Red-88
97Pinnacle Tot Cert Mirror Platinum Gold-88
97Score-197
97SP Authentic-22
98Be A Player-262
Press Release-262
98BAP Gold-262
98BAP Autographs-262
98BAP Autographs Gold-262
98Black Diamond-70
Double Diamond-70
Triple Diamond-70
Quadruple Diamond-70
98Crown Royale-112
Limited Series-112
98Pacific-127
Ice Blue-127
Red-127
98Panini Stickers-178
98SP Authentic-68
Power Shift-68
98UD Choice-30
Prime Choice Reserve-30
Reserve-30
98Upper Deck-346
Exclusives-346
Exclusives 1 of 1-346
Gold Reserve-346
98Upper Deck MVP-169
Gold Script-169
Silver Script-169
Super Script-169
99BAP Memorabilia-96
Gold-96
Silver-96
99Pacific-348
Copper-348
Emerald Green-348
Gold-348
Ice Blue-348
Premiere Date-348
Red-348
99Pacific Dynagon Ice-164
Blue-164
Copper-164
Gold-164
Premiere Date-164
99Pacific Omega-192
Copper-192
Gold-192
Ice Blue-192
Premiere Date-192
99Panini Stickers-139
99Paramount-193
Copper-193
Emerald-193
Gold-193
Holographic Emerald-193
Holographic Gold-193
Holographic Silver-193
Ice Blue-193
Premiere Date-193
Red-193
Silver-193
99SPx-123
Radiance-123
Spectrum-123
99Upper Deck MVP-167
Gold Script-167
Silver Script-167
Super Script-167
99Upper Deck Victory-242
00BAP Memorabilia-407
Emerald-407
Ruby-407
Sapphire-407
00O-Pee-Chee-143
00O-Pee-Chee Parallel-143
00Pacific-175
Copper-175
Gold-175
Ice Blue-175
Premiere Date-175
00Panini Stickers-159
00Topps/OPC-143
Parallel-143
00Upper Deck-233
Exclusives Tier 1-233
Exclusives Tier 2-233
00Upper Deck Vintage-1
02BAP Sig Series Auto Buybacks 1998-262
02Pacific-9
Blue-9
Red-9
03Russian Hockey League-99

Titus, Scott

99Ohio State Buckeyes-18
00Ohio State Buckeyes-6
01Ohio State Buckeyes-17
02Ohio State Buckeyes-14

Titus, Stephen

86London Knights-27

Titzhoff, Guido

94German First League-586

Tiumenev, Viktor

81Swedish Semic Hockey VM Stickers-48
87Russian National Team-21

Tjallden, Mikael

92Swedish Semic Elitserien Stickers-352
98Finnish Kerailysarja-170
00UK Sekonda Superleague-75
00UK Sekonda Superleague-191

Tjarnqvist, Daniel

93Swedish Semic Elitserien-226
93Swedish Semic Elitserien-314
94Swedish Leaf-209
Rookie Rockets-6
95SP-186
95Swedish Leaf-116
95Swedish Upper Deck-175
95Signature Rookies-49
Signatures-49
97Swedish Collector's Choice-40
Crash the Game Exchange-C3
Crash the Game Redemption-R3
Stick'Ums-S14
98Swedish UD Choice-53
99Swedish Upper Deck-39
00Swedish Upper Deck-49
01BAP Signature Series-202
Autographs-202
Autographs Gold-202
01Parkhurst-300
01Parkhurst Beckett Promos-300
01Titanium Draft Day Edition-109
02BAP Sig Series Auto Buybacks 2001-202
02Pacific-22
Blue-22
Red-22
02Upper Deck Vintage-16
03ITG Action-13
03Pacific Complete-196
Red-196
03Thrashers Postcards-22
04Swedish Alfabilder Alfa Stars-36
04Swedish Alfabilder Autographs-126
04Swedish Alfabilder Limited Autographs-126
04Swedish Alfabilder Proof Parallels-36
04Swedish Djurgardens Postcards-10
04Swedish Elitset-159
Dominators-8
Gold-159
04Swedish Pure Skills-9
Parallel-9
Professional Power-DT
05Swedish SHL Elitset-15

Tjarnqvist, Mathias

98Black Diamond-113
Double Diamond-113
Triple Diamond-113
Quadruple Diamond-113
98SPx Top Prospects-83
Radiance-83
Spectrum-83
99Swedish Upper Deck-48
99Swedish Upper Deck-203
00Swedish Upper Deck-54
03Stars Postcards-25
03Swedish Elite-19
Silver-19
04Swedish Elitset-197
Gold-197
Signatures Series B-8
05Iowa Stars-15

Tjernstrom, Leif

69Swedish Hockey-92

Tjitjurin, Juri

73Swedish Stickers-136
74Swedish Stickers-56

Tkach, Stanislav

92Nashville Knights-9
95Madison Monsters-18

Tkachenko, Ivan

00Russian Hockey League-389
02Russian World Championships-5

Tkachenko, Sergei

95Central Hockey League-53
96Louisiana Ice Gators II-18
97Anchorage Aces-20
98Anchorage Aces-9

Tkachuck, Pete

51Laval Dairy QSHL-34

Tkachuk, Alexei

98Russian Hockey League-100
99Russian Hockey League-215
99Russian Stars Postcards-27
00Russian Hockey League-261

Tkachuk, Grant

84Saskatoon Blades Stickers-18
86Saskatoon Blades Photos-22
88ProCards AHL-251
89ProCards IHL-105
90ProCards AHL/IHL-281

Tkachuk, Keith

91Parkhurst-424
French-424
91Upper Deck-698
French-698
91Upper Deck Czech World Juniors-85
92O-Pee-Chee-346
92OPC Premier-43
92Parkhurst-206
Emerald Ice-206
92Pinnacle-222
French-222
92Pro Set-243
92Score-450
Canadian-450
Young Superstars-29
92Stadium Club-116
92Topps-102
Gold-102G
92Ultra-446
92Upper Deck-364
92Upper Deck-398
92Upper Deck-419
Ameri/Can Holograms-2
Calder Candidates-CC15
Gordie Howe Selects-G18
93Donruss-390
93Jets Readers Club-20
93Jets Ruffles-25
93Leaf-105
Gold Rookies-11
93OPC Premier-27
93OPC Premier-502
Gold-27
Gold-502
93Panini Stickers-193
93Parkhurst-228
Emerald Ice-228
93Pinnacle-33
Canadian-33
Captains-26
Captains Canadian-26
93PowerPlay-276
Rising Stars-8
93Score-195
Canadian-195
93Stadium Club-135
Members Only Master Set-135
OPC-135
First Day Issue-135
First Day Issue OPC-135
93Topps/OPC Premier-27
93Topps/OPC Premier-502
Gold-27
Gold-502
93Ultra-111
93Upper Deck-195
Next In Line-NL5
SP-178
94Be A Player-R36
94Canada Games NHL POGS-256
94Donruss-192
94Finest-19
Super Team Winners-19
Refractors-19
Bowman's Best-B17
Bowman's Best Refractors-B17
94Flair-211
94Fleer-246
Franchise Futures-8
94Kraft-29
94Leaf-94
94Leaf Limited-108
94OPC Premier-242
94OPC Premier-300
Special Effects-242
Special Effects-300
94Parkhurst-264
Gold-264
SE Vintage-38
94Pinnacle-103
Artist's Proofs-103
Rink Collection-103
Gamers-GR18
Northern Lights-NL12
94Score Check It-CI14
94Select-75
Gold-75
94SP-132
Die Cuts-132
94Stadium Club-5
Members Only Master Set-5
First Day Issue-5
Super Team Winner Cards-5
94Topps/OPC Premier-242
94Topps/OPC Premier-300
Special Effects-242
Special Effects-300
94Topps Finest Inserts-18
94Ultra-247
Power-10
94Upper Deck-145
Electric Ice-145
SP Inserts-SP89
SP Inserts Die Cuts-SP89
95Bashan Super Stickers-136
95Be A Player-215
Signatures-S215
Signatures Die Cuts-S215
Lethal Lines-LL1
95Bowman-69
All-Foil-69
95Canada Games NHL POGS-16
95Canada Games NHL POGS-293
95Collector's Choice-168
95Collector's Choice-356
95Collector's Choice-382
Player's Club-168
Player's Club-356
Player's Club-382
Player's Club Platinum-168
Player's Club Platinum-356
Player's Club Platinum-382
95Donruss-78
Pro Pointers-7
95Donruss Elite-81
Die Cut Stars-81
Die Cut Uncut-81
95Emotion-197
Ntense Power-9
95Finest-123
Refractors-123
95Hoyle Western Playing Cards-23
95Imperial Stickers-136
95Jets Readers Club-11
95Jets Team Issue-24
95Kraft-48
95Leaf-79
95Leaf Limited-57
95Metal-166
Iron Warriors-14
95NHL Aces Playing Cards-11S
95Panini Stickers-214
95Parkhurst International-501
Emerald Ice-501
95Pinnacle Full Contact-11
95Playoff One on One-109
95Playoff One on One-220
95Post Upper Deck-23
95Pro Magnets-64
95Score Promos-33
95Score-33
Black Ice Artist's Proofs-33
Black Ice-33
Check It-11
95Select Certified-37
Mirror Gold-37
Double Strike-17
Double Strike Gold-17
95SkyBox Impact-185
95SkyBox Impact-239
95SP-164
Stars/Etoiles-E30
Stars/Etoiles Gold-E30
95Stadium Club Members Only-39
95Stadium Club-90
Members Only Master Set-90
Fearless-F9
Fearless Members Only Master Set-F9
95Summit-152
Artist's Proofs-152
Ice-152
GM's Choice-6
95Topps-152
OPC Inserts-152
Home Grown USA-HGA5
Mystery Finest-M14
Mystery Finest Refractors-M14
Power Lines-2PL
Rink Leaders-7RL
95Topps SuperSkills-51
Platinum-51
95Ultra-184
Gold Medallion-184
Crease Crashers-20
95Upper Deck-243
95Upper Deck-464
Electric Ice-243
Electric Ice-464
Electric Ice Gold-243
Electric Ice Gold-464
Special Edition-SE88
Special Edition Gold-SE88
95Zenith-74
Gifted Grinders-1
96Headliners Hockey-20
96Be A Player Biscuit In The Basket-6
96Black Diamond-153
Gold-153
96Collector's Choice-201
96Collector's Choice-295
96Collector's Choice-327
MVP-UD16
MVP Gold-UD16
Crash the Game-C26A
Crash the Game-C26B
Crash the Game-C26C
Crash the Game Gold-C26A
Crash the Game Gold-C26B
Crash the Game Gold-C26C
Crash the Game Exchange-CR26
Crash the Game Exchange Gold-CR26
96Coyotes Coca-Cola-30
96Coyotes Coca-Cola-31
96Donruss-134
Press Proofs-134
Dominators-8
Hit List-10
96Donruss Canadian Ice-22
Gold Press Proofs-22
Red Press Proofs-22
96Donruss Elite-61
Die Cut Stars-61
Status-2
96Duracell All-Cherry Team-DC18
96Duracell L'Equipe Beliveau-JB18
96Flair-73
Blue Ice-73
96Fleer-92
96Fleer-141
Art Ross-22
96Fleer Picks-18
Captain's Choice-7
Dream Lines-5
Fabulous 50-44
96Kraft Upper Deck-2
96Leaf-133
Press Proofs-133
96Leaf Leather And Laces Promos-P2
96Leaf Leather And Laces-2
96Leaf The Best Of...-5
96Leaf Limited-3
Gold-3
96Leaf Limited Bash the Boards Promos-P5
96Leaf Limited Bash The Boards-5
96Leaf Limited Bash The Boards Ltd Ed-5
96Leaf Preferred-89
96Leaf Preferred-148
Press Proofs-89
Press Proofs-148
Vanity Plates-12
Vanity Plates Gold-12
96Metal Universe-122
Cool Steel-11
Cool Steel Super Power-11
Lethal Weapons-19
Lethal Weapons Super Power-19
96NHL Aces Playing Cards-47
96NHL Pro Stamps-64
96Pinnacle-114
Artist's Proofs-114
Foil-114
Premium Stock-114
Rink Collection-114
96Pinnacle Mint-19
Bronze-19
Gold-19
Silver-19
Coins Brass-19
Coins Solid Gold-19
Coins Gold Plated-19
Coins Nickel-19
Coins Silver-19
96Playoff One on One-351
96Score-47
Artist's Proofs-47
Dealer's Choice Artist's Proofs-47
Special Artist's Proofs-47
Check It-3
Golden Blades-47
96Select Certified-24
Artist's Proofs-24
Blue-24
Mirror Blue-24
Mirror Gold-24
Mirror Red-24
Red-24
Cornerstones-10
96SkyBox Impact-107
BladeRunners-22
96SP-118
Inside Info-IN2
Inside Info Gold-IN2
Game Film-GF5
96SPx-35
Gold-35
96Summit-104
Artist's Proofs-104
Ice-104
Metal-104
Premium Stock-104
96Team Out-14
96Ultra-136
Gold Medallion-136
Clear the Ice-10
96Upper Deck-313
Generation Next-X15
Hart Hopefuls Bronze-HH8
Hart Hopefuls Gold-HH8
Hart Hopefuls Silver-HH8
Lord Stanley's Heroes Finals-LS17
Lord Stanley's Heroes Quarterfinals-LS17
Lord Stanley's Heroes Semifinals-LS17
Superstar Showdown-SS6A
96Upper Deck Ice-100
Parallel-100
Stanley Cup Foundation-S8
Stanley Cup Foundation Dynasty-S8
96Zenith-6
Artist's Proofs-6
Z-Team-12
96Swedish Semic Wien-168
97SLU Hockey Canadian-18
97SLU Hockey American-20
97Headliners Hockey-27
97Be A Player-22
Autographs-22
Autographs Die-Cuts-22
Autographs Prismatic Die-Cuts-22
One Timers-2
97Beehive-14
Golden Portraits-14
Team-17
Team Gold-17
97Black Diamond-110
Double Diamond-110
Triple Diamond-110
Quadruple Diamond-110
Premium Cut-PC14
Premium Cut Double Diamond-PC14
Premium Cut Quadruple Diamond Horiz-PC14
Premium Cut Triple Diamond-PC14
Premium Cut Quadruple Diamond Verticals-PC14
97Collector's Choice-194
Crash the Game-C27A
Crash the Game-C27B
Crash the Game-C27C
Crash the Game Exchange-CR27
Star Quest-SQ87
97Coyotes Face-Off Luncheon -22
97Crown Royale-107
Emerald Green-107
Ice Blue-107
Silver-107
Hat Tricks Die-Cuts-14
Lamplighters Cel-Fusion Die-Cuts-16
97Donruss-83
97Donruss-227
Press Proofs Silver-83
Press Proofs Silver-227
Press Proofs Gold-83
Press Proofs Gold-227
Red Alert-4
97Donruss Canadian Ice-16
Dominion Series-16
Provincial Series-16
97Donruss Elite-112
Aspirations-112
Status-112
Craftsmen-28
Master Craftsmen-28
97Donruss Limited-83
97Donruss Limited-133
97Donruss Limited-138
97Donruss Limited-140
Exposure-83
Exposure-133
Exposure-138
Exposure-140
Fabric of the Game-18
97Donruss Preferred-6
97Donruss Preferred-191
Cut to the Chase-6
Cut to the Chase-191
Line of the Times-3B
97Donruss Preferred Line of Times Promos-3B
97Donruss Priority-3
97Donruss Priority-202
Stamp of Approval-3
Stamp of Approval-202
Direct Deposit-17
Postcards-26
Postcards Opening Day Issues-3
Stamps-26
Stamps Bronze-26
Stamps Gold-26
Stamps Silver-26
97Esso Olympic Hockey Heroes-23
97Esso Olympic Hockey Heroes French-23
97Katch-113
Gold-113
Silver-113
97Kenner Starting Lineup Cards-20
97Kraft-25
97Leaf-73
97Leaf-185
Fractal Matrix-73
Fractal Matrix-185
Fractal Matrix Die Cuts-73
Fractal Matrix Die Cuts-185
Banner Season-14
97Leaf International-73
Universal Ice-73
97McDonald's Upper Deck-7
97NHL Aces Playing Cards-8
97Pacific-28
Copper-28
Emerald Green-28
Ice Blue-28
Red-28
Silver-28
Card-Supials-17
Card-Supials Minis-17
Slap Shots Die-Cuts-7A
97Pacific Dynagon-98
Copper-98
Dark Grey-98
Emerald Green-98
Ice Blue-98
Red-98
Silver-98
Best Kept Secrets-76
Dynamic Duos-12B
Tandems-6
97Pacific Invincible-109
Copper-109
Emerald Green-109
Ice Blue-109
Red-109
Silver-109
NHL Regime-156
Off The Glass-16
97Pacific Omega-177
Copper-177
Dark Gray-177
Emerald Green-177
Gold-177
Gold-245
Ice Blue-177
Game Face-15
97Panini Stickers-123
97Panini Stickers-162
97Paramount-144
Copper-144
Dark Grey-144
Emerald Green-144
Ice Blue-144
Red-144
Silver-144
Big Numbers Die-Cuts-16
Photoengravings-16
97Pinnacle-40
Artist's Proofs-40
Rink Collection-40
Epix Game Emerald-6
Epix Game Orange-6
Epix Game Purple-6
Epix Moment Emerald-6
Epix Moment Orange-6
Epix Moment Purple-6
Epix Play Emerald-6
Epix Play Orange-6
Epix Play Purple-6
Epix Season Emerald-6
Epix Season Orange-6
Epix Season Purple-6
Press Plates Back Black-40
Press Plates Back Cyan-40
Press Plates Back Magenta-40
Press Plates Back Yellow-40
Press Plates Front Black-40
Press Plates Front Cyan-40
Press Plates Front Magenta-40
Press Plates Front Yellow-40
Team Pinnacle-6
Team Mirror-6
Team Parallel-6
Team Parallel Mirror-6
97Pinnacle Certified-37
Red-37
Mirror Blue-37
Mirror Gold-37
Mirror Red-37
Team-11
Gold Team Promo-11
Gold Team-11
97Pinnacle Inside-5
Coach's Collection-5
Executive Collection-5
Track-24
Cans-7
Cans Gold-7
97Pinnacle Mint-21
Bronze-21
Gold Team-21
Silver Team-21
Coins Brass-21
Coins Brass Proofs-21
Coins Gold Plated-21
Coins Gold Plated Proofs-21
Coins Nickel Silver-21
Coins Nickel Silver Proofs-21
Coins Solid Gold-21
Coins Solid Silver-21
97Pinnacle Power Pack Blow-Ups-6
97Pinnacle Tot Cert Platinum Blue-37
97Pinnacle Tot Certi Platinum Gold-37
97Pinnacle Totally Certified Platinum Red-37
97Pinnacle Tot Cert Mirror Platinum Gold-37
97Revolution-109
Copper-109
Emerald-109
Ice Blue-109
Silver-109
Team Checklist Laser Cuts-19
97Score-87
Artist's Proofs-87
Golden Blades-87
Check It-4
97SP Authentic-119
Icons-I23
Icons Die-Cuts-I23
Icons Embossed-I23
97SPx-40
Bronze-40
Gold-40
Silver-40
Steel-40
Dimension-SPX15
Grand Finale-40
97Studio-8
Press Proofs Silver-8
Press Proofs Gold-8
Hard Hats-7
Portraits-8
Silhouettes-18
Silhouettes 8x10-18
97Upper Deck-126
Blow-Ups 3 x 5-1-9
Blow-Ups 5 x 7-4C
Game Dated Moments-126
Sixth Sense Masters-SS23
Sixth Sense Wizards-SS23
Smooth Grooves-SG37
The Specialists-15
The Specialists Level 2 Die Cuts-15
Three Star Selects-6C
97Upper Deck Crash the All-Star Game-11
97Upper Deck Crash the All-Star Game-AR11
97Upper Deck Diamond Vision-18
Signature Moves-18
97Upper Deck Ice-70
Parallel-70
Champions-IC15
Champions 2 Die Cuts-IC15
Lethal Lines-L3A
Lethal Lines 2-L3A
Power Shift-70
97Zenith-7
Z-Gold-7
Z-Silver-7
97Zenith 5 x 7-18
Gold Impulse-18
Silver Impulse-18
98SLU Hockey One on One-6
98Aurora-148
Championship Fever-38
Championship Fever Copper-38
Championship Fever Ice Blue-38
Championship Fever Red-38
Championship Fever Silver-38
98Be A Player-256
Press Release-256
98BAP Gold-256
98BAP Autographs-256
98BAP Autographs Gold-256
98Black Diamond-66
Double Diamond-66
Triple Diamond-66
Quadruple Diamond-66
Myriad-M4
Myriad 2-M4
Winning Formula Gold-WF23
Winning Formula Platinum-WF23
98Bowman's Best-6
Refractors-6
Atomic Refractors-6
Mirror Image Fusion-F12
Mirror Image Fusion Refractors-F12
Mirror Image Fusion Atomic Refractors-F12
98Crown Royale-105
Limited Series-105
Pillars of the Game-20
Pivotal Players-20
98Donruss Elite Promos-5
98Finest-80
No Protectors-80
No Protectors Refractors-80
Refractors-80
Double Sided Mystery Finest-M42
Double Sided Mystery Finest-M45
Double Sided Mystery Finest-M48
Double Sided Mystery Finest-M50
Double Sided Mystery Refractors-M42
Double Sided Mystery Refractors-M45
Double Sided Mystery Refractors-M48
Double Sided Mystery Refractors-M50
Red Lighters-R17
Red Lighters Refractors-R17
98OPC Chrome-154
Refractors-154
Season's Best-SB18
Season's Best Refractors-SB18
98Pacific-344
Ice Blue-344
Red-344
Gold Crown Die-Cuts-27
Team Checklists-20
Timelines-15
98Pacific Dynagon Ice-145
Blue-145
Red-145
Team Checklists-20
98Pacific Omega-188
Red-188
Opening Day Issue-188
EO Portraits-17
EO Portraits 1 of 1-17
Face to Face-5
Online-29
Planet Ice-18
Planet Ice Parallel-18
Prism-17
98Panini Photocards-84
98Panini Stickers-144
98Paramount-186
Copper-186
Emerald Green-186
Holo-Electric-186
Ice Blue-186
Silver-186
Special Delivery Die-Cuts-15
Team Checklists Die-Cuts-20
98Revolution-112
Ice Shadow-112
Red-112
All-Star Die Cuts-29
Chalk Talk Laser-Cuts-15
Showstoppers-30
Three Pronged Attack-7
Three Pronged Attack Parallel-7
98SP Authentic-66
Power Shift-66
Authentics-13
Authentics-14
Sign of the Times-KT
Sign of the Times Gold-KT
Snapshots-SS25
Stat Masters-S11
98SPx Finite-64
Radiance-64
Spectrum-64
98SPx Top Prospects-46
Radiance-46
Spectrum-46
Highlight Heroes-H23
Lasting Impressions-L4
Premier Stars-PS29
98Topps-154
O-Pee-Chee-154
Autographs-A6
Mystery Finest Bronze-M13
Mystery Finest Bronze Refractors-M13
Mystery Finest Gold-M13
Mystery Finest Gold Refractors-M13
Mystery Finest Silver-M13
Mystery Finest Silver Refractors-M13
Season's Best-SB18
98Topps Gold Label Class 1-12
Black-12
Black One of One-12
One of One-12
Red-12
Red One of One-12
98Topps Gold Label Class 2-12
98Topps Gold Label Class 2 Black-12
98Topps Gold Label Class 2 Black 1 of 1-12
98Topps Gold Label Class 2 One of One-12
98Topps Gold Label Class 2 Red-12
98Topps Gold Label Class 2 Red One of One-12
98Topps Gold Label Class 3-12
98Topps Gold Label Class 3 Black-12
98Topps Gold Label Class 3 Black 1 of 1-12
98Topps Gold Label Class 3 One of One-12
98Topps Gold Label Class 3 Red-12
98Topps Gold Label Class 3 Red One of One-12
98Topps Gold Label Goal Race '99-GR6
98Topps Gold Label Goal Race '99 Black-GR6
98Topps Gold Label Goal '99 Black 1 of 1-GR6
98Topps Gold Label Goal Race 99 1 of 1-GR6
98Topps Gold Label Goal Race '99 Red-GR6
98Topps Gold Label GoalRace 99 Red 1 of 1-GR6
98UD Choice-160
Mini Bobbing Head-BH2
Prime Choice Reserve-160
Reserve-160
StarQuest Blue-SQ30
StarQuest Gold-SQ30
StarQuest Green-SQ30
StarQuest Red-SQ30
98UD3-52
98UD3-112
98UD3-172
Die-Cuts-52
Die-Cuts-112
Die-Cuts-172
98Upper Deck-154
Exclusives-154
Exclusives 1 of 1-154
Fantastic Finishers-FF9
Fantastic Finishers Quantum 1-FF9
Fantastic Finishers Quantum 2-FF9
Fantastic Finishers Quantum 3-FF9
Frozen In Time-FT19
Frozen In Time Quantum 1-FT19
Frozen In Time Quantum 2-FT19
Frozen In Time Quantum 3-FT19
Lord Stanley's Heroes-LS21
Lord Stanley's Heroes Quantum 1-LS21
Lord Stanley's Heroes Quantum 2-LS21
Lord Stanley's Heroes Quantum 3-LS21
Gold Reserve-154
98Upper Deck MVP-156
Gold Script-156
Silver Script-156
Super Script-156
OT Heroes-OT12
Power Game-PG2
99Aurora-113
Striped-113
Premiere Date-113
Premiere Date Striped-113
Styrotechs-16
99BAP Memorabilia-291
Gold-291
Silver-291
99BAP Millennium-188
Emerald-188
Ruby-188
Sapphire-188
Signatures-188
Signatures Gold-188
99Black Diamond-66
Diamond Cut-66
Final Cut-66
A Piece of History-KT
A Piece of History Double-KT
A Piece of History Triple-KT
Diamonation-D13
Diamond Might-DM6
99Crown Royale-110
Limited Series-110
Premiere Date-110
International Glory-20
International Glory Parallel-20
Team Captain Die-Cuts-6
99O-Pee-Chee-4
99O-Pee-Chee All-Topps-AT9
99O-Pee-Chee Chrome-4
99O-Pee-Chee Chrome All Topps-AT9
99O-Pee-Chee Chrome All-Topps Refractors-AT9
99O-Pee-Chee Chrome Ice Masters-IM17
99O-Pee-Chee Chrome Ice Masters Refractor-IM17
99O-Pee-Chee Chrome Refractors-4
99O-Pee-Chee Ice Masters-IM17
99O-Pee-Chee Top of the World-TW11
99Pacific-328
Copper-328
Emerald Green-328
Gold-328
Ice Blue-328
Premiere Date-328
Red-328
Gold Crown Die-Cuts-30
Team Leaders-21
99Pacific Dynagon Ice-155
Blue-155
Copper-155
Gold-155
Premiere Date-155
2000 All-Star Preview-17
Checkmates American-11
Checkmates American-26
Checkmates Canadian-11
99Pacific Omega-185
Copper-185
Gold-185
Ice Blue-185
Premiere Date-185
EO Portraits-15
EO Portraits 1/1-15
5 Star Talents-10
5 Star Talents Parallel-10
99Pacific Prism-110
Holographic Blue-110
Holographic Gold-110
Holographic Mirror-110

Holographic Purple-110
Premiere Date-110
Sno-Globe Die-Cuts-18
99Panini Stickers-276
99Paramount-184
Copper-184
Emerald-184
Gold-184
Holographic Emerald-184
Holographic Gold-184
Holographic Silver-184
Ice Blue-184
Premiere Date-184
Red-184
Silver-184
Ice Alliance-21
Personal Best-30
99Revolution-114
Premiere Date-114
Red-114
Shadow Series-114
NHL Icons-16
Showstoppers-29
Top of the Line-8
Copper-114
Gold-114
CSC Silver-114
99SP Authentic-66
Supreme Skill-SS10
99SPx-115
Radiance-115
Spectrum-115
Prolifics-P6
SPXcitement-X12
SPXtreme-XT2
Starscape-S10
99Stadium Club-15
First Day Issue-15
One of a Kind-15
Printing Plates Black-15
Printing Plates Cyan-15
Printing Plates Magenta-15
Printing Plates Yellow-15
Capture the Action-CA16
Capture the Action Game View-CAG16
Chrome-14
Chrome Refractors-14
99Topps/OPC-4
All-Topps-AT9
Ice Masters-IM17
Top of the World-TW11
99Topps/OPC Chrome-4
Refractors-4
All-Topps-AT9
All-Topps Refractors-AT9
Ice Masters-IM17
Ice Masters Refractors-IM17
99Topps Gold Label Class 1-6
Black-6
Black One of One-6
One of One-6
Red-6
Red One of One-6
99Topps Gold Label Class 2-6
99Topps Gold Label Class 2 Black-6
99Topps Gold Label Class 2 Black 1 of 1-6
99Topps Gold Label Class 2 One of One-6
99Topps Gold Label Class 2 Red-6
99Topps Gold Label Class 2 Red One of One-6
99Topps Gold Label Class 3-6
99Topps Gold Label Class 3 Black-6
99Topps Gold Label Class 3 Black 1 of 1-6
99Topps Gold Label Class 3 One of One-6
99Topps Gold Label Class 3 Red-6
99Topps Gold Label Class 3 Red One of One-6
99Topps Gold Label Quest for the Cup-QC2
99Topps Gold Label Quest for the Cup One of One -QC2
99Topps Gold Label Quest 4 the Cup Black-QC2
99Topps Gold Label Quest for the Cup Black One of One -QC2
99Topps Gold Label Quest for the Cup Red-QC2
99Topps Gold Label Quest for the Cup Red One of One -QC2
99Topps Premier Plus-63
Parallel-63
Code Red-CR1
99Ultimate Victory-67
1/1-67
Parallel-67
Parallel 100-67
Stature-S10
99Upper Deck-100
99Upper Deck-146
Exclusives-100
Exclusives-146
Exclusives 1 of 1-100
Exclusives 1 of 1-146
All-Star Class-AS6
All-Star Class Quantum Gold-AS6
All-Star Class Quantum Silver-AS6
Crunch Time-CT26
Crunch Time Quantum Gold-CT26
Crunch Time Quantum Silver-CT26
Fantastic Finishers-FF8
Fantastic Finishers Quantum Gold-FF8
Fantastic Finishers Quantum Silver-FF8
Game Jersey Patch Series II-KTP
Marquee Attractions-MA14
Marquee Attractions Quantum Gold-MA14
Marquee Attractions Quantum Silver-MA14
Sixth Sense-SS19
Sixth Sense Quantum Gold-SS19
Sixth Sense Quantum Silver-SS19
99Upper Deck Century Legends-64
Century Collection-64
Essence of the Game-E8
99Upper Deck Gold Reserve-100
99Upper Deck Gold Reserve-146
99Upper Deck HoloGrFx-45
Ausome-45
99Upper Deck MVP-158
Gold Script-158
Silver Script-158
Super Script-158
Game-Used Souvenirs-GU10
Game-Used Souvenirs-GU24
99Upper Deck MVP SC Edition-139
Gold Script-139
Silver Script-139
Super Script-139
Great Combinations-GCTR
Great Combinations Parallel-GCTR
Second Season Snipers-SS9
Stanley Cup Talent-SC16
99Upper Deck Ovation-44
Standing Ovation-44
Lead Performers-LP7
99Upper Deck Retro-61
Gold-61
Platinum-61
Generation-G2C
Generation Level 2-G2C
99Upper Deck Victory-222
99Upper Deck Victory-224
99Wayne Gretzky Hockey-129
Elements of the Game-EG12
00Aurora-113
Pinstripes-113
Pinstripes Premiere Date-113
Premiere Date-113
00BAP Memorabilia-244
00BAP Memorabilia-499
Emerald-244
Ruby-244
Sapphire-244
Promos-244
00BAP Mem Chicago Sportsfest Copper-244
00BAP Memorabilia Chicago Sportsfest Blue-244
00BAP Memorabilia Chicago Sportsfest Gold-244
00BAP Memorabilia Chicago Sportsfest Ruby-244
00BAP Memorabilia Chicago Sun-Times Ruby-244
00BAP Memorabilia Chicago Sun-Times Gold-244
00BAP Mem Chicago Sun-Times Sapphire-244
00BAP Mem Toronto Fall Expo Copper-244
00BAP Memorabilia Toronto Fall Expo Gold-244
00BAP Memorabilia Toronto Fall Expo Ruby-244
00BAP Mem Update Heritage Jersey Cards-H10
00BAP Mem Update Heritage Jersey Gold-H10
00BAP Memorabilia Update Teammates-TM5
00BAP Memorabilia Update Teammates-TM30
00BAP Memorabilia Update Teammates Gold-TM5
00BAP Memorabilia Update Teammates Gold-TM30
00BAP Parkhurst 2000-P130
00BAP Signature Series-21
Emerald-21
Ruby-21
Sapphire-21
Franchise Players-F23
He Shoots-He Scores Prizes-25
Jersey Cards-J40
Jersey and Stick Cards-GSJ40
Jersey Cards Autographs-J40
Jersey Emblems-E40
Jersey Numbers-IN40
00BAP Ultimate Memorabilia Captain's C-C2
00BAP Ultimate Mem Game-Used Jerseys-GJ47
00BAP Ultimate Mem Game-Used Emblems-E39
00BAP Ultimate Mem Game-Used Numbers-N39
00BAP Ultimate Mem Game-Used Sticks-GS47
00BAP Ultimate Mem Journey Jerseys-JJ11
00BAP Ultimate Mem Journey Emblems-JE11
00BAP Ultimate Mem Journey Numbers-JI11
00BAP Ultimate Memorabilia Teammates-TM5
00BAP Ultimate Memorabilia Teammates-TM33
00Black Diamond-46
Gold-46
00Crown Royale-85
Ice Blue-85
Limited Series-85
Premiere Date-85
Red-85
00O-Pee-Chee-146
00O-Pee-Chee Parallel-146
00Pacific-322
Copper-322
Gold-322
Ice Blue-322
Premiere Date-322
Gold Crown Die Cuts-26
00Panini Stickers-190
00Paramount-194
Copper-194
Gold-194
Holo-Gold-194
Holo-Silver-194
Ice Blue-194
Premiere Date-194
00Private Stock-77
Gold-77
Premiere Date-77
Retail-77
Silver-77
PS-2001 Action-45
00Revolution-115
Blue-115
Premiere Date-115
Red-115
HD NHL-28
00SP Authentic-68
Special Forces-SF6
00SP Game Used-47
Patch Cards-P-KT
Tools of the Game-KT
Tools of the Game Exclusives-KT
Tools of the Game Combos-C-RT
00SPx-53
00SPx-77
00SPx-147
Spectrum-53
Spectrum-77
Winning Materials-KT
Winning Materials-WTK
Winning Materials Autographs-SKT
00Stadium Club-100
Special Forces-SF19
00Titanium-74
Blue-74
Gold-74
Premiere Date-74
Red-74
Retail-74
00Topps/OPC-146
Parallel-146
00Topps Chrome-106
OPC Refractors-106
Refractors-106
00Topps Gold Label Class 1-41
Gold-41
00Topps Gold Label Class 2-41
00Topps Gold Label Class 2 Gold-41
00Topps Gold Label Class 3-41
00Topps Gold Label Class 3 Gold-41
00Topps Gold Label Bullion-B7
00Topps Gold Label Bullion One to One-B7
00Topps Gold Label Game-Worn Jerseys-GLJ-KT
00Topps Gold Label Golden Greats-GG9
00Topps Gold Label Golden Greats 1 to 1-GG9
00Topps Heritage-20
Chrome Parallel-20
Heroes-HH15
00Topps Premier Plus-67
Blue Ice-67
World Premier-WP11
00Topps Stars-43
Blue-43
Game Gear-GGKT
00UD Heroes-92
NHL Leaders-L8
00UD Pros and Prospects-67
Game Jersey Autograph Exclusives-S-KT
Game Jersey Autographs-S-KT
00UD Reserve-67
Buyback Autographs-94
Buyback Autographs-95
Buyback Autographs-96
Buyback Autographs-97
Buyback Autographs-98
Buyback Autographs-99
Buyback Autographs-100
00Upper Deck-363
Exclusives Tier 1-363
Exclusives Tier 2-363
All-Star Class-A8
Fantastic Finishers-FF8
Game Jerseys-KT
Game Jersey Autographs-HKT
Game Jersey Autographs Exclusives-EKT
Game Jersey Autographs Exclusives-ESKT
Game Jersey Patches-KTP
Game Jersey Patches-PKT
Game Jersey Patch Autographs Exclusives-KTP
Game Jersey Patch Exclusives Series II-EKT
Number Crunchers-NC5
Signs of Greatness-SKT
Triple Threat-TT6
UD Flashback-UD7
00Upper Deck Ice-72
00Upper Deck Legends-103
00Upper Deck Legends-104
Legendary Collection Bronze-103
Legendary Collection Bronze-104
Legendary Collection Gold-103
Legendary Collection Gold-104
Legendary Collection Silver-103
Legendary Collection Silver-104
Epic Signatures-KT
Legendary Game Jerseys-JKT
00Upper Deck MVP-135
First Stars-135
Game-Used Souvenirs-GSKT
Second Stars-135
Super Game-Used Souvenirs-GSKT
Third Stars-135
Top Draws-TD9
00Upper Deck Victory-177
00Upper Deck Victory-316
00Upper Deck Vintage-276
00Upper Deck Vintage-283
00Upper Deck Vintage-284
00Vanguard-77
High Voltage-28
High Voltage Gold-28
High Voltage Green-28
High Voltage Red-28
High Voltage Silver-28
Holographic Gold-77
Holographic Purple-77
Pacific Proofs-77
01Atomic-83
Blue-83
Gold-83
Premiere Date-83
Red-83
Power Play-29
01BAP Memorabilia-140
Emerald-140
Ruby-140
Sapphire-140
All-Star Jerseys-ASJ41
All-Star Emblems-ASE41
All-Star Numbers-ASN41
Country of Origin-CO20
He Shoots-He Scores Prizes-31
01BAP Sig Series He Shoots/Scores Prizes-37
01BAP Signature Series Jerseys-GJ-77
01BAP Signature Series Teammates-TM-26
01BAP Ultimate Memorabilia Autographs-4
01BAP Ultimate Mem Autographs Gold-4
01BAP Ultimate Memorabilia Dynamic Duos-14
01BAP Ultimate Memorabilia Emblems-7
01BAP Ultimate Memorabilia Jerseys-7
01BAP Ultimate Mem Jerseys and Sticks-7
01BAP Ultimate Mem Journey Jerseys-14
01BAP Ultimate Mem Journey Emblems-14
01BAP Ultimate Memorabilia Numbers-6
01BAP Ultimate Memorabilia Name Plates-25
01BAP Ultimate Mem Scoring Leaders-16
01BAP Update Heritage-H6
01BAP Update Travel Plans-TP5
01Bowman YoungStars-37
Gold-37
Ice Cubed-37
01Crown Royale-121
Blue-121
Premiere Date-121
Red-121
Retail-121
Jewels of the Crown-26
01eTopps-24
01O-Pee-Chee-38
01O-Pee-Chee Heritage Parallel-38
01O-Pee-Chee Heritage Parallel Limited-38
01O-Pee-Chee Premier Parallel-38
01Pacific-332
Extreme LTD-332
Hobby LTD-332
Premiere Date-332
Retail LTD-332
Gold Crown Die-Cuts-18
01Pacific Adrenaline-163
Blue-163
Premiere Date-163
Red-163
Retail-163
World Beaters-17
01Pacific Arena Exclusives-332
01Pacific Heads-Up-81
Blue-81
Premiere Date-81
Red-81
Silver-81
Stat Masters-15
01Parkhurst-19
Gold-19
Silver-19
Sticks-PS48
Waving the Flag-28
01Private Stock-82
Gold-82
Premiere Date-82
Retail-82
Silver-82
01Private Stock Pacific Nights-82
01Private Stock PS-2002-62
01Private Stock Reserve-S16
01SP Authentic-77
Limited-77
Limited Gold-77
01SP Game Used-48
01SPx-59
01Sports Illustrated for Kids III-108
01Stadium Club-54
Award Winners-54
Master Photos-54
Gallery-G19
Gallery Gold-G19
Perennials-P11
01Titanium-119
Hobby Parallel-119
Premiere Date-119
Retail-119
Retail Parallel-119
01Topps-38
Heritage Parallel-38
Heritage Parallel Limited-38
OPC Parallel-38
01Topps Chrome-38
Refractors-38
Black Border Refractors-38
01Topps Heritage-9
Refractors-9
01Topps Reserve-33
01UD Challenge for the Cup-78
01UD Honor Roll Playoff Matchups-HS-HT
01UD Honor Roll Playoff Matchups Gold-HS-HT
01UD Mask Collection-83
Gold-83
Gloves-GGTK
01UD Playmakers-86
01UD Premier Collection-44
01UD Top Shelf-39
Sticks-SKT
Sticks Gold-SKT
01Upper Deck-150
Exclusives-150
Crunch Timers-CT12
Fantastic Finishers-FF6
Gate Attractions-GA3
Skilled Stars-SS7
Tandems-T9
01Upper Deck Ice-38
01Upper Deck MVP-163
Souvenirs-S-KT
Souvenirs Gold-S-KT
01Upper Deck Victory-303
01Upper Deck Victory-406
Gold-303
Gold-406
01Upper Deck Vintage-219
01Upper Deck Vintage-226
01Vanguard-83
Blue-83
Red-83
One of Ones-83
Premiere Date-83
Proofs-83
02Atomic-84
Blue-84
Gold-84
Red-84
Hobby Parallel-84
National Pride-U9
Power Converters-17
Super Colliders-13
02BAP All-Star Edition-93
Jerseys-93
Jerseys Gold-93
Jerseys Silver-93
02BAP First Edition-69
02BAP First Edition-331
02BAP First Edition-430H
Debut Jerseys-19
He Shoots-He Scores Prizes-29
Jerseys-69
02BAP Memorabilia-178
Emerald-178
Ruby-178
Sapphire-178
All-Star Jerseys-ASJ-57
All-Star Teammmates-AST-13
NHL All-Star Game-178
NHL All-Star Game Blue-178
NHL All-Star Game Green-178
NHL All-Star Game Red-178
Stanley Cup Playoffs-SC-22
Teammates-TM-17
02BAP Memorabilia Toronto Fall Expo-178
02BAP Signature Series-170
Autographs-170
Autograph Buybacks 1998-256
Autograph Buybacks 1999-188
Autographs Gold-170
Jerseys-SGJ27
Jersey Autographs-SGJ27
Team Quads-TQ15
02BAP Ultimate Memorabilia Hat Tricks-5
02BAP Ultimate Memorabilia Numerology-9
02Blues Team Issue-22
02Bowman YoungStars-27
Gold-27
Silver-27
02Crown Royale-82
Blue-82
Red-82
Retail-82
02ITG Used-69
02ITG Used-169
Jerseys-GUJ27
Jersey Autographs-GUJ27
Jerseys Gold-GUJ27
Emblems-E27
Jersey and Stick-SJ27
Jersey and Stick Gold-SJ27
Teammates-T8
Teammates Gold-T8
02O-Pee-Chee-39
02O-Pee-Chee Premier Blue Parallel-39
02O-Pee-Chee Premier Red Parallel-39
02O-Pee-Chee Factory Set-39
02Pacific-329
Blue-329
Red-329
Main Attractions-17
02Pacific Complete-470
Red-470
02Pacific Exclusive-146
Jerseys-21
Jerseys Gold-21
02Pacific Heads-Up-105
Blue-105
Purple-105
Red-105
Quad Jerseys-23
Quad Jerseys Gold-23
02Pacific Quest for the Cup-84
Gold-84
02Parkhurst-27
Bronze-27
Gold-27
Silver-27
College Ranks-CR3
College Ranks Jerseys-CRM3
He Shoots-He Scores Prizes-27
02Parkhurst Retro-10
Minis-10
02Private Stock Reserve-140
Red-140
Retail-140
Patches-140
02SP Authentic-79
02SP Authentic-103
Beckett Promos-79
02SP Game Used-44
Authentic Fabrics-CFDT
Authentic Fabrics-CFTL
Authentic Fabrics Gold-CFDT
Authentic Fabrics Gold-CFTL
Authentic Fabrics Rainbow-CFDT
Authentic Fabrics Rainbow-CFTL
First Rounder Patches-KT
Tools of the Game-KT
02SPx-64
Spectrum Gold-64
Spectrum Silver-64
02Stadium Club-49
Silver Decoy Cards-49
Proofs-49
02Titanium Jerseys-59
02Titanium Jerseys Retail-59
02Titanium Patches-59
02Topps-39
OPC Blue Parallel-39
OPC Red Parallel-39
Factory Set-39
02Topps Chrome-35
Black Border Refractors-35
Refractors-35
02Topps Heritage-12
Chrome Parallel-12
02Topps Total-279
Team Checklists-TTC26
02UD Artistic Impressions-78
Gold-78
02UD Artistic Impressions Beckett Promos-78
02UD Artistic Impressions Retrospectives-R78
02UD Artistic Impressions Retrospect Gold-R78
02UD Artistic Impress Retrospect Silver-R78
02UD Honor Roll-61
Students of the Game-SG27
02UD Piece of History-77
02UD Premier Collection-47A
02UD Top Shelf-77
All-Stars-ASKT
Clutch Performers-CPKT
Sweet Sweaters-SWKT
02Upper Deck-154
Exclusives-154
Good Old Days-GOKT
Number Crunchers-NC12
Reaching Fifty-50KT
Reaching Fifty Gold-50KT
02Upper Deck Classic Portraits-87
Starring Cast-CKT
Starring Cast Limited-CKT
02Upper Deck MVP-160
Gold-160
Classics-160
Golden Classics-160
02Upper Deck Rookie Update-84
02Upper Deck Rookie Update-160B
02Upper Deck Victory-188
Bronze-188
Gold-188
Silver-188
National Pride-NP59
02Upper Deck Vintage-220
Tall Boys-T56
Tall Boys Gold-T56
02Vanguard Jerseys-39
02Vanguard Jerseys Gold-39
02UD SuperStars *-235
Gold-235
City All-Stars Triple Jersey-JMK
03BAP Memorabilia-44
Emerald-44
Gold-44
Ruby-44
Sapphire-44
Gloves-GUG11
He Shoots-He Scores Prizes-25
03BAP Ultimate Memorabilia Autographs-48
Gold-48
03BAP Ultimate Mem Auto Jerseys-48
03BAP Ultimate Mem Auto Emblems-48
03BAP Ultimate Memorabilia Dynamic Duos-6
03BAP Ultimate Memorabilia Hat Tricks-1
03BAP Ultimate Memorabilia Jerseys-27
03BAP Ultimate Memorabilia Jerseys Gold-27
03BAP Ultimate Mem Jersey and Emblems-20
03BAP Ultimate Mem Jersey and Emblem Gold-20
03BAP Ultimate Mem Jersey and Numbers-20
03BAP Ultimate Mem Jersey and Number Gold-20
03BAP Ultimate Mem Jersey and Stick-10
03BAP Ultimate Mem Jersey and Stick Gold-10
03BAP Ultimate Memorabilia Triple Threads-20
03Beehive-170
Variations-170
Gold-170
Silver-170
Jumbo Jerseys-BH13
Jerseys-JT10
Sticks Beige Border-BE3
Sticks Red Border-RE16
03Black Diamond-22
Black-22
Green-22
Red-22
03Blues Team Set-26
03Crown Royale-83
Blue-83
Retail-83
Lords of the Rink-19
03ITG Action-531
Jerseys-M148
03ITG Used Signature Series-46
Gold-46
Autographs-KT
Autographs Gold-KT
Jerseys-20
Jerseys Gold-20
Jersey Autos-20
Jersey and Stick-20
Jersey and Stick Gold-20
Teammates-8
Teammates Gold-8
Triple Memorabilia-27
Triple Memorabilia Gold-27
03NHL Sticker Collection-275
03O-Pee-Chee-235
03OPC Blue-235
03OPC Gold-235
03OPC Red-235
03Pacific-290
Blue-290
Red-290
Jerseys-33
Jerseys Gold-33
03Pacific Calder-84
Silver-84
03Pacific Complete-244
Red-244
03Pacific Exhibit-125
Blue Backs-125
Yellow Backs-125
03Pacific Prism-86
Blue-86
Gold-86
Red-86
03Pacific Quest for the Cup-86
Blue-86
03Pacific Supreme-83
Blue-83
Red-83
Retail-83
03Parkhurst Rookie-22
Jerseys-GJ-19
Jersey Autographs-GUJ-KT
Jerseys Gold-GJ-19
Teammates Gold-RT14
Teammates-RT14
03Private Stock Reserve-87
Blue-87
Red-87
Retail-87
03SP Authentic-76
Limited-76
Breakout Seasons-B16
Breakout Seasons Limited-B16
03SP Game Used-41
03SP Game Used-112
Gold-41
Gold-112
Authentic Fabrics-DFWT
Authentic Fabrics Gold-DFWT
03SPx-85
Radiance-85
Spectrum-85
Fantasy Franchise-FF-TWM
Fantasy Franchise Limited-FF-TWM
Style-SPX-BS
Style Limited-SPX-BS
03Titanium-85
Hobby Jersey Number Parallels-85
Retail-85
Retail Jersey Number Parallels-85
03Topps-235
Blue-235
Gold-235
Red-235
Topps/OPC Idols-UI9
03UD Honor Roll-76
03UD Premier Collection-49
Skills-SK-BT
Skills Patches-SK-BT
Teammates-PT-SB
Teammates Patches-PT-SB
03Upper Deck-166
Canadian Exclusives-166
HG-166
NHL Best-NB-KT
Power Zone-PZ-2
03Upper Deck Classic Portraits-84
03Upper Deck Classic Portraits-138
03Upper Deck Ice-74
Gold-74
Breakers-IB-KT
Breaker Patches-IB-KT
Frozen Fabrics-FF-KT
Frozen Fabric Patches-FF-KT
03Upper Deck MVP-363
Gold Script-363
Silver Script-363
Canadian Exclusives-363
SportsNut-SN76
03Upper Deck Rookie Update-77
Super Stars-SSKT
03Upper Deck Trilogy-84
Authentic Patches-AP36
Limited-84
03Upper Deck Victory-166
Bronze-166
Gold-166
Silver-166
Freshman Flashback-FF41
Game Breakers-GB34
03Toronto Star-81
04Pacific-224
Blue-224
Red-224
Philadelphia-14
04SP Authentic-78
04SP Authentic-140
04Ultimate Collection-36
04Ultimate Collection-84
Dual Logos-UL2-WT
Patches-UP-TK
04Upper Deck-152
04Upper Deck-197
Big Playmakers-BP-KT
Canadian Exclusives-152
Canadian Exclusives-197
HG Glossy Gold-152
HG Glossy Gold-197
HG Glossy Silver-152
HG Glossy Silver-197
World's Best-WB30
World Cup Tribute-KTDWBH
05Be A Player-78
First Period-78
Second Period-78
Third Period-78
Overtime-78
Class Action-CA1
Dual Signatures-KC
Dual Signatures-ST
Outtakes-OT42
Quad Signatures-BLUE
Signatures-KT
Signatures Gold-KT
Triple Signatures-HGT
Triple Signatures-STL
World Cup Salute-WCS3
05Beehive-79
05Beehive-212
Beige -79
Blue -79
Gold-79
Red -79
Matte-79
Matted Materials-MMKT
05Black Diamond-146
Emerald-146
Gold-146
Onyx-146
Ruby-146
05Blues Team Set-19
05Hot Prospects-87
En Fuego-87
Red Hot-87
White Hot-87
05Panini Stickers-334
05Parkhurst-419
05Parkhurst-696
Facsimile Auto Parallel-419
Facsimile Auto Parallel-696
True Colors-TCSTL
True Colors-TCSTL
05SP Authentic-87
Limited-87
Prestigious Pairings-PPTW
05SP Game Used-85
Gold-85
Authentic Fabrics-AF-KT
Authentic Fabrics Dual-WT
Authentic Fabrics Gold-AF-KT
Authentic Fabrics Quad-TRGL
Authentic Patches Quad -TRGL
Authentic Patches-AP-KT
Authentic Patches Dual-WT
Awesome Authentics-AA-KT
Awesome Authentics Gold-DA-KT
Game Gear-GG-KT
05SPx-78
Spectrum-78
Winning Combos-WC-WT
Winning Combos Gold-WC-WT
Winning Combos Spectrum-WC-WT
Winning Materials-WM-KT
Winning Materials Gold-WM-KT
Winning Materials Spectrum-WM-KT
Xcitement Superstars-XS-KT
Xcitement Superstars Gold-XS-KT
Xcitement Superstars Spectrum-XS-KT
05The Cup-88
Gold-88
Black Rainbow-88
Dual NHL Shields-DSWT
Masterpiece Pressplates-88
Masterpiece Pressplates (Rookie Update)-210
Noble Numbers-NNMT
Noble Numbers Dual-DNNTG
Patch Variation-P88
05UD Artifacts-88
05UD Artifacts-192
Blue-88
Blue-192
Gold-88
Gold-192
Green-88
Green-192
Pewter-88
Pewter-192
Red-88
Red-192
Gold Autographed-88
Gold Autographed-192
05UD PowerPlay-78
Rainbow-78
05Ultimate Collection-78
Gold-78
National Heroes Jerseys-NHJKT
National Heroes Patches-NHPKT
05Ultra-167
Gold-167
Ice-167
Scoring Kings-SK32
Scoring Kings Jerseys-SKJ-KT
Scoring Kings Patches-SKP-KT
05Upper Deck-164
05Upper Deck All-Time Greatest-43
05Upper Deck Big Playmakers-B-KT
05Upper Deck HG Glossy-164
05Upper Deck Hometown Heroes-HH14
05Upper Deck Jerseys-J-KT
05Upper Deck Majestic Materials-MMKT
05Upper Deck Patches-P-KT
05Upper Deck Shooting Stars-S-KT
05Upper Deck Ice-84
Rainbow-84
Frozen Fabrics-FFKT
Frozen Fabrics Glass-FFKT
Frozen Fabrics Patches-FFPKT
05Upper Deck MVP-331
Gold-331
Platinum-331
05Upper Deck Rookie Update-85
05Upper Deck Rookie Update-210
Inspirations Patch Rookies-210
05Upper Deck Trilogy-79
05Upper Deck Trilogy-153
Crystal-153
Honorary Patches-HP-TK
Honorary Patch Scripts-HSP-TK
Honorary Swatches-HS-TK
Honorary Swatch Scripts-HSS-TK
05Upper Deck Toronto Fall Expo-164
05Upper Deck Victory-167
Black-167
Gold-167
Silver-167
Game Breakers-GB39
Stars on Ice-SI37
05Czech Stadion-680
06Be A Player Portraits-87
06Beehive-13
Blue-13
Gold-13
Matte-13
Red Facsimile Signatures-13
Wood-13
06Black Diamond-72
Black-72
Gold-72
Ruby-72
Jerseys-JKT
Jerseys Black-JKT
Jerseys Gold-JKT
Jerseys Ruby-JKT
06Flair Showcase-86
06Flair Showcase-161
Parallel-86
Parallel-161
Stitches-SSKT
06Fleer-166
Tiffany-166
Fabricology-FKT
06Hot Prospects-82
Red Hot-82
White Hot-82
06ITG Ultimate Memorabilia Blades of Steel-21
06ITG Ultimate Memorabilia Blades of Steel Gold-21
06ITG Ultimate Memorabilia Going For Gold-27
06ITG Ultimate Memorabilia Going For Gold Gold-27
06ITG Ultimate Memorabilia Jerseys Autos-68
06ITG Ultimate Memorabilia Jerseys Autos Gold-68
06ITG Ultimate Memorabilia Triple Thread Jerseys-9
06ITG Ultimate Memorabilia Triple Thread Jerseys Gold-9
06McDonald's Upper Deck-40
06O-Pee-Chee-422
06O-Pee-Chee-668
06O-Pee-Chee-696
Rainbow-422
Rainbow-668
Rainbow-696
06Panini Stickers-346
06SP Authentic-14
Limited-14
06SP Game Used-88
Gold-88
Rainbow-88
Authentic Fabrics Triple-AF3STL
Authentic Fabrics Triple Patches-AF3STL
By The Letter-BLKT
06SPx-87
Spectrum-87
SPxcitement-X86
SPxcitement Spectrum-X86
Winning Materials-WMKT
Winning Materials Spectrum-WMKT
06The Cup NHL Shields Duals-DSHTW
06UD Artifacts-14
Blue-14
Gold-14
Platinum-14
Radiance-14
Red-14
Treasured Patches Black-TSKT
Treasured Patches Blue-TSKT
Treasured Patches Gold-TSKT
Treasured Patches Platinum-TSKT
Treasured Patches Red-TSKT
Treasured Swatches-TSKT
Treasured Swatches Black-TSKT
Treasured Swatches Blue-TSKT
Treasured Swatches Gold-TSKT
Treasured Swatches Platinum-TSKT
Treasured Swatches Red-TSKT
Tundra Tandems-TTTG
Tundra Tandems-TTTW
Tundra Tandems Black-TTTG
Tundra Tandems Black-TTTW
Tundra Tandems Blue-TTTG
Tundra Tandems Blue-TTTW
Tundra Tandems Gold-TTTG
Tundra Tandems Gold-TTTW
Tundra Tandems Platinum-TTTG
Tundra Tandems Platinum-TTTW
Tundra Tandems Red-TTTG
Tundra Tandems Red-TTTW
Tundra Tandems Dual Patches Red-TTTG
Tundra Tandems Dual Patches Red-TTTW
06UD Mini Jersey Collection-86
06UD Powerplay-86
Impact Rainbow-86
06Ultra-167
Gold Medallion-167
Ice Medallion-167
Uniformity-UKT
Uniformity Patches-UPKT
06Upper Deck Arena Giveaways-STL1
06Upper Deck-168
Exclusives Parallel-168
High Gloss Parallel-168
Game Jerseys-JKT
Game Patches-PKT
Masterpieces-168
Walmart Tins Oversize-168
06Upper Deck MVP-250
Gold Script-250
Super Script-250
Jerseys-OJNT
Jerseys-OJTH
06Upper Deck Ovation-43
06Upper Deck Trilogy-85
06Upper Deck Victory-171
06Upper Deck Victory Black-171
06Upper Deck Victory Gold-171
06Russian Sport Collection Olympic Stars-52
07Upper Deck Victory-76
Black-76
Gold-76

Tkacs, Wojciech

92Finnish Semic-287

Tkacz, Andrzej

70Swedish Masterserien-194

Tkaczuk, Daniel

92Quebec Pee-Wee Tournament-495
93Quebec Pee-Wee Tournament-562
95Slapshot-17
95Barrie Colts-24
96Black Diamond-38
Gold-38
96Upper Deck-387
96Barrie Colts-27
97Beehive-65
Authentic Autographs-65
Golden Portraits-65
97Black Diamond-55
Double Diamond-55
Triple Diamond-55
Quadruple Diamond-55
97Collector's Choice-298
97Barrie Colts-24
97Bowman CHL-8
97Bowman CHL-152
OPC-8
OPC-152
Bowman's Best-4
Bowman's Best Atomic Refractors-4
Bowman's Best Refractor-4
98Black Diamond-93
Double Diamond-93
Triple Diamond-93
Quadruple Diamond-93
98Bowman's Best-146
Refractors-146
Atomic Refractors-146
98OPC Chrome-227
Refractors-227
98SPx Top Prospects-65
Radiance-65
Spectrum-65
98Topps-227
O-Pee-Chee-227
98UD Choice-254
Prime Choice Reserve-254
Reserve-254
98Upper Deck Game Jerseys-GJ11
98Barrie Colts-6
98Bowman CHL-34
Golden Anniversary-34
OPC International-34
Scout's Choice-SC3
98Bowman Chrome CHL-34
Golden Anniversary-34
Golden Anniversary Refractors-34
OPC International-34
OPC International Refractors-34
Refractors-34
99O-Pee-Chee-249
99O-Pee-Chee Chrome-249
99O-Pee-Chee Chrome Refractors-249
99Topps/OPC-249
99Topps/OPC Chrome-249
Refractors-249
99Quebec PeeWee Tournament Coll Souv-9
99Bowman CHL-133
Gold-133
OPC International-133
Scout's Choice-SC14
00BAP Parkhurst 2000-P203
00BAP Signature Series-298
Emerald-298
Ruby-298
Sapphire-298
00Black Diamond-93
00Topps Premier Plus-96
Blue Ice-96
01BAP Memorabilia-208

Emerald-208
Ruby-208
Sapphire-208
01O-Pee-Chee-287
01O-Pee-Chee Premier Parallel-287
01Pacific-66
Extreme LTD-66
Hobby LTD-66
Premiere Date-66
Retail LTD-66
01Pacific Arena Exclusives-66
01Topps-287
OPC Parallel-287
01Worcester Icecats-11
04Barrie Colts 10th Anniversary-1
06German DEL New Arrivals-NA14

Tkaczuk, Walt
69O-Pee-Chee-43
69Topps-43
70Dad's Cookies-128
70Esso Power Players-193
70O-Pee-Chee-180
Deckle-41
70Sargent Promotions Stamps-117
71Bazooka-31
71Colgate Heads-14
71Letraset Action Replays-4
71O-Pee-Chee-75
71Sargent Promotions Stamps-120
71Topps-75
71Toronto Sun-185
72O-Pee-Chee-110
Player Crests-14
72Sargent Promotions Stamps-149
72Topps-14
72Finnish Semic World Championship-212
72Swedish Semic World Championship-212
73O-Pee-Chee-25
73Topps-25
74Lipton Soup-12
74NHL Action Stamps-192
74O-Pee-Chee NHL-119
74Topps-119
75O-Pee-Chee NHL-128
75Topps-128
76O-Pee-Chee NHL-220
76Topps-220
77O-Pee-Chee NHL-90
77Topps-90
78O-Pee-Chee-235
78Topps-235
79O-Pee-Chee-15
79Topps-15
80O-Pee-Chee-211
80Topps-211
03Parkhurst Original Six New York-58
03Parkhurst Original Six New York-76
Autographs-15
06Parkhurst-131
06Parkhurst-218
Autographs-131

Tkatch, Stas
96Madison Monsters-21
97Quad-City Mallards-13

Tlacil, Jan
00Czech OFS-4

Tlusty, Jiri
05ITG Heroes and Prospects He Shoots-He Scores Prizes-58
06Czech OFS Jagr Team-3
06Toronto Marlies-30
06ITG Heroes and Prospects-132
Autographs-AJTL
Complete Jerseys-CJ12
Complete Jerseys Gold-CJ12

Toal, Mike
88Oilers Tenth Anniversary-111

Tobia, Eric
02Belleville Bulls-20
02Belleville Bulls-25
03Belleville Bulls-6
04Belleville Bulls-6

Tobin, Jim
94Anchorage Aces-9

Tobin, Mark
02Rimouski Oceanic-19
03Rimouski Oceanic-19
03Rimouski Oceanic Sheets-3
04Rimouski Oceanic-20
05Rimouski Oceanic-5

Tobin, Mike
98San Antonio Iguanas-8
00Rockford IceHogs-18

Tobler, Michael
03Swiss EV Zug Postcards-26

Tobler, Ryan
96Swift Current Broncos-18
99Milwaukee Admirals Keebler-17
00Milwaukee Admirals Keebler-18
00Milwaukee Admirals Postcards-15
01BAP Memorabilia-445
Emerald-445
Ruby-445
Sapphire-445
01SP Authentic-173
Limited-173
Limited Gold-173
01SP Game Used-97
01UD Challenge for the Cup-132
01Upper Deck-440
Exclusives-440
01Upper Deck Ice-83
02Chicago Wolves-23
03Colorado Eagles-18
04Colorado Eagles-19
05Colorado Eagles-18
06Colorado EaglesÂ -21

Tocchet, Rick
81Sault Ste. Marie Greyhounds-22
82Sault Ste. Marie Greyhounds-21
83Sault Ste. Marie Greyhounds-22
85Flyers Postcards-29
86Flyers Postcards-27
87Flyers Postcards-22
87O-Pee-Chee-2
87Panini Stickers-134
87Topps-2
87Sault Ste. Marie Greyhounds-26
88Flyers Postcards-17
88O-Pee-Chee-177
88O-Pee-Chee Stickers-99
88Panini Stickers-326
88Topps-177
89Flyers Postcards-26
89Kraft-57
89Kraft All-Stars Stickers-2
89O-Pee-Chee-80
89O-Pee-Chee Stickers-108
89Panini Stickers-295
89Topps-80
90Bowman-108
Tiffany-108
90Bowman Hat Tricks-14
Tiffany-14
90Flyers Postcards-24
90Kraft-58
90O-Pee-Chee-26
90OPC Premier-120
90Panini Stickers-121
90Pro Set-225
90Pro Set-374
90Score-80
Canadian-80
90Score Hottest/Rising Stars-40
90Topps-26
Tiffany-26
Team Scoring Leaders-9
Team Scoring Leaders Tiffany-9
90Upper Deck-263
90Upper Deck-488
French-263
French-488
91Pro Set Platinum-88
91Bowman-230
91Flyers J.C. Penney-24
91Kraft-45
91McDonald's Upper Deck-2
91O-Pee-Chee-160
91OPC Premier-63
91Panini Stickers-229
91Panini Stickers-331
91Parkhurst-129
91Parkhurst-354
French-129
French-354
91Penguins Foodland-5
91Pinnacle-20
French-20
91Pro Set-177
91Pro Set-311
91Pro Set-580
French-177
French-311
French-580
91Score American-9
91Score American-302
91Score American-334
91Score Canadian Bilingual-9
91Score Canadian Bilingual-306
91Score Canadian Bilingual-364
91Score Canadian English-9
91Score Canadian English-306
91Score Canadian English-364
91Score Kellogg's-2
91Stadium Club-35
91Topps-160
Team Scoring Leaders-13
91Upper Deck-91
91Upper Deck-122
91Upper Deck-503
French-91
French-122
French-503
92Bowman-159
92O-Pee-Chee-148
92Panini Stickers-226
92Panini Stickers French-226
92Parkhurst-139
Emerald Ice-139
Cherry Picks-CP12
92Penguins Coke/Clark-24
92Penguins Foodland-4
92Penguins Foodland Coupon Stickers-12
92Pinnacle-282
French-282
92Pro Set-138
92Score-245
Canadian-245
92Seasons Patches-37
92Stadium Club-76
92Topps-70
Gold-70G
92Ultra-172
92Upper Deck-238
92Upper Deck-454
92Finnish Semic-96
93Donruss-267
93Leaf-109
93OPC Premier-72
Gold-72
93Panini Stickers-80
93Parkhurst-428
Emerald Ice-428
93Penguins Foodland-4
93Pinnacle-174
Canadian-174
All-Stars-14
All-Stars Canadian-14
93PowerPlay-196
93Score-340
Canadian-340
93Stadium Club-329
Members Only Master Set-329
First Day Issue-329
All-Stars-20
All-Stars Members Only-20
All-Stars OPC-20
93Topps/OPC Premier-72
Gold-72
93Ultra-225
93Upper Deck-179
93Upper Deck-233
Hat Tricks-HT12
SP-126
93Upper Deck Locker All-Stars-16
93Swedish Semic World Champ Stickers-200
94Be A Player 99 All-Stars-G18
94Finest-52
Super Team Winners-52
Refractors-52
94Flair-83
94Fleer-100
94Hockey Wit-58
94Leaf-100
94Leaf-474
94Leaf Limited-117
94OPC Premier-281
94OPC Premier-346
Special Effects-281
Special Effects-346
94Parkhurst Vintage-V25
94Parkhurst SE-SE79
Gold-SE79
94Pinnacle-371
Artist's Proofs-371
Rink Collection-371
Boomers-BR18
Gamers-GR12
94Score Check It-CI11
94Select-2
Gold-2
94SP-55
Die Cuts-55
94Stadium Club-160
Members Only Master Set-160
First Day Issue-160
Super Team Winner Cards-160
94Topps/OPC Premier-281
94Topps/OPC Premier-346
Special Effects-281
Special Effects-346
94Ultra-309
94Upper Deck-224
Electric Ice-224
SP Inserts-SP129
SP Inserts Die Cuts-SP129
94Finnish Jaa Kiekko-95
94Finnish Jaa Kiekko-358
95Bashan Super Stickers-59
95Be A Player-82
Signatures-S82
Signatures Die Cuts-S82
95Bowman-36
All-Foil-36
95Canada Games NHL POGS-137
95Collector's Choice-254
Player's Club-254
Player's Club Platinum-254
95Donruss-41
95Emotion-86
Ntense Power-10
95Finest-133
Refractors-133
95Hoyle Western Playing Cards-24
95Imperial Stickers-59
95Leaf-29
95Leaf Limited-112
95Metal-74
Iron Warriors-15
95Panini Stickers-271
95Parkhurst International-287
Emerald Ice-287
95Playoff One on One-161
95Pro Magnets-70
95Score-37
Black Ice Artist's Proofs-37
Black Ice-37
95Select Certified-98
Mirror Gold-98
95SkyBox Impact-83
95SkyBox Impact-247
95Stadium Club-32
Members Only Master Set-32
Fearless-F5
Fearless Members Only Master Set-F5
95Summit-103
Artist's Proofs-103
Ice-103
95Topps-264
OPC Inserts-264
Hidden Gems-15HG
95Topps SuperSkills-64
Platinum-64
95Ultra-79
Gold Medallion-79
Crease Crashers-19
95Upper Deck-274
Electric Ice-274
Electric Ice Gold-274
Special Edition-SE40
Special Edition Gold-SE40
95Zenith-118
Gifted Grinders-5
95Finnish Semic World Championships-98
95Swedish Globe World Championships-92
96Black Diamond-55
Gold-55
96Collector's Choice-18
96Donruss-122
Press Proofs-122
96Duracell All-Cherry Team-DC14
96Fleer-8
96Leaf-90
Press Proofs-90
96Maggers-102
96Metal Universe-11
96NHL Pro Stamps-70
96Pinnacle-23
Artist's Proofs-23
Foil-23
Premium Stock-23
Rink Collection-23
96Playoff One on One-376
96Score-92
Artist's Proofs-92
Dealer's Choice Artist's Proofs-92
Special Artist's Proofs-92
Golden Blades-92
96SkyBox Impact-9
96SP-12
96Team Out-38
96Topps Picks-111
OPC Inserts-111
96Ultra-12
Gold Medallion-12
96Upper Deck-10
Generation Next-X32
96Upper Deck Ice-4
Parallel-4
96Swedish Semic Wien-89
97Be A Player-127
Autographs-127
Autographs Die-Cuts-127
Autographs Prismatic Die-Cuts-127
97Donruss-45
Press Proofs Silver-45
Press Proofs Gold-45
97Donruss Limited-83
Exposure-83
97Donruss Priority-148
Stamp of Approval-148
97Pacific-311
Copper-311
Emerald Green-311
Ice Blue-311
Red-311
Silver-311
97Pacific Omega-178
Copper-178
Dark Gray-178
Emerald Green-178
Gold-178
Ice Blue-178
97Paramount-145
Copper-145
Dark Grey-145
Emerald Green-145
Ice Blue-145
Red-145
Silver-145
97Pinnacle Inside-174
97Score-246
97SP Authentic-121
97Upper Deck-339
98Aurora-149
98Be A Player-105
Press Release-105
98BAP Gold-105
98BAP Autographs-105
98BAP Autographs Gold-105
98BAP Tampa Bay All Star Game-105
98Bowman's Best-38
Refractors-38
Atomic Refractors-38
98Crown Royale-106
Limited Series-106
98OPC Chrome-34
Refractors-34
98Pacific-92
Ice Blue-92
Red-92
98Pacific Dynagon Ice-146
Blue-146
Red-146
98Pacific Omega-189
Red-189
Opening Day Issue-189
98Paramount-187
Copper-187
Emerald Green-187
Holo-Electric-187
Ice Blue-187
Silver-187
98Post-4
98Revolution-113
Ice Shadow-113
Red-113
98Topps-34
O-Pee-Chee-34
98Topps Gold Label Class 1-48
Black-48
Black One of One-48
One of One-48
Red-48
Red One of One-48
98Topps Gold Label Class 2-48
98Topps Gold Label Class 2 Black-48
98Topps Gold Label Class 2 Black 1 of 1-48
98Topps Gold Label Class 2 One of One-48
98Topps Gold Label Class 2 Red-48
98Topps Gold Label Class 2 Red One of One-48
98Topps Gold Label Class 3-48
98Topps Gold Label Class 3 Black-48
98Topps Gold Label Class 3 Black 1 of 1-48
98Topps Gold Label Class 3 One of One-48
98Topps Gold Label Class 3 Red-48
98Topps Gold Label Class 3 Red One of One-48
98Upper Deck-341
Exclusives-341
Exclusives 1 of 1-341
Gold Reserve-341
98Upper Deck MVP-162
Gold Script-162
Silver Script-162
Super Script-162
99Aurora-112
Premiere Date-112
99BAP Memorabilia-276
99BAP Memorabilia-329
Gold-276
Gold-329
Silver-276
Silver-329
99O-Pee-Chee-117
99O-Pee-Chee Chrome-117
99O-Pee-Chee Chrome Refractors-117
99Pacific-329
Copper-329
Emerald Green-329
Gold-329
Ice Blue-329
Premiere Date-329
Red-329
99Pacific Dynagon Ice-156
Blue-156
Copper-156
Gold-156
Premiere Date-156
99Pacific Prism-111
Holographic Blue-111
Holographic Gold-111
Holographic Mirror-111
Holographic Purple-111
Premiere Date-111
99Panini Stickers-282
99Paramount-185
Copper-185
Emerald-185
Gold-185
Holographic Emerald-185
Holographic Gold-185
Holographic Silver-185
Ice Blue-185
Premiere Date-185
Red-185
Silver-185
99Revolution-115
Premiere Date-115
Red-115
Shadow Series-115
99SPx-116
Radiance-116
Spectrum-116
99Stadium Club-94
First Day Issue-94
One of a Kind-94
Printing Plates Black-94
Printing Plates Cyan-94
Printing Plates Magenta-94
Printing Plates Yellow-94
99Topps/OPC-117
99Topps/OPC Chrome-117
Refractors-117
99Upper Deck MVP-159
Gold Script-159
Silver Script-159
Super Script-159
99Upper Deck Victory-231
00BAP Memorabilia-370
Emerald-370
Ruby-370
Sapphire-370
Promos-370
00BAP Mem Chicago Sportsfest Copper-370
00BAP Memorabilia Chicago Sportsfest Blue-370
00BAP Memorabilia Chicago Sportsfest Gold-370
00BAP Memorabilia Chicago Sportsfest Ruby-370
00BAP Memorabilia Chicago Sun-Times Ruby-370
00BAP Memorabilia Chicago Sun-Times Gold-370
00BAP Mem Chicago Sun-Times Sapphire-370
00BAP Mem Toronto Fall Expo Copper-370
00BAP Memorabilia Toronto Fall Expo Gold-370
00BAP Memorabilia Toronto Fall Expo Ruby-370
00BAP Parkhurst 2000-P161
00O-Pee-Chee-220
00O-Pee-Chee Parallel-220
00Pacific-308
Copper-308
Gold-308
Ice Blue-308
Premiere Date-308
00Paramount-186
Copper-186
Gold-186
Holo-Gold-186
Holo-Silver-186
Ice Blue-186
Premiere Date-186
00Private Stock Game Gear-86
00SPx-50
Spectrum-50
00Topps/OPC-220
Parallel-220
00Topps Heritage-163
00Upper Deck-131
Exclusives Tier 1-131
Exclusives Tier 2-131
00Upper Deck Vintage-261
00Upper Deck Vintage-271
00Czech Stadion-198
01BAP Signature Series-141
Autographs-141
Autographs Gold-141
01Flyers Postcards-21
01O-Pee-Chee-176
01O-Pee-Chee Premier Parallel-176
01Pacific-295
Extreme LTD-295
Hobby LTD-295
Premiere Date-295
Retail LTD-295
01Pacific Arena Exclusives-295
01SP Authentic Jerseys-NNRT
01Topps-176
OPC Parallel-176
02BAP Sig Series Auto Buybacks 1998-105
02BAP Sig Series Auto Buybacks 2001-141

Tocher, Ryan
917th Inn. Sketch OHL-204
95Slapshot-235
00Johnstown Chiefs-24
01Fresno Falcons-18

Todd, Alex
01Fresno Falcons-19
02Fresno Falcons-6

Todd, Brody
00Kingston Frontenacs-22
01Sudbury Wolves-22
01Sudbury Wolves Police-4
03Ottawa 67's-20

Todd, Daine
04Medicine Hat Tigers-21
05Medicine Hat Tigers-23
06Medicine Hat Tigers-22

Todd, Dick
89Peterborough Petes-123
897th Inn. Sketch OHL-123
907th Inn. Sketch OHL-376
91Peterborough Petes-23
917th Inn. Sketch OHL-123

Todd, Kevin
88ProCards AHL-329
89ProCards AHL-205
90ProCards AHL/IHL-570
91Pro Set Platinum-260
91Gillette-40
91O-Pee-Chee-400
91OPC Premier-22
91Parkhurst-97
91Parkhurst-444
French-97
French-444
91Pinnacle-308
French-308
91Pro Set-548
French-548
91Score American-397
91Score Canadian Bilingual-287
91Score Canadian English-287
91Topps-400
91Upper Deck-401
French-401
92Bowman-21
92Oilers Team Issue-19
92O-Pee-Chee-1
92Panini Stickers-275
92Panini Stickers-O
92Panini Stickers French-275
92Panini Stickers French-O
92Parkhurst-94
92Parkhurst-238
92Parkhurst-285
Emerald Ice-94
Emerald Ice-238
Emerald Ice-285
92Pinnacle-272
French-272
Team 2000-22
Team 2000 French-22
92Pro Set-94
Rookie Goal Leaders-7
92Score-162
Canadian-162
Young Superstars-19
92Stadium Club-465
92Topps-15
92Topps-228
Gold-15G
Gold-228G
92Ultra-121
Rookies-8
92Upper Deck-11
92Upper Deck-303
92Upper Deck-365
All-Rookie Team-AR3
All-Rookie Team-AR7
93Blackhawks Coke-18
93Leaf-15
93Parkhurst-37
Emerald Ice-37
93Pinnacle-270
Canadian-270
93PowerPlay-318
93Score-338
93Score-507
Gold-507
Canadian-338
Canadian-507
Canadian Gold-507
93Stadium Club-8
Members Only Master Set-8
OPC-8
First Day Issue-8
First Day Issue OPC-8
93Ultra-294
93Upper Deck-88
93Upper Deck-440
SP-33
94Be A Player Signature Cards-74
94Leaf-350
94Parkhurst-108
Gold-108
94Upper Deck-120
Electric Ice-120
95Parkhurst International-374
Emerald Ice-374
95Upper Deck-364
Electric Ice-364
Electric Ice Gold-364
96Be A Player-101
Autographs-101
Autographs Silver-101
96Collector's Choice-127
96Ducks Team Issue-4
96Upper Deck Ice-1
Parallel-1
97Collector's Choice-11
97Pacific-182
Copper-182
Emerald Green-182
Ice Blue-182
Red-182
Silver-182
97Score Mighty Ducks-6
Platinum-6
Premier-6
97Upper Deck-3
98Swiss Power Play Stickers-221

Toews, A.J.
02Chicago Steel-23

Toews, Brent
04Columbus Cottonmouths-6

Toews, Jonathan
06ITG Ultimate Memorabilia Future Star Autos-25
06ITG Ultimate Memorabilia Future Star Autos Gold-25
06ITG Ultimate Memorabilia Future Star Patches Autos-26
06ITG Ultimate Memorabilia Future Star Patches Autos Gold-26
07ITG Going For Gold World Juniors-21
Autographs-21
Emblems-GUE21
Jerseys-GUJ21
Numbers-GUN21

Toews, Krister
03Portland Winter Hawks-23

Toews, Lorne
907th Inn. Sketch WHL-36
917th Inn. Sketch WHL-316
94Wheeling Thunderbirds-17
94Wheeling Thunderbirds Photo Album-14
95Wheeling Thunderbirds-10
95Wheeling Thunderbirds Series II-15

Toews, Warren
04Peoria Rivermen-2

Toffey, John
05Johnstown Chiefs-19

Toffolo, Mark
78Saginaw Gears-19
79Rochester Americans-21

Toft, Henrik
98Danish Hockey League-172

Togni, Stefano
93Swiss HNL-155
95Swiss HNL-152
96Swiss HNL-170
98Swiss Power Play Stickers-306

Tognini, Omar
95Swiss HNL-207
96Swiss HNL-96
98Swiss Power Play Stickers-23
00Swiss Panini Stickers-24
01Swiss HNL-232
02Swiss HNL-362

Toivola, Marko
94Finnish SISU-303
95Finnish SISU-119

Toivola, Tero
93Finnish SISU-75

Toivonen, Hannu
01Finnish Cardset-213
02BAP Memorabilia Draft Redemptions-29
02Finnish Cardset-280
Bound for Glory-10
Signatures-10
03Finnish Cardset D-Day-DD15
03AHL Top Prospects-38
03Pacific AHL Prospects-69
Gold-69
03Providence Bruins-19
04SP Authentic Rookie Redemptions-RR3
04AHL Top Prospects-44
04Providence Bruins-22
04ITG Heroes and Prospects-2
Autographs-HT
04ITG Heroes/Prospects Toronto Expo '05-2
04ITG Heroes/Prospects Expo Heroes/Pros-2
05ITG Heroes/Prosp Toronto Expo Parallel -97
05Beehive-109
Beige -109
Blue -109
Gold-109
Red -109
Matte-109
05Black Diamond-205
Emerald-205
Gold-205
Onyx-205
Ruby-205
05Bruins Boston Globe-2
05Hot Prospects-221
En Fuego-221
Hot Materials-HMHT
Red Hot-221
White Hot-221
05Parkhurst-606
Facsimile Auto Parallel-606
True Colors-TCBOS
True Colors-TCBOS
05SP Authentic-135
Limited-135
Exquisite Endorsements-EEHT
Rarefied Rookies-RRHT
Rookie Authentics-RAHT
Sign of the Times Duals-DRT
Sign of the Times Fives-TWLDH
05SP Game Used-152
Autographs-152
Gold-152
Auto Draft-AD-HT
Game Gear-GG-HT
Game Gear Autographs-AG-HT
Rookie Exclusives-HT
Rookie Exclusives Silver-RE-HT
Significant Numbers-SN-HT
05SPx-158
Spectrum-158
Xcitement Rookies-XR-HT
Xcitement Rookies Gold-XR-HT
Xcitement Rookies Spectrum-XR-HT
05The Cup-108
Autographed Rookie Patches Gold Rainbow-108
Black Rainbow Rookies-108
Dual NHL Shields-DSRT
Dual NHL Shields Autographs-ADSRT
Masterpiece Pressplates (Artifacts)-203
Masterpiece Pressplates (Bee Hive)-109
Masterpiece Pressplates (Black Diamond)-205
Masterpiece Pressplates (Ice)-108
Masterpiece Pressplates (MVP)-399
Masterpiece Pressplates (Power Play)-135
Masterpiece Pressplates Rookie Upd Auto-258
Masterpiece Pressplates SPA Autos-135
Masterpiece Pressplates (SP Game Used)-152
Masterpiece Pressplates SPx Autos-158
Masterpiece Pressplates (Trilogy)-175
Masterpiece Pressplates Ult Coll Autos-98
Masterpiece Pressplates (Victory)-259
Masterpiece Pressplates Autographs-108
Platinum Rookies-108
05UD Artifacts-203
Gold-RED3
05UD PowerPlay-135
05UD Rookie Class-25
05Ultimate Collection-98
Autographed Patches-98
Autographed Shields-98
Jerseys-JHT
Jerseys Dual-DJTL
Marquee Attractions-MA6
Marquee Attractions Signatures-SMA6
Premium Patches-PPHT
Premium Swatches-PSHT
Ultimate Debut Threads Jerseys-DTJHT
Ultimate Debut Threads Jerseys Autos-DAJHT
Ultimate Debut Threads Patches-DTPHT
Ultimate Debut Threads Patches Autos-DAPHT
Ultimate Patches-PHT
Ultimate Patches Dual-DPTL
Ultimate Signatures-USHT
Ultimate Signatures Logos-SLHT
Ultimate Signatures Pairings-UPLT
Ultimate Signatures Pairings-UPRT
Ultimate Signatures Trios-UTLTD
05Ultra-258
Gold-258
Fresh Ink-FI-HT
Fresh Ink Blue-FI-HT
Ice-258
Rookie Uniformity Jerseys-RU-HT
Rookie Uniformity Jersey Autographs-ARU-HT
Rookie Uniformity Patches-RUP-HT
Rookie Uniformity Patch Autographs-ARP-HT
05Upper Deck-241
HG Glossy-241
Majestic Materials-MMHT
Rookie Ink-RIHT
05Upper Deck Rookie Showcase-RS3
05Upper Deck Rookie Showcase Promos-RS3
05Upper Deck Rookie Threads-RTHT
05Upper Deck Rookie Threads Autographs-ARTHT
05Upper Deck Stars in the Making-SM9
05Upper Deck Ice-108
Cool Threads-CTHT
Cool Threads Autographs-ACTHT
Cool Threads Glass-CTHT
Cool Threads Patches-CTPHT
Cool Threads Patch Autographs-CAPHT
Glacial Graphs-GGHT
Glacial Graphs Labels-GGHT
Premieres Auto Patches-AIPHT
05Upper Deck MVP-399
Gold-399
Platinum-399
Rookie Breakthrough-RB12
05Upper Deck Rookie Update-258
05Upper Deck Trilogy-175
05Upper Deck Toronto Fall Expo-241
05Upper Deck Victory-259
Black-259
Gold-259
Silver-259
05ITG Heroes and Prospects-97
Autographs-A-HT
06Be A Player Portraits-11
First Exposures-FEHT
Signature Portraits-SPHT
06Beehive-92
Matte-92
Matted Materials-MMHT
Remarkable Matted Materials-MMHT
06Between The Pipes-16
06Between The Pipes-109
Autographs-AHT2
Autographs-AHT
Double Memorabilia-DM18
Double Memorabilia Gold-DM18
Emblems-GUE14
Emblems Gold-GUE14
Emblems Autographs-GUE14
Gloves-GG17
Gloves Gold-GG17
Jerseys-GUJ14
Jerseys Gold-GUJ14
Jerseys Autographs-GUJ14
Numbers-GUN14
Numbers Gold-GUN14
Numbers Autographs-GUN14
Playing For Your Country-PC23
Playing For Your Country Gold-PC23
Prospect Trios-PT01
Prospect Trios Gold-PT01
Shooting Gallery-SG03
Shooting Gallery Gold-SG03
Stick and Jersey-SJ35
Stick and Jersey Gold-SJ35
Stick and Jersey Autographs-SJ35
The Mask-M27
The Mask Gold-M27
The Mask Silver-M27
The Mask Game-Used-MGU20
The Mask Game-Used Gold-MGU20
06Black Diamond-6
Black-6
Gold-6
Ruby-6
06Flair Showcase Hot Gloves-HG3
06Fleer-16
Tiffany-16
06Hot Prospects-8
Red Hot-8
White Hot-8
Hot Materials -HMHT
Hot Materials Red Hot-HMHT
Hot Materials White Hot-HMHT
06ITG Ultimate Memorabilia Future Star Patches Autos-17
06ITG Ultimate Memorabilia Future Star Patches Autos Gold-17
06O-Pee-Chee-35
Rainbow-35
Autographs-A-HT
Swatches-S-HT
06SP Authentic Sign of the Times Duals-STCT
06SP Game Used-9
Gold-9
Rainbow-9
Authentic Fabrics-AFHT
Authentic Fabrics Parallel-AFHT
Authentic Fabrics Patches-AFHT
Authentic Fabrics Dual-AF2TT
Authentic Fabrics Dual Patches-AF2TT
Autographs-9
Inked Sweaters-ISHT
Inked Sweaters Patches-ISHT
SIGnificance-SHT
06The Cup Autographed NHL Shields Duals-DASCT
06The Cup NHL Shields Duals-DSHTT
06UD Powerplay-9
Impact Rainbow-9
06Ultimate Collection Premium Patches-PS-HT
06Ultimate Collection Premium Swatches-PS-HT
06Upper Deck Arena Giveaways-BOS2
06Upper Deck-19
Exclusives Parallel-19
High Gloss Parallel-19
Generations Triples-G3KTL
Generations Patches Triple-G3PKTL
Masterpieces-19
Signature Sensations-SSHT
06Upper Deck MVP-21
Gold Script-21
Super Script-21
Last Line of Defense-LL24
06Upper Deck Ovation-5
06Upper Deck Trilogy-7
06Upper Deck Victory-234
06ITG Heroes and Prospects Net Prospects-NPR11
06ITG Heroes and Prospects Sticks and Jerseys-SJ18
06ITG Heroes and Prospects Sticks and Jerseys Gold-SJ18

Toivonen, Harri
78Finnish SM-Liiga-121
80Finnish Mallasjuoma-76

Toivonen, Juha
05Finnish Cardset -201
06Finnish Cardset-26

Toivonen, Kalevi
66Finnish Jaakiekkosarja-179

Toivonen, Kari-Pekka
70Finnish Jaakiekko-204
72Finnish Panda Toronto-44

Toivonen, Marko
98Finnish Kerailysarja-168
99Finnish Cardset-285
00Finnish Cardset-64
01Finnish Cardset-87
04Finnish Cardset-311
05Finnish Cardset -166
06Finnish Cardset-170
06Finnish Porin Assat Pelaajakortit-5

Toivonen, Timo
72Finnish Jaakiekko-355

Tok, Chris
95Fort Wayne Komets-20
99Missouri River Otters-22
99Missouri River Otters Sheet-21
00Missouri River Otters-3
04Waterloo Blackhawks-14

Tokarczyk, Trevor
95Slapshot-367
95Sault Ste. Marie Greyhounds-22
96Sault Ste. Marie Greyhounds-25
96Sault Ste. Marie Greyhounds Autographed-25

Tokarz, Leszek
73Finnish Jaakiekko-101
74Finnish Jenkki-88
74Finnish Typotor-92
79Panini Stickers-135

Tokarz, Wieslav
73Finnish Jaakiekko-102
74Finnish Jenkki-89

Toljanich, Mark
917th Inn. Sketch WHL-300
93Red Deer Rebels-24

Tolkunov, Dmitri
98Quebec Remparts-21
Signed-21
98Bowman CHL-117
Golden Anniversary-117
OPC International-117
98Bowman Chrome CHL-117
Golden Anniversary-117
Golden Anniversary Refractors-117
OPC International-117
OPC International Refractors-117
Refractors-117
99Cleveland Lumberjacks-22
99Bowman CHL-48
Gold-48
OPC International-48
01Norfolk Admirals-7
02Norfolk Admirals-21

Toll, Christian
03Minnesota State Mavericks-19

Toll, Steven
98Fayetteville Force-4
99Indianapolis Ice-18

Tollefsen, Ole-Kristian
02Brandon Wheat Kings-20
03Brandon Wheat Kings-14
04Syracuse Crunch-6
05Beehive-95
Matte-95
05Black Diamond-229
05Hot Prospects-197
Autographed Patch Variation-197
Autographed Patch Variation Gold-197
Hot Materials-HMOT
Red Hot-197
05Parkhurst Signatures-OK
05SP Authentic-209
05SP Game Used-205
05SPx-227
Spectrum-227
05The Cup-161
Autographed Rookie Patches Gold Rainbow-161
Black Rainbow Rookies-161
Masterpiece Pressplates (Artifacts)-267
Masterpiece Pressplates (Bee Hive)-95
Masterpiece Pressplates (Black Diamond)-229
Masterpiece Pressplates (Ice)-193
Masterpiece Pressplates (Rookie Update)-241
Masterpiece Pressplates SPA Autos-209
Masterpiece Pressplates (SP Game Used)-205
Masterpiece Pressplates SPx Autos-227
Masterpiece Pressplates (Trilogy)-244
Masterpiece Pressplates Ult Coll-202
Masterpiece Pressplates Autographs-161
Platinum Rookies-161
05UD Artifacts-267
05Ultimate Collection-202
Gold-202
05Upper Deck Ice-193
05Upper Deck Rookie Update-241
Inspirations Patch Rookies-241
05Upper Deck Trilogy-244
05Syracuse Crunch-17
06Hot Prospects Hotagraphs-HOT

Tolpeko, Dennis
05Regina Pats-25
06Philadelphia Phantoms-6

Tolsa, Jari
00Swedish Upper Deck-70

02Swedish SHL-118
Parallel-118
03Swedish Elite-29
Silver-29
04Swedish Elitset-29
Gold-29
05Swedish SHL Elitset-29
Gold-29
06Finnish Cardset-189

Tolstik, Pavel
99Danish Hockey League-121

Tolvanen, Ismo
71Finnish Suomi Stickers-337

Tolvanen, Jarmo
95German DEL-168

Tolzer, Steffen
04German Augsburg Panthers Postcards-26
05German DEL-304

Tom, Chris
93Quebec Pee-Wee Tournament-1314

Tomajko, Jan
95Upper Deck-544
Electric Ice-544
Electric Ice Gold-544
95Czech APS Extraliga-122
96Czech APS Extraliga-277
97Czech APS Extraliga-48
97Czech DS Extraliga-64
97Czech DS Stickers-185
98Czech DS-82
98Czech DS Stickers-181
98Czech OFS-111
99Czech DS-135
99Czech OFS-67
99Czech OFS-272
00Czech OFS-335
01Czech DS-21
01Czech OFS-25
02Czech OFS Plus-18
Duos-D3
03Czech OFS Plus-165
04Czech OFS-81
05Czech HC Liberec-14
06Czech HC Liberec Postcards-9

Tomalty, Sean
91Nashville Knights-25

Toman, Ilmar
94German DEL-419

Toman, Milan
02Czech OFS Plus-122
04Czech OFS-302
05Czech HC Sparta Praha-13
06Czech HC Ceske Budejovice Postcards-9
06Czech OFS-17

Tomanek, Robert
01Czech OFS-24

Tomans, Janis
97Flint Generals EBK-6

Tomaras, Alexandre
92Quebec Pee-Wee Tournament-913
93Quebec Pee-Wee Tournament-132

Tomas, Roman
04Russian Legion-15
06Czech OFS-169

Tomasek, Ales
94Czech APS Extraliga-6
95Czech APS Extraliga-301
96Czech APS Extraliga-194
97Czech APS Extraliga-224
97Czech DS Extraliga-15
97Czech DS Stickers-195
98Czech DS-102
98Czech DS Stickers-30
98Czech OFS-68
98Czech OFS-358
98Czech OFS-476
99Czech DS-48
99Czech OFS-295
00Czech OFS-271

Tomasek, Martin
96Red Deer Rebels-12
97Czech APS Extraliga-144
99Czech DS-181
99Czech OFS-430
00Czech OFS-257
02Russian Hockey League-87
03Czech OFS Plus-23
03Czech National Team Postcards-13
04Czech OFS-240
05Czech HC Vitkovice-16
06Czech OFS-65

Tomasoni, Dick
72Finnish Semic World Championship-137
72Swedish Semic World Championship-137

Tomassoni, Dave
82Swedish Semic VM Stickers-128
83Swedish Semic VM Stickers-128

Tomassoni, Matt
06Cedar Rapids RoughRiders-18

Tomassoni, Ron
92Harvard Crimson-29

Tomberlin, Justin
92Maine Black Bears-30
93Maine Black Bears-50
94Raleigh Icecaps-19
98Fayetteville Force-5

Tomek, Michal
94Czech APS Extraliga-245
95Czech APS Extraliga-23
96Czech APS Extraliga-225
97Czech APS Extraliga-113
97Czech DS Extraliga-25
98Czech DS Stickers-56
98Czech OFS-26
99Czech DS-11
99Czech OFS-217

Tomica, Marek
99Czech OFS-393
00Czech OFS-104
01Czech OFS-281
02Czech OFS Plus-252
03Czech OFS Plus-193
04Czech OFS-175
06Czech OFS All Stars-16

Tomik, Robert
00Czech DS Extraliga-131
00Czech OFS-176
01Czech OFS All Stars-37
02Czech OFS Plus-19
02Slovakian Kvarteto-18
03German DEL-210
03German Nuremberg Ice Tigers Postcards-26
04Czech OFS-37
04Finnish Cardset-297
04German DEL Update-341
06Czech HC Zlin Hame Postcards-12
06Czech OFS-243
06Swedish SHL Elitset-100

Tomilin, Vitali
92Classic-53
Gold-53
92Classic Four-Sport *-191
Gold-191
93Upper Deck-278

Tomko, Slavomir
02Topeka Scarecrows-2

Tomlak, Mike
89Whalers Junior Milk-21
900-Pee-Chee-95
90Panini Stickers-46
90Pro Set-452
90Topps-95
Tiffany-95
90Upper Deck-343
French-343
90Whalers Jr. 7-Eleven-24
90ProCards AHL/IHL-176
91Bowman-14
910-Pee-Chee-410
91Panini Stickers-319
91Score Canadian Bilingual-538
91Score Canadian English-538
91Stadium Club-266
91Topps-410
91Upper Deck-310
French-310
91ProCards-114
94Milwaukee Admirals-24
95Milwaukee Admirals-18
95Milwaukee Admirals Postcards-16
96Milwaukee Admirals-25
97Milwaukee Admirals-18

Tomlinson, Dave
91ProCards-346
92St. John's Maple Leafs-22
93Classic Pro Prospects-12
95Cincinnati Cyclones-18
96German DEL-170
96Collector's Edge Ice-114
Prism-114
98German DEL-227
99German Adler Mannheim Eagles Postcards-6
99German DEL-7
00German DEL-2
Star Attractions-S9
01German Upper Deck-178
02German DEL City Press-276
03German DEL-120
04German DEL-137
04German Hamburg Freezers Postcards-19

Tomlinson, Jeff
92Raleigh Icecaps-16
94German First League-572
00German Berlin Polar Bears Postcards-20
01German Berlin Polar Bears Postcards-26
01UK Manchester Storm Retro-5
02German Berlin Polar Bears Postcards-27
02German DEL City Press-40
03German Berlin Polar Bears Postcards-30
04German Berlin Eisbarens 50th Anniv-34

Tomlinson, Kirk
88Kitchener Rangers-22
88ProCards IHL-40
91ProCards-122
93Las Vegas Thunder-28
95Peoria Rivermen-23
98Colorado Gold Kings-23
98Colorado Gold Kings Postcards-11
99Colorado Gold Kings Taco Bell-20
99Colorado Gold Kings Wendy's-20
01Flint Generals-22
03Lubbock Cotton Kings-19

Tomlinson, Mike
89Peterborough Petes-108
897th Inn. Sketch OHL-108
907th Inn. Sketch OHL-373
91Peterborough Petes-10
917th Inn. Sketch OHL-126
99Corpus Christi IceRays-22

Tomlinson, Shayne
93Northern Michigan Wildcats-27
05Port Huron Flags-23
06Port Huron Flags-20

Tommila, Esa
92Finnish Jyvas-Hyva Stickers-46
93Finnish Jyvas-Hyva Stickers-89
93Finnish SISU-126
94Finnish SISU-285
95Finnish SISU-188

Tommila, Tero
71Finnish Suomi Stickers-375

Tompkins, Dan
95Seattle Thunderbirds-29
99Missouri River Otters-23
99Missouri River Otters Sheet-22

Toms, C.
10C56-29

Toms, Jeff
917th Inn. Sketch OHL-334
93Sault Ste. Marie Greyhounds-23
93Sault Ste. Marie Greyhound Memorial Cup-25
94Atlanta Knights-19
95Atlanta Knights-20
97Pacific-342
Copper-342
Emerald Green-342
Ice Blue-342
Red-342
Silver-342
98Portland Pirates-13
00Topps Gold Label Class 1-98
Gold-98
00Topps Gold Label Class 2-98
00Topps Gold Label Class 2 Gold-98
00Topps Gold Label Class 3-98
00Topps Gold Label Class 3 Gold-98

Ton, Andy
91Finnish Semic World Champ Stickers-190
91Swedish Semic World Champ Stickers-190
92Finnish Semic-207
93Swedish Semic World Champ Stickers-118
93Swiss HNL-180
95Swedish World Championships Stickers-133
95Swiss HNL-153
95Swiss HNL-520
96Swiss HNL-171

Ton, Petr
94Czech APS Extraliga-62
95Czech APS Extraliga-95
96Czech APS Extraliga-89
97Czech APS Extraliga-206
97Czech DS Extraliga-11
97Czech DS Stickers-148
98Czech DS Stickers-237
98Finnish Keraílysarja-21
99Finnish Cardset-279
00Finnish Cardset-51
01Finnish Cardset-276
01Finnish Cardset Dueling Aces-6
02Finnish Cardset-127
03Czech OFS Plus-159
04Czech HC Sparta Praha Postcards-23
04Czech OFS-202
05Czech HC Sparta Praha-14
06Czech HC Sparta Praha Postcards-12
06Czech OFS-69
Goals Leaders-1
Points Leaders-4

Tonaj, Mark
75HCA Steel City Vacuum-15

Tonelli, John
75Houston Aeros WHA-19
79Islanders Transparencies-20
790-Pee-Chee-146
79Topps-146
800-Pee-Chee-305
810-Pee-Chee-218
820-Pee-Chee-213
820-Pee-Chee Stickers-49
82Post Cereal-12
82Topps Stickers-49
83Islanders Team Issue-17
83NHL Key Tags-82
830-Pee-Chee-20
830-Pee-Chee Stickers-74
830-Pee-Chee Stickers-75
83Puffy Stickers-21
83Topps Stickers-74
83Topps Stickers-75
84Islanders News-14
840-Pee-Chee-138
840-Pee-Chee Stickers-80
840-Pee-Chee Stickers-81
84Topps-103
85Islanders News-15
850-Pee-Chee-41
850-Pee-Chee Box Bottoms-O
850-Pee-Chee Stickers-80
850-Pee-Chee Stickers-116
85Topps-41
85Topps Box Bottoms-O
85Topps Sticker Inserts-7
86Flames Red Rooster-28
860-Pee-Chee-132
860-Pee-Chee Stickers-81
86Topps-132
87Flames Red Rooster-29
870-Pee-Chee-84
870-Pee-Chee Stickers-47
87Topps-84
88Esso All-Stars-45
88Kings Postcards-15
88Kings Smokey-23
880-Pee-Chee Stickers-87
89Kings Smokey-13
890-Pee-Chee-8
89Panini Stickers-90
89Topps-8
90Bowman-148
Tiffany-148
90Kings Smokey-14
900-Pee-Chee-281
90Panini Stickers-235
90Pro Set-129A
90Pro Set-129B
90Score-89
Canadian-89
90Topps-281
Tiffany-281
90Upper Deck-95
French-95
91Pro Set Platinum-22
91Pro Set Platinum-142
91Blackhawks Coke-27
91Bowman-175
910-Pee-Chee-161
91OPC Premier-37
91OPC Premier-159
91Panini Stickers-90
91Pinnacle-284
French-284
91Pro Set-373
French-373
91Score American-172
91Score Canadian Bilingual-172
91Score Canadian Bilingual-567
91Score Canadian English-172
91Score Canadian English-567
91Score Rookie/Traded-17T
91Stadium Club-189
91Topps-161
92Pro Set-263
92Score-342
Canadian-342
92Stadium Club-159
92Topps-119
Gold-119G
93Islanders Chemical Bank Alumni-9

Toninato, Jim
84Minnesota-Duluth Bulldogs-26
85Minnesota-Duluth Bulldogs-12

Tookey, Tim
81Fredericton Express-8
82Fredericton Express-8
88ProCards AHL-191
89ProCards AHL-353
90ProCards AHL/IHL-51
91ProCards-281
94Classic Pro Prospects-84
98Hershey Bears-39

Toomey, Dick
72Finnish Semic World Championship-134
72Swedish Semic World Championship-134

Toomey, Sean
84Minnesota-Duluth Bulldogs-9
85Minnesota-Duluth Bulldogs-24

Toor, Gary
93Quebec Pee-Wee Tournament-1447
95Tri-City Americans-27
98Prince George Cougars-22
99Prince George Cougars-7
01Idaho Steelheads-21
02Arkansas Riverblades-20
03Muskegon Fury-20

Tootoo, Jordin
98OCN Blizzard-12
99Brandon Wheat Kings-21
00Brandon Wheat Kings-1
00UD CHL Prospects-45
01Brandon Wheat Kings-22
01UD Prospects-34
Jerseys-J-JT
Jerseys-C-RT
Jerseys Gold-J-JT
Jerseys Gold-C-RT
02SPx Rookie Redemption-R220
02Brandon Wheat Kings-17
03BAP Memorabilia-172
Emerald-172
Gold-172
Ruby-172
Sapphire-172
Super Rookies-SR14
Super Rookies Gold-SR14
Super Rookies Silver-SR14
03BAP Ultimate Memorabilia Autographs-114
Gold-114
03BAP Ultimate Mem Auto Jerseys-114
03BAP Ultimate Mem Auto Emblems-114
03BAP Ultimate Mem Auto Numbers-114
03BAP Ultimate Mem Franch Present Future-17
03BAP Ultimate Mem Magnificent Prospects-8
03BAP Ultimate Mem Magnif Prospect Autos-8
03BAP Ultimate Mem Rookie Jersey Emblems-15
03BAP Ultimate Mem Rookie Jsy Emblem Gold-15
03BAP Ultimate Mem Rookie Jersey Numbers-15
03BAP Ultimate Mem Rookie Jsy Number Gold-15
03BAP Ultimate Memorabilia Triple Threads-32
03Beehive-221
Gold-221
Silver-221
03Black Diamond-194
Black-194
Green-194
Red-194
03Bowman-154
Gold-154
03Bowman Chrome-154
Refractors-154
Gold Refractors-154
Xfractors-154
03Crown Royale-124
Red-124
Retail-124
Royal Portraits-6
03eTopps-48
03ITG Action-619
03ITG Toronto Spring Expo Class of 2004-8
03ITG Used Signature Series-135
Autographs Gold-135
03ITG VIP Rookie Debut-25
03Kraft-10
03McDonald's Pacific-60
030-Pee-Chee-338
03OPC Blue-338
03OPC Gold-338
03OPC Red-338
03Pacific-357
03Pacific Calder-169
03Pacific Complete-567
Red-567
03Pacific Heads-Up-123
Hobby LTD-123
Retail LTD-123
Jerseys-17
Prime Prospects-14
Prime Prospects LTD-14
03Pacific Invincible-117
Blue-117
Red-117
Retail-117
03Pacific Luxury Suite-92
Gold-92
03Pacific Prism-158
03Pacific Quest for the Cup-123
Calder Contenders-13
03Pacific Supreme-125
03Pacific Supreme-125A
Blue-125
Red-125
Retail-125
03Parkhurst Toronto Expo Rookie Preview-PRP-2
03Parkhurst Rookie-174
Calder Candidates-CMC-11
Calder Candidates Gold-CMC-11
Rookie Emblems-RE-9
Rookie Emblems Gold-RE-9
Rookie Jerseys-RJ-9
Rookie Jerseys Gold-RJ-9
Rookie Numbers-RN-9
Rookie Numbers Gold-RN-9
Teammates Gold-RT13
Teammates-RT13
03Private Stock Reserve-126
Blue-126
Red-126
Retail-126
Class Act-7
03SP Authentic-148
Limited-148
Signed Patches-JT
03SP Game Used-89
Gold-89
Rookie Exclusives-RE10
03SPx-226
Radiance-226
Spectrum-226
03Titanium-212
Patches-212
Right on Target-10
03Topps-338
Blue-338
Gold-338
Red-338
03Topps C55-133
Minis-133
Minis American Back-133
Minis American Back Red-133
Minis Bazooka Back-133
Minis Brooklyn Back-133
Minis Hat Trick Back-133
Minis O Canada Back-133
Minis O Canada Back Red-133
Minis Stanley Cup Back-133
03Topps Pristine-188
03Topps Pristine-189
03Topps Pristine-190
Gold Refractor Die Cuts-188
Gold Refractor Die Cuts-189
Gold Refractor Die Cuts-190
Refractors-188
Refractors-189
Refractors-190
Mini-PM-JTO
Press Plates Black-188
Press Plates Black-189
Press Plates Black-190
Press Plates Cyan-188
Press Plates Cyan-189
Press Plates Cyan-190
Press Plates Magenta-188
Press Plates Magenta-189
Press Plates Magenta-190
Press Plates Yellow-188
Press Plates Yellow-189
Press Plates Yellow-190
03UD Honor Roll-186
03UD Premier Collection-112
Signatures-PS-TOO
Stars-ST-JT
Stars Patches-ST-JT
03Upper Deck-225
Canadian Exclusives-225
HG-225
Magic Moments-MM-15
Rookie Threads-RT-10
03Upper Deck Classic Portraits-172
03Upper Deck Ice-128
Glass Parallel-128
03Upper Deck MVP-470
03Upper Deck Rookie Update-165
03Upper Deck Trilogy-178
Limited-178
03Upper Deck Victory-206
04Pacific-150
Blue-150
Red-150
Gold Crown Die-Cuts-6
04Pacific Montreal International-5
Gold-5
04Pacific Montreal International Gold-5
04Pacific NHL All-Star FANtasy-6
04Pacific NHL All-Star FANtasy Gold-6
04Pacific Toronto Spring Expo-5
Gold-5
04SP Authentic-50
04UD Toronto Fall Expo Priority Signings-JT
04Ultimate Collection Dual Logos-UL2-VT
04Upper Deck All-Star Promos-TO
04AHL Top Prospects-35
04Milwaukee Admirals-16
05ITG Heroes/Prosp Toronto Expo Parallel -75
05Be A Player-51
First Period-51
Second Period-51
Third Period-51
Overtime-51
05Black Diamond-48
Emerald-48
Gold-48
Onyx-48
Ruby-48
05UD Artifacts-56
Blue-56
Gold-56
Green-56
Pewter-56
Red-56
Gold Autographed-56
05Upper Deck-109
HG Glossy-109
Jerseys-J-TO
Patches-P-JTO
05Upper Deck MVP-227
Gold-227
Platinum-227
05Upper Deck Toronto Fall Expo-109
05Milwaukee Admirals Choice-15
05Milwaukee Admirals Pepsi-19
05ITG Heroes and Prospects-75
Autographs-A-JTO
Jerseys-GUJ-99
Jerseys Gold-GUJ-99
06Fleer Fabricology-FTO
060-Pee-Chee-279
Rainbow-279
06Upper Deck-113
Exclusives Parallel-113
High Gloss Parallel-113
Masterpieces-113
06Upper Deck MVP-164
Gold Script-164
Super Script-164

Tootoo, Terence
97OCN Blizzard-5
98OCN Blizzard-2
99OCN Blizzard-21
00OCN Blizzard-19
01Roanoke Express-20

Topatigh, Lucio
92Finnish Semic-261
93Swedish Semic World Champ Stickers-221
95Finnish Semic World Championships-175
95Swedish World Championships Stickers-88

Topazzini, Ted
52Juniors Blue Tint-145

Topilko, Jeff
02Brandon Wheat Kings-21
03Brandon Wheat Kings-18
04Brandon Wheat Kings-21
05Brandon Wheat Kings-22

Topol, Miloslav
02Czech OFS Plus-325

Topoli, Marek
92Quebec Pee-Wee Tournament-1747
02Czech OFS Plus-295

Topolnisky, Craig
94German DEL-147

Toporowski, Brad
917th Inn. Sketch WHL-14
97Louisiana Ice Gators-12
98Colorado Gold Kings-22
98Colorado Gold Kings Postcards-2

Toporowski, Kerry
89Spokane Chiefs-17
907th Inn. Sketch WHL-206
91ProCards-499
917th Inn. Sketch Memorial Cup-85
91Ultimate Draft-48
91Ultimate Draft French-48
92Indianapolis Ice-24
93Indianapolis Ice-22
93Las Vegas Thunder-29
94Las Vegas Thunder-29
95Adirondack Red Wings-22
97Quad-City Mallards-21
00Quad-City Mallards-24
01Quad-City Mallards-22

Toporowski, Shayne
93Prince Albert Raiders-18
94Prince Albert Raiders-18
95St. John's Maple Leafs-18
96St. John's Maple Leafs-23
96Collector's Edge Ice-84
Prism-84
97Donruss-224
Press Proofs Silver-224
Press Proofs Gold-224
00Finnish Cardset-252
01UK Belfast Giants-23
02German DEL City Press-146
03Finnish Cardset-125
04Finnish Cardset-118
Parallel-88
05Finnish Cardset -287
06Finnish Cardset-115

Toppazzini, Jerry
44Beehive Group II Photos-71
53Parkhurst-98
54Topps-21
55Bruins Photos-17
57Bruins Photos-20
57Topps-5
58Bruins Photos-15
58Topps-45
59Topps-38
60NHL Ceramic Tiles-17
60Shirriff Coins-110
60Topps-28
61Shirriff/Salada Coins-9
61Topps-9
62Topps-13
Hockey Bucks-22
63Topps-18
91Ultimate Original Six-55
French-55
92Parkhurst Parkie Reprints-PR27
94Parkhurst Missing Link-1

Toppazzini, Zellio
44Beehive Group II Photos-72
52Parkhurst-73

Topping, Brad
00Brampton Batalion-25
03Brampton Batallion-23

Torchetti, John
94Central Hockey League-88
94San Antonio Iguanas-16

Torchia, Mike
88Kitchener Rangers-6
89Kitchener Rangers-6
897th Inn. Sketch OHL-191
897th Inn. Sketch OHL-192
90Kitchener Rangers-6
907th Inn. Sketch OHL-244
907th Inn. Sketch Memorial Cup-31
917th Inn. Sketch OHL-75
917th Inn. Sketch CHL Award Winners-6
917th Inn. Sketch Memorial Cup-131
91Star Pics-26
91Ultimate Draft-50
91Ultimate Draft French-50
91Ultimate Draft Promos-3
93Classic Pro Prospects-119
95Donruss-143
95Leaf-213
95Score-311
Black Ice Artist's Proofs-311
Black Ice-311
95Ultra-43
Gold Medallion-43
97Milwaukee Admirals-19
00UK Sekonda Superleague-203
00UK Sheffield Steelers-25
01UK Manchester Storm-14
01UK Manchester Storm-20
02UK Guildford Flames-12
02UK Guildford Flames-26
02UK Manchester Storm-16
02UK Manchester Storm-19

Tordjman, Josh
03Victoriaville Tigers-26
04Victoriaville Tigres-9
05Moncton Wildcats-28
05Victoriaville Tigres-5

Torgajev, Pavel
93Finnish SISU-46
94Finnish SISU-309
95Parkhurst International-302
Emerald Ice-302
95Ultra-215
98Swiss Power Play Stickers-99
00Russian Hockey League-199

Torkkel, Kari
66Finnish Jaakiekkosarja-62
70Finnish Jaakiekko-151
71Finnish Suomi Stickers-202
72Finnish Jaakiekko-239
73Finnish Jaakiekko-274

Torkkeli, Jorma
78Finnish SM-Liiga-151
80Finnish Mallasjuoma-106

Torkkeli, Veikko
78Finnish SM-Liiga-143
80Finnish Mallasjuoma-103

Torkki, Jari
88ProCards IHL-117
89ProCards IHL-55
91Finnish Semic World Champ Stickers-22
91Finnish Jyvas-Hyva Stickers-45
91Swedish Semic World Champ Stickers-22
92Finnish Jyvas-Hyva Stickers-130
93Finnish Jyvas-Hyva Stickers-239
93Finnish SISU-194
94Finnish SISU-13
94Finnish SISU Fire On Ice-20
95Finnish SISU-104
95Finnish SISU-189
95Finnish SISU Limited-34
96Finnish SISU Redline-107
96German DEL-194

Torkki, Sami
00Finnish Cardset-67
01Finnish Cardset-91
02Finnish Cardset-281
03Finnish Cardset-108
04Finnish Cardset-121
Parallel-90
05Swedish SHL Elitset-225
Gold-225
06Swedish SHL Elitset-77

Torma, Hannu
65Finnish Hellas-29
66Finnish Jaakiekkosarja-3

Tormanen, Antti
93Finnish SISU-16
94Finnish SISU-63
94Finnish SISU Magic Numbers-7
94Finnish SISU NHL Draft-8
94Finnish Jaa Kiekko-28
95Bowman-117
All-Foil-117
95Donruss-347
Rated Rookies-15
95Finest-118
Refractors-118
95Metal-196
95Parkhurst International-415
95Parkhurst International-522
Emerald Ice-415
Emerald Ice-522
95Select Certified-111
Mirror Gold-111
95Senators Team Issue-22
95SP-105
95Stadium Club-156
Members Only Master Set-156
95Summit-174
Artist's Proofs-174
Ice-174
95Topps SuperSkills Super Rookies-SR13
95Ultra-360
95Upper Deck-347
Electric Ice-347
Electric Ice Gold-347
95Zenith-135
Rookie Roll Call-4
95Finnish SISU Gold Cards-23
95Finnish SISU Limited-17
95Finnish Karjala World Champ Labels-22
95Finnish Semic World Championships-49
96Collector's Choice-184
96Score-265
Artist's Proofs-265
Dealer's Choice Artist's Proofs-265
Special Artist's Proofs-265
Golden Blades-265
96Summit-161
Artist's Proofs-161
Ice-161
Metal-161
Premium Stock-161
96Upper Deck-114
96Zenith-78
Artist's Proofs-78
96Swedish Semic Wien-15
98Finnish Kerailysarja Leijonat-45
98Swedish UD Choice-110
99Finnish Cardset-200
Aces High-H-9
99Swedish Upper Deck-96
00Finnish Cardset-163
01Finnish Cardset-54
02Finnish Cardset-133
02Swedish SHL-254
Dynamic Duos-7
Parallel-254
Signatures Series II-16
03Swedish Elite-117
Signatures-1
Silver-117
Stars of the Game-8

Tornberg, Johan
93Swedish Semic Elitserien-30
94Swedish Leaf-212
95Swedish Leaf-294
95Swedish Upper Deck-190
97Swedish Collector's Choice-186
98Swedish UD Choice-154
99Swedish Upper Deck-152
SHL Signatures-14
00Swedish Upper Deck-140

Tornberg, Ove
85Swedish Panini Stickers-189

Torney, Mike
02Pee Dee Pride RBI-148
03Florence Pride-159

Tornlund, Inge
67Swedish Hockey-211

Tornquist, Michael
98Odessa Jackalopes-14
99Odessa Jackalopes-1

Tornqvist, Alf
84Swedish Semic Elitserien-126

Tornqvist, Gusten
02Swedish SHL-217
Parallel-217
02Swiss SCL Tigers-5
03Swedish Elite-78
Silver-78
04Swedish Elitset-70
Gold-70
Masks-6
05Swedish SHL Elitset-82
Series One Signatures-14

Tornqvist, Johan
86Swedish Panini Stickers-16
87Swedish Panini Stickers-38

Tornvall, Ilkka
06Finnish Cardset-349
06Finnish Porin Assat Pelaajakortit-12

Toropchenko, Leonid
93Cleveland Lumberjacks-14
93Cleveland Lumberjacks Postcards-22
93Classic Pro Prospects-95
93Classic Four-Sport *-250
Gold-250
94Classic Pro Prospects-212
00Russian Hockey League-203

Torquato, Zack
05Saginaw Spirit-23
06Erie Otters-13
06Saginaw Spirit-17

Torrel, Doug
92Hamilton Canucks-26

Torres, Raffi
99Brampton Battalion-11
99Brampton Battalion-30
99UD Prospects-23
00SPx Rookie Redemption-RR19
00Brampton Battalion-11
00Brampton Battalion-29
00UD CHL Prospects-34
Autographs-A-RT
Future Leaders-FL2
Game Jersey Autographs-S-RT
Game Jerseys-RT
Game Jerseys-S-T
Game Jerseys-T-Z
Great Desire-GD4
Supremacy-CS3
01BAP Memorabilia-350
Emerald-350
Ruby-350
Sapphire-350
01Bowman YoungStars-146
Gold-146
Ice Cubed-146
01Crown Royale-170
010-Pee-Chee-360
01Parkhurst-329
01SP Authentic-180
Limited-180
Limited Gold-180
01SP Game Used-86
01SPx-210
Rookie Treasures-RTRT
01Titanium-170
Retail-170
Rookie Team-9
Three-Star Selections-29
01Titanium Draft Day Edition-151
01Topps-360
01Topps Chrome-179
Refractors-179
Black Border Refractors-179
01UD Challenge for the Cup-124
01UD Honor Roll-94
01UD Mask Collection-154
Gold-154
01UD Playmakers-128
01UD Premier Collection-112
Signatures-RT
Signatures Black-RT
01UD Top Shelf-133
01Upper Deck-436
Exclusives-436
01Upper Deck Ice-143
01Upper Deck MVP-228
01Upper Deck Victory-448
01Vanguard-121
Blue-121
Red-121
One of Ones-121
Premiere Date-121
Proofs-121
01UD Prospects Autographs-A-RT
02BAP First Edition-258
020-Pee-Chee-308
020-Pee-Chee Premier Blue Parallel-308
020-Pee-Chee Premier Red Parallel-308
020-Pee-Chee Factory Set-308
02Pacific-244
Blue-244
Red-244
02Pacific Calder-70
Silver-70
02Pacific Complete-54
Red-54
02Pacific Entry Draft-7
02Pacific Heads-Up Head First-9
02Pacific Toronto Spring Expo Rookie Coll-8
02SP Authentic-123
02SP Game Used First Rounder Patches-RT
02Topps-308
OPC Blue Parallel-308
OPC Red Parallel-308
Factory Set-308
02UD Top Shelf Signatures-RT
02Upper Deck Victory-133
Bronze-133
Gold-133
Silver-133
02Upper Deck Vintage-156
Green Backs-156
03Beehive-80
Variations-80
Gold-80
Silver-80
03Oilers Postcards-21
03Pacific Calder-43
Silver-43
03Pacific Complete-282
Red-282
03Pacific Quest for the Cup-44
Blue-44
03SP Authentic-33
Limited-33
03Titanium-40
Hobby Jersey Number Parallels-40
Retail-40
Retail Jersey Number Parallels-40
03Topps Traded-TT41
Blue-TT41
Gold-TT41
Red-TT41
03UD Premier Collection-23
Teammates-PT-EO2
Teammates Patches-PT-EO2
03Upper Deck-318
Canadian Exclusives-318
HG-318
UD Exclusives-318
03Upper Deck Ice-35
Gold-35
Breakers-IB-RT
Breaker Patches-IB-RT
Frozen Fabrics-FF-RT
Frozen Fabric Patches-FF-RT
03Upper Deck MVP-171
Gold Script-171
Silver Script-171
Canadian Exclusives-171
03Upper Deck Rookie Update-35
YoungStars-YS16
04Pacific-107
Blue-107
Red-107
04Upper Deck-72
Canadian Exclusives-72
Heritage Classic-CC-RT
HG Glossy Gold-72
HG Glossy Silver-72
YoungStars-YS-RT
05Parkhurst-192
Facsimile Auto Parallel-192
05SP Game Used Authentic Fabrics Dual-RA
05SP Game Used Authentic Patches Dual-RA
05SP Game Used Game Gear-GG-RT
05SP Game Used Significant Numbers-SN-RT
05UD Toronto Fall Expo Priority Signings-PS-RT
05Ultra-83
Gold-83
Ice-83
05Upper Deck-75
HG Glossy-75
Jerseys-J-RT
Jerseys Series II-J2RT
Ice Fresh Ice-FIRT
Ice Fresh Ice Glass-FIRT
Ice Fresh Ice Glass Patches-FIPRT
05Upper Deck MVP-160
Gold-160
Platinum-160
05Upper Deck Toronto Fall Expo-75
05Upper Deck Victory-78
Black-78
Gold-78
Silver-78
06Flair Showcase Stitches-SSRT
06Fleer Fabricology-FRT
06Gatorade-23
060-Pee-Chee-202
Rainbow-202
06Panini Stickers-274
06SP Game Used Authentic Fabrics Dual-AF2TP
06SP Game Used Authentic Fabrics Dual Patches-AF2TP
06The Cup NHL Shields Duals-DSHPT
06Upper Deck-81
Exclusives Parallel-81
High Gloss Parallel-81
Masterpieces-81
06Upper Deck MVP-119
Gold Script-119
Super Script-119
06Upper Deck Ovation-121
06Upper Deck Victory-82
06Upper Deck Victory Black-82
06Upper Deck Victory Gold-82
07Upper Deck Victory-161
Black-161
Gold-161

Torresan, Eric
93Quebec Pee-Wee Tournament-1681

Torretti, Dominic
99Des Moines Buccaneers-1

Torrey, Bill
84Islanders News-28
85Islanders News-28
00Panthers Team Issue-1

Torrey, Jeff
92Richmond Renegades-19

Torri, Chris
93Quebec Pee-Wee Tournament-830

Torstensson, Sverker
69Swedish Hockey-182
73Swedish Stickers-63
74Swedish Stickers-193

Torstensson, Ulf
65Swedish Coralli ISHockey-178
67Swedish Hockey-129
69Swedish Hockey-109
70Swedish Hockey-87
71Swedish Hockey-192

72Swedish Stickers-178
74Swedish Stickers-267
Torti, Sloan
86Kingston Canadians-27
Tortorella, Andrew
95Waterloo Blackhawks -20
99Knoxville Speed-21
00Knoxville Speed-21
Tortorella, John
88ProCards AHL-202
89Sabres Campbell's-25
90Sabres Campbell's-26
95Rochester Americans-25
96Rochester Americans-23
03Lightning Team Issue-3
05Lightning Team Issue-1
Tortunov, Boris
98Russian Hockey League-18
99Russian Hockey League-19
99Russian Metallurg Magnetogorsk-33
00Russian Hockey League-219
01Russian Hockey League-123
02Russian Hockey League-183
05Russian Hockey League RHL-45
Tory, Jeff
91British Columbia JHL-88
91British Columbia JHL-159
92British Columbia JHL-138
98IHL All-Star Western Conference-11
01German Upper Deck-135
02German DEL City Press-104
All-Stars-AS9
03German Deg Metro Stars-18
03German DEL-40
All-Stars-AS22
04German DEL-55
04German Dusseldorf Metro Stars Postcards-20
05German DEL-74
06German DEL-101
Tosi, Didier
93Swiss HNL-265
95Swiss HNL-462
96Swiss HNL-363
98Swiss Power Play Stickers-339
Tosio, Renato
91Finnish Semic World Champ Stickers-177
91Swedish Semic World Champ Stickers-177
92Finnish Semic-195
93Swedish Semic World Champ Stickers-109
93Swiss HNL-60
95Finnish Semic World Championships-189
95Swedish Globe World Championships-209
95Swedish World Championships Stickers-117
95Swiss HNL-87
96Swiss HNL-29
98Swiss Power Play Stickers-29
99Swiss Panini Stickers-30
00Swiss Panini Stickers-30
00Swiss Slapshot Mini-Cards-SCB1
Toskala, Vesa
95Collector's Choice-335
Player's Club-335
Player's Club Platinum-335
95Finnish SISU-230
Drafted Dozen-7
95Finnish SISU Limited-100
96Finnish SISU Redline-27
96Finnish SISU Redline Foil Parallels-27
96Finnish SISU Redline Mighty Adversaries-6
96Finnish SISU Redline Promos-3
96Finnish SISU Redline Rookie Energy-8
96Finnish SISU Redline Silver Signatures-5
98Finnish Kerailysarja-74
Mad Masks-4
99Finnish Cardset-180
Par Avion-10
99Swedish Upper Deck-52
00Finnish Cardset-111
00Kentucky Thoroughblades-23
01Between the Pipes-86
01Titanium Draft Day Edition-166
01Finnish Cardset Haltmeisters-4
01Cleveland Barons-20
02Between the Pipes-100
Gold-100
Silver-100
02Pacific Calder-95
Silver-95
02Pacific Complete-598
Red-598
02UD Mask Collection-73
02UD Mask Collection Beckett Promos-73
02Finnish Cardset-128
02Cleveland Barons-22
03BAP Memorabilia-169
Emerald-169
Gold-169
Ruby-169
Sapphire-169
03ITG Action-426
03Pacific-302
Blue-302
Red-302
03Pacific Complete-441
Red-441
04Pacific-234
Blue-234
Red-234
05Parkhurst-399
Facsimile Auto Parallel-399
05Upper Deck-405
05Upper Deck MVP-327
Gold-327
Platinum-327
05Finnish Cardset -39
Finnish Cardset Super Snatchers-6
06Be A Player-21
Autographs-21
Signatures-VT
Signatures 10-23
Signatures Trios-TTBM
Signatures Foursomes-FLTKG
06Beehive-18
Matte-18
Signature Scrapbook-SSVT
06Between The Pipes The Mask-M37
06Between The Pipes The Mask Gold-M37
06Between The Pipes The Mask Silver-M37
06Black Diamond-71
Black-71
Gold-71
Ruby-71
Gemography-GVT
06Flair Showcase Hot Gloves-HG27
06Fleer-162
Tiffany-162
Netminders-N23
06Hot Prospects-86
06O-Pee-Chee-419
Rainbow-419
06Panini Stickers-328
06SP Authentic-19
Limited-19
Sign of the Times-STVT
06SP Game Used Inked Sweaters-ISVT
06SP Game Used Inked Sweaters Patches-ISVT
06SP Game Used SIGnificance-SVT
06The Cup Autographed NHL Shields Duals-DASLT
06The Cup Enshrinements-EVT
06The Cup Limited Logos-LLVT
06UD Artifacts-19
Blue-19
Gold-19
Platinum-19
Radiance-19
Red-19
06UD Mini Jersey Collection-83
06Ultimate Collection Signatures-US-VT
06Ultra-163
Gold Medallion-163
Ice Medallion-163
06Upper Deck Arena Giveaways-SJS2
06Upper Deck-162
Exclusives Parallel-162
High Gloss Parallel-162
Masterpieces-162
Signature Sensations-SSVT
06Upper Deck MVP-241
Gold Script-241
Super Script-241
Last Line of Defense-LL16
06Upper Deck Ovation-142
06Upper Deck Sweet Shot Signature Shots/Saves-SSVT
06Upper Deck Trilogy-82
06Upper Deck Victory-167
06Upper Deck Victory Black-167
06Upper Deck Victory Gold-167
07Upper Deck Ovation-60
07Upper Deck Victory-175
Black-175
Gold-175
Toth, Anthony
91Air Canada SJHL-E50
92Saskatchewan JHL-164
Toth, Kaleb
94Prince Albert Raiders-19
97Lethbridge Hurricanes-20
Toth, Radek
94Czech APS Extraliga-251
95Czech APS Extraliga-126
97Czech APS Extraliga-195
97Czech DS Extraliga-89
98Czech DS Stickers-227
99German DEL-353
00German DEL-113
Tottle, Scott
85Fredericton Express-1
Touchette, Alexandre
06Gatineau Olympiques-22
Touchette, Jean-Francois
99Quebec Remparts-10
Signed-10
Tougas, Vincent
01Drummondville Voltigeurs-16
Touhey, Bill
33O-Pee-Chee V304A-26
33V252 Canadian Gum-48
Touhimaa, Harri
83Swedish Semic VM Stickers-49
Toujikov, Rouslan
94Roanoke Express-10
Toulmin, Grant
05Swift Current Broncos-16
06Swift Current Broncos-4
Touminen, Jani
03UK London Racers-16
Toupal, Kamil
94Czech APS Extraliga-31
95Czech APS Extraliga-61
96Czech APS Extraliga-244
97Czech APS Extraliga-271
97Czech DS Stickers-77
98Czech DS Stickers-73
98Czech OFS-197
99German EV Landshut-9
Toupal, Radek
91Finnish Semic World Champ Stickers-117
91Swedish Semic World Champ Stickers-117
92Finnish Jyvas-Hyva Stickers-28
94German DEL-377
95Czech APS Extraliga-65
95Finnish Semic World Championships-149
95Swedish World Championships Stickers-209
96Czech APS Extraliga-250
97Czech APS Extraliga-276
97Czech DS Extraliga-31
97Czech DS Stickers-86
98Czech DS-34
98Czech DS Stickers-74
98Czech OFS-201
98Czech OFS-466
99Czech DS-38
99Czech OFS-190
Toupin, Maxime
92Quebec Pee-Wee Tournament-1899
93Quebec Pee-Wee Tournament-1596
Toupin, Simon
907th Inn. Sketch QMJHL-129
917th Inn. Sketch QMJHL-177
Tournier, Marc
83Sault Ste. Marie Greyhounds-7
Tousignant, Dan
85Minnesota-Duluth Bulldogs-23
Tousignant, Jean-Francois
93Quebec Pee-Wee Tournament-96
Touzimsky, Zdenek
94Czech APS Extraliga-73
95Czech APS Extraliga-182
96Czech APS Extraliga-316
97Czech DS Stickers-155
98Czech OFS-363
99German DEL-344
00Czech OFS-64
Tovall, Trevor
89Spokane Chiefs-18
907th Inn. Sketch WHL-192
917th Inn. Sketch Memorial Cup-86
Tower, George
92Norwegian Elite Series-180
Towns, Mike
04Penticton Vees-11
05Penticton Vees-18
06Penticton Vees-21
Townsend, Andrew
93Quebec Pee-Wee Tournament-1285
03Fort Wayne Komets-13
04Fort Wayne Komets-16
Townsend, Ryan
01Johnstown Chiefs-24
02Johnstown Chiefs-20
Townsend, Scott
907th Inn. Sketch WHL-37
917th Inn. Sketch WHL-325
93Lethbridge Hurricanes-18
93Spokane Chiefs-27
Townshend, Graeme
89Bruins Sports Action Update-10
89ProCards AHL-70
90ProCards AHL/IHL-133
91ProCards-456
93Senators Kraft Sheets-23
95Houston Aeros-20
01Greensboro Generals-19
Towriss, Jeff
98Halifax Mooseheads-24
Toye, Randy
917th Inn. Sketch WHL-20
Toykkala, Joni
04Finnish Cardset-9
04Finnish Cardset Signatures-1
05Finnish Cardset -4
06Finnish Cardset-188
Traber, Patrik
95Swiss HNL-457
Trabichet, Cyril
92Quebec Pee-Wee Tournament-1201
93Quebec Pee-Wee Tournament-1485
Trach, Jordan
06Prince Albert Raiders-15
Trachta, David
94Czech APS Extraliga-161
95Czech APS Extraliga-262
Trachta, Karel
94Czech APS Extraliga-289
95Czech APS Extraliga-242
97Czech APS Extraliga-219
98Czech OFS-81
Trachta, Tomas
96Czech APS Extraliga-83
97Czech APS Extraliga-213
99Czech Score Blue 2000-18
99Czech Score Red Ice 2000-18
Tracy, Joe
91Swedish Semic Elitserien Stickers-247
Tracy, Tripp
92Harvard Crimson-30
96Richmond Renegades-23
Tracze, Steve
95Slapshot-42
Trader, Larry
83Canadian National Juniors-15
86Canadiens Postcards-27
87Canadiens Postcards-33
87Canadiens Vachon Stickers-44
88ProCards AHL-71
Trafford, Mark
93Quebec Pee-Wee Tournament-1690
Tragust, Thomas
06Texas Tornados-23
Trainer, Chris
83Kitchener Rangers-28
05Quad City Mallards-23
Trakhanov, Pavel
00Russian Hockey League-331
02Russian Hockey League-108
Trampuh, Robbie
92British Columbia JHL-131
Tranholm, Soren
98Danish Hockey League-92
99Danish Hockey League-125
Tranmer, Zach
02Barrie Colts-4
02London Knights-16
Tranvik, Isak
05Waterloo Blackhawks-23
Trapp, Barry
82Regina Pats-24
83Regina Pats-24
Trapp, Bob
23V128-1 Paulin's Candy-42
Trapp, Doug
82Regina Pats-6
83Regina Pats-6
Trattner, Jurgen
94German First League-534
98German DEL-197
Trattnig, Matthias
02Swedish SHL-163
Parallel-163
03German DEL-164
04Syracuse Crunch-8
Traub, Puss
23V128-1 Paulin's Candy-23
Traverse, Patrick
90Montreal-Bourassa AAA-25
917th Inn. Sketch QMJHL-63
95PEI Senators-21
98Pacific Omega-171
Red-171
Opening Day Issue-171
98Senators Team Issue-21
99Senators Team Issue-19
00Topps Heritage-206
01BAP Signature Series-79
Autographs-79
Autographs Gold-79
01Canadiens Postcards-27
02BAP Sig Series Auto Buybacks 2001-79
02Canadiens Postcards-18
02NHL Power Play Stickers-54
04Houston Aeros-17
05Iowa Stars-18
06Hamilton Bulldogs-25
Travis, Shannon
89ProCards IHL-174
Travnicek, Michal
98Czech OFS-16
99Czech DS-70
99Czech OFS-340
00St. John's Maple Leafs-27
01St. John's Maple Leafs-24
02Czech OFS Plus-333
03Czech OFS Plus-105
03Czech OFS Plus MS Praha-SE28
04Czech OFS-109
Czech/Slovak-20
05Czech HC Hame Zlin-15
06Czech OFS-149
All Stars-18
Travnicek, Zdenek
94German DEL-300
95German DEL-389
96German DEL-72
99German Bundesliga 2-87
Traylen, Dustin
06Port Huron Flags-18
Traynor, Paul
94Kitchener Rangers-8
95Slapshot-139
96Kitchener Rangers-25
97Albany River Rats-18
97Bowman CHL-39
OPC-39
00Rochester Americans-22
01South Carolina Stingrays-17
03Syracuse Crunch-8
04German Cologne Sharks Postcards-27
04German DEL Update-321A
05German DEL-216
06German DEL-116
Trboyevich, Dean
91Richmond Renegades Set 2-13
94Anchorage Aces-25
96Anchorage Aces-15
97Grand Rapids Griffins-19
98Anchorage Aces-2
Trebil, Dan
92Minnesota Golden Gophers-21
93Minnesota Golden Gophers-25
94Minnesota Golden Gophers-27
95Minnesota Golden Gophers-27
97Donruss-105
Press Proofs Silver-105
Press Proofs Gold-105
98Cincinnati Mighty Ducks-18
99AHL All-Stars-10
99Cincinnati Mighty Ducks-9
Trebil, Ryan
96Minnesota Golden Gophers-26
97Minnesota Golden Gophers-17
98Minnesota Golden Gophers-21
99Minnesota Golden Gophers-26
Trefilov, Andrei
91O-Pee-Chee Inserts-45R
91Star Pics-49
92Upper Deck-345
92Upper Deck-514
92Finnish Semic-99
92Russian Stars Red Ace-4
92Salt Lake Golden Eagles-22
93Donruss-409
93Parkhurst-29
Emerald Ice-29
93PowerPlay-311
93Score-599
Gold-599
Canadian-599
Canadian Gold-599
93Classic-95
93Classic Pro Prospects-30
BCs-BC2
93Classic Four-Sport *-248
Gold-248
94Donruss-244
94Leaf-87
94OPC Premier-166
Special Effects-166
94Parkhurst-36
Gold-36
94Topps/OPC Premier-166
Special Effects-166
94Ultra-271
94Finnish Jaa Kiekko-136
94Saint John Flames-25
94Classic Pro Prospects-181
Jumbos-PP9
95Donruss-273
95Parkhurst International-296
Emerald Ice-296
95Upper Deck-277
Electric Ice-277
Electric Ice Gold-277
95Swedish Globe World Championships-163
96Upper Deck-225
98Indianapolis Ice-11
99Chicago Wolves-21
00German DEL-58
Profiles-P11
01German Upper Deck-58
Goalies in Action-G3
Jersey Cards-AT-J
02German DEL City Press-60
03German Deg Metro Stars-19
03German DEL-41
All-Stars-AS2
04German DEL-56
All-Stars-AS2
04German Dusseldorf Metro Stars Postcards-21
05German DEL-75
Tregunna, Scott
05Owen Sound Attack-10
06Owen Sound Attack-10
Treille, Yorick
93Quebec Pee-Wee Tournament-1483
02Norfolk Admirals-22
03Norfolk Admirals-19
04Providence Bruins-18
Trembecky, Jeff
98Peoria Rivermen-18
Tremblay, Alexandre
93Quebec Pee-Wee Tournament-281
99Rimouski Oceanic-7
Signed-7
99Bowman CHL-77
Gold-77
OPC International-77
03Finnish Cardset-79
Tremblay, Andre
93Quebec Pee-Wee Tournament-1363
Tremblay, Clement
51Bas Du Fleuve-4
52Bas Du Fleuve-32
Tremblay, Dave
907th Inn. Sketch QMJHL-29
917th Inn. Sketch QMJHL-80
Tremblay, David
02Hull Olympiques-22
03Gatineau Olympiques-24
03Hull Olympiques Memorial Cup-18
04Gatineau Olympiques-1
05Gatineau Olympiques-1
Tremblay, Denis
79Montreal Juniors-27
Tremblay, Devyn
04Medicine Hat Tigers-22
Tremblay, Didier
93Quebec Pee-Wee Tournament-1333
95Halifax Mooseheads-6
96Halifax Mooseheads I-21
96Halifax Mooseheads II-21
97Halifax Mooseheads I-21
98Val d'Or Foreurs-7
98Bowman CHL-84
Golden Anniversary-84
OPC International-84
98Bowman Chrome CHL-84
Golden Anniversary-84
Golden Anniversary Refractors-84
OPC International-84
OPC International Refractors-84
Refractors-84
99Bowman CHL-68
Gold-68
OPC International-68
00Peoria Rivermen-2
04St Georges de Beauce Garaga-21
Tremblay, Eric
99Baie-Comeau Drakkar-23
99Bowman CHL-46
Gold-46
OPC International-46
Tremblay, Erick
02Rimouski Oceanic-20
03Rimouski Oceanic-20
03Rimouski Oceanic Sheets-2
04Rimouski Oceanic-21
05Rimouski Oceanic-2
06Victoriaville Tigres-7
Tremblay, Frank
85London Knights-16
Tremblay, Gilles
44Beehive Group II Photos-290A
44Beehive Group II Photos-290B
60NHL Ceramic Tiles-16
60York Photos-36
61Shirriff/Salada Coins-112
61York Yellow Backs-4
62Parkhurst-46
62Shirriff Coins-24
62York Iron-On Transfers-34
63Chex Photos-53
63Parkhurst-21
63Parkhurst-80
63Toronto Star-38
63York White Backs-21
64Beehive Group III Photos-117A
64Beehive Group III Photos-117B
64Canadiens Postcards-19
64Coca-Cola Caps-70
64Topps-2
65Canadiens Steinberg Glasses-10
65Coca-Cola-69
66Canadiens IGA-8
66Topps-4
66Topps USA Test-4
67Canadiens IGA-5
67Post Flip Books-9
67Topps-5
68Canadiens IGA-5
68Canadiens Postcards BW-17
68O-Pee-Chee-66
68Post Marbles-25
68Shirriff Coins-81
68Topps-66
69O-Pee-Chee-168
80Quebec Remparts-22
94Parkhurst Tall Boys-77
95Parkhurst '66-67-71
Coins-71
Tremblay, Hunter
02Barrie Colts-9
03Barrie Colts-9
04Barrie Colts-11
06Barrie Colts-9
Tremblay, J.C.
44Beehive Group II Photos-291A
44Beehive Group II Photos-291B
60NHL Ceramic Tiles-34
60Shirriff Coins-36
61Shirriff/Salada Coins-118
61York Yellow Backs-34
62Parkhurst-54
62Shirriff Coins-30
62York Iron-On Transfers-6
63Chex Photos-54
63Parkhurst-31
63Parkhurst-90
63Toronto Star-39
63York White Backs-24
64Beehive Group III Photos-118
64Canadiens Postcards-20
64Coca-Cola Caps-57
64Topps-88
64Toronto Star-46
65Canadiens Steinberg Glasses-11
65Coca-Cola-57
65Topps-69
66Canadiens IGA-1
66Topps-5
66Topps USA Test-5
67Canadiens IGA-3
67Post Flip Books-3
67Post Flip Books-10
67Topps-73
67York Action Octagons-9
67York Action Octagons-12
67York Action Octagons-13
67York Action Octagons-19
67York Action Octagons-24
68Canadiens IGA-3
68Canadiens Postcards BW-18
68O-Pee-Chee-59
68O-Pee-Chee-206
68Post Marbles-26
68Shirriff Coins-79
68Topps-59
69Canadiens Postcards Color-30
69O-Pee-Chee-5
69Topps-5
70Canadiens Pins-16
70Colgate Stamps-64
70Dad's Cookies-129
70Esso Power Players-3
70O-Pee-Chee-178
70Post Shooters-16
70Sargent Promotions Stamps-99
71Canadiens Postcards-24
71Frito-Lay-5
71O-Pee-Chee-130
71O-Pee-Chee-252
71Sargent Promotions Stamps-97
71Topps-130
71Toronto Sun-165
72Nordiques Postcards-21
72O-Pee-Chee-293
727-Eleven Slurpee Cups WHA-18
73Nordiques Team Issue-21
73O-Pee-Chee WHA Posters-2
73Quaker Oats WHA-30
74O-Pee-Chee WHA-18
75O-Pee-Chee WHA-62
75O-Pee-Chee WHA-130
76Nordiques Marie Antoinette-12
76Nordiques Postcards-19
76O-Pee-Chee WHA-2
76O-Pee-Chee WHA-40
76O-Pee-Chee WHA-62
77O-Pee-Chee WHA-44
81TCMA-3
94Parkhurst Tall Boys-74
95Parkhurst '66-67-67
Coins-67
02Parkhurst Reprints-282
02Parkhurst Reprints-288
02Parkhurst Reprints-297
Tremblay, J.F.
96Roanoke Express-11
98Roanoke Express-17
00UK Sekonda Superleague-186
00Muskegon Fury-5
Tremblay, Jacques
87Kingston Canadians-4
Tremblay, Jean
50Quebec Citadelles-19
Tremblay, Jerome
92Quebec Pee-Wee Tournament-438
92Quebec Pee-Wee Tournament-678
93Quebec Pee-Wee Tournament-289
93Quebec Pee-Wee Tournament-534
97Bowman CHL-75
OPC-75
99Rouyn-Noranda Huskies-20
99Bowman CHL-74
Gold-74
OPC International-74
00QMJHL All-Star Program Inserts-18
Tremblay, Johnathan
04Johnstown Chiefs-19
05Cleveland Barons-24
05Quad City Mallards-17
Tremblay, Jules
51Laval Dairy Lac St. Jean-42
Tremblay, Ludger
51Laval Dairy QSHL-11
52St. Lawrence Sales-49
56Quebec Aces-16
Tremblay, Luis
00Baie-Comeau Drakkar-8
Signed-8
01Baie-Comeau Drakkar-7
02Baie Comeau Drakkar-9
03Baie Comeau Drakkar-11
04Bakersfield Condors-19
Tremblay, Marc-Aurele
51Laval Dairy Lac St. Jean-34
Tremblay, Mario
74Canadiens Postcards-25
75Canadiens Postcards-19
75O-Pee-Chee NHL-223
75Topps-223
76Canadiens Postcards-22
76O-Pee-Chee NHL-97
76Topps-97
77Canadiens Postcards-24
77O-Pee-Chee NHL-163
77Topps-163
78Canadiens Postcards-26
78O-Pee-Chee-376
79Canadiens Postcards-25
79O-Pee-Chee-123
79Topps-123
80Canadiens Postcards-25
80O-Pee-Chee-297
80Pepsi-Cola Caps-59
81Canadiens Postcards-26
81O-Pee-Chee-192
81Post Standups-23
82Canadiens Postcards-25
82Canadiens Steinberg-20
82O-Pee-Chee-193
82O-Pee-Chee Stickers-30
82Post Cereal-10
82Topps Stickers-30
83Canadiens Postcards-28
83Esso-20
83NHL Key Tags-66
83O-Pee-Chee-199
83O-Pee-Chee Stickers-69
83Puffy Stickers-5
83Topps Stickers-69
83Vachon-57
84Canadiens Postcards-28
84Kellogg's Accordion Discs-5A
84Kellogg's Accordion Discs-5B
84Kellogg's Accordion Discs Singles-37
84O-Pee-Chee-274
84O-Pee-Chee Stickers-161
85Canadiens Placemats-6
85Canadiens Placemats-7
85Canadiens Postcards-38
85Canadiens Postcards-39
85Canadiens Provigo-24
85O-Pee-Chee-245
85O-Pee-Chee Stickers-134
86O-Pee-Chee-223
86O-Pee-Chee Stickers-9
95Canadiens Postcards-19
96Canadiens Postcards-31
Tremblay, Michel
98Bowman CHL-93
Golden Anniversary-93
OPC International-93
98Bowman Chrome CHL-93
Golden Anniversary-93
Golden Anniversary Refractors-93
OPC International-93
OPC International Refractors-93
Refractors-93
Tremblay, Nelson
67Columbus Checkers-14
Tremblay, Nils
51Laval Dairy QSHL-51
51Laval Dairy Subset-51
52Bas Du Fleuve-31
52St. Lawrence Sales-80
Tremblay, Paul
51Laval Dairy Lac St. Jean-29
Tremblay, Philippe
92Quebec Pee-Wee Tournament-436
93Amos Les Forestiers-21
Tremblay, Regis
907th Inn. Sketch Memorial Cup-65
Tremblay, Remy
01Val d'Or Foreurs-4
Tremblay, Sebastien
907th Inn. Sketch QMJHL-246
917th Inn. Sketch QMJHL-269
92Quebec Pee-Wee Tournament-680
93Quebec Pee-Wee Tournament-388
96Rimouski Oceanic Quebec Police-25
Tremblay, Sebastien (Goon)
907th Inn. Sketch QMJHL-246
917th Inn. Sketch QMJHL-269
Tremblay, Shayne
04Chicoutimi Sagueneens-22
05Chicoutimi Sagueneens-7
06Saint Johns Sea Dogs-12
Tremblay, Simon
92Quebec Pee-Wee Tournament-444
98Quebec Remparts-20
Signed-20
99Bowman CHL-45
Gold-45
OPC International-45
00Sherbrooke Castors-3
Signed-3
02ECHL All-Star Northern-37
02Reading Royals-7
02Reading Royals RBI Sports-186
04Florida Everblades-5
Tremblay, Tommy
06Chicoutimi Sagueneens-20
Tremblay, Trevor
90Rayside-Balfour Jr. Canadians-21
91Rayside-Balfour Jr. Canadians-19
Tremblay, Vincent
81Maple Leafs Postcards-22
82Maple Leafs Postcards-35
82O-Pee-Chee-334
82O-Pee-Chee Stickers-70
82Topps Stickers-70
93Drummondville Voltigeurs-13
Tremblay, Yannick
96St. John's Maple Leafs-24
97Pacific Omega-226
Copper-226
Dark Gray-226
Emerald Green-226
Gold-226
Ice Blue-226
98Pacific-423
Ice Blue-423
Red-423
98Upper Deck-190
Exclusives-190
Exclusives 1 of 1-190
Gold Reserve-190
99Panini Stickers-19
99Upper Deck MVP SC Edition-12
Gold Script-12
Silver Script-12
Super Script-12
00O-Pee-Chee-251B
00O-Pee-Chee Parallel-251B
00Pacific-26
Copper-26
Gold-26
Ice Blue-26
Premiere Date-26
00Stadium Club-60
00Topps/OPC-251B
Parallel-251B
00Upper Deck Vintage-16
01BAP Signature Series-149
Autographs-149
Autographs Gold-149
01Upper Deck-238
Exclusives-238
02BAP Sig Series Auto Buybacks 2001-149
02Pacific Complete-193
Red-193
02Topps Total-189
03ITG Action-95
03NHL Sticker Collection-7
03O-Pee-Chee-261
03OPC Blue-261
03OPC Gold-261
03OPC Red-261
03Pacific Complete-157
Red-157
03Topps-261
Blue-261
Gold-261
Red-261
03Upper Deck-11
Canadian Exclusives-11
HG-11
03Upper Deck MVP-20
Gold Script-20
Silver Script-20
Canadian Exclusives-20
04German DEL Superstars-SU04
05German DEL-364
06Manitoba Moose-24
Trempe, Martin
02Cape Breton Screaming Eagles-21
Trendl, Markus
94German First League-322
Trepanier, Pascal
917th Inn. Sketch QMJHL-107
93Sherbrooke Faucons-11
98Bowman's Best-128
Refractors-128
Atomic Refractors-128
99Pacific Omega-7
Copper-7
Gold-7
Ice Blue-7
Premiere Date-7
00Upper Deck NHLPA-PA3
01Avalanche Team Issue-16
01BAP Signature Series-87
Autographs-87
Autographs Gold-87
02BAP Sig Series Auto Buybacks 2001-87
02Milwaukee Admirals-24
02Milwaukee Admirals Postcards-15
03Hershey Bears-6
03Hershey Bears Patriot News-24
04German DEL-261
05German DEL All-Star Jerseys-AS20
05German DEL Star Attack-ST08
06German DEL-154
Team Leaders-TL12
Trepanier, Serge
93Amos Les Forestiers-22
Tresk, Ryan
97Seattle Thunderbirds-18
Tresl, Ladislav
88ProCards AHL-102
89Halifax Citadels-26
89ProCards AHL-175
90ProCards AHL/IHL-433
91ProCards-614
95Czech APS Extraliga-208
Tretiak, Doug
92Hamilton Canucks-27
97Las Vegas Thunder-13
06Rio Grande Valley Killer Bees-21
Tretiak, Vladislav
70Finnish Jaakiekko-18
70Russian National Team Postcards-20
70Swedish Hockey-160
70Swedish Hockey-161
70Swedish Hockey-230
70Swedish Hockey-314
70Swedish Masterserien-131
71Finnish Suomi Stickers-17
71Swedish Hockey-27
72Finnish Jaakiekko-37
72Finnish Hellas-79
72Finnish Panda Toronto-62
72Finnish Semic World Championship-20
72Swedish Stickers-27
72Swedish Semic World Championship-20
73Finnish Jaakiekko-17
73Russian National Team-2
73Swedish Stickers-77
74Finnish Jenkki-57
74Finnish Typotor-73
74Russian National Team-20
74Swedish Stickers-1
74Swedish Semic World Champ Stickers-26
77Finnish Sportscasters-78-1861
79Panini Stickers-140
79Russian National Team-4
80USSR Olympic Team Mini Pics-9
81Swedish Semic Hockey VM Stickers-37
82Swedish Semic VM Stickers-51
83Swedish Semic VM Stickers-51
84Russian National Team-20
90Alberta International Team Canada-20
90Blackhawks Coke-28
91Future Trends Canada '72-5
91Future Trends Canada '72-11
91Future Trends Canada '72-31
91Future Trends Canada '72-71
91Future Trends Canada '72 French-5
91Future Trends Canada '72 French-11
91Future Trends Canada '72 French-71
91Finnish Semic World Champ Stickers-241
91Russian Sports Unite Hearts-10
91Russian Stars in NHL-10
91Swedish Semic World Champ Stickers-241
92Alberta International Team Canada-21
92Blackhawks Coke-13
92Future Trends '76 Canada Cup-103
92Future Trends '76 Canada Cup-109
92Future Trends '76 Canada Cup-110
92Future Trends '76 Canada Cup-163
92Future Trends '76 Canada Cup-163A
92Future Trends Promo Sheet-1
95Swedish Globe World Championships-235
99Upper Deck Retro-102
Gold-102
Platinum-102
Distant Replay-DR15
Distant Replay Level 2-DR15
Inkredible-VT
Inkredible Level 2-VT
99Russian Stars of Hockey-36
00BAP Memorabilia Goalie Memorabilia-G7
00BAP Memorabilia Goalie Memorabilia-G16
00BAP Memorabilia Goalie Memorabilia-G22
00BAP Sig Ser Goalie Memorabilia Autos-GLS2
00BAP Ultimate Mem Goalie Memorabilia-GM17
00BAP Ultimate Mem Goalie Mem Autos-UG2
01Between the Pipes-133
Vintage Memorabilia-VM10
01Parkhurst Heroes-H11
02BAP Ultimate Memorabilia Numerology-23
02BAP Ultimate Mem Vintage Jerseys-40
02Between the Pipes Goalie Autographs-30
02Between the Pipes Inspirations-I6
02Between the Pipes Trappers-GT1
02Between the Pipes Vintage Memorabilia-18
02Parkhurst Vintage Memorabilia-VM17
02Parkhurst Vintage Teammates-VT15
03BAP Memorabilia Gloves-GUG9
03BAP Ultimate Memorabilia Heroes-12
03BAP Ultimate Mem Vintage Jerseys-23
03BAP Ultimate Mem Vintage Jerseys Gold-23
03Blackhawks Postcards-28
03ITG Used Signature Series Goalie Gear-31
03ITG Used Sig Series Goalie Gear Autos-31
03ITG Used Sig Series Goalie Gear Gold-31
03ITG Used Sig Series Intl Experience-18
03ITG Used Sig Ser Intl Exper Emblem Gold-18
03ITG Used Sig Ser Intl Experience Emblem-18
03ITG Used Sig Ser Intl Experience Gold-18
03Parkhurst Rookie Jerseys-GJ-48
03Parkhurst Rookie Jerseys Gold-GJ-48
03Czech Stadion-557
04UD All-World-90
04UD All-World-112
Gold-90
Autographs-90
Autographs-112
Triple Autographs-AT-LTZ
Quad Autographs-AQ-RUS
Five Autographs-AF-AST
Five Autographs-AF-GOL
04ITG Heroes and Prospects-161
Autographs-VT
04ITG Heroes/Prospects Toronto Expo '05-161
04ITG Heroes/Prospects Expo Heroes/Pros-161
05ITG Heroes/Prosp Toronto Expo Parallel -20
05Between the Pipes-22
Autographs-A-VT
Double Memorabilia-DM-7
Gloves-GUG-4
Jerseys-GUJ-5
05ITG Ultimate Memorabilia Level 1-99
05ITG Ultimate Memorabilia Level 2-99
05ITG Ultimate Memorabilia Level 3-99
05ITG Ultimate Memorabilia Level 4-99
05ITG Ultimate Memorabilia Level 5-99
05ITG Ultimate Memorabilia Double Autos-4
05ITG Ultimate Mem Double Autos Gold-4
05ITG Ultimate Mem Double Mem-3
05ITG Ultimate Mem Double Mem Autos-18
05ITG Ultimate Mem Double Mem Autos Gold-18
05ITG Ultimate Mem Double Mem Gold-3
05ITG Ultimate Memorabilia Jersey Autos-28
05ITG Ultimate Mem Jersey Autos Gold-28
05ITG Ultimate Mem Retro Teammate Jerseys-30
05ITG Ult Mem Retro Teammates Jersey Gold-30
05ITG Ultimate Memorabilia Triple Autos-4
05ITG Ultimate Memorabilia Triple Autos-12
05ITG Ultimate Mem Triple Autos Gold-4
05ITG Ultimate Mem Triple Autos Gold-12
05ITG Ultimate Memorabilia Ultimate Autos-4
05ITG Ultimate Mem Ultimate Autos Gold-4
05ITG Heroes and Prospects-20
Autographs-A-VT
Autographs Series II-YC2
Hero Memorabilia-HM-11
06Between The Pipes-104
Autographs-AVT
Complete Jersey-CJ11
Complete Jersey Gold-CJ11
Double Jerseys-DJ09
Double Jerseys-DJ20
Double Jerseys Gold-DJ09
Double Jerseys Gold-DJ20
Double Memorabilia-DM19
Double Memorabilia Gold-DM19
Emblems-GUE40
Emblems Gold-GUE40
Emblems Autographs-GUE40
Jerseys-GUJ40
Jerseys Gold-GUJ40
Jerseys Autographs-GUJ40
Numbers-GUN40
Numbers Gold-GUN40
Numbers Autographs-GUN40
Pads-GP08
Pads Gold-GP08
Playing For Your Country-PC24
Playing For Your Country Gold-PC24
Shooting Gallery-SG08
Shooting Gallery Gold-SG08
06ITG International Ice-1
06ITG International Ice-25
Gold-1
Gold-25
Autographs-AVT
Autographs-AVT2

Best of the Best-BB01
Best of the Best Gold-BB01
Cornerstones-IC02
Cornerstones-IC07
Cornerstones-IC10
Cornerstones Gold-IC02
Cornerstones Gold-IC07
Cornerstones Gold-IC10
Emblem Autographs-GUE04
Emblem Autographs Gold-GUE04
Emblems-GUE04
Emblems Gold-GUE04
Goaltending Glory-GG15
Goaltending Glory Gold-GG15
Greatest Moments-GM01
Greatest Moments Gold-GM01
Hockey Passport-HP02
Hockey Passport Gold-HP02
International Rivals-IR01
International Rivals Gold-IR01
Jersey Autographs-GUJ04
Jersey Autographs Gold-GUJ04
Jerseys-GUJ04
Jerseys Gold-GUJ04
Numbers-GUN04
Numbers Autographs-GUN04
Numbers Autographs Gold-GUN04
Numbers Gold-GUN04
Passing The Torch-PTT8
Passing The Torch Gold-PTT8
Quad Patch-QP04
Quad Patch Gold-QP04
Teammates-IT18
Teammates Gold-IT18
Triple Memorabilia-TM02
Triple Memorabilia Gold-TM02
06ITG Ultimate Memorabilia-147
Artist Proof-147
Autos-32
Autos Gold-32
Autos Dual-9
Autos Dual Gold-9
Autos Triple-3
Autos Triple Gold-3
Boys Will Be Boys-27
Boys Will Be Boys Gold-27
Cornerstones-1
Cornerstones Gold-1
Double Memorabilia-22
Double Memorabilia Gold-22
Going For Gold-25
Going For Gold Gold-25
Jerseys Autos-59
Jerseys Autos Gold-59
Retro Teammates-11
Retro Teammates Gold-11

Tretowicz, Dave
92Phoenix Roadrunners-23
92Classic-112
Gold-112
92Classic Four-Sport *-218
Gold-218
93Fort Wayne Komets-20

Trettenes, Steffen
92Norwegian Elite Series-143

Trevelyan, T.J.
06Providence Bruins-22

Trevisani, Carter
01Ottawa 67's-4
02Ottawa 67's-3

Trew, Bill
97El Paso Buzzards-14
98El Paso Buzzards-6
99German Bundesliga 2-131
99German EHC Straubing-10
06German DEL-181
Team Leaders-TL9

Trew, Jordan
01Flint Generals-18
02Kalamazoo Wings-11

Trewin, Jim
71Johnstown Jets Acme-13

Triano, Jeff
98Abilene Aviators-2

Tribuntsovs, Atvars
98Finnish Kerailysarja-165
03Russian Hockey League-151
03Russian SL-26
03Russian World Championship Stars-6
04Russian Legion-41
05Swedish SHL Elitset-255
Gold-255
06Finnish Cardset-273
06Swedish SHL Elitset-117

Trick, Chris
04Notre Dame Fighting Irish-22

Trifonov, Lev
00Russian Hockey League-356
02Russian Hockey League-265

Trigg, Jeff
98Idaho Steelheads-20

Trigubov, Vitali
01Russian Hockey League-157

Trihey, Harry
83Hall of Fame Postcards-F14
85Hall of Fame-88

Trim, Lee
84Brandon Wheat Kings-13
85Brandon Wheat Kings-13

Trimper, Tim
80Blackhawks White Border-14
80Jets Postcards-23
80O-Pee-Chee-357
81Jets Postcards-22
81O-Pee-Chee-376
82O-Pee-Chee-394
82Post Cereal-21
84Springfield Indians-12

Trineer, Neil
81Kingston Canadians-8

Tripp, John
95Slapshot-238
95Classic-55
95Classic-91
97Saint John Flames-22
97Bowman CHL-9
OPC-9
99Johnstown Chiefs-15
01Hartford Wolf Pack-23
02BAP Memorabilia-336
02BAP Ultimate Memorabilia-84
02Upper Deck Rookie Update-131
02Hartford Wolf Pack-22
03Manchester Monarchs-18
03Manchester Monarchs Team Issue-18
04German Adler Mannheim Eagles Postcards-29
04German DEL-18
05German DEL-254

Triulzi, Roberto
93Swiss HNL-79
95Finnish Semic World Championships-194
95Swedish World Championships Stickers-134

95Swiss HNL-106
96Swiss HNL-50
98Swiss Power Play Stickers-49

Trlicik, Mojmir
99Czech OFS-418
00Czech OFS-238

Trmavski, Artem
00Sherbrooke Castors-13
Signed-13

Trnka, Pavel
94Czech APS Extraliga-49
97Pacific Omega-9
Copper-9
Dark Gray-9
Emerald Green-9
Gold-9
Ice Blue-9
97SP Authentic-170
98Upper Deck-35
Exclusives-35
Exclusives 1 of 1-35
Gold Reserve-35
99BAP Millennium-7
Emerald-7
Ruby-7
Sapphire-7
Signatures-7
Signatures Gold-7
99Panini Stickers-184
99Cincinnati Mighty Ducks-22
00Stadium Club-181
00Upper Deck-235
Exclusives Tier 1-235
Exclusives Tier 2-235
02BAP Sig Series Auto Buybacks 1999-7
02Pacific Complete-396
Red-396
02Topps Total-195
03ITG Action-288
03Pacific Complete-333
Red-333
03Panthers Team Issue-16
04Czech HC Plzen Postcards-21
04Czech OFS-155
05Czech HC Plzen-13
06Czech OFS-285
06Czech NHL ELH Postcards-12

Trofimenkoff, David
917th Inn. Sketch WHL-353
93Lethbridge Hurricanes-19
00UK Sekonda Superleague-90
01UK London Knights-24
01UK Manchester Storm Retro-14
02UK London Knights-16
04UK Edinburgh Capitals-14

Trofimov, Alexander
98Russian Hockey League-56
99Russian Hockey League-78

Troha, Tine
93Quebec Pee-Wee Tournament-1797

Troini, Jason
96Halifax Mooseheads I-22
96Halifax Mooseheads II-22
97Halifax Mooseheads I-22
97Halifax Mooseheads II-21
98Halifax Mooseheads-14
98Halifax Mooseheads Second Edition-15

Trojan, Richard
94German DEL-418
95German DEL-390
96German DEL-298

Trojovsky, Matej
00Lincoln Stars-17
01Regina Pats-22
02Regina Pats-2
03Swift Current Broncos-20
04Swift Current Broncos-23
05Czech HC Plzen-14

Troliga, Tomas
03Calgary Hitmen-18

Trombley, Rhett
91Saskatoon Blades-7
917th Inn. Sketch WHL-99
93Sault Ste. Marie Greyhounds-16
94Toledo Storm-22
95Las Vegas Thunder-20
96Las Vegas Thunder-21
99Bakersfield Condors-19
00Fort Wayne Komets Shoe Carnival-1

Tronrud, Oystein
92Norwegian Elite Series-94

Tront, Kyle
06Sarnia Sting-12

Tropp, Corey
06Sioux Falls Stampede -24

Tropper, Marc
98ECHL All-Star Northern Conference-9
99Charlotte Checkers-18
99Charlotte Checkers-24
99Charlotte Checkers-31
99ECHL All-Star Northern Conference-16
00Charlotte Checkers-4
01BC Icemen-24

Troschinsky, Alexei
91Upper Deck Czech World Juniors-6
98Russian Hockey League-155
99Russian Dynamo Moscow-9
00Russian Champions-2
00Russian Hockey League-123
01Russian Dynamo Moscow-2
01Russian Dynamo Moscow Mentos-8
01Russian Legions-1
03Russian Hockey League-31
04Russian Moscow Dynamo-31
04Russian Super League All-Stars-4
05Russian Hockey League RHL-15

Troschinsky, Andrei
00Worcester Icecats-10
01Worcester Icecats-18

Trotta, Joe
99Indianapolis Ice-21

Trotter, Brock
04Lincoln Stars-18

Trottier, Bryan
75Heroes Stand-Ups-18
76O-Pee-Chee NHL-67
76O-Pee-Chee NHL-115
76O-Pee-Chee NHL-216
76Topps-67
76Topps-115
76Topps-216
76Topps Glossy Inserts-15
77O-Pee-Chee NHL-105
77Sportscasters-4621
77Sportscasters-4716
77Topps-105
77Finnish Sportscasters-49-1197
78O-Pee-Chee-10
78O-Pee-Chee-64
78O-Pee-Chee-65
78O-Pee-Chee-325
78Topps-10
78Topps-64
78Topps-65
79Islanders Transparencies-21
79O-Pee-Chee-2
79O-Pee-Chee-3
79O-Pee-Chee-7
79O-Pee-Chee-100
79O-Pee-Chee-165
79Topps-2
79Topps-3
79Topps-7
79Topps-100
79Topps-165
80O-Pee-Chee-40
80Topps-40
81O-Pee-Chee-200
81O-Pee-Chee-210
81O-Pee-Chee Stickers-152
81O-Pee-Chee Stickers-160
81Topps-41
81Topps-E132
82McDonald's Stickers-25
82O-Pee-Chee-5
82O-Pee-Chee-214
82O-Pee-Chee-215
82O-Pee-Chee Stickers-47
82O-Pee-Chee Stickers-48
82Post Cereal-12
82Topps Stickers-47
82Topps Stickers-48
83Islanders Team Issue-18
83NHL Key Tags-79
83O-Pee-Chee-21
83O-Pee-Chee Stickers-76
83O-Pee-Chee Stickers-77
83Puffy Stickers-21
83Topps Stickers-76
83Topps Stickers-77
84Islanders News-15
84Islanders News-37
84O-Pee-Chee-139
84O-Pee-Chee-214
84O-Pee-Chee Stickers-86
84O-Pee-Chee Stickers-87
847-Eleven Discs-34
84Topps-104
84Topps-160
84Kelowna Wings-26
85Islanders News-16
85Islanders News-35
85Islanders News Trottier-1
85Islanders News Trottier-2
85Islanders News Trottier-3
85Islanders News Trottier-4
85Islanders News Trottier-5
85Islanders News Trottier-6
85Islanders News Trottier-7
85Islanders News Trottier-8
85Islanders News Trottier-9
85Islanders News Trottier-10
85Islanders News Trottier-11
85Islanders News Trottier-12
85Islanders News Trottier-13
85Islanders News Trottier-14
85Islanders News Trottier-15
85Islanders News Trottier-16
85Islanders News Trottier-17
85Islanders News Trottier-18
85Islanders News Trottier-19
85Islanders News Trottier-20
85Islanders News Trottier-21
85Islanders News Trottier-22
85Islanders News Trottier-23
85Islanders News Trottier-24
85Islanders News Trottier-25
85Islanders News Trottier-26
85Islanders News Trottier-27
85Islanders News Trottier-28
85Islanders News Trottier-29
85Islanders News Trottier-30
85Islanders News Trottier-31
85Islanders News Trottier-32
85Islanders News Trottier-33
85O-Pee-Chee-60
85O-Pee-Chee Stickers-65
857-Eleven Credit Cards-12
85Topps-60
86Islanders Team Issue-9
86O-Pee-Chee-155
86O-Pee-Chee Box Bottoms-P
86O-Pee-Chee Stickers-216
86Topps-155
86Topps Box Bottoms-P
87O-Pee-Chee-60
87O-Pee-Chee Box Bottoms-O
87O-Pee-Chee Minis-41
87O-Pee-Chee Stickers-240
87Panini Stickers-96
87Topps-60
87Topps Box Bottoms-O
88Esso All-Stars-46
88Frito-Lay Stickers-2
88O-Pee-Chee-97
88O-Pee-Chee Stickers-112
88Panini Stickers-293
88Topps-97
89Islanders Team Issue-19
89O-Pee-Chee-149
89O-Pee-Chee Stickers-118
89Panini Stickers-269
89Panini Stickers-382
89Topps-149
90O-Pee-Chee-6
90O-Pee-Chee-291
90OPC Premier-121
90Panini Stickers-83
90Penguins Foodland-15
90Pro Set-192
90Pro Set-511
90Score-270
Canadian-270
90Score Rookie/Traded-106T
90Topps-6
90Topps-291
Tiffany-6
Tiffany-291
90Upper Deck-137
90Upper Deck-425
French-137
French-425
91Pro Set Platinum-216
91Bowman-93
91O-Pee-Chee-472
91Parkhurst-208
91Parkhurst-360
91Parkhurst-431
91Parkhurst-461
French-208
French-360
French-431
91Penguins Coke/Elby's-19
91Penguins Foodland-12
91Penguins Foodland Coupon Stickers-1
91Pinnacle-241
French-241
91Pro Set-192
91Pro Set-319
French-192
Platinum PC-PC19
91Score American-229
91Score Canadian Bilingual-229
91Score Canadian English-229
91Stadium Club-91
91Topps-472
91Upper Deck-329
French-329
92Bowman-152
92Bowman-243
92O-Pee-Chee-107
92O-Pee-Chee-130
25th Anniv. Inserts-9
92Panini Stickers-227
92Panini Stickers French-227
92Score-157
92Score-518
Canadian-157
92Stadium Club-26
92Topps-416
Gold-416G
93Donruss-268
93Leaf-318
93OPC Premier-296
Gold-296
93Parkhurst-431
Emerald Ice-431
93Penguins Foodland-12
93Pinnacle-411
Canadian-411
93PowerPlay-416
93Score-567
Gold-567
Canadian-567
Canadian Gold-567
93Topps/OPC Premier-296
Gold-296
93Ultra-398
93Upper Deck Locker All-Stars-50
94Hockey Wit-44
96Penguins Tribune-Review-4
96Swedish Semic Wien Hockey Legends-HL9
97SP Authentic Mark of a Legend-M4
97SP Authentic Tradition-T4
97Portland Pirates-24
99Upper Deck 500 Goal Club-500BT
99Upper Deck 500 Goal Club-500BT
99Upper Deck Century Legends-30
Century Collection-30
00Topps Stanley Cup Heroes-SHBT
00Topps Stanley Cup Heroes Autographs-SHBT
00UD Heroes-131
Signs of Greatness-BT
00Upper Deck Legends-82
00Upper Deck Legends-88
Legendary Collection Bronze-82
Legendary Collection Bronze-88
Legendary Collection Gold-82
Legendary Collection Gold-88
Legendary Collection Silver-82
Legendary Collection Silver-88
Epic Signatures-BT
Legendary Game Jerseys-JBT
Playoff Heroes-PH11
00Upper Deck Vintage Dynasty: A Piece of History-TP
00Upper Deck Vintage Dynasty: A Piece of History Gold-TP
01BAP Memorabilia 500 Goal Scorers-GS20
01BAP Signature Series 500 Goal Scorers-19
01BAP Signature Series Vintage Autographs-VA-34
01BAP Ultimate Mem All-Star History-29
01BAP Ultimate Memorabilia Calder Trophy-19
01BAP Ultimate Mem Dynasty Jerseys-17
01BAP Ultimate Mem Dynasty Emblems-17
01BAP Ultimate Mem Dynasty Numbers-17
01BAP Ultimate Memorabilia Emblem Attic-20
01BAP Ultimate Mem 500 Goal Scorers-16
01BAP Ultimate Mem 500 Goal Scorers Autos-2
01BAP Ultimate Mem 500 Goal Jerseys/Stick-16
01BAP Ultimate Mem 500 Goal Emblems-16
01BAP Ultimate Mem Retro Teammates-5
01BAP Ultimate Mem Stanley Cup Winners-9
01Fleer Legacy-7
01Fleer Legacy-52
Ultimate-7
Ultimate-52
Memorabilia-24
Memorabilia Autographs-8
01Greats of the Game-29
Retro Collection-9
Autographs-29
01Parkhurst Autographs-PA30
01Parkhurst 500 Goal Scorers-PGS20
01Topps Archives-12
Arena Seats-ASBT
Autographs-19
01UD Stanley Cup Champs-22
Jerseys-T-BT
Pieces of Glory-G-BT
Sticks-S-BT
01Upper Deck Legends-43
Epic Signatures-BT
Fiorentino Collection-FCBT
Jerseys-TTBT
Jerseys-TTST
Jerseys Platinum-TTBT
Jerseys Platinum-TTST
Milestones-MBT
Milestones Platinum-MBT
Sticks-PHBT
01Upper Deck Vintage Jerseys-SCBT
02BAP Memorabilia Mini Stanley Cups-18
02BAP NHL All-Star History-29
02BAP Ultimate Memorabilia Conn Smythe-11
02BAP Ultimate Memorabilia Numerology-22
02BAP Ultimate Mem Playoff Scorers-16
02BAP Ultimate Memorabilia Retro Trophies-18
02BAP Ultimate Mem Scoring Leaders-15
02BAP Ultimate Mem Vintage Jerseys-8
02Parkhurst Heroes-NH4
02Parkhurst Vintage Teammates-VT10
02UD Foundations 1000 Point Club-BT
02UD Foundations 1000 Point Club-TR
02UD Foundations 1000 Point Club Gold-BT
02UD Foundations 1000 Point Club Silver-BT
02UD Foundations Calder Winners-TBT
02UD Foundations Calder Winners Gold-TBT
02UD Foundations Calder Winners Silver-T-BT
02UD Foundations Canadian Heroes-CBT
02UD Foundations Canadian Heroes Gold-CBT
02UD Foundations Canadian Heroes Silver-C-BT
02UD Foundations Milestones-NBT
02UD Foundations Milestones Gold-NBT
02UD Foundations Milestones Silver-N-BT
02UD Foundations Playoff Performers-PBT
02UD Foundations Playoff Performers Gold-PBT
02UD Foundations Playoff Performer Silver-P-BT
02UD Piece of History Historical Swatches-HSBT
02UD Piece of History Mark of Distinction-BT
03BAP Ultimate Memorabilia Cornerstones-8
03BAP Ultimate Memorabilia Heroes-4
03BAP Ultimate Mem Jersey and Stick-28
03BAP Ultimate Mem Jersey and Stick Gold-28
03BAP Ultimate Memorabilia Linemates-7
03BAP Ultimate Mem Raised to the Rafters-19
03BAP Ultimate Mem Retro Teammates-6
03BAP Ultimate Mem Vintage Jerseys-27
03BAP Ultimate Mem Vintage Jerseys Gold-27
03ITG VIP MVP-21
03Parkhurst Rookie ROYalty-VR-14
03Parkhurst Rookie ROYalty Gold-VR-14
03SP Authentic Sign of the Times-BTG
04ITG NHL AS FANtasy AS History Jerseys-SB29
04ITG Franchises He Shoots/Scores Prizes-40
04ITG Franchises Update Linemates-ULI3
04ITG Franchises Update Linemates Gold-ULI3
04ITG Franchises US East-374
Autographs-A-BT
Double Memorabilia-EDM11
Double Memorabilia Autographs-EDM-BT
Double Memorabilia Gold-EDM11
Memorabilia-ESM17
Memorabilia Autographs-ESM-BT
Memorabilia Gold-ESM17
Teammates-ETM2
Teammates Gold-ETM2
Trophy Winners-ETW4
Trophy Winners Gold-ETW4
04ITG Ultimate Memorabilia-166
04ITG Ultimate Memorabilia-178
Gold-166
Gold-178
Art Ross Trophy-5
Autographs-43
Autographs Gold-43
Calder Trophy-3
Conn Smythe Trophy-6
Cornerstones-9
Cornerstones Gold-9
Day In History-34
Day In History Gold-34
Heroes Mario Lemieux-6
Jersey Autographs-53
Jersey Autographs Gold-53
Retro Teammates-5
Seams Unbelievable-5
Stick Autographs-15
Stick Autographs Gold-15
Triple Threads-12
04SP Authentic Octographs-OS-CAP
04SP Authentic Octographs-OS-ART
04SP Authentic Sign of the Times-DS-BT
04SP Authentic Sign of the Times-TS-BTG
04SP Authentic Sign of the Times-FS-CTR
04UD Legendary Signatures-15
Autographs-BT
Linemates-CGBTMB
04UD Legends Classics-10
04UD Legends Classics-68
04UD Legends Classics-97
Gold-10
Gold-68
Gold-97
Platinum-10
Platinum-68
Platinum-97
Silver-10
Silver-68
Silver-97
Signature Moments-M43
Signatures-CS41
Signatures-DC5
Signatures-TC5
Signatures-QC4
04Ultimate Collection Jerseys-UGJ-BT
04Ultimate Collection Jerseys Gold-UGJ-BT
04Ultimate Collection Jersey Autographs-UGJA-BT
04Ultimate Collection Patches-UP-BT
04Ultimate Collection Signatures-US-BT
04Ultimate Collection Signature Logos-ULA-BT
04Ultimate Collection Signature Patches-SP-BT
05Beehive-240
05Black Diamond-188
Emerald-188
Gold-188
Onyx-188
Ruby-188
05Canada Post-35
05Canada Post Autographs-35
05ITG Ultimate Mem Cornerstones Jerseys-8
05ITG Ultimate Mem Cornerst Jerseys Gold-8
05ITG Ultimate Memorabilia Jerseys-7
05ITG Ultimate Memorabilia Jerseys Gold-7
05ITG Ultimate Mem Pass the Torch Jerseys-19
05ITG Ultimate Mem Passing Torch Jsy Gold-19
05ITG Ultimate Mem Record Breaker Jerseys-10
05ITG Ultimate Mem RecBreak Jerseys Gold-10
05ITG Ultimate Mem Retro Teammate Jerseys-1
05ITG Ult Mem Retro Teammates Jersey Gold-1
05ITG Ult Mem 3 Star of the Game Jsy-16
05ITG Ult Mem 3 Star of the Game Jsy Gold-16
05NHL Legends Medallions-22
05SP Authentic Exquisite Endorsements-EEBT
05SP Authentic Immortal Inks-IIBT
05SP Authentic Octographs-OH
05SP Authentic Prestigious Pairings-PPTB
05SP Authentic Sign of the Times Quads-QTBNP
05SP Authentic Six Star Signatures-SSHF
05SP Game Used Authentic Fabrics Dual-NY
05SP Game Used Authentic Fabric Dual Auto-DT
05SP Game Used Authentic Fabrics Quad-TBYS
05SP Game Used Authentic Patches Quad -TBYS
05SP Game Used Authentic Patches Dual-NY
05SP Game Used Authentic Patch Dual Autos-DT
05SP Game Used Game Gear-GG-BT
05SP Game Used Signature Sticks-SS-BT
05SP Game Used Statscriptions-ST-BT
05SPx-96
Spectrum-96
Winning Combos-WC-MT
Winning Combos-WC-NY
Winning Combos Autographs-AWC-NY
Winning Combos Gold-WC-MT
Winning Combos Gold-WC-NY
Winning Combos Spectrum-WC-MT
Winning Combos Spectrum-WC-NY
Winning Materials-WM-BT
Winning Materials Gold-WM-BT
Winning Materials Spectrum-WM-BT
Xcitement Legends-XL-BT
Xcitement Legends Gold-XL-BT
Xcitement Legends Spectrum-XL-BT
05The Cup-67
Gold-67
Black Rainbow-67
Hardware Heroes-HHBT
Honorable Numbers-HNBT
Masterpiece Pressplates-67
Noble Numbers Dual-DNNTB
Patch Variation-P67
Patch Variation Autographs-AP67
Stanley Cup Titlists-TBT1
Stanley Cup Titlists-TBT2
05UD Artifacts-150
Blue-150
Gold-150
Green-150
Pewter-150
Red-150
Frozen Artifacts-FA-BT
Frozen Artifacts Autographed-FA-BT
Frozen Artifacts Copper-FA-BT
Frozen Artifacts Dual-FAD-BT
Frozen Artifacts Dual Autographed-FAD-BT
Frozen Artifacts Dual Copper-FAD-BT
Frozen Artifacts Dual Gold-FAD-BT
Frozen Artifacts Dual Maroon-FAD-BT
Frozen Artifacts Dual Pewter-FAD-BT
Frozen Artifacts Dual Silver-FAD-BT
Frozen Artifacts Gold-FA-BT
Frozen Artifacts Maroon-FA-BT
Frozen Artifacts Patches-FP-BT
Frozen Artifacts Patches Autographed-FP-BT
Frozen Artifacts Patches Dual-FPD-BT
Frozen Artifacts Patches Dual Autos-FPD-BT
Frozen Artifacts Patches Pewter-FP-BT
Frozen Artifacts Patches Silver-FP-BT
Frozen Artifacts Pewter-FA-BT
Frozen Artifacts Silver-FA-BT
Gold Autographed-150
Remarkable Artifacts-RA-BT
Remarkable Artifacts Dual-RA-BT
05Ultimate Collection Jerseys-JBT
05Ultimate Collection Ultimate Patches-PBT
05Upper Deck Jerseys-J-BT
05Upper Deck Patches-P-BT
06ITG International Ice-116
Gold-116
Autographs-ABT
06ITG Ultimate Memorabilia-23
Artist Proof-23
Autos-33
Autos Gold-33
Boys Will Be Boys-20
Boys Will Be Boys Gold-20
Gloves Are Off-4
Gloves Are Off Gold-4
Jerseys Autos-60
Jerseys Autos Gold-60
Retro Teammates-15
Retro Teammates Gold-15
Road to the Cup-6
Road to the Cup Gold-6
Stick Rack-8
Stick Rack-24
Stick Rack Gold-8
Stick Rack Gold-24
06SPx Winning Materials-WMBT
06SPx Winning Materials Spectrum-WMBT
06Upper Deck Sweet Shot Sweet Stitches-SSBT
06Upper Deck Sweet Shot Sweet Stitches Duals-SSBT
06Upper Deck Sweet Shot Sweet Stitches Triples-SSBT
06ITG Heroes and Prospects-7
Autographs-ABTR

Trottier, Dave
33O-Pee-Chee V304B-62
33V252 Canadian Gum-47
34Beehive Group I Photos-208
34Sweet Caporal-26
36O-Pee-Chee V304D-126
37O-Pee-Chee V304E-168
37V356 Worldwide Gum-70
05ITG Ultimate Mem Marvelous Maroons Auto-3
06ITG Ultimate Memorabilia Marvelous Maroons Autos-8

Trottier, Eric
93Quebec Pee-Wee Tournament-52

Trottier, Guy
70Esso Power Players-25
70Maple Leafs Postcards-14
71Bazooka-23
71Maple Leafs Postcards-20
71O-Pee-Chee-5
71Toronto Sun-273
72O-Pee-Chee-326
73Quaker Oats WHA-40

Trottier, Joel
95Slapshot-273
97Bowman CHL-10
OPC-10
98Providence Bruins-22
98Bowman CHL-40
Golden Anniversary-40
OPC International-40
98Bowman Chrome CHL-40
Golden Anniversary-40
Golden Anniversary Refractors-40
OPC International-40
OPC International Refractors-40
Refractors-40

Trottier, Monty
81Indianapolis Checkers-20
82Indianapolis Checkers-21
84Springfield Indians-19

Trottier, Rocky
82Medicine Hat Tigers-20
83Medicine Hat Tigers-13
89ProCards AHL-356

Trotz, Barry
81Regina Pats-21
90ProCards AHL/IHL-218
91ProCards-572
93Portland Pirates-3
95Portland Pirates-22
96Portland Pirates-NNO

Troumbly, Stacy
04Minnesota Golden Gophers Women-8

Troymark, T.
74Finnish Typotor-84

Trubachev, Yuri
01Russian Hockey League-55
02Russian Future Stars-9
02Russian Hockey League-171
02Russian Hockey League-184B
02Russian Hockey League-282
03Russian SL-14

Trudeau, Francis
92Quebec Pee-Wee Tournament-639
93Quebec Pee-Wee Tournament-130

Trudeau, Roger
95Waterloo Blackhawks -21
01Greenville Grrrowl-6

Trudel, Francis
00Sherbrooke Castors-7
Signed-7
01Sherbrooke Castors-10
03Lewiston Maineiacs-20

Trudel, Guillaume
03Victoriaville Tigers-27

Trudel, Jean-Guy
917th Inn. Sketch QMJHL-190
95Slapshot Memorial Cup-64
96Peoria Rivermen-23
96Peoria Rivermen Photo Album-23
97Peoria Rivermen-11
98Kansas City Blades-14
00BAP Memorabilia-260
Emerald-260
Ruby-260
Sapphire-260
Promos-260
00BAP Mem Chicago Sportsfest Copper-260
00BAP Memorabilia Chicago Sportsfest Blue-260
00BAP Memorabilia Chicago Sportsfest Gold-260
00BAP Memorabilia Chicago Sportsfest Ruby-260
00BAP Memorabilia Chicago Sun-Times Ruby-260
00BAP Memorabilia Chicago Sun-Times Gold-260
00BAP Mem Chicago Sun-Times Sapphire-260
00BAP Mem Toronto Fall Expo Copper-260
00BAP Memorabilia Toronto Fall Expo Gold-260
00BAP Memorabilia Toronto Fall Expo Ruby-260
00Black Diamond-83
Gold-83
00SP Authentic-158
00SPx-107
Spectrum-107
00Upper Deck-224
Exclusives Tier 1-224
Exclusives Tier 2-224
00Upper Deck Ice-99

Trudel, Louis
34Beehive Group I Photos-83
34Beehive Group I Photos-185
34Diamond Matchbooks Silver-59
35Diamond Matchbooks Tan 1-67
35Diamond Matchbooks Tan 2-62
35Diamond Matchbooks Tan 3-57
35Diamond Matchbooks Tan 4-14
35Diamond Matchbooks Tan 5-13
37Diamond Matchbooks Tan 6-13
37V356 Worldwide Gum-71

Trudel, Martin
907th Inn. Sketch QMJHL-65
917th Inn. Sketch QMJHL-11
92Quebec Pee-Wee Tournament-33

Trudell, Brett
02Guelph Storm-18
03Guelph Storm-14
04Oshawa Generals-6
04Oshawa Generals Autographs-6

Trudelle, Jean-Sebastien
99Shawinigan Cataractes-9
Signed-9

True, Mads
92Saskatchewan JHL-5
98Danish Hockey League-33
99Danish Hockey League-211

True, Soren
89ProCards IHL-47
90ProCards AHL/IHL-530
91ProCards-311
95San Diego Barracudas RHI-7
98Danish Hockey League-31
99Danish Hockey League-209

True, Stuart
90ProCards AHL/IHL-531

Truelson, Kevin
03ECHL All-Stars-281
03Fresno Falcons-22
04Fresno Falcons-20
04Gwinnett Gladiators-25
05Bakersfield Condors-19
06Bakersfield Condors-6

Truitt, Jeff
01Kelowna Rockets-25
03Kelowna Rockets-25
04Kelowna Rockets-12
05Kelowna Rockets-27

Truitt, Jim
93Quebec Pee-Wee Tournament-613
02Kelowna Rockets-27

Trukhno, Leonid
91O-Pee-Chee Inserts-61R
98Danish Hockey League-32
99Danish Hockey League-210

Trukhno, Viatcheslav
04P.E.I. Rocket-21
05PEI Rocket-8
06Gatineau Olympiques-5

Trumbley, Peter
03Fort Worth Brahmas-14

Trumbley, Rob
95Wheeling Thunderbirds-1
95Wheeling Thunderbirds Series II-17
96Wheeling Nailers-20
00UK Sekonda Superleague-107

Trummer, Peter
93Swiss HNL-258

Trunchion, Wayne
94UK Guildford Flames-2
95UK Guildford Flames-2

Trunov, Vladimir
73Swedish Stickers-105

Truntschka, Bernd
89Swedish Semic World Champ Stickers-120
91Finnish Semic World Champ Stickers-164
91Swedish Semic World Champ Stickers-164
93Swedish Semic World Champ Stickers-162
94German DEL-95
95German DEL-96
96German DEL-285

Truntschka, Gerd
83Swedish Semic VM Stickers-108
89Swedish Semic World Champ Stickers-115
91Finnish Semic World Champ Stickers-163
91Swedish Semic World Champ Stickers-163
93Swedish Semic World Champ Stickers-157
94Swedish Olympics Lillehammer*-328

Trupp, Evan
05Penticton Vees-19
06Penticton Vees-22

Truvacheev, Yuri
00Russian Hockey League-76

Trvaj, Jiri
98Czech OFS-114
99Czech DS-170
99Czech OFS-543
00Czech DS Extraliga-158
00Czech OFS-240
01Czech OFS-42
01Czech OFS H Inserts-H7
02Czech OFS Plus-299
02Czech OFS Plus All-Star Game-H19
02Czech OFS Plus Checklists-C11
02Czech OFS Plus Masks-M4
02Czech OFS Plus Trios-T18
02Czech OFS Plus Duos-D6
03Czech OFS Plus-14
03Czech OFS Plus Checklists-1
03Czech OFS Plus Insert B-B5
03Czech OFS Plus Insert H-H2
03Czech OFS Plus Insert P-P6
03Czech OFS Plus MS Praha-SE20
03Russian Hockey League-246
04Czech OFS Goals-Against Leaders-4
04Czech OFS Save Percentage Leaders-6
04Russian Legion-16
05Czech HC Znojmo-13
06Czech OFS-216
Goalies I-5
Goalies II-5
Stars-24
Team Cards-14

Trygg, Marius
99Norwegian National Team-9
02Swedish SHL-172
Parallel-172

Trygg, Mats
99Norwegian National Team-16
02Swedish SHL-24
Parallel-24
03Swedish Elite-36
Silver-36
04Swedish Elitset-183
Gold-183
05German DEL-178

Trzcinski, Jason
91Lake Superior State Lakers-24
92Lake Superior State Lakers-29

Tsareev, Andrei
99Russian Hockey League-137
99Russian Stars Postcards-28
00Russian Goalkeepers-4
00Russian Hockey League-394
01Russian Hockey League-108
02Russian Hockey League-7
02Russian Hockey League-66
02Russian SL-23
04Russian RHL-18

Tschanz, Oliver
96Swiss Power Play Stickers-13
01Swiss HNL-268
02Swiss HNL-152

Tschemernjak, Klaus
93Quebec Pee-Wee Tournament-1523

Tschichoflos, Martin
94German First League-140

Tschiemer, Stefan
95Swiss HNL-364
96Swiss HNL-337
98Swiss Power Play Stickers-149
99Swiss Panini Stickers-149
00Swiss Panini Stickers-193
01Swiss HNL-320

Tschour, Sandro
99Swiss Panini Stickers-298
99Swiss Panini Stickers-317

Tschudy, Marc
01Swiss HNL-289
02Swiss HNL-356

Tschumi, Mike
93Swiss HNL-409
95Swiss HNL-284

Tschumi, Rick
91Finnish Semic World Champ Stickers-181
91Swedish Semic World Champ Stickers-181
92Finnish Semic-197
93Swedish Semic World Champ Stickers-114
93Swiss HNL-145
95Swedish Globe World Championships-216
95Swiss HNL-144
96Swiss HNL-160
98Swiss Power Play Stickers-159
99Swiss Panini Stickers-159
00Swiss Panini Stickers-204
01Swiss HNL-33

Tschuor, Sandro
00Swiss Panini Stickers-94
00Swiss Slapshot Mini-Cards-EHCC13
01Swiss HNL-254

Tschupp, Chris
94Erie Panthers-12

Tselios, Nikos
93Quebec Pee-Wee Tournament-704
97Black Diamond-91
Double Diamond-91
Triple Diamond-91
Quadruple Diamond-91
97Bowman CHL-138
OPC-138
Autographs-18
98UD Choice-304
Prime Choice Reserve-304
Reserve-304
99Upper Deck Victory-373
99Cincinnati Cyclones-19
00Cincinnati Cyclones-1
02Lowell Lock Monsters-2
03Springfield Falcons Postcards-7
04Springfield Falcons-21

Tseplis, Gatis
97Fort Worth Brahmas-19
99Fort Worth Brahmas-20
01New Mexico Scorpions-19

Tsimikalis, Peter
02Ottawa 67's-14
03Ottawa 67's-21
04Oshawa Generals-8
04Oshawa Generals Autographs-8
05OHL Bell All-Star Classic-19
06Albany River Rats-20

Tsirkounov, Oleg
95Owen Sound Platers-11
99Topeka Scarecrows-3

Tsujiura, Steve
83Springfield Indians-6
88ProCards AHL-159
93Swiss HNL-234

Tsulygin, Nikolai
92Upper Deck-614
93Parkhurst-526
Emerald Ice-526
93Pinnacle-507
Canadian-507
93Classic-46
93Classic Four-Sport *-206
Gold-206
94Classic-78
Gold-78
Tri-Cards-T1
94Signature Rookies Gold Standard *-94
95Swedish World Championships Stickers-28
95Signature Rookies-33
Signatures-33
96Ducks Team Issue-14
96Collector's Edge Ice-16
Prism-16
99Russian Hockey League-125
00Russian Hockey League-250
03Russian Hockey League-252
04Russian Super League All-Stars-22

Tsvetkov, Alexei
00Russian Hockey League-78
03Russian Hockey League-84

Tsybouk, Evgeni
96Lethbridge Hurricanes-23
97Lethbridge Hurricanes-21

98Michigan K-Wings-17
99Michigan K-Wings-9
00Utah Grizzlies-23

Tsygankov, Gennady

71Finnish Suomi Stickers-18
71Swedish Hockey-28
72Finnish Jaakiekko-38
72Finnish Hellas-67
72Finnish Semic World Championship-7
72Swedish Stickers-28
72Swedish Semic World Championship-7
73Finnish Jaakiekko-18
73Russian National Team-11
73Swedish Stickers-81
74Finnish Jenkki-58
74Finnish Typotor-74
74Russian National Team-21
74Swedish Stickers-2
74Swedish Semic World Champ Stickers-29
79Panini Stickers-145
79Russian National Team-8
91Future Trends Canada '72-67
91Future Trends Canada '72 French-67
99Russian Fetisov Tribute-16

Tsygurov, Denis

94Donruss-200
94Flair-23
94Leaf-161
94OPC Premier-29
Special Effects-29
94Pinnacle-258
Artist's Proofs-258
Rink Collection-258
Rookie Team Pinnacle-3
94Topps/OPC Premier-29
Special Effects-29
94Ultra-267
96Czech APS Extraliga-106
97Czech DS Stickers-266
99Russian Hockey League-104

Tsygurov, Dmitri

96Swiss HNL-87

Tsyplakov, Alexander

96Czech APS Extraliga-151
98Czech DS Stickers-134
98Czech OFS-376

Tsyplakov, Vladimir

93Fort Wayne Komets-21
94Classic Pro Prospects-103
95Parkhurst International-377
Emerald Ice-377
95Las Vegas Thunder-21
96Black Diamond-8
Gold-8
97Be A Player-197
Autographs-197
Autographs Die-Cuts-197
Autographs Prismatic Die-Cuts-197
97Collector's Choice-122
97Pacific-82
Copper-82
Emerald Green-82
Ice Blue-82
Red-82
Silver-82
97Pacific Dynagon-61
Copper-61
Dark Grey-61
Emerald Green-61
Ice Blue-61
Red-61
Silver-61
Tandems-43
97Pacific Invincible-69
Copper-69
Emerald Green-69
Ice Blue-69
Red-69
Silver-69
97Pacific Omega-115
Copper-115
Dark Gray-115
Emerald Green-115
Gold-115
Ice Blue-115
97Panini Stickers-218
97Revolution-68
Copper-68
Emerald-68
Ice Blue-68
Silver-68
97SP Authentic-74
97Upper Deck-289
98Aurora-91
98Be A Player-213
Press Release-213
98BAP Gold-213
98BAP Autographs-213
98BAP Autographs Gold-213
98OPC Chrome-14
Refractors-14
98Pacific-247
Ice Blue-247
Red-247
98Pacific Dynagon Ice-92
Blue-92
Red-92
98Pacific Omega-115
Red-115
Opening Day Issue-115
98Panini Stickers-204
98Paramount-110
Copper-110
Emerald Green-110
Holo-Electric-110
Ice Blue-110
Silver-110
98SPx Finite-40
Radiance-40
Spectrum-40
98Topps-14
O-Pee-Chee-14
98UD Choice-101
98UD Choice Preview-101
98UD Choice Prime Choice Reserve-101
98UD Choice Reserve-101
98Upper Deck-287
Exclusives-287
Exclusives 1 of 1-287
Gold Reserve-287
99Pacific-200
Copper-200
Emerald Green-200
Gold-200
Ice Blue-200
Premiere Date-200
Red-200
99Upper Deck-65
Exclusives-65
Exclusives 1 of 1-65
99Upper Deck Gold Reserve-65
99Upper Deck MVP-98
Gold Script-98
Silver Script-98
Super Script-98
99Upper Deck Victory-135
00BAP Memorabilia-31
Emerald-31
Ruby-31
Sapphire-31
Promos-31
00BAP Mem Chicago Sportsfest Copper-31
00BAP Memorabilia Chicago Sportsfest Blue-31
00BAP Memorabilia Chicago Sportsfest Gold-31
00BAP Memorabilia Chicago Sportsfest Ruby-31
00BAP Memorabilia Chicago Sun-Times Ruby-31
00BAP Memorabilia Chicago Sun-Times Gold-31
00BAP Mem Chicago Sun-Times Sapphire-31
00BAP Mem Toronto Fall Expo Copper-31
00BAP Memorabilia Toronto Fall Expo Gold-31
00BAP Memorabilia Toronto Fall Expo Ruby-31
00O-Pee-Chee-253A
00O-Pee-Chee Parallel-253A
00Pacific-58
Copper-58
Gold-58
Ice Blue-58
Premiere Date-58
00Topps/OPC-253A
Parallel-253A
01Russian Legions-3
02BAP Sig Series Auto Buybacks 1998-213
02Russian Hockey League-252
04Russian Legion-8

Tsyplakov, Yuri

95Swedish World Championships Stickers-47

Tsyrkunov, Oleg

95Slapshot-287

Tucciarone, Mike

06Austin Ice Bats-10

Tucek, Petr

99Czech OFS-550
99Czech Score Blue 2000-121
99Czech Score Red Ice 2000-121
00Czech OFS-351
01Czech OFS-84
01Czech OFS H Inserts-H9
02Czech OFS Plus-40
Checklists-C9
02Czech OFS Plus Masks-M3
02Czech OFS Plus Trios-T23
02Czech OFS Plus Duos-D17
03Czech OFS Plus-143
03Czech OFS Plus Checklists-7
03Czech OFS Plus Insert B-B11
03Czech OFS Plus Insert P-P12
04Slovakian Skalica Team Set-26
06Czech OFS-310

Tucker, Brian

98OCN Blizzard-24
99Muskegon Fury-18
01Memphis RiverKings-16
03Memphis RiverKings-20

Tucker, Chris

91Upper Deck Czech World Juniors-67
94Richmond Renegades-18

Tucker, Darcy

917th Inn. Sketch WHL-88
93Kamloops Blazers-22
94Finest-164
Super Team Winners-164
Refractors-164
94Pinnacle-537
Artist's Proofs-537
Rink Collection-537
94Upper Deck-503
Electric Ice-503
94Kamloops Blazers-1
95Donruss Canadian World Junior Team-13
95Topps Canadian World Juniors-16CJ
95Fredericton Canadiens-27
95Slapshot Memorial Cup-12
96Canadiens Postcards-32
96Canadiens Sheets-24
96Donruss Canadian Ice-143
Gold Press Proofs-143
Red Press Proofs-143
96Fleer Picks-148
96Leaf Gold Rookies-8
96Leaf Preferred-134
Press Proofs-134
96Summit Metal-176
96Upper Deck-281
96Upper Deck Ice-33
Parallel-33
96Zenith-130
Artist's Proofs-130
96Collector's Edge Future Legends-23
96Collector's Edge Ice-42
Platinum Club-5
Prism-42
97Be A Player-119
Autographs-119
Autographs Die-Cuts-119
Autographs Prismatic Die-Cuts-119
97Canadiens Postcards-24
97Donruss-182
Press Proofs Silver-182
Press Proofs Gold-182
97Donruss Canadian Ice-111
Dominion Series-111
Provincial Series-111
97Donruss Limited-34
97Donruss Limited-53
Exposure-34
Exposure-53
97Donruss Preferred-28
Cut to the Chase-28
97Leaf-77
Fractal Matrix-77
Fractal Matrix Die Cuts-77
97Leaf International-77
Universal Ice-77
97Pacific-83
Copper-83
Emerald Green-83
Ice Blue-83
Red-83
Silver-83
97Pinnacle-140
Press Plates Back Black-140
Press Plates Back Cyan-140
Press Plates Back Magenta-140
Press Plates Back Yellow-140
Press Plates Front Black-140
Press Plates Front Cyan-140
Press Plates Front Magenta-140
Press Plates Front Yellow-140
97Score-202
97Score Canadiens-13
Platinum-13
Premier-13
97Upper Deck-88
98OPC Chrome-183
Refractors-183
98Pacific-407
Ice Blue-407
Red-407
98Pacific Omega-222
Red-222
Opening Day Issue-222
98Topps-183
O-Pee-Chee-183
99Aurora-133
Premiere Date-133
99BAP Memorabilia-58
Gold-58
Silver-58
99Maple Leafs Pizza Pizza-17
99O-Pee-Chee-239
99O-Pee-Chee Chrome-239
99O-Pee-Chee Chrome Refractors-239
99Pacific-398
Copper-398
Emerald Green-398
Gold-398
Ice Blue-398
Premiere Date-398
Red-398
99Pacific Dynagon Ice-183
Blue-183
Copper-183
Gold-183
Premiere Date-183
99Pacific Prism-133
Holographic Blue-133
Holographic Gold-133
Holographic Mirror-133
Holographic Purple-133
Premiere Date-133
99Panini Stickers-151
99Paramount-220
Copper-220
Emerald-220
Gold-220
Holographic Emerald-220
Holographic Gold-220
Holographic Silver-220
Ice Blue-220
Premiere Date-220
Red-220
Silver-220
99Revolution-134
Premiere Date-134
Red-134
Shadow Series-134
99Stadium Club-87
First Day Issue-87
One of a Kind-87
Printing Plates Black-87
Printing Plates Cyan-87
Printing Plates Magenta-87
Printing Plates Yellow-87
99Topps/OPC-239
99Topps/OPC Chrome-239
Refractors-239
99Upper Deck-288
Exclusives-288
Exclusives 1 of 1-288
99Upper Deck Gold Reserve-288
99Upper Deck MVP-192
Gold Script-192
Silver Script-192
Super Script-192
99Upper Deck Victory-276
99Wayne Gretzky Hockey-155
00BAP Memorabilia-134
Emerald-134
Ruby-134
Sapphire-134
Promos-134
00BAP Mem Chicago Sportsfest Copper-134
00BAP Memorabilia Chicago Sportsfest Blue-134
00BAP Memorabilia Chicago Sportsfest Gold-134
00BAP Memorabilia Chicago Sportsfest Ruby-134
00BAP Memorabilia Chicago Sun-Times Ruby-134
00BAP Memorabilia Chicago Sun-Times Gold-134
00BAP Mem Chicago Sun-Times Sapphire-134
00BAP Mem Toronto Fall Expo Copper-134
00BAP Memorabilia Toronto Fall Expo Gold-134
00BAP Memorabilia Toronto Fall Expo Ruby-134
00O-Pee-Chee-235
00O-Pee-Chee Parallel-235
00Pacific-401
Copper-401
Gold-401
Ice Blue-401
Premiere Date-401
00Panini Stickers-96
00Paramount-235
Copper-235
Gold-235
Holo-Gold-235
Holo-Silver-235
Ice Blue-235
Premiere Date-235
00Revolution-141
Blue-141
Premiere Date-141
Red-141
00Stadium Club-193
00Topps/OPC-235
Parallel-235
00Topps Chrome-145
OPC Refractors-145
Refractors-145
00Upper Deck-163
Exclusives Tier 1-163
Exclusives Tier 2-163
00Upper Deck MVP-166
First Stars-166
Second Stars-166
Third Stars-166
00Upper Deck Victory-218
00Upper Deck Vintage-341
01BAP Signature Series-102
Autographs-102
Autographs Gold-102
01Crown Royale-135
Blue-135
Premiere Date-135
Red-135
Retail-135
01O-Pee-Chee-145
01O-Pee-Chee Premier Parallel-145
01Pacific-375
Extreme LTD-375
Hobby LTD-375
Premiere Date-375
Retail LTD-375
01Pacific Adrenaline-186
Blue-186
Premiere Date-186
Red-186
Retail-186
01Pacific Arena Exclusives-375
01Titanium-133
Hobby Parallel-133
Premiere Date-133
Retail-133
Retail Parallel-133
01Topps-145
OPC Parallel-145
01Topps Chrome-115
Refractors-115
Black Border Refractors-115
01UD Mask Collection-90
Gold-90
01Upper Deck-165
Exclusives-165
01Upper Deck MVP-177
01Upper Deck Victory-332
Gold-332
01Upper Deck Vintage-238
01Upper Deck Vintage-243
02Atomic Jerseys-23
02Atomic Jerseys Gold-23
02Atomic Patches-23
02BAP First Edition-11
Jerseys-11
02BAP Memorabilia-188
Emerald-188
Ruby-188
Sapphire-188
NHL All-Star Game-188
NHL All-Star Game Blue-188
NHL All-Star Game Green-188
NHL All-Star Game Red-188
02BAP Memorabilia Toronto Fall Expo-188
02BAP Signature Series-64
Autographs-64
Autograph Buybacks 2001-102
Autographs Gold-64
02Crown Royale Dual Patches-21
02Maple Leafs Platinum Collection-20
02Maple Leafs Team Issue-14
02NHL Power Play Stickers-137
02O-Pee-Chee-171
02O-Pee-Chee Premier Blue Parallel-171
02O-Pee-Chee Premier Red Parallel-171
02O-Pee-Chee Factory Set-171
02O-Pee-Chee Factory Set Hometown Heroes-HHC19
02Pacific-371
Blue-371
Red-371
Jerseys-48
Jerseys Holo-Silver-48
02Pacific Complete-405
Red-405
02Pacific Exclusive-164
02Pacific Heads-Up Quad Jerseys-26
02Pacific Heads-Up Quad Jerseys Gold-26
02Parkhurst-53
Bronze-53
Gold-53
Silver-53
02Parkhurst Retro-91
Minis-91
02Private Stock Reserve-94
Blue-94
Red-94
Retail-94
02Stadium Club-60
Silver Decoy Cards-60
Proofs-60
02Titanium Jerseys-68
02Titanium Jerseys Retail-68
02Topps-171
OPC Blue Parallel-171
OPC Red Parallel-171
Topps/OPC Hometown Heroes-HHC19
Factory Set-171
02Topps Total-311
02Upper Deck MVP-173
Gold-173
Classics-173
Golden Classics-173
02Upper Deck Victory-204
Bronze-204
Gold-204
Silver-204
02Upper Deck Vintage-239
02Vanguard Jerseys-45
02Vanguard Jerseys Gold-45
03ITG Action-587
03NHL Sticker Collection-135
03O-Pee-Chee-106
03OPC Blue-106
03OPC Gold-106
03OPC Red-106
03Pacific-326
Blue-326
Red-326
03Pacific Complete-334
Red-334
03Pacific Exhibit-139
Blue Backs-139
Yellow Backs-139
03Parkhurst Original Six Toronto-26
Memorabilia-TM4
Memorabilia-TM16
Memorabilia-TM58
03Private Stock Reserve-96
Blue-96
Red-96
Retail-96
03Titanium-94
Hobby Jersey Number Parallels-94
Retail-94
Retail Jersey Number Parallels-94
03Topps-106
Blue-106
Gold-106
Red-106
03Upper Deck-179
Canadian Exclusives-179
HG-179
03Upper Deck MVP-396
Gold Script-396
Silver Script-396
Canadian Exclusives-396
03Czech Stadion-537
04Pacific-252
Blue-252
Red-252
05Panini Stickers-166
05Parkhurst-452
Facsimile Auto Parallel-452
05Upper Deck-180
HG Glossy-180
05Upper Deck MVP-357
Gold-357
Platinum-357
05Upper Deck Toronto Fall Expo-180
05Upper Deck Victory-188
Black-188
Gold-188
Silver-188
06Be A Player-20
Autographs-20
Signatures-DT
Signatures 10-22
Signatures 25-22
Signatures Duals-DRT
Signatures Trios-TTWS
Up Close and Personal-UC13
Up Close and Personal Autographs-UC13
06Beehive Signature Scrapbook-SSDT
06Black Diamond-79
Black-79
Gold-79
Ruby-79
06Fleer-185
Tiffany-185
06Gatorade-63
06Hot Prospects-93
Red Hot-93
White Hot-93
06McDonald's Upper Deck-44
Jerseys-JDT
Patches-PDT
06O-Pee-Chee-455
Rainbow-455
Swatches-S-DT
06Panini Stickers-164
06SP Authentic Chirography-DT
06SP Game Used Authentic Fabrics Dual-AF2PT
06SP Game Used Authentic Fabrics Dual Patches-AF2PT
06SP Game Used Inked Sweaters-ISDT
06SP Game Used Inked Sweaters Patches-ISDT
06SP Game Used Inked Sweaters Dual-IS2PT
06SP Game Used Inked Sweaters Dual Patches-IS2PT
06SP Game Used SIGnificance-STU
06The Cup Limited Logos-LLTU
06The Cup NHL Shields Duals-DSHTP
06UD Artifacts-7
Blue-7
Gold-7
Platinum-7
Radiance-7
Red-7
Tundra Tandems-TTMT
Tundra Tandems Black-TTMT
Tundra Tandems Blue-TTMT
Tundra Tandems Gold-TTMT
Tundra Tandems Platinum-TTMT
Tundra Tandems Red-TTMT
Tundra Tandems Dual Patches Red-TTMT
06UD Mini Jersey Collection-94
06Ultra-185
Gold Medallion-185
Ice Medallion-185
06Upper Deck Arena Giveaways-TOR2
06Upper Deck-182
Exclusives Parallel-182
High Gloss Parallel-182
Game Jerseys-J2DT
Game Patches-P2DT
Hometown Heroes-HH41
Masterpieces-182
06Upper Deck MVP-277
Gold Script-277
Super Script-277
Autographs-OAPT
06Upper Deck Ovation-96
06Upper Deck Sweet Shot-95
06Upper Deck Victory-188
06Upper Deck Victory Black-188
06Upper Deck Victory Gold-188
07Upper Deck Victory-57
Black-57
Gold-57

Tucker, Gib

89Kitchener Rangers-22
90Kitchener Rangers-20
907th Inn. Sketch OHL-245
907th Inn. Sketch Memorial Cup-43
917th Inn. Sketch OHL-85

Tucker, Jeremy

06Port Huron Flags-8

Tucker, John

82Kitchener Rangers-24
83Kitchener Rangers-20
84Sabres Blue Shield-20
85O-Pee-Chee Stickers-184
85Sabres Blue Shield-27
85Sabres Blue Shield Small-27
86O-Pee-Chee-67
86O-Pee-Chee Stickers-48
86Sabres Blue Shield-28
86Sabres Blue Shield Small-28
86Topps-67
87O-Pee-Chee-154
87O-Pee-Chee Stickers-145
87Panini Stickers-30
87Sabres Blue Shield-27
87Sabres Wonder Bread/Hostess-29
87Topps-154
88O-Pee-Chee-74
88Panini Stickers-229
88Sabres Blue Shield-26
88Sabres Wonder Bread/Hostess-29
88Topps-74
89Capitals Kodak-12
89O-Pee-Chee-37
89Panini Stickers-212
89Topps-37
90O-Pee-Chee-374
90OPC Premier-122
90Panini Stickers-157
90Pro Set-322
90Pro Set-420
90Sabres Blue Shield-23
90Sabres Campbell's-27
90Topps-374
Tiffany-374
90Upper Deck-387
French-387
91Stadium Club-335
92Lightning Sheraton-23
92Parkhurst-405
Emerald Ice-405
92Ultra-414
92Upper Deck-548
93Donruss-328
93Leaf-21
93Lightning Season in Review-26
93OPC Premier-473
Gold-473
93Panini Stickers-212
93Parkhurst-462
Emerald Ice-462
93Pinnacle-144
Canadian-144
93PowerPlay-235
93Score-354
Canadian-354
93Stadium Club-38
Members Only Master Set-38
OPC-38
First Day Issue-38
First Day Issue OPC-38
93Topps/OPC Premier-473
Gold-473
93Ultra-211
93Upper Deck-409
94Canada Games NHL POGS-226
94Donruss-87
94Leaf-38
94Lightning Photo Album-25
94OPC Premier-132
Special Effects-132
94Parkhurst SE-SE170
Gold-SE170
94Pinnacle-226
Artist's Proofs-226
Rink Collection-226
94Score-23
Gold-23
Platinum-23
94Topps/OPC Premier-132
Special Effects-132
94Ultra-210
95Be A Player-120
Signatures-S120
Signatures Die Cuts-S120
95Canada Games NHL POGS-249
95Collector's Choice-104
Player's Club-104
Player's Club Platinum-104
95Donruss-311
95Leaf-269
95Lightning Team Issue-18
95Panini Stickers-125
95Parkhurst International-192
Emerald Ice-192
95Playoff One on One-312
95Score-191
Black Ice Artist's Proofs-191
Black Ice-191
95Upper Deck-78
Electric Ice-78
Electric Ice Gold-78
03Lightning Team Issue-18

Tucker, Kevin

01Peoria Rivermen-7

Tucker, Travis

96Quad-City Mallards-3
97Quad-City Mallards-11

Tuckey, Kevin

04Saginaw Spirit-8

Tuckey, Trevor

93Quebec Pee-Wee Tournament-1427

Tuckwell, Harry

23V128-1 Paulin's Candy-51

Tudin, Dan

95Slapshot-266
03Columbus Cottonmouths-18
04Las Vegas Wranglers-10
05Las Vegas Wranglers-22

Tuer, Al

81Regina Pats-22
82Regina Pats-9
83Regina Pats-9
88ProCards AHL-66
89ProCards AHL-289
90ProCards AHL/IHL-313
91ProCards-367
92Cincinnati Cyclones-23

Tugnutt, Ron

87Nordiques General Foods-30
87Nordiques Team Issue-29
88Nordiques General Foods-36
88Nordiques Team Issue-39
88ProCards AHL-117
89Nordiques Team Issue-38
89Nordiques General Foods-29
89Nordiques Police-27
89O-Pee-Chee-263
89Panini Stickers-332
90Nordiques Petro-Canada-25
90Nordiques Team Issue-25
90O-Pee-Chee-367
90Panini Stickers-142
90Pro Set-258
90Score-126
Canadian-126
90Topps-367
Tiffany-367
90Upper Deck-27
French-27
91Pro Set Platinum-98
91Bowman-151
91Nordiques Panini Team Stickers-22
91Nordiques Petro-Canada-30
91O-Pee-Chee-181
91Panini Stickers-267
91Parkhurst-149
91Parkhurst-277
French-149
French-277
91Pinnacle-124
French-124
91Pro Set-202
French-202
91Score American-41
91Score Canadian Bilingual-41
91Score Canadian English-41
91Score Young Superstars-33
91Stadium Club-115
91Topps-181
91Upper Deck-277
French-277
92Oilers IGA-24
92O-Pee-Chee-211
92Parkhurst-290
Emerald Ice-290
92Pinnacle-366
French-366
92Score-387
Canadian-387
92Ultra-298
93Donruss-12
93Donruss-453
Special Print-A
93Leaf-277
93OPC Premier-286
Gold-286
93Pinnacle-187
Canadian-187
93PowerPlay-13
93Score-368
93Score-504
Gold-504
Canadian-368
Canadian-504
Canadian Gold-504
93Stadium Club-325
Members Only Master Set-325
First Day Issue-325
93Topps/OPC Premier-286
Gold-286
93Ultra-263
93Upper Deck-426
SP-5
94Canadiens Postcards-27
94Donruss-69
94Leaf-46
94OPC Premier-523
Special Effects-523
94Pinnacle-172
Artist's Proofs-172
Rink Collection-172
94Score-21
Gold-21
Platinum-21
94Topps/OPC Premier-523
Special Effects-523
94Upper Deck-321
Electric Ice-321
95Score-70
Black Ice Artist's Proofs-70
Black Ice-70
95Portland Pirates-23
96Senators Pizza Hut-24
96Collector's Edge Ice-57
Prism-57
97Be A Player-36
Autographs-36
Autographs Die-Cuts-36
Autographs Prismatic Die-Cuts-36
97Collector's Choice-181
97Crown Royale-93
Emerald Green-93
Ice Blue-93
Silver-93
97Donruss-103
Press Proofs Silver-103
Press Proofs Gold-103
97Donruss Canadian Ice-63
Dominion Series-63
Provincial Series-63
97Donruss Priority-76
Stamp of Approval-76
97Gatorade Stickers-3
97Pacific-87
Copper-87
Emerald Green-87
Ice Blue-87
Red-87
Silver-87
97Pacific Invincible-96
Copper-96
Emerald Green-96
Ice Blue-96
Red-96
Silver-96
97Pacific Omega-158
Copper-158
Dark Gray-158
Emerald Green-158
Gold-158
Ice Blue-158
97Pinnacle-99
Artist's Proofs-99
Rink Collection-99
Press Plates Back Black-99
Press Plates Back Cyan-99
Press Plates Back Magenta-99
Press Plates Back Yellow-99
Press Plates Front Black-99
Press Plates Front Cyan-99
Press Plates Front Magenta-99
Press Plates Front Yellow-99
97Pinnacle Certified-29
Red-29
Mirror Blue-29
Mirror Gold-29
Mirror Red-29
97Pinnacle Inside-82
Coach's Collection-82
Executive Collection-82
97Pinnacle Tot Cert Platinum Blue-29
97Pinnacle Tot Cert Platinum Gold-29
97Pinnacle Totally Certified Platinum Red-29
97Pinnacle Tot Cert Mirror Platinum Gold-29
97Revolution-95
Copper-95
Emerald-95
Ice Blue-95
Silver-95
97Score-49
Artist's Proofs-49
Golden Blades-49
97Upper Deck-113
98Be A Player-244
Press Release-244
98BAP Gold-244
98BAP Autographs-244
98BAP Autographs Gold-244
98NHL Aces Playing Cards-20
98Pacific-316
Ice Blue-316
Red-316
98Pacific Omega-169
Red-169
Opening Day Issue-169
98Paramount-167
Copper-167
Emerald Green-167
Holo-Electric-167
Ice Blue-167
Silver-167
98Senators Team Issue-22
99Aurora-101
Premiere Date-101
Glove Unlimited-14
99BAP Memorabilia-84
99BAP Memorabilia-351
Gold-84
Gold-351
Silver-84
Silver-351
99BAP Millennium-172
Emerald-172
Ruby-172
Sapphire-172
Signatures-172
Signatures Gold-172
99Crown Royale-99
Limited Series-99
Premiere Date-99
99Jell-O Goalie Collection-1
99O-Pee-Chee-129
99O-Pee-Chee Chrome-129
99O-Pee-Chee Chrome Refractors-129
99Pacific-296
Copper-296
Emerald Green-296
Gold-296
Ice Blue-296
Premiere Date-296
Red-296
In the Cage Net-Fusions-13
99Pacific Dynagon Ice-141
Blue-141
Copper-141
Gold-141
Premiere Date-141
99Pacific Omega-163
Copper-163
Gold-163
Ice Blue-163
Premiere Date-163
99Pacific Prism-98
Holographic Blue-98
Holographic Gold-98
Holographic Mirror-98
Holographic Purple-98
Premiere Date-98
99Panini Stickers-117
99Panini Stickers-348
99Paramount-166
Copper-166
Emerald-166
Gold-166
Holographic Emerald-166
Holographic Gold-166
Holographic Silver-166
Ice Blue-166
Premiere Date-166
Red-166
Silver-166
Glove Side Net Fusions-14
99Revolution-104
Premiere Date-104
Red-104
Shadow Series-104
Copper-104
Gold-104
CSC Silver-104
99Senators Team Issue-20
99SPx-104
Radiance-104
Spectrum-104
99Stadium Club-91
First Day Issue-91
One of a Kind-91
Printing Plates Black-91
Printing Plates Cyan-91
Printing Plates Magenta-91
Printing Plates Yellow-91
Goalie Cam-GC6
99Topps/OPC-129
99Topps/OPC Chrome-129
Refractors-129
99Topps Gold Label Class 1-41
Black-41
Black One of One-41
One of One-41
Red-41
Red One of One-41
99Topps Gold Label Class 2-41
99Topps Gold Label Class 2 Black-41
99Topps Gold Label Class 2 Black 1 of 1-41
99Topps Gold Label Class 2 One of One-41
99Topps Gold Label Class 2 Red-41
99Topps Gold Label Class 2 Red One of One-41
99Topps Gold Label Class 3-41
99Topps Gold Label Class 3 Black-41
99Topps Gold Label Class 3 Black 1 of 1-41
99Topps Gold Label Class 3 One of One-41
99Topps Gold Label Class 3 Red-41
99Topps Gold Label Class 3 Red One of One-41
99Topps Premier Plus-27
Parallel-27
99Ultimate Victory-62
1/1-62
Parallel-62
Parallel 100-62
99Upper Deck-263
Exclusives-263
Exclusives 1 of 1-263
99Upper Deck Gold Reserve-263
99Upper Deck MVP-142
Gold Script-142
Silver Script-142
Super Script-142
ProSign-RT
99Upper Deck MVP SC Edition-127
Gold Script-127
Silver Script-127
Super Script-127
99Upper Deck Victory-207
99Wayne Gretzky Hockey-120
00SLU Hockey-220
00SLU Hockey-221
00BAP Memorabilia-169
00BAP Memorabilia-489
Emerald-169
Emerald-489
Ruby-169
Ruby-489
Sapphire-169
Sapphire-489
Promos-169
00BAP Mem Chicago Sportsfest Copper-169
00BAP Memorabilia Chicago Sportsfest Blue-169
00BAP Memorabilia Chicago Sportsfest Gold-169
00BAP Memorabilia Chicago Sportsfest Ruby-169
00BAP Memorabilia Chicago Sun-Times Ruby-169
00BAP Memorabilia Chicago Sun-Times Gold-169
00BAP Mem Chicago Sun-Times Sapphire-169
00BAP Mem Toronto Fall Expo Copper-169
00BAP Memorabilia Toronto Fall Expo Gold-169
00BAP Memorabilia Toronto Fall Expo Ruby-169
00BAP Parkhurst 2000-P113
00BAP Signature Series-177
Emerald-177
Ruby-177
Sapphire-177
Autographs-16
Autographs Gold-16
Franchise Players-F9
00Crown Royale-33
Ice Blue-33
Limited Series-33
Premiere Date-33
Red-33
00Kraft-29
00O-Pee-Chee-248
00O-Pee-Chee Parallel-248
00Pacific-338
Copper-338
Gold-338
Ice Blue-338
Premiere Date-338
00Panini Stickers-138
00Paramount-72
Copper-72
Gold-72
Holo-Gold-72
Holo-Silver-72
Ice Blue-72
Premiere Date-72
00SP Authentic-26
Sign of the Times-RT
00SP Game Used-17
00SPx-18
Spectrum-18
00Stadium Club-210
00Titanium-26
Blue-26
Gold-26
Premiere Date-26
Red-26

Retail-26
Game Gear-13
00Topps/OPC-248
Parallel-248
00Topps Chrome-221
OPC Refractors-221
Refractors-221
00Topps Gold Label Class 1-50
Gold-50
00Topps Gold Label Class 2-50
00Topps Gold Label Class 2 Gold-50
00Topps Gold Label Class 3-50
00Topps Gold Label Class 3 Gold-50
00Topps Heritage-106
00Topps Premier Plus-25
Blue Ice-25
00Topps Stars-97
Blue-97
Game Gear-GGRT
00UD Heroes-34
00UD Reserve-25
00Upper Deck-54
00Upper Deck-278
Exclusives Tier 1-54
Exclusives Tier 1-278
Exclusives Tier 2-54
Exclusives Tier 2-278
00Upper Deck Victory-189
00Upper Deck Vintage-102
00Upper Deck Vintage-111
00Vanguard-32
Holographic Gold-32
Holographic Purple-32
Pacific Proofs-32
01BAP Memorabilia-35
Emerald-35
Ruby-35
Sapphire-35
01Between the Pipes-3
He Shoots-He Saves Prizes-2
Jerseys-GJ27
Jersey and Stick Cards-GSJ28
Masks-36
Masks Silver-36
Masks Gold-36
01Blue Jackets Donatos Pizza-12
01Blue Jackets Donatos Pizza-19
01Crown Royale-45
Blue-45
Premiere Date-45
Red-45
Retail-45
01O-Pee-Chee-166
01O-Pee-Chee Premier Parallel-166
01Pacific-118
Extreme LTD-118
Hobby LTD-118
Premiere Date-118
Retail LTD-118
01Pacific Adrenaline-56
Blue-56
Premiere Date-56
Red-56
Retail-56
Power Play-11
01Pacific Arena Exclusives-118
01Parkhurst-105
01Private Stock-27
Gold-27
Premiere Date-27
Retail-27
Silver-27
01Private Stock Pacific Nights-27
01SP Authentic-21
Limited-21
Limited Gold-21
01SP Game Used-13
01SPx-18
01Stadium Club-21
Award Winners-21
Master Photos-21
01Titanium-41
Hobby Parallel-41
Premiere Date-41
Retail-41
Retail Parallel-41
01Titanium Draft Day Edition-31
01Topps-166
OPC Parallel-166
01Topps Reserve-29
01UD Mask Collection-109
Gold-109
Double Patches-DPRT
Goalie Jerseys-MMRT
Goalie Jerseys-SSRT
Jerseys-J-RT
Jersey and Patch-JPRT
01UD Playmakers Jerseys-J-RT
01UD Playmakers Jerseys Gold-J-RT
01Upper Deck-49
Exclusives-49
01Upper Deck Ice-11
01Upper Deck MVP-55
01Upper Deck Victory-96
01Upper Deck Victory-100
Gold-96
Gold-100
01Upper Deck Vintage-71
01Upper Deck Vintage-78
01Vanguard-30
Blue-30
Red-30
One of Ones-30
Premiere Date-30
Proofs-30
02BAP All-Star Edition-94
Jerseys-94
Jerseys Gold-94
Jerseys Silver-94
02BAP First Edition-107
Jerseys-107
02BAP Signature Series-103
Autographs-103
Autograph Buybacks 1998-244
Autograph Buybacks 1999-172
Autograph Buybacks 2000-16
Autographs Gold-103
02Between the Pipes-59
Gold-59
Silver-59
Jerseys-45
Tandems-19
02O-Pee-Chee-216
02O-Pee-Chee Premier Blue Parallel-216
02O-Pee-Chee Premier Red Parallel-216
02O-Pee-Chee Factory Set-216
02Pacific-107
Blue-107
Red-107
Jerseys-13
Jerseys Holo-Silver-13
02Pacific Complete-410
Red-410
02Pacific Heads-Up Quad Jerseys-10
02Pacific Heads-Up Quad Jerseys Gold-10
02Parkhurst-143
Bronze-143
Gold-143
Silver-143
02Stars Postcards-20
02Titanium Jerseys-21
02Titanium Jerseys Retail-21
02Titanium Patches-21
02Topps-216
OPC Blue Parallel-216
OPC Red Parallel-216
Factory Set-216
02Topps Heritage-180
02Topps Total-276
02UD Mask Collection-26
02UD Mask Collection-27
02UD Mask Collection Beckett Promos-26
02UD Mask Collection Beckett Promos-27
02UD Mask Collection Career Wins-CWRT
02UD Piece of History Patches-PHRT
02UD Top Shelf Stopper Jerseys-SSRT
02Upper Deck-300
Exclusives-300
02Upper Deck Beckett UD Promos-300
02Upper Deck CHL Graduates-CGRT
02Upper Deck CHL Graduates Gold-CGRT
02Upper Deck Saviors Jerseys-SVTU
02Upper Deck Classic Portraits Hockey Royalty-KTK
02Upper Deck Classic Portraits Hockey Royalty Limited-KTK
02Upper Deck MVP Skate Around Jerseys-SDTD
02Upper Deck MVP Skate Around Jerseys-STWKT
02Upper Deck MVP Souvenirs-S-RT
02Upper Deck Victory-62
Bronze-62
Gold-62
Silver-62
02Upper Deck Vintage Jerseys-EERT
02Upper Deck Vintage Jerseys Gold-EE-RT
03BAP Memorabilia-160
Emerald-160
Gold-160
Ruby-160
Sapphire-160
Tandems-T-6
03ITG Action-129
03Pacific-110
Blue-110
Red-110
03Pacific Complete-495
Red-495
03Pacific Invincible Jerseys-9
03Stars Postcards-26
03Upper Deck-307
Canadian Exclusives-307
HG-307
UD Exclusives-307
03Upper Deck MVP-141
Gold Script-141
Silver Script-141
Canadian Exclusives-141

Tukio, Arto
99Finnish Cardset-245
00Finnish Cardset-31
00Finnish Cardset Next Generation-6
01Finnish Cardset-234
02Finnish Cardset-129
03Finnish Cardset-62
04Swedish Elitset-171
Gold-171
05Swedish SHL Elitset-174
Gold-174
06Swedish SHL Elitset-29

Tukonen, Lauri
04Finnish Cardset-12
04Finnish Cardset Signatures-3
05ITG Heroes/Prosp Toronto Expo Parallel -251
05Finnish Cardset -7
05AHL Top Prospects-44
05Manchester Monarchs-20
05ITG Heroes and Prospects-251
Autographs Series II-LT
06Manchester Monarchs-12
06ITG Heroes and Prospects-47
Autographs-ALT
07Upper Deck Victory-230
Black-230
Gold-230

Tuli, Jukka
70Finnish Jaakiekko-343

Tuli, Raimo
66Finnish Jaakiekkosarja-22

Tulik, Brian
92Raleigh Icecaps-17
92Raleigh Icecaps-31

Tulli, Nate
93Quebec Pee-Wee Tournament-780

Tully, Brent
907th Inn. Sketch OHL-374
91Peterborough Petes-5
917th Inn. Sketch OHL-130
92Upper Deck-592
93Donruss Team Canada-21
93Pinnacle-464
Canadian-464
93Upper Deck-530
93Peterborough Petes-9
93Classic-31
95Upper Deck World Junior Alumni-9
96Syracuse Crunch-44
98German DEL-184
99German DEL-184
00German DEL-115
01German Upper Deck-89

Tulupov, Kirill
06Chicoutimi Sagueneens-21

Tuma, Martin
02Czech OFS Plus-353
03Sault Ste. Marie Greyhounds-23
04Sault Ste. Marie Greyhounds-22
05Florida Everblades-2

Tuma, Zbynek
01Czech OFS-275

Tumbach, Troy
94German DEL-144
95German DEL-41

Tunik, Evgeny
03Russian Hockey League-80
04Russian World Junior Team-18

Tunikov, Vadim
92Norwegian Elite Series-85

Tuohimaa, Harri
71Finnish Suomi Stickers-376
78Finnish SM-Liiga-110
80Finnish Mallasjuoma-128
91Finnish Jyvas-Hyva Stickers-4

Tuohimaa, Juha
78Finnish SM-Liiga-136
80Finnish Mallasjuoma-94
83Swedish Semic Elitserien-158
85Swedish Panini Stickers-205
86Swedish Panini Stickers-173
87Swedish Panini Stickers-172
91Finnish Jyvas-Hyva Stickers-35
92Finnish Jyvas-Hyva Stickers-94

Tuohimaa, Pasi
71Finnish Suomi Stickers-377
80Finnish Mallasjuoma-118

Tuokko, Marco
98Finnish Kerailysarja-240
99Finnish Cardset-143
00Finnish Cardset-218
01Finnish Cardset-143
02Finnish Cardset-282
03Finnish Cardset-163
04Finnish Cardset-175
Parallel-129
05Swedish SHL Elitset-261
Gold-261
06Swedish SHL Elitset-257

Tuokkola, Pekka
05Finnish Cardset -315
06Finnish Cardset-248

Tuomainen, Marko
91Upper Deck-675
French-675
91Upper Deck Czech World Juniors-38
92Clarkson Knights-23
95Collector's Choice-121
Player's Club-121
Player's Club Platinum-121
95Donruss-56
95Leaf-171
95Topps-189
OPC Inserts-189
95Upper Deck-12
Electric Ice-12
Electric Ice Gold-12
96Collector's Edge Ice-36
Prism-36
98Finnish Kerailysarja-50
Leijonat-44
99Pacific Omega-114
Copper-114
Gold-114
Ice Blue-114
Premiere Date-114
99Upper Deck MVP SC Edition-89
Gold Script-89
Silver Script-89
Super Script-89
99Finnish Cardset-199
Aces High-S-J
Blazing Patriots-6
Par Avion-7
00Finnish Cardset-118
00Lowell Lock Monsters-8
02Finnish Cardset-283
03Finnish Cardset-13
04Swiss Lausanne HC Postcards-19

Tuomainen, Miikka
05Finnish Cardset -288
06Finnish Cardset-117
Signature Sensations-22

Tuomainen, Teemu
98Finnish Kerailysarja-148

Tuomainen, Timo
66Finnish Jaakiekkosarja-132
70Finnish Jaakiekko-270

Tuomanen, Teppo
06Finnish Cardset-226
06Finnish Ilves Team Set-25

Tuomenoksa, Antti
92Finnish Jyvas-Hyva Stickers-98
93Finnish Jyvas-Hyva Stickers-170
93Finnish SISU-167
94Finnish SISU-89
94Finnish SISU Horoscopes-3
95Finnish SISU-190

Tuomi, Michael
02Barrie Colts-5

Tuomi, Niko
02Sault Ste. Marie Greyhounds-18
03Guelph Storm-9
04St. Francis Xavier X-Men-21

Tuomi, Risto
80Finnish Mallasjuoma-209

Tuominen, Aki
99Finnish Cardset-227
00Finnish Cardset-133
01Finnish Cardset-13

Tuominen, Jouni
94Finnish SISU-331
95Finnish SISU-144
05Finnish Cardset -305

Tuominen, Olli
78Finnish SM-Liiga-165
80Finnish Mallasjuoma-119

Tuominen, Pasi
95Finnish SISU-364
96Finnish SISU Redline-158
98Finnish Kerailysarja-215
99Finnish Cardset-320
00Finnish Cardset-206
01Finnish Cardset-114
03Finnish Cardset-177
04Finnish Cardset-194
Parallel-143
05Swedish SHL Elitset-246
Gold-246
06Swedish SHL Elitset-109

Tuomisto, Martti
80Finnish Mallasjuoma-46

Tuomisto, Pekka
70Finnish Jaakiekko-382
80Finnish Mallasjuoma-101
91Finnish Jyvas-Hyva Stickers-3
92Finnish Jyvas-Hyva Stickers-12
93Finnish Jyvas-Hyva Stickers-24
93Finnish SISU-102
93Swedish Semic World Champ Stickers-81
94Finnish SISU-18
95Finnish SISU-214

Tupa, Martin
95Czech APS Extraliga-185
96Czech APS Extraliga-317
97Czech APS Extraliga-295
98Czech DS Stickers-111
98Czech OFS-51
99Czech Score Blue 2000-32
99Czech Score Red Ice 2000-32
00Czech OFS-142
01Czech OFS-155
02Czech OFS Plus-210
03Czech OFS Plus-396
04Czech OFS-110

Tuplin, Darcy
02Belleville Bulls-21

Tuppurainen, Jani
05Finnish Cardset -260
06Finnish Cardset-86

Turan, Miroslav
04Slovakian Poprad Team Set-7

Turbide, Patrick
01Drummondville Voltigeurs-2

Turcer, Michal
95Slovakian-Quebec Pee-Wee Tournament-26

Turco, Marty
98IHL All-Star Eastern Conference-6
98Michigan K-Wings-19
99IHL All-Stars-9
99Michigan K-Wings-10
00BAP Memorabilia-440
Emerald-440
Ruby-440
Sapphire-440
00BAP Parkhurst 2000-P210
00BAP Signature Series-288
Emerald-288
Ruby-288
Sapphire-288
Autographs-250
Autographs Gold-250
00Black Diamond-117
00Crown Royale-122
21st Century Rookies-9
00Private Stock-117
Gold-117
Premiere Date-117
Retail-117
Silver-117
PS-2001 Rookies-8
00SP Authentic-102
Sign of the Times-MT
00SP Game Used-67
00SPx-159
00Stadium Club-259
00Stars Postcards-24
00Titanium-116
Retail-116
00Titanium Draft Day Edition-116
00Titanium Draft Day Promos-116
00Topps Chrome-243
Blue-243
Red-243
OPC Refractors-243
OPC Refractors Blue-243
OPC Refractors Red-243
Refractors-243
Refractors Blue-243
Refractors Red-243
00Topps Gold Label Class 1-105
Gold-105
00Topps Gold Label Class 2-105
00Topps Gold Label Class 2 Gold-105
00Topps Gold Label Class 3-105
00Topps Gold Label Class 3 Gold-105
00Topps Gold Label Autographs-GLA-MT
00Topps Heritage-75
Chrome Parallel-75
00Topps Premier Plus-126
Blue Ice-126
Game-Used Memorabilia-GPMT
Game-Used Memorabilia-GPEBMT
Private Signings-PSMT
00Topps Stars-112
00Topps Stars-147
Blue-112
Blue-147
Progression-P5
00UD Pros and Prospects-102
00UD Reserve-93
00Upper Deck-428
Exclusives Tier 1-428
Exclusives Tier 2-428
00Upper Deck Ice-69
00Vanguard-117
Pacific Proofs-117
01BAP Memorabilia-151
Emerald-151
Ruby-151
Sapphire-151
01BAP Update He Shoots-He Scores Prizes-16
01Between the Pipes-26
Goalie Gear-GG13
He Shoots-He Saves Prizes-4
Jerseys-GJ28
Tandems-GT7
01Crown Royale Toronto Expo Rookie Coll-G1
01Pacific-136
01Pacific-446
Extreme LTD-136
Hobby LTD-136
Premiere Date-136
Retail LTD-136
01Pacific Adrenaline-61
Blue-61
Premiere Date-61
Red-61
Retail-61
Power Play-13
01Pacific Arena Exclusives-136
01Pacific Heads-Up Breaking the Glass-9
01Parkhurst Teammates-T21
01Private Stock PS-2002-25
01SP Authentic Buybacks-21
01SPx Hockey Treasures Autographed-STTU
01Sports Illustrated for Kids III-330
01Stadium Club New Regime-NR1
01Stadium Club New Regime-NRAMT
01Stadium Club Souvenirs-MT
01Stadium Club Souvenirs-MTEB
01Stars Postcards-23
01Titanium Double-Sided Jerseys-53
01Titanium Double-Sided Jerseys-57
01Titanium Double-Sided Patches-53
01Titanium Double-Sided Patches-57
01Topps Heritage-78
01Topps Heritage-129
Refractors-78
01Topps Reserve Emblems-MT
01Topps Reserve Jerseys-MT
01Topps Reserve Name Plates-MT
01Topps Reserve Numbers-MT
01Topps Reserve Patches-MT
01UD Mask Collection Double Patches-DPMT
01UD Mask Collection Goalie Jerseys-MMMT
01UD Mask Collection Goalie Jerseys-VCMT
01UD Mask Collection Jerseys-J-MT
01UD Mask Collection Jersey and Patch-JPMT
01UD Top Shelf Jerseys-MT
01UD Top Shelf Jersey Autographs-MT
01Upper Deck Game Jerseys-GJMT
01Upper Deck Game Jerseys-NGMT
01Upper Deck Victory-118
Gold-118
01Upper Deck Vintage-268
01Upper Deck Vintage-269
02Atomic-34
Blue-34
Gold-34
Red-34
Denied-6
Hobby Parallel-34
02BAP All-Star Edition-104
Gold-104
Silver-104
02BAP First Edition-68
02BAP First Edition-376
02BAP First Edition-377
Jerseys-68
02BAP Memorabilia-104
Emerald-104
Ruby-104
Sapphire-104
NHL All-Star Game-104
NHL All-Star Game Blue-104
NHL All-Star Game Green-104
NHL All-Star Game Red-104
02BAP Memorabilia Toronto Fall Expo-104
02BAP Signature Series-165
Autographs-165
Autographs Gold-165
Defensive Wall-DW5
Jerseys-SGJ68
Jersey Autographs-SGJ68
Team Quads-TQ16
02BAP Ultimate Memorabilia Jerseys-23
02BAP Ultimate Mem Jersey and Stick-11
02BAP Ultimate Memorabilia Numerology-30
02Between the Pipes-23
02Between the Pipes-130
Gold-23
Silver-23
Behind the Mask-1
Blockers-7
Complete Package-CP5
Double Memorabilia-9
Emblems-19
Future Wave-10
Goalie Autographs-24
He Shoots-He Saves Points-10
He Shoots-He Saves Prizes-4
Jerseys-19
Masks II-10
Masks II Gold-10
Masks II Silver-10
Numbers-19
Pads-3
Stick and Jerseys-19
Tandems-19
Trappers-GT15
02Crown Royale-31
Blue-31
Red-31
Retail-31
Jerseys-5
Jerseys Gold-5
Coats of Armor-2
02eTopps-35
02ITG Used-20
02ITG Used-120
Goalie Pad and Jersey-GP11
Goalie Pad and Jersey Gold-GP11
Teammates-T13
Teammates Gold-T13
02O-Pee-Chee-85
02O-Pee-Chee Premier Blue Parallel-85
02O-Pee-Chee Premier Red Parallel-85
02O-Pee-Chee Factory Set-85
02Pacific-119
Blue-119
Red-119
02Pacific Calder-36
Silver-36
Chasing Glory-5
Hart Stoppers-5
02Pacific Complete-7
Red-7
02Pacific Exclusive-58
Advantage-6
02Pacific Heads-Up-40
Blue-40
Purple-40
Red-40
Quad Jerseys-11
Quad Jerseys Gold-11
Showstoppers-7
02Pacific Quest for the Cup-30
02Pacific Quest for the Cup-30AU
Gold-30
Chasing the Cup-5
Jerseys-8
02Pacific Toronto Fall Expo-8
Gold-8
02Parkhurst-26
Bronze-26
Gold-26
Silver-26
02Parkhurst Retro-82
Minis-82
He Shoots-He Scores Points-8
He Shoots-He Scores Prizes-19
Hopefuls-HH4
Hopefuls-VH2
Jerseys-RJ11
Jersey and Sticks-RSJ8
Memorabilia-RM12
02Private Stock Reserve-33
Blue-33
Red-33
Retail-33
InCrease Security-7
02SP Authentic-29
Beckett Promos-29
02SP Game Used Future Fabrics-FFMT
02SP Game Used Future Fabrics Gold-FFMT
02SP Game Used Future Fabrics Rainbow-FFMT
02SPx-24
Spectrum Gold-24
Spectrum Silver-24
Xtreme Talents-MT
Xtreme Talents Gold-MT
Xtreme Talents Silver-MT
02Stadium Club-66
Silver Decoy Cards-66
Proofs-66
Puck Stops Here-PSH7
02Stars Postcards-19
02Titanium-33
Blue-33
Red-33
Retail-33
Jerseys-22
Jerseys Retail-22
Patches-22
Masked Marauders-2
02Topps-85
OPC Blue Parallel-85
OPC Red Parallel-85
Factory Set-85
02Topps Chrome-53
Black Border Refractors-53
Refractors-53
02Topps Heritage-72
Chrome Parallel-72
Crease Piece-MT
Crease Piece Patches-MT
02Topps Total-204
02UD Artistic Impressions-28
Gold-28
02UD Artistic Impressions Beckett Promos-28
02UD Artistic Impressions Retrospectives-R28
02UD Artistic Impressions Retrospect Gold-R28
02UD Artistic Impress Retrospect Silver-R28
02UD Honor Roll-22
02UD Mask Collection-26
02UD Mask Collection-27
02UD Mask Collection-28
02UD Mask Collection-29
02UD Mask Collection-95
02UD Mask Collection Beckett Promos-26
02UD Mask Collection Beckett Promos-27
02UD Mask Collection Beckett Promos-28
02UD Mask Collection Beckett Promos-29
02UD Mask Collection Great Gloves-GGMT
02UD Mask Collection Masked Marvels-MMMT
02UD Mask Collection Nation's Best-NJBT
02UD Mask Collection Patches-PWMT
02UD Mask Collection View from the Cage-VMT
02UD Piece of History-30
Patches-PHMT
02UD Premier Collection-20
02UD Top Shelf-28
02Upper Deck-58
Exclusives-58
Blow-Ups-C12
Goaltender Threads-MT
Goaltender Threads Gold-MT
Patchwork-PWMT
Playbooks Series II-MT
Saviors Jerseys-SVMT
Super Saviors-SA5
02Upper Deck Classic Portraits-31
02Upper Deck MVP-57
Gold-57
Classics-57
Golden Classics-57
Skate Around Jerseys-SDMT
Skate Around Jerseys-SDTBE
Souvenirs-S-MT
02Upper Deck Rookie Update-33
02Upper Deck Victory-66
Bronze-66
Gold-66
Silver-66
02Upper Deck Vintage-82
02Upper Deck Vintage-270
02Upper Deck Vintage-317
Green Backs-82
Jerseys-EEMT
Jerseys Gold-EE-MT
02Vanguard-34
LTD-34
East Meets West-10
Stonewallers-2
V-Team-2
03McFarlane Hockey NHL 2-Pack-20
03BAP Memorabilia-140
Emerald-140
Gold-140
Ruby-140
Sapphire-140
Gloves-GUG3
Jersey and Stick-SJ-10
Jerseys-GJ-11
Jersey Autographs-GJ-11
Masks III-15
Masks III Gold-15
Masks III Silver-15
Masks III Autographs-M-MT
Masks III Memorabilia-15
Stanley Cup Playoffs-SCP-18
Tandems-T-6
03BAP Ultimate Memorabilia Autographs-64
Gold-64
03BAP Ultimate Mem Auto Emblems-64
03BAP Ultimate Mem Complete Package-7
03BAP Ultimate Mem Complete Package Gold-7
03BAP Ultimate Memorabilia Jerseys-36
03BAP Ultimate Memorabilia Jerseys Gold-36
03BAP Ultimate Mem Jersey and Emblems-26
03BAP Ultimate Mem Jersey and Emblem Gold-26
03BAP Ultimate Mem Jersey and Numbers-26
03BAP Ultimate Mem Jersey and Number Gold-26
03BAP Ultimate Memorabilia Triple Threads-4
03Beehive-67
Variations-67
Gold-67
Silver-67
Jumbos-10
Jumbo Variations-10
Jumbo Jerseys-BH2
Jerseys-JT21
03Black Diamond-98
Black-98
Green-98
Red-98
Signature Gems-SG-21
Threads-DT-MT
Threads Green-DT-MT
Threads Red-DT-MT
Threads Black-DT-MT
03Bowman-90
Gold-90
Future Rivals-AT
Future Rivals Patches-AT
03Bowman Chrome-90
Refractors-90
Gold Refractors-90
Xfractors-90
03Crown Royale-34
Blue-34
Retail-34
Gauntlet of Glory-8
03Duracell-4
03ITG Action-157
First Time All-Star-FT3
Highlight Reel-HR11
Homeboys-HB2
Jerseys-M180
Jerseys-M228
League Leaders-L5
03ITG Toronto Fall Expo Jerseys-FE11
03ITG Used Signature Series-37
Gold-37
Autographs-MT
Autographs Gold-MT
Goalie Gear-6
Goalie Gear Autographs-6
Goalie Gear Gold-6
Jerseys-26
Jerseys Gold-26
Jersey Autos-26
Emblems-19
Emblems Gold-19
Jersey and Stick-26
Jersey and Stick Gold-26
Teammates-19
Teammates Gold-19
Triple Memorabilia-9
Triple Memorabilia Gold-9
03ITG VIP Netminders-5
03McDonald's Pacific-16
Patches Silver-9
Patches Gold-9
Patches and Sticks-9
03NHL Sticker Collection-210
03O-Pee-Chee-216
03O-Pee-Chee-294
03OPC Blue-216
03OPC Blue-294
03OPC Gold-216
03OPC Gold-294
03OPC Red-216
03OPC Red-294
03Pacific-111
Blue-111
Red-111
In the Crease-4
Jerseys-14
Jerseys Gold-14
Marty Turco-1
Marty Turco-2
Marty Turco-3
Marty Turco-4
Marty Turco-5
Marty Turco-6
Marty Turco Autographs-1
Marty Turco Autographs-2
Marty Turco Autographs-3
Marty Turco Autographs-4
Marty Turco Autographs-5
Marty Turco Autographs-6
Milestones-4
03Pacific Calder-33
03Pacific Calder-148
Silver-33
03Pacific Complete-416
Red-416
03Pacific Exhibit-166
03Pacific Exhibit-206
Blue Backs-166
Standing on Tradition-4
03Pacific Heads-Up-33
Hobby LTD-33
Retail LTD-33
Stonewallers-4
Stonewallers LTD-4
03Pacific Invincible-31
Blue-31
Red-31
Retail-31
Freeze Frame-6
Jerseys-10
03Pacific Luxury Suite-32A
03Pacific Luxury Suite-32B
03Pacific Luxury Suite-32C
03Pacific Prism-115
Blue-115
Patches-115
Red-115
Retail-115
Crease Police-3
03Pacific Quest for the Cup-33
Blue-33
Chasing the Cup-6
Jerseys-8
03Pacific Supreme-31
Blue-31
Red-31
Retail-31
Standing Guard-5
03Parkhurst Rookie-7
Jerseys-GJ-40
Jerseys Gold-GJ-40
Jersey and Sticks-SJ-11
Jersey and Sticks Gold-SJ-11
03Private Stock Reserve-164
Blue-164
Patches-164
Red-164
Retail-164
Increase Security-6
03SP Authentic-27
Limited-27
Foundations-F7
Foundations Limited-F7
Sign of the Times-MT
03SP Game Used-15
03SP Game Used-119
Gold-15
Gold-119
Authentic Fabrics-DFMT
Authentic Fabrics-QMGTM
Authentic Fabrics-QRGBT
Authentic Fabrics Gold-DFMT
Authentic Fabrics Gold-QMGTM
Authentic Fabrics Gold-QRGBT
Double Threads-DTMT
Game Gear-GGMT
Limited Threads-LTMT
Limited Threads Gold-LTMT
Premium Patches-PPMT
Signers-SPSMT
Team Threads-TTMGT
03SPx-30
03SPx-139
Radiance-30
Radiance-139
Spectrum-30
Spectrum-139
Big Futures-BF-MT
Big Futures Limited-BF-MT
Fantasy Franchise-FF-MGT
Fantasy Franchise Limited-FF-MGT
Signature Threads-ST-MT
Style-SPX-BT
Style Limited-SPX-BT
Winning Materials-WM-MT
Winning Materials Limited-WM-MT
03Stars Postcards-27
03Titanium-152
Hobby Jersey Number Parallels-152
Patches-152
Retail-152
Masked Marauders-3
03Topps-216
03Topps-294
Blue-216
Blue-294
Gold-216
Gold-294
Red-216
Red-294
Topps/OPC Idols-CI9
03Topps C55-60
Minis-60
Minis American Back-60
Minis American Back Red-60
Minis Bazooka Back-60
Minis Brooklyn Back-60
Minis Hat Trick Back-60
Minis O Canada Back-60
Minis O Canada Back Red-60
Minis Stanley Cup Back-60
Relics-TRMTA
03Topps Pristine-10
Gold Refractor Die Cuts-10
Refractors-10
Autographs-PE-MT
Autographs Gold-PE-MT
Jersey Portions-PPJ-MT
Jersey Portion Refractors-PPJ-MT
Mini-PM-MT
Patches-PP-MT
Patch Refractors-PP-MT
Press Plates Black-10
Press Plates Cyan-10
Press Plates Magenta-10
Press Plates Yellow-10
03Topps Traded Franchise Fabrics-FF-MT
03UD Honor Roll-25
03UD Honor Roll-98
Grade A Jerseys-GATM
Signature Class-SC27
03UD Premier Collection-18
NHL Shields-SH-MT
Signatures-PS-MT
Signatures Gold-PS-MT
Teammates-PT-DS1
Teammates Patches-PT-DS1
03Upper Deck-65
All-Star Class-AS-7
Big Playmakers-BP-MT
Canadian Exclusives-65
Franchise Fabrics-FF-MT
HG-65
Patches-SV4
Super Saviors-SS-MT
Three Stars-TS9
03Upper Deck Classic Portraits-30
03Upper Deck Ice-27
Gold-27
Authentics-IA-MT
Breakers-IB-MT
Breaker Patches-IB-MT
Frozen Fabrics-FF-MT
Frozen Fabric Patches-FF-MT
03Upper Deck MVP-139
Gold Script-139
Silver Script-139
Canadian Exclusives-139
Masked Men-MM10
SportsNut-SN27
03Upper Deck Rookie Update-27
All-Star Lineup-AS7
Skills-SKMT
Super Stars-SSMT
03Upper Deck Trilogy-30
Limited-30
Scripts-S2MT
Scripts Limited-S2MT
Scripts Red-S2MT
03Upper Deck Victory-61
Bronze-61
Gold-61
Silver-61
Game Breakers-GB9
03Toronto Star-27
04Pacific-88
Blue-88
Red-88
All-Stars-6
In The Crease-4
04Pacific NHL All-Star Nets-2
Gold-2
04Pacific NHL Draft All-Star Nets-3
04SP Authentic-30
Limited-30
Buybacks-135
Buybacks-136
Buybacks-137
Buybacks-138
Buybacks-139
Buybacks-140
Rookie Review-RR-MT
Sign of the Times-ST-MT
Sign of the Times-DS-MT
Sign of the Times-TS-RBT
04UD All-World-49
04UD All-World-97
Gold-49
Autographs-97
Five Autographs-AF-GOL
04UD Toronto Fall Expo Priority Signings-MT
04Ultimate Collection Buybacks-60
04Ultimate Collection Buybacks-61
04Ultimate Collection Buybacks-62
04Ultimate Collection Dual Logos-UL2-MT
04Ultimate Collection Patch Autographs-UPA-MT
04Ultimate Collection Signature-US-MT
04Ultimate Collection Signature Logos-ULA-MT
04Ultimate Collection Signature Patches-SP-MT
04Upper Deck-59
Canadian Exclusives-59
HG Glossy Gold-59
HG Glossy Silver-59
Jersey Autographs-GJA-MT
Jersey Autographs-GJA-MT/JG
04Michigan Wolverines TK Legacy-1996A
04Michigan Wolverines TK Legacy-H5
04Michigan Wolverines TK Legacy-HL1
04Michigan Wolverines TK Legacy-VH3
05Be A Player-27
First Period-27
Second Period-27
Third Period-27
Overtime-27
Dual Signatures-TL
Outtakes-OT19
Quad Signatures-TLAL
Signatures-TU
Signatures Gold-TU
Triple Signatures-DAL
Triple Signatures-TGR
05Beehive-30
Matte-30
Matted Materials-MMMT
Matted Materials Remarkable-RMMT
PhotoGraphs-PGMT
Signature Scrapbook-SSMT
05Black Diamond-94
Emerald-94
Gold-94
Onyx-94
Ruby-94
05Hot Prospects-31
En Fuego-31

Red Hot-31
White Hot-31
05McDonalds Upper Deck Goalie Factory-GF4
05McDonalds Upper Deck Goalie Gear-MG8
05Panini Stickers-258
05Parkhurst-163
05Parkhurst-563
Facsimile Auto Parallel-163
Facsimile Auto Parallel-563
True Colors-TCDAL
True Colors-TCDAL
True Colors-TCMIDA
True Colors-TCMIDA
05SP Authentic-32
Limited-32
Prestigious Pairings-PPTZ
Sign of the Times Fives-MMZTJ
05SP Game Used-33
Autographs-33
Gold-33
Authentic Fabrics-AF-MT
Authentic Fabrics Autographs-AAF-MT
Authentic Fabrics Dual-TM
Authentic Fabrics Dual Autographs-TM
Authentic Fabrics Gold-AF-MT
Authentic Fabrics Quad-MTGA
Authentic Patches Quad -MTGA
Authentic Fabrics Triple-BBT
Authentic Fabrics Triple-KRT
Authentic Patches-AP-MT
Authentic Patches Autographs-AAP-MT
Authentic Patches Dual-TM
Authentic Patches Dual Autographs-TM
Authentic Patches Triple-BBT
Authentic Patches Triple-KRT
Awesome Authentics-AA-MT
Awesome Authentics Gold-DA-MT
By the Letter-LM-MT
Endorsed Equipment-EE-MT
Game Gear-GG-MT
Game Gear Autographs-AG-MT
SIGnificance-MT
SIGnificance Gold-S-MT
SIGnificance Extra-MT
SIGnificance Extra-TA
SIGnificance Extra Gold-MT
SIGnificance Extra Gold-TA
Significant Numbers-SN-MT
Statscriptions-ST-MT
05SPx-27
Spectrum-27
Winning Combos-WC-EM
Winning Combos-WC-ST
Winning Combos-WC-TM
Winning Combos Autographs-AWC-TM
Winning Combos Gold-WC-EM
Winning Combos Gold-WC-ST
Winning Combos Gold-WC-TM
Winning Combos Spectrum-WC-EM
Winning Combos Spectrum-WC-ST
Winning Combos Spectrum-WC-TM
Winning Materials-WM-TU
Winning Materials Autographs-AWM-MT
Winning Materials Gold-WM-TU
Winning Materials Spectrum-WM-TU
Xcitement Superstars-XS-MT
Xcitement Superstars Gold-XS-MT
Xcitement Superstars Spectrum-XS-MT
05The Cup-36
Gold-36
Black Rainbow-36
Dual NHL Shields-DSMT
Dual NHL Shields Autographs-ADSMT
Emblems of Endorsement-EEMT
Honorable Numbers-HNMT
Limited Logos-LLMT
Masterpiece Pressplates-36
Masterpiece Pressplates Rookie Upd Auto-262
Noble Numbers-NNGT
Patch Variation-P36
Patch Variation Autographs-AP36
Scripted Numbers-SNET
Scripted Numbers-SNGT
Scripted Swatches-SSMT
Signature Patches-SPMT
05UD Artifacts-35
05UD Artifacts-165
Blue-35
Blue-165
Gold-35
Gold-165
Green-35
Green-165
Pewter-35
Pewter-165
Red-35
Red-165
Auto Facts-AF-MT
Auto Facts Blue-AF-MT
Auto Facts Copper-AF-MT
Auto Facts Pewter-AF-MT
Auto Facts Silver-AF-MT
Frozen Artifacts-FA-MT
Frozen Artifacts Autographed-FA-MT
Frozen Artifacts Copper-FA-MT
Frozen Artifacts Dual-FAD-MT
Frozen Artifacts Dual Autographed-FAD-MT
Frozen Artifacts Dual Copper-FAD-MT
Frozen Artifacts Dual Gold-FAD-MT
Frozen Artifacts Dual Maroon-FAD-MT
Frozen Artifacts Dual Pewter-FAD-MT
Frozen Artifacts Dual Silver-FAD-MT
Frozen Artifacts Gold-FA-MT
Frozen Artifacts Maroon-FA-MT
Frozen Artifacts Pewter-FA-MT
Frozen Artifacts Silver-FA-MT
Goalie Gear-FG-MT
Goalie Gear Autographed-FG-MT
Goalie Gear Dual-FGD-MT
Goalie Gear Dual Autographed-FGD-MT
Goalie Gear Pewter-FG-MT
Goalie Gear Silver-FG-MT
Gold Autographed-35
Gold Autographed-165
Remarkable Artifacts-RA-MT
Remarkable Artifacts Dual-RA-MT
05UD PowerPlay-31
05UD PowerPlay-131
Rainbow-31
Specialists-TSMT
Specialists Patches-SPMT
05UD Toronto Fall Expo Priority Signings-PS-MT
05Ultimate Collection-31
Gold-31
Jerseys-JMT
Marquee Attractions-MA19
National Heroes Jerseys-NHJMT
National Heroes Patches-NHPMT
Premium Patches-PPMT
Premium Swatches-PSMT
Ultimate Achievements-UAMT
Ultimate Patches-PMT
Ultimate Signatures-USMT
Ultimate Signatures Pairings-UPMT
05Ultra-67
Gold-67
Fresh Ink-FI-MT
Fresh Ink Blue-FI-MT
Ice-67
05Upper Deck-306
Big Playmakers-B-MT
Jerseys Series II-J2MT
Majestic Materials-MMMT
NHL Generations-DTC
Notable Numbers-N-MT
Patches-P-MT
05Upper Deck Ice-29
Rainbow-29
Frozen Fabrics-FFMT
Frozen Fabrics Autographs-AFFMT
Frozen Fabrics Glass-FFMT
Frozen Fabrics Patches-FFPMT
Frozen Fabrics Patch Autographs-FAPMT
Glacial Graphs-GGMT
05Upper Deck MVP-128
Gold-128
Platinum-128
05Upper Deck Rookie Update-32
05Upper Deck Rookie Update-262
05Upper Deck Trilogy-31
05Upper Deck Trilogy-136
Crystal-136
Honorary Patches-HP-MT
Honorary Patch Scripts-HSP-MT
Honorary Swatches-HS-MT
Honorary Swatch Scripts-HSS-MT
Ice Scripts-IS-MT
Scripts-SCS-MT
05Upper Deck Victory-62
Black-62
Gold-62
Silver-62
Stars on Ice-SI17
06Be A Player-19
Autographs-19
Signatures-MT
Signatures 10-21
Signatures 25-21
Signatures Duals-DTL
Signatures Trios-TTLO
Signatures Foursomes-FLTFR
Unmasked Warriors-UM3
Unmasked Warriors Autographs-UM3
Up Close and Personal-UC35
Up Close and Personal Autographs-UC35
06Be A Player Portraits-36
Dual Signature Portraits-DSMT
Sensational Six-SSGOL
Signature Portraits-SPMT
06Beehive-69
06Beehive-209
Blue-69
Gold-69
Matte-69
Red Facsimile Signatures-69
Wood-69
Matted Materials-MMMT
Remarkable Matted Materials-MMMT
06Between The Pipes The Mask-M20
06Between The Pipes The Mask Gold-M20
06Between The Pipes The Mask Silver-M20
06Between The Pipes The Mask Game-Used-MGU18
06Between The Pipes The Mask Game-Used Gold-MGU18
06Black Diamond-101
Black-101
Gold-101
Ruby-101
Gemography-GMT
06Flair Showcase-35
06Flair Showcase-124
06Flair Showcase-226
Parallel-35
Parallel-124
Parallel-226
Hot Gloves-HG10
Inks-IMT
06Fleer-63
Tiffany-63
Fabricology-FMT
Netminders-N9
06Hot Prospects-35
Red Hot-35
White Hot-35
06ITG Ultimate Memorabilia-99
Artist Proof-99
Autos-59
Autos Gold-59
Complete Jersey-26
Complete Jersey Gold-26
Emblems-11
Emblems Gold-11
In The Numbers-17
In The Numbers Gold-17
Jerseys Autos-61
Jerseys Autos Gold-61
Passing The Torch-13
Passing The Torch Gold-13
06McDonald's Upper Deck-14
Autographs-AMT
Hot Gloves-HG8
Jerseys-JMT
Patches-PMT
06O-Pee-Chee-156
Rainbow-156
Swatches-S-MT
06Panini Stickers-244
06SP Authentic-69
Chirography-MT
Limited-69
Sign of the Times-STMT
Sign of the Times Duals-STET
Sign of the Times Triples-ST3MTM
06SP Game Used-32
Gold-32
Rainbow-32
Authentic Fabrics Dual-AF2TM
Authentic Fabrics Dual Patches-AF2TM
Authentic Fabrics Triple-AF3DAL
Authentic Fabrics Triple Patches-AF3DAL
Authentic Fabrics Quads-AF4BJTW
Authentic Fabrics Quads Patches-AF4BJTW
Autographs-32
By The Letter-BLMT
Inked Sweaters-ISMT
Inked Sweaters Patches-ISMT
Inked Sweaters Dual-IS2MT
Inked Sweaters Dual Patches-IS2MT
Letter Marks-LMMT
SIGnificance-SMT
06SPx-32
Spectrum-32
SPxcitement-X30
SPxcitement Spectrum-X30
SPxcitement Autographs-X30
Winning Materials-WMMT
Winning Materials Spectrum-WMMT
Winning Materials Autographs-WMMT
06Stars Team Postcards-23
06The Cup Autographed Foundations-CQMT
06The Cup Autographed Foundations Patches-CQMT
06The Cup Autographed NHL Shields Duals-DASMT
06The Cup Foundations-CQMT
06The Cup Foundations Patches-CQMT
06The Cup Enshrinements-EMT
06The Cup Honorable Numbers-HNMT
06The Cup Limited Logos-LLMT
06The Cup Property of-POMT
06The Cup Scripted Swatches-SSMT
06The Cup Signature Patches-SPMT
06UD Artifacts-68
06UD Artifacts-165
Blue-68
Blue-165
Gold-68
Gold-165
Platinum-68
Platinum-165
Radiance-68
Radiance-165
Autographed Radiance Parallel-68
Autographed Radiance Parallel-165
Red-68
Red-165
Treasured Patches Black-TSMT
Treasured Patches Blue-TSMT
Treasured Patches Gold-TSMT
Treasured Patches Platinum-TSMT
Treasured Patches Red-TSMT
Treasured Patches Autographed Black Tag Parallel-TSMT
Treasured Swatches-TSMT
Treasured Swatches Black-TSMT
Treasured Swatches Blue-TSMT
Treasured Swatches Gold-TSMT
Treasured Swatches Platinum-TSMT
Treasured Swatches Red-TSMT
Treasured Swatches Autographed Black-TSMT
Tundra Tandems-TTTM
Tundra Tandems Black-TTTM
Tundra Tandems Blue-TTTM
Tundra Tandems Gold-TTTM
Tundra Tandems Platinum-TTTM
Tundra Tandems Red-TTTM
Tundra Tandems Dual Patches Red-TTTM
06UD Mini Jersey Collection-34
Jerseys-MT
Jersey Autographs-MT
06UD Powerplay-34
Impact Rainbow-34
Goal Robbers-GR7
Specialists-SMT
Specialists Patches-PMT
06Ultimate Collection-21
Autographed Jerseys-AJ-MT
Autographed Patches-AJ-MT
Premium Patches-PS-MT
Premium Swatches-PS-MT
Signatures-US-MT
06Ultra-62
Gold Medallion-62
Ice Medallion-62
Difference Makers-DM12
06Upper Deck Arena Giveaways-DAL6
06Upper Deck-61
Exclusives Parallel-61
High Gloss Parallel-61
Game Jerseys-J2MT
Game Patches-P2MT
Generations Triples-G3BTW
Generations Patches Triple-G3PBTW
Masterpieces-61
Walmart Tins Oversize-61
Zero Men-ZM5
06Upper Deck MVP-92
Gold Script-92
Super Script-92
Jerseys-OJTG
Last Line of Defense-LL4
06Upper Deck Ovation-164
06Upper Deck Sweet Shot-36
Endorsed Equipment-EEMT
Signature Shots/Saves-SSMT
Signature Shots/Saves Ice Signings-SSIMT
Signature Shots/Saves Sticks-SSSMT
Signature Sticks-STMT
Sweet Stitches-SSMT
Sweet Stitches Duals-SSMT
Sweet Stitches Triples-SSMT
06Upper Deck Trilogy-33
Combo Autographed Jerseys-CJTM
Combo Autographed Patches-CJTM
Combo Clearcut Autographs-C3MTM
Honorary Scripted Patches-HSPMT
Honorary Scripted Swatches-HSSMT
Honorary Swatches-HSMT
Scripts-S3MT
06Upper Deck Victory-61
06Upper Deck Victory Black-61
06Upper Deck Victory Gold-61
06Upper Deck Victory GameBreakers-GB15
06Upper Deck Victory Oversize Cards-MT
07Upper Deck All-Star Game Redemptions-AS6
07Upper Deck Victory-182
Black-182
Gold-182
GameBreakers-GB37
Stars on Ice-SI35

Turcot, Jonatan
93Quebec Pee-Wee Tournament-1396

Turcotte, Alain
99Rouyn-Noranda Huskies-21

Turcotte, Alex
00Chicoutimi Sagueneens-2
Signed-2
00Val d'Or Foreurs-11
Signed-11

Turcotte, Alfie
83Canadiens Postcards-29
84Canadiens Postcards-29
84Canadiens Postcards-30
84Kelowna Wings-25
89ProCards AHL-81
90ProCards AHL/IHL-200
94German DEL-440
97Indianapolis Ice-25

Turcotte, Darren
89Rangers Marine Midland Bank-8
90Bowman-216
Tiffany-216
90O-Pee-Chee-48
90O-Pee-Chee Box Bottoms-K
90OPC Premier-123
90Panini Stickers-107
90Pro Set-208
90Pro Set-400
90Score-241
Canadian-241
90Score Young Superstars-16
90Topps-48
Tiffany-48
90Topps Box Bottoms-K
90Upper Deck-274
90Upper Deck-475
French-274
French-475
91Bowman-62
91McDonald's Upper Deck-7
91O-Pee-Chee-71
91Panini Stickers-285
91Parkhurst-118
French-118
91Pinnacle-47
French-47
91Pro Set-160
91Pro Set-310
French-160
French-310
91Score American-196
91Score Canadian Bilingual-196
91Score Canadian English-196
91Score Young Superstars-28
91Stadium Club-346
91Topps-71
91Upper Deck-90
91Upper Deck-155
91Upper Deck-513
French-90
French-155
French-513
91Finnish Semic World Champ Stickers-139
91Swedish Semic World Champ Stickers-139
92Bowman-156
92O-Pee-Chee-387
92Panini Stickers-235
92Panini Stickers French-235
92Parkhurst-345
Emerald Ice-345
92Pinnacle-33
French-33
92Pro Set-114
92Score-224
Canadian-224
92Stadium Club-360
92Topps-203
Gold-203G
92Ultra-143
92Upper Deck-169
93Donruss-224
93Leaf-45
93OPC Premier-246
Gold-246
93Panini Stickers-94
93Parkhurst-356
Emerald Ice-356
93Pinnacle-386
Canadian-386
93PowerPlay-166
93PowerPlay-357
93Score-24
93Score-570
Gold-570
Canadian-24
Canadian-570
Canadian Gold-570
93Stadium Club-476
Members Only Master Set-476
First Day Issue-476
93Topps/OPC Premier-246
Gold-246
93Ultra-341
93Upper Deck SP-66
93Whalers Coke-22
94Be A Player-R14
94Be A Player-R124
Signature Cards-35
94Canada Games NHL POGS-119
94Donruss-286
94Flair-75
94Fleer-90
94Hockey Wit-30
94Leaf-210
94OPC Premier-2
Special Effects-2
94Parkhurst SE-SE75
Gold-SE75
94Pinnacle-161
Artist's Proofs-161
Rink Collection-161
94Score-169
Gold-169
Platinum-169
94SP-49
Die Cuts-49
94Stadium Club-201
Members Only Master Set-201
First Day Issue-201
Super Team Winner Cards-201
94Topps/OPC Premier-2
Special Effects-2
94Ultra-94
94Upper Deck-84
Electric Ice-84
SP Inserts-SP123
SP Inserts Die Cuts-SP123
95Collector's Choice-24
Player's Club-24
Player's Club Platinum-24
95Donruss-43
95Donruss-295
Pro Pointers-10
95Emotion-79
95Hoyle Eastern Playing Cards-24
95Jets Team Issue-25
95Leaf-173
95Metal-167
95Panini Stickers-27
95Parkhurst International-93
95Parkhurst International-498
Emerald Ice-93
Emerald Ice-498
95Pinnacle-20
Artist's Proofs-20
Rink Collection-20
95Playoff One on One-267
95Pro Magnets-130
95Score-224
Black Ice Artist's Proofs-224
Black Ice-224
95SkyBox Impact-186
95Stadium Club-27
Members Only Master Set-27
95Summit-22
Artist's Proofs-22
Ice-22
95Topps-251
OPC Inserts-251
Home Grown USA-HGA7
95Ultra-72
95Ultra-328
Gold Medallion-72
95Upper Deck-481
Electric Ice-481
Electric Ice Gold-481
Special Edition-SE37
Special Edition-SE180
Special Edition Gold-SE37
Special Edition Gold-SE180
95Swedish Globe World Championships-123
96Be A Player-70
Autographs-70
Autographs Silver-70
96Collector's Choice-235
96Collector's Choice-330
96Donruss-59
Press Proofs-59
96Leaf-184
Press Proofs-184
96Metal Universe-141
96NHL Pro Stamps-130
96Pinnacle-165
Artist's Proofs-165
Foil-165
Premium Stock-165
Rink Collection-165
96Playoff One on One-413
96Score-219
Artist's Proofs-219
Dealer's Choice Artist's Proofs-219
Special Artist's Proofs-219
Golden Blades-219
96SP-142
96Summit-54
Artist's Proofs-54
Ice-54
Metal-54
Premium Stock-54
96Ultra-154
Gold Medallion-154
96Upper Deck-333
97Collector's Choice-219
97Donruss-176
Press Proofs Silver-176
Press Proofs Gold-176
97Donruss Limited-191
Exposure-191
97Pacific-229
Copper-229
Emerald Green-229
Ice Blue-229
Red-229
Silver-229
97Score-251
97Score Blues-8
Platinum-8
Premier-8
98Aurora-105
98Be A Player-74
Press Release-74
98BAP Gold-74
98BAP Autographs-74
98BAP Autographs Gold-74
98BAP Tampa Bay All Star Game-74
98Pacific-373
Ice Blue-373
Red-373
98Pacific Dynagon Ice-105
Blue-105
Red-105
98Panini Stickers-139
98Paramount-128
Copper-128
Emerald Green-128
Holo-Electric-128
Ice Blue-128
Silver-128
98Predators Team Issue-21
98Upper Deck-297
Exclusives-297
Exclusives 1 of 1-297
Gold Reserve-297
99BAP Memorabilia-272
Gold-272
Silver-272
02BAP Sig Series Auto Buybacks 1998-74

Turcotte, Hugo
93Sherbrooke Faucons-18
03St. Georges de Beauce Garaga-18

Turcotte, Pascal
93Quebec Pee-Wee Tournament-532

Turcotte, Patrick
02Belleville Bulls-22

Turcotte, Stephane
93Quebec Pee-Wee Tournament-948

Turcotte, Yannick
93Quebec Pee-Wee Tournament-1072
01Quebec Remparts-3

Turek, Filip
94Czech APS Extraliga-109
95Czech APS Extraliga-68
96Czech APS Extraliga-253
97Czech APS Extraliga-280
97Czech DS Stickers-89
98Czech DS-35
98Czech DS Stickers-77
98Czech OFS-202
99Czech DS-36
99Czech OFS-286
00Czech DS Extraliga-79
00Czech OFS-16
01Finnish Cardset-193
02Czech OFS Plus-188
03Czech OFS Plus-275
03Czech OFS Plus-352
04Czech OFS-241

Turek, Matt
917th Inn. Sketch OHL-341
96Knoxville Cherokees-6
99Alexandria Warthogs-16
02Greensboro Generals RBI-17
03Greensboro Generals-191

Turek, Roman
93Swedish Semic World Champ Stickers-90
94Czech APS Extraliga-93
95Czech APS Extraliga-354
95Finnish Semic World Championships-142
95German DEL-289
95Swedish World Championships Stickers-187
96Black Diamond-1
Gold-1
96Collector's Choice-358
96Flair-106
Blue Ice-106
96SP-175
96Upper Deck Generation Next-X28
96Czech APS Extraliga-338
96Swedish Semic Wien-102
All-Stars-AS1
Super Goalies-SG6
96Michigan K-Wings-20
97Be A Player-35
Autographs-35
Autographs Die-Cuts-35
Autographs Prismatic Die-Cuts-35
97Donruss-64
Press Proofs Silver-64
Press Proofs Gold-64
97Donruss Limited-42
97Donruss Limited-113
Exposure-42
Exposure-113
97Donruss Priority-29
Stamp of Approval-29
97Leaf-56
Fractal Matrix-56
Fractal Matrix Die Cuts-56
97Leaf International-56
Universal Ice-56
97Pacific Invincible NHL Regime-66
97Pinnacle Inside-79
Coach's Collection-79
Executive Collection-79
Stoppers-9
97Score-36
Artist's Proofs-36
Golden Blades-36
97Upper Deck-53
97Upper Deck Ice-35
Parallel-35
Power Shift-35
98Be A Player-41
Press Release-41
98BAP Gold-41
98BAP Autographs-41
98BAP Autographs Gold-41
98BAP Tampa Bay All Star Game-41
98NHL Aces Playing Cards-43
98Pacific-184
Ice Blue-184
Red-184
98Pacific Omega-76
Red-76
Opening Day Issue-76
98Paramount-71
Copper-71
Emerald Green-71
Holo-Electric-71
Ice Blue-71
Silver-71
99BAP Memorabilia-161
Gold-161
Silver-161
Selects Silver-SL18
Selects Gold-SL18
99Blues Taco Bell-18
99Crown Royale-120
Limited Series-120
Premiere Date-120
99Pacific-130
Copper-130
Emerald Green-130
Gold-130
Ice Blue-130
Premiere Date-130
Red-130
99Pacific Dynagon Ice-168
Blue-168
Copper-168
Gold-168
Premiere Date-168
99Pacific Omega-201
Copper-201
Gold-201
Ice Blue-201
Premiere Date-201
World All-Stars-8
99Pacific Prism-121
Holographic Blue-121
Holographic Gold-121
Holographic Mirror-121
Holographic Purple-121
Premiere Date-121
99Panini Stickers-285
99SP Authentic-76
99Ultimate Victory-77
1/1-77
Parallel-77
Parallel 100-77
Net Work-NW6
99Upper Deck-283
Exclusives-283
Exclusives 1 of 1-283
Ultimate Defense-UD6
Ultimate Defense Quantum Gold-UD6
Ultimate Defense Quantum Silver-UD6
99Upper Deck Gold Reserve-283
99Upper Deck MVP SC Edition-162
Gold Script-162
Silver Script-162
Super Script-162
99Upper Deck Victory-268
99Wayne Gretzky Hockey-144
99Czech DS Premium-P2
00Aurora-124
Pinstripes-124
Pinstripes Premiere Date-124
Premiere Date-124
00BAP Memorabilia-152
Emerald-152
Ruby-152
Sapphire-152
Promos-152
00BAP Mem Chicago Sportsfest Copper-152
00BAP Memorabilia Chicago Sportsfest Blue-152
00BAP Memorabilia Chicago Sportsfest Gold-152
00BAP Memorabilia Chicago Sportsfest Ruby-152
00BAP Memorabilia Chicago Sun-Times Ruby-152
00BAP Memorabilia Chicago Sun-Times Gold-152
00BAP Mem Chicago Sun-Times Sapphire-152
00BAP Mem Toronto Fall Expo Copper-152
00BAP Memorabilia Toronto Fall Expo Gold-152
00BAP Memorabilia Toronto Fall Expo Ruby-152
00BAP Parkhurst 2000-P27
00BAP Signature Series-6
Emerald-6
Ruby-6
Sapphire-6
Autographs-63
Autographs Gold-63
00BAP Ultimate Memorabilia Autographs-32
Gold-32
00BAP Ultimate Mem Game-Used Jerseys-GJ4
00BAP Ultimate Mem Game-Used Emblems-E3
00BAP Ultimate Mem Game-Used Numbers-N3
00BAP Ultimate Mem Game-Used Sticks-GS4
00BAP Ultimate Mem Goalie Memorabilia-GM13
00BAP Ultimate Memorabilia Goalie Sticks-G25
00BAP Ultimate Mem Plante Jersey Cards-PJ11
00BAP Ultimate Mem Plante Skate Cards-PS11
00Black Diamond-52
Gold-52
Game Gear-LTU
00Crown Royale-90
Ice Blue-90
Limited Series-90
Premiere Date-90
Red-90
00McDonald's Pacific-29
Blue-29
00O-Pee-Chee-100
00O-Pee-Chee Parallel-100
00Pacific-352
Copper-352
Gold-352
Ice Blue-352
Premiere Date-352
Autographs-352
Euro-Stars-8
Gold Crown Die Cuts-30
00Panini Stickers-196
00Paramount-209
Copper-209
Gold-209
Holo-Gold-209
Holo-Silver-209
Ice Blue-209
Premiere Date-209
Freeze Frame-31
Glove Side Net Fusions-16
Glove Side Net Fusions Platinum-16
00Private Stock-85
Gold-85
Premiere Date-85
Retail-85
Silver-85
PS-2001 New Wave-20
00Revolution-125
Blue-125
Premiere Date-125
Red-125
HD NHL-30
Stat Masters-18
00SP Authentic-78
Super Stoppers-SS5
00SP Game Used-52
00SPx-61
Spectrum-61
SPXcitement-X12
00Stadium Club-47
Glove Save-GS6
00Titanium-82
Blue-82
Gold-82
Premiere Date-82
Red-82
Retail-82
Game Gear-45
Three-Star Selections-7
00Topps/OPC-100
Parallel-100
Autographs-ART
Own the Game-OTG12
00Topps Chrome-78
OPC Refractors-78
Refractors-78
00Topps Gold Label Class 1-44
Gold-44
00Topps Gold Label Class 2-44
00Topps Gold Label Class 2 Gold-44
00Topps Gold Label Class 3-44
00Topps Gold Label Class 3 Gold-44
00Topps Gold Label Behind the Mask-BTM6
00Topps Gold Label Behind the Mask 1 to 1-BTM6
00Topps Gold Label Bullion-B5
00Topps Gold Label Bullion One to One-B5
00Topps Heritage-35
00Topps Heritage-227
00Topps Heritage-231
00Topps Heritage-237
00Topps Heritage-241
Chrome Parallel-35
00Topps Premier Plus-55
Blue Ice-55
Masters of the Break-MB17
00Topps Stars-82
Blue-82
00UD Heroes-104
Player Idols-PI6
Signs of Greatness-RT
00UD Pros and Prospects-75
00UD Reserve-76
Golden Goalies-GG9
00Upper Deck-154
Exclusives Tier 1-154
Exclusives Tier 2-154
Rise to Prominence-RP7
Triple Threat-TT10
00Upper Deck Ice-35
Immortals-35
Legends-35
Stars-35
Clear Cut Autographs-RT
00Upper Deck Legends-116
Legendary Collection Bronze-116
Legendary Collection Gold-116
Legendary Collection Silver-116
00Upper Deck MVP-158
Excellence-ME6
First Stars-158
Mark of Excellence-SGTB
Masked Men-MM8
ProSign-RT
Second Stars-158
Third Stars-158
00Upper Deck Victory-205
00Upper Deck Victory-258
00Upper Deck Victory-324
00Upper Deck Vintage-315
00Upper Deck Vintage-320
00Upper Deck Vintage-321
Great Gloves-GG16
00Vanguard-84
Holographic Gold-84
Holographic Purple-84
Pacific Proofs-84
00Czech DS Extraliga Team Jagr-JT1
00Czech DS Extraliga Team Jagr Parallel-JT1
00Czech OFS-378
00Czech Stadion-13
00Czech Stadion-109
01Atomic-15
Blue-15
Gold-15
Premiere Date-15
Red-15
Team Nucleus-2
01BAP Memorabilia-5
01BAP Memorabilia-392
Emerald-5
Emerald-392
Ruby-5
Ruby-392
Sapphire-5
Sapphire-392
All-Star Jerseys-ASJ35
All-Star Emblems-ASE35
All-Star Numbers-ASN35
All-Star Teammates-AST18
Goalies Jerseys-GJ17
Stanley Cup Playoffs-SC15
01BAP Signature Series Certified 100-C37
01BAP Signature Series Certified 50-C37
01BAP Signature Series Certified 1 of 1's-C37
01BAP Signature Series Autographs-LRT
01BAP Signature Series Autographs Gold-LRT
01BAP Signature Series Jerseys-GJ-92
01BAP Signature Series Teammates-TM-5
01BAP Ultimate Mem Journey Jerseys-21
01BAP Ultimate Mem Journey Emblems-21
01BAP Update Heritage-H24
01BAP Update Travel Plans-TP3
01Between the Pipes-65
All-Star Jerseys-ASJ14
Double Memorabilia-DM22
Goalie Gear-GG19
He Shoots-He Saves Points-10
He Shoots-He Saves Prizes-11
Jerseys-GJ17
Emblems-GUE5
Jersey and Stick Cards-GSJ16
Masks-12
Masks Silver-12
Masks Gold-12
Tandems-GT8
01Bowman YoungStars-42
Gold-42
Ice Cubed-42
01Crown Royale-24
Blue-24
Premiere Date-24
Red-24
Retail-24
All-Star Honors-2
Jewels of the Crown-4
Triple Threads-2
Triple Threads-12
01O-Pee-Chee-105
01O-Pee-Chee-105U
01O-Pee-Chee Heritage Parallel-105
01O-Pee-Chee Heritage Parallel Limited-105
01O-Pee-Chee Premier Parallel-105
01Pacific-333
Extreme LTD-333
Hobby LTD-333
Premiere Date-333
Retail LTD-333
Steel Curtain-17
01Pacific Adrenaline-29
Blue-29
Premiere Date-29
Red-29
Retail-29
Jerseys-6
Power Play-6
01Pacific Arena Exclusives-333
01Pacific Heads-Up-14
Blue-14
Premiere Date-14
Red-14
Silver-14
HD NHL-11
Showstoppers-3
01Parkhurst-221
Sticks-PS56
01Private Stock-13
Gold-13
Premiere Date-13
Retail-13
Silver-13
Game Gear-17
Game Gear Patches-17
01Private Stock Pacific Nights-13
01SP Authentic-12
Limited-12
Limited Gold-12
01SP Game Used-6
01SPx-160
01Titanium-22
Hobby Parallel-22
Premiere Date-22
Retail-22
Retail Parallel-22
Double-Sided Jerseys-5
Double-Sided Jerseys-6
Three-Star Selections-1
01Titanium Draft Day Edition-17
01Topps-105
01Topps-105U
Heritage Parallel-105
Heritage Parallel Limited-105
OPC Parallel-105
01Topps Chrome-105
Refractors-105
Black Border Refractors-105
01Topps Heritage-168
01Topps Reserve-61
01UD Challenge for the Cup-10
Backstops-BB1
01UD Mask Collection-105
01UD Mask Collection-173
Gold-105
Gold-173
01UD Playmakers-15
01UD Top Shelf-82
01Upper Deck-256
Exclusives-256
01Upper Deck Ice-89
01Vanguard-14
Blue-14
Red-14
Memorabilia-5
Memorabilia-41
One of Ones-14
Patches-5
Patches-41
Premiere Date-14
Proofs-14
Stonewallers-4
V-Team-1
02McFarlane Hockey-90
02McFarlane Hockey-92
02Atomic-14
Blue-14
Gold-14
Red-14
Denied-2

Hobby Parallel-14
Jerseys-2
Jerseys Gold-2
Patches-2
02BAP All-Star Edition-95
Jerseys-95
Jerseys Gold-95
Jerseys Silver-95
02BAP First Edition-28
Jerseys-28
02BAP Memorabilia-183
02BAP Memorabilia-256
Emerald-183
Emerald-256
Ruby-183
Ruby-256
Sapphire-183
Sapphire-256
NHL All-Star Game-183
NHL All-Star Game-256
NHL All-Star Game Blue-183
NHL All-Star Game Blue-256
NHL All-Star Game Green-183
NHL All-Star Game Green-256
NHL All-Star Game Red-183
NHL All-Star Game Red-256
Teammates-TM-20
02BAP Memorabilia Toronto Fall Expo-183
02BAP Memorabilia Toronto Fall Expo-256
02BAP Signature Series-123
Autographs-123
Autograph Buybacks 1998-41
Autograph Buybacks 2000-63
Autograph Buybacks 2001-LRT
Autographs Gold-123
Golf-GS79
02BAP Ultimate Memorabilia Number Ones-6
02BAP Ultimate Memorabilia Numerology-2
02Between the Pipes-34
02Between the Pipes-125
Gold-34
Silver-34
All-Star Stick and Jersey-12
Blockers-14
Double Memorabilia-10
Emblems-28
Goalie Autographs-25
He Shoots-He Saves Points-11
He Shoots-He Saves Prizes-11
Jerseys-28
Masks II-5
Masks II Gold-5
Masks II Silver-5
Numbers-28
Stick and Jerseys-28
02Bowman YoungStars-82
Gold-82
Silver-82
02Crown Royale-15
Blue-15
Red-15
Retail-15
02ITG Used Goalie Pad and Jersey-GP9
02ITG Used Goalie Pad and Jersey Gold-GP9
02ITG Used International Experience-IE25
02ITG Used International Experience Gold-IE25
02McDonald's Pacific-7
02NHL Power Play Stickers-6
02O-Pee-Chee-98
02O-Pee-Chee Jumbos-3
02O-Pee-Chee Premier Blue Parallel-98
02O-Pee-Chee Premier Red Parallel-98
02O-Pee-Chee Factory Set-98
02O-Pee-Chee Factory Set Hometown Heroes-HHC12
02Pacific-60
Blue-60
Red-60
Jerseys-5
Jerseys Holo-Silver-5
Maximum Impact-1
02Pacific Complete-12
Red-12
02Pacific Exclusive-24
Advantage-2
02Pacific Heads-Up-18
Blue-18
Purple-18
Red-18
Quad Jerseys-5
Quad Jerseys Gold-5
Showstoppers-3
02Pacific Quest for the Cup-13
Gold-13
02Pacific Toronto Fall Expo-3
Gold-3
02Parkhurst-129
Bronze-129
Gold-129
Silver-129
02Parkhurst Retro-166
Minis-166
02Private Stock Reserve-107
Red-107
Retail-107
InCrease Security-2
Patches-107
02SP Authentic-13
Beckett Promos-13
02SP Game Used Piece of History-PHRT
02SP Game Used Piece of History Gold-PHRT
02SP Game Used Piece of History Rainbow-PHRT
02SPx-9
Spectrum Gold-9
Spectrum Silver-9
Xtreme Talents-RT
Xtreme Talents Gold-RT
Xtreme Talents Silver-RT
02Stadium Club-86
Silver Decoy Cards-86
Proofs-86
02Titanium-16
Blue-16
Red-16
Retail-16
Jerseys-12
Jerseys Retail-12
02Topps-98
OPC Blue Parallel-98
OPC Red Parallel-98
Topps/OPC Hometown Heroes-HHC12
Factory Set-98
02Topps Chrome-62
Black Border Refractors-62
Refractors-62
02Topps Heritage-90
02Topps Heritage-115
Chrome Parallel-90
02Topps Total-7
02UD Artistic Impressions-12
Gold-12
02UD Artistic Impressions Beckett Promos-12
02UD Artistic Impressions Retrospectives-R12
02UD Artistic Impressions Retrospect Gold-R12
02UD Artistic Impress Retrospect Silver-R12
02UD Mask Collection-13
02UD Mask Collection-14
02UD Mask Collection-15
02UD Mask Collection-16
02UD Mask Collection Beckett Promos-13
02UD Mask Collection Beckett Promos-14
02UD Mask Collection Beckett Promos-15
02UD Mask Collection Beckett Promos-16
02UD Mask Collection Career Wins-CWTU
02UD Mask Collection Great Gloves-GGRT
02UD Mask Collection Masked Marvels-MMRT
02UD Mask Collection Patches-PWRT
02UD Mask Collection Super Stoppers-SSRT
02UD Mask Collection View from the Cage-VRT
02UD Piece of History-15
02UD Top Shelf-13
02Upper Deck-24
Exclusives-24
Blow-Ups-C4
Difference Makers-RT
Goaltender Threads-RT
Goaltender Threads Gold-RT
Saviors Jerseys-SVRT
Super Saviors-SA2
02Upper Deck Classic Portraits-13
Hockey Royalty-SIT
Hockey Royalty Limited-SIT
02Upper Deck MVP-26
Gold-26
Classics-26
Golden Classics-26
02Upper Deck Rookie Update-18
Jerseys-DRT
Jerseys Gold-DRT
02Upper Deck Victory-30
Bronze-30
Gold-30
Silver-30
02Upper Deck Vintage-36
02Upper Deck Vintage-265
Green Backs-36
Tall Boys-T9
Tall Boys Gold-T9
02Vanguard-16
LTD-16
02Czech Stadion Olympics-347
03BAP Memorabilia-159
Emerald-159
Gold-159
Ruby-159
Sapphire-159
03BAP Ultimate Memorabilia Autographs-60
Gold-60
03BAP Ultimate Mem Auto Jerseys-60
03Beehive-32
Gold-32
Silver-32
03Black Diamond-58
Black-58
Green-58
Red-58
03Bowman-41
Gold-41
03Bowman Chrome-41
Refractors-41
Gold Refractors-41
Xfractors-41
03Crown Royale-15
Blue-15
Retail-15
03ITG Action-72
Jerseys-M65
03ITG Used Signature Series-79
Gold-79
Autographs-RT
Autographs Gold-RT
Goalie Gear-14
Goalie Gear Autographs-14
Goalie Gear Gold-14
03NHL Sticker Collection-170
03O-Pee-Chee-203
03OPC Blue-203
03OPC Gold-203
03OPC Red-203
03Pacific-56
Blue-56
Red-56
03Pacific Complete-467
Red-467
03Pacific Exhibit-25
Blue Backs-25
Yellow Backs-25
03Pacific Invincible-14
Blue-14
Red-14
Retail-14
Jerseys-5
03Pacific Prism-19
Blue-19
Gold-19
Red-19
03SP Authentic-13
Limited-13
03SPx-14
Radiance-14
Spectrum-14
03Topps-203
Blue-203
Gold-203
Red-203
03Topps C55-33
Minis-33
Minis American Back-33
Minis American Back Red-33
Minis Bazooka Back-33
Minis Brooklyn Back-33
Minis Hat Trick Back-33
Minis O Canada Back-33
Minis O Canada Back Red-33
Minis Stanley Cup Back-33
03Topps Pristine-5
Gold Refractor Die Cuts-5
Refractors-5
Mini-PM-RT
Press Plates Black-5
Press Plates Cyan-5
Press Plates Magenta-5
Press Plates Yellow-5
03UD Honor Roll-11
03Upper Deck-33
Canadian Exclusives-33
HG-33
03Upper Deck Classic Portraits-14
03Upper Deck Ice-12
Gold-12
03Upper Deck MVP-74
Gold Script-74
Silver Script-74
Canadian Exclusives-74
SportsNut-SN14
03Upper Deck Trilogy-14
Limited-14
Limited Threads-LT5
03Upper Deck Victory-30
Bronze-30
Gold-30
Silver-30
04UD All-World-1
Gold-1
Autographs-1
05UD Powerplay Power Marks-PMZP
05UD Powerplay Specialists-TSRT
05UD Powerplay Specialists Patches-SPRT
05Upper Deck Notable Numbers-N-RT
05Czech HC Ceske Budejovice-14
06Czech HC Ceske Budejovice Postcards-10
06Czech OFS-18
Goalies I-15
Goalies II-8
Stars-13
Team Cards-1

Turgeon, Charles

93Quebec Pee-Wee Tournament-1125

Turgeon, Dean

93Lakeland Ice Warriors-24

Turgeon, Jeremy

02Rimouski Oceanic-21

Turgeon, Kevin

03Lewiston Maineiacs-21

Turgeon, Luc

77Granby Vics-20

Turgeon, Pierre

87Sabres Blue Shield-28
87Sabres Wonder Bread/Hostess-30
88O-Pee-Chee-194
88O-Pee-Chee Stickers-69
88O-Pee-Chee Stickers-133
88O-Pee-Chee Stickers-198
88Panini Stickers-230
88Sabres Blue Shield-27
88Sabres Wonder Bread/Hostess-30
88Topps-194
89O-Pee-Chee-25
89O-Pee-Chee Box Bottoms-P
89O-Pee-Chee Stickers-262
89Panini Stickers-204
89Sabres Blue Shield-23
89Sabres Campbell's-26
89Topps-25
89Topps Box Bottoms-P
90Bowman-241
Tiffany-241
90Kraft-59
90Kraft-91
90O-Pee-Chee-66
90O-Pee-Chee Box Bottoms-M
90OPC Premier-124
90Panini Stickers-28
90Pro Set-31
90Pro Set-366
90Sabres Blue Shield-24
90Sabres Campbell's-28
90Score-110
Canadian-110
90Score Hottest/Rising Stars-53
90Score Young Superstars-1
90Topps-66
Tiffany-66
90Topps Box Bottoms-M
90Topps Team Scoring Leaders-20
90Topps Team Scoring Leaders Tiffany-20
90Upper Deck-43
90Upper Deck-318
French-43
French-318
91Pro Set Platinum-10
91Bowman-27
91Gillette-35
91O-Pee-Chee-416
91OPC Premier-59
91Panini Stickers-303
91Parkhurst-106
French-106
91Pinnacle-30
French-30
91Pro Set-15
91Pro Set-433
French-15
French-433
91Score American-4
91Score American-377
91Score American-416
91Score Canadian Bilingual-4
91Score Canadian Bilingual-267
91Score Canadian Bilingual-332
91Score Canadian English-4
91Score Canadian English-267
91Score Canadian English-332
91Score Rookie/Traded-101T
91Score Kellogg's-6
91Stadium Club-77
91Topps-416
91Upper Deck-176
91Upper Deck-554
French-176
French-554
91Finnish Semic World Champ Stickers-66
91Swedish Semic World Champ Stickers-66
92Bowman-23
92Durivage Panini-11
92O-Pee-Chee-47
92Panini Stickers-196
92Panini Stickers French-196
92Parkhurst-103
Emerald Ice-103
92Pinnacle Canadian Promo Panels-2
92Pinnacle-165
French-165
Team 2000-17
Team 2000 French-17
92Pro Set-104
92Score-325
92Score-430
Canadian-325
Canadian-430
Sharpshooters-25
Sharpshooters Canadian-25
Young Superstars-27
92Seasons Patches-53
92Stadium Club-276
92Topps-289
Gold-289G
92Ultra-132
92Upper Deck-175
93Donruss-209
Special Print-N
93Durivage Score-30
93Kraft-24
93Leaf-25
Hat Trick Artists-5
93McDonald's Upper Deck-27
93OPC Premier-190
Gold-190
93Panini Stickers-F
93Parkhurst-389
Emerald Ice-389
East/West Stars-E10
First Overall-F7
93Pinnacle-160
93Pinnacle-225
Canadian-160
Canadian-225
All-Stars-5
All-Stars Canadian-5
Nifty Fifty-7
Team 2001-13
Team 2001 Canadian-13
93PowerPlay-155
Point Leaders-19
93Score Samples-6
93Score-6
Canadian-6
Dream Team-15
Dynamic Duos Canadian-9
Franchise-12
93Stadium Club-145
93Stadium Club-380
Members Only Master Set-145
Members Only Master Set-380
OPC-145
First Day Issue-145
First Day Issue-380
First Day Issue OPC-145
All-Stars-21
All-Stars Members Only-21
All-Stars OPC-21
Master Photos-20
Master Photos Winners-20
93Topps/OPC Premier-190
Gold-190
93Topps Premier Black Gold-20
93Topps Premier Finest-7
93Ultra-197
All-Stars-3
Premier Pivots-9
Scoring Kings-5
93Upper Deck-224
93Upper Deck-297
93Upper Deck-347
Award Winners-AW7
Hat Tricks-HT11
Silver Skates-H7
Silver Skates Gold-H7
SP-96
93Upper Deck Locker All-Stars-17
94Be A Player-R80
94Canada Games NHL POGS-160
94Donruss-23
94EA Sports-81
94Finest-78
Super Team Winners-78
Refractors-78
Bowman's Best-B9
Bowman's Best Refractors-B9
94Flair-109
94Fleer-130
94Hockey Wit-27
94Leaf-367
Limited Inserts-14
94Leaf Limited-52
94McDonald's Upper Deck-McD26
94OPC Premier-115
Special Effects-115
94Parkhurst-135
Gold-135
Crash the Game Green-14
Crash the Game Blue-14
Crash the Game Gold-14
Crash the Game Red-14
SE Vintage-31
94Pinnacle-78
Artist's Proofs-78
Rink Collection-78
94Score-166
Gold-166
Platinum-166
Franchise-TF14
90 Plus Club-14
94Select-46
Gold-46
94SP-61
Die Cuts-61
94Stadium Club Members Only-38
94Topps/OPC Premier-115
Special Effects-115
94Ultra-133
94Upper Deck-77
Electric Ice-77
SP Inserts-SP48
SP Inserts Die Cuts-SP48
94Upper Deck NHLPA/Be A Player-37
95SLU Hockey American-19
95Bashan Super Stickers-63
Die-Cut-1
95Be A Player-152
Signatures-S152
Signatures Die Cuts-S152
95Bowman-6
All-Foil-6
95Canada Games NHL POGS-145
95Canadiens Postcards-20
95Canadiens Sheets-12
95Collector's Choice-131
Player's Club-131
Player's Club Platinum-131
Crash The Game-C15A
Crash The Game-C15B
Crash The Game-C15C
Crash The Game Gold-C15A
Crash The Game Gold-C15B
Crash The Game Gold-C15C
Crash the Game Silver Redeemed-C15
Crash the Game Silver Bonus-C15
Crash the Game Gold Redeemed-C15
Crash the Game Gold Bonus-C15
95Donruss-61
Igniters-4
95Donruss Elite-90
Die Cut Stars-90
Die Cut Uncut-90
Cutting Edge-10
95Emotion-93
95Finest-46
95Finest-182
Refractors-46
Refractors-182
95Imperial Stickers-63
Die Cut Superstars-1
95Kenner Starting Lineup Cards-21
95Kraft-4
95Leaf-90
Freeze Frame-2
95Leaf Limited-102
95McDonald's Pinnacle-MCD-13
95Metal-80
95NHL Aces Playing Cards-8H
95Panini Stickers-37
95Parkhurst International-109
Emerald Ice-109
Parkie's Trophy Picks-PP50
95Pinnacle-34
Artist's Proofs-34
Rink Collection-34
Clear Shots-14
Roaring 20s-20
95Playoff One on One-56
95Pro Magnets-25
95Score-90
Black Ice Artist's Proofs-90
Black Ice-90
Border Battle-1
Lamplighters-6
95Select Certified-49
Mirror Gold-49
95SkyBox Impact-89
95SP-71
Stars/Etoiles-E15
Stars/Etoiles Gold-E15
95Stadium Club Members Only-20
95Stadium Club-175
Members Only Master Set-175
Extreme North-EN7
Extreme North Members Only Master Set-EN7
Power Streak-PS1
Power Streak Members Only Master Set-PS1
95Summit-43
Artist's Proofs-43
Ice-43
95Topps-21
95Topps-224
OPC Inserts-21
OPC Inserts-224
Canadian Gold-7CG
Home Grown Canada-HGC3
Marquee Men Power Boosters-21
Power Lines-9PL
95Topps SuperSkills-9
Platinum-9
95Ultra-85
Gold Medallion-85
95Upper Deck-389
Electric Ice-389
Electric Ice Gold-389
NHL All-Stars-AS15
NHL All-Stars Jumbo-AS15
Special Edition-SE44
Special Edition Gold-SE44
95Zenith-38
96Black Diamond-135
Gold-135
96Canadiens Sheets-25
96Collector's Choice-133
96Collector's Choice-321
Stick'Ums-S19
96Collector's Choice Blow-Ups-133
96Collector's Choice Blow-Ups Bi-Way-5
96Donruss-17
Press Proofs-17
Dominators-6
96Donruss Canadian Ice-110
Gold Press Proofs-110
Red Press Proofs-110
96Donruss Elite-112
Die Cut Stars-112
96Duracell L'Equipe Beliveau-JB14
96Fleer-57
Art Ross-23
96Fleer Picks-32
Fabulous 50-45
96Leaf-186
Press Proofs-186
96Leaf Leather And Laces Promos-P18
96Leaf Leather And Laces-18
96Leaf Limited-38
Gold-38
96Leaf Preferred-70
Press Proofs-70
Steel-26
Steel Gold-26
96Maggers-103
96McDonald's Pinnacle-19
96Metal Universe-84
96NHL Aces Playing Cards-48
96NHL Pro Stamps-25
96Pinnacle-22
Artist's Proofs-22
Foil-22
Premium Stock-22
Rink Collection-22
96Score-71
Artist's Proofs-71
Dealer's Choice Artist's Proofs-71
Special Artist's Proofs-71
Golden Blades-71
Sudden Death-1
96Select Certified-82
Artist's Proofs-82
Blue-82
Mirror Blue-82
Mirror Gold-82
Mirror Red-82
Red-82
96SkyBox Impact-66
BladeRunners-23
96SP-137
96SPx-22
Gold-22
96Stadium Club Members Only-39
96Summit-90
Artist's Proofs-90
Ice-90
Metal-90
Premium Stock-90
96Team Out-24
96Ultra-148
Gold Medallion-148
96Upper Deck Ice-61
Parallel-61
96Zenith-39
Artist's Proofs-39
Assailants-12
97Headliners Hockey-28
97Be A Player Take A Number-14
97Black Diamond-100
Double Diamond-100
Triple Diamond-100
Quadruple Diamond-100
97Collector's Choice-226
Star Quest-SQ58
97Crown Royale-118
Emerald Green-118
Ice Blue-118
Silver-118
97Donruss-28
Press Proofs Silver-28
Press Proofs Gold-28
97Donruss Canadian Ice-24
Dominion Series-24
Provincial Series-24
National Pride-24
97Donruss Elite-105
Aspirations-105
Status-105
97Donruss Limited-158
97Donruss Limited-172
Exposure-158
Exposure-172
97Donruss Preferred-117
Cut to the Chase-117
97Donruss Priority-41
Stamp of Approval-41
97Katch-131
Gold-131
Silver-131
97Leaf-43
Fractal Matrix-43
Fractal Matrix Die Cuts-43
97Leaf International-43
Universal Ice-43
97NHL Aces Playing Cards-32
97Pacific-32
Copper-32
Emerald Green-32
Ice Blue-32
Red-32
Silver-32
Slap Shots Die-Cuts-9B
97Pacific Dynagon-108
Copper-108
Dark Grey-108
Emerald Green-108
Ice Blue-108
Red-108
Silver-108
Best Kept Secrets-83
Tandems-59
97Pacific Invincible-122
Copper-122
Emerald Green-122
Ice Blue-122
Red-122
Silver-122
NHL Regime-173
97Pacific Omega-199
Copper-199
Dark Gray-199
Emerald Green-199
Gold-199
Ice Blue-199
97Panini Stickers-164
97Paramount-161
Copper-161
Dark Grey-161
Emerald Green-161
Ice Blue-161
Red-161
Silver-161
97Pinnacle-75
Artist's Proofs-75
Rink Collection-75
Press Plates Back Black-75
Press Plates Back Cyan-75
Press Plates Back Magenta-75
Press Plates Back Yellow-75
Press Plates Front Black-75
Press Plates Front Cyan-75
Press Plates Front Magenta-75
Press Plates Front Yellow-75
97Pinnacle Certified-62
Red-62
Mirror Blue-62
Mirror Gold-62
Mirror Red-62
97Pinnacle Inside-122
97Pinnacle Tot Cert Platinum Blue-62
97Pinnacle Tot Cert Platinum Gold-62
97Pinnacle Totally Certified Platinum Red-62
97Pinnacle Tot Cert Mirror Platinum Gold-62
97Revolution-122
Copper-122
Emerald-122
Ice Blue-122
Silver-122
97Score-118
Artist's Proofs-118
Golden Blades-118
97Score Blues-2
Platinum-2
Premier-2
97SP Authentic-141
97Studio-64
Press Proofs Silver-64
Press Proofs Gold-64
97Upper Deck-353
Game Dated Moments-353
97Zenith-23
Z-Gold-23
Z-Silver-23
97Zenith 5 x 7-61
Gold Impulse-61
Silver Impulse-61
98Aurora-164
Championship Fever-42
Championship Fever Copper-42
Championship Fever Ice Blue-42
Championship Fever Red-42
Championship Fever Silver-42
98Be A Player-275
Press Release-275
98BAP Gold-275
98BAP Autographs-275
98BAP Autographs Gold-275
98Bowman's Best-86
Refractors-86
Atomic Refractors-86
98Crown Royale-117
Limited Series-117
98Finest-125
No Protectors-125
No Protectors Refractors-125
Refractors-125
98Katch-130
98OPC Chrome-208
Refractors-208
98Pacific-374
Ice Blue-374
Red-374
98Pacific Dynagon Ice-163
Blue-163
Red-163
98Pacific Omega-206
Red-206
Opening Day Issue-206
98Panini Photocards-85
98Panini Stickers-154
98Paramount-207
Copper-207
Emerald Green-207
Holo-Electric-207
Ice Blue-207
Silver-207
98Revolution-125
Ice Shadow-125
Red-125
98SP Authentic-73
Power Shift-73
98SPx Finite-74
Radiance-74
Spectrum-74
98Topps-208
O-Pee-Chee-208
98Topps Gold Label Class 1-30
Black-30
Black One of One-30
One of One-30
Red-30
Red One of One-30
98Topps Gold Label Class 2-30
98Topps Gold Label Class 2 Black-30
98Topps Gold Label Class 2 Black 1 of 1-30
98Topps Gold Label Class 2 One of One-30
98Topps Gold Label Class 2 Red-30
98Topps Gold Label Class 2 Red One of One-30
98Topps Gold Label Class 3-30
98Topps Gold Label Class 3 Black-30
98Topps Gold Label Class 3 Black 1 of 1-30
98Topps Gold Label Class 3 One of One-30
98Topps Gold Label Class 3 Red-30
98Topps Gold Label Class 3 Red One of One-30
98UD Choice-184
Prime Choice Reserve-184
Reserve-184
98Upper Deck-172
Exclusives-172
Exclusives 1 of 1-172
Gold Reserve-172
98Upper Deck MVP-181
Gold Script-181
Silver Script-181
Super Script-181
99Aurora-128
Premiere Date-128
99BAP Memorabilia-158
Gold-158
Silver-158
99BAP Millennium-205
Emerald-205
Ruby-205
Sapphire-205
Signatures-205
Signatures Gold-205
99Blues Taco Bell-4
99Crown Royale-121
Limited Series-121
Premiere Date-121
99Kraft Face Off Rivals-3
99Kraft Overtime Winners-4
99O-Pee-Chee-223
99O-Pee-Chee Chrome-223
99O-Pee-Chee Chrome Refractors-223
99Pacific-364
Copper-364
Emerald Green-364
Gold-364
Ice Blue-364
Premiere Date-364
Red-364
99Pacific Dynagon Ice-169
Blue-169
Copper-169
Gold-169
Premiere Date-169
99Pacific Omega-202
Copper-202
Gold-202
Ice Blue-202
Premiere Date-202
99Pacific Prism-122
Holographic Blue-122
Holographic Gold-122
Holographic Mirror-122
Holographic Purple-122
Premiere Date-122
99Panini Stickers-292
99Paramount-201
Copper-201
Emerald-201
Gold-201
Holographic Emerald-201
Holographic Gold-201
Holographic Silver-201
Ice Blue-201
Premiere Date-201
Red-201
Silver-201
Ice Alliance-23
99Revolution-125
Premiere Date-125
Red-125
Shadow Series-125
99SP Authentic-77
99SPx-134
Radiance-134
Spectrum-134
99Stadium Club-112
First Day Issue-112
One of a Kind-112
Printing Plates Black-112
Printing Plates Cyan-112
Printing Plates Magenta-112
Printing Plates Yellow-112
99Topps/OPC-223
99Topps/OPC Chrome-223
Refractors-223
99Topps Gold Label Class 1-65
Black-65
Black One of One-65
One of One-65
Red-65
Red One of One-65
99Topps Gold Label Class 2-65
99Topps Gold Label Class 2 Black-65
99Topps Gold Label Class 2 Black 1 of 1-65
99Topps Gold Label Class 2 One of One-65
99Topps Gold Label Class 2 Red-65
99Topps Gold Label Class 2 Red One of One-65
99Topps Gold Label Class 3-65
99Topps Gold Label Class 3 Black-65
99Topps Gold Label Class 3 Black 1 of 1-65
99Topps Gold Label Class 3 One of One-65
99Topps Gold Label Class 3 Red-65
99Topps Gold Label Class 3 Red One of One-65
99Topps Premier Plus-20
Parallel-20
99Upper Deck-287
Exclusives-287
Exclusives 1 of 1-287
99Upper Deck Gold Reserve-287
99Upper Deck MVP-184
Gold Script-184
Silver Script-184
Super Script-184
99Upper Deck MVP SC Edition-161
Gold Script-161
Silver Script-161
Super Script-161
99Upper Deck Victory-266
99Wayne Gretzky Hockey-143
00Aurora-125
Premiere Date-125
00BAP Memorabilia-108
Emerald-108
Ruby-108
Sapphire-108
Promos-108
00BAP Mem Chicago Sportsfest Copper-108
00BAP Memorabilia Chicago Sportsfest Blue-108
00BAP Memorabilia Chicago Sportsfest Gold-108
00BAP Memorabilia Chicago Sportsfest Ruby-108
00BAP Memorabilia Chicago Sun-Times Ruby-108
00BAP Memorabilia Chicago Sun-Times Gold-108
00BAP Mem Chicago Sun-Times Sapphire-108
00BAP Mem Toronto Fall Expo Copper-108
00BAP Memorabilia Toronto Fall Expo Gold-108
00BAP Memorabilia Toronto Fall Expo Ruby-108
00BAP Parkhurst 2000-P74
00BAP Signature Series-181
Emerald-181
Ruby-181
Sapphire-181
Autographs-56
Autographs Gold-56
00BAP Ultimate Memorabilia Autographs-48
Gold-48
00Crown Royale-91
Ice Blue-91
Limited Series-91
Premiere Date-91
Red-91
00O-Pee-Chee-205
00O-Pee-Chee Parallel-205
00Pacific-353
Copper-353
Gold-353
Ice Blue-353
Premiere Date-353
00Panini Stickers-194
00Paramount-210
Copper-210
Gold-210
Holo-Gold-210
Holo-Silver-210
Ice Blue-210
Premiere Date-210
00Private Stock-86
Gold-86
Premiere Date-86
Retail-86
Silver-86
PS-2001 Action-53
PS-2001 Stars-23
00Revolution-126
Blue-126
Premiere Date-126
Red-126
00SP Authentic-76
00Stadium Club-56
00Titanium-83
Blue-83
Gold-83
Premiere Date-83
Red-83
Retail-83
00Topps/OPC-205
Parallel-205
1000 Point Club-PC14
00Topps Chrome-135
OPC Refractors-135
Refractors-135
1000 Point Club Refractors-14
00Topps Gold Label Class 1-35
Gold-35
00Topps Gold Label Class 2-35
00Topps Gold Label Class 2 Gold-35
00Topps Gold Label Class 3-35
00Topps Gold Label Class 3 Gold-35
00Topps Heritage-48
Chrome Parallel-48
00Topps Premier Plus-24
Blue Ice-24
00Topps Stars-31
Blue-31
00UD Heroes-105
00UD Pros and Prospects-76
00Upper Deck-379
Exclusives Tier 1-379
Exclusives Tier 2-379
00Upper Deck MVP-157
First Stars-157
Second Stars-157
Third Stars-157
00Upper Deck Victory-207
00Upper Deck Vintage-319
00Vanguard-85
High Voltage-30
High Voltage Gold-30
High Voltage Green-30
High Voltage Red-30
High Voltage Silver-30
Holographic Gold-85
Holographic Purple-85
Pacific Proofs-85
Press East/West-10
01Atomic-34
Blue-34
Gold-34
Premiere Date-34
Red-34
01BAP Memorabilia-296
01BAP Memorabilia-353
Emerald-296
Emerald-353
Ruby-296
Ruby-353
Sapphire-296
Sapphire-353
01BAP Signature Series Certified 100-C34
01BAP Signature Series Certified 50-C34
01BAP Signature Series Certified 1 of 1's-C34
01BAP Signature Series Autographs-LPT
01BAP Signature Series Autographs Gold-LPT
01BAP Signature Series Jerseys-GJ-11
01BAP Signature Series Jersey Autographs-GUPT

01BAP Sig Series Jersey and Stick Cards-GSJ-11
01Bowman YoungStars-60
Gold-60
Ice Cubed-60
01Crown Royale-50
Blue-50
Premiere Date-50
Red-50
Retail-50
Triple Threads-8
Triple Threads-19
01O-Pee-Chee-79
01O-Pee-Chee-79U
01O-Pee-Chee Heritage Parallel-79
01O-Pee-Chee Heritage Parallel Limited-79
01O-Pee-Chee Premier Parallel-79
01Pacific-334
01Pacific-420
01Pacific-440
Extreme LTD-334
Gold-420
Gold-440
Hobby LTD-334
Premiere Date-334
Retail LTD-334
Top Draft Picks-9
01Pacific Top Draft Picks Draft Day Promo-9
01Pacific Adrenaline-62
Blue-62
Premiere Date-62
Red-62
Retail-62
Jerseys-14
01Pacific Arena Exclusives-334
01Pacific Arena Exclusives-420
01Pacific Arena Exclusives-440
01Pacific Heads-Up-33
Blue-33
Premiere Date-33
Red-33
Silver-33
01Parkhurst-62
Gold-62
Silver-62
Sticks-PS55
01Private Stock-31
Gold-31
Premiere Date-31
Retail-31
Silver-31
Game Gear-40
Game Gear Patches-40
01Private Stock Pacific Nights-31
01SP Authentic-25
Limited-25
Limited Gold-25
01SP Game Used-16
01SPx-21
01Stadium Club-106
Award Winners-106
Master Photos-106
01Stars Postcards-24
01Titanium-47
Hobby Parallel-47
Premiere Date-47
Retail-47
Retail Parallel-47
Double-Sided Jerseys-52
Double-Sided Jerseys-65
Double-Sided Patches-52
Double-Sided Patches-65
01Titanium Draft Day Edition-35
01Topps-79
01Topps-79U
Heritage Parallel-79
Heritage Parallel Limited-79
OPC Parallel-79
01Topps Chrome-79
Refractors-79
Black Border Refractors-79
01Topps Heritage-163
01Topps Reserve-60
01UD Challenge for the Cup-23
01UD Mask Collection-28
Gold-28
01UD Playmakers-32
01Upper Deck-57
Exclusives-57
01Upper Deck Ice-94
01Upper Deck MVP-63
01Upper Deck Victory-310
01Upper Deck Victory-412
Gold-310
Gold-412
01Upper Deck Vintage-81
01Vanguard-33
Blue-33
Red-33
Memorabilia-30
One of Ones-33
Premiere Date-33
Proofs-33
02BAP First Edition-58
02BAP First Edition-428R
Jerseys-58
02BAP Memorabilia-175
Emerald-175
Ruby-175
Sapphire-175
NHL All-Star Game-175
NHL All-Star Game Blue-175
NHL All-Star Game Green-175
NHL All-Star Game Red-175
02BAP Memorabilia Toronto Fall Expo-175
02BAP Signature Series-154
Autographs-154
Autograph Buybacks 1998-275
Autograph Buybacks 1999-205
Autograph Buybacks 2000-56
Autograph Buybacks 2001-LPT
Autographs Gold-154
02Crown Royale Dual Patches-8
02ITG Used Jerseys-GUJ50
02ITG Used Jersey Autographs-GUJ50
02ITG Used Jerseys Gold-GUJ50
02ITG Used Jersey and Stick-SJ50
02ITG Used Jersey and Stick Gold-SJ50
02O-Pee-Chee-113
02O-Pee-Chee Premier Blue Parallel-113
02O-Pee-Chee Premier Red Parallel-113
02O-Pee-Chee Factory Set-113
02Pacific-120
Blue-120
Red-120
02Pacific Complete-449
Red-449
02Pacific Exclusive-59
Jerseys-6
Jerseys Gold-6
02Pacific Heads-Up Quad Jerseys-11
02Pacific Heads-Up Quad Jerseys Gold-11
02Pacific Quest for the Cup-31
Gold-31
02Parkhurst-14
Bronze-14
Gold-14
Silver-14
02Parkhurst Retro-81
Minis-81
02Private Stock Reserve-34
Blue-34
Red-34
Retail-34
02SPx-134
02Stars Postcards-18
02Titanium-34
Blue-34
Red-34
Retail-34
02Topps-113
OPC Blue Parallel-113
OPC Red Parallel-113
Factory Set-113
02Topps Chrome-73
Black Border Refractors-73
Refractors-73
02Topps Total-187
02Upper Deck-302
Exclusives-302
02Upper Deck Beckett UD Promos-302
02Upper Deck Victory-71
Bronze-71
Gold-71
Silver-71
02Upper Deck Vintage-80
02Upper Deck Vintage-270
Green Backs-80
02Vanguard Jerseys-16
02Vanguard Jerseys Gold-16
03ITG Action Jerseys-M86
03NHL Sticker Collection-206
03Pacific-112
Blue-112
Red-112
03Pacific Complete-55
Red-55
03Stars Postcards-28
03Upper Deck-304
Canadian Exclusives-304
HG-304
UD Exclusives-304
04Pacific-89
Blue-89
Red-89
05Be A Player Signatures-PT
05Be A Player Signatures Gold-PT
05Panini Stickers-232
05Parkhurst-125
Facsimile Auto Parallel-125
True Colors-TCCOL
True Colors-TCCOL
05The Cup Master Pressplate Rookie Update-214
05Ultra-60
Gold-60
Ice-60
05Upper Deck-293
Jerseys-J-PT
Jerseys Series II-J2PT
Notable Numbers-N-PT
05Upper Deck Hockey Showcase-HS19
05Upper Deck Showcase Promos-HS19
05Upper Deck MVP-106
Gold-106
Platinum-106
05Upper Deck Rookie Update-214
Inspirations Patch Rookies-214
05Upper Deck Victory-212
Black-212
Gold-212
Silver-212
06Avalanche Team Postcards-19
06Fleer-54
Tiffany-54
Fabricology-FPT
Hockey Headliners-HL12
06Hot Prospects Hot Materials -HMPT
06Hot Prospects Hot Materials Red Hot-HMPT
06Hot Prospects Hot Materials White Hot-HMPT
06O-Pee-Chee-133
Rainbow-133
06Panini Stickers-224
06SP Game Used Authentic Fabrics-AFPT
06SP Game Used Authentic Fabrics Parallel-AFPT
06SP Game Used Authentic Fabrics Patches-AFPT
06SP Game Used Authentic Fabrics Dual-AF2TS
06SP Game Used Authentic Fabrics Dual Patches-AF2TS
06SP Game Used Authentic Fabrics Sixes-AF6500
06SP Game Used Authentic Fabrics Sixes Patches-AF6500
06SPx Winning Materials-WMPT
06SPx Winning Materials Spectrum-WMPT
06The Cup Property of-POPT
06Ultra-53
Gold Medallion-53
Ice Medallion-53
06Upper Deck-50
Exclusives Parallel-50
High Gloss Parallel-50
Game Dated Moments-GD14
Masterpieces-50
06Upper Deck MVP-77
Gold Script-77
Super Script-77
Jerseys-OJMT

Turgeon, Sylvain
83Canadian National Juniors-16
83Whalers Junior Hartford Courant-20
84O-Pee-Chee-79
84O-Pee-Chee-372
84O-Pee-Chee Stickers-191
84O-Pee-Chee Stickers-192
847-Eleven Discs-23
84Topps-62
84Whalers Junior Wendy's-20
85O-Pee-Chee-43
85O-Pee-Chee Stickers-165
85Topps-43
85Whalers Junior Wendy's-21
86O-Pee-Chee-103
86O-Pee-Chee Stickers-53
86Topps-103
86Whalers Junior Thomas'-22
87O-Pee-Chee-70
87O-Pee-Chee Stickers-203
87Panini Stickers-50
87Topps-70
87Whalers Jr. Burger King/Pepsi-20
88O-Pee-Chee-24
88Panini Stickers-245
88Topps-24
88Whalers Junior Ground Round-17
89Devils Caretta-26
90Bowman-81
Tiffany-81
90Canadiens Postcards-32
90O-Pee-Chee-73
90Panini Stickers-71
90Pro Set-177
90Pro Set-474
90Score-116
Canadian-116
90Score Rookie/Traded-108T
90Topps-73
Tiffany-73
90Upper Deck-70
French-70
91Canadiens Postcards-31
91O-Pee-Chee-231
91OPC Premier-184
91Parkhurst-91
French-91
91Pinnacle-226
French-226
91Pro Set-416
French-416
91Score American-208
91Score American-377
91Score Canadian Bilingual-208
91Score Canadian Bilingual-267
91Score Canadian English-208
91Score Canadian English-267
91Topps-231
91Upper Deck-579
French-579
92Bowman-167
92Durivage Panini-29
92O-Pee-Chee-315
92OPC Premier-116
92Parkhurst-121
Emerald Ice-121
92Pinnacle-373
French-373
92Pro Set-123
92Score-367
92Score-516
Canadian-367
Canadian-516
92Senators Team Issue-15
92Stadium Club-59
92Topps-375
Gold-375G
92Ultra-149
92Upper Deck-107
92Quebec Pee-Wee Tournament-441
93Donruss-235
93Donruss Score-36
93Leaf-74
93OPC Premier-97
Gold-97
93Panini Stickers-K
93Parkhurst-136
Emerald Ice-136
93Pinnacle-64
Canadian-64
93PowerPlay-176
93Score-46
Canadian-46
93Senators Kraft Sheets-24
93Stadium Club-482
Members Only Master Set-482
First Day Issue-482
93Topps/OPC Premier-97
Gold-97
93Ultra-190
93Upper Deck-44
93Quebec Pee-Wee Tournament-288
94Be A Player-R60
94Canada Games NHL POGS-173
94Donruss-105
94EA Sports-94
94Fleer-148
94Leaf-191
94OPC Premier-23
Special Effects-23
94Parkhurst-153
Gold-153
Vintage-V51
94Pinnacle-288
Artist's Proofs-288
Rink Collection-288
94Senators Team Issue-26
94Topps/OPC Premier-23
Special Effects-23
94Ultra-341
94Upper Deck-336
Electric Ice-336
SP Inserts-SP146
SP Inserts Die Cuts-SP146
95Leaf-33
95Panini Stickers-52
95Parkhurst International-146
Emerald Ice-146
95Playoff One on One-290
95Upper Deck-177
Electric Ice-177
Electric Ice Gold-177
95Houston Aeros-21
99German DEL-187
00German DEL-127
All-Star Class-A10

Turgeon, Tyson
02Kalamazoo Wings-3
03Kalamazoo Wings-5
04Kalamazoo Wings-6

Turgeon, Yan
00Rockford IceHogs-19

Turikov, Vladimir
91Finnish Semic World Champ Stickers-85
91Swedish Semic World Champ Stickers-85

Turkiewicz, Jim
76O-Pee-Chee WHA-18
79Rochester Americans-22

Turkovski, Vasili
99Russian Stars Postcards-29
00Russian Hockey League-258
02Russian Hockey League-146
02Russian Hockey League-166
02Russian Hockey League-214
02Russian SL-43
03Russian Hockey League-155
03Russian World Championship Team 2003-21
04Russian World Championship Team-12

Turkulainen, Raimo
66Finnish Jaakiekkosarja-127
70Finnish Jaakiekko-271

Turler, Julien
00Swiss Panini Stickers-72
00Swiss Slapshot Mini-Cards-HCCF14
02Swiss HNL-133
04Swiss Lausanne HC Postcards-10

Turler, Michel
72Finnish Semic World Championship-161
72Swedish Semic World Championship-161

Turmel, Eric
93Quebec Pee-Wee Tournament-325

Turmel, Guy
99Baie-Comeau Drakkar-24
00Baie-Comeau Drakkar-16
Signed-16

Turmel, Nicolas
917th Inn. Sketch QMJHL-114

Turmel, Richard
83Fredericton Express-15

Turnbull, Dale
87Sault Ste. Marie Greyhounds-9
89Sault Ste. Marie Greyhounds-17
95Central Hockey League-86

Turnbull, Ian
73Maple Leafs Postcards-27
74Maple Leafs Postcards-24
74NHL Action Stamps-259
74O-Pee-Chee NHL-289
75Maple Leafs Postcards-25
75Maple Leafs Postcards-26
75O-Pee-Chee NHL-41
75Topps-41
76Maple Leafs Postcards-19
76Maple Leafs Postcards-20
76O-Pee-Chee NHL-39
76Topps-39
77Maple Leafs Postcards-16
77O-Pee-Chee NHL-186
77O-Pee-Chee NHL-215
77Topps-186
77Topps-215
78Maple Leafs Postcards-21
78O-Pee-Chee-127
78Topps-127
79Maple Leafs Postcards-31
79O-Pee-Chee-228
79Topps-228
80Maple Leafs Postcards-27
80O-Pee-Chee-133
80O-Pee-Chee Super-21
80Pepsi-Cola Caps-99
80Topps-133
81O-Pee-Chee-309
81O-Pee-Chee Stickers-100
81Topps-42
02Maple Leafs Platinum Collection-38
04ITG Franchises Canadian-104
Autographs-IT
04UD Legendary Signatures-45
Autographs-IT
Rearguard Retrospectives-BSIT

Turnbull, Perry
80O-Pee-Chee-169
80Topps-169
81O-Pee-Chee-298
81Topps-W123
82O-Pee-Chee-312
82O-Pee-Chee Stickers-203
82Post Cereal-17
82Topps Stickers-203
83Canadiens Postcards-30
83O-Pee-Chee-321
83O-Pee-Chee Stickers-124
83Topps Stickers-124
84Jets Police-20
84O-Pee-Chee-349
85Jets Police-20
85O-Pee-Chee-254
86Jets Postcards-23
86Kraft Drawings-76
86O-Pee-Chee-170
86Topps-170
87Blues Kodak-25
92Blues UD Best of the Blues-26
96St. Louis Vipers RHI-4

Turnbull, Travis
04Sioux City Musketeers-22

Turner, Bart
92Michigan State Spartans-25
93Michigan State Spartans-24

Turner, Bob
44Beehive Group II Photos-143A
44Beehive Group II Photos-143B
44Beehive Group II Photos-292
55Parkhurst-54
Quaker Oats-54
57Parkhurst-M13
58Parkhurst-40
59Parkhurst-43
60Parkhurst-43
60Shirriff Coins-37
60York Photos-37
61Parkhurst-41
61Shirriff/Salada Coins-37
61Topps-41
62Topps-29
63Topps-32
64Beehive Group III Photos-57
94Parkhurst Missing Link-81
00London Knights-2
01Mississauga Ice Dogs-17

Turner, Bobby
00London Knights-2
01Mississauga Ice Dogs-17

Turner, Brad
90Richmond Renegades-1
91ProCards-381
93OPC Premier Team Canada-10
93Ultra-475
94Finnish SISU-302

Turner, Dan
82Medicine Hat Tigers-21
83Medicine Hat Tigers-11

Turner, Ian
98Kingston Frontenacs-22
00London Knights-16
01London Knights-21
03Reading Royals-18
03Reading Royals RBI Sports-304
04Reading Royals-14

Turner, Jack
66Columbus Checkers-15
67Columbus Checkers-15

Turner, Jeff
03Kalamazoo Wings-11

Turner, Lloyd
83Hall of Fame-29
83Hall of Fame Postcards-B15
85Hall of Fame-29

Turner, Mark
85Sudbury Wolves-18
86Sudbury Wolves-18
87Kingston Canadians-11
88Sudbury Wolves-21
90Cincinnati Cyclones-31
91ProCards-245
93Muskegon Fury-19
95Muskegon Fury-8
99Mobile Mysticks-12
02ECHL Update-U-24
03Greensboro Generals-192
04Richmond Riverdogs-11

Turner, Scott
91Peterborough Petes-3
917th Inn. Sketch OHL-124
03Peoria Rivermen-21
04Peoria Rivermen-10

Turner, Tim
03Kalamazoo Wings-14
04Kalamazoo Wings-13
05Kalamazoo Wings-10

Turner, Trever
04Williams Lake Timberwolves-18

Turnipseed, Mark
93Quebec Pee-Wee Tournament-891

Turon, David
03Memphis RiverKings-21
06Czech OFS-217

Turpeinen, Untu
71Finnish Suomi Stickers-274

Turple, Dan
03Oshawa Generals-1
04Kitchener Rangers-6
05ITG Heroes/Prosp Toronto Expo Parallel -293
05Kitchener Rangers-1
05ITG Heroes and Prospects-293
Autographs Series II-DT

Turtiainen, Kimo
72Finnish Jaakiekko-297

Turunen, Jyrki
66Finnish Jaakiekkosarja-131
70Finnish Jaakiekko-272

Turunen, Kimmo
70Finnish Jaakiekko-322

Turunen, Martti
70Finnish Jaakiekko-273

Turunen, Mikko
04Finnish Cardset-211
05Finnish Cardset -12
06Finnish Cardset-16

Turunen, Olli-Pekka
71Finnish Suomi Stickers-354
72Finnish Jaakiekko-338

Turunen, Timo
70Finnish Jaakiekko-188
71Finnish Suomi Stickers-109
72Finnish Jaakiekko-76
72Finnish Jaakiekko-153
72Finnish Hellas-17
73Finnish Jaakiekko-81
73Finnish Jaakiekko-122
73Swedish Stickers-36
74Finnish Typotor-17

Turunen, Tommi
95Finnish SISU-305
96Finnish SISU Redline-103
98Finnish Keraillysarja-135
99Finnish Cardset-300
00Finnish Cardset-74
01Finnish Cardset-320
02Finnish Cardset-130
03Finnish Cardset-67
04Finnish Cardset-59
Parallel-44
05Finnish Cardset -121

Turvey, Ward
23Crescent Selkirks-10

Turville, Rob
04Vernon Vipers-13

Tustian, Rob
90Michigan Tech Huskies-25
91ProCards-42

Tustin, Norm
34Beehive Group I Photos-295

Tuten, Audley
34Beehive Group I Photos-84

Tutschek, Brad
98Kootenay Ice-24

Tutt, Brian
89ProCards AHL-91
92Norwegian Elite Series-190
92Norwegian Elite Series-192
93Finnish SISU-363
93Swedish Semic Elitserien-80
94Finnish SISU-318
96German DEL-297
98German DEL-245
99German DEL-239

Tutt, Thayer
83Hall of Fame Postcards-I15
85Hall of Fame-134

Tuttle, Steve
87Blues Team Issue-24
88Blues Kodak-24
88Blues Team Issue-24
89Blues Kodak-35
89O-Pee-Chee-157
89Panini Stickers-126
89Topps-157
90Blues Kodak-24
90O-Pee-Chee-278
90Pro Set-273
90Topps-278
Tiffany-278
90Upper Deck-195
French-195
90ProCards AHL/IHL-84
91ProCards-41
92Ultra-205
94Milwaukee Admirals-25
95Milwaukee Admirals-19
95Milwaukee Admirals Postcards-15
96Milwaukee Admirals-26
97Milwaukee Admirals-20

Tuulola, Marko
92Finnish Jyvas-Hyva Stickers-26
93Finnish Jyvas-Hyva Stickers-235
93Finnish SISU-187
94Finnish SISU-6
94Finnish Jaa Kiekko-7
95Finnish SISU-248
95Finnish Semic World Championships-25
96Finnish SISU Redline-43
98Swedish UD Choice-35
99Swedish Upper Deck-29
00Swedish Upper Deck-34
01Finnish Cardset-219
02Finnish Cardset-131
03Finnish Cardset-34
06Finnish Cardset-238

Tuyl, Clyde
93UK Sheffield Steelers-16
94UK Sheffield Steelers-2
95UK Sheffield Steelers-9
97UK Sheffield Steelers-25

Tuzzolino, Nick
03Lincoln Stars-6
03Lincoln Stars Update-46
05Sudbury Wolves-19

Tuzzolino, Tony
93Michigan State Spartans-25
97Kentucky Thoroughblades-16
98Cincinnati Mighty Ducks-24
99Hartford Wolf Pack-20
00Hartford Wolf Pack-20
01BAP Memorabilia-453
Emerald-453
Ruby-453
Sapphire-453
01UD Playmakers-106
01Upper Deck Ice-129
01Providence Bruins-8
02Louisiana Ice Gators-21
03Binghamton Senators-20

Tverdovsky, Oleg
93Parkhurst-531
Emerald Ice-531
93Pinnacle-506
Canadian-506
93Classic-111
94Be A Player-R160
94Ducks Carl's Jr.-24
94Finest-2
Super Team Winners-2
Refractors-2
Bowman's Best-R2
Bowman's Best-X24
Bowman's Best Refractors-R2
Bowman's Best Refractors-X24
94Fleer-8
Rookie Sensations-10
94Leaf Phenoms-6
94Leaf Limited-24
94OPC Premier-464
Special Effects-464
94Pinnacle-261
Artist's Proofs-261
Rink Collection-261
Rookie Team Pinnacle-2
94Score-214
Gold-214
Platinum-214
Top Rookie Redemption-4
94Select-169
Gold-169
Youth Explosion-YE2
94SP-2
Die Cuts-2
Premier-5
Premier Die-Cuts-5
94Topps/OPC Premier-464
Special Effects-464
94Ultra Prospects-9
94Upper Deck-243
94Upper Deck-540
Electric Ice-243
Electric Ice-540
Predictor Canadian-C14
94Upper Deck Predictor Canadian Exch Gold-C14
94Upper Deck Predictor Cdn Exch Silver-C14
94Upper Deck SP Inserts-SP93
94Upper Deck SP Inserts Die Cuts-SP93
94Brandon Wheat Kings-22
94Classic-2
Gold-2
Picks-CP12
Previews-HK5
ROY Sweepstakes-R19
Tri-Cards-T1
94Classic Pro Prospects-208
94Classic Four-Sport *-116
Gold-116
High Voltage-HV8
Printers Proofs-116
95Bashan Super Stickers-1
95Bashan Super Stickers-4
95Be A Player-61
Signatures-S61
Signatures Die Cuts-S61
95Bowman-88
All-Foil-88
95Collector's Choice-81
Player's Club-81
Player's Club Platinum-81
95Donruss-3
Rookie Team-6
95Donruss Elite-6
Die Cut Stars-6
Die Cut Uncut-6
95Emotion-4
95Imperial Stickers-4
95Leaf-28
Studio Rookies-6
95Leaf Limited-46
95McDonald's Pinnacle-MCD-35
95Metal-5
95Panini Stickers-231
95Parkhurst International-9
95Parkhurst International-496
Emerald Ice-9
Emerald Ice-496
95Pinnacle-60
Artist's Proofs-60
Rink Collection-60
Global Gold-11
95Playoff One on One-4
95Pro Magnets-44
95Score-16
Black Ice Artist's Proofs-16
Black Ice-16
95Select Certified-79
Mirror Gold-79
Future-9
95SkyBox Impact-5
95SkyBox Impact-236
95SP-166
95Stadium Club-113
Members Only Master Set-113
95Summit-37
Artist's Proofs-37
Ice-37
95Topps-365
OPC Inserts-365
New To The Game-4NG
Young Stars-YS7
95Topps SuperSkills-12
Platinum-12
95Ultra-6
Gold Medallion-6
95Upper Deck-408
Electric Ice-408
Electric Ice Gold-408
Special Edition-SE2
Special Edition Gold-SE2
95Zenith-71
95Images Four-Sport *-95
95Signature Rookies Tetrad Autobilia *-49
96Black Diamond-102
Gold-102
96Collector's Choice-199
96Collector's Choice-327
96Coyotes Coca-Cola-32
96Donruss-105
Press Proofs-105
96Flair-74
Blue Ice-74
96Fleer-93
96Leaf-3
Press Proofs-3
96Leaf Preferred-71
Press Proofs-71
96Metal Universe-123
96NHL Pro Stamps-44
96Pinnacle-145
Artist's Proofs-145
Foil-145
Premium Stock-145
Rink Collection-145
96Playoff One on One-332
96Score-89
Artist's Proofs-89
Dealer's Choice Artist's Proofs-89
Special Artist's Proofs-89
Golden Blades-89
96SkyBox Impact-109
96SP-121
96Summit-129
Artist's Proofs-129
Ice-129
Metal-129
Premium Stock-129
96Topps Picks-97
OPC Inserts-97
96Ultra-137
Gold Medallion-137
96Upper Deck-129
Superstar Showdown-SS25A
96Upper Deck Ice-99
Parallel-99
96Zenith-70
Artist's Proofs-70
97Collector's Choice-198
Star Quest-SQ28
97Coyotes Face-Off Luncheon -24
97Donruss-54
Press Proofs Silver-54
Press Proofs Gold-54
Line 2 Line-6
Line 2 Line Die Cut-6
97Donruss Canadian Ice-62
Dominion Series-62
Provincial Series-62
97Donruss Elite-109
Aspirations-109
Status-109
97Donruss Limited-93
Exposure-93
97Donruss Preferred-137
Cut to the Chase-137
97Donruss Priority-53
Stamp of Approval-53
97Katch-114
Gold-114
Silver-114
97Leaf-92
Fractal Matrix-92
Fractal Matrix Die Cuts-92
97Leaf International-92
Universal Ice-92
97Pacific-252
Copper-252
Emerald Green-252
Ice Blue-252
Red-252
Silver-252
97Pacific Dynagon-99
Copper-99
Dark Grey-99
Emerald Green-99
Ice Blue-99
Red-99
Silver-99
Tandems-66
97Pacific Invincible-110
Copper-110
Emerald Green-110
Ice Blue-110
Red-110
Silver-110
97Pacific Omega-179
Copper-179
Dark Gray-179
Emerald Green-179
Gold-179
Ice Blue-179
97Panini Stickers-163
97Paramount-146
Copper-146
Dark Grey-146
Emerald Green-146
Ice Blue-146
Red-146
Silver-146
97Pinnacle-166
Press Plates Back Black-166
Press Plates Back Cyan-166
Press Plates Back Magenta-166
Press Plates Back Yellow-166
Press Plates Front Black-166
Press Plates Front Cyan-166
Press Plates Front Magenta-166
Press Plates Front Yellow-166
97Pinnacle Certified-103
Red-103
Mirror Blue-103
Mirror Gold-103
Mirror Red-103
97Pinnacle Inside-132
97Pinnacle Tot Cert Platinum Blue-103
97Pinnacle Tot Cert Platinum Gold-103
97Pinnacle Totally Certified Platinum Red-103
97Pinnacle Tot Cert Mirror Platinum Gold-103
97Score-195
97Studio-38
Press Proofs Silver-38
Press Proofs Gold-38
97Upper Deck-335
Game Dated Moments-335
Smooth Grooves-SG42
98Aurora-150
98Be A Player-258
Press Release-258
98BAP Gold-258
98BAP Autographs-258
98BAP Autographs Gold-258
98Crown Royale-107
Limited Series-107
98Finest-104
No Protectors-104
No Protectors Refractors-104
Refractors-104
98Katch-112
98Pacific-345
Ice Blue-345
Red-345
98Pacific Dynagon Ice-147
Blue-147
Red-147
98Pacific Omega-190
Red-190
Opening Day Issue-190
98Panini Photocards-86
98Panini Stickers-146
98Paramount-188
Copper-188
Emerald Green-188
Holo-Electric-188
Ice Blue-188
Silver-188
98UD Choice-159
98UD Choice Preview-159
98UD Choice Prime Choice Reserve-159
98UD Choice Reserve-159
98Upper Deck-153
Exclusives-153
Exclusives 1 of 1-153
Gold Reserve-153
98Upper Deck MVP-161
Gold Script-161
Silver Script-161
Super Script-161
ProSign-OT
99BAP Memorabilia-140
Gold-140
Silver-140
99BAP Millennium-3
Emerald-3
Ruby-3
Sapphire-3
Signatures-3
Signatures Gold-3
99Pacific-330
Copper-330
Emerald Green-330
Gold-330
Ice Blue-330
Premiere Date-330
Red-330
99Pacific Dynagon Ice-13
Blue-13
Copper-13
Gold-13
Premiere Date-13
99Panini Stickers-183
99SPx-7
Radiance-7
Spectrum-7
99Stadium Club-156
First Day Issue-156
One of a Kind-156
Printing Plates Black-156
Printing Plates Cyan-156
Printing Plates Magenta-156
Printing Plates Yellow-156
99Topps Arena Giveaways-ANA-OT
99Upper Deck-102
99Upper Deck-173
Exclusives-102
Exclusives-173
Exclusives 1 of 1-102
Exclusives 1 of 1-173
99Upper Deck Gold Reserve-102
99Upper Deck Gold Reserve-173
99Upper Deck MVP-9
Gold Script-9
Silver Script-9
Super Script-9
99Upper Deck MVP SC Edition-4
Gold Script-4
Silver Script-4
Super Script-4
99Upper Deck Victory-6
99Wayne Gretzky Hockey-5
99Russian Fetisov Tribute-13
00BAP Memorabilia-135
Emerald-135
Ruby-135
Sapphire-135
Promos-135
00BAP Mem Chicago Sportsfest Copper-135
00BAP Memorabilia Chicago Sportsfest Blue-135
00BAP Memorabilia Chicago Sportsfest Gold-135
00BAP Memorabilia Chicago Sportsfest Ruby-135
00BAP Memorabilia Chicago Sun-Times Ruby-135
00BAP Memorabilia Chicago Sun-Times Gold-135
00BAP Mem Chicago Sun-Times Sapphire-135
00BAP Mem Toronto Fall Expo Copper-135
00BAP Memorabilia Toronto Fall Expo Gold-135
00BAP Memorabilia Toronto Fall Expo Ruby-135
00BAP Parkhurst 2000-P83
00BAP Signature Series-96
Emerald-96
Ruby-96
Sapphire-96
00O-Pee-Chee-86
00O-Pee-Chee Parallel-86
00Pacific-12
Copper-12
Gold-12
Ice Blue-12
Premiere Date-12
00Panini Stickers-114
00Paramount-8
Copper-8
Gold-8
Holo-Gold-8
Holo-Silver-8
Ice Blue-8
Premiere Date-8
00SP Authentic-3
00Stadium Club-137
00Topps/OPC-86
Parallel-86
00Topps Chrome-68
OPC Refractors-68
Refractors-68
00UD Heroes-3
00Upper Deck-3
Exclusives Tier 1-3
Exclusives Tier 2-3
00Upper Deck MVP-3
First Stars-3
Second Stars-3
Third Stars-3
00Upper Deck Victory-5
00Upper Deck Vintage-4
01BAP Memorabilia-87
Emerald-87

Ruby-87
Sapphire-87
01BAP Signature Series-148
Autographs-148
Autographs Gold-148
Department of Defense-DD-4
International Medals-IB-5
01Crown Royale Triple Threads-1
01O-Pee-Chee-111
01O-Pee-Chee Premier Parallel-111
01Pacific-12
Extreme LTD-12
Hobby LTD-12
Premiere Date-12
Retail LTD-12
01Pacific Adrenaline-6
Blue-6
Premiere Date-6
Red-6
Retail-6
Jerseys-1
01Pacific Arena Exclusives-12
01Parkhurst-106
01Private Stock Game Gear-5
01Private Stock Game Gear Patches-5
01Titanium Double-Sided Jerseys-2
01Titanium Double-Sided Patches-2
01Titanium Draft Day Edition-3
01Topps-111
OPC Parallel-111
01Topps Chrome-111
Refractors-111
Black Border Refractors-111
01Upper Deck-232
01Upper Deck MVP-4
01Upper Deck Victory-3
Gold-3
01Upper Deck Vintage-4
01Upper Deck Vintage-9
01Vanguard Memorabilia-1
02Atomic Jerseys-13
02Atomic Jerseys Gold-13
02Atomic Patches-13
02BAP First Edition-48
Jerseys-48
02BAP Memorabilia-126
02BAP Memorabilia-269
Emerald-126
Emerald-269
Ruby-126
Ruby-269
Sapphire-126
Sapphire-269
NHL All-Star Game-126
NHL All-Star Game-269
NHL All-Star Game Blue-126
NHL All-Star Game Blue-269
NHL All-Star Game Green-126
NHL All-Star Game Green-269
NHL All-Star Game Red-126
NHL All-Star Game Red-269
02BAP Memorabilia Toronto Fall Expo-126
02BAP Memorabilia Toronto Fall Expo-269
02BAP Signature Series-93
Autographs-93
Autograph Buybacks 1998-258
Autograph Buybacks 1999-3
Autograph Buybacks 2001-148
Autographs Gold-93
02Devils Team Issue-8
02O-Pee-Chee-207
02O-Pee-Chee Premier Blue Parallel-207
02O-Pee-Chee Premier Red Parallel-207
02O-Pee-Chee Factory Set-207
02Pacific-10
Blue-10
Red-10
02Pacific Complete-147
Red-147
02Pacific Heads-Up Quad Jerseys-1
02Pacific Heads-Up Quad Jerseys Gold-1
02Parkhurst-156
Bronze-156
Gold-156
Silver-156
02Parkhurst Retro-170
Minis-170
02Topps-207
OPC Blue Parallel-207
OPC Red Parallel-207
Factory Set-207
02Topps Heritage-179
02Upper Deck-347
Exclusives-347
02Upper Deck Beckett UD Promos-347
02Upper Deck Victory-5
Bronze-5
Gold-5
Silver-5
03Pacific-207
Blue-207
Red-207
03Russian Avangard Omsk-6
03Russian Hockey League-89
03Russian National Team-23
03Russian Postcards-9
04Russian World Championship Team-20
05Panini Stickers-47
05Parkhurst-95
Facsimile Auto Parallel-95
05Ultra-44
Gold-44
Ice-44
05Upper Deck-285
05Upper Deck MVP-81
Gold-81
Platinum-81
06O-Pee-Chee-236
Rainbow-236
06Upper Deck-344
Exclusives Parallel-344
High Gloss Parallel-344
Masterpieces-344

Tveten, Erik
92Norwegian Elite Series-3
95Swedish World Championships Stickers-254

Tvohy, Brandan
93Quebec Pee-Wee Tournament-1282

Tvrdek, Kamil
01Czech OFS Update-303
02Czech OFS Plus-296
06Czech OFS-43

Tvrdik, Michal
98Czech OFS-381
99Czech OFS-99
00Czech DS Extraliga-96
00Czech OFS-48
01Czech OFS-258
02Czech OFS Plus-321
03Czech OFS Plus-82
04Czech OFS-135
05Czech HC Pardubice-16
06Czech HC Pardubice Postcards-22
06Czech OFS-314

Tvrdon, Roman
99Spokane Chiefs-27
00Spokane Chiefs-28
03ITG VIP Rookie Debut-143
03Parkhurst Rookie-74
03UD Premier Collection-101
03Upper Deck Rookie Update-184
04Pacific-300
Blue-300
Red-300
04UK Nottingham Panthers-18
05Czech HC Plzen-15

Tvrznik, Martin
00Czech OFS-155

Twerdin, Dwayne
99OCN Blizzard-22

Twerdun, Chris
97Moose Jaw Warriors-16
04Bakersfield Condors-20

Twist, Tony
86Saskatoon Blades Photos-23
88ProCards IHL-79
89Blues Kodak-6
90Nordiques Petro-Canada-38
90ProCards AHL/IHL-85
91Nordiques Petro-Canada-31
91Score Canadian Bilingual-396
91Score Canadian English-396
92Nordiques Petro-Canada-34
93Score-400
Canadian-400
94Leaf-13
94Leaf-454
95Be A Player-214
Signatures-S214
Signatures Die Cuts-S214
95Topps-203
OPC Inserts-203
96Blues Dispatch 30th Anniversary-5
96Collector's Choice-231
96Score-207
Artist's Proofs-207
Dealer's Choice Artist's Proofs-207
Special Artist's Proofs-207
Golden Blades-207
97Collector's Choice-230
97Katch-132
Gold-132
Silver-132
97Pacific-254
Copper-254
Emerald Green-254
Ice Blue-254
Red-254
Silver-254
97Paramount-162
Copper-162
Dark Grey-162
Emerald Green-162
Ice Blue-162
Red-162
Silver-162
97Score-157
Artist's Proofs-157
Golden Blades-157
97Score Blues-10
Platinum-10
Premier-10
97Upper Deck-201
98Aurora-165
98Pacific-375
Ice Blue-375
Red-375
98Pacific Omega-207
Red-207
Opening Day Issue-207
98Paramount-208
Copper-208
Emerald Green-208
Holo-Electric-208
Ice Blue-208
Silver-208
98Revolution Three Pronged Attack-8
98Revolution 3 Pronged Attack Parallel-8
98Upper Deck-177
Exclusives-177
Exclusives 1 of 1-177
Gold Reserve-177
98Upper Deck MVP-184
Gold Script-184
Silver Script-184
Super Script-184
99Pacific-365
Copper-365
Emerald Green-365
Gold-365
Ice Blue-365
Premiere Date-365
Red-365
01Fleer Legacy-51
Ultimate-51
In the Corners-12
02Fleer Throwbacks-68
Gold-68
Platinum-68
Autographs-23
Drop the Gloves-3
Scraps-7
Tie Downs-7
Squaring Off-7
Squaring Off Memorabilia-7
02UD Foundations-86
Canadian Heroes-CTT
Canadian Heroes Gold-CTT
Canadian Heroes Silver-C-TT
Power Stations-STT
Power Stations Gold-STT
Power Stations Silver-S-TT
04UD Legendary Signatures-33
AKA Autographs-AKA-TW
Autographs-TW

Twomey, Christian
92British Columbia JHL-209

Twordik, Brad
96Brandon Wheat Kings-12
98Brandon Wheat Kings-21
99Brandon Wheat Kings-22
99Bowman CHL-94
Gold-94
OPC International-94
00Fort Wayne Komets-22
00Fort Wayne Komets Shoe Carnival-14

Twordik, Brent
97Brandon Wheat Kings-24
97Swift Current Broncos-17
98Swift Current Broncos-10
99Swift Current Broncos-21
01Swift Current Broncos-16

Tyacke, Jay
92Quebec Pee-Wee Tournament-1277
93Quebec Pee-Wee Tournament-1250

Tyers, Shawn
85Kitchener Rangers-19

Tyler, Bret
04Maine Black Bears-27
05Maine Black Bears-26

Tymchak, Josh
99Asheville Smoke-17
99Asheville Smoke-22

Tymchuk, Greg
95Slapshot-200

Tymchyshyn, Darren
91British Columbia JHL-40
92British Columbia JHL-56

Tynkkynen, Matti
78Finnish SM-Liiga-168
80Finnish Mallasjuoma-123

Tyorikov, Vladimir
00Russian Hockey League-18

Tyrin, Denis
03Russian Hockey League-2

Tysk, Evert
56Swedish Alfabilder-91
67Swedish Hockey-148
69Swedish Hockey-163

Tyulyapkin, Denis
00Russian Hockey League-200

Tyulyapkin, Mikhail
03Russian Hockey League-165
04Russian World Junior Team-11

Tyurikov, Vladimir
99Russian Hockey League-30
99Russian Stars Postcards-30
03Russian Hockey League-96
04Russian Super League All-Stars-5

Tyurin, Denis
00Russian Hockey League-191

Tyutin, Fedor
00Russian Hockey League-77
01Guelph Storm-1
01Guelph Storm Memorial Cup-1
02Russian Future Stars-5
02Russian Hockey League-185
02Russian Young Lions-16
03BAP Memorabilia-229
03BAP Ultimate Mem Franch Present Future-20
03BAP Ultimate Mem Rookie Jersey Emblems-21
03BAP Ultimate Mem Rookie Jsy Emblem Gold-21
03BAP Ultimate Mem Rookie Jersey Numbers-21
03BAP Ultimate Mem Rookie Jsy Number Gold-21
03ITG Toronto Spring Expo Class of 2004-6
03ITG Used Signature Series-193
Gold-193
03ITG VIP Rookie Debut-120
03Parkhurst Toronto Expo Rookie Preview-PRP-4
03Parkhurst Rookie-131
Rookie Emblems-RE-2
Rookie Emblems Gold-RE-2
Rookie Jerseys-RJ-2
Rookie Jerseys Gold-RJ-2
Rookie Numbers-RN-2
Rookie Numbers Gold-RN-2
03SP Game Used-123
03Topps Traded-TT129
Blue-TT129
Gold-TT129
Red-TT129
03UD Premier Collection-118
03Upper Deck Rookie Update-93
03Upper Deck Trilogy-189
03Russian Hockey League-91
03AHL Top Prospects-39
03Hartford Wolf Pack-24
03Pacific AHL Prospects-35
Gold-35
04Pacific-180
Blue-180
Red-180
04Russian Back to Russia-31
04ITG Heroes and Prospects-46
Autographs-FT
Emblems-14
Emblems Gold-14
He Shoots-He Scores Prizes-23
Jersey Autographs-14
Jerseys-14
Jerseys Gold-14
Numbers-14
Numbers Gold-14
04ITG Heroes/Prospects Toronto Expo '05-46
04ITG Heroes/Prospects Expo Heroes/Pros-46
05Beehive Signature Scrapbook-SSFT
05Parkhurst-326
Facsimile Auto Parallel-326
05SP Authentic Scripts to Success-SSFT
05SP Authentic Sign of the Times-FT
05SP Game Used Auto Draft-AD-FT
05SP Game Used Statscriptions-ST-FT
05UD Rookie Class-28
05Ultimate Coll National Heroes Jersey-NHJFT
05Ultimate Coll National Heroes Patch-NHPFT
05Upper Deck-378
Jerseys Series II-J2FT
Notable Numbers-N-FT
05Upper Deck MVP-261
Gold-261
Platinum-261
06O-Pee-Chee-324
Rainbow-324
06Upper Deck MVP-200
Gold Script-200
Super Script-200
06Upper Deck Victory-134
06Upper Deck Victory Black-134
06Upper Deck Victory Gold-134
06Russian Sport Collection Olympic Stars-14
06Russian Torino Olympic Team-5

Tyznych, Alexander
89ProCards AHL-144
90ProCards AHL/IHL-236

Tyznych, Sergei
74Swedish Stickers-40

Tzountzouris, Alex
93Quebec Pee-Wee Tournament-1477

Ubriaco, Gene
69O-Pee-Chee-149
92Finnish Semic-242
92Atlanta Knights-24
93Atlanta Knights-23

Uchaikin, Dmitri
00Russian Hockey League-19

Uchevatov, Victor
01Albany River Rats-22
02Albany River Rats-23
02Albany River Rats AAP-25
03Albany River Rats-27
03Albany River Rats Kinko's-26
04San Antonio Rampage-20
04ITG Heroes and Prospects-32
Autographs-VU
04ITG Heroes/Prospects Toronto Expo '05-32
04ITG Heroes/Prospects Expo Heroes/Pros-32
06Milwaukee Admirals -18

Udiansky, Stanislav
01Russian Hockey League-135

Udle, Clark
96Halifax Mooseheads I-23
96Halifax Mooseheads II-23

Udovicic, Nick
04Fort Worth Brahmas-15

Udvari, Frank
83Hall of Fame-240
83Hall of Fame Postcards-N16
85Hall of Fame-240
06Parkhurst-133
Autographs-133

Udvari, Steve
87Sault Ste. Marie Greyhounds-12
89Niagara Falls Thunder-20
897th Inn. Sketch OHL-138

Udyachski, Stanislav
00Russian Hockey League-207

Uens, Jim
81Oshawa Generals-20

Ugolnikov, Oleg
99Russian Hockey League-175

Uher, Zdenek
95Czech APS Extraliga-352
96Czech APS Extraliga-336

Uhlback, Jaakko
98Finnish Kerailysarja-160
99Finnish Cardset-325
00Finnish Cardset-90
01Finnish Cardset-131
03Finnish Cardset-82
04Finnish Cardset-89
Parallel-66
05Finnish Cardset -186

Uhrstedt, Martin
05Swedish SHL Elitset-147

Uitus, Pekka
66Finnish Jaakiekkosarja-175
70Finnish Jaakiekko-256
71Finnish Suomi Stickers-221
72Finnish Jaakiekko-169
73Finnish Jaakiekko-237

Ujcik, Viktor
91Upper Deck Czech World Juniors-92
94Czech APS Extraliga-175
95Czech APS Extraliga-136
95Czech APS Extraliga-378
96Czech APS Extraliga-19
96Czech APS Extraliga-347
97Czech APS Extraliga-159
97Czech APS Extraliga-360
97Czech DS Extraliga-12
97Czech DS Stickers-14
97Czech DS Stickers-129
98Czech DS-8
98Czech DS Stickers-19
98Czech DS Stickers-196
98Czech OFS-184
98Czech OFS-428
99Czech DS National Stars-NS9
99Czech OFS-203
99Czech OFS-273
99Czech OFS-529
All-Star Game Blue-529
All-Star Game Gold-529
All-Star Game Red-529
All-Star Game Silver-529
00Czech DS Extraliga-68
00Czech OFS-224
00Czech OFS-412
00Czech OFS Star Emerald-25
00Czech OFS Star Pink-25
00Czech OFS Star Violet-25
01Czech DS-22
01Czech DS-55
01Czech National Team Postcards-14
01Czech OFS-12
01Czech OFS Red Inserts-RE1D
02Czech DS-30
02Czech DS-83
02Czech OFS Plus-253
02Czech OFS Plus-359
02Czech OFS Plus All-Star Game-H40
02Czech OFS Plus Trios-T13
02Czech OFS Plus Duos-D5
03Czech OFS Plus Insert G-G7
04Finnish Cardset-98
Parallel-72
05Finnish Cardset -94
06Czech Super Six Postcards-15
06Finnish Cardset-98

Ujvary, Lubomir
70Finnish Jaakiekko-60
70Swedish Hockey-352
70Swedish Masterserien-144

Ukkola, Timo
80Finnish Mallasjuoma-18

Ukkonen, Veikko
65Finnish Hellas-123
66Finnish Jaakiekkosarja-16

Ulander, Mats
82Swedish Semic VM Stickers-18
83Swedish Semic Elitserien-15
83Swedish Semic VM Stickers-18

Ulanov, Igor
91O-Pee-Chee Inserts-62R
91Parkhurst-421
French-421
91Upper Deck-590
French-590
92Bowman-392
92O-Pee-Chee-229
92Parkhurst-440
Emerald Ice-440
92Pro Set-216
92Score-467
Canadian-467
92Stadium Club-366
92Topps-468
Gold-468G
92Upper Deck-300
Euro-Stars-E15
93Jets Readers Club-21
93Jets Ruffles-26
93PowerPlay-477
94Be A Player Signature Cards-70
94Leaf-416
94OPC Premier-179
Special Effects-179
94Topps/OPC Premier-179
Special Effects-179
94Ultra-397
95Finnish Semic World Championships-129
96Collector's Choice-252
97Be A Player-209
Autographs-209
Autographs Die-Cuts-209
Autographs Prismatic Die-Cuts-209
97Collector's Choice-239
97Panini Stickers-106
98Canadiens Team Issue-23
99Paramount-121
Copper-121
Emerald-121
Gold-121
Holographic Emerald-121
Holographic Gold-121
Holographic Silver-121
Ice Blue-121
Premiere Date-121
Red-121
Silver-121
00Upper Deck-69
Exclusives Tier 1-69
Exclusives Tier 2-69
01Hartford Wolf Pack-24
03ITG Action-250
05Upper Deck MVP-163
Gold-163
Platinum-163

Ulanski, Kevin
06Rockford IceHogs -21

Ulcar, Anze
93Quebec Pee-Wee Tournament-1781

Ulehla, Petr
99Czech OFS-128

Uliasz, Nicole
04Wisconsin Badgers Women-20

Ulin, Patrik
92Swedish Semic Elitserien Stickers-297

Ulion, Gretchen
94Classic Women of Hockey-W29

Ullbors, Daniel
98Danish Hockey League-204

Ullman, David
00Medicine Hat Tigers-23

Ullman, Norm
44Beehive Group II Photos-215
57Topps-46
58Topps-65
59Topps-45
60Parkhurst-26
60Shirriff Coins-45
61Parkhurst-26
61Shirriff/Salada Coins-76
62Parkhurst-21
62York Iron-On Transfers-29
63Chex Photos-55
63Parkhurst-52
63Toronto Star-40
63York White Backs-47
64Beehive Group III Photos-95
64Coca-Cola Caps-42
64Topps-15
64Toronto Star-47
65Coca-Cola-42
65Topps-49
66Topps-52
66Topps USA Test-52
67Topps-101
67Topps-132
68O-Pee-Chee-131
68Post Marbles-27
68Shirriff Coins-168
68Topps-131
69Maple Leafs White Border Glossy-35
69Maple Leafs White Border Matte-6
69O-Pee-Chee-54
Stamps-25
69Topps-54
70Colgate Stamps-12
70Dad's Cookies-130
70Esso Power Players-24
70O-Pee-Chee-110
Deckle-48
70Sargent Promotions Stamps-204
70Topps-110
71Bazooka-18
71Colgate Heads-15A
71Colgate Heads-15B
71Frito-Lay-10
71Letraset Action Replays-17
71Maple Leafs Postcards-21
71O-Pee-Chee-30
Posters-11
71Sargent Promotions Stamps-193
71Topps-30
71Toronto Sun-274
72Maple Leafs Postcards-29
72Maple Leafs Postcards-30
72O-Pee-Chee-147
72Sargent Promotions Stamps-197
72Topps-168
72Finnish Semic World Championship-163
72Swedish Semic World Championship-163
73Mac's Milk-29
73Maple Leafs Postcards-28
73O-Pee-Chee-27
73Topps-148
74Lipton Soup-1
74Maple Leafs Postcards-25
74NHL Action Stamps-261
74O-Pee-Chee NHL-219
74O-Pee-Chee NHL-236
74Topps-219
74Topps-236
76O-Pee-Chee WHA-126
81TCMA-1
83Hall of Fame-104
83Hall of Fame Postcards-G15
85Hall of Fame-104
88Esso All-Stars-47
91Ultimate Original Six-72
91Ultimate Original Six-78
French-72
French-78
92Hall of Fame Legends-17
92Parkhurst Parkie Reprints-PR25
94Parkhurst Missing Link-45
94Parkhurst Tall Boys-58
Mail-Ins-AS4
Mail-Ins-SL3
94Zeller's Masters of Hockey-8
94Zeller's Masters of Hockey Signed-8
95Parkhurst '66-67-45
Coins-45
99BAP Memorabilia AS Retail-R10
99BAP Memorabilia AS Retail Autographs-R10
01Greats of the Game-43
Autographs-43
01Topps Archives-11
Arena Seats-ASNU
Autographs-7
01Topps Heritage Autographs-ANU
01Topps Heritage Salute-S6
02Maple Leafs Platinum Collection-69
02Parkhurst Reprints-253
02Parkhurst Reprints-266
02Parkhurst Reprints-277
03Parkhurst Original Six Detroit-50
03Parkhurst Original Six Detroit-88
Autographs-OS-NU
03Parkhurst Original Six Toronto-50
04ITG Franchises US West-222
Autographs-A-NU
Complete Jerseys-WCJ8
Complete Jerseys Gold-WCJ8
Double Memorabilia-WDM16
Double Memorabilia Gold-WDM16
Memorabilia-WSM27
Memorabilia Gold-WSM27
Teammates-WTM6
Teammates Gold-WTM6
04ITG Ultimate Memorabilia-28
04ITG Ultimate Memorabilia-43
Gold-28
Gold-43
Jerseys-15
Jerseys Gold-15
Original Six-16
Original Six-20
05ITG Ultimate Mem Decades Jerseys-2
05ITG Ultimate Mem Decades Jerseys Gold-2
05ITG Ultimate Memorabilia Emblem Attic-5
05ITG Ultimate Mem Emblem Attic Gold-5
05ITG Ultimate Mem Retro Teammate Jerseys-24
05ITG Ult Mem Retro Teammates Jersey Gold-24
05ITG Ultimate Mem 3 Star of the Game Jsy-7
05ITG Ult Mem 3 Star of the Game Jsy Gold-7
05ITG Ultimate Mem Triple Threads Jerseys-6
05ITG Ultimate Mem Triple Thread Jsy Gold-6
06ITG Ultimate Memorabilia Boys Will Be Boys-9
06ITG Ultimate Memorabilia Boys Will Be Boys
Gold-9
06ITG Ultimate Memorabilia Decades-5
06ITG Ultimate Memorabilia Decades Gold-5
06ITG Ultimate Memorabilia Retro Teammates-8
06ITG Ultimate Memorabilia Retro Teammates Gold-
8

Ullmann, Christoph
02German DEL City Press-210
03German DEL-15
03German Mannheim Eagles Postcards-7
03German Mannheim Eagles Postcards-33
04German Adler Mannheim Eagles Postcards-30
04German DEL-21
05German DEL-260
05German DEL-377
06German DEL-155

Ullrich, Mike
04Vernon Vipers-12
05Vernon Vipers-20

Ullrych, Tomas
99Czech OFS-174

Ulmer, Alexander
94German First League-158

Ulmer, Jason
00Quad-City Mallards-10
01Quad-City Mallards-23
04Portland Pirates-5
05German DEL-197
06German DEL-90

Ulmer, Jeff
00SPx-183
00Titanium Draft Day Edition-167
00Titanium Draft Day Promos-167
00Upper Deck Ice-116
00Hartford Wolf Pack-26
01BAP Memorabilia-184
Emerald-184
Ruby-184
Sapphire-184
01Upper Deck Victory-381
Gold-381
01Grand Rapids Griffins-12
04Hershey Bears Patriot News-28
05German DEL-117
06German DEL-64

Ulmer, Layne
97Swift Current Broncos-15
98Swift Current Broncos-19
99Swift Current Broncos-22
02Hartford Wolf Pack-23
03Hartford Wolf Pack-25
03Pacific AHL Prospects-36
Gold-36
04SP Authentic-93
04Ultimate Collection-45
04Hartford Wolf Pack-23
05AHL All-Stars-40
06Finnish Cardset-339

Ulrich, Martin
93Swedish Semic World Champ Stickers-273
94Finnish Jaa Kiekko-237
95Austrian National Team-28
95Swedish Globe World Championships-184
95Swedish World Championships Stickers-259
96German DEL-166
99German DEL-288
00German DEL-42
01German Upper Deck-59
02German DEL City Press-61
03German Deg Metro Stars-20
03German DEL-42
04German DEL-57
04German Dusseldorf Metro Stars Postcards-22

Ulrich, Mike
04Lethbridge Hurricanes-19

Ulrich, Shawn
95Alaska Gold Kings-19
96Alaska Gold Kings-14
99Asheville Smoke-18
00Asheville Smoke-14
01Asheville Smoke-24

Ulweback, Borje
69Swedish Hockey-254

Ulwelling, Matt
02Columbia Inferno-112
03Columbia Inferno Update-55

Ulyanov, Anton
99Russian Hockey League-48

Umberger, R.J.
00Ohio State Buckeyes-15
01BAP Memorabilia Draft Redemptions-16
01Ohio State Buckeyes-18
02Ohio State Buckeyes-15
04AHL Top Prospects-38
04Philadelphia Phantoms-23
04ITG Heroes and Prospects-199
04ITG Heroes/Prospects Toronto Expo '05-199
05ITG Heroes/Prosp Toronto Expo Parallel -49
05Beehive-134
Beige -134
Blue -134
Gold-134
Red -134
Matte-134
05Black Diamond-267
05Flyers Team Issue-25
05Hot Prospects-259
En Fuego-259
Hot Materials-HMRU
Red Hot-259
White Hot-259
05Parkhurst-654
Facsimile Auto Parallel-654
05SP Authentic-192
Limited-192
Rarefied Rookies-RRRJ
05SP Game Used-183
Gold-183
05SPx-237
Spectrum-237
05The Cup-103
Autographed Rookie Patches Gold Rainbow-103
Black Rainbow Rookies-103
Masterpiece Pressplates (Artifacts)-307
Masterpiece Pressplates (Bee Hive)-134
Masterpiece Pressplates (Black Diamond)-267
Masterpiece Pressplates (Ice)-124
Masterpiece Pressplates (Rookie Update)-225
Masterpiece Pressplates SPA Autos-192
Masterpiece Pressplates (SP Game Used)-183
Masterpiece Pressplates SPx Autos-237
Masterpiece Pressplates (Trilogy)-287
Masterpiece Pressplates Ult Coll-161
Masterpiece Pressplates (Victory)-273
Masterpiece Pressplates Autographs-103
Platinum Rookies-103
05UD Artifacts-307
05UD Rookie Class-24
05Ultimate Collection-161
Gold-161
Ultimate Debut Threads Jerseys-DTJRJ
Ultimate Debut Threads Patches-DTPRJ
05Upper Deck-449
Rookie Ink-RIRU
05Upper Deck Ice-124
05Upper Deck Rookie Update-225
Inspirations Patch Rookies-225
05Upper Deck Trilogy-287
05Upper Deck Victory-273
Black-273
Gold-273
Silver-273
05Philadelphia Phantoms-23
05ITG Heroes and Prospects-49
Autographs-A-RJU
06Be A Player-18
Autographs-18
Signatures-RU
Signatures 25-20
Signatures Duals-DRU
Portraits Dual Signature Portraits-DSRU
Portraits First Exposures-FERU
Portraits Signature Portraits-SPRJ
06Black Diamond Jerseys-JRU
06Black Diamond Jerseys Black-JRU
06Black Diamond Jerseys Gold-JRU
06Black Diamond Jerseys Ruby-JRU
06Fleer-147
Tiffany-147
06Flyers Postcards-10
06O-Pee-Chee-361
Rainbow-361
06UD Toronto Fall Expo Priority Signings -PSRU
06Upper Deck-147
Exclusives Parallel-147
High Gloss Parallel-147
Game Dated Moments-GD36
Game Jerseys-JRU
Game Patches-PRU
Masterpieces-147
Signature Sensations-SSRU
06Upper Deck MVP-214
Gold Script-214
Super Script-214

Umicevic, Dragan
04Swedish Pure Skills-88
Parallel-88
05Swedish SHL Elitset-277
Gold-277
06Swedish SHL Elitset-170
Performers-2

Umisevic, Dragan
05Swedish SHL Elitset Star Potential-15

Umunna, George
99Odessa Jackalopes-18

Underhill, Jason
907th Inn. Sketch QMJHL-206

Underhill, Matt
02ECHL All-Star Southern-56
02Pee Dee Pride RBI-149
03ITG Action-668
03ITG VIP Rookie Debut-130
03Parkhurst Rookie-70
03Upper Deck Rookie Update-205
03Florence Pride-160

Undershute, Kevin
04Medicine Hat Tigers-23
05Medicine Hat Tigers-24
06Medicine Hat Tigers-23

Underwood, Jim
04Columbus Cottonmouths-21

Underwood, Joe
06Guelph Storm-3

Unger, Garry
68O-Pee-Chee-142
68Shirriff Coins-42
69O-Pee-Chee-159
70Colgate Stamps-7
70Dad's Cookies-131
70Esso Power Players-132
70O-Pee-Chee-26
Deckle-16
70Red Wings Marathon-10
70Sargent Promotions Stamps-61
70Topps-26
Topps/OPC Sticker Stamps-30
71Bazooka-19
71Blues Postcards-25
71Blues Postcards-26
71Colgate Heads-16
71Letraset Action Replays-6
71O-Pee-Chee-26
O-Pee-Chee/Topps Booklets-14
Posters-20
71Sargent Promotions Stamps-178
71Topps-26
71Toronto Sun-251
72Blues White Border-22
72O-Pee-Chee-120
72Sargent Promotions Stamps-184
72Topps-35
72Finnish Semic World Championship-191
72Swedish Semic World Championship-191
73Blues White Border-22
73Blues White Border-23
73O-Pee-Chee-15
73Topps-15
74Lipton Soup-5
74Nabisco Sugar Daddy-14
74NHL Action Stamps-252
74O-Pee-Chee NHL-197
74O-Pee-Chee NHL-237
74Topps-197
74Topps-237
75O-Pee-Chee NHL-40
75O-Pee-Chee NHL-327
75Topps-40
75Topps-327
76O-Pee-Chee NHL-68
76O-Pee-Chee NHL-260
76O-Pee-Chee NHL-393
76Topps-68
76Topps-260
77O-Pee-Chee NHL-35
77Sportscasters-1823
77Topps-35
77Finnish Sportscasters-52-1232
78Blues Postcards-24
78O-Pee-Chee-5
78O-Pee-Chee-110
78Topps-5
78Topps-110
79Flames Postcards-19
79Flames Team Issue-21
79O-Pee-Chee-33
79Topps-33
80Kings Card Night-13
80O-Pee-Chee-273
81Oilers Red Rooster-77
81O-Pee-Chee-123
82Oilers Red Rooster-77
82O-Pee-Chee-120
88Oilers Tenth Anniversary-1
89ProCards IHL-112
90ProCards AHL/IHL-368
92Blues UD Best of the Blues-27
92Tulsa Oilers-16
94Central Hockey League-108
95Central Hockey League-72
97New Mexico Scorpions-27
01Topps Archives-56
02Topps Rookie Reprints-13
02Topps Rookie Reprint Autographs-13
04ITG Franchises Canadian-33
Autographs-GU2
04ITG Franchises US West-292
Autographs-A-GU
Barn Burners-WBB4
Barn Burners Gold-WBB4
Double Memorabilia-WDM17
Double Memorabilia Gold-WDM17
Memorabilia-WSM31
Memorabilia Gold-WSM31
Original Sticks-WOS6
Original Sticks Gold-WOS6
Teammates-WTM3
Teammates Gold-WTM3
06Parkhurst-146
Autographs-146

Unger, James
02Topeka Scarecrows-12

Uniac, John
87Sudbury Wolves-14
88Kitchener Rangers-8
89Kitchener Rangers-8
90Kitchener Rangers-8
907th Inn. Sketch OHL-246
907th Inn. Sketch Memorial Cup-36
92Wheeling Thunderbirds-18
95Tallahassee Tiger Sharks-11

Uniacke, Richard
93Sault Ste. Marie Greyhounds-10
95Slapshot-361
95Sault Ste. Marie Greyhounds-23
96Sault Ste. Marie Greyhounds-26
96Sault Ste. Marie Greyhounds Autographed-26
97Austin Ice Bats-20

Unkila, Mauri
72Finnish Jaakiekko-339

Unser, Cory
98Brandon Wheat Kings-22
99Brandon Wheat Kings-23

Unsinn, Xavier
89Swedish Semic World Champ Stickers-102

Unterluggauer, Gerhard
95Swedish World Championships Stickers-263
95Brandon Wheat Kings-23
96Brandon Wheat Kings-5
01German Upper Deck-239
02German DEL City Press-62
03German Deg Metro Stars-21
03German DEL-43

Uotila, Ilmo
78Finnish SM-Liiga-68
80Finnish Mallasjuoma-61

Uotila, Pentti
65Finnish Hellas-116
66Finnish Jaakiekkosarja-199

Upshall, Randy
00Halifax Mooseheads-23
01Halifax Mooseheads-16
02Halifax Mooseheads-16
03Halifax Mooseheads-15

Upshall, Scottie
96Quebec Pee-Wee Tournament-1406
97Quebec Pee-Wee Tournament-290
00Kamloops Blazers-23
01SPx Rookie Redemption-R17
02Atomic-117
Blue-117
Gold-117
Red-117
Hobby Parallel-117
02BAP All-Star Edition-149
Gold-149
Silver-149
02BAP First Edition-439R
02BAP Memorabilia-298
Emerald-298
Ruby-298
Sapphire-298
Draft Redemptions-6
NHL All-Star Game-298
NHL All-Star Game Blue-298
NHL All-Star Game Green-298
NHL All-Star Game Red-298
02BAP Memorabilia Toronto Fall Expo-298
02BAP Signature Series-188

Autographs-188
Autographs Gold-188
Jerseys-SGJ61
Jersey Autographs-SGJ61
02BAP Ultimate Memorabilia-19
Autographs-12
Autographs Gold-12
02Bowman YoungStars-162
Gold-162
Silver-162
02Crown Royale-125
Blue-125
Purple-125
Red-125
Retail-125
Rookie Royalty-14
02ITG Used-96
02Pacific Calder-130
Silver-130
02Pacific Complete-572
Red-572
02Pacific Exclusive-183
Blue-183
Gold-183
02Pacific Heads-Up-139
02Pacific Quest for the Cup-130
Gold-130
02Parkhurst-219
Bronze-219
Gold-219
Silver-219
Jerseys-GJ58
02Parkhurst Retro-219
Minis-219
02Private Stock Reserve-170
Blue-170
Red-170
Retail-170
02SP Authentic-199
Signed Patches-PSU
02SP Game Used-85
02SPx-155
02Titanium-125
Blue-125
Red-125
Retail-125
Right on Target-14
02Topps Chrome-168
Black Border Refractors-168
Refractors-168
02Topps Heritage-151
02Topps Total-403
02UD Artistic Impressions-117
Gold-117
Common Ground-CG17
Common Ground Gold-CG17
02UD Honor Roll-158
02UD Mask Collection-176
02UD Premier Collection-75
Gold-75
Signatures Bronze-SSU
Signatures Gold-SSU
Signatures Silver-SSU
02UD Top Shelf-132
02Upper Deck-440
Exclusives-440
02Upper Deck Classic Portraits-121
02Upper Deck Rookie Update-169
02Vanguard-123
LTD-123
Prime Prospects-15
02Kamloops Blazers-16
02UD SuperStars *-276
Gold-276
03BAP Memorabilia-84
Emerald-84
Gold-84
Ruby-84
Sapphire-84
Future of the Game-FG-1
03Black Diamond-53
Black-53
Green-53
Red-53
03Crown Royale-57
Blue-57
Retail-57
03ITG Action-384
Jerseys-M87
03ITG VIP Making the Bigs-3
03Pacific-193
Blue-193
Red-193
03Pacific Calder-60
Silver-60
03Pacific Invincible-53
Blue-53
Red-53
Retail-53
03Pacific Prism-58
Blue-58
Gold-58
Red-58
03Parkhurst Rookie Road to the NHL-RNJ-10
03Parkhurst Rookie Road to the NHL Gold-RTN-10
03Parkhurst Rookie Road to the NHL Emblem-RTNE-10
03Parkhurst Rookie Road NHL Emblem Gold-RTNE-10
03Private Stock Reserve-57
Blue-57
Red-57
Retail-57
03SP Game Used Limited Threads-LTSU
03SP Game Used Limited Threads Gold-LTSU
03Upper Deck-109
Canadian Exclusives-109
HG-109
03Upper Deck MVP-244
Gold Script-244
Silver Script-244
Canadian Exclusives-244
03Upper Deck Victory-105
Bronze-105
Gold-105
Silver-105
03AHL Top Prospects-40
03Milwaukee Admirals-14
03Milwaukee Admirals Postcards-22
03Pacific AHL Prospects Gold-60
04Pacific-288
Blue-288
Red-288
04AHL Top Prospects-34
04Milwaukee Admirals-17
04ITG Heroes and Prospects-26
Autographs-SU
Combos-8
Emblems-58
Emblems Gold-58
He Shoots-He Scores Prizes-20
Jersey Autographs-58
Jerseys-58
Jerseys Gold-58
Numbers-58
Numbers Gold-58
04ITG Heroes/Prospects Toronto Expo '05-26
04ITG Heroes/Prospects Expo Heroes/Pros-26
05Parkhurst-279
Facsimile Auto Parallel-279
True Colors-TCNSH
True Colors-TCNSH
05Upper Deck Jerseys-J-SU
05Milwaukee Admirals Pepsi-20
05ITG Heroes/Prospects He Shoots/Scores-32
05ITG Heroes and Prospects Making the Big-MTB-12
06Black Diamond Jerseys-JSU
06Flyers Postcards-5
06UD Artifacts Tundra Tandems-TTHU
06UD Artifacts Tundra Tandems Black-TTHU
06UD Artifacts Tundra Tandems Blue-TTHU
06UD Artifacts Tundra Tandems Gold-TTHU
06UD Artifacts Tundra Tandems Platinum-TTHU
06UD Artifacts Tundra Tandems Red-TTHU
06UD Artifacts Tundra Tandems Dual Patches Red-TTHU
06Upper Deck Game Jerseys-JSU
06Upper Deck Game Patches-PUP

Upton, Derrell
01El Paso Buzzards-8
03Fort Worth Brahmas-15
04Fort Worth Brahmas-16

Urakin, Alexander
00Russian Hockey League-119

Uram, Marek
99Czech OFS-462
00Czech OFS-199
00Czech OFS Star Emerald-34
00Czech OFS Star Pink-34
00Czech OFS Star Violet-34
01Czech OFS-119
All Stars-7
01Czech OFS Red Inserts-RE16D
02Czech OFS Plus-123
02Czech OFS Plus All-Star Game-H20
02Czech OFS Plus Trios-T25
02Czech OFS Plus Duos-D12
02Slovakian Kvarteto-27
03Czech OFS Plus-378
03Czech OFS Plus All-Star Game-H43
03Czech OFS Plus Insert G-G9
04Czech OFS-304
Assist Leaders-12
Czech/Slovak-21
Goals Leaders-3
Points Leaders-6
05Czech HC Znojmo-14

Urbanik, Joe
03Huntsville Channel Cats-16

Urick, Brian
00Hamilton Bulldogs-13

Urkewicz, Terry
61Hamilton Red Wings-20

Uronen, Jesse
06Finnish Cardset-65

Urpalainen, Seppo
72Finnish Jaakiekko-188
80Finnish Mallasjuoma-151

Urquhart, Cory
00Quebec Remparts-23
Signed-23
01Quebec Remparts-24
03P.E.I. Rocket-24
06Hamilton Bulldogs-26

Urquhart, Mike
99UK Guildford Flames-30
00UK Guildford Flames-24
01UK Guildford Flames-22
02UK Guildford Flames-18

Urvikko, Jouko
78Finnish SM-Liiga-47
80Finnish Mallasjuoma-27

Usenko, Ivan
01Swift Current Broncos-19

Usjmakov, Slava
74Swedish Stickers-86

Uski, Jani
92Finnish Jyvas-Hyva Stickers-153
93Finnish Jyvas-Hyva Stickers-269
93Finnish SISU-298

Usov, Alexander
74Swedish Stickers-93

Ustorf, Peter
96German DEL-246

Ustorf, Stefan
92Upper Deck-371
92Classic-29
Gold-29
92Classic Four-Sport *-178
Gold-178
93Swedish Semic World Champ Stickers-159
94Portland Pirates-23
94Signature Rookies Gold Standard *-95
95Bowman-147
All-Foil-147
95Capitals Team Issue-27
95Donruss-294
95Parkhurst International-520
95Parkhurst International-538
Emerald Ice-520
Emerald Ice-538
95SP-161
95Upper Deck-502
Electric Ice-502
Electric Ice Gold-502
95Swedish Globe World Championships-224
95Portland Pirates-24
95Signature Rookies-28
Club Promos-2
Signatures-28
96Collector's Choice-284
96Collector's Edge Ice-55
Prism-55
98Las Vegas Thunder-21
99Cincinnati Cyclones-20
00Cincinnati Cyclones-7
01German Adler Mannheim Eagles Postcards-9
01German Upper Deck-180
Gate Attractions-GA9
02German DEL City Press-256
Top Scorers-TS10
03German DEL-192
03German Mannheim Eagles Postcards-8
04German Berlin Polar Bears Postcards-27
04German DEL-76
05German DEL-35
05German DEL-292
06German DEL-24
Team Leaders-TL10

Ustrnul, Libor
99UD Prospects-13
00UD CHL Prospects-22
01Plymouth Whalers-1
02Czech DS-42
02Czech DS-63
02Chicago Wolves-24
03Chicago Wolves-21
04Chicago Wolves-7
05Czech HC Karlovy Vary-16
06Czech OFS-44

Ustyugov, Anatoli
98Russian Hockey League-73
99Russian Hockey League-92
00Russian Hockey League-12

Ustyuzhanin, Dmitry
99Knoxville Speed-22
00Knoxville Speed-14

Uusikartano, Aki
99Finnish Cardset-228
00Finnish Cardset-17
01Finnish Cardset-304
02Finnish Cardset-284
03Finnish Cardset-139
04Finnish Cardset-199
Parallel-146
05Finnish Cardset -173
06Finnish Cardset-219

Uusikartano, Jari
72Finnish Jaakiekko-319

Uusimaa, Veli-Matti
71Finnish Suomi Stickers-355
72Finnish Jaakiekko-356

Uusitalo, Per-Olof
70Swedish Hockey-97
71Swedish Hockey-180

Uusitalo, Ville
06Finnish Cardset-297

Uvajev, Vjatjeslav
91Finnish Semic World Champ Stickers-86
91Swedish Semic World Champ Stickers-86

Uvira, Eduard
82Swedish Semic VM Stickers-86
83Swedish Semic VM Stickers-86
94German DEL-251
95German DEL-245
99German EV Landshut-4

Vaahtoluoto, Timo
71Finnish Suomi Stickers-338

Vaananen, Auvo
78Finnish SM-Liiga-97
80Finnish Mallasjuoma-30

Vaananen, Jani
01Finnish Cardset-375

Vaananen, Jarkko
98Finnish Kerailysarja-115
99Finnish Cardset-61
00Finnish Cardset-229
01Finnish Cardset-316

Vaananen, Ossi
98Finnish Kerailysarja-105
99Finnish Cardset-259
00BAP Memorabilia-484
Emerald-484
Ruby-484
Sapphire-484
00BAP Signature Series-258
Emerald-258
Ruby-258
Sapphire-258
Autographs-249
Autographs Gold-249
00Private Stock-139
Gold-139
Premiere Date-139
Retail-139
Silver-139
PS-2001 Rookies-18
00SP Authentic-159
00SPx-184
00Stadium Club-252
00Titanium Draft Day Edition-171
00Titanium Draft Day Promos-171
00Topps Premier Plus-116
Blue Ice-116
00Upper Deck-425
Exclusives Tier 1-425
Exclusives Tier 2-425
00Upper Deck Ice-119
00Vanguard-141
Pacific Proofs-141
00Finnish Cardset-39
01BAP Memorabilia-102
Emerald-102
Ruby-102
Sapphire-102
01BAP Signature Series-105
Autographs-105
Autographs Gold-105
01Coyotes Team Issue-21
01Parkhurst-142
01Finnish Cardset-164
02BAP Sig Series Auto Buybacks 2001-105
02Bowman YoungStars-112
Gold-112
Silver-112
Autographs-OV
Jerseys-OV
Patches-OV
Double Stuff-OV
Triple Stuff-OV
Rivals-OVHT
Rivals Patches-5
Sticks-OV
02Coyotes Team Issue-3
02Pacific Complete-185
Red-185
02Finnish Cardset-295
02Finnish Cardset Solid Gold Six-Pack-3
03Coyotes Postcards-26
03O-Pee-Chee-36
03OPC Blue-36
03OPC Gold-36
03OPC Red-36
03Topps-36
Blue-36
Gold-36
Red-36
03Topps C55-84
Minis-84
Minis American Back-84
Minis American Back Red-84
Minis Bazooka Back-84
Minis Brooklyn Back-84
Minis Hat Trick Back-84
Minis O Canada Back-84
Minis O Canada Back Red-84
Minis Stanley Cup Back-84
03Topps Traded-TT42
Blue-TT42
Gold-TT42
Red-TT42
04Finnish Cardset-242
04Swedish Pure Skills-118
Parallel-118
Professional Power-OV
05Finnish Cardset -56
Finnish Cardset Magicmakers-10
06Avalanche Team Postcards-20

Vaarasuo, Ilkka
04Finnish Cardset-249
05Finnish Cardset -98

Vaatamoinen, Antero
70Finnish Jaakiekko-275
80Finnish Mallasjuoma-145

Vaatamoinen, Matti
72Finnish Jaakiekko-189

Vaatamoinen, Timo
65Finnish Hellas-91
66Finnish Jaakiekkosarja-91
72Finnish Jaakiekko-190

Vacatko, Vladimir
82Swedish Semic VM Stickers-115

Vacca, Pietro
94German First League-34

Vacheron, Alexis
98Swiss Power Play Stickers-137
99Swiss Panini Stickers-286
00Swiss Panini Stickers-62
00Swiss Slapshot Mini-Cards-HCCF7
01Swiss HNL-290
02Swiss HNL-200

Vachon, Alexandre
02Rimouski Oceanic-22
03Rimouski Oceanic-21
03Rimouski Oceanic Sheets-4
04Rimouski Oceanic-2
04Victoriaville Tigres-30

Vachon, Luc
93Quebec Pee-Wee Tournament-912

Vachon, Marc
89Johnstown Chiefs-32
93Flint Generals-16
98Huntsville Channel Cats-18
99Tupelo T-Rex-5
06Drummondville Voltigeurs-20

Vachon, Mathieu
03St. Georges de Beauce Garaga-19
04St Georges de Beauce Garaga-11

Vachon, Nicholas
93Knoxville Cherokees-19
95Phoenix Roadrunners-19
97Long Beach Ice Dogs-16

Vachon, Pat
85London Knights-25
86London Knights-7

Vachon, Rogie
64Canadiens Postcards-22
67Canadiens IGA-30
67Post Flip Books-2
67Topps-75
67York Action Octagons-5
67York Action Octagons-9
67York Action Octagons-10
67York Action Octagons-11
67York Action Octagons-15
67York Action Octagons-31
67York Action Octagons-36
68Canadiens IGA-30
68Canadiens Postcards BW-19
68O-Pee-Chee-164
68O-Pee-Chee-212
68Post Marbles-28
68Shirriff Coins-76
69Canadiens Postcards Color-31
69O-Pee-Chee-165
70Canadiens Pins-17
70Colgate Stamps-85
70Dad's Cookies-132
70Esso Power Players-1
70O-Pee-Chee-49
Deckle-22
70Sargent Promotions Stamps-100
70Topps-49
71Canadiens Postcards-25
71Letraset Action Replays-1
71O-Pee-Chee-156
71Sargent Promotions Stamps-68
71Toronto Sun-166
72O-Pee-Chee-100
72Sargent Promotions Stamps-87
72Topps-51
72Finnish Semic World Championship-232
72Swedish Semic World Championship-232
73O-Pee-Chee-64
73Topps-64
74Lipton Soup-7
74NHL Action Stamps-116
74O-Pee-Chee NHL-235
74Topps-235
75O-Pee-Chee NHL-160
75O-Pee-Chee NHL-213
75O-Pee-Chee NHL-297
75Topps-160
75Topps-213
75Topps-297
76O-Pee-Chee NHL-40
76Topps-40
77Coca-Cola-27
77O-Pee-Chee NHL-8
77O-Pee-Chee NHL-160
77Sportscasters-4306
77Topps-8
77Topps-160
77Topps/O-Pee-Chee Glossy-21
Square-21
77Finnish Sportscasters-50-1197
78O-Pee-Chee-20
78Topps-20
79O-Pee-Chee-235
79Red Wings Postcards-17
79Topps-235
80O-Pee-Chee-110
80O-Pee-Chee-168
80Topps-110
80Topps-168
81O-Pee-Chee-10
81O-Pee-Chee Stickers-47
81Topps-E74
82O-Pee-Chee-23
82Post Cereal-1
91Pinnacle-387
French-387
92Future Trends '76 Canada Cup-154
92Future Trends '76 Canada Cup-185
92Future Trends '76 Canada Cup-195
93Kings Forum-8
94Hockey Wit-24
94Parkhurst Tall Boys Future Stars-FS5
95Parkhurst '66-67-75
Coins-75
98Kings LA Times Coins-6
01Between the Pipes Vintage Memorabilia-VM18
01Greats of the Game-68
Autographs-68
01Upper Deck Legends-29
01Upper Deck Vintage Jerseys-GGRV
02BAP Ultimate Mem Storied Franchise-20
02Between the Pipes Goalie Autographs-36
03Parkhurst Original Six Montreal-50
04ITG Franchises Canadian-46
Autographs-RV2
Original Sticks-OS9
Original Sticks Gold-OS9
04ITG Franchises He Shoots/Scores Prizes-32
04ITG Franchises US East-333
04ITG Franchises US West-235
Autographs-A-RV1
04ITG Ultimate Memorabilia-144
04ITG Ultimate Memorabilia-157
Gold-144
Gold-157
04UD Legendary Signatures-76
Autographs-RV
04ITG Heroes and Prospects-145
Autographs-RV
Hero Memorabilia-22
04ITG Heroes/Prospects Toronto Expo '05-145
04ITG Heroes/Prospects Expo Heroes/Pros-145
05Beehive Signature Scrapbook-SSRV
05Between the Pipes-23
Autographs-A-RV
Gloves-GUG-6
05ITG Ultimate Memorabilia Level 1-84
05ITG Ultimate Memorabilia Level 2-84
05ITG Ultimate Memorabilia Level 3-84
05ITG Ultimate Memorabilia Level 4-84
05ITG Ultimate Memorabilia Level 5-84
05SP Authentic Sign of the Times Quads-QGTVD
05SP Game Used Statscriptions-ST-RV
05SPx-122
Spectrum-122
Xcitement Legends-XL-RV
Xcitement Legends Gold-XL-RV
Xcitement Legends Spectrum-XL-RV
05The Cup-51
Gold-51
Black Rainbow-51
Emblems of Endorsement-EERV
Limited Logos-LLRV
Masterpiece Pressplates-51
Noble Numbers Dual-DNNCV
Noble Numbers Dual-DNNDV
Patch Variation-P51
Patch Variation Autographs-AP51
05Upper Deck Notable Numbers-N-RV
05ITG Heroes and Prospects Hero Mem-HM-55
06Between The Pipes-100
06Between The Pipes-138
Autographs-ARV
Complete Jersey-CJ16
Complete Jersey Gold-CJ16
Double Memorabilia-DM01
Double Memorabilia Gold-DM01
Emblems-GUE01
Emblems Gold-GUE01
Emblems Autographs-GUE01
Jerseys-GUJ01
Jerseys Gold-GUJ01
Jerseys Autographs-GUJ01
Numbers-GUN01
Numbers Gold-GUN01
Numbers Autographs-GUN01
Playing For Your Country-PC14
Playing For Your Country Gold-PC14
Shooting Gallery-SG01
Shooting Gallery Gold-SG01
Stick and Jersey-SJ36
Stick and Jersey Gold-SJ36
Stick and Jersey Autographs-SJ36
06ITG International Ice-135
Gold-135
Autographs-ARV
Cornerstones-IC09
Cornerstones Gold-IC09
Goaltending Glory-GG10
Goaltending Glory Gold-GG10
Quad Patch-QP03
Quad Patch Gold-QP03
Triple Memorabilia-TM01
Triple Memorabilia Gold-TM01
06ITG Ultimate Memorabilia-123
Artist Proof-123
Autos-34
Autos Gold-34
Jerseys Autos-62
Jerseys Autos Gold-62
Sticks and Jerseys-13
Sticks and Jerseys Gold-13
06SP Authentic Sign of the Times Duals-STDV
06SP Authentic Sign of the Times Quads-ST4ECVP
06SP Game Used Authentic Fabrics Quads-AF4FCSW
06SP Game Used Authentic Fabrics Quads Patches-AF4FCSW
06SP Game Used Letter Marks-LMRV
06SP Game Used SIGnificance-SRV
06SPx SPxcitement-X49
06SPx SPxcitement Spectrum-X49
06The Cup-41
Autographed Foundations-CQRV
Black Rainbow-41
Foundations-CQRV
Gold-41
Limited Logos-LLRV
Masterpiece Pressplates-41
Signature Patches-SPRV
Stanley Cup Signatures-CSRV
06Ultimate Collection Autographed Jerseys-AJ-RV
06Ultimate Collection Autographed Patches-AJ-RV
06Ultimate Collection Jerseys Dual-UJ2-DV
06Ultimate Collection Patches Dual-UJ2-DV
06Upper Deck Sweet Shot Sweet Stitches-SSRV
06Upper Deck Sweet Shot Sweet Stitches Duals-SSRV
06Upper Deck Sweet Shot Sweet Stitches Triples-SSRV
06Upper Deck Trilogy Scripts-TSRV

Vachon, Sebastien
93Quebec Pee-Wee Tournament-927

Vachulka, Josef
99Czech Score Blue 2000-110
99Czech Score Red Ice 2000-110

Vadenberghe, Mike
907th Inn. Sketch WHL-225A
907th Inn. Sketch WHL-225B

Vadnais, Carol
64Canadiens Postcards-21
67Canadiens IGA-17
67Topps-9
68O-Pee-Chee-81
68Shirriff Coins-114
68Topps-81
69O-Pee-Chee-82
Four-in-One-4
Stamps-26
69Topps-82
70Colgate Stamps-86
70Dad's Cookies-133
70Esso Power Players-95
70O-Pee-Chee-70
Deckle-36
70Sargent Promotions Stamps-130
70Topps-70
Topps/OPC Sticker Stamps-31
71O-Pee-Chee-46
71Sargent Promotions Stamps-137
71Topps-46
71Toronto Sun-60
72O-Pee-Chee-39
72Sargent Promotions Stamps-25
72Topps-85
72Finnish Semic World Championship-181
72Swedish Semic World Championship-181
73O-Pee-Chee-58
73Topps-58
74NHL Action Stamps-23
74O-Pee-Chee NHL-165
74Topps-165
75O-Pee-Chee NHL-27A
75O-Pee-Chee NHL-27B
75Topps-27
76O-Pee-Chee NHL-257
76O-Pee-Chee NHL-390
76Topps-257
77O-Pee-Chee NHL-154
77Topps-154
78O-Pee-Chee-85
78Topps-85
79O-Pee-Chee-145
79Topps-145
80O-Pee-Chee-57
80Topps-57
81O-Pee-Chee-236
82O-Pee-Chee-148
83O-Pee-Chee Stickers-224
83Topps Stickers-224
04ITG Franchises US West-261
Autographs-A-CV

Vadnais, John
03Lincoln Stars Update-31
03Waterloo Blackhawks-13
04Lincoln Stars-3

Vafides, Tim
93Quebec Pee-Wee Tournament-650

Vagner, Martin
01Hull Olympiques-13
02Hull Olympiques-13
03Gatineau Olympiques-25
03Hull Olympiques Memorial Cup-19
06Czech HC Ceske Budejovice Postcards-11
06Czech OFS-19

Vaha-Ruohola, Kimmo
00Finnish Cardset-155
01Finnish Cardset-44

Vahalahti, Ville
99Finnish Cardset-142
00Finnish Cardset-341
01Finnish Cardset-145
02Finnish Cardset-134
03Finnish Cardset-166
04Finnish Cardset-179
Parallel-133
05Finnish Cardset -159
06Finnish Cardset-162

Vahanen, Kim
93Finnish SISU-238
03UK Basingstoke Bison-7

Vahanen, Timo
70Finnish Jaakiekko-383

Vaic, Lubomir
97Paramount-191
Copper-191
Dark Grey-191
Emerald Green-191
Ice Blue-191
Red-191
Silver-191
95Syracuse Crunch-12
00German Berlin Polar Bears Postcards-21
00German DEL-68
02Finnish Cardset-285
03Russian Metallurg Magnitogorsk-9
03Russian SL-37
04Czech OFS-82
05Czech HC Liberec-15
06Czech HC Liberec Postcards-10
06Czech OFS-105
All Stars-12
Goals Leaders-7
Points Leaders-2

Vaihinen, Kari
80Finnish Mallasjuoma-181

Vaihinen, Risto
70Finnish Jaakiekko-358

Vail, Eric
74NHL Action Stamps-1
74O-Pee-Chee NHL-391
75O-Pee-Chee NHL-135
75O-Pee-Chee NHL-313
75Topps-135
75Topps-313
76O-Pee-Chee NHL-51
76Topps-51
77O-Pee-Chee NHL-168
77Topps-168
78Flames Majik Market-27
78O-Pee-Chee-129
78Topps-129
79Flames Postcards-20
79Flames Team Issue-22
79O-Pee-Chee-188
79Topps-188
80Flames Postcards-22
80O-Pee-Chee-15
80Pepsi-Cola Caps-19
80Topps-15
81O-Pee-Chee-38
81O-Pee-Chee Stickers-220
81Topps-43
82O-Pee-Chee-97
04ITG Franchises US East-305
Autographs-A-EV

Vaillancourt, Denis
93Quebec Pee-Wee Tournament-1073

Vaillancourt, Mike
99Sudbury Wolves-24
99Sudbury Wolves-26
00Sudbury Wolves-9

Vaillancourt, Nicolas
93Quebec Pee-Wee Tournament-1034

Vaillancourt, Sarah
04Canadian Womens World Championship Team-21
06ITG Going For Gold-18
06ITG Going For Gold Samples-18
06ITG Going For Gold Autographs-AV
06ITG Going For Gold Jerseys-GUJ18

Vaillullin, Marat
03Russian Hockey League-236

Vainio, Niko
04Peterborough Petes Postcards-10

Vainio, Risto
66Finnish Jaakiekkosarja-66
70Finnish Jaakiekko-152
71Finnish Suomi Stickers-203
72Finnish Jaakiekko-240
73Finnish Jaakiekko-275

Vainio, Seppo
65Finnish Hellas-21

Vainiola, Ville-Vesa
06Finnish Cardset-113

Vair, Steve
10Sweet Caporal Postcards-18
11C55-18
12C57-10

Vaisanen, Hannu
04Finnish Cardset-38
Parallel-28
05Finnish Cardset -32
06Finnish Cardset-36

Vaisanen, Matti
70Finnish Jaakiekko-117
71Finnish Suomi Stickers-127
72Finnish Jaakiekko-99
72Finnish Panda Toronto-16
73Finnish Jaakiekko-147

Vaisanen, Pertti
70Finnish Jaakiekko-345

Vaive, Jeff
81Ottawa 67's-24
82Ottawa 67's-25
94German First League-59

Vaive, Rick
79Canucks Royal Bank-22
80Maple Leafs Postcards-28
80O-Pee-Chee-242
80Pepsi-Cola Caps-100
80Topps-242
81Maple Leafs Postcards-23
81O-Pee-Chee-310
81O-Pee-Chee Stickers-101
81Topps-44
82Maple Leafs Postcards-36
82Maple Leafs Postcards-37
82O-Pee-Chee-314
82O-Pee-Chee-335
82O-Pee-Chee-336
82O-Pee-Chee Stickers-62
82O-Pee-Chee Stickers-63
82Post Cereal-18
82Topps Stickers-62
82Topps Stickers-63
83Esso-21
83Maple Leafs Postcards-26
83NHL Key Tags-117
83O-Pee-Chee-323
83O-Pee-Chee-324
83O-Pee-Chee-343
83O-Pee-Chee Stickers-25
83O-Pee-Chee Stickers-26
83Puffy Stickers-2
83Topps Stickers-25
83Topps Stickers-26
83Vachon-100
84Kellogg's Accordion Discs-6
84Kellogg's Accordion Discs Singles-38
84Maple Leafs Postcards-24
84O-Pee-Chee-313
84O-Pee-Chee-368
84O-Pee-Chee Stickers-11
84O-Pee-Chee Stickers-12
84O-Pee-Chee Stickers-139
847-Eleven Discs-47
84Topps-138
85Maple Leafs Postcards-30
85Maple Leafs Postcards-31
85O-Pee-Chee-106
85O-Pee-Chee Stickers-6
857-Eleven Credit Cards-18
85Topps-106
86Kraft Drawings-77
86Maple Leafs Postcards-21
86O-Pee-Chee-191
86O-Pee-Chee Stickers-138
86Topps-191
87Blackhawks Coke-26
87O-Pee-Chee-155
87O-Pee-Chee Stickers-155
87Panini Stickers-228
87Pro-Sport All-Stars-9
87Topps-155
88Blackhawks Coke-21
88O-Pee-Chee-77
88O-Pee-Chee Stickers-9
88Panini Stickers-31
88Sabres Blue Shield-28
88Topps-77
89O-Pee-Chee-125
89O-Pee-Chee Stickers-256
89Panini Stickers-206
89Sabres Blue Shield-24
89Sabres Campbell's-27
89Topps-125
90Bowman-250
Tiffany-250
90O-Pee-Chee-148
90Panini Stickers-23
90Pro Set-30
90Sabres Blue Shield-25
90Sabres Campbell's-29
90Score-103
Canadian-103
90Topps-148
Tiffany-148
90Upper Deck-376
French-376
91Bowman-39
91O-Pee-Chee-457
91Panini Stickers-297
91Pro Set-26
French-26
91Sabres Blue Shield-23
91Sabres Pepsi/Campbell's-23
91Score American-26
91Score Canadian Bilingual-26
91Score Canadian English-26
91Stadium Club-13
91Topps-457
91Upper Deck-179
French-179
92Hamilton Canucks-28
95South Carolina Stingrays-1
96South Carolina Stingrays-NNO
00Mississauga Ice Dogs-26
01Upper Deck Legends-61
02Maple Leafs Platinum Collection-74
Autographs-74
02UD Foundations Canadian Heroes-CRV
02UD Foundations Canadian Heroes Gold-CRV
02UD Foundations Canadian Heroes Silver-C-RV
02UD Foundations Power Stations-SRV
02UD Foundations Power Stations Gold-SRV
02UD Foundations Power Stations Silver-S-RV
03ITG Toronto Fall Expo Forever Rivals-FR4
03Parkhurst Original Six Toronto-41
03Parkhurst Original Six Toronto-77
03Parkhurst Original Six Toronto-96
Autographs-12
Memorabilia-TM58
Memorabilia-TM62
04ITG Franchises Canadian-109
Autographs-RVA
Barn Burners-BB4
Barn Burners Gold-BB4
Memorabilia-SM31
Memorabilia Gold-SM31
04ITG Franchises Update-498
04ITG Ultimate Memorabilia Original Six-7
05ITG Ultimate Mem 3 Star of the Game Jsy-21
05ITG Ult.Mem 3 Star of the Game Jsy Gold-21
05SP Game Used Heritage Classic-HC-RV
05SP Game Used Heritage Classic Autos-HCA-RV
05SP Game Used Heritage Classic Patches-HCP-RV
05SP GameUsed Heritage Classic Patch Auto-HAP-RV
06Parkhurst-148
06Parkhurst-210
Autographs-148
Autographs-210
Autographs Dual-DADR
Autographs Dual-DASV
06UD Artifacts-138
Blue-138
Gold-138
Platinum-138
Radiance-138
Red-138
Treasured Patches Black-TSRV
Treasured Patches Blue-TSRV
Treasured Patches Gold-TSRV
Treasured Patches Platinum-TSRV
Treasured Patches Red-TSRV
Treasured Swatches-TSRV
Treasured Swatches Black-TSRV
Treasured Swatches Blue-TSRV
Treasured Swatches Gold-TSRV
Treasured Swatches Platinum-TSRV
Treasured Swatches Red-TSRV
Treasured Swatches Autographed Black-TSRV
Tundra Tandems-TTSV
Tundra Tandems Black-TTSV
Tundra Tandems Blue-TTSV
Tundra Tandems Gold-TTSV
Tundra Tandems Platinum-TTSV
Tundra Tandems Red-TTSV
Tundra Tandems Dual Patches Red-TTSV
06Upper Deck Sweet Shot Signature Shots/Saves Sticks-SSSRV
06Upper Deck Trilogy Scripts-TSVA

Vak, Tomas
98Czech OFS-382
99Czech OFS-100
01Czech OFS-257
02Czech OFS Plus-79
03Czech OFS Plus-37
04Czech OFS-261
05Czech HC Ceski Budejovice-15
06Czech HC Ceske Budejovice Postcards-12
06Czech OFS-20

Vakhrushev, Alexei
99Russian Hockey League-103

Vakiparta, Erkki
70Finnish Jaakiekko-207
71Finnish Suomi Stickers-95
72Finnish Jaakiekko-260
72Finnish Panda Toronto-47
73Finnish Jaakiekko-258
78Finnish SM-Liiga-234
80Finnish Mallasjuoma-210

Vakkilainen, Juuso
01Finnish Cardset-332

Vala, Ales
99Czech Score Blue 2000-74
99Czech Score Red Ice 2000-74
02Czech OFS Plus-341

Vala, Petr
97Seattle Thunderbirds-17
98Czech OFS-32
99Czech DS-14
99Czech OFS-218
00Czech DS Extraliga-58
00Czech OFS-363
01Czech OFS-243
02Czech OFS Plus All-Star Game-H21
03Czech OFS Plus-15
04Czech OFS-20

Valabik, Boris
03Kitchener Rangers-24
04ITG Top Prospects Spring Expo-14
04Kitchener Rangers-3
04ITG Heroes and Prospects-56
Autographs-BV
Top Prospects-14
04ITG Heroes/Prospects Toronto Expo '05-56
04ITG Heroes/Prospects Expo Heroes/Pros-56
05Extreme Top Prospects Signature Edition-S29
05Kitchener Rangers-10
06AHL Top Prospects-10

Valaitis, Paul
99Prince George Cougars-22

Valasek, Horst
94Czech APS Extraliga-297
95Czech APS Extraliga-1
96Czech APS Extraliga-25

Valcak, Patrik
04Lincoln Stars-22

Valcic, Mark
93Quebec Pee-Wee Tournament-1410

Valdix, Andreas
02Swedish Malmo Red Hawks-19
03Swedish Elite-247
Silver-247
04Swedish Elitset-232
Future Stars-7
Gold-232
Signatures-2
04Swedish Malmo Red Hawks-17

Valecko, Tomas
04Slovakian Poprad Team Set-13

Valeev, Igor
99Swift Current Broncos-23

01Worcester Icecats-6
02Worcester IceCats-18

Valek, Oldrich
89Swedish Semic World Champ Stickers-197
92Norwegian Elite Series-68
92Norwegian Elite Series-196
93Finnish SISU-289
94Czech APS Extraliga-179

Valenta, Peter
907th Inn. Sketch QMJHL-6
917th Inn. Sketch QMJHL-224

Valente, Stephen
05Quebec Remparts-3
05Quebec Remparts Signature Series-3
06Drummondville Voltigeurs-17

Valenti, Maren
98German DEL-157

Valenti, Ronny
03St. Jean Mission-26

Valenti, Sven
94German DEL-294
95German DEL-285
98German DEL-262
99German Bundesliga 2-38
02German DEL City Press-188
04German DEL-199
05German DEL-191

Valentine, Chris
81Capitals Team Issue-17
82Capitals Team Issue-24
820-Pee-Chee-373
820-Pee-Chee Stickers-155
82Post Cereal-20
82Topps Stickers-155
94German DEL-82
95German DEL-88
98German DEL-86
99German Adler Mannheim Eagles Postcards-26
99German DEL-24

Valette, Craig
03Cleveland Barons-21
04Cleveland Barons-24
05Cleveland Barons-25

Valicevic, Chris
93Greensboro Monarchs-14
95Louisiana Ice Gators-18
96Louisiana Ice Gators-18
96Louisiana Ice Gators II-19
98ECHL All-Star Southern Conference-14
98Louisiana Ice Gators-20
99ECHL All-Star Southern Conference-4
99Louisiana Ice Gators-16
01Louisiana Ice Gators-24

Valicevic, Rob
91Lake Superior State Lakers-25
92Lake Superior State Lakers-30
95Louisiana Ice Gators-19
95Louisiana Ice Gators Playoffs-20
98IHL All-Star Western Conference-10
99Black Diamond-50
Diamond Cut-50
Final Cut-50
99Pacific Prism-78
Holographic Blue-78
Holographic Gold-78
Holographic Mirror-78
Holographic Purple-78
Premiere Date-78
99SP Authentic-48
99Topps Premier Plus-85
Parallel-85
99Ultimate Victory-49
1/1-49
Parallel-49
Parallel 100-49
99Upper Deck MVP SC Edition-99
Gold Script-99
Silver Script-99
Super Script-99
00Paramount-138
Copper-138
Gold-138
Holo-Gold-138
Holo-Silver-138
Ice Blue-138
Premiere Date-138
00Upper Deck-98
Exclusives Tier 1-98
Exclusives Tier 2-98
01Manchester Monarchs-11B
02Cincinnati Mighty Ducks-B-8
03Stars Postcards-29
05German DEL-341
06German DEL-102

Valiharju, Sakari
70Finnish Jaakiekko-384

Valikangas, Matti
66Finnish Jaakiekkosarja-220

Valila, Mika
92Finnish Jyvas-Hyva Stickers-129
93Finnish Jyvas-Hyva Stickers-238
93Finnish SISU-197
95Finnish Semic World Championships-34

Valimaki, Jyrki
70Finnish Jaakiekko-364

Valimaki, Teppo
72Finnish Jaakiekko-359

Valimont, Carl
89ProCards IHL-184
90ProCards AHL/IHL-325
91ProCards-603
95Houston Aeros-22

Valioja, Esa
80Finnish Mallasjuoma-165

Valiots, Jaak
91Rayside-Balfour Jr. Canadians-20

Valipirtti, Ole
98Danish Hockey League-45
99Danish Hockey League-27

Valiquette, Jack
76Maple Leafs Postcards-21
760-Pee-Chee NHL-294
77Maple Leafs Postcards-17
770-Pee-Chee NHL-64
77Topps-64
780-Pee-Chee-391
790-Pee-Chee-229
79Rockies Team Issue-23
79Topps-229
800-Pee-Chee-108
80Topps-108
04ITG Franchises US West-192
Autographs-A-JVA

Valiquette, Steve
94Sudbury Wolves Police-27
95Slapshot-382
95Sudbury Wolves-18
95Sudbury Wolves Police-23
96Sudbury Wolves-23
96Sudbury Wolves Police-25
97Sudbury Wolves Police-23
98Hampton Roads Admirals-23
99Lowell Lock Monsters-20
00BAP Memorabilia-5
Emerald-5
Ruby-5
Sapphire-5
Promos-5
00BAP Mem Chicago Sportsfest Copper-5
00BAP Memorabilia Chicago Sportsfest Blue-5
00BAP Memorabilia Chicago Sportsfest Gold-5
00BAP Memorabilia Chicago Sportsfest Ruby-5
00BAP Memorabilia Chicago Sun-Times Ruby-5
00BAP Memorabilia Chicago Sun-Times Gold-5
00BAP Mem Chicago Sun-Times Sapphire-5
00BAP Mem Toronto Fall Expo Copper-5
00BAP Memorabilia Toronto Fall Expo Gold-5
00BAP Memorabilia Toronto Fall Expo Ruby-5
00Black Diamond-81
Gold-81
000-Pee-Chee-321
000-Pee-Chee Parallel-321
00Pacific-256
Copper-256
Gold-256
Ice Blue-256
Premiere Date-256
00Paramount-158
Copper-158
Gold-158
Holo-Gold-158
Holo-Silver-158
Ice Blue-158
Premiere Date-158
00Revolution-93
Blue-93
Premiere Date-93
Red-93
00SPx-102
Spectrum-102
00Topps/OPC-321
Parallel-321
00Topps Chrome-216
OPC Refractors-216
Refractors-216
00Upper Deck-191
Exclusives Tier 1-191
Exclusives Tier 2-191
00Upper Deck Ice-60
Immortals-60
Legends-60
Stars-60
00Upper Deck MVP-199
First Stars-199
Second Stars-199
Third Stars-199
00Upper Deck Victory-266
00Upper Deck Vintage-386
02Between the Pipes-107
Gold-107
Silver-107
03Pacific AHL Prospects-91
Gold-91
04Hartford Wolf Pack-24
06Hartford Wolf Pack-11

Valis, Lindsay
907th Inn. Sketch WHL-10

Valivaara, Jyrki
98Finnish Kerailysarja-125
99Finnish Cardset-69
00Finnish Cardset-48
01Finnish Cardset-339
02Finnish Cardset-294
03Swedish Elite-214
Silver-214
04Swedish Elitset-63
Gold-63
05Swedish SHL Elitset-73
06Swedish SHL Elitset-72

Valk, Garry
90Canucks Mohawk-29
90Upper Deck-530
French-530
90ProCards AHL/IHL-322
91Bowman-314
91Canucks Autograph Cards-24
910-Pee-Chee-117
91Pinnacle-291
French-291
91Pro Set-499
French-499
91Score American-195
91Score Canadian Bilingual-195
91Score Canadian English-195
91Stadium Club-318
91Topps-117
91Upper Deck-152
French-152
92Canucks Road Trip Art-22
92Pinnacle-181
French-181
92Score-355
Canadian-355
92Stadium Club-493
92Topps-383
Gold-383G
92Upper Deck-114
92North Dakota Fighting Sioux-39
93Donruss-401
93OPC Premier-354
Gold-354
93Parkhurst-4
Emerald Ice-4
93PowerPlay-286
93Score-641
Gold-641
Canadian-641
Canadian Gold-641
93Stadium Club-407
Members Only Master Set-407
First Day Issue-407
93Topps/OPC Premier-354
Gold-354
93Upper Deck-515
94Be A Player-R116
Signature Cards-118
94Canada Games NHL POGS-370
94Donruss-198
94Ducks Carl's Jr.-8
94Flair-7
94Leaf-206
94OPC Premier-372
Special Effects-372
94Parkhurst Vintage-V19
94Parkhurst SE-SE7
Gold-SE7
94Pinnacle-119
Artist's Proofs-119
Rink Collection-119
94Stadium Club-89
Members Only Master Set-89
First Day Issue-89
Super Team Winner Cards-89
94Topps/OPC Premier-372
Special Effects-372
94Ultra-253
94Upper Deck-282
Electric Ice-282
Ice Gallery-IG12
SP Inserts-SP3
SP Inserts Die Cuts-SP3
95Ducks Team Issue-5
95Parkhurst International-5
Emerald Ice-5
95Pro Magnets-45
96Be A Player-155
Autographs-155
Autographs Silver-155
96Ducks Team Issue-28
96NHL Pro Stamps-45
97Score Penguins-12
Platinum-12
Premier-12
99Kraft Overtime Winners-2
99Maple Leafs Pizza Pizza-4
99Pacific-418
Copper-418
Emerald Green-418
Gold-418
Ice Blue-418
Premiere Date-418
Red-418
00Topps Gold Label Class 1-100
Gold-100
00Topps Gold Label Class 2-100
00Topps Gold Label Class 2 Gold-100
00Topps Gold Label Class 3-100
00Topps Gold Label Class 3 Gold-100
01Topps Reserve-84

Valk, Phil
91British Columbia JHL-92
92British Columbia JHL-115
97Mobile Mysticks-12
97Mobile Mysticks Kellogg's-19
99Corpus Christi IceRays-23

Valkeapaa, Pertti
72Finnish Jaakiekko-77
72Finnish Jaakiekko-207
72Finnish Hellas-18
73Finnish Jaakiekko-171
74Finnish Jenkki-21
74Swedish Semic World Champ Stickers-95
78Finnish SM-Liiga-4
78Finnish SM-Liiga-180
80Finnish Mallasjuoma-158
05Finnish Tappara Legendat-18

Valko, Lukas
01Czech OFS-70
02Czech OFS Plus-80

Valko, Pavol
99Czech OFS-219
99Czech OFS-461
00Czech OFS-194

Valkonen, Pertti
66Finnish Jaakiekkosarja-108

Vallant, Rene
93Quebec Pee-Wee Tournament-1539

Vallee, Sebastien
95Signature Rookies-55
Signatures-55
98Thetford Mines Coyotes-8

Vallerand, Marc-Olivier
06Quebec Remparts-24

Valley, Mike
00Louisiana Ice Gators-16
03Peoria Rivermen-18

Valliere, Michel
93Swedish Semic World Champ Stickers-250
94Finnish Jaa Kiekko-211
94French National Team-32
95Swedish Globe World Championships-200
95Swedish World Championships Stickers-97
96German DEL-316
96Swedish Semic Wien-184
98German DEL-263

Vallieres, David
97Peoria Rivermen-18
98Kansas City Blades-21
99Kansas City Blades Supercuts-19
00UK Sekonda Superleague-84
00Florida Everblades-24

Vallieres, Mario
93Quebec Pee-Wee Tournament-1028

Vallin, Ari
98Finnish Kerailysarja-56
99Finnish Cardset-316
00Finnish Cardset-141
01Finnish Cardset-249
02Finnish Cardset-135
03Finnish Cardset-86
04Finnish Cardset-94
Parallel-70
05Finnish Cardset -268
06Finnish Cardset-94

Valliquette, Brett
06Plymouth Whalers-24

Vallis, Lindsay
91ProCards-82
92Fredericton Canadiens-26
93Fredericton Canadiens-28
93Classic Pro Prospects-41
97Bakersfield Fog-17
98UHL All-Stars-13
99Asheville Smoke-19
99UHL All-Stars East-18T

Valois, Richard
88Richelieu Riverains-29

Valois, Stephane
88Richelieu Riverains-30

Valton, Julien
93Quebec Pee-Wee Tournament-1642

Valtonen, Jorma
65Finnish Hellas-16
70Finnish Jaakiekko-78
70Finnish Jaakiekko-205
70Swedish Hockey-294
70Swedish Masterserien-157
70Swedish Masterserien-163
71Finnish Suomi Stickers-77
71Finnish Suomi Stickers-93
71Swedish Hockey-59
72Finnish Jaakiekko-78
72Finnish Jaakiekko-258
72Finnish Hellas-19
72Finnish Panda Toronto-45
72Finnish Panda Toronto-110
72Finnish Semic World Championship-90
72Swedish Stickers-33
72Swedish Semic World Championship-90
73Finnish Jaakiekko-82
73Finnish Jaakiekko-123
74Finnish Typotor-18
74Swedish Stickers-103
74Swedish Semic World Champ Stickers-76
77Finnish Sportscasters-16-364
77Finnish Sportscasters-107-2559
78Finnish SM-Liiga-198

Valtonen, Tomek
99Finnish Cardset-264
00Finnish Cardset-282
01Finnish Cardset-52
02Finnish Cardset-286
03Finnish Cardset-63
04Finnish Cardset-70
Parallel-53
05Finnish Cardset -234
06Finnish Cardset-60

Valui, Vitali
99Russian Hockey League-200

Vampola, Petr
00Czech OFS-345
01Czech OFS-69
02Czech OFS Plus-81
03Czech OFS Plus-38
04Czech OFS-340
05Czech HC Liberec-16
06Czech OFS-106

Van Acker, Eric
01Greenville Grrrowl-5
02Greenville Grrrowl-21

Van Allen, Shaun
86Saskatoon Blades Photos-24
88ProCards AHL-87
89ProCards AHL-151
90ProCards AHL/IHL-223
910-Pee-Chee-414
91Topps-414
91Upper Deck-52
French-52
91ProCards-221
92Oilers IGA-25
92Parkhurst-288
Emerald Ice-288
92Ultra-299
93Donruss-14
93OPC Premier-396
Gold-396
93Parkhurst-278
Emerald Ice-278
93PowerPlay-15
93Stadium Club-361
Members Only Master Set-361
First Day Issue-361
93Topps/OPC Premier-396
Gold-396
93Ultra-264
93Upper Deck-506
93Classic Pro Prospects-64
93Classic Pro Prospects-150
94Canada Games NHL POGS-31
94Ducks Carl's Jr.-7
94Leaf-338
94OPC Premier-432
Special Effects-432
94Stadium Club-207
Members Only Master Set-207
First Day Issue-207
Super Team Winner Cards-207
94Topps/OPC Premier-432
Special Effects-432
94Upper Deck-312
Electric Ice-312
95Collector's Choice-173
Player's Club-173
Player's Club Platinum-173
95Donruss-26
95Emotion-5
95Leaf-248
95Panini Stickers-223
95Parkhurst International-8
Emerald Ice-8
95Pinnacle-102
Artist's Proofs-102
Rink Collection-102
95Playoff One on One-115
95Score-166
Black Ice Artist's Proofs-166
Black Ice-166
95SkyBox Impact-6
95Topps-297
OPC Inserts-297
95Ultra-7
Gold Medallion-7
95Upper Deck-488
Electric Ice-488
Electric Ice Gold-488
96Be A Player-163
Autographs-163
Autographs Silver-163
96Collector's Choice-6
96Donruss-86
Press Proofs-86
96Score-227
Artist's Proofs-227
Dealer's Choice Artist's Proofs-227
Special Artist's Proofs-227
Golden Blades-227
96Senators Pizza Hut-25
97Pacific Invincible NHL Regime-138
98Be A Player-245
Press Release-245
98BAP Gold-245
98BAP Autographs-245
98BAP Autographs Gold-245
98Pacific-317
Ice Blue-317
Red-317
98Senators Team Issue-23
99Pacific Omega-164
Copper-164
Gold-164
Ice Blue-164
Premiere Date-164
99Senators Team Issue-21
99Upper Deck MVP SC Edition-130
Gold Script-130
Silver Script-130
Super Script-130
00Stars Postcards-25
00Upper Deck Vintage-117
01BAP Memorabilia-500
Emerald-500
Ruby-500
Sapphire-500
01Canadiens Postcards-2
02BAP Sig Series Auto Buybacks 1998-245
02Pacific Complete-373
Red-373
030-Pee-Chee-213
03OPC Blue-213
03OPC Gold-213
03OPC Red-213
03Pacific Complete-81
Red-81
03Senators Postcards-15
03Topps-213
Blue-213
Gold-213
Red-213
03Upper Deck MVP-296
Gold Script-296
Silver Script-296
Canadian Exclusives-296

Van Amburg, Sean
90Rayside-Balfour Jr. Canadians-22
91Rayside-Balfour Jr. Canadians-21

Van Boxmeer, John
74Canadiens Postcards-26
760-Pee-Chee NHL-330
76Rockies Coke Cans-20
770-Pee-Chee NHL-315
77Rockies Coke Cans-19
780-Pee-Chee-224
78Topps-224
790-Pee-Chee-96
79Sabres Bells-9
79Topps-96
800-Pee-Chee-183
80Topps-183
810-Pee-Chee-26
810-Pee-Chee Stickers-58
81Sabres Milk Panels-2
81Topps-E80
820-Pee-Chee-36
820-Pee-Chee-37
820-Pee-Chee Stickers-121
82Post Cereal-2
82Sabres Milk Panels-4
82Topps Stickers-121
83NHL Key Tags-9
830-Pee-Chee-73
830-Pee-Chee Stickers-244
83Puffy Stickers-9
83Topps Stickers-244
83Vachon-78
88ProCards AHL-268
89ProCards AHL-266
90Sabres Campbell's-30
92Rochester Americans Kodak-1
93Rochester Americans Kodak-1
98Long Beach Ice Dogs-19
99Long Beach Ice Dogs-10

Van Bruggen, A.J.
97Seattle Thunderbirds-24

Van Burskirk, Ryan
03Florida Everblades-24
03Florida Everblades RBI Sports-175
04Gwinnett Gladiators-26

Van Buskirk, Parker
06Sarnia Sting-8

Van den Thillart, Leo
98German DEL-36

Van Der Gulik, David
03Boston University Terriers-17

Van Der Horst, Jamie
94UK Solihul Barons-13
95UK Solihull Barons-1
97UK Sheffield Steelers-16

Van Der Sloot, Adrian
88Niagara Falls Thunder-18

Van der Velden, Matt
03UK London Racers-18
04UK Milton Keynes Lightning-15

Van Dorp, Wayne
87Penguins Kodak-25
88Oilers Tenth Anniversary-164
88ProCards AHL-260
89Blackhawks Coke-15
90Nordiques Petro-Canada-40
900-Pee-Chee-527
91Nordiques Petro-Canada-32
92Nordiques Petro-Canada-35

Van Drunen, David
93Prince Albert Raiders-19
94Prince Albert Raiders-20
95Prince Albert Raiders-19
96Prince Albert Raiders-21
99Grand Rapids Griffins-25
99Mobile Mysticks-2
01Grand Rapids Griffins-19
02Grand Rapids Griffins-26
03Grand Rapids Griffins-21
05Muskegon Fury-18

Van Dyk, Chris
94Windsor Spitfires-6
95Slapshot-409
95Classic Five-Sport *-150
Autographs-150

Van Dyke, Jeff
98Sioux City Musketeers-23
99Sioux City Musketeers-21
00Sioux City Musketeers-5

Van Guilder, Mark
02Tri-City Stormfront-20
04Notre Dame Fighting Irish-4

Van Hauten, Mike
94German First League-514

van Hellemond, Andy
90Pro Set-701
01Upper Deck Legends-52
Jerseys-TTVH
Jerseys Platinum-TTVH

Van Herpt, Ed
01Kingston Frontenacs-23

Van Herpt, Nick
01Kingston Frontenacs-24
03Mississauga Ice Dogs-22
04Ottawa 67's-11

Van Hiltgen, Kelly
99Columbus Cottonmouths-17

Van Hoof, Jeremy
99Ottawa 67's-21
00Ottawa 67's-3
03ECHL Update RBI Sports-144
04Johnstown Chiefs-20

Van Horlick, Matt
96Red Deer Rebels-17
97Wheeling Nailers-10
97Wheeling Nailers Photo Pack-10

Van Horlick, Quinten
97Wheeling Nailers-20
97Wheeling Nailers Photo Pack-20
99Corpus Christi IceRays-24
01Rockford IceHogs-19
02Rockford Ice Hogs-13
04Missouri River Otters-11

Van Impe, Darren
90Prince Albert Raiders-21
907th Inn. Sketch WHL-268
91Prince Albert Raiders-23
917th Inn. Sketch WHL-258
917th Inn. Sketch Memorial Cup-117
93Red Deer Rebels-25
95Leaf-138
96Ducks Team Issue-16
96Metal Universe-193
96SP-4
96Ultra-7
Gold Medallion-7
96Upper Deck-213
96Collector's Edge Ice-12
Prism-12
97Collector's Choice-4
97Pacific-286
Copper-286
Emerald Green-286
Ice Blue-286
Red-286
Silver-286
97Pacific Invincible-5
Copper-5
Emerald Green-5
Ice Blue-5
Red-5
Silver-5
97Panini Stickers-185
97Score Mighty Ducks-9
Platinum-9
Premier-9
97Upper Deck-4
98Be A Player-159
Press Release-159
98BAP Gold-159
98BAP Autographs-159
98BAP Autographs Gold-159
99Ultimate Victory-9
1/1-9
Parallel-9
Parallel 100-9
00Pacific-44
Copper-44
Gold-44
Ice Blue-44
Premiere Date-44
02BAP Sig Series Auto Buybacks 1998-159
03German DEL-106
04German DEL-138
04German Hamburg Freezers Postcards-20
05German DEL-118
All-Star Jerseys-AS04
06German DEL-51

Van Impe, Ed
63Topps-30
64Beehive Group III Photos-58
680-Pee-Chee-91
68Topps-91
690-Pee-Chee-92
Four-in-One-18
69Topps-92
70Colgate Stamps-78
70Dad's Cookies-134
70Esso Power Players-200
700-Pee-Chee-80
Deckle-34
70Sargent Promotions Stamps-159
70Topps-80
Topps/OPC Sticker Stamps-32
71Bazooka-3
71Letraset Action Replays-11
710-Pee-Chee-126
71Sargent Promotions Stamps-150
71Topps-126
71Toronto Sun-207
72Flyers Mighty Milk-8
720-Pee-Chee-33
72Sargent Promotions Stamps-160
72Topps-9
73Flyers Linnett-16
730-Pee-Chee-206
74NHL Action Stamps-207
740-Pee-Chee NHL-85
74Topps-85
75Flyers Canada Dry Cans-19
750-Pee-Chee NHL-38
75Topps-38
760-Pee-Chee NHL-157
76Topps-157
92Parkhurst-479
Emerald Ice-479
95Parkhurst '66-67-36
Coins-36

Van Kessel, John
89ProCards AHL-26
897th Inn. Sketch OHL-162
90ProCards AHL/IHL-348
91ProCards-400
93Wheeling Thunderbirds-UD3
94Cape Breton Oilers-19
98German DEL-28

Van Lare, Ben
03Saskatoon Blades-9
04Saskatoon Blades-9

Van Leusen, Aaron
99Brampton Battalion-21
00Brampton Battalion-18

Van Leyen, Thorsten
94German DEL-90

Van Nynatten, Jeff
06Rio Grande Valley Killer Bees-15

Van Oene, Darren
94Brandon Wheat Kings-23
95Bowman Draft Prospects-P34
95Upper Deck-511
Electric Ice-511
Electric Ice Gold-511
95Brandon Wheat Kings-24
95Slapshot Memorial Cup-44
96Brandon Wheat Kings-19
97Brandon Wheat Kings-25
98Rochester Americans-16
00Rochester Americans-23
02Providence Bruins-14
03Providence Bruins-20

van Olphen, Jeroen
05Dutch Vadeko Flyers -18

Van Oosten, Steve
04Williams Lake Timberwolves-19

Van Parys, Justin
01El Paso Buzzards-10
02Lexington Men O'War-3

Van Rohr, Andre
95Swiss HNL-458

Van Rooyen, Keith
85Sudbury Wolves-23

Van Ryn, Mike
96Upper Deck-378
98Black Diamond-95
Double Diamond-95
Triple Diamond-95
Quadruple Diamond-95
98SPx Top Prospects-63
Radiance-63
Spectrum-63
98UD Choice-266
Prime Choice Reserve-266
Reserve-266
99Upper Deck-332
Exclusives-332
Exclusives 1 of 1-332
99Upper Deck Gold Reserve-332
99UD Prospects-20
Signatures of Tradition-MV
00Private Stock-142
Gold-142
Premiere Date-142
Retail-142
Silver-142
00Worcester Icecats-8
01SP Authentic-115
Limited-115
Limited Gold-115
01Upper Deck Victory-387
Gold-387
01Worcester Icecats-8
02Blues Team Issue-23
020-Pee-Chee-302
020-Pee-Chee Premier Blue Parallel-302
020-Pee-Chee Premier Red Parallel-302
020-Pee-Chee Factory Set-302
02Pacific Complete-172
Red-172
02Topps-302
OPC Blue Parallel-302
OPC Red Parallel-302
Factory Set-302
03Pacific Complete-241
Red-241
03Panthers Team Issue-17
04Pacific-116
Blue-116
Red-116
04Upper Deck-74
Canadian Exclusives-74
HG Glossy Gold-74
HG Glossy Silver-74
05Parkhurst-211
Facsimile Auto Parallel-211
05SP Game Used Statscriptions-ST-VR
05Upper Deck-81
HG Glossy-81
Notable Numbers-N-VR
05Upper Deck MVP-175
Gold-175
Platinum-175
05Upper Deck Toronto Fall Expo-81
05Upper Deck Victory-87
Black-87
Gold-87
Silver-87
06Be A Player-17
Autographs-17
Signatures-MV
Signatures 25-19
Signatures Duals-DVB
06Black Diamond Gemography-GMV
06Hot Prospects Hotagraphs-HMV
060-Pee-Chee-212
Rainbow-212
06UD Powerplay Power Marks-PMMV
06Upper Deck-334
Exclusives Parallel-334
High Gloss Parallel-334
Masterpieces-334
Victory-87
Victory Black-87
Victory Gold-87

Van Slooten, Mike
86Regina Pats-28
87Regina Pats-27

Van Tassel, Colby
96Madison Monsters-15
99Alexandria Warthogs-17

Van Tassel, Miles
93Waterloo Black Hawks-26
99Alexandria Warthogs-18

Van Tighem, Travis
01New Mexico Scorpions-14
02New Mexico Scorpions-21

Van Volsen, Joe
93Sault Ste. Marie Greyhounds-17
93Sault Ste. Marie Greyhound Memorial Cup-26
95Slapshot-51
95Sault Ste. Marie Greyhounds-24
97Austin Ice Bats-21
99Tupelo T-Rex-7
01Fort Worth Brahmas-16
02Fort Worth Brahmas-14

Van Volsen, Mike
95Slapshot-33

Van Wagner, Mike
03Chicago Steel-4

Vanballegooie, Dustin
03St. Michael's Majors-21
04Fresno Falcons-21
05Fresno Falcons-18

Vanbiesbrouck, John
80Sault Ste. Marie Greyhounds-13
81Sault Ste. Marie Greyhounds-23
82Sault Ste. Marie Greyhounds-22
850-Pee-Chee Stickers-88
860-Pee-Chee-9
860-Pee-Chee Stickers-114
860-Pee-Chee Stickers-190
860-Pee-Chee Stickers-218
86Topps-9
86Topps Sticker Inserts-1
870-Pee-Chee-36
870-Pee-Chee Stickers-33
87Panini Stickers-106
87Topps-36
87Sault Ste. Marie Greyhounds-16
880-Pee-Chee-102
880-Pee-Chee Minis-42
880-Pee-Chee Stickers-241
88Panini Stickers-300
88Topps-102
890-Pee-Chee-114
890-Pee-Chee Stickers-246
89Panini Stickers-282
89Rangers Marine Midland Bank-34
89Topps-114
89Swedish Semic World Champ Stickers-154
90SLU Kenner Club Pieces *-18
90Bowman-222
Tiffany-222
90Kraft-60
900-Pee-Chee-75
90Panini Stickers-108
90Pro Set-209
90Score-175
Canadian-175
90Score Hottest/Rising Stars-76
90Topps-75
Tiffany-75
90Upper Deck-279
French-279
91Bowman-68
910-Pee-Chee-353
91Panini Stickers-282
91Parkhurst-338
French-338
91Pinnacle-121
91Pinnacle-367
French-121
French-367
91Pro Set-447
French-447
Platinum PC-PC1
91Score American-10
91Score Canadian Bilingual-10
91Score Canadian English-10
91Stadium Club-323
91Topps-353
91Upper Deck-324
French-324
91Finnish Semic World Champ Stickers-127
91Swedish Semic World Champ Stickers-127
92Bowman-132
92Kraft-34
920-Pee-Chee-275
92Panini Stickers-232
92Panini Stickers French-232
92Parkhurst-349
Emerald Ice-349
92Pinnacle-186
French-186
92Score-160
Canadian-160
USA Greats-7
92Sports Illustrated for Kids II-338
92Stadium Club-58
92Topps-169
Gold-169G
92Ultra-144
92Upper Deck-44
92Finnish Semic-147
93Donruss-132
93High Liner Greatest Goalies-5
93Kraft-25
93Leaf-371
Painted Warriors-8
93OPC Premier-160
93OPC Premier-314
Gold-160
Gold-314
93Panini Stickers-98
93Parkhurst-73
Emerald Ice-73
93Pinnacle-148
Canadian-148
Expansion-1
Masks-9
93PowerPlay-102
93Score-162
93Score-445
93Score-492
93Score-501
Gold-501
Canadian-162
Canadian-445
Canadian-492
Canadian-501
Canadian Gold-501
93Stadium Club-85
93Stadium Club-330
Members Only Master Set-85
Members Only Master Set-330
OPC-85
First Day Issue-85
First Day Issue-330
First Day Issue OPC-85
Master Photos-10
Master Photos Winners-10
93Topps/OPC Premier-160
93Topps/OPC Premier-314
Gold-160
Gold-314
93Ultra-333
93Upper Deck-8
NHLPA/Roots-27
SP-60
94Action Packed Big Picture Promos-BP2
94Be A Player-R20
94Be A Player-R135
Signature Cards-20
94Canada Games NHL POGS-261
94Canada Games NHL POGS-280
94Donruss-176
Dominators-3
Ice Masters-10
Masked Marvels-10
94EA Sports-54
94Finest-40
Super Team Winners-40
Refractors-40
Bowman's Best-B8
Bowman's Best Refractors-B8
94Flair-69
94Fleer-83
Netminders-10
94Kraft-55
94Kraft Goalie Masks-8
94Leaf-70
Crease Patrol-5
Gold Stars-13
Limited Inserts-9
94Leaf Limited-72
94NHLPA Phone Cards-8
94OPC Premier-82
94OPC Premier-360
Special Effects-82
Special Effects-360
94Panthers Pop-ups-2
94Parkhurst Crash the Game Green-9
94Parkhurst Crash the Game Blue-9
94Parkhurst Crash the Game Gold-9
94Parkhurst Crash the Game Red-9
94Parkhurst Vintage-V13
94Parkhurst SE-SE67
Gold-SE67
94Pinnacle-100
Artist's Proofs-100
Rink Collection-100
Goaltending Greats-GT3
Masks-MA2
94Score Franchise-TF9
94Select Promos-7
94Select-7
Gold-7
94SP-44

Die Cuts-44
94Stadium Club Members Only-40
94Stadium Club-95
Members Only Master Set-95
First Day Issue-95
Super Team Winner Cards-95
94Topps/OPC Premier-82
94Topps/OPC Premier-360
Special Effects-82
Special Effects-360
94Ultra-86
94Upper Deck-46
Electric Ice-46
Predictor Canadian-C20
94Upper Deck Predictor Canadian Exch Gold-C20
94Upper Deck Predictor Hobby-H32
94Upper Deck Predictor Hobby Exch Gold-H32
94Upper Deck SP Inserts-SP31
94Upper Deck SP Inserts Die Cuts-SP31
95Bashan Super Stickers-46
95Bashan Super Stickers-47
95Bowman-30
All-Foil-30
95Canada Games NHL POGS-123
95Collector's Choice-253
95Collector's Choice-368
Player's Club-253
Player's Club-368
Player's Club Platinum-253
Player's Club Platinum-368
95Donruss-106
95Donruss Elite-83
Die Cut Stars-83
Die Cut Uncut-83
Painted Warriors-6
95Emotion-72
95Finest-20
95Finest-188
Refractors-20
Refractors-188
95Hoyle Eastern Playing Cards-25
95Imperial Stickers-47
95Kraft-32
95Leaf-172
95Leaf Limited-47
Stick Side-6
95Metal-62
95NHL Aces Playing Cards-7S
95Panini Stickers-79
95Parkhurst International-85
Emerald Ice-85
Crown Collection Silver Series 2-12
Crown Collection Gold Series 2-12
Goal Patrol-7
Parkie's Trophy Picks-PP5
Parkie's Trophy Picks-PP29
95Pinnacle FANtasy-16
95Playoff One on One-44
95Pro Magnets-90
95Score-241
95Score-322
Black Ice Artist's Proofs-241
Black Ice Artist's Proofs-322
Black Ice-241
Black Ice-322
95Select Certified-85
Mirror Gold-85
95SkyBox Impact-70
Deflectors-6
95SP-56
95Stadium Club Members Only-7
95Stadium Club-35
Members Only Master Set-35
95Summit-130
Artist's Proofs-130
Ice-130
In The Crease-15
95Topps-252
OPC Inserts-252
Home Grown USA-HGA8
Profiles-PF9
95Topps SuperSkills-78
Platinum-78
95Ultra-64
95Ultra-378
Gold Medallion-64
Premier Pad Men-11
Premier Pad Men Gold Medallion-11
95Upper Deck-321
Electric Ice-321
Electric Ice Gold-321
NHL All-Stars-AS19
NHL All-Stars Jumbo-AS19
Predictor Hobby-H19
Predictor Hobby Exchange-H19
Special Edition-SE122
Special Edition Gold-SE122
95Zenith-36
95Finnish Semic World Championships-102
95Finnish Semic World Championships-217
95Swedish Globe World Championships-101
96Headliners Hockey-21
96Be A Player Link to History-10B
96Be A Player Link to History Autographs-10B
96Be A Player Link to History Auto Silver-10B
96Be A Player Stacking the Pads-4
96Black Diamond-165
Gold-165
Run for the Cup-RC6
96Collector's Choice-101
96Collector's Choice-318
MVP-UD12
MVP Gold-UD12
96Donruss-187
Press Proofs-187
Between the Pipes-4
Dominators-1
96Donruss Canadian Ice-84
Gold Press Proofs-84
Red Press Proofs-84
96Donruss Elite-74
Die Cut Stars-74
Painted Warriors-4
Painted Warriors Promos-P4
96Flair-40
Blue Ice-40
Hot Gloves-12
96Fleer-44
Vezina-10
96Fleer Picks-88
Dream Lines-8
Fabulous 50-46
96Kraft Upper Deck-19
96Leaf-193
Press Proofs-193
Shut Down-2
Sweaters Away-4
Sweaters Home-4
96Leaf Limited-30
Gold-30
96Leaf Preferred-41
Press Proofs-41
Masked Marauders-3
Vanity Plates-2
Vanity Plates Gold-2
96Maggers-104
96McDonald's Pinnacle-35
96Metal Universe-64
Armor Plate-12
Armor Plate Super Power-12
Cool Steel-12
Cool Steel Super Power-12
96NHL Aces Playing Cards-49
96NHL Pro Stamps-90
96Pinnacle-203
Artist's Proofs-203
Foil-203
Premium Stock-203
Rink Collection-203
Masks-3
Masks Die Cuts-3
Team Pinnacle-8
96Pinnacle Fantasy-FC9
96Pinnacle Mint-26
Bronze-26
Gold-26
Silver-26
Coins Brass-26
Coins Solid Gold-26
Coins Gold Plated-26
Coins Nickel-26
Coins Silver-26
96Playoff One on One-425
96Post Upper Deck-23
96Score Samples-63
96Score-63
Artist's Proofs-63
Dealer's Choice Artist's Proofs-63
Special Artist's Proofs-63
Golden Blades-63
Net Worth-8
Sudden Death-7
96Select Certified-59
Artist's Proofs-59
Blue-59
Mirror Blue-59
Mirror Gold-59
Mirror Red-59
Red-59
Freezers-4
96SkyBox Impact-50
Zero Heroes-10
96SP-61
Clearcut Winner-CW9
Game Film-GF8
96Stadium Club Members Only-34
96Summit-66
Artist's Proofs-66
Ice-66
Metal-66
Premium Stock-66
In The Crease-10
In The Crease Premium Stock-10
96Team Out-63
96Topps Picks Ice D-ID12
96Ultra-70
Gold Medallion-70
96Upper Deck-63
Game Jerseys-GJ7
Generation Next-X7
Hart Hopefuls Bronze-HH6
Hart Hopefuls Gold-HH6
Hart Hopefuls Silver-HH6
Superstar Showdown-SS2B
96Upper Deck Ice-110
Parallel-110
Stanley Cup Foundation-S3
Stanley Cup Foundation Dynasty-S3
96Zenith-91
Artist's Proofs-91
Z-Team-17
96Swedish Semic Wien-156
97SLU Hockey Canadian-19
97SLU Hockey American-21
97Headliners Hockey-29
97NHL Pro Zone-60
97Be A Player Stacking the Pads-8
97Be A Player Take A Number-6
97Beehive-27
Golden Portraits-27
Team-5
Team Gold-5
97Black Diamond-42
Double Diamond-42
Triple Diamond-42
Quadruple Diamond-42
97Collector's Choice-102
97Collector's Choice-317
Star Quest-SQ84
Stick'Ums-S2
97Crown Royale-60
Emerald Green-60
Ice Blue-60
Silver-60
Freeze Out Die-Cuts-9
97Donruss-58
Press Proofs Silver-58
Press Proofs Gold-58
Between The Pipes-3
Elite Inserts-8
97Donruss Canadian Ice-7
Dominion Series-7
Provincial Series-7
Stanley Cup Scrapbook-16
97Donruss Elite-3
97Donruss Elite-126
Aspirations-3
Aspirations-126
Status-3
Status-126
Craftsmen-1
Master Craftsmen-1
Prime Numbers-8A
Prime Numbers-8B
Prime Numbers-8C
Prime Numbers Die-Cuts-8A
Prime Numbers Die-Cuts-8B
Prime Numbers Die-Cuts-8C
97Donruss Limited-5
97Donruss Limited-62
97Donruss Limited-113
Exposure-5
Exposure-62
Exposure-113
Fabric of the Game-7
97Donruss Preferred-9
97Donruss Preferred-182
Cut to the Chase-9
Cut to the Chase-182
Color Guard-4
Color Guard Promos-4
Precious Metals-13
97Donruss Priority-5
97Donruss Priority-193
Stamp of Approval-5
Stamp of Approval-193
Postcards-11
Postcards Opening Day Issues-5
Postmaster General-2
Postmaster Generals Promos-2
Stamps-11
Stamps Bronze-11
Stamps Gold-11
Stamps Silver-11
97Esso Olympic Hockey Heroes-34
97Esso Olympic Hockey Heroes French-34
97Highland Mint Mint-Coins-16
97Katch-66
Gold-66
Silver-66
97Kenner Starting Lineup Cards-21
97Leaf-5
97Leaf-172
Fractal Matrix-5
Fractal Matrix-172
Fractal Matrix Die Cuts-5
Fractal Matrix Die Cuts-172
Pipe Dreams-2
97Leaf International-5
Universal Ice-5
97McDonald's Upper Deck-24
97NHL Aces Playing Cards-51
97Pacific-34
Copper-34
Emerald Green-34
Ice Blue-34
Red-34
Silver-34
Card-Supials-9
Card-Supials Minis-9
Gold Crown Die-Cuts-13
In The Cage Laser Cuts-10
Team Checklists-11
97Pacific Dynagon-57
Copper-57
Dark Grey-57
Emerald Green-57
Ice Blue-57
Red-57
Silver-57
Best Kept Secrets-43
Kings of the NHL-5
Stonewallers-10
Tandems-13
97Pacific Invincible-64
Copper-64
Emerald Green-64
Ice Blue-64
Red-64
Silver-64
Feature Performers-17
NHL Regime-89
97Pacific Omega-102
Copper-102
Dark Gray-102
Emerald Green-102
Gold-102
Ice Blue-102
No Scoring Zone-5
97Paramount-86
Copper-86
Dark Grey-86
Emerald Green-86
Ice Blue-86
Red-86
Silver-86
Big Numbers Die-Cuts-11
Glove Side Laser Cuts-9
Photoengravings-11
97Pinnacle-37
97Pinnacle-NNO
Artist's Proofs-37
Rink Collection-37
Epix Game Emerald-2
Epix Game Orange-2
Epix Game Purple-2
Epix Moment Emerald-2
Epix Moment Orange-2
Epix Moment Purple-2
Epix Play Emerald-2
Epix Play Orange-2
Epix Play Purple-2
Epix Season Emerald-2
Epix Season Orange-2
Epix Season Purple-2
Press Plates Back Black-37
Press Plates Back Cyan-37
Press Plates Back Magenta-37
Press Plates Back Yellow-37
Press Plates Front Black-37
Press Plates Front Cyan-37
Press Plates Front Magenta-37
Press Plates Front Yellow-37
Masks-1
Masks Die Cuts-1
Masks Jumbos-1
97Pinnacle Masks Promos 1
97Pinnacle Team Pinnacle-10
97Pinnacle Team Pinnacle Mirror-10
97Pinnacle Team Pinnacle Parallel-10
97Pinnacle Team Pinnacle Parallel Mirror-10
97Pinnacle Tins-10
97Pinnacle Certified-6
Red-6
Mirror Blue-6
Mirror Gold-6
Mirror Red-6
Team-3
Gold Team Promo-3
Gold Team-3
97Pinnacle Inside-19
Coach's Collection-19
Executive Collection-19
Stand Up Guys-2A/B
Stand Up Guys-2C/D
Stand Up Guys Promos-2A/B
Stand Up Guys Promos-2C/D
Stoppers-2
Track-7
Cans-20
Cans Gold-20
97Pinnacle Mint-4
Bronze-4
Gold Team-4
Silver Team-4
Coins Brass-4
Coins Brass Proofs-4
Coins Gold Plated-4
Coins Gold Plated Proofs-4
Coins Nickel Silver-4
Coins Nickel Silver Proofs-4
Coins Solid Gold-4
Coins Solid Silver-4
97Pinnacle Power Pack Blow-Ups-13
97Pinnacle Power Pack Blow-Ups-P13
97Pinnacle Replica Masks-6
97Pinnacle Tot Cert Platinum Blue-6
97Pinnacle Tot Certi Platinum Gold-6
97Pinnacle Totally Certified Platinum Red-6
97Pinnacle Tot Cert Mirror Platinum Gold-6
97Revolution-62
Copper-62
Emerald-62
Ice Blue-62
Silver-62
Return to Sender Die-Cuts-9
Team Checklist Laser Cuts-11
97Score-34
Artist's Proofs-34
Golden Blades-34
Net Worth-15
97SP Authentic-69
Icons-I5
Icons Die-Cuts-I5
Icons Embossed-I5
97SPx-20
Bronze-20
Gold-20
Silver-20
Steel-20
DuoView-8
Grand Finale-20
97Studio-17
Press Proofs Silver-17
Press Proofs Gold-17
Portraits-17
Silhouettes-16
Silhouettes 8x10-16
97Upper Deck-72
Blow-Ups 3 x 5-1-10
Blow-Ups 5 x 7-5D
Game Dated Moments-72
Smooth Grooves-SG54
The Specialists-7
The Specialists Level 2 Die Cuts-7
Three Star Selects-2C
97Upper Deck Diamond Vision-7
Signature Moves-7
97Upper Deck Ice-74
Parallel-74
Champions-IC17
Champions 2 Die Cuts-IC17
Power Shift-74
97Zenith-9
Z-Gold-9
Z-Silver-9
97Zenith 5 x 7-4
Gold Impulse-4
Silver Impulse-4
97Pinnacle Collector's Club Team Pinnacle-H6
98Headliners Hockey In the Crease-5
98Headliners Hockey XL-8
98SLU Hockey Extended-215
98Aurora-142
98Be A Player-252
Press Release-252
98BAP Gold-252
98BAP Autographs-252
98BAP Autographs Gold-252
98BAP Playoff Highlights-H11
98Black Diamond-64
Double Diamond-64
Triple Diamond-64
Quadruple Diamond-64
Myriad-M2
Myriad 2-M2
98Bowman's Best-82
Refractors-82
Atomic Refractors-82
98Crown Royale-101
Limited Series-101
Pillars of the Game-19
Pivotal Players-19
98Finest-55
No Protectors-55
No Protectors Refractors-55
Refractors-55
98Kenner Starting Lineup Cards-32
98NHL Aces Playing Cards-39
98OPC Chrome-215
Refractors-215
98Pacific-34
Ice Blue-34
Red-34
Team Checklists-11
98Pacific Dynagon Ice-140
Blue-140
Red-140
Watchmen-7
98Pacific Omega-180
Red-180
Opening Day Issue-180
Online-27
Planet Ice-12
Planet Ice Parallel-12
98Panini Photocards-87
98Panini Stickers-60
98Paramount-178
Copper-178
Emerald Green-178
Holo-Electric-178
Ice Blue-178
Silver-178
98Revolution-107
Ice Shadow-107
Red-107
Showstoppers-27
Three Pronged Attack-17
Three Pronged Attack Parallel-17
98SP Authentic-62
Power Shift-62
Snapshots-SS16
Stat Masters-S10
98SPx Top Prospects-45
Radiance-45
Spectrum-45
Highlight Heroes-H20
Lasting Impressions-L2
Premier Stars-PS10
Winning Materials-JV
98Topps-215
O-Pee-Chee-215
98Topps Gold Label Class 1-59
Black-59
Black One of One-59
One of One-59
Red-59
Red One of One-59
98Topps Gold Label Class 2-59
98Topps Gold Label Class 2 Black-59
98Topps Gold Label Class 2 Black 1 of 1-59
98Topps Gold Label Class 2 One of One-59
98Topps Gold Label Class 2 Red-59
98Topps Gold Label Class 2 Red One of One-59
98Topps Gold Label Class 3-59
98Topps Gold Label Class 3 Black-59
98Topps Gold Label Class 3 Black 1 of 1-59
98Topps Gold Label Class 3 One of One-59
98Topps Gold Label Class 3 Red-59
98Topps Gold Label Class 3 Red One of One-59
98UD Choice-89
98UD Choice-247
Mini Bobbing Head-BH10
98UD Choice Preview-89
98UD Choice Prime Choice Reserve-89
98UD Choice Prime Choice Reserve-247
98UD Choice Reserve-89
98UD Choice Reserve-247
98UD3-54
98UD3-114
98UD3-174
Die-Cuts-54
Die-Cuts-114
Die-Cuts-174
98Upper Deck-148
Exclusives-148
Exclusives 1 of 1-148
Profiles-P7
Profiles Quantum 1-P7
Profiles Quantum 2-P7
Profiles Quantum 3-P7
Gold Reserve-148
98Upper Deck MVP-149
Gold Script-149
Silver Script-149
Super Script-149
99SLU Hockey Pro Action Deluxe-60
99Aurora-108
Striped-108
Premiere Date-108
Premiere Date Striped-108
Glove Unlimited-15
99BAP Memorabilia-44
Gold-44
Silver-44
AS Heritage Ruby-H4
AS Heritage Sapphire-H4
AS Heritage Emerald-H4
99BAP Millennium Prototypes-6
99BAP Millennium-185
Emerald-185
Ruby-185
Sapphire-185
Signatures-185
Signatures Gold-185
99Crown Royale-106
Limited Series-106
Premiere Date-106
Card-Supials-17
Card-Supials Minis-17
International Glory-19
International Glory Parallel-19
99Jell-O Partners of Power-3
99O-Pee-Chee-201
99O-Pee-Chee Chrome-201
99O-Pee-Chee Chrome Refractors-201
99Pacific-313
Copper-313
Emerald Green-313
Gold-313
Ice Blue-313
Premiere Date-313
Red-313
Gold Crown Die-Cuts-28
In the Cage Net-Fusions-14
Past and Present-18
99Pacific Dynagon Ice-150
Blue-150
Copper-150
Gold-150
Premiere Date-150
Masks-4
Masks-9
Masks Holographic Blue-4
Masks Holographic Blue-9
Masks Holographic Gold-4
Masks Holographic Gold-9
Masks Holographic Purple-4
Masks Holographic Purple-9
99Pacific Omega-176
Copper-176
Gold-176
Ice Blue-176
Premiere Date-176
EO Portraits-14
EO Portraits 1/1-14
Game-Used Jerseys-8
5 Star Talents-29
5 Star Talents Parallel-29
99Pacific Prism-105
Holographic Blue-105
Holographic Gold-105
Holographic Mirror-105
Holographic Purple-105
Premiere Date-105
Sno-Globe Die-Cuts-17
99Panini Stickers-128
99Panini Stickers-337
99Paramount-176
Copper-176
Emerald-176
Gold-176
Holographic Emerald-176
Holographic Gold-176
Holographic Silver-176
Ice Blue-176
Premiere Date-176
Red-176
Silver-176
Glove Side Net Fusions-15
Personal Best-28
99Revolution-110
Premiere Date-110
Red-110
Shadow Series-110
NHL Icons-15
Showstoppers-27
Copper-110
Gold-110
CSC Silver-110
99SPx-109
Radiance-109
Spectrum-109
99Stadium Club-126
First Day Issue-126
One of a Kind-126
Printing Plates Black-126
Printing Plates Cyan-126
Printing Plates Magenta-126
Printing Plates Yellow-126
99Topps/OPC-201
99Topps/OPC Chrome-201
Refractors-201
99Topps Premier Plus Imperial Guard-IG6
99Upper Deck-268
Exclusives-268
Exclusives 1 of 1-268
99Upper Deck Gold Reserve-268
99Upper Deck MVP-155
Gold Script-155
Silver Script-155
Super Script-155
Last Line-LL7
99Upper Deck Victory-219
99Upper Deck Victory-385
99Wayne Gretzky Hockey-128
00SLU Hockey-230
00Aurora-91
Premiere Date-91
Dual Game-Worn Jerseys-2
Game-Worn Jerseys-6
Game-Worn Jersey Patches-6
00BAP Memorabilia-101
00BAP Memorabilia-413
Emerald-101
Emerald-413
Ruby-101
Ruby-413
Sapphire-101
Sapphire-413
Promos-101
Georges Vezina-V14
00BAP Mem Chicago Sportsfest Copper-101
00BAP Memorabilia Chicago Sportsfest Blue-101
00BAP Memorabilia Chicago Sportsfest Gold-101
00BAP Memorabilia Chicago Sportsfest Ruby-101
00BAP Memorabilia Chicago Sun-Times Ruby-101
00BAP Memorabilia Chicago Sun-Times Gold-101
00BAP Mem Chicago Sun-Times Sapphire-101
00BAP Mem Toronto Fall Expo Copper-101
00BAP Memorabilia Toronto Fall Expo Gold-101
00BAP Memorabilia Toronto Fall Expo Ruby-101
00BAP Parkhurst 2000-P189
00BAP Signature Series-168
Emerald-168
Ruby-168
Sapphire-168
Autographs-180
Autographs Gold-180
00BAP Ultimate Memorabilia Active Eight-AE5
00BAP Ultimate Mem Goalie Memorabilia-GM15
00BAP Ultimate Memorabilia Goalie Sticks-G19
00Black Diamond Game Gear-BJV
00Black Diamond Game Gear-CJV
00Black Diamond Game Gear-LJV
00Crown Royale-68
Ice Blue-68
Limited Series-68
Premiere Date-68
Red-68
00O-Pee-Chee-265A
00O-Pee-Chee Parallel-265A
00Pacific-309
Copper-309
Gold-309
Ice Blue-309
Premiere Date-309
00Paramount Jersey and Patches-7
00Private Stock-63
Gold-63
Premiere Date-63
Retail-63
Silver-63
Game Gear-72
Game Gear Patches-72
00SP Game Used-39
00Stadium Club-227
00Titanium-59
Blue-59
Gold-59
Premiere Date-59
Red-59
Retail-59
00Topps/OPC-265A
Parallel-265A
00Topps Chrome-159
OPC Refractors-159
Refractors-159
00Topps Heritage-103
00Topps Premier Plus Club Signings-CS-2
00Topps Premier Plus Club Signings-CSC-1
00Topps Premier Plus GameUsed Memorabilia-GPJV
00Topps Premier Plus GameUsed Memorabilia-GPJVTP
00Topps Stars-94
Blue-94
00UD Heroes-77
00UD Reserve-55
Golden Goalies-GG8
00Upper Deck-339
Exclusives Tier 1-339
Exclusives Tier 2-339
00Upper Deck Legends-57
Legendary Collection Bronze-57
Legendary Collection Gold-57
Legendary Collection Silver-57
00Upper Deck Vintage-230
00Upper Deck Vintage-233
00Upper Deck Vintage-234
00Vanguard-63
Dual Game-Worn Jerseys-9
Holographic Gold-63
Holographic Purple-63
Pacific Proofs-63
01Between the Pipes-153
Masks-6
Masks Silver-6
Masks Gold-6
01Fleer Legacy-64
Ultimate-64
Memorabilia-25
01Pacific-240
Extreme LTD-240
Hobby LTD-240
Premiere Date-240
Retail LTD-240
01Pacific Arena Exclusives-240
01Parkhurst-387
01UD Top Shelf Goalie Gear-LPJV
02BAP Sig Series Auto Buybacks 1998-252
02BAP Sig Series Auto Buybacks 1999-185
02BAP Sig Series Auto Buybacks 2000-180
02BAP Ultimate Memorabilia Cup Duels-17
02Pacific-231
Blue-231
Red-231
03Parkhurst Original Six New York-52
04ITG Franchises Update Goalie Gear-UGG4
04ITG Franchises Update Goalie Gear Gold-UGG4
04ITG Franchises Update Trophy Winners-UTW4
04ITG Franchises Update Trophy Win Gold-UTW4
04ITG Franchises US East-350
Autographs-A-JV
Memorabilia-ESM32
Memorabilia Gold-ESM32
04ITG Ultimate Mem Archives 1st Edition-18
04ITG Ultimate Mem Archives 1st Edition-33
06Between The Pipes Autographs-AJV
06Between The Pipes Double Jerseys-DJ27
06Between The Pipes Double Jerseys Gold-DJ27
06Between The Pipes Playing For Your Country-PC12
06Between The Pipes Playing For Your Country Gold-PC12
06Between The Pipes Shooting Gallery-SG05
06Between The Pipes Shooting Gallery Gold-SG05
06Between The Pipes Stick and Jersey-SJ37
06Between The Pipes Stick and Jersey Gold-SJ37
06ITG International Ice-56
Gold-56
Autographs-AJV
Cornerstones-IC08
Cornerstones Gold-IC08
Goaltending Glory-GG14
Goaltending Glory Gold-GG14
Teammates-IT14
Teammates Gold-IT14

Vanclief, Chris

89Oshawa Generals-33

Vandal, Jean-Paul

51Bas Du Fleuve-15

Vandal, Steve

93Quebec Pee-Wee Tournament-1358
99Rouyn-Noranda Huskies-22

Vandale, Duane

92Saskatchewan JHL-94

Vande Velde, Chris

04Lincoln Stars Update-33

Vandekamp, Mike

03Vernon Vipers-20

Vandenberghe, Mike

88Brandon Wheat Kings-4
89Brandon Wheat Kings-5
90Brandon Wheat Kings-3
917th Inn. Sketch WHL-334
94Dayton Bombers-19
96Knoxville Cherokees-19
98San Angelo Outlaws-18
99Corpus Christi IceRays-25
99Odessa Jackalopes-14
00Knoxville Speed-10

VandenBussche, Ryan

907th Inn. Sketch OHL-49
91Cornwall Royals-7
917th Inn. Sketch OHL-22
93St. John's Maple Leafs-24
94St. John's Maple Leafs-22
95Binghamton Rangers-24
96Binghamton Rangers-21
97Be A Player-223
Autographs-223
Autographs Die-Cuts-223
Autographs Prismatic Die-Cuts-223
97Hartford Wolf Pack-26
98Indianapolis Ice-3
00BAP Memorabilia-98
Emerald-98
Ruby-98
Sapphire-98
Promos-98
00BAP Mem Chicago Sportsfest Copper-98
00BAP Memorabilia Chicago Sportsfest Blue-98
00BAP Memorabilia Chicago Sportsfest Gold-98
00BAP Memorabilia Chicago Sportsfest Ruby-98
00BAP Memorabilia Chicago Sun-Times Ruby-98
00BAP Memorabilia Chicago Sun-Times Gold-98
00BAP Mem Chicago Sun-Times Sapphire-98
00BAP Mem Toronto Fall Expo Copper-98
00BAP Memorabilia Toronto Fall Expo Gold-98
00BAP Memorabilia Toronto Fall Expo Ruby-98
00BAP Memorabilia Update Tough Materials-T20
00BAP Mem Update Tough Materials Gold-T20
00Pacific-104
Copper-104
Gold-104
Ice Blue-104
Premiere Date-104
01BAP Update Tough Customers-TC21
01BAP Update Tough Customers-TC35
01Upper Deck Victory-82
Gold-82
02Blackhawks Postcards-6
02Upper Deck Vintage-54
03Blackhawks Postcards-29
03ITG Action-132
03Parkhurst Original Six Chicago-30
Memorabilia-CM9
06Finnish Cardset-245
Enforcers-3

vander Holst, Ruud

05Dutch Vadeko Flyers -17

Vander Wal, Wes

95Slapshot-148

Vanderbreggen, Josh

03Yarmouth Mariners-22

Vanderklok, Ben

98Barrie Colts-22

Vanderkracht, Bram

89Spokane Chiefs-19
907th Inn. Sketch WHL-211
917th Inn. Sketch WHL-194
917th Inn. Sketch Memorial Cup-88

Vandermeer, Dan

97Spokane Chiefs-25
98Spokane Chiefs-27
00Richmond Renegades-7
04Idaho Steelheads-12

Vandermeer, Jim

98Red Deer Rebels-20
00Red Deer Rebels-20
Signed-20
02BAP Memorabilia-329
02BAP Ultimate Memorabilia-66
02Pacific Calder-137
Silver-137
02Pacific Complete-543
Red-543
02Pacific Quest for the Cup-137
Gold-137
02Parkhurst Retro-242
Minis-242
02UD Artistic Impressions-133
Gold-133
02UD Honor Roll-138
02UD Mask Collection-157
02UD Premier Collection-89
Gold-89
02Philadelphia Phantoms-13
03Flyers Postcards-22
03O-Pee-Chee-326
03OPC Blue-326
03OPC Gold-326
03OPC Red-326
03Topps-326
Blue-326
Gold-326
Red-326
03Topps C55-87
Minis-87
Minis American Back-87
Minis American Back Red-87
Minis Bazooka Back-87
Minis Brooklyn Back-87
Minis Hat Trick Back-87
Minis O Canada Back-87
Minis O Canada Back Red-87
Minis Stanley Cup Back-87
03Topps Traded-TT7
Blue-TT7
Gold-TT7
Red-TT7
03Upper Deck-143
Canadian Exclusives-143
HG-143
04Norfolk Admirals-19
05Parkhurst-114
Facsimile Auto Parallel-114
06Blackhawks Postcards-12
06O-Pee-Chee-110
Rainbow-110

Vandermeer, Joe

00Richmond Renegades-8
02Lexington Men O'War-19
03Peoria Rivermen-12
03Worcester Ice Cats-3

Vandermeer, Pete

93Red Deer Rebels-26
95Red Deer Rebels-16
98BC Icemen-2
98BC Icemen II-4
99ECHL All-Star Northern Conference-19
00Providence Bruins-11
02Philadelphia Phantoms-11
03Philadelphia Phantoms-20
05Hamilton Bulldogs-26

Vandermeer, Ted

03Red Deer Rebels-13
05Red Deer Rebels-20

Vanderveeken, Jamie

03St. Michael's Majors-3
04Ottawa 67's-16
04St. Michael's Majors-3
05London Knights-6

Vanderveer, Erika

06Ohio State Buckeyes Women-5

Vanderweer, Erika

04Ohio State Buckeyes Women-14

Vanderydt, Rob

91Richmond Renegades-1
91Richmond Renegades Set 2-18

Vanecek, Filip

96Czech APS Extraliga-319
97Czech APS Extraliga-274
01Czech OFS-133

Vanek, Thomas

97Quebec Pee-Wee Tournament-1118
00Sioux Falls Stampede-18
01Sioux Falls Stampede-15
02Minnesota Golden Gophers-25
03BAP Memorabilia Draft Redemptions-5
03Minnesota Golden Gophers-3
04SP Authentic Rookie Redemptions-RR4
04AHL Top Prospects-46
04Rochester Americans-25
04Rochester Americans-29
04ITG Heroes and Prospects-185
Autographs-U-TV
04ITG Heroes/Prospects Toronto Expo '05-185
05ITG Heroes/Prosp Toronto Expo Parallel -59
05ITG Heroes/Prosp Toronto Expo Parallel -369
05Beehive-120
Beige -120
Blue -120
Gold-120
Red -120
Matte-120
Signature Scrapbook-SSTV
05Black Diamond-197
Emerald-197
Gold-197
Onyx-197
Ruby-197
05Hot Prospects-224
En Fuego-224
Hot Materials-HMTV
Red Hot-224
White Hot-224
05ITG Ultimate Mem Future Stars Autos-10
05ITG Ultimate Mem Future Star Autos Gold-10
05ITG Ultimate Mem Future Stars Jerseys-10
05ITG Ultimate Mem Fut Stars Jerseys Gold-10
05ITG Ultimate Mem Future Stars Mem Autos-10
05ITG Ultimate Mem Fut Star Mem Auto Gold-10
05ITG Ultimate Mem Pass the Torch Jerseys-20
05ITG Ultimate Mem Passing Torch Jsy Gold-20
05ITG Ultimate Memorabilia R.O.Y. Autos-3
05ITG Ultimate Mem R.O.Y. Autos Gold-3
05ITG Ultimate Memorabilia R.O.Y. Emblems-15
05ITG Ultimate Mem R.O.Y. Emblems Gold-15
05ITG Ultimate Memorabilia R.O.Y. Jerseys-15
05ITG Ultimate Mem R.O.Y. Jerseys Gold-15
05ITG Ultimate Memorabilia R.O.Y. Numbers-15
05ITG Ultimate Mem R.O.Y. Numbers Gold-15
05Panini Stickers-40
05Parkhurst-610
Facsimile Auto Parallel-610
True Colors-TCBUF
True Colors-TCBUF
05SP Authentic-139
Limited-139
Exquisite Endorsements-EETV
Octographs-OR
Prestigious Pairings-PPPV
Rarefied Rookies-RRTV
Rookie Authentics-RATV
Sign of the Times Duals-DDV
Sign of the Times Triples-TDBV
Six Star Signatures-SSRO
05SP Game Used-118
Autographs-118
Gold-118
Auto Draft-AD-TV
Game Gear-GG-TV
Game Gear Autographs-AG-TV
Rookie Exclusives-TV
Rookie Exclusives Silver-RE-TV
Significant Numbers-SN-TV
05SPx-177
Spectrum-177
Xcitement Rookies-XR-TV
Xcitement Rookies Gold-XR-TV
Xcitement Rookies Spectrum-XR-TV
05The Cup-175
Autographed Rookie Patches Gold Rainbow-175
Black Rainbow Rookies-175

Masterpiece Pressplates (Artifacts)-204
Masterpiece Pressplates (Bee Hive)-120
Masterpiece Pressplates (Black Diamond)-197
Masterpiece Pressplates (Ice)-102
Masterpiece Pressplates (MVP)-422
Masterpiece Pressplates (Power Play)-144
Masterpiece Pressplates (Power Play)-144
Masterpiece Pressplates Rookie Upd Auto-259
Masterpiece Pressplates SPA Autos-139
Masterpiece Pressplates (SP Game Used)-118
Masterpiece Pressplates SPx Autos-177
Masterpiece Pressplates (Trilogy)-178
Masterpiece Pressplates Ult Coll Autos-100
Masterpiece Pressplates (Victory)-292
Masterpiece Pressplates Autographs-175
Platinum Rookies-175
Scripted Swatches-SSTV
Signature Patches-SPTV
05UD Artifacts-204
Gold-RED4
05UD PowerPlay-144
05UD Rookie Class-5
Commemorative Boxtoppers-CC-4
05Ultimate Collection-100
Autographed Patches-100
Autographed Shields-100
Jerseys-JVA
Marquee Attractions-MA9
Marquee Attractions Signatures-SMA9
Premium Patches-PPTV
Premium Swatches-PSTV
Ultimate Debut Threads Jerseys-DTJTV
Ultimate Debut Threads Jerseys Autos-DAJTV
Ultimate Debut Threads Patches-DTPTV
Ultimate Debut Threads Patches Autos-DAPTV
Ultimate Patches-PVA
Ultimate Signatures-USTV
Ultimate Signatures Logos-SLTV
Ultimate Signatures Pairings-UPPV
05Ultra-271
Gold-271
Fresh Ink-FI-TV
Fresh Ink Blue-FI-TV
Ice-271
Rookie Uniformity Jerseys-RU-TV
Rookie Uniformity Jersey Autographs-ARU-TV
Rookie Uniformity Patches-RUP-TV
Rookie Uniformity Patch Autographs-ARP-TV
05Upper Deck-457
Majestic Materials-MMVA
Rookie Ink-RITV
05Upper Deck Rookie Showcase-RS4
05Upper Deck Rookie Showcase Promos-RS4
05Upper Deck Rookie Threads-RTTV
05Upper Deck Rookie Threads Autographs-ARTTV
05Upper Deck Stars in the Making-SM5
05Upper Deck Ice-102
Cool Threads-CTTV
Cool Threads Autographs-ACTTV
Cool Threads Glass-CTTV
Cool Threads Patches-CTPTV
Cool Threads Patch Autographs-CAPTV
Glacial Graphs-GGTV
Glacial Graphs Labels-GGTV
Premieres Auto Patches-AIPTV
05Upper Deck MVP-422
Gold-422
Platinum-422
Rookie Breakthrough-RB11
05Upper Deck Rookie Update-259
05Upper Deck Trilogy-178
05Upper Deck Victory-292
Black-292
Gold-292
Silver-292
05ITG Heroes and Prospects-59
05ITG Heroes and Prospects-369
Autograph Memorabilia-GA-05
Autograph Memorabilia Gold-GA-05
Autographs-A-TV
Autographs Series II-TV2
Complete Jerseys-CJ-27
Complete Jerseys Gold-CJ-27
Jerseys-GUJ-114
Jerseys Gold-GUJ-114
Emblems-GUE-97
Emblems Gold-GUE-97
Numbers-GUN-97
Numbers Gold-GUN-97
Spectrum-STM-06
Spectrum Gold-STM-06
06Be A Player-16
Autographs-16
Profiles-PP2
Profiles Autographs-PP2
Signatures-TV
Signatures 10-18
Signatures Duals-DBU
Signatures Trios-TDBV
Portraits First Exposures-FETV
Portraits Signature Portraits-SPTV
06Black Diamond-12
Black-12
Gold-12
Ruby-12
06Flair Showcase-15
06Flair Showcase-112
Parallel-15
Parallel-112
Wave of the Future-WF22
06Fleer-26
Tiffany-26
Signing Day-SDTV
06Hot Prospects-12
06ITG Ultimate Memorabilia Autos-71
06ITG Ultimate Memorabilia Autos Gold-71
06ITG Ultimate Memorabilia Jerseys Autos-69
06ITG Ultimate Memorabilia Jerseys Autos Gold-69
06McDonald's Upper Deck Rookie Review-RR6
06O-Pee-Chee-62
06O-Pee-Chee-638
Rainbow-62
Rainbow-638
06Panini Stickers-33
06SP Game Used Letter Marks-LMVA
06SP Game Used SIGnificance-SVA
06The Cup Enshrinements-EVA
06The Cup Property of-POTV
06UD Artifacts Auto-Facts-AFTV
06UD Artifacts Auto-Facts Gold-AFTV
06UD Mini Jersey Collection-10
Jerseys-TV
Jersey Variations-TV
Jersey Autographs-TV
06UD Toronto Fall Expo Priority Signings -PSTV
06Ultra-21
Gold Medallion-21
Ice Medallion-21
06Upper Deck Arena Giveaways-BUF2
06Upper Deck-22
Exclusives Parallel-22
High Gloss Parallel-22
Masterpieces-22
Signatures-STV
06Upper Deck MVP-34
Gold Script-34
Super Script-34
06Upper Deck Ovation-6
06Upper Deck Trilogy Combo Clearcut Autographs-C2MV
06Upper Deck Trilogy Ice Scripts-ISTV
06Upper Deck Victory-22
06Upper Deck Victory Black-22
06Upper Deck Victory Gold-22
06Upper Deck Victory Next In Line-NL9
06ITG Heroes and Prospects Quad Emblems-QE10
06ITG Heroes and Prospects Quad Emblems Gold-QE10
07Upper Deck Ovation-44
3x5s-XL24
Autographed 3x5s-XLATV
07Upper Deck Victory-35
Black-35
Gold-35
GameBreakers-GB43
Oversize Cards-OS11

VanHerzele, Larry
83Brantford Alexanders-10
84Belleville Bulls-14

Vani, Carmine
81Kingston Canadians-10
82Kingston Canadians-6
83Kitchener Rangers-17
93Swedish Semic World Champ Stickers-222
94Finnish Jaa Kiekko-310
94Italian Milano-5

Vanik, Milos
94German DEL-142
95German DEL-140
96German DEL-335
99German Bundesliga 2-45

Vanin, Jeremy
98El Paso Buzzards-7
01El Paso Buzzards-7
03Fort Worth Brahmas-16

Vankka, Leo
66Finnish Jaakiekkosarja-115

Vanmoerkerke, Luke
06London Knights-19

Vann, Cody
06Prince Albert Raiders-7

Vanne, Antti
70Finnish Jaakiekko-359

Vanne, Ari
70Finnish Jaakiekko-360

Vannelli, Mike
01Sioux Falls Stampede-16
03Minnesota Golden Gophers-4
04Minnesota Golden Gophers-27
05Minnesota Golden Gophers-24
06Minnesota Golden Gophers-22

VanSchagen, Casey
01Missouri River Otters-7

Vanscoy, Rachel
04Ohio State Buckeyes Women-18

Vanstaalduinen, Bart
91Air Canada SJHL-B37
91Air Canada SJHL-D17
91Air Canada SJHL All-Stars-22
91Air Canada SJHL All-Stars-49
92Michigan State Spartans-26
93Michigan State Spartans-26

Vanthuyne, Brendan
99Swift Current Broncos-24

Vantighem, Travis
91Air Canada SJHL-D12
92Saskatchewan JHL-78

Vantroba, Miroslav
03Czech OFS Plus-85
03Czech OFS Plus All-Star Game-H9

Vanttinen, Tuomas
04Finnish Cardset-291
05Finnish Cardset -133
06Finnish Cardset-253

Vantuch, Lukas
05Calgary Hitmen-21

Vanyasov, Dmitri
98Russian Hockey League-77

Vapola, Ari
00Finnish Cardset-223

Varada, Vaclav
95Signature Rookies-1
Signatures-1
96Flair-102
Blue Ice-102
96SP-171
96Upper Deck-224
96Rochester Americans-12
97Donruss-217
Press Proofs Silver-217
Press Proofs Gold-217
97Donruss Canadian Ice-141
Dominion Series-141
Provincial Series-141
97Donruss Limited-23
97Donruss Limited-178
Exposure-23
Exposure-178
97Donruss Preferred-159
Cut to the Chase-159
97Leaf-48
97Leaf-166
Fractal Matrix-48
Fractal Matrix-166
Fractal Matrix Die Cuts-48
Fractal Matrix Die Cuts-166
97Leaf International-48
Universal Ice-48
97Upper Deck-229
97Rochester Americans-3-1
98Pacific-111
Ice Blue-111
Red-111
98Pacific Dynagon Ice-22
Blue-22
Red-22
98Paramount-23
Copper-23
Emerald Green-23
Holo-Electric-23
Ice Blue-23
Silver-23
98UD Choice-20
Prime Choice Reserve-20
Reserve-20
98UD3-24
98UD3-84
98UD3-144
Die-Cuts-24
Die-Cuts-84
Die-Cuts-144
98Upper Deck-48
Exclusives-48
Exclusives 1 of 1-48
Gold Reserve-48
99BAP Millennium-34
Emerald-34
Ruby-34
Sapphire-34
Signatures-34
Signatures Gold-34
99Pacific-47
Copper-47
Emerald Green-47
Gold-47
Ice Blue-47
Premiere Date-47
Red-47
99Panini Stickers-41
99Czech OFS-38
99Czech OFS-233
99Czech OFS Jagr Team Embossed-38
99Slovakian Challengers-21
00Pacific-59
Copper-59
Gold-59
Ice Blue-59
Premiere Date-59
00Panini Stickers-21
00Upper Deck-253
Exclusives Tier 1-253
Exclusives Tier 2-253
00Czech DS Extraliga Team Jagr-JT16
00Czech OFS-392
01BAP Signature Series-54
Autographs-54
Autographs Gold-54
01Upper Deck-23
Exclusives-23
01Czech DS-48
02BAP Sig Series Auto Buybacks 1999-34
02BAP Sig Series Auto Buybacks 2001-54
02Pacific Complete-266
Red-266
02Czech DS-59
02Czech DS-73
03ITG Action-407
03Pacific-244
Blue-244
Red-244
03Pacific Complete-197
Red-197
03Private Stock Reserve-73
Blue-73
Red-73
Retail-73
03Senators Postcards-19
03Upper Deck MVP-300
Gold Script-300
Silver Script-300
Canadian Exclusives-300
04Czech OFS-242
Stars-33
04Czech Zuma-26
05Parkhurst-346
Facsimile Auto Parallel-346
05Upper Deck-135
HG Glossy-135
05Upper Deck MVP-275
Gold-275
Platinum-275
05Upper Deck Toronto Fall Expo-135
05Czech World Champions Postcards-8
05Czech Pexeso Mini Red Set-8
06Czech NHL ELH Postcards-13

Varady, Jay
03Everett Silvertips-28
04Everett Silvertips-28
05Everett Silvertips-28

Vardale, Duane
91Air Canada SJHL-D38

Varga, Chris
907th Inn. Sketch OHL-21
917th Inn. Sketch OHL-38

Varga, John
917th Inn. Sketch WHL-150
92Tacoma Rockets-27
93Donruss Team USA-21
93Pinnacle-500
Canadian-500
93Upper Deck-559
93Tacoma Rockets-27
96Louisiana Ice Gators-19
96Wheeling Nailers-21
96Wheeling Nailers Photo Pack-10
97Louisiana Ice Gators-6
98ECHL All-Star Southern Conference-8
98Louisiana Ice Gators-21
99Florida Everblades-18

Vargas, Ernie
86Sherbrooke Canadiens-28
89ProCards IHL-170

Vargo, Jamie
89Windsor Spitfires-19

Varhaug, Mike
97Lethbridge Hurricanes-22
01Flint Generals-19

Varholik, Jan
94Finnish Jaa Kiekko-194
95Slovakian APS National Team-11

Varianov, Nikolai
94German First League-101

Varickij, Igor
98Czech OFS-126

Varis, Petri
92Finnish Jyvas-Hyva Stickers-199
93Finnish Jyvas-Hyva Stickers-109
93Finnish SISU-23
93Finnish SISU-393
93Swedish Semic World Champ Stickers-82
94Finnish SISU-248
94Finnish SISU-376
94Finnish Jaa Kiekko-46
95Finnish SISU-259
95Finnish SISU Limited-18
95Finnish SISU Painkillers-7
95Finnish SISU Specials-1
95Finnish Semic World Championships-28
95Swedish World Championships Stickers-180
96Finnish SISU Redline-47
96Finnish SISU Redline-180
At The Gala-1
97Indianapolis Ice-26
98German DEL-92
99Finnish Cardset-268
Aces High-S-9
00Finnish Cardset-43
01Finnish Cardset-261
01Swiss HNL-23
02Finnish Cardset-136
02Swiss HNL-386
03Finnish Cardset-149
03Finnish Cardset Globetrotters-GR7
04Finnish Cardset-73
Parallel-55
05Finnish Cardset -61
06Finnish Cardset-64

Varitsky, Igor
95German DEL-162
95Swedish World Championships Stickers-43
99Russian Hockey League-185
00Russian Hockey League-370
01Russian Hockey League-49
01Russian Lightnings-2
02Russian Hockey League-130
03Russian Hockey League-131
04Russian Super League All-Stars-26

Varjamo, Riku
98Finnish Kerailysarja-9
99Finnish Cardset-9
00Finnish Cardset-171
03Las Vegas Wranglers-19
04Missouri River Otters-9

Varjanen, Kari
66Finnish Jaakiekkosarja-82
70Finnish Jaakiekko-171

Varjanov, Nikolai
90O-Pee-Chee-504

Varjonen, Tommi
92Finnish Jyvas-Hyva Stickers-29
93Finnish Jyvas-Hyva Stickers-52
93Finnish SISU-251
94Finnish SISU-74

Varlamov, Evgeni
98Russian Hockey League-50
99Russian Hockey League-74
00Russian Hockey League-42
02Russian Hockey League-143
02Russian SL-6

Varlamov, Sergei
95Swift Current Broncos-19
96Swift Current Broncos-23
97Beehive-73
Authentic Autographs-73
Golden Portraits-73
97Swift Current Broncos-22
97Bowman CHL-120
OPC-120
98Bowman's Best-142
Refractors-142
Atomic Refractors-142
98OPC Chrome-231
Refractors-231
98Pacific-58
Ice Blue-58
Red-58
98Topps-231
O-Pee-Chee-231
98Bowman CHL-79
Golden Anniversary-79
OPC International-79
Scout's Choice-SC9
98Bowman Chrome CHL-79
Golden Anniversary-79
Golden Anniversary Refractors-79
OPC International-79
OPC International Refractors-79
Refractors-79
00BAP Memorabilia-70
Emerald-70
Ruby-70
Sapphire-70
Promos-70
00BAP Mem Chicago Sportsfest Copper-70
00BAP Memorabilia Chicago Sportsfest Blue-70
00BAP Memorabilia Chicago Sportsfest Gold-70
00BAP Memorabilia Chicago Sportsfest Ruby-70
00BAP Memorabilia Chicago Sun-Times Ruby-70
00BAP Memorabilia Chicago Sun-Times Gold-70
00BAP Mem Chicago Sun-Times Sapphire-70
00BAP Mem Toronto Fall Expo Copper-70
00BAP Memorabilia Toronto Fall Expo Gold-70
00BAP Memorabilia Toronto Fall Expo Ruby-70
00O-Pee-Chee-286
00O-Pee-Chee Parallel-286
00Pacific-77
Copper-77
Gold-77
Ice Blue-77
Premiere Date-77
00Topps/OPC-286
Parallel-286
00Topps Chrome-181
OPC Refractors-181
Refractors-181
01Titanium Draft Day Edition-163
02Crown Royale Jerseys-19
02Crown Royale Jerseys Gold-19
02O-Pee-Chee-270
02O-Pee-Chee Premier Blue Parallel-270
02O-Pee-Chee Premier Red Parallel-270
02O-Pee-Chee Factory Set-270
02Pacific Complete-67
Red-67
02Pacific Heads-Up Quad Jerseys-23
02Pacific Heads-Up Quad Jerseys Gold-23
02Titanium Jerseys-60
02Titanium Jerseys Retail-60
02Titanium Patches-60
02Topps-270
OPC Blue Parallel-270
OPC Red Parallel-270
Factory Set-270
02Worcester IceCats-21
03Worcester Ice Cats-25

Varnakov, Mikhail
81Swedish Semic Hockey VM Stickers-54
87Russian National Team-22
04Russian RHL-10

Varolik, Marian
01Slovakian Kvarteto-8D

Varone, Phil
06Kitchener Rangers-23

Varpela, Matti
66Finnish Jaakiekkosarja-45

Vartiainen, Eero
78Finnish SM-Liiga-146

Vartiainen, Matti
66Finnish Jaakiekkosarja-123

Vartiainen, Seppo
72Finnish Jaakiekko-320
73Finnish Jaakiekko-124

Varty, Brent
00London Knights-10

Varvio, Jarkko
91Upper Deck-676
French-676
91Upper Deck Czech World Juniors-39
92Finnish Jyvas-Hyva Stickers-24
92Classic-30
Gold-30
92Classic Four-Sport *-179
Gold-179
93Donruss-90
Rated Rookies-6
93Leaf-383
Freshman Phenoms-8
93Parkhurst-252
Emerald Ice-252
Calder Candidates-C8
Calder Candidates Gold-C8
93Pinnacle-430
Canadian-430
93Score-620
Gold-620
Canadian-620
Canadian Gold-620
93Ultra-302
Wave of the Future-19
93Upper Deck-422
SP-40
93Finnish SISU-371
93Swedish Semic World Champ Stickers-83
94Donruss-129
94Leaf-199
94Parkhurst SE-SE40
Gold-SE40
94Ultra-281
94Upper Deck-429
Electric Ice-429
94Finnish SISU-349
94Finnish SISU Guest Specials-12
94Finnish Jaa Kiekko-44
94Classic Pro Prospects-125
95Finnish SISU-306
95Finnish SISU Limited-89
95Finnish Semic World Championships-44
96Finnish SISU Redline-108
98Finnish Kerailysarja Leijonat-46
98Swedish UD Choice-115
99Finnish Cardset Aces High-H-10
99Swedish Upper Deck-12
00Finnish Cardset-220

Vary, John
897th Inn. Sketch OHL-155
907th Inn. Sketch OHL-75
907th Inn. Sketch OHL-320
917th Inn. Sketch OHL-237
94Central Hockey League-123
95Louisiana Ice Gators-20
95Louisiana Ice Gators Playoffs-21
98Muskegon Fury-16
98UHL All-Stars-7
99Topeka Scarecrows-2
01Bakersfield Condors-19
03Port Huron Beacons-22

Vary, Marc-Olivier
01Cape Breton Screaming Eagles-10

Vas, Janos
02Swedish Malmo Red Hawks-15
05Idaho Steelheads-22
05Iowa Stars-20
06Iowa Stars-22

Vasicek, Josef
00BAP Memorabilia-429
Emerald-429
Ruby-429
Sapphire-429
00BAP Signature Series-264
Emerald-264
Ruby-264
Sapphire-264
Autographs-226
Autographs Gold-226
00Black Diamond-70
Gold-70
00Crown Royale-115
00Private Stock-108
Gold-108
Premiere Date-108
Retail-108
Silver-108
PS-2001 Rookies-5
00SP Authentic-96
00SP Game Used-64
00SPx-155
00Stadium Club-254
00Titanium-109
Retail-109
00Titanium Draft Day Edition-109
00Titanium Draft Day Promos-109
00Topps Gold Label Class 1-108
Gold-108
00Topps Gold Label Class 2-108
00Topps Gold Label Class 2 Gold-108
00Topps Gold Label Class 3-108
00Topps Gold Label Class 3 Gold-108
00Topps Heritage-86
Chrome Parallel-86
00Topps Premier Plus-106
Blue Ice-106
Rookies-PR6
Rookies Blue Ice-PR6
00Topps Stars-114
Blue-114
00UD Pros and Prospects-97
00UD Reserve-90
00Upper Deck-205
Exclusives Tier 1-205
Exclusives Tier 2-205
00Upper Deck Ice-50
00Upper Deck Ice-66
Immortals-50
Legends-50
Stars-50
00Upper Deck MVP-212
First Stars-212
Second Stars-212
Third Stars-212
00Vanguard-108
Pacific Proofs-108
01BAP Memorabilia-172
Emerald-172
Ruby-172
Sapphire-172
01O-Pee-Chee-227
01O-Pee-Chee Premier Parallel-227
01Parkhurst-244
01Topps-227
OPC Parallel-227
01Topps Chrome-76
Refractors-76
Black Border Refractors-76
01Topps Heritage-77
Refractors-77
01Upper Deck-35
Exclusives-35
01Upper Deck Victory-68
Gold-68
02BAP Memorabilia-134
Emerald-134
Ruby-134
Sapphire-134
NHL All-Star Game-134
NHL All-Star Game Blue-134
NHL All-Star Game Green-134
NHL All-Star Game Red-134
02BAP Memorabilia Toronto Fall Expo-134
02BAP Sig Series Auto Buybacks 2000-226
02BAP Signature Series Golf-GS45
02O-Pee-Chee-146
02O-Pee-Chee Premier Blue Parallel-146
02O-Pee-Chee Premier Red Parallel-146
02O-Pee-Chee Factory Set-146
02Pacific-71
Blue-71
Red-/1
02Pacific Complete-337
Red-337
02Pacific Exclusive-33
02Topps-146
OPC Blue Parallel-146
OPC Red Parallel-146
Factory Set-146
02Topps Total-267
02Upper Deck-29
Exclusives-29
02Upper Deck Vintage-48
02Czech Stadion Cup Finals-492
03Bowman-29
Gold-29
03Bowman Chrome-29
Refractors-29
Gold Refractors-29
Xfractors-29
03Hurricanes Postcards-19
03ITG Action-148
03O-Pee-Chee-134
03OPC Blue-134
03OPC Gold-134
03OPC Red-134
03Pacific Calder-17
Silver-17
03Pacific Complete-123
Red-123
03Pacific Heads-Up-18
Hobby LTD-18
Retail LTD-18
03Titanium-22
Hobby Jersey Number Parallels-22
Retail-22
Retail Jersey Number Parallels-22
03Topps-134
Blue-134
Gold-134
Red-134
03Topps C55-41
Minis-41
Minis American Back-41
Minis American Back Red-41
Minis Bazooka Back-41
Minis Brooklyn Back-41
Minis Hat Trick Back-41
Minis O Canada Back-41
Minis O Canada Back Red-41
Minis Stanley Cup Back-41
03Czech National Team Postcards-14
04Pacific-51
Blue-51
Red-51
04Czech HC Slavia Praha Postcards-10
04Czech OFS-176
Stars-20
05Beehive Signature Scrapbook-SSJV
05Parkhurst-100
Facsimile Auto Parallel-100
Signatures-JV
05SP Game Used Auto Draft-AD-JV
05SP Game Used Statscriptions-ST-JV
05UD PowerPlay-18
Rainbow-18
05Upper Deck-33
HG Glossy-33
Notable Numbers-N-JV
05Upper Deck MVP-73
Gold-73
Platinum-73
05Upper Deck Toronto Fall Expo-33
05Upper Deck Victory-38
Black-38
Gold-38
Silver-38
05Czech World Champions Postcards-6
05Czech Kvarteto Bonaparte-7b
05Czech Pexeso Mini Blue Set-22
05Czech Pexeso Mini Red Set-7
06O-Pee-Chee-278
Rainbow-278
06Ultra Fresh Ink-IJV
06Upper Deck MVP Autographs-OAVV
06Czech NHL ELH Postcards-15

Vasicek, Michal
98Czech OFS-289

Vasicek, Tomas
94Czech APS Extraliga-116
96Czech APS Extraliga-192

Vasie, Valeri
96UK Guildford Flames-22

Vasilev, Ivan
95Czech APS Extraliga-336

Vasilevski, Alex
95Images-11
Gold-11
95Slapshot Memorial Cup-49
96Collector's Edge Ice-98
Prism-98
99Muskegon Fury-11

Vasilevski, Andrei
00Russian Hockey League-147

Vasiliev, Alexei
03Russian SL-32

Vasiliev, Mikhael
83Swedish Semic VM Stickers-70
84Russian National Team-21

Vasiliev, Valeri
70Finnish Jaakiekko-19
70Russian National Team Postcards-14
70Swedish Hockey-320
72Finnish Jaakiekko-39
72Finnish Hellas-68
73Finnish Jaakiekko-19
73Russian National Team-5
73Swedish Stickers-85
74Finnish Jenkki-59
74Finnish Typotor-75
74Russian National Team-22
74Swedish Stickers-3
79Panini Stickers-144
79Russian National Team-7
80USSR Olympic Team Mini Pics-10
82Swedish Semic VM Stickers-56
91Future Trends Canada '72-68
91Future Trends Canada '72 French-68
92Future Trends '76 Canada Cup-132
96Swedish Semic Wien Hockey Legends-HL4
99Russian Stars of Hockey-38
05ITG Ultimate Memorabilia Ultimate Autos-3
05ITG Ultimate Mem Ultimate Autos Gold-3
06ITG International Ice-40
Gold-40
Autographs-AVV
Cornerstones-IC07
Cornerstones Gold-IC07

Vasilijevs, Herbert
94German DEL-230
95Slapshot-94
95Guelph Storm-10
96Carolina Monarchs-24
98Kentucky Thoroughblades-20
00Pacific-28
Copper-28
Gold-28
Ice Blue-28
Premiere Date-28
00SPx-91
Spectrum-91
00Upper Deck-216
Exclusives Tier 1-216
Exclusives Tier 2-216
01BAP Memorabilia-268
Emerald-268
Ruby-268
Sapphire-268
02Manitoba Moose-15
03Russian Hockey League-273
04German DEL Update-339
05German DEL-233
06German DEL-141

Vasilyev, Alexei
95Upper Deck-555
Electric Ice-555
Electric Ice Gold-555
95Signature Rookies Tetrad Autobilia *-53
98Hartford Wolf Pack-21
99Hartford Wolf Pack-21
00BAP Memorabilia-304
Emerald-304
Ruby-304
Sapphire-304
Promos-304
00BAP Mem Chicago Sportsfest Copper-304
00BAP Memorabilia Chicago Sportsfest Blue-304
00BAP Memorabilia Chicago Sportsfest Gold-304
00BAP Memorabilia Chicago Sportsfest Ruby-304
00BAP Memorabilia Chicago Sun-Times Ruby-304
00BAP Memorabilia Chicago Sun-Times Gold-304
00BAP Mem Chicago Sun-Times Sapphire-304
00BAP Mem Toronto Fall Expo Copper-304
00BAP Memorabilia Toronto Fall Expo Gold-304
00BAP Memorabilia Toronto Fall Expo Ruby-304
00Milwaukee Admirals Keebler-19
00Milwaukee Admirals Postcards-16

Vasilyev, Andrei
95Parkhurst International-513
Emerald Ice-513
95Upper Deck-412
Electric Ice-412
Electric Ice Gold-412
97Long Beach Ice Dogs-17
98Grand Rapids Griffins-20
99German DEL-88
01German Upper Deck-19

Vaske, Dennis
90ProCards AHL/IHL-508
91O-Pee-Chee-230
91Score American-310
91Score Canadian Bilingual-340
91Score Canadian English-340
91Topps-230
91Upper Deck-49
French-49
91ProCards-460
92Bowman-28
92Parkhurst-335
Emerald Ice-335
92Stadium Club-362
92Topps-87
Gold-87G
92Upper Deck-50
92Upper Deck-383
93OPC Premier-438
Gold-438
93PowerPlay-387
93Stadium Club-358
Members Only Master Set-358
First Day Issue-358
93Topps/OPC Premier-438
Gold-438
94Parkhurst-141
Gold-141
94Pinnacle-456
Artist's Proofs-456
Rink Collection-456
94Ultra-134
95Emotion-110
95Panini Stickers-100
95Playoff One on One-170
95SkyBox Impact-106
95Ultra-272
96Islander Postcards-21
97Be A Player-120
Autographs-120
Autographs Die-Cuts-120
Autographs Prismatic Die-Cuts-120
97Pacific Invincible NHL Regime-122

Vasko, Elmer
44Beehive Group II Photos-144
57Topps-27
58Topps-12
59Topps-3
60Shirriff Coins-73
60Topps-23
Stamps-50
61Shirriff/Salada Coins-26
61Topps-25
62Topps-27
Hockey Bucks-23
63Chex Photos-56
63Topps-26
63Toronto Star-41
64Beehive Group III Photos-59
64Coca-Cola Caps-22
64Topps-5
64Toronto Star-48
65Coca-Cola-22
65Topps-114
68O-Pee-Chee-147
Puck Stickers-8
91Ultimate Original Six-64
French-64
94Parkhurst Missing Link-31
94Parkhurst Tall Boys-30
94Parkhurst Tall Boys-141
04ITG Franchises US West-165

Vaskovic, Lubomir
06Czech OFS-218

Vassiliev, Vladimir
94German DEL-198

Vassos, Chris
04Langley Hornets-18
06Westside Warriors-13

Vasut, Martin
04Czech OFS-262
05Missouri River Otters-5

Vasyuchkov, Maxim
99Russian Hockey League-131

Vasyunov, Alexander
06ITG Heroes and Prospects-137
Autographs-AAV

Vater, Matthias
93Quebec Pee-Wee Tournament-1771
98German DEL-216

Vatri, Josh
05Erie Otters-13
06Erie Otters-9

Vauclair, Geoffrey
96Swiss HNL-515
98Swiss Power Play Stickers-174
99Swiss Panini Stickers-174
99Swiss Panini Stickers-273
00Swiss Panini Stickers-217
01Swiss HNL-48

Vauclair, Julien
92Quebec Pee-Wee Tournament-1385
96Swiss HNL-503
98Swiss Power Play Stickers-160
98Swiss Power Play Stickers-289
99Swiss Panini Stickers-160
99Swiss Panini Stickers-287
00Swiss Slapshot Mini-Cards-HCL6
01Grand Rapids Griffins-1
03ITG VIP Rookie Debut-51
03Pacific Complete-524
Red-524
03Parkhurst Rookie-71
03SP Authentic-123
Limited-123
03Topps Traded-TT158
Blue-TT158
Gold-TT158
Red-TT158
03UD Honor Roll-164
03UD Premier Collection-83
03Upper Deck-453
Canadian Exclusives-453
HG-453
UD Exclusives-453
03Upper Deck Ice-105
Glass Parallel-105
03Upper Deck Rookie Update-142
03Binghamton Senators-21
03Binghamton Senators Postcards-3
03Pacific AHL Prospects-8
Gold-8
04ITG Heroes and Prospects Emblems-38
04ITG Heroes and Prospects Emblems Gold-38
04ITG Heroes/Prospects He Shoots/Scores-39
04ITG Heroes and Prospects Jerseys-38
04ITG Heroes and Prospects Jerseys Gold-38
04ITG Heroes and Prospects Numbers-38
04ITG Heroes and Prospects Numbers Gold-38
06Binghamton Senators 5th Anniversary-32

Vaughan, Doug
52Juniors Blue Tint-117

Vaughan, Kevin
93Oshawa Generals-17

Vaughan, Lyle
91Air Canada SJHL-C40

Vaughan, R.
83Belleville Bulls-8
84Belleville Bulls-2

Vauhkonen, Jonni
92Upper Deck-619
92Finnish Jyvas-Hyva Stickers-146
93Parkhurst-525
Emerald Ice-525
93Finnish Jyvas-Hyva Stickers-262
93Finnish SISU-296
93Finnish SISU-392
93Finnish SISU Autographs-296
94Finnish SISU-174
95Finnish Semic World Championships-234
96Finnish SISU Redline-105
98Finnish Kerailysarja-173
99Finnish Cardset-86
00Finnish Cardset-190
01Finnish Cardset-204

Vautour, Yvon
81O-Pee-Chee-84
81Rockies Postcards-28
84Fredericton Express-26

Vavra, Kamil
03Regina Pats-13

Vavrecka, Jan
94Czech APS Extraliga-8
95Czech APS Extraliga-31

Vavroch, Robert
99Czech Score Blue 2000-54
99Czech Score Red Ice 2000-54

Veale, Brian
91British Columbia JHL-105
91British Columbia JHL-147
92British Columbia JHL-113

Veasey, Bill
00Arizona Icecats-23

Veber, Jiri
94Finnish SISU-337
95Czech APS Extraliga-10
95Finnish Semic World Championships-147
95Swedish World Championships Stickers-196
96Czech APS Extraliga-218
96Czech APS Extraliga-340
97Czech APS Extraliga-32
97Czech APS Extraliga-348
97Czech DS Stickers-2
97Czech DS Stickers-23
98Czech DS-77
98Czech OFS-100
98Czech OFS-422
98Czech OFS-472
99Czech DS-131
99Czech OFS-445
03Czech OFS Plus-368

Veber, Roman
96Czech APS Extraliga-268
97Czech DS Stickers-176
04German DEL-280

Vecchiarelli, John
93Swedish Semic World Champ Stickers-219
94Finnish Jaa Kiekko-303
95Buffalo Stampedes RHI-19

95Buffalo Stampedes RHI-19
99UHL All-Stars East-10T
Veccia, Rob
84Sault Ste. Marie Greyhounds-21
Vehanen, Petri
99Finnish Cardset-79
00Finnish Cardset-300
01Finnish Cardset-292
02Finnish Cardset-149
02Finnish Cardset-287
03Finnish Cardset-100
04Finnish Cardset-109
Parallel-80
05Swedish SHL Elitset-253
Catchers-10
Catchers Gold-10
Gold-253
06Swedish SHL Elitset-116
Goal Patrol-16
In The Crease-9
Vehmanen, Hannu
70Finnish Jaakiekko-361
Vehmanen, Jorma
66Finnish Jaakiekkosarja-14
70Finnish Jaakiekko-79
70Finnish Jaakiekko-240
70Swedish Hockey-312
70Swedish Masterserien-167
71Finnish Suomi Stickers-78
71Finnish Suomi Stickers-163
71Swedish Hockey-74
72Finnish Jaakiekko-115
72Finnish Semic World Championship-89
72Swedish Semic World Championship-89
73Finnish Jaakiekko-83
73Finnish Jaakiekko-213
74Finnish Typotor-24
78Finnish SM-Liiga-164
80Finnish Mallasjuoma-117
96Finnish SISU Redline-194
Vehvilainen, Simo
06Czech OFS-195
Veijalainen, Ari
71Finnish Suomi Stickers-378
Veilleux, Eric
917th Inn. Sketch QMJHL-245
94Classic Pro Prospects-67
98Kentucky Thoroughblades-21
99Manitoba Moose-9
00Lowell Lock Monsters-9
Veilleux, Guillaume
03Rimouski Oceanic-22
03Rimouski Oceanic Sheets-4
04Moncton Wildcats-24
04Quebec Remparts-24
05Quebec Remparts-21
05Quebec Remparts Signature Series-21
06Quebec Remparts-25
Veilleux, Hubert
03Rimouski Oceanic-23
03Rimouski Oceanic Sheets-5
Veilleux, Julien
93Quebec Pee-Wee Tournament-393
Veilleux, Keven
06Victoriaville Tigres-2
Veilleux, Simon
93Quebec Pee-Wee Tournament-401
Veilleux, Stephane
00Val d'Or Foreurs-23
Signed-23
02Atomic-127
02BAP All-Star Edition-129
Gold-129
Silver-129
02BAP Memorabilia-352
02BAP Signature Series-187
Autographs-187
Autographs Gold-187
02BAP Ultimate Memorabilia-40
Autographs-27
02Crown Royale-120
Blue-120
Purple-120
Red-120
Retail-120
02ITG Used-189
02Pacific Calder-125
Silver-125
02Pacific Complete-533
Red-533
02Pacific Quest for the Cup-125
Gold-125
02Parkhurst-240
Bronze-240
Gold-240
Silver-240
02Private Stock Reserve-166
Blue-166
Red-166
Retail-166
02SP Authentic-148
02SP Game Used-100
02Titanium-120
Blue-120
Red-120
Retail-120
02Topps Total-437
02UD Honor Roll-116
02UD Mask Collection-124
02UD Premier Collection-57B
Gold-57
02UD Top Shelf-115
02Upper Deck-439
Exclusives-439
02Vanguard-119
LTD-119
03AHL Top Prospects-41
03Houston Aeros-18
04Houston Aeros-18
06Be A Player-15
Autographs-15
Signatures-VE
Veilleux, Steve
89ProCards IHL-167
90ProCards AHL/IHL-332
91ProCards-79
92Fredericton Canadiens-27
Veinot, Nathan
02Cape Breton Screaming Eagles-4
03Cape Breton Screaming Eagles-8
Veisor, Jon
93Quebec Pee-Wee Tournament-825
Veisor, Mike
75O-Pee-Chee NHL-385
77O-Pee-Chee NHL-393
79Blackhawks Postcards-20
80O-Pee-Chee-361
82Whalers Junior Hartford Courant-21
83Whalers Junior Hartford Courant-21
Veitch, Darren
81Capitals Team Issue-18
82Capitals Team Issue-25
82Post Cereal-20
85Capitals Pizza Hut-15
87O-Pee-Chee-114
87Panini Stickers-239
87Red Wings Little Caesars-28
87Topps-114
88Maple Leafs PLAY-22
88Panini Stickers-39
89ProCards AHL-123
90Newmarket Saints-25
90ProCards AHL/IHL-155
91Moncton Hawks-28
92Peoria Rivermen-25
93Peoria Rivermen-27
96Collector's Edge Ice-180
Prism-180
98Phoenix Mustangs-21
Vejvoda, Martin
99Czech OFS-175
Vejvoda, Otakar
94Czech APS Extraliga-59
95Czech APS Extraliga-96
95Czech APS Extraliga-372
96Swedish Semic Wien-115
97Swedish Collector's Choice-15
98Czech OFS-408
99Czech OFS-161
00Czech OFS-134
Velebny, Lubos
01Belleville Bulls Update-9
Velemirovich, Tim
06Fayetteville FireAntz-19
Velikov, Maxim
00Russian Hockey League-221
02Russian Hockey League-115
Velischek, Randy
83North Stars Postcards-26
84North Stars Postcards-29
85Springfield Indians-4
85Devils Postcards-9
86Devils Police-18
88Devils Caretta-28
89Devils Caretta-27
89O-Pee-Chee-245
89Panini Stickers-259
90Nordiques Petro-Canada-39
90O-Pee-Chee-453
90OPC Premier-125
90Pro Set-518
90Score Rookie/Traded-64T
90Upper Deck-392
French-392
91Bowman-152
91Nordiques Panini Team Stickers-23
91Nordiques Petro-Canada-33
91O-Pee-Chee-377
91Panini Stickers-265
91Pro Set-206
French-206
91Score American-257
91Score Canadian Bilingual-477
91Score Canadian English-477
91Stadium Club-27
91Topps-377
91Upper Deck-484
French-484
92Bowman-131
92Durivage Panini-45
92O-Pee-Chee-288
92Stadium Club-460
92Topps-430
Gold-430G
94Milwaukee Admirals-26
Vellan, Per Kristian
92Norwegian Elite Series-124
92Norwegian Elite Series-206
Vellinga, Mike
95Slapshot-92
95Guelph Storm-21
96Guelph Storm-19
96Guelph Storm Premier Collection-3
97Guelph Storm-12
99Johnstown Chiefs-20
00Johnstown Chiefs-19
03Laredo Bucks-19
Vellucci, Mike
83Belleville Bulls-17
88ProCards AHL-54
91Michigan Falcons-11
01Plymouth Whalers-25
03Plymouth Whalers-25
Venalainen, Sami
00Finnish Cardset-332
01Finnish Cardset-344
03Finnish Cardset-152
04Finnish Cardset-163
Parallel-120
05Finnish Cardset -148
06Finnish Cardset-153
Venard, Dave
04Notre Dame Fighting Irish-10
Venasky, Aaron
00Sioux City Musketeers-28
Venasky, Vic
74O-Pee-Chee NHL-389
75O-Pee-Chee NHL-312
75Topps-312
76O-Pee-Chee NHL-211
76Topps-211
77O-Pee-Chee NHL-187
77Topps-187
78O-Pee-Chee-321
79O-Pee-Chee-269
80O-Pee-Chee-290
92Quebec Pee-Wee Tournament-1238
Vendette, Steve
93Quebec Pee-Wee Tournament-1345
Venedam, Sean
93Sudbury Wolves-11
93Sudbury Wolves Police-24
94Sudbury Wolves-10
94Sudbury Wolves Police-17
95Slapshot-393
95Sudbury Wolves-1
95Sudbury Wolves Police-24
96Sudbury Wolves-24
96Sudbury Wolves Police-26
97Sudbury Wolves Anniversary-21
97Toledo Storm-7
99ECHL All-Star Southern Conference-17
01Greenville Grrrowl-8
02Fort Wayne Komets-21
02Fort Wayne Komets Shoe Carnival-9
03Fort Wayne Komets-4
03Fort Wayne Komets 2003 Champions-4
03Fort Wayne Komets Shoe Carnival-12
04Fort Wayne Komets-17
04Fort Wayne Komets Shoe Carnival-14
05Bakersfield Condors-20
06Bakersfield Condors-1
Venera, Zdenek
98Czech OFS-17
00Czech OFS-348
06Czech OFS Coaches-12
Veneruzzo, Gary
68O-Pee-Chee-119
68Topps-119
70O-Pee-Chee-101
70Topps-101
72Los Angeles Sharks WHA-16
72O-Pee-Chee-330
73Quaker Oats WHA-32
74O-Pee-Chee WHA-55
75Stingers Kahn's-14
76O-Pee-Chee WHA-21
76San Diego Mariners WHA-13
Venis, Ken
93Memphis RiverKings-16
94Central Hockey League-89
94San Antonio Iguanas-17
Venkrbec, Miroslav
96Czech APS Extraliga-264
98Czech OFS-98
99Czech OFS-437
00Czech OFS-319
Venne, Maxime
93Quebec Pee-Wee Tournament-37
Venne, Stephane
93Wichita Thunder-15
Venneruzzo, Gary
66Tulsa Oilers-11
Venters, Daryl
96UK Fife Flyers-12
97UK Fife Flyers-10
Vento, Jouni
92Finnish Jyvas-Hyva Stickers-195
93Finnish Jyvas-Hyva Stickers-355
93Finnish SISU-214
93Finnish SISU-215C
94Finnish SISU-53
94Finnish SISU-177
95Finnish SISU-354
96German DEL-231
99German Bundesliga 2-99
Veravainen, Heikki
65Finnish Hellas-67
66Finnish Jaakiekkosarja-18
Verbeek, Brian
84Kingston Canadians-23
85Kingston Canadians-23
Verbeek, Pat
83Canadian National Juniors-17
83Devils Postcards-25
84Devils Postcards-12
84O-Pee-Chee-121
84O-Pee-Chee Stickers-73
84Topps-90
85O-Pee-Chee-56
85Topps-56
86Devils Police-19
86O-Pee-Chee-46
86O-Pee-Chee Stickers-202
86Topps-46
87O-Pee-Chee-6
87O-Pee-Chee Stickers-58
87Panini Stickers-81
87Topps-6
88Devils Caretta-29
88O-Pee-Chee-29
88O-Pee-Chee Minis-43
88O-Pee-Chee Stickers-81
88Panini Stickers-278
88Topps-29
89O-Pee-Chee-32
89Topps-32
89Whalers Junior Milk-22
90Bowman-257
Tiffany-257
90O-Pee-Chee-112
90Panini Stickers-36
90Pro Set-112
90Score-35
Canadian-35
90Score Hottest/Rising Stars-18
90Topps-112
Tiffany-112
90Upper Deck-172
French-172
90Whalers Jr. 7-Eleven-25
91Pro Set Platinum-44
91Bowman-12
91Gillette-24
91Kraft-23
91O-Pee-Chee-499
91OPC Premier-5
91Panini Stickers-313
91Parkhurst-64
French-64
91Pinnacle-43
French-43
91Pro Set-86
91Pro Set-303
French-86
French-303
Puck Candy Promos-3
Puck Candy-10
91Score American-70
91Score Canadian Bilingual-70
91Score Canadian English-70
91Stadium Club-102
91Topps-499
Team Scoring Leaders-1
91Upper Deck-193
French-193
91Whalers Jr. 7-Eleven-26
92Bowman-112
92Humpty Dumpty II-24
92O-Pee-Chee-197
92Panini Stickers-256
92Panini Stickers French-256
92Parkhurst-58
Emerald Ice-58
92Pinnacle-348
French-348
92Pro Set-58
92Score-282
Canadian-282
92Seasons Patches-44
92Stadium Club-197
92Topps-493
Gold-493G
92Ultra-305
92Upper Deck-7
92Upper Deck-204
92Whalers Dairymart-22
93Donruss-148
93Kraft-39
93Leaf-144
93OPC Premier-47
Gold-47
93Panini Stickers-124
93Parkhurst-353
Emerald Ice-353
93Pinnacle-243
Canadian-243
Captains-10
Captains Canadian-10
93PowerPlay-110
93Score-10
Canadian-10
93Stadium Club-36
Members Only Master Set-36
OPC-36
First Day Issue-36
First Day Issue OPC-36
93Topps/OPC Premier-47
Gold-47
93Ultra-175
93Upper Deck-331
SP-67
93Whalers Coke-23
94Be A Player-R61
Signature Cards-71
94Canada Games NHL POGS-120
94Donruss-299
94EA Sports-59
94Flair-76
94Fleer-91
94Leaf-172
94Leaf Limited-27
94OPC Premier-390
Special Effects-390
94Parkhurst-92
Gold-92
SE Vintage-7
94Pinnacle-37
Artist's Proofs-37
Rink Collection-37
94Score Check It-CI18
94Select-76
Gold-76
94SP-72
Die Cuts-72
94Stadium Club-120
Members Only Master Set-120
First Day Issue-120
Super Team Winner Cards-120
94Topps/OPC Premier-390
Special Effects-390
94Ultra-95
94Upper Deck-278
Electric Ice-278
SP Inserts-SP124
SP Inserts Die Cuts-SP124
94Upper Deck NHLPA/Be A Player-38
95Canada Games NHL POGS-182
95Collector's Choice-55
Player's Club-55
Player's Club Platinum-55
95Donruss-29
95Donruss Elite-76
Die Cut Stars-76
Die Cut Uncut-76
95Emotion-120
95Finest-131
Refractors-131
95Leaf-16
95Metal-101
95Panini Stickers-108
95Parkhurst International-407
Emerald Ice-407
95Pinnacle-111
Artist's Proofs-111
Rink Collection-111
95Playoff One on One-70
95Score-122
Black Ice Artist's Proofs-122
Black Ice-122
95Select Certified-108
Mirror Gold-108
95SkyBox Impact-115
95SP-93
95Stadium Club-17
Members Only Master Set-17
95Summit-107
Artist's Proofs-107
Ice-107
95Topps-37
OPC Inserts-37
Power Lines-3PL
95Topps SuperSkills-43
Platinum-43
95Ultra-107
Gold Medallion-107
95Upper Deck-98
Electric Ice-98
Electric Ice Gold-98
NHL All-Stars-AS13
NHL All-Stars Jumbo-AS13
95Zenith-82
95Swedish World Championships Stickers-17
96Be A Player-38
Autographs-38
Autographs Silver-38
96Black Diamond-136
Gold-136
96Collector's Choice-170
96Donruss-200
Press Proofs-200
96Donruss Canadian Ice-48
Gold Press Proofs-48
Red Press Proofs-48
96Donruss Elite-42
Die Cut Stars-42
96Flair-25
Blue Ice-25
96Fleer Picks Dream Lines-10
96Leaf-59
Press Proofs-59
96Leaf Limited-33
Gold-33
96Leaf Preferred-8
Press Proofs-8
Steel-14
Steel Gold-14
96Maggers-105
96Metal Universe-43
96Pinnacle-68
Artist's Proofs-68
Foil-68
Premium Stock-68
Rink Collection-68
96Playoff One on One-359
96Score-94
Artist's Proofs-94
Dealer's Choice Artist's Proofs-94
Special Artist's Proofs-94
Golden Blades-94
96Select Certified-49
Artist's Proofs-49
Blue-49
Mirror Blue-49
Mirror Gold-49
Mirror Red-49
Red-49
96SP-41
96Stadium Club Members Only-35
96Stars Postcards-26
96Stars Score Sheet-94
96Summit-5
Artist's Proofs-5
Ice-5
Metal-5
Premium Stock-5
96Topps Picks-69
OPC Inserts-69
96Ultra-47
Gold Medallion-47
96Upper Deck-249
96Upper Deck Ice-17
Parallel-17
96Zenith-93
Artist's Proofs-93
97Collector's Choice-66
Star Quest-SQ16
97Crown Royale-43
Emerald Green-43
Ice Blue-43
Silver-43
97Donruss-23
Press Proofs Silver-23
Press Proofs Gold-23
97Donruss Canadian Ice-27
Dominion Series-27
Provincial Series-27
97Donruss Limited-75
Exposure-75
97Donruss Preferred-57
Cut to the Chase-57
97Leaf-78
Fractal Matrix-78
Fractal Matrix Die Cuts-78
97Leaf International-78
Universal Ice-78
97Pacific-162
Copper-162
Emerald Green-162
Ice Blue-162
Red-162
Silver-162
97Pacific Invincible-44
Copper-44
Emerald Green-44
Ice Blue-44
Red-44
Silver-44
97Pacific Omega-76
Copper-76
Dark Gray-76
Emerald Green-76
Gold-76
Ice Blue-76
97Panini Stickers-137
97Paramount-63
Copper-63
Dark Grey-63
Emerald Green-63
Ice Blue-63
Red-63
Silver-63
97Pinnacle-173
Press Plates Back Black-173
Press Plates Back Cyan-173
Press Plates Back Magenta-173
Press Plates Back Yellow-173
Press Plates Front Black-173
Press Plates Front Cyan-173
Press Plates Front Magenta-173
Press Plates Front Yellow-173
97Pinnacle Certified-111
Red-111
Mirror Blue-111
Mirror Gold-111
Mirror Red-111
97Pinnacle Inside-157
97Pinnacle Tot Cert Platinum Blue-111
97Pinnacle Tot Cert Platinum Gold-111
97Pinnacle Totally Certified Platinum Red-111
97Pinnacle Tot Cert Mirror Platinum Gold-111
97Score-124
Artist's Proofs-124
Golden Blades-124
Check It-18
97Upper Deck-262
97Sudbury Wolves Anniversary-22
98Finest-69
No Protectors-69
No Protectors Refractors-69
Refractors-69
98OPC Chrome-120
Refractors-120
98Pacific-185
Ice Blue-185
Red-185
98Panini Stickers-126
98Topps-120
O-Pee-Chee-120
98Upper Deck-257
Exclusives-257
Exclusives 1 of 1-257
Gold Reserve-257
99Pacific-131
Copper-131
Emerald Green-131
Gold-131
Ice Blue-131
Premiere Date-131
Red-131
99Pacific Omega-86
Copper-86
Gold-86
Ice Blue-86
Premiere Date-86
99Upper Deck MVP SC Edition-69
Gold Script-69
Silver Script-69
Super Script-69
00Aurora-53
Pinstripes-53
Premiere Date-53
00BAP Memorabilia-302
Emerald-302
Ruby-302
Sapphire-302
Promos-302
00BAP Mem Chicago Sportsfest Copper-302
00BAP Memorabilia Chicago Sportsfest Blue-302
00BAP Memorabilia Chicago Sportsfest Gold-302
00BAP Memorabilia Chicago Sportsfest Ruby-302
00BAP Memorabilia Chicago Sun-Times Ruby-302
00BAP Memorabilia Chicago Sun-Times Gold-302
00BAP Mem Chicago Sun-Times Sapphire-302
00BAP Mem Toronto Fall Expo Copper-302
00BAP Memorabilia Toronto Fall Expo Gold-302
00BAP Memorabilia Toronto Fall Expo Ruby-302
00BAP Parkhurst 2000-P238
00O-Pee-Chee-218
00O-Pee-Chee Parallel-218
00Pacific-159
Copper-159
Gold-159
Ice Blue-159
Premiere Date-159
00Paramount-90
Copper-90
Gold-90
Holo-Gold-90
Holo-Silver-90
Ice Blue-90
Premiere Date-90
00Topps/OPC-218
Parallel-218
1000 Point Club-PC16
00Topps Chrome-140
OPC Refractors-140
Refractors-140
1000 Point Club Refractors-16
00Topps Heritage-187
00UD Heroes-45
00Upper Deck 500 Goal Club-500PV
00Upper Deck 500 Goal Club-500PV
00Upper Deck Legends Epic Signatures-PV
00Upper Deck MVP-68
Excellence-ME5
First Stars-68
Mark of Excellence-SGYV
Second Stars-68
Third Stars-68
00Upper Deck Victory-87
00Upper Deck Victory-250
01BAP Memorabilia 500 Goal Scorers-GS24
01BAP Signature Series-155
Autographs-155
Autographs Gold-155
500 Goal Scorers-18
500 Goal Scorers Autographs-18
01BAP Ultimate Mem 500 Goal Scorers-27
01BAP Ultimate Mem 500 Goal Scorers Autos-20
01BAP Ultimate Mem 500 Goal Scorers Jersey/Stick-27
01BAP Ultimate Mem 500 Goal Emblems-27
01O-Pee-Chee-126
01O-Pee-Chee Premier Parallel-126
01Pacific-150
Extreme LTD-150
Hobby LTD-150
Premiere Date-150
Retail LTD-150
01Pacific Arena Exclusives-150
01Parkhurst 500 Goal Scorers-PGS24
01Private Stock PS-2002-26
01Stars Postcards-25
01Topps-126
OPC Parallel-126
02BAP First Edition-202
02BAP Sig Series Auto Buybacks 2001-155
02BAP Signature Series Golf-GS67
02Pacific-121
Blue-121
Red-121
02UD Top Shelf Milestones Jerseys-MSYVR
03Parkhurst Original Six Detroit-57
03Parkhurst Original Six New York-67
04ITG Franchises Update-479
Autographs-PV1
04ITG Franchises US East Autographs-A-PV2
04ITG Franchises US East Memorabilia-ESM31
04ITG Franchises US East Mem Autos-ESM-PV
04ITG Franchises US East Memorabilia Gold-ESM31
05ITG Ultimate Mem 3 Star of the Game Jsy-20
05ITG Ult Mem 3 Star of the Game Jsy Gold-20
Verbeek, Tim
96Kitchener Rangers-26
98Barrie Colts-9
04Barrie Colts 10th Anniversary-21
04Idaho Steelheads-22
06Stockton Thunder-16
Verchota, Phil
80USA Olympic Team Mini Pics-7
81Swedish Semic Hockey VM Stickers-107
95Signature Rookies Miracle on Ice-37
95Signature Rookies Miracle on Ice-38
95Signature Rook Miracle on Ice Sigs-37
95Signature Rook Miracle on Ice Sigs-38
Vercik, Rudolf
03Czech OFS Plus-129
04Czech OFS-21
Verdule, Jimmy
92Quebec Pee-Wee Tournament-1027
02Florida Everblades-20
02Florida Everblades RBI-131
Vereker, John
93Quebec Pee-Wee Tournament-643
Verge, Brandon
03Lewiston Maineiacs-22
04Chicoutimi Sagueneens-4
Verizjnikov, Viktor
74Swedish Stickers-78
Vermette, Alexandre
96Quebec Pee-Wee Tournament-992
Vermette, Antoine
95Quebec Pee-Wee Tournament-278
98Quebec Remparts-22
Signed-22
99UD Prospects-57
99UD Prospects-79
00Victoriaville Tigres-8
Signed-8
00UD CHL Prospects-83
02SPx Rookie Redemption-R207
03BAP Memorabilia-191
Emerald-191
Gold-191
Ruby-191
Sapphire-191
03BAP Ultimate Memorabilia Autographs-128
Gold-128
03BAP Ultimate Mem Auto Jerseys-128
03BAP Ultimate Mem Auto Emblems-128
03BAP Ultimate Mem Auto Numbers-128
03BAP Ultimate Mem Rookie Jersey Emblems-17
03BAP Ultimate Mem Rookie Jsy Emblem Gold-17
03BAP Ultimate Mem Rookie Jersey Numbers-17
03BAP Ultimate Mem Rookie Jsy Number Gold-17
03Black Diamond-151
Black-151
Green-151
Red-151
03Bowman-153
Gold-153
Premier Performance-PP-AV
Premier Performance Patches-PP-AV
Signs of the Future-SOF-AV
03Bowman Chrome-153
Refractors-153
Gold Refractors-153
Xfractors-153
03Crown Royale-126
Red-128
Retail-128
Jerseys-18
Patches-18
03ITG Action-613
03ITG Used Signature Series-123
Autographs Gold-123
03ITG VIP Rookie Debut-12
03Pacific Calder-171
03Pacific Complete-527
Red-527
03Pacific Heads-Up-127
Hobby LTD-127
Retail LTD-127
Jerseys-21
Prime Prospects-15
Prime Prospects LTD-15
03Pacific Invincible-119
Blue-119
Red-119
Retail-119
03Pacific Luxury Suite-94
Gold-94
03Pacific Prism-159
03Pacific Quest for the Cup-128
Calder Contenders-15
03Pacific Supreme-130
03Pacific Supreme-130A
Blue-130
Red-130
Retail-130
03Parkhurst Toronto Expo Rookie Preview-PRP-18
03Parkhurst Rookie-195
Rookie Emblems-RE-45
Rookie Emblem Autographs-RE-AV
Rookie Emblems Gold-RE-45
Rookie Jerseys-RJ-45
Rookie Jersey Autographs-RJ-AV
Rookie Jerseys Gold-RJ-45
Rookie Numbers-RN-45
Rookie Number Autographs-RN-AV
Rookie Numbers Gold-RN-45
Teammates Gold-RT8
Teammates-RT8
03Private Stock Reserve-131
Blue-131
Red-131
Retail-131
03SP Authentic-140
Limited-140
03SP Game Used-73
Gold-73
03SPx-217
Radiance-217
Spectrum-217
03Titanium-213
Patches-213
03Topps C55-145
Minis-145
Minis American Back-145
Minis American Back Red-145
Minis Bazooka Back-145
Minis Brooklyn Back-145
Minis Hat Trick Back-145
Minis O Canada Back-145
Minis O Canada Back Red-145
Minis Stanley Cup Back-145
03Topps Pristine-179
03Topps Pristine-180
03Topps Pristine-181
Gold Refractor Die Cuts-179
Gold Refractor Die Cuts-180
Gold Refractor Die Cuts-181
Refractors-179
Refractors-180
Refractors-181
Press Plates Black-179
Press Plates Black-180
Press Plates Black-181
Press Plates Cyan-179
Press Plates Cyan-180
Press Plates Cyan-181
Press Plates Magenta-179
Press Plates Magenta-180
Press Plates Magenta-181
Press Plates Yellow-179
Press Plates Yellow-180
Press Plates Yellow-181
03Topps Traded-TT131
Blue-TT131
Gold-TT131
Red-TT131
Future Phenoms-FP-AV
03UD Honor Roll-177
03UD Premier Collection-77
03Upper Deck-231
Canadian Exclusives-231
HG-231
03Upper Deck Classic Portraits-178
03Upper Deck Ice-97
Glass Parallel-97
03Upper Deck MVP-450
03Upper Deck Trilogy-162
Limited-162
03Binghamton Senators-22
03Binghamton Senators Postcards-11
03Pacific AHL Prospect Destined Greatness-2
04Pacific Montreal International-6
Gold-6
04Pacific Montreal International Gold-6
04Pacific Toronto Spring Expo-6
Gold-6
04AHL Top Prospects-4
04Binghamton Senators-20
04Binghamton Senators Hess-6
05Black Diamond Gemography-G-AV
05Black Diamond Gemography Emerald-G-AV
05Black Diamond Gemography Gold-G-AV
05Black Diamond Gemography Onyx-G-AV
05Black Diamond Gemography Ruby-G-AV
05Parkhurst-343
Facsimile Auto Parallel-343
05Upper Deck-384
05Upper Deck MVP-277
Gold-277
Platinum-277
06Be A Player-14
Autographs-14
Signatures-AV
Signatures Duals-DEV
06Fleer-134
Tiffany-134
06Gatorade-52
06O-Pee-Chee-351
Rainbow-351
06Upper Deck-140
Exclusives Parallel-140
High Gloss Parallel-140
Masterpieces-140
06Binghamton Senators 5th Anniversary-33
Vermette, Frederic
03St. Georges de Beauce Garaga-20
Vermette, Mark
88Nordiques General Foods-37
88Nordiques Team Issue-32
89Halifax Citadels-25
89ProCards AHL-163
90Nordiques Petro-Canada-41
90Halifax Citadels-28
90ProCards AHL/IHL-450
91Nordiques Petro-Canada-34
91Upper Deck-470
French-470
92Nordiques Petro-Canada-36
93Las Vegas Thunder-30
Vermeulen, Amy
04Wisconsin Badgers Women-21
Vernace, Michael
04Brampton Battalion-4
05Brampton Battalion-7
Vernarsky, Kris
96Quebec Pee-Wee Tournament-680
00UD CHL Prospects-24
01Plymouth Whalers-18
02BAP Memorabilia-371
02BAP Ultimate Memorabilia-77
02Pacific Calder-105
Silver-105
02Pacific Complete-558
Red-558
02Parkhurst Retro-244
Minis-244
02UD Mask Collection-156
02UD Premier Collection-94
Gold-94
02Providence Bruins-9
03O-Pee-Chee-323
03OPC Blue-323
03OPC Gold-323
03OPC Red-323
03Parkhurst Original Six Boston-17
03Topps-323
Blue-323
Gold-323
Red-323
03Providence Bruins-21
04Florida Everblades-10
04Providence Bruins-19
06Port Huron Flags-6
Vernelli, Nick
02Plymouth Whalers-23
03Plymouth Whalers-13
Verner, Andrew
89Peterborough Petes-121
897th Inn. Sketch OHL-121
907th Inn. Sketch OHL-375
91Upper Deck-74
French-74
91Peterborough Petes-12
917th Inn. Sketch OHL-143
917th Inn. Sketch Memorial Cup-132
91Arena Draft Picks-25
91Arena Draft Picks French-25
91Arena Draft Picks Autographs-25
91Arena Draft Picks Autographs French-25
91Classic-30
91Star Pics-21
91Ultimate Draft-26
91Ultimate Draft French-26
91Classic Four-Sport *-30
Autographs-30A
93Classic Pro Prospects-84
97Swedish Collector's Choice-134
98Swedish UD Choice-149
99German DEL-118
00German DEL-234
01German Upper Deck-103
Goalies in Action-G4
Jersey Cards-AV-J
02German DEL City Press-124
02German DEL City Press-125
Verner, Brandon
00Owen Sound Attack-22
Vernikov, Stanislav
05Dutch Vadeko Flyers -19
Vernon, Mike
83Canadian National Juniors-18
84Moncton Golden Flames-20
85Flames Red Rooster-29
86Flames Red Rooster-29
86Kraft Drawings-78
87Flames Red Rooster-30
87O-Pee-Chee-215
87O-Pee-Chee Stickers-41
87Panini Stickers-203
88Flames Postcards-7
88O-Pee-Chee-261
88O-Pee-Chee Minis-44
88O-Pee-Chee Stickers-86
88Panini Stickers-4
89Kraft-62
89Kraft All-Stars Stickers-4
89O-Pee-Chee-163
89O-Pee-Chee-300
89O-Pee-Chee Stickers-76
89O-Pee-Chee Stickers-94
89O-Pee-Chee Stickers-167
89O-Pee-Chee Stickers-215
89Panini Stickers-6
89Panini Stickers-7
89Panini Stickers-34
89Panini Stickers-178
89Topps-163
89Topps Sticker Inserts-12
90Bowman-94
Tiffany-94
90Flames IGA/McGavin's-28
90Kraft-61
90Kraft-76
90O-Pee-Chee-351
90O-Pee-Chee Box Bottoms-L
90OPC Premier-126
90Panini Stickers-175
90Panini Stickers-329
90Pro Set-47
90Pro Set-338
90Score-52
Canadian-52
90Score Hottest/Rising Stars-23
90Topps-351
Tiffany-351
90Topps Box Bottoms-L

90Upper Deck-254
90Upper Deck-495
French-254
French-495
91Pro Set Platinum-21
91Bowman-253
91Flames Panini Team Stickers-23
91Flames IGA-24
91Kraft-19
91McDonald's Upper Deck-20
91O-Pee-Chee-107
91O-Pee-Chee-247
91OPC Premier-9
91Panini Stickers-55
91Panini Stickers-328
91Parkhurst-27
French-27
91Pinnacle-132
French-132
91Pro Set-35
91Pro Set-277
French-35
French-277
91Score American-80
91Score Canadian Bilingual-80
91Score Canadian English-80
91Stadium Club-269
91Topps-107
91Upper Deck-163
French-163
92Bowman-86
92Flames IGA-10
92Kraft-36
92O-Pee-Chee-247
92Panini Stickers-39
92Panini Stickers French-39
92Parkhurst-24
Emerald Ice-24
92Pinnacle-318
French-318
92Pro Set-25
92Score-60
Canadian-60
92Seasons Patches-61
92Stadium Club-345
92Topps-20
Gold-20G
92Ultra-31
92Upper Deck-112
93Donruss-54
93Kraft-66
93Leaf-83
Painted Warriors-7
93OPC Premier-15
Gold-15
Black Gold-5
93Panini Stickers-188
93Parkhurst-301
Emerald Ice-301
93Pinnacle-231
Canadian-231
All-Stars-40
All-Stars Canadian-40
Masks-2
93PowerPlay-45
93Score-43
Canadian-43
93Stadium Club-319
Members Only Master Set-319
First Day Issue-319
All-Stars-13
All-Stars Members Only-13
All-Stars OPC-13
93Topps Premier Promo Sheet-15
93Topps/OPC Premier-15
Gold-15
93Ultra-207
93Upper Deck-177
94Canada Games NHL POGS-278
94EA Sports-24
94Finest-36
Super Team Winners-36
Refractors-36
94Flair-53
94Fleer-66
94Hockey Wit-45
94Kraft-56
94Leaf-464
94OPC Premier-302
94OPC Premier-348
Special Effects-302
Special Effects-348
94Parkhurst SE-SE52
Gold-SE52
94Pinnacle-377
Artist's Proofs-377
Rink Collection-377
Goaltending Greats-GT10
94Select-54
Gold-54
94Stadium Club-79
94Stadium Club-189
Members Only Master Set-79
Members Only Master Set-189
First Day Issue-79
First Day Issue-189
Super Team Winner Cards-79
Super Team Winner Cards-189
94Topps/OPC Premier-302
94Topps/OPC Premier-348
Special Effects-302
Special Effects-348
94Ultra-287
94Upper Deck-141
Electric Ice-141
SP Inserts-SP115
SP Inserts Die Cuts-SP115
95Canada Games NHL POGS-104
95Collector's Choice-100
Player's Club-100
Player's Club Platinum-100
95Donruss Between The Pipes-3
95Emotion-59
95Kraft-31
95Leaf-8
95Panini Stickers-188
95Parkhurst International-334
Emerald Ice-334
95Pinnacle Masks-6
95Playoff One on One-255
95Pro Magnets Iron Curtain Insert-5
95Score-219
95Score-319
Black Ice Artist's Proofs-219
Black Ice Artist's Proofs-319
Black Ice-219
Black Ice-319
95Select Certified-42
Mirror Gold-42
95Stadium Club-12
Members Only Master Set-12
95Summit-114
Artist's Proofs-114
Ice-114
95Topps-11
95Topps-160
OPC Inserts-11
OPC Inserts-160
Marquee Men Power Boosters-11
95Topps SuperSkills-84
Platinum-84
95Ultra-50
Gold Medallion-50
Premier Pad Men-12
Premier Pad Men Gold Medallion-12
95Upper Deck-4
Electric Ice-4
Electric Ice Gold-4
95Zenith-60
96Donruss-52
Press Proofs-52
96Donruss Canadian Ice-94
Gold Press Proofs-94
Red Press Proofs-94
96Donruss Elite-86
Die Cut Stars-86
96Fleer-144
96Kraft Upper Deck-51
96Leaf-147
Press Proofs-147
Preferred Steel-57
Preferred Steel Gold-57
96Maggers-106
96Pinnacle-16
Artist's Proofs-16
Foil-16
Premium Stock-16
Rink Collection-16
96Red Wings Detroit News/Free Press-3
96Red Wings Detroit News/Free Press-4
96Score-164
Artist's Proofs-164
Dealer's Choice Artist's Proofs-164
Special Artist's Proofs-164
Golden Blades-164
Net Worth-14
96Summit-101
Artist's Proofs-101
Ice-101
Metal-101
Premium Stock-101
96Collector's Edge Ice Livin' Large-L8
97Collector's Choice-77
Star Quest-SQ53
97Crown Royale-123
Emerald Green-123
Ice Blue-123
Silver-123
Freeze Out Die-Cuts-18
97Donruss-73
Press Proofs Silver-73
Press Proofs Gold-73
97Donruss Canadian Ice-118
Dominion Series-118
Provincial Series-118
National Pride-28
Stanley Cup Scrapbook-31
97Donruss Limited-188
Exposure-188
Fabric of the Game-17
97Donruss Preferred-82
Cut to the Chase-82
Color Guard-12
Color Guard Promos-12
97Donruss Priority-159
Stamp of Approval-159
Postmaster General-11
Postmaster Generals Promos-11
97Flames Collector's Photos-1
97Katch-126
Gold-126
Silver-126
97Leaf-94
Fractal Matrix-94
Fractal Matrix Die Cuts-94
97Leaf International-94
Universal Ice-94
97NHL Aces Playing Cards-2
97Pacific-24
Copper-24
Emerald Green-24
Ice Blue-24
Red-24
Silver-24
In The Cage Laser Cuts-8
97Pacific Dynagon-45
Copper-45
Dark Grey-45
Emerald Green-45
Ice Blue-45
Red-45
Silver-45
Stonewallers-8
Tandems-44
97Pacific Invincible-52
Copper-52
Emerald Green-52
Ice Blue-52
Red-52
Silver-52
Feature Performers-15
97Pacific Omega-207
Copper-207
Dark Gray-207
Emerald Green-207
Gold-207
Ice Blue-207
97Paramount-170
Copper-170
Dark Grey-170
Emerald Green-170
Ice Blue-170
Red-170
Silver-170
Glove Side Laser Cuts-19
97Pinnacle-36
Artist's Proofs-36
Rink Collection-36
Press Plates Back Black-36
Press Plates Back Cyan-36
Press Plates Back Magenta-36
Press Plates Back Yellow-36
Press Plates Front Black-36
Press Plates Front Cyan-36
Press Plates Front Magenta-36
Press Plates Front Yellow-36
97Pinnacle Certified-8
Red-8
Mirror Blue-8
Mirror Gold-8
Mirror Red-8
97Pinnacle Inside-84
Coach's Collection-84
Executive Collection-84
Stand Up Guys-1A/B
Stand Up Guys-1C/D
Stand Up Guys Promos-1A/B
Stand Up Guys Promos-1C/D
Stoppers-11
Cans-5
Cans Gold-5
Promos-84
97Pinnacle Tot Cert Platinum Blue-8
97Pinnacle Tot Cert Platinum Gold-8
97Pinnacle Totally Certified Platinum Red-8
97Pinnacle Tot Cert Mirror Platinum Gold-8
97Revolution-128
Copper-128
Emerald-128
Ice Blue-128
Silver-128
Return to Sender Die-Cuts-18
Team Checklist Laser Cuts-22
97Score-4
Artist's Proofs-4
Golden Blades-4
97SP Authentic-133
97Studio-69
Press Proofs Silver-69
Press Proofs Gold-69
97Upper Deck-60
97Upper Deck-356
Game Dated Moments-60
98SLU Hockey Classic Doubles-2
98SLU Hockey One on One-4
98Aurora-172
Championship Fever-44
Championship Fever Copper-44
Championship Fever Ice Blue-44
Championship Fever Red-44
Championship Fever Silver-44
98Black Diamond-74
Double Diamond-74
Triple Diamond-74
Quadruple Diamond-74
98Bowman's Best-17
Refractors-17
Atomic Refractors-17
98Crown Royale-122
Limited Series-122
98Finest-135
No Protectors-135
No Protectors Refractors-135
Refractors-135
98NHL Aces Playing Cards-21
98OPC Chrome-86
Refractors-86
98Pacific-393
Ice Blue-393
Red-393
98Pacific Dynagon Ice-170
Blue-170
Red-170
Team Checklists-23
98Pacific Omega-216
Red-216
Opening Day Issue-216
98Panini Photocards-88
98Panini Stickers-211
98Paramount-216
Copper-216
Emerald Green-216
Holo-Electric-216
Ice Blue-216
Silver-216
Glove Side Laser Cuts-18
98Post-17
98Revolution-130
Ice Shadow-130
Red-130
98Topps-86
O-Pee-Chee-86
98UD Choice-177
98UD Choice Preview-177
98UD Choice Prime Choice Reserve-177
98UD Choice Reserve-177
98Upper Deck-167
Exclusives-167
Exclusives 1 of 1-167
Gold Reserve-167
98Upper Deck MVP-176
Gold Script-176
Silver Script-176
Super Script-176
99Aurora-123
Premiere Date-123
99BAP Memorabilia-251
99BAP Memorabilia-323
Gold-251
Gold-323
Silver-251
Silver-323
99Crown Royale-63
Limited Series-63
Premiere Date-63
99Jell-O Partners of Power-12
99O-Pee-Chee-159
99O-Pee-Chee Chrome-159
99O-Pee-Chee Chrome Refractors-159
99Pacific-384
Copper-384
Emerald Green-384
Gold-384
Ice Blue-384
Premiere Date-384
Red-384
In the Cage Net-Fusions-18
Team Leaders-24
99Pacific Dynagon Ice-178
Blue-178
Copper-178
Gold-178
Premiere Date-178
99Pacific Omega-102
Copper-102
Gold-102
Ice Blue-102
Premiere Date-102
99Panini Stickers-305
99Paramount-212
Copper-212
Emerald-212
Gold-212
Holographic Emerald-212
Holographic Gold-212
Holographic Silver-212
Ice Blue-212
Premiere Date-212
Red-212
Silver-212
99Revolution-130
Premiere Date-130
Red-130
Shadow Series-130
Copper-130
Gold-130
CSC Silver-130
99SPx-131
Radiance-131
Spectrum-131
99Topps/OPC-159
99Topps/OPC Chrome-159
Refractors-159
99Upper Deck MVP SC Edition-79
Gold Script-79
Silver Script-79
Super Script-79
99Upper Deck Victory-257
00BAP Memorabilia-458
Emerald-458
Ruby-458
Sapphire-458
00BAP Parkhurst 2000-P168
00BAP Signature Series-125
Emerald-125
Ruby-125
Sapphire-125
00BAP Ultimate Memorabilia Active Eight-AE5
00BAP Ultimate Mem Dynasty Jerseys-D20
00BAP Ultimate Mem Dynasty Emblems-D20
00BAP Ultimate Mem Goalie Memorabilia-GM3
00BAP Ultimate Memorabilia Goalie Sticks-G5
00BAP Ultimate Memorabilia Teammates-TM31
00O-Pee-Chee-65
00O-Pee-Chee Parallel-65
00Pacific-188
Copper-188
Gold-188
Ice Blue-188
Premiere Date-188
In the Cage Net-Fusions-4
00Stadium Club-214
00Titanium-13
Blue-13
Gold-13
Premiere Date-13
Red-13
Retail-13
00Topps/OPC-65
Parallel-65
00UD Pros and Prospects-15
00Upper Deck-257
Exclusives Tier 1-257
Exclusives Tier 2-257
00Upper Deck Vintage-52
01BAP Memorabilia Goalies Jerseys-GJ3
01BAP Signature Series Certified 100-C56
01BAP Signature Series Certified 50-C56
01BAP Signature Series Certified 1 of 1's-C56
01BAP Signature Series Autographs-XLMV
01BAP Signature Series Autographs Gold-LMV
01BAP Signature Series Emblems-GUE-9
01BAP Signature Series Numbers-ITN-9
01BAP Ultimate Memorabilia Active Eight-2
01Between the Pipes-54
Double Memorabilia-DM2
Goalie Gear-GG3
Jerseys-GJ3
Jersey and Stick Cards-GSJ3
Tandems-GT8
01O-Pee-Chee-152
01O-Pee-Chee Premier Parallel-152
01Pacific-67
Extreme LTD-67
Hobby LTD-67
Premiere Date-67
Retail LTD-67
01Pacific Adrenaline-30
Blue-30
Premiere Date-30
Red-30
Retail-30
01Pacific Arena Exclusives-67
01Topps-152
OPC Parallel-152
01UD Stanley Cup Champs-27
01Upper Deck Victory-48
Gold-48
02BAP Ultimate Memorabilia Conn Smythe-25
02BAP Ultimate Memorabilia Cup Duels-10
02BAP Ultimate Memorabilia Cup Duels-13
02BAP Ultimate Memorabilia Cup Duels-16
02BAP Ultimate Mem Dynasty Jerseys-14
02BAP Ultimate Mem Dynasty Emblems-14
02BAP Ultimate Mem Dynasty Numbers-14
02Pacific-61
Blue-61
Red-61
03Parkhurst Original Six Detroit-33
Memorabilia-DM63
04ITG Franchises Canadian Forever Rivals-FR3
04ITG Franchises Cdn Forever Rivals Gold-FR3
04ITG Franchises Canadian Goalie Gear-GG7
04ITG Franchises Cdn Goalie Gear Gold-GG7
04ITG Franchises Canadian Teammates-TM3
04ITG Franchises Canadian Teammates Gold-TM3
04ITG Franchises US West Memorabilia-WSM33
04ITG Franchises US West Memorabilia Gold-WSM33
04ITG Ultimate Mem Archives 1st Edition-15
04ITG Ultimate Mem Archives 1st Edition-18
04ITG Ultimate Mem Archives 1st Edition-37
04ITG Ultimate Memorabilia Day In History-3
04ITG Ultimate Memorabilia Day In History-26
04ITG Ultimate Mem Day In History Gold-3
04ITG Ultimate Mem Day In History Gold-26
04ITG Ultimate Memorabilia Original Six-6
06Between The Pipes Shooting Gallery-SG06
06Between The Pipes Shooting Gallery Gold-SG06

Verot, Darcy
00Wilkes-Barre Scranton Penguins-24
01Wilkes-Barre Scranton Penguins-7
03ITG VIP Rookie Debut-96
03Parkhurst Rookie-66
03Topps Traded-TT159
Blue-TT159
Gold-TT159
Red-TT159
03Upper Deck Rookie Update-125
04Portland Pirates-20
05Syracuse Crunch-4
06Syracuse Crunch-5

Verpaelst, Hugues
01Chicoutimi Sagueneens-17

Verreault, Bryan
05Sudbury Wolves-24
06Sudbury Wolves-27

Verreault, Francis
04Chicoutimi Sagueneens-8
05Chicoutimi Sagueneens-6
06Chicoutimi Sagueneens-23

Verreault, Jonathan
93Quebec Pee-Wee Tournament-459

Verret, Claude
95Swiss HNL-258
96Swiss HNL-416

Verret, Frederick
93Quebec Pee-Wee Tournament-278

Vershinin, Alex
92Cornell Big Red-28
93Cornell Big Red-25

Vershinin, Dmitri
98Russian Hockey League-133
99Russian Hockey League-33
01Russian Hockey League-147
03Russian Hockey League-97

Versteeg, Kris
03Lethbridge Hurricanes-6
04Lethbridge Hurricanes-6
05Red Deer Rebels-21
06Providence Bruins-23

Versteeg-Lytwyn, Mark
04Guelph Storm-11
05Sudbury Wolves-16

Vertala, Timo
97Black Diamond-25
Double Diamond-25
Triple Diamond-25
Quadruple Diamond-25
98UD Choice-277
Prime Choice Reserve-277
Reserve-277
98Finnish Kerailysarja-136
99Finnish Cardset-324
00Finnish Cardset-213
01Finnish Cardset-119
01Quebec Citadelles-22
02Finnish Cardset-137
03Finnish Cardset-66
04Finnish Cardset-75
04Finnish Cardset-300
Parallel-57
05Finnish Cardset -325
06Swedish SHL Elitset-200

Ververgaert, Dennis
73Canucks Royal Bank-19
74Canucks Royal Bank-20
74NHL Action Stamps-275
74O-Pee-Chee NHL-117
74O-Pee-Chee NHL-207
74Topps-117
74Topps-207
75Canucks Royal Bank-22
75O-Pee-Chee NHL-42
75Topps-42
76Canucks Royal Bank-21
76O-Pee-Chee NHL-175
76O-Pee-Chee NHL-395
76Topps-175
77Canucks Canada Dry Cans-16
77Canucks Royal Bank-20
77O-Pee-Chee NHL-56
77Topps-56
78Canucks Royal Bank-22
78O-Pee-Chee-52
78Topps-52
79O-Pee-Chee-214
79Topps-214
80O-Pee-Chee-99
80Topps-99
81O-Pee-Chee-356

Verville, Dave
98Val d'Or Foreurs-20
99Shawinigan Cataractes-13
Signed-13
00Chicoutimi Sagueneens-19
Signed-19

Verwey, Roland
99German DEL-352
02German DEL City Press-166
03German DEL-150
04German DEL-178
05German DEL-234
06German DEL-142

Vesa, Kimmo
93Finnish SISU-184
94Finnish SISU-245
98Finnish Kerailysarja-162
99Finnish Cardset-257
03Swedish Elite-248
Silver-248

Vesce, Ryan
05ITG Heroes/Prosp Toronto Expo Parallel -246
05AHL All-Stars-41
05AHL Top Prospects-45
05Springfield Falcons-22
05ITG Heroes and Prospects-246
Autographs Series II-RVE
06Binghamton Senators-21
06ITG Heroes and Prospects-58
Autographs-ARVE
Jerseys-GUJ54
Jerseys Gold-GUJ54
Emblems-GUE54
Emblems Gold-GUE54
Numbers-GUN54
Numbers Gold-GUN54

Vescio, Brian
71Johnstown Jets Acme-14
72Johnstown Jets-9

Vescio, Kevin
82North Bay Centennials-22
83North Bay Centennials-22

Vesel, Jesse
03Waterloo Blackhawks-14
04Waterloo Blackhawks-10

Veselovsky, Peter
94Czech APS Extraliga-149
94Finnish Jaa Kiekko-201

Vesely, Eric
02Topeka Scarecrows-16

Vesely, Ondrej
98Czech OFS-280
99Czech DS-13
99Czech OFS-456
00Czech DS Extraliga-24
00Czech OFS-341
02Czech OFS Plus-41
02Czech OFS Plus All-Star Game-H22
03Czech OFS Plus-144
04Czech OFS-268
04Czech OFS-400
Goals Leaders-15
06Czech HC Ceske Budejovice Postcards-13
06Czech OFS-21

Vesey, Jim
88ProCards IHL-91
89ProCards IHL-16
91Bruins Sports Action-20
93Phoenix Roadrunners-24

Vessio, Rob
03Cape Fear Fire Antz-15
03Lubbock Cotton Kings-18

Vesslin, Esa
66Finnish Jaakiekkosarja-32

Vestberg, Jan
71Swedish Hockey-376

Vestergaard, Chad
91British Columbia JHL-115
92British Columbia JHL-177

Vetchy, Ondrej
01Czech OFS-68

Vetter, Jesse
04Wisconsin Badgers Women-22

Vettraino, Scott
90Michigan Tech Huskies-26
91Michigan Tech Huskies-27
96Dayton Ice Bandits-21

Veuger, Jared
03Camrose Kodiaks-4

Vevcherenko, Oleg
98Russian Hockey League-108
99Russian Hockey League-116
00Russian Hockey League-22
02Russian Hockey League-92

Vey, Shaun
04Vancouver Giants-11

Vezina, Benoit
93Quebec Pee-Wee Tournament-902

Vezina, Georges
10Sweet Caporal Postcards-38
11C55-38
12C57-1
23V145-1-19
24Anonymous NHL-3
24C144 Champ's Cigarettes-60
24V130 Maple Crispette-13
24V145-2-43
25Dominion Chocolates-120
27La Patrie-21
27La Presse Photos-15
55Parkhurst-56
Quaker Oats-56
60Topps-19
Stamps-51
83Hall of Fame-30
83Hall of Fame Postcards-B16
85Hall of Fame-30
907th Inn. Sketch QMJHL-44
91Pro Set-333
French-333
92Hall of Fame Legends-26
93O-Pee-Chee Canadiens Hockey Fest-28
94Parkhurst Missing Link Pop-Ups-P3
00BAP Memorabilia Georges Vezina-V1
00BAP Memorabilia Georges Vezina-V2
00BAP Memorabilia Georges Vezina-V3
00BAP Memorabilia Georges Vezina-V4
00BAP Memorabilia Georges Vezina-V5
00BAP Memorabilia Georges Vezina-V6
00BAP Memorabilia Georges Vezina-V7
00BAP Memorabilia Georges Vezina-V8
00BAP Memorabilia Georges Vezina-V9
00BAP Memorabilia Georges Vezina-V10
00BAP Memorabilia Georges Vezina-V11
00BAP Memorabilia Georges Vezina-V12
00BAP Memorabilia Georges Vezina-V13
00BAP Memorabilia Georges Vezina-V14
00BAP Memorabilia Georges Vezina-V15
00BAP Memorabilia Georges Vezina-V16
00BAP Ultimate Mem Goalie Memorabilia-GM20
01Between the Pipes-132
Vintage Memorabilia-VM13
01Parkhurst Reprints-PR43
02BAP Ultimate Mem Blades of Steel-2
02BAP Ultimate Mem Storied Franchise-24
02Between the Pipes-115
03BAP Ultimate Memorabilia Cornerstones-1
03BAP Ultimate Mem Redemption Cards-1
03BAP Ultimate Mem Vintage Blade of Steel-2
03BAP Ultimate Mem Vintage Lumber-4
03ITG VIP Collages-31
03ITG VIP Vintage Memorabilia-2
03Parkhurst Original Six Montreal-53
03Parkhurst Original Six Montreal-82
Memorabilia-MM35
04ITG Franchises Canadian-44
Double Memorabilia-DM4
Double Memorabilia Gold-DM4
04ITG Ultimate Memorabilia-23
Gold-23
Blades of Steel-18
Cornerstones-10
Cornerstones Gold-10
Goalie Gear-20
Nicknames-30
Original Six-17
Vintage Lumber-16
04ITG Heroes and Prospects-176
04ITG Heroes/Prospects Toronto Expo '05-176
04ITG Heroes/Prospects Expo Heroes/Pros-176
05Between the Pipes-24
05ITG Ultimate Memorabilia Level 1-40
05ITG Ultimate Memorabilia Level 2-40
05ITG Ultimate Memorabilia Level 3-40
05ITG Ultimate Memorabilia Level 4-40
05ITG Ultimate Memorabilia Level 5-40
05ITG Ultimate Mem Blades of Steel-15
05ITG Ultimate Mem Blades of Steel Gold-15
05ITG Ultimate Memorabilia Vintage Lumber-2
05ITG Ultimate Mem Vintage Lumber Gold-2
06Between The Pipes-127
Shooting Gallery-SG01
Shooting Gallery Gold-SG01
06ITG Ultimate Memorabilia-53
Artist Proof-53
Stick Rack-20
Stick Rack Gold-20
Vintage Lumber-9
Vintage Lumber Gold-9

Vezina, J.J.
79Montreal Juniors-28

Vezina, Steve
97Macon Whoopee-1
97Macon Whoopee Autographs-1
99Colorado Gold Kings Taco Bell-12
99Colorado Gold Kings Wendy's-17
03St. Jean Mission-27

Vial, Dennis
88Niagara Falls Thunder-7
89ProCards AHL-32
90Pro Set-628
91Red Wings Little Caesars-16
91Score Canadian Bilingual-428
91Score Canadian English-428
93Parkhurst-406
Emerald Ice-406
93Senators Kraft Sheets-25
94Senators Team Issue-27
95Be A Player-131
Signatures-S131
Signatures Die Cuts-S131
95Senators Team Issue-23
96Senators Pizza Hut-26
98Chicago Wolves-18
98Chicago Wolves Turner Cup-16
99UK Sheffield Steelers-19
00UK Sekonda Superleague-149
00UK Sheffield Steelers-26
02Columbia Inferno-113
03Columbia Inferno-112
04UK Thommo's Top 10-9
04Richmond Riverdogs-18

Vicari, Dominic
06Toledo Storm-10

Vicars, Thomas
01Prince Albert Raiders-22

Vichorek, Mark
88Flint Spirits-20
90ProCards AHL/IHL-590

Vickar, Aaron
99Columbus Cottonmouths-1
01Missouri River Otters-2

Vickers, Chris
84Ottawa 67's-26

Vickers, Jim
03Louisiana Ice Gators-21
04UK London Racers-8
04UK London Racers Playoffs-17

Vickers, Steve
72O-Pee-Chee-254
73O-Pee-Chee-57
73Topps-57
74Lipton Soup-34
74NHL Action Stamps-198
74O-Pee-Chee NHL-29
74Topps-29
75O-Pee-Chee NHL-19
75O-Pee-Chee NHL-295
75O-Pee-Chee NHL-324
75Topps-19
75Topps-295
75Topps-324
76O-Pee-Chee NHL-75
76O-Pee-Chee NHL-390
76Topps-75
77O-Pee-Chee NHL-136
77Topps-136
78O-Pee-Chee-55
78Topps-55
79O-Pee-Chee-195
79Topps-195
80O-Pee-Chee-23
80Topps-23
82Post Cereal-13

Victor, David
03OCN Blizzard-22
04Cape Breton Screaming Eagles-20
05Cape Breton Screaming Eagles-4

Videll, Linus
04Swedish Elitset Future Stars-3
05Swedish SHL Elitset Star Potential-16

Vidgren, Simo
04Finnish Cardset-61
04Finnish Cardset Signatures-14
05Finnish Cardset -49

Vidman, Hermani
01Finnish Cardset-303

Vienneau, Justin
02Shawinigan Cataractes-18
03Shawinigan Cataractes-23
05Shawinigan Cataractes-6

Vienonen, Jussi
93Finnish SISU-22
93Finnish SISU-22B
99Finnish Cardset-104

Viens, Christian
93Quebec Pee-Wee Tournament-953

Viens, Stephan
917th Inn. Sketch QMJHL-121

Vierimaa, Hannu
80Finnish Mallasjuoma-129

Vieten, Oliver
94German First League-392

Vig, Mitch
99Mobile Mysticks-3

Vigano, Luca
93Swiss HNL-156
95Swiss HNL-209
96Swiss HNL-98
98Swiss Power Play Stickers-348

Viggiano, Tom
91Michigan Falcons-16

Vigier, J.P.
00Upper Deck Ice-107
01Pacific-26
Extreme LTD-26
Hobby LTD-26
Premiere Date-26
Retail LTD-26
01Pacific Arena Exclusives-26
01Parkhurst-353
01Upper Deck Victory-362
Gold-362
01Chicago Wolves-23
02Thrashers Postcards-20
02AHL Top Prospects-42
02Chicago Wolves-25
03Pacific Complete-496
Red-496
03Thrashers Postcards-23
04Chicago Wolves-12
06Thrashers Postcards-1

Vigilante, John
02Plymouth Whalers-8
03Plymouth Whalers-14
05OHL Bell All-Star Classic-6
05Plymouth Whalers-A-01
06Milwaukee Admirals -19

Vigilante, Mike `
03Gwinnett Gladiators-21
03Gwinnett Gladiators RBI Sports-208
04Gwinnett Gladiators-27

Viglasi, Ron
82Victoria Cougars-23
84Kelowna Wings-9

Vigneault, Alain
87Hull Olympiques-20
917th Inn. Sketch QMJHL-222
97Canadiens Postcards-25
98Canadiens Team Issue-24
04P.E.I. Rocket-31
06Canucks Postcards-23

Vigneault, Alexandre
92Quebec Pee-Wee Tournament-866
95Quebec Pee-Wee Tournament-527

Vigneault, Eric
93Quebec Pee-Wee Tournament-110

Vignola, Rejean
83Fredericton Express-19

Vihanto, Pentti
66Finnish Jaakiekkosarja-53
70Finnish Jaakiekko-153
71Finnish Suomi Stickers-204
72Finnish Jaakiekko-241
73Finnish Jaakiekko-276
74Finnish Typotor-41

Viherva, Teemu
01Finnish Cardset-313

Vihko, Joonas
00Finnish Cardset-263
01Finnish Cardset-202
02Finnish Cardset-138
03Finnish Cardset-23
04Finnish Cardset-22
Parallel-15
05Finnish Cardset -17
06Finnish Cardset-218

Viilma, Olli
70Finnish Jaakiekko-291
71Finnish Suomi Stickers-165

Viinanen, Mika
01Finnish Cardset-300
01Finnish Cardset Dueling Aces-4
02Finnish Cardset-139
03Finnish Cardset-106
04Finnish Cardset-159
Parallel-118
05Finnish Cardset -143
06Finnish Cardset-151

Viinikainen, Juha
95Collector's Choice-329
Player's Club-329
Player's Club Platinum-329
96Finnish SISU Redline-66
98Finnish Kerailysarja-130
99Finnish Cardset-72
01Finnish Cardset-153

Viita, Mauri
71Finnish Suomi Stickers-356

Vitakahti, Kari
71Finnish Suomi Stickers-275

Viitakoski, Matti
96Finnish SISU Redline-109

Viitakoski, Vesa
91Finnish Jyvas-Hyva Stickers-58
93Donruss-60
93Leaf-433
93Parkhurst-263
Emerald Ice-263
Calder Candidates-C20
Calder Candidates Gold-C20
93Pinnacle-444
Canadian-444
93Score-622
Gold-622
Canadian-622
Canadian Gold-622
93Upper Deck-344
SP-26
93Swedish Semic World Champ Stickers-84
93Classic-47
94Donruss-295
94Leaf-34
94OPC Premier-472
Special Effects-472
94Topps/OPC Premier-472
Special Effects-472
94Ultra-272
94Finnish Jaa Kiekko-22
94Swedish Olympics Lillehammer*-302
94Saint John Flames-26
94Classic-45
Gold-45
Tri-Cards-T10
94Classic Pro Prospects-42
95Finnish Semic World Championships-45
95Saint John Flames-25
98Finnish Keraiilysarja-91
99Finnish Cardset-55
00Finnish Cardset-159
01Finnish Cardset-242
02Finnish Cardset-140
03Finnish Cardset-55
04Swedish Elitset-155
Gold-155
04Swedish Pure Skills Signatures-1
05Finnish Cardset-215
05Swedish SHL Elitset-12
Gold-12
06Finnish Cardset-51
06Finnish Ilves Team Set-26

Viitala, Jari
70Finnish Jaakiekko-323
78Finnish SM-Liiga-61
80Finnish Mallasjuoma-38

Viitalahti, Kari
73Finnish Jaakiekko-238
78Finnish SM-Liiga-95

Viitaluoma, Ville
04Finnish Cardset-149
Parallel-111
05Finnish Cardset -135
06Finnish Cardset-191

Viitanen, Mikko
03Hershey Bears Patriot News-25
04Hershey Bears Patriot News-29
04Reading Royals-23

Viitanen, Pentti
71Finnish Suomi Stickers-296
73Finnish Jaakiekko-214

Vikingstad, Tore
99Norwegian National Team-20
99Swedish Upper Deck-65
00Swedish Upper Deck-117
01German Upper Deck-50
02German DEL City Press-63
03German Deg Metro Stars-22
03German DEL-44
04German DEL-58
04German Dusseldorf Metro Stars Postcards-23
05German DEL-76
06German DEL-52

Viklund, Tobias
04Swedish MoDo Postcards-20
05Swedish SHL Elitset-244
Gold-244
Series One Signatures-6
06Swedish SHL Elitset-108

Vikstrom, Seppo
66Finnish Jaakiekkosarja-63

Viktorsson, Jan
83Swedish Semic Elitserien-97
84Swedish Semic Elitserien-93
85Swedish Panini Stickers-87
86Swedish Panini Stickers-80
87Swedish Panini Stickers-83
89Swedish Semic Elitserien Stickers-63
90Swedish Semic Elitserien Stickers-285
91Finnish Semic World Champ Stickers-41

91Swedish Semic Elitserien Stickers-67
91Swedish Semic Elitserien Stickers-352
91Swedish Semic World Champ Stickers-41
92Swedish Semic Elitserien Stickers-99
95Swedish Leaf-191
Champs-15
95Swedish Upper Deck-55
97Swedish Collector's Choice-48
98Swedish UD Choice-62

Vikulov, Vladimir
69Russian National Team Postcards-17
69Swedish Hockey-17
70Finnish Jaakiekko-20
70Russian National Team Postcards-18
70Swedish Hockey-332
70Swedish Masterserien-73
70Swedish Masterserien-132
70Swedish Masterserien-135
71Finnish Suomi Stickers-19
71Swedish Hockey-41
72Finnish Jaakiekko-40
72Finnish Hellas-77
72Finnish Semic World Championship-18
72Swedish Stickers-32
72Swedish Stickers-48
72Swedish Semic World Championship-18
73Finnish Jaakiekko-20
73Swedish Stickers-102
74Finnish Jenkki-60
74Swedish Semic World Champ Stickers-49
91Future Trends Canada '72-47
91Future Trends Canada '72 French-47
92Future Trends '76 Canada Cup-164

Vilander, Jukka
89Swedish Semic World Champ Stickers-47
91Finnish Jyvas-Hyva Stickers-63
92Finnish Jyvas-Hyva Stickers-186
93Finnish Jyvas-Hyva Stickers-317
93Finnish SISU-42
98Danish Hockey League-8

Vilasek, Daniel
97Czech APS Extraliga-143
99Czech OFS-296
99Czech Score Blue 2000-99
99Czech Score Red Ice 2000-99

Vilen, Jaska
05Finnish Cardset -309
06Finnish Cardset-141

Vilen, Jorma
66Finnish Jaakiekkosarja-180
70Finnish Jaakiekko-257
71Finnish Suomi Stickers-222
72Finnish Jaakiekko-170
73Finnish Jaakiekko-239

Vilen, Petri
93Finnish SISU-235

Vilgrain, Claude
89ProCards AHL-211
90Upper Deck-250
French-250
90ProCards AHL/IHL-558
91Pro Set Platinum-195
91Parkhurst-321
French-321
91Pro Set-425
French-425
92Bowman-191
92O-Pee-Chee-133
92Score-326
Canadian-326
Sharpshooters-14
Sharpshooters Canadian-14
92Stadium Club-422
92Topps-187
Gold-187G
95Swiss HNL-412
96Swiss HNL-358
96Swiss HNL-581
98German DEL-204
99Swiss Panini Stickers-305

Vililante, Mike
93Quebec Pee-Wee Tournament-847

Viljanen, Risto
72Finnish Jaakiekko-357

Viljanen, Timo
78Finnish SM-Liiga-209

Villa, Ismo
73Finnish Jaakiekko-322
77Finnish Sportscasters-90-2165
78Finnish SM-Liiga-167
80Finnish Mallasjuoma-121

Villandre, Stephane
93Quebec Pee-Wee Tournament-1400

Villard, Alain
96Swiss HNL-391

Ville, Christophe
92Finnish Semic-238
93Swedish Semic World Champ Stickers-267
94Finnish Jaa Kiekko-225
95Finnish Semic World Championships-199
95Swedish Globe World Championships-203

Villemure, Gilles
63Topps-46
64Topps-74
67Topps-86
70Colgate Stamps-89
70Esso Power Players-198
70O-Pee-Chee-183
71Bazooka-10
71O-Pee-Chee-18
71O-Pee-Chee-248
71Sargent Promotions Stamps-127
71Topps-18
71Toronto Sun-186
72O-Pee-Chee-132
72O-Pee-Chee-286
72Topps-64
72Topps-137
73O-Pee-Chee-119
73Topps-153
74NHL Action Stamps-194
74O-Pee-Chee NHL-179
74Topps-179
75O-Pee-Chee NHL-379
76O-Pee-Chee NHL-61
76Topps-61
03Parkhurst Orig Six New York Mem-NM35

Villeneuve, Andre
86Sherbrooke Canadiens-29

Villeneuve, Bruno
907th Inn. Sketch QMJHL-145
91Knoxville Cherokees-15
92Raleigh Icecaps-18
92Raleigh Icecaps-21
93Knoxville Cherokees-20

Villeneuve, Daniel
93Sherbrooke Faucons-7
98Halifax Mooseheads-26
00Fort Worth Brahmas-16
01Fort Worth Brahmas-17

Villeneuve, Dany
93Amos Les Forestiers-23

Villeneuve, Jonathan
01Shawinigan Cataractes-8
02Shawinigan Cataractes-15

Villeneuve, Martin
97New Orleans Brass-7
99Quad-City Mallards-18
00Quad-City Mallards-20

Villeneuve, Mathieu
92Quebec Pee-Wee Tournament-789
93Quebec Pee-Wee Tournament-1051

Villeneuve, Michael
93Quebec Pee-Wee Tournament-1365

Villeneuve, Samuel
02Drummondville Voltigeurs-19

Villeneuve, Simon
93Quebec Pee-Wee Tournament-256

Villeneuve, Steeve
01Cape Breton Screaming Eagles-1
02Cape Breton Screaming Eagles-22
02Halifax Mooseheads-22
03Cape Breton Screaming Eagles-4

Villiger, Samuel
98Swiss Power Play Stickers-222
99Swiss Panini Stickers-223
00Swiss Panini Stickers-73
00Swiss Slapshot Mini-Cards-HCCF15
01Swiss HNL-278
02Swiss HNL-206

Vilneff, Mark
907th Inn. Sketch OHL-296
94Muskegon Fury-7
95Muskegon Fury-2
98Muskegon Fury-25
99Muskegon Fury-12
00Muskegon Fury-14
03Kalamazoo Wings-3
04Kalamazoo Wings-4
05Kalamazoo Wings-4

Vilonen, Mikko
70Finnish Jaakiekko-324
80Finnish Mallasjuoma-156

Vimmer, Josef
94German First League-626

Vince, Bill
82Brandon Wheat Kings-10

Vince, Ryan
03UK Guildford Flames-6

Vincelette, Dan
87Blackhawks Coke-27
88Blackhawks Coke-22
89ProCards IHL-59
90Nordiques Petro-Canada-26
91ProCards-480
92Atlanta Knights-17

Vincent, Alexandre
04Chicoutimi Sagueneens-2
04ITG Heroes and Prospects-204
04ITG Heroes/Prospects Toronto Expo '05-204
05ITG Heroes/Prosp Toronto Expo Parallel -155
05Chicoutimi Sagueneens-9
05ITG Heroes and Prospects-155
Autographs-A-AVI
Complete Logos-CHL-14
Jerseys-GUJ-78
Jerseys Gold-GUJ-78
Emblems-GUE-78
Emblems Gold-GUE-78
Numbers-GUN-78
Numbers Gold-GUN-78
06Between The Pipes Prospect Trios-PT11
06Between The Pipes Prospect Trios Gold-PT11

Vincent, Andre
01Drummondville Voltigeurs-8
02Drummondville Voltigeurs-6
03Drummondville Voltigeurs-22
04Drummondville Voltigeurs-10

Vincent, Dominic
92Quebec Pee-Wee Tournament-53
93Quebec Pee-Wee Tournament-231
93Quebec Pee-Wee Tournament-424

Vincent, Pascal
907th Inn. Sketch QMJHL-70
917th Inn. Sketch QMJHL-246

Vincent, Paul
92Quebec Pee-Wee Tournament-1005
93Seattle Thunderbirds-27
93Classic Four-Sport *-226
Gold-226
94Signature Rookies Gold Standard *-96
95St. John's Maple Leafs-19
95Signature Rookies-34
Signatures-34
96Peoria Rivermen-24
96Peoria Rivermen Photo Album-24
96Collector's Edge Ice-85
Prism-85
99Odessa Jackalopes-2
03Florida Everblades-20

Vincent, Robert
51Laval Dairy Lac St. Jean-30

Vincent, Steve
01Sorel Royaux-23

Vines, Mark
90Pro Set-702

Vinet, Claude
52Juniors Blue Tint-137

Vinogradov, Alexander
95Swedish World Championships Stickers-46
00Russian Hockey League-392

Vinokurov, Denis
91Upper Deck Czech World Juniors-4

Violy, Jonathan
93Quebec Pee-Wee Tournament-1590

Vipond, Kelly
91Peterborough Petes-27
917th Inn. Sketch OHL-142
92Windsor Spitfires-20

Virag, Dustin
94North Bay Centennials-16
95Slapshot-222
01Fort Wayne Komets-6
01Fort Wayne Komets Shoe Carnival-1
02Fort Wayne Komets-22
02Fort Wayne Komets Shoe Carnival-12
03Fort Wayne Komets-8
03Fort Wayne Komets 2003 Champions-3
03Fort Wayne Komets 2003 Champions-9
03Fort Wayne Komets 2003 Champions-13
03Fort Wayne Komets Shoe Carnival-16
04Fort Wayne Komets-18
04Fort Wayne Komets Shoe Carnival-15
05Kalamazoo Wings-13

Virhimo, Tapio
70Finnish Jaakiekko-258
71Finnish Suomi Stickers-223
72Finnish Jaakiekko-171
73Finnish Jaakiekko-193
74Finnish Typotor-12
78Finnish SM-Liiga-43
80Finnish Mallasjuoma-44

Virkgunen, Tommi
91British Columbia JHL-170
91British Columbia JHL-NNO

Virkki, Jarno
04Finnish Cardset-219
06Finnish Cardset-305

Virkku, Kalevi
65Finnish Hellas-18

Virkkunen, Teemu
04Finnish Cardset-196
04Finnish Cardset Signatures-40
05Finnish Cardset -324
06Finnish Cardset-330

Virkkunnen, Teemu
98Black Diamond-101
Double Diamond-101
Triple Diamond-101
Quadruple Diamond-101
98SPx Top Prospects-69
Radiance-69
Spectrum-69
00Finnish Cardset-128
01Finnish Cardset-8

Virmanen, Matti
80Finnish Mallasjuoma-56

Virolainen, Mikko
93Finnish SISU-55
93Finnish SISU-55B

Virolainen, Petri
01Finnish Cardset-271
04Finnish Cardset-248

Virta, Hannu
82Sabres Milk Panels-16
84Sabres Blue Shield-21
85Sabres Blue Shield-28
85Sabres Blue Shield Small-28
89Swedish Semic World Champ Stickers-34
91Finnish Semic World Champ Stickers-6
91Finnish Jyvas-Hyva Stickers-66
91Swedish Semic World Champ Stickers-6
92Finnish Jyvas-Hyva Stickers-183
93Finnish Jyvas-Hyva Stickers-315
93Finnish SISU-37
95Finnish SISU Gold Cards-11
95Finnish SISU Limited-2
Leaf Gallery-7
95Finnish Karjala World Champ Labels-23
95Finnish Kellogg's-3
95Finnish Semic World Championships-23
95Swedish Globe World Championships-132
95Swedish World Championships Stickers-168
95Swiss HNL-295
96Swedish Semic Wien-23
98Finnish Kerailysarja Leijonat-18
99Finnish Cardset Aces High-H-2
02Finnish Cardset-289

Virta, Heikki
70Finnish Jaakiekko-362

Virta, Pasi
78Finnish SM-Liiga-118
80Finnish Mallasjuoma-180

Virta, Pekka
94Finnish SISU-212
94Finnish SISU Magic Numbers-6
95Finnish SISU-146
95Finnish SISU-360
96Finnish SISU Redline-157
99German Bundesliga 2-301

Virta, Seppo
80Finnish Mallasjuoma-172

Virta, Tony
92Finnish Jyvas-Hyva Stickers-33
93Finnish Jyvas-Hyva Stickers-53
93Finnish SISU-243
94Finnish SISU-46
95Finnish SISU-224
96German DEL-56
98Finnish Kerailysarja-237
99Finnish Cardset-137
99Finnish Cardset-172
00Finnish Cardset-98
00Finnish Cardset-239
01BAP Memorabilia-454
Emerald-454
Ruby-454
Sapphire-454
01Parkhurst-319
01UD Mask Collection-149
Gold-149
01Finnish Cardset-178
02SPx-113
02Upper Deck MVP-206
Gold-206
Classics-206
Golden Classics-206
02Upper Deck Victory-108
Bronze-108
Gold-108
Silver-108
02Finnish Cardset-141
03Finnish Cardset-37
03Finnish Cardset Globetrotters-GR8
05Finnish Cardset -232
06Finnish Cardset-59

Virtanen, Anto
65Finnish Hellas-33
66Finnish Jaakiekkosarja-38
70Finnish Jaakiekko-206
71Finnish Suomi Stickers-94
72Finnish Jaakiekko-259
72Finnish Panda Toronto-46
73Finnish Jaakiekko-257

Virtanen, Antti
65Finnish Hellas-147
66Finnish Jaakiekkosarja-165
98Finnish Kerailysarja-70
99Finnish Cardset-36
00Finnish Cardset-177
01Finnish Cardset-70
02Finnish Cardset-290
03Finnish Cardset-83
04Finnish Cardset-90
Parallel-67
05Finnish Cardset -74

Virtanen, Arttu
04Finnish Cardset-183
Parallel-136
05Finnish Cardset -162
06Finnish Cardset-165

Virtanen, Hannu
70Finnish Jaakiekko-363

Virtanen, Jaakko
70Finnish Jaakiekko-325

Virtanen, Jani
03Bakersfield Condors-19

Virtanen, Janne
91Finnish Jyvas-Hyva Stickers-68
92Finnish Jyvas-Hyva Stickers-193
93Finnish Jyvas-Hyva Stickers-348
93Finnish SISU-219
94Finnish SISU-67
95Finnish SISU-157
95Finnish SISU-281
00Finnish Cardset-143
01Finnish Cardset-185

Virtanen, Jari
78Finnish SM-Liiga-141
93Finnish SISU-133
94Finnish SISU-72
95Finnish SISU-39

Virtanen, Jorma
72Finnish Jaakiekko-98
72Finnish Panda Toronto-15
73Finnish Jaakiekko-146
74Finnish Typotor-6
78Finnish SM-Liiga-111

Virtanen, Juha
94Finnish SISU-264
95Finnish SISU-142
95Finnish SISU Limited-98
98Finnish Kerailysarja-62
99Finnish Cardset-35
00Finnish Cardset-164

Virtanen, Jukka
70Finnish Jaakiekko-344
80Finnish Mallasjuoma-203
92Finnish Jyvas-Hyva Stickers-184
93Finnish SISU-385

Virtanen, Marko
92Finnish Jyvas-Hyva Stickers-75
93Finnish Jyvas-Hyva Stickers-148
93Finnish SISU-150
93Finnish SISU-173B
93Finnish SISU Autographs-173
93Swedish Semic World Champ Stickers-85
94Finnish SISU-249
94Finnish SISU Horoscopes-18
94Finnish Jaa Kiekko-49
95Finnish SISU-67
95Finnish SISU Limited-53
95Finnish SISU Painkillers-8
97Swedish Collector's Choice-172
98Finnish Kerailysarja-139
99Finnish Cardset-77

Virtanen, Petteri
04Finnish Cardset-223

Virtanen, Timo
71Finnish Suomi Stickers-357
72Finnish Jaakiekko-358

Virtue, Terry
907th Inn. Sketch WHL-107
907th Inn. Sketch WHL-329
93Wheeling Thunderbirds-14
98Providence Bruins-23
99Hartford Wolf Pack-22
00Hartford Wolf Pack-27
01Hartford Wolf Pack-25
02Worcester IceCats-2
03Worcester Ice Cats-4
03Worcester Ice Cats 10th Anniversary-6
06Austin Ice Bats-11

Viscovich, Peter
84Kingston Canadians-17
85Kingston Canadians-17

Visek, Jan
02Czech OFS Plus-330
04Czech OFS-341
06Czech HC Liberec Postcards-11
06Czech OFS-107

Visheau, Mark
907th Inn. Sketch OHL-147
917th Inn. Sketch OHL-378
94Classic Pro Prospects-101
97Milwaukee Admirals-21
98Pacific Omega-116
Red-116
Opening Day Issue-116

Vishedkevich, Sergei
01Russian Dynamo Moscow-22
01Russian Dynamo Moscow Mentos-1

Vishnevskiy, Yvan
05ITG Heroes and Prospects-417
Team Orr-TO19
06ITG Heroes and Prospects-98
Autographs-AIV
CHL Top Prospects-TP04
CHL Top Prospects Gold-TP04

Vishnevsky, Vitali
97Black Diamond-93
Double Diamond-93
Triple Diamond-93
Quadruple Diamond-93
98UD Choice-285
Prime Choice Reserve-285
Reserve-285
99BAP Memorabilia-330
Gold-330
Silver-330
99Pacific Omega-8
Copper-8
Gold-8
Ice Blue-8
Premiere Date-8
99Russian Fetisov Tribute-18
99Cincinnati Mighty Ducks-30
00BAP Memorabilia-243
Emerald-243
Ruby-243
Sapphire-243
Promos-243
00BAP Mem Chicago Sportsfest Copper-243
00BAP Memorabilia Chicago Sportsfest Blue-243
00BAP Memorabilia Chicago Sportsfest Gold-243
00BAP Memorabilia Chicago Sportsfest Ruby-243
00BAP Memorabilia Chicago Sun-Times Ruby-243
00BAP Memorabilia Chicago Sun-Times Gold-243
00BAP Mem Chicago Sun-Times Sapphire-243
00BAP Mem Toronto Fall Expo Copper-243
00BAP Memorabilia Toronto Fall Expo Gold-243
00BAP Memorabilia Toronto Fall Expo Ruby-243
00BAP Parkhurst 2000-P16
00BAP Signature Series-141
Emerald-141
Ruby-141
Sapphire-141
Autographs-161
Autographs Gold-161
00O-Pee-Chee-309
00O-Pee-Chee Parallel-309
00Pacific-13
Copper-13
Gold-13
Ice Blue-13
Premiere Date-13
00Panini Stickers-113
00Topps/OPC-309
Parallel-309
00Topps Chrome-204
OPC Refractors-204
Refractors-204
00Upper Deck-234
Exclusives Tier 1-234
Exclusives Tier 2-234
00Upper Deck MVP-184
First Stars-184
Second Stars-184
Third Stars-184
00Upper Deck Victory-3
01BAP Memorabilia-55
Emerald-55
Ruby-55
Sapphire-55
01BAP Signature Series-126
Autographs-126
Autographs Gold-126
01Crown Royale Triple Threads-10
01Parkhurst-116
01Upper Deck-236
Exclusives-236
01Upper Deck Victory-5
Gold-5
02BAP Sig Series Auto Buybacks 2001-126
02Ducks Team Issue-6
02Topps Total-179
02Upper Deck-1
Exclusives-1
02Upper Deck Victory-1
Bronze-1
Gold-1
Silver-1
02Upper Deck Vintage-1
02Upper Deck Vintage-261
03ITG Action-98
04Russian Back to Russia-26
05Ducks Team Issue-21
05Parkhurst-14
05Upper Deck MVP-11
Gold-11
Platinum-11
06O-Pee-Chee-21
Rainbow-21
06Russian Torino Olympic Team-6

Vishnyakov, Albert
02Russian Hockey League-71
04Russian Moscow Dynamo-5

Viskari, Esa
66Finnish Jaakiekkosarja-137

Viskari, Timo
66Finnish Jaakiekkosarja-126
70Finnish Jaakiekko-274

Viskovich, Peter
86Kingston Canadians-18

Visnak, Bohdan
06Saskatoon Blades-20

Visnovsky, Lubomir
00BAP Memorabilia-451
Emerald-451
Ruby-451
Sapphire-451
00BAP Parkhurst 2000-P228
00Black Diamond-120
00Private Stock-123
Gold-123
Premiere Date-123
Retail-123
Silver-123
00SP Authentic-109
00Titanium-125
Retail-125
00Titanium Draft Day Edition-125
00Titanium Draft Day Promos-125
00Topps Heritage-87
Chrome Parallel-87
00Topps Premier Plus-139
Blue Ice-139
00Upper Deck-430
Exclusives Tier 1-430
Exclusives Tier 2-430
00Vanguard-125
Pacific Proofs-125
01BAP Memorabilia-51
Emerald-51
Ruby-51
Sapphire-51
01BAP Signature Series-107
Autographs-107
Autographs Gold-107
01O-Pee-Chee-149
01O-Pee-Chee Premier Parallel-149
01Pacific-191
Extreme LTD-191
Hobby LTD-191
Premiere Date-191
Retail LTD-191
01Pacific Arena Exclusives-191
01Parkhurst-140
01Stadium Club-62
Award Winners-62
Master Photos-62
01Topps-149
OPC Parallel-149
Own The Game-OTG14
01Topps Heritage-109
Refractors-108
01Upper Deck-311
Exclusives-311
01Upper Deck MVP-90
01Slovakian Kvarteto-5B
02BAP Sig Series Auto Buybacks 2001-107
02Kings Game Sheets-29
02Kings Game Sheets-30
02Topps Total-305
02Slovakian Kvarteto-11
03ITG Action-245
03NHL Sticker Collection-239
03Pacific Complete-183
Red-183
03Upper Deck MVP-195
Gold Script-195
Silver Script-195
Canadian Exclusives-195
05Black Diamond-40
Emerald-40
Gold-40
Onyx-40
Ruby-40
05Kings Team Issue-9
05Panini Stickers-291
05Parkhurst-219
Facsimile Auto Parallel-219
05UD PowerPlay-43
Rainbow-43
05Upper Deck-88
HG Glossy-88
05Upper Deck MVP-180
Gold-180
Platinum-180
05Upper Deck Toronto Fall Expo-88
05Upper Deck Victory-94
Black-94
Gold-94
Silver-94
06Fleer-92
Tiffany-92
06NHL POG-49
06O-Pee-Chee-227
Rainbow-227
06Panini Stickers-284
06Ultra-94
Gold Medallion-94
Ice Medallion-94
06Upper Deck Arena Giveaways-LAK2
06Upper Deck-91
Exclusives Parallel-91
High Gloss Parallel-91
Masterpieces-91
06Upper Deck MVP-137
Gold Script-137
Super Script-137
06Upper Deck Ovation-23
06Upper Deck Victory-95
06Upper Deck Victory Black-95
06Upper Deck Victory Gold-95
07Upper Deck Victory-190
Black-190
Gold-190

Visnovsky, Tibor
04Slovakian Skalica Team Set-3

Vit, Pavel
95German DEL-425
96German DEL-62

Vit, Radek
99German Bundesliga 2-246
05German DEL-56

Vitale, Joe
04Sioux Falls Stampede-2-4

Vitale, Phil
51Laval Dairy Subset-72
52St. Lawrence Sales-28

Vitarelli, Cory
02St. Michaels Majors-21
03St. Michael's Majors-20
04St. Michael's Majors-21

Vitek, Jiri
95Czech APS Extraliga-214

Vitek, Josef
03Czech OFS Plus-301
04Czech OFS-315

Viteli, Jarmo
70Finnish Jaakiekko-326
71Finnish Suomi Stickers-358
72Finnish Jaakiekko-340

Viteli, Petri
71Finnish Suomi Stickers-359

Vitolinsh, Harijs
90O-Pee-Chee-521
92Thunder Bay Thunder Hawks-26
93Parkhurst-496
Emerald Ice-496
93Upper Deck-428
94Classic Pro Prospects-197
95Swedish Leaf-285
95Swedish Upper Deck-183
96Swiss HNL-467
98Swiss Power Play Stickers-312
00Swiss Panini Stickers-95
01Swiss HNL-459
02Swiss HNL-438

Vittenberg, Andre
94French National Team-33

Vitucci, Nick
91Greensboro Monarchs-14
92Hampton Roads Admirals-17
93Peoria Rivermen-28
93Toledo Storm-7
94Toledo Storm-23
95Buffalo Stampedes RHI-36
95Roller Hockey Magazine RHI-3
96Charlotte Checkers-17
97Toledo Storm-13
01Greenville Grrrowl-2
02Greenville Grrrowl-20
06Toledo Storm-23

Viuhkola, Jari
00Finnish Cardset-61
01Finnish Cardset-82
02Finnish Cardset-291
03Finnish Cardset-97
04Finnish Cardset-102
Parallel-76
05Finnish Cardset -273
Finnish Cardset Magicmakers-14
06Czech Super Six Postcards-16
06Finnish Cardset-102

Viveiros, Emanuel
84Prince Albert Raiders Stickers-22
88ProCards IHL-29
90ProCards AHL/IHL-183
96German DEL-314

Vizzutti, Chad
92British Columbia JHL-159

Vlach, Ladislav
02Czech OFS Plus Trios-T23

Vlach, Rostislav
89Swedish Semic World Champ Stickers-194
91Finnish Jyvas-Hyva Stickers-38
94Czech APS Extraliga-246
95Czech APS Extraliga-18
95Czech APS Extraliga-390
96Czech APS Extraliga-224
97Czech APS Extraliga-36
97Czech APS Extraliga-365
97Czech DS Extraliga-66
97Czech DS Stickers-29
98Czech DS Stickers-174
98Czech OFS-329
01Czech OFS-67
01Czech OFS Red Inserts-RE15D
02Czech OFS Plus-42
Duos-D17
03Czech OFS Plus-145
04Czech OFS-263
06Czech OFS Coaches-13

Vlaisavljevich, Eli
04Lincoln Stars-9
05Lincoln Stars-10
05Lincoln Stars Update Traded-9T
05Lincoln Stars Update Traded-16T

Vlasak, Tomas
93Parkhurst-515
Emerald Ice-515
94Czech APS Extraliga-218
95Czech APS Extraliga-169
96Czech APS Extraliga-183
97Czech APS Extraliga-87
97Czech DS Extraliga-45
97Czech DS Stickers-52
98Czech DS Stickers-95
98Finnish Kerailysarja-72
99Czech OFS-274
99Finnish Cardset-42
99Finnish Cardset-160
00BAP Memorabilia-441
Emerald-441
Ruby-441
Sapphire-441
00BAP Signature Series-196
Emerald-196
Ruby-196
Sapphire-196
Autographs-210
Autographs Gold-210
00Czech DS Extraliga National Team-NT9
00Czech DS Extraliga Team Jagr-JT15
00Czech DS Extraliga World Champions-WCH9
00Czech OFS-396
00Finnish Cardset-268
01Czech National Team Postcards-15
01Swiss HNL-233
02BAP Sig Series Auto Buybacks 2000-210
02Czech DS-31
02Czech DS-88
02Finnish Cardset-142
02Russian Hockey League-121
02Russian SL-37
03Russian Avangard Omsk-5
03Russian Hockey League-223
04Czech HC Slavia Praha Postcards-11
04Czech OFS-352
Stars II-8
05Czech Kvarteto Bonaparte-8d
05Czech Pexeso Mini Blue Set-11
05Czech HC Slavia Praha-13
06Czech HC Slavia Praha Postcards-15
06Czech OFS-306
Points Leaders-13
Team Cards-8

Vlasanek, Petr
99Czech OFS-248

Vlasic, Marc-Edouard
03Quebec Remparts-26
04Quebec Remparts-12
05ITG Heroes/Prosp Toronto Expo Parallel -149
05Quebec Remparts-22
05Quebec Remparts Signature Series-22
05ITG Heroes and Prospects-149
Autographs-A-MEV
06Be A Player-232
06Be A Player Portraits-122
06Beehive-150
Matte-150
06Black Diamond-158A
Black-158A
Gold-158A
Ruby-158A
06Flair Showcase-325
06Hot Prospects-132
Red Hot-132
White Hot-132
Hot Materials -HMMV
Hot Materials Red Hot-HMMV
Hot Materials White Hot-HMMV
06O-Pee-Chee-551
Rainbow-551
06SP Authentic-202
Limited-202
06SP Game Used-151
Gold-151
Rainbow-151
Autographs-151
Rookie Exclusives Autographs-REMV
06SPx-183
Spectrum-183
06The Cup-154
Autographed Rookie Masterpiece Pressplates-154
Gold Rainbow Autographed Rookie Patches-154
Masterpiece Pressplates (Be A Player Portraits)-122
Masterpiece Pressplates (Bee Hive)-150
Masterpiece Pressplates (Black Diamond)-158
Masterpiece Pressplates (Marquee Rookies)-551
Masterpiece Pressplates (MVP)-310
Masterpiece Pressplates (SP Authentic Autographs)-202
Masterpiece Pressplates (SP Game Used)-151
Masterpiece Pressplates (SPx Autographs)-183
Masterpiece Pressplates (Sweet Beginnings)-150
Masterpiece Pressplates (Trilogy)-151
Masterpiece Pressplates (Ultimate Collection Autographs)-129
Masterpiece Pressplates (Victory)-297
NHL Shields Duals-DSHCV
Rookies Black-154
Rookies Platinum-154
06UD Artifacts-255
06UD Mini Jersey Collection-113
06Ultimate Collection-129
Rookies Autographed NHL Shields-129
Rookies Autographed Patches-129
Ultimate Debut Threads Jerseys-DJ-MV
Ultimate Debut Threads Jerseys Autographs-DJ-MV
Ultimate Debut Threads Patches-DJ-MV
Ultimate Debut Threads Patches Autographs-DJ-MV
06Ultra-237
Gold Medallion-237
Ice Medallion-237
06Upper Deck-242
Exclusives Parallel-242
High Gloss Parallel-242
Masterpieces-242
Rookie Game Dated Moments-RGD25
Rookie Headliners-RH12
Rookie Materials-RMMV
Rookie Materials Patches-RMMV
06Upper Deck MVP-310
Gold Script-310
Super Script-310
06Upper Deck Sweet Shot-150
Rookie Jerseys Autographs-150
06Upper Deck Trilogy-151
06Upper Deck Victory-297
06ITG Heroes and Prospects-189
Autographs-AMEV
Memorial Cup Champions-MC06
Update Autographs-AMEV
07Upper Deck Rookie Class -27

Vlasidis, Nick
93Quebec Pee-Wee Tournament-731

Vlasov, Igor
95Swedish Upper Deck 1st Division Stars-DS2

Vlassenkov, Dmitri
97Black Diamond-124
Double Diamond-124
Triple Diamond-124
Quadruple Diamond-124
98UD Choice-287
Prime Choice Reserve-287
Reserve-287
99Russian Stars of Hockey-20
02Russian Hockey League-211

Vlcek, Ivan
94Czech APS Extraliga-147
96Czech APS Extraliga-290
97Czech APS Extraliga-175
97Czech DS Extraliga-51
97Czech DS Stickers-212
98Czech DS Stickers-150
98Czech OFS-287
98Czech OFS-453
99Czech DS-88
99Czech OFS-129
00Czech DS Extraliga-29
00Czech OFS-61
00Czech OFS Star Emerald-18
00Czech OFS Star Pink-18
00Czech OFS Star Violet-18
01Czech OFS-206
All Stars-39
02Czech OFS Plus-270
Trios-T11

Vlcek, Ladislav
99Czech OFS-334
00Czech DS Extraliga-143
00Czech OFS-125
01Czech OFS-268
02Czech OFS Plus-43
02Czech OFS Plus-350
05Czech HC Kladno-13

Vlcek, Tomas
03Czech OFS Plus-315

Vlk, Petr
89Swedish Semic World Champ Stickers-189
91Finnish Semic World Champ Stickers-123
91Swedish Semic World Champ Stickers-123
93Swiss HNL-359
95Czech APS Extraliga-187
96Czech APS Extraliga-322
97Czech APS Extraliga-301
97Czech DS Extraliga-36
97Czech DS Stickers-163
98Czech DS-38
98Czech DS Stickers-115
98Czech OFS-56

Vlk, Vladimir
99Czech OFS-415
00Czech DS Extraliga-65
00Czech OFS-215

Vlzek, Ivan
95Finnish SISU-276
95Finnish SISU-384
Double Trouble-7
96Finnish SISU Redline-72

Voakes, Craig
04Kitchener Rangers-5
05Kitchener Rangers-19

Voboril, Milan
02Czech OFS Plus-271
03Czech OFS Plus-207
06Czech OFS-286

Voce, Tony
94Quebec Pee-Wee Tournament-46
03Boston College Eagles-2
04Philadelphia Phantoms-24
05Philadelphia Phantoms-24
06Philadelphia Phantoms-12
06ITG Heroes and Prospects-31
Autographs-ATV
Jerseys-GUJ14
Jerseys Gold-GUJ14
Emblems-GUE14
Emblems Gold-GUE14
Numbers-GUN14
Numbers Gold-GUN14

Vodak, Jiri
96Czech APS Extraliga-26

Vodden, Mark
02Medicine Hat Tigers-22

Vodila, Jan
89Swedish Semic World Champ Stickers-192

Vodnjov, Matjaz
93Quebec Pee-Wee Tournament-1795

Vodrazka, Jan
95Slapshot-72
96Detroit Whalers-18
99Kansas City Blades Supercuts-20
00Kansas City Blades-2

Vodrazka, Milan
05Bossier-Shreveport Mudbugs-19

Voegele, Stefan
01Swiss EV Zug Postcards-16
02Swiss EV Zug Postcards-16
02Swiss HNL-73

Voevodin, Nikolai
00Russian Hockey League-92

Vogel, Daniel
94German First League-350

Vogel, Gerd
94German First League-564

Vogel, Jason
92Cornell Big Red-29

Vogel, Ron
02Pee Dee Pride RBI-150
03Rockford Ice Hogs-17
05Rockford Ice Hogs-22

Vogel, Tony
81Regina Pats-23
82Regina Pats-11
83Regina Pats-11
92Finnish Semic-192
94German DEL-303
95German DEL-183

Vogeltanz, Petr
96Czech APS Extraliga-94

Vogl, Sebastian
05German DEL-154

Vogl, Thomas
95German DEL-250
99German EV Landshut-8

Vohralik, Karel
73Finnish Jaakiekko-62
74Finnish Jenkki-84

Voigt, Benjamin
01German Upper Deck-259
04German Augsburg Panthers Postcards-27

Voigt, Dieter
04German Berlin Eisbarens 50th Anniv-70

Voillat, Yann
93Swiss HNL-273
96Swiss HNL-504
00Swiss Panini Stickers-291

01Swiss HNL-420
02Swiss HNL-175

Voisard, Gaetan

91Upper Deck-664
French-664
91Upper Deck Czech World Juniors-25
93Swiss HNL-69
95Swiss HNL-95
96Swiss HNL-37
96Swiss HNL-517
96Swiss HNL-534
98Swiss Power Play Stickers-161
99Swiss Panini Stickers-161
00Swiss Panini Stickers-205
00Swiss Slapshot Mini-Cards-HCL7
01Swiss HNL-34
02Swiss EV Zug Postcards-14
02Swiss HNL-224
03Swiss EV Zug Postcards-27
04Swiss EV Zug Postcards-13

Vojta, Jakub

05Ottawa 67's-10
06Ottawa 67s-17

Vojtek, Martin

99Czech Score Blue 2000-97
99Czech Score Red Ice 2000-97
01Czech OFS-130
01Czech OFS H Inserts-H4
03Czech OFS Plus-346
04Czech OFS-373
Goals-Against Leaders-11
Save Percentage Leaders-9
05Czech HC Trinec-14

Vojtynek, Henryk

73Finnish Jaakiekko-103
74Finnish Jenkki-90

Vokes, Jeremy

01Rockford IceHogs-14

Vokey, Jared

02Cape Breton Screaming Eagles-16
03Halifax Mooseheads-10

Vokoun, Tomas

94Czech APS Extraliga-48
95Wheeling Thunderbirds-5
95Wheeling Thunderbirds Series II-18
96Fredericton Canadiens-22
97Donruss-209
Press Proofs Silver-209
Press Proofs Gold-209
Rated Rookies-1
Medallist-1
97Donruss Canadian Ice-138
Dominion Series-138
Provincial Series-138
97Leaf-157
Fractal Matrix-157
Fractal Matrix Die Cuts-157
97Pinnacle Inside-72
Coach's Collection-72
Executive Collection-72
98Pacific Omega-133
Red-133
Opening Day Issue-133
98Predators Team Issue-22
98Revolution-81
Ice Shadow-81
Red-81
98Milwaukee Admirals Postcards-11
99BAP Millennium-139
Emerald-139
Ruby-139
Sapphire-139
Signatures-139
Signatures Gold-139
99O-Pee-Chee-72
99O-Pee-Chee Chrome-72
99O-Pee-Chee Chrome Refractors-72
99Pacific-232
Copper-232
Emerald Green-232
Gold-232
Ice Blue-232
Premiere Date-232
Red-232
99Pacific Omega-129
Copper-129
Gold-129
Ice Blue-129
Premiere Date-129
99Topps Arena Giveaways-NAS-TV
99Topps/OPC-72
99Topps/OPC Chrome-72
Refractors-72
99Upper Deck-245
Exclusives-245
Exclusives 1 of 1-245
99Upper Deck Gold Reserve-245
99Upper Deck Victory-163
00BAP Memorabilia-394
Emerald-394
Ruby-394
Sapphire-394
Promos-394
00BAP Mem Chicago Sportsfest Copper-394
00BAP Memorabilia Chicago Sportsfest Blue-394
00BAP Memorabilia Chicago Sportsfest Gold-394
00BAP Memorabilia Chicago Sportsfest Ruby-394
00BAP Memorabilia Chicago Sun-Times Ruby-394
00BAP Memorabilia Chicago Sun-Times Gold-394
00BAP Mem Chicago Sun-Times Sapphire-394
00BAP Mem Toronto Fall Expo Copper-394
00BAP Memorabilia Toronto Fall Expo Gold-394
00BAP Memorabilia Toronto Fall Expo Ruby-394
00Pacific-227
Copper-227
Gold-227
Ice Blue-227
Premiere Date-227
00Paramount-139
Copper-139
Gold-139
Holo-Gold-139
Holo-Silver-139
Ice Blue-139
Premiere Date-139
00Topps Heritage-212
00UD Reserve-49
00Upper Deck-329
Exclusives Tier 1-329
Exclusives Tier 2-329
00Czech Stadion-122
01Between the Pipes-15
Jersey and Stick Cards-GSJ34
01Pacific-222
Extreme LTD-222
Hobby LTD-222
Premiere Date-222
Retail LTD-222
01Pacific Adrenaline-108
Blue-108
Premiere Date-108
Red-108
Retail-108
01Pacific Arena Exclusives-222
01Topps Reserve Emblems-TV
01Topps Reserve Jerseys-TV
01Topps Reserve Name Plates-TV
01Topps Reserve Numbers-TV
01Topps Reserve Patches-TV
01Upper Deck-329
Exclusives-329
01Upper Deck Victory-204
Gold-204
01Czech DS-26
Ice Heroes-IH1
02BAP Sig Series Auto Buybacks 1999-139
02Between the Pipes-36
02Between the Pipes-137
Gold-36
Silver-36
02Bowman YoungStars-19
Gold-19
Silver-19
02Crown Royale-55
Blue-54
Red-55
Retail-55
02ITG Used Goalie Pad and Jersey-GP14
02ITG Used Goalie Pad and Jersey Gold-GP14
02Pacific-215
Blue-215
Red-215
02Pacific Complete-332
Red-332
02Pacific Quest for the Cup-55
Gold-55
02Parkhurst Retro-191
Minis-191
02SP Authentic-50
Beckett Promos-50
02Titanium-61
Blue-61
Red-61
Retail-61
02Topps Total-370
02UD Artistic Impressions-51
Gold-51
02UD Artistic Impressions Beckett Promos-51
02UD Artistic Impressions Retrospectives-R51
02UD Artistic Impressions Retrospect Gold-R51
02UD Artistic Impress Retrospect Silver-R51
02UD Honor Roll-43
02UD Mask Collection-48
02UD Mask Collection-49
02UD Mask Collection Beckett Promos-48
02UD Mask Collection Beckett Promos-49
02Upper Deck-98
Exclusives-98
02Upper Deck Rookie Update-57
02Czech DS-42
02Czech DS-56
02Czech DS-79
03BAP Memorabilia-166
Emerald-166
Gold-166
Ruby-166
Sapphire-166
Deep in the Crease-D6
03BAP Ultimate Memorabilia Autographs-39
Gold-39
03BAP Ultimate Mem Auto Jerseys-39
03Beehive-110
Variations-110
Gold-110
Silver-110
03Black Diamond-116
Black-116
Green-116
Red-116
03Bowman-26
Gold-26
03Bowman Chrome-26
Refractors-26
Gold Refractors-26
Xfractors-26
03Crown Royale-58
Blue-58
Retail-58
03ITG Action-380
Jerseys-M239
03ITG Used Signature Series-2
Gold-2
Autographs-TV
Autographs Gold-TV
Franchise-17
Franchise Autographs-17
Goalie Gear-10
Goalie Gear Autographs-10
Goalie Gear Gold-10
03NHL Sticker Collection-260
03O-Pee-Chee-230
03OPC Blue-230
03OPC Gold-230
03OPC Red-230
03Pacific-194
Blue-194
Red-194
03Pacific Calder-61
Silver-61
03Pacific Complete-412
Red-412
03Pacific Exhibit-82
Blue Backs-82
Yellow Backs-82
03Pacific Invincible-54
Blue-54
Red-54
Retail-54
Freeze Frame-11
Jerseys-17
03Pacific Luxury Suite-39A
03Pacific Luxury Suite-39B
03Pacific Luxury Suite-39C
03Pacific Luxury Suite-39D
03Pacific Prism-59
Blue-59
Gold-59
Red-59
03Pacific Quest for the Cup-62
Blue-62
03Pacific Supreme-56
Blue-56
Red-56
Retail-56
03Private Stock Reserve-177
Blue-177
Patches-177
Red-177
Retail-177
03SP Authentic-50
Limited-50
03SP Game Used-26
03SP Game Used-108
Gold-26
Gold-108
03SPx-54
Radiance-54
Spectrum-54
03Titanium-59
Hobby Jersey Number Parallels-59
Retail-59
Retail Jersey Number Parallels-59
03Topps-230
Blue-230
Gold-230
Red-230
03Topps C55-101
Minis-101
Minis American Back-101
Minis American Back Red-101
Minis Bazooka Back-101
Minis Brooklyn Back-101
Minis Hat Trick Back-101
Minis O Canada Back-101
Minis O Canada Back Red-101
Minis Stanley Cup Back-101
03Topps Pristine-53
Gold Refractor Die Cuts-53
Refractors-53
Jersey Portions-PPJ-TV
Jersey Portion Refractors-PPJ-TV
Mini-PM-TV
Press Plates Black-53
Press Plates Cyan-53
Press Plates Magenta-53
Press Plates Yellow-53
03Topps Traded Franchise Fabrics-FF-TV
03UD Honor Roll-47
03UD Premier Collection-30
03Upper Deck-110
Canadian Exclusives-110
HG-110
03Upper Deck Classic Portraits-55
03Upper Deck Ice-50
Gold-50
03Upper Deck MVP-245
Gold Script-245
Silver Script-245
Canadian Exclusives-245
SportsNut-SN49
03Upper Deck Rookie Update-50
03Upper Deck Trilogy-55
Limited-55
03Upper Deck Victory-106
Bronze-106
Gold-106
Silver-106
03Czech National Team Postcards-15
03Russian World Championship Stars-32
04Pacific-151
Blue-151
Red-151
04SP Authentic-51
04UD All-World-14
Gold-14
04Ultimate Collection-24
Dual Logos-UL2-VT
04Upper Deck-101
Canadian Exclusives-101
HG Glossy Gold-101
HG Glossy Silver-101
World's Best-WB11
World Cup Tribute-RCTV
World Cup Tribute-MHSKTV
04Czech OFS-311
Stars-44
04Czech Zuma-5
04Czech World Championship Postcards-22
04Finnish Cardset-210
04Swedish Pure Skills-100
Parallel-100
05Be A Player-49
First Period-49
Second Period-49
Third Period-49
Overtime-49
Outtakes-OT29
World Cup Salute-WCS12
05Beehive-51
Matte-51
05Black Diamond-49
Emerald-49
Gold-49
Onyx-49
Ruby-49
05Hot Prospects-56
En Fuego-56
Red Hot-56
White Hot-56
05McDonalds Upper Deck Goalie Factory-GF7
05Panini Stickers-309
05Parkhurst-269
Facsimile Auto Parallel-269
True Colors-TCNSH
True Colors-TCNSH
05SP Authentic-56
Limited-56
Chirography-SPTV
Prestigious Pairings-PPHV
05SP Game Used-57
Gold-57
Authentic Fabrics-AF-TV
Authentic Fabrics Dual-KV
Authentic Fabrics Gold-AF-TV
Authentic Fabrics Quad-KLHV
Authentic Patches Quad -KLHV
Authentic Fabrics Triple-VKL
Authentic Patches-AP-TV
Authentic Patches Dual-KV
Authentic Patches Triple-VKL
Awesome Authentics-AA-TV
05SPx-48
Spectrum-48
Winning Combos-WC-VH
Winning Combos Gold-WC-VH
Winning Combos Gold-WC-VK
Winning Combos Spectrum-WC-VH
05The Cup-60
Gold-60
Black Rainbow-60
Dual NHL Shields-DSKV
Emblems of Endorsement-EETV
Honorable Numbers-HNTV
Limited Logos-LLTV
Masterpiece Pressplates-60
Masterpiece Pressplates (Rookie Update)-205
Noble Numbers-NNGV
Noble Numbers Dual-DNNKV
Patch Variation-P60
Patch Variation Autographs-AP60
Scripted Numbers-SNGV
Scripted Numbers Dual-DSNHV
Signature Patches-SPVO
05UD Artifacts-57
05UD Artifacts-174
Blue-57
Blue-174
Gold-57
Gold-174
Green-57
Green-174
Pewter-57
Pewter-174
Red-57
Red-174
Gold Autographed-57
Gold Autographed-174
05UD PowerPlay-51
05UD PowerPlay-110
Rainbow-51
05Ultimate Collection-52
Gold-52
Jerseys-JTV
Jerseys Dual-DJKV
National Heroes Jerseys-NHJTV
National Heroes Patches-NHPTV
Premium Patches-PPVO
Premium Swatches-PSVO
Ultimate Patches-PTV
Ultimate Patches Dual-DPKV
05Ultra-110
Gold-110
Ice-110
05Upper Deck-105
05Upper Deck All-Time Greatest-34
05Upper Deck Big Playmakers-B-TV
05Upper Deck HG Glossy-105
05Upper Deck Jerseys Series II-J2TV
05Upper Deck Majestic Materials-MMTV
05Upper Deck NHL Generations-DHV
05Upper Deck Patches-P-TV
05Upper Deck Ice-55
Rainbow-55
Cool Threads-CTVO
Cool Threads Glass-CTVO
Cool Threads Patches-CTPVO
05Upper Deck MVP-215
Gold-215
Platinum-215
05Upper Deck Rookie Update-55
05Upper Deck Rookie Update-205
Inspirations Patch Rookies-205
05Upper Deck Trilogy-51
05Upper Deck Trilogy-143
Crystal-143
05Upper Deck Toronto Fall Expo-105
05Upper Deck Victory-111
Black-111
Gold-111
Silver-111
05Czech World Champions Postcards-21
05Czech Kvarteto Bonaparte-1d
05Czech Pexeso Mini Blue Set-1
05Czech Pexeso Mini Red Set-20
05Czech Stadion-677
05Finnish Cardset Super Snatchers-2
06Be A Player Portraits-61
Dual Signature Portraits-DSKV
Quadruple Signature Portraits-QHVHH
Signature Portraits-SPVO
Timeless Tens-TTNET
06Beehive-45
06Beehive-188
Blue-45
Gold-45
Matte-45
Red Facsimile Signatures-45
Wood-45
5 X 7 Black and White-45
Matted Materials-MMTV
06Between The Pipes The Mask-M39
06Between The Pipes The Mask Gold-M39
06Between The Pipes The Mask Silver-M39
06Black Diamond-111
Black-111
Gold-111
Ruby-111
06Flair Showcase-58
06Flair Showcase-139
Parallel-58
Parallel-139
Hot Gloves-HG17
Inks-ITV
06Fleer-111
Tiffany-111
Netminders-N14
06Hot Prospects-56
Red Hot-56
White Hot-56
Hot Materials -HMTV
Hot Materials Red Hot-HMTV
Hot Materials White Hot-HMTV
06O-Pee-Chee-275
Rainbow-275
Swatches-S-TV
06Panini Stickers-307
06SP Authentic-47
06SP Authentic-158
Chirography-TV
Limited-47
Limited-158
Sign of the Times-STTV
Sign of the Times Duals-STVA
Sign of the Times Duals-STVH
06SP Game Used-58
Gold-58
Rainbow-58
Authentic Fabrics-AFTV
Authentic Fabrics Parallel-AFTV
Authentic Fabrics Patches-AFTV
Authentic Fabrics Dual-AF2KV
Authentic Fabrics Dual Patches-AF2KV
Authentic Fabrics Triple-AF3NAS
Authentic Fabrics Triple Patches-AF3NAS
Autographs-58
By The Letter-BLTV
Inked Sweaters-ISTV
Inked Sweaters Patches-ISTV
Inked Sweaters Dual-IS2HV
Inked Sweaters Dual-IS2VW
Inked Sweaters Dual Patches-IS2HV
Inked Sweaters Dual Patches-IS2VW
SIGnificance-STV
06SPx-57
Spectrum-57
SPxcitement-X59
SPxcitement Spectrum-X59
Winning Materials-WMTV
Winning Materials Spectrum-WMTV
Winning Materials Autographs-WMTV
06The Cup-51
Autographed Foundations-CQTV
Autographed Foundations Patches-CQTV
Autographed NHL Shields Duals-DASHV
Autographed NHL Shields Duals-DASVS
Autographed Patches-51
Black Rainbow-51
Foundations-CQTV
Foundations Patches-CQTV
Enshrinements-ETV
Gold-51
Gold Patches-51
Honorable Numbers-HNTV
Jerseys-51
Limited Logos-LLTV
Masterpiece Pressplates-51
NHL Shields Duals-DSHVK
Scripted Swatches-SSTV
Signature Patches-SPTV
06UD Artifacts-46
06UD Artifacts-178
Blue-46
Blue-178
Gold-46
Gold-178
Platinum-46
Platinum-178
Radiance-46
Radiance-178
Autographed Radiance Parallel-46
Autographed Radiance Parallel-178
Red-46
Red-178
Auto-Facts-AFVO
Auto-Facts Gold-AFVO
Frozen Artifacts-FATV
Frozen Artifacts Black-FATV
Frozen Artifacts Blue-FATV
Frozen Artifacts Gold-FATV
Frozen Artifacts Platinum-FATV
Frozen Artifacts Red-FATV
Frozen Artifacts Autographed Black-FATV
Frozen Artifacts Patches Black-FATV
Frozen Artifacts Patches Blue-FATV
Frozen Artifacts Patches Gold-FATV
Frozen Artifacts Patches Platinum-FATV
Frozen Artifacts Patches Red-FATV
Frozen Artifacts Patches Autographed Black Tag Parallel-FATV
Tundra Tandems-TTVE
Tundra Tandems Black-TTVE
Tundra Tandems Blue-TTVE
Tundra Tandems Gold-TTVE
Tundra Tandems Platinum-TTVE
Tundra Tandems Red-TTVE
Tundra Tandems Dual Patches Red-TTVE
06UD Mini Jersey Collection-59
06UD Powerplay-58
Impact Rainbow-58
Goal Robbers-GR11
06Ultimate Collection-35
Autographed Jerseys-AJ-TV
Autographed Patches-AJ-TV
Jerseys-UJ-TV
Patches-UJ-TV
Signatures-US-TV
Ultimate Achievements-UA-TV
Ultimate Signatures Logos-SL-TV
06Ultra-109
Gold Medallion-109
Ice Medallion-109
06Upper Deck Arena Giveaways-NSH1
06Upper Deck-108
Exclusives Parallel-108
High Gloss Parallel-108
All-Time Greatest-ATG12
All World-AW17
Game Jerseys-J2TV
Game Patches-P2TV
Generations Duals-G2VH
Generations Patches Dual-G2PVH
Masterpieces-108
Walmart Tins Oversize-108
06Upper Deck MVP-167
Gold Script-167
Super Script-167
Autographs-OAVV
International Icons-II13
Jerseys-OJHV
Last Line of Defense-LL12
06Upper Deck Ovation-128
06Upper Deck Sweet Shot-61
Signature Shots/Saves-SSTV
Signature Shots/Saves Ice Signings-SSITV
Signature Shots/Saves Sticks-SSSTV
Signature Sticks-STTV
Sweet Stitches-SSTV
Sweet Stitches Duals-SSTV
Sweet Stitches Triples-SSTV
06Upper Deck Trilogy-55
Combo Autographed Jerseys-CJVH
Combo Autographed Patches-CJVH
Combo Clearcut Autographs-C2VS
Honorary Scripted Patches-HSPTV
Honorary Scripted Swatches-HSSTV
Ice Scripts-ISVO
Scripts-S3TV
Scripts-TSTV
06Upper Deck Victory-110
06Upper Deck Victory Black-110
06Upper Deck Victory Gold-110
06Upper Deck Victory GameBreakers-GB27
06Russian Sport Collection Olympic Stars-28
07Upper Deck Victory-105
Black-105
Gold-105
GameBreakers-GB27

Volak, Milan

94Czech APS Extraliga-151
95Czech APS Extraliga-258
96Czech APS Extraliga-298
97Czech APS Extraliga-185
97Czech DS Extraliga-56
97Czech DS Stickers-215
98Czech DS-63
98Czech DS Stickers-159
98Czech OFS-45
99Czech DS-98
99Czech OFS-375
00Czech DS Extraliga-33
00Czech OFS-69
01Czech OFS-222
02Czech OFS Plus-272
03Czech OFS Plus-208

Volcan, Mickey

82Whalers Junior Hartford Courant-22
83NHL Key Tags-43
83O-Pee-Chee-94
83Vachon-20
84Moncton Golden Flames-13
85Nova Scotia Oilers-24
90ProCards AHL/IHL-365

Volchenkov, Anton

00Russian Hockey League-47
00Russian Hockey League-302
02Atomic-120
Blue-120
Gold-120
Red-120
Hobby Parallel-120
02BAP All-Star Edition-140
Gold-140
Silver-140
02BAP First Edition-434R
02BAP Memorabilia-296
Emerald-296
Ruby-296
Sapphire-296
NHL All-Star Game-296
NHL All-Star Game Blue-296
NHL All-Star Game Green-296
NHL All-Star Game Red-296
02BAP Memorabilia Toronto Fall Expo-296
02BAP Signature Series-198
Autographs-198
Autographs Gold-198
02BAP Ultimate Memorabilia-26
Autographs-3
Autographs Gold-3
Calder Candidates-5
02Bowman YoungStars-122
Gold-122
Silver-122
Autographs-AV
Jerseys-AV
Patches-AV
Double Stuff-AV
Triple Stuff-AV
Rivals-RKAV
Rivals Patches-7
Sticks-AV
02Crown Royale-128
Blue-128
Purple-128
Red-128
Retail-128
02ITG Used-94
Calder Jerseys-C17
Calder Jerseys Gold-C17
02NHL Power Play Stickers-122
02Pacific Calder-134
Silver-134
02Pacific Complete-574
Red-574
02Pacific Exclusive-186
Blue-186
Gold-186
02Pacific Heads-Up-142
02Pacific Quest for the Cup-134
Gold-134
02Parkhurst-226
Bronze-226
Gold-226
Silver-226
02Parkhurst Retro-226
Minis-226
02Private Stock Reserve-174
Blue-174
Red-174
Retail-174
02Senators Team Issue-15
02Senators Team Issue-16
02SP Authentic-162
02SP Game Used-86
02SPx-163
02Titanium-127
Blue-127
Red-127
Retail-127
02Topps Chrome-167
Black Border Refractors-167
Refractors-167
02Topps Heritage-154
02Topps Total-404
02UD Artistic Impressions-103
Gold-103
02UD Foundations-160
02UD Honor Roll-161
02UD Mask Collection-166
02UD Piece of History-142
02UD Premier Collection-61
Gold-61
Jerseys Bronze-AV
Jerseys Gold-AV
Jerseys Silver-AV
02UD Top Shelf-98
02Upper Deck-444
Exclusives-444
02Upper Deck Classic Portraits-122
02Upper Deck Rookie Update-161A
02Upper Deck Rookie Update-161B
02Upper Deck Rookie Update-161C
02Vanguard-125
LTD-125
03ITG Action-494
Jerseys-M88
03Senators Postcards-17
03Upper Deck Shooting Stars-ST-AV
03Upper Deck MVP-301
Gold Script-301
Silver Script-301
Canadian Exclusives-301
04AHL All-Stars-44
04AHL Top Prospects-5
04Binghamton Senators-21
04Binghamton Senators Hess-11
05ITG Heroes/Prosp Toronto Expo Parallel -90
05Upper Deck-385
05ITG Heroes and Prospects-90
Autographs-A-AV
06O-Pee-Chee-353
Rainbow-353
06Senators Postcards-2
06Russian Sport Collection Olympic Stars-3
06Russian Torino Olympic Team-24
06Binghamton Senators 5th Anniversary-34

Volchkov Jr., Alexander

95Slapshot-16
95Slapshot-431
95Barrie Colts-25
96Collect Edge Ice Sign Sealed Delivered-1
96Collect Edge Ice Sign Sealed Delivered-NNO
96All-Sport PPF *-73
96All Sport PPF Gold *-73
96Visions Signings *-62
Autographs-62A
Autographs Silver-62A
97Barrie Colts-25
97Portland Pirates-22
97Bowman CHL-12
OPC-12
97Autographed Collection *-48
Game Breakers-GB30
97Players Club *-65
99Black Diamond-90
Diamond Cut-90
Final Cut-90
99Pacific Dynagon Ice-205
Blue-205
Copper-205
Gold-205
Premiere Date-205
99Pacific Omega-247
Copper-247
Gold-247
Ice Blue-247
Premiere Date-247
99SP Authentic-121
99Upper Deck-303
Exclusives-303
Exclusives 1 of 1-303
99Upper Deck Gold Reserve-303
99Wayne Gretzky Hockey-178
99AHL All-Stars-11
99Portland Pirates-23
04Barrie Colts 10th Anniversary-15

Volchkov Sr., Alexander

73Finnish Jaakiekko-21
73Russian National Team-13
73Swedish Stickers-96
74Finnish Jenkki-61
91Future Trends Canada '72-59
91Future Trends Canada '72 French-59

Volek, Ales

94German First League-369

Volek, Dave

89Islanders Team Issue-20
89O-Pee-Chee-85
89O-Pee-Chee-309
89O-Pee-Chee Stickers-43
89O-Pee-Chee Stickers-113
89O-Pee-Chee Stickers-187
89Panini Stickers-267
89Topps-85
90Bowman-127
Tiffany-127
90O-Pee-Chee-300
90Pro Set-193
90Score-12
Canadian-12
90Topps-300
Tiffany-300
90Upper Deck-1
French-1
91Pro Set Platinum-75
91Bowman-223
91O-Pee-Chee-488
91Panini Stickers-241
91Parkhurst-104
French-104
91Pinnacle-198
French-198
91Pro Set-147
French-147
91Score American-88
91Score Canadian Bilingual-88
91Score Canadian English-88
91Stadium Club-204
91Topps-488
91Upper Deck-89
91Upper Deck-173
French-89
French-173
91Finnish Semic World Champ Stickers-221
91Swedish Semic World Champ Stickers-221
92Bowman-196
92O-Pee-Chee-3
92Panini Stickers-200
92Panini Stickers French-200
92Parkhurst-340
Emerald Ice-340
92Pinnacle-188
French-188
92Score-166
Canadian-166
92Stadium Club-319
92Topps-204
Gold-204G
92Ultra-350
92Upper Deck-313
93OPC Premier-371
Gold-371
93Parkhurst-395
Emerald Ice-395
93Pinnacle-423
Canadian-423
93PowerPlay-388
93Score-495
Canadian-495
93Stadium Club-324
Members Only Master Set-324
First Day Issue-324
93Topps/OPC Premier-371
Gold-371
93Upper Deck-370
93Swedish Semic World Champ Stickers-108
94Parkhurst-139
Gold-139
95Czech APS Extraliga-270
99Czech OFS-39
99Czech OFS Jagr Team Embossed-39
00Czech DS Extraliga Team Jagr-JT10
00Czech OFS-395

Volk, Christian

02German DEL City Press-105

Volk, Dreu

96Swift Current Broncos-14
97Moose Jaw Warriors-17

Volk, John

93Quebec Pee-Wee Tournament-81

Volk, Josef

72Finnish Hellas-45
72Finnish Semic World Championship-96
72Swedish Semic World Championship-96

Volkle, Jorg

94German First League-630

Volkov, Alexei

98Black Diamond-104
Double Diamond-104
Triple Diamond-104
Quadruple Diamond-104
98SPx Top Prospects-78
Radiance-78
Spectrum-78
98Halifax Mooseheads-1
98Halifax Mooseheads Second Edition-18
99Black Diamond-104
Diamond Cut-104
Final Cut-104
99Upper Deck-328
Exclusives-328
Exclusives 1 of 1-328
99Upper Deck Sobey's Memorial Cup-1
99Upper Deck Gold Reserve-328
99Upper Deck Ovation-74
Standing Ovation-74
99Halifax Mooseheads-1
99Bowman CHL-42
Gold-42
OPC International-42
99UD Prospects-58
International Stars-IN4
Signatures of Tradition-AV
00QMJHL All-Star Program Inserts-23
01Russian Hockey League-85
02Russian Future Stars-16
02Russian Transfert-22
02Russian Transfert Promos-5
02Russian Ultimate Line-10
03Russian Hockey League-27

Volkov, Igor

01Russian Hockey League-62
03Russian National Team-17
03Russian Postcards-10

Volkov, Mikhail

91Upper Deck Czech World Juniors-5
93Rochester Americans Kodak-24
94Classic Pro Prospects-104
95Rochester Americans-20
95South Carolina Stingrays-5
99Swiss Panini Stickers-335
00Russian Hockey League-262

Volkov, Oleg

00Russian Hockey League-360
02Russian Hockey League-36

Volland, Andreas

94German DEL-188
95German DEL-188

Vollertzen, Dan

99Danish Hockey League-189

Vollhoffer, Troy

84Saskatoon Blades Stickers-19
88Flint Spirits-21
88ProCards IHL-63

Vollmer, Bruno

93Swiss HNL-170
95Swiss HNL-52
96Swiss HNL-197

Vollmer, Jochen

99German DEL-355

Volmar, Doug

73O-Pee-Chee-215

Vologjaninov, Ivan

93Lethbridge Hurricanes-21
94Kamloops Blazers-5
95Slapshot Memorial Cup-6

Voloshenko, Roman

04Russian Under-18 Team-12
05ITG Heroes/Prosp Toronto Expo Parallel -224
05AHL Top Prospects-46
05ITG Heroes and Prospects-224
Autographs Series II-RV
06ITG Heroes and Prospects-37
Autographs-ARV

Volp, Jon

03Minnesota State Mavericks-20

Volpatti, Aaron

03Vernon Vipers-16
04Vernon Vipers-11
05Vernon Vipers-21

Volpe, Mike

85Kitchener Rangers-10

Volrab, Daniel

01Saskatoon Blades-14
02Saskatoon Blades-11

Volstad, Craig

91Air Canada SJHL-C17

Voltera, Rob

01BC Icemen-25
02Hershey Bears-24
03Hershey Bears-13
03Hershey Bears Patriot News-26
05Rockford Ice Hogs-17
06Rio Grande Valley Killer Bees-5

Vomela, Lukas

03Czech OFS Plus-255

von Arb, Alexandre

96Swiss HNL-508
96Swiss HNL-558

Von Arx, Jan

96Swiss HNL-112
98Swiss Power Play Stickers-62
98Swiss Power Play Stickers-290
99Swiss Panini Stickers-62
00Swiss Panini Stickers-110
00Swiss Slapshot Mini-Cards-HCD6
01Swiss HNL-107
02Swiss HNL-4
04Swiss Davos Postcards-28

Von Arx, Reto

95Swiss HNL-130
96Swiss HNL-122
96Swiss HNL-545
98Swiss Power Play Stickers-73
98Swiss Power Play Stickers-271
99Swiss Panini Stickers-75
99Swiss Panini Stickers-274
00BAP Memorabilia-459
Emerald-459
Ruby-459
Sapphire-459
00BAP Signature Series-269
Emerald-269
Ruby-269
Sapphire-269
Autographs-231
Autographs Gold-231
00SP Authentic-97
00Topps Heritage-79
Chrome Parallel-79
00Topps Premier Plus-107
Blue Ice-107
00UD Pros and Prospects-98
00Upper Deck-413
Exclusives Tier 1-413
Exclusives Tier 2-413
00Upper Deck Vintage-376
00Swiss Panini Stickers National Team-P24
01BAP Memorabilia-215
Emerald-215
Ruby-215
Sapphire-215
02BAP Sig Series Auto Buybacks 2000-231
02Swiss HNL-10
02Swiss HNL-478
04Swiss Davos Postcards-29

von der Geest, Mikael

03Swedish Elite-219
Silver-219

von Gunten, Mischa

02Swiss HNL-226

Von Rohr, Andre

93Swiss HNL-259
96Swiss HNL-445

96Swiss HNL-446
98Swiss Power Play Stickers-348
01Swiss HNL-379

Von Stefenelli, Phil
91ProCards-604
92Hamilton Canucks-25
96Detroit Vipers-19
98German DEL-145
99German DEL-142
01German Upper Deck-165
02German DEL City Press-106
03German DEL-89
04German DEL-97
04German Ingolstadt Panthers-24
05German DEL-157

Von Trzcinski, A.
95German DEL-198

Vonachen, Yann
93Quebec Pee-Wee Tournament-1643

Vondra, Michal
03Czech OFS Plus-276

Vondracek, Roman
02Czech OFS Plus-20
03Czech OFS Plus-166

Vondrka, Michal
00Czech OFS-27
01Czech OFS-142
02Czech OFS Plus-189
04Czech OFS-177
05Czech HC Slavia Praha-14
06Czech OFS-307

Voorhees, K.J.
04Knoxville Ice Bears-24
05Knoxville Ice Bears-18
06Fort Wayne Komets-21

Vopat, Jan
91Upper Deck Czech World Juniors-95
92Upper Deck-601
92Classic-36
Gold-36
Four-Sport Autographs-NNO
94Czech APS Extraliga-211
94Finnish Jaa Kiekko-171
95Czech APS Extraliga-362
95Finnish Semic World Championships-143
95Swedish World Championships Stickers-193
95Phoenix Roadrunners-20
96Leaf-222
Press Proofs-222
96Pinnacle-214
Artist's Proofs-214
Foil-214
Premium Stock-214
Rink Collection-214
96Ultra-83
Gold Medallion-83
96Swedish Semic Wien-108
96Collector's Edge Ice-186
Prism-186
97Collector's Choice-126
97Pacific-271
Copper-271
Emerald Green-271
Ice Blue-271
Red-271
Silver-271
97Upper Deck-79
98Panini Stickers-137
98Predators Team Issue-23
98Upper Deck-299
Exclusives-299
Exclusives 1 of 1-299
Gold Reserve-299
99Upper Deck Victory-164
99Czech OFS-40
99Czech OFS Jagr Team Embossed-40

Vopat, Roman
94Signature Rookies Gold Standard *-97
95Bowman-139
All-Foil-139
95Donruss-307
95Parkhurst International-447
Emerald Ice-447
95SkyBox Impact-219
95Upper Deck-440
Electric Ice-440
Electric Ice Gold-440
95Prince Albert Raiders-20
95Signature Rookies-2
Signatures-2
96Donruss-216
Press Proofs-216
96Fleer-135
Calder Candidates-10
96Metal Universe-194
96Score-252
Artist's Proofs-252
Dealer's Choice Artist's Proofs-252
Special Artist's Proofs-252
Golden Blades-252
96SkyBox Impact-162
96Summit Metal-193
97Be A Player-103
Autographs-103
Autographs Die-Cuts-103
Autographs Prismatic Die-Cuts-103
97Collector's Choice-124
97Donruss-147
Press Proofs Silver-147
Press Proofs Gold-147
97Donruss Limited-129
97Donruss Limited-180
Exposure-129
Exposure-180
97Leaf-69
Fractal Matrix-69
Fractal Matrix Die Cuts-69
97Leaf International-69
Universal Ice-69
97Upper Deck-78
99Stadium Club-39
First Day Issue-39
One of a Kind-39
Printing Plates Black-39
Printing Plates Cyan-39
Printing Plates Magenta-39
Printing Plates Yellow-39
00Finnish Cardset-196
01Finnish Cardset-237
02Finnish Cardset-292
04Finnish Cardset-29
Parallel-21
05Czech HC Sparta Praha-15

Voracek, Jakub
06Halifax Mooseheads-14
06ITG Heroes and Prospects-199
Autographs-AJV
Complete CHL Logos-CHL14
Jerseys-GUJ69
Emblems-GUE69
Numbers-GUN69
Quad Emblems-QE12
Quad Emblems-QE15

Voracek, Tomas
06Czech OFS-319

Vorderbruggen, Reiner
94German DEL-335

Vorel, Marek
95Czech APS Extraliga-346
97Czech APS Extraliga-73
98Czech OFS-173
99Czech DS-193
99Czech OFS-85
00Czech OFS-205
01Czech OFS-264
02Czech OFS Plus-124
02Czech National Team Postcards-14
03Finnish Cardset-53
04Czech OFS-303
05Czech HC Plzen-16

Vorlicek, Frantisek
74Swedish Stickers-113
94Czech APS Extraliga-295
95Czech APS Extraliga-174
96Czech APS Extraliga-309

Vorobel, Slavomir
95Slovakian APS National Team-14

Vorobiev, Alexei
00Russian Hockey League-99

Vorobiev, Dmitri
03Russian Hockey League-120

Vorobiev, Ilya
02German DEL City Press-257
03Russian Hockey League-140

Vorobiev, Pavel
00Russian Hockey League-295
02SPx Rookie Redemption-R195
03BAP Memorabilia-188
Emerald-188
Gold-188
Ruby-188
Sapphire-188
Super Rookies-SR18
Super Rookies Gold-SR18
Super Rookies Silver-SR18
03BAP Ultimate Memorabilia Autographs-104
Gold-104
03Beehive-205
Gold-205
Silver-205
03Black Diamond-185
Black-185
Green-185
Red-185
03Blackhawks Postcards-30
03Bowman-129
Gold-129
03Bowman Chrome-129
Refractors-129
Gold Refractors-129
Xfractors-129
03Crown Royale-109
Red-110
Retail-109
Retail-110
03ITG Action-608
03ITG Used Signature Series-125
Autographs Gold-125
03ITG VIP Rookie Debut-41
03Pacific-354
03Pacific Calder-109
Silver-109
03Pacific Complete-600
Red-600
03Pacific Invincible-107
Blue-107
Red-107
Retail-107
03Pacific Luxury Suite-57
Gold-57
03Pacific Quest for the Cup-109
03Pacific Supreme-112
Blue-112
Red-112
Retail-112
03Parkhurst Original Six Chicago-11
03Parkhurst Rookie-163
03Private Stock Reserve-112
Blue-112
Red-112
Retail-112
03SP Authentic-138
Limited-138
03SP Game Used-86
Gold-86
03SPx-211
Radiance-211
Spectrum-211
03Titanium-109
Hobby Jersey Number Parallels-109
Retail-109
Retail Jersey Number Parallels-109
03Topps Traded-TT93
Blue-TT93
Gold-TT93
Red-TT93
03UD Honor Roll-171
03UD Premier Collection-71
03Upper Deck-208
Canadian Exclusives-208
HG-208
03Upper Deck Classic Portraits-175
03Upper Deck Ice-91
Glass Parallel-91
03Upper Deck MVP-469
03Upper Deck Rookie Update-212
03Upper Deck Trilogy-175
Limited-175
03Norfolk Admirals-20
04Norfolk Admirals-20
05Parkhurst-105
Facsimile Auto Parallel-105
05UD Rookie Class-16
05Upper Deck-287
05Upper Deck MVP-96
Gold-96
Platinum-96
05Upper Deck Victory-211
Black-211
Gold-211
Silver-211
05ITG Heroes and Prospects Complete Logos-AHL-3
05ITG Heroes/Prospects He Shoots/Scores-24
05ITG Heroes and Prospects Jerseys-GUJ-30
05ITG Heroes and Prospects Jerseys Gold-GUJ-30
05ITG Heroes and Prospects Emblems-GUE-30
05ITG Heroes and Prospects Emblems Gold-GUE-30
05ITG Heroes and Prospects Numbers-GUN-30
05ITG Heroes and Prospects Numbers Gold-GUN-30
06Upper Deck MVP-63
Gold Script-63
Super Script-63
06Upper Deck Victory-46
06Upper Deck Victory Black-46
06Upper Deck Victory Gold-46
06ITG Heroes and Prospects-69
Autographs-APV

Vorobiev, Petr
02Russian Hockey League-45
02Russian SL-42
03Russian Hockey League-138

Vorobiev, Vladimir
96Binghamton Rangers-22
97Collector's Choice-164
97Donruss-210
Press Proofs Silver-210
Press Proofs Gold-210
97Donruss Canadian Ice-139
Dominion Series-139
Provincial Series-139
97Donruss Limited-97
97Donruss Limited-121
97Donruss Limited-197
Exposure-97
Exposure-121
Exposure-197
97Pinnacle-188
Press Plates Back Black-188
Press Plates Back Cyan-188
Press Plates Back Magenta-188
Press Plates Back Yellow-188
Press Plates Front Black-188
Press Plates Front Cyan-188
Press Plates Front Magenta-188
Press Plates Front Yellow-188
97Pinnacle Inside-123
97Score-75
Artist's Proofs-75
Golden Blades-75
97Score Rangers-13
Platinum-13
Premier-13
97Hartford Wolf Pack-27
98Pacific-304
Ice Blue-304
Red-304
98Hartford Wolf Pack-22
99Hamilton Bulldogs-8
00Russian Hockey League-235
02Russian SL-41
02Russian Transfert-10
02Russian Transfert Promos-1
03Russian Hockey League-52
04Russian Moscow Dynamo-6
04Russian Super League All-Stars-15
05Russian Hockey League RHL-25

Vorobjev, Ilja
94German DEL-109
96German DEL-57
98German DEL-136
99German DEL-129
00German DEL-147

Vorobjev, Piotr
94German DEL-103
95German DEL-110

Voronov, Sergei
95Hampton Roads Admirals-22
98Russian Hockey League-142
00Russian Hockey League-105
00Russian Hockey League-278
02Russian SL-49
03Russian Hockey League-280

Voros, Aaron
04Albany River Rats-23
04ITG Heroes and Prospects-192
04ITG Heroes/Prospects Toronto Expo '05-192
05Albany River Rats-26

Voroshilov, Igor
06Moncton Wildcats-21

Voroshin, Pavel
02Mississauga Ice Dogs-11
03Owen Sound Attack-15

Vos, Ralph
96German DEL-222

Vosatko, Lubomir
03Czech OFS Plus-390
06Czech OFS-244

Vosatko, Martin
04Czech OFS-289

Voschenikin, Oleg
01Russian Hockey League-156

Voshakov, Juri
95Swiss HNL-415

Voskar, Jozef
00Czech DS Extraliga-144
00Czech OFS-126
02Czech OFS Plus-273

Voss, Carl
34Beehive Group I Photos-128
35Diamond Matchbooks Tan 1-68
35Diamond Matchbooks Tan 2-63
35Diamond Matchbooks Tan 3-58
37O-Pee-Chee V304E-175
37V356 Worldwide Gum-66
83Hall of Fame Postcards-O16
85Hall of Fame-225
04ITG Ultimate Mem Marvelous Maroons-5
04ITG Ultimate Memorabilia Paper Cuts-19

Voss, Dirk
94German First League-455

Vossen, Dale
917th Inn. Sketch WHL-236

Vossen, Jamie
95Slapshot-211
98OCN Blizzard-11

Vost, Oliver
94German First League-162

Vosta, Ondrej
94Czech APS Extraliga-108
95Czech APS Extraliga-69
96Czech APS Extraliga-256
97Czech APS Extraliga-281
98Czech DS Stickers-79

Vostrak, Pavel
96Czech APS Extraliga-308
97Czech APS Extraliga-186
97Czech DS Stickers-224
98Czech DS-60
98Czech DS Stickers-163
98Czech OFS-46
99Czech DS-94
99Czech OFS-130
00Czech DS Extraliga-31
00Czech OFS-67
01Czech DS-23
01Czech OFS-221
All Stars-40
02Finnish Cardset-143
04Czech OFS-359

Vostrikov, Artem
03Russian Hockey League-249

Vostrikov, Sergei
91O-Pee-Chee Inserts-27R
99German DEL-152
00German DEL-16
All-Star Class-A4
01German Upper Deck-15
Gate Attractions-GA1
02German DEL City Press-21

Voth, Brad
97Medicine Hat Tigers-21
98Medicine Hat Tigers-22
99Medicine Hat Tigers-13
00Medicine Hat Tigers-24
01Peoria Rivermen-17
01Worcester Icecats-24
02Peoria Rivermen-15
02Peoria Rivermen RBI Sports-168
03Columbus Cottonmouths-16
05UK Cardiff Devils-8
Gold-8
Silver-8
05UK Cardiff Devils Challenge Cup-2

Voth, Curtis
01Missouri River Otters-9

Vourela, Janne
00Finnish Cardset-329

Voutilainen, Jukka
02Finnish Cardset-293
02Finnish Cardset Dynamic Duos-5
04Finnish Cardset-43
Parallel-31
05Finnish Cardset -210
06Swedish SHL Elitset-201

Voytechek, Keith
04Vancouver Giants-10
06Moose Jaw Warriors-7

Vozar, Patrick
94German DEL-122
95German DEL-122
99German Bundesliga 2-124

Vozar, Robert
94German First League-393

Vozdecky, Martin
99Czech OFS-68

Vozka, Tomas
99Czech Score Blue 2000-76
99Czech Score Red Ice 2000-76

Vrabec, Thomas
91Finnish Semic World Champ Stickers-200
91Swedish Semic World Champ Stickers-200
92Finnish Semic-215
93Swiss HNL-80
95Swiss HNL-107
95Swiss HNL-507

Vrabel, Michal
04UK Coventry Blaze-20

Vrana, Petr
02Halifax Mooseheads-11
03Halifax Mooseheads-7
03Halifax Mooseheads-NNO
04Halifax Mooseheads-20
05Albany River Rats-27
05Extreme Top Prospects Signature Edition-S10

Vrataric, Rich
95Slapshot-196

Vrba, Tomas
06Czech OFS-170

Vrbata, David
00Calgary Hitmen-24
03Czech OFS Plus-160
04Czech OFS-321
06Czech HC Sparta Praha Postcards-3
06Czech OFS-68

Vrbata, Radim
99O-Pee-Chee-256
99O-Pee-Chee Chrome-256
99O-Pee-Chee Chrome Refractors-256
99Topps/OPC-256
99Topps/OPC Chrome-256
Refractors-256
99Hull Olympiques-12
Signed-12
99Bowman CHL-21
Gold-21
OPC International-21
Autographs-BA20
Autographs Gold-BA20
Autographs Silver-BA20
00QMJHL All-Star Program Inserts-35
00Shawinigan Cataractes-10
Signed-10
00UD CHL Prospects-86
Future Leaders-FL9
01Avalanche Team Issue-8
01BAP Memorabilia-338
Emerald-338
Ruby-338
Sapphire-338
01Bowman YoungStars-137
Gold-137
Ice Cubed-137
01Parkhurst-351
01SPx-170
01Titanium-38
Hobby Parallel-38
Premiere Date-38
Retail-38
Retail Parallel-38
Rookie Team-5
Three-Star Selections-25
01Titanium Draft Day Edition-117
01Upper Deck Ice-91
01Hershey Bears-28
02BAP First Edition-212
02BAP Memorabilia-193
02BAP Memorabilia-379
Emerald-193
Ruby-193
Sapphire-193
NHL All-Star Game-193
NHL All-Star Game Blue-193
NHL All-Star Game Green-193
NHL All-Star Game Red-193
02BAP Memorabilia Toronto Fall Expo-193
02BAP Signature Series-60
Autographs-60
Autographs Gold-60
02Bowman YoungStars-138
Gold-138
Silver-138
02O-Pee-Chee-83
02O-Pee-Chee Premier Blue Parallel-83
02O-Pee-Chee Premier Red Parallel-83
02O-Pee-Chee Factory Set-83
02Pacific-98
Blue-98
Red-98
Shining Moments-4
02Pacific Complete-375
Red-375
02Pacific Exclusive-48
Great Expectations-5
02Pacific Toronto Spring Expo Rookie Coll-4
02Parkhurst-162
Bronze-162
Gold-162
Silver-162
02Parkhurst Retro-194
Minis-194
02Private Stock Reserve-29
Blue-29
Red-29
Retail-29
02SP Authentic-113
02Topps-83
OPC Blue Parallel-83
OPC Red Parallel-83
Signs of the Future-RV
Factory Set-83
02Topps Chrome-52
Black Border Refractors-52
Refractors-52
Chromographs-CGRV
Chromograph Refractors-CGRV
02Topps Heritage-78
Chrome Parallel-78
02Topps Total-61
Signatures-RV
02Upper Deck-44
Exclusives-44
02Upper Deck Victory-51
Bronze-51
Gold-51
Silver-51
03Hurricanes Postcards-20
03ITG Action-120
03Pacific-66
Blue-66
Red-66
03Pacific Complete-36
Red-36
03Pacific Supreme-17
Blue-17
Red-17
Retail-17
Generations-1
03Topps C55 Autographs-TA-RV
03Upper Deck-280
Canadian Exclusives-280
HG-280
UD Exclusives-280
03Upper Deck MVP-80
Gold Script-80
Silver Script-80
Canadian Exclusives-80
03Czech National Team Postcards-16
04Pacific-52
Blue-52
Red-52
04Czech OFS-83
Stars-3
05Parkhurst-109
Facsimile Auto Parallel-109
05Upper Deck-34
HG Glossy-34
05Upper Deck MVP-74
Gold-74
Platinum-74
05Upper Deck Toronto Fall Expo-34
05Czech World Champions Postcards-12
05Czech Pexeso Mini Red Set-11
06Be A Player-13
Autographs-13
Signatures-RV
06Blackhawks Postcards-17
06O-Pee-Chee-120
Rainbow-120
06Panini Stickers-212
06Upper Deck-43
Exclusives Parallel-43
High Gloss Parallel-43
Masterpieces-43
06Czech NHL ELH Postcards-14
07Upper Deck Victory-122
Black-122
Gold-122

Vrla, Daniel
94Czech APS Extraliga-232
95Czech APS Extraliga-11

Vrolyk, Kris
93Quebec Pee-Wee Tournament-821

Vrolyk, Robbie
06Sioux Falls Stampede -10

Vroman, Bob
71Johnstown Jets Acme-15

Vsetecka, David
04Czech OFS-314
05Czech HC Trinec-13

Vuillemin, Frank
93Swiss HNL-498

Vujtek Sr., Vladimir
00Czech OFS-210
02Russian SL-5

Vujtek, Vladimir
917th Inn. Sketch WHL-303
92Oilers IGA-22
92Oilers Team Issue-20
92Pinnacle-396
French-396
92Upper Deck-417
92Upper Deck-496
93OPC Premier-459
Gold-459
93Parkhurst-339
Emerald Ice-339
93PowerPlay-343
93Score-465
Canadian-465
93Stadium Club-278
Members Only Master Set-278
First Day Issue-278
93Topps/OPC Premier-459
Gold-459
93Ultra-319
93Upper Deck-168
94OPC Premier-503
Special Effects-503
94Topps/OPC Premier-503
Special Effects-503
94Ultra-293
94Czech APS Extraliga-131
94Czech APS Extraliga-293
95Czech APS Extraliga-27
95Czech APS Extraliga-303
96Czech APS Extraliga-189
97Be A Player-113
Autographs-113
Autographs Die-Cuts-113
Autographs Prismatic Die-Cuts-113
97Czech APS Extraliga-123
97Czech APS Extraliga-362
98Czech DS-5
98Czech OFS-119
98Czech OFS-349
98Czech OFS-430
99Czech OFS-221
99Czech OFS-402
99Czech OFS-492
All-Star Game Blue-492
All-Star Game Gold-492
All-Star Game Red-492
All-Star Game Silver-492
00Czech DS Extraliga-7
National Team-NT4
00Czech OFS-302
01Czech National Team Postcards-16
01Czech OFS All Stars-41
01Finnish Cardset-223
01Finnish Cardset Dueling Aces-5
02Czech DS-34
02Finnish Cardset-144
02Russian Hockey League-213
03Finnish Cardset-38
03Finnish Cardset Globetrotters-GR9
03Russian Hockey League-167
04Czech OFS-354
Stars II-6

Vukonich, Mike
91ProCards-391
92Phoenix Roadrunners-24
92Classic-110
Gold-110
92Classic Four-Sport *-219
Gold-219
93Phoenix Cobras RHI-19
98Indianapolis Ice-6

Vukota, Mick
84Kelowna Wings-22
89Islanders Team Issue-21
90O-Pee-Chee-10
90Pro Set-488
90Topps-10
Tiffany-10
90Upper Deck-39
French-39
91O-Pee-Chee-25
91Score Canadian Bilingual-387
91Score Canadian English-387
91Stadium Club-309
91Topps-25
91Upper Deck-135
French-135
92Score-549A
Canadian-549A
94Parkhurst SE-SE101
Gold-SE101
95Upper Deck-380
Electric Ice-380
Electric Ice Gold-380
96Islander Postcards-22
97Be A Player-56
Autographs-56
Autographs Die-Cuts-56
Autographs Prismatic Die-Cuts-56
98Pacific-259
Ice Blue-259
Red-259
99Utah Grizzlies-18
99Utah Grizzlies-28
02Fleer Throwbacks-83
Gold-83
Platinum-83

Vukovic, Nick
98Owen Sound Platers-23
99Owen Sound Platers-28
00Owen Sound Attack-23

Vuorela, Janne
98Finnish Kerailysarja-213
99Finnish Cardset-121

Vuori, Ari
89Swedish Semic World Champ Stickers-49
92Finnish Jyvas-Hyva Stickers-187
93Finnish Jyvas-Hyva Stickers-319
93Finnish SISU-51
94Finnish SISU-109
95Finnish SISU-191

Vuorinen, Jarmo
80Finnish Mallasjuoma-22

Vuorinen, Jukka-Pekka
78Finnish SM-Liiga-108

Vuorinen, Teemu
94Finnish SISU-222
95Finnish SISU-234
96Finnish SISU Redline-28

Vuorio, Jari
80Finnish Mallasjuoma-67

Vuorio, Matti
93Finnish SISU-282

Vuorio, Mikael
04Finnish Cardset-264

Vuorivirta, Juha
94Finest-141
Super Team Winners-141
Refractors-141
94Finnish SISU-290
95Finnish SISU-120
Drafted Dozen-10
95Signature Rookies-29
Signatures-29
98Finnish Kerailysarja-218

Vuoti, Arto
94Finnish SISU-204

Vyazmikin, Igor
98Russian Hockey League-151

Vyborny, David
92Upper Deck-600
93Classic-48
94Finnish Jaa Kiekko-185
94Cape Breton Oilers-20
94Classic-77
Gold-77
95Czech APS Extraliga-280
95Finnish Semic World Championships-148
96Czech APS Extraliga-135
97Czech APS Extraliga-361
97Czech DS Stickers-11
97Czech DS Stickers-71
97Swedish Collector's Choice-165
98Czech DS-11
98Czech OFS-137
98Czech OFS-427
98Czech OFS-456
99Czech DS-147
National Stars-NS21
99Czech OFS-113
99Czech OFS-275
99Czech OFS-493
All-Star Game Blue-493
All-Star Game Gold-493
All-Star Game Red-493
All-Star Game Silver-493
00BAP Memorabilia-410
Emerald-410
Ruby-410
Sapphire-410
00Black Diamond-95
00Crown Royale-121
00Private Stock-114
Gold-114
Premiere Date-114
Retail-114
Silver-114
PS-2001 Rookies-7
00Titanium-115
Retail-115
00Titanium Draft Day Edition-115
00Titanium Draft Day Promos-115
00Topps Chrome-230
OPC Refractors-230
Refractors-230
00UD Heroes-36
00Vanguard-115
Pacific Proofs-115
00Czech DS Extraliga World Champions-WCH10
01BAP Memorabilia-108
Emerald-108
Ruby-108
Sapphire-108
01BAP Signature Series-131
Autographs-131
Autographs Gold-131
01Blue Jackets Donatos Pizza-14
01O-Pee-Chee-195
01O-Pee-Chee Premier Parallel-195
01Pacific-119
Extreme LTD-119
Hobby LTD-119
Premiere Date-119
Retail LTD-119
01Pacific Arena Exclusives-119
01Parkhurst-154
01Topps-195
OPC Parallel-195
Own The Game-OTG20
01Topps Heritage-105
Refractors-105
01Upper Deck-280
Exclusives-280
01Upper Deck Victory-99
Gold-99
01Czech DS-43
Ice Heroes-IH9
02BAP Memorabilia-79
Emerald-79
Ruby-79
Sapphire-79
NHL All-Star Game-79
NHL All-Star Game Blue-79
NHL All-Star Game Green-79
NHL All-Star Game Red-79
02BAP Memorabilia Toronto Fall Expo-79
02BAP Sig Series Auto Buybacks 2001-131
02O-Pee-Chee-221
02O-Pee-Chee Premier Blue Parallel-221
02O-Pee-Chee Premier Red Parallel-221
02O-Pee-Chee Factory Set-221
02Pacific-108
Blue-108
Red-108
02Pacific Complete-186
Red-186
02Topps-221
OPC Blue Parallel-221
OPC Red Parallel-221
Factory Set-221
02Topps Total-23
02Upper Deck Vintage-72
02Czech DS-33
02Czech DS-48
02Czech DS-62
02Czech National Team Postcards-15
03ITG Action-181
03Pacific-99
Blue-99
Red-99
03Pacific Complete-21
Red-21
03Pacific Heads-Up-30
Hobby LTD-30
Retail LTD-30
03Titanium-32
Hobby Jersey Number Parallels-32
Retail-32
Retail Jersey Number Parallels-32
03Upper Deck-298
Canadian Exclusives-298
HG-298
UD Exclusives-298
03Upper Deck MVP-117
Gold Script-117
Silver Script-117
Canadian Exclusives-117
03Czech National Team Postcards-17
04Pacific-80
Blue-80
Red-80
04Czech HC Sparta Praha Postcards-24
04Czech NHL ELH Postcards-16
04Czech OFS-203
Stars-25
04Czech Zuma-41
04Czech World Championship Postcards-23
05Panini Stickers-245
05Parkhurst-134
Facsimile Auto Parallel-134
05Upper Deck-54
HG Glossy-54
05Upper Deck MVP-115
Gold-115
Platinum-115
05Upper Deck Toronto Fall Expo-54
05Czech World Champions Postcards-3
05Czech Kvarteto Bonaparte-7c
05Czech Pexeso Mini Blue Set-9
05Czech Pexeso Mini Red Set-28
06Be A Player-12
Autographs-12
Signatures-DV
Signatures 25-14
Signatures Duals-DBV
Signatures Trios-TFVB
06Fleer-61
Tiffany-61
06O-Pee-Chee-142
Rainbow-142
06Panini Stickers-235
06Ultra-61
Gold Medallion-61
Ice Medallion-61
06Upper Deck-310
Exclusives Parallel-310
High Gloss Parallel-310
Masterpieces-310
06Upper Deck MVP-87
Gold Script-87
Super Script-87
06Upper Deck Ovation-14
06Upper Deck Victory-55
06Upper Deck Victory Black-55
06Upper Deck Victory Gold-55
06Czech IIHF World Championship Postcards-23
06Czech OFS Jagr Team-18
07Upper Deck Ovation-34
07Upper Deck Victory-125
Black-125
Gold-125

Vyborny, Frantisek
94Czech APS Extraliga-283
95Czech APS Extraliga-267
98Czech OFS-361
99Czech OFS-394
00Czech OFS-288
06Czech OFS Coaches-14

Vyborny, Martin
99Czech Score Blue 2000-75
99Czech Score Red Ice 2000-75
01Czech OFS-210
02Czech OFS Plus-274
Duos-D14
03Czech OFS Plus-306
04Czech HC Plzen Postcards-22
04Czech OFS-156

Vychodil, David
00Sioux City Musketeers-29

Vydareny, Rene
99Rimouski Oceanic-13
Signed-13
02Manitoba Moose-24
03Manitoba Moose-14
04ITG Heroes and Prospects-201
Autographs-U-RV
04ITG Heroes/Prospects Toronto Expo '05-201
05Czech HC Ceski Budejovice-16
06Czech HC Ceske Budejovice Postcards-14
06Czech OFS-22

Vyhlidal, Michael
94Czech APS Extraliga-169
95Czech APS Extraliga-179
96Czech APS Extraliga-315
97Czech APS Extraliga-293
97Czech DS Extraliga-35
97Czech DS Stickers-153
98Czech DS-66
98Czech DS Stickers-109
98Czech OFS-316
99Czech DS-45
99Czech OFS-249
00Czech DS Extraliga-147
00Czech OFS-266
01Czech OFS-247
All Stars-8
02Czech OFS Plus-232
Trios-T9
Duos-D10

Vykoukal, Jiri
90ProCards AHL/IHL-214
91ProCards-562
94Swedish Leaf-279
Foreign Affairs-6
95Czech APS Extraliga-271
95Czech APS Extraliga-360
95Swedish Globe World Championships-152
95Swedish World Championships Stickers-195
96Czech APS Extraliga-123
96Czech APS Extraliga-346
96Swedish Semic Wien-107
97Czech APS Extraliga-24
97Czech APS Extraliga-347
97Czech DS Extraliga-6
97Czech DS Stickers-3
97Czech DS Stickers-61
98Czech DS Stickers-12
98Czech DS Stickers-209
98Czech OFS-421
98Finnish Keralysarja-10
99Czech OFS-276
99Finnish Cardset-8
00Finnish Cardset-7
01Finnish Cardset-186
01Finnish Cardset Dueling Aces-7
02Finnish Cardset-145
03Finnish Cardset-160
04Finnish Cardset-173
Parallel-127
05Czech HC Sparta Praha-16
06Czech OFS-67
Stars-19

Vymazal, Martin
00Red Deer Rebels-21
Signed-21
00Saskatoon Blades-30

Vyrubalik, Martin
03Czech OFS Plus-43

Vyshedkevich, Sergei
96Albany River Rats-21
97Albany River Rats-19
98Albany River Rats-19
99Russian Fetisov Tribute-12
00BAP Memorabilia-252
Emerald-252
Ruby-252
Sapphire-252
Promos-252
00BAP Mem Chicago Sportsfest Copper-252
00BAP Memorabilia Chicago Sportsfest Blue-252
00BAP Memorabilia Chicago Sportsfest Gold-252
00BAP Memorabilia Chicago Sportsfest Ruby-252
00BAP Memorabilia Chicago Sun-Times Ruby-252
00BAP Memorabilia Chicago Sun-Times Gold-252
00BAP Mem Chicago Sun-Times Sapphire-252
00BAP Mem Toronto Fall Expo Copper-252
00BAP Memorabilia Toronto Fall Expo Gold-252
00BAP Memorabilia Toronto Fall Expo Ruby-252
00BAP Signature Series-274
Emerald-274
Ruby-274
Sapphire-274
Autographs-150
Autographs Gold-150
00O-Pee-Chee-298
00O-Pee-Chee Parallel-298
00Pacific-28
Copper-28
Gold-28
Ice Blue-28
Premiere Date-28
00SPx-112

Spectrum-112
00Topps/OPC-298
Parallel-298
00Topps Chrome-193
OPC Refractors-193
Refractors-193
00Upper Deck-217
Exclusives Tier 1-217
Exclusives Tier 2-217
02BAP Sig Series Auto Buybacks 2000-150
02Russian Hockey League-248
02Russian World Championships-18
03Russian Hockey League-46
03Russian World Championship Team 2003-14
04Russian Moscow Dynamo-7
Vyskocil, Tomas
99Czech Score Blue 2000-71
99Czech Score Red Ice 2000-71
Vytisk, Jan
99Czech OFS-234
00Czech OFS-249
01Czech OFS-43
02Czech OFS Plus-300
03Czech OFS Plus-167
03Czech OFS Plus All-Star Game-H39
04Czech HC Plzen Postcards-23
04Czech OFS-157
06Czech OFS-171
Team Cards-10
Vyukhin, Alexander
98Russian Hockey League-126
99Russian Hockey League-258
99Russian Stars Postcards-31
00Russian Hockey League-223
01Russian Hockey League-79
Waatchorn, Jeff
89Kamloops Blazers-22
Wacker, Becky
04Minnesota Golden Gophers Women-9
Waddell, Don
87Flint Spirits-19
88Flint Spirits-22
91ProCards-332
Waddell, Matt
03Ohio State Buckeyes-18
04Ohio State Buckeyes-14
05Ohio State Buckeyes-15
06Ohio State Buckeyes-14
Waddell, Trevor
04Oshawa Generals-4
04Oshawa Generals Autographs-4
Wadden, Sean
03Yarmouth Mariners-23
Wade, Ryan
98Kelowna Rockets-26
Wadel, Jason
917th Inn. Sketch OHL-238
Wagar, Blair
91Air Canada SJHL-A41
Wager, Roman
91Finnish Semic World Champ Stickers-193
91Swedish Semic World Champ Stickers-193
93Swedish Semic World Champ Stickers-123
93Swiss HNL-29
95Swiss HNL-27
95Swiss HNL-522
95Swiss HNL-534
96Swiss HNL-25
98Swiss Power Play Stickers-360
Waghorn, Graham
94Finnish Jaa Kiekko-317
Waghorne, Fred C
83Hall of Fame Postcards-H15
85Hall of Fame-119
Waginger, Michael
05German DEL-54
06German DEL-103
German Forwards-GF14
Wagner, Bernd
91Finnish Semic World Champ Stickers-161
91Swedish Semic World Champ Stickers-161
94German DEL-250
Wagner, Chad
00San Diego Gulls-19
01Asheville Smoke-5
Wagner, Ryan
05Penticton Vees-20
06Penticton Vees-23
Wagner, Steve
02Tri-City Stormfront-15
Wagner, Thomas
94German DEL-403
95German DEL-422
Wagstaff, Kory
97Arizona Icecats-22
Wagstrom, Daniel
01Swedish Brynas Tigers-26
02Swedish SHL-154
Parallel-154
Wahl, Christoph
93Swiss HNL-86
95Swiss HNL-264
96Swiss HNL-383
Wahl, Greg
91Air Canada SJHL-C33
92Saskatchewan JHL-138
Wahl, Henrik
70Finnish Jaakiekko-289
Wahlberg, Bo
72Swedish Stickers-278
Wahlberg, Mikael
92Swedish Semic Elitserien Stickers-65
93Swedish Semic Elitserien-38
94Swedish Leaf-163
95Swedish Leaf-21
95Swedish Upper Deck-30
98German DEL-171
99German DEL-58
02German DEL City Press-189
02Swedish Malmo Red Hawks-13
02Swedish SHL-235
Parallel-235
03German DEL-165
03Swedish Elite-245
Silver-245
04Swedish Elitset-91
Gold-91
04Swedish Malmo Red Hawks-11
05Swedish SHL Elitset-156
Gold-156
Series Two Signatures-2
06Swedish SHL Elitset-99
Wahlgren, Thomas
99Danish Hockey League-194
Wahlsten, Jali
92Finnish Jyvas-Hyva Stickers-67
93Finnish Jyvas-Hyva Stickers-118
93Swedish Semic World Champ Stickers-86
Wahlsten, Juhani
65Finnish Hellas-8
66Finnish Jaakiekkosarja-78
69Swedish Hockey-383
70Swedish Masterserien-87
Wahlsten, Sami
93Swedish Semic World Champ Stickers-87
94Finnish SISU-308
94Finnish Jaa Kiekko-45
Wahlsten, Veijo
73Finnish Jaakiekko-302
Waibel, Harald
94German DEL-308
95German DEL-145
99German Bundesliga 2-163
Waibel, Jon
00Minnesota Golden Gophers-26
01Minnesota Golden Gophers-12
02Minnesota Golden Gophers-26
03Minnesota Golden Gophers-5
Waidlich, Michael
03Lincoln Stars-21
Wainio, Patrik
78Finnish SM-Liiga-66
Wainwright, David
97Columbus Cottonmouths-19
Waite, Jim
88Blackhawks Coke-23
89ProCards IHL-73
90O-Pee-Chee-214
90Score-407A
90Score-407B
Canadian-407A
Canadian-407B
90Topps-214
Tiffany-214
90ProCards AHL/IHL-401
91Blackhawks Coke-28
91Bowman-396
91O-Pee-Chee-127
91Pinnacle-316
French-316
91Pro Set-530
French-530
91Score Canadian Bilingual-632
91Score Canadian English-632
91Score Rookie/Traded-82T
91Topps-127
91Upper Deck-443
French-443
92Blackhawks Coke-18
92Bowman-120
92Parkhurst-270
Emerald Ice-270
92Stadium Club-35
92Topps-100
Gold-100G
92Upper Deck-67
93Donruss-302
93Durivage Score-49
93Leaf-324
93OPC Premier-388
Gold-388
93Parkhurst-181
Emerald Ice-181
93Pinnacle-371
Canadian-371
93PowerPlay-438
93Score-365
93Score-539
Gold-539
Canadian-365
Canadian-539
Canadian Gold-539
93Topps/OPC Premier-388
Gold-388
93Ultra-419
93Upper Deck-501
94Be A Player Signature Cards-126
94Leaf-405
94OPC Premier-496
Special Effects-496
94Parkhurst-214
Gold-214
94Pinnacle Masks-MA9
94Topps/OPC Premier-496
Special Effects-496
95Indianapolis Ice-21
98Be A Player-260
Press Release-260
98BAP Gold-260
98BAP Autographs-260
98BAP Autographs Gold-260
98Pacific-346
Ice Blue-346
Red-346
98Pacific Omega-191
Red-191
Opening Day Issue-191
98Revolution-114
Ice Shadow-114
Red-114
99St. John's Maple Leafs-24
00St. John's Maple Leafs-28
01German Upper Deck-74
Jersey Cards-JW-J
02BAP Sig Series Auto Buybacks 1998-260
02German DEL City Press-167
03German DEL-90
All-Stars-AS1
04German DEL-98
All-Stars-AS1
04German Ingolstadt Panthers-25
05German DEL-158
Goalies-G13
06German DEL-104
Wakaluk, Darcy
84Kelowna Wings-2
88ProCards AHL-257
89ProCards AHL-258
90ProCards AHL/IHL-288
91Bowman-33
91Parkhurst-306
French-306
91Score Canadian Bilingual-653
91Score Canadian English-653
92Bowman-148
92O-Pee-Chee-63
92Parkhurst-315
Emerald Ice-315
92Score-313
Canadian-313
92Stadium Club-153
92Topps-108
Gold-108G
92Ultra-99
93Donruss-420
93OPC Premier-399
Gold-399
93PowerPlay-327
93Score-432
Canadian-432
93Stadium Club-276
Members Only Master Set-276
First Day Issue-276
93Topps/OPC Premier-399
Gold-399
94Donruss-17
94Leaf-152
94OPC Premier-424
Special Effects-424
94Parkhurst SE-SE44
Gold-SE44
94Pinnacle-157
Artist's Proofs-157
Rink Collection-157
94Stadium Club-187
Members Only Master Set-187
First Day Issue-187
Super Team Winner Cards-187
94Stars HockeyKaps-24
94Stars Pinnacle Sheet-157
94Stars Pinnacle Sheet-NNO
94Stars Postcards-21
94Topps/OPC Premier-81
94Topps/OPC Premier-424
Special Effects-424
94Ultra-282
94Upper Deck-459
Electric Ice-459
95Be A Player-90
Signatures-S90
Signatures Die Cuts-S90
95Finest-156
Refractors-156
95Parkhurst International-331
Emerald Ice-331
95Score-197
Black Ice Artist's Proofs-197
Black Ice-197
95Stars Score Sheet-197
95Topps-313
OPC Inserts-313
95Ultra-231
95Images Platinum Players-PL9
96Coyotes Coca-Cola-33
96Score-210
Artist's Proofs-210
Dealer's Choice Artist's Proofs-210
Special Artist's Proofs-210
Golden Blades-210
97Coyotes Face-Off Luncheon -25
Wakefield, Lance
91Air Canada SJHL-D50
Wakeham, Randy
93Michigan Tech Huskies-23
Wakely, Ernie
70Colgate Stamps-92
70Esso Power Players-252
70O-Pee-Chee-97
70Sargent Promotions Stamps-181
70Topps-97
71Blues Postcards-27
71Letraset Action Replays-12
71O-Pee-Chee-81
71Sargent Promotions Stamps-185
71Topps-81
71Toronto Sun-252
73Quaker Oats WHA-41
75O-Pee-Chee WHA-132
76O-Pee-Chee WHA-92
76San Diego Mariners WHA-14
Waker, Nolan
03Kelowna Rockets-21
04Prince Albert Raiders-12
05Brampton Battalion-18
Wala, Martin
96Slovakian Quebec Pee-Wee Tournament-29
Walby, Steffon
92British Columbia JHL-61
92British Columbia JHL-246
93St. John's Maple Leafs-25
94St. John's Maple Leafs-23
94Classic Pro Prospects-97
95St. John's Maple Leafs-20
97Fort Wayne Komets-10
98Rochester Americans-25
00Hershey Bears-19
02ECHL All-Star Southern-57
03ECHL All-Stars-282
03Mississippi Sea Wolves-15
Walbye, Knut
92Norwegian Elite Series-40
92Norwegian Elite Series-198
Walbye, Per Oddvar
92Norwegian Elite Series-45
Walcot, Brad
82Kingston Canadians-22
83Oshawa Generals-13
85Sudbury Wolves-24
Walcott, Richie
91ProCards-564
93Hampton Roads Admirals-19
98Fort Worth Brahmas-12
99Asheville Smoke-20
Walde, Oliver
94German First League-438
Walder, Raymond
91Finnish Semic World Champ Stickers-191
91Swedish Semic World Champ Stickers-191
92Finnish Semic-205
93Swiss HNL-106
96Swiss HNL-172
98Swiss Power Play Stickers-312
00Swiss Panini Stickers-96
00Swiss Slapshot Mini-Cards-EHCC14
Walder, Remo
95Swiss HNL-154
Waldrop, Merit
01Sioux Falls Stampede-17
Wales, Michael
04UK Milton Keynes Lightning-3
06UK Coventry Blaze-17
Walford, Clarke
93Quebec Pee-Wee Tournament-1412
Walitalo, Gote
82Swedish Semic VM Stickers-2
83Swedish Semic Elitserien-26
83Swedish Semic VM Stickers-2
84Swedish Semic Elitserien-26
85Swedish Panini Stickers-26
86Swedish Panini Stickers-3
87Swedish Panini Stickers-26
Walker, Adam
04UK Guildford Flames-8
04UK U-20 Team-17
Walker, Ben
93London Knights-21
93London Knights-24
Walker, Brent
03Swift Current Broncos-21
Walker, Darby
917th Inn. Sketch WHL-312
00UK Sekonda Superleague-85
Walker, Francis
04Lakehead University Thunderwolves-8
Walker, Geoff
06PEI Rocket-2
Walker, Geoffrey
04Gatineau Olympiques-22
05PEI Rocket-7
Walker, Gordie
84Kamloops Blazers-24
88ProCards AHL-222
89ProCards AHL-22
Walker, Howard
81Capitals Team Issue-20
82O-Pee-Chee-59
Walker, Jack
83Hall of Fame Postcards-E16
85Hall of Fame-75
Walker, Jared
02Red Deer Rebels-13
03Red Deer Rebels-10
Walker, Jeff
89Niagara Falls Thunder-21
897th Inn. Sketch OHL-148
907th Inn. Sketch OHL-272
91Peterborough Petes-17
917th Inn. Sketch OHL-133
Walker, John
93Quebec Pee-Wee Tournament-521
Walker, Johnny
88ProCards AHL-325
94German DEL-242
95German DEL-236
96German DEL-87
98German DEL-23
99German DEL-138
00German DEL-78
01German Upper Deck-90
Walker, Jordan
98Prince George Cougars-23
99Kamloops Blazers-23
Walker, Kelly
90Arizona Icecats-14
91Arizona Icecats-3
91Arizona Icecats-18
92Arizona Icecats-2
Walker, Kurt
76Maple Leafs Postcards-22
77Maple Leafs Postcards-18
78O-Pee-Chee-282
Walker, Matt
97Portland Winter Hawks-22
00Worcester Icecats-12
01Worcester Icecats-19
02BAP Memorabilia-311
02BAP Ultimate Memorabilia-60
02Pacific Calder-142
Silver-142
02Pacific Complete-565
Red-565
02Pacific Quest for the Cup-143
Gold-143
02Parkhurst Retro-212
Minis-212
02SP Authentic-165
02UD Honor Roll-142
02Worcester IceCats-19
03Blues Team Set-27
03Worcester Ice Cats 10th Anniversary-7
05Blues Team Set-20
Walker, Scott
917th Inn. Sketch OHL-274
93Owen Sound Platers-31
94Classic Pro Prospects-165
95Bowman-143
All-Foil-143
95Donruss-303
95Leaf-108
95Parkhurst International-484
Emerald Ice-484
95Upper Deck-418
Electric Ice-418
Electric Ice Gold-418
96Canucks Postcards-24
96Upper Deck-351
96Collector's Edge Ice-90
Prism-90
97Be A Player-33
Autographs-33
Autographs Die-Cuts-33
Autographs Prismatic Die-Cuts-33
97Pacific Invincible NHL Regime-205
98Be A Player-224
Press Release-224
98BAP Gold-224
98BAP Autographs-224
98BAP Autographs Gold-224
98Pacific-435
Ice Blue-435
Red-435
98Panini Stickers-142
98Paramount-129
Copper-129
Emerald Green-129
Holo-Electric-129
Ice Blue-129
Silver-129
98Predators Team Issue-24
99Aurora-82
Premiere Date-82
99Pacific-233
Copper-233
Emerald Green-233
Gold-233
Ice Blue-233
Premiere Date-233
Red-233
99Pacific Dynagon Ice-112
Blue-112
Copper-112
Gold-112
Premiere Date-112
99Panini Stickers-266
99Paramount-129
Copper-129
Emerald-129
Gold-129
Holographic Emerald-129
Holographic Gold-129
Holographic Silver-129
Ice Blue-129
Premiere Date-129
Red-129
Silver-129
99Revolution-82
Premiere Date-82
Red-82
Shadow Series-82
00BAP Parkhurst 2000-P174
00BAP Signature Series-4
Emerald-4
Ruby-4
Sapphire-4
Autographs-43
Autographs Gold-43
00Pacific-228
Copper-228
Gold-228
Ice Blue-228
Premiere Date-228
00Titanium Draft Day Edition-58
Patches-58
00Topps Heritage-194
00Upper Deck Vintage-205
01Atomic Jerseys-36
01Atomic Patches-36
01BAP Memorabilia-113
Emerald-113
Ruby-113
Sapphire-113
01BAP Signature Series-64
Autographs-64
Autographs Gold-64
01Crown Royale-83
Blue-83
Premiere Date-83
Red-83
Retail-83
Triple Threads-16
01Pacific-223
Extreme LTD-223
Hobby LTD-223
Premiere Date-223
Retail LTD-223
01Pacific Adrenaline-109
Blue-109
Premiere Date-109
Red-109
Retail-109
01Pacific Arena Exclusives-223
01Pacific Heads-Up Quad Jerseys-13
01Parkhurst-127
01UD Challenge for the Cup-49
01Upper Deck-326
Exclusives-326
01Upper Deck MVP-108
01Upper Deck Victory-196
Gold-196
01Upper Deck Vintage-142
01Upper Deck Vintage-144
02BAP Signature Series-37
Autographs-37
Autograph Buybacks 1998-224
Autograph Buybacks 2000-43
Autograph Buybacks 2001-64
Autographs Gold-37
Golf-GS85
02Pacific-216
Blue-216
Red-216
02Pacific Complete-140
02Pacific Complete-286
Red-140
Red-286
02Pacific Heads-Up Quad Jerseys-16
02Pacific Heads-Up Quad Jerseys Gold-16
02Titanium Jerseys-38
02Titanium Jerseys Retail-38
02Titanium Patches-38
02Topps Total-218
02Vanguard Jerseys-25
02Vanguard Jerseys Gold-25
03ITG Action-372
03Pacific-195
Blue-195
Red-195
Jerseys-22
Jerseys Gold-22
03Pacific Complete-108
Red-108
03Pacific Exhibit-83
Blue Backs-83
Yellow Backs-83
03Pacific Luxury Suite-39A
03Pacific Luxury Suite-39B
03Pacific Luxury Suite-39C
03Pacific Luxury Suite-39D
03Pacific Prism-60
Blue-60
Gold-60
Red-60
03Pacific Quest for the Cup Jerseys-11
03Private Stock Reserve-58
Blue-58
Red-58
Retail-58
03Titanium-165
Hobby Jersey Number Parallels-165
Patches-165
Retail-165
03Upper Deck-352
Canadian Exclusives-352
HG-352
UD Exclusives-352
03Upper Deck MVP-241
Gold Script-241
Silver Script-241
Canadian Exclusives-241
04Pacific-152
Blue-152
Red-152
05Be A Player Signatures-WA
05Be A Player Signatures Gold-WA
06Black Diamond-50
Emerald-50
Gold-50
Onyx-50
Ruby-50
05Panini Stickers-315
05Parkhurst-283
Facsimile Auto Parallel-283
05Ultra-115
Gold-115
Ice-115
05Upper Deck-359
05Upper Deck MVP-219
Gold-219
Platinum-219
05Upper Deck Victory-110
Black-110
Gold-110
Silver-110
06Be A Player-11
Autographs-11
Signatures-WA
Signatures 25-13
06Hurricanes Postcards-23
06O-Pee-Chee-102
Rainbow-102
Walker, Steve
94Muskegon Fury-14
95Muskegon Fury-13
96Detroit Vipers-20
97Detroit Vipers-8
98Detroit Vipers-16
98Detroit Vipers Freschetta-12
98IHL All-Star Eastern Conference-13
99Detroit Vipers-4
99Detroit Vipers Kid's Club-5
00German Berlin Polar Bears Postcards-22
00German DEL-67
01German Berlin Polar Bears Postcards-27
01German Upper Deck-45
02German Berlin Polar Bears Postcards-28
02German DEL City Press-41
03German Berlin Polar Bears Postcards-31
03German DEL-75
04German Berlin Polar Bears Postcards-28
04German DEL-77
05German DEL-28
All-Star Jerseys-AS19
06German DEL-25
Walker, Todd
91Cornwall Royals-11
917th Inn. Sketch OHL-9
Walkington, Troy
00UK Sekonda Superleague-50
Wall, Bob
61Hamilton Red Wings-18
64Beehive Group III Photos-96
66Topps-49
68O-Pee-Chee-156
68Shirriff Coins-52
69O-Pee-Chee-140
Four-in-One-10
70Dad's Cookies-135
70Esso Power Players-236
70O-Pee-Chee-98
70Sargent Promotions Stamps-191
70Topps-98
71Sargent Promotions Stamps-50
72O-Pee-Chee-323
Wall, Kyosti
65Finnish Hellas-62
Wall, Lyndsay
04Minnesota Golden Gophers Women-10
Wall, Mike
03Everett Silvertips-5
04Everett Silvertips-14
05Hot Prospects-103
Red Hot-103
White Hot-103
05SP Authentic-221
Limited-221
05SP Game Used-175
Gold-175
05SPx-207
Spectrum-207
05The Cup Masterpiece Pressplate Artifact-245
05The Cup Masterpiece Pressplates (Ice)-186
05The Cup Master Pressplate Rookie Update-102
05The Cup Masterpiece Pressplates SPA-221
05The Cup Masterpiece Pressplates SP GU-175
05The Cup Masterpiece Pressplates (SPx)-207
05The Cup Masterpiece Pressplates Trilogy-223
05The Cup Masterpiece Pressplate Ult Coll-133
05UD Artifacts-245
05Ultimate Collection-133
Gold-133
05Upper Deck Ice-186
05Upper Deck Rookie Update-102
05Upper Deck Trilogy-223
06Portland Pirates-23
Wallace, Adam
98Sioux City Musketeers-24
Wallace, Ben
04Odessa Jackalopes-18
05Johnstown Chiefs-20
Wallace, Bruce
52Juniors Blue Tint-58
Wallace, Buddy
01South Carolina Stingrays-18
Wallace, Greg
85Kamloops Blazers-26
Wallace, Jackie
93Quebec Pee-Wee Tournament-654
Wallace, Paul
02UK Hull Thunder-11
Wallace, Scott
04Vernon Vipers-10
Wallace, Stephen
01UK Hull Thunder-15
Wallace, Tim
04Notre Dame Fighting Irish-18
Walleitner, Christian
94German First League-182
Wallen, Peter
87Swedish Panini Stickers-265
89Swedish Semic Elitserien Stickers-129
Wallenberg, Patrik
93Swedish Semic Elitserien-318
95Collector's Choice-352
Player's Club-352
Player's Club Platinum-352
95Upper Deck-563
Electric Ice-563
Electric Ice Gold-563
95Swedish Upper Deck-70
97Swedish Collector's Choice-66
98Finnish Kerailysarja-161
00Swedish Upper Deck-162
01UK Nottingham Panthers-4
02Swedish SHL-266
Parallel-266
05Swedish SHL Elitset-209
Gold-209
Teammates-6
Wallenius, Juhani
78Finnish SM-Liiga-173
80Finnish Mallasjuoma-131
Wallgren, Tomas
06Swedish SHL Elitset-217
Wallin Jr., Peter
95Collector's Choice-354
Player's Club-354
Player's Club Platinum-354
95Swedish Leaf-161
Rookies-1
95Signature Rookies Auto-Phonex-40
95Signature Rook Auto-Phonex Phone Cards-40
95Signature Rookies Tetrad Autobilia *-54
Wallin Sr., Peter
83Swedish Semic Elitserien-213
84Swedish Semic Elitserien-237
85Swedish Panini Stickers-236
Wallin, Anders
83Swedish Semic Elitserien-9
Wallin, Claes Goran
57Swedish Alfabilder-137
64Swedish Coralli ISHockey-119
65Swedish Coralli ISHockey-119
73Swedish Stickers-219
74Swedish Stickers-268
91Swedish Semic Elitserien Stickers-311
Wallin, Daniel
99Swedish Upper Deck-101
Wallin, Esa
80Finnish Mallasjuoma-122
Wallin, Hans
86Swedish Panini Stickers-126
87Swedish Panini Stickers-118
Wallin, Jesse
95Bowman Draft Prospects-P35
95Red Deer Rebels-17
96Upper Deck Ice-128
96Red Deer Rebels-4
96Red Deer Rebels-25
97Red Deer Rebels-20
97Bowman CHL-104
OPC-104
98UD Choice-262
Prime Choice Reserve-262
Reserve-262
99Cincinnati Mighty Ducks-17
00Pacific-160
Copper-160
Gold-160
Ice Blue-160
Premiere Date-160
00Paramount-91
Copper-91
Gold-91
Holo-Gold-91
Holo-Silver-91
Ice Blue-91
Premiere Date-91
01BAP Memorabilia-228
Emerald-228
Ruby-228
Sapphire-228
02Pacific Calder-67
Silver-67
02Pacific Complete-552
Red-552
03Lowell Lock Monsters-11
03Lowell Lock Monsters Photo Album-2
Wallin, Justin
98Red Deer Rebels-21
00Red Deer Rebels-22
Signed-22
00Saskatoon Blades-15
Wallin, Magnus
89Swedish Semic Elitserien Stickers-257
Wallin, Mason
98Spokane Chiefs-28
99Spokane Chiefs-28
00Spokane Chiefs-29
01Spokane Chiefs-22
02Spokane Chiefs-23
Wallin, Niclas
93Swedish Semic Elitserien-319
96Swedish Brynas Tigers-12
97Swedish Collector's Choice-25
98Swedish UD Choice-39
99Swedish Upper Deck-23
00BAP Memorabilia-419
Emerald-419
Ruby-419
Sapphire-419
00Stadium Club-243
00Titanium Draft Day Edition-156
00Titanium Draft Day Promos-156
00Topps Premier Plus-132
Blue Ice-132
00Topps Stars-103
Blue-103
00Upper Deck-421
Exclusives Tier 1-421
Exclusives Tier 2-421
01BAP Memorabilia-280
Emerald-280
Ruby-280
Sapphire-280
01Upper Deck MVP-192
02Pacific Complete-484
Red-484
02Upper Deck-30
Exclusives-30
02Upper Deck Vintage-47
03Hurricanes Postcards-21
03O-Pee-Chee-51
03OPC Blue-51
03OPC Gold-51
03OPC Red-51
03Topps-51
Blue-51
Gold-51
Red-51
04Swedish Elitset-215
Gold-215
04Swedish Pure Skills-49
Parallel-49
05Upper Deck-35
HG Glossy-35
05Upper Deck MVP-75
Gold-75
Platinum-75
05Upper Deck Toronto Fall Expo-35
06Hurricanes Postcards-24
Wallin, Per
90Swedish Semic Elitserien Stickers-24
91Swedish Semic Elitserien Stickers-270
92Swedish Semic Elitserien Stickers-270
93Swedish Semic Elitserien-228
94Swedish Leaf-21
95Swedish Leaf-118
95Swedish Upper Deck-177
Wallin, Rickard
02BAP Memorabilia-338
02BAP Ultimate Memorabilia-69
02Parkhurst-228
Bronze-228
Gold-228
Silver-228
02Parkhurst Retro-220
Minis-220
02SP Authentic-164
02UD Artistic Impressions-113
Gold-113
02UD Honor Roll-143
02UD Premier Collection-58B
Gold-58
02Swedish SHL-30
Parallel-30
Signatures-6
03Houston Aeros-19
04Houston Aeros-19
05Swedish SHL Elitset-186
Gold-186
06Swedish SHL Elitset-47
Playmakers-6
Wallingford, Justin
03Oshawa Generals-20
04Kingston Frontenacs-21
05Kingston Frontenacs-14
06Kingston Frontenacs-21
Wallinheimo, Sinuhe
97Mississippi Sea Wolves-1
98Finnish Kerailysarja-163
Mad Masks-8
Off Duty-8
99German Bundesliga 2-247
00German DEL-210
01German Upper Deck-224
Goalies in Action-G10
Jersey Cards-SW-J
02Swedish SHL-167
02Swedish SHL-285
Masks-1
Parallel-167
Parallel-285
03Swedish Elite-34
Global Impact-GI4
Jerseys-2
Masks-1
Masks II-4
Signatures II-1
Silver-34
Zero Hero-5
04Finnish Cardset-80
Parallel-61
04Swedish Elitset In The Crease-4
04Swedish Elitset Jerseys Series 1-3
04Swedish Pure Skills-122
Parallel-122
05Finnish Cardset -240
Finnish Cardset Super Snatchers-8
06Finnish Cardset-67
Between the Pipes-11
Signature Sensations-12
Superior Snatchers-10
Superior Snatchers Gold-10
Superior Snatchers Silver-10
Wallmann, Mark
01OCN Blizzard-21
02OCN Blizzard-26
03OCN Blizzard-23
Wallmann, Paul
02OCN Blizzard-6
03OCN Blizzard-24
Wallner, Stig
56Swedish Alfabilder-54
Wallton, Mats
73Swedish Stickers-24
73Swedish Stickers-68
74Swedish Stickers-194
Wallwork, Bobby
91Cincinnati Cyclones-25
93Memphis RiverKings-17
94Central Hockey League-54
95Muskegon Fury-11
99Memphis RiverKings All-Time-11
Walrod, Kevin
06Westside Warriors-10
Walser, Derrick
96Rimouski Oceanic Update-10
97Rimouski Oceanic-91
97Bowman CHL-68
OPC-68
98Bowman's Best-144
Refractors-144
Atomic Refractors-144
98OPC Chrome-229
Refractors-229
98Topps-229
O-Pee-Chee-229
98Bowman CHL-119
Golden Anniversary-119
OPC International-119
98Bowman Chrome CHL-119
Golden Anniversary-119
Golden Anniversary Refractors-119
OPC International-119
OPC International Refractors-119
Refractors-119
99ECHL All-Star Northern Conference-9
99Johnstown Chiefs-10
01Syracuse Crunch-15
02Bowman YoungStars-164
Gold-164
Silver-164
03ITG Action-178
03Pacific Complete-346
Red-346
03Syracuse Crunch-14
04German Berlin Polar Bears Postcards-29
04German DEL-78
05German DEL-36
06Syracuse Crunch-20
Walser, Thomas
01Swiss HNL-398
02Swiss HNL-102
Walsh, Brendan
93Omaha Lancers-28
00Jackson Bandits-11
00Jackson Bandits Promos-8
03Providence Bruins-22
04Providence Bruins-20
Walsh, Chris
03Chicago Steel-10
Walsh, Ed
68SCFS Old Timers-54
76Nova Scotia Voyageurs-18
79Rochester Americans-23
Walsh, Gord
93Kingston Frontenacs-7
95Slapshot-112
95Classic-86
Walsh, Jonathan
00Baie-Comeau Drakkar-1
Signed-1
Walsh, Julien
03Baie Comeau Drakkar-18
Walsh, Keith
95Slapshot-150
Walsh, Kurt
95Bowman Draft Prospects-P36
95Slapshot-249
95Slapshot-304
95Slapshot-437
96Owen Sound Platers-11
Walsh, Marty
10C56-7
10Sweet Caporal Postcards-11
11C55-11

12C57-49
83Hall of Fame-89
83Hall of Fame Postcards-F15
85Hall of Fame-89

Walsh, Mike
88ProCards AHL-314
89ProCards AHL-230
91ProCards-52
04Notre Dame Fighting Irish-20
06Toledo Storm-21

Walsh, Rory
04Notre Dame Fighting Irish-17

Walsh, Ryan
92Quebec Pee-Wee Tournament-1791
00St. Michaels Majors-27
03St. Francis Xavier X-Men-19
04St. Francis Xavier X-Men-22

Walsh, Shawn
93Classic-59

Walsh, Tim
97New Hampshire Wildcats-19
98New Hampshire Wildcats-15

Walsh, Trevor
89Windsor Spitfires-20
907th Inn. Sketch OHL-194

Walski, Aaron
03Lincoln Stars-23

Walter, Ben
05ITG Heroes/Prosp Toronto Expo Parallel -382
05Black Diamond-217
05Hot Prospects-190
Red Hot-190
05Parkhurst-609
Facsimile Auto Parallel-609
Signatures-BW
05SP Authentic-288
05SP Game Used-193
05SPx-245
05The Cup-191
Black Rainbow Rookies-191
Masterpiece Pressplates (Artifacts)-249
Masterpiece Pressplates (Black Diamond)-217
Masterpiece Pressplates (Ice)-231
Masterpiece Pressplates (Rookie Update)-108
Masterpiece Pressplates (SP Authentic)-288
Masterpiece Pressplates (SP Game Used)-193
Masterpiece Pressplates (SPx)-245
Masterpiece Pressplates (Trilogy)-226
Masterpiece Pressplates Ult Coll-194
Masterpiece Pressplates Autographs-191
Platinum Rookies-191
05UD Artifacts-249
05Ultimate Collection-194
Gold-194
05Upper Deck Ice-231
05Upper Deck Rookie Update-108
05Upper Deck Trilogy-226
05AHL Top Prospects-47
05Providence Bruins-22
06ITG Heroes and Prospects-382
06UD Artifacts Auto-Facts-AFBW
06UD Artifacts Auto-Facts Gold-AFBW
06Providence Bruins-24
06ITG Heroes and Prospects-60
Autographs-ABW
Jerseys-GUJ56
Jerseys Gold-GUJ56
Emblems-GUE56
Emblems Gold-GUE56
Numbers-GUN56
Numbers Gold-GUN56

Walter, Jaroslav
95Czech APS Extraliga-198

Walter, Martin
04German DEL-142
04German Hamburg Freezers Postcards-21
05German DEL-120

Walter, Owen
03Rockford Ice Hogs-18

Walter, Rafael
04Swiss EV Zug Postcards-7

Walter, Ryan
78Capitals Team Issue-17
79Capitals Team Issue-23
79O-Pee-Chee-236
79Topps-236
80O-Pee-Chee-154
80Topps-154
81Capitals Team Issue-21
81O-Pee-Chee-352
81O-Pee-Chee Stickers-192
81Topps-E122
82Canadiens Postcards-26
82Canadiens Steinberg-21
82O-Pee-Chee-189
82O-Pee-Chee Stickers-152
82Post Cereal-20
82Topps Stickers-152
83Canadiens Postcards-31
83O-Pee-Chee-200
83O-Pee-Chee Stickers-62
83O-Pee-Chee Stickers-63
83Puffy Stickers-3
83Topps Stickers-62
83Topps Stickers-63
83Vachon-58
84Canadiens Postcards-31
84O-Pee-Chee-275
84O-Pee-Chee Stickers-159
84Kelowna Wings-36
85Canadiens Postcards-40
85Canadiens Provigo-25
86Canadiens Postcards-25
86Kraft Drawings-79
86O-Pee-Chee-224
87Canadiens Postcards-34
87Canadiens Vachon Stickers-24
87Canadiens Vachon Stickers-25
87O-Pee-Chee-231
87O-Pee-Chee Stickers-17
88Canadiens Postcards-30
88O-Pee-Chee-262
88O-Pee-Chee Stickers-40
88Panini Stickers-262
89Canadiens Kraft-24
89Canadiens Postcards-32
89O-Pee-Chee-240
90Canadiens Postcards-33
90O-Pee-Chee-296
90Pro Set-475
90Topps-296
Tiffany-296
91Canadiens Panini Team Stickers-24
91Canucks Autograph Cards-23
91Canucks Team Issue 8x10-23
91Parkhurst-401
French-401
91Pro Set-504
French-504
91Score Canadian Bilingual-591
91Score Canadian English-591
91Score Rookie/Traded-41T
92Canucks Road Trip Art-23
92Pinnacle-255
French-255
93Stadium Club-185
Members Only Master Set-185
OPC-185
First Day Issue-185
First Day Issue OPC-185
02UD Foundations-56
04ITG Franchises US East-448
Autographs-A-RW
06Parkhurst-158
Autographs-158

Walters, Dominic
93Quebec Pee-Wee Tournament-1167

Walters, Greg
897th Inn. Sketch OHL-50
90Newmarket Saints-26
90ProCards AHL/IHL-147
91ProCards-349
96Rochester Americans-21
97Rochester Americans-3-4
98Rochester Americans-2
99Houston Aeros-18

Walters, Jeremy
94Arizona Icecats-19

Walters, Mark
05Penticton Vees-21

Walters, Ron
72O-Pee-Chee-301

Walters, S.
28V128-2 Paulin's Candy-69

Walterson, Ian
94Brandon Wheat Kings-24
98Prince George Cougars-24
99Greensboro Generals-1
01Atlantic City Boardwalk Bullies-21
02Atlantic City Boardwalk Bullies-22
03Atlantic City Boardwalk Bullies-25
03Atlantic City Boardwalk Bullies RBI-31
04Atlantic City Boardwalk Bullies-2
04Atlantic City Boardwalk Bullies Kinko's-8

Walther, Daniel
94German First League-535

Waltin, Mats
74Swedish Semic World Champ Stickers-18
79Panini Stickers-188
81Swedish Semic Hockey VM Stickers-7
82Swedish Semic VM Stickers-6
83Swedish Semic Elitserien-82
83Swedish Semic VM Stickers-6
89Swedish Semic Elitserien Stickers-57
90Swedish Semic Elitserien Stickers-56
93Swiss HNL-211
95Swiss HNL-110
96Swiss HNL-150

Walton, Graeme
03UK Belfast Giants-18

Walton, John
98Cincinnati Mighty Ducks-4

Walton, Mike
64Beehive Group III Photos-188
65Coca-Cola-100
65Topps-86
66Topps-14
66Topps USA Test-14
67Topps-7
67York Action Octagons-2
67York Action Octagons-10
67York Action Octagons-11
67York Action Octagons-12
67York Action Octagons-13
67York Action Octagons-23
68O-Pee-Chee-132
68Post Marbles-29
68Shirriff Coins-163
68Topps-132
69Maple Leafs White Border Glossy-36
69Maple Leafs White Border Glossy-37
69O-Pee-Chee-50
Four-in-One-15
69Topps-50
70Colgate Stamps-3
70Dad's Cookies-136
70Esso Power Players-28
70Maple Leafs Postcards-15
70O-Pee-Chee-109
70Sargent Promotions Stamps-206
70Topps-109
71Bruins Postcards-8
71O-Pee-Chee-171
71Sargent Promotions Stamps-12
71Toronto Sun-20
72O-Pee-Chee-94
72Sargent Promotions Stamps-24
73O-Pee-Chee WHA Posters-15
74Minnesota Fighting Saints WHA-23
74O-Pee-Chee WHA-10
74Team Canada L'Equipe WHA-23
75O-Pee-Chee WHA-26
76Canucks Royal Bank-22
76O-Pee-Chee NHL-23
76Topps-23
77Canucks Canada Dry Cans-15
77Canucks Royal Bank-21
77O-Pee-Chee NHL-350
78O-Pee-Chee-38
78Topps-38
79Topps-141
95Parkhurst '66-67-101
Coins-101
07Maple Leafs 1967 Commemorative-27
French-123
91ProCards-48
93Donruss-57
93Leaf-393
93Parkhurst-305
Emerald Ice-305
93Ultra-287
93Upper Deck-431
94Canada Games NHL POGS-62
94Donruss-319
94Leaf-154
94OPC Premier-137
Special Effects-137
94Parkhurst-38
Gold-38
94Topps/OPC Premier-137
Special Effects-137
94Ultra-37
94Upper Deck-350
Electric Ice-350
95Adirondack Red Wings-23
96Swiss HNL-75
98Swiss Power Play Stickers-223
00Topps Gold Label Class 1-95
Gold-95
00Topps Gold Label Class 2-95
00Topps Gold Label Class 2 Gold-95
00Topps Gold Label Class 3-95
00Topps Gold Label Class 3 Gold-95
01BAP Memorabilia-156
Emerald-156
Ruby-156
Sapphire-156
01BAP Signature Series-78
Autographs-78
Autographs Gold-78
01Pacific-201
Extreme LTD-201
Hobby LTD-201
Premiere Date-201
Retail LTD-201
01Pacific Adrenaline-95
Blue-95
Premiere Date-95
Red-95
Retail-95
01Pacific Arena Exclusives-201
01Parkhurst-108
01Upper Deck-315
Exclusives-315
01Upper Deck MVP-93
01Upper Deck Victory-173
Gold-173
01Upper Deck Vintage-127
01Upper Deck Vintage-130
02BAP Sig Series Auto Buybacks 2001-78
02Pacific-188
Blue-188
Red-188
02Pacific Complete-79
Red-79
02Topps Total-98
02Upper Deck-86
Exclusives-86
02Upper Deck MVP-92
Gold-92
Classics-92
Golden Classics-92
02Upper Deck Victory-105
Bronze-105
Gold-105
Silver-105
03Beehive-97
Gold-97
Silver-97
03ITG Action-263
03Pacific-171
Blue-171
Red-171
03Upper Deck-95
Canadian Exclusives-95
HG-95
03Upper Deck MVP-212
Gold Script-212
Silver Script-212
Canadian Exclusives-212
03Upper Deck Victory-94
Bronze-94
Gold-94
Silver-94
03Wild Law Enforcement Cards-9
05Panini Stickers-306
05Parkhurst-240
05Parkhurst-529
Facsimile Auto Parallel-240
05Wild Crime Prevention-6
06O-Pee-Chee-245
Rainbow-245
06Panini Stickers-297
06Upper Deck-95
Exclusives Parallel-95
High Gloss Parallel-95
Masterpieces-95
06Upper Deck MVP-145
Gold Script-145
Super Script-145
06Upper Deck Victory-100
06Upper Deck Victory Black-100
06Upper Deck Victory Gold-100

Wamsley, Rick
81Canadiens Postcards-27
82Canadiens Postcards-27
82Canadiens Steinberg-22
82McDonald's Stickers-5
82O-Pee-Chee-195
82O-Pee-Chee Stickers-37
82Topps Stickers-37
83Canadiens Postcards-32
83O-Pee-Chee-201
83O-Pee-Chee Stickers-72
83Topps Stickers-72
83Vachon-59
84O-Pee-Chee Stickers-157
86O-Pee-Chee-240
86O-Pee-Chee Stickers-179
87Blues Kodak-26
87O-Pee-Chee-65
87O-Pee-Chee Stickers-22
87Panini Stickers-305
87Topps-65
88Flames Postcards-6
89O-Pee-Chee-204
89O-Pee-Chee Stickers-93
90Bowman-98
Tiffany-98
90Flames IGA/McGavin's-29
90O-Pee-Chee-409
90Panini Stickers-186
90Pro Set-48
90Score-309C
Canadian-309C
90Upper Deck-10
French-10
91Bowman-268
91Flames Panini Team Stickers-24
91Flames IGA-25
91O-Pee-Chee-459
91Parkhurst-394
French-394
91Pro Set-367
French-367
91Score Canadian Bilingual-232
91Score Canadian English-232
91Stadium Club-294
91Topps-459
91Upper Deck-130
French-130
92Bowman-97
92Maple Leafs Kodak-33
92O-Pee-Chee-310
92Stadium Club-53
92Topps-425
Gold-425G

Wanchuk, Mike
77Kalamazoo Wings-10

Wanchulak, Brad
01Notre Dame Fighting Irish-11
03Notre Dame Fighting Irish-4

Wanchulak, Chris
03Camrose Kodiaks-19

Wandell, Tom
06Finnish Cardset-352
06Finnish Porin Assat Pelaajakortit-16

Wandler, Bryce
98Swift Current Broncos-4
99Swift Current Broncos-25
00Charlotte Checkers-35

Wandler, Dion
99San Angelo Outlaws-18

Wanhainen, Rolf
92Upper Deck-223
02Swedish SHL-89
Netminders-NM4
Parallel-89
Signatures-13
03Swedish Elite-257
Hot Numbers-HN6
Silver-257
Zero Hero-2
04Swedish Elitset-156
Gold-156
In The Crease-9
Signatures-4
05German DEL-16
Goalies-G14
05Swedish SHL Elitset Stoppers-3
06German DEL-13

Wanner, Simon
01Swiss HNL-399
02Swiss HNL-153

Wannstrom, Jorgen
89Swedish Semic Elitserien Stickers-212

Wansborough, Shawn
98Las Vegas Thunder-22
98Orlando Solar Bears-9
00Idaho Steelheads-21
02Columbia Inferno-114

Wanvig, Kyle
98SP Authentic-133
Power Shift-133
98Upper Deck-410
Exclusives-410
Exclusives 1 of 1-410
Gold Reserve-410
98Kootenay Ice-17
99Bowman CHL-7
Gold-7
OPC International-7
Autographs BA27
Autographs Gold-BA27
Autographs Silver-BA27
00Red Deer Rebels-23
Signed-23
02Crown Royale-121
Blue-121
Purple-121
Red-121
Retail-121
02Pacific Calder-74
Silver-74
02Pacific Complete-591
Red-591
02Titanium-121
Blue-121
Red-121
Retail-121
02AHL Top Prospects-43
03AHL Top Prospects-42
03Houston Aeros-20
03Pacific AHL Prospects-41
Gold-41
04Houston Aeros-20

Ward, Aaron
91Michigan Wolverines-22
93Donruss-93
93Leaf-359
93OPC Premier-484
Gold-484
93Parkhurst-262
Emerald Ice-262
93Pinnacle-432
Canadian-432
93Stadium Club-423
Members Only Master Set-423
First Day Issue-423
93Topps/OPC Premier-484
Gold-484
93Upper Deck-479
93Classic-85
94Leaf-312
94Score-229
Gold-229
Platinum-229
94Upper Deck-153
Electric Ice-153
94Classic Autographs-NNO
94Classic Pro Prospects-120
95Parkhurst International-71
Emerald Ice-71
95Adirondack Red Wings-24
95Images-98
Gold-98
Autographs-98A
96Collector's Edge Ice-5
Prism-5
97Be A Player-200
Autographs-200
Autographs Die-Cuts-200
Autographs Prismatic Die-Cuts-200
97Pacific Invincible NHL Regime-74
97Upper Deck-270
99BAP Millennium-92
Emerald-92
Ruby-92
Sapphire-92
Signatures-92
Signatures Gold-92
99Pacific-150
Copper-150
Emerald Green-150
Gold-150
Ice Blue-150
Premiere Date-150
Red-150
00Upper Deck NHLPA-PA33
01Pacific-151
Extreme LTD-151
Hobby LTD-151
Premiere Date-151
Retail LTD-151
01Pacific Arena Exclusives-151
02BAP Sig Series Auto Buybacks 1999-92
02Pacific Complete-458
Red-458
03Hurricanes Postcards-22
03ITG Action-170
03Pacific Complete-73
Red-73
03Upper Deck MVP-87
Gold Script-87
Silver Script-87
Canadian Exclusives-87
04Upper Deck-33
Canadian Exclusives-33
HG Glossy Gold-33
HG Glossy Silver-33
04German DEL Superstars-SU13
04German Ingolstadt Panthers-26
05Parkhurst-97
Facsimile Auto Parallel-97
06Be A Player-10
Autographs-10
Signatures-AW
Signatures Duals-DCW
06O-Pee-Chee-334
Rainbow-334

Ward, Adam
92Quebec Pee-Wee Tournament-1048
02Saskatoon Blades-21
03Saskatoon Blades-4

Ward, Blake
98Tri-City Americans-24
99UD Prospects-48
99UD Prospects-89
00Lethbridge Hurricanes-22
01Lethbridge Hurricanes-19

Ward, Brett
05Saskatoon Blades-22
06Saskatoon Blades-21

Ward, Caleb
94Windsor Spitfires-23
95Slapshot-26
96Barrie Colts-26

Ward, Cam
01Red Deer Rebels-19
02BAP Memorabilia Draft Redemptions-25
02Red Deer Rebels-1
02Red Deer Rebels-25
03Red Deer Rebels-20
04SP Authentic Rookie Redemptions-RR6
04Lowell Lock Monsters-23
04Lowell Lock Monsters Photo Album-23
04ITG Heroes and Prospects-62
Autographs-CW
04ITG Heroes/Prospects Toronto Expo '05-62
04ITG Heroes/Prospects Expo Heroes/Pros-62
05ITG Heroes/Prosp Toronto Expo Parallel -41
05ITG Heroes/Prosp Toronto Expo Parallel -335
05Beehive-117
Beige -117
Blue -117
Gold-117
Red -117
Matte-117
Signature Scrapbook-SSCW
05Black Diamond-152
Emerald-152
Gold-152
Onyx-152
Ruby-152
05Hot Prospects-227
En Fuego-227
Hot Materials-HMCW
Red Hot-227
White Hot-227
05ITG Ultimate Mem First Rounders Jerseys-7
05ITG Ultimate Mem 1st Round Jersey Gold-7
05ITG Ultimate Mem Future Star Autos-5
05ITG Ultimate Mem Future Star Autos Gold-5
05ITG Ultimate Mem Future Stars Jerseys-5
05ITG Ultimate Mem Fut Stars Jerseys Gold-5
05ITG Ultimate Mem Future Stars Mem Auto-5
05ITG Ultimate Mem Fut Star Mem Auto Gold-5
05ITG Ultimate Memorabilia R.O.Y. Autos-4
05ITG Ultimate Mem R.O.Y. Autos Gold-4
05ITG Ultimate Memorabilia Triple Autos-3
05ITG Ultimate Mem Triple Autos Gold-3
05Parkhurst-614
Facsimile Auto Parallel-614
True Colors-TCCAR
True Colors-TCCAR
05SP Authentic-142
Limited-142
Rarefied Rookies-RRCW
Rookie Authentics-RACW
Sign of the Times Duals-DGW
Sign of the Times Fives-TWLDH
05SP Game Used-132
Autographs-132
Gold-132
Auto Draft-AD-CW
Rookie Exclusives-CW
Rookie Exclusives Silver-RE-CW
Significant Numbers-SN-CW
05SPx-166
Spectrum-166
Xcitement Rookies-XR-CW
Xcitement Rookies Gold-XR-CW
Xcitement Rookies Spectrum-XR-CW
05The Cup-104
Autographed Rookie Patches Gold Rainbow-104
Black Rainbow Rookies-104
Masterpiece Pressplates (Artifacts)-206
Masterpiece Pressplates (Bee Hive)-117
Masterpiece Pressplates (Black Diamond)-152
Masterpiece Pressplates (Ice)-110
Masterpiece Pressplates (MVP)-408
Masterpiece Pressplates (Power Play)-158
Masterpiece Pressplates (Power Play)-158
Masterpiece Pressplates Rookie Upd Auto-262
Masterpiece Pressplates SPA Autos-142
Masterpiece Pressplates (SP Game Used)-132
Masterpiece Pressplates SPx Autos-166
Masterpiece Pressplates (Trilogy)-181
Masterpiece Pressplates Ult Coll Autos-107
Masterpiece Pressplates (Victory)-274
Masterpiece Pressplates Autographs-104
Platinum Rookies-104
05UD Artifacts-206
Gold-RED6
05UD PowerPlay-158
05UD Rookie Class-50
05Ultimate Collection-107
Autographed Patches-107
Autographed Shields-107
Jerseys Dual-DJWN
Premium Patches-PPCW
Premium Swatches-PSCW
Ultimate Debut Threads Jerseys-DTJCW
Ultimate Debut Threads Jerseys Autos-DAJCW
Ultimate Debut Threads Patches-DTPCW
Ultimate Debut Threads Patches Autos-DAPCW
Ultimate Patches Dual-DPWN
Ultimate Signatures-USCW
Ultimate Signatures Logos-SLCW
05Ultra-263
Gold-263
Fresh Ink-FI-CW
Fresh Ink Blue-FI-CW
Ice-263
Rookie Uniformity Jerseys-RU-CW
Rookie Uniformity Jersey Autographs-ARU-CW
Rookie Uniformity Patches-RUP-CW
Rookie Uniformity Patch Autographs-ARP-CW
05Upper Deck-229
HG Glossy-229
Rookie Ink-RICW
05Upper Deck Rookie Showcase-RS6
05Upper Deck Rookie Showcase Promos-RS6
05Upper Deck Rookie Threads-RTCW
05Upper Deck Rookie Threads Autographs-ARTCW
05Upper Deck Ice-110
Cool Threads-CTCW
Cool Threads Autographs-ACTCW
Cool Threads Glass-CTCW
Cool Threads Patches-CTPCW
Cool Threads Patch Autographs-CAPCW
Glacial Graphs-GGCW
Glacial Graphs Labels-GGCW
Premieres Auto Patches-AIPCW
Signature Swatches-SSCW
05Upper Deck MVP-408
Gold-408
Platinum-408
05Upper Deck Rookie Update-262
05Upper Deck Trilogy-181
05Upper Deck Toronto Fall Expo-229
05Upper Deck Victory-274
Black-274
Gold-274
Silver-274
05ITG Heroes and Prospects-41
05ITG Heroes and Prospects-335
AHL Grads-AG-9
AHL Grads Gold-AG-9
Autographs-A-CW
Autographs Series II-CW2
Complete Jerseys-CJ-20
Complete Jerseys Gold-CJ-20
Future Teammates-FT6
He Shoots-He Scores Prizes-23
Jerseys-GUJ-23
Jerseys Gold-GUJ-23
Emblems-GUE-23
Emblems Gold-GUE-23
Numbers-GUN-23
Numbers Gold-GUN-23
Measuring Up-MU1
Measuring Up Gold-MU1
Nameplates-N-8
Nameplates Gold-N-08
Net Prospects-NP-9
Net Prospects Dual-NPD6
Net Prospects Dual Gold-NPD6
Net Prospects Gold-NP-09
06Be A Player-9
Autographs-9
Signatures-CW
Signatures 10-11
Unmasked Warriors-UM7
Unmasked Warriors Autographs-UM7
06Be A Player Portraits-23
Dual Signature Portraits-DSWS
First Exposures-FECW
Sensational Six-SSGOL
Signature Portraits-SPCW
Timeless Tens-TTNET
Triple Signature Portraits-TLWF
06Beehive-83
06Beehive-220
Blue-83
Gold-83
Matte-83
Red Facsimile Signatures-83
Wood-83
5 X 7 Black and White-83
Matted Materials-MMCW
06Between The Pipes-58
06Between The Pipes-106
Aspiring-AS01
Aspiring Gold-AS01
Autographs-ACW2
Autographs-ACW
Complete Jersey-CJ01
Complete Jersey Gold-CJ01
Double Jerseys-DJ04
Double Jerseys Gold-DJ04
Emblems-GUE64
Emblems Gold-GUE64
Emblems Autographs-GUE64
Jerseys-GUJ64
Jerseys Gold-GUJ64
Jerseys Autographs-GUJ64
Numbers-GUN64
Numbers Gold-GUN64
Numbers Autographs-GUN64
The Mask-M13
The Mask Gold-M13
The Mask Silver-M13
The Mask Game-Used-MGU19
The Mask Game-Used Gold-MGU19
06Black Diamond-132
Black-132
Gold-132
Ruby-132
Jerseys-JCW
Jerseys Black-JCW
Jerseys Gold-JCW
Jerseys Ruby-JCW
06Flair Showcase-20
06Flair Showcase-115
06Flair Showcase-215
Parallel-20
Parallel-115
Parallel-215
Hot Gloves-HG11
06Fleer-37
Tiffany-37
Hockey Headliners-HL4
Netminders-N6
Signing Day-SDCW
06Hot Prospects-20
Red Hot-20
White Hot-20
Hot Materials -HMCW
Hot Materials Red Hot-HMCW
Hot Materials White Hot-HMCW
06Hurricanes Postcards-25
06ITG Ultimate Memorabilia-26
Artist Proof-26
Autos-60
Autos Gold-60
Jerseys Autos-63
Jerseys Autos Gold-63
06McDonald's Upper Deck Hardware Heroes-HH5
06McDonald's Upper Deck Rookie Review-RR15
06O-Pee-Chee-100
Rainbow-100
Autographs-A-CW
06Panini Stickers-40
06SP Authentic-83
06SP Authentic-107
Limited-83
Limited-107
Sign of the Times-STCW
Sign of the Times Duals-STBW
Sign of the Times Duals-STSW
Sign of the Times Triples-ST3RBW
Sign of the Times Triples-ST3WSW
06SP Game Used-18
Gold-18
Rainbow-18
Authentic Fabrics-AFCW
Authentic Fabrics Parallel-AFCW
Authentic Fabrics Patches-AFCW
Authentic Fabrics Dual-AF2SW
Authentic Fabrics Dual Patches-AF2SW
Authentic Fabrics Triple-AF3CAR
Authentic Fabrics Triple Patches-AF3CAR
Authentic Fabrics Quads-AF4BJTW
Authentic Fabrics Quads Patches-AF4BJTW
Authentic Fabrics Sevens-AF7CON
Authentic Fabrics Sevens Patches-AF7CON
Inked Sweaters-ISCW
Inked Sweaters Patches-ISCW
Inked Sweaters Dual-IS2WR
Inked Sweaters Dual Patches-IS2WR
Letter Marks-LMCW
SIGnificance-SCW
06SPx-17
Spectrum-17
Winning Materials-WMCW
Winning Materials Spectrum-WMCW
06The Cup-18
Autographed Foundations-CQCW
Autographed Foundations Patches-CQCW
Autographed NHL Shields Duals-DASEC
Autographed Patches-18
Black Rainbow-18
Foundations-CQCW
Foundations Patches-CQCW
Enshrinements-ECW
Gold-18
Gold Patches-18
Hardware Heroes Patches-HHCW
Honorable Numbers-HNCW
Jerseys-18
Limited Logos-LLCW
Masterpiece Pressplates-18
NHL Shields Duals-DSHWB
Scripted Swatches-SSCW
Signature Patches-SPCW
Stanley Cup Signatures-CSCW
Stanley Cup Titlists Patches-TCW
06UD Artifacts-82
Blue-82
Gold-82
Platinum-82
Radiance-82
Red-82
Frozen Artifacts-FACW
Frozen Artifacts Black-FACW
Frozen Artifacts Blue-FACW
Frozen Artifacts Gold-FACW
Frozen Artifacts Platinum-FACW
Frozen Artifacts Red-FACW
Frozen Artifacts Patches Black-FACW
Frozen Artifacts Patches Blue-FACW
Frozen Artifacts Patches Gold-FACW
Frozen Artifacts Patches Platinum-FACW
Frozen Artifacts Patches Red-FACW
Tundra Tandems-TTSW
Tundra Tandems Black-TTSW
Tundra Tandems Blue-TTSW
Tundra Tandems Gold-TTSW
Tundra Tandems Platinum-TTSW
Tundra Tandems Red-TTSW
Tundra Tandems Dual Patches Red-TTSW
06UD Mini Jersey Collection-18
06UD Powerplay-19
Impact Rainbow-19
Cup Celebrations-CC2
Goal Robbers-GR5
06Ultimate Collection-14
Autographed Jerseys-AJ-CW
Autographed Patches-AJ-CW
Jerseys-UJ-CW
Jerseys Dual-UJ2-SW
Patches-UJ-CW
Patches Dual-UJ2-SW
Premium Patches-PS-CW
Premium Swatches-PS-CW
Signatures-US-CW
Ultimate Achievements-UA-CW
Ultimate Signatures Logos-SL-CW
06Ultra-35
Gold Medallion-35
Ice Medallion-35
06Upper Deck Arena Giveaways-CAR2
06Upper Deck-36
Exclusives Parallel-36
High Gloss Parallel-36
Award Winners-AW7
Award Winners Canadian Exclusive-DAW2
Game Dated Moments-GD12
Game Dated Moments-GD32
Game Jerseys-J2CW
Game Patches-P2CW
Generations Duals-G2BW
Generations Triples-G3BTW
Generations Patches Dual-G2PBW
Generations Patches Triple-G3PBTW
Hometown Heroes-HH46
Masterpieces-36
Walmart Tins Oversize-36
Zero Men-ZM6
06Upper Deck MVP-51
Gold Script-51
Super Script-51
Clutch Performers-CP1
Jerseys-OJWD
Jerseys-OJWL
Last Line of Defense-LL8
06Upper Deck Ovation-59
06Upper Deck Sweet Shot-21
Signature Shots/Saves-SSCW
Signature Shots/Saves Ice Signings-SSICW
Signature Sticks-STCW
Sweet Stitches-SSCW
Sweet Stitches Duals-SSCW
Sweet Stitches Triples-SSCW
06Upper Deck Trilogy-19
Honorary Swatches-HSCW
06Upper Deck Victory-34
06Upper Deck Victory Black-34
06Upper Deck Victory Gold-34
06Upper Deck Victory Next In Line-NL13
06ITG Heroes and Prospects-25
Autographs-ACW
Complete AHL Logos-AHL01
Complete Jerseys-CJ09
Complete Jerseys Gold-CJ09
Making The Bigs-MTB03
Making The Bigs Gold-MTB03
Net Prospects-NPR04
Net Prospects Gold-NPR04
Quad Emblems-QE04
Quad Emblems Gold-QE04
07Upper Deck Victory-80
Black-80
Gold-80
GameBreakers-GB21

Ward, Colin
92Western Michigan Broncos-24
93Western Michigan Broncos-26
00UK Sekonda Superleague-27
01UK Belfast Giants-5
03UK Belfast Giants-19

Ward, Dixon
91UND Fighting Sioux Sports Collectors Card Set -14
92Canucks Road Trip Art-24
92OPC Premier-67
92Parkhurst-194
Emerald Ice-194
92Ultra-431
92Upper Deck-580
Calder Candidates-CC1
92North Dakota Fighting Sioux-40
92Classic-84
Gold-84
93Donruss-449
93Leaf-97
93OPC Premier-58
93OPC Premier-127
Gold-58
Gold-127
93Parkhurst-209
Emerald Ice-209
93Pinnacle-176
Canadian-176
93PowerPlay-257
93PowerPlay-365
93Score-210
93Score-654
Gold-654
Canadian-210
Canadian-654
Canadian Gold-654
93Stadium Club-454
Members Only Master Set-454
First Day Issue-454
93Topps/OPC Premier-58
93Topps/OPC Premier-127
Gold-58
Gold-127
93Ultra-102
93Upper Deck-62
SP-167
94Canucks Program Inserts-21
94Maple Leafs Kodak-27
94OPC Premier-112
Special Effects-112
94Parkhurst-102
Gold-102
94Pinnacle-239
Artist's Proofs-239
Rink Collection-239
94Topps/OPC Premier-112
Special Effects-112
95Rochester Americans-21
96Be A Player-130
Autographs-130
Autographs Silver-130
97Pacific Invincible NHL Regime-24
97Score Sabres-3
Platinum-3
Premier-3
97Upper Deck-21
98Aurora-21
98Be A Player-16
Press Release-16
98BAP Gold-16
98BAP Autographs-16
98BAP Autographs Gold-16
98BAP Tampa Bay All Star Game-16
98Pacific-112
Ice Blue-112
Red-112
98Pacific Omega-29
Red-29
Opening Day Issue-29
98Paramount-24
Copper-24
Emerald Green-24
Holo-Electric-24
Ice Blue-24
Silver-24
98Revolution-17
Ice Shadow-17
Red-17
99BAP Millennium-36
Emerald-36
Ruby-36
Sapphire-36
Signatures-36
Signatures Gold-36
99Pacific-48
Copper-48
Emerald Green-48
Gold-48
Ice Blue-48
Premiere Date-48
Red-48
99Paramount-32

Copper-32
Emerald-32
Gold-32
Holographic Emerald-32
Holographic Gold-32
Holographic Silver-32
Ice Blue-32
Premiere Date-32
Red-32
Silver-32
99Revolution-21
Premiere Date-21
Red-21
Shadow Series-21
99Stadium Club-57
First Day Issue-57
One of a Kind-57
Printing Plates Black-57
Printing Plates Cyan-57
Printing Plates Magenta-57
Printing Plates Yellow-57
99Upper Deck-25
Exclusives-25
Exclusives 1 of 1-25
99Upper Deck Gold Reserve-25
99Upper Deck MVP-27
Gold Script-27
Silver Script-27
Super Script-27
99Upper Deck Victory-36
01O-Pee-Chee-256
01O-Pee-Chee Premier Parallel-256
01Topps-256
OPC Parallel-256
02BAP Sig Series Auto Buybacks 1998-16
02BAP Sig Series Auto Buybacks 1999-36
02Hartford Wolf Pack-24

Ward, Don
69Seattle Totems-8

Ward, Ed
94Classic Pro Prospects-196
95Bowman-105
All-Foil-105
95Parkhurst International-305
Emerald Ice-305
97Be A Player-172
Autographs-172
Autographs Die-Cuts-172
Autographs Prismatic Die-Cuts-172
97Pacific Invincible NHL Regime-33
98Upper Deck MVP-31
Gold Script-31
Silver Script-31
Super Script-31
99Upper Deck MVP SC Edition-9
Gold Script-9
Silver Script-9
Super Script-9
00Upper Deck NHLPA-PA54
00Albany River Rats-21
01Pacific-241
Extreme LTD-241
Hobby LTD-241
Premiere Date-241
Retail LTD-241
01Pacific Arena Exclusives-241
02Swedish SHL-110
Parallel-110

Ward, Geoff
94Kitchener Rangers-27
95Slapshot-155
96Kitchener Rangers-27
98Guelph Storm-24
01Hamilton Bulldogs-24

Ward, Jason
95Slapshot-186
96Upper Deck-388
97Collector's Choice-303
97Bowman CHL-129
OPC-129
Autographs-129
Bowman's Best-5
Bowman's Best Atomic Refractors-5
Bowman's Best Refractor-5
98UD Choice-272
Prime Choice Reserve-272
Reserve-272
98Bowman CHL-9
Golden Anniversary-9
OPC International-9
98Bowman Chrome CHL-9
Golden Anniversary-9
Golden Anniversary Refractors-9
OPC International-9
OPC International Refractors-9
Refractors-9
99Pacific Omega-125
Copper-125
Gold-125
Ice Blue-125
Premiere Date-125
99Quebec Citadelles-8
99Bowman CHL-154
Gold-154
OPC International-154
00BAP Signature Series-77
Emerald-77
Ruby-77
Sapphire-77
Autographs-20
Autographs Gold-20
00Quebec Citadelles-6
Signed-6
01Quebec Citadelles-5
02BAP Sig Series Auto Buybacks 2000-20
02Hamilton Bulldogs-8
03Canadiens Postcards-28
03ITG Action-335
03Parkhurst Original Six Montreal-11
04Hamilton Bulldogs-28
05Parkhurst-324
Facsimile Auto Parallel-324
05Upper Deck MVP-264
Gold-264
Platinum-264
06O-Pee-Chee-337
Rainbow-337

Ward, Jimmy
28La Presse Photos-14
33O-Pee-Chee V304B-56
33V252 Canadian Gum-49
33V357 Ice Kings-37
34Beehive Group I Photos-209
34Sweet Caporal-27
37O-Pee-Chee V304E-170
37V356 Worldwide Gum-2
38Quaker Oats Photos-29

Ward, Joel
97Owen Sound Platers-19
98Owen Sound Platers-8
99Owen Sound Platers-8
00Owen Sound Attack-24

Ward, Lance
95Bowman Draft Prospects-P37
95Red Deer Rebels-18
96Red Deer Rebels-19
96Red Deer Rebels-26
97Red Deer Rebels-21
98New Haven Beast-18
99Louisville Panthers-24
00Panthers Team Issue-32
00SP Authentic-145
00SPx-139
05Binghamton Senators-21
05Binghamton Senators Quickway-21
06Swedish SHL Elitset-196

Ward, Nathan
06Odessa Jackalopes-19

Ward, Ron
66Tulsa Oilers-12
69Maple Leafs White Border Glossy-38
71Canucks Royal Bank-8
71Toronto Sun-292
72O-Pee-Chee-332
72 7-Eleven Slurpee Cups WHA-19
73Quaker Oats WHA-34
74O-Pee-Chee WHA-21
75O-Pee-Chee WHA-73
76O-Pee-Chee WHA-35

Ward, Spencer
92British Columbia JHL-192

Ward, Steve
03Sarnia Sting-21
05Plymouth Whalers-A-04
06Plymouth Whalers-25

Ward, Troy
00Trenton Titans-12

Ward, Wes
94Windsor Spitfires-13
95Slapshot-417

Warde, Michael
94Anchorage Aces-11

Warden, Jim
79Panini Stickers-207

Warden, Tom
92Thunder Bay Thunder Hawks-23
93Thunder Bay Senators-14
98Thunder Bay Thunder Cats-20

Ware, Jeff
94Parkhurst SE-SE257
Gold-SE257
94Select-163
Gold-163
94SP-188
Die Cuts-188
95Slapshot-246
95Classic-15
95Classic-91
Ice Breakers-BK14
Ice Breakers Die Cuts-BK14
95Images-86
Gold-86
96Upper Deck Ice-131
97Donruss Canadian Ice-129
Dominion Series-129
Provincial Series-129
97Upper Deck-370
97St. John's Maple Leafs-25
99Louisville Panthers-25
00Syracuse Crunch-17
01Syracuse Crunch-16

Ware, Mike
88Oilers Tenth Anniversary-151
88ProCards AHL-81
90ProCards AHL/IHL-232
92Michigan State Spartans-27
93Michigan State Spartans-27
95St. John's Maple Leafs-21
97UK Sheffield Steelers-18
98German DEL-196
99UK London Knights-16
00UK Cardiff Devils-10
00UK Sekonda Superleague-68
01UK Cardiff Devils-14
01UK London Knights-22
02UK Cardiff Devils-14
03UK Cardiff Devils-13

Wares, Eddie
34Beehive Group I Photos-129
39O-Pee-Chee V301-1-73

Warg, Fredrik
02Swedish SHL-245
Parallel-245
03Swedish Elite-253
Silver-253
04Swedish Elitset-98
Gold-98
04Swedish MoDo Postcards-26
05Swedish SHL Elitset-288
Gold-288
06Swedish SHL Elitset-144

Wargh, Tommy
06Swedish SHL Elitset-239

Waring, Corey
01El Paso Buzzards-19

Warkus, T.J.
00Sudbury Wolves-4
02Fort Worth Brahmas-15

Warming, Thomas
65Swedish Coralli ISHockey-75

Warner, Jim
79Panini Stickers-221
79O-Pee-Chee-384

Warning, Lars-Ake
64Swedish Coralli ISHockey-148
65Swedish Coralli ISHockey-148
69Swedish Hockey-56
70Swedish Hockey-16

Warr, Andrew
97Halifax Mooseheads II-22

Warren, Morgan
00St. John's Maple Leafs-29
01St. John's Maple Leafs-25

Warrener, Rhett
93Saskatoon Blades-21
94Signature Rookies Gold Standard *-98
95Bowman-108
All-Foil-108
95Donruss-358
Elite World Juniors-9
95Stadium Club-140
Members Only Master Set-140
95Topps-272
OPC Inserts-272
95Upper Deck-528
Electric Ice-528
Electric Ice Gold-528
95Signature Rookies-35
Signatures-35
96Be A Player-138
Autographs-138
Autographs Silver-138
96Upper Deck-266
96Saskatoon Blades-24
99Pacific Omega-32
Copper-32
Gold-32
Ice Blue-32
Premiere Date-32
99Upper Deck Victory-41
00Upper Deck Vintage-46
01Upper Deck Vintage-31
02BAP First Edition-166
02Sabres Team Issue-14
02Upper Deck-266
Exclusives-266
02Upper Deck Beckett UD Promos-266
05Parkhurst-80
Facsimile Auto Parallel-80
06Panini Stickers-202

Warrener, Trevor
91Air Canada SJHL-B7
92Saskatchewan JHL-129

Warriner, Mike
92British Columbia JHL-146

Warriner, Todd
90 7th Inn. Sketch OHL-195
91 7th Inn. Sketch OHL-173
92Windsor Spitfires-17
92Windsor Spitfires-31
93Alberta International Team Canada-21
93OPC Premier Team Canada-19
93PowerPlay-496
93Ultra-476
93Kitchener Rangers-15
94Be A Player-R163
94Maple Leafs Kodak-28
94Score Team Canada-CT3
94St. John's Maple Leafs-24
94Classic-109
Gold-109
Pro Prospects Ice Ambassadors-IA7
Pro Prospects International Heroes-LP20
95Bowman-106
All-Foil-106
95Donruss-85
95Leaf-101
95Parkhurst International-472
Emerald Ice-472
95Pinnacle-219
Artist's Proofs-219
Rink Collection-219
95Score-296
Black Ice Artist's Proofs-296
Black Ice-296
95Topps-45
OPC Inserts-45
95St. John's Maple Leafs-22
96Be A Player-122
Autographs-122
Autographs Silver-122
96Black Diamond-93
Gold-93
96Upper Deck-163
97Collector's Choice-254
97Donruss-91
Press Proofs Silver-91
Press Proofs Gold-91
97Donruss Limited-162
Exposure-162
97Pacific-257
Copper-257
Emerald Green-257
Ice Blue-257
Red-257
Silver-257
97Panini Stickers-177
97Pinnacle Inside-166
97Score-207
97Score Maple Leafs-9
Platinum-9
Premier-9
97Upper Deck-163
99BAP Millennium-225
Emerald-225
Ruby-225
Sapphire-225
Signatures-225
Signatures Gold-225
99Stadium Club-30
First Day Issue-30
One of a Kind-30
Printing Plates Black-30
Printing Plates Cyan-30
Printing Plates Magenta-30
Printing Plates Yellow-30
99Upper Deck MVP SC Edition-170
Gold Script-170
Silver Script-170
Super Script-170
00Paramount-225
Copper-225
Gold-225
Holo-Gold-225
Holo-Silver-225
Ice Blue-225
Premiere Date-225
00Upper Deck-157
Exclusives Tier 1-157
Exclusives Tier 2-157
00Upper Deck Vintage-300
02BAP Sig Series Auto Buybacks 1999-225
02NHL Power Play Stickers-163
05German DEL-136
06German DEL-91
Team Leaders-TL11

Warring, Jeremy
90 7th Inn. Sketch WHL-102
91 7th Inn. Sketch WHL-22

Warschaw, Shane
92Quebec Pee-Wee Tournament-1557
93Quebec Pee-Wee Tournament-1245

Warset, Jon
92Norwegian Elite Series-224

Warus, Mike
88ProCards AHL-178

Warwick, F.
75HCA Steel City Vacuum-16

Warwick, Grant
34Beehive Group I Photos-296
44Beehive Group II Photos-73
44Beehive Group II Photos-316
45Quaker Oats Photos-113
48Exhibits Canadian-26
51Buffalo Bison-19

Wasama, Jarmo
65Finnish Hellas-124
96Finnish SISU Redline-190

Waschuk, Daniel
01Regina Pats-23
02Regina Pats-17
03Regina Pats-11
04Regina Pats-11
04Saskatoon Blades-7

Wasden, Scott
05Medicine Hat Tigers-25
06Medicine Hat Tigers-24

Washbrook, Jeff
02Fort Worth Brahmas-16

Washburn, Steve
91 7th Inn. Sketch OHL-308
92Ottawa 67's-22
95Classic-92
95Images-36
Gold-36
Autographs-36A
96Leaf-237
Press Proofs-237
96Leaf Preferred-138
Press Proofs-138
96Pinnacle-232
Artist's Proofs-232
Foil-232
Premium Stock-232
Rink Collection-232
96Ultra-71
Gold Medallion-71
96Carolina Monarchs-25
96Collector's Edge Ice-25
Prism-25
97Be A Player-139
Autographs-139
Autographs Die-Cuts-139
Autographs Prismatic Die-Cuts-139
97Collector's Choice-107
97Donruss-115
Press Proofs Silver-115
Press Proofs Gold-115
97Pacific Invincible NHL Regime-90
97Pacific Omega-103
Copper-103
Dark Gray-103
Emerald Green-103
Gold-103
Ice Blue-103
98OPC Chrome-158
Refractors-158
98Pacific-229
Ice Blue-229
Red-229
98Topps-158
O-Pee-Chee-158
00Swiss Slapshot Mini-Cards-EHCK15
02German DEL City Press-168

Washkurak, Joel
90 7th Inn. Sketch OHL-72
01Mississauga Ice Dogs-25

Wasley, Charlie
92Minnesota Golden Gophers-22
93Minnesota Golden Gophers-26
94Minnesota Golden Gophers-28
95Minnesota Golden Gophers-28

Waslowski, Norman
99Fort Wayne Komets Points Leaders-13

Wasmuth, Andrew
04Swift Current Broncos-24
05Swift Current Broncos-5

Wasnie, Nick
28V128-2 Paulin's Candy-64
33O-Pee-Chee V304A-47
33V252 Canadian Gum-50
33V288 Hamilton Gum-1

Wassberger, Joakin
96Mississippi Sea Wolves-19

Wassermann, Sepp
94German DEL-339
95German DEL-306

Wasylko, Steve
95Bowman Draft Prospects-P38
95Slapshot-71
96Detroit Whalers-19

Wasyluk, Trevor
95Bowman Draft Prospects-P39
95Upper Deck-512
Electric Ice-512
Electric Ice Gold-512
95Medicine Hat Tigers-21
96Medicine Hat Tigers-24
96Visions Signings *-63
Autographs-63A
Autographs Silver-63A
97Lethbridge Hurricanes-23
97Medicine Hat Tigers-22
98Kootenay Ice-13

Watchorn, Jeff
90 7th Inn. Sketch WHL-292
90 7th Inn. Sketch Memorial Cup-13
91 7th Inn. Sketch WHL-92

Wathen, Trevor
91Air Canada SJHL-A16
92Saskatchewan JHL-61

Wathier, Francis
01Hull Olympiques-6
02Hull Olympiques-7
03Gatineau Olympiques-26
03Hull Olympiques Memorial Cup-20
04Gatineau Olympiques-6
05Iowa Stars-22
06Idaho Steelheads-12
06Iowa Stars-23

Wathier, Mathieu
00Victoriaville Tigres-10
Signed-10
01Sherbrooke Castors-13
03Moncton Wildcats-15
06Quad City Mallards-18

Watkins, Joe
99UK Basingstoke Bison-19
00UK Sekonda Superleague-32
03Bakersfield Condors-20
03ECHL Update RBI Sports-59
04UK London Racers-6
04UK London Racers Playoffs-18
05UK Guildford Flames-15
06UK Guildford Flames-15

Watkins, Larry
90 7th Inn. Sketch WHL-258
91 7th Inn. Sketch WHL-320

Watkins, Matt
04Vernon Vipers-5

Watkins, Tom
99UK Hull Thunder-10
00Lincoln Stars-3
02UK Coventry Blaze-14
03UK Coventry Blaze-12
04UK Coventry Blaze-21
04UK Coventry Blaze Champions-18
05UK Coventry Blaze-8
06UK Coventry Blaze-7

Watson, Bill
84Minnesota-Duluth Bulldogs-22
85Blackhawks Team Issue-14
86Blackhawks Coke-22
86O-Pee-Chee-151
86Topps-151
87Blackhawks Coke-28
87Panini Stickers-232
88ProCards IHL-118
04Minnesota-Duluth Bulldogs-31

Watson, Blake
24Crescent Falcon-Tigers-14

Watson, Brent
90 7th Inn. Sketch OHL-223
91 7th Inn. Sketch OHL-351

Watson, Bruce
98Port Huron Border Cats-16
99Asheville Smoke-21
99Asheville Smoke-22
00Asheville Smoke-25
05Rockford Ice Hogs-18
06Rockford IceHogs-22

Watson, Bryan
64Canadiens Postcards-23
64Quebec Aces-18
65Topps-45
66Topps-48
68O-Pee-Chee-173
69O-Pee-Chee-112
69Topps-112
70Dad's Cookies-137
70Esso Power Players-221
70O-Pee-Chee-204
70Sargent Promotions Stamps-164
71O-Pee-Chee-132
71Penguins Postcards-20
71Sargent Promotions Stamps-164
71Toronto Sun-229
72O-Pee-Chee-90
72O-Pee-Chee-268
72Sargent Promotions Stamps-172
72Topps-65
72Topps-116
72Finnish Semic World Championship-217
72Swedish Semic World Championship-217
73O-Pee-Chee-14
73Topps-144
74NHL Action Stamps-95
74O-Pee-Chee NHL-5
74O-Pee-Chee NHL-259
74Topps-5
74Topps-259
75O-Pee-Chee NHL-31
75Topps-31
76O-Pee-Chee NHL-4
76O-Pee-Chee NHL-228
76O-Pee-Chee NHL-385
76Topps-4
76Topps-228
77O-Pee-Chee NHL-342
78O-Pee-Chee-316
88Oilers Tenth Anniversary-124
02Fleer Throwbacks-72
Gold-72
Platinum-72

Watson, Curtis
98Windsor Spitfires-9

Watson, Dan
99Bowman CHL-160
Gold-160
OPC International-160
00Syracuse Crunch-6
01Syracuse Crunch-3
02Syracuse Crunch-4
02Syracuse Crunch Sheets-16
03Kalamazoo Wings-20
06Toledo Storm-16

Watson, Greg
00Prince Albert Raiders-25
00UD CHL Prospects-59
00UD CHL Prospects-98
01Prince Albert Raiders-23
01UD Prospects-35
Autographs-A-GW
Jersey Autographs-S-GW
Jerseys-J-GW
Jerseys-C-KW
Jerseys Gold-J-GW
Jerseys Gold-C-KW
02Brandon Wheat Kings-18
02Prince Albert Raiders-22
03Binghamton Senators-23
04Binghamton Senators-22
04ITG Heroes and Prospects-17
Autographs-GW
04ITG Heroes/Prospects Toronto Expo '05-17
04ITG Heroes/Prospects Expo Heroes/Pros-17

Watson, Harry
24V-122-43
25Dominion Chocolates-114
34Beehive Group I Photos-257
44Beehive Group II Photos-459
45Quaker Oats Photos-58A
45Quaker Oats Photos-58B
45Quaker Oats Photos-58C
45Quaker Oats Photos-60A
51Parkhurst-70
52Parkhurst-46
53Parkhurst-12
54Parkhurst-17
83Hall of Fame Postcards-G16
85Hall of Fame-105
91Ultimate Original Six-46
French-46
93Parkhurst Parkie Reprints Case Inserts-11
94Parkhurst Missing Link-36
02Maple Leafs Platinum Collection-70
03BAP Ultimate Mem Maple Leafs Forever-13
04ITG Ultimate Memorabilia Autographs-60
04ITG Ultimate Mem Autographs Gold-60

Watson, Jim
67Topps-107
67Topps-107
68Shirriff Coins-48
68Shirriff Coins-48
70Esso Power Players-74
70Esso Power Players-74
70O-Pee-Chee-144
70O-Pee-Chee-144
70Sargent Promotions Stamps-32
70Sargent Promotions Stamps-32
71O-Pee-Chee-165
71O-Pee-Chee-165
71Sabres Postcards-71
71Sabres Postcards-71
71Sargent Promotions Stamps-21
71Sargent Promotions Stamps-21
71Toronto Sun-40
71Toronto Sun-40
72Los Angeles Sharks WHA-17
72Los Angeles Sharks WHA-17
72 7-Eleven Slurpee Cups WHA-20
72 7-Eleven Slurpee Cups WHA-20
73Flyers Linnett-17
74NHL Action Stamps-208
74O-Pee-Chee NHL-303
75Flyers Canada Dry Cans-20
75O-Pee-Chee NHL-202
75Topps-202
77Coca-Cola-28
77O-Pee-Chee NHL-43
77Topps-43
78O-Pee-Chee-247
78Topps-247
79O-Pee-Chee-26
79Topps-26
80O-Pee-Chee-224
80Topps-224
82O-Pee-Chee-259
82Post Cereal-14
90Upper Deck-514

Watson, Joe
66Topps-33
68O-Pee-Chee-90
68Topps-90
69O-Pee-Chee-93
69Topps-93
70Dad's Cookies-138
70Esso Power Players-209
70O-Pee-Chee-79
70Sargent Promotions Stamps-156
70Topps-79
71Sargent Promotions Stamps-158
71Toronto Sun-208
72O-Pee-Chee-62
72Sargent Promotions Stamps-159
72Topps-156
73Flyers Linnett-18
73O-Pee-Chee-91
73Topps-91
74NHL Action Stamps-214
74O-Pee-Chee NHL-217
74Topps-217
75Flyers Canada Dry Cans-21
75O-Pee-Chee NHL-281
75Topps-281
76O-Pee-Chee NHL-45
76O-Pee-Chee NHL-247
76Topps-45
76Topps-247
77Coca-Cola-29
77O-Pee-Chee NHL-247
77Topps-247
78O-Pee-Chee-43
78Topps-43
92Parkhurst-474
Emerald Ice-474
95Parkhurst '66-67-3
Coins-3
01BAP Ultimate Mem Dynasty Jerseys-18
01BAP Ultimate Mem Dynasty Emblems-18
01BAP Ultimate Mem Dynasty Numbers-18
01Parkhurst Autographs-PA41
04ITG Franchises US East-413
Autographs-A-JW1
04ITG Franchises US West-187
04ITG Ultimate Mem Broad St Bullie Jersey-8
04ITG Ult Mem Broad St Bullie Jersey Auto-8
04ITG Ultimate Mem Broad St Bullie Emblem-8
04ITG Ult Mem Broad St Bullie Emblem Auto-8
04ITG Ultimate Mem Broad St Bullie Number-8
04ITG Ult Mem Broad St Bullie Number Auto-8

Watson, Jordon
02Belleville Bulls-23

Watson, Phil
34Beehive Group I Photos-297
37V356 Worldwide Gum-80
39O-Pee-Chee V301-1-83
43Parade Sportive *-83
52Juniors Blue Tint-80
61Shirriff/Salada Coins-19
61Topps-1
62Topps-1
94Parkhurst Missing Link-108

Watson, Ross
52Juniors Blue Tint-159

Watson, Ryan
03Oklahoma City Blazers-21

Watt, J.D.
04Vancouver Giants-7
05ITG Heroes/Prosp Toronto Expo Parallel -176
05Vancouver Giants-24
05ITG Heroes and Prospects-176
Autographs-A-JDW

Watt, Jim
02Spokane Chiefs-24
04Spokane Chiefs Magnets-5
05Saskatoon Blades-23

Watt, Jordan
98Red Deer Rebels-22

Watt, Mike
95Donruss Elite World Juniors-21
95Upper Deck-536
Electric Ice-536
Electric Ice Gold-536
98Bowman's Best Mirror Image Fusion-F11
98Bowmans Best Mirror Im Fusion Ref-F11
98Bowmans Best Mirror Im Fusion Atom Ref-F11
98Islanders Power Play-NY13
98Pacific Omega-153
Red-153
Opening Day Issue-153
98Revolution-91
Ice Shadow-91
Red-91
98SP Authentic-103
Power Shift-103
98SPx Finite-138
Radiance-138
Spectrum-138
98Upper Deck-14
98Upper Deck-316
Exclusives-14
Exclusives-316
Exclusives 1 of 1-14
Exclusives 1 of 1-316
Generation Next-GN15
Generation Next Quantum 1-GN15
Generation Next Quantum 2-GN15
Generation Next Quantum 3-GN15
Gold Reserve-14
Gold Reserve-316
98Upper Deck MVP-128
Gold Script-128
Silver Script-128
Super Script-128
99Aurora-92
Premier Date-92
99Pacific-266
Copper-266
Emerald Green-266
Gold-266
Ice Blue-266
Premiere Date-266
Red-266
99Paramount-147
Copper-147
Emerald-147
Gold-147
Holographic Emerald-147
Holographic Gold-147
Holographic Silver-147
Ice Blue-147
Premiere Date-147
Red-147
Silver-147
99Revolution-94
Premiere Date-94
Red-94
Shadow Series-94
99SPx-90
Radiance-90
Spectrum-90
99Upper Deck MVP-125
Gold Script-125
Silver Script-125
Super Script-125
99Upper Deck Victory-185
00Upper Deck NHLPA-PA51
00Milwaukee Admirals Keebler-20
00Milwaukee Admirals Postcards-17
02Lowell Lock Monsters-12
03Russian Hockey League-77
05Swedish SHL Elitset-210
Gold-210

Watt, Nicky
03UK Basingstoke Bison-16

Watt, Sylvain
00Chicoutimi Sagueneens-8
Signed-8

Watt, Tom
81Jets Postcards-23
82Jets Postcards-26
88Flames Postcards-27
90Pro Set-677
91Maple Leafs PLAY-29
95St. John's Maple Leafs-23
97Sudbury Wolves Police-6

Watters, Tim
81Jets Postcards-24
81Swedish Semic Hockey VM Stickers-78
82Jets Postcards-27
82O-Pee-Chee-395
82Post Cereal-21
83Jets Postcards-23
83O-Pee-Chee-394
83Vachon-139
84Jets Police-21
84O-Pee-Chee-350
85Jets Police-21
86Jets Postcards-24
87Jets Postcards-22
87O-Pee-Chee-219
88Kings Postcards-9
88Kings Smokey-24
89Kings Smokey-2
89O-Pee-Chee-212
90Kings Smokey-4
90O-Pee-Chee-461
90Pro Set-458
90Score-204
Canadian-204
90Upper Deck-117
French-117
90Michigan Tech Huskies-27
91Score Canadian Bilingual-523
91Score Canadian English-523
91Upper Deck-471
French-471
92Phoenix Roadrunners-25
93OPC Premier-298
Gold-298
93Topps/OPC Premier-298
Gold-298
04ITG Franchises Canadian-149
Autographs-TWA

Watts, Morgan
85London Knights-8

Waugh, Geoff
04Northern Michigan Wildcats-26
06Springfield Falcons-27

Waugh, Thomas
03St. Michael's Majors-17

Waver, Jeff
84Brandon Wheat Kings-16
85Brandon Wheat Kings-16
88ProCards IHL-64
90ProCards AHL/IHL-523

Wavra, Matt
00Lincoln Stars-5
01Lincoln Stars-23

Way, Clint
03Austin Ice Bats-19

Way, Jim
86Sudbury Wolves-9

Way, Shawn
89 7th Inn. Sketch OHL-84

Weasler, Dean
02South Carolina Stingrays-19

Weatherston, Katie
06ITG Going For Gold-19
06ITG Going For Gold Samples-19
06ITG Going For Gold Autographs-AW
06ITG Going For Gold Jerseys-GUJ19

Weathon, John
02Owen Sound Attack-18

Weaver, Dave
92Western Michigan Broncos-25

Weaver, Jason
90 7th Inn. Sketch OHL-348
91Oshawa Generals-18
91Oshawa Generals Sheet-11
91 7th Inn. Sketch OHL-160
97Grand Rapids Griffins-20
99UK Sheffield Steelers-20
00UK Sekonda Superleague-159
00UK Sheffield Steelers-27
01Fresno Falcons-20
02Fresno Falcons-21
03Fresno Falcons-23
04Fresno Falcons-22

Weaver, Jonathan
99Mississippi Sea Wolves-12
00UK Sekonda Superleague-20
02UK Hull Thunder-16

Weaver, Mike
01BAP Memorabilia-400
Emerald-400
Ruby-400
Sapphire-400
01UD Honor Roll-62
01UD Playmakers-103
01Chicago Wolves-24
02Upper Deck MVP-192
Gold-192
Classics-192
Golden Classics-192
03Chicago Wolves-22
04Manchester Monarchs-16
04Manchester Monarchs Tobacco-16
05Manchester Monarchs-47

Weaver, Scott
91Air Canada SJHL-D23

Webb, Jonathan
02Brandon Wheat Kings-1
03Brandon Wheat Kings-21
04Brandon Wheat Kings-2

Webb, Steve
92Windsor Spitfires-22
95Muskegon Fury-10
96Kentucky Thoroughblades-18
97Pacific-248
Copper-248
Emerald Green-248
Ice Blue-248
Red-248
Silver-248
97Upper Deck-308
97Kentucky Thoroughblades-17
98Muskegon Fury-18
99O-Pee-Chee-73
99O-Pee-Chee Chrome-73
99O-Pee-Chee Chrome Refractors-73
99Topps/OPC-73
99Topps/OPC Chrome-73
Refractors-73
00BAP Signature Series-180
Emerald-180
Ruby-180
Sapphire-180
Autographs-46
Autographs Gold-46
00Upper Deck NHLPA-PA57
02BAP Memorabilia-161
Emerald-161
Ruby-161
Sapphire-161
NHL All-Star Game-161
NHL All-Star Game Blue-161
NHL All-Star Game Green-161
NHL All-Star Game Red-161
02BAP Memorabilia Toronto Fall Expo-161
02BAP Sig Series Auto Buybacks 2000-46
02Upper Deck-110
Exclusives-110
02Upper Deck MVP-118
Gold-118
Classics-118
Golden Classics-118
03Wilkes-Barre Scranton Penguins-27

Webber, Mike
83North Bay Centennials-23
06Barrie Colts-14

Weber, Alexis
02Swiss HNL-387

Weber, Christian
91Finnish Semic World Champ Stickers-196
91Swedish Semic World Champ Stickers-196
92Finnish Semic-212
93Swedish Semic World Champ Stickers-125
93Swiss HNL-181
95Swedish Globe World Championships-212
95Swiss HNL-131
95Swiss HNL-507
95Swiss HNL-508
96Swiss HNL-123
96Swiss HNL-546
98Swiss Power Play Stickers-246
99Swiss Panini Stickers-248
01Swiss HNL-381
02Swiss HNL-375

Weber, Daniel
93Swiss HNL-17
95Swiss HNL-14
96Swiss HNL-13
98Swiss Power Play Stickers-111

Weber, Jason
93Cornell Big Red-26

Weber, Jeff
02Plymouth Whalers-24
04Barrie Colts-1
05Stockton Thunder-19

Weber, Marc
91Upper Deck-666
French-666
91Upper Deck Czech World Juniors-27
93Swiss HNL-207
95Swiss HNL-234
96Swiss HNL-147
98Swiss Power Play Stickers-50
99Swiss Panini Stickers-50
00Swiss Panini Stickers-49
00Swiss Slapshot Mini-Cards-SCB16
01Swiss HNL-97

Weber, Matt
93Quebec Pee-Wee Tournament-678
99Des Moines Buccaneers-5
04New Mexico Scorpions-10
04New Mexico Scorpions-25

Weber, Mike
05ITG Heroes/Prosp Toronto Expo Parallel -409
05ITG Heroes and Prospects-409
Team Cherry-TC2

Weber, Patrik
94Czech APS Extraliga-42
95Czech APS Extraliga-329
99Czech Score Blue 2000-19
99Czech Score Red Ice 2000-19

Weber, Pius
95Swiss HNL-447

Weber, Randall
00UK Nottingham Panthers-7
00UK Sekonda Superleague-141
01UK Nottingham Panthers-5

Weber, Shea
02Kelowna Rockets-11
03Kelowna Rockets Memorial Cup-20
03Kelowna Rockets-22
04Kelowna Rockets-2
05ITG Heroes/Prosp Toronto Expo Parallel -161
05Milwaukee Admirals Choice-16
05Milwaukee Admirals Pepsi-21
05ITG Heroes and Prospects-161
Aspiring-ASP9
Autographs-A-SW
Complete Logos-CHL-8
Jerseys-GUJ-26
Jerseys Gold-GUJ-26
Emblems-GUE-26
Emblems Gold-GUE-26
Numbers-GUN-26
Numbers Gold-GUN-26
Nameplates-N-4

Nameplates Gold-N-04
06Be A Player-207
Autographs-207
Signatures 25-207
Signatures Trios-TCWB
06Be A Player Portraits-111
06Beehive-132
Blue-132
Matte-132
Red Facsimile Signatures-132
Wood-132
06Black Diamond-196
Black-196
Gold-196
Ruby-196
06Flair Showcase-59
06Flair Showcase-137
Parallel-59
Parallel-137
06Fleer-201
Tiffany-201
06Hot Prospects-120
Red Hot-120
White Hot-120
Hot Materials -HMSW
Hot Materials Red Hot-HMSW
Hot Materials White Hot-HMSW
Hotagraphs-HSW
06O-Pee-Chee-525
06O-Pee-Chee-630
Rainbow-525
Rainbow-630
06SP Authentic-187
Limited-187
Sign of the Times Duals-STWR
06SP Game Used-128
Gold-128
Rainbow-128
Autographs-128
Inked Sweaters-ISSW
Inked Sweaters Patches-ISSW
Inked Sweaters Dual-IS2VW
Inked Sweaters Dual Patches-IS2VW
Rookie Exclusives Autographs-RESW
06SPx-174
Spectrum-174
06The Cup-139
Autographed Rookie Masterpiece Pressplates-139
Gold Rainbow Autographed Rookie Patches-139
Honorable Numbers-HNSW
Masterpiece Pressplates (Artifacts)-222
Masterpiece Pressplates (Be A Player Portraits)-111
Masterpiece Pressplates (Bee Hive)-132
Masterpiece Pressplates (Marquee Rookies)-525
Masterpiece Pressplates (MVP)-354
Masterpiece Pressplates (Power Play)-110
Masterpiece Pressplates (SP Authentic Autographs)-187
Masterpiece Pressplates (SP Game Used)-128
Masterpiece Pressplates (SPx Autographs)-174
Masterpiece Pressplates (Sweet Beginnings)-135
Masterpiece Pressplates (Trilogy)-124
Masterpiece Pressplates (Ultimate Collection Autographs)-118
Masterpiece Pressplates (Victory)-215
NHL Shields Duals-DSHCW
Rookies Black-139
Rookies Platinum-139
06UD Artifacts-222
Blue-222
Gold-222
Platinum-222
Radiance-222
Red-222
06UD Mini Jersey Collection-110
06UD Powerplay-110
Impact Rainbow-110
06Ultimate Collection-118
Rookies Autographed NHL Shields-118
Rookies Autographed Patches-118
Ultimate Debut Threads Jerseys-DJ-SW
Ultimate Debut Threads Jerseys Autographs-DJ-SW
Ultimate Debut Threads Patches-DJ-SW
Ultimate Debut Threads Patches Autographs-DJ-SW
06Ultra-211
Gold Medallion-211
Ice Medallion-211
06Upper Deck-222
Exclusives Parallel-222
High Gloss Parallel-222
Masterpieces-222
Rookie Game Dated Moments-RGD14
Rookie Materials-RMSW
Rookie Materials Patches-RMSW
06Upper Deck MVP-354
Gold Script-354
Super Script-354
06Upper Deck Ovation-178
06Upper Deck Sweet Shot-135
Rookie Jerseys Autographs-135
06Upper Deck Trilogy-124
06Upper Deck Victory-215
06Upper Deck Victory Black-215
06Upper Deck Victory Gold-215
06ITG Heroes and Prospects Quad Emblems-QE03
06ITG Heroes and Prospects Quad Emblems Gold-QE03
07Upper Deck Rookie Class -1

Weber, Travis
01Minnesota Golden Gophers-28
02Minnesota Golden Gophers-27

Weber, Yannick
06Kitchener Rangers-21

Webster, Chris
87Brockville Braves-19
88Brockville Braves-23

Webster, Dave
82Kitchener Rangers-30

Webster, Glen
89Brandon Wheat Kings-14
90Brandon Wheat Kings-10
907th Inn. Sketch WHL-230

Webster, Jeff
93Quebec Pee-Wee Tournament-1231

Webster, Tom
70Dad's Cookies-139
70Esso Power Players-133
70O-Pee-Chee-155
70Red Wings Marathon-11
70Sargent Promotions Stamps-57
71O-Pee-Chee-78
71Sargent Promotions Stamps-135
71Topps-78
72Whalers New England WHA-16
74O-Pee-Chee WHA-8
74Team Canada L'Equipe WHA-24
75O-Pee-Chee WHA-95
76O-Pee-Chee WHA-14
77O-Pee-Chee WHA-55
90Pro Set-667

Weckerle, Georg
94German First League-241

Weckstrom, Kari
80Finnish Mallasjuoma-150

Wedderburn, Tim
98Prince George Cougars-25
99Prince George Cougars-2
00Prince George Cougars-3
02Hershey Bears-25
04Chicago Wolves-15
05Chicago Wolves-23
06Rockford IceHogs -23

Weder, Matt
96Flint Generals-20

Wedl, Alexander
94German DEL-107
95German DEL-152
96German DEL-230
98German DEL-54
99German Bundesliga 2-273

Weekes, Kevin
93Owen Sound Platers-6
93Owen Sound Platers-32
93Owen Sound Platers-33
96Carolina Monarchs-26
96Collector's Edge Ice-26
Prism-26
97Crown Royale-61
Emerald Green-61
Ice Blue-61
Silver-61
97Donruss Priority-177
Stamp of Approval-177
97Pacific Omega-104
Copper-104
Dark Gray-104
Emerald Green-104
Gold-104
Ice Blue-104
97SP Authentic-183
97Fort Wayne Komets-20
98Pacific-230
Ice Blue-230
Red-230
98Upper Deck-100
Exclusives-100
Exclusives 1 of 1-100
Gold Reserve-100
98Detroit Vipers-20
98Detroit Vipers Freschetta-1
99BAP Memorabilia-196
Gold-196
Silver-196
99Pacific-434
Copper-434
Emerald Green-434
Gold-434
Ice Blue-434
Premiere Date-434
Red-434
99Pacific Dynagon Ice-198
Blue-198
Copper-198
Gold-198
Premiere Date-198
99Pacific Omega-145
Copper-145
Gold-145
Ice Blue-145
Premiere Date-145
99Upper Deck-128
Exclusives-128
Exclusives 1 of 1-128
99Upper Deck Gold Reserve-128
99Upper Deck MVP-208
Gold Script-208
Silver Script-208
Super Script-208
99Upper Deck Victory-297
00Aurora-135
Premiere Date-135
00Crown Royale-98
Ice Blue-98
Limited Series-98
Premiere Date-98
Red-98
00O-Pee-Chee-29
00O-Pee-Chee Parallel-29
00Pacific-257
Copper-257
Gold-257
Ice Blue-257
Premiere Date-257
00Topps/OPC-29
Parallel-29
00Topps Heritage-118
00UD Pros and Prospects-77
01BAP Memorabilia-471
Emerald-471
Ruby-471
Sapphire-471
01BAP Signature Series-170
Autographs-170
Autographs Gold-170
01Between the Pipes-40
01Between the Pipes-155
01O-Pee-Chee-20
01O-Pee-Chee Heritage Parallel-20
01O-Pee-Chee Heritage Parallel Limited-20
01O-Pee-Chee Premier Parallel-20
01Pacific-359
Extreme LTD-359
Hobby LTD-359
Premiere Date-359
Retail LTD-359
01Pacific Adrenaline-178
Blue-178
Premiere Date-178
Red-178
Retail-178
01Pacific Arena Exclusives-359
01Topps-20
Heritage Parallel-20
Heritage Parallel Limited-20
OPC Parallel-20
01Upper Deck Victory-314
01Upper Deck Victory-319
Gold-314
Gold-319
02BAP First Edition-248
02BAP Memorabilia-158
Emerald-158
Ruby-158
Sapphire-158
NHL All-Star Game-158
NHL All-Star Game Blue-158
NHL All-Star Game Green-158
NHL All-Star Game Red-158
02BAP Memorabilia Toronto Fall Expo-158
02BAP Sig Series Auto Buybacks 2001-170
02Between the Pipes-19
Gold-19
Silver-19
Masks II-6
Masks II Gold-6
Masks II Silver-6
02Bowman YoungStars-60
Gold-60
Silver-60
02Hurricanes Postcards-6
02Pacific-72
Blue-72
Red-72
02Pacific Complete-143
Red-143
02Parkhurst-41
Bronze-41
Gold-41
Silver-41
02Parkhurst Retro-102
Minis-102
02Titanium-20
Blue-20
Red-20
Retail-20
02Topps Heritage-40
Chrome Parallel-40
02Topps Total-287
02UD Mask Collection-17
02UD Mask Collection-18
02UD Mask Collection Beckett Promos-17
02UD Mask Collection Beckett Promos-18
02Upper Deck-274
Exclusives-274
02Upper Deck Beckett UD Promos-274
02Vanguard-20
LTD-20
03BAP Memorabilia-132
Emerald-132
Gold-132
Ruby-132
Sapphire-132
Masks III-7
Masks III Gold-7
Masks III Silver-7
Masks III Autographs-M-KW
Masks III Memorabilia-7
03BAP Ultimate Memorabilia Autographs-43
Gold-43
03Black Diamond-82
Black-82
Green-82
Red-82
03Bowman-103
Gold-103
03Bowman Chrome-103
Refractors-103
Gold Refractors-103
Xfractors-103
03Crown Royale-18
Blue-18
Retail-18
03Hurricanes Postcards-23
03ITG Action-160
Jerseys-M118
03ITG Used Signature Series-82
Gold-82
Autographs-KW
Autographs Gold-KW
03NHL Sticker Collection-40
03O-Pee-Chee-22
03OPC Blue-22
03OPC Gold-22
03OPC Red-22
03Pacific-67
Blue-67
Red-67
03Pacific Complete-443
Red-443
03Pacific Heads-Up-19
Hobby LTD-19
Retail LTD-19
03Private Stock Reserve-20
Blue-20
Red-20
Retail-20
03Titanium-23
Hobby Jersey Number Parallels-23
Retail-23
Retail Jersey Number Parallels-23
03Topps-22
Blue-22
Gold-22
Red-22
03Topps Pristine-6
Gold Refractor Die Cuts-6
Refractors-6
Mini-PM-KW
Press Plates Black-6
Press Plates Cyan-6
Press Plates Magenta-6
Press Plates Yellow-6
03Upper Deck-39
Canadian Exclusives-39
HG-39
03Upper Deck MVP-89
Gold Script-89
Silver Script-89
Canadian Exclusives-89
04Pacific-53
Blue-53
Red-53
05Be A Player Signatures-KW
05Be A Player Signatures Gold-KW
05Black Diamond-56
Emerald-56
Gold-56
Onyx-56
Ruby-56
05Panini Stickers-109
05Parkhurst-321
Facsimile Auto Parallel-321
05SP Authentic Sign of the Times-KW
05SP Authentic Sign of the Times Duals-DWL
05SP Game Used-66
Gold-66
Auto Draft-AD-KW
Statscriptions-ST-KW
05SPx-59
Spectrum-59
05Ultra-128
Gold-128
Fresh Ink-FI-KW
Fresh Ink Blue-FI-KW
Ice-128
05Upper Deck-129
HG Glossy-129
Notable Numbers-N-KW
05Upper Deck Ice-63
Rainbow-63
05Upper Deck MVP-259
Gold-259
Platinum-259
05Upper Deck Trilogy-56
05Upper Deck Toronto Fall Expo-129
05Upper Deck Victory-233
Black-233
Gold-233
Silver-233
06Between The Pipes The Mask-M30
06Between The Pipes The Mask Gold-M30
06Between The Pipes The Mask Silver-M30
06O-Pee-Chee-331
Rainbow-331
06Upper Deck-130
Exclusives Parallel-130
High Gloss Parallel-130
Masterpieces-130

Weeks, Steve
82O-Pee-Chee-234
82O-Pee-Chee Stickers-141
82Post Cereal-13
82Topps Stickers-141
84Whalers Junior Wendy's-21
85Whalers Junior Wendy's-22
86Whalers Junior Thomas' -23
87Panini Stickers-39
87Whalers Jr. Burger King/Pepsi-21
88Canucks Mohawk-24
89Canucks Mohawk-24
89O-Pee-Chee-262
89Panini Stickers-150
90O-Pee-Chee-407
90Upper Deck-107
French-107
90ProCards AHL/IHL-331
92Bowman-274
92Pinnacle-380
French-380
92Score-547
Canadian-547
92Stadium Club-273
92Topps-461
Gold-461G
06Thrashers Postcards-5

Weenk, Heath
89Regina Pats-22
907th Inn. Sketch WHL-185
917th Inn. Sketch WHL-220

Wegener, John
90Arizona Icecats-15

Wegleitner, Mike
84Kelowna Wings-11

Wegmann, Stefan
94German First League-331

Wegmuller, Marco
98Swiss Power Play Stickers-55
99Swiss Panini Stickers-55
01Swiss HNL-302

Wehrli, Remo
96Swiss HNL-129
98Swiss Power Play Stickers-179
99Swiss Panini Stickers-179

Wehrmann, Mike
94German First League-580

Wehrs, Kevin
06Cedar Rapids RoughRiders-19

Wehrstedt, Michael
99Kitchener Rangers-11
00Mississauga Ice Dogs-27
01Mississauga Ice Dogs-9
04Lakehead University Thunderwolves-14

Weibel, Lars
93Swiss HNL-85
95Swiss HNL-136
95Swiss HNL-507
95Swiss HNL-510
95Swiss HNL-511
95Swiss HNL-514
96Swiss HNL-152
98Swiss Power Play Stickers-154
99Swiss Panini Stickers-154
00Swiss Panini Stickers-103
00Swiss Slapshot Mini-Cards-HCD1
01Swiss HNL-100
02Swiss HNL-1
02Swiss HNL-491
04Swiss EV Zug Postcards-6

Weibel, Sacha
96Swiss HNL-359
01Swiss HNL-279
02Swiss HNL-92
04Swiss Lausanne HC Postcards-22

Weidenbach, Andy
907th Inn. Sketch OHL-124
96Hampton Roads Admirals-HRA11

Weidenbach, John
92Michigan State Spartans-28
93Michigan State Spartans-28

Weidlich, Steve
03Laredo Bucks-20

Weight, Doug
91Pro Set Platinum-263
91OPC Premier-32
91OPC Premier-139
91Parkhurst-116
French-116
91Pinnacle-310
91Pinnacle-383
French-310
French-383
91Pro Set-549
French-549
91Score American-396
91Score Canadian Bilingual-286
91Score Canadian English-286
91Upper Deck-440
91Upper Deck-444
French-440
French-444
92Bowman-36
92Oilers Team Issue-21
92O-Pee-Chee-114
92Panini Stickers-236
92Panini Stickers French-236
92Parkhurst-115
92Parkhurst-229
Emerald Ice-115
Emerald Ice-229
92Pinnacle-189
French-189
92Score-314
Canadian-314
92Stadium Club-380
92Topps-477
Gold-477G
92Ultra-358
92Upper Deck-279
93Donruss-118
93Leaf-184
93OPC Premier-136
Gold-136
93Panini Stickers-235
93Parkhurst-69
Emerald Ice-69
93Pinnacle-17
Canadian-17
93PowerPlay-87
93Score-253
Canadian-253
93Stadium Club-382
Members Only Master Set-382
First Day Issue-382
93Topps/OPC Premier-136
Gold-136
93Ultra-195
93Upper Deck-442
SP-53
94Be A Player-R118
Signature Cards-117
94Canada Games NHL POGS-101
94Donruss-3
94EA Sports-45
94Flair-62
94Leaf-40
94Leaf Limited-53
94OPC Premier-8
Special Effects-8
94Parkhurst-74
Gold-74
SE Vintage-23
94Pinnacle-18
Artist's Proofs-18
Rink Collection-18
94Score-58
Gold-58
Platinum-58
94Select-27
Gold-27
94SP-39
Die Cuts-39
94Topps/OPC Premier-8
Special Effects-8
94Ultra-77
94Upper Deck-44
94Upper Deck-549
Electric Ice-44
Electric Ice-549
SP Inserts-SP28
SP Inserts Die Cuts-SP28
94Upper Deck NHLPA/Be A Player-39
95Bashan Super Stickers-43
95Bowman-68
All-Foil-68
95Canada Games NHL POGS-105
95Collector's Choice-172
Player's Club-172
Player's Club Platinum-172
95Donruss-25
95Donruss Elite-5
Die Cut Stars-5
Die Cut Uncut-5
95Emotion-67
95Finest-104
Refractors-104
95Hoyle Western Playing Cards-25
95Imperial Stickers-43
95Kraft-68
95Leaf-145
95Leaf Limited-110
95Metal-57
95Panini Stickers-259
95Parkhurst International-346
Emerald Ice-346
95Playoff One on One-259
95Pro Magnets-85
95Score-263
Black Ice Artist's Proofs-263
Black Ice-263
95Select Certified-109
Mirror Gold-109
95SkyBox Impact-65
95SP-50
Holoviews-FX9
Holoviews Special FX-FX9
95Stadium Club-74
Members Only Master Set-74
95Summit-110
Artist's Proofs-110
Ice-110
95Topps-158
OPC Inserts-158
95Ultra-58
Gold Medallion-58
95Upper Deck-280
Electric Ice-280
Electric Ice Gold-280
NHL All-Stars-AS16
NHL All-Stars Jumbo-AS16
Special Edition-SE31
Special Edition Gold-SE31
95German DEL-449
95Swedish Globe World Championships-125
95Swedish World Championships Stickers-231
96Be A Player-174
Autographs-174
Autographs Silver-174
96Black Diamond-172
Gold-172
96Collector's Choice-91
96Collector's Choice-317
MVP-UD9
MVP Gold-UD9
Crash the Game-C9A
Crash the Game-C9B
Crash the Game-C9C
Crash the Game Gold-C9A
Crash the Game Gold-C9B
Crash the Game Gold-C9C
Crash the Game Exchange-CR9
Crash the Game Exchange Gold-CR9
96Donruss-85
Press Proofs-85
Elite Inserts-3
Elite Inserts Gold-3
Hit List-5
96Donruss Canadian Ice-14
Gold Press Proofs-14
Red Press Proofs-14
96Donruss Elite-25
Die Cut Stars-25
Status-4
96Flair-36
Blue Ice-36
96Fleer-38
Art Ross-24
Picks Fabulous 50-47
Picks Jagged Edge-4
96Kraft Upper Deck-21
96Kraft Upper Deck-71
96Leaf-136
Press Proofs-136
Fire On Ice-6
The Best Of ...-7
96Leaf Limited-71
Gold-71
96Leaf Preferred-54
Press Proofs-54
Steel-49
Steel Gold-49
96McDonald's Pinnacle-16
96Metal Universe-56
Lethal Weapons-20
Lethal Weapons Super Power-20
96NHL Aces Playing Cards-50
96NHL Pro Stamps-85
96Oilers Postcards-39
96Pinnacle-158
Artist's Proofs-158
Foil-158
Premium Stock-158
Rink Collection-158
By The Numbers-5
By The Numbers Premium-5
Team Pinnacle-4
96Playoff One on One-434
96Score-170
Artist's Proofs-170
Dealer's Choice Artist's Proofs-170
Special Artist's Proofs-170
Check It-14
Golden Blades-170
Superstitions-2
96Select Certified-50
Artist's Proofs-50
Blue-50
Mirror Blue-50
Mirror Gold-50
Mirror Red-50
Red-50
96SkyBox Impact-43
BladeRunners-24
96SP-57
Clearcut Winner-CW10
Holoview Collection-HC24
96SPx-17
Gold-17
96Stadium Club Members Only-12
96Summit-92
Artist's Proofs-92
Ice-92
Metal-92
Premium Stock-92
Untouchables-11
96Topps Picks-23
OPC Inserts-23
96Ultra-63
Gold Medallion-63
96Upper Deck-260
Generation Next-X13
Superstar Showdown-SS17A
96Upper Deck Ice-87
Parallel-87
Stanley Cup Foundation-S9
Stanley Cup Foundation Dynasty-S9
96Zenith-12
Artist's Proofs-12
96Swedish Semic Wien-172
97Beehive-34
Golden Portraits-34
97Black Diamond-84
Double Diamond-84
Triple Diamond-84
Quadruple Diamond-84
97Collector's Choice-87
97Collector's Choice-319
Crash the Game-C3A
Crash the Game-C3B
Crash the Game-C3C
Crash the Game Exchange-CR3
Star Quest-SQ68
97Crown Royale-55
Emerald Green-55
Ice Blue-55
Silver-55
97Donruss-32
Press Proofs Silver-32
Press Proofs Gold-32
97Donruss Canadian Ice-86
Dominion Series-86
Provincial Series-86
97Donruss Elite-103
Aspirations-103
Status-103
97Donruss Limited-173
97Donruss Limited-191
Exposure-173
Exposure-191
97Donruss Preferred-74
97Donruss Preferred-181
Cut to the Chase-74
Cut to the Chase-181
97Donruss Priority-161
Stamp of Approval-161
97Esso Olympic Hockey Heroes-26
97Esso Olympic Hockey Heroes French-26
97Katch-60
Gold-60
Silver-60
97Kraft-26
97Kraft 3-D World's Best-1
97Leaf-131
Fractal Matrix-131
Fractal Matrix Die Cuts-131
97Leaf International-131
Universal Ice-131
97McDonald's Upper Deck-18
97NHL Aces Playing Cards-21
97Pacific-138
Copper-138
Emerald Green-138
Ice Blue-138
Red-138
Silver-138
97Pacific Dynagon-52
Copper-52
Dark Grey-52
Emerald Green-52
Ice Blue-52
Red-52
Silver-52
Tandems-46
97Pacific Invincible-59
Copper-59
Emerald Green-59
Ice Blue-59
Red-59
Silver-59
97Pacific Omega-96
Copper-96
Dark Gray-96
Emerald Green-96
Gold-96
Ice Blue-96
97Panini Stickers-215
97Paramount-78
Copper-78
Dark Grey-78
Emerald Green-78
Ice Blue-78
Red-78
Silver-78
97Pinnacle-54
Artist's Proofs-54
Rink Collection-54
Press Plates Back Black-54
Press Plates Back Cyan-54
Press Plates Back Magenta-54
Press Plates Back Yellow-54
Press Plates Front Black-54
Press Plates Front Cyan-54
Press Plates Front Magenta-54
Press Plates Front Yellow-54
97Pinnacle Certified-66
Red-66
Mirror Blue-66
Mirror Gold-66
Mirror Red-66
97Pinnacle Inside-48
Coach's Collection-48
Executive Collection-48
97Pinnacle Tot Cert Platinum Blue-66
97Pinnacle Tot Cert Platinum Gold-66
97Pinnacle Totally Certified Platinum Red-66
97Pinnacle Tot Cert Mirror Platinum Gold-66
97Revolution-57
Copper-57
Emerald-57
Ice Blue-57
Silver-57
97Score-100
Artist's Proofs-100
Golden Blades-100
97SP Authentic-58
Icons-I32
Icons Die-Cuts-I32
Icons Embossed-I32
Sign of the Times-DW
97SPx-17
Bronze-17
Gold-17
Silver-17
Steel-17
DuoView-7
DuoView Autographs-6
Grand Finale-17
97Studio-95
Press Proofs Silver-95
Press Proofs Gold-95
97Upper Deck-65
Game Jerseys-GJ12
Sixth Sense Masters-SS10
Sixth Sense Wizards-SS10
Smooth Grooves-SG20
Three Star Selects-13B
97Upper Deck Diamond Vision-15
Signature Moves-15
97Upper Deck Ice-9
Parallel-9
Power Shift-9
97Zenith-62
Z-Gold-62
Z-Silver-62
97Zenith 5 x 7-50
Gold Impulse-50
Silver Impulse-50
98Aurora-77
Championship Fever-21
Championship Fever Copper-21
Championship Fever Ice Blue-21
Championship Fever Red-21
Championship Fever Silver-21
98Black Diamond-34
Double Diamond-34
Triple Diamond-34
Quadruple Diamond-34
98Bowman's Best-46
Refractors-46
Atomic Refractors-46
98Crown Royale-55
Limited Series-55
98Finest-133
No Protectors-133
No Protectors Refractors-133
Refractors-133
98Katch-57
98Kraft Fearless Forwards-12
98OPC Chrome-8
Refractors-8
98Pacific-217
Ice Blue-217
Red-217
98Pacific Dynagon Ice-77
Blue-77
Red-77
98Pacific Omega-97
Red-97
Opening Day Issue-97
98Panini Photocards-89
98Panini Stickers-197
98Paramount-93
Copper-93
Emerald Green-93
Holo-Electric-93
Ice Blue-93
Silver-93
98Revolution-58
Ice Shadow-58
Red-58
98SP Authentic-33
Power Shift-33
Authentics-4
Sign of the Times-DW
Sign of the Times Gold-DW
Stat Masters-S5
98SPx Finite-34
98SPx Finite-113
Radiance-34
Radiance-113
Spectrum-34
Spectrum-113
98SPx Top Prospects-27
Radiance-27
Spectrum-27
Premier Stars-PS28
98Topps-8
O-Pee-Chee-8
98Topps Gold Label Class 1-18
Black-18
Black One of One-18
One of One-18
Red-18
Red One of One-18
98Topps Gold Label Class 2-18
98Topps Gold Label Class 2 Black-18
98Topps Gold Label Class 2 Black 1 of 1-18
98Topps Gold Label Class 2 One of One-18
98Topps Gold Label Class 2 Red-18
98Topps Gold Label Class 2 Red One of One-18
98Topps Gold Label Class 3-18
98Topps Gold Label Class 3 Black-18
98Topps Gold Label Class 3 Black 1 of 1-18
98Topps Gold Label Class 3 One of One-18
98Topps Gold Label Class 3 Red-18
98Topps Gold Label Class 3 Red One of One-18
98UD Choice-85
98UD Choice Preview-85
98UD Choice Prime Choice Reserve-85
98UD Choice Reserve-85
98Upper Deck-90
Exclusives-90
Exclusives 1 of 1-90
Fantastic Finishers-FF21
Fantastic Finishers Quantum 1-FF21
Fantastic Finishers Quantum 2-FF21
Fantastic Finishers Quantum 3-FF21
Lord Stanley's Heroes-LS22
Lord Stanley's Heroes Quantum 1-LS22
Lord Stanley's Heroes Quantum 2-LS22
Lord Stanley's Heroes Quantum 3-LS22
Profiles-P22
Profiles Quantum 1-P22
Profiles Quantum 2-P22
Profiles Quantum 3-P22
Gold Reserve-90
98Upper Deck MVP-77
Gold Script-77
Silver Script-77
Super Script-77
ProSign-DW
99Aurora-60
Striped-60
Premiere Date-60
Premiere Date Striped-60
99BAP Memorabilia-204
Gold-204
Silver-204
99BAP Millennium-96
Emerald-96
Ruby-96
Sapphire-96
Signatures-96
Signatures Gold-96
99Black Diamond-40
Diamond Cut-40
Final Cut-40
99Crown Royale-58
Limited Series-58
Premiere Date-58
99Jell-O Partners of Power-8
99McDonald's Upper Deck-MCD11
99McDonald's Upper Deck-MCD11R
99O-Pee-Chee-104
99O-Pee-Chee Chrome-104
99O-Pee-Chee Chrome Refractors-104
99Pacific-167
Copper-167
Emerald Green-167
Gold-167
Ice Blue-167
Premiere Date-167
Red-167
Center Ice-12
Center Ice Proofs-12
99Pacific Dynagon Ice-86
Blue-86
Copper-86
Gold-86
Premiere Date-86
99Pacific Omega-96
Copper-96
Gold-96
Ice Blue-96
Premiere Date-96
99Pacific Prism-59
Holographic Blue-59
Holographic Gold-59
Holographic Mirror-59
Holographic Purple-59
Premiere Date-59
99Panini Stickers-243
99Paramount-97
Copper-97
Emerald-97
Gold-97
Holographic Emerald-97
Holographic Gold-97
Holographic Silver-97
Ice Blue-97
Premiere Date-97
Red-97
Silver-97
Ice Advantage-11
Ice Advantage Proofs-11
99Revolution-61
Premiere Date-61
Red-61
Shadow Series-61
Showstoppers-18
Copper-61
Gold-61
CSC Silver-61
99SP Authentic-34
99SPx-62
Radiance-62
Spectrum-62
99Stadium Club-81
First Day Issue-81
One of a Kind-81
Printing Plates Black-81
Printing Plates Cyan-81
Printing Plates Magenta-81
Printing Plates Yellow-81
Chrome-29
Chrome Refractors-29
99Topps/OPC-104
99Topps/OPC Chrome-104
Refractors-104
99Topps Gold Label Class 1-28
Black-28
Black One of One-28
One of One-28
Red-28
Red One of One-28
99Topps Gold Label Class 2-28
99Topps Gold Label Class 2 Black-28
99Topps Gold Label Class 2 Black 1 of 1-28
99Topps Gold Label Class 2 One of One-28
99Topps Gold Label Class 2 Red-28
99Topps Gold Label Class 2 Red One of One-28
99Topps Gold Label Class 3-28

99Topps Gold Label Class 3 Black-28
99Topps Gold Label Class 3 Black 1 of 1-28
99Topps Gold Label Class 3 One of One-28
99Topps Gold Label Class 3 Red-28
99Topps Gold Label Class 3 Red One of One-28
99Topps Premier Plus-18
Parallel-18
Game Pieces-GPDW
99Ultimate Victory-35
1/1-35
Parallel-35
Parallel 100-35
99Upper Deck-229
Exclusives-229
Exclusives 1 of 1-229
99Upper Deck Gold Reserve-229
99Upper Deck HoloGrFx-24
Ausome-24
99Upper Deck MVP-79
Gold Script-79
Silver Script-79
Super Script-79
99Upper Deck MVP SC Edition-72
Gold Script-72
Silver Script-72
Super Script-72
99Upper Deck Ovation-25
Standing Ovation-25
99Upper Deck Retro-31
Gold-31
Platinum-31
Inkredible-DW
Inkredible Level 2-DW
99Upper Deck Victory-108
99Upper Deck Victory-113
99Wayne Gretzky Hockey-67
Tools of Greatness-TGDW
00Aurora-59
Premiere Date-59
00BAP Memorabilia-73
Emerald-73
Ruby-73
Sapphire-73
Promos-73
00BAP Mem Chicago Sportsfest Copper-73
00BAP Memorabilia Chicago Sportsfest Blue-73
00BAP Memorabilia Chicago Sportsfest Gold-73
00BAP Memorabilia Chicago Sportsfest Ruby-73
00BAP Memorabilia Chicago Sun-Times Ruby-73
00BAP Memorabilia Chicago Sun-Times Gold-73
00BAP Mem Chicago Sun-Times Sapphire-73
00BAP Mem Toronto Fall Expo Copper-73
00BAP Memorabilia Toronto Fall Expo Gold-73
00BAP Memorabilia Toronto Fall Expo Ruby-73
00BAP Parkhurst 2000-P133
00BAP Signature Series-209
Emerald-209
Ruby-209
Sapphire-209
Autographs-86
Autographs Gold-86
Franchise Players-F12
00BAP Ultimate Memorabilia Autographs-38
Gold-38
00Black Diamond-24
Gold-24
00Crown Royale-44
Ice Blue-44
Limited Series-44
Premiere Date-44
Red-44
Jewels of the Crown-15
00Kraft-6
00McDonald's Pacific-16
Blue-16
Checklists-2
00O-Pee-Chee-81
00O-Pee-Chee Parallel-81
00Pacific-176
Copper-176
Gold-176
Ice Blue-176
Premiere Date-176
00Panini Stickers-158
00Paramount-101
Copper-101
Gold-101
Holo-Gold-101
Holo-Silver-101
Ice Blue-101
Premiere Date-101
Freeze Frame-17
Game Used Sticks-11
00Private Stock-41
Gold-41
Premiere Date-41
Retail-41
Silver-41
Game Gear-50
Game Gear Patches-50
PS-2001 Action-24
00Revolution-60
Blue-60
Premiere Date-60
Red-60
00SP Authentic-35
00SP Game Used-25
00SPx-26
Spectrum-26
00Stadium Club-4
00Titanium-38
Blue-38
Gold-38
Premiere Date-38
Red-38
Retail-38
00Titanium Draft Day Edition-45
Patches-45
00Topps/OPC-81
Parallel-81
00Topps Chrome-64
OPC Refractors-64
Refractors-64
00Topps Heritage-22
Chrome Parallel-22
00Topps Premier Plus-39
Blue Ice-39
00Topps Stars-18
Blue-18
00UD Heroes-47
00UD Pros and Prospects-35
00UD Reserve-35
00Upper Deck-296
Exclusives Tier 1-296
Exclusives Tier 2-296
00Upper Deck Ice-19
Immortals-19
Legends-19
Stars-19
00Upper Deck Legends-53
00Upper Deck Legends-54
Legendary Collection Bronze-53
Legendary Collection Bronze-54
Legendary Collection Gold-53
Legendary Collection Gold-54
Legendary Collection Silver-53
Legendary Collection Silver-54
00Upper Deck MVP-74
First Stars-74
Second Stars-74
Third Stars-74
00Upper Deck Victory-92
00Upper Deck Victory-97
00Upper Deck Victory-303
00Upper Deck Vintage-138
00Upper Deck Vintage-148
00Upper Deck Vintage-149
00Vanguard-44
Dual Game-Worn Jerseys-7
Dual Game-Worn Patches-7
High Voltage-15
High Voltage Gold-15
High Voltage Green-15
High Voltage Red-15
High Voltage Silver-15
Holographic Gold-44
Holographic Purple-44
Pacific Proofs-44
01Atomic-84
Blue-84
Gold-84
Premiere Date-84
Red-84
01BAP Memorabilia-282
01BAP Memorabilia-371
Emerald-282
Emerald-371
Ruby-282
Ruby-371
Sapphire-282
Sapphire-371
All-Star Jerseys-ASJ9
All-Star Emblems-ASE9
All-Star Numbers-ASN9
All-Star Teammates-AST4
All-Star Teammates-AST8
Country of Origin-CO17
01BAP Signature Series Certified 100-C12
01BAP Signature Series Certified 50-C12
01BAP Signature Series Certified 1 of 1's-C12
01BAP Signature Series Autographs-LDW
01BAP Signature Series Autographs Gold-LDW
01BAP Signature Series Franchise Jerseys-FP-26
01BAP Sig Series He Shoots/Scores Prizes-30
01BAP Sig Series International Medals-IS-4
01BAP Signature Series Jerseys-GJ-56
01BAP Signature Series Jersey Autographs-GUDW
01BAP Sig Series Jersey and Stick Cards-GSJ-56
01BAP Signature Series Emblems-GUE-25
01BAP Signature Series Numbers-ITN-25
01BAP Signature Series Teammates-TM-26
01BAP Ultimate Memorabilia Dynamic Duos-15
01BAP Ultimate Memorabilia Emblems-25
01BAP Ultimate Memorabilia Gloves Are Off-15
01BAP Ultimate Memorabilia Jerseys-25
01BAP Ultimate Mem Jerseys and Sticks-25
01BAP Ultimate Memorabilia Numbers-25
01BAP Ultimate Memorabilia Name Plates-40
01BAP Update Travel Plans-TP12
01Bowman YoungStars-30
Gold-30
Ice Cubed-30
01Crown Royale-122
Blue-122
Premiere Date-122
Red-122
Retail-122
All-Star Honors-18
01eTopps-35
01McDonald's Pacific-34
Cosmic Force-3
01O-Pee-Chee-24
01O-Pee-Chee-24U
01O-Pee-Chee Heritage Parallel-24
01O-Pee-Chee Heritage Parallel Limited-24
01O-Pee-Chee Premier Parallel-24
01Pacific-167
01Pacific-430
Extreme LTD-167
Gold-430
Hobby LTD-167
Premiere Date-167
Retail LTD-167
All-Stars-NA7
Jerseys-15
01Pacific Adrenaline-164
Blue-164
Premiere Date-164
Red-164
Retail-164
Jerseys-41
01Pacific Arena Exclusives-167
01Pacific Arena Exclusives-430
01Pacific Heads-Up-82
Blue-82
Premiere Date-82
Red-82
Silver-82
All-Star Net-3
Quad Jerseys-22
01Parkhurst-233
He Shoots-He Scores Prizes-27
Sticks-PS57
Waving the Flag-22
01Private Stock-83
Gold-83
Premiere Date-83
Retail-83
Silver-83
Game Gear-89
Game Gear Patches-89
01Private Stock Pacific Nights-83
01Private Stock PS-2002-63
01SP Authentic-76
Limited-76
Limited Gold-76
Buybacks-9
Sign of the Times-DW
Sign of the Times-WM
Sign of the Times-GWA
01SP Game Used-51
Inked Sweaters-DSWM
01SPx-60
Signs of Xcellence-DW
01Stadium Club-107
Award Winners-107
Master Photos-107
01Titanium-120
Hobby Parallel-120
Premiere Date-120
Retail-120
Retail Parallel-120
01Topps-24
01Topps-24U
Heritage Parallel-24
Heritage Parallel Limited-24
OPC Parallel-24
Own The Game-OTG8
01Topps Chrome-24
Refractors-24
Black Border Refractors-24
01Topps Heritage-161
01Topps Reserve-100
01UD Challenge for the Cup-74
Jerseys-FPDW
Jersey Autographs-FPWE
01UD Honor Roll Jerseys-J-DW
01UD Honor Roll Jerseys Gold-J-DW
01UD Mask Collection-85
Gold-85
01UD Playmakers-87
01UD Premier Collection Signatures-DW
01UD Premier Collection Signatures Black-DW
01UD Top Shelf-117
Jerseys-DW
Jersey Autographs-DW
01Upper Deck-155
Exclusives-155
Game Jersey Autographs-SDW
Leaders of the Pack-LP13
Patches-PDW
Pride of a Nation-PNDW
Pride of a Nation-TPAWL
01Upper Deck Ice-119
Jerseys-J-DW
01Upper Deck MVP-166
01Upper Deck Victory-139
01Upper Deck Victory-422
Gold-139
Gold-422
01Upper Deck Vintage-220
01Vanguard-84
Blue-84
Red-84
Memorabilia-47
One of Ones-84
Premiere Date-84
Proofs-84
Quebec Tournament Heroes-9
02BAP All-Star Edition-96
Jerseys-96
Jerseys Gold-96
Jerseys Silver-96
02BAP First Edition-26
Jerseys-26
02BAP Memorabilia-103
Emerald-103
Ruby-103
Sapphire-103
All-Star Jerseys-ASJ-58
NHL All-Star Game-103
NHL All-Star Game Blue-103
NHL All-Star Game Green-103
NHL All-Star Game Red-103
Teammates-TM-17
02BAP Memorabilia Toronto Fall Expo-103
02BAP Signature Series-163
Autographs-163
Autograph Buybacks 1999-96
Autograph Buybacks 2001-LDW
Autographs Gold-163
Jerseys-SGJ43
Jersey Autographs-SGJ43
Team Quads-TQ15
02BAP Ultimate Memorabilia Hat Tricks-12
02Blues Magnets-3
02Blues Team Issue-24
02Bowman YoungStars-10
Gold-10
Silver-10
02Crown Royale-83
Blue-83
Red-83
Retail-83
02ITG Used-68
02ITG Used-168
Jerseys-GUJ43
Jersey Autographs-GUJ43
Jerseys Gold-GUJ43
Jersey and Stick-SJ43
Jersey and Stick Gold-SJ43
Triple Memorabilia-TM14
Triple Memorabilia Gold-TM14
02O-Pee-Chee-257
02O-Pee-Chee Premier Blue Parallel-257
02O-Pee-Chee Premier Red Parallel-257
02O-Pee-Chee Factory Set-257
02Pacific-330
Blue-330
Red-330
02Pacific Complete-34
Red-34
02Pacific Exclusive-147
02Pacific Heads-Up-106
Blue-106
Purple-106
Red-106
02Pacific Quest for the Cup-85
Gold-85
Jerseys-19
02Parkhurst-126
Bronze-126
Gold-126
Silver-126
College Ranks-CR11
College Ranks Jerseys-CRM11
Jerseys-GJ26
Stick and Jerseys-SJ26
Teammates-TT16
02Parkhurst Retro-47
Minis-47
02Private Stock Reserve-85
Blue-85
Red-85
Retail-85
02SP Authentic-77
Beckett Promos-77
02SP Game Used Authentic Fabrics-CFWD
02SP Game Used Authentic Fabrics Gold-CFWD
02SP Game Used Authentic Fabrics Rainbow-CFWD
02Stadium Club-79
Silver Decoy Cards-79
Proofs-79
02Titanium-85
Blue-85
Red-85
Retail-85
02Topps-257
OPC Blue Parallel-257
OPC Red Parallel-257
Topps/OPC Hometown Heroes-HHU16
Factory Set-257
Factory Set Hometown Heroes-HHU16
02Topps Chrome-140
Black Border Refractors-140
Refractors-140
02Topps Heritage-38
Chrome Parallel-38
02Topps Total-131
02UD Artistic Impressions-77
Gold-77
02UD Artistic Impressions Beckett Promos-77
02UD Artistic Impressions Retrospectives-R77
02UD Artistic Impressions Retrospect Gold-R77
02UD Artistic Impress Retrospect Silver-R77
02UD Top Shelf Clutch Performers-CPDW
02UD Top Shelf Signatures-DW
02Upper Deck-151
Exclusives-151
02Upper Deck Classic Portraits-86
Hockey Royalty-GWA
Hockey Royalty Limited-GWA
02Upper Deck MVP-159
Gold-159
Classics-159
Golden Classics-159
02Upper Deck Rookie Update-83
02Upper Deck Victory-187
Bronze-187
Gold-187
Silver-187
National Pride-NP60
02Upper Deck Vintage-221
Green Backs-221
02Vanguard-84
LTD-84
03BAP Memorabilia-24
Emerald-24
Gold-24
Ruby-24
Sapphire-24
Stanley Cup Playoffs-SCP-3
03BAP Ultimate Memorabilia Autographs-79
Gold-79
03BAP Ultimate Mem Auto Jerseys-79
03BAP Ultimate Mem Auto Emblems-79
03BAP Ultimate Memorabilia Hat Tricks-17
03BAP Ultimate Memorabilia Triple Threads-19
03Beehive-169
Gold-169
Silver-169
Jerseys-JT34
03Black Diamond-39
Black-39
Green-39
Red-39
Threads-DT-DW
Threads Green-DT-DW
Threads Red-DT-DW
Threads Black-DT-DW
03Blues Team Set-28
03Crown Royale-84
Blue-84
Retail-84
03ITG Action-546
Jerseys-M149
03ITG Used Signature Series-66
Gold-66
Autographs-DW
Autographs Gold-DW
Teammates-8
Teammates Gold-8
03NHL Sticker Collection-276
03O-Pee-Chee-125
03OPC Blue-125
03OPC Gold-125
03OPC Red-125
03Pacific-291
Blue-291
Red-291
03Pacific Calder-85
Silver-85
03Pacific Complete-294
Red-294
03Pacific Exhibit-126
Blue Backs-126
Yellow Backs-126
03Pacific Invincible-82
Blue-82
Red-82
Retail-82
03Pacific Luxury Suite-46A
03Pacific Luxury Suite-46B
03Pacific Luxury Suite-46C
03Pacific Prism-140
Blue-140
Patches-140
Red-140
Retail-140
03Pacific Quest for the Cup-87
Blue-87
03Parkhurst Original Six New York-32
03Private Stock Reserve-198
Blue-198
Patches-198
Red-198
Retail-198
03SP Authentic-75
Limited-75
03SP Game Used-101
Gold-101
Authentic Fabrics-DFWT
Authentic Fabrics Gold-DFWT
03SPx Fantasy Franchise-FF-TWM
03SPx Fantasy Franchise Limited-FF-TWM
03SPx Origins-O-DW
03Titanium-180
Hobby Jersey Number Parallels-180
Patches-180
Retail-180
03Topps-125
Blue-125
Gold-125
Red-125
Topps/OPC Idols-UI3
03Topps C55-23
Minis-23
Minis American Back-23
Minis American Back Red-23
Minis Bazooka Back-23
Minis Brooklyn Back-23
Minis Hat Trick Back-23
Minis O Canada Back-23
Minis O Canada Back Red-23
Minis Stanley Cup Back-23
03Topps Pristine Stick Portions-PPS-DW
03Topps Pristine Stick Portion Refractors-PPS-DW
03UD Honor Roll-75
03UD Premier Collection-48
Stars-ST-DW
Stars Patches-ST-DW
Teammates-PT-SB
Teammates Patches-PT-SB
03Upper Deck-412
Canadian Exclusives-412
HG-412
UD Exclusives-412
Classic Portraits Classic Colors-CC-DW
03Upper Deck Ice-76
Gold-76
03Upper Deck MVP-361
Gold Script-361
Silver Script-361
Canadian Exclusives-361
03Upper Deck Rookie Update-75
Skills-SKDW
Super Stars-SSDW
03Upper Deck Victory-165
Bronze-165
Gold-165
Silver-165
03Toronto Star-80
04Pacific-225
Blue-225
Red-225
04SP Authentic-77
04SP Authentic-141
Limited-77
Limited-141
Buybacks-44
Buybacks-45
Buybacks-46
Buybacks-47
Rookie Review-RR-DW
Sign of the Times-ST-DW
Sign of the Times-DS-PW
Sign of the Times-SS-USA
04Ultimate Collection Dual Logos-UL2-WT
04Upper Deck World Cup Tribute-DWMOCD
04Upper Deck World Cup Tribute-KTDWBH
04German DEL Superstars-SU09
05Be A Player-77
First Period-77
Second Period-77
Third Period-77
Overtime-77
05Beehive-78
05Beehive-213
Beige -78
Blue -78
Gold-78
Red -78
Matte-78
Matted Materials-MMDW
Matted Materials Remarkable-RMDW
PhotoGraphs-PGDW
05Black Diamond-115
Emerald-115
Gold-115
Onyx-115
Ruby-115
05Blues Team Set-21
05Hot Prospects-19
En Fuego-19
Red Hot-19
White Hot-19
05Panini Stickers-333
05Parkhurst-90
Facsimile Auto Parallel-90
True Colors-TCCAR
True Colors-TCCAR
05SP Authentic-18
05SP Authentic-130
Limited-18
Limited-130
Marks of Distinction-MDDW
Prestigious Pairings-PPTW
Sign of the Times-DW
05SP Game Used-86
Autographs-86
Gold-86
Authentic Fabrics-AF-DW
Authentic Fabrics Autographs-AAF-DW
Authentic Fabrics Dual-WT
Authentic Fabrics Gold-AF-DW
Authentic Patches-AP-DW
Authentic Patches Autographs-AAP-DW
Authentic Patches Dual-WT
Awesome Authentics-AA-DW
Significant Numbers-SN-DW
Statscriptions-ST-DW
05SPx-79
05SPx-99
Spectrum-79
Spectrum-99
Winning Combos-WC-WM
Winning Combos-WC-WT
Winning Combos Gold-WC-WM
Winning Combos Gold-WC-WT
Winning Combos Spectrum-WC-WM
Winning Combos Spectrum-WC-WT
Winning Materials-WM-DW
Winning Materials Autographs-AWM-DW
Winning Materials Gold-WM-DW
Winning Materials Spectrum-WM-DW
05The Cup-22
Gold-22
Black Rainbow-22
Dual NHL Shields-DSWT
Emblems of Endorsement-EEDW
Honorable Numbers-HNDW
Limited Logos-LLDW
Masterpiece Pressplates-22
Patch Variation-P22
Patch Variation Autographs-AP22
Scripted Numbers Dual-DSNSW
Scripted Swatches-SSDW
Signature Patches-SPDW
05UD Artifacts-87
Blue-87
Gold-87
Green-87
Pewter-87
Red-87
Frozen Artifacts-FA-DW
Frozen Artifacts Autographed-FA-DW
Frozen Artifacts Copper-FA-DW
Frozen Artifacts Dual-FAD-DW
Frozen Artifacts Dual Autographed-FAD-DW
Frozen Artifacts Dual Copper-FAD-DW
Frozen Artifacts Dual Gold-FAD-DW
Frozen Artifacts Dual Maroon-FAD-DW
Frozen Artifacts Dual Pewter-FAD-DW
Frozen Artifacts Dual Silver-FAD-DW
Frozen Artifacts Gold-FA-DW
Frozen Artifacts Maroon-FA-DW
Frozen Artifacts Patches-FP-DW
Frozen Artifacts Patches Autographed-FP-DW
Frozen Artifacts Patches Dual-FPD-DW
Frozen Artifacts Patches Dual Autos-FPD-DW
Frozen Artifacts Patches Pewter-FP-DW
Frozen Artifacts Patches Silver-FP-DW
Frozen Artifacts Pewter-FA-DW
Frozen Artifacts Silver-FA-DW
Gold Autographed-87
Remarkable Artifacts-RA-DW
Remarkable Artifacts Dual-RA-DW
05UD PowerPlay-77
Rainbow-77
Specialists-TSDW
Specialists Patches-SPDW
05Ultimate Collection-17
Gold-17
Endorsed Emblems-EEDW
Jerseys-JDW
National Heroes Jerseys-NHJDW
National Heroes Patches-NHPDW
Premium Patches-PPDW
Premium Swatches-PSDW
Ultimate Achievements-UADW
Ultimate Patches-PDW
Ultimate Signatures-USDW
05Ultra-166
Gold-166
Fresh Ink-FI-DW
Fresh Ink Blue-FI-DW
Ice-166
Scoring Kings-SK19
Scoring Kings Jerseys-SKJ-DW
Scoring Kings Jersey Autographs-KAJ-DW
Scoring Kings Patches-SKP-DW
Scoring Kings Patch Autographs-KAP-DW
05Upper Deck-410
05Upper Deck All-Time Greatest-49
05Upper Deck Big Playmakers-B-DW
05Upper Deck Jerseys-J-DW
05Upper Deck Jerseys Series II-J2DW
05Upper Deck Majestic Materials-MMDW
05Upper Deck Notable Numbers-N-DW
05Upper Deck Patches-P-DW
05Upper Deck Ice-85
Rainbow-85
Frozen Fabrics-FFDW
Frozen Fabrics Autographs-AFFDW
Frozen Fabrics Glass-FFDW
Frozen Fabrics Patches-FFPDW
Frozen Fabrics Patch Autographs-FAPDW
Signature Swatches-SSDW
05Upper Deck MVP-334
Gold-334
Platinum-334
ProSign-P-DW
05Upper Deck Rookie Update-18
05Upper Deck Trilogy-78
05Upper Deck Trilogy-152
Crystal-152
Honorary Patches-HP-DW
Honorary Patch Scripts-HSP-DW
Honorary Swatches-HS-DW
Honorary Swatch Scripts-HSS-DW
05Upper Deck Victory-166
Black-166
Gold-166
Silver-166
Stars on Ice-SI38
06Be A Player-8
Autographs-8
Signatures-DW
Signatures 10-10
Signatures 25-10
Signatures Duals-DWB
Signatures Trios-TWBS
Up Close and Personal-UC16
Up Close and Personal Autographs-UC16
06Be A Player Portraits-88
Dual Signature Portraits-DSWG
Signature Portraits-SPDW
06Beehive-14
Gold-14
Matte-14
06Black Diamond-123
Black-123
Gold-123
Ruby-123
Gemography-GDW
Jerseys-JDW
Jerseys Black-JDW
Jerseys Gold-JDW
Jerseys Ruby-JDW
Jerseys Black Autographs -JDW
06Flair Showcase-23
Parallel-23
06Fleer-168
Tiffany-168
Fabricology-FDW
06Hot Prospects-80
Red Hot-80
White Hot-80
06O-Pee-Chee-437
06O-Pee-Chee-667
Rainbow-437
Rainbow-667
Swatches-S-DW
06Panini Stickers-340
06SP Authentic-13
06SP Authentic-111
Limited-13
Limited-111
06SP Game Used-87
Gold-87
Rainbow-87
Authentic Fabrics-AFDW
Authentic Fabrics Parallel-AFDW
Authentic Fabrics Patches-AFDW
Authentic Fabrics Dual-AF2WG
Authentic Fabrics Dual Patches-AF2WG
Authentic Fabrics Triple-AF3STL
Authentic Fabrics Triple Patches-AF3STL
Authentic Fabrics Quads-AF4MWGD
Authentic Fabrics Quads Patches-AF4MWGD
06SPx-88
Spectrum-88
SPxcitement-X85
SPxcitement Spectrum-X85
SPxcitement Autographs-X85
Winning Materials-WMDW
Winning Materials Spectrum-WMDW
Winning Materials Autographs-WMDW
06The Cup NHL Shields Duals-DSHTW
06The Cup NHL Shields Duals-DSHWG
06UD Artifacts-15
Blue-15
Gold-15
Platinum-15
Radiance-15
Autographed Radiance Parallel-15
Red-15
Treasured Patches Black-TSWE
Treasured Patches Blue-TSWE
Treasured Patches Gold-TSWE
Treasured Patches Platinum-TSWE
Treasured Patches Red-TSWE
Treasured Patches Autographed Black Tag
Parallel-TSWE
Treasured Swatches-TSWE
Treasured Swatches Black-TSWE
Treasured Swatches Blue-TSWE
Treasured Swatches Gold-TSWE
Treasured Swatches Platinum-TSWE
Treasured Swatches Red-TSWE
Treasured Swatches Autographed Black-TSWE
Tundra Tandems-TTTW
Tundra Tandems-TTWG
Tundra Tandems Black-TTTW
Tundra Tandems Black-TTWG
Tundra Tandems Blue-TTTW
Tundra Tandems Blue-TTWG
Tundra Tandems Gold-TTTW
Tundra Tandems Gold-TTWG
Tundra Tandems Platinum-TTTW
Tundra Tandems Platinum-TTWG
Tundra Tandems Red-TTTW
Tundra Tandems Red-TTWG
Tundra Tandems Dual Patches Red-TTTW
Tundra Tandems Dual Patches Red-TTWG
06UD Powerplay-85
Impact Rainbow-85
Power Marks-PMDW
Specialists-SDW
Specialists Patches-PDW
06Ultra-169
Gold Medallion-169
Ice Medallion-169
06Upper Deck Arena Giveaways-STL6
06Upper Deck-416
Exclusives Parallel-416
High Gloss Parallel-416
Game Jerseys-JDW
Game Patches-PDW
Hometown Heroes-HH54
Masterpieces-416
Oversized Wal-Mart Exclusives-417
Signatures-SDW
Signature Sensations-SSDW
06Upper Deck MVP-256
Gold Script-256
Super Script-256
Jerseys-OJKW
Jerseys-OJWA
Jerseys-OJWC
06Upper Deck Ovation-158
06Upper Deck Sweet Shot-89
Sweet Stitches-SSDW
Sweet Stitches Duals-SSDW
Sweet Stitches Triples-SSDW
06Upper Deck Trilogy-86
Honorary Scripted Patches-HSPDW
Honorary Scripted Swatches-HSSDW
Scripts-TSDW
06Upper Deck Victory-37
06Upper Deck Victory-272
06Upper Deck Victory Black-37
06Upper Deck Victory Gold-37
07Upper Deck Victory-114
Black-114
Gold-114

Weiland, Ralph

33O-Pee-Chee V304A-27
33V129-24
33V357 Ice Kings-65
34Beehive Group I Photos-36
34Sweet Caporal-39
37V356 Worldwide Gum-69
39O-Pee-Chee V301-1-92
83Hall of Fame Postcards-H16
85Hall of Fame-120
91Bruins Sports Action Legends-33
06ITG Ultimate Memorabilia Beantown's Best Autos-4
06ITG Ultimate Memorabilia Sensational Sens Autos-2

Weilleux, Eric

98Finnish Keraliysarja-203

Weiman, Shawn

03Augusta Lynx-48
04Oklahoma City Blazers-18
05Fresno Falcons-19

Weiman, Tyler

04Colorado Eagles-20
06Albany River Rats-21

Weimer, Marty

86Saskatoon Blades Photos-20

Weinberger, Randy

95Saskatoon Blades-22

Weinfurter, Michael

94German DEL-338
95German DEL-295
99German Bundesliga 2-248

Weingartner, Rob

93Wichita Thunder-16
94Central Hockey League-124
95Central Hockey League-87
95Oklahoma Coyotes RHI-17
96Louisiana Ice Gators-20
96Louisiana Ice Gators II-20
98Louisiana Ice Gators-22

Weinhandl, Mattias

98Black Diamond-112
Double Diamond-112
Triple Diamond-112
Quadruple Diamond-112
98SPx Top Prospects-82
Radiance-82
Spectrum-82
99Black Diamond-118
Diamond Cut-118
Final Cut-118
99Upper Deck-327
Exclusives-327
Exclusives 1 of 1-327
99Upper Deck Gold Reserve-327
99Upper Deck Ovation-80
Standing Ovation-80
99Swedish Upper Deck-178
99Swedish Upper Deck-214
Snapshots-13
00Swedish Upper Deck-160
00Swedish Upper Deck-207
00Swedish Upper Deck-219
SHL Excellence-S5
SHL Signatures-MI
Top Draws-T10
Top Playmakers-P8
02Bowman YoungStars-156
Gold-156
Silver-156
Autographs-MW
Jerseys-MW
Patches-MW
Double Stuff-MW
Triple Stuff-MW
Rivals-AHMW
Rivals Patches-11
Sticks-MW
02Crown Royale Blue-126
02Crown Royale Purple-126
02Crown Royale Red-126
02Crown Royale Retail-126
02Pacific Calder-83
Silver-83
02Pacific Complete-520
Red-520
02Private Stock Reserve-172
Blue-172
Red-172
02Swedish SHL Promos-TCC8
02Swedish SHL Sharpshooters-SS8
03Bowman Future Fabrics-FF-MW
03Bowman Future Fabric Patches-MW
03Bowman Future Rivals-WL
03Bowman Future Rivals Patches-WL
03eTopps-17
03ITG Action-385
03O-Pee-Chee-165
03OPC Blue-165
03OPC Gold-165
03OPC Red-165
03Pacific-217
Blue-217
Red-217
03Pacific Complete-477
Red-477
03Pacific Invincible New Sensations-17
03Private Stock Reserve-67
Blue-67
Red-67
Retail-67
03Topps-165
Blue-165
Gold-165
Red-165
Traded Future Phenoms-FP-MW
03Upper Deck MVP-272
Gold Script-272
Silver Script-272
Canadian Exclusives-272
03Pacific AHL Prospects-12
Gold-12
04Swedish Alfabilder Alfa Stars-25
04Swedish Alfabilder Autographs-128
04Swedish Alfabilder Limited Autographs-128
04Swedish Alfabilder Proof Parallels-25
04Swedish Elitset-244
Gold-244
04Swedish MoDo Postcards-4
04Swedish Pure Skills-66
Parallel-66
Signatures-12
05Be A Player Signatures-MW
05Be A Player Signatures Gold-MW
05Swedish SHL Elitset-98
Gold-98

Weinrich, Alexander

99Danish Hockey League-9

Weinrich, Eric

88ProCards AHL-345
89Devils Caretta-28
89ProCards AHL-222
90Bowman-90
Tiffany-90
90Devils Team Issue-30
90O-Pee-Chee-416
90Pro Set-622
90Score-389
Canadian-389
90Upper Deck-245
French-245
91Bowman-278
91O-Pee-Chee-10
91O-Pee-Chee-92
91Panini Stickers-223
91Parkhurst-318
French-318
91Pinnacle-89
French-89
91Pro Set-133
French-133
Platinum PC-PC10
91Score American-131
91Score American-350
91Score Canadian Bilingual-131
91Score Canadian Bilingual-380
91Score Canadian English-131
91Score Canadian English-380
91Score Young Superstars-26
91Stadium Club-339
91Topps-10
91Topps-92
91Upper Deck-44
91Upper Deck-344
91Upper Deck-509
French-44
French-344
French-509
92Bowman-343
92O-Pee-Chee-95
92OPC Premier-63
92Parkhurst-56
Emerald Ice-56
92Pinnacle-297
French-297
92Score-308
Canadian-308
92Stadium Club-165
92Topps-399
Gold-399G
92Ultra-76
92Ultra-306
92Upper Deck-195
92Upper Deck-553
92Whalers Dairymart-23
92Finnish Semic-154
93Blackhawks Coke-16
93Donruss-136
93Donruss-416
93Leaf-271
93OPC Premier-195
Gold-195
93Panini Stickers-130
93Parkhurst-311
Emerald Ice-311
93Pinnacle-281
Canadian-281
93PowerPlay-111
93PowerPlay-319
93Score-227
93Score-573
Gold-573
Canadian-227
Canadian-573
Canadian Gold-573
93Topps/OPC Premier-195
Gold-195
93Ultra-295
93Upper Deck-497
94Be A Player-R19
Signature Cards-139

94Blackhawks Coke-21
94Donruss-302
94EA Sports-56
94Leaf-221
94OPC Premier-106
Special Effects-106
94Parkhurst-43
Gold-43
Vintage-V83
94Pinnacle-186
Artist's Proofs-186
Rink Collection-186
94Topps/OPC Premier-106
Special Effects-106
94Upper Deck-119
Electric Ice-119
94Finnish Jaa Kiekko-112
95Blackhawks Coke-19
95Collector's Choice-63
Player's Club-63
Player's Club Platinum-63
95Parkhurst International-310
Emerald Ice-310
95Pinnacle-182
Artist's Proofs-182
Rink Collection-182
95Topps-289
OPC Inserts-289
95Upper Deck-45
Electric Ice-45
Electric Ice Gold-45
95Swedish Globe World Championships-108
96Be A Player-71
Autographs-71
Autographs Silver-71
96Collector's Choice-51
96Upper Deck-34
Generation Next-X4
96Upper Deck Ice-12
Parallel-12
97Collector's Choice-52
97Pacific Invincible NHL Regime-49
97Panini Stickers-134
97Upper Deck-246
98Be A Player-30
Press Release-30
98BAP Gold-30
98BAP Autographs-30
98BAP Autographs Gold-30
98BAP Tampa Bay All Star Game-30
98Canadiens Team Issue-25
98Pacific-153
Ice Blue-153
Red-153
98Panini Stickers-117
98Paramount-50
Copper-50
Emerald Green-50
Holo-Electric-50
Ice Blue-50
Silver-50
98Upper Deck-67
Exclusives-67
Exclusives 1 of 1-67
Gold Reserve-67
98Upper Deck MVP-107
Gold Script-107
Silver Script-107
Super Script-107
99Pacific-213
Copper-213
Emerald Green-213
Gold-213
Ice Blue-213
Premiere Date-213
Red-213
99Panini Stickers-74
99Upper Deck-68
Exclusives-68
Exclusives 1 of 1-68
99Upper Deck Gold Reserve-68
99Upper Deck MVP-103
Gold Script-103
Silver Script-103
Super Script-103
99Upper Deck Victory-147
99Wayne Gretzky Hockey-89
00BAP Memorabilia-320
Emerald-320
Ruby-320
Sapphire-320
Promos-320
00BAP Mem Chicago Sportsfest Copper-320
00BAP Memorabilia Chicago Sportsfest Blue-320
00BAP Memorabilia Chicago Sportsfest Gold-320
00BAP Memorabilia Chicago Sportsfest Ruby-320
00BAP Memorabilia Chicago Sun-Times Ruby-320
00BAP Memorabilia Chicago Sun-Times Gold-320
00BAP Mem Chicago Sun-Times Sapphire-320
00BAP Mem Toronto Fall Expo Copper-320
00BAP Memorabilia Toronto Fall Expo Gold-320
00BAP Memorabilia Toronto Fall Expo Ruby-320
00Canadiens Postcards-29
00Pacific-216
Copper-216
Gold-216
Ice Blue-216
Premiere Date-216
00Private Stock Game Gear-60
00Titanium Game Gear-29
00Titanium Game Gear-101
00Titanium Game Gear Patches-101
00Titanium Draft Day Edition-9
Patches-9
00Upper Deck-322
Exclusives Tier 1-322
Exclusives Tier 2-322
00Upper Deck Legends-70
Legendary Collection Bronze-70
Legendary Collection Gold-70
Legendary Collection Silver-70
00Upper Deck Victory-120
00Upper Deck Vintage-187
01BAP Signature Series-120
Autographs-120
Autographs Gold-120
01Flyers Postcards-22
01Pacific-41
Extreme LTD-41
Hobby LTD-41
Premiere Date-41
Retail LTD-41
Jerseys-2
01Pacific Arena Exclusives-41
01Parkhurst-249
01Topps Heritage-181
01Upper Deck Victory-32
Gold-32
01Vanguard Memorabilia-21
01Vanguard Patches-21
02BAP Sig Series Auto Buybacks 1998-30
02BAP Sig Series Auto Buybacks 2001-120
02Flyers Postcards-1
02Pacific-289
Blue-289
Red-289
02Pacific Complete-192
Red-192
02Topps Total-343
02Upper Deck-128
Exclusives-128
02Upper Deck Vintage-190
03Flyers Postcards-23
03ITG Action-475
03Pacific Complete-90
Red-90
03Upper Deck-142
Canadian Exclusives-142
HG-142
03Upper Deck MVP-317
Gold Script-317
Silver Script-317
Canadian Exclusives-317
05Be A Player Quad Signatures-BLUE
05Be A Player Signatures-EW
05Be A Player Signatures Gold-EW
05Blues Team Set-22
05Parkhurst Facsimile Auto Parallel-422
06Portland Pirates-2

Weinrich, Jason
92Maine Black Bears-6
93Maine Black Bears-39
94Huntington Blizzard-21
99Tallahassee Tiger Sharks-18

Weinstock, Ulf
71Swedish Hockey-162
72Swedish Stickers-155
73Swedish Stickers-44
74Swedish Stickers-195
79Panini Stickers-187
81Swedish Semic Hockey VM Stickers-3
83Swedish Semic Elitserien-129

Weir, Bert
84Ottawa 67's-27

Weir, Bill
98Quad-City Mallards-22
99Alexandria Warthogs-22

Weir, Matt
01London Knights-24
02London Knights-10
03Lincoln Stars Update-37

Weir, Nolan
91Air Canada SJHL-C38
92Saskatchewan JHL-16
02Macon Trax-10

Weir, Stan
74NHL Action Stamps-63
74O-Pee-Chee NHL-355
75Maple Leafs Postcards-27
75O-Pee-Chee NHL-132
75O-Pee-Chee NHL-316
75Topps-132
75Topps-316
76Maple Leafs Postcards-23
76O-Pee-Chee NHL-270
77O-Pee-Chee NHL-356
79Oilers Postcards-23
79O-Pee-Chee-331
80O-Pee-Chee-153
80Pepsi-Cola Caps-40
80Topps-153
81Oilers Red Rooster-21
81Oilers West Edmonton Mall-9
81O-Pee-Chee-124
88Oilers Tenth Anniversary-66

Weir, Wally
76Nordiques Marie Antoinette-14
76Nordiques Postcards-20
79O-Pee-Chee-388
80Nordiques Postcards-28
80Pepsi-Cola Caps-79
81Nordiques Postcards-21
81O-Pee-Chee-284
82Nordiques Postcards-25
82O-Pee-Chee-297
82Post Cereal-16
83Nordiques Postcards-31
83O-Pee-Chee-306
83Vachon-79

Weis, Rudiger
94German First League-200

Weisbrod, John
92Kansas City Blades-17

Weise, Dale
05Swift Current Broncos-17
06Swift Current Broncos-9

Weisenbach, Heinz
72Finnish Semic World Championship-106
72Swedish Semic World Championship-106

Weisenbach, Michael
94German First League-195

Weishaar, Toby
917th Inn. Sketch WHL-166
92Tacoma Rockets-28

Weishaupt, Erich
79Panini Stickers-96
82Swedish Semic VM Stickers-101
83Swedish Semic VM Stickers-101

Weising, Rocky
98Kansas City Blades-13

Weismann, Paul
99German DEL-260

Weiss, Alfred
94German First League-62

Weiss, Ben
93Quebec Pee-Wee Tournament-683

Weiss, Dave
84Kitchener Rangers-10
85Kitchener Rangers-6
86Kitchener Rangers-6
87Kingston Canadians-9
96Arizona Icecats-21

Weiss, Doug
88ProCards AHL-324
89Johnstown Chiefs-31
91Johnstown Chiefs-7

Weiss, Ken
93Richmond Renegades-1

Weiss, Markus
94German First League-277

Weiss, Shaun
92Disney Mighty Ducks Movie-6

Weiss, Stephen
00UD CHL Prospects-21
00UD CHL Prospects-92
Future Leaders-FL4
01BAP Memorabilia-448
Emerald-448
Ruby-448
Sapphire-448
Draft Redemptions-4
01Parkhurst-318
01Titanium Draft Day Edition-133
01UD Mask Collection-145
Gold-145
01UD Premier Collection-63
01UD Top Shelf-137
01Plymouth Whalers-3
01Plymouth Whalers-28
01UD Prospects-27
Autographs-A-SW
Jersey Autographs-S-SW
Jerseys-J-SW
Jerseys-C-BW
Jerseys-C-HW
Jerseys-C-SW
Jerseys-C-WM
Jerseys Gold-J-SW
Jerseys Gold-C-BW
Jerseys Gold-C-HW
Jerseys Gold-C-SW
Jerseys Gold-C-WM
02Atomic-47
Blue-47
Gold-47
Red-47
Hobby Parallel-47
02BAP First Edition-282
02BAP First Edition-424R
02BAP Memorabilia-139
Emerald-139
Ruby-139
Sapphire-139
NHL All-Star Game-139
NHL All-Star Game Blue-139
NHL All-Star Game Green-139
NHL All-Star Game Red-139
02BAP Memorabilia Toronto Fall Expo-139
02BAP Signature Series-156
All-Rookie-AR4
Autographs-156
Autographs Gold-156
Team Quads-TQ5
02BAP Ultimate Mem Calder Candidates-15
02Bowman YoungStars-157
Gold-157
Silver-157
Autographs-SW
Jerseys-SW
Patches-SW
Double Stuff-SW
Triple Stuff-SW
Rivals-SCSW
Rivals Patches-10
Sticks-SW
02Crown Royale Rookie Royalty-12
02ITG Used Calder Jerseys-C4
02ITG Used Calder Jerseys Gold-C4
02O-Pee-Chee-305
02O-Pee-Chee Premier Blue Parallel-305
02O-Pee-Chee Premier Red Parallel-305
02O-Pee-Chee Factory Set-305
02Pacific-161
Blue-161
Red-161
Shining Moments-7
02Pacific Calder-72
Silver-72
Reflections-12
02Pacific Complete-238
Red-238
02Pacific Exclusive-78
Destined-8
Great Expectations-9
02Pacific Heads-Up-54
Blue-54
Purple-54
Red-54
Head First-5
02Parkhurst-169
Bronze-169
Gold-169
Silver-169
Hardware-C9
Heroes-NH12
Jerseys-GJ53
02Parkhurst Retro-183
Minis-183
02Private Stock Reserve-43
Blue-43
Red-43
Retail-43
Class Act-9
Moments in Time-4
02SPx-111
02Stadium Club-115
Silver Decoy Cards-115
Proofs-115
Lone Star Signatures Blue-LSSW
Lone Star Signatures Red-LSSW
02Titanium Right on Target-10
02Topps-305
OPC Blue Parallel-305
OPC Red Parallel-305
Factory Set-305
02Topps Chrome-147
Black Border Refractors-147
Refractors-147
Chromographs-CGSW
Chromograph Refractors-CGSW
02Topps Heritage-55
Chrome Parallel-55
Autographs-SW
Autographs Black-SW
Autographs Red-SW
02Topps Total-128
Signatures-SW
02UD Foundations-130
02UD Piece of History-131
02UD Premier Collection-26
02Upper Deck-205
Exclusives-205
02Upper Deck MVP-202
Gold-202
Classics-202
Golden Classics-202
02Upper Deck Victory-89
Bronze-89
Gold-89
Silver-89
02Upper Deck Vintage-273
02Upper Deck Vintage-333
Tall Boys-T31
Tall Boys Gold-T31
02Vanguard Prime Prospects-12
03Black Diamond-101
Black-101
Green-101
Red-101
03ITG Action-210
Homeboys-HB12
Jerseys-M119
03NHL Sticker Collection-46
03O-Pee-Chee-8
03OPC Blue-8
03OPC Gold-8
03OPC Red-8
03Pacific-149
Blue-149
Red-149
03Pacific Complete-184
Red-184
03Pacific Exhibit-65
Blue Backs-65
Yellow Backs-65
03Pacific Prism-46
Blue-46
Gold-46
Red-46
Paramount Prodigies-12
03Panthers Team Issue-18
03Private Stock Reserve-44
Blue-44
Red-44
Retail-44
03SPx-40
Radiance-40
Spectrum-40
Big Futures-BF-SW
Big Futures Limited-BF-SW
Winning Materials-WM-SW
Winning Materials Limited-WM-SW
03Titanium-44
Hobby Jersey Number Parallels-44
Retail-44
Retail Jersey Number Parallels-44
03Topps-8
Blue-8
Gold-8
Red-8
Signs of Youth-SW
C55 Autographs-TA-SW
Traded Future Phenoms-FP-SW
03Upper Deck-83
Canadian Exclusives-83
HG-83
03Upper Deck All-Star Promos-AS5
03Upper Deck Classic Portraits-40
03Upper Deck MVP-182
Gold Script-182
Silver Script-182
Canadian Exclusives-182
SportsNut-SN40
03Upper Deck Trilogy-40
Limited-40
03Upper Deck Victory-80
Bronze-80
Gold-80
Silver-80
03AHL Top Prospects-43
04Pacific-117
Blue-117
Red-117
04SP Authentic Buybacks-189
04SP Authentic Rookie Review-RR-SW
04SP Authentic Sign of the Times-ST-SW
04SP Authentic Sign of the Times-DS-WL
04SP Authentic Sign of the Times-TS-LWH
04SP Authentic Sign of the Times-FS-SES
04Upper Deck-76
Canadian Exclusives-76
HG Glossy Gold-76
HG Glossy Silver-76
04AHL Top Prospects-47
04San Antonio Rampage-8
04ITG Heroes and Prospects-111
Autographs-U-SW
He Shoots-He Scores Prizes-17
04ITG Heroes/Prospects Toronto Expo '05-111
04ITG Heroes/Prospects Expo Heroes/Pros-111
05Be A Player Dual Signatures-LW
05Be A Player Signatures-WE
05Be A Player Signatures Gold-WE
05Be A Player Triple Signatures-PAN
05Black Diamond-35
Emerald-35
Gold-35
Onyx-35
Ruby-35
05Panini Stickers-64
05Parkhurst-210
Facsimile Auto Parallel-210
True Colors-TCFLA
True Colors-TCFLA
True Colors-TCFLTB
True Colors-TCFLTB
05SP Game Used-42
Autographs-42
Gold-42
Authentic Fabrics-AF-SW
Authentic Fabrics Autographs-AAF-SW
Authentic Fabrics Dual-WH
Authentic Fabrics Dual Autographs-WH
Authentic Fabrics Gold-AF-SW
Authentic Patches-AP-SW
Authentic Patches Autographs-AAP-SW
Authentic Patches Dual-WH
Authentic Patches Dual Autographs-WH
SIGnificance-SW
SIGnificance Gold-S-SW
SIGnificance Extra-WH
SIGnificance Extra Gold-WH
05SPx-36
Spectrum-36
Winning Combos-WC-WH
Winning Combos Autographs-AWC-WH
Winning Combos Gold-WC-WH
Winning Combos Spectrum-WC-WH
Winning Materials-WM-SW
Winning Materials Gold-WM-SW
Winning Materials Spectrum-WM-SW
05The Cup Limited Logos-LLSW
05UD Artifacts-43
Blue-43
Gold-43
Green-43
Pewter-43
Red-43
Auto Facts-AF-SW
Auto Facts Blue-AF-SW
Auto Facts Copper-AF-SW
Auto Facts Pewter-AF-SW
Auto Facts Silver-AF-SW
Gold Autographed-43
Remarkable Artifacts-RA-SW
Remarkable Artifacts Dual-RA-SW
05Ultra-88
Gold-88
Ice-88
05Upper Deck-327
Jerseys Series II-J2SW
Majestic Materials-MMSW
Notable Numbers-N-LO
Patches-P-SW
05Upper Deck Ice-43
Rainbow-43
05Upper Deck MVP-170
Gold-170
Platinum-170
Materials-M-SW
05Upper Deck Trilogy-41
Ice Scripts-IS-SW
05Upper Deck Victory-84
Black-84
Gold-84
Silver-84
06Black Diamond Jerseys-JSW
06Black Diamond Jerseys Black-JSW
06Black Diamond Jerseys Gold-JSW
06Black Diamond Jerseys Ruby-JSW
06Black Diamond Jerseys Black Autographs -JSW
06Flair Showcase Stitches-SSSW
06Fleer Fabricology-FSW
06O-Pee-Chee-210
Rainbow-210
Autographs-A-SW
06SP Game Used SIGnificance-SSW
06UD Artifacts Auto-Facts-AFSW
06UD Artifacts Auto-Facts Gold-AFSW
06UD Artifacts Frozen Artifacts-FASW
06UD Artifacts Frozen Artifacts Black-FASW
06UD Artifacts Frozen Artifacts Blue-FASW
06UD Artifacts Frozen Artifacts Gold-FASW
06UD Artifacts Frozen Artifacts Platinum-FASW
06UD Artifacts Frozen Artifacts Red-FASW
06UD Artifacts Frozen Artifacts Autographed Black-FASW
06UD Artifacts Frozen Artifacts Patches Black-FASW
06UD Artifacts Frozen Artifacts Patches Blue-FASW
06UD Artifacts Frozen Artifacts Patches Gold-FASW
06UD Artifacts Frozen Artifacts Patches Platinum-FASW
06UD Artifacts Frozen Artifacts Patches Red-FASW
06UD Artifacts Frozen Artifacts Patches Autographed Black Tag Parallel-FASW
06Ultra Uniformity-USW
06Ultra Uniformity Patches-UPSW
06Ultra Uniformity Autographed Jerseys-UASW
06Upper Deck Arena Giveaways-FLA3
06Upper Deck-87
Exclusives Parallel-87
High Gloss Parallel-87
Game Jerseys-JSW
Game Patches-PSW
Masterpieces-87
06Upper Deck MVP-124
Gold Script-124
Super Script-124
Jerseys-OJWW
06Upper Deck Trilogy Scripts-TSSW
07Upper Deck Victory-89
Black-89
Gold-89

Weissemann, Erik
03Czech OFS Plus-149
03Czech OFS Plus All-Star Game-H22

Weissenberger, Oliver
94German First League-160

Weisser, Cuno
93Swiss HNL-459
95Swiss HNL-339
96Swiss HNL-313
98Swiss Power Play Stickers-330

Weissman, Mika
72Finnish Jaakiekko-321

Weissman, Ondrej
94Czech APS Extraliga-296
97Czech APS Extraliga-75
98Czech OFS-1
00Czech OFS-82

Weistche, Ryan
02OCN Blizzard-17

Weisz, Mike
93Quebec Pee-Wee Tournament-1479

Weitzel, Jason
97Moose Jaw Warriors-18

Welch, Dan
99Minnesota Golden Gophers-28
02Macon Trax-2
02Minnesota Golden Gophers-28
03Manchester Monarchs-19
03Manchester Monarchs Team Issue-19
04Manchester Monarchs-4
04Manchester Monarchs Tobacco-5
04Reading Royals-17
05UK Coventry Blaze-10

Welch, Jason
91Lake Superior State Lakers-28
92Lake Superior State Lakers-31
93Northern Michigan Wildcats-28
97El Paso Buzzards-9
98El Paso Buzzards-8

Welch, Noah
05ITG Heroes/Prosp Toronto Expo Parallel -211
05AHL All-Stars-42
05AHL Top Prospects-48
05WBS Penguins-26
05ITG Heroes and Prospects-211
Autographs Series II-NW
06Be A Player-215
06Be A Player Portraits-123
06Beehive-148
Matte-148
06Black Diamond-195
Black-195
Gold-195
Ruby-195
06Flair Showcase-81
06Flair Showcase-156
Parallel-81
Parallel-156
06Fleer-202
Tiffany-202
06Hot Prospects-128
Red Hot-128
White Hot-128
Hot Materials -HMNW
Hot Materials Red Hot-HMNW
Hot Materials White Hot-HMNW
Hotagraphs-HNW
06O-Pee-Chee-523
06O-Pee-Chee-629
Rainbow-523
Rainbow-629
06SP Authentic-197
Limited-197
06SP Game Used-145
Gold-145
Rainbow-145
Autographs-145
Rookie Exclusives Autographs-RENW
06SPx-173
Spectrum-173
06The Cup-150
Autographed Rookie Masterpiece Pressplates-150
Gold Rainbow Autographed Rookie Patches-150
Masterpiece Pressplates (Artifacts)-220
Masterpiece Pressplates (Be A Player Portraits)-123
Masterpiece Pressplates (Bee Hive)-148
Masterpiece Pressplates (Marquee Rookies)-523
Masterpiece Pressplates (MVP)-350
Masterpiece Pressplates (Power Play)-123
Masterpiece Pressplates (SP Authentic Autographs)-197
Masterpiece Pressplates (SP Game Used)-145
Masterpiece Pressplates (SPx Autographs)-173
Masterpiece Pressplates (Sweet Beginnings)-147
Masterpiece Pressplates (Trilogy)-145
Masterpiece Pressplates (Ultimate Collection Autographs)-128
Masterpiece Pressplates (Victory)-210
NHL Shields Duals-DSHBW
NHL Shields Duals-DSHOW
Rookies Black-150
Rookies Platinum-150
06UD Artifacts-220
Blue-220
Gold-220
Platinum-220
Radiance-220
Red-220
06UD Mini Jersey Collection-123
06UD Powerplay-123
Impact Rainbow-123
06Ultimate Collection-128
Rookies Autographed NHL Shields-128
Rookies Autographed Patches-128
Ultimate Debut Threads Jerseys-DJ-NW
Ultimate Debut Threads Jerseys Autographs-DJ-NW
Ultimate Debut Threads Patches-DJ-NW
Ultimate Debut Threads Patches Autographs-DJ-NW
06Ultra-223
Gold Medallion-223
Ice Medallion-223
06Upper Deck-237
Exclusives Parallel-237
High Gloss Parallel-237
Masterpieces-237
Rookie Game Dated Moments-RGD24
Rookie Headliners-RH5
Rookie Materials-RMNW
Rookie Materials Patches-RMNW
06Upper Deck MVP-350
Gold Script-350
Super Script-350
06Upper Deck Sweet Shot-147
Rookie Jerseys Autographs-147
06Upper Deck Trilogy-145
06Upper Deck Victory-210
06Upper Deck Victory Black-210
06Upper Deck Victory Gold-210
06Wilkes-Barre Scranton Penguins-15
06Wilkes-Barre Scranton Penguins Jerseys-8
06ITG Heroes and Prospects-45
AHL Shooting Stars-AS03
Autographs-ANW
Jerseys-GUJ21
Jerseys Gold-GUJ21
Emblems-GUE21
Emblems Gold-GUE21
Numbers-GUN21
Numbers Gold-GUN21
07Upper Deck Rookie Class -13

Welcher, Wesley
04Moncton Wildcats-1

Welik, Jeremy
93Quebec Pee-Wee Tournament-87

Wellar, Patrick
02Calgary Hitmen-14
03Calgary Hitmen-19
04Peoria Rivermen-17

Weller, Craig
00Kootenay Ice-24
02Charlotte Checkers-94
03Hartford Wolf Pack-26
04Hartford Wolf Pack-25
05Hartford Wolf Pack-23
06Hartford Wolf Pack-23

Weller, Jody
91Air Canada SJHL-E19

Welling, Jesse
99Rockford IceHogs-21
00Finnish Cardset-274
01Finnish Cardset-333
04Finnish Cardset-134
Parallel-99

Wellman, Casey
06Cedar Rapids RoughRiders-20

Wells, Brad
83Brandon Wheat Kings-9

Wells, Bryan
83Brandon Wheat Kings-1
92Thunder Bay Thunder Hawks-14
93Thunder Bay Senators-7
94Central Hockey League-125
95Central Hockey League-88
98Wichita Thunder-24
99Wichita Thunder-23

Wells, Chris
917th Inn. Sketch WHL-141
93Seattle Thunderbirds-28
94Classic-20
Gold-20
Tri-Cards-T52
94Classic Four-Sport *-137
Gold-137
Printers Proofs-137
Tri-Cards-TC4
95Bowman-136
All-Foil-136
95Penguins Foodland-3
95Images-19
Gold-19
95Images Four-Sport *-111
95Signature Rookies-15
Signatures-15
97Be A Player-62
Autographs-62
Autographs Die-Cuts-62
Autographs Prismatic Die-Cuts-62
97Pacific Invincible NHL Regime-91
99Louisville Panthers-14
00Utah Grizzlies-17

Wells, J.C.
01Indianapolis Ice-21

Wells, Jay
80Kings Card Night-14
82Post Cereal-8
84Kings Smokey-17
85O-Pee-Chee-178
86Kings 20th Anniversary Team Issue-22
86O-Pee-Chee-217
86O-Pee-Chee Stickers-92
87O-Pee-Chee-151
87O-Pee-Chee Stickers-212
87Panini Stickers-274
87Topps-151
88Flyers Postcards-7
88Panini Stickers-72
89Flyers Postcards-27
90Sabres Blue Shield-26
90Sabres Campbell's-31
91Bowman-35
91Sabres Blue Shield-24
91Sabres Pepsi/Campbell's-24
92Score-548A
Canadian-548A
93Score-416
Canadian-416
94OPC Premier-249
Special Effects-249
94Pinnacle-507
Artist's Proofs-507
Rink Collection-507
94Topps/OPC Premier-249
Special Effects-249
95Be A Player-29
Signatures-S29
Signatures Die Cuts-S29
97Pacific Invincible NHL Regime-189
97Portland Pirates-23
98Hershey Bears-23
02Fleer Throwbacks-40
Gold-40
Platinum-40
Stickwork-7

Wells, Jeff
95Birmingham Bulls-4
95Cincinnati Cyclones-19
96Cincinnati Cyclones-5
97Cincinnati Cyclones-18
98Cincinnati Cyclones-22
98Cincinnati Cyclones 2-18
99Providence Bruins-24

Wells, Marc
95Signature Rookies Miracle on Ice-39
95Signature Rookies Miracle on Ice-40
95Signature Rook Miracle on Ice Sigs-39
95Signature Rook Miracle on Ice Sigs-40
04UD Legendary Signatures Miracle Men-USA13
04UD Legendary Sigs Miracle Men Autos-USA-MW

Wells, Marty
96Dayton Ice Bandits-22

Wellwood, Kyle
00Belleville Bulls-23
00UD CHL Prospects-33
01Belleville Bulls-24
01Belleville Bulls-28
02Windsor Spitfires-30
03BAP Ultimate Memorabilia Autographs-130
Gold-130
03Beehive-215
Gold-215
Silver-215
03ITG Action-658
03ITG Used Signature Series-190
Gold-190
03ITG VIP Rookie Debut-104
03Pacific Calder-135
Silver-135
03Pacific Complete-571
Red-571
03Parkhurst Rookie-161
03SP Authentic-161
03Topps Traded-TT151
Blue-TT151
Gold-TT151
Red-TT151
03UD Premier Collection-66
03Upper Deck Rookie Update-133
03AHL Top Prospects-44
03Pacific AHL Prospects-83
Gold-83
04AHL All-Stars-45
04AHL Top Prospects-51
04ITG Heroes and Prospects-190
Autographs-U-KW
04ITG Heroes/Prospects Toronto Expo '05-190
05Parkhurst-453
Facsimile Auto Parallel-453
05UD Rookie Class-27
05Upper Deck-427
05Upper Deck MVP-359
Gold-359
Platinum-359
05Upper Deck Trilogy-87
06Be A Player-7
Autographs-7
Signatures-KW
Signatures 25-8
Signatures Duals-DWS
Signatures Trios-TTWS
06Flair Showcase Wave of the Future-WF39
06Fleer-181
Tiffany-181
06Gatorade-64
06McDonald's Upper Deck Rookie Review-RR1
06O-Pee-Chee-456
Rainbow-456
06Ultra-184
Gold Medallion-184
Ice Medallion-184
06Upper Deck-429
Exclusives Parallel-429
High Gloss Parallel-429
Masterpieces-429
06Upper Deck MVP-275
Gold Script-275
Super Script-275
06Upper Deck Ovation-146
06Upper Deck Victory-278
06Upper Deck Victory Next In Line-NL50
06ITG Heroes and Prospects-26
AHL All-Star Jerseys-AJ12
AHL All-Star Jerseys Gold-AJ12
AHL All-Star Emblems-AE12
AHL All-Star Emblems Gold-AE12
AHL All-Star Numbers-AN12
AHL All-Star Numbers Gold-AN12
Autographs-AKW

Welser, Daniel
06Swedish SHL Elitset-132

Welsh, Devin
03Everett Silvertips-18
04Kootenay Ice-23
05Kootenay Ice-21
06Okotoks Oilers -21

Welsh, Hugo
93Quebec Pee-Wee Tournament-458

Welsh, Jorin
04Fort Worth Brahmas-17

Welsh, Keith
94Kitchener Rangers-17
96Kitchener Rangers-28

Welsh, Thomas
02Ohio State Buckeyes-16
03Ohio State Buckeyes-15
04Ohio State Buckeyes-15

Welsing, Rocky
99Charlotte Checkers-3

Welte, Wade
91Air Canada SJHL-D14
92Saskatchewan JHL-80
97Bakersfield Fog-18
99Adirondack IceHawks-19

Welter, Josh
92Saskatchewan JHL-92
06Fayetteville FireAntz-20

Welton, Nathan
03Quebec Remparts-27
05Moncton Wildcats-18
06Moncton Wildcats-11

Welz, Markus
96German DEL-332
99German Bundesliga 2-193

Wen, Ting
79Panini Stickers-355

Wenaas, Jeff
85Medicine Hat Tigers-13
88Salt Lake Golden Eagles-21
89ProCards IHL-194

Wendell, Erik
98Minnesota Golden Gophers-4
99Minnesota Golden Gophers-29
00Minnesota Golden Gophers-27
01Minnesota Golden Gophers-8
02Rockford Ice Hogs-7

Wendell, Krissy
04Minnesota Golden Gophers Women-2

Wendt, Michael
93Quebec Pee-Wee Tournament-640

Wennberg, Peter
92Swedish Semic Elitserien Stickers-269

Wennerberg, Mattias
02Swedish SHL-87
Parallel-87
03Swedish Elite-110
Signatures-15
Silver-110
03Swedish MoDo Postcards-4
04Swedish Elitset High Expectations-8
04Swedish MoDo Postcards-23
05Swedish SHL Elitset-285
Gold-285
Series Two Signatures-28
06Swedish SHL Elitset-142

Wensink, John
78O-Pee-Chee-133
78Topps-133
79O-Pee-Chee-182
79Topps-182
80Nordiques Postcards-29
80O-Pee-Chee-390
80Pepsi-Cola Caps-80
81Rockies Postcards-29
82Post Cereal-11
02Fleer Throwbacks-38
Gold-38
Platinum-38

Wensley, Clint
91Air Canada SJHL-E45
01Rockford IceHogs-2
02Rockford Ice Hogs-12
03New Mexico Scorpions-7

Wentworth, Marvin
33O-Pee-Chee V304B-61
33V357 Ice Kings-43
34Beehive Group I Photos-187
34Beehive Group I Photos-210
34Sweet Caporal-28
36O-Pee-Chee V304D-116
37O-Pee-Chee V304E-163
37V356 Worldwide Gum-19
38Quaker Oats Photos-30
39O-Pee-Chee V301-1-30
04ITG Ultimate Mem Marvelous Maroons-4
04ITG Ultimate Memorabilia Paper Cuts-14
05ITG Ultimate Mem Marvelous Maroons Auto-10
06ITG Ultimate Memorabilia Chi-Town Immortals Autos-3
06ITG Ultimate Memorabilia Paper Cuts Autos-8

Wentzell, Jamie
95Slapshot-161
95Sault Ste. Marie Greyhounds-25

Wenzel, Jeremy
93Quebec Pee-Wee Tournament-493

Wenzel, Sheldon
03Lewiston Maineiacs-23

Werder, Marco
93Swiss HNL-384
95Swiss HNL-235
96Swiss HNL-173

Werenka, Brad
92Oilers Team Issue-22
92Parkhurst-289
Emerald Ice-289
92Classic-99
Gold-99
92Classic Four-Sport *-212
Gold-212
93Parkhurst-68
Emerald Ice-68
93Score-438
Canadian-438
93Upper Deck-41
SP-54
94Score Team Canada-CT21
94Milwaukee Admirals-27
95Indianapolis Ice-22
97Be A Player-41
Autographs-41
Autographs Die-Cuts-41
Autographs Prismatic Die-Cuts-41
98Be A Player-264
Press Release-264
98BAP Gold-264
98BAP Autographs-264
98BAP Autographs Gold-264
99Pacific-349
Copper-349
Emerald Green-349
Gold-349
Ice Blue-349
Premiere Date-349
Red-349
00Upper Deck-259
Exclusives Tier 1-259
Exclusives Tier 2-259

02BAP Sig Series Auto Buybacks 1998-264

Werenka, Darcy
89Lethbridge Hurricanes-23
907th Inn. Sketch WHL-122
917th Inn. Sketch WHL-351
917th Inn. Sketch Memorial Cup-101
91Arena Draft Picks-28
91Arena Draft Picks French-28
91Arena Draft Picks Autographs-28
91Arena Draft Picks Autographs French-28
91Classic-33
91Star Pics-54
91Ultimate Draft-29
91Ultimate Draft French-29
91Classic Four-Sport *-33
Autographs-33A
92Upper Deck-594
92Brandon Wheat Kings-23
94Binghamton Rangers-23
94Classic Pro Prospects-96
99Utah Grizzlies-32
00Finnish Cardset-266
01German Upper Deck-240
02German DEL City Press-211

Werenka, Derek
02Brandon Wheat Kings-10
03Kamloops Blazers-23

Werenka, Nigel
91Air Canada SJHL-D25
92Saskatchewan JHL-162

Werlen, Marc
96Swiss HNL-213
98Swiss Power Play Stickers-88
98Swiss Power Play Stickers-291
99Swiss Panini Stickers-87
00Swiss Panini Stickers-135
00Swiss Slapshot Mini-Cards-HCFG7
01Swiss HNL-130
02Swiss HNL-298

Wernblom, Magnus
91Swedish Semic Elitserien Stickers-215
92Swedish Semic Elitserien Stickers-235
93Swedish Semic Elitserien-204
94Swedish Leaf-68
95Swedish Leaf-110
95Swedish Upper Deck-160
Ticket to North America-NA20
97Swedish Collector's Choice-157
Select-UD14
98Swedish UD Choice-174
99Swedish Upper Deck-176
Snapshots-12
00Swedish Upper Deck-157
00Swedish Upper Deck-206
SHL Excellence-S5
SHL Signatures-MW
02Swedish SHL-81
Parallel-81
Signatures Series II-11
03Swedish Elite-252
Enforcers-EF12
Signatures-12
Silver-252
06Swedish SHL Elitset-268
Performers-15

Werner, Eric
00Sioux Falls Stampede-19
02Michigan Wolverines-30
03Michigan Wolverines-16
05Manchester Monarchs-48
05Reading Royals-16
06Manchester Monarchs-6

Werner, Frank
01Michigan Tech Huskies-32

Werner, Kyle
96Saskatoon Blades-25

Werner, Sascha
94German First League-348

Werner, Stephen
97Quebec Pee-Wee Tournament-284

Werner, Thomas
91Finnish Semic World Champ Stickers-172
91Swedish Semic World Champ Stickers-172
94German DEL-133
95German DEL-134

Werthan, Patrick
95Swiss HNL-435
96Swiss HNL-468

Wesenberg, Brian
94Guelph Storm-16
95Slapshot-96
95Guelph Storm-15
95Classic-26
95Classic-85
96Guelph Storm-14
96Guelph Storm Premier Collection-2
97Bowman CHL-33
OPC-33
99Upper Deck MVP-154
Gold Script-154
Silver Script-154
Super Script-154
99Upper Deck Victory-220

Wesley, Blake
82O-Pee-Chee-133
82Post Cereal-7
82Whalers Junior Hartford Courant-23
83NHL Key Tags-110
83Nordiques Postcards-32
83O-Pee-Chee-307
83Vachon-80
84O-Pee-Chee-294
84Fredericton Express-28
85Maple Leafs Postcards-32
03Portland Winter Hawks-27

Wesley, Glen
86Portland Winter Hawks-23
88Bruins Sports Action-22
88Bruins Postcards-20
88O-Pee-Chee-166
88O-Pee-Chee Stickers-85
88O-Pee-Chee Stickers-215
88Panini Stickers-207
88Topps-166
89Bruins Sports Action-22
89O-Pee-Chee-51
89O-Pee-Chee Stickers-27
89Panini Stickers-200
89Topps-51
90Bruins Sports Action-25
90O-Pee-Chee-379
90Panini Stickers-6
90Pro Set-16
90Score-97
Canadian-97
90Score Hottest/Rising Stars-57
90Score Young Superstars-8
90Topps-379
Tiffany-379
90Upper Deck-377
French-377
91Pro Set Platinum-7
91Bowman-350
91Bruins Sports Action-21
91O-Pee-Chee-452
91Panini Stickers-182
91Parkhurst-5
French-5
91Pinnacle-112
French-112
91Pro Set-1
French-1
91Score American-273
91Score Canadian Bilingual-493
91Score Canadian English-493
91Stadium Club-190
91Topps-452
91Upper Deck-370
French-370
92Bowman-15
92Bruins Postcards-12
92O-Pee-Chee-150
92Panini Stickers-145
92Panini Stickers French-145
92Parkhurst-6
Emerald Ice-6
92Pinnacle-326
French-326
92Pro Set-10
92Score-230
Canadian-230
92Stadium Club-279
92Topps-346
Gold-346G
92Ultra-11
92Upper Deck-244
93Donruss-19
93Leaf-268
93OPC Premier-114
Gold-114
93Panini Stickers-6
93Parkhurst-17
Emerald Ice-17
93Pinnacle-383
Canadian-383
93PowerPlay-25
93Score-243
Canadian-243
93Stadium Club-222
Members Only Master Set-222
OPC-222
First Day Issue-222
First Day Issue OPC-222
93Topps/OPC Premier-114
Gold-114
93Ultra-272
93Upper Deck-208
94Donruss-232
94Finest-60
Super Team Winners-60
Refractors-60
94Fleer-92
94Leaf-6
94Leaf-460
94Leaf Limited-13
94OPC Premier-357
Special Effects-357
94Parkhurst-17
Gold-17
94Pinnacle-388
Artist's Proofs-388
Rink Collection-388
94Select-81
Gold-81
94Stadium Club-210
Members Only Master Set-210
First Day Issue-210
Super Team Winner Cards-210
94Topps/OPC Premier-357
Special Effects-357
94Ultra-18
94Ultra-303
94Upper Deck-89
Electric Ice-89
SP Inserts-SP125
SP Inserts Die Cuts-SP125
95Be A Player-116
Signatures-S116
Signatures Die Cuts-S116
95Canada Games NHL POGS-130
95Collector's Choice-315
Player's Club-315
Player's Club Platinum-315
95Donruss-186
95Leaf-231
95Metal-68
95Parkhurst International-98
Emerald Ice-98
95Pinnacle-80
Artist's Proofs-80
Rink Collection-80
95Playoff One on One-158
95Score-194
Black Ice Artist's Proofs-194
Black Ice-194
95SkyBox Impact-77
95Stadium Club-4
Members Only Master Set-4
95Summit-73
Artist's Proofs-73
Ice-73
95Topps-213
OPC Inserts-213
95Topps SuperSkills-39
Platinum-39
95Ultra-248
95Upper Deck-137
Electric Ice-137
Electric Ice Gold-137
95Whalers Bob's Stores-26
96Team Out-50
96Topps Picks-155
OPC Inserts-155
96Whalers Kid's Club-13
97Collector's Choice-114
97Hurricanes Team Issue-26
97Pacific-244
Copper-244
Emerald Green-244
Ice Blue-244
Red-244
Silver-244
97Pinnacle-132
Press Plates Back Black-132
Press Plates Back Cyan-132
Press Plates Back Magenta-132
Press Plates Back Yellow-132
Press Plates Front Black-132
Press Plates Front Cyan-132
Press Plates Front Magenta-132
Press Plates Front Yellow-132
97SP Authentic-23
97Upper Deck-244
98Be A Player-26
Press Release-26
98BAP Gold-26
98BAP Autographs-26
98BAP Autographs Gold-26
98BAP Tampa Bay All Star Game-26
98Hurricanes Team Issue-2
98Pacific-141
Ice Blue-141
Red-141
98UD Choice-41
98UD Choice Preview-41
98UD Choice Prime Choice Reserve-41
98UD Choice Reserve-41
98Upper Deck-59
Exclusives-59
Exclusives 1 of 1-59
Gold Reserve-59
99BAP Memorabilia-230
Gold-230
Silver-230
99O-Pee-Chee-27
99O-Pee-Chee Chrome-27
99O-Pee-Chee Chrome Refractors-27
99Pacific-82
Copper-82
Emerald Green-82
Gold-82
Ice Blue-82
Premiere Date-82
Red-82
99Panini Stickers-48
99Topps/OPC-27
99Topps/OPC Chrome-27
Refractors-27
99Upper Deck Victory-63
00Paramount-47
Copper-47
Gold-47
Holo-Gold-47
Holo-Silver-47
Ice Blue-47
Premiere Date-47
00Stadium Club-158
00Upper Deck Vintage-72
02BAP Sig Series Auto Buybacks 1998-26
02Hurricanes Postcards-7
02Pacific Complete-328
Red-328
02Topps Total-273
03Hurricanes Postcards-24
03Pacific Complete-343
Red-343
05Panini Stickers-53
05Parkhurst-99
Facsimile Auto Parallel-99
05Ultra-43
Gold-43
Ice-43
05Upper Deck-284
05Upper Deck MVP-72
Gold-72
Platinum-72
06Hurricanes Postcards-26
06O-Pee-Chee-87
Rainbow-87
06Upper Deck-38
Exclusives Parallel-38
High Gloss Parallel-38
Masterpieces-38

Wesslau, Gustaf
06Swedish SHL Elitset-95

Wesslin, Samu
99Finnish Cardset-340
00Finnish Cardset-109
01Finnish Cardset-380
02Finnish Cardset-188
03Finnish Cardset-174
04Finnish Cardset-190
Parallel-141

West, Dan
93Windsor Spitfires-21

West, Joseph
94German First League-159
96German DEL-213
98German DEL-183
99German DEL-223

West, Marc
83Brantford Alexanders-9
99German Bundesliga 2-16
02UK Hull Thunder-22

West, Nathan
96Detroit Whalers-20

West, Russ
907th Inn. Sketch WHL-142
917th Inn. Sketch WHL-282

West, Steve
78Jets Postcards-23

Westblom, Kristofer
04Kelowna Rockets-6
05ITG Heroes/Prosp Toronto Expo Parallel -168
05Kelowna Rockets-25
05ITG Heroes and Prospects-168
Autographs-A-KW
Complete Logos-CHL-19
He Shoots-He Scores Prizes-17
Jerseys-GUJ-43
Jerseys Gold-GUJ-43
Emblems-GUE-43
Emblems Gold-GUE-43
Numbers-GUN-43
Numbers Gold-GUN-43
Nameplates-N-27
Nameplates Gold-N-27
Net Prospects-NP-21
Net Prospects Dual-NPD4
Net Prospects Dual Gold-NPD4
Net Prospects Gold-NP-21
06Between The Pipes Prospect Trios-PT09
06Between The Pipes Prospect Trios Gold-PT09

Westcott, Duvie
01BAP Memorabilia-417
Emerald-417
Ruby-417
Sapphire-417
01UD Premier Collection-60
01Syracuse Crunch-6
02AHL Top Prospects-44
02Syracuse Crunch Sheets-7
03ITG Action-174
04Finnish Cardset-82
04Finnish Cardset Signatures-17
05Parkhurst-140
Facsimile Auto Parallel-140
05Finnish Cardset -65
06O-Pee-Chee-146
Rainbow-146

Westerby, Bob
93Kamloops Blazers-23
94Kamloops Blazers-18
95Rochester Americans-22
95Slapshot Memorial Cup-20
98Baton Rouge Kingfish-18
99San Antonio Iguanas-9

Westerling, Jonas
04Swedish Elitset-107
Gold-107
05Swedish SHL Elitset-111
Gold-111

Westerlund, Gosta
64Swedish Coralli ISHockey-133
65Swedish Coralli ISHockey-133

Westerlund, Kjell
67Swedish Hockey-77
67Swedish Hockey-229
69Swedish Hockey-273

Westermark, Johan
98Danish Hockey League-135
99Danish Hockey League-152

Westfall, Ed
63Topps-8
64Beehive Group III Photos-28
64Coca-Cola Caps-13
64Topps-51
65Coca-Cola-11
65Topps-37
66Topps-32
66Topps USA Test-32
67Topps-95
68O-Pee-Chee-135
68Shirriff Coins-2
69O-Pee-Chee-129
69Topps-29
70Bruins Postcards-11
70Bruins Team Issue-9
70Esso Power Players-67
70O-Pee-Chee-139
70Sargent Promotions Stamps-7
71Bruins Postcards-13
71O-Pee-Chee-169
71Sargent Promotions Stamps-2
71Toronto Sun-21
72O-Pee-Chee-104
Player Crests-13
72Sargent Promotions Stamps-127
72Topps-159
73O-Pee-Chee-67
73Topps-67
74Lipton Soup-47
74NHL Action Stamps-180
74O-Pee-Chee NHL-32
74Topps-32
75Heroes Stand-Ups-19
75O-Pee-Chee NHL-302
75Topps-302
76O-Pee-Chee NHL-11
76Topps-11
77Coca-Cola-30
77O-Pee-Chee NHL-153
77Topps-153
78O-Pee-Chee-232
78Topps-232
91Bruins Sports Action Legends-34
91Ultimate Original Six-56
French-56
93Islanders Chemical Bank Alumni-10
94Parkhurst Tall Boys-6
95Parkhurst '66-67-4
Coins-4
01Topps Archives-51
Autographs-28
Relics-JEW

Westin, Zack
94Anchorage Aces-3

Westling, Bo
71Swedish Hockey-289
72Swedish Stickers-70

Westling, Mikael
83Swedish Semic Elitserien-77

Westlund, Alex
00Milwaukee Admirals Postcards-18
02Russian Hockey League-63
02Russian SL-38
02Russian Transfert-14
03Russian SL-24

Westlund, Olle
57Swedish Alfabilder-140
64Swedish Coralli ISHockey-118
65Swedish Coralli ISHockey-118
67Swedish Hockey-179

Westlund, Todd
91Minnesota Golden Gophers-25
92Minnesota Golden Gophers-29

Westlund, Tommy
96Swedish Brynas Tigers-9
97Swedish Collector's Choice-23
98New Haven Beast-20
99BAP Memorabilia-345
Gold-345
Silver-345
99Pacific Dynagon Ice-45
Blue-45
Copper-45
Gold-45
Premiere Date-45
99Pacific Omega-50
Copper-50
Gold-50
Ice Blue-50
Premiere Date-50
99Panini Stickers-51
99Upper Deck MVP SC Edition-42
Gold Script-42
Silver Script-42
Super Script-42
00BAP Memorabilia-371
Emerald-371
Ruby-371
Sapphire-371
Promos-371
00BAP Mem Chicago Sportsfest Copper-371
00BAP Memorabilia Chicago Sportsfest Blue-371
00BAP Memorabilia Chicago Sportsfest Gold-371
00BAP Memorabilia Chicago Sportsfest Ruby-371
00BAP Memorabilia Chicago Sun-Times Ruby-371
00BAP Memorabilia Chicago Sun-Times Gold-371
00BAP Mem Chicago Sun-Times Sapphire-371
00BAP Mem Toronto Fall Expo Copper-371
00BAP Memorabilia Toronto Fall Expo Gold-371
00BAP Memorabilia Toronto Fall Expo Ruby-371
00O-Pee-Chee-234
00O-Pee-Chee Parallel-234
00Pacific-91
Copper-91
Gold-91
Ice Blue-91
Premiere Date-91
00Topps/OPC-234
Parallel-234
00Upper Deck-262
Exclusives Tier 1-262
Exclusives Tier 2-262
01BAP Signature Series-56
Autographs-56
Autographs Gold-56
01Upper Deck Victory-69
Gold-69
02BAP Sig Series Auto Buybacks 2001-56
02Lowell Lock Monsters-17
03Swedish Elite-203
Silver-203

Westner, Dave
76Saginaw Gears-12
78Saginaw Gears-20

Westover, Nathan
04Langley Hornets-19

Westrum, Erik
97Minnesota Golden Gophers-20
98Minnesota Golden Gophers-28
99Minnesota Golden Gophers-30
00Minnesota Golden Gophers-28
02Springfield Falcons-23
03BAP Memorabilia-235
03ITG VIP Rookie Debut-134
03Parkhurst Rookie-80
03UD Premier Collection-92
03Upper Deck Rookie Update-127
03Springfield Falcons Postcards-4
05ITG Heroes/Prosp Toronto Expo Parallel -201
05AHL All-Stars-43
05ITG Heroes and Prospects-201
Autographs Series II-EW
06Toronto Marlies-31
06ITG Heroes and Prospects-73
AHL Shooting Stars-AS06
Autographs-AEW

Westrum, Patrick
79Panini Stickers-211

Westrum, Ryan
98Minnesota Golden Gophers-14

Westwick, Harry
83Hall of Fame-135
83Hall of Fame Postcards-I16
85Hall of Fame-135

Wetherill, Darren
91Lake Superior State Lakers-26
92Lake Superior State Lakers-32
94Richmond Renegades-12
95Richmond Renegades-7
97Cleveland Lumberjacks-26
97Cleveland Lumberjacks Postcards-3
00Fresno Falcons-20
01Fresno Falcons-21

Wetter, Markus
93Swiss HNL-348
96Swiss HNL-480

Wetzel, Carl
72Minnesota Fighting Saints Postcards WHA-25
72Finnish Semic World Championship-117
72Swedish Semic World Championship-117

Wetzel, Todd
907th Inn. Sketch OHL-273
917th Inn. Sketch OHL-213
94Anaheim Bullfrogs RHI-19
95Anaheim Bullfrogs RHI-8
95Toledo Storm-8
96Anaheim Bullfrogs RHI-16
98German DEL-8
99UK London Knights-17
00Swiss Panini Stickers-294
01UK Guildford Flames-7

Wetzell, Stig
70Finnish Jaakiekko-290
71Finnish Suomi Stickers-164
72Finnish Jaakiekko-79
72Finnish Jaakiekko-116
73Finnish Jaakiekko-148
74Swedish Stickers-28
78Finnish SM-Liiga-21
80Finnish Mallasjuoma-1

Wever, Alwin
94German First League-404

Wevers, Mike
91Air Canada SJHL-E25
92Saskatchewan JHL-132

Weyermann, Michael
93Quebec Pee-Wee Tournament-1277

Wharram, Ken
44Beehive Group II Photos-145
52Juniors Blue Tint-176
58Topps-14
60Shirriff Coins-70
61Shirriff/Salada Coins-32
61Topps-30
61Topps-43
62Topps-39
63Chex Photos-57
63Topps-38
63Toronto Star-42
64Beehive Group III Photos-60
64Coca-Cola Caps-31
64Topps-28
64Topps-108
65Coca-Cola-32
65Topps-61
66Topps-117
66Topps USA Test-44
67Topps-117
67Topps-125
68Blackhawks Team Issue-8
68O-Pee-Chee-22
68Shirriff Coins-21
68Topps-22
69O-Pee-Chee-74
69Topps-74
94Parkhurst Tall Boys-23
94Parkhurst Tall Boys-137
94Parkhurst Tall Boys-150
95Parkhurst '66-67-29
Coins-29
03BAP Ultimate Memorabilia Linemates-1
03Parkhurst Original Six Chicago-40
03Parkhurst Original Six Chicago-70
Autographs-16
04ITG Ultimate Memorabilia-74
Gold-74

Wharton, Kyle
02Ottawa 67's-16
03Ottawa 67's-22
05Guelph Storm-D-02

Wheat, Torrie
01Swift Current Broncos-17
02Swift Current Broncos-21
03Everett Silvertips-16
04Everett Silvertips-13
05Everett Silvertips-25

Wheatcroft, Jim
88Lethbridge Hurricanes-23

Wheaton, Chris
01South Carolina Stingrays-19
03Las Vegas Wranglers-20

Wheaton, David
91Pro Set Platinum-294

Wheaton, John
01Owen Sound Attack-23

Wheeldon, Simon
83Victoria Cougars-24
89ProCards IHL-39
90Jets IGA-33
90Moncton Hawks-24
90ProCards AHL/IHL-246
91Baltimore Skipjacks-14
91ProCards-553
99German DEL-321
00German DEL-174
Game Jersey-SW
01German Upper Deck-195

Wheeler, Blake
04Green Bay Gamblers-23
05Minnesota Golden Gophers-25
06Minnesota Golden Gophers-23

Wheeler, Shawn
91Greensboro Monarchs-15
92Peoria Rivermen-27
93Hampton Roads Admirals-20
94Classic Pro Prospects-235
96Charlotte Checkers-18
97Charlotte Checkers-21
98Charlotte Checkers-19

Whelan, Shane
86London Knights-24

Whelan, Tobias
03Oshawa Generals-28
04Lakehead University Thunderwolves-23

Whidden, Jarrett
00Tacoma Sabercats-4

Whidden, Robert
72Cleveland Crusaders WHA-14

Whistle, Bill
88Brandon Wheat Kings-11

Whistle, David
00UK Sekonda Superleague-22
01UK Belfast Giants-3
03UK Cardiff Devils-20
05UK Sheffield Steelers-17
Gold-17
Silver-17

Whistle, Rob
88ProCards AHL-33

Whitacre, James
93Quebec Pee-Wee Tournament-1664

Whitaker, Gord
87Moncton Hawks-24

Whitchurch, Jed
00Trenton Titans-9

Whitcroft, Fred
83Hall of Fame-45
83Hall of Fame Postcards-C16
85Hall of Fame-45

White, Al
67Columbus Checkers-16

White, Alex
00Belleville Bulls-12
01Belleville Bulls-25
01London Knights-25

White, Alton
66Columbus Checkers-16
72Los Angeles Sharks WHA-18

White, Alvin
77Kalamazoo Wings-18

White, Andrew
06Halifax Mooseheads-15

White, Ben
01Missouri River Otters-8
03Missouri River Otters-14

White, Bill
68O-Pee-Chee-37
68Shirriff Coins-53
68Topps-37
69O-Pee-Chee-101
69Topps-101
70Blackhawks Postcards-14
70Esso Power Players-110
71O-Pee-Chee-11
71Sargent Promotions Stamps-47
71Topps-11
71Toronto Sun-82
72O-Pee-Chee-158
72O-Pee-Chee-248
Player Crests-6
Team Canada-28
72Sargent Promotions Stamps-62
72Topps-40
72Topps-128
73Mac's Milk-30
73O-Pee-Chee-78
73Topps-180
74NHL Action Stamps-75
74O-Pee-Chee NHL-90
74O-Pee-Chee NHL-136
74Topps-90
74Topps-136
75O-Pee-Chee NHL-157
75Topps-157
76O-Pee-Chee NHL-235
76Topps-235
91Future Trends Canada '72-15
91Future Trends Canada '72 French-15
04ITG Franchises US West-162
Autographs-A-BW
04UD Legendary Signatures-6
Autographs-BW
Summit Stars-CDN12
Summit Stars Autographs-CDN-BW

White, Brian
98Hershey Bears-31
00Hershey Bears-20
01Cincinnati Mighty Ducks-23
03Providence Bruins-23
04German DEL-179
05Finnish Cardset -316

White, Clucker
23V128-1 Paulin's Candy-55

White, Colin
95Slapshot Memorial Cup-67
97Albany River Rats-20
98Albany River Rats-20
99Albany River Rats-25
00BAP Signature Series-270
Emerald-270
Ruby-270
Sapphire-270
Autographs-117
Autographs Gold-117
00Black Diamond-80
Gold-80
00Crown Royale-131
21st Century Rookies-14
00Devils Team Issue-24
00O-Pee-Chee-288
00O-Pee-Chee Parallel-288
00Pacific-246
Copper-246
Gold-246
Ice Blue-246
Premiere Date-246
00Paramount-151
Copper-151
Gold-151
Holo-Gold-151
Holo-Silver-151
Ice Blue-151
Premiere Date-151
00Private Stock-130
Gold-130
Premiere Date-130
Retail-130
Silver-130
PS-2001 Rookies-13
00SPx-99
Spectrum-99
00Topps/OPC-288
Parallel-288
00Topps Chrome-183
OPC Refractors-183
Refractors-183
00Topps Heritage-92
Chrome Parallel-92
00Topps Premier Plus-134
Blue Ice-134
00UD Heroes-169
00UD Pros and Prospects-112
00Upper Deck-189
Exclusives Tier 1-189
Exclusives Tier 2-189
00Upper Deck Ice-59
Immortals-59
Legends-59
Stars-59
00Upper Deck MVP-196
First Stars-196
Second Stars-196
Third Stars-196
00Upper Deck Vintage-385
00Vanguard-132
Pacific Proofs-132
01BAP Memorabilia-226
Emerald-226
Ruby-226
Sapphire-226
01McDonald's Pacific Hometown Pride-9
01O-Pee-Chee-214
01O-Pee-Chee Premier Parallel-214
01Pacific-414
Gold-414
01Pacific Arena Exclusives-414
01Topps-214
OPC Parallel-214
02BAP Sig Series Auto Buybacks 2000-117
02Devils Team Issue-3
02Pacific Complete-490
Red-490
02Topps Total-399
02Upper Deck-352
Exclusives-352
02Upper Deck Beckett UD Promos-352
03Devils Team Issue-5
03ITG Action-312
03Upper Deck MVP-258
Gold Script-258
Silver Script-258
Canadian Exclusives-258
05Devils Team Issue-29
05Parkhurst-299
Facsimile Auto Parallel-299
06Devils Team Set-25
06O-Pee-Chee-296
Rainbow-296
06Panini Stickers-81
06Upper Deck-367
Exclusives Parallel-367
High Gloss Parallel-367
Masterpieces-367

White, Danny
03St. Francis Xavier X-Men-11
04St. Francis Xavier X-Men-23
06Richmond Renegades-15

White, Geoff
92British Columbia JHL-187

White, George
84Moncton Golden Flames-5
85Moncton Golden Flames-6

White, Goalie
85Sudbury Wolves-26
86Sudbury Wolves-33

White, Ian
00Swift Current Broncos-21
01Swift Current Broncos-5
02Swift Current Broncos-22
03Swift Current Broncos-22
06Be A Player-235
06Be A Player Portraits-128
06Beehive-154
Matte-154
06Black Diamond-193
Black-193
Gold-193
Ruby-193
06Flair Showcase-90
06Flair Showcase-165
Parallel-90
Parallel-165
06Fleer-210
Tiffany-210
06Gatorade-70
06Hot Prospects-137
Red Hot-137
White Hot-137
Hot Materials -HMIW
Hot Materials Red Hot-HMIW
Hot Materials White Hot-HMIW
Hotagraphs-HIW
06O-Pee-Chee-520
06O-Pee-Chee-640
Rainbow-520
Rainbow-640
06SP Authentic-205
Limited-205
06SP Game Used-156
Gold-156
Rainbow-156
Autographs-156
Rookie Exclusives Autographs-REIW
06SPx-170
Spectrum-170
06The Cup-161
Autographed NHL Shields Duals-DASWW
Autographed Rookie Masterpiece Pressplates-161
Gold Rainbow Autographed Rookie Patches-161
Masterpiece Pressplates (Artifacts)-217
Masterpiece Pressplates (Be A Player Portraits)-128
Masterpiece Pressplates (Bee Hive)-154
Masterpiece Pressplates (Marquee Rookies)-520
Masterpiece Pressplates (MVP)-337
Masterpiece Pressplates (Power Play)-128
Masterpiece Pressplates (SP Authentic Autographs)-205
Masterpiece Pressplates (SP Game Used)-156
Masterpiece Pressplates (SPx Autographs)-170
Masterpiece Pressplates (Sweet Beginnings)-155
Masterpiece Pressplates (Trilogy)-156
Masterpiece Pressplates (Ultimate Collection)-96
Masterpiece Pressplates (Victory)-212
Rookies Black-161
Rookies Platinum-161
06UD Artifacts-217
Blue-217
Gold-217
Platinum-217
Radiance-217
Red-217
06UD Mini Jersey Collection-128
06UD Powerplay-128
Impact Rainbow-128
06Ultimate Collection-96
Ultimate Debut Threads Jerseys-DJ-IW
Ultimate Debut Threads Jerseys Autographs-DJ-IW
Ultimate Debut Threads Patches-DJ-IW
Ultimate Debut Threads Patches Autographs-DJ-IW
06Ultra-228
Gold Medallion-228
Ice Medallion-228
06Upper Deck-246
Exclusives Parallel-246
High Gloss Parallel-246
Masterpieces-246
Rookie Game Dated Moments-RGD27
Rookie Headliners-RH15
Rookie Materials-RMIW
Rookie Materials Patches-RMIW
06Upper Deck MVP-337
Gold Script-337
Super Script-337
06Upper Deck Ovation-97
06Upper Deck Sweet Shot-155
Rookie Jerseys Autographs-155
06Upper Deck Trilogy-156
06Upper Deck Victory-212
06Upper Deck Victory Black-212
06Upper Deck Victory Gold-212
06Toronto Marlies-32
06ITG Heroes and Prospects-43
Autographs-AIW
Complete AHL Logos-AHL04
Jerseys-GUJ16
Jerseys Gold-GUJ16
Emblems-GUE16
Emblems Gold-GUE16
Numbers-GUN16
Numbers Gold-GUN16
07Upper Deck Rookie Class -30

White, Jason
90Brandon Wheat Kings-22
907th Inn. Sketch WHL-157
907th Inn. Sketch WHL-234
91British Columbia JHL-143
93Dallas Freeze-17
97Bakersfield Fog-19

White, Jeff
02UK Guildford Flames-15

White, Jim
74Sioux City Musketeers-20

White, Jordan
05Penticton Vees-22

White, Justin
02Topeka Scarecrows-9
04Sioux Falls Stampede-2-5
05Notre Dame Freshmen-2

White, K.J.
89Windsor Spitfires-21

White, Kam
94North Bay Centennials-6
94Sarnia Sting-4
95Slapshot-208
96Johnstown Chiefs-22
00Trenton Titans-21
01Trenton Titans-2-11
02Trenton Titans-A-8
03Atlantic City Boardwalk Bullies-26
03Atlantic City Boardwalk Bullies RBI-32
04Atlantic City Boardwalk Bullies Kinko's-6
05Port Huron Flags-7

White, Kevin
907th Inn. Sketch OHL-321

White, Mark
92Quebec Pee-Wee Tournament-1476
01Johnstown Chiefs-27
02Orlando Seals-10

White, Mike
95Slapshot-27
95Barrie Colts-27

White, Peter
93Donruss-431
93PowerPlay-344
93Score-629
Gold-629
Canadian-629
Canadian Gold-629
94Cape Breton Oilers-21
95Ultra-240
96Collector's Edge Ice-37
Prism-37
00Topps Gold Label Class 1-94
Gold-94
00Topps Gold Label Class 2-94
00Topps Gold Label Class 2 Gold-94
00Topps Gold Label Class 3-94
00Topps Gold Label Class 3 Gold-94
01BAP Signature Series-46
Autographs-46
Autographs Gold-46
01Norfolk Admirals-17
02BAP Sig Series Auto Buybacks 2001-46
02Philadelphia Phantoms-6
03Philadelphia Phantoms-21
05Philadelphia Phantoms All-Decade Team-7

White, Robert
52Juniors Blue Tint-106

White, Ryan
00Halifax Mooseheads-24
01Halifax Mooseheads-16
03St. Francis Xavier X-Men-1
04Calgary Hitmen-20
04St. Francis Xavier X-Men-24
05ITG Heroes/Prosp Toronto Expo Parallel -329

05Calgary Hitmen-22
05Kamloops Blazers-6
05ITG Heroes and Prospects-329
Autographs Series II-RWH
Team Orr-TO20
06Kamloops Blazers-23
06ITG Heroes and Prospects-127
Autographs-ARW
White, Scott
90Kansas City Blades-11
91Greensboro Monarchs-16
93Classic Pro Prospects-56
02ECHL Update-U-25
White, Sherman
51Laval Dairy QSHL-35
White, Stephane
93Quebec Pee-Wee Tournament-23
White, Todd
97Indianapolis Ice-27
98Pacific-154
Ice Blue-154
Red-154
98Pacific Omega-57
Red-57
Opening Day Issue-57
99Cleveland Lumberjacks-23
99IHL All-Stars-12
00Grand Rapids Griffins-22
01Crown Royale-103
Blue-103
Premiere Date-103
Red-103
Retail-103
01Senators Team Issue-27
01Titanium-102
Hobby Parallel-102
Premiere Date-102
Retail-102
Retail Parallel-102
01Upper Deck-355
Exclusives-355
02BAP First Edition-206
02BAP Signature Series Golf-GS96
02NHL Power Play Stickers-114
02O-Pee-Chee-204
02O-Pee-Chee Premier Blue Parallel-204
02O-Pee-Chee Premier Red Parallel-204
02O-Pee-Chee Factory Set-204
02Pacific-274
Blue-274
Red-274
02Pacific Complete-229
Red-229
02Senators Team Issue-19
02Topps-204
OPC Blue Parallel-204
OPC Red Parallel-204
Factory Set-204
02Topps Total-144
02Upper Deck-120
Exclusives-120
02Upper Deck Victory-153
Bronze-153
Gold-153
Silver-153
03ITG Action-427
03Pacific-245
Blue-245
Red-245
03Pacific Complete-341
Red-341
03Pacific Exhibit-107
Blue Backs-107
Yellow Backs-107
03Pacific Prism-75
Blue-75
Gold-75
Red-75
03Private Stock Reserve-74
Blue-74
Red-74
Retail-74
03Senators Postcards-20
03Upper Deck-382
Canadian Exclusives-382
HG-382
UD Exclusives-382
03Upper Deck MVP-290
Gold Script-290
Silver Script-290
Canadian Exclusives-290
03Upper Deck Victory-132
Bronze-132
Gold-132
Silver-132
05Be A Player Signatures-TW
05Be A Player Signatures Gold-TW
05Parkhurst-238
Facsimile Auto Parallel-238
05Upper Deck-344
06Be A Player-6
Autographs-6
Signatures-TW
06O-Pee-Chee-246
Rainbow-246
06Panini Stickers-299
06Upper Deck-99
Exclusives Parallel-99
High Gloss Parallel-99
Masterpieces-99
06Upper Deck MVP-150
Gold Script-150
Super Script-150
White, Tony
76O-Pee-Chee NHL-279
76O-Pee-Chee NHL-396
77O-Pee-Chee NHL-314
00Amarillo Rattlers-17
01Missouri River Otters-23
03Missouri River Otters-10
Whitecotton, Dustin
01Missouri River Otters-4
Whitehead, Duane
04Williams Lake Timberwolves-20
06Richmond Renegades-16
Whitehead, Tim
04Maine Black Bears-31
05Maine Black Bears-28
Whitehead, Tyler
04Cape Breton Screaming Eagles-21
Whitely, Steve
04St. Michael's Majors-2
05Saginaw Spirit-24
06Belleville Bulls-20
06Plymouth Whalers-26
Whitfield, Jeff
03Sarnia Sting-22
04London Knights-22
Whitfield, Ryan
04Vernon Vipers-9
Whitfield, Trent
94Spokane Chiefs-4
95Spokane Chiefs-9
96Upper Deck Ice-127
96Spokane Chiefs-8
97Spokane Chiefs-11
97Bowman CHL-89
OPC-89
98Portland Pirates-18
98Bowman CHL-50
Golden Anniversary-50
OPC International-50
98Bowman Chrome CHL-50
Golden Anniversary-50
Golden Anniversary Refractors-50
OPC International-50
OPC International Refractors-50
Refractors-50
99Portland Pirates-24
00Titanium-150
Retail-150
00Titanium Draft Day Edition-150
00Titanium Draft Day Promos-150
04Portland Pirates-21
05Peoria Rivermen-15
06Peoria Rivermen-20
Whiting, Reed
01Ohio State Buckeyes-19
02Ohio State Buckeyes-17
03Ohio State Buckeyes-16
Whitley, Brian
94North Bay Centennials-15
95Slapshot-221
Whitley, Chris
04Lakehead University Thunderwolves-24
Whitlock, Bob
74O-Pee-Chee WHA-12
75O-Pee-Chee WHA-93
Whitlock, Dan
02Arizona Icecats-23
03Arizona Icecats-22
Whitlock, Riley
05Saint John's Sea Dogs-18
Whitmarsh, Joel
01Sudbury Wolves-23
01Sudbury Wolves Police-25
Whitmore, Derek
03Lincoln Stars Update-33
Whitmore, Kay
88ProCards AHL-52
89ProCards AHL-303
90O-Pee-Chee-232
90Pro Set-610
90Score-402
Canadian-402
90Topps-232
Tiffany-232
91Pro Set Platinum-178
91Bowman-3
91OPC Premier-182
91Parkhurst-58
French-58
91Pinnacle-22
French-22
91Score Canadian Bilingual-625
91Score Canadian English-625
91Score Rookie/Traded-75T
91Upper Deck-291
French-291
91Whalers Jr. 7-Eleven-27
92Bowman-155
92Canucks Road Trip Art-25
92OPC Premier-87
92Panini Stickers-255
92Panini Stickers French-255
92Parkhurst-423
Emerald Ice-423
92Score-304
Canadian-304
92Stadium Club-459
92Topps-381
Gold-381G
92Upper Deck-76
93Donruss-359
93OPC Premier-514
Gold-514
93Parkhurst-478A
Emerald Ice-478A
93Pinnacle-138
Canadian-138
93PowerPlay-462
93Score-360
Canadian-360
93Stadium Club-60
Members Only Master Set-60
OPC-60
First Day Issue-60
First Day Issue OPC-60
93Topps/OPC Premier-514
Gold-514
93Ultra-443
94Canucks Program Inserts-22
94Leaf-524
94OPC Premier-134
Special Effects-134
94Pinnacle-438
Artist's Proofs-438
Rink Collection-438
94Topps/OPC Premier-85
94Topps/OPC Premier-134
Special Effects-134
95Canucks Building the Dream Art-2
97Long Beach Ice Dogs-18
98Hartford Wolf Pack-23
98Milwaukee Admirals-13
99Providence Bruins-25
00Topps Heritage-200
00Providence Bruins-1
00Providence Bruins-22
Whitmore, Keith
907th Inn. Sketch OHL-297
91Hampton Roads Admirals-18
93Flint Generals-11
94Flint Generals-22
Whitney, Dean
93Prince Albert Raiders-20
Whitney, Mike
95Red Deer Rebels-19
96Red Deer Rebels-24
97Red Deer Rebels-22
Whitney, Ray
89Spokane Chiefs-20
907th Inn. Sketch WHL-201
91Parkhurst-454
French-454
917th Inn. Sketch CHL Award Winners-20
917th Inn. Sketch Memorial Cup-82
91Classic-20
91Classic Four-Sport *-20
Autographs-20A
92Parkhurst-160
Emerald Ice-160
92Pinnacle-227
French-227
92Pro Set-241
92Score-475
Canadian-475
92Stadium Club-490
92Topps-205
Gold-205G
92Upper Deck-407
92Classic-119
Gold-119
Promos-3
92Classic Four-Sport *-223
Gold-223
93Parkhurst-182
Emerald Ice-182
93PowerPlay-439
93Score-324
Canadian-324
93Ultra-420
93Upper Deck-4
94Donruss-117
94Fleer-202
94Leaf-448
94OPC Premier-33
Special Effects-33
94Parkhurst SE-SE163
Gold-SE163
94Pinnacle-316
Artist's Proofs-316
Rink Collection-316
94SP-106
Die Cuts-106
94Stadium Club-149
Members Only Master Set-149
First Day Issue-149
Super Team Winner Cards-149
94Topps/OPC Premier-33
Special Effects-33
94Upper Deck-149
Electric Ice-149
SP Inserts-SP163
SP Inserts Die Cuts-SP163
95Be A Player-125
Signatures-S125
Signatures Die Cuts-S125
95Canada Games NHL POGS-225
95Collector's Choice-225
Player's Club-225
Player's Club Platinum-225
95Donruss-308
95Emotion-161
95Leaf-208
Road To The Cup-1
95Panini Stickers-280
95Parkhurst International-183
Emerald Ice-183
95Playoff One on One-304
95Score-84
Black Ice Artist's Proofs-84
Black Ice-84
95Stadium Club-86
Members Only Master Set-86
95Topps-68
OPC Inserts-68
95Ultra-150
Gold Medallion-150
95Upper Deck-62
Electric Ice-62
Electric Ice Gold-62
96Collector's Choice-240
96Pinnacle-20
Artist's Proofs-20
Foil-20
Premium Stock-20
Rink Collection-20
96Summit-83
Artist's Proofs-83
Ice-83
Metal-83
Premium Stock-83
96Upper Deck-150
97Be A Player-105
Autographs-105
Autographs Die-Cuts-105
Autographs Prismatic Die-Cuts-105
97Pacific Omega-105
Copper-105
Dark Gray-105
Emerald Green-105
Gold-105
Ice Blue-105
97Revolution-63
Copper-63
Emerald-63
Ice Blue-63
Silver-63
97SP Authentic-66
98Aurora-84
98Be A Player-56
Press Release-56
98BAP Gold-56
98BAP Autographs-56
98BAP Autographs Gold-56
98BAP Tampa Bay All Star Game-56
98Finest-138
No Protectors-138
No Protectors Refractors-138
Refractors-138
98Pacific-231
Ice Blue-231
Red-231
98Pacific Omega-107
Red-107
Opening Day Issue-107
98Panini Stickers-58
98Paramount-101
Copper-101
Emerald Green-101
Holo-Electric-101
Ice Blue-101
Silver-101
98SPx Finite-37
Radiance-37
Spectrum-37
98Topps Gold Label Class 1-26
Black-26
Black One of One-26
One of One-26
Red-26
Red One of One-26
98Topps Gold Label Class 2-26
98Topps Gold Label Class 2 Black-26
98Topps Gold Label Class 2 Black 1 of 1-26
98Topps Gold Label Class 2 One of One-26
98Topps Gold Label Class 2 Red-26
98Topps Gold Label Class 2 Red One of One-26
98Topps Gold Label Class 3-26
98Topps Gold Label Class 3 Black-26
98Topps Gold Label Class 3 Black 1 of 1-26
98Topps Gold Label Class 3 One of One-26
98Topps Gold Label Class 3 Red-26
98Topps Gold Label Class 3 Red One of One-26
98UD Choice-87
98UD Choice Preview-87
98UD Choice Prime Choice Reserve-87
98UD Choice Reserve-87
98Upper Deck-97
Exclusives-97
Exclusives 1 of 1-97
Gold Reserve-97
98Upper Deck MVP-89
Gold Script-89
Silver Script-89
Super Script-89
99Aurora-66
Premiere Date-66
99BAP Memorabilia-20
Gold-20
Silver-20
99BAP Millennium-112
Emerald-112
Ruby-112
Sapphire-112
Signatures-112
Signatures Gold-112
99Crown Royale-62
Limited Series-62
Premiere Date-62
99O-Pee-Chee-83
99O-Pee-Chee Chrome-83
99O-Pee-Chee Chrome Refractors-83
99Pacific-183
Copper-183
Emerald Green-183
Gold-183
Ice Blue-183
Premiere Date-183
Red-183
99Pacific Dynagon Ice-93
Blue-93
Copper-93
Gold-93
Premiere Date-93
99Pacific Omega-103
Copper-103
Gold-103
Ice Blue-103
Premiere Date-103
99Pacific Prism-64
Holographic Blue-64
Holographic Gold-64
Holographic Mirror-64
Holographic Purple-64
Premiere Date-64
99Paramount-106
Copper-106
Emerald-106
Gold-106
Holographic Emerald-106
Holographic Gold-106
Holographic Silver-106
Ice Blue-106
Premiere Date-106
Red-106
Silver-106
99Revolution-66
Premiere Date-66
Red-66
Shadow Series-66
99Stadium Club-71
First Day Issue-71
One of a Kind-71
Printing Plates Black-71
Printing Plates Cyan-71
Printing Plates Magenta-71
Printing Plates Yellow-71
99Topps/OPC-83
99Topps/OPC Chrome-83
Refractors-83
99Upper Deck MVP-87
Gold Script-87
Silver Script-87
Super Script-87
99Upper Deck MVP SC Edition-81
Gold Script-81
Silver Script-81
Super Script-81
00Aurora-64
Premiere Date-64
00BAP Memorabilia-93
Emerald-93
Ruby-93
Sapphire-93
Promos-93
00BAP Mem Chicago Sportsfest Copper-93
00BAP Memorabilia Chicago Sportsfest Blue-93
00BAP Memorabilia Chicago Sportsfest Gold-93
00BAP Memorabilia Chicago Sportsfest Ruby-93
00BAP Memorabilia Chicago Sun-Times Ruby-93
00BAP Memorabilia Chicago Sun-Times Gold-93
00BAP Mem Chicago Sun-Times Sapphire-93
00BAP Mem Toronto Fall Expo Copper-93
00BAP Memorabilia Toronto Fall Expo Gold-93
00BAP Memorabilia Toronto Fall Expo Ruby-93
00BAP Parkhurst 2000-P78
00BAP Signature Series-29
Emerald-29
Ruby-29
Sapphire-29
Autographs-42
Autographs Gold-42
00Crown Royale-47
Ice Blue-47
Limited Series-47
Premiere Date-47
Red-47
00O-Pee-Chee-88
00O-Pee-Chee Parallel-88
00Pacific-189
Copper-189
Gold-189
Ice Blue-189
Premiere Date-189
00Panini Stickers-35
00Panthers Team Issue-17
00Paramount-109
Copper-109
Gold-109
Holo-Gold-109
Holo-Silver-109
Ice Blue-109
Premiere Date-109
00Revolution-65
Blue-65
Premiere Date-65
Red-65
00SP Authentic-39
00Stadium Club-123
00Topps/OPC-88
Parallel-88
00Topps Chrome-70
OPC Refractors-70
Refractors-70
00Topps Heritage-185
00Topps Stars-76
Blue-76
00UD Heroes-51
00UD Pros and Prospects-37
00UD Reserve-37
00Upper Deck-75
Exclusives Tier 1-75
Exclusives Tier 2-75
00Upper Deck MVP-80
First Stars-80
Second Stars-80
Third Stars-80
00Upper Deck Victory-106
00Upper Deck Vintage-151
00Vanguard-47
Holographic Gold-47
Holographic Purple-47
Pacific Proofs-47
01Blue Jackets Donatos Pizza-20
01Pacific-120
Extreme LTD-120
Hobby LTD-120
Premiere Date-120
Retail LTD-120
01Pacific Arena Exclusives-120
01Titanium-42
Hobby Parallel-42
Premiere Date-42
Retail-42
Retail Parallel-42
01UD Challenge for the Cup-22
01UD Mask Collection-26
Gold-26
Double Patches-DPRW
Jerseys-J-RW
Jersey and Patch-JPRW
01UD Playmakers-29
01Upper Deck-50
Exclusives-50
01Upper Deck MVP-53
02Atomic-30
Blue-30
Gold-30
Red-30
Hobby Parallel-30
02BAP First Edition-217
02BAP Memorabilia-45
Emerald-45
Ruby-45
Sapphire-45
NHL All-Star Game-45
NHL All-Star Game Blue-45
NHL All-Star Game Green-45
NHL All-Star Game Red-45
02BAP Memorabilia Toronto Fall Expo-45
02BAP Signature Series-45
Autographs-45
Autograph Buybacks 1998-56
Autograph Buybacks 1999-112
Autograph Buybacks 2000-42
Autographs Gold-45
02Bowman YoungStars-103
Gold-103
Silver-103
02O-Pee-Chee-191
02O-Pee-Chee Premier Blue Parallel-191
02O-Pee-Chee Premier Red Parallel-191
02O-Pee-Chee Factory Set-191
02Pacific-109
Blue-109
Red-109
02Pacific Complete-209
Red-209
02Pacific Exclusive-53
02Pacific Heads-Up-36
Blue-36
Purple-36
Red-36
02Pacific Quest for the Cup-26
Gold-26
02Parkhurst-198
Bronze-198
Gold-198
Silver-198
02Parkhurst Retro-28
Minis-28
02Private Stock Reserve-32
Blue-32
Red-32
Retail-32
02SP Authentic-25
Beckett Promos-25
02SP Game Used Authentic Fabrics-AFRW
02SP Game Used Authentic Fabrics Gold-AFRW
02SP Game Used Authentic Fabrics Rainbow-AFRW
02Topps-191
OPC Blue Parallel-191
OPC Red Parallel-191
Factory Set-191
02Topps Total-397
02UD Honor Roll-19
02UD Honor Roll-79
02UD Top Shelf Dual Player Jerseys-STKW
02Upper Deck-52
Exclusives-52
Hot Spots-HSRW
02Upper Deck MVP-54
Gold-54
Classics-54
Golden Classics-54
Skate Around Jerseys-STWKT
02Upper Deck Victory-58
Bronze-58
Gold-58
Silver-58
02Upper Deck Vintage-75
03BAP Memorabilia-74
Emerald-74
Gold-74
Ruby-74
Sapphire-74
03BAP Ultimate Memorabilia Autographs-4
Gold-4
03Crown Royale-38
Blue-38
Retail-38
03ITG Action-121
03ITG Used Signature Series-84
Gold-84
Autographs-RW
Autographs Gold-RW
03NHL Sticker Collection-196
03O-Pee-Chee-243
03OPC Blue-243
03OPC Gold-243
03OPC Red-243
03Pacific-100
Blue-100
Red-100
03Pacific Complete-227
Red-227
03Pacific Exhibit-45
Blue Backs-45
Yellow Backs-45
03Pacific Prism-33
Blue-33
Gold-33
Red-33
03Pacific Supreme-34
Blue-34
Red-34
Retail-34
03Parkhurst Original Six Detroit-9
03Topps-243
Blue-243
Gold-243
Red-243
03Topps Traded-TT13
Blue-TT13
Gold-TT13
Red-TT13
03Upper Deck-310
Canadian Exclusives-310
HG-310
UD Exclusives-310
03Upper Deck MVP-114
Gold Script-114
Silver Script-114
Canadian Exclusives-114
Souvenirs-S5
03Upper Deck Victory-50
Bronze-50
Gold-50
Silver-50
05Be A Player Signatures-RW
05Be A Player Signatures Gold-RW
05Panini Stickers-52
05Parkhurst-91
Facsimile Auto Parallel-91
05Upper Deck MVP-80
Gold-80
Platinum-80
06Hurricanes Postcards-27
06O-Pee-Chee-97
Rainbow-97
06Panini Stickers-45
06Upper Deck-41
Exclusives Parallel-41
High Gloss Parallel-41
Masterpieces-41
06Upper Deck MVP-59
Gold Script-59
Super Script-59
Whitney, Ryan
97Quebec Pee-Wee Tournament-1165
02BAP Memorabilia Draft Redemptions-5
03Boston University Terriers-16
04AHL Top Prospects-57
04Wilkes-Barre Scranton Penguins-6
04ITG Heroes and Prospects-187
Autographs-U-RW
Emblems-63
Emblems Gold-63
Jerseys-63
Jerseys Gold-63
Numbers-63
Numbers Gold-63
04ITG Heroes/Prospects Toronto Expo '05-187
05ITG Heroes/Prosp Toronto Expo Parallel -73
05Beehive-137
Beige -137
Blue -137
Gold-137
Red -137
Matte-137
Signature Scrapbook-SSRW
05Black Diamond-271
05Hot Prospects-263
En Fuego-263
Hot Materials-HMRW
Red Hot-263
White Hot-263
05Parkhurst-659
Facsimile Auto Parallel-659
True Colors-TCPIT
True Colors-TCPIT
05SP Authentic-191
Rarefied Rookies-RRRW
05SP Game Used-186
Gold-186
05SPx-239
Spectrum-239
05The Cup-102
Autographed Rookie Patches Gold Rainbow-102
Black Rainbow Rookies-102
Masterpiece Pressplates (Artifacts)-315
Masterpiece Pressplates (Bee Hive)-137
Masterpiece Pressplates (Black Diamond)-271
Masterpiece Pressplates (Ice)-138
Masterpiece Pressplates (Rookie Update)-229
Masterpiece Pressplates SPA Autos-191
Masterpiece Pressplates (SP Game Used)-186
Masterpiece Pressplates SPx Autos-239
Masterpiece Pressplates (Trilogy)-292
Masterpiece Pressplates Ult Coll-178
Masterpiece Pressplates (Victory)-284
Masterpiece Pressplates Autographs-102
Platinum Rookies-102
05UD Artifacts-315
05UD Rookie Class-31
05Ultimate Collection-178
Gold-178
Ultimate Debut Threads Jerseys-DTJRW
Ultimate Debut Threads Patches-DTPRW
Ultimate Signatures-USRW
05Upper Deck-461
Rookie Ink-RIRW
05Upper Deck Ice-138
05Upper Deck Rookie Update-229
Inspirations Patch Rookies-229
05Upper Deck Trilogy-292
05Upper Deck Victory-284
Black-284
Gold-284
Silver-284
05WBS Penguins-27
05ITG Heroes and Prospects-73
Complete Logos-AHL-11
He Shoots-He Scores Prizes-37
Jerseys-GUJ-14
Jerseys Gold-GUJ-14
Emblems-GUE-14
Emblems Gold-GUE-14
Numbers-GUN-14
Numbers Gold-GUN-14
Nameplates-N-11
Nameplates Gold-N-11
06Be A Player Portraits Dual Signature Portraits-DSFW
06Be A Player Portraits First Exposures-FERW
06Be A Player Portraits Signature Portraits-SPRW
06Beehive Signature Scrapbook-SSRW
06Black Diamond-67
Black-67
Gold-67
Ruby-67
06O-Pee-Chee-393
06O-Pee-Chee-629
Rainbow-393
Rainbow-629
06Panini Stickers-143
06SP Game Used SIGnificance-SRW
06UD Toronto Fall Expo Priority Signings -PSRW
06Ultra-158
Gold Medallion-158
Ice Medallion-158
06Upper Deck-159
Exclusives Parallel-159
High Gloss Parallel-159
Masterpieces-159
Signature Sensations-SSRW
06Upper Deck MVP-234
Gold Script-234
Super Script-234
06Upper Deck Victory-162
06Upper Deck Victory Black-162
06Upper Deck Victory Gold-162
07Upper Deck Victory-12
Black-12
Gold-12
Whitten, Damon
00Michigan State Spartans-18
01Greenville Grrrowl-15
Whitten, Erin
92Sports Illustrated for Kids II-551
93Toledo Storm-27
94Classic Women of Hockey-W40
94Classic Pro Prospects-249
Autographs-AU8
95Flint Generals-1
Whitten, Wade
89Sault Ste. Marie Greyhounds-16
907th Inn. Sketch OHL-175
917th Inn. Sketch OHL-347A
917th Inn. Sketch Memorial Cup-8
Whittle, Jeff
917th Inn. Sketch WHL-167
94Flint Generals-23
95Flint Generals-23
96Flint Generals-21
97Flint Generals-22
97Flint Generals EBK-15
98Detroit Vipers-15
98Flint Generals-6
Whittman, Don
97Pinnacle Hockey Night in Canada-13
Whittom, Dave
917th Inn. Sketch QMJHL-283
917th Inn. Sketch Memorial Cup-58
93Quebec Pee-Wee Tournament-1017
Whitton, Damon
02Arkansas Riverblades-21
Whitton, Mike
92Western Michigan Broncos-26
93Western Michigan Broncos-27
95Toledo Storm-13
96Toledo Storm-25
Whitwell, David
02UK Peterborough Phantoms-3
Whitwell, John
01Augusta Lynx-8
Whitworth, Dave
92British Columbia JHL-129
99Greensboro Generals-5
00Trenton Titans-23
01Greensboro Generals-7
02Greensboro Generals RBI-18
Whynot, Craig
95Slapshot-258
Whyte, Darryl
93Kitchener Rangers-3
94Kitchener Rangers-3
Whyte, Dean
84Belleville Bulls-21
Whyte, George
52Juniors Blue Tint-63
Whyte, Noah
05Quad City Mallards-18
Whyte, Sandra
94Classic Women of Hockey-W30
Whyte, Sean
90ProCards AHL/IHL-346
91ProCards-401
92Phoenix Roadrunners-26
93Classic Pro Prospects-101
95Central Hockey League-16
95Fort Worth Fire-8
98Phoenix Mustangs-22
Wiberg, Jan-Ove
74Swedish Stickers-196
Wiberg, Joakin
96Madison Monsters-22
Wibner, Christian
98Odessa Jackalopes-15
Wichser, Adrian
93Quebec Pee-Wee Tournament-1621
98Swiss Power Play Stickers-124
98Swiss Power Play Stickers-292
99Swiss Panini Stickers-125
99Swiss Panini Stickers-299
00Swiss Panini Stickers-167
00Swiss Slapshot Mini-Cards-EHCK16
01Swiss HNL-73
02Swiss HNL-99
Wick, Marcel
93Swiss HNL-470
95Swiss HNL-246
Wick, Roman
05Lethbridge Hurricanes-20
05Red Deer Rebels-22
Wickberg, Hakan
64Swedish Coralli ISHockey-23
64Swedish Coralli ISHockey-77
65Swedish Coralli ISHockey-23
65Swedish Coralli ISHockey-77
67Swedish Hockey-23
67Swedish Hockey-59
69Swedish Hockey-74
70Finnish Jaakiekko-40
70Swedish Hockey-35
70Swedish Hockey-292
70Swedish Masterserien-106
71Finnish Suomi Stickers-60
71Swedish Hockey-25
71Swedish Hockey-113
72Finnish Jaakiekko-59
72Finnish Hellas-41
72Finnish Panda Toronto-79
72Finnish Semic World Championship-52
72Swedish Stickers-20
72Swedish Stickers-92
72Swedish Semic World Championship-52
73Finnish Jaakiekko-39
73Swedish Stickers-13
73Swedish Stickers-163
74Finnish Jenkki-37
74Swedish Stickers-269
74Swedish Semic World Champ Stickers-9
81Swedish Semic Hockey VM Stickers-116
Wickberg, Jan
83Swedish Semic Elitserien-121
Wickenheiser, Chris
93Red Deer Rebels-27
95Red Deer Rebels-20
98ECHL All-Star Southern Conference-20
99Tallahassee Tiger Sharks-13
Wickenheiser, Doug
80Canadiens Postcards-26
80Pepsi-Cola Caps-60
81Canadiens Postcards-28
81O-Pee-Chee-193
82Canadiens Postcards-28
82Canadiens Steinberg-23
82McDonald's Stickers-26
82O-Pee-Chee-196
83Canadiens Postcards-33
83NHL Key Tags-68
83O-Pee-Chee-202
83O-Pee-Chee Stickers-67
83Topps Stickers-67
83Vachon-60
84O-Pee-Chee-193
84O-Pee-Chee Stickers-58
85O-Pee-Chee-229
85O-Pee-Chee Stickers-52
87Canucks Shell Oil-24
87O-Pee-Chee-193
87Panini Stickers-318
87Topps-193
88O-Pee-Chee-263
88O-Pee-Chee Stickers-56
89Capitals Team Issue-23
92Peoria Rivermen-26
93Fort Wayne Komets-22
Wickenheiser, Hayley
94Classic Women of Hockey-W13
97Collector's Choice-279
97Esso Olympic Hockey Heroes-58
97Esso Olympic Hockey Heroes French-58
04Canadian Womens World Championship Team-22
06ITG Going For Gold-20
06ITG Going For Gold Samples-20
06ITG Going For Gold Autographs-AWI
06ITG Going For Gold Jerseys-GUJ20
Wickenheiser, Kurt
82Regina Pats-16
83Regina Pats-16
94German First League-410
99Corpus Christi IceRays-26
99Corpus Christi IceRays-34
Wicks, Ron
91Ultimate Original Six-87
French-87
Wickstrom, Kjell-Arne
67Swedish Hockey-166
69Swedish Hockey-93
71Swedish Hockey-132
73Finnish Jaakiekko-40
73Swedish Stickers-11
73Swedish Stickers-71
74Finnish Jenkki-38
74Swedish Stickers-270
Wickstrom, Per-Allan
72Swedish Stickers-107
74Swedish Stickers-271
Wickware, Randy
81Victoria Cougars-16
Wicky, Michel
95Swiss HNL-506
96Swiss HNL-248
99Swiss Panini Stickers-341
02Swiss HNL-305
Widauer, Christian
03UK Basingstoke Bison-17
Wideman, Dennis
99Sudbury Wolves-7
00Sudbury Wolves-8
01London Knights-3
02London Knights-2
03London Knights-9
04AHL All-Stars-46
04Worcester IceCats-17
04ITG Heroes and Prospects-70
Autographs-DW
04ITG Heroes/Prospects Toronto Expo '05-70
04ITG Heroes/Prospects Expo Heroes/Pros-70
05Beehive-96
Matte-96
05Black Diamond-281
05Blues Team Set-23
05Hot Prospects-164
En Fuego-164
Red Hot-164
White Hot-164
05Parkhurst-429
Facsimile Auto Parallel-429
05SP Authentic-240
Limited-240
05SP Game Used-233
05SPx-282
05The Cup Masterpiece Pressplate Artifact-325
05The Cup Masterpiece Pressplate Bee Hive-96
05The Cup Master Pressplate Black Diamond-281
05The Cup Masterpiece Pressplates (Ice)-206
05The Cup Master Pressplate Rookie Update-174
05The Cup Masterpiece Pressplates SPA-240
05The Cup Masterpiece Pressplates SP GU-233
05The Cup Masterpiece Pressplates (SPx)-282
05The Cup Masterpiece Pressplates Trilogy-300
05The Cup Masterpiece Pressplate Ult Coll-225
05UD Artifacts-325
05Ultimate Collection-225
Gold-225
05Upper Deck-484
05Upper Deck Ice-206
05Upper Deck Rookie Update-174
05Upper Deck Trilogy-300
05ITG Heroes and Prospects Complete Logos-AHL-19
05ITG Heroes and Prospects Jerseys-GUJ-101
05ITG Heroes and Prospects Jerseys Gold-GUJ-101
05ITG Heroes and Prospects Nameplates-N-55
05ITG Heroes and Prospects Nameplate Gold-N-55
05ITG Heroes and Prospects Shooting Stars-AS-3
06O-Pee-Chee-435
Rainbow-435

06Upper Deck-417
Exclusives Parallel-417
High Gloss Parallel-417
Masterpieces-417

Widenborg, Michael
99Danish Hockey League-176

Widing, Daniel
00Swedish Upper Deck-114
02Swedish SHL Dynamic Duos-4
03Finnish Cardset-120
04Finnish Cardset-128
Parallel-94
05Finnish Cardset -336

Widing, Juha
70Colgate Stamps-11
70Dad's Cookies-140
70Esso Power Players-155
70Sargent Promotions Stamps-76
710-Pee-Chee-86
O-Pee-Chee/Topps Booklets-19
71Sargent Promotions Stamps-65B
71Topps-86
71Toronto Sun-124
720-Pee-Chee-46
72Sargent Promotions Stamps-93
72Topps-108
730-Pee-Chee-159
73Topps-156
74NHL Action Stamps-123
740-Pee-Chee NHL-258
74Topps-258
750-Pee-Chee NHL-142
750-Pee-Chee NHL-320
75Topps-142
75Topps-320
760-Pee-Chee NHL-354
770-Pee-Chee WHA-33

Widmark, Bjorn
98UK Kingston Hawks-7

Widmark, Christer
98UK Kingston Hawks-9

Widmark, Per
93Swedish Semic Elitserien-132

Widmer, Jason
907th Inn. Sketch WHL-136
917th Inn. Sketch WHL-357
917th Inn. Sketch Memorial Cup-129
93Lethbridge Hurricanes-22
95Leaf-287
96Kentucky Thoroughblades-19
97Kentucky Thoroughblades-18

Widmer, Thomas
00Swiss Panini Stickers-168
01Swiss HNL-74
02Swiss HNL-44

Wiebe, Art
34Beehive Group I Photos-85
35Diamond Matchbooks Tan 1-69
35Diamond Matchbooks Tan 2-64
35Diamond Matchbooks Tan 3-59
35Diamond Matchbooks Tan 4-15
35Diamond Matchbooks Tan 5-14
360-Pee-Chee V304D-113
37Diamond Matchbooks Tan 6-14
37V356 Worldwide Gum-124
390-Pee-Chee V301-1-49

Wiebe, Dan
92Toledo Storm-15

Wieckowski, Krzystof
98SP Authentic-134
Power Shift-134
98Upper Deck-411
Exclusives-411
Exclusives 1 of 1-411
Gold Reserve-411
02Greenville Grrrowl-19

Wieczorek, Dariusz
89Swedish Semic World Champ Stickers-130

Wiegand, Chuck
91Nashville Knights-12
93Johnstown Chiefs-13

Wiegand, Jake
02Notre Dame Fighting Irish-1

Wiegand, Josh
93Michigan State Spartans-29

Wieland, Markus
94German DEL-370
95German DEL-362
96German DEL-137
98German DEL-78
99German Adler Mannheim Eagles Postcards-17
99German DEL-16
05German SC Bietigheim-Bissingen Steelers-3

Wiele, Sven
99German DEL-328

Wielgus, Janusz
94German First League-655

Wieloch, Slawomir
92Finnish Semic-284

Wiemer, Jason
93Upper Deck Program of Excellence-E3
93Portland Winter Hawks-26
94Finest Bowman's Best-R16
94Finest Bowman's Best-X25
94Finest Bowman's Best Refractors-R16
94Finest Bowman's Best Refractors-X25
94Flair-176
94Fleer-211
94Leaf-489
Phenoms-4
94Leaf Limited-119
94Lightning Photo Album-26
94Lightning Postcards-18
94OPC Premier-463
Special Effects-463
94Parkhurst SE-SE172
Gold-SE172
94Pinnacle-484
Artist's Proofs-484
Rink Collection-484
94Select-171
Gold-171
94Topps/OPC Premier-463
Special Effects-463
94Ultra-374
Prospects-10
94Upper Deck-262
Electric Ice-262
SP Inserts-SP166
SP Inserts Die Cuts-SP166
94Classic-8
Gold-8
Tri-Cards-T64
94Classic Four-Sport *-122
Gold-122
Printers Proofs-122
95Donruss-11
95Leaf-23
Studio Rookies-19
95Lightning Team Issue-19
95Parkhurst International-193
Emerald Ice-193
95Pinnacle-77
Artist's Proofs-77
Rink Collection-77
95Score-149
Black Ice Artist's Proofs-149
Black Ice-149
95Ultra-156
Gold Medallion-156
95Upper Deck-391
Electric Ice-391
Electric Ice Gold-391
95Images Four-Sport *-101
96Be A Player-26
Autographs-26
Autographs Silver-26
96Upper Deck-157
97Pacific Dynagon Best Kept Secrets-90
98Be A Player-21
Press Release-21
98BAP Gold-21
98BAP Autographs-21
98BAP Autographs Gold-21
98BAP Tampa Bay All Star Game-21
98Pacific-128
Ice Blue-128
Red-128
98Pacific Omega-36
Red-36
Opening Day Issue-36
99Pacific-63
Copper-63
Emerald Green-63
Gold-63
Ice Blue-63
Premiere Date-63
Red-63
000-Pee-Chee-254B
000-Pee-Chee Parallel-254B
00Pacific-76
Copper-76
Gold-76
Ice Blue-76
Premiere Date-76
00Topps/OPC-254B
Parallel-254B
00Upper Deck Vintage-61
01Pacific-68
01Pacific-405
Extreme LTD-68
Gold-405
Hobby LTD-68
Premiere Date-68
Retail LTD-68
01Pacific Arena Exclusives-68
01Pacific Arena Exclusives-405
01Parkhurst-216
01Upper Deck-306
Exclusives-306
02BAP Sig Series Auto Buybacks 1998-21
02Pacific-162
Blue-162
Red-162
02Pacific Complete-349
Red-349
03ITG Action-309
05Upper Deck MVP-70
Gold-70
Platinum-70
06Devils Team Set-26

Wiemer, Jim
88Oilers Tenth Anniversary-25
88ProCards AHL-95
89Bruins Sports Action Update-11
89New Haven Nighthawks-13
900-Pee-Chee-439
90Pro Set-413
91Bowman-363
91Bruins Sports Action-22
910-Pee-Chee-475
91Score Canadian Bilingual-535
91Score Canadian English-535
91Stadium Club-16
91Topps-475

Wienke, Steve
86Kamloops Blazers-22

Wiens, Luke
05Kootenay Ice-22

Wieren, Van
79Panini Stickers-279

Wierzba, Nick
93Quebec Pee-Wee Tournament-802

Wiesel, Adam
95Fredericton Canadiens-28
95Classic-81
Autographs-23
95Classic Five-Sport *-152
96Fredericton Canadiens-23

Wieser, Josef
94German First League-170

Wieser, Mathias
94German First League-175

Wieser, Nando
93Swiss HNL-213
96Swiss HNL-103
99Swiss Panini Stickers-315
00Swiss Panini Stickers-79
00Swiss Slapshot Mini-Cards-EHCC1
01Swiss HNL-236

Wiesmann, Robert
93Swiss HNL-447
95Swiss HNL-327
96Swiss HNL-303
99Swiss Panini Stickers-350

Wiesser, Nando
95Swiss HNL-113

Wiest, Matt
04South Surrey Eagles-28
04Surrey Eagles-23
04Surrey Eagles-23

Wiest, Rich
86Kamloops Blazers-23

Wiggins, Chris
06UK Guildford Flames-17

Wiggins, Mike
05Roanoke Valley Vipers-12

Wight, David
96Sault Ste. Marie Greyhounds-27
96Sault Ste. Marie Greyhounds Autographed-27

Wight, Travis
04Maine Black Bears-4
05Maine Black Bears-27
06Idaho Steelheads-21

Wigle, Dennis
84Ottawa 67's-28

Wigren, Ulf
67Swedish Hockey-130
69Swedish Hockey-143
70Swedish Hockey-88
71Swedish Hockey-181
72Swedish Stickers-170

Wiikman, Miika
04Finnish Cardset-30
Parallel-22
05Finnish Cardset -25
Finnish Cardset Super Snatchers-4
06Finnish Cardset-210
Between the Pipes-6
Signature Sensations-3
Superior Snatchers-11
Superior Snatchers Gold-11
Superior Snatchers Silver-11
Trophy Winners-6

Wiita, Martin
91Swedish Semic Elitserien Stickers-148
92Norwegian Elite Series-107
93Swedish Semic Elitserien-137
98Swedish UD Choice-28
99German Bundesliga 2-307
01UK Dundee Stars-17
02UK Dundee Stars-17

Wikberg, Anders
85Swedish Panini Stickers-212
86Swedish Panini Stickers-208
87Swedish Panini Stickers-202

Wikegard, Niklas
01Swiss HNL-234

Wikgren, Ulf
83Swedish Semic Elitserien-45
84Swedish Semic Elitserien-45

Wiklander, Lars-Goran
95Swedish Leaf-203
Rookies-4
95Swedish Upper Deck-217
97Swedish Collector's Choice-67
98Swedish UD Choice-60
99Swedish Upper Deck-45

Wiklander, Mikael
93Swedish Semic Elitserien-34
94Swedish Leaf-191
95Swedish Leaf-179
95Swedish Upper Deck-22
98Danish Hockey League-186
99Danish Hockey League-68

Wiklund, Gote
57Swedish Alfabilder-77

Wikman, Juha
72Finnish Jaakiekko-298

Wikman, Sven
56Swedish Alfabilder-45

Wikner, John
05Brandon Wheat Kings-23

Wikstrom, Jorgen
93Swedish Semic Elitserien-3
98Swedish UD Choice-17

Wikstrom, Kjell-Arne
72Swedish Stickers-210

Wikstrom, Michael
83Swedish Semic Elitserien-19
84Swedish Semic Elitserien-17

Wikstrom, Sami
92Finnish Jyvas-Hyva Stickers-143
93Finnish Jyvas-Hyva Stickers-264
93Finnish SISU-295
99Danish Hockey League-65

Wikstrom, Seppo
70Finnish Jaakiekko-307
71Finnish Suomi Stickers-205
72Finnish Jaakiekko-242

Wikstrom, Terje
92Norwegian Elite Series-176

Wikulow, Sergej
94German DEL-168

Wilchynski, Chad
96Medicine Hat Tigers-25
99Alexandria Warthogs-23
00Amarillo Rattlers-18
02Charlotte Checkers-95

Wilcox, Archie
330-Pee-Chee V304B-57
33V357 Ice Kings-9

Wilcox, Chad
06Fayetteville FireAntz-21

Wilcox, Dayle
97Moose Jaw Warriors-19

Wilcox, George
87Hull Olympiques-21
97Anchorage Aces-21
98Anchorage Aces-8
99Anchorage Aces-12

Wild, Leonard
00German DEL-167
01German Upper Deck-247
02German DEL City Press-212
04German DEL-139

Wild, Martin
79Panini Stickers-104

Wilde, Martin
01Providence Bruins-19
03Swedish Elite-103
Silver-103
03Providence Bruins-24
04Hershey Bears Patriot News-30
04Reading Royals-22
05Hershey Bears-17

Wilder, Archie
34Beehive Group I Photos-131
400-Pee-Chee V301-2-145

Wildfong, Dan
01Bossier-Shreveport Mudbugs-22
02Bossier-Shreveport Mudbugs-19
03Bossier-Shreveport Mudbugs-18
05Bossier-Shreveport Mudbugs-20

Wildfong, Jack
61Hamilton Red Wings-19

Wildgoose, Lyle
91Richmond Renegades Set 2-4
92Raleigh Icecaps-19
92Raleigh Icecaps-34
93Raleigh Icecaps-19
94Raleigh Icecaps-20
94Classic Pro Prospects-242

Wilejto, Dave
99Tupelo T-Rex-10

Wilejto, Steve
96Prince Albert Raiders-22
97Prince Albert Raiders-21

Wilenius, Bengt
66Finnish Jaakiekkosarja-110
71Finnish Suomi Stickers-241
72Finnish Jaakiekko-225
73Finnish Jaakiekko-303

Wiley, Jim
74NHL Action Stamps-279
76Canucks Royal Bank-23
96Kentucky Thoroughblades-20
97Kentucky Thoroughblades-22
02Lexington Men O'War-2

Wilford, Marty
95Slapshot-233
97Indianapolis Ice-28
97Bowman CHL-18
OPC-18
98Indianapolis Ice-4
99Houston Aeros-2
01St. John's Maple Leafs-26
02Norfolk Admirals-23
03Norfolk Admirals-21
04Norfolk Admirals-21
05Manchester Monarchs-21
06Iowa Stars-24

Wilgosh, Curtis
99ECHL All-Star Northern Conference-8

Wilgosh, Kiel
02OCN Blizzard-13
03OCN Blizzard-25

Wilhelmy, Jonathan
98Quebec Remparts-23
Signed-23

Wilk, Gregor
94German First League-553

Wilkens, Jake
01Sioux Falls Stampede-18
03Vernon Vipers-17

Wilkey, Jim
97Arizona Icecats-24

Wilkie, Bob
89ProCards AHL-307
90ProCards AHL/IHL-477
91Score American-328
91Score Canadian Bilingual-358
91Score Canadian English-358
94Parkhurst-171
Gold-171
95German DEL-11
95Cincinnati Cyclones-20
98Pensacola Ice Pilots-4
99Anchorage Aces-1

Wilkie, Brian
86Regina Pats-29

Wilkie, David
907th Inn. Sketch WHL-11
917th Inn. Sketch WHL-95
92Classic-11
Gold-11
LPs-LP7
92Classic Four-Sport *-160
Gold-160
93Donruss Team USA-22
93Pinnacle-487
Canadian-487
93Upper Deck-558
93Kamloops Blazers-24
94Leaf-458
94OPC Premier-481
Special Effects-481
94Topps/OPC Premier-481
Special Effects-481
94UK Solihul Barons-14
94Fredericton Canadiens-30
95Leaf-259
95UK Solihull Barons-7
96Be A Player-108
Autographs-108
Autographs Silver-108
96Canadiens Postcards-33
96Canadiens Sheets-26
96Flair-113
Blue Ice-113
96Hockey Greats Coins-25
Gold-25
96Metal Universe-195
96SP-82
96Topps Picks-173
OPC Inserts-173
96Ultra-91
Gold Medallion-91
Rookies-19
96Upper Deck-282
96Collector's Edge Ice-43
Prism-43
97Canadiens Postcards-26
97Pacific-54
Copper-54
Emerald Green-54
Ice Blue-54
Red-54
Silver-54
99Houston Aeros-15
00Upper Deck NHLPA-PA60

Wilkie, Max
97Arizona Icecats-23

Wilkins, Andrew
05London Knights-16
06London Knights-14

Wilkins, Barry
70Canucks Royal Bank-18
70Esso Power Players-40
71Canucks Royal Bank-14
710-Pee-Chee-230
71Sargent Promotions Stamps-221
71Toronto Sun-293
72Canucks Nalley's-6
72Canucks Royal Bank-19
720-Pee-Chee-109
72Sargent Promotions Stamps-217
72Topps-102
73Canucks Royal Bank-20
74NHL Action Stamps-273
74NHL Action Stamps Update-29
740-Pee-Chee NHL-182
74Topps-182
750-Pee-Chee NHL-148
75Topps-148
76Topps-102
94SLU Basketball-27

Wilkins, Jon
93Quebec Pee-Wee Tournament-1249

Wilkinson, Bill
92Western Michigan Broncos-27
93Western Michigan Broncos-28

Wilkinson, Derek
917th Inn. Sketch OHL-48
94Atlanta Knights-23
95Atlanta Knights-21
96Cleveland Lumberjacks-25
96Cleveland Lumberjacks Multi-Ad-27
96Collector's Edge Future Legends-44
96Collector's Edge Ice-103
Prism-103
97Donruss-213
Press Proofs Silver-213
Press Proofs Gold-213
97Cleveland Lumberjacks-27
97Cleveland Lumberjacks Postcards-20
98Cleveland Lumberjacks-23
99Charlotte Checkers-13
00UK Sekonda Superleague-181
01UK Belfast Giants-24

Wilkinson, Mark
95Waterloo Blackhawks -22

Wilkinson, Neil
88ProCards IHL-39
89ProCards IHL-91
90Bowman-184
Tiffany-184
900-Pee-Chee-443
90Pro Set-465
90Upper Deck-547
French-547
91Pro Set Platinum-229
910-Pee-Chee-348
91OPC Premier-110
91Parkhurst-382
French-382
91Pinnacle-108
French-108
91Pro Set-328
91Pro Set-483
French-328
French-483
91Score American-369
91Score Canadian Bilingual-328
91Score Canadian Bilingual-558
91Score Canadian English-328
91Score Canadian English-558
91Score Rookie/Traded-8T
91Sharks Sports Action-19
91Stadium Club-293
91Topps-348
91Upper Deck-55
91Upper Deck-95
French-55
French-95
92Humpty Dumpty II-25
92Panini Stickers-128
92Panini Stickers French-128
92Parkhurst-165
Emerald Ice-165
92Pinnacle-27
French-27
92Pro Set-168
92Score-235
Canadian-235
92Stadium Club-219
92Topps-76
Gold-76G
92Ultra-198
92Upper Deck-30
93Blackhawks Coke-15
93Donruss-62
93Leaf-357
93Parkhurst-315
Emerald Ice-315
93Pinnacle-354
Canadian-354
93Score-138
93Score-523
Gold-523
Canadian-138
Canadian-523
Canadian Gold-523
93Upper Deck-378
94Be A Player-R70
Signature Cards-44
94EA Sports-116
94Upper Deck-392
Electric Ice-392
95Parkhurst International-439
Emerald Ice-439
97Upper Deck-347

Wilkinson, Peter
92Western Michigan Broncos-28
93Western Michigan Broncos-29

Wilks, Brian
82Kitchener Rangers-15
83Kitchener Rangers-9
84Kitchener Rangers-15
88ProCards AHL-220
89ProCards AHL-148

Will, Andrew
97Mobile Mysticks-16
97Mobile Mysticks Kellogg's-1
98Mobile Mysticks-21

Will, Colby
04Columbus Cottonmouths-11

Willard, Craig
97Macon Whoopee-13
97Macon Whoopee Autographs-13
98Oklahoma City Blazers-4

Willard, Rod
83Springfield Indians-18

Willberg, Esa
70Finnish Jaakiekko-292

Willenius, Bengt
78Finnish SM-Liiga-211

Willers, Greg
93Quebec Pee-Wee Tournament-481
01Austin Ice Bats-18
02Odessa Jackalopes-18

Willerton, Larry
97OCN Blizzard-4
98OCN Blizzard-4

Willett, Paul
91ProCards-368
95Fort Wayne Komets-21
98Muskegon Fury-19
98UHL All-Stars-8
99Bakersfield Condors-20
00Bakersfield Condors-20
00Bakersfield Condors-21
01Bakersfield Condors-20
02Bakersfield Condors-19
03Bakersfield Condors-21
04Bakersfield Condors-23

Williams, Barry
74Penguins Postcards-22

Williams, Blake
02Chicago Steel-22

Williams, Bobby
03Swift Current Broncos-23

Williams, Brian
86Sherbrooke Canadiens-30

Williams, Colin
04Penticton Vees-10

Williams, Dan
89Johnstown Chiefs-26

Williams, Danny
03Odessa Jackalopes-19

Williams, Darryl
88ProCards AHL-194
89ProCards AHL-25
90ProCards AHL/IHL-416
91ProCards-369
92Phoenix Roadrunners-27
93Phoenix Roadrunners-25
97Long Beach Ice Dogs-19
98Long Beach Ice Dogs-18
02Cincinnati Mighty Ducks-B-2
03Cincinnati Mighty Ducks-A13

Williams, Dave
74Maple Leafs Postcards-26
75Heroes Stand-Ups-31
75Maple Leafs Postcards-28
75Maple Leafs Postcards-29
76Maple Leafs Postcards-24
760-Pee-Chee NHL-373
760-Pee-Chee NHL-394
77Maple Leafs Postcards-19
770-Pee-Chee NHL-4
770-Pee-Chee NHL-383
77Topps-4
78Maple Leafs Postcards-22
780-Pee-Chee-66
780-Pee-Chee-359
78Topps-66
79Maple Leafs Postcards-32
790-Pee-Chee-4
790-Pee-Chee-97
79Topps-4
79Topps-97
80Canucks Silverwood Dairies-24
80Canucks Team Issue-22
800-Pee-Chee-105
800-Pee-Chee-164
80Pepsi-Cola Caps-120
80Topps-105
80Topps-164
81Canucks Team Issue-20
810-Pee-Chee-345
810-Pee-Chee-385
810-Pee-Chee Stickers-247
81Post Standups-10
82Canucks Team Issue-22
820-Pee-Chee-358
82Post Cereal-19
83Canucks Team Issue-22
83NHL Key Tags-122
830-Pee-Chee-363
83Puffy Stickers-4
83Vachon-120
847-Eleven Discs-12
86Kings 20th Anniversary Team Issue-23
860-Pee-Chee-6
860-Pee-Chee Stickers-94
86Topps-6
87Panini Stickers-283
95Vancouver VooDoo RHI-2
01BAP Update Tough Customers-TC1
01Greats of the Game-39
Autographs-39
01Parkhurst Autographs-PA44
01Saskatoon Blades-16
02BAP Signature Series Famous Scraps-FS1
02BAP Ultimate Mem Retro Teammates-1
02Maple Leafs Platinum Collection-39
03Parkhurst Orig Six He Shoots/Scores-6
03Parkhurst Orig Six He Shoots/Scores-6A
03Parkhurst Original Six Toronto-36
Autographs-13
Memorabilia-TM31
Memorabilia-TM54
04ITG Franchises Canadian-101
04ITG Franchises Canadian-117
Autographs-TW1
Autographs-TW2
04ITG Franchises US East-354
04ITG Ultimate Memorabilia Original Six-8
04ITG Ultimate Mem Retro Teammates-4
04ITG Ultimate Memorabilia Triple Threads-10
04UD Legendary Signatures-24
Autographs-TI
Linemates-TISSTT
04UD Legends Classics-14
04UD Legends Classics-61
Gold-14
Gold-61
Platinum-14
Platinum-61
Silver-14
Silver-61
Jersey Redemptions-JY28
Signature Moments-M40
Signatures-CS38
Signatures-DC15
05ITG Tough Customers-TW
Autographs-TW
Famous Battles Autographs-WS
Jerseys-TW
Signed Memorabilia-TW
05ITG Ultimate Mem Record Breaker Jerseys-19
05ITG Ultimate Mem RecBreak Jerseys Gold-19
05ITG Ultimate Mem 3 Star of the Game Jsy-19
05ITG Ult Mem 3 Star of the Game Jsy Gold-19
05SP Game Used Heritage Classic-HC-DW
05SP Game Used Heritage Classic Autos-HCA-DW
05SP Game Used Heritage Classic Patches-HCP-DW
05SP GameUsed Heritage Classic Patch Auto-HAP-DW
05SP Game Used Oldtimer's Challenge-OC-DW
05SP Game Used Oldtimer's Challenge Autos-OCA-DW
05SP Game Used Oldtimer's Challenge Patch-OCP-DW
05SP Game Used Oldtime Chall Patch Autoa-OAP-DW
05SPx-128
Xcitement Legends-XL-TW
Xcitement Legends Gold-XL-TW
Xcitement Legends Spectrum-XL-TW
05The Cup Emblems of Endorsement-EETI
05The Cup Signature Patches-SPTI
06ITG Ultimate Memorabilia-137
Artist Proof-137
Stick Rack-22
Stick Rack Gold-22
06Parkhurst-149
06Parkhurst-229
06Parkhurst-230
06Parkhurst-248
Autographs-149
Autographs-229
Autographs-230
Autographs-248
Autographs Dual-DATB
Autographs Dual-DAWS
06SP Game Used Inked Sweaters Dual-IS2WP
06SP Game Used Inked Sweaters Dual Patches-IS2WP
06SP Game Used Letter Marks-LMDW
06SPx-121
Spectrum-121
06The Cup Honorable Numbers-HNTW
06The Cup Scripted Swatches-SSDW
06UD Artifacts-149
Blue-149
Gold-149
Platinum-149
Radiance-149
Autographed Radiance Parallel-149
Red-149
Auto-Facts-AFWI
Auto-Facts Gold-AFWI
Treasured Patches Black-TSDW
Treasured Patches Blue-TSDW
Treasured Patches Gold-TSDW
Treasured Patches Platinum-TSDW
Treasured Patches Red-TSDW
Treasured Patches Autographed Black Tag Parallel-TSDW
Treasured Swatches-TSDW
Treasured Swatches Black-TSDW
Treasured Swatches Blue-TSDW
Treasured Swatches Gold-TSDW
Treasured Swatches Platinum-TSDW
Treasured Swatches Red-TSDW
Treasured Swatches Autographed Black-TSDW
Tundra Tandems-TTDR
Tundra Tandems Black-TTDR
Tundra Tandems Blue-TTDR
Tundra Tandems Gold-TTDR
Tundra Tandems Platinum-TTDR
Tundra Tandems Red-TTDR
Tundra Tandems Dual Patches Red-TTDR
06Upper Deck Game Jerseys-J2DW
06Upper Deck Game Patches-P2DW
06Upper Deck Trilogy Scripts-TSWI

Williams, David
90Knoxville Cherokees-101
91Kansas City Blades-4
92Bowman-377
920-Pee-Chee-250
92Pro Set-172
92Score-539
Canadian-539
92Stadium Club-461
92Topps-372
Gold-372G
92Upper Deck-51
92Kansas City Blades-2
94Ducks Carl's Jr.-25
94Leaf-538
97Cincinnati Cyclones-19

Williams, Dunc
04ITG Ultimate Memorabilia Original Six-8

Williams, Gordie
83Springfield Indians-7

Williams, Greg
02Peterborough Petes-14
04Kingston Frontenacs-23
04Peterborough Petes Postcards-23

Williams, Jack
89Kitchener Rangers-9
90Kitchener Rangers-28
907th Inn. Sketch OHL-247
907th Inn. Sketch Memorial Cup-48
917th Inn. Sketch OHL-57
93Wichita Thunder-17
94Central Hockey League-126
95Central Hockey League-89
96Louisiana Ice Gators II-21
97Louisiana Ice Gators-10

Williams, Jason
00BAP Memorabilia-510
00Black Diamond-118
00SP Authentic-104
01BAP Memorabilia-25
Emerald-25
Ruby-25
Sapphire-25
01BAP Signature Series-211
Autographs-211
Autographs Gold-211
010-Pee-Chee-307
010-Pee-Chee Premier Parallel-307
01Parkhurst-299
01Parkhurst Beckett Promos-299
01Private Stock-104
Gold-104
Premiere Date-104
Retail-104
Silver-104
01Private Stock Pacific Nights-104
01Private Stock PS-2002-81
01Stadium Club-119
Award Winners-119
Master Photos-119
01Topps-307
OPC Parallel-307
01Upper Deck Victory-369
Gold-369
01Cincinnati Mighty Ducks-24
02BAP Memorabilia Stanley Cup Champions-SCC-12
02BAP Sig Series Auto Buybacks 2001-211
02Pacific-136
Blue-136
Red-136
Jerseys-18
Jerseys Holo-Silver-18
02Pacific Complete-163
Red-163
02Pacific Heads-Up Quad Jerseys-12
02Pacific Heads-Up Quad Jerseys Gold-12
02Titanium Jerseys-27
02Titanium Jerseys Retail-27
02Titanium Patches-27
02Upper Deck Playbooks Series II-LW
03ITG Action-299
03Parkhurst Original Six Detroit-26
04Finnish Cardset-198
04Finnish Cardset Signatures-41
04Swedish Pure Skills-144
Parallel-144
05Topps Lux Box Trinity Triple Relics 25-WWP
05Topps Luxury Box Trinity Triple Relic 1-WWP
05Topps Luxury Box Trinity Triple Relics-WWP
05Topps Luxury Box Trinity Triple Relics-WWW
05Topps Luxury Box Trinity Triple Relic 1-WWW
05Topps Lux Box Trinity Triple Relics 25-WWW
05Beehive Matted Materials-MMJW
05Parkhurst-172
Facsimile Auto Parallel-172
05Upper Deck-316
Jerseys Series II-J2JW
05Upper Deck Victory-217
Black-217
Gold-217
Silver-217
05Finnish Cardset -172
Finnish Cardset Magicmakers-18
06Upper Deck Trilogy-75
Gold-75
06Upper Deck Trilogy Blue-75
06Flair Showcase Stitches-SSWI
060-Pee-Chee-180
Rainbow-180
06SP Game Used Authentic Fabrics-AFJW
06SP Game Used Authentic Fabrics Parallel-AFJW
06SP Game Used Authentic Fabrics Patches-AFJW
06UD Artifacts Tundra Tandems-TTDW
06UD Artifacts Tundra Tandems Black-TTDW
06UD Artifacts Tundra Tandems Blue-TTDW
06UD Artifacts Tundra Tandems Gold-TTDW
06UD Artifacts Tundra Tandems Platinum-TTDW
06UD Artifacts Tundra Tandems Red-TTDW
06UD Artifacts Tundra Tandems Dual Patches Red-TTDW
06Upper Deck-72
Exclusives Parallel-72
High Gloss Parallel-72
Game Jerseys-JJW
Game Patches-PJW
Masterpieces-72
Shootout Artists-SA9
06Upper Deck MVP-111
Gold Script-111
Super Script-111
07Upper Deck Victory-119
Black-119
Gold-119

Williams, Jeff
93Guelph Storm-17
94Guelph Storm-18
95Slapshot-98
95Guelph Storm-11
97Albany River Rats-21
98Albany River Rats-21
99Albany River Rats-26
00Syracuse Crunch-13

Williams, Jeremy
02Swift Current Broncos-23
03Swift Current Broncos-24
05AHL Top Prospects-49
06Be A Player Portraits-129
06Black Diamond-154A
Black-154A
Gold-154A
Ruby-154A
06Flair Showcase-94
Parallel-94
06Hot Prospects-138
Red Hot-138
White Hot-138
Hotagraphs-HJW
060-Pee-Chee-521
Rainbow-521
06SP Authentic-204
Limited-204
06SP Game Used Rookie Exclusives Autographs-REJW
06SPx-171
Spectrum-171
06The Cup-163
Autographed NHL Shields Duals-DASWW
Autographed Rookie Masterpiece Pressplates-163
Gold Rainbow Autographed Rookie Patches-163
Masterpiece Pressplates (Artifacts)-218
Masterpiece Pressplates (Be A Player Portraits)-129
Masterpiece Pressplates (Black Diamond)-154
Masterpiece Pressplates (Marquee Rookies)-521
Masterpiece Pressplates (MVP)-339
Masterpiece Pressplates (Power Play)-129
Masterpiece Pressplates (SP Authentic Autographs)-204
Masterpiece Pressplates (SPx Autographs)-171
Masterpiece Pressplates (Sweet Beginnings)-156
Masterpiece Pressplates (Trilogy)-157
Masterpiece Pressplates (Victory)-227
Rookies Black-163
Rookies Platinum-163
06UD Artifacts-218
Blue-218
Gold-218
Platinum-218
Radiance-218
Red-218
06UD Mini Jersey Collection-129
06UD Powerplay-129
Impact Rainbow-129
06Ultimate Collection Ultimate Debut Threads Jerseys-DJ-JW
06Ultimate Collection Ultimate Debut Threads Jerseys Autographs-DJ-JW
06Ultimate Collection Ultimate Debut Threads Patches-DJ-JW
06Ultimate Collection Ultimate Debut Threads Patches Autographs-DJ-JW
06Ultra-229
Gold Medallion-229
Ice Medallion-229
06Upper Deck-247
Exclusives Parallel-247
High Gloss Parallel-247
Masterpieces-247
Rookie Materials-RMJW
Rookie Materials Patches-RMJW
06Upper Deck MVP-339
Gold Script-339
Super Script-339
06Upper Deck Sweet Shot-156
Rookie Jerseys Autographs-156
06Upper Deck Trilogy-157
06Upper Deck Victory-227
06Upper Deck Victory Black-227
06Upper Deck Victory Gold-227
06Toronto Marlies-33
06ITG Heroes and Prospects-44
Autographs-AJW
07Upper Deck Rookie Class -26

Williams, Justin
95Quebec Pee-Wee Tournament-692
99OCN Blizzard-16
00BAP Memorabilia-444
Emerald-444
Ruby-444
Sapphire-444
00BAP Parkhurst 2000-P226
00BAP Signature Series-260
Emerald-260
Ruby-260
Sapphire-260
Autographs-222
Autographs Gold-222
00Black Diamond-129
00Crown Royale-136
21st Century Rookies-19
00Private Stock-136
Gold-136
Premiere Date-136
Retail-136
Silver-136
PS-2001 Rookies-16
00SP Authentic-118
00SP Game Used-79

00SPx-120
Spectrum-120
00Stadium Club-245
00Titanium-138
Retail-138
00Titanium Draft Day Edition-138
00Titanium Draft Day Promos-138
00Topps Chrome-241
Blue-241
Red-241
OPC Refractors-241
OPC Refractors Blue-241
OPC Refractors Red-241
Refractors-241
Refractors Blue-241
Refractors Red-241
00Topps Gold Label Class 1-106
Gold-106
00Topps Gold Label Class 2-106
00Topps Gold Label Class 2 Gold-106
00Topps Gold Label Class 3-106
00Topps Gold Label Class 3 Gold-106
00Topps Gold Label Autographs-GLA-JW
00Topps Heritage-97
Chrome Parallel-97
00Topps Premier Plus-128
Blue Ice-128
Private Signings-PSJW
Rookies-PR5
Rookies Blue Ice-PR5
00Topps Stars-109
Blue-109
00UD Heroes-174
00UD Pros and Prospects-119
Now Appearing-NA6
00UD Reserve-109
00Upper Deck-214
Exclusives Tier 1-214
Exclusives Tier 2-214
00Upper Deck Ice-97
00Upper Deck Vintage-389
00Vanguard-138
Pacific Proofs-138
00OCN Blizzard-15
01BAP Memorabilia-101
Emerald-101
Ruby-101
Sapphire-101
01Bowman YoungStars-155
Gold-155
Ice Cubed-155
Autographs-JW
Relics-JJW
Relics-SJW
Relics-DSJW
Rivals-R7
01Flyers Postcards-23
01O-Pee-Chee-33
01O-Pee-Chee Heritage Parallel-33
01O-Pee-Chee Heritage Parallel Limited-33
01O-Pee-Chee Premier Parallel-33
01Pacific-296
Extreme LTD-296
Hobby LTD-296
Premiere Date-296
Retail LTD-296
01Pacific Adrenaline-144
Blue-144
Premiere Date-144
Red-144
Retail-144
01Pacific Arena Exclusives-296
01SP Authentic-114
Limited-114
Limited Gold-114
01SPx Hidden Treasures-DTGW
01Topps-33
Heritage Parallel-33
Heritage Parallel Limited-33
OPC Parallel-33
Heritage Autographs-AJW
01UD Mask Collection Double Patches-DPJW
01UD Mask Collection Jerseys-J-JW
01UD Mask Collection Jersey and Patch-JPJW
01Upper Deck-129
Exclusives-129
Game Jerseys-NGJW
Game Jerseys Series II-GNJW
01Upper Deck MVP-139
01Upper Deck Victory-257
Gold-257
01OCN Blizzard-17
02BAP Memorabilia-156
Emerald-156
Ruby-156
Sapphire-156
Future of the Game-FG-20
NHL All-Star Game-156
NHL All-Star Game Blue-156
NHL All-Star Game Green-156
NHL All-Star Game Red-156
02BAP Memorabilia Toronto Fall Expo-156
02Flyers Postcards-6
02O-Pee-Chee-184
02O-Pee-Chee Premier Blue Parallel-184
02O-Pee-Chee Premier Red Parallel-184
02O-Pee-Chee Factory Set-184
02Pacific-290
Blue-290
Red-290
02Pacific Complete-131
Red-131
02Parkhurst Retro-156
Minis-156
02SP Authentic Sign of the Times-JW
02SP Authentic Sign of the Times-LW
02SP Game Used Authentic Fabrics-AFJW
02SP Game Used Authentic Fabrics Gold-AFJW
02SP Game Used Authentic Fabrics Rainbow-AFJW
02SP Game Used First Rounder Patches-JW
02SP Game Used Signature Style-JW
02Stadium Club YoungStars Relics-S11
02Stadium Club YoungStars Relics-DS5
02Topps-184
OPC Blue Parallel-184
OPC Red Parallel-184
Factory Set-184
02Topps Total-185
02UD Artistic Impressions Right Track-RTJW
02UD Artistic Impression Right Track Gold-RTJW
02UD Premier Collection Signatures Bronze-SJW
02UD Premier Collection Signatures Gold-SJW
02UD Premier Collection Signatures Silver-SJW
02UD Top Shelf Dual Player Jerseys-RIW
02Upper Deck-131
Exclusives-131
02Upper Deck MVP-137
Gold-137
Classics-137
Golden Classics-137
Skate Around Jerseys-SDWF
Skate Around Jerseys-SDWG
Souvenirs-S-JW
02Upper Deck Victory-160
Bronze-160
Gold-160
Silver-160
02Upper Deck Vintage-187
Green Backs-187
Jerseys-HSJW
Jerseys Gold-HS-JW
03Beehive-141
Gold-141
Silver-141
Sticks Blue Border-BL4
03Black Diamond-128
Black-128
Green-128
Red-128
Signature Gems-SG-31
03Crown Royale-76
Blue-76
Retail-76
03ITG Action-463
03O-Pee-Chee-163
03OPC Blue-163
03OPC Gold-163
03OPC Red-163
03Pacific Calder-18
Silver-18
03Pacific Complete-99
Red-99
03Pacific Heads-Up-75
Hobby LTD-75
Retail LTD-75
03SPx-170
Radiance-170
Spectrum-170
03Topps-163
Blue-163
Gold-163
Red-163
Pristine Jersey Portions-PPJ-JW
Pristine Jersey Portion Refractors-PPJ-JW
Pristine Patches-PP-JW
Pristine Patch Refractors-PP-JW
03Topps Traded-TT5
Blue-TT5
Gold-TT5
Red-TT5
03UD Premier Collection-10
03Upper Deck-387
Canadian Exclusives-387
HG-387
Shooting Stars-ST-JW
UD Exclusives-387
03Upper Deck Ice-14
Gold-14
03Upper Deck MVP-316
Gold Script-316
Silver Script-316
Canadian Exclusives-316
03Upper Deck Rookie Update-14
03Upper Deck Trilogy Scripts-S2JW
03Upper Deck Trilogy Scripts Limited-S2JW
03Upper Deck Trilogy Scripts Red-S2JW
04Pacific-54
Blue-54
Red-54
04UD All-World-61
Gold-61
Autographs-61
Triple Autographs-AT-CWR
Quad Autographs-AQ-SWE
Quad Autographs-AQ-YFW
Six Autographs-AS-SWD
04Swedish Elitset-220
Dominators-5
Gold-220
04Swedish Pure Skills-53
Parallel-53
05Be A Player Signatures-JW
05Be A Player Signatures Gold-JW
05Black Diamond-26
Emerald-26
Gold-26
Onyx-26
Ruby-26
05Panini Stickers-46
05Parkhurst-87
Facsimile Auto Parallel-87
True Colors-TCCAR
True Colors-TCCAR
05SP Game Used Auto Draft-AD-JW
05SP Game Used Awesome Authentics-AA-JW
05SP Game Used Awesome Authentics Gold-DA-JW
05SPx Winning Combos-WC-EJ
05SPx Winning Combos-WC-SW
05SPx Winning Combos Autographs-AWC-SW
05SPx Winning Combos Gold-WC-EJ
05SPx Winning Combos Gold-WC-SW
05SPx Winning Combos Spectrum-WC-EJ
05SPx Winning Combos Spectrum-WC-SW
05SPx Winning Materials-WM-JW
05SPx Winning Materials Autographs-AWM-JW
05UD Artifacts-19
Blue-19
Gold-19
Green-19
Pewter-19
Red-19
Auto Facts-AF-JW
Auto Facts Blue-AF-JW
Auto Facts Copper-AF-JW
Auto Facts Pewter-AF-JW
Auto Facts Silver-AF-JW
Frozen Artifacts-FA-JW
Frozen Artifacts Autographed-FA-JW
Frozen Artifacts Copper-FA-JW
Frozen Artifacts Dual-FAD-JW
Frozen Artifacts Dual Autographed-FAD-JW
Frozen Artifacts Dual Copper-FAD-JW
Frozen Artifacts Dual Gold-FAD-JW
Frozen Artifacts Dual Maroon-FAD-JW
Frozen Artifacts Dual Pewter-FAD-JW
Frozen Artifacts Dual Silver-FAD-JW
Frozen Artifacts Gold-FA-JW
Frozen Artifacts Maroon-FA-JW
Frozen Artifacts Patches-FP-JW
Frozen Artifacts Patches Autographed-FP-JW
Frozen Artifacts Patches Dual-FPD-JW
Frozen Artifacts Patches Dual Autos-FPD-JW
Frozen Artifacts Patches Pewter-FP-JW
Frozen Artifacts Patches Silver-FP-JW
Frozen Artifacts Pewter-FA-JW
Frozen Artifacts Silver-FA-JW
Gold Autographed-19
05UD Powerplay Power Marks-PMJW
05Ultra-42
Gold-42
Ice-42
05Upper Deck-36
Big Playmakers-B-JW
HG Glossy-36
Jerseys-J-JW
Jerseys Series II-J2JU
Notable Numbers-N-JW
Patches-P-JW
05Upper Deck MVP-79
Gold-79
Platinum-79
05Upper Deck Trilogy Honorary Patches-HP-JW
05Upper Deck Tril Honorary Patch Script-HSP-JW
05Upper Deck Trilogy Honorary Swatches-HS-JW
05Upper Deck Tril Honorary Swatch Scripts-HSS-JW
05Upper Deck Toronto Fall Expo-36
05Upper Deck Victory-209
Black-209
Gold-209
Silver-209
06Be A Player-5
Autographs-5
Signatures-JW
Signatures 10-5
Signatures 25-5
Up Close and Personal-UC2
Up Close and Personal Autographs-UC2
06Black Diamond-16
Black-16
Gold-16
Ruby-16
06Flair Showcase-21
Parallel-21
Stitches-SSJW
06Fleer-36
Tiffany-36
Fabricology-FJW
06Hurricanes Postcards-28
06O-Pee-Chee-98
Rainbow-98
06Panini Stickers-46
06SP Authentic Sign of the Times-STJW
06SP Authentic Sign of the Times Triples-ST3WSW
06SP Game Used Authentic Fabrics Dual-AF2WB
06SP Game Used Authentic Fabrics Dual Patches-AF2WB
06SP Game Used Inked Sweaters-ISJW
06SP Game Used Inked Sweaters Patches-ISJW
06SP Game Used Inked Sweaters Dual-IS2SW
06SP Game Used Inked Sweaters Dual Patches-IS2SW
06SPx Winning Materials-WMJW
06SPx Winning Materials Spectrum-WMJW
06The Cup Autographed NHL Shields Duals-DASSW
06UD Artifacts Tundra Tandems-TTWB
06UD Artifacts Tundra Tandems Black-TTWB
06UD Artifacts Tundra Tandems Blue-TTWB
06UD Artifacts Tundra Tandems Gold-TTWB
06UD Artifacts Tundra Tandems Platinum-TTWB
06UD Artifacts Tundra Tandems Red-TTWB
06UD Artifacts Tundra Tandems Dual Patches Red-TTWB
06Ultra-38
Gold Medallion-38
Ice Medallion-38
Uniformity-UJW
Uniformity Patches-UPJW
06Upper Deck Arena Giveaways-CAR3
06Upper Deck-37
Exclusives Parallel-37
High Gloss Parallel-37
Game Jerseys-J2JW
Game Patches-P2JW
Masterpieces-37
Signatures-SJW
06Upper Deck MVP-58
Gold Script-58
Super Script-58
Jerseys-OJWW
06Upper Deck Ovation-159
06Upper Deck Trilogy Honorary Scripted Patches-HSPJW
06Upper Deck Trilogy Honorary Scripted Swatches-HSSJW
06Upper Deck Trilogy Honorary Swatches-HSJW
06Upper Deck Victory-38
06Upper Deck Victory Black-38
06Upper Deck Victory Gold-38
07Upper Deck Ovation-40
07Upper Deck Victory-82
Black-82
Gold-82

Williams, Justin (Minors)
02Fort Worth Brahmas-17
03Fort Worth Brahmas-17

Williams, Justin (NCAA)
04Minnesota-Duluth Bulldogs-26

Williams, Martin
94German First League-394
98German DEL-146
99German Bundesliga 2-172

Williams, Mike
90Cincinnati Cyclones-23
92Toledo Storm Team Issue-7
93Oklahoma City Blazers-17
93Peterborough Petes-18
94Central Hockey League-90
94San Antonio Iguanas-18
95Slapshot-322
95Central Hockey League-106
98Oklahoma City Blazers-17

Williams, Nathanael
04UK Coventry Blaze-22
04UK Coventry Blaze Champions-17

Williams, Paul
97Anchorage Aces-22
98Anchorage Aces-17
99Anchorage Aces-3
01Anchorage Aces-15
07Absolute Memorabilia Rookie Premiere Materials Autographs AFC/NFC Spectrum Platinum-277

Williams, Richard
93Quebec Pee-Wee Tournament-1684

Williams, Rod
84Kelowna Wings-14
85Brandon Wheat Kings-21
86Regina Pats-30

Williams, Sean
88ProCards IHL-119
89ProCards IHL-50
90ProCards AHL/IHL-393
91ProCards-488
92Indianapolis Ice-25
94Minnesota Moose-14
95Minnesota Moose-6

Williams, Steve
91British Columbia JHL-95
92British Columbia JHL-130
93Quebec Pee-Wee Tournament-1682

Williams, Tom
44Beehive Group II Photos-74
51Cleveland Barons-10
60Cleveland Barons-18
61Shirriff/Salada Coins-17
62Topps-21
63Topps-12
64Beehive Group III Photos-29
64Coca-Cola Caps-8
64Topps-58
65Coca-Cola-7
65Topps-35
66Topps-38
66Topps USA Test-38
67Topps-40
68O-Pee-Chee-11
68Shirriff Coins-16
68Topps-11
69O-Pee-Chee-128
69Topps-128
70Colgate Stamps-5
70Dad's Cookies-141
70Esso Power Players-172
70North Stars Postcards-9
70O-Pee-Chee-169
70Sargent Promotions Stamps-83
71O-Pee-Chee-31
71Sargent Promotions Stamps-130
71Topps-31
71Toronto Sun-61
72Whalers New England WHA-17
74Capitals White Borders-25
74NHL Action Stamps-118
74O-Pee-Chee NHL-394
75O-Pee-Chee NHL-79
75O-Pee-Chee NHL-179
75O-Pee-Chee NHL-330
75Topps-79
75Topps-179
75Topps-330
76O-Pee-Chee NHL-319
77O-Pee-Chee NHL-5
77O-Pee-Chee NHL-44
77Topps-5
77Topps-44
78O-Pee-Chee-314
93Quebec Pee-Wee Tournament-681
94Parkhurst Tall Boys-4
95Parkhurst '66-67-11
Coins-11
02Parkhurst Vintage Teammates-VT20

Williams, Vince
00Trenton Titans-10
01Florida Everblades-4
02Trenton Titans-B-11
03Trenton Titans-367

Williams, Warren
75O-Pee-Chee NHL-217
75Topps-217

Williams-Kovacs, Matt
04Notre Dame Fighting Irish-13

Williamson, Andrew
95Slapshot-55
95Slapshot-199
96Owen Sound Platers-12
97Toledo Storm-23
98ECHL All-Star Northern Conference-8
99ECHL All-Star Northern Conference-2
02Augusta Lynx-78

Williamson, Brad
94Thunder Bay Flyers-21
99Houston Aeros-13
01South Carolina Stingrays-20
02ECHL All-Star Southern-58
02South Carolina Stingrays-20
02South Carolina Stingrays RBI-222
03Colorado Eagles-19
04Colorado Eagles-21
05Colorado Eagles-19
06Colorado EaglesÂ -22

Williamson, Drew
02Arizona Icecats-24
03Arizona Icecats-23

Williamson, Glen
91Jets IGA-33

Williamson, Mike
917th Inn. Sketch WHL-28
93Portland Winter Hawks-27
97Portland Winter Hawks-26
03Portland Winter Hawks-26

Willie, Travis
97Medicine Hat Tigers-23

Williman, U.
74Finnish Typotor-111

Willis, B.J.
98Sioux City Musketeers-25

Willis, Jordan
93London Knights-22
93London Knights-25
96Dayton Bombers-8
96Collector's Edge Ice-143
Prism-143
98Baton Rouge Kingfish-19
00UK Nottingham Panthers-2
00UK Sekonda Superleague-126
01Roanoke Express-21

Willis, Ralph
52Juniors Blue Tint-98

Willis, Rick
91Michigan Wolverines-23
93Michigan Wolverines-26
95Binghamton Rangers-25
96Binghamton Rangers-23

Willis, Shane
94Prince Albert Raiders-21
95Prince Albert Raiders-21
95Classic-48
96Black Diamond-26
Gold-26
96Upper Deck Ice-126
96Prince Albert Raiders-23
97Collector's Choice-300
97Lethbridge Hurricanes-24
97Bowman CHL-113
OPC-113
98New Haven Beast-7
98Bowman CHL-75
Golden Anniversary-75
OPC International-75
98Bowman Chrome CHL-75
Golden Anniversary-75
Golden Anniversary Refractors-75
OPC International-75
OPC International Refractors-75
Refractors-75
99BAP Memorabilia-28
Gold-28
Silver-28
99O-Pee-Chee-163
99O-Pee-Chee Chrome-163
99O-Pee-Chee Chrome Refractors-163
99Paramount-51
Copper-51
Emerald-51
Gold-51
Holographic Emerald-51
Holographic Gold-51
Holographic Silver-51
Ice Blue-51
Premiere Date-51
Red-51
Silver-51
99Topps/OPC-163
99Topps/OPC Chrome-163
Refractors-163
99Upper Deck MVP-41
Gold Script-41
Silver Script-41
Super Script-41
99Cincinnati Cyclones-21
99IHL All-Stars-4
00BAP Parkhurst 2000-P152
00BAP Signature Series-265
Emerald-265
Ruby-265
Sapphire-265
Autographs-72
Autographs Gold-72
00Crown Royale-116
21st Century Rookies-5
00O-Pee-Chee-308
00O-Pee-Chee Parallel-308
00Private Stock-109
Gold-109
Premiere Date-109
Retail-109
Silver-109
00SPx-134
00Titanium-110
Retail-110
Three-Star Selections-21
00Titanium Draft Day Edition-110
00Titanium Draft Day Promos-110
00Topps/OPC-308
Parallel-308
00Topps Chrome-203
OPC Refractors-203
Refractors-203
00Topps Heritage-120
00Topps Premier Plus Aspirations-PA8
00Upper Deck Ice-65
00Vanguard-109
Pacific Proofs-109
01BAP Memorabilia-11
01BAP Memorabilia-489
Emerald-11
Emerald-489
Ruby-11
Ruby-489
Sapphire-11
Sapphire-489
01BAP Signature Series-6
Autographs-6
Autographs Gold-6
01O-Pee-Chee-165
01O-Pee-Chee Premier Parallel-165
01Pacific-81
Extreme LTD-81
Hobby LTD-81
Premiere Date-81
Retail LTD-81
01Pacific Adrenaline-37
Blue-37
Premiere Date-37
Red-37
Retail-37
01Pacific Arena Exclusives-81
01Pacific Heads-Up Breaking the Glass-4
01Parkhurst-66
Gold-66
Silver-66
01Stadium Club-64
Award Winners-64
Master Photos-64
01Topps-165
OPC Parallel-165
Own The Game-OTG12
01Topps Heritage-101
Refractors-101
01Upper Deck-33
Exclusives-33
01Upper Deck MVP-31
01Upper Deck Victory-67
Gold-67
01Upper Deck Vintage-46
02BAP Memorabilia-100
Emerald-100
Ruby-100
Sapphire-100
NHL All-Star Game-100
NHL All-Star Game Blue-100
NHL All-Star Game Green-100
NHL All-Star Game Red-100
02BAP Memorabilia Toronto Fall Expo-100
02BAP Signature Series-151
Autographs-151
Autograph Buybacks 2000-72
Autograph Buybacks 2001-6
Autographs Gold-151
02Pacific-356
Blue-356
Red-356
02Pacific Complete-30
Red-30
02Pacific Exclusive-158
02Upper Deck-405
Exclusives-405
02Upper Deck Beckett UD Promos-405
02Upper Deck MVP-170
Gold-170
Classics-170
Golden Classics-170
02Upper Deck Vintage-228
02Springfield Falcons-24
03Lightning Team Issue-24
03Hershey Bears-12
03Hershey Bears Patriot News-27
04Springfield Falcons-24
06Albany River Rats-22

Willis, Tyler
92British Columbia JHL-71
95Swift Current Broncos-20
96Seattle Thunderbirds-9
97Bowman CHL-87
OPC-87
00Peoria Rivermen-8
00Worcester Icecats-24
01Augusta Lynx-4
03Kalamazoo Wings-10
04Kalamazoo Wings-10
05Kalamazoo Wings-8

Willman, Jay
99San Angelo Outlaws-34

Willman, Timo
98Finnish Kerailysarja-76
99Finnish Cardset-338
00Finnish Cardset-104
00Finnish Cardset-245
01Finnish Cardset-369
02UK Sheffield Steelers-19

Willmann, Dieter
94German DEL-287

Willmann, Peter
99German DEL-229

Willner, Brad
91Lake Superior State Lakers-27
92Lake Superior State Lakers-33
03St. Cloud State Huskies-28
04St. Cloud State Huskies-30

Willsie, Brian
95Slapshot-100
95Guelph Storm-14
96Guelph Storm-18
96Guelph Storm Premier Collection-7
97Guelph Storm-21
98UD Choice-273
Prime Choice Reserve-273
Reserve-273
98Hershey Bears-29
98Bowman CHL-8
Golden Anniversary-8
OPC International-8
98Bowman Chrome CHL-8
Golden Anniversary-8
Golden Anniversary Refractors-8
OPC International-8
OPC International Refractors-8
Refractors-8
99BAP Memorabilia-388
Gold-388
Silver-388
99Pacific Omega-69
Copper-69
Gold-69
Ice Blue-69
Premiere Date-69
00O-Pee-Chee-322
00O-Pee-Chee Parallel-322
00Topps/OPC-322
Parallel-322
00Topps Chrome-217
OPC Refractors-217
Refractors-217
01Avalanche Team Issue-6
01Crown Royale Rookie Royalty-6
01Titanium Draft Day Edition-118
02Avalanche Postcards-13
02Pacific Complete-173
Red-173
02Hershey Bears-26
04Pacific-268
Blue-268
Red-268
05Parkhurst-488
Facsimile Auto Parallel-488
05Ultra-199
Gold-199
Ice-199
05Upper Deck MVP-391
Gold-391
Platinum-391

Wilm, Clarke
93Saskatoon Blades-22
95Saskatoon Blades-23
96Saint John Flames-20
97Saint John Flames-23
98Bowman's Best-129
Refractors-129
Atomic Refractors-129
98Pacific Omega-37
Red-37
Opening Day Issue-37
99Pacific-64
Copper-64
Emerald Green-64
Gold-64
Ice Blue-64
Premiere Date-64
Red-64
99Stadium Club Promos-PP6
99Stadium Club-51
First Day Issue-51
One of a Kind-51
Printing Plates Black-51
Printing Plates Cyan-51
Printing Plates Magenta-51
Printing Plates Yellow-51
00BAP Signature Series-14
Emerald-14
Ruby-14
Sapphire-14
Autographs-145
Autographs Gold-145
00Paramount-40
Copper-40
Gold-40
Holo-Gold-40
Holo-Silver-40
Ice Blue-40
Premiere Date-40
00Upper Deck-29
Exclusives Tier 1-29
Exclusives Tier 2-29
00Upper Deck Vintage-54
01Upper Deck-258
Exclusives-258
01Upper Deck Victory-57
Gold-57
02BAP Sig Series Auto Buybacks 2000-145
02Pacific Complete-365
Red-365

Wilmert, Sean
95Madison Monsters-5

Wilmot, Lefty
54UK A and BC Chewing Gum-41

Wilmshofer, Andre
94German First League-407

Wilson, Aaron
06Austin Ice Bats-22

Wilson, Andrew
05Kingston Frontenacs-12

Wilson, Behn
79O-Pee-Chee-111
79Topps-111
80O-Pee-Chee-145
80Topps-145
81O-Pee-Chee-239
81O-Pee-Chee Stickers-175
81Topps-45
82O-Pee-Chee-260
82Post Cereal-14
83Blackhawks Postcards-24
83Puffy Stickers-12
85Blackhawks Team Issue-6
86Blackhawks Coke-23
87Blackhawks Coke-29
02Fleer Throwbacks-86
Gold-86
Platinum-86

Wilson, Bert
74O-Pee-Chee NHL-384
75O-Pee-Chee NHL-338
76O-Pee-Chee NHL-378
78O-Pee-Chee-369
80Flames Postcards-23
80Pepsi-Cola Caps-20

Wilson, Bob
52Juniors Blue Tint-171

Wilson, Bryan
04Gatineau Olympiques-21
05Drummondville Voltigeurs-25
05Gatineau Olympiques-9
06Drummondville Voltigeurs-2

Wilson, Carey
85Flames Red Rooster-30
85O-Pee-Chee-191
85O-Pee-Chee Stickers-213
86Flames Red Rooster-30
86Kraft Drawings-80
86O-Pee-Chee-166
86Topps-166
87O-Pee-Chee-211
87O-Pee-Chee Stickers-45
87Panini Stickers-211
88O-Pee-Chee-75
88O-Pee-Chee Minis-45
88O-Pee-Chee Stickers-266
88Panini Stickers-246
88Topps-75
88Whalers Junior Ground Round-18
89O-Pee-Chee-66
89O-Pee-Chee Stickers-239
89Panini Stickers-280
89Rangers Marine Midland Bank-17
89Topps-66
90Bowman-214
Tiffany-214
90O-Pee-Chee-54
90OPC Premier-128
90Panini Stickers-105
90Pro Set-210
90Pro Set-453
90Score-254
Canadian-254
90Score Rookie/Traded-42T
90Topps-54
Tiffany-54
90Whalers Jr. 7-Eleven-26
91Bowman-265
91Flames IGA-26
91O-Pee-Chee-85
91Panini Stickers-56
91Pinnacle-364
French-364
91Pro Set-36
French-36
91Score American-227
91Score Canadian Bilingual-227
91Score Canadian English-227
91Stadium Club-301
91Topps-85
91Upper Deck-538
French-538
92Flames IGA-11
92Pinnacle-369
French-369
92Score-127
Canadian-127
92Ultra-272

Wilson, Chad
92British Columbia JHL-151
93Cornell Big Red-28

Wilson, Clay
01Michigan Tech Huskies-33
05Muskegon Fury-19
06Portland Pirates-7

Wilson, Colin
91Peterborough Petes-20
917th Inn. Sketch OHL-125
92Windsor Spitfires-8

Wilson, Craig
897th Inn. Sketch OHL-69
96UK Fife Flyers-11
04UK Edinburgh Capitals-6

Wilson, Cully
23V128-1 Paulin's Candy-67

Wilson, Devin
99Prince George Cougars-8
00Prince George Cougars-8
03Everett Silvertips-8

Wilson, Doug
78O-Pee-Chee-168
78Topps-168
79Blackhawks Postcards-21
80O-Pee-Chee-12
80Topps-12
81Blackhawks Borderless Postcards-28
81O-Pee-Chee-66
81Topps-W78
82Blackhawks Postcards-23
82McDonald's Stickers-36
82O-Pee-Chee-77
82O-Pee-Chee-78
82O-Pee-Chee Stickers-163
82O-Pee-Chee Stickers-172
82O-Pee-Chee Stickers-254
82Post Cereal-4
82Topps Stickers-163
82Topps Stickers-172
82Topps Stickers-254
83Blackhawks Postcards-25
83NHL Key Tags-26
83O-Pee-Chee-114
83O-Pee-Chee Stickers-112
83O-Pee-Chee Stickers-165
83Puffy Stickers-14
83Topps Stickers-112
83Topps Stickers-165
84Kellogg's Accordion Discs-6
84Kellogg's Accordion Discs Singles-39
84O-Pee-Chee-48
84O-Pee-Chee Stickers-27
84Topps-37
85Blackhawks Team Issue-26
85O-Pee-Chee-45
85O-Pee-Chee Box Bottoms-P
85O-Pee-Chee Stickers-25
85O-Pee-Chee Stickers-122
857-Eleven Credit Cards-4
85Topps-45
85Topps Box Bottoms-P
85Topps Sticker Inserts-11
86Blackhawks Coke-24
86O-Pee-Chee-106
86O-Pee-Chee Stickers-153
86Topps-106
87Blackhawks Coke-30
87O-Pee-Chee-14
87O-Pee-Chee Stickers-77
87Panini Stickers-222
87Topps-14
88Blackhawks Coke-24
88O-Pee-Chee-89
88O-Pee-Chee Stickers-6
88Panini Stickers-24
88Topps-89
89Blackhawks Coke-4
89O-Pee-Chee-112
89O-Pee-Chee Stickers-14
89Panini Stickers-45
89Topps-112
90Blackhawks Coke-4
90Bowman-2
Tiffany-2
90Kraft-62
90Kraft-77
90O-Pee-Chee-111
90O-Pee-Chee-203
90O-Pee-Chee-363
90O-Pee-Chee Box Bottoms-N
90OPC Premier-129
90Panini Stickers-189
90Pro Set-63A
90Pro Set-63B
90Pro Set-346
90Score-280
90Score-320
Canadian-280
Canadian-320
90Score Hottest/Rising Stars-68
90Topps-111
90Topps-203
90Topps-363
Tiffany-111
Tiffany-203
90Topps Box Bottoms-N
90Upper Deck-223
French-223
91Pro Set Platinum-107
91Pro Set Platinum-141
91Bowman-400
91Kraft-34
91O-Pee-Chee-49
91OPC Premier-6
91Panini Stickers-18
91Parkhurst-168
French-168
91Pinnacle-13
91Pinnacle-369
French-13
French-369
91Pro Set-52
91Pro Set-478
91Pro Set-584
French-52
French-478
French-584
91Score American-35
91Score Canadian Bilingual-35
91Score Canadian Bilingual-551
91Score Canadian English-35
91Score Canadian English-551
91Score Rookie/Traded-1T
91Score Kellogg's-19
91Sharks Sports Action-20
91Stadium Club-131
91Topps-49
92Bowman-75
92Bowman-219
92O-Pee-Chee-281
92Panini Stickers-129
92Panini Stickers French-129
92Parkhurst-167
Emerald Ice-167
92Pinnacle-52
French-52
92Pro Set-165
92Score-15
Canadian-15
92Seasons Patches-63
92Stadium Club-470
92Topps-482
Gold-482G
92Ultra-199
92Upper Deck-150
93OPC Premier-77
Gold-77
93Panini Stickers-264
93Score-115
Canadian-115
93Topps/OPC Premier-77
Gold-77
93Ultra-230
94EA Sports-115
00Ottawa 67's-28
01Topps Archives-68
Arena Seats-ASDWI
03Parkhurst Original Six Chicago-48
03Parkhurst Original Six Chicago-68
Autographs-17
04UD Legendary Signatures-32
Autographs-DW
Rearguard Retrospectives-DWKB
04UD Legends Classics-20
Gold-20
Platinum-20
Silver-20
Signature Moments-M38
Signatures-CS36
Signatures-DC22
Signatures-TC15
04Arizona Icecats-22
06Parkhurst-184
06SP Authentic Sign of the Times Quads-ST4EHSW
06The Cup Honorable Numbers-HNDW
06The Cup Limited Logos-LLDW
06The Cup Signature Patches-SPDW
06UD Artifacts-140
Blue-140
Gold-140
Platinum-140
Radiance-140
Autographed Radiance Parallel-140
Red-140
Auto-Facts-AFDW
Auto-Facts Gold-AFDW
Tundra Tandems-TTWS
Tundra Tandems Black-TTWS
Tundra Tandems Blue-TTWS
Tundra Tandems Gold-TTWS
Tundra Tandems Platinum-TTWS
Tundra Tandems Red-TTWS
Tundra Tandems Dual Patches Red-TTWS
06Upper Deck Sweet Shot Signature Shots/Saves

Sticks-SSSDW
06Upper Deck Trilogy Honorary Scripted Patches-HSPWI
06Upper Deck Trilogy Honorary Scripted Swatches-HSSWI
06Upper Deck Trilogy Scripts-TSDO
Wilson, Dunc
70Canucks Royal Bank-19
70Esso Power Players-54
71Canucks Royal Bank-15
71Letraset Action Replays-20
71O-Pee-Chee-24
71Sargent Promotions Stamps-222
71Toronto Sun-294
72Canucks Royal Bank-20
72O-Pee-Chee-18
72Sargent Promotions Stamps-213
72Topps-91
73Maple Leafs Postcards-29
73O-Pee-Chee-257
74Maple Leafs Postcards-27
74NHL Action Stamps-265
74O-Pee-Chee NHL-327
76O-Pee-Chee NHL-102
77O-Pee-Chee NHL-8
77O-Pee-Chee NHL-224
77Penguins Puck Bucks-29
77Topps-8
77Topps-224
Wilson, Jay
98Madison Monsters-14
Wilson, Jeff
87Kingston Canadians-6
907th Inn. Sketch OHL-196
93Quebec Pee-Wee Tournament-1184
Wilson, Jesse
907th Inn. Sketch WHL-12
917th Inn. Sketch WHL-132
Wilson, Johnny
44Beehive Group II Photos-216
44Beehive Group II Photos-460
52Parkhurst-89
53Parkhurst-51
54Parkhurst-44
54Topps-4
57Topps-47
58Topps-22
59Parkhurst-13
60Parkhurst-14
60Shirriff Coins-15
61Shirriff/Salada Coins-100
76Rockies Coke Cans-21
77Penguins Puck Bucks-NNO
81Red Wings Oldtimers-17
91Ultimate Original Six-65
French-65
Wilson, Kelsey
03Sarnia Sting-23
05Guelph Storm-B-04
06Milwaukee Admirals -20
Wilson, Kevin
97OCN Blizzard-3
98OCN Blizzard-3
Wilson, Landon
95Bowman-95
All-Foil-95
95Parkhurst International-526
Emerald Ice-526
95Select Certified-134
Mirror Gold-134
95Upper Deck-424
Electric Ice-424
Electric Ice Gold-424
96Be A Player-106
Autographs-106
Autographs Silver-106
96Leaf-215
Press Proofs-215
96Metal Universe-196
96Score-257
Artist's Proofs-257
Dealer's Choice Artist's Proofs-257
Special Artist's Proofs-257
Golden Blades-257
96Summit-188
Artist's Proofs-188
Ice-188
Metal-188
Premium Stock-188
96Ultra-41
Gold Medallion-41
Rookies-20
96Upper Deck-242
96Zenith-142
Artist's Proofs-142
96Collector's Edge Future Legends-24
96Collector's Edge Ice-30
Prism-30
97Donruss-87
Press Proofs Silver-87
Press Proofs Gold-87
97Donruss Limited-52
Exposure-52
97Leaf-147
Fractal Matrix-147
Fractal Matrix Die Cuts-147
97Leaf International-147
Universal Ice-147
97Pacific-105
Copper-105
Emerald Green-105
Ice Blue-105
Red-105
Silver-105
97Upper Deck-10
97Providence Bruins-21
98Providence Bruins-24
99BAP Memorabilia-143
Gold-143
Silver-143
99Pacific-31
Copper-31
Emerald Green-31
Gold-31
Ice Blue-31
Premiere Date-31
Red-31
00Upper Deck NHLPA-PA68
01BAP Signature Series-34
Autographs-34
Autographs Gold-34
01Coyotes Team Issue-22
01Pacific-309
Extreme LTD-309
Hobby LTD-309
Premiere Date-309
Retail LTD-309
01Pacific Arena Exclusives-309
01Upper Deck MVP-146
01Upper Deck Victory-269
Gold-269
01Upper Deck Vintage-197
02BAP Sig Series Auto Buybacks 2001-34
02Coyotes Team Issue-14
02Pacific Complete-394
Red-394
03Coyotes Postcards-27
03ITG Action-443
03Pacific Complete-170
Red-170
04Finnish Cardset-6
Parallel-6
04Swedish Pure Skills-97
Parallel-97
Wilson, Larry
44Beehive Group II Photos-146
52Parkhurst-92
53Parkhurst-74
54Parkhurst-85
54Topps-40
Wilson, Mark
03Vernon Vipers-18
Wilson, Michael
06Swift Current Broncos-12
Wilson, Mike
92Sudbury Wolves-6
93Sudbury Wolves-6
93Sudbury Wolves Police-6
93Classic-32
94Sudbury Wolves-4
94Sudbury Wolves Police-24
95Bowman-94
All-Foil-94
95Parkhurst International-534
Emerald Ice-534
95Rochester Americans-23
96Be A Player-23
Autographs-23
Autographs Silver-23
96Collector's Edge Future Legends-45
96Collector's Edge Ice-66
Prism-66
97Pacific Invincible NHL Regime-25
97Score Sabres-20
Platinum-20
Premier-20
97Sudbury Wolves Anniversary-23
98Las Vegas Thunder-23
00BAP Memorabilia-232
Emerald-232
Ruby-232
Sapphire-232
Promos-232
00BAP Mem Chicago Sportsfest Copper-232
00BAP Memorabilia Chicago Sportsfest Blue-232
00BAP Memorabilia Chicago Sportsfest Gold-232
00BAP Memorabilia Chicago Sportsfest Ruby-232
00BAP Memorabilia Chicago Sun-Times Ruby-232
00BAP Memorabilia Chicago Sun-Times Gold-232
00BAP Mem Chicago Sun-Times Sapphire-232
00BAP Mem Toronto Fall Expo Copper-232
00BAP Memorabilia Toronto Fall Expo Gold-232
00BAP Memorabilia Toronto Fall Expo Ruby-232
00Panthers Team Issue-11
00Upper Deck-78
Exclusives Tier 1-78
Exclusives Tier 2-78
01Wilkes-Barre Scranton Penguins-6
02Hartford Wolf Pack-25
02Wilkes-Barre Scranton Penguins-4
03Springfield Falcons Postcards-21
Wilson, Mike BCJHL
04Langley Hornets-20
Wilson, Mitch
88ProCards IHL-65
89ProCards IHL-149
90ProCards AHL/IHL-376
Wilson, Murray
72Canadiens Postcards-22
72Dimanche/Derniere Heure *-176
72Dimanche/Derniere Heure *-177
73Canadiens Postcards-24
74Canadiens Postcards-27
74NHL Action Stamps-160
74O-Pee-Chee NHL-359
75Canadiens Postcards-20
75O-Pee-Chee NHL-162
75Topps-162
76Canadiens Postcards-23
76O-Pee-Chee NHL-254
76Topps-254
77Canadiens Postcards-25
77O-Pee-Chee NHL-69
77Topps-69
Wilson, Phat
23V128-1 Paulin's Candy-16
83Hall of Fame Postcards-J16
85Hall of Fame-195
Wilson, Rick
74NHL Action Stamps-238
74O-Pee-Chee NHL-284
75O-Pee-Chee NHL-356
76O-Pee-Chee NHL-293
77O-Pee-Chee NHL-57
77Topps-57
81Kingston Canadians-17
94Stars HockeyKaps-25
Wilson, Rob
85Sudbury Wolves-25
86Sudbury Wolves-25
87Sudbury Wolves-25
94UK Sheffield Steelers-21
97UK Sheffield Steelers-3
99UK Sheffield Steelers-21
00UK Sekonda Superleague-116
00UK Sheffield Steelers Centurions-4
01UK Manchester Storm-23
02UK Manchester Storm-9
Wilson, Ron
77Kalamazoo Wings-2
Wilson, Ron Lawrence
76Nova Scotia Voyageurs-19
78Maple Leafs Postcards-23
79Maple Leafs Postcards-33
87North Stars Postcards-30
87Panini Stickers-291
89ProCards IHL-188
96Ducks Team Issue-27
Wilson, Ron Lee
77Nova Scotia Voyageurs-24
79Jets Postcards-27
80Jets Postcards-24
80O-Pee-Chee-243
80Pepsi-Cola Caps-140
80Topps-243
81O-Pee-Chee-377
81O-Pee-Chee Stickers-140
83Jets Postcards-24
84Jets Police-22
85Jets Police-22
86Jets Postcards-25
87Jets Postcards-23
87O-Pee-Chee-224
88ProCards AHL-175
89ProCards AHL-51
90Blues Kodak-25
90Pro Set-529
91Blues Postcards-21
91Bowman-382
91O-Pee-Chee-120
91Panini Stickers-34
91Pro Set-220
French-220
91Score Canadian Bilingual-533
91Score Canadian English-533
91Stadium Club-347
91Topps-120
92Bowman-364
92Panini Stickers-18
92Panini Stickers French-18
92Score-365
Canadian-365
92Stadium Club-429
92Topps-78
Gold-78G
93Canadiens Postcards-26
93Leaf-316
93OPC Premier-194
Gold-194
93Panini Stickers-162
93PowerPlay-373
93Score-431
93Score-657
Gold-657
Canadian-431
Canadian-657
Canadian Gold-657
93Topps/OPC Premier-194
Gold-194
93Ultra-356
95Wheeling Thunderbirds-19
95Wheeling Thunderbirds Series II-19
97Springfield Falcons-24
04Hamilton Bulldogs-29
05Hamilton Bulldogs-29
Wilson, Ross
89ProCards AHL-17
90ProCards AHL/IHL-437
91ProCards-389
96Flint Generals-22
97Flint Generals-23
97Flint Generals EBK-22
98Flint Generals-19
98UHL All-Stars-1
99UHL All-Stars East-19T
Wilson, Ryan
03St. Michael's Majors-4
04St. Michael's Majors-4
06Sarnia Sting-7
Wilson, Stacy
94Classic Women of Hockey-W9
97Collector's Choice-287
97Esso Olympic Hockey Heroes-60
97Esso Olympic Hockey Heroes French-60
06ITG Going For Gold-24
06ITG Going For Gold Samples-24
06ITG Going For Gold Autographs-AWIL
Wilson, Steve
92Dayton Bombers-24
93Cornell Big Red-27
93Dayton Bombers-3
94Dayton Bombers-3
94Dayton Bombers-23
94Los Angeles Blades RHI-4
95Peoria Rivermen-24
95Phoenix Roadrunners-21
98German DEL-101
99German DEL-102
00Jackson Bandits-20
01German Upper Deck-104
02German DEL City Press-125
03German DEL-135
04German DEL-159
04German Hannover Scorpions Postcards-29
Wilson, Tom
97Columbus Cottonmouths-20
98Columbus Cottonmouths-19
00Asheville Smoke-19
01Asheville Smoke-7
Winborg, Jorgen
86Swedish Panini Stickers-270
Winch, Jason
89Niagara Falls Thunder-22
897th Inn. Sketch OHL-135
907th Inn. Sketch OHL-274
91ProCards-14
91Rochester Americans Kodak-26
92Rochester Americans Kodak-25
Winchester, Brad
04SP Authentic Rookie Redemptions-RR12
04AHL Top Prospects-12
05ITG Heroes/Prosp Toronto Expo Parallel -389
05Beehive-177
Matte-177
05Black Diamond-240
05Hot Prospects-238
En Fuego-238
Hot Materials-HMBW
Red Hot-238
White Hot-238
05Parkhurst Signatures-WI
05SP Authentic-157
Limited-157
Rarefied Rookies-RRBW
Rookie Authentics-RABW
Sign of the Times Quads-QPSCW
05SP Game Used-106
Autographs-106
Gold-106
Auto Draft-AD-BW
Rookie Exclusives-BW
Rookie Exclusives Silver-RE-BW
05SPx-152
Spectrum-152
05The Cup-133
Autographed Rookie Patches Gold Rainbow-133
Black Rainbow Rookies-133
Masterpiece Pressplates (Artifacts)-212
Masterpiece Pressplates (Bee Hive)-177
Masterpiece Pressplates (Black Diamond)-240
Masterpiece Pressplates (Ice)-129
Masterpiece Pressplates (Power Play)-141
Masterpiece Pressplates (Rookie Update)-210
Masterpiece Pressplates SPA Autos-157
Masterpiece Pressplates (SP Game Used)-106
Masterpiece Pressplates (SPx)-152
Masterpiece Pressplates (SPx)-152
Masterpiece Pressplates (Trilogy)-254
Masterpiece Pressplates Ult Coll Autos-116
Masterpiece Pressplates (Victory)-262
Masterpiece Pressplates Autographs-133
Platinum Rookies-133
05UD Artifacts-212
Gold-RED12
05UD PowerPlay-141
05Ultimate Collection-116
Autographed Patches-116
Autographed Shields-116
Ultimate Debut Threads Jerseys-DTJBW
Ultimate Debut Threads Jerseys Autos-DAJBW
Ultimate Debut Threads Patches-DTPBW
Ultimate Debut Threads Patches Autos-DAPBW
05Ultra-218
Gold-218
Ice-218
Rookie Uniformity Jerseys-RU-BW
Rookie Uniformity Jersey Autographs-ARU-BW
Rookie Uniformity Patches-RUP-BW
Rookie Uniformity Patch Autographs-ARP-BW
05Upper Deck-447
Rookie Ink-RIBW
05Upper Deck Rookie Showcase-RS12
05Upper Deck Rookie Showcase Promos-RS12
05Upper Deck Rookie Threads-RTBW
05Upper Deck Rookie Threads Autographs-ARTBW
05Upper Deck Ice-129
Fresh Ice-FIBW
Fresh Ice Glass-FIBW
Fresh Ice Glass Patches-FIPBW
Premieres Auto Patches-AIPBW
05Upper Deck Rookie Update-210
Inspirations Patch Rookies-210
05Upper Deck Trilogy-254
05Upper Deck Victory-262
Black-262
Gold-262
Silver-262
05Hamilton Bulldogs-27
05ITG Heroes and Prospects-389
06Be A Player Portraits First Exposures-FEBW
06Be A Player Portraits Signature Portraits-SPBW
06Black Diamond Gemography-GBW
06O-Pee-Chee-200
06O-Pee-Chee-635
Rainbow-200
Rainbow-635
06Upper Deck Signature Sensations-SSBW
Windle, Jason
01Greenville Grrrowl-7
Windler, Harald
94German DEL-68
Windsor, Nicholas
98Roanoke Express-19
Windsor, Pat
75HCA Steel City Vacuum-17
Wing, Johnny
37V356 Worldwide Gum-102
Winge, Goran
67Swedish Hockey-113
Wingels, Tommy
06Cedar Rapids RoughRiders-22
Wingerter, Mark
84Kelowna Wings-21
Wingfield, Brad
92British Columbia JHL-8
97New Mexico Scorpions-23
99Corpus Christi IceRays-27
99Corpus Christi IceRays-33
00UK Sekonda Superleague-48
05Danbury Trashers-22
Wingren, Eddie
64Swedish Coralli ISHockey-122
65Swedish Coralli ISHockey-122
67Swedish Hockey-78
Winkler, Benjamin
95Swiss HNL-340
96Swiss HNL-314
98Swiss Power Play Stickers-112
99Swiss Panini Stickers-112
99Swiss Panini Stickers-263
00Swiss Panini Stickers-157
01Swiss HNL-108
02Swiss HNL-253
04Swiss Davos Postcards-30
Winkler, Chris
92Saskatchewan JHL-127
94German First League-306
Winkler, Hal
23V128-1 Paulin's Candy-46
Winkler, Wade
03Port Huron Beacons-23
Winnes, Chris
91Bruins Sports Action-23
91Pinnacle-351
French-351
91Pro Set-522
French-522
91Upper Deck-514
French-514
92Upper Deck-380
97Hartford Wolf Pack-28
98Hartford Wolf Pack-24
Winnet, Ben
05Salmon Arm Silverbacks-21
Winstanley, Jeff
96German DEL-119
Winstanley, John
01Sudbury Wolves-24
01Sudbury Wolves Police-10
Winsth, Walter
69Swedish Hockey-236
71Swedish Hockey-363
Winter, Jeff
24Diaz Cigarettes-78
96Madison Monsters-23
98Cincinnati Mighty Ducks-22
99UHL All-Stars West-4T
Wintoneak, Walker
06Saskatoon Blades-22
Wires, John
03Owen Sound Attack-20
Wires, Mark
03Bowling Green Falcons-8
Wirl, Torbjorn
84Swedish Semic Elitserien-176
Wirll, Mike
98Brandon Wheat Kings-23
99Brandon Wheat Kings-24
99UD Prospects-30
99UD Prospects-80
01Prince Albert Raiders-24
03Charlotte Checkers-80
Wirtanen, Petteri
05Finnish Cardset -30
06Finnish Cardset-33
Playmakers Rookies-6
Playmakers Rookies Gold-6
Playmakers Rookies Silver-6
Signature Sensations-5
06Portland Pirates-18
Wirtz, Arthur M
83Hall of Fame Postcards-F16
85Hall of Fame-90
Wirtz, William W
70Blackhawks Postcards-3
83Hall of Fame Postcards-M15
85Hall of Fame-179
Wirz, Valentin
99Swiss Panini Stickers-329
02Swiss HNL-172
Wirzenius, Olli
65Finnish Hellas-115
Wise, Tony
24Crescent Falcon-Tigers-10
Wiseman, Brian
91Michigan Wolverines-24
93Michigan Wolverines-27
94Classic-63
Gold-63
96St. John's Maple Leafs-25
98IHL All-Star Western Conference-17
99Houston Aeros-6
06Houston Aeros RetroÂ -4
Wiseman, Carl
917th Inn. Sketch QMJHL-100
Wiseman, Chad
00Mississauga Ice Dogs-28
00UD CHL Prospects-12
01Cleveland Barons-21
02BAP Memorabilia-335
02BAP Ultimate Memorabilia-62
02Upper Deck Rookie Update-135
02Cleveland Barons-23
03Pacific Calder-128
Silver-128
03Pacific Complete-516
Red-516
03Hartford Wolf Pack-27
03Pacific AHL Prospects-37
Gold-37
04Hartford Wolf Pack-26
05Hartford Wolf Pack-24
Wiseman, Eddie
34Beehive Group I Photos-258
40O-Pee-Chee V301-2-149
03BAP Ultimate Mem Linemates Autos-13
Wiseman, Lyall
51Laval Dairy QSHL-63
51Laval Dairy Subset-121
52St. Lawrence Sales-100
Wishart, Gary
97UK Fife Flyers-17
01UK Fife Flyers-8
05ITG Heroes and Prospects-321
Autographs Series II-TW
Team Cherry-TC1
Wishart, Ty
06ITG Heroes and Prospects-92
Autographs-ATW
Class of 2006-CL10
Wishloff, Peter
00Ohio State Buckeyes-13
Wismer, Chris
94Owen Sound Platers-21
95Slapshot-302
95Owen Sound Platers-24
96Owen Sound Platers-22
97Owen Sound Platers-20
98Dayton Bombers-17
98Roanoke Express-25
00Jackson Bandits-7
Wisniewski, James
01Plymouth Whalers-19
01Plymouth Whalers-32
02Plymouth Whalers-21
03Plymouth Whalers-21
04Norfolk Admirals-22
04ITG Heroes and Prospects-77
Autographs-JWI
04ITG Heroes/Prospects Toronto Expo '05-77
04ITG Heroes/Prospects Expo Heroes/Pros-77
05Black Diamond-226
05Hot Prospects-119
En Fuego-119
Red Hot-119
White Hot-119
05SPx-253
05The Cup Masterpiece Pressplate Artifact-263
05The Cup Master Pressplate Black Diamond-226
05The Cup Master Pressplate Rookie Update-121
05The Cup Masterpiece Pressplates (SPx)-253
05The Cup Masterpiece Pressplates Trilogy-239
05The Cup Masterpiece Pressplate Ult Coll-199
05UD Artifacts-263
05Ultimate Collection-199
Gold-199
05Upper Deck Rookie Update-121
05Upper Deck Trilogy-239
05Norfolk Admirals-14
06Blackhawks Postcards Glossy-3
Wisocki, Todd
98Florida Everblades-25
00Florida Everblades-25
04Florida Everblades-26
Wissmann, Oliver
96Swiss HNL-275
98Swiss Power Play Stickers-315
99Swiss Panini Stickers-280
99Swiss Panini Stickers-321
Wiste, Jim
70Canucks Royal Bank-20
70Dad's Cookies-142
70Sargent Promotions Stamps-223
72Cleveland Crusaders WHA-15
73Quaker Oats WHA-1
74O-Pee-Chee WHA-34
Wistling, Bengt
71Swedish Hockey-377
Witehall, Johan
96Swedish Semic Elitserien Stickers-48
97Swedish Collector's Choice-110
98Hartford Wolf Pack-25
99Hartford Wolf Pack-23
00Canadiens Postcards-28
00Pacific-271
Copper-271
Gold-271
Ice Blue-271
Premiere Date-271
00SPx-105
Spectrum-105
00Upper Deck-222
Exclusives Tier 1-222
Exclusives Tier 2-222
01Swiss HNL-255
03Swedish Elite-205
Silver-205
05Swedish SHL Elitset-180
Gold-180
Witkowski, Byron
92Western Michigan Broncos-29
Witschen, Shaun
04Williams Lake Timberwolves-21
05Salmon Arm Silverbacks-22
Witschi, Adrian
02Swiss HNL-399
Witt, Brendan
917th Inn. Sketch WHL-129
93Donruss Team Canada-22
93Pinnacle-465
Canadian-465
93Upper Deck-544
93Seattle Thunderbirds-29
94Score-205
Gold-205
Platinum-205
94Classic-90
Gold-90
CHL All-Stars-C10
Tri-Cards-T73
95Bowman-127
All-Foil-127
95Capitals Team Issue-28
95Collector's Choice-400
95Donruss-361
Pro Pointers-18
95Emotion generatioNext-6
95Finest-106
Refractors-106
95Leaf Limited-117
95Metal-197
95Parkhurst International-258
Emerald Ice-258
95Pro Magnets-35
95Select Certified-119
Mirror Gold-119
95SkyBox Impact-225
95SP-162
95Stadium Club-193
Members Only Master Set-193
95Summit-189
Artist's Proofs-189
Ice-189
95Topps-346
OPC Inserts-346
95Ultra-361
High Speed-20
95Upper Deck-265
Electric Ice-265
Electric Ice Gold-265
95Zenith-124
Rookie Roll Call-3
96Collector's Choice-283
96Collector's Choice-345
96Donruss Elite-83
Die Cut Stars-83
96Fleer-120
96Leaf Preferred-74
Press Proofs-74
96Metal Universe-168
96NHL Pro Stamps-35
96Score-270
Artist's Proofs-270
Dealer's Choice Artist's Proofs-270
Special Artist's Proofs-270
Golden Blades-270
96SkyBox Impact-143
96Summit-162
Artist's Proofs-162
Ice-162
Metal-162
Premium Stock-162
96Upper Deck-177
96Zenith-50
Artist's Proofs-50
97Be A Player-162
Autographs-162
Autographs Die-Cuts-162
Autographs Prismatic Die-Cuts-162
97Pacific Invincible NHL Regime-214
97Upper Deck-384
98Pacific-450
Ice Blue-450
Red-450
99BAP Memorabilia-210
Gold-210
Silver-210
99BAP Millennium-247
Emerald-247
Ruby-247
Sapphire-247
Signatures-247
Signatures Gold-247
00Upper Deck Vintage-368
02BAP Sig Series Auto Buybacks 1999-247
02BAP Signature Series Defensive Wall-DW9
02Capitals Team Issue-8
02O-Pee-Chee-104
02O-Pee-Chee Premier Blue Parallel-104
02O-Pee-Chee Premier Red Parallel-104
02O-Pee-Chee Factory Set-104
02Pacific Complete-471
Red-471
02Parkhurst-184
Bronze-184
Gold-184
Silver-184
02Topps-104
OPC Blue Parallel-104
OPC Red Parallel-104
Factory Set-104
02Topps Total-332
02Upper Deck Vintage-252
03ITG Action-563
03O-Pee-Chee-53
03O-Pee-Chee-286
03OPC Blue-53
03OPC Blue-286
03OPC Gold-53
03OPC Gold-286
03OPC Red-53
03OPC Red-286
03Pacific Complete-311
Red-311
03Topps-53
03Topps-286
Blue-53
Blue-286
Gold-53
Gold-286
Red-53
Red-286
04Pacific-269
Blue-269
Red-269
04Upper Deck-177
Canadian Exclusives-177
HG Glossy Gold-177
HG Glossy Silver-177
05Be A Player Signatures-BW
05Be A Player Signatures Gold-BW
05Beehive Matted Materials-MMBW
05Black Diamond-83
Emerald-83
Gold-83
Onyx-83
Ruby-83
05Hot Prospects Hot Materials-HMWI
05Panini Stickers-183
05Parkhurst-284
Facsimile Auto Parallel-495
True Colors-TCWAS
True Colors-TCWAS
05SP Game Used-100
Gold-100
05Ultra-200
Gold-200
Ice-200
05Upper Deck-194
HG Glossy-194
Jerseys-J-BW
05Upper Deck MVP-385
Gold-385
Platinum-385
05Upper Deck Toronto Fall Expo-194
05Upper Deck Victory-200
Black-200
Gold-200
Silver-200
06O-Pee-Chee-311
Rainbow-311
06Panini Stickers-93
06Upper Deck-376
Exclusives Parallel-376
High Gloss Parallel-376
Game Jerseys-J2BW
Game Patches-P2BW
Masterpieces-376
MVP Jerseys-OJRW
Witt, Jared
92Saskatchewan JHL-136
Wittbrock, Marc
94German DEL-145
95German DEL-132
Wittenberg, Tom
92British Columbia JHL-1
Wittig, Andreas
94German First League-302
Witting, Kristen
04Wisconsin Badgers Women-23
Witting, Markus
05German DEL-235
Wittliff, Phil
95Milwaukee Admirals-21
96Milwaukee Admirals-27
Wittmann, Gerd
94German First League-146
99German EHC Straubing-22
Wittmann, Theo
93Swiss HNL-157
95Swedish World Championships Stickers-135
95Swiss HNL-210
96Swiss HNL-96
98Swiss Power Play Stickers-24
99Swiss Panini Stickers-317
00Swiss Panini Stickers-97
00Swiss Slapshot Mini-Cards-EHCC15
01Swiss HNL-256
02Swiss HNL-350
Wittwer, Alan
92Quebec Pee-Wee Tournament-1620
96Swiss HNL-550
Wittwer, Bruno
72Finnish Semic World Championship-141
72Swedish Semic World Championship-141
Wittwer, Christian
98Swiss Power Play Stickers-353
Wiwchar, Tim
90Fort Saskatchewan Traders-20
Wlasow, Leo
93Maine Black Bears-54
Wobmann, Daniel
01Swiss HNL-439
02Swiss HNL-463
Wochele, Kenny
05Waterloo Blackhawks-24
Wochok, Tim
02Arizona Icecats-23
03Arizona Icecats-24
04Arizona Icecats-23
Wochy, Steve
51Cleveland Barons-8
Wohl, Pavel
89Swedish Semic World Champ Stickers-177
Wohlers, Nick
92St. John's Maple Leafs-23
Wohlin, Folke
32Swedish Marabou-147
Wohlmann, Rainer
94German First League-49
Woit, Benny
44Beehive Group II Photos-217
51Parkhurst-58
52Parkhurst-62
53Parkhurst-45
54Parkhurst-38
54Topps-9
94Parkhurst Missing Link-40
Woitas, Joshua
93Quebec Pee-Wee Tournament-180
96Brandon Wheat Kings-6
97Brandon Wheat Kings-26
Wojciak, Richard
04UK Nottingham Panthers-19
05UK Nottingham Panthers-5
Wojcik, Adam
00Victoriaville Tigres-15
Signed-15
Wojcinski, Scott
93Quebec Pee-Wee Tournament-800
Wojtynek, Henryk
79Panini Stickers-118
Wolak, Casey
92Quebec Pee-Wee Tournament-914
96Sarnia Sting-27
Wolak, Mike
85Kitchener Rangers-16
89ProCards IHL-13
Wolanin, Chris
91Greensboro Monarchs-17
92Greensboro Monarchs-2
Wolanin, Craig
84Kitchener Rangers-7
85Devils Postcards-10
86Devils Police-20
87Panini Stickers-77
88Devils Caretta-30
88Panini Stickers-270
89Devils Caretta-29
90Bowman-166
Tiffany-166
90Nordiques Petro-Canada-27
90O-Pee-Chee-40
90Pro Set-519
90Score-167
Canadian-167
90Topps-40
Tiffany-40
91Bowman-138
91Nordiques Panini Team Stickers-24
91Nordiques Petro-Canada-35
91O-Pee-Chee-199
91Panini Stickers-264
91Parkhurst-369
French-369
91Pinnacle-217
French-217
91Pro Set Preview-203
91Pro Set-203
French-203
91Score American-74
91Score Canadian Bilingual-74
91Score Canadian English-74
91Stadium Club-4
91Topps-199
91Upper Deck-486
French-486
92Bowman-41
92Nordiques Petro-Canada-37
92Pinnacle-107
French-107
92Score-21
Canadian-21
92Stadium Club-317
92Topps-487
Gold-487G
93Score-406
Canadian-406
94Nordiques Burger King-26
94OPC Premier-228
Special Effects-228
94Pinnacle-445
Artist's Proofs-445
Rink Collection-445
94Topps/OPC Premier-228
Special Effects-228
94Finnish Jaa Kiekko-109
95Be A Player-59
Signatures-S59
Signatures Die Cuts-S59
95Finnish Semic World Championships-103
95Swedish Globe World Championships-110
95Swedish World Championships Stickers-218
97Pacific Dynagon Best Kept Secrets-94
97Pacific Invincible NHL Regime-197
97Upper Deck-373
Wolanski, Paul
88Niagara Falls Thunder-3
89Niagara Falls Thunder-23
897th Inn. Sketch OHL-136
907th Inn. Sketch OHL-275
917th Inn. Sketch OHL-383
Wolbeck, Derek
04Camrose Kodiaks-8
Wolcott, Brad
93Quebec Pee-Wee Tournament-670
Wold, Ketil
99Norwegian National Team-17
Wold, Vidar
92Norwegian Elite Series-153
Wolf, Manfred
82Swedish Semic VM Stickers-116
83Swedish Semic VM Stickers-116
89Swedish Semic World Champ Stickers-121
Wolf, Rudolf
94Czech APS Extraliga-119
95Czech APS Extraliga-296
Wolf, Thorsten
94German First League-384
Wolf, Tom
01Arizona Icecats-21
Wolfe, Bernie
76O-Pee-Chee NHL-227
76Topps-227
77O-Pee-Chee NHL-138
77Topps-138A
77Topps-138B
78Capitals Team Issue-18
78O-Pee-Chee-81
78Topps-81
Wolfe, Dwight
97Halifax Mooseheads I-23
97Halifax Mooseheads II-23
98Val d'Or Foreurs-23
Wolfe, Harry
81Sault Ste. Marie Greyhounds-24
82Sault Ste. Marie Greyhounds-23
83Sault Ste. Marie Greyhounds-23
84Sault Ste. Marie Greyhounds-22
87Sault Ste. Marie Greyhounds-31
Wolfe, Jason
03Roanoke Express-320
04Bakersfield Condors-21
Wolfe, John
96UK Guildford Flames-1
Wolff, Chris
93Quebec Pee-Wee Tournament-1283
93Quebec Pee-Wee Tournament-1740
Wolfgang, Reinhard
93Quebec Pee-Wee Tournament-1533
Wolfgramm, Christian
94German First League-84
Wolgin, German
94German First League-47
Wolhwend, Christian
96Swiss HNL-148
Wolitski, Sheldon
91British Columbia JHL-4
Wolke, Benji
99Ohio State Buckeyes-19
Wolkow, Alexander
94German First League-518
Wolkowski, Chad
00Calgary Hitmen-26
01Calgary Hitmen-26
01Calgary Hitmen Autographed-26
03Portland Winter Hawks-11
Wollard, Chad
05Quad City Mallards-19
Wolsch, Sebastian
04German Weiden Blue Devils-24
Wolski, Wojtek
03Brampton Battalion-24
04ITG Top Prospects Spring Expo-1
04SP Authentic Rookie Redemptions-RR8
04Brampton Battalion-1

04ITG Heroes and Prospects-110
Autographs-WW
Complete Emblems-10
Emblems-54
Emblems-66
Emblems Gold-54
Emblems Gold-66
He Shoots-He Scores Prizes-13
Jersey Autographs-54
Jerseys-54
Jerseys-66
Jerseys Gold-54
Jerseys Gold-66
Numbers-54
Numbers-66
Numbers Gold-54
Numbers Gold-66
Top Prospects-1
04ITG Heroes/Prospects Toronto Expo '05-110
04ITG Heroes/Prospects Expo Heroes/Pros-110
05ITG Heroes/Prosp Toronto Expo Parallel -380
05Beehive-110
Beige -110
Blue -110
Gold-110
Red -110
Matte-110
05Black Diamond-203
Emerald-203
Gold-203
Onyx-203
Ruby-203
05Hot Prospects-232
En Fuego-232
Hot Materials-HMWW
Red Hot-232
White Hot-232
05Parkhurst-620
Facsimile Auto Parallel-620
05SP Authentic-149
Limited-149
Rarefied Rookies-RRWW
Rookie Authentics-RAWW
Sign of the Times Triples-TTHW
05SP Game Used-107
Autographs-107
Gold-107
Game Gear-GG-WW
Game Gear Autographs-AG-WW
Rookie Exclusives-WW
Rookie Exclusives Silver-RE-WW
05SPx-154
Spectrum-154
Xcitement Rookies-XR-WW
Xcitement Rookies Gold-XR-WW
Xcitement Rookies Spectrum-XR-WW
05The Cup-114
Autographed Rookie Patches Gold Rainbow-114
Black Rainbow Rookies-114
Masterpiece Pressplates (Artifacts)-208
Masterpiece Pressplates (Bee Hive)-110
Masterpiece Pressplates (Black Diamond)-203
Masterpiece Pressplates (Ice)-111
Masterpiece Pressplates (MVP)-396
Masterpiece Pressplates (Power Play)-134
Masterpiece Pressplates Rookie Upd Auto-263
Masterpiece Pressplates SPA Autos-149
Masterpiece Pressplates (SP Game Used)-107
Masterpiece Pressplates SPx Autos-154
Masterpiece Pressplates (Trilogy)-185
Masterpiece Pressplates Ult Coll Autos-112
Masterpiece Pressplates (Victory)-252
Masterpiece Pressplates Autographs-114
Platinum Rookies-114
05UD Artifacts-208
Gold-RED8
05UD PowerPlay-134
05UD Rookie Class-40
05Ultimate Collection-112
Autographed Patches-112
Autographed Shields-112
Ultimate Debut Threads Jerseys-DTJWW
Ultimate Debut Threads Jerseys Autos-DAJWW
Ultimate Debut Threads Patches-DTPWW
Ultimate Debut Threads Patches Autos-DAPWW
Ultimate Signatures-USWW
05Ultra-256
Gold-256
Fresh Ink-FI-WW
Fresh Ink Blue-FI-WW
Ice-256
Rookie Uniformity Jerseys-RU-WW
Rookie Uniformity Jersey Autographs-ARU-WW
Rookie Uniformity Patches-RUP-WW
Rookie Uniformity Patch Autographs-ARP-WW
05Upper Deck-240
HG Glossy-240
Rookie Ink-RIWW
05Upper Deck Rookie Showcase-RS8
05Upper Deck Rookie Showcase Promos-RS8
05Upper Deck Rookie Threads-RTWW
05Upper Deck Rookie Threads Autographs-ARTWW
05Upper Deck Stars in the Making-SM14
05Upper Deck Ice-111
Glacial Graphs-GGWW
Glacial Graphs Labels-GGWW
Premieres Auto Patches-AIPWW
05Upper Deck MVP-396
Gold-396
Platinum-396
Rookie Breakthrough-RB5
05Upper Deck Rookie Update-263
05Upper Deck Trilogy-185
05Upper Deck Toronto Fall Expo-240
05Upper Deck Victory-252
Black-252
Gold-252
Silver-252
05Brampton Battalion-1
05Extreme Top Prospects Signature Edition-S27
05OHL Bell All-Star Classic-3
05ITG Heroes and Prospects-380
He Shoots-He Scores Prizes-25
Jerseys-GUJ-45
Jerseys Gold-GUJ-45
Emblems-GUE-45
Emblems Gold-GUE-45
Numbers-GUN-45
Numbers Gold-GUN-45
Nameplates-N-61
Nameplates Gold-N-61
Spectrum-STM-07
Spectrum Gold-STM-07
06Avalanche Team Postcards-21
06Be A Player Portraits First Exposures-FEWW
06Be A Player Portraits Signature Portraits-SPWW
06Black Diamond-22
Black-22
Gold-22
Ruby-22
06Fleer-50
Tiffany-50
06ITG Ultimate Memorabilia Autos Triple-5
06ITG Ultimate Memorabilia Autos Triple Gold-5
06ITG Ultimate Memorabilia Future Star-4
06ITG Ultimate Memorabilia Future Star Gold-4
06ITG Ultimate Memorabilia Future Star Autos-18
06ITG Ultimate Memorabilia Future Star Autos Gold-18
06ITG Ultimate Memorabilia Future Star Patches Autos-18
06ITG Ultimate Memorabilia Future Star Patches Autos Gold-18
06ITG Ultimate Memorabilia R.O.Y. Autos-5
06ITG Ultimate Memorabilia R.O.Y. Autos Gold-5
06ITG Ultimate Memorabilia R.O.Y. Emblems-5
06ITG Ultimate Memorabilia R.O.Y. Emblems Gold-5
06ITG Ultimate Memorabilia R.O.Y. Jerseys-5
06ITG Ultimate Memorabilia R.O.Y. Jerseys Gold-5
06ITG Ultimate Memorabilia R.O.Y. Numbers-5
06ITG Ultimate Memorabilia R.O.Y. Numbers Gold-5
06O-Pee-Chee-131
Rainbow-131
Autographs-A-WW
06The Cup Property of-POWW
06Upper Deck Arena Giveaways-COL2
06Upper Deck-52
Exclusives Parallel-52
High Gloss Parallel-52
Masterpieces-52
Signature Sensations-SSWW
06Upper Deck MVP-75
Gold Script-75
Super Script-75
06Upper Deck Victory-238
06ITG Heroes and Prospects Jerseys-GUJ42
06ITG Heroes and Prospects Jerseys Gold-GUJ42
06ITG Heroes and Prospects Emblems-GUE42
06ITG Heroes and Prospects Emblems Gold-GUE42
06ITG Heroes and Prospects Numbers-GUN42
06ITG Heroes and Prospects Numbers Gold-GUN42
06ITG Heroes and Prospects Making The Bigs-MTB01
06ITG Heroes and Prospects Making The Bigs Gold-MTB01
06ITG Heroes and Prospects Quad Emblems-QE07
06ITG Heroes and Prospects Quad Emblems Gold-QE07
07Upper Deck Ovation-90
07Upper Deck Victory-155
Black-155
Gold-155

Wong, Randy
97Medicine Hat Tigers-24
98Medicine Hat Tigers-24

Wonschweski, Darius
94German First League-417
94German First League-509

Woo, Larry
89Victoria Cougars-20
907th Inn. Sketch WHL-250

Wood, Dan
81Kingston Canadians-14
84Fredericton Express-9

Wood, Derek
93Lethbridge Hurricanes-23
98Fort Wayne Komets-22
01BC Icemen-27

Wood, Dody
907th Inn. Sketch WHL-13
917th Inn. Sketch WHL-134
91Classic-38
91Star Pics-12
91Ultimate Draft-33
91Ultimate Draft French-33
91Classic Four-Sport *-38
Autographs-38A
92Kansas City Blades-11
93Parkhurst-186
Emerald Ice-186
93Upper Deck-238
93Kansas City Blades-9
93Classic Four-Sport *-251
Gold-251
94Kansas City Blades-11
95Bowman-161
All-Foil-161
95Upper Deck-415
Electric Ice-415
Electric Ice Gold-415
97Pacific Dynagon Best Kept Secrets-87
98Kansas City Blades-11
99Kansas City Blades Supercuts-21
00Kansas City Blades-8
02UK Nottingham Panthers-6

Wood, Doug
96South Carolina Stingrays-19
99German EV Landshut-3

Wood, Dustin
01Peterborough Petes-2
02ECHL All-Star Northern-39
02ECHL Update-U-26
02Trenton Titans-A-9
03Springfield Falcons Postcards-5
06Manitoba Moose-16

Wood, Eric
93Quebec Pee-Wee Tournament-693

Wood, Fraser
81Ottawa 67's-13
81Ottawa 67's-25

Wood, Gary
71Johnstown Jets Acme-16
72Johnstown Jets-12

Wood, Ian
84Nova Scotia Oilers-19
95German DEL-310
96German DEL-93
99German Bundesliga 2-227

Wood, Jason
92British Columbia JHL-109
92Quebec Pee-Wee Tournament-1454

Wood, Martin
81Regina Pats-24

Wood, Pryce
88Brandon Wheat Kings-22
89Brandon Wheat Kings-4

Wood, Randy
88O-Pee-Chee-140
88O-Pee-Chee Stickers-107
88O-Pee-Chee Stickers-202
88Panini Stickers-294
88Topps-140
89Islanders Team Issue-22
89O-Pee-Chee-35
89Topps-35
90Bowman-121
Tiffany-121
90O-Pee-Chee-97
90Panini Stickers-79
90Pro Set-194
90Score-119
Canadian-119
90Topps-97
Tiffany-97
90Upper Deck-16
French-16
91Pro Set Platinum-160
91Bowman-227
91O-Pee-Chee-205
91Panini Stickers-244
91Parkhurst-13
French-13
91Pinnacle-104
French-104
91Pro Set Preview-151
91Pro Set-151
91Pro Set-359
French-151
French-359
91Sabres Blue Shield-25
91Sabres Pepsi/Campbell's-25
91Score American-281
91Score Canadian Bilingual-501
91Score Canadian English-501
91Score Rookie/Traded-42T
91Stadium Club-221
91Topps-205
91Upper Deck-289
French-289
92Bowman-246
92Panini Stickers-251
92Panini Stickers French-251
92Pinnacle-133
92Pinnacle-234
French-133
French-234
92Pro Set-20
92Sabres Blue Shield-25
92Sabres Jubilee Foods-16
92Score-73
Canadian-73
92Stadium Club-206
92Topps-170
Gold-170G
92Ultra-265
92Upper Deck-245
92Finnish Semic-168
93Leaf-226
93OPC Premier-119
Gold-119
93Panini Stickers-105
93Parkhurst-297
Emerald Ice-297
93Pinnacle-177
Canadian-177
93PowerPlay-35
93Score-55
Canadian-55
93Stadium Club-89
Members Only Master Set-89
OPC-89
First Day Issue-89
First Day Issue OPC-89
93Topps/OPC Premier-119
Gold-119
93Ultra-279
93Upper Deck-22
94Canada Games NHL POGS-51
94EA Sports-196
94Leaf-544
94Maple Leafs Kodak-29
94Maple Leafs Pin-up Posters-16
94OPC Premier-61
Special Effects-61
94Parkhurst-25
Gold-25
94Pinnacle-218
Artist's Proofs-218
Rink Collection-218
94Topps/OPC Premier-61
Special Effects-61
95Be A Player-35
Signatures-S35
Signatures Die Cuts-S35
95Canada Games NHL POGS-262
95Collector's Choice-74
Player's Club-74
Player's Club Platinum-74
95Donruss-154
95Leaf-168
95Pinnacle-164
Artist's Proofs-164
Rink Collection-164
95Playoff One on One-205
95Score-63
Black Ice Artist's Proofs-63
Black Ice-63
96Islander Postcards-23
96Playoff One on One-395

Wood, Ryan
98Huntsville Channel Cats-8

Wood, Stephen
06Peoria Rivermen-21

Wood, Tim
92Quebec Pee-Wee Tournament-1132
93Quebec Pee-Wee Tournament-687

Wood, Tom
00Arizona Icecats-24
01Arizona Icecats-22

Wood, Travis
00Connecticut Huskies-15

Wood, Wayne
76O-Pee-Chee WHA-31
77O-Pee-Chee WHA-42

Woodall, Frank
23Crescent Selkirks-12
24Holland Creameries-4

Woodburn, Steven
92Finnish Semic-226
94French National Team-34
95Swedish World Championships Stickers-104

Woodcock, Tom
71Blues Postcards-28

Woodcroft, Craig
91ProCards-492
92Indianapolis Ice-26
93Alberta International Team Canada-22
93OPC Premier Team Canada-5
93PowerPlay-497
93Ultra-477
94Finnish Jaa Kiekko-103
98German DEL-99
99German DEL-192
01German Upper Deck-75
01UK Manchester Storm Retro-2

Woodcroft, Jay
00Missouri River Otters-22

Wooderson, Phil
04UK Milton Keynes Lightning-4

Woodford, Michael
02Michigan Wolverines-14
03Michigan Wolverines-24

Woodgate, Peter
82North Bay Centennials-23
83North Bay Centennials-24

Woodley, Dan
86Portland Winter Hawks-24
87Flint Spirits-20
89ProCards AHL-190
90ProCards AHL/IHL-64
90ProCards AHL/IHL-528
93Muskegon Fury-6

Woodley, Darrell
95Slapshot-19
95Barrie Colts-28
97Barrie Colts-26
97Louisiana Ice Gators-8

Woodman, Lance
03Gatineau Olympiques-27

Woods, Bob
88Brandon Wheat Kings-2
89ProCards AHL-218
90ProCards AHL/IHL-560
91Johnstown Chiefs-9
93Johnstown Chiefs-4
95Hampton Roads Admirals-21
99Mississippi Sea Wolves-9
99Mississippi Sea Wolves Kelly Cup-7
05Hershey Bears-19

Woods, Brad
88Brandon Wheat Kings-5
94Tampa Bay Tritons RHI-21
99Brampton Battalion-10

Woods, Brad (OHL)
99Brampton Battalion-10

Woods, Brock
907th Inn. Sketch OHL-73
917th Inn. Sketch OHL-279
92Greensboro Monarchs-4
93Wheeling Thunderbirds-6
93Wheeling Thunderbirds-UD10
94Wheeling Thunderbirds-3
95Wheeling Thunderbirds-8
95Wheeling Thunderbirds Series II-20

Woods, Martin
917th Inn. Sketch QMJHL-255
96Johnstown Chiefs-23
97Johnstown Chiefs-15
97New Orleans Brass-8
01Flint Generals-20

Woods, Nick
01Arizona Icecats-23
02Arizona Icecats-26

Woods, Paul
76Nova Scotia Voyageurs-20
78O-Pee-Chee-159
78Topps-159
79O-Pee-Chee-48
79Red Wings Postcards-18
79Topps-48
80O-Pee-Chee-148
80Topps-148
81O-Pee-Chee-104
82O-Pee-Chee-98
82O-Pee-Chee Stickers-187
82Post Cereal-5
82Topps Stickers-187
83O-Pee-Chee-133
84O-Pee-Chee-66
89Red Wings Little Caesars-23

Woods, Rob
00Saskatoon Blades-24
01Saskatoon Blades-24
02Saskatoon Blades-15
03Saskatoon Blades-11

Woods, Steve
907th Inn. Sketch OHL-224

Woodward, Rob
92Michigan State Spartans-29

Woog, Dan
92Minnesota Golden Gophers-24
93Minnesota Golden Gophers-27
94Minnesota Golden Gophers-29
95Minnesota Golden Gophers-29
96Minnesota Golden Gophers-27

Woog, Doug
92Minnesota Golden Gophers-25
93Minnesota Golden Gophers-28
94Minnesota Golden Gophers-30
95Minnesota Golden Gophers-2
96Minnesota Golden Gophers-2
97Minnesota Golden Gophers-2
98Minnesota Golden Gophers-2

Woog, Steve
92Northern Michigan Wildcats-27
93Northern Michigan Wildcats-29

Woolf, Mark
907th Inn. Sketch WHL-200
917th Inn. Sketch Memorial Cup-92
92Thunder Bay Thunder Hawks-29
94Huntington Blizzard-22
99San Diego Gulls-16
00San Diego Gulls-20

Woolger, Brian
03Portland Winter Hawks-9
04Portland Winter Hawks-9

Woolhouse, Geoff
03UK Nottingham Panthers-11
04UK Nottingham Panthers-20
04UK U-20 Team-22
05UK Nottingham Panthers-2
06UK Nottingham Panthers-18

Woollard, Chad
96Sault Ste. Marie Greyhounds-28
96Sault Ste. Marie Greyhounds Autographed-28
98Owen Sound Platers-17
00Fort Worth Brahmas-17
01Fort Worth Brahmas-18
02Fort Worth Brahmas-18
03Fort Worth Brahmas-18
04Fort Worth Brahmas-18
06Quad City Mallards-19

Woolley, Jason
91Alberta International Team Canada-23
92Capitals Kodak-25
92OPC Premier-98
92Parkhurst-429
Emerald Ice-429
92Pinnacle-415
French-415
92Score Canadian Olympians-7
92Upper Deck-422
92Classic-97
Gold-97
93Donruss-364
93Leaf-273
93Parkhurst-490
Emerald Ice-490
93Score-435
Canadian-435
93Upper Deck-462
93Portland Pirates-8
95Donruss-260
95Leaf-307
95Parkhurst International-89
Emerald Ice-89
95Ultra-244
95Upper Deck-335
Electric Ice-335
Electric Ice Gold-335
Special Edition-SE124
Special Edition Gold-SE124
95Images-90
Gold-90
96Be A Player-58
Autographs-58
Autographs Silver-58
96Fleer Picks-62
97Collector's Choice-203
97Pacific-279
Copper-279
Emerald Green-279
Ice Blue-279
Red-279
Silver-279
97Score Sabres-17
Platinum-17
Premier-17
97Upper Deck-138
98Be A Player-13
Press Release-13
98BAP Gold-13
98BAP Autographs-13
98BAP Autographs Gold-13
98BAP Tampa Bay All Star Game-13
98OPC Chrome-9
Refractors-9
98Pacific-113
Ice Blue-113
Red-113
98Topps-9
O-Pee-Chee-9
99BAP Memorabilia-125
Gold-125
Silver-125
99O-Pee-Chee-122
99O-Pee-Chee Chrome-122
99O-Pee-Chee Chrome Refractors-122
99Pacific-49
Copper-49
Emerald Green-49
Gold-49
Ice Blue-49
Premiere Date-49
Red-49
99Panini Stickers-36
99Paramount-33
Copper-33
Emerald-33
Gold-33
Holographic Emerald-33
Holographic Gold-33
Holographic Silver-33
Ice Blue-33
Premiere Date-33
Red-33
Silver-33
99Stadium Club-104
First Day Issue-104
One of a Kind-104
Printing Plates Black-104
Printing Plates Cyan-104
Printing Plates Magenta-104
Printing Plates Yellow-104
99Topps/OPC-122
99Topps/OPC Chrome-122
Refractors-122
99Upper Deck MVP SC Edition-26
Gold Script-26
Silver Script-26
Super Script-26
00BAP Memorabilia-109
Emerald-109
Ruby-109
Sapphire-109
Promos-109
00BAP Mem Chicago Sportsfest Copper-109
00BAP Memorabilia Chicago Sportsfest Blue-109
00BAP Memorabilia Chicago Sportsfest Gold-109
00BAP Memorabilia Chicago Sportsfest Ruby-109
00BAP Memorabilia Chicago Sun-Times Ruby-109
00BAP Memorabilia Chicago Sun-Times Gold-109
00BAP Mem Chicago Sun-Times Sapphire-109
00BAP Mem Toronto Fall Expo Copper-109
00BAP Memorabilia Toronto Fall Expo Gold-109
00BAP Memorabilia Toronto Fall Expo Ruby-109
00O-Pee-Chee-139
00O-Pee-Chee Parallel-139
00Pacific-60
Copper-60
Gold-60
Ice Blue-60
Premiere Date-60
00Topps/OPC-139
Parallel-139
01BAP Memorabilia-126
Emerald-126
Ruby-126
Sapphire-126
02BAP Sig Series Auto Buybacks 1998-13
02Pacific Complete-158
Red-158
02Topps Total-40
03ITG Action-287
03Pacific Complete-338
Red-338
03Parkhurst Original Six Detroit-7
03Upper Deck MVP-151
Gold Script-151
Silver Script-151
Canadian Exclusives-151

Worden, Scott
92Michigan State Spartans-30
93Michigan State Spartans-30

Worle, Tobias
05German DEL-200

Worlton, Jeff
01Austin Ice Bats-19
02Louisiana Ice Gators-22
04Fort Wayne Komets-19
04Fort Wayne Komets Shoe Carnival-16
05Fort Wayne Komets Choice-2

Wormald, Brent
92British Columbia JHL-226

Worrell, Peter
95Slapshot Memorial Cup-71
97Bowman CHL-56
OPC-56
98Pacific-232
Ice Blue-232
Red-232
98Pacific Omega-108
Red-108
Opening Day Issue-108
98Upper Deck-99
Exclusives-99
Exclusives 1 of 1-99
Gold Reserve-99
98Upper Deck MVP-90
Gold Script-90
Silver Script-90
Super Script-90
99Pacific-184
Copper-184
Emerald Green-184
Gold-184
Ice Blue-184
Premiere Date-184
Red-184
99Upper Deck Victory-129
00BAP Memorabilia-355
Emerald-355
Ruby-355
Sapphire-355
Promos-355
00BAP Mem Chicago Sportsfest Copper-355
00BAP Memorabilia Chicago Sportsfest Blue-355
00BAP Memorabilia Chicago Sportsfest Gold-355
00BAP Memorabilia Chicago Sportsfest Ruby-355
00BAP Memorabilia Chicago Sun-Times Ruby-355
00BAP Memorabilia Chicago Sun-Times Gold-355
00BAP Mem Chicago Sun-Times Sapphire-355
00BAP Mem Toronto Fall Expo Copper-355
00BAP Memorabilia Toronto Fall Expo Gold-355
00BAP Memorabilia Toronto Fall Expo Ruby-355
00BAP Memorabilia Update Tough Materials-T10
00BAP Mem Update Tough Materials Gold-T10
00Pacific-190
Copper-190
Gold-190
Ice Blue-190
Premiere Date-190
00Panthers Team Issue-12
00Upper Deck Vintage-160
01BAP Signature Series-61
Autographs-61
Autographs Gold-61
01BAP Update Tough Customers-TC4
01BAP Update Tough Customers-TC12
01O-Pee-Chee-167
01O-Pee-Chee Premier Parallel-167
01Pacific-178
01Pacific-412
Extreme LTD-178
Gold-412
Hobby LTD-178
Premiere Date-178
Retail LTD-178
01Pacific Arena Exclusives-178
01Pacific Arena Exclusives-412
01Topps-167
OPC Parallel-167
01Upper Deck Victory-156
Gold-156
01Upper Deck Vintage-266
02BAP First Edition-375
02BAP Sig Series Auto Buybacks 2001-61
02BAP Signature Series Famous Scraps-FS4
02O-Pee-Chee-241
02O-Pee-Chee Premier Blue Parallel-241
02O-Pee-Chee Premier Red Parallel-241
02O-Pee-Chee Factory Set-241
02Pacific-163
Blue-163
Red-163
02Pacific Complete-45
Red-45
02Topps-241
OPC Blue Parallel-241
OPC Red Parallel-241
Factory Set-241
02Topps Heritage-96
02Topps Heritage-114
Chrome Parallel-96
02Upper Deck Vintage-112
02Upper Deck Vintage-273
02Upper Deck Vintage-313
03Avalanche Team Issue-20
03ITG Action-291
Jerseys-M89
03O-Pee-Chee-135
03OPC Blue-135
03OPC Gold-135
03OPC Red-135
03Pacific-150
Blue-150
Red-150
03Pacific Complete-444
Red-444
03Topps-135
Blue-135
Gold-135
Red-135
Own the Game-OTG20
Signs of Toughness-PW
Tough Materials-PW
Tough Materials-PWDL
Tough Materials Signed-PW
03Topps Traded-TT10
Blue-TT10
Gold-TT10
Red-TT10
03Upper Deck MVP-187
Gold Script-187
Silver Script-187
Canadian Exclusives-187
04SP Authentic Sign of the Times-ST-PW
04SP Authentic Sign of the Times-DS-LW
05SP Game Used Authentic Fabrics Dual-WB
05SP Game Used Authentic Patches Dual-WB
05SPx Winning Combos-WC-WL
05SPx Winning Combos Autographs-AWC-WL
05SPx Winning Combos Gold-WC-WL
05SPx Winning Combos Spectrum-WC-WL
05UD Artifacts Auto Facts-AF-PW
05UD Artifacts Auto Facts Blue-AF-PW
05UD Artifacts Auto Facts Copper-AF-PW
05UD Artifacts Auto Facts Pewter-AF-PW
05UD Artifacts Auto Facts Silver-AF-PW
05Upper Deck Notable Numbers-N-PW

Worsley, Gump
44Beehive Group II Photos-294
44Beehive Group II Photos-369
53Parkhurst-53
54Topps-10
57Topps-53
58Topps-39
59Topps-15
59Topps-54
60NHL Ceramic Tiles-18
60Topps-36
Stamps-52
61Shirriff/Salada Coins-85
61Topps-50
61Topps-64
61Topps-65
62Topps-45
Hockey Bucks-24
63Chex Photos-58
63Parkhurst-39
63Parkhurst-98
63York White Backs-22
63Quebec Aces-23
64Beehive Group III Photos-119
64Canadiens Postcards-24
64Quebec Aces-19
65Canadiens Steinberg Glasses-12
65Coca-Cola-72
65Topps-2
66Canadiens IGA-10
66Post Cereal Box Backs-1
66Topps-2
66Topps-65
66Topps-130
66Topps USA Test-2
67Canadiens IGA-1
67Post Flip Books-1
67Topps-1
67York Action Octagons-2
67York Action Octagons-17
67York Action Octagons-18
67York Action Octagons-22
67York Action Octagons-24
67York Action Octagons-35
68Canadiens IGA-1
68Canadiens Postcards BW-20
68O-Pee-Chee-56
68O-Pee-Chee-199
68O-Pee-Chee-212
Puck Stickers-6
68Post Marbles-30
68Shirriff Coins-75
68Topps-56
69O-Pee-Chee-1
Four-in-One-9
69Topps-1
70Canadiens Pins-22
70Dad's Cookies-143
70Esso Power Players-163
70North Stars Postcards-10
70O-Pee-Chee-40
70Sargent Promotions Stamps-84
70Topps-40
71Letraset Action Replays-4
71O-Pee-Chee-241
Posters-23
71Sargent Promotions Stamps-96
71Toronto Sun-145
72O-Pee-Chee-28
72O-Pee-Chee-189
72O-Pee-Chee-286
72Sargent Promotions Stamps-105
72Topps-55
72Topps-64
72Finnish Semic World Championship-201
72Swedish Semic World Championship-201
73North Stars Postcards-20
73O-Pee-Chee-230
77Sportscasters-607
81TCMA-2
83Hall of Fame Postcards-M16
85Hall of Fame-180
88Esso All-Stars-48
91Ultimate Original Six-17
French-17
92Hall of Fame Legends-30
92Parkhurst Parkie Reprints-PR4
93O-Pee-Chee Canadiens Hockey Fest-64
93Parkhurst Parkie Reprints-PR41
93Zeller's Masters of Hockey-8
93Zeller's Masters of Hockey Signed-8
94Hockey Wit-14
94Parkhurst Missing Link-92
94Parkhurst Missing Link-165
Autographs-4
94Parkhurst Tall Boys-81
95Parkhurst '66-67-76
95Parkhurst '66-67-131
Coins-76
00Topps Heritage Arena Relics-OSA-LW
00Topps Heritage Arena Relics-HAA-LW
00Topps Heritage Autographs-HA-LW
00Topps Heritage Autoproofs-10
01BAP Signature Series Vintage Autographs-VA-18
01Between the Pipes-120
01Between the Pipes-131
Double Memorabilia-DM28
Vintage Memorabilia-VM16
01Greats of the Game-88
01Parkhurst Autographs-PA38
01Parkhurst Reprints-PR116
01Parkhurst Reprints-PR132
01Parkhurst Reprints-PR143
01Topps Archives-59
02BAP Memorabilia-234
Emerald-234
Ruby-234
Sapphire-234
Mini Stanley Cups-4
NHL All-Star Game-234
NHL All-Star Game Blue-234
NHL All-Star Game Green-234
NHL All-Star Game Red-234
02BAP Memorabilia Toronto Fall Expo-234
02BAP Ultimate Memorabilia Cup Duels-6
02BAP Ultimate Mem Storied Franchise-13
02Between the Pipes Goalie Autographs-31
02Parkhurst Retro Nicknames-RN9
02Topps Rookie Reprints-5
02Topps Rookie Reprint Autographs-5
03BAP Ultimate Memorabilia Emblem Attic-10
03BAP Ultimate Mem Emblem Attic Gold-10
03BAP Ultimate Mem Jersey and Stick-26
03BAP Ultimate Mem Jersey and Stick Gold-26
03BAP Ultimate Mem Retro Teammates-7
03BAP Ultimate Mem Vintage Jerseys-28
03BAP Ultimate Mem Vintage Jerseys Gold-28
03ITG Used Signature Series Goalie Gear-29
03ITG Used Sig Series Goalie Gear Autos-29
03ITG Used Sig Series Goalie Gear Gold-29
03ITG Used Sig Series Vintage Mem -17
03ITG Used Sig Series Vintage Mem Autos-17
03ITG Used Sig Series Vintage Mem Gold-17
03Parkhurst Orig Six He Shoots/Scores-7
03Parkhurst Orig Six He Shoots/Scores-7A
03Parkhurst Original Six Montreal-48
Autographs-18
Memorabilia-MM27
03Parkhurst Original Six New York-59
Autographs-16
Inserts-N6
03Parkhurst Rookie Before the Mask-BTM-4
03Parkhurst Rookie Before the Mask Gold-BTM-4
03Parkhurst Rookie ROYalty-VR-26
03Parkhurst Rookie ROYalty Autographs-VR-GW
03Parkhurst Rookie ROYalty Gold-VR-26
04ITG All-Star FANtasy Hall Minnesota-9
04ITG Franchises Canadian-45
Autographs-GW3
Double Memorabilia-DM9
Double Memorabilia Gold-DM9
Goalie Gear-GG6
Goalie Gear Autographs-GG6
Goalie Gear Gold-GG6
Memorabilia-SM12
Memorabilia Autographs-SM12
Memorabilia Gold-SM12
Teammates-TM9
Teammates Gold-TM9
Trophy Winners-TW3
Trophy Winners Gold-TW3
04ITG Franchises He Shoots/Scores Prizes-8
04ITG Franchises US East-389
Autographs-A-GW1
04ITG Franchises US West-246
Autographs-A-GW2
04ITG Ultimate Memorabilia-146
04ITG Ultimate Memorabilia-149
04ITG Ultimate Memorabilia-170
Gold-146
Gold-149
Gold-170
Goalie Gear-1
Jersey Autographs-52
Jersey Autographs Gold-52
Nicknames-20
Nickname Autographs-11
Original Six-3
Original Six-6
Retro Teammates-15
Stick Autographs-17
Stick Autographs Gold-17
Triple Threads-3
04UD Legendary Signatures-54
AKA Autographs-AKA-LW
Autographs-LW
04UD Legends Classics-38
Gold-38
Platinum-38
Silver-38
Signature Moments-M20
Signatures-CS20
Signatures-TC1
Signatures-TC12
04ITG Heroes and Prospects-156
Autographs-LW
Hero Memorabilia-3
04ITG Heroes/Prospects Toronto Expo '05-156
04ITG Heroes/Prospects Expo Heroes/Pros-156
05Between the Pipes-25
Autographs-A-GW
05ITG Ultimate Memorabilia Level 1-45
05ITG Ultimate Memorabilia Level 2-45
05ITG Ultimate Memorabilia Level 3-45
05ITG Ultimate Memorabilia Level 4-45
05ITG Ultimate Memorabilia Level 5-45
05ITG Ultimate Mem Decades Jerseys-8
05ITG Ultimate Mem Decades Jerseys Gold-8
05ITG Ultimate Memorabilia Emblem Attic-4
05ITG Ultimate Mem Emblem Attic Gold-4
05ITG Ultimate Memorabilia Goalie Gear-9
05ITG Ultimate Mem Goalie Gear Gold-9
05ITG Ultimate Memorabilia Jersey Autos-29
05ITG Ultimate Mem Jersey Autos Gold-29
05ITG Ultimate Memorabilia Sextuple Autos-1
05ITG Ultimate Memorabilia Stick Autos-24
05ITG Ultimate Mem Stick Autos Gold-24
05ITG Ultimate Mem Sticks and Jerseys-21
05ITG Ultimate Mem Stick and Jerseys Gold-21
05ITG Ultimate Mem 3 Star of the Game Jsy-8
05ITG Ult Mem 3 Star of the Game Jsy Gold-8
05ITG Ultimate Memorabilia Triple Autos-15
05ITG Ultimate Mem Triple Autos Gold-15
05ITG Ultimate Memorabilia Ultimate Autos-2
05ITG Ultimate Mem Ultimate Autos Gold-2
05ITG Ultimate Memorabilia Vintage Lumber-29
05ITG Ultimate Mem Vintage Lumber Gold-29
05UD Artifacts Auto Facts-AF-GW
05UD Artifacts Auto Facts Blue-AF-GW
05UD Artifacts Auto Facts Copper-AF-GW
05UD Artifacts Auto Facts Pewter-AF-GW
05UD Artifacts Auto Facts Silver-AF-GW
05ITG Heroes and Prospects Hero Mem-HM-34
06Between The Pipes-93
06Between The Pipes-138
Autographs-AGW
Double Jerseys-DJ13
Double Jerseys Gold-DJ13
Emblems-GUE15
Emblems Gold-GUE15
Emblems Autographs-GUE15
Gloves-GG18
Gloves Gold-GG18
Jerseys-GUJ15
Jerseys Gold-GUJ15
Jerseys Autographs-GUJ15
Numbers-GUN15
Numbers Gold-GUN15
Numbers Autographs-GUN15
Stick and Jersey-SJ38
Stick and Jersey Gold-SJ38
Stick and Jersey Autographs-SJ38
Stick Work-SW04
Stick Work Gold-SW04
06ITG Ultimate Memorabilia-59
Artist Proof-59
Autos-35
Autos Gold-35
R.O.Y. Autos-20
R.O.Y. Autos Gold-20
R.O.Y. Emblems-20
R.O.Y. Emblems Gold-20
R.O.Y. Jerseys-20
R.O.Y. Jerseys Gold-20
R.O.Y. Numbers-20
R.O.Y. Numbers Gold-20
Retro Teammates-6
Retro Teammates Gold-6
Stick Rack-14
Stick Rack-25
Stick Rack Gold-14
Stick Rack Gold-25
06Parkhurst-134
06SP Game Used Authentic Fabrics Quads-AF4FCSW
06SP Game Used Authentic Fabrics Quads Patches-AF4FCSW
06The Cup-62
Autographed Patches-62
Black Rainbow-62
Gold-62
Gold Patches-62
Jerseys-62
Masterpiece Pressplates-62

06Ultimate Collection Jerseys-UJ-GW
06Ultimate Collection Patches-UJ-GW
06Ultimate Collection Premium Patches-PS-GW
06Ultimate Collection Premium Swatches-PS-GW

Worters, Roy
24Anonymous NHL-47
330-Pee-Chee V304A-45
33V357 Ice Kings-11
34Beehive Group I Photos-259
34Diamond Matchbooks Silver-60
35Diamond Matchbooks Tan 1-70
35Diamond Matchbooks Tan 2-65
35Diamond Matchbooks Tan 3-60
36Triumph Postcards-10
37V356 Worldwide Gum-7
83Hall of Fame-60
83Hall of Fame Postcards-D16
85Hall of Fame-60
94Hall of Fame Tickets-8
01Between the Pipes-150
02BAP Ultimate Memorabilia Emblem Attic-6
02BAP Ultimate Mem Vintage Jerseys-33
02Between the Pipes-120
He Shoots-He Saves Prizes-22
Vintage Memorabilia-13
02ITG Used Vintage Memorabilia-VM3
02ITG Used Vintage Memorabilia Gold-VM3
02Parkhurst Retro Nicknames-RN15
03BAP Ultimate Memorabilia Emblem Attic-3
03BAP Ultimate Mem Emblem Attic Gold-3
03BAP Ultimate Memorabilia Paper Cuts-40
03BAP Ultimate Mem Retro-Active Trophies-7
03BAP Ultimate Memorabilia Triple Threads-9
03BAP Ultimate Mem Vint Complete Jersey-6
03BAP Ultimate Mem Vint Comp Jersey Gold-6
03BAP Ultimate Mem Vintage Jerseys-4
03BAP Ultimate Mem Vintage Jerseys Gold-4
03ITG VIP MVP-2
03Parkhurst Rookie Before the Mask-BTM-1
03Parkhurst Rookie Before the Mask Gold-BTM-1
04ITG Franchises He Shoots/Scores Prizes-49
04ITG Franchises US East-367
Memorabilia-ESM20
Memorabilia Gold-ESM20
04ITG Franchises US West-282
04ITG Ultimate Memorabilia-164
Gold-164
Emblem Attic-7
Emblem Attic Gold-7
Jerseys-12
Jerseys Gold-12
Seams Unbelievable-10
Triple Threads-4
05ITG Ultimate Mem Amazing Amerks Autos-3
05ITG Ultimate Memorabilia Emblem Attic-8
05ITG Ultimate Mem Emblem Attic Gold-8
05ITG Ultimate Mem Pass the Torch Jerseys-9
05ITG Ultimate Mem Passing Torch Jsy Gold-9
06Between The Pipes-131
Double Jerseys-DJ26
Double Jerseys Gold-DJ26
Forgotten Franchises-FF09
06ITG Ultimate Memorabilia Emblem Attic-7
06ITG Ultimate Memorabilia Emblem Attic Gold-7

Worthman, Kevin
91ProCards-578

Worthy, Chris
69Seattle Totems-16

Wortman, Kevin
92Salt Lake Golden Eagles-23
92Classic-116
Gold-116
92Classic Four-Sport *-220
Gold-220
94Kansas City Blades-4
95Fort Wayne Komets-22
98Finnish Kerailysarja-123
99German DEL-196
00German DEL-165

Wothe, Chris
01Sioux Falls Stampede-19

Wotton, Mark
89Saskatoon Blades-6
90Saskatoon Blades-16
907th Inn. Sketch WHL-86
91Saskatoon Blades-16
917th Inn. Sketch WHL-115
93Saskatoon Blades-23
95Leaf-296
96Canucks Postcards-4
96Syracuse Crunch-4
99Michigan K-Wings-14
00Utah Grizzlies-33
01Utah Grizzlies-15
02Utah Grizzlies-26
05Hershey Bears-27

Wotton, Scott
91Air Canada SJHL-A48

Wourns, Darren
84Nanaimo Clippers-22

Wouters, Micah
92Quebec Pee-Wee Tournament-1551
93Quebec Pee-Wee Tournament-1253

Woytiuk, Mark
93Quebec Pee-Wee Tournament-1141

Woytowich, Bob
61Sudbury Wolves-18
62Sudbury Wolves-22
65Coca-Cola-5
65Topps-100
66Topps-34
68Bauer Ads-21
680-Pee-Chee-49
680-Pee-Chee-192
68Shirriff Coins-63
68Topps-49
690-Pee-Chee-151
Four-in-One-14
69Topps-113
70Dad's Cookies-144
70Esso Power Players-219
700-Pee-Chee-88
Deckle-8
70Sargent Promotions Stamps-163
70Topps-88
Topps/OPC Sticker Stamps-33
71Letraset Action Replays-7
710-Pee-Chee-28
71Penguins Postcards-21
71Sargent Promotions Stamps-165
71Topps-28
71Toronto Sun-230
720-Pee-Chee-325
750-Pee-Chee WHA-123
94Parkhurst Tall Boys-13
95Parkhurst '66-67-8
Coins-8

Woywitka, Jeff
00Red Deer Rebels-24
Signed-24
00UD CHL Prospects-54
01BAP Memorabilia Draft Redemptions-27
01UD Prospects-4
Jerseys-J-JW
Jerseys-C-WA
Jerseys Gold-J-JW
Jerseys Gold-C-WA
02Red Deer Rebels-5
03AHL Top Prospects-45
03Philadelphia Phantoms-9
04SP Authentic Rookie Redemptions-RR26
04ITG Heroes and Prospects-10
Autographs-JW
04ITG Heroes/Prospects Toronto Expo '05-10
04ITG Heroes/Prospects Expo Heroes/Pros-10
05Beehive-111
Beige -111
Blue -111
Gold-111
Red -111
Matte-111
05Black Diamond-167
Emerald-167
Gold-167
Onyx-167
Ruby-167
05Hot Prospects-266
En Fuego-266
Hot Materials-HMJW
Red Hot-266
White Hot-266
05Parkhurst Signatures-JW
05Parkhurst True Colors-TCSTL
05Parkhurst True Colors-TCSTL
05SP Authentic-187
Limited-187
Rarefied Rookies-RRJW
Rookie Authentics-RAJW
05SP Game Used-151
Autographs-151
Gold-151
Rookie Exclusives-JW
Rookie Exclusives Silver-RE-JW
Significant Numbers-SN-JW
05SPx-157
Spectrum-157
Xcitement Rookies-XR-JW
Xcitement Rookies Gold-XR-JW
Xcitement Rookies Spectrum-XR-JW
05The Cup-142
Autographed Rookie Patches Gold Rainbow-142
Black Rainbow Rookies-142
Masterpiece Pressplates (Artifacts)-226
Masterpiece Pressplates (Bee Hive)-111
Masterpiece Pressplates (Black Diamond)-167
Masterpiece Pressplates (Ice)-142
Masterpiece Pressplates (MVP)-398
Masterpiece Pressplates (Power Play)-137
Masterpiece Pressplates (Rookie Update)-232
Masterpiece Pressplates SPA Autos-187
Masterpiece Pressplates (SP Game Used)-151
Masterpiece Pressplates SPx Autos-157
Masterpiece Pressplates (Trilogy)-214
Masterpiece Pressplates Ult Coll Autos-132
Masterpiece Pressplates (Victory)-257
Masterpiece Pressplates Autographs-142
Platinum Rookies-142
05UD Artifacts-226
Gold-RED26
05UD PowerPlay-137
05Ultimate Collection-132
Autographed Patches-132
Autographed Shields-132
Ultimate Debut Threads Jerseys-DTJJW
Ultimate Debut Threads Jerseys Autos-DAJJW
Ultimate Debut Threads Patches-DTPJW
Ultimate Debut Threads Patches Autos-DAPJW
05Ultra-257
Gold-257
Fresh Ink-FI-JW
Fresh Ink Blue-FI-JW
Ice-257
Rookie Uniformity Jerseys-RU-JW
Rookie Uniformity Jersey Autographs-ARU-JW
Rookie Uniformity Patches-RUP-JW
Rookie Uniformity Patch Autographs-ARP-JW
05Upper Deck-220
HG Glossy-220
Rookie Ink-RIJW
05Upper Deck Rookie Showcase-RS26
05Upper Deck Rookie Showcase Promos-RS26
05Upper Deck Rookie Threads-RTJW
05Upper Deck Rookie Threads Autographs-ARTJW
05Upper Deck Ice-142
Premieres Auto Patches-AIPJW
05Upper Deck MVP-398
Gold-398
Platinum-398
05Upper Deck Rookie Update-232
Inspirations Patch Rookies-232
05Upper Deck Trilogy-214
05Upper Deck Toronto Fall Expo-220
05Upper Deck Victory-257
Black-257
Gold-257
Silver-257
05Peoria Rivermen-23
06Upper Deck MVP Autographs-OALW
06Peoria Rivermen-22

Wozney, Paul
90Fort Saskatchewan Traders-21

Wozniewski, Andy
03Wisconsin Badgers-28
04SP Authentic Rookie Redemptions-RR44
05Beehive-140
Beige -140
Blue -140
Gold-140
Red -140
Matte-140
05Black Diamond-149
Emerald-149
Gold-149
Onyx-149
Ruby-149
05Hot Prospects-216
Autographed Patch Variation-216
Autographed Patch Variation Gold-216
Red Hot-216
05SP Authentic-189
Limited-189
Rarefied Rookies-RRAW
05SP Game Used-149
Autographs-149
Gold-149
Rookie Exclusives-AW
Rookie Exclusives Silver-RE-AW
05SPx-146
Spectrum-146
Xcitement Rookies-XR-AW
Xcitement Rookies Gold-XR-AW
Xcitement Rookies Spectrum-XR-AW
05The Cup-164
Autographed Rookie Patches Gold Rainbow-164
Black Rainbow Rookies-164
Masterpiece Pressplates (Artifacts)-333
Masterpiece Pressplates (Bee Hive)-140
Masterpiece Pressplates (Black Diamond)-149
Masterpiece Pressplates (Ice)-172
Masterpiece Pressplates (MVP)-412
Masterpiece Pressplates (Rookie Update)-235
Masterpiece Pressplates SPA Autos-189
Masterpiece Pressplates (SP Game Used)-149
Masterpiece Pressplates (SPx)-146
Masterpiece Pressplates (Trilogy)-219
Masterpiece Pressplates Ult Coll-175
Masterpiece Pressplates Autographs-164
Platinum Rookies-164
05UD Artifacts-333
05Ultimate Collection-175
Gold-175
05Ultra-249
Gold-249
Fresh Ink-FI-AW
Fresh Ink Blue-FI-AW
Ice-249
Rookie Uniformity Jerseys-RU-AW
Rookie Uniformity Jersey Autographs-ARU-AW
Rookie Uniformity Patches-RUP-AW
Rookie Uniformity Patch Autographs-ARP-AW
05Upper Deck-212
HG Glossy-212
Rookie Ink-RIAW
Rookie Threads-RTAW
Rookie Threads Autographs-ARTAW
05Upper Deck Ice-172
Premieres Auto Patches-AIPAW
05Upper Deck MVP-412
Gold-412
Platinum-412
05Upper Deck Rookie Update-235
Inspirations Patch Rookies-235
05Upper Deck Trilogy-219
05Upper Deck Toronto Fall Expo-212
05ITG Heroes and Prospects-261
Autographs Series II-AW
06Toronto Marlies-34

Woznikoski, Joel
06Westside Warriors-6

Wray, Brennen
04Moose Jaw Warriors-14
05Moose Jaw Warriors-21

Wray, Dick
51Laval Dairy QSHL-28
51Laval Dairy Subset-118

Wray, Jeremy
04Memphis RiverKings-10

Wray, Scott
96Owen Sound Platers-18
00Charlotte Checkers-33
01Fort Worth Brahmas-19
06Port Huron Flags-15

Wregget, Ken
84Maple Leafs Postcards-25
84Kelowna Wings-53
85Maple Leafs Postcards-33
86Kraft Drawings-81
86Maple Leafs Postcards-22
87Maple Leafs PLAY-29
87Maple Leafs Postcards-20
87Maple Leafs Postcards Oversized-20
870-Pee-Chee-242
870-Pee-Chee Stickers-164
87Panini Stickers-322
88Maple Leafs PLAY-29
880-Pee-Chee-264
880-Pee-Chee Stickers-177
88Panini Stickers-117
89Flyers Postcards-28
890-Pee-Chee-255
90Flyers Postcards-25
900-Pee-Chee-80
900-Pee-Chee-415
90Panini Stickers-112
90Pro Set-226
90Score-263
Canadian-263
90Upper Deck-89
French-89
91Pro Set Platinum-210
91Bowman-231
91Flyers J.C. Penney-25
910-Pee-Chee-136
91Panini Stickers-236
91Parkhurst-357
French-357
91Pro Set-450
French-450
91Score American-141
91Score Canadian Bilingual-141
91Score Canadian English-141
91Stadium Club-8
91Topps-136
91Upper Deck-206
French-206
92Bowman-182
92Parkhurst-371
Emerald Ice-371
92Penguins Coke/Clark-25
92Pinnacle-356
French-356
92Score-399
Canadian-399
92Stadium Club-130
92Topps-494
Gold-494G
92Ultra-383
930PC Premier-277
Gold-277
93Penguins Foodland-10
93Pinnacle-325
Canadian-325
93PowerPlay-417
93Score-329
Canadian-329
93Topps/OPC Premier-277
Gold-277
93Ultra-399
94Fleer-172
94Leaf-76
940PC Premier-328
Special Effects-328
94Parkhurst SE-SE139
Gold-SE139
94Penguins Foodland-16
94Pinnacle-230
Artist's Proofs-230
Rink Collection-230
94SP-88
Die Cuts-88
94Stadium Club-133
Members Only Master Set-133
First Day Issue-133
Super Team Winner Cards-133
94Topps/OPC Premier-84
94Topps/OPC Premier-328
Special Effects-328
94Ultra-353
94Upper Deck-362
Electric Ice-362
95Be A Player-67
Signatures-S67
Signatures Die Cuts-S67
95Canada Games NHL POGS-220
95Collector's Choice-314
Player's Club-314
Player's Club Platinum-314
95Donruss-182
95Emotion-143
95Leaf-19
95Panini Stickers-68
95Parkhurst International-167
Emerald Ice-167
95Penguins Foodland-9
95Pinnacle-107
Artist's Proofs-107
Rink Collection-107
95Playoff One on One-80
95Score-126
Black Ice Artist's Proofs-126
Black Ice-126
95SkyBox Impact-136
95Summit-112
Artist's Proofs-112
Ice-112
95Topps-190
OPC Inserts-190
95Ultra-128
Gold Medallion-128
95Upper Deck-108
Electric Ice-108
Electric Ice Gold-108
96Collector's Choice-220
96Donruss-136
Press Proofs-136
96Leaf-40
Press Proofs-40
96Score-183
Artist's Proofs-183
Dealer's Choice Artist's Proofs-183
Special Artist's Proofs-183
Golden Blades-183
96Summit-60
Artist's Proofs-60
Ice-60
Metal-60
Premium Stock-60
96Upper Deck-135
97Collector's Choice-210
97Donruss-27
Press Proofs Silver-27
Press Proofs Gold-27
97Donruss Canadian Ice-76
Dominion Series-76
Provincial Series-76
97Donruss Limited-188
Exposure-188
97Donruss Preferred-118
Cut to the Chase-118
97Leaf-82
Fractal Matrix-82
Fractal Matrix Die Cuts-82
97Leaf International-82
Universal Ice-82
97Pacific-201
Copper-201
Emerald Green-201
Ice Blue-201
Red-201
Silver-201
97Pinnacle-96
Artist's Proofs-96
Rink Collection-96
Press Plates Back Black-96
Press Plates Back Cyan-96
Press Plates Back Magenta-96
Press Plates Back Yellow-96
Press Plates Front Black-96
Press Plates Front Cyan-96
Press Plates Front Magenta-96
Press Plates Front Yellow-96
97Pinnacle Certified-17
Red-17
Mirror Blue-17
Mirror Gold-17
Mirror Red-17
97Pinnacle Inside-32
Coach's Collection-32
Executive Collection-32
97Pinnacle Tot Cert Platinum Blue-17
97Pinnacle Tot Certi Platinum Gold-17
97Pinnacle Totally Certified Platinum Red-17
97Pinnacle Tot Cert Mirror Platinum Gold-17
97Score-32
Artist's Proofs-32
Golden Blades-32
97Score Penguins-2
Platinum-2
Premier-2
97Upper Deck-344
98Be A Player-169
Press Release-169
98BAP Gold-169
98BAP Autographs-169
98BAP Autographs Gold-169
98Crown Royale-21
Limited Series-21
98NHL Aces Playing Cards-15
98Pacific-360
Ice Blue-360
Red-360
98Pacific Dynagon Ice-29
Blue-29
Red-29
98Upper Deck-230
Exclusives-230
Exclusives 1 of 1-230
Gold Reserve-230
99BAP Memorabilia-114
Gold-114
Silver-114
99Pacific-65
Copper-65
Emerald Green-65
Gold-65
Ice Blue-65
Premiere Date-65
Red-65
99Pacific Omega-87
Copper-87
Gold-87
Ice Blue-87
Premiere Date-87
00Pacific-161
Copper-161
Gold-161
Ice Blue-161
Premiere Date-161
00Paramount-92
Copper-92
Gold-92
Holo-Gold-92
Holo-Silver-92
Ice Blue-92
Premiere Date-92
00Manitoba Moose-22
02BAP Sig Series Auto Buybacks 1998-169
04ITG Franchises Update Autographs-KW
06Between The Pipes-96
Autographs-AKW

Wren, Bob
917th Inn. Sketch OHL-37
93Detroit Jr. Red Wings-25
93Classic-33
93Classic Four-Sport *-216
Gold-216
98Cincinnati Mighty Ducks-19
99AHL All-Stars-12
99Cincinnati Mighty Ducks-31
00SPx Rookie Redemption-RR28
01BAP Memorabilia-406
Emerald-406
Ruby-406
Sapphire-406
01Pacific-13
Extreme LTD-13
Hobby LTD-13
Premiere Date-13
Retail LTD-13
01Pacific Arena Exclusives-13
01SP Authentic-174
Limited-174
Limited Gold-174
01SPx-129
01Upper Deck Ice-70
01Upper Deck Vintage-299
01St. John's Maple Leafs-27
02Milwaukee Admirals-8
03German DEL-30

Wren, Chad
05Vernon Vipers-22

Wretling, Sune
57Swedish Alfabilder-102

Wright, Ben
05Lethbridge Hurricanes-21

Wright, Billy
907th Inn. Sketch OHL-322
917th Inn. Sketch OHL-63

Wright, Darren
82Kitchener Rangers-22
83Kitchener Rangers-7
84Kingston Canadians-21
85Kingston Canadians-21
93Prince Albert Raiders-21
94Prince Albert Raiders-22
95Prince Albert Raiders-22
96Kamloops Blazers-28
97New Mexico Scorpions-4
99San Angelo Outlaws-19

Wright, Dave
93Lakeland Ice Warriors-25

Wright, Doug
03Las Vegas Wranglers-21
03Las Vegas Wranglers RBI-240
04Las Vegas Wranglers-16

Wright, Erik
93Quebec Pee-Wee Tournament-1300

Wright, Jamie
93Guelph Storm-11
94Guelph Storm-12
95Donruss Elite World Juniors-22
95Slapshot-93
95Upper Deck-535
Electric Ice-535
Electric Ice Gold-535
95Guelph Storm-27
96Michigan K-Wings-11
98Bowman's Best-121
Refractors-121
Atomic Refractors-121
Mirror Image Fusion-F12
Mirror Image Fusion Refractors-F12
Mirror Image Fusion Atomic Refractors-F12
98Pacific-186
Ice Blue-186
Red-186
98Pacific Omega-78
Red-78
Opening Day Issue-78
98Upper Deck-253
Exclusives-253
Exclusives 1 of 1-253
Gold Reserve-253
99Michigan K-Wings-1
00Utah Grizzlies-32
02NHL Power Play Stickers-7
02Upper Deck-273
Exclusives-273
02Upper Deck Beckett UD Promos-273
05Finnish Cardset -285

Wright, Jason
93Michigan Tech Huskies-20
96Richmond Renegades-24
98Fayetteville Force-8
00UK Sekonda Superleague-182
01UK Belfast Giants-30
04Langley Hornets-21

Wright, John
72Canucks Royal Bank-21
73Canucks Royal Bank-21
74NHL Action Stamps-291
740-Pee-Chee NHL-156
74Topps-156

Wright, Kory
94Anchorage Aces-4

Wright, Larry
74NHL Action Stamps-62
780-Pee-Chee-360

Wright, Mark
93UK Sheffield Steelers-10
94UK Sheffield Steelers-16
95UK Sheffield Steelers-9

Wright, Nate
03St. Cloud State Huskies-26

Wright, Peter
51Laval Dairy QSHL-41
52St. Lawrence Sales-85

Wright, Shayne
93Owen Sound Platers-34
94Owen Sound Platers-14
94Owen Sound Platers-28
95Rochester Americans-24
96Rochester Americans-8
96Collector's Edge Ice-67
Prism-67
97Rochester Americans-4-2
99German DEL-132
00German DEL-148
01German Upper Deck-134
02German DEL City Press-190
03German DEL-193
04German DEL-240
04German Krefeld Penguins Postcards-23

Wright, Tyler
907th Inn. Sketch WHL-56
91Upper Deck-67
91Upper Deck-686
French-67
French-686
91Upper Deck Czech World Juniors-60
917th Inn. Sketch WHL-191
917th Inn. Sketch Memorial Cup-112
91Arena Draft Picks-9
91Arena Draft Picks French-9
91Arena Draft Picks Autographs-9
91Arena Draft Picks Autographs French-9
91Classic-10
91Star Pics-16
91Star Pics-36
91Ultimate Draft-10
91Ultimate Draft-66
91Ultimate Draft French-10
91Classic Four-Sport *-10
Autographs-10A
920PC Premier-32
92Upper Deck-558
92Upper Deck-584
93Leaf-347
93Parkhurst-340
Emerald Ice-340
93Pinnacle-214
Canadian-214
93Score-463
Canadian-463
93Ultra-240
Prospects-10
93Upper Deck-256
94Cape Breton Oilers-22
94Classic Pro Prospects-140
95Upper Deck World Junior Alumni-8
95SkyBox Impact-199
95Upper Deck-327
Electric Ice-327
Electric Ice Gold-327
97Be A Player-64
Autographs-64
Autographs Die-Cuts-64
Autographs Prismatic Die-Cuts-64
99Pacific Omega-193
Copper-193
Gold-193
Ice Blue-193
Premiere Date-193
00BAP Memorabilia-130
Emerald-130
Ruby-130
Sapphire-130
Promos-130
00BAP Mem Chicago Sportsfest Copper-130
00BAP Memorabilia Chicago Sportsfest Blue-130
00BAP Memorabilia Chicago Sportsfest Gold-130
00BAP Memorabilia Chicago Sportsfest Ruby-130
00BAP Memorabilia Chicago Sun-Times Ruby-130
00BAP Memorabilia Chicago Sun-Times Gold-130
00BAP Mem Chicago Sun-Times Sapphire-130
00BAP Mem Toronto Fall Expo Copper-130
00BAP Memorabilia Toronto Fall Expo Gold-130
00BAP Memorabilia Toronto Fall Expo Ruby-130
00BAP Parkhurst 2000-P108
00BAP Signature Series-45
Emerald-45
Ruby-45
Sapphire-45
Autographs-206
Autographs Gold-206
00Stadium Club-211
00Topps Chrome-228
OPC Refractors-228
Refractors-228
00UD Heroes-35
00UD Pros and Prospects-26
01Blue Jackets Donatos Pizza-7
01Pacific-121
Extreme LTD-121
Hobby LTD-121
Premiere Date-121
Retail LTD-121
01Pacific Arena Exclusives-121
01Upper Deck-281
Exclusives-281
01Upper Deck MVP-56
01Upper Deck Victory-102
Gold-102
01Upper Deck Vintage-74
02BAP Sig Series Auto Buybacks 2000-206
02Pacific Complete-357
Red-357
02Topps Total-232
02Upper Deck-298
Exclusives-298
02Upper Deck Beckett UD Promos-298
03ITG Action-102
030-Pee-Chee-251
030PC Blue-251
030PC Gold-251
030PC Red-251
03Pacific-101
Blue-101
Red-101
03Pacific Complete-22
Red-22
03Topps-251
Blue-251
Gold-251
Red-251
03Upper Deck MVP-121
Gold Script-121
Silver Script-121
Canadian Exclusives-121
05Upper Deck MVP-117
Gold-117
Platinum-117

Wrigley, David
05Muskegon Fury-20

Wrobel, J.J.
01Anchorage Aces-16
02Bakersfield Condors-20
04Richmond Riverdogs-17
05Quad City Mallards-20
06Richmond Renegades-17

Wroble, Brian
92Quebec Pee-Wee Tournament-1444
93Quebec Pee-Wee Tournament-1583

Wroblewski, John
01Notre Dame Fighting Irish-15
02Notre Dame Fighting Irish-5
03Fresno Falcons-24
04Fresno Falcons-23
05Fresno Falcons-20

Wuchterl, Michael
03Everett Silvertips-6
04Everett Silvertips-6
05Lethbridge Hurricanes-22

Wudrick, Geordie
06Swift Current Broncos-8

Wuest, Mathias
99Swiss Panini Stickers-113

Wuhrer, Marc
93Quebec Pee-Wee Tournament-1769

Wunsch, Alexander
94German DEL-112
95German DEL-314

Wunsche, Lars
94German First League-581

Wust, Harald
94German First League-135

Wust, Mathias
00Swiss Panini Stickers-169
01Swiss HNL-61
02Swiss HNL-327

Wuthrich, Markus
98Swiss Power Play Stickers-136
98Swiss Power Play Stickers-293
99Swiss Panini Stickers-137
01Swiss HNL-408
02Swiss HNL-170

Wuthrich, Martin
02Swiss HNL-475

Wuthrich, Olivier
95Swiss HNL-388

Wuthrich, Stefan
01Swiss HNL-370
02Swiss HNL-419

Wuttunee, Wally
960CN Blizzard-13
970CN Blizzard-12

Wycherly, Ralph
34Beehive Group I Photos-260

Wycisk, Austin
04Lakehead University Thunderwolves-16

Wynes, Deuce
98El Paso Buzzards-9

Wynia, Sjon
91British Columbia JHL-50
92British Columbia JHL-93

Wynn, Keith
05Mississauga Ice Dogs-6

Wynne, Derek
91Air Canada SJHL-B44
92Saskatchewan JHL-62

Wynne, John
907th Inn. Sketch OHL-121
917th Inn. Sketch OHL-28

Wynne, Teeder
92North Dakota Fighting Sioux-30
99UK Sheffield Steelers-22
00UK Sekonda Superleague-21
01UK Dundee Stars-7
02UK Dundee Stars-7

Wyrozub, Randy
700-Pee-Chee-141
70Sargent Promotions Stamps-31
72Sabres Postcards-20

Wyssen, Raymond
93Swiss HNL-420
95Swiss HNL-247

Wywrot, Pete
51Laval Dairy Subset-46
52St. Lawrence Sales-76

Wyzansky, Ben
92Richmond Renegades-20
94Johnstown Chiefs-19

Wyzgowski, David
02Michigan Wolverines-4
03Michigan Wolverines-27

Yablonski, Jeremy
98Kootenay Ice-21
01Idaho Steelheads-22
02Peoria Rivermen-19
03ITG VIP Rookie Debut-93
03Parkhurst Rookie-77
04Milwaukee Admirals-2
05Milwaukee Admirals Choice-17
05Milwaukee Admirals Pepsi-22
06Idaho Steelheads-13

Yacboski, Darryl
01Regina Pats-24
02Regina Pats-5A
03Calgary Hitmen-20
04Calgary Hitmen-21

Yachanov, Dmitri
99Russian Hockey League-70
00Russian Hockey League-34
01Russian Hockey League-160
02Russian Hockey League-15
02Russian SL-36
03Russian Hockey League-266

Yachimel, Bert
83Moncton Alpines-16

Yachmenev, Vitali
93North Bay Centennials-22
93North Bay Centennials-25
94Parkhurst SE-SE229
Gold-SE229
94SP-167
Die Cuts-167
94Upper Deck-513
Electric Ice-513
94North Bay Centennials-24
94Classic CHL Previews-CP5
94Signature Rookies Gold Standard *-99
94Signature Rookies Tetrad *-117
Signatures-117
95Be A Player-181
Signatures-S181
Signatures Die Cuts-S181
95Bowman-115
All-Foil-115
Bowman's Best-BB20
Bowman's Best Refractors-BB20
95Collector's Choice-409
95Donruss-318
Rated Rookies-9
95Donruss Elite-52
Die Cut Stars-52
Die Cut Uncut-52
Rookies-2
95Finest-157
Refractors-157
95Leaf Limited-115
Rookie Phenoms-5
95Metal-198
International Steel-22
95Parkhurst International-266
95Parkhurst International-506
Emerald Ice-266
Emerald Ice-506
Parkie's Trophy Picks-PP37
95Select Certified-130
Mirror Gold-130
95SkyBox Impact-205
95SP-68
Holoviews-FX11
Holoviews Special FX-FX11
95Stadium Club-190
Members Only Master Set-190
95Summit-180
Artist's Proofs-180
Ice-180
95Topps-351
OPC Inserts-351
SuperSkills Super Rookies-SR15
95Ultra-362
95Upper Deck-263
Electric Ice-263
Electric Ice Gold-263
Predictor Hobby-H21
Predictor Hobby Exchange-H21
95Zenith-131
Rookie Roll Call-11
95Classic-90
95Signature Rookies Club Promos-5
96Black Diamond-43
Gold-43
96Collector's Choice-125
96Collector's Choice-320
MVP Gold-UD32
Crash the Game-C8A
Crash the Game-C8B
Crash the Game-C8C
Crash the Game Gold-C8A
Crash the Game Gold-C8B
Crash the Game Gold-C8C
Crash the Game Exchange-CR8
Crash the Game Exchange Gold-CR8
96Donruss-233
Press Proofs-233
96Donruss Canadian Ice-80
Gold Press Proofs-80
Red Press Proofs-80
96Donruss Elite-94
Die Cut Stars-94
96Fleer-51
Rookie Sensations-10
96Fleer Picks-142
96Leaf-157
Press Proofs-157
96Leaf Limited-34
Gold-34
96Leaf Preferred-99
Press Proofs-99
Steel-41
Steel Gold-41
96Metal Universe-78
96Pinnacle-206
Artist's Proofs-206
Foil-206
Premium Stock-206
Rink Collection-206
96Score-241
Artist's Proofs-241
Dealer's Choice Artist's Proofs-241
Special Artist's Proofs-241
Golden Blades-241
96SkyBox Impact-59
96SkyBox Impact-173
NHL on Fox-20
96SP-78
96SPx-20
96SPx-GF1
Gold-20
96Stadium Club Members Only-48
96Summit-171
Artist's Proofs-171
Ice-171
Metal-171
Premium Stock-171
96Topps Picks Rookie Stars-RS3
96Topps Picks Rookie Stars OPC-RS3
96Ultra-84
Gold Medallion-84
96Upper Deck-77
Generation Next-X20
Superstar Showdown-SS24A
96Zenith-52
Artist's Proofs-52
97Collector's Choice-123
Star Quest-SQ43
97Pacific-167
Copper-167
Emerald Green-167
Ice Blue-167
Red-167
Silver-167
97Panini Stickers-222
97Pinnacle Inside-144
97Score-212
97Upper Deck-291
Smooth Grooves-SG43
98Predators Team Issue-25
98Milwaukee Admirals Postcards-10
990-Pee-Chee-139
990-Pee-Chee Chrome-139
990-Pee-Chee Chrome Refractors-139
99Panini Stickers-272
99Topps/OPC-139
99Topps/OPC Chrome-139
Refractors-139
00BAP Memorabilia-368
Emerald-368
Ruby-368
Sapphire-368
Promos-368
00BAP Mem Chicago Sportsfest Copper-368
00BAP Memorabilia Chicago Sportsfest Blue-368
00BAP Memorabilia Chicago Sportsfest Gold-368
00BAP Memorabilia Chicago Sportsfest Ruby-368
00BAP Memorabilia Chicago Sun-Times Ruby-368
00BAP Memorabilia Chicago Sun-Times Gold-368
00BAP Mem Chicago Sun-Times Sapphire-368
00BAP Mem Toronto Fall Expo Copper-368
00BAP Memorabilia Toronto Fall Expo Gold-368
00BAP Memorabilia Toronto Fall Expo Ruby-368
00Crown Royale-61
Ice Blue-61
Limited Series-61
Premiere Date-61
Red-61
00Panini Stickers-179
00Paramount-140
Copper-140
Gold-140

Holo-Gold-140
Holo-Silver-140
Ice Blue-140
Premiere Date-140
00Stadium Club-180
00Upper Deck-328
Exclusives Tier 1-328
Exclusives Tier 2-328
00Upper Deck MVP-100
First Stars-100
Second Stars-100
Third Stars-100
00Vanguard Dual Game-Worn Jerseys-11
00Vanguard Dual Game-Worn Patches-11
01Pacific-224
Extreme LTD-224
Hobby LTD-224
Premiere Date-224
Retail LTD-224
01Pacific Arena Exclusives-224
01Upper Deck-330
Exclusives-330
01Upper Deck Victory-195
Gold-195
01Upper Deck Vintage-146
01Vanguard Memorabilia-16
02Pacific-217
Blue-217
Red-217
02Pacific Complete-169
Red-169
02Predators Team Issue-6
02Topps Total-254
03ITG Action-377
03Russian National Team-16
03Russian Postcards-11

Yaganiski, Jason
91Air Canada SJHL-C19

Yager, Cam
91Air Canada SJHL-A37

Yakabuski, Mark
92Ottawa 67's-23

Yake, Terry
85Brandon Wheat Kings-14
88ProCards AHL-55
89ProCards AHL-304
90Score-419
Canadian-419
90ProCards AHL/IHL-186
91Bowman-4
91O-Pee-Chee-169
91Stadium Club-374
91Topps-169
91Upper Deck-323
French-323
92Parkhurst-293
Emerald Ice-293
92Stadium Club-496
92Topps-432
Gold-432G
92Upper Deck-512
92Whalers Dairymart-24
93Donruss-4
93Ducks Milk Caps-4
93Leaf-406
93OPC Premier-432
Gold-432
93Panini Stickers-125
93Parkhurst-271
Emerald Ice-271
93Pinnacle II Samples-340
93Pinnacle-340
Canadian-340
93PowerPlay-14
93Score-259
93Score-511
Gold-511
Canadian-259
Canadian-511
Canadian Gold-511
93Stadium Club-490
Members Only Master Set-490
First Day Issue-490
93Topps/OPC Premier-432
Gold-432
93Ultra-221
93Ultra-265
93Upper Deck-311
SP-6
93Classic Pro Prospects-148
94Donruss-124
94EA Sports-3
94EA Sports-201
94Leaf-88
94Maple Leafs Kodak-30
94Maple Leafs Pin-up Posters-13
94Parkhurst Vintage-V10
94Pinnacle-282
Artist's Proofs-282
Rink Collection-282
94Score-93
Gold-93
Platinum-93
94Stadium Club-226
Members Only Master Set-226
First Day Issue-226
Super Team Winner Cards-226
94Ultra-9
94Upper Deck NHLPA/Be A Player-40
95Milwaukee Admirals-20
95Milwaukee Admirals Postcards-8
96Rochester Americans-14
96Collector's Edge Future Legends-49
97Be A Player-190
Autographs-190
Autographs Die-Cuts-190
Autographs Prismatic Die-Cuts-190
98Pacific-376
Ice Blue-376
Red-376
98Upper Deck-360
Exclusives-360
Exclusives 1 of 1-360
Gold Reserve-360
99Upper Deck MVP SC Edition-193
Gold Script-193
Silver Script-193
Super Script-193
02German DEL City Press-277
All-Stars-AS16
03German DEL-194
All-Stars-AS15

Yakhanov, Andrei
95Swedish World Championships Stickers-34
97Providence Bruins-22
00Russian Hockey League-245
02Russian Hockey League-138

Yakimishyn, Shawn
89Saskatoon Blades-19
90Saskatoon Blades-23
907th Inn. Sketch WHL-80
91Saskatoon Blades-22
917th Inn. Sketch WHL-119
99Adirondack IceHawks-10

Yakimovich, Sergei
00Russian Hockey League-74

Yakiwchuk, Dale
81Milwaukee Admirals-8

Yakovenko, Alexander
01Russian Hockey League-2

Yakovenko, Andrei
91O-Pee-Chee Inserts-63R
92Greensboro Monarchs-9
92Rochester Americans Dunkin' Donuts-8
92San Diego Gulls-12
95Czech APS Extraliga-131
96Czech APS Extraliga-9
97Czech APS Extraliga-152
98Czech DS-71
98Czech DS Stickers-190
98Czech OFS-252
99Czech OFS-239

Yakubov, Mikhail
00Russian Hockey League-197
00Russian Hockey League-293
01Red Deer Rebels-20
02Norfolk Admirals-24
03Beehive-240
Gold-240
Silver-240
03ITG Action-640
03ITG Used Signature Series-173
Gold-173
03ITG VIP Rookie Debut-68
03Pacific Complete-590
Red-590
03Pacific Heads-Up-108
Hobby LTD-108
Retail LTD-108
03Pacific Luxury Suite-58
Gold-58
03Pacific Quest for the Cup-110
03Parkhurst Rookie-120
03SP Authentic-103
Limited-103
03Titanium-110
Hobby Jersey Number Parallels-110
Retail-110
Retail Jersey Number Parallels-110
03Upper Deck-456
Canadian Exclusives-456
HG-456
UD Exclusives-456
03Upper Deck Classic Portraits-191
03Upper Deck Ice-96
Glass Parallel-96
03Upper Deck Rookie Update-209
03Upper Deck Trilogy-182
03Norfolk Admirals-22
04AHL Top Prospects-36
04Norfolk Admirals-23
05Norfolk Admirals-23

Yakubov, Rafik
98Russian Hockey League-52
99Russian Hockey League-61
00Russian Hockey League-387

Yakubov, Ravil
91O-Pee-Chee Inserts-46R
92Upper Deck-349
92Russian Stars Red Ace-32
92Russian Stars Red Ace-29
95Swedish World Championships Stickers-44
96Saint John Flames-21
97Swedish Collector's Choice-164
98Russian Hockey League-37
99Russian Hockey League-145
00Russian Hockey League-136
00Russian Hockey League-333
01Russian Dynamo Moscow-12
01Russian Dynamo Moscow Mentos-9
02Russian Hockey League-125
02Russian Transfert-23
03Russian Hockey League-176
03Russian SL-15

Yakushev, Alexander
69Russian National Team Postcards-13
69Swedish Hockey-4
70Finnish Jaakiekko-4
70Russian National Team Postcards-15
70Swedish Hockey-17
70Swedish Hockey-324
70Swedish Masterserien-121
70Swedish Masterserien-123
70Swedish Masterserien-131
70Swedish Masterserien-132
72Finnish Jaakiekko-25
72Finnish Hellas-74
73Finnish Jaakiekko-5
73Russian National Team-19
73Swedish Stickers-91
74Finnish Jenkki-46
74Finnish Typotor-68
74Russian National Team-23
74Swedish Stickers-9
74Swedish Semic World Champ Stickers-38
77Sportscasters-10308
77Finnish Sportscasters-71-1686
77Finnish Sportscasters-84-2015
91Future Trends Canada '72-70
91Future Trends Canada '72-97
91Future Trends Canada '72 French-70
91Future Trends Canada '72 French-97
92Future Trends '76 Canada Cup-106
95Swiss HNL-183
96Swiss HNL-77
99Russian Stars of Hockey-33
03Czech Stadion-647
05ITG Ultimate Memorabilia Level 1-3
05ITG Ultimate Memorabilia Level 2-3
05ITG Ultimate Memorabilia Level 3-3
05ITG Ultimate Memorabilia Level 4-3
05ITG Ultimate Memorabilia Level 5-3
05ITG Ultimate Memorabilia Triple Autos-4
05ITG Ultimate Mem Triple Autos Gold-4
05ITG Ultimate Memorabilia Ultimate Autos-26
05ITG Ultimate Mem Ultimate Autos Gold-26
06ITG International Ice-19
Gold-19
Autographs-AAY
Emblem Autographs-GUE02
Emblem Autographs Gold-GUE02
Emblems-GUE02
Emblems Gold-GUE02
International Rivals-IR03
International Rivals Gold-IR03
Jersey Autographs-GUJ02
Jersey Autographs Gold-GUJ02
Jerseys-GUJ02
Jerseys Gold-GUJ02
Numbers-GUN02
Numbers Autographs-GUN02
Numbers Autographs Gold-GUN02
Numbers Gold-GUN02
Passing The Torch-PTT13
Passing The Torch Gold-PTT13
Teammates-IT18
Teammates Gold-IT18
Triple Memorabilia-TM03
Triple Memorabilia Gold-TM03
06ITG Ultimate Memorabilia Retro Teammates-11
06ITG Ultimate Memorabilia Retro Teammates Gold-11

Yakushin, Dmitri
99BAP Memorabilia-390
Gold-390
Silver-390
99Pacific Omega-230
Copper-230
Gold-230
Ice Blue-230
Premiere Date-230
99St. John's Maple Leafs-25
00O-Pee-Chee-277
00O-Pee-Chee Parallel-277
00Topps/OPC-277
Parallel-277
00Topps Chrome-172
OPC Refractors-172
Refractors-172
00St. John's Maple Leafs-30

Yakutsenya, Maxim
03Russian Hockey League-132
03Russian Hockey League-214
05Russian Hockey League RHL-44

Yamada, Mineki
93Quebec Pee-Wee Tournament-151

Yandle, Keith
05ITG Heroes/Prosp Toronto Expo Parallel -416
05Moncton Wildcats-9
05ITG Heroes and Prospects-416
06Be A Player-229
06Beehive-143
Matte-143
06Black Diamond-157A
Black-157A
Gold-157A
Ruby-157A
06Hot Prospects-127
Red Hot-127
White Hot-127
Hot Materials -HMKY
Hot Materials Red Hot-HMKY
Hot Materials White Hot-HMKY
Hotagraphs-HRB
06O-Pee-Chee-559
06O-Pee-Chee-617
Rainbow-559
Rainbow-617
06SP Authentic-195
Limited-195
06SP Game Used-143
Gold-143
Rainbow-143
Autographs-143
Rookie Exclusives Autographs-REKY
06SPx-194
Spectrum-194
06The Cup-148
Autographed Rookie Masterpiece Pressplates-148
Gold Rainbow Autographed Rookie Patches-148
Masterpiece Pressplates (Bee Hive)-143
Masterpiece Pressplates (Black Diamond)-157
Masterpiece Pressplates (Marquee Rookies)-559
Masterpiece Pressplates (MVP)-328
Masterpiece Pressplates (SP Authentic Autographs)-195
Masterpiece Pressplates (SP Game Used)-143
Masterpiece Pressplates (SPx Autographs)-194
Masterpiece Pressplates (Sweet Beginnings)-143
Masterpiece Pressplates (Trilogy)-134
Masterpiece Pressplates (Ultimate Collection Autographs)-124
Masterpiece Pressplates (Victory)-311
Rookies Black-148
Rookies Platinum-148
06UD Mini Jersey Collection-121
06Ultimate Collection-124
Rookies Autographed NHL Shields-124
Rookies Autographed Patches-124
Ultimate Debut Threads Jerseys-DJ-KY
Ultimate Debut Threads Jerseys Autographs-DJ-KY
Ultimate Debut Threads Patches-DJ-KY
Ultimate Debut Threads Patches Autographs-DJ-KY
06Ultra-238
Gold Medallion-238
Ice Medallion-238
06Upper Deck-485
Exclusives Parallel-485
High Gloss Parallel-485
Masterpieces-485
Rookie Materials-RMKY
Rookie Materials Patches-RMKY
06Upper Deck MVP-328
Gold Script-328
Super Script-328
06Upper Deck Sweet Shot-143
Rookie Jerseys Autographs-143
06Upper Deck Trilogy-134
06Upper Deck Victory-311
07Upper Deck Rookie Class -28

Yannetti, Mark
95Central Hockey League-107
97Johnstown Chiefs-16

Yannick, Robert
93Swiss HNL-204

Yardley, Shaun
02UK Peterborough Phantoms-17

Yarema, Brendan
94Sarnia Sting-16
95Slapshot-344
95Sarnia Sting-14
97Kentucky Thoroughblades-19
98Kansas City Blades-8
99Kansas City Blades Supercuts-22
00UK Sekonda Superleague-86
00UK Sekonda Superleague-192
03Chicago Wolves-23
04Milwaukee Admirals-10
05German DEL-18

Yaremchuk, Gary
81Maple Leafs Postcards-24

Yaremchuk, Ken
83Blackhawks Postcards-26
85Blackhawks Team Issue-19
88ProCards AHL-236
93Swiss HNL-131
95Swiss HNL-180
95Swiss HNL-516
95Swiss HNL-528
95Swiss HNL-538
96Swiss HNL-124
98Swiss Power Play Stickers-198

Yaremko, Chad
99Lethbridge Hurricanes-25

Yari, J.D.
81Sault Ste. Marie Greyhounds-25

Yarosh, Troy
98Wichita Thunder-23
99Wichita Thunder-22

Yasakov, Sergei
98Russian Hockey League-71
99Russian Hockey League-94
99Russian Stars Postcards-32
00Russian Hockey League-3
01Russian Hockey League-86

Yasechko, Stanislav
02Russian Hockey League-34

Yashin, Alexei
91Upper Deck-651
French-651
91Upper Deck Czech World Juniors-12
92Upper Deck-334
92Russian Stars Red Ace-33
92Russian Stars Red Ace-27
92Classic-2
92Classic-60
Gold-2
Gold-60
LPs-LP2
92Classic Four-Sport *-152
Gold-152
LPs-LP25
93Donruss-238
Elite Inserts-U5
Rated Rookies-7
93Leaf-386
Freshman Phenoms-9
93OPC Premier-317
Gold-317
93Parkhurst-254
Emerald Ice-254
Calder Candidates-C10
Calder Candidates Gold-C10
East/West Stars-E7
93Pinnacle-455
Canadian-455
Super Rookies-5
Super Rookies Canadian-5
93PowerPlay-403
Global Greats-10
Rookie Standouts-16
93Score-603
Gold-603
Canadian-603
Canadian Gold-603
Dynamic Duos Canadian-3
93Senators Kraft Sheets-26
93Stadium Club-359
Members Only Master Set-359
First Day Issue-359
93Topps/OPC Premier-317
Gold-317
93Ultra-384
Wave of the Future-20
93Upper Deck-277
93Upper Deck-349
NHLPA/Roots-14
Silver Skates-H8
Silver Skates Gold-H8
SP-112
93Swedish Semic World Champ Stickers-136
93Classic-34
93Classic-96
Previews-HK5
94Be A Player-R92
94Be A Player-R172
Signature Cards-150
94Canada Games NHL POGS-174
94Donruss-63
94Finest-5
94Finest-56
Super Team Winners-5
Super Team Winners-56
Refractors-5
Refractors-56
94Flair-124
Scoring Power-10
94Fleer-149
Franchise Futures-9
94Kraft-30
94Leaf-19
Gold Rookies-3
Gold Stars-5
Limited Inserts-16
94Leaf Limited-80
94McDonald's Upper Deck-McD3
94OPC Premier-192
94OPC Premier-365
94O-Pee-Chee Finest Inserts-15
94OPC Premier Special Effects-192
94OPC Premier Special Effects-365
94Parkhurst-273
Gold-273
Crash the Game Green-16
Crash the Game Blue-16
Crash the Game Gold-16
Crash the Game Red-16
94Parkhurst SE-SE123
Gold-SE123
Vintage-21
94Pinnacle-28
94Pinnacle-465
Artist's Proofs-28
Artist's Proofs-465
Rink Collection-28
Rink Collection-465
Northern Lights-NL7
World Edition-WE17
94Post Box Backs-24
94Score-253
Gold-253
Platinum-253
94Select-135
Gold-135
94Senators Team Issue-28
94SP-79
Die Cuts-79
94Stadium Club Members Only-42
94Stadium Club-116
94Stadium Club-175
Members Only Master Set-116
Members Only Master Set-175
First Day Issue-116
First Day Issue-175
Super Team Winner Cards-116
Super Team Winner Cards-175
94Topps/OPC Premier-192
94Topps/OPC Premier-365
Special Effects-192
Special Effects-365
94Ultra-152
All-Rookies-10
All-Rookies Parallel-10
Global Greats-10
94Upper Deck-129
94Upper Deck-554
Electric Ice-129
Electric Ice-554
SP Inserts-SP55
SP Inserts Die Cuts-SP55
94Upper Deck NHLPA/Be A Player-17
94Finnish Jaa Kiekko-147
94Classic All-Rookie Team-AR3
94Classic Pro Prospects-40
94Classic Pro Prospects-NNO
Autographs-AU9
International Heroes-LP25
Jumbos-PP2
94Images *-125
94Images *-130
Chrome-CC13
95Canada Games NHL POGS-191
95Collector's Choice-189
Player's Club-189
Player's Club Platinum-189
Crash The Game-C18A
Crash The Game-C18B
Crash The Game-C18C
Crash The Game Gold-C18A
Crash The Game Gold-C18B
Crash The Game Gold-C18C
Crash the Game Silver Redeemed-C18
Crash the Game Silver Bonus-C18
Crash the Game Gold Redeemed-C18
Crash the Game Gold Bonus-C18
95Donruss-107
95Donruss Elite-79
Die Cut Stars-79
Die Cut Uncut-79
95Emotion-128
Xcel-5
Xcited-7
95Finest-151
Refractors-151
95Hoyle Eastern Playing Cards-54
95Leaf-153
95Leaf Limited-50
95NHL Aces Playing Cards-8S
95Panini Stickers-48
95Parkhurst International-151
95Parkhurst International-242
Emerald Ice-151
Emerald Ice-242
95Playoff One on One-74
95Score-230
Black Ice Artist's Proofs-230
Black Ice-230
Golden Blades-7
95Select Certified-36
Mirror Gold-36
95Senators Team Issue-24
95SkyBox Impact-122
95SP-101
95Stadium Club Members Only-14
95Stadium Club-182
Members Only Master Set-182
95Stadium Club Master Photo Test-9
95Summit-101
Artist's Proofs-101
Ice-101
Mad Hatters-12
95Topps-170
OPC Inserts-170
Canadian Gold-2CG
Young Stars-YS5
95Ultra-114
Gold Medallion-114
Rising Stars-9
Rising Stars Gold Medallion-9
95Upper Deck-15
Electric Ice-15
Electric Ice Gold-15
Special Edition-SE59
Special Edition Gold-SE59
95Finnish Semic World Championships-136
95Swedish Globe World Championships-172
96Be A Player-48
Autographs-48
Autographs Silver-48
96Black Diamond-159
Gold-159
96Collector's Choice-179
96Collector's Choice-325
96Donruss-124
Press Proofs-124
96Donruss Canadian Ice-61
Gold Press Proofs-61
Red Press Proofs-61
96Donruss Elite-41
Die Cut Stars-41
96Flair-65
Blue Ice-65
96Fleer-77
96Fleer Picks-48
Fabulous 50-48
Jagged Edge-5
96Kraft Upper Deck-10
96Kraft Upper Deck-72
96Leaf-101
Press Proofs-101
96Leaf Limited-31
Gold-31
96Leaf Preferred-17
Press Proofs-17
Steel-16
Steel Gold-16
96Maggers-107
96Metal Universe-108
96NHL Aces Playing Cards-51
96Pinnacle-121
Artist's Proofs-121
Foil-121
Premium Stock-121
Rink Collection-121
96Post Upper Deck-24
96Score-181
Artist's Proofs-181
Dealer's Choice Artist's Proofs-181
Special Artist's Proofs-181
Golden Blades-181
96Select Certified-83
Artist's Proofs-83
Blue-83
Mirror Blue-83
Mirror Gold-83
Mirror Red-83
Red-83
96Senators Pizza Hut-27
96SkyBox Impact-91
96SP-108
Holoview Collection-HC13
96SPx-31
Gold-31
96Summit-34
Artist's Proofs-34
Ice-34
Metal-34
Premium Stock-34
96Team Out-27
96Ultra-120
Gold Medallion-120
96Upper Deck-110
96Upper Deck Ice-96
Parallel-96
96Zenith-23
Artist's Proofs-23
Assailants-1
96Swedish Semic Wien-148
97Beehive-21
Golden Portraits-21
97Black Diamond-111
Double Diamond-111
Triple Diamond-111
Quadruple Diamond-111
97Collector's Choice-173
Crash the Game-C15A
Crash the Game-C15B
Crash the Game-C15C
Crash the Game Exchange-CR15
Star Quest-SQ72
97Crown Royale-94
Emerald Green-94
Ice Blue-94
Silver-94
97Donruss-19
Press Proofs Silver-19
Press Proofs Gold-19
97Donruss Canadian Ice-127
Dominion Series-127
Provincial Series-127
Stanley Cup Scrapbook-11
97Donruss Elite-27
Aspirations-27
Status-27
97Donruss Limited-69
97Donruss Limited-71
97Donruss Limited-189
Exposure-69
Exposure-71
Exposure-189
97Donruss Preferred-42
Cut to the Chase-42
97Donruss Priority-147
97Donruss Priority-213
Stamp of Approval-147
Stamp of Approval-213
97Esso Olympic Hockey Heroes-37
97Esso Olympic Hockey Heroes French-37
97Katch-102
Gold-102
Silver-102
97Kraft-15
97Kraft 3-D World's Best-3
97Leaf-59
Fractal Matrix-59
Fractal Matrix Die Cuts-59
97Leaf International-59
Universal Ice-59
97NHL Aces Playing Cards-34
97Pacific-120
Copper-120
Emerald Green-120
Ice Blue-120
Red-120
Silver-120
97Pacific Dynagon-87
Copper-87
Dark Grey-87
Emerald Green-87
Ice Blue-87
Red-87
Silver-87
Tandems-70
97Pacific Invincible-97
Copper-97
Emerald Green-97
Ice Blue-97
Red-97
Silver-97
97Pacific Omega-159
Copper-159
Dark Gray-159
Emerald Green-159
Gold-159
Ice Blue-159
97Panini Stickers-43
97Paramount-129
Copper-129
Dark Grey-129
Emerald Green-129
Ice Blue-129
Red-129
Silver-129
97Pinnacle-126
Epix Game Emerald-4
Epix Game Orange-4
Epix Game Purple-4
Epix Moment Emerald-4
Epix Moment Orange-4
Epix Moment Purple-4
Epix Play Emerald-4
Epix Play Orange-4
Epix Play Purple-4
Epix Season Emerald-4
Epix Season Orange-4
Epix Season Purple-4
Press Plates Back Black-126
Press Plates Back Cyan-126
Press Plates Back Magenta-126
Press Plates Back Yellow-126
Press Plates Front Black-126
Press Plates Front Cyan-126
Press Plates Front Magenta-126
Press Plates Front Yellow-126
97Pinnacle Certified-78
Red-78
Mirror Blue-78
Mirror Gold-78
Mirror Red-78
97Pinnacle Inside-57
Coach's Collection-57
Executive Collection-57
97Pinnacle Tot Cert Platinum Blue-78
97Pinnacle Tot Certi Platinum Gold-78
97Pinnacle Totally Certified Platinum Red-78
97Pinnacle Tot Cert Mirror Platinum Gold-78
97Post Pinnacle-23
97Revolution-96
Copper-96
Emerald-96
Ice Blue-96
Silver-96
97Score-116
Artist's Proofs-116
Golden Blades-116
97SP Authentic-105
97SPx-35
Bronze-35
Gold-35
Silver-35
Steel-35
Grand Finale-35
97Studio-31
Press Proofs Silver-31
Press Proofs Gold-31
97Upper Deck-321
Smooth Grooves-SG23
97Upper Deck Ice-28
Parallel-28
Power Shift-28
97Zenith-72
Z-Gold-72
Z-Silver-72
98SLU Hockey-220
98Aurora-134
Championship Fever-34
Championship Fever Copper-34
Championship Fever Ice Blue-34
Championship Fever Red-34
Championship Fever Silver-34
98Be A Player-246
Press Release-246
98BAP Gold-246
98BAP Autographs-246
98BAP Autographs Gold-246
98BAP Playoff Game Used Jerseys-G24
98BAP Playoff Game Used Jersey Autographs-G22
98BAP Playoff Practice Used Jerseys-P23
98Black Diamond-59
Double Diamond-59
Triple Diamond-59
Quadruple Diamond-59
Winning Formula Gold-WF20
Winning Formula Platinum-WF20
98Bowman's Best-37
Refractors-37
Atomic Refractors-37
98Crown Royale-96
Limited Series-96
Pivotal Players-17
98Finest-96
No Protectors-96
No Protectors Refractors-96
Refractors-96
Centurion-C5
Centurion Refractors-C5
Red Lighters-R12
Red Lighters Refractors-R12
98Katch-101
98Kenner Starting Lineup Cards-33
98Kraft Fearless Forwards-13
98McDonald's Upper Deck-9
98OPC Chrome-5
Refractors-5
98Pacific-318
Ice Blue-318
Red-318
Team Checklists-18
98Pacific Dynagon Ice-132
Blue-132
Red-132
Team Checklists-18
98Pacific Omega-170
Red-170
Opening Day Issue-170
Online-24
Planet Ice-6
Planet Ice Parallel-6
Prism-14
98Panini Photocards-90
98Panini Stickers-43
98Paramount-168
Copper-168
Emerald Green-168
Holo-Electric-168
Ice Blue-168
Silver-168
Ice Galaxy-8
Ice Galaxy Gold-8
Ice Galaxy Silver-8
Team Checklists Die-Cuts-18
98Revolution-102
Ice Shadow-102
Red-102
All-Star Die Cuts-30
Chalk Talk Laser-Cuts-12
Showstoppers-24
98Senators Team Issue-24
98SP Authentic-59
Power Shift-59
98SPx Finite-57
98SPx Finite-98
Radiance-57
Radiance-98
Spectrum-57
Spectrum-98
98SPx Top Prospects-42
Radiance-42
Spectrum-42
98Topps-5
O-Pee-Chee-5
98Topps Gold Label Class 1-11
Black-11
Black One of One-11
One of One-11
Red-11
Red One of One-11
98Topps Gold Label Class 2-11
98Topps Gold Label Class 2 Black-11
98Topps Gold Label Class 2 Black 1 of 1-11
98Topps Gold Label Class 2 One of One-11
98Topps Gold Label Class 2 Red-11
98Topps Gold Label Class 2 Red One of One-11
98Topps Gold Label Class 3-11
98Topps Gold Label Class 3 Black-11
98Topps Gold Label Class 3 Black 1 of 1-11
98Topps Gold Label Class 3 One of One-11
98Topps Gold Label Class 3 Red-11
98Topps Gold Label Class 3 Red One of One-11
98UD Choice-141
98UD Choice Preview-141
98UD Choice Prime Choice Reserve-141
98UD Choice Reserve-141
98UD Choice StarQuest Blue-SQ10
98UD Choice StarQuest Gold-SQ10
98UD Choice StarQuest Green-SQ10
98UD Choice StarQuest Red-SQ10
98UD3-49
98UD3-109
98UD3-169
Die-Cuts-49
Die-Cuts-109
Die-Cuts-169
98Upper Deck-139
Exclusives-139
Exclusives 1 of 1-139
Fantastic Finishers-FF18
Fantastic Finishers Quantum 1-FF18
Fantastic Finishers Quantum 2-FF18
Fantastic Finishers Quantum 3-FF18
Gold Reserve-139
98Upper Deck MVP-139
Gold Script-139
Silver Script-139
Super Script-139
98Slovakian Eurotel-27
99SLU Hockey One On One-3
99Aurora-102
Striped-102
Premiere Date-102
Premiere Date Striped-102
Styrotechs-13
99BAP Memorabilia-244
Gold-244
Silver-244
Jersey Cards-J17
Jersey Emblems-E17
Jersey Numbers-I17
Jersey and Stick Cards-S17
99Crown Royale-100
Limited Series-100
Premiere Date-100
99Kraft Dinner-14
99McDonald's Upper Deck Signatures-AY
99O-Pee-Chee-2
99O-Pee-Chee Autographs-TA4
99O-Pee-Chee Chrome-2
99O-Pee-Chee Chrome Ice Masters-IM14
99O-Pee-Chee Chrome Ice Masters Refractor-IM14
99O-Pee-Chee Chrome Refractors-2
99O-Pee-Chee Chrome Fantastic Finishers-FF4
99OPC Chrome Fantastic Finishers Ref-FF4
99O-Pee-Chee Ice Masters-IM14
99O-Pee-Chee Fantastic Finishers-FF4
99O-Pee-Chee Top of the World-TW7
99Oscar Mayer Lunchables-12
99Pacific-297
Copper-297
Emerald Green-297
Gold-297
Ice Blue-297
Premiere Date-297
Red-297
Center Ice-15
Center Ice Proofs-15
Gold Crown Die-Cuts-24
Team Leaders-19
99Pacific Dynagon Ice-142
Blue-142
Copper-142
Gold-142
Premiere Date-142
99Pacific Omega-165
Copper-165
Gold-165
Ice Blue-165
Premiere Date-165
99Pacific Prism-99
Holographic Blue-99
Holographic Gold-99
Holographic Mirror-99
Holographic Purple-99
Premiere Date-99
99Panini Stickers-322
99Paramount-167
Copper-167
Emerald-167
Gold-167
Holographic Emerald-167
Holographic Gold-167
Holographic Silver-167
Ice Blue-167
Premiere Date-167
Red-167
Silver-167
Ice Alliance-19
Personal Best-24
99Revolution-105
Premiere Date-105
Red-105
Shadow Series-105
Showstoppers-25
Top of the Line-17
99SPx-102
Radiance-102
Spectrum-102
99Stadium Club-28
First Day Issue-28
One of a Kind-28
Printing Plates Black-28
Printing Plates Cyan-28
Printing Plates Magenta-28
Printing Plates Yellow-28
Co-Signers-CS5
Co-Signers-CS7
Co-Signers-CS9
Lone Star Signatures-LS2
99Topps/OPC-2
Autographs-TA4
Fantastic Finishers-FF4
Ice Masters-IM14
Top of the World-TW7
99Topps/OPC Chrome-2
Refractors-2
Fantastic Finishers-FF4
Fantastic Finishers Refractors-FF4
Ice Masters-IM14
Ice Masters Refractors-IM14
99Upper Deck-90
99Upper Deck-147
Exclusives-90
Exclusives-147
Exclusives 1 of 1-90
Exclusives 1 of 1-147
Crunch Time-CT12
Crunch Time Quantum Gold-CT12
Crunch Time Quantum Silver-CT12
Fantastic Finishers-FF7
Fantastic Finishers Quantum Gold-FF7
Fantastic Finishers Quantum Silver-FF7
Marquee Attractions-MA7
Marquee Attractions Quantum Gold-MA7
Marquee Attractions Quantum Silver-MA7
99Upper Deck Century Legends-68
Century Collection-68
99Upper Deck Gold Reserve-90
99Upper Deck Gold Reserve-147
99Upper Deck MVP-138
Gold Script-138
Silver Script-138
Super Script-138
Game-Used Souvenirs-GU13

Game-Used Souvenirs-GU26
99Upper Deck Retro-54
Gold-54
Platinum-54
99Upper Deck Victory-199
99Upper Deck Victory-201
99Upper Deck Victory-329
99Russian Stars of Hockey-26
99Russian Fetisov Tribute-11
99Slovakian Challengers-5
00BAP Parkhurst 2000-P155
00BAP Signature Series-20
Emerald-20
Ruby-20
Sapphire-20
Autographs-207
Autographs Gold-207
He Shoots-He Scores Prizes-5
00BAP Ultimate Mem Game-Used Jerseys-GJ49
00BAP Ultimate Mem Game-Used Emblems-E40
00BAP Ultimate Mem Game-Used Numbers-N40
00BAP Ultimate Mem Game-Used Sticks-GS49
00Black Diamond-104
Game Gear-GYA
00Crown Royale-77
Ice Blue-77
Limited Series-77
Premiere Date-77
Red-77
Game-Worn Jerseys-18
Game-Worn Jersey Patches-18
Premium-Sized Game-Worn Jerseys-18
00Pacific-288
Copper-288
Gold-288
Ice Blue-288
Premiere Date-288
00Senators Team Issue-24
00SP Authentic-61
00SP Game Used-43
00SPx-142
00Titanium-67
Blue-67
Gold-67
Premiere Date-67
Red-67
Retail-67
Game Gear-120
Game Gear Patches-120
00Titanium Draft Day Edition-71
Patches-71
00Topps Gold Label Class 1-76
Gold-76
00Topps Gold Label Class 2-76
00Topps Gold Label Class 2 Gold-76
00Topps Gold Label Class 3-76
00Topps Gold Label Class 3 Gold-76
00Topps Heritage-6
Chrome Parallel-6
00Topps Premier Plus-84
Blue Ice-84
00UD Heroes-82
NHL Leaders-L6
00UD Pros and Prospects-60
Great Skates-GS6
00UD Reserve-61
00Upper Deck Ice-74
00Upper Deck Vintage-258
00Vanguard-70
Holographic Gold-70
Holographic Purple-70
Pacific Proofs-70
Press East/West-16
00Czech Stadion-72
01Atomic-62
Blue-62
Gold-62
Premiere Date-62
Red-62
Blast-7
Core Players-11
Power Play-21
Statosphere-16
Team Nucleus-9
01BAP Memorabilia-291
01BAP Memorabilia-394
Emerald-291
Emerald-394
Ruby-291
Ruby-394
Sapphire-291
Sapphire-394
All-Star Jerseys-ASJ42
All-Star Emblems-ASE42
All-Star Numbers-ASN42
All-Star Jersey Doubles-DASJ29
All-Star Teammates-AST27
Country of Origin-CO35
01BAP Signature Series-139
Autographs-139
Autographs Gold-139
Franchise Jerseys-FP-20
He Shoots-He Scores Prizes-38
International Medals-IB-4
Jerseys-GJ-43
Jersey Autographs-GUAY
Jersey and Stick Cards-GSJ-43
Emblems-GUE-42
Numbers-ITN-42
Teammates-TM-20
01BAP Ultimate Memorabilia Autographs-1
01BAP Ultimate Mem Autographs Gold-1
01BAP Ultimate Memorabilia Dynamic Duos-5
01BAP Ultimate Memorabilia Emblems-24
01BAP Ultimate Memorabilia Gloves Are Off-19
01BAP Ultimate Memorabilia Jerseys-24
01BAP Ultimate Mem Jerseys and Sticks-24
01BAP Ultimate Mem Journey Jerseys-3
01BAP Ultimate Mem Journey Emblems-3
01BAP Ultimate Memorabilia Numbers-24
01BAP Update He Shoots-He Scores Points-8
01BAP Update He Shoots-He Scores Prizes-23
01BAP Update Travel Plans-TP9
01Bowman YoungStars-67
Gold-67
Ice Cubed-67
01Crown Royale-93
Blue-93
Premiere Date-93
Red-93
Retail-93
All-Star Honors-14
Jewels of the Crown-20
01O-Pee-Chee-14
01O-Pee-Chee-14U
01O-Pee-Chee Heritage Parallel-14
01O-Pee-Chee Heritage Parallel Limited-14
01O-Pee-Chee Premier Parallel-14
01Pacific-281
01Pacific-436
Extreme LTD-281
Gold-436
Hobby LTD-281
Premiere Date-281
Retail LTD-281
01Pacific Adrenaline-123
Blue-123
Premiere Date-123
Red-123
Retail-123
World Beaters-11
01Pacific Arena Exclusives-281
01Pacific Arena Exclusives-436
01Pacific Heads-Up-62
Blue-62
Premiere Date-62
Red-62
Silver-62
01Parkhurst-35
Gold-35
Silver-35
World Class Jerseys-WCJ8
World Class Emblems-WCE8
World Class Numbers-WCN8
Waving the Flag-29
01Private Stock-60
Gold-60
Premiere Date-60
Retail-60
Silver-60
Game Gear Patches-65
01Private Stock Pacific Nights-60
01Private Stock PS-2002-46
01Private Stock Reserve-S10
01SP Authentic-52
Limited-52
Limited Gold-52
01SP Game Used-33
01SPx-181
01Stadium Club-102
Award Winners-102
Master Photos-102
01Titanium-91
Hobby Parallel-91
Premiere Date-91
Retail-91
Retail Parallel-91
All-Stars-14
01Topps-14
01Topps-14U
Heritage Parallel-14
Heritage Parallel Limited-14
OPC Parallel-14
Shot Masters-SM16
01Topps Chrome-14
Refractors-14
Black Border Refractors-14
01Topps Heritage-170
01Topps Reserve-68
01UD Challenge for the Cup-54
01UD Mask Collection-61
Gold-61
01UD Playmakers-61
01UD Premier Collection-33
01UD Top Shelf-101
Jerseys-AY
01Upper Deck-338
Exclusives-338
Crunch Timers-CT8
Shooting Stars-SS11
01Upper Deck Ice-104
01Upper Deck Victory-413
Gold-413
01Vanguard-62
Blue-62
Red-62
East Meets West-5
One of Ones-62
Premiere Date-62
Proofs-62
01Czech Stadion-243
02Atomic-65
Blue-65
Gold-65
Red-65
Hobby Parallel-65
Jerseys-14
Jerseys Gold-14
Patches-14
Power Converters-12
02BAP All-Star Edition-97
He Shoots-He Scores Points-8
He Shoots-He Score Prizes-29
Jerseys-97
Jerseys Gold-97
Jerseys Silver-97
02BAP First Edition-146
02BAP First Edition-334
02BAP First Edition-359
02BAP First Edition-407R
Jerseys-146
Scoring Leaders-11
02BAP Memorabilia-56
02BAP Memorabilia-219
Emerald-56
Emerald-219
Ruby-56
Ruby-219
Sapphire-56
Sapphire-219
All-Star Jerseys-ASJ-59
All-Star Teammates-AST-15
Franchise Players-FP-19
NHL All-Star Game-56
NHL All-Star Game-219
NHL All-Star Game Blue-56
NHL All-Star Game Blue-219
NHL All-Star Game Green-56
NHL All-Star Game Green-219
NHL All-Star Game Red-56
NHL All-Star Game Red-219
Stanley Cup Playoffs-SC-4
02BAP Memorabilia Toronto Fall Expo-56
02BAP Memorabilia Toronto Fall Expo-219
02BAP Signature Series-26
Autographs-26
Autograph Buybacks 1998-246
Autograph Buybacks 2001-139
Autographs Gold-26
Golf-GS6
Jerseys-SGJ18
Jersey Autographs-SGJ18
02BAP Ultimate Memorabilia Hat Tricks-8
02Bowman YoungStars-15
Gold-15
Silver-15
02Crown Royale-62
Blue-62
Red-62
Retail-62
Dual Patches-15
02eTopps-28
02ITG Used-44
02ITG Used-144
Franchise Players-F19
Franchise Players Autographs-F19
Franchise Players Gold-F19
International Experience-IE13
International Experience Gold-IE13
Jerseys-GUJ18
Jersey Autographs-GUJ18
Jerseys Gold-GUJ18
Emblems-E18
Jersey and Stick-SJ18
Jersey and Stick Gold-SJ18
Triple Memorabilia-TM15
Triple Memorabilia Gold-TM15
02McDonald's Pacific-25
02O-Pee-Chee-233
02O-Pee-Chee Premier Blue Parallel-233
02O-Pee-Chee Premier Red Parallel-233
02O-Pee-Chee Factory Set-233
02Pacific-245
Blue-245
Red-245
Jerseys-33
Jerseys Holo-Silver-33
Lamplighters-8
Main Attractions-12
02Pacific Calder-44
Silver-44
02Pacific Complete-246
Red-246
02Pacific Exclusive-111
Maximum Overdrive-13
02Pacific Heads-Up-76
Blue-76
Purple-76
Red-76
Bobble Heads-14
Inside the Numbers-14
Quad Jerseys-18
Quad Jerseys-30
Quad Jerseys Gold-18
Quad Jerseys Gold-30
02Pacific Quest for the Cup-62
Gold-62
Chasing the Cup-9
02Parkhurst-101
Bronze-101
Gold-101
Silver-101
Franchise Players-FP19
Jerseys-GJ48
Stick and Jerseys-SJ48
02Parkhurst Retro-17
Minis-17
02Private Stock Reserve-132
Red-132
Retail-132
02SP Authentic-56
Beckett Promos-56
02SP Game Used-31
Authentic Fabrics-AFAY
Authentic Fabrics Gold-AFAY
Authentic Fabrics Rainbow-AFAY
First Rounder Patches-AY
Piece of History-PHAY
Piece of History Gold-PHAY
Piece of History Rainbow-PHAY
02SPx-46
Spectrum Gold-46
Spectrum Silver-46
Winning Materials-WMAY
Winning Materials Gold-AY
Winning Materials Silver-AY
02Stadium Club-76
Silver Decoy Cards-76
Proofs-76
World Stage-WS11
02Titanium-67
Blue-67
Red-67
Retail-67
Jerseys-42
Jerseys Retail-42
Patches-42
02Topps-233
OPC Blue Parallel-233
OPC Red Parallel-233
Factory Set-233
02Topps Chrome-127
Black Border Refractors-127
Refractors-127
02Topps Heritage-30
Chrome Parallel-30
02Topps Total-224
02UD Artistic Impressions-55
Gold-55
02UD Artistic Impressions Beckett Promos-55
02UD Artistic Impressions Retrospectives-R55
02UD Artistic Impressions Retrospect Gold-R55
02UD Artistic Impress Retrospect Silver-R55
02UD Honor Roll-44
Students of the Game-SG19
02UD Mask Collection Instant Offense-IOAY
02UD Piece of History-55
02UD Top Shelf-54
02Upper Deck-111
02Upper Deck-237
Exclusives-111
Exclusives-237
02Upper Deck Classic Portraits-61
02Upper Deck MVP-115
Gold-115
Classics-115
Golden Classics-115
02Upper Deck Rookie Update-61
02Upper Deck Rookie Update-150A
02Upper Deck Rookie Update-159B
Jerseys-DAY
Jerseys Gold-DAY
02Upper Deck Victory-134
Bronze-134
Gold-134
Silver-134
National Pride-NP36
02Upper Deck Vintage-163
02Upper Deck Vintage-279
02Upper Deck Vintage-309
02Vanguard-65
LTD-65
02UD SuperStars Leg Leaders Triple Jersey-MCA
03BAP Memorabilia-8
Emerald-8
Gold-8
Ruby-8
Sapphire-8
Stanley Cup Playoffs-SCP-10
03BAP Ultimate Memorabilia Autographs-18
Gold-18
03BAP Ultimate Mem Franch Present Future-19
03BAP Ultimate Memorabilia Hat Tricks-3
03Beehive-124
Gold-124
Silver-124
Jerseys-JT8
03Black Diamond-146
Black-146
Green-146
Red-146
03Bowman-69
Gold-69
Goal to Goal-AY
03Bowman Chrome-69
Refractors-69
Gold Refractors-69
Xfractors-69
03ITG Action-369
Homeboys-HB8
Jerseys-M150
Jerseys-M259
03ITG Used Signature Series-12
Gold-12
Autographs-AY
Autographs Gold-AY
International Experience-20
International Experience Autographs-20
International Experience Emblems Gold-20
International Experience Emblems-20
International Experience Gold-20
Jerseys-2
Jerseys Gold-2
Jersey Autos-2
Jersey and Stick-2
Jersey and Stick Gold-2
Triple Memorabilia-28
Triple Memorabilia Gold-28
03NHL Sticker Collection-77
03O-Pee-Chee-69
03OPC Blue-69
03OPC Gold-69
03OPC Red-69
03Pacific-218
Blue-218
Red-218
Jerseys-24
Jerseys Gold-24
03Pacific Complete-117
Red-117
03Pacific Exhibit-179
Blue Backs-179
03Pacific Heads-Up-64
Hobby LTD-64
Retail LTD-64
03Pacific Invincible-63
Blue-63
Red-63
Retail-63
03Pacific Luxury Suite-41A
03Pacific Luxury Suite-41B
03Pacific Prism-129
Blue-129
Patches-129
Red-129
Retail-129
03Pacific Quest for the Cup-68
Blue-68
03Pacific Supreme-64
Blue-64
Red-64
Retail-64
03Private Stock Reserve-181
Blue-181
Patches-181
Red-181
Retail-181
03SP Authentic-55
Limited-55
Breakout Seasons-B24
Breakout Seasons Limited-B24
03SP Game Used-28
03SP Game Used-104
Gold-28
Gold-104
Authentic Fabrics-DFYP
Authentic Fabrics Gold-DFYP
Authentic Patches-APAY
Limited Threads-LTAY
Limited Threads Gold-LTAY
03SPx-60
03SPx-142
Radiance-60
Radiance-142
Spectrum-60
Spectrum-142
Origins-O-AY
03Titanium-169
Hobby Jersey Number Parallels-169
Patches-169
Retail-169
03Topps-69
03Topps-PP6
Blue-69
Gold-69
Red-69
First Round Fabrics-AY
First Round Fabrics-TBAY
Topps/OPC Idols-II5
03Topps C55-79
Minis-79
Minis American Back-79
Minis American Back Red-79
Minis Bazooka Back-79
Minis Brooklyn Back-79
Minis Hat Trick Back-79
Minis O Canada Back-79
Minis O Canada Back Red-79
Minis Stanley Cup Back-79
Relics-TRAY
03Topps Pristine-21
Gold Refractor Die Cuts-21
Refractors-21
Popular Demand Relics-PD-AY
Popular Demand Relic Refractors-PD-AY
Press Plates Black-21
Press Plates Cyan-21
Press Plates Magenta-21
Press Plates Yellow-21
03Topps Traded Franchise Fabrics-FF-AY
03UD Honor Roll-51
03UD Honor Roll-122
Grade A Jerseys-GAAY
03UD Premier Collection-33
03Upper Deck-365
All-Star Class-AS-17
Canadian Exclusives-365
Franchise Fabrics-FF-AY
HG-365
Three Stars-TS4
UD Exclusives-365
03Upper Deck Classic Portraits-60
03Upper Deck Ice-56
Gold-56
03Upper Deck MVP-263
Gold Script-263
Silver Script-263
Canadian Exclusives-263
SportsNut-SN54
03Upper Deck Rookie Update-55
Skills-SKAY
03Upper Deck Trilogy-60
Limited-60
Limited Threads-LT26
03Upper Deck Victory-114
Bronze-114
Gold-114
Silver-114
Game Breakers-GB8
03Toronto Star-56
04Pacific-171
Blue-171
Red-171
04SP Authentic-126
04UD Toronto Fall Expo Priority Signings-AY
04Upper Deck Jersey Autographs-GJA-AY
04Upper Deck World Cup Tribute-AKAYSS
04Russian Back to Russia-36
04Russian World Championship Team-2
05Beehive-57
05Beehive-200
Beige -57
Blue -57
Gold-57
Red -57
Matte-57
Matted Materials-MMAY
05Black Diamond-104
Emerald-104
Gold-104
Onyx-104
Ruby-104
05Hot Prospects-62
En Fuego-62
Red Hot-62
White Hot-62
05Panini Stickers-91
05Parkhurst-301
05Parkhurst-517
05Parkhurst-689
Facsimile Auto Parallel-301
Facsimile Auto Parallel-517
Facsimile Auto Parallel-689
True Colors-TCNYI
True Colors-TCNYI
True Colors-TCNYNY
True Colors-TCNYNY
05SP Authentic-62
Limited-62
Chirography-SPAY
Marks of Distinction-MDAY
Sign of the Times-AY
Sign of the Times Duals-DYS
Sign of the Times Triples-TYPN
05SP Game Used-62
Gold-62
Authentic Fabrics-AF-AY
Authentic Fabrics Autographs-AAF-AY
Authentic Fabrics Gold-AF-AY
Authentic Fabrics Quad-SDYH
Authentic Fabrics Quad-TBYS
Authentic Patches Quad -SDYH
Authentic Patches Quad -TBYS
Authentic Fabrics Triple-YSP
Authentic Patches-AP-AY
Authentic Patches Autographs-AAP-AY
Authentic Patches Triple-YSP
Awesome Authentics-AA-AY
SIGnificance-AY
SIGnificance Gold-S-AY
Significant Numbers-SN-AY
Statscriptions-ST-AY
05SPx-54
Spectrum-54
Winning Combos-WC-JY
Winning Combos Gold-WC-JY
Winning Combos Spectrum-WC-JY
05The Cup-64
Gold-64
Black Rainbow-64
Dual NHL Shields-DSAM
Dual NHL Shields-DSYP
Dual NHL Shields Autographs-ADSAM
Dual NHL Shields Autographs-ADSYP
Emblems of Endorsement-EEAY
Honorable Numbers-HNAY
Limited Logos-LLAY
Masterpiece Pressplates-64
Masterpiece Pressplates Rookie Upd Auto-268
Patch Variation-P64
Patch Variation Autographs-AP64
Scripted Swatches-SSAY
Signature Patches-SPAY
05UD Artifacts-67
05UD Artifacts-180
Blue-67
Blue-180
Gold-67
Gold-180
Green-67
Green-180
Pewter-67
Pewter-180
Red-67
Red-180
Gold Autographed-67
Gold Autographed-180
05UD Powerplay Specialists-TSAY
05UD Powerplay Specialists Patches-SPAY
05UD Toronto Fall Expo Priority Signings-PS-AY
05Ultimate Collection-57
Gold-57
Endorsed Emblems-EEAY
Jerseys-JAY
National Heroes Jerseys-NHJAY
National Heroes Patches-NHPAY
Premium Patches-PPAY
Premium Swatches-PSAY
Ultimate Achievements-UAAY
Ultimate Patches-PAY
Ultimate Signatures-USAY
Ultimate Signatures Pairings-UPYS
05Ultra-123
Gold-123
Fresh Ink-FI-AY
Fresh Ink Blue-FI-AY
Ice-123
05Upper Deck-118
05Upper Deck All-Time Greatest-38
05Upper Deck Big Playmakers-B-AY
05Upper Deck HG Glossy-118
05Upper Deck Hometown Heroes-HH23
05Upper Deck Jerseys-J-AY
05Upper Deck Majestic Materials-MMAY
05Upper Deck Notable Numbers-N-AY
05Upper Deck Ice-59
Rainbow-59
Frozen Fabrics-FFAY
Frozen Fabrics Autographs-AFFAY
Frozen Fabrics Glass-FFAY
Frozen Fabrics Patches-FFPAY
Frozen Fabrics Patch Autographs-FAPAY
05Upper Deck MVP-242
Gold-242
Platinum-242
05Upper Deck Rookie Update-60
05Upper Deck Rookie Update-268
05Upper Deck Trilogy-57
05Upper Deck Trilogy-165
Crystal-165
Scripts-SCS-AY
05Upper Deck Toronto Fall Expo-118
05Upper Deck Victory-122
Black-122
Gold-122
Silver-122
Game Breakers-GB27
06Be A Player-3
Autographs-3
Signatures-AY
Signatures 10-3
Signatures 25-3
Signatures Duals-DSY
Signatures Trios-TYSS
Up Close and Personal-UC4
Up Close and Personal Autographs-UC4
06Be A Player Portraits-65
06Beehive-38
Blue-38
Gold-38
Matte-38
Red Facsimile Signatures-38
Wood-38
06Black Diamond-113
Black-113
Gold-113
Ruby-113
06Flair Showcase-62
06Flair Showcase-141
06Flair Showcase-245
Parallel-62
Parallel-141
Parallel-245
Hot Numbers-HN28
Hot Numbers Parallel-HN28
06Fleer-121
Tiffany-121
06Hot Prospects-61
Red Hot-61
White Hot-61
06NHL POG-52
06O-Pee-Chee-314
Rainbow-314
Swatches-S-AY
06Panini Stickers-90
06SP Authentic-42
Limited-42
06SP Game Used-63
Gold-63
Rainbow-63
Authentic Fabrics-AFAY
Authentic Fabrics Parallel-AFAY
Authentic Fabrics Patches-AFAY
Authentic Fabrics Triple-AF3NYI
Authentic Fabrics Triple Patches-AF3NYI
Autographs-63
Inked Sweaters-ISAY
Inked Sweaters Patches-ISAY
Inked Sweaters Dual-IS2SY
Inked Sweaters Dual Patches-IS2SY
06SPx-65
Spectrum-65
SPxcitement-X65
SPxcitement Spectrum-X65
Winning Materials-WMAY
Winning Materials Spectrum-WMAY
Winning Materials Autographs-WMAY
06The Cup-54
Autographed Foundations-CQAY
Autographed Foundations Patches-CQAY
Autographed NHL Shields Duals-DASYS
Autographed Patches-54
Black Rainbow-54
Foundations-CQAY
Foundations Patches-CQAY
Gold-54
Gold Patches-54
Jerseys-54
Limited Logos-LLAY
Masterpiece Pressplates-54
NHL Shields Duals-DSHDY
06UD Artifacts-41
Blue-41
Gold-41
Platinum-41
Radiance-41
Autographed Radiance Parallel-41
Red-41
06UD Mini Jersey Collection-62
06UD Powerplay-63
Impact Rainbow-63
Power Marks-PMAY
06Ultimate Collection-38
Premium Patches-PS-AY
Premium Swatches-PS-AY
06Ultra-121
Gold Medallion-121
Ice Medallion-121
Action-UA17
06Upper Deck Arena Giveaways-NYI5
06Upper Deck-371
Exclusives Parallel-371
High Gloss Parallel-371
Game Jerseys-JAY
Game Patches-PAY
Masterpieces-371
06Upper Deck MVP-186
Gold Script-186
Super Script-186
06Upper Deck Ovation-79
06Upper Deck Sweet Shot-66
06Upper Deck Trilogy-63
06Upper Deck Victory-122
06Upper Deck Victory Black-122
06Upper Deck Victory Gold-122
06Russian Sport Collection Olympic Stars-15
06Russian Torino Olympic Team-8
07Upper Deck Ovation-71
07Upper Deck Victory-19
Black-19
Gold-19

Yashin, Oleg

91O-Pee-Chee Inserts-64R
93Roanoke Express-21
94Roanoke Express-14
95Fort Wayne Komets-23
95Roller Hockey Magazine RHI-1
95San Diego Barracudas RHI-10
01Russian Hockey League-40
01Russian Hockey League-169

Yashin, Sergei

87Russian National Team-23
89Russian National Team-24
89Swedish Semic World Champ Stickers-88
90O-Pee-Chee-482
94German First League-634
04German Berlin Eisbaren 50th Anniv-13

Yates, Brock

00Kitchener Rangers-28

Yates, Joel

917th Inn. Sketch OHL-239
93Niagara Falls Thunder-7

Yates, Ross

94German DEL-151
96German DEL-157
99German Bundesliga 2-165
00Syracuse Crunch-23

Yawney, Trent

83Saskatoon Blades-2
84Saskatoon Blades Stickers-20
88Blackhawks Coke-25
89Blackhawks Coke-9
89O-Pee-Chee-222
89Panini Stickers-53
90Blackhawks Coke-9
90O-Pee-Chee-297
90Panini Stickers-187
90Pro Set-64
90Score-292
Canadian-292
90Topps-297
Tiffany-297
90Upper Deck-82
French-82
91Bowman-393
91O-Pee-Chee-255
91Parkhurst-245
French-245
91Score Canadian Bilingual-439
91Score Canadian English-439
91Stadium Club-205
91Topps-255
91ProCards-491
92Flames IGA-12
92Parkhurst-262
Emerald Ice-262
92Pinnacle-174
French-174
92Score-216
Canadian-216
93Pinnacle-123
Canadian-123
93Score-332
Canadian-332
93Stadium Club-472
Members Only Master Set-472
First Day Issue-472
94Pinnacle-245
Artist's Proofs-245
Rink Collection-245
94Stadium Club-44
Members Only Master Set-44
First Day Issue-44
Super Team Winner Cards-44
95Be A Player-146
Signatures-S146
Signatures Die Cuts-S146
95Upper Deck Electric Ice Gold-308
97Pacific Dynagon Best Kept Secrets-84
99Blackhawks Chicago Sun-Times-10
01Norfolk Admirals-26
02Norfolk Admirals-25
03Norfolk Admirals-23
04Norfolk Admirals-24

Yderstrom, Dick

67Swedish Hockey-196
69Swedish Hockey-201
69Swedish Hockey-255
70Swedish Hockey-145
71Swedish Hockey-239
72Swedish Stickers-224
73Finnish Jaakiekko-41
73Swedish Stickers-18
73Swedish Stickers-74
74Finnish Jenkki-39
74Swedish Stickers-272
74Swedish Semic World Champ Stickers-13

Yeatman, D.

28V128-2 Paulin's Candy-67

Yeats, Matthew

02Atlantic City Boardwalk Bullies-23
03ITG Action-671
03ITG VIP Rookie Debut-144
03Parkhurst Rookie-67
03UD Premier Collection-102
03Upper Deck Rookie Update-185
05Idaho Steelheads-23

Yegorov, Alexei

95Kansas City Blades-20
96Fleer Picks-174
96Leaf-216
Press Proofs-216
96SkyBox Impact-163
96Summit-195
Artist's Proofs-195
Ice-195
Metal-195
Premium Stock-195
96Upper Deck-192
96Kentucky Thoroughblades-21
97Sharks Fleer All-Star Sheet-8
97Kentucky Thoroughblades-20
98Russian Hockey League-144
99Russian Dynamo Moscow-26
99Adirondack IceHawks-20
00German DEL-219
00Russian Dynamo Moscow-1
00Russian Goalkeepers-8
01Russian Hockey League-155
02Russian Hockey League-157
02Russian Transfert-25
03Russian Hockey League-59
03Russian National Team-8
03Russian SL-3

Yelle, Stephane

91Oshawa Generals-6
91Oshawa Generals Sheet-7
917th Inn. Sketch OHL-161
92Oshawa Generals Sheet-24
93Oshawa Generals-10
95Bowman-124
All-Foil-124
95Donruss-350
95Parkhurst International-539
Emerald Ice-539
95Ultra-363
96Be A Player-15
Autographs-15
Autographs Silver-15
96Collector's Choice-61
96Donruss-220
Press Proofs-220
96Donruss Canadian Ice-45
Gold Press Proofs-45
Red Press Proofs-45
96Leaf-150
Press Proofs-150
96Summit-156
Artist's Proofs-156
Ice-156
Metal-156
Premium Stock-156
96Upper Deck-40
97Pacific-344
Copper-344
Emerald Green-344
Ice Blue-344
Red-344
Silver-344
97Score Avalanche-19
Platinum-19
Premier-19
97Upper Deck-49
98Avalanche Team Issue-11
98Pacific-170
Ice Blue-170
Red-170
99Avalanche Team Issue-24
99Pacific-116
Copper-116
Emerald Green-116
Gold-116
Ice Blue-116
Premiere Date-116
Red-116
00Pacific-124
Copper-124
Gold-124
Ice Blue-124
Premiere Date-124
00Panini Stickers-133
00Titanium Game Gear-10
00Upper Deck-277
Exclusives Tier 1-277
Exclusives Tier 2-277
01Avalanche Team Issue-2
01Upper Deck Avalanche NHL All-Star Game-CA6
02BAP First Edition-60
Jerseys-60
02NHL Power Play Stickers-20
02Pacific Complete-443
Red-443
02Topps Total-345
02Upper Deck-41
02Upper Deck-272
Exclusives-41
Exclusives-272
02Upper Deck Beckett UD Promos-272
02Upper Deck Vintage-62
03ITG Action-90
03NHL Sticker Collection-167
03Pacific-57
Blue-57
Red-57
03Pacific Complete-160
Red-160
05Parkhurst-77
Facsimile Auto Parallel-77
05Upper Deck-279
05Upper Deck MVP-66
Gold-66
Platinum-66
06Gatorade-10
06O-Pee-Chee-76
Rainbow-76
06Upper Deck-285
Exclusives Parallel-285
High Gloss Parallel-285
Masterpieces-285

Yellow Horn, Colton

04Lethbridge Hurricanes-10
05ITG Heroes and Prospects-423

Yellowaga, Kevin

88Saskatoon Blades-14

Yellowhorn, Colton

05Lethbridge Hurricanes-23

Yellowhorn, Shane

96Lethbridge Hurricanes-24

Yemelin, Alexei

04Russian Under-18 Team-21

Yemelin, Andrei

01Russian Hockey League-168

Yenedam, Sean

97Bowman CHL-11
OPC-11

Yeo, Brad

01Plymouth Whalers-9

Yeo, Dylan

03Prince George Cougars-12
04Calgary Hitmen-22
05Calgary Hitmen-23

Yeo, Mike

907th Inn. Sketch OHL-396
90Sudbury Wolves-23
917th Inn. Sketch OHL-253
91Sudbury Wolves-23
92Sudbury Wolves-20
93Sudbury Wolves-22
93Sudbury Wolves Police-22
95Houston Aeros-23
00Wilkes-Barre Scranton Penguins-25
01Wilkes-Barre Scranton Penguins-24
02Wilkes-Barre Scranton Penguins-26
03Wilkes-Barre Scranton Penguins-29
04Wilkes-Barre Scranton Penguins-29

Yeo, Theran

04Brandon Wheat Kings-5
05Brandon Wheat Kings-24

Yeoman, Justin

98Brandon Wheat Kings-24

Yeomans, Derek

03Kelowna Rockets-23
04Kelowna Rockets-17
05Kelowna Rockets-26

Yeremenko, Alexander

00Russian Dynamo Moscow-3
01Russian Ultimate Line-5
02Russian Ultimate Line-3
03Russian Hockey League-28
04Russian Moscow Dynamo-13

Yeremeyev, Vitali

99Russian Dynamo Moscow-25
99Russian Hockey League-188
00Black Diamond-126
00SP Authentic-153
00Russian Champions-6

00Charlotte Checkers-30
00Hartford Wolf Pack-28
01BAP Memorabilia-281
Emerald-281
Ruby-281
Sapphire-281
01Between the Pipes-77
01Upper Deck Game Jerseys-GJVY
01Upper Deck Victory-381
Gold-381
01Russian Dynamo Moscow-20
01Russian Ultimate Line-1
02Russian Hockey League-234
02Russian Ultimate Line-13
03Russian Hockey League-26
03Russian SL-36
04Russian Moscow Dynamo-12
06Russian Sport Collection Olympic Stars-53

Yeremin, Vladimir
93Swiss HNL-182

Yerkovich, Sergei
96Las Vegas Thunder-22
97Las Vegas Thunder-10
99Hamilton Bulldogs-22
00Russian Hockey League-359
01Russian Hockey League-89
03Russian Hockey League-95

Yermelin, Yuri
03Russian Avangard Omsk-16

Yershov, Andrei
01Russian Hockey League-18

Yesmantovich, Igor
89Swedish Semic World Champ Stickers-97

Yetman, Patrick
01Augusta Lynx-1
02ECHL All-Star Southern-59
02ECHL Update-U-27
02Hartford Wolf Pack-26

Yetman, Steve
03Yarmouth Mariners-24
05Rockford Ice Hogs-19

Yevdokimov, Dmitri
01Russian Hockey League-17

Yewchuk, Marty
95Louisiana Ice Gators-21
96Anaheim Bullfrogs RHI-7

Yingst, Doug
88ProCards AHL-145

Yingst, Matt
94Johnstown Chiefs-20

Ylaja, Mikko
73Finnish Jaakiekko-323

Ylanen, Veijo
73Finnish Jaakiekko-324

Yli-Junnila, Juhamatti
04Finnish Cardset-271
05Finnish Cardset -111
06Finnish Cardset-118

Yli-Maenpaa, Kari
89Swedish Semic Elitserien Stickers-196

Yli-Maenpaa, Mika
93Finnish SISU-185
94Finnish SISU-45
95Finnish SISU-98

Yli-Torkko, Joni
00Finnish Cardset-205
01Finnish Cardset-119
04Finnish Cardset-272
05Finnish Cardset -290
06Finnish Cardset-343

Ylitite, Paivi
99Finnish Cardset Aces High-C-Q

Ylonen, Antti
05Finnish Cardset -267
06Finnish Cardset-275

Ylonen, Juha
91Upper Deck-673
French-673
91Upper Deck Czech World Juniors-36
92Finnish Jyvas-Hyva Stickers-23
93Finnish Jyvas-Hyva Stickers-114
93Finnish SISU-21
94Finnish SISU-220
95Finnish SISU-254
Gold Cards-24
95Finnish Karjala World Champ Labels-24
96Finnish SISU Redline-53
96Swedish Semic Wien-21
96Springfield Falcons-15
97Be A Player-240
Autographs-240
Autographs Die-Cuts-240
Autographs Prismatic Die-Cuts-240
97Coyotes Face-Off Luncheon -26
97Pacific Omega-180
Copper-180
Dark Gray-180
Emerald Green-180
Gold-180
Ice Blue-180
97Upper Deck-192
98Pacific-347
Ice Blue-347
Red-347
98UD Choice-164
Prime Choice Reserve-164
Reserve-164
98Upper Deck-151
Exclusives-151
Exclusives 1 of 1-151
Gold Reserve-151
98Finnish Keraliysarja Leijonat-47
99O-Pee-Chee-177
99O-Pee-Chee Chrome-177
99O-Pee-Chee Chrome Refractors-177
99Pacific-331
Copper-331
Emerald Green-331
Gold-331
Ice Blue-331
Premiere Date-331
Red-331
99Panini Stickers-275
99Topps/OPC-177
99Topps/OPC Chrome-177
Refractors-177
99Finnish Cardset Aces High-H-6
00Upper Deck NHLPA-PA69
01BAP Memorabilia-470
Emerald-470
Ruby-470
Sapphire-470
01Finnish Cardset-179
01Finnish Cardset Salt Lake City-8
02Finnish Cardset-296

Ylonen, Petri
92Finnish Semic-220
93Swedish Semic World Champ Stickers-249
94Finnish Jaa Kiekko-212
94French National Team-35
95Finnish Semic World Championships-195
95Swedish Globe World Championships-199
95Swedish World Championships Stickers-96
96Swedish Semic Wien-183

Ylonen, Urpo
66Finnish Jaakiekkosarja-71
69Swedish Hockey-384
70Finnish Jaakiekko-80
70Finnish Jaakiekko-154
70Swedish Hockey-293
70Swedish Masterserien-14
70Swedish Masterserien-164
71Finnish Suomi Stickers-79
71Finnish Suomi Stickers-206
71Swedish Hockey-60
72Finnish Jaakiekko-243
72Finnish Panda Toronto-111
72Finnish Semic World Championship-71
72Swedish Semic World Championship-71
73Finnish Jaakiekko-277
74Finnish Typotor-42
78Finnish SM-Liiga-197
79Panini Stickers-162
91Finnish Semic World Champ Stickers-226
91Swedish Semic World Champ Stickers-226
96Finnish SISU Redline-192

Yobin, Ildar
00Russian Hockey League-46

Yoder, C.J.
96St. Louis Vipers RHI-11

Yoder, Jami
98Hampton Roads Admirals-6
01Anchorage Aces-17
02Odessa Jackalopes-19
03Odessa Jackalopes-20
05Quad City Mallards-21
06Quad City Mallards-20

Yokoyama, Garrett
93Quebec Pee-Wee Tournament-1257

Yonkman, Nolan
98Kelowna Rockets-27
99O-Pee-Chee-267
99O-Pee-Chee Chrome-267
99O-Pee-Chee Chrome Refractors-267
99Topps/OPC-267
99Topps/OPC Chrome-267
Refractors-267
99Kelowna Rockets-12
99Bowman CHL-3
Gold-3
OPC International-3
Autographs-BA23
Autographs Gold-BA23
Autographs Silver-BA23
00Brandon Wheat Kings-9
01BAP Memorabilia-401
Emerald-401
Ruby-401
Sapphire-401
04Portland Pirates-22
05Parkhurst Facsimile Auto Parallel-482
05Milwaukee Admirals -21

Yonkman, Travis
05Swift Current Broncos-8
06Swift Current Broncos-1

York, Harry
96Be A Player Link to History-2A
96Be A Player Link to History Autographs-2A
96Be A Player Link to History Auto Silver-2A
96Donruss Elite-130
Die Cut Stars-130
96Flair-122
Blue Ice-122
96Select Certified-96
Artist's Proofs-96
Blue-96
Mirror Blue-96
Mirror Gold-96
Mirror Red-96
Red-96
96SP-134
96Ultra-149
Gold Medallion-149
96Upper Deck-329
96Zenith-131
Artist's Proofs-131
97Collector's Choice-229
97Donruss-138
Press Proofs Silver-138
Press Proofs Gold-138
97Donruss Limited-1
97Donruss Limited-158
Exposure-1
Exposure-158
97Donruss Preferred-50
Cut to the Chase-50
97Donruss Priority-156
Stamp of Approval-156
97Leaf-133
Fractal Matrix-133
Fractal Matrix Die Cuts-133
97Leaf International-133
Universal Ice-133
97Pacific-176
Copper-176
Emerald Green-176
Ice Blue-176
Red-176
Silver-176
97Pacific Dynagon-109
Copper-109
Dark Grey-109
Emerald Green-109
Ice Blue-109
Red-109
Silver-109
Tandems-61
97Pinnacle-161
Press Plates Back Black-161
Press Plates Back Cyan-161
Press Plates Back Magenta-161
Press Plates Back Yellow-161
Press Plates Front Black-161
Press Plates Front Cyan-161
Press Plates Front Magenta-161
Press Plates Front Yellow-161
97Score-192
97Score Blues-5
Platinum-5
Premier-5
97Upper Deck-140
99Stadium Club-64
First Day Issue-64
One of a Kind-64
Printing Plates Black-64
Printing Plates Cyan-64
Printing Plates Magenta-64
Printing Plates Yellow-64
99Ultimate Victory-86
1/1-86
Parallel-86
Parallel 100-86

York, Jason
907th Inn. Sketch OHL-197
907th Inn. Sketch Memorial Cup-32
91ProCards-139
94Donruss-115
94Flair-54
94Leaf-275
94Parkhurst SE-SE56
Gold-SE56
94Ultra-288
95Upper Deck-306
Electric Ice-306
Electric Ice Gold-306
96Senators Pizza Hut-28
96Upper Deck-5
97Be A Player-95
Autographs-95
Autographs Die-Cuts-95
Autographs Prismatic Die-Cuts-95
97Pacific Dynagon Best Kept Secrets-67
98Be A Player-247
Press Release-247
98BAP Gold-247
98BAP Autographs-247
98BAP Autographs Gold-247
98Pacific-319
Ice Blue-319
Red-319
99BAP Millennium-175
Emerald-175
Ruby-175
Sapphire-175
Signatures-175
Signatures Gold-175
99Pacific-298
Copper-298
Emerald Green-298
Gold-298
Ice Blue-298
Premiere Date-298
Red-298
99Senators Team Issue-22
99Upper Deck MVP SC Edition-129
Gold Script-129
Silver Script-129
Super Script-129
00BAP Signature Series-190
Emerald-190
Ruby-190
Sapphire-190
Autographs-148
Autographs Gold-148
00Pacific-289
Copper-289
Gold-289
Ice Blue-289
Premiere Date-289
00Senators Team Issue-25
00Upper Deck-351
Exclusives Tier 1-351
Exclusives Tier 2-351
00Upper Deck Vintage-250
01Upper Deck-235
Exclusives-235
02BAP Sig Series Auto Buybacks 1998-247
02BAP Sig Series Auto Buybacks 1999-175
02BAP Sig Series Auto Buybacks 2000-148
02Pacific-11
Blue-11
Red-11
02Pacific Complete-175
Red-175
02Upper Deck MVP-5
Gold-5
Classics-5
Golden Classics-5
03ITG Action-308
03Pacific Complete-147
Red-147
03Upper Deck-355
Canadian Exclusives-355
HG-355
UD Exclusives-355
06O-Pee-Chee-50
Rainbow-50

York, Mike
92Quebec Pee-Wee Tournament-1576
95Donruss Elite World Juniors-44
96Upper Deck Ice-147
99BAP Memorabilia-327
Gold-327
Silver-327
99BAP Millennium-167
Emerald-167
Ruby-167
Sapphire-167
Signatures-167
Signatures Gold-167
Calder Candidates Ruby-C11
Calder Candidates Emerald-C11
Calder Candidates Sapphire-C11
99Crown Royale-93
Limited Series-93
Premiere Date-93
Prospects Parallel-93
99Pacific-460
99Pacific Dynagon Ice-135
Blue-135
Copper-135
Gold-135
Premiere Date-135
99Pacific Omega-154
Copper-154
Gold-154
Ice Blue-154
Premiere Date-154
99Pacific Prism-93
Holographic Blue-93
Holographic Gold-93
Holographic Mirror-93
Holographic Purple-93
Premiere Date-93
99SP Authentic-57
99Topps Arena Giveaways-NYR-MY
99Topps Premier Plus-126
Parallel-126
99Upper Deck-262
Exclusives-262
Exclusives 1 of 1-262
99Upper Deck Arena Giveaways-NR1
99Upper Deck Gold Reserve-262
99Upper Deck MVP SC Edition-119
Gold Script-119
Silver Script-119
Super Script-119
00BAP Memorabilia-96
Emerald-96
Ruby-96
Sapphire-96
Promos-96
00BAP Mem Chicago Sportsfest Copper-96
00BAP Memorabilia Chicago Sportsfest Blue-96
00BAP Memorabilia Chicago Sportsfest Gold-96
00BAP Memorabilia Chicago Sportsfest Ruby-96
00BAP Memorabilia Chicago Sun-Times Ruby-96
00BAP Memorabilia Chicago Sun-Times Gold-96
00BAP Mem Chicago Sun-Times Sapphire-96
00BAP Mem Toronto Fall Expo Copper-96
00BAP Memorabilia Toronto Fall Expo Gold-96
00BAP Memorabilia Toronto Fall Expo Ruby-96
00BAP Parkhurst 2000-P9
00BAP Signature Series-5
Emerald-5
Ruby-5
Sapphire-5
Autographs-53
Autographs Gold-53
00O-Pee-Chee-61
00O-Pee-Chee Parallel-61
00Pacific-272
Copper-272
Gold-272
Ice Blue-272
Premiere Date-272
Autographs-272
00Paramount-168
Copper-168
Gold-168
Holo-Gold-168
Holo-Silver-168
Ice Blue-168
Premiere Date-168
00Revolution-100
Blue-100
Premiere Date-100
Red-100
00SP Authentic BuyBacks-82
00SP Authentic Sign of the Times-MY
00SP Authentic Sign of the Times-B/Y
00SP Game Used Tools of the Game Combos-C-GY
00SPx-44
Spectrum-44
00Stadium Club-44
Co-Signers-CO4
Lone Star Signatures-LS9
11 X 14 Autographs-MY
00Titanium Draft Day Edition-69
Patches-69
00Topps/OPC-61
Parallel-61
Own the Game-OTG23
00Topps Chrome-49
OPC Refractors-49
Refractors-49
00Topps Gold Label Autographs-GLA-MY
00Topps Heritage-142
00Topps Stars Autographs-AMY
00UD Heroes-79
Signs of Greatness-MY
Timeless Moments-TM7
00Upper Deck-116
Exclusives Tier 1-116
Exclusives Tier 2-116
Game Jersey Autographs-HMY
Game Jersey Autographs Exclusives-EMY
Game Jersey Combos-DYL
Game Jersey Patches-MYP
Game Jersey Patch Autographs Exclusives-MYP
Prospects In Depth-P7
Signs of Greatness-SMY
00Upper Deck Ice-27
Immortals-27
Legends-27
Stars-27
Clear Cut Autographs-MY
00Upper Deck MVP-118
Excellence-ME9
First Stars-118
Mark of Excellence-SGMY
ProSign-MY
Second Stars-118
Third Stars-118
00Upper Deck Victory-157
00Upper Deck Vintage-241
Original 6: A Piece of History-OMY
Original 6: A Piece of History Gold-OMY
01Atomic Jerseys-41
01Atomic Patches-41
01BAP Memorabilia-18
01BAP Memorabilia-477
Emerald-18
Emerald-477
Ruby-18
Ruby-477
Sapphire-18
Sapphire-477
01Bowman YoungStars-58
Gold-58
Ice Cubed-58
01O-Pee-Chee-92
01O-Pee-Chee Heritage Parallel-92
01O-Pee-Chee Heritage Parallel Limited-92
01O-Pee-Chee Premier Parallel-92
01Pacific-268
Extreme LTD-268
Hobby LTD-268
Premiere Date-268
Retail LTD-268
01Pacific Arena Exclusives-268
01Pacific Heads-Up Quad Jerseys-25
01Parkhurst-159
01Parkhurst-377
01SP Game Used Authentic Fabric-AFMY
01SP Game Used Authentic Fabric Gold-AFMY
01SPx-174
Hidden Treasures-DTYL
01Titanium-97
Hobby Parallel-97
Premiere Date-97
Retail-97
Retail Parallel-97
Double-Sided Jerseys-28
Three-Star Selections-17
01Topps-92
Heritage Parallel-92
Heritage Parallel Limited-92
OPC Parallel-92
Autographs-AMY
Game-Worn Jersey-JMY
Jumbo Jersey Autographs-JJA-MY
01Topps Chrome-92
Refractors-92
Black Border Refractors-92
01Topps Reserve Emblems-MY
01Topps Reserve Jerseys-MY
01Topps Reserve Name Plates-MY
01Topps Reserve Numbers-MY
01Topps Reserve Patches-MY
01UD Mask Collection Double Patches-DPMY
01UD Mask Collection Jerseys-J-MY
01UD Mask Collection Jersey and Patch-JPMY
01Upper Deck-345
Exclusives-345
Game Jerseys-NGMY
Game Jerseys Series II-GNMY
01Upper Deck Victory-231
Gold-231
01Vanguard Memorabilia-20
02BAP First Edition-246
02BAP Memorabilia-151
Emerald-151
Ruby-151
Sapphire-151
NHL All-Star Game-151
NHL All-Star Game Blue-151
NHL All-Star Game Green-151
NHL All-Star Game Red-151
02BAP Memorabilia Toronto Fall Expo-151
02BAP Signature Series-21
Autographs-21
Autograph Buybacks 1999-167
Autographs Gold-21
02NHL Power Play Stickers-41
02Oilers Postcards-5
02O-Pee-Chee-259
02O-Pee-Chee Premier Blue Parallel-259
02O-Pee-Chee Premier Red Parallel-259
02O-Pee-Chee Factory Set-259
02O-Pee-Chee Factory Set Hometown Heroes-HHC4
02Pacific-150
Blue-150
Red-150
02Pacific Complete-223
Red-223
02Pacific Exclusive-74
02Parkhurst-160
Bronze-160
Gold-160
Silver-160
02Parkhurst Retro-60
Minis-60
02Private Stock Reserve-40
Blue-40
Red-40
Retail-40
02SP Game Used Piece of History-PHMY
02SP Game Used Piece of History Gold-PHMY
02SP Game Used Piece of History Rainbow-PHMY
02Topps-259
OPC Blue Parallel-259
OPC Red Parallel-259
Topps/OPC Hometown Heroes-HHC4
Factory Set-259
02Topps Chrome-142
Black Border Refractors-142
Refractors-142
02Topps Total-297
02UD Top Shelf Goal Oriented-GOMY
02UD Top Shelf Shooting Stars-SHMY
02Upper Deck-318
Exclusives-318
02Upper Deck Beckett UD Promos-318
02Upper Deck Bright Futures-MY
02Upper Deck Rookie Update-153B
02Upper Deck Victory-87
Bronze-87
Gold-87
Silver-87
02Upper Deck Vintage-101
Green Backs-101
03Black Diamond-1
Black-1
Green-1
Red-1
03ITG Action-273
03NHL Sticker Collection-226
03Oilers Postcards-22
03O-Pee-Chee-157
03OPC Blue-157
03OPC Gold-157
03OPC Red-157
03Pacific-139
Blue-139
Red-139
03Pacific Calder-44
Silver-44
03Pacific Complete-296
Red-296
03Pacific Exhibit-61
Blue Backs-61
Yellow Backs-61
03Private Stock Reserve-39
Blue-39
Red-39
Retail-39
03Titanium-41
Hobby Jersey Number Parallels-41
Retail-41
Retail Jersey Number Parallels-41
03Topps-157
Blue-157
Gold-157
Red-157
Topps/OPC Idols-UI15
03Upper Deck-75
Canadian Exclusives-75
HG-75
03Upper Deck MVP-162
Gold Script-162
Silver Script-162
Canadian Exclusives-162
04Pacific-108
Blue-108
Red-108
04UD All-World-22
Gold-22
04German DEL-180
Superstars-SU14
05Panini Stickers-100
05Parkhurst-303
Facsimile Auto Parallel-303
05Upper Deck-372
05Upper Deck Hockey Showcase-HS25
05Upper Deck Showcase Promos-HS25
05Upper Deck MVP-252
Gold-252
Platinum-252
05Upper Deck Victory-83
Black-83
Gold-83
Silver-83
05German DEL Star Attack-ST09
06Flyers Postcards-22
06O-Pee-Chee-319
Rainbow-319
06Panini Stickers-91
06UD Artifacts Tundra Tandems-TTNY
06UD Artifacts Tundra Tandems Black-TTNY
06UD Artifacts Tundra Tandems Blue-TTNY
06UD Artifacts Tundra Tandems Gold-TTNY
06UD Artifacts Tundra Tandems Platinum-TTNY
06UD Artifacts Tundra Tandems Red-TTNY
06UD Artifacts Tundra Tandems Dual Patches Red-TTNY
06Upper Deck-374
Exclusives Parallel-374
High Gloss Parallel-374
Game Jerseys-J2MY
Game Patches-P2MY
Masterpieces-374
06Upper Deck Ovation-80
06Upper Deck Victory-126
06Upper Deck Victory Black-126
06Upper Deck Victory Gold-126

York, Shawn
91British Columbia JHL-59
92British Columbia JHL-100

Young, Adam
92Windsor Spitfires-11
93Windsor Spitfires-10
94Windsor Spitfires-12
95Slapshot-414
96Louisville Riverfrogs-6

Young, Alan
94German DEL-420
95German DEL-394
96German DEL-302

Young, Allen
90Fort Saskatchewan Traders-22

Young, Andrew
92British Columbia JHL-162

Young, B.J.
95Red Deer Rebels-21
96Red Deer Rebels-15
97Bowman CHL-112
OPC-112
99Cincinnati Mighty Ducks-19
01Anchorage Aces-18

Young, Barry
89Sudbury Wolves-22
907th Inn. Sketch OHL-397
90Sudbury Wolves-3
917th Inn. Sketch OHL-248
91Sudbury Wolves-11

Young, Bill
72Los Angeles Sharks WHA-19
72Minnesota Fighting Saints Postcards WHA-24

Young, Bobby
93Quebec Pee-Wee Tournament-688

Young, Bryan
04Peterborough Petes Postcards-19
06Stockton Thunder-18
07Upper Deck Victory-239
Black-239
Gold-239

Young, C.J.
90ProCards AHL/IHL-617
92Parkhurst-246
Emerald Ice-246
92Upper Deck-395
93OPC Premier-347
Gold-347
93Stadium Club-316
Members Only Master Set-316
First Day Issue-316
93Topps/OPC Premier-347
Gold-347
93Ultra-248

Young, Clayton
89Kamloops Blazers-23
907th Inn. Sketch Memorial Cup-19
91Michigan Falcons-20
99German Bundesliga 2-197
03German Deg Metro Stars-23
03German DEL-45
04German DEL-59
04German DEL Update-308
04German Dusseldorf Metro Stars Postcards-24
04German Hamburg Freezers Postcards-22

Young, Colin
93Quebec Pee-Wee Tournament-1685

Young, Don
82North Bay Centennials-24

Young, Doug
34Beehive Group I Photos-132
34Beehive Group I Photos-188
37V356 Worldwide Gum-49
39O-Pee-Chee V301-1-58

Young, Erik
99Minnesota Golden Gophers-29

Young, Geordie
91British Columbia JHL-45

Young, Harry
05Guelph Storm-D-05

Young, Howie
44Beehive Group II Photos-147
44Beehive Group II Photos-218
61Shirriff/Salada Coins-74
62York Iron-On Transfers-35
63Topps-29
67Topps-49
68O-Pee-Chee-82
68O-Pee-Chee-151
68Shirriff Coins-121
68Topps-82
74Phoenix Roadrunners WHA Pins-9

Young, Ian
91Oshawa Generals-30
94German DEL-324
95German DEL-300

Young, Jamie
98Kingston Frontenacs-23

Young, Jason
89Sudbury Wolves-20
907th Inn. Sketch OHL-398
90Sudbury Wolves-16
917th Inn. Sketch OHL-251
91Sudbury Wolves-24
91Classic-45
91Star Pics-65
91Ultimate Draft-40
91Ultimate Draft French-40
91Classic Four-Sport *-45
Autographs-45A
92Rochester Americans Dunkin' Donuts-20
92Rochester Americans Kodak-26
93Rochester Americans Kodak-25
94Classic Pro Prospects-226
97Sudbury Wolves Anniversary-24
98German DEL-234
99German DEL-116
00German DEL-134
01German Upper Deck-150
02German DEL City Press-147
03German DEL-105
04German DEL-118
05German DEL-96
Star Attack-ST10
06German DEL-65
Team Leaders-TL14

Young, Joey
917th Inn. Sketch WHL-151

Young, John
90Michigan Tech Huskies-28
90Michigan Tech Huskies-29
91Michigan Tech Huskies-28
93Greensboro Monarchs-15
94Minnesota Moose-3

Young, Kevin
94Owen Sound Platers-3
96Dayton Ice Bandits-23
98Medicine Hat Tigers-23
01Kelowna Rockets-22

Young, Liam
94UK Solihul Barons-15
95UK Solihull Barons-12

Young, Matt
917th Inn. Sketch WHL-182

Young, Michael
99OCN Blizzard-11
00OCN Blizzard-10
01OCN Blizzard-13
02OCN Blizzard-11
03OCN Blizzard-26

Young, Robert
06UK Guildford Flames-9

Young, Ryan
00Lincoln Stars-16

Young, Scott
89O-Pee-Chee-209
89O-Pee-Chee Stickers-44
89O-Pee-Chee Stickers-96
89O-Pee-Chee Stickers-233
89O-Pee-Chee Stickers-264
89Panini Stickers-224
89Whalers Junior Milk-23
89ProCards AHL-13
90Bowman-253
Tiffany-253
90O-Pee-Chee-84
90Panini Stickers-34
90Pro Set-113
90Score-21
Canadian-21
90Score Hottest/Rising Stars-12
90Score Young Superstars-14
90Topps-84
Tiffany-84
90Upper Deck-87
French-87
90Whalers Jr. 7-Eleven-27
90ProCards AHL/IHL-438
91Bowman-86
91O-Pee-Chee-235
91Panini Stickers-273
91Pro Set-195
French-195
91Score American-287
91Score Canadian Bilingual-507
91Score Canadian English-507
91Stadium Club-74
91Topps-235
92Nordiques Petro-Canada-38
92Parkhurst-383
Emerald Ice-383
92Ultra-391
92Upper Deck-397
93Donruss-284
93Leaf-108
93Panini Stickers-73
93Pinnacle-129
Canadian-129
93PowerPlay-206
93Score-56
Canadian-56
93Stadium Club-261
Members Only Master Set-261
First Day Issue-261
94Canada Games NHL POGS-200
94Donruss-310
94Leaf-118
94Nordiques Burger King-27
94OPC Premier-519
Special Effects-519
94Pinnacle-361
Artist's Proofs-361
Rink Collection-361
94Stadium Club-153
Members Only Master Set-153
First Day Issue-153
Super Team Winner Cards-153
94Topps/OPC Premier-519
Special Effects-519
94Ultra-181
94UK Humberside Hawks-5
95Be A Player-107
Signatures-S107
Signatures Die Cuts-S107
95Canada Games NHL POGS-78
95Collector's Choice-271
Player's Club-271
Player's Club Platinum-271
95Donruss-36
95Leaf-317
95Panini Stickers-250
95Parkhurst International-322
Emerald Ice-322
95Score-278
Black Ice Artist's Proofs-278
Black Ice-278
95Stadium Club-47
Members Only Master Set-47
95Ultra-226
95Finnish Semic World Championships-110
95German DEL-450
95Swedish Globe World Championships-124
95Swedish World Championships Stickers-227
96Black Diamond-48
Gold-48
96Donruss-129
Press Proofs-129
96Donruss Canadian Ice-30
Gold Press Proofs-30
Red Press Proofs-30
96Leaf-181
Press Proofs-181
96Leaf Preferred-98
Press Proofs-98
96Pinnacle-197
Artist's Proofs-197
Foil-197
Premium Stock-197
Rink Collection-197
96Score-140
Artist's Proofs-140
Dealer's Choice Artist's Proofs-140
Special Artist's Proofs-140
Golden Blades-140
96Summit-78
Artist's Proofs-78
Ice-78
Metal-78
Premium Stock-78
96Topps Picks-113
OPC Inserts-113
96Upper Deck-42
96Zenith-115
Artist's Proofs-115
96Swedish Semic Wien-173
97Be A Player-143
Autographs-143
Autographs Die-Cuts-143
Autographs Prismatic Die-Cuts-143
97Katch-6
Gold-6
Silver-6
97Pacific-187
Copper-187
Emerald Green-187
Ice Blue-187
Red-187
Silver-187
97Paramount-8
Copper-8
Dark Grey-8
Emerald Green-8
Ice Blue-8
Red-8
Silver-8
97Score Mighty Ducks-10
Platinum-10
Premier-10
98Be A Player-278
Press Release-278
98BAP Gold-278
98BAP Autographs-278
98BAP Autographs Gold-278
98Katch-131
98Pacific-48
Ice Blue-48
Red-48
99Blues Taco Bell-5
99Pacific-366
Copper-366
Emerald Green-366
Gold-366
Ice Blue-366
Premiere Date-366
Red-366
99Pacific Dynagon Ice-170
Blue-170
Copper-170
Gold-170
Premiere Date-170
99Panini Stickers-288
99Paramount-202
Copper-202
Emerald-202
Gold-202
Holographic Emerald-202
Holographic Gold-202
Holographic Silver-202
Ice Blue-202
Premiere Date-202
Red-202
Silver-202
99Stadium Club-86
First Day Issue-86
One of a Kind-86
Printing Plates Black-86
Printing Plates Cyan-86
Printing Plates Magenta-86
Printing Plates Yellow-86
99Upper Deck MVP SC Edition-166
Gold Script-166
Silver Script-166
Super Script-166
00BAP Parkhurst 2000-P235
00Crown Royale-92
Ice Blue-92
Limited Series-92
Premiere Date-92
Red-92
00O-Pee-Chee-189
00O-Pee-Chee Parallel-189
00Pacific-354
Copper-354
Gold-354
Ice Blue-354
Premiere Date-354
00Paramount-211
Copper-211
Gold-211
Holo-Gold-211
Holo-Silver-211
Ice Blue-211
Premiere Date-211
00Topps/OPC-189
Parallel-189
00Topps Gold Label Class 1-57
Gold-57
00Topps Gold Label Class 2-57
00Topps Gold Label Class 2 Gold-57
00Topps Gold Label Class 3-57
00Topps Gold Label Class 3 Gold-57
00Topps Heritage-143
00UD Reserve-75
00Upper Deck-152
Exclusives Tier 1-152
Exclusives Tier 2-152
01BAP Memorabilia-187
Emerald-187
Ruby-187
Sapphire-187
01BAP Signature Series-111
Autographs-111
Autographs Gold-111
01Crown Royale Triple Threads-18
01O-Pee-Chee-125
01O-Pee-Chee Premier Parallel-125
01Pacific-335
Extreme LTD-335
Hobby LTD-335
Premiere Date-335
Retail LTD-335
Adrenaline Jerseys-42
01Pacific Arena Exclusives-335
01Parkhurst-132
01Private Stock Game Gear-90
01Private Stock Game Gear Patches-90
01Titanium Double-Sided Jerseys-38
01Titanium Double-Sided Patches-38
01Topps-125
OPC Parallel-125
01Topps Heritage-84
Refractors-84
01Upper Deck-153
Exclusives-153
01Upper Deck MVP-164
01Upper Deck Victory-306

Gold-306
01Upper Deck Vintage-225
01Vanguard Memorabilia-31
02Atomic Jerseys-5
02Atomic Jerseys Gold-5
02Atomic Patches-5
02BAP Memorabilia-159
Emerald-159
Ruby-159
Sapphire-159
NHL All-Star Game-159
NHL All-Star Game Blue-159
NHL All-Star Game Green-159
NHL All-Star Game Red-159
02BAP Memorabilia Toronto Fall Expo-159
02BAP Signature Series-168
Autographs-168
Autograph Buybacks 1998-278
Autograph Buybacks 2001-111
Autographs Gold-168
02O-Pee-Chee-248
02O-Pee-Chee Premier Blue Parallel-248
02O-Pee-Chee Premier Red Parallel-248
02O-Pee-Chee Factory Set-248
02Pacific-331
Blue-331
Red-331
02Pacific Complete-225
Red-225
02Stadium Club-106
Silver Decoy Cards-106
Proofs-106
02Stars Postcards-13
02Topps-248
OPC Blue Parallel-248
OPC Red Parallel-248
Factory Set-248
02Topps Chrome-135
Black Border Refractors-135
Refractors-135
02Topps Heritage-162
02Topps Total-44
02Upper Deck-301
Exclusives-301
02Upper Deck Beckett UD Promos-301
02Upper Deck Victory-189
Bronze-189
Gold-189
Silver-189
03ITG Action-135
Jerseys-M90
03NHL Sticker Collection-207
03Pacific-113
Blue-113
Red-113
03Pacific Complete-374
Red-374
03Stars Postcards-30
03Upper Deck MVP-133
Gold Script-133
Silver Script-133
Canadian Exclusives-133
05Be A Player Signatures-YO
05Be A Player Signatures Gold-YO
05Blues Team Set-24
05Panini Stickers-340
05Parkhurst-415
Facsimile Auto Parallel-415
05Upper Deck-414
05Upper Deck MVP-341
Gold-341
Platinum-341
06Upper Deck Ovation-92
06Upper Deck Victory-172
06Upper Deck Victory Black-172
06Upper Deck Victory Gold-172

Young, Scott (UK)

00UK Sekonda Superleague-11
01UK Dundee Stars-3
02UK Dundee Stars-3
02UK Hull Thunder-6
03Cape Fear Fire Antz-16

Young, Steve

89Portland Winter Hawks-21
98SLU Football Classic Doubles-6

Young, Tim

76O-Pee-Chee NHL-158
76O-Pee-Chee NHL-387
76Topps-158
77O-Pee-Chee NHL-223
77Topps-223
77Topps/O-Pee-Chee Glossy-22
Square-22
78North Stars Cloverleaf Dairy-8
78O-Pee-Chee-138
78Topps-138
79North Stars Postcards-19
79O-Pee-Chee-36
79Topps-36
80North Stars Postcards-22
80O-Pee-Chee-174
80Topps-174
81North Stars Postcards-24
81O-Pee-Chee-169
81O-Pee-Chee Stickers-94
81Topps-W113
82North Stars Postcards-24
82O-Pee-Chee-177
82Post Cereal-9
83Jets Postcards-25
83O-Pee-Chee-395
83Vachon-140
84O-Pee-Chee-351

Young, Travis

00Brandon Wheat Kings-6
01Brandon Wheat Kings-24
03Prince Albert Raiders-25

Young, Warren

82Birmingham South Stars-15
85O-Pee-Chee-152
85O-Pee-Chee Stickers-100
85Topps-152
86O-Pee-Chee-209
86Penguins Kodak-25
96Louisville Riverfrogs-23
96Louisville Riverfrogs-29
97Louisville Riverfrogs-23

Young, Wendell

82Kitchener Rangers-8
84Fredericton Express-18
85Fredericton Express-12
86Canucks Team Issue-24
89Penguins Foodland-14
90Bowman-203
Tiffany-203
90O-Pee-Chee-309
90Panini Stickers-127
90Pro Set-512
90Score-298
Canadian-298
90Topps-80
90Topps-309
Tiffany-309
90Upper Deck-102
French-102
91Penguins Coke/Elby's-1
92Kraft-25
92Lightning Sheraton-24
92OPC Premier-76
92Parkhurst-170
Emerald Ice-170
92Pinnacle-381
French-381
92Score-511
Canadian-511
92Ultra-206
93Lightning Kash n'Karry-6
93Lightning Season in Review-27
93OPC Premier-166
Gold-166
93Panini Stickers-221
93Pinnacle Masks-7
93Score-341
Canadian-341
93Topps/OPC Premier-166
Gold-166
94EA Sports-132
94Signature Rookies Tetrad *-118
Signatures-118
96Collector's Edge Ice-109
Prism-109
The Wall-TW6
98Chicago Wolves-14
98Chicago Wolves Turner Cup-1
99Chicago Wolves-2
00Chicago Wolves-23

Youngclaus, Phil

06Richmond Renegades-18

Younghans, Tom

78North Stars Cloverleaf Dairy-9
78O-Pee-Chee-295
79Panini Stickers-218
79North Stars Postcards-20
79O-Pee-Chee-177
79Topps-177
80North Stars Postcards-23
80O-Pee-Chee-343
81O-Pee-Chee-173

Yovanic, Paul

05Drummondville Voltigeurs-22
06Texas Tornados-20

Yrjola, Juha

72Finnish Jaakiekko-360

Ysebaert, Paul

88ProCards AHL-326
89ProCards AHL-209
90O-Pee-Chee-49
90Pro Set-607
90Score-406
Canadian-406
90Topps-49
Tiffany-49
90Upper Deck-375
French-375
91Pro Set Platinum-167
91Bowman-53
91Kraft-46
91O-Pee-Chee-248
91Parkhurst-42
91Parkhurst-435
French-42
French-435
91Pinnacle-36
French-36
91Pro Set-59
91Pro Set-608
French-59
French-608
91Red Wings Little Caesars-17
91Score American-166
91Score Canadian Bilingual-166
91Score Canadian English-166
91Stadium Club-171
91Topps-248
91Upper Deck-278
French-278
92Bowman-376
92O-Pee-Chee-46
92Panini Stickers-118
92Panini Stickers French-118
92Parkhurst Previews-PV1
92Parkhurst-43
Emerald Ice-43
92Pinnacle-93
French-93
92Pro Set-41
92Pro Set-248
92Score-95
92Score-414
Canadian-95
Canadian-414
Young Superstars-35
92Stadium Club-378
92Topps-58
92Topps-314
Gold-58G
Gold-314G
92Ultra-54
92Upper Deck-176
93Donruss-376
93Donruss-417
93Jets Readers Club-22
93Jets Ruffles-27
93Leaf-388
93Panini Stickers-248
93Parkhurst-504
Emerald Ice-504
93Pinnacle-348
Canadian-348
93PowerPlay-277
93Score-239
93Score-517
Gold-517
Canadian-239
Canadian-517
Canadian Gold-517
93Stadium Club-360
Members Only Master Set-360
First Day Issue-360
93Ultra-457
93Upper Deck-365
SP-179
94Donruss-2
94Leaf-202
94Lightning Photo Album-27
94Lightning Postcards-19
94OPC Premier-368
Special Effects-368
94Parkhurst-48
Gold-48
94Pinnacle-301
Artist's Proofs-301
Rink Collection-301
94Topps/OPC Premier-368
Special Effects-368
94Ultra-277
94Upper Deck-491
Electric Ice-491
95Be A Player-139
Signatures-S139
Signatures Die Cuts-S139
95Canada Games NHL POGS-250
95Collector's Choice-27
Player's Club-27
Player's Club Platinum-27
95Donruss-258
95Emotion-167
95Leaf-185
95Lightning Team Issue-20
95Panini Stickers-129
95Parkhurst International-191
Emerald Ice-191
95Pinnacle-17
Artist's Proofs-17
Rink Collection-17
95Playoff One on One-313
95Pro Magnets-74
95Score-116
Black Ice Artist's Proofs-116
Black Ice-116
95Topps-320
OPC Inserts-320
95Ultra-157
Gold Medallion-157
95Upper Deck-109
Electric Ice-109
Electric Ice Gold-109
Special Edition-SE165
96Collector's Choice-251
96Kraft Upper Deck-36
96NHL Pro Stamps-74
96Upper Deck-159
97Be A Player-163
Autographs-163
Autographs Die-Cuts-163
Autographs Prismatic Die-Cuts-163
97Crown Royale-127
Emerald Green-127
Ice Blue-127
Silver-127
97Pacific-178
Copper-178
Emerald Green-178
Ice Blue-178
Red-178
Silver-178
97Pacific Invincible-134
Copper-134
Emerald Green-134
Ice Blue-134
Red-134
Silver-134
97Pacific Omega-215
Copper-215
Dark Gray-215
Emerald Green-215
Gold-215
Ice Blue-215
97Paramount-177
Copper-177
Dark Grey-177
Emerald Green-177
Ice Blue-177
Red-177
Silver-177
97Revolution-131
Copper-131
Emerald-131
Ice Blue-131
Silver-131
97Upper Deck-159
98Aurora-177
98Finest-73
No Protectors-73
No Protectors Refractors-73
Refractors-73
98Pacific-408
Ice Blue-408
Red-408
98Pacific Dynagon Ice-175
Blue-175
Red-175
98Panini Stickers-101
98Paramount-222
Copper-222
Emerald Green-222
Holo-Electric-222
Ice Blue-222
Silver-222
98UD Choice-194
Prime Choice Reserve-194
Reserve-194
99Swiss Panini Stickers-199

Ytfeldt, David

99Swedish Upper Deck-107
99Swedish Upper Deck-208

Ytfeldt, Fredrik

98German DEL-123
99German DEL-269

Ytter, Mats

84Swedish Semic Elitserien-75
85Swedish Panini Stickers-70
89Swedish Semic Elitserien Stickers-240
90Swedish Semic Elitserien Stickers-150
91Swedish Semic Elitserien Stickers-252
92Swedish Semic Elitserien Stickers-274
93Swedish Semic Elitserien-242
94Swedish Leaf-134
95Swedish Leaf-126
Spidermen-12
95Swedish Upper Deck-186

Yubin, Ildar

96Dayton Bombers-5

Yudin, Alexander

91O-Pee-Chee Inserts-47R
92Upper Deck-336
99Russian Hockey League-239
99Russian Hockey League-252
99Russian Hockey League-264
00Russian Hockey League-125
00Russian Hockey League-161
01Russian Dynamo Moscow Mentos-15
01Russian Hockey League-43
01Russian Hockey League-44
01Russian Hockey League-45
01Russian Hockey League-121
02Russian Hockey League-49
02Russian Hockey League-62
02Russian Hockey League-169
02Russian World Championships-2
03Russian Hockey League-22
03Russian Hockey League-23
04Russian Super League All-Stars-6
05Russian Hockey League RHL-54

Yuldashev, Ramil

93Swiss HNL-208
96Swiss HNL-492

Yule, Steve

88Kamloops Blazers-24
89Kamloops Blazers-24
907th Inn. Sketch WHL-286
907th Inn. Sketch Memorial Cup-22
917th Inn. Sketch WHL-78
96Mississippi Sea Wolves-20
97Mississippi Sea Wolves-19

Yulzari, Thomas

93Quebec Pee-Wee Tournament-1657

Yunkov, Alexander

05Russian Hockey League RHL-53

Yunkov, Mikhail

04Russian Under-18 Team-18
05Russian Hockey League RHL-53

Yuresko, Yuri

97Hampton Roads Admirals-21

Yushkevich, Dimitri

92Flyers J.C. Penney-22
92Flyers Upper Deck Sheets-10
92Flyers Upper Deck Sheets-31
92Flyers Upper Deck Sheets-43
92OPC Premier-65
92Parkhurst-133
Emerald Ice-133
92Pinnacle-394
French-394
92Ultra-161
92Upper Deck-333
92Upper Deck-350
92Upper Deck-570
Calder Candidates-CC20
Euro-Rookies-ER12
92Russian Stars Red Ace-34
92Russian Stars Red Ace-35
93Donruss-254
93Flyers J.C. Penney-23
93Flyers Lineup Sheets-34
93Flyers Lineup Sheets-35
93Leaf-82
93OPC Premier-18
Gold-18
93Parkhurst-145
Emerald Ice-145
93Pinnacle-146
Canadian-146
93PowerPlay-186
93Score-216
Canadian-216
93Stadium Club-492
Members Only Master Set-492
First Day Issue-492
93Topps/OPC Premier-18
Gold-18
93Ultra-198
93Upper Deck-127
SP-119
93Swedish Semic World Champ Stickers-144
93Classic-97
94Donruss-308
94EA Sports-98
94Fleer-160
94Leaf-37
94OPC Premier-468
Special Effects-468
94Parkhurst-163
Gold-163
94Pinnacle-227
Artist's Proofs-227
Rink Collection-227
94Stadium Club-78
Members Only Master Set-78
First Day Issue-78
Super Team Winner Cards-78
94Topps/OPC Premier-468
Special Effects-468
94Ultra-161
94Upper Deck-349
Electric Ice-349
95Be A Player-7
Signatures-S7
Signatures Die Cuts-S7
95Collector's Choice-249
Player's Club-249
Player's Club Platinum-249
95Donruss-387
95Leaf-291
95Panini Stickers-121
95Parkhurst International-469
Emerald Ice-469
95Topps-192
OPC Inserts-192
95Upper Deck-81
95Upper Deck-376
Electric Ice-81
Electric Ice-376
Electric Ice Gold-81
Electric Ice Gold-376
95Finnish Semic World Championships-126
95Swedish Globe World Championships-171
96Collector's Choice-263
96Upper Deck-164
96Swedish Semic Wien-137
97Pacific-153
Copper-153
Emerald Green-153
Ice Blue-153
Red-153
Silver-153
97Panini Stickers-173
97Score Maple Leafs-16
Platinum-16
Premier-16
98Finest-115
No Protectors-115
No Protectors Refractors-115
Refractors-115
98Panini Stickers-161
99BAP Memorabilia-6
Gold-6
Silver-6
00BAP Memorabilia-87
Emerald-87
Ruby-87
Sapphire-87
Promos-87
00BAP Mem Chicago Sportsfest Copper-87
00BAP Memorabilia Chicago Sportsfest Blue-87
00BAP Memorabilia Chicago Sportsfest Gold-87
00BAP Memorabilia Chicago Sportsfest Ruby-87
00BAP Memorabilia Chicago Sun-Times Ruby-87
00BAP Memorabilia Chicago Sun-Times Gold-87
00BAP Mem Chicago Sun-Times Sapphire-87
00BAP Mem Toronto Fall Expo Copper-87
00BAP Memorabilia Toronto Fall Expo Gold-87
00BAP Memorabilia Toronto Fall Expo Ruby-87
00BAP Signature Series-241
Emerald-241
Ruby-241
Sapphire-241
Autographs-157
Autographs Gold-157
Department of Defense-DD18
00Pacific-402
Copper-402
Gold-402
Ice Blue-402
Premiere Date-402
00Stadium Club-11
00Titanium Game Gear-147
00Titanium Game Gear Patches-147
00Upper Deck-166
Exclusives Tier 1-166
Exclusives Tier 2-166
00Upper Deck MVP-171
First Stars-171
Second Stars-171
Third Stars-171
00Upper Deck Vintage-340
01Atomic Jerseys-49
01Atomic Patches-49
01Pacific Adrenaline Jerseys-48
01Titanium Draft Day Edition-91
01Topps Reserve Emblems-DY
01Topps Reserve Jerseys-DY
01Topps Reserve Name Plates-DY
01Topps Reserve Numbers-DY
01Topps Reserve Patches-DY
01Upper Deck Victory-336
Gold-336
02BAP First Edition-33
Jerseys-33
02BAP Memorabilia-244
Emerald-244
Ruby-244
Sapphire-244
NHL All-Star Game-244
NHL All-Star Game Blue-244
NHL All-Star Game Green-244
NHL All-Star Game Red-244
02BAP Memorabilia Toronto Fall Expo-244
02BAP Sig Series Auto Buybacks 2000-157
02Kings Game Sheets-3
02Kings Game Sheets-4
02Pacific-372
Blue-372
Red-372
02Pacific Complete-422
Red-422
02Topps Total-41
02Upper Deck-321
Exclusives-321
02Upper Deck Beckett UD Promos-321
03ITG Action-472
03Russian Hockey League-232
03Russian National Team-28
04Russian World Championship Team-22

Yuzda, Jason

90Fort Saskatchewan Traders-23

Yzerman, Steve

83Canadian National Juniors-19
84O-Pee-Chee-67
84O-Pee-Chee-385
84O-Pee-Chee Stickers-37
847-Eleven Discs-11
84Topps-49
85O-Pee-Chee-29
85O-Pee-Chee Stickers-23
85O-Pee-Chee Stickers-30
857-Eleven Credit Cards-5
85Topps-29
86O-Pee-Chee-11
86O-Pee-Chee Stickers-161
86Topps-11
87O-Pee-Chee-56
87O-Pee-Chee Box Bottoms-C
87O-Pee-Chee Stickers-111
87Panini Stickers-243
87Red Wings Little Caesars-29
87Topps-56
87Topps Box Bottoms-C
88Frito-Lay Stickers-3
88O-Pee-Chee-196
88O-Pee-Chee Box Bottoms-L
88O-Pee-Chee Stickers-253
88Panini Stickers-47
88Red Wings Little Caesars-23
88Topps-196
88Topps Box Bottoms-L
89Action Packed Prototypes-4
89Kraft-63
89Kraft All-Stars Stickers-3
89O-Pee-Chee-83
89O-Pee-Chee Box Bottoms-L
89O-Pee-Chee Stickers-254
89Panini Stickers-57
89Red Wings Little Caesars-17
89Sports Illustrated for Kids I-25
89Topps-83
89Topps Box Bottoms-L
89Swedish Semic World Champ Stickers-72
90Bowman-233
Tiffany-233
90Bowman Hat Tricks-5
Tiffany-5
90Kraft-63
90Kraft-78
90O-Pee-Chee-133
90O-Pee-Chee-222
90O-Pee-Chee Box Bottoms-J
90OPC Premier-130
90Panini Stickers-208
90Pro Set-79
90Pro Set-347
90Score-3
90Score-339
Canadian-3
Canadian-339
90Score Hottest/Rising Stars-4
90Topps-133
90Topps-222
Tiffany-222
90Topps Box Bottoms-J
90Topps Team Scoring Leaders-19
90Topps Team Scoring Leaders Tiffany-19
90Upper Deck-56
90Upper Deck-303
90Upper Deck-477
French-56
French-303
French-477
90Upper Deck Holograms-7
90Upper Deck Holograms-8
90Upper Deck Holograms-9
91Pro Set Platinum-32
91Bowman-41
91Bowman-42
91Kraft-68
91McDonald's Upper Deck-19
91O-Pee-Chee-60
91O-Pee-Chee-424
91OPC Premier-73
91OPC Premier-142
91Panini Stickers-134
91Parkhurst-44
91Parkhurst-434
French-44
French-434
91Pinnacle-75
91Pinnacle-383
French-75
French-383
91Pro Set-62
91Pro Set-281
91Pro Set-571
French-62
French-281
French-571
Puck Candy-8
91Red Wings Little Caesars-18
91Score National-7
91Score Ntnl Candy Wholesalers Convention-7
91Score Fanfest-7
91Score American-190
91Score American-419
91Score Canadian Bilingual-190
91Score Canadian Bilingual-335
91Score Canadian English-190
91Score Canadian English-335
91Score Kellogg's-14
91Stadium Club-81
91Topps-424
Topps/Bowman Preview Sheet-8
Team Scoring Leaders-3
91Upper Deck-146
91Upper Deck-626
French-146
French-626
Box Bottoms-5
91Finnish Semic World Champ Stickers-65
91Swedish Semic World Champ Stickers-65
92Bowman-103
92Bowman-220
92Humpty Dumpty I-24
92Kraft-48
92McDonald's Upper Deck-14
92O-Pee-Chee-61
92O-Pee-Chee-321
25th Anniv. Inserts-17
92Panini Stickers-112
92Panini Stickers French-112
92Parkhurst-44
92Parkhurst-456
Emerald Ice-44
Emerald Ice-456
92Pinnacle-241
92Pinnacle-258
92Pinnacle-350
French-241
French-258
French-350
92Pro Set-39
92Pro Set-247
Gold Team Leaders-3
92Score-400
92Score-423
Canadian-400
Canadian-423
92Seasons Patches-6
92Sports Illustrated for Kids II-474
92Stadium Club-19
92Stadium Club-254
92Topps-207
Gold-207G
92Ultra-55
92Upper Deck-155
Gordie Howe Selects-G10
World Junior Grads-WG7
92Finnish Semic-87
93SLU Hockey Canadian-11
93SLU Hockey American-12
93Donruss-95
Special Print-G
93Kenner Starting Lineup Cards-12
93Kraft-49
93Leaf-162
Hat Trick Artists-10
Studio Signature-5
93McDonald's Upper Deck-13
93OPC Premier-280
Gold-280
Black Gold-23
93Panini Stickers-V
93Parkhurst-326
Emerald Ice-326
East/West Stars-W5
93Pinnacle-175
Canadian-175
All-Stars-36
All-Stars Canadian-36
Captains-7
Captains Canadian-7
Nifty Fifty-8
93PowerPlay-77
Gamebreakers-10
Point Leaders-20
93Score-310
93Score-448
Canadian-310
Canadian-448
Dream Team-16
Dynamic Duos U.S.-9
Franchise-6
93Seasons Patches-20
93Stadium Club-70
Members Only Master Set-70
OPC-70
First Day Issue-70
First Day Issue OPC-70
All-Stars-5
All-Stars Members Only-5
All-Stars OPC-5
93Topps/OPC Premier-280
Gold-280
93Topps Premier Black Gold-16
93Topps Premier Black Gold-B
93Ultra-201
All-Stars-12
Premier Pivots-10
Scoring Kings-6
93Upper Deck-227
93Upper Deck-290
93Upper Deck-388
Hat Tricks-HT6
Next In Line-NL3
NHLPA/Roots-4
Program of Excellence-E14
Silver Skates-R6
Silver Skates Gold-R6
SP-47
93Upper Deck Locker All-Stars-36
93Swedish Semic World Champ Stickers-203
94Hockey Canadian-13
94SLU Hockey Canadian-13
94SLU Hockey American-20
94Action Packed Big Picture Promos-BP4
94Be A Player-R29
94Be A Player-R115
99 All-Stars-G19
Signature Cards-115
Up Close and Personal-UC5
94Canada Games NHL POGS-92
94Donruss-1
94EA Sports-39
94Finest-84
Super Team Winners-84
Refractors-84
94Flair-55
Hot Numbers-10
94Fleer-67
94Hockey Wit-108
94Kenner Starting Lineup Cards-21
94Kraft-14
94Leaf-148
94Leaf Limited-120
94OPC Premier-235
Special Effects-235
94Parkhurst-299
Gold-299
Vintage-V57
94Parkhurst SE-SE55
Gold-SE55
94Pinnacle-271
Artist's Proofs-271
Rink Collection-271
94Score-150
Gold-150
Platinum-150
Dream Team-DT20
94Select-35
Gold-35
94SP-34
Die Cuts-34
94Topps/OPC Premier-235
Special Effects-235
The Go To Guy-12
94Ultra-67
Premier Pivots-10
Scoring Kings-7
94Upper Deck-300
94Upper Deck-550
Electric Ice-300
Electric Ice-550
Ice Gallery-IG1
Predictor Hobby-H22
94Upper Deck Predictor Hobby Exch Gold-H22
94Upper Deck Predictor Hobby Exch Silver-H22
94Upper Deck Predictor Retail-R24
94Upper Deck Predictor Retail-R43
94Upper Deck Predictor Retail Exchange-R24
94Upper Deck Predictor Retail Exchange-R43
94Upper Deck SP Inserts-SP25
94Upper Deck SP Inserts Die Cuts-SP25
94Upper Deck NHLPA/Be A Player-18
95Bashan Super Stickers-37
Die-Cut-25
95Bowman-21
All-Foil-21
95Canada Games NHL POGS-96
95Collector's Choice-266
Player's Club-266
Player's Club Platinum-266
Crash The Game-C26A
Crash The Game-C26B
Crash The Game-C26C
Crash The Game Gold-C26A
Crash The Game Gold-C26B
Crash The Game Gold-C26C
Crash the Game Silver Redeemed-C26
Crash the Game Silver Bonus-C26
Crash the Game Gold Redeemed-C26
Crash the Game Gold Bonus-C26
95Donruss-96
Igniters-8
95Donruss Elite-99
Die Cut Stars-99
Die Cut Uncut-99
95Emotion-60
95Finest-162
Refractors-162
95Hoyle Western Playing Cards-53
95Imperial Stickers-37
Die Cut Superstars-25
95Leaf-60
95Leaf Limited-105
95Metal-51
95NHL Aces Playing Cards-3S
95Panini Stickers-179
95Parkhurst International-70
Emerald Ice-70
95Playoff One on One-147
95Pro Magnets-105
95Score-240
Black Ice Artist's Proofs-240
Black Ice-240
Golden Blades-12
95Select Certified-94
Mirror Gold-94
95SkyBox Impact-58
95SP-46
Holoviews-FX7
Holoviews Special FX-FX7
Stars/Etoiles-E14
Stars/Etoiles Gold-E14
95Stadium Club-20
Members Only Master Set-20
95Summit-154
Artist's Proofs-154
Ice-154
95Topps-237
OPC Inserts-237
Home Grown Canada-HGC16
95Topps SuperSkills-10
Platinum-10
95Ultra-51
Gold Medallion-51
Extra Attackers-20
95Upper Deck-113
95Upper Deck-218
Electric Ice-113
Electric Ice-218
Electric Ice Gold-113
Electric Ice Gold-218
95Upper Deck All-Star Game Predictors-15
Redemption Winners-15
95Upper Deck Predictor Retail-R15
95Upper Deck Predictor Retail-R58
95Upper Deck Predictor Retail Exchange-R15
95Upper Deck Predictor Retail Exchange-R58
95Upper Deck Special Edition-SE30
95Upper Deck Special Edition Gold-SE30
95Zenith-93
95Swedish Globe World Championships-89
95Swedish World Championships Stickers-280
96Be A Player Biscuit In The Basket-13
96Be A Player Link to History-9B
96Be A Player Link to History Autographs-9B
96Be A Player Link to History Auto Silver-9B
96Black Diamond-162
Gold-162
Run for the Cup-RC9
96Collector's Choice-79
96Collector's Choice-292
MVP-UD14
MVP Gold-UD14
Stick'Ums-S22
Crash the Game-C10A
Crash the Game-C10B
Crash the Game-C10C
Crash the Game Gold-C10A
Crash the Game Gold-C10B
Crash the Game Gold-C10C
Crash the Game Exchange-CR10
Crash the Game Exchange Gold-CR10
96Donruss-171
96Donruss-240
Press Proofs-171
Press Proofs-240
96Donruss Canadian Ice-39
Gold Press Proofs-39
Red Press Proofs-39
96Donruss Elite-38
Die Cut Stars-38
Perspective-3
96Duracell All-Cherry Team-DC15
96Flair-31
Blue Ice-31
Center Ice Spotlight-10
96Fleer-35
Art Ross-25
Picks Captain's Choice-2
Picks Fabulous 50-49
96Hockey Greats Coins-20
Gold-20
96Kraft Upper Deck-38
96Leaf-13
96Leaf-239
Press Proofs-13
Press Proofs-239
Fire On Ice-12
96Leaf Limited-40
Gold-40
Stubble-14
96Leaf Preferred-102
Press Proofs-102
Vanity Plates-4
Vanity Plates Gold-4
96Maggers-108
96McDonald's Pinnacle-17
96Metal Universe-51
96NHL Aces Playing Cards-52
96NHL Pro Stamps-105
96Pinnacle-25
Artist's Proofs-25
Foil-25
Premium Stock-25
Rink Collection-25
96Pinnacle Mint-12
Bronze-12
Gold-12
Silver-12
Coins Brass-12
Coins Solid Gold-12
Coins Gold Plated-12
Coins Nickel-12
Coins Silver-12
96Playoff One on One-366
96Score-60
Artist's Proofs-60
Dealer's Choice Artist's Proofs-60
Special Artist's Proofs-60
Golden Blades-60
Sudden Death-2
96Select Certified-41
Artist's Proofs-41
Blue-41
Mirror Blue-41
Mirror Gold-41
Mirror Red-41
Red-41
Cornerstones-14
96SkyBox Impact-40
BladeRunners-25
96SP-47
Clearcut Winner-CW15
Inside Info-IN8
Inside Info Gold-IN8
96SPx-14
Gold-14
Holoview Heroes-HH3
96Summit-76
Artist's Proofs-76
Ice-76
Metal-76
Premium Stock-76
96Team Out-28
96Topps Picks-31
500 Club-FC7
OPC Inserts-31
Top Shelf-TS15
96Ultra-56
Gold Medallion-56
Mr. Momentum-10
96Upper Deck-50
96Upper Deck Blow-Ups-1
96Upper Deck Game Jerseys-GJ1
96Upper Deck Generation Next-X13
96Upper Deck Hart Hopefuls Bronze-HH19
96Upper Deck Hart Hopefuls Gold-HH19
96Upper Deck Hart Hopefuls Silver-HH19
96Upper Deck Superstar Showdown-SS16B
96Upper Deck Ice-109
Parallel-109
Stanley Cup Foundation-S2
Stanley Cup Foundation Dynasty-S2
96Zenith-5
Artist's Proofs-5
Z-Team-6
96Swedish Semic Wien-101
97SLU Hockey One on One-5
97Headliners Hockey-30
97Beehive-11
Golden Portraits-11
Team-16
Team Gold-16
97Black Diamond-123
Double Diamond-123
Triple Diamond-123
Quadruple Diamond-123
Premium Cut-PC7

Premium Cut Double Diamond-PC7
Premium Cut Quadruple Diamond Horiz-PC7
Premium Cut Triple Diamond-PC7
Premium Cut Quadruple Diamond Verticals-PC7
97Collector's Choice-78
97Collector's Choice-313
Crash the Game-C19A
Crash the Game-C19B
Crash the Game-C19C
Crash the Game Exchange-CR19
Star Quest-SQ67
Stick'Ums-S29
World Domination-W3
97Crown Royale-51
Emerald Green-51
Ice Blue-51
Silver-51
Blades of Steel Die-Cuts-10
Cramer's Choice Jumbos-6
Cramer's Choice Jumbos Gold-6
Cramer's Choice Jumbos Signed-6
Hat Tricks Die-Cuts-8
Lamplighters Cel-Fusion Die-Cuts-9
97Donruss-2
Press Proofs Silver-2
Press Proofs Gold-2
Elite Inserts-6
Line 2 Line-5
Line 2 Line-P5
Line 2 Line Die Cut-5
97Donruss Canadian Ice-4
Dominion Series-4
Provincial Series-4
National Pride-4
Stanley Cup Scrapbook-19
97Donruss Elite-15
97Donruss Elite-122
Aspirations-15
Aspirations-122
Status-15
Status-122
Back to the Future-8
Back to the Future Autographs-8
Craftsmen-16
Master Craftsmen-16
Prime Numbers-10A
Prime Numbers-10B
Prime Numbers-10C
Prime Numbers Die-Cuts-10A
Prime Numbers Die-Cuts-10B
Prime Numbers Die-Cuts-10C
97Donruss Limited-41
97Donruss Limited-115
97Donruss Limited-165
Exposure-41
Exposure-115
Exposure-165
Fabric of the Game-49
Fabric of the Game-70
97Donruss Preferred-41
97Donruss Preferred-179
Cut to the Chase-41
Cut to the Chase-179
Line of the Times-6B
97Donruss Preferred Line of Times Promos-6B
97Donruss Preferred Precious Metals-14
97Donruss Priority-4
97Donruss Priority-209
Stamp of Approval-4
Stamp of Approval-209
Direct Deposit-2
Postcards-3
Postcards Opening Day Issues-4
Stamps-3
Stamps Bronze-3
Stamps Gold-3
Stamps Silver-3
97Highland Mint Mint-Cards Topps-27
97Highland Mint Mint-Cards Topps-28
97Highland Mint Mint-Coins-17
97Katch-54
97Katch-161
Gold-54
Gold-161
Silver-54
Silver-161
97Kraft-9
97Kraft Team Canada-12
97Leaf-4
97Leaf-171
Fractal Matrix-4
Fractal Matrix-171
Fractal Matrix Die Cuts-4
Fractal Matrix Die Cuts-171
Banner Season-5
Fire On Ice-4
97Leaf International-4
Universal Ice-4
97McDonald's Team Canada Coins-10
97McDonald's Upper Deck-19
Game Film-3
97Pacific-19
Copper-19
Emerald Green-19
Ice Blue-19
Red-19
Silver-19
Card-Supials-8
Card-Supials Minis-8
Cramer's Choice-6
Gold Crown Die-Cuts-11
Slap Shots Die-Cuts-3C
Team Checklists-9
97Pacific Dynagon-46
97Pacific Dynagon-139
Copper-46
Copper-139
Dark Grey-46
Dark Grey-139
Emerald Green-46
Emerald Green-139
Ice Blue-46
Ice Blue-139
Red-46
Red-139
Silver-46
Silver-139
Best Kept Secrets-36
Dynamic Duos-6B
Tandems-7
Tandems-26
97Pacific Invincible-53
Copper-53
Emerald Green-53
Ice Blue-53
Red-53
Silver-53
Attack Zone-11
Feature Performers-16
NHL Regime-75
Off The Glass-9
97Pacific Omega-88
Copper-88
Dark Gray-88
Emerald Green-88
Gold-88
Ice Blue-88
Game Face-8
Silks-6
Stick Handle Laser Cuts-9
Team Leaders-9
97Panini Stickers-149
97Paramount-71
Copper-71
Dark Grey-71
Emerald Green-71
Ice Blue-71
Red-71
Silver-71
Big Numbers Die-Cuts-10
Canadian Greats-7
Photoengravings-10
97Pinnacle-71
Artist's Proofs-71
Rink Collection-71
Epix Game Emerald-9
Epix Game Orange-9
Epix Game Purple-9
Epix Moment Emerald-9
Epix Moment Orange-9
Epix Moment Purple-9
Epix Play Emerald-9
Epix Play Orange-9
Epix Play Purple-9
Epix Season Emerald-9
Epix Season Orange-9
Epix Season Purple-9
Press Plates Back Black-71
Press Plates Back Cyan-71
Press Plates Back Magenta-71
Press Plates Back Yellow-71
Press Plates Front Black-71
Press Plates Front Cyan-71
Press Plates Front Magenta-71
Press Plates Front Yellow-71
Team Pinnacle-9
Team Mirror-9
Team Parallel-9
Team Parallel Mirror-9
97Pinnacle Certified-38
Red-38
Mirror Blue-38
Mirror Gold-38
Mirror Red-38
Team-13
Gold Team Promo-13
Gold Team-13
97Pinnacle Inside-24
Coach's Collection-24
Executive Collection-24
Track-9
Cans-9
Cans Gold-9
97Pinnacle Mint-5
Bronze-5
Gold Team-5
Silver Team-5
Coins Brass-5
Coins Brass Proofs-5
Coins Gold Plated-5
Coins Gold Plated Proofs-5
Coins Nickel Silver-5
Coins Nickel Silver Proofs-5
Coins Solid Gold-5
Coins Solid Silver-5
97Pinnacle Power Pack Blow-Ups-18
97Pinnacle Tot Cert Platinum Blue-38
97Pinnacle Tot Cert Platinum Gold-38
97Pinnacle Totally Certified Platinum Red-38
97Pinnacle Tot Cert Mirror Platinum Gold-38
97Post Pinnacle-10
97Revolution-52
Copper-52
Emerald-52
Ice Blue-52
Silver-52
NHL Icons-5
Team Checklist Laser Cuts-9
97Score-86
97Score-263
97Score-PR86
Artist's Proofs-86
Golden Blades-86
97Score Red Wings-2
Platinum-2
Premier-2
97SP Authentic-52
Icons-I21
Icons Die-Cuts-I21
Icons Embossed-I21
Sign of the Times-SY
97SPx-14
Bronze-14
Gold-14
Silver-14
Steel-14
DuoView-5
Grand Finale-14
97Studio-10
97Studio-106
Press Proofs Silver-10
Press Proofs Silver-106
Press Proofs Gold-10
Press Proofs Gold-106
Hard Hats-10
Portraits-10
Silhouettes-10
Silhouettes 8x10-10
97Upper Deck-57
Blow-Ups 3 x 5-1-2
Game Dated Moments-57
Sixth Sense Masters-SS20
Sixth Sense Wizards-SS20
Smooth Grooves-SG19
The Specialists-19
The Specialists Level 2 Die Cuts-19
Three Star Selects-3B
97Upper Deck Crash the All-Star Game-5
97Upper Deck Crash the All-Star Game-AR5
97Upper Deck Diamond Vision-4
Signature Moves-4
Defining Moments-DM3
97Upper Deck Ice-89
Parallel-89
Champions-IC19
Champions 2 Die Cuts-IC19
Lethal Lines-L5B
Lethal Lines 2-L5B
Power Shift-89
97Zenith-5
Z-Gold-5
Z-Silver-5
97Zenith 5 x 7-21
Gold Impulse-21
Silver Impulse-21
97Zenith Chasing The Cup-15
97Pinnacle Collector's Club Team Pinnacle-H8
98SLU Hockey-235
98Aurora-69
Atomic Laser Cuts-11
Championship Fever-20
Championship Fever Copper-20
Championship Fever Ice Blue-20
Championship Fever Red-20
Championship Fever Silver-20
Cubes-10
Front Line Copper-5
Front Line Ice Blue-5
Front Line Red-5
Man Advantage-10
NHL Command-6
98Be A Player-46
Press Release-46
98BAP Gold-46
98BAP Autographs-46
98BAP Autographs Gold-46
98BAP AS Game Used Stick Cards-S9
98BAP AS Game Used Jersey Cards-AS9
98BAP AS Milestones-M4
98BAP AS Milestones-M10
98BAP Playoff Game Used Jerseys-G15
98BAP Playoff Game Used Jersey Autographs-G15
98BAP Playoff Highlights-H7
98BAP Playoff Practice Used Jerseys-P5
98BAP Tampa Bay All Star Game-46
98Black Diamond-30
Double Diamond-30
Triple Diamond-30
Quadruple Diamond-30
Myriad-M19
Myriad 2-M19
Winning Formula Gold-WF11
Winning Formula Platinum-WF11
98Bowman's Best-1
Refractors-1
Atomic Refractors-1
Scotty Bowman's Best-SB7
Scotty Refractors-SB7
Scotty Atomic Refractors-SB7
98Crown Royale-49
Limited Series-49
Cramer's Choice Jumbos-6
Cramer's Choice Jumbos Dark Blue-6
Cramer's Choice Jumbos Green-6
Cramer's Choice Jumbos Red-6
Cramer's Choice Jumbos Light Blue-6
Cramer's Choice Jumbos Gold-6
Cramer's Choice Jumbos Purple-6
Living Legends-6
Master Performers-11
Pillars of the Game-14
98Donruss Elite Promos-15
98Finest-72
No Protectors-72
No Protectors Refractors-72
Refractors-72
Double Sided Mystery Finest-M31
Double Sided Mystery Finest-M35
Double Sided Mystery Finest-M36
Double Sided Mystery Finest-M37
Double Sided Mystery Refractors-M31
Double Sided Mystery Refractors-M35
Double Sided Mystery Refractors-M36
Double Sided Mystery Refractors-M37
Oversize-5
Oversize Refractors-5
Red Lighters-R7
Red Lighters Refractors-R7
98Katch-160
98Kenner Starting Lineup Cards-34
98McDonald's Upper Deck-6
98OPC Chrome-175
Refractors-175
98Pacific-19
Ice Blue-19
Red-19
Dynagon Ice Inserts-10
Titanium Ice-10
Gold Crown Die-Cuts-16
Team Checklists-9
Timelines-8
Trophy Winners-10
98Pacific Dynagon Ice-69
Blue-69
Red-69
Adrenaline Rush Bronze-7
Adrenaline Rush Ice Blue-7
Adrenaline Rush Red-7
Adrenaline Rush Silver-7
Forward Thinking-11
Preeminent Players-6
Team Checklists-9
98Pacific Omega-88
Red-88
Opening Day Issue-88
Championship Spotlight-4
Championship Spotlight Green-4
Championship Spotlight Red-4
Championship Spotlight Gold-4
EO Portraits-11
EO Portraits 1 of 1-11
Face to Face-6
Online-16
Planet Ice-24
Planet Ice Parallel-24
Prism-10
Toronto Spring Expo-88
98Panini Photocards-91
98Panini Photocards-92
98Panini Stickers-135
98Paramount-83
Copper-83
Emerald Green-83
Holo-Electric-83
Ice Blue-83
Silver-83
Hall of Fame Bound-5
Hall of Fame Bound Proofs-5
Ice Galaxy-5
Ice Galaxy Gold-5
Ice Galaxy Silver-5
Special Delivery Die-Cuts-9
Team Checklists Die-Cuts-9
98Post-9
98Revolution-53
Ice Shadow-53
Red-53
Chalk Talk Laser-Cuts-10
NHL Icons-6
Showstoppers-18
Three Pronged Attack-26
Three Pronged Attack Parallel-26
98SP Authentic-31
Power Shift-31
Authentics-3
Authentics-15
Authentics-16
Authentics-17
Sign of the Times-SY
Sign of the Times Gold-SY
Snapshots-SS3
Stat Masters-S23
Stat Masters-S24
Stat Masters-S25
98SPx Finite-30
98SPx Finite-93
98SPx Finite-156
98SPx Finite-175
Radiance-30
Radiance-93
Radiance-156
Radiance-175
Spectrum-30
Spectrum-93
Spectrum-156
Spectrum-175
98SPx Top Prospects-21
Radiance-21
Spectrum-21
Highlight Heroes-H14
Lasting Impressions-L19
Premier Stars-PS26
98Topps-175
O-Pee-Chee-175
98Topps Gold Label Class 1-31
Black-31
Black One of One-31
One of One-31
Red-31
Red One of One-31
98Topps Gold Label Class 2-31
98Topps Gold Label Class 2 Black-31
98Topps Gold Label Class 2 Black 1 of 1-31
98Topps Gold Label Class 2 One of One-31
98Topps Gold Label Class 2 Red-31
98Topps Gold Label Class 2 Red One of One-31
98Topps Gold Label Class 3-31
98Topps Gold Label Class 3 Black-31
98Topps Gold Label Class 3 Black 1 of 1-31
98Topps Gold Label Class 3 One of One-31
98Topps Gold Label Class 3 Red-31
98Topps Gold Label Class 3 Red One of One-31
98UD Choice-73
98UD Choice-310
Blow-Ups-2
Mini Bobbing Head-BH27
98UD Choice Preview-73
98UD Choice Prime Choice Reserve-73
98UD Choice Prime Choice Reserve-310
98UD Choice Reserve-73
98UD Choice Reserve-310
98UD Choice StarQuest Blue-SQ18
98UD Choice StarQuest Gold-SQ18
98UD Choice StarQuest Green-SQ18
98UD Choice StarQuest Red-SQ18
98UD3-60
98UD3-120
98UD3-180
Die-Cuts-60
Die-Cuts-120
Die-Cuts-180
98Upper Deck-85
98Upper Deck-209
98Upper Deck-389
98Upper Deck-390
Exclusives-85
Exclusives-209
Exclusives-389
Exclusives-390
Exclusives 1 of 1-85
Exclusives 1 of 1-209
Exclusives 1 of 1-389
Exclusives 1 of 1-390
Blow-Ups 5 x 7-85
Blow-Ups 5 x 7-P3
Blow-Ups 5 x 7-FF20
Blow-Ups 5 x 7-FT1
Blow-Ups 5 x 7-LS14
Fantastic Finishers-FF20
Fantastic Finishers Quantum 1-FF20
Fantastic Finishers Quantum 2-FF20
Fantastic Finishers Quantum 3-FF20
Frozen In Time-FT1
Frozen In Time Quantum 1-FT1
Frozen In Time Quantum 2-FT1
Frozen In Time Quantum 3-FT1
Generation Next-GN4
Generation Next-GN5
Generation Next-GN6
Generation Next Quantum 1-GN4
Generation Next Quantum 1-GN5
Generation Next Quantum 1-GN6
Generation Next Quantum 2-GN4
Generation Next Quantum 2-GN5
Generation Next Quantum 2-GN6
Generation Next Quantum 3-GN4
Generation Next Quantum 3-GN5
Generation Next Quantum 3-GN6
Lord Stanley's Heroes-LS14
Lord Stanley's Heroes Quantum 1-LS14
Lord Stanley's Heroes Quantum 2-LS14
Lord Stanley's Heroes Quantum 3-LS14
Profiles-P3
Profiles Quantum 1-P3
Profiles Quantum 2-P3
Profiles Quantum 3-P3
Gold Reserve-85
Gold Reserve-209
Gold Reserve-389
Gold Reserve-NNO2
98Upper Deck MVP-69
Gold Script-69
Silver Script-69
Super Script-69
Game Souvenirs-SY
Game Souvenirs-SYA
OT Heroes-OT1
ProSign-SY
Snipers-S11
Special Forces-F7
98Slovakian Eurotel-28
99SLU Hockey Classic Doubles-4
99SLU Hockey-17
99SLU Hockey Pro Action-70
99Aurora-55
Striped-55
Premiere Date-55
Premiere Date Striped-55
Canvas Creations-6
Championship Fever-13
Championship Fever Copper-13
Championship Fever Ice Blue-13
Championship Fever Silver-13
Complete Players-7
Complete Players Parallel-7
Complete Players Retail-7
Complete Players Retail Parallel-7
Styrotechs-10
99BAP Memorabilia-141
Gold-141
Silver-141
99BAP Update Teammates Jersey Cards-TM14
99BAP Update Teammates Jersey Cards-TM37
99BAP Update Teammates Jersey Cards-TM39
99BAP Update Teammates Jersey Cards-TM40
99BAP Millennium-88
Emerald-88
Ruby-88
Sapphire-88
Signatures-88
Signatures Gold-88
Jerseys-J30
Jersey Autographs-J30
Jersey and Stick Cards-JS30
Jersey Emblems-E30
Jersey Numbers-N30
Pearson-P8
Pearson Autographs-P8
Players of the Decade-D10
Players of the Decade Autographs-D10
99Black Diamond-36
Diamond Cut-36
Final Cut-36
A Piece of History-SY
A Piece of History Double-SY
A Piece of History Triple-SY
Diamonation-D19
Myriad-M7
99Crown Royale-53
Limited Series-53
Premiere Date-53
Card-Supials-11
Card-Supials Minis-11
Cramer's Choice Jumbos-6
Cramer's Choice Jumbos Dark Blue-6
Cramer's Choice Jumbos Gold-6
Cramer's Choice Jumbos Green-6
Cramer's Choice Jumbos Light Blue-6
Cramer's Choice Jumbos Purple-6
Cramer's Choice Jumbos Red-6
Gold Crown Die-Cuts Jumbos-4
Ice Elite-12
Ice Elite Parallel-12
Team Captain Die-Cuts-4
99Hasbro Starting Lineup Cards-17
99Jell-O Partners of Power-10
99Kraft Dinner-15
99Kraft Face Off Rivals-5
99McDonald's Upper Deck-MCD4
99McDonald's Upper Deck-MCD4R
Signatures-SY
99O-Pee-Chee-14
99O-Pee-Chee-286A
99O-Pee-Chee-286B
99O-Pee-Chee-286C
99O-Pee-Chee-286D
99O-Pee-Chee-286E
99O-Pee-Chee All-Topps-AT12
99O-Pee-Chee Chrome-14
99O-Pee-Chee Chrome-286A
99O-Pee-Chee Chrome-286B
99O-Pee-Chee Chrome-286C
99O-Pee-Chee Chrome-286D
99O-Pee-Chee Chrome-286E
99O-Pee-Chee Chrome All Topps-AT12
99O-Pee-Chee Chrome All-Topps Refractors-AT12
99O-Pee-Chee Chrome Ice Masters-IM15
99O-Pee-Chee Chrome Ice Masters Refractor-IM15
99O-Pee-Chee Chrome Refractors-14
99O-Pee-Chee Chrome Refractors-286A
99O-Pee-Chee Chrome Refractors-286B
99O-Pee-Chee Chrome Refractors-286C
99O-Pee-Chee Chrome Refractors-286D
99O-Pee-Chee Chrome Refractors-286E
99O-Pee-Chee Ice Masters-IM15
99Pacific-151
Copper-151
Emerald Green-151
Gold-151
Ice Blue-151
Premiere Date-151
Red-151
Center Ice-11
Center Ice Proofs-11
Cramer's Choice-7
Gold Crown Die-Cuts-18
Home and Away-7
Home and Away-7
Past and Present-13
Team Leaders-10
99Pacific Dynagon Ice-79
Blue-79
Copper-79
Gold-79
Premiere Date-79
2000 All-Star Preview-6
Checkmates American-7
Checkmates American-22
Checkmates Canadian-22
Lamplighter Net-Fusions-5
Lords of the Rink-7
99Pacific Omega-88
Copper-88
Gold-88
Ice Blue-88
Premiere Date-88
Cup Contenders-10
EO Portraits-9
EO Portraits 1/1-9
Game-Used Jerseys-3
NHL Generations-6
North American All-Stars-6
5 Star Talents-21
5 Star Talents Parallel-21
99Pacific Prism-54
Holographic Blue-54
Holographic Gold-54
Holographic Mirror-54
Holographic Purple-54
Premiere Date-54
Clear Advantage-9
Dial-a-Stats-7
Sno-Globe Die-Cuts-11
99Panini Stickers-231
99Paramount-88
Copper-88
Emerald-88
Gold-88
Holographic Emerald-88
Holographic Gold-88
Holographic Silver-88
Ice Blue-88
Premiere Date-88
Red-88
Silver-88
Hall of Fame Bound-6
Hall of Fame Bound Proofs-6
Ice Advantage-10
Ice Advantage Proofs-10
Ice Alliance-10
Personal Best-18
Toronto Fall Expo '99-88
99Revolution-56
Premiere Date-56
Red-56
Shadow Series-56
Ice Sculptures-5
NHL Icons-11
Ornaments-11
Top of the Line-14
Copper-56
Gold-56
CSC Silver-56
99SP Authentic-30
Buyback Signatures-66
Buyback Signatures-67
Buyback Signatures-68
Buyback Signatures-69
Honor Roll-HR3
Sign of the Times-SY
Sign of the Times Gold-SY
Special Forces-SF4
99SPx-55
Radiance-55
Spectrum-55
Prolifics-P9
SPXcitement-X4
Winning Materials-WM3
99Stadium Club-145
First Day Issue-145
One of a Kind-145
Printing Plates Black-145
Printing Plates Cyan-145
Printing Plates Magenta-145
Printing Plates Yellow-145
Capture the Action-CA25
Capture the Action Game View-CAG25
Chrome-40
Chrome Refractors-40
Chrome Oversized-16
Chrome Oversized Refractors-16
99Topps/OPC-14
99Topps/OPC-286A
99Topps/OPC-286B
99Topps/OPC-286C
99Topps/OPC-286D
99Topps/OPC-286E
All-Topps-AT12
Ice Masters-IM15
99Topps Stanley Cup Heroes-SC7
99Topps Stanley Cup Heroes Refractors-SC7
99Topps/OPC Chrome-14
99Topps/OPC Chrome-286A
99Topps/OPC Chrome-286B
99Topps/OPC Chrome-286C
99Topps/OPC Chrome-286D
99Topps/OPC Chrome-286E
Refractors-14
Refractors-286A
Refractors-286B
Refractors-286C
Refractors-286D
Refractors-286E
All-Topps-AT12
All-Topps Refractors-AT12
Ice Masters-IM15
Ice Masters Refractors-IM15
99Topps Gold Label Class 1-4
Black-4
Black One of One-4
One of One-4
Red-4
Red One of One-4
99Topps Gold Label Class 2-4
99Topps Gold Label Class 2 Black-4
99Topps Gold Label Class 2 Black 1 of 1-4
99Topps Gold Label Class 2 One of One-4
99Topps Gold Label Class 2 Red-4
99Topps Gold Label Class 2 Red One of One-4
99Topps Gold Label Class 3-4
99Topps Gold Label Class 3 Black-4
99Topps Gold Label Class 3 Black 1 of 1-4
99Topps Gold Label Class 3 One of One-4
99Topps Gold Label Class 3 Red-4
99Topps Gold Label Class 3 Red One of One-4
99Topps Gold Label Quest for the Cup-QC1
99Topps Gold Label Quest for the Cup One of One - QC1
99Topps Gold Label Quest 4 the Cup Black-QC1
99Topps Gold Label Quest for the Cup Black One of One -QC1
99Topps Gold Label Quest for the Cup Red-QC1
99Topps Gold Label Quest for the Cup Red One of One -QC1
99Topps Premier Plus-4
Parallel-4
Code Red-CR4
Feature Presentations-FP3
Premier Team-PT7
Premier Team Parallel-PT7
99Ultimate Victory-31
1/1-31
Parallel-31
Parallel 100-31
Frozen Fury-FF10
The Victors-V3
UV Extra-UV7
99Upper Deck-49
99Upper Deck-140
99Upper Deck-304
Exclusives-49
Exclusives-140
Exclusives-304
Exclusives 1 of 1-49
Exclusives 1 of 1-140
Exclusives 1 of 1-304
500 Goal Club-500SY
500 Goal Club-500SY
All-Star Class-AS10
All-Star Class Quantum Gold-AS10
All-Star Class Quantum Silver-AS10
Crunch Time-CT2
Crunch Time Quantum Gold-CT2
Crunch Time Quantum Silver-CT2
Fantastic Finishers-FF14
Fantastic Finishers Quantum Gold-FF14
Fantastic Finishers Quantum Silver-FF14
Game Jerseys-SY
Game Jerseys-SYS
Game Jerseys Series II-SY
Game Jerseys Series II-SYC
Game Jerseys Series II-SYS
Game Jersey Patch-SYP
Game Jersey Patch Series II-SYP
Game Jersey Patch Series II 1 of 1-SY-P1
Headed for the Hall-HOF4
Headed for the Hall Quantum Gold-HOF4
Headed for the Hall Quantum Silver-HOF4
Marquee Attractions-MA9
Marquee Attractions Quantum Gold-MA9
Marquee Attractions Quantum Silver-MA9
NHL Scrapbook-SB3
NHL Scrapbook Quantum Gold-SB3
NHL Scrapbook Quantum Silver-SB3
PowerDeck Inserts-PD4
Sixth Sense-SS8
Sixth Sense Quantum Gold-SS8
Sixth Sense Quantum Silver-SS8
99Upper Deck Century Legends-56
Century Collection-56
99Upper Deck Gold Reserve-49
99Upper Deck Gold Reserve-140
99Upper Deck Gold Reserve-304
Game-Used Souvenirs-GRSY
UD Authentics-SY
99Upper Deck HoloGrFx-21
Ausome-21
99Upper Deck MVP-69
Gold Script-69
Silver Script-69
Super Script-69
90's Snapshots-S7
Draw Your Own Trading Card-W5
Game-Used Souvenirs-GU11
Game-Used Souvenirs-GU28
Hands of Gold-H10
ProSign-SY
Talent-MVP6
99Upper Deck MVP SC Edition-65
Gold Script-65
Gold Script-220
Silver Script-65
Silver Script-220
Super Script-65
Super Script-220
Clutch Performers-CP4
Game-Used Souvenirs-GUSY
Golden Memories-GM5
Great Combinations-GCYO
Great Combinations Parallel-GCYO
ProSign-SY
99Upper Deck Ovation-24
99Upper Deck Ovation-87
Standing Ovation-24
Standing Ovation-87
Lead Performers-LP14
99Upper Deck PowerDeck-11
Auxiliary-11
Auxiliary 1 of 1-11
Time Capsule-T8
Time Capsule Auxiliary-T8
Time Capsule Auxiliary 1 of 1-T8
99Upper Deck Retro-27
Gold-27
Platinum-27
Distant Replay-DR5
Distant Replay Level 2-DR5
Inkredible-SY
Inkredible Level 2-SY
Turn of the Century-TC5
99Upper Deck Victory-96
99Upper Deck Victory-98
99Upper Deck Victory-320
99Wayne Gretzky Hockey-60
Great Heroes-GH6
Will to Win-W2
99Slovakian Challengers-18
00McFarlane Hockey-60
00SLU Hockey-240
00Aurora-54
Pinstripes-54
Pinstripes Premiere Date-54
Premiere Date-54
Canvas Creations-5
Championship Fever-12
Championship Fever Copper-12
Championship Fever Platinum Blue-12
Championship Fever Silver-12
Dual Game-Worn Jerseys-3
Game-Worn Jerseys-3
Game-Worn Jersey Patches-3
Styrotechs-6B
00BAP Memorabilia-124
Emerald-124
Ruby-124
Sapphire-124
Promos-124
Jersey Cards-J29
Jersey Emblems-E29
Jersey Numbers-N29
Jersey and Stick Cards-JS29
Patent Power Jerseys-PP2
00BAP Mem Chicago Sportsfest Copper-124
00BAP Memorabilia Chicago Sportsfest Blue-124
00BAP Memorabilia Chicago Sportsfest Gold-124
00BAP Memorabilia Chicago Sportsfest Ruby-124
00BAP Memorabilia Chicago Sun-Times Ruby-124
00BAP Memorabilia Chicago Sun-Times Gold-124
00BAP Mem Chicago Sun-Times Sapphire-124
00BAP Mem Toronto Fall Expo Copper-124
00BAP Memorabilia Toronto Fall Expo Gold-124
00BAP Memorabilia Toronto Fall Expo Ruby-124
00BAP Memorabilia Update Teammates-TM13
00BAP Memorabilia Update Teammates-TM29
00BAP Memorabilia Update Teammates Gold-TM13
00BAP Memorabilia Update Teammates Gold-TM29
00BAP Parkhurst 2000-P146
00BAP Signature Series-11
Emerald-11
Ruby-11
Sapphire-11
Autographs-114
Autographs Gold-114
Franchise Players-F11
He Shoots-He Scores Points-20
He Shoots-He Scores Prizes-6
Jersey Cards-J30
Jersey and Stick Cards-GSJ30
Jersey Cards Autographs-J30
Jersey Emblems-E30
Jersey Numbers-IN30
00BAP Ultimate Memorabilia Autographs-30
Gold-30
00BAP Ultimate Memorabilia Active Eight-AE1
00BAP Ultimate Memorabilia Active Eight-AE2
00BAP Ultimate Memorabilia Captain's C-C1
00BAP Ultimate Mem Dynasty Jerseys-D13
00BAP Ultimate Mem Dynasty Emblems-D13
00BAP Ultimate Mem Game-Used Jerseys-GJ30
00BAP Ultimate Mem Game-Used Emblems-E26
00BAP Ultimate Mem Game-Used Numbers-N26
00BAP Ultimate Mem Game-Used Sticks-GS30
00BAP Ultimate Mem Magnificent Ones-ML1
00BAP Ultimate Mem Magnificent Ones Autos-ML1
00BAP Ultimate Memorabilia Retro-Active-RA5
00BAP Ultimate Memorabilia Teammates-TM1
00BAP Ultimate Memorabilia Teammates-TM3
00BAP Ultimate Memorabilia Teammates-TM4
00BAP Ultimate Memorabilia Teammates-TM31
00Black Diamond-23
00Black Diamond-87
Gold-23
Gold-87
Diamond Skills-IC3
00Crown Royale-41
Ice Blue-41
Limited Series-41
Premiere Date-41
Red-41
Jewels of the Crown-14
Landmarks-5
Now Playing-8
00Kraft-12
00McDonald's Pacific-15
Blue-15
Dial-A-Stats-2
Game Jerseys-5
00O-Pee-Chee-22
00O-Pee-Chee-329
00O-Pee-Chee Parallel-22
00O-Pee-Chee Parallel-329
00Pacific-162
Copper-162
Gold-162
Ice Blue-162
Premiere Date-162
2001: Ice Odyssey-9
Cramer's Choice-5
Jerseys-8
Jersey Patches-8
Gold Crown Die Cuts-15
North American Stars-6
Reflections-10
00Pacific 2001: Ice Odyssey Anaheim Ntnl-9
00Panini Stickers-156
00Paramount-93
Copper-93
Gold-93
Holo-Gold-93
Holo-Silver-93
Ice Blue-93
Premiere Date-93
Epic Scope-11
Freeze Frame-16
Hall of Fame Bound-6
Hall of Fame Bound Canvas Proofs-6
Hall of Fame Bound Proofs-6
Sub Zero-5
Sub Zero Gold-5
Sub Zero Red-5
00Private Stock-38
Gold-38
Premiere Date-38
Retail-38
Silver-38
Artist's Canvas-12
Artist's Canvas Proofs-12
Extreme Action-9
PS-2001 Action-23
PS-2001 Stars-13
Reserve-10
00Revolution-55
Blue-55
Premiere Date-55
Red-55
Ice Immortals-11
NHL Game Gear-6
NHL Icons-12
Stat Masters-6
00SP Authentic-31
BuyBacks-102
BuyBacks-103
BuyBacks-104
BuyBacks-105
BuyBacks-106
BuyBacks-107
BuyBacks-108
BuyBacks-109
BuyBacks-110
BuyBacks-111
BuyBacks-112
BuyBacks-113
Sign of the Times-SY
Sign of the Times-Y/L
Sign of the Times-HLY
Significant Stars-ST3
00SP Game Used-21
Patch Cards-P-SY
Tools of the Game-SY
Tools of the Game Exclusives-SY
Tools of the Game Combos-C-YH
Tools of the Game Autographed Bronze-A-SY
Tools of the Game Autographed Silver-A-SY
Tools of the Game Autographed Gold-A-SY
00SPx-25
00SPx-86
Spectrum-25
Spectrum-86
Prolifics-P4
Winning Materials-SY
Winning Materials-WYZ
Winning Materials Autographs-SSY
00Stadium Club-24
Beam Team-BT4
Special Forces-SF6
00Titanium-35
Blue-35
Gold-35
Premiere Date-35
Red-35
Retail-35
Game Gear-17
Game Gear-98
Game Gear Patches-98
00Titanium Draft Day Edition-42
00Topps/OPC-22
00Topps/OPC-329
Parallel-22
Parallel-329
Combos-TC9
Combos Jumbos-TC9
Hobby Masters-HM10
Own the Game-OTG10
1000 Point Club-PC2
00Topps Chrome-21
OPC Refractors-21
Refractors-21
Combos-TC9
Combos Refractors-TC9
Hobby Masters Refractors-HM10
1000 Point Club Refractors-2
00Topps Gold Label Class 1-79
Gold-79
00Topps Gold Label Class 2-79
00Topps Gold Label Class 2 Gold-79
00Topps Gold Label Class 3-79
00Topps Gold Label Class 3 Gold-79
00Topps Gold Label Bullion-B3

00Topps Gold Label Bullion One to One-B3
00Topps Gold Label Golden Greats-GG5
00Topps Gold Label Golden Greats 1 to 1-GG5
00Topps Heritage-10
00Topps Heritage-216
00Topps Heritage-238
Chrome Parallel-10
Arena Relics-OSA-SY
Heroes-HH3
Original Six Relics-OSS-SY
00Topps Premier Plus-58
Blue Ice-58
Trophy Tribute-TT9
World Premier-WP14
00Topps Stars-4
00Topps Stars-139
Blue-4
Blue-139
All-Star Authority-ASA8
Progression-P3
Walk of Fame-WF7
00UD Heroes-146
Game-Used Twigs-T-SY
Game-Used Twigs Gold-C-HY
NHL Leaders-L4
Second Season Heroes-SS5
Signs of Greatness-SY
00UD Pros and Prospects-32
00UD Pros and Prospects-90
Championship Rings-CR3
Game Jersey Autograph Exclusives-S-SY
Game Jersey Autographs-S-SY
NHL Passion-NP3
00UD Reserve-32
Buyback Autographs-11
Buyback Autographs-12
Buyback Autographs-13
Buyback Autographs-14
Buyback Autographs-15
Buyback Autographs-16
Buyback Autographs-17
Buyback Autographs-18
Buyback Autographs-19
Buyback Autographs-20
Buyback Autographs-21
Buyback Autographs-22
Power Portfolios-PP3
The Big Ticket-BT4
00Upper Deck-179
00Upper Deck-293
00Upper Deck-409
Exclusives Tier 1-179
Exclusives Tier 1-293
Exclusives Tier 1-409
Exclusives Tier 2-179
Exclusives Tier 2-293
Exclusives Tier 2-409
Dignitaries-D5
e-Cards-EC3
e-Card Prizes-ASY
e-Card Prizes-ESY
e-Card Prizes-SESY
Fantastic Finishers-FF5
Frozen in Time-FT4
Game Jersey Autographs-HSY
Game Jersey Autographs-HSY
Game Jersey Autographs Exclusives-ESY
Game Jersey Autographs Exclusives-ESSY
Game Jersey Combos-DYS
Game Jersey Patches-PSY
Game Jersey Patches-SYP
Game Jersey Patch Autographs Exclusives-SYP
Game Jersey Patch Autographs Exclusives-PSSY
Game Jersey Patch Exclusives Series II-ESY
Gate Attractions-GA6
Lord Stanley's Heroes-L4
Triple Threat-TT5
00Upper Deck Ice-18
Immortals-18
Legends-18
Stars-18
Champions-IC3
Clear Cut Autographs-SY
Rink Favorites-FP5
00Upper Deck Legends-46
00Upper Deck Legends-47
00Upper Deck Legends-135
Legendary Collection Bronze-46
Legendary Collection Bronze-47
Legendary Collection Bronze-135
Legendary Collection Gold-46
Legendary Collection Gold-47
Legendary Collection Gold-135
Legendary Collection Silver-46
Legendary Collection Silver-47
Legendary Collection Silver-135
Epic Signatures-SY
Essence of the Game-EG8
Legendary Game Jerseys-JSY
Playoff Heroes-PH2
Supreme Milestones-SM5
00Upper Deck MVP-70
00Upper Deck MVP-220
Excellence-ME5
First Stars-70
Game-Used Souvenirs-GSSY
Mark of Excellence-SGYV
Second Stars-70
Super Game-Used Souvenirs-GSSY
Third Stars-70
Third Stars-220
Top Playmakers-TP5
Valuable Commodities-VC5
00Upper Deck Victory-81
00Upper Deck Victory-83
00Upper Deck Victory-249
00Upper Deck Victory-300
00Upper Deck Vintage-125
00Upper Deck Vintage-136
00Upper Deck Vintage-137
All UD Team-UD7
Dynasty: A Piece of History-YO
Dynasty: A Piece of History Gold-YO
National Heroes-NH11
Original 6: A Piece of History-OSY
Original 6: A Piece of History Gold-OSY
Star Tandems-S3A
00Vanguard-41
Cosmic Force-5
High Voltage-14
High Voltage Gold-14
High Voltage Green-14
High Voltage Red-14
High Voltage Silver-14
Holographic Gold-41
Holographic Purple-41
In Focus-9
Pacific Proofs-41
Press East/West-7
00Czech Stadion-85
01McFarlane Hockey Inserts-60
01McFarlane Hockey Inserts-65
01Atomic-40
Blue-40
Gold-40
Premiere Date-40
Red-40
Blast-4
Core Players-5
Jerseys-26
Patches-26
Power Play-14
Team Nucleus-6
01BAP Memorabilia-15
Emerald-15
Ruby-15
Sapphire-15
All-Star Jerseys-ASJ36
All-Star Emblems-ASE36
All-Star Numbers-ASN36
All-Star Jersey Doubles-DASJ15
All-Star Teammates-AST19
All-Star Teammates-AST22
All-Star Teammates-AST24
All-Star Teammates-AST43
Country of Origin-C09
500 Goal Scorers-GS7
He Shoots-He Scores Points-17
He Shoots-He Scores Prizes-4
Patented Power-PP6
01BAP Signature Series Certified 100-C44
01BAP Signature Series Certified 50-C44
01BAP Signature Series Certified 1 of 1's-C44
01BAP Signature Series Autographs-LSY
01BAP Signature Series Autographs Gold-LSY
01BAP Signature Series 500 Goal Scorers-2
01BAP Signature Series 500 Goal Scorers-SY
01BAP Sig Series 500 Goal Scorers Autos-2
01BAP Signature Series Franchise Jerseys-FP-11
01BAP Sig Series He Shoots/Scores Points-20
01BAP Sig Series He Shoots/Scores Prizes-1
01BAP Sig Series International Medals-IG-8
01BAP Signature Series Jerseys-GJ-23
01BAP Signature Series Jersey Autographs-GUSY
01BAP Sig Series Jersey and Stick Cards-GSJ-23
01BAP Signature Series Emblems-GUE-22
01BAP Signature Series Numbers-ITN-22
01BAP Signature Series Teammates-TM-11
01BAP Ultimate Memorabilia Active Eight-3
01BAP Ultimate Memorabilia Active Eight-8
01BAP Ultimate Mem All-Star History-36
01BAP Ultimate Memorabilia Autographs-33
01BAP Ultimate Mem Autographs Gold-33
01BAP Ultimate Memorabilia Captain's C-15
01BAP Ultimate Memorabilia Cornerstones-4
01BAP Ultimate Memorabilia Dynamic Duos-6
01BAP Ultimate Memorabilia Emblems-22
01BAP Ultimate Mem 500 Goal Scorers-13
01BAP Ultimate Mem 500 Goal Scorers Autos-24
01BAP Ultimate Mem 500 Goal Jerseys/Stick-13
01BAP Ultimate Mem 500 Goal Emblems-13
01BAP Ultimate Memorabilia Jerseys-22
01BAP Ultimate Mem Jerseys and Sticks-22
01BAP Ultimate Memorabilia Numbers-22
01BAP Ultimate Memorabilia Name Plates-15
01BAP Ultimate Mem Prototypical Players-7
01BAP Ultimate Memorabilia Retro Trophies-13
01BAP Update Passing the Torch-PTT3
01Bowman YoungStars-35
Gold-35
Ice Cubed-35
01Crown Royale-57
Blue-57
Premiere Date-57
Red-57
Retail-57
All-Star Honors-10
Crowning Achievement-15
Jewels of the Crown-12
Legendary Heroes-4
Triple Threads-11
01EA Sports-9
01eTopps-16
01McDonald's Pacific-15
Hockey Greats-5
Jersey Patches Silver-11
Jersey Patches Gold-11
01O-Pee-Chee-2
01O-Pee-Chee Heritage Parallel-2
01O-Pee-Chee Heritage Parallel Limited-2
01O-Pee-Chee Premier Parallel-2
01O-Pee-Chee Jumbos-2
01Pacific-152
01Pacific-410
Extreme LTD-152
Gold-410
Hobby LTD-152
Premiere Date-152
Retail LTD-152
Cramer's Choice-5
Gold Crown Die-Cuts-10
01Pacific Adrenaline-70
Blue-70
Premiere Date-70
Red-70
Retail-70
Blade Runners-5
Jerseys-16
World Beaters-6
01Pacific Arena Exclusives-152
01Pacific Arena Exclusives-410
01Pacific Heads-Up-39
Blue-39
Premiere Date-39
Red-39
Silver-39
HD NHL-5
Rink Immortals-6
Stat Masters-7
01Parkhurst-31
Gold-31
Silver-31
500 Goal Scorers-PGS7
He Shoots-He Scores Points-15
He Shoots-He Scores Prizes-13
Heroes-H2
Jerseys-PJ18
Jersey and Stick-PSJ1
Milestones-M14
Milestones-M17
Milestones-M22U
Milestones-M33
Sticks-PS18
Teammates-T1
Teammates-T23
Teammates-T28
World Class Jerseys-WCJ1
World Class Emblems-WCE1
World Class Numbers-WCN1
Waving the Flag-3
01Private Stock-38
Gold-38
Premiere Date-38
Retail-38
Silver-38
Game Gear-45
Game Gear Patches-45
01Private Stock Pacific Nights-38
01Private Stock PS-2002-30
01Private Stock Reserve-S5
01SP Authentic-28
01SP Authentic-97
Limited-28
Limited-97
Limited Gold-28
Limited Gold-97
Buybacks-32
Buybacks-33
Buybacks-34
Jerseys-NNSY
Sign of the Times-SY
Sign of the Times-HY
Sign of the Times-YA
Sign of the Times-HGY
01SP Game Used-18
Authentic Fabric-AFSY
Authentic Fabric-DFYO
Authentic Fabric-TFYSF
Authentic Fabric-GYSL
Authentic Fabric-YSFO
Authentic Fabric Gold-AFSY
Inked Sweaters-SSY
Inked Sweaters-ISSY
Inked Sweaters-DSYH
Patches-PSY
Patches-CPSY
Patches-CPYF
Patches-TPKYB
Patches-TPLGY
Patches Signed-SPSY
Tools of the Game-TSY
Tools of the Game Signed-STSY
Tools of the Game Signed-SCPY
Tools of the Game Signed-SCTY
01SPx-22
01SPx-75
01SPx-85
01SPx-NNO
Hidden Treasures-TTYLS
Hockey Treasures-HTSY
Hockey Treasures Autographed-STSY
Yzerman Tribute-SY1
Yzerman Tribute-SY2
Yzerman Tribute-SY3
Yzerman Tribute-SY4
Yzerman Tribute-SY5
Yzerman Tribute-SY6
Yzerman Tribute-SY7
Yzerman Tribute-SY8
Yzerman Tribute-SY9
Yzerman Tribute-SY10
Yzerman Tribute-SY11
Yzerman Tribute-SY12
Yzerman Tribute-SY13
Yzerman Tribute-SY14
Yzerman Tribute-SY15
Yzerman Tribute-SY16
Yzerman Tribute-SY17
Yzerman Tribute-SY18
Yzerman Tribute-SY19
Yzerman Tribute-SY20
Yzerman Tribute-SY21
Yzerman Tribute-SY22
Yzerman Tribute-SY23
Yzerman Tribute-SY24
Yzerman Tribute-SY25
Yzerman Tribute-SY26
01Stadium Club-24
Award Winners-24
Master Photos-24
Gallery-G37
Gallery Gold-G37
Heart and Soul-HS3
NHL Passport-NHLP20
Perennials-P8
01Titanium-54
Hobby Parallel-54
Premiere Date-54
Retail-54
Retail Parallel-54
Saturday Knights-7
Three-Star Selections-15
01Topps-2
Heritage Parallel-2
Heritage Parallel Limited-2
OPC Parallel-2
Shot Masters-SM6
01Topps Chrome-2
Refractors-2
Black Border Refractors-2
01Topps Heritage-38
Refractors-38
01Topps Reserve-6
01UD Challenge for the Cup-28
Century Men-CM3
Cornerstones-CR5
Future Famers-FF5
Jerseys-FPSY
Jerseys-UCSY
Jersey Autographs-FPYZ
01UD Honor Roll-20
01UD Honor Roll-50
Defense First-DF3
Student of the Game-SG4
01UD Mask Collection-33
Gold-33
Double Patches-DPSY
Dual Jerseys-PMYR
Jerseys-J-SY
Jersey and Patch-JPSY
01UD Playmakers-38
01UD Premier Collection-21
Dual Jerseys-DSY
Dual Jerseys Black-DSY
Jerseys-GSY
Jerseys Black-G-SY
Signatures-SY
Signatures Black-SY
01UD Stanley Cup Champs-57
Jerseys-T-SY
Pieces of Glory-G-SY
Sticks-S-SY
01UD Top Shelf-15
Jerseys-SY
Jersey Autographs-SY
Patches-PSY
Sticks-SSY
Sticks Gold-SSY
01Upper Deck-61
01Upper Deck-179
01Upper Deck-216
Exclusives-61
Exclusives-179
Exclusives-216
Crunch Timers-CT6
Franchise Cornerstones-FC10
Game Jerseys-YSF
Game Jerseys Series II-FJSY
Game Jerseys Series II-SSSY
Game Jerseys Series II-DJYL
Game Jerseys Series II-TJYFS
Game Jersey Autographs-SSY
Game Jersey Autographs-SJSY
Gate Attractions-GA12
Leaders of the Pack-LP5
Patches-PSY
Patches Series II-PLSY
Patches Series II-FN3Y
Patches Series II-NASY
Pride of a Nation-PNSY
Pride of a Nation-DPYS
Pride of a Nation-TPYRL
Skilled Stars-SS15
Tandems-T3
EA Sports Gold-9
01Upper Deck Ice-15
Autographs-SY
Combos-C-SY
Combos Gold-G-SY
First Rounders-F-SY
01Upper Deck Legends Milestones-MSY
01Upper Deck Legends Milestones Platinum-MSY
01Upper Deck MVP-64
01Upper Deck MVP-219
Souvenirs-S-SY
Souvenirs Gold-S-SY
Talent-MT6
Valuable Commodities-VC1
01Upper Deck Victory-123
01Upper Deck Victory-404
Gold-123
Gold-404
01Upper Deck Vintage-88
01Upper Deck Vintage-96
Jerseys-SCSY
Next In Line-NLHY
01Vanguard-38
Blue-38
Red-38
East Meets West-7
In Focus-5
Memorabilia-13
Memorabilia-38
One of Ones-38
Patches-38
Premiere Date-38
Proofs-38
Quebec Tournament Heroes-4
V-Team-14
02McFarlane Hockey Team Canada-20
02Atomic-41
Blue-41
Gold-41
Red-41
Cold Fusion-12
Hobby Parallel-41
National Pride-C7
02BAP All-Star Edition-98
02BAP All-Star Edition-99
He Shoots-He Scores Points-20
He Shoots-He Score Prizes-30
Jerseys-98
Jerseys-99
Jerseys Gold-98
Jerseys Gold-99
Jerseys Silver-98
Jerseys Silver-99
02BAP First Edition-151
02BAP First Edition-315
02BAP First Edition-351
02BAP First Edition-426H
Debut Jerseys-10
He Shoots-He Score Points-16
He Shoots-He Scores Prizes-7
Jerseys-151
02BAP Memorabilia-1
02BAP Memorabilia-211
Emerald-1
Emerald-211
Ruby-1
Ruby-211
Sapphire-1
Sapphire-211
All-Star Jerseys-ASJ-60
All-Star Emblems-ASE-25
All-Star Numbers-ASN-25
All-Star Teammates-AST-7
All-Star Teammates-AST-17
Franchise Players-FP-11
He Shoots-He Scores Points-20
He Shoots-He Scores Prizes-1
Mini Stanley Cups-35
NHL All-Star Game-1
NHL All-Star Game-211
NHL All-Star Game Blue-1
NHL All-Star Game Blue-211
NHL All-Star Game Green-1
NHL All-Star Game Green-211
NHL All-Star Game Red-1
NHL All-Star Game Red-211
Stanley Cup Champions-SCC-5
Stanley Cup Playoffs-SC-14
Stanley Cup Playoffs-SC-31
Teammates-TM-1
02BAP Memorabilia Toronto Fall Expo-1
02BAP Memorabilia Toronto Fall Expo-211
02BAP NHL All-Star History-36
02BAP Signature Series-112
Autographs-112
Autograph Buybacks 1998-46
Autograph Buybacks 1999-88
Autographs Gold-112
Complete Jersey-CJ3
Franchise Players-FJ11
Golf-GS90
Jerseys-SGJ2
Jersey Autographs-SGJ2
Team Quads-TQ13
Triple Memorabilia-TM3
02BAP Ultimate Memorabilia Active Eight-1
02BAP Ultimate Memorabilia Active Eight-4
02BAP Ultimate Memorabilia Active Eight-5
02BAP Ultimate Memorabilia Active Eight-8
02BAP Ultimate Memorabilia Captains-7
02BAP Ultimate Memorabilia Conn Smythe-26
02BAP Ultimate Memorabilia Dynamic Duos-4
02BAP Ultimate Mem Dynasty Jerseys-18
02BAP Ultimate Mem Dynasty Emblems-18
02BAP Ultimate Mem Dynasty Numbers-18
02BAP Ultimate Mem Global Dominators-7
02BAP Ultimate Memorabilia Hat Tricks-18
02BAP Ultimate Memorabilia Jerseys-36
02BAP Ultimate Mem Jersey and Stick-22
02BAP Ultimate Mem Lifetime Achievers-15
02BAP Ultimate Mem Magnificent Ones-2
02BAP Ultimate Mem Magnificent Ones Autos-2
02BAP Ultimate Memorabilia Nameplates-9
02BAP Ultimate Memorabilia Numbers-18
02BAP Ultimate Memorabilia Numerology-21
02BAP Ultimate Mem Playoff Scorers-5
02BAP Ultimate Mem Playoff Scorers-20
02BAP Ultimate Memorabilia Retro Trophies-7
02Between the Pipes Nightmares-GN4
02Bowman YoungStars-47
Gold-47
Silver-47
02Crown Royale-37
Blue-37
Red-37
Retail-37
Lords of the Rink-10
Royal Portraits-6
02eTopps-21
02ITG Used-30
02ITG Used-130
Franchise Players-F11
Franchise Players Autographs-F11
Franchise Players Gold-F11
International Experience-IE4
International Experience Gold-IE4
Jerseys-GUJ2
Jersey Autographs-GUJ2
Jerseys Gold-GUJ2
Emblems-E2
Jersey and Stick-SJ2
Jersey and Stick Gold-SJ2
Teammates-T5
Teammates Gold-T5
Triple Memorabilia-TM17
Triple Memorabilia Gold-TM17
02McDonald's Pacific-13
Atomic-4
Salt Lake Gold-5
02O-Pee-Chee-4
02O-Pee-Chee Jumbos-7
02O-Pee-Chee Premier Blue Parallel-4
02O-Pee-Chee Premier Red Parallel-4
02O-Pee-Chee Factory Set-4
02Pacific-137
Blue-137
Red-137
Cramer's Choice-7
Lamplighters-7
Main Attractions-7
Maximum Impact-13
02Pacific Calder-29
Silver-29
Hardware Heroes-6
02Pacific Chicago National *-6
02Pacific Complete-500
Red-500
02Pacific Exclusive-68
Etched in Stone-6
Maximum Overdrive-10
02Pacific Heads-Up-48
Blue-48
Purple-48
Red-48
Etched in Time-10
Postseason Picks-8
Stat Masters-9
02Pacific Quest for the Cup-37
Gold-37
Raising the Cup-8
02Parkhurst-100
Bronze-100
Gold-100
Silver-100
Franchise Players-FP11
Heroes-NH2
Heroes-NH4
Heroes-NH10
He Shoots-He Scores Points-17
He Shoots-He Scores Prizes-14
Jerseys-GJ5
Mario's Mates-MM2
Patented Power-PP2
Stick and Jerseys-SJ5
Teammates-TT4
02Parkhurst Retro-22
Minis-22
Franchise Players-RF11
He Shoots-He Scores Points-20
He Shoots-He Scores Prizes-1
Jerseys-RJ22
Jersey and Sticks-RSJ15
Memorabilia-RM14
Nicknames-RN22
02Private Stock Reserve-121
Red-121
Retail-121
Elite-4
Patches-121
02SP Authentic-36
02SP Authentic-96
Beckett Promos-36
Sign of the Times-SY
Sign of the Times-YH
Sign of the Times-YZ
Super Premiums-SPSY
Super Premiums-DPYS
Super Premiums-TPGLY
02SP Game Used-17
Authentic Fabrics-AFSY
Authentic Fabrics-CFYR
Authentic Fabrics Gold-AFSY
Authentic Fabrics Gold-CFYR
Authentic Fabrics Rainbow-AFSY
Authentic Fabrics Rainbow-CFYR
First Rounder Patches-SY
Piece of History-PHSY
Piece of History Gold-PHSY
Piece of History Rainbow-PHSY
Signature Style-SY
02SPx-26
02SPx-90
02SPx-128
Spectrum Gold-26
Spectrum Gold-90
Spectrum Silver-26
Spectrum Silver-90
Milestones-MSY
Milestones Gold-SY
Milestones Silver-SY
Smooth Skaters-SY
Smooth Skaters Gold-SY
Smooth Skaters Silver-SY
Winning Materials-WMSY
Winning Materials Gold-SY
Winning Materials Silver-SY
Xtreme Talents-SY
Xtreme Talents Gold-SY
Xtreme Talents Silver-SY
02Stadium Club-38
Silver Decoy Cards-38
Proofs-38
Beam Team-BT1
02Titanium-40
Blue-40
Red-40
Retail-40
Saturday Knights-4
Shadows-5
02Topps-4
OPC Blue Parallel-4
OPC Red Parallel-4
Topps/OPC Hometown Heroes-HHU4
Factory Set-4
Factory Set Hometown Heroes-HHU4
02Topps Chrome-4
Black Border Refractors-4
Refractors-4
02Topps Heritage-32
Chrome Parallel-32
USA Test Parallel-32
02Topps Total-289
Team Checklists-TTC10
Topps-TT11
02UD Artistic Impressions-31
Gold-31
02UD Artistic Impressions Beckett Promos-31
02UD Artistic Impressions Common Ground-CG19
02UD Artistic Impress Common Ground Gold-CG19
02UD Artistic Impressions Great Depiction-GD8
02UD Artistic Impress Great Depiction Gld-GD8
02UD Artistic Impressions Performers-SSSY
02UD Artistic Impressions Performers Gold-SSSY
02UD Artistic Impressions Retrospectives-R31
02UD Artistic Impressions Retrospect Gold-R31
02UD Artistic Impress Retrospect Silver-R31
02Upper Deck Collectors Club-NHL7
Jerseys-SY-J
02UD Foundations-28
02UD Foundations-113
1000 Point Club-SY
1000 Point Club-YZ
1000 Point Club Gold-SY
1000 Point Club Silver-SY
Canadian Heroes-CSY
Canadian Heroes Gold-CSY
Canadian Heroes Silver-C-SY
Milestones-NSY
Milestones Gold-NSY
Milestones Silver-N-SY
Playoff Performers-PSY
Playoff Performers Gold-PSY
Playoff Performers Silver-P-SY
02UD Honor Roll-24
02UD Honor Roll-81
Grade A Jerseys-TYFS
Signature Class-SY
Students of the Game-SG13
02UD Mask Collection-32
02UD Mask Collection Beckett Promos-32
02UD Mask Collection Instant Offense-IOSY
02UD Mask Collection Patches-PGSY
02UD Piece of History-32
02UD Piece of History-95
Awards Collection-AC12
Hockey Beginnings-HB3
Marks of Distinction-SY
Patches-PHSY
Simply the Best-SB4
Stellar Stitches-SSSY
02UD Premier Collection-21
Jerseys Bronze-SY
Jerseys Bronze-SY
Jerseys Gold-SY
Jerseys Gold-SY
Jerseys Silver-SY
Jerseys Silver-SY
NHL Patches-SY1
Patches-PSY
Signatures Bronze-SSY
Signatures Gold-SSY
Signatures Silver-SSY
02UD Top Shelf-29
Clutch Performers-CPSY
Dual Player Jerseys-RYK
Goal Oriented-GOSY
Hardware Heroes-HFYGC
Hardware Heroes-HYNLR
Milestones Jerseys-MGBYM
Milestones Jerseys-MGHLY
Milestones Jerseys-MMHYR
Milestones Jerseys-MSYVR
Shooting Stars-SHSY
Signatures-SY
Sweet Sweaters-SWSY
Triple Jerseys-HTKYI
Triple Jerseys-TSSYH
02Upper Deck-61
02Upper Deck-180
02Upper Deck-186
Exclusives-61
Exclusives-180
Exclusives-186
Blow-Ups-C13
CHL Graduates-CGSY
CHL Graduates Gold-CGSY
Difference Makers-SY
First Class-UDSY
First Class Gold-UDSY
Game Jersey Autographs-SY
Game Jersey Series II-GJSY
Gifted Greats-GG8
Letters of Note-LNSY
Letters of Note Gold-LNSY
Patch Card Numbers-SY
Patchwork-PWSY
Playbooks Series II-YF
Reaching Fifty-50SY
Reaching Fifty Gold-50SY
Shooting Stars-SS7
02Upper Deck Classic Portraits-34
Etched in Time-ET5
Genuine Greatness-GG4
Headliners-YH
Headliners Limited-YH
Hockey Royalty-SYL
Hockey Royalty Limited-SYL
Starring Cast-CSY
Starring Cast Limited-CSY
02Upper Deck MVP-67
02Upper Deck MVP-190
Gold-67
Gold-190
Classics-67
Classics-189
Golden Classics-67
Golden Classics-190
Vital Forces-VF9
02Upper Deck Rookie Update-34
02Upper Deck Rookie Update-108
Autographs-SY
Jerseys-DSY
Jerseys-SYS
Jerseys Gold-DSY
Jerseys Gold-SYS
02Upper Deck Victory-77
Bronze-77
Gold-77
Silver-77
National Pride-NP6
02Upper Deck Vintage-88
02Upper Deck Vintage-271
02Upper Deck Vintage-295
Jerseys-FSSY
Jerseys-OSSY
Jerseys Gold-FS-SY
Tall Boys-T24
Tall Boys Gold-T24
02Vanguard-40
LTD-40
East Meets West-3
In Focus-6
V-Team-10
02UD SuperStars *-82
Gold-82
City All-Stars Triple Jersey-JSB
Keys to the City-K9
Legendary Leaders Dual Jersey-SYJH
Legendary Leaders Triple Jersey-MPS
03McFarlane Hockey Red Wings-10
03McFarlane Hockey-90
03BAP Memorabilia-92
Emerald-92
Gold-92
Ruby-92
Sapphire-92
All-Star Complete Jerseys-ASCJ10
All-Star Emblems-ASE-20
All-Star Jerseys-ASJ-39
All-Star Numbers-ASN-20
Brush with Greatness-24
Brush with Greatness Contest Cards-24
He Shoots-He Scores Points-9
He Shoots-He Scores Prizes-20
Jersey and Stick-SJ-29
Jerseys-GJ-38
Jersey Autographs-GJ-38
Practice Jerseys-PMP11
Stanley Cup Playoffs-SCP-1
03BAP Ultimate Memorabilia Autographs-131
Gold-131
03BAP Ultimate Mem Auto Jerseys-131
03BAP Ultimate Mem Auto Emblems-131
03BAP Ultimate Mem Auto Sticks-131
03BAP Ultimate Memorabilia Active Eight-6
03BAP Ultimate Memorabilia Active Eight-8
03BAP Ultimate Memorabilia Career Year-6
03BAP Ultimate Mem Complete Jersey-8
03BAP Ultimate Mem Complete Jersey Gold-8
03BAP Ultimate Mem Complete Package-2
03BAP Ultimate Mem Complete Package Gold-2
03BAP Ultimate Memorabilia Cornerstones-7
03BAP Ultimate Memorabilia Dynamic Duos-3
03BAP Ultimate Memorabilia Emblems-28
03BAP Ultimate Memorabilia Emblems Gold-28
03BAP Ultimate Mem Franch Present Future-11
03BAP Ultimate Memorabilia Great Moments-4
03BAP Ultimate Memorabilia Hat Tricks-12
03BAP Ultimate Memorabilia Heroes-2
03BAP Ultimate Memorabilia Heroes-4
03BAP Ultimate Memorabilia Heroes-18
03BAP Ultimate Mem Heroes Autos-1
03BAP Ultimate Mem Heroes Autos-8
03BAP Ultimate Memorabilia Jerseys-7
03BAP Ultimate Memorabilia Jerseys Gold-7
03BAP Ultimate Mem Jersey and Emblems-39
03BAP Ultimate Mem Jersey and Emblem Gold-39
03BAP Ultimate Mem Jersey and Numbers-39
03BAP Ultimate Mem Jersey and Number Gold-39
03BAP Ultimate Mem Jersey and Stick-9
03BAP Ultimate Mem Jersey and Stick Gold-9
03BAP Ultimate Mem Lifetime Achievers-8
03BAP Ultimate Memorabilia Nameplates-14
03BAP Ultimate Mem Nameplates Gold-14
03BAP Ultimate Memorabilia Numbers-6
03BAP Ultimate Memorabilia Numbers Gold-6
03BAP Ultimate Mem Retro-Active Trophies-18
03BAP Ultimate Mem Seams Unbelievable-3
03BAP Ultimate Memorabilia Triple Threads-21
03Beehive-75
Variations-75
Gold-75
Silver-75
Jumbos-12
Jumbo Jerseys-BH20
Jerseys-JT27
03Black Diamond-137
Black-137
Green-137
Red-137
Signature Gems-SG-35
03Crown Royale-39
Blue-39
Retail-39
Jerseys-9
Patches-9
Lords of the Rink-11
03ITG Action-211
Center of Attention-CA2
Jerseys-M200
Jerseys-M220
Jerseys-M251
Oh Canada-OC3
03ITG Toronto Fall Expo Jerseys-FE30
03ITG Used Signature Series-101
Gold-101
Autographs-SY
Autographs Gold-SY
Franchise-11
Franchise Autographs-11
Franchise Gold-11
Game-Day Jerseys-3
Game-Day Jerseys Gold-3
International Experience-3
International Experience Autographs-3
International Experience Emblems Gold-3
International Experience Emblems-3
International Experience Gold-3
Jerseys-43
Jerseys Gold-43
Jersey Autos-43
Emblems-4
Emblems Gold-4
Jersey and Stick-43
Jersey and Stick Gold-43
Oh Canada-11
Oh Canada Gold-11
Oh Canada Emblems-11
Oh Canada Emblems Gold-11
Retrospectives-13A
Retrospectives-13B
Retrospectives-13C
Retrospectives-13D
Retrospectives-13E
Retrospectives-13F
Retrospectives Gold-13A
Retrospectives Gold-13B
Retrospectives Gold-13C
Retrospectives Gold-13D
Retrospectives Gold-13E
Retrospectives Gold-13F
Teammates-13
Teammates Gold-13
03ITG VIP Brightest Stars-8
03ITG VIP Collages-3
03ITG VIP Collage Autographs-3
03ITG VIP International Experience-10
03ITG VIP Jerseys-21
03ITG VIP Jersey Autographs-21
03ITG VIP Jersey and Emblems-15
03ITG VIP Jersey and Numbers-15
03ITG VIP MVP-19
03McDonald's Pacific-19
Etched in Time-4
Patches Silver-11
Patches Gold-11
Patches and Sticks-11
03NHL Sticker Collection-216
03Pacific-127
Blue-127
Red-127
Cramer's Choice-5
Jerseys-16
Jerseys Gold-16
Main Attractions-6
03Pacific Calder-41
Silver-41
03Pacific Complete-216
Red-216
03Pacific Exhibit-169
03Pacific Exhibit-217
Blue Backs-169
History Makers-5
03Pacific Heads-Up-38
Hobby LTD-38
Retail LTD-38
Jerseys-10
Mini Sweaters-5
Rink Immortals-6
Rink Immortals LTD-6
03Pacific Invincible-36
Blue-36
Red-36
Retail-36
Featured Performers-11
Top Line-6
03Pacific Luxury Suite-10A
03Pacific Luxury Suite-10B
03Pacific Luxury Suite-10C
03Pacific Luxury Suite-10D
03Pacific Prism-118
Blue-118
Patches-118
Red-118
Retail-118
Stat Masters-6
03Pacific Quest for the Cup-41
Blue-41
Conquest-4
Jerseys-9
Raising the Cup-11
03Pacific Supreme-35
Blue-35
Red-35
Retail-35
Generations-4
Jerseys-12
Team-5
03Parkhurst Original Six Detroit-27
03Parkhurst Original Six Detroit-68
03Parkhurst Original Six Detroit-71
03Parkhurst Original Six Detroit-91
03Parkhurst Original Six Detroit-92
03Parkhurst Original Six Detroit-93
03Parkhurst Original Six Detroit-96
Inserts-D-14
Inserts-D-15
Memorabilia-DM5
Memorabilia-DM15
Memorabilia-DM53
03Parkhurst Orig Six He Shoots/Scores-27
03Parkhurst Orig Six He Shoots/Scores-27A
03Parkhurst Rookie-1
Jerseys-GJ-12
Jersey Autographs-GUJ-SY
Jerseys Gold-GJ-12
Jersey and Sticks-SJ-2
Jersey and Sticks Gold-SJ-2
03Private Stock Reserve-166
Blue-166
Patches-166
Red-166
Retail-166
Moments in Time-8
03SP Authentic-31
Limited-31
10th Anniversary-SP3
10th Anniversary Limited-SP3
Breakout Seasons-B1
Breakout Seasons Limited-B1
Foundations-F5
Foundations Limited-F5
Honors-H28
Honors Limited-H28
03SP Game Used-17
03SP Game Used-114
Gold-17
Gold-114
Authentic Fabrics-DFHY
Authentic Fabrics-DFYH
Authentic Fabrics-QYBHH
Authentic Fabrics Gold-DFHY
Authentic Fabrics Gold-DFYH
Authentic Fabrics Gold-QYBHH
Double Threads-DTYZ
Limited Threads-LTSY
Limited Threads Gold-LTSY
Premium Patches-PPSY
Team Threads-TTYZH
Top Threads-YZHH
03SPx-34
03SPx-120
03SPx-179
Radiance-34
Radiance-120
Radiance-179
Spectrum-34
Spectrum-120
Spectrum-179
Fantasy Franchise-FF-HYS
Fantasy Franchise-FF-HYZ
Fantasy Franchise Limited-FF-HYS
Fantasy Franchise Limited-FF-HYZ

Signature Threads-ST-SY
VIP-VIP-YS
VIP Limited-VIP-YS
03Titanium-199
Patches-199
Highlight Reels-6
03Topps/OPC Idols-CI10
03Topps Lost Rookies-SY
03Topps C55 Award Winners-9
03Topps Pristine Stick Portions-PPS-SY
03Topps Pristine Stick Portion Refractors-PPS-SY
03Topps Traded-TT71
Blue-TT71
Gold-TT71
Red-TT71
03UD Honor Roll-29
03UD Honor Roll-127
Grade A Jerseys-TDET
03UD Premier Collection-22
Skills-SK-SY
Skills Patches-SK-SY
Stars-ST-SY
Stars Patches-ST-SY
Teammates-PT-DR1
Teammates-PT-DR2
Teammates Patches-PT-DR1
Teammates Patches-PT-DR2
03Upper Deck-72
All-Star Class-AS-9
Canadian Exclusives-72
Fan Favorites-FF6
HG-72
Magic Moments-MM-4
Patches-LD1
Performers-PS3
Superstar Spotlight-SS5
Team Essentials-TL-SY
03Upper Deck Classic Portraits-33
03Upper Deck Classic Portraits-105
03Upper Deck Classic Portraits-158
Classic Stitches-CS-SY
Genuine Greatness-GG-SY
Hockey Royalty-LYG
Hockey Royalty-YHS
Premium Portraits-PP-SY
03Upper Deck Ice-32
Gold-32
Breakers-IB-SY
Breaker Patches-IB-SY
Clear Cut Winners-CC-SY
Icons-I-SY
Icons Jerseys-I-SY
03Upper Deck MVP-156
Gold Script-156
Silver Script-156
Canadian Exclusives-156
Clutch Performers-CP7
Lethal Lineups-LL6
SportsNut-SN31
Talent-MT7
Winning Formula-WF4
03Upper Deck Rookie Update-32
03Upper Deck Rookie Update-152
Skills-SKSY
Super Stars-SSSY
Top Draws-TD15
03Upper Deck Trilogy-33
03Upper Deck Trilogy-104
Authentic Patches-AP5
Crest Variations-104
Limited-33
Limited-104
Limited Threads-LT7
03Upper Deck Victory-68
Bronze-68
Gold-68
Silver-68
03Toronto Star-36
Foil-2
04ITG NHL AS FANtasy AS History Jerseys-SB36
04ITG Franchises He Shoots/Scores Prizes-25
04ITG Franchises Update Memorabilia-USM3
04ITG Franchises Update Memorabilia Gold-USM3
04ITG Franchises Update Trophy Winners-UTW2
04ITG Franchises Update Trophy Win Gold-UTW2
04ITG Franchises US West-210
Autographs-A-SY
Barn Burners-WBB9
Barn Burners Gold-WBB9
Complete Jersey-WCJ5
Complete Jerseys Gold-WCJ5
Double Memorabilia-WDM13
Double Memorabilia Autographs-WDMSY
Double Memorabilia Gold-WDM13
Forever Rivals-WFR1
Forever Rivals Gold-WFR1
Memorabilia-WSM21
Memorabilia-WSM28
Memorabilia Autographs-WSMSY
Memorabilia Gold-WSM21
Memorabilia Gold-WSM28
Original Sticks-WOS3
Original Sticks Autographs-WOSSY
Original Sticks Gold-WOS3
Teammates-WTM8
Teammates Gold-WTM8
Triple Memorabilia Autographs-WTMSY
Triple Memorabilia Gold-WTM7
Trophy Winners-WTW9
Trophy Winners Gold-WTW9
04ITG Ultimate Memorabilia-134
Gold-134
Archives 1st Edition-2
Archives 1st Edition-5
Archives 1st Edition-8
Archives 1st Edition-15
Archives 1st Edition-17
Archives 1st Edition-21
Archives 1st Edition-36
Autographs-28
Autographs Gold-28
Changing the Game-9
Complete Jerseys-13
Complete Logo-27
Complete Logo-28
Conn Smythe Trophy-3
Cornerstones-1
Cornerstones Gold-1
Country of Origin-7
Country of Origin Gold-7
Day In History-7
Day In History-9
Day In History-18
Day In History-22
Day In History Gold-7
Day In History Gold-9
Day In History Gold-18
Day In History Gold-22
Gloves are Off-3
Heroes Steve Yzerman-1
Heroes Steve Yzerman-2
Heroes Steve Yzerman-3
Heroes Steve Yzerman-4
Heroes Steve Yzerman-5
Heroes Steve Yzerman-6
Heroes Steve Yzerman-7
Heroes Steve Yzerman-8
Heroes Steve Yzerman-9
Heroes Steve Yzerman-10
Jerseys-11
Jerseys Gold-11
Jersey Autographs-2
Jersey Autographs Gold-2
Jersey and Sticks-8
Jersey and Sticks Gold-8
Nicknames-7
Nickname Autographs-3
Original Six-3
Original Six-15
Seams Unbelievable-2
Stick Autographs-21
Stick Autographs Gold-21
Triple Threads-11
04Pacific-99
Blue-99
Red-99
Cramer's Choice-6
Milestones-1
Philadelphia-6
04SP Authentic-34
04SP Authentic-113
04SP Game Used Hawaii Conference Patch-PP30
04Ultimate Collection-16
Dual Logos-UL2-SY
Jerseys-UGJ-SY
Jerseys Gold-UGJ-SY
Patches-UP-SY
04Upper Deck-66
04Upper Deck-186
Canadian Exclusives-66
Canadian Exclusives-186
HG Glossy Gold-66
HG Glossy Gold-186
HG Glossy Silver-66
HG Glossy Silver-186
Patches-GJPA-SY
Patches-GJPL-SY
Patches-GJPN-SY
Swatch of Six-SS-SY
Three Stars-AS1
05ITG Heroes/Prosp Toronto Expo Parallel -19
05ITG Heroes/Prosp Toronto Expo Parallel -183
05Be A Player-33
First Period-33
Second Period-33
Third Period-33
Overtime-33
Class Action-CA10
Ice Icons-ICE5
Outtakes-OT22
05Beehive-31
05Beehive-187
Beige -31
Blue -31
Gold-31
Red -31
Matte-31
Matted Materials-MMSY
05Black Diamond-175
Emerald-175
Gold-175
Onyx-175
Ruby-175
Jerseys-J-SY
Jerseys Ruby-J-SY
Jersey Duals-DJ-SY
Jersey Triples-TJ-SY
Jersey Quads-QJ-SY
05Hot Prospects-33
En Fuego-33
Red Hot-33
White Hot-33
05ITG Ultimate Memorabilia Level 1-89
05ITG Ultimate Memorabilia Level 2-89
05ITG Ultimate Memorabilia Level 3-89
05ITG Ultimate Memorabilia Level 4-89
05ITG Ultimate Memorabilia Level 5-89
05ITG Ultimate Mem Complete Jersey-19
05ITG Ultimate Mem Complete Jersey Gold-19
05ITG Ultimate Mem Complete Package-19
05ITG Ultimate Mem Complete Package Gold-19
05ITG Ultimate Mem Cornerstones Jerseys-4
05ITG Ultimate Mem Cornerst Jerseys Gold-4
05ITG Ultimate Memorabilia Double Autos-10
05ITG Ultimate Mem Double Autos Gold-10
05ITG Ultimate Mem Double Mem-16
05ITG Ultimate Mem Double Mem Autos-6
05ITG Ultimate Mem Double Mem Autos Gold-6
05ITG Ultimate Mem Double Mem Gold-16
05ITG Ultimate Memorabilia Emblems-25
05ITG Ultimate Memorabilia Emblems Gold-25
05ITG Ultimate Mem First Rounders Jerseys-3
05ITG Ultimate Mem First Rounders Jerseys-10
05ITG Ultimate Mem 1st Round Jersey Gold-3
05ITG Ultimate Mem 1st Round Jersey Gold-10
05ITG Ultimate Memorabilia Gloves Are Off-6
05ITG Ultimate Mem Gloves Are Off Gold-6
05ITG Ultimate Memorabilia In The Numbers-15
05ITG Ultimate Mem In The Numbers Gold-15
05ITG Ultimate Mem Jersey and Emblem-5
05ITG Ultimate Memorabilia Jersey Autos-30
05ITG Ultimate Mem Jersey Autos Gold-30
05ITG Ultimate Mem Jersey Emblems Gold-5
05ITG Ultimate Memorabilia Jerseys-36
05ITG Ultimate Memorabilia Jerseys Gold-36
05ITG Ultimate Mem Pass the Torch Jerseys-10
05ITG Ultimate Mem Passing Torch Jsy Gold-10
05ITG Ultimate Mem Retro Teammate Jerseys-25
05ITG Ult Mem Retro Teammates Jersey Gold-25
05ITG Ultimate Mem Seams Unbelievable-4
05ITG Ultimate Mem Seam Unbelievable Gold-4
05ITG Ultimate Memorabilia Sextuple Autos-3
05ITG Ultimate Memorabilia Stick Autos-25
05ITG Ultimate Mem Stick Autos Gold-25
05ITG Ultimate Mem Sticks and Jerseys-2
05ITG Ultimate Mem Stick and Jerseys Gold-2
05ITG Ultimate Mem 3 Star of the Game Jsy-22
05ITG Ult Mem 3 Star of the Game Jsy Gold-22
05ITG Ultimate Memorabilia Trifecta Autos-8
05ITG Ultimate Mem Trifecta Autos Gold-8
05ITG Ultimate Memorabilia Triple Autos-20
05ITG Ultimate Mem Triple Autos Gold-20
05ITG Ultimate Mem Triple Threads Jerseys-3
05ITG Ultimate Mem Triple Thread Jsy Gold-3
05ITG Ultimate Memorabilia Ultimate Autos-1
05ITG Ultimate Mem Ultimate Autos Gold-1
05ITG Ultimate Mem Ult Hero Double Jersey-8
05ITG Ult Mem Ult Hero Double Jersey Gold-8
05ITG Ultimate Mem Ult Hero Single Jersey-8
05ITG Ult Mem Ult Hero Single Jersey Gold-8
05ITG Ultimate Mem Ult Hero Triple Jersey-8
05ITG Ult Mem Ult Hero Triple Jersey Gold-8
05McDonalds Upper Deck-26
Jerseys-MJ7
Top Scorers-TS6
05Panini Stickers-259
05Parkhurst-173
05Parkhurst-511
05Parkhurst-681
Facsimile Auto Parallel-173
Facsimile Auto Parallel-511
Facsimile Auto Parallel-681
True Colors-TCDET
True Colors-TCDET
True Colors-TCDECO
True Colors-TCDECO
05SP Authentic-35
05SP Authentic-107
Limited-35
Limited-107
05SP Game Used-35
Gold-35
Authentic Fabrics-AF-SY
Authentic Fabrics Dual-YS
Authentic Fabrics Gold-AF-SY
Authentic Fabrics Quad-MLYS
Authentic Fabrics Quad-YDSL
Authentic Patches Quad -MLYS
Authentic Patches Quad -YDSL
Authentic Fabrics Triple-GLY
Authentic Fabrics Triple-TSY
Authentic Patches-AP-SY
Authentic Patches Dual-YS
Authentic Patches Triple-GLY
Authentic Patches Triple-TSY
Awesome Authentics-AA-SY
By the Letter-LM-SY
Game Gear-GG-SY
05SPx-28
Spectrum-28
Winning Combos-WC-SY
Winning Combos Gold-WC-SY
Winning Combos Spectrum-WC-SY
Winning Materials-WM-SY
Winning Materials Gold-WM-SY
Winning Materials Spectrum-WM-SY
Xcitement Superstars-XS-SY
Xcitement Superstars Gold-XS-SY
Xcitement Superstars Spectrum-XS-SY
05The Cup-38
Gold-38
Black Rainbow-38
Masterpiece Pressplates-38
Noble Numbers-NNYS
Noble Numbers-NNYT
Noble Numbers Dual-DNNYL
Noble Numbers Dual-DNNYS
Patch Variation-P38
Property of-POSY
05UD Artifacts-39
05UD Artifacts-167
Blue-39
Blue-167
Gold-39
Gold-167
Green-39
Green-167
Pewter-39
Pewter-167
Red-39
Red-167
Gold Autographed-39
Gold Autographed-167
Treasured Patches-TP-SY
Treasured Patches Autographed-TP-SY
Treasured Patches Dual-TPD-SY
Treasured Patches Dual Autographed-TPD-SY
Treasured Patches Pewter-TP-SY
Treasured Patches Silver-TP-SY
Treasured Swatches-TS-SY
Treasured Swatches Autographed-TS-SY
Treasured Swatches Blue-TS-SY
Treasured Swatches Copper-TS-SY
Treasured Swatches Dual-TSD-SY
Treasured Swatches Dual Autographed-TSD-SY
Treasured Swatches Dual Blue-TSD-SY
Treasured Swatches Dual Copper-TSD-SY
Treasured Swatches Dual Maroon-TSD-SY
Treasured Swatches Dual Pewter-TSD-SY
Treasured Swatches Dual Silver-TSD-SY
Treasured Swatches Maroon-TS-SY
Treasured Swatches Pewter-TS-SY
Treasured Swatches Silver-TS-SY
05UD PowerPlay-34
05UD PowerPlay-97
05UD PowerPlay-125
Rainbow-34
05UD Toronto Fall Expo Priority Signings-PS-SY
05Ultimate Collection-32
Gold-32
Jerseys-JSY
Jerseys Dual-DJHY
Premium Patches-PPSY
Premium Swatches-PSSY
Ultimate Patches-PSY
Ultimate Patches Dual-DPHY
Ultimate Patches Dual-DPSY
05Ultra-74
Gold-74
Difference Makers-DM3
Difference Makers Jerseys-DMJ-SY
Difference Makers Patches-DMP-SY
Ice-74
Scoring Kings-SK7
Scoring Kings Jerseys-SKJ-SY
Scoring Kings Patches-SKP-SY
05Upper Deck-66
05Upper Deck All-Time Greatest-22
05Upper Deck All-Time Greatest-71
05Upper Deck Big Playmakers-B-SY
05Upper Deck Destined for the Hall-DH1
05Upper Deck Goal Rush-GR4
05Upper Deck HG Glossy-66
05Upper Deck Hometown Heroes-HH6
05Upper Deck Jerseys-J-SY
05Upper Deck Jerseys Series II-J2SY
05Upper Deck Majestic Materials-MMSY
05Upper Deck NHL Generations-DYS
05Upper Deck NHL Generations-TGYS
05Upper Deck Patches-P-SY
05Upper Deck Scrapbooks-HS19
05Upper Deck Shooting Stars-S-SY
05Upper Deck Ice-31
Rainbow-31
Frozen Fabrics-FFSY
Frozen Fabrics Glass-FFSY
Frozen Fabrics Patches-FFPSY
05Upper Deck MVP-139
05Upper Deck MVP-441
Gold-139
Gold-441
Platinum-139
Platinum-441
Materials-M-SY
Monumental Moments-MM4
Rising to the Occasion-RO6
05Upper Deck Rookie Update-33
05Upper Deck Trilogy-35
05Upper Deck Trilogy-111
Crystal-111
Honorary Patches-HP-SY
Honorary Swatches-HS-SY
05Upper Deck Toronto Fall Expo-66
05Upper Deck Victory-67
Black-67
Gold-67
Silver-67
Blow-Ups-BU14
Game Breakers-GB17
Stars on Ice-SI21
05ITG Heroes and Prospects-19
05ITG Heroes and Prospects-183
Aspiring-ASP17
Autographs-A-SY
Autographs Series II-SY2
CHL Grads-CG-7
CHL Grads Gold-CG-7
He Shoots-He Scores Prizes-7
He Shoots-He Scores Prizes-43
He Shoots-He Scores Prizes-53
Hero Memorabilia-HM-16
Hero Memorabilia Dual-HDM-8
National Pride-NPR-19
Spectrum-STM-10
Spectrum Gold-STM-10
06Black Diamond Black-155B
06Flair Showcase-38
06Flair Showcase-182
06Flair Showcase-228
06Flair Showcase-280
Parallel-38
Parallel-182
Parallel-228
Parallel-280
Hot Numbers-HN19
Hot Numbers Parallel-HN19
Stitches-SSSY
06ITG International Ice-8
06ITG International Ice-26
Gold-8
Gold-26
Autographs-ASY
Autographs-ASY2
Complete Jersey-CJ06
Complete Jersey Gold-CJ06
Cornerstones-IC01
Cornerstones Gold-IC01
Emblem Autographs-GUE15
Emblem Autographs Gold-GUE15
Emblems-GUE15
Emblems Gold-GUE15
International Rivals-IR12
International Rivals Gold-IR12
Jersey Autographs-GUJ15
Jersey Autographs Gold-GUJ15
Jerseys-GUJ15
Jerseys Gold-GUJ15
My Country My Team-MC3
My Country My Team Gold-MC3
Numbers-GUN15
Numbers Autographs-GUN15
Numbers Autographs Gold-GUN15
Numbers Gold-GUN15
Quad Patch-QP05
Quad Patch Gold-QP05
Stick and Jersey-SJ04
Stick and Jersey Gold-SJ04
Teammates-IT07
Teammates Gold-IT07
Triple Memorabilia-TM05
Triple Memorabilia Gold-TM05
06ITG Ultimate Memorabilia-132
Artist Proof-132
Autos-61
Autos Gold-61
Autos Dual-2
Autos Dual Gold-2
Autos Triple-2
Autos Triple-8
Autos Triple Gold-2
Autos Triple Gold-8
Bowman Factor-16
Bowman Factor Gold-16
Bowman Factor Autos-14
Bowman Factor Autos Gold-14
Captain-C-1
Captain-C Gold-1
Complete Jersey-3
Complete Jersey Gold-3
Complete Package-15
Complete Package Gold-15
Cornerstones-5
Cornerstones Gold-5
Decades-5
Decades Gold-5
Double Memorabilia-5
Double Memorabilia Gold-5
Double Memorabilia Autos-6
Double Memorabilia Autos Gold-6
Emblems-19
Emblems Gold-19
First Round Picks-17
First Round Picks Gold-17
Gloves Are Off-20
Gloves Are Off Gold-20
Going For Gold-23
Going For Gold Gold-23
In The Numbers-9
In The Numbers Gold-9
Jerseys-10
Jerseys Gold-10
Jerseys and Emblems-16
Jerseys and Emblems Gold-16
Jerseys Autos-64
Jerseys Autos Gold-64
Legendary Captains-4
Legendary Captains Gold-4
Passing The Torch-5
Passing The Torch Gold-5
Raised to the Rafters-10
Raised to the Rafters Gold-10
Retro Teammates-24
Retro Teammates-25
Retro Teammates Gold-24
Retro Teammates Gold-25
Ring Leaders-3
Ring Leaders Gold-3
Road to the Cup-10
Road to the Cup Gold-10
Stick Rack-5
Stick Rack Gold-5
Sticks and Jerseys-3
Sticks and Jerseys Gold-3
Sticks Autos-30
Sticks Autos Gold-30
Trifecta Autos-6
Trifecta Autos Gold-6
Triple Thread Jerseys-3
Triple Thread Jerseys Gold-3
Ultimate Hero Single Jerseys-4
Ultimate Hero Single Jerseys Gold-4
Ultimate Hero Double Jerseys-4
Ultimate Hero Double Jerseys Gold-4
Ultimate Hero Triple Jerseys-4
Ultimate Hero Triple Jerseys Gold-4
06McDonald's Upper Deck-15
06NHL POG-32
06Ultra-75
Gold Medallion-75
Ice Medallion-75
06Upper Deck Trilogy Frozen In Time-FT18
06Upper Deck National NHL VIP-5
06Upper Deck Victory-68
06Upper Deck Victory Black-68
06Upper Deck Victory Gold-68
06ITG Heroes and Prospects Heroes Memorabilia-HM03
06ITG Heroes and Prospects Heroes Memorabilia Gold-HM03

Z'berg, Dominik
01Swiss HNL-469

Zabawa, Andrezei
79Panini Stickers-132

Zabel, Norbert
94German DEL-182

Zabka, Boris
00Czech OFS-359
02Czech OFS Plus-102
03Czech OFS Plus-302
04Czech OFS-178
05Czech HC Slavia Praha-15
06Czech OFS-109

Zabkowicz, Sam
06Sioux Falls Stampede -15

Zabkowicz, Tom
04Maine Black Bears-2
05Rockford Ice Hogs-20

Zabolotnev, Andrei
01Russian Hockey League-170

Zaborowski, Roman
94German First League-70

Zaborsky, Tomas
06Saginaw Spirit-8

Zabransky, Libor
94Czech APS Extraliga-104
95Czech APS Extraliga-60
97Score Blues-17
Platinum-17
Premier-17
97Upper Deck-144
98Czech OFS-348
99Czech DS-130
99Czech OFS-446
99Czech OFS-486
99Czech OFS-530
All-Star Game Blue-530
All-Star Game Gold-530
All-Star Game Red-530
All-Star Game Silver-530
00Czech DS Extraliga-3
00Czech OFS-293
01Czech DS-11
01Czech OFS-99
03Czech OFS Plus-380
04Czech OFS Czech/Slovak-22

Zabrodsky, Jan
70Swedish Hockey-61

Zabrodsky, Vladimir
01Czech DS Legends-L5
03Czech Stadion-622

Zach, Hans
94German DEL-77
95German DEL-146
96German DEL-64
98German DEL-339
99German DEL-194
99German DEL-392
04German Cologne Sharks Postcards-28

Zach, Johann
79Panini Stickers-112

Zacha, Ales
01Czech OFS-66

Zacharias, Mark
00Fort Worth Brahmas-18

Zacharias, Michael
02Topeka Scarecrows-22
04Green Bay Gamblers-24

Zacharie, Carl
01Drummondville Voltigeurs-19

Zachary, Travis
98Quebec Remparts-24
Signed-24

Zachrisson, Erik
03UK London Racers-19

Zachurla, Jan
05Russian Hockey League RHL-C2

Zadina, Marek
94Czech APS Extraliga-38
95Czech APS Extraliga-235
96Czech APS Extraliga-65
97Czech APS Extraliga-95
97Czech DS Extraliga-118
97Czech DS Stickers-240
98Czech DS Stickers-281
98Czech OFS-277
98Czech OFS-487
99Czech DS-106
99Czech OFS-204
00Czech DS Extraliga-63
00Czech OFS-228
01Czech OFS-56
02Czech OFS Plus-100
03Czech OFS Plus-303
03Czech OFS Plus All-Star Game-H35
03Czech OFS Plus Insert G-G4
03Czech OFS Plus Insert S-S7
04Czech OFS-264

Zadrazil, Jiri
95Czech APS Extraliga-24
96Czech APS Extraliga-110

Zafrani, Andre
92Arizona Icecats-16

Zagitov, Ilnaz
03Russian Hockey League-231

Zagrapan, Marek
04Chicoutimi Sagueneens-14
04ITG Heroes and Prospects-216
04ITG Heroes/Prospects Toronto Expo '05-216
05ITG Heroes/Prosp Toronto Expo Parallel -141
05Chicoutimi Sagueneens-3
05Extreme Top Prospects Signature Edition-S22
05ITG Heroes and Prospects-141
Autographs-A-MZ
Complete Logos-CHL-9
Jerseys-GUJ-35
Jerseys Gold-GUJ-35
Emblems-GUE-35
Emblems Gold-GUE-35
Numbers-GUN-35
Numbers Gold-GUN-35
Nameplates-N-24
Nameplates Gold-N-24
06Rochester Americans-23

Zaharko, Miles
80Blackhawks Postcards-16
81Blackhawks Brown Background-17

Zahn, Teigan
06Saskatoon Blades-23

Zahnd, Raymond
01Swiss HNL-440

Zahorovsky, Martin
02Czech OFS Plus-44
03Czech OFS Plus-146
04Czech OFS-290
05Czech HC Hame Zlin-16
06Czech HC Zlin Hame Postcards-14
06Czech OFS-245

Zaichkowski, Jason
92British Columbia JHL-143

Zaine, Rod
71Sabres Postcards-81
71Toronto Sun-41

Zainullin, Ruslan
00Russian Hockey League-268
03Russian Hockey League-54
03Russian SL-38

Zajac, Darcy
04Salmon Arm Silverbacks-9
05Salmon Arm Silverbacks-23

Zajac, Martin
04Czech OFS-22

Zajac, Travis
03Salmon Arm Silverbacks-21
04North Dakota Fighting Sioux-26
06Be A Player-212
06Be A Player Portraits-117
06Beehive-133
Blue-133
Gold-133
Matte-133
Red Facsimile Signatures-133
Wood-133
06Black Diamond-201
Black-201
Gold-201
Ruby-201
06Devils Team Set-27
06Flair Showcase-318
06Hot Prospects-122
Red Hot-122
White Hot-122
Hot Materials -HMTZ
Hot Materials Red Hot-HMTZ
Hot Materials White Hot-HMTZ
Hotagraphs-HTZ
06O-Pee-Chee-541
06O-Pee-Chee-628
Rainbow-541
Rainbow-628
06SP Authentic-189
Limited-189
06SP Game Used-132
Gold-132
Rainbow-132
Autographs-132
Rookie Exclusives Autographs-RETZ
06SPx-180
Spectrum-180
06The Cup-141
Autographed NHL Shields Duals-DASEZ
Autographed Rookie Masterpiece Pressplates-141
Enshrinements-ETZ
Gold Rainbow Autographed Rookie Patches-141
Masterpiece Pressplates (Be A Player Portraits)-117
Masterpiece Pressplates (Bee Hive)-133
Masterpiece Pressplates (Marquee Rookies)-541
Masterpiece Pressplates (MVP)-307
Masterpiece Pressplates (SP Authentic Autographs)-189
Masterpiece Pressplates (SP Game Used)-132
Masterpiece Pressplates (SPx Autographs)-180
Masterpiece Pressplates (Sweet Beginnings)-137
Masterpiece Pressplates (Trilogy)-128
Masterpiece Pressplates (Ultimate Collection Autographs)-119
Masterpiece Pressplates (Victory)-287
NHL Shields Duals-DSHZD
Rookies Black-141
Rookies Platinum-141
06UD Artifacts-248
06UD Mini Jersey Collection-111
06Ultimate Collection-119
Rookies Autographed NHL Shields-119
Rookies Autographed Patches-119
Ultimate Debut Threads Jerseys-DJ-TZ
Ultimate Debut Threads Jerseys Autographs-DJ-TZ
Ultimate Debut Threads Patches-DJ-TZ
Ultimate Debut Threads Patches Autographs-DJ-TZ
06Ultra-234
Gold Medallion-234
Ice Medallion-234
06Upper Deck-225
Exclusives Parallel-225
High Gloss Parallel-225
Masterpieces-225
Rookie Game Dated Moments-RGD16
Rookie Headliners-RH6
Rookie Materials-RMTZ
Rookie Materials Patches-RMTZ
06Upper Deck MVP-307
Gold Script-307
Super Script-307
06Upper Deck Sweet Shot-137
Rookie Jerseys Autographs-137
06Upper Deck Trilogy-128
06Upper Deck Victory-287
07Upper Deck Ovation-19
07Upper Deck Rookie Class -15
07Upper Deck Victory-6
Black-6
Gold-6

Zajankala, George
917th Inn. Sketch WHL-124
92Cleveland Lumberjacks-11
94Knoxville Cherokees-17
95Dayton Bombers-22
99German DEL-112

Zajgla, Petr
99Czech OFS-69
00Czech OFS-343

Zajic, Josef
94Czech APS Extraliga-35
95Czech APS Extraliga-97
96Czech APS Extraliga-85
97Czech APS Extraliga-204
97Czech DS Extraliga-92
97Czech DS Stickers-143
98Czech DS Stickers-235
99German DEL-354
00German DEL-205
01German Upper Deck-225
04Czech OFS-67
05Czech HC Kladno-14

Zajic, Leos
94German First League-78

Zajic, Vladimir
98Czech OFS-39

Zajicek, Jan
79Panini Stickers-81

Zajkowski, Michael
04Swedish MoDo Postcards-21
05Swedish SHL Elitset-92
Gold-92
06Swedish SHL Elitset-238

Zajonc, Petr
95Czech APS Extraliga-232
96Czech APS Extraliga-63
97Czech APS Extraliga-141
97Czech DS Stickers-245
98Czech DS Stickers-263

Zak, Robert
99Czech Score Blue 2000-112
99Czech Score Red Ice 2000-112

Zak, Roman
00Czech DS Extraliga-126
00Czech OFS-168

Zak, Zdenek
00Czech OFS-154

Zakall, Brian
91British Columbia JHL-74

Zakharov, Evgeni
98Russian Hockey League-78
99Russian Hockey League-128

Zakharov, Konstantin
03Moncton Wildcats-18
06Peoria Rivermen-23

Zakiyev, Radik
05Russian Hockey League RHL-48

Zalapski, Zarley
89O-Pee-Chee-168
89O-Pee-Chee Stickers-2
89O-Pee-Chee Stickers-45
89O-Pee-Chee Stickers-232
89Panini Stickers-318
89Penguins Coke/Elby's-5
89Penguins Foodland-3
89Topps-168
89Swedish Semic World Champ Stickers-60
90Bowman-207
Tiffany-207
90O-Pee-Chee-78
90Panini Stickers-126
90Penguins Foodland-12
90Pro Set-242
90Score-218
Canadian-218
90Topps-78
Tiffany-78
90Upper Deck-33
French-33
91Pro Set Platinum-47
91Bowman-15
91O-Pee-Chee-344
91Panini Stickers-322
91Parkhurst-61
French-61
91Pinnacle-110
French-110
91Pro Set-91
French-91
91Score American-111
91Score Canadian Bilingual-111
91Score Canadian English-111
91Stadium Club-228
91Topps-344
91Upper Deck-231
French-231
91Whalers Jr. 7-Eleven-28
91Finnish Semic World Champ Stickers-60
91Swedish Semic World Champ Stickers-60
92Bowman-173
92Humpty Dumpty I-25
92O-Pee-Chee-248
92Panini Stickers-263
92Panini Stickers French-263
92Parkhurst-59
Emerald Ice-59
92Pinnacle-271
French-271
92Pro Set-59
92Score-238
Canadian-238
92Stadium Club-25
92Topps-82
Gold-82G
92Ultra-77
92Upper Deck-316
92Whalers Dairymart-25
93Donruss-149
93Donruss-410
93Leaf-8
93OPC Premier-20
Gold-20
93Panini Stickers-129
93Parkhurst-88
Emerald Ice-88
93Pinnacle-257
Canadian-257
All-Stars-2
All-Stars Canadian-2
93PowerPlay-112
93Score-104
Canadian-104
93Stadium Club-102
Members Only Master Set-102
OPC-102
First Day Issue-102
First Day Issue OPC-102
All-Stars-14
All-Stars Members Only-14
All-Stars OPC-14
93Topps/OPC Premier-20
Gold-20
93Ultra-234
93Upper Deck-213
93Upper Deck Locker All-Stars-18
93Whalers Coke-24
94Canada Games NHL POGS-64
94Donruss-248
94EA Sports-55
94Flair-30
94Leaf-294
94OPC Premier-379
Special Effects-379
94Parkhurst-31
Gold-31
94Pinnacle-342
Artist's Proofs-342
Rink Collection-342
94Select-140
Gold-140
94Stadium Club-141
Members Only Master Set-141
First Day Issue-141
Super Team Winner Cards-141
94Topps/OPC Premier-379
Special Effects-379
94Ultra-38
94Upper Deck-110
Electric Ice-110
95Bashan Super Stickers-19
95Be A Player-108
Signatures-S108
Signatures Die Cuts-S108
95Canada Games NHL POGS-58
95Collector's Choice-123
Player's Club-123
Player's Club Platinum-123
95Donruss-177
95Emotion-26
95Imperial Stickers-19
95Leaf-225
95Panini Stickers-242
95Parkhurst International-31
Emerald Ice-31
95Playoff One on One-132
95Score-69
Black Ice Artist's Proofs-69
Black Ice-69
95SkyBox Impact-26
95Stadium Club-96
Members Only Master Set-96
95Topps-263
OPC Inserts-263
95Ultra-29
Gold Medallion-29
95Upper Deck-480
Electric Ice-480
Electric Ice Gold-480
96Collector's Choice-41
96Donruss-4
Press Proofs-4
96Leaf-95
Press Proofs-95
96Pinnacle-119
Artist's Proofs-119
Foil-119
Premium Stock-119
Rink Collection-119
96Score-205
Artist's Proofs-205
Dealer's Choice Artist's Proofs-205
Special Artist's Proofs-205
Golden Blades-205
96SP-25
96Team Out-89
96Upper Deck-24
97Be A Player-68
Autographs-68
Autographs Die-Cuts-68
Autographs Prismatic Die-Cuts-68
97Pacific Dynagon Best Kept Secrets-15
98OPC Chrome-196
Refractors-196
98Topps-196
O-Pee-Chee-196
98Upper Deck-321
Exclusives-321
Exclusives 1 of 1-321
Gold Reserve-321
99Utah Grizzlies-33

Zalasky, Lee
01Moose Jaw Warriors-13
03Calgary Hitmen-21

Zalba, Bill
99Owen Sound Platers-9
00Owen Sound Attack-25
05Muskegon Fury-21

Zalesak, Miroslav
00Kentucky Thoroughblades-24
00QMJHL All-Star Program Inserts-31
01Cleveland Barons-22
02BAP Memorabilia-330
02BAP Ultimate Memorabilia-57
02Upper Deck Rookie Update-145
02Cleveland Barons-24
03Bowman Signs of the Future-SOF-MZ
03ITG Action-413
03O-Pee-Chee-315
03OPC Blue-315
03OPC Gold-315
03OPC Red-315
03Topps-315
Blue-315
Gold-315
Red-315
03Cleveland Barons-22
03Pacific AHL Prospects-23
Gold-23
04Czech OFS-371
04Slovakian Skalica Team Set-8

Zaleski, Chris
01El Paso Buzzards-6
02El Paso Buzzards-3

Zaleski, Tom
00Sioux Falls Stampede-20

Zaltkovskis, Edgar
98Tacoma Sabercats-21
99Tacoma Sabercats-18
01Idaho Steelheads-23

Zaltsev, Sergei
90O-Pee-Chee-487
94German First League-522

Zambon, Mike
91British Columbia JHL-34

Zamec, Adam
06Kitchener Rangers-18

Zamick, Chick
54UK A and BC Chewing Gum-35

Zamojski, Jacek
89Swedish Semic World Champ Stickers-131
92Finnish Semic-273

Zamuner, Rob
89ProCards IHL-40
90ProCards AHL/IHL-1
91ProCards-204
92Lightning Sheraton-25
92OPC Premier-69
92Parkhurst-171

Emerald Ice-171
92Pinnacle-414
French-414
92Stadium Club-439
92Topps-426
Gold-426G
92Ultra-415
92Upper Deck-583
Calder Candidates-CC4
92Classic-98
Gold-98
92Classic Four-Sport *-211
Gold-211
93Donruss-329
93Leaf-173
93Lightning Season in Review-28
93OPC Premier-19
Gold-19
93Panini Stickers-214
93Parkhurst-194
Emerald Ice-194
93Pinnacle-121
Canadian-121
93PowerPlay-236
93Score-291
Canadian-291
93Stadium Club-376
Members Only Master Set-376
First Day Issue-376
93Topps/OPC Premier-19
Gold-19
93Ultra-199
93Upper Deck-202
SP-154
94Be A Player-R175
Signature Cards-147
94Leaf-427
94Lightning Photo Album-28
94Lightning Postcards-20
94Parkhurst-224
Gold-224
94Stadium Club-48
Members Only Master Set-48
First Day Issue-48
Super Team Winner Cards-48
94Upper Deck-468
Electric Ice-468
95Lightning Team Issue-21
95Playoff One on One-200
95Pro Magnets-174
96Be A Player-114
Autographs-114
Autographs Silver-114
96Collector's Choice-248
96NHL Pro Stamps-75
96Upper Deck-158
97Collector's Choice-238
97Donruss Limited-88
Exposure-88
97Donruss Priority-112
Stamp of Approval-112
97Kraft Team Canada-10
97McDonald's Team Canada Coins-12
97Pacific-204
Copper-204
Emerald Green-204
Ice Blue-204
Red-204
Silver-204
97Pacific Omega-216
Copper-216
Dark Gray-216
Emerald Green-216
Gold-216
Ice Blue-216
97Panini Stickers-108
97Revolution-132
Copper-132
Emerald-132
Ice Blue-132
Silver-132
Team Checklist Laser Cuts-23
97Score-200
97Upper Deck-364
98Aurora-178
Championship Fever-45
Championship Fever Copper-45
Championship Fever Ice Blue-45
Championship Fever Red-45
Championship Fever Silver-45
98Be A Player-132
Press Release-132
98BAP Gold-132
98BAP Autographs-132
98BAP Autographs Gold-132
98BAP Tampa Bay All Star Game-132
98Crown Royale-127
Limited Series-127
98Finest-20
No Protectors-20
No Protectors Refractors-20
Refractors-20
98OPC Chrome-43
Refractors-43
98Pacific-409
Ice Blue-409
Red-409
Team Checklists-24
98Pacific Dynagon Ice-176
Blue-176
Red-176
98Pacific Omega-223
Red-223
Opening Day Issue-223
98Panini Stickers-99
98Paramount-223
Copper-223
Emerald Green-223
Holo-Electric-223
Ice Blue-223
Silver-223
Team Checklists Die-Cuts-24
98Post-21
98Revolution-135
Ice Shadow-135
Red-135
98Topps-43
O-Pee-Chee-43
98UD Choice-196
Prime Choice Reserve-196
Reserve-196
98Upper Deck MVP-191
Gold Script-191
Silver Script-191
Super Script-191
99BAP Millennium-177
Emerald-177
Ruby-177
Sapphire-177
Signatures-177
Signatures Gold-177
99Pacific-399
Copper-399
Emerald Green-399
Gold-399
Ice Blue-399
Premiere Date-399
Red-399
99Pacific Dynagon Ice-143
Blue-143
Copper-143
Gold-143
Premiere Date-143
99Panini Stickers-111
99Senators Team Issue-23
99Upper Deck MVP SC Edition-128
Gold Script-128
Silver Script-128
Super Script-128
00Pacific-290
Copper-290
Gold-290
Ice Blue-290
Premiere Date-290
00Senators Team Issue-26
00Upper Deck-354
Exclusives Tier 1-354
Exclusives Tier 2-354
01Pacific-282
Extreme LTD-282
Hobby LTD-282
Premiere Date-282
Retail LTD-282
01Pacific Arena Exclusives-282
01Parkhurst-203
01Upper Deck-247
Exclusives-247
02BAP Sig Series Auto Buybacks 1998-132
02BAP Sig Series Auto Buybacks 1999-177
02Pacific Complete-95
Red-95
03Pacific Complete-463
Red-463
03Parkhurst Original Six Boston-11

Zancanaro, Brad
03Boston University Terriers-14

Zaniboni, Bill
04Northern Michigan Wildcats-27

Zanier, Mike
83Moncton Alpines-4
84Nova Scotia Oilers-18
88Oilers Tenth Anniversary-4
92Finnish Semic-244
92Dallas Freeze-19

Zankovets, Eduard
00Rockford IceHogs-20

Zanon, Brad
03Kootenay Ice-6

Zanon, Greg
03Milwaukee Admirals-21
03Milwaukee Admirals Postcards-23
04Milwaukee Admirals-21
05Hot Prospects-147
En Fuego-147
Red Hot-147
White Hot-147
05SPx-270
05The Cup Masterpiece Pressplate Artifact-293
05The Cup Masterpiece Pressplates (Ice)-250
05The Cup Master Pressplate Rookie Update-154
05The Cup Masterpiece Pressplates (SPx)-270
05UD Artifacts-293
05Upper Deck Ice-250
05Upper Deck Rookie Update-154
05Milwaukee Admirals Choice-18
05Milwaukee Admirals Pepsi-23

Zanoski, Tom
01Owen Sound Attack-24
02Owen Sound Attack-9
03Mississauga Ice Dogs-23
04Mississauga Ice Dogs-11

Zanussi, Joe
76O-Pee-Chee NHL-324

Zanussi, Ron
78North Stars Cloverleaf Dairy-9
78O-Pee-Chee-252
78Topps-252
79North Stars Postcards-21
79O-Pee-Chee-22
79Topps-22
80North Stars Postcards-24
80O-Pee-Chee-192
80Topps-192
81Maple Leafs Postcards-25
81O-Pee-Chee-325

Zanutto, Chris
93London Knights-23

Zanutto, Mike
95Slapshot-245
97Rochester Americans-2-5

Zaore, Vincent
05Cape Breton Screaming Eagles-21

Zaore-Vanie, Vincent
02Cape Breton Screaming Eagles-7
03Cape Breton Screaming Eagles-13
04Cape Breton Screaming Eagles-22
05Cape Breton Screaming Eagles-21
06Victoriaville Tigres-18

Zapletal, Jan
04Regina Pats-19

Zapletal, Tomas
98Czech OFS-330
99Czech OFS-250

Zaporzan, Terry
84Kelowna Wings-12

Zapotocny, Daniel
97Czech APS Extraliga-299
98Czech OFS-297
99Czech Score Blue 2000-47
99Czech Score Red Ice 2000-47
01Czech OFS-44
02Czech OFS Plus-301
03Czech OFS Plus-21

Zappala, Joe
06Reading Royals-8

Zappe, Tobias
92Quebec Pee-Wee Tournament-1674
93Quebec Pee-Wee Tournament-1776

Zapt, Bill
92British Columbia JHL-240

Zareba, Zdzislaw
93Quebec Pee-Wee Tournament-1512

Zarillo, Bruno
94Finnish Jaa Kiekko-308
95Swedish Globe World Championships-231

Zaripov, Danis
98Swift Current Broncos-6
99Russian Hockey League-260
01Russian Hockey League-102
02Russian Hockey League-145
03Russian Hockey League-14
03Russian National Team-2

Zarowny, Aaron
93Lethbridge Hurricanes-24

Zarrillo, Bruno
92Finnish Semic-254
93Swedish Semic World Champ Stickers-225
95Swedish World Championships Stickers-90
96German DEL-352
98German DEL-89
99German DEL-109
00German DEL-129
Game Jersey-BZ
01German Upper Deck-210
02Swiss HNL-476

Zaryk, Steve
95Slapshot-269

Zasitko, Brennan
04Everett Silvertips-12
05Saskatoon Blades-24

Zasowski, Tony
02Notre Dame Fighting Irish-4

Zatkoff, Jeff
04Sioux City Musketeers-23

Zatonski, Dmitri
98Russian Hockey League-38
99Russian Hockey League-174
00Russian Hockey League-227
01Russian Hockey League-80
01Russian Hockey League-118
02Russian Hockey League-123
02Russian Hockey League-242
02Russian Hockey League-262
02Russian World Championships-19
02Russian Avangard Omsk-4
03Russian Postcards-12

Zatopek, Libor
95Czech APS Extraliga-239

Zatopek, Lukas
98Czech OFS-354
99Czech OFS-235
00Czech OFS-247
00Czech OFS Plus-310

Zatovic, Martin
06Czech OFS-322

Zattlin, Ake
64Swedish Coralli ISHockey-109

Zaugg, Jinelle
04Wisconsin Badgers Women-24

Zavacky, Pavol
04Slovakian Poprad Team Set-19

Zavakhin, Alexander
02Russian Hockey League-227

Zavarukhin, Nikolai
93Parkhurst-530
Emerald Ice-530
93Classic-49
94Parkhurst SE-SE230
Gold-SE230
94SP-163
Die Cuts-163
94Upper Deck-516
Electric Ice-516
99Russian Hockey League-127
00Russian Hockey League-162
02Russian Hockey League-222

Zavediuk, Tom
92Quebec Pee-Wee Tournament-1352
95Tri-City Americans-28

Zavisha, Brad
907th Inn. Sketch WHL-14
917th Inn. Sketch WHL-358
94Cape Breton Oilers-23

Zavisha, Colby
02Spokane Chiefs-25

Zavoral, Vaclav
01Flint Generals-21
05UK Guildford Flames-13
06UK Guildford Flames-13

Zavrtalek, Pavel
03Czech OFS Plus-150

Zavyalov, Alexander
98Russian Hockey League-107
99Russian Hockey League-76
00Russian Hockey League-39
02Russian Hockey League-142
03Russian Hockey League-143
04Russian RHL-8

Zavyalov, Vladimir
99Russian Hockey League-138

Zawatsky, Ed
91Rochester Americans Postcards-21
94German First League-344

Zayonce, Dean
907th Inn. Sketch WHL-118
91Greensboro Monarchs-18
93Greensboro Monarchs-16
94Greensboro Monarchs-1
95Central Hockey League-100
98Charlotte Checkers-18
99Greensboro Generals-14

Zbontar, Miha
93Quebec Pee-Wee Tournament-1801

Zboril, Tomas
02Czech OFS Plus-101
03Czech OFS Plus-304
04Czech OFS-374
05Czech HC Trinec-15

Zbriger, Mike
06Bloomington PrairieThunder-7

Zbynek, Michalek
00Shawinigan Cataractes Signed-2

Zdrahal, Pavel
95Czech APS Extraliga-307
96Czech OFS-78
99Czech DS-54
99Czech OFS-302
00Czech OFS-280
01Czech OFS-244
All Stars-10
01Czech OFS Red Inserts-RE13D
03Czech OFS Plus-353

Zdunek, Piotr
89Swedish Semic World Champ Stickers-138
92Finnish Semic-279

Zednik, Richard
96Donruss Canadian Ice-125
Gold Press Proofs-125
Red Press Proofs-125
96Leaf Preferred-133
Press Proofs-133
96Metal Universe-197
96Select Certified-110
Artist's Proofs-110
Blue-110
Mirror Blue-110
Mirror Gold-110
Mirror Red-110
Red-110
96Upper Deck-356
96Zenith-120
Artist's Proofs-120
96Portland Pirates-14
97Be A Player One Timers-17
97Black Diamond-51
Double Diamond-51
Triple Diamond-51
Quadruple Diamond-51
97Crown Royale-144
Emerald Green-144
Ice Blue-144
Silver-144
97Katch-156
Gold-156
Silver-156
97Pacific Omega-244
Copper-244
Dark Gray-244
Emerald Green-244
Gold-244
Ice Blue-244
97SP Authentic-197
97Upper Deck-388
97Upper Deck Ice-55
Parallel-55
Power Shift-55
97Zenith-83
Z-Gold-83
Z-Silver-83
97Zenith 5 x 7-72
Gold Impulse-72
Silver Impulse-72
97Zenith Rookie Reign-15
97Zenith Z-Team-17
97Zenith Z-Team Gold-17
98Aurora-200
98Black Diamond-90
Double Diamond-90
Triple Diamond-90
Quadruple Diamond-90
98OPC Chrome-92
Refractors-92
98Pacific-451
Ice Blue-451
Red-451
98Pacific Dynagon Ice-200
Blue-200
Red-200
98Pacific Omega-250
Red-250
Opening Day Issue-250
98Paramount-250
Copper-250
Emerald Green-250
Holo-Electric-250
Ice Blue-250
Silver-250
98Revolution-150
Ice Shadow-150
Red-150
98SPx Finite-135
Radiance-135
Spectrum-135
98Topps-92
O-Pee-Chee-92
98UD Choice-218
Prime Choice Reserve-218
Reserve-218
98UD3-7
98UD3-67
98UD3-127
Die-Cuts-7
Die-Cuts-67
Die-Cuts-127
98Upper Deck-206
Exclusives-206
Exclusives 1 of 1-206
Generation Next-GN23
Generation Next Quantum 1-GN23
Generation Next Quantum 2-GN23
Generation Next Quantum 3-GN23
Gold Reserve-206
98Upper Deck MVP-215
Gold Script-215
Silver Script-215
Super Script-215
99O-Pee-Chee-93
99O-Pee-Chee Chrome-93
99O-Pee-Chee Chrome Refractors-93
99Pacific-449
Copper-449
Emerald Green-449
Gold-449
Ice Blue-449
Premiere Date-449
Red-449
99Pacific Dynagon Ice-206
Blue-206
Copper-206
Gold-206
Premiere Date-206
99Panini Stickers-172
99Paramount-250
Copper-250
Emerald-250
Gold-250
Holographic Emerald-250
Holographic Gold-250
Holographic Silver-250
Ice Blue-250
Premiere Date-250
Red-250
Silver-250
99SPx-156
Radiance-156
Spectrum-156
99Topps Arena Giveaways-WAS-RZ
99Topps/OPC-93
99Topps/OPC Chrome-93
Refractors-93
99Upper Deck MVP-212
Gold Script-212
Silver Script-212
Super Script-212
99Upper Deck Victory-310
99Slovakian Challengers-3
00BAP Memorabilia-331
Emerald-331
Ruby-331
Sapphire-331
Promos-331
00BAP Mem Chicago Sportsfest Copper-331
00BAP Memorabilia Chicago Sportsfest Blue-331
00BAP Memorabilia Chicago Sportsfest Gold-331
00BAP Memorabilia Chicago Sportsfest Ruby-331
00BAP Memorabilia Chicago Sun-Times Ruby-331
00BAP Memorabilia Chicago Sun-Times Gold-331
00BAP Mem Chicago Sun-Times Sapphire-331
00BAP Mem Toronto Fall Expo Copper-331
00BAP Memorabilia Toronto Fall Expo Gold-331
00BAP Memorabilia Toronto Fall Expo Ruby-331
00BAP Signature Series-156
Emerald-156
Ruby-156
Sapphire-156
Autographs-57
Autographs Gold-57
00O-Pee-Chee-200
00O-Pee-Chee Parallel-200
00Pacific-430
Copper-430
Gold-430
Ice Blue-430
Premiere Date-430
00Paramount-250
Copper-250
Gold-250
Holo-Gold-250
Holo-Silver-250
Ice Blue-250
Premiere Date-250
00Stadium Club-189
00Topps/OPC-200
Parallel-200
00Upper Deck-175
Exclusives Tier 1-175
Exclusives Tier 2-175
00Upper Deck Vintage-366
01BAP Memorabilia-261
Emerald-261
Ruby-261
Sapphire-261
01BAP Signature Series-108
Autographs-108
Autographs Gold-108
01Canadiens Postcards-28
01O-Pee-Chee-168
01O-Pee-Chee Premier Parallel-168
01Pacific-214
Extreme LTD-214
Hobby LTD-214
Premiere Date-214
Retail LTD-214
01Pacific Adrenaline-102
Blue-102
Premiere Date-102
Red-102
Retail-102
01Pacific Arena Exclusives-214
01Parkhurst-170
01Topps-168
OPC Parallel-168
01Upper Deck-91
Exclusives-91
01Upper Deck MVP-101
01Upper Deck Victory-183
Gold-183
01Upper Deck Vintage-137
02BAP First Edition-259
02BAP Memorabilia-127
Emerald-127
Ruby-127
Sapphire-127
NHL All-Star Game-127
NHL All-Star Game Blue-127
NHL All-Star Game Green-127
NHL All-Star Game Red-127
02BAP Memorabilia Toronto Fall Expo-127
02BAP Signature Series-25
Autographs-25
Autograph Buybacks 2001-108
Autographs Gold-25
02Canadiens Postcards-4
02Crown Royale-53
Blue-53
Red-53
Retail-53
02NHL Power Play Stickers-68
02O-Pee-Chee-194
02O-Pee-Chee Premier Blue Parallel-194
02O-Pee-Chee Premier Red Parallel-194
02O-Pee-Chee Factory Set-194
02Pacific-204
Blue-204
Red-204
02Pacific Complete-215
Red-215
02Pacific Exclusive-95
02Pacific Quest for the Cup-53
Gold-53
02Parkhurst-161
Bronze-161
Gold-161
Silver-161
02Parkhurst Retro-199
Minis-199
02Private Stock Reserve-55
Blue-55
Red-55
Retail-55
02Stadium Club-85
Silver Decoy Cards-85
Proofs-85
02Titanium-58
Blue-58
Red-58
Retail-58
02Topps-194
OPC Blue Parallel-194
OPC Red Parallel-194
Factory Set-194
02Topps Total-377
02UD Top Shelf-47
02Upper Deck-94
Exclusives-94
02Upper Deck MVP-95
Gold-95
Classics-95
Golden Classics-95
02Upper Deck Vintage-133
03BAP Memorabilia-75
Emerald-75
Gold-75
Ruby-75
Sapphire-75
03Canadiens Postcards-29
03ITG Action-396
03NHL Sticker Collection-54
03O-Pee-Chee-84
03OPC Blue-84
03OPC Gold-84
03OPC Red-84
03Pacific-184
Blue-184
Red-184
03Pacific Complete-348
Red-348
03Pacific Exhibit-79
Blue Backs-79
Yellow Backs-79
03Pacific Montreal International-4
03Pacific Prism-125
Blue-125
Patches-125
Red-125
Retail-125
03Pacific Supreme-53
Blue-53
Red-53
Retail-53
03Parkhurst Original Six Montreal-27
03Private Stock Reserve-175
Blue-175
Patches-175
Red-175
Retail-175
03Titanium-163
Hobby Jersey Number Parallels-163
Patches-163
Retail-163
03Topps-84
Blue-84
Gold-84
Red-84
03Topps Pristine-19
Gold Refractor Die Cuts-19
Refractors-19
Press Plates Black-19
Press Plates Cyan-19
Press Plates Magenta-19
Press Plates Yellow-19
03Upper Deck-103
Canadian Exclusives-103
HG-103
03Upper Deck MVP-222
Gold Script-222
Silver Script-222
Canadian Exclusives-222
03Upper Deck Victory-96
Bronze-96
Gold-96
Silver-96
03Russian World Championship Stars-22
04Pacific-144
Blue-144
Red-144
04UD All-World-88
Gold-88
Autographs-88
05Black Diamond-45
Emerald-45
Gold-45
Onyx-45
Ruby-45
05Canadiens Team Issue-24
05Panini Stickers-76
05Parkhurst-260
Facsimile Auto Parallel-260
True Colors-TCMTL
True Colors-TCMTL
05SP Authentic Sign of the Times-RZ
05SP Game Used Awesome Authentics-AA-RZ
05SP Game Used Statscriptions-ST-RZ
05SPx Winning Materials-WM-RZ
05SPx Winning Materials Autographs-AWM-RZ
05SPx Winning Materials Gold-WM-RZ
05SPx Winning Materials Spectrum-WM-RZ
05UD Artifacts Auto Facts-AF-RZ
05UD Artifacts Auto Facts Blue-AF-RZ
05UD Artifacts Auto Facts Copper-AF-RZ
05UD Artifacts Auto Facts Pewter-AF-RZ
05UD Artifacts Auto Facts Silver-AF-RZ
05Ultimate Collection Endorsed Emblems-EERZ
05Ultra-109
Gold-109
Fresh Ink-FI-RZ
Fresh Ink Blue-FI-RZ
Ice-109
05Upper Deck-99
HG Glossy-99
Notable Numbers-N-RZ
05Upper Deck MVP-201
Gold-201
Platinum-201
05Upper Deck Toronto Fall Expo-99
05Upper Deck Victory-107
Black-107
Gold-107
Silver-107
06Flair Showcase Stitches-SSRZ
06Fleer-200
Tiffany-200
06O-Pee-Chee-497
Rainbow-497
06Panini Stickers-173
06SP Game Used Authentic Fabrics Triple-AF3WAS
06SP Game Used Authentic Fabrics Triple Patches-AF3WAS
06The Cup NHL Shields Duals-DSHKZ
06Ultra Uniformity-URZ
06Ultra Uniformity Patches-UPRZ
06Ultra Uniformity Autographed Jerseys-UARZ
06Upper Deck Arena Giveaways-WSH4
06Upper Deck-444
Exclusives Parallel-444
High Gloss Parallel-444
Masterpieces-444
06Upper Deck MVP-294
Gold Script-294
Super Script-294
06Russian Sport Collection Olympic Stars-46

Zehnder, Andreas
93Swiss HNL-171
95Swedish World Championships Stickers-124
95Swiss HNL-40
96Swiss HNL-187
96Swiss HNL-535
98Swiss Power Play Stickers-236
99Swiss Panini Stickers-237
00Swiss Panini Stickers-277
00Swiss Slapshot Mini-Cards-ZSCL6
01Swiss HNL-243
02Swiss HNL-443

Zehnder, Lukas
93Swiss HNL-471

Zehr, Jeff
95Slapshot-416
97Bowman CHL-149
OPC-149
Autographs-29
99BAP Memorabilia-380
Gold-380
Silver-380
02Columbus Cottonmouths-19

Zeibaq, Mike
03Indianapolis Ice-19

Zeidel, Larry
44Beehive Group II Photos-219
52Parkhurst-91
53Parkhurst-73
68O-Pee-Chee-92
68Topps-92

Zeiler, John
00Sioux City Musketeers-30
06Manchester Monarchs-10
07Upper Deck Victory-234
Black-234
Gold-234

Zeiter, Michel
93Swiss HNL-183
95Swiss HNL-53
96Swiss HNL-198
96Swiss HNL-547
98Swiss Power Play Stickers-247
98Swiss Power Play Stickers-272
99Swiss Panini Stickers-249
99Swiss Panini Stickers-275
00Swiss Panini Stickers-289
00Swiss Panini Stickers National Team-P25
00Swiss Slapshot Mini-Cards-ZSCL16
01Swiss HNL-24
02Swiss HNL-275

Zelenbaba, Jovica
06Saginaw Spirit-19

Zelenchev, Igor
98Russian Hockey League-92
99Russian Hockey League-207

Zelenewich, Brent
03Indianapolis Ice-20

Zelenka, Jiri
94Czech APS Extraliga-83
95Czech APS Extraliga-279
96Czech APS Extraliga-133
97Czech APS Extraliga-11
97Czech DS Extraliga-84
98Czech DS-94
98Czech DS Stickers-16
98Czech DS Stickers-215
98Czech OFS-136
98Czech OFS-458
99Czech DS-153
99Czech OFS-114
00Czech OFS-309
00Czech OFS Star Emerald-8
00Czech OFS Star Pink-8
00Czech OFS Star Violet-8
01Czech OFS Update-286
01Czech OFS Red Inserts-RE5D
01Finnish Cardset-189
02Czech OFS Plus-21
02Czech OFS Plus All-Star Game-H42
02Czech OFS Plus Duos-D2
03German DEL-60
06Czech HC Plzen Postcards-5
06Czech OFS-287
Goals Leaders-14
Team Cards-7

Zelenko, Boris
98Russian Hockey League-164
98Hampton Roads Admirals-18
99Russian Dynamo Moscow-24
00Russian Dynamo Moscow-23

Zelepukin, Valeri
91Pro Set Platinum-261
91O-Pee-Chee Inserts-65R
91Parkhurst-324
French-324
91Pinnacle-354
French-354
91Upper Deck-589
French-589
91ProCards-427
92Bowman-430
92Panini Stickers-177
92Panini Stickers French-177
92Parkhurst-228
92Parkhurst-327
Emerald Ice-228
Emerald Ice-327
92Pinnacle-286
French-286
92Pro Set Rookie Goal Leaders-10
92Score-206
Canadian-206
92Stadium Club-99
92Topps-462
Gold-462G
92Ultra-122
92Upper Deck-295
Euro-Stars-E12
92Russian Stars Red Ace-7
92Russian Tri-Globe From Russia With Puck-15
92Russian Tri-Globe From Russia With Puck-16
93Donruss-193
93Kraft-26
93Leaf-104
93Panini Stickers-38
93Parkhurst-383
Emerald Ice-383
93Pinnacle-94
Canadian-94
93PowerPlay-145
93Score-278
Canadian-278
93Stadium Club-314
Members Only Master Set-314
First Day Issue-314
93Ultra-222
93Upper Deck-369
94Canada Games NHL POGS-149
94Donruss-291
94Flair-101
94Leaf-17
94OPC Premier-58
Special Effects-58
94Parkhurst-124
Gold-124
94Pinnacle-49
Artist's Proofs-49
Rink Collection-49
94Score-49
Gold-49
Platinum-49
94Stadium Club-225
Members Only Master Set-225
First Day Issue-225
Super Team Winner Cards-225
94Topps/OPC Premier-58
Special Effects-58
94Ultra-124
94Upper Deck-143
Electric Ice-143
95Be A Player-207
Signatures-S207
Signatures Die Cuts-S207
95Donruss-320
95Leaf-260
95Parkhurst International-391
Emerald Ice-391
95Pinnacle-194
Artist's Proofs-194
Rink Collection-194
Global Gold-25
95Playoff One on One-168
95Score-179
Black Ice Artist's Proofs-179
Black Ice-179
96Devils Team Issue-25
96Upper Deck Ice-38
Parallel-38
97Devils Team Issue-20
97Pacific-299
Copper-299
Emerald Green-299
Ice Blue-299
Red-299
Silver-299
97Panini Stickers-67
97Score Devils-9
Platinum-9
Premier-9
97Upper Deck-303
98Be A Player-254
Press Release-254
98BAP Gold-254
98BAP Autographs-254
98BAP Autographs Gold-254
98OPC Chrome-187
Refractors-187
98Pacific-218
Ice Blue-218
Red-218
98Topps-187
O-Pee-Chee-187
99Pacific-314
Copper-314
Emerald Green-314
Gold-314
Ice Blue-314
Premiere Date-314
Red-314
99Panini Stickers-123
00O-Pee-Chee-209
00O-Pee-Chee Parallel-209
00Pacific-310
Copper-310
Gold-310
Ice Blue-310
Premiere Date-310
00Panini Stickers-79
00Topps/OPC-209
Parallel-209
00Upper Deck-271
Exclusives Tier 1-271
Exclusives Tier 2-271
00Upper Deck Vintage-81
01Norfolk Admirals-24
02BAP Sig Series Auto Buybacks 1998-254
02Russian Transfert-8
03Russian Hockey League-82
03Russian National Team-27
04Russian Super League All-Stars-11
04Russian World Championship Team-15

Zelezny, Otto
95Czech APS Extraliga-199

Zeliska, Lukas
06Prince Albert Raiders-14

Zellhuber, Stefan
94German First League-103

Zeman, Jiri
03Czech OFS Plus-231
04Czech OFS-328
05Czech HC Kladno-15
06Czech OFS-268

Zemchenok, Sergei
98Russian Hockey League-2
99Russian Hockey League-20
99Russian Metallurg Magnetogorsk-34

Zemlak, Garrett
06Saskatoon Blades-24

Zemlak, Richard
85Nordiques Team Issue-27
86Nordiques General Foods-28
87North Stars Postcards-31
89ProCards IHL-154
90ProCards AHL/IHL-623
91ProCards-590
94Classic Enforcers Promo-PR1

Zemlicka, Richard
91Finnish Semic World Champ Stickers-125
91Swedish Semic World Champ Stickers-125
92Finnish Semic-134
93Swedish Semic World Champ Stickers-95
94Finnish Jaa Kiekko-180
94German DEL-47
95Czech APS Extraliga-290
95Czech APS Extraliga-366
95Finnish Semic World Championships-151
95Swedish Globe World Championships-154
95Swedish World Championships Stickers-198
96Czech APS Extraliga-132
96Swedish Semic Wien-120
97Czech APS Extraliga-12
97Czech APS Extraliga-367
97Czech APS Extraliga-372
97Czech DS Extraliga-83
97Czech DS Stickers-67
98Czech DS-92
98Czech DS Stickers-214
98Czech OFS-367
99Czech DS-152
99Czech OFS-115
00Czech DS Extraliga-12
00Czech OFS-308
00Czech OFS Star Emerald-9
00Czech OFS Star Pink-9
00Czech OFS Star Violet-9
01Czech OFS-118
02Czech OFS Plus-22
Trios-T14
03Czech OFS Plus-102
03Czech OFS Plus Insert C-C5
03Czech OFS Plus Insert H-H13
04Slovakian Poprad Team Set-25

Zemlyanoi, Igor
98Russian Hockey League-13
99Russian Hockey League-2
99Russian Metallurg Magnetogorsk-30

Zenette, Bill
75HCA Steel City Vacuum-18

Zenhausern, Bruno
99Swiss Panini Stickers-356

Zenhausern, Gerd
93Swiss HNL-360
95Swiss HNL-259
96Swiss HNL-199
98Swiss Power Play Stickers-100
99Swiss Panini Stickers-100
00Swiss Panini Stickers-105
00Swiss Slapshot Mini-Cards-HCFG15
01Swiss HNL-280

02Swiss HNL-306
04Swiss Lausanne HC Postcards-11

Zent, Jason
94Classic-117
Gold-117
95PEI Senators-22
95Images-54
Gold-54
Autographs-54A
96Senators Pizza Hut-29
96Collector's Edge Ice-50
Prism-50

Zepp, Rob
00UD CHL Prospects-23
Autographs-A-RZ
CHL Class-CC5
Game Jersey Autographs-S-RZ
Game Jerseys-RZ
Game Jerseys-B-Z
Game Jerseys-S-Z
Game Jerseys-T-Z
Supremacy-CS4
02ECHL All-Star Southern-60
02Florida Everblades-22
02Florida Everblades RBI-132
03Florida Everblades-25
03Florida Everblades RBI Sports-176
04Florida Everblades-21
05Finnish Cardset -302
06Finnish Cardset-304
Between the Pipes-19
Superior Snatchers-12
Superior Snatchers Gold-12
Superior Snatchers Silver-12

Zerwesz, Rainer
94German DEL-101
95German DEL-212
96German DEL-356
98German DEL-102
99German Adler Mannheim Eagles Postcards-13
99German DEL-13
01German Upper Deck-60

Zerzuben, Martin
00Swiss Panini Stickers-175
01Swiss HNL-303
02Swiss HNL-135

Zessak, Christian
94German First League-37

Zetariuk, Jesse
02Red Deer Rebels-23
03Red Deer Rebels-18
05Moose Jaw Warriors-22

Zetek, Ondrej
94Czech APS Extraliga-212
95Czech APS Extraliga-154
96Czech APS Extraliga-59
97Czech APS Extraliga-179
97Czech DS Stickers-232
99Czech DS-111
99Czech OFS-410
99Czech OFS-420
00Czech OFS-219

Zettel, Michael
94German DEL-223
96Swiss HNL-382

Zetterberg, Bertz
55Swedish Alfabilder-4

Zetterberg, Bo
64Swedish Coralli ISHockey-108
65Swedish Coralli ISHockey-108
67Swedish Hockey-180

Zetterberg, Henrik
00Swedish Upper Deck-175
00Swedish Upper Deck-208
SHL Signatures-HZ
01SPx Rookie Redemption-R11
01UD Top Shelf Rookie Redemption-TS3
02Atomic-107
Blue-107
Gold-107
Red-107
Hobby Parallel-107
02BAP All-Star Edition-139
Gold-139
Silver-139
02BAP Memorabilia-286
Emerald-286
Ruby-286
Sapphire-286
NHL All-Star Game-286
NHL All-Star Game Blue-286
NHL All-Star Game Green-286
NHL All-Star Game Red-286
02BAP Memorabilia Toronto Fall Expo-286
02BAP Signature Series-190
All-Rookie-AR11
Autographs-190
Autographs Gold-190
02BAP Ultimate Memorabilia-16
Autographs-29
Calder Candidates-1
Customer Appreciation Card-1
02Bowman YoungStars-137
Gold-137
Silver-137
02Crown Royale-113
Blue-113
Purple-113
Red-113
Retail-113
Rookie Royalty-9
02eTopps-41
02ITG Used-198
02O-Pee-Chee-331
02O-Pee-Chee Premier Blue Parallel-331
02O-Pee-Chee Premier Red Parallel-331
02O-Pee-Chee Factory Set-331
02Pacific-405
02Pacific Calder-116
Silver-116
Reflections-9
02Pacific Complete-521
Red-521
02Pacific Exclusive-197
Blue-197
Gold-197
02Pacific Heads-Up-132
02Pacific Quest for the Cup-117
Gold-117
Calder Contenders-7
02Parkhurst-216
Bronze-216
Gold-216
Silver-216
Hardware-C2
02Parkhurst Retro-216
Minis-216
02Private Stock Reserve-160
Blue-160
Red-160
Retail-160
Class Act-7
02SP Authentic-186
Sign of the Times-HZ
Sign of the Times-SZ
Sign of the Times-YZ
Sign of the Times-SZB
Signed Patches-PHZ
02SP Game Used-75
02SPx-151
02Stadium Club-127
Silver Decoy Cards-127
Proofs-127
02Titanium-114
Blue-114
Red-114
Retail-114
Right on Target-7
02Topps-331
OPC Blue Parallel-331
OPC Red Parallel-331
Factory Set-331
02Topps Chrome-182
Black Border Refractors-182
Refractors-182
02Topps Heritage-131
02Topps Total-426
02UD Artistic Impressions-92
Gold-92
Common Ground-CG12
Common Ground-CG21
Common Ground Gold-CG12
Common Ground Gold-CG21
02UD Foundations-151
02UD Honor Roll-151
Signature Class-HZ
02UD Mask Collection-162
02UD Piece of History-128
02UD Premier Collection-81
Gold-81
Signatures Bronze-SHZ
Signatures Gold-SHZ
Signatures Silver-SHZ
02UD Top Shelf-127
02Upper Deck-234
Exclusives-234
Game Jersey Autographs-HZ
Game Jersey Series II-GJHZ
02Upper Deck Classic Portraits-111
02Upper Deck Rookie Update-168
Autographs-HZ
02Vanguard-113
LTD-113
Prime Prospects-9
02Swedish SHL-108
02Swedish SHL-143
Parallel-108
Parallel-143
02Swedish SHL Promos-TCC10
02Swedish SHL Signatures-15
02UD SuperStars *-268
Gold-268
03BAP Memorabilia-30
Emerald-30
Gold-30
Ruby-30
Sapphire-30
Brush with Greatness-9
Brush with Greatness Contest Cards-9
Future of the Game-FG-6
Jerseys-GJ-5
Jersey Autographs-GJ-5
03BAP Ultimate Memorabilia Autographs-150
Gold-150
03BAP Ultimate Mem Auto Jerseys-150
03BAP Ultimate Mem Auto Emblems-150
03BAP Ultimate Mem Blades of Steel-2
03BAP Ultimate Mem Complete Jersey-14
03BAP Ultimate Mem Complete Jersey Gold-14
03BAP Ultimate Memorabilia Emblems-5
03BAP Ultimate Memorabilia Emblems Gold-5
03BAP Ultimate Memorabilia Hat Tricks-2
03BAP Ultimate Memorabilia Jerseys-23
03BAP Ultimate Memorabilia Jerseys Gold-23
03BAP Ultimate Memorabilia Linemates-9
03BAP Ultimate Mem Linemates Autos-12
03BAP Ultimate Memorabilia Made to Order-Z1
03BAP Ultimate Memorabilia Made to Order-Z2
03BAP Ultimate Memorabilia Made to Order-Z3
03BAP Ultimate Memorabilia Made to Order-Z4
03BAP Ultimate Memorabilia Nameplates-23
03BAP Ultimate Mem Nameplates Gold-23
03BAP Ultimate Memorabilia Numbers-18
03BAP Ultimate Memorabilia Numbers Gold-18
03BAP Ultimate Memorabilia Triple Threads-23
03Beehive-74
Variations-74
Gold-74
Silver-74
Signatures-RF19
03Black Diamond-90
Black-90
Green-90
Red-90
Signature Gems-SG-20
03Bowman-20
Gold-20
03Bowman Chrome-20
Refractors-20
Gold Refractors-20
Xfractors-20
03Crown Royale Lords of the Rink-12
03ITG Action-233
League Leaders-L6
03ITG Toronto Fall Expo Jerseys-FE12
03ITG Used Signature Series-14
Gold-14
Autographs-HZ
Autographs Gold-HZ
Jerseys-10
Jerseys Gold-10
Jersey Autos-10
Emblems-1
Emblems Gold-1
Jersey and Stick-10
Jersey and Stick Gold-10
Teammates-4
Teammates Gold-4
Triple Memorabilia-1
Triple Memorabilia Gold-1
03ITG VIP Collages-18
03ITG VIP Collage Autographs-18
03ITG VIP Jerseys-13
03ITG VIP Jersey Autographs-13
03ITG VIP Sophomores-4
03McDonald's Pacific-20
03O-Pee-Chee-103
03OPC Blue-103
03OPC Gold-103
03OPC Red-103
03Pacific-128
Blue-128
Red-128
Cramer's Choice-6
03Pacific Atlantic City National-2
03Pacific Calder Contenders Entry Draft-7
03Pacific Calder Collection NHL All-Star Block Party
Gold-5
03Pacific Complete-149
Red-149
03Pacific Exhibit-56
Blue Backs-56
Yellow Backs-56
Pursuing Prominence-5
03Pacific Heads-Up-39
Hobby LTD-39
Retail LTD-39
In Focus-7
In Focus LTD-7
03Pacific Invincible-37
Blue-37
Red-37
Retail-37
Afterburners-5
New Sensations-11
03Pacific Montreal Olympic Stadium Show-4
Gold-4
03Pacific Prism-39
Blue-39
Gold-39
Red-39
Paramount Prodigies-8
Rookie Revolution-6
03Pacific Supreme-36
Blue-36
Red-36
Retail-36
Generations-5
03Pacific Toronto Spring Expo-4
Gold-4
03Parkhurst Original Six Detroit-16
Memorabilia-DM21
Memorabilia-DM57
Memorabilia-DM60
03Parkhurst Rookie-31
Jerseys-GJ-14
Jersey Autographs-GUJ-HZ
Jerseys Gold-GJ-14
03Private Stock Reserve-35
Blue-35
Red-35
Retail-35
Rising Stock-6
03SP Authentic-30
Limited-30
Sign of the Times-HZ
Sign of the Times-NSZ
03SP Game Used-102
Gold-102
Authentic Fabrics-DFZH
Authentic Fabrics-QSNZH
Authentic Fabrics Gold-DFZH
Authentic Fabrics Gold-QSNZH
Authentic Patches-APHZ
Double Threads-DTYZ
Signers-SPSHZ
Team Threads-TTYZH
Top Threads-YZHH
03SPx-32
03SPx-146
03SPx-160
Radiance-32
Radiance-146
Radiance-160
Spectrum-32
Spectrum-146
Spectrum-160
Big Futures-BF-HZ
Big Futures Limited-BF-HZ
Fantasy Franchise-FF-HYZ
Fantasy Franchise-FF-NSZ
Fantasy Franchise Limited-FF-HYZ
Fantasy Franchise Limited-FF-NSZ
Origins-O-HZ
Signature Threads-ST-HZ
Style-SPX-NZ
Style Limited-SPX-NZ
03Titanium-38
Hobby Jersey Number Parallels-38
Retail-38
Retail Jersey Number Parallels-38
Right on Target-5
03Topps-103
Blue-103
Gold-103
Red-103
Box Toppers-12
Own the Game-OTG6
03Topps All-Star Block Party-4
03Topps C55-7
03Topps C55-7B
Minis-7
Minis American Back-7
Minis American Back Red-7
Minis Bazooka Back-7
Minis Brooklyn Back-7
Minis Hat Trick Back-7
Minis O Canada Back-7
Minis O Canada Back Red-7
Minis Stanley Cup Back-7
Autographs-TA-HZ
03Topps Pristine-46
Gold Refractor Die Cuts-46
Refractors-46
Press Plates Black-46
Press Plates Cyan-46
Press Plates Magenta-46
Press Plates Yellow-46
03UD Honor Roll-28
03UD Honor Roll-101
Grade A Jerseys-TDET
03UD Premier Collection Signatures-PS-HZ
03UD Premier Collection Signatures Gold-PS-HZ
03Upper Deck-69
All-Star Lineup-AS8
Canadian Exclusives-69
Franchise Fabrics-FF-HZ
HG-69
03Upper Deck All-Star Promos-AS12
03Upper Deck Classic Portraits-32
03Upper Deck Ice-31
Gold-31
Authentics-IA-HZ
Under Glass Autographs-UG-HZ
03Upper Deck MVP-148
Gold Script-148
Silver Script-148
Canadian Exclusives-148
ProSign-PS-HZ
Winning Formula-WF10
03Upper Deck Rookie Update-30
Super Stars-SSHZ
03Upper Deck Trilogy-105
Crest Variations-105
Limited-105
Limited Threads-LT18
Scripts-S1HZ
Scripts Limited-S1HZ
03Upper Deck Victory-67
Bronze-67
Gold-67
Silver-67
Freshman Flashback-FF17
Game Breakers-GB23
03Russian World Championship Stars-10
03Toronto Star-33
Foil-7
04Pacific Global Connection-5
04Pacific Gold Crown Die-Cuts-4
04SP Authentic-35
Limited-35
Buybacks-63
Buybacks-64
Buybacks-65
Buybacks-66
Rookie Review-RR-HZ
Sign of the Times-ST-HZ
Sign of the Times-DS-MZ
04UD All-World-76
Gold-76
Autographs-76
Six Autographs-AS-SWD
04Ultimate Collection Signatures-US-HZ
04Ultimate Collection Signature Patches-SP-HZ
04Upper Deck World Cup Tribute-HZTSNL
04Swedish Alfabilder Alfa Stars-40
04Swedish Alfabilder Autographs-102
04Swedish Alfabilder Limited Autographs-102
04Swedish Alfabilder Next In Line-4
04Swedish Alfabilder Proof Parallels-40
04Swedish Elitset-286
Dominators-2
Gold-286
04Swedish Pure Skills-94
Parallel-94
Professional Power-HZ
Signatures-13
Signatures Limited-3
05Be A Player Signatures-HZ
05Be A Player Signatures Gold-HZ
05Beehive Matted Materials-MMHZ
05Beehive Matted Materials Remarkable-RMHZ
05Beehive Signature Scrapbook-SSHZ
05Black Diamond-30
Emerald-30
Gold-30
Onyx-30
Ruby-30
05Hot Prospects-36
En Fuego-36
Red Hot-36
White Hot-36
05Panini Stickers-270
05Parkhurst-168
Facsimile Auto Parallel-168
True Colors-TCDET
True Colors-TCDET
True Colors-TCDECO
True Colors-TCDECO
05SP Authentic-36
Limited-36
Scripts to Success-SSHZ
Sign of the Times-HZ
Sign of the Times Duals-DZF
Sign of the Times Triples-TZFD
05SP Game Used-37
Autographs-37
Gold-37
Authentic Fabrics-AF-HZ
Authentic Fabrics Autographs-AAF-HZ
Authentic Fabrics Dual-ZD
Authentic Fabrics Gold-AF-HZ
Authentic Fabrics Quad-LZDC
Authentic Fabrics Quad-NSZB
Authentic Patches Quad -LZDC
Authentic Patches Quad -NSZB
Authentic Patches-AP-HZ
Authentic Patches Autographs-AAP-HZ
Authentic Patches Dual-ZD
Awesome Authentics-AA-HZ
By the Letter-LM-HZ
Game Gear-GG-HZ
Game Gear Autographs-AG-HZ
SIGnificance-HZ
SIGnificance Gold-S-HZ
Significant Numbers-SN-HZ
Statscriptions-ST-HZ
05SPx-30
Spectrum-30
Winning Combos-WC-RW
Winning Combos-WC-ZD
Winning Combos-WC-ZL
Winning Combos Autographs-AWC-ZD
Winning Combos Autographs-AWC-ZL
Winning Combos Gold-WC-RW
Winning Combos Gold-WC-ZD
Winning Combos Gold-WC-ZL
Winning Combos Spectrum-WC-RW
Winning Combos Spectrum-WC-ZD
Winning Combos Spectrum-WC-ZL
Winning Materials-WM-HZ
Winning Materials Autographs-AWM-HZ
Winning Materials Gold-WM-HZ
Winning Materials Spectrum-WM-HZ
Xcitement Superstars-XS-HZ
Xcitement Superstars Gold-XS-HZ
Xcitement Superstars Spectrum-XS-HZ
05The Cup-43
Gold-43
Black Rainbow-43
Dual NHL Shields-DSDZ
Dual NHL Shields-DSNZ
Dual NHL Shields Autographs-ADSNZ
Emblems of Endorsement-EEHZ
Masterpiece Pressplates-43
Masterpiece Pressplates (Rookie Update)-209
Noble Numbers-NNZS
Noble Numbers Dual-DNNDZ
Patch Variation-P43
Patch Variation Autographs-AP43
Property of-POHZ
Scripted Numbers-SNZS
Scripted Numbers Dual-DSNZN
05UD Artifacts-40
Blue-40
Gold-40
Green-40
Pewter-40
Red-40
Auto Facts-AF-HZ
Auto Facts Blue-AF-HZ
Auto Facts Copper-AF-HZ
Auto Facts Pewter-AF-HZ
Auto Facts Silver-AF-HZ
Frozen Artifacts-FA-HZ
Frozen Artifacts Autographed-FA-HZ
Frozen Artifacts Copper-FA-HZ
Frozen Artifacts Dual-FAD-HZ
Frozen Artifacts Dual Autographed-FAD-HZ
Frozen Artifacts Dual Copper-FAD-HZ
Frozen Artifacts Dual Gold-FAD-HZ
Frozen Artifacts Dual Maroon-FAD-HZ
Frozen Artifacts Dual Pewter-FAD-HZ
Frozen Artifacts Dual Silver-FAD-HZ
Frozen Artifacts Gold-FA-HZ
Frozen Artifacts Maroon-FA-HZ
Frozen Artifacts Patches-FP-HZ
Frozen Artifacts Patches Autographed-FP-HZ
Frozen Artifacts Patches Dual-FPD-HZ
Frozen Artifacts Patches Dual Autos-FPD-HZ
Frozen Artifacts Patches Pewter-FP-HZ
Frozen Artifacts Patches Silver-FP-HZ
Frozen Artifacts Pewter-FA-HZ
Frozen Artifacts Silver-FA-HZ
Gold Autographed-40
Remarkable Artifacts-RA-HZ
Remarkable Artifacts Dual-RA-HZ
05UD Powerplay Power Marks-PMHZ
05Ultimate Collection-37
Gold-37
Endorsed Emblems-EEHZ
Jerseys Dual-DJFZ
Marquee Attractions-MA21
Marquee Attractions Signatures-SMA21
National Heroes Jerseys-NHJHZ
National Heroes Patches-NHPHZ
Ultimate Achievements-UAHZ
Ultimate Patches Dual-DPFZ
Ultimate Signatures-USHZ
Ultimate Signatures Pairings-UPZF
05Ultra-79
Gold-79
Fresh Ink-FI-HZ
Fresh Ink Blue-FI-HZ
Ice-79
05Upper Deck-73
HG Glossy-73
Jerseys Series II-J2HZ
Majestic Materials-MMHZ
NHL Generations-DNZ
NHL Generations-TSFZ
Notable Numbers-N-HZ
Patches-P-HZ
Shooting Stars-S-HZ
05Upper Deck Ice-35
Rainbow-35
Fresh Ice-FIHZ
Fresh Ice Glass-FIHZ
Fresh Ice Glass Patches-FIPHZ
Signature Swatches-SSHZ
05Upper Deck MVP-149
Gold-149
Platinum-149
05Upper Deck Rookie Update-35
05Upper Deck Rookie Update-209
Inspirations Patch Rookies-209
05Upper Deck Trilogy-36
05Upper Deck Trilogy-112
Crystal-112
Crystal Autographs-111
05Upper Deck Toronto Fall Expo-73
05Upper Deck Victory-71
Black-71
Gold-71
Silver-71
Game Breakers-GB19
05Swedish SHL Elitset-142
Gold-142
Playmakers-12
06Be A Player Portraits-42
06Beehive-64
06Beehive-205
Blue-64
Gold-64
Matte-64
Red Facsimile Signatures-64
Wood-64
5 X 7 Black and White-64
5 X 7 Dark Wood-64
Matted Materials-MMHZ
06Black Diamond-135
Black-135
Gold-135
Ruby-135
Gemography-GHZ
Jerseys-JHZ
Jerseys Black-JHZ
Jerseys Gold-JHZ
Jerseys Ruby-JHZ
Jerseys Black Autographs -JHZ
06Flair Showcase-40
06Flair Showcase-127
06Flair Showcase-231
06Flair Showcase-282
Parallel-40
Parallel-127
Parallel-231
Parallel-282
Hot Numbers-HN16
Hot Numbers Parallel-HN16
Inks-IHZ
Wave of the Future-WF13
06Fleer-71
Oversized-71
Tiffany-71
Total 0-09
06Hot Prospects-39
Red Hot-39
White Hot-39
06ITG International Ice-154
Gold-154
Autographs-AHZ
Stick and Jersey-SJ25
Stick and Jersey Gold-SJ25
06ITG Ultimate Memorabilia-65
Artist Proof-65
Autos-62
Autos Gold-62
Autos Dual-6
Autos Dual Gold-6
Autos Triple-2
Autos Triple Gold-2
Blades of Steel-15
Blades of Steel Gold-15
Decades-5
Decades Gold-5
Double Memorabilia-25
Double Memorabilia Gold-25
Going For Gold-10
Going For Gold Gold-10
In The Numbers-19
In The Numbers Gold-19
Jerseys Autos-65
Jerseys Autos Gold-65
06McDonald's Upper Deck Autographs-AHZ
06McDonald's Upper Deck Jerseys-JHZ
06McDonald's Upper Deck Patches-PHZ
06NHL POG-53
06O-Pee-Chee-190
Rainbow-190
06Panini Stickers-260
06SP Authentic-65
06SP Authentic-116
Limited-65
Limited-116
Sign of the Times Triples-ST3LHZ
06SP Game Used-35
Gold-35
Rainbow-35
Authentic Fabrics-AFHZ
Authentic Fabrics Parallel-AFHZ
Authentic Fabrics Patches-AFHZ
Authentic Fabrics Dual-AF2HZ
Authentic Fabrics Dual Patches-AF2HZ
Authentic Fabrics Triple-AF3DET
Authentic Fabrics Triple Patches-AF3DET
Authentic Fabrics Quads-AF4SFSZ
Authentic Fabrics Quads Patches-AF4SFSZ
Authentic Fabrics Fives-AF5GWG
Authentic Fabrics Fives Patches-AF5GWG
Authentic Fabrics Eights-AF8SWE
Authentic Fabrics Eights Patches-AF8SWE
Autographs-35
Inked Sweaters Dual-IS2ZH
Inked Sweaters Dual Patches-IS2ZH
SIGnificance-SHZ
06SPx-36
Spectrum-36
SPxcitement-X34
SPxcitement Spectrum-X34
SPxcitement Autographs-X34
Winning Materials-WMHZ
Winning Materials Spectrum-WMHZ
Winning Materials Autographs-WMHZ
06The Cup-28
Autographed Foundations-CQHZ
Autographed Foundations Patches-CQHZ
Autographed NHL Shields Duals-DASHZ
Autographed NHL Shields Duals-DASZN
Autographed Patches-28
Black Rainbow-28
Foundations-CQHZ
Foundations Patches-CQHZ
Enshrinements-EHZ
Gold-28
Gold Patches-28
Honorable Numbers-HNHZ
Jerseys-28
Limited Logos-LLHZ
Masterpiece Pressplates-28
Scripted Swatches-SSHZ
Scripted Swatches Duals-DSZL
Signature Patches-SPHZ
06UD Artifacts-63
06UD Artifacts-166
Blue-63
Blue-166
Gold-63
Gold-166
Platinum-63
Platinum-166
Radiance-63
Radiance-166
Autographed Radiance Parallel-63
Autographed Radiance Parallel-166
Red-63
Red-166
Auto-Facts-AFHZ
Auto-Facts Gold-AFHZ
Frozen Artifacts-FAHZ
Frozen Artifacts Black-FAHZ
Frozen Artifacts Blue-FAHZ
Frozen Artifacts Gold-FAHZ
Frozen Artifacts Platinum-FAHZ
Frozen Artifacts Red-FAHZ
Frozen Artifacts Autographed Black-FAHZ
Frozen Artifacts Patches Black-FAHZ
Frozen Artifacts Patches Blue-FAHZ
Frozen Artifacts Patches Gold-FAHZ
Frozen Artifacts Patches Platinum-FAHZ
Frozen Artifacts Patches Red-FAHZ
Frozen Artifacts Patches Autographed Black Tag
Parallel-FAHZ
Tundra Tandems-TTNH
Tundra Tandems Black-TTNG
Tundra Tandems Black-TTNH
Tundra Tandems Blue-TTNH
Tundra Tandems Gold-TTNH
Tundra Tandems Platinum-TTNH
Tundra Tandems Red-TTNH
Tundra Tandems Dual Patches Red-TTNH
06UD Mini Jersey Collection-36
06UD Powerplay-36
Impact Rainbow-36
In Action-IA4
Power Marks-PMHZ
06Ultimate Collection-22
Jerseys-UJ-HZ
Jerseys Dual-UJ2-ZD
Patches-UJ-HZ
Patches Dual-UJ2-ZD
06Ultra-70
Gold Medallion-70
Ice Medallion-70
Action-UA9
Difference Makers-DM14
Scoring Kings-SK8
06Upper Deck Arena Giveaways-DET4
06Upper Deck-323
Exclusives Parallel-323
High Gloss Parallel-323
All World-AW13
Game Jerseys-J2HZ
Game Patches-P2HZ
Generations Duals-G2NZ
Generations Triples-G3NZS
Generations Patches Dual-G2PNZ
Generations Patches Triple-G3PNZS
Hometown Heroes-HH34
Masterpieces-323
Oversized Wal-Mart Exclusives-323
Signatures-SHZ
06Upper Deck MVP-106
Gold Script-106
Super Script-106
Autographs-OALZ
Clutch Performers-CP16
Jerseys-OJKZ
Jerseys-OJZN
06Upper Deck Ovation-67
06Upper Deck Sweet Shot-37
Signature Shots/Saves-SSHZ
Signature Shots/Saves Ice Signings-SSIHZ
Signature Shots/Saves Sticks-SSSHZ
Signature Sticks-STHZ
Sweet Stitches-SSHZ
Sweet Stitches Duals-SSHZ
Sweet Stitches Triples-SSHZ
06Upper Deck Trilogy-36
Combo Autographed Jerseys-CJLZ
Combo Autographed Patches-CJLZ
Combo Clearcut Autographs-C2LZ
Combo Clearcut Autographs-C3LDZ
Honorary Scripted Patches-HSPHZ
Honorary Scripted Swatches-HSSHZ
Honorary Swatches-HSHZ
Scripts-S2HZ
Scripts-S3HZ
Scripts-TSHZ
06Upper Deck Victory-73
06Upper Deck Victory Black-73
06Upper Deck Victory Gold-73
06Upper Deck Victory GameBreakers-GB16
06Upper Deck Victory Next In Line-NL20
06Upper Deck Victory Oversize Cards-HZ
06Russian Sport Collection Olympic Stars-17
07Upper Deck Victory-104
Black-104
Gold-104
GameBreakers-GB8
Oversize Cards-OS27
Stars on Ice-SI40

Zetterberg, Kent
71Swedish Hockey-378

Zetterberg, Patrik
94Swedish Leaf-254
95Swedish Leaf-292
98Swedish UD Choice-90
99Swedish Upper Deck-194
00German DEL-101
01German Upper Deck-105
02Swedish SHL-259
Parallel-259
03Swedish Elite-121
Silver-121

Zetterberg, Stig-Olof
67Swedish Hockey-245

Zetterholm, Peter
84Swedish Semic Elitserien-9

Zetterstrom, Lars
74Swedish Stickers-197
78Canucks Royal Bank-23
79Panini Stickers-190

Zetterstrom, Lasse
73Swedish Stickers-189

Zettler, Rob
84Sault Ste. Marie Greyhounds-23
87Sault Ste. Marie Greyhounds-14
88ProCards IHL-25
89ProCards IHL-81
90O-Pee-Chee-289
90Topps-289
Tiffany-289
91O-Pee-Chee-272
91OPC Premier-21
91Pinnacle-213
French-213
91Pro Set-330
French-330
91Score American-370
91Score Canadian Bilingual-643
91Score Canadian English-643
91Score Rookie/Traded-93T
91Sharks Sports Action-21
91Stadium Club-194
91Topps-272
91Upper Deck-61
French-61
92Bowman-84
92O-Pee-Chee-366
92Panini Stickers-127
92Panini Stickers French-127
92Pinnacle-89
French-89
92Score-191
Canadian-191
92Stadium Club-225
92Topps-227
Gold-227G
93Flyers Lineup Sheets-36
93Score-413
Canadian-413
94Parkhurst-164
Gold-164
94Stadium Club-109
Members Only Master Set-109
First Day Issue-109
Super Team Winner Cards-109
94Upper Deck-454
Electric Ice-454
96Be A Player-64
Autographs-64
Autographs Silver-64
97Pacific-101
Copper-101
Emerald Green-101
Ice Blue-101
Red-101
Silver-101
99Portland Pirates-25
00Portland Pirates-15

Zettlin, Ake
65Swedish Coralli ISHockey-109

Zevakhin, Alexander
98Black Diamond-106
Double Diamond-106
Triple Diamond-106
Quadruple Diamond-106
98SPx Top Prospects-77
Radiance-77
Spectrum-77
99Russian Hockey League-123
00Wilkes-Barre Scranton Penguins-26
01Wilkes-Barre Scranton Penguins-11
02Russian SL-52
02Wilkes-Barre Scranton Penguins-9
03Russian Hockey League-21

Zezel, Peter
85Flyers Postcards-30
85O-Pee-Chee-24
85O-Pee-Chee Stickers-94
85Topps-24
86Flyers Postcards-28
86O-Pee-Chee-190
86O-Pee-Chee Stickers-245
86Topps-190
87Flyers Postcards-25
87O-Pee-Chee-71
87O-Pee-Chee Stickers-96
87Panini Stickers-129
87Topps-71
88Blues Kodak-25
88O-Pee-Chee-146
88O-Pee-Chee Stickers-102
88Topps-146
89Blues Kodak-9
89O-Pee-Chee-27
89O-Pee-Chee Stickers-23
89Panini Stickers-118
89Topps-27
90Bowman-19
Tiffany-19
90O-Pee-Chee-15
90OPC Premier-131
90Panini Stickers-264
90Pro Set-274
90Pro Set-556
90Score-24
Canadian-24
90Score Rookie/Traded-6T
90Topps-15
Tiffany-15
90Upper Deck-17
French-17
91Pro Set Platinum-232
91Bowman-164
91Maple Leafs PLAY-30
91O-Pee-Chee-445
91Panini Stickers-103
91Parkhurst-174
French-174
91Pinnacle-174
91Pinnacle-414
French-174
French-414
91Pro Set-227
French-227
91Score American-269
91Score Canadian Bilingual-489
91Score Canadian English-489
91Stadium Club-104
91Topps-445
91Upper Deck-241
French-241
92Bowman-263
92Maple Leafs Kodak-22
92O-Pee-Chee-337
92Panini Stickers-81
92Panini Stickers French-81
92Parkhurst-410
Emerald Ice-410
92Pinnacle-283
French-283
92Pro Set-187
92Score-174
Canadian-174
92Stadium Club-433
92Topps-319
Gold-319G
92Ultra-216
92Upper Deck-389
93Donruss-338
93Leaf-107
Maple Leafs Score Black's-4
93OPC Premier-454
Gold-454
93Parkhurst-206
Emerald Ice-206
93Pinnacle-297
Canadian-297
93PowerPlay-455
93Score-31
Canadian-31
93Stadium Club-116
Members Only Master Set-116
OPC-116
First Day Issue-116
First Day Issue OPC-116
93Topps/OPC Premier-454
Gold-454
93Ultra-436
93Upper Deck-199
94Be A Player Signature Cards-100
94Leaf-533
94OPC Premier-22
Special Effects-22
94Pinnacle-109
Artist's Proofs-109
Rink Collection-109
94Stars Postcards-22
94Topps/OPC Premier-22
Special Effects-22
94Upper Deck-140
Electric Ice-140
95Upper Deck-377
Electric Ice-377
Electric Ice Gold-377
96Be A Player-94
Autographs-94
Autographs Silver-94
97Albany River Rats-22
98Be A Player-294
Press Release-294
98BAP Gold-294
98BAP Autographs-294
98BAP Autographs Gold-294
98OPC Chrome-56
Refractors-56
98Pacific-436
Ice Blue-436
Red-436
98Topps-56
O-Pee-Chee-56
02BAP Sig Series Auto Buybacks 1998-294

Zhadeleyenov, Sergei
00Russian Hockey League-213

Zhamnov, Alexei
91O-Pee-Chee Inserts-48R
91Upper Deck-2
French-2
91Finnish Semic World Champ Stickers-95
91Swedish Semic World Champ Stickers-95
92OPC Premier-13
92Parkhurst-210
Emerald Ice-210
92Pinnacle-416
French-416
92Ultra-447
92Upper Deck-578
Euro-Rookies-ER8
92Finnish Semic-110
92Russian Stars Red Ace-35
92Russian Stars Red Ace-2
92Russian Tri-Globe From Russia With Puck-7
92Russian Tri-Globe From Russia With Puck-8
93Donruss-380
93Jets Readers Club-23
93Jets Ruffles-28
93Leaf-84
Gold Rookies-5
93OPC Premier-128
93OPC Premier-420
Gold-128
Gold-420
93Panini Stickers-190
93Parkhurst-243
93Parkhurst-503
Emerald Ice-243
Emerald Ice-503
93Pinnacle-56
Canadian-56
93PowerPlay-278
Rising Stars-9
Second Year Stars-12
93Score-256
Canadian-256
Dynamic Duos Canadian-2
93Stadium Club-56
Members Only Master Set-56
OPC-56
First Day Issue-56
First Day Issue OPC-56
93Topps/OPC Premier-128
93Topps/OPC Premier-420
Gold-128
Gold-420
93Topps Premier Black Gold-8
93Ultra-128
93Upper Deck-162
SP-180

93Upper Deck Locker All-Stars-60
94Be A Player Signature Cards-21
94Canada Games NHL POGS-375
94Donruss-73
94EA Sports-147
94Finest-102
Super Team Winners-102
Refractors-102
94Flair-212
94Fleer-247
94Leaf-97
94Leaf Limited-113
94McDonald's Upper Deck-McD27
94OPC Premier-217
Special Effects-217
94Parkhurst-260
Gold-260
SE Vintage-45
94Pinnacle-147
Artist's Proofs-147
Rink Collection-147
94Score-154
Gold-154
Platinum-154
94Select-51
Gold-51
94SP-133
Die Cuts-133
94Stadium Club Super Teams-26
94Stadium Club Super Team MemberOnly Set-26
94Topps/OPC Premier-217
Special Effects-217
94Ultra-398
94Upper Deck-7
Electric Ice-7
SP Inserts-SP90
SP Inserts Die Cuts-SP90
94Finnish Jaa Kiekko-150
94Finnish Jaa Kiekko-356
95Bashan Super Stickers-135
95Bowman-60
All-Foil-60
95Canada Games NHL POGS-15
95Canada Games NHL POGS-289
95Collector's Choice-49
95Collector's Choice-383
Player's Club-49
Player's Club-383
Player's Club Platinum-49
Player's Club Platinum-383
Crash The Game-C8A
Crash The Game-C8B
Crash The Game-C8C
Crash The Game Gold-C8A
Crash The Game Gold-C8B
Crash The Game Gold-C8C
Crash the Game Silver Redeemed-C8
Crash the Game Silver Bonus-C8
Crash the Game Gold Redeemed-C8
Crash the Game Gold Bonus-C8
95Donruss-155
Elite Inserts-1
Igniters-6
95Donruss Elite-29
Die Cut Stars-29
Die Cut Uncut-29
95Emotion-198
Xcel-10
Xcited-17
95Finest-78
Refractors-78
95Hoyle Western Playing Cards-54
95Imperial Stickers-135
95Jets Readers Club-12
95Jets Team Issue-26
95Kraft-47
95Kraft-76
95Leaf-104
Fire On Ice-3
Freeze Frame-5
Gold Stars-4
95Leaf Limited-116
95McDonald's Pinnacle-MCD-3
95Metal-168
International Steel-23
Winners-9
95NHL Aces Playing Cards-13H
95Panini Stickers-212
95Parkhurst International-226
95Parkhurst International-241
Emerald Ice-226
Emerald Ice-241
95Pinnacle-23
Artist's Proofs-23
Rink Collection-23
Roaring 20s-11
95Playoff One on One-110
95Playoff One on One-330
95Pro Magnets-65
95Score-85
Black Ice Artist's Proofs-85
Black Ice-85
Border Battle-12
Lamplighters-10
95Select Certified-6
Mirror Gold-6
Double Strike-20
Double Strike Gold-20
95SkyBox Impact-187
Ice Quake-12
95SP-167
95Stadium Club-95
Members Only Master Set-95
95Summit-3
Artist's Proofs-3
Ice-3
Mad Hatters-5
95Topps-22
95Topps-331
OPC Inserts-22
OPC Inserts-331
Marquee Men Power Boosters-22
Power Lines-2PL
95Topps SuperSkills-70
Platinum-70
95Ultra-185
95Ultra-398
Gold Medallion-185
Premier Pivots-10
Premier Pivots Gold Medallion-10
Red Light Specials-10
Red Light Specials Gold Medallion-10
Ultraview-10
Ultraview Hot Pack-10
95Upper Deck-64
95Upper Deck-234
Electric Ice-64
Electric Ice-69
Electric Ice-234
Electric Ice Gold-64
Electric Ice Gold-234
Freeze Frame-F13
Freeze Frame Jumbo-F13
Predictor Retail-R28
Predictor Retail Exchange-R28
95Zenith-26
95Swedish Globe World Championships-173
96Be A Player-11
96Black Diamond-106
Gold-106
96Collector's Choice-203
96Collector's Choice-327
Crash the Game-C11A
Crash the Game-C11B
Crash the Game-C11C
Crash the Game Gold-C11A
Crash the Game Gold-C11B
Crash the Game Gold-C11C
Crash the Game Exchange-CR11
Crash the Game Exchange Gold-CR11
96Donruss-89
Press Proofs-89
96Donruss Canadian Ice-88
Gold Press Proofs-88
Red Press Proofs-88
96Donruss Elite-65
Die Cut Stars-65
96Flair-17
Blue Ice-17
96Fleer-94
96Fleer Picks-56
Fabulous 50-50
Jagged Edge-14
96Leaf-107
Press Proofs-107
96Leaf Preferred-95
Press Proofs-95
96Metal Universe-29
96NHL Pro Stamps-65
96Pinnacle-13
Artist's Proofs-13
Foil-13
Premium Stock-13
Rink Collection-13
96Score-128
Artist's Proofs-128
Dealer's Choice Artist's Proofs-128
Special Artist's Proofs-128
Golden Blades-128
96SkyBox Impact-21
96SP-30
96SPx-36
Gold-36
96Summit-37
Artist's Proofs-37
Ice-37
Metal-37
Premium Stock-37
96Upper Deck-125
96Upper Deck-233
Superstar Showdown-SS24B
96Zenith-108
Artist's Proofs-108
96Swedish Semic Wien-143
97Be A Player-99
Autographs-99
Autographs Die-Cuts-99
Autographs Prismatic Die-Cuts-99
97Black Diamond-56
Double Diamond-56
Triple Diamond-56
Quadruple Diamond-56
97Collector's Choice Star Quest-SQ46
97Donruss-96
Press Proofs Silver-96
Press Proofs Gold-96
97Donruss Canadian Ice-91
Dominion Series-91
Provincial Series-91
97Donruss Priority-62
Stamp of Approval-62
97Pacific-316
Copper-316
Emerald Green-316
Ice Blue-316
Red-316
Silver-316
97Pacific Invincible-32
Copper-32
Emerald Green-32
Ice Blue-32
Red-32
Silver-32
97Pacific Omega-53
Copper-53
Dark Gray-53
Emerald Green-53
Gold-53
Ice Blue-53
97Panini Stickers-128
97Paramount-47
Copper-47
Dark Grey-47
Emerald Green-47
Ice Blue-47
Red-47
Silver-47
97Pinnacle-123
Press Plates Back Black-123
Press Plates Back Cyan-123
Press Plates Back Magenta-123
Press Plates Back Yellow-123
Press Plates Front Black-123
Press Plates Front Cyan-123
Press Plates Front Magenta-123
Press Plates Front Yellow-123
97Pinnacle Certified-101
Red-101
Mirror Blue-101
Mirror Gold-101
Mirror Red-101
97Pinnacle Inside-107
97Pinnacle Tot Cert Platinum Blue-101
97Pinnacle Tot Cert Platinum Gold-101
97Pinnacle Totally Certified Platinum Red-101
97Pinnacle Tot Cert Mirror Platinum Gold-101
97Score-175
97SP Authentic-32
97Upper Deck-42
Three Star Selects-19C
98Aurora-44
98Be A Player-29
Press Release-29
98BAP Gold-29
98BAP Autographs-29
98BAP Autographs Gold-29
98BAP Tampa Bay All Star Game-29
98Finest-134
No Protectors-134
No Protectors Refractors-134
Refractors-134
98Katch-36
98OPC Chrome-135
Refractors-135
98Pacific-155
Ice Blue-155
Red-155
98Pacific Omega-56
Red-56
Opening Day Issue-56
98Panini Stickers-112
98Paramount-51
Copper-51
Emerald Green-51
Holo-Electric-51
Ice Blue-51
Silver-51
98Topps-135
O-Pee-Chee-135
98UD Choice-48
Prime Choice Reserve-48
Reserve-48
98Upper Deck-245
Exclusives-245
Exclusives 1 of 1-245
Game Jerseys-GJ23
Gold Reserve-245
98Slovakian Eurotel-29
99Aurora-34
Premiere Date-34
99BAP Memorabilia-118
Gold-118
Silver-118
99Blackhawks Lineup Cards-10
99O-Pee-Chee-247
99O-Pee-Chee Chrome-247
99O-Pee-Chee Chrome Refractors-247
99Pacific-98
Copper-98
Emerald Green-98
Gold-98
Ice Blue-98
Premiere Date-98
Red-98
99Pacific Dynagon Ice-53
Blue-53
Copper-53
Gold-53
Premiere Date-53
99Pacific Omega-57
Copper-57
Gold-57
Ice Blue-57
Premiere Date-57
99Pacific Prism-36
Holographic Blue-36
Holographic Gold-36
Holographic Mirror-36
Holographic Purple-36
Premiere Date-36
99Panini Stickers-200
99Paramount-59
Copper-59
Emerald-59
Gold-59
Holographic Emerald-59
Holographic Gold-59
Holographic Silver-59
Ice Blue-59
Premiere Date-59
Red-59
Silver-59
99Revolution-36
Premiere Date-36
Red-36
Shadow Series-36
Copper-36
Gold-36
CSC Silver-36
99Stadium Club-107
First Day Issue-107
One of a Kind-107
Printing Plates Black-107
Printing Plates Cyan-107
Printing Plates Magenta-107
Printing Plates Yellow-107
99Topps/OPC-247
99Topps/OPC Chrome-247
Refractors-247
99Upper Deck-208
Exclusives-208
Exclusives 1 of 1-208
99Upper Deck Gold Reserve-208
99Upper Deck MVP-50
Gold Script-50
Silver Script-50
Super Script-50
99Upper Deck MVP SC Edition-46
Gold Script-46
Silver Script-46
Super Script-46
99Upper Deck Victory-72
99Wayne Gretzky Hockey-44
99Slovakian Challengers-30
00Aurora-35
Premiere Date-35
00BAP Memorabilia-236
Emerald-236
Ruby-236
Sapphire-236
Promos-236
00BAP Mem Chicago Sportsfest Copper-236
00BAP Memorabilia Chicago Sportsfest Blue-236
00BAP Memorabilia Chicago Sportsfest Gold-236
00BAP Memorabilia Chicago Sportsfest Ruby-236
00BAP Memorabilia Chicago Sun-Times Ruby-236
00BAP Memorabilia Chicago Sun-Times Gold-236
00BAP Mem Chicago Sun-Times Sapphire-236
00BAP Mem Toronto Fall Expo Copper-236
00BAP Memorabilia Toronto Fall Expo Gold-236
00BAP Memorabilia Toronto Fall Expo Ruby-236
00BAP Parkhurst 2000-P92
00BAP Signature Series-138
Emerald-138
Ruby-138
Sapphire-138
Autographs-130
Autographs Gold-130
00Crown Royale-25
Ice Blue-25
Limited Series-25
Premiere Date-25
Red-25
00O-Pee-Chee-50
00O-Pee-Chee Parallel-50
00Pacific-105
Copper-105
Gold-105
Ice Blue-105
Premiere Date-105
00Panini Stickers-125
00Paramount-55
Copper-55
Gold-55
Holo-Gold-55
Holo-Silver-55
Ice Blue-55
Premiere Date-55
00Private Stock-21
Gold-21
Premiere Date-21
Retail-21
Silver-21
Game Gear-17
Game Gear Patches-17
00Revolution-33
Blue-33
Premiere Date-33
Red-33
00Stadium Club-113
00Titanium Game Gear-6
00Titanium Game Gear-73
00Titanium Game Gear Patches-73
00Titanium Draft Day Edition-22
Patches-22
00Topps/OPC-50
Parallel-50
00Topps Heritage-160
Original Six Relics-OSJ-AZ
Original Six Relics-OSJ
00UD Heroes-26
00UD Pros and Prospects-20
00UD Reserve-19
00Upper Deck-42
Exclusives Tier 1-42
Exclusives Tier 2-42
00Upper Deck MVP-41
First Stars-41
Second Stars-41
Third Stars-41
00Upper Deck Victory-56
00Upper Deck Vintage-82
00Vanguard-24
Dual Game-Worn Jerseys-10
Dual Game-Worn Patches-10
Holographic Gold-24
Holographic Purple-24
Pacific Proofs-24
01O-Pee-Chee-186
01O-Pee-Chee Premier Parallel-186
01Pacific-94
Extreme LTD-94
Hobby LTD-94
Premiere Date-94
Retail LTD-94
Jerseys-7
01Pacific Adrenaline-43
Blue-43
Premiere Date-43
Red-43
Retail-43
Jerseys-8
01Pacific Arena Exclusives-94
01Pacific Heads-Up Quad Jerseys-7
01Parkhurst-191
Jerseys-PJ32
01Private Stock Game Gear-27
01Private Stock Game Gear Patches-27
01Stadium Club Souvenirs-AZ
01Titanium-33
Hobby Parallel-33
Premiere Date-33
Retail-33
Retail Parallel-33
Double-Sided Jerseys-10
01Topps-186
OPC Parallel-186
Reserve Emblems-AZ
Reserve Jerseys-AZ
Reserve Name Plates-AZ
Reserve Numbers-AZ
Reserve Patches-AZ
01Upper Deck-270
Exclusives-270
01Upper Deck MVP-42
01Upper Deck Victory-76
Gold-76
01Upper Deck Vintage-54
01Upper Deck Vintage-61
02BAP All-Star Edition-100
Jerseys-100
Jerseys Gold-100
Jerseys Silver-100
02BAP First Edition-21
Jerseys-21
02BAP Memorabilia-15
02BAP Memorabilia-252
Emerald-15
Emerald-252
Ruby-15
Ruby-252
Sapphire-15
Sapphire-252
NHL All-Star Game-15
NHL All-Star Game-252
NHL All-Star Game Blue-15
NHL All-Star Game Blue-252
NHL All-Star Game Green-15
NHL All-Star Game Green-252
NHL All-Star Game Red-15
NHL All-Star Game Red-252
02BAP Memorabilia Toronto Fall Expo-15
02BAP Memorabilia Toronto Fall Expo-252
02BAP Signature Series-2
Autographs-2
Autograph Buybacks 1998-29
Autograph Buybacks 2000-130
Autographs Gold-2
02Blackhawks Postcards-7
02Bowman YoungStars-32
Gold-32
Silver-32
02Crown Royale-22
Blue-22
Red-22
Retail-22
Dual Patches-4
02O-Pee-Chee-121
02O-Pee-Chee Premier Blue Parallel-121
02O-Pee-Chee Premier Red Parallel-121
02O-Pee-Chee Factory Set-121
02Pacific-85
Blue-85
Red-85
02Pacific Complete-219
Red-219
02Pacific Exclusive-38
02Pacific Heads-Up-27
Blue-27
Purple-27
Red-27
02Pacific Quest for the Cup-19
Gold-19
02Parkhurst-87
Bronze-87
Gold-87
Silver-87
Teammates-TT13
02Parkhurst Retro-30
Minis-30
02Private Stock Reserve-22
Blue-22
Red-22
Retail-22
02SP Authentic-17
Beckett Promos-17
02SP Game Used Piece of History-PHAZ
02SP Game Used Piece of History Gold-PHAZ
02SP Game Used Piece of History Rainbow-PHAZ
02Topps-121
OPC Blue Parallel-121
OPC Red Parallel-121
Factory Set-121
02Topps Chrome-77
Black Border Refractors-77
Refractors-77
02Topps Heritage-97
Chrome Parallel-97
02Topps Total-91
02UD Artistic Impressions-17
Gold-17
02UD Artistic Impressions Beckett Promos-17
02UD Artistic Impressions Retrospectives-R17
02UD Artistic Impressions Retrospect Gold-R17
02UD Artistic Impress Retrospect Silver-R17
02UD Honor Roll-77
02UD Top Shelf-20
02Upper Deck-36
Exclusives-36
Specialists-SAZ
02Upper Deck Classic Portraits-20
Headliners-DZ
Headliners Limited-DZ
Hockey Royalty-DZT
Hockey Royalty Limited-DZT
02Upper Deck MVP-38
Gold-38
Classics-38
Golden Classics-38
02Upper Deck Victory-43
Bronze-43
Gold-43
Silver-43
National Pride-NP33
02Upper Deck Vintage-60
02Upper Deck Vintage-267
02Vanguard Jerseys-12
02Vanguard Jerseys Gold-12
03BAP Memorabilia-9
Emerald-9
Gold-9
Ruby-9
Sapphire-9
03Beehive-119B
Gold-119
Silver-119
03Black Diamond-9
Black-9
Green-9
Red-9
Threads-DT-AZ
Threads Green-DT-AZ
Threads Red-DT-AZ
Threads Black-DT-AZ
03Blackhawks Postcards-31
03ITG Action-171
03ITG Action-672
03NHL Sticker Collection-175
03Pacific-78
Blue-78
Red-78
03Pacific Complete-144
Red-144
03Pacific Exhibit-34
Blue Backs-34
Yellow Backs-34
03Pacific Invincible-19
Blue-19
Red-19
Retail-19
03Pacific Prism-26
Blue-26
Gold-26
Red-26
03Parkhurst Original Six Chicago-18
03Parkhurst Original Six Chicago-71
Memorabilia-CM4
Memorabilia-CM13
Memorabilia-CM58
03Private Stock Reserve-23
Blue-23
Red-23
Retail-23
03SP Authentic-16
Limited-16
03SP Game Used Authentic Fabrics-DFZT
03SP Game Used Authentic Fabrics Gold-DFZT
03SP Game Used Double Threads-DTZT
03SPx-18
Radiance-18
Spectrum-18
03Titanium-27
Hobby Jersey Number Parallels-27
Retail-27
Retail Jersey Number Parallels-27
03Topps Pristine Popular Demand Relics-PD-AZ
03Topps Pristine Popular Demand Relic Ref-PD-AZ
03Topps Traded-TT52
Blue-TT52
Gold-TT52
Red-TT52
03Upper Deck-40
Canadian Exclusives-40
HG-40
03Upper Deck Classic Portraits-17
03Upper Deck Ice-17
Gold-17
03Upper Deck MVP-91
Gold Script-91
Silver Script-91
Canadian Exclusives-91
03Upper Deck Rookie Update-66
03Upper Deck Trilogy-17
Limited-17
03Upper Deck Victory-38
Bronze-38
Gold-38
Silver-38
04UD All-World-41
Gold-41
05Bruins Boston Globe-11
05Upper Deck Hockey Showcase-HS40
05Upper Deck Showcase Promos-HS40
05Upper Deck MVP-35
Gold-35
Platinum-35

Zhavaliuk, Vyacheslav

98Russian Hockey League-88
99Russian Hockey League-250
00Russian Hockey League-53
02Russian Hockey League-9
02Russian Hockey League-10
03Russian Hockey League-68

Zhavyalov, Vladimir

00Russian Hockey League-64

Zhdan, Alexander

93Richmond Renegades-3
99Russian Hockey League-43
00Russian Hockey League-36
00Russian Hockey League-311
02Russian SL-18
02Russian Transfert-17
03Russian Hockey League-42
03Russian World Championship Team 2003-13

Zhelenchev, Igor

00Russian Hockey League-174

Zherdev, Nikolai

01Russian Young Lions-8
02Russian Hockey League-92
02Russian Hockey League-197
02Russian Hockey League-261
02Russian SL-44
02Russian Transfert-9
02Russian Young Lions-15
03BAP Memorabilia-210
Draft Redemptions-4
03BAP Ultimate Memorabilia Autographs-109
Gold-109
03BAP Ultimate Mem Auto Jerseys-109
03BAP Ultimate Mem Auto Emblems-109
03BAP Ultimate Mem Auto Numbers-109
03BAP Ultimate Mem Calder Candidates-10
03BAP Ultimate Mem Calder Candidates Gold-10
03BAP Ultimate Mem Franch Present Future-9
03BAP Ultimate Mem Magnificent Prospects-10
03BAP Ultimate Mem Magnif Prospect Autos-10
03BAP Ultimate Mem Rookie Jersey Emblems-19
03BAP Ultimate Mem Rookie Jsy Emblem Gold-19
03BAP Ultimate Mem Rookie Jersey Numbers-19
03BAP Ultimate Mem Rookie Jsy Number Gold-19
03BAP Ultimate Memorabilia Triple Threads-34
03Beehive-230
Gold-230
Silver-230
03Bowman-142
Gold-142
03Bowman Chrome-142
Refractors-142
Gold Refractors-142
Xfractors-142
03Crown Royale-113
Red-105
Retail-105
Retail-106
Retail-113
03ITG Action-644
03ITG Toronto Spring Expo Class of 2004-7
03ITG Used Signature Series-150
Autographs Gold-150
03ITG VIP Rookie Debut-74
03Pacific-363
03Pacific Calder-113
Silver-113
03Pacific Complete-563
Red-563
03Pacific Exhibit-230
03Pacific Heads-Up-111
Hobby LTD-111
Retail LTD-111
Prime Prospects-7
Prime Prospects LTD-7
03Pacific Luxury Suite-62
Gold-62
03Pacific Prism-155
03Pacific Quest for the Cup-112
Calder Contenders-7
03Parkhurst Toronto Expo Rookie Preview-PRP-15
03Parkhurst Rookie-199
All-Rookie-ART-11
All-Rookie Gold-ART-11
Calder Candidates-CMC-10
Calder Candidates Gold-CMC-10
Rookie Emblems-RE-28
Rookie Emblem Autographs-RE-NZ
Rookie Emblems Gold-RE-28
Rookie Jerseys-RJ-28
Rookie Jerseys Gold-RJ-28
Rookie Numbers-RN-28
Rookie Numbers Gold-RN-28
Teammates Gold-RT4
Teammates-RT4
03SP Authentic-124
Limited-124
03SP Game Used-129
03SPx-236
03Titanium-114
Hobby Jersey Number Parallels-114
Retail-114
Retail Jersey Number Parallels-114
03Topps Traded-TT102
Blue-TT102
Gold-TT102
Red-TT102
03UD Premier Collection-108
Stars-ST-NZ
Stars Patches-ST-NZ
Teammates-PT-CB2
Teammates Patches-PT-CB2
03Upper Deck-451
Canadian Exclusives-451
HG-451
UD Exclusives-451
03Upper Deck Classic Portraits-194
03Upper Deck Ice-125
Glass Parallel-125
03Upper Deck Rookie Update-163
Top Draws-TD9
YoungStars-YS17
YoungStars-YS17A
03Upper Deck Trilogy-186
03Russian Hockey League-6
03Russian SL-16
04Pacific-81
Blue-81
Red-81
04SP Authentic-27
Limited-27
Octographs-OS-ROK
Sign of the Times-ST-NZ
Sign of the Times-DS-NZ
Sign of the Times-TS-LRZ
Sign of the Times-TS-SHZ
Sign of the Times-QS-FSHZ
04UD All-World-31
Gold-31
Autographs-31
Dual Autographs-AD-FZ
Triple Autographs-AT-LTZ
Triple Autographs-AT-ZFA
Five Autographs-AF-YGN
Six Autographs-AS-RUS
04Ultimate Collection Dual Logos-UL2-NZ
04Ultimate Collection Jerseys-UGJ-NZ
04Ultimate Collection Jerseys Gold-UGJ-NZ
04Ultimate Collection Jersey Autographs-UGJA-NZ
04Ultimate Collection Patches-UP-NZ
04Ultimate Collection Patch Autographs-UPA-NZ
04Ultimate Collection Signatures-US-NZ
04Ultimate Collection Signature Logos-ULA-NZ
04Ultimate Collection Signature Patches-SP-NZ
04Upper Deck-52
Canadian Exclusives-52
HG Glossy Gold-52
HG Glossy Silver-52
YoungStars-YS-NZ
04Upper Deck All-Star Promos-NZ
04Russian Back to Russia-10
05Be A Player-25
First Period-25
Second Period-25
Third Period-25
Overtime-25
Outtakes-OT16
05Beehive Signature Scrapbook-SSNZ
05Black Diamond-24
Emerald-24
Gold-24
Onyx-24
Ruby-24
Gemography-G-NZ
Gemography Emerald-G-NZ
Gemography Gold-G-NZ
Gemography Onyx-G-NZ
Gemography Ruby-G-NZ
05Panini Stickers-238
05Parkhurst-135
Facsimile Auto Parallel-135
True Colors-TCCLB
True Colors-TCCLB
05SP Authentic Prestigious Pairings-PPNZ
05SP Game Used-29
Autographs-29
Gold-29
Authentic Fabrics-AF-NZ
Authentic Fabrics Autographs-AAF-NZ
Authentic Fabrics Gold-AF-NZ
Authentic Fabrics Quad-NZDF
Authentic Patches Quad -NZDL
Authentic Patches-AP-NZ
Authentic Patches Autographs-AAP-NZ
Awesome Authentics-AA-NZ
SIGnificance-NZ
SIGnificance Gold-S-NZ
SIGnificance Extra-ZN
SIGnificance Extra Gold-ZN
Significant Numbers-SN-NZ
Statscriptions-ST-NZ
05SPx-24
Spectrum-24
Winning Combos-WC-NZ
Winning Combos Autographs-AWC-NZ
Winning Combos Gold-WC-NZ
Winning Combos Spectrum-WC-NZ
Winning Materials-WM-NZ
Winning Materials Autographs-AWM-NZ
Winning Materials Gold-WM-NZ
Winning Materials Spectrum-WM-NZ
05The Cup Noble Numbers-NNDZ
05UD Artifacts-31
Blue-31
Gold-31
Green-31
Pewter-31
Red-31
Auto Facts-AF-NZ
Auto Facts Blue-AF-NZ
Auto Facts Copper-AF-NZ
Auto Facts Pewter-AF-NZ
Auto Facts Silver-AF-NZ
Gold Autographed-31
Remarkable Artifacts-RA-NZ
Remarkable Artifacts Dual-RA-NZ
05UD PowerPlay-27
Rainbow-27
05UD Toronto Fall Expo Priority Signings-PS-NZ
05Ultimate Collection Endorsed Emblems-EENZ
05Ultimate Collection Ultimate Signatures-USNZ
05Ultimate Coll Ultimate Sigs Trios-UTNBZ
05Ultra-63
Gold-63
Fresh Ink-FI-NZ
Fresh Ink Blue-FI-NZ
Ice-63
05Upper Deck-298
Jerseys Series II-J2NZ
Majestic Materials-MMNZ
NHL Generations-DKZ
Notable Numbers-N-NZ
Patches-P-NZ
Ice Signature Swatches-SSNZ
05Upper Deck MVP-119
Gold-119
Platinum-119
05Upper Deck Trilogy-28
05Upper Deck Trilogy-106
Crystal-106
Honorary Patches-HP-NZ
Honorary Patch Scripts-HSP-NZ
Honorary Swatches-HS-NZ
Honorary Swatch Scripts-HSS-NZ
Scripts-SFS-NZ
05Upper Deck Victory-57
Black-57
Gold-57
Silver-57
06Be A Player-2
Autographs-2
Signatures-NZ
Signatures 10-2
Signatures Duals-DFZ
Portraits Signature Portraits-SPNZ
Portraits Triple Signature Portraits-TCLB
06Hot Prospects-32
Red Hot-32
White Hot-32
Hotagraphs-HNZ
06O-Pee-Chee-140
Rainbow-140
06Panini Stickers-239
06SP Game Used Inked Sweaters-ISNZ
06SP Game Used Inked Sweaters Patches-ISNZ
06SP Game Used SIGnificance-SNZ
06The Cup Autographed NHL Shields Duals-DASNZ
06The Cup Honorable Numbers-HNNZ
06The Cup Limited Logos-LLNZ
06The Cup NHL Shields Duals-DSHFZ
06UD Mini Jersey Collection-31
06Ultimate Collection Ultimate Signatures Logos-SL-NZ
06Ultra-56
Gold Medallion-56
Ice Medallion-56
06Upper Deck-308
Exclusives Parallel-308
High Gloss Parallel-308
Masterpieces-308
06Upper Deck MVP-89
Gold Script-89
Super Script-89
06Upper Deck Ovation-65
06Upper Deck Sweet Shot Signature Shots/Saves-SSNZ
06Upper Deck Sweet Shot Signature Shots/Saves Sticks-SSSNZ
06Upper Deck Sweet Shot Signature Sticks-STNZ
06Upper Deck Trilogy Combo Clearcut Autographs-C3NZB
06Upper Deck Victory-57
06Upper Deck Victory Black-57
06Upper Deck Victory Gold-57
06Upper Deck Victory Next In Line-NL17

Zhitnik, Alexei

91Upper Deck-660
French-660
91Upper Deck Czech World Juniors-21
91Star Pics-38
92OPC Premier-125
92Parkhurst-71
Emerald Ice-71
92Pinnacle-392
French-392
92Ultra-314
92Upper Deck-566
Calder Candidates-CC7
Euro-Rookies-ER13
92Russian Stars Red Ace-36
93Donruss-165
93Leaf-123
Gold Rookies-8
93OPC Premier-2
Gold-2
93Parkhurst-92
Emerald Ice-92
93Pinnacle-23
Canadian-23
93PowerPlay-123
93Score-148
Canadian-148
93Stadium Club-221
Members Only Master Set-221
OPC-221
First Day Issue-221
First Day Issue OPC-221
93Topps/OPC Premier-2
Gold-2
93Ultra-87
93Upper Deck-161
SP-75
94Canada Games NHL POGS-131
94Donruss-279
94Leaf-8
94Leaf Limited-111
94OPC Premier-57
Special Effects-57
94Parkhurst-101
Gold-101
94Pinnacle-87
Artist's Proofs-87
Rink Collection-87
94Score-171
Gold-171
Platinum-171
94SP-16
Die Cuts-16
94Topps/OPC Premier-57
Special Effects-57
94Ultra-104
94Upper Deck SP Inserts-SP38
94Upper Deck SP Inserts Die Cuts-SP38
95Bashan Super Stickers-13
95Be A Player-28
Signatures-S28
Signatures Die Cuts-S28
95Canada Games NHL POGS-47
95Collector's Choice-303
Player's Club-303
Player's Club Platinum-303
95Donruss-50
95Emotion-19
95Imperial Stickers-13
95Leaf-4
95Metal-17
95Panini Stickers-20
95Parkhurst International-19
Emerald Ice-19
All-Stars-3
95Pinnacle-64
Artist's Proofs-64
Rink Collection-64
95Playoff One on One-14
95Pro Magnets-110
95Score-47
Black Ice Artist's Proofs-47
Black Ice-47
95SkyBox Impact-19
95SP-15
95Stadium Club-143
Members Only Master Set-143
95Topps-49
OPC Inserts-49
95Ultra-22
Gold Medallion-22
Rising Stars-10
Rising Stars Gold Medallion-10
95Upper Deck-187
Electric Ice-187
Electric Ice Gold-187
Special Edition-SE11
Special Edition Gold-SE11
95Finnish Semic World Championships-128
95Swedish Globe World Championships-169
96Collector's Choice-26
96Collector's Choice-311
96Donruss-11
Press Proofs-11
96Donruss Elite-115
Die Cut Stars-115
96Flair-10
Blue Ice-10
96Fleer Picks-152
96Leaf-155
Press Proofs-155
96NHL Pro Stamps-110
96Pinnacle-180
Artist's Proofs-180
Foil-180
Premium Stock-180
Rink Collection-180
96Score-70
Artist's Proofs-70
Dealer's Choice Artist's Proofs-70
Special Artist's Proofs-70
Golden Blades-70
96Select Certified-45
Artist's Proofs-45
Blue-45
Mirror Blue-45
Mirror Gold-45
Mirror Red-45
Red-45
96SP-19
96Summit-69
Artist's Proofs-69
Ice-69
Metal-69
Premium Stock-69
96Team Out-76
96Upper Deck-17
96Swedish Semic Wien-134
97Black Diamond-1
Double Diamond-1
Triple Diamond-1

Quadruple Diamond-1
97Collector's Choice-29
97Katch-18
Gold-18
Silver-18
97Pacific-236
Copper-236
Emerald Green-236
Ice Blue-236
Red-236
Silver-236
97Panini Stickers-11
97Score Sabres-18
Platinum-18
Premier-18
97SP Authentic-17
98Aurora-22
98Be A Player-166
Press Release-166
98BAP Gold-166
98BAP Autographs-166
98BAP Autographs Gold-166
98Bowman's Best-88
Refractors-88
Atomic Refractors-88
98Finest-33
No Protectors-33
No Protectors Refractors-33
Refractors-33
98Katch-16
98Kraft Peanut Butter-5
98OPC Chrome-192
Refractors-192
98Pacific-114
Ice Blue-114
Red-114
98Panini Stickers-22
98Paramount-25
Copper-25
Emerald Green-25
Holo-Electric-25
Ice Blue-25
Silver-25
98Topps-192
O-Pee-Chee-192
98UD Choice-26
Prime Choice Reserve-26
Reserve-26
98Upper Deck-226
Exclusives-226
Exclusives 1 of 1-226
Gold Reserve-226
99BAP Memorabilia-122
Gold-122
Silver-122
99O-Pee-Chee-232
99O-Pee-Chee Chrome-232
99O-Pee-Chee Chrome Refractors-232
99Pacific-50
Copper-50
Emerald Green-50
Gold-50
Ice Blue-50
Premiere Date-50
Red-50
99Panini Stickers-35
99Paramount-34
Copper-34
Emerald-34
Gold-34
Holographic Emerald-34
Holographic Gold-34
Holographic Silver-34
Ice Blue-34
Premiere Date-34
Red-34
Silver-34
99SPx-16
Radiance-16
Spectrum-16
99Topps/OPC-232
99Topps/OPC Chrome-232
Refractors-232
99Topps Premier Plus-39
Parallel-39
99Upper Deck-191
Exclusives-191
Exclusives 1 of 1-191
99Upper Deck Gold Reserve-191
99Upper Deck Victory-42
99Wayne Gretzky Hockey-23
00BAP Memorabilia-8
Emerald-8
Ruby-8
Sapphire-8
Promos-8
00BAP Mem Chicago Sportsfest Copper-8
00BAP Memorabilia Chicago Sportsfest Blue-8
00BAP Memorabilia Chicago Sportsfest Gold-8
00BAP Memorabilia Chicago Sportsfest Ruby-8
00BAP Memorabilia Chicago Sun-Times Ruby-8
00BAP Memorabilia Chicago Sun-Times Gold-8
00BAP Mem Chicago Sun-Times Sapphire-8
00BAP Mem Toronto Fall Expo Copper-8
00BAP Memorabilia Toronto Fall Expo Gold-8
00BAP Memorabilia Toronto Fall Expo Ruby-8
00BAP Parkhurst 2000-P217
00Panini Stickers-22
00Titanium Game Gear-63
00Titanium Game Gear Patches-63
00Upper Deck-251
Exclusives Tier 1-251
Exclusives Tier 2-251
00Upper Deck Vintage-45
01Crown Royale Triple Threads-5
01Pacific-55
Extreme LTD-55
Hobby LTD-55
Premiere Date-55
Retail LTD-55
01Pacific Arena Exclusives-55
01Pacific Heads-Up Quad Jerseys-23
01Parkhurst Teammates-T11
01Titanium Double-Sided Jerseys-4
01Titanium Double-Sided Patches-4
01Upper Deck-255
Exclusives-255
01Upper Deck Victory-44
Gold-44
02BAP Sig Series Auto Buybacks 1998-166
02Pacific-49
Blue-49
Red-49
02Pacific Complete-423
Red-423
02Topps Total-257
02Upper Deck Vintage-35
03Beehive-23
Gold-23
Silver-23
03ITG Action-17
03Pacific-46
Blue-46
Red-46
03Pacific Complete-236
Red-236
03Upper Deck-25
Canadian Exclusives-25
HG-25
03Upper Deck MVP-59
Gold Script-59
Silver Script-59
Canadian Exclusives-59
04Russian Back to Russia-39
05Panini Stickers-101
05Parkhurst-307
Facsimile Auto Parallel-307
05Upper Deck-371
05Upper Deck MVP-244
Gold-244
Platinum-244
05Upper Deck Victory-231
Black-231
Gold-231
Silver-231
06Flyers Postcards-23
06O-Pee-Chee-316
Rainbow-316
06Panini Stickers-94
06Upper Deck-123
Exclusives Parallel-123
High Gloss Parallel-123
Masterpieces-123
06Upper Deck MVP-188
Gold Script-188
Super Script-188
06Upper Deck Victory-127
06Upper Deck Victory Black-127
06Upper Deck Victory Gold-127

Zhluktov, Viktor
74Swedish Stickers-47
79Panini Stickers-149
79Russian National Team-19
82Swedish Semic VM Stickers-64
83Swedish Semic VM Stickers-64
84Russian National Team-23
92Future Trends '76 Canada Cup-138

Zhmakin, Stanislav
03Russian Hockey League-134

Zholotov, Sergei
98Russian Hockey League-75
99Russian Hockey League-45
00Russian Hockey League-30
00Russian Hockey League-299
02Russian Hockey League-26
02Russian Hockey League-235

Zholtok, Sergei
91Upper Deck-659
French-659
91Upper Deck Czech World Juniors-20
92Parkhurst-482
Emerald Ice-482
92Classic-50
Gold-50
93Leaf-376
93Parkhurst-281
Emerald Ice-281
93PowerPlay-294
93Score-475
Canadian-475
93Upper Deck-244
94Leaf-508
94Parkhurst SE-SE10
Gold-SE10
94Stadium Club-254
Members Only Master Set-254
First Day Issue-254
Super Team Winner Cards-254
94Upper Deck-419
Electric Ice-419
94Classic Pro Prospects-227
95Las Vegas Thunder-22
96Senators Pizza Hut-30
96Las Vegas Thunder-23
97Be A Player-192
Autographs-192
Autographs Die-Cuts-192
Autographs Prismatic Die-Cuts-192
97Collector's Choice-177
97Pacific-328
Copper-328
Emerald Green-328
Ice Blue-328
Red-328
Silver-328
97Panini Stickers-39
97Upper Deck-116
98Canadiens Team Issue-26
98Pacific-320
Ice Blue-320
Red-320
98Pacific Dynagon Ice-99
Blue-99
Red-99
99Pacific-214
Copper-214
Emerald Green-214
Gold-214
Ice Blue-214
Premiere Date-214
Red-214
99Upper Deck MVP SC Edition-95
Gold Script-95
Silver Script-95
Super Script-95
00BAP Memorabilia-359
Emerald-359
Ruby-359
Sapphire-359
Promos-359
00BAP Mem Chicago Sportsfest Copper-359
00BAP Memorabilia Chicago Sportsfest Blue-359
00BAP Memorabilia Chicago Sportsfest Gold-359
00BAP Memorabilia Chicago Sportsfest Ruby-359
00BAP Memorabilia Chicago Sun-Times Ruby-359
00BAP Memorabilia Chicago Sun-Times Gold-359
00BAP Mem Chicago Sun-Times Sapphire-359
00BAP Mem Toronto Fall Expo Copper-359
00BAP Memorabilia Toronto Fall Expo Gold-359
00BAP Memorabilia Toronto Fall Expo Ruby-359
00BAP Signature Series-113
Emerald-113
Ruby-113
Sapphire-113
Autographs-131
Autographs Gold-131
00O-Pee-Chee-159
00O-Pee-Chee Parallel-159
00Pacific-217
Copper-217
Gold-217
Ice Blue-217
Premiere Date-217
00Panini Stickers-42
00Stadium Club-96
00Titanium Game Gear-102
00Titanium Game Gear Patches-102
00Titanium Draft Day Edition-51
Patches-51
00Topps/OPC-159
Parallel-159
00Upper Deck-320
Exclusives Tier 1-320
Exclusives Tier 2-320
00Upper Deck MVP-95
First Stars-95
Second Stars-95
Third Stars-95
00Upper Deck Victory-119
00Upper Deck Vintage-188
01Atomic Jerseys-30
01Atomic Patches-30
01Pacific Heads-Up Quad Jerseys-12
01Parkhurst-380
01Upper Deck-318
Exclusives-318
01Wild Crime Prevention-21
02O-Pee-Chee-165
02O-Pee-Chee Premier Blue Parallel-165
02O-Pee-Chee Premier Red Parallel-165
02O-Pee-Chee Factory Set-165
02Pacific-189
Blue-189
Red-189
02Pacific Complete-231
Red-231
02Topps-165
OPC Blue Parallel-165
OPC Red Parallel-165
Factory Set-165
02Topps Total-191
03ITG Action-208
03NHL Sticker Collection-246
03Pacific-172
Blue-172
Red-172
03Pacific Complete-54
Red-54
03Upper Deck-339
Canadian Exclusives-339
HG-339
UD Exclusives-339
03Upper Deck MVP-211
Gold Script-211
Silver Script-211
Canadian Exclusives-211
03Wild Law Enforcement Cards-10

Zhuev, Yuri
98Russian Hockey League-89
00Russian Hockey League-176

Zhukov, Alexander
03Russian Hockey League-230

Zhukov, Sergei
01Russian Hockey League-128
02Russian World Championships-20
06Russian Torino Olympic Team-19

Zhurik, Alexander
93Kingston Frontenacs-10
93Phoenix Cobras RHI-20
98Russian Hockey League-161
99Hamilton Bulldogs-13
00Russian Hockey League-129
02Russian Hockey League-148

Zhurikov, Sergei
02Russian Hockey League-2
04Russian RHL-11

Zib, Lukas
95Czech APS Extraliga-57
96Czech APS Extraliga-246
97Czech APS Extraliga-272
98Czech OFS-411
99Czech OFS-281
00Czech OFS-358
02German DEL City Press-298
03Russian Hockey League-267
04Russian Legion-21
06Czech CP Cup Postcards-22
06Czech HC Liberec Postcards-12
06Czech OFS-108

Zibin, Alexander
99Russian Hockey League-67

Zidlicky, Marek
94Czech APS Extraliga-56
95Czech APS Extraliga-86
96Czech APS Extraliga-80
97Czech APS Extraliga-198
97Czech DS Stickers-137
98Czech DS-97
98Czech DS Stickers-230
98Czech OFS-163
99Finnish Cardset-221
00Finnish Cardset-14
01Finnish Cardset-15
01Finnish Cardset Dueling Aces-7
02SPx Rookie Redemption-R204
02Czech DS-36
02Finnish Cardset-146
03BAP Memorabilia-202
03BAP Ultimate Memorabilia Autographs-124
Gold-124
03BAP Ultimate Mem Rookie Jersey Emblems-6
03BAP Ultimate Mem Rookie Jsy Emblem Gold-6
03BAP Ultimate Mem Rookie Jersey Numbers-6
03BAP Ultimate Mem Rookie Jsy Number Gold-6
03Black Diamond-166
Black-166
Green-166
Red-166
03Bowman-139
Gold-139
03Bowman Chrome-139
Refractors-139
Gold Refractors-139
Xfractors-139
03Crown Royale-125
Red-125
Retail-125
03ITG Action-610
03ITG Used Signature Series-132
Autographs Gold-132
03ITG VIP Rookie Debut-26
03Pacific Calder-124
Silver-124
03Pacific Complete-575
Red-575
03Pacific Heads-Up-124
Hobby LTD-124
Retail LTD-124
03Pacific Luxury Suite-69
Gold-69
03Pacific Quest for the Cup-124
03Pacific Supreme-126
Blue-126
Red-126
Retail-126
03Parkhurst Rookie-182
Rookie Emblems-RE-36
Rookie Emblems Gold-RE-36
Rookie Jerseys-RJ-36
Rookie Jerseys Gold-RJ-36
Rookie Numbers-RN-36
Rookie Numbers Gold-RN-36
03Private Stock Reserve-127
Blue-127
Red-127
Retail-127
03SP Authentic-105
Limited-105
03SP Game Used-68
Gold-68
03SPx-202
Radiance-202
Spectrum-202
03Titanium-125
Hobby Jersey Number Parallels-125
Retail-125
Retail Jersey Number Parallels-125
03Topps Traded-TT120
Blue-TT120
Gold-TT120
Red-TT120
03UD Honor Roll-142
03UD Premier Collection-75
03Upper Deck-226
Canadian Exclusives-226
HG-226
03Upper Deck Ice-95
Glass Parallel-95
03Upper Deck Rookie Update-215
03Upper Deck Trilogy-157
Limited-157
03Finnish Cardset D-Day-DD16
04Pacific-153
Blue-153
Red-153
04Upper Deck-99
Canadian Exclusives-99
HG Glossy Gold-99
HG Glossy Silver-99
04Finnish Cardset-15
04Finnish Cardset Signatures-4
04Finnish Cardset Stars of the Game-14
04Swedish Pure Skills-101
Parallel-101
Professional Power-MZ
05Panini Stickers-311
05Parkhurst-274
Facsimile Auto Parallel-274
05Czech World Champions Postcards-16
05Czech Kvarteto Bonaparte-4c
05Czech Pexeso Mini Blue Set-3
05Czech Pexeso Mini Red Set-30
05Finnish Cardset -11
06Black Diamond Gemography-GMZ
06O-Pee-Chee-277
Rainbow-277
06Panini Stickers-308
06Ultra Fresh Ink-IMZ
06Upper Deck-110
Exclusives Parallel-110
High Gloss Parallel-110
Masterpieces-110
06Upper Deck MVP-168
Gold Script-168
Super Script-168

Ziedins, Maris
03Rockford Ice Hogs-19
05Stockton Thunder-20

Zieffle, Kirk
99OCN Blizzard-9
00OCN Blizzard-8
01OCN Blizzard-11

Ziegelmann, Nate
01Lincoln Stars-24
02Lincoln Stars-24
02Lincoln Stars-39
02Lincoln Stars-47
03North Dakota Fighting Sioux-2

Ziegler, John A
85Hall of Fame-257

Ziegler, Rolf
93Swiss HNL-472
95Swiss HNL-296
98Swiss Power Play Stickers-162
99Swiss Panini Stickers-88
00Swiss Panini Stickers-38
00Swiss Panini Stickers National Team-P12
00Swiss Slapshot Mini-Cards-SC87
01Swiss HNL-84
02Swiss HNL-262
02Swiss HNL-492

Ziegler, Thomas
95Swiss HNL-312
98Swiss Power Play Stickers-25
98Swiss Power Play Stickers-294
99Swiss Panini Stickers-25
00Swiss Panini Stickers-25
00Swiss Panini Stickers National Team-P21
01BAP Memorabilia-450
Emerald-450
Ruby-450
Sapphire-450
01Pacific-360
Extreme LTD-360
Hobby LTD-360
Premiere Date-360
Retail LTD-360
01Pacific Arena Exclusives-360
01SPx-127
01UD Top Shelf-64
01UD Top Shelf-64B
01Upper Deck-208
Exclusives-208
01Upper Deck MVP-217
01Upper Deck Victory-388
Gold-388
01Upper Deck Vintage-298
02Swiss HNL-282

Zieri, Daniel
96Swiss HNL-411

Ziesche, Jens
04German Berlin Eisbaren 50th Anniv-57

Ziesche, Joachim
70Finnish Jaakiekko-100
70Swedish Hockey-384
04German Berlin Eisbaren 50th Anniv-69

Ziesche, Steffen
91Upper Deck-679
French-679
91Upper Deck Czech World Juniors-42
95German DEL-111
01German Upper Deck-154
02German DEL City Press-234
03German DEL-195
04German Berlin Eisbaren 50th Anniv-14
04German DEL-241
04German Krefeld Penguins Postcards-24
05German DEL-192

Zietara, Walenty
73Finnish Jaakiekko-104
74Finnish Jenkki-91
74Finnish Typotor-93
79Panini Stickers-129

Ziffzer, Youri
04German Berlin Polar Bears Postcards-30
04German DEL-79
05German DEL-38
06German DEL-26

Zigardy, Stefan
03Czech OFS Plus-362
06Czech OFS-172

Zigomanis, Mike
98SP Authentic-135
Power Shift-135
Sign of the Times-MZ
Sign of the Times Gold-MZ
98Upper Deck-412
Exclusives-412
Exclusives 1 of 1-412
Gold Reserve-412
98Kingston Frontenacs-24
99Black Diamond-94
Diamond Cut-94
Final Cut-94
99Upper Deck-334
Exclusives-334
Exclusives 1 of 1-334
99Upper Deck Gold Reserve-334
99Upper Deck MVP SC Edition-215
Gold Script-215
Silver Script-215
Super Script-215
99Kingston Frontenacs-23
99Bowman CHL-36
99Bowman CHL-134
Gold-36
Gold-134
OPC International-36
OPC International-134
Autographs-BA5
Autographs Gold-BA5
Autographs Silver-BA5
Scout's Choice-SC7
99UD Prospects-8
00Kingston Frontenacs-23
00UD CHL Prospects-10
CHL Class-CC2
Future Leaders-FL5
02Lowell Lock Monsters-5
03ITG Action-165
03Lowell Lock Monsters-17
03Lowell Lock Monsters Photo Album-6
03Pacific AHL Prospects-44
Gold-44
04Lowell Lock Monsters-24
04Lowell Lock Monsters Photo Album-24
05ITG Heroes/Prosp Toronto Expo Parallel -98
05ITG Heroes and Prospects-98
Autographs-A-MZI

Ziliotto, Mark
89ProCards AHL-64

Zilka, Ken
917th Inn. Sketch WHL-195

Zilka, Roman
94German First League-372

Zilliotto, Larry
61Hamilton Red Wings-21

Zima, Ales
94Czech APS Extraliga-19
95Czech APS Extraliga-116
95Czech APS Extraliga-383
96Czech APS Extraliga-39
97Czech APS Extraliga-63
97Czech DS Extraliga-105
97Czech DS Stickers-108
98Czech DS-123
98Czech DS Stickers-296
98Czech OFS-188
99Czech OFS-303

Zimakov, Sergei
95Upper Deck-558
Electric Ice-558
Electric Ice Gold-558
99Russian Hockey League-160
00Russian Hockey League-256

Zimin, Yevgeny
69Russian National Team Postcards-9
69Swedish Hockey-18
70Swedish Masterserien-75
71Finnish Suomi Stickers-20
71Swedish Hockey-42
72Finnish Panda Toronto-63
72Finnish Semic World Championship-9
72Swedish Semic World Championship-9
73Swedish Stickers-117
74Swedish Semic World Champ Stickers-47
91Future Trends Canada '72-14
91Future Trends Canada '72 French-14

Zimmer, Brad
89Lethbridge Hurricanes-24
907th Inn. Sketch WHL-125
917th Inn. Sketch WHL-349
917th Inn. Sketch Memorial Cup-127
93Red Deer Rebels-28

Zimmer, Devin
91Air Canada SJHL-D8

Zimmer, Michael J
93Quebec Pee-Wee Tournament-179

Zimmer, Myles
03Prince George Cougars-19

Zimmerman, Dan
03St. Jean Mission-28

Zimmerman, Jason
92Saskatchewan JHL-34

Zimmerman, Lynn
71Rochester Americans-18

Zimmerman, Scott
03Mississauga Ice Dogs-24
04Guelph Storm-14

Zimmerman, Shawn
92Saskatchewan JHL-38
93Western Michigan Broncos-30

Zimmermann, Jacques
01Swiss HNL-460

Zimmermann, Marc
94German First League-363
01Swiss HNL-343
02Swiss HNL-389

Zimmermann, Yvan
93Swiss HNL-510

Zinck, Gary
99Halifax Mooseheads-20
00Halifax Mooseheads-25

Zinevych, Alex
00Albany River Rats-26
01Macon Whoopee-19

Zinger, Darrin
95UK Guildford Flames-15
96UK Guildford Flames-15
97UK Guildford Flames-16

Zinger, Dwayne
01Cincinnati Mighty Ducks-25
03ITG VIP Rookie Debut-82
03Parkhurst Rookie-67
03Topps Traded-TT153
Blue-TT153
Gold-TT153
Red-TT153
03Upper Deck Rookie Update-94
04Portland Pirates-23
05Hershey Bears-28
06Providence Bruins-25

Zinger, Viktor
69Russian National Team Postcards-1
69Swedish Hockey-19
70Swedish Masterserien-27
70Swedish Masterserien-29
73Swedish Stickers-108

Zingoni, Peter
06Philadelphia Phantoms-29

Zinine, Dimitri
93Finnish Jyvas-Hyva Stickers-169
93Finnish SISU-172

Zinkovs, Andrejs
98Danish Hockey League-113

Zinnecker, Jorg
94German First League-123

Zinovjev, Sergei
99Russian Hockey League-224
01Russian Hockey League-126
02Russian Future Stars-17
02Russian Hockey League-240
03BAP Memorabilia-249
03Beehive-241
Gold-241
Silver-241
03Bowman-136
Gold-136
03Bowman Chrome-136
Refractors-136
Gold Refractors-136
Xfractors-136
03Crown Royale-104
Red-104
Retail-104
03ITG Used Signature Series-160
Gold-160
03ITG VIP Rookie Debut-49
03Pacific Complete-536
Red-536
03Pacific Luxury Suite-53
Gold-53
03Parkhurst Original Six Boston-19
03Parkhurst Rookie-134
03SP Authentic-122
Limited-122
03SPx-231
03Titanium-103
Hobby Jersey Number Parallels-103
Retail-103
Retail Jersey Number Parallels-103
03Topps Traded-TT87
Blue-TT87
Gold-TT87
Red-TT87
03UD Honor Roll-163
03UD Premier Collection-82
03Upper Deck-452
03Upper Deck-475
Canadian Exclusives-452
Canadian Exclusives-475
HG-452
HG-475
UD Exclusives-452
UD Exclusives-475
03Upper Deck Ice-104
Glass Parallel-104
03Upper Deck Rookie Update-108
03Russian World Championship Team 2003-7

Zinovyev, Dimitri
90O-Pee-Chee-478

Zion, Jonathan
98SP Authentic-122
Power Shift-122
98Upper Deck-399
Exclusives-399
Exclusives 1 of 1-399
Gold Reserve-399
99Ottawa 67's-22
00Ottawa 67's-4
00UD CHL Prospects-17
01Ottawa 67's-5
02ECHL All-Star Northern-39
03ECHL All-Stars-261
03Greenville Grrrowl-21
03Reading Royals-7
04Idaho Steelheads-15
05Idaho Steelheads-24

Zirnis, Karlis
03Colorado Eagles-20
04Colorado Eagles-22

Ziska, Jakub
99Czech Score Blue 2000-16
99Czech Score Red Ice 2000-16

Zittlau, Alexander
94German First League-201

Zivic, Jerald
01Arizona Icecats-24
04Arizona Icecats-24

Zivny, Martin
94Czech APS Extraliga-154
95Czech APS Extraliga-257
99Czech Score Blue 2000-93
99Czech Score Red Ice 2000-93

Zizka, Tomas
97Czech APS Extraliga-74
98Czech OFS-24
99Czech DS-6
99Czech OFS-220
00Czech DS Extraliga-51
00Czech OFS-352
01Manchester Monarchs-10A
02BAP Memorabilia-386
02BAP Ultimate Memorabilia-71
02UD Premier Collection-92
Gold-92
02AHL Top Prospects-45
02Manchester Monarchs-30
03ITG Action-260
03Manchester Monarchs-20
03Manchester Monarchs Team Issue-20
04Czech HC Slavia Praha Postcards-22
04Czech OFS-353
05Czech HC Slavia Praha-16
06Czech CP Cup Postcards-23
06Czech HC Slavia Praha Postcards-16
06Czech OFS-308

Zjulin, Pjotr
74Swedish Stickers-38

Zlov, Yuri
00Russian Hockey League-366

Zmolek, Doug
91O-Pee-Chee Inserts-9S
91Minnesota Golden Gophers-26
92OPC Premier-18
92Parkhurst-393
Emerald Ice-393
92Ultra-405
92Upper Deck-509
92Classic-88
Gold-88
92Classic Four-Sport *-207
Gold-207
Autographs-207A
93Donruss-313
93Leaf-112
93OPC Premier-143
Gold-143
93Panini Stickers-263
93Parkhurst-457
Emerald Ice-457
93Pinnacle-117
Canadian-117
93Score-327
Canadian-327
93Stadium Club-171
Members Only Master Set-171
OPC-171
First Day Issue-171
First Day Issue OPC-171
93Topps/OPC Premier-143
Gold-143
93Upper Deck-193
94Leaf-453
94Stars Postcards-23
96Be A Player-151
Autographs-151
Autographs Silver-151
97Pacific-297
Copper-297
Emerald Green-297
Ice Blue-297
Red-297
Silver-297
99Blackhawks Chicago Sun-Times-9
99O-Pee-Chee-85
99O-Pee-Chee Chrome-85
99O-Pee-Chee Chrome Refractors-85
99Topps/OPC-85
99Topps/OPC Chrome-85
Refractors-85

Zmrhal, Pavel
94Czech APS Extraliga-166

Zmudczynski, Steve
04Guelph Storm-13

Zmudczynski, Steve
02Guelph Storm-16
03Guelph Storm-12

Znarok, Oleg
90O-Pee-Chee-477
91Finnish Jyvas-Hyva Stickers-70
94German First League-203
99German Bundesliga 2-109

Znojemsky, Martin
98Czech OFS-263

Zobel, Tauno
94German First League-113

Zohil, Jason
89Windsor Spitfires-22
907th Inn. Sketch OHL-198
907th Inn. Sketch OHL-243
917th Inn. Sketch OHL-268
91Sudbury Wolves-25

Zohorna, Tomas
05Drummondville Voltigeurs-11
06Drummondville Voltigeurs-8

Zol, Diano
92British Columbia JHL-53

Zolotov, Roman
92Classic-55
Gold-55
99Russian Dynamo Moscow-5
00Russian Dynamo Moscow-5

Zombo, Mike
85London Knights-19

Zombo, Rick
87Red Wings Little Caesars-30
88Red Wings Little Caesars-24
89Panini Stickers-64
89Red Wings Little Caesars-18
90O-Pee-Chee-21
90Panini Stickers-206
90Pro Set-80
90Score-101
Canadian-101
90Score Hottest/Rising Stars-49
90Topps-21
Tiffany-21
90Upper Deck-115
French-115
91Blues Postcards-22
91Bowman-54
91O-Pee-Chee-454
91Panini Stickers-137
91Parkhurst-380
French-380
91Pinnacle-259
91Pinnacle-393
91Pinnacle-410
French-259
French-393
French-410
91Pro Set-64
91Pro Set-474
French-64
French-474
91Score American-177
91Score Canadian Bilingual-177
91Score Canadian English-177
91Score Rookie/Traded-60T
91Stadium Club-32
91Topps-454
91Upper Deck-395
French-395
92Bowman-87
92O-Pee-Chee-97
92Pinnacle-129
French-129
92Score-154
Canadian-154
92Stadium Club-100
92Topps-288
Gold-288G
93Pinnacle-306
Canadian-306
93Score-211
Canadian-211
94Pinnacle-447
Artist's Proofs-447
Rink Collection-447
94Score-75
Gold-75
Platinum-75
95Be A Player-136
Signatures-S136
Signatures Die Cuts-S136
95Upper Deck-319
Electric Ice-319
Electric Ice Gold-319

Zorger, Dan
93Quebec Pee-Wee Tournament-788

Zorica, Joe
52Juniors Blue Tint-2

Zorkin, Vladimir
98Russian Hockey League-26
99Russian Hockey League-106

Zorn, Jeff
98Prince George Cougars-26
99Prince George Cougars-4

Zoryk, Steve
93Sault Ste. Marie Greyhounds-11
01New Mexico Scorpions-18
05Florida Seals Team Issue-17

Zounimbiat, Christian
93Quebec Pee-Wee Tournament-257

Zruna, Mike
99Alexandria Warthogs-19

Zubicek, Pavel
95Czech APS Extraliga-205
97Czech APS Extraliga-42
98Czech DS Stickers-173
98Czech OFS-104
99Czech DS-140
99Czech OFS-70
00Czech OFS-327
01Czech OFS-134
02Czech OFS Plus-45
03Czech OFS Plus-147
04Czech OFS-291
06Czech HC Zlin Hame Postcards-15
06Czech OFS-246

Zubkov, Andrei
99Russian Hockey League-261

Zubkov, Vladimir
82Swedish Semic VM Stickers-72
83Swedish Semic VM Stickers-75
84Russian National Team-24

Zubkus, Jason
93Cornell Big Red-29

Zubov, Ilya
03Russian Hockey League-278
05Russian Hockey League RHL-39

Zubov, Sergei
91O-Pee-Chee Inserts-28R
91O-Pee-Chee Inserts-30R
92Parkhurst-351
Emerald Ice-351
92Ultra-359
92Upper Deck-516
92Binghamton Rangers-10
93Donruss-225
93Leaf-164
93OPC Premier-217
Gold-217
93Parkhurst-133
Emerald Ice-133
93Pinnacle-156
Canadian-156
93PowerPlay-167
Rising Stars-10
93Score-313
Canadian-313
93Stadium Club-312
Members Only Master Set-312
First Day Issue-312
93Topps/OPC Premier-217
Gold-217
93Ultra-243
93Upper Deck-181
93Classic Pro Prospects-70
93Classic Pro Prospects-74
BCs-BC6
94Canada Games NHL POGS-172
94Donruss-219
94Flair-118
94Fleer-140
Franchise Futures-10
94Leaf-111
94Leaf Limited-65
94OPC Premier-221
94OPC Premier-382
94OPC Premier-493
Special Effects-221
Special Effects-382
Special Effects-493
94Parkhurst-144
Gold-144
94Pinnacle-36
Artist's Proofs-36
Rink Collection-36
94Select-14
Gold-14
94SP-78
Die Cuts-78
94Topps/OPC Premier-221
94Topps/OPC Premier-382
94Topps/OPC Premier-493
Special Effects-221
Special Effects-382
Special Effects-493
94Ultra-144
94Upper Deck-100
Electric Ice-100
SP Inserts-SP142
SP Inserts Die Cuts-SP142
94Finnish Jaa Kiekko-140
94Classic Pro Prospects-115
95Bashan Super Stickers-99
95Canada Games NHL POGS-217
95Collector's Choice-10
Player's Club-10
Player's Club Platinum-10
95Donruss-130
95Donruss-357
Dominators-3
95Donruss Elite-37
Die Cut Stars-37
Die Cut Uncut-37
95Emotion-144
95Finest-171
Refractors-171
95Hoyle Eastern Playing Cards-53
95Imperial Stickers-99
95Leaf-126
95Leaf Limited-74
95Metal-121
International Steel-24
Winners-8
95Panini Stickers-111
95Parkhurst International-434
Emerald Ice-434
All-Stars-3
Parkie's Trophy Picks-PP27
95Penguins Foodland-12
95Playoff One on One-187
95Pro Magnets-95
95Score-188
Black Ice Artist's Proofs-188
Black Ice-188
95Select Certified-67
Mirror Gold-67
95SkyBox Impact-137
95SP-117

95Stadium Club-92
Members Only Master Set-92
95Summit-74
Artist's Proofs-74
Ice-74
95Topps-333
OPC Inserts-333
95Ultra-108
95Ultra-295
Gold Medallion-108
95Upper Deck-474
Electric Ice-474
Electric Ice Gold-474
Predictor Hobby-H37
Predictor Hobby Exchange-H37
Special Edition-SE155
Special Edition Gold-SE155
95Zenith-66
95Swedish Globe World Championships-165
96Black Diamond-56
Gold-56
96Collector's Choice-214
96Donruss-91
Press Proofs-91
96Donruss Elite-111
Die Cut Stars-111
96Fleer-28
96Fleer Picks-26
96Leaf-130
Press Proofs-130
96Leaf Preferred-63
Press Proofs-63
96Metal Universe-44
96NHL Pro Stamps-95
96Pinnacle-122
Artist's Proofs-122
Foil-122
Premium Stock-122
Rink Collection-122
96Playoff One on One-383
96Score-171
Artist's Proofs-171
Dealer's Choice Artist's Proofs-171
Special Artist's Proofs-171
Golden Blades-171
96SkyBox Impact-32
96SP-43
96Stars Postcards-27
96Stars Score Sheet-171
96Summit-119
Artist's Proofs-119
Ice-119
Metal-119
Premium Stock-119
96Ultra-48
Gold Medallion-48
96Upper Deck-246
Generation Next-X39
96Upper Deck Ice-16
Parallel-16
96Zenith-38
Artist's Proofs-38
96Swedish Semic Wien-136
96Collector's Edge Ice Crucibles-C16
97Crown Royale-44
Emerald Green-44
Ice Blue-44
Silver-44
97Donruss Limited-93
Exposure-93
97Donruss Preferred-91
Cut to the Chase-91
97Donruss Priority-51
Stamp of Approval-51
97Pacific-76
Copper-76
Emerald Green-76
Ice Blue-76
Red-76
Silver-76
97Pacific Dynagon-40
Copper-40
Dark Grey-40
Emerald Green-40
Ice Blue-40
Red-40
Silver-40
Tandems-44
97Pacific Invincible-45
Copper-45
Emerald Green-45
Ice Blue-45
Red-45
Silver-45
97Pacific Omega-77
Copper-77
Dark Gray-77
Emerald Green-77
Gold-77
Ice Blue-77
97Panini Stickers-138
97Revolution-45
Copper-45
Emerald-45
Ice Blue-45
Silver-45
97SP Authentic-46
97Upper Deck-263
98Aurora-61
98Be A Player-43
Press Release-43
98BAP Gold-43
98BAP Autographs-43
98BAP Autographs Gold-43
98BAP Tampa Bay All Star Game-43
98OPC Chrome-176
Refractors-176
Board Members-B7
Board Members Refractors-B7
98Pacific-56
Ice Blue-56
Red-56
98Pacific Dynagon Ice-61
Blue-61
Red-61
98Pacific Omega-77
Red-77
Opening Day Issue-77
98Panini Stickers-124
98Paramount-72
Copper-72
Emerald Green-72
Holo-Electric-72
Ice Blue-72
Silver-72
98Topps-176
O-Pee-Chee-176
Board Members-B7
98UD Choice-66
Prime Choice Reserve-66
Reserve-66
98Upper Deck-254
Exclusives-254
Exclusives 1 of 1-254
Gold Reserve-254
98Upper Deck MVP-65
Gold Script-65
Silver Script-65
Super Script-65
99BAP Memorabilia-24
Gold-24
Silver-24
99Pacific-132
Copper-132
Emerald Green-132
Gold-132
Ice Blue-132
Premiere Date-132
Red-132
99Pacific Omega-77
Copper-77
Gold-77
Ice Blue-77
Premiere Date-77
99Panini Stickers-221
99Paramount-78
Copper-78
Emerald-78
Gold-78
Holographic Emerald-78
Holographic Gold-78
Holographic Silver-78
Ice Blue-78
Premiere Date-78
Red-78
Silver-78
99Stars Postcards-27
99Upper Deck-218
Exclusives-218
Exclusives 1 of 1-218
99Upper Deck Gold Reserve-218
99Upper Deck Victory-95
00BAP Memorabilia-32
Emerald-32
Ruby-32
Sapphire-32
Promos-32
00BAP Mem Chicago Sportsfest Copper-32
00BAP Memorabilia Chicago Sportsfest Blue-32
00BAP Memorabilia Chicago Sportsfest Gold-32
00BAP Memorabilia Chicago Sportsfest Ruby-32
00BAP Memorabilia Chicago Sun-Times Ruby-32
00BAP Memorabilia Chicago Sun-Times Gold-32
00BAP Mem Chicago Sun-Times Sapphire-32
00BAP Mem Toronto Fall Expo Copper-32
00BAP Memorabilia Toronto Fall Expo Gold-32
00BAP Memorabilia Toronto Fall Expo Ruby-32
00BAP Parkhurst 2000-P46
00BAP Signature Series-7
Emerald-7
Ruby-7
Sapphire-7
Autographs-74
Autographs Gold-74
Department of Defense-DD11
00BAP Ultimate Memorabilia Teammates-TM27
00O-Pee-Chee-128
00O-Pee-Chee Parallel-128
00Pacific-143
Copper-143
Gold-143
Ice Blue-143
Premiere Date-143
00Panini Stickers-146
00Paramount-82
Copper-82
Gold-82
Holo-Gold-82
Holo-Silver-82
Ice Blue-82
Premiere Date-82
00Private Stock Game Gear-42
00Private Stock Game Gear Patches-42
00Stars Postcards-26
00Titanium Game Gear-93
00Titanium Game Gear Patches-93
00Topps/OPC-128
Parallel-128
00Topps Chrome-97
OPC Refractors-97
Refractors-97
00Topps Heritage-193
00Topps Premier Plus World Premier-WP4
00Topps Stars Game Gear-GGSZ
00UD Heroes-40
00Upper Deck-285
Exclusives Tier 1-285
Exclusives Tier 2-285
00Upper Deck MVP-62
First Stars-62
Second Stars-62
Third Stars-62
00Upper Deck Victory-73
00Upper Deck Vintage-115
01Atomic Jerseys-20
01Atomic Patches-20
01BAP Memorabilia-74
Emerald-74
Ruby-74
Sapphire-74
01Crown Royale Triple Threads-3
01O-Pee-Chee-17
01O-Pee-Chee Heritage Parallel-17
01O-Pee-Chee Heritage Parallel Limited-17
01O-Pee-Chee Premier Parallel-17
01Pacific-137
Extreme LTD-137
Hobby LTD-137
Premiere Date-137
Retail LTD-137
Jerseys-12
01Pacific Arena Exclusives-137
01Parkhurst-139
01Private Stock Game Gear-41
01Private Stock Game Gear Patches-41
01Stars Postcards-26
01Titanium Draft Day Edition-36
01Topps-17
Heritage Parallel-17
Heritage Parallel Limited-17
OPC Parallel-17
01Topps Chrome-17
Refractors-17
Black Border Refractors-17
01Topps Heritage-104
Refractors-104
01Topps Reserve Emblems-SZ
01Topps Reserve Jerseys-SZ
01Topps Reserve Name Plates-SZ
01Topps Reserve Numbers-SZ
01Topps Reserve Patches-SZ
01UD Challenge for the Cup-26
01UD Mask Collection-31
Gold-31
01UD Stanley Cup Champs-49
01Upper Deck-284
Exclusives-284
01Upper Deck MVP-59
01Upper Deck Victory-113
Gold-113
01Upper Deck Vintage-83
01Upper Deck Vintage-87
02BAP First Edition-62
Jerseys-62
02BAP Memorabilia-246
Emerald-246
Ruby-246
Sapphire-246
NHL All-Star Game-246
NHL All-Star Game Blue-246
NHL All-Star Game Green-246
NHL All-Star Game Red-246
02BAP Memorabilia Toronto Fall Expo-246
02BAP Sig Series Auto Buybacks 1998-43
02BAP Sig Series Auto Buybacks 2000-74
02BAP Signature Series Defensive Wall-DW5
02O-Pee-Chee-225
02O-Pee-Chee Premier Blue Parallel-225
02O-Pee-Chee Premier Red Parallel-225
02O-Pee-Chee Factory Set-225
02Pacific-122
Blue-122
Red-122
02Pacific Complete-124
Red-124
02Parkhurst-152
Bronze-152
Gold-152
Silver-152
02Parkhurst Retro-158
Minis-158
Hopefuls-NH5
02Stadium Club Champions Fabric-FC9
02Stadium Club Champions Patches-PC-9
02Stars Postcards-6
02Topps-225
OPC Blue Parallel-225
OPC Red Parallel-225
Captain's Cloth-CC3
Factory Set-225
02Topps Total-346
02Upper Deck-57
Exclusives-57
02Upper Deck Victory-68
Bronze-68
Gold-68
Silver-68
03BAP Memorabilia-88
Emerald-88
Gold-88
Ruby-88
Sapphire-88
03Beehive-63
Gold-63
Silver-63
03ITG Action-112
Jerseys-M120
03NHL Sticker Collection-208
03O-Pee-Chee-56
03OPC Blue-56
03OPC Gold-56
03OPC Red-56
03Pacific-114
Blue-114
Red-114
03Pacific Complete-143
Red-143
03Parkhurst Orig Six New York Mem-NM62
03Stars Postcards-31
03Topps-56
Blue-56
Gold-56
Red-56
03Topps C55-56
Minis-56
Minis American Back-56
Minis American Back Red-56
Minis Bazooka Back-56
Minis Brooklyn Back-56
Minis Hat Trick Back-56
Minis O Canada Back-56
Minis O Canada Back Red-56
Minis Stanley Cup Back-56
03Upper Deck-60
Canadian Exclusives-60
HG-60
03Upper Deck MVP-128
Gold Script-128
Silver Script-128
Canadian Exclusives-128
04Pacific-90
Blue-90
Red-90
04Upper Deck-55
Canadian Exclusives-55
HG Glossy Gold-55
HG Glossy Silver-55
05Beehive Signature Scrapbook-SSSZ
05Black Diamond-28
Emerald-28
Gold-28
Onyx-28
Ruby-28
05Panini Stickers-249
05Parkhurst-165
Facsimile Auto Parallel-165
True Colors-TCDAL
True Colors-TCDAL
05SP Authentic Prestigious Pairings-PPTZ
05SP Authentic Sign of the Times-SZ
05SP Authentic Sign of the Times Fives-MMZTJ
05SP Game Used Auto Draft-AD-SZ
05SP Game Used SIGnificance-SZ
05SP Game Used SIGnificance Gold-S-SZ
05SP Game Used Statscriptions-ST-SZ
05Ultra-71
Gold-71
Ice-71
05Upper Deck-60
Big Playmakers-B-SZ
HG Glossy-60
Jerseys-J-SZ
Notable Numbers-N-SZ
Ice Frozen Fabrics-FFSZ
Ice Frozen Fabrics Autographs-AFFSZ
Ice Frozen Fabrics Glass-FFSZ
Ice Frozen Fabrics Patches-FFPSZ
Ice Frozen Fabrics Patch Autographs-FAPSZ
05Upper Deck MVP-127
Gold-127
Platinum-127
05Upper Deck Toronto Fall Expo-60
05Upper Deck Victory-66
Black-66
Gold-66
Silver-66
Stars on Ice-SI18
06Beehive Matted Materials-MMSZ
06Black Diamond-27
Black-27
Gold-27
Ruby-27
06Fleer-68
Tiffany-68
06O-Pee-Chee-164
Rainbow-164
06Panini Stickers-247
06SP Game Used Authentic Fabrics Fives-AF5DPT
06SP Game Used Authentic Fabrics Fives Patches-AF5DPT
06SP Game Used Authentic Fabrics Eights-AF8RUS
06SP Game Used Authentic Fabrics Eights Patches-AF8RUS
06Stars Team Postcards-24
06The Cup NHL Shields Duals-DSHLZ
06The Cup NHL Shields Duals-DSHZG
06Ultimate Collection Premium Patches-PS-SZ
06Ultimate Collection Premium Swatches-PS-SZ
06Ultra-64
Gold Medallion-64
Ice Medallion-64
06Upper Deck Arena Giveaways-DAL3
06Upper Deck Arena Giveaways-DAL3
06Upper Deck-64
Exclusives Parallel-64
High Gloss Parallel-64
Game Jerseys-J2SZ
Game Patches-P2SZ
Masterpieces-64
Shootout Artists-SA14
06Upper Deck MVP-94
Gold Script-94
Super Script-94
Jerseys-OJLZ
06Upper Deck Ovation-66
06Upper Deck Sweet Shot Sweet Stitches-SSSZ
06Upper Deck Sweet Shot Sweet Stitches Duals-SSSZ
06Upper Deck Sweet Shot Sweet Stitches Triples-SSSZ
06Upper Deck Victory-64
06Upper Deck Victory Black-64
06Upper Deck Victory Gold-64

Zubrus, Dainius

92Quebec Pee-Wee Tournament-1464
96Black Diamond-68
Gold-68
96Donruss Canadian Ice-147
Gold Press Proofs-147
Red Press Proofs-147
96Donruss Elite-141
Die Cut Stars-141
Aspirations-15
96Flair-119
Blue Ice-119
96Flyers Postcards-24
96Leaf Limited Rookies-6
96Leaf Limited Rookies Gold-6
96Leaf Preferred-128
Press Proofs-128
96Metal Universe-198
96Select Certified-120
Artist's Proofs-120
Blue-120
Mirror Blue-120
Mirror Gold-120
Mirror Red-120
Red-120
96SP-117
96Ultra-129
Gold Medallion-129
96Upper Deck-309
96Zenith-123
Artist's Proofs-123
96All-Sport PPF *-98
96All-Sport PPF *-170
96All Sport PPF Gold *-98
96All Sport PPF Gold *-170
97Be A Player-26
Autographs-26
Autographs Die-Cuts-26
Autographs Prismatic Die-Cuts-26
97Black Diamond-8
Double Diamond-8
Triple Diamond-8
Quadruple Diamond-8
97Collector's Choice-187
97Crown Royale-101
Emerald Green-101
Ice Blue-101
Silver-101
Lamplighters Cel-Fusion Die-Cuts-15
97Donruss-75
Press Proofs Silver-75
Press Proofs Gold-75
97Donruss Elite-50
97Donruss Elite-135
Aspirations-50
Aspirations-135
Status-50
Status-135
97Donruss Limited-109
97Donruss Limited-195
Exposure-109
Exposure-195
Fabric of the Game-3
97Donruss Preferred-59
97Donruss Preferred-190
Cut to the Chase-59
Cut to the Chase-190
Line of the Times-8C
97Donruss Preferred Line of Times Promos-8C
97Donruss Priority-23
Stamp of Approval-23
Direct Deposit-29
Postcards-34
Stamps-34
Stamps Bronze-34
Stamps Gold-34
Stamps Silver-34
97Katch-108
Gold-108
Silver-108
97Leaf-124
97Leaf-186
Fractal Matrix-124
Fractal Matrix-186
Fractal Matrix Die Cuts-124
Fractal Matrix Die Cuts-186
Banner Season-22
Fire On Ice-13
97Leaf International-124
Universal Ice-124
97Pacific-303
Copper-303
Emerald Green-303
Ice Blue-303
Red-303
Silver-303
97Pacific Dynagon-94
Copper-94
Dark Grey-94
Emerald Green-94
Ice Blue-94
Red-94
Silver-94
Dynamic Duos-11B
Tandems-9
97Pacific Invincible-105
Copper-105
Emerald Green-105
Ice Blue-105
Red-105
Silver-105
Off The Glass-15
97Pacific Omega-171
Copper-171
Dark Gray-171
Emerald Green-171
Gold-171
Ice Blue-171
Game Face-14
97Panini Stickers-95
97Panini Stickers-249
97Paramount-138
Copper-138
Dark Grey-138
Emerald Green-138
Ice Blue-138
Red-138
Silver-138
97Pinnacle-105
Press Plates Back Black-105
Press Plates Back Cyan-105
Press Plates Back Magenta-105
Press Plates Back Yellow-105
Press Plates Front Black-105
Press Plates Front Cyan-105
Press Plates Front Magenta-105
Press Plates Front Yellow-105
97Pinnacle Certified-116
Red-116
Mirror Blue-116
Mirror Gold-116
Mirror Red-116
97Pinnacle Inside-33
Coach's Collection-33
Executive Collection-33
Track-30
97Pinnacle Tot Cert Platinum Blue-116
97Pinnacle Tot Certi Platinum Gold-116
97Pinnacle Totally Certified Platinum Red-116
97Pinnacle Tot Cert Mirror Platinum Gold-116
97Revolution-104
Copper-104
Emerald-104
Ice Blue-104
Silver-104
97Score-249
97Score Flyers-12
Platinum-12
Premier-12
97SP Authentic-117
Sign of the Times-DZ
97Studio-26
Press Proofs Silver-26
Press Proofs Gold-26
Hard Hats-5
Portraits-27
97Upper Deck-122
Smooth Grooves-SG59
Three Star Selects-15B
97Upper Deck Ice-49
Parallel-49
Power Shift-49
97Autographed Collection Autographs *-52
97Autographed Collection AutosGold *-52
97Players Club *-32
Play Backs-PB8
97Talk N' Sports *-46
Phone Cards $1-46
Phone Cards $20-10
97Visions Signings *-40
Artistry-A20
Artistry Autographs-A20
Autographs-65
98Aurora-143
Championship Fever-37
Championship Fever Copper-37
Championship Fever Ice Blue-37
Championship Fever Red-37
Championship Fever Silver-37
98Be A Player-102
Press Release-102
98BAP Gold-102
98BAP Autographs-102
98BAP Autographs Gold-102
98BAP Tampa Bay All Star Game-102
98Crown Royale-102
Limited Series-102
98Finest-14
No Protectors-14
No Protectors Refractors-14
Refractors-14
98OPC Chrome Season's Best-SB30
98OPC Chrome Season's Best Refractors-SB30
98Pacific-333
Ice Blue-333
Red-333
Gold Crown Die-Cuts-26
98Pacific Dynagon Ice-141
Blue-141
Red-141
98Pacific Omega-181
Red-181
Opening Day Issue-181
98Panini Stickers-92
98Paramount-179
Copper-179
Emerald Green-179
Holo-Electric-179
Ice Blue-179
Silver-179
98Revolution-108
Ice Shadow-108
Red-108
98Topps Season's Best-SB30
98Upper Deck-145
Exclusives-145
Exclusives 1 of 1-145
Gold Reserve-145
98Upper Deck MVP-102
Gold Script-102
Silver Script-102
Super Script-102
99Pacific-215
Copper-215
Emerald Green-215
Gold-215
Ice Blue-215
Premiere Date-215
Red-215
99Panini Stickers-73
99Paramount-122
Copper-122
Emerald-122
Gold-122
Holographic Emerald-122
Holographic Gold-122
Holographic Silver-122
Ice Blue-122
Premiere Date-122
Red-122
Silver-122
99Upper Deck MVP SC Edition-92
Gold Script-92
Silver Script-92
Super Script-92
99Quebec PeeWee Tournament Coll Souv-7
00BAP Memorabilia-78
Emerald-78
Ruby-78
Sapphire-78
Promos-78
00BAP Mem Chicago Sportsfest Copper-78
00BAP Memorabilia Chicago Sportsfest Blue-78
00BAP Memorabilia Chicago Sportsfest Gold-78
00BAP Memorabilia Chicago Sportsfest Ruby-78
00BAP Memorabilia Chicago Sun-Times Ruby-78
00BAP Memorabilia Chicago Sun-Times Gold-78
00BAP Mem Chicago Sun-Times Sapphire-78
00BAP Mem Toronto Fall Expo Copper-78
00BAP Memorabilia Toronto Fall Expo Gold-78
00BAP Memorabilia Toronto Fall Expo Ruby-78
00BAP Parkhurst 2000-P60
00BAP Signature Series-127
Emerald-127
Ruby-127
Sapphire-127
Autographs-18
Autographs Gold-18
00Canadiens Postcards-30
00O-Pee-Chee-201
00O-Pee-Chee Parallel-201
00Pacific-218
Copper-218
Gold-218
Ice Blue-218
Premiere Date-218
00Panini Stickers-44
00Paramount-133
Copper-133
Gold-133
Holo-Gold-133
Holo-Silver-133
Ice Blue-133
Premiere Date-133
00Private Stock Game Gear-61
00Private Stock Game Gear Patches-61
00Titanium Draft Day Edition-100
00Topps/OPC-201
Parallel-201
00Upper Deck-92
Exclusives Tier 1-92
Exclusives Tier 2-92
00Upper Deck MVP-91
First Stars-91
Second Stars-91
Third Stars-91
00Upper Deck Victory-125
00Upper Deck Vintage-189
01Pacific-400
Extreme LTD-400
Hobby LTD-400
Premiere Date-400
Retail LTD-400
Jerseys-36
01Pacific Arena Exclusives-400
01Pacific Heads-Up Quad Jerseys-12
01Parkhurst-192
01Titanium Double-Sided Jerseys-43
01Titanium Double-Sided Patches-43
01Upper Deck-409
Exclusives-409
01Upper Deck Victory-359
Gold-359
01Czech Stadion-248
02BAP First Edition-223
02BAP Sig Series Auto Buybacks 1998-102
02BAP Sig Series Auto Buybacks 2000-18
02Capitals Team Issue-9
02Pacific-400
Blue-400
Red-400
02Pacific Complete-312
Red-312
02Pacific Exclusive-175
02Private Stock Reserve-100
Blue-100
Red-100
Retail-100
02Topps Total-325
02Upper Deck-178
Exclusives-178
02Upper Deck Victory-216
Bronze-216
Gold-216
Silver-216
03ITG Action-526
03NHL Sticker Collection-148
03Pacific-350
Blue-350
Red-350
03Pacific Complete-13
Red-13
03Upper Deck-443
Canadian Exclusives-443
HG-443
UD Exclusives-443
04Pacific-270
Blue-270
Red-270
04Upper Deck-175
Canadian Exclusives-175
HG Glossy Gold-175
HG Glossy Silver-175
04Russian Legion-10
05Panini Stickers-179
05Parkhurst-484
Facsimile Auto Parallel-484
05Upper Deck-196
HG Glossy-196
05Upper Deck MVP-387
Gold-387
Platinum-387
05Upper Deck Toronto Fall Expo-196
06Be A Player-1
Autographs-1
Signatures-DZ
Signatures 10-1
06Black Diamond-83
Black-83
Gold-83
Ruby-83
06Fleer-197
Tiffany-197
06O-Pee-Chee-490
Rainbow-490
06Panini Stickers-174
06Ultra-198
Gold Medallion-198
Ice Medallion-198
06Upper Deck Arena Giveaways-WSH5
06Upper Deck-447
Exclusives Parallel-447
High Gloss Parallel-447
Masterpieces-447
06Upper Deck MVP-295
Gold Script-295
Super Script-295
06Upper Deck Ovation-50
06Upper Deck Victory-198
06Upper Deck Victory Black-198
06Upper Deck Victory Gold-198

Zubyck, John

96Guelph Storm-4
97Guelph Storm-22

Zuccolini, Reto

95Swiss HNL-417
96Swiss HNL-450

Zuger, Simon

01Swiss HNL-147
02Swiss HNL-177

Zuk, Greg

84Kelowna Wings-5

Zuk, Wayne

76Saginaw Gears-13

Zuke, Mike

80O-Pee-Chee-209
80Topps-209
81O-Pee-Chee-299
81O-Pee-Chee Stickers-132
81Topps-W124
82O-Pee-Chee-313
82Post Cereal-17
83O-Pee-Chee-322
83Whalers Junior Hartford Courant-22
84O-Pee-Chee-80
84O-Pee-Chee Stickers-195
84Topps-63
84Whalers Junior Wendy's-22
85O-Pee-Chee-19
85Topps-19
85Whalers Junior Wendy's-23
89Sault Ste. Marie Greyhounds-26
93Sault Ste. Marie Greyhounds-30
93Sault Ste. Marie Greyhound Memorial Cup-32
96Sault Ste. Marie Greyhounds-29
96Sault Ste. Marie Greyhounds Autographed-29

Zukiwsky, Jarret

89Victoria Cougars-21
907th Inn. Sketch WHL-247
917th Inn. Sketch WHL-284
94Tampa Bay Tritons RHI-12

Zukiwsky, Jon

93Red Deer Rebels-29
95Bowman Draft Prospects-P40
95Red Deer Rebels-22
96Red Deer Rebels-7
96Visions Signings *-66
Autographs-66A
Autographs Silver-66A
97Red Deer Rebels-23

Zulianello, Colin

02Charlotte Checkers-96
04Idaho Steelheads-21

Zultek, Matt

93Quebec Pee-Wee Tournament-1441
97Bowman CHL-132
OPC-132
Autographs-132
99Ottawa 67's-2
00Black Diamond-64
Gold-64
00Upper Deck-199
Exclusives Tier 1-199
Exclusives Tier 2-199
00Upper Deck Ice-44
Immortals-44
Legends-44
Stars-44
00Upper Deck MVP-213
First Stars-213
Second Stars-213
Third Stars-213
01Trenton Titans-1-12
02Trenton Titans-A-10
03Trenton Titans-368
06Toledo Storm-22

Zulyniak, Andy

02Prince Albert Raiders-23
03Vernon Vipers-19
04Vernon Vipers-8
05Vernon Vipers-23

Zulyniak, Shane

90Prince Albert Raiders-22
90 7th Inn. Sketch WHL-278
91Prince Albert Raiders-24
91 7th Inn. Sketch WHL-264
93Prince Albert Raiders-22
94Prince Albert Raiders-23
99German EHC Straubing-8

Zunic, David

94Owen Sound Platers-9

Zupancic, Nik

99Finnish Cardset-275
00Swedish Upper Deck-172

Zurba, Peter

91British Columbia JHL-13
92British Columbia JHL-189
97Central Texas Stampede-19
98Bakersfield Condors-21

Zurbriggen, Marc

96Swiss HNL-370
99Swiss Panini Stickers-358
01Swiss HNL-349
02Swiss HNL-393

Zurbriggen, Natal

96Swiss HNL-380

Zurek, Jan

97Czech DS Stickers-282
04German DEL-281

Zurek, Jiri

97Czech APS Extraliga-117
98Czech OFS-77
99Czech OFS-205
00Czech OFS-78

Zurenko, Joe

03Notre Dame Fighting Irish-1
04Notre Dame Fighting Irish-23

Zurfluh, Ken

01Swiss HNL-360
02Swiss HNL-400

Zuurmond, Jerry

93Swiss HNL-473
95Swiss HNL-297
96Swiss HNL-161

Zvachkin, Leonid

01Guelph Storm-4
01Guelph Storm Memorial Cup-3
02Guelph Storm-17

Zvyagin, Sergei

96Quad-City Mallards-17
97Quad-City Mallards-3
98Quad-City Mallards-1
02Russian Hockey League-31
02Russian Hockey League-136
02Russian Ultimate Line-1
05Russian Hockey League RHL-34

Zwakman, Greg

92Minnesota Golden Gophers-21
93Minnesota Golden Gophers-29
94Minnesota Golden Gophers-31
95Minnesota Golden Gophers-30

Zweng, Christopher

94German First League-109

Zwijack, Tim

80Sault Ste. Marie Greyhounds-11

Zwyer, Dave

92Saskatchewan JHL-148

Zygulski, Scott

93Fort Worth Fire-17

Zytynsky, Taras

79Montreal Juniors-29
83Springfield Indians-24

Zyuzin, Andrei

95Classic-69
Autographs-24
96Collect Edge Ice Sign Sealed Delivered-8
96All-Sport PPF *-77
96All Sport PPF Gold *-77
97Pacific Omega-208
Copper-208
Dark Gray-208
Emerald Green-208
Gold-208
Ice Blue-208
97Kentucky Thoroughblades-21
97Autographed Collection *-50
Autographs-53
Autographs Gold-53
97Visions Signings Autographs *-66
98Be A Player-116
Press Release-116
98BAP Gold-116
98BAP Autographs-116
98BAP Autographs Gold-116
98BAP Tampa Bay All Star Game-116
98Black Diamond-73
Double Diamond-73
Triple Diamond-73
Quadruple Diamond-73
98Pacific-394
Ice Blue-394
Red-394
98Panini Stickers-213
98SPx Finite-134
Radiance-134
Spectrum-134
98UD Choice-179
98UD Choice Preview-179
98UD Choice Prime Choice Reserve-179
98UD Choice Reserve-179
98UD3-18
98UD3-78
98UD3-138
Die-Cuts-18
Die-Cuts-78
Die-Cuts-138
98Upper Deck-168
Exclusives-168
Exclusives 1 of 1-168
Gold Reserve-168
98Upper Deck MVP-171
Gold Script-171
Silver Script-171
Super Script-171
98Kentucky Thoroughblades-22
99BAP Memorabilia-214
Gold-214
Silver-214
Selects Silver-SL16
Selects Gold-SL16
99Panini Stickers-149
99SPx-140
Radiance-140
Spectrum-140
99Upper Deck-289
Exclusives-289
Exclusives 1 of 1-289
99Upper Deck Arena Giveaways-TL2
99Upper Deck Gold Reserve-289
99Wayne Gretzky Hockey-157
00BAP Memorabilia-279
Emerald-279
Ruby-279
Sapphire-279
Promos-279
00BAP Mem Chicago Sportsfest Copper-279
00BAP Memorabilia Chicago Sportsfest Blue-279
00BAP Memorabilia Chicago Sportsfest Gold-279
00BAP Memorabilia Chicago Sportsfest Ruby-279
00BAP Memorabilia Chicago Sun-Times Ruby-279
00BAP Memorabilia Chicago Sun-Times Gold-279
00BAP Mem Chicago Sun-Times Sapphire-279
00BAP Mem Toronto Fall Expo Copper-279
00BAP Memorabilia Toronto Fall Expo Gold-279
00BAP Memorabilia Toronto Fall Expo Ruby-279
00BAP Signature Series-38
Emerald-38
Ruby-38
Sapphire-38
Autographs-134
Autographs Gold-134
00Upper Deck-389
Exclusives Tier 1-389
Exclusives Tier 2-389
01Upper Deck Victory-321
Gold-321
02BAP Sig Series Auto Buybacks 1998-116
03ITG Action-276
03O-Pee-Chee-186
03OPC Blue-186
03OPC Gold-186
03OPC Red-186
03Pacific Complete-91
Red-91
03Topps-186
Blue-186
Gold-186
Red-186
03Upper Deck MVP-218
Gold Script-218
Silver Script-218
Canadian Exclusives-218
05Upper Deck MVP-194
Gold-194
Platinum-194

Zywitza, Sven

94German DEL-13
95German DEL-14
96German DEL-14
99German Bundesliga 2-201

Index

Minors, Juniors & European

ACKNOWLEDGMENTS

A great deal of diligence, hard work, and dedicated effort went into this year's volume. The high standards to which we hold ourselves, however, could not have been met without the expert input and generous amount of time contributed by many people. Our sincere thanks are extended to each and every one of you.

Each year we refine the process of developing the most accurate and up-to-date information for this book. I believe this year's Price Guide is our best yet. Thanks again to all of the contributors nationwide (listed below) as well as our staff here in Dallas.

Those who have worked closely with us on this and many other books, have again proven themselves invaluable in every aspect of producing this book: Mike Aronstein, Pete Belanger, Erwin Borau, Bill Bossert, John Brenner, Cartomania (Joseph E. Filion), Collection de Sport AZ (Ronald Villanueve), Bill and Diane Dodge, Gervise Ford, Steve Freedman, Larry and Jeff Fritsch, John Furniss, Gary Gagen, Dick Gariepy, Dick Gilkeson, Mike and Howard Gordon, George Grauer, Gene Guarnere, Jerry and Etta Hersh, Mike Hersh, Gerald Higgs, In The Game, Sean Isaacs, Dennis Kannokko, Paul and Anna Kannokko, Lew Lipset, Paul Marchant, Michael Moretto, Jean-Guy Pichette, Jack Pollard, Gavin Riley, Rotman Productions, John Rumierz, Kevin Savage, Angelo Savelli, Mike Schechter (MSA), Richard Sherman, Brad Shrabin, Gary Silkstone, Gerry Sobie, John Spalding, Phil and Joan Spector, Nigel Spill, Murvin Sterling, Topps, Upper Deck, Rob Unlus, Michel Vaillancourt, Shirl Volk, Pete Wooten, Kit Young, and Robert Zanze. Finally, we give a special acknowledgment to Dennis W. Eckes, Mr. Sport Americana, whose untimely passing in 1991 was a real loss to the hobby and to me personally. The success of the Beckett Price Guides has always been the result of a team effort.

Many other individuals have provided price input, illustrative material, checklist verifications, errata, and/or background information. At the risk of inadvertently overlooking or omitting these many contributors, we should like to personally thank Ab D Cards (Dale Wesolewski), Jerry Adamic, Bren Adams, Murray Akbart, Neil Armstrong, Alan Applegate, Roland J. Atlas, Art Baker, Brent Barnes, Frank and Vivian Barning, Robert Beaudoin, Al Beharrell, Todd Bellerose, Gary Benton, Beulah Sports (Jeff Blatt), Ki Billy, Chad Blick, Michel Bolduc, Joseph Bonett, Peter Borkowski, Luc Boucher, B. Jack Bourland III, Tony Bouwman, Jim Boyne, Elio Brandelli, Tim Brahmer, Marco Brizuela, Douglas Brown, Bob Bruner, Dan Bruner, Jacey Buel, Dave Bullis, Eric Burgoyne, Scott Burke, Jason Caines, Jim Cappello, Danny Cariseo, Greg Caskey, Rick Chambers, Dwight Chapin, Jeff Chapman, Michael Chark, Steve Chiaramonte, Susan Christensen, Larry Ciancone, Scott Coates, Allan E. Cohen, Shane Cohen (Grand Slam), Barry Colla, Matt Collett, Ken Collins, Shelby Colson, Joe Conte, Dan Conway, Ryan Cope, Michael J. Cox, Taylor Crane, Wil Curtis, Allen Custer, Kenneth Daniels, Steven Danver, Leo Davis, Scott Dean, Jim Decorso, Mary Dempster, Deerquotes Baseball Cards, Normand Desroches, Larry DeTienne, Dave Deveney, Karlos Diego, Leon Dill, Mario DiPastena, Marc Dixon, Gerard Dolci, Benoit Doyon, Michel Dubois, Charles Dugre, John Duplisea, Don Ellis, Danny Ellwood, Michael Esposito, Bryan Epstein, Doak Ewing, Dave Feltham, Larry Fleming, Don Forsey, Frank Fox, Craig Frank, Mark Franke, Kathryn Friedlander, Bob Friedman, Bob Frye, James Funke Jr., Tom Galanis, Jim Galusha, Richard, Gariepy, Neil Garvey, Ron and Dave Gibara, Michael R. Gionet, Dave Giove, Mike Gogal, Harvey Goldfarb, Brian Goldstein, Jeff Goldstein, Renvel Gonsalves, Rynel Gonsalves, Seth Gordon, John Gosney, Erik Gravel, Pierre-Luc Gravel, Great Canadian Sportcard Co., Hall's Nostalgia, Gerald Hamelin, Tom Harrett, Ron Heller, Bill Henderson, Tom Hendrickson, Wayne Hepburn, Chick Hershberger, Clay Hill, Gary Hlady, Shawn Hoagland, Keith Holtzmann, Joseph Horgan, Dan Horton, Teresa Horton, D. Howery Jr., Richard Irving, Torstein H. Jacobsen, John James, Robert Jansing, Cliff Janzen, Peter Jeffrey, Leslie Jezuit, Scott Jugan, Robert Kantor, Jay and Mary Kasper, Sam Kassam, John Kelly, Rick Keplinger, Larry Kerrigan, John Killan, Dean Konieczka, Bob Krawetz, Chuck Kucera, George Kumagai, Rob Kuhlman, Thomas Kunnecke, Roger Lampert, Ted Larkins, Brent Lee, Scott LeLievre, Irv Lerner, Howie Levy, Mike Lewandoski, Stephane Lizotte, Nicholas LoCasto, The Locker Room, Tim Loop, Frank Lopez, Karoline K. Lowry, Doug Lowther, Steven J. Loy, Thierry Lubenec, Jim Macie, Joe Marasco, Adam Martin, Jason Martin, Chris Mayhew, Michael McDonald, Blake Meyer, John Meyer, Dick Millerd, Ben Mitchell, Paul V. Mohrle, Joe Morano, Michael Moretto, Michel Morin, Brian Morris, Kevin Mudrak, Larry Murray, Todd Nelkin, Rob Nicholls, Dave Nicklas, Paul Noble, Leandre Normand, David Nystrom, John O'Hara, John O' Mara, Glenn Olson, Nelson Paine, Andrew Pak, David Paolicelli, Tom Parker, Clay Pasternack, Alan Peace, Joe Pellicio, Alan Philpot, Dale Pinney, Richard Plett, Len Pottie, Red River Coins and Cards, Randall Reese, Tom Reid, Dave and Shawn Redden, Paula Reinke, Ralph Reitsma, Ron Ressler, Dorothy Reznik, Owen Ricker, Mark Rogers, John Wayne Roman, Paul Romero, Charles Rooke, Jim Routly, Grant Rowland, Joe Rubert II, Terry Sack, Joe Sak, Linda Santiago, Cheryl Sauve, Mike Shafer, Chris Sklener, Lyle Skrapek, Slapshot Sports Collectibles, Steve Smith, Don Spagnola, Carl Specht, Dave Stallings, Cary Stephenson, Dan Stickney, Andy Stoltz, Ray Stonehouse, Cheryl Suave, Mark Suchawericz, Dave Sularz, Walt Suski, Fred Suzman, Danny Tarquini, Paul S. Taylor, Lee Temanson, Teresa Tewell, Chuck Thomas, Tim Thompson, Joe Tomasik, Darren Turcotte, Michel Vaillancourt, Variete Sports, Rob Veres, Verville Enr., Ernie Vickers, Clayton Vigent, Shirl Volk, Jonathan Waldman, Jonathan Watts, David Weiner, Andrew B. Weisenfeld, Kermit B. Wells, Brian Wentz, Bill Wesslund, Frank and Jason Wilder, Kelly Wionzek, Brian Wobbeking, Ted Woo, Thomas L. Wujek, Andre Yip Hoi, Yaz's Sports Memorabilia, Gerard Yodice, Christina Zawadzki, and Bill Zimpleman.

A special thanks also goes out to those who graciously donated their knowledge and expertise (and their cards) in adding to the comprehensiveness of this year's volume: Ralph Slate (Whose web site www.hockeydb.com is one of the hobby's great minor league resources), Vinnie Montalbano and Dale Sprenger (for their efforts in improving the scope of our minor league and college coverage), Caspar Friberg (Finnish issues), Marek Pandoscak (Slovakian issues), Jiri Kuca and Jiri Peterka (Czech issues), Holger Petersen (German issues), Hockey Heaven, Christian Olander, and Per Vedin (Swedish issues), Joe Bonnett, Stewart Etlinger, Dino Fazio, Steve Fraser, CTM Ste-Foy, Gerry Garland, Gary Giovane, Ian Green (Armchair Sports UK), John Ignato, Chad Kitzman, Troy Moore, Jeremy Poclitar, J.D. Porter, Gus Saunders, Andre Yip Hoi (Time-Out Sportscards), Dave Weselowski.

Every year we make active solicitations for expert input. We are particularly appreciative of the help (however extensive or cursory) provided for this volume. We receive many inquiries, comments and questions regarding material within this book. In fact, each and every one is read and digested. Time constraints, however, prevent us from personally replying. But keep sharing your knowledge. Even though we cannot respond to each letter, you are making significant contributions to the hobby through your interest and comments.

The effort to continually refine and improve this book also involves a growing number of people and types of expertise on our home team. Our company boasts a substantial Sports Collectibles Publishing team, which strengthens our ability to provide comprehensive analysis of the marketplace. Our hockey analysts played a major part in compiling this years book, travelling thousands of miles during the past year to attend sports card shows and visit card shops around the United States and Canada. Their baseline analysis and careful proofreading were key contributions to the accuracy of this annual.

In the years since this guide debuted, Beckett.com has grown beyond any rational expectation. A great many talented and hard working individuals have been instrumental in this growth and success. Our whole team is to be congratulated for what we together have accomplished.

The whole Beckett Publications team has my thanks for jobs well done. Thank you, everyone.

- Al Muir, Editor